VideoHound's GOLDEN MOVIE RETRIEVER

VideoHound's GOLDEN MOVIE RETRIEVER®

Jim Craddock, Editor

101872 — Oct. 2008

GALE
CENGAGE Learning™

Detroit • New York • San Francisco • New Haven, Conn • Waterville, Maine • London

GALE
CENGAGE Learning

VideoHound's® Golden Movie Retriever 2009

Project Editor: Jim Craddock

Editorial: Tom Burns, Michael J. Tyrkus

Editorial Support Systems: Wayne Fong

Manufacturing: Rita Wimberley

For product information and technology assistance, contact us at
Gale Customer Support, 1-800-877-4253.

For permission to use material from this text or product,
submit all requests online at www.cengage.com/permissions.
Further permissions questions can be emailed to
permissionrequest@cengage.com

While every effort has been made to ensure the reliability of the information presented in this publication, Gale, a part of Cengage Learning, does not guarantee the accuracy of the data contained herein. Gale accepts no payment for listing; and inclusion in the publication of any organization, agency, institution, publication, service, or individual does not imply endorsement of the editors or publisher. Errors brought to the attention of the publisher and verified to the satisfaction of the publisher will be corrected in future editions.

Gale
27500 Drake Rd.
Farmington Hills, MI, 48331-3535

ISBN-13: 978-1-4144-004-4
ISSN 1095-371X
This title is also available as an e-book.
ISBN-13: 978-1-4144-3848-1
ISBN-10: 1-4144-3848-6

Contact your Gale sales representative for ordering information.

3 5944 00101 8728

Printed in the United States of America
1 2 3 4 5 6 7 12 11 10 09 08

Credits: or Who Does What

Project Editor
Jim Craddock

Editorial Coordinator
Terri Schell

Editorial
Tom Burns
Michael J. Tyrkus

Editorial Support Services
Wayne Fong

Product Design
Pam Galbreath

Manufacturing
Rita Wimberley

Also Starring:

Animal Control Officer
Kathy Nolan

Review Crew
Tom Burns
James A. Cook
Martin Craddock
Dawn Desjardins

Lisa DeShantz-Cook
Scott Estes
Beth A. Fhaner
Jeff Hermann
Lynne Konstantin
Peter Tigger Lunney
Stuart Mammel
Robyn Parton
Joel Potrykus
Chris Scanlon
Amanda Scheid
Chris Tomassini
Mike Tyrkus
Hilary White

Special Assignment Research
Keith Lindsay

Typesetter Extraordinaire:
Michael Boyd, ATLIS
Publishing Services, Inc.

Makin' Copy:
PJ Butland

Licensing/Special Markets
Jerry Moore

Contents

Introduction Ix
It's really worth reading, y'know

Using VideoHound xi
And then you don't even call!

Alternate Titles Index 1
A film by any other name will be found here

Videos A-Z 41
Why we do what we do

Category Index 1063
Flicks that flock together

Kibbles and Series Index 1267
Adaptations, quality check, recurring characters, successful screen partnerships

Awards Index 1293
Egomaniacal acceptance speeches not included, but nominations are.

Cast Index 1329
Hey, what else has she been in?

Director Index 1723
Cut! Print it, that was perfect!

Writer Index 1785
Does spelling count?

Cinematographer Index 1839
If a movie looks good, these are the people to thank

Composer Index 1873
They make the music that makes the movies

Video Sources Guide 1905
When renting just won't do, find out where to buy your favorites

Web Site Guide 1907
If you're going surfing, check here for the best locations

"It's like, how much more black could this be? And the answer is none. None more black."

Were the boys from Spinal Tap discussing their album cover, or 2007's movie slate? The world may never know...okay, we do know, but it's a funny quote and it fits what we wanted to say, so we copped it.

The vampires from *30 Days of Night* would have been quite at home in movie theaters in 2007. In fact, anyone who likes it dark should have enjoyed the past year in movies. Besides all the milkshake-drinking and coin-flipping, any year that requires the *Hound* to add such new categories as "Genocide/Ethnic Cleansing" and "Killing Sprees," and counts a movie about an unwed teenage mother as the "feel-good" movie of the year (*Juno*), probably qualifies as "angsty."

The two most decorated films of the year, Paul Thomas Anderson's sweeping epic *There Will Be Blood* and the Coen brothers' *No Country for Old Men* offered compelling characters inhabiting dark places who did horrible things to their fellow man. In fact, a quick look at the award nominations lists reveals a plethora of dramas that deal either in bad people doing bad things, or ordinary people struggling with difficult, and usually harrowing or heartbreaking circumstances. Sure, these things are the essence of drama, but this year seemed to have more than its fair share of it.

Besides *Blood* and *Country*, there was the corporate shenanigans of *Michael Clayton*, people dealing with disease or disability in *Away from Her*, *The Diving Bell and the Butterfly*, and *The Savages*, and of course there was the now-standard tragic biopics *La Vie en Rose* and *Into the Wild*. The epic period romance *Atonement* turned on a moment of spite, and spent the remainder of its running time showing the consequences. Even musicals got into the act, with the always-gothic Tim Burton bringing *Sweeney Todd* to the big screen, in the form of long-time collaborator Johnny Depp. Crime dramas, always reliably dark and brooding, didn't disappoint on those counts, with *Eastern Promises* leading the way; mostly on the strength of the most disturbing frontal nudity since Harvey Keitel in *Bad Lieutenant*. *American Gangster* and *The Assassination of Jesse James by the Coward Robert Ford* explored America's fascination with the criminal element. Ben Affleck revived his career by directing a gut-punch of a movie focusing on child abduction and parental neglect in *Gone Baby Gone*.

Not much of an escape for audiences looking for a break from rising prices, a tanking economy, and an unpopular war, the latter of which Hollywood was only too happy to remind us about and try to discuss. Apparently, the movie-going public wasn't in the mood, judging by the boxoffice for such films as *In the Valley of Elah*, *Lions for Lambs*, and *Grace is Gone*.

Of course, all the doom and gloom on screen could may have been a reflection of the mood in Hollywood itself, what with diminishing boxoffice, a declining home-video market, and a protracted writers strike that put a lot of major projects on hold and decimated the TV season. Too much reality TV can make anyone grumpy.

But fear not! For not all the news was bad. *Superbad* and *Enchanted* charmed audiences of vastly different stripes, and last summer did witness the long-awaited big-screen debut of *The Simpsons Movie*, and Homer and company did not disappoint. Another animated TV icon, *The Transformers* made a very big (number three at the boxoffice at $319 mil), and very loud live-action debut. In fact, plenty of familiar faces populated the top of the boxoffice list, including Spider-Man, Shrek, Harry Potter, Jason Bourne...and—Yippee-Ky-Ay—John McClane.

In news of the weird, John Travolta wore a dress for *Hairspray*, an animated culinary-arts obsessed rat may have provided the most enjoyable pure movie experience of the year (okay, not TOO surprising, considering it was a Pixar flick), and Uwe Boll kept his WOOF! streak intact with two more "masterpieces" and threatened/promised to go away if 1,000,000 people signed an online petition asking him to stop making movies.

Speaking of online, things around the *VideoHound* compound have been hopping as well, as we prepare to unveil our foray into cyberspace...um, are the kids still calling it that? Anyway, we decided to give you, our loyal readers, a way to waste time (er, we mean find important valuable information) while at work, when you are away from your beloved copy of this tome. Just go to www.movieretriever.com to find our usual irreverent yet knowledgeable take on movies, plus the cast and crew information and exhaustive categorization that you've come to depend on. But wait! That's not all! You'll also be able to sign in and create your own page, rate and review movies and cast people, join discussions, read hilarious blog entries from the *VideoHound* staff, and suggest new categories.

But don't think for a minute that we have neglected the book. We put in the same love and dedication, blood, sweat, and tears as always. Then we wiped it off and shipped it to a bookstore near you. Along with the aforementioned bodily fluids, we included new categories such as "Milwaukee," "Brains!" "Joke and Dagger," "Chefs," and "Teen Musicals," and some interesting new Kibbles stuff such as breaking out the Marvel and DC comic book adaptations, as well as highlighting such recurring characters as Philip Marlowe, Mister Moto, and—Yippee-Ky-Ay again!—John McClane. There's also new director/star and screen team collaborations, for your knowledge-expanding pleasure. Plus there's the usual cast of theatrical releases, direct-to-video, foreign, niche, and documentary releases. Because we care, and we know that you do, too. And in that spirit, as always, we want to hear from you. Questions? Comments? Something we missed (it has been known to happen)? Just want to say 'Hi?' Here's how to contact us:

VideoHound's Golden Movie Retriever
27500 Drake Rd.
Farmington Hills, MI 48331-3535
or email at jim.craddock@cengage.com or at the website (once again, that's www.movieretriever.com)

Thanks for your continued support and assistance.

P.S. For those of you who have asked, Robert De Niro is indeed listed in the Cast Index. He is under De(space)N, not DeN.

Alphabetization

Titles are arranged on a word-by-word basis, including articles and prepositions. Leading articles (A, An, The) are ignored in English-language titles. The equivalent foreign articles are not ignored, however: *The Abyss* appears under "A," while *Les Misérables* appears under "L." **Other points to keep in mind:**

- Acronyms appear alphabetically as if regular words. For example, *C.H.U.D.* is alphabetized as "Chud"; *M*A*S*H* as "Mash."

- Common abbreviations in titles file as if they were spelled out, so *St. Elmo's Fire* will be found under "Saint Elmo's Fire" and *Mr. Holland's Opus* will be alphabetized as "Mister Holland's Opus."

- Proper names in titles are alphabetized beginning with the individual's first name; for instance, *Monty Python's The Meaning of Life* is under "M"; *Eddie Murphy: Raw* is under "E."

- Titles with numbers (*2001: A Space Odyssey*) are alphabetized as if the number were spelled out under the appropriate letter, in this case "Two Thousand One." When numeric titles gather in close proximity to each other (*2000 Year Old Man, 2001, 2010: The Year We Make Contact*), the titles will be arranged in a low (2000) to high (2010) numeric sequence.

Indexes

Alternate Title Index. A number of videos, particularly older, foreign, or B-type releases, may have variant titles. Alternate titles are listed alphabetically and refer the reader to the title under which the entry is listed. The alternate titles are also noted within the review.

Category Index. Subject categories ranging from the orthodox to slightly eccentric permit you to video sleuth from broad type to significant themes to signature scenes. The mix, arranged alphabetically by category, includes hundreds of traditional film genres and sub-genres as well as a feast of *VideoHound* exclusives. Integrated into the index are cross references, while preceding the index is a list of definitions. Release year will help differentiate between titles of the same name. A tipped triangle (▶) indicates a movie rated three bones or above.

Kibbles and Series Index. Not your everyday categories, Kibbles span the literary side of movie-making (Adapted from a Play, Books to Film; Ernest Hemingway) and point out key producers and special effects masters. Yearly box-office winners (that are now on video) since 1939 are listed, along with classic movies, four-bone delights, trash films, modern Shakespeare, Disney fare, significant on-screen and director/actor pairings. The Series portion of this index provides listings of major movie series, ranging from James Bond to National Lampoon to Indiana Jones. Recurring cinematic collaborations and partnerships of note are also listed, including Hope & Crosby, Abbott & Costello, De Niro & Scorsese, and Rafelson & Nicholson. A complete list of the categories precedes the index. Release year will help differentiate between titles of the same name. **As in the Category Index, tipped triangles (▶) indicate quality views.**

Awards Index. The Awards Index lists almost 7,000 films honored by national and international award bodies, representing some 90 categories of competition. This information is also contained in the review following the credits. Nominations are once again (thanks to popular demand) included in this index. A star (?) denotes the winner. **Only features are listed in this index; movies not yet released on video are not covered.**

As award-winning and nominated films find their way to video, they will be added to the review section and covered in this index. Awards listed include the American Academy Awards; British Academy of Film and Television Arts; Golden Globe; Directors Guild of America; Screen Actors Guild; Writers Guild; Independent Spirit; National Film Registry; and the Golden Raspberries.

Cast/Director Indexes. The Cast Index provides full videographies for all actors and actresses listed in *VideoHound* with more than two movies on their resume. The Director Index lists the works of any director who has made it to video and to *VideoHound*. Although listed in a first name, last name sequence, the names are alphabetized by last name. Film titles, complete with initial year of release, are arranged in chronological order, starting with their most recent. A (V) designation after a film title indicates that the actor lent only vocal talents to that movie, as in animation features. An (N) depicts narration duties. Birth and death dates (year only) have been added to the citations. While they are not yet complete, they will continue to be updated, with more added to every edition. **Cross-references for actors and actresses who have appeared under more than one name are also included.**

Writer Index. Screenwriters and script doctors are listed with their vital works. Names are arranged alphabetically by last name. Works are arranged chronologically.

Cinematographer Index. Directors of Photography are listed alphabetically by last name, along with their work, which is arranged chronologically.

Composer Index. Videographies of movie music composers, arrangers, lyricists, and so on are listed. Arranged alphabetically by last name.

The **Video Sources Guide:** Lists a number of mail order and independent video dealers where videos and DVDs can be obtained.

Web Site Guide. Lists Internet web sites for studios; general entertainment information; film festivals; and filmmaker resources; as well as sites for gossip, upcoming releases, video ordering outlets, and trivia.

Sample Review

Each *VideoHound* review contains up to 19 items, ranging from title, to the review, to cast listings, to awards received. The information in these reviews is designed to help you choose a video you'll like, increase your enjoyment of a movie as you watch (especially by answering that nagging question of "What else have I seen that guy in?"), and increase your knowledge of movie trivia.

1. Title
2. One- to four-bone rating (or *Woof!*)
3. Alternate Title (we made this up)
4. Year released
5. MPAA rating
6. Description/review
7. Songs (made these up, too)
8. Length (in minutes)
9. Black & White (B) or Color (C)
10. Format (VHS, DVD, CD-I, UMD, Blu-Ray, HD DVD, Widescreen, closed captioned, or 8mm)
11. Country of origin (made up)
12. Cast (*V:* indicates voiceovers; also includes cameos)
13. Director
14. Writer(s)
15. Cinematographer(s)
16. Composer(s)/Lyricist(s)
17. Narrator (made up)
18. Awards (yet again, made up)
19. Made-for-Television/Cable/Video identification

The movie used in this sample is a real movie, it was filmed in Detroit, released by Troma, and is available from Thomas Video.

1 Tainted **2** 🦴🦴 **3** *Angry Young Vampires* **4** 1998 **5** (R) **6** Ever wonder what would happen if the guys from "Clerks" fell in with a bunch of vampires? Well, lucky you. Now you can find out. Video clerks Ryan and J.T. hitch a ride to the midnight movie with their new co-worker Alex, who just happens to be a vampire whose ex is shacking up with the new vamp in town, who wants to taint the city's blood supply with undead blood. Script has many laughs, lots of attitude, and plenty of pop-culture knowledge, but gets a bit windy at times. Sometimes the actors seem to be trying a little too hard, but it doesn't detract from the story. Filmed in Detroit with lots of excellent local product placement. **7** ♫Bottoms Up; Rats!; One More for the Road.

8&9 64m/C **10** VHS, DVD. **11** *GB* **12** Brian Evans, Sean Farley, Dusan "Dean" Cechvala, Greg James, Jason Brouwer, Tina Kapousis; **13** *D:* Brian Evans; **14** *W:* Sean Farley; **15** *C:* Brian Evans; **16** *M:* Jessie McClear. **17** *Nar:* Bela Lugosi. **18** Academy Awards '98: Best Adapted Screenplay; Independent Spirit Awards '99: Best First Feature; Writers Guild of America '98: Best Original Screenplay. **19** VIDEO

The Alternate Titles Index provides variant and foreign titles for movies with more than one name. Titles are listed in alphabetical order, followed by a cross-reference to the appropriate entry in the main video review section. If you don't find a movie you're looking for in the main section, this is the best place to look next.

A-009 Missione Hong Kong See Code Name Alpha (1967)

A Bout de Souffle See Breathless (1959)

Abar, the First Black Superman See In Your Face (1977)

Abbie See Steal This Movie! (2000)

Abbott and Costello in the Navy See In the Navy (1941)

Abbott and Costello Meet the Ghosts See Abbott and Costello Meet Frankenstein (1948)

Abbott and Costello Meet the Killer See Abbott and Costello Meet the Killer, Boris Karloff (1949)

ABC Murders See The Alphabet Murders (1965)

Abdullah's Harem See Abdulla the Great (1956)

Abismos de Pasion See Wuthering Heights (1953)

The Abominable Snowman of the Himalayas See The Abominable Snowman (1957)

Abraxas See Abraxas: Guardian o' the Universe (1990)

Abre Los Ojos See Open Your Eyes (1997)

Abril Despedacado See Behind the Sun (2001)

Absent-Minded See The Daydreamer (1975)

Absinthe See Madame X (1966)

L'Accompagnatrice See The Accompanist (1993)

L'Accordeur de tremblements de terre See Piano Tuner of Earthquakes (2005)

The Accused See The Mark of the Hawk (1957)

Ace See The Great Santini (1980)

Ace Ventura Goes to Africa See Ace Ventura: When Nature Calls (1995)

Aces Go Places 3: Our Man From Bond Street See Mad Mission 3 (1984)

Acia See Acia's Descent into Floristella (1987)

Across Five Aprils See Civil War Diary (1990)

Act of Violence See Deadline Assault (1990)

Acts of Love See Carried Away (1995)

Adam & Eve See National Lampoon's Adam & Eve (2005)

Adam Wants to Be a Man See Accamas Nori Buti Zmogumi (1959)

Adams Aebler See Adam's Apples (2005)

Addict See Born to Win (1971)

Addio, Fratello, Crudele See 'Tis a Pity She's a Whore (1973)

Adieu, l'ami See Honor Among Thieves (1968)

Adorable Idiot See Ravishing Idiot (1964)

Adorenarin Doraibu See Adrenaline Drive (1999)

The Adventure See L'Avventura (1960)

Adventure for Two See The Demi-Paradise (1943)

The Adventure of Lyle Swan See Timerider (1983)

The Adventurer See The Rover (1967)

Adventures at Rugby See Tom Brown's School Days (1940)

The Adventures of Chatran See The Adventures of Milo & Otis (1989)

The Adventures of Galgameth See Galgameth (1996)

The Adventures of Hercules See Hercules 2 (1985)

The Adventures of Jack London See Jack London (1944)

The Adventures of the Great Mouse Detective See The Great Mouse Detective (1987)

Adventures of the Great North See Legends of the North (1995)

The Adventuress See I See a Dark Stranger (1946)

Aelita: The Revolt of the Robots See Aelita: Queen of Mars (1924)

Aerobicide See Killer Workout (1986)

The Affair Gleiwitz See The Gleiwitz Case (1961)

Agent 38-24-36 See Ravishing Idiot (1964)

An Affair at the Heart See The Love Affair, or The Case of the Missing Switchboard Operator (1967)

An Affair of the Heart See Body and Soul (1947)

Affairs of the Vampire See Curse of the Undead (1959)

AFO See Air Force One (1997)

African Fury See Cry, the Beloved Country (1951)

After Jenny Died See Revenge (1971)

After You See Apres-Vous (2003)

Afula Express See Pick a Card (1997)

Afurika Monogatari See Green Horizon (1980)

Ageguk: Shadow of the Wolf See Shadow of the Wolf (1992)

Against All Odds See Kiss and Kill (1968)

Against All Hope See One for the Road (1982)

Against All Enemies See The Siege (1998)

Agatha Christie's Endless Night See Endless Night (1971)

Agatha Christie's Miss Marple: A Murder Is Announced See A Murder Is Announced (1987)

Agatha Christie's Miss Marple: A Pocketful of Rye See A Pocketful of Rye (1987)

Agatha Christie's Miss Marple: The Body in the Library See The Body in the Library (1984)

Agatha Christie's Ten Little Indians See Ten Little Indians (1989)

The Age of Beauty See Belle Epoque (1992)

Age of Gold See L'Age D'Or (1930)

Agent Provocateur See Provocateur

L'Agente Federale Lemmy Caution See Your Turn Darling (1963)

Agenten Kennen Keine Tranen See The Uranium Conspiracy (1978)

The Agitators See The Fix (1984)

Agnes und Seine Bruder See Agnes and His Brothers (2004)

Agoniya See Rasputin (1985)

Agostino di Ippona See Augustine of Hippo (1972)

L'Agression See Act of Aggression (1973)

Aguirre, der Zorn Gottes See Aguirre, the Wrath of God (1972)

Ahava Colombianit See Colombian Love (2004)

Ahava Ilemeth See Secret of Yolanda (1982)

Ai-Fak See The Judgement (2004)

Ai No Corrida See In the Realm of the Senses (1976)

Aideista Parhain See Mother of Mine (2005)

Aime ton pere See A Loving Father (2002)

Aimez-Vous Brahms See Goodbye Again (1961)

Ain't No Way Back See No Way Back (1990)

Aiqing Wansui See Vive l'Amour (1994)

Airport '79 See The Concorde: Airport '79 (1979)

Akage See Red Lion (1969)

Akahige See Red Beard (1965)

Akarui mirai See Bright Future (2003)

Akasen Chitai See Street of Shame (1956)

Akira Kurosawa's The Quiet Duel See A Quiet Duel (1949)

Al DI La Della Legge See Beyond the Law (1968)

Al-Jenna-An See Paradise Now (2005)

Al-Massir See Destiny (1997)

Al-Ris-Alah See The Message (1977)

Ai 33 di Via Orologio fa Sempre Freddo See Shock (1979)

Alas de Mariposa See Butterfly Wings (1991)

Alem Da Paixao See Happily Ever After (1986)

Alfie Darling See Oh, Alfie (1975)

Ali Baba et les Quarante Voleurs See Ali Baba and the 40 Thieves (1954)

Alias Bulldog Drummond See Bulldog Jack (1935)

The Alibi See Lies & Alibis (2006)

Alice and Martin See Alice et Martin (1998)

Alicja See Alice (1986)

Alien 2 See Aliens (1986)

Alien P.I. See Alien Private Eye (1987)

The Alien Within See Unknown Origin (1995)

Alien Terror See The Sinister Invasion (1968)

Alien Women See Zeta One (1969)

Alien Zone See House of the Dead (1978)

Alien Thunder See Dan Candy's Law (1973)

Alien Within See Evil Spawn (1987)

The Alien's Return See The Return (1980)

Alistair MacLean's Death Train See Detonator (1993)

Alistair MacLean's Night Watch See Detonator 2: Night Watch (1995)

Alive by Night See Evil Spawn (1987)

All for Love See St. Ives (1998)

All for One See Return to Paradise (1998)

All Forgotten See Lover's Prayer (1999)

All Good Citizens See All My Good Countrymen (1968)

All That Money Can Buy See The Devil & Daniel Webster (1941)

All in Place and Time See All Screwed Up (1974)

All the Mornings of the World See Tous les Matins du Monde (1992)

All Monsters Attack See Destroy All Monsters (1968)

All the Rage See It's the Rage (1999)

All Night Long See Toute Une Nuit (1982)

All the Way See The Night We Called It a Day (2003)

All Our Fault See Nothing Personal (1995)

All This and Glamour Too See Vogues of 1938 (1937)

All Weekend Lovers See The Killing Game (1967)

Alla vi barn I Bullerby See The Children of Noisy Village (1986)

Aller-Simple Pour Manhattan See Petty Crimes (2002)

Alles Auf Zucker! See Go for Zucker (2005)

The Alley of Miracles See Midaq Alley (1995)

Alley of Nightmares See She-Freak (1967)

Alligators See The Great Alligator (1981)

Almok a hazrol See 25 Fireman's Street (1973)

Almost Human See Shock Waves (1977)

Alone See Horton Foote's Alone (1997)

Alone See Solas (1999)

Alone Together See Crisscross (1992)

Alphaville, a Strange Case of Lemmy Caution See Alphaville (1965)

Alphaville, Une Etrange Aventure de Lemmy Caution See Alphaville (1965)

Alter Ego See Murder by the Book (1987)

The Alternate See Agent of Death (1999)

The Alzheimer Affair See The Memory of a Killer (2003)

Amantes See Lovers: A True Story (1990)

Amanti d'Oltretomba See Nightmare Castle (1965)

Amarelo Manga See Mango Yellow (2002)

Amateur Hour See I Was a Teenage TV Terrorist (1987)

The Amateurs See The Moguls (2005)

Amator See Camera Buff (1979)

The Amazing Panda Rescue See The Amazing Panda Adventure (1995)

The Amazing Quest of Ernest Bliss See Amazing Adventure (1937)

Amazon: Savage Adventure See Cut and Run (1985)

Amazon Women See Gold of the Amazon Women (1979)

Amazonia: The Catherine Miles Story See White Slave (1986)

Ambush in Waco See In the Line of Duty: Ambush in Waco (1993)

Amelia and the King of Plants See Bed of Roses (1995)

Amelie from Montmartre See Amelie (2001)

American Beauty Hostages See She Devils in Chains (1976)

An American Daughter See Trial by Media (2000)

American Dragons See Double Edge (1997)

American Nightmares See Combat Shock (1984)

American Pie 3 See American Wedding (2003)

American Pie 5: The Naked Mile See American Pie Presents: The Naked Mile (2006)

American Raspberry See Prime Time (1977)

American Rickshaw See American Tiger (1989)

American Warrior See American Ninja (1985)

The American Way See Riders of the Storm (1988)

Amerikaner Shadkhn See American Matchmaker (1940)

L'Ami de Mon Ami See Boyfriends & Girlfriends (1988)

Amigo/Amado See Beloved/Friend (1999)

Amityville 3-D See Amityville 3: The Demon (1983)

The Amityville Horror: The Evil Escapes, Part 4 See Amityville 4: The Evil Escapes (1989)

Amok See Schizo (1977)

Amor Estranho Amor See Love Strange Love (1982)

Amor Perjudica Seriamente la Salud See Love Can Seriously Damage Your Health (1996)

Amore In Citta See Love in the City (1953)

Amores Passivels See Possible Loves (2000)

The Amorous General See Waltz of the Toreadors (1962)

The Amorous Sex See Sweet Beat (1959)

L'Amour a Mort See Love Unto Death (1984)

Amour de Poche See Girl in His Pocket (1957)

L'Amour l'Apres-midi See Chloe in the Afternoon (1972)

Amy Fisher: My Story See Lethal Lolita—Amy Fisher: My Story (1992)

Amy Foster See Swept from the Sea (1997)

Amy's Orgasm See Amy's O (2002)

Anacardium See Deranged (2001)

Anatomie See Anatomy (2000)

Anatomie de L'Enfer See Anatomy of Hell (2004)

And Comes the Dawn...But Colored Red See Web of the Spider (1970)

And Life Goes On ... See Life and Nothing More ... (1992)

And Once Upon a Love See Fantasies (1973)

And Then There Were None See Ten Little Indians (1975)

...And They Lived Happily Ever After See Happily Ever After (2004)

And Woman...Was Created See And God Created Woman (1957)

And Your Mother Too See Y Tu Mama Tambien (2001)

An Andalusian Dog See Un Chien Andalou (1928)

Anders Als du und Ich See The Third Sex (1957)

Anderson's Angels See Chesty Anderson USN (1976)

Andrews' Raiders See The Great Locomotive Chase (1956)

Andy Colby's Incredibly Awesome Adventure See Andy and the Airwave Rangers (1989)

Andy Warhol's Flesh See Flesh (1968)

Andy Warhol's Heat See Heat (1972)

An Angel Passed Over Brooklyn See The Man Who Wagged His Tail (1957)

Andy Warhol's Young Dracula See Andy Warhol's Dracula (1974)

Angel See Danny Boy (1982)

Angel in Red See Uncaged (1991)

Angel of Vengeance See Ms. 45 (1981)

Angel of Vengeance See WarCat (1988)

Angel Sharks See Marie Baie des Anges (1997)

Angel Street See Gaslight (1940)

Angelos See Angel (1982)

Angels for Kicks See Wild Riders (1971)

Angels in the Attic See The Robin Hood Gang (1998)

Anglagard See House of Angels (1992)

Angst Essen Selle auf See Ali: Fear Eats the Soul (1974)

Angst vor der Angst See Fear of Fear (1975)

Animal House See National Lampoon's Animal House (1978)

Anita—Tanze des Lasters See Anita, Dances of Vice (1987)

Anna: From Six Till Eighteen See Anna (1993)

Anna: Ot Shesti do Vosemnadtsati See Anna (1993)

Anne and Muriel See Two English Girls (1972)

Anne of Green Gables: The Sequel See Anne of Avonlea (1987)

Annie's Coming Out See A Test of Love (1984)

Anno Domini See A.D. (1985)

Anno Zero - Guerra Nello Spazio See War in Space (1977)

Anoche Sone Contigo See Dreaming About You (1992)

Ansikte mot Ansikte See Face to Face (1976)

The Anti-Extortion Woman See Minbo—Or the Gentle Art of Japanese Extortion (1992)

The Antichrist See The Tempter (1974)

L'Anticristo See The Tempter (1974)

Antikorper See Antibodies (2005)

Antinea, l'Amante Della Citta Sepolta See Journey Beneath the Desert (1961)

Anton der Zauberer See Anton, the Magician (1978)

The Anxious Years See Dark Journey (1937)

Any Special Way See Business is Business (1971)

Anyone for Venice? See The Honey Pot (1967)

Anything for Love See 11 Harrowhouse (1974)

Apa See Father (1967)

Apache Vengeance See The Desperados (1970)

The Apartment on the 13 Floor See Cannibal Man (1971)

Apocalipsis Canibal See Hell of the Living Dead (1983)

The Apprentices See Les Apprentis (1995)

L'Argent de Poche See Small Change (1976)

Apres l'Amour See Love After Love (1994)

Apres-Ski See Snowballin' (1971)

April One See Stand Off (1993)

Apu Sansat See The World of Apu (1959)

Apur Sansar See The World of Apu (1959)

The Aqua Sex See The Mermaids of Tiburon (1962)

Aranyer Din Ratri See Days and Nights in the Forest (1970)

Arctic Heat See Born American (1986)

L'Armee des Ombres See Army of Shadows (1969)

Are You Dying Young Man? See Beast in the Cellar (1970)

Armored Attack See The North Star (1943)

Armour of God See Operation Condor 2: The Armour of the Gods (1986)

Arms and the Woman See Mr. Winkle Goes to War (1944)

Army in the Shadows See Army of Shadows (1969)

Army Mystery See Criminals Within (1941)

The Arrangement See Blood Money (1998)

Arriva Dorellik See How to Kill 400 Duponts (1968)

Arizona Ripper See Terror at London Bridge (1985)

Artaud See My Life and Times with Antonin Artaud (1993)

Arthur et les Minimoys See Arthur and the Invisibles (2006)

Arthur the King See Merlin and the Sword (1985)

Artie Lange's Beer League See Beer League (2006)

Arven See The Inheritance (2003)

As Tres Marias See The 3 Marias (2003)

Ascenseur pour L'Echafaud See Frantic (1958)

Ascent to Heaven See Mexican Bus Ride (1951)

Ashani Sanket See Distant Thunder (1973)

Ashanti See Ashanti, Land of No Mercy (1979)

Asian Adam See Lion Man (1975)

Asphalt Zahov See Yellow Asphalt (2001)

The Assassination Team See Wardogs (1987)

Assault Force See flolkes (1980)

Assault on Devil's Island See Shadow Warriors (1997)

Assault on Paradise See Maniac (1977)

Assignment: Istanbul See The Castle of Fu Manchu (1971)

Assignment: Kill Castro See The Mercenaries (1980)

Assignment: Terror See Dracula vs. Frankenstein (1969)

Asylum of Insane See Flesh and Blood Show (1973)

Asylum Erotica See Slaughter Hotel (1971)

At First Sight See Entre-Nous (1983)

At First Sight See Love at First Sight (1976)

At Sachem Farm See Uncorked (1998)

At the Villa Rose See House of Mystery (1941)

Atame! See Tie Me Up! Tie Me Down! (1990)

Atenarjuat, the Fast Runner See The Fast Runner (2001)

Atlantic City U.S.A. See Atlantic City (1981)

The Atlantis Interceptors See Raiders of Atlantis (1983)

Atlas Against the Cyclops See Atlas in the Land of Cyclops (1961)

Atoll K See Utopia (1951)

Atomic Monster See Man Made Monster (1941)

Atomic Rocketship See Flash Gordon: Rocketship (1940)

Ator the Invincible See Blade Master (1984)

Atrapadas See Condemned to Hell (1984)

Attack of the 5 Ft. 2 Women See National Lampoon's Attack of the 5 Ft. 2 Women (1994)

Attack of the Giant Horny Gorilla See A*P*E* (1976)

Attack of the Killer Shrews See the Killer Shrews (1959)

Attack of the Monsters See Gamera vs. Guiron (1969)

Attack of the Normans See Conquest of the Normans (1962)

Attack of the Phantoms See KISS Meets the Phantom of the Park (1978)

Attack of the Rebel Girls See Assault of the Rebel Girls (1959)

Attention! Une Femme Peut en Cacher une Autre See My Other Husband (1985)

Au-Dela de la Peur See Beyond Fear (1975)

Au-Dela des Grilles See The Walls of Malapaga (1949)

L'Auberge Rouge See The Red Inn (1951)

Auf der Sonnenseite See On the Sunny Side (1962)

Auggie Rose See Beyond Suspicion (2000)

Aura See The Witch (1966)

Aurora by Night See Aurora (1984)

Austerlitz See The Battle of Austerlitz (1960)

Austria 1700 See Mark of the Devil (1969)

Autopsia de un Fantasma See Autopsy of a Ghost (1967)

Avazhaye Sarzamine Madariyam See Marooned in Iraq (2002)

The Avenger See Texas, Adios (1966)

The Avengers See The Day Will Dawn (1942)

Avenging Godfather See Avenging Disco Godfather (1976)

Aventis See If They Tell You I Fell (1989)

L'Aventure Sauvage See Trap (1966)

AvP See Alien vs. Predator (2004)

A.W.O.L. See Lionheart (1990)

An Axe for the Honeymoon See Hatchet for the Honeymoon (1970)

Ax en XX, Szzazadon See My Twentieth Century (1990)

Azulo Scuro Casi Negro See Dark Blue Almost Black (2006)

Azucar Amarga See Bitter Sugar (1996)

Ba Xian Fan Dian Zhi Ren Rou Cha Shao Bao See The Untold Story (1992)

Baby Blood See The Evil Within (1989)

Baby Cart 1: Lend a Child...Lend an Arm See Lone Wolf and Cub: Baby Cart at the River Styx (1972)

Baby Cart 2 See Lone Wolf and Cub: Baby Cart at the River Styx (1972)

Baby Cart to Hades See Lone Wolf and Cub: Baby Cart to Hades (1972)

The Baby Vanishes See Broadway Limited (1941)

Bachelor Girl Apartment See Any Wednesday (1966)

Bachelor Knight See The Bachelor and the Bobby-Soxer (1947)

Back to Even See The Debt (1998)

Backwoods Massacre See Midnight (1981)

Bad Blood See Mauvais Sang (1986)

Bad Boy See Dawg (2002)

Bad Boyz See Valley Girl (1983)

Bad Company See Mayalunta (1996)

Bad Genres See Transfixed (2001)

Bad Girl See Teenage Bad Girl (1959)

Bad Girls See Delinquent School Girls (1984)

Bad Girls See Whore 2 (1994)

Bad Karma See Hell's Gate (2001)

Bad Man of Harlem See Harlem on the Prairie (1938)

Bad Seed See Mauvaise Graine (1933)

Badkonake Sefid See The White Balloon (1995)

The Bailiff See Sansho the Bailiff (1954)

Baisers Voles See Stolen Kisses (1968)

The Baited Trap See The Trap (1959)

The Bait See L'Appat (1994)

Bakterion See Panic (1976)

Bakuto Gaijin Butai See Sympathy for the Underdog (1971)

Bakushu See Early Summer (1951)

The Ballad of Billie Blue See Jailbreakin' (1972)

Ballad of Django See Fistful of Death (1971)

Ballade o Soldate See Ballad of a Soldier (1960)

Balzac et la petite tailleuse Chinois See Balzac and the Little Chinese Seamstress (2002)

Bamboo Dolls House See The Big Doll House (1971)

The Banana Monster See Schlock (1973)

Band Camp See American Pie Presents Band Camp (2005)

Bande a Part See Band of Outsiders (1964)

Banditi a Orgosolo See Bandits of Orgosolo (1961)

Bang Bang See Bang Bang Kid (1967)

Bangiku See Late Chrysanthemums (1954)

Banjo Hackett: Roamin' Free See Banjo Hackett (1976)

The Bank Detective See The Bank Dick (1940)

The Bar Sinister See It's a Dog's Life (1955)

Banner in the Sky See Third Man on the Mountain (1959)

Banlieue 13 See District B13 (2004)

The Barbaric Beast of Boggy Creek, Part II See Boggy Creek II (1983)

The Barbarians and Co. See The Barbarians (1987)

The Bare Breasted Contessa See Female Vampire (1973)

Bargain Basement See Department Store (1935)

Baron Blood See Torture Chamber of Baron Blood (1972)

Baron Munchausen See Fabulous Adventures of Baron Munchausen (1961)

Baron Prasil See Fabulous Adventures of Baron Munchausen (1961)

Baron of Terror See The Brainiac (1961)

Barbados Quest See Murder on Approval (1956)

Barbarella, Queen of the Galaxy See Barbarella (1968)

Batalla En El Cielo See Battle in Heaven (2005)

Batman: The Animated Movie See Batman: Mask of the Phantasm (1993)

Batmen of Africa See Darkest Africa (1936)

The Battle for Anzio See Anzio (1968)

Battle of the Astros See Godzilla vs. Monster Zero (1968)

The Battle of the Mareth Line See Battleforce (1978)

The Battle of the River Plate See Pursuit of the Graf Spee (1957)

Battle of the Stars See War in Space (1977)

Battle Beyond the Stars See The Green Slime (1968)

Battle Stripe See The Men (1950)

Bettletruck See Warlords of the 21st Century (1982)

The Battling Bellhop See Kid Galahad (1937)

Battling Hoofer See Something to Sing About (1937)

Bawang Bie Ji See Farewell My Concubine (1993)

Bay of Blood See Twitch of the Death Nerve (1971)

The Bay of Saint Michel See Pattern for Plunder (1962)

Bayou See Poor White Trash (1957)

Be Beautiful and Shut Up See Sois Belle et Tais-Toi (1958)

Be Beautiful but Shut Up See Just Another Pretty Face (1958)

Be Beautiful but Shut Up See Sois Belle et Tais-Toi (1958)

Be My Valentine, Or Else... See Hospital Massacre (1981)

Be Rforingen See The Touch (1971)

A Beach Called Desire See Emmanuelle on Taboo Island (1976)

The Beans of Egypt, Maine See Forbidden Choices (1994)

The Beast See Equinox (1971)

The Beast in the Heart See Don't Tell (2005)

The Beast of War See The Beast (1988)

Beasts See Twilight People (1972)

The Beating of the Butterfly's Wings See Happenstance (2000)

Beatlemania See Beatlemania! The Movie (1981)

Beatsville See The Rebel Set (1959)

Beaumarchais L'insolent See Beaumarchais the Scoundrel (1996)

A Beautiful Place to Kill See Paranoia (1969)

The Beautiful Troublemaker See La Belle Noiseuse (1990)

Beautiful But Dangerous See She Couldn't Say No (1952)

Beautiful But Deadly See The Don Is Dead (1973)

Because He's My Friend See Love Under Pressure (1978)

Beethoven's Great Love See Beethoven (1936)

Before It Had a Name See The Black Widow (2005)

Beggars' Opera See The Threepenny Opera (1931)

The Beginners See The First Time (1969)

The Beginners Three See The First Time (1969)

Behind Enemy Lines See The P.O.W. Escape (1986)

Behind Locked Doors See Human Gorilla (1948)

Behind the Blue See L'Enfant d'Eau (1995)

Behind the Forbidden City See East Palace, West Palace (1996)

Behind the Iron Mask See The Fifth Musketeer (1979)

Bela Martha See Mostly Martha (2001)

Believe Me See Hollow Reed (1995)

The Beloved See Restless (1972)

Belleville Rendez-Vous See The Triplets of Belleville (2002)

Bells See Murder by Phone (1982)

Below Utopia See Body Count (1997)

Berlinguer Ti Voglio Bene See Berlinguer I Love You (1977)

Berry Gordy's The Last Dragon See The Last Dragon (1985)

The Best Way to Walk See The Best Way (1976)

Beta House See American Pie Presents: Beta House (2007)

Bethune See Dr. Bethune (1990)

Bethune, The Making of a Hero See Dr. Bethune (1990)

Betrayal See Lady Jayne Killer (2003)

Betrayal See Trahir (1993)

Betty Fisher and Other Stories See Alias Betty (2001)

Betty Fisher et Autres Histoires See Alias Betty (2001)

Between Us See Entre-Nous (1983)

Betzilo Shel Helem Krav See Shell Shock (1963)

Beverly Hills Nightmare See Housewife (1972)

Bewitching Scatterbrain *See* Ravishing Idiot (1964)

Beyond Bedlam *See* Nightscare (1993)

Beyond Control *See* The Amy Fisher Story (1993)

Beyond Justice *See* Guardian Angel (1994)

Beyond Obsession *See* Beyond the Door (1975)

Beyond the City Limits *See* Rip It Off (2002)

Beyond the Door 2 *See* Shock (1979)

Beyond the Fog *See* Tower of Evil (1972)

Beyond the Gates *See* Shooting Dogs (2005)

Beyond the Living *See* Hospital of Terror (1978)

Beyond the Living Dead *See* The Hanging Woman (1972)

Beyond the Rising Moon *See* Star Quest (1989)

Bez Konca *See* No End (1984)

Bez Znieczulenia *See* Without Anesthesia (1978)

Blandan, Guniang *See* So Close to Paradise (1998)

The Big Bang Theory *See* Big Bang (1995)

The Big Bankroll *See* The King of the Roaring 20s: The Story of Arnold Rothstein (1961)

The Big Boss *See* Fists of Fury (1973)

The Big Boss *See* Rulers of the City (1976)

The Big Carnival *See* Ace in the Hole (1951)

The Big Dance *See* DC 9/11: Time of Crisis (2004)

The Big Day *See* Jour de Fete (1948)

Big Deal at Dodge City *See* A Big Hand for the Little Lady (1966)

Big Duel in the North *See* Godzilla vs. the Sea Monster (1966)

Big Enough and Old Enough *See* Savages from Hell (1968)

The Big Escape *See* Eagles Attack at Dawn (1970)

The Big Grab *See* Any Number Can Win (1963)

The Big Heart *See* Miracle on 34th Street (1947)

The Big Lobby *See* Rosebud Beach Hotel (1985)

Big Monster on Campus *See* Boltneck (1998)

The Big One: The Great Los Angeles Earthquake *See* The Great Los Angeles Earthquake (1991)

The Big Payoff *See* Win, Place, or Steal (1972)

The Big Search *See* East of Kilimanjaro (1957)

Big Time Operators *See* The Smallest Show on Earth (1957)

Big Town Scandal *See* Underworld Scandal (1947)

Billy the Kid in Texas *See* Battling Outlaw (1940)

Billy the Kid's Fighting Pals *See* Trigger Men (1941)

Bijo to Ekitainigen *See* H-Man (1959)

Bikini Genie *See* Wildest Dreams (1990)

Bikur Ha-Tizmoret *See* The Band's Visit (2007)

Billy the Kid's Law and Order *See* Law and Order (1942)

Billy the Kid's Range War *See* Texas Trouble (1941)

Bio-Force I *See* Mutant Species (1995)

The Bird with the Glass Feathers *See* The Bird with the Crystal Plumage (1970)

Birds of a Feather *See* The Birdcage (1995)

Birds of a Feather *See* La Cage aux Folles (1978)

Birds of Prey *See* Beaks: The Movie (1987)

Birthmark *See* The Omen (1976)

Birumano Tategoto *See* The Burmese Harp (1956)

Bis ans Ende der Welt *See* Until the End of the World (1991)

The Bitch *See* La Chienne (1931)

The Bitter End *See* Love Walked In (1997)

Bitter Harvest *See* How Harry Became a Tree (2001)

Bittere Ernte *See* Angry Harvest (1985)

Black Angels *See* Black Bikers from Hell (1970)

Black Arrow Strikes *See* Black Arrow (1948)

The Black Book *See* Reign of Terror (1949)

The Black Bounty Hunter *See* Boss (1974)

The Black Bounty Killer *See* Boss (1974)

The Black Buccaneer *See* The Black Pirate (1926)

Black Christmas *See* Black Sabbath (1964)

Black Dragon *See* Miracles (1989)

Black Eliminator *See* Kill Factor (1978)

Black Emmanuelle *See* Emmanuelle, the Queen (1979)

Black Emmanuelle, White Emmanuelle *See* Naked Paradise (1978)

Black Evil *See* Ganja and Hess (1973)

Black Fist *See* Fist (1976)

Black Flowers for the Bride *See* Something for Everyone (1970)

Black Forest: Rage in Space *See* Hyper Space (1989)

Black Frankenstein *See* Blackenstein (1973)

Black Gauntlet *See* Black Starlet (1974)

Black Jack *See* Captain Blackjack (1951)

Black Jesus *See* Super Brother (1968)

Black Kingpin *See* Hit Men (1973)

Black Love, White Love *See* Sweet Love, Bitter (1967)

Black Out *See* Midnight Heat (1995)

Black Out: The Moment of Terror *See* Ganja and Hess (1973)

The Black Streetfighter *See* Fist (1976)

Black Valor *See* Savage! (1973)

Black Vampire *See* Ganja and Hess (1973)

Black Velvet *See* Naked Paradise (1978)

The Black Velvet Gown *See* Catherine Cookson's The Black Velvet Gown (1992)

Black Vengeance *See* Poor Pretty Eddie (1973)

Black Werewolf *See* The Beast Must Die (1975)

Blackboard Massacre *See* Massacre at Central High (1976)

Blackout *See* Contraband (1940)

Blackout in Rome *See* Era Notte a Roma (1960)

Blade of Steel *See* The Far Pavilions (1984)

Blair Witch 2 *See* Book of Shadows: Blair Witch 2 (2000)

Blake Edwards' Son of the Pink Panther *See* Son of the Pink Panther (1993)

Blast-Off *See* Those Fantastic Flying Fools (1967)

Blazing Arrows *See* Fighting Caravans (1931)

Blazing Magnums *See* Strange Shadows in an Empty Room (1976)

Bless 'Em All *See* The Act (1982)

Blikende Lygter *See* Flickering Lights (2001)

Blind Alley *See* Perfect Strangers (1984)

The Blind Dead *See* Tombs of the Blind Dead (1972)

Blind Fairies *See* His Secret Life (2001)

Blind Man's Bluff *See* Cauldron of Blood (1967)

The Blind Swordsman: Zatoichi *See* Zatoichi (2003)

Blind Terror *See* See No Evil (1971)

Blink of an Eye *See* Blink of an Eye (1992)

BI..m *See* Bloom (2003)

Blonde Bombshell *See* Bombshell (1933)

Blonde for Danger *See* Sois Belle et Tais-Toi (1958)

The Blonde From Peking *See* The Peking Blond (1968)

A Blonde in Love *See* Loves of a Blonde (1965)

Blondie Has Servant Trouble *See* Blondie Has Trouble (1940)

Blood and Bullets *See* Rulers of the City (1976)

Blood and Sand *See* Sand and Blood (1987)

The Blood Baron *See* Torture Chamber of Baron Blood (1972)

Blood Bath *See* Track of the Vampire (1966)

Blood Beast from Outer Space *See* Night Caller from Outer Space (1966)

Blood Brides *See* Hatchet for the Honeymoon (1970)

The Blood Brother *See* Texas Pioneers (1932)

The Blood Cult of Shangri-La *See* The Thirsty Dead (1974)

Blood Demon *See* The Torture Chamber of Dr. Sadism (1969)

Blood Castle *See* The Blood Spattered Bride (1972)

Blood Ceremony *See* The Legend of Blood Castle (1972)

Blood Couple *See* Ganja and Hess (1973)

Blood Creature *See* Terror Is a Man (1959)

The Blood Crowd *See* The McMasters (1970)

Blood Doctor *See* Mad Doctor of Blood Island (1968)

The Blood Drinkers *See* The Vampire People (1966)

Blood Evil *See* Demons of the Mind (1972)

Blood Feast *See* Night of a Thousand Cats (1972)

Blood Fiend *See* Theatre of Death (1967)

Blood for Dracula *See* Andy Warhol's Dracula (1974)

Blood Freaks *See* Blood Freak (1972)

Blood Hunger *See* Vampyres (1974)

Blood Hunt *See* The Thirsty Dead (1974)

Blood Is My Heritage *See* Blood of Dracula (1957)

Blood Mad *See* The Glove (1978)

Blood Money *See* The Killer's Edge (1990)

Blood Money *See* Requiem for a Heavyweight (1962)

Blood Money *See* Under Oath (1997)

Blood Moon *See* The Werewolf vs. the Vampire Woman (1970)

Blood Oath *See* Prisoners of the Sun (1991)

Blood of Frankenstein *See* Dracula vs. Frankenstein (1971)

Blood of Fu Manchu *See* Kiss and Kill (1968)

Blood of the Demon *See* Blood of Dracula (1957)

Blood of the Man Devil *See* House of the Black Death (1965)

Blood of the Undead *See* Schizo (1977)

Blood on His Lips *See* Hideous Sun Demon (1959)

Blood Orange *See* Three Stops to Murder (1953)

Blood Orgy *See* The Gore-Gore Girls (1972)

The Blood Seekers *See* Cain's Cutthroats (1971)

Blood Song *See* Haunted Symphony (1994)

Blood Splash *See* Nightmare (1982)

The Blood Suckers *See* Alien Massacre (1967)

The Blood Suckers *See* Dr. Terror's House of Horrors (1965)

Blood Thirst *See* Salem's Lot (1979)

Blood Waters of Dr. Z *See* Attack of the Swamp Creature (1975)

Blood Will Have Blood *See* Demons of the Mind (1972)

Bloodline *See* Hush (1998)

Bloodline *See* Sidney Sheldon's Bloodline (1979)

Bloodrage *See* Never Pick Up a Stranger (1979)

Bloodsilver *See* Beyond the Law (1968)

Bloodsucking Nazi Zombies *See* Oasis of the Zombies (1982)

The Bloody Bushido Blade *See* The Bushido Blade (1980)

Bloody Fiance *See* The Blood Spattered Bride (1972)

Bloody Pom Poms *See* Cheerleader Camp (1988)

The Bloody Scream of Dracula *See* Dracula, Prince of Darkness (1966)

Bloody Weekend *See* Loaded (1994)

Bloomfield *See* The Hero (1971)

The Blow-Out *See* La Grande Bouffe (1973)

Blue Jean Cop *See* Shakedown (1988)

Blue Manhattan *See* Hi, Mom! (1970)

Blue *See* Trois Couleurs: Bleu (1993)

Blue and the Gold *See* An Annapolis Story (1955)

Blue Beach *See* Beach Hotel (1992)

Blue Eyes of the Broken Doll *See* House of Psychotic Women (1973)

Blue Heat *See* The Last of the Finest (1990)

Blue Sierra *See* Courage of Lassie (1946)

Blue Vision *See* In Dreams (1998)

Blues for Lovers *See* Ballad in Blue (1966)

Blues La-Chofesh Ha-Godol *See* Late Summer Blues (1987)

Bluff Storia di Truffe e di Imbroglioni *See* The Switch (1976)

Blut an den Lippen *See* Daughters of Darkness (1971)

The Boat *See* Das Boot (1981)

Bob the Gambler See Bob le Flambeur (1995)

Boca a Boca See Mouth to Mouth (1995)

Bodas de Sangre See Blood Wedding (1981)

Bodies Bear Traces of Carnal Violence See Torso (1973)

Body Parts See Harold Robbins' Body Parts (1999)

The Body Stealers See Invasion of the Body Stealers (1969)

The Bodyguards See La Scorta (1994)

Bogus Bandits See The Devil's Brother (1933)

Bohemian Life See La Vie de Boheme (1992)

A Bold Affair See Interlocked (1998)

The Bold Cavalier See The Bold Caballero (1936)

Bolero: An Adventure in Ecstasy See Bolero (1984)

Bolt See Rebel Run (1994)

Bombsight Stolen See Cottage to Let (1941)

Bone See Housewife (1972)

Bookworm See The Edge (1997)

Bor Lei Jun See Gorgeous (1999)

Bordello of Blood See Tales from the Crypt Presents Bordello of Blood (1996)

Border Heat See Deadly Stranger (1988)

Born Natturunnar See Children of Nature (1991)

Born to Kill See Cockfighter (1974)

Born to the West See Helltown (1938)

Bosambo See Sanders of the River (1935)

Boss Nigger See Boss (1974)

Boudu Sauve des Eaux See Boudu Saved from Drowning (1932)

Bourbon St. Shadows See The Invisible Avenger (1958)

Bowfinger's Big Thing See Bowfinger (1999)

The Boxer See Blade Boxer (1997)

The Boxer See Counter Punch (1971)

The Boy in the Golden Kimono See Karate Warrior (1968)

The Boy Who Had Everything See Winner Takes All (1984)

The Boyfriend School See Don't Tell Her It's Me (1990)

Boylchi and the Supermonster See Gamera vs. Gaos (1967)

The Boynton Beach Bereavement Club See The Boynton Beach Club (2005)

The Boys From Brooklyn See Bela Lugosi Meets a Brooklyn Gorilla (1952)

The Boys From County Clare See The Boys and Girl From County Clare (2003)

Brain Damage See Brain of Blood (1971)

The Brain Machine See Mind Warp (1972)

The Brain of Frankenstein See Abbott and Costello Meet Frankenstein (1948)

Braindead See Dead Alive (1993)

The Brainsnatchers See The Man Who Lived Again (1936)

Brainwash See Circle of Power (1983)

Bram Stoker's Burial of the Rats See Burial of the Rats (1995)

Bram Stoker's Count Dracula See Count Dracula (1971)

Bram Stoker's Dracula See Dracula (1973)

Branded See Bad Boy (1939)

Brandy Ashore See Green Grow the Rushes (1951)

Brat See Brother (1997)

The Brave and the Beautiful See Up the Academy (1980)

The Brave Young Men of Weinberg See Family of Cops 2: Breach of Faith (1997)

Breach of Faith: A Family of Cops 2 See Family of Cops 2: Breach of Faith (1997)

Break In See Loophole (1983)

Breakdance See Breakin' (1984)

Breakdance 2: Electric Boogaloo See Breakin' 2: Electric Boogaloo (1984)

The Breakup See La Rupture (1970)

Brenn, Hexe, Brenn See Mark of the Devil (1969)

Brennendes Geheimnis See Burning Secret (1989)

Briar Patch See Plain Dirty (2004)

Bride of Fengriffen See And Now the Screaming Starts (1973)

Bride of the Atom See Bride of the Monster (1955)

Brides of Blood See Brides of the Beast (1968)

Bridge Across Time See Terror at London Bridge (1985)

The Bride of the Lake See Lily of Killarney (1934)

Brodre See Brothers (2005)

Broken April See Behind the Sun (2001)

Broken Hearts and Noses See Crimewave (1985)

Broken Lizard's Club Dread See Club Dread (2004)

Broken Lizard's Super Troopers See Super Troopers (2001)

Bronenosets Potemkin See The Battleship Potemkin (1925)

Bronx Warriors See 1990: The Bronx Warriors (1983)

Brooklyn Love Story See Who Shot Pat? (1992)

Brothel 8 See Sandakan No. 8 (1974)

Brotherhood of the Yakuza See The Yakuza (1975)

Bruce Brown's The Endless Summer See The Endless Summer (1994)

Bruce Brown's The Endless Summer 2 See The Endless Summer 2 (1994)

Bruce Lee's Game of Death See Game of Death (1979)

Bruno See The Dress Code (1999)

The Brute See El Bruto (1952)

Brutti, Sporchi, e Cattivi See Down & Dirty (1976)

Bu san See Goodbye, Dragon Inn (2003)

Buck Rogers See Destination Saturn (1939)

Buckaroo Banzai See The Adventures of Buckaroo Banzai Across the Eighth Dimension (1984)

Bud Abbott and Lou Costello in Hollywood See Abbott and Costello in Hollywood (1945)

Budbringeren See Junk Mail (1997)

Budding Love See L'Amour en Herbe (1977)

The Buddy Factor See Swimming with Sharks (1994)

The Bug See The Bug (1975)

Build a Fort Set it on Fire See Basquiat (1996)

Build My Gallows High See Out of the Past (1947)

A Bullet from God See God's Gun (1975)

Bullfighter See Torero (1956)

Bump in the Night See The Final Terror (1983)

Bunman See The Untold Story (1993)

The Bunny Caper See Games Girls Play (1975)

Buon Funerale, Amigos! See Gunslinger (1970)

The Burden of Proof See Scott Turow's The Burden of Proof (1992)

Bure Baruta See Cabaret Balkan (1998)

Buried on Sunday See Northern Extremes (1993)

Burn, Hollywood, Burn See An Alan Smithee Film: Burn, Hollywood, Burn (1997)

Burn Out See Journey into Fear (1974)

Burn, Witch, Burn See Mark of the Devil (1969)

Burning Cross See The Klansman (1974)

Burning Hearts See Kolberg (1945)

The Burning Man See Dangerous Summer (1982)

The Burning Question See Reefer Madness (1938)

The Bus is Coming See Ghetto Revenge (1971)

Bush Christmas See Prince and the Great Race (1983)

Bushwhacked See French Twist (1995)

Bustin' Bonaparte: The Story of an African Farm See The Story of an African Farm (2004)

The Butcher See Le Boucher (1969)

The Butcher See Psycho from Texas (1981)

Butcher Baker (Nightmare Maker) See Night Warning (1982)

The Butterfly Affair See Queen of Diamonds (1970)

Butterfly on a Wheel See Shattered (2007)

The Butterfly Revolution See Summer Camp Nightmare (1986)

Butterfly's Tongue See Butterfly (1998)

Bvongiorno, Elefante See Pardon My Trunk (1952)

By Hook or By Crook See I Dood It (1943)

By Rocket to the Moon See Woman in the Moon (1929)

Ca Va Barder See There Goes Barder (1954)

Caballos Salvajes See Wild Horses (1995)

Cabiria See Nights of Cabiria (1957)

Caccia Al Violenti See One Step to Hell (1967)

Caccia alla Volpe See After the Fox (1966)

Caceria See Manhunt (2001)

Cache See Hidden (2005)

Cactus Jack See The Villain (1979)

Cafe of the Seven Sinners See Seven Sinners (1940)

The Cage See My Sister, My Love (1978)

Caged Females See Caged Heat (1974)

Caged Heart See L'Addition (1985)

Cain's Way See Cain's Cutthroats (1971)

Calhoun See Nightstick (1987)

California Axe Massacre See Axe (1974)

The California Dolls See ...All the Marbles (1981)

California Holiday See Spinout (1966)

California Hot Wax See The Bikini Car Wash Company (1990)

California in 1878 See Fighting Thru (1930)

California Man See Encino Man (1992)

The Californian See The Gentleman from California (1937)

Call Harry Crown See 99 & 44/100 Dead (1974)

Call It Love See She's So Lovely (1997)

Call It Murder See Midnight (1934)

The Call of the Savage See Savage Fury (1935)

The Call of the Wild: Dog of the Yukon See Jack London's The Call of the Wild (1997)

The Call the Cops See Find the Lady (1976)

The Calling See Murder by Phone (1982)

Calling Northside 777 See Call Northside 777 (1948)

Campanadas a Medianoche See Chimes at Midnight (1967)

Camper John See Gentle Savage (1973)

Campsite Massacre See The Final Terror (1983)

Cana Adentro See Live-in Maid (2004)

A Candle for the Devil See It Happened at Nightmare Inn (1970)

Canicule See Dog Day (1983)

Cannibal Orgy, or the Maddest Story Ever Told See Spider Baby (1964)

Cannibals in the City See Cannibal Apocalypse (1980)

Cannibals in the Streets See Cannibal Apocalypse (1980)

The Cannibal's Daughter See Lucia, Lucia (2003)

Can't Be Heaven See Forever Together (2000)

Capitaine Morgan See Morgan the Pirate (1960)

Capitalismo Salvaje See Savage Capitalism (1993)

Captain Conan See Capitaine Conan (1996)

Captain Mephisto and the Transformation Machine See Manhunt of Mystery Island (1945)

Captain Midnight See On the Air Live with Captain Midnight (1979)

Captain Yankee See Jungle Raiders (1985)

Captive See Sex and the Other Man (1995)

Captive Women 3: Sweet Sugar See Sweet Sugar (1972)

Captured See Agent Red (2000)

The Car See El Carro (2004)

Caravan See Himalaya (1999)

Caravans West See Wagon Wheels (1934)

Cardigan's Last Case See State's Attorney (1931)

Care of the Spitfire Grill See The Spitfire Grill (1995)

A Caribbean Mystery See Agatha Christie's A Caribbean Mystery (1983)

Caricies See Caresses (1997)

Carlo Collodi's Pinocchio See The Adventures of Pinocchio (1996)

Carnage See Twitch of the Death Nerve (1971)

Carne per Frankenstein See Andy Warhol's Frankenstein (1974)

Carne Tremula See Live Flesh (1997)

Carnival of Fools See Death Wish Club (1983)

Carnival of Thieves See Caper of the Golden Bulls (1967)

Carquake See Cannonball (1976)

Carrie 2 See The Rage: Carrie 2 (1999)

Carry On Follow That Camel See Follow That Camel (1967)

Carry On 'Round the Bend See Carry On at Your Convenience (1971)

The Cars That Eat People See The Cars That Ate Paris (1974)

Cartagine in Flamme See Carthage in Flames (1960)

Cartas del Parque *See* Letters from the Park (1988)

Carter's Army *See* Black Brigade (1969)

Cartes sur Table *See* Attack of the Robots (1966)

Carthage en Flammes *See* Carthage in Flames (1960)

Casa de Areia *See* House of Sand (2005)

Casa Privata per le SS *See* SS Girls (1977)

Casanova Falling *See* Giving It Up (1999)

Case of Evil *See* Sherlock: Case of Evil (2002)

The Case of Jonathan Drew *See* The Lodger (1926)

The Case of the Hillside Stranglers *See* The Hillside Strangler (1989)

Case of the Missing Switchboard Operator *See* The Love Affair, or The Case of the Missing Switchboard Operator (1967)

Cash *See* If I Were Rich (1933)

Cash Crop *See* Harvest (1998)

Cassanova and Co. *See* Sex on the Run (1978)

Castle in the Sky *See* Yidl Mitn Fidl (1936)

Castle of Doom *See* Vampyr (1931)

Castle of Dracula *See* Blood of Dracula's Castle (1969)

Castle of Terror *See* Castle of Blood (1964)

Castle of Terror *See* The Virgin of Nuremberg (1965)

The Castle of the Spider's Web *See* Throne of Blood (1957)

Castle of the Walking Dead *See* The Torture Chamber of Dr. Sadism (1969)

The Cat *See* Le Chat (1975)

The Cat Ate the Parakeet *See* Pot, Parents, and Police (1971)

The Cat in the Hat *See* Dr. Seuss' The Cat in the Hat (2003)

A Cause d'un Garcon *See* You'll Get Over It (2002)

Cause Toujours, Mon Lapin *See* Keep Talking Baby (1961)

Cavalleria Commandos *See* Cavalry Command (1963)

The Cave Dwellers *See* One Million B.C. (1940)

Cave Man *See* One Million B.C. (1940)

Cavegirl *See* Cave Girl (1985)

Cell Block Girls *See* Women's Prison Escape (1974)

Celos *See* Jealousy (1999)

Cemetery Girls *See* The Vampire Hookers (1978)

Cemetery Girls *See* The Velvet Vampire (1971)

Cento Dollari D'Odio *See* Uncle Tom's Cabin (1969)

Central Do Brasil *See* Central Station (1998)

Ceremonia Sangrienta *See* The Legend of Blood Castle (1972)

Cerny Petr *See* Black Peter (1963)

A Certain Mr. Scratch *See* The Devil & Daniel Webster (1941)

Ces Dames Preferent le Mambo *See* Dishonorable Discharge (1957)

C'est Arrive pres de Chez Vous *See* Man Bites Dog (1991)

Cet Obscur Objet du Desir *See* That Obscure Object of Desire (1977)

Ceux Qui M'Aiment Predront le Train *See* Those Who Love Me Can Take the Train (1998)

Chacun Cherche Son Chat *See* When the Cat's Away (1996)

Chacun sa Nuit *See* One to Another (2006)

Chained Heat 3 *See* Chained Heat 3: Hell Mountain (1998)

Chained Heat 3: The Horror of Hell Mountain *See* Chained Heat 3: Hell Mountain (1998)

Chaingang Girls *See* Sweet Sugar (1972)

Challapin: Adventures of Don Quixote *See* Don Quixote (1935)

The Challenge *See* It Takes a Thief (1959)

The Challenge of Rin Tin Tin *See* Courage of Rin Tin Tin (1957)

Chamber of Fear *See* The Fear Chamber (1968)

Chamber of Tortures *See* Torture Chamber of Baron Blood (1972)

The Chambermaid *See* The Chambermaid on the Titanic (1997)

Champ d'Honneur *See* Field of Honor (1987)

Changes *See* Danielle Steel's Changes (1991)

Chaos *See* Kaos (1985)

Charades *See* First Degree (1998)

Charles: Mort ou Vif *See* Charles: Dead or Alive (1969)

Charlie's Ghost Story *See* Charlie's Ghost: The Secret of Coronado (1994)

Charterhouse at Parma *See* La Chartreuse de Parme (1948)

Chastnaya Zhizn *See* Private Life (1982)

The Chautauqua *See* The Trouble with Girls (and How to Get into It) (1969)

Che? *See* Diary of Forbidden Dreams (1973)

Cheaters *See* Tricheurs (1984)

Cheeseburger Film Sandwich *See* Amazon Women on the Moon (1987)

Chelovek s Kinoapparatom *See* The Man with the Movie Camera (1929)

Chernobyl: The Final Warning *See* Final Warning (1990)

Cherry Pink *See* Just Looking (1999)

Cheun Gwong Tsa Sit *See* Happy Together (1996)

Cheung Fo *See* The Mission (1999)

Chevy Van *See* The Van (1977)

Chi l'Ha Vista Morire *See* Who Saw Her Die? (1972)

Chi Sel *See* Beyond the Door (1975)

The Chief Wants No Survivors *See* No Survivors, Please (1963)

Chikamatsu Monogatari *See* The Crucified Lovers (1954)

Chikto Gouyeung *See* Naked Killer (1992)

Chikyu Boelgun *See* The Mysterians (1958)

Child of Satan *See* To the Devil, a Daughter (1976)

Child of the Night *See* What the Peeper Saw (1972)

Childhood of Maxim Gorky *See* My Childhood (1938)

Childish Things *See* Confessions of Tom Harris (1972)

The Children of Bullerby Village *See* The Children of Noisy Village (1986)

Children of the Dust *See* A Good Day to Die (1995)

Child's Play *See* Love Me If You Dare (2003)

Chin gel bin *See* Vampire Effect (2003)

China 9, Liberty 37 *See* Gunfire (1978)

China Ranch *See* Shell Shock (1963)

Chinchero *See* The Last Movie (1971)

Chine, Ma Douleur *See* China, My Sorrow (1989)

Chocolate for Breakfast *See* Four and a Half Women (2005)

Chongqing Senlin *See* Chungking Express (1995)

A Christmas Memory *See* ABC Stage 67: Truman Capote's A Christmas Memory (1966)

Christmas Miracle in Caulfield, U.S.A. *See* The Christmas Coal Mine Miracle (1977)

Christmas Mountains *See* Story of a Cowboy Angel (1981)

The Christmas Tree *See* When Wolves Cry (1969)

Christmas Vacation *See* National Lampoon's Christmas Vacation (1989)

Christmas Vacation 2: Cousin Eddie *See* National Lampoon's Christmas Vacation 2: Cousin Eddie's Big Island Adventure (2003)

Christmas Vacation 2: Cousin Eddie's Island Adventure *See* National Lampoon's Christmas Vacation 2: Cousin Eddie's Big Island Adventure (2003)

A Christmas Wish *See* The Great Rupert (1950)

Chrome Hearts *See* C.C. & Company (1970)

Chronicle of a Lonely Child *See* Chronicle of a Boy Alone (1964)

Chronos *See* Cronos (1994)

Chuck Norris vs. the Karate Cop *See* Slaughter in San Francisco (1981)

Chul Ma Lau *See* Drunken Monkey (2002)

Chungon Sattuk Linggel *See* Organized Crime & Triad Bureau (1993)

Chupacabra: Dark Seas *See* Chupacabra Terror (2005)

Ciao! Manhattan *See* Edie in Ciao! Manhattan (1972)

Cica Tomina Koliba *See* Uncle Tom's Cabin (1969)

Cidade de Deus *See* City of God (2002)

Cidade des Homens *See* City of Men (2007)

The Cinder Path *See* Catherine Cookson's The Cinder Path (1994)

Cinq fois deux *See* 5x2 (2004)

Cipolla Colt *See* Spaghetti Western (1975)

The Circle *See* The Fraternity (2001)

The Circle *See* The Vicious Circle (1957)

The Circle *See* Woman in Brown (1948)

Circuit Breaker *See* Inhumanoid (1996)

Circuitry Man 2 *See* Plughead Rewired: Circuitry Man 2 (1994)

The Cisco Kid in Old New Mexico *See* In Old New Mexico (1945)

Citadel of Crime *See* Wheel of Fortune (1941)

The Citizen Rebels *See* Street Law (1974)

Citizen's Band *See* FM (1978)

City in Fear *See* A Place Called Today (1972)

The City Jungle *See* The Young Philadelphians (1959)

The City of the Dead *See* Horror Hotel (1960)

City of the Living Dead *See* Gates of Hell (1980)

Ciudad de M *See* City of M (2001)

Civility *See* Malicious Intent (1999)

The Clairvoyant *See* The Evil Mind (1934)

The Clairvoyant *See* Killing Hour (1984)

The Clansman *See* The Birth of a Nation (1915)

Class of '86 *See* National Lampoon's Class of '86 (1986)

Class Reunion *See* National Lampoon's Class Reunion (1982)

Claude *See* The Two of Us (1968)

Claude et Greta *See* Her and She and Him (1969)

Claudine's Return *See* Kiss of Fire (1998)

Claustrophobia *See* Serial Slayer (2003)

Clean Slate *See* Coup de Torchon (1981)

The Cleaner *See* The Professional (1994)

Cleo de 5 a 7 *See* Cleo from 5 to 7 (1961)

Clickety Clickety *See* Dodes 'ka-den (1970)

Clinton & Nadine *See* Blood Money: The Story of Clinton and Nadine (1988)

Clive Barker's Lord of Illusions *See* Lord of Illusions (1995)

The Cloak *See* The Overcoat (1959)

The Closer You Get *See* American Women (2000)

The Closest of Kin *See* All the Lovin' Kinfolk (1970)

Club Dead *See* Terror at Red Wolf Inn (1972)

Clubland *See* Introducing the Dwights (2007)

Coast of Terror *See* Summer City (1977)

Coastwatcher *See* The Last Warrior (1989)

Cobra Nero *See* The Black Cobra (1987)

Cobweb Castle *See* Throne of Blood (1957)

Cockles and Muscles *See* Cote d'Azur (2005)

Cocozza's Way *See* Strictly Sinatra (2001)

Code Inconnu: Recit Incomplet De Divers Voyages *See* Code Unknown (2000)

Code Name: Operation Crossbow *See* Operation Crossbow (1965)

Code Name: Trixie *See* The Crazies (1973)

Code Name: Wolverine *See* Wolverine (1996)

Code 645 *See* G-Men Never Forget (1948)

Code Unknown: Incomplete Tales of Several Journeys *See* Code Unknown (2000)

Codename: The Soldier *See* The Soldier (1982)

Coeurs *See* Private Fears in Public Places (2006)

Coffin of Terror *See* Castle of Blood (1964)

Cold Night Into Dawn *See* Bomb Squad (1997)

Colin Nuttley's House of Angels *See* House of Angels (1992)

Collision Course *See* The Bamboo Saucer (1968)

Colonel Blimp *See* The Life and Death of Colonel Blimp (1943)

Colorado Ranger See Guns of Justice (1950)

Colossus and the Amazons See Colossus and the Amazon Queen (1964)

Colour Blind See Catherine Cookson's Colour Blind (1998)

Combien Tu M'Aimes? See How Much Do You Love Me? (2005)

Come Back to Me See Doll Face (1946)

Come Dance with Me See Voulez-Vous Danser avec Moi? (1959)

Come 'n' Get It See Lunch Wagon (1981)

Come On Ranger See Come on Rangers (1938)

A Comedia de Deus See God's Comedy (1995)

Comedie de L'Innocence See Comedy of Innocence (2000)

Comizi d'Amore See Love Meetings (1964)

Comme un Frere See Like a Brother (2005)

Comme un Poisson Hors de l'Eau See Like a Fish Out of Water (1999)

Comme une image See Look at Me (2004)

Comment J'ai Tue Mon Pere See How I Killed My Father (2003)

Comment le Desir Vient aux Filles See I Am Frigid... Why? (1972)

Communion See Alice Sweet Alice (1973)

Como Agua para Chocolate See Like Water for Chocolate (1993)

Como Era Gostoso O Meu Frances See How Tasty Was My Little Frenchman (1971)

Como ser Mujer y No Morir en El See How to Be a Woman and Not Die in the Attempt (1991)

Compagna di Viaggio See Traveling Companion (1996)

The Company of Strangers See Strangers in Good Company (1991)

Complicity See Retribution (1998)

Computer Killers See Horror Hospital (1973)

The Con Man See The Con Artists (1980)

Con Man See Freelance (1971)

Concerto See I've Always Loved You (1946)

Concierto a la Laura See Confessing to Laura (1990)

Concendados a Vivir See Bronson's Revenge (1972)

A Condemned Man Has Escaped See A Man Escaped (1957)

Comradeship See Kameradschaft (1931)

Comrades See The Organizer (1964)

The Confession See Quick, Let's Get Married (1971)

Confession See Repentance (1987)

Confidential Report See Mr. Arkadin (1955)

Conflagration See Enjo (1958)

The Conflict See Catholics (1973)

Confessions of A Peeping John See Hi, Mom! (1970)

Confessions of a Prostitute See The Immoral One (1980)

Confessions of a Sex Maniac See The Slasher (1972)

Confidences trop Intimes See Intimate Strangers (2004)

Conqueror of the Desert See The Conquero (1956)

Conquest See El Barbaro (1984)

The Conquests of Peter the Great See Peter the First, Part 2 (1938)

The Conspiracy See Le Complot (1973)

Contamination See Alien Contamination (1981)

Conte d'Automne See Autumn Tale (1998)

Conte d'Ete See A Summer's Tale (1996)

Conte D'Hiver See A Tale of Winter (1992)

Continuavamo A Chiamarlo Trinita See Trinity Is Still My Name (1975)

Contra el Viento See Against the Wind (1990)

Control See Kontroll (2003)

Convention City See Sons of the Desert (1933)

Conviene far Bene L'Amore See The Sex Machine (1975)

The Cook in Love See A Chef in Love (1996)

Coolangatta Gold See The Gold & Glory (1984)

Coonskin See Streetfight (1975)

A Cop for the Killing See In the Line of Duty: A Cop for the Killing (1990)

Cop Killers See Corrupt (1984)

Cop Tips Waitress $2 Million See It Could Happen to You (1994)

Copenhagen's Psychic Loves See The Psychic (1968)

Copland See Cop Land (1997)

Cord See Hide and Seek (2000)

The Corporation See Subliminal Seduction (1996)

A Corps Perdu See Straight for the Heart (1988)

The Corpse See Crucible of Horror (1969)

Corpse Bride See Tim Burton's Corpse Bride (2005)

A Corpse Hangs in the Web See Horrors of Spider Island (1959)

Corta Notte delle Bambole di Vetro See Short Night of Glass Dolls (1971)

Cosi Dolce...Cosi Perversa See Kiss Me, Kill Me (1969)

The Cosmic Man Appears in Tokyo See Warning from Space (1956)

Cosmo 2000: Planet Without a Name See Cosmos: War of the Planets (1980)

Cottonmouth See Lethal Force (2000)

Count Dracula and His Vampire Bride See The Satanic Rites of Dracula (1973)

Count Dracula's Great Love See Dracula's Great Love (1972)

Country Blue See On the Run (1973)

Country Music See Las Vegas Hillbillys (1966)

Country Music Daughter See Nashville Girl (1976)

Country Nurse See Emmanuelle in the Country (1978)

Country of My Skull See In My Country (2004)

Coup de Foudre See Entre-Nous (1983)

Coup de Tete See Hothead (1978)

Courage See Raw Courage (1984)

The Courage of Kavik, the Wolf Dog See Kavik the Wolf Dog (1980)

The Courier See Outta Time (2001)

Cours Toujours See Dad On the Run (2000)

The Court See Bamako (2006)

Court Martial See Carrington, V.C. (1954)

Courtesan See Dangerous Beauty (1998)

The Courtneys of Curzon Street See The Courtney Affair (1947)

Covek Nije Tica See Man Is Not a Bird (1965)

Covert One: The Hades Factor See The Hades Factor (2006)

Cows See Vacas (1991)

Coyote Moon See Desert Heat (1999)

Crack See Strike Force (1975)

Crackerjack 2: Hostage Train See Crackerjack 2 (1997)

Cradle of Crime See Dead End (1937)

Crash Landing: The Rescue of Flight 232 See A Thousand Heroes (1992)

Crash of Silence See Mandy (1953)

Crawlers See They Crawl (2001)

The Crawling Monster See Creeping Terror (1964)

Crazy Doll Trick See Murders in the Doll House (1979)

Crazy for You See Vision Quest (1985)

Crazy Horse See Friends, Lovers & Lunatics (1989)

Crazy House See Night of the Laughing Dead (1975)

Crazy Joe See Dead Center (1994)

Crazy Knights See Ghost Crazy (1944)

Crazy Streets See Forever, Lulu (1987)

Crazy World See Mondo Cane 2 (1964)

Crazy Jack and the Boy See Silence (1973)

Created to Kill See Embryo (1976)

Creature from Galaxy 27 See Night of the Blood Beast (1958)

The Creature's Revenge See Brain of Blood (1971)

The Creature Wasn't Nice See Spaceship (1981)

Creatures of the Devil See Dead Men Walk (1943)

Creatures of the Prehistoric Planet See Horror of the Blood Monsters (1970)

Creatures of the Red Planet See Horror of the Blood Monsters (1970)

Creatures See From Beyond the Grave (1973)

The Creeper See Dark Side of Midnight (1986)

The Creeper See Rituals (1979)

Creepers See Bloody Birthday (1980)

Creeps See Night of the Creeps (1986)

Creeps See They Live (1988)

The Creepers See Assault (1970)

The Creepers See Island of Terror (1966)

The Creeping Unknown See The Quatermass Experiment (1956)

Cria Cuervos See Cria (1976)

The Cricket See La Cicada (1983)

Crime and Punishment See Dostoevsky's Crime and Punishment (1999)

Crime Boss See New Mafia Boss (1972)

Crime et Chatiment See Crime and Punishment (1935)

Crimen Ferpecto See El Crimen Perfecto (2004)

Crimes, Inc. See Gangs, Inc. (1941)

Crimes in the Wax Museum See Nightmare in Wax (1969)

The Crimes of Dr. Mabuse See Testament of Dr. Mabuse (1962)

The Criminal See The Concrete Jungle (1982)

The Crimson Altar See The Crimson Cult (1968)

The Crimson Executioner See The Bloody Pit of Horror (1965)

The Crimson Ghost See Cyclotrode "X" (1946)

Crocodile See Blood Surf (2000)

Cronaca di un Amore See Story of a Love Affair (1950)

Cronica de un Nino Solo See Chronicle of a Boy Alone (1964)

Cronicamente Inviavel See Chronically Unfeasible (2000)

Crooked River See Last Bullet (1950)

Crooks in Clover See Penthouse (1933)

Crossed Swords See The Prince and the Pauper (1978)

Crossfire See The Bandits (1967)

Crossing the Line See The Big Man: Crossing the Line (1991)

The Crown Caper See The Thomas Crown Affair (1968)

The Cry See Il Grido (1957)

Crying Out Loud See Cotton Queen (1937)

Crypt of Dark Secrets See Mardi Gras Massacre (1978)

Crypt of the Blind Dead See Tombs of the Blind Dead (1972)

Cruel Swamp See Swamp Women (1955)

Crustaces et Coquillages See Cote d'Azur (2005)

C.S. Lewis Through the Shadowlands See Shadowlands (1985)

Csillagosok, Katonak See The Red and the White (1968)

C't'a Ton Tour, Laura Cadieux See It's My Turn, Laura Cadieux (1998)

Cuba Crossing See The Mercenaries (1980)

Cuban Rebel Girls See Assault of the Rebel Girls (1959)

Cult of the Dead See The Snake People (1968)

Cumbres Borrascosas See Wuthering Heights (1953)

Cupid in the Rough See Aggie Appleby, Maker of Men (1933)

Curley and His Gang in the Haunted Mansion See Who Killed Doc Robbin? (1948)

Curse of Dark Shadows See Night of Dark Shadows (1971)

The Curse of Demon Mountain See Shadow of Chikara (1977)

The Curse of Dr. Phibes See The Abominable Dr. Phibes (1971)

The Curse of Dracula See Return of Dracula (1958)

Curse of Green Eyes See Cave of the Living Dead (1964)

The Curse of Melissa See The Touch of Satan (1970)

The Curse of the Blood-Ghouls See The Slaughter of the Vampires (1962)

The Curse of the Crimson Altar See The Crimson Cult (1968)

The Curse of the Dragon See Bruce Lee: Curse of the Dragon (1993)

The Curse of the Living Dead See Kill, Baby, Kill (1966)

Curse of the Ghouls See The Slaughter of the Vampires (1962)

Curse of the Mushroom People See Attack of the Mushroom People (1963)

The Cusp See Falling Fire (1997)

Cut-Throats Nine See Bronson's Revenge (1972)

Cutter and Bone See Cutter's Way (1981)

Cybele See Sundays & Cybele (1962)

Cyber-Chic See Robo-Chic (1989)

Cyberjack See Virtual Assassin (1995)

Cyborg Cop 2 See Cyborg Soldier (1994)

Cyborg 2: Glass Shadow See Cyborg 2 (1993)

D-Day on Mars See The Purple Monster Strikes (1945)

D-Tox See Eye See You (2001)

Da Bancarella a Bancarotta See Peddlin' in Society (1947)

Da Wan See Big Shot's Funeral (2001)

Da Zdravstvuyet Meksika See Que Viva Mexico (1932)

Daddy See Danielle Steel's Daddy (1991)

Daddy Nostalgie *See* Daddy Nostalgia (1990)

Daddy's Deadly Darling *See* Pigs (1973)

Dad's Week Off *See* National Lampoon's Dad's Week Off (1997)

Dagboek Van Een Oude Dwaas *See* Diary of a Mad Old Man (1988)

Dagora *See* Dagora, the Space Monster (1965)

Dai Koesu Yongkari *See* Yongkari Monster of the Deep (1967)

Daibosatsu Toge *See* Sword of Doom (1967)

Daikaiju Baran *See* Varan the Unbelievable (1961)

Daikaiju Gamera *See* Gamera, the Invincible (1966)

Daikaiju Masura *See* Mothra (1962)

Daikyoju Gappa *See* Gappa the Trifibian Monster (1967)

Dairy Queens *See* Drop Dead Gorgeous (1999)

Dakhtaran-e Khorshid *See* Daughters of the Sun (2000)

Dalle Ardenne All'Inferno *See* Dirty Heroes (1971)

The Dalton Gang *See* Outlaw Gang (1949)

Dance Academy *See* Body Beat (1988)

Dance of the Dwarfs *See* Jungle Heat (1984)

Dance of the Vampires *See* The Fearless Vampire Killers (1967)

Dancer *See* Billy Elliot (2000)

Dancing about Architecture *See* Playing by Heart (1998)

Dandelion *See* Tampopo (1986)

Danger Rides the Range *See* Three Texas Steers (1939)

Dangerous Charter *See* Creeping Terror (1964)

Dangerous Female *See* The Maltese Falcon (1931)

A Dangerous Friend *See* The Todd Killings (1971)

Dangerous Kiss *See* True Crime (1995)

Dangerous Love Affairs *See* Dangerous Liaisons (1960)

Danny the Dog *See* Unleashed (2005)

Danny Travis *See* The Last Word (1980)

Dans la Ville Blanche *See* In the White City (1983)

Dans les Griffes du Maniaque *See* The Diabolical Dr. Z (1965)

Dans Paris *See* Inside Paris (2006)

Danza Macabra *See* Castle of Blood (1964)

Daoma Zei *See* The Horse Thief (1987)

Dare mo shiranai *See* Nobody Knows (2004)

The Daring Caballero *See* Guns of Fury (1949)

Dario Argento's Phantom of the Opera *See* The Phantom of the Opera (1998)

Dark Angel *See* I Come in Peace (1990)

The Dark Avenger *See* The Warriors (1955)

Dark Empire *See* Dark City (1997)

Dark Encounters *See* The Black Gate (1995)

Dark Eyes *See* Demon Rage (1982)

Dark Eyes of London *See* Dead Eyes of London (1961)

Dark Eyes of London *See* The Human Monster (1939)

Dark Prince: Intimate Tales of Marquis de Sade *See* Marquis de Sade (1996)

Dark Prince: The True Story of Dracula *See* Dracula: The Dark Prince (2001)

Dark Sands *See* Jericho (1938)

Dark Summer *See* Innocents (2000)

Dark Waters *See* Dead Waters (1994)

Dark World *See* Dark City (1997)

The Darkening *See* The Black Gate (1995)

Darkness Falling *See* Dark Side (2002)

Darkness in Tallinn *See* City Unplugged (1995)

D'Artagnan *See* The Three Musketeers (1916)

D'Artagnan and the Three Musketeers *See* The 4 Musketeers (2005)

D'Artagnan et les Trois Mousquetaires *See* The 4 Musketeers (2005)

D'Artagnan's Daughter *See* Revenge of the Musketeers (1994)

Das Amulett des Todes *See* Cold Blood (1975)

Das Bildnes des Dorian Gray *See* Dorian Gray (1970)

Das Blaue Licht *See* The Blue Light (1932)

Das Boot Ist Voll *See* The Boat Is Full (1981)

Das Cabinet des Dr. Caligari *See* The Cabinet of Dr. Caligari (1919)

Das Indische Grabmal *See* The Indian Tomb (1959)

Das Kabinett des Doktor Caligari *See* The Cabinet of Dr. Caligari (1919)

Das Leben der Anderen *See* The Lives of Others (2006)

Das Phantom von Soho *See* The Phantom of Soho (1964)

Das Schlangenei *See* The Serpent's Egg (1978)

Das Schloss *See* The Castle (1968)

Das Schreckliche Madchen *See* The Nasty Girl (1990)

Das tagebuch einer verlorenen *See* Diary of a Lost Girl (1929)

Das Ungeheuer von London City *See* The Monster of London City (1964)

Das Versprechen *See* The Promise (1994)

Das Zweite Erwachen der Christa Klages *See* The Second Awakening of Christa Klages (1978)

Das Zweite Gleis *See* The Second Track (1962)

Dashiell Hammett's The Dain Curse *See* The Dain Curse (1978)

The Daughter of Frankenstein *See* Lady Frankenstein (1972)

Daughter of the Werewolf *See* The Legend of the Wolf Woman (1977)

Daughters of Dracula *See* Vampyres (1974)

David Lynch's Hotel Room *See* Hotel Room (1993)

Day of the Woman *See* I Spit on Your Grave (1977)

The Day the Hot Line Got Hot *See* The Hot Line (1969)

The Day the Screaming Stopped *See* The Comeback (1977)

The Day They Gave the Babies Away *See* All Mine to Give (1956)

A Day to Remember *See* Two Bits (1996)

Daybreak *See* Le Jour Se Leve (1939)

Dayereh *See* The Circle (2000)

De Aanslag *See* The Assault (1986)

De battre mon coeur s'est arrete *See* The Beat My Heart Skipped (2005)

De Eso No Se Habla *See* I Don't Want to Talk About It (1994)

De Gronne Slagtere *See* The Green Butchers (2003)

De la Part des Copains *See* Cold Sweat (1971)

De Noche Vienes, Esmeralda *See* Esmeralda Comes by Night (1998)

De Sable et de Sang *See* Sand and Blood (1987)

De Stilte Rond Christine M *See* Question of Silence (1983)

De Wisselwachter *See* The Pointsman (1986)

De Zaak Alzheimer *See* The Memory of a Killer (2003)

Dead Alm *See* Born in America (1990)

Dead Aviators *See* Restless Spirits (1999)

Dead Drop *See* Chain Reaction (1996)

Dead Innocent *See* Eye (1996)

Dead Kids *See* Strange Behavior (1981)

Dead Man's Curve *See* The Curve (1997)

Dead Man's Walk *See* Larry McMurtry's Dead Man's Walk (1996)

Dead of Night *See* Deathdream (1972)

Dead of Night *See* Mirror of Death (1987)

Dead on Course *See* Wings of Danger (1952)

Dead or Alive *See* A Minute to Pray, a Second to Die (1967)

Dead or Alive *See* The Tracker (1988)

Dead People *See* Messiah of Evil (1974)

Dead Scared *See* The Hazing (2004)

Dead Tired *See* Grosse Fatigue (1994)

Deadlocked: Escape from Zone 14 *See* Deadlock 2 (1994)

Deadly Companion *See* The Double Negative (1980)

Deadly Desire *See* Maybe I'll Be Home in the Spring (1970)

Deadly Desires *See* Home for the Holidays (1972)

Deadly Encounter *See* The Meal (1975)

A Deadly Game *See* Charlie Muffin (1979)

Deadly Harvest *See* Children of the Corn 4: The Gathering (1996)

Deadly Is the Female *See* Gun Crazy (1949)

The Deadly Rays from Mars *See* Flash Gordon: Mars Attacks the World (1939)

Deadly Rivals *See* Rivals (1972)

The Deadly Spawn *See* Return of the Aliens: The Deadly Spawn (1983)

Deadly Sting *See* Evil Spawn (1987)

The Deadly Three *See* Enter the Dragon (1973)

The Deadly Tower *See* Sniper (1975)

Deadly Treasure of the Piranha *See* Killer Fish (1979)

Deadly Visions *See* Possessed (2005)

Dear Diary *See* Caro Diario (1993)

Dear Inspector *See* Dear Detective (1977)

Dear Mr. Wonderful *See* Ruby's Dream (1982)

Dearest Love *See* Murmur of the Heart (1971)

Dearly Devoted *See* Devil in the Flesh (1998)

Death and the Green Slime *See* The Green Slime (1968)

Death Bite *See* Spasms (1982)

Death by Pizza *See* Delivered (1998)

Death Collector *See* Family Enforcer (1976)

Death Corps *See* Shock Waves (1977)

Death Dimension *See* Kill Factor (1978)

Death Force *See* Lights! Camera! Murder! (1989)

Death From Outer Space *See* The Day the Sky Exploded (1957)

Death Game *See* Seducers (1977)

Death House *See* Silent Night, Bloody Night (1973)

Death Ride *See* Haunted Highway (2005)

Death Ride to Osaka *See* Girls of the White Orchid (1985)

Death Rides a Carousel *See* Carnival of Blood (1971)

Death Scream *See* The Deadly Trap (1971)

Death Screams *See* House of Death (1982)

Death Train *See* Detonator (1993)

Death Trap *See* Eaten Alive (1976)

Death Vengeance *See* Fighting Back (1982)

The Death Wheelers *See* Psychomania (1973)

Deathline *See* Redline (1997)

Deathshead Vampire *See* Blood Beast Terror (1967)

Deathstalker 3: The Warriors From Hell *See* Deathstalker 3 (1989)

Debajo del Mundo *See* Under the Earth (1986)

The Debt *See* Veronico Cruz (1987)

Decalage Horaire *See* Jet Lag (2002)

Decoy for Terror *See* Playgirl Killer (1966)

Dedee *See* Dedee d'Anvers (1949)

Deep Red *See* Deep Red: Hatchet Murders (1975)

The Defender *See* The Bodyguard from Beijing (1994)

The Definite Maybe *See* No Money Down (1997)

Delirios de Um Anormal *See* Hallucinations of a Deranged Mind (1978)

Deliver Them from Evil: The Taking of Alta View *See* Take Down (1992)

Dellamorte Delamore *See* Cemetery Man (1995)

Delta Pi *See* Mugsy's Girls (1985)

Deluxe Combo Platter *See* Love on the Side (2004)

Dem Khann's Zindi *See* The Cantor's Son (1937)

Demanty Noci *See* Diamonds of the Night (1964)

Dementia *See* Daughter of Horror (1955)

Demolition Day *See* Captain Nuke and the Bomber Boys (1995)

Demon *See* God Told Me To (1976)

The Demon *See* Onibaba (1964)

The Demon Doctor *See* The Awful Dr. Orloff (1962)

Demon House *See* Night of the Demons 3 (1997)

Demon Island *See* Survival Island (2002)

Demon Keeper *See* Tales from the Crypt Presents Demon Knight (1994)

Demon Knight *See* Tales from the Crypt Presents Demon Knight (1994)

Demon Master *See* Craze (1974)

The Demon Planet *See* Planet of the Vampires (1965)

Demoni *See* Demons (1986)

Demonios En El Jardin *See* Demons in the Garden (1982)

The Demon's Mask *See* Black Sunday (1960)

Demons of the Swamp *See* Attack of the Giant Leeches (1959)

Den Tuchtigen Gehart die Welt *See* The Uppercrust (1981)

Den Underbara Lognen *See* The True and the False (1955)

Den Vita Lejoninnan *See* The White Lioness (1996)

Denial *See* Something About Sex (1998)

Depraved Indifference *See* New Best Friend (2002)

Depuis Qu'Otar est Parti *See* Since Otar Left... (2003)

The Deputy *See* El Diputado (1978)

Der Amerikanische Freund *See* The American Friend (1977)

Der Amerikanische Soldat *See* The American Soldier (1970)

Der Bewegte Mann *See* Maybe... Maybe Not (1994)

Der Blaue Engel *See* The Blue Angel (1930)

Der Chef Wuenscht Keine Zeugen *See* No Survivors, Please (1963)

Der Dibuk *See The Dybbuk* (1937)

Der Dirnenmoerder von London *See* Jack the Ripper (1976)

Der Dritte *See* The Third (1972)

Der Fall Furtwangler *See* Taking Sides (2001)

Der Fall Gleiwitz *See* The Gleiwitz Case (1961)

Der Fluch Der Gruenen Augen *See* Cave of the Living Dead (1965)

Der Fussgaenger *See* The Pedestrian (1973)

Der Golem, wie er in die Welt kam *See* The Golem (1920)

Der Hauptmann von Koepenick *See* The Captain from Koepenick (1956)

Der Henker Von London *See* The Mad Executioners (1965)

Der Himmel Uber Berlin *See* Wings of Desire (1988)

Der Joker *See* Lethal Obsession (1987)

Der Kongress Tanzt *See* Congress Dances (1931)

Der Krieger und die Kaiserin *See* The Princess and the Warrior (2000)

Der Letzte Mann *See* The Last Laugh (1924)

Der Morder Dimitri Karamasoff *See* The Brothers Karamazov (1958)

Der Mude Tod *See* Destiny (1921)

Der Neunte Tag *See* The Ninth Day (2004)

Der Prozess *See* The Trial (1963)

Der Schweigende Stern *See* First Spaceship on Venus (1960)

Der Tunnel *See* The Tunnel (2001)

Der Unhold *See* The Ogre (1996)

Der Untergang *See* Downfall (2004)

Der Verlorne Sohn *See* The Kaiser's Lackey (1951) *

Der Verlone *See* The Lost One (1951)

Der Vilner Shtot Khazn *See* Overture to Glory (1940)

Der Wurger kommt auf leisen Socken *See* The Mad Butcher (1972)

Deranged *See* Idaho Transfer (1973)

Desert Patrol *See* Sea of Sand (1958)

The Deserter *See* Ride to Glory (1971)

Desire in Motion *See* Mouvements du Desir (1994)

Desires of a Housewife *See* When a Man Falls in the Forest (2007)

Desperate Siege *See* Rawhide (1950)

The Destroyers *See* Devastator (1985)

Destruction, Inc. *See* Just for the Hell of It (1968)

Destry Rides Again *See* Justice Rides Again (1932)

Det Sjunde Inseglet *See* The Seventh Seal (1956)

Det Stora Aventyret *See* The Great Adventure (1953)

The Detective *See* Ring of Death (1969)

Detective Geronimo *See* The Mad Bomber (1972)

The Detective Kid *See* The Gumshoe Kid (1989)

Detention: The Siege at Johnson High *See* Hostage High (1997)

Detroit Heat *See* Detroit 9000 (1973)

Deus e o Diabo na Terra do Sol *See* Black God, White Devil (1964)

Deutschland, Bleiche Mutter *See* Germany, Pale Mother (1980)

Deutschland im Herbst *See* Germany in Autumn (1978)

Deux ou Trois Choses Que Je Sais d'Elle *See* Two or Three Things I Know about Her (1966)

Deux Secondes *See* 2 Seconds (1998)

The Devil and Dr. Frankenstein *See* Andy Warhol's Frankenstein (1974)

The Devil and the Dead *See* Lisa and the Devil (1975)

The Devil and the Nun *See* Mother Joan of the Angels (1960)

The Devil in the House of Exorcism *See* Lisa and the Devil (1975)

Devil Master *See* The Demon Lover (1977)

Devil Rider *See* Master's Revenge (1971)

The Devil Walks at Midnight *See* The Devil's Nightmare (1971)

The Devil within Her *See* Beyond the Door (1975)

The Devil Within Her *See* I Don't Want to Be Born (1975)

The Devil Woman *See* Onibaba (1964)

The Devil's Bride *See* The Devil Rides Out (1968)

The Devil's Commandment *See* I, Vampiri (1956)

Devil's Doll *See* The Devil's Hand (1961)

The Devil's Envoys *See* Les Visiteurs du Soir (1942)

Devil's Express *See* Gang Wars (1975)

The Devil's Men *See* Land of the Minotaur (1977)

Devil's Odds *See* The Wild Pair (1987)

The Devils of Loudun *See* The Devils (1971)

The Devil's Own *See* The Witches (1966)

The Devil's Plot *See* Counterblast (1948)

The Devil's Undead *See* Nothing But the Night (1972)

The Devil's Weed *See* She Shoulda Said No (1949)

Devil's Witch *See* Kiss Me, Kill Me (1969)

Dia de los Muertos *See* All Souls Day (2005)

Diabolica Malicia *See* What the Peeper Saw (1972)

The Diabolical Dr. Mabuse *See* The Thousand Eyes of Dr. Mabuse (1960)

Diabolik *See* Danger: Diabolik (1968)

Diaboliquement Votre *See* Diabolically Yours (1967)

Dial 999 *See* The Way Out (1956)

Dial Rat for Terror *See* Housewife (1972)

Diamond Alley *See* Little Ladies of the Night (1977)

Diamond Earrings *See* The Earrings of Madame De... (1954)

Diamond Skulls *See* Dark Obsession (1990)

Diamond Thieves *See* The Squeeze (1980)

Diamonds and Crime *See* Hi Diddle Diddle (1943)

Dian Zhi Gong Fu Gan Chian Chan *See* Half a Loaf of Kung Fu (1978)

Diario Segreto Di Un Carcere Femminele *See* Women in Cell Block 7 (1977)

Diarios de motocicleta *See* The Motorcycle Diaries (2004)

Diary of a Hooker *See* Business is Business (1971)

Diary of Oharu *See* Life of Oharu (1952)

Dias Contados *See* Running Out of Time (1994)

Dick Tracy Meets Karloff *See* Dick Tracy Meets Gruesome (1947)

Dick Tracy's Amazing Adventure *See* Dick Tracy Meets Gruesome (1947)

The Abenteuer des Werner Holt *See* The Adventures of Werner Holt (1965)

Die Angst Tormannes beim Elfmeter *See* The Goalie's Anxiety at the Penalty Kick (1971)

Die Bitteren Traenen der Petra von Kant *See* The Bitter Tears of Petra von Kant (1972)

Die Blechtrommel *See* The Tin Drum (1979)

Die Bleierne Zeit *See* Marianne and Juliane (1982)

Die Brucke *See* The Bridge (1959)

Die Buechse der Pandora *See* Pandora's Box (1928)

Die Dreigroschenoper *See* The Three Penny Opera (1962)

Die Dreigroschenoper *See* The Threepenny Opera (1931)

Die Ehe Der Maria Braun *See* The Marriage of Maria Braun (1979)

Die Erotische Geschichten *See* Tales of Erotica (1993)

Die Falscher *See* The Counterfeiters (2007)

Die Fetten Jahre sind vorbei *See* The Edukators (2004)

Die Flambierte Frau *See* A Woman in Flames (1984)

Die Folterkammer des Dr. Fu Manchu *See* The Castle of Fu Manchu (1968)

Die Freudlosse Gasse *See* Joyless Street (1925)

Die Geschichte vom Weinenden Kamel *See* The Story of the Weeping Camel (2003)

Die Geschwister Oppermann *See* The Oppermann Family (1982)

Die Hard 3 *See* Die Hard: With a Vengeance (1995)

Die Holle von Macao *See* The Corrupt Ones (1967)

Die Holle von Manitoba *See* A Place Called Glory (1966)

Die Legende von Paul und Paula *See* The Legend of Paul and Paula (1973)

Die Letzte Brucke *See* The Last Bridge (1954)

Die Lustigen Weiber von Windsor *See* The Merry Wives of Windsor (1950)

Die Marquise Von O *See* The Marquise of O (1976)

Die Morder Sind Unter Uns *See* The Murderers Are Among Us (1946)

Die Nibelungen *See* Kriemhilde's Revenge (1924)

Die Regenschirme von Cherbourg *See* The Umbrellas of Cherbourg (1964)

Die Reise nach Kafiristan *See* The Journey to Kafiristan (2001)

Die Saege des Todes *See* Bloody Moon (1983)

Die Schachnovelle *See* Brainwashed (1960)

Die Schlangengrube und das Pendel *See* The Torture Chamber of Dr. Sadism (1969)

Die Sehns Ucht Der Veronika Voss *See* Veronika Voss (1982)

Die Siebtelbauern *See* The Inheritors (1998)

Die Stille Nach Dem Schuss *See* The Legend of Rita (1999)

Die Tausend Augen des Dr. Mabuse *See* The Thousand Eyes of Dr. Mabuse (1960)

Die Toten Augen von London *See* Dead Eyes of London (1961)

Die Unsichtbaren Krallen des Dr. Mabuse *See* The Invisible Dr. Mabuse (1962)

Die Verlorene Ehre Der Katharina Blum *See* The Lost Honor of Katharina Blum (1975)

Die Vierde Man *See* The 4th Man (1979)

Die Weisse Rose *See* The White Rose (1983)

Die Xue Jie Tou *See* A Bullet in the Head (1990)

Die Xue Shuang Xiong *See* The Killer (1990)

Die Zartlichkeit der Wolfe *See* Tenderness of the Wolves (1973)

Die Zwolfte Stunde *See* Nosferatu (1922)

The Digital Prophet *See* Cyberstalker (1996)

Dillinger 70 *See* Carbon Copy (1969)

Dillo con Parole Mie *See* Ginger and Cinnamon (2003)

Dimensions in Death *See* Castle of Blood (1964)

Dio Mio, Come Sono Caduta in Basso *See* Till Marriage Do Us Part (1974)

Dio, Sei Proprio un Padrenterno! *See* Escape from Death Row (1973)

Direktoren for Det Hele *See* The Boss of It All (2006)

Dirty Hands *See* Innocents with Dirty Hands (1976)

A Dirty Knight's Work *See* Choice of Weapons (1976)

Dirty Mary *See* A Very Curious Girl (1969)

Dirty, Mean and Nasty *See* Down & Dirty (1976)

The Dirty Mob *See* Mean Machine (1973)

Dirty Work *See* Bad City (2006)

The Disappearance of Nora *See* High Stakes (1993)

Disaster at Valdez *See* Dead Ahead: The Exxon Valdez Disaster (1992)

Disciple of Dracula *See* Dracula, Prince of Darkness (1966)

Disco Godfather *See* Avenging Disco Godfather (1976)

Disco Madness *See* Toga Party (1977)

The Discreet *See* La Discrete (1990)

Disney's Blank Check *See* Blank Check (1993)

Disparen a Matar *See* Outrage (1993)

Disparen a Matar *See* Shoot to Kill (1990)

Distant Cousins *See* Desperate Motives (1992)

Dites-Lui Que Je L'Aime *See* This Sweet Sickness (1977)

Divertimento *See* La Belle Noiseuse (1990)

Divine Emmanuelle *See* Love Camp (1981)

Divine Obsession *See* Dangerous Obsession (1988)

Divorzio All'Italiana See Divorce—Italian Style (1962)

Django 2: il Grande Ritorno See Django Strikes Again (1987)

Django Spara per Primo See Django Shoots First (1974)

Djavulens Oga See The Devil's Eye (1960)

Djoflaeyjan See Devil's Island (1996)

Dnevnol Dozor: Mei Sudbi See Day Watch (2006)

Do Not Disturb See Silent Witness (1999)

Do You Want to Dance with Me? See Voulez-Vous Danser avec Moi? (1959)

Doches Froices See Cold Showers (2005)

The Dock Brief See Trial & Error (1962)

Docteur Chance See Doctor Chance (1997)

Docteur M. See Club Extinction (1989)

Docteur Popaul See High Heels (1972)

Doctor Beware See Teresa Venerdi (1941)

Dr. Black and Mr. White See Dr. Black, Mr. Hyde (1976)

The Doctor from Seven Dials See Corridors of Blood (1958)

Doctor Gore See The Body Shop (1972)

Dr. Jekyll vs. the Werewolf See Dr. Jekyll and the Wolfman (1971)

Dr. Jekyll y el Hombre Lobo See Dr. Jekyll and the Wolfman (1971)

Dr. Jekyll's Dungeon of Darkness See Dr. Tarr's Torture Dungeon (1975)

Dr. Sleep See Close Your Eyes (2002)

Dr. Terror's Gallery of Horrors See Alien Massacre (1967)

Doctors Wear Scarlet See The Bloodsuckers (1970)

A Dog, a Mouse, and a Sputnik See Sputnik (1961)

Dog Soldiers See Who'll Stop the Rain? (1978)

Dogboys See Tracked (1998)

A Dog's Life See Mondo Cane (1963)

Dogwater See Since You've Been Gone (1997)

Doin' It See The First Time (1969)

Doin' It See First Time (1982)

Doing Life See Truth or Die (1986)

Doing Time See Porridge (1991)

Doktor Mabuse der Spieler See Dr. Mabuse, The Gambler (1922)

Dolwyn See The Last Days of Dolwyn (1949)

Don Durakov See House of Fools (2002)

Don Za Vesanje See Time of the Gypsies (1990)

Domicile Conjugal See Bed and Board (1970)

Dominick Dunne Presents Murder in Greenwich See Murder in Greenwich (2002)

The Domino Killings See The Domino Principle (1977)

Don Juan See Private Life of Don Juan (1934)

Don Juan 73 See Don Juan (Or If Don Juan Were a Woman) (1973)

Don Juan, Mi Querido Fantasma See Don Juan, My Love (1990)

Don Kikhot See Don Quixote (1957)

Dona Flor e Seus Dois Maridos See Dona Flor and Her Two Husbands (1978)

Dona Herlinda y Su Hijo See Dona Herlinda & Her Son (1986)

Donato and Daughter See Dead to Rights (1993)

Dong Fang San Xia See The Heroic Trio (1993)

Donggong, Xigong See East Palace, West Palace (1996)

The Don's Analyst See National Lampoon's The Don's Analyst (1997)

Don't Go Near the Park See Nightstalker (1981)

Don't Look Now, We've Been Shot At See La Grande Vadrouille (1966)

Don't Tempt Me! See No News from God (2001)

Don't Touch the Axe See The Duchess of Langeais (2007)

Donzoko See The Lower Depths (1957)

Doomed See Ikiru (1952)

The Doomsday Machine See Escape from Planet Earth (1967)

The Door with Seven Locks See Chamber of Horrors (1940)

Dope Addict See Reefer Madness (1938)

Doped Youth See Reefer Madness

Dopo mezzanotte See After Midnight (2004)

Doppelganger See Journey to the Far Side of the Sun (1969)

Dos Tipos Duros See Two Tough Guys

Dos Veces Judas See Twice a Judas (1969)

The Double See Kagemusha (1980)

Double Cross See Motorcycle Squad (1941)

Double Down See Stacy's Knights (1983)

Double Hit See The Arab Conspiracy (1976)

Double Possession See Ganja and Hess (1973)

Double Trouble See No Deposit, No Return (1976)

Down Among the Z Men See Goon Movie (1952)

Down Went McGinty See The Great McGinty (1940)

Down See The Shaft (2001)

Douce Violence See Sweet Ecstasy (1962)

Doulos—The Finger Man See Le Doulos (1961)

Drunken Master 2 See The Legend of Drunken Master (1994)

The Drum See Drums (1938)

Du Riffi Chez les Hommes See Rififi (1954)

Duck, You Sucker See A Fistful of Dynamite (1972)

The Duckweed Story See Drifting Weeds (1959)

Due Er Ikke Alene See You Are Not Alone (1978)

Due Notti Con Cleopatra See Two Nights with Cleopatra (1954)

Due Occhi Diabolici See Two Evil Eyes (1990)

Duel of the Space Monsters See Frankenstein Meets the Space Monster (1965)

Duel of the Gargantuas See War of the Gargantuas (1970)

Duello Nel Texas See Gunfight at Red Sands (1963)

Dumb Dicks See Detective School Dropouts (1985)

Dumbo Drop See Operation Dumbo Drop (1995)

Dracula: The Bloodline Continues... See The Saga of the Draculas (1972)

Dracula: The Love Story See To Die For (1989)

Dracula, the Terror of the Living Dead See The Hanging Woman (1972)

Dracula Today See Dracula A.D. 1972 (1972)

Dracula vs. Frankenstein See The Screaming Dead (1972)

Dracula Vuole Vivere: Cerca Sangue de Vergina See Andy Warhol's Dracula (1974)

Dracula's Castle See Blood of Dracula's Castle (1969)

Dracula's Dog See Zoltan... Hound of Dracula (1978)

Dracula's Virgin Lovers See Dracula's Great Love (1972)

Dragon Lady See G.I. Executioner (1971)

The Dragon and the Cobra See Fist of Fear, Touch of Death (1980)

Dragonfly See One Summer Love (1976)

Dragon's Food See Drachenfutter (1987)

Dragon Chow See Drachenfutter (1987)

Dragon Forever See Dragons Forever

Drawing Blood See Sergio Lapel's Drawing Blood (1999)

Draws See American Tickler (1976)

The Dreaded Persuasion See The Narcotics Story (1955)

Dream Slayer See Blood Song (1982)

The Dreamcatcher See The Dream Catcher (1999)

Dreaming of Julia See Cuban Blood (2003)

Dreams See Akira Kurosawa's Dreams (1990)

Dreamworld See Covergirl (1983)

Drei Sterne See Mostly Martha (2001)

Dripping Deep Red See Deep Red: Hatchet Murders (1975)

Drivers to Hell See Wild Ones on Wheels (1962)

Droid Gunner See Cyberzone (1995)

Droie de Drama See Bizarre Bizarre (1939)

Drole de Felix See The Adventures of Felix (1999)

Drops of Blood See Mill of the Stone Women (1960)

The Drug See Kids in the Hall: Brain Candy (1996)

D'Une Femme a L'Autre See A Business Affair (1993)

Dungeons and Dragons See Mazes and Monsters (1982)

Duoluo Tianshi See Fallen Angels (1995)

Dusting Cliff Seven See The Last Assassins (1996)

Dutchess of Doom See Blacksnake! (1973)

Duvar See The Wall (1983)

The Dwelling Place See Catherine Cookson's The Dwelling Place (1994)

Dynamite Women See The Great Texas Dynamite Chase (1976)

Dyrygent See The Conductor (1980)

E Dio Disse a Caino See And God Said to Cain (1969)

E Tu Vivrai Nel Terrore—L'atdila See The Beyond (1982)

E venne il giorno dei limoni neri See Black Lemons (1970)

Each Man For Himself See The Ruthless Four (1970)

Each One For Himself See The Ruthless Four (1970)

The Eagle with Two Heads See The Eagle Has Two Heads (1946)

Earth See Tierra (1995)

Earth Defense Forces See The Mysterians (1958)

East of the Bowery See Follow the Leader (1944)

East of the Rising Sun See Malaya (1949)

Easy Go See Free and Easy (1930)

Eaten Alive See Emerald Jungle (1980)

Eaten Alive by Cannibals See Emerald Jungle (1980)

Eaters of the Dead See The 13th Warrior (1999)

East Great Falls High See American Pie (1999)

East of Shanghai See Rich and Strange (1932)

Eating Pattern See Tales from a Parallel Universe: Eating Pattern (1997)

Ebirah, Terror of the Deep See Godzilla vs. the Sea Monster (1966)

Eboli See Christ Stopped at Eboli (1979)

Ebony, Ivory, and Jade See She Devils in Chains (1976)

Echte Kerle See Regular Guys (1996)

Ecks vs. Sever See Ballistic: Ecks vs. Sever (2002)

Edgar Allan Poe's Conqueror Worm See The Conqueror Worm (1968)

Edgar Allen Poe's House of Usher See The House of Usher (1988)

Edgar Allan Poe's The Oblong Box See The Oblong Box (1969)

The Edge of Hell See Rock 'n' Roll Nightmare (1985)

Edipo Re See Oedipus Rex (1967)

Edison See Edison Force (2005)

Edwards & Hunt: The First American Road Trip See Almost Heroes (1997)

Etter the Wedding See After the Wedding (2006)

Etter Brylupet See After the Wedding (2006)

Etter Repetitionen See After the Rehearsal (1984)

Eight Arms to Hold You See Help! (1965)

8 Crazy Nights See Adam Sandler's 8 Crazy Nights (2002)

8 femmes See 8 Women (2002)

800 Balas See 800 Bullets (2002)

18 Shades of Dust See Hitman's Journal (1999)

Ein Lied von Liebe und Tod See Gloomy Sunday (2002)

Ein Mann wie Eva See A Man Like Eva (1983)

Ein Toter Hing im Netz See Horrors of Spider Island (1959)

Eine Liebe in Deutschland See A Love in Germany (1984)

Eine Reise ins Licht See Despair (1978)

Einer Frisst den Anderen See Dog Eat Dog (1964)

Einer Trage des Anderen Last... See Bear Ye One Another's Burden... (1988)

Ekstase See Ecstasy (1933)

El Abrazo Partido See Lost Embrace (2004)

El Angel exterminador See The Exterminating Angel (1962)

El Ataud Del Vampiro See The Vampire's Coffin (1958)

El Ataque de los Muertos Sin Ojos See Return of the Evil Dead (1975)

El Baron del Terror See The Brainiac (1961)

El Beso Que Me Diste See The Kiss You Gave Me (2000)

El Buque Maldito See Horror of the Zombies (1974)

El Callejon de los Milagros See Midaq Alley (1995)

El Camino See The Road (2000)

El Cazador de la Muerte See Deathstalker (1983)

El Che Guevara See Diary of a Rebel (1968)

El Cobra See The Cobra (1968)

El Coleccionista de Cadaveres See Cauldron of Blood (1967)

El Crimen del Padre Amaro See The Crime of Father Amaro (2002)

El Crimen Ferpecto See El-Crimen Perfecto (2004)

El Dedo En El Gatillo See Finger on the Trigger (1965)

El Dia Que Murio el Silencio See The Day Silence Died (1998)

El Diablo se Lleva a los Muertos See Lisa and the Devil (1975)

El Espanto Surge de la Tumba See Horror Rises from the Tomb (1972)

El Espinazo del Diablo See The Devil's Backbone (2001)

El Espiritu de la Colmena See Spirit of the Beehive (1973)

El Grito de la Muerte See The Living Coffin (1958)

El Hijo de la Novia See The Son of the Bride (2001)

El la Nave Va See And the Ship Sails On (1983)

El Laberinto del Fauno See Pan's Labyrinth (2006)

El Lado Oscuro del Corazon See The Dark Side of the Heart (1992)

El Lago de los Muertos Vivientes See Zombie Lake (1980)

El Lazarillo de Tormes See Lazarillo (1959)

El Maquinista See The Machinist (2004)

El Mariachi 2 See Desperado (1995)

El Marido Perfecto See The Perfect Husband (1992)

El Mas Fabuloso Golpe del Far West See The Boldest Job in the West (1971)

El Metodo See The Method (2005)

El Nido See The Nest (1980)

El Orfanato See The Orphanage (2007)

El Otro Lado de la Cama See The Other Side of the Bed (2003)

El Patrullero See Highway Patrolman (1991)

El Pecado de Adan y Eva See Sin of Adam & Eve (1967)

El Rapto de las Sabinas See The Rape of the Sabines (1961)

El Retorno de la Walpurgis See Curse of the Devil (1973)

El Retorno del Hombre-Lobo See The Craving (1980)

El Retorno de la Drequessa Dracula See Devil's Wedding Night (1973)

El Robot Humano See The Robot vs. the Aztec Mummy (1959)

El Rubio de las dos Caras See The Hot Line (1969)

El Sonido de la Muerte See Sound of Horror (1964)

El Suero de Ibiza See Ibiza Dream (2002)

El Tesoro del Amazonas See The Treasure of the Amazon (1984)

El Verano de la Senora Forbes See The Summer of Miss Forbes (1988)

El Zorro See Zorro (1974)

El Zorro la belva del Colorado See Zorro (1974)

Eldorado See The Midas Touch (1989)

Electric Boogaloo "Breakin' 2" See Breakin' 2: Electric Boogaloo (1994)

The Electric Man See Man Made Monster (1941)

The Electric Monster See The Electronic Monster (1957)

Elena et les Hommes See Elena and Her Men (1956)

Eleni See Weeping Meadow (2004)

Elevator to the Gallows See Frantic (1958)

The 11th Commandment See Body Count (1987)

Elisa, My Life See Elisa, Vida Mia (1977)

Elisa, My Love See Elisa, Vida Mia (1977)

Elke See Friend of the Family (1995)

Ella See Monkey Shines (1988)

Elles See Women (1997)

Eloge de L'Amour See In Praise of Love (2001)

Emanuele and the Last Cannibals See Trap Them & Kill Them (1977)

Emanuelle e Gli Ultimi Cannibali See Trap Them & Kill Them (1977)

Emanuelle's Amazon Adaventure See Trap Them & Kill Them (1977)

Emergency Landing See Robot Pilot (1941)

Emil Und Die Detektive See Emil and the Detectives (1964)

Emma Mae See Black Sister's Revenge (1976)

Emmanuelle l'Antivierge See Emmanuelle, the Joys of a Woman (1976)

Emmanuelle 2 See Emmanuelle, the Joys of a Woman (1976)

Emmanuelle's 7th Heaven See Emmanuelle, the Joys of a Woman (1976)

Emmett's Mark See Killing Emmett Young (2002)

L'Emploi du Temps See Time Out (2001)

Emporte-Moi See Set Me Free (1999)

The Empress Yang Kwei Fei See Princess Yang Kwei Fei (1955)

En Compagnie d'Antonin Artaud See My Life and Times with Antonin Artaud (1993)

En Effeuillant la Marguerite See Plucking the Daisy (1956)

En el Aire See On the Air (1995)

En el Hoyo See In the Pit (2006)

En el Pais de No Pasa Nada See In the Country Where Nothing Happens (1999)

En Enda Natt See Only One Night (1942)

En Garde See On Guard! (2003)

En Kaerlighedshistorie See Kira's Reason—A Love Story (2001)

En Kvinnas Ansikte See A Woman's Face (1938)

En Lektion i Karlek See Lesson in Love (1954)

En Medio de la Nada See In the Middle of Nowhere (1993)

En Sang for Martin See A Song for Martin (2001)

Enchanted See Incantato (2003)

Encounters of the Spooky Kind See Spooky Encounters (1980)

Endangered See Uncivilized (1994)

End of the Rainbow See Northwest Outpost (1947)

End of the World See Panic in the Year Zero! (1962)

End of the World (in Our Usual Bed in a Night Full of Rain) See A Night Full of Rain (1978)

L'Enfant See The Child (2005)

Enfer Dans la Peau See Sexus (1964)

The Enforcer See Jet Li's The Enforcer (1995)

The Engagement See Fiances (1963)

The Enigma of Kaspar Hauser See Every Man for Himself & God Against All (1975)

Enormous Changes at the Last Minute See Enormous Changes (1983)

Enrico Caruso: Leggenda di Una Voce See Young Caruso (1951)

Ensayo de un Crimen See The Criminal Life of Archibaldo de la Cruz (1955)

Entebbe: Operation Thunderbolt See Operation Thunderbolt (1977)

Enter Three Dragons See The Three Avengers (1980)

Entity Force See One Dark Night (1982)

Entre las Piernas See Between Your Legs (1999)

Entre Tinieblas See Dark Habits (1984)

Eonios Fhitis See Ghost of a Chance (2001)

Episoda Del Mare See La Terra Trema (1948)

Epsilon See Alien Visitor (1995)

The Era of the Vampires See Tsui Park's Vampire Hunters (2002)

Ercole al Centro Della Terra See Hercules in the Haunted World (1964)

Ercole e la Regina de Lidia See Hercules Unchained (1959)

Ercole Alla Conquista di Atlantide See Hercules and the Captive Women (1963)

Ercole Contro i Figli del Sole See Hercules vs. the Sons of the Sun (1964)

Ercole Contro Molock See Conquest of Mycene (1963)

Eric the Conqueror See The Invaders (1963)

Ermanno Olmi's I Fadanzati See Fiances (1963)

Ernest Hemingway's the Killers See The Killers (1964)

Eroi All'Inferno See Heroes in Hell (1973)

Eroina See Fatal Fix (1980)

Erotic Rites of Frankenstein See Rites of Frankenstein (1972)

Erotikill See Female Vampire (1973)

Erzebeth See Daughters of Darkness (1971)

Escalofrio See Satan's Blood (1977)

Escapade See Utopia (1951)

The Escape of Megagodzilla See Terror of Mechagodzilla (1978)

Escape by Night See Era Notte a Roma (1960)

Escape If You Can See St. Benny the Dip (1951)

Escape Route See I'll Get You (1953)

Escape from the Dark See The Littlest Horse Thieves (1976)

Escape to Freedom See Judgment in Berlin (1988)

Escapement See The Electronic Monster (1957)

Escort Girl See Half Moon Street (1986)

The Escort See L'Escorte (1996)

The Escorts See La Scorta (1994)

Escuadron See Counterforce (1987)

Espiritismo See Spiritism (1961)

L'esquive See Games of Love and Chance (2003)

Est-Ouest See East-West (1999)

Et Dieu Crea la Femme See And God Created Woman (1957)

Etz Hadomim Tafus See Under the Domim Tree (1995)

The Eternal Kiss of the Mummy See The Eternal (1999)

Etat de Siege See State of Siege (1973)

Eu Tu Eles See Me You Them (2000)

Eulogy of Love See In Praise of Love (2001)

Euro Pudding See L'Auberge Espagnole (2002)

Europa See Zentropa (1992)

European Vacation See National Lampoon's European Vacation (1985)

Eva the Devil's Woman See Eva (1962)

Every Day's a Holiday See Seaside Swingers (1965)

Every Home Should Have One See Think Dirty (1970)

Every Man For Himself See The Ruthless Four (1967)

Every Woman's Man See The Prizefighter and the Lady (1933)

Everybody Loves Sunshine See B.U.S.T.E.D. (1999)

Everybody's Cheering See Take Me Out to the Ball Game (1949)

Everything's on Ice See Frolics on Ice (1939)

Evidence of Love See A Killing in a Small Town (1990)

Evil Angels See A Cry in the Dark (1988)

Evil Dead 3 See Army of Darkness (1992)

Evil Eden See Death in the Garden (1956)

The Evil Eye See The Girl Who Knew Too Much (1963)

Evil in the Swamp See All the Kind Strangers (1974)

Evil Woman See Saving Silverman (2001)

The Evils of Dorian Gray See Dorian Gray (1970)

Ewiger Walzer See The Eternal Waltz (1954)

Except for Me and Thee *See* Friendly Persuasion (1956)

Excite Me *See* Your Vice is a Closed Room and Only I Have the Key (1972)

Exorcismo *See* Exorcism (1974)

Expedition Moon *See* Rocketship X-M (1950)

Exploring the Kinsey Report *See* One Plus One (1961)

Expose *See* Footsteps (1998)

Expose *See* The House on Straw Hill (1976)

Exquisite Tenderness *See* The Surgeon (1994)

Extase *See* Ecstasy (1933)

Extenuating Circumstances *See* Circonstances Attenuantes (1936)

Extreme Close-Up *See* Sex Through a Window (1972)

An Eye for an Eye *See* Psychopath (1973)

An Eye for an Eye *See* Talion (1966)

Eye of the Black Cat *See* Your Vice is a Closed Room and Only I Have the Key (1972)

Eyes of Hell *See* The Mask (1961)

Eyes without a Face *See* The Horror Chamber of Dr. Faustus (1959)

Fabula de la Bella Palomera *See* The Fable of the Beautiful Pigeon Fancier (1988)

The Fabulous Baron Munchausen *See* Fabulous Adventures of Baron Munchausen (1961)

The Fabulous Baron Munchausen *See* The Original Fabulous Adventures of Baron Munchausen (1961)

The Fabulous Destiny of Amelie Poulain *See* Amelie (2001)

Face of a Stranger *See* The Promise (1979)

Face of Fear *See* Peeping Tom (1960)

Face the Music *See* Black Glove (1954)

The Faceless Monsters *See* Nightmare Castle (1965)

Fag Hag *See* Okoge (1993)

Fair Trade *See* Skeleton Coast (1989)

Fairytales *See* Fairy Tales (1976)

Fakebook *See* American Blue Note (1989)

Fallen *See* Falling (2006)

Fallen Knight *See* The Minion (1998)

Falltime *See* Fall Time (1994)

False Face *See* Scalpel (1976)

False Faces *See* Let 'Em Have It (1935)

Falstaff *See* Chimes at Midnight (1967)

Familia Rodante *See* Rolling Family (2004)

The Familiar Stranger *See* My Husband's Double Life (2001)

Family Resemblances *See* Un Air de Famille (1996)

Fanatic *See* Die! Die! My Darling! (1965)

Fanfan the Tulip *See* Fanfan la Tulipe (1951)

Fang Shi Yu *See* Kick of Death: The Prodigal Boxer (1973)

Fangelse *See* Devil's Wanton (1949)

Fanny by Gaslight *See* Man of Evil (1948)

Fanny Och Alexander *See* Fanny and Alexander (1983)

Fan's Video *See* Otaku No Video (1991)

The Fantastic Disappearing Man *See* Return of Dracula (1958)

The Far Country *See* Nevil Shute's The Far Country (1985)

Farewell, Friend *See* Honor Among Thieves (1968)

Farewell, My Love *See* Murder, My Sweet (1944)

Farinelli Il Castrato *See* Farinelli (1994)

Farinelli the Castrato *See* Farinelli (1994)

The Farm *See* The Curse (1987)

Farm Girl *See* The Farmer's Other Daughter (1965)

Farm of the Year *See* Miles from Home (1988)

The Farmhouse *See* Eye of the Storm (1998)

Fashion House of Death *See* Blood and Black Lace (1964)

Fashions *See* Fashions of 1934 (1934)

Fast Fortune *See* 11 Harrowhouse (1974)

Fast on the Draw *See* Sudden Death (1950)

Fast Track *See* The Ex (2007)

Fatal Affair *See* Stalker (1998)

Fatal Assassin *See* African Rage (1978)

Fatal Woman *See* Femme Fatale (1990)

Fate Ignoranti *See* His Secret Life (2001)

The Father *See* Baba (1973)

Father Jackleg *See* Sting of the West (1972)

Father & Son: Dangerous Relations *See* Dangerous Relations (1993)

Father Brown *See* The Detective (1954)

Father Damien: The Leper Priest *See* Damien: The Leper Priest (1980)

Father Goose *See* Fly Away Home (1996)

The Father Kino Story *See* Mission to Glory (1980)

Father Master *See* Padre Padrone (1977)

Father, Son and the Mistress *See* For Richer, for Poorer (1992)

Faust-Eine deutsche Volkssage *See* Faust (1926)

Faustrecht der Freiheit *See* Fox and His Friends (1975)

Fauteuils d'Orchestre *See* Avenue Montaigne (2006)

The FBI Murders *See* In the Line of Duty: The FBI Murders (1988)

Fear *See* Night Creature (1979)

The Fear *See* Gates of Hell (1980)

Fear 2 *See* The Fear: Halloween Night (1999)

fear dot com *See* Feardotcom (2002)

Fear Eats the Soul *See* Ali: Fear Eats the Soul (1974)

Fear in the City of the Living Dead *See* Gates of Hell (1980)

Fear in the Night *See* Dynasty of Fear (1972)

Fear: Resurrection *See* The Fear: Halloween Night (1999)

Fearless *See* Jet Li's Fearless (2006)

Fearless Little Soldier *See* Fanfan la Tulipe (1951)

The Feast of All Saints *See* Anne Rice's The Feast of All Saints (2001)

Feast of Flesh *See* Blood Feast (1963)

Feast of Satan *See* Feast for the Devil (1971)

Federico Fellini: Sono un gran bugiardo *See* Fellini: I'm a Born Liar (2003)

Federico Fellini's 8 1/2 *See* 8 1/2 (1963)

Federico Fellini's Intervista *See* Intervista (1987)

Feel the Heat *See* Catch the Heat (1987)

Fei Ying *See* Silver Hawk (2004)

Fellini: Je suis un grand menteur *See* Fellini: I'm a Born Liar (2003)

Fellini: Sono un gran bugiardo *See* Fellini: I'm a Born Liar (2003)

Felons *See* First Degree (1998)

Female *See* The Violent Years (1956)

The Female Butcher *See* The Legend of Blood Castle (1972)

Female Fiend *See* Theatre of Death (1967)

Femmine Infernali *See* Escape from Hell (1979)

Feng Yue *See* Temptress Moon (1996)

Fengriffen *See* And Now the Screaming Starts (1973)

Perpect Crime *See* El Crimen Perfecto (2004)

Festen *See* The Celebration (1998)

Feux rouges *See* Red Lights (2004)

A Few Days in the Life of I.I. Oblomov *See* Oblomov (1981)

Fibra Optica *See* Optic Fiber (1997)

The Fiend with the Atomic Brain *See* Blood of Ghastly Horror (1972)

The Fiend with the Electronic Brain *See* Blood of Ghastly Horror (1972)

Fiendish Ghouls *See* The Flesh and the Fiends (1960)

Fierce *See* Fighting Mad (1977)

The Fifteen Streets *See* Catherine Cookson's The Fifteen Streets (1990)

The Fifth Chair *See* It's in the Bag (1945)

The Fifth Season *See* Profile for Murder (1996)

The 51st State *See* Formula 51 (2001)

50 Violins *See* Music of the Heart (1999)

50 Ways to Leave Your Lover *See* How to Lose Your Lover (2004)

Figaros Hochzeit *See* The Marriage of Figaro (1949)

The Fighting Phantom *See* The Mysterious Rider (1933)

The Fighting Pimpernel *See* The Elusive Pimpernel (1950)

The Fighting Seventh *See* Little Big Horn (1951)

Fighting Thru *See* Fightin' Ranch (1930)

Figli de Annibale *See* Children of Hannibal (1998)

The Final Crash *See* Steelyard Blues (1973)

Final Cut *See* Death Games (1980)

Finally, Sunday *See* Confidentially Yours (1983)

Fine and Dandy *See* The West Point Story (1950)

Fine Things *See* Danielle Steel's Fine Things (1990)

Fire Festival *See* Himatsuri (1985)

Fire in Eden *See* Tusks (1989)

Fire on the Mountain *See* Volcano: Fire on the Mountain (1997)

The Firebird *See* Phoenix (1978)

The First and the Last *See* 21 Days (1937)

The First Great Train Robbery *See* The Great Train Robbery (1979)

The First Hello *See* High Country (1981)

The First of the Few *See* Spitfire (1942)

The First Rebel *See* Allegheny Uprising (1939)

First Strike *See* Jackie Chan's First Strike (1996)

The First Time *See* The Fighter (1952)

First Woman into Space *See* Space Monster (1964)

Fischia Il sesso *See* Loose in New York (1974)

Fish Out of Water *See* The Witness (1999)

A Fist Full of Chopsticks *See* They Call Me Bruce? (1982)

Fist of Fear *See* Fist of Fear, Touch of Death (1980)

Fist of Fury *See* Chinese Connection (1973)

Fist Right of Freedom *See* Fox and His Friends (1975)

A Fistful of Feathers *See* Fowl Play (1975)

Fistful of the Dragon *See* Chinese Connection 2 (1977)

Fists of Fury 2 *See* Chinese Connection 2 (1977)

Five Angles on Murder *See* The Woman in Question (1950)

The Five at the Funeral *See* House of Terror (1972)

Five Bloody Days to Tombstone *See* Gun Riders (1969)

Five Bloody Graves *See* Gun Riders (1969)

The Five Day Lover *See* Time Out for Love (1961)

Five Days *See* Paid to Kill (1954)

Five Minutes to Live *See* Door to Door Maniac (1961)

Five Savage Men *See* The Desperados (1970)

Five Times Two *See* 5x2 (2004)

Five Women Around Utamaro *See* Utamaro and His Five Women (1946)

Fixing the Shadow *See* Beyond the Law (1992)

Flagrant Desir *See* Trade Secrets (1986)

The Flame of Torment *See* Enjo (1958)

Flanagan *See* Walls of Glass (1985)

Flash Gordon: Rocketship *See* Rocketship (1936)

Flash Gordon's Trip to Mars *See* Flash Gordon: Mars Attacks the World (1939)

Flatbed Annie *See* Flatbed Annie and Sweetiepie: Lady Truckers (1979)

The Flesh Creatures *See* Horror of the Blood Monsters (1970)

Flesh Creatures of the Red Planet *See* Horror of the Blood Monsters (1970)

Flesh for Frankenstein *See* Andy Warhol's Frankenstein (1974)

The Flight *See* The Taking of Flight 847: The Uli Derickson Story (1988)

Flight of the Dove *See* The Spy Within (1994)

The Flight of the White Stallions *See* The Miracle of the White Stallions (1963)

Flip Out *See* Get Crazy (1983)

Flipper and the Pirates *See* Flipper's New Adventure (1964)

Floating Weeds *See* Drifting Weeds (1959)

Flood *See* Hard Rain (1997)

Flower of the Arabian Nights *See* Arabian Nights (1974)

Flying Aces *See* The Flying Deuces (1939)

The Flying Dutchman *See* Frozen in Fear (2000)

Flying Wild *See* Fly Away Home (1996)

Focus *See* Shot (2001)

Fog *See* A Study in Terror (1966)

Folles Bourgeoises *See* Twist (1976)

The Folks at Red Wolf Inn *See* Terror at Red Wolf Inn (1974)

Follow That Bird *See* Sesame Street Presents: Follow That Bird (1985)

Follow the Hunter See Fangs of the Wild (1954)

Follow Your Dreams See Independence Day (1983)

Fontane Effi Briest See Effi Briest (1974)

Footprints See Primal Impulse (1974)

For a Few Bullets More See Any Gun Can Play (1967)

For Better or For Worse See Honeymoon Academy (1990)

For Love or Money See If I Were Rich (1933)

For Men Only See Tall Le (1953)

For the Cause See Final Encounter (2000)

For We Too Do Not Forgive See Death Is Called Engelchen (1963)

Forbidden Alliance See The Barretts of Wimpole Street (1934)

Forbidden Love See Freaks (1932)

Forbidden Paradise See Hurricane (1979)

Forbidden Passions See The Sensuous Teenager (1970)

Forbidden Son See Buildance (1988)

The Forbin Project See Colossus: The Forbin Project (1970)

Forbrydelsens Element See The Element of Crime (1984)

Ford Fairlane See The Adventures of Ford Fairlane (1990)

A Foreign Affair See 2 Brothers & a Bride (2003)

Foreign Skin See Unveiled (2005)

The Forest Primeval See The Final Terror (1983)

Forgotten Prisoners: The Amnesty Files See Forgotten Prisoners (1990)

The Forsyte Saga See That Forsyte Woman (1950)

Fortune in Diamonds See The Adventurers (1951)

The Fortunes and Misfortunes of Moll Flanders See Moll Flanders (1996)

47 Samurai See 47 Ronin, Part 1 (1942)

Forward March See Doughboys (1930)

The Fotographer of Panic See Peeping Tom (1960)

The Four Just Men See The Secret Four (1940)

Foxforce See She Devils in Chains (1976)

4. Luni, 3 Saptamani si 2 Zile See 4 Months, 3 Weeks, 2 Days (2007)

F.P. 1 Antwortet Nicht See F.P. 1 Doesn't Answer (1933)

A Fourth for Marriage See What's Up Front (1963)

4...3...2...1...Morte See Mission Stardust (1968)

Frameup See ...on Jost's Frameup (1993)

Francesco, giullare di Dio See The Flowers of St. Francis (1950)

Francis See Francis the Talking Mule (1949)

Francis, God's Jester See The Flowers of St. Francis (1950)

Frank Herbert's Dune See Dune (2000)

Frank Miller's Sin City See Sin City (2005)

Frankenstein See Andy Warhol's Frankenstein (1974)

Frankenstein See Mary Shelley's Frankenstein (1994)

Frankenstein '88 See The Vindicator (1985)

The Frankenstein Experiment See Andy Warhol's Frankenstein (1974)

Frankenstein Made Woman See Frankenstein Created Woman (1966)

Frankenstein Meets the Spacemen See Frankenstein Meets the Space Monster (1965)

Frankenstein Monsters: Sanda vs. Gairath See War of the Gargantuas (1970)

Frasier the Lovable Lion See Frasier the Sensuous Lion (1973)

Fraternally Yours See Sons of the Desert (1933)

The Freak from Suckweasel Mountain See Geek Maggot Bingo (1983)

Freak Talks About Sex See Blowin' Smoke (1999)

Freddie as F.R.O.7 See Freddie the Frog (1992)

Free to Live See Holiday (1938)

Freedom for Us See A Nous la Liberte (1931)

The Freedom Seekers See The Bloodsuckers (1970)

Freetall See Firefall (1994)

The Freeze Bomb See Kill Factor (1978)

Freie Haut See Unveiled (2005)

Frenzy See Torment (1944)

Fresa y Chocolate See Strawberry and Chocolate (1993)

Fresh Bait See L'Appat (1994)

Freylekhe Kabtsonim See The Jolly Paupers (1938)

A Friday Night Date See Road Rage (2001)

The Fright See Visiting Hours (1982)

The Frightened Lady See The Case of the Frightened Lady (1939)

Frightmare 2 See Frightmare (1974)

Frissons See They Came from Within (1975)

Fritz Freleng's Looney Looney Looney Bugs Bunny Movie See Looney Looney Looney Bugs Bunny Movie (1981)

The Frog Prince See The French Lesson (1986)

Froken Julie See Miss Julie (1950)

From a Whisper to a Scream See The Offspring (1987)

From Broadway to Cheyenne See Broadway to Cheyenne (1932)

From Hell to Victory See Eagles Attack at Dawn (1970)

From the Mixed-Up Files of Mrs. Basil E. Frankweiler See The Hideaways (1973)

The Fruit Machine See Wonderland (1988)

Fruhlingssinfonie See Spring Symphony (1986)

Frozen Terror See Macabre (1980)

Fu Gui Lie Che See The Millionaire's Express (1986)

Fugitive Lovers See Runaways (1975)

Fukkatsu no Hi See Virus (1982)

Fukusho Suruwa Ware Ni Ari See Vengeance Is Mine (1979)

The Fulfillment of Mary Gray See Fulfillment (1989)

Full Moon of the Virgins See Devil's Wedding Night (1973)

The Fun House See Last House on Dead End Street (1977)

Fun Loving See Quackser Fortune Has a Cousin in the Bronx (1970)

Funeral Rites See The Funeral (1984)

Funf Patronenhulsen See Five Cartridges (1960)

Fungus of Terror See Attack of the Mushroom People (1963)

Funny Little Dirty War See Funny, Dirty Little War (1983)

Fuoco Fatuo See The Fire Within (1964)

Fuori dal Mondo See Not of This World (1999)

Furankenshutain No Kaiju: Sanda tai Gaiiah See War of the Gargantuas (1970)

Furin Kazan See Samurai Banners (1969)

The Further Adventures of Ma and Pa Kettle See Ma and Pa Kettle (1949)

A Further Gesture See The Break (1997)

Fury Is a Woman See Siberian Lady Macbeth (1961)

Fury of Samson See The Fury of Hercules (1961)

Fury of the Succubus See Demon Rage (1982)

Fury of the Vikings See The Invaders (1963)

Future Cop See Trancers (1984)

Future Ninja See Cyber Ninja (1994)

Gadjo Dilo See The Crazy Stranger (1998)

A Gal Waak See Project A (1983)

The Gallery Murders See The Bird with the Crystal Plumage (1970)

Gallery of Horror See Alien Massacre (1967)

Gambara vs. Barugon See Gamera vs. Barugon (1966)

The Game of Death See Robert Louis Stevenson's The Game of Death (1999)

Gamblin' Man See Cockfighter (1974)

Gamblers in Okinawa See Sympathy for the Underdog (1971)

Gambling Man See Cockfighter (1974)

Gamera See Gamera, the Invincible (1966)

Gamera Tai Barugon See Gamera vs. Barugon (1966)

Gamera Tai Daiakaju Bairasu See Destroy All Planets (1968)

Gamera Tai Gaos See Gamera vs. Gaos (1967)

Gamera Tai Guiron See Gamera vs. Guiron (1969)

Gamera Tai Shinkai Kaiju Jigara See Gamera vs. Zigra (1971)

Gamera Tai Uchukaiju Bairasu See Destroy All Planets (1968)

Gamera Tai Viras See Destroy All Planets (1968)

Gamera Vs. Gyaos See Gamera vs. Gaos (1967)

Gamera Vs. Viras See Destroy All Planets (1968)

Gamera vs. Outer Space Monster Viras See Destroy All Planets (1968)

Gamera vs. the Deep Sea Monster Zigra See Gamera vs. Zigra (1971)

Gamera, the Invincible (1966)

Gammera See Gamera, the Invincible (1966)

Gamma 3 See The Green Slime (1968)

Gamma Sango Uchu Daisakusen See The Green Slime (1968)

Gamma 693 See The Chilling (1989)

Gamma 693 See Night of the Zombies (1981)

Gang War See Odd Man Out (1947)

Gangland Boss See A Better Tomorrow, Part 1 (1986)

Gangland See Mean Machine (1973)

The Gangster's Moll See Minbo—Or the Gentle Art of Japanese Extortion (1992)

Gangster See Hoodlum (1996)

The Gardener See Seeds of Evil (1976)

The Gargon Terror See Teenagers from Outer Space (1959)

Garou Garou le Passe Muraille See Mr. Peek-A-Boo (1950)

Gas-s-s-s... or, It May Become Necessary to Destroy the World in Order to Save It See Gas-s-s-s! (1970)

A Gathering of Old Men See Murder on the Bayou (1991)

Gatto Rossi in Un Labirinto Do Vetro See Eyeball (1978)

The Gay Divorce See The Gay Divorcee ('1934)

The Gay Mrs. Trexel See Susan and God (1940)

The Gaze of Ulysses See Ulysses' Gaze (1995)

Gazon Maudit See French Twist (1995)

Gebroken Spiegels See Broken Mirrors

Gegen die Wand See Head On (2004)

Geheimecode Wildganse See Codename: Wildgeese (1984)

Gei Ba Ba de Xin See Jet Li's The Enforcer (1995)

The Gemini Twins See Twins of Evil (1971)

Genealogies d'un Crime See Genealogies of a Crime (1997)

Genie of Darkness See Curse of Nostradamus (1960)

A Gentle Creature See A Gentle Woman (1969)

The Gentleman Tramp See La Collectionneuse (1967)

Gentlemen Don't Eat Poets See Grave Indiscretions (1996)

Gently Before She Dies See Your Vice is a Closed Room and Only I Have the Key (1972)

George A. Romero's Diary of the Dead See Diary of the Dead (2007)

George McKenna Story See Hard Lessons (1986)

Georgia's Friends See Four Friends (1981)

The German Sisters See Marianne and Juliane (1982)

Gestapo See Night Train to Munich (1940)

Get Down and Boogie See Darktown Strutters (1974)

Get Rita See Lady of the Evening (1975)

Get Well Soon See Visiting Hours (1982)

Get Even See Fight for Your Life (1977)

Getting Even See Utilities (1983)

Getting Married in Buffalo Jump See Buffalo Jump (1990)

Ghidorah Sandai Kaiju Chikyu Saidai No Kessan See Ghidrah the Three Headed Monster (1965)

Ghidorah, the Three-Headed Monster See Ghidrah the Three Headed Monster (1965)

Ghare Baire See The Home and the World (1984)

Gharbar See The Householder (1963)

Ghidora, the Three-Headed Monster See Ghidrah the Three Headed Monster (1965)

The Ghost Creeps See Boys of the City (1940)

The Ghost of Fletcher Ridge See Ain't No Way Back (1989)

The Ghost of John Holling See Mystery Liner (1934)

Ghost Rider (1934)

Ghost Riders of the West See The Phantom Rider (1946)

The Ghost Steps Out See The Time of Their Lives (1946)

Ghost Story See Madhouse Mansion (1974)

Ghosthouse 2 See Witchery (1988)

The Ghostly Rental See The Haunting of Hell House (1999)

Ghosts from the Past See Ghosts of Mississippi (1996)

Ghosts of Mars See John Carpenter's Ghosts of Mars (2001)

The Ghoul in School See Werewolf in a Girl's Dormitory (1961)

The Giant Leeches *See* Attack of the Giant Leeches (1959)

Giga Shadow *See* Tales from a Parallel Universe: Giga Shadow (1997)

Gigantis, the Fire Monster *See* Godzilla Raids Again (1955)

Gilbert Grape *See* What's Eating Gilbert Grape (1993)

Gill Woman *See* Voyage to the Planet of Prehistoric Women (1968)

Gill Women of Venus *See* Voyage to the Planet of Prehistoric Women (1968)

Ging Chaat Goo Si *See* Police Story (1985)

Ginger Snaps 2: The Sequel *See* Ginger Snaps: Unleashed (2004)

Ginger Snaps 3 *See* Ginger Snaps Back: The Beginning (2004)

Gingerbread House *See* Who Slew Auntie Roo? (1971)

Gion Bayashi *See* A Geisha (1953)

Gion Festival Music *See* A Geisha (1953)

Gion No Shimai *See* Sisters of the Gion (1936)

Giormi *See* Days (2002)

The Girl *See* Catherine Cookson's The Girl (1996)

The Girl Gets Moe *See* Love to Kill (1997)

Girl in Pawn *See* Little Miss Marker (1934)

Girl in the Leather Suit *See* Hell's Belles (1969)

Girl in the Moon *See* Woman in the Moon (1929)

Girl in the Park *See* Sanctuary of Fear (1979)

Girl in the Street *See* London Melody (1937)

The Girl of the Nile *See* Emerald of Artama (1967)

The Girl Was Young *See* Young and Innocent (1937)

The Girl You Want *See* Boys (1995)

The Girls *See* Les Bonnes Femmes (1960)

Girls for Rent *See* I Spit on Your Corpse (1974)

The Girls He Left Behind *See* The Gang's All Here (1943)

Girls in Uniform *See* Maedchen in Uniform (1931)

Girls Will Be Girls *See* Fish Without a Bicycle (2003)

Giro City *See* And Nothing But the Truth (1982)

Giu la Testa *See* A Fistful of Dynamite (1972)

Giu la Testa...Hombre *See* Fistful of Death (1971)

Giulietta Degli Spiriti *See* Juliet of the Spirits (1965)

Give Me Back My Skin *See* Rendez-Moi Ma Peau (1981)

Gladiatorerna *See* The Gladiators (1970)

Glass Bottle *See* Gorgeous (1999)

The Glass Cage *See* Glass Tomb (1955)

The Glass Virgin *See* Catherine Cookson's The Glass Virgin (1995)

Glen or Glenda: The Confessions of Ed Wood *See* Glen or Glenda? (1953)

Gli Amori di Ercole *See* The Loves of Hercules (1960)

Gli Indifferenti *See* Time of Indifference (1964)

Gli Invasori *See* The Invaders (1963)

Gli Orrori del Castello di Norimberga *See* Torture Chamber of Baron Blood (1972)

Global Heresy *See* Rock My World (2002)

Glorious Sacrifice *See* The Glory Trail (1936)

Glory at Sea *See* The Gift Horse (1952)

Glory Glory *See* Hooded Angels (2000)

The Glove: Lethal Terminator *See* The Glove (1978)

Glump *See* Please Don't Eat My Mother (1972)

G'mar Giviya *See* Cup Final (1992)

Gnaw: Food of the Gods 2 *See* Food of the Gods: Part 2 (1988)

A Gnome Named Gnorm *See* The Adventures of a Gnome Named Gnorm (1993)

Go and See *See* Come and See (1985)

The Goat *See* La Chevre (1981)

The Goddess *See* Devi (1960)

God's Gift *See* Wend Kuuni (1982)

Godson *See* Le Samourai (1967)

Godzilla Fights the Giant Moth *See* Godzilla vs. Mothra (1964)

Godzilla Versus the Bionic Monster *See* Godzilla vs. the Cosmic Monster (1974)

Godzilla vs. Gigan *See* Godzilla on Monster Island (1972)

Godzilla vs. Hedora *See* Godzilla vs. the Smog Monster (1972)

Godzilla vs. Mechagodzilla *See* Godzilla vs. the Cosmic Monster (1974)

Godzilla vs. the Giant Moth *See* Godzilla vs. Mothra (1964)

Godzilla vs. the Thing *See* Godzilla vs. Mothra (1964)

Godzilla's Counter Attack *See* Godzilla Raids Again (1955)

Gohatto *See* Taboo (1999)

Going Ape *See* Where's Poppa? (1970)

Going Back *See* Under Heavy Fire (2001)

Going West in America *See* Switchback (1997)

Gojira *See* Godzilla, King of the Monsters (1956)

Gojira no Musuko *See* Son of Godzilla (1966)

Gojira tai Biorante *See* Godzilla vs. Biollante (1989)

Gojira Tai Hedora *See* Godzilla vs. the Smog Monster (1972)

Gojira tai Megaro *See* Godzilla vs. Megalon (1976)

Gojira Tai Meka-Gojira *See* Godzilla vs. the Cosmic Monster (1974)

Goke, Body Snatcher from Hell *See* Body Snatcher from Hell (1969)

Goke the Vampire *See* Body Snatcher from Hell (1969)

Gokiburi *See* Twilight of the Cockroaches (1990)

Gokudo kyofu dai-gekijo *See* Gozu (2003)

Gold Coast *See* Elmore Leonard's Gold Coast (1997)

The Golden Age *See* L'Age D'Or (1930)

Golden Hands of Kurigal *See* Federal Agents vs. Underworld, Inc. (1949)

The Golden Heist *See* Inside Out (1975)

The Golden Hour *See* Pot o' Gold (1941)

Golden Ivory *See* White Huntress (1957)

Golden Marie *See* Casque d'Or (1952)

The Golden Trail *See* Riders of the Whistling Skull (1937)

Golden Virgin *See* The Story of Esther Costello (1957)

Golden Years *See* Stephen King's Golden Years (1991)

Golemata voda *See* The Great Water (2004)

Goliat Contra Los Gigantes *See* Goliath Against the Giants (1963)

Goliath and the Giants *See* Goliath Against the Giants (1963)

Goliath and the Golden City *See* Samson and the 7 Miracles of the World (1962)

Goliath Contro I Giganti *See* Goliath Against the Giants (1963)

Goliathon *See* The Mighty Peking Man (1977)

Golpes a Mi Puerta *See* Knocks at My Door (1993)

Gomar the Human Gorilla *See* Night of the Bloody Apes (1968)

Gone are the Days! *See* Purlie Victorious (1963)

Gong fu *See* Kung Fu Hustle (2004)

Gonggongui Jeog 2 *See* Another Public Enemy (2005)

The Good Girls *See* Les Bonnes Femmes (1960)

Good Idea *See* It Seemed Like a Good Idea at the Time (1975)

Good Luck, Miss Wyckoff *See* The Shaming (1971)

A Good Marriage *See* Le Beau Mariage (1982)

Good Morning Babilonia *See* Good Morning, Babylon (1987)

Good Ole Boy: A Delta Boyhood *See* The River Pirates (1988)

The Good Shepherd *See* The Confessor (2004)

Good to Go *See* Short Fuse (1988)

Goodbye Bafana *See* The Color of Freedom (2007)

Goodbye Bruce Lee: His Last Game of Death *See* Game of Death (1979)

Goodbye, Children *See* Au Revoir les Enfants (1987)

Goodbye Gemini *See* Twinsanity (1970)

Goodbye to the Hill *See* Paddy (1970)

Gordon II Pirata Nero *See* The Black Pirate (1926)

Gorilla *See* Nabonga (1944)

Gosta Berling's Saga *See* The Atonement of Gosta Berling (1924)

Gotter der Pest *See* Gods of the Plague (1969)

Gouttes d'Eau sur Pierres Brulantes *See* Water Drops on Burning Rocks (1999)

Grace Under Pressure *See* Something to Talk About (1995)

The Grail *See* Lancelot of the Lake (1974)

Gran Amore del Conde Dracula *See* Dracula's Great Love (1972)

The Grand Highway *See* Le Grand Chemin (1987)

The Grand Maneuvers *See* Les Grandes Manoeuvres (1955)

Grandmother's House *See* Grandma's House (1988)

The Grass is Singing *See* Killing Heat (1984)

The Grasshopper *See* The Passing of Evil (1970)

Grave Desires *See* Brides of the Beast (1968)

Grave Robbers from Outer Space *See* Plan 9 from Outer Space (1956)

The Graveside Story *See* The Comedy of Terrors (1964)

Graveyard Tramps *See* Invasion of the Bee Girls (1973)

The Great Adventure *See* The Adventurers (1951)

The Great Balloon Adventure *See* Olly Olly Oxen Free (1978)

The Great Day *See* A Special Day (1977)

The Great Decision *See* Men of America (1932)

Great Freedom No. 7 *See* Die Grosse Freiheit Nr. 7 (1945)

The Great Georgia Bank Hoax *See* Great Bank Hoax (1978)

The Great Hope *See* Submarine Attack (1954)

The Great Lester Boggs *See* Hootch Country Boys (1975)

The Great Manhunt *See* The Doolins of Oklahoma (1949)

Great Moments in Aviation *See* Shades of Fear (1993)

The Great Monster War *See* Godzilla vs. Monster Zero (1968)

Great Monster Yongkari *See* Yongkari Monster of the Deep (1967)

The Great Ride *See* Greedy Terror (1978)

The Great Schnozzle *See* Palooka (1934)

The Great Spy Mission *See* Operation Crossbow (1965)

The Great Wall is a Great Wall *See* A Great Wall (1986)

The Greatest Battle *See* Battleforce (1978)

The Greatest Battle on Earth *See* Ghidran the Three Headed Monster (1965)

The Greatest Love *See* Europa '51 (1952)

Greed *See* Axe (2006)

The Greeks Had a Word for Them *See* Three Broadway Girls (1932)

The Green Carnation *See* The Trials of Oscar Wilde (1960)

Green Monkey *See* Blue Monkey (1987)

The Green Ray *See* Summer (1986)

The Greenhouse *See* The Green House (1996)

Greta the Mad Butcher *See* Ilsa, the Wicked Warden (1978)

Grey Knight *See* The Ghost Brigade (1993)

Grey Matter *See* Mind Warp (1972)

Greystoke 2: Tarzan and Jane *See* Tarzan and the Lost City (1998)

Gridlock *See* Great American Traffic Jam (1980)

Grijpstra and de Gier *See* Fatal Error (1983)

Grim Weekend *See* S.I.C.K. Serial Insane Clown Killer (2003)

Grimm Brothers' Snow White *See* Snow White: A Tale of Terror (1997)

The Grinch *See* Dr. Seuss' How the Grinch Stole Christmas (2000)

Grindhouse: Death Proof *See* Death Proof (2007)

Grindhouse: Planet Terror *See* Planet Terror (2007)

Grine Felder *See* Green Fields (1937)

Gringo *See* Gunfight at Red Sands (1963)

The Grip of the Strangler *See* The Haunted Strangler (1958)

The Grip of the Vampire *See* Curse of the Undead (1959)

Gritos en la Noche *See* The Awful Dr. Orloff (1962)

The Groove Room *See* A Man with a Maid (1973)

The Grotesque *See* Grave Indiscretions (1996)

The Grudge *See* Ju-On: The Grudge (2003)

Gruner Felder *See* Green Fields (1937)

Gruppo di Famiglia in un Interno *See* Conversation Piece (1975)

Guardian of the Wilderness *See* Mountain Man (1977)

Guardians of the Deep *See* Shark Hunter (1979)

Guerreros *See* Warriors (2002)

Guilty Assignment *See* Big Town (1947)

Guizi Laile See Devils on the Doorstep (2000)

Gun Man from Bodie See Gunman from Bodie (1941)

Gun Moll See Jigsaw (1949)

Gun Moll See Lady of the Evening (1975)

Guney's The Wall See The Wall (1983)

Gunki hatameku motoni See Under the Flag of the Rising Sun (1972)

Gunpoint See At Gunpoint (1955)

Guns in the Afternoon See Ride the High Country (1962)

Guns, Sin and Bathtub Gin See Lady in Red (1979)

Gwendoline See The Perils of Gwendoline (1984)

Gweomul See The Host (2006)

Gycklarnas Afton See Sawdust & Tinsel (1953)

The Gypsy See Le Gitan (1975)

Ha Buah See The Bubble (2006)

Haakon Haakonsen See Shipwrecked (1990)

Hab Og Karlighed See Twist & Shout (1984)

Habitaciones para Turistas See Rooms for Tourists (2004)

Hable con Ella See Talk to Her (2002)

Habricha el Hashemesh See Escape to the Sun (1972)

Hachigatsu no Kyoshikyoku See Rhapsody in August (1991)

Hacks See Sink or Swim (1997)

Hadaka No Shima See The Island (1961)

Hadduta Misriya See An Egyptian Story (1982)

Hail to the Chief See Hall (1973)

The Hairy Bird See All I Wanna Do (1998)

Hairshirt See Too Smooth (1998)

Haishang Hua See Flowers of Shanghai (1998)

Hak Hap See Black Mask (1996)

Ha'Kohavim Shel Shlomi See Bonjour Monsieur Shlomi (2003)

Half a Sinner See Half a Soldier (1940)

The Half Life of Timofey Berezin See PU-239 (2006)

Half Slave, Half Free 2 See Charlotte Forten's Mission: Experiment in Freedom (1985)

Hallelujah, I'm a Tramp See Hallelujah, I'm a Bum (1933)

Halloween 7 See Halloween: H20 (1998)

Halloween: H20 (Twenty Years Later) See Halloween: H20 (1998)

Halloween Night See Hack O'Lantern (1987)

Halloween: The Origin of Michael Myers See Halloween 6: The Curse of Michael Myers (1995)

Hallucination Generation See Hallucination (1967)

Ham Ham See Jamon, Jamon (1993)

Hamam: Il Bagno Turco See Steam: A Turkish Bath (1996)

Ha'Matarah Tiran See Sinai Commandos (1968)

The Hammond Mystery See The Undying Monster (1942)

Hana-Bi See Fireworks (1997)

Hand of Night See Beast of Morocco (1966)

Handgun See Deep in the Heart (1983)

Handle With Care See Citizens Band (1977)

Hands of a Killer See Planets Against Us (1961)

Hands of a Strangler See The Hands of Orlac (1960)

The Hands of Orlac See Mad Love (1935)

Hands of the Strangler See The Hands of Orlac (1960)

Handsome Antonio See Il Bell'Antonio (1960)

Handsome Serge See Le Beau Serge (1958)

The Hengover See The Female Jungle (1956)

Hans Christian Andersen's Thumbelina See Thumbelina (1994)

Hanzo the Razor: Sword of Justice See The Razor: Sword of Justice (1972)

Hao xi a See Last Hurrah for Chivalry (1978)

Happiness See Le Bonheur (1965)

Happiness See Le Bonheur Est Dans le Pre (1995)

Happiness Is in the Fields See Le Bonheur Est Dans le Pre (1995)

Happy as the Grass Was Green See Hazel's People (1973)

Happy Go Lucky See Hallelujah, I'm a Bum (1933)

Happy Mother's Day, Love, George See Run, Stranger, Run (1973)

The Happy New Year Caper See Happy New Year (1973)

Happy Times See The Inspector General (1949)

Hard Driver See The Last American Hero (1973)

Hard Knocks See Mid Knight Rider (1979)

Hard Stick See A Real American Hero (1978)

Hard Times for Vampires See Uncle Was a Vampire (1959)

Hard to Die See Crime Story (1993)

Hard Way Out See Bloodfist 8: Hard Way Out (1996)

The Hardcore Life See Hardcore (1979)

Hardball See Bounty Hunters 2: Hardball (1997)

Harem Holiday See Harum Scarum (1965)

Harem Suare See Harem (1999)

Harlem Hot Shot See The Black King (1932)

Harlequin See Dark Forces (1983)

Harold Robbins' The Betsy See The Betsy (1978)

Harp of Burma See The Burmese Harp (1956)

Harrison Bergeron See Kurt Vonnegut's Harrison Bergeron (1995)

Harry, A Friend Who Wishes You Well See With a Friend Like Harry (2000)

Harry Black See Harry Black and the Tiger (1958)

Harry, He's Here to Help See With a Friend Like Harry (2000)

Harry Potter and the Philosopher's Stone See Harry Potter and the Sorcerer's Stone (2001)

Harry Tracy—Desperado See Harry Tracy (1983)

Harvest See Cash Crop (2001)

Hasta Cierto Punto See Up to a Certain Point (1983)

The Hatchet Murders See Deep Red: Hatchet Murders (1975)

Hatouna Mehuheret See Late Marriage (2001)

Hatred See Hate (1995)

The Haunted See Curse of the Demon (1957)

The Haunted and the Hunted See Dementia 13 (1963)

The Haunted Planet See Planet of the Vampires (1965)

The Haunting of Hamilton High See Hello Mary Lou: Prom Night 2 (1987)

The Haunting of Hill House See The Haunting (1999)

The Haunting of Julia See Full Circle (1977)

Haunted tension See High Tension (2003)

Haus Der Tausend Freuden See The House of 1000 Dolls (1967)

Haut Bas Fragile See Up/Down/Fragile (1995)

Haute tension See High Tension (2003)

Hauru no ugoku shiro See Howl's Moving Castle (2004)

Have a Nice Funeral See Gunslinger (1970)

The Hawk See Hawk and Castile (1967)

The Hawk of Castile See Hawk and Castile (1967)

Haxan See Haxan: Witchcraft through the Ages (1922)

A Heart in Winter See Un Coeur en Hiver (1993)

The Head that Wouldn't Die See The Brain that Wouldn't Die (1963)

Head On See Fatal Attraction (1980)

Head Over Heels See Chilly Scenes of Winter (1979)

He Lived to Kill See Night of Terror (1933)

He Loved an Actress See Mad About Money (1937)

He Ni Zaiyiqi See Together (2002)

He or She See Glen or Glenda? (1953)

He, She or It See The Doll (1962)

The Heart Is Elsewhere See Incantato (2003)

The Heart of New York See Hallelujah, I'm a Bum (1933)

Heartbeat See Le Schpountz (1938)

Heartbeat See Danielle Steel's Heartbeat (1993)

Heartbreak Motel See Poor Pretty Eddie (1973)

Hearts and Minds See Master Touch (1974)

Hearst Castle See Demonstone (1989)

Heaven on a Shoestring See The Night of Nights (1939)

Heaven Only Knows See For Heaven's Sake (1979)

Heavenly Pursuits See The Gospel According to Vic (1987)

Heaven's Pond See Devil's Pond (2003)

Hector Servadac's Ark See On the Comet (1968)

Hei Ma See A Mongolian Tale (1994)

Heimat-Eine deutsche Chronik See Heimat 1 (1984)

Heisser Sommer See Hot Summer (1968)

The Heir to Genghis Khan See Storm over Asia (1928)

Held Hostage See Fight for Your Life (1977)

Heldcrado See Heldorado (1946)

The Heist See Carbon Copy (1999)

The Heist See Dollars (1971)

The Heist See The Squeeze (1980)

Heidi Bent for Glory See Lafayette Escadrille (1958)

Hell Creatures See Invasion of the Saucer Men (1957)

Hell Fire See They (1977)

Hell in Normandy See Special Forces (1968)

Hell to Macao See The Corrupt Ones (1967)

Hellborn See Asylum of the Damned (2003)

Hellcab See Chicago Cab (1998)

Helicamp See Opposing Force (1987)

Hellbound: Hellraiser 2 See Hellraiser 2 (1988)

Hellfire See Haunted Symphony (1994)

Hellfire See Primal Scream (1987)

Hellfire on Ice, Part 2: Escape from Hell See Escape from Hell (1979)

Hell's Beacon See Predator Island (2005)

Hemoglobin See Bleeders (1997)

Hello Elephant See Perdon My Trunk (1952)

Henry: Portrait of a Serial Killer See Henry: Portrait of a Serial Killer (1986)

Henry James' The Ghostly Rental See The Haunting of Hell House (1999)

Her Bridal Night See The Bride Is Much Too Beautiful (1958)

Her Majesty, Mrs. Brown See Mrs. Brown (1997)

Her Mad Night See Held for Murder (1932)

Her Secret Life See Code Name: Dancer (1987)

Her Third See The Third (1972)

Her Wicked Ways See Lethal Charm (1990)

Hercules 2: See Hercules vs. the Sons of the Sun (1964)

Hercules Against the Sons of the Sun See Hercules vs. the Sons of the Sun (1964)

Hercules and the Captive Women See Hercules and the Captive Women (1963)

Hercules and the Conquest of Atlantis See Hercules and the Captive Women (1963)

Hercules and the Haunted Women See Hercules and the Captive Women (1963)

Hercules and the Hydra See The Loves of Hercules (1960)

Hercules and the Ten Avengers See The Triumph of Hercules (1964)

Hercules Goes Bananas See Hercules in New York (1970)

Hercules: The Movie See Hercules in New York (1970)

Hercules vs. the Giant Warriors See The Triumph of Hercules (1964)

Hercules vs. the Hydra See The Loves of Hercules (1960)

Hercules vs. the Molach See Conquest of Mycene (1963)

Here Come the Tigers See Manny's Orphans (1978)

Here Is a Man See The Devil & Daniel Webster (1941)

Here Lies Love See The Second Woman (1951)

Here We Go Again See Pride of the Bowery (1941)

The Hero of Pine Ridge See Yodelin' Kid from Pine Ridge (1937)

The Heroes See The Invincible Six (1968)

The Heroes Die Hard See Mr. Kingstreet's War (1971)

The Heterosexuals See Les Biches (1968)

Hets See Torment (1944)

Hex See The Shrieking (1973)

Hexen bis aufs Blut Gequault See Mark of the Devil (1969)

Herz aus Glas See Heart of Glass (1974)

Herzbube See King, Queen, Knave (1972)

H.G. Wells' New Invisible Man See The New Invisible Man (1958)

Hi No Tori See Phoenix (1978)

Hidden Face *See* Jail Bait (1954)

Hidden Power *See* Sabotage (1936)

Hidden Rage *See* Perfect Victims (1987)

The Hidden Room of 1,000 Horrors *See* The Tell-Tale Heart (1960)

Hidden Vision *See* Night Eyes (1990)

Hide and Shriek *See* American Gothic (1988)

Hideous Mutant Freekz *See* Freaked (1993)

Hifazaat *See* In Custody (1994)

High Risk *See* Meltdown (1995)

High Rolling *See* High Rolling in a Hot Corvette (1977)

Highbinders *See* The Medallion (2003)

Higher Love *See* Uncorked (1998)

The Highest Bidder *See* Woman Hunt (1972)

Highlander 2: Renegade Version *See* Highlander 2: The Quickening (1991)

Highlander 3: The Magician *See* Highlander: The Final Dimension (1994)

Highlander 3: The Sorcerer *See* Highlander: The Final Dimension (1994)

Highway to Hell *See* Running Hot (1983)

Hillbillys in a Haunted House *See* Hillbillies in a Haunted House (1967)

Him *See* Only You (1994)

Himalaya - L'Enfance d'un Chef *See* Himalaya (1999)

Himalaya - The Youth of a Chief *See* Himalaya (1999)

The Hindu *See* Sabaka (1955)

His Other Woman *See* Desk Set (1957)

Histoires Extraordinaires *See* Spirits of the Dead (1968)

History is Made at Night *See* Spy Games (1999)

Hit & Run *See* Hot Blooded (1998)

Hit Man *See* La Scoumoune (1972)

Hitlerjunge Salomon *See* Europa, Europa (1991)

Hitler's Gold *See* Inside Out (1975)

Hitman *See* American Commandos (1984)

HMS Defiant *See* Damn the Defiant (1962)

The Hoary Legends of the Caucasus *See* Ashik Kerib (1988)

Hol Volt, Hol Nem Volt *See* A Hungarian Fairy Tale (1987)

The Hole *See* Le Trou (1959)

Holiday *See* Jour de Fete (1948)

Hollow Point *See* The Wild Pair (1987)

Hollow Triumph *See* The Scar (1948)

Hollyweird *See* Flicks (1985)

Hollywood Cowboy *See* Hearts of the West (1975)

Hollywood Hoodlum *See* Hollywood Mystery (1934)

Hollywood Knight *See* Mid Knight Rider

Hollywood Strangler *See* Don't Answer the Phone (1980)

Hollywood Stunt Man *See* Movie Stuntmen (1953)

Hollywood Thrillmakers *See* Movie Stuntmen (1953)

Hollywood Vixens *See* Beyond the Valley of the Dolls (1970)

Holocaust 2000 *See* The Chosen (1977)

The Holy Child *See* Holy Girl (2004)

Holy Terror *See* Alice Sweet Alice (1976)

Holy Week *See* Angel of Death (2002)

Holy Year *See* L'Annee Sainte (1976)

Homa ke Nero *See* Earth & Water (1999)

Hombre Mirando Al Sudeste *See* Man Facing Southeast (1986)

Home Fires Burning *See* The Turning (1992)

Home Front *See* Morgan Stewart's Coming Home (1987)

Home in Oklahoma *See* Big Show (1937)

Home Is Where the Heart Is *See* Where the Heart Is (2000)

Home Is Where the Heart Is *See* Square Dance (1987)

Homeboy *See* Fist (1976)

Homecoming Night *See* Night of the Creeps (1986)

L'Homme de Sa Vie *See* The Man of My Life (2006)

L'Homme du Minnesota *See* Minnesota Clay (1965)

The Honest Courtesan *See* Dangerous Beauty (1998)

Honeymoon in Bali *See* My Love For Yours (1939)

Honeymoon of Fear *See* Dynasty of Fear (1972)

Hong Kong Express. *See* Chungking Express (1995)

Hong Ying Tao *See* Red Cherry (1995)

Hongfen *See* Blush (1995)

Honor Betrayed *See* Fear (1988)

The Honorary Consul *See* Beyond the Limit (1983)

Honour Among Thieves *See* Grisbi (1953)

Hoodlum Girls *See* Youth Aflame (1944)

Hoods *See* Hoodlum (1996)

The Hooker Cult Murders *See* The Pyx (1973)

Hopalong Cassidy Enters *See* Hopalong Cassidy (1935)

The Hopeless Ones *See* The Round Up (1966)

A Hora Da Estrela *See* The Hour of the Star (1985)

Horem Padem *See* Up and Down (2004)

Horí, ma panenko *See* The Firemen's Ball (1968)

L'Horloger de Saint-Paul *See* The Clockmaker (1973)

The Horrible House on the Hill *See* Devil Times Five (1974)

The Horrible Mill Women *See* Mill of the Stone Women (1960)

Horror Castle *See* The Virgin of Nuremberg (1965)

Horror Convention *See* Nightmare in Blood (1975)

Horror Creatures of the Prehistoric Planet *See* Horror of the Blood Monsters (1970)

Horror High *See* Twisted Brain (1974)

Horror Hotel Massacre *See* Eaten Alive (1976)

Horror in the Midnight Sun *See* Invasion of the Animal People (1962)

Horror Maniacs *See* The Greed of William Hart (1948)

Horror Planet *See* Inseminoid (1980)

Hors de Prix *See* Priceless (2006)

Horse, My Horse *See* The Horse (1982)

A Horse Named Comanche *See* Tonka (1958)

Horsie *See* Queen for a Day (1951)

Horton Hears a Who! *See* Dr. Seuss' Horton Hears a Who! (2008)

Hostage *See* Savage Attraction (1983)

Hostage: Dallas *See* Getting Even (1986)

Hostage: The Christine Maresch Story *See* Savage Attraction (1983)

Hostage Train *See* Crackerjack 2 (1997)

Hostages in the Gulf *See* Eagles Attack at Dawn (1970)

Hostile Country *See* Outlaw Fury (1950)

Hostile Force *See* The Heist (1996)

Hostsonaten *See* Autumn Sonata (1978)

Hot and Cold *See* Weekend at Bernie's (1989)

Hot Car Girl *See* Hot Rod Girl (1956)

Hot Lead *See* Run of the Arrow (1956)

The Hot One *See* Corvette Summer (1978)

Hot Seat *See* The Chair (1987)

Hot Sex in Bangkok *See* Inn of Temptation (1973)

Hot Spot *See* I Wake Up Screaming (1941)

The Hot Spur *See* Love Desperados (1968)

Hot Sweat *See* Katie Tippel (1975)

Hotaru no Haka *See* Grave of the Fireflies (1988)

Hotel Paraiso *See* Zus & Zo (2001)

Hotel Sorrento *See* Sorrento Beach (1995)

The Houghland Murder Case *See* Murder by Television (1935)

The Hounds of Zaroff *See* The Most Dangerous Game (1932)

Hour of Glory *See* The Small Back Room (1949)

The Hour of the Pig *See* The Advocate (1993)

House 3 *See* The Horror Show (1989)

The House Across the Lake *See* Heat Wave (1954)

House by the Lake *See* Death Weekend (1976)

House in Nightmare Park *See* Night of the Laughing Dead (1975)

House of Crazies *See* Asylum (1972)

House of Doom *See* The Black Cat (1934)

House of Evil *See* Dance of Death (1968)

House of Evil *See* The House on Sorority Row (1983)

The House of Exorcism *See* Lisa and the Devil (1975)

House of Fear *See* Fearmaker (1989)

House of Fright *See* Black Sunday (1960)

House of Fright *See* The Two Faces of Dr. Jekyll (1960)

House of Insane Women *See* Exorcism's Daughter (1974)

House of Mortal Sin *See* The Confessional (1975)

House of Mystery *See* Night Monster (1942)

House of Pleasure *See* Le Plaisir (1952)

House of Terror *See* Face of the Screaming Werewolf (1959)

House of Terror *See* The Hanging Woman (1972)

House of the Damned *See* Spectre (1996)

House of the Dark Stairway *See* A Blade in the Dark (1983)

House of the Screaming Virgins *See* Bloodsucking Freaks (1975)

House of Usher *See* The Fall of the House of Usher (1960)

The House on Turk Street *See* No Good Deed (2002)

House Transformations *See* The Heirloom (2005)

The House Where Death Lives *See* Delusion (1984)

The House Where Hell Froze Over *See* Keep My Grave Open (1980)

House Without Windows *See* Seven Alone (1975)

How Is It Going? *See* Comment Ca Va? (1976)

How Long Can You Fall? *See* Till Marriage Do Us Part (1974)

How the Grinch Stole Christmas *See* Dr. Seuss' How the Grinch Stole Christmas (2000)

How to Be a Player *See* Def Jam's How to Be a Player (1997)

How to Be a Woman and Not Die Trying *See* How to Be a Woman and Not Die in the Attempt (1991)

How to Get the Man's Foot Outta Your Asss! *See* Baadasssss! (2003)

How to Irritate People *See* John Cleese on How to Irritate People (1968)

How to Steal a Diamond in Four Easy Lessons *See* The Hot Rock (1970)

How to Steal a Million Dollars and Live Happily Ever After *See* How to Steal a Million (1966)

Howard Beach: Making the Case for Murder *See* Skin (1989)

Howard Stern's Private Parts *See* Private Parts (1996)

Howling 2: Stirba—Werewolf Bitch *See* Howling 2: Your Sister Is a Werewolf (1985)

Howling 7 *See* The Howling: New Moon Rising (1995)

H.P. Lovecraft's Beyond the Wall of Sleep *See* Beyond the Wall of Sleep (2006)

H.P. Lovecraft's The Unnamable Returns *See* The Unnamable 2: The Statement of Randolph Carter (1992)

Hrafninn Flygur *See* Revenge of the Barbarians (1985)

Hsi Yen *See* The Wedding Banquet (1993)

Hua Pi Zhi Yinyang Fawang *See* Painted Skin (1993)

Huang Jia Zhan Shi *See* Royal Warriors (1986)

Huang Tudi *See* Yellow Earth (1989)

Huggers *See* Crazy Moon (1987)

The Human Beast *See* La Bete Humaine (1938)

Human Cargo *See* Escape: Human Cargo (1998)

Human Meat Pies *See* The Untold Story (1993)

The Human Tornado *See* Dolemite 2: Human Tornado (1976)

Hunchback *See* The Hunchback of Notre Dame (1982)

Hungry Pets *See* Please Don't Eat My Mother (1972)

Hungry Wives *See* Season of the Witch (1973)

Hunt to Kill *See* The White Buffalo (1977)

The Hunted *See* Touch Me Not (1974)

Hunter of the Apocalypse *See* The Last Hunter (1980)

Hunters Are For Killing *See* Hard Frame (1970)

Huo Shao Dao *See* The Prisoner (1990)

Huo Yuan Jia *See* Jet Li's Fearless (2006)

Huozhe *See* To Live (1994)

Hurricane Streets *See* Hurricane Streets (1996)

Hustler Squad *See* The Doll Squad (1973)

Hydra *See* Attack of the Swamp Creature (1975)

Hypercube *See* Cube 2: Hypercube (2002)

Hypnotic *See* Close Your Eyes (2002)

I Accuse *See* J'Accuse (1937)

I Am a Fugitive From the Chain Gang *See* I Am a Fugitive from a Chain Gang (1932)

I Bambini Ci Guardano *See* The Children Are Watching Us (1944)

I Became a Criminal *See* They Made Me a Criminal (1939)
I Became a Criminal *See* They Made Me a Fugitive (1947)
I Breathe *See* Respiro (2002)
I Call First *See* Who's That Knocking at My Door? (1968)
I Can Make You Love Me *See* Stalking Laura (1993)
I Changed My Sex *See* Glen or Glenda? (1953)
I Cinque Della Vendetta *See* Five Giants from Texas (1966)
I Coltelli Del Vendicatore *See* Knives of the Avenger (1965)
I Compagni *See* The Organizer (1963)
I Giorni Dell'Inferno *See* Days of Hell (1984)
I Corpi Presentano Tracce Di Violenza Carnale *See* Torso (1973)
I Crossed the Line *See* The Black Klansmar (1966)
I Fak *See* The Judgement (1999)
I Fidanzati *See* Fiances (1963)
I Fought the Law *See* Dead Heat (2001)
I Led Two Lives *See* Glen or Glenda? (1953)
I Love a Man in Uniform *See* A Man in Uniform (1993)
I Hate Your Guts *See* Shame (1961)
I Have a New Master *See* Passion for Life (1948)
I Have a Stranger's Face *See* Face of Another (1966)
I Have Lived *See* After Midnight (1953)
I Have No Mouth But I Must Scream *See* And Now the Screaming Starts (1973)
I Love to Kill *See* Impulse (1974)
I Married a Shadow *See* I Married a Dead Man (1982)
I Married Too Young *See* Married Too Young (1962)
I Masnadieri *See* The Mercenaries (1962)
I Nuovi Barbari *See* Warriors of the Wasteland (1983)
I Padroni della Citta *See* Rulers of the City (1976)
I Pianeti Contro di Noi *See* Planets Against Us (1961)
I Racconti di Canterbury *See* The Canterbury Tales (1971)
I Remember *See* Amarcord (1974)
I Saw a Dream Like This *See* Akira Kurosawa's Dreams (1990)
I Skiachtra *See* The Enchantress (1985)
I Soliti Ignoti *See* Big Deal on Madonna Street (1958)
I Tre Volti della Paura *See* Black Sabbath (1964)
I Want Her Dead *See* W (1974)
I Was a Teenage Boy *See* Something Special (1986)
I Was a Teenage Teenager *See* Clueless (1995)
I Worship His Shadow *See* Tales from a Parallel Universe: I Worship His Shadow (1997)
I You She He *See* Je Tu Il Elle (1974)
The Iceberg *See* L'Iceberg (2005)
Ich und Er *See* Me and Him (1999)
Ich War Neunzehn *See* I Was Nineteen (1968)
Ich Will Doch Nur, Dass Ihr Mich Liebt *See* I Only Want You to Love Me (1976)
Ici et Ailleurs *See* Here and Elsewhere (1976)
Identificazione di una Donna *See* Identification of a Woman (1982)
Identikit *See* Driver's Seat (1973)
Idi I Smotri *See* Come and See (1985)
Idl *See* L'Idiot
The Idiot *See* L'Idiot (1946)

Idioterne *See* The Idiots (1999)
Iedereen Beroemdi *See* Everybody's Famous! (2000)
Ieri, Oggi E Domani *See* Yesterday, Today and Tomorrow (1964)
If He Hollers, Let Him Go *See* Dead Right (1968)
If You Can't Say It, Just See It *See* Whore (1991)
If You Feel Like Singing *See* Summer Stock (1950)
Ignorant Fairies *See* His Secret Life (2001)
Ike: The War Years *See* Ike (1979)
Iklimler *See* Climates (2006)
Il Bois Scarlato *See* The Bloody Pit of Horror (1965)
Il Buco *See* Le Trou (1959)
Il Cacciatore di Squali *See* Shark Hunter (1979)
Il Castello de Morti Vivi *See* Castle of the Living Dead (1964)
Il Cielo Cade *See* The Sky is Falling (2000)
Il Citadino si Ribella *See* Street Law (1974)
Il Cobra *See* The Cobra (1968)
Il Conformista *See* The Conformist (1971)
Il Conte Dracula *See* Count Dracula (1971)
Il Cristo Proibito *See* The Forbidden Christ (1950)
Il Diario di una Cameriera *See* Diary of a Chambermaid (1964)
Il Deserto Rosso *See* The Red Desert (1964)
Il Deserto dei Tartari *See* The Desert of the Tartars (1976)
Il Decameron *See* The Decameron (1970)
Il Cuore Altrove *See* Incantato (2003)
Il Crudeli *See* Hellbenders (1967)
Il Diavolo e i Morti *See* Lisa and the Devil (1975)
Il Diavolo in Corpo *See* Devil in the Flesh (1987)
Il Dio Chiamato a Dorian Gray *See* Dorian Gray (1970)
Il Disprezzo *See* Contempt (1964)
Il Etait une Fois un Pays *See* Underground (1995)
Il Fantasma dell'Opera *See* The Phantom of the Opera (1998)
Il Figlio del Capitano Blood *See* Son of Captain Blood (1962)
Il Fiore delle Mille e Una Notte *See* Arabian Nights (1974)
Il Flume del Grande Caimano *See* The Great Alligator (1981)
Il Gatto Nero *See* The Black Cat (1981)
Il Gatto Dagli Occhi di Giada *See* Watch Me When I Kill (1977)
Il Gattopardo *See* The Leopard (1963)
Il Generale Della-Rovere *See* Generale Della Rovere (1960)
Il Giardino Del Finzi-Contini *See* The Garden of the Finzi-Contins (1971)
Il Gladiatore Invincible *See* The Invincible Gladiator (1963)
Il Gigante Di Metropolis *See* The Giant of Metropolis (1961)
Il Giorno e L'Ora *See* The Day and the Hour (1963)
Il Gladiatore Di Roma *See* Gladiator of Rome (1963)
Il Gladiatore (1933)
Il Ladro Di Bagdad *See* Thief of Baghdad (1961)
Il Ladro di Bambini *See* The Stolen Children (1992)

Il Lago di Satana *See* The She-Beast (1965)
Il Mercante di Pietre *See* The Stone Merchant (2006)
Il Messia *See* The Messiah (1975)
Il Mio Nome e Nessuno *See* My Name is Nobody (1974)
Il Mlo West *See* Gunslinger's Revenge (1998)
Il Mondo Di Yor *See* Yor, the Hunter from the Future (1983)
Il Monstro *See* The Monster (1996)
Il Mostro e in Tavola...Barone Frankenstein *See* Andy Warhol's Frankenstein (1974)
Il Montagna di Dio Cannibale *See* Mountain of the Cannibal God (1979)
Il Mulino delle Donne di Pietra *See* Mill of the Stone Women (1960)
Il Natale Che Quasi Non Fu *See* The Christmas That Almost Wasn't (1966)
Il Pianeta Degli Uomini Spenti *See* Battle of the Worlds (1961)
Il Portiere de Notte *See* The Night Porter (1974)
Il Positino *See* The Postman (1994)
Il Processo *See* The Trial (1963)
Il Quartetto Basileus *See* Basileus Quartet (1982)
Il Ragno *See* The Killer Must Kill Again (1975)
Il Re Del Criminali *See* Superargo (1967)
Il Rosso Segmo della Follia *See* Hatchet for the Honeymoon (1970)
Il Sale Anche di Notte *See* Night Sun (1990)
Il Segreto del Vestito Rosso *See* Assassination in Rome (1965)
Il Sicario *See* The Hit Man (1960)
Il Sigillo de Pechino *See* The Corrupt Ones (1967)
Il sorriso di mia madre *See* My Mother's Smile (2002)
Il Terror Del Barabesi *See* Goliath and the Barbarians (1960)
Il Testimone dello Sposo *See* The Best Man (1997)
Il Tigre *See* Tiger and the Pussycat (1967)
Il Treno *See* The Train (1965)
Il Trionfo di Ercole *See* The Triumph of Hercules (1966)
Il tuo vizio e una stanza chiusa e solo io ne ho la chiave *See* Your Vice is a Closed Room and Only I Have the Key (1972)
Il Vangelo Secondo Matteo *See* The Gospel According to St. Matthew (1964)
Ill Met By Moonlight *See* Night Ambush (1957)
Illicit Dreams 2 *See* Death and Desire (1997)
Illicit Interlude *See* Summer Interlude (1950)
Illuminacja *See* Illumination (1973)
Illumination *See* FairyTale: A True Story (1997)
Ilsa, the Absolute Power *See* Ilsa, the Wicked Warden (1978)
Ilya Mourometz *See* Sword & the Dragon (1956)
Im Lauf der Zeit *See* Kings of the Road—In the Course of Time (1976)
Im Stahlnetz Des Dr. Mabuse *See* The Return of Dr. Mabuse (1961)
L'Imbalsamatore *See* The Embalmer (2003)
Immediate Disaster *See* The Stranger from Venus (1954)
Immorale *See* The Immoral One (1980)
Immortal Ad Vitam *See* Immortal (2004)

Immortal France *See* Heart of a Nation (1943)
The Imp *See* Sorority Babes in the Slimeball Bowl-A-Rama (1987)
The Important Story of Alcoholism *See* One Too Many (1951)
Impossible Object *See* The Story of a Love Story (1973)
In a Year with 13 Moons *See* In a Year of 13 Moons (1978)
In Bed with Madonna *See* Truth or Dare (1991)
In Bed *See* En la Cama (2005)
In Deadly Heat *See* Stuff Stephanie in the Incinerator (1989)
In Einem Jahr Mit 13 Monden *See* In a Year of 13 Moons (1978)
In Fashion *See* A la Mode (1994)
In Love *See* Falling in Love Again (1980)
In Old Oklahoma *See* War of the Wildcats (1943)
In Pursuit of Honor *See* G.I. Jane (1997)
In the Bleak Midwinter *See* A Midwinter's Tale (1995)
In the Devil's Garden *See* Assault (1970)
In the Empty City *See* Hollow City (2004)
In the Grip of the Spider *See* Web of the Spider (1970)
In the Line of Duty *See* Royal Warriors (1986)
In the Line of Duty: Manhunt in the Dakotas *See* Midnight Murders (1991)
In the Line of Duty: Siege at Marion *See* Children of Fury (1994)
In the Realm of Passion *See* The Empire of Passion (1976)
In the Woods *See* Flashoman (1951)
In Weiter Ferne, So Nah! *See* Faraway, So Close! (1993)
Incautos *See* Swindled (2004)
Incense for the Damned *See* The Bloodsuckers (1970)
Incident at Victoria Falls *See* Sherlock Holmes and the Incident at Victoria Falls (1991)
Inconvenienced *See* Held Up (2000)
The Incredible Invasion *See* The Sinister Invasion (1968)
The Incredible Praying Mantis *See* The Deadly Mantis (1957)
The Incredible Torture Show *See* Bloodsucking Freaks (1975)
The Incredibly Strange Creatures *See* Incredibly Strange Creatures Who Stopped Living and Became Mixed-Up Zombies (1963)
L'Incroyable Mme. Ritchie *See* The Incredible Mrs. Ritchie (2003)
Incubo Sulla Citta Contaminata *See* City of the Walking Dead (1980)
Indagine su un Delitto Perfetto *See* Perfect Crime (1979)
Independence *See* Best Men (1998)
An Indian in the City *See* Little Indian, Big City (1995)
Indian Summer *See* Alive and Kicking (1996)
Indian Love Call *See* Rose Marie (1936)
Indigenes *See* Days of Glory (2006)
Indiscretion *See* Christmas in Connecticut (1945)
Indiscretion *See* Dangerous Beauty (1998)
Indiscretion *See* Indiscretion of an American Wife (1954)
L'Infermiera di Campagna *See* Emmanuelle in the Country (1978)
The Internal Idol *See* Craze (1974)
Inferno *See* Desert Heat (1999)

Inferno in Diretta *See* Cut and Run (1985)

Infested *See* Ticks (1993)

The Infra Superman *See* Infra-Man (1976)

Inn of the Frightened People *See* Revenge (1971)

Innocence Is Bliss *See* Miss Grant Takes Richmond (1949)

The Innocent and the Damned *See* Girls' Town (1959)

Insane World *See* Mondo Cane 2 (1964)

The Insect *See* The Insect Woman (1963)

Inside I'm Dancing *See* Rory O'Shea Was Here (2004)

The Insolent *See* The Insolent Killer (1973)

L'Insoumis *See* Fight for Us (1989)

Intensivstation Deutschland *See* Terror 2000 (1992)

Interlude *See* Intermezzo (1936)

Intermezzo: A Love Story *See* Intermezzo (1939)

Intern Academy *See* White Coats (2004)

International Spy *See* The Spy Ring (1938)

Intimi Osvetleni *See* Intimate Lighting (1965)

Intramuros *See* The Walls of Hell (1964)

Intruder *See* Intruso (1993)

The Intruder *See* The Innocent (1976)

The Intruder *See* Shame (1961)

L'Intrus *See* The Intruder (2004)

The Invader *See* Old Spanish Custom (1936)

The Invaders *See* The Forty-Ninth Parallel (1941)

Invasion *See* Robin Cook's Invasion (1997)

Invasion Earth 2150 A.D. *See* Daleks—Invasion Earth 2150 A.D. (1966)

Invasion Force *See* Hangar 18 (1980)

Invasion from Inner Earth *See* They (1977)

Invasion of Mars *See* The Angry Red Planet (1959)

Invasion of Planet X *See* Godzilla vs. Monster Zero (1968)

The Invasion of the Astro-Monsters *See* Godzilla vs. Monster Zero (1968)

Invasion of the Astros *See* Godzilla vs. Monster Zero (1968)

Invasion of the Flesh Hunters *See* Cannibal Apocalypse (1980)

Invasion of the Flying Saucers *See* Earth vs. the Flying Saucers (1956)

Invasion of the Zombies *See* Horror of Party Beach (1964)

Invasion Siniestra *See* The Sinister Invasion (1968)

Investigating Sex *See* Intimate Affairs (2001)

An Investigation of Murder *See* The Laughing Policeman (1974)

The Invisible Dead *See* Orloff and the Invisible Man (1970)

The Invisible Horror *See* The Invisible Dr. Mabuse (1962)

The Invisible Killer *See* Curse of the Undead (1959)

An Invited Guest *See* Uninvited Guest (1999)

Io Non Ho Paura *See* I'm Not Scared (2003)

Io Speriamo Che Me La Cavo *See* Ciao, Professore! (1994)

The Iron Hand *See* Chinese Connection (1973)

The Iron Kiss *See* Naked Kiss (1964)

Iron Monkey: The Young Wong Feihung *See* Iron Monkey (1993)

The Ironman *See* Tetsuo: The Iron Man (1992)

Irving Berlin's Alexander's Ragtime Band *See* Alexander's Ragtime Band (1938)

Irving Berlin's Second Fiddle *See* Second Fiddle (1939)

Iskanderija, Kaman oue Kaman *See* Alexandria Again and Forever (1990)

Island of Monte Cristo *See* Sword of Venus (1953)

Island of Shame *See* The Young One (1961)

Island of the Alive *See* It's Alive 3: Island of the Alive (1987)

Island of the Burning Damned *See* Island of the Burning Doomed (1967)

Island of the Fishmen *See* Screamers (1980)

The Island of the Last Zombies *See* Doctor Butcher M.D. (1980)

Island of the Living Dead *See* Zombie (1980)

Island of the Living Horror *See* Brides of the Beast (1968)

Isle of Lost Women *See* 99 Women (1969)

Isle of the Living Dead *See* The Snake People (1968)

Isle of the Snake People *See* The Snake People (1968)

Isn't Life A Bitch? *See* La Chienne (1931)

istanbul, Keep Your Eyes Open *See* Istanbul (1990)

It Ain't No Sin *See* Belle of the Nineties (1934)

It Comes Up Murder *See* The Honey Pot (1967)

It Fell from the Sky *See* Alien Dead (1979)

It Happened at Lakewood Manor *See* Ants (1977)

It Happened in Paris *See* The Lady in Question (1940)

It Happened One Summer *See* State Fair (1945)

It Hurts Only When I Laugh *See* Only When I Laugh (1981)

It Lives Again *See* It's Alive 2: It Lives Again (1978)

It Lives By Night *See* The Bat People (1974)

It Only Take Five Minutes *See* Five Minutes to Love (1963)

It Runs in the Family *See* My Summer Story (1994)

It Stalked the Ocean Floor *See* Monster from the Ocean Floor (1954)

It! The Vampire from Beyond Space *See* It! The Terror from Beyond Space (1958)

It Won't Rub Off, Baby *See* Sweet Love, Bitter (1967)

Italia ultimo atto *See* Could It Happen Here? (1977)

The Italian Connection *See* Hired to Kill (1973)

The Italian Connection *See* Manhunt (1973)

Italianetz *See* The Italian (2005)

Italiensk for Begyndere *See* Italian for Beginners (2001)

It's Hot in Hell *See* Un Singe en Hiver (1962)

It's Hot in Paradise *See* Horrors of Spider Island (1959)

It's My Life *See* My Life to Live (1962)

It's Only Money *See* Double Dynamite (1951)

Ivan Groznyi *See* Ivan the Terrible, Part 1 (1944)

Ivan Groznyi 2 *See* Ivan the Terrible, Part 2 (1946)

Ivan the Terrible, Part 2: The Boyars' Plot *See* Ivan the Terrible, Part 2 (1946)

Ivan's Childhood *See* My Name Is Ivan (1962)

L'Ivresse du Pouvoir *See* Comedy of Power (2006)

Ja Cuba *See* I Am Cuba (1964)

Ja Zuster Nee Zuster *See* Yes Nurse! No Nurse! (2002)

Jack London's Klondike Fever *See* Klondike Fever (1979)

Jackals *See* American Justice (1986)

Jackie Chan Is the Prisoner *See* The Prisoner (1990)

Jackie Chan's Police Force *See* Police Story (1985)

Jackie Chan's Police Story *See* Police Story (1985)

Jackie Chan's Project A *See* Project A (1983)

Jackie Chan's Project A2 *See* Project A: Part 2 (1987)

Jackie, Ethel, Joan: Women of Camelot *See* Jackie, Ethel, Joan: The Kennedy Women (2001)

Jack's Wife *See* Season of the Witch (1973)

Jacqueline Susann's Once Is Not Enough *See* Once Is Not Enough (1975)

Jacquot de Nantes *See* Jacquot (1991)

Jag ar nyfiken-film i guit *See* I Am Curious (Yellow) (1967)

Jag ar nyfiken-gul *See* I Am Curious (Yellow) (1967)

Jag, en Kvinna *See* I, a Woman (1966)

Jahrgang '45 *See* Born in '45 (1965)

J'ai Epouse une Ombre *See* I Married a Dead Man (1982)

J'al Pas Sommeil *See* I Can't Sleep (1993)

Jail Birds *See* Pardon Us (1931)

Jakob der Lugner *See* Jacob the Liar (1974)

James A. Michener's Texas *See* Texas (1994)

James Clavell's Shogun *See* Shogun (1980)

James Dean: Race with Destiny *See* James Dean: Live Fast, Die Young (1997)

Jana Aranya *See* The Middleman (1976)

Jane Austen's Emma *See* Emma (1997)

Jane Austen's Mafia! *See* Mafia! (1998)

Janghwa, Hongryeon *See* A Tale of Two Sisters (2003)

The Janitor *See* Eyewitness (1981)

Japan Sinks *See* Tidal Wave (1975)

Jatszani Kell *See* Lily in Love (1985)

Jaws 3-D *See* Jaws 3 (1983)

Jayne Mansfield: A Symbol of the '50s *See* The Jayne Mansfield Story (1980)

J.C. *See* Iron Horsemen (1971)

Je Rentre a la Maison *See* I'm Going Home (2000)

Je Suis Frigide...Pourquoi? *See* I Am Frigid... Why? (1972)

Je Veux Rentrer a la Maison *See* I Want to Go Home (1989)

Je Vous Salue Marie *See* Hail Mary (1985)

Jealousy *See* L'Enfer (1993)

Jean de Florette 2 *See* Manon of the Spring (1987)

Jeanne et le Garcon Formidable *See* Jeanne and the Perfect Guy (1998)

Jeanne la Pucelle: Les Batailles *See* Jeanne la Pucelle (1994)

Jeanne la Purcelle: Les Prisons *See* Jeanne la Pucelle (1994)

Jeder fur Sich und Gott gegen Alle *See* Every Man for Himself & God Against All (1975)

Jekyll's Inferno *See* The Two Faces of Dr. Jekyll (1960)

Jennie *See* Portrait of Jennie (1948)

Jennifer (The Snake Goddess) *See* Jennifer (1978)

Jennifer's Shadow *See* Chronicle of the Raven (2004)

Jenseits der Stille *See* Beyond Silence (1996)

Jerome Bixby's Man from Earth *See* The Man from Earth (2007)

Jerry Springer's Ringmaster *See* Ringmaster (1998)

Jesse James, Jr. *See* Sundown Fury (1942)

The Jester *See* Der Purimshpiler (1937)

Jesus de Montreal *See* Jesus of Montreal (1989)

The Jesus Video *See* Ancient Relic (2002)

Jette un Sort *See* Rough Magic (1995)

Jeu de Massacre *See* The Killing Game (1967)

Jeux D'Enfants *See* Love Me if You Dare (2003)

Jew Suss *See* Power (1934)

The Jewish Jester *See* Der Purimshpiler (1937)

The Jezebels *See* Switchblade Sisters (1975)

Jian Gui *See* The Eye (2002)

Jian Yu Feng Yun Xu Ji *See* Prison on Fire 2 (1991)

Jiang-Hu: Between Love and Glory *See* The Bride with White Hair (1993)

Jiang-Hu: Between Love and Glory 2 *See* The Bride with White Hair 2 (1993)

Jie Quan Ying Zhao Gong *See* Chinese Connection 2 (1977)

Jigokumen *See* Gate of Hell (1954)

Jilly Cooper's Riders *See* Riders (1988)

Jilly Cooper's The Man Who Made Husbands Jealous *See* The Man Who Made Husbands Jealous (1998)

Jim Buck *See* Portrait of a Hitman (1977)

Jim Henson's Jack and the Beanstalk *See* Jack and the Beanstalk: The Real Story (2001)

Jing Wu Men *See* Chinese Connection (1973)

Jisatsu Sakuru *See* Suicide Club (2002)

Joan the Mad *See* Mad Love (2001)

Joan the Maid: The Battles *See* Jeanne la Pucelle (1994)

Joan the Maid: The Prisons *See* Jeanne la Pucelle (1994)

Job Lazadasa *See* The Revolt of Job (1984)

Joe Palooka *See* Palooka (1934)

John Carpenter Presents Body Bags *See* Body Bags (1993)

John Carpenter's Escape from L.A. *See* Escape from L.A. (1996)

John Le Carre's A Perfect Spy *See* A Perfect Spy (1988)

John Travis, Solar Survivor *See* Omega Cop (1990)

Johnnie Mae Gibson: FBI *See* Johnnie Gibson F.B.I. (1987)

Johnny Vagabond *See* Johnny Come Lately (1943)

Johnny Zombie *See* My Boyfriend's Back (1993)

A Joke of Destiny *See* A Joke of Destiny, Lying in Wait Around the Corner Like a Bandit (1984)

Joker's Wild *See* Body Trouble (1992)

Jonas—Qui Aura 25 Ans en l'An 2000 *See* Jonah Who Will Be 25 in the Year 2000 (1976)

Joseon Namnyeo Sangyeol Ji Sa See Untold Scandal (2003)

Joseph Conrad's Nostromo See Nostromo (1996)

Joseph Conrad's The Secret Agent See The Secret Agent (1996)

Joshua Tree See Woman Undone (1995)

Journey into Autumn See Dreams (1955)

Journey of the Hyena See Touki Bouki (1973)

Journey to Planet Four See The Angry Red Planet (1959)

Journey to the Beginning of the World See Voyage to the Beginning of the World (1996)

Joyous Laughter See Passionate Thief (1960)

Joy Girls See Story of a Prostitute (1965)

J.R. See Who's That Knocking at My Door? (1968)

Juana la Loca See Mad Love (2001)

Jude the Obscure See Jude (1996)

Jules et Jim See Jules and Jim (1962)

Jules Verne's Rocket to the Moon See Those Fantastic Flying Fools (1967)

A Judgement in Stone See The Housekeeper (1986)

Judgment See Hitz (1989)

A Judgment in Stone See La Ceremonie (1995)

July Pork Bellies See For Pete's Sake (1974)

Jui Kun 2 See The Legend of Drunken Master (1994)

Jumbo See Billy Rose's Jumbo (1962)

Jump See Fury on Wheels (1971)

Jungfrauennaschine See Virgin Machine (1988)

Jungle Wolf 2 See Return Fire (1991)

Jungle Woman See Nabonga (1944)

Jungfrukallan See The Virgin Spring (1959)

Juninatten See June Night (1940)

Junior Pilot See Final Approach (2004)

Jurassic Park 2 See The Lost World: Jurassic Park 2 (1997)

Jury Duty See The Great American Sex Scandal (1994)

Jusqu'au Bout du Monde See Until the End of the World (1991)

Just Another Day at the Races See Win, Place, or Steal (1972)

Just Ask for Diamond See Diamond's Edge (1988)

Just in Time See Only You (1994)

Just One of the Girls See Anything for Love (1993)

Justice See Backlash (1999)

Justice Cain See Cain's Cutthroats (1971)

Justice Rides Again See Destry Rides Again (1939)

Jutai See Traffic Jam (1991)

Kabale und Liebe See Intrigue and Love (1959)

Kabloonak See The Stranger: Kabloonak (1995)

Kaena: La Prophetie See Kaena: The Prophecy (2003)

Kaiju Daisenso See Godzilla vs. Monster Zero (1968)

Kaiju Soshingeki See Destroy All Monsters (1968)

Kairo See Pulse (2001)

Kaitei Daisenso See Terror Beneath the Sea (1966)

Kakushi Ken: Oni No Tsume See The Hidden Blade (2004)

Kakushi Toride No San Akunin See The Hidden Fortress (1958)

Kaleidoscope See Danielle Steel's Kaleidoscope (1990)

Kamakazi See Attack Squadron (1963)

Kamala Koshiri-Kyoku See Fall Guy (1982)

Kamui No Ken See The Dagger of Kamui (1985)

Kanzo Sensei See Dr. Akagi (1998)

Karamazov See The Brothers Karamazov (1958)

Karate Cop See Slaughter in San Francisco (1981)

Karbid und Sauerampfer See Carbide and Sorrel (1963)

Kat and Allison See Lip Service (2000)

Katie's Passion See Katie Tippel (1975)

Kavkazsky Plennik See Prisoner of the Mountains (1996)

Kayitz Shel Aviya See The Summer of Aviya (1988)

Kazoku gaimu See The Family Game (1983)

Kazoku Game See The Family Game (1983)

Keep It Up, Jack See Auntie (1973)

Keep the Aspidistra Flying See A Merry War (1997)

Keetje Tippel See Katie Tippel (1975)

Kekexili See Mountain Patrol: Kekexili (2004)

The Kent Chronicles See The Bastard (1978)

Kenka Ereji See Fighting Elegy (1966)

Kenka Ereji See Fighting Elegy (1966)

Kessen Nankai No Daikaiju See Yog, Monster from Space (1971)

Kette Creek See Mountain Justice (1930)

Kevin of the North See Chilly Dogs (2001)

The Key See Odd Obsession (1960)

Key West Crossing See The Mercenaries (1980)

KGOD See Pray TV (1980)

Khaneh-Je Doost Kojast? See Where Is My Friend's House? (1987)

Khamosh Pani See Silent Waters (2003)

The Kid See La Vie en Rose (2007)

The Kidnap of Mary Lou See Almost Human (1979)

The Kids See Les Mistons (1957)

Kilian's Chronicle See The Magic Stone (1995)

Kill and Go Hide See Tha Child (1976)

Kill Castro See The Mercenaries (1980)

Kill My Wife... Please! See I Wonder Who's Killing Her Now? (1976)

Kill Squad See Code of Honor (1982)

Kill Two Birds See Cry Terror (1976)

Killbots See Chopping Mall (1986)

Killer See Bulletproof Heart (1995)

Killer See This Man I Must Die (1970)

Killer Bait See Too Late for Tears (1949)

Killer Bats See The Devil Bat (1941)

The Killer Behind the Mask See Savage Weekend (1980)

Killer Grizzly See Grizzly (1976)

Killer Instinct See Homicidal Impulse (1992)

Killer of Killers See The Mechanic (1972)

The Killer Whale See Orca (1977)

Killer With a Label See One Too Many (1951)

The Killers See Pigs (1973)

Killers of the Wild See Children of the Wild (1937)

The Killing Box See The Ghost Brigade (1993)

Killing Cars See Blitz (1985)

Killing Edgar See Plain Dirty (2004)

Killing Mrs. Tingle See Teaching Mrs. Tingle (1999)

Kilometer Zero See Km. 0 (2000)

Kilronan See Hush (1998)

Kimono No Kiroku See I Live in Fear (1955)

Kin Folk See All the Lovin' Kinfolk (1970)

Kinfolk See All the Lovin' Kinfolk (1970)

Kinfolks See Parental Guidance (1998)

King Cobra See Jaws of Satan (1981)

King Gun See The Gatling Gun (1972)

King Kong tai Godzilla See King Kong vs. Godzilla (1963)

King of Africa See Men of Two Words (1946)

King of the Jungleland See Darkest Africa (1936)

Kings Ransom See Devastator (1985)

KinguKongu tai Gojira See King Kong vs. Godzilla (1963)

Kisenga, Man of Africa See Men of Two Words (1946)

Kiss My Butterfly See I Love You, Alice B. Toklas! (1968)

A Kiss from Eddie See The Arousers (1970)

Kiss of Evil See Kiss of the Vampire (1962)

The King of Criminals See Supergargo (1967)

Kjaerlighetens Kjotere See Zero Degrees Kelvin (1995)

KKK See The Klansman (1974)

The Knack...and How to Get It See The Knack (1965)

Knatayim Shvurot See Broken Wings (2002)

The Knock-Out Cop See Flatfoot (1978)

Ko Zapram Oci See When I Close My Eyes (1993)

Kohi Jikou See Cafe Lumiere (2005)

Koka I Kullssen See Ladies on the Rocks (1983)

Komissar See Commissar (1968)

Kommissar X - Drei Goldene Schlangen See Island of Lost Girls (1968)

Kondom des Grauens See Killer Condom (1995)

Koneko Monogatari See The Adventures of Milo & Otis (1989)

Konig der Diebe See King of Thieves (2004)

Kanjiki Yasha See Golden Demon (1953)

Konna Yume Wo Mita See Akira Kurosawa's Dreams (1990)

Kootenai Brown See Showdown at Williams Creek (1991)

Kopek and Broom See Find the Lady (1976)

Koroshi no Rakuin See Branded to Kill (1967)

Koukaku Kidoutai See Ghost in the Shell (1995)

Krajobraz Po Bitwie See Landscape After Battle (1970)

Krampack See Nico and Dani (2000)

Kriget ar Slut See La Guerre Est Finie (1966)

Krokodillen in Amsterdam See Crocodiles in Amsterdam (1993)

Kronos See Captain Kronos: Vampire Hunter (1974)

Kronprinz Rudolf See The Crown Prince (2006)

Krug and Company See Last House on the Left (1972)

Kuchisake-onna See Carved (2007)

Kumonosujo, Kumonosu-djo See Throne of Blood (1957)

Kung Fu Master See Le Petit Amour (1987)

Kung Fu: The Head Crusher See Tough Guy (1970)

Kung Fu: The Punch of Death See Kick of Death: The Prodigal Boxer (1973)

Kunisada Chuji See The Gambling Samurai (1960)

Kurai Ame See Black Rain (1988)

Kurotokage See Black Lizard (1968)

Kushka See The Cuckoo (2002)

Kvia See Because of You (1995)

Kvish L'Lo Motzah See Dead End Street (1983)

Kyoko See Because of You (1995)

Kyuketsuki Gokemidoro See Body Snatcher from Hell (1969)

Kvinnm odrom See Dreams (1955)

Kvinn odrom See Dreams (1955)

Kvinnorna pa Taket See The Women on the Roof (1989)

Kvinnors Vantan See Secrets of Women (1952)

La Ardilla Roja See The Red Squirrel (1993)

La Banda J.&S. Cronaca Criminale del Far West See Sonny and Jed (1973)

La Bataille d'Alger See The Battle of Algiers (1966)

La Battaglia di Algeri See The Battle of Algiers (1966)

La Bataille du Rail See Battle of the Rails (1946)

La Beaute du Diable See Beauty and the Devil (1950)

La Belle et la Bete See Beauty and the Beast (1946)

La Bestia Uccide a Sangue Freddo See Slaughter Hotel (1971)

La Bestia nel Cuore See Don't Tell (2005)

La Bete See The Beast (1975)

La Bionda See The Blonde (1992)

La Bonne Annee See Happy New Year (1973)

La Bride sur le Cou See Please Not Now! (1961)

La Cabeza Viviente See The Living Head (1959)

La Camara del Terror See The Fear Chamber (1968)

La Casa See Witchery (1988)

La Casa 4 See Witchery (1988)

La Casa con la Scala Nel Buio See A Blade in the Dark (1983)

La Casa Del Terror See Face of the Screaming Werewolf (1959)

La Casa Dell'Esorcismo See Lisa and the Devil (1975)

La Casa Embrujada See The Curse of the Crying Woman (1961)

La Casa Nel Parco See House on the Edge of the Park (1984)

La Casa de L'Oncle Tom See Uncle Tom's Cabin (1959)

La Caza See The Hunt (1965)

La Chambre Ardente See The Burning Court (1962)

La Chambre Verte See The Green Room (1978)

La Chasse aux Papillons *See* Chasing Butterflies (1994)
La Chiesa *See* The Church (1998)
La Ciel Sur la Tete *See* Times Have Been Better (2006)
La Ciociara *See* Two Women (1961)
La Cite des Enfants Perdus *See* The City of Lost Children (1995)
La Citte delle Donne *See* City of Women (1981)
La Ciudad y los Perros *See* The City and the Dogs (1985)
La Coda dello Scorpione *See* The Case of the Scorpion's Tail (1971)
La Commare Secca *See* The Grim Reaper (1962)
La Comtesse Perverse *See* The Perverse Countess (1973)
La Confusion des Genres *See* Confusion of Genders (2000)
La Curee *See* The Game Is Over (1966)
La Decade Prodigieuse *See* Ten Days Wonder (1972)
La Decima Vittima *See* 10th Victim (1965)
La Demoiselle d'Honneur *See* The Bridesmaid (2004)
La Dentelliere *See* The Lacemaker (1977)
La Desenchantee *See* The Disenchanted (1990)
La Diagonale du Fou *See* Dangerous Moves (1984)
La Dixieme Victime *See* 10th Victim (1965)
La Donna E Donna *See* A Woman Is a Woman (1960)
La Double Vie de Veronique *See* The Double Life of Veronique (1991)
La Doublure *See* The Valet (2006)
La Dueda Interna *See* Veronico Cruz (1987)
La Face Cachee de la Lune *See* Far Side of the Moon (2003)
La Famiglia *See* The Family (1987)
La Faute a Fidel *See* Blame It on Fidel (2006)
La Femme De Mon Pote *See* My Best Friend's Girl (1984)
La Femme du Boulanger *See* The Baker's Wife (1933)
La Femme Mariee *See* A Married Woman (1965)
La Femme de L'Aviateur *See* The Aviator's Wife (1980)
La Fiancee du Pirate *See* A Very Curious Girl (1969)
La Figlia di Frankenstein *See* Lady Frankenstein (1972)
La Fille De D'Artagnan *See* Revenge of the Musketeers (1994)
La Fille Du Puisatier *See* Well-Digger's Daughter (1946)
La Fille Seule *See* A Single Girl (1996)
La Finestra di Fronte *See* Facing Windows (2003)
La Flor de My Secreto *See* The Flower of My Secret (1995)
A la Folie *See* Six Days, Six Nights (1994)
A la Folie...Pas de Tout *See* He Loves Me ... He Loves Me Not (2002)
La Folle des Grandeurs *See* Delusions of Grandeur (1976)
La Fortuna di Essere Donna *See* What a Woman! (1956)
La Fracture du Myocarde *See* Cross My Heart (1991)

La Francaise et L'Amour *See* Love and the Frenchwoman (1960)
La Fuente Amarilla *See* The Yellow Fountain (1999)
La Furia del Hombre Lobo *See* The Fury of the Wolfman (1970)
La Furia Di Ercole *See* The Fury of Hercules (1961)
La Gangster del Pupa *See* Lady of the Evening (1975)
La Giffe *See* The Slap (1976)
La Gloire de Mon Pere *See* My Father's Glory (1991)
La Grande Guerre *See* The Great War (1959)
La Grande Illusion *See* Grand Illusion (1937)
La Grande Seduction *See* Seducing Doctor Lewis (2003)
La Grande Speranza *See* Submarine Attack (1954)
La Grande Strada Azzurra *See* The Wide Blue Road (1957)
La Grieta *See* Endless Descent (1990)
La Haine *See* Hate (1995)
La Hija del Canibal *See* Lucia, Lucia (2003)
La Historia Oficial *See* The Official Story (1985)
La Horriplante Bestia Humana *See* Night of the Bloody Apes (1968)
La Illusion Viaja en Tranvia *See* The Illusion Travels by Streetcar (1953)
La Invasion de Los Vampiros *See* Invasion of the Vampires (1961)
La Isla Del Tersoro *See* Treasure Island (1972)
La Joven *See* The Young One (1961)
La Kermesse Heroique *See* Carnival in Flanders (1935)
La Legge *See* Where the Hot Wind Blows (1959)
La Leggenda del Pianista Sull'Oceano *See* The Legend of 1900 (1998)
La Lengua Asesina *See* Killer Tongue (1996)
La Lengua de las Mariposas *See* Butterfly (1998)
La Ley del Deseo *See* Law of Desire (1986)
La Linea Del Cielo *See* Skyline (1984)
La Llorona *See* The Wailer (2006)
La Loi *See* Where the Hot Wind Blows (1959)
La Lune Dans le Caniveau *See* Moon in the Gutter (1983)
La Lunga Notte del '43 *See* That Long Night in 43 (1960)
La Macchina Ammazzacattivi *See* Machine to Kill Bad People (1948)
La Mala Educacion *See* Bad Education (2004)
La Mala Ordina *See* Hit Men (1973)
La Mala Ordina *See* Manhunt (1973)
La Maldicion de a Llorona *See* The Curse of the Crying Woman (1961)
La Maldicion de la Bestia *See* Night of the Howling Beast (1975)
La Maldicion de la Momia Azteca *See* The Curse of the Aztec Mummy (1959)
La Maman et la Putain *See* The Mother and the Whore (1973)
La Marca del Muerto *See* Creature of the Walking Dead (1960)
La Mariee Est Trop Belle *See* The Bride Is Much Too Beautiful (1958)
La Mariee Etait en Noir *See* The Bride Wore Black (1968)
La Maschera del Demonio *See* Black Sunday (1960)
La Matriarca *See* The Libertine (1969)

La Meglio Gioventu *See* Best of Youth (2003)
La Meilleure Facon de Marcher *See* The Best Way (1976)
La Misma Luna *See* Under the Same Moon (2007)
La Mitad del Cielo *See* Half of Heaven (1986)
La Mogile Vergine *See* You've Got to Have Heart (1977)
La Mome *See* La Vie en Rose (2007)
La Momia Azteca Contra el Robot Humano *See* The Robot vs. the Aztec Mummy (1959)
La Mort en Ce Jardin *See* Death in the Garden (1956)
La Morte Vestita di Dollar *See* Dog Eat Dog (1964)
La Morte Viene Dalla Spazio *See* The Day the Sky Exploded (1957)
La Morte Vivante *See* The Living Dead Girl (1982)
La Motocyclette *See* The Girl on a Motorcycle (1968)
La Muerte de un Burocrata *See* Death of a Bureaucrat (1966)
La Muerte Viviente *See* The Snake People (1968)
La nina de tus ojos *See* The Girl of Your Dreams (1999)
La Nina Santa *See* Holy Girl (2004)
La Nipote del Vampiro *See* Fangs of the Living Dead (1968)
La Noche de la Muerta Ciega *See* Tombs of the Blind Dead (1972)
La Noche de los Mil Gatos *See* Night of a Thousand Cats (1972)
La Noche de Walpurgis *See* The Werewolf vs. the Vampire Woman (1970)
La Noche dell Terror Ciego *See* Tombs of the Blind Dead (1972)
La Noia: L'Ennui Et Sa Diversion, L'Erotisme *See* Empty Canvas (1964)
La Notte Che Evelyn Usca Dalla Tomba *See* The Night Evelyn Came Out of the Grave (1971)
La Notte di San Lorenzo *See* The Night of the Shooting Stars (1982)
La Nouvelle Eve *See* The New Eve (1998)
La Novia Esangrentada *See* The Blood Spattered Bride (1972)
La Nuit Americaine *See* Day for Night (1973)
La Nuit de Generaux *See* Night of the Generals (1967)
La Nuit Des Espions *See* Double Agents (1959)
La Nuit Fantastique *See* The Fantastic Night (1942)
La Orgia de los Muertos *See* Tombs of the Blind Dead (1972)
La Padrona e Servita *See* The Boss Is Served (1976)
La Passante du Sans Souci *See* La Passante (1983)
La Passion Beatrice *See* Beatrice (1988)
La Patinoire *See* The Ice Rink (1999)
La Permission *See* The Story of a Three Day Pass (1968)
La Pianiste *See* The Piano Teacher (2001)
La Planete Sauvage *See* Fantastic Planet (1973)
La Polizia vuole Giustizia *See* Violent Professionals (1973)
La Poupee *See* The Doll (1962)
La Prise de Pouvoir Par Louis XIV *See* The Rise of Louis XIV (1966)
La Provinciale *See* The Wayward Wife (1952)
La Puppa del Gangster *See* Get Rita (1975)

La Ragazza Che Sapeva Troppo *See* The Girl Who Knew Too Much (1963)
La Ragazza con la Valgia *See* The Girl with a Suitcase (1960)
La Recreation *See* Love Play (1960)
La Regina delle Amazzoni *See* Colossus and the Amazon Queen (1964)
La Reine Margot *See* Queen Margot (1994)
La Rivolta del Barbari *See* Revolt of the Barbarians (1964)
La Romana *See* A Woman of Rome (1956)
La Rosa di Bagdad *See* The Singing Princess (1949)
La Ruee Des Vikings *See* The Invaders (1963)
La Semana del Asesino *See* Cannibal Man (1971)
La Signora Senza Camelie *See* The Lady Without Camelias (1953)
La Sindrome di Stendhal *See* The Stendahl Syndrome (1995)
La Sirene des Tropiques *See* Siren of the Tropics (1927)
La Sorella de Satan *See* The She-Beast (1965)
La Sorgente del fiume *See* Weeping Meadow (2004)
La Souffle au Coeur *See* Murmur of the Heart (1971)
La Spada del Cid *See* The Sword of El Cid (1962)
La Spettatrice *See* The Spectator (2004)
La Spiaggia del Desiderio *See* Emmanuelle on Taboo Island (1976)
La Spina Dorsale del Diavolo *See* Ride to Glory (1971)
La Stanza del Figlio *See* The Son's Room (2000)
La Strega in Amore *See* The Witch (1966)
La Tabla de Flandes *See* Uncovered (1994)
La Tarantola dal Ventre Nero *See* The Black Belly of the Tarantula (1971)
La Tarea *See* Homework (1990)
La Tarea Prohibida *See* Forbidden Homework (1992)
La Tatiche de Ercole *See* Hercules (1958)
La Terre qui pleure *See* Weeping Meadow (2004)
La Tigre e la Neve *See* The Tiger and the Snow (2005)
La Tourneuse de Pages *See* The Page Turner (2006)
La Tragedia di un Uomo Ridicolo *See* The Tragedy of a Ridiculous Man (1981)
La Tragedie de la Mine *See* Kameradschaft (1931)
La Tregua *See* The Truce (1996)
La Vallee *See* The Valley Obscured by the Clouds (1970)
La Vendetta dei Barbari *See* Revenge of the Barbarians (1964)
La Vendetta di Ercole *See* Goliath and the Dragon (1961)
La Venganza de la Momia *See* The Mummy's Revenge (1973)
La Vergine de Norimberga *See* The Virgin of Nuremberg (1965)
La Veuve de Saint-Pierre *See* The Widow of Saint-Pierre (2000)
La Victoire en Chantant *See* Black and White in Color (1997)
La Vida Segun Muriel *See* Life According to Muriel (1997)
La Vie a L'Envers *See* Life Upside Down (1964)
La Vie de Jesus *See* The Life of Jesus (1996)

La Vie Devant Soi See Madame Rosa (1977)

La Vie est Rien d'Autre See Life and Nothing But (1989)

La Vie est un Roman See Life is a Bed of Roses (1983)

La Vie Est Une Longue Fleuve Tranquille See Life is a Long Quiet River (1991)

La Vie Privee See A Very Private Affair (1962)

La Vie Revee des Anges See The Dreamlife of Angels (1998)

La Vie Sexuelle des Belges See The Sexual Life of the Belgians (1994)

La Vieille qui Merchait dans la Mer See The Old Lady Who Walked in the Sea (1991)

La Virgen de los Sicarios See Our Lady of the Assassins (2001)

La Vita E Bella See Life Is Beautiful (1998)

Laberinto de Pasiones See Labyrinth of Passion (1982)

Labyrinth See A Reflection of Fear (1972)

Ladies Man See Your Turn Darling (1963)

Ladies of the Park See The Ladies of the Bois de Bologne (1944)

The Lady Dances See The Merry Widow (1934)

Ladri di Biciclette See The Bicycle Thief (1948)

Ladri di Saponette See The Icicle Thief (1989)

Lady Beware (1974)

Lady Dracula See Lemora, Lady Dracula (1973)

Lady Godiva Meets Tom Jones See Lady Godiva Rides (1963)

Lady Hamilton See That Hamilton Woman (1941)

Lady in the Fog See Scotland Yard Inspector (1952)

Lady Jane Grey See Nine Days a Queen (1936)

Lady Killers See National Lampoon's Gold Diggers (2004)

The Lady Killers See The Ladykillers (1955)

Lady of Deceit See Born to Kill (1947)

Lady of the Shadows See The Terror (1963)

Ladykiller See Lady Killer (1997)

Laererinden See All Things Fair (1995)

Laitakaupungin Valot See Lights in the Dusk (2006)

The Lake of the Living Dead See Zombie Lake (1980)

L'Aigle a Deux Tetes See The Eagle Has Two Heads (1948)

L'Albero Degli Zoccoli See The Tree of Wooden Clogs (1978)

L'Amant See The Lover (1992)

L'Amant de Lady Chatterley See Lady Chatterley's Lover (1955)

The Lament of the Path See Pather Panchali (1954)

L'Amour en Fuite See Love on the Run (1978)

The Lamp See The Outing (1987)

Lan Feng Zheng See The Blue Kite (1993)

Lancelot and Guinevere See Sword of Lancelot (1963)

Lancelot du Lac See Lancelot of the Lake (1974)

Land of the Dead See George A. Romero's Land of the Dead (2005)

Landru See Bluebeard (1963)

The Lane Frost Story See 8 Seconds (1994)

L'Anee Derniere a Marienbad See Last Year at Marienbad (1961)

L'Anglaise et le Duc See The Lady and the Duke (2001)

The Langoliers See Stephen King's The Langoliers (1995)

Larceny Lane See Blonde Crazy (1931)

Large as Life See Larger Than Life (1996)

Larsen, Wolf of the Seven Seas See The Legend of the Sea Wolf (1958)

Las Cartas de Alou See Letters from Alou (1990)

Las Luchadoras Contra la Momia See Wrestling Women vs. the Aztec Mummy (1959)

Las Vegas Strip War See The Vegas Strip Wars (1984)

Lasbou Shentan See Hard-Boiled (1992)

Lasky Jedne Plavovlasky See Loves of a Blonde (1965)

The Last Adventurers See Down to the Sea in Ships (1922)

L'Associe See The Associate (1979)

The Last Battle See Le Dernier Combat (1984)

The Last Chance For a Born Loser See Stateline Motel (1975)

The Last Days of John Dillinger See Dillinger (1991)

The Last Days of Man on Earth See The Final Programme (1973)

The Last Days of Sodom and Gomorrah See Sodom and Gomorrah (1962)

The Last Elephant See Ivory Hunters (1990)

The Last Frontier See Savage Wilderness (1955)

The Last Great Treasure See Mother Lode (1982)

The Last Horror Film See Fanatic (1932)

Last House on the Left, Part 2 See Twitch of the Death Nerve (1971)

Last Man Standing See Circle Man (1987)

Last Message From Saigon See Operation C.I.A. (1965)

Last of the Cowboys See Great Smokey Roadblock (1976)

The Last Outpost See Cavalry Charge (1951)

The Last Page See Man Bait (1952)

Last Resurrection See Haunted Symphony (1994)

The Last Rites See Dracula's Last Rites (1979)

The Last Shot See Carbon Copy (1969)

The Last Train of the Night See Night Train Murders (1975)

The Last Victim See Forced Entry (1975)

The Last Warrior See The Final Executioner (1983)

The Last Will of Dr. Mabuse See Crimes of Dr. Mabuse (1932)

The Last Will of Dr. Mabuse See Testament of Dr. Mabuse (1932)

The Last Witness See Caracara (2000)

The Late Edwina Black See The Obsessed (1951)

Latin Love See Greek Street (1930)

Latin Quarter See Frenzy (1946)

Laughterhouse See Singleton's Pluck (1984)

Laure See Forever Emmanuelle (1975)

The Law See Tilai (1990)

The Law See Where the Hot Wind Blows (1959)

Law Breakers See Les Assassins de L'Ordre (1971)

Lawless: Beyond Justice See Beyond Justice (2001)

Lawless: Dead Evidence See Dead Evidence (2000)

The Lay of the Land See The Student Affair (1997)

Lazarus and the Hurricane See The Hurricane (1999)

Lazy Bones See Hallelujah, I'm a Bum (1933)

LD 50 Lethal Dose See Lethal Dose (2003)

Le Battement d'Ailes du Papillon See Happenstance (2000)

Le Blonde de Pekin See The Peking Blond (1968)

Le Bossu See On Guard! (2003)

Le Caporal Epingle See The Elusive Corporal (1962)

Le Carrosse D'Or See The Golden Coach (1952)

Le Cerveau See The Brain (1969)

Le Charme Discret de la Bourgeoisie See The Discreet Charm of the Bourgeoisie (1972)

Le Chat et la Souris See Cat and Mouse (1975)

Le Chateau de Ma Mere See My Mother's Castle (1991)

Le Cheval D'Orgueil See The Horse of Pride (1980)

Le Ciel et le Boue See The Sky Above, the Mud Below (1961)

Le Coeur au Poing See Street Heart (1998)

Le Comte de Monte Cristo See The Count of Monte Cristo (1999)

Le Confessional See The Confessional (1995)

Le Corniauds See The Sucker (1965)

Le Cri du Hibou See The Cry of the Owl (1987)

Le Crime de Monsieur Lange See The Crime of Monsieur Lange (1936)

Le Danger Vient de l'Escape See The Day the Sky Exploded (1957)

Le Declin De L'Empire Americain See The Decline of the American Empire (1986)

Le Dejeuner sur l'Herbe See Picnic on the Grass (1959)

Le Dernier Metro See The Last Metro (1980)

Le Dernier Tango a Paris See Last Tango in Paris (1973)

Le Desert des Tartares See The Desert of the Tartars (1976)

Le Diable au Corps See Devil in the Flesh (1946)

Le Diable, Probablement See The Devil, Probably (1977)

Le Diner de Cons See The Dinner Game (1998)

Le Distrait See The Daydreamer (1975)

Le Docteur Petiot See Dr. Petiot (1990)

Le Fabuleux Destin d'Amelie Poulain See Amelie (2001)

Le Fantome de la Liberte See Phantom of Liberty (1974)

Le Fantome D'henri Langlois See Henri Langlois: The Phantom of the Cinematheque (2004)

Le Feu Follet See The Fire Within (1964)

Le Fille sure le Pont See The Girl on the Bridge (1998)

Le Fils du Requin See The Son of the Shark (1993)

Le Fils Prefere See The Favorite Son (1994)

Le Fruit Defendu See Forbidden Fruit (1952)

Le Gai Savoir See The Joy of Knowledge (1969)

Le Geant de la Vallee Das Rois See Son of Samson (1962)

Le Genou de Claire See Claire's Knee (1971)

Le Gentleman d'Epsom See Duke of the Derby (1962)

Le Gout des Autres See The Taste of Others (2000)

Le Graal See Lancelot of the Lake (1974)

Le Grand Bleu See The Big Blue (1988)

Le Grand Blond avec une Chassure Noire See The Tall Blond Man with One Black Shoe (1972)

Le Grand Meaulnes See The Wanderer (1967)

Le Grand Role See The Grand Role (2004)

Le Hussard sur le Toit See The Horseman on the Roof (1995)

Le Huitieme Jour See The Eighth Day (1995)

Le Jour et L'Heure See The Day and the Hour (1963)

Le Journal du Seducteur See Diary of a Seducer (1995)

Le Journal d'un Cure de Campagne See Diary of a Country Priest (1950)

Le Journal d'une Femme de Chambre See Diary of a Chambermaid (1964)

Le Juge et L'assassin See The Judge and the Assassin (1975)

Le Locataire See The Tenant (1976)

Le Maitre de Musique See The Music Teacher (1988)

Le Mari de la coiffeuse See The Hairdresser's Husband (1992)

Le Mepris See Contempt (1964)

Le Meraviglie Di Aladino See The Wonders of Aladdin (1961)

Le Moine et la Sorciere See Sorceress (1988)

Le Monstre See The Monster (1996)

Le Mur See The Wall (1983)

Le Mura di Malapaga See The Walls of Malapaga (1949)

Le Neveu de Beethoven See Beethoven's Nephew (1988)

Le Notti di Cabiria See Nights of Cabiria (1957)

Le Notti Bianche See White Nights (1957)

Le Nouveau Monde See New World (1995)

Le Pacte des Loups See Brotherhood of the Wolf (2001)

Le Papillon See The Butterfly (2002)

Le Pays Bleu See Blue Country (1977)

Le Peau Douce See The Soft Skin (1964)

Le Petit Monde de Don Camillo See The World of Don Camillo (1951)

Le Peuple Migrateur See Winged Migration (2001)

Le Placard See The Closet (2000)

Le Plus Vieux Metier du Monde See Oldest Profession (1967)

Le Proces See The Trial (1963)

Le Quatrieme Sexe See The Fourth Sex (1961)

Le Rayon Vert See Summer (1986)

Le Regle du Jeu See The Rules of the Game (1939)
Le Retour de Martin Guerre See The Return of Martin Guerre (1983)
Le Retour du Grand Blond See Return of the Tall Blond Man with One Black Shoe (1974)
Le Roi de Coeur See The King of Hearts (1966)
Le Rouble a Deux Faces See The Hot Line (1969)
Le Rouge aux Levres See Daughters of Darkness (1971)
Le Rouge et le Noir See The Red and the Black (1957)
Le Salaire de la Peur See The Wages of Fear (1955)
Le Sang d'un Poete See The Blood of a Poet (1930)
Le Sant de l'Ange See Cobra (1971)
Le Sauvage See Lovers Like Us (1975)
Le Scaphandre et le Papillon See The Diving Bell and the Butterfly (2007)
Le Sirene du Mississippi See Mississippi Mermaid (1969)
Le Temps des Loups See Carbon Copy (1969)
Le Temps du Loup See Time of the Wolf (2003)
Le Temps Retrouve See Time Regained (1999)
Le Testament D'Orphee See The Testament of Orpheus (1959)
Le Testament du Docteur Cordelier See The Testament of Dr. Cordelier (1959)
Le Teur Invisible See Curse of the Undead (1959)
Le Tournoi dans la Cite See Tournament (1929)
Le Train See The Train (1965)
Le Trio Infernal See The Infernal Trio (1974)
Le Trou See Night Watch (1972)
Le Trou Normand See Crazy for Love (1952)
Le Vieil Homme Et L'Enfant See The Two of Us (1968)
Le Violon Rouge See The Red Violin (1998)
Le Voleur De Bagdad See Thief of Baghdad (1961)
Le Voyage du Ballon Rouge See Flight of the Red Balloon (2008)
Leader of the Pack See Unholy Rollers (1972)
The Leather Girls See Faster, Pussycat! Kill! Kill! (1965)
The Leatherboys See The Leather Boys (1963)
Lebenszeichen See Signs of Life (1968)
L'eclisse See The Eclipse (1966)
L'Ecole Buissonniere See Passion for Life (1948)
Legacy of Blood See Blood Legacy (1973)
The Legacy of Maggie Walsh See The Legacy (1979)
The Legend See James Dean (1976)
Legend in Leotards See Return of Captain Invincible (1983)
Legend of Cougar Canyon See The Secret of Navajo Cave (1976)
The Legend of Gosta Berling See The Atonement of Gosta Berling (1924)
The Legend of Machine Gun Kelly See Melvin Purvis: G-Man (1974)
Legend of the Bayou See Eaten Alive (1976)
Legend of the Mummy See Bram Stoker's The Mummy (1997)
The Legend of the Pianist on the Ocean See The Legend of 1900 (1998)

The Legend of the Zaat Monster See Attack of the Swamp Creature (1975)
Legend of Witch Hollow See The Witchmaker (1969)
Legenda Del Rudio Malese See Jungle Raiders (1985)
Legenda Suramskol Kreposti See The Legend of Suram Fortress (1985)
The Legendary Curse of Lemora See Lemora, Lady Dracula (1973)
Legion of the Damned See Battle of the Commandos (1971)
Lejonsommar See Vibration (1968)
Lemon Popsicle V See Baby Love (1983)
Lemora: A Child's Tale of the Supernatural See Lemora, Lady Dracula (1973)
Len Deighton's Bullet to Beijing See Bullet to Beijing (1995)
Lenexa, 1 Mile See Full Count (2006)
L'Enfant Sauvage See The Wild Child (1970)
Leo Tolstoy's Anna Karenina See Leo Tolstoy's Anna Karenina (1996)
Leon See The Professional (1994)
Leona Helmsley: The Queen of Mean See The Queen of Mean (1990)
Lepa Sela, Lepo Gore See Pretty Village, Pretty Flame (1996)
Lepassager de la Pluie See Rider on the Rain (1970)
L'Eredita Ferramonti See The Inheritance (1976)
Les Adventures de Rabbi Jacob See The Mad Adventures of Rabbi Jacob (1973)
Les Amants Criminels See Criminal Lovers (1999)
Les Amants du Pont-Neuf See The Lovers on the Bridge (1991)
Les Amities Particulieres See This Special Friendship (1967)
Les Avaleuses See Female Vampire (1973)
Les Aventuriers See The Last Adventure (1967)
Les Bananes Mecaniques See Erotic Escape (1972)
Les Bas Fonds See The Lower Depths (1936)
Les Belles de Nuit See Beauties of the Night (1952)
Les Bijoutiers du Clair de Lune See The Night Heaven Fell (1957)
Les Boys See The Boys (1997)
Les Bronzes See French Fried Vacation (1979)
Les Cent et Une Nuits See One Hundred and One Nights (1995)
Les Cent et Une Nuits de Simon Cinema See One Hundred and One Nights (1995)
Les Chansons d'Amour See Love Songs (2007)
Les Choristes See The Chorus (2004)
Les Choses De La Vie See The Things of Life (1970)
Les Collegiennes See The Twilight Girls (1957)
Les Corrompus See The Corrupt Ones (1967)
Les Cousins See The Cousins (1959)
Les Dames du Bois de Bologne See The Ladies of the Bois de Bologne (1944)
Les Demoiselles de Rochefort See The Young Girls of Rochefort (1968)
Les Demons See The Demons (1974)
Les Destinees Sentimentales See Les Destinees (2000)
Les Deux Anglaises et le Continent See Two English Girls (1972)
Les Deux Rivales See Time of Indifference (1964)
Les Diabolique See Diabolique (1955)

Les Dimanches de Ville d'Arvay See Sundays & Cybele (1962)
Les Egares See Strayed (2003)
Les Enfants du Paradis See Children of Paradise (1944)
Les Enfants du Siecle See Children of the Century (1999)
Les Enfants Gates See Spoiled Children (1977)
Les Felins See Joy House (1964)
Les Feluettes See Lilies (1996)
Les Femmes See The Women (1968)
Les Filles Ne Savent Pas Nager See Girls Can't Swim (1999)
Les Fils de Gascogne See Son of Gascogne (1985)
Les Fils du Vent See The Great Challenge (2004)
Les Gaspards See The Holes (1972)
Les Grandes Gueules See Jailbird's Vacation (1965)
Les Grandes Personnes See Time Out for Love (1961)
Les Griffes du Vampire See Curse of the Undead (1959)
Les Innocents aux Mains Sales See Innocents with Dirty Hands (1976)
Les Invasions Barbares See The Barbarian Invasions (2003)
Les Jeux Interdits See Forbidden Games (1952)
Les Liaisons Dangereuses See Dangerous Liaisons (1960)
Les Liaisons dangereuses See Dangerous Liaisons (2003)
Les Liens de Sang See Blood Relatives (1977)
Les Louves See Letters to an Unknown Lover (1984)
Les Mille Et Une Nuits See The Wonders of Aladdin (1961)
Les Mille et Une Recettes du Cuisinier Amoureux See A Chef in Love (1996)
Les Mongols See The Mongols (1960)
Les Noces de Papier See A Paper Wedding (1989)
Les Nuits de la Pleine See Full Moon in Paris (1984)
Les Orgueilleux See The Proud Ones (1953)
Les Parapluies de Cherbourg See Umbrellas of Cherbourg (1964)
Les Parents Terribles See The Storm Within (1948)
Les Passagers See Intruder (1976)
Les Possedes See The Possessed (1988)
Les Poupees Russes See Russian Dolls (2005)
Les Predateurs de la Nuit See Faceless (1988)
Les Quartre Cents Coups See The 400 Blows (1959)
Les Rendez-vous de Paris See Rendezvous in Paris (1995)
Les Repos du Guerrier See Love on a Pillow (1962)
Les Revenants See They Came Back (2004)
Les Ripoux See My New Partner (1984)
Les Rivieres Pourpres See The Crimson Rivers (2001)
Les Rivieres Pourpres II: Les Anges de L'apocalypse See Crimson Rivers 2: Angels of the Apocalypse (2005)
Les Roseaux Sauvages See Wild Reeds (1994)
Les Routes du Sud See Roads to the South (1978)
Les Silences du Palais See The Silences of the Palace (1994)
Les Somnambules See Mon Oncle d'Amerique (1980)

Les Sorcieres de Salem See The Crucible (1957)
Les Temps Qui Changent See Changing Times (2004)
Les Temps Qui Reste See Time to Leave (2005)
Les Triplettes de Belleville See The Triplets of Belleville (2002)
Les Trois Visages de la Peur See Black Sabbath (1964)
Les Vacances de Monsieur Hulot See Mr. Hulot's Holiday (1953)
Les Valseuses See Going Places (1974)
Les Visiteurs See The Visitors (1995)
Les Yeux Noirs See Dark Eyes (1987)
Les Yeux sans Visage See The Horror Chamber of Dr. Faustus (1959)
Lesbian Twins See The Virgin Witch (1970)
L'Ete Meurtrier See One Deadly Summer (1983)
L'Ete Prochain See Next Summer (1984)
L'Eternel Retour See Eternal Return (1943)
Lethal See The KGB: The Secret War (1986)
Let's Kill Bobby Z See Bobby Z (2007)
Letter to Daddy See Jet Li's The Enforcer (1995)
A Letter to Mama See A Brivele der Mamen (1938)
A Letter to Mother See A Brivele der Mamen (1938)
Letyat Zhuravit See The Cranes Are Flying (1957)
L'Evangile Selon Saint-Matthieu See The Gospel According to St. Matthew (1964)
Levres de Sang See Lips of Blood (1975)
L'Histoire d'Adele H. See The Story of Adele H. (1975)
L'Homme de Rio See That Man from Rio (1964)
L'Homme du Train See The Man on the Train (2002)
L'Homme Qui Aimait les Femmes See The Man Who Loved Women (1977)
L'Homme Qui J'aime See The Man I Love (1997)
L'Humanite See Humanity (1999)
L'Hypothese du Tableau Vole See The Hypothesis of the Stolen Painting (1978)
Liar See Deceiver (1997)
Libido See The Sensuous Teenager (1970)
Licensed to Kill See Second Best Secret Agent in the Whole Wide World (1965)
The Lie Detector See Le Polygraphe (1996)
Liebe Ist Kalter Als Der Tod See Love Is Colder Than Death (1969)
The Life and Adventures of Nicholas Nickleby See Nicholas Nickleby (1946)
The Life and Death of Bobby Z See Bobby Z (2007)
The Life and Death of King Richard III See Richard III (1912)
The Life and Loves of Beethoven See Beethoven (1936)
The Life and Music of Giuseppe Verdi See Verdi (1953)
Life at Stake See The Key Man (1957)
Life/Drawing See Apartment 12 (2006)
Life During Wartime See The Alarmist (1998)
Life in the Food Chain See Age Isn't Everything (1991)
Life Is a Fairy Tale See Life Is a Bed of Roses (1983)
Life Is Rosy See La Vie Est Belle (1987)
Life of Brian See Monty Python's Life of Brian (1979)

The Life of Jack London See Jack London (1944)

Lifebreath See Last Breath (1996)

Lifesavers See Mixed Nuts (1994)

The Light Fantastic See Love is Better Than Ever (1952)

Lighthouse See Dead of Night (1999)

Lights of Variety See Variety Lights (1951)

Like a Crow on a June Bug See Sixteen (1972)

Like Father, Like Son See The Executioner (1978)

Like Minds See Murderous Intent (2006)

Lila See Mantis in Lace (1968)

Lila Dit Ca See Lila Says (2004)

Lilacs in the Spring See Let's Make Up (1955)

The Limit See Gone Dark (2003)

Limonadovy Joe aneb Konska Opera See Lemonade Joe (1964)

L'inafferrabile Invincibile See Mr. Super-invisible (1973)

Lincoln See Gore Vidal's Lincoln (1988)

L'Innocente See The Innocent (1976)

The Lion's Den See La Boca del Lobo (1989)

Lisa See Lila and the Devil (1975)

Lisa e il Diavolo See Lisa and the Devil (1975)

Lisa, Lisa See Axe (1974)

Lisbon See Lisboa (1999)

L'Isola Degli Uomini Pesce See Screamers (1980)

Little Fellas See Petits Freres (2000)

Little Lili See La Petite Lili (2003)

The Little Martyr See The Children Are Watching Us (1944)

The Little Mermaid See La Petite Sirene (1980)

Little Miss Millions See Home for Christmas (1993)

Little Mother See Mamele (1938)

Little Pal See Healer (1935)

The Little Panda See The Amazing Panda Adventure (1995)

The Little Sister See The Tender Age (1984)

Live a Little, Steal a Lot See Murph the Surf (1975)

Live Bait See L'Appat (1994)

Live to Love See The Devil's Hand (1961)

Live Virgin See American Virgin (1998)

The Liver Eaters See Spider Baby (1964)

Livers Ain't Cheap See The Real Thing (1997)

Living See Ikiru (1952)

The Living Dead at Manchester Morgue See Let Sleeping Corpses Lie (1974)

Ljubarni Slucaj See The Love Affair, or The Case of the Missing Switchboard Operator (1967)

Lo Chiamavano Trinita See They Call Me Trinity (1972)

Lo Que Vendra See Times to Come (1981)

Lo Sbarco di Anzio See Anzio (1968)

Lo Scatenato See Catch as Catch Can (1968)

Lo Sceicco Bianco See The White Sheik (1952)

Lo Spettro See Dr. Hitchcock See The Ghost (1963)

Lo Squartatore de New York See New York Ripper (1982)

Lo Strangolatore di Vienna See The Mad Butcher (1972)

Lo Strano Vizio della Signora Ward See Blade of the Ripper (1970)

Lo Strano Vizio Della Signora Wardh See The Next Victim (1971)

Lo Zio Indegno See The Sleazy Uncle (1989)

L'Oeuvre au Noir See The Abyss (1988)

Loaded Weapon 1 See National Lampoon's Loaded Weapon 1 (1993)

Lock Your Doors See The Ape Man (1943)

The Ledger: A Case of London Fog See The Ledger (1926)

Lockin' Italian See Showdown (1994)

The Loner See Ruckus (1981)

Lonely Man See Gun Riders (1969)

The Lonely Wife See Charulata (1964)

The Lonely Woman See Voyage in Italy (1953)

The Lonely Hearts Killers See Honeymoon Killers (1970)

Lonesome Dove: Streets of Laredo See Larry McMurtry's Streets of Laredo (1995)

The Long, Dark Night See The Pack (1977)

The Long Arm See The Third Key (1957)

The Long Night of '43 See That Long Night in '43 (1960)

Long John Silver Returns to Treasure Island See Long John Silver (1954)

The Long Night See Long John Silver (1954)

The Long Ride See Brady's Escape (1977)

The Long Shot See African Rage (1978)

Long Time, Nothing New See No Looking Back (1998)

Long Way Home See Raising Victor Vargas (2003)

Longshot See Long Shot Kids (1981)

Longxiong Hudi See Operation Condor 2: The Armour of the Gods (1986)

L'Opera De Quat'Sous See The Threepenny Opera (1931)

Looters See Trespass (1992)

Loose Joints See Flicks (1985)

Loonies on Broadway See Zombies on Broadway (1944)

The Look of Ulysses See Ulysses' Gaze (1995)

Look Down and Die See Steel (1980)

Look Beautiful and Shut Up See Sois Belle et Tais-Toi (1958)

Lords of Treason See Secret Honor (1985)

Lord Mountbatten: The Last Viceroy See The Last Viceroy (1986)

Lorca and the Outlaws See Starship (1987)

Lorca See The Disappearance of Garcia Lorca (1996)

L'Oro Di Napoli See The Gold of Naples (1954)

...'Orribile Segreto del Dr. Hichcock See The Horrible Dr. Hichcock (1962)

Los Amantes del Circulo Polar See Lovers of the Arctic Circle (1998)

Los Ambiciosos See Fever Mounts at El Pao (1959)

Los Demonios See The Demons (1974)

Los Despiadados See Hellbenders (1967)

Los Lunes al Sol See Mondays in the Sun (2002)

Los Ojos Azules de la Muneca Rota See House of Psychotic Women (1973)

Los Santos Inocentes See The Holy Innocents (1984)

Loser Take All See Strike It Rich (1990)

The Lost Glory of Troy See The Avenger (1962)

The Lost Illusion See The Fallen Idol (1949)

Lost in Time See Waxwork 2: Lost in Time (1991)

Lost Island of Kioga See Hawk of the Wilderness (1938)

Lost Planet Airmen See King of the Rocketmen (1949)

Lost Women See Mesa of Lost Women (1952)

Lost Women of Zarpa See Mesa of Lost Women (1952)

The Lost World See Sir Arthur Conan Doyle's The Lost World (1998)

The Loudest Whisper See The Children's Hour (1961)

Louis L'Amour's Conagher See Conagher (1991)

Louis L'Amour's "The Shadow Riders" See The Shadow Riders (1982)

Louis 19, le Roi des Ondes See King of the Airwaves (1994)

Love and Death in Saigon See A Better Tomorrow, Part 3 (1989)

Love and Hate: The Story of Colin and Joanne Thatcher See Love and Hate: A Marriage Made in Hell (1990)

Love and the Midnight Auto Supply See Midnight Auto Supply (1978)

The Love Cage See Joy House (1964)

Love Eternal See Eternal Return (1943)

The Love Factor See Zeta One (1969)

Love in Las Vegas See Viva Las Vegas (1963)

Love is Blind See Love at First Sight (1976)

Love Lessons See All Things Fair (1995)

Love Letter See When I Close My Eyes (1995)

Love Madness See Reefer Madness (1938)

The Love Maniac See Blood of Ghastly Horror (1972)

The Love of a Man See Amor de Hombre (1997)

A Love Story See Song of Love (1947)

Love, the Magician See El Amor Brujo (1986)

Love Scenes See Ecstasy (1984)

Love Trap See Curse of the Black Widow (1977)

Love You to Death See Deadly Illusion (1987)

Lovelorn Minstrel See Ashik Kerib (1988)

Lover of the Great Bear See Smugglers (1975)

Lover, Wife See Wifemistress (1979)

Lovers from Beyond the Tomb See Nightmare Castle (1965)

Lovers Must Learn See Rome Adventure (1962)

The Lovers of Montparnasse See Modigliani (1958)

The Lovers of Isadora See Isadora (1968)

Love's a Bitch See Amores Perros (2000)

Loves of a Scoundrel See Death of a Scoundrel (1956)

The Loves of Count Yorga, Vampire See Count Yorga, Vampire (1970)

The Loves of Irina See Female Vampire (1973)

Loving Moments See Bleak Moments (1971)

Low Rent See Apartment 12 (2006)

The Loyal 47 Ronin See 47 Ronin, Part 1 (1942)

Luce Del Miel Occhi See Light of My Eyes (2001)

L'Uccello dalle Plume di Cristallo See The Bird with the Crystal Plumage (1970)

Luci del Varieta See Variety Lights (1951)

Lucia y el Sexo See Sex and Lucia (2001)

Lucky Boots See Gun Play (1936)

Lucky Break See Paperback Romance (1996)

Lucky 13 See Running Hot (1983)

Lucky to Be a Woman See What a Woman! (1956)

The Lucifer Project See Barracuda (1978)

The Lullaby See The Sin of Madelon Claudet (1931)

L'Ultimo Uomo Della Terra See The Last Man on Earth (1964)

L'Une Chante, l'Autre Pas See One Sings, the Other Doesn't (1977)

L'Uomo Dalle Due Ombre See Cold Sweat (1971)

L'Uomo di Rio See That Man from Rio (1964)

Lulu See Pandora's Box (1928)

Lunch on the Grass See Picnic on the Grass (1959)

Lunch Wagon Girls See Lunch Wagon (1981)

Lust for Evil See Purple Noon (1960)

Lust och Fägring Stor See All Things Fair (1995)

Lust of the Vampires See I Vampiri (1956)

Lycanthropus See Werewolf in a Girl's Dormitory (1961)

Lysets Hjerte See Heart of Light (1997)

M. Hire See Monsieur Hire (1989)

Ma Femme est une Actrice See My Wife is an Actress (2001)

Ma Nuit Chez Maud See My Night at Maud's (1969)

Ma Vie Sexuelle...Comment Je Me Suis Dispute See My Sex Life... Or How I Got into an Argument (1996)

Ma Vraie Vie a Rouen See My Life on Ice (2002)

Maboroshi no Hikari See Maborosi (1995)

Macabra See Demonoid, Messenger of Death (1981)

Macabre Serenade See Dance of Death (1968)

Maccheroni See Macaroni (1985)

M:i:2 See Mission: Impossible 2 (2000)

M:i:III See In This World (2003)

Maciste at the Court of the Great Khan See Samson and the 7 Miracles of the World (1962)

Maciste Alla Corte Del Gran Khan See Samson and the 7 Miracles of the World (1962)

Maciste Contro i Mostri See Fire Monsters Against the Son of Hercules (1962)

Maciste Contro lo Sceicco See Samson Against the Sheik (1962)

Maciste Nella Terra del Ciclopi See Atlas in the Land of the Cyclops (1961)

Maciste, L'Eroe Piu Grande Del Mondo See Goliath and the Sins of Babylon (1964)

Maciste la Regina di Samar See Hercules against the Moon Men (1964)

Maciste, Il Gladiatore piu Forte del Monte See Colossus of the Arena (1962)

The Mad Butcher of Vienna See The Mad Butcher (1972)

Mad Dog See Mad Dog Morgan (1976)

Mad Dog Time See Trigger Happy (1996)

Mad Dogs and Englishmen *See* Shameless (1994)

The Mad Hatter *See* Breakfast in Hollywood (1946)

Mad Jake *See* Blood Salvage (1990)

Mad Magazine's Up the Academy *See* Up the Academy (1980)

Mad Max 2 *See* The Road Warrior (1982)

Mad Trapper of the Yukon *See* Challenge To Be Free (1976)

Mad Wednesday *See* The Sin of Harold Diddlebock (1947)

Madame De... *See* The Earrings of Madame De... (1954)

Madame Frankenstein *See* Lady Frankenstein (1972)

Madeleine Tel. 13 62 11 *See* Naked in the Night (1958)

Mademoiselle France Reunion in France (1942)

Mademoiselle Striptease *See* Plucking the Daisy (1956)

Madmen of Mandoras *See* They Saved Hitler's Brain (1964)

Madness of Love *See* Mad Love (2001)

Madonna Truth or Dare *See* Truth or Dare (1991)

Mafia Docks *See* Desperate Crimes (1993)

Mafia Junction *See* Super Bitch (1973)

The Mafu Cage *See* My Sister, My Love (1978)

The Magic Hour *See* Twilight (1998)

The Magic Roundabout *See* Doogal (2005)

The Magnificent One *See* Le Magnifique (1976)

The Magnificent Seven *See* Seven Samurai (1954)

The Magnificent Showman *See* Circus World (1964)

Mahanagar *See* The Big City (1963)

Making It *See* Going Places (1974)

Mamba Snakes *See* Fair Game (1989)

Man Against the Mob: The Chinatown Murders *See* The Chinatown Murders: Man against the Mob (1989)

Man and His Mate *See* One Million B.C. (1940)

A Man Betrayed *See* Wheel of Fortune (1941)

Man Cheng Jin Dai Huang Jin Jia *See* Curse of the Golden Flower (2006)

Man-Eater *See* Shark! (1968)

A Man Escaped, or the Wind Bloweth Where It Listeth *See* A Man Escaped (1957)

The Man from C.O.T.T.O.N. *See* Purlie Victorious (1963)

The Man From C.O.T.T.O.N., Purlie Victorious *See* Gone Are the Days (1963)

Man from Music Mountain *See* Texas Legionnaires (1943)

The Man From Nevada *See* The Nevadan (1950)

Man in a Cocked Hat *See* Carlton Browne of the F.O. (1959)

A Man in Mommy's Bed *See* With Six You Get Eggroll (1968)

The Man in Possession *See* Personal Property (1937)

The Man in the Middle *See* 48 Hours to Live (1960)

Man Looking Southeast *See* Man Facing Southeast (1986)

Man of Bronze *See* Jim Thorpe: All American (1951)

Man of the Frontier *See* Red River Valley (1936)

Man of the Hour *See* Colonel Effingham's Raid (1945)

Man on the Move *See* Jigsaw (1971)

The Man Who Changed His Mind *See* The Man Who Lived Again (1936)

The Man Who Cried *See* Catherine Cookson's The Man Who Cried (1993)

The Man Who Watched Trains Go By *See* Paris Express (1953)

The Man With The Deadly Lens *See* Wrong Is Right (1982)

The Man with the Green Carnation *See* The Trials of Oscar Wilde (1960)

The Man with the Synthetic Brain *See* Blood of Ghastly Horror (1972)

The Man with the X-Ray Eyes *See* X: The Man with X-Ray Eyes (1963)

The Man with the Yellow Eyes *See* Planets Against Us (1961)

The Man with Thirty Sons *See* The Magnificent Yankee (1950)

Manchester Prep *See* Cruel Intentions 2 (1999)

Manen Pa Taket *See* The Man on the Roof (1976)

Mangiati Vivi dal Cannibali *See* Emerald Jungle (1980)

Manhattan Project: The Deadly Game *See* The Manhattan Project (1986)

Manhunt *See* Hit Men (1972)

Manhunt in the Dakotas *See* Midnight Murders (1991)

Manhunt: The Search for the Night Stalker *See* The Hunt for the Night Stalker (1991)

The Maniacs Are Loose *See* The Thrill Killers (1965)

Manifesto *See* A Night of Love (1987)

Manly Love *See* Amor de Hombre (1997)

Mannen fran Mallorca *See* Man from Mallorca (1984)

Mannequins for Rio *See* Party Girls for Sale (1954)

Manner wie wir *See* Guys and Balls (2004)

Manon des Sources *See* Manon of the Spring (1987)

Mansion of Madness *See* Dr. Tarr's Torture Dungeon (1975)

Mansquito *See* Mosquitoman (2005)

The Manster—Half Man, Half Monster *See* The Manster (1959)

Manuela's Loves *See* Le Jupon Rouge (1987)

Mar Adentro *See* The Sea Inside (2004)

Marc Bolan and T-Rrex: Born to Boogie *See* Born to Boogie (1972)

Marc Mato, Agent S.077 *See* Espionage in Tangiers (1965)

Marcelino *See* The Miracle of Marcelino (1955)

Marcelino, Pan y Vino *See* The Miracle of Marcelino (1955)

Marching Along *See* Stars and Stripes Forever (1952)

Marco Polo Junior Versus the Red Dragon *See* Marco Polo, Jr. (1972)

Margaret Bourke-White *See* Double Exposure: The Story of Margaret Bourke-White (1989)

Maria di Mi Corazon *See* Mary, My Dearest (1983)

Maria, Ilena eres de gracia *See* Maria Full of Grace (2004)

Maria Marten *See* Murder in the Old Red Barn (1936)

Maria-nap *See* Maria's Day (1984)

Marie Bay of Angels *See* Marie Baie des Anges (1997)

Marie Walewska *See* Conquest (1937)

Marijuana the Devil's Weed *See* She Shoulda Said No (1949)

Marijuana: The Devil's Weed *See* Marihuana (1936)

Marijuana, Weed with Roots in Hell *See* Marihuana (1936)

Marilyn *See* Roadhouse Girl (1953)

Marine Issue *See* Instant Justice (1986)

Mario Puzo's The Last Don *See* The Last Don (1997)

Mario Puzo's The Last Don 2 *See* The Last Don 2 (1998)

Marius et Jeannette: Un Conte de L'Estaque *See* Marius and Jeannette (1997)

Mark of Terror *See* Drums of Jeopardy (1931)

Mark of the Avenger *See* The Mysterious Rider (1938)

Mark of the Beast *See* Curse of the Undead (1959)

Mark of the Claw *See* Dick Tracy's Dilemma (1947)

Mark of the Vampire *See* The Vampire (1957)

Mark of the West *See* Curse of the Undead (1959)

Mark Twain *See* The Adventures of Mark Twain (1985)

Married in Haste *See* Consolation Marriage (1931)

Marrionnier: Doll Horror Movie *See* Marrionnier (2005)

Mars Invades Puerto Rico *See* Frankenstein Meets the Space Monster (1965)

The Marseille Contract *See* The Destructors (1974)

Marshal of Heldorado *See* Blazing Guns (1950)

The Marsupials: Howling 3 *See* Howling 3: The Marsupials (1987)

Marte, Dio Della Guerra *See* Venus Against the Son of Hercules (1962)

Martha, Meet Frank, Daniel and Laurence *See* The Very Thought of You (1998)

Martin Lawrence You So Crazy *See* You So Crazy (1994)

Marusa No Onna *See* A Taxing Woman (1987)

Marusa No Onna II *See* A Taxing Woman's Return (1988)

The Marvelous Visit *See* La Merveilleuse Visite (1974)

The Marx Brothers at the Circus *See* At the Circus (1939)

Marx Brothers Go West *See* Go West (1940)

Mary Bryant *See* The Incredible Journey of Mary Bryant (2005)

Mary Jane's Last Dance *See* New Best Friend (2002)

Mascskajatek *See* Cat's Play (1974)

Masculin Feminin *See* Masculine Feminine (1966)

Mask of Dust *See* Race for Life (1955)

Mask of Fury *See* First Yank into Tokyo (1945)

Mask of Satan *See* Black Sunday (1960)

Massacre at Fort Holman *See* A Reason to Live, a Reason to Die (1973)

Massacre Hill *See* Eureka Stockade (1949)

Massacre Mafia Style *See* The Executioner (1978)

Massa'ot James Be'eretz Hakodesh *See* James' Journey to Jerusalem (2003)

Master of Evil *See* The Demon Lover (1977)

Master of Lassie *See* The Hills of Home (1948)

Master of the Crimson Armor *See* The Promise (2005)

Mat i Syn *See* Mother and Son (1997)

Matango *See* Attack of the Mushroom People (1963)

Matar al Abuelito *See* Killing Grandpa (1991)

Mater Dolorosa *See* The Torture of Silence (1917)

The Mating of the Sabine Women *See* The Rape of the Sabines (1961)

Matir Moina *See* The Clay Bird (2002)

Matka Joanna Od Aniolow *See* Mother Joan of the Angels (1960)

Matt Riker *See* Mutant Hunt (1987)

A Matter of Life and Death *See* Stairway to Heaven (1946)

Mauri *See* Big Mo (1973)

Maurice Richard *See* The Rocket (2005)

Mausoleum *See* One Dark Night (1982)

Mauvaises Genres *See* Transfixed (2001)

Mauvaises Frequentations *See* Bad Company (1999)

Mavri Emmanouella *See* Emmanuelle, the Queen (1979)

Max, My Love *See* Max, Mon Amour (1986)

Mayerling to Sarajevo *See* De Mayerling a Sarajevo (1940)

The Mayfair Bank Caper *See* The Big Scam (1979)

Mazel Tov Ou le Marriage *See* Marry Me, Marry Me (1969)

McKlusky *See* White Lightning (1973)

The McMasters...Tougher Than the West Itself *See* The McMasters (1970)

M.D.C. Maschera di Cera *See* Wax Mask (1997)

Me Faire ca a Moi *See* It Means That to Me (1960)

Meachorel Hasoragim *See* Beyond the Walls (1984)

Meat Is Meat *See* The Mad Butcher (1972)

Mecaniques Celestes *See* Celestial Clockwork (1994)

Mechanical Bananas *See* Erotic Escape (1972)

The Medicine Hat Stallion *See* Peter Lundy and the Medicine Hat Stallion (1977)

The Medieval Dead *See* Army of Darkness (1992)

Medusa *See* Medusa Against the Son of Hercules

Medusa vs. the Son of Hercules *See* Medusa Against the Son of Hercules (1962)

Meet Miss Marple *See* Murder She Said (1962)

Meet Ruth Stoops *See* Citizen Ruth (1996)

Meet the Applegates *See* The Applegates (1989)

Meet the Browns *See* Tyler Perry's Meet the Browns (2008)

Meet the Ghosts *See* Abbott and Costello Meet Frankenstein (1948)

Meet Whiplash Willie *See* The Fortune Cookie (1966)

The Meetings of Anna *See* Les Rendezvous D'Anna (1978)

Mega Snake *See* Megasnake (2007)

Megall Az Ido *See* Time Stands Still (1982)

A Mela-Noite Levarei Sua Alma *See* At Midnight, I'll Take Your Soul (1963)

Mekagojira No Gyakushu See Terror of Mechagodzilla (1978)

Melanie Rose See High Stakes (1989)

Melodie en Sous-Sol See Any Number Can Win (1963)

Melody of Youth See They Shall Have Music (1939)

Mem om oss barn i Bullerby See More about the Children of Noisy Village (1987)

Memorias del Subdesarrollo See Memories of Underdevelopment (1968)

The Men See Killing in the Sun (1973)

Men Don't Quit See Grilled (2006)

Men in Tights See Robin Hood: Men in Tights (1993)

Men of Steel See Steel (1980)

Men with Guns See Hombres Armados (1997)

Meng zhong ren See Dream Lovers (1986)

The Mercenaries See Dark of the Sun (1968)

Merry Christmas See Joyeux Noel (1965)

Merchant of Death See Mission of Death (1997)

Mermaid Chronicles Part 1: She Creature See The Creature (2001)

Mery per Sempre See Forever Mary (1989)

Meteor Monster See Teenage Monster (1957)

Metempsycose See Tomb of Torture (1965)

Metalmeccanico e Parrucchiera in un Turbine di Sesso e di Politica See The Worker and the Hairdresser (1996)

Messer im Kopf See Knife in the Head (1978)

Meteoro Kai Skia See Meteor & Shadow (1985)

Mettisse See Cate au Lait (1994)

Meurtre en 45 Tours See Murder at 45 R.P.M. (1965)

MIB See Men in Black (1997)

Mia Eoniotita Ke Mia Mera See Eternity and a Day (1997)

Mi Casa, Su Casa See Loco Love (2003)

Mi Familia See My Family (1994)

A mi madre le gustan las mujeres See My Mother Likes Women (2002)

Microscopia See Fantastic Voyage (1966)

Midare Karakuri See Murders in the Doll House (1979)

Midnight at Madame Tussaud's See The External (1999)

Michael Almereyda's The Mummy See The Mummy (1999)

Michael Angel See The Apostate (1998)

Mickey Spillane's Margin for Murder See Margin for Murder (1981)

Midnight at the Wax Museum (1936)

Midnight Heat See Sunset Heat (1992)

Midnight Man See Jack Higgins' Midnight Man (1996)

Midnight Movie Massacre See Attack from Mars (1988)

A Midsummer Night's Dream See William Shakespeare's A Midsummer Night's Dream (1999)

Miel et Cendres See Honey & Ashes (1996)

Mies Vailla Menneisyytta See The Man Without a Past (2002)

Mifune's Last Song See Mifune (1999)

Mifunes Sidste Sang See Mifune (1999)

The Mighty Ducks 2 See D2: The Mighty Ducks (1994)

The Mighty Thunder See Tundra (1936)

The Mighty Ursus See Ursus in the Valley of the Lions (1962)

The Mighty Warrior See The Trojan Horse (1962)

Mit Eva Fing Die Sunde An See The Bellboy and the Playgirls (1962)

Mikan No Taikyoku See The Go-Masters (1982)

Mike Leigh's Naked See Naked (1993)

Mikres Aphrodites See Young Aphrodites (1963)

Milagro en Roma See Miracle in Rome (1988)

Milczaca Gwiazda See First Spaceship on Venus (1960)

Mile a Minute Love See Roaring Speedboats (1937)

Miliou en Mai See May Fools (1990)

Miliou in May See May Fools (1990)

Mimi Metallurgico Ferito Nell'Onore See Seduction of Mimi (1972)

Minaccia d'Amore See Dial Help (1983)

Minbo No Onna See Minbo—Or the Gentle Art of Japanese Extortion (1992)

Mind Games See The Agency (1981)

Mind Rage See Mind Lies (2000)

Mind Ripper See Wes Craven Presents Mind Ripper (1995)

Mindwarp: An Infinity of Terror See Galaxy of Terror (1981)

Minna von Barnheim oder das Soldatengluck See Minna von Barnhelm or The Soldier's Fortune (1962)

Miracolo a Milano See Miracle in Milan (1951)

The Miracle of Fatima See Miracle of Our Lady of Fatima (1952)

A Miracle Can Happen See On Our Merry Way (1948)

Mio in the Land of Faraway See The Land of Faraway (1987)

Miracle of Life See Our Daily Bread (1934)

Mirai Ninja See Cyber Ninja (1994)

Mirage See Matorosi (1951)

The Mischief-Makers See Les Mistons (1957)

Miss Castaway and the Island Girls See Miss Cast Away (2004)

Miss Europe See Prix de Beaute (1930)

Miss Muerte See The Diabolical Dr. Z (1965)

Miss Shumway See Rough Magic (1995)

The Mission of the Yogi See The Indian Tomb (1921)

Mrs. Bradley Mysteries: Speedy Death See Speedy Death (1999)

Mrs. Parker and the Round Table See Mrs. Parker and the Vicious Circle (1994)

Mr. Ashton was Indiscreet See The Senator Was Indiscreet (1947)

Mr. Bug Goes to Town See Hoppity Goes to Town (1941)

Mr. Celebrity See Turf Boy (1942)

Mr. Forbush and the Penguins See Cry of the Penguins (1971)

Mr. Fox of Venice See The Honey Pot (1967)

Mr. Invisible See Mr. Superinvisible (1973)

Mr. Murder See Dean Koontz's Mr. Murder (1998)

Mr. Quilp See The Old Curiosity Shop (1975)

Mister Scarface See Rulers of the City (1976)

Mr. Sebastian See Sebastian (1968)

Mr. 247 See A Modern Affair (1994)

Mister V See Pimpernel Smith (1942)

Mr. Wrong See Dark of the Night (1985)

Misterios del Ultratumba See Black Pit of Dr. M (1947)

Mitt Liv Som Hund See My Life As a Dog (1985)

Miyazaki's Spirited Away See Spirited Away (2001)

Mme. Olga's Massage Parlor See Olga's Massage Parlor (1965)

Moartea Domnului Lazarescu See The Death of Mr. Lazarescu (2005)

The Model Killer See The Hollywood Strangler Meets the Skid Row Slasher (1979)

Model Massacre See Color Me Blood Red (1964)

Modelo Antiguo See Vintage Model

A Modern Hero See Knute Rockne: All American (1940)

A Modern Bluebeard See Boom in the Moon (1946)

Modesty Blaise: The Beginning See My Name is Modesty: A Modesty Blaise Adventure (2004)

Modigliani of Montparnasse See Modigliani (1958)

Mogliamante See Wifemistress (1979)

The Mogul See Ratings Game (1984)

Mohammad: Messenger of God See The Message (1977)

Morgan Do See Infernal Affairs (2002)

Moise: L'Affaire Roch Theriault See Savage Messiah (2002)

Molly Louvain See The Strange Love of Molly Louvain (1932)

Mon Pere, Ma Mere, Mes Freres et Mes Soeurs See My Father, My Mother, My Brothers and My Sisters (1999)

Mon Meilleur Ami See My Best Friend (2006)

Mon tresor See Or (My Treasure) (2004)

Monday Morning See Class of Fear (1991)

Mondo Pazzo See Mondo Cane 2 (1964)

Mondo Insanity See Mondo Cane 2 (1964)

Money See L'Argent (1983)

Monique and Julie See Sweet Young Thing (1979)

Monkey Shines: An Experiment in Fear See Monkey Shines (1988)

Monsieur Hulot's Holiday See Mr. Hulot's Holiday (1953)

Monsieur Ibrahim and the Flowers of the Koran See Monsieur Ibrahim (2003)

Monsieur Ibrahim et les Fleurs du Coran See Monsieur Ibrahim (2003)

Monsoon See Isle of Forgotten Sins (1943)

Monster See Humanoids from the Deep (1980)

The Monster Baran See Varan the Unbelievable (1961)

The Monster Demolisher See Curse of Nostradamus (1960)

Monster from a Prehistoric Planet See Gappa the Trifibian Monster (1967)

Monster from Mars See Robot Monster (1953)

Monster from the Surf See The Beach Girls and the Monster (1965)

Monster in the Surf See The Beach Girls and the Monster (1965)

Monster in the Night See Monster on the Campus (1959)

Monster Island's Decisive Battle: Godzilla's Son See Son of Godzilla (1966)

Monster Maker See Monster from the Ocean Floor (1954)

The Monster Meets the Gorilla See Bela Lugosi Meets a Brooklyn Gorilla (1952)

Monster of Monsters See Ghidrah the Three Headed Monster (1965)

Monster of Terror See Die, Monster, Die! (1965)

Monster of the Island See Island Monster (1953)

The Monster Show See Freaks (1932)

The Monster Walked See The Monster Walks (1932)

The Monster with Green Eyes See Planets Against Us (1961)

The Monster from the Moon See Robot Monster (1953)

Monster Yongkari See Yongkari Monster of the Deep (1967)

Monster Zero See Godzilla vs. Monster Zero (1968)

Monsters from the Unknown Planet See Terror of Mechagodzilla (1976)

Monsters of the Night See Navy vs. the Night Monsters (1966)

The Monsters Are Loose See The Thrill Killers (1965)

Monsters from the Deep See Robot Monster (1953)

Monstrosity See The Atomic Brain (1964)

Montana Justice See Man from Montana (1941)

Monte Carlo or Bust See Those Daring Young Men in Their Jaunty Jalopies (1969)

Montenegro—Or Pigs and Pearls See Montenegro (1981)

Montparnasse 19 See Modigliani (1958)

More About the Children of Bullerby Village See More about the Children of Noisy Village (1987)

More Tales of the City See Armistead Maupin's More Tales of the City (1997)

Morgan! See Morgan: A Suitable Case for Treatment (1966)

Morgan il Pirata See Morgan the Pirate (1960)

Morgen Grauen See Time Troopers (1989)

Morte a Venezia See Death in Venice (1971)

Mortal Sins See Dangerous Obsession (1988)

Mortras en Chafarinas See Zafarinas (1994)

The Mormon Peril See Trapped by the Mormons (1922)

Morning Terror See Time Troopers (1989)

The Moscow Chronicle See Final Assignment (1980)

Mosaic See Frankenstein '80 (1979)

Moscow Distrusts Tears See Moscow Does Not Believe in Tears (1980)

Moscow Nights See Stand Condemned (1936)

Moskwa Sljesam Nje Jerit See Moscow Does Not Believe in Tears (1980)

The Most Desired Man See Maybe... Maybe Not (1994)

Motel See Pink Motel (1982)

Motel Vacancy See Talking Walls (1985)

Motevalede Mahe Mehr See Born Under Libra (2001)

The Moth See Catherine Cookson's The Moth (1996)

Mother Goose A Go-Go See The Unkissed Bride (1966)

Mother Riley Meets the Vampire See My Son, the Vampire (1952)

A Mother's Fight for Justice See Crash Course (2000)

Mosura See Mothra (1962)

Mosura 2 See Rebirth of Mothra 2 (1997)

Mosura tai Gojira See Godzilla vs. Mothra (1964)

Mothra See Mothra (1962)

Mothra 2 See Rebirth of Mothra 2 (1997)

Mothra vs. Godzilla See Godzilla vs. Mothra (1964)

Motor Rods and Rockers See Motor Psycho (1965)

The Moustache See La Moustache (2005)

Movie Struck See Pick a Star (1937)

The Moving Target See Harper (1966)

Mowgli and Baloo: Jungle Book 2 See Rudyard Kipling's the Second Jungle Book: Mowgli and Baloo (1997)

Mr. Scarface See Big Boss (1977)

Ms. Don Juan See Don Juan (Or If Don Juan Were a Woman) (1973)

Mua Len Trau See Buffalo Boy (2004)

Much Ado about Murder See Theatre of Blood (1973)

Mud See The Stick-Up (1977)

Muhomatsu no Issho See Rikisha-Man (1958)

Mui du du Xanh See The Scent of Green Papaya (1993)

Mujeres al Borde de un Ataque de Nervios See Women on the Verge of a Nervous Breakdown (1988)

The Mummy See Bram Stoker's The Mummy (1997)

Mumsy, Nanny, Sonny, and Girly See Girly (1970)

Mundo Depravados See World of the Depraved (1967)

Munkbrogreven See The Count of the Old Town (1934)

Mur See Wall (2004)

Murder by Mail See Schizoid (1980)

Murder by Proxy See Blackout (1954)

Murder: By Reason of Insanity See My Sweet Victim (1985)

Murder in the Ring See Counter Punch (1971)

The Murder in Thorton Square See Gaslight (1944)

Murder, Inc. See The Enforcer (1951)

Murder is Easy See Agatha Christie's Murder is Easy (1982)

Murder Near Perfect See Dagger Eyes (1983)

Murder on Diamond Row See The Squeaker (1937)

Murder One See Death Sentence (1974)

The Murder Room See P.D. James: The Murder Room (2004)

Murder Rooms: The Dark Origins of Sherlock Holmes See Dr. Bell and Mr. Doyle: The Dark Beginnings of Sherlock Holmes (2000)

Murder with Mirrors See Agatha Christie's Murder with Mirrors (1985)

Murder with Music See Mistaken Identity (1941)

The Murderer Dmitri Karamazov See The Brothers Karamazov (1958)

Muriel, Or the Time of Return See Muriel (1963)

Muriel, Ou le Temps d'Un Retour See Muriel (1963)

The Murri Affair See La Grande Bourgeoise (1974)

Music in Darkness See Night Is My Future (1947)

The Music Room See Jalsaghar (1958)

Musime si Pomahat See Divided We Fall (2000)

Mussolini: The Decline and Fall of Il Duce See Mussolini & I (1985)

Mutant See Forbidden World (1982)

The Mutation See The Freakmaker (1973)

Mutations See The Freakmaker (1973)

Mute Love See Secret of Yolanda (1982)

The Mutilator See The Dark (1979)

The Mutineers See Pirate Ship (1949)

Mutter Kusters Fahrt Zum Himmel See Mother Kusters Goes to Heaven (1976)

Mutter und Sohn See Mother and Son (1997)

Mutters Courage See My Mother's Courage (1995)

MVP 3 See MXP: Most Xtreme Primate (2003)

My Brother, the Outlaw See My Outlaw Brother (1951)

My Brother's Keeper See Brother's Keeper (2002)

My Brother's Wife See La Mujer de Mi Hermano (2006)

My Crazy Life See Mi Vida Loca (1994)

My Darling Shiksa See Over the Brooklyn Bridge (1983)

My Father Is a Hero See Jet Li's The Enforcer (1995)

My Father, My Master See Padre Padrone (1977)

My Favorite Season See Ma Saison Preferee (1993)

My Favourite Year See My Favorite Year (1982)

My Forgotten Man See Flynn (1996)

My Girlfriend's Boyfriend See Boyfriends & Girlfriends (1988)

My Hero See A Southern Yankee (1948)

My Life in Pink See Ma Vie en Rose (1997)

My Love Letters See Love Letters (1983)

My Man See Mon Homme (1996)

My Name is John See The Legend of Hillbilly John (1973)

My Name Is Zora See Zora Is My Name! (1990)

My Neighbor's Daughter See Angel Blue (1997)

My Night with Maud See My Night at Maud's (1969)

My Palikari See Silent Rebellion (1982)

My Posse Don't Do Homework See Dangerous Minds (1995)

My Son Alone See American Empire (1942)

My Teenage Daughter See Teenage Bad Girl (1959)

My Uncle See Mon Oncle (1958)

My Uncle, Mr. Hulot See Mon Oncle (1958)

My World Dies Screaming See Terror in the Haunted House (1958)

Mystere See Dagger Eyes (1983)

Mystere Alexina See The Mystery of Alexina (1986)

Mysterious Invader See The Astounding She-Monster (1958)

The Mysterious Rider See Badmen of Nevada (1933)

The Mysterious Satellite See Warning from Space (1956)

The Mystery of Kaspar Hauser See Every Man for Himself & God Against All (1975)

The Mystery of Spoon River See The Ghost of Spoon River (2000)

Mystery of the Black Jungle See The Black Devils of Kali (1955)

The Mystery of the Marie Celeste See The Mystery of the Mary Celeste (1935)

Mystique See Circle of Power (1983)

Na Cidade Vazia See Hollow City (2004)

Na Komete See On the Comet (1968)

Na Samyn Dnie See Deep End (1970)

Nachts wenn Dracula Erwacht See Count Dracula (1971)

Nagooa See Drifting (1982)

The Naked Goddess See The Devil's Hand (1961)

Naked Island See The Island (1961)

Naked Massacre See Born for Hell (1976)

The Naked Night See Sawdust & Tinsel (1953)

Naked Space See The Creature Wasn't Nice (1981)

Naked Space See Spaceship (1981)

Naked under Leather See The Girl on a Motorcycle (1968)

Naked Warriors See The Arena (1973)

The Naked Weekend See Circle of Power (1983)

Naked Youth See The Cruel Story of Youth (1960)

Nam's Angels See The Losers (1970)

Namu, My Best Friend See Namu, the Killer Whale (1966)

Nanguo Zaijian, Nanguo See Goodbye South, Goodbye (1996)

Nankai No Daikaiju See Yog, Monster from Space (1971)

Nankai No Kai Ketto See Godzilla vs. the Sea Monster (1966)

NaPolA See Before the Fall (2004)

Nara Livet See Brink of Life (1957)

Narayama-Bushi-Ko See The Ballad of Narayama (1983)

Nathaniel Hawthorne's "Twice Told Tales" See Twice-Told Tales (1963)

National Lampoon's Cousin Eddie's Christmas Vacation See National Lampoon's Christmas Vacation 2: Cousin Eddie's Big Island Adventure (2003)

Nattens Engel See Angel of the Night (1998)

Nattvardsgaesterna See The Winter Light (1962)

Nature's Mistakes See Freaks (1932)

Naughty Girl See Mam'zelle Pigalle (1958)

Navy Cross See G.I. Jane (1997)

Navy Diver See Men of Honor (2000)

The Navy Steps Out See A Girl, a Guy and a Gob (1941)

Ne Touchez pas la Hache See The Duchess of Langeais (2007)

Neat and Tidy See Adventures Beyond Belief (1987)

Neco Z Alenky See Alice (1988)

Necromancy See The Witching (1972)

Necronomicon See H.P. Lovecraft's Necronomicon: Book of the Dead (1993)

Ned Blessing: The Story of My Life and Times See Lone Justice 2 (1993)

Ned Kelly, Outlaw See Ned Kelly (1970)

Neil Simon's Biloxi Blues See Biloxi Blues (1988)

Neil Simon's Brighton Beach Memoirs See Brighton Beach Memoirs (1986)

Neil Simon's Broadway Bound See Broadway Bound (1992)

Neil Simon's Lost in Yonkers See Lost in Yonkers (1993)

Neil Simon's The Slugger's Wife See The Slugger's Wife (1985)

Nella Stretta M Orsa Del Ragno See Web of the Spider (1970)

Nelly and Mr. Arnaud See Nelly et Monsieur Arnaud (1995)

Nemesis 3: Prey Harder See Nemesis 3: Time Lapse (1996)

The Neptune Disaster See Neptune Factor (1973)

Neskolko Dnei Iz Zhizni I.I. Oblomov See Oblomov

Nettoyage a Sec See Dry Cleaning (1997)

Neurosis See Revenge in the House of Usher (1982)

Nevada Heat See Fake Out (1982)

Never Cry Devil See Night Visitor (1989)

The Never Dead See Phantasm (1979)

Never Ever See Circle of Passion (1997)

Never Give an Inch See Sometimes a Great Notion (1971)

NeverWhere See Neil Gaiman's Never-Where (1996)

The New Adventures of Don Juan See Adventures of Don Juan (1949)

New Adventures of Tarzan See Tarzan and the Green Goddess (1938)

The New Barbarians See Warriors of the Wasteland (1983)

New Girl in Town See Nashville Girl (1976)

New Tales of the Taira Clan See Shin Heike Monogatari (1955)

New Wave See Nouvelle Vague (1990)

New Wine See Melody Master (1941)

The Newcomers See The Wild Country (1971)

Next! See Blade of the Ripper (1970)

The Next Man See The Arab Conspiracy (1976)

The Next Victim See Blade of the Ripper (1970)

Ngo Hai Sui See Jackie Chan's Who Am I (1998)

Nicholas Nickleby See The Life and Adventures of Nicholas Nickleby (1981)

Nickel and Dime See Larger Than Life (1996)

The Niece of the Vampire See Fangs of the Living Dead (1968)

Niewinni Czarodzieje See Innocent Sorcerers (1959)

Night After Night After Night See He Kills Night After Night After Night (1969)

Night After Night After Night See Night Slasher (1969)

The Night Andy Came Home See Deathdream (1972)

Night Beauties See Beauties of the Night (1952)

The Night Caller See Night Caller from Outer Space (1966)

Night Comes Too Soon See The Ghost of Rashmon Hall (1947)

Night Encounter See Double Agents (1959)

The Night Flier See Stephen King's The Night Flier (1996)

Night Hair Child See What the Peeper Saw (1972)

Night Is the Phantom See The Whip and the Body (1963)

Night is the Time for Killing See Murder on the Midnight Express (1974)

Night Legs See Fright (1971)

The Night of San Lorenzo See The Night of the Shooting Stars (1982)

Night of the Anubis See Night of the Living Dead (1968)

Night of the Beast See House of the Black Death (1965)

Night of the Big Heat See Island of the Burning Doomed (1967)

Night of the Blind Dead See Tombs of the Blind Dead (1972)

Night of the Bloodsuckers See The Vampire Hookers (1978)

Night of the Claw See Island Claw (1980)

Night of the Dark Full Moon See Silent Night, Bloody Night (1973)

Night of the Demon See Curse of the Demon (1957)

Night of the Demon See The Touch of Satan (1970)

Night of the Doomed See Nightmare Castle (1965)

Night of the Eagle See Burn Witch, Burn! (1962)

Night of the Flesh Eaters See Night of the Living Dead (1968)
Night of the Seagulls See Night of the Death Cult (1975)
Night of the Seagulls See Terror Beach (1975)
Night of the Silicates See Is and of Terror (1966)
Night of the Vampire See Cave of the Living Dead (1965)
Night of the Wenrmacht Zombies See Night of the Zombies (1981)
Night of the Zombies See Hell of the Living Dead (1983)
Night of Walpurgis See The Werewolf vs. the Vampire Woman (1970)
No Man's Land See No Man's Range (1935)
Night Passage See Jesse Stone: Night Passage (2006)
Night Scare See Nightscare (1993)
Night Shadows See Mutant (1983)
The Night They Invented Striptease See The Night They Raided Minsky's (1966)
Night Train See Night Train to Munich (1940)
Night Train Murders See Torture Train (1975)
Night Trap See Mardi Gras for the Devil (1993)
Night Walk See Deathdream (1972)
Night Watch See Detonator 2: Night Watch (1995)
The Night Watch See Le Trou (1959)
Nightcap See Merci pour le Chocolat (2000)
Nighttall See Isaac Asimov's Nightfall (2000)
Nightingale See The Young Nurses (1973)
A Nightingale Sang in Berkeley Square See The Big Scam (1979)
Nightmare Beach See Welcome to Spring Break (1988)
Nightmare Circus See Barn of the Naked Dead (1973)
Nightmare City See City of the Walking Dead (1980)
Nightmare See Nightmare in Badham County (1976)
Nightmare at Shadow Woods See Blood Rage (1987)
Nightmare Hotel See It Happened at Nightmare Inn (1970)
Nightmare House See Scream, Baby, Scream (1969)
Nightmare in a Damaged Brain See Nightmare (1982)
Nightmare Island See Night Warning (1982)
Nightmare Maker See Night Warning (1982)
A Nightmare on Elm Street 6: Freddy's Dead See Freddy's Dead: The Final Nightmare (1991)
Nightmare on Elm Street 7 See Wes Craven's New Nightmare (1994)
Nights in a Harem See Son of Sinbad (1955)
The Nights of Dracula See Count Dracula (1971)
Nijushi No Hitomi See Twenty-Four Eyes (1954)
Nikutai No Mon See Gate of Flesh (1964)
9/30/55 See September 30, 1955 (1977)
1990 I Guerrieri del Bronx See 1990: The Bronx Warriors (1983)
1999—Nen No Natsu Yasumi See Summer Vacation: 1999 (1988)
Ningen No Joken See The Human Condition: Road to Eternity (1959)
Ninja Dragons See Magic Kid (1992)
Nippon Chinbotsu See Tidal Wave (1975)

Nippon Konchuki See The Insect Woman (1963)
Nirgendwo in Afrika See Nowhere in Africa (2002)
Nizza See A Propos de Nice (1929)
No Comebacks See Two by Forsyth (1986)
No Exit See Fatal Combat (1996)
No Fear See Fear (1996)
No Greater Love See The Human Condition: Road to Eternity (1959)
No Hambra mas Penas ni Olvido See Funny, Dirty Little War (1983)
No Knife See The Frisco Kid (1979)
No Man's Land See No Man's Range (1935)
No Mercy Man See Trained to Kill, U.S.A. (1975)
No Place Like Homicide See What a Carve-Up! (1962)
No Place to Hide See Rebel (1970)
The No-Tell Hotel See Rosebud Beach Hotel (1985)
No Worries See Clueless (1995)
Nobi See Fires on the Plain (1959)
Noce in Galilee See A Wedding in Galilee (1987)
Nochnoi Dozor See Night Watch (2004)
Nocturna, Granddaughter of Dracula See Nocturna (1979)
Noi Albinoi See Noi (2003)
Noi the Albino See Noi (2003)
Non Si Sevizia un Paperino See Don't Torture a Duckling (1972)
Nora Roberts' Blue Smoke See Blue Smoke (2007)
Nora Roberts' Carolina Moon See Carolina Moon (2007)
Normal Adolescent Behavior See Havoc 2: Normal Adolescent Behavior (2007)
The Northfield Cemetery Massacre See Northville Cemetery Massacre (1976)
Northwest Frontier See Flame Over India (1960)
Nosferatu, A Symphony of Horror See Nosferatu (1922)
Nosferatu, A Symphony of Terror See Nosferatu (1922)
Nosferatu, Eine Symphonie des Grauens See Nosferatu (1922)
Nosferatu: Phantom der Nacht See Nosferatu, the Vampyre (1979)
Nosferatu, the Vampire See Nosferatu, the Vampyre (1979)
Nostradamus No Daiyogen See Last Days of Planet Earth (1974)
Not against the Flesh See Vampyr (1931)
Not Me See Sous Sol (1996)
Not Quite Jerusalem See Not Quite Paradise (1986)
Not Wanted See Streets of Sin (1949)
Nothing in Order See All Screwed Up (1974)
Nothing to Lose See Death in Brunswick (1990)
Nothing to Lose See Ten Benny (1998)
Notre Dame de Paris See The Hunchback of Notre Dame (1957)
Novecento See 1900 (1976)
Novembermond See November Moon (1985)
Novia Que Te Vea See Like A Bride (1994)
Nowhere to Hide See Fatal Chase (1977)

Noz w Wodzie See Knife in the Water (1962)
Nuclear Run See Chain Reaction (1980)
Nuclear Terror See Golden Rendezvous (1977)
Nude in His Pocket See Girl in His Pocket (1957)
Nue Propriete See Private Property (2006)
Nueve Reinas See Nine Queens (2000)
Nuit et Jour See Night and Day (1991)
Nuit le Plus Longue See Sexus (1964)
Nulyan, Selsap See Summer Snow (1994)
Number Two See Numero Deux (1975)
Numbered Days See Cycle Psycho (1972)
Numbered Days See Running Out of Time (1994)
Nuovo Cinema Paradiso See Cinema Paradiso (1988)
Nurse Sherri See Hospital of Terror (1978)
The Nutcracker See George Balanchine's The Nutcracker (1993)
Nyba See Night Watch (1973)
Nyoka and the Lost Secrets of Hippocrates See Nyoka and the Tigermen (1942)
O Beijo da Mulher Aranha See Kiss of the Spider Woman (1985)
O Dragao da Maldade contra o Santo Guerreiro See Antonio Das Mortes (1968)
O Estranho Mundo de Ze do Caixao See Strange World of Coffin Joe (1968)
O Thiassos See The Travelling Players (1975)
Obch Od Na Korze See The Shop on Main Street (1965)
Obecna Skola See The Elementary School (1991)
Occhi senza Volto See The Horror Chamber o' Dr. Faustus (1959)
Occhi Dalle Stelle See Eyes Behind the Stars (1972)
Ochoa See 8-A (1992)
Oci Ciornie See Dark Eyes (1987)
Octane See Pulse (2003)
October See Ten Days That Shook the World (1927)
The Odd Couple 2 See Neil Simon's The Odd Couple 2 (1998)
Odete See Two Drifters (2005)
Odio le Blonde See I Hate Blondes (1983)
Odishon See Audition (1999)
Of a Thousand Delights See Sandra of a Thousand Delights (1965)
Of Death, of Love See Cemetery Man (1995)
Office Party See Hostile Takeover (1988)
The Official History See The Official Story (1985)
The Official Version See The Official Story (1985)
Oh, Charlie See Hold That Ghost (1941)
Oh Woe is Me See Helas pour Moi (1994)
Ohayo See Good Morning (1959)
Ojos Que No Ven See What Your Eyes Don't See (1999)
Okasan See Mother (1952)
Oktyabr See Ten Days That Shook the World (1927)
The Old and the New See The General Line (1929)
The Old Corral See Song of the Gringo (1936)
Old Friends See As Good As It Gets (1997)

Old Greatheart See Way Back Home (1932)
Old Heidelberg See The Student Prince in Old Heidelberg (1927)
Old Man See William Faulkner's Old Man (1997)
The Old Man and the Boy See The Two of Us (1968)
Old Mother Riley Meets the Vampire See My Son, the Vampire (1952)
Old Shatterhand See Apache's Last Battle (1964)
Oielikezo Tekintetek See Another Way (1982)
Olga's Massage Parlor See Olga's Girls (1964)
Olga's Parlor See Olga's Girls (1964)
Oltre la Porta See Beyond Obsession (1982)
Omar Mukhtar See Lion of the Desert (1981)
Omen 3: The Final Conflict See The Final Conflict (1981)
On Connait la Chanson See Same Old Song (1997)
On Dangerous Ground See Jack Higgins' On Dangerous G-round (1995)
On Eagle's Wings See Black Horizon (2001)
On the Great White Trail See Renfrew on the Great White Trail (1938)
On the Road Again See Honeysuckle Rose (1980)
On the Run See Nowhere to Hide (1983)
On to Mars See Abbott and Costello Go to Mars (1953)
Once Upon a Texas Train See Texas Guns (1991)
Once Upon a Time There Was a Country See Underground (1995)
Ondskan See Evil (2003)
One and a Two... See Yi Yi (2000)
One Born Every Minute See Flim-Flam Man (1967)
One Cup of Coffee See Pastime (1991)
One For All See The President's Mystery (1936)
One for Sorrow, Two for Joy See Signs of Life (1989)
One for the Money, Two for the Show See On the Run (1973)
One Horse Town See Small Town Girl (1953)
One Hundred Percent Pure See The Girl from Missouri (1934)
One in a Million See Dangerous Appointment (1934)
One-Man Mutiny See The Court Martial of Billy Mitchell (1955)
One Man Out See Erik (1990)
One Plus One See Sympathy for the Devil (1970)
One Point O See Paranoia 1.0 (2004)
One Silver Dollar See Blood for a Silver Dollar (1966)
One Way Out See Crazed Cop (1988)
Onkel Toms Hutta See Uncle Tom's Cabin (1969)
Only Blackness See The Bloodstained Shadow (1978)
Only for Love See Please Not Now! (1961)
Only the French Can! See French Can-Can (1955)
Onna Ga Kaidan O Agaru Toki See When a Woman Ascends the Stairs (1960)
Oopsie Poopsie See Get Rita (1975)
Oopsie Poopsie See The Lady of the Evening (1975)
OpenCam See Open Cam (2005)

Operacione Paura See Kill, Baby, Kill (1966)

Operation Cicero See Five Fingers (1952)

Operation Kid Brother See Secret Agent 00 (1967)

Operation Monsterland See Destroy All Monsters (1968)

Operation Overthrow See Power Play (1981)

Operation Serpent See Fer-De-Lance (1974)

Operation Snafu See On the Fiddle (1961)

Operation Undercover See Report to the Commissioner (1974)

Operation Warhead See On the Fiddle (1961)

Operazione Goldman See Lightning Bolt (1967)

Opium Connection See The Poppy Is Also a Flower (1966)

Oprah Winfrey Presents: Mitch Albom's For One More Day See For One More Day (2007)

L'ora di religione See My Mother's Smile (2002)

The Oracle See The Horse's Mouth (1958)

Orazi e Curiazi See Duel of Champions (1961)

Orca—Killer Whale See Orca (1977)

Ore Ni Sawaru to Abunaize See Black Tight Killers (1966)

Orchestra Seats See Avenue Montaigne (2006)

Order of Death See Corrupt (1984)

Orfeu Negro See Black Orpheus (1958)

Orgasmo See Paranoia (1969)

Orgy of the Dead See The Hanging Woman (1972)

The Original Fabulous Adventures of Baron Munchausen See Fabulous Adventures of Baron Munchausen (1961)

Orkobefogadas See Adoption (1975)

Orlacs Hände See The Hands of Orlac (1925)

Orloff Against the Invisible Man See Dr. Orloff and the Invisible Man (1972)

Orloff Against the Invisible Man See Orloff and the Invisible Man (1970)

Orphee See Orpheus (1949)

Orson Welles's Othello See Othello (1952)

Oru Kaiju Daishingeki See Godzilla's Revenge (1969)

Oscar See Forbidden Passion: The Oscar Wilde Movie (1985)

Osenny Marafon See Autumn Marathon (1979)

Ososhiki See The Funeral (1984)

OSS 177 - Double Agent See Murder for Sale (1968)

Ost und West See East and West (1924)

Ostre Sledovane Vlaky See Closely Watched Trains (1966)

Otac na Sluzbenom Putu See When Father Was Away on Business (1985)

Otets I Syn See Father and Son (2003)

Other People's Business See Way Back Home (1932)

The Other Side of Paradise See Foxtrot (1976)

Otto E Mezzo See 8 1/2 (1963)

Our Daily Bread See City Girl (1930)

Our Girl Friday See The Adventures of Sadie (1955)

Our Music See Our Music (2004)

Our Story See Notre Histoire (1984)

L'Ours See The Bear (1989)

Ourselves Alone See River of Unrest (1936)

Out of Omaha See California Dreaming (2007)

Out of Rosenheim See Bagdad Cafe (1988)

Out of Sight, Out of Mind See Out of Sight, Out of Her Mind (1989)

Out of Synch See Lip Service (2000)

Out of the Darkness See Night Creature (1979)

Out of the Darkness See Teenage Caveman (1958)

Out of the Frying Pan See Young and Willing (1942)

Out of the Night See Strange Illusion (1945)

Out of the Shadow See Murder on the Campus (1952)

Out of Time See Iris (1989)

Out on Probation See Daddy-O (1959)

Outback Vampires See The Wicked (1989)

The Outcast See Man in the Saddle (1951)

The Outcry See Il Grido (1957)

Outlaw Gun See Spaced Out (1980)

Outlaw Gun See A Minute to Pray, a Second to Die (1967)

The Outlawed Planet See Planet of the Vampires (1965)

Outomlionnye Solntsem See Burnt by the Sun (1994)

Outside In See Red, White & Busted (1975)

The Outsider See Fatal Error (1983)

The Outsider See The Guinea Pig (1948)

Outsider in Amsterdam See Fatal Error (1983)

The Outsiders See Band of Outsiders (1964)

Over Her Dead Body See Enid Is Sleeping (1990)

Pamela Principle 2 See Seduce Me: Pamela Principle 2 (1994)

Pan Jin Lian Zhi Qian Shi Jin Sheng See The Reincarnation of Golden Lotus (1989)

Pane e Cioccolata See Bread and Chocolate (1973)

Pane e Tulipani See Bread and Tulips (2001)

Panga See Curse 3: Blood Sacrifice (1990)

Panic See Panique (1947)

Panic at Lakewood Manor See Ants (1977)

Panic in the Trans-Siberian Train See Horror Express (1972)

Panic on the Trans-Siberian Express See Horror Express (1972)

Panico en el Transiberiano See Horror Express (1972)

Panny z Wilka See Maids of Wilko (1979)

Panther Squadron See Men of the Fighting Lady (1954)

Paoda Shuang Deng See Red Firecracker, Green Firecracker (1993)

Paper Bullets See Gangs, Inc. (1941)

Par-dela les Nuages See Beyond the Clouds (1995)

Paralyzed See Short Night of Glass Dolls (1971)

The Parasite Murders See They Came from Within (1975)

Pardon Me, Your Teeth Are in My Neck See The Fearless Vampire Killers (1967)

Parfait Amour See Perfect Love (1996)

The Pariah See La Scoumoune (1972)

Paris Brule-t-il? See Is Paris Burning? (1966)

Paris Does Strange Things See Elena and Her Men (1956)

Paris, I Love You See Paris, je t'aime (2006)

Paris Is Ours See Paris Belongs to Us (1960)

Paris Nous Appartient See Paris Belongs to Us (1960)

Paris Qui Dort See The Crazy Ray (1922)

Paris vu Par See Six in Paris (1968)

Park Plaza See Norman Conquest (1953)

Paroxismus See Venus in Furs (1970)

Parts: The Clonus Horror See The Clonus Horror (1979)

The Party See Can't Hardly Wait (1998)

The Party at Kitty and Stud's See The Italian Stallion (1973)

Party Girls See Party Incorporated (1989)

Pas de Probleme! See No Problem (1975)

Pasazerka See Passenger (1961)

Pasqualino Settebellezze See Seven Beauties (1976)

Pasqualino: Seven Beauties See Seven Beauties (1976)

The Pass See Highway Hitcher (1998)

Passages from "Finnegans Wake" See Finnegan's Wake (1965)

Passages from James Joyce's "Finnegans Wake" See Finnegan's Wake (1965)

The Passerby See La Passante (1983)

Passions See The Passing of Evil (1970)

Passport to Shame See Room 43 (1958)

The Passion Flower Hotel See Boarding School (1983)

Passion Play See Love Letters (1983)

Passione d'Amore See Passion of Love (1982)

The Patsy See L'Addition (1985)

Patterns of Power See Patterns (1956)

Patton: A Salute to a Rebel See Patton (1970)

Patton—Lust for Glory See Patton (1970)

Paul Bowles: Halfmoon See Halfmoon (1995)

Pauline a la Plage See Pauline at the Beach (1983)

Paura in citta See Street War (1976)

Paura Nella Citta Dei Morti Viventi See Gates of Hell (1980)

Pavillon 6 See Ward Six (1978)

Pay the Devil See Man in the Shadow (1957)

P.D. James: A Mind to Murder See A Mind to Murder (1996)

P. D. James: Devices & Desires See Devices and Desires (1991)

The Peace Game See The Gladiators (1970)

Peace Virus See Terminal Error (2002)

Peacemaker See The Ambassador (1984)

Peau d'Ane See Donkey Skin (1970)

Peccato Che Sia una Canaglia See Too Bad She's Bad (1954)

The Peking Medallion See The Corrupt Ones (1967)

Pellet See El Bola (2000)

Pelvis See Toga Party (1977)

Penn of Pennsylvania See The Courageous Mr. Penn (1941)

Pensionat Oskar See Like It Never Was Before (1995)

People Toys See Devil Times Five (1974)

People's Enemy See Prison Train (1938)

Pepi, Luci, Bom y Otras Chicas del Monton See Pepi, Luci, Bom and Other Girls on the Heap (1980)

Per Saldo Mord See Swiss Conspiracy (1977)

Perceval Le Gallois See Perceval (1978)

Perche Quelle Strane Gocce di Sangre sul Corpo di Jennifer? See The Case of the Bloody Iris (1972)

Percy's Progress See It's Not the Size That Counts (1974)

Perdita Durango See Dance with the Devil (1997)

The Perfect Man See Heartstrings (1993)

The Perfect Model See Sweet Perfection (1990)

Perfect Strangers See Almost Strangers (2001)

The Perfect You See Crazy Little Thing (2002)

The Perfumed Garden See Tales of the Kama Sutra: The Perfumed Garden (1998)

Peril en la Demeure See Peril (1985)

Perils from Planet Mongo See Flash Gordon: Rocketship (1940)

The Perils of Gwendoline in the Land of the Yik-Yak See The Perils of Gwendoline (1984)

Perils of Nyoka See Nyoka and the Tigermen (1942)

Persecution See The Graveyard (1974)

Perseo l'Invincibile See Medusa Against the Son of Hercules (1962)

Perseus the Invincible See Medusa Against the Son of Hercules (1962)

Persons Unknown See Big Deal on Madonna Street (1958)

Peter and Pavla See Black Peter (1963)

Peter Benchley's The Beast See The Beast (1996)

Peter Rabbit and Tales of Beatrix Potter See Tales of Beatrix Potter (1971)

Petersen See Jock Petersen (1974)

Petroleum Girls See Legend of Frenchie King (1971)

Phantom See O Fantasma (2000)

Phantom Fiend See The Return of Dr. Mabuse (1961)

The Phantom of Terror See The Bird with the Crystal Plumage (1970)

Phantom of the Air See The Phantom Broadcast (1933)

The Phantom Ship See The Mystery of the Mary Celeste (1935)

Phar Lap: Heart of a Nation See Phar Lap (1984)

Phenomena See Creepers (1985)

Philo Vance Returns See Infamous Crimes (1947)

Phoebe See Zelly & Me (1988)

Phoenix See War of the Wizards (1983)

Phorpa See The Cup (1999)

The Piano Player See The Target (2002)

Picking up the Pieces See Bloodsucking Pharaohs of Pittsburgh (1990)

Pickup on 101 See Where the Eagle Flies (1972)

Pictures of Baby Jane Doe See Jane Doe (1996)

Pigsty See Porcile (1969)

Pilgrimage to Rome See L'Annee Sainte (1976)

The Pill See Test Tube Babies (1948)

The Pilot See Danger in the Skies (1979)

Pin Down Girl See Pin Down Girls (1951)

The Pinata: Survival Island See Survival Island (2002)

Pinball Pick-Up See Pick-Up Summer (1979)

Pinball Summer See Pick-Up Summer (1979)

Pinocchio See The Adventures of Pinocchio (1996)

Pinochet in Suburbia See Pinochet's Last Stand (2006)

Pioneers See Pioneer Woman (1973)

Pippi Langstrump Pa de Sju Haven See Pippi in the South Seas (1970)

Piranha 2: Flying Killers See Piranha 2: The Spawning (1982)

Pirate's Fiancee See A Very Curious Girl (1969)

Pirate's Harbor See Haunted Harbor (1944)

Pistol Blues See Machine Gun Blues (1995)

Pitch Black 2: Chronicles of Riddick See The Chronicles of Riddick (2004)

Pixote: A Lei do Mais Fraco See Pixote (1981)

The Pizza Connection See The Sicilian Connection (1985)

The Plains of Heaven See Panic Station (1982)

Plane Dead See Flight of the Living Dead: Outbreak on a Plane (2007)

Planet of Blood See Planet of the Vampires (1965)

Planet of Horrors See Galaxy of Terror (1981)

Planet of Incredible Creatures See Fantastic Planet (1973)

The Planet of Junior Brown See Junior's Groove (1997)

Planet of Love See Galaxies Are Colliding (1992)

Planet of Terror See Planet of the Vampires (1965)

Planet of the Damned See Planet of the Vampires (1965)

Planet of the Lifeless Men See Battle of the Worlds (1961)

Plankton See Creatures from the Abyss (1994)

The Plants Are Watching See The Kirlian Witness (1978)

Plata Quemada See Burnt Money (2000)

Play of the Month: MacBeth See Macbeth (1970)

Playa Azul See Beach Hotel (1992)

Players See The Club (1981)

Playgirl Gang See Switchblade Sisters (1975)

The Playgirls and the Bellboy See The Bellboy and the Playgirls (1962)

Playing for Keeps See Lily in Love (1985)

Playtime See Love Play (1960)

Please! Mr. Balzac See Plucking the Daisy (1956)

The Pleasure of Your Company See Wedding Daze (2006)

Pledge of Allegiance See Players (2003)

Plein Soleil See Purple Noon (1960)

Plein Sud See Heat of Desire (1984)

Pluck of the Irish See Great Guy (1936)

Po Deziu See Before the Rain (1994)

Pocomania See The Devil's Daughter (1939)

Podranki See The Orphans (1977)

Poe's Tales of Terror See Tales of Terror (1962)

Poisoned by Love: The Kern County Murders See Murder So Sweet (1993)

Pokayaniye See Repentance (1987)

Poketto Monsutaa: Maboroshi No Pokemon X: Lugia Bakudan See Pokemon the Movie 2000: The Power of One (2000)

Pokolenie See A Generation (1954)

Police Assassins See Royal Warriors (1986)

Police Connection See The Mad Bomber (1972)

Police Force See Police Story (1985)

Police Story 3, Part 2 See Supercop 2 (1993)

Police Story 3: Supercop See Supercop (1992)

Police Story 4 See Jackie Chan's First Strike (1996)

Police Woman See Young Tiger (1974)

Polk County Pot Plane See In Hot Pursuit (1977)

Polly Tix in Washington See Kid 'n' Hollywood anc Polly Tix in Washington (1933)

Pony Express See Peter Lundy and the Medicine Hat Stallion (1977)

Pookie See The Sterile Cuckoo (1969)

Poopsie See Get Rita (1975)

Poor Albert and Little Annie See I Dismember Mama (1974)

Poor Boy's Game See Poor Man's Game (2006)

The Poor Outlaws See The Round Up (1966)

The Pope Must Die See The Pope Must Diet (1991)

Popiol i Diament See Ashes and Diamonds (1958)

Poppies Are Also Flowers See The Poppy Is Also a Flower (1966)

Popsy Pop See Queen of Diamonds (1970)

Por Que Lo Llaman Amor Cuando Quieren Decir Sexo? See Why Do They Call It Love When They Mean Sex? (1992)

Porcherie See Porcile (1969)

A Pornographic Liaison See An Affair of Love (1999)

Porte Aperte See Open Doors (1989)

Portrait of a Woman, Nude See Nudo di Donna (1933)

Portrait of Allison See Postmark for Danger (1956)

Portrait of Maria See Maria Candelaria (1946)

Portraits of Innocence See Portraits of a Killer (1995)

Post Coitum See After Sex (1997)

Post Coitum, Animal Triste See After Sex (1997)

Postal Worker See Going Postal (1998)

Potemkin See The Battleship Potemkin (1925)

Potop See The Deluge (1973)

The Powder Keg See Cabaret Balkan (1998)

Practice Makes Perfect See Le Cavaleur (1978)

Prague Duet See Lies and Whispers (1998)

Prairie Outlaws See Wild West (1946)

Pratidwandi See The Adversary (1971)

Pre See Without Limits (1997)

Precious See Citizen Ruth (1996)

Pred dozhdot See Before the Rain (1994)

Prega Il Morto e Ammazza Il Vivo See Shoot the Living, Pray for the Dead (1970)

The Prehistoric Sound See Sound of Horror (1964)

Prehistoric World See Teenage Caveman (1958)

Prenom: Carmen See First Name: Carmen (1983)

Preparez Vous Mouchoirs See Get Out Your Handkerchiefs (1978)

Preppies See Making the Grade (1984)

The President's Women See Foreplay (1975)

Presque Rien See Come Undone (2000)

Preston Tylk See Bad Seed (2000)

Pret-a-Porter See Ready to Wear (1994)

Pretty When You Cry See Seduced: Pretty When You Cry (2001)

Pride of Kentucky See The Story of Seabiscuit (1949)

Prima della Rivoluzione See Before the Revolution (1965)

Prince of Jutland See Royal Deceit (1994)

Priority Red One See Delta Force Commando 2 (1990)

Prison See Devil's Wanton (1949)

The Prisoner See Cold Room (1984)

Prisoner of the Caucasus See Prisoner of the Mountains (1996)

Prisoner of Zenda, Inc. See Double Play (1996)

Private House of the SS See SS Girls (1977)

Private Snuffy Smith See Snuffy Smith, Yard Bird (1942)

The Private Lives of Elizabeth and Essex See Elizabeth, the Queen (1968)

The Private Life of Paul Joseph Goebbels See Enemy of Women (1944)

The Private Wore Skirts See Never Wave at a WAC (1952)

Pro Urodov I Lyudei See Of Freaks and Men (1998)

The Prodigal Boxer See Kick of Death: The Prodigal Boxer (1973)

The Prodigious Hickey See The Lawrenceville Stories (1988)

Profession: Reporter See The Passenger (1975)

The Professional See Le Professionnel (1981)

The Profile of Terror See The Sadist (1963)

Profumo di Donna See The Scent of a Woman (1975)

Profondo Rosso See Deep Red: Hatchet Murders (1975)

Profondo Carmesi See Deep Crimson (1996)

Project Greenlight's Stolen Summer See Stolen Summer (2002)

Project Greenlight's The Battle of Shaker Heights See The Battle of Shaker Heights (2003)

Project Shadowchaser 2 See Night Siege Project: Shadowchaser 2 (1994)

Prom Night 2 See Hello Mary Lou: Prom Night 2 (1987)

Promenons Nous dans les Bois See Deep in the Woods (2000)

The Promise See La Promesse (1996)

Promise Her Anything See Promises! Promises! (1963)

A Promise Kept See The Gunman (2003)

The Promise of Red Lips See Daughters of Darkness (1971)

The Promised Land See Legal Deceit (1995)

The Promised Life See La Vie Promise (2002)

Prophecies of Nostradamus See Last Days of Planet Earth (1974)

A Proposito Luciano See Lucky Luciano (1974)

Prorva See Moscow Parade (1992)

Protection See Moolaade (2004)

The Protectors, Book One See Angel of H.E.A.T. (1982)

Proud, Damned, and Dead See The Proud and the Damned (1972)

Prova d'Orchestra See Orchestra Rehearsal (1978)

Przesluchanie See The Interrogation (1982)

Psycho a Go Go! See Blood of Ghastly Horror (1972)

Psycho-Circus See Circus of Fear (1967)

Psycho Killers See The Flesh and the Fiends (1960)

Psycho Puppet See Delirium (1977)

Psycho Sex Fiend See The House that Vanished (1973)

Psycho Sisters See The Sibling (1972)

Psychotic See Driver's Seat (1973)

Ptang, Yang, Kipperbang See Kipperbang (1982)

Public Be Damned See The World Gone Mad (1933)

The Public Be Hanged See The World Gone Mad (1933)

Puo Una Morta Rivivere Per Amore? See Venus in Furs (1970)

The Pupil See L'Eleve (1995)

The Purim Player See Der Purimshpiler (1937)

Purple Death from Outer Space See Flash Gordon Conquers the Universe (1940)

The Purple Riders See Purple Vigilantes (1938)

The Purple Shadow Strikes See The Purple Monster Strikes (1945)

Pursuit See Apache Blood (1975)

Pussycat See Faster, Pussycat! Kill! Kill! (1965)

Putyovka V Zhizn See The Road to Life (1931)

Q See Q (The Winged Serpent) (1982)

Q Planes See Clouds over Europe (1939)

Qian Li Zou Dan Ji See Riding Alone for Thousands of Miles (2005)

Qiji See Miracles (1989)

Qin Song See The Emperor's Shadow (1996)

Qiu Ju Da Guansi See The Story of Qiu Ju (1991)

Qiuyue See Autumn Moon (1992)

Quai des Orfevres See Jenny Lamour (1947)

Qualcosa di Biondo See Aurora (1984)

Quality of Life See Against the Wall (1994)

Quando De Donne Avevando La Coda See When Women Had Tails (1970)

Quante Volte...Quella Notte See Four Times That Night (1969)

Que He Hecho Yo Para Merecer Esto!? See What Have I Done to Deserve This? (1985)

Que La Bete Meure See This Man Must Die (1970)

Queen of Blood See Planet of Blood (1966)

Queen of Broadway See Kid Dynamite (1943)

Queen of the Cannibals See Doctor Butcher M.D. (1980)

Queen of the Gorillas See The Bride & the Beast (1958)

The Queen's Husband See The Royal Bed (1931)

Quel Tennerari Suite Loro Pazze, Scatenate, Scaicnate Carriole See Those Daring Young Men in Their Jaunty Jalopies (1969)

Quel Maledetto Treno Blindato See Deadly Mission (1978)

Quella Villa Accanto Al Cimitero See The House by the Cemetery (1983)

Quelqu' Un Derriere la Porte See Someone Behind the Door (1971)

Quelques Jours en Septembre *See* A Few Days in September (2006)

Quemimada! *See* Burn! (1970)

Quentin Tarantino's Death Proof *See* Death Proof (2007)

The Quest *See* The Captive: The Longest Drive 2 (1976)

The Quest *See* The Longest Drive (1976)

Qui a tu Bambi? *See* Who Killed Bambi? (2003)

Quien Sabe? *See* A Bullet for the General (1968)

A Quiet Little Neighborhood, A Perfect Little Murder *See* A Perfect Little Murder (1990)

A Quiet Place to Kill *See* Paranoia (1969)

Quoi De Neuf, Pussycat? *See* What's New Pussycat? (1965)

Race for the Yankee Zephyr *See* Treasure of the Yankee Zephyr (1983)

The Rag Nymph *See* Catherine Cookson's The Rag Nymph (1996)

Rage *See* Rabid (1977)

Rage of the Buccaneers *See* The Black Pirate (1926)

Ragewar *See* Dungeonmaster (1983)

Ragged Angels *See* They Shall Have Music (1939)

The Raging Moon *See* Long Ago Tomorrow (1971)

Raging Waters *See* The Green Promise (1949)

Ragno Gelido *See* Dial Help (1988)

Rags to Riches *See* Callie and Son (1981)

Rain *See* Baran (2001)

Rainbow Boys *See* The Rainbow Gang (1973)

Rainbow on the River *See* The Color of Paradise (1999)

Rang-e Khoda *See* The Color of Paradise (1999)

The Rainmaker *See* John Grisham's The Rainmaker (1997)

The Ranger, the Cook and a Hole in the Sky *See* Hole in the Sky (1995)

Ransom *See* Maniac (1977)

Ramblin' Man *See* The Concrete Cowboys (1979)

Rane *See* The Wounds (1998)

Rape Me *See* Baise Moi (2000)

Rape of Innocence *See* Dupont Lajoie (1974)

The Rape of Richard Beck *See* Broken Badge (1985)

Rape Squad *See* Act of Vengeance (1974)

Rasputin: The Mad Monk *See* Rasputin and the Empress (1933)

Rat Pfink and Boo Boo *See* Rat Pfink a Boo-Boo (1966)

The Rats *See* Deadly Eyes (1982)

Rats: Night of Terror *See* Rats (1983)

The Rats of Tobruk *See* The Fighting Rats of Tobruk (1944)

The Raven *See* Le Corbeau (1943)

Raye Makhfi *See* Secret Ballot (2001)

Re-Animator 2 *See* Bride of Re-Animator (1989)

RE: Lucky Luciano *See* Lucky Luciano (1974)

The Reader *See* La Lectrice (1988)

Real Men *See* Regular Guys (1996)

The Rebel *See* The Bushwackers (1952)

Rebel of the Road *See* Hot Rod (1979)

Rebel with a Cause *See* The Loneliness of the Long Distance Runner (1962)

Rebellion *See* Samurai Rebellion (1967)

Rece do Gory *See* Hands Up (1981)

Record of a Living Being *See* I Live in Fear (1955)

Red *See* Trois Couleurs: Rouge (1994)

Red Blooded American Girl 2 *See* Hot Blooded (1998)

The Red Circle *See* Le Cercle Rouge (1970)

Red Dragon *See* Code Name Alpha (1967)

Red Dragon *See* Manhunter (1986)

The Red Hangman *See* The Bloody Pit of Horror (1965)

The Red Head *See* Poil de Carotte (1931)

Red Hot Tires *See* Racing Luck (1935)

Red Hot Wheels *See* To Please a Lady (1950)

Red-Light District *See* Street of Shame (1956)

The Red Lips *See* Daughters of Darkness (1971)

Red Nightmare *See* The Commies Are Coming, the Commies Are Coming (1957)

Red on Red *See* Scarred (1984)

The Red Sign of Madness *See* Hatchet for the Honeymoon (1970)

The Red Tide *See* Blood Tide (1982)

The Redeemer *See* Class Reunion Massacre (1977)

Redheads *See* Desperate Prey (1994)

Redneck County *See* Hooch County (1975)

Redneck County *See* Poor Pretty Eddie (1973)

Reed, Mexico Insurgente *See* Reed: Insurgent Mexico (1973)

Reflections on a Crime *See* Reflections in the Dark (1994)

The Refugee *See* Three Faces West (1940)

Regain *See* Harvest (1937)

Regeneration *See* Behind the Lines (1997)

Regina Roma *See* Regina (1983)

Rehearsal for a Crime *See* The Criminal Life of Archibaldo de la Cruz (1955)

Rejuvenatrix *See* The Rejuvenator (1988)

Rekopis Znaleziony W Saragossie *See* The Saragossa Manuscript (1965)

Religious Racketeers *See* Mystic Circle Murder (1939)

Remando al Viento *See* Rowing with the Wind (1988)

The Remarkable Mr. Kipps *See* Kipps (1941)

Remembrance of Love *See* Holocaust Survivors... Remembrance of Love (1983)

Remo: Unarmed and Dangerous *See* Remo Williams: The Adventure Begins (1985)

Remorques *See* Stormy Waters (1941)

Remove Lum & Abner *See* So This Is Washington (1943)

Renacer *See* Reborn (1981)

Renegade Girls *See* Caged Heat (1974)

Renfrew of the Royal Mounted on the Great White Trail *See* Renfrew on the Great White Trail (1938)

Reprieved *See* Sing Sing Nights (1935)

Requiem fur Dominic *See* Requiem for Dominic (1991)

The Rescue *See* Let's Get Harry (1987)

Rescue Force *See* Terminal Force (1988)

Respectable Families *See* Un Air de Famille (1996)

Respiro: Grazia's Island *See* Respiro (2002)

The Rest of the Warrior *See* Love on a Pillow (1962)

The Resurrection Syndicate *See* Nothing But the Night (1972)

Retaliator *See* Programmed to Kill (1986)

Retik, the Moon Menace *See* Radar Men from the Moon (1952)

Return from the Past *See* Alien Massacre (1967)

The Return of Captain America *See* Captain America (1944)

The Return of Maxwell Smart *See* The Nude Bomb (1980)

The Return of Mr. H. *See* They Saved Hitler's Brain (1964)

The Return of She *See* The Vengeance of She (1968)

Return of the Blind Dead *See* Return of the Evil Dead (1975)

The Return of the Duchess Dracula *See* Devil's Wedding Night (1973)

The Return of the Giant Monsters *See* Gamera vs. Gaos (1967)

Return of the Living Dead *See* Messiah of Evil (1974)

Return of the Seven *See* Return of the Magnificent Seven (1966)

Return of the Texas Chainsaw Massacre *See* The Texas Chainsaw Massacre 4: The Next Generation (1995)

Return of the Wolfman *See* The Craving (1980)

Return of the Zombies *See* The Hanging Woman (1972)

Return to Sender *See* Convicted (2004)

Reunion *See* Reunion in France (1942)

Revelations of a Sex Maniac to the Head ot the Criminal Investigation Division *See* The Slasher (1974)

Revenant *See* Modern Vampires (1998)

The Revenge *See* Zemsta (2002)

Revenge *See* Blood Feud (1979)

Revenge *See* Fallen Angel (1999)

Revenge of a Kabuki Actor *See* An Actor's Revenge (1963)

The Revenge of Al Capone *See* Capone (1989)

Revenge of Dracula *See* Dracula, Prince of Darkness (1966)

Revenge of Dracula *See* Dracula vs. Frankenstein (1971)

The Revenge of Milady *See* The Four Musketeers (1975)

The Revenge of the Blood Beast *See* The She-Beast (1965)

Revenge of the Dead *See* Night of the Ghouls (1959)

Revenge of the Dead *See* Zeder (1983)

Revenge of the Innocents *See* South Bronx Heroes (1985)

Revenge of the Living Dead *See* Children Shouldn't Play with Dead Things (1972)

Revenge of the Ninja Warrior *See* The Dagger of Kamui (1985)

Revenge of the Savage Bees *See* Terror Out of the Sky (1978)

Revenge of the Screaming Dead *See* Messiah of Evil (1974)

Revenge of the Vampire *See* Black Sunday (1960)

Revenge of the Zombie *See* Kiss Daddy Goodbye (1981)

Revenge! The Killing Fist *See* Hit & Run (1982)

Revenge! The Killing Fist *See* The Street Fighter's Last Revenge (1974)

The Revengers' Comedies *See* Sweet Revenge (1998)

Rex: Le cyber chien *See* Cybermutt (2002)

Rhodes of Africa *See* Rhodes (1936)

Rhosyn A Rhith *See* Coming Up Roses (1987)

Rhythm on the Ranch *See* Rootin' Tootin' Rhythm (1938)

Ricco *See* Mean Machine (1973)

Rice, Beans and Ketchup *See* Manhattan Merenquel (1995)

Rich, Young, and Deadly *See* Platinum High School (1960)

Riches and Romance *See* Amazing Adventure (1937)

The Richest Man in the World: The Story of Aristotle Onassis *See* Onassis (1988)

Richie *See* The Death of Richie (1976)

Rickshaw Man *See* Rikisha-Man (1958)

Ride a Dark Horse *See* Man & Boy (1971)

Riders *See* Guerilla Brigade (1939)

Rien ne va plus *See* The Swindle (1997)

Riffraff *See* Riff Raff (1935)

Riget *See* The Kingdom (1995)

Riget II *See* The Kingdom 2 (1997)

The Right Man *See* Her First Romance (1940)

Rih Essed *See* Man of Ashes (1986)

Ring of Fire *See* Cowboy Up (2000)

Rinjin 13-go *See* The Neighbor No. Thirteen (2005)

Rio Vengeance *See* Motor Psycho (1965)

Riot *See* Riot in the Streets (1996)

Rip-Off *See* The Squeeze (1980)

Ripped Off *See* Counter Punch (1971)

The Ripper *See* New York Ripper (1982)

Risate de Gioia *See* Passionate Thief (1960)

Risate di Gioia *See* Joyful Laughter (1960)

The Rise of Catherine the Great *See* Catherine the Great (1934)

The Rise of Helga *See* Susan Lenox: Her Fall and Rise (1931)

Rising to Fame *See* Susan Lenox: Her Fall and Rise (1931)

Riten *See* The Rite (1969)

Riso Amaro *See* Bitter Rice (1949)

The Ritual *See* The Rite (1969)

Ritoru Champion *See* My Champion (1981)

Ritual Dos Sadicos *See* Awakenings of the Beast (1968)

Ritual of the Maniacs *See* Awakenings of the Beast (1968)

Rivelazioni di un Maniaco Sessuale al Capo Della Squadra Mobile *See* The Slasher (1972)

The Road *See* La Strada (1954)

The Road to Frisco *See* They Drive by Night (1940)

Roaring Timber *See* Come and Get It (1936)

Rob-B-Hood *See* Robin-B-Hood (2006)

Rob Roy *See* Rob Roy—The Highland Rogue (1953)

Robert A. Heinlein's The Puppet Masters *See* The Puppet Masters (1994)

Robert B. Parker's Jesse Stone: Death in Paradise *See* Jesse Stone: Death in Paradise (2006)

Robert B. Parker's Jesse Stone: Night Passage *See* Jesse Stone: Night Passage (2006)

Robert B. Parker's Jesse Stone: Stone Cold *See* Jesse Stone: Stone Cold (2005)

- Robert B. Parker's Thin Air See Thin Air (2000)
- Robert Louis Stevenson's St. Ives See St. Ives (1998)
- Robert Louis Stevenson's The Suicide Club See Robert Louis Stevenson's The Game of Death (1999)
- Robert Ludlum's Covert One: The Hades Factor See The Hades Factor (2006)
- Robert Ludlum's the Apocalypse Watch See The Apocalypse Watch (1997)
- Robert Rodriguez's Planet Terror See Planet Terror (2007)
- Robinson Crusoeland See Utopia (1951)
- Robo Ninja See Cyber Ninja (1994)
- Rocco E I Suoi Fratelli See Rocco and His Brothers and (1960)
- Rocco et Ses Freres See Rocco and His Brothers (1960)
- Rock and Roll Wrestling Women vs. the Aztec Mummy See Wrestling Women vs. the Aztec Mummy (1959)
- Rocket and Roll See Abbott and Costello Go to Mars (1953)
- Rocket Man See RocketMan (1997)
- Rocket to the Moon See Cat Women of the Moon (1953)
- Rocky Mountain Mystery See The Fighting Westerner (1935)
- Rodents See Ratas, Ratones, Rateros (1999)
- Rodgers & Hammerstein's Cinderella See Cinderella (1997)
- Rois et reine See Kings and Queen (2004)
- Rolt See Last Mercenary (1984)
- Roma See Fellini's Roma (1972)
- Roma, Citta Aperta See Open City
- Romance and Riches See Amazing Adventure (1937)
- Romance da Empregada See The Story of Fausta (1983)
- Romauid et Juliet See Mama, There's a Man in Your Bed (1989)
- Rome, Open City See Open City (1945)
- Romeo and Juliet See William Shakespeare's Romeo and Juliet (1996)
- Romeo in Pyjamas See Parlor, Bedroom and Bath (1931)
- Romeo, Giulia e Tma See Sweet Light in a Dark Room (1960)
- Romeo, Juliet and Darkness See Sweet Light in a Dark Room (1960)

- Roger Corman Presents: Alien Avengers See Alien Avengers (1996)
- Roger Corman Presents: Black Scorpion See Black Scorpion (1995)
- Roger Corman Presents Burial of the Rats See Burial of the Rats (1995)
- Roger Corman Presents: House of the Damned See Spectre (1996)
- Roger Corman Presents: Humanoids from the Deep See Humanoids from the Deep (1996)
- Roger Corman Presents: Inhumanoid See Inhumanoid (1996)
- Roger Corman Presents Last Exit to Earth See Last Exit to Earth (1996)
- Roger Corman Presents Subliminal Seduction See The Corporation (1996)
- Roger Corman Presents: Subliminal Seduction See Subliminal Seduction (1996)
- Roger Corman Presents: Suspect Device See Suspect Device (1995)
- Roger Corman Presents: The Alien Within See Unknown Origin (1995)
- Roger Corman Presents: Vampirella See Vampirella (1996)
- Roger Corman's Frankenstein Unbound See Frankenstein Unbound (1990)

- Rommel—Desert Fox See The Desert Fox (1951)
- Rona Jaffe's Mazes and Monsters See Mazes and Monsters (1982)
- The Rook See Something for Everyone (1970)
- Rookies See Buck Privates (1941)
- Rookies Come Home See Buck Privates Come Home (1947)
- The Rose and the Sword See Flesh and Blood (1985)
- The Rose of Baghdad See The Singing Princess (1949)
- Rose Red See Stephen King's Rose Red (2002)
- Roseanna's Grave See For Roseanna (1996)
- Rosemary's Killer See The Prowler (1981)
- The Rotten Apple See Five Minutes to Love (1963)
- Rouge Baiser See Red Kiss (1985)
- Rough Company See The Violent Men (1955)
- Rough Treatment See Without Anesthesia (1978)
- The Round Tower See Catherine Cookson's The Round Tower (1998)
- Roveh Hulliot See The Wooden Gun (1979)
- Roxanne: The Prize Pulitzer See The Prize Pulitzer (1989)
- The Royal Game See Brainwashed (1960)
- Ruang rak noi nid mahasan See Last Life in the Universe (2003)
- Ruby Cairo See Deception (1992)
- Rudyard Kipling's Jungle Book See The Jungle Book (1942)
- Rue Cases Negres See Sugar Care Alley (1983)
- Rukajarven Tie See Ambush (1999)
- Rules of Obsession See A Passion to Kill (1994)
- Rumble in Hong Kong See Young Tiger (1974)
- Rumpo Kid See Carry On Cowboy (1966)
- Run for the Money See Hard Cash (2001)
- Run, Simon, Run See Savage Run (1970)
- The Runaways See South Bronx Heroes (1985)
- Russ Meyer's SuperVixens See Supervixens (1975)
- Russkium See Third Solution (1989)
- Rustler's Roundup See Rustler's Hideout (1944)
- The Rutles See All You Need Is Cash (1978)

- S21: La Machine De Mort Khmere Rouge See S21: The Khmer Rouge Killing Machine (2003)
- S21: The Khmer Rouge Death Machine See S21: The Khmer Rouge Killing Machine (2003)
- Sababa See Private Manoeuvres (1983)
- Saboteur: Code Name Morituri See The Saboteur: Code Name Morituri (1965)
- The Saboteur: Code Name Morituri See Morituri (1965)
- The Sabre and the Arrow See Last of the Comanches (1952)
- The Sabre Tooth Tiger See Deep Red: Hatchet Murders (1975)
- Sabrina Fair See Sabrina (1954)
- Sacco e Vanzetti See Sacco & Vanzetti (1971)
- Sadie & Son See Detective Sadie & Son (1984)
- Sadko See The Magic Voyage of Sinbad (1952)

- The Saga of Dracula See The Saga of the Draculas (1972)
- The Saga of Gosta Berling See The Atonement of Gosta Berling (1924)
- The Saga of the Road See Pather Panchali (1954)
- Saikaku Ichidai Onna See Life of Oharu (1952)
- St. George and the Dragon See The Magic Sword (1962)
- St. George and the Seven Curses See The Magic Sword (1962)
- St. Martin's Lane See Sidewalks of London (1938)
- Sakima and the Masked Marvel See The Masked Marvel (1943)
- The Salamander See La Salamandre (1971)
- Salem's Ghost See Witchcraft 8: Salem's Ghost (1995)
- Salerno Beachhead See A Walk in the Sun (1946)
- Salmui chueok See Memories of Murder (2003)
- Sally Lockhart Mysteries: Ruby in the Smoke See Ruby in the Smoke (2006)
- Salmer fra Kjokkenet See Kitchen Stories (2003)
- The Salute of the Jugger See The Blood of Heroes (1989)
- Salvation! Have You Said Your Prayers Today? See Salvation! (1987)
- Sam Cooper's Gold See The Ruthless Four (1970)
- Sam Marlowe, Private Eye See The Man with Bogart's Face (1980)
- Sam's Song See The Swap (1971)
- The Samurai See Le Samourai (1967)
- San Fernando Valley See San Fernando Valley (1944)
- San Ging Chaat Goo Si See New Police Story (2004)
- San Michele Aveva un Gallo See St. Michele Had a Rooster (1972)
- Sanda tai Gailah See War of the Gargantuas (1970)
- Sandakan House 8 See Sandakan No. 8 (1974)
- Sandkings See The Outer Limits: Sandkings (1995)
- Sandok alla Riscossa See The Conqueror & the Empress (1964)
- The Sandpit Generals See Defiant (1970)
- Sandra See Sandra of a Thousand Delights (1965)
- Sanma No Aji See An Autumn Afternoon (1962)
- Sans Toit Ni Loi See Vagabond (1985)
- Sansho Dayu See Sansho the Bailiff (1954)
- Santa Claus Defeats the Aliens See Santa Claus Conquers the Martians (1964)
- Santo en el Museo de Cera See Samson in the Wax Museum (1963)
- Santo in the Wax Museum See Samson in the Wax Museum (1963)
- The Sasquatch Dumpling Gang See The Sasquatch Gang (2006)
- Satan See Mark of the Devil (1969)
- Satan See Sheitan (2006)
- Satanic Mechanic See Perfect Killer (1977)
- Satan's Bloody Freaks See Dracula vs. Frankenstein (1971)
- Satan's Claw See The Blood on Satan's Claw (1971)

- Satan's Daughters See Vampyres (1974)
- Satan's Dog See Play Dead (1981)
- Satan's Mistress See Demon Rage (1982)
- Satan's Satellites See Zombies of the Stratosphere (1952)
- Satan's Skin See The Blood on Satan's Claw (1971)
- Satan's Supper See Cataclysm (1981)
- Satansbraten See Satan's Brew (1976)
- Satellite of Blood See First Man into Space (1959)
- Satin Vengeance See Naked Vengeance (1985)
- Satyricon See Fellini Satyricon (1969)
- Saturday Island See Island of Desire (1952)
- Saturn See Speed of Life (1999)
- Satsujin-ken 2 See Return of the Street Fighter (1974)
- Satsujin-ken See The Street Fighter (1974)
- Saul e David See Saul and David (1964)
- Savage Nights See Les Nuits Fauves (1992)
- The Savage State See L'Etat Sauvage (1978)
- Sayat Nova See The Color of Pomegranates (1969)
- The Savage Planet See Fantastic Planet (1973)
- The Savage See In Hell (2003)
- The Savage See Lovers Like Us (1975)
- Savage Abduction See Cycle Psycho (1972)
- Savage Apocalypse See Cannibal Apocalypse (1980)
- Savage Beasts See The Wild Beasts (1985)
- The Scalpel See Just the Ticket (1998)
- Scaramouche See Loves & Times of Scaramouche (1976)

- Scared Stiff See Treasure of Fear (1945)
- The Scaremaker See Girls Night Out (1983)
- Scarface: The Shame of a Nation See Scarface (1931)
- The Scarlet Buccaneer See Swashbuckler (1976)
- Scary Movie See Scream (1996)
- The Scavengers See Rebel Vixens (1969)
- Schatten der Engel See Shadow of Angels (1976)
- Scherben See Shattered (1921)
- Schlates Bruder See Brother of Sleep (1995)
- Schloss Vogelod See The Haunted Castle (1921)
- The School That Ate My Brain See Zombie High (1987)
- Schrei - denn ich werde dich toten! See School's Out (1999)
- Schwestern Oder die Balance des Glucks See Sisters, Or the Balance of Happiness (1979)
- Scotland Yard Mystery See The Living Dead (1933)
- Scoundrel in White See High Heels (1972)
- The Scoundrel's Wife See The Home Front (2002)
- Scream See The Night God Screamed (1971)
- Scream Again See Scream 2 (1997)
- Scream and Die See The House that Vanished (1973)
- Scream Bloody Murder See House of Terror (1972)

Scream Bloody Murder *See* My Brother Has Bad Dreams (1972)

Scream Free! *See* Free Grass (1969)

Screamer *See* Scream and Scream Again (1970)

Screwface *See* Marked for Death (1990)

Scrooge *See* A Christmas Carol (1951)

Scum of the Earth *See* Poor White Trash 2 (1975)

Se, Jie *See* Lust, Caution (2007)

Sea Change *See* Jesse Stone: Sea Change (2007)

Sea Wyf and Biscuit *See* Sea Wife (1957)

Search for the Mother Lode *See* Mother Lode (1982)

Searchers of the Voodoo Mountain *See* Warriors of the Apocalypse (1985)

Season of Dreams *See* Stacking (1987)

Seated At His Right *See* Black Jesus (1968)

The Second Arrival *See* The Arrival 2 (1998)

Second Chances *See* Probation (1932)

The Second Coming *See* Messiah of Evil (1974)

The Second Jungle Book: Mowgli and Baloo *See* Rudyard Kipling's the Second Jungle Book: Mowgli and Baloo (1997)

The Second Lieutenant *See* The Last Lieutenant (1994)

Secondloitnanten *See* The Last Lieutenant (1994)

Seconds to Live *See* Viva Knievel (1977)

The Secret *See* Catherine Cookson's The Secret (2000)

The Secret Cinema *See* Paul Bartel's The Secret Cinema (1969)

Secret File: Hollywood *See* Secret File of Hollywood (1962)

Secret Honor: A Political Myth *See* Secret Honor (1985)

Secret Honor: The Last Testament of Richard M. Nixon *See* Secret Honor (1985)

The Secret of Dr. Mabuse *See* The Thousand Eyes of Dr. Mabuse (1960)

The Secret of Dorian Gray *See* Dorian Gray (1970)

The Secret Pact *See* The Pact (1999)

Secret Paper WB1 *See* Geheimakte WB1 (1942)

Secret Service in Darkest Africa *See* Manhunt in the African Jungles (1943)

The Secret Stranger *See* Rough Riding Ranger (1935)

Secret Weapon *See* Sherlock Holmes and the Secret Weapon (1942)

Secretos del Corazon *See* Secrets of the Heart (1997)

Secrets of the Red Bedroom *See* Secret Weapons (1985)

Seddok, l'Erede di Satana *See* Atom Age Vampire (1961)

Sedotta e Abbandonata *See* Seduced and Abandoned (1964)

The Seducer's Diary *See* Diary of a Seducer (1995)

The Seductress *See* The Teacher (1974)

Seduta Alla Sua Destra *See* Black Jesus (1968)

Seed of Terror *See* Grave of the Vampire (1972)

Seeds of Wrath *See* Man in the Shadow (1957)

The Seekers *See* Land of Fury (1955)

Segunda Piel *See* Second Skin (1999)

Sei Donne per l'Assassino *See* Blood and Black Lace (1964)

Seishun Zanoku Monogatari *See* The Cruel Story of Youth (1960)

Semana Santa *See* Angel of Death (2002)

Sen to Chihiro—No Kamikakushi *See* Spirited Away (2001)

Sengoku Gunto-Den *See* Saga of the Vagabond (1959)

Senior Trip *See* National Lampoon's Senior Trip (1995)

Sensations *See* Sensations of 1945 (1944)

Sensuous Vampires *See* The Vampire Hookers (1978)

Sentimental Destinies *See* Les Destinees (2000)

The Sentinel *See* La Sentinelle (1992)

Seom *See* The Isle (2001)

Separate Beds *See* The Wheeler Dealers (1963)

Separate Rooms *See* Notre Histoire (1984)

Separation *See* Don't Hang Up (1990)

Seppuku *See* Harakiri (1962)

Sept Fois Femme *See* Woman Times Seven (1967)

Sergeant Steiner *See* Breakthrough (1978)

Serial Killing 4 Dummys *See* Serial Killing 101 (2004)

The Serpent *See* Night Flight from Moscow (1973)

Seryozha *See* A Summer to Remember (1961)

Sette Volte Donna *See* Woman Times Seven (1967)

Seul contre tous *See* I Stand Alone (1998)

Seunlau Ngaklau *See* Time and Tide (2000)

Se7en *See* Seven (1995)

Seven Bad Men *See* Rage at Dawn (1955)

The Seven Brothers Meet Dracula *See* The Legend of the 7 Golden Vampires (1973)

Seven Different Ways *See* Quick, Let's Get Married (1971)

Seven Doors of Death *See* The Beyond (1982)

Seven Graves for Rogan *See* Time to Die (1983)

Seven Sisters *See* The House on Sorority Row (1983)

Seven Waves Away *See* Abandon Ship (1957)

75 Degrees in July *See* 75 Degrees (2000)

Sex Crime of the Century *See* Last House on the Left (1972)

The Sex of the Stars *See* Le Sexe des Etoiles (1993)

Sex Play *See* Games Girls Play (1975)

The Sex Racketeers *See* Man of Violence (1971)

Sexton Blake and the Hooded Terror *See* The Hooded Terror (1938)

Shadow *See* Unsane (1982)

The Shadow *See* Webmaster (1998)

The Shadow Army *See* Army of Shadows (1969)

Shadow of the Werewolf *See* The Werewolf vs. the Vampire Woman (1970)

Shadow Play *See* Portraits Chinois (1996)

The Shadow Versus the Thousand Eyes of Dr. Mabuse *See* The Thousand Eyes of Dr. Mabuse (1960)

The Shadow Warrior *See* Kagemusha (1980)

Shadow Zone: My Teacher Ate My Homework *See* My Teacher Ate My Homework (1998)

Shadowbuilder *See* Bram Stoker's Shadowbuilder (1998)

Shadows in an Empty Room *See* Strange Shadows in an Empty Room (1976)

Shadows of Our Ancestors *See* Shadows of Forgotten Ancestors (1964)

Shadows of Our Forgotten Ancestors *See* Shadows of Forgotten Ancestors (1964)

Shadows of the Peacock *See* Echoes of Paradise (1986)

Shaft Returns *See* Shaft (2000)

Shakespeare's Sister *See* The Proposition (1997)

Shalimar *See* Deadly Thief (1978)

Shall We Dansu? *See* Shall We Dance? (1996)

Shame of the Sabine Women *See* The Rape of the Sabines (1961)

Shanghai Express *See* The Millionaire's Express (1986)

Shao Nian Huang Fei Hong Zhi Tie Ma Liu *See* Iron Monkey (1993)

Shark: Red on the Ocean *See* Devilfish (1984)

Shark Reef *See* She Gods of Shark Reef (1956)

Shatter *See* Call Him Mr. Shatter (1974)

Shatterhand *See* Apache's Last Battle (1964)

She Demons of the Swamp *See* Attack of the Giant Leeches (1959)

She Devil *See* Drums O'Voodoo (1934)

She Devils of the S.S. *See* The Cut Throats (1969)

She Drives Me Crazy *See* Friends, Lovers & Lunatics (1989)

She Got What She Asked For *See* Yesterday, Today and Tomorrow (1964)

She Knew No Other Way *See* Last Resort (1986)

She Monster of the Night *See* Frankenstein's Daughter (1958)

She Should Have Stayed in Bed *See* I Am Frigid... Why? (1972)

She Was a Hippy Vampire *See* The Wild World of Batwoman (1966)

She-Wolf *See* The Legend of the Wolf Woman (1977)

Sheba *See* The Graveyard (1974)

Sheer Bliss *See* Winter Break (2002)

Shelf Life *See* Subhuman (2004)

She'll Be Sweet *See* Magee and the Lady (1978)

Shenanigans *See* Great Bank Hoax (1978)

Sherlock Holmes *See* The Adventures of Sherlock Holmes (1939)

Sherlock Holmes and the Prince of Crime *See* Hands of a Murderer (1990)

Sherlock Holmes and the Scarlet Claw *See* Scarlet Claw (1944)

Sherlock Holmes and the Spider Woman *See* Spider Woman (1944)

Sherlock Holmes and the Woman in Green *See* The Woman in Green (1945)

Sherlock Holmes Grosster Fall *See* A Study in Terror (1966)

Sherlock Holmes in The Hound of London *See* The Hound of London (1993)

Sherlock Holmes: The Silver Blaze *See* Murder at the Baskervilles (1937)

Sherlock Holmes Und Das Halsband des Todes *See* Sherlock Holmes and the Deadly Necklace (1962)

She's De Lovely *See* De-Lovely (2004)

She's De Lovely *See* She's So Lovely (1997)

Shi gan *See* Time (2006)

Shi qi sui de tian kong *See* Formula 17 (2004)

Shichinin No Samurai *See* Seven Samurai (1954)

Shifshuf Naim *See* Hot Bubblegum (1981)

Shijie *See* The World (2004)

Shimian Maifu *See* House of Flying Daggers (2004)

Shimmering Light *See* Mutual Respect (1977)

Shin Jingi No Hakaba *See* Graveyard of Honor (2002)

Shin Kanashiki Hittoman *See* Another Lonely Hitman (1995)

Shinel *See* The Overcoat (1959)

Shinju Ten No Amijima *See* Double Suicide (1969)

Ship of Fools *See* The Imposters (1998)

The Ship was Loaded *See* Carry On Admiral (1957)

Ships of the Night *See* Ships in the Night (1928)

Shiqisuide Danche *See* Beijing Bicycle (2001)

Shiver *See* Night Train to Terror (1984)

Shivers *See* They Came from Within (1975)

Shiza *See* Schizo (2004)

Shizuka Naru Ketto *See* A Quiet Duel (1949)

Shnat Effes *See* Year Zero (2004)

Shock (Transfer Suspense Hypnos) *See* Shock (1979)

Shocked *See* Mesmerized (1984)

Shockwave *See* The Arrival (1996)

Shogun Island *See* Raw Force (1981)

Shoot the Pianist *See* Shoot the Piano Player (1962)

The Shooter *See* Hidden Assassin (1994)

Shootout *See* Shoot Out (1971)

The Shop on High Street *See* The Shop on Main Street (1965)

Shu Dan Long Wei *See* Meltdown (1995)

Shu Shan Zu: Warriors from the Magic Mountain (1983)

Shuang Long Hui *See* Twin Dragons (1992)

Shuang Tong *See* Double Vision (2002)

Shuban *See* Scandal (1950)

Shunpuden *See* Story of a Prostitute (1965)

Shut Up and Dance *See* Dance with Me (1998)

The Shuttered Room *See* Blood Island (1968)

Shvil Hahalav *See* The Milky Way (1997)

Si Don Juan Etait une Femme *See* Don Juan (Or If Don Juan Were a Woman) (1973)

Si Te Dicen Que Cai *See* If They Tell You I Fell (1989)

Sibirska Ledi Magbet *See* Siberian Lady Macbeth (1961)

Sid & Nancy: Love Kills *See* Sid & Nancy (1986)

Sidney Sheldon's Windmills of the Gods *See* Windmills of the Gods (1988)

Siegfried's Death *See* Siegfried (1924)

Siegfrieds Tod *See* Siegfried (1924)

Signal One *See* Bullet Down Under (1994)

Signe Charlotte *See* Sincerely Charlotte (1986)

Significant Other *See* When a Man Loves a Woman (1994)

The Silence After the Shot *See* The Legend of Rita (1999)

The Silence of the Sea *See* La Silence de la Mer (1947)

Silencio de Neto *See* The Silence of Neto (1994)

Silencio Roto *See* Broken Silence (2001)

The Silent Flute *See* Circle of Iron (1978)

Silent Night, Evil Night See Black Christmas (1975)

Silken Skin See The Soft Skin (1964)

Silver Blaze See Murder at the Baskervilles (1937)

The Silver Brumby See The Silver Stallion: King of the Wild Brumbies (1993)

Silver Devil See Wild Horse (1931)

Simon del Deserto See Simon of the Desert (1966)

Simon Magus See Simon the Magician (1999)

Simone Barbes ou la Vertu See Simone Barbes (1980)

Simoom: A Passion in the Desert See Passion in the Desert (1997)

Simple Lies See Rx (2006)

The Sin See The Shaming (1971)

Sin Eater See The Order (2003)

Sin Noticias de Dios See No News from God (2001)

Sinai Commandos: The Story of the Six Day War See Sinai Commandos (1968)

The Singing Musketeer See The Three Musketeers (1939)

Sinister House See Who Killed Doc Robbin? (1948)

The Sinners See La Piscine (1969)

Sins of Love See Test Tube Babies (1948)

Siren's Kiss See Body Strokes (1995)

Sista Dansen See The Last Dance (1993)

The Sister of Satan See The She-Beast (1965)

Sisters See Some Girls (1988)

Sitting Bull's History Lesson See Buffalo Bill & the Indians (1976)

Siu lam juk kau See Shaolin Soccer (2001)

Siulam Chukkau See Shaolin Soccer (2001)

Siunin Woang Fei-hung Tsi Titmalau See Iron Monkey (1993)

Six Inches Tall See Attack of the Puppet People (1958)

Six Women for the Murderer See Blood and Black Lace (1964)

The Sixth of June See D-Day, the Sixth of June (1956)

Skatel See Blades of Courage (1988)

Ski Lift to Death See Snowblind (1978)

Skip Tracer See Deadly Business (1977)

Skipper See The Todd Killings (1971)

Sky is Falling See Bloodbath (1976)

Skyggen See Webmaster (1998)

Skyggen af Emma See Emma's Shadow (1988)

Skylark See Sarah, Plain and Tall: Skylark (1993)

The Slammer See Short Eyes (1979)

The Slasher See Cosh Boy (1931)

Slasher in the House See Home Sweet Home (1980)

The Slaughterers See Cannibal Apocalypse (1980)

Slaves of the Invisible Monster See The Invisible Monster (1950)

Slaves See Blacksnake! (1973)

Slave Coast See Cobra Verde (1988)

Slave Girls See Prehistoric Women (1967)

Slave of the Cannibal God See Mountain of the Cannibal God (1979)

Sleep No More See Invasion of the Body Snatchers (1956)

Slip Slide Adventures See Water Babies (1979)

Slit-Mouthed Woman See Carved (2007)

Stay It Again, Sam See Codename: Foxfire (1935)

A Small Miracle See Simon Birch (1998)

Small Town Massacre See Strange Behavior (1981)

Smart Alec See Movie Maker (1986)

Smokey and the Bandit Ride Again See Smokey and the Bandit 2 (1980)

Smorgasbord See Cracking Up (1983)

Smultron-Stallet See Wild Strawberries (1957)

Snake Eyes See Dangerous Game (1993)

Snake Fist Fighter See Master with Cracked Fingers (1971)

The Snake King See Snakeman (2005)

Snapshot See The Night After Halloween (1979)

Snitch See Monument Ave. (1998)

Snow Days See Let It Snow (1999)

Snow White and the Three Clowns See Snow White and the Three Stooges (1961)

Snow White in the Black Forest See Snow White: A Tale of Terror (1997)

Snuff See Thesis (1996)

Snuffy Smith See Snuffy Smith, Yard Bird (1942)

So This is Romance? See Romance and Rejection (1996)

So Sweet, So Perverse See Kiss Me, Kill Me (1969)

So Sweet, So Dead See The Slasher (1972)

So Sad About Gloria See Visions of Evil (1975)

So Naked, So Dead See The Slasher (1972)

So Evil, My Sister See The Sibling (1972)

Social Suicide See Pre-Madonnas: Rebels Without a Clue (1995)

Sodome et Gomorrhe See Sodom and Gomorrah (1962)

Soldier Duroc See Soldat Duroc... Ca Va Etre Ta Fete! (1975)

Soldier in Skirts See Triple Echo (1977)

The Soldier Who Declared Peace See Tribes (1970)

The Soldiers See Les Carabiniers (1963)

Solamente Nero See The Bloodstained Shadow (1978)

Soldaat van Oranje See Soldier of Orange (1978)

Solo de Otono See Autumn Sun (1998)

Solomon Northrup's Odyssey See Half Slave, Half Free (1985)

Solyaris See Solaris (1972)

Sombra, the Spider Woman See The Black Widow (1947)

Some Like It Cool See Sex on the Run (1978)

Some Like It Hot See Rhythm Romance (1938)

Some Like It Sexy See The Seducer (1969)

Someone is Killing the Great Chefs of Europe See Who is Killing the Great Chefs of Europe? (1978)

Someone's Killing the World's Greatest Models See She's Dressed to Kill (1979)

Something Fishy See Pas Tres Catholique (1993)

Something is Out There See Day of the Animals (1977)

Something Like the Truth See The Offence (1973)

Something to Hide See Shattered (1972)

Something Waits in the Dark See Screamers (1980)

Something's Gotta Give See Move Over, Darling (1963)

Somewhere in France See The Foreman Went to France (1942)

Somewhere in Paris See The Spy Ring (1938)

Sommariek See Summer Interlude (1950)

Sommarnattens Leende See Smiles of a Summer Night (1955)

Son of Blob See Beware! The Blob (1972)

Son of Darkness: To Die For 2 See To Die For 2: Son of Darkness (1991)

Sondagsengier See The Other Side of Sunday (1996)

The Song of the Road See Pather Panchali (1954)

Song of the Sierra See Springtime in the Sierras (1947)

The Songs of My Homeland See Marooned in Iraq (2002)

Sono Otoko, Kyobo ni Tsuki See Violent Cop (1989)

Sons and Warriors See Some Mother's Son (1996)

Sons of the Legion See Sons of the Desert (1933)

Sons of the Musketeers See At Sword's Point (1951)

Sons of the Wind See The Great Challenge (2004)

Sophie Scholl: Die Letzten Tage See Sophie Scholl: The Final Days (2005)

Sophie's Place See Crooks & Coronets (1969)

Sorstalansag See Fateless (2005)

So's Your Aunt Emma See Meet the Mob (1942)

Sotto gli Occhi dell'Assassino See Unsane (1982)

Soul See Earth (1930)

Soul Man 2 See Far Out Man (1989)

Soulmates See Evil Lives (1992)

Sound From a Million Years Ago See Sound of Horror (1964)

Sound of Fury See Try and Get Me (1950)

Soup to Nuts See Waitress (1981)

Sous le Sable See Under the Sand (2000)

Sous le Soleil de Satan See Under Satan's Sun (1987)

Sous les Toits de Paris See Under the Roofs of Paris (1929)

South of Panama See Panama Menace (1941)

South Pacific See Rodgers & Hammerstein's South Pacific (2001)

South Sea Woman See Pearl of the South Pacific (1955)

South Seas See South Seas Massacre (1974)

Southside See Cock & Bull Story (2003)

Southwest to Sonora See The Appaloosa (1966)

Soy Cuba See I Am Cuba (1964)

Space 2074 See Star Quest (1989)

Space: 2100 See Destination Moonbase Alpha (1975)

The Space Amoeba See Yog, Monster from Space (1971)

Space Avenger See Alien Space Avenger (1991)

Space Invasion from Lapland See Invasion of the Animal People (1962)

Space Invasion of Lapland See Invasion of the Animal People (1962)

Space Men See Assignment Outer Space (1961)

Space Men Appear in Tokyo See Warning from Space (1956)

Space Mission of the Lost Planet See Horror of the Blood Monsters (1970)

Space Monster Dagora See Dagora, the Space Monster (1965)

Space Mutants See Planet of the Vampires (1965)

Space Soldiers See Flash Gordon: Rocketship (1940)

Space Station See Black Horizon (2001)

Space Travellers See Marooned (1969)

The Space Vampires See The Astro-Zombies (1967)

Spacemen Saturday Night See Invasion of the Saucer Men (1957)

Spaceship to the Unknown See Flash Gordon: Rocketship (1940)

Spaceship See The Creature Wasn't Nice (1981)

Spanish Rose See Point of Impact (1993)

The Spanish Apartment See L'Auberge Espagnole (2002)

Spara Forte, Piu Forte... Non Capisco See Shoot Loud, Louder, I Don't Understand! (1966)

Sparkling Cyanide See Agatha Christie's Sparkling Cyanide (1983)

Spawn See Todd McFarlane's Spawn (1997)

Spawn of the Slithis See Slithis (1978)

The Spawning See Piranha 2: The Spawning (1982)

The Specter of Freedom See Phantom of Liberty (1974)

The Spectre See The Ghost (1963)

Speed Brent Wins See Breed of the Border (1933)

Spell of Amy Nugent See Spellbound (1941)

Spell of the Hypnotist See Fright (1956)

Spettri See Specters (1987)

The Spider See Earth vs. the Spider (1958)

Spider Baby, or the Maddest Story Ever Told See Spider Baby (1964)

Spider-Man See The Amazing Spider-Man (1977)

Spies-A-Go-Go See Nasty Rabbit (1964)

Spies, Lies, and Alibis See Code Name: Chaos (1990)

Spinal Tap See This Is Spinal Tap (1984)

The Spider See The Killer Must Kill Again (1975)

Spione See Spies (1928)

Spivs See Vitelloni (1953)

Spoorloos See The Vanishing (1988)

Spot See Dog Pound Shuffle (1975)

Spotlight on Scandal See Spotlight Scandals (1943)

Spotlight Revue See Spotlight Scandals (1943)

Spotswood See The Efficiency Expert (1992)

The Spooky Movie Show See The Mask (1961)

The Split See The Manster (1959)

Spring Break USA See Lauderdale (1989)

Spring Fever USA See Lauderdale (1989)

Spur der Steine See Trace of Stones (1966)

The Spy in White See Secret of Stamboul (1936)

Spyder See Blackbelt 2: Fatal Force (1993)

Spymaker See Spymaker: The Secret Life of Ian Fleming (1990)

Spymaster See Goldeneye: The Secret Life of Ian Fleming (1989)

Squadron of Doom See Ace Drummond (1936)

Stacey and Her Gangbusters See Stacey (1973)

Stadt ohne Mitleid See Town without Pity (1961)

Stakeout 2 See Another Stakeout (1993)

The Stand See Stephen King's The Stand (1994)

Stand and Deliver See Bowery Blitzkrieg (1941)

Stand Easy See Goon Movie (1952)

Standard Time See Anything But Love (2002)

Stanno Tutti Bene See Everybody's Fine (1990)

Star See Danielle Steel's Star (1993)

Star Child See Space Raiders (1983)

The Star Man See The Star Maker (1995)

Star Runner See The Kumite (2003)

Star Wars: Episode 4—A New Hope See Star Wars (1977)

Star Wars: Episode 5—The Empire Strikes Back See The Empire Strikes Back (1980)

Star Wars: Episode 6—Return of the Jedi See Return of the Jedi (1983)

Stardust See Mad About Money (1937)

Starflight: the Plane that Couldn't Land See Starflight One (1983)

Starknight See Star Knight (1985)

Starlight Slaughter See Eaten Alive (1976)

The Statutory Affair See Lola (1969)

Stay See Sleeping Dogs Lie (2006)

Staying Alive See Fight for Your Life (1977)

Steiner—Das Eiserne Kreuz See Cross of Iron (1976)

Stella Star See Star Crash (1978)

Stepfather See Beau Pere (1981)

Stephen King's Cat's Eye See Cat's Eye (1985)

Stephen King's Graveyard Shift See Graveyard Shift (1990)

Stephen King's Silver Bullet See Silver Bullet (1985)

Stephen King's Sleepwalkers See Sleepwalkers (1992)

Steven Spielberg Presents: Taken See Taken (2002)

Still Smokin' See Cheech and Chong: Still Smokin' (1983)

Stinky See Fistful of Death (1971)

Sto Dnej Do Pri Kaza See 100 Days Before the Command (1990)

Stolen Hearts See Two If by Sea (1995)

Stone Cold See Jesse Stone: Stone Cold (2005)

Storia de Ragazzi e di Ragazze See The Story of Boys & Girls (1991)

Storm See Storm Tracker (1999)

Storm of the Century See Stephen King's The Storm of the Century (1999)

Stormbreaker See Alex Rider: Operation Stormbreaker (2006)

Stormy Crossing See Black Tide (1958)

Story of a Marriage See On Valentine's Day (1986)

The Story of Gosta Berling See The Atonement of Gosta Berling (1924)

The Story of Robin Hood See The Story of Robin Hood & His Merrie Men (1952)

A Story of the Cruelties of Youth See The Cruel Story of Youth (1960)

The Story Without A Name See Without Warning (1952)

Strafsache 4 Ks 2/63: Auschwitz Vor Dem Frankfurter Schwurgericht See Verdict on Auschwitz: The Frankfurt Auschwitz Trial 1963—1965 (1993)

Straight Jacket See Dark Sanity (1982)

Straight on Till Morning See Dressed for Death (1974)

Straight to Hell See Cut and Run (1985)

Straightheads See Closure (2007)

Stranded See Black Horizon (2001)

A Strange Adventure See Wayne Murder Case (1932)

The Strange Adventure of David Gray See Vampyr (1931)

The Strange Case of Dr. Jekyll and Mr. Hyde See Dr. Jekyll and Mr. Hyde (1968)

The Strange Case of Madeleine See Madeleine (1950)

Strange Deception See The Accused (1948)

Strange Hearts See Road to Riches (2001)

Strange Incident See The Ox-Bow Incident (1943)

Strange Interval See Strange Interlude (1932)

Strange Journey See Fantastic Voyage (1966)

The Strange Ones See Les Enfants Terrible (1950)

Strange Skirts See When Ladies Meet (1941)

The Strange World of Planet X See The Cosmic Monsters (1958)

Strangeland See Dee Snider's Strangeland (1998)

The Stranger See Shame (1961)

A Stranger Came Home See Unholy Four (1954)

The Stranger from Afar See Marebito (2004)

Stranger in Our House See Summer of Fear (1978)

Stranger in the House See Black Christmas (1975)

Stranger in the House See Cop-Out (1967)

Stranger on the Campus See Monster on the Campus (1959)

A Stranger Walked In See Love from a Stranger (1947)

Strangers See Voyage in Italy (1953)

Stranger's Face See Face of Another (1966)

Stranger's Gold See Gunslinger (1970)

Strangest Dreams: Invasion of the Space Preachers See Invasion of the Space Preachers (1990)

The Strangler of Vienna See The Mad Butcher (1972)

Strangler's Morgue See The Crimes of Stephen Hawke (1936)

Stray Dogs See U-Turn (1997)

Street Fighter Counterattacks See The Street Fighter's Last Revenge (1974)

Street Gang See Vigilante (1983)

Street Kill See Death Scream (1975)

Street Legal See The Last of the Finest (1990)

Street Love See Scarred (1984)

Street of Shadows See The Shadow Man (1953)

Street of Sorrow See Joyless Street (1925)

Streets of New York See The Abe Lincoln of Ninth Avenue (1939)

Streetwise See Jailbait (1993)

Strictly Confidential See Broadway Bill (1934)

Strictly for Pleasure See The Perfect Furlough (1959)

Strike! See All I Wanna Do (1998)

Strike the Tent See The Last Confederate: The Story of Robert Adams (2005)

Striking Back See Search and Destroy (1981)

Strip Poker See The Big Switch (1970)

Striptease See Insanity (1976)

Striptease Lady See Lady of Burlesque (1943)

Struktura Krysztalu See The Structure of Crystals (1969)

Stryker's War See Thou Shalt Not Kill...Except (1987)

Student Body See Getting In (1994)

Subarashiki Nichiyobi See One Wonderful Sunday (1947)

Subida Al Cielo See Mexican Bus Ride (1951)

Subliminal Seduction See The Corporation (1996)

The Submersion of Japan See Tidal Wave (1975)

Subspecies 2 See Bloodstone: Subspecies 2 (1992)

Subspecies 3 See Bloodlust: Subspecies 3 (1993)

Subspecies 4 See Bloodstorm: Subspecies 4 (1998)

Subspecies 4: Bloodstorm—The Master's Revenge See Bloodstorm: Subspecies 4 (1998)

Succubus See The Devil's Nightmare (1971)

Such Men are Dangerous See The Racers (1955)

Sud pralad See Tropical Malady (2004)

Sudden Terror See Eye Witness (1970)

The Suicide Club See Robert Louis Stevenson's The Game of Death (1999)

Suicide Run See Too Late the Hero (1970)

Suicide Squadron See Dangerous Moonlight (1941)

A Suitable Case for Treatment See Morgan: A Suitable Case for Treatment (1966)

Sukkar Banat See Caramel (2007)

The Sullivans See The Fighting Sullivans (1942)

Sullivan's Marauders See Commandos (1973)

Summer of Innocence See Big Wednesday (1978)

Suit See Hunger (1966)

Summer Camp See A Pig's Tale (1994)

Summer Fling See The Last of the High Kings (1996)

Summer Madness See Summertime (1955)

Summer Manoeuvers See Les Grandes Manoeuvres (1955)

Summer with Monika See Monika (1952)

Summerplay See Summer Interlude (1950)

Summertime Killer See Ricco (1974)

Sumurun See One Arabian Night (1921)

The Sun Demon See Hideous Sun Demon (1959)

Suna No Onna See Woman in the Dunes (1964)

Sunburst See Slashed Dreams (1974)

Sunless See Sans Soleil (1982)

Sunrise—A Song of Two Humans See Sunrise (1927)

Sunset of a Clown See Sawdust & Tinsel (1953)

The Sunset Warrior See Heroes Shed No Tears (1986)

Sunshine Even by Night See Night Sun (1990)

Super Dragon See Secret Agent Super Dragon (1966)

Super Fly T.N.T. See Superfly T.N.T. (1973)

The Super Inframan See Infra-Man (1976)

Super Nova See Tales from a Parallel Universe: Super Nova (1997)

Superargo the Giant See Superargo (1967)

Superchicken See Fowl Play (1975)

Supercock See Fowl Play (1975)

Superfantagenio See Aladdin (1986)

Superman and the Strange People See Superman & the Mole Men (1951)

Supersnooper See Super Fuzz (1981)

SuperVixens Eruption See Supervixens (1975)

Sur Mes Levres See Read My Lips (2001)

Surf 2: The End of the Trilogy See Surf 2 (1984)

Surf Warriors See Surf Ninjas (1993)

Susan's Plan See Dying to Get Rich (1998)

Suspected Alibi See Suspended Alibi (1956)

Suspense See Shock (1979)

Svenska Hjaltar See Expectations (1997)

Svitati See Screw Loose (1999)

Swamp Diamonds See Swamp Women (1955)

Swedish Heroes See Expectations (1997)

Swedish Wildcats See A Man with a Maid (1973)

Sweeney Todd: The Demon Barber of Fleet Street See Demon Barber of Fleet Street (1936)

Sweet Candy See Candy Stripe Nurses (1974)

Sweet Dirty Tony See The Mercenaries (1980)

Sweet Kill See The Arousers (1970)

Sweet Revenge See Code of Honor (1984)

Sweet Savior See Love Thrill Murders (1971)

Sweet Smell of Woman See The Scent of a Woman (1975)

Sweet Suzy See Blacksnake! (1973)

Sweet Trash See Corruption (1970)

Sweet Violence See Sweet Ecstasy (1962)

Sweeter Song See Snapshot (1977)

Sweetheart! See Canada's Sweetheart: The Saga of Hal C. Banks (1985)

Switchboard Operator See The Love Affair, or The Case of the Missing Switchboard Operator (1967)

Swordkill See Ghostwarrior (1986)

Swords of Blood See Cartouche (1962)

Sydney See Hard Eight (1996)

Sylvia and the Ghost See Sylvia and the Phantom (1945)

Sylvia Kristel's Beauty School See Beauty School (1993)

Symphony of Love See Ecstasy (1933)

The System See The Girl Getters (1966)

Szegenylegenyek Nehezeletuck See The Round Up (1966)

Szerelem See Love (1971)

Szerelmesfilm See Love Film (1970)

Szerencses Daniel See Daniel Takes a Train (1983)

- T & A See H.O.T.S. (1979)
- T & A Academy 2 See Gimme an F (1985)
- A Table for One See Wicked Ways (1999)
- Tacones Lejanos See High Heels (1991)
- Taepung See Typhoon (2006)
- Tahara See God's Sandbox (2002)
- The Tai-Chi Master See Twin Warriors (1993)
- Tai Ji Zhang San Feng See Twin Warriors (1993)
- Taiaye Sorgh See Crimson Gold (2003)
- Tai! Det as sa Morkt See Speak Up! It's So Dark (1993)
- Tainted Money See Show Them No Mercy (1935)
- A Tale of Africa See Green Horizon (1980)
- A Tale of the Cock See Confessions of Tom Harris (1972)
- Tale of the Mummy See Russell Mulcahy's Tale of the Mummy (1999)
- The Tale of Zatoichi See Zatoichi: The Life and Opinion of Masseur Ichi (1962)
- A Talent for Loving See Gun Crazy (1969)
- Talaye Sorgh See Crimson Gold (2003)
- Tales from the Crypt II See Vault of Horror (1973)
- Tales of Mystery See Spirits of the Dead (1968)
- Tales of Mystery and Imagination See Spirits of the Dead (1968)
- Tales of the City See Armistead Maupin's Tales of the City (1993)
- Talos the Mummy See Russell Mulcahy's Tale of the Mummy (1999)
- Ta'm e Guilass See The Taste of Cherry (1996)
- Talvisota See The Winter War (1989)
- Tang Shan da Xiong See Fists of Fury (1973)
- Tangled Trails See Sands of Sacrifice (1921)
- Tanin no kao See Face of Another (1966)
- Tanner: A Political Fable See Tanner '88 (1988)
- Tao Fan See Prison on Fire 2 (1991)
- Target: Embassy See Embassy (1972)
- Target in the Sun See The Man Who Would Not Die (1975)
- Target of an Assassin See African Rage (1978)
- Tarot See Autopsy (1974)
- Tartu See The Adventures of Tartu (1943)
- Tarzan and Jane See Tarzan and the Lost City (1998)
- Tarzan and the Green Goddess See The New Adventures of Tarzan (1935)
- Tarzan and the Jungle Mystery See Green Inferno (1972)
- Tasogare Seibei See The Twilight Samurai (2002)
- Taste of Cherries See The Taste of Cherry (1996)
- Taste of Fear See Scream of Fear (1961)
- Te Day Mis Ojos See Take My Eyes (2003)
- Te Deum See Sting of the West (1972)
- Teacher's Pet: The Movie See Disney's Teacher's Pet (2004)
- Teacher's Pet See Devil in the Flesh 2 (2000)
- The Tears of Julian Po See Julian Po (1997)
- Teen Kanya See Two Daughters (1961)
- Teen Monster See Boltneck (1998)
- The Teenage Psycho Meets Bloody Mary See Incredibly Strange Creatures Who Stopped Living and Became Mixed-Up Zombies (1963)
- Tejing Xinrenlei See Gen-X Cops (1999)
- The Telegian See The Secret of the Telegian (1961)
- Tell It To the Marines See Here Come the Marines (1952)
- Tell Your Children See Reefer Madness (1938)
- Tema See The Theme (1979)
- Templ Duri per i Vampiri See Uncle Was a Vampire (1959)
- Tempo di Ucc.dere See Time to Kill (1989)
- Tempo di Charleston - Chicago 1929 See They Paid with Bullets: Chicago 1929 (1969)
- Temporada de patos See Duck Season (2004)
- Tempting Fate See The Proposition (1997)
- Tender Love See L'Amour en Herbe (1977)
- The Tenderfoot See Bushwhacked (1995)
- Tenderfoots See Bushwhacked (1995)
- Tendre Poulet See Dear Detective (1977)
- Tenebrae See Unsane (1982)
- Tenebre See Unsane (1982)
- Tengoku To Jigoku See High & Low (1962)
- Tennessee Valley See The Only Thrill (1997)
- Tennessee Williams: The Roman Spring of Mrs. Stone See The Roman Spring of Mrs. Stone (2003)
- Tentacoli See Tentacles (1977)
- Tenue de Soiree See Menage (1986)
- Terminal Station Indiscretion See Indiscretion of an American Wife (1954)
- Terminal Station See Indiscretion of an American Wife (1954)
- Terminus Station See Indiscretion of an American Wife (1954)
- Terminal See Robin Cook's Terminal (1996)
- Terra Estrangeira See Foreign Land (1996)
- Terra em Transe See Earth Entranced (1966)
- Terreur dans l'Espace See Planet of the Vampires (1965)
- Terror at the Opera See Opera (1988)
- Terror Castle See The Virgin of Nuremberg (1965)
- Terror Circus See Barn of the Naked Dead (1973)
- Terror Eyes See Night School (1931)
- Terror from the Sun See Hideous Sun Demon (1959)
- Terror House See Terror at Rec Wolf Inn (1972)
- Terror House See The Night Has Eyes (1942)
- Terror Hospital See Hospital of Terror (1978)
- Terror in Space See Planet of the Vampires (1965)
- Terror in the Midnight Sun See Invasion of the Animal People (1962)
- Terror in Toyland See Christmas Evil (1980)
- Terror of Dracula See Nosferatu (1922)
- Terror of Sheba See The Graveyard (1974)
- Terror Strikes See The War of the Colossal Beast (1953)
- Terror under the House See Revenge (1971)
- Terrore nello Spazio See Planet of the Vampires (1965)
- Tesis See Thesis (1996)
- Testament in Evil See The Testament of Dr. Mabuse (1959)
- The Testament of Dr. Mabuse See Crimes of Dr. Mabuse (1932)
- Texas Blood Money See From Dusk Till Dawn 2: Texas Blood Money (1998)
- Texas Chainsaw Massacre 3: Leatherface See Leatherface: The Texas Chainsaw Massacre 3 (1989)
- Texas Desperadoes See Drift Fence (1936)
- Texas Layover See Blazing Stewardesses (1975)
- Texas Road Agent See Road Agent (1926)
- Texas Serenade See Old Corral (1936)
- Teyve der Milkhiker See Tevye (1939)
- Thank God He Met Lizzie See The Wedding Party (1997)
- Thanksgiving Family Reunion See National Lampoon's Holiday Reunion (2003)
- That Man Mr. Jones See The Fuller Brush Man (1948)
- That They May Live See J'Accuse (1937)
- That's the Way of the World See Shining Star (1975)
- These Dangerous Years See Dangerous Youth (1953)
- These Foolish Things See Daddy Nostalgia (1990)
- They Call Me Hallelujah See Guns for Dollars (1973)
- They Call Me Macho Woman See Savage Instinct (1989)
- They Don't Wear Pajamas at Rosie's See The First Time (1969)
- They Loved Life See Kanal (1956)
- They Made Me a Criminal See They Made Me a Fugitive (1947)
- They Made Me a Fugitive See They Made Me a Criminal (1939)
- They May Watch See They (2002)
- They See Wes Craven Presents: They (2002)
- They See They Watch (1993)
- They Passed This Way See Four Faces West (1948)
- They Who Step on the Tiger's Tail See The Men Who Tread on the Tiger's Tail (1945)
- They're Coming to Get You See Dracula vs. Frankenstein (1971)
- Thieves Holiday See A Scandal in Paris (1946)
- Thieves See Les Voleurs (1996)
- Thin Air See Invasion of the Body Stealers (1969)
- The Thing from Another World See The Thing (1951)
- Thinner See Stephen King's Thinner (1996)
- Thirst See Three Strange Loves (1949)
- The Thirst of Baron Blood See Torture Chamber of Baron Blood (1972)
- Thirteen at Dinner See Agatha Christie's Thirteen at Dinner (1985)
- The Thirteen Chairs See 12 Plus 1 (1970)
- This and That See Zus & Zo (2001)
- This Strange Passion See El (1952)
- 37.2 Degrees in the Morning See Betty Blue (1986)
- 37.2 le Matin See Betty Blue (1986)
- 36 Hours See Terror Street (1954)
- Thomas Crown and Company See The Thomas Crown Affair (1968)
- Thomas Est Amoureux See Thomas in Love (2001)
- Thoroughbred See Run for the Roses (1978)
- Those Dear Departed See Ghosts Can Do It (1987)
- Those Were the Happy Times See Star! (1968)
- Thou Shall Not Kill See Avenging Conscience (1914)
- Thou Shalt Honour Thy Wife See Master of the House (1925)
- A Thousand and One Nights See Arabian Nights (1974)
- Thrills See Blood Angels (2005)
- 3x Jugatsu See Boiling Point (1990)
- Three Colors: White See Trois Couleurs: Blanc (1994)
- Three Colors: Blue See Trois Couleurs: Bleu (1993)
- Three Colors: Red See Trois Couleurs: Rouge (1994)
- Three Bad Men in the Hidden Fortress See The Hidden Fortress (1958)
- Three Crazy Legionnaires See Three Legionnaires (1937)
- The Three Faces of Fear See Black Sabbath (1964)
- The Three Faces of Terror See Black Sabbath (1964)
- Three For the Money See Win, Place, or Steal (1972)
- Three Golden Serpents See Island of Lost Girls (1968)
- Three Moves to Freedom See Brainwashed (1960)
- Three Ninjas: Showdown at Mega Mountain See 3 Ninjas: High Noon at Mega Mountain (1957)
- Three of a Kind See Cooking Up Trouble (1944)
- Three Rascals in the Hidden Fortress See The Hidden Fortress (1958)
- Three Steps to the Gallows See White Fire (1953)
- The Three Stooges Go Around the World in a Daze See Around the World in a Daze (1963)
- Three Way Split See 3-Way (2004)
- The Threepenny Opera See Mack the Knife (1989)
- Thriller: An Echo of Teresa See Anatomy of Terror (1974)
- Thriller: Kill Two Birds See Cry Terror (1976)
- Through the Looking Glass See The Velvet Vampire (1971)
- Through the Magic Pyramid See Tut & Tuttle (1981)
- Thunder on the Trail See Thundering Trail (1951)
- Thunder Point See Jack Higgins' Thunder Point (1997)
- Thunder County See Woman's Prison Escape (1974)
- Thunder Mountain See Shadow of Chikara (1977)
- Thunder Warrior See Thunder Warrior (1985)
- Thursday the 12th See Pandemonium (1982)
- Thy Neighbor's Wife See Poison (2001)
- Ti Kniver i Hjertet See Cross My Heart and Hope to Die (1994)
- Tian di ying xiong See Warriors of Heaven and Earth (2003)
- Tian Yu See Xiu Xiu: The Sent Down Girl (1997)
- Tianguo Niezi See The Day the Sun Turned Cold (1994)
- Tidal Wave See Portrait of Jennie (1948)
- The Tide of Life See Catherine Cookson's The Tide of Life (1996)
- The Ties That Blind See The Unsaid (2001)
- The Tiger See Tiger Warsaw (1987)
- Tiger in the Sky See The McConnell Story (1955)

Tiger of Bengal See Journey to the Lost City (1958)
The Tiger of Eschanapur See The Indian Tomb (1921)
The Tiger Woman See Perils of the Darkest Jungle (1944)
Tigers Don't Cry See African Rage (1978)
Tight Little Island See Whiskey Galore (1948)
The Tigress See Ilsa, the Tigress of Siberia (1979)
'Til Christmas See Breathing Room (1996)
Til Dawn Do Us Part See Dressed for Death (1974)
Till Death Us Do Part See The Blood Spattered Bride (1972)
Till Gladje See To Joy (1950)
Tilly Trotter See Catherine Cookson's Tilly Trotter (1999)
Tim Burton's The Nightmare before Christmas See The Nightmare before Christmas (1993)
Timber Tramps See The Big Push (1975)
Time Flyers See The Blue Yonder (1986)
A Time For Caring See Generation (1969)
The Time of Return See Muriel (1963)
Time of the Beast See Mutator (1990)
Time of the Wolves See Carbon Copy (1969)
Time Raiders See Warriors of the Apocalypse (1985)
Time Trap See The Time Travelers (1964)
Time Warp Terror See Bloody New Year (1987)
Timecode See Time Code (2000)
The Timeshifters See Thrill Seekers (1999)
Timeslip See The Atomic Man (1956)
Timewarp See Day Time Ended (1980)
Tini Zabutykh Predkiv See Shadows of Forgotten Ancestors (1964)
Tintorera See Tintorera... Tiger Shark (1978)
Tintorera...Bloody Waters See Tintorera... Tiger Shark (1978)
Tirez sur le Pianiste See Shoot the Piano Player (1962)
Titan Find See Creature (1985)
Tito and I See Tito and Me (1992)
Tito I Ja See Tito and Me (1992)
To Be a Man See Cry of Battle (1963)
To Catch a Spy See Catch Me a Spy (1971)
To Die For See Heaven's a Drag (1994)
To Elvis, With Love See Touched by Love (1980)
To Have and to Hold See When a Man Loves a Woman (1994)
To Koritsi Me Ta Mavra See Girl in Black (1956)
To Live See Ikiru (1952)
To Love a Vampire See Lust for a Vampire (1971)
To Our Loves See A Nos Amours (1984)
To Return See Volver (2006)
To Telefteo Psemma See A Matter of Dignity (1957)
To Vienna Tou Odyssea See Ulysses' Gaze (1995)
Toca Para Mi See Play for Me (2001)
Today We Live See The Day and the Hour (1963)
Todo Sobre Mi Madre See All About My Mother (1999)
A Toi de Faire, Mignonne See Your Turn Darling (1963)

Tokyo Monogatari See Tokyo Story (1953)
Tokyo Nagaremono See Tokyo Drifter (1966)
Tomb of the Cat See Tomb of Ligeia (1964)
Tomb of the Living Dead See Mad Doctor of Blood Island (1968)
Tomb Raider See Lara Croft: Tomb Raider (2001)
The Tommyknockers See Stephen King's The Tommyknockers (1993)
Ton Kero Ton Hellinon See When the Greeks (1981)
Tong Nien Wang Shi See A Time to Live and a Time to Die (1985)
Too Many Chefs See Who Is Killing the Great Chefs of Europe? (1978)
Too Much See Wish You Were Here (1987)
Top of the Food Chain See Invasion! (1999)
Topio Stin Omichli See Landscape in the Mist (1988)
Tora No O Wo Fumu Otokotachi See The Men Who Tread on the Tiger's Tail (1945)
Torment See L'Enfer (1993)
Torpedo Zone See Submarine Attack (1954)
Torture Chamber See The Fear Chamber (1968)
Torture Zone See The Fear Chamber (1968)
Toto the Hero See Toto le Heros (1991)
The Touch of Flesh See You've Ruined Me, Eddie (1958)
The Touch of Melissa See The Touch of Satan (1970)
Touchez Pas Au Grisbi See Grisbi (1953)
Touchez pas au Grisbi See Grisbi (1953)
Tough Guy See Counter Punch (1971)
Tout Contre Leo See Close to Leo (2002)
A Toute Vitesse See Full Speed (1996)
Tower of Terror See Assault (1970)
Tower of Terror See Hard to Die (1990)
A Town Called Bastard See A Town Called Hell (1972)
The Town That Cried Terror See Maniac (1977)
Train 2419 See The Return of Casey Jones (1934)
Traitement de Choc See Shock Treatment (1981)
Trance See The External (1999)
Trancers See Future Cop (1976)
Transport Z Raje See Transport from Paradise (1965)
The Transvestite See Glen or Glenda? (1953)
Tras el Cristal See In a Glass Cage (1986)
Trauma See Dario Argento's Trauma (1993)
Trauma See The House on Straw Hill (1976)
Traveling Birds See Winged Migration (2001)
Travels with Anita See Lovers and Liars (1981)
Tre Fratelli See Three Brothers (1980)

Tre Passi nel Delirio See Spirits of the Dead (1968)
Treasure of the Living Dead See Oasis of the Zombies (1982)
Tredowata See Leper (1976)
The Tree of Hands See Innocent Victim (1990)
Tree of Liberty See The Howards of Virginia (1940)
Trial by Combat See Choice of Weapons (1976)
Trick of the Eye See Primal Secrets (1994)
Trilogia: To Livadi pou dakryzei See Weeping Meadow (2004)
Trilogy: The Weeping Meadow See Weeping Meadow (2004)
A Trip with Anita See Lovers and Liars (1981)
Triple Trouble See Kentucky Kernels (1934)
Tristan and Isolde See Lovespell (1979)
Triumph des Willens See Triumph of the Will (1934)
Trmavomodry Svet See Dark Blue World (2001)
Trois Histoires Extraordinaires d'Edgar Poe See Spirits of the Dead (1968)
Trois Hommes et un Couffin See Three Men and a Cradle (1985)
Trois Vies et Une Seule Mort See Three Lives and Only One Death (1996)
The Trojan Brothers See Murder in the Footlights (1946)
The Trojan War See The Trojan Horse (1962)
The Trollenberg Terror See The Crawling Eye (1958)
Trolosa See Faithless (2000)
Tromba See Tromba, the Tiger Man (1952)
Trop Belle pour Tol See Too Beautiful for You (1988)
Trop Jolie pour Etre Honette See Too Pretty to Be Honest (1972)
Tropicana See The Heat's On (1943)
Trottie True See The Gay Lady (1949)
Trouble at 16 See Platinum High School (1960)
Trouble Chaser See Li'l Abner (1940)
The Trout See La Truite (1983)
The Truth About Tully See Tully (2000)
Try and Find It See Hi Diddle Diddle (1943)
Try Seventeen See All I Want (2002)
Tsarskaya Nevesta See The Tsar's Bride (1966)
Tsubaki Sanjuro See Sanjuro (1962)
Tsvet Granata See The Color of Pomegranates (1969)
Tudor Rose See Nine Days a Queen (1936)
Tueur de Ch Icago See Scarface Mob (1962)
Tulitkkutehtaan Tytto See The Match Factory Girl (1990)
The Tunnel See Transatlantic Tunnel (1935)
Tunnels See Criminal Act (1988)
Turkey Shoot See Escape 2000 (1981)
Turn Your Pony Around See Mortal Danger (1994)

Turnaround See The Big Turnaround (1988)
Turtle Beach See The Killing Beach (1992)
Tuzolto utca 25 See 25 Fireman's Street (1973)
Twee Vrouwen See Twice a Woman (1979)
Twelve Miles Out See The Second Woman (1951)
Twenty-One Days Together See 21 Days (1937)
24 Hours See Trapped (2002)
Twice Bitten See The Vampire Hookers (1978)
Twilight of the Dead See Gates of Hell (1980)
Twinkle, Twinkle, Killer Kane See The Ninth Configuration (1979)
Twinky See Lola (1969)
The Twins Effect See Vampire Effect (2003)
Twins of Dracula See Twins of Evil (1971)
Twist of Fate See Psychopath (1997)
Twisted See Medusa (1974)
The Twisted Road See They Live by Night (1949)
2 Cries in the Night See Funeral Home (1982)
Two If By Sea See Stolen Hearts (1995)
Two Guys Talkin' About Girls See At First Sight (1995)
The Two-Headed Monster See The Manster (1959)
Two Minds for Murder See Someone Behind the Door (1971)
2 S.I.C.K. (Serial Insane Clown Killer) See Mr. Jingles (2006)
2002: The Rape of Eden See Bounty Hunter 2002 (1994)
Two Weeks in September See A Coeur Joie (1967)
2BPerfectlyHonest See 2B Perfectly Honest (2004)
Tyler Perry's Daddy's Little Girls See Daddy's Little Girls (2007)
Tystnaden See The Silence (1963)
Tyubeu See Tube (2003)
U-Boat See In Enemy Hands (2004)
U-Boat 29 See Spy in Black (1939)
U-238 and the Witch Doctor See Jungle Drums of Africa (1953)
Uccellacci e Uccellini See The Hawks & the Sparrows (1967)
Uccidero Un Uomo See This Man Must Die (1970)
Uchu Daikaiju Dogora See Dagora, the Space Monster (1965)
Uchudal Dogora See Dagora, the Space Monster (1965)
Uchujin Tokyo Ni Arawaru See Warning from Space (1956)
Ugetsu Monogatari See Ugetsu (1953)
Ugly, Dirty and Bad See Down & Dirty (1976)
Ukigusa See Drifting Weeds (1959)
Ulisse See Ulysses (1955)
The Ultimate Chase See The Ultimate Thrill (1974)
Ultimate Desires See Beyond the Silhouette (1990)
The Ultimate Solution of Grace Quigley See Grace Quigley (1984)
Ultimi Giorni di Pompeii See The Last Days of Pompeii (1960)
L'Ultimo Tango a Parigi See Last Tango in Paris (1973)
L'Ultimo Treno della Notte See Night Train Murders (1975)
Ultra Force See Royal Warriors (1986)

Umarete Wa Mita Keredo See I Was Born But.. (1932)

The Umbrella Woman See The Good Wife (1986)

Un Amour De Swann See Swann in Love (1984)

Un Angelo En Allemagne See A Love in Germany (1984)

Un Angelo e Scesso a Brooklyn See The Man Who Wagged His Tail (1957)

Un Ano Perdido See A Lost Year (1993)

Un Ano Sin Amor See A Year Without Love (2005)

Un Arma de Dos Filos See Sharki (1968)

Un Autre Homme, Une Autre Chance See Another Man, Another Chance (1977)

Un Chapeau de Paille d'Italie See Italian Straw Hat (1927)

Un Complicato Intrigo Di Donne, Vicoli E Delitti See Camorra: The Naples Connection (1985)

Un Condamne a Mort s'est Echappe, Ou Le Vent Souffle ou il Vent See A Man Escaped (1956)

Un Dimanche a la Campagne See A Sunday in the Country (1984)

Un Divan a New York See A Couch in New York (1995)

Un, Deux, Trois, Quatre! See Black Tights (1960)

Un dia sin mexicanos See A Day Without a Mexican (2004)

Un Dollar Troue See Blood for a Silver Dollar (1966)

Un Elephant a Trompe Enormement See Pardon Mon Affaire (1976)

Un Grand Amour de Beethoven See Beethoven (1936)

Un Heros Tres Discret See A Self-Made Hero (1995)

Un Hombre vino a matar See Rattler Kid (1968)

Un Homme Amoureux See A Man in Love (1987)

Un Homme Est Mort See The Outside Man (1973)

Un Homme et Un Femme See A Man and a Woman (1966)

Un Homme Et Une Femme: Vingt Ans Deja See A Man and a Woman: 20 Years Later (1986)

Un Indien dans la Ville See Little Indian, Big City (1995)

Un long dimanche de fiancailles See A Very Long Engagement (2004)

Un Minuto Per Pregare, Un Istante Per Morire See A Minute to Pray, a Second to Die (1967)

Un monde presque paisible See Almost Peaceful (2002)

Un Paraiso Bajo las Estrellas See A Paradise Under the Stars (1999)

Un Partie de Plaisir See A Piece of Pleasure ('974)

Un Senor Muy Viejo Con Unas Alas Enormes See A Very Old Man with Enormous Wings (1988)

Un Tipo con Una Faccia Strana ti Cerca per Ucciderti See Mean Machine (1973)

Un Trem Para as Estrelas See Subway to the Stars (1987)

Un Uomo da Rispettare See Master Touch (1974)

Un Week-end sur Deux See Every Other Weekend (1991)

Un Zoo, La Nuit See Night Zoo (1987)

Una Bruja Sin Escoba See A Witch Without a Broom ('968)

Una Giornata Speciale See A Special Day (1977)

Una Hacha para la Luna de Miel See Hatchet for the Honeymoon (1970)

Una Lucertola con la Pelle di Donna See A Lizard in a Woman's Skin (1971)

Una Pura Formalita See A Pure Formality (1994)

Una Ragione Per Vivere e Una Per Morire See A Reason to Live, a Reason to Die (1973)

Una Sombra Ya Pronto Seras See A Shadow You Soon Will Be (1994)

Unagi See The Eel (1996)

Unakrsna Vatra See Operation Cross Eagles (1969)

Uncle Harry See The Strange Affair of Uncle Harry (1945)

Uncle Silas See Inheritance (1947)

Unconventional Linda See Holiday (1938)

Under California Skies See Under California Stars (1948)

Under Siege See Hostages (1980)

Under Solen See Under the Sun (1998)

Under the Banner of Samurai See Samural Banners (1969)

Under the Clock See The Clock (1945)

Under the Olive Trees See Through the Olive Trees (1994)

Under the Sun of Satan See Under Satan's Sun (1987)

An Underwater Odyssey See Neptune Factor (1973)

Underworld See Transmutations (1985)

Underworld After Dark See Big Town After Dark (1947)

Une Affaire de Femmes See The Story of Women (1988)

Une Femme de Menage See The Housekeeper (2002)

Une Femme Douce See A Gentle Woman (1969)

Une Femme Est Une Femme See A Woman Is a Woman (1960)

Une Femme ou Deux See One Woman or Two ('985)

Une Hirondelle a Fait le Printemps See The Girl from Paris (2002)

Une Histoire Simple See A Simple Story (1979)

Une Liaison d'Amour See An Affair of Love (1999)

Une Liaison Pornographique See An Affair of Love (1999)

Une Partie de Campagne See A Day in the Country (1946)

Une Pure Formalite See A Pure Formality (1994)

The Unfaithful Wife See La Femme Infidele (1969)

The Ungodly See The Perfect Witness (2007)

The Unknown See Clawed: The Legend of Sasquatch (2005)

Unknown Satellite Over Tokyo See Warning from Space ('956)

The Unnamable Returns See The Unnamable 2: The Statement of Randolph Carter (1992)

Unseen Evil 2 See Alien 3000 (2004)

Untel Pere et Fils See Heart of a Nation (1943)

Unterm Birnbaum See Under the Pear Tree (1973)

The Untold Story See Sasquatch (2002)

The Untold Story: Human Meat Roast Pork Buns See The Untold Story (1993)

The Unvanquished See Aparajito (1958)

Uomo Dalla Pelle Dura See Counter Punch (1971)

L'Uomo delle Stelle See The Star Maker (1995)

Up Frankenstein See Andy Warhol's Frankenstein (1974)

Up in the Cellar See Three in the Cellar (1970)

Up in Smoke See Cheech and Chong's Up in Smoke (1979)

Up 'n Coming See Cassie (1983)

Up the Chastity Belt See Naughty Knights (1971)

Up to a Point See Up to a Certain Point (1983)

The Upstate Murders See Savage Weekend (1980)

Urban Justice See Under Oath (1997)

Urga See Close to Eden (1990)

Ursus See Ursus in the Valley of the Lions (1962)

The Usual Unidentified Thieves See Big Deal on Madonna Street (1958)

Utamaro O Meguru Gonin No Onna See Utamaro and His Five Women (1946)

Utvandrarna See The Emigrants (1972)

Uvidet Parizi I Umeret See To See Paris and Die (1993)

Vacation See National Lampoon's Vacation (1983)

Vagabond Violinist See Broken Melody (1934)

Vaghe Stelle Dell'Orsa See Sandra of a Thousand Delights (1965)

Valborgsmassoafton See Walpurgis Night (1941)

The Valdez Horses See Chino (1975)

Valdez the Half Breed See Chino (1975)

Vale Abraao See Abraham's Valley (1993)

Valentine's Day See Protector (1997)

Valley of Abraham See Abraham's Valley (1993)

Valley of Fear See Sherlock Holmes and the Deadly Necklace (1962)

Valley of the Swords See The Castillian (1963)

The Vampire See Vampyr (1931)

The Vampire and the Robot See My Son, the Vampire (1952)

The Vampire-Beast Craves Blood See Blood Beast Terror (1967)

Vampire Castle See Captain Kronos: Vampire Hunter (1974)

Vampire Conspiracy See Vampire Centerfolds (1998)

Vampire Hunters See Tsui Hark's Vampire Hunters (2002)

Vampire Men of the Lost Planet See Horror of the Blood Monsters (1970)

Vampire Orgy See Vampyres (1974;

Vampire Over London See My Son, the Vampire (1952)

The Vampire's Niece See Fangs of the Living Dead (1968)

Vampire Playgirls See Dracula's Great Love (1972)

Vampires See John Carpenter's Vampires (1997)

Vampires: Los Muertos See John Carpenter Presents Vampires: Los Mueros (2002)

Vampires of Prague See Mark of the Vampire (1935)

Vampire's Thirst See The Body Beneath (1970)

Vampyr, Der Traum des David Gray See Vampyr (1931)

Vampyr, Ou l'Etrange Aventure de David Gray See Vampyr (1931)

Vampyres, Daughters of Dracula See Vampyres (1974)

Van Wilder See National Lampoon's Van Wilder (2002)

Van Wilder 2: The Rise of Taj See National Lampoon's Van Wilder 2: The Rise of Taj (2006)

Vanishing Body See The Black Cat (1934)

Vargtimmen See Hour of the Wolf (1968)

Variete See Variety (1925)

The Varrow Mission See Teen Alien (1978)

Vasectomy See Vasectomy: A Delicate Matter (1986)

Vaudeville See Variety (1925)

V.C. Andrews' Rain See Rain (2006)

Vegas, Baby See Bachelor Party Vegas (2005)

The Veil See Haunts (1977)

Veillees d'armes See The Troubles We've Seen (1994)

Velka voda See The Great Water (2004)

Velocity See The Wild Ride (1960)

The Velocity of Gary* (*Not His Real Name) See The Velocity of Gary (1998)

Velvet House See Crucible of Horror (1969)

Vendetta: Secrets of a Mafia Bride See A Family Matter (1991)

A Vendre See For Sale (1958)

Vendredi Soir See Friday Night (2002)

Vengeance See The Brain (1962)

Vengeance of a Soldier See Soldier's Revenge (1984)

Vengeance: The Demon See Pumpkinhead (1988)

Vengeance: The Story of Tony Cimo See Vengeance (1989)

The Vengeful Dead See K ss Daddy Goodbye (1981)

Venice See Dangerous Beauty (1998)

Venus in Peltz See Venus in Furs (1970)

The Venusian See The Stranger from Venus (1954)

Vercingetorix See Druids (2001)

Verdi See Life of Verdi (1982)

The Veritas Project: Hangman's Curse See Hangman's Curse (2003)

Vers le Sud See Heading South (2005)

A Very Big Weekend See A Man, a Woman, and a Bank (1979)

A Very Discreet Hero See A Self-Made Hero (1995)

Vesnicko Ma Strediskova See My Sweet Little Village ('986)

Vessel of Wrath See Beachcomber (1938)

The Veteran See Deathdream (1972)

Viagem ao Principio do Mundo See Voyage to the Beginning of the World (1996)

Viaggio in Italia See Voyage in Italy (1953)

Viaje Fantastico en Globo See Fantastic Balloon Voyage (1976)

The Vicious Circle See Woman in Brown (1948)

Victims of the Beyond See Sucker Money (1934)

Viehjud Levi See Jew-Boy Levi (1999)

The Vienna Strangler See The Mad Butcher (1972)

Vig See Morey Kings (1998)

Viking Massacre See Knives of the Avenger (1965)

Viktor Vogel: Commercial Artist See Advertising Rules! (2001)

Vincent, Francois, Paul et les Autres See Vincent, Francois, Paul and the Others (1976)

Vindicator *See* Wheels of Fire (1984)

Violated *See* Party Girls for Sale (1954)

Violence et Passion *See* Conversation Piece (1975)

Violent City *See* The Family (1970)

Violent Journey *See* The Fool Killer (1965)

Violent Midnight *See* Psychomania (1963)

Violent Rage *See* Fearmaker (1989)

Violent Streets *See* Thief (1981)

Violette Noziere *See* Violette (1978)

Viperes *See* Posers (2002)

Virgin Hunters *See* Test Tube Teens from the Year 2000 (1993)

The Virgin Vampires *See* Twins of Evil (1971)

The Virgin Wife *See* You've Got to Have Heart (1977)

The Virtuous Tramps *See* The Devil's Brother (1933)

Virus *See* Cannibal Apocalypse (1980)

Viskingar Och Rop *See* Cries and Whispers (1972)

Vita Privata *See* A Very Private Affair (1962)

Vital Parts *See* Harold Robbins' Body Parts (1999)

Vitelloni *See* I Vitelloni (1953)

Viva Las Nowhere *See* Dead Simple (2001)

Vivement Dimanche! *See* Confidentially Yours (1983)

The Vivero Letter *See* Forgotten City (1998)

Viviamo Oggi *See* The Day and the Hour (1963)

Vivid *See* Luscious (1997)

Vivre Sa Vie *See* My Life to Live (1962)

The Vixen *See* The Women (1968)

Vixens *See* Supervixens (1975)

Vici Jama *See* Wolf Trap (1957)

Voor een Verloren Soldaat *See* For a Lost Soldier (1993)

Vor *See* The Thief (1997)

Voros Fold *See* Red Earth (1982)

Vortex *See* Day Time Ended (1980)

Voskhozhdeniye *See* The Ascent (1976)

Voyage beyond the Sun *See* Space Monster (1964)

Voyage to a Prehistoric Planet *See* Voyage to the Prehistoric Planet (1965)

Voyage to Italy *See* Voyage in Italy (1953)

Vrazda Po Cesky *See* Murder Czech Style (1966)

Vredens Dag *See* Day of Wrath (1943)

Vsichni Moji Blizci *See* All My Loved Ones (2000)

Vudu Sangriento *See* Voodoo Black Exorcist (1973)

Vulcan, Son of Jupiter *See* Vulcan God of Fire (1962)

Vzlomschik *See* Burglar (1987)

W Pustyni I W Puszczy *See* In Desert and Wilderness (2001)

Wages of Fear *See* Sorcerer (1977)

Waiting Women *See* Secrets of Women (1952)

Wajda: Czlowiek Z Zelaza *See* Man of Iron (1981)

The Waking Hour *See* The Velvet Vampire (1971)

Waldo Warren: Private Dick Without a Brain *See* Maximum Thrust (1988)

Walkers on the Tiger's Tail *See* The Men Who Tread on the Tiger's Tail (1945)

Wandafuru Raifu *See* After Life (1998)

Wannseekonferenz *See* The Wannsee Conference (1984)

Want a Ride, Little Girl? *See* Impulse (1974)

Wanted *See* Crime Spree (2003)

Wanted Women *See* Jessi's Girls (1975)

The Wanton Contessa *See* Senso (1954)

War Between the Planets *See* Planet on the Prowl (1965)

War Games *See* Suppose They Gave a War and Nobody Came? (1970)

The War Is Over *See* La Guerre Est Finie (1966)

The War of the Monsters *See* Gamera vs. Barugon (1966)

War of the Monsters *See* Godzilla vs. Monster Zero (1968)

War of the Planets *See* Cosmos: War of the Planets (1980)

War of the Robots *See* Reactor (1985)

War Shock *See* Battle Shock (1956)

Ward 13 *See* Hospital Massacre (1981)

Warlock *See* Skulduggery (1979)

The Warm-Blooded Spy *See* Ravishing Idiot (1964)

Warnung Vor Einer Heiligen Nutte *See* Beware of a Holy Whore (1970)

Warrior *See* Mexican Blow (2002)

The Warrior of Waverly Street *See* Star Kid (1997)

Warrior's Rest *See* Le Repos du Guerrier (1962)

Waru Yatsu Hodo Yoku Nemuru *See* The Bad Sleep Well (1960)

Warum Lauft Herr R Amok? *See* Why Does Herr R. Run Amok? (1969)

Was Tun, Wenn's Brennt? *See* What to Do in Case of Fire (2002)

Washington, B.C. *See* Hail (1973)

Watch That Man *See* The Man Who Knew Too Little (1997)

Watchtower *See* Cruel and Unusual (2001)

Water Child *See* L'Enfant d'Eau (1995)

Water Cyborgs *See* Terror Beneath the Sea (1966)

The Watts Monster *See* Dr. Black, Mr. Hyde (1976)

The Way *See* Yol (1982)

The Way Ahead *See* Immortal Battalion (1944)

The Way of Life *See* They Call It Sin (1932)

The Way We Are *See* Quiet Days in Hollywood (1997)

Ways of Love *See* The Miracle (1948)

We Met on the Vineyard *See* The Big Day (1999)

We Will All Meet in Paradise *See* Pardon Mon Affaire, Tool (1977)

Wedding Bells *See* Royal Wedding (1951)

Wedding Breakfast *See* The Catered Affair (1956)

A Wedding for Bella *See* The Bread, My Sweet (2001)

Wednesday's Child *See* Family Life (1971)

Week of the Killer *See* Cannibal Man (1971)

Weekend Babysitter *See* Weekend with the Babysitter (1970)

Welcome Home Brother Charles *See* Soul Vengeance (1975)

Welcome to Jericho *See* Last Man Standing (1996)

Welcome to Oblivion *See* Ultra Warrior (1992)

Welcome to Planet Earth *See* Alien Avengers (1996)

The Well-Made Marriage *See* Le Beau Mariage (1982)

Wendy Cracked a Walnut *See* ...Almost (1990)

We're in the Army Now *See* Pack Up Your Troubles (1932)

The Werewolf and the Yeti *See* Night of the Howling Beast (1975)

Werewolf Woman *See* The Legend of the Wolf Woman (1977)

Wes Craven Presents Carnival of Souls *See* Carnival of Souls (1998)

Wes Craven Presents: Don't Look Down *See* Don't Look Down (1998)

Wes Craven Presents Dracula 2: Ascension *See* Dracula 2: Ascension (2003)

Wes Craven Presents: Dracula 2000 *See* Dracula 2000 (2000)

Wes Craven Presents Wishmaster *See* Wishmaster (1997)

West Beyrouth *See* West Beirut (1998)

West of the Badlands *See* The Border Legion (1940)

West of the Brazos *See* Rangeland Empire (1950)

The Westing Game *See* Get a Clue! (1998)

Whare Are Those Strange Drops of Blood on the Body of Jennifer? *See* The Case of the Bloody Iris (1972)

What *See* The Whip and the Body (1963)

What? *See* Diary of Forbidden Dreams (1973)

What a Chassis! *See* Belle Americaine (1961)

What a Drag *See* Pedale Douce (1996)

What a Man *See* Never Give a Sucker an Even Break (1941)

What Changed Charley Farthing *See* Bananas Boat (1978)

What Ever Happened to Baby Jane *See* What Ever Happened To... (1993)

What Happened to Tully *See* Tully (2000)

What Lola Wants *See* Damn Yankees (1958)

What the Swedish Butler Saw *See* A Man with a Maid (1973)

What We Did That Night *See* Murder at Devil's Glen (1999)

The Wheelchair *See* El Cochecito (1960)

Wheels of Terror *See* The Misfit Brigade (1987)

When Knighthood Was in Flower *See* The Sword & the Rose (1953)

When Michael Calls *See* Shattered Silence (1971)

When the Girls Meet the Boys *See* Girl Crazy (1943)

When the Raven Flies *See* Revenge of the Barbarians (1985)

When Youth Conspires *See* Old Swimmin' Hole (1940)

Where is the Friend's Home? *See* Where is My Friend's House? (1987)

Where the Hell's the Gold? *See* Dynamite and Gold (1988)

Where the River Bends *See* Bend of the River (1952)

While Plucking the Daisy *See* Plucking the Daisy (1956)

The Whipping Boy *See* Prince Brat and the Whipping Boy (1995)

White *See* Trois Couleurs: Blanc (1994)

White Paws *See* Pattes Blanches (1949)

The White River Kid *See* White River (1999)

White Trash on Moonshine Mountain *See* Moonshine Mountain (1964)

A White White Boy *See* The Mirror (1975)

Whiteboys *See* White Boyz (1999)

Who? *See* Roboman (1975)

Who Am I *See* Jackie Chan's Who Am I (1998)

Who Dares Wins *See* The Final Option (1982)

Who Fears the Devil *See* The Legend of Hillbilly John (1973)

Who Is Killing the Stuntman *See* Stunts (1977)

Who Killed Atlanta's Children? *See* Echo of Murder (2000)

Who Knows? *See* Va Savoir (2001)

Who Murdered Joy Morgan? *See* Killjoy (1981)

Who Not? *See* Eijanaika (1981)

Who Shot Patakango? *See* Who Shot Pat? (1992)

Whoever Slew Auntie Roo? *See* Who Slew Auntie Roo? (1971)

The Who's Tommy *See* Tommy (1975)

Why Did I Get Married? *See* Tyler Perry's Why Did I Get Married? (2007)

The Wicked Caresses of Satan *See* Devil's Kiss (1981)

Wide-Eyed and Legless *See* The Wedding Gift (1993)

The Widow and the Gigolo *See* Roman Spring of Mrs. Stone (1961)

Wilbur Falls *See* Dead Silence (1998)

Wild Beds *See* Tigers in Lipstick (1980)

Wild Drifters *See* Cockfighter (1974)

Wild Flower *See* Fiorile (1993)

Wild Flower *See* Flor Silvestre (1958)

Wild Flowers *See* Wildflowers (1999)

Wild for Kicks *See* Beat Girl (1960)

Wild Geese *See* Mistress (1953)

Wild Horse Mesa *See* When the West Was Young (1932)

Wild Horses of Fire *See* Shadows of Forgotten Ancestors (1964)

The Wild McCullochs *See* The McCullochs (1975)

Wild Oats *See* The Errors of Youth (1978)

The Wild Pack *See* Defiant (1970)

The Wild Side *See* Suburbia (1983)

Wild Weed *See* She Shoulda Said No (1949)

Wild West Comedy Show *See* Vince Vaughn's Wild West Comedy Show (2006)

Wild Youth *See* Naked Youth (1959)

Wildcat *See* Great Scout & Cathouse Thursday (1976)

Wildchild 2 *See* Silk 'n' Sabotage (1994)

Wilderness Family, **Part 2** *See* Further Adventures of the Wilderness Family, Part 2 (1977)

A Wilderness Station *See* Edge of Madness (2002)

William Shakespeare's **The Merchant of Venice** *See* The Merchant of Venice (2004)

Willy Milly *See* Something Special (1986)

Witt *See* The Misadventures of Mr. Witt (1990)

Wind-Fire-Forest-Mountain *See* Samurai Banners (1969)

The Wind in the Willows *See* Mr. Toad's Wild Ride (1996)

A Window in London *See* Lady in Distress (1939)

A Window to the Sky *See* The Other Side of the Mountain (1975)

The Windsor Protocol *See* Jack Higgins' The Windsor Protocol (1997)

The Winged Serpent *See* Q (The Winged Serpent) (1982)

The Wingless Bird *See* Catherine Cookson's The Wingless Bird (1997)

Wings of the Apache *See* Fire Birds (1990)

Winter Rates *See* Out of Season (1975)

Winter's End *See* Serah, Plain and Tall: Winter's End (1999)

Winterschlafer *See* Winter Sleepers (1997)

The Wisdom of Crocodiles *See* Immortality (1997)

Wise Girls (1998) *See* Wisegirls (2002)

The Wistful Widow *See* The Wistful Widow of Wagon Gap (1947)

The Witch *See* Superstition (1982)

Witch Doctor *See* Men of Two Worlds (1946)

Witchcraft (1988) *See* Witchery (1988)

Witchcraft through the Ages *See* Haxan: Witchcraft through the Ages (1922)

Wit's End *See* G.I. Executioner (1971)

The Witches of Salem *See* The Crucible (1957)

Witchfinder General *See* The Conqueror Worm (1968)

Witchkill *See* The Witchmaker (1969)

Witch's Curse *See* Maciste in Hell (1960)

With a Vengeance *See* Undesirable No. (1937)

With Words and Music *See* The Girl Said No (1937)

Within *See* The Cavern (2005)

Witness to a Kill *See* Queen's Messenger II (2001)

The Wizard of Mars *See* Horrors of the Red Planet (1964)

Wo Do Fu Qin Mu Qin *See* The Road Home (2001)

Wolf Larsen *See* The Legend of Sea Wolf (1975)

Wolf (1958) *See* The Legend of the Sea Wolf

Wo Die Grunen Ameisen Traumen *See* Where the Green Ants Dream (1984)

Wo Do I Gotta Kill? *See* Me and the Mob (1994)

Wolf Larsen *See* The Legend of Sea Wolf (1975)

A Woman Alone *See* Sabotage (1936)

A Woman Destroyed *See* Smash-Up: The Story of a Woman (1947)

Woman, Forty *See* Summer Snow (1994)

The Woman in His House *See* The Animal Kingdom (1932)

Woman of Antwerp *See* Dedee d'Anvers (1949)

Woman of Dolwyn *See* The Last Days of Dolwyn (1949)

Woman of Osaka *See* Osaka Elegy (1936)

Woman of Summer *See* The Stripper (1963)

Woman of the Dunes *See* Woman in the Dunes (1964)

A Woman Scorned: The Betty Broderick Story *See* Till Murder Do Us Part (1992)

A Woman's Devotion *See* Battle Shock (1956)

A Woman's Revenge *See* La Vengeance d'une Femme (1989)

Women Gladiators *See* Thor and the Amazon Women (1960)

Women in Cages *See* The Big Doll House (1971)

Women in Prison *See* Ladies They Talk About (1933)

Women of Nazi Germany *See* Hitler (1962)

Women of Paris *See* Femmes de Paris (1953)

Women Prefer the Mambo *See* Dishonorable Discharge (1957)

Women Unchained *See* Escape from Cell Block 3 (1974)

Women without Names *See* Women in Prison (1949)

Women's Penitentiary 1 *See* The Big Doll House (1971)

Women's Penitentiary 2 *See* The Big Bird Cage (1972)

Women's Penitentiary 4 *See* Caged Women (1984)

Wonder Women *See* The Deadly and the Beautiful (1973)

Wong Fei-hung Tsi Sam: Siwong Tsangba *See* Once Upon a Time in China III (1993)

Wong Fei-hung Ji Yi: Naam Yi Dong Ji Keung *See* Once Upon a Time in China II (1992)

The World and His Wife *See* State of the Union (1948)

The Word *See* Ordet (1955)

The World of Yor *See* Yor, the Hunter from the Future (1983)

The Worlds of Gulliver *See* The Three Worlds of Gulliver (1959)

The Worse You Are, the Better You Sleep *See* The Bad Sleep Well (1960)

Worthy Deceivers *See* Big Bluff (1955)

The Wounded Man *See* L'Homme Blesse (1983)

Wrestling Women vs. the Aztec Ape *See* Doctor of Doom (1962)

Wrong Bet *See* Lionheart (1990)

The Wrong Kind of Girl *See* Bus Stop (1956)

Wrony *See* Crows (1994)

Wszyskio na Sprzedaz *See* Everything for Sale (1968)

Wu Ji *See* The Promise (2005)

Wu jian dao *See* Infernal Affairs (2002)

Wuthering Heights *See* Emily Bronte's Wuthering Heights (1992)

Wuthering Heights *See* MTV's Wuthering Heights (2003)

Wuya Yu Maque *See* Crows and Sparrows (1949)

WW3 *See* Winds of Terror (2001)

X *See* X: The Man with X-Ray Eyes (1963)

X Change *See* Xchange (2000)

The X-Files: Fight the Future *See* The X-Files (1998)

X-Men 2 *See* X2: X-Men United (2003)

X-Men 3 *See* X-Men: The Last Stand (2006)

X-Ray *See* Hospital Massacre (1981)

X-Treme Fighter *See* Sci-Fighter (2004)

Xia dao Gao Fei *See* Full Contact (1992)

Xiao cai feng *See* Balzac and the Little Chinese Seamstress (2002)

Xich Lo *See* Cyclo (1995)

Xin Ching-wu Men *See* New Fist of Fury (1976)

Xingfu Shiguang *See* Happy Times (2000)

Xiyan *See* The Wedding Banquet (1993)

Xizao *See* Shower (2000)

Xochimilco *See* Maria Candelaria (1946)

XX Beautiful Beast *See* Beautiful Beast (1995)

XX Beautiful Hunter *See* Beautiful Hunter (1994)

XX: Utukushiki Gakuen *See* Beautiful Beast (1995)

The XYZ Murders *See* Crimewave (1985)

...Y No Se Lo Trago La Tierra *See* ...And the Earth Did Not Swallow Him (1994)

Yaju No Seishun *See* Youth of the Beast (1963)

Yangtse Incident *See* Battle Hell (1956)

A Yank in London *See* I Live in Grosvenor Square (1946)

A Yankee in King Arthur's Court *See* A Connecticut Yankee in King Arthur's Court (1949)

Yao a Yao Yao Dao Waipo Qiao *See* Shanghai Triad (1995)

Yatgo Ho Yan *See* Mr. Nice Guy (1998)

Y'aura t'il de la Niege a Noel? *See* Will It Snow for Christmas? (1996)

Ye Bang Ga Sheng *See* The Phantom Lover (1995)

Ye Ben *See* Fleeing by Night (2000)

The Year of the Jellyfish *See* L'Annee des Meduses (1986)

Year Zero - War in Sace *See* War in Space (1977)

Yellow Faced Tiger *See* Slaughter in San Francisco (1981)

Yellow Hair and the Pecos Kid *See* Yellow Hair & the Fortress of Gold (1984)

Yeojaneun namjaui miraeda *See* Woman is the Future of Man (2004)

Yi Ge Dou Bu Neng Shao *See* Not One Less (1999)

Yiddle with a Fiddle *See* Yidl Mitn Fidl (1936)

Yihe Yuan *See* Summer Palace (2006)

Ying Huang Boon Sik *See* A Better Tomorrow, Part 1 (1986)

Ying Xiong *See* Hero (2003)

Ying Xiong Wei Lei *See* Heroes Shed No Tears (1986)

Yinghung Bunsik 2 *See* A Better Tomorrow, Part 2 (1988)

Yo, la Peor de Todas *See* I, the Worst of All (1990)

Yokihi *See* Princess Yang Kwei Fei (1955)

Yosei Gorasu *See* Gorath (1962)

You Better Watch Out *See* Christmas Evil (1980)

You Can't Steal Love *See* Murph the Surf (1975)

You Don't Need Pajamas at Rosie's *See* Tha First Time (1969)

The Young and the Damned *See* Los Olvicados (1950)

The Young and the Immortal *See* Tha Sinister Urge (1960)

The Young and the Passionate *See* I Vitelloni (1953)

Young Commandos *See* Delta Force 3: The Killing Game (1991)

The Young Cycle Girls *See* Cycle Vixens (1979)

Young Dracula *See* Andy Warhol's Dracula (1974)

Young Dracula *See* Son of Dracula (1943)

Young Hearts *See* Promised Land (1988)

Young Hellions *See* High School Confidential (1958)

Young Invaders *See* Darby's Rangers (1958)

Young L.A. Nurses 1 *See* Private Duty Nurses (1971)

Young L.A. Nurses 2 *See* Night Cell Nurses (1972)

Young L.A. Nurses 3 *See* The Young Nurses (1973)

The Young Ladies of Wilko *See* Maids of Wilko (1979)

The Young Lieutenant *See* Le Petit Lieutenant (2005)

Young Scarface *See* Brighton Rock (1947)

Youngest Godfather *See* Bonanno: A Godfather's Story (1999)

The Youngest Spy *See* My Name Is Ivan (1962)

Your Past is Showing *See* The Naked Truth (1958)

Your Red Wagon *See* They Live by Night (1949)

Your Witness *See* Eye Witness (1949)

You're Killing Me *See* The Killing Club (2001)

Youth Takes a Hand *See* Behind Prison Walls (1943)

Yukinojo Henge *See* An Actor's Revenge (1963)

Yume *See* Akira Kurosawa's Dreams (1990)

Yup-Yup Man *See* Dark Justice (2000)

Zaat *See* Attack of the Swamp Creature (1975)

Zabudnite na Mozarta *See* Forget Mozart (1985)

Zambo, King of the Jungle *See* Jungle Inferno (1972)

Zamri Ouml Voskresani *See* Freeze-Die-Come to Life (1990)

Zatoichi and the Fugitives *See* Zato-ichi: The Blind Swordsman and the Fugitives (1968)

Zatoichi Meets Yojimbo *See* Zatoichi vs. Yojimbo (1970)

Zatoichi's Vengeance *See* Zatoichi: The Blind Swordsman's Vengeance (1966)

Zayn Vayps Lubovnik *See* His Wife's Lover (1931)

Zazie in the Subway *See* Zazie dans le Metro (1961)

Zazie in the Underground *See* Zazie dans le Metro (1961)

Zato ichi To Yojimbo *See* Zatoichi vs. Yojimbo (1970)

Zeder: Voices from Beyond *See* Zeder (1983)

Zee & Co. *See* X, Y & Zee (1972)

Zeiram *See* Zeiram (1991)

Zeiram 2 *See* Zeiram 2 (1994)

Zeiramu *See* Zeiram (1991)

Zeiramu 2 *See* Zeiram 2 (1994)

Zeisters *See* Fat Guy Goes Nutzoid (1986)

Zemiya *See* Earth (1930)

Zendegi Va Digar Hich ... *See* Life and Nothing More... (1992)

Zero Kelvin *See* Zero Degrees Kelvin (1995)

Zerkalo *See* The Mirror (1975)

Zero de Conduit *See* Zero for Conduct (1933)

Zhaibian *See* The Heirloom (2005)

Zhitu *See* Uniform (2003)

Zhong Nan Hai Bao Biao *See* The Bodyguard from Beijing (1994)

Zhou Yu de Huoche *See* Zhou Yu's Train (2002)

Zi Hudie *See* Purple Butterfly (2003)

Ziemia Obiecana *See* Land of Promise (1974)

Zigs *See* Double Down (2001)

Zire Darakhtan Zeyton *See* Through the Olive Trees ('994)

Zombi *See* Dawn of the Dead (1978)

Zombi 2 *See* Zombie (1980)

Zombie *See* Dawn of the Dead (1978)

Zombie *See* I Eat Your Skin (1964)

Zombie 5 *See* Revenge in the House of Usher (1982)

Zombie Creeping Flesh *See* Hell of the Living Dead (1983)

Zombie Flesh-Eaters *See* Zombie (1980)

Zombie Holocaust *See* Doctor Butcher M.D. (1980)

Zombie ja Kummitusjuna *See* Zombie and the Ghost Train (1991)

Zombies *See* Dawn of the Dead (1978)

Zombies *See* I Eat Your Skin (1964)

Zong Heng Si Hai *See* Once a Thief (1990)

Zoot Suit Jesus *See* Greaser's Palace (1972)

Zormba *See* Zorba the Greek (1964)

Zorro *See* The Mask of Zorro (1998)

Z.P.G. *See* Zero Population Growth (1972)

Zuckerbaby *See* Sugarbaby (1985)

Zuihaode Shiguang *See* Three Times (2005)

Zwartboek *See* Black Book (2006)

Zycle Rodzinne *See* Family Life (1971)

A Coeur Joie ♂♂ *Two Weeks in September* 1967 Beautiful 30-something Cecile is married to a much older Englishman. She's content with her peaceful life until she meets a young man who rekindles her passions. Will Cecile run off with her new lover or stay with the man who makes her secure? French with subtitles. **96m/C VHS, DVD, GB FR** Brigitte Bardot, Laurent Terzieff, Jean Rochefort, James Robertson Justice, Michael Sarne, Murray Head; *D:* Serge Bourguignon; *W:* Serge Bourguignon, Pascal Jardin.

A.I.: Artificial Intelligence ♂♂ 2001 (PG-13) Definitely an acquired taste—the uneasy melding of a long-cherished idea by late director Stanley Kubrick and the homage director Steven Spielberg. Global warming has submerged the world's coastal cities but advanced humanoid robots, or "mechas," keep things going. Professor Hobby (Hurt) has made a child mecha, Davic (Osment), designed to be loving and extremely loyal—in this case to his human mother Monica (O'Connor) who eventually abandons him to the cruel wide world. Having heard the Pinocchio story, David (and his mecha bear Teddy) go in search of the Blue Fairy who can make David a "real" boy. Along the way, David meets mecha Gigolo Joe (Law), who profers good advice about the perfidity of human beings. It's long, it's dark, it's confusing, it's sometimes boring, and sometimes touching. Law's role is small but, as usual, Osment carries the picture. Based on the 1969 short story "Supertoys Last All Summer Long" by Brian Aldiss. **145m/C VHS, DVD, US** Haley Joel Osment, Jude Law, Frances O'Connor, Sam Robards, Brendan Gleeson, William Hurt, Jake Thomas, Clara Bellar, Enrico Colantoni, Adrian Grenier, Emmanuelle Chriqui; *D:* Steven Spielberg; *W:* Steven Spielberg; *C:* Janusz Kaminski; *M:* John Williams; *V:* Robin Williams, Chris Rock, Meryl Streep, Jack Angel; *Nar:* Ben Kingsley.

A la Mode ♂♂½ *In Fashion* 1994 (R) It's Paris in the '60s as shy 17-year-old orphan Fausto (Higelin) is apprenticed to fatherly Jewish tailor Mietek (Yanne). But Fausto is transfixed by lovely mechanic Tonie (Dare) and decides what he really wants (besides the girl) is to design women's fashions. Very frothy coming-of-age tale, anchored by Yanne's veteran charm. Based on the novel "Fausto" by Richard Morgieve. French with subtitles. **89m/C VHS, DVD, FR** Ken Higelin, Jean Yanne, Florence Darel, Francois Hautesserre; *D:* Remy Duchemin; *W:* Remy Duchemin, Richard Morgieve; *M:* Denis Barbier.

A Lot Like Love ♂ 2005 (PG-13) More like "A Lot Like a Million Other Disposable Romantic Comedies." On a plane from New York to L.A., shy Oliver (Kutcher) meets aggressive Emily (Peet), who goads Oliver into joining the Mile High Club and unceremoniously cumps him once they land, claiming that he's just not her type. Apparently the universe and the writers (who've obviously seen "When Harry Met Sally" a few times) disagree, because over the next seven years, Oliver and Emily's paths keep crossing, making them both wonder if they've found their true love. Kutcher and Peet do their best to fake on-screen chemistry, but instead come off as the poor man's Tom Hanks and Meg Ryan. **95m/C DVD, US** Ashton Kutcher, Amanda Peet, Kathryn Hahn, Kal Penn, Taryn Manning, James Read, Molly Cheek, Gabriel Mann, Tyrone Giordano, Aimee Garcia, Ali Larter, Amy Aquino, Jeremy Sisto, Hames Osborne, Lee Garlington, Linda Hunt, Melissa van der Schyft; *D:* Nigel Cole; *W:* Colin Patrick Lynch; *C:* John de Borman; *M:* Alex Wurman.

A Nos Amours ♂♂♂ *To Our Loves* 1984 (R) Craving the attention she is denied at home, a young French girl searches for love and affection from numerous boyfriends in hopes of eradicating her unhappy home. Occasional lapses in quality and slow pacing hamper an otherwise excellent effort. The characterization of the girl Suzanne is especially memorable. In French with English subtitles. **99m/C VHS, DVD, FR** Sandrine Bonnaire, Dominique Besnehard, Maurice Pialat, Evelyne Ker; *D:* Maurice Pialat; *W:* Arlette Langmann, Maurice Pialat; *C:* Jacques Loiseleux; *M:* Henry Purcell.

A Nous la Liberte ♂♂♂ *Freedom for Us* 1931 Two tramps encounter industrialization and automation, making one into a wealthy leader, the other into a nature-loving iconoclast. A poignant, fantastical masterpiece by Clair, made before he migrated to Hollywood. Though the amount of automation may be dated, it influenced such films as Chaplin's "Modern Times." In French with English subtitles. **97m/B VHS, DVD, FR** Henri Marchand, Raymond Cordy, Rolla France, Paul Olivier, Jacques Shelly, Andre Michaud; *D:* Rene Clair; *W:* Rene Clair; *C:* Georges Perinal; *M:* Georges Auric.

A Propos de Nice ♂♂♂ *Nizza* 1929 First film by French director Vigo, the silent film parodies French travelogues in a manner that indicates the director's later brilliance. **25m/B VHS, FR** *D:* Jean Vigo; *W:* Jean Vigo; *C:* Boris Kaufman.

Aaron Loves Angela ♂♂ 1975 (R) Puerto Rican girl falls in love with a black teen amidst the harsh realities of the Harlem ghetto. "Romeo and Juliet" meets "West Side Story" in a cliched comedy-drama. **99m/C VHS,** Kevin Hooks, Irene Cara, Moses Gunn, Robert Hooks; *Cameos:* Jose Feliciano; *D:* Gordon Parks Jr.; *C:* Richard Kratina; *M:* Jose Feliciano.

Abandon ♂♂½ 2002 (PG-13) "Traffic" screenwriter Stephen Gaghan makes his directorial debut in this psychological thriller that centers on bookworm college student Katie (Holmes) and her mysteriously missing boyfriend Embry (Hunnam). When police detective Wade (Bratt) arrives to question Katie two years after the disappearance of the eccentric Embry, she begins to see glimpses of him all over campus. The "twist" ending is fairly predictable, but the cast, particularly Union, Mann and Deschanel as Katie's classmates, get the most out of the script. Based on the book "Adam's Fall" by Sean Desmond. **99m/C VHS, DVD, US** Katie Holmes, Benjamin Bratt, Charlie Hunnam, Zooey Deschanel, Gabrielle Union, Gabriel Mann, Mark Feuerstein, Melanie Lynskey, Will McCormack, Philip Bosco, Tony Goldwyn, Fred Ward; *D:* Stephen Gaghan; *W:* Stephen Gaghan; *C:* Matthew Libatique; *M:* Clint Mansell.

Abandon Ship ♂♂½ *Seven Waves Away* 1957 A luxury liner hits a derelict mine and sinks within minutes, leaving 27 survivors clinging to one tiny lifeboat. Ship's officer Alex Holmes (Power) knows that the injured stand little chance, so he must decide who will survive. **97m/B VHS, GB** Tyrone Power, Mai Zetterling, Lloyd Nolan, Stephen Boyd, Moira Lister, James Hayter, Marie Lohr, Gordon Jackson, Laurence Naismith, John Stratton, Victor Maddern, Eddie Byrne, Noel Willman, Ralph Michael, David Langton, Ferdinand "Ferdy" Mayne, Austin Trevor, Finlay Currie, Jill Melford; *D:* Richard Sale; *W:* Richard Sale; *C:* Wilkie Cooper; *M:* Arthur Bliss.

The Abandoned ♂♂ 2006 (R) Euro-horror. Marie and her twin brother Nicolai were abandoned as babies and only meet again when they must deal with their parents abandoned farmhouse, located in a creepy Russian forest. The haunted house is the site of the 40-year-old murder of their mother, and the siblings soon find themselves trapped by ghostly images that want to re-create the past and make sure that this time they die. **99m/C DVD, EL SP** Anastasia Hille, Karel Roden, Valentin Ganev, Carlos Reig-Plaza; *D:* Nacho Cerda; *W:* Richard Stanley, Nacho Cerda, Karim Hussani; *C:* Xavi Gimenez; *M:* Alfons Conde.

Abbott and Costello Go to Mars ♂½ *On to Mars; Rocket and Roll* 1953 Poor parody of sci-fi finds the frantic duo aboard a rocket ship and accidentally heading off into outer space. They don't land on Mars, but Venus, which is populated by lots of pretty women and no men. Even this duo looks good to the ladies. Cheapie production and uninspired buffoonery. **77m/B VHS, DVD,** Bud Abbott, Lou Costello, Mari Blanchard, Robert Paige, Martha Hyer, Horace McMahon, Jack Kruschen, Anita Ekberg, Jean Willes, Joe (Joseph) Kirk, Jackie Loughery, James Flavin; **W:** John Grant, D.D. Beauchamp; **C:** Clifford Stine; **M:** Joseph Gershenson.

Abbott and Costello in Hollywood 1945 Bud and Lou appear as a barber and porter of a high-class tonsorial parlor in Hollywood. A rather sarcastic look at backstage Hollywood, Abbott & Costello style. Ball makes a guest appearance. 111m/B VHS, DVD. Bud Abbott, Lou Costello, Frances Rafferty, Warner Anderson, Jean Porter, Robert Stanton, Mike Mazurki; **D:** S. Sylvan Simon; **M:** George Bassman.

Abbott and Costello in the Foreign Legion 1950 Fight promoters Jonesy and Max trail their runaway fighter to Algiers where they're tricked into joining the French Foreign Legion. They have to cope with a sadistic sergeant, a sexy spy, and still find their man. Most amusement comes from Lou's wild desert mirages. 80m/B VHS, DVD. Bud Abbott, Lou Costello, Walter Slezak, Patricia Medina, Douglass Dumbrille, Leon Belasco, Marc Lawrence, Tor Johnson; **D:** Charles Lamont; **W:** John Grant, Martin Ragaway, Leonard Stern; **C:** George Robinson.

Abbott and Costello Meet Captain Kidd 1952 With pirates led by Captain Kidd (Charles Laughton) on their trail, Abbott and Costello follow a treasure map. Bland A&C swashbuckler spoof with a disinterested Laughton impersonating the Kidd. One of the duo's few color films 70m/C VHS. Bud Abbott, Lou Costello, Charles Laughton, Hillary Brooke, Fran Warren, Bill (William) Shirley, Leif Erickson; **D:** Charles Lamont.

Abbott and Costello Meet Dr. Jekyll and Mr. Hyde 1952 Slim (Abbott) and Tubby (Costello) are a couple of cops sent to London, who become involved with crazy Dr. Jekyll (Karloff), who has transformed himself into Mr. Hyde via an experimental serum, and is terrorizing London. Naturally, he goes after the boys. A lame attempt at recapturing the success of "Abbott and Costello Meet Frankenstein" but Karloff is top-notch as always. 77m/B VHS, DVD. Bud Abbott, Lou Costello, Boris Karloff, Craig Stevens, Helen Westcott, Reginald Denny, John Dierkes, Marjorie Bennett, Lucille Lamar, Patti McKay; **D:** Charles Lamont; **W:** John Grant, Leo Loeb, Howard Dimsdale; **C:** George Robinson.

Abbott and Costello Meet the Invisible Man 1951 Abbott and Costello play newly graduated detectives who take on the murder case of a boxer (Franz) accused of killing his manager. Using a serum that makes people invisible, the boxer helps Costello in a prizefight that will frame the real killers, who killed the manager because the boxer refused to throw a fight. Great special effects and hilarious gags make this one of the best from the crazy duo. 82m/B VHS, DVD. Bud Abbott, Lou Costello, Nancy Guild, Adele Jergens, Sheldon Leonard, William Frawley, Gavin Muir, Arthur Franz, Syd Saylor, Bobby Barber; **D:** Charles Lamont; **W:** Frederic Rinaldo, John Grant, Robert Lees; **C:** George Robinson; **M:** Hans J. Salter.

Abbott and Costello Meet the Keystone Kops 1954 It's 1912 and the boys are bilked into buying a fake movie studio by a clever con man. When they find out they've been tricked, the duo head to Hollywood to track him down and find out the crook is trying to cheat Sennett's film company. Sennett himself trained A&C and the new Keystone Kops in their recreations of his silent screen routines. Good final chase sequence but the earlier work is tired. 79m/B VHS, DVD. Bud Abbott, Lou Costello, Fred Clark, Lynn Bari, Mack Sennett, Maxie "Slapsie" Rosenbloom, Frank Wilcox, Harold Goodwin; **D:** Charles Lamont; **W:** John Grant; **C:** Reggie Lanning; **M:** Joseph Gershenson.

Abbott and Costello Meet the Killer, Boris Karloff 1949 Unremarkable Abbott and Costello murder mystery. Karloff plays a psychic who tries to frame Lou for murder. Pleasant enough but not one of their best. 84m/B VHS, DVD. Bud Abbott, Lou Costello, Boris Karloff, Lenore Aubert, Gar Moore, Donna (Dona Martel) Martell, Alan Mowbray, James Flavin, Roland Winters, Nicholas Joy, Mikel Conrad, Morgan Farley, Victoria Horne; **D:** Charles T. Barton; **W:** John Grant, Hugh Wedlock Jr., Howard Snyder; **C:** Charles Van Enger; **M:** Milton Schwarzwald.

Abbott and Costello Meet the Mummy 1955 Okay comedy from the duo has them stranded in Egypt with a valuable medallion which will lead to secret treasure and the mummy who guards the tomb. The last of the films the twosome made for Universal. 90m/B VHS, DVD. Bud Abbott, Lou Costello, Marie Windsor, Michael Ansara, Dan Seymour, Kurt Katch, Richard Deacon, Mel Welles, Edwin Parker, Richard Karlan, George Khoury; **D:** Charles Lamont; **W:** John Grant; **C:** George Robinson; **M:** Joseph Gershenson, Hans J. Salter.

ABC Stage 67: Truman Capote's A Christmas Memory 1966 *Truman Capote's A Christmas Memory; A Christmas Memory* 1966 Capote narrates his remembered childhood experience of baking dozens of fruitcakes for friends at Christmas with his elderly distant cousin, Miss Sook Faulk (Page). She is quiet, lovely, and true in this sensitive portrait of why we give and what we have to be thankful for. Adapted from a short story by Capote and Eleanor Perry. 51m/B VHS. Geraldine Page, Donnie Melvin; **D:** Frank Perry; **W:** Truman Capote; **Nar:** Truman Capote. TV

Abducted 1986 (PG) A woman jogger is abducted by a crazed mountain man in the Canadian Rockies. Weird and unbelievably tedious film is nevertheless highlighted by some spectacular wilderness footage of the Vancouver area, a travelogue bonus for those in the mood. 87m/C VHS. CA Dan Haggerty, Roberta Weiss, Lawrence King Phillips; **D:** Boon Collins.

Abducted 2: The Reunion 1994 (R) Three girlfriends decide to go camping for their reunion trip. Oops—psycho mountain man alert! 91m/C VHS. Dan Haggerty, Jan-Michael Vincent, Donna Jason, Raquel Bianca, Debbie Rochon, Lawrence King; **D:** Boon Collins; **W:** Boon Collins; **C:** Danny Nowak.

Abduction 1975 (R) Exploitative account of the Patty Hearst kidnapping, loosely adapted from the Harrison James novel written before the kidnapping. A young woman from a wealthy capitalist family is kidnapped by black radicals and held for an unusual ransom. Oh, and she tangles with lesbians, too. 100m/C VHS. Judith-Marie Bergan, David Pendleton, Gregory Rozakis, Leif Erickson, Dorothy Malone, Lawrence Tierney; **D:** Joseph Zito.

The Abduction 1996 Fact-based melodrama about Kate Olavsky (Principal) and her abusive marriage to cop Paul (Hays). Afraid to press charges, she finally manages to leave him and get on with her life. But Paul refuses to let Kate go, constantly hounding her, until he takes Kate hostage at gunpoint. 91m/C VHS, DVD. Victoria Principal, Robert Hays, Christopher Lawford, William Greenblatt; **D:** Larry Peerce; **M:** Marshall Goldberg; **C:** Tony Imi; **W:** Fred Mollin. CABLE

The Abduction of Allison Tate 1992 (R) Rich developer takes land belonging to a group of Native Americans. Three young tribe members retaliate by kidnapping the developer's daughter. But when their plans go awry and one of the trio is killed, Allison finds herself sympathizing more with them than with her father's ambitions. 95m/C VHS. Leslie Hope, Bernie (Bernard) White; **D:** Paul Leder.

The Abduction of Kari Swenson 1987 An account of the true-life (it really happened) kidnapping of Olympic biathalon hopeful Swensen by a pair of mischievous Montana mountain men with matrimony in mind. As the put-upon Kari, Pollan exceeds script expectations in this exercise in stress avoidance. 100m/C VHS. Joe Don Baker, M. Emmet Walsh, Ronny Cox, Michael Bowen, Geoffrey Blake, Dorothy Fielding, Tracy Pollan; **D:** Stephen Gyllenhaal. TV

Abduction of St. Anne 1975 An almost interesting mystical thriller about a detective and a bishop trying to track down a gangster's daughter, who may have nifty supernatural healing powers the Church would be very interested in having documented. 78m/C VHS. Robert Wagner, E.G. Marshall, William Windom, Lloyd Nolan; **D:** Harry Falk; **M:** George Duning. TV

The Abductors 1972 (R) Caffaro's super-agent takes on international white slavery, a worthy target for any exploitation effort. While the novelty is a tough and intelligent on-screen heroine, sufficient sleaze and violence bring it all down to the proper level of swampland video. Sequel to the never-to-be-forgotten "Ginger." 90m/C VHS, DVD. Cheri Caffaro, William Grannel, Richard Smedley, Patrick Wright, Laurie Rose, Jeramie Rain; **D:** Don Schain; **W:** Don Schain; **C:** R. Kent Evans; **M:** Robert G. Orpin.

Abdulla the Great *Abdullah's Harem* 1956 A dissolute Middle Eastern monarch falls for a model, who spurns him for an army officer. While distracted by these royal shenanigans, the king is blissfully unaware of his subjects' disaffection—until they revolt. Dares to lampoon Egypt's dead King Farouk, going against conventional Hollywood wisdom ("Farouk in film is boxoffice poison"). 89m/C VHS. GB Gregory Ratoff, Kay Kendall, Sydney Chaplin, Alexander D'Arcy; **D:** Gregory Ratoff; **C:** Lee Garmes; **M:** Georges Auric.

Abe Lincoln in Illinois 1940 Massey considered this not only his finest film but a part he was "born to play." Correct on both counts, this Hollywood biography follows Lincoln from his log cabin days to his departure for the White House. The Lincoln-Douglass debate scene and Massey's post-presidential election farewell to the citizens of Illinois are nothing short of brilliant. Written by Sherwood from his Pulitzer-Prize winning play. Contrasted with the well-known "Young Mr. Lincoln" (Henry Fonda), its relative anonymity is perplexing. 110m/B VHS. Raymond Massey, Gene Lockhart, Ruth Gordon, Mary Howard, Dorothy Tree, Harvey Stephens, Minor Watson, Alan Baxter, Howard da Silva, Maurice Murphy, Clem Bevans, Herbert Rudley; **D:** John Cromwell; **W:** Robert Sherwood; **C:** James Wong Howe; **M:** Roy Webb.

The Abe Lincoln of Ninth Avenue *Streets of New York* 1939 All-American tale of a poor young man making good in New York. His role model is Abraham Lincoln. Cooper is exceptional, supported by effective performances by the rest of the cast. 68m/B VHS, DVD. Jackie Cooper, Martin Spelling, Marjorie Reynolds, Dick Purcell, George Cleveland, George Irving; **D:** William Nigh.

Aberdeen 2000 Ambitious London attorney Kaisa (Headey) gets a call from her terminally ill mother Helen (Rampling), who lives in Aberdeen, Scotland. Helen wants Kaisa to travel to Oslo and retrieve Tomas (Skargard), her alcoholic and estranged father, so Helen and he can have a deathbed reconciliation. Assertive Kaisa tracks the drunk down and makes him come with her on a nightmare trip back. Lead performances are utterly unsentimental. 103m/C VHS, DVD. NO GB Stellan Skarsgard, Lena Headey, Ian Hart, Charlotte Rampling; **D:** Hans Petter Moland; **W:** Hans Petter Moland, Kristin Amundsen; **C:** Philip Ogaard; **M:** Zbigniew Preisner.

Aberration 1997 (R) Amy (Gidley) has traveled to her parents remote cabin and notices a lizard infestation. So she heads to the store for some exterminating equipment and meets biologist Marshall (Bossell), who studies eco-abnormalities. Seems the lizards are vicious mutants who eat Amy's cat and are working their way up the food chain. Doesn't offer many scares. 93m/C VHS. AU GB Pamela Gidley, Simon Bossell, Valery (Valeri Nikolayev) Nikolaev; **D:** Tim Boxell; **W:** Darrin Oura, Scott Lew; **C:** Allen Guilford. VIDEO

Abigail's Party 1977 Steadman plays the hostess for a very ill-fated dinner party, especially when she realizes her husband has just died on her new carpet. 105m/C VHS, DVD. GB Alison Steadman; **D:** Mike Leigh. VIDEO

Abilene Town 1946 In a post-Civil War Kansas town far from the freeway, Scott is the tough marshal trying to calm the conflict between cattlemen and homesteaders. He also finds time to participate in a romantic triangle with dance hall vixen Dvorak and heart-of-gold Fleming. Snappy pace keeps it interesting. Based on a novel by Ernest Haycox. 90m/B VHS, DVD. Randolph Scott, Ann Dvorak, Edgar Buchanan, Rhonda Fleming, Lloyd Bridges; **D:** Edwin L. Marin; **W:** Harold Shumate; **C:** Archie Stout.

Ablaze 2000 (R) Greedy developer Wendell Mays (Arnold) arranges for his industrial refinery to be torched and the ensuing fire and explosion taxes both the fire fighters and the hospital that has to deal with the casualties. Wynorski directs under the pseudonym Jay Andrews. 97m/C VHS, DVD. John Bradley, Tom Arnold, Michael Dudikoff, Ice-T, Amanda Pays, Cathy Lee Crosby, Pat Harrington, Edward Albert, Mary Jo Catlett, Richard Biggs; **D:** Jim Wynorski; **W:** Steve Latshaw; **C:** Andrea V. Rossotto; **M:** Neal Acree. VIDEO

The Abominable Dr. Phibes *Dr. Phibes; The Curse of Dr. Phibes* 1971 (PG) After being disfigured in a freak car accident that killed his wife, an evil genius decides that the members of a surgical team let his wife die and shall each perish by a different biblical plague. High camp with the veteran cast in top form. 90m/C VHS, DVD. GB Vincent Price, Joseph Cotten, Hugh Griffith, Terry-Thomas, Virginia North, Susan Travers, Alex Scott, Caroline Munro, Peter Jeffrey, Peter Gilmore, Edward Burnham, Sean Bury, David Hutcheson, Maurice Kaufmann, Charles Farrell; **D:** Robert Fuest; **W:** William Goldstein, James Whiton; **C:** Norman Warwick; **M:** Basil Kirchin, Jack Nathan.

The Abominable Snowman *The Abominable Snowman of the Himalayas* 1957 Corny Hammer horror about adventurer Tom Friend (Tucker), Dr. John Rollason (Cushing), and guide Ed Shelley (Brown) searching for the legendary Yeti. The harsh conditions cause the explorers to lose their grip begins to suspect that the creatures practice mind control. 91m/B VHS, DVD. GB Peter Cushing, Forrest Tucker, Robert Brown, Richard Wattis, Maureen Connell; **D:** Val Guest; **W:** Nigel Kneale; **C:** Arthur Grant; **M:** Humphrey Searle.

The Abomination 1988 (R) After a 5,000-year-old creature possesses him during a nightmare, a boy goes on an eye-gouging frenzy. Only the audience gets hurt. 100m/C VHS. Van Connery, Victoria Chaney, Gaye Bottoms, Suzy Meyer, Jude Johnson, Blue Thompson, Scott Davis; **D:** Max Raven.

About a Boy 2002 (PG-13) After "Bridget Jones's Diary," Grant continues to take on the role of charming cad. This time, he's Will, a 38-year-old bachelor who doesn't work thanks to a legacy from his father and has never made a lasting emotional commitment to anyone.

Will's latest dating scheme is to pretend to be a single parent and join support groups so he can hit on the single mums. This is how he meets Marcus (Hoult), the 12-year-old misfit son of the seriously depressed Fiona (Collette). Will likes Marcus despite himself and becomes his confidante. And he finds a romance with single mum Rachel (Weitz) but that's almost besides the point. Adapted from the novel by Nick Hornby. **100m/C VHS, DVD, US GB** Hugh Grant, Rachel Weisz, Toni Collette, Nicholas Hoult, Isabel Brook, Victoria Smurfit; **D:** Chris Weitz, Paul Weitz; **C:** Remi Adefarasin; **M:** Badly Drawn Boy.

About Adam ★★ 2000 (R) Adam (Townsend) is a duplicitous Dublin charmer who worms his way into the Owens family. Waitress Lucy (Hudson) falls in love with Adam and takes him to meet her family and before anyone realizes what's happening, Adam seduces both her sisters, telling each woman exactly what she needs to hear. And no one holds a grudge! **99m/C VHS, DVD, IR GB** Stuart Townsend, Kate Hudson, Frances O'Connor, Charlotte Bradley, Rosaleen Linehan, Brendan F. Dempsey, Alan Maher, Tommy Tiernan, Cathleen Bradley; **C:** Bruno de Keyzer. **M:** Adrian Johnston.

About Last Night... ★★★½ 1986 (R) Semi-realistic comedy-drama which explores the ups and downs of one couple's (Lowe, Moore) relationship. Mostly quality performances, especially Perkins, and Belushi as friends of the young lovers. Based on David Mamet's play "Sexual Perversity in Chicago," but considerably softened so that more people would buy tickets at the box office. the film acts as a historical view of contemporary mating rituals before the onset of the AIDS crisis. **113m/C VHS, DVD,** Rob Lowe, Demi Moore, Elizabeth Perkins, James Belushi, George DiCenzo, Robin Thomas, Michael Alldredge; **D:** Edward Zwick; **W:** Tim Kazurinsky, Denise DeClue; **C:** Andrew Dintenfass; **M:** Miles Goodman.

About Schmidt ★★★ 2002 (R) Jack's back and playing against type as Warren Schmict, a man left with virtually no identy once he retires from his home insurance job. Left only with time to reflect on a meaningless life, he questions everything he once took for granted, including Helen (Squibb), his wife of 42 years. The day after his retirement, his couple shares breakfast before Helen suddenly dies. With nothing left to lose, Schmic hits the road in a Winnebago to visit his daughter and try to find some meaning in his poorly thought-out life. In Denver, he meets and immediately hates his daughter's cheesy salesman fiance Randall (Mulroney), while Randall's flowsy mother Roberta (Bates) tries to seduce the lonely introvert in a hot tuz. Combines humor, pathos, and hope with a first rate performance by Nicholson, who quashes any of his characteristic animation. Davis, excellent. **124m/C VHS, DVD, US** Jack Nicholson, Hope Davis, Dermot Mulroney, Kathy Bates, Len Carou, Howard Hesseman, June Squibb; **D:** Alexander Payne; **W:** Alexander Payne, Jim Taylor; **C:** James Gemior; **M:** Rolfe Kent. Golden Globes '03: Actor—Drama; Screenplay; L.A. Film Critics '02: Actor (Nicholson); Film, Screenplay; Natl. Bd. of Review '02: Support. Actress (Bates).

Above and Beyond ★★★ 1953 Good performance by Taylor as Col. Paul Tibbets, the man who piloted the Enola Gay, which dropped the atomic bomb on Hiroshima. Focuses on the secrecy of the mission and the strain this puts on Tibbets' marriage. Exciting action sequences at the mission itself. **122m/B VHS,** Robert Taylor, Eleanor Parker, James Whitmore, Larry Keating, Larry Gates, Robert Burton, Jim Backus, Marilyn Erskine, Steve (Stephen) Dunne, John Pickard, Hayden Rorke, Lawrence (Larry) Dobkin, Jack Raine, Jeff Richards, Barbara Ruick, Harlan Warde, John Close, Frank Gerstle, Dabbs Greer, Ewing Mitchell, Gregory Walcott, John Baer, Jonathon Cott, Dick Simmons, John McKee, G. Pat Collins, John Hadlee, Mack Williams, Dorothy Kennedy; **D:** Melvin Frank, Norman Panama, Beirne Lay Jr.; **C:** Ray June; **M:** Hugo Friedhofer.

Above Suspicion ★★ 1943 MacMurray and Crawford are American honeymooners (poor Fred!) asked to assist an international intelligence organization. They engage the Nazis in a tense battle of wits. Well-made and engaging. **91m/B VHS,** Joan Crawford, Fred MacMurray, Conrad Veidt, Basil Rathbone, Reginald Owen, Richard Ainley, Cecil Cunningham; **D:** Richard Thorpe; **W:** Patricia Coleman; **C:** Robert Planck; **M:** Bronislau Kaper.

Above Suspicion ★★ 1995 (R) Dempsey. Cain (Reeve) seems to be the perfect cop, as well as a loving husband and father and a mentor to his younger brother. But when Cain is paralyzed by a drug dealer's bullet, he begins to notice just how sexy his wife (Cattrall) and brother are. There's adultery, there's murder, and there's the cop who just may be a cold-blooded killer. Unnervingly, Reeve plays a paraplegic in the last movie he made before his own paralyzing riding accident. **92m/C VHS, DVD,** Christopher Reeve, Kim Cattrall, Joe Mantegna, Edward Kerr; **D:** Steven Schachter. C.A.B.L.E.

Above Suspicion ★★ 2000 (R) Stockton (Bakula) seems like the perfect family man but his wife Lisa (Sciorra) starts becoming suspicious of his past—fearing that he's a killer. **99m/C VHS, DVD,** Scott Bakula, Annabella Sciorra, George Dzundza, Ed Asner, Jack Blessing; **D:** Steven La Rocque.

Above the Law ★★ 1988 (R) In his debut, Seagal does his wooden best to portray a tough Chicago police detective. Unfortunately, the FBI has ordered him to back off one of the state. The reasons are almost as complex as Seagal's character, and like most details of the flick, stupid. However, people don't watch these movies for the acting or the plot, but for the fight scenes, which are well-choreographed and violent. Watch it with someone you love. **99m/C VHS, DVD,** Steven Seagal, Pam Grier, Henry Silva, Sharon Stone, Ron Dean, Daniel Faraldo, Chelcie Ross, Thalmus Rasulala, Michael Rooker; **D:** Andrew Davis; **W:** Andrew Davis, Steven Pressfield; **C:** Robert Steadman; **M:** David Michael Frank.

Above the Rim ★★½ 1994 (R) Vulgar, violent hoopster drama about a fiercely competitive inner-city playground game. Kyle-Lee Watson (Martin), a self-involved high school star raised by a saintly single mom (Pinkins), is torn between the lure of the streets and his college recruiting chances. His odds aren't made any easier by homeboy hustler Birdie (Shakur), who wants to improve his chances of making money on the local games by making sure Watson plays for his team. Energetic b-ball sequences, strong performances lose impact amid formulaic melodrama and the usual obscenities. Debut for director Pollack. **97m/C VHS, DVD,** Duane Martin, Tupac Shakur, Leon, Marlon Wayans, Tonya Pinkins, Bernie Mac; **D:** Jeff Pollack; **W:** Jeff Pollack, Barry Michael Cooper; **M:** Marcus Miller.

Above Us the Waves ★★ 1956 During WWII, the British navy immobilizes a huge German battleship off the coast of Norway. Effectively dramatizes the British naval preparations for what seemed a suicidal mission: using midget submarines to plant underwater explosives on the hull of the German vessel and detonating them before the Germans could detect the danger. **92m/C VHS, GB** John Mills, John Gregson, Donald Sinden, James Robertson Justice, Lee Patterson, Lyndon Brook, Anthony Newley; **D:** Ralph Thomas.

Abraham ★★½ 1994 Biblical epic chronicling the Old Testament story of humble shepherd Abraham (Harris), who's commanded by God to lead his family into the promised land of Canaan. Among his family's many trials will be God's command that Abraham sacrifice his son Isaac as a test of faith and obedience. Filmed on location in Morocco with a commanding performance by Harris that somewhat redeems the film's dullness. **175m/C VHS.** Richard Harris, Barbara Hershey, Maximilian Schell, Vittorio Gassman, Carolina Rosi, Gottfried John, Kevin McNally; **D:** Joseph Sargent; **W:** Robert McKee; **C:** Raffaele Mertes; **M:** Ennio Morricone.

Abraham Lincoln ★★½ 1930 Griffith's first talking movie takes Abraham Lincoln from his birth through his assassination. This restored version includes the original slavery sequences which were believed to be lost, but obviously were not. Musical score included. **97m/B VHS, DVD,** Walter Huston, Una Merkel, Kay Hammond, E. Alyn (Fred) Warren, Hooart Bosworth, Henry B. Walthall, Russell Simpson, Ian Keith, Frank Campeau; **D:** D.W. Griffith; **C:** Karl Struss.

Abraham's Valley ★★ Vale Abraao Valley of Abraham 1993 Beautiful Ema (Silveira) is forced into a wealthy marriage to a friend of her father's and they move to the vineyards of Abraham's Valley where the bride knows no one. Unhappy, Ema refuses to submit to her husband and decides to take a lover of her own. Based on the novel by Augustina Bessa-Luis. Portuguese with subtitles. **180m/C VHS, DVD, PT** Leonor Silveira, Luis Miguel Cintra, Diogo Doria, Ruy de Carvalho, Luis Lima Barreto, Micheline Larpin, Cecile Sanz de Alba, Isabel Ruth; **D:** Manoel de Oliveira; **W:** Manoel de Oliveira; **C:** Mario Barroso.

Abraxas: Guardian of the Universe ★½ 1990 (R) Good space cop versus bad space cop with an ecological twist. Good-guy Abraxas (Ventura) has the task of stopping planets from destroying their environments and fighting senseless wars. His ex-partner Secundas (Ole-Thorsen) has his own mission, seeking to rule Earth as the battleground. Also available in an edited PG-13 version. **90m/C VHS, DVD,** Jesse Ventura, Sven-Ole Thorsen, Marjorie Bransfield, Ken Quinn, Marilyn Ightstone, Moses Znaimer, Layne Coleman, Sonja Belliveau, James Belushi; **D:** Damian Lee; **W:** Damian Lee; **C:** Curtis Petersen.

Abroad with Two Yanks ★★ 1944 Two Marine buddies on furlough exhibit slapstick tendencies while competing for the same girl. Along the way a big chase ensues with the two soldiers in drag. Typical wartime shenanigans likely to incite only weak chuckling if inspired snoozing. **81m/B VHS,** William Bendix, Dennis O'Keefe, Helen Walker, John Loder, George Cleveland, Janet Lambert, James Flavin, Arthur Hunnicutt; **D:** Allan Dwan.

Absence of Malice ★★½ 1981 (PG) High-minded story about the harm that the news media can inflict. Field is the earnest reporter who, after being fed some facts by an unscrupulous federal investigator, writes a story implicating Newman in a murder he didn't commit. Field hides behind journalistic confidentiality and privilege to put off the outraged Newman, who loses a friend to suicide during the debacle. Interesting performances by Field and Newman. **116m/C VHS, DVD,** Paul Newman, Sally Field, Bob Balaban, Melinda Dillon, Luther Adler, Barry Primus, Josef Sommer, John Harkins, Don Hood, Wilford Brimley; **D:** Sydney Pollack; **W:** Kurt Luedtke; **C:** Owen Roizman; **M:** Dave Grusin.

Absence of the Good ★★ 1999 (R) Homicide detective Caleb Barnes (Baldwin) is mourning the accidental death of his only child while investigating a series of murders in Salt Lake City. He's under pressure to solve the case, even as his home life is disintegrating, and Caleb's investigation leads to a tyrannical priest over the edge of sanity. As a result, bad things (including murder) occur. Burton's death, maybe due to something interesting in sadistic character study. Not released in the U.S. until 1988 following. **95m/C VHS, DVD,** Stephen Baldwin, Tyne Daly, Allen (Goorwitz) Garfield, Robert Knepper; **D:** John Flynn; **W:** James Reid.

The Absent-Minded Professor ★★★½ 1961 Classic dumb Disney fantasy of the era. A professor accidentally invents an anti-gravity substance called flubber, causing inanimate objects and people to become airborne. Great sequence of the losing school basketball team taking advantage of flubber during a game. MacMurray is convincing as the absent-minded genius in this newly colored version. Followed by "Son of Flubber." **97m/C VHS, DVD,** Fred MacMurray, Nancy Olson, Keenan Wynn, Tommy Kirk, Leon Ames, Ed Wynn, Edward Andrews, Wally Brown, Wendell Holmes; **D:** Robert Stevenson; **W:** Bill Walsh; **C:** Edward Colman; **M:** George Bruns.

Absent Without Leave ★★½ 1996 Ed (McLachlan) marries his pregnant girlfriend Daisy (Hobbs) in 1942 before joining the army. When Daisy miscarries, Ed pledges to take her home even though it means leaving the army without permission. As the newlyweds travel across the New Zealand countryside, they struggle with the new demands of their relationship. **104m/C VHS, NZ** Craig McLachlan, Katrina Hobbs; **D:** John Lang.

Absolute Beginners ★★ 1986 (PG) Fervently stylish camp musical exploring the lives of British teenagers in the 1950s never gets untracked, although MTV video moments fill out a spare plotline. Based on a novel by Colin MacInnes. "Absolute Beginners." That's Motivation; Volare; Killer Blow; Have You Ever Been Blue?; Quiet Life; Having It All; Selling Out; Va Va Voom. **107m/C VHS, DVD, GB** David Bowie, Ray Davies, Mandy Rice-Davies, James Fox, Eddie O'Connell, Patsy Kensit, Anita Morris, Sade, Sandie Shaw, Julien Temple; **W:** Richard Burridge, Don MacPherson; **C:** Oliver Stapleton.

Absolute Power ★★½ 1997 (R) Eastwood is "In the Line of Fire," (against the very agents he previously glorified) as an expert thief being pursued by rogue Secret Service men in this fast-paced thriller. While lifting a Washington official's jewels, Luther (Eastwood) inadvertently witnesses a murder committed by none other than U.S. President Richmond (Hackman) and his goons. Immediately, a cover-up is organized by his unbalanced chief-of-staff (Davis) and Luther becomes the prime suspect. Harris gives his usual solid performance as the homicide detective. Eastwood's simple directorial style keeps up the suspense and propels the film steadily forward, alongside a generally solid plot that gets a bit improbable near the end. Baser, son the novel by David Baldacci. **120m/C VHS, DVD,** Clint Eastwood, Gene Hackman, Ed Harris, Laura Linney, Judy Davis, Scott Glenn, Dennis Haysbert, E.G. Marshall, Melora Hardin; **D:** Clint Eastwood; **W:** William Goldman; **C:** Jack N. Green; **M:** Lennie Niehaus.

Absolutely Fabulous: The Last Shout ★★ 1996 The first TV movie from the British comedy series finds Edina (Saunders) selling her fashion PR business after a near-death experience and doing some soul-searching. AbFab style, which involves shopping, travel, and champagne. Naturally, Patsy (Lumley) goes along for the ride. The interesting character designer Christian LaCroix even has a cameo. **99m/C VHS, GB** Jennifer Saunders, Joanna Lumley; Cameos: Marianne Faithfull. TV

Absolution ★★ 1981 (R) Two English boys trapped in a Catholic boarding school conspire to drive a tyrannical priest written in this student filmmaker. **95m/C VHS, DVD, GB** Richard Burton, Dominic Guard, Dai Bradley, Andrew Burton, Billy Connolly, Willoughby Gray, Preston Lockwood, James Ottaway, Brook Williams, Jon Plowman, Robin Soans, Trevor Martin; **D:** Anthony Page; **W:** Anthony Shaffer; **C:** John Coquillon; **M:** Stanley Myers.

Abuse ★★ 1982 Fourteen-year-old Tommy (Stargte) is the victim of child abuse. After a beating causes convulsions, his parents rush him to a New York hospital where the intern on duty phones his student filmmaker friend Larry (Ryder), who's doing a documentary on child abuse as his master thesis. When Tommy learns that Larry is also gay, he agrees to discuss his problems but their continuing contact leads the duo to fall in love and Larry to worry about exploiting Tommy's affections. Interspersed with their story are interviews and photos of child abuse victims and their abusers. Not necessarily for the squeamish. **33m/B VHS,** Richard Ryder...

der, Raphael Sbarge; **D:** Arthur J. Bressan Jr.; **W:** Arthur J. Bressan Jr.; **C:** Douglas Dickinson; **M:** Shawn Phillips.

The Abyss ♂♂♂ 1989 (PG-13) Underwater sci-fi adventure about a team of oil-drilling divers pressed into service by the navy to locate and disarm an inoperative nuclear submarine. A high-tech thriller with fab footage underwater and pulsating score. **140m/C VHS, DVD.** Ed Harris, Mary Elizabeth Mastrantonio, Todd Graff, Michael Biehn, John Bedford Lloyd, J.C. Quinn, Leo Burmester, Kidd Brewer Jr., Kimberly Scott, Adam Nelson, George Robert Kirk, Chris Elliott, Jimmie Ray Weeks; **D:** James Cameron; **W:** James Cameron; **C:** Mikael Salomon; **M:** Alan Silvestri. Oscars '89: Visual FX.

Acapulco Gold ♂♪½ 1978 (PG) Mockumentary follows Gortner as he's framed for drug smuggling and becomes entangled in a Hawaiian drug deal. Not worth the time it'll take to track down a copy. **105m/C DVD.** Marjoe Gortner, Robert Lansing, Ed Nelson, John Harkins, Lawrence Casey, Phil Hoover; **D:** Burt Brinckerhoff; **W:** Don Enright; **C:** Robert Steadman; **M:** Craig Safan.

Accatone! ♂♂♂ 1961 Accatone (Citti), a failure as a pimp, tries his luck as a thief. Hailed as a return to Italian neorealism, this is a gritty, despairing, and dark look at the lives of the street people of Rome. Pasolini's first outing, adapted by the director from his novel, "A Violent Life." Pasolini served as mentor to Bernardo Bertolucci, listed in the credits as an assistant director. **116m/B VHS, DVD. IT** Franco Citti, Franca Pasut, Roberto Scaringelli, Silvana Corsini, Paolo Guidi, Adriana Asti; **D:** Pier Paolo Pasolini; **W:** Pier Paolo Pasolini; **C:** Tonino Delli Colli.

Acceptable Risk ♂♂ 2001 Pharmaceutical scientist Edward Wells (Lowe) discovers a strange fungus in a walled-in part of his basement. He takes it into the lab, finds unusual healing properties in the substance, and immediately begins to test it on himself. At first, he feels superhuman, but monstrous side effects quickly surface. There is some suspense in this TV movie, but the inconsistent story and poor performances are hard to get past. **92m/C DVD.** Chad Lowe, Kelly Rutherford, Sean Patrick Flanery, Patty McCormack, Danielle von Zerneck; **D:** William A. Graham; **W:** Michael J. Murray; **C:** Eyal Gordin. **TV**

Acceptable Risks ♂♪½ 1986 (R) Toxic disaster strikes when a plant manager is ordered to cut costs and sacrifice safety at the Citichem plant. Predictable plot stars Dennehy as the plant manager who risks all and fights politicians to reinstate the safety standards. Meanwhile, Tyson is the city manager who tries to warn the town of a possible chemical accident that could have devastating effects on the community. TV drama that shamelessly preys on audience fears. **97m/C VHS.** Brian Dennehy, Cicely Tyson, Kenneth McMillan, Christine Ebersole, Beah Richards, Richard Gilliland; **D:** Rick Wallace. **TV**

Accepted ♂♪½ 2006 (PG-13) Flunky campus farce about what to do after getting one too many thin envelopes from college admissions offices: create your own university. Bartleby (Long) and his buds pretend to matriculate at the fictitious South Harmon Institute of Technology. So-so jokes about beer and babes and that oh-so-hilarious acronym abound, until the tale attempts to take an unexpectedly touching turn. Ultimately lands on the failing side of the campus-movie bell curve (with "Animal House" and "Back to School" at the top of the class). **92m/C DVD.** Justin Long, Blake Lively, Mark Derwin, Anthony Heald, Adam Herschman, Jonah Hill, Columbus Short, Maria Thayer, Lewis Black, Ann Cusack, Travis Van Winkle, Hannah Marks; **D:** Steve Pink; **W:** Mark Perez, Adam Cooper, Bill Collage; **C:** Matthew F. Leonetti; **M:** David Schommer.

Access Code ♂♪ 1984 Government agents attempt to uncover a private organization that has gained control of nuclear weapons for the purpose of world domination. A ragged patchwork of disconnected scenes meant to test the virtue of patience. **90m/C VHS.** Martin Landau, Michael Ansara, MacDonald Carey; **D:** Mark Sobel.

Accident ♂♂♂ 1967 A tangled web of guilt, remorse, humor and thwarted sexuality is unravelled against the background of the English countryside in this complex story of an Oxford love triangle. An inside view of English repression at the university level adapted for the screen by Pinter from the novel by Nicholas Mosley. Long-winded but occasionally engrossing character study with interesting performances. **100m/C VHS, DVD. GB** Dirk Bogarde, Michael York, Stanley Baker, Jacqueline Sassard, Delphine Seyrig, Alexander Knox, Vivien Merchant, Freddie Jones, Harold Pinter; **D:** Joseph Losey; **W:** Harold Pinter; **C:** Gerry Fisher; **M:** John Dankworth. Cannes '67: Grand Jury Prize.

Accident ♂♪½ 1983 Skate for your life. A hockey game turns into a nightmare when the roof over the arena collapses under the weight of too much ice and snow. One of the few hockey disaster films. **104m/C VHS.** Terence Kelly, Fiona Reid, Frank Perry; **D:** Donald Brittain.

The Accidental Husband 2008 (PG-13) Easygoing New York firefighter Patrick Sullivan (Morgan) thinks his engagement to Sophia (Machado) is going fine, but then she seeks couples advice from uptight radio host Dr. Emma Lloyd (Thurman) and gets the idea that romantic love is not a basis for marriage. So the engagement is off. Patrick wants revenge on the meddler and plays a prank that gets him "accidentally" hitched to the no-nonsense doc, which is a big problem for HER fiance, Richard (Firth). Not yet reviewed. **90m/C** Uma Thurman, Jeffrey Dean Morgan, Colin Firth, Justina Machado, Sam Shepard, Lindsay Sloane, Isabella Rossellini; **D:** Griffin Dunne; **W:** Mimi Hare, Clare Naylor; **C:** William Rexer; **M:** Andrea Guerra.

Accidental Meeting ♂♪½ 1993 (R) A female version of "Strangers on a Train." Two women meet because of an auto accident and wind up talking about their lives. The main topic is men trouble and both "jokingly" plot to murder each other's man. Only, one woman does the deed and the other soon finds herself in the murderess' hit list. **91m/C VHS.** Linda Gray, Linda Purl, Leigh McCloskey, David Hayward, Ernie Lively, Leigh McCord; **D:** Michael Zinberg; **W:** Pete Best; Christopher Homer.

The Accidental Spy ♂♂½ 1993 2001 (R) Salesman Bei (Chan) longs for some excitement in his life but gets more than anticipated when he foils the plans of two bank robbers. The resulting publicity leads Bei to discover that he's the long-lost son of a wealthy Korean businessman who also turns out to be a spy and Bei decides to join the family profession. **87m/ C VHS, DVD. HK** Jackie Chan, Eric Tsang, Vivian Hsu, Alfred Cheung, Min-jeong Kim, Hsing-kuo Wu; **D:** Teddy Chen; **W:** Ivy Ho; **C:** Wing-Hung Wong; **M:** Peter Kam.

The Accidental Tourist ♂♂♂½ 1988 (PG) A bittersweet and subtle story, adapted faithfully from Anne Tyler's novel, of an introverted, grieving man who learns to love again. After meeting an unconventional woman. After his son's death and subsequent separation from wife Turner, Macon Leary (Hurt) avoids emotional confrontation, burying himself in routines with the aid of his obsessive-compulsive siblings. Kooky dog-trainer Muriel Pritchett (an exuberant Davis) wins his attention, but not without struggle. Hurt effectively uses small gestures to describe Macon's emotional journey, while Davis grabs hearts with her open performance. Outstanding supporting cast. **121m/C VHS, DVD.** William Hurt, Geena Davis, Kathleen Turner, Ed Begley Jr., David Ogden Stiers, Bill Pullman, Amy Wright; **D:** Lawrence Kasdan; **W:** Lawrence Kasdan; **C:** John Bailey; **M:** John Williams. Oscars '88: Support. Actress (Davis); N.Y. Film Critics '88: Film.

Accidents ♂♪ 1989 (R) A scientist discovers that his invention has been stolen and is going to be used to cause worldwide havoc. He becomes concerned and spends the remainder of the movie trying to relieve himself of anxiety. **90m/C VHS.** Edward Albert, Leigh Taylor-Young, Jon Cypher; **D:** Gideon Amir.

The Accompanist ♂♂♂ 1993 (PG) L'Accompagnatrice 1993 Centers around a Parisian diva Irene's (Safonova) relationship with her talented pianist Sophie (Romane Bohringer), amidst the clamor of WWII Europe. Sophie impresses Irene with her musical abilities, and takes on additional work as her housekeeper. Meanwhile, Charles (Richard Bohringer), Irene's husband, schmoozes with the Nazis to line his own pockets while she helps the war effort by having an affair with a member of the resistance (Labarthe). Unfortunately, Sophie starts to resent living in Irene's shadow. Adapted from the novel by Nina Berberouva. The Bohringers are father and daughter. French with subtitles. **111m/C VHS. FR** Elena Safonova, Romane Bohringer, Richard Bohringer, Samuel Labarthe, Nelly Borgeaud, Julien Rassam; **D:** Claude Miller; **W:** Claude Miller, Luc Beraud, Claude Rich; **C:** Yves Angelo; **M:** Alain Jomy.

Accomplice ♂♪½ 1946 Plodding whodunit with Arlen as a shy, bookish private eye hired by his old flame to locate her missing husband. His investigations uncover several murders and long after the viewers have put 2 + 2 together, the P.I. smells a rat. The missing husband was a ruse to divert him from the real scam—a bank heist. Painfully low-level excitement. **66m/B VHS.** Richard Arlen, Veda Ann Borg, Tom Dugan, Francis Ford; **D:** Walter Colmes.

Accused ♂♂½ 1936 Married dancers Fairbanks and Del Rio are working in a Parisian revue when the show's sultry leading lady (Desmond) makes a pass at Fairbanks. Though he's turned her down, through a series of misunderstandings Del Rio believes the worst and the two women get into a vicious argument. When the star is found dead guess who gets the blame? Del Rio is lovely, Desmond is spiteful, and Fairbanks serves as a fine object of two women's affections. **83m/B VHS. GB** Douglas Fairbanks Jr., Dolores Del Rio, Florence Desmond, Basil Sydney, Athole Stewart, Esme Percy, Googie Withers, Cecil Humphreys; **D:** Thornton Freeland.

The Accused ♂♂♂ 1948 (R) Provocative treatment of a true story involving a young woman gang raped in a bar while onlookers cheer. McGillis is the assistant district attorney who takes on the case and must contend with the victim's questionable past and a powerful lawyer hired by a wealthy defendant's parents. As the victim with a past, Foster gives an Oscar-winning performance that won raves for its strength and complexity. **110m/C VHS, DVD.** Jodie Foster, Kelly McGillis, Bernie Coulson, Leo Rossi, Ann Hearn, Carmen Argenziano, Steve Antin, Tom O'Brien, Peter Van Norden, Woody Brown; **D:** Jonathan Kaplan; **W:** Tom Topor; **C:** Ralf Bode; **M:** Brad Fiedel. Oscars '88: Actress (Foster); Golden Globes '89: Actress—Drama (Foster); Natl. Bd. of Review '88: Actress (Foster).

Ace Drummond ♂♂ 1936 The complete 13-chapter serial about a murder organization that tries to stop several countries from forming a worldwide clipper ship air service and government troubleshooter Ace Drummond who's out to stop them. **260m/B VHS.** John "Dusty" King, Jean Rogers, Noah Beery Jr.; **D:** Ford Beebe.

Ace High ♂♪½ 1968 Spaghetti western about a ruthless outlaw named Cat Stevens trying to save himself from the noose. Patterned after the famous Sergio Leone-Clint Eastwood westerns, with less of a budget and more camp tendencies. **120m/C VHS, DVD. IT** Eli Wallach, Terence Hill, Bud Spencer, Brock Peters, Kevin McCarthy; **D:** Giuseppe Colizzi.

Ace in the Hole ♂♂♂ The Big Carnival 1951 Moralist Wilder brilliantly captures a cynical media circus. Alcoholic SOB reporter Chuck Tatum (Douglas) is bored crazy working a podunk paper in New Mexico when he gets a big scoop. Unhappy Lorraine (Sterling) tells Tatum her husband Leo (Benedict) was searching for Indian artifacts and is now trapped in a cave-in. Tatum teams up with corrupt local sheriff Gus Kretzer (Teal) to delay rescue operations while poor Leo suffers for maximum exposure while the public come to gawk. Based on the Floyd Collins mining disaster of the 1920s. **111m/B DVD.** Kirk Douglas, Richard Benedict, Ray Teal, Jan Sterling, Bob Arthur, Porter Hall, Frank Cady, Gene Evans, Lewis Martin, Harry Harvey, Richard Gaines; **D:** Billy Wilder; **W:** Billy Wilder, Lesser Samuels, Walter Newman; **C:** Charles B(ryant) Lang Jr.; **M:** Hugo Friedhofer.

Ace of Aces ♂♂ 1933 An American sculptor is reviled, particularly by his girlfriend, when he does not join fellows in enlisting in what becomes WWI. Out to prove he's not lacking testosterone, he becomes a pilot in France, but is embittered by his experiences. Dated but well-acted war melodrama. **77m/B VHS.** Richard Dix, Elizabeth Allan, Theodore Newton, Ralph Bellamy, William Cagney, Frank Conroy; **D:** J. Walter Ruben; **C:** Henry Cronjager; **M:** Max Steiner.

Ace of Hearts ♂ 1985 A seedy story about a rich guy in the South Pacific who pays heavily to have himself killed. **90m/C VHS.** Mickey Rooney, Chris Robinson, Pilar Velasquez.

Ace Ventura: Pet Detective ♂♂ 1993 (PG-13) Shamelessly silly comedy casts human cartoon Carrey, he of the rubber limbs and spasmodic facial muscles, as Ace, the guy who'll find missing pets, big or small. When the Miami Dolphins' mascot 'Snowflake is kidnapped, he abandons his search for an albino pigeon to save the lost dolphin just in time for the Super Bowl. This is brain candy, running full throttle with juvenile humor, some charm, and the hyper-energetic Carrey, not to mention Young as the police chief with a secret. Critically trashed boxoffice smash catapulted Carrey into nearly instant stardom after seven seasons as the geeky white guy on "In Living Color." **87m/C VHS, DVD.** Jim Carrey, Courteney Cox, Sean Young, Tone Loc, Noble Willingham, Troy Evans, Udo Kier; **Cameos:** Dan Marino; **D:** Tom Shadyac; **W:** Tom Shadyac, Jack Bernstein, Jim Carrey; **C:** Julio Macat; **M:** Ira Newborn. Blockbuster '95: Male Newcomer, V. (Carrey), Comedy Actor, V. (Carrey).

Ace Ventura: When Nature Calls ♂♂ Ace Ventura Goes to Africa 1995 (PG-13) Ace is back on the case as the pet dick (Carrey) ventures to Africa to restore peace among rival tribes by finding an albino bat that's M.I.A. Plot is secondary, however, to multi-million dollar man Carrey's outrageous brand of physical comedy combined with his unique ability to deliver junior high level lines with pseudosuave savoir-faire. Contains only a handful of outstanding gags, the best with Ace and a mechanical rhino. Mainly for Carrey aficionados (of which there are many) and original "Ace" fans—the low-brow humor runs a bit thin by the end. **94m/C VHS, DVD.** Jim Carrey, Ian McNeice, Simon Callow, Maynard Eziashi, Bob Gunton, Sophie Okonedo, Tommy Davidson; **D:** Steve Oedekerk; **W:** Steve Oedekerk; **C:** Donald E. Thorin; **M:** Robert Folk. MTV Movie Awards '96: Male Perf. (Carrey), Comedic Perf. (Carrey); Blockbuster '96: Comedy Actor, T. (Carrey).

Aces and Eights ♂♂½ 1936 Gambler McCoy catches a fellow card-sharp cheating and the marshal runs the cheater out of town. When the cheater is murdered, the lawman suspects McCoy, who sets out to prove his innocence. Title refers to the "death hand" held by Wild Bill Hickok, killed while playing poker. Film opens with a shot of Hickok and a speech about gambler's luck. **62m/B VHS, DVD.** Tim McCoy, Jimmy Aubrey, Luana Walters, Wheeler Oakman, Earle Hodgins, Frank Glennon, Rex Lease, Joseph Girard, John Merton; **D:** Sam Newfield.

Aces: Iron Eagle 3 ♂♂ 1992 (R) Colonel "Chappy" Sinclair returns once again in this air adventure. He's been keeping busy flying in air shows when he stumbles across the nefarious activities of a Peruvian drug baron working out of a remote village. Sinclair recruits a team of maverick air circus pilots and they "borrow" a fleet of WWII vintage aircraft to raid the village, coming up against a fellow Air Force officer who turns out to be another villain. Lots of action and a stalwart cast. **98m/C VHS, DVD.** Louis Gossett Jr., Rachel McLish, Paul Freeman, Horst Buchholz, Christopher Cazenove, Sonny Chiba, Fred Dalton Thompson, Mitchell Ryan, Robert Estes, J.E. Freeman; **D:** John Glen.

Across 110th Street ♂♂ 1972 (R) Gritty, violent cop thriller in the blaxploitation genre. Both the Mafia and the cops hunt down three black hoods who, in a display of extremely bad judgment, knocked over a mob-controlled bank while disguised as police. Lots of bullets create buckets of blood. Filmed on location in Harlem. **102m/C VHS, DVD.** Anthony Quinn, Yaphet Kotto, Anthony (Tony) Franciosa, Paul Benjamin, Ed Bernard, Antonio Farças, Tim O'Connor, Lewis Gilbert, Richard Ward; **D:** Barry Shear; **W:** Luther Davis; **C:** Jack Priestley.

Acqua e Sapone ♂1/2 1983 (PG) A young innocent model goes to Rome under the watchful eyes of an appointed priest-chaperon, but finds love, fun and other sinful things. Sudsy/romantic comedy. **97m/C** VHS. Carlo Verdone, Natasha Hovey, Florinda Bolkan, Elena Bolkan; **D:** Carlo Verdone.

Acorn People ♂♂ 1982 An unemployed teacher takes a summer job at a camp for handicapped children and learns sensitivity. Weeper adapted by Tewkesbury from the book by Ron Jones. **97m/C** VHS. Ted Bessell, Cloris Leachman, LeVar Burton, Dolph Sweet, Cheryl Anderson; **D:** Joan Tewkesbury. TV

Acla's Descent into Floristella ♂♂ Acla 1987 Twelve-year-old Acla (Cusmano) is sold by his father to work underground in the sulfur mines 'or eight years. Repeatedly beaten by his overlord, Acla runs away, but there are dire consequences for him and his family. Set in 1930s Sicily. Italian with subtitles. **66m/C VHS.** //Francesco Cusimano, Tony Sperandeo; **D:** Aurelio Grimaldi; **W:** Aurelio Grimaldi; **C:** Maurizio Calvesi; **M:** Dario Lucantoni.

The Acid House ♂♂1/2 1998 Trilogy of tales written by Irving Welsh, author of "Trainspotting," similarly centers on down-on-their-luck Scottish hooligans ravaged by drugs and drink. Its tone, however, makes its predecessor look like a light-hearted romp in the countryside. In "The Grantan Star Cause," freeloading loser Boab (McCole) gets turned into a fly by God during a trip to the pub. He proceeds to exact some disgusting revenge on those he feels have wronged him. "A Soft Touch" depicts the twisted relationship between brow-beaten (McKidd) and kinky wife Catriona (Gomez), who is sleeping with psycho neighbor Larry (McCormack). In the last chapter, "The Acid House," tripped-out rave party boy Coco (Bremner) exchanges personalities with the newborn baby of suburban couple Rory (Clunes) and Jenny (Redgrave). First-time director McGuigan does a good job of translating the material to the screen, but sometimes goes over the top in showing these skanky Scots. Also, be warned that the Scottish accents are so thick that the movie ran with subtitles during its limited U.S. theatre run. If you liked "Trainspotting," however, you'll probably like this similar entry in the "if it's Scottish it's crap!" genre. **118m/C VHS, DVD.** Stephen McCole, Maurice Roeves, Garry Sweeney, Kevin McKidd, Ewen Bremner, Martin Clunes, Jemma Redgrave, Arlene Cockburn, Jenny McDonnie, Michelle Gomez, Jane Stabler; **D:** Paul McGuigan; **W:** Irvine Welsh; **C:** Alasdair Walker.

Across the Pacific ♂♂♂1/2 1942 Classic Bogie/Huston vehicle made on the heels of "The Maltese Falcon." Bogie is an American Army officer booted out of the service on false charges of treason. When no other military will accept him, he sails to China (via the Panama Canal) to offer his services to Chiang Kai-Shek. On board, he meets a variety of seedy characters who plan to blow up the canal. Huston turned over direction to Vincent Sherman. Also available colorized. **97m/B VHS, DVD.** Humphrey Bogart, Mary Astor, Sydney Greenstreet, Charles Halton, Victor Sen Yung, Roland Got, Keye Luke, Richard Loo, Frank Wilcox, Paul Stanton, Lester Matthews, Tom Stevenson, Roland (Walter Goss) Drew, Monte Blue, Rudy Robles, Lee Tung Foo, Chester Gan, Kam Tong, Spencer Chan, Philip Ahn, Frank Faylen, Frank Mayo; **D:** John Huston; **W:** Richard Macaulay; **C:** Arthur Edeson; **M:** Adolph Deutsch.

Across the Plains ♂♂ 1939 Predictable oater about two brothers who are raised separately after their parents are murdered by outlaws. One is brought up by Indians, the other by the outlaws responsible for wiping out the folks, who tell the boy that Indians did in his ma and pa. Eventually the brothers meet and fight. Odds favor the good one winning, aided by Indian pals. **59m/B VHS.** Addison "Jack" Randall, Frank Yaconelli, Joyce Bryant, Hal Price, Dennis Moore, Glenn Strange, Bud Osborne; **D:** Spencer Gordon Bennet.

Across the Tracks ♂♂ 1989 (PG-3) Two brothers, Billy (Schroder), a juvie-home rebel, and Joe (Pitt), a straight-A jock, are at odds when the black sheep is pressured into selling drugs. In an attempt to save his brother from a life of crime, saintly Joe convinces Billy to join him on the school track team, and the brothers are forced to face off in a big meet. Fairly realistic good guy/bad guy drama. **101m/C VHS, DVD.** Rick Schroder, Brad Pitt, Carrie Snodgress; **D:** Sandy Tung; **C:** Michael Delahoussaye; **M:** Joel Goldsmith.

Across the Universe ♂♂ 2007 (PG-13) Director Julie Taymor has certainly crafted a mystical tool, from middle America to bohemian Greenwich Village to Vietnam. Whether this portrayal of the Vietnam era, using gorgeous visuals, a styl-ized 60s aesthetic, a nice chunk of the Beatles songbook, and surprisingly little spoken dialogue, is also magical is debatable. Lucy Even (Wood) moves from a small town to New York City, where she and her brother Max (Anderson) meet and befriend a number of predictable characters including Juce (Sturgess), a Brit from—where else?—Liverpool. The music has been tasked with propelling the plot along via a vision of this revolutionary time from hippie idealism through the duty of military service to the anti-war counter culture, which is where the message of the film finally lands. See it for the stunning visuals and its fresh interpretation of Beatles classics. **133m/C DVD, Blu-ray Disc.** Evan Rachel Wood, Joe Anderson, Jim Sturgess, Dara Fuchs, Martin Luther McCoy, T.V. Carpio; **Cameos:** Bono; **D:** Julie Taymor; **W:** Dick Clement, and Ian La Frenais; **C:** Bruno Delbonnel; **M:** Elliot Goldenthal.

Across the Wide Missouri ♂♂1/2 1951 Pioneer epic stars Gable as a rugged fur trapper who marries an Indian woman (Marques) so he can trap beaver pelts on her people's rich land. On the journey to the Indian territory however, the trapper truly falls in love with his bride. Superior historical drama is provided by Howard Keel. Look for lively performances from Menjou as a French tipper and Naish as the quirky Indian Chief. Beautiful scenery filmed in the spectacular Rocky Mountains. **78m/C VHS.** Clark Gable, Ricardo Montalban, John Hodiak, Adolphe Menjou, Maria Elena Marques, J. Carrol Naish, Jack Holt, Alan Napier; **D:** William A. Wellman; **C:** William Mellor; **Nar:** Howard Keel.

The Act ♂♂ Bless 'Em All 1982 (R) A muddled satire about political double dealing and union corruption further muddled by a twangy musical score manufactured by folksy Sebastian. **90m/C VHS.** Jill St. John, Eddie Albert, Pat Hingle, Robert Ginty, Sarah Langenfeld, Nicolas Surovy; **D:** Sig Shore; **M:** John Sebastian.

Act of Aggression ♂♂ L'Agression 1973 (R) When a Parisian man finds his wife and daughter murdered at a summer resort, he takes the law into his own hands, with predictable results. **90m/C VHS, FR** Jean-Louis Trintignant, Catherine Deneuve, Claude Brasseur, Milena Vukotic, Jacques Rispal, Philippe Brigaud, Michele Grellier, Robert Charlebois, Franco Fabrizi; **D:** Gerard Pires; **C:** Silvano Ippoliti.

Act of Passion: The Lost Honor of Kathryn Beck ♂♂1/2 1983 A woman meets a man at a party and has the proverbial one-night stand. Her privacy is shattered when she discovers that he's a terrorist under surveillance by the police and press. Strong performances by Thomas and Kristofferson help turn this into an interesting American TV remake of the German "Lost Honor of Katharina Blum," based loosely on a novel by Heinrich Boll. **100m/C VHS.** Marlo Thomas, Kris Kristofferson, George Dzundza, Jon (John) DeVries; **D:** Simon Langton. TV

Act of Piracy ♂1/2 1988 (R) A bankrupt contractor reunites with his estranged wife to track down the brutal terrorists who have kidnapped their son. **105m/C VHS.** Gary Busey, Belinda Bauer, Ray Sharkey, Nancy Mulford, Dennis Casey Park, Arnold Vosloo, Ken Gampu; **D:** John Cardos; **W:** Hal Reed; **C:** Vincent Cox; **M:** Morton Stevens.

Act of Vengeance ♂♂ Rape Squad 1974 (R) A group of women band together to hunt down and exact revenge on the man who raped them. Exploitative action-filled thriller. **90m/C VHS.** Jo Ann Harris, Peter Brown, Jennifer Lee, Lisa Moore, Connie Strickland, Pat Estrin; **D:** Bob Kelljan.

Act of Vengeance ♂♂1/2 1986 Drama about Jock Yablonski, a United Mine Workers official who challenged the president. Based on fact, showing the events that led to the murder of Yablonski and his family. Intriguing story lacking cinematic drive. **97m/C VHS.** Charles Bronson, Ellen Burstyn, Wilford Brimley, Hoyt Axton, Roger Schenkkan, Ellen Barkin, Keanu Reeves; **D:** John Mackenzie; **W:** Scott Spencer. CABLE

Act of Violence ♂♂♂1/2 1948 Postwar melodrama. Small-town businessman and war hero Frank Enley (Heflin) has a pretty wife (Leigh), a young son, and a good life that gets him recognition. But this brings Frank to the attention of embittered, crippled vet Joe Parkson (Ryan), who's got a beef. Seems both were POWs in a German camp and Enley informed on the man's escape plans, which got everyone but Parkson killed. As Parkson pursues Enley through the seedier sides of L.A. Astor enters the picture as a down-heels dame at a dive bar who offers Enley some assistance that results in a lot more trouble. **82m/B DVD.** Van Heflin, Robert Ryan, Janet Leigh, Mary Astor, Phyllis Thaxter, Berry Kroeger, Taylor Holmes; **D:** Fred Zinnemann; **W:** Robert ... Richards; **C:** Robert L. Surtees; **M:** Bronislau Kaper.

Acting on Impulse ♂♂ 1993 (R) Impulsive, troublemaking movie star (Fiorentino) becomes a murder suspect when she takes over a remote nuclear missile site pressing the button on a missile aimed directly at the White House. Lots of action should hold viewers' interest. **100m/C VHS, DVD. CA** C.Z. Jack Scalia, Ingrid Torrance, Douglas Arthurs; **D:** Robert Lee; **W:** Michael Bafaro; **C:** David Pelletier; **M:** Peter Allen. VIDEO

Act of War ♂♂ 1956 Disgraced diplomat/spy Jack Gracey (Scalia) has to stop renegade communists who've taken over a ... slow major party attitude and manages to seduce a conservative businessman (Howell) and his junior exec (Allen) into helping her forget her troubles. And then the businessman's fiancee turns up dead. Any connection? **54m/C VHS.** Linda Fiorentino, C. Thomas Howell, Nancy Allen, Adam Ant, Judith Hoag, Patrick Bauchau, Isaac Hayes, Paul Bartel, Dorley Most, Miles O'Keeffe, Dick Sargent, Charles Lane, Mary Woronov, Zelda Rubinstein, Nicholas Sadler, Peter Lupus, Kim McGuire, Cassandra Peterson, Brinke Stevens, Michael Talbot, er, Scott Thompson; Stevens; **D:** Sam Irvin; **W:** Mark Pittman, Alan Moskowitz; **C:** Dear Lent; **M:** Daniel Licht. CABLE

Action for Slander ♂♂ 1938 A British army officer sporting the typical stiff upper lip is accused of cheating during a card game, and the slander mars his reputation until the case is taken to court. Dryly earnest and honest in its depiction of class differences in pre-war England. Based on a novel by Mary Borden. **84m/B VHS. GB** Clive Brook, Ann Todd Margaretta Scott, Francis L. Sullivan, Felix Aylmer, Googie Withers; **D:** Tim Whelan.

Action in Arabia ♂♂ 1944 A newsman uncovers a Nazi plot to turn the Arabs against the Allies while investigating a colleague's murder in Damascus. The desert teems with spies, double agents, and sheiks as suave Sanders goes about his investigative business. Quintessential wartime B-movie. **75m/B VHS.** George Sanders, Virginia Bruce, Lenore Aubert, Gene Lockhart, Robert Armstrong, H.B. Warner, Alan Napier, Michael Ansara; **D:** Leonide Moguy.

Action in the North Atlantic ♂♂ 1943 Massey and Bogart are the captain and first mate of a Merchant Marine vessel running the lone supply route to the Soviet Union. Eventually they wind up locking horns with a Nazi U-boat. Plenty of action and strenuous flag waving in this propaganda-drama. Gordon fans won't want to miss her as Massey's wife. Also available colorized. **126m/B VHS, DVD.** Humphrey Bogart, Raymond Massey, Alan Hale, Julie Bishop, Ruth Gordon, Sam Levene, Dane Clark, Peter Whitney...

Levene, Dane Clark, Peter Whitney, Minor Watson, J.M. Kerrigan, Dick Hogan, Kane Richmond, Chick Chandler, Donald Douglas, Creighton Hale, Iris Adrian, Elliott Sullivan, Glenn Strange; **D:** Lloyd Bacon; **W:** A(lbert) I(saac) Bezzerides, W.R. Burnett, John Howard Lawson; **C:** Ted D. McCord; **M:** Adolph Deutsch.

Action Jackson 🐾🐾 1988 (R)
Power-hungry auto tycoon Nelson tries to frame rebellious black police sergeant Weathers for murder. Being a graduate of Harvard and a tough guy, the cop doesn't go for it. Nelson eats up the screen as the heavy with no redeeming qualities, while Weathers is tongue-in-cheek as the resourceful good guy who keeps running afoul of the law in spite of his best efforts. Lots of action, violence, and a few sexy women help cover the plot's lack of common sense. **96m/C VHS, DVD.** Carl Weathers, Vanity, Craig T. Nelson, Sharon Stone, Thomas F. Wilson, Mary Ellen Trainor; **D:** Craig R. Baxley; **W:** Robert Reneau; **C:** Matthew F. Leonetti; **M:** Herbie Hancock, Michael Kamen.

Action U.S.A. 🐾1/2 1989 A young woman witnesses the murder of her boyfriend by gangsters, who then pursue her to make sure she will never tell what she saw. Throughout Texas she rambles with the mob sniffing at her heels, grateful for the opportunity to participate in numerous stunts and car crashes. **90m/C VHS.** Barri Murphy, Gregory Scott Cummins, William Knight, William (Bill) Smith, Cameron Mitchell; **D:** John Stewart; **W:** David Reskin; **C:** Thomas Callaway.

Actor: The Paul Muni Story 🐾🐾 1978 Musical biography of Paul Muni, from his beginnings as a traveling actor in Hungary to his New York theatre and movie career. **105m/C VHS.** Herschel Bernardi, Georgia Brown, Harold Gould.

Actors and Sin 🐾🐾1/2 1952 Two-part film casting a critical eye toward actors and Hollywood. "Actor's Blood" is the melodramatic story of Shakespearean actor Robinson and his unhappy actress daughter. She commits suicide and Now, it's up to Jefferson Pike (Baldwin) to lead a team into the Central American jungles to retrieve the military's property. **99m/C VHS, DVD.** Daniel Baldwin, Fred Williamson, Hannes Jaenicke, Chick Vennera, Lisa Vidal; **D:** Fred Olen Ray. **VIDEO**

Lighter and more entertaining is "Woman of Sin," which relates a Hollywood satire involving a theatrical agent and his newest client, a precocious nine-year-old. **82m/B VHS.** Edward G. Robinson, Marsha Hunt, Eddie Albert, Alan Reed, Dan O'Herlihy, Tracey Roberts, Rudolph Anders, Paul Guilfoyle, Alice Key, Douglas Evans, Rick Roman, Jenny Hecht, Jody Gilbert, John Crawford; **D:** Lee Garmes, Ben Hecht; **C:** Lee Garmes; **M:** George Antheil.

An Actor's Revenge 🐾🐾 *Yukinojo Henge; Revenge of a Kabuki Actor* 1963 In the early 19th century, a female impersonator in a Kabuki troupe takes revenge on the three men who killed his parents. Fascinating study of opposites—male/female, stage/life, love/hate. In Japanese with English subtitles. **110m/C VHS.** JP Kazuo Hasegawa, Fujiko Yamamoto, Ayako Wakao, Ganjiro Nakamura; **D:** Kon Ichikawa; **W:** Teinosuke Kinugasa, Daisuke Ito, Natto Wada; **C:** Setsuo Kobayashi; **M:** Yashushi Akutagawa.

Acts of Betrayal 🐾🐾 1998 Alonso is about to divulge wise guy secrets so is about to divulge wise guy secrets and agent McColm to make certain the bad guys don't silence her first. **112m/C VHS.** Maria Conchita Alonso, Matt McColm, Muse Watson, David Groh, Gregory Alan Williams, Susan Egsard; **W:** Patrick Highsmith; **C:** Joakim (Jack) Ersgard; **D:** Jerry Sidell; **M:** Roger Neill. **VIDEO**

Acts of Worship 🐾🐾1/2 2001 (R)
Kicked out by her boyfriend, junkie Alix finds a safe haven with Digna, a former addict. But her attempt to straighten Alix out leads Digna back to her old, bad habits. **94m/C VHS, DVD.** Ana Reeder, Michael Hyatt, Nestor Rodriguez, Christopher Kadish; **D:** Rose-

mary Rodriguez; **W:** Rosemary Rodriguez; **C:** Luke Geissbuhler; **M:** Jim Coleman. **VIDEO**

A.D. 🐾🐾1/2 *Anno Domini* 1985 Set shortly after Jesus' death, this rather low-budget miniseries chronicles the life and adventures of Christ's disciples (especially Peter and Paul) and the growing conflicts between Jewish zealots, early Christians, and the power of the Roman empire. Based on the Acts of the Apostles. **540m/C VHS, DVD.** Denis Quilley, Philip Sayer, Anthony Andrews, Colleen Dewhurst, Ava Gardner, Richard Kiley, James Mason, David Hedison, John Houseman, John McEnery, Ian McShane, Jennifer O'Neill, Fernando Rey, Richard Roundtree, Ben Vereen, Susan Sarandon, Diane Venora, Anthony Zerbe, Jack Warden, Amanda Pays, Millie Perkins, Michael Wilding Jr.; **D:** Stuart Cooper; **W:** Anthony Burgess; **C:** Ennio Guarnieri; **M:** Lalo Schifrin. **TV**

Adam 🐾🐾1/2 1983 Docu-drama based on a tragic, true story. John and Reve Williams (Travanti and Williams) desperately search for their six-year-old son abducted during an outing. During their long search and struggle, they lobby Congress for use of the FBI's crime computer. Eventually their efforts led to the creation of the Missing Children's Bureau. Sensitive, compelling performances by Travanti and Williams as the agonized, courageous parents. **100m/C VHS.** Daniel J. Travanti, JoBeth Williams, Martha Scott, Richard Masur, Paul Regina, Mason Adams; **D:** Michael Tuchner. **TV**

Adam & Steve 🐾🐾 2005 Contrived but generally amusing gay romance begins in 1987 when shy goth boy Adam (writer/director Chester) meets glittery party boy Steve (Gets) and their trick turns into disaster. They meet cute 17 years later, don't recognize each other, and start a romance fraught with individual neuroses that stem from that fateful night. Each man also comes complete with the prerequisite straight best friend: for Adam, it's former-fatty turned skinny comic Rhonda (Posey) and for Steve it's caustic roommate Michael (Kattan). A couple of musical fantasy sequences provide some unexpected distraction. **99m/C DVD.** *US* Craig Chester, Malcolm Gets, Parker Posey, Chris Kattan, Sally Kirkland, Noah Segan; **D:** Craig Chester; **W:** Craig Chester; **C:** Carl F. Bartels; **M:** Roddy Bottum.

Adam at 6 a.m. 🐾🐾 1970 (PG)
Douglas is a young college professor who decides to spend a summer laboring in Missouri, where life, he thinks, is simpler. Of course, he learns that life in the boonies has its own set of problems, but unfortunately it takes him the entire movie before he catches the drift. **100m/C VHS, DVD.** Michael Douglas, Lee Purcell, Joe Don Baker, Charles Aidman, Marge Redmond, Louise Latham, Grayson Hall, Dana Elcar, Meg Foster, Richard Derr, Anne Gwynne; **D:** Robert Scheerer.

Adam Had Four Sons 🐾🐾 1941 Satisfying character study involving the typical turn-of-the-century family nearly consumed by love, jealousy, and hatred. In the early part of the century, a goodly governess (Bergman in her second U.S. film) watches sympathetically over four sons of an American businessman after their mother dies. Economic necessity separates Bergman from the family for several years. Upon her return, she tangles with scheming bride-to-be Hayward, a bad girl intent on dividing and conquering the family before walking down the aisle with one of the sons. Based on a novel by Charles Bonner. **81m/B VHS, DVD.** Ingrid Bergman, Warner Baxter, Susan Hayward, Fay Wray, Richard Denning, June Lockhart, Robert Shaw, Johnny Downs; **D:** Gregory Ratoff.

Adam Sandler's 8 Crazy Nights 🐾🐾 *8 Crazy Nights* 2002 (PG-13)
Parents should be warned that Adam Sandler's foray into animated holiday fare is more for the big kids than the tiny tots. When eyes are aglow, it's usually after he goes on a spree of booze-soaked vandalism, the judge is about to throw the book at him until Whitey, the ref of a youth basketball league, intercedes for him. Davey proceeds to torment Whitey

and his sister Eleanor (both also voiced by Sandler) until the last act less-than-believably transforms him into a good guy. At turns offensive and interesting, this foul-mouthed cartoon does manage to set a record for animated product placement. **71m/C VHS, DVD.** *US D:* Seth Kearsley; **W:** Adam Sandler, Allen Covert, Brooks Arthur, Brad Isaacs; **V:** Adam Sandler, Kevin Nealon, Rob Schneider, Norm Crosby, Jackie Titone, Austin Stout, Jon Lovitz.

Adam's Apples 🐾🐾 *Adams Aebler* 2005 (R) Danish black comedy about a Neo-Nazi forced to finish a prison sentence doing community service at a church. Adam (Thomsen) is EVIL and meets his opposite in the positive-to-a-fault priest Ivan (Mikkelsen). Adam promises Ivan that he'll make a pie from the apples that grow in the churchyard, but as crows and disease peck away at the apples, Adam decides to break Ivan down, mentally and physically. Alternately bleak and ludicrous, the movie is mostly style over substance and rarely digs deeper than the basic absurdity of its premise. **93m/C DVD.** *CZ* Ulrich Thomsen, Mads Mikkelsen, Paprika Steen, Nikolaj Lie Kaas, Nicolas Bro, Ali Kazim, Ole Thestrup; **D:** Anders Thomas Jensen; **W:** Anders Thomas Jensen; **C:** Sebastian Blenkov; **M:** Jeppe Kaas.

Adam's Rib 🐾🐾🐾🐾 1950 Classic war between the sexes cast Tracy and Hepburn as married attorneys on opposite sides of the courtroom in the trial of blonde bombshell Holliday, charged with attempted murder of the lover of her philandering husband. The battle in the courtroom soon takes its toll at home as the couple is increasingly unable to leave their work at the office. Sharp, snappy dialogue by Gordon and Kanin with superb direction by Cukor. Perhaps the best of the nine movies pairing Tracy and Hepburn. Also available colorized. **101m/B VHS, DVD.** Spencer Tracy, Katharine Hepburn, Judy Holliday, Tom Ewell, David Wayne, Jean Hagen, Hope Emerson, Polly Moran, Marvin Kaplan, Paula Raymond, Tommy Noonan; **D:** George Cukor; **W:** Garson Kanin, Ruth Gordon; **C:** George J. Folsey; **M:** Miklos Rozsa. Natl. Film Reg. 92.

Adaptation 🐾🐾🐾 2002 (R)
Quirky but highly entertaining comedy about blocked L.A. screenwriter Charlie Kaufman (Cage), hired to adapt author Susan Orlean's (Streep) book "The Orchid Thief." The book recounts the story of orchid-obsessed con men who schemes to steal the desirable plants from the Florida Everglades. At a loss as to how to treat the story, the neurotic Charlie becomes obsessed with Orlean, gazing at her picture while his lesser twin brother Donald (also Cage), breezily announces the sales of his own million dollar screenplay, which he wrote after one seminar. Meanwhile, Orlean travels to Florida to interview the gap-toothed Laroche (Cooper), one of a breed of orchid-obsessed con men who schemes and Cooper turns in a career-making performance. Deftly directed by Jonze. **114m/C VHS, DVD.** *US* Nicolas Cage, Meryl Streep, Chris Cooper, Tilda Swinton, Cara Seymour, Brian Cox, Judy Greer, Maggie Gyllenhaal, Ron Livingston, Stephen Tobolowsky, Jay Tavare, Litefoot, Gary Farmer, Peter Jason, Curtis Hanson; **D:** Spike Jonze; **W:** Charlie Kaufman; **C:** Lance Acord; **M:** Carter Burwell. Oscars '02: Support. Actor (Cooper); British Acad. '02: Adapt. Screenplay; Golden Globes '03: Support. Actor (Cooper), Support. Actress (Streep); L.A. Film Critics '02: Support. Actor (Cooper), Support. Actress (Streep); Natl. Bd. of Review '02: Screenplay, Support. Actor (Cooper); N.Y. Film Critics '02: Screenplay.

The Addams Family 🐾🐾1/2 1991 (PG-13) Everybody's favorite family of ghouls hits the big screen, but something is lost in the translation. An imposter claiming to be long-lost Uncle Fester (Lloyd), who says he was in the Bermuda Triangle for 25 years, shows up at the Addams' home to complete a dastardly deed—raid the family's immense fortune. Although Fester's plan is foiled, a series of

plot twists highlight the ghoulish family's eccentricities. Darkly humorous but eventually disappointing; Julia, Huston, and Ricci (as Gomez, Morticia, and Wednesday, respectively) are great in their roles and the sets look good, but the plot is thin. Much closer to the original comic strip by Charles Addams than the popular TV show ever was. **102m/C VHS, DVD.** Anjelica Huston, Raul Julia, Christopher Lloyd, Dan Hedaya, Elizabeth Wilson, Judith Malina, Carel Struycken, Dana Ivey, Paul Benedict, Christina Ricci, Jimmy Workman, Christopher Hart, John Franklin; *Cameos:* Marc Shaiman; **D:** Barry Sonnenfeld; **W:** Caroline Thompson, Larry Thompson; **C:** Owen Roizman; **M:** Marc Shaiman. Golden Raspberries '91: Worst Song ("Addams Groove").

Addams Family Values 🐾🐾1/2 1993 (PG-13) The creepy Addams' are back, but this time they leave the dark confines of the mansion to meet the "real" world. New baby Pubert causes homicidal jealousy in sibs Wednesday and Pugsley, causing Mom and Dad to hire a gold-digging, serial-killing nanny (Cusack) with designs on Uncle Fester to watch over the tot. A step above its predecessor, chock full of black humor, sub-plots, and one-liners. Cusack fits right in with an outrageously over the top performance and Ricci nearly steals the show again as the deadpan Wednesday. **93m/C VHS, DVD.** Anjelica Huston, Raul Julia, Christopher Lloyd, Joan Cusack, Carol Kane, Christina Ricci, Jimmy Workman, Kaitlyn Hooper, Kristen Hooper, Carel Struycken, David Krumholtz, Christopher Hart, Dana Ivey, Peter MacNichol, Christine Baranski, Mercedes McNab; **D:** Barry Sonnenfeld; **W:** Paul Rudnick; **M:** Marc Shaiman. Golden Raspberries '93: Worst Song ("WHOOMP! There It Is").

Addicted to Love 🐾🐾1/2 1996 (R)
Warning: Do not rent this movie with your significant other if you're thinking about breaking up with them. After they're both dumped, mild-mannered Sam (Broderick) and wild woman Maggie (Ryan) discover they have a lot in common. First of all, their exes Linda (Preston) and Anton (Karyo) are dating each other. Secondly, they're both stalkers! Yep! A romantic comedy about stalking. Sam wants nothing more than to reclaim Linda as his own. Maggie wants nothing less than Anton's head on a plate. Interesting comedy wavers between dark and light moments, aided by the rather murky sets and lighting. Directorial debut for Dunne, who makes his father eat a bug in one scene. **100m/C VHS, DVD.** Meg Ryan, Matthew Broderick, Kelly Preston, Tchéky Karyo, Maureen Stapleton, Remak Ramsay, Nesbitt Blaisdell, Dominick Dunne; **D:** Griffin Dunne; **W:** Robert Gordon; **C:** Andrew Dunn; **M:** Rachel Portman. **VIDEO**

Addicted to Murder 🐾🐾1/2 1995
Joel Winter (McCleery) was abused as a child and now takes his anger out on women by killing them. Then he meets vampire Angie (Graham), who decides to transform him since he's already a predator. But Joel develops a conscience and tries to reform, which ticks Angie off and she intends to put a stop to it. And just around for — more laughs — is Joel (McCleery)—the serial killer turned vampire turned vampire hunter. **90m/C VHS, DVD.** Michael (Mick) McCleery, Sasha Graham, Laura McLaughlin; **D:** Kevin J. Lindenmuth; **W:** Kevin J. Lindenmuth. **VIDEO**

Addicted to Murder 2: Tainted Blood 🐾🐾1/2 1997 It's a case of diminishing returns as is usual with sequels in this plotwise mishmash. New York City is the happy hunting grounds for a rogue vamp who's turning others whom Angie (Graham) doesn't consider worthy of getting "The Gift." So she intends to put a stop to it. **80m/C VHS, DVD.** Sasha Graham, Michael (Mick) McCleery, Sarah K. Lippmann, Robbi Firestone, Ted Grayson, Joe Moretti, Jon D. Wynkoop, Tom NonDorf; **W:** Kevin J. Lindenmuth. **VIDEO**

Addicted to Murder 3: Bloodlust 🐾🐾1/2 1999 Serial killer Joel Winter (McCleery) continues his quest to eliminate vampires in revenge for his own

The Addiction 🐾🐾½ 1995 (R) ... transformation. One master vamp thinks he has a secure haven but he's very wrong. **85m/C VHS, DVD**. Michael (Mick) McCleery, Sarah < Lippmann, Nick Kostopoulos, Cloud Michaels, Grant Cramer, Frank Lopez, Joe Zaso, Jon Sanborne, Reid Ostrowski; **D:** Kevin J. Lincenmuth, Tom Vollmann. **W:** Kevin J. Lincenmuth, Tom Vollmann. **VIDEO**

The Adjuster 🐾🐾½ 1991 (R) Critics either loved or hated this strange film. An insurance adjuster Noah Render's clients look to him for all sorts of comfort, so much so that his own identity becomes a blurred reflection of their tragedies. Wife Hera is a film censor who secretly tapes the pornographic videos she watches at work. Their carefully organized lives are invaded by Bubba and Mimi, a wealthy couple who pass themselves off as filmmakers who want to use the Render house as a movie set. They are instead looking to involve the Renders in their latest and most elaborate erotic fantasy. Lots of symbolism, but little substance. **102m/C VHS, DVD. CA** Elias Koteas, Arsinee Khanjian, Maury Chaykin, Gabrielle Rose, David Hemblen, Jennifer Dale, Don McKellar, Raoul Trujillo; **D:** Atom Egoyan; **W:** Atom Egoyan; **C:** Paul Sarossy; **M:** Mychael Danna. Toronto-City '91: Feature Film.

Adios, Sabata 🐾🐾½ 1971 (PG-13) Brynner took over the role for one sequel. In 1873, Sabata comes to the aid of a band of Mexican revolutionaries who want to steal a wagonload of gold from sadistic Austrian interloper, Colonel Von Skimmel. **102m/C DVD. IT** Yul Brynner, Ignazio Spalla, Gerard Herter, Dean Reed, Sal Borgese, Franco Fantasia; **D:** Gianfranco Parolini; **W:** Gianfranco Parolini; **C:** Sandro Mancori; **M:** Bruno Nicolai.

Adios, Hombre 🐾 1968 An innocent man was imprisoned for murder escapes from prison and seeks revenge. You'll be saying adios as well. **90m/C VHS. IT** Craig Hill, Giulia Rubini; **D:** Mario Caiano.

Adios Amigo 🐾 1975 (PG) Off-beat western comedy has ad-libbing Pryor hustling as a perennially inept con man. Script and direction (both provided by Williamson) are not up to Pryor's level, although excessive violence and vulgarity are avoided in a boring attempt to provide good clean family fare. **87m/C VHS, DVD.** Fred Williamson, Richard Pryor, Thalmus Rasulala, James Brown, Robert Phillips, Mike Henry; **D:** Fred Williamson; **W:** Fred Williamson.

Adelheid 🐾🐾 1969 Viktor, a Czech soldier, returns home after WWII and is told to inventory the contents of a mansion that was owned by a wealthy German family. Adelheid, the daughter of the previous owner, is now a servant there and Viktor falls in love, the lingering bitterness of the war ruins the romance. Czech with subtitles. **99m/C DVD. CZ** Petr Cepek, Emma Cerna; **D:** Frantisek Vlacil; **W:** Frantisek Vlacil; **C:** Frantisek Uldrich; **M:** Zdenek Liska.

Address Unknown 🐾🐾½ 1996 (PG) A ten-year-old letter and a priceless stamp provide a teenager with clues to dad's mysterious death. **92m/C VHS.** Kyle Howard, Johna Stewart, Patrick Renna, Corbin Allred, Michael Flynn; **C:** Ken Kelsch; **M:** Joe Delia.

Adrenaline Drive 🐾🐾 1999 Sad sack Suzuki (Ando), who's working for a car rental company, accidentally plows a car into the jaguar of yakuza big guy Kuroiwa (Matushige). Before punishment can be exacted, there's an explosion that lands them in the hospital. There shy nurse Shizuko (Ishida) latches on to Suzuki and to a yakuza suitcase full of money and drags both on a road trip to freedom. Silly, good-natured comedy. Japanese with subtitles. **111m/C VHS, DVD. JP** Hikari Ishida, Masanobu Ando, Yutaka Matushige, Kazue Tsunogae; **D:** Shinobu Yaguchi; **W:** Shinobu Yaguchi; **C:** Takashi Hamada; **M:** Seiichi Yamamoto.

Adrift 🐾🐾½ 1993 Yet another couple-in-terror-from-psychos-on-the-high-seas flick. Katie and Guy Nast (Jackson and Welsh) are on an anniversary sailing adventure intended to shore up their shaky marriage. They discover a boat adrift with two survivors (Greenwood and Rowan) who have a suspicious story but they help them nonetheless. Big mistake. **92m/C VHS.** Kate Jackson, Kenneth Welsh, Bruce Greenwood, Kelly Rowan; **D:** Christian Duguay. **TV**

The Admirable Crichton 🐾🐾½ 1957 Social satire about an aristocratic family and their butler who are marooned on a tropical island. Crichton (More), the butler, has a good deal more practical experience and sense of their survival. Filmed in Bermuda and based on the play by James M. Barrie. **93m/C VHS. GB** Kenneth More, Cecil Parker, Sally Ann Howes, Diane Cilento, Martita Hunt, Jack Watling, Peter Graves, Gerald Harper, Sally Nesbitt; **D:** Lewis Gilbert; **W:** Vernon Harris; **C:** Wilkie Cooper; **M:** Douglas Gamley.

The Admiral Was a Lady 🐾🐾 1950 Four ex-GIs try to get by in life without going to work. Hendrix walks into their lives as an ex-Wave gifted with a knack for repartee who is disgusted by their collective lack of ambition. Nevertheless, she is pursued by the zany quartet with predictable results. **87m/B VHS, DVD.** Edmond O'Brien, Wanda Hendrix, Rudy Vallee, Steve Brodie; **D:** Albert Rogell.

Adomas Nori Buti Zmogumi 🐾🐾 *Adam Wants to Be a Man* 1959 Soviet Lithuanian feature in its original form, with dialogue in Lithuanian. A young worker scrapes together money for a ticket to Buenos Aires, but the money is stolen by the manager of the travel office. **90m/B VHS. RU, LI** Donatas Banionis, Juozas Miltinis; **D:** V. Zhalakyavichus; **W:** V. Zhalakyavichus; **C:** Algimantas Mockus.

Adoption 🐾🐾 *Orkokotogadras* 1975 The third of Meszaros's trilogy, involving a middle-aged Hungarian woman who longs for a child and instead forms a deep friendship with a 19-year-old orphan. Hungarian with English subtitles. **89m/B VHS, DVD. HU** Kati Berek, Laszlo Szabo, Gyongyver Vigh, Dr. Arpad Perlaky; **D:** Marta Meszaros; **W:** Marta Meszaros, Gyula Hernadi; **C:** Lajos Koltai; **M:** Gyorgy Kovacs. Berlin Intl. Film Fest. '75: Golden Berlin Bear.

The Adorable Cheat 🐾🐾 1928 A low-budget, late-silent melodrama about a young woman who tries to get involved in the family business, despite her father's refusal of her help. Once in the business, she finds love. **76m/B VHS.** Lila Lee, Cornelius Keefe, Burr McIntosh; **D:** Burton King.

Adorable Julia 🐾🐾 1962 When an actress takes on a lover many years younger than herself, the laughs begin to fly in this sex comedy based on W. Somerset Maugham's novel. **97m/C VHS. FR** Lilli Palmer, Charles Boyer; **D:** Alfred Weidenmann.

Adrenalin: Fear the Rush 🐾 1996 (R) Dull future thriller in the deadly virus category. In 2007, a plague in Eastern Europe causes those that survive to turn into cannibalistic killers. The U.S. has started quarantine camps, one of which is in Boston, and two cops (Henstridge and Lambert) must track down an infected killer who's escaped. Not worth your time. **77m/C VHS, DVD.** Christopher Lambert, Natasha Henstridge, Norbert Weisser, Craig Davis, Elizabeth Barondes, Xavier Declie; **D:** Albert Pyun; **W:** Albert Pyun; **C:** George Mooradian; **M:** Tony Riparetti.

Adrift in Manhattan 🐾🐾 2007 (R) Chance encounters change the lives of three lonely New Yorkers. Simon (Rasuk) is a young man with a passion for photography. Snapping street pics, he finds his muse in depressed optometrist Rose (Graham), who's estranged from her husband (Baldwin) after their young child's death. Rose's patient Tommaso (Chianese), a painter, is going blind and she encourages him to find comfort with someone, deciding to take her own advice after Simon gets the courage to introduce himself. **91m/C DVD.** Heather Graham, William Baldwin, Victor Rasuk, Dominic Chianese, Elizabeth Pena, Marta Colon, Erika Michels; **D:** Alfredo de Villa; **W:** Alfredo de Villa, Nat Moss; **C:** John Foster; **M:** Michael A. Levine.

The Adultress 🐾 1977 (R) When a husband and wife cannot satisfy their desire to have a family, they hire a young man to help them in this dumb melodrama. **85m/C VHS.** Tyne Daly, Eric (Hans Gudegast) Braeder, Gregory Morton; **D:** Norbert Meisel.

Adventure 🐾🐾 1945 Gable's first postwar film has him as a roughneck sailor romancing a shy and reserved librarian (Garson). Dull and disappointing—both stars deserve better. However, there is a touching scene of Gable with newborn child that might be of interest to some. Based on the novel by Clyde Brion Davis. **130m/B VHS.** Clark Gable, Greer Garson, Joan Blondell, Thomas Mitchell, Tom Tully, John Qualen, Richard Haydn, Lina Romay; **D:** Victor Fleming; **W:** Vincent Lawrence, Frederick Hazlitt Brennan; **C:** Joseph Ruttenberg.

Adventure Island 🐾½ 1947 En route to Australia, a small ship stops at a remote island for supplies. The crew is greeted by a crazed, tyrannical leader who makes their lives difficult. Dull low-budget remake of 1937's "Ebb Tide." **66m/C VHS.** Rory Calhoun, Rhonda Fleming, Paul Kelly, John Abbott, Alan Napier; **D:** Sam Newfield.

Adventure of the Action Hunters 🐾 1987 (PG) A dying sailor leaves a tourist couple a message leading to a treasure, and they vie for it along with gangsters, mercenaries and other unsavory types. **81m/C VHS.** Ronald Hunter, Sean Murphy, Joe Cimino; **D:** Lee Bonner.

The Adventurer 🐾🐾½ 1917 An escaped convict saves two weaving women from death. They mistake him for a gentleman and bring him home. Early Chaplin silent with music track. **20m/B VHS, DVD.** Charlie Chaplin, Charlie Hatton; **D:** Charlie Chaplin.

The Adventurers 🐾🐾 1970 (R) amorous: *The Great Adventure* 1951 At the turn of the century, two Boers and an English officer set out to recover stolen jewels hidden in the jungles of South Africa. On the way, greed and anger take their toll in a less convincing scale. **82m/B VHS, GB** Dennis Price, Jack Hawkins, Siobhan McKenna, Peter Hammond, Bernard Lee; **D:** David MacDonald.

The Adventurers WOOF! 1970 (R) Sleazy Harold Robbins novel retains its trashy aura on film. Unfortunately, this turkey is also long and boring. Set in South America, it tells the tale of a rich playboy who uses and destroys everyone who crosses his path. His vileness results from having seen his mother murdered by outlaws, but his obsession is to avenge his father's murder. Blood, gore, revolutions, and exploitive sex follow him everywhere. Watch and be amazed at the number of stars who signed on for this one. **171m/C VHS, DVD.** Candice Bergen, Olivia de Havilland, Bekim Fehmiu, Charles Aznavour, Alan Badel, Ernest Borgnine, Leigh Taylor-Young, Fernando Rey, Thommy Berggren, John Ireland, Sydney Tafler, Rossano Brazzi, Anna Moffo, Christian Roberts, Yorgo Voyagis, Angela Scoular, Yolande Donlan, Ferdinand "Ferdy" Mayne, Jaclyn Smith, Peter Graves, Roberta Haynes; **D:** Lewis Gilbert.

Adventures Beyond Belief 🐾 *Neat and Tidy* 1987 An irreverent motorcyclist is chased across Europe for a murder he didn't commit. Firmly within the boundaries of belief. **95m/C VHS.** Elke Sommer, Jill

Adventures

Adventures in Babysitting 🐾🐾½ 1987 (PG-13) Pleasant comedy has its moments when a babysitter and her charges leave a peaceful suburb for downtown Chicago to rescue a friend in trouble. After a flat tire strands them on the freeway, trouble takes on a new meaning. Shue is charming as the hapless sitter, unexpectedly dateless, who finds herself in charge of a trio of kids. Ludicrous at times, but still fun to watch. **102m/C VHS, DVD.** Elisabeth Shue, Keith Coogan, Maia Brewton, Anthony Rapp, Calvin Levels, Vincent D'Onofrio, Penelope Ann Miller, George Newbern, John Ford Noonan, Lolita (David) Davidovich Albert Collins; **D:** Chris Columbus; **W:** David Simkins; **C:** Ric Waite; **M:** Michael Kamen.

Adventures in Dinosaur City 🐾🐾 1992 (PG) Expect to see lots of movies riding on the coattails of dino mania sweeping the land. Some will be good, others will not. "Adventures" falls into the latter category. Mode-n-day preteen siblings are transported back in time to the stone age. There they meet their favorite TV characters (they're dinosaurs). Family film may arrouse kids, but adults should stick to "Jurassic Park." **88m/C VHS.** Omri Katz, Shawn Hoffman, Tiffanie Poston, Pete Koch, Megan Hughes, Tony Doyle, Mimi Maynard; **D:** Brett Thompson; **W:** Willie Baronet, Lisa Norton; **M:** Fredric Teetsel.

Adventures in Spying 🐾🐾 1992 (PG-13) Brian McNichols is just trying to enjoy his summer vacation when he discovers that a notorious drug lord is living in his neighborhood. After realizing there is a $50,000 reward for his capture, he enlists the help of his friend (Scholen) to get the man's picture for the police. Action-packed film is geared towards the junior high set, but relies too heavily on coincidence and other plot contrivances to compete with espionage flicks directed at an older market. **92m/C VHS.** Jill Schoelen, Bernie Coulson, Seymour Cassel, & Gordon Liddy, Michael Emil; **D:** Hil Covington; **W:** Hil Covington; **M:** James Stemple.

The Adventures of a Gnome Named Gnorm 🐾🐾½ 1990 (PG) Silly cop caper finds LAPD detective Casey (Hall) stuck with a very strange new partner—a dark-wearing gnome named Gnorm. The two team up go after a diamond smuggling ring. The special-effects creature may hold the kiddies interest. **86m/C VHS.** Anthony Michael Hall, Jerry Orbach, Claudia Christian; **D:** Stan Winston.

Adventures of a Private Eye 🐾 1987 A self-mocking British detective farce about an inept private eye who takes his time tracking down a beautiful girl's blackmailer, bedding down with all the women he meets along the way. **96m/C VHS. GB** Christopher Neil, Suzy Kendall, Irene Handl; **D:** Stanley Long.

Adventures of a Taxi Driver WOOF! 1976 Cabbie finds sex, crime, sex, adventure and sex on the road in this off-duty comedy. **89m/C VHS.** Barry Evans, Judy Geeson, Adrienne Posta, Diana Dors, Liz Fraser; **D:** Stanley Long.

The Adventures of Baron Munchausen 🐾🐾½ 1989 (PG) From the director of "Time Bandits," "Brazil," and "The Fisher King" comes an ambitious, imaginative, chaotic, and underappreciated marvel based on the tall (and often confused) tales of the Baron. Munchausen encounters the King of the Moon, Venus, and other odd and fascinating characters during what might be described as a circular narrative in which flashbacks dovetail into the present and place and time are never quite what they seem. Wonderful special effects and visually stunning sets occasionally dwarf the actors and prove what Gilliam can do with a big budget. **125m/C VHS, DVD. GB GE** John Neville, Eric Idle, Sarah Polley, Valentina Cortese, Oliver Reed, Uma Thurman, Sting, Jonathan Pryce, Bill Paterson, Peter Jeffrey, Alison Stead-

Adventures

man, Charles McKeown, Winston Dennis, Jack Purvis, Don Henderson, Andrew MacLachlan; *Cameos:* Robin Williams; *D:* Terry Gilliam; *W:* Terry Gilliam, Charles McKeown; *C:* Giuseppe Rotunno; *M:* Michael Kamen.

The Adventures of Buckaroo Banzai Across the Eighth Dimension 🐶🐶🐶

Buckaroo Banzai **1984 (PG)** A man of many talents, Buckaroo Banzai (Weller) travels through the eighth dimension in a jet-propelled Ford Fiesta to battle Planet 10 aliens led by the evil Lithgow. Buckaroo incorporates his vast knowledge of medicine, science, music, racing, and foreign relations to his advantage. Offbeat and often humorous cult sci-fi trip. **100m/C VHS, DVD.** Peter Weller, Ellen Barkin, Jeff Goldblum, Christopher Lloyd, John Lithgow, Lewis Smith, Rosalind Cash, Robert Ito, Pepe Serna, Vincent Schiavelli, Dan Hedaya, Yakov Smirnoff, Jamie Lee Curtis, Ronald Lacey, Matt Clark, Clancy Brown, Carl Lumbly, Boyd 'Red' Morgan, Damon Hines, Billy Vera, Bill Henderson, Jonathan Banks, John Ashton, James Saito; *D:* W.D. Richter; *W:* Earl MacRauch; *C:* Fred W. Koenekamp; *M:* Michael Boddicker.

The Adventures of Bullwhip Griffin 🐶🐶½

1966 A rowdy, family-oriented comedy-adventure set during the California Gold Rush. Light Disney farce catches Russell at the tail end of his teenage star days. Pleshette and McDowall embark on an ocean trip from Boston to San Francisco to find her brother, Russell, who's out west digging for gold. Assorted comedic adventures take place. **110m/C VHS, DVD.** Roddy McDowall, Suzanne Pleshette, Karl Malden, Harry Guardino, Bryan Russell; *C:* Edward Colman; *M:* George Bruns.

Adventures of Captain Fabian 🐶½

1951 When the captain of the "China Sea" learns that a beautiful woman has been falsely imprisoned, he comes to her rescue. Not one of Flynn's better swashbucklers, with typically low-quality Republic production. **100m/B VHS.** Errol Flynn, Vincent Price, Agnes Moorehead, Micheline Presle; *D:* William Marshall.

The Adventures of Captain Marvel 🐶🐶🐶½

1941 A 12-episode cliff-hanging serial based on the comic book character. Details the adventures of klutzy Billy Batson, who transforms into superhero Captain Marvel by speaking the magic word, "Shazam!" **240m/B VHS, DVD.** Tom Tyler, Frank "Junior" Coghlan, Louise Currie; *D:* William Witney.

Adventures of Don Juan 🐶🐶½

Don Juan **1949** Flynn's last spectacular epic features elegant costuming and loads of action. Don Juan saves Queen Margaret from her evil first minister. He then swashbuckles his way across Spain and England in an effort to win her heart. Grand, large-scale fun and adventure with Flynn at his self-mocking best. **111m/C VHS, DVD.** Errol Flynn, Viveca Lindfors, Robert Douglas, Romney Brent, Alan Hale, Raymond Burr, Aubrey Mather, Ann Rutherford; *D:* Vincent Sherman; *M:* Max Steiner. Oscars '49: Costume Des. (C).

The Adventures of Eliza Fraser 🐶½

1976 A young shipwrecked couple move from bawdy pleasures to cannibalism after being captured by aborigines. **114m/C VHS.** Susannah York, Trevor Howard, Leon Lissek, Abigail, Noel Ferrier, Carole Skinner; *D:* Tim Burstall.

The Adventures of Felix 🐶🐶

Drôle de Felix **1999** Felix (Bouajila) is a gay, HIV-positive Frenchman of Arab descent who decides to go on a road trip to Marseilles after finding some old letters from the father he never knew. Felix has a number of adventures while hitchhiking that he meets along the way, which leads him to wonder if he really needs to meet his biological dad after all. French with subtitles. **95m/C VHS, DVD.** *FR* Sami Bouajila, Patachou, Ariane Ascaride, Pierre-Loup Rajot, Charly Sergue, Clement Reverend, Maurice Benichou; *D:* Olivier Ducastel, Jacques Martineau; *W:* Olivier Ducastel, Jacques Martineau; *C:* Mathieu Poirot-Delpech.

The Adventures of Ford Fairlane 🐶

Ford Fairlane **1990 (R)** The Diceman plays an unusual detective specializing in rock 'n' roll cases. When a heavy metal singer dies on stage, he takes the case in his own inimitable fashion, pursuing buxom gals, sleazy record executives, and even his ex-wife. Not surprisingly, many of his stand-up bits are worked into the movie. Clay, the ever-so-controversial comic in his first (and likely last) starring role 'apparently sneers his way through this rock 'n' roll dud of a comedy thriller. A quick effort to cash in on Clay's fading star. Forget about it. **101m/C VHS, DVD.** Andrew (Dice Clay) Silverstein, Wayne Newton, Priscilla Presley, Morris Day, Lauren Holly, Maddie Corman, Gilbert Gottfried, David Patrick Kelly, Brandon Call, Robert Englund, Ed O'Neill, Sheila E, Karl Wuhrer, Tone Loc; *D:* Renny Harlin; *W:* David Arnott, Daniel Waters, James Cappe. Golden Raspberries '90: Worst Picture, Worst Actor (Silverstein), Worst Screenplay.

The Adventures of Frank and Jesse James 🐶🐶

1948 The bad brothers of the Wild West are trying to make good for rip-offs committed in their names, so they're hoping to hit pay-dirt with a silver mine. A 13-episode serial on two cassettes. **180m/B VHS.** Steve Darrell, Clayton Moore, Noel Neill, Stanley Andrews; *D:* Yakima Canutt.

The Adventures of Frontier Fremont 🐶🐶

1975 A rough and tumble story of a man who leaves the city, grows a beard, and makes the wilderness his home (and the animals his friends). Almost indistinguishable from Haggerty's "Grizzly Adams," with the usual redeeming panoramic shots of majestic mountains. **95m/C VHS.** Dan Haggerty, Denver Pyle; *D:* Richard Friedenberg.

The Adventures of Gallant Bess 🐶🐶

1948 The time-honored story of a rodeo man torn between his girl and his talented horse (the Bess of the title). **73m/C VHS, DVD.** Cameron Mitchell, Audrey Long, Fuzzy Knight, James Millican; *D:* Lew Landers.

The Adventures of Huck Finn 🐶🐶🐶

1993 (PG) Decent Disney attempt at adapting an American favorite by Mark Twain. Mischievious Huck and runaway slave Jim travel down the muddy Mississippi, working on life and friendship and getting into all sorts of adventures in the pre-Civil War era. Fast-paced and amusing with good performances by Wood (in the title role) and Broadway trained Vance (as Jim). Racial epithets and minstrel show dialect have been eliminated in this version. Some material, including Jim's close call with a lynch mob and Huck's drunken, brutal father may be too strong for immature children. **108m/C VHS, DVD.** Elijah Wood, Courtney B. Vance, Robbie Coltrane, Jason Robards Jr., Ron Perlman, Dana Ivey, Anne Heche, James Gammon, Paxton Whitehead, Tom Aldredge, Curtis Armstrong, Mary Louise Wilson, Frances Conroy; *D:* Stephen Sommers; *W:* Stephen Sommers; *C:* Janusz Kaminski; *M:* Bill Conti.

The Adventures of Huckleberry Finn 🐶🐶🐶

1939 Mark Twain's classic story about a boy who runs away and travels down the Mississippi on a raft, accompanied by a runaway slave, is done over in MGM-style. Rooney is understated as Huck (quite a feat), while the production occasionally floats aimlessly down the Mississippi. An entertaining follow-up to "The Adventures of Tom Sawyer." **89m/B VHS.** Mickey Rooney, Lynne Carver, Rex Ingram, William Frawley, Walter Connolly; *D:* Richard Thorpe.

The Adventures of Huckleberry Finn 🐶🐶½

1960 A lively adaptation of the Twain saga in which Huck and runaway slave Jim raft down the Mississippi in search of freedom and adventure. Miscasting of Hodges as Huck hampers the proceedings, but Randall shines as the treacherous King. Strong supporting cast includes Keaton as a lion-tamer and boxing champ Moore as Jim. **107m/C VHS, DVD.** Tony Randall, Eddie Hodges, Archie Moore, Patty McCormack, Neville Brand, Mickey Shaughnessy, Judy Canova, Andy Devine, Sherry Jackson, Buster Keaton, Finlay Currie, Josephine Hutchinson, Parley Baer, John Carradine, Royal Dano, Sterling Holloway, Harry Dean Stanton; *D:* Michael Curtiz.

The Adventures of Huckleberry Finn 🐶🐶

1978 The classic adventure by Mark Twain of an orphan boy and a runaway slave done again as a TV movie and starring "F-Troop" regulars Tucker and Storch. Lacks the production values of earlier versions. **100m/C VHS.** Forrest Tucker, Larry Storch, Kurt Ida, Mike Mazurki, Brock Peters; *D:* Jack B. Hively. **TV**

The Adventures of Huckleberry Finn 🐶🐶½

1985 An adaptation of the Mark Twain story about the adventures encountered by Huckleberry Finn and a runaway slave as they travel down the Mississippi River. Top-notch cast makes this an entertaining version. Originally made in a much longer version for PBS's "American Playhouse." **121m/C VHS, DVD.** Sada Thompson, Lillian Gish, Richard Kiley, Jim Dale, Barnard Hughes, Patrick Day, Frederic Forrest, Geraldine Page, Butterfly McQueen, Samm-Art Williams; *D:* Peter H. Hunt. **TV**

The Adventures of Ichabod and Mr. Toad 🐶🐶🐶½

1949 Disney's wonderfully animated versions of Kenneth Grahame's "The Wind in the Willows" and "The Legend of Sleepy Hollow" by Washington Irving. Rathbone narrates the story of Mr. Toad, who suffers from arrogance and eventually must defend himself in court after being charged with driving a stolen vehicle (Disney did take liberties with the story). Crosby provides all the voices for "Ichabod," which features the all-time great animated sequences—Ichabod riding in a frenzy through the forest while being pursued by the headless horseman. A treat for all ages. **68m/C VHS, DVD.** *D:* James Nelson Algar, Clyde Geronimi; *W:* Winston Hibler, Erdman Penner, Joe Rinaldi, Ted Sears, Homer Brightman, Harry Reeves; *M:* Oliver Wallace; *V:* Eric Blore, Pat O'Malley, Jack Kinney, Bing Crosby; *Nar:* Basil Rathbone.

The Adventures of Marco Polo 🐶🐶½

1938 Lavish Hollywood production based on the exploits of 13th-century Venetian explorer Marco Polo (Cooper). He becomes the first white man to record his visit to the Eastern court of Kublai Khan, where he falls for a beautiful princess also desired by the evil Rathbone. Lots of action, though its hard to picture the laconic Cooper in the title role. **100m/B VHS, DVD.** Gary Cooper, Sigrid Gurie, Basil Rathbone, Ernest Truex, George Barbier, Binnie Barnes, Alan Hale, H.B. Warner; *D:* Archie Mayo; *W:* Robert Sherwood; *M:* Hugo Friedhofer.

The Adventures of Mark Twain 🐶🐶🐶

1944 March stars as Mark Twain, the nom de plume of Samuel Clemens, the beloved humorist and writer. His travels and adventures along the Mississippi and on to the California gold rush would later result in the books and stories which would make him so well-known. March attains a quiet nobility as he goes from young man to old sage, along with Smith, who plays Olivia, Twain's beloved wife. **130m/B VHS.** Fredric March, Alexis Smith, Donald Crisp, Alan Hale, Sir C. Aubrey Smith, John Carradine, William Henry, Robert Barrat, Walter Hampden, Percy Kilbride; *D:* Irving Rapper; *W:* Alan LeMay, Harry Chandlee; *M:* Max Steiner.

The Adventures of Mark Twain 🐶🐶🐶

Mark Twain **1985 (G)** A clay-animated fantasy based on, and radically departing from, the life and work of Mark Twain. Story begins with Twain flying into outer space in a blimp with stowaways Huck Finn, Tom Sawyer and Becky Thatcher and takes off from there. Above average entertainment for kids and their folks. **86m/C VHS, DVD.** *D:* Will Vinton; *W:* Susan Shadburne; *V:* James Whitmore, Chris Ritchie, Gary Krug, Michele Mariana.

The Adventures of Milo & Otis 🐶🐶½

Koneko Monogatari; The Adventures of Chatran **1989 (G)** Delightful Japanese children's film about a farm-dwelling dog and cat and their odyssey after the cat is accidentally swept away on a river. No table since no humans appear in the film. A record-breaking success in its homeland. Well received by U.S. children. Narrated by Dudley Moore. **76m/C VHS, DVD.** *JP D:* Masanori Hata; *W:* Mark Saltzman; *C:* Hideo Fujii, Shinji Tomita; *M:* Michael Boddicker; *Nar:* Dudley Moore.

The Adventures of Nellie Bly 🐶

1981 "Classics Illustrated" story of Nellie Bly, a strong-willed female reporter doing her best to expose wrongdoings in the late 19th century. A decent performance by Purl is overshadowed by the general lack of direction. **100m/C VHS.** Linda Purl, Gene Barry, John Randolph, Raymond Buktenica, J.D. Cannon, Elayne Heilveil, Cliff Osmond; *D:* Henning Schellerup. **TV**

The Adventures of Picasso 🐶🐶

1980 A Swedish satire on the life of Picasso, dubbed in English. Don't look for art or facts here, or, for that matter, many laughs. **88m/C VHS.** *SW* Gosta Ekman Jr., Lena Nyman, Hans Alfredson, Margareta Krook, Bernard Cribbins, Wilfrid Brambell; *D:* Tage Danielsson.

The Adventures of Pinocchio 🐶🐶½

Pinocchio; Carlo Collodi's Pinocchio **1996 (G)** Live-action version of Carlo Collodi's story about woodcarver Gepetto (Landau) who carves himself a puppet son (Thomas) who longs to be a real boy. Story differs from the Disney cartoon version in that it's a little darker and the cat, the fox, and the cricket have larger roles. Jim Henson's Creature Shop provided the animatronic magic to bring Pinocchio to life. His head alone was jammed with wiring and 18 tiny motors to give the "boy" a full range of facial expressions. It took as many as five puppeteers at a time to animate the character. So lifelike was the puppet that some of the crew actually spoke to it as they did the human actors. **88m/C VHS, DVD.** Martin Landau, Jonathan Taylor Thomas, Rob Schneider, Bebe Neuwirth, Udo Kier; *D:* Steven Barron; *W:* Steven Barron, Tom Benedek, Sherry Mills; *C:* Juan Ruiz-Anchia; *M:* Rachel Portman.

The Adventures of Pluto Nash woof!

2002 (PG-13) Pluto Nash (Murphy) owns a nightclub on the moon in the year 2087, and some gangsters want it. Murphy should save us all a lot of time, trouble, and wasted effort and hand it over. On the shelf for two years (and some good reasons), this steaming pile of "action-comedy" has nothing going for it. The performances are "collecting-a-paycheck" quality, the script and direction are a mess, and it's howlingly unfunny. If you avoid seeing one movie this year, make it this one. **97m/C VHS, DVD.** *US* Eddie Murphy, Rosario Dawson, Randy Quaid, Joe Pantoliano, Jay Mohr, John Cleese, James Rebhorn, Burt Young, Miguel A. Nunez Jr., Illeana Douglas, Victor Varnado; *D:* Ron Underwood; *W:* Neil Cuthbert; *C:* Oliver Wood; *M:* John Powell.

The Adventures of Priscilla, Queen of the Desert 🐶🐶🐶

1994 (R) Quirky down-under musical-comedy follows two drag queens and a transsexual across the Australian Outback on their way to a gig in a small resort town. They make the drive in a pink bus nicknamed Priscilla. Along the way they encounter, and perform for, the usual unusual assortment of local characters. Scenes depicting homophobic natives play out as expected. Finest moments occur on the bus or onstage (all hail ABBA). Strong performances, especially by usually macho Stamp as the widowed Bernadette, rise above the cliches in what is basically a bitchy, cross-dressing road movie, celebrating drag as art and the nonconformity of its heroes. Costumes (by Lizzy Gardner and Tim Chappel) are a lark, the photography's surreal, and the soundtrack fittingly campy. **102m/C VHS, DVD.** *AU* Terence Stamp, Hugo Weaving, Guy Pearce, Bill Hunter, Sarah Chadwick, Mark Holmes, Julia Cortez, Rebel Russell, June Marie Bennett, Alan Dargin, Al Clark, Margaret Pomeranz; *D:* Stephan Elliott; *W:* Stephan Elliott; *C:* Brian J. Breheny; *M:* Guy Gross. Oscars '94: Costume Des.; Australian Film Inst. '94: Costume Des.

The Adventures of Red Ryder 1940 The thrills of the rugged West are presented in this 12-episode serial. Based on the then-famous comic strip character. 240m/B VHS, DVD. Tommy Cook, Harry Worth, Wally Wales, William Farnum, Carleton Young, Donald (Don "Red") Barry, Noah Beery Sr.; *D:* John English; *W:* Frank (Franklyn) Adreon, Norman S. Hal, Barney A. Saredky; *C:* William Nobles; *M:* Cy Feuer.

The Adventures of Robin Hood 1938 Rollicking technicolor tale of the legendary outlaw, regarded as the swashbuckler standard-bearer. The justice-minded Saxon knight battles the Normans, outwits evil Prince John, and gallantly romances Maid Marian. Grand Castle sets and lush forest photography display ample evidence of the huge (for 1938) budget of $2 million plus. Just entering his prime, Flynn gives enthusiastically performed most of his own stunts, including intricate swordplay and advanced tree climbing. His Robin brims with charm and bravura. The rest of the cast is very merry men. Based on the many Robin Hood legends, as well as Sir Walter Scott's "Ivanhoe" and the opera "Robin Hood" by De Koven-Smith. 102m/C VHS, DVD, HD DVD. Errol Flynn, Olivia de Havilland, Claude Rains, Basil Rathbone, Alan Hale, Una O'Connor, Patric Knowles, Eugene Pallette, Herbert Mundin, Melville Cooper, Ian Hunter, Montagu Love; *D:* Michael Curtiz; *W:* Seton I. Miller, Norman Reilly Raine; *C:* Gaetano Antonio (Tony) Gaudio, Sol Polito; *M:* Erich Wolfgang Korngold. Oscars '38: Film Editing, Orig. Score, Natl. Film Reg. '95.

The Adventures of Rocky & Bullwinkle 2000 (PG) Flying squirrel and his moose pal, who have been living on residuals since their TV show was cancelled, discover that their old enemies, spies Boris Badenov (Alexander), Natasha Fatale (Russo) and their Fearless Leader (De Niro), have escaped from their two-dimensional existence. Now the trio are headed for Hollywood and a plot to—what else—take over the world. Someone seriously miscalculated in aiming this one at the Pokemon set (the show is 35 years old, and the majority of the jokes were always aimed at adults anyway), but it still provides a few good laughs, and is much more effective back on the small screen. 88m/C VHS, DVD. Robert De Niro, Jason Alexander, Rene Russo, Janeane Garofalo, Randy Quaid, Piper Perabo, Carl Reiner, Jonathan Winters, John Goodman, Kenan Thompson, Kel Mitchell, James Rebhorn, David Alan Grier, Norman Lloyd, John Polito, Whoopi Goldberg, Billy Crystal, Don Novello, Harrison Young, Dian Bachar, Faget Brewster; *D:* Des McAnuff; *W:* Kenneth Lonergan; *C:* Thomas Ackerman; *M:* Mark Mothersbaugh; *V:* June Foray, Keith Scott.

The Adventures of Rusty 1945 Forties family film series begins with this classic boy-meets-dog story. Danny's dog dies in an accident and his widowed father has just remarried so the kid's feeling pretty bad. Then he meets neglected German Shepherd Rusty, a former police dog with an undeservedly bad rep. Naturally, boy and dog bond and even capture a couple of escaped convicts (and Danny learns to love his stepmom too). 67m/B VHS. Ted Donaldson, Margaret Lindsay, Conrad Nagel, Gloria Holden; *D:* Paul Burnford; *W:* Aubrey Wisberg.

The Adventures of Sadie *Our Girl Friday* 1955 Collins is stranded on a desert island with three men, two of whom continuously chase her around. Naturally, she falls for the guy who ignores her. Obvious sex comedy which plays on Collins' scantily clad physical assets. Based on the novel "The Cautious Amorist" by Norman Lindsay. 87m/C VHS. GB Joan Collins, George Cole, Kenneth Mcre, Robertson Hare, Hermione Gingold, Walter Fitzgerald; *D:* Noel Langley.

The Adventures of Sebastian Cole 1999 (R) Sebastian (Grenier) is a misfit highschooler in upstate New York in 1983. Not only does he have to deal with the usual trials of adolescence but there's his unusual family problems. His mother, Joan (Colin), returns to her native England upon learning that Sebastian's stepdad, Hank (Gregg), has decided to become a woman. Sebastian eventually winds up living with Hank, who is now known as Henrietta, and who's still the most stable adult in the teen's fractured world. 99m/C VHS, DVD. Adrian Grenier, Clark Gregg, Aleksa Palladino, Margaret Colin, John Shea, Joan Copeland, Marni Lustig, Tom Lacy; *D:* Tod Williams; *W:* Tod Williams; *C:* John Foster; *M:* Lynne Geller.

The Adventures of Sharkboy and Lavagirl in 3-D 2005 (PG) Multi-hyphenate Rodriguez uses a story from son Racer as the basis for this kid-friendly adventure. Ten year-old misfit Max (Boyd) dreams up a couple of young superheroes and finds them computer-ready. Sharkboy (Lautner) and Lavagirl (Dooley) need Max's help to save their home world, Planet Drool, from the evil Mr. Electric (Lopez). The cartoonish geewizardry will no doubt appeal to its target audience, but might struggle to hold the attention of older fans. 94m/C DVD, UMD. US Kristen Davis, David Arquette, George Lopez, Taylor Lautner, Taylor Dooley, Cayden Boyd, Jacob Davich, Sasha Pieterse, Rico Torres, Rebel Rodriguez, Racer Rodriguez, Rocket Rodriguez; *D:* Robert Rodriguez; *W:* Robert Rodriguez; *C:* Robert Rodriguez; *M:* John Debney, Graeme Revell.

The Adventures of Sherlock Holmes *Sherlock Holmes* 1939 The immortal Sherlock Holmes and his assistant Dr. Watson conflict with Scotland Yard as they both race to stop arch-criminal Professor Moriarty. The Yard is put to shame as Holmes, a mere amateur sleuth, uses his brilliant deductive reasoning to save the damsel in distress and to stop Moriarty from stealing the Crown Jewels. Second in the series. 83m/B VHS, DVD. Basil Rathbone, Nigel Bruce, Ida Lupino, George Zucco, E.E. Clive, Mary Gordon; *D:* Alfred Werker; *W:* Edwin Blum; *C:* Leon Shamroy.

The Adventures of Sherlock Holmes' Smarter Brother 1978 (PG) The unknown brother of the famous Sherlock Holmes takes on some of his brother's more disposable excess cases and makes some hilarious moves. Moments of engaging farce borrowed from the Mel Brooks school of parody (and parts of the Mel Brooks ensemble as well). 91m/C VHS, DVD. Gene Wilder, Madeline Kahn, Marty Feldman, Dom DeLuise, Leo McKern, Roy Kinnear, John Le Mesurier, Douglas Wilmer, Thorley Walters; *D:* Gene Wilder; *W:* Gene Wilder.

Adventures of Smilin' Jack 1943 WWII flying ace Smilin' Jack Martin comes to life in this action-packed serial. Character from the Zack Mosley comic strip about air force fighting over China. 90m/B VHS, DVD. Tom Brown, Sidney Toler; *D:* Ray Taylor.

The Adventures of Tartu *Tartu* 1943 A British secret agent, sent to blow up a Nazi poison gas factory in Czechoslovakia, poses as a Romanian. One of Donat's lesser films, in the style of "The 39 Steps." 103m/B VHS, DVD. GB Robert Donat, Valerie Hobson, Glynis Johns; *D:* Harold Bucquet.

The Adventures of Tarzan 1921 The screen's first Tarzan in an exciting jungle thriller. Silent. 153m/B VHS. Elmo Lincoln, Louise Lorraine, Lillian Worth, Frank Whitson, Frank Merrill; *D:* Robert F. "Bob" Hill; *W:* Robert F. "Bob" Hill.

The Adventures of the Wilderness Family 1976 (G) The story of a modern-day pioneer family who becomes bored with the troubles of city life and heads for life in the wilderness. There, they find trouble in paradise. Family-oriented adventure offering pleasant scenery. Followed by "The Wilderness Family, Part 2." 100m/C VHS, DVD. Robert F. Logan, Susan Damante-Shaw; *D:* Stewart Raffill; *W:* Stewart Raffill.

Advise and Consent 1962 An interesting political melodrama with a fascinating cast, based upon Allen Drury's novel. The President chooses a candidate for the Secretary of State position which divides the Senate and causes the suicide of a senator. Controversial in its time, though somewhat turgid today. 139m/B VHS, DVD. Don Murray, Charles Laughton, Henry Fonda, Walter Pidgeon, Lew Ayres, Burgess Meredith, Gene Tierney, Franchot Tone, Paul Ford, George Grizzard, Betty White, Peter Lawford, Edward Andrews; *D:* Otto Preminger; *W:* Wendell Mayes; *C:* Sam Leavitt. Natl. Bd. of Review '62: Support. Actor (Meredith).

The Advocate *The Hour of the Pig* 1993 (R) Bizarre black comedy about 15th-century Paris lawyer Richard Courtois (Firth) who decides to ply his trade in the country, only to find things stranger than he can imagine. His first case turns out to be defending a pig that's accused of murdering a child. And the pig is owned by beautiful gypsy Samira (Annabi), so the idealistic lawyer can fall in love (or lust). There's religion and superstition, there's power struggles, there's ignorance versus knowledge—things sound very modern indeed. 102m/C VHS, DVD. GB Colin Firth, Amina Annabi, Nicol Williamson, Ian Holm, Lysette Anthony, Donald Pleasence, Michael Gough, Harriet Walter, Jim Carter, Dave Atkins; *D:* Leslie Megahey; *W:* Leslie Megahey.

Aelita: Queen of Mars *Aelita; The Revolt of the Robots* 1924 Though the title has blockbuster potential, "Aelita" is a little-known silent Soviet sci-fi flick destined to remain little known. After building a rocket to fly to Mars, a Russian engineer finds it's no Martian holiday on the fourth planet from the sun, with the Martians in the midst of a revolution. Silent, with a piano score. 113m/B VHS, DVD. RU Yulia Solntseva, Nikolai Batalov, Nikolai Tsereteli, Vera Orlova, Pavel Pol, Konstantin Eggert, Yuri Zavadski, Valentina Kuindzi, N. Tretyakova; *D:* Yakov Protazanov; *W:* Fedor Otsep, Aleksei Faiko; *C:* Yuri Zhelyabuzhski, Emil Schoneman.

The Adventures of Tom Sawyer 1938 The vintage Hollywood adaptation of the Mark Twain classic, with art direction by William Cameron Menzies. Not a major effort from the Selznick studio, but quite detailed and the best Tom so far. 91m/C VHS. Tommy Kelly, Walter Brennan, Victor Jory, May Robson, Victor Kilian, Jackie Moran, Donald Meek, Ann Gillis, Marcia Mae Jones, David Holt, Margaret Hamilton, James Wong Howe; *M:* Max Steiner.

The Adventures of Tom Sawyer 1973 Tom Sawyer is a mischievous Missouri boy who gets into all kinds of trouble in this white-washed made for TV adaptation of the Mark Twain classic. 76m/C VHS. Jane Wyatt, Buddy Ebsen, Vic Morrow, John McGiver, Josh Albee, Jeff Tyler; *D:* James Neilson. TV

The Adventures of Werner Holt *Die Abenteuer des Werner Holt* 1965 Two teenagers, Werner Holt and Gilbert Wolzow, are taken out of school and conscripted into Hitler's army. Gilbert is a fanatical soldier, while the horrors of the war make Werner question. But when Gilbert is executed by the SS, Werner turns his gun on his own side. Based on the novel by Dieter Noll. German with subtitles. 163m/B VHS. GE Klaus-Peter Thiele, Manfred Karge, Arno Wyzniewski, Gunter Junghans, Peter Reusse, Wolfgang Langhoff; *D:* Joachim Kunzel.

The Adventurous Knights WOOF! 1935 An athlete learns he is the heir to a Transylvanian throne. 60m/B VHS. David Sharpe, Mary Kornman, Mickey Daniels, Gertrude Messinger; *D:* Edward Roberts.

The Adversary *Pratidwandi* 1971 A young man must quit college because of his father's death. He struggles to find employment in Calcutta but his hardships are magnified by the impersonal society. In Bengali with English subtitles. 110m/C VHS. IN Dhritiman Chatterjee, Jayshree Roy, Jonraj Roy, Krishna Bose; *D:* Satyajit Ray; *W:* Satyajit Ray; *C:* Soumendu Roy, Purnendu Bose; *M:* Satyajit Ray.

Advertising Rules! *Viktor Vogel: Commercial Artist* 2001 (R) Graphic artist Viktor Vogel actualy lands a job after sneaking into an ad agency board meeting. And his luck continues when he meets sexy artist Rosa and helps her with an idea for her debut art exhibition. Then Viktor inadvertently pitches the same idea for the ad campaign and has to find a way to satisfy both work and Rosa. German with subtitles. 109m/C VHS, DVD. GE Gudrun Landgrebe, Alexander Scheer, Goetz George, Chulpan Khamatova, Maria Schrader, Vadim Glowna; *D:* Lars Kraume; *W:* Lars Kraume, Tom Schlessinger; *C:* Andreas Daub; *M:* Robert Jan Meyer.

The Affair 1973 Songwriter/polio victim Wood falls in love for the first time with attorney Wagner. Delicate situation handled well by a fine cast. 74m/C VHS. DVD Natalie Wood, Robert Wagner, Bruce Davison, Kent Smith, Frances Reid, Pat Harrington; *D:* Gilbert Cates. TV

The Affair 1995 (R) It's 1944 in a small English town, where a troop of black American soldiers are billeted prior to the D-Day invasion. Travis (Vance) falls for the married Maggie (Fox)—whose husband, Edward (Hinds), is supposed to be away at sea—and they begin an affair. Unfortunately Edward arrives home unexpectedly and accuses Travis of raping his wife. If Maggie denies the accusation, she'll lose her home and family but if she confirms it, Travis, according to Army law, will be condemned to death. 105m/C VHS, DVD. GB Courtney B. Vance, Kerry Fox, Ciaran Hinds, Beatie Edney, Leland Gantt, Bill Nunn, Ned Beatty; *D:* Paul Seed; *W:* Pablo F. Fenjves, Bryan Goulubelf; *C:* Ivan Strasburg; *M:* Christopher Gunning. CABLE.

An Affair in Mind 1989 A professional writer falls in love with a beautiful woman who tries to convince him to assist her in murdering her husband. 88m/C VHS. Amanda Donohoe, Stephen (Dillon) Dillane, Matthew Marsh, Jean-Laurent Cochot; *D:* Michael Baker. TV

Affair in Trinidad 1952 Fun in the tropics as nightclub singer Hayworth enlists the help of brother-in-law Ford to find her husband's murderer. The trail leads to international thieves and espionage in a romantic thriller that reunites the stars of "Gilda." Hayworth sings (with Jo Ann Greer's voice) "I've Been Kissed Before." 98m/B VHS. Rita Hayworth, Glenn Ford, Alexander Scourby, Torin Thatcher, Valerie Bettis, Steven Geray; *D:* Vincent Sherman.

An Affair of Love *Une Liaison Pornographique; A Pornographic Liaison* 1999 (R) French love story sounds like "Last Tango in Paris" but really owes more to "sex, lies and videotape." Elle (Baye) places an ad in a sex magazine and arranges to meet a respondent, Lui (Lopez), for afternoon sexual encounters in a hotel. Virtually all of the physical action takes place behind a closed door. The point is emotional and so, in after-the-fact monologues, they both discuss (separately) what's happened. French with subtitles. **80m/C VHS, DVD.** *FR BE LU* Nathalie Baye, Sergi Lopez, Paul Pavel; *D:* Frederic Fonteyne; *W:* Philippe Blasband; *C:* Virginie Saint-Martin; *M:* Andre Dziezuk, Marc Mergen, Jeannot Sanavia.

The Affair of the Necklace

🦴🦴½ 2001 (R) Louis XVI-era history is given a tabloid treatment in this costume drama concerning the vengeful efforts of orphaned Jeanne de la Motte-Valois to restore nobility to her family name. She conspires with a court rogue to hatch a sophisticated scam involving the cardinal of France, Marie Antoinette, German Illuminati, and the fabulous necklace of the title, paving the way for the French Revolution. Excessive narration and flashbacks bog the plot; film offers little other than eye candy in the form of intricate set pieces and fancy dress. Intriguing story potential is mishandled, and Swank is terribly miscast but looks nice in a corset. The remaining actors are underused, except Walken in a scene-chewing role as a Svengali-like mesmerist. **120m/C VHS, DVD.** *US* Hilary Swank, Jonathan Pryce, Simon Baker, Adrien Brody, Brian Cox, Joely Richardson, Christopher Walken, Paul Brooke, Peter Eyre, Simon Kunz, Hayden Panettiere; *D:* Charles Shyer; *W:* John Sweet; *C:* Ashley Rowe; *M:* David Newman.

An Affair to Remember

🦴🦴½ 1957 McCarey remakes his own "Love Affair," with less success. Nightclub singer Kerr and wealthy bachelor Grant discover love on an ocean liner and agree to meet six months later on top of the Empire State Building to see if their feelings are the same. Not as good as the original, but a winner of a fairy tale just the same. Notable for causing many viewers to sob uncontrollably. "Affair" was gathering dust on store shelves until "Sleepless in Seattle" used it as a plot device and rentals skyrocketed. In 1994 real life couple Warren Beatty and Annette Bening attempted a third "Love Affair" remake. **115m/C VHS, DVD.** Cary Grant, Deborah Kerr, Richard Denning, Cathleen Nesbitt, Neva Patterson, Robert C. Lewis, Fortunio Bonanova, Matt Moore, Nora Marlowe, Sarah Selby; *D:* Leo McCarey; *W:* Leo McCarey, Delmer Daves, Donald Ogden Stewart; *C:* Milton Krasner; *M:* Hugo Friedhofer.

Affairs of Anatol

🦴🦴 1921 Philandering playboy Anatol Spencer (Reid) finds no luck with women. He's robbed by one (Ayres), two-timed by another (Hawley), and even what she seems. Then Anatol decides to return to his wife, Vivian (Swanson), only to discover that she's being amusing herself with another. Based on a play by Arthur Schnitzler. **117m/B VHS, DVD.** Wallace Reid, Gloria Swanson, Bebe Daniels, Wanda (Petit) Hawley, Agnes Ayres, Monte Blue, Theodore Roberts, Elliott Dexter; *D:* Cecil B. DeMille; *W:* Beulah Marie Dix; *C:* Karl Struss, Alvin Wyckoff.

The Affairs of Dobie Gillis

🦴🦴½ 1953 Light musical-comedy about a group of college kids and their carefree antics. Complete with big-band tunes, dance numbers, and plenty of collegiate shenanigans, this "50s classic inspired a hit TV series, "The Many Loves of Dobie Gillis." ♪I'm Through with Love; All I Do Is Dream of You; You Can't Do Wrong Doing Right; Those Endearing Young Charms. **72m/B VHS.** Debbie Reynolds, Bobby Van, Barbara Ruick, Bob Fosse, Lurene Tuttle, Hans Conried, Charles Lane; *D:* Don Weis; *W:* Max Shulman; *C:* William Mellor.

Affliction

🦴🦴🦴½ 1997 (R) Nolte, Schrader, and Coburn turn in the finest work of their careers in this bleak tale of one man's battle with the demons of his past and the failures of the present. Nolte is small-town, small-time sheriff Wade Whitehouse, who wants to do the right things, but never does. Damaged beyond repair by his abusive alcoholic father (Coburn), he alienates or scares away anyone who might care for him, including his daughter (Tierney) and his girlfriend (Spacek). When a local businessman dies under mysterious circumstances, Wade sees a chance at redemption, but the investigation turns out to be the catalyst for his final degradation. Schrader has studied the beaten-down male psyche before, but never with this much discipline or effect. He adapted the screenplay from Russell Banks' 1989 novel. **113m/C VHS, DVD.** Nick Nolte, James Coburn, Sissy Spacek, Willem Dafoe, Mary Beth Hurt, Jim True-Frost, Marian Seldes, Brigid Tierney, Sean McCann, Wayne Robson, Holmes Osborne; *D:* Paul Schrader; *W:* Paul Schrader; *C:* Paul Sarossy; *M:* Michael Brook. Oscars '98: Support. Actor (Coburn); N.Y. Film Critics '98: Actor (Nolte); Natl. Soc. Film Critics '98: Actor (Nolte).

Afghan Knights

🦴½ 2007 (R) An ex-Navy SEAL recruits some former comrades to go back to Afghanistan as mercenaries in order to sneak a warlord out of the country. They meet some opposition and are forced to hide out in a cave where they find some weapons that contain the spirit of Genghis Khan and his Mongol warriors. Said ghostly hordes are looking for some new recruits. Surprisingly, not as ridiculous as it sounds. **90m/C DVD.** Francesco Quinn, Steve Bacic, Gary Stretch, Michael Madsen, Chris Kramer; *D:* Allan Harmon; *W:* Christine Stringer; *C:* Randal Platt; *M:* Jon Lee, Stu Goldberg. **VIDEO**

Afraid of the Dark

🦴🦴 1992 (R) Convoluted psycho-thriller from a child's point of view. Young Lucas is fearful for his blind mother. It seems a vicious slasher has been attacking blind women and Lucas' father, a policeman, has yet to apprehend the criminal. But...Lucas it seems has a problem with reality. With his fantasies and realities mixed, all the people in his life also play entirely different roles. Characters are so detached and unreal that a viewer is prevented from a clear understanding of anything that may, or may not, be going on. Directorial debut of Peploe. **91m/C VHS, DVD.** *FR GB* Ben Keyworth, James Fox, Fanny Ardant, Paul McGann, Clare Holman, Robert Stephens; *D:* Mark Peploe; *W:* Mark Peploe; *C:* Bruno de Keyzer.

Africa Screams

🦴🦴½ 1949 Abbott and Costello go on an African safari in possession of a secret map. Unheralded independent A&C film is actually quite good in the stupid vein, with lots of jungle slapstick, generally good production values, and a supporting cast of familiar comedy faces. **79m/B VHS, DVD.** Lou Costello, Bud Abbott, Shemp Howard, Hillary Brooke, Joe Besser, Clyde Beatty, Max Baer Sr.; *D:* Charles T. Barton; *W:* Earl Baldwin; *M:* Walter Schumann.

Africa Texas Style

🦴🦴 1967 An East African rancher hires an American cowboy and his Navajo sidekick to help run his wild game ranch. Decent family adventure which served as the pilot for the short-lived TV series "Cowboy in Africa." Features lots of wildlife footage and a cameo appearance by Hayley Mills. **109m/C VHS.** Hugh O'Brian, John Mills, Nigel Green, Tom Nardini, Adrienne Corri; *Cameos:* Hayley Mills; *D:* Andrew Marton; *M:* Malcolm Arnold. **TV**

An African Dream

🦴🦴½ 1990 (PG) A period tale about a black man and a white woman fighting against repression in South Africa. **94m/C VHS.** Kitty Aldridge, John Kani, Dominic Jephcott, John Carson, Richard Haines, Joy Stewart Spence; *D:* John Smallcombe.

African Journey

1989 A moving, cross-cultural drama of friendship. A young black American goes to Africa for the summer to be with his divorced father who is working in the diamond mines. There he meets a young black African like himself; they overcome cultural clashes and learn respect for one another. Beautiful scenery, filmed in Africa. Part of the "Wonderworks" series. **174m/C VHS.** Jason Blicker, Pedzisai Sithole.

The African Queen

🦴🦴🦴 1951 After Bible-thumping spinster Hepburn's missionary brother is killed in WWI Africa, hard-drinking, dissolute steamer captain Bogart offers her safe passage. Not satisfied with sanctuary, she persuades him to destroy a German gunboat blocking the British advance. The two spend most of their time battling aquatic obstacles and each other, rather than the Germans. Time alone on an African river turns mistrust and adventure to love, a transition effectively counterpointed by the continuing suspense of their daring mission. Classic war of the sexes script adapted from C.S. Forester's novel makes wonderful use of natural dialogue and humor. Shot on location in Africa. **105m/C VHS, DVD.** *GB* Humphrey Bogart, Katharine Hepburn, Robert Morley, Theodore Bikel, Peter Bull, Walter Gotell, Peter Swanwick, Richard Mamer; *D:* John Huston; *W:* John Huston, James Agee; *C:* Jack Cardiff. Oscars '51: Actor (Bogart); AFI '98: Top 100. Natl. Film Reg. '94.

African Rage

🦴🦴 *Tigers Don't Cry; The Long Shot; Target of an Assassin; Fatal Assassin* 1978 Little known release about an aging male nurse (yes, Quinn) who discovers he's dying of an incurable disease. With nothing left to lose, he plans the kidnapping of an African leader, hoping that the ransom will support his family. Meanwhile, another man is plotting the same leader's death. Decent performances help move along the improbable plot. **90m/C VHS, DVD.** *SA* Anthony Quinn, John Phillip Law, Simon Sabela, Ken Gampu, Marius Weyers, Sandra Prinsloo; *D:* Peter Collinson.

After Dark, My Sweet

🦴🦴🦴 1990 (R) A troubled young man in search of a little truth ends up entangled in a kidnapping scheme. Muddled direction is overcome by above average performances and gritty realism. Based on the novel by Jim Thompson. **114m/C VHS, DVD.** Jason Patric, Rachel Ward, Bruce Dern, George Dickerson, James Cotton, Corey Carrier, Rocky Giordani; *D:* James Foley; *W:* Robert Redlin, James Foley; *C:* Mark Plummer; *M:* Maurice Jarre.

After Darkness

🦴 1985 Slow-moving psycho-suspenser about a man obsessed with a desire to remedy his twin brother's schizophrenia. **104m/C VHS.** *SI GB* John Hurt, Julian Sands, Victoria Abril, Pamela Salem; *D:* Dominique Othenin-Girard.

After Hours

🦴🦴🦴½ 1985 (R) An absurd, edgy black comedy that's filled with novel twists and turns and often more disturbing than funny. An isolated uptown New York yuppie (Dunne) takes a late night stroll downtown and meets a sexy woman in an all-night coffee shop. From there he wanders through a series of threatening and surreal misadventures, leading to his pursuit by a vigilante mob stirred by ice cream dealer O'Hara. Something like "Blue Velvet" with more Catholicism and farce. Or similar to "Something Wild" without the high school reunion. Great cameos from the large supporting cast, including Cheech and Chong as burglars. A dark view of a small hell-hole in the Big Apple. **97m/C VHS, DVD.** Griffin Dunne, Rosanna Arquette, John Heard, Teri Garr, Catherine O'Hara, Verna Bloom, Linda Fiorentino, Dick Miller, Bronson Pinchot, Will Patton, Rockets Redglare, Rocco Sisto, Larry Block, Victor Argo; *Cameos:* Richard "Cheech" Marin, Thomas Chong, Martin Scorsese; *D:* Martin Scorsese; *W:* Joe Minion; *C:* Michael Ballhaus; *M:* Howard Shore. Cannes '86: Director (Scorsese); Ind. Spirit '86: Director (Scorsese), Film.

After Innocence

🦴🦴🦴 2005 Sanders explores the cracks in the criminal justice system by examining the cases of seven men—four white and three black—who were convicted on murder and rape charges. Eventually, after spending many years in prison, each was exonerated because of DNA evidence. Also examined are the roadblocks thrown up by authorities who don't seem to admit to mistakes, the question of compensation after wrongful imprisonment, and life after release. Documentary was made in collaboration with the nonprofit legal clinic, the Innocence Project, now expanded into the Innocence Network. Since its founding in 1992 more than 160 people have been exonerated through DNA testing. **95m/C DVD.** *US D:* Jessica Sanders; *W:* Jessica Sanders; *C:* Buddy Squires, Shana Hagan; *M:* Charles Bernstein.

After Julius

🦴🦴 1978 Twenty years after Julius Grace's death, his memory still hovers over his wife's and daughters' lives. British soap opera moves with glacier-like speed. Adapted from the book by Elizabeth Jane Howard. **150m/C VHS.** *GB* Faith Brook, John Carson, Cyd Hayman; *D:* John Glenister.

After Life

🦴🦴 *Wandafuru Raifu* 1998 A drab office building turns out to be a metaphysical doorway and those who pass through are the recently deceased. Each person is assigned a caseworker and told that they have three days to decide on one particular memory to take with them into the after life. If they cannot chose, they will be forced to remain in the limbo of the processing center until they can do so. Japanese with subtitles. **118m/C VHS, DVD.** *JP* Takeotoshi Naito, Susumu Terajima, Arata, Erika Oda, Takashi Naito, Hisako Hara; *C:* Yutaka Yamazaki, Masayoshi Sukita; *M:* Yasuhiro Kasamatsu.

After Midnight

🦴 *I Have Lived* 1933 An aspiring playwright tries to get his work produced, only to meet with dead ends. Eventually, he hooks up with a talented young actress with whom he finds romance and success. **69m/B VHS.** Alan Dinehart, Anita Page, Allen Vincent, Gertrude Astor; *D:* Richard Thorpe.

After Midnight

🦴🦴 1989 (R) Suspended in a central story about an unorthodox professor who preys upon the deepest fears of his students, a trio of terror tales come to life. From the writers of "The Fly II" and "Nightmare on Elm Street 4." Some chills, few thrills. **90m/C VHS, DVD.** Marg Helgenberger, Marc McClure, Alan Rosenberg, Pamela Segall, Nadine Van Der Velde, Ramy Zada, Jillian McWhirter, Billy Ray Sharkey, Judie Aronson, Tracy Wells, Ed Monaghan, Monique Salcido, Penelope Sudrow; *D:* Jim Wheat, Ken Wheat; *W:* Jim Wheat, Ken Wheat; *M:* Marc Donahue.

After Midnight

🦴🦴🦴 *Dopo mezzanotte* 2004 Quiet Martino lives a simple life as the night watchman for the National Museum of Cinema at the Mole Antonelliana in Turin, Italy, with the film aficionado spending his spare time dabbling on a pieced-together project of the city's history on film. But the entrance of eye-catching Amanda—on the lam from the police for scalding her boss with hot cooking fat—changes all that, especially once she's cleared of the charges and free to return to her car-thief boyfriend. The romantic triangle, in Italian, with English subtitles. **99m/C** zle. Giorgio Pasotti, Silvio Orlando, Francesca Inaudi, Fabio Troiano, Francesca Picozza; *D:* Davide Ferrario; *W:* Davide Ferrario; *M:* Banda Ionica, Daniele Sepe, Fabio Barovero.

After Pilkington

🦴🦴 1988 Thriller about an uptight Oxford professor who runs into his bewitching childhood sweetheart after many years. She persuades him to help search for a missing archaeologist. **100m/C VHS.** *GB* Bob Peck, Miranda Richardson, Barry Foster; *D:* Christopher Morahan. **TV**

After Sex

🦴🦴 *Post Coïtum, Animal Triste; Post Coïtum* 1997 Passion and madness—French style. Confident, middleaged Diane (Rouan) has a successful career and a complacent marriage. Then she meets twentysomething hunk Emilio (Terral) and all bets are off. The twosome have a delirious affair but Diane's passion teeters towards obsession, with reckless disregard for her family. Then the affair ends and Diane falls apart. French with subtitles. **97m/C VHS.** *FR* Brigitte Rouan, Boris Terral, Patrick Chesnais, Nils (Niels) Tavernier, Jean-Louis Richard, Françoise Arnoul; *D:* Brigitte Rouan; *W:* Santiago Amigorena, Guy Zilberstein, Brigitte Rouan, Jean-Louis Richard; *C:* Pierre Dupouey; *M:* Michel Musseau, Umberto Tozzi.

After the Deluge

🦴🦴🦴 2003 Dogged with their own problems, three brothers must deal with their distant father's decline from Alzheimer's while he is

After the Fall of New
York WOOF! 1985 (R) Dim-witted post-apocalyptic tale set in New York after the fall of the "Big Bomb." A man, driven in search for the last normal woman, has reason to believe she is frozen alive and kept in the heart of the city. His mission: locate her, thaw her, and engage in extremely limited foreplay with her, and repopulate the planet. A poorly dubbed dating allegory. **95m/C VHS, DVD.** *IT FR* Michael Sopkiw, Valentine Monnier, George Eastman; **D:** Sergio Martino.

After the Promise 1987 During the Depression, a poor carpenter tries to regain custody of his four sons following the death of his wife. Maudlin melodrama based on a true story. **100m/C VHS.** Mark Harmon, Diana Scarwid, Rosemary Dunsmore, Donnelly Rhodes, Mark Hildreth, Trey Ames, Richard Billingsley; **D:** David Greene. **M:** Ralph Burns. **TV**

After the Rain 𝄞𝄞 1999 (R) Hard-hitting apartheid story that unfortunately descends into melodrama. In 1970s South Africa, Steph (Bettany) is a conflicted soldier in love with dancer Emma (Lombard). After his brigade is posted, lonely Emma befriends a black co-worker, Joseph (Bakare). Upon learning that he is living on the streets, Emma invites Joseph to stay with her. Of course that just happens to be when Steph, who's deserted, returns and assumes the worst. Writer/director Kettle adapted the film from his play "Soweto's Burning." **110m/C DVD.** *SA* Paul Bettany, Louise Lombard, Ariyon Bakare; **D:** Ross Kettle; **W:** Ross Kettle; **C:** Koos Roets; **M:** Hummie Mann.

After the Rehearsal 𝄞𝄞𝄞 Efter Repetitionen 1984 (R) Two actresses, one young, the other at the end of her career, challenge their director with love and abuse. Each questions his right to use them on stage and off. A thoughtful discussion of the meaning and reason for art originally made for Swedish TV. In Swedish with English subtitles. **72m/C VHS.** *SW* Erland Josephson, Ingrid Thulin, Lena Olin; **D:** Ingmar Bergman; **W:** Ingmar Bergman; **C:** Sven Nykvist. **TV**

After the Revolution 𝄞𝄞 1990 A struggling novelist decides to write his next book from the viewpoint of his cat. In Hungarian with English subtitles. **82m/C VHS.** *HU* D: Tibor Wright; **D:** Andras Szirtes.

After the Shock 𝄞𝄞 1990 (PG) Documentary-like dramatization of the San Francisco-Oakland earthquake of October 1989 and, of course, its aftermath. Incorporates actual footage of the disaster. **92m/C VHS.** Yaphet Kotto, Rue McClanahan, Jack Scalia, Scott Valentine; **D:** Gary Sherman. **CABLE**

After the Storm 𝄞𝄞½ 2001 (R) Beachcomber Amo (Bratt) discovers a sunken yacht but can't salvage the loot, even with the help of girlfriend Coquina (Avital). So he hooks up with Jean-Pierre (Assante) and his wife Janine (Girard), but greed gets the best of everyone. Based on a story by Ernest Hemingway; filmed in Belize. **103m/C VHS, DVD.** Benjamin Bratt, Armand Assante, Mili Avital, Simone-Elise Girard; **C:** Gregory Middleton; **M:** Bill Wandel.

pained by flashbacks of his WWII tour of duty. **103m/C VHS, DVD.** David Wenham, Hugo Weaving, Samuel Johnson, Aden Young, Catherine McClements, Ray Barrett, Rachel Griffiths, Essie Davis, Kate Beahan, Vince Colosimo, Marta Dusseldorp, Bob Franklin, Marco Chiappi, Simon Burke; **D:** Brendan Maher; **W:** Jeb Cox, Andrew Knight; **C:** Geoff Burton; **M:** Cezary Skubiszwski. **TV**

After the Fox 1966 Sellers is a con artist posing as a film director to carry out a bizarre plan to steal gold from Rome. Features occasional backhand slaps at Hollywood, with Mature turning in a memorable performance as the has-been actor starring in Sellers' movie. Though the laughs are marginal. **103m/C VHS, DVD.** *IT FR* Michael Sopkiw, Victor Mature, Martin Balsam, Britt Ekland; **C:** Leonida Barboni; **M:** Burt Bacharach.

Afterburn 𝄞𝄞 1992 (R) When Ted, her Air Force pilot husband, is killed in a crash of his F-16 fighter, Janet Harduval learns the official explanation is pilot error. Convinced that something was wrong with his plane, Janet sets out to investigate, and eventually sue, military contractor General Dynamics. Dern turns in a great performance as the tough widow determined to clear her husband's name. Based on a true story. **103m/C VHS, DVD.** Laura Dern, Robert Loggia, Vincent Spano, Michael Rooker, Andy Romano; **D:** Robert Markowitz; **W:** Elizabeth Chandler. **CABLE**

Afterglow 𝄞𝄞 1997 (R) Romantic quadrangle skates by on the performances of its two veterans. Lucky Mann (Nolte) is experiencing marital boredom with his longtime wife Phyllis (the ever-beautiful Christie), a former B-movie actress. Meanwhile twentysomething Marianne Byron (Boyle), who is desperate to have a baby, is sexually frustrated by her workaholic hubby, Jeffrey (Miller). Repairman Lucky happens to come along to work on the Byron's apartment and Marianne decides to throw herself at him. Then Jeffrey meets the sophisticated Phyllis and soon both couples have uncoupled and re-formed. **113m/C VHS, DVD.** Nick Nolte, Julie Christie, Lara Flynn Boyle, Jonny Lee Miller, Jay Underwood, Domini Blythe; **D:** Alan Rudolph; **W:** Alan Rudolph; **C:** Toyomichi Kurita; **M:** Mark Isham. Ind. Spirit '98: Actress (Christie). N.Y. Film Critics '97: Actress (Christie); Natl. Soc. Film Critics '97: Actress (Christie). **TV**

Aftermath 𝄞𝄞½ 1985 Three astronauts return to Earth and are stricken to discover that the planet has been ravaged by a nuclear war. Quickly they make new plans. **96m/C VHS.** Steve Barkett, Larry Latham, Lynne Margulies, Sid Haig, Forrest J Ackerman; **D:** Ted V. Mikels.

After the Sunset 𝄞𝄞 2004 (PG-13) Lightweight crime caper is as memorable as a soap bubble, although the scenery (Hayek in a variety of skimpy attire and the sun-drenched island setting) is appealing. Max (Brosnan) is a suave thief who, with partner Lola (Hayek), has pulled off a successful diamond heist that runs the career of FBI agent Stan ("arrestson). The thieves then retire to the Bahamas where Max is soon bored, bored, bored, and ready for some action when an ocean liner docks in port with a priceless jewel exhibit onboard. Stan, of course, shows up, determined to finally outwit Max. Hayek plays another firecracker while Brosnan slums charmingly; Cheadle assorted evilness) is good deeds and responsibly. Nifty special effects though. **93m/C VHS, DVD.** *US* Pierce Brosnan, Salma Hayek, Woody Harrelson, Don Cheadle, Naomie Harris, Christopher Penn, Mykelti Williamson, Obba Babatunde, Russell Hornsby, Rex Linn, Kate Walsh, Troy Garity; **D:** Brett Ratner; **W:** Craig Rosenberg, Paul Zbyszewski; **C:** Dante Spinotti; **M:** Lalo Schifrin.

After the Thin Man 𝄞𝄞𝄞 1936 Second in a series of six "Thin Man" films, this one finds Nick, Nora and Asta, the lovable terrier, seeking out a murderer from Nora's own blue-blooded relatives. Fast-paced mystery with a witty script and the popular Powell/Loy charm. Sequel to "The Thin Man," followed by "Another Thin Man." **113m/B VHS, DVD.** William Powell, Myrna Loy, James Stewart, Elissa Landi, Joseph Calleia, Jessie Ralph, Alan Marshal; **D:** Woodbridge S. Van Dyke.

After the Wedding 𝄞𝄞𝄞 Efter Brylluppet 2006 (R) Jacob (Mikkelsen), director of a struggling Indian orphanage, is given the opportunity to solve all his problems via a rich benefactor back in Denmark. Once he returns home, however, he finds things much more complicated than he expected, and he must choose between the world he knows in India and the obligations towards an ex-girlfriend and illegitimate daughter in Denmark. An fine line between melodrama and soap opera. **120m/C DVD.** *CZ* Mads Mikkelsen, Rolf Lassgard, Sidse Babett Knudsen, Stine Fischer Christensen, Christian Tafdrup; **D:** Suzanne (dianne) Bier; **W:** Anders Thomas Jensen; **C:** Morten Soborg; **M:** Johan Soderqvist.

Against All Odds 𝄞𝄞½ 1984 (R) An interesting love triangle evolves when recently cut quarterback Terry Brogan (Bridges) is asked by his nightclub owner buddy, Jack (Woods), to travel to Mexico and bring back Jack's sultry girlfriend, Jessie (Ward). Then Terry discovers that Jessie is the daughter of Mrs. Wyler, the football team owner. Contains complicated plot, numerous double crosses, sensual love scenes, and a chase scene along Sunset Boulevard. As the good friend sans his conscience, Woods stars. A remake of 1947's "Out of the Past." **122m/C VHS, DVD.** Jeff Bridges, Rachel Ward, James Woods, Alex Karras, Jane Greer, Richard Widmark, Dorian Harewood, Swoosie Kurtz, Bill McKinney, Saul Rubinek; **D:** Taylor Hackford; **W:** Eric Hughes; **C:** Donald E. Thorin; **M:** Larry Carlton, Michel Colombier.

Against the Law 𝄞𝄞½ 1998 Criminal Rex (Grieco) prides himself on his abilities with a gun—leaving a trail of dead cops in his wake. His wants notoriety and, after spotting detective John Shepard (Mancuso) on a news show, decides that TV is the perfect medium to get his 15 minutes of infamy. **85m/C VHS.** Richard Grieco, Nick Mancuso, Nancy Allen, Steven Ford; **D:** Jim Wynorski; **W:** Steve Mitchell, Bob Sheridan; **C:** Andrea V. Rossotto; **M:** Kevin Kiner. **VIDEO**

Against the Ropes 𝄞𝄞 2004 (PG-13) "Erin Brockovich" meets "Rocky" in this biopic loosely based on the life of Detroit boxing manager Jackie Kallen (a-though for some reason, they set it in Cleveland). Jackie (Ryan) is a tough, harried secretary for the Cleveland Coliseum who's smarter than the boxing world she would indicate. She sees her chance to go somewhere in the boxing world when she buys cracknead/boxer "Luther's" contract from mobbed-up manager Sam (Shalhoub) for a dollar. Ryan plays Jackie as a walking cliche spouting lousy dialogue. Shalhoub injects the movie with a bit of fun doing his best Snidley Whiplash. Dutton does better playing Luther's trainer, Felix, than he does directing fight scenes that don't show the action with much clarity. There's no clear winner here, but the audience is definitely the loser. Paramount shelved the movie for a year and a half. **111m/C VHS, DVD.** *US* Meg Ryan, Charles S. Dutton, Kerry Washington, Joe Cortese; **D:** Charles S. Dutton; **W:** Cheryl Edwards; **C:** Jack N. Green; **M:** Michael Kamen.

Aftershock 𝄞½ 1988 (R) A beautiful alien and a mysterious stranger battle the Earth's repressive, evil government **90m/C VHS, DVD.** Jay Roberts Jr, Elizabeth Kaitan, Chris Mitchum, Richard Lynch, John Saxon, Russ Tamblyn, Michael Berryman, Chris De Rose, Chuck Jeffreys; **D:** Frank Harris; **W:** Michael Standing; **M:** Kevin Klinger, Bob Mamet.

Aftershock: Earthquake in
New York 𝄞½ 1999 Typical TV disaster movie based on the novel by Chuck Scarborough. You're introduced to a bunch of nice people (there's quite a good cast), disaster strikes, death and destruction are everywhere and it all brings out (rather than hysteria, looting, violence and cues. **139m/C VHS, DVD.** Tom Skerritt, Sharon Lawrence, Charles S. Dutton, Lisa Nicole Carson, Cicely Tyson, Jennifer Garner, Rachel Ticotin, Frederick Weller, Erika Eleniak, Michael Ryan; **D:** Mikael Salomon; **W:** David Stevens, Paul Eric Meyers, Loren Boothby; **C:** Jon Joffin; **M:** Irwin Fisch. **TV**

Against a Crooked Sky 𝄞𝄞 1975 (G) A young boy sets out with an elderly trapper to find his sister, who was captured by the Indians. Similar story to "The Searchers," but no masterpiece. **89m/C VHS, DVD.** Richard Boone, Stewart Petersen, Jewel Blanch, Geoffrey Land, Henry Wilcoxon; **D:** Earl Bellamy.

Against All Flags 𝄞𝄞 1952 An enjoyable Flynn swashbuckler about a British soldier slashing his way through the Spanish fleet at the turn of the 18th century. Though the story has been told before, tight direction and good performances win out. O'Hara is a tarty eyeful as a hot-tempered pirate moll. **81m/C VHS, DVD.** Errol Flynn, Maureen O'Hara, Anthony Quinn, Mildred Natwick; **D:** George Sherman.

Agatha 𝄞𝄞½ 1979 (PG) A speculative period drama about Agatha Christie's still unexplained disappearance in 1926, and a fictional American reporter's efforts to find her. Beautiful but lackluster mystery. Unfortunately Hoffman and Redgrave generate few sparks. **98m/C VHS.** Dustin Hoffman, Vanessa Redgrave, Timothy Dalton, Helen Morse, Tony Britton, Timothy West, Celia Gregory; **D:** Michael Apted.

Agatha Christie: A Life in
Pictures 𝄞𝄞½ 2004 In 2004, famed mystery writer Agatha Christie (Williams) went missing for 11 days. She was found at a hotel and couldn't remember what had happened to her, although hypnosis revealed that Christie knew her husband Archie (Coulthard) was an unfaithful wastrel. But Christie also left clues in her writings and, in 1962, the aged Agatha (Massey) speaks of her disappearance to journalist. **90m/C DVD, GB** Olivia Williams, Anthony O'Donnell, Bill Coulthard, Stephen Boxer, Anthony Massey, Raymond Coulthard; **D:** Richard Curson Smith; **C:** Jef Baynes; **M:** Andrew Phillips. **TV**

Agatha Christie's A
Caribbean Mystery 𝄞𝄞 1983 Miss Marple's vacation turns into another sleuthing adventure when she must solve the murder of a retired British Army officer. Faithful adaptation updates the action form the 1950s to the '80s in fine fashion. **96m/C VHS, DVD.** Helen Hayes, Barnard Hughes, Jameson Parker, Season Hubley, Swoosie Kurtz, Cassie Yates, Zakes Mokae, Stephen Macht, Maurice Evans, Lynne Moody, George Innes, Brock Peters; **D:** Robert Lewis; **W:** Sue Grafton, Steve Humphrey; **C:** Ted Voightlander; **M:** Lee Holdridge. **TV**

Agatha Christie's Murder is
Easy 𝄞𝄞 Murder is Easy 1982 Luke Williams (Bixby), an American computer expert, is on a train to London when he meets an old woman (Hayes) who confides that she is going to Scotland Yard to report some mysterious deaths in her village. When she is killed by a hit-and-run driver after leaving the train, he decides to

Against the Wall 𝄞𝄞½ 1948 A motley crew is trained for a mission into Nazi Germany to blow up records and restrain efforts. Unfortunately they win only a pyrrhic victory. A well-done production with solid performances from the cast. **96m/B VHS, DVD.** Robert Beatty, Jack Warner, Simone Signoret, Gordon Jackson, Paul Dupuis, Peter Illing; **D:** Charles Crichton.

Against the Wind 𝄞𝄞½ 1992 Contra el Viento 1990 Juan (Banderas) takes refuge in a remote area of Andalusia in an effort to get away from a mutually obsessive love. But his exile is in vain when his lover appears—his sister (Suarez). Spanish with subtitles. **117m/C VHS, DVD.** *SP* Antonio Banderas, Emma Suarez; **D:** Paco Periman.

Against the Wall 𝄞𝄞𝄞 1994 Compelling and tense dramatization of the 1971 Attica, New York prison uprising in which 10 guards were held hostage and state troopers and the National Guard killed 29 prisoners before regaining control. Partially fictionalized version of the story told from the viewpoints of a young prison guard (MacLachlan) and a politicized prisoner (Jackson). Filmed at a prison in Clarksville, Tennessee. **115m/C VHS, DVD.** Kyle MacLachlan, Samuel L. Jackson, Clarence Williams III, Frederic Forrest, Harry Dean Stanton, Tom Bower, Philip Bosco, Anne Heche, David Ackroyd; **D:** John Frankenheimer; **W:** Ron Hutchinson; **M:** Gary Chang. **CABLE**

investigate. When he reaches the village, he is aided by a local girl who also suspects foul play. So-so mystery suffers from attempts to update the mystery with computer technology. Adapted from the Agatha Christie novel "Easy to Kill." **95m/C VHS, DVD.** Bill Bixby, Lesley-Anne Down, Olivia de Havilland, Helen Hayes, Patrick Allen, Freddie Jones, Shane Briant, Leigh Lawson, Jonathan Pryce, Carol MacReady; **D:** Claude Whatham; **W:** Carmen Culver; **C:** Brian Tufano; **M:** Gerald Fried. **TV**

Agatha Christie's Murder with Mirrors 🐾🐾 *Murder with Mirrors* 1985 Lightweight TV mystery has Miss Marple (Hayes) once again sleuthing about to help an old friend (Davis) who thinks she's going to be killed for her estate. Hayes is once again dignified, but things begin to fade about half way through. Look for Tm Roth spicing things up in an early ro e. **96m/C VHS, DVD.** Helen Hayes, Bette Davis, Leo McKern, John Mills, John Laughlin, Dorothy Tutin, Anton Rodgers, John Woodvine, James Coombes, Tim Roth; **D:** Dick Lowry; **W:** George Eckstein; **C:** Brian West; **M:** Richard Rodney Bennett. **TV**

Agatha Christie's Sparkling Cyanide 🐾🐾 *Sparkling Cyanide* 1983 Somebody spiked the champagne—with cyanide! This really brings down a socialite couple's anniversary party as they have to set aside the ho r's douvres o solve the whodunit. Cheesy but enjoyable, the twist ending adds to the fun. **96m/C VHS.** Anthony Andrews, Deborah Raffin, Pamela Bellwood, Nancy Marchand, Josef Sommer, David Huffman, Christine Belford, June Chadwick, Harry (Henry) Morgan, Michael Woods; **D:** Robert Lewis; **W:** Robert M. Young, Sue Grafton, Steve Humphrey; **C:** Ted Voightlander. **TV**

Agatha Christie's The Pale Horse 🐾🐾½ *The Pale Horse* 1996 When writer Mark Easterbrook is accused of murdering a priest, the only clue to clearing himself is a mysterious list of names. Now he has to figure out the connection between the names if he expects to clear himself. **100m/C VHS, DVD.** *GB* Michael Byrne, Ruth Madoc, Leslie Phillips, Jean Marsh; **D:** Charles Beeson. **TV**

Agatha Christie's Thirteen at Dinner 🐾🐾 *Thirteen at Dinner* 1985 Hercule Poirot must solve the case when an actress's ex-husband dies shortly after granting her a divorce. Lack of character development hurt this otherwise solid outing. Fine cast is highlighted by Ustinov and Dunaway. **91m/C VHS, DVD.** Peter Ustinov, Faye Dunaway, David Suchet, Jonathan Cecil, Bill Nighy, Lee Horsley, Diane Keen, Allan Cuthbertson, John Barron, Amanda Pays, Lesley Dunlop; **Cameos:** David Frost; **D:** Lou Antonic; **W:** Rod Browning; **C:** Curtis Clark; **M:** John Addison. **TV**

The Age of Innocence 🐾🐾🐾 1993 (PG) Magnificently lavish adaptation of Edith Wharton's novel of passion thwarted by convention is visually stunning, but don't expect action since these people kill with a word or gesture. In 1870s New York, proper lawyer Newland Archer (Day-Lewis) is engaged to the equally proper May Welland (Ryder). He discovers unexpected romance when May's cousin, the rather scandalous Ellen Olenska (Pfeiffer), returns to the city from Europe but his hesitancy costs them dearly. Woodward's narration of Wharton's observations helps sort out what goes on behind the facades. Although slow, see this one for the beautiful period authenticity, thanks to Scorsese, who obviously labored over the small details. He shows up as a photographer; his parents appear in a scene on a train. **138m/C VHS, DVD.** Martin Scorsese, Daniel Day-Lewis, Michelle Pfeiffer, Wi-

nona Ryder, Richard E. Grant, Alec McCowen, Miriam Margolyes, Mary Beth Hurt, Geraldine Chaplin, Stuart Wilson, Michael Gough, Alexis Smith, Jonathan Pryce, Robert Sean Leonard; **D:** Martin Scorsese; **W:** Martin Scorsese, Jay Cocks; **C:** Michael Ballhaus; **M:** Elmer Bernstein; **Nar:** Joanne Woodward. Oscars '93: Costume Des.; British Acad. '93: Support. Actress (Margolyes); Golden Globes '94: Support. Actress (Ryder); Natl. Bd. of Review '93: Director (Scorsese); Support. Actress (Ryder).

Age Old Friends 🐾🐾🐾½ 1989 Crusty octogenarian Cronyn must choose. His daughter (played by real-life offspring Tandy) wants him to move out of a retirement home and into her house. But he's struggling to keep neighbor and increasingly senile friend Gardenia from slipping into "zombieland." An emotional treat with two fine actors deploying dignity and wit in the battle against old age. Originally adapted for HBO from the Broadway play, "A Month of Sundays" by Bob Larbey. **89m/C VHS, DVD.** Vincent Gardenia, Hume Cronyn, Tandy Cronyn, Esther Rolle, Michelle Scarabelli; **D:** Allen Kroeker.

The Agency 🐾🐾 *Mind Games* 1981 (R) An advertising agency attempts to manipulate public behavior and opinion through the use of subliminal advertising. A good premise is bogged down by a dull script and plodding performances by a dull concerned. Based on a Paul Gottlieb novel. **94m/C VHS, DVD.** *CA* Robert Mitchum, Lee Majors, Valerie Perrine, Saul Rubinek, Alexandra Stewart; **D:** George Kaczender; **M:** Lewis Furey.

Agent Cody Banks 🐾🐾½ 2003 (PG) Muniz is Cody Banks, a seemingly normal 15-year-old kid who lives a secret life as a CIA spy. After training for a few years at a "junior spy" summer camp, he's given his first mission: talk to a girl He must befriend and protect classmate Natalie (Duff), the daughter of a scientist (Donovan) who's created a nanotechnology that could help villains McShane and Vosloo CONTROL THE WORLD!!! Much junior 007 action ensues, mixed with some quirky comedy and innocent teen romance. "Spy Kids" had more charm, but the target audience probably won't mind the difference. Harmon keeps things interesting for the older set with her vavoomish wardrobe and surprising knack for comedy. If the characters aren't exactly fleshed out, at least the actors playing them seem to be enjoying themselves. **95m/C VHS, DVD.** *US* Frankie Muniz, Hilary Duff, Angie Harmon, Keith David, Cynthia Stevenson, Arnold Vosloo, Martin Donovan, Daniel Roebuck, Ian McShane, Darrell Hammond; **D:** Harald Zwart; **W:** Scott M. Alexander, Ashley Edward Miller, Zack Stentz, Larry Karaszewski; **C:** Denis Crossan; **M:** John Powell.

Agent Cody Banks 2: Destination London 🐾🐾 2004 (PG) Banks is back to take on more evildoers who want to RULE THE WORLD!!! AGAIN!!! Now it's British industrialist Lord Kenworth (Faulkner) and Diaz (Allen) Banks's CIA camp commander turned traitor, who have a device that allows them to control what people do and say. Off to London for the big showdown, Cody goes undercover in a youth symphony where he meets his handler (the funny Anderson, who's not given much to work with) and Hilary Duff fill-in Spearritt as Emily, the prerequisite pretty girl (albeit a drab one here). While the first effort thrived on the normal-teenager-becomes-secret-agent concept the second surprisingly ignores the first part and focuses on the at-times hard-to-follow action scenes. Muniz puts in another fine performance and the kids will probably still find it a fun ride, but a trilogy is probably not needed. **98m/C VHS, DVD.** *US* Frankie Muniz, Anthony Anderson, Cynthia Stevenson, Daniel Roebuck, Hannah Spearritt, Anna Chancellor, Keith Allen, James Faulkner, David Kelly, Santiago Segura, Connor Widdows; **D:** Kevin Allen; **W:** Don Rhymer, Harald Zwart; **C:** Denis Crossan; **M:** Mark Thomas.

Agent of Death 🐾🐾 *The Alternate* 1999 (R) Philandering President Beck is not Mr. Popularity and there's an election coming up. So his PR head arranges for a fake kidnapping to garner sympathy. But the plans goes wrong and he winds up in

the hands of a psycho Secret Service agent (Genesse). And the one man (Roberts) who might be able to rescue the Prez doesn't want the job. **105m/C VHS, DVD.** Ice-T, Eric Roberts, Michael Madsen, Bryan Genesse, John Beck; **D:** Sam Firstenberg; **W:** Bryan Genesse. **VIDEO**

Agent on Ice 🐾🐾 1986 (R) Hockey team is stalked by lawyers. No, wait. An ex-CIA agent is stalked for cover-up purposes by the agency and the mob. One slippery fellow. **96m/C VHS.** Tom Ormeny, Clifford David, Louis Pastore, Matt Craven; **D:** Clark Worswick.

Agent Red 🐾½ *Captured* 2000 (R) Oh so typical story done in a less-than-enthralling manner. Naval Specials Ops Commander Matt Hendricks (Lundgren) is aboard a U.S. sub, escorting a deadly chemical weapon to a safe storage facility. Then the sub is boarded by Russian terrorists who want to unleash the virus on New York City. Naturally, Hendricks must prevent that. **95m/C VHS, DVD.** Dolph Lundgren, Randolph Mantooth, Meilani Paul, Alexander Kuznitsov, Natalie Radford, Steve Eastin, Tony Becker; **D:** Damian Lee; **W:** Damian Lee; **C:** Ken Blakey; **M:** David Wurst. **VIDEO**

Aggie Appleby, Maker of Men 🐾½ *Cupid in the Rough* 1933 A wimpy society boy transforms himself into a tough guy, all for the love of a dame. Based on a play by Joseph O. Kesselring. Very slight comedy. **73m/B VHS.** Charles Farrell, Wynne Gibson, William Gargan, Zasu Pitts, Betty Furness; **D:** Mark Sandrich; **M:** Max Steiner.

Agnes and His Brothers 🐾🐾 *Agnes und Seine Bruder* 2004 Transsexual Agnes has little in common with her two brothers, Hans-Jorg and Werner, except for their loathing of their weirdo recluse father, Gunther. Agnes has man trouble (she's always a victim) and Hans-Jorg and Werner are sexually desperate, albeit for different reasons. These are strange, unlikable people and you will be very glad they're not part of your family. German with subtitles. **115m/C DVD.** *GE* Moritz Bleibtreu, Herbert Knaup, Vadim Glowna, Katja Riemann, Martin Weiss, Tom Schilling; **D:** Oskar Roehler; **C:** Carl F. Koschnick; **M:** Martin Todsharow.

Agnes Browne 🐾🐾 1999 (R) Sentimental, old-fashioned saga concerning recent widow Agnes Browne (Huston), who's trying to cope with her seven children under difficult circumstances in Dublin in 1967. Agnes, who works a market stall, has some personal dream—she wants to see Tom Jones in an upcoming concert. Guess what happens. Director Huston does try to keep the bathos under control. Based on the novel "The Mammy" of Brendan O'Carroll. **91m/C VHS, DVD.** Anjelica Huston, Ray Winstone, Arno Chevrier, Marion O'Dwyer, Ciaran Owens, Tom Jones; **D:** Anjelica Huston; **W:** John Goldsmith, Brendan O'Carroll; **C:** Anthony B. Richmond; **M:** Paddy Moloney.

Agnes of God 🐾🐾 1985 (PG-13) Stage to screen translation of John Pielmeier's play loses something in the translation. Coarse chain-smoking psychiatrist Fonda is sent to a convent to investigate whether young nun Tilly is fit to stand trial. Seems that the nun may have given birth to and then strangled her baby, although she denies ever having sexual relations and knows nothing about an infant. Naive Tilly is frightened by probing Bancroft, while worldly mother-superior Bancroft is distrusting. Melodramatic stew of Catholicism, religious fervor, and science features generally good performances, although Fonda often seems to be acting (maybe it's the cigarettes). **98m/C VHS, DVD.** Jane Fonda, Anne Bancroft, Meg Tilly, Anne Pitoniak, Winston Rekert, Gratien Gelinas; **D:** Norman Jewison; **W:** John Pielmeier; **C:** Sven Nykvist; **M:** Georges Delerue. Golden Globes '86: Support. Actress (Tilly).

The Agony and the Ecstasy 🐾🐾½ 1965 Big-budget (for

cess and the hours (it seems literal due to movie length) of painting flat on his back. Heston exudes quiet strength in his sincere interpretation of the genius artist, while Harrison has a fling as the Pope. Slow script is not up to the generally good performances. Disappointing at the boxoffice, but worth a look on the small screen for the sets alone. **136m/C VHS, DVD.** Charlton Heston, Rex Harrison, Harry Andrews, Diane Cilento, Alberto Lupo, Adolfo Celi; **D:** Carol Reed; **W:** Philip Dunne; **C:** Leon Shamroy; **M:** Jerry Goldsmith, Alex North. Natl. Bd. of Review '65: Support. Actor (Andrews).

Agony of Love 🐾 1966 An unhappy homemaker rents a nearby apartment to live out her wildest fantasies and bring some excitement into her otherwise dull life. **?m/C VHS, DVD.** Pat (Barringer) Barrington, William Rotsler; **D:** William Rotsler; **W:** William Rotsler.

Aguirre, the Wrath of God 🐾🐾🐾½ *Aguirre, der Zorn Gottes* 1972 Herzog at his best, combining brilliant poetic images and an intense narrative dealing with power, irony, and death. Spanish conquistadors in 1590 search for the mythical city of gold in Peru. Instead, they descend into the hell of the jungle. Kinski is fabulous as Aguirre, succumbing to insanity while leading a continually diminishing crew in this compelling, extraordinary drama shot in the jungles of South America. Both English- and German-language versions available. **94m/C VHS, DVD.** *GE* Klaus Kinski, Ruy Guerra, Del Negro, Helena Rojo, Cecilia Rivera, Peter Berling, Danny Ades; **D:** Werner Herzog; **W:** Werner Herzog; **C:** Thomas Mauch; **M:** Popul Vuh. Natl. Soc. Film Critics '77: Cinematog.

Ah, Wilderness! 🐾🐾🐾½ 1935 Delightful tale of a teen boy coming of age in small town America. Watch for the hilarious high school graduation scene. Based on the play by Eugene O'Neill. Remade in 1948 as "Summer Holiday," a musical with Mickey Rooney in the lead. **101m/B VHS.** Wallace Beery, Lionel Barrymore, Aline MacMahon, Eric Linden, Cecilia Parker, Spring Byington, Mickey Rooney, Charley Grapewin, Frank Albertson; **D:** Clarence Brown; **C:** Clyde De Vinna.

Aileen: Life and Death of a Serial Killer 🐾🐾 2003 Documentary studies the life and crimes of serial killer Aileen Wuornos. In-depth work recounts her horrible childhood and the psychoses that led to her murderous spree. Chilling. **89m/C VHS, DVD.** *US* Joan Churchill, Nick Broomfield; **C:** Joan Churchill; **M:** Robert (Rob) Lane.

Aimee & Jaguar 🐾🐾 1998 In 1943 Berlin, Jewish Felice (Schrader) is hiding her identity and working for a Nazi newspaper where she can gather information to leak to the resistance. She leads a hedonistic night life with a group of lesbian friends and, one night, encounters Lilly (Koehler), the unfaithful wife of an SS soldier who's away at the Russian front. The odd couple begin a risky love affair (the title refers to the nicknames the women gave each other) until the inevitable discovery. Based on a true story from the 1994 book by Erica Fischer. German with subtitles. **125m/C VHS, DVD.** *GE* Maria Schrader, Juliane Kohler, Johanna Wokalek, Heike Makatsch, Elisabeth Degen, Detlev Buck; **D:** Max Farberbock; **W:** Rona Munro, Max Farberbock; **C:** Tony Imi; **M:** Jan A.P. Kaczmarek.

Ain't No Way Back 🐾 1990 (R) It's the Vietnam War and the CIA is operating a secret drug smuggling operation in Southeast Asia to finance the effort. Flyboys Gibson and Downey drop opium and glib lines all over Laos. Big-budget Gibson vehicle with sufficient action but lacking much of a story, which was adapted from a book by Christopher Robbins. **113m/C VHS, DVD.** Mel Gibson, Robert Downey Jr., Marshall Bell, Nancy Travis, David Marshall Grant, Tim Thomerson, Lane Smith; **D:** Roger Spottiswoode;

Air Bud 🐾🐾½ 1997 (PG) Buddy's a basketball-playing golden retriever (no relation) who befriends lonely misfit Josh (Zegers) and teaches him the nuances of the layup, fade-away J, and pick-and-roll. It's good to see cog athletes getting to stretch beyond the usual frisbee and stick-fetching roles. Teaming animals (especially canines) with kids usually adds up to success. This one's no exception, especially 'for the grade school crowd. 92m/C VHS, DVD. Kevin Zegers, Michael Jeter, Bill Cobbs, Wendy Makkena, Eric Christmas, Brendan Fletcher, Jay Brazeau, Stephen E. Miller, Nicola Cavendish; D: Charles Martin Smith; W: Paul Tamasy, Aaron Mendelsohn; C: Mike Southon; M: Brahm Wenger.

Air Bud 2: Golden Receiver 🐾🐾 1998 (G) Buddy, the canine Michael Jordan of last year's "Air Bud," is back for more organized team sports with small children. His owner, Josh (Zegers) is still mourning the death of his father and isn't ready to deal with his mother's budding romance with the new veterinarian in town (Harrison). Meanwhile, Josh joins the school's football team and finds himself thrust into the spotlight as the team's quarterback when the starter is injured (big surprise!), only to be balled out by his multi-sport pooch. Actually, Buddy is played by four different Golden Retrievers, as the original died shortly after completing the original. This rehash tries to take itself seriously, with lessons about overcoming tragedy and adjusting to change, but isn't much more than sappy melodrama and cute dog tricks. 90m/C VHS, DVD. Kevin Zegers, Cynthia Stevenson, Gregory Harrison, Nora Dunn, Robert Costanzo, Tim Conway, Dick Martin, Perry Anzilotti, Suzanne Ristic, Jay B'azeau; D: Richard Martin; W: Paul Tamasy, Aaron Mendelsohn; C: Mike Southon; M: Brahm Wenger. VIDEO

Air Bud 3: World Pup 🐾🐾½ 2000 (G) Buddy went from basketball to football and now to soccer in this third installment. This time he teams up with the U.S. Women's Soccer Team and also becomes a dad. And wouldn't you know—just before the championship game, dad Buddy must rescue one of his pups from a gang of dog-nappers. 83m/C VHS, DVD. Kevin Zegers, Dale Midkiff, Caitlin Wachs, Martin Ferrero, Duncan Regehr, Brittany Paige Bouck, Briana Scurry, Brandi Chastain, Tisha Venturini; D: Bill Banneman. VIDEO

Air Bud 4: Seventh Inning Fetch 🐾🐾½ 2002 (G) Since Josh is off at college, it's his little sis Andrea who needs Buddy's help on her baseball team. But Buddy's got other problems—Rocky the Raccoon has kidnapped Buddy's puppies! 93m/C VHS, DVD. Richard Karn, Cynthia Stevenson, Kevin Zegers, Caitlin Wachs; D: Robert Vince. VIDEO

Air Bud 5: Buddy Spikes Back 🐾🐾 2003 (G) After her best friend moves to California, Andrea (Wachs) takes up volleyball so she can win a chance to visit. Naturally, all-around sports dog Buddy can do a little spiking of his own. 87m/C VHS, DVD, CA Caitlin Wachs, Molly Pevsin, Jake D. Smith, Tyler Boissonnault, Edie McCurg, Patrick Cranshaw, Cynthia Stevenson, Rob Tinkler; D: Mike Southon; C: Adam Sliwinski. VIDEO

Air Bud 6: Air Buddies 🐾🐾 2006 (PG) When doggie parents Buddy and Moly are abducted, their five talking puppies—B-Dawg, RoseBud, Buddha, Mudbud, and Budderball—must come to the rescue. Yeah, it's cute—you expected more? 82m/C DVD. Slade Pearce, Trevor Wright; D: Robert Vince; W: Robert Vince, Anna McRoberts; C: Mike Southon; M: Brahm Wenger. V: Abigail Breslin, Spencer Breslin, Josh Flitter, Spencer Fox, Michael Clarke Duncan, Don Knotts, Mike Southon.

Air Force 🐾🐾🐾½ 1943 One of the finest c' the WWII movies, Hawks' exciting classic has worn well through the years, in spite of the Japanese propaganda. It follows the hazardous exploits of a Boeing B-17 bomber crew who fight over Pearl Harbor, Manila, and the Coral Sea. Ex

tremely realistic dogfight sequences and powerful, introspective real guy interfacing by the ensemble cast are masterfully combined by Hawks. 124m/B VHS, DVD. John Garfield, John Ridgely, Gig Young, Arthur Kennedy, Charles Drake, Harry Carey Sr., George Tobias, Ray Montgomery, James Brown, Stanley Ridges, Willard Robertson, Moroni Olsen, Edward Brophy, Richard Lane, Faye Emerson, Addison Richards, James Flavin, Ann Doran, Dorothy Peterson, William Forrest, Ward Wood; D: Howard Hawks; W: Dudley Nichols, William Faulkner, C: James Wong Howe, Elmer Dyer, Charles A. Marshall; M: Franz Waxman. Oscars '43: Film Editing.

Air Force One 🐾🐾🐾 1997 (R) Ford stars as U.S. President James Marshall, who is not only tough on crime but with terrorists. Then Air Force One, with aboard is hijacked by Russian nationalists, led by ice cold Ivan (Oldman). Close is first woman Veep, Kathryn Bennett, stuck in D.C. coping with the situation. Ford is in fine form as the President who's forced to kick some Commie butt to save the day. Director Petersen ("In The Line of Fire") is becoming a master of building tension in confined places and puts his strong cast to good use. Nail-biting suspense and breath-taking action sequences cap off tour-de-force adventure. 124m/C VHS, DVD, UMD. Harrison Ford, Gary Oldman, Glenn Close, Dean Stockwell, William H. Macy, Wendy Crewson, Xander Berkeley, Paul Guilfoyle, Liesl Matthews, Bill Smitrovich, Elya Baskin, David Vadim, Tom Everett, Philip Baker Hall, Spencer Garrett, Donna Bullock; Cameos: Jurgen Prochnow; D: Wolfgang Petersen; W: Andrew Marlowe; C: Michael Ballhaus; M: Jerry Goldsmith.

Air Guitar Nation 🐾🐾🐾 2006 (R) Suit up, grab your guitars...wait, you don't need them. First time director (and reality TV vet) Lipsitz follows David "C. Diddy" Jung and Dan "Bjorn Turoque" Crane as they air guitar-battle their way from American competitions to the World Championships in Finland. Lipsitz doesn't push many boundaries with her direction or narrative, but still manages to create a film that's often hilarious without making its subjects the butt of the joke. 81m/C DVD. US D: Alexandra Lipsitz; C: Anthony Sacco; M: Dan Crane.

Air Hawk 🐾 1984 Australian made for TV release details the adventures of an outback pilot involved with stolen diamonds. 90m/C VHS. AU Eric Oldfield, Louise Howitt, Ellie MacLure, David Rooson, David Baker; D: David Baker. TV

The Air I Breathe 🐾🐾 2007 (R) Four interlocking stories are delivered in the form of an allegorical gangster movie that ends up an overwrought mess. Characters Happiness (Whitaker), Pleasure (Fraser), Sorrow (Gellar), and Love (Bacon), named for the key emotions of a Chinese proverb, muddle through individual challenges while the menacing gangster Finger's (Garcia) casts a shadow over all their lives. Standout cast 'ails to overcome the challenges presented by such a poorly executed, pretentious movie. 97m/C DVD. US Forest Whitaker, Brendan Fraser, Sarah Michelle Gellar, Kevin Bacon, Andy Garcia, Emile Hirsch, Julie Delpy; D: Jieho Lee; W: Jieho Lee, Bob DeRosa; C: Walt Lloyd; M: Marcelo Zarvos.

Air Rage 🐾🐾 2001 (R) General Prescott (Cord) screwed over five Marines, setting them up and sending them to prison in order to advance his career. Now they're out and have just hijacked a 747 with revenge on board—they not only want Marshall (Ice-T) and his team are sent on a rescue mission but things go wrong and Marshall is left to tackle the bad guys on his own. Familiar O'Reilly, Steve Hytner, Gil Gerard, Alex Cord, Cyril O'Reilly, Steve Hytner, Gil Gerard, Alex Cord, Kim Oja; D: Fred One Riley; W: Sean O'Bannon; C: Mac Ahlberg.

Air Raid Wardens 🐾🐾½ 1943 Laurel & Hardy play a couple of small-town failures who become the local air raid warders during WWII. They even manage to make a mess of this but redeem themselves when they overhead a spy plot and

save the town's munitions factory from a German spy ring. A so-so effort from the comic duo. 67m/B VHS, DVD. Stan Laurel, Oliver Hardy, Edgar Kennedy, Jacqueline White, Stephen McNally, Russell Hicks, Howard Freeman, Donald Meek, Henry O'Neill; D: Edward Sedgwick.

The Air Up There 🐾🐾 1994 (PG) Assistant basketball coach Jimmy Dolan (Bacon) heads to the African village of Winabi to recruit talented (and tall) Saleh (Maina) to play b-ball in the U.S. But Saleh is next in line to be the tribe's king and doesn't want to leave. Stupid American in foreign country learning from the natives story is lighthearted, but relies heavily on formula—and borders on the stereotypical, though clinical game is a lot of fun. 108m/C VHS, DVD, Kevin Bacon, Charles Gitona chael Glaser; W: Max Apple; C: Elliot Davis; M: Maina, Sean McCann, Dennis Patrick; D: Paul MiDavid Newman.

Airborne 🐾½ 1993 (PG) Cool California rollerblade dude gets transplanted to Cincinnati for a school year, and has to prove himself when those good ol' midwestern boys come after him. Nothing short of a skate vehicle appealing largely, if not solely, to the high school contingent. 91m/C VHS. Jack Black, Chris Conrad, Alanna Ubach, Jacob Vargas, Shane McDermott, Seth Green, Brittney Powell, Edie McClurg; D: Rob Bowman; W: Bill Apablasaa; M: Stewart Copeland.

Airboss 🐾½ 1997 (R) A special forces team of FBI agents and the military must track down a hijacked shipment of plutonium before it falls into terrorist hands. When a team member is killed, fighter pilot Frank White (Zagarino) s called in. Lots of machinery, guns, and explosions make up for the lack of believable story. 90m/C VHS, DVD. Frank Zagarino, John Christian, Kayte Watson, Caroline Strong, Jerry Kakch; D: J. Christian Ingvordsen. VIDEO

Airborne 🐾🐾 1998 (R) Members of a covert Special Forces team are targeted for assassination after recovering a biochemical weapon from terrorists. But their leader (Guttenberg) decides to use the virus as bait to find out who wants them dead. Guttenberg tries but can't convince as a tough guy but there's lots of action to make up for this casting quirk. 94m/C VHS, DVD. Steve Guttenberg, Sean Bean, Colm Feore; D: Julian Grant. VIDEO

Airheads 🐾🐾½ 1994 (PG-13) "Wayne's World" meets "Dog Day Afternoon." "Silly farce has three metal heads (Buscemi, Fraser, Sandler) holding a radio station hostage in order to get their demo tape played. Events snowball and they receive instant fame. Cast and crew rich with subversive comedic talents, including Sandler and Farley from "Saturday Night Live." Soundtrack authenticity supplied by White Zombie and The Galatic Cowboys. 81m/C VHS, DVD. Brendan Fraser, Steve Buscemi, Adam Sandler, Chris Farley, Michael McKean, Judd Nelson, Joe Mantegna, Michael Richards, Ernie Hudson, Amy Locane, Nina Siemaszko, John Melendez; D: Michael Lehmann; M: Carter Burwell.

Airplane! 🐾🐾🐾½ 1980 (PG) Classic lampoon of disaster flicks is stupid but funny and launched a bevy of wanna-be spoofs. Pilot Peter Graves, Steve Buscewho's lost both his stewardess girlfriend Elaine (Hagerty) and his nerve, takes over the controls of a jet when the crew is hit with food poisoning. The passengers become increasingly crazed and ground support more surreal as our hero struggles to land the plane. Clever, fast-paced, and very funny parody mangles every Hollywood cliché within reach. The gags are so furiously paced that when one bombs it's hardly noticeable. Launched Nielsen's second career as a comic actor. And it ain't over till it's over; don't miss the amusing final credits. Followed by "Airplane 2: The Sequel." 88m/C VHS, DVD. Jerry Zucker, Jim Abrahams, David Zucker, Robert Hays, Julie Hagerty, Lloyd Bridges, Peter Graves, Robert Stack, Kareem Abdul-Jabbar, Leslie Nielsen, Stephen Stucker, Ethel Merman, Barbara Billingsley, Lorna Patterson, Joyce Bulifant, James Hong, Maureen McGovern, Jimmie Walker, Rosse (Ross) Harris; D: Jerry Zucker, Jim Abrahams, David Zucker; W: Jerry Zucker, Jim Abrahams David

Zucker; C: Joseph Biroc; M: Elmer Bernstein. Writers Guild '80: Adapt. Screenplay.

Airplane 2: The Sequel 🐾🐾 1982 (PG) Not a Zucker, Abrahams and Zucker effort, and sorely missing their slapstick and script finesse. The first passenger space shuttle has taken off for the moon and there's a mad bomber on board. Given the number of stars mugging, it's more of a loveboat in space than a fitting sequel to "Airplane." Nonetheless, some funny laughs and gags. 84m/C VHS, DVD. Robert Hays, Julie Hagerty, Lloyd Bridges, Raymond Burr, Peter Graves, William Shatner, Sonny Bono, Chuck Connors, Chad Everett, Stephen Stucker, Rip Torn, Ken McCord, Sandahl Bergman, Jack Jones, John Dehner, Richard Jaeckel; Cameos: Ken Finkleman; C: Ken Finkleman; W: Ken Finkleman; C: Joseph Biroc; M: Elmer Bernstein.

Airport 🐾🐾🐾 1970 (G) Old-fashioned disaster thriller built around an all-star cast; fairly moronic script, and an unavoidable accident during the flight of a passenger airliner. A boxoffice hit that paved the way for many lesser disaster flicks (including its many sequels) detailing the reactions of the passengers and crew as they cope with impending doom. Considered to be the best of the "Airport" series; adapted from the Arthur Hailey novel. 137m/C VHS, DVD, Dean Martin, Jean Seberg, Burt Lancaster, Jean Seberg, Jacqueline Bisset, George Kennedy, Helen Hayes, Van Heflin, Maureen Stapleton, Barry Nelson, Lloyd Nolan, Dana Wynter, Barbara Hale, Gary Collins, Jessie Royce Landis; D: George Seaton; C: Ernest Laszlo; M: Alfred Newman. Oscars '70: Support. Actress (Hayes); Golden Globes '71: Support. Actress (Stapleton).

Airport '75 🐾🐾 1975 (PG) After a mid-air collision, a jumbo 747 is left pilotless. Airline attendant Black must fly da plane. She does her cross-eyed best in this absurd sequel to "Airport" built around a lesser "all-star cast." Safe on the ground, Heston tries to talk the airline hostess/pilot into landing, while the impatient Kennedy continues to grouse as a leader of the tram-ready ground crew. A slick, insincere attempt to find box office magic again (which unfortunately worked, leading to two more sequels). 107m/C VHS, DVD, Charlton Heston, Karen Black, George Kennedy, Gloria Swanson, Helen Reddy, Sid Caesar, Efrem Zimbalist Jr., Susan Clark, Dana Andrews, Linda Blair, Nancy Olson, Roy Thinnes, Myrna Loy; Ed Nelson, Larry Storch; D: Jack Smight; W: Don Ingalls; C: Philip Lathrop; M: John Cacavas.

Airport '77 🐾🐾 1977 (PG) Billionaire Stewart fills his converted passenger jet with priceless art and sets off to Palm Beach for a museum opening, joined by an uninvited garg of hijackers. Twist to this in-flight disaster is that the bad time in the air occurs underwater, a novel (and some might say desperate) twist to the old panic in the plane we're all gonna die formula. With a cast of familiar faces, some of them stars and some of them just familiar faces, this is yet another sequel to "Airport" and another boxoffice success, leading to the last of the tired series in 1979. 114m/C VHS, DVD. Jack Lemmon, James Stewart, Lee Grant, Brenda Vaccaro, Joseph Cotten, Olivia de Havilland, Darren McGavin, Christopher Lee, George Kennedy, Kathleen Quinlan, Monte Markham; D: Jack Smight.

AKA 🐾🐾 2002 (R) Unhappy with his family life, young man Dean leeches off of rich socialite Lady Gryfforn until her son, Alex, smells a rat and Dean scampers away to Paris. Unable to forgo his taste for the good life, he opts to pass himself off as Alex–causing him to face his sexuality. British writer-director Roy uses offbeat three-screen device to tell his own real-life tale. 107m/C VHS, DVD, GE Diana Quick, Blake Ritson, Bill Nighy, Geoff Bell, Matthew Leitch, George Asprey, Lindsey Coulson; D: Duncan Roy. VIDEO

Akeelah and the Bee 🐾🐾½ 2006 (PG) Inspirational story focuses on 11-year-old Akeelah (Palmer), a vocabulary whiz (thanks to ner late father's Scrabble prowass) who doesn't want to be humiliated as a brainiac at her tough South Central L.A. school. But after a couple of spelling bee wins, and the coaching

Akeelah (cont.) of no-nonsense UCLA English professor Larabee (Fishburne), Akeelah is encouraged to dream big and head for the National Spelling Bee. Bassett plays her overworked widow mom, who has too many other worries to help her daughter (at least at first). Palmer's character is both sweet and determined although the film may seem overly familiar. 107m/C DVD. *US* Laurence Fishburne, Angela Bassett, Keke Palmer, Curtis Armstrong, Tzi Ma, Lee Thompson Young, Sahara Garey, J.R. Villarreal, Sean Michael Afable; *D:* Doug Atchison; *W:* Doug Atchison; *C:* M. David Mullen; *M:* Aaron Zigman.

Akira (2 bones) 1989 Secret government experiments on children with ESP go awry, resulting in an cataclysmic explosion on Tokyo. The city in turn builds itself up into a Megalopolis and the experiments continue. Animated; in Japanese with English subtitles or dubbed. 124m/C VHS, DVD, UMD. *JP D:* Katsuhiro Otomo, Sheldon Renan; *W:* Katsuhiro Otomo, Izo Hashimoto; *C:* Katsuji Misawa; *M:* Shoji Yamashiro; *V:* Mitsuo Iwata, Nozomu Sasaki, Mami Koyama.

Akira Kurosawa's Dreams (2.5 bones) *Dreams; Yume; I Saw a Dream Like This; Konna Yume Wo Mita* 1990 (PG) An anthological lesson regarding the simultaneous loss of humanity and nature that threatens us all from the renowned Japanese director. Although the startling and memorable imagery is still present, Kurosawa's lessons are strangely trite and consequently lack the power that is normally associated with his work. Watch for Scorsese as Van Gogh. With English subtitles. 104m/C VHS, DVD. *JP* Akira Kurosawa, Martin Scorsese; *D:* Akira Kurosawa; *W:* Akira Kurosawa; *C:* Kazutami Hara, Takao Saito, Masaharu Ueda; *M:* Shinichiro Ikebe.

Al Capone (2 bones) 1959 Film noir character study of one of the most colorful gangsters of the Roaring '20s. Sort of an underworld "How to Succeed in Business." Steiger chews scenes and bullets as they fly by, providing the performance of his career. Plenty of gangland violence and mayhem and splendid cinematography keep the fast-paced period piece sailing. 104m/C VHS, DVD. Rod Steiger, Fay Spain, Murvyn Vye, Nehemiah Persoff, Martin Balsam, Al Ruscio, Joe De Santis; *D:* Richard Wilson.

Alabama's Ghost (1 bone) 1972 (PG) Musician steals a dead master magician's secrets, incurring the wrath of the paranormal underworld. Far from the best of the "blaxploitation" films of the '70s. 96m/C VHS. Christopher Brooks, E. Kerrigan Prescott; *D:* Fredric Hobbs.

Aladdin (3 bones) *Superfantagenio* 1986 (PG) A comedic Italian modernization of the Aladdin fable. 97m/C VHS, DVD. *IT* Bud Spencer, Luca Venantini, Janet Agren, Julian Voloshin, Umberto Raho; *D:* Richard Wilson.

Aladdin (3.5 bones) 1992 (G) Boy meets princess, loses her, finds her, wins her from evil vizier and nasty parrot, while being aided by big blue genie. Superb animation triumphs over average songs and storyline by capitalizing on Williams' talent for ad-lib with lightning speed genie changes, lots of celebrity spoofs, and even a few pokes at Disney itself. Adults will enjoy the 1,001 impersonations while kids will get a kick out of the big blue genie and the songs, three of which are the late Ashman's legacy. Kane and Salonga are responsible for the singing voices of Aladdin and Jasmine; Gottfried is a riot as the obnoxious parrot sidekick. Be forewarned: small children may be frightened by some of the scarier sequences. ♫A Whole New World; Prince Ali; Friend Like Me; One Jump Ahead; Arabian Nights. 90m/C VHS, DVD. *D:* Ron Clements, John Musker; *W:* Ron Clements, John Musker, Ted Elliott, Terry Rossio; *M:* Alan Menken, Howard Ashman, Tim Rice; *V:* Robin Williams, Scott Weinger, Linda Larkin, Jonathan Freeman, Frank Welker, Gilbert Gottfried, Douglas Seale, Brad Kane, Lea Salonga. Oscars '92: Song ("A Whole New World"), Orig. Score; Golden Globes '93: Song ("A Whole New World"), Score; MTV Movie Awards '93: Comedic Perf. (Williams).

Aladdin and His Wonderful Lamp (2.5 bones) 1984 The story of Aladdin, a young man who finds a magical oil lamp when he is trapped in a tiny cave. From the "Faerie Tale Theatre" series and director of "Beetlejuice" and "Batman" Tim Burton. 60m/C VHS, DVD. Valerie Bertinelli, Robert Carradine, Leonard Nimoy, James Earl Jones; *D:* Tim Burton.

Aladdin and the King of Thieves (2 bones) 1996 Second-direct-to-video saga (following "The Return of Jafar") once again features Williams as the voice of the genie (after settling a dispute with Disney). On the eve of Aladdin's marriage to Jasmine, thieves try to steal a magic talisman, sending Aladdin on a mission to find the thieves—and his father. Disney had such terrific success with "Return" that it was inevitable they would try again. 82m/C VHS, DVD. *D:* Ted Stones; *W:* Mark McCorkle, Robert Schooley; *M:* Mark Watters; *V:* Robin Williams, Scott Weinger, Jerry Orbach, John Rhys-Davies, Gilbert Gottfried, Linda Larkin, CCH Pounder, Frank Welker.

The Alamo (3 bones) 1960 Old-fashioned patriotic battle epic recounts the real events of the 1836 fight for independence in Texas. The usual band of diverse and contentious personalities, including Wayne as a coonskin-capped Davy Crockett, defend a small fort against a very big Mexican raiding party outside of San Antonio. Before meeting mythic death, they fight with each other, learn the meaning of life, and ultimately come to respect each other. Just to make it more entertaining, Avalon sings. Big-budget production features an impeccable musical score by Tiomkin and an impressive 7,000 extras for the Mexican army alone. Wayne reportedly received directorial assistance from John Ford, particularly during the big massacre finale. 161m/C VHS, DVD. John Wayne, Richard Widmark, Laurence Harvey, Frankie Avalon, Richard Boone, Carlos Arruza, Chill Wills, Veda Ann Borg, Linda Cristal, Patrick Wayne, Joan O'Brien, Joseph Calleia, Ken Curtis, Jester Hairston, Denver Pyle, Jim Dierkes, Guinn "Big Boy" Williams, Olive Carey, William Henry, Hank Worden, Ruben Padilla, Jack Pennick; *D:* John Wayne; *W:* James Edward Grant; *C:* William Clothier; *M:* Dimitri Tiomkin, Paul Francis Webster. Oscars '60: Sound; Golden Globes '61: Score.

The Alamo (2.5 bones) 2004 (PG-13) Dry and so greatest in a dozen odd big-screen tries of dubious success at depicting the historic Texas battle. Thornton stars as Davy Crockett along with Wilson, Patric, and Quaid as William Travis, Jim Bowie, and Sam Houston who, along with 189 others, form the "Texican" holdouts who, after nearly two weeks of anxious waiting, battle the Mexican army of nearly 2,500 and their General, Santa Anna (Echevarría). Mostly tedious waiting, while the actual battle is surprisingly sterile. Thornton (if not his character) emerges unscathed with an excellent performance, especially in the winning rooftop fiddle serenade scene. Supporting work is more uneven. Big-budgeter looks great and is exacting in historical accuracy but ultimately lacks dramatic punch and a cohesive plot. 137m/C DVD. Dennis Quaid, Billy Bob Thornton, Jason Patric, Patrick Wilson, Emilio Echeverría, Jordi Molla, Leon Rippy, Marc Blucas, Tom Davidson, Robert Prentiss, Ken Page, Joe Stevens, Steven Prince, Tom Everett, Brandon Smith, Rance Howard, Stephen Bruton, Emily Deschanel, Laura Clifton, Edward "Blue" Deckert; *D:* John Lee Hancock; *W:* John Lee Hancock, Leslie Bohem, Stephen Gaghan; *C:* Dean Semler, John O'Connor; *M:* Carter Burwell.

Alamo Bay (2.5 bones) 1985 A slow-moving but sincere tale of contemporary racism. An angry Vietnam veteran and his red-neck buddies feel threatened by Vietnamese refugees who want to go into the fishing business. Set in Texas, filled with Texas-sized characters, and based on a true Texas story, as interpreted by the French Malle. 99m/C VHS. Ed Harris, Ho Nguyen, Amy Madigan, Donald Moffat, Cynthia Carle, Truyen V. Tran, Rudy Young; *D:* Louis Malle; *W:* Alice Arlen; *M:* Ry Cooder.

The Alamo: Thirteen Days to Glory (2 bones) 1987 The legendary Davy Crockett (Keith), Colonel William Travis (Baldwin), and Jim Bowie (Arness) overcome personal differences to unite against the Mexican Army, vowing to hold down the fort or die. It takes a true Texan to fully appreciate the merits of this rather pedestrian retelling of a familiar story, but the battle scenes are pretty heady (although they lose some of their froth on the small screen). If nothing else, the ever-versatile Julia is worth seeing as Santa Anna in this made-for-TV rendering of J. Lon Tinkle's "Thirteen Days to Glory." You may not want to remember the Alamo this way. 180m/C VHS. James Arness, Lorne Greene, Alec Baldwin, Brian Keith, Raul Julia, Laura Elena Harrison; *D:* Peter Werner; *M:* Peter Bernstein.

Alamut Ambush (1 bone) 1986 A federal agent is stalked by assassins, and decides to hunt them in return. Sequel to "Cold War Killer." 94m/C VHS, DVD. *GB* Terence Stamp, Michael Culver; *D:* Ken Grieve.

Alan & Naomi (2.5 bones) 1992 (PG) In 1944, 14-year-old Alan Silverman is more concerned with his Brooklyn stickball team than the war raging across Europe. All changes when his upstairs neighbor offers refuge to a French-Jewish mother and her young daughter and he is asked to befriend the girl. Naomi witnessed the brutal death of her father by the Nazis and retreated into a world of her own. Together the two build a sweet, if unlikely, friendship. Fine performances save this average coming of age tale. Based on the novel by Myron Levoy. 95m/C VHS. Lukas Haas, Vanessa Zaoui, Michael Gross, Amy Aquino, Kevin Connolly, Zohra Lampert; *D:* Sterling Van Wagenen; *W:* Jordan Horowitz; *M:* Dick Hyman.

An Alan Smithee Film: Burn, Hollywood, Burn (1.5 bones) *Burn, Hollywood, Burn* 1997 (R) Follows a British director (Idle), whose given name is Alan Smithee, as he kidnaps the reels of his own picture when he realizes he hates the movie but can't remove his name from it since the Directors Guild of America's official pseudonym for disputed films is "Alan Smithee." O'Neal stars as the boorish producer who drives Smithee to the desperate act. This extended in-joke ran into its own problem when director Arthur Hiller, in what seemed like a publicity stunt, repudiated the version producer/writer Eszterhas re-cut and had his own name removed from the film, thus making it "An Alan Smithee Film" one of the more than 30 Alan Smithee films in existence. The tedious mockumentary style is relentless in narrating the story to the audience, who is never allowed to just watch what happens. Only interest is the parade of star cameos, including Stallone, Goldberg, and Chan (as themselves), along with writer Eszterhas in a scene with the director who declined credit for the film. Hiller. 86m/C VHS, DVD. Eric Idle, Ryan O'Neal, Coolio, Richard Jeni, Sandra Bernhard, Cherie Lunghi, Harvey Weinstein, M.C. Lyte, Stephen Tobolowsky, Chuck D, Leslie Stefanson, Gavin Polone, Marcello Thedford, Nicole Nagel, Dina Spybey; *Cameos:* Joe Eszterhas, Sylvester Stallone, Whoopi Goldberg, Jackie Chan, Larry King, Billy Bob Thornton, Dominick Dunne, Robert Evans, Shane Black; *D:* Arthur Hiller; *W:* Joe Eszterhas; *C:* Reynaldo Villalobos; *M:* Gary G-Wiz. Golden Raspberries '98: Worst Picture, Worst Support. Actor (Eszterhas), Worst Screenplay, Worst Song ("I Wanna Be Mike Ovitz!"), Worst New Star (Eszterhas).

The Alarmist (2 bones) *Life During Wartime* 1998 Tommy Hudler (Arquette) is the eager beaver new employee at the L.A. home-security company owned by slick supersalesman Heinrich Grigoris (Tucci). But Tommy's soon shocked to learn that Heinrich makes certain clients continue to need his services by breaking into their homes. Tommy makes his first sale to fortysomething widow Gale (Capshaw), who enjoys seducing the boyish innocent, and the two embark on a torrid affair. Then Gale and her teenaged son are murdered after a home break-in and Tommy suspects Heinrich went a little too far. Arquette's amusingly geeky but Tucci steals the film as his sleazy boss. 93m/C VHS, DVD. Stanley Tucci, David Arquette, Kate Capshaw, Ryan Reynolds, Mary McCormack, Tricia Vessey; *D:* Evan Dunsky; *W:* Evan Dunsky; *C:* Alex Nepomniaschy; *M:* Christophe Beck.

Alaska (2.5 bones) 1996 (PG) Fourteen-year-old Vincent Barnes (Kartheiser) and his 12-year-old sister Jessie (Birch) try to rescue their bush pilot father Jake (Benedict) whose plane has crashed in the wilderness. They also rescue an orphaned polar bear cub from an evil poacher (Heston) that manages to help them out along the way. See this flick if only to enjoy the lush backdrop of Alaska and British Columbia and, of course, the absolutely adorable polar cub. Director Fraser C. Heston directs dad Charlton, appropriate payback for landing him the role as the infant Moses in "The Ten Commandments." 109m/C VHS, DVD. Thora Birch, Vincent Kartheiser, Dirk Benedict, Charlton Heston; *D:* Fraser Heston; *W:* Andy Burg, Carol Fuchs; *C:* Tony Westman.

Alberto Express (2 bones) 1992 Black comedy explores the debts children owe their parents—literally. Alberto's family has a peculiar tradition. It seems that now he's married and about to become a father, he's expected to pay back every cent spent on his own upbringing. Cash poor (and panicky) Alberto hops a train from Paris to Rome and frantically tries to raise the necessary cash by preying, in a series of increasingly bizarre ways, on his fellow passengers before he faces his father once again. In French and Italian with English subtitles. 90m/C VHS. *FR* Sergio Castellito, Nino Manfredi, Marie Trintignant, Jeanne Moreau, Michel Aumont, Dominique Pinon, Marco Messeri, Eugenia Marruzzo; *D:* Arthur Joffe; *W:* Arthur Joffe.

Albino WOOF! 1976 (R) Albino chief leads African terrorists to murder white settlers, one of whom is an ex-policeman's fiancee. So the ex-cop pursues the bad guys, who are fairly easy to identify (just look for the big group hanging with the albino). Danning, Lee, and Howard only briefly show faces and collect checks. 85m/C VHS. Christopher Lee, Trevor Howard, Sybil Danning, Horst Frank, James Faulkner; *D:* Jurgen Goslar.

Albino Alligator (2 bones) 1996 (R) Three small-time crooks bungle a robbery and inadvertently run down a federal officer in Academy Award-winning actor Spacey's directorial debut. The trio, consisting of leader Dova (Dillon), brains Milo (Sinise) and brawn Law (Fichtner) hole up in a seedy bar and grab the occupants as hostages. The police soon surround the dive, and the crooks begin arguing among themselves and with brash barmaid Janet (Dunaway) about their chances and means for escape. All, however, is not as it seems. The claustrophobic setting seems more suitable for the stage than the screen, and the plot twists don't bend very far from predictable. Screenwriter Forte is the son of '60s teen idol Fabian. 94m/C VHS, DVD. Matt Dillon, Gary Sinise, Faye Dunaway, William Fichtner, Joe Mantegna, Viggo Mortensen, John Spencer, Skeet Ulrich, M. Emmet Walsh; *D:* Kevin Spacey; *W:* Christian Forte; *C:* Mark Plummer; *M:* Michael Brook.

The Alchemist WOOF! 1981 (R) See humans transformed into murderous zombies! A bewitched man seeks revenge upon the evil magician who placed a curse on him, causing him to live like an animal. Painfully routine, with a few chills along the way. Amonte is an alias for Charles Band. Filmed in 1981 and released four years later. 86m/C VHS. Robert Ginty, Lucinda Dooling, John Sanderford, Viola Kate Stimpson, Bob Glaudini; *D:* Charles Band; *W:* Alan J. Adler; *M:* Richard Band.

The Alchemists (2.5 bones) 1999 (PG-13) The world's leading pharmaceutical company is covering up the fact that their fertility drug has some serious side effects. Employees Show and Gemmell try to expose the corporate conspiracy. Based on the novel by Peter James. 150m/C VHS, DVD. Grant Show, Ruth Gemmell, Edward Hardwicke; *D:* Peter Smith; *C:* Peter Middleton; *M:* Rick Wentworth.

Alchemy 🐾🐾½ 2005 (PG-13) Slight romantic comedy that gets a little extra oomph from its appealing leads. Professor software to woo struggling actress Samantha Rose (Chalke) based on the responses the program generates. 85m/C DVD. Sarah Chalke, Tom Cavanagh, James Oppenheimer; **W:** Evan Oppenheimer; **C:** Luke Geissbuhler; **M:** Peter Lurye.

Alex Rider: Operation Stormbreaker 🐾🐾
2006 (PG) Horowitz adapted the story from the first book in his own young adult series Stormbreaker... follow up his recent hit (in real life, "Bob & Carol & Ted & Alice") with a picture of some integrity that will keep the mass audience away. The confused plot provides obvious parallels to Fellini (who appears in a cameo), and some sharp, often bitter insights into the Hollywood of the early '60s. Strong performances by Sutherland and Burstyn compensate somewhat for the patience-trying self-indulgent airy whining of the script. 109m/C VHS. Donald Sutherland, Ellen Burstyn, Paul Mazursky; **Cameos:** Jeanne Moreau, Federico Fellini; **D:** Paul Mazursky; **W:** Jeremy Lerner; **C:** Gavin Finney. **M:** Marc Shaiman.

Alex in Wonderland 🐾🐾½
1970 (R) A semi-autobiographical and satirical look at Hollywood from the standpoint of a young director who's trying to... 2006 (PG) Horowitz adapted the story from the first book in his own young adult series Petyfen), who's basically an Alex Rider (newcomer Bond. Alex is orphaned and living with his spy uncle Ian (McGregor), who's quickly killed off, thus leaving Alex himself to be recruited by MI-6 boss Blunt (Nighy). Good thing the teen's already had all that spec-al ops training. The villain is the ever-creepy Rourke, here playing some evil ty-

Alex & Emma 🐾🐾½ 2003 (PG-13)
The original unwieldy title was "Loosely Based on a True Love Story" because it's loosely based on writer Fyodor Dostoyevsky's story "The Gambler," which was based on a true incident in his life. Or at least that's what the original hype for the movie maintained. Writer Alex (Wilson) has big gambling debts so he takes an advance from his publisher (Reiner) in exchange for churning out a book in 30 days. He hires stenographer Emma (Hudson) to take dictation of his very bad novel, which is set in 1924 and comes to life as Alex spins a story that Emma heartily criticizes. Lame romantic comedy wastes its leads, who have been much more charming in other films (and who have no chemistry together). Lovely blond Hudson is forced into a drab brunette persona that's as unappealing as her wardrobe. 96m/C DVD. **D:** Luke Wilson, Kate Hudson, Sophie Marceau, David Paymer, Francois Giroday, Rob Reiner; **D:** Rob Reiner; **C:** Cloris Leachman, Rip Taylor; **D:** Rob Reiner. **W:** Jeremy Lerner; **C:** Gavin Finney. **M:** Marc Shaiman.

Alex 🐾🐾🐾½ 1992 Inspirational story about 15-year-old New Zealand swimmer Alex Archer (Jackson), who is working towards a spot at the 1960 Rome Olympics. But her goal is threatened by an accident and a new rival and Alex struggles to overcome her obstacles with the help of her boyfriend Andy (Picker). Based on the novel by Tessa Ducer. 92m/C VHS. AU Lauren Jackson, Chris Haywood, Josh Picker, Catherine Godbold, Elizabeth Hawthorne; **D:** Megan Simpson.

Aldrich Ames: Traitor Within 🐾🐾½ 1998 (PG) Hutton stars as Aldrich Ames, a longtime, second-rate CIA employee with an expensive Colombian-born second wife, Rosario (Peña), and a lot of debts. So Ames turns weasel and begins to sell secrets to the Russians in the mid-'80s, which resulted in the deaths of at least 10 agents. Plowright is the CIA analyst in charge of plugging the leak. Both Ames were arrested and sent to prison in 1994; Rosario was released in 1999 and returned to Bogota. 97m/C VHS. Timothy Hutton, Joan Plowright, Elizabeth Peña, Eugene Lipinski; **C:** David Johnson; **D:** John MacKenzie; **W:** Michael Burton; **C:** Walter McGill. CABLE

Alexander 🐾🐾 2004 (R) Looooong and somewhat farcical bio of Macedonian conqueror Alexander the Great. In Stone's depiction, Alexander (Farrell) is the pawn in a marital war between his swaggering drunken father Philip (Kilmer) and his snake-worshipping mother Olympias (a sultry Jolie), who implies that her boy is really the progeny of the god Zeus. Tutored by Aristotle (Plummer), Alexander believes it's his destiny to subjugate as much of the known world as is possible. Lots of big battles ensue as Alexander forcibly unites the squabbling Greek citystates before challenging the might of the Persian empire. He takes some time out to marry a hot-blooded Eastern princess, Roxanne (Dawson), while the ruler's relationship with constant companion Hephaistion (Leto) is reduced to meaningful glances. Farrell cannot overcome the fact that he isn't forceful enough to portray an epic figure. 175m/C VHS, DVD. US Colin Farrell, Angelina Jolie, Val Kilmer, Christopher Plummer, Jared Leto, Rosario Dawson, Anthony Hopkins, Brian Blessed, Jonathan Rhys Meyers, Tim Pigott-Smith, Gary Stretch, John Kavanagh, Ian Beattie, Fedor Atkine, Connor Paolo, Nick Dunning, Denis Conway, Jessie Kamm, Neil Jackson, Rory McCann, Raz Degan, Annelise Hesme; **D:** Oliver Stone; **W:** Oliver Stone, Laeta Kalogridis, Christopher Kyle; **C:** Rodrigo Prieto; **M:** Vangelis.

Alexander Nevsky 🐾🐾🐾½ 1938
A story of the invasion of Russia in 1241 by the Teutonic Knights of Germany and the defense of the region by good old Prince Nevsky. Eisenstein's first completed project in nearly ten years, it was widely regarded as an artistic disappointment upon release and as pro-war propaganda for the looming conflict with the Nazis. Fabulous Prokofiev score illuminates the classic battle scenes, which used thousands of Russian army regulars. Russian with subtitles. 110m/B VHS, DVD. RU Nikolai Cherkassov, Nikolai P. Okhlopkov, Andrei Abrikosov, Alexandra Danilova, Dmitri Orlov, Vera Ivasheva, Sergei Blinnikov, Lev Fenin, Vladimir Yershov, Nikolai Arsky, Naum Rogozhin, Varvara O. Massalitinova, Vasili Novikov, Ivan Lagutin; **D:** Sergei Eisenstein; **W:** Sergei Eisenstein, Pyotr Pavlenko; **C:** Eduard Tisse; **M:** Sergei Prokofiev.

Alexander the Great 🐾🐾🐾½
1955 A lavish epic about the legendary Greek conqueror of the fourth century B.C., which provides Burton a rare chance at an adventure role. Here we find Alexander as the product of a dysfunctional royal family who hopes to create an idealized world modeled after Greek culture to make up for the love he lacks from daddy. This he does by conquering everything before dying at the age of 33. The great cast helps to overcome the sluggish pacing of the spectacle, while numerous battle scenes featuring loads of spears and arrows are staged effectively. 135m/C VHS, DVD. Richard Burton, Fredric March, Claire Bloom, Harry Andrews, Peter Cushing, Danielle Darrieux, Helmut Dantine; **D:** Robert Rossen; **C:** Robert Krasker.

Alexander: The Other Side of Dawn 🐾🐾🐾 1977 Tired sequel to the television movie "Dawn: Portrait of a Teenage Runaway." A young man turns to prostitution to support himself on the street of Los Angeles. 100m/C VHS. Leigh McCloskey, Eve Plumb, Earl Holliman, Juliet Mills, Jean Hagen, Lonny (Lonnie) Chapman; **D:** John Erman. TV

Alexander's Ragtime Band 🐾🐾🐾
1938 Energetic musical that Ragtime Band 1938 Energetic musical that spans 1915 to 1938 and has Power and Ameche battling for Faye's affections. Power is a society nabob who takes up ragtime to... *Irving Berlin's Alexander's*

coon with a grudge, and Silverstone is the title, and finds a singer (Faye). Ameche is a struggling composer who brings a Broadway producer to listen to star in a show and becomes an offer to lose success, marry and divorce, and finally end up happy. Corny but charming. ♪Alexander's Ragtime Band; All Alone; Blue Skies; Easter Parade; Everybody's Doin' It; Everybody Step; For Your Country and My Country; Heat Wave; I Can Always Find a Little Sunshine at the YMCA. 106m/B VHS, DVD. Tyrone Power, Alice Faye, Don Ameche, Ethel Merman, Jack Haley, Jean Hersholt, Helen Westley, John Carradine, Paul Hurst, Joe King, Ruth Terry; **D:** Henry King; **W:** Kathryn Scola, Lamar Trotti; **M:** Irving Berlin. Oscars '38: Score.

Alexandria... Why? 🐾🐾 1978
Schoolboy (director Chahine uses his adolescent remembrances) tries to ignore the war in Alexandria in 1942 by escaping into the movies and his dreams of becoming a star. He also witnesses two love affairs—one between a Muslim man and a Jewish woman and the second between an Arab nationalist and an English soldier. Part 1 of Chahine's Alexandria trilogy, and "An Egyptian Story" and "Alexandria Again and Forever." Arabic with subtitles. 133m/C VHS, DVD. EG Gerry Sundquist, Naglaa Fathi, Farid Shawki, Mohsen Mohieldine; **D:** Youssef Chahine; **C:** Mohsen Nasr; **M:** Foad El Zaheri.

Alexandria Again and Forever 🐾🐾 1989 *Iskandariya, Kaman oue Kaman* 1990 Yehia (Chahine) remembers his win as best director at the Berlin Film Festiva a decade before for his political film "Alexandria...Why?" and thinks about that film's leading man with whom he fell in love. But when he meets and falls for Nadia, Yehia decides he will launch her career as the star of his new film. The final part of Chahine's Alexandria trilogy, following "Alexandria...Why?" and "An Egyptian Story." Arabic with subtitles. 105m/C VHS, DVD. EG Youssef Chahine, Yousra, Hussein Fahmy; **D:** Youssef Chahine; **W:** Youssef Chahine; **M:** Mohammed Nouh.

Alfie 🐾🐾🐾 1966 (PG) What's it all about, Alfie? Caine, in his first starring role, plays the British playboy out of control in mod London. Alfie is a despicable, unscrupulous and vile sort of guy who uses women after woman to fulfill his basic needs and then casts them aside until...tragedy strikes. Though this box office hit was seen as a sophisticated take on current sexual mores upon release, it now seems a dated but engaging comedy, notable chiefly for its performances. From the play by Bill Naughton. The title song "Alfie," sung by Dionne Warwick, was a top ten hit. 114m/C VHS, DVD. GB Michael Caine, Shelley Winters, Millicent Martin, Vivien Merchant, Julia Foster, Jane Asher, Shirley Anne Field, Eleanor Bron, Denholm Elliott, Alfie Bass, Graham Stark, Murray Melvin, Sydney Tafler; **D:** Lewis Gilbert; **W:** Bill Naughton; **C:** Otto Heller; **M:** Burt Bacharach, Sonny Rollins. Cannes '66: Jury Prize; Golden Globes '67: Foreign Film; Natl. Bd. of Review '66: Support. Actress (Merchant); Natl. Soc. Film Critics '66: Actor (Caine).

Alfie 🐾🐾½ 2004 (R) Law plays a Kinsier, gentler lothario in this contemporary update of the 1966 film (which helped make Michael Caine a star), although Alfie still engages in a somewhat self-conscious running commentary directed to the camera. The charming, handsome Alfie is now a limo driver in New York who indulges himself with as many beautiful birds as will put up with him. These include the heavy-drinking Dorie (Krakowski), single mom Julie (Tomei) who kicks him out after realizing Alfie is a horn-dog; sexy, self-destructive party girl Nikki (Miller); and foxy Lonette (Long), the ex-girlfriend of his best friend Marlon (Eps). But when he suffers a bout of impotence and then meets his sexual match in worldly mature beauty Liz (Sarandon), Alfie re mains a narcissist (though ever-so-ap

the group after a piece of music (hence pealing as played by Law) at least the women characters are no longer complaisant or compliant. 106m/C VHS, DVD. US Jude Law, Marisa Tomei, Omar Epps, Nia Long, Renee Taylor, Dick Latessa, Jefferson Mays, Gedde Watanabe; **D:** Charles Shyer; **W:** Charles Shyer, Elaine Pope; **C:** Ashley Rowe; **M:** Mick Jagger, David A. Stewart, John Powell; Golden Globes '05: Song ("Old Habits Die Hard").

Alfredo, Alfredo 🐾🐾½ 1972 (R) Hoffman plays a mild-mannered bank clerk who regrets marrying a sexy woman. Lightweight domestic comedy. In Italian with English subtitles. (Hoffman's voice was dubbed). 97m/C VHS. IT Dustin Hoffman, Stefania Sandrelli, Carla Gravina, Clara Colosimo, Daniele Patella, Duilio Del Prete; **D:** Pietro Germi; **W:** Pietro Germi, Leonardo Benvenuti; **C:** Aiace Parolin; **M:** Carlo Rustichelli.

Algiers 🐾🐾🐾 1938 Nearly a scene-for-scene Americanized remake of the 1937 French "Pepe Le Moko" about a beautiful rich girl (Lamarr) who meets and falls in love with a notorious thief (Boyer, in a leading sex symbol). Pursued by French police and hiding in the underworld-controlled Casbah, Boyer meets up with Lamarr in a tragically fated romance done in the best tradition of Hollywood. Boyer provides a measured performance as Le Moko, while Lamarr is appropriately sultry in her American film debut (which made her a star). Later remade as the semi-musical "Casbah." 96m/B DVD. Charles Boyer, Hedy Lamarr, Sigrid Gurie, Gene Lockhart, Joseph Calleia, Alan Hale; **D:** John Cromwell; **C:** James Wong Howe.

Ali 🐾🐾🐾 2001 (R) Mann, a notorious obsessive, couldn't have picked a more ambitious topic. The herculean task proves too much, yielding a film that lacks focus or insight into its subject. Ali is depicted during a contentious decade (1964–1974), in which he converted to Islam, befriended Malcolm X, refused the draft, was stripped of his title, married three times, and blurred lines between sport, ethics and society. Perhaps it's no coincidence that screenwriter Roth, who previously penned "Forrest Gump," was chosen to chronicle Ali amid such historic happenings. Mann's visual skills are apparent, and Smith gives an inspired performance in and out of the ring. Other noteworthies include Foxx as cornerman "Bundini" Brown, and Voight as verbose sportscaster Cosell. Despite the charisma of its subject (and its lead), film feels distant and subdued. Lance's a few clear blows, but certainly not a knockout. 158m/C VHS, DVD. US Will Smith, Jamie Foxx, Jon Voight, Mario Van Peebles, Ron Silver, Jeffrey Wright, Mykelti Williamson, Jada Pinkett Smith, Michael Michele, Joe Morton, Paul Rodriguez, Nona Gaye, Bruce McGill, Barry (Shabaka) Henley, Giancarlo Esposito, Laurence Mason, LeVar Burton, Albert Hall, David Cubitt, Ted Levine, David Elliott, Michael Bent, James N. Toney, Charles Shufford, Malick Bowens, Shari Watson, Victoria Dillard, Kim Robillard, Gailard Sartain, Rufus Dorsey, Robert Sale, Damien "Bolo" Wills, Michael Dorn; **D:** Michael Mann; **W:** Michael Mann, Stephen J. Rivele, Christopher Wilkinson, Eric Roth; **C:** Emmanuel Lubezki; **M:** Lisa Gerrard, Pieter Bourke.

Ali Baba and the Forty Thieves 🐾🐾🐾 1943 Ali Baba and his gang of thieves do battle against Hulagu Khan, leader of the Mongols, to save Baghdad and its citizens from ruin and death. 87m/C VHS. Jon Hall, Turhan Bey, Maria Montez, Andy Devine, Kurt Katch, Frank Puglia, Fortunio Bonanova, Moroni Olsen, Scotty Beckett; **D:** Arthur Lubin; **W:** Edmund Hartmann; **C:** William Howard Greene.

Ali Baba and the 40 Thieves 🐾🐾🐾 *Ali Baba et les Quarante Voleurs* 1954 French adaptation of the popular tale novel "A Thousand and One Nights." Servant boy Ali Baba discovers the magic cave holding the stolen treasure of Abdul and his 40 thieves. Shot on location in Morocco. Also available dubbed. 92m/C VHS. FR Samia Gamal, Dieter Borsche, Henri Vilbert; **D:** Jacques Becker; **W:** Jacques Becker.

Ali: Fear Eats the Soul 🐾🐾🐾 *Fear Eats the Soul; Angst Essen Seele auf* 1974 A widow cleaning woman in her 60s has a love affair with a Moroccan man 30 years her junior. To no one's surprise, both encounter racism and moral hypocrisy in West Germany. Serious melodrama from Fassbinder, who wrote it and appears as the squirmy son-in-law. In German with English subtitles. **88m/C VHS, DVD, GE** Brigitte Mira, El Hedi Ben Salem, Irm Hermann; **D:** Rainer Werner Fassbinder; **W:** Rainer Werner Fassbinder; **C:** Jurgen Jurges.

Alias Betty ✓✓ *Betty Fisher et Autres Histoires* **2001** Stories; Betty Fisher et... Writer Betty (Kiberlain) has recently returned to Paris after separating from her lover. She is uneasily waiting for the arrival of her mother Margot (Garcia), a disturbed woman who abused Betty as a child. Betty's own young son Joseph (Serbon) suddenly dies in an accidental fall and she suffers a breakdown. Jose (Chatrian) is the abused young son of single mother Carole (Seigner). When Margot notices Jose alone in the streets, she takes him back to Betty as a replacement child—and Betty debates whether to go along or go to the cops. Based on the book "The Tree of Hands" by Ruth Rendell. French with subtitles. **101m/C VHS, DVD, FR CA** Sandrine Kiberlain, Nicole Garcia, Mathilde Seigner, Alexis Chatrian, Edouard Baer, Arthur Setbon, Luck Mervil, Stephane Freiss; **D:** Claude Miller; **W:** Claude Miller; **C:** Christophe Pollock.

Alias Billy the Kid ✓✓ **1946** Western adventure with Carson posing as a famous outlaw to find out who's behind the scam involving the Denton City cattle trade. **54m/B VHS.** Sunset Carson, Peggy Stewart, Tom London, Roy Barcroft; **D:** Thomas Carr; **C:** Bud Thackery.

Alias Jesse James ✓✓ **1959 (PG)** Insurance agent Milford Farnsworth (Hope) is an eastern tenderfoot who holds a policy on Jesse James (Corey). So he heads west to make certain the outlaw doesn't get killed. Only Jesse sets Milford up as himself, hoping to collect on his own policy. Fleming's the local beauty. A number of western stars have cameos, coming to Hope's rescue. **92m/C VHS.** Bob Hope, Rhonda Fleming, Wendell Corey, Jim Davis, Gloria Talbott, Will Wright, Mary (Marsden) Young, Joseph (Joe) Vitale; *Cameos:* Hugh O'Brian, Ward Bond, James Arness, Roy Rogers, Fess Parker, Gail Davis, James Garner, Gene Autry, Jay Silverheels, Bing Crosby, Gary Cooper; **D:** Norman Z. McLeod; **W:** William Bowers, D.D. Beauchamp; **C:** Lionel Lindon.

Alias John Law ✓ **1935** The Good Guy fights for oil rights against the bad guys. Confused program western with an especially convoluted plot. **54m/B VHS, DVD.** Bob Steele; **D:** Robert North Bradbury.

Alias, La Gringa ✓✓ **1991** Follows the adventures of La Gringa, a likeable criminal capable of escaping from any Peruvian jail. After being aided in his latest escape by a political prisoner, La Gringa decides to return in disguise to pay back the favor. But the prison is rocked by rioting and La Gringa finds himself in a situation out of his control. Spanish with subtitles. **100m/C VHS.** *Pv* Orlando Sacha, Alberto Gonzalez, Elsa Olivero, Juan Manuel Ochoa; **D:** Alberto Durant; **C:** Mario Garcia Joya; **M:** Pochi Marambio.

Alibi ✓✓ **1929** Low-budget crime drama from independent producer/director West. Gangster Chick Williams (Morris) reclaims his mob role after being released from prison. But when a cop is killed during a robbery, Williams is suspected of the crime and the detective squad will employ its methods to bring him to justice. Noted for its experimental use of sound, its dazzling Art Deco sets, and its eccentric composition. **84m/B VHS.** Chester Morris, Mae

Busch, Regis Toomey, Harry Stubbs; **D:** Roland West; **W:** Roland West, C. Gardner Sullivan; **C:** Ray June; **M:** Hugo Riesenfeld.

Alibi Ike ✓✓ **1935** Baseball comedy about rookie Cubs pitcher Frank Farrell (rubbery-faced comedian Brown), who is known as "Alibi Ike" because he's always making excuses, driving his manager Cap (Frawley) and his teammates crazy. He can't even be straight with his gal, Dolly (de Havilland). Next, Frank gets into trouble with gamblers who want him to throw games but he comes through in the end. Adapted from a story by Ring Lardner. **73m/B VHS.** Joe E. Brown, Olivia de Havilland, William Frawley, Ruth Donnelly, Roscoe Karns, Joseph King, Paul Harvey, Selmer Jackson; **D:** Ray Enright; **W:** William Wister Haines; **C:** Arthur L. Todd.

Alice ✓✓ *Alicja* **1986** A twist on the "Alice in Wonderland" tale. Alice witnesses an attempted murder, faints, and awakens in a weird, yet strangely familiar environment. Adapted from the stage production. **80m/C VHS, DVD.** Sophie Barjac, Susannah York, Jean-Pierre Cassel, Paul Nicholas; **D:** Jacek Bromski; Jerzy Gruza.

Alice ✓✓✓ *Neco Z Alenky* **1988** An acclaimed surreal version of Lewis Carroll's already surreal "Alice in Wonderland," with the emphasis on Carroll's obsessiveness. Utilizing animated puppets and a live actor for Alice, Czech director Svankmajer injects grotesque images and black comedy into English adventure. Not for the kids. **84m/C VHS, DVD.** *CZ SI GB GE* Kristina Kohoutova; **D:** Jan Svankmajer; **W:** Jan Svankmajer; **C:** Svatopluk Maly.

Alice ✓✓✓ **1990 (PG-13)** Farrow is "Alice," a woman plagued with doubts about her lifestyle, her religion, and her happiness. Her perfect children, husband, and apartment don't prevent her backaches, and she turns to an Oriental "herbalist" for aid. She finds his methods unusual and the results of the treatments surprising. Lightweight fairytale of Yuppiedom gone awry. Fine performances, but superficial and pointed story that may leave the viewer looking for more. (Perhaps that's Allen's point.) Farewell performance from character actor Luke, unbilled cameo from Judith Ivey, and first time out for Dylan O'Sullivan Farrow, adopted daughter of Allen and Farrow, as Kate. **106m/C VHS, DVD.** Mia Farrow, William Hurt, Joe Mantegna, Keye Luke, Alec Baldwin, Cybill Shepherd, Blythe Danner, Gwen Verdon, Bernadette Peters, Judy Davis, Patrick O'Neal, Julie Kavner, Caroline Aaron, Holland Taylor, Robin Bartlett, David Spielberg, Bob Balaban, Dylan O'Sullivan Farrow, Elle Macpherson; **D:** Woody Allen; **W:** Woody Allen; **C:** Carlo Di Palma. Natl. Bd. of Review '90: Actress (Farrow).

The Alice ✓✓ **2004** A disparate group of characters come from all corners of Australia to the outback town of Alice Springs in order to witness a total eclipse of the sun in hopes that it will changes their lives. Apparently intended as an Australian TV pilot although it never went any farther. **98m/C DVD.** *AU* Erik Thomson, Jessica Napier, Brett Stiller, Simon Burke, Caitlin McDougall, Luke Carroll, Kyas Sherriff; **D:** Kate Dennis; **W:** Justin Mongo; **C:** Louis Irving. TV

Alice Adams ✓✓½ **1935** Based on the classic Booth Tarkington novel about a poor girl from a small Midwestern town who falls in love with a man from the upper level of society. She tries desperately to fit in and nearly alienates her family and friends. The sets may be dated, but the insight on human behavior is timeless. **99m/B VHS, DVD.** Katharine Hepburn, Fred MacMurray, Evelyn Venable, Fred Stone, Frank Albertson, Ann Shoemaker, Charley Grapewin, Grady Sutton, Hedda Hopper, Hattie McDaniel; **D:** George Stevens; **M:** Max Steiner.

Alice Doesn't Live Here Anymore ✓✓½ **1974 (PG)** Scorsese marries road opera with pseudo-feminist semi-realistic melodrama and produces uneven but interesting results. When Alice's husband dies suddenly, leaving her with their 11-year-old son, she leaves for California, but finds herself stranded in Phoenix, down to her last few bucks. There she lands a job as a waitress in a diner where she meets kindly rancher

Kristofferson. Notable for its female point of view, it was also the basis for the once-popular TV show "Alice." Burstyn and Ladd lend key performances, while Kristofferson is typically wooden. **105m/C VHS, DVD.** Ellen Burstyn, Kris Kristofferson, Diane Ladd, Jodie Foster, Harvey Keitel, Vic Tayback, Billy Green Bush, Laura Dern; **D:** Martin Scorsese; **W:** Robert Getchell; **C:** Kent Wakeford; **M:** Richard LaSalle. Oscars '74: Actress (Burstyn); British Acad. '75: Actress (Burstyn); Film, Screenplay, Support, Actress (Ladd).

Alice et Martin ✓✓½ *Alice and Martin* **1998 (R)** Director Andre Techine examines the complexity of relationships through the lives of nervous violinist Alice (Binoche) and psychologically fragile model Martin (Loret). The story opens in Martin's childhood, when he is sent by his free-spirited mother to live with his cold and distant father Victor (Maguelon). Martin flees his father's house after an unrevealed trauma, showing up at the door of his half-brother Benjamin (Amalric), who is Alice's roommate. Despite initial reluctance from Alice, the pair become lovers. During a trip to Spain Alice tells Martin that she's pregnant, and he goes off the deep end, haunted by memories of his father and the fateful event that will continue to affect their lives. Slow-moving but beautifully filmed. **123m/C VHS.** *FR SP* Juliette Binoche, Alexis Loret, Carmen Maura, Pierre Maguelon, Mathieu Amalric; **D:** Andre Techine; **W:** Andre Techine, Gilles Taurand, Olivier Assayas; **C:** Caroline Champetier; **M:** Philippe Sarde.

Alice in the Cities ✓✓½ **1974** American and German culture are compared and contrasted in this early Wenders road work about a German journalist in the USA on assignment who suddenly finds himself custodian to a worldly nine-year-old girl abandoned by her mother. Together they return to Germany and search for the girl's grandmother. Along the way they learn about each other, with many distinctive and graceful Wenders moments. **110m/B VHS.** Rudiger Vogler, Yella Rottlaender, Elisabeth (Lisa) Kreuzer, Edda Kochi; **D:** Wim Wenders; **W:** Wim Wenders.

Alice in Wonderland ✓✓½ **1950** Another version of the Lewis Carroll classic which combines the useage of Lou Bunin's puppets and live action to tell the story. Released independently to cash in on the success of the Disney version. Takes a more adult approach to the story and is worth viewing on its own merits. **83m/C VHS.** *FR* Carol Marsh, Stephen Murray, Pamela Brown, Felix Aylmer, Ernest Milton; **D:** Dallas Bower.

Alice in Wonderland ✓✓✓ **1951 (G)** Classic Disney dream version of Lewis Carroll's famous children's story about a girl who falls down a rabbit hole into a magical world populated by strange creatures. Beautifully animated with some startling images, but served with a strange dispassion warmed by a fine batch of songs. Wynn's Mad Hatter and Holloway's Cheshire Cat are among the treats in store. ♪Alice in Wonderland; I'm Late; A Very Merry Un-Birthday; **75m/C VHS, DVD.** ♪Hamilton Luske, Wilfred Jackson, Clyde Geronimi; **W:** Carol Marsh, Robert Morley, Sammy Williams, Jerry Colonna.

Alice in Wonderland ✓✓½ **1985** All-star updated adaptation of the Lewis Carroll classic. This time instead of Alice falling down a rabbit hole she falls through her television set. But her adventures still include the White Rabbit, Mad Hatter, March Hare, Cheshire Cat, and the King and Queen of Hearts. Followed by "Alice Through the Looking Glass." **99m/C VHS, DVD.** Red Buttons, Ann Jillian, Scott Baio, Sid Caesar, Ernest Borgnine, Beau Bridges, Lloyd Bridges, Tom McLoughlin, Harvey Korman, Patrick Duffy, Donald O'Connor, Arte Johnson, Carol Channing, Sherman Hemsley, Roddy McDowall, Donna Mills, Imogene Coca, Karl Malden, Noriyuki "Pat" Morita, Sally Struthers, Martha Raye, Merv Griffin, Jack Warden, Louis Nye, Shelley Winters, John Stamos, Jonathan Winters, George Savalas; **D:** Harry Harris; **W:** Paul Zindel; **C:** Fred W. Koenekamp; **M:** Morton Stevens. TV

Alice in Wonderland ✓✓½ **1999** Visually elaborate but somewhat tedious version of the popular Lewis Carroll tale filled with scenery chewing by the real actors and the welcome presence of animatronic wonders from the Jim Henson Creature Shop. This time Alice is the poised Majorino, who seems more annoyed by the denizens of Wonderland than amazed at her adventures. **129m/C VHS, DVD.** Tina Majorino, Martin Short, Miranda Richardson, Whoopi Goldberg, Ben Kingsley, Gene Wilder, Christopher Lloyd, Pete Postlethwaite, Peter Ustinov, George Wendt, Robbie Coltrane; **D:** Nick Willing; **W:** Peter Barnes; **C:** Giles Nutgens; **M:** Richard Hartley. TV

Alice Sweet Alice ✓✓½ *Holy Terror; Communion* **1976 (R)** Mediocre, gory who-killed-her, best remembered as the debut of Shields (in a small role). **112m/C VHS, DVD.** Linda Miller, Paula Sheppard, Mildred Clinton, Niles McMaster, Jane Lowry, Rudolph Willrich, Brooke Shields, Alphonso de Noble, Gary Allen, Tom Signorelli, Lillian Roth; **D:** Alfred Sole; **W:** Alfred Sole, Rosemary Ritvo; **C:** John Friberg, Chuck Hall; **M:** Stephen Lawrence.

Alice Through the Looking Glass ✓✓ **1966** Based on Lewis Carroll's classic adventure. Follows the further adventures of young Alice. After a chess piece comes to life, it convinces Alice that excitement and adventure lie through the looking glass. **72m/C VHS.** Judi Rolin, Ricardo Montalban, Nanette Fabray, Robert Coote, Agnes Moorehead, Jack Palance, Jimmy Durante, Tom Smothers, Roy Castle, Richard Denning; **D:** Alan Handley.

Alice to Nowhere ✓✓ **1986** Concerns a running argument in the Outback over a fortune in gems unknowingly carried by a young woman. Based on a novel by Evan Green. **210m/C VHS.** *AU* Rosie Jones, Steve Jacobs, John Waters, Ruth Cracknell; **D:** John Power. TV

Alice's Restaurant ✓✓½ **1969 (PG)** Based on the popular and funny 20-minute Arlo Guthrie song "Alice's Restaurant Massacre" about a Flower Child during the Last Big War who gets hassled for littering, man. Step back in time and study the issues of the hippie era, including avoiding the draft, dropping out of college, and dealing with the local pigs. Sort of a modern movie in the cinematic ambling genre, in that nothing really happens. **111m/C VHS, DVD.** Arlo Guthrie, James Broderick, Pat Quinn, Geoff Outlaw, Pete Seeger, Lee Hays, Michael McClanathan, Tina Chen, Kathleen Dabney, William Obanhein, Graham Jarvis, M. Emmet Walsh; **D:** Arthur Penn; **W:** Arthur Penn, Venabel Herndon; **C:** Michael Nebbia; **M:** Garry Sherman, Arlo Guthrie.

Alien ✓✓✓✓ **1979 (R)** Terse direction, stunning sets and special effects, and a well-seasoned cast save this from being another "Slimy monster from Outerspace" story. Instead it's a grisly rollercoaster of suspense and fear (and a huge boxoffice hit). Intergalactic freighter's crew is invaded by an unstoppable carnivorous alien intent on picking off the crew one by one. While the cast mostly bitches and banters while awaiting the horror of their imminent departure, Weaver is exceptional as Ripley, a self-reliant survivor who goes toe to toe with the Big Ugly. Futuristic, in the belly of the beast/starship design creates a vivid sense of claustrophobic doom enhanced further by the ominous score. Oscar-winning special effects include the classic baby alien busting out of the guy's chest routine, a rib-splitting ten on the gore meter. Successfully followed by "Aliens" and "Alien 3." **116m/C VHS, DVD, UMD.** *GB* Tom Skerritt, Sigourney Weaver, Veronica Cartwright, Yaphet Kotto, Harry Dean Stanton, Ian Holm, John Hurt, Bolaji Badejo; **D:** Ridley Scott; **W:** Dan O'Bannon; **C:** Derek Vanlint; **M:** Jerry Goldsmith; **V:** Helen Horton. Oscars '79: Visual FX; Natl. Film Reg. '02.

Alien 3 ✓✓ **1992 (R)** Picks up where "Aliens" left off as Ripley crash lands on Fiorina 161, a planet that serves as a penal colony for 25 celibate but horny men who smell bad. Ripley is forced to shave her head because of the planet's lice problem, and she sets out to survive on the cold, unfriendly planet until a rescue ship can come for her. Fending off sexual

The Alien Agenda: Endangered Species 🌀 *1997* Tabloid TV reporter Megar Cross has a too-close encounter with extraterrestrials that frighten her enough to have her join a secret organization that keeps tabs on alien activity. Along with mercenary Cope Ransom and operative Fritz, Megan is sent to infiltrate the mutant wasteland that used to be Florida and see what the aliens are plotting. 102m/C VHS, DVD. Deabie Rochon, Joel D. Wynkoop, Joe Zaso, Candice Meade; D: Kevin J. Lindenmuth, Ron Ford, Gabriel Campisi, Tim Ritter. VIDEO

The Alien Agenda: Out of the Darkness WOOF! *1996* Cheesy sci-fi with a narrator who ruminates about mysterious aliens who enjoy tormenting humans and can travel through time (and send humans back and forth). You won't care. 80m/C VHS, Sasha Graham, Michael (Mick) McCleery, Scooter McCrae, T.J. Miller, Marcus Zanders; D: Michael (Mick) McCleery, Kevin J. Lindenmuth; W: Michael (Mick) McCleery, Kevin J. Lindenmuth. VIDEO

The Alien Agenda: Under the Skin 🌀½ *1997* Scientist Alfred Malone is kidnapped by the mystery guys in black and taken to their hideaway in Puerto Rico, where vicious aliens roam around outside just looking for a tasty earthling snack. Then there's Victor who's a small-time hood who's not only got the cops after him but the new head of Chicago's crime syndicate, who's exactly what he seems. 75m/C VHS, Nick Kostopoulos, Arthur Lundquist, Leslie Body, Steven Jon White, Conrad Brooks; D: Kevin J. Lindenmuth, Mike Legge; W: Kevin J. Lindenmuth, Mike Legge. VIDEO

Alien Agent 🌀½ *2007 (R)* Agent Rykker (Dacascos) is sent to stop a renegade military unit that is building a portal between itself and Earth. Seem Saylon (Zane), Isis (Cooke), and their band have decided they will exterminate the humans and move in. Good fights (director Johnson got his start as a stunt coordinator) but not much true sci-fi despite the plot. 95m/C DVD. Mark Dacascos, Billy Zane, Kim Coates, Amelia Cooke, Emma Lahana; D: Jesse Johnson; W: Vilady Pildysh; C: C. Kim Miles; M: Michael Richard Plowman. VIDEO

Alien Avengers 🌀½ *1996 (R)* Roger Corman Presents: Alien Avengers' Welcome to Planet Earth. Naive, poor Joseph Collins (Brown) inherits a rundown rooming-house and before he knows it, he has his first tenants—Charlie (Wendy), Rhonda (Reed), and their teenaged daughter Daphne (Sakelaris). What Joseph doesn't know is the friendly trio are aliens (on vacation), who are fond of killing lowlifes and bringing home human parts for snacks. Goofy and gory cable movie. 89m/C VHS, DVD. George Wendt, Shanna Reed, Christopher Brown, Anastasia Sakelaris; D: Lev L. Spiro; W: Michae James McDonald; C: Christopher Baffa; M: Tyler Bates.

Alien Cargo 🌀 *1999 (PG)* The crew of a Mars transport ship has just awakened from eight months in hypersleep to discover something they're off-course and in big trouble. Standard issue plot makes for boring entertainment. 89m/C VHS. Jason London; C: (Liz) Alexander; D: Mark Haber. TV

Alien Chaser 🌀 *1996 (R)* Alien android Zagarino, who crashed in the African desert 5000 years ago, returns to life thanks to the unwitting aid of archeologists Jensen and MacDonald. They literally hold the key to stopping his destruction of mankind. 95m/C VHS, DVD, Frank Zagarino, Todd Jensen, Jennifer MacDonald, Brian O'Shaughnessy; D: Mark Roper; W: B.J. Nelson; C: Rick Stewart; M: Robert O. Ragland.

Alien Contamination WOOF! Contamination *1981 (R)* Tale of two astronauts who return to Earth from an expedition on Mars carrying some deadly bacterial eggs. Controlled by a Martian intent on conquering the world, the eggs squirt a gloppy juice that makes people explode on contact (a special effect). A cheap and sloppy attempt to cash in on the success of "Alien." Dubbed. 90m/C VHS, DVD. /Tian McCulloch, Louise Monroe, Martin Mase, Siegfried Rauch, Lisa Hahn, Louise Marleau, Al Cliver, Carlo De Mejo, Gisela Hahn; D: Lewis (Luigi Cozzi) Coates; W: Lewis (Luigi Cozzi) Coates; M: The Goblins.

Alien Dead 🌀 *It Fell from the Sky 1979 (R)* The teenage victims of a bizarre meteor crash reincarnate as flesh-eating ghouls anxious to cut a group of human food in this extremely low-budget sleep in a Baltimore. The grotesque extraterrestrials jolt a small town out of its sleepy state by wreaking havoc (except for the good one, of course). Decent special effects. 82m/C VHS, DVD. Don Leifert, Tom Griffith, Mary Mertens, Richard Dyszel, Richard Geiwitz, Eleanor Herman, Anne Frith, Christopher Gummer, George Stover, John Walker, Donald M. Dohler; D: Donald M. Dohler; W: Donald M. Dohler; M: Ken Walker.

Alien from L.A. WOOF! *1987 (PG)* Awesomely inept comedy about a California girl who unwittingly stumbles onto the famed continent of Atlantis and can't find a yogurt stand. Weakly plotted and acted and filmed. Like, really. 88m/C VHS, DVD. Kathy Ireland, Thom Mathews, Don Michael Paul, Linda Kerridge, William R. Moses, Richard Haines, Janie de Plessis, Russel Savadier, Simon Poland, Locher de Kock, Deep Roy; D: Albert Pyun; W: Albert Pyun, Debra Ricci, Regina Davis; C: Tom Fraser; M: James Saad.

Alien Fury: Countdown to Invasion 🌀 *2000 (PG-13)* Bill Templer (Midkiff) is upset when budget cuts threaten to close his government defense office, which sends probes into space looking for aliens. So he fakes some satellite photos of an alien armada poised to attack Earth from the dark side of the moon. Only, ha ha, the threat turns out to be real. This movie is so lame, you'll hope the aliens do attack and make these fools out. 88m/C VHS, DVD. Dale Midkiff, Stephen Tobolowsky, Dondre T. Whitfield, Joanie Laurer, Grace Phillips, Scott Lowell, Paul Schulze, Troy Evans; D: Rob Hedden; W: Rob Hedden; C: John Newby; M: John Beal.

Alien Intruder 🌀 *1993 (R)* What happens when an evil demon appears before the soldiers of the future in the guise of a beautiful woman? Futuristic trash "B"-movie emerges from the depths. 90m/C VHS, DVD. Billy Dee Williams, Tracy Scoggins, Maxwell Caulfield; D: Ricardo Jacques Gale.

Alien Massacre WOOF! Dr. Terror's Gallery of Horrors; Return from the Past; The Blood Suckers; Gallery of Horror *1967* One of the worst films of all time—five short horror stories about zombies and vampires. Goes by many names—stinks in all of them. 90m/C VHS, DVD. Lon Chaney Jr., John Carradine, Rochelle Hudson, Roger Gentry, Mitch Evans, Joey Benson, Vic McGee; D: David L. Hewitt; W: Gary Heacock, David Prentiss; C: Austin McKinney.

Alien Nation 🌀🌀 *1988 (R)* A few hundred thousand alien workers land accidentally on Earth and slowly become part of its society, although widely discriminated against. One of the "newcomers" teams with a surly and bigoted human cop to solve a racially motivated murder. An inconsistent and occasionally transparent script looks at race conflicts and includes some humorous parallels with contemporary American life. Basis for the TV series. Producer Hurd was also the force behind "The Terminator" and "Aliens." 89m/C VHS, DVD. James Caan, Mandy Patinkin, Terence Stamp, Kevyn Major Howard, Peter Jason, Jeff Kober, Leslie Bevis; D: Graham Baker; W: Rockine S. O'Bannon; C: Adam Greenberg; M: Curt Sobel.

Alien Nation: Body and Soul 🌀🌀½ *1995* The second TV movie sequel to the series finds detectives Francisco (Pierpoint) and Sykes (Graham) painfully aware of the sexual differences between humans and Newcomers. 2m/C VHS. Gary (Rand) Graham, Eric Pierpoint, Terri Treas, Michelle Scarabelli, Sean Six, Lauren Woodland, Kristen Davis, Tiny Ron; D: Kenneth Johnson; M: David Kurtz.

Alien Nation: Dark Horizon 🌀🌀½ *1994 (PG)* The alien Newcomer's have successfully adapted to life on Earth but face continuing dangers when a human-supremacy group develops a virus to wipe them out and an alien infiltrator is plotting to return them to slavery on Tencton. Naturally, it's up to detectives Sykes and Francisco to save the day. Based on the TV series. 90m/C VHS. Gary (Rand) Graham, Eric Pierpoint, Scott Patterson, Terri Treas, Michelle Scarabelli, Lee Bryant, Sean Six, Kerrie Keane, Michelle Scarabelli, Jeff Marcus, Jenny Gago, David Faustino; D: Kenneth Johnson; W: Kenneth Johnson; C: Shelly Johnson; M: David Kurtz.

Alien Nation: Millennium 🌀🌀½ *1996* In this third movie sequel to the series, and George's very close to the Francisco home. Rebellious teenager Buck (Six) gets involved with a suspicious cult, lead by Newcomer Jennifer (Keane), that offers spiritual enlightenment at a very heavy price. 2m/C VHS. Eric Pierpoint, Gary (Rand) Graham, Sean Six, Kerrie Keane, Michelle Scarabelli, Terri Treas, Lauren Woodland, Jeff Marcus, Jenny Gago, David Faustino; D: Kenneth Johnson; W: Kenneth Johnson; M: David Kurtz.

Alien Nation: The Enemy Within 🌀🌀½ *1996* George (Pierpont) must deal with his own bigotry when he and Matt (Graham) investigate the death of an Eenos Newcomer. The underground-dwelling Eenos are shunned as ignorant and savage subclass by other Newcomers but the detectives gradually discover some sinister goings-on involving a fierce Eenos/Newcomer mutant. Meanwhile, George's wife Susan (Scarabelli) is feeling neglected and Cathy (Treas) and Matt find living together causes a strain on their relationship. The fourth TV movie from the series. 90m/C VHS. Eric Pierpoint, Gary (Rand) Graham, Gary (Rand) Graham, Sean Six, Lauren Woodland, Joe Lando, Kerria Keane, Tiny Ron, Ron Fassler; D: Kenneth Johnson; C: Shelly Johnson; M: David Kurtz.

Alien Predators WOOF! *1980 (F)* Three friends encounter a malevolent alien in this dull reworking of the plot of "The Andromeda Strain" with laughable special effects tossed in for those outwitted by the script. 92m/C VHS. Dennis Christopher, Martin Hewitt, Lynn-Holly Johnson, Luis Prendes; D: Deran Saralian.

Alien Prey 🌀½ *1983 (R)* Two lesbians are making love when they are unexpectedly devoured by a hungry and indiscreet alien. No safe sex there. Graphic sex, violence, and cannibalism produce an interesting twist to the old eat 'em and leave 'em genre. 85m/C VHS, DVD Barry Stokes, Sally Faulkner; D: Norman J. Warren.

Alien: Resurrection 🌀🌀 *1997 (R)* Despite her fiery end in the last film, Ripley is brought back, through cloning, by a team of scientist anxious to get their hands on the alien embryo that invaded her. A more buffed and equally strange Ripley (Weaver) results as some of her DNA gets mixed with her alien friend. Injecting new life into the franchise, director Jeunet creates a freaky and macabre journey as she and the aliens get loose on board the mysterious space craft Auriga and create messy havoc for new alien appetizers including Call (Ryder), who has a personal agenda of her own with Ripley. Ryder may be somewhat out of place, but the humor and energy from the supporting cast, along with the film's dank look raises the one from the bowels of formulaic action/ horror. Includes some decent scares with a tense underwater sequence. 108m/C VHS, DVD. Sigourney Weaver, Winona Ryder, Ron Perlman, Dominique Pinon, Michael Wincott, Kim Flowers, Leland Orser, Brad Dourif, Dan Hedaya, J.E. Freeman, Raymond Cruz; D: Jean-Pierre Jeunet; W: Joss Whedon; C: Darius Khondji; M: John (Gianni) Frizzel.

Alien Seed 🌀 *1989* Aliens kidnap a woman and impregnate her. Estrada is the government scientist hot on her trail. (How fat could a woman carrying alien offspring wander?) 88m/C VHS, DVD. Erik Estrada, Heidi Paine, Steven Blade; D: Bob James.

Alien Siege 🌀½ *2005 (R)* Aliens descend upon Earth seeking human blood, which is the only cure for a virus killing their race. They destroy some cities to show they mean business. Since they need 8 million bodies, a lottery system is devised and the unlucky get to become alien vaccine. Scientist Steven Chase (Johnson) decides no fair when his only child, Heather (Ross), is chosen. Naturally, there's a resistance group that feels earthlings should be fighting the aliens and Steve joins. A Sci-Fi Channel original. 90m/C DVD. Brad Johnson, Carl Weathers, Nathan Anderson, Erin Foss, Lilas Lane; D: Robert Stadd; W: Robert Stadd; C: Lorenzo Senetor; M: Matthias Weber, Chris Walden. CABLE

Alien Space Avenger 🌀½ *1989* Space Avenger 1991 A spaceship piloted by four alien convicts crash lands in New York City. Stalked by an intergalactic bounty hunter whose job is to kill them, the aliens attack and hide inside human bodies to avoid discovery. It's a race against time as the preservation of the human race depends on the avenger's ability to seek and destroy the alien invaders. Bland ripoff of "Aliens" is reminiscent of old-time "B" sci-fi flicks, with more gore and violence. Shot with the old 3-strip Technicolor method. 88m/C VHS. Robert Prichard, Mike McClerie, Charity Staley, Gina Mastrogiacomo, Kick Fairbanks Fogg, Angela Nicholas, Marty Roberts, James Gillis; D: Richard W. Haines; W: Richard W. Haines, Linwood Sawyer; M: Richard Fiocca.

Alien Terminator 🌀 *1995 (R)* Scientists experimenting with DNA find themselves creating an organism capable of instant regeneration that also likes to nosh on living flesh. To make matters worse, the scientists are trapped in their lab complex, which happens to be located five miles below Los Alamos. 95m/C VHS, DVD. Maria Ford, Kevin Alber, Rodger Halston, Cassandra Leigh, Emia Levisetti; D: Dave Payne.

Alien 3000 WOOF! Unseen Evil 2/2004 (R) Sci-entists experimenting with DNA find themselves creating an organism capable of instant regeneration that also likes to nosh on living flesh. To make matters worse, the scientists are trapped in their lab complex, which happens to be located five miles below Los Alamos. Ummm, maybe that's because it's really hard to tell what's going on and not worth the effort anyway. 81m/C DVD. Lorenzo Lamas, Priscilla Barnes, Corbin Timbrook, Scott Schwartz; D: Jeff Leroy; W: Sarrett Clancy; C: Rachel Wyn Dune; M: Collin Simon. VIDEO

Alien Visitor 🌀🌀 Epsilon *1995 (PG-13)* Beautiful alien woman lands on commando ...rit is sent into the forest to search for an invisible alien creature that is supposed to be guarding an unknown treasure in a cave no one can find. Umm, that it's because it's really backwards. But he manages to show her some things that make Earth life worth living. 92m/C VHS, DVD. AU Syd Brisbane, Alethea McGrath, Chloe Ferguson, Phoebe Ferguson, Ulli Birve; D: Rolf de Heer; W: Rolf de Heer; C: Tony Clark; M: Graham Tardif.

Alien vs. Predator 🦴 AvP 2004 (PG-13) How to classify "AvP?" Is it an "Alien" or "Predator" movie? It doesn't really matter since it's the worst offering that either franchise has produced to date. Predictable, effects-laden prequel to the two-part "Alien" saga and a sequel to the two "Predator" films has a bunch of humans finding an arctic training base for adolescent Predators that uses Aliens as their prey. Of course, the silly humans get caught between them and bad things happen. Monster fest fails to enhance either franchise. **110m/C VHS, DVD, Blu-ray Disc, UMD.** *US* Sanaa Lathan, Raoul Bova, Lance Henriksen, Ewen Bremner, Colin Salmon, Tommy Flanagan, Joseph Rye, Agathe de la Boulaye, Carsten Norgaard, Sam Troughton, Ian Whyte; **D:** Paul W.S. Anderson; **W:** Paul W.S. Anderson, Dan O'Bannon; **C:** David C(lark) Johnson; **M:** Harald Kloser.

Alien Warrior woof! 1985 (R) An extraterrestrial fights a street pimp to save a crime-ridden Earth neighborhood. Low-brain rip-off of Superman. **92m/C VHS.** Brett (Baxter) Clark, Pamela Saunders; **D:** Ed(ward) Hunt.

Alienator 🦴 1989 (R) In the improbable future, an unstoppable android killer is sent after an intergalactic villain. An intentional "Terminator" rip-off. **93m/C VHS, DVD.** Jan-Michael Vincent, John Phillip Law, Ross Hagen, Dyana Ortelli, Dawn Wildsmith, P.J. Soles, Teagan Clive, Robert Clarke, Leo Gordon, Robert Quarry, Fox Harris, Hoke Howell, Jay Richardson; **D:** Fred Olen Ray.

Aliens 🦴🦴🦴½ 1986 (R) The bitch is back, some 50 years later. Popular sequel to "Alien" amounts to non-stop, ravaging combat in space. Contact with a colony on another planet has mysteriously stopped. Fresh from deep space sleep, Ripley and a slew of pulsar-equipped Marines return to confront the mother alien at her nest, which is also inhabited by a whole bunch of the nasty critters spewing for a fight. Something's gotta give, and the Oscar-winning special effects are especially inventive (and messy) in the alien demise department. Dimension (acting biz talk) is given to our hero Ripley, as she discovers maternal instincts lurking within her space suit while looking after a young girl, the lone survivor of the colony. Tension-filled gore blaster. Followed by "Aliens 3." **138m/C VHS, DVD.** Sigourney Weaver, Michael Biehn, Lance Henriksen, Bill Paxton, Paul Reiser, Carrie Henn, Jenette Goldstein, William Hope, Al Matthews, Mark Rolston, Ricco Ross, Colette Hiller; **D:** James Cameron; **W:** James Cameron, Walter Hill; **C:** Adrian Biddle; **M:** James Horner. Oscars '86: Sound FX Editing, Visual FX.

Aliens Are Coming 🦴½ 1980 A spaceship crash-lands on Earth, and its devious denizens begin invading human bodies. TV movie that's a dull echo of "Invasion of the Body Snatchers." **100m/C VHS.** Tom Mason, Melinda Fee, Max Gail, Eric (Hans Gudegast) Braeden, Matthew Laborteaux; **D:** Harvey Hart; **M:** William Goldstein.

Aliens from Spaceship Earth 🦴½ 1977 Are strange, celestial forces invading our universe? If they are, is man prepared to defend his planet against threatening aliens of unknown strength? Lame docudrama featuring the Hurdy Gurdy man himself, Donovan. **107m/C VHS.** Donovan, Lynda Day George; **D:** Don Como.

Aliens vs. Predator: Requiem 🦴½ 2007 (R) In this sequel to the 2004 flick, the extraterrestrial beasties are cool and the humans are interchangeable incubators and fodder. A mutant alien-predator crash-lands near a small Colorado town and begins using convenient humans for procreation vessels and a super-Predator shows up to dispatch the new critters. The locals are collateral damage. Everything moves along at a snappy pace and there's some action pieces that are watchable, which means if you're a fan you probably won't be disappointed. **86m/C DVD.** *US* Reiko Aylesworth, John Ortiz, Johnny Lewis, Ariel Gade, Steven Pasquale, Sam Trammell, Robert Joy; **D:** Colin Strause, Greg Strause; **W:** Shane Salerno; **C:** Daniel Pearl; **M:** Brian Tyler.

Alison's Birthday 🦴🦴 1979 A teenage girl learns that some of her family and friends are Satan worshipers at a terrifying birthday party. Meanwhile, the ghost of her dad hovers about, asking for more lines. **99m/C VHS.** *AU* Joanne Samuel, Lou Brown, Bunny Brooke; **D:** Ian Coughlan.

Alive 🦴🦴½ 1993 (R) Recounts the true-life survival story of a group of Uruguayan rugby players in 1972. After their plane crashes in the remote, snowy Andes (in a spectacular sequence) they're forced to turn to cannibalism during a 10-week struggle to stay alive. Marshall doesn't focus on the gruesome idea, choosing instead to focus on all aspects of their desperate quest for survival. The special effects are stunning, but other parts of the film are never fully realized, including the final scene. Based on the nonfiction book by Piers Paul Read. **127m/C VHS, DVD.** Ethan Hawke, Vincent Spano, Josh Hamilton, Bruce Ramsay, John Haymes Newton, David Kriegel, Kevin Breznahan, Sam Behrens, Illeana Douglas, Jack Noseworthy, Christian Meoli, Jake Carpenter; **D:** Frank Marshall; **W:** John Patrick Shanley; **C:** Peter James; **M:** James Newton Howard; **Nar:** John Malkovich.

Alive and Kicking 🦴🦴½ Indian Summer 1996 (R) Tonio (Flemyng) is a handsome, vain ballet dancer with AIDS, who hides his emotions beneath a witty facade and his work. At a club he meets the older, equally driven Jack (Sher), an AIDS counselor, who pursues him. Though they become lovers, Tonio's obsession with his latest (and last) dance role causes a rift between them. Subplot between Tonio and lesbian dancer Millie (Parish) is self-conscious and Tonio's theatrics can become annoying but both Flemyng and Sher do their best in somewhat one-note roles. **100m/C VHS, DVD.** *GB* Jason Flemyng, Anthony Sher, Dorothy Tutin, Anthony (Corlan) Higgins, Diane Parish, Bill Nighy; **D:** Nancy Meckler; **W:** Martin Sherman; **C:** Chris Seager; **M:** Peter Salem.

All About Eve 🦴🦴🦴🦴 1950 One of the wittiest (and most cynical) flicks of all time follows aspiring young actress Eve Harrington (Baxter) as she ingratiates herself with a prominent group of theatre people so she can become a Broadway star without the usual years of work. The not-so-innocent babe becomes secretary to aging star Margo Channing (Davis) and ruthlessly uses everyone in her climb to the top, much to Davis' initial disbelief and eventual displeasure. Satirical, darkly funny view of the theatre world features exceptional work by Davis, Sanders, and Ritter. Based on "The Wisdom of Eve" by Mary Orr. Later staged as the musical "Applause." **138m/B VHS, DVD.** Bette Davis, Anne Baxter, George Sanders, Celeste Holm, Gary Merrill, Thelma Ritter, Marilyn Monroe, Hugh Marlowe, Gregory Ratoff, Eddie Fisher; **D:** Joseph L. Mankiewicz; **W:** Joseph L. Mankiewicz; **C:** Milton Krasner; **M:** Alfred Newman. Oscars '50: Costume Des. (B&W), Director (Mankiewicz), Picture, Screenplay, Sound, Support. Actor (Sanders); AFI '98: Top 100; British Acad. '50: Film; Cannes '51: Actress (Davis), Grand Jury Prize; Directors Guild '50: Director (Mankiewicz); Golden Globes '51: Screenplay, Natl. Film Reg. '90; N.Y. Film Critics '50: Actress (Davis), Director (Mankiewicz), Film.

All About My Mother 🦴🦴🦴 Todo Sobre Mi Madre 1999 (R) Manuela (Roth) is a single mom, emotionally dependent on her 17-year-old son, Esteban (Azorin). After seeing him killed in a car accident, the grief-stricken mom seeks to find Esteban's father—now a transvestite named Lola (Canto)—and meets an old friend, transvestite prostitute Agrado (San Juan), who offers comfort. Adding to the female roundelay are Huma Rojo (Paredes), Esteban's favorite actress, and Sister Rosa (Cruz), a pregnant nun who runs a shelter. As Manuela encounters each of them, they help give her a renewed sense of hope and the strength to carry on. Spanish with subtitles. **102m/C VHS, DVD.** *SP* Cecilia (Celia) Roth, Penelope Cruz, Marisa Paredes, Eloy Azorin, Toni Canto, Antonia San Juan, Candela Pena; **D:** Pedro Almodovar; **W:** Pedro Almodovar; **C:** Alfonso Beato; **M:** Alberto Iglesias. Oscars '99: Foreign Film; British Acad. '99: Director (Almodovar), Foreign Film; Cannes '99: Director for (Almodovar); Cesar '00: Foreign Film; Golden Globes '00: Foreign Film; L.A. Film Critics '99: Foreign Film; N.Y. Film Critics '99: Foreign Film; Broadcast Film Critics '99: Foreign Film.

All About the Benjamins 🦴🦴 2002 (R) Cube and Epps re-team ("Next Friday") as bounty hunter Bucum (Ice Cube) and two-bit con Reggie (Epps) who meet mobsters and mayhem in Miami in this hip-hop buddy flick. Bucum, who dreams of opening his own private-eye agency, is sent to track down Reggie, who seeks a lost lottery tickets which gets the mismatched duo mixed up in a diamond heist. As usual, Cube, straight man to Epps's clown, have the usual chemistry and deliver some amusing moments in this light caper comedy, but the director's penchant for gory violence interrupts the otherwise slapstick mood. The two leads would shine if not for being stuck in this nod to "Miami Vice" and Elmore Leonard without the character development and plot. Cube co-wrote with Levy. **98m/C VHS, DVD.** *US* Ice Cube, Mike Epps, Tommy Flanagan, Eva Mendes, Carmen Chaplin, Roger Guenveur Smith, Anthony Michael Hall, Valarie Rae Miller, Bow Wow; **D:** Kevin Bray; **W:** Ice Cube, Ronald Lang; **C:** Glen MacPherson; **M:** John Murphy.

All About You 🦴½ 2001 (PG) Tired tale takes Nicole from lost love Robbie in L.A. to blossoming romance with Brian in San Fran. Naturally the new guy is the old guy's alienated brother. **100m/C VHS, DVD.** Terron Brooks, Debbie Allen, Lisa-Raye, Renee Goldsberry, Lou Myers, Vanessa Bell Calloway, Bobby Hosea, Chris Spencer, Tico Wells, Adam Lazarre-White, Emily Liu; **D:** Christine Swanson; **W:** Christine Swanson; **C:** Wolf Baschung, David Scardina; **M:** John Bickerton. VIDEO

All-American Murder 🦴🦴 1991 (R) A rebellious young man is enrolled in a typical, all-American college for one last shot at mainstream life. Things start out okay, as he meets an attractive young coed. Hours later, he finds himself accused of her grisly murder. The youth is then given 24 hours to prove his innocence by a canny homicide detective. Average performances highlight this film, which isn't able to rise above the mediocre. **94m/C VHS, DVD.** Christopher Walken, Charlie Schlatter, Josie Bissett, Joanna Cassidy, Richard Kind, Woody Watson, J.C. Quinn, Amy Davis; **D:** Anson Williams; **C:** Peter Suschitzky; **M:** Wilfred Josephs.

All Creatures Great and Small 🦴🦴🦴 1974 Taken from James Herriot's bestselling novels, this is a delightful, quiet drama of a veterinarian's apprentice in rural England. Fine performance by Hopkins. Followed by "All Things Bright and Beautiful" and a popular British TV series. **92m/C VHS, DVD.** *GB* Simon Ward, Anthony Hopkins, Lisa Harrow, Brian Stirner, Freddie Jones, T.P. McKenna; **D:** Claude Whatham; **W:** Hugh Whitemore; **C:** Peter Suschitzky; **M:** Wilfred Josephs.

All Dogs Go to Heaven 🦴🦴 1989 (G) Somewhat heavy-handed animated musical (Reynolds sings) about a gangster dog who is killed by his partner in business. On the way to Heaven, he discovers how to get back to Earth to seek his revenge. When he returns to Earth, he is taken in by a little girl and learns about something he missed in the first time around: Love. Expertly animated, but the plot may not keep the grown-ups engrossed, and the kids may notice its lack of charm. **85m/C VHS, DVD.** **D:** Don Bluth; **W:** Don Bluth, David N. Weiss; **M:** Ralph Burns; **V:** Burt Reynolds, Judith Barsi, Dom DeLuise, Vic Tayback, Charles Nelson Reilly, Melba Moore, Candy Devine, Loni Anderson.

All Dogs Go to Heaven 2 🦴½ 1995 (G) Animated musical finds lovable scamp Charlie (Sheen) the dog discovering that the afterlife is not all it's cracked up to be and pining for dysfunction aplenty back on earth. He gets his chance when Gabriel's Horn is stolen and Charlie is assigned to retrieve it. Charlie teams up again with old buddy Itchy (Deluise) as the two come down from Dog Heaven to stop the villainous Carface (Borgnine) and demonic cat Red (Hearn). Along the way, Charlie falls in love with sexy Irish Setter Sasha (Easton), and finds a chance for redemption by helping a little boy in trouble. Animation not outstanding, but should keep the attention of small children. **82m/C VHS, DVD.** **D:** Paul Sabella, Larry Leker; **W:** Arne Olsen, Kelly Ward, Mark Young; **M:** Mark Watters, Barry Mann, Cynthia Weil; **V:** Charlie Sheen, Sheena Easton, Ernest Borgnine, Dom DeLuise, George Hearn, Bebe Neuwirth, Hamilton Camp, Wallace Shawn, Bobby DiCicco, Adam Wylie.

All Fall Down 🦴🦴½ 1962 A young man (de Wilde) idolizes his callous older brother (Beatty) until a tragedy forces him to grow up. Saint plays the older woman taken in by the brother's family, who is seduced and abandoned. When she finds herself pregnant and alone, she commits suicide causing the younger brother, who loved her from afar, to vow to kill his older sibling. A well-acted melodrama. Also available colorized. **111m/B VHS.** Eva Marie Saint, Brandon de Wilde, Warren Beatty, Karl Malden, Angela Lansbury, Constance Ford, Barbara Baxley; **D:** John Frankenheimer; **W:** William Inge; **C:** Lionel Lindon; **M:** Alex North.

All God's Children 🦴🦴½ 1980 Drama about the controversial forced busing issue and two families who must face it. Top-notch cast is occasionally mislead by meandering script attempting to stay true to a sensitive issue. **100m/C VHS.** Richard Widmark, Ned Beatty, Ossie Davis, Ruby Dee, Mariclare Costello, George Spell, Trish Van Devere, Ken Swofford; **D:** Jerry Thorpe; **M:** Billy Goldenberg. TV

All Hat 🦴½ 2007 (R) And no particular brains or heart. Hot-head Ray Doakes (Kirby) just got out of prison. He returns to his Ontario hometown to find that lowdown land developer Sonny Stanton (Jenkins), who helped put Ray away, is still up to no good. When an expensive thoroughbred from Stanton's racing stables goes missing, the scumball uses it as an excuse to squeeze the local farmers into selling their property for his golf resort. Only Ray comes up with a plan to stop him. **91m/C DVD.** *CA* Rachael Leigh Cook, Luke Kirby, Noam Jenkins, Keith Carradine, Ernie Hudson, David Alpay, Graham Greene, Gary Farmer, Lisa Ray, Stephen McHattie, Michelle Nolden; **D:** Leonard Farlinger; **W:** Brad Smith; **C:** Paul Sarossy; **M:** Bill Frisell. VIDEO

All I Desire 🦴🦴½ 1953 Estranged wife and mother (Stanwyck) returns to her hometown after fleeing years ago to pursue a stage career. She desires a new beginning with her family, but finds things have changed in her absence. The story examines the will of a strong woman and small town values. Director Sirk disagreed with the happy ending demanded by producers, but the drama is still noteworthy. **80m/B VHS.** Barbara Stanwyck, Richard Carlson, Lyle Bettger, Maureen O'Sullivan; **D:** Douglas Sirk; **W:** James Gunn, Robert Blees, Carl Guthrie, Gina Kaus; **M:** Joseph Gershenson.

All I Wanna Do 🦴🦴½ 1998 (PG-13) The Hairy Bird; Strike! 1998 (PG-13) The students of an exclusive, and financially troubled, East Coast girls' school, circa 1963, are vigorously opposed to the merger of their school with a boys' academy. So they decide to stage a protest strike. Rather typical coming of age tale with a notable cast of up-and-comers. Film was briefly released in 1998 at 110 minutes under the title "Strike" and then re-edited and re-released under its current title in 2000. **94m/C VHS, DVD.** Kirsten Dunst, Gaby Hoffman, Heather Matarazzo, Rachael Leigh Cook, Monica Keena, Merritt Wever, Lynn Redgrave, Vincent Kartheiser, Tom Guiry, Matthew Lawrence, Robert Bockstael; **D:** Sarah Kernochan; **W:** Sarah Kernochan; **C:** Anthony C. "Tony" Jannelli; **M:** Graeme Revell.

All I Want 🦴🦴 Try Seventeen 2002 (R) Jones Dillon (Wood) is a 17-year-old wide-eyed Kansas university freshman who soon decides that dorm life is not for him. So he moves into the boarding house of Ma Mabley (Harry) and is soon pining after a couple of his neighbors—sweet would-be actress Lisa (Moore) and experienced photographer Jane (Potente). Coming of ager hasn't do well with their limited material. **96m/C VHS, DVD.** Elijah Wood, Franka Potente, Mandy Moore, Deborah Harry, Aaron Pearl,

All I Want for Christmas ⅆⅆ 1991 (G) Low-budget, sappy holiday tale of a young girl (Birch) who wants to reunite her divorced parents. Determined to fulfill her Christmas wish, Hallie seeks out the Santa Claus at Macy's department store to tell him the one thing she truly wants for Christmas. Birch is charming and Nielsen as her grandmother and Nielsen as Santa but the story is too squishy and bland to be believable. **92m/C VHS, DVD.** Thora Birch, Leslie Nielsen, Lauren Bacall, Jamey Sheridan, Hallie Jane Kozak, Ethan (Randall) Embry, Kevin Nealon, Andrea Martin; **D:** Robert Lieberman; **W:** Richard Kramer, Thom Eberhardt, Neal Israel, Gail Parent. **C:** Robbie Greenberg; **M:** Bruce Broughton.

All In ⅆ 2006 (R) Alice "Ace" Anderson (Swain) has been raised by her poker-playing father (Madsen) in the world of backstreet gambling. With mounting debts from med school, Ace decides to "recruit" some fellow students to take on the best players and win at the World Series of Poker. Lame effort with some confusing and unnecessary subplots. **?m/C VHS, DVD.** Dominique Swain, Michael Madsen, James Russo, Louis Gossett Jr., Kristen Miller, Colleen Porch, Scott Whyte, Michelle Lombardo, Chris Backus, Johann Urb, Hayley DuMont; **D:** Nick Vallelonga; **W:** Loren Conroy; **C:** Jeff Bausert; **M:** Harry Manfredini.

All in a Night's Work ⅆⅆ 1961 The founder of a one-man publishing empire is found dead with a smile on his face. His nephew inherits the business and finds himself caught in a series of big and small business misunderstandings. He's also falling in love with the woman he suspects was responsible for his uncle's demise. Nicely paced sex and business comedy with warm performances. **94m/C VHS, DVD.** Dean Martin, Shirley MacLaine, Cliff Robertson, Charlie Ruggles; **D:** Joseph Anthony; **W:** Sidney Sheldon; **M:** Andre Previn.

All Mine to Give ⅆⅆ½ 1956 The Day They Gave the Babies Away. Sad saga of a Scottish family of eight who braved frontier hardships, epidemics, and death in the Wisconsin wilderness more than a century ago. Midway through, mom and dad die, leaving the oldest child struggling to keep the family together. A strange, through often effective, combination of pioneer adventures and tearjerking moments that avoids be-coming hopelessly soapy due to fine performances. Unless you're pretty weathered, you'll need some hankies. Based on the reminiscences of Dale and Katherine Eunson as detailed in a "Cosmopolitan" magazine article. **102m/C VHS.** Glynis Johns, Cameron Mitchell, Rex Thompson, Patty McCormack, Ernest Truex, Hope Emerson, Alan Hale Jr., Royal Dano, Reta Shaw, Rita Johnson; **D:** Allen Reisner; **M:** Max Steiner.

All My Good Countrymen ⅆⅆ½ 1968 A lyrical, funny film about the eccentric denizens of a small Moravan village soon after the socialization of Czechoslovakia in 1948. Completed during the Soviet invasion of 1968 and immediately banned. In Czech with English subtitles. **115m/C VHS.** CZ Vladimir Mensik, Radoslav Brzobohaty, Pavel Pavlovsky; **D:** Vojtech Jasny. Cannes '59: Director (Jasny).

All My Loved Ones ⅆⅆ 2000 Moj Blizzi Vsichni Moi Blizci. Moving fictionalized account by director Minac of his mother's recollections of a small Jewish children saved in the Kindertransport trains. Briton Nicholas Winton (Graves) is on holiday in Prague in 1938, recognizing the worsening situation for the Jews in Czechoslovakia, he discovers that both Sweden and Britain are willing to take in child refugees if he can transport them out of the country. One of these potential transportees is 10-year-old David (Holicek), a member of a wealthy family who fail to recognize the seriousness of their situation. Czech with subtitles. **91m/C VHS, DVD.** CZ Rupert Graves, Libuse Safrankova, Josef Abrham, Jiri Bartoska, Branó Holicek, Jiri Menzel; **D:** Matej Minac; **W:** Jiri Hubac; **C:** Dodo Simoncic.

All Night Long ⅆⅆ½ 1981 (R) Offbeat middle-age crisis comedy about a burned-out and recently demoted drug-store executive (Hackman) in L.A. who leaves his wife, takes up with his fourth cousin by marriage, and begins a humorous rebellion, becoming an extremely free ance inventor while joining the drifters, weirdos and thieves of the night. An obscure, sometimes uneven little gem with Hackman in top form and an appealing supporting performance by Streisand. Highlighted by delightful malapropisms and satiric invasion of the usual cliches. **100m/C VHS, DVD.** Gene Hackman, Barbra Streisand, Diane Ladd, Dennis Quaid, Kevin Dobson, William Daniels; **D:** Jean-Claude Tramont; **W:** W.D. Richter; **M:** Ira Newborn.

All of Me ⅆⅆ½ 1984 (PG) A wealthy woman (Tomlin) dies and her guru accidentally transfers her soul to the right side of her lawyer's body, a modern version of existential hell. Lawyer Martin indulges in some funny slapstick as he discovers that his late client is waging an internal war for control of his body. Flat and cliched at times, but redeemed by the inspired clowning of Martin and witty Martin/Tomlin repartee. Based on the novel "Me Too" by Ed Davis. **93m/C VHS, DVD.** Steve Martin, Lily Tomlin, Victoria Tennant, Madolyn Smith, Richard Libertini, Dana Elcar, Selma Diamond, Jason Bernard, Eric Christmas, Peggy Feury; **D:** Carl Reiner; **W:** Phil Alden Robinson; **C:** Richard H. Kline; **M:** Patrick Williams. N.Y. Film Critics '84: Actor (Martin); Natl. Soc. Film Critics '84: Actor (Martin).

All or Nothing ⅆⅆ 2002 (R) A depressing tale about depressed and despondent people set in a grotty housing project in South London. Hangdog minicab driver Phil (Spall) can't even earn a decent wage to support his family, cashier common-law wife Penny (Manville), and their layabout son Rory (Corden) and misfit daughter Rachel (Garland). Their neighbors aren't any better off—stuck with abusive boyfriends, unplanned pregnancy, alcoholism, and the general dreariness of their daily lives. Leigh is known for his slice-of-life dramas but this just stays one-dimensional. **128m/C VHS, DVD.** GB FR Timothy Spall, Leslie Manville, Alison Garland, James Corden, Paul Jesson, Ruth Sheen, Marion Bailey, Sally Hawkins, Ben Crompton, Helen Coker; Daniel Mays; **D:** Mike Leigh; **W:** Mike Leigh; **C:** Dick Pope; **M:** Andrew Dickson.

All My Sons ⅆⅆ 1943 Joe Keller (Robinson) is a small-town manufacturer who during the profits he made from his WWII contracts. But his family is pulled apart by guilt and shame when son Chris (Lancaster) discovers his father sold defective parts to the military that resulted in loss of life and then covered up the crime. Excellent performances; adapted from the play by Arthur Miller. Remade in 1986 with James Whitmore and Aidan Quinn. **94m/B VHS.** Edward G. Robinson, Burt Lancaster, Mady Christians, Louisa Horton, Howard Duff, Frank Conroy, Arlene Francis, Harry (Henry) Morgan; **D:** Irving Reis; **W:** Chester Erskine; **C:** Russell Metty; **M:** Leith Horton.

All My Sons ⅆⅆ 1986 A wealthy family is distraught when their eldest son is listed as missing-in-action during WWII. They must cope with guilt, as well as grief, because the father's business reaped profits from his war. Adapted from the acclaimed Arthur Miller play. **122m/C VHS.** James Whitmore, Aidan Quinn, Joan Allen, Michael Learned; **D:** John Power. TV

All New Adventures of Laurel and Hardy: For Love or Mummy ⅆⅆ½ 1998 (PG) Stan Laurel (Pinchot) and Oliver Hardy (Sartain) are the equally bumbling nephews of the original comedic duo. The would-be movers are hired to transport an Egyptian mummy to an American museum, where archeologist Leslie (Danford) is the unwitting object of an ancient curse that foretells her marrying the reanimated corpse. **84m/C VHS, DVD.** Bronson Pinchot, Gailard Sartain, F. Murray Abraham, Susan Danford; **D:** John R. Cherry III; Larry Harmon.

All Over Me ⅆⅆ 1996 (R) Teen angst/coming of age set in New York's Hell's Kitchen. Ungainly wanna-be guitarist, 15-year-old Claudia-AKA-Claude (Folland), is best friends with flirty blonde Ellen when Ellen begins dating the macho older Mark (Hauser) and is soon into sex and drugs, while Claude's sexual quandries lead her to a lesbian bar and an interest in singer Lucy (Hailey). Good performances and a moody and somewhat awkward first feature from Sichel, whose sister wrote the screenplay. **90m/C VHS, DVD.** Alison Folland, Tara Subkoff, Cole Hauser, Wilson Cruz, Leisha Hailey, Pat Briggs, Ann Dowd; **D:** Alex Sichel; **W:** Sylvia Sichel; **C:** Joe DeSalvo; **M:** Miki Navazio.

All Over the Guy ⅆⅆ½ 2001 (R) Writer/director Roos served as executive producer on this film, which re-unites some of the personnel from his hit "The Opposite of Sex." Unfortunately, the quality of that film isn't reproduced here. Eli (writer Bucatinsky adapted from his play) and Tom (Ruccolo) are two gay men who are set up on a blind date by Brett (Goldberg) and Jackie (Alexander). They don't really get along, but they find themselves very attracted to one another. The film then explores the ups and downs of their courtship, as each tries to deal with their baggage from the past which keeps them from succeeding in the present. The problem is it's incredibly unoriginal. There doesn't seem to be any real chemistry between the couple, so whether or not they stay together may become a moot point to some viewers. Some of the performances are good (Goldberg has some good lines), but Ruccolo looks very uncomfortable at times. **95m/C VHS, DVD.** Dan Bucatinsky, Richard Ruccolo, Adam Goldberg, Sasha Alexander, Doris Roberts, Andrea Martin, Tony Abatemarco, Joanna Kerns, Nicolas Surovy, Christina Ricci, Lisa Kudrow; **D:** Julie Davis; **W:** Dan Bucatinsky; **C:** Goran Pavicevic; **M:** Peter Stuart, Andrew Williams.

All Over Town ⅆⅆ½ 1937 Two vaudevillians with a trained seal find themselves involved in a murder when they are kidnapped by a gang of thugs. A lesser Olsen and Johnson comedy with scattered funny moments. **52m/B VHS, DVD.** Ole Olsen, Chic Johnson, Mary Howard, Franklin Pangborn, James Finlayson; **D:** James W. Horne; **W:** Jack Townley, Jerome Chodorov.

All Quiet on the Western Front ⅆⅆⅆ 1930 Extraordinary and realistic anti-war epic based on the novel by Erich Maria Remarque. Seven patriotic German youths go together from school to the battlefields of WWI. They experience the horrors of war first-hand, stuck in the trenches and facing gradual extermination. Centers on experiences of one of the young men, Paul Baumer, who changes from enthusiastic war endorser to battle-weary veteran in an emotionally exact performance by Ayres. Boasts a gigantic budget (for the time) of $1.25 million, and features more than 2000 extras swarming about battlefields set up on ranchland in California. Relentless anti-war message is emotionally draining and starting with both graphic shots and haunting visual poetry. Extremely controversial in the U.S. and Germany upon release, the original version was 140 minutes long (some versions are available with 'restored footage') and featured ZaSu Pitts as Ayres mother (later reshot with Western Front, was eventually forced to leave Germany for the U.S. due to the film's ongoing controversy). **103m/B VHS, DVD.** Lew Ayres, Louis Wolheim, John Wray, Slim Summerville, Russell Gleason, Raymond Griffith, Ben Alexander, Beryl Mercer, Arnold Lucy, William "Billy" Bakewell, Scott Kolk, Owen Davis Jr., Walter Rodgers, Richard Alexander, Harold Goodwin, G. Pat Collins, Edmund Breese; **D:** Lewis Milestone; **W:** Maxwell Anderson, George Abbott, Del Andrews; **C:** Arthur Edeson, Karl Freund; **M:** David Broekman; Oscars '30: Director (Milestone), Picture; AFI '98: Top 100, Natl. Film Reg. '90.

All or Nothing at All ⅆⅆ 1993 Leo Hopkins (Laurie) is a charming con man with a successful career and a wife and kids. He's also a gambling addict who can't help living life on the edge, until he finds himself about to fall off. **150m/C DVD.** GB Hugh Laurie, Bob Monkhouse, Pippa Guard, Caroline Quentin, Jessica Turner, Steve Steen, Phyllida Law; **D:** Andrew Grieve; **W:** Guy Andrews. TV

All Screwed Up ⅆⅆ 1974 All in Place; Nothing in Order 1974. A group of young immigrants come to Milan and try to adjust to city life; they soon find that everything is in city life, but nothing is in order. Wertmuller in a lighter vein than usual. **82m/C VHS, DVD.** Luigi Diberti, Lina Polito; **D:** Lina Wertmuller; **W:** Lina Wertmuller.

All Saint's Day ⅆⅆ 1998 Tired of his going-nowhere life, Marco (Blatt) recruits four of his screw-up friends to help him rob the Brooklyn fish market where he works. Of course, since they're all losers this doesn't work out as planned. **83m/C VHS, DVD.** Mickey Blatt, Thomas J. La Sosa, James Patrick McArdle, Mark Love, Christopher Lynn, Anthony Mangaro, Ray Garvey, Howard Simon; **D:** Thomas J. La Sosa; **W:** Thomas J. La Sosa, Christopher Lynn; **C:** Daniel Marracino.

All Souls Day ⅆ½ Dia de los Muertos 2005 Vargas Diaz's 1892 brutal rampage in a small Mexican town on the symbolic "Day of the Dead" causes his murderous soul to haunt the locals for years, leading them to perform certain acts to keep the zombies at bay. First up to be terrorized is a 1950's family with a sick boy and a hot teenaged girl who takes the long-standing rite and must flee the same creepy hotel. Sci-Fi Channel original should have let the walking dead lie. **90m/C DVD.** Travis Wester, Nichole Hiltz, Laz Alonso, Laura Elena Harring, Marisa Ramirez, David Keith, Jeffrey Combs, Elle Cornell, Julia Vera, Daniel Bungio, Mircea Monroe, Danny Trejo, Noah Luke; **D:** Jeremy Kasten; **W:** Mark Altman; **C:** Christopher Gutowski. CABLE

All Quiet on the Western Front ⅆⅆ½ 1979 A big-budget TV remake of the 1930 masterpiece starring John Boy. Sensitive German youth Thomas plunges excitedly into WWI and discovers its terror and degradation. Nowhere near the original's quality. **150m/C VHS, DVD.** Richard Thomas, Ernest Borgnine, Donald Pleasence, Patricia Neal; **D:** Delbert Mann; **W:** Paul Monash; **C:** John Coquillon; **M:** Allyn Ferguson. TV

All That Heaven Allows ⅆⅆⅆ 1955 Attractive wealthy middle-aged widow Cary Scott (Wyman) falls for her 15-years-younger gardener Ron Kirby (Hudson), and becomes the target of small-minded gossips and her disapproving family. Ron's no gigolo or fortune-hunter but societal pressure still gets to Cary and she breaks things off. But loneliness makes her realize what she's missing and she decides to make things up with Ron and forget her critics. Hopeful Sirk romance that still takes some jabs at conformity. **89m/B VHS, DVD.** Jane Wyman, Rock Hudson, Conrad Nagel, Agnes Moorehead, Virginia Grey, Gloria Talbott, William Reynolds; **D:** Douglas Sirk; **W:** Peggy Fenwick; **C:** Russell Metty; **M:** Frank Skinner; Joseph Gershenson. Natl. Film Reg. '95.

All That Jazz ⅆⅆ½ 1979 Fosse's autobiographical portrait with Scheider fully occupying his best role as the obsessed, pill-popping, chain-smoking choreographer/director dancing simultaneously with love and death. But even while dying, he creates some great dancing. Vivid and imaginative with exact editing, and an eerie footnote to Fosse's similar death almost ten years later. Egocentric and self-indulgent for sure, but that's entertainment. ♪On Broadway; Everything Old is New Again; After You've Gone; There'll Be Some Changes Made; Some of These Days; Bye Bye Love. **120m/C VHS, DVD.** Roy Scheider, Jessica Lange, Ann Reinking, Leland Palmer, Cliff Gorman, Ben Vereen, Erzsebet Foldi, John Lithgow, Max Wright, Deborah Geffner, Michael (Lawrence) Gordon, David Margulies, Nicole Fosse, Anthony Holland; **D:** Bob Fosse; **W:** Bob Fosse, Robert

Alan Aurthur; **C:** Giuseppe Rotunno; **M:** Ralph Burns. Oscars '79: Art Dir/Set Dec.; Costume Des., Film Editing, Orig. Song Score and/or Adapt.; Cannes '80: Film. Natl. Film Reg. '01.

All the Brothers Were Valiant ⊘⊘½ 1953 Brothers Taylor and Granger are New England whaling captains but Granger decides to treasure hunt instead. He finds a priceless cache of black pearls on an island but angers the locals who regard the gems as sacred. When Taylor rescues him, Granger promptly turns his brother's crew into mutineers in order to return to the island and retrieve his prize. Lots of brawling and there's an incidental love story with Blyth desired by both men (she's married Taylor and just happens to be aboard). Last role for Stone. Based on the novel by Ben Ames Williams. **101m/C VHS.** Robert Taylor, Stewart Granger, Ann Blyth, Betta St. John, Keenan Wynn, James Whitmore, Kurt Kasznar, Lewis Stone, Robert Burton, Peter Whitney, John Lupton, Billie Dove; **D:** Richard Thorpe; **W:** Harry Brown; **C:** George J. Folsey; **M:** Miklos Rozsa.

All the Kind Strangers ⊘⊘ *Evil in the Swamp* 1974 Traveling photographer Keach picks up a young hitchhiker and takes him to the boy's home. He discovers six other children there who want him as a father, his alternative being death. He and "Mother" Eggar plot their escape from the dangerous orphans. **72m/C VHS, DVD.** Stacy Keach, Robby Benson, John Savage, Samantha Eggar; **D:** Burt Kennedy. TV

All the King's Men ⊘⊘⊘⊘ 1949 Grim and graphic classic set in the Depression follows the rise of a Louisiana farm-boy from angry and honest political hopeful to powerful but corrupt governor. Loosely based on the life (and death) of Huey Long and told by a newsman who's followed his career (Ireland). Willy Stark (Crawford, in his break-through role) is the politician who, while appearing to improve the state, rules dictatorially, betraying friends and constituents and proving once again that power corrupts. In her first major role, McCambridge delivers a powerful performance as the cunning political aide. Potent morality play based on the Robert Penn Warren book. **109m/B VHS, DVD.** Broderick Crawford, Mercedes McCambridge, John Ireland, Joanne Dru, John Derek, Anne Seymour, Shepperd Strudwick; **D:** Robert Rossen; **W:** Robert Rossen; **C:** Burnett Guffey; **M:** Louis Gruenberg. Oscars '49: Actor (Crawford), Picture, Support. Actress (McCambridge); Golden Globes '50: Actor—Drama (Crawford), Director (Rossen), Film—Drama, Support. Actress (McCambridge). Natl. Film Reg. '01; N.Y. Film Critics '49: Actor (Crawford), Film.

All the King's Men ⊘⊘½ 1999 In 1915, Frank Beck (Jason), the manager of the royal estate of Sandringham, trains a company of servants to be volunteer soldiers. Unfortunately, the raw recruits are posted to the disaster of Gallipoli and a battle against the Turks. The true fate of the company was unknown for many years and their disappearance became the stuff of myth (recent discoveries proved much grimmer) but the storyline is muddled and it's not easy to distinguish one youthful character from another (although the veterans do a notable job). Based on the novel by Nigel McCrery. **110m/C VHS, DVD. GB** David Jason, Maggie Smith, Stuart Bunce, William Ash, James Murray, Sonya Walger, Eamon Boland, David Troughton, Emma Cunniffe, Adam Kotz, Patrick Malahide, Ed Waters, Tom Burke, Ben Crompton, Jo Stone-Fewings, James Hillier, Ian McDiarmid, Phyllis Logan; **D:** Julian Jarrold; **W:** Alma Cullen; **C:** David Odd; **M:** Adrian Johnston. TV

All the King's Men ⊘⊘½ 2006 (PG-13) Based on Robert Penn Warren's 1946 novel, this bungled remake of the 1949 film focuses on the rise and fall of a Huey P. Long-like politician, with Penn all bug-eyed sputterings as southern demagogue Willie Stark. Besides the out-of-place Penn, there's a bunch of miscast Brits, including narrator Law as boozy journalist Jack Burden, Winslet as Stark's unrequited love Anne, and Hopkins as a judge that Willie wants dirt on. Louisiana native Clarkson and former child actor Ha-

ley are about the only two actors who probably won't make you squirm. **128m/C Blu-ray Disc. US** Sean Penn, Jude Law, Kate Winslet, James Gandolfini, Mark Ruffalo, Patricia Clarkson, Kathy Baker, Jackie Earle Haley, Anthony Hopkins, Kevin Dunn, Frederic Forrest, Talia Balsam, Glenn Morshower; **D:** Steven Zaillian; **W:** Steven Zaillian; **C:** Pawel Edelman; **M:** James Horner.

All the Little Animals ⊘⊘½ 1998 (R) Twenty-four-year old Bobby (Bale) is brain damaged from a childhood accident. After his mother's death, he's left in the less-than-tender care of his malevolent stepfather, De Winter (Benzali), who's only interested in Bobby's inheritance. So Bobby runs away and is taken in by hermit, Mr. Summers (Hurt), who is devoted to burying the remains of animals killed in road accidents. But Bobby's idyll cannot last when his stepfather finds him—and Mr. Summers is also not quite what he seems. Based on the novel by Walker Hamilton. **104m/C VHS, DVD. GB** John Hurt, Christian Bale, Daniel Benzali, James Faulkner, Amy Robbins; **D:** Jeremy Thomas; **W:** Eski Thomas; **C:** Mike Molloy; **M:** Richard Hartley.

...All the Marbles ⊘⊘ *The California Dolls* 1981 (R) A manager of two beautiful lady wrestlers has dreams of going to the top. Aldrich's last film, and an atypical one, with awkward pacing and a thin veil of sex exploitation. Falk provides needed grace and humor as the seedy manager, with Young controlling his usual competent bit as a hustling promoter dabbling in criminal activity. One of the few tag-team women wrestling pictures, it builds to a rousing finale match in the "Rocky" tradition, although the shift in tone and mountainous cliches effectively body slam the intent. **113m/C VHS.** Peter Falk, Burt Young, Vicki Frederick, Richard Jaeckel, Claudette Nevins; **D:** Robert Aldrich; **C:** Joseph Biroc.

All the President's Men ⊘⊘⊘½ 1976 (PG) True story of the Watergate break-in that led to the political scandal of the decade, based on the best-selling book by Washington Post reporters Bob Woodward and Carl Bernstein. Intriguing, terse thriller is a nail-biter even though the ending is no secret. Expertly paced by Pakula with standout performances by Hoffman and Redford as the reporters who slowly uncover and connect the seemingly isolated facts that ultimately lead to criminal indictments of the Nixon Administration. Deep Throat Holbrook and Robards as executive editor Ben Bradlee lend authenticity to the endeavor, a realistic portrayal of the stop and go of journalistic investigations. **135m/C VHS, DVD.** Dominic Chianese, David Arkin, Polly Holliday, James Karen, Robert Redford, Dustin Hoffman, Jason Robards Jr., Martin Balsam, Jane Alexander, Hal Holbrook, F. Murray Abraham, Stephen Collins, Lindsay Crouse, Meredith Baxter, Ned Beatty, Penny Fuller; **D:** Alan J. Pakula; **W:** William Goldman; **C:** Gordon Willis; **M:** David Shire. Oscars '76: Adapt. Screenplay, Art Dir./Set Dec. Sound. Support. Actor (Robards); Natl. Bd. of Review '76: Director (Pakula), Support. Actor (Robards); N.Y. Film Critics '76: Director (Pakula), Film, Support. Actor (Robards); Natl. Soc. Film Critics '76: Film. Support. Actor (Robards); Writers Guild '76: Adapt. Screenplay.

All the Pretty Horses ⊘⊘ 2000 (PG-13) John Grady Cole (Damon) is a dispossessed Texas cowboy in the late 1940s who, along with his buddy Lacey Rawlins (Thomas) and teen misfit Blevins (Black), crosses the border for he, hopes, a better life in Mexico. What he finds is an ill-fated romance with the beautiful daughter (Cruz) of a possessive rancher (Blades). It's pretty, all right. But thanks to Thornton's uneven pacing and inability to settle on a visual style, the story, and splendor, of the book is lost somewhere along the way. Of the young (and also pretty) cast, Damon and especially Black

fare the best. Based on the first book of Cormac McCarthy's Border Trilogy. **117m/C VHS. DVD.** Matt Damon, Penelope Cruz, Ruben Blades, Lucas Black, Henry Thomas, Robert Patrick, Julio Oscar Mechoso, Miriam Colon, Bruce Dern, Sam Shepard; **D:** Billy Bob Thornton; **W:** Ted Tally; **C:** Barry Markowitz; **M:** Marty Stuart. Natl. Bd. of Review '00: Screenplay.

All the Queen's Men ⊘⊘ 2002 After his mission to steal a German Enigma encoding machine is torpedoed by an arrogant British officer, American OSS agent O'Rourke (LeBlanc) is assigned to multinational commando team to try again. Only this time they'll be infiltrating a Nazi factory—as female workers. Cross-dressing comic Izzard, as team member Tony, is invaluable here, as he's the only one who looks comfortable in a dress or supplies any comic flair. Jumbled plot and bumbled comedic opportunities combine to thwart a good premise and excellent cast. **99m/C VHS, DVD.** Matt LeBlanc, Eddie Izzard, James Cosmo, Udo Kier, Edward Fox, Nicolette Krebitz, David Birkin, Oliver Korittke, Karl Markovics; **D:** Stefan Ruzowitzky; **W:** David Schneider; **C:** Wedigo von Schultzendorff; **M:** Joern-ewe Fahrenkrog-Petersen.

All the Real Girls ⊘⊘⊘½ 2003 (R) Sophomore effort of writer-director Green is a sincere and poignant look at youthful love. Paul (Schneider), a twenty-something Romeo who's broken more than a few hearts in town, finds the real thing in Noel (played wonderfully by Deschanel), the 18-year-old sister of his best friend, fresh out of boarding school. Fully captures the real and often awkward moments of young love and the pain and confusion that can come with it. Schneider also helped conceive and write the story. **108m/C VHS, DVD.** Paul Schneider, Zooey Deschanel, Patricia Clarkson, Maurice Compte, Benjamin Mouton, Shea Whigham, Danny McBride; **D:** David Gordon Green; **W:** Paul Schneider, David Gordon Green; **C:** Tim Orr; **M:** David Wingo, Michael Linnen.

All the Right Moves ⊘⊘½ 1983 (R) Cruise is the high school football hero hoping for a scholarship so he can vacate pronto the dying Pennsylvania mill town where he grew up. At least he thinks that's what he wants to do. Further mixing up his own mixed feelings are his pushy, ambitious coach (Nelson, doing what he does best), his understanding dad (Cioffi) and supportive girlfriend (Thompson, in a notable early role). Strong performances push the relatively cliched melodrama into field goal range. **90m/C VHS, DVD.** Tom Cruise, Lea Thompson, Craig T. Nelson, Christopher Penn, Charles Cioffi, Paul Carafotes, Dick Miller; **D:** Michael Chapman; **W:** Michael Kane; **C:** Jan De Bont; **M:** David (Richard) Campbell.

All the Rivers Run 1984 First made-for-cable miniseries. A young Australian girl spends her inheritance on a river boat and becomes the first female river captain in Australian history. Directed by George Miller of "Man from Snowy River" fame. **400m/C VHS. AU** Sigrid Thornton, John Waters, Diane Craig, Charles "Bud" Tingwell, Gus Mercurio; **D:** George Miller, Pino Amenta; **C:** David Connell. CABLE

All the Vermeers in New York ⊘⊘⊘½ 1991 A stressed-out Wall Street broker flees to the soothing recesses of the Metropolitan Museum's Vermeer Room. There he meets a beautiful, manipulative French actress dreaming of success in Manhattan. Amidst the opulent art world of New York, the two pursue their relationship to an ultimately tragic end. Jost offers an inside look at the collision of commerce and art and the corrupt underside of New York in this elegant contemporary film. **87m/C VHS, DVD.** Emmanuelle Chaulet, Stephen Lack, Gracie Phillips, Katherine Bean, Laurel Lee Kiefer, Gracie Mansion, Gordon Joseph Weiss, Roger Ruffin; **D:** Jon Jost; **W:** Jon Jost.

All the Way, Boys ⊘½ 1973 (PG) Two inept adventurers crash-land a plane in the Andes in the hope of discovering "Trinity" cast up to no good. **105m/C VHS. IT** Terence

Hill, Bud Spencer, Cyril Cusack, Michel Antoine; **D:** Giuseppe Colizzi.

All the Wrong Places ⊘½ 2000 Twenty-somethings Marisa (Hillis) and Paul (Klavens), the children of successful parents, are struggling to find their own identities and careers. Marisa is trying to make it as a filmmaker, while spending much of her time on her therapist's couch, while Paul is working on his first novel. They've got a lot in common but most of it is little above slacker whining. **95m/C DVD. US** Ali Hillis, Alyce LaTourelle, Brian Patrick Sullivan, Jeremy Klavens, Judy Del Guidice; **D:** Martin Edwards; **W:** Martin Edwards; **C:** Bing Rao; **M:** Jody Elff.

All the Young Men ⊘⊘ 1960 Fairly powerful men-uniting-in-battle story with an interesting cast, highlighted by Poitier in an early role. A tiny marine squadron overrun by the Chinese in the Korean War attempts to resist the numerous attackers. In their spare time, the men confront racial prejudice when a black man (guess who) is put in command. **86m/B VHS.** Alan Ladd, Sidney Poitier, James Darren, Glenn Corbett, Mort Sahl, Ana St. Clair, Paul (E.) Richards, Richard (Dick) Davalos, Lee Kinsolving, Joseph (Joe) Gallison, Paul Baxley, Charles Quinlivan, Michael Davis; **D:** Hall Bartlett; **W:** Hall Bartlett; **C:** Daniel F. Fapp; **M:** George Duning.

All Things Fair ⊘⊘½ *Lust och Fagring Stor; Love Lessons; Laerarinden* 1995 Coming of age story set in neutral Sweden in 1943. Fifteen-year-old Stig (Widerberg, the director's son) has just arrived in Malmo to begin classes at his all-male school—a situation filled with sexual curiosity and repression. Stig is attracted to his beautiful teacher Viola (Lagercrantz), whose marriage to alcoholic traveling salesman Frank (von Bromssen) is less than ideal, and the duo begin an affair. Frank not only seems not to care but befriends his wife's youthful lover, although the situation is ripe for tragedy. Excellent performances, sensual air, though somewhat lacking in logical narrative. Swedish with subtitles. **128m/C VHS, DVD. DK SW** Johan Widerberg, Marika Lagercrantz, Tomas von Bromssen, Bjorn Kjellman, Charles A. Palmer; **D:** Bo Widerberg; **W:** Bo Widerberg; **C:** Morten Bruus.

All This and Heaven Too ⊘⊘⊘ 1940 When a governess arrives at a Parisian aristocrat's home in the 1840s, she causes jealous tension between the husband and his wife. The wife is soon found murdered. Based on Rachel Field's best-seller. **141m/B VHS.** Charles Boyer, Bette Davis, Barbara O'Neil, Virginia Weidler, Jeffrey Lynn, Helen Westley, Henry Daniell, Harry Davenport, June Lockhart, Montagu Love, Anne Howard; **D:** Anatole Litvak; **M:** Max Steiner.

All Through the Night ⊘⊘⊘ 1942 A very funny spy spoof as well as a thrilling crime story with Bogart playing a gambler who takes on a Nazi spy ring. Features memorable double-talk and a great auction scene that inspired the one with Cary Grant in "North by Northwest." Suspense builds throughout the film as Lorre appears in a sinister role as Pepi and Veidt gives a fine performance as the spymaster. **107m/B VHS, DVD.** Humphrey Bogart, Conrad Veidt, Karen Verne, Jane Darwell, William Demarest, Jackie Gleason, Phil Silvers, Barton MacLane, Martin Kosleck, Wallace Ford; **D:** Vincent Sherman; **C:** Sid Hickox; **M:** Adolph Deutsch.

All Tied Up ⊘⊘½ 1992 (R) Ladies man Brian (Galligan) thinks he's found true love with Linda (Hatcher) but that doesn't mean he's stopped seeing other women. And when Linda finds out, she breaks it off. So Brian goes over to her house to work things out and gets tied up—literally—by Linda and her girlfriends. Talk about teaching a guy a lesson. **90m/C VHS, DVD.** Zach Galligan, Teri Hatcher, Tracy Griffith, Lara Harris; **D:** John Mark Robinson; **W:** Robert Madero, I. Markie Lane; **M:** Bernardo Bonezzi.

All You Need Is Cash ⊘⊘⊘ *The Rutles* 1978 "The Beatles" star in this parody of The Beatles' legend, from the early days of the "Pre-Fab Four" in Liverpool to their worldwide success. A marvelous pseudo-documentary, originally shown on NBC-TV and with various SNL alumni, which captures the development of the Beatles and '60s rock with devastating effect. Served as the inspiration for "This is Spinal Tap." **70m/C VHS.** *GB* Eric Idle, Neil Innes, Ricky Fataar, Dan Aykroyd, Gilda Radner, John Belushi, George Harrison, Paul Simon, Mick Jagger, Bill Murray, Michael Palin, Bianca Jagger, Gwen Taylor, Ron Wood, Jeannette Charles, Al Franken, Lorne Michaels, Tom Davis; *D:* Gary Weis, Eric Idle; *W:* Eric Idle; *C:* Gary Weis & Neil Innes. **TV**

Allan Quatermain and the Lost City of Gold ✗½ **1986 (PG)** While trying to find his brother, Quatermair discovers a lost African civilization. Ramon devours the animal remains of a this weak adaptation of an H. Rider Haggard adventure. An ostensible sequel to the equally shallow "King Solomon's Mines." **100m/C VHS, DVD.** *W:* Gene Quintano, Lee Reynolds; *C:*

Allegheny Uprising ✗½ **The** ... 1759, the story of a frontiersman who clashes with a British military commander (in order to stop the sale of firearms to Indians. The stars of "Stagecoach" are back on board in this lesser effort. Also available colorized. **81m/** **B VHS.** John Wayne, Claire Trevor, George Sanders, Brian Donlevy, Chill Wills, Moroni Olsen; *D:* William A. Seiter.

Allegro ✗½ **2005** Emotionally frigid pianist Zetterstrom (Thomsen) is unable to tell his girlfriend Andrea (Christensen) that he loves her, which causes some bizarre time rupture. He loses his memories, which are sealed-off in a special section of Copenhagen called the Zone. When Zetterstrom returns to Copenhagen after ten years, he's instructed to go to Zone and see if he can recapture his past. Since the romantic leads have zero chemistry, this doesn't seem too important but the visual effects are kinda cool. Danish with subtitles. **88m/C DVD, CZ** Ulrich Thomsen, Henning Moritzen, Helena Christensen, Svetoslav Korolev; *D:* Christoffer Boe; *W:* Christoffer Boe, Mikael Wulff; *C:* Manuel Alberto Claro; *M:* Thomas Knak.

Allegro Non Troppo ✗✗✗ **1976 (PG)** An energetic and bold collection of animated skits set to classical music in this Italian version of Disney's "Fantasia." Watch for, or better yet, watch the whole dam movie. Features Nichetti (often referred to as the Italian Woody Allen, particularly by people in Italy) in the non-animated segments, who went on to write, direct, and star (he may have sold concessions in the lobby as well) in "The Icicle Thief." **75m/C VHS, DVD.** *IT* Maurizio Nichetti; *D:* Bruno Bozzetto, Guido Manuli, Maurizio Nichetti; *C:* Mario Masini.

Alley Cat ✗ **1984 (R)** Woman uses martial arts to fight back against a street gang that attacked her. **82m/C VHS, DVD.** Karin Mani, Robert Torti, Britt Helfer, Michael Wayne, Jon Greene; *D:* Edward Victor.

The Alley Cats ✗✗ **1965** Leslie, a part of Berlin's swinging '60s set, is being ignored by fiancé Logan in favor of his affair with her friend Agnes. So Leslie decides to retaliate by having an affair with a painter, Christian, but since Leslie just can't stand to be alone, when Christian is called away on business, she succumbs to the charms of socialite Irena. **83m/B VHS, DVD.** Anna Arthur, Sabrina Koch, Karin (Karen) Field, Chaz Hickman, Harold Baerow, Uta Levka; *D:* Radley Metzger; *W:* Radley Metzger.

Alley Cats Strike ✗✗½ **2000** Four teen misfits have an interest in bowling that makes them outcasts among their hipper classmates. But then their skills could win them a major trophy and school glory. **88m/C VHS,** Robert Richard, Kyle Schmid, Kaley Cuoco, Mimi Paley, Daphne Maxwell; *D:* Rod Daniel. **CABLE**

Allie & Me ✗✗ **1997** Gullible beautician Allie (Baron) wants to make some changes in her life but doesn't quite expect what happens when she teams up with wronged wife Michelle (Benson). They decide to take out their frustrations

by committing a burglary but find the Beverly Hills abode occupied by stud Rodney (Wilder), whom they take as a hostage, and then Allie decides to fall in love with him. Lots of recognizable faces but the comedy doesn't quite come together. **86m/ C VHS, DVD.** Joanne Baron, Lyndie Benson, James Wilder, Steven Prince, Ed Lauter, Lainie Kazan, Dyan Cannon, Harry Hamlin, Julianne Phillips; *D:* Michael Rymer; *W:* Michael Rymer; *C:* Rex Nicholson.

Alligator ✗✗✗ **1980 (R)** Dumped down a toilet 12 long years ago, lonely alligator Ramon resides in the city sewers, quietly eating and sleeping. In addition to feasting on the occasional stray human, chemical plant's experiment involving growth hormones and eventually begins to swell at an enormous rate. Nothing seems to satisfy Ramon's ever-widening appetite; not all the people of the buildings in the whole town, but he keeps trying, much to the regret of the guilt-ridden cop and lovely scientist who get to know each other while trying to nab the gator. Mediocre special effects are only a distraction in this witty eco-monster tale. **94m/C VHS, DVD.** Robert Forster, Robin Riker, Jack Carter, Henry Silva, Dean Jagger, Michael V. Gazzo, Perry Lang, Bart Braverman, Angel Tompkins, Sue Lyon, Sydney Lassick, James Ingersoll, John Lisbon Wood, Robert Doyle, Frank Ray Perilli; *C:* Joseph Mangine; *M:* Craig Hundley.

Alligator 2: The Mutation ✗✗ **1990 (PG-13)** Not a sequel to 1980's surprisingly good "Alligator," but a bland rehash with a decent cast. Once again an toxic alligator grows to enormous size and menaces a community. A Donald-Trump-like villain and pro wrestlers (!) bring this up to date, but it's all on the PG-13 rating is a bit too harsh. **92m/C VHS.** Steve Railsback, Dee Wallace Stone, Joseph Bologna, Woody Brown, Bill Daily, Brock Peters, Richard Lynch, Holly Gagnier; *D:* Jon Hess; *W:* Curt Allen; *C:* Joseph Mangine.

Alligator Alley ✗ **1972** When two young divers witness a major drug deal, they become entangled in a web of danger they never expected. **92m/C VHS.** Steve Alaimo, John Davis Chandler, Willie Pastrano, Jeremy Slate, Cece Stone; *D:* William Grefe.

Alligator Eyes ✗✗½ **1990 (R)** Stranger wearing trouble like a cheap perfume enters the midst of a vacationing trio of New Yorkers. Their vulnerabilities are exposed by a young hitchhiker sporting a slinky polka dot ensemble and way cool sunglasses who insinuates herself into their vacation plans (not to mention their private lives), before the three realize she's blind and full of manipulative and vindictive tricks, thanks to the usual brutal childhood. Psycho-sexo-logical thriller has some fine performances and a promising beginning before fizzling into celluloid cottoh candy. **101m/C VHS,** Annabelle Larsen, Roger Kabler, Mary McLain, Allen McCullough; *D:* John Feldman; *W:* John Feldman; *M:* Sheila Silver.

The Allnighter ✗ **1987 (PG-13)** A college coed searches through the hyper-sexed beach-party milieu of her senior year for Mr. Right. Bangle Hoffs is directed by her mom, to no avail. **95m/C VHS, DVD.** Susanna Hoffs, John Terlesky, Joan Cusack, Michael Ontkean; *D:* Tamar Simon Hoffs; *W:* Tamar Simon Hoffs; *C:* Joseph D. Urbanczyk; *M:* Charles Bernstein.

Allonsanfan ✗✗½ **1973** Early Taviani, in which a disillusioned Jacobin aristocrat in 1816, after Napoleon has fallen, struggles with his revolutionary ideals and his accustomed lifestyle. Exciting score. In Italian with English subtitles. **115m/C VHS.** *IT* Marcello Mastroianni, Laura Betti, Renato de Carmine, Lea Massari, Mimsy Farmer, Claudio Cassinelli, Bruno Cirino, Michael Berger; *D:* Paolo Taviani, Vittorio Taviani; *W:* Paolo Taviani, Vittorio Taviani; *C:* Giuseppe Ruzzolini; *M:* Ennio Morricone.

All's Fair ✗ **1989** Silly and predictable comedy about executives who take on their spouses at weekend war games. An unfortunate waste of a good cast. **89m/** *C VHS.* George Segal, Sally Kellerman, Robert

...Almost ✗✗ *Wendy Cracked a Walnut.*

...Almost an Angel ✗✗½ **1990 (PG)** Another in a recent spate of angels and ghosts assigned back to earth by the head office. A life-long criminal (Hogan) commits a heroic act and finds himself a probationary angel returned to earth to gain permanent angel status. He befriends a wheelchair-bound man, falls in love with the guy's sister, and helps her out at a center for potential juvenile delinquents. Melodramatic and hokey in places, relying too much on Hogan's crocodilian charisma. **98m/C VHS.** Paul Hogan, Linda Kozlowski, Elias Koteas, Doreen Lang, Charlton Heston; *D:* John Cornell; *W:* Paul Hogan; *C:* Russell Boyd.

Almost Blue ✗½ **1993 (R)** A gigantic, slow-moving movie cliche. Madsen is a sulky, hard-living sax player going off the deep end because of his wife's death. Walden is the good woman who comes along to save him from himself. Tenor saxman Ernie Watts doubles for Madsen. Do yourself a favor—skip the movie and listen to some good jazz instead. **98m/C VHS.** Michael Madsen, Lynette Walden, Garrett Morris, Dale Mayron, Yaphet Kotto; *D:* Keoni Waxman.

Almost Dead ✗✗½ **1994** Psychiatrist Katherine Roshak's (Doherty) mother committed suicide four years ago and er suddenly her corpse is appearing to Katherine. When she visits Mom's grave, Katherine finds an empty coffin. So she teams up with a skeptical cop (Mancylo') to figure out what's going on. Lots of loose ends. Based on the novel "Resurrection" by William Valtos. **92m/C VHS.** Shannen Doherty, Costas Mandylor, John Diehl, William R. Moses; *D:* Ruben Preuss; *W:* Miguel Tejada-Flores; *C:* Zoran Hochstatter.

Almost Famous ✗✗✗ **2000 (R)** Fifteen-year-old budding rock critic William Miller's (Fugit) dream comes true after he bluffs his way into a Rolling Stone writing assignment covering a rising '70s rock band on tour. This ode to the music and youth culture of that decade may lack grit, but its sympathetic treatment of young Miller's coming-of-age amid groupies, drugs, rock and roll, and a worried, uncupable mother (McDormand) achieves director Crowe's ends. The film's adoration of the music's energy and emotion appear performs its devotion to character and represents the headliner here, but it never outlightarg. Delicate performances by first-timer Fugit, and by Hudson as the more-then-a-groupie groupie, plus a memorable portrayal of the wise and slightly surly critic Lester Bangs by Hoffman. Based on Crowe's own experiences. **202m/C VHS, DVD.** Patrick Fugit, Philip Seymour Hoffman, Frances McDormand, Jason Lee, Billy Crudup, Kate Hudson, John Fedevich, Mark Kozelek, Fairuza Balk, Bijou Phillips, Anna Paquin, Noah Taylor, Jimmy Fallon, Zooey Deschanel, Liz Stauber, Eion Bailey, Mark Pellington, Terry Chen, Peter Frampton, Zack (Zach) Ward; *Cameos:* Jann Wenner; *D:* Cameron Crowe; *W:* Cameron Crowe; *C:* John Toll; *M:* Nancy Wilson. Oscars '00: Orig. Screenplay; Golden Globes '01: Film—Mus./Comedy; L.A. Film Critics '00:

Almanac of Fall ✗✗ **1985** Set in a claustrophic apartment, where the occupants reveal all their deepest hostilities, fears, and obsessions. In Hungarian with English subtitles. **119m/C VHS, DVD.** *HU* Hédi Temessy, Erika Bodnar, Miklos B. Szekely, Pal Hetenyi, Janos Derzsi; *D:* Bela Tarr; *W:* Bela Tarr.

Almost Angels ✗✗ **1962** Two boys romp in Austria as members of the Vienna Boys Choir. Lesser sentimental Disney effort that stars the actual members of the Choir; not much of a draw 'or today's Nintendo-jaded young viewers. **85m/C VHS.** Vincent Winter, Peter Weck, Hans Holt; *D:* Steve Previn.

Almost Heroes ✗½ *Edwards &* *Hunt: The First American Road Trip* **1997 (PG-13)** Farley's last screen appearance teams him with Perry as explorers Edwards and Hunt, who are racing Lewis and Clark to the Pacific Ocean in 1804. Edwards is a glory-seeking fop who's totally out of his league. Hunt (Farley) is a slovenly, clumsy tracker with a soft spot for toilet (or would that be outhouse?) humor. Along with a team of misfits and losers, the duo wreaks havoc on the American frontier. Perry and Farley show some flashes of comic chemistry, but their left to fend for themselves by a script that's lost in the wilderness, sadly relying too much on Farley's patented self-destructive schtick. (check your weapons at the door). **90m/C VHS, DVD.** *IT* Henry Silva, Tiziana Milian, Laura Belli; *D:* Umberto Lenzi; *M:* Ennio Morricone.

Almost Human woof! *The Kidnap of* *Mary Lou* **1979 (R)** A1 Italian Mafia gorefest about ashes are in trouble. His urn and remains have been stolen. Fortunately, his teenage granddaughter and a detective are on the case. From the PBS "Wonderworks" series. **58m/C VHS,** Paul Scrvino, Royana Black, Mary Wickes; *D:* Alan Kingsberg. **TV**

Almost Partners ✗✗ **1987** Grandpa's ashes are in trouble. His urn and remains have been stolen. Fortunately, his teenage granddaughter and a detective are on the case. From the PBS "Wonderworks" series. **58m/C VHS,** Paul Scrvino, Royana Black, Mary Wickes; *D:* Alan Kingsberg. **TV**

Almost Peaceful ✗✗✗ **1987** *Un monde presque paisible* **2002** In 1946, a Jewish tailor is restarting his business and attempting to regain a life of normalcy. Deville quietly follows the extended employees—some who have survived the camps, some who have escaped the horrors but have fought their war—as they stitch, sew, and try to restore themselves. Intertwined stories flow marvelously, providing poignant observation of the Holocaust aftermath. **90m/ C DVD, FR** Simon Abkarian, Zabou Breitman, Denis Podalydes, Vincent Elbaz, Lubna Azabal, Stanislas Merhar, Clotilde Courau, Julie Gaynet, Malik Zidi; *D:* Michel Deville; *C:* Andre Diot.

An Almost Perfect Affair ✗✗ **1979 (PG)** Taxing romantic comedy about an ambitious independent American filmmaker who, after finishing a movie about an executed murderer, travels to the Cannes festival and proceeds to fall in love or lust with the wife of an Italian producer. Numerous inside jokes and capable performances nearly overcome script weaknesses. **92m/C VHS, DVD.** Keith Carradine, Monica Vitti, Raf Vallone, Christian de Sica, Dick Anthony Williams; *D:* Michael Ritchie; *W:* Walter Bernstein; *M:* Georges Delerue.

Almost Pregnant ✗✗½ **1991 (R)** Linda Anderson (Roberts) desperately wants a baby, but her husband, Charlie (Conaway) is unable to get her pregnant. Dead set against artificial insemination, Linda decides to take a lover. Charlie doesn't want to lose her, so he goes along with her idea. Linda falls in love with the new guy, discovers he's had a vasectomy and takes yet another lover while continuing to see the other two guys. Hilarious complications abound in her outrageous quest for a baby. An unrated version containing explicit scenes is also available. **90m/C VHS.** Tanya Roberts, Joan Severance, Dom DeLuise; *D:* Michael DeLuise; *W:* Fred Stroppel.

Almost Strangers ✗✗✗ **2001** Compelling thriller about family ties. Ernest Symon (Howell) arranges a complicated three-day family reunion at a London hotel, which is reluctantly attended by black sheep Raymond (Gambon) and his curious son Daniel (Macfadyen). Both see family photos of events neither of them can remember and then Daniel meets his up-to-no-good cousins Rebecca (Skinner) and Charles

Carradine, Jennifer Edwards, Jane Kaczmarek, John Kapelos, Lou Ferrigno; *D:* Rocky Lane; *C:* Peter -yons Collister.

Actor (Douglas), Support. Actress (McDormand); Broadcast Film Critics '00: Orig. Screenplay, Support. Actress (McDormand).

Almost

(Stephens). Are those family skeletons we hear rattling? 237m/C DVD. *GB* Michael Gambon, Matthew MacFadyen, Claire Skinner, Toby Stephens, Lindsay Duncan, Peter Howell, Anton Lesser; *D:* Stephen Poliakoff; *W:* Stephen Poliakoff; *C:* Cinders Forshaw; *M:* Adrian Johnston. TV

Almost You ♂♂ 1985 (R) Normal marital conflicts and uncertainties grow exponentially when a wealthy New York City 30-something couple hires a lovely young nurse to help care for the wife after a car accident. An unsentimental marital comedy with a good cast that still misses. 91m/C VHS, DVD. Brooke Adams, Griffin Dunne, Karen Young, Marty Watt, Christine Estabrook, Josh Mostel, Laura Dean, Dana Delany, Miguel Piñero, Joe Silver, Suzzy Roche, Spalding Gray; *D:* Adam Brooks; *M:* Jonathan Elias.

Aloha, Bobby and Rose ♂♂½ 1974 (PG) A mechanic and his girlfriend in L.A. become accidentally involved in an attempted robbery and murder and go on the run for Mexico, of course. Semi-satisfying drama in the surf, with fine location photography. 90m/C VHS, DVD. Paul LeMat, Dianne Hull, Robert Carradine, Tim McIntire, Noble Willingham, Leigh French; *D:* Floyd Mutrux; *W:* Floyd Mutrux; *C:* William A. Fraker.

Aloha Summer ♂♂ 1988 (PG) Six surfing teenagers of various ethnic backgrounds learn of love and life in 1959 Hawaii while riding the big wave of impending adulthood, with a splash of Kung Fu thrown in for good measure. Sensitive and bland. 97m/C VHS. Chris Makepeace, Lorie Griffin, Don Michael Paul, Sho Kosugi, Yuji Okumoto, Tia Carrere; *D:* Tommy Lee Wallace; *M:* Bob Benedetto.

Alone Against Rome ♂½ 1962 A muscle-bound warrior takes on the forces of Rome to avenge himself against a scornful woman. 100m/B VHS. *IT* Lang Jeffries, Rossana Podesta, Philippe LeRoy; *D:* Herbert Wise.

Alone in the Dark ♂♂ 1982 (R) Slash and dash horror attempt featuring four escaped patients from a mental hospital who decide that they must kill their doctor because they don't like him. Conveniently, a city-wide blackout provides the opportunity, as the good doctor defends home and family against the aging stars intent on chewing up as much scenery as possible. 92m/C VHS, DVD. Jack Palance, Donald Pleasence, Martin Landau, Dwight Schultz; *D:* Jack Sholder; *W:* Jack Sholder.

Alone in the Dark woof! 2005 (R) If there's any justice, Tim Burton's grandson will one day film a lovingly campy biopic about director Uwe Boll. Heir apparent to Ed Wood, Boll follows up 2003's "House of the Dead" with yet another incoherent video game adaptation. Paranormal detective Edward Camby (Slater) represses memories of an orphanage trauma as he travels the globe collecting mystical chotchkies and fighting poorly-lit bad guys. When his fellow orphans start disappearing, Camby and his scientist girlfriend (Reid) team up to battle bargain-basement CGI terror dogs. The monsters are somehow tied in with an extinct Indian tribe, but you'll be too busy groaning at Reid's phonetically sounded-out science talk or the ridiculously inane opening crawl to care. 96m/C DVD. *US US CA GE* Christian Slater, Tara Reid, Stephen Dorff, Matthew (Matt) Walker, Will Sanderson, Darren Shahlavi, Karin Konoval, Ed Anders, Frank C. Turner, Mark Acheson, Clough Bruhnanski, Kwesi Ameyaw, Catherine Lough Haggquist; *D:* Uwe Boll; *W:* Elan Mastai, Michael Roesch, Peter Scheerer; *C:* Mathias Neumann; *M:* Bernd Wendlandt.

Alone in the Neon Jungle ♂♂ 1987 A glamorous big-city police captain is assigned to clean up the most corrupt precinct in town. Pleshette is untypically cast but still manages to make her role believable in a serviceable TV cop drama with more dialogue than action. 90m/C VHS, DVD. Suzanne Pleshette, Danny Aiello, Georg Stanford Brown, Frank Converse, Joe Morton; *D:* Georg Stanford Brown.

Alone in the T-Shirt Zone ♂ 1986 A maniacal T-shirt designer lands in a mental institution. 81m/C VHS. Michael Barrack, Taylor Gilbert, Bill Barron; *D:* Mikel B. Anderson; *W:* Mikel B. Anderson.

Alone in the Woods ♂♂ 1995 (PG) Ten-year-old Justin mistakenly gets into the wrong van while on his way to his family's annual mountain vacation. Turns out the duo in the van are would-be kidnappers after Chelsea Stuart, the daughter of a toy magnate and now Justin must escape and rescue Chelsea. 81m/C VHS, DVD. Brady Bluhm, Chick Vennera, Mathias Hues, Laraine Newman, Daniel McVicar, Krystee Clark; *D:* John Putch; *W:* J. Riley Lagesen; *C:* Frank Johnson; *M:* David Lawrence. VIDEO

Alone with a Stranger ♂♂ 1999 (R) Long lost Evil Twin (Moses) learns that he has a rich brother. Evil Twin and girlfriend (Peeples) plan to kidnap Good Twin, sell his company, and scoot with the loot. But what about Good Twin's wife (Niven) and family? 90m/C DVD. William R. Moses, Barbara Niven, Priscilla Barnes, Nia Peeples, Mindy Cohn; *D:* Peter Paul Liapis; *W:* Peter Paul Liapis, Richard Dana Smith; *C:* M. David Mullen; *M:* Alan Howarth.

Alone With Her ♂♂½ 2007 Clumsy thriller with camera as voyeur. Doug (Hanks) is obsessed with Amy (Talancon) and sets up surveillance on her hidden cameras after breaking into her apartment. He orchestrates nasty little surprises and then turns up as Amy's concerned friend but the tension never particularly increases, even when Doug goes to what should have been more creepy extremes. 78m/C DVD. *US* Ana Claudia Talancon, Colin Hanks, Jordana Spiro, Jonathan Trent; *D:* Eric Nicholas; *W:* Eric Nicholas; *C:* Nathan Wilson; *M:* David E. Russo.

Along Came a Spider ♂♂♂ 2001 (R) Sequel to 1997's "Kiss the Girls" is actually a prequel storywise but Freeman does reprise his character of Detective Alex Cross. This time he must save a U.S. Senator's daughter who's been kidnapped by a serial killer. Freeman is easily the best thing in this convoluted, plot-deficient, murky mess. He makes every "yeah, right" moment (and there are many) palatable. Based on the novel by James Patterson. 103m/C VHS, DVD. *US* Morgan Freeman, Monica Potter, Michael Wincott, Penelope Ann Miller, Michael Moriarty, Dylan Baker, Billy Burke, Jay O. Sanders, Kim Tamahorne, Mika Boorem, Anton Yelchin; *D:* Lee Tamahori; *W:* Marc Moss; *C:* Matthew F. Leonetti; *M:* Jerry Goldsmith.

Along Came Jones ♂♂♂ 1945 Cowboy Cooper, who can't handle a gun and is saddled with grumpy sidekick Demarest, is the victim of mistaken identity as both the good guys and the bad guys pursue him thinking he is a vicious killer. Young is the woman who rides to his defense. Offbeat and charming western parody based on a novel by Alan Le May. 93m/B VHS, DVD. Gary Cooper, Loretta Young, Dan Duryea, William Demarest; *D:* Stuart Heisler; *W:* Nunnally Johnson; *C:* Milton Krasner; *M:* Arthur Lange.

Along Came Polly ♂♂½ 2004 (PG-13) There's something about Polly. Neurotic risk analyst (Stiller) meets wild child Polly (Aniston) and learns to let loose. Has the requisite number of sight gags involving bodily fluids and embarrassing situations (Stiller is a master at squeezing the humor out of both), but breaks no new ground and quickly become formulaic. Generic romantic comedy with a few laughs is otherwise forgettable. 91m/C VHS, DVD. *US* Ben Stiller, Jennifer Aniston, Philip Seymour Hoffman, Debra Messing, Alec Baldwin, Hank Azaria, Bryan Brown, Michele Lee, Jsu Garcia, Bob (Robert) Dishy, Missi Pyle, Judah Friedlander, Kym E. Whitley, Kevin Hart; *D:* John Hamburg; *W:* John Hamburg; *C:* Seamus McGarvey; *M:* Theodore Shapiro.

Along for the Ride ♂½ 2000 (R) Seriously disturbed Lulu (Griffith) checks herself out of the mental hospital and informs old boyfriend Ben (Swayze) that when she was a teen, she gave birth to their son and put him up for adoption. Somehow she manages to persuade him or a cross-country journey to Wisconsin to meet the now-teenaged kid. Naturally, this idea doesn't sit that well with Ben's wife Claire (Miller) who decides to put a stop to the nonsense. Goopy sentiment. 99m/C VHS, DVD. Melanie Griffith, Patrick Swayze, Penelope Ann Miller, Joseph Gordon-Levitt, Richard Schiff, Annie Corley, Lee Garlington, Michael J. Pollard, Steven Bauer, Dion Beebe; *W:* John Kaye; *C:* Dion Beebe; *M:* Serge Colbert.

Along the Great Divide ♂♂ 1951 A U.S. marshal and his deputy battle pursuing vigilantes and the untamed frontier to bring a falsely accused murderer to trial (and of course, find the real bad guy). Douglas' first western has the usual horse opera cliches supported by excellent cinematography. 88m/B VHS. Kirk Douglas, John Agar, Walter Brennan, Virginia Mayo; *D:* Raoul Walsh.

Along the Navaho Trail ♂♂ 1945 A cattle syndicate is threatening the local ranchers and Roy, aided by a band of gypsies, helps thwart the bad guys. 66m/B VHS. Roy Rogers, Dale Evans, George "Gabby" Hayes, Douglas Fowley; *D:* Frank McDonald; *W:* Gerald Geraghty; *C:* William Bradford.

Along the Sundown Trail ♂½ 1942 Standard western escapades as cowboy G-men round up the villains. 59m/B VHS. William Boyd, Art Davis, Lee Powell, Julie Duncan, Kermit Maynard, Charles "Blackie" King; *D:* Sam Newfield.

Alpha Beta ♂♂½ 1973 A stage production set to film studying the breakup of a marriage, where all the husband and wife have in common is the children. Finney and Roberts efficiently carry the load. 70m/C VHS. Albert Finney, Rachel Roberts; *D:* Anthony Page.

Alpha Dog ♂♂ 2006 (R) True crime saga resulting from sheer stupidity. Wannabe white gangsta drug dealer Johnny Truelove (Hirsch) feels dissed when customer Jake (Foster) refuses to pay his tab. So Johnny and his equally wasted posse take advantage of a run-in with Jake's naive 15-year-old half brother Zack (Yelchin) and decide to hold him as collateral. Cohort Frankie (a convincing Timberlake) becomes Zack's de-facto babysitter and introduces him to their indulgent SoCal life—that is until someone finally realizes that kidnapping is a serious crime. A "River's Edge" for 21st-century teens. 117m/C DVD, HD DVD. *US* Emile Hirsch, Justin Timberlake, Ben Foster, Sharon Stone, David Thornton, Bruce Willis, Shawn Hatosy, Amanda Seyfried, Dominique Swain, Olivia Wilde, Lukas Haas, Vincent Kartheiser, Harry Dean Stanton, Alex Kingston, Heather Wahlquist; *D:* Nick Cassavetes; *W:* Nick Cassavetes; *C:* Robert Fraisse; *M:* Aaron Zigman.

The Alpha Incident ♂½ 1976 (PG) Time-worn doomsday drama about an alien organism with the potential to destroy all living things. Government works hard to cover up. 86m/C VHS. Ralph Meeker, Stafford Morgan, John Goff, Carol Irene Newell, John Alderman; *D:* Bill Rebane.

Alpha Male ♂♂½ 2006 The time switch between the present and 10 years in the past can be confusing but this is an otherwise decent family drama. Wealthy Jim (Huston) has made a good life for wife Alice (Ehle) and their two children, despite his temper and domineering attitude. After Jim dies from cancer, officious son Jack (Wells) takes it badly when Alice decides to remarry, especially since widower Clive (Baladi) is his father's polar opposite. The situation comes to a boil when Alice throws Jack a lavish 21st birthday party. 100m/C DVD. *GB* Danny Huston, Jennifer Ehle, Amelia Warner, Christopher Egan, Mark Wells, Patrick Baladi, Trudie Styler; *D:* Dan Wilde; *W:* Dan Wilde; *C:* Shane Daly; *M:* Stephen Warbeck.

Alphabet City ♂♂ 1984 (R) A drug kingpin who runs New York's Lower East Side has decided to turn over a new leaf, but first he must survive his last night as a criminal while figuring out a way to pay off his large debts. Very stylish and moody, but light on content and plot. 85m/C VHS, DVD. Vincent Spano, Michael Winslow, Kate Vernon, Jami Gertz, Zohra Lampert, Raymond Serra, Ken Marino, Daniel Jordano, Miguel Piñero; *D:* Amos Poe; *W:* Amos Poe.

The Alphabet Murders ♂♂ *ABC Murders* 1965 Picture this: Randall playing Agatha Christie's famous Belgian sleuth, Hercule Poirot, and Rutherford—in a cameo—as Miss Marple. As if that wouldn't be enough to make Dame Agatha roll over in her grave, there's plenty of cloying wisecracking and slapsticking throughout. An adaptation of "The ABC Murders" in which Poirot stalks a literate killer who snuffs out his victims in alphabetical order. Hardly a must-see, unless you're hellbent on viewing the entire Randall opus. 90m/B VHS. Tony Randall, Anita Ekberg, Robert Morley, Maurice Denham, Guy Rolfe, Sheila Allen, Margaret Rutherford, Julian Glover; *D:* Frank Tashlin.

Alphaville ♂♂ *Alphaville, a Strange Case of Lemmy Caution; Alphaville, Une Etrange Aventure de Lemmy Caution* 1965 Engaging and inimitable Godard attempt at science fiction mystery. P.I. Lemmy Caution searches for a scientist in a city (Paris as you've never seen it before) run by robots and overseen by a dictator. The futuristic techno-conformist society must be upended so that Caution may save the scientist as well as nonconformists everywhere. In French with subtitles. 100m/B VHS, DVD. *FR* Eddie Constantine, Anna Karina, Akim Tamiroff, Howard Vernon, Laszlo Szabo, Michel Delahaye, Jean-Pierre Leaud; *D:* Jean-Luc Godard; *W:* Jean-Luc Godard; *C:* Raoul Coutard; *M:* Paul Misraki. Berlin Intl. Film Fest. '65: Golden Berlin Bear.

Alpine Fire ♂♂½ 1989 (R) Coming of age story about an adolescent girl and her deaf-mute brother living in an isolated life in the Swiss Alps. When life on the mountain overwhelms them, they turn to each other for love. Sharply observed with a naturalistic style, elevating the proceedings above mere voyeurism. 119m/C VHS. *SI* Thomas Knock, Johanna Lier, Dorothea Moritz, Rolf Illig; *D:* Fredi M. Murer.

Already Dead ♂♂½ 2007 (R) Thomas Archer (Eidard) has a great job and a beautiful wife and son. Then the Archer home is robbed, his wife is brutalized, and his son is killed. The police can't find the criminals so Archer turns to a shadow group that promises to deliver those responsible and then give Archer the opportunity to deal with them as he sees fit. 93m/C DVD. Ron Eldard, Til Schweiger, Christopher Plummer, Patrick Kilpatrick, Marisa Coughlan; *D:* Joe Otting; *W:* Joe Chappelle; *C:* Eric Trageser; *M:* Nathan Furst. VIDEO

Alsino and the Condor ♂♂ 1982 (R) An acclaimed Nicaraguan drama about a young boy, caught in war-torn Nicaragua between the Somoza government and the Sandinista rebels, who dreams of flying above the human strife. In Spanish with English subtitles. 89m/C VHS. *NI* Dean Stockwell, Alan Esquivel; *D:* Miguel Littin.

Altered States ♂♂♂ 1980 (R) Obsessed with the task of discovering the inner man, Hurt's ambitious researcher ignores his family while consuming hallucinogenic drugs and floating in an immersion tank. He gets too deep inside, slipping way back through the evolutionary order and becoming a menace in the process. Confusing script based upon Chayefsky's (alias Sidney Aaron) confusing novel is supported by great special effects and the usual self-indulgent and provocative Russell direction. Chayefsky eventually washed his hands of the project after artistic differences with the producers. Others who departed the film include initial director William Penn and special effects genius John Dykstra (relieved ably by Bran Ferren). Hurt's a solemn hoot in his first starring role. 103m/C VHS, DVD. William Hurt, Blair Brown, Bob Balaban, Charles Haid, Dori Brenner, Drew Barrymore, Miguel Godreau, Thaao Penghlis, Peter Brandon, Charles White Eagle, Meghan Jeffers, Jack Murdock, John Larroquette; *D:* Ken Russell; *W:* Paddy Chayefsky, Sidney Aaron; *C:* Jordan Cronenweth; *M:* John Corigliano.

Alternative ♂♂ 1976 'A female magazine editor finds herself unmarried and quite pregnant. She is caught in a tug-of-war between the baby's father and her current lover. Dated liberated woman and career snoozer. **90m/C VHS, AU** Wendy Hughes, Peter Adams, Alwyn Kurts, Carla Hoogeveen; Tony Bonner; **D:** Paul Eddy; **W:** Tony Morphet; **M:** Bob Young.

Alvarez Kelly ♂♂½ **1966** Offbeat western with Holden as the Mexican-Irish Kelly who has just sold a herd of cattle to the North during the Civil War. Confederate officer Widmark kidnaps Holden in an effort to have the cattle redirected to the South. Aided by the traditional women in the midst of men intent on double-crossing each other, a fierce hatred develops between the two, erupting into violence. Sleepy performance by Holden is countered by an intensive Widmark. Based on a true Civil War incident, the script occasionally wanders far afield with the excitement by who cleverly heightens the excitement by stampeding. **109m/C VHS, DVD,** William Holden, Richard Widmark, Janice Rule, Patrick O'Neal, Harry Carey Jr., Victoria Shaw, Roger C. Carmel, Indus Arthur; **D:** Edward Dmytryk; **W:** Elliott Arnold, Franklin Coen; **C:** Joe MacDonald; **M:** Johnny Green.

Always ♂♂½ **1989 (PG)** A hotshot pilot (Dreyfuss) meets a fiery end and finds that his spirit is destined to become a guardian angel to the greenhorn fire-fighting "flyboy (Johnson) who steals his girl's heart. Warm remake of "A Guy Named Joe," one of Spielberg's favorite movies.

Alvin and the Chipmunks ♂♂½ **2007 (PG)** Alvin, Simon, and Theodore (now digitally rendered) bring their chipmunk schtick into the twenty-first century, and mostly pull it off. Dave Seville (Lee) finds the trio in a muffin basket, quickly discovering their ability not only to speak, but to sing. Soon enough a hustling promoter (Cross) takes their act on the road, where, sadly, the chipmunks fall victim to burn-out and must lip-sync the rest of their shows. (It ain't the '50s.) Lots of fun for nostalgic baby-boomers and kiddies alike; featuring techno and hip-hop remixes of the Chipmunks' classics. **92m/C DVD, US** Jason Lee, David Cross, Cameron Richardson, Jane Lynch; **D:** Tim Hill; **W:** Jon Vitti, Will McRob, Chris Viscardi; **V:** Justin Long, Matthew Grey Gubler, Jesse McCartney.

Alvin Purple ♂♂ **1973 (R)** Pedestrian comedy about a Mr. Purple, an ordinary Aussie who sells waterbeds and is for some reason constantly being pursued by sexually insatiable women. Fortunately, he too enjoys sex, even though complications abound. Sexual situations, double entendres, and a script that aims for cleverness (but rarely attains it) somehow made the lust romp a hit in its native Australia while worldwide it helped establish a market for Down Under cinema. Shot in Melbourne, and followed by "Alvin Rides Again"; George Whaley, Ellie Maclure, Penne Hackforth-Jones; **D:** Tim Burstall; **W:** Alan Finney, Alan Hopgood Tim Burstall.

Alvin Rides Again ♂♂ **1974** The sexually insatiable Alvin Purple is asked to impersonate an American gangster who was accidentally killed. Another Aussie sex farce from the original writers, who conspire to create a decent sequel to "Alvin Purple," with much of the same cast and crew. **89m/C VHS, AU** Graeme Blundell, Alan Finney, Briony Behets, Frank Thring Jr., Jeff Ashby, Chantal Contouri; **D:** David Bilcock, Robin Copping; **W:** Tim Burstall, Alan Hopgood, Alan Finney; **C:** Robin Copping.

Always ♂♂♂ **1985 (R)** Jaglom fictionally documents his own divorce and reconciliation with Patrice Townsend; set in the director's home and starring his friends and family, the film provides comic insight into the dynamics of married/about-to-be-married/and used-to-be-married relationships. Set at a Fourth of July barbecue, this bittersweet romantic comedy is a veritable testfest for Jaglom fans, but not everyone will find the director's free-form narrative to their taste. **105m/C VHS, DVD,** Henry Jaglom, Patrice Townsend, Bob Rafelson, Melissa Leo, Andre Gregory, Michael Emil, Joanna Frank, Alan Rachins, Jonathan Kaufer; **D:** Henry Jaglom; **C:** Hanania Baer.

Sparks between Dreyfuss and Hunter eventually ignite, but Goodman delivers the most heat. Hepburn makes an appearance as the angel who guides Dreyfuss. An old-fashioned tear-burner romance that includes actual footage of the 1988 Yellowstone fire. **123m/C VHS, DVD** Holly Hunter, Richard Dreyfuss, John Goodman, Audrey Hepburn, Brad Johnson, Marg Helgenberger, Keith David, Roberts Blossom, Dale Dye; **D:** Steven Spielberg; **W:** Jerry Belson; **C:** Mikael Salomon; **M:** John Williams.

Always Outnumbered Always Outgunned ♂♂♂ **1998 (R)** Character study follows ex-con Socrates Fortlow (Fishburne) in a dynamic performance). A convicted murderer, he's now trying to lead a non-violent life on the violent streets of L.A.'s Watts, maintain his dignity, and find a job. But none of this is easy. Adapted from the book by Mosley, who wrote the teleplay. **110m/C VHS, DVD,** Laurence Fishburne, Bill Cobbs, Natalie Cole, Daniel Williams, Laurie Metcalf, Bill Nunn, Cicely Tyson, Isaiah Washington IV; **D:** Michael Apted; **W:** Walter Mosley; **C:** John Bailey; **M:** Michael Franti. **CABLE**

Always Will ♂♂½ **2006 (PG)** High-school senior Will discovers his elementary school's 'time capsule and it allows him to revisit his past and change decisions the now regrets. But his changes impact his present in unexpected ways and Will wonders if selfishness is the true problem and if he needs to accept his past and move on. **95m/C DVD,** Andrew Baglini, John Schmidt, Mark Schroeder, Noelle Meixell, Barr Meilland, Jody Seymour; **D:** Michael Sammaciccia; **M:** Michael Sammaciccia. **VIDEO**

Amadeus ♂♂♂½ **1984 (PG)** Entertaining adaptation by Shaffer of 'his play about the intense rivalry between 18th century composers Antonio Salieri and Wolfgang Amadeus Mozart. Abraham's Salieri is a man who desires greatness but is tortured by envy and sorrow. His worst attacks of angst occur when he comes into contact with Hulce's Mozart, an immature, boorish genius who, despite his gifts, remains unaffected and delighted by the beauty he creates while irking the hell out of everyone around him. Terrific period piece filmed on location in Prague; excellent musical score, beautiful sets, nifty billowy costumes, and realistic American accents for the 18th century Europeans. Concert No. 27 for Pianoforte and Orchestra in B Flat Major; Ave Verum Corpus; A Quintet For Strings in E Flat. A Concerto for Clarinet and Orchestra in A Major; Number 39 in E Flat Major; Number 40 in G Minor; Number 41 in C Major. **158m/C VHS, DVD,** F. Murray Abraham, Tom Hulce, Elizabeth Berridge, Simon Callow, Roy Dotrice, Christine Ebersole, Jeffrey Jones, Kenny Baker, Cynthia Nixon, Vincent Schiavelli; **D:** Milos Forman; **W:** Peter Shaffer; **C:** Miroslav Ondricek; **M:** John Strauss. Oscars '84: Actor (Abraham), Adapt. Screenplay, Art Dir./Set Dec., Costume Des., Director (Forman), Makeup, Picture, Sound; AF '98: Top 100; Cesar '85: Foreign Film; Directors Guild '84: Director (Forman); Golden Globes '85: Actor—Drama (Abraham), Director (Forman), Film—Drama, Screenplay; L.A. Film Critics '84: Director (Forman), Film, Screenplay.

Amanda and the Alien ♂½ **1995 (R)** Dumb saga finds flaky Californian Amanda (Eggert) taking care of a sex-starved, shape-changing extraterrestrial (Meneses) while a couple of feds hunt him down. Based on a story by Robert Silverberg. **94m/C VHS,** Alex Meneses, Nicole Eggert, Michael Dorn, Stacy Keach, Michael C. Bendetti, Richard Speight Jr., David Millbern; **D:** Jon Kroll; **W:** Jon Kroll. **CABLE**

Amarcord ♂♂♂½ *I Remember* **1974 (R)** Semi-autobiographical Fellini fantasy which takes place in the village of Rimini, his birthplace. Focusing on the young Zanin's impressions of his town's colorful slices of life, Fellini takes aim at fascism, family life, and religion in 1930s Italy. Visually ripe, delivering a generous, occasionally uneven mix of satire, burlesque, drama, and tragicomedic lyricism. Considered by people in the know as one of Fellini's best films and the topic of meaningful discussions among art film students ev-

erywhere. **124m/C VHS, DVD, /T** Magali Noel, Bruno Zanin, Pupella Maggio, Armando Brancia; **D:** Federico Fellini; **W:** Federico Fellini, Tonino Guerra; **C:** Giuseppe Rotunno; **M:** Nino Rota. Oscars '74: Foreign Film; N.Y. Film Critics '74: Director (Fellini), Film.

The Amazing Colossal Man ♂♂ **1957** A standard '50s sci-fi film about atomic radiation. Colonel Manning is exposed to massive doses of plutonium when an experiment backfires (literally). The former good-guy grows to 70 feet and starts taking out his anger on a helpless Las Vegas. Can anything stop his murderous rampages? Followed by "War of the Colossal Beast." **79m/B VHS** Glenn Langan, Cathy Downs, William (Bill) Hudson, James Seay, Russ Bender, Lyn Osborn, Frank Jenks, Hank Patterson; **D:** Bert I. Gordon; **W:** Bert I. Gordon, Mark Hanna; **C:** Joseph Biroc; **M:** Albert Glasser.

The Amazing Dobermans ♂♂ **1976 (G)** Family-oriented pooch performance piece featuring Astaire in one of his lesser roles. Ex-con man Astaire and his five trained Dobermans assist an undercover agent in foiling a small-time criminal's gambling and extortion racket. The last in a series that includes "The Daring Dobermans" and "The Doberman Gang." **96m/C VHS,** Fred Astaire, Barbara Eden, James Franciscus, Jack Carter, Billy Barty, Parley Baer; **D:** Byron Ross Chudnow; **M:** Alan Silvestri.

The Amazing Howard Hughes ♂♂♂ **1977** Reveals the full story of the legendary millionaire's life and career, from daring test pilot to inventor to Hollywood film producer to isolated weakthy paranoiac with a germ phobia. Lingers on the rich guy with big problems theme. Big-budget TV drama with a nice performance by Jones. **119m/C VHS, DVD,** Tommy Lee Jones, Ed Flanders, James Hampton, Tovah Feldshuh, Lee Purcell; **D:** William A. Graham. **TV**

The Amazing Mrs. Holiday ♂♂½ **1943** Pleasant Durbin outing finds the star playing the daughter of missionaries working in China. Ruth accompanies a group of Chinese orphans aboard a ship bound for San Francisco, aided by steward Timothy (Fitzgerald).

Amarilly of Clothesline Alley ♂♂½ **1918** Amarilly (Pickford) gets a job as a New York dance hall cigarette girl and is around to help wealthy slumming playboy Gordon Phillips (Kerry) after he gets into a fight. Phillips becomes convinced he loves Amarilly, despite her social inferiority, but Amarilly comes to realize she should stick with those that know her best, including neighborhood beau, Terry (Scott). **77m/B VHS, DVD,** Mary Pickford, William Scott, Norman Kerry, Ida Waterman, Kate Price, Margaret Landis; **D:** Marshall Neilan; **W:** Frances Marion; **C:** Walter Strading.

The Amateur ♂½ **1982 (R)** Computer technologist for the CIA dives into a plot of international intrigue behind the Iron Curtain when he investigates the death of his girlfriend, murdered by terrorists. Confused and ultimately disappointing spy drama cursed with a wooden script, written by Littell, based on his novel. **112m/C VHS, DVD,** John Savage, Christopher Plummer, Marthe Keller, Arthur Hill, Ed Lauter; **D:** Charles Jarrott; **W:** Robert Littell.

Amateur ♂½ **1994 (R)** Former nun Huppert, trying to make a living writing pornography, hooks up with an amnesiac (Donovan) who turns out to have a criminal past and a porno actress wife (Lowensohn) who wants him dead. Blackmail plot has oddball characters racing through dark and evocative settings while unfolding a tale loaded with offbeat oppositions and an irresistibly bizarre romantic triangle. Lively and playful without becoming pretentious, Hartley's self-described "eccentric thriller... with one flat line" evokes his typical deadpan subtle style. **105m/C VHS, DVD,** Isabelle Huppert, Martin Donovan, Elina Lowensohn, Damian Young, Chuck Montgomery, David Simonds, Pamela Stewart, Terry Alexander; **D:** Hal Hartley; **W:** Hal Hartley; **C:** Michael Spiller; **W:** Tom Dempsey.

Amateur Night ♂ **1985** Sloppy musical comedy about the backstage bickering occurring during the amateur night at a famous nightclub. **91m/C VHS,** Geoffrey Deuel, Dennis Cole, Allen Kirk; **D:** Eddie Beverly Jr.; **W:** Tom Dempsey.

Amazing Adventure" ♂♂ *Romance and Riches; The Amazing Quest of Ernest Bliss; Riches and Romance* **1937** A millionaire wins a bet when he rises from a chauffeur's position to the executive board room without using his wealth. Though not particularly amazing, lightweight English comedy has Grant working hard to charm over and above the demands of the dated formula, a performance he undertook during a vacation from Hollywood. Adapted from a novel by E. Phillips Oppenheim. **61m/C VHS, DVD,** Cary Grant, Mary Brian, Henry Kendall, Leon M. Lion, Ralph Richardson; **D:** Alfred Zeisler.

Amazing Dr. Clitterhouse ♂♂♂ **1938** Satirical gangster saga has criminologist Dr. Clitterhouse (Robinson) so fascinated by crime that he commits a few jewel robberies just to test out that bad guy rush. He contacts a fence, luscious Jo Keller (Trevor), who gets Clitterhouse an in with gangster Rocks Valentine (Bogart). Clitterhouse successfully masterminds some heists for Valentine—who becomes jealous of Clitterhouse's brain power and things just get more wacky from there (including a farcical trial). This s definitely Robinson's show. **87m/B VHS,** Edward G. Robinson, Claire Trevor, Humphrey Bogart, Gale Page, Donald Crisp, Maxie "Slapsie" Rosenbloom, Thurston Hall, Allen Jenkins, John Litel, Henry O'Neill, Ward Bond, Curt Bois; **D:** Anatole Litvak; **W:** John Huston, John Wexley; **C:** Gaetano Antonio "Tony" Gaudio; **M:** Max Steiner.

Amazing Grace ♂♂♂ **1974** Some righteous mothers led by Morris Mabley go up against corrupt city politics in this extremely dated comedy that was cast with a sense of the absurd. **99m/C VHS, DVD,** Moms Mabley, Slappy (Melvin) White, Moses Gunn, Rosalind Cash, Dolph Sweet, Butterfly McQueen, Stepin Fetchit; **D:** Stan Lathan; **W:** Matt Robinson; **C:** Edward R. Brown, Sol Negrin.

Amazing Grace ♂♂ **1992** Eighteen-year-old Jonathan leaves home to share his friend Mickey's apartment. He meets Thomas, who has just returned to Israel after years in New York, and they begin a tentative relationship. But Thomas is hiding the fact that he may be HIV-positive and tries to keep a distance from his eager Jonathan. Hebrew with subtitles. **95m/C VHS, IS** Rivka Michaely, Sharon Alexander, Gal Rozovska; **M:** Max Steiner.

Amazing Grace ♂♂♂ **2006 (PG)** Sincere and forceful bio of evangelical Christian William Wilberforce (Gruffudd), a member of the House of Commons, who spent his years in the British Parliament introducing antislavery legislation. Tells the crusader's story with flashbacks, introducing both foes and friends, including former slave trader John Newton (Finney), who wrote the title hymn 'rousingly sung' by Gruffudd), as part of his atonement. Senegalese singer N'Dour makes his film debut as freed slave and author Olaudah Equiano. **111m/C DVD, GB** can Gruffudd, Romola Garai, Albert Finney, Michael Gambon, Rufus Sewell, Ciaran Hinds, Toby Jones, Nicholas Farrell, Sylvestra Le Touzel, Stephan Campbell Moore, Benedict Cumberbatch, Youssou N'Dour, Senegal; **M:** David Arnold.

Amazing Grace & Chuck ♂♂ **1987 (PG)** Perhaps the only anti-war/sports fantasy ever made. After a visit to a Minuteman missile site in Montana, 12-year-old Little Leaguer Chuck learns of the dangers of nuclear arms. He begins a protest by refusing to play until the nations come to a peace agreement. In a sudden surge of social conscience, athletes worldwide put down their equipment and join in droves, starting with pro-basketball star Amazing Grace Smith (Denver Nugget English). Capra-like fantasy with pro-disarmament intentions but ultimately lacks two key elements: coherency and plausibility. **115m/C VHS,** Jamie Lee Curtis, Gregory Peck, William L. Petersen, Joshua Zuehlke, Alex English; **D:** Mike Newell; **C:** Robert Elswit; **M:** Elmer Bernstein.

She wants the children to stay together, so Timothy passes Ruth off as the wife of a shipping magnate, who's been lost at sea. Ruth admits her deception to the man's grandson Tom (O'Brien) and convinces him that it's okay that she and the children stay in the family mansion. **98m/B VHS.** Deanna Durbin, Edmond O'Brien, Barry Fitzgerald, Arthur Treacher, Harry Davenport, Grant Mitchell, Frieda Inescort, Elisabeth Risdon; **C:** Elwood "Woody" Bredell; **M:** Frank Skinner, Hans J. Salter.

Amazing Mr. Blunden 1972 (G) Solid kidvid about two youngsters aided by a ghost who travel back in time to save the lives of two murdered children. Adapted by Jeffries from Antonia Barber's novel, "The Ghosts." **100m/C VHS.** Laurence Naismith, Lynne Frederick, Garry Miller, Marc Granger, Rosalyn London, Diana Dors; **D:** Lionel Jeffries; **M:** Elmer Bernstein.

The Amazing Mr. X *The Spiritualist* 1948 When a woman's husband dies, she tries to contact him via a spiritualist. Things are not as they seem however, and the medium may just be part of an intricate scheme to defraud the woman. **79m/B VHS, DVD.** Turhan Bey, Lynn Bari, Cathy O'Donnell, Richard Carlson, Donald Curtis, Virginia Gregg; **D:** Bernard Vorhaus; **W:** Ian McLellan Hunter, Muriel Roy Boulton; **C:** John Alton.

The Amazing Panda Adventure *Little Panda; The Amazing Panda Rescue* 1995 (PG) Ryan (Slater) is off to China during his spring break to visit dad Michael (Lang), who's working on a project to rescue the dwindling panda population. But there's poacher trouble and Ryan and young translator Ling (Ding) decide to rescue the animal-napped cub, which has been animal-napped (where's Ace Ventura when you need him). Family fare, with a mixture of totally adorable real and animatronic pandas, filmed in the Sichuan province of China, home to the Wolong Nature Reserve which is famous for its successful breeding of the endangered giant pandas. Slater, in his first starring role, is the younger brother of Christian. **84m/C VHS, DVD.** Ryan Slater, Stephen Lang, Yi Ding, Wang Fei; **D:** Christopher Cain; **W:** Laurice Elehwany, Jeff Rothberg; **C:** Jack N. Green; **M:** William Ross.

The Amazing Spider-Man *Spider-Man* 1977 The Marvel Comics superhero's unique powers are put to the test when he comes to the rescue of the government by preventing an evil scientist from blackmailing the government for big bucks. The wall-walking web-slinger has his origins probed (a grad student bit by a radioactive spider develops super-human powers) in his live-action debut, which led to a short-lived TV series. **94m/C VHS.** Nicholas Hammond, David White, Lisa Eilbacher, cheal Pataki; **D:** E.W. Swackhamer. **TV**

Amazing Stories 1985 From the Steven Spielberg produced TV series. "The Mission" sees a WWII turret gunner trapped in an unusual predicament. In "The Wedding Ring," a man gives his wife a strange ring and bizarre situations ensue. **70m/C VHS.** Kevin Costner, Casey Siemaszko, Kiefer Sutherland, Danny DeVito, Rhea Perlman; **D:** Danny DeVito, Steven Spielberg. **TV**

The Amazing Transparent Man WOOF! 1960 A mad scientist makes a crook invisible in order to steal the radioactive materials he needs. The crook decides to rob banks instead. Shot at the Texas State Fair for that elusive futuristic look. For Ulmer fans only. **58m/B VHS, DVD.** Douglas Kennedy, Marguerite Chapman, James J. Griffith, Ivan Triesault, Boyd 'Red' Morgan, Carmel Daniel, Jonathan Ledford, Norman Smith, Patrick Cranshaw, Kevin Kelly; **D:** Edgar G. Ulmer; **W:** Jack Lewis; **C:** Meredith Nicholson; **D:** Darrell Calker.

The Amazing Transplant WOOF! 1970 A sleazebag psycho has a "love enhancing" transplant, much to the pleasure of his sexual partners. Much to their and our dismay, however, he then kills them and bores us. **90m/C VHS, DVD.** Juan Fernandez, Linda Southern, Larry Hunter, Kim Pope; **D:** Doris Wishman; **W:** Doris Wishman; **C:** C. Davis Smith.

Amazon 1990 (R) An adventure movie filmed in the Brazilian rainforest with an environmental message. A businessman being chased by the police in the Amazon jungle is rescued by a bush pilot who dreams of mining the Amazon's riches. A Brazilian woman enters the picture and persuades the businessman to help save the rainforest. Portions of the proceeds from the sale of this film go to the Rainforest Action Network. **88m/C VHS.** Kari Vaananen, Robert Davi, Rae Dawn Chong; **D:** Mika Kaurismaki.

Amazon Jail 1985 Scantily clad women go over the wall and promptly get caught by devil worshiping men in the jungle. They should have known better. Redeemed only by lingerie selection. **94m/C VHS, DVD.** Elisabeth Hartmann, Maurício Do Valle, Sondra Graffi; **D:** Oswald De Oliveira.

Amazon Warrior 1997 Tara is a mercenary in a future world ruled by violence. The last survivor of her Amazon tribe, she sells her fighting skills to the highest bidder while searching for the leader of the rebel Marauder army, which massacred her people. Tara's well-equipped when that final showdown comes. **85m/C VHS.** J.J. Rodgers, Christine Lydon, Jimmy Jerman, Al Spencer, Raymond Storti; **D:** Dennis Devine; **W:** Steve Jarvis; **M:** David De Palo.

Amazon Women on the Moon *Cheeseburger Film Sandwich* 1987 (R) A plotless, irreverent media spoof, depicting the programming of a slipshod TV station as it crams weird commercials and shorts around a comical '50s science fiction film. Inconsistent, occasionally funny anthology hangs together very loosely. Produced by Landis, with the usual amount of in-joke cameos and allusions to his other works of art. **85m/C VHS, DVD.** Rosanna Arquette, Steve Guttenberg, Steve Allen, B.B. King, Michelle Pfeiffer, Arsenio Hall, Andrew (Dice Clay) Silverstein, Howard Hesseman, Lou Jacobi, Carrie Fisher, Griffin Dunne, Sybil Danning, Henny Youngman, Monique Gabrielle, Paul Bartel, Kelly Preston, Ralph Bellamy, Russ Meyer, Steve Forrest, Joey Travolta, Ed Begley Jr., Forrest J Ackerman, Archie Hahn, Phil Hartman, Peter Horton, Charlie Callas, T.K. Carter, Dick Miller, Roxie Roker; **D:** John Landis, Joe Dante, Carl Gottlieb, Robert Weiss, Peter Horton; **W:** Michael Barrie, Jim Mulholland; **C:** Daniel Pearl; **M:** Ira Newborn.

The Amazons 1984 Goofy drama about a beautiful doctor who discovers an underground organization of Amazon-descended women bent on taking over the world or at least making life hard for men while investigating a Congressman's mysterious death. **100m/C VHS.** Tamara Dobson, Jack Scalia, Stella Stevens, Madeleine Stowe, Jennifer Warren; **D:** Paul Michael Glaser; **M:** Basil Poledouris. **TV**

Amazons 1986 (R) Tall, strong women who occasionally wander around nude search for a magical talisman that will overthrow an evil magician. **76m/C VHS, DVD.** Mindi Miller, Penelope Reed, Joseph Whipp, Willie Nelson, Danitza Kingsley; **D:** Alex Sessa.

Amazons and Gladiators 2001 (R) The title says it all, doesn't it? Beautiful slave girl joins up with an Amazon queen and her band of warriors to fight an evil Roman governor. **89m/C VHS, DVD. US GE** Jennifer Rubin, Patrick Bergin, Nichole Hiltz, Wendi Winburn, Melanie Gutteridge, Richard Norton; **C:** Zachary Weintraub; **M:** Zachary Weintraub; **C:** Thomas Hencz; **M:** Timothy S. (Tim) Jones. **VIDEO**

The Ambassador *Peacemaker* 1984 An American ambassador (Mitchum) is sent to the Middle East to try to solve the area's deep political problems. He quickly becomes the target of terrorist attacks, and is blamed for the nation's unrest. To make matters worse, his wife is having an affair with a PLO leader. The President ignores him, forcing the ambassador to fend for himself. Talk about your bad days. Hudson's last feature. Based on Elmore Leonard's "52 Pickup," and remade a year later under its own title. **97m/C VHS, DVD.** Robert Mitchum, Ellen Burstyn, Rock Hudson, Fabio Testi, Donald Pleasence; **D:** J. Lee Thompson.

Ambassador Bill 1931 An Oklahoma rancher is appointed ambassador to a country in revolt. Rogers, of course, saves the day with his rustic witticisms. Based on the story "Ambassador from the United States" by Vincent Sheean. **68m/B VHS.** Will Rogers, Marguerite Churchill, Greta Nissen, Ray Milland, Tad Alexander, Gustav von Seyffertitz; **D:** Sam Taylor.

The Ambassador's Daughter 1956 The Parisian adventures of an American ambassador's daughter De Havilland and soldier Forsythe, who, unaware of her position, falls in love with her. Faltering comedy is supported by an expert cast (although nearly 40, De Havilland is charming as the young woman) with especially good performances from Menjou and Loy. **102m/C VHS.** Olivia de Havilland, John Forsythe, Myrna Loy, Adolphe Menjou, Edward Arnold, Francis Lederer, Tommy Noonan, Minor Watson; **D:** Norman Krasna; **W:** Norman Krasna.

Amber Waves 1982 Credible drama about a generation-gap conflict between a Midwestern farmer (Weaver) and an irresponsible male model (Russell) who has coasted through life on con and charm. **98m/C VHS.** Dennis Weaver, Kurt Russell, Rossie (Ross) Harris, Mare Winningham, Wilford Brimley; **D:** Joseph Sargent. **TV**

Ambition 1991 (R) Scriptwriter/star Phillips gets a bone for chutzpah by taking an unsavory lead role; his character torments a paroled psycho so that the killer will kill again and inspire a true-crime bestseller. The plot looks good on paper, but onscreen it's padded and unconvincing. **99m/C VHS.** Lou Diamond Phillips, Clancy Brown, Cecilia Peck, Richard Bradford, Willard Pugh, Grace Zabriskie, Katherine Armstrong, John David (J.D.) Cullum, Haing S. Ngor; **D:** Scott Goldstein; **W:** Lou Diamond Phillips; **M:** Leonard Rosenman.

The Ambulance 1990 (R) A New York cartoonist witnesses a mysterious ambulance at work and decides to investigate. His probings uncover a plot to sell the bodies of dying diabetics. A surprisingly good no-money feature from low-budget king Cohen. Includes an appearance by Marvel Comics' Stan Lee as himself. **95m/C VHS.** Eric Roberts, James Earl Jones, Megan Gallagher, Red Buttons, Laurene Landon, Jill Gatsby, Nicholas Chinlund, James Dixon, Stan Lee; **D:** Larry Cohen; **W:** Larry Cohen; **C:** Jacques Haitkin; **M:** Jay Chattaway.

Ambush *Rukajarven Tie* 1999 Young lieutenant Eero is serving in the Finnish Army in 1941 pursuing Russian troops along the border. During his mission, Eero is able to briefly spend some soon leave to go on a recon. He receives word that Irina has been killed by Russian soldiers and seeks revenge on any Russians he finds—turning from innocent soldier to dehumanized killer. Co-writer Tuuri adapted from his novel. Finnish with subtitles. **117m/C VHS, DVD. FI** Peter Franzen, Irina Bjorklund, Kari Vaananen, Kari Heiskanen, Taisto Reimaluoto; **D:** Olli Saarela; **W:** Olli Saarela, Antti Tuuri; **C:** Kjell Lagerroos; **M:** Tuomas Kantelinen.

Ambush at Tomahawk Gap 1953 Three released prisoners go in search of hidden loot and tempers rise when the goods don't turn up. Then the Apaches show up. **73m/C VHS.** John Hodiak, John Derek, David Brian, Maria Elena Marques, Ray Teal; **D:** Fred F. Sears.

The Ambush Murders 1982 True story of a stalwart white attorney defending a black activist accused of killing two cops. Not the compelling TV drama it could be, but still enjoyable. From Ben Bradlee Jr.'s novel. **100m/C VHS.** James Brolin, Dorian Harewood, Alfre Woodard, Louis Gossett Jr., John McLiam, Teddy Wilson, Antonio Fargas, Amy Madigan; **D:** Steven Hilliard Stern. **TV**

Ambush Trail 1946 Stranger-in-town Steele metes out justice to help local ranchers while sidekick Saylor leaves 'em laughing. **60m/B VHS.** Bob Steele, Syd Saylor, I. Stanford Jolley, Lorraine Miller, Charles "Blackie" King, Kermit Maynard; **D:** Harry Fraser.

The Ambushers WOOF! 1967 Martin's third Matt Helm farce finds him handling a puzzling case involving the first United States spacecraft. When the craft is hijacked with Rule on board, it's Matt to the rescue, regaining control before unfriendly forces can take it back to Earth. Tired formula seems to have worn Martin out while the remainder of the cast goes to camp. Followed by "The Wrecking Crew." **102m/C VHS, DVD.** Dean Martin, Janice Rule, James Gregory, Albert Salmi, Senta Berger, Kurt Kasznar, Beverly Adams; **D:** Henry Levin; **W:** Herbert Baker; **C:** Burnett Guffey, Edward Colman; **M:** Hugo Montenegro.

Amelia Earhart: The Final Flight 1994 Investigates the mysterious disappearance of pioneering aviatrix Amelia Earhart's 1937 flight to become the first pilot to circumnavigate the globe. Earhart (Keaton) and her navigator Fred Noonan (Hauer) disappeared over the Pacific Ocean and their fate has never been determined. Dern plays Earhart's husband, publisher George B. Putnam, who served as Amelia's manager and publicist. Based on the biography by Doris L. Rich. **95m/C VHS.** Diane Keaton, Rutger Hauer, Bruce Dern, Paul Guilfoyle, Denis Arndt, David Carpenter, Diana Bellamy; **D:** Yves Simoneau; **W:** Anna Sandor; **M:** George S. Clinton. **TV**

Amelie *Amelie from Montmartre; The Fabulous Destiny of Amelie Poulain; Le Fabuleux Destin d'Amelie Poulain* 2001 (R) Paris waitress Amelie (Tautou) has led a solitary, but not wholly unpleasant, existence. When she finds a box of childhood treasures behind a wall in her apartment, she sets out to return them to their original owner. Accomplishing this, she begins to secretly intervene in the lives of neighbors and coworkers, helping some find romance, others retribution for past wrongs. When her "missions" bring her into contact with a quirky local (Kassovitz), she begins a roundabout courtship involving a treasure hunt instead of approaching him directly. Director Jeunet leaves intact his stunning, and very stylized visual talents, but marshals them in service of a fresh, lighthearted comedy, in contrast to his previous, downcast work. Tautou has no problem carrying the movie and has the look of a budding major star. **120m/C VHS, DVD. FR GE** Audrey Tautou, Mathieu Kassovitz, Rufus, Yolande Moreau, Dominique Pinon, Maurice Benichou, Artus de Penguem, Urbain Cancellier, Isabelle Nanty, Claire Maurier, Claude Perron, Clothilde Mollet, Serge Merlin, Jamel Debbouze, Flora Guiet; **D:** Jean-Pierre Jeunet; **W:** Jean-Pierre Jeunet, Guillaume Laurant; **C:** Bruno Delbonnel; **M:** Yann Tiersen; **Nar:** Andre Dussollier. British Acad. '01: Orig. Screenplay; Cesar '01: Art Dir./Set Dec., Director (Jeunet), Film, Score; Broadcast Film Critics '01: Foreign Film.

Amen 2002 (R) Costa-Gavras dramatizes a Holocaust story with a somewhat heavy hand. SS. Lt. Kurt Gerstein (Tukur) is a chemist who uses prussic acid Zyklon B for fumigating camp barracks. Sent to a Polish concentration camp, he witnesses the deaths of Jewish prisoners by the gas. Appalled, Gerstein rishes reprisals by informing various church leaders, although no one is willing to speak out until he reaches the young Italian priest, Father Riccardo Fontana (Kassovitz), who has family ties to Pope Pius XII (lures). As head of the Hygiene Institute, the SS expects Gerstein to continue to eliminate vermin of all kinds while Father Fontana heads to the Vatican in the hopes of getting the Pope to expose the genocide. An adaptation of Rolf Hochhuth's 1963 play, "The Deputy." **130m/C DVD. FR** Ulrich Tukur, Mathieu Kassovitz, Marcel lures, Ulrich Muhe, Michel Duchaussoy, Ion Caramitru; **D:** Constantin Costa-Gavras; **W:** Constantin Costa-Gavras, Jean-Claude Grumberg; **C:** Patrick Blossier; **M:** Armand Amar.

America 1924 Young patriot Nathan Holden (Hamilton) is torn between his political beliefs and his love for the daughter of a Virginia Tory (Dempster). Meanwhile, evil redcoat Captain Butler (Barrymore) and his band of murderous Mohawks ruthlessly attack the colonists.

141m/B VHS, DVD. Neil Hamilton, Carol Demp- ster, Lionel Barrymore, Emilie Alderson, Charles Bennett, Arthur Donaldson, Charles Mack, Frank McGlynn, Henry O'Neill, Ed Rossman, Harry Sem- els, Louis Wolheim, Hugh Baird, Lee Beggs, Downing Clarke, Sydney Deane, Arthur Dewey, Michael Donavan, Paul Doucet, John Dunton, Ri- ley Hatch, Emil Hoch, Edwin Holland, W.W. Jones, William S. Rising, Frank Walsh; *D:* D.W. Griffith; *W:* Robert W. Chambers; *C:* Marcel Le Picard, Hendrik Sartov, Billy (G.W.) Bitzer.

America ☆☆½ **1986** (R) New York ca- ble station receives worldwide fame when their signal bounces off of the moon. Unin- spired piece of fluff from otherwise talent- ed director Downey. **83m/C VHS.** Zack Nor- man, Tammy Grimes, Michael J. Pollard, Monroe Arnold, Richard Belzer, Liz Torres, Howard Tho- mashefsky, Laura Ashton, Robert Downey; *D:* Robert Downey.

America at the Movies ☆☆½ 1976 Scenes from more than 80 of the fin- est American motion pictures fly by in an effort to tell the story of the cinema and provide a portrait of America as it has been seen on screen for half a century. Clips from "The Birth of a Nation," "Citizen Kane," "Dr. Strangelove," "East of Eden," "Here to Eternity," and "From Here to Eternity" are among the many in- cluded. Some black-and-white scenes; produced by the American Film Institute. **116m/C VHS.** John Wayne, Orson Welles, Peter Sellers, James Dean, Gene Hackman, Burt Lan- caster, Julie Harris, Deborah Kerr, Al Pacino, Rob- ert De Niro; *M:* Nelson Riddle; *Narr:* Charlton He- ston.

America First ☆☆½ 1970 A group of seven travelers try to build an "Eden" with the inhabitants of an Appalachian hol- low. **90m/C VHS.** Michael Kennedy, Walter Keller, Pat Estrin, Lois McGuire; *D:* Joseph L. Anderson.

America 3000 ☆ 1986 (PG-13) Hun- dreds of years in the holocaust-torn future, men rebel against a brutal, overpowering race of women, with predictable results. **94m/C VHS.** Chuck Wagner, Laurene Landon; *D:* David Engelbach.

The American ☆☆ 2001 Heavy- handed adaptation of Henry James's 1877 novel. Christopher Newman (Modine) bring its flavors together. As it does the quire both culture and a wife. He hopes to ac- Paris in the 1870s where he hopes to ac- quire both culture and a wife, the mysterious widow Claire de Cintre (Sulli- van) but his proposal is rejected by her snobby aristocratic "family," which is head- ed by Claire's imperious mother, Madame de Bellegarde (Rigg). Then Newman learns a family secret that could win him Claire's hand. **90m/C VHS, DVD.** Matthew Mod- ine, Aisling O'Sullivan, Diana Rigg, Brenda Fricker, Andrew Scott, Eva Birthistle; *D:* Paul Unwin; *W:* Michael Hastings. TV

American Adobo ☆☆½ 2002 (R) An adobo is the Philippines' national dish, a savory concoction that must marinate to bring its flavors together. As it does the Filipino-American long-time friends around a dinner table in Queens. They are all do- ing well professionally but their personal lives could definitely use work. **99m/C VHS, DVD.** Dina Bonnevie, Randy Becker, Cherry Pie Picache, Sol Ocoa, Christopher De Leon, Susan Valdez-LeGoff, Ricky Davao, Wayne Maugans, Paolo Montalban, Gloria Romero; *D:* Laurice Guil- len; *W:* Vincent R. Nebrida; *C:* Lee Meily.

An American Affair ☆☆ 1999 Washington, D.C., District Attorney Sam Brady (Berrsen) marries Genevieve (D'Abo) even though he's having an affair with her best friend, Barbara (Heitmeyer). But after Genevieve is murdered, her ghost begins to haunt him. And to make things more complicated a senator seems to have it in for Sam. The two plotlines take too long to intersect, so the story nev- er makes much sense. **90m/C VHS, DVD. CA** Corbin Bensen, Maryam D'Abo, Jayne Heitmeyer, Robert Vaughn; *D:* Sebastian Shah. **VIDEO**

The American Angels: Baptism of Blood ☆ 1989 (R) Three beautiful young women, each with a personal dream, strive to make it in the world of professional wrestling. Hack- neyed pot devices, but those simply watching the wrestling scenes won't be disappointed. **99m/C VHS.** Jan MacKenzie, Tray Loren, Mimi Lesseos, Trudy Adams, Patricia

---

American Anthem ☆ 1986 (PG-13) A young gymnast must choose between Olympic gymnast Gaylord makes his mov- Olympic gymnast Gaylord makes his mov- ie debut but doesn't get the gold. Good fare for young tumblers, but that's about it. Followed by two of the films' music videos and tape-ads featuring Max Headroom. **100m/C VHS.** Mitch Gaylord, Janet Jones, Mic- helle Phillips, Michael Pataki; *D:* Albert Magnoli; *W:* Evan P. Archerd, Jeff Benjamin; *M:* Alan Silves- tri.

American Aristocracy ☆☆½ 1917 A silent comic romp in which Fair- banks, an old moneyed dandy, wreaks havoc on an island resort whose clientele is composed of the nouveau well-to-do. **52m/B VHS.** Douglas Fairbanks Sr., Jewel Car- men, Albert Parker; *D:* Lloyd Ingraham.

American Autobahn ☆☆½ 1984 A low-budget independent actioner about a journalist who discovers an underworld weapons ring that hits the highway in pur- suit of him. **90m/C VHS.** Jan Jalenak, Michael von der Goltz, Jim Jarmusch; *D:* Andre Degas.

American Beauty ☆☆☆½ 1999 (R) Lester Burnham (Spacey) is dead. This isn't any shock—Lester tells you this himself in his opening narration. It's the time leading up to his death Lester wants to remember. Lester is a middle-aged drone with a brittle, status-conscious wife, Carolyn (Bening), and a sullen teenaged daughter, Jane (Birch). Lester's world is rocked when he meets Jane's Lolita-like friend, Angela (Suvari) and his fantasies about bedding her lead him to quitting his job, pumping iron, and smoking dope with Ricky (Bentley), the voyeuristic kid next door who has a thing for videotaping Jane. It's a suburban nightmare writ large with an excellent cast and some unexpected twists. **118m/C VHS, DVD.** Kevin Spacey, Annette Bening, Mena Suvari, Thora Birch, Wes Bentley, Peter Gallagher, Chris Cooper, Allison Janney, Scott Bakula, Sam Ro- bards; *D:* Sam Mendes; *W:* Alan Ball; *C:* Conrad L. Hall; *M:* Thomas Newman. Oscars '99: Actor (Spa- cey), Cinematog., Director (Mendes), Film, Orig. Screenplay; British Acad. '99: Actor (Spacey), Ac- tress (Bening), Cinematog., Film, Film Editing, Score; Directors Guild '99: Director (Mendes); Golden Globes '00: Director (Mendes), Film—Dra- ma, Screenplay; L.A. Film Critics '99: Director (Mendes); Natl. Bd. of Review '99: Film; Screen Actors Guild '99: Actor (Spacey), Actress (Bening), Cast; Writers Guild '99: Orig. Screenplay; Broad- cast Film Critics '99: Director (Mendes), Film, Orig. Screenplay.

American Blue Note ☆☆ 1989 Fake- book 1989 (PG-13) Loosely plotted, bitter- sweet account of a struggling jazz quartet in the early 1960s, as its leader (MacNicol) must decide if their fruitless tours of sleazy bars and weddings are still worth it. The debut of director Topor off. **96m/C VHS.** Peter MacNichol, Carl Capotorto, Tim Guinee, Bill Chris- topher-Myers, Jonathan Walker, Charlotte d'Amboise, Louis Guss, Zohra Lampert, Trini Alva- rado, Sam Behrens; *D:* Ralph Toporoff; *W:* Gilbert Girion, Larry Schanker.

American Born ☆☆ 1989 Murder inc. returns to the dismay of one idealist who embarks on a battle he doesn't intend to lose. The mob had better look out. **90m/ C VHS.** Joey Travolta, Andrew Zeller; *D:* Raymond Martino; *W:* Raymond Martino.

American Boyfriends ☆☆ 1989 (PG-3) An ostensible sequel to "My Amer- ican Cousin" in which two Canadian girls go to California and discover innocent ro- mance and friendship. **90m/C VHS. CA** Mar- gare Langrok, John Wildman, Jason Blicker, Lisa Repo Martell; *D:* Sandy Wilson; *W:* Sandy Wilson; *C:* Brenton Spencer.

American Buffalo ☆☆½ 1995 (R) Somewhat lackluster but decent screen adaptation of a classic American drama. Franz's junk shop owner Donny plans to steal back a rare Buffalo-head nickel that he feels he was swindled out of, with the help of his protege Bobby (Nelson). Hoff- man's ferret-like Teach, one of Donny's card-playing buddies and an arrogant op- portunist, tries to weasel in on the plan that never comes to fruition. Set in Cor- rente's hometown of Pawtucket, the direc-

---

tor's reverence for the material is obvious and he plays it too safe. Top-notch perfor- mances raise the level. Mamet adapts his play for the screen. **88m/C VHS, DVD.** Dustin Hoffman, Dennis Franz, Sean Nelson; *D:* Michael Corrente; *W:* David Mamet; *C:* Richard Crudo; *M:* Thomas Newman.

American Chinatown ☆½ 1996 Orphaned tough guy is taken in by a pow- erful Chinatown mob family but a pow- trouble when he falls for the head man's sister. He has a chance to redeem himself when he learns about a plot to overthrow the triad clan but will he take it? **90m/C VHS, DVD.** Henry Lee, Robert D'Zar, Liat Goodson; *D:* Richard M. Park.

An American Christmas Carol ☆☆ 1979 Charles Dickens' classic story is retold with limited charm in a TV effort. This time a greedy American financier (Winkler) learns about the true meaning of Christmas. **98m/C VHS, DVD.** Henry Winkler, David Wayne, Dorian Harewood; *D:* Eric Till; *M:* Hagood Hardy. TV

American Commandos ☆ Hi- man 1984 (R) An ex-Green Beret slaughters a vacation, when his layover in the Mos- cow airport becomes a lesson in mistaken identities. He teams up with the pre-requi- site beautiful woman to outwit and outrun the Russian mafia. **91m/C VHS.** Wayne Craw- ford, Ashley Laurence, Daniel Quinn, William Katt, Olga Vodin, Vladimir Shpoudeiko, Nickolai Neco- wdin; *D:* Wayne Crawford; *W:* Carlos Brooks; *C:* Nicholas Josef von Sternberg.

American Cop ☆☆½ 1994 (PG-13) Elmo LaGrange is an ordinary cop taking an moo while in Europe and are instructed to lay low in Glasgow with their distant cousin Roberto. Roberto is a mild-man- nered, stamp-collecting fish & chips shop proprietor, who is clueless about his American cousins' true business. But they decide to repay his hospitality by helping Roberto out with some local thugs who are trying to muscle in on his business. Light-hearted culture clash comedy. **89m/C VHS, DVD.** GB Danny Nucci, Dan Hedaya, Shirley Her- derson, Vincent Pastore, Gerald Lepkowski, Rus- sell Hunter, Stevan Remkus; *D:* Donald Couts; *W:* Sergio Casci; *C:* Jerry Kalogeratos; *M:* Don Shew.

American Cousins ☆☆½ 2002 New Jersey gangsters Gino and Settimo Bazaglia get into trouble with the Ukraini- an mob while in Europe and are instructed to lay low in Glasgow with their distant cousin Roberto. Roberto is a mild-man- nered, stamp-collecting fish & chips shop proprietor, who is clueless about his American cousins' true business. **89m/C VHS, DVD.** Kevin Spacey, Annette Bening, Mena Suvari, Thora Birch, Wes Bentley, Peter Gallagher, Chris Cooper.

American Cyborg: Steel Warrior ☆☆½ 1994 (R) Basic evil- machine-bent-on-mankind's-destruction movie—with a hero bent on rescuing the world. **95m/C VHS.** Joe Lara, John P. Ryan; *D:* Boaz Davidson; *W:* Bill Crounse.

American Dream ☆☆☆ 1981 A midwestern family leaves the suburbs and moves into a Chicago inner-city neighbor- hood. Good TV-movie pilot for the short- lived series that was Emmy nominated for direction and writing. **90m/C VHS.** Stephen Macht, Karen Carlson, John Karlen, Andrea Smith, John Malkovich, John McIntire; *D:* Mel Damski *M:* Artie Butler. TV

American Dreamer ☆☆ 1984 (PG) A housewife wins a trip to Paris as a prize from a mystery writing contest. Silly from a blow on the head, she begins living the fictional life of her favorite literary adven- ture. Sporadic comedy with a good cast wandering about courtesy of a clumsy screenplay. **105m/C VHS, DVD.** JoBeth Wil- liams, Tom Conti, Giancarlo Giannini, Coral Browne, James Staley; *D:* Rick Rosenthal; *M:* Lewis Furey.

American Dreamz ☆☆ 2006 (PG-13) Weitz's obvious satire has self- loathing, smarmy Brit Martin Tweed (Grant) hosting the universally popular re- ality show of the title. This latest version will be highlighted by the appearance of dim-witted affable American President Staton (Quaid) as a guest judge. He has the time because the country is actually being run by his power-hungry chief of staff (Dafoe). Vying for celebrity status are

---

small-town blonde Sally Kendoo (Moore), who hides her unholy ambitions behind a girl-next-door smile, and Omer (Golzari), a showtune-loving Iraqi who has been cho- sen as a suicide bomber. Grant and Moore fare best as conniving players who recognize and respect the dark streak in each other. **107m/C DVD, US** Hugh Grant, Dan- nis Quaid, Mandy Moore, William Dafoe, Chris Klein, Jennifer Coolidge, Marcia Gay Harden, John Cho, Sam Golzari, Seth Meyers, Judy Greer, Shohreh Aghdashloo, Jennie (Bernard) White, Tony Yalda, Marley Shelton, Lawrence Pressman, Noureen DeWulf; *D:* Paul Weitz; *W:* Paul Weitz; *C:* Robert Elswit; *M:* Stephen Trask.

American Eagle ☆☆ 1990 (R) A veteran goes crazy and seeks sadistic, bloody revenge on his war buddies. Now his war buddies are the only ones who can stop him. **92m/C VHS, DVD.** Asher Brauner, Robert F. Lyons, Vernon Wells, Kai Baker; *D:* Rob- ert J. Smawley.

American Empire ☆☆ 1942 My Son Alone 1942 Two Civil War heroes struggle to build a cattle empire in Texas and are hampered by rustlers, one of whom was their partner. A fine, veteran cast and a tight script keep things moving, including the cattle. **82m/B VHS, DVD.** Preston Foster, Richard Dix, Frances Gifford, Leo Carrillo; *D:* Wil- liam McGann.

American Fabulous ☆☆½ 1992 The posthumously released autobiogra- phy of an eccentric homosexual who lived life in the fast lane. Jeffrey Strouth per- forms his monologue from the back seat of a 1957 Cadillac, where the images of small-town America are seen to contrast sharply with his flamboyant style. His gro- tesque and candid recollections include his alcoholic Elvis-impersonator father, a stint as a teenage prostitute, drag queen friends, and drug addiction in New York. Strouth puts a comic twist on even the most brutal of his memories. He died of AIDS at the age of 33 in 1992. **105m/C VHS.** Jeffrey Strouth; *D:* Reno Dakota; *W:* Jeffrey Strouth.

American Flyers ☆☆ 1985 (PG-13) Two competitive brothers train for a grueling three-day bicycle race in Colo- rado while tangling with personal drama, including the spectre that one of them may have inherited dad's tendency for cerebral aneurisms and is sure to drop dead during a bike race soon. Written by bike movie specialist Tesich ("Breaking Away") with a lot of the usual cliches (the last bike ride, batting bros., eventual understanding) which are gracefully overridden by fine bike-racing photography. Interesting per- formances, especially Chong as a patient girlfriend and Amos as the trainer. **113m/C VHS, DVD.** Kevin Costner, David Marshall Grant, Rae Dawn Chong, Alexandra Paul, John Amos, Janice Rule, Robert Kevin Townsend, Jennifer Grey, Luca Barcovici; *D:* John Badham; *W:* Steve Tesich; *M:* Lee Ritenour; Greg Mathieson.

The American Friend ☆☆☆½ Der Amerikanische Freund 1977 Tribute to the American gangster film helped introduce Wenders to American moviegoers. Young Hamburg picture framer thinks he has a terminal disease and is easily set up by a hired assassin in West Germany. The lure is a promise of quick money that the suppos- edly dying man can then leave his wife and child. After the first assassination, the two bond Hopper is the typical Wenders protagonist, a strange man in a strange land looking for a connection. Great, creepy thriller adapted from Patricia Hi- ghsmith's novel "Ripley's Game." Fuller and Ray (better known as directors) ap- pear briefly as gangsters. **127m/C VHS, DVD.** FR GE Bruno Ganz, Dennis Hopper, Elisa- beth (Lisa) Kreuzer, Gerard Blain, Jean Eustache, Samuel Fuller, Nicholas Ray, Daniel Schmid, Lou Castel, Rudolf Schundler, Sandy Whitelaw; *Cam- eos:* Wim Wenders; *D:* Wim Wenders; *W:* Wim Wenders; *C:* Robby Muller; *M:* Jurgen Knieper.

American Friends ☆☆ 1991 (PG) Genteel story masquerades as high com- edy. Pair is a fussy middle-aged Oxford classics tutor. On a holiday he meets American Hartley (Booth) and her adopted daughter, Elinor (Alvarado). Both women are immensely attracted to the don (for reasons that are unclear) and follow him back to Oxford, where he's engaged in a battle of succession with his rival Molira. Dismal screenplay lacks logic and urgency, making it difficult to care about the story or the characters. Script is said to have been inspired by an incident in the life of Palin's great-grandfather. If this sounds like your cup of tea, save your time and watch a Merchant Ivory film instead. **89m/C VHS, GB** Michael Palin, Connie Booth, Trini Alvarado, Alfred Molina; **D:** Tristram Powell; **W:** Michael Palin, Tristram Powell; **M:** Georges Delerue.

American Gangster 🐾🐾🐾 **2007 (R)** Director Ridley Scott's shot at the gangster genre hits the mark, transcending the tough-guy norm in its purposeful juxtaposition of the two main characters Frank Lucas (Washington), the near-perfect, respectable, yet cold-blooded criminal genius who is pursued by the unkempt, womanizing, but razor-straight cop, Ritchie Roberts (Crowe). Washington and Crowe are mesmerizing in this powerful story of the brutality and excess of the '70s era Harlem drug trade that would be over-the-top if it weren't true, and that revolutionized both the drug trade and the law enforcement of the period. **157m/C DVD. US** Denzel Washington, Russell Crowe, Chiwetel Ejiofor, Cuba Gooding Jr., Josh Brolin, Ted Levine, Armand Assante, Clarence Williams III, Lymari Nadal, John Ortiz, RZA, Ruby Dee, Idris Elba, Carla Gugino, Common, Joe Morton, Jon Polito, Kevin Corrigan, Ruben Santiago-Hudson, Roger Bart, KaDee Strickland; **D:** Ridley Scott; **W:** Steven Zaillian; **C:** Harris Savides; **M:** Marc Streitenfeld. Screen Actors Guild '07: Support. Actress (Dee).

American Gigolo 🐾🐾 **1979 (R)** *Hide and Shriek* A Los Angeles loner who sexually services the rich women of Beverly Hills becomes involved with the wife of a California state senator and is then framed for a murder he did not commit. A highly stylized but empty view of seamy low lives marred by a contrived plot, with decent romp in the hay readiness displayed by Gere. **117m/C VHS, DVD.** Richard Gere, Lauren Hutton, Hector Elizondo, Nina Van Pallandt, Bill Duke, K. Callan; **Cameos:** Paul Schrader; **D:** Paul Schrader; **W:** Paul Schrader; **C:** John Bailey; **M:** Giorgio Moroder.

American Gothic woof! **1988 (R)** *Shriek* Three couples headed for a vacation are instead stranded on an island and captured by a demented family headed by Steiger and De Carlo, a scary enough proposition in itself. Even worse, Ma and Pa have three middle-aged moronic offspring who still dress as children and are intent on killing the thwarted vacationers (who are none too bright themselves) one by bloody one. A stultifying career low for all involved. **89m/C VHS, DVD. CA GB** Rod Steiger, Yvonne De Carlo, Michael J. Pollard, Sarah Torgov, Fiona Hutchinson, William Hootkins, Terry Kelly, Mark Ericksen, Caroline Barclay, Mark Lindsay Chapman; **D:** John Hough; **W:** Michael Vines, Bert Wetanson; **C:** Harvey Harrison; **M:** Alan Parker.

American Graffiti 🐾🐾🐾½ **1973 (PG).** Atmospheric, episodic look at growing up in the innocence of America before the Kennedy assassination and the Vietnam War. It all takes place on one hectic but typical night in the life of a group of recent California high school grads unsure of what the next big step in life is. So they spend their time cruising, listening to Wolfman Jack, and meeting at the drive-in. Slice of '60s life boasts a prudent script, great set design, authentic soundtrack, and consistently fine performances by the young cast. Catapulted Dreyfuss, Ford, and Somers to stardom, branded Lucas a hot directorial commodity with enough leverage to launch "Star Wars," and steered Howard and Williams towards continued age-of-innocence nirvana on "Happy Days." **112m/C VHS, DVD.** Richard Dreyfuss, Ron Howard, Cindy Williams, MacKenzie Phillips, Paul LeMat, Charles Martin Smith, Suzanne Somspano, Kathleen Quinlan, Wolfman Jack; **D:** George Lucas; **W:** George Lucas, Gloria Katz, Willard Huyck; **C:** Jan D'Alquen, Ron Eversiage. AFI '98: Top 100; Golden Globes '74: Film—Mus./

Comedy, Natl. Film Reg. '95; N.Y. Film Critics '73: Screenplay; Natl. Soc. Film Critics '73: Screenplay.

American Gun 🐾🐾🐾 **2002 (R)** Coburn, in his last performance, is Martin Tillman, an anguished father whose daughter has recently been killed during a violent crime. He decides to trace the history of the gun that was used, and along the way deals with an incident from his service in the Korean War that still haunts him. Coburn's performance is magnificent, even if the material itself is a little uneven. **89m/C VHS, DVD.** James Coburn, Barbara Bain, Virginia Madsen, Alexandra Holden; **D:** Alan Jacobs; **W:** Alan Jacobs; **C:** Phil Parmet; **M:** Anthony Marinelli.

American Gun 🐾🐾½ **2005 (R)** Three generally uninvolving stories about guns from debuting director Avelino. In Oregon, Janet (Harden) and her teen son David (Marquette) are guilt-wracked community outcasts three years after her older son participated in a high school shooting rampage. At a gang-ridden Chicago school, Principal Carter (Whitaker) expels student Jay (Escarpeta) for having a handgun, and the pic follows the teen to his convenience store job where he tries to use the (fake) weapon as intimidation against would-be thieves. In Virginia, coed Mary Ann (Cardellini) sets aside her dislike of firearms and learns to shoot after a friend is date-raped. **94m/C DVD. US** Donald Sutherland, Forest Whitaker, Marcia Gay Harden, Linda Cardellini, Tony Goldwyn, Christopher Marquette, Nikki Reed, Garcelle Beauvais, Amanda Seyfried, Melissa Leo, Arlen Escarpeta; **D:** Aric Avelino; **W:** Aric Avelino, Steven Bagatourian; **C:** Nancy Schreiber; **M:** Peter Golub.

An American Haunting 🐾🐾½ **2005 (PG-13)** Fictionalized account of Tennessee's "Bell Witch," adapted from Brent Monahan's novel. In 1818, a neighbor curses the prosperous Bell family for their greed and soon they are haunted by a poltergeist that eventually takes possession of pretty teen daughter Betsy (Hurd-Ward). Parents John (Sutherland) and Lucy (Spacek) try to fight the evil spirit. Lots of hokum, not many frights. **82m/C DVD. US** Donald Sutherland, Sissy Spacek, Rachel Hurd-Wood, James D'Arcy, Matthew Marsh, Thom Fell, Gaye Brown; **D:** Courtney Solomon; **W:** Courtney Solomon; **C:** Adrian Biddle; **M:** Caine Davidson.

American Heart 🐾🐾🐾½ **1992 (R)** Jack (Bridges) is a suspicious ex-con, newly released from prison, with few prospects and little hope. He also has a teenage son, Nick (Furlong), he barely remembers but who desperately wants to have his father back in his life. Jack is reluctantly persuaded to let Nick stay with him in his cheap hotel where Nick befriends fellow resident, Molly (Kapilsky), a teenage hooker, and other castoff street kids. Superb performances by both male leads—Furlong, both yearning and frustrated as he pursues his dream of having a family, and Bridges as the tough parolee, unwilling to open his heart. Hardboiled, poignant, and powerful. **114m/C VHS, DVD.** Jeff Bridges, Edward Furlong, Lucinda Jenney, Tracey Kapisky, Don Harvey, Margaret Welsh; **D:** Martin Bell; **W:** Peter Silverman; **C:** James R. Bagdonas; **M:** James Newton Howard. Ind. Spirit '94: Actor (Bridges).

American History X 🐾🐾🐾½ **1998 (R)** Former skinhead Derek (Norton) is released from prison after a three-year stint for killing two black teens. He returns home having renounced his neo-Nazi ideology and lifestyle, only to find his younger brother Danny (Furlong) involved in a skinhead gang. Controversial not only due to its touchy subject matter and startling violence, but also because director Kaye waged a public war with New Line to remove his name from the film, believing his vision had been compromised by the studio. Ultimately, the fuss is much ado about not much, as the film falls short of expectations. The story is predictable and rather simplistic, the script uneven and sometimes preachy, and most of the characters are wafer-thin. Only Norton's mesmerizing, forceful performance and a commendable job by Furlong as the impressionable younger brother lend credibility. **118m/C VHS, DVD.** Edward Norton, Edward Fur-

long, Fairuza Balk, Beverly D'Angelo, Avery Brooks, Stacy Keach, Jennifer Lien, Elliott Gould, Guy Torry, Giuseppe Andrews, Jordan Marder, Anne Lambton, Paul LeMat; **D:** Tony Kaye; **W:** David McKenna; **C:** Tony Kaye; **M:** Anne Dudley.

An American in Paris 🐾🐾🐾🐾 **1951** Lavish, imaginative musical features a sweeping score, and knockout choreography by Kelly. Ex-G.I. Kelly stays on in Paris after the war to study painting, supported in his efforts by rich American Foch, who hopes to acquire a little extra attention. But Kelly loves the lovely Caron, unfortunately engaged to an older gent. Highlight is an astonishing 17-minute ballet which holds the record for longest movie dance number—and one of the most expensive, pegged at over half a million for a month of filming. For his efforts, the dance king won a special Oscar citation. While it sure looks like Paris, most of it was filmed in MGM studios. ♫'S Wonderful; I Got Rhythm; Embraceable You; Love Is Here To Stay; Tra-La-La; I'll Build a Stairway to Paradise; Nice Work If You Can Get It; By Strauss; Concerto in F (3rd Movement). **113m/C VHS, DVD.** Gene Kelly, Leslie Caron, Oscar Levant, Nina Foch, Georges Guetary; **D:** Vincente Minnelli; **W:** Alan Jay Lerner; **C:** John Alton; **M:** Ira Gershwin. Oscars '51: Art Dir./Set Dec., Color, Color Cinematog., Costume Dec. (C), Picture, Story & Screenplay, Scoring/Musical; AFI '98: Top 100; Golden Globes '52: Film—Mus./Comedy, Natl. Film Reg. '93.

American Justice 🐾🐾 *Jackals* **1986 (R)** Two cops, one of whom looks suspiciously like a Simon of "Simon and Simon," fight political corruption and white slavery near the Mexican border. The chief white slaver bears a full resemblance to the other Simon. Sufficient action but less than original. **96m/C VHS, DVD.** Jameson Parker, Gerald McRaney, Wilford Brimley, Jack Lucarelli; **D:** Gary Grillo.

American Kickboxer 1 🐾🐾½ **1991 (R)** Barrett stars as B.J. Quinn, a down on his luck kickboxing champion who spends much of his time onscreen aimlessly wandering (apparently searching for the meaning of his life). Lackluster script and performances will make this one trying—even for kickboxing fans. Barrett is Chuck Norris' former workout partner, but there isn't enough action often enough for him to show of its formidable skills. **93m/C VHS.** John Barrett, Keith Vitali, Brad Morris, Terry Norton, Ted Leplat; **D:** Frans Nel; **W:** Emil Kolbe; **M:** Frank Becker.

American Kickboxer 2: To the Death 🐾🐾½ **1993 (R)** Lillian must find a way to get her cop ex-husband and her kickboxer ex-lover to work together to save her kidnapped daughter's life. **91m/C VHS, DVD.** Dale "Apollo" Cook, Evan Lurie, Kathy Shower, Ted Markland; **D:** Jeno Hodi.

American Madness 🐾🐾½ **1932** Benevolent banker Dickson (Huston) has been making loans without sufficient collateral. The bank's board of directors give him a warning and then a robbery causes a run on the bank. The directors are ready to oust Dickson when the small businessman he's helped rally to his defense. Tedious romantic subplot has Dickson's unhappy wife (Johnson) accusing him of neglect and dallying with unscrupulous bank clerk Cluett (Gordon). **75m/B VHS, DVD.** Walter Huston, Pat O'Brien, Kay Johnson, Gavin Gordon, Constance Cummings, Robert Ellis, Walter Walker, Arthur Hoyt; **D:** Frank Capra; **W:** Robert Riskin; **C:** Joseph Walker.

American Matchmaker 🐾🐾½ *Amerikaner Shadkin* **1940** Nat Silver decides to go into the matchmaking business, after his own marriages fail miserably, hoping to experience happiness vicariously. However, he soon begins to realize that one of his clients is a better match for him than the man he chose for her. In Yiddish with English subtitles. **87m/B VHS, DVD.** Leo Fuchs, Judith Abarbanel, Rosetta Bialis, Yudel Dubinsky, Abe Lax; **D:** Edgar G. Ulmer; **W:** S. (Shirley Ulmer) Castle; **C:** Edgar G. Ulmer.

American Me 🐾🐾🐾 **1992 (R)** Violent and brutal depiction of more than 30 years of gang wars and drugs in East Los Angeles. Santana founded a street gang as a teenager, but has spent the last 18 years in prison, where he's the boss of the so-called Mexican Mafia, which oversees the drugs, scams, murders, and violence that are an everyday fact of prison life. Released from Folsom, Santana goes back to his old neighborhood and attempts to distance himself from his old life but finds his gang ties are stronger than any other alliance. Unsparing and desolate directorial debut from Olmos. **119m/C VHS, DVD, HD DVD.** Edward James Olmos, William Forsythe, Pepe Serna, Danny De La Paz, Evelina Fernandez, Sal Lopez, Daniel Villarreal, Cary-Hiroyuki Tagawa; **D:** Edward James Olmos; **W:** Floyd Mutrux, Desmond Nakano; **C:** Reynaldo Villalobos; **M:** Dennis Lambert.

American Movie 🐾🐾🐾 **1999 (R)** Would-be filmmaker Mark Borchardt's American Dream is to make his own independent film in his home of Menomonee Falls, Wisconsin. He doesn't have the money (or a particularly workable idea) but he does have lots of self-confidence and enthusiasm, as well as his mom, his 82-year-old Uncle Bill, and a cast of eccentrics. Smith's unlimited access shows Borchardt's almost limitless failures and obstacles, making the whole affair seem like a "Spinal Tap"-esque spoof, even though the people are painfully, sometimes hilariously real. **104m/C VHS, DVD.** Mike Schank, Mark Borchardt; **D:** Chris Smith; **C:** Chris Smith; **M:** Mike Schank.

American Nightmare 🐾½ **1981** Young man searches for his missing sister against a background of pornography, drug peddling, and prostitution in the slums of a city. The usual titillating squalid urban drama. **85m/C VHS.** Lawrence S. Day, Lora Staley, Lenore Zann, Michael Ironside, Alexandra Paul; **D:** Don McBrearty.

American Nightmare 🐾½ **2000 (R)** To commemorate the killings of four college students on Halloween the year before, pirate radio show "American Nightmare" is broadcasting all night. The program's host, Caligari (Ryan), has listeners calling in with their worst fears and seven friends take turns calling. Too bad, the killer is also listening and decides to make their nightmares come true. **91m/C VHS, DVD.** Debbie Rochon, Brandy Little, Johnny Sneed, Christopher Ryan, Brinke Stevens; **D:** Jon Keeyes; **W:** Jon Keeyes; **C:** Brad Walker; **M:** Peter Gannan, David Rosenblad.

American Ninja 🐾🐾 *American Warrior* **1985 (R)** American Dudikoff is G.I. Joe, a martial-arts expert stationed in the Philippines who alienates most everyone around him (he's a rebel). Deadly blackbelt war begins with Joe confronting the army who is selling stolen weapons to the South American black market. Aided by one faithful pal, Joe uses his head-kicking martial arts skills to stop hundreds of ninja combatants working for the corrupt arms dealer. In his spare time he romances the base chief's daughter. Efficient rib-crunching chop-socky action wrapped in no-brainer plot and performed by nonactors. Cannon epic mercilessly followed by at least three sequels. **96m/C VHS, DVD.** Michael Dudikoff, Guich Koock, Judie Aronson, Steve James; **D:** Sam Firstenberg; **W:** Gideon Amir; **C:** Hanania Baer; **M:** Michael Linn.

American Ninja 2: The Confrontation 🐾🐾½ **1987 (R)** Soldiers Dudikoff and James are back again using their martial arts skills (in lieu of any acting) to take on a Caribbean drug-lord. Apparently he has been kidnapping Marines and taking them to his island, where he genetically alters them to become fanatical ninja assassins eager to do his dirty work. The script hardly gets in the way of the rib-crunching action, but is an improvement upon Ninja Number One. **90m/C VHS.** Michael Dudikoff, Steve James, Larry Poindexter, Gary Conway; **D:** Sam Firstenberg; **W:** Gary Conway, James Booth.

American Ninja 3: Blood Hunt *woof!* 1989 (R) Second sequel in the American Ninja series. Bradley replaces Dudikoff as the martial arts good guy fighting the martial arts bad guys on a Caribbean island. He's pursued by ex-evangelist Marjoe, who wants to inject him with a nasty virus before unloading the germs to bad buys before his death. For the best of this series, see ninjitsu; more uninspired martial arts. **90m/C VHS, DVD.** *D:* David Bradley, Steve James, Marjoe Gortner, Michele Chan, Calvin Jung; *D:* Cedric Sundstrom; *W:* Paul DeMielche, Gary Conway; *M:* George S. Clinton.

American Ninja 4: The Annihilation *woof!* 1991 (R) Dudikoff returns after noticeable absence in last sequel. He should have stayed away from #4—it's a rehash of tired ideas that never gets off the ground. Forget this and see "American Ninja 2: The Confrontation," the best of this series. **95m/C VHS, DVD.** Michael Dudikoff, David Bradley, James Booth, Dwayne Alexandre, Robin Stille, Ken Gampu; *D:* Cedric Sundstrom; *W:* Steve James. Nicolas Tenbroek.

American Outlaws ✔ 2001 (PG-13) Look kids, it's N'Sync as the James Gang! Remember "Young Guns" (1988)? By the end of this, you'll be begging for Emilio Estevez's constant mugging and Kiefer Sutherland's ridiculous brooding. Jesse (Farrell) and Frank James (Macht), along with cousins Cole (Caan), Bob (McCormack) and Jim Younger (Smith) return from the Civil War to find Ma (Bates) and the family farm threatened by the railroad. So they commence to robbin' banks to help out the poor folk who been done wrong. Along the way Jesse courts purty young filly Zee (Larter). People have been writing the obituary of the Western for a few years now, but "Outlaws" may be the bullet in the genre's back. **95m/C VHS, DVD, UMD.** Colin Farrell, Gabriel Macht, Scott Caan, Gregory Edward Smith, Will McCormack, Timothy Dalton, Kathy Bates, Nathaniel Arcand, Ali Larter, Ronny Cox, Harris Yulin, Terry O'Quinn, Ty O'Neal, Joe Stevens; *D:* Les Mayfield; *W:* Roderick Taylor; *C:* Russell Boyd; *M:* Trevor Rabin.

American Pie ✔✔✔ East Great Falls High 1999 (R) And you thought you loved dessert Four high school seniors led by pastry molesting Jim (Biggs) vow to lose their virginity before the Prom. Unfortunately for them, the girls that they're chasing aren't your usual teenage sex comedy tarts. These smart little cookies make sure that the boys' quest is chock full of humiliation. The sensitivity to the female point-of-view is balanced by a heapin' helpin' of crude and disgusting humor for the guys. An absolute must-see for baked goods and the men who love them. **95m/C VHS, DVD, UMD.** Jason Biggs, Thomas Ian Nicholas, Chris Owen, Chris Klein, Natasha Lyonne, Tara Reid, Mena Suvari, Alyson Hannigan, Shannon Elizabeth, Eugene Levy, Seann William Scott, Jennifer Coolidge, Eddie Kaye Thomas, Lawrence Pressman; *D:* Chris Weitz, Paul Weitz; *W:* Adam Herz; *C:* Richard Crudo; *M:* David Lawrence.

American Pie 2 ✔✔½ 2001 (R) No pie is abused in this movie, although everyone (including exec producers Chris and Paul Weitz) is back for a second helping. The story picks up a year later while everyone is on summer vacation from college and sharing a beach house. Jim (Biggs) is nervously anticipating a visit from Nadia, while getting sex tips from band camp geek Michelle (Hannigan). Entertaining sequel shares the original's appealing and effective combination of gross-out situations and sweet silliness, and while it's not quite as good, it doesn't miss by much. **105m/C VHS, DVD, UMD. US** Jason Biggs, Shannon Elizabeth, Alyson Hannigan, Chris Klein, Natasha Lyonne, Thomas Ian Nicholas, Tara Reid, Chris Owen, Seann William Scott, Mena Suvari, Eddie Kaye Thomas, Eugene Levy, Jennifer Coolidge, Christopher Penn, Eli Marienthal, Casey Affleck, Denise Faye, Molly Cheek; *D:* James B. Rogers; *W:* Adam Herz; *C:* Mark Irwin; *M:* David Lawrence.

American Pie Presents Band Camp ✔ Band Camp 2005 Stiffie's equally obnoxious and horny younger brother Matt (Hilgenbrink) is sent to summer band camp as punishment for a prank gone wrong. He decides to liven up his stay by shooting "girls gone wild"-type videos of the band chicks, only to have a change of heart when he hooks up with old friend Elyse (Kebbel). Levy's the only original cast member to sheepishly show up in this drivel. **94m/C DVD.** Tad Hilgenbrink, Arielle Kebbel, Crystle Lighting, Eugene Levy, Jason Earles; *D:* Steve Rash; *W:* Brad Riddell; *C:* Victor Kemper; *M:* Robert Folk. **VIDEO**

American Pie Presents: Beta House ✔ Beta House 2007 (R) And the franchise just gets lamer and grosser. Dwight Stifler is the head of the infamous Beta frat, just begging by his cousin Erik and his buds. But their house superiority is challenged by newcomer Geek House and power-hungry nerd Edgar. **89m/C DVD.** John White, Steven Talley, Meghan Heffern, Nic Nac, Tyrone Savage, Sarah Power, Eugene Levy, Christopher McDonald; *D:* Andrew Waller; *W:* Erik Lindsay; *M:* Jeff Cardoni. **VIDEO**

American Pie Presents: The Naked Mile ✔✔ American Pie 5: The Naked Mile 2306 (R) Raunchy and surprisingly funny sex comedy. Erik Stifler (White) is a high school virgin since sweet girlfriend Tracy (Schram) won't put out. Erik and his buddies are visiting his cousin Dwight (Talley) at college for the weekend in order to run in the annual naked mile. Feeling guilty, Tracy gives him a free pass to do whatever he wants—and then worries that what Erik wants is sex with some other girl. Humiliation and a wide variety of bodily fluids follow. Also available unrated. **97m/C DVD.** John White, Steven Talley, Ross Thomas, Christopher McDonald, Jessy Schram, Jake Siegel, Eugene Levy, Candace Kroslak; *D:* Joe Nussbaum; *W:* Erik Lindsay; *C:* Eric Haase; *M:* Jeff Cardoni. **VIDEO**

American Pluck ✔✔ 1925 Before he can inherit anything, a playboy millionaire's son must go out into the world and prove he can make his own way. He meets a beautiful princess, who is pursued by a villainous count. Walsh, as the dashing hero, was the younger brother of director Raoul. Silent with original organ music. **91m/B VHS.** George Walsh, Wanda Hawley, Frank Leigh, Sidney De Grey; *D:* Richard Stanton.

American Pop ✔✔ 1981 (R) Animated story of four generations of men told in music. Immigrant Zalmie starts off in vaudeville and winds up involved in the mob, his pianist son Benny gets killed in WWII. Benny's son Tony winds up in the early psychedelic rock scene in Haight-Asbury, and Tony's son Little Pete becomes a rock idol. ♪A Hard Rain's A-Gonna Fall; Don't Think Twice It's All Right; People Are Strange; Purple Haze; Hell is for Children; Free Bird; I'm Waiting for the Man; Night Moves; You Send Me. **95m/C VHS, DVD.** *D:* Ralph Bakshi; *W:* Ron Thomson, Marya Small, Lisa Jane Persky, Roz Kelly, Richard Singer, Jeffrey Lippa.

The American President ✔✔✔ 1995 (PG-13) Widower president Andrew Shepherd (Douglas) decides it's time to get back into the dating game. But just what woman wants is in for romance in the public eye? Well, it turns out to be feisty environmental lobbyist Sydney Wade (the ever-charming Bening). But the Prez also has a run up with nasty opponent Bob Rumson (Dreyfuss), who's using the courtship as political fodder, approval ratings, and a nosy press. Glossy fairytale material expertly handled by both cast and director. **114m/C VHS, DVD.** Michael Douglas, Annette Bening, Martin Sheen, Michael J. Fox, David Paymer, Samantha Mathis, John Mahoney, Anna Deavere Smith, Nina Siemaszko, Wendie Malick, Shawna Waldron, Richard Dreyfuss, Gabe Jarret, Anne Haney, Gail Strickland, Joshua Malina, Ron Canada, Jennifer Crystal Foley, Taylor Nichols; *D:* Rob Reiner; *W:* Aaron Sorkin; *C:* John Seale; *M:* Marc Shaiman.

American Psycho ✔✔✔ 1999 (R) Trimmed-down and (slightly) cleaned-up version of Bret Easton Ellis's widely hated 1991 novel has Bale as '80s hotshot Wall Street exec and apparent serial-killer Patrick Bateman is the poster child for Reagan-era excess and preference for style over substance a theme with which you over the head. Like the decade it portrays, "Psycho" is far from subtle, and the characters barely register as two-dimensional, let alone three. They got the look right, but then, that's the point, isn't it? The production drew protests in Toronto, where some scenes were shot, and Leo DiCaprio was rumored to be in line to play the lead for a time. **103m/C VHS, DVD, Blu-ray Disc, UMD.** Christian Bale, Willem Dafoe, Jared Leto, Reese Witherspoon, Samantha Mathis, Chloe Sevigny, Justin Theroux, Joshua Lucas, Guinevere Turner, Matt Ross, William Sage, Cara Seymour; *D:* Mary Harron; *W:* Mary Harron, Guinevere Turner; *C:* Andrzej Sekula; *M:* John Cale.

American Psycho 2: All American Girl ✔✔ 2002 (R) Racehelle Newman (Kunis) is the only victim who managed to escape from serial killer Patrick Bateman. But her ordeal left her obsessed with such killers and when she learns that college prof Robert Strickland (Shatner) was an FBI profiler specializing in the subject, Rachelle is determined to become his teaching assistant. Even if it means killing the competition. **88m/C VHS, DVD.** Mila Kunis, William Shatner, Geraint Wyn Davies, Lindy Booth, Robin Dunne; *D:* Morgan J. Freeman; *W:* Karen Craig, Alex Sanger; *C:* Vania Cernjul; *M:* Norman Orenstein. **VIDEO**

An American Rhapsody ✔✔✔ 2001 (PG-13) A mother/daughter conflict steeped in history and based on the experiences of writer/director Gardos. Margit (Kinski) and her family flee Hungary currently in the communist takeover of the 1950s but she is forced to leave her infant daughter behind. While the family settles in L.A., Suzanne is being raised in the country by adoptive parents and knows nothing of her origins. She gets a rude awakening at the age of 6 when her grandmother Helen (Banfalvy) makes arrangements to reunite Suzy with her unknown "real" family. The child grows into a sullen teenager (Johansson) who longs to return to Budapest. Her father finally agrees to a solo trip and Suzanne learns just what her family suffered and where she truly belongs. **106m/C VHS, DVD, US HU.** Nastassja Kinski, Scarlett Johansson, Tony Goldwyn, Kelly Endresz-Banlaki, Agnes Banfalvy, Zsuzsi Csrikoczi, Balazs Galko, Zoltan Seress, Mae Whitman, Lisa Jane Persky, Emmy Rossum; *D:* Eva Gardos; *W:* Eva Gardos; *C:* Elemer Ragalyi; *M:* Cliff Eidelman.

American Roulette ✔ 1988 (R) Garcia is the exiled president of a Latin American country living in London in this thin political thriller. A plot riddled with weaknesses and poor direction make this potentially interesting film dull and lifeless. **102m/C VHS, GB AU Andy Garcia, Kitty Aldridge, Robert Stephens, Al Matthews, Susannah York; *D:* Maurice Hatton; *M:* Michael Gibbs.

American Samurai ✔½ 1992 (R) Drew is the adopted son of a Japanese samurai, who gives him the family's sacred sword This gesture angers his stepbrother who gets involved with Japanese gangsters and illegal live-blade fighting, and who also vows revenge on this American. Lots of sword play to go with the chop-socky action. **89m/C VHS, DVD.** David Bradley, Mark Dacascos, John Fujioka, Valarie Trapp; *D:* Sam Firstenberg; *W:* John Corcoran.

The American Scream ✔½ 1987 An innocent family vacationing in the mountains stumbles on to a satanic cult. And that can really ruin a vacation. **85m/C VHS.** Jennifer Darling, Pons Marr, Blaxkie Dammett, Kimberly Kramer, Jean Sapienza, Kevin Kaye, Matt Borlenghi, James Cooper; *D:* Mitchell Linden.

American Shaolin: King of the Kickboxers 2 ✔½ 1992 (PG-13) When Drew gets his butt kicked in a karate tournament he decides to head to China and learn some fight-winning moves from a group of warrior monks. **103m/C VHS.** Reese Madigan, Trent Bushy, Daniel Dae Kim, Billy Chang, Cliff Lenderman, Zhang Sh Yen, Kim Chan, Alice Zhang Hung; *D:* Lucas Lowe.

American Soldiers *woof!* 2005 (R) Incompetent mess mangles a serious subject and is only worth a groan for its ineptitude. In April 2004, an army platoon is ambushed by insurgents in Iraq and the surviving soldiers must make their way back to base through enemy territory. Filmed in Hamilton, Ontario, which cannot in any way pass for Iraq. **103m/C DVD, CA** Curtis Morgan, Zan Calabretta, Jordan Brown, Curtis Morgan; *D:* Sidney J. Furie; *W:* Greg Mellott. **VIDEO**

An American Story ✔✔½ 1992 (PG) Earnest but predictable story based on an actual incident. Six WWII vets return to their small Texas town as heroes. But when they find a corrupt mayor and a brutal sheriff running things they decide to campaign to unseat the local politicos. In spite of some dire warnings. Meade Blount (G.W. Bailey, John M. Jackson; *D:* John Gray; *W:* John Gray; *C:* Johnny E. Jensen. **TV**

American Strays ✔✔½ 1996 (R) Episodic black comedy about various oddballs (most of them violent) who cross paths (usually in Kane's roadside diner) in an isolated desert town. There's a masochist who wants help committing suicide, an unemployed family man on the verge of a breakdown, a serial killer, and more—mostly strange. **97m/C VHS, DVD.** Jack Kehler, Eric Roberts, John Savage, Vonte Sweet, Sam Jones, Bron James, Russo, Luke Perry, Joe (Johnny) Viterelli, James Toni Kalem, Melora Walters; *D:* Michael Covert; *W:* Michael Covert; *C:* Sead Muhtarevic; *M:* Graham.

American Streetfighter ✔✔ 1992 Martial arts expert Jake Tanner gets involved with an illegal streetfighting ring to rescue his brother, Randy, who's the target of a drug courier. But what happens

The American Soldier ✔✔½ Der Amerikanische Soldat 1970 Fassbinder's homage to the American gangster film tells the story of Ricky, a charismatic hit man. Ricky always wears a gun in a shoulder holster, sports a fedora and a white double-breasted suit, and drinks Scotch straight from the bottle. He also carries out his assigned murders with German efficiency and no emotion. In German with English subtitles. **80m/C VHS, DVD. GE** Rainer Werner Fassbinder, Karl Scheydt, Elga Sorbas, Jan George, Ingrid Caven, Ulli Lommel, Kurt Raab; *D:* Rainer Werner Fassbinder; *C:* Dietrich Lohmann; *M:* Peer Raben.

American Splendor ✔✔✔ ½ 2003 (R) Giamatti is brilliant as Harvey Pekar, a life-long file clerk in Cleveland who authored the R. Crumb-illustrated autobiographical graphic novels of the film's title. The unlikely courtship of misfits Pekar and his third wife Joyce Brabner (Davis) is comically portrayed as the two kindred souls mysteriously come together. Their unlikely romance mirrors the unlikelihood that a comic filled with the pessimism, cynicism, and wry comic observations of Pekar's admitted hum-drum life would somehow translate hum-drum to the big screen. But it does. Documentarian directors Berman and Pulcini weave fiction with frequent appearances and footage from Pekar's frequent appearances on David Letterman's show. Also makes use of illustrated sections as well onto the big screen, and the real Pekar narrates and comic segments and footage from Pekar's frequent appearances on David Letterman's show. **101m/C VHS, DVD. US** Paul Giamatti, Hope Davis, Harvey Pekar, Joyce Brabner, Earl Billings, James Urbaniak, Judah Friedlander, Donal Logue, Molly Shannon, James McCaffrey, Shari Springer Berman, Robert Pulcini; *D:* Shari Springer Berman, Robert Pulcini; *W:* Shari Springer Berman, Robert Pulcini; *C:* Terry Stacey; *M:* Mark Suozzo. L.A. Film Critics '03: Actress (Davis); Natl. Soc. Film Critics '03: Film, Screenplay; Writers Guild '03: Adapt. Screenplay.

when his next opponent is his sibling? **80m/C VHS, DVD.** Gary Daniels, Ian Jacklin, Tracy Dali; **D:** Steve Austin.

American Streetfighter 2: The Full Impact ✓✓½ 1997 Ex-cop becomes a bounty hunter tracking a serial killer who likes to kill his victims with his bare hands. **90m/C VHS, DVD.** Gary Daniels, Graciela Casillas; **D:** Marc Messenger. **VIDEO**

An American Summer ✓✓ 1990 A Chicago kid spends a summer with his aunt in beach-rich Los Angeles in this coming-of-age tale filled with '90s teen idols. **100m/C VHS, DVD.** Brian (Austin) Green, Joanna Kerns, Michael Landes, Tony Crane, Brian Krause, Wayne Pere, Amber Susa; **D:** James Slocum; **W:** James Slocum; **C:** Bruce Dorfman; **M:** Roger Neill.

An American Tail ✓✓½ 1986 (G) While emigrating to New York in the 1880s, a young Russian mouse (Fievel) is separated from his family. He matures as he learns to live on the Big Apple's dirty boulevards. The bad guys are of course cats. Excellent animation and a high-minded (though sentimental and stereotypical) plot keep it interesting for adults. Produced by Spielberg and the first big hit for the Bluth factory, a collection of expatriate Disney artists. Knowing better than to let a money-making mouse tale languish, Bluth followed with "An American Tale: Fievel Goes West." **81m/C VHS, DVD.** **D:** Don Bluth; **M:** James Horner; **V:** Dom DeLuise, Madeline Kahn, Phillip Glasser, Christopher Plummer, Nehemiah Persoff, Will Ryan, John Finnegan, Cathianne Blore.

An American Tail: Fievel Goes West ✓✓ 1991 (G) Fievel and the Mousekewitz family continue their pursuit of the American dream by heading West, where the intrepid mouse seeks to become a famous lawman while his sister looks to make it big as a dance hall singer. The score is performed by the London Symphony Orchestra. Unfortunately released at the same time as "Beauty and the Beast," "Fievel Goes West" suffers from comparison. Worthwhile viewing for the whole family, but it won't ever reach the heights of "B&B." The laser edition is letterboxed and features chapter stops. **75m/C VHS, DVD.** **D:** Phil Nibbelink, Simon Wells; **W:** Flint Dille; **M:** James Horner; **V:** John Cleese, Dom DeLuise, Phillip Glasser, Amy Irving, Jon Lovitz, Catherine Cavadini, Nehemiah Persoff, Erica Yohn, James Stewart.

American Tickler ✓½ 1976 (R) A thigh-slappin' (or is it head-whacking?) series of satirical pastiches in the grand style of "Kentucky Fried Movie," only more sophomoric. A tasteless collection of yearning to be funny sketches about American institutions. **77m/C VHS.** Mitch Gaylord, Joan Sumner, Marlow Ferguson, Jeff Allin, Joe Piscopo; **D:** Chuck Vincent.

American Tiger ✓✓ 2000 *American Rickshaw* 1989 (R) The collegiate hero of "American Tiger" is, like so many college students, framed for murder, and he applies himself to clearing his sullied name. Somewhere during this process, he finds himself in the middle of a battle between good and evil on a football field. About what you'd expect from a supernatural kung-fu teen-action drama. **93m/C VHS, DVD.** Donald Pleasence, Daniel Greene, Victoria Prouty; **D:** Sergio Martino.

American Tragedy ✓✓½ 2000 (PG-13) Remember the O.J. Simpson trial? Well, if you don't, this cable drama is here to remind you as it explores the egos and infighting of Simpson's four defense lawyers: Johnny Cochran (Rhames), Bob Shapiro (Silver), F. Lee Bailey (Plummer), and Barry Scheck (Kirby). Based on the book by Schiller, who also directed. **170m/C VHS, DVD.** Ving Rhames, Ron Silver, Christopher Plummer, Bruno Kirby, Nicholas Pryor, Robert LaPone, Ruben Santiago-Hudson, Richard Cox, Clyde Kusatsu, Jeff Kober; **C:** Lawrence Schiller; **W:** Norman Mailer; **C:** Bruce Surtees; **M:** Bill Conti. **CABLE**

American Vampire ✓✓½ 1997 (R) Teenager Frankie (Lussauer) has been left alone while his parents are on vacation. One night on the beach, he and his friend Bogie (Hitt) meet Moondoggie (Venokur), who promises to help them party the summer away. He soon reappears with two babes (Electra and Xavier) who appear to be undead. Frankie must turn to The Big Kahuna (West) to stop the vampires. Yes, the plot strictly follows the formula, but the effects are not bad for a low-budget production; the photography is better than it needs to be; and the humor is intentional. **99m/C VHS, DVD.** Trevor Lissauer, Danny Hitt, Johnny Venokur, Carmen Electra, Debora Xavier, Adam West, Sydney Lassick; **D:** Luis Esteban; **W:** Rollin Jarrett; **C:** Jurgen Baum, Goran Pavicevic. **VIDEO**

American Virgin ✓✓ *Live Virgin* 1998 (R) Ronny Bartoloti (Loggia) is a successful Hollywood adult film director who has upset his virginal 18-year-old daughter, Katrina (Suvari), with his double-standard attitudes. So she decides to get even by sharing her first sexual experience with millions—by going live on camera on closed-circuit—with the help of Ronny's rival Joey Quinn (Hoskins). But can daddy get his determined little darling to change her mind? Exploitative would-be satire falls flat. **87m/C VHS, DVD.** Mena Suvari, Robert Loggia, Bob Hoskins, Gabriel Mann, Sally Kellerman, Bobbie Phillips, Lamont Johnson, Rick Peters, O-lan Jones, Alexandra Wentworth; **D:** Jean Pierre Marois; **W:** Jean Pierre Marois, Ira Israel; **C:** Eagle Egilsson.

American Wedding ✓✓½ 2003 *American Pie 3* (R) In the finale of the epic trilogy Annakin and Amidala, no, wait. Frodo and Gollum...no, Neo and Trinity...that's not it either. Jim and Michelle are getting married, with the dubious help of most of the gang. Kevin and Finch are still around, but it's Stifler who has the biggest impact, throwing the bachelor party, battling Finch for the affections of Michelle's sister Cadence (Jones), and almost putting the kibosh on the whole wedding. Like the other two, it's pretty gross in parts, uproarious in others, but still has its sweet, charming moments. Levy and Willard make the most of their scenes as the father of the groom and bride, respectively. **96m/C VHS, DVD, UMD.** *US* Jason Biggs, Alyson Hannigan, Seann William Scott, Eddie Kaye Thomas, January Jones, Eugene Levy, Thomas Ian Nicholas, Fred Willard, Molly Cheek, Eric Allen Kramer, Deborah Rush, Jennifer Coolidge, Angela Paton, Lawrence Pressman, Amanda Swisten, Nikki Schieler Ziering; **D:** Jesse Dylan; **W:** Adam Herz; **C:** Lloyd Ahern II; **M:** Christophe Beck.

An American Werewolf in London ✓✓✓ 1981 (R) Strange, darkly humorous version of the classic man-into-wolf horror tale became a cult hit, but never clicked with most American critics. Two American college students, David (Naughton) and Jack (Dunne), are backpacking through England when they're viciously attacked by a werewolf one foggy night. Jack is killed, but keeps appearing (in progressively decomposed form) before the seriously wounded David, warning him of impending werewolfdom when the moon is full; Jack advises suicide. Seat-jumping horror and gore, highlighted by intensive metamorphosis sequences orchestrated by Rick Baker, are offset by wry humor, though the shifts in tone don't always work. Great moon songs permeate the soundtrack, including CCR's "Bad Moon Rising" and Van Morrison's "Moondance." Followed by "An American Werewolf in Paris" (1997). **97m/C VHS, DVD, HD DVD.** *GB* David Naughton, Griffin Dunne, Jenny Agutter, Frank Oz, Brian Glover, Lila Kaye, David Schofield, John Woodvine, Don McKillop, Paul Kember, Colin Fernandes, Rik Mayall, Paddy Ryan; **D:** John Landis; **W:** John Landis; **C:** Robert Paynter; **M:** Elmer Bernstein. Oscars '81: Makeup.

An American Werewolf in Paris ✓✓½ 1997 (R) More of a remake than a sequel, horror-comedy fails to live up to the wit and quirkiness of the original. Andy (Scott) is on a daredevil tour of Europe along with buddies Brad (Vieluf) and Chris (Buckman). As he attempts to bungee jump off the Eiffel Tower, he spots a French femme attempting to plunge jump nearby. He saves her and immediately falls in love with her. The girl, Serafine (Delpy) warns him to stay away, but he keeps sniffing around. They tail her to a creepy house she shares with a guy named Claude (Cosso), where Andy secures a date and his friends are invited to a dinner party. Claude, however, is top dog in a pack of racist werewolves, and Andy's pals end up as the main course. Bitten himself, Andy learns that he's now a werewolf. Brad and the other victims pop up now and again to remind Andy that they're doomed to walk the earth until the werewolves that killed them are destroyed. Special effects have advanced a long way since the original and it shows, although the computer generated wolves are difficult to tell apart. **100m/C VHS, DVD.** Anthony Waller, Julie Delpy, Tom Everett Scott, Julie Bowen, Pierre Cosso, Thierry Lhermitte, Vince Vieluf, Phil Buckman, Tom Novembre, Isabelle Constantini; **D:** Anthony Waller; **W:** Anthony Waller, Tim Burns, Tom Stern; **C:** Egon Werdin; **M:** Wilbert Hirsch.

American Women ✓✓ *The Closer You Get* 2000 (PG-13) Poor schlub County Donegal lads, weary of their lack of female companionship, send an ad to the Miami Herald, looking for young, nubile American women to come over and "see what happens." Hoping to see the American lasses in time for the social event of the season, the St. Martha's Day dance, they're disappointed when the day arrives but the girls don't. To make matters worse, the local ladies have brought in some Spanish fishermen to play music at the dance. Old fashioned ethnic comedy tries to cash in on the successes of "The Full Monty" and "Waking Ned Devine," but contains a wee bit too many Irish cliches, and the charm is squeezed out by the patronizing view of what is supposed to be modern-day Ireland. **90m/C VHS, DVD.** *IR GB* Ian Hart, Sean McGinley, Niamh Cusack, Ruth McCabe, Ewan Stewart, Maureen O'Brien, Pat Laffan, Britta Smith, Pat Shortt, Cathleen Bradley, Sean McDonagh, Risteard Cooper; **D:** Aileen Ritchie; **W:** William Ivory; **C:** Robert Alazraki; **M:** Rachel Portman.

American Yakuza ✓✓ 1994 (R) FBI agent Nick Davis (Mortensen) is sent to L.A. to infiltrate the American arm of the Yakuza, Japan's dangerous criminal underworld. He rises through the ranks and is adopted into the powerful Tendo family. Now Davis finds himself caught between the FBI, the Yakuza, and the vengeful American mafia. **95m/C VHS, DVD.** Viggo Mortensen, Michael Nouri, Ryo Ishibashi, Franklin Ajaye; **D:** Frank Cappello; **W:** Max Strom, John Allen Nelson; **C:** Richard Clabaugh; **M:** David Williams.

Americana ✓✓½ 1981 (PG) A troubled Vietnam vet tries to restore himself by rebuilding a merry-go-round in a small midwestern town, while dealing with opposition from the local residents. Offbeat, often effective post-Nam editorial that was produced and directed in 1973 by Carradine and then shelved. Hershey and Carradine were a couple back then. **90m/C VHS, DVD.** David Carradine, Barbara Hershey, Michael Greene, John Drew (Blythe) Barrymore Jr.; **D:** David Carradine; **W:** Richard Carr.

The Americanization of Emily ✓✓½ 1964 American naval officer (Garner) with no appetite for war discovers to his horror that he may be slated to become the first casualty of the Normandy invasion as part of a military PR effort in this black comedy-romance. Meanwhile, he spreads the charisma in an effort to woo and uplift Emily (Andrews), a depressed English woman who has suffered the loss of her husband, father, and brother during the war. A cynical, often funny look at military maneuvers and cultural drift that was adapted by Paddy Chayefsky from William Bradford Huie's novel. Also available colorized. **117m/B VHS, DVD.** James Garner, Julie Andrews, Melvyn Douglas, James Coburn, Joyce Grenfell, Keenan Wynn, Edward Binns, Liz Fraser, William Windom; **D:** Arthur Hiller; **W:** Paddy Chayefsky.

The Americano ✓✓½ 1917 Ever-suave Fairbanks frees a South American politician locked in a dungeon, returns him to political success, and captures the heart of his beautiful daughter. Based on Eugene P. Lyle Jr.'s "Blaze Derringer." **58m/B VHS.** Douglas Fairbanks Sr., Alma Rubens, Spottiswoode Aitken, Lillian Langdon, Carl Stockdale, Tom Wilson; **D:** John Emerson.

Americano ✓✓ 1955 A cowboy travelling to Brazil with a shipment of Brahma bulls discovers the rancher he's delivering them to has been murdered. An odd amalgam of western cliches and a South American setting. **85m/C VHS.** Glenn Ford, Frank Lovejoy, Abbe Lane, Cesar Romero; **D:** William Castle.

Americano ✓✓ 2005 (R) Recent college grad Chris (Jackson) and his friends Ryan (Sharp) and Michelle (Ruthanna Hopper) have been backpacking through Europe and wind up at the end of their trip in Pamplona, Spain, for the annual running of the bulls. Chris meets beautiful Adela (Varela), who takes pity on him and lets Chris stay at her house after his backpack is stolen. His feelings quickly turn romantic. Dennis Hopper plays an ex-pat bar owner proffering advice when Chris wonders if he's really ready to return home. **95m/C DVD.** Joshua Jackson, Leonor Varela, Dennis Hopper, Timm Sharp, Ruthanna Hopper; **D:** Kevin Noland; **W:** Kevin Noland; **C:** Robert Christopher Webb; **M:** Peter Golub.

America's Deadliest Home Video ✓✓ 1991 Camp spoof about America's obsession with videotaping everything in sight. Video enthusiast Doug is taken hostage by the Clint Dryer gang who want him to tape their crime spree. Every aspect is only seen through the lens of the video camera. **90m/C VHS.** Danny Bonaduce, Mick Wynhoff, Mollena Williams, Melora Walters; **D:** Jack Perez; **W:** Jack Perez.

America's Dream ✓✓✓ 1995 (PG-13) Trilogy of short stories covering black life from 1938 to 1958. In "Long Black Song," based on a short story by Richard Wright, Alabama farmer Silas (Glover) lives with lonely wife Sarah (Lifford), who succumbs to the charms of white travelling salesman, David (Donovan). "The Boy Who Painted Christ Black" is young Aaron (Golden), who gives the drawing to his teacher, Miss Williams (Calloway). But the portrait causes a great deal of controversy in Aaron's 1948 Georgia school, especially for ambitious principal George Du Vaul (Snipes). Based on a story by John Henrich Clarke. The last story is Maya Angelou's "The Reunion," about Chicago jazz pianist Philomena (Toussaint), who encounters her childhood nemesis, Beth Ann (Thompson), the daughter of the white family who employed her parents as servants. **87m/C VHS, DVD.** Danny Glover, Tina Lifford, Tate Donovan, Dan Karnin, Wesley Snipes, Jasmine Guy, Vanessa Bell Calloway, Norman D. Golden II, Timothy Carhart, Yolanda King, Rae'Ven (Alyla Larrymore) Kelly, Lorraine Toussaint, Susanna Thompson, Carl Lumbly, Phyllis Cicero; **D:** Bill Duke, Kevin Rodney Sullivan, Paris Barclay; **W:** Ron Stacker Thompson, Ashley Tyler; **C:** Karl Herrmann; **M:** Patrice Rushen.

America's Heart and Soul ✓✓ 2004 (PG) Series of vignettes seeks to capture the diversity and indomitable spirit of America, as a saccharine and ineffective answer to "Fahrenheit 9/11." Viewers literally fly over the U.S. and swoop down to meet a cowboy in Colorado, a rug weaver in Appalachia, a dairy farmer in Vermont, a trombone prodigy in Louisiana, a Methodist pastor in San Francisco, an Olympic boxer in Chicago and so on. Although the scenery is gorgeous and the people compelling, you're never with them for very long or reach any sort of depth. **84m/C DVD.** **D:** Louis Schwartzberg; **C:** Louis Schwartzberg; **M:** Joel McNeely.

America's Sweethearts ✓✓ 2001 (PG-13) This just in: Hollywood is shallow and fake, Julia Roberts is pretty, and entertainment reporters are freeloading numbskulls. These are the themes covered in this disappointing romantic comedy in which America's favorite on- and off-screen couple Eddie (Cusack) and Gwen (Zeta-Jones) pretend to reconcile during a disaster-filled press junket cooked up by desperate publicist Lee (Crystal). Complicating matters are the developing relationship between Gwen's sis-

Americathon WOOF! **1979 (PG)** It is the year 1998 and the United States is almost bankrupt, so President Chet Roosevelt decides to stage a telethon to keep the country from going broke. Interesting satiric premise with a diverse cast, but a poor script and slack pacing spoil all the fun. The soundtrack features music by The Beach Boys and Elvis Costello while the narration is by George Carlin. **85m/C VHS.** Terence McGovern, Allan Arbus, David Opatoshu, John Lone, Cybill Shepherd, Dorothy Stratten, Peter Riegert, John Ritter, Nancy Morgan, Harvey Korman, Fred Willard, Meat Loaf Aday, Elvis Costello, Chief Dan George, Howard Hesseman; *Cameos:* Tommy Lasorda, Peter Marshall; *D:* Neal Israel; *W:* Monica Johnson, Neal Israel; *M:* Ea1 Brown Jr.; *Nar:* George Carlin.

Amin: The Rise and Fall WOOF! **1982** Excessively violent and ultimately pointless dramatization of Idi Amin's eight-year reign of terror in Uganda, which resulted in the deaths of a half million people and the near ruin of a nation. **10m/C VHS.** Joseph Olita, Geoffrey Keen; *D:* Sharad Patel.

Amistad ♦♦♦ **1997 (R)** Spielberg again creates an epic from another historic example of man's inhumanity, although not quite as effectively this time around. In 1839, African captives aboard the slaveship Amistad, led by a Mende tribesman named Cinque (Hounsou), free themselves and take over the ship in a bloody mutiny. Property attorney Robert Baldwin (McConaughey) must prove in lengthy court battles that the Africans were rightfully freed individuals in the eyes of law. John Quincy Adams (Hopkins) presents the Africans' defense to the Supreme Court. Sequences depicting the horrors of slavery are bogged down with heavy handed musical orchestrations that elicit emotion, but at the price of storytelling. McConaughey seems a bit too Californian in a too colonial and Morgan Freeman is reduced to periodic cameos as an abolitionist. Fortunately, thanks to an eye for rich detail and a superb acting by dynamic newcomer Hounsou, the film nearly escapes the clutches of melodrama to emerge educational and moving. Film's release was marred by a French author accusing Spielberg and his Dreamworks studio of plagiarism. **152m/C VHS, DVD, DIm-on** Housou, Anthony Hopkins, Matthew McConaughey, Morgan Freeman, Nigel Hawthorne, David Paymer, Pete Postlethwaite, Stellan Skarsgard, Anna Paquin, Austin Pendleton, Tomas Milian, Paul Guilfoyle; *D:* Steven Spielberg; *W:* David Franzoni; *C:* Janusz Kaminski; *M:* John Williams. *Broadcast Film Critics '97. Support. Actor (Hopkins).*

The Amityville Horror ♦♦ **1979 (R)** Sometimes a house is not a home. Ineffective chiller that became a boxoffice biggie, based on a supposedly real-life occurrence in Amityville, Long Island. The Lutz family moves into the house of their dreams only to find it full of nightmares. Once the scene of a grisly mass murder, the house takes on a devilish attitude, plunging the family into supernatural terror. Pipes and walls ooze icky stuff, flies manifest in the strangest places, and doors mysteriously slam while exorcist Steiger staggers from room to room in scene-chewing prayer. Based on the Jay Anson book and followed by a number of sequels. **117m/C VHS.** James Brolin, Margot Kidder, Roc Steiger, Don Stroud, Murray Hamilton, Helen Shaver, Amy Wright, Val Avery, Natasha Ryan, John Larch, K.C. Martel, Meeno Peluce; *D:* Stuart Rosenberg; *W:* Sandor Stern; *C:* Fred W. Koenekamp; *M:* Lalo Schifrin.

ter and assistant Kiki (Roberts) and Eddie Roth hasn't directed a film in over 10 years, and it shows here. But beneath the rust, there are some funny moments, mostly including Walken as the crazy director who has taken his own film hostage. **103m/C VHS, DVD, US** Julia Roberts, Catherine Zeta-Jones, John Cusack, Billy Crystal, Hank Azaria, Christopher Walken, Seth Green, Stanley Tucci; *Cameos:* Larry King; *D:* Joe Roth; *W:* Billy Crystal, Peter Tolan; *C:* Phedon Papamichael; *M:* James Newton Howard.

Amityville 2: The Possession WOOF! **1982 (R)** More of a prequel than a sequel to "The Amityville Horror" (1979). Relates the story of the house's early years on driving a father to demonic forces intent on driving a father to beat the kids, a mother to prayer, and a brother to lust; after his sister. (before he murders them all). Young etc. portray an obnoxious family that you're actually glad to see wasted by the possessed son. A stupid, clumsy attempt to cash in on the success of the first film, which was also stupid and clumsy but could at least claim novelty in the bad housing development genre. Followed by "Amityville 3: The Demon" in 1983. **110m/C VHS.** James Olson, Burt Young, Andrew Prine, Moses Gunn, Rutanya Alda, Jack Magner, Diane Franklin; *D:* Damiano Damiani; *W:* Tommy Lee Wallace; *C:* Franco Di Giacomo.

Amityville 3: The Demon ♦½ **1983 (R)** America's worst real-estate value dupes another funky buyer. The infamous Amityville house is once again restless with terror and gore, though supported with even less plot than the usual smidgin. Cynical reporter Roberts moves in while trying to get to the bottom of the story by way of the basement. Courtesy of 3-D technology, monsters sprang at theatre patrons but the video version is strictly two-dimensional, forcing the viewer to press his or her face directly onto the TV screen in order to derive similar effect. **96m/C VHS, DVD.** Tony Roberts, Tess Harper, Robert Joy, Candy Clark, John Beal, Leora Dana, John Harkins, Lori Loughlin, Meg Ryan, Rikke Borge, Jack Cardiff; *D:* Richard Fleischer; *W:* William Wales, David Ambrose; *C:* Fred Schuler; *M:* Howard Blake.

Amityville 1992: It's About Time ♦♦ **1992 (R)** Time is of the essence in the sixth installment of the Amityville flicks. A vintage clock (from Amityville, of course), causes creepy goings-on in a family's house. Actually a halfway decent horror film with high-grade special effects, and much, much better than previous Amityville sequels, which isn't saying much. **95m/C VHS, DVD.** Stephen Macht, Shawn Weatherly, Megan Ward, Damon Martin, Nita Talbot, Dick Miller; *D:* Tony Randel; *W:* Christopher DeFaria, Antonio Toro.

Amityville 3-D 1983 (R) America's worst real-estate value dupes another funky buyer.

Amityville 4: The Evil Escapes ♦½ *The Amityville Horror: The Evil Escapes, Part 4* **1989 (R)** It's an unusual case of house-to-house transference as the horror from Amityville continues, now lodged in a Californian residence. The usual good-house-gone-bad story has the place creating a lot of unusual creaks and rattles before deciding to use its inherited powers to attack and possess a little girl. Special effects stand out somewhat. ("The Lost Boys" and "Jaws"). **95m/C VHS, DVD.** Patty Duke, Jane Wyatt, Norman Lloyd, Frederic Lehne, Brandy Gold; *D:* Sandor Stern; *M:* Rick Conrad. *TV*

Amityville: A New Generation ♦½ **1993 (R)** And the bad sequels just go on and on and on. Terry is a young photographer who's given an old mirror by a crazy homeless man (tell me why he took it). He shares a loft with three friends and all begin experiencing vivid and terrifying dreams of murder. Seems the mirror is tied to Amityville and its evil legacy and Terry is the designated inheritor. **92m/C VHS, DVD.** Ross Partridge, Julia Nickson-Soul, David Naughton, Richard Roundtree, Terry O'Quinn; *D:* John Murowski; *W:* Christopher DeFaria, Antonio Toro.

The Amityville Curse WOOF! **1990 (F)** The possessed house is yet again purchased by a pathetically uninformed family. The usual ghostly shenanigans occur with low-budget regularity in this fifth entry in the series. Never released theatrically, for good reason. **92m/C VHS, CA** Kim Coates, Dawna Wightman, Helen Hughes, Jan Rubes; *D:* Tom Berry.

Amityville Dollhouse ♦½ **1996 (R)** Family moves into their Victorian dream home in Amityville, which comes complete with a replica dollhouse that charms the daughter. But the Amityville curse inhabits the plaything and soon the poltergeists make their nasty appearance. At the farm, he meets an older woman and compromises his virtue. Postlethwaite does a fine job as the unlikely romantic lead, though. **93m/C VHS, DVD.** Robin Thomas, Starr Andreeff, Allen (Cutler) Cutler, Rachel Duncan, Jarrett Lennon, Clayton Murray, Frank Ross, Lenora Kardorf, Lisa Robin Kelly; *D:* Steve White; *W:* Joshua Michael Stern; *C:* Thomas Callaway.

The Amityville Horror ♦♦½ **2005 (R)** Revamp of the Amityville tale swaps the understated chills of the original 1979 film with faster editing, more gore, and lots of goth imagery. George and Kathy Lutz (Reynolds and George) learn the

meaning of "buyer beware" when they move their family into a lakeside colonial home, a real bargain thanks to the house's history of bone-chilling mass murders. After a series of strange incidents and ghostly visitations, Kathy begins catching on, just in time to watch her husband start channeling Jack Nicholson in "The Shining." The scares are familiar, but Douglas does an admirable job of creating a pervasively creepy, claustrophobic atmosphere throughout. **89m/C DVD, Blu-ray Disc, UMD, US** Ryan Reynolds, Melissa George, Jesse James, Jimmy Bennett, Rachel Nichols, Philip Baker Hall, Rich Komenich, Scott Kosar, Brendan Donaldson, Annabel Armour, Chloe Grace Moretz, Isabel Conner, Jose Taitano, David Gee, Danny McCarthy, Nancy Lollar; *D:* Andrew Douglas; *C:* Peter Lyons Collister; *M:* Steve Jablonsky.

Amnesia ♦♦ **1996 (R)** Minister Paul Keller (Walker) is having an affair with his son's teacher, Veronica Dow (Tomanovich). Paul decides to fake his death, leaving wife Martha (Sheedy) with the insurance money and allowing him to start a new life with Veronica. Only he has an accident that causes amnesia and runs into more trouble than he can imagine. Has more humor than you might imagine, thanks to its wacky characters, but as usual Kirkland is way over the top as a love-starved motel owner. **92m/C VHS, DVD.** Nicholas Walker, Ally Sheedy, Sally Kirkland, John Savage, Dara Tomanovich, Vincent Berry; *D:* Kurt Voss.

Among Brothers ♦♦ **2005 (R)** "what if" based on a true crime from 1994. South Carolina frat boy Ethan doesn't take it well when co-ed Jennifer just wants to be friends, and she winds up dead in her apartment. Ethan whines to frat brothers Miles and Billy that it was an accident, so they torch the place to cover things up. Only the cops figure out Jennifer was murdered, so the boys try to shift the blame elsewhere. The real crime remains unsolved. **85m/C DVD.** Matt Mercer, Lauren Schneder, Corey Cicci, Daniel J. Watts, Lindsay Ayliffe; *D:* John Schwert; *W:* John Schwert; *C:* Brad Hoover.

Among Giants ♦♦ **1998 (R)** Post-leftwate is Ray, the foreman of a crew of painters assigned to slap a new coat on the electrical towers that line the Yorkshire countryside. When a female Australian rock climber (Griffiths) wanders into town, Ray, she causes static between him and his best friend (Thornton). Understated to the point of being comatose, nothing much happens with the romance or the dangerous occupation angle. Postlethwaite does a fine job as the unlikely romantic lead, though. **93m/C VHS, GB** Pete Postlethwaite, Rachel Griffiths, James Thornton, Lennie James, Andy Serkis, Rob Jarvis; *D:* Sam Miller; *W:* Simon Beaufoy; *C:* Witold Stok; *M:* Tim Atack.

Among the Cinders ♦♦ **1983** Sometimes interesting coming of age drama about a 16-year-old New Zealand boy who runs away to his grandfather's farm to forget about his friend's accidental death. At the farm, he meets an older woman and compromises his virtue. **103m/C VHS, GE NZ** Paul O'Shea, Derek Hardwick, Rebecca Gibney, Yvonne Lawley, Amanda Jones; *D:* Rolf Haedrich.

Amongst Friends ♦♦ **1993 (F)** Three boyhood buddies, Trevor (McGaw), Billy (Lindsey), and Andy (Pantaevecchio), from a nice Long Island neighborhood turn to crime out of boredom. Trevor gets busted and goes to prison for two years. Upon getting out, he finds his old cronies still share the taste for crime and general aim-

lessness but also still want thet one big score. Trevor finally agrees to join Andy and Billy in a drug deal but the jealous Billy, who wants Trevor's old girlfriend Laura (Sorvino), plans a double-cross that will affect them all. Filled with cutting attacks on the society that spawns aimless youth. Debut of the 1 26-year-old writer/director Weiss. **88m/C VHS, DVD.** Louis Lombardi, Patrick McGaw, Steve Parlavecchio, Joseph Lindsey, Mira Sorvino, David Stepkin, Michael Artura; *D:* Rob Weiss; *W:* Rob Weiss; *C:* Michael Bonvillain; *M:* Mick Jones.

Amor de Hombre ♦♦ *The Love of a Man; Man's Love* **1997** Ramon is a gay man with a lot of bedroom action. His best friend is Esperanza, who goes home alone, speaking to her lover on the telephone. Based on Jean Cocteau's one-act drama. In "The Miracle," she is a simple peasant girl who believes her illegitimate child is equally the new Messiah. Italian with English subtitles. **78m/B VHS.** *It* Anna Magnani; *D:* Roberto Rossellini.

Amore ♦♦♦ **1948** Rossellini's tribute to actress Magnani consists of the short films "The Human Voice" and "The Miracle." In "The Human Voice," Magnani is by a woman leading man material under the name of Salvatore Guiliano III, but promptly winds up falling for Rucol/(Ireland), who couldn't care less. **95m/C VHS.** Jack Scalia, Kathy Ireland, Elliott Gould, George Hamilton, Brenda Epperson, James Doohan, Katherine Helmond, Betsy Russell, Norm Crosby, Frank Gorshin; *D:* Lorenzo Doumani; *W:* Lorenzo Dourani.

Amore! ♦♦½ **1993 (PG-13)** Wealthy investment banker Saul Schwartz (Scala) hates his job, his wife, and his life. The telephone is by watching movies starring Italian matinee idol Rucol/. So Saul gets dreaming of Hollywood and becoming an actor like his debonair idol. With the help of some newfound friends he transforms himself into suave leading man material under the name of Salvatore Guiliano III, but promptly winds up falling for Rucol/(Ireland), who couldn't care less. **95m/C VHS.** Jack Scalia, Kathy Ireland, Elliott Gould, George Hamilton, Brenda Epperson, James Doohan, Katherine Helmond, Betsy Russell, Norm Crosby, Frank Gorshin; *D:* Lorenzo Doumani; *W:* Lorenzo Dourani.

Amor Bandido ♦♦ **1979** When cab drivers in Rio are turning up dead, a young prostitute is torn between her detective father and her prime suspect boyfriend. Drama based on a true story. In Portuguese with English subtitles. **95m/C VHS, BR** Paulo Gracindo, Cristina Ache, Paulo Guarnero; *D:* Bruno Barreto.

Amores Perros ♦♦♦ *Love's a Bitch* **2000 (R)** A Mexico City car accident and the fortunes of a cog bring together three stories of love, loss, and redemption in director/producer Gonzalez Inarritu's impressive feature debut. Octavio's love for his brother's wife leads him to enter his dog. Cofi, in a dogfight for elopement money. When Cofi is wounded, it leads to a car chase, and the central accident. A woman, Valeria, is injured and permanently scarred in the accident. This affects her life by. She has just left his family to live with her. A homeless man, a former revolutionary 'turned hitman, witnesses the crash and rescues the dog, who becomes a part of his search for his estranged daughter. The plot structure invites comparisons to Tarantino, but these characters inhabit a more consequences-end-morality-oriented word than Q's characters ever did. Film came under fire from animal rights activists for the dogfight scenes, although it was made clear from the start that no animals were actually harmed. **153m/C VHS, DVD, MX** Vanessa Bauche, Emilio Echeverria, Gael Garcia Bernal, Goya Toledo, Alvaro Guerrero, Jorge Salinas Marco Perez, Rodrigo Murray, Humberto Busto, Gerardo Campbell, Rossa Maria Bianchi, Dunia Saldivar, Adriana Barraza; *D:* Alejandro Gonzalez Inarritu; *W:* Guillermo Arriaga; *C:* Rodrigo Prieto; *M:* Gustavo vo Santaolalla. British Acad. '01: Foreign Film; Natl. Bd. of Review '01: Foreign Film.

The Amorous Adventures of Moll Flanders 1965 An amusing romp set in 18th century England focusing on a poor orphan girl who seeks wealth. Moll plots to get ahead through an advantageous series of romances and marriages. Her plan is ruined when she falls in love and he turns out to be a wanted highwayman, landing her in prison. Not surprisingly, love (and money) conquers all. Based on the novel by Daniel Defoe. Novak tries in this female derivative of "Tom Jones," but this period piece isn't her style. 126m/C VHS. Kim Novak, Richard Johnson, Angela Lansbury, Vittorio De Sica, Leo McKern, George Sanders, Lilli Palmer; **D:** Terence Young; **C:** Ted Moore; **M:** John Addison.

Amos 1985 Douglas is Amos, an aging baseball coach confined most reluctantly to a nursing home. He's disturbed by recent suspicious events there his concern causing him to take on Montgomery, the staunch head nurse. Well-acted drama produced by Douglas's son Peter, offering an echo of "One Flew Over the Cuckoo's Nest," which Dad starred in on Broadway and son Michael helped produced as a movie classic. 100m/C VHS. Kirk Douglas, Elizabeth Montgomery, Dorothy McGuire, Noriyuki "Pat" Morita, James Sloyan, Ray Walston; **D:** Michael Tuchner; **M:** Georges Delerue.

Amos and Andrew 1993 (PG-13) Embarrassing attempt at comedy stops short of endorsing the stereotypes it tries to parody. Prizewinning African-American author Andrew Sterling (Jackson) is seen moving into a house on an island previously reserved for the uptight white, and the neighbors call the cops, assuming he's a thief. Chief of police (Coleman) eagerly gets into the act, then exploits drifter Amos (Cage) in a cover-up attempt when he realizes his mistake. Talented cast can't overcome lame jokes and transparent plot that serves as an opportunity to bring black and white together for a "see how much we have in common" bonding session. 96m/C VHS, DVD. Nicolas Cage, Samuel L. Jackson, Michael Lerner, Margaret Colin, Giancarlo Esposito, Dabney Coleman, Bob Balaban, Aimee Graham, Brad Dourif, Chelcie Ross, Jodi Long; **D:** E. Max Frye; **W:** E. Max Frye; **M:** Richard Gibbs.

The Amphibian Man 1961 What does a scientist do once he's created a young man with gills? Plunge him in the real world of aqua pura to experience life and love, albeit underwater. Trouble is, the protagonist, who's come to be known as the Sea Devil, takes a dive for a young pretty he's snatched from the jaws of death. A '60s Soviet sci-fi romance originally seen on American TV. 93m/C VHS, DVD. RU K. Korienev, M. Virzinskaya, Mikhail Kozakov, Vladlen Davydov; **D:** Y. Kasancki; **W:** Aleksei Kapler.

The Amsterdam Connection 1978 Film company acts as a cover for prostitution and drug smuggling, with the girls acting as international couriers. 90m/C VHS, DVD. HK Chen Shing, Kid Sherrif, Yeung Sze, Jason Pai Piu, Fang Mui San; **D:** Fang Mui San, Lo Ke.

The Amsterdam Kill 1978 (R) A washed-up ex-agent of the U.S. Drug Enforcement Agency is hired by a desperate U.S. Drug Enforcement Agency to hunt down the kingpin of a narcotics syndicate in Hong Kong. Tedious pace with occasional spells of Mitchum. Shot on location in Hong Kong. 93m/C VHS. HK Robert Mitchum, Richard Egan, Keye Luke, Leslie Nielsen, Bradford Dillman; **D:** Robert Clouse; **W:** Robert Clouse.

Amsterdamned 1988 (R) A crime thriller taking place on the canals of Amsterdam featuring a serial skindiver killer who surfaces periodically to slash and splash. A steely detective fishes for clues. Dubbed. 114m/C VHS. NL Monique Van De Ven, Huub Stapel, Hidde Maas, Serge-Henri Valcke, Wim Zomer, Tatum Dagelet; **D:** Dick Maas; **W:** Dick Maas; **M:** Marc Felperlaan.

Amuck! 1971 Vintage early '70s Euro-sleaze makes a belated debut on home video. Greta (Bouchet) is hired to be a secretary to world-famous author Richard Stuart (Granger). But Stuart's wife Eleanora (Neri) has designs on the young woman, and Greta has secrets of her own. 98m/C DVD. IT Farley Granger, Barbara Bouchet, Rosalba Neri, Umberto Raho, Patrizia Viotti, Dino Mele, Petar Martinovic, Nino Segurini; **D:** Silvio Amandio; **W:** Silvio Amandio; **C:** Aldo Giordani; **M:** Teo Usuelli.

Amy 1981 (G) Set in the early 1900s, the story follows the experiences of a woman after she leaves her well-to-do husband to take a teaching position at a school for the deaf and blind. Eventually she organizes a football game between the handicapped kids and the other children in the neighborhood. Good Disney family fare. 100m/C VHS. Jenny Agutter, Barry Newman, Kathleen Nolan, Margaret O'Brien, Nanette Fabray, Chris Robinson, Louis Fant; **D:** Vincent McEveety; **M:** Robert F. Brunner.

Amy 1998 Quirky to say the least. Nine-year-old Amy (Davis) has been an elective deaf-mute since witnessing the death of her rock star father Will (Barker), who was electrocuted during a concert. The only way Amy does communiate is through music—something discovered by luckless musician Robert (Mendelsohn). Meanwhile, Amy's bitter mom Tanya (Griffiths) is trying to avoid the welfare authorities who want to take charge of Amy's schooling and treatment. Uneasy mix of genres by Australian director de Roma is remarkable. 103m/C VHS. AU Rachel Griffiths, Alana De Roma, Ben Mendelsohn, Nick Barker, Kerry Armstrong; **D:** Nadia Tass; **W:** David Parker; **C:** David Parker; **M:** Phil Judd.

The Amy Fisher Story *Beyond Control* 1993 Amy Fisher wishes she looked this good. Perhaps if she did, she could be acting in TV movies like Barrymore instead of providing fodder from them. The ABC account draws from a variety of sources to dramatize the relationship between Amy and her married, ahem, friend, and Amy's subsequent attack on his wife. Although it tries not to take sides, it does include some pretty hot sex scenes which could be why this docudrama garnered the highest ratings of the three network productions released on TV. See also: "Casualties of Love: The Long Island Lolita' Story" and "Lethal Lolita—Amy Fisher: My Story". 93m/C VHS, DVD. Drew Barrymore, Anthony John (Tony) Denison, Harley Jane Kozak, Tom Mason, Laurie Paton, Ken Pogue, Linda Darlow, Garry Davey, Dwight McFee, Gabe Khouth, Philip Granger, Stephen Cooper; **D:** Andy Tennant; **W:** Janet Brownell; **C:** Glen MacPherson; **M:** Michael Hoenig. TV

Amy's O *Amy's Orgasm* 2002 Amy (Davis) is a twentysomething L.A. single who has penned a self-help book about why women don't need men to feel complete. She's successful but doesn't believe her own word and is lonely and looking. She meets radio shock jock Matthew Starr (Chinlund), who turns out to be a pretty decent guy, although he's got some personal quirks Amy comes to resent. And Matthew finds some things about Amy he could live without. Of course, they're meant to be together if they could just get past their own egos. 87m/C VHS, DVD. Julie Davis, Nicholas Chinlund, Caroline Aaron, Mitchell Whitfield, Mary Ellen Trainor, Charles Cioffi, Tina Lifford, Jennifer Bransford; **D:** Julie Davis; **W:** Julie Davis; **C:** Mark Mervis, Goran Pavicenic.

Anaconda 1996 (PG-13) Snakes—lots and lots of snakes. Teeny baby snakes, little snakes, medium-sized snakes, large snakes, and one gigantic 40-foot long snake that likes to swallow people and then vomit them up again (the better to have room to swallow somebody else). Oh yeah, the minimal plot concerns a documentary film crew traveling the Amazon River looking for a legendary Indian tribe. They not only have to contend with the snakes but with crazy, snake-obsessed guide Paul Sarone (Voight). The actors react appropriately to becoming snake food. 90m/C VHS, DVD. Jon Voight, Jennifer Lopez, Ice Cube, Eric Stoltz, Owen Wilson, Kari Wuhrer, Jonathan Hyde, Vincent Castellanos, Danny Trejo; **D:** Luis Llosa; **W:** Jim Cash, Jack Epps Jr., Hans Bauer; **C:** Bill Butler; **M:** Randy Edelman.

Anacondas: The Hunt for the Blood Orchid 2004 (PG-13) An enjoyably trashy quasi-sequel to the 1997 flick finds even more (and bigger) snakes to swallow the generally no-name cast. A pharmaceutical company sponsors a scientific expedition along a Borneo river to hunt for the rare title flower, which may extend life and youth. There's the usual mix of characters: fearless riverboat captain (Messner), arrogant scientist (Marsden), computer geek (Byrd), babe (Strickland), etc., and the standard situations: ramshackle boat, dense jungle, hungry snakes, and a really clever monkey for a little variety. The director and cast handle their parts efficiently and they know enough not to take it too seriously. Neither should you. 93m/C VHS, DVD, UMD. US Johnny Messner, KaDee Strickland, Matthew Marsden, Eugene Byrd, Denis Arndt, Morris Chestnut, Salli Richardson, Nicholas Gonzalez; **D:** Dwight Little; **W:** Michael Miner, John Claflin, Daniel Zelman, Edward Neumeier; **C:** Stephen Windon; **M:** Nerida Tyson-Chew.

Analyze That 2002 (R) Woefully inferior sequel finds shrink Dr. Sobel (Crystal, becoming more irritating with every film), who's trying to deal with his family (De Niro), whose life is being threatened after Vitti fakes a breakdown in order to escape jailhouse hitmen, Sobel is forced by the FBI to house and rehabilitate him, incurring the wrath of his loving but running-out-of patience wife Laura (the sadly underused Kudrow). There are a few laughs to be had, mostly compliments of De Niro, but not enough to keep the inevitable "Analyze the Other Thing" off the Least Wanted list. 95m/C VHS, DVD. US Billy Crystal, Robert De Niro, Lisa Kudrow, Joe (Johnny) Viterelli, Reg Rogers, Cathy Moriarty, John Finn, Kyle Sabihy, Callie (Calliope) Thorne, Pat Cooper, Frank Gio, Donnamarie Recco; **D:** Harold Ramis; **W:** Harold Ramis, Peter Steinfeld, Peter Tolan; **C:** Ellen Kuras; **M:** David Holmes.

Analyze This 1998 (R) Robert De Niro stars as anxiety-stricken mob boss Paul Vitti. He begins to see suburban shrink Ben (Crystal), and is so pleased with the results that he strong-arms the doc into seeing him whenever he wants. Unfortunately for Ben and fiance Laura (Kudrow), that usually happens to be when they're trying to get married. Palminteri is a rival gangster with whom Vitti "seeks closure." De Niro expertly winks at the mob genre (which he helped create) without losing the air of menace that surrounds the good fella character. His performance carries the movie despite the somewhat hokey ending. It's De Niro's underworld, Billy's just living in it. 110m/C VHS, DVD. Robert De Niro, Billy Crystal, Lisa Kudrow, Chazz Palminteri, Joe (Johnny) Viterelli, Bill Macy, Leo Rossi, Rebecca Schull, Molly Shannon, Max Casella, Pat Cooper, Richard C. Castellano, Jimmie Ray Weeks, Elizabeth Bracco, Tony Darrow, Kyle Sabihy, Donnamarie Recco; **D:** Harold Ramis; **W:** Harold Ramis, Peter Tolan, Kenneth Lonergan; **C:** Stuart Dryburgh; **M:** Howard Shore.

Anastasia 1956 Bergman won her second Oscar, and deservedly so, for her classic portrayal of the amnesia victim chosen by Russian expatriate Brynner to impersonate Anastasia, the last surviving member of the Romanoff dynasty. As such, she becomes part of a scam to collect millions of rubles deposited in a foreign bank by her supposed father, the now-dead Czar. But is she just impersonating the princess? Brynner as the scheming White General and Hayes as the Grand Duchess who needs to be convinced turn in fine performances as well. Based on Marcelle Maurette's play. 105m/C VHS, DVD. Ingrid Bergman, Yul Brynner, Helen Hayes, Akim Tamiroff, Martita Hunt, Felix Aylmer, Ivan Desny, Sacha (Sascha) Pitoeff; **D:** Anatole Litvak; **W:** Arthur Laurents; **C:** Jack Hildyard. Oscars '56: Actress (Bergman); Golden Globes '57: Actress—Drama (Bergman); N.Y. Film Critics '56: Actress (Bergman).

Anastasia 1997 (G) Let's face it, this is a pretty weird story to turn into a cartoon fairy tale. Fox's first entry into the Disney-dominated full-length animated musical fray is the story of Princess Anastasia and the fall of the Romanov empire. She has been missing ever since the evil Rasputin put a curse on the Romanov family and started the Russian Revolution (Lenin must have flunked the screen test. Not "toon" enough). Ten years later, con artist Dimitri and ex-aristocrat Vladimir try to convince orphaned 18-year-old Anya that she's the ex-royal so they can claim a reward from the princess' grandmother. Little do they know that she actually is the lost princess, but they must battle Rasputin and his albino bat henchman to put things right. Among the big names lending their voices are Meg Ryan, John Cusack (Cossack?), and Christopher Lloyd. Now let me tell you how the Katzenjammer Kids started WWIII... 90m/C VHS, DVD. **D:** Don Bluth, Gary Goldman; **W:** Bruce Graham, Susan Gauthier, Bob Tzudiker, Noni White; **M:** David Newman; **V:** Meg Ryan, John Cusack, Kelsey Grammer, Angela Lansbury, Christopher Lloyd, Hank Azaria, Bernadette Peters, Kirsten Dunst.

Anastasia: The Mystery of Anna 1986 Irving stars as Anna Anderson, a woman who claimed to be the Grand Duchess Anastasia, the sole surviving daughter of Russian Czar Nicholas II. A powerful epic reliving her experience of royalty, flight from execution, and struggle to retain her heritage. The story of Anastasia remains as one of the greatest dramatic mysteries of the 20th century. Adapted from the book "Anastasia: The Riddle of Anna Anderson" by Peter Kurth. 190m/C VHS, DVD. Amy Irving, Olivia de Havilland, Jan Niklas, Nicolas Surovy, Susan Lucci, Elke Sommer, Edward Fox, Claire Bloom, Omar Sharif, Rex Harrison; **D:** Marvin J. Chomsky; **W:** James Goldman. CABLE

Anatomy *Anatomie* 2000 (R) Medical student Paula Henning (Potente) is accepted into a prestigious Heidelberg anatomy class. She's carrying on the family tradition of her grandfather, who's dying in the hospital he built, and her father, with whom she disagrees on almost everything. But when she gets to the new university, she finds that very creepy stuff is going on. Medical horror/thriller is right up there with "Coma." It's inventive, grotesque, and the special effects work very well. Franka Potente shows that the impression she made in "Run, Lola, Run" was no fluke. 100m/C VHS, DVD. GE Franka Potente, Benno Furmann, Anna Loos, Holger Speckhann, Sebastian Blomberg; **D:** Stefan Ruzowitzky; **W:** Stefan Ruzowitzky; **C:** Peter von Haller; **M:** Marius Ruhland.

Anatomy of a Murder 1959 Considered by many to be the best courtroom drama ever made. Small-town lawyer in northern Michigan faces an explosive case as he defends an army officer who has killed a man he suspects was his philandering wife's rapist. Realistic, cynical portrayal of the court system isn't especially concerned with guilt or innocence, focusing instead on the interplay between the various courtroom characters. Classic performance by Stewart as the down home but brilliant defense lawyer who matches wits with Scott, the sophisticated prosecutor; terse and clever direction by Preminger. Though tame by today's standards, the language used in the courtroom was controversial. Filmed in upper Michigan; based on the bestseller by judge Robert Traver. 161m/B VHS, DVD. James Stewart, Lee Remick, Orson Bean, Eve Arden, Ben Gazzara, Arthur O'Connell, Duke Ellington, Kathryn Grant, Murray Hamilton, Joseph Welch; **D:** Otto Preminger; **W:** Wendell Mayes; **C:** Sam Leavitt; **M:** Duke Ellington. N.Y. Film Critics '59: Actor (Stewart), Screenplay.

Anatomy of a Psycho 1961 A man plans to avenge his gas chambered brother by committing mass murder. Very cheaply and poorly produced. 75m/B VHS, DVD. Ronnie Burns, Pamela Lincoln, Darrell Howe, Russ Bender; **D:** Boris L. Petroff.

Anatomy of a Seduction 🦴🦴 1979 TV formula melodrama of a middle-aged divorcee's affair with her son's best friend. Age knows no boundaries when it comes to television lust. 100m/C VHS. Susan Flannery, Jameson Parker, Rita Moreno, Ed Nelson, Michael LeClair; D: Steven Hilliard Stern; M: Hagood Hardy. TV

Anchors Aweigh 🦴🦴🦴 1945 Snappy, big-budget (for then) musical about two horny sailors, one a girl-happy dancer and the other a shy singer. While on leave in Hollywood they return a lost urchin to his sister. The four of them try to infiltrate a movie studio to win an audition for the girl from maestro Iturbi. Kelly's famous dance with Jerry the cartoon Mouse (of "Tom and Jerry" fame) is the second instance of combining live action and animation. The young and handsome Sinatra's easy crooning and Grayson's near operatic soprano are blessed with music and lyrics by Styne and Cahn. Lots of fun, with conductor-pianist Iturbi contributing and Hollywood-style Little Mexico also in the brew. ♪We Hate to Leave; I Fall in Love Too Easily; The Charm of You; The Worry Song; Jacousie; All of a Sudden My Heart Sings; I Begged Her; What Makes the Sun Set?; Waltz Serenade. 139m/C VHS, DVD. Frank Sinatra, Gene Kelly, Kathryn Grayson, Jose Iturbi, Dean Stockwell, Carlos Ramirez; D: Pamela Britton, Sharon McManus, Leon Ames; D: George Sidney; M: Julie Styne, Sammy Cahn. Oscars '45: Scoring/Musical.

Anatomy of Hell WOOF! Anatomie de L'Enfer 2004 French pretentiousness at its most full-blown. An unnamed straight woman (Casar)—bored, stupid, mentally unbalanced or all three—slits her wrists in a gay disco and is attended to by a homeless gay man (Italian porn stud Siffredi) whom she then propositions. She'll pay him to accompany her to her creepy isolated house and look at her naked. This will help her confront her problems with intimacy or sexuality or something. Unless you're as masochistic as the characters, you won't care. Oh, and Casar has a body double for the more, ummm, close-up views but that's all Siffredi all the time. Adapted from Breillat's novel "Pornocratie"; French with subtitles. 87m/C DVD, FR. Amira Casar, Rocco Siffredi, Catherine Breillat; D: Catherine Breillat; C: Yorgos Arvanitis, Guillaume Schiffman, Miguel Malherios, Pedro da Santos; M: D'juz.

Anatomy of Terror 🦴 Thriller: An army vet going bonkers (what? really?) and revealing espionage secrets in his home life. 73m/C VHS. Paul Burke, Polly Bergen, Dinsdale Landen, Basil Henson, Roger Hume, William Job; D: Brian Clemens, Peter Jeffries; M: Laurie Johnson. TV

Anchorman: The Legend of Ron Burgundy 🦴🦴½ 2004 (PG-13) Back in the '80s, Chevy Chase specialized in clueless all-American goofs who thought they were smarter than they were. The crown has been passed to Ferrell. Here, he plays Ron Burgundy, the top-rated anchorman in '70s-era San Diego. Ron is the booze swilling, cigarette smoking, female ogling, narcissistic leader of an all-male news team whose world is rocked by the arrival of a new female reporter—beautiful, talented, and ambitious Veronica Corningstone (Applegate). Ron falls for the babe even as he tries to retain his chauvinistic place at the top of the news chain. It's amusing shtick and a fair send-up of a time when men were men were pigs and women decided to bring home the bacon themselves. Besides Applegate, Ferrell is well supported by Koechner, Carell, and Rudd as his equally macho-wannabe news boys. 91m/C DVD, HD DVD, Will Ferrell, Christina Applegate, David Koechner, Steven Carell, Paul Rudd, Fred Willard, Vince Vaughn, Chad Everett, Tara Subkoff, Stephen (Steve) Root, Danny Trejo, Jack Black, Ben Stiller, Missi Pyle, Chris Parnell, Tim Robbins, Luke Wilson, Laura Kightlinger, Kevin Corrigan, Fred Armisen; D: Adam McKay; W: Will Ferrell, Adam McKay; C: Thomas Ackerman.

Ancient Evil: Scream of the Mummy 🦴½ 2000 (R) Six archeology students discover accidentally revive an Aztec mummy and unleash a deadly curse that could destroy mankind. 86m/C VHS, DVD. Ariauna Albright, Jeff Peterson, Russell Richardson, Christopher Cullen; D: David DeCoteau. VIDEO

Ancient Relic 🦴½ The Jesus Video 2002 (R) Confusing German miniseries focuses on a startling archeological discovery. Steffen Vogt is helping out at a dig site in Israel when he finds a 2,000-year-old skeleton holding instructions for a video camera. He leaps to the conclusion that the skeleton belongs to a time traveler who got actual footage of Jesus. His crackpot idea is given credence by expert Kaun, who's convinced the camera is hidden somewhere in Jerusalem's Wailing Wall. Then Steffen is abducted by your basic secret Vatican society who doesn't want the status quo upset. German with subtitles. 182m/C DVD, GE Naike Rivelli, Hans Diehl, Matthias Koeberlin, Heinrich Giskes; D: Sebastian Niemann; W: Martin Ritzenhoff; C: Gerhard Schirlo; M: Egon Riedel. TV

And a Nightingale Sang 🦴🦴½ 1991 WWII England is the scene of this sweet romance, a sad and humorous tale of a woman who gives everything for the war effort. Stunning recreation of the final days of the Blitzkrieg. Originally produced for Masterpiece Theatre. 90m/C VHS, GB Joan Plowright, Tom Watt, Phyllis Logan, John Woodvine, Pippa Hinchley, Stephen Tompkinson; D: Robert Knights. TV

And Baby Makes Six 🦴🦴½ 1979 An unexpected pregnancy creates new challenges for a couple with grown children. Dewhurst is excellent as usual. Followed by "Baby Comes Home." 100m/C VHS. Colleen Dewhurst, Warren Oates, Maggie Cooper, Mildred Dunnock, Timothy Hutton, Allyn Ann McLerie; D: Waris Hussein; M: Shelley List. TV

And God Created Woman 🦴🦴½ 1988 (R) Loose, dull remake by Vadim of his own 1957 softcore favorite about a free-spirited woman dogging men and the law while yearning for rock and roll stardom. DeMornay is the one who hopes to marry one of the local hunks (Spano) so she can be paroled. They marry, she strips, he frets, while political hopeful Langella smacks his lips in anticipation. Available in an unrated 100-minute version. 98m/C VHS, DVD. Rebecca DeMornay, Vincent Spano, Frank Langella, Donovan Leitch, Judith Chapman, Thelma Houston, Benjamin Mouton; M: Tom Chase, Steve Rucker.

And God Created Woman 🦴🦴🦴 And Woman... Was Created; Et Dieu Crea la Femme 1957 (PG) Launching pad for Bardot's career as a sex siren, as she flits across the screen in a succession of scanty outfits and hangs out at the St. Tropez beach in what is euphemistically known as a swimsuit while turning up the heat for the males always in attendance. The plot concerns an 18-year-old nymphomaniac who is given a home by a local family with three handsome young sons. A cutting-edge sex film in its time that was boffo at the boxoffice. In French with English subtitles. 93m/C VHS, DVD, FR. Brigitte Bardot, Curt Jurgens, Jean-Louis Trintignant, Christian Marquand; D: Roger Vadim; W: Roger Vadim, Raoul Levy; C: Armand Thirard; M: Paul Misraki.

And God Said to Cain 🦴 E Dio Disse a Caino 1969 Another Biblically titled western from the prolific Kinski, about a put-upon gunman who must fight for his life. 95m/C VHS. IT Klaus Kinski, Antonio Cantafora, Peter Carsten, Marcella Michelangeli, Alan Collins, Giuliano Raffaelli; D: Anthony M. Dawson.

...And God Spoke 🦴🦴 1994 (R) Low budget spoof takes on both religion and moviemaking with two schlockmeisters filming a biblical epic. Since the duo have no budget and are basic hacks with pretensions, they have to settle...so Sales plays Moses, "The Incredible Hulk" Ferrigno gets cast as Cain, while Plumb ("Jan" on "The Brady Bunch") does Mrs. Noah. Has some lulls but also covers very recognizable territory. Directorial debut of Borman. 82m/C VHS, DVD, Michael Riley, Stephen Rappaport, Soupy Sales, Lou Ferrigno, Eve Plumb, Andy Dick, Richard (Clarios) Bates, Fred Kaz, Cannel Tisman; D: Arthur Borman; W: Gregory S. Malins, Michael Curtis; C: Lee Daniel.

And Now Ladies and Gentlemen 🦴🦴 2002 (PG-13) English Valentin (Irons) is a jewel thief who likes disguises and is suffering from mysterious blackouts. In Paris, jazz singer Jane Lester (Kaas) is also suffering from blackouts. They both wind up in Morocco, staying at the same hotel and seeing the same doctor (both turn out to have brain tumors). They flirt, there's a robbery at the hotel, a cop investigates...and the film continues to meander on...and on. It all looks lovely but doesn't amount to much. English and French with subtitles. 126m/C VHS, DVD, FR GB Jeremy Irons, Patricia Kaas, Alessandra Martines, Thierry Lhermitte, Ticky Holgado, Yvan Attal, Claudia Cardinale, Amidou, Jean-Marie Bigard; D: Claude Lelouch; W: Claude Lelouch, Pierre Uytterhoeven, Pierre Leroux; C: Pierre William Glenn; M: Michel Legrand.

And Now for Something Completely Different 🦴🦴🦴 1972 (PG) A compilation of skits from BBC-TV's "Monty Python's Flying Circus" featuring Monty Python's own weird, hilarious brand of humor. Sketches include the "Upper Class Twit of the Year Race," "Hell's Grannies," and "The Townsmen's Guild Reconstruction of Pearl Harbor." A great intro to Python for the uninitiated, or a chance for the converted to see their favorite sketches again. 89m/C VHS, DVD, GB John Cleese, Michael Palin, Eric Idle, Graham Chapman, Terry Gilliam, Terry Jones, Carol Cleveland, Connie Booth; D: Ian McNaughton; W: John Cleese, Michael Palin, Terry Jones, Eric Idle, Graham Chapman, Terry Gilliam.

And Nothing But the Truth 🦴🦴½ Giro City 1982 A muckraking-national corporation is out to ruin the investigative TV report team trying to do a story on the company. 120m/C VHS, GB Glenda Jackson, Jon Finch, Kenneth Colley, James Donnelly; D: Karl Francis.

And Hope to Die 🦴🦴½ 1972 95m/C VHS, FR Robert Ryan, Jean-Louis Trintignant, Aldo Ray, Tisa Farrow, Lea Massari; D: Rene Clement.

And I Alone Survived 🦴🦴 1978 True story of a woman who survives a leisure-plane crash in the Sierra Nevadas and her struggle to get to the village below. Brown does her best to elevate the usual 1-hope-I-don't-die clichés. 96m/C VHS. Blair Brown, David Ackroyd, Vera Miles, G.D. Spradlin; D: William A. Graham; C: Jordan Cronenweth. TV

And Justice for All 🦴🦴½ 1979 (R) Earnest attorney Pacino questions the law and battles for justice in and out of the courtroom. He's hired to defend a detested judge from a rape charge, while dealing with a lost-soul caseload of eccentric, dramatic, and pitiful clients. Overly melodramatic, an odd mix of satire, cynicism, and seemingly sincere drama that fits with a club when a stick will do. Jewison aims for black surrealism, permitting both Pacino and Warden to veer into histrionics, to the detriment of what is essentially a gripping courtroom story. Excellent cast, including Lahti in her film debut. And Baltimore never looked lovelier. 120m/C VHS, DVD. Al Pacino, Jack Warden, Christine Lahti, Thomas G. Waites, Craig T. Nelson, John Forsythe, Lee Strasberg, Jeffrey Tambor; D: Norman Jewison; W: Barry Levinson, Valerie Curtin; C: Victor Kemper; M: Dave Grusin.

And Now My Love 🦴🦴 1974 (PG) A French couple endeavor to maintain their romance despite interfering socio-economic factors—she's a millionaire and he's an ex-con thief. Keller plays three roles spanning three generations as Lelouch invests autobiographical details to invent a highly stylized, openly sentimental view of French folks in love with love. Along the way he comments on social mores and changing attitudes through the years. Dubbed in English. 121m/C VHS, DVD, FR Marthe Keller, Andre Dussollier, Carla Gravina; D: Claude Lelouch; W: Claude Lelouch. LA. Film Critics '75: Foreign Film.

And Now the Screaming Starts 🦴🦴½ Bride of Fengriffen; Fengriffen; I Have No Mouth But I Must Scream 1973 (R) The young bride-to-be of the lord of a British manor house is greeted by a bloody, severed hand, and faces death at the window, a severed hand, and other corpses. Then Cushing shows up to investigate. Good-looking, sleek production with genuine chills. 91m/C VHS, DVD, GB Peter Cushing, Herbert Lom, Patrick Magee, Ian Ogilvy, Stephanie Beacham, Rosalie Crutchley, Guy Rolfe, Janet Key, Gillian Lind; D: Roy Ward Baker; W: Roger Marshall; C: Denys Coop; M: Douglas Gamley.

And Soon the Darkness 🦴🦴 1970 (PG) One of two vacationing young nurses disappears in France where a murderer was once murdered and the search is on. Predictable, ineffective suspense. 94m/C VHS, DVD, GB Pamela Franklin, Michele Dotrice, Sandor Eles, John Nettleton, Claire Kelly, Hanna-Marie Pravda; D: Robert Fuest; W: Terry Nation, Brian Clemens; C: Ian Wilson; M: Laurie Johnson.

And Starring Pancho Villa as Himself 🦴🦴🦴 2003 (PG-13) It's 1914, and Mexican revolutionary Pancho Villa finds himself in dire need of funding for his campaign against the military-run government. He strikes a deal with American filmmakers D.W. Griffith (Feore) and Harry Aiken (Broadbent) that provides them with full access to his war. Based upon actual events, their efforts resulted in the first feature length film. Splendid portrayal by the charismatic and superbly-cast Banderas in the title role of the complex and compelling Villa. 115m/C VHS, DVD, Antonio Banderas, Eion Bailey, Alan Arkin, Jim Broadbent, Matthew Day, Colm Feore, Michael McKean, Alexa Davalos, Anthony Head, Kyle Chandler, Saul Rubinek, Damian Alcazar, Pedro Armendariz Jr.; D: Bruce Beresford; W: Larry Gelbart; C: Andre Fleuren, Peter James; M: Joseph Vitarelli. CABLE.

And the Band Played On 🦴🦴🦴 1993 (PG-13) Randy Shilts's monumental, sad and controversial, 1987 book on the AIDS epidemic comes to TV in an equally controversial cable movie. Details the intricate medical research undertaken by doctors in France and the U.S. who fought to isolate and identify the mystery virus despite governmental neglect, red tape, clashing egos, and lack of funding. Various aspects of gay life are shown objectively, without sensationalizing. Celebrity cameos are somewhat distracting through most acquit themselves well. The script went through numerous rewrites; director Spottiswoode reportedly objected to HBO interference at the editing stage. 140m/C VHS, DVD. Matthew Modine, Alan Alda, Ian McKellen, Lily Tomlin, Glenne Headly, Richard Masur, Saul Rubinek, Charles Martin Smith, Patrick Bauchau, Nathalie Baye, Christian Clemenson. Cameos: Richard Gere, David Clennon, Phil Collins, Alex Courtney, David Dukes, David Marshall Grant, Ronald Guttman, Anjelica Huston, Ken Jenkins, Richard Jenkins, Tchéky Karyo, Swoosie Kurtz, Jack Laufer, Steve Martin, Dakin Matthews, Peter McRobbie, Lawrence Monoson, B.D. Wong, Donal Logue, Jeffrey Nording, Stephen Spinella; D: Roger Spottiswoode.

And Now Miguel 🦴🦴 1966 Plodding tale of a young boy who wants to take over as head shepherd of his family's flock. Filmed in New Mexico, with long outdoor shots make it drag a bit in spite of Cardi's competent performance. 95m/C VHS. Pat Cardi, Michael Ansara, Guy Stockwell, Clu Gulager, Joe De Santis, Pilar Del Rey, Buck Taylor; D: James B. Clark.

And

woode; **W:** Arnold Schuman; **C:** Paul Elliott; **M:** Carter Burwell. **C.A.B.L.E**

...And the Earth Did Not Swallow Him 🐾🐾½ *...Y No Se Lo Trago La Tierra* 1994 Family trials of migrant farm workers from the perspective of 12-year-old Marcos, who travels with his parents on their annual (it's 1952) move from Texas throughout the midwest during harvest season. Balances their struggles with the strong family bonds that allow them to endure. Based on the semi-autobiographical novel by Tomas Rivera. **99m/C VHS.** Jose Alcala, Rose Portillo, Marco Rodriguez; **D:** Severo Perez; **W:** Severo Perez; **C:** Virgil Harper; **M:** Marcos Loya.

And the Ship Sails On 🐾🐾🐾 *E la Nave Va* 1983 (PG) On the eve of WWI, a group of devoted opera lovers take a luxury cruise to pay their respects to a recently deceased opera diva. A charming and absurd autumnal homage-to-life by Fellini shot entirely in the studio. **130m/C VHS, DVD.** *IT* Freddie Jones, Barbara Jefford, Janet Suzman, Peter Cellier, Philip Locke, Victor Poletti, Norma West; **D:** Federico Fellini; **W:** Federico Fellini, Tonino Guerra; **C:** Giuseppe Rotunno; **M:** Gianfranco Plenizio.

And Then Came Love 🐾🐾 2007 When Julie (Williams) decides to search for the anonymous sperm donor father of her six-year old son, her idyllic world is suddenly turned upside-down. This color-blind romantic comedy provides unadulterated insight into complex relationships without being overly sappy or contrary. **98m/C DVD.** Vanessa Williams, Kevin Daniels, Ben Vereen, Michael Boatman, Eartha Kitt, Tommy Nelson, Stephen Spinella; **D:** Richard Schenkman; **W:** Caytha Jentis; **C:** Timothy Naylor; **M:** Rebecca Lloyd.

And Then There Were None 🐾🐾½ 1945 An all-star cast makes up the ten colorful guests invited to a secluded estate in England by a mysterious host. What the invitations do not say, however, is the reason they have been specifically chosen to visit—to be murdered, one by one. Cat and mouse classic based on Agatha Christie's book with an entertaining mix of suspense and black comedy. Remade in 1966 and again in 1975 as "Ten Little Indians," but lacking the force and gloss of the original. **97m/B VHS, DVD.** Louis Hayward, Barry Fitzgerald, Walter Huston, Roland Young, Sir C. Aubrey Smith, Judith Anderson, Mischa Auer, June Duprez; **D:** Rene Clair; **W:** Rene Clair, Dudley Nichols; **C:** Lucien N. Andriot; **M:** Mario Castelnuovo-Tedesco.

And Then You Die 🐾🐾🐾 1988 (R) An intense crime drama about a Canadian drug lord who amasses a fortune from the cocaine and marijuana trade. His empire is threatened as the Mafia, Hell's Angels, and the police try to bring him down. **115m/C VHS.** *CA* Kenneth Welsh, R.H. Thomson, Wayne Robson, Tom Harvey, George Bloomfield, Graeme Campbell; **D:** Francis Mankiewicz.

And You Thought Your Parents Were Weird! 🐾🐾½ 1991 (PG) A pair of introverted, whiz kid brothers invent a lovable robot to provide fatherly guidance as well as companionship for their widowed mother. Surprisingly charming, sentimental film is only slightly hampered by low-budget special effects. **92m/C VHS.** Marcia Strassman, Joshua John Miller, Edan Gross, John Quade, Sam Behrens, Susan Gibney, Gustav Vintas, Eric Walker; **D:** Tony Cookson; **W:** Tony Cookson; **C:** Paul Elliott; **M:** Randy Miller; **V:** Alan Thicke, Richard Libertini.

The Anderson Tapes 🐾🐾🐾 1971 (PG) Newly released from prison, an ex-con assembles his professional pals and plans the million-dollar robbery of an entire luxury apartment house on NYC's upper east side. Of course, he's unaware that a hoard of law men from federal, state, and local agencies are recording their activities for a wide variety of reasons, though none of the surveillance is coordinated and it has nothing to do with the intricate caper. Based on the novel by Lawrence Sanders, the intricate caper is effectively shaped by Lumet, who skill-

fully integrates broad satire with suspense. Shot on location in New York City. Walken is The Kid, his first major role. **100m/C VHS.** Sean Connery, Dyan Cannon, Martin Balsam, Christopher Walken, Alan King, Ralph Meeker, Garrett Morris, Margaret Hamilton, Val Avery, Dick Anthony Williams, Richard B. Shull, Conrad Bain, Paul Benjamin; **D:** Sidney Lumet; **W:** Frank Pierson; **M:** Quincy Jones.

Andersonville 🐾🐾🐾 1995 Andersonville was an infamous Confederate prison camp in Georgia that by August, 1864 contained more than 32,000 Union POWs—and was planned to hold 8,000 men. One in four soldiers died in the camp. The story is told through the eyes of Massachusetts Corporal Josiah Day (Emick), who is captured in 1864 and struggles to survive the hellish conditions. The commander of the Andersonville was a deranged German-Swiss captain named Wirz (Triska)—who became the only Civil War soldier to be hanged for war crimes (depicted in "The Andersonville Trial"). The TV miniseries was filmed some 150 miles from the original site. **168m/C VHS, DVD.** Thomas F. Wilson, Jarrod Emick, Frederic Forrest, Ted Marcoux, Jan Triska, Cliff DeYoung, Tom Aldredge, Frederick Coffin, Justin Henry, Kris Kamm, William H. Macy, Gabriel Olds, William Sanderson, Bud Davis, Carmen Argenziano, Peter Murnik; **D:** John Frankenheimer; **W:** David W. Rintels; **C:** Ric Waite; **M:** Gary Chang. **TV**

The Andersonville Trial 🐾🐾½ 1970 Details the atrocities experienced by captured Union soldiers who were held in the Confederacy's notorious Andersonville prison during the American Civil War. Provides an interesting account of the war-crimes trial of the Georgia camp's officials, under whom more than 14,000 prisoners died. Moving, remarkable TV drama based on the book by Pulitzer prize-winner MacKinlay Kantor. **150m/C VHS, DVD.** Martin Sheen, William Shatner, Buddy Ebsen, Jack Cassidy, Richard Basehart, Cameron Mitchell; **D:** George C. Scott. **TV**

Andre 🐾🐾½ 1994 (PG) More human-animal interaction from "the director of "The Man from Snowy River," telling the true story of an orphaned seal that was adopted by the local Maine harbormaster (Carradine) and his family. As they raise their houseguest, the question arises whether Andre should be returned to the wild. It'll remind you of "Free Willy" with an appealing smaller sea mammal and the equally appealing Majorino, as the youngster who befriends Andre. For those who are sticklers for accuracy, Andre is actually portrayed by a sea lion and not a seal. **94m/C VHS, DVD.** Keith Carradine, Tina Majorino, Chelsea Field, Keith Szarabajka, Shane Meier, Joshua Jackson; **D:** George Miller; **W:** Dana Baratta; **C:** Thomas Burstyn; **M:** Bruce Rowland.

Andrei Rublev 🐾🐾🐾🐾 1966 A 15th-century Russian icon painter must decide whether to record history or participate in it as Tartar invaders make life miserable. During the black and white portion, he becomes involved in a peasant uprising, killing a man in the process. After a bout of pessimism and a vow of silence, he goes forth to create artistic beauty as the screen correspondingly blazes with color. A brilliant historical drama censored by Soviet authorities until 1971. In Russian with English subtitles. **185m/C VHS, DVD.** *RU* Anatoli (Otto) Solonitzin, Ivan Lapikov, Nikolai Grinko, Nikolai Sergeyev; **D:** Andrei Tarkovsky; **W:** Andrei Tarkovsky, Andrei Konchainovsky; **C:** Vadim Yusov; **M:** Vyacheslav Ovchinnikov.

Androcles and the Lion 🐾🐾½ 1952 Stage-bound Hollywood version of the George Bernard Shaw story about a tailor in Imperial Rome who saves Christians from a hungry lion he had previously befriended. Sharp dialogue and a plot that's relatively (within the bounds of Hollywood) faithful help a great play become a semi-satisfying cinematic morsel. Harpo Marx was originally cast as Androcles, but was fired by producer Howard Hughes five weeks into the shooting. **105m/B VHS.** Jean Simmons, Alan Young, Victor Mature, Robert Newton, Maurice Evans, Elsa Lanchester; **D:** Chester Erskine; **C:** Harry Stradling Sr.

Android 🐾🐾🐾 1982 (PG) When an android who has been assisting a quirky scientist in space learns that he is about to be permanently retired, he starts to take matters into his own synthetic hands. Combines science fiction, suspense and cloned romance. A must for Kinski fans. **80m/C VHS, DVD.** Klaus Kinski, Don Opper, Brie Howard, Norbert Weisser, Crofton Hardester, Ray Kirchner; **D:** Aaron Lipstadt; **W:** James Reigle, Don Opper; **D:** Tim Suhrstedt; **M:** Don Preston.

The Android Affair 🐾🐾½ 1995 (PG-13) Karen Garrett (Kozak) is studying at the Institute for Surgical Research where doctors practice experimental techniques on lifelike androids. Her next patient is William (Dunne), a handsome and charming android with a heart defect, who doesn't want to "die" during Karen's risky surgical procedure. What's worse is Karen finds this 'droid all too humanly appealing and decides to help him escape the Institute. From a story by Isaac Asimov and screenwriter Kletter. **90m/C VHS.** Harley Jane Kozak, Griffin Dunne, Ossie Davis, Saul Rubinek, Peter Outerbridge, Natalie Radford; **D:** Richard Kletter; **W:** Richard Kletter; **C:** Bernard Salzmann; **M:** Simon Boswell.

The Andromeda Strain 🐾🐾½ 1971 (G) A satellite falls back to earth carrying a deadly bacteria that must be identified in time to save the population from extermination. The tension inherent in the bestselling Michael Crichton novel is talked down by a boring cast. Also available in letterbox format. **131m/C VHS, DVD.** Arthur Hill, David Wayne, James Olson, Kate Reid, Paula Kelly, Ramon Bieri, George Mitchell; **D:** Robert Wise; **W:** Nelson Gidding; **C:** Richard H. Kline; **M:** Gil Melle.

Andy and the Airwave Rangers 🐾🐾 *Awesome Adventure* 1989 Andy is whisked into the TV!! He finds adventure and excitement—car chases, intergalactic battles, and cartoons. **75m/C VHS, DVD.** Dianne Kay, Vince Edwards, Bo Svenson, Richard Thomas, Erik Estrada, Randy Josselyn, Jessica Puscas, Chuck Kovacic; **D:** Deborah Brock.

Andy Hardy Gets Spring Fever 🐾🐾 1939 Andy falls for a beautiful acting teacher, and then goes into a funk when he finds she's engaged. Judge Hardy and the gang help heal the big wound in his heart. A lesser entry (and the seventh) from the popular series. **88m/B VHS.** Mickey Rooney, Lewis Stone, Ann Rutherford, Fay Holden, Cecilia Parker, Sara Haden, Helen Gilbert; **D:** Woodbridge S. Van Dyke.

Andy Hardy Meets Debutante 🐾🐾½ 1940 Seems like there should be an article in that title. Garland's second entry in series, wherein Andy meets and falls foolishly for glamorous debutante Lewis with Betsy's help while family is on visit to New York. Judy Betsy sings "I'm Nobody's Baby" and "Singing in Rain." **86m/B VHS.** Mickey Rooney, Judy Garland, Lewis Stone, Ann Rutherford, Fay Holden, Sara Haden, Cecilia Parker, Diana Lewis, Tom Neal; **D:** George B. Seitz.

Andy Hardy's Double Life 🐾🐾🐾 1942 In this entertaining installment from the Andy Hardy series, Andy proposes marriage to two girls at the same time and gets in quite a pickle when they both accept. Williams makes an early screen splash. **91m/B VHS.** Mickey Rooney, Lewis Stone, Ann Rutherford, Fay Holden, Sara Lundigan, Susan Peters, Robert (Bobby) Blake; **D:** George B. Seitz; **C:** George J. Folsey.

Andy Hardy's Private Secretary 🐾🐾½ 1941 After Andy fails high school finals he gets help from a sympathetic faculty member. As the secretary, Grayson makes a good first impression in one of her early screen appearances. The Hardy series was often used as a training ground for new MGM talent. **101m/B VHS.** Mickey Rooney, Kathryn Grayson, Lewis Stone, Fay Holden, Ian Hunter, Gene Reynolds, Ann Rutherford; **D:** George B. Seitz.

Andy Warhol's Bad 🐾🐾🐾 1977 (R) In the John Waters' school of "crime is beauty," a Queens housewife struggles to make appointments for both her home

electrolysis clinic and her all-female murder-for-hire operation, which specializes in children and pets (who are thrown out of windows and knived, respectively). Her life is further complicated by a boarder (King) who's awaiting the go-ahead for his own assignment, an autistic child unwanted by his mother. One of Warhol's more professional-appearing films, and very funny if your tastes run to the tasteless. **100m/C VHS, DVD.** Perry King, Carroll Baker, Susan Tyrrell, Stefania Casini, Cyrinda Foxe, Lawrence Tierney, Tito Goya; **D:** Jed Johnson; **C:** Alan Metzger; **M:** Michael Bloomfield.

Andy Warhol's Dracula 🐾🐾🐾 *Blood for Dracula; Young Dracula; Dracula Cerca Sangue di Vergine e...Morì da Sete; Dracula Vuole Vivere: Cerca Sangue de Vergina; Andy Warhol's Young Dracula* 1974 (R) Sex and camp humor, as well as a large dose of blood, highlight Warhol's treatment of the tale. As Dracula can only subsist on the blood of pure, untouched maidens ("were-gins"), gardener Dallesandro rises to the occasion in order to make as many women as he can ineligible for Drac's purposes. Very reminiscent of Warhol's "Frankenstein," but with a bit more spoofery. Look for Roman Polanski in a cameo peek as a pub patron. Available in R and unrated versions. **106m/C VHS, DVD.** *IT* Udo Kier, Arno Juerging, Maxine McKendry, Joe Dallesandro, Vittorio De Sica, Milena Vukotic, Dominique Darel, Stefania Casini, Silvia Dionisio; **Cameos:** Roman Polanski; **D:** Paul Morrissey; **W:** Paul Morrissey; **M:** Claudio Gizzi.

Andy Warhol's Frankenstein 🐾🐾½ *Flesh for Frankenstein; The Frankenstein Experiment; Up Frankenstein; Came per Frankenstein; Frankenstein; Il Mostro e in Tavola...Barone Frankenstein* 1974 (X) A most outrageous parody of Frankenstein, featuring plenty of gore, sex, and bad taste in general. Baron von Frankenstein (Kier) derives sexual satisfaction from his corpses (he delivers a particularly thought-provoking philosophy on life as he lustfully fondles a gall bladder); his wife seeks her pleasure from the monster himself (Dallesandro). Originally made in 3-D, this is one of Warhol's campiest outings. Also available on video in an R-rated version. **95m/C VHS, DVD. GE FR IT** Udo Kier, Monique Van Vooren, Joe Dallesandro, Dalila di Lazzaro, Arno Juerging, Srdjan Zelenovic, Nicoletta Elmi, Marco Liofredi, Cristina Gajoni, Carla Mancini, Liu Bozizio; **D:** Paul Morrissey; **W:** Paul Morrissey; **C:** Luigi Kuveiller; **M:** Claudio Gizzi.

Angel 🐾🐾½ 1937 Melodrama finds Maria Barker (Dietrich) the bored wife of British diplomat Sir Frederick (Marshall). So she heads off to Paris to visit a friend and meets the dashing Anthony Halton (Douglas), with whom she has a fling. Too bad Halton's next stop is jolly old England when he runs into an old military chum (Sir Fred, of course). High gloss but no heart. **91m/B VHS.** Marlene Dietrich, Herbert Marshall, Melvyn Douglas, Edward Everett Horton, Laura Hope Crews; **D:** Ernst Lubitsch; **W:** Guy Bolton, Samson Raphaelson, Russell Medcroft; **C:** Charles Bryant) Lang Jr.; **M:** Frederick "Friedrich" Hollander.

Angel 🐾🐾🐾 1982 *Angelos* 1982 Angel (Maniatis) falls for a sailor (Xanthos) who promises a better life away from his abusive father and the poverty that surrounds him. Instead, Angel winds up on the Athens' streets as a transvestite prostitute, a situation that eventually lead the distraught young man to a shocking act of violence. Explicit but not prurient and based on a true story. Greek with subtitles. **126m/C VHS, DVD.** *GR* Michael Maniatis, Dionyssis Xanthos, Maria Alkeou, Katerina Helmi; **D:** George Katakouzinos; **W:** Stamatis Spanoudakis; **C:** Tassos Alexakis; **M:** Stamatis Spanoudakis.

Angel 🐾½ 1984 (R) Low-budget leerer about a 15-year-old honor student who attends an expensive Los Angeles private school during the day and by night becomes Angel, a streetwise prostitute making a living amid the slime and sleaze of Hollywood Boulevard. But wait, all is not perfect. A psycho is following her, looking for an opportunity. **94m/C VHS, DVD.** Donna Wilkes, Cliff Gorman, Susan Tyrrell, Dick Shawn,

Angel 3: The Final Chapter WOOF! 1988 (R) Former hooker Angel hits the streets to save her newly discovered sister from a life of prostitution. Trashy sequel with a better cast to tepid "Avenging Angel" which was the inept "1985 follow-up to 1984's tasteless "Angel." 100m/C VHS, DVD. Maud Adams, Mitzi Kapture, Richard Roundtree, Mark Blankfield, Kin Shriner, Tawny Ellis; Fere, Toni Basil; *D:* "om De Simone; *M:* Eric Allaman.

Angel-A 🐾🐾 2005 (R) Andre (Debbouze), a small-time crook, owes thugs all over Paris and he's at the end of the line. Contemplating a leap from a bridge to end his woes, a gorgeous blonde in a miniskirt beats him to it and leaps first. Of course he saves her. Of course she's his angel (a la "It's a Wonderful Life") and it's really her mission to save him. The spectacular Angela (Rasmussen) and Andre then traipse around town fixing Andre's mistakes as well as Andre himself. Shot in black and white, with stunning images of Paris; the film's plot and actors, alas, do not fare as well. 91m/B DVD, FR Jamel Debbouze, Rie Rasmussen, Gilbert Melki, Serge Riaboukine; *D:* Luc Besson; *W:* Luc Besson; *C:* Thierry Arbogast.

Angel and the Badman 🐾🐾🐾 1947 When notorious gunslinger Wayne is wounded during a shoot-out, a pacifist family takes him in and nurses him back to health. While he's recuperating, the daughter in the family (Russell) falls for him. She begs him not to return to his previous life. But Wayne, though smitten, thinks that a Duke's gotta do. And that means finding the dirty outlaw (Cabot) who killed his pa. Predictable but nicely done, with a good cast and script. Wayne provides one of his better performances (and also produced). 100m/B VHS, DVD. John Wayne, Gail Russell, Irene Rich, Harry Carey Sr., Bruce Cabot; *C:* James Edward Grant; *W:* James Edward Grant; *C:* Archie Stout; *M:* Richard Hageman.

An Angel at My Table 🐾🐾🐾 1989 (R) New Zealand TV miniseries chronicling the life of Janet Frame, New Zealand's premiere writer/poet. At once whimsical and tragic, the film tells of how a mischievous, free-spirited young girl was wrongly placed in a mental institution for eight years, yet was ultimately able to cultivate her incredible storytelling gifts, achieving success, fame and happiness. Adapted from three of Frame's novels: "To the Is-land," "An Angel at My Table," and "The Envoy From Mirror City." Highly acclaimed the world over, winner of over 20 major international awards. 157m/C VHS, DVD, NZ Kerry Fox, Alexia Keogh, Karen Fergusson, Iris Churn, K.J. Wilson, Martyn Sanderson; *D:* Jane Campion; *W:* Laura Jones; *C:* Stuart Dryburgh; Ind. Spirit '92. Foreign Film. TV

Angel Baby 🐾🐾🐾 1995 (R) Psychiatric out patients Kate (McKenzie) and Harry (Lynch) fall in love and move in together despite some misgivings from family and the medical bureaucracy. When Kate becomes pregnant, they decide to stop taking their medication so the baby has a better chance of being born healthy. Kate's doctors believe she's not capable of dealing with a child, although she is equally determined to have her baby, while Harry struggles to make a life for all of them. Strong performances and an assured debut by writer/director Rymer. Film won all seven of the Australian Film Institute Awards for which it was nominated. 101m/C VHS, AU John Lynch, Jacqueline McKenzie, Colin Friels, Deborra-Lee Furness, Robyn Nevin; *D:* Michael Rymer; *W:* Michael Rymer; *C:* Ellery Ryan; *M:* John Clifford Ryan. Australian Film

Angel Face 🐾🐾🐾 1952 An angel's face with a devil's heart is psycho rich girl Diane (Simmons), who wants to get rid of her hated stepmommy (O'Neil) so she can have daddy (Marshall) all to herself. Diane is infatuated with new chauffeur Frank (Mitchum) and he becomes an unwitting accomplice in her deadly scheme. Both are brought up on murder charges but Frank doesn't realize how far this crazy chick will go to keep what—and who—she wants. Wild noir melodrama from Preminger that gave good girl Simmons a chance to unleash her inner bad femme. Mitchum is his usual cool self. 92m/B DVD. Jean Simmons, Robert Mitchum, Herbert Marshall, Mona Freeman, Leon Ames, Barbara O'Neil, Kenneth Tobey; *D:* Otto Preminger; *W:* Frank Nugent, Oscar Millard; *C:* Harry Stradling Sr.; *M:* Dimitri Tiomkin.

An Angel for Satan 🐾🐾 gelo per Satan 1966 Steele plays a dual role in her last major, Italian horror film. She gives a strong performance as a woman possessed by the spirit of a statue. In Italian with no subtitles. 90m/B VHS, DVD. IT Barbara Steele, Anthony Steffen, Aldo Berti, Mario Brega, Ursula Davis, Claudio Gora; *D:* Camillo Mastrocinque; *W:* Camillo Mastrocinque; *M:* Francesco De Masi.

Angel Blue 🐾½ 1997 *My Neighbor's Daughter* 1997 All-around nice guy Dennis Cromwell (Bottoms) lives with his wife, Jill (Eichhorn) and newborn child in his California hometown. He befriends newcomer Enrique (Rodriguez) and soon Enrique's daughter Angela (Behrens) is babysitting for the infant Cornwell. David should really know better when his friendship with the teen turns sexual and their secret gets out. 91m/C VHS, DVD, Karen Black, Sandor "ecsy, Sam Behrens, Yeniffer Behrens, Lisa Eichhorn, Marco Rodriguez; *D:* Steven Kovacs; *W:* Steven Kovacs; *C:* Nickey Freeman; *M:* Joel Goldsmith. **CABLE**

Angel City 🐾½ 1980 A Florida labor camp is the setting for this made-for-TV drama. A family of rural West Virginia migrant workers find themselves trapped inside the camp and exploited by the boss-man. Adapted from Patricia Smith's book. 96m/C VHS, Ralph Waite, Paul Winfield, Jennifer Warren, Jennifer Jason Leigh, Mitchell Ryan; *D:* Philip Leacock; *W:* James Lee Barrett.

Angel Dust 🐾🐾 1996 Nightmare noir about a serial killer who haunts Tokyo's subways. Setsuko (Minami) is a criminal psychologist investigating the murders of several young women, all committed during rush hour at various commuter stops. Each victim has been killed with a poisonous injection. Setsuko learns the first victim was psychologically deprogrammed after leaving a religious cult and contacts her ex-lover, Rei (Wakamatsu), who runs a clinic specializing in such deprogramming. But Rei also becomes the chief suspect when he begins to play sadistic mind games with Setsuko. Is she paranoid or truly in danger? Japanese with subtitles. 116m/C VHS. JP Kaho Minami, Takeshi Wakamatsu; *D:* Sogo Ishii; *W:* Sogo Ishii, Yorozu Ikuta; *C:* Norimichi Kasamatsu; *M:* Hiroyuki Nagashime.

Angel Eyes 🐾🐾½ 2001 (R) Although the film's marketing campaign implied some supernatural elements, there's nothing unworldly about this romantic drama. And despite some capable performances by the leads, the film is utterly predictable as well. Tough Chicago police officer Sharon Pogue (Lopez) is still dealing with the effects of an abusive childhood when she meets another lost soul, Catch (Caviezel), who's grasping with the death of his wife and child. He saves her life, they fall for each other, but things are hardly that simple. They both have emotional issues and a past connection that's all too easy to determine. 104m/C VHS, DVD. Jennifer Lopez, James (Jim) Caviezel, Sonia Braga, Terrence Howard, Jeremy Sisto, Monet Mazur, Victor Argo, Shirley Knight, Jeremy Ratchford, Peter MacNeill, Stephen Kay; *D:* Luis Mandoki; *W:* Gerald Di Pego; *C:* Piotr Sobocinski; *M:* Marco Beltrami.

Angel Heart 🐾🐾½ 1987 (R) Exotic, controversial look at murder, voodoo cults, and sex in 1955 New Orleans. Bonet defiantly sheds her image as a young innocent (no more Cosby Show for you, young lady). Rourke is slimy as marginal NYC private eye Angel, hired by the devilish De Niro to track a missing big band singer who violated a "contract." His investigation leads him to the bizarre world of drips to a different beat. Visually stimulant- ing with a provocative sex scene between Bonet and Rourke, captured in both R-rat- ed and unrated versions. Adapted by Parker from "Falling Angel" by William Hjorts- berg. 112m/C VHS, DVD. Mickey Rourke, Robert De Niro, Lisa Bonet, Charlotte Rampling, Michael Higgins, Charles Gordone, Kathleen Wilhoite, Stocker Fountelieu, Brownie McGhee, Elizabeth Whitcraft, Eliott Keener, Dann Florek; *D:* Alan Parker; *W:* Alan Parker; *C:* Michael Seresin; *M:* Trevor Jones.

Angel in a Taxi 🐾🐾 1959 A six-year-old boy in an orphanage decides to choose his own mother, a beautiful ballerina he sees in a magazine, when an ugly couple try to adopt him. Italian film dubbed in English. 89m/B VHS. IT Wera Cecova, Ettore Manni, Vittorio De Sica, Marietto, Gabriele Ferzetti; *D:* Antonio Leonviola.

The Angel Levine 🐾🐾 1970 (PG) Morris (Mostel) is an old Jewish men of personal and professional losses. Alexander Levine (Belafonte) is a black angel who can earn his wings if he can convince Morris that his life does have meaning. As sentimental as it sounds but the leads are pros. Based on a story by Bernard Mala- mud. 104m/C VHS, DVD. Zero Mostel, Harry Be- lafonte, Ida Kaminska, Milo O'Shea, Gloria Foster, Eli Wallach, Anne Jackson; *D:* Jan Kadar; *W:* Bill Gunn, Ronald Ribman; *C:* Richard Kratina; *M:* William Eaton.

Angel of Death WOOF! 1986 (R) A small mercenary band of Nazi hunters attempt to track down Josef Mengele in South America. Stupid entry in the minor causes trouble" genre. Director Franco is also known as A. Frank Drew White. 92m/C VHS. Chris Mitchum, Fernando Rey, Susan Andrews; *D:* Jess (Jesus) Franco.

Angel of Death 🐾 *Semana Santa;* Holy Week 2002 Detective Maria Delgado (Sorvino) comes to Seville during Holly Week to investigate a series of ritual killings. With cops Quemada (Martinez) and Torillo (Atkine) assisting, Maria discovers a mysterious religious order. The Brotherhood of Christ, and an old woman (Vail) keeping a secret since the Spanish Civil War. Lackluster, miscast thriller adapted from the novel by David Hewson. 94m/C DVD. GE SP GB FR IT DK Mira Sorvino, Olivier Martinez, Feodor Atkine, Alida Valli, Luis Tosar; *D:* Pepe Darquart; *W:* Roy Mitchell; *C:* Ciro Cappellari; *M:* Andrea Guerra.

Angel of Destruction 🐾½ 1994 (R) Undercover cop is assigned to protect controversial rock star from psycho fan. Cop gets killed and star's sister decides to go after the killer. 80m/C VHS, DVD. Maria Ford, Charlie Spradling; *D:* Charles Philip Moore.

Angel of Fury 🐾🐾½ 1993 (R) Rothrock plays the head of security of a computer corporation who must battle terrorists after the company's top-secret computer. And there's no one she can trust. Lots of martial arts action with the competent Rothrock. 91m/C VHS. Cynthia Rothrock, Christopher Barnes, Peter O'Brian; *D:* Ackyl Anwary.

Angel of H.E.A.T. 🐾 WOOF! *The Protectors, Book One* 1982 (R) Porn-star Chambers is Angel, a female super-agent on a mission to save the world from total destruction. Sex and spies abound with trashy nonchalance. 90m/C VHS, DVD. Marilyn Chambers, Mary Woronov, Steve Johnson; *D:* Helen Sanford, Myrt A. Schreibman.

Angel of the Night 🐾🐾 *Engel 1998* (R) Rebecca inherits her grandmother's creepy mansion and invites her best friend and her boyfriend for a visit. While exploring, Rebecca discovers that great-grandpa Rico was a vampire and

Angel on My Shoulder 🐾🐾🐾 1946 A murdered convict makes a deal with the Devil (Rains) and returns to earth for revenge as a respected judge who's been thinning Hell's waiting list. Occupying the good judge, the murderous Muni has significant problems adjusting. Amusing fantasy with Muni in a rare and successful comic role. Co-written by Segall, who scripted "Here Comes Mr. Jordan," in which Rains played an angel. Remade in 1980. 101m/B VHS, DVD. Paul Muni, Claude Rains, Anne Baxter, Onslow Stevens; *D:* Archie Mayo; *W:* Harry Segall; *C:* James Van Trees; *M:* Dimitri Tiomkin.

Angel Rodriguez 🐾🐾½ 2005 Unsentimental story about the problems facing the trouble-prone title character, Angel (Everett) is a smart Brooklyn high schooler whose temper often gets the best of him. After getting into a fight with his dad's girlfriend, he's thrown out of the house and taken in for the night by his pregnant guidance counselor Nicole (Griffiths). But good intentions have a way of going wrong. 87m/C DVD. Rachel Griffiths, Jonan Everett, Walter Denis O'Hare, David Zayas, Jonan Everett, Walter Little, Jon Norman Schneider, Denise Burse, Tony Valentino, Peter Kwong, Mike Morott; *D:* Jim McKay.

Angel Square 🐾🐾 1992 A Canadian production from the director of the acclaimed "Bye Bye Blues." When the father of a neighborhood boy is brutally attacked, the community bands together to search for the culprit. 106m/C VHS, CA Ned Beatty; *D:* Anne Wheeler; *W:* James DeFelice.

Angel Town 🐾🐾 1989 (R) A foreign exchange student, who happens to be a champion kick-boxer, is forced into combat with LA street gangs. 90m/C VHS, DVD. Olivier Gruner, Theresa Saldana, Frank Aragon, Tony Valentino, Peter Kwong, Mike Morott; *D:* Eric Karson.

Angel Unchained 🐾 1970 Typical biker exploitation flick has bikers and hippies joining together to fend off small-town redneck hostility. 92m/C VHS, DVD. Don Stroud, Tyne Daly, Luke Askew, Larry Bishop, Aldo Ray, Bill McKinnay; *D:* Lee Madden; *W:* Jeffrey Alladin Fiskin.

Angel with the Trumpet 🐾🐾 1950 Depressing character study of a woman who marries to please her family, rather than herself. When the Gestapo finds out about her Jewish ancestry, she must make the most important decision of her life. 98m/B VHS. GB Eileen Herlie, Basil Sydney, Norman Wooland, Maria Schell, Olga Edwards, Oskar Werner, Anthony Bushell, Wilfrid Hyde-White; *D:* Anthony Bushell.

Angela 🐾 1977 Twisted love story about a young man (Railsback) who jumps the bones of an older woman, unaware that she is the mother he's been separated from for 23 long years. Seems that way back when, the boy was kidnapped by crime boss Huston from mom Loren, an ex-prostitute, who then turned in the boy's dad, who was something of a criminal. Mom thought son was dead, dad vowed revenge from prison, and son went about his unwitting business. It all comes together insipidly, at the expense of the cast and viewer. 91m/C VHS, CA Sophia Loren, Steve Railsback, John Huston, John Vernon; *D:* Boris Sagal; *M:* Henry Marcini.

Angela 🐾 1994 Exceedingly mystical film focuses on religiously obsessed 10-year-old Angela (Rhyne), who tells her six-year-old sister Ellie (Blythe) that unless they are very good the Devil will come to take them away. Meanwhile, she tries to cope with volatile family relationships, including their unstable mother. Good performances in a sometimes sluggish and abstract drama. **105m/C VHS, DVD.** Miranda Stuart Rhyne, Charlotte Blythe, Anna Thomson; **W:** Rebecca Miller; **C:** Ellen Kuras; **M:** Michael Rohatyn. *Sundance '95: Cinematog., Filmmakers Trophy.*

Angela ♦♦ **2002 (R)** Angela (Finocchiarro) is married to the older Saro (Pupella), who runs the mob in Palermo. Angea helps out by using her shoe store as a front for his drug deals, but she's frustrated by being shut out of all the business decisions. Then hunky hood Masino (di Stefano) is hired and the two are soon hitting the sheets. A bad idea, not only because of what Saro will do but because it gives the cops, who have the mobsters under surveillance, the leverage they need to take Saro down. Italian with subtitles. **100m/C DVD.** *IT* Andrea Di Stefano, Donnatella Finochiaro, Mario Pupella, Toni Gambino; **D:** Roberta Torre; **W:** Roberta Torre, Massimo D'Anolfi; **C:** Daniele Cipri; **M:** Andrea Guerra.

Angela's Ashes ♦♦½ **1999 (R)** Frank McCourt's devastating memoir covers growing up poverty-stricken in Limerick during the 1930s, with an alcoholic father (Carlyle) and a mother (Watson) struggling to hold the family together while dealing with her own deep depression. The book had the saving graces of lyricism and wit. Unfortunately, the film misses all that and is merely bleak despite the talented cast (including the three actors who play Frank through the years). **145m/C VHS, DVD.** Emily Watson, Robert Carlyle, Joe Breen, Ciaran Owens, Michael Legge, Ronnie Masterson, Pauline McLynn; **D:** Alan Parker; **W:** Robert Carlyle, Laura Jones; **C:** Michael Seresin; **M:** John Williams; **Nar:** Andrew Bennett.

Angele ♦♦♦ **1934** A lovely, naive country girl is lured to the city by a cunning pimp who knows that she wants to escape her oppressive father. With her illegitimate baby, she's discovered in a whorehouse and taken in disgrace back home to dad, who promptly locks her in the barn. One special guy, however, appreciates her purity and plots to rescue her. What he lacks in material resources he makes up for in character. An overlong but moving story of lost innocence and intolerance. In French with English subtitles. Based on the novel "Un de Baumugnes" by Jean Giono. **130m/B VHS.** *FR* Orane Demazis, Fernandel, Henri Poupon, Édouard Delmont; **D:** Marcel Pagnol.

Angelo My Love ♦♦♦ **1983 (R)** Compassionate docudrama about New York's modern gypsy community. Follows the adventures of 12-year-old Angelo Evans, the streetwise son of a fortune teller, who, with a fresh view, explores the ups and downs of his family's life. Duvall financed the effort and cast non-professional actors in this charming tale of reality and fairy-tale. **91m/C VHS.** Angelo Evans, Michael Evans, Cathy Kitchen, Millie Tsiginoff; **D:** Robert Duvall; **M:** Michael Kamen.

Angels and Insects ♦♦♦ **1995 (R)** Very strange Victorian-era romantic drama is definitely an acquired taste. The mysteries of nature are nothing compared to the mysteries of human life as naturalist William Adamson (Rylance) comes to discover when he takes up a position at the home of amateur insect collector, Sir Harald Alabaster (Kemp). He falls in love and quickly marries blondly beautiful Eugenia (Kensit), whose outward propriety hides a sensual nature and some decadent family secrets. Based on A.S. Byatt's novella "Morpho Eugenia." Take particular note of the costumes by Paul Brown, which mimic the exoticness of insects. **116m/C VHS, DVD.** *GB* Mark Rylance, Patsy Kensil, Kristin Scott Thomas, Jeremy Kemp, Douglas Henshall, Chris Larkin, Annette Badland, Anna Massey, Saskia Wickham; **C:** Bernard Zitzermann; **M:** Alexander Balanescu.

Angel's Brigade ♦♦ **1979 (PG)** Seven models get together to stop a big drug operation. Drive-in vigilante movie fare fit for a rainy night. **97m/C VHS.** Jack Palance, Peter Lawford, Jim Backus, Arthur God-frey; **D:** Greydon Clark; **W:** Greydon Clark; **C:** Dean Cundey.

Angel's Dance ♦♦½ **1999 (R)** Tony (Chandler) works for mobster Uncle Vinnie (Polito) and wants to be a hit man. So, Vinnie sends him to L.A. for training with Stevie Rosselini (Belushi) who, despite appearances, is an expert. Part of Tony's education is to choose and kill a victim at random and he selects Angel (Lee). This is Tony's big mistake, since this Angel is turns out to be the avenging kind. Gets a little too goofy but does provide some action. **102m/C VHS, DVD.** James Belushi, Sheryl Lee, Kyle Chandler, Jon Polito, Ned Bellamy, Mac Davis, Frank John Hughes, Mark Carlton; **D:** David Corley; **W:** David Corley; **C:** Michael G. Wojciechowski; **M:** Tim Truman.

Angels Die Hard ♦♦ **1984 (R)** Novel biker story with the cyclists as the good guys intent on helping a town during a mining disaster. Grizzly Adams makes an early film appearance. **86m/C VHS.** Tom Baker, R.G. Armstrong, Dan Haggerty, William (Bill) Smith; **D:** Richard Compton.

Angels Don't Sleep Here ♦♦ **2000** Forensic pathologist Michael Daniels returns to his hometown when his twin brother disappears. He gets involved with district attorney Kate, who was his brother's childhood girlfriend, and whose father is the town's mayor. Michael thinks his brother is stalking him and when the mayor is killed, he believes his brother is the culprit. But local detective Russell Stark thinks Michael is the real criminal. **97m/C VHS, DVD.** Dana Ashbrook, Robert Patrick, Roy Scheider, Susan Allison, Gary Farmer, Kelly Rutherford, Christina Pickles; **D:** Paul Cade. **VIDEO**

Angels Fall ♦♦½ **2007** Reece Gilmore (Locklear) was the sole survivor of a mass killing at the Boston restaurant where she worked. Desperate for a fresh start, Reece hits the road until her car breaks down in a Wyoming town and she takes a diner job to get some cash. Settling in, Reece becomes interested in writer Brody (Schaech), who is the only one to help her when Reece claims she witnessed a murder, although the cops don't find any evidence of a crime. A Lifetime original movie based on the novel by Nora Roberts. **95m/C VHS.** Heather Locklear, Johnathon Schaech, Gary Hudson, Derek Hamilton, Linda Darlow; **D:** Ralph Hameckler; **W:** Janet Brownell; **C:** Joel Ransom; **M:** Chris P. Bacon, Stuart M. Thomas. **CABLE**

Angels from Hell ♦♦ **1968** Early application in the nutso 'Nam returnee genre. Disillusioned Vietnam veteran forms a massive biker gang for the sole purpose of wreaking havoc upon the Man, the Establishment and anyone else responsible for sending him off to war. The big gang invades a town, with predictably bloody results. Sort of a follow-up to "Hell's Angels on Wheels." **86m/C VHS.** Tom Stern, Arlene Martel, Ted Markland, Stephen Oliver, Paul Bertoya, James Murphy, Jack Starrett, Pepper Martin, Luana Talltree; **D:** Bruce Kessler.

Angels Hard As They Come ♦♦ **1971 (R)** Opposing Hell's Angels leaders clash in a hippie-populated ghost town. A semi-satiric spoof of the biker genre's clichés features an early Glenn appearance and Busey's film debut. **86m/C VHS, DVD.** Gary Busey, Scott Glenn, James Iglehart, Gary Littlejohn, Charles Dierkop, Larry Tucker, Gilda Texter, Janet Wood, Brendan Kelly; **D:** Joe Viola; **W:** Jonathan Demme, Joe Viola; **M:** Richard Hieronymous.

Angels in America ♦♦♦ **2003** Kushner exquisitely adapts his two-part award-winning play into this six-part miniseries that vividly intertwines the lives and sufferings of several New Yorkers as they grapple with such issues as AIDS, drug addiction, homosexuality, and abandonment during the mid-80s. Masterfully directed by Nichols, it presents a spiritual perspective featuring Thompson as an angel of mercy to a man dying of AIDS while Streep appears as an apparition to another. **360m/C DVD.** Meryl Streep, Emma Thompson, Justin Kirk, Ben Shenkman, Mary-Louise Parker, Jeffrey Wright, Patrick Wilson, James Cromwell, Michael Gambon, Simon Callow, Brian Markinson; **D:** Mike Nichols; **W:** Al Pacino, Tony Kushner; **C:** Stephen Goldblatt; **M:** Thomas Newman. **CABLE**

Angels in the Endzone ♦♦½ **1998** TV follow-up to Disney's 1994 "Angels in the Outfield" finds the heavenly troops trying to aid a failing high school football squad, especially the leading players (Gallagher and Lawrence) who are also trying to also handle the death of their father. **85m/C VHS, DVD.** Matthew Lawrence, David Gallagher, Paul Dooley, Christopher Lloyd; **D:** Gary Nadeau. **TV**

Angels in the Infield ♦♦½ **2000** Third in the Disney series finds former baseball player Bob "The Bungler" Bugler (Grier) trying to earn his Guardian Angels wings by looking out for pitcher Eddie Everett (Warburton) who's lost his self-confidence. But with daughter Laurel (Irvin) praying for some heavenly intervention, things are certainly looking up. **93m/C VHS, DVD.** David Alan Grier, Patrick Warburton, Kurt Fuller, Rebecca Jenkins, Colin Fox, Peter Keleghan, Duane Davis, Brittney Irvin; **D:** Robert King. **TV**

Angels in the Outfield ♦♦♦ **1951** Enjoyable comedy fantasy about the lowly Pittsburgh Pirates who get a little celestial help from a new friend in their race for the pennant. Naturally, it takes the prayers of young Bridget (Corcoran) to get the angel Gabriel to assist. Oh yeah, only the kid can actually see the angels (no special effects in this movie). Great performances all around, especially Douglas as gruff/losing manager Guffy McGovern, with Janet Leigh as the reporter he makes a play for. Based on a story by Richard Conlin. **102m/C VHS, DVD.** Paul Douglas, Janet Leigh, Keenan Wynn, Donna Corcoran, Lewis Stone, Spring Byington, Bruce Bennett, Marvin Kaplan, Ellen Corby, Jeff Richards; **D:** Clarence Brown; **W:** Dorothy Kingsley, George Wells; **C:** Paul Vogel.

Angels in the Outfield ♦♦½ **1994 (PG)** Remake of the 1951 fantasy about a lowly baseball team who, along with some heavenly animated help find themselves on a winning streak. The new lineup includes Glover as manager of the hapless California Angels, Danza as a washed-up pitcher, and Lloyd as captain of the celestial spirits. Gordon-Levitt plays the foster child who believes he'll get his family back together if the Angels win the pennant. Familiar ground still yields good, heartfelt family fare. Oakland A's third baseman Carney Lansford served as technical advisor, molding actors into fair semblance of baseball team. **105m/C VHS, DVD.** Danny Glover, Tony Danza, Christopher Lloyd, Brenda Fricker, Ben Johnson, Joseph Gordon-Levitt, Jay O. Sanders, Dermot Mulroney; **D:** William Dear; **W:** Holly Goldberg Sloan; **C:** Matthew F. Leonetti; **M:** Randy Edelman.

Angels of the City ♦♦ **1989** What's a girl got to do to join a sorority? A house prank turns vicious when two coeds take a walk on the wild side and accidentally observe a murder, making them the next targets. Credible exploitation effort, if that's not an oxymoron. **90m/C VHS.** Lawrence-Hilton Jacobs, Cynthia Cheston, Kelly Galindo; **D:** Lawrence-Hilton Jacobs; **W:** Lawrence-Hilton Jacobs, Raymond Martino, Joseph Merhi.

Angels One Five ♦♦ **1954** A worm's-eye view of British air power in WWII. What little "excitement" there is, is generated by flashing lights, plotting maps, and status boards. Hawkins and Denison are the only bright spots. **97m/B VHS.** *GB* Jack Hawkins, Michael Denison, Dulcie Gray, John Gregson, Cyril Raymond, Veronica Hurst, Geoffrey Keen, Vida Hope, Andrew Osborn; **D:** George More O'Ferrall; **W:** Derek Twist; **C:** Christopher Challis, Stanley Grant; **M:** John Wooldridge.

Angels Over Broadway ♦♦♦ **1940** Slick, fast-paced black comedy about con man Fairbanks, who plans to hustle suicidal thief Qualen during a poker game, but has a change of heart. With the help of call-girl Hayworth and drunken playwright Mitchell, he helps Qualen turn his life around. Ahead of its time with an offbeat morality, but a delight in the '90s. **80m/B VHS, DVD.** Douglas Fairbanks Jr., Rita Hayworth, Thomas Mitchell, John Qualen, George Watts; **D:** Ben Hecht, Lee Garmes; **W:** Ben Hecht; **C:** Lee Garmes.

Angels' Wild Women *woof!* **1972** From the man who brought you "Dracula vs. Frankenstein" comes an amalgamation of hippies, motorcycle dudes, evil desert gurus and precious little plot. **85m/C VHS, DVD.** Kent Taylor, Regina Carrol, Ross Hagen, Maggie Bemby, Vicki Volante; **D:** Al Adamson.

Angels with Dirty Faces ♦♦♦½ **1938** Rousing classic with memorable Cagney twitches and the famous long walk from the cell to the chair. Two young hoods grow up on NYC's lower East Side with diverse results—one enters the priesthood and the other opts for crime and prison. Upon release from the pen, famed gangster Cagney sets up shop in the old neighborhood, where Father O'Brien tries to keep a group of young toughs (the Dead End Kids) from following in his footsteps. Bogart's his unscrupulous lawyer and Bancroft a crime boss intent on double-crossing Cagney. Reportedly they were blasting real bullets during the big shootout, no doubt helping Cagney's intensity. Adapted from a story by Rowland Brown. **97m/B VHS, DVD.** James Cagney, Pat O'Brien, Humphrey Bogart, Ann Sheridan, George Bancroft, Billy Halop, Leo Gorcey, Huntz Hall, Bobby Jordan, Bernard Punsley, Gabriel Dell, Adrian Morris; **D:** Michael Curtiz; **W:** John Wexley, Warren Duff, Rowland Brown; **C:** Sol Polito; **M:** Max Steiner. *N.Y. Film Critics '38: Actor (Cagney).*

Anger Management ♦♦ **2003 (PG-13)** Disappointing comedy has mild-mannered, confrontation-averse Dave (Sandler) forced to attend anger management therapy after a misunderstanding on an airplane. Crazed anger therapist Dr. Buddy Rydell (Nicholson) is of the opinion that Dave isn't angry enough on the outside, so he proceeds, in increasingly ridiculous ways, to make him...angry, disrupting Dave's life and his relationship with girlfriend Linda (Tomei). While attempting to play off the two leads' screen and public personas, it succeeds only rarely, due mainly to a weak script that takes the easy way out whenever it's offered, and by-the-numbers direction. Nicholson's obvious glee at not having to be restrained makes some scenes work on a pure comic level, while Sandler seems right at home, back in his element, after the smart comedy of "Punch-Drunk Love." **101m/C VHS, DVD, UMD.** *US* Adam Sandler, Jack Nicholson, Marisa Tomei, Luis Guzman, Allen Covert, Lynne Thigpen, Kurt Fuller, Jonathan Loughran, Krista Allen, January Jones, Woody Harrelson, John Turturro, Heather Graham, John C. Reilly, Kevin Nealon, Harry Dean Stanton; **Cameos:** Bobby Knight, John McEnroe; **D:** Peter Segal; **W:** David Dorfman; **C:** Donald McAlpine; **M:** Teddy Castellucci.

Angi Vera ♦♦♦ **1978** Naive 18-year-old Angi (Papp) is living in 1948 Hungary during the early days of socialism. Sent to a re-education school, she falls in love with her married Party leader but gradually loses her personal integrity to a corrupt system. Hungarian with subtitles. **96m/C VHS.** *HU* Veronika Papp, Erszi Pasztor, Eva Szabo, Tamas Dunai, Laszlo Horvath; **D:** Pal Gabor; **W:** Pal Gabor; **C:** Lajos Koltai; **M:** Gyorgy Selmeczi.

Angie ♦♦ **1994 (R)** Brassy Angie finds herself pregnant and unmarried. Tired of the advice and criticism she receives from her close knit neighborhood she strikes out of Brooklyn to find a new life for herself. Average "woman's movie" wrought with messages of pregnancy, childbirth, friendship, love, and family has far too much going on and relies too heavily on formula soap. Davis, in what could have been a juicy (read "Oscar") role is strong, but her performance is drowned by all the melodrama. Madonna was originally cast as Angie, but was bounced when the filming of "Snake Eyes" conflicted. Adapted from the book "Angie, I Says" by Avra Wing. **108m/C VHS, DVD.** Geena Davis, Aida Turturro, Stephen Rea, Philip Bosco, James Gandolfini, Jenny O'Hara; **D:** Martha Coolidge; **W:** Todd Graff;

AngKor: Cambodia Express 🐾 **1981** An American journalist travels back to Vietnam to search for his long lost love. **96m/C VHS, DVD.** Robert Walker Jr., Christopher George. **D:** Lek Kitipara-pon.

Angry Harvest 🐾🐾🐾 **1985** During the WWII German occupation of Poland, a gentile farmer shelters a young Jewish woman on the run, and a serious, ultimately interdependent relationship forms. Acclaimed; Holland's first film since her native Poland's martial law imposition made her an exile to Sweden. In German with English subtitles. Contains nudity and violence **102m/C VHS, DVD.** GE Armin Mueller-Stahl, Elisabeth Trissenaar, Wojciech Pszoniak, Margit Carstensen, Kurt Raab, Kathe Jaenicke, Hans Beenherle, Isa Haller. **D:** Agnieszka Holland. **W:** Agnieszka Holland. Montreal World Film Fest. '85. *Bittere Ernte*

Angry Joe Bass 🐾 **1976** Contemporary Native American Joe Bass faces government officials who continually usurp his fishing rights. Something like "Billy Jack" without the intelligence. **82m/C VHS,** Henry Bal, **D:** Mery Mershon; **D:** Thomas G. Reeves.

The Angry Red Planet 🐾🐾 *Invasion of Mars; Journey to Planet Four* **1959** An unintentionally amusing sci-fi adventure about astronauts on Mars fighting off aliens and giant, ship-swallowing amoebas. Filmed using bizarre "Cinemagic" process, which turns almost everything pink. Wild effects have earned the film cult status. **83m/C VHS, DVD.** Gerald Mohr, Les Tremayne, Jack Kruschen, Nora Hayden, Paul Hahn, J. Edward McKinley, Tom Daly, Don Lamond; **D:** Ib Melchior, Sidney W. Pink; **C:** Stanley Cortez. **M:** Paul Dunlap.

Anguish 🐾🐾½ **1988 (R)** Well-done horror thriller about a lunatic who, inspired to duplicate the overweight Angus (Talbert), a friendly kid tormented by the usual school bullies. He's best bud is twerp Troy (Owen), murders in a popular film, murders a movie audience as they watch the movie. Violence and gore abound. **89m/C VHS, DVD.** SP Zelda Rubinstein, Michael Lerner, Talia Paul, Clara Pastor; **D:** Bigas Luna; **W:** Bigas Luna; **C:** Josep Civit; **M:** (Jose) (Manuel) Pagar.

Angus 🐾🐾 **1995 (PG-13)** Dull teen comedy about self-esteem revolves around the overweight Angus (Talbert), a friendly kid tormented by the usual school bullies. He's best bud is twerp Troy (Owen), and tries to help Angus with his crush on cute blonde Melissa (Ariana). There's even a schmaltzy prom scene. The profanity, though mild, and the boys sexual interests make this questionable for the pre-teen audience that could actually enjoy it. **87m/C VHS,** Charlie Talbert, Kathy Bates, George C. Scott, Chris Owen, Ariana Richards, Lawrence Pressman, Rita Moreno, James Van Der Beek, Anna Thomson; **D:** Patrick Read Johnson; **W:** Jill Gordon; **C:** Alexander Gruysynski; **M:** (Jose) E. Russo.

The Animal 🐾🐾 **2001 (PG-13)** Meek clerk Schneider is injured in a serious car accident and is rescued by a mad scientist who surgically replaces his damaged organs with animal parts. These animalistic traits tend to surface at the worst possible time for Schneider, just as he's realizing his dream of becoming a super-cop. Haskell (from TV's first "Survivor") is pleasant in her big screen debut as the animal-rights advocate girlfriend, but Schneider is the one who makes this surprisingly enjoyable comedy work with his affable loser persona and willingness to go with the joke. **83m/C VHS, DVD. US** Rob Schneider, Guy Torry, John C. McGinley, Colleen Haskell, Michael Caton, Louis Lombardi, Ed Asner, Michael (Mike) Papajohn; **D:** Luke Greenfield; **W:** Rob Schneider; Tom Brady; **C:** Peter Lyons Collister. **M:** Teddy Castellucci.

Anima 🐾🐾 **1998** Sam and Iris have long left their pasts in Nazi Germany behind them for a secluded life in a New England farmhouse. At least until young journalist Bill discovers them while researching an article on taxidermy and mummification and sees that their bizarre private world. **88m/C VHS, DVD.** Bray Poor, George Bartenieff, Jacqueline Bertrand; **D:** Craig Richardson; **W:** Craig Richardson; **M:** Joel Diamond, Adam Hurst.

Anima 🐾🐾 **2005 (R)** James "Animal" Allen is a violent gangsta sent to prison, leaving behind young son Darius (Horton), who grows up following in pop's footsteps. When Animal emerges from prison reformed, he attempts to get Darius out of the life. Thoughtful and intelligent, with excellent performances by leads Howard and Rhames. **93m/C VHS, DVD.** Ving Rhames, Terrence Howard, Jim Brown, Chazz Palminteri, Paula Jai Parker, Faizon Love, Wes Studi, Beverly Todd; **D:** David J. Burke; **W:** David Clark) Johnson. VIDEO

Animal 2 🐾🐾½ **2007** Lifer James "Animal" Allen's (Rhames) prison transfer finds him doing time with younger son James Jr. (Collins), who was framed for murder by Animal's old foe Kasada (Dunn), who wants Animal to get back into the prison fight game. On the outside, either son Darius (Shannon) is trying to find the evidence to clear his bro. **93m/C DVD.** Ving Rhames, Vicelous Shannon, Conrad Dunn, K.C. Collins; **D:** Ryan Combs; **W:** Jacob L. Adams; **M:** Craig McConnell. VIDEO

Animal Behavior 🐾 **1989 (PG)** An animal researcher and a music professor fall in love on a college campus. Bower's (she actually released it under the alias Riley H. Anne) comedy was filmed in 1985 and edited/shelved for over four years, and finally released with good reason. **79m/C VHS.** Karen Allen, Armand Assante, Holly Hunter, Josh Mostel, Richard Libertini; **D:** Jenny (H. Anne Riley) Bowen; **W:** Susan Rice; **C:** Richard Bowen; **M:** Cliff Eidelman.

Animal Called Man 🐾 **1987** Two crooked buddies join a big western gang in pillaging a small town and get in too deep. **83m/C VHS.** Vassili Karis, Craig Hill, Gillian Bray. **D:** Carlo (Roberto) Mauri.

Animal Crackers 🐾🐾🐾 **1930 (G)** The second and possibly the funniest of the 13 Marx Brothers films, "Animal Crackers" is a screen classic. Groucho is a guest at the house of wealthy matron Margaret Dumont and he, along with Zeppo, Chico, and Harpo, destroy the tranquility of the estate. Complete with the Harry Ruby music score—including Groucho's "Hooray for Captain Spaulding" with more quotable lines than any other Marx Brothers film: "One morning I shot an elephant in my pajamas. How he got in my pajamas, I'll never know." Based on a play by George S. Kaufman. **98m/B VHS, DVD.** Groucho Marx, Chico Marx, Harpo Marx, Zeppo Marx, Lillian Roth, Margaret Dumont, Louis Sorin, Hal Thompson, Robert Greig, Margaret Irving, Edward Metcalf, Kathryn Reece; **D:** Victor Heerman; **W:** Morrie Ryskind; **C:** George J. Folsey; **M:** Bert Kalmar, Harry Ruby.

Animal Factory 🐾🐾½ **2000 (R)** When first-time felon Ron Decker (Furlong) is sentenced to two years in a decaying prison, he is introduced to a world where violence is a way of life. After witnessing a riot, Ron is taken under the wing of Earl Copen (Dafoe), the main-man on the cellblock, but the younger man soon discovers that life in prison is not about rehabilitation, it's about survival. Bunker wrote the screenplay based on his novel of the same name. **94m/C VHS, DVD.** Edward (Eddie) Bunker, Willem Dafoe, Edward Furlong, Danny Trejo, John Heard, Mickey Rourke, Tom Arnold, Mark Boone Jr., Steve Buscemi, Seymour Cassel; **D:** Steve Buscemi; **W:** Edward (Eddie) Bunker, John Steppling; **C:** Phil Parmet; **M:** John Lurie.

Animal Instincts 🐾🐾 **1992 (R)** A woman takes a prescription drug that makes her a nymphomaniac, and her police officer husband discovers that he's turned on by videotaping her in bed with other men and women. One of the many in her constant stream of lovers is a politician whose campaign is based on shutting down all the town's sex clubs. Another in the string of sexual thrillers riding on the coattails of "Basic Instinct." **94m/C VHS, DVD.** Maxwell Caulfield, Jan-Michael Vincent, Mitch Gaylord, Shannon Whirry, Delia Sheppard, John Saxon, David Carradine; **W:** Jon Robert Samsel, Georges des Essarnies; **C:** Paul Desatoff; **M:** Joseph Smith.

Animal Instincts 2 🐾🐾 **1994 (R)** Joanna leaves her overbearing husband and moves into a supposedly quiet community. Neighbor Steve is a security expert—and a voyeur. He's hidden a camera in Joanna's bedroom but she knows he's watching. **92m/C VHS, DVD.** Shannon Whirry, Woody Brown, Elizabeth Sandifer, Al Sapienza; **C:** Alexander Gray (Gregory Dark) Hippolyte.

Animal Instincts 3: The Seductress 🐾 **1995 (R)** Joanna (Schumacher) finds a new kind of sexual excitement when she gets involved with rock music promoter Alex (Matthew), whose kicks include feining blindness. The unrated version contains 12 more minutes of footage. **96m/C VHS, DVD.** Wendy Schumacher, James Matthew, Marcus Graham, John Bates, Anthony Lesa; **D:** Alexander Gray (Gregory Dark) Hippolyte. **W:** Selwyn Harris; **C:** Ernest Paul Roebuck.

The Animal Kingdom 🐾🐾🐾 **1932** A romantic triangle develops when Howard, married to Loy, has an affair with Harding. The problem is Harding acts more like a wife and Loy a mistress. Intelligently written and directed, with a marvelous performance from veteran character actor Gargan. **95m/B VHS, DVD.** Ann Harding, Leslie Howard, Myrna Loy, Neil Hamilton, William Gargan, Henry Stephenson, Ilka Chase; **D:** Edward H. Griffith; **W:** Horace Jackson; **C:** George J. Folsey.

Animal Room 🐾🐾 **1995** When high school student Arnold Mosk (Harris) is caught using drugs, he's place in the school's controversial isolation program that's nicknamed "The Animal Room." There are no rules and Arnold's life is threatened by delinquent thug Doug (Lillard). But if Arnold expects to survive, he's going to have to learn how to fight. **93m/C VHS, DVD.** Neil Patrick Harris, Matthew Lillard, Gabriel Olds, Catherine Hicks, Brian Vincent; **D:** George J. Folsey. **C:** Craig Slinger.

Anita, Dances of Vice 🐾🐾 *Anita—Tanze des Lasters* **1987** German avant-garde film celebrates Anita Berber, the "most scandalous woman in 1920s Berlin." Berber was openly bisexual, used drugs, and danced nude in public. In von Praunheim's film, she rises from the dead and creates yet more scandal. **85m/C VHS.** GE Lotti Huber, Ina Blum, Mikhael Honessenau; **D:** Rosa von Praunheim.

Animal Farm 🐾🐾🐾 **1955** An animated version of George Orwell's classic political satire about a barnyard full of animals who parallel the growth of totalitarian dictatorships. Not entirely successful, but probably best translation of Orwell to film. **73m/C VHS, DVD.** Gordon Heath. **V:** Maurice Denham, Gordon Heath.

Animal Farm 🐾½ **1999** Orwell's political satire is given the "Babe" treatment in this live-action version. Drunken farmer Mr. Jones (Postlethwaite) has his power overthrown by his barnyard animals, who in turn are ruled by the pig population. Only porker Napoleon (Stewart) turns out to be as big a tyrant as his human counterpart. Far beyond the scope of children, this retelling of the familiar story is clunky and its propaganda value has certainly come and gone. (Orwell was originally satirizing Stalinist Russia.) **91m/C VHS, DVD.** Pete Postlethwaite; **D:** John Stephenson; **W:** Martyn Burke, Alan James; **C:** Mike Brewster; **M:** Richard Harvey; **V:** Patrick Stewart, Kelsey Grammer, Ian Holm, Julia Ormond, Louis-Dreyfus, Paul Scofield, Peter Ustinov. CABLE

Ann Vickers 🐾🐾½ **1933** A dashing young army captain wins over the heart of a dedicated social worker. Okay adaptation of a Sinclair Lewis novel, with Dunne suffering more than usual. **76m/B VHS.** Irene Dunne, Walter Huston, Bruce Cabot, Conrad Nagel, Edna May Oliver; **D:** John Cromwell; **M:** Max Steiner.

The Ann Jillian Story 🐾½ **1988** Jillian stars as herself in this melodrama recounting her battle with breast cancer. Several musical numbers are included. **96m/C VHS.** Ann Jillian, Tony LoBianco, Viveca Lindfors, Leighton Bewley; **D:** Corey Allen. TV

Anna 🐾🐾🐾 **1987 (PG-13)** Age, envy, and the theatrical world receive their due in an uneven but engrossing drama about aging Czech film star Anna making a sad living in New York doing commercials and trying to land off-Broadway roles. She takes in Krystyna, a young Czech peasant girl who eventually rockets to model stardom. Mo-dern, strongly acted "All About Eve" with a story partially based on a real Polish actress. Kirkland drew quite a bit of flak for shamelessly self-promoting for the Oscar. She still lost. **101m/C VHS, DVD.** Sally Kirkland, Paulina Porizkova, Robert Fields, Stefan Schnabel, Larry Pine, Ruth Maleczech; **D:** Yurek Bogayevicz. **W:** Yurek Bogayevicz, Agnieszka Holland; **C:** Bobby Bukowski; **M:** Greg Hawkes. Golden Globes '88. Actress (Kirkland); Ind. Spirit '88. Actress (Kirkland); L.A. Film Critics '87. Actress (Kirkland).

Anna 🐾🐾🐾 *Anna: From Six, Till Eighteen; Anna: Ot Shesti do Vosemnadtsati* **1993** Director Nikhalkov follows Russian history from the early 1990s through the next 13 years of the West. The film looks stunning (it was filmed in Malaysia) and Yun-Fat is regal and charismatic but Foster is too stiff upper-lipped and remote and there's respect rather than any hint of romance. Previously filmed as 1946's "Anna and the King of Siam" and the 1956 musical "The King and I." **147m/C VHS, DVD.** Jocie Foster, Chow Yun-Fat, Bai Ling, Tom Felton, Syed Alwi; **D:** Andy Tennant; **W:** Steve Meerson, Peter Krikes; **C:** Caleo Deschanel; **M:** George Fenton.

Anna and the King 🐾🐾½ **1999 (PG-13)** Based on the story of English widow and schoolteacher Anna Leonowens (Foster) who, in 1862, is hired by the King Mongkut of Siam (Yun-Fat) to introduce his 58 children to the ideas of the West. The film looks stunning (it was filmed in Malaysia) and Yun-Fat is regal and charismatic but Foster is too stiff upper-lipped and remote and there's respect rather than any hint of romance. Previously filmed as 1946's "Anna and the King of Siam" and the 1956 musical "The King and I." **147m/C VHS, DVD.** Jocie Foster, Chow Yun-Fat, Bai Ling, Tom Felton, Syed Alwi; **D:** Andy Tennant; **W:** Steve Meerson, Peter Krikes; **C:** Caleo Deschanel; **M:** George Fenton.

Anna and the King of Siam 🐾🐾🐾 **1946** Splendid adaptation, from the true life adventures of 33-year-old English widow Anna Leonowens. In 1862 Anna and her son travelled to the exotic kingdom of Siam to educate the harem and children of the king. Dunne is splendid as the strong-willed governess as is Harrison (in his first American film) as the authoritarian eastern ruler. Remade as the musical "The King and I." **128m/B VHS.** Irene Dunne, Rex Harrison, Linda Darnell, Lee J. Cobb, Gale Sondergaard, Mikhail Rasumny, Dennis Hoey, Richard Lyon, John Abbott; **D:** John Cromwell; **W:** Sally Benson, Talbot Jennings; **C:** Arthur C. Miller; **M:** Bernard Herrmann. Oscars '46. Art Dir/Set Dec., B&W, B&W Cinematog.

Anna Christie 🐾🐾🐾½ **1923** Silent production of Eugene O'Neill's play about the love a young girl is sent away by her father, a seaman, and finds her way to Chicago, where she becomes a prostitute. Later she visits her father's barge and falls for a sailor. She shares her past life story hoping they will understand. This film was acclaimed when it was released, and still remains a touching work of art. Remade in 1930. **75m/B VHS.** Blanche Sweet, George F. Marion Sr., William Russell, Eugenie Besserer, Chester Conklin, George Siegmann, Victor Potel, Fred Kohler Sr.; **D:** John Griffith Wray.

Anna Christie 🐾🐾½ **1930** Garbo is the ex-prostitute who finds love with a sailor Bickford. Bickford is unaware of the lover's tarnished past and she does her best to keep it that way. Garbo's first sound effort was advertised with the slogan "Garbo talks!" Remade from the 1923 version; also the basis for a 1930 German version, also starring Garbo. Garbo is seriously injured former fiancee is brought to the hospital where she is a nurse. Anna must finally deal with her feelings and decide which path her life will take. Dubbed in English. **111m/B VHS.** IT Silvana Mangano, Raf Vallone, Vittorio Gassman; **D:** Alberto Lattuada; **C:** Otello Martelli; **M:** Nino Rota.

---

gan "Garbo Talks." Adapted from the classic Eugene O'Neill play, the film is a slow but rewarding romantic drama. **90m/B VHS, DVD.** Greta Garbo, Marie Dressler, Charles Bickford, George F. Marion Sr.; **D:** Clarence Brown; **C:** William H. Daniels.

Anna Karenina 🦴🦴🦴½ **1935** Cinematic Tolstoy with Garbo as sad, moody, married Anna willing to give up everything to be near Vronsky (March), the cavalry officer she's obsessed with. And since it's Russian, expect tragedy. A classic Garbo vehicle with March and Rathbone (as the cuckhold husband) providing excellent support. Interestingly, a remake of the Garbo and John Gilbert silent, "Love." **85m/B VHS, DVD.** Greta Garbo, Fredric March, Freddie Bartholomew, Maureen O'Sullivan, May Robson, Basil Rathbone, Reginald Owen, Reginald Denny; **D:** Clarence Brown; **W:** S.N. Behrman, Clemence Dane, Salka Viertel; **C:** William H. Daniels; **M:** Herbert Stothart. N.Y. Film Critics '35: Actress (Garbo).

Anna Karenina 🦴🦴½ **1948** Stiff version of Tolstoy's passionate story of illicit love between a married woman and a military officer. In spite of exquisite costumes, and Leigh and Richardson as leads, still tedious. **123m/C VHS, DVD. GB** Vivien Leigh, Ralph Richardson, Kieron Moore, Sally Ann Howes, Niall MacGinnis, Martita Hunt, Michael Gough; **D:** Julien Duvivier; **W:** Julien Duvivier; **C:** Henri Alekan; **M:** Constant Lambert.

Anna Karenina 🦴🦴½ **2000** Well-done British adaptation of the familiar Tolstoy drama although, frankly, Anna (McCrory) is a pill. Less tragic than headstrong, this willful Russian beauty runs from her passionless marriage to Karenin (Dillane) straight into the arms of dashing seducer Vronsky (McKidd). Of course, once they turn each other's lives to misery, what else is left but a tragic end. This version also includes the secondary love affair of Kitty (Baeza) and Levin (Henshall). **240m/C VHS, DVD.** Helen McCrory, Kevin McKidd, Stephen (Dillon) Dillane, Douglas Henshall, Paloma Baeza, Amanda Root, Mark Strong; **D:** David Blair; **W:** Allan Cubitt; **C:** Ryszard Lenczewski; **M:** John Keane. **TV**

Anna to the Infinite Power 🦴🦴½ **1984** Sci fi based on the book of the same name follows a young girl with telepathic powers. When the girl discovers that she has sisters as the result of a strange scientific experiment, she sets out to find them, drawing on her own inner strength. **101m/C VHS.** Dina Merrill, Martha Byrne, Mark Patton; **D:** Robert Wiemer.

Annapolis 🦴 **1928** Life's in the pink for two guys at the U.S. naval academy until jealousy rears its loathsome head when they fall for the same gal. Just when it's beginning to look like love and honor is an either-or proposition, the lovelorn rivals find that although love transcends all, a guy's gotta do what a guy's gotta do, even if it means sticking up for his romantic nemesis. Lots of sub-par male bonding. **63m/B VHS.** Johnny Mack Brown, Hugh Allan, Holly "Billy" Bakewell, Charlotte Walker, Jeanette Loff; **D:** Christy Cabanne.

Annapolis 🦴🦴½ **2006 (PG-13)** Predictable military/boxing flick finds hot-headed, working-class Jake Huard (Franco) set on entering the U.S. Naval Academy at Annapolis. He's finally accepted and disciplinarian Lt. Cole (Gibson), who is certain Jake doesn't have what it takes. However, Jake is a really good boxer and starts training for the Academy's Brigades competition, hoping for a shot at the reigning champ—Cole. The fetching Brewster serves as Jake's superior officer, questionable trainer, and romantic object. **108m/C VHS, DVD, Blu-ray Disc.** US James Franco, Tyrese Gibson, Jordana Brewster, Donnie Wahlberg, Vicellous Shannon, Roger Fan, Chi McBride, Brian Goodman, Charles Napier, Zachery Ty Bryan; **D:** Justin Lin; **W:** Dave Collard; **C:** Phil Abraham; **M:** Brian Tyler.

An Annapolis Story 🦴🦴½ *Blue and the Gold* **1955** Cliche-ridden WWII drama about two naval cadets romancing the same lucky girl. Low-rent time for director Siegel which wastes a decent cast. **81m/C VHS.** John Derek, Kevin McCarthy, Diana Lynn, Pat Conway, L.Q. Jones, Alvy Moore, Betty Lou Gerson, Robert Osterloh, George Eldredge, Dabbs Greer, Sam Peckinpah, William Schallert; **D:** Donald Siegel; **W:** Daniel Mainwaring, Daniel Ullman; **C:** Sam Leavitt; **M:** Martin Skiles.

Anne of Avonlea 🦴🦴🦴½ *Anne of Green Gables: The Sequel* **1987** Equally excellent miniseries sequel to "Anne of Green Gables" in which the romantic heroine grows up and discovers romance. The same cast returns and Sullivan continues his tradition of lavish filming on Prince Edward Island and beautiful costumes. Based on the characters from L.M. Montgomery's classic novels "Anne of Avonlea," "Anne of the Island," and "Anne of Windy Poplars." CBC, PBS, and Disney worked together on this WonderWorks production. **224m/C VHS, DVD. CA** Megan Follows, Colleen Dewhurst, Wendy Hiller, Frank Converse, Patricia Hamilton, Rosemary Dunsmore; **D:** Kevin Sullivan; **W:** Kevin Sullivan; **M:** Hagood Hardy.

Anne of Green Gables 🦴🦴🦴 **1934** A lonely Canadian couple adopts an orphan who keeps them on their toes with her animated imagination, and wins a permanent place in their hearts. Warm (but loose) adaptation of Lucy Maud Montgomery's popular novel is entertaining although 1985 remake is far superior. Followed by "Anne of Windy Poplars." **79m/B VHS.** Anne Shirley, Tom Brown, O.P. Heggie, Helen Westley, Sara Haden, Charley Grapewin; **D:** George Nicholls Jr.; **M:** Max Steiner.

Anne of Green Gables 🦴🦴🦴½ **1985** Splendid production of the famous Lucy Maud Montgomery classic about a young orphan girl growing to young adulthood with the help of a crusty brother and sister duo. The characters come to life under Sullivan's direction, and the movie is enhanced by the beautiful Prince Edward Island scenery and wonderful costumes. One of the few instances where an adaptation lives up to (if not exceeds) the quality of the original novel. A WonderWorks presentation that was made with the cooperation of the Disney channel, CBC, and PBS. Followed by "Anne of Avonlea." On two tapes. **197m/C VHS, DVD. CA** Megan Follows, Colleen Dewhurst, Richard Farnsworth, Patricia Hamilton, Schuyler Grant, Jonathan Crombie, Marilyn Lightstone, Charmion King, Rosemary Radcliffe, Jackie Burroughs, Robert E. Collins, Joachim Hansen, Cedric Smith, Paul Bown, Miranda de Pencier, Jennifer Inch, Wendy Lyon, Christiane Kruger, Trish Nettleton, Morgan Chapman; **D:** Kevin Sullivan; **W:** Kevin Sullivan, Joe Wiesenfeld; **C:** Rene Ohashi; **M:** Hagood Hardy. **TV**

Anne of Green Gables: The Continuing Story 🦴🦴½ **1999** (Follows) learns that fiance Gilbert (Blythe) has accepted a job in a New York hospital. She takes a job in a publishing house where she meets fast-living journalist Jack Garrison (Daddo). Gilbert and Anne return to Avonlea to marry just before WWI and Gilbert joins the army as a doctor and is sent to France. When he's declared MIA, Anne heads overseas with the Red Cross to search for him and runs into Jack again, who leads Anne into numerous intrigues. This far-fetched story is not based on one of Lucy Maud Montgomery's books but Anne at least retains her spunkiness and determination. **185m/C VHS, DVD. CA** Megan Follows, Jonathan Crombie, Cameron Daddo, Schuyler Grant, Patricia Hamilton, Rosemary Radcliffe, Hannah-Leanne Green, Barry Morse, Martha Henry, Janet-Laine Green, Nigel Bennett, Shannon Lawson; **D:** Stefan Scaini; **W:** Kevin Sullivan, Laurie Pearson; **C:** Robert Saad; **M:** Peter Breiner. **TV**

Anne of the Thousand Days 🦴🦴🦴 **1969 (PG)** Lavish retelling of the life and loves of Henry the VIII. In 1526, Henry tosses aside his current wife for the young and devastatingly beautiful Anne Boleyn (Bujold). But after the birth of Princess Elizabeth, Henry tires of Anne and wishes to marry another. So he decides to rid himself of her presence—permanently. Burton's performance of the amoral king garnered him an Oscar nomination. Based on the 1948 play by Maxwell Anderson. Watch for Elizabeth Taylor as a masked courtesan at the costume ball. **145m/C VHS.** Richard Burton, Genevieve Bujold, Irene Papas, Anthony Quayle, John Colicos, Michael Hordern, Michael Johnson; **D:** Charles Jarrott; **W:** Bridget Boland, John Hale; **M:** Georges Delerue. Oscars '69: Costume Des.; Directors Guild '70: Director (Jarrott); Golden Globes '70: Actress—Drama (Bujold), Director (Jarrott), Film—Drama, Screenplay.

Anne Rice's The Feast of All Saints 🦴🦴🦴 **2001** It's not about vampires. Rice's novel is set in pre-Civil War New Orleans among free people of color. They enjoy certain privileges of middleclass society while still dealing with class, race, and sex. Cecil St. Marie (Rueben) is the mistress of white plantation owner Philippe Ferronnaire (Gallagher). He makes certain promises to his children (Ri'chard) and Marie (Lyn)—which he fails to keep, thus causing family dissension. As the children grow into adults they face romantic and societal dilemmas of their own. Excellent cast does well by the sometimes melodramatic story. Title refers to the day for remembering the dead. **212m/C VHS, DVD.** Robert Ri'chard, Peter Gallagher, Gloria Reuben, Nicole Lyn, Jennifer Beals, Ossie Davis, Ruby Dee, Pam Grier, Jasmine Guy, Victoria Rowell, James Earl Jones, Eartha Kitt, Ben Vereen, Forest Whitaker, Bianca Lawson, Daniel Sunjata; **D:** Peter Medak; **W:** John Wilder; **C:** Edward Pei; **M:** Patrick Seymour. **CABLE**

Annie 🦴🦴 **1982 (PG)** Stagy big-budget adaptation of the Broadway musical, which was an adaptation of the comic strip. A major financial disaster upon release, still it's an entertaining enterprise curiously directed by Huston and engagingly acted by Finney and Quinn. 🎵Tomorrow; It's the Hard Knock Life; Maybe; I Think I'm Gonna Like It Here; Little Girls; We Got Annie; Let's Go to the Movies; You're Never Fully Dressed Without a Smile; Easy Street. **128m/C VHS, DVD.** Aileen Quinn, Carol Burnett, Albert Finney, Bernadette Peters, Ann Reinking, Tim Curry; **D:** John Huston; **W:** Thomas Meehan; **C:** Richard Moore; **M:** Ralph Burns. Golden Raspberries '82: Worst Support. Actress (Quinn).

Annie 🦴🦴🦴 **1999** Lively and amusing adaptation of the smash Broadway musical that will make you forget that dud (newcomer Morton) is incarcerated in a Depression-era orphanage run by despotic Miss Hannigan (Bates) when she's offered the chance to spend the holidays with chilly moneybags Oliver Warbucks (Garber). Naturally, Annie thaws his frosty demeanor. Able support is provided by Warbucks' faithful assistant Grace (McDonald) and Miss Hannigan's wastrel brother Rooster (Cumming) and his floozy Lily (Chenoweth). **120m/C VHS, DVD.** Alicia Morton, Victor Garber, Kathy Bates, Alan Cumming, Audra McDonald, Kristin Chenoweth; **Cameos:** Andrea McArdle; **D:** Rob Marshall; **W:** Irene Mecchi; **C:** Ralf Bode; **M:** Charles Strouse, Martin Charnin. **TV**

Annie: A Royal Adventure 🦴🦴½ **1995** TV sequel to "Annie" finds the red-haired heroine (Johnson) traveling to England with her Daddy Warbucks (Hearn), who's about to be knighted in London. But the evil Lady Edwina Hogbottom (played to a high-camp hilt by Collins) has a plan to blow up Buckingham Palace and take over as queen. Naturally, it's up to Annie to defeat her and have a happy ending. **92m/C VHS, DVD.** Ashley Johnson, George Hearn, Joan Collins, Emily Ann Lloyd, Camilla Belle, Ian McDiarmid; **D:** Ian Toynton; **W:** Trish Soodik; **C:** Alan Hume; **M:** David Michael Frank.

Annie Get Your Gun 🦴🦴🦴 **1950** A lavish production of Irving Berlin's Broadway hit musical. Sharpshooting Annie Oakley (Hutton) is the queen of Buffalo Bill's Wild West show though her talents leave her loveless. Seems fellow marksman Frank Butler's (Keel) ego can't handle the fact that Annie keeps beating him. Lots of singing, with an enthusiastic lead performance by Hutton. 🎵There's No Business Like Show Business; My Defenses Are Down; I'm an Indian Too; Doin' What Comes Naturlly; Colonel Buffalo Bill; The Girl That I Marry; You Can't Get a Man with a Gun; They Say It's Wonderful; I Got the Sun in the Morning. **107m/C VHS, DVD.** Betty Hutton, Howard Keel, Edward Arnold, Louis Calhern, J. Carrol Naish, Edward Arnold, Clinton Sundberg; **D:** George Sidney; **W:** Sidney Sheldon; **C:** Charles Rosher; **M:** Irving Berlin. Oscars '50: Scoring/Musical.

Annie Hall 🦴🦴🦴🦴 **1977 (PG)** Acclaimed coming-of-cinematic-age film for Allen is based in part on his own life. His love affair with Hall/Keaton is chronicled as an episodic, wistful comedy commenting on family, love, loneliness, communicating, maturity, driving, city life, careers, and various other topics. Abounds with classic scenes, including future star Goldblum and his mantra at a cocktail party; Allen and the lobster pot; and Allen, Keaton, a bathroom, a tennis racket, and a spider. The film operates on many levels, as does Keaton's wardrobe, which started a major fashion trend. Don't blink or you'll miss several future stars in bit parts. Expertly shot by Gordon Willis. **94m/C VHS, DVD.** Woody Allen, Diane Keaton, Tony Roberts, Carol Kane, Paul Simon, Colleen Dewhurst, Janet Margolin, Shelley Duvall, Christopher Walken, Marshall McLuhan, Dick Cavett, John Glover, Jeff Goldblum, Beverly D'Angelo; **D:** Woody Allen; **W:** Woody Allen, Marshall Brickman; Director (Allen), Orig. Screenplay; Picture; AFI '98: Top 100; British Acad. '77: Actress (Keaton), Director (Allen); Film, Screenplay; Directors Guild '77: Director (Allen); Golden Globes '78: Actress—Mus./Comedy (Keaton); L.A. Film Critics '77: Actress (Keaton), Natl. Film Reg. '92; N.Y. Film Critics '77: Actress (Keaton), Director (Allen), Film, Screenplay; Natl. Soc. Film Critics '77: Actress (Keaton), Film, Screenplay; Writers Guild '77: Orig. Screenplay.

Annie O 🦴🦴½ **1995** 15-year-old Annie Rojas (Yares) runs into problems when she joins the boys' basketball team (since her school doesn't have a girls team). Her teammates are jealous and so are her brother and boyfriend. **93m/C VHS.** Coco Yares, Chad Willet, Robert Stewart; **C:** Michael McClary.

Annie Oakley 🦴🦴🦴 **1935** Energetic biographical drama based on the life and legend of sharpshooter Annie Oakley and her on-off relationship with Wild Bill Hickok. Stanwyck makes a great Oakley. Later musicalized as "Annie Get Your Gun." **90m/B VHS.** Barbara Stanwyck, Preston Foster, Melvyn Douglas, Pert Kelton, Andy Clyde, Moroni Olsen, Chief Thundercloud; **D:** George Stevens.

The Annihilators woof! **1985 (R)** A group of Vietnam vets band together in an extremely violent manner to protect their small town from a gang of thugs. **87m/C VHS.** Gerrit Graham, Lawrence-Hilton Jacobs, Paul Koslo, Christopher Stone, Andy Wood, Sid Conrad, Dennis Redfield; **D:** Charles E. Seiller.

The Anniversary 🦴🦴 **1968** One-eyed monster mom Mrs. Taggart (Bette at her baddest) gives new meaning to the word "possessive." Thoroughly cowing her three grown sons, she manages to get them to come home each year on the wedding anniversary to the husband she despised. Only this time, the trio tell her they're going to live their own lives. That is, not if mom has anything to do with it. Based on the play by Bill MacIlwraith. **93m/C VHS, DVD. GB** Bette Davis, Jack Hedley, James Cossins, Christian Roberts, Sheila Hancock, Elaine Taylor; **D:** Roy Ward Baker; **W:** Jimmy Sangster; **C:** Henry Waxman; **M:** Philip Martell.

The Anniversary Party 🎬🎬🎬 2001 (R) Leigh and Cumming co-write, co-direct, and star as the central couple in this impressive ensemble comedy-drama about a group of Hollywood friends celebrating said couple's sixth anniversary. Amid much career and personal angst, drug use, and the characters are fleshed out nicely and the dialogue remains sharp throughout. The air is thick with genuine personal dread and interpersonal tension. Among the uniformly excellent performances, two especially stand out: Leigh as the aging actress on the cusp of career oblivion, and Cates as a former actress who's given up her career to focus on being a wife to just-beyond-leading-man-status hubby Kline) and mother. Filmed in digital video in 19 days under the Dogme 95 guidelines. **117m/C VHS, DVD.** *C:* John Bailey. *M:* Michael Penn.

Another Chance 🎬🎬 1988 (R) Girl-crazy bachelor is returned from heaven for a second chance and has to choose between a "bad" girl and a "good" girl. What a choice! **99m/C VHS.** *D:* Jerry Vint.

Another Country 🎬🎬1/2 1984 Mitchell's adaptation of his play based on the life of Guy Burgess, who became a spy for the Soviet Union. Guy Bennett (Everett) is an English boarding school upperclassman whose affected mannerisms and barely disguised homosexuality cause dissension among his schoolmates, while his one friend, Tommy Judd (Firth), is a fervent Marxist. Rather fancifully depicted and loving recreation of 1930s English life. Although the film is interior to the award-winning play, director Kanievska manages to transform a piece into a solid film, and Everett's performance as Bennett/Burgess is outstanding. **90m/C VHS, DVD, GB** *C:* Rupert Everett; Colin Firth; Michael Jenn; Robert Addie; Anna Massey; Betsy Brantley; Rupert Wainwright; Cary Elwes; Arthur Howard; Tristan Oliver; Frederick Alexander; Adrian Ross-Magenty; Geoffrey Bateman; Philip Dupuy; Jeffrey Wickham; Gideon Bouring; Ivor Howard; Charles Spencer; *M:* Marek Kanievska; *V:* Julian Mitchel; *C:* Peter Biziou.

Another Day in Paradise 🎬🎬 1998 (R) Tulsa teen junkies Eobbie (Kartheiser) and Rosie (Wagner) team up with older junkie couple Mel (Woods) and Sidney (G-iffith) and go from bed to worse. Mel's is a dealer and thief and is glad to add two would-be partners in crime to his and Sidney's traveling road to hell. Woods is all sly confidence while Griffith shows some seductive tough-chick grit and the younger twosome manage :o hold their own nicely. Not a pic for the faint of heart or queasy of stomach. Based on the book by Eddie Little. **101m/C VHS, DVD.** *C:* James Woods, Melanie Griffith, Vincent Kartheiser, Natasha Gregson Wagner, Paul Hipp, Brent Briscoe, Lou Diamond Phillips; *D:* Larry Clark; *W:* Christopher Landon; Stephen Chin; *C:* Eric Alan Edwards.

Another 48 Hrs. 🎬1/2 1990 (R) Continuing chemistry between Nolte and Murphy is one of the few worthwhile items in this stodgy rehash. Any innovation is murdered among the drag out stale of any other cop thriller, and violence and car chases abound. Pointlessly energetic and occasionally fun for only the true devotee. **98m/C VHS, DVD.** Eddie Murphy, Nick

Anonymous Rex 🎬🎬 2004 So dinosaurs didn't actually die off, they adapted and live side-by-side with humans. They wear holographic suits as disguises. Dino-detectives Vince Rubio and Ernie Watson are out to stop a mutant sect that wants to wipe out mankind. Based on the comic mysteries by Eric Garcia. **89m/C DVD.** Sam Trammell; Daniel Baldwin; Faye Dunaway, Isaac Hayes, Tamara Gorski, Stephanie Lemelin; *D:* Julian Jarrold; *W:* Joe Menosky; *C:* Albert J. Dunk, Kit Whitmore; *M:* David Bergeaud. **CABLE.**

Another Man, Another Chance 🎬🎬 1977 (PG) Remake of Lelouch's "A Man and a Woman," set in the turn-of-the-century American West, pales by comparison to the original. Slow-moving tale casts Caan and widow Bujold as two lovers. French. **132m/C VHS, FR** James Caan, Genevieve Bujold, Francis Huster, Jennifer Warren, Susan Tyrrell; *D:* Claude Lelouch; *W:* Claude Lelouch.

Another Man's Poison 🎬🎬1/2 1952 Melodramatic crime drama with a showy, if stereotypical role, for Davis. She's mystery writer Janet Frobisher and lives on a secluded Yorkshire farm. Too bad her escaped con husband suddenly shows up (and gets killed by Janet). Her troubles aren't over. Hubby's partner, George Bates (Merrill), comes a-lookin' and agrees to dispose of the body if Janet will let him hide out. She tries to kill Bates as well but her scheming comes to an unexpected conclusion. Adapted from the play "Deadlock" by Leslie Sands. **90m/B VHS, DVD, GB** Bette Davis, Gary Merrill, Emlyn Williams, Anthony Steel, Barbara Murray, Reginald Beckwith, Edna Morris; *D:* Irving Rapper; *W:* Val Guest; *C:* Robert Krasker; *M:* Paul Sawell.

Another 9 1/2 Weeks WOOF! 1996 (R) Unintersting sequel finds suicidal John (Rourke) overwhelmed by his kinky memories of Elizabeth, so he flies to Paris determined to find her. Instead, he meets fashion designer Lea (Everhart), who claims to be Elizabeth's friend and who puts the sexual tease on the S/M devotee. Monotony sets in early and there's no real heat generated between the duo. Available for TV. Sequel to "9 1/2 Weeks." **104m/C VHS, DVD.** Mickey Rourke, Angie Everhart, Steven Berkoff, Agathe de la Fontaine, Georay Scott; *D:* Anne Goursaud; *W:* Nick Davis; *C:* Robert Alazraki; *M:* Stephen Parsons, Francis Haines.

Another Pair of Aces: Three of a Kind 🎬🎬🎬 1991 Nelson and Kristofferson team up to clear the name of Tom, a Texas Ranger accused of murder. Video contains some scenes deemed too racy for TV. Sequel to "A Pair of Aces." **93m/C VHS, DVD.** Willie Nelson, Kris Kristofferson, Joan Severance, Rip Torn, Dan Kamin, Ken Farmer, Richard Jones; *D:* Bill Bixby. **TV**

Another Public Enemy 🎬🎬 2005 (R) Gonggongui Jeog 2 2005 (R) Prosecutor Kang investigates corrupt businessman Han, who is laundering his ill-gotten real estate gains in the U.S. Only his superiors suspect Kang's motives since the two were bitter high school rivals. Really, really, really long, which dilutes any action and suspense. Korean with subtitles. **148m/C DVD.** K:N Kyungyu Sol, Jun-ho Jeong, Shin-il Kang; *D:* Woo-suk Kang; *W:* Woo-suk Kang; *M:* Jawe-kwon Han.

Another Stakeout 🎬🎬1/2 1993 Sequel six years after the original finds Dreyfuss and Estevez partnered again for another stakeout, this time to keep an eye on Moriarty, a reluctant witness against the mob. The two spying detectives find themselves in a an upscale neighborhood where blending in is a hard thing to do. O'Donnell is a breath of fresh air as a wisecracking assistant district attorney. Stowe briefly reprises her role as Dreyfuss' girlfriend. Writer Kouf reportedly had difficulty penning the script, surprising. **109m/C VHS, DVD.** Richard Dreyfuss, Emilio Estevez, Rosie O'Donnell, Cathy Moriarty, Madeleine Stowe, John Rubinstein, Marcia Strassman, Dennis Farina, Miguel Ferrer; *D:* John Badham; *W:* Jim Kouf; *C:* Roy Wagner.

Another Woman's Husband 🎬🎬 2000 Traumatized as a child by the drowning death of her brother, Laurel (Rinna) finally decides to get over her fear of water by taking swimming lessons. Susan (O'Grady) is her swimming instructor and they become best friends. Until the women realize they also share the same man (Midkiff), who happens to be Susan's husband. Based on the novel "Swimming Lessons" by Anna Villegas and Lynne Hugo. **91m/C VHS, DVD.** Lisa Rinna, Gail O'Grady, Dale Midkiff, Sally Kirkland, Charlotte Rae; *D:* Noel Nossack; *W:* Susan Amori; Mark Smith; *C:* Alan Caso; *M:* Mark Snow. **CABLE.**

Another You 🎬 1991 (R) Con man Wilder takes pathological liar Pryor under his care and decides to use his talents to his fullest advantage. Posing as success-ful businessmen, the duo initiate a scam so complicated that they may end up being double-crossed or worse yet, dead! Can the pair see their plan through without losing their lives? Sad to see how far these two gifted comedians have fallen. Their collaboration is tired and the movie

Another Lonely Hitman 🎬🎬 Shin Kanashiki Hittoman 1995 Character study rather than a typical gangster flick. Old-school yakuza and former junkie Tachibana (Ishibashi) finds his ways badly out of date after he's released from a 13-year prison stretch. He tries to do the right thing by helping young druggie/hooker Yuki (Sawada), clean up (and the withdrawal scenes aren't pretty) and teach the younger hoods some manners. Based on the book by Yamanouchi, who did the screenplay. Japanese with subtitles. **105m/C DVD.** JP Ryo Ishibashi, Asami Sawada, Kazuhiko Kanayama Tatsuo Yamada; *D:* Rokuro Mochizuki; *W:* Yukio Yamanouchi; *C:* Naoki Imazumi; *M:* Kazuo Umezu.

Another Time, Another Place 🎬🎬 1958 Sappy melodrama about an American journalist who suffers an emotional meltdown when her married British lover is killed during WWII. So she heads for Cornwall to console the widow and family. **98m/B VHS, DVD, GB** Lana Turner, Barry Sullivan, Glynis Johns, Sean Connery, Terence Longdon; *D:* Lewis Allen; *C:* Jack Hildyard.

Another Time, Another Place 🎬🎬🎬 1983 (R) Bored young Scottish housewife married to an older fellow falls in love with an Italian prisoner-of-war who works on her farm during WWI. Occasionally quirky, always finely crafted view of wartime Britain and the little-known life of POWs in England. **101m/C VHS.** GB Phyllis Logan, Giovanni Mauriello, Gian Luca Favila, Paul Young, Tom Watson; *D:* Michael Radford; *W:* Michael Radford; *C:* Roger Deakins.

Another Way 🎬🎬🎬 Olelkezo Tekintek 1982 The director of 1971's much-lauded "Love" sets this politically charged love story in Hungary in 1958. Opening with a view of a female corpse, the story flashes backward to look at the woman's journalistic career and her relationship with a women colleague. Candid love scenes between women in Hungary of 1958, considered a cinematic novelty in many places outside Hungary. In Hungarian with English subtitles. **100m/C VHS, DVD.** HU Jadwiga Jankowska Cieslak, Grazyna Szapolowska, Josef Kroner, Hemadi Judit, Andoral Peter; *D:* Karoly Makk Cannes '82: Actress (Cieslak).

Another Woman 🎬🎬🎬 1988 (PG) The study of an intellectual woman whose life is changed when she begins to eavesdrop. What she hears provokes her to examine every relationship in her life, finding things quite different than she had believed. Heavy going, with Rowlands effective as a woman coping with an entirely new vision of herself. Farrow plays the catalyst. Although Allen's comedies are more popular than his dramas, this one deserves a look. **81m/C VHS, DVD.** Gena Rowlands, Gene Hackman, Mia Farrow, Ian Holm, Betty Buckley, Martha Plimpton, Blythe Danner, Harris Yulin, Sandy Dennis, David Ogden Stiers, John Houseman, Philip Bosco, Frances Conroy; Kenneth Welsh, Michael Kirby; *D:* Woody Allen; *W:* Woody Allen; *C:* Sven Nykvist.

Another Thin Man 🎬🎬1/2 1939 Powell and Loy team up for the third in the delightful "Thin Man" series. Slightly weaker series entry takes its time, but has both Powell and Loy providing stylish performances. Nick Jr. is also introduced as the newest member of the sleuthing team. Sequel to "After the Thin Man," followed by "Shadow of the Thin Man." **105m/B VHS, DVD.** William Powell, Myrna Loy, Virginia Grey, Otto Kruger, Sir C. Aubrey Smith, Ruth Hussey; *D:* W.S. Van Dyke.

Antarctica 🎬🎬 1984 Due to unfortunate circumstances, a group of scientists must leave their pack of huskies behind on a frozen glacier in the Antarctic. The film focuses on the dogs' subsequent struggle for survival. Dubbed. **112m/C VHS.** JP Ken Takakura, Masako Natsume, Keiko Oginome; *D:* Koreyoshi Kurahara; *M:* Vangelis.

Anthony Adverse 🎬🎬1/2 1936 March is a young man in the 19th century who searches for manhood across America and Mexico. He grows slowly as he battles foes, struggles against adversity and returns home to find his lover in this romantic swashbuckler. A star-studded cast, lush costuming, and an energetic musical score. Highly acclaimed in its time, but now seems dated. Based on the novel by Hervey Allen. **141m/B VHS.** Frederic March, Olivia de Havilland, Anita Louise, Gale Sondergaard, Claude Rains, Edmund Gwenn, Louis Hayward, Anne Howard; *D:* Mervyn LeRoy; *C:* Gaetano Antonio "Tony" Gaudio; *M:* Erich Wolfgang Korngold. Oscars '36: Cinematog., Film Editing, Support. Actress (Sondergaard), Score.

The Ant Bully 🎬🎬1/2 2006 (PG) Warner Bros. entry in the CGI-created insect category comes eight years after Pixar and DreamWorks set the standard with "A Bug's Life" and "Antz," respectively. It's, and delivers nothing new. New kid on the block and neighborhood punching-bag Lucas vents his frustration by picking on something smaller than him—an ant colony in his yard—only to be magically shrunken and transported into the ant's world to face his victims. Predictable life lessons about acceptance and teamwork, along with uninspired voice work from the star-studded cast drag down this visually impressive but all too familiar story. Based on the book by John Nickle. **88m/C DVD, Blu-ray Disc.** US *D:* John A. Davis; *W:* John A. Davis, Nicolas Cage, Bruce Campbell, Meryl Streep, Julia Roberts, Paul Giarnatti, Myles Jeffrey, Regina King, Cheri Oteri, Lily Tomlin, Rob Paul-sen, Allison Mack, Ricardo Montalban, Larry Miller, Austin Majors, Mark DeCarlo, Frank Welker, Nicole Sullivan, Vernee Watson-Johnson.

Antibodies 🎬🎬 Antikorper 2005 Captured serial killer Gabriel Engel (Hennicke) admits to the murders of 13 boys and is suspected in the death of a young girl in a rural community. Naive local cop Michael Martens (Mohring) travels to the city to question the now wheelchair-bound Engel and close his case. But Engel tries to convince him that someone else killed the girl, and Michael learns more about the killer and himself that he could have imagined. German with subtitles. **128m/C DVD.** GE Andre Hennicke, Wotan Wilke Mohring, Heinz Hoenig, Ulrike Kriumbiegel, Jurgen Schonagel *D:* Christian Alvart; *W:* Christian Alvart; *C:* Hager Bogdanski; *M:* Michi Britsch.

Antibody 🎬🎬 2002 (R) Terrorist Morgan (Vergov) has a nuclear bomb and the detonator chip is inside his body. He's shot and it dies, the chip will go off. So it's up to security expert Richard Gaynes (Henriksen) and a team of scientists to send an experimental tracking craft inside Moran's bloodstream to find and extract the chip in time. **90m/C VHS, DVD.** Lance Henriksen, Robin Givens, William Zabka, Julian Vergov; *D:* Christian McIntire; *W:* Michael Baldwin; *C:* Adolfo Bartoli; *M:* Scott Clausen. **VIDEO**

Antitrust 🎬1/2 2001 (PG-13) Super-nerd code writer Milo (Philippe) leaves the garage for a Pacific Northwest software giant only to discover the company's mega-monied leader, Winston (Robbins) may not be on the up and up—in fact, the things he's doing to maintain industry supremacy could be downright evil. Robbins's bespectacled techie villain is spot-on Bill Gates, but the film borrows heavily from its paranoid predecessors and offers little of its own to hold. A mediocre thriller among other mediocre thrillers. **120m/C VHS, DVD.** Ryan Phillippe, Tim Robbins, Rachael Leigh Cook, Claire Forlani, Douglas McFerran, Richard Roundtree, Yee Jee Tso, Tygh generally dreadful. **98m/C VHS, DVD.** Richard Pryor, Gene Wilder, Mercedes Ruehl, Vanessa Williams, Stephen Lang, Kevin Polak; *D:* Maurice Phillips.

Runyan; **D:** Peter Howitt; **W:** Howard Franklin; **C:** John Bailey; **M:** Don Davis.

Antoine et Antoinette 🦴🦴½ *1947* Antoine (Pigaut) is a shop foreman and his wife, Antoinette (Maffei), a clerk, who lead a somewhat tempestuous life in Paris. Then the situation worsens when Antoine loses the couple's winning lottery ticket. The first of Becker's romantic trilogy, followed by "Rendez-vous de Juillet" and "Edward and Caroline." French with subtitles; originally released at 95 minutes. **78m/B VHS, FR** Roger Pigaut, Claire Maffei, Noel Roquevert; **D:** Jacques Becker; **W:** Jacques Becker, Maurice Griffe, Francoise Giroud; **C:** Pierre Montazel; **M:** Jean Jacques Grunenwald.

Anton, the Magician 🦴🦴 *Anton der Zauberer 1978* Anton likes to live by his wits. A car mechanic, he marries the boss' daughter, Liesel, and uses his skills to make a pile of illegal dough that he hides at the home of the widowed Sabine, with whom he's also involved. When Anton's schemes catch up with him, he ends up in prison, and Sabine takes off to Switzerland with the cash. But this isn't the end of their story. German with subtitles. **101m/C VHS. GE** Ulrich Thein, Barbara Dittus, Anna Dymna, Erwin Geschonneck, Erik S. Klein; **D:** Guenther Reisch; **W:** Guenther Reisch, Karl-Georg Egel; **C:** Gunter Haubold; **M:** Wolfram Heicking.

Antonia and Jane 🦴🦴🦴 *1991 (R)* Enjoyable film tells the story of a longstanding, heavily tested friendship between two women. From the very beginning, they are a study in contrasts—Jane as rather plain, frumpy, and insecure; Antonia as glamorous, elegant, and successful. Both believe that each other's lives are more interesting and exciting than their own. Kidron, who directed this smart witty comedy for British TV, offers an honest look into the often complex world of adult friendships. **75m/C VHS. GB** Imelda Staunton, Saskia Reeves, Patricia Leventon, Alfred Hoffman, Maria Charles, John Bennett, Richard Hope, Alfred Marks, Lila Kaye, Bill Nighy, Brenda Bruce; **D:** Beeban Kidron; **W:** Marcy Kahan; **C:** Rex Maidment; **M:** Rachel Portman. TV

Antonio 🦴🦴 *1973* A Texas millionaire on the run from his wife and her divorce lawyer alights in a small Chilean village and turns his life upside down. **89m/C VHS.** Larry Hagman, Trini Lopez, Noemi Guerrero, Pedro Becker; **D:** Claudio Guzman.

Antonio Das Mortes 🦴🦴½ *O Dragao da Maldade contra o Santo Guerreiro 1968* Antonio is a savage mercenary hired to kill rebels against the Brazilian government. Belatedly he realizes he sympathizes with the targets and turns his guns the other way for an incredible shootout climax. A visually lavish political polemic, espousing revolutionary guerrilla action within the format of a South American western. In Portuguese with English subtitles. **100m/C VHS. BR** Mauricio Do Valle, Odete Lara, Jofre Soares, Othon Bastos; **D:** Glauce Rocha; **W:** Glauce Rocha; **C:** Alfonso Beato.

Antony and Cleopatra 🦴🦴 *1973 (PG)* Heston wrote, directed, and starred in this long, dry adaptation of the Shakespeare play that centers on the torrid romance between Mark Antony and Cleopatra. **150m/C VHS, DVD.** Charlton Heston, Hildegard(e) Neil, Fernando Rey, Eric Porter, John Castle, Freddie Jones, Warren Clarke, Julian Glover; **D:** Charlton Heston.

Ants 🦴½ *Panic at Lakewood Manor; It Happened at Lakewood Manor 1977* A mad bug parable for our planet-obsessed society. Insecticide-infected ants turn militant and check into a local hotel to vent their chemically induced foul mood on the unsuspecting clientele. The guest register includes a gaggle of celebrities who probably wish they'd signed on the Love Boat instead. Made for TV (an ant farm would probably be just too horrible on the big screen). **100m/C VHS, DVD.** Suzanne Somers, Robert Foxworth, Myrna Loy, Lynda Day George, Gerald Gordon, Bernie Casey, Barry Van Dyke, Karen Lamm, Anita Gillette, Moosie Drier, Steve Franken, Brian Dennehy, Bruce French, Stacy Keach Sr., Rene Enriquez, James Storm; **D:** Robert Scheerer; **W:** Guerdon (Gordon) Trueblood; **C:** Bernie Abramson; **M:** Ken Richmond. TV

Antwone Fisher 🦴🦴🦴 *2002 (PG-13)* Washington's directorial debut is a drama based on the true story of Antwone Fisher, who also wrote the screenplay. Washington also stars as Jerome Davenport, the naval psychiatrist who helps the angry young Fisher (Luke) get past the demons of his foster childhood. The two knock heads and are both forced to change their own ideas, slowly coming to understand and trust one another. Davenport learns that Fisher was born in prison, his father murdered and his mother a convict. Davenport urges Fisher to confront his past, and some of the best scenes are with Fisher's aunt (Johnson), uncle (Billings) and mother (Davis), which resonate. Subplot with Davenport and wife Berta (Richardson) shows they have their own issues to work out, as well. A tearjerker in the best sense, the simply told tale is a triumph for Luke, who is impressive in his debut role. **113m/C VHS, DVD. US** Derek Luke, Denzel Washington, Joy Bryant, Salli Richardson, Earl Billings, Kevin Connolly, Viola Davis, Rainoldo Gooding, Novella Nelson, Vernee Watson-Johnson, Kente Scott, Yolonda Ross, Stephen Snedden; **D:** Denzel Washington; **W:** Antwone Fisher; **C:** Philippe Rousselot; **M:** Mychael Danna. Ind. Spirit '03: Actor (Luke).

Antz 🦴🦴🦴 *1998 (PG)* Malcontent worker ant, Z (Allen), moans to his therapist about his insignificance and the depressing anonymity of "being born in the middle of five million." But after meeting the colony's princess, Bala (Stone), who is facing her own bleak future thanks to an arranged marriage with the colony's power-hungry General Mandible (Hackman), Z and Princess Bala embark on a dangerous mission to the surface in search of the mythical "Insectopia." Only the second film ever created entirely through computer animation ("Toy Story" being the first), the film is visually amazing. The fact that the ant characters do not resemble their performers' appearances make this one fun for all ages. **83m/C VHS, DVD. D:** Eric Darnell, Tim Johnson; **W:** Chris Weitz, Paul Weitz, Todd Alcott; **M:** Harry Gregson-Williams. **V:** Woody Allen, Sharon Stone, Sylvester Stallone, Anne Bancroft, Danny Glover, Christopher Walken, Jane Curtin, Jennifer Lopez, John Mahoney, Dan Aykroyd, Paul Mazursky, Gene Hackman.

Any Given Sunday 🦴🦴🦴 *1999 (R)* Stone sets aside his conspiracy theories on war and politics and effectively shines a spotlight on a different kind of battlefield to come up with the most commerical and entertaining film of his career. Pacino leads an all-star cast as the battered, yet wise and resilient coach of a struggling Miami football team who locks horns with not only young quarterback Foxx, but ruthless, ballbuster team owner Diaz. Epic-like runtime (which sprints along thanks to Stone's potent mix of raw camera work and hip-hop soundtrack) allows much of the cast plenty of room, with comedian Foxx holding his own with the big boys in a star-making performance as the hotdog player with a bad case of ego. With an intelligent script and a perfect cast, Stone creates the most realistic look at pro football since 1979's "North Dallas Forty." **170m/B VHS, DVD.** Al Pacino, Dennis Quaid, Cameron Diaz, Jamie Foxx, Charlton Heston, James Woods, Matthew Modine, Ann-Margret, Lauren Holly, Lela Rochon, LL Cool J, Aaron Eckhart, Jim Brown, Bill Bellamy, Elizabeth Berkley, John C. McGinley; **D:** Oliver Stone; **W:** Oliver Stone, John Logan; **C:** Salvatore Totino; **M:** Robbie Robertson.

Any Gun Can Play 🦴 *For a Few Bullets More 1967* Typical spaghetti western. Three men (banker, thief, and bounty hunter) compete for a treasure of gold while wandering around the Spanish countryside. **103m/C VHS, DVD. IT SP** Edd Byrnes, Gilbert Roland, George Hilton, Kareen O'Hara, Pedro Sanchez, Gerard Herter; **D:** Enzo G. Castellari.

Any Man's Death 🦴🦴 *1990 (R)* Savage is a globe-trotting reporter on the trail of a worldwide conspiracy who accidentally uncovers a Nazi war criminal in Africa. Well-meaning but confused tale. **105m/C VHS.** John Savage, William Hickey, Mia Sara, Ernest Borgnine, Michael Lerner; **D:** Tom Clegg.

Any Number Can Play 🦴🦴½ *1949* Fast-moving drama about an ailing gambler who faces a series of crises. Gable gives a commanding performance as the noble dice-roller. Based on the novel by Edward Harris Heath. **102m/B VHS.** Clark Gable, Alexis Smith, Wendell Corey, Audrey Totter, Frank Morgan, Mary Astor, Lewis Stone, Barry Sullivan; **D:** Mervyn LeRoy; **W:** Richard Brooks.

Any Number Can Win 🦴🦴 *Melodie en Sous-Sol; The Big Grab 1963* Two ex-convicts, aging Charles (Gabin) and his former cellmate Francis (Delon), risk their lives and freedom for one last major heist: a gambling casino on the French Riviera. French with English subtitles. **118m/B VHS, DVD. FR** Claude Cerval, Jean Gabin, Alain Delon, Viviane Romance, Maurice Biraud, Carla Marlier, Jose-Luis De Villalonga, Jean Carmet; **D:** Henri Verneuil; **W:** Henri Verneuil, Michel Audiard, Albert Simonin; **C:** Louis Page; **M:** Michel Magne.

Any Place But Home 🦴🦴½ *1997 (PG-13)* Roberta (Keller) and Lucas (Lando) Dempsey find themselves in big trouble when Roberta's sister Carrie Miller (Conway) and her low-life hubby Carl (Midkiff) try to involve them in a plan to kidnap 12-year-old John Danforth (Norris), figuring John's rich dad August (Thicke) will be happy to pay the ransom. Roberta manages to get the kid and the money away from the Millers but she and Lucas discover John is an abused child and terrified of his father. The threesome go on the run with the Millers, August's hired help, and the FBI on their trail. **90m/C VHS.** Joe Lando, Mary Page Keller, Alan Thicke, Dale Midkiff, Cristie Conway, Richard Roundtree; **D:** Rob Hedden; **W:** Bart Baker. CABLE

Any Wednesday 🦴🦴½ *Bachelor Girl Apartment 1966* Okay sex farce about powerful industrialist Robards' use of his mistress's apartment as a tax write-off. When a young company executive learns of the "company" apartment, along with excellent voice performances (even Stallone) make this one fun for all ages. **110m/C VHS.** Jane Fonda, Jason Robards Jr., Dean Jones, Rosemary Murphy; **D:** Robert Ellis Miller; **W:** Julius J. Epstein; **M:** George Duning.

Any Which Way You Can 🦴🦴 *1980 (PG)* Bad brawler Philo Beddoe and his buddy Clyde, the orangutan, are back again in the sequel to "Every Which Way But Loose." This time Philo is tempted to take part in a big bout for a large cash prize. Clyde steals scenes, brightening up the no-brainer story. **116m/C VHS, DVD.** Clint Eastwood, Sondra Locke, Ruth Gordon, Harry Guardino, William (Bill) Smith, Geoffrey Lewis, Barry Corbin; **D:** Buddy Van Horn; **W:** Stanford Sherman; **C:** David Worth.

Anything But Love 🦴🦴½ *Standard Time 2002 (PG-13)* Predictable Hollywood love story. Writer/actor Isabel Rose plays Billie Golden, a not-so-young wanna-be torch singer wrestling with the choice of whether to marry her old high school crush (Bancroft) for security, or stay with her anguished true love (McCarthy), who better understands her. Meager budget is best spent on the elaborate dream sequences. Eartha Kitt appears as herself, providing crucial advice and a shining example of a true star. **99m/C VHS, DVD. US** Isabel Rose, Andrew McCarthy, Cameron Bancroft, Alix Korey, Victor Argo, Ilana Levine, Sean Arbuckle, Eartha Kitt; **D:** Robert Cary; **W:** Isabel Rose, Robert Cary; **C:** Horacio Marquinez; **M:** Andrew Hollander, Steven Lutvak.

Anything Else 🦴🦴½ *2003 (R)* With his last few outings, Allen has shown that he's a shadow of his former creative self, so he's logically picked Biggs to play a shadow of his former self. Biggs doesn't seem comfortable in his role as a neurotic psychoanalyst-dependent joke-writer trying to break up with the quirky, torturing girlfriend (Ricci) he's smitten with. The Woodman shows up as his alter-ego's paranoid, mean-spirited mentor and confidant. Flick is so short on new ideas that the young couple can only agree on their love of Bogie and old jazz records. Ricci spends most of the film walking around her apartment in her underwear, which isn't bad if you can keep the image of Allen leering just off-camera out of your head. If you insist on a Woody Allen movie, make it almost anything else but this mess. **108m/C VHS, DVD. US** Jason Biggs, Christina Ricci, Woody Allen, Stockard Channing, Danny DeVito, Jimmy Fallon, Erica Leerhsen, David Conrad, KaDee Strickland, Adrian Grenier; **D:** Woody Allen; **W:** Woody Allen; **C:** Darius Khondji.

Anything for a Thrill 🦴 *1937* Two kids save a cameraman's career, make friends with a millionairess, and foil some crooks. **59m/B VHS.** Frankie Darro, Kane Richmond; **D:** Leslie Goodwins.

Anything for Love 🦴½ *Just One of the Girls 1993* Teen musician is the object of a school bully's rage so he decides to dress up as a girl to escape the guy's fists. **90m/C VHS, DVD. CA** Corey Haim, Nicole Eggert, Cameron Bancroft, Kevin McNulty, Wendy Van Riesen, Lochlyn Munro, Frank Hayward, Molly Parker; **D:** Michael Keusch; **M:** Amin Bhatia.

Anywhere But Here 🦴🦴½ *1999 (PG-13)* Just who's the Mom here? It certainly doesn't seem to be flaky Adele (Sarandon), who suddenly uproots teen daughter Ann (Portman) from provincial Wisconsin to relocate in sunny L.A., where Adele wants Ann to become an actress. Ann's definitely the practical one of the duo and she tries to rein in Adele's loopier flights of fantasy. Of course, Ann does have some plans (and dreams) of her own. The leads are both pros and there are enough tear-jerking moments to satisfy in this somewhat stereotypical drama. Based on the 1986 novel by Mona Simpson. **114m/C VHS, DVD.** Susan Sarandon, Natalie Portman, Shawn Hatosy, Hart Bochner, Bonnie Bedelia, Eileen Ryan, Ray Baker, John Diehl, Caroline Aaron, Paul Guilfoyle, Mary Ellen Trainor, Ashley Johnson; **D:** Wayne Wang; **W:** Alvin Sargent; **C:** Roger Deakins; **M:** Danny Elfman.

Anzacs: The War Down Under 🦴🦴 *1985* Well-made Australian TV miniseries about the Australian and New Zealand Army Corps during WWI. Follows the men from the time they enlist to the campaigns in Gallipoli and France. **165m/C VHS. AU** Paul Hogan, Andrew Clarke, Jon Blake, Megan Williams; **D:** George Miller. TV

Anzio 🦴🦴 *The Battle for Anzio; Lo Sbarco di Anzio 1968* The historic Allied invasion of Italy during WWII as seen through the eyes of American war correspondent Mitchum. Fine cast waits endlessly to leave the beach, though big battle scenes are effectively rendered. Based on the book by Wynford Vaughan Thomas. **117m/C VHS, DVD.** Giancarlo Giannini, Robert Mitchum, Peter Falk, Arthur Kennedy, Robert Ryan, Earl Holliman, Mark Damon, Reni Santoni, Patrick Magee; **D:** Edward Dmytryk; **W:** H.A.L. Craig, Frank De Felitta; **C:** Giuseppe Rotunno; **M:** Riz Ortolani.

Apache 🦴🦴 *1954* Lancaster is the only Indian in Geronimo's outfit who refuses to surrender in this chronicle of a bitter battle between the Indians and the U.S. cavalry in the struggle for the West. First western for Aldrich is a thoughtful piece for its time that had the original tragic ending (against Aldrich's wishes) to make it more happy. Adapted from "Bronco Apache" by Paul I. Wellman. 91m/C VHS, DVD. Burt Lancaster, John McIntire, Jean Peters, Charles Bronson, John Dehner, Paul Guilfoyle; *D:* Robert Aldrich; *C:* Ernest Laszlo.

Apache Blood ♂1/2 *Pursuit 1975* (R) An Indian massacre by the U.S. Army, squares off with a cavalry scout in the foreboding desert. 92m/C VHS. Ray Danton, DeWitt Lee, Troy Neighbors, Diane Taylor, Eva Kovacs, Jason Clark; *D:* Thomas Quillen.

Apache Chief ♂1/2 *1950* Two Apache tribe leaders, one good, the other evil, clash. Ultimately, and perhaps predictably, they face each other in hand-to-hand combat and peace prevails. 60m/B VHS. Alan Curtis, Tom Neal, Russell Hayden, Carol Thurston, Fuzzy Knight; *D:* Frank McDonald.

Apache Kid's Escape ♂ *1930* The Apache Kid leads the cavalry on a wild chase across the plains in this saga of the old west. 60m/B VHS. Jack Perrin, Fred Church, Josephine Hill, Virginia Ashcroft, Bud Osborne, Henry Roquemore, Buzz Barton; *D:* Robert J. Horner.

Apache Rose ♂1/2 *1947* Gambling boat owner plots to gain control of oil found on Vegas Ranch. Roy and Dale oppose the idea. First of the series in color; the original, unedited version of the film. 75m/B VHS, DVD. Roy Rogers, Dale Evans, Olin Howlin, George Meeker; *D:* William Witney.

Apache Uprising ♂1/2 *1966* A standard western with Calhoun as the lawman up against gunfighters and stagecoach robbers as well as the usual Indians. 90m/C VHS. Rory Calhoun, Corinne Calvet, DeForest Kelley, John Russell, Lon Chaney Jr., Gene Evans, Richard Arlen, Robert H. Harris, Arthur Hunnicutt, Jean Parker, Johnny Mack Brown; *D:* R.G. Springsteen.

Apache Woman ♂1/2 *1955* Bridges stars as a government agent sent to investigate some crimes committed by a group of Apache Indians. As he tries to calm the townspeople, Bridges discovers that the group is made up of white people led by an educated half-breed. He instigates the help of the half-breed's sister (and also Bridges' love interest) to stop the gang. Some good action, but lots of dull spots. 82m/C VHS. Lloyd Bridges, Joan Taylor, Lance Fuller, Morgan Jones, Paul Birch, Jonathan Haze, Paul Dubov, Lou Place; *D:* Roger Corman.

Apache's Last Battle ♂♂ *Old Shatterhand 1964* A boundary scout discovers the ward of an Apache chief has been framed for murder by a cavalry officer who wants to start an Indian war in this exciting Euro western. 122m/C VHS. GE YU FR IT Lex Barker, Pierre Brice, Daliah Lavi, Guy Madison, Ralf Wolter, Gustavo Rojo, Rick Battaglia, Bill Ramsey; *D:* Hugo Fregonese.

Aparajito ♂♂♂ *1958* The second of the Apu trilogy, about a boy growing up in India, after "Pather Panchali," and before "The World of Apu." Apu is brought to Benares and his education seriously begins. The work of a master; in Bengali with English subtitles. 108m/B VHS, DVD. IN Pinaki Sen Gupta, Karuna Banerjee, Kanu Barnerjee, Ramani Sen Gupta; *D:* Satyajit Ray. *W:* Satyajit Ray; *C:* Subrata Mitra; *M:* Ravi Shankar. Venice Film Fest. '57: Film.

Apart from Hugh ♂♂ *1994* Collin and Hugh have been living together for a year and to celebrate the occasion, Hugh decides to plan an anniversary party. Unfortunately, Collin hasn't told Hugh he's "loaning" his apartment out to corporate executives. Problems arise, however, when he unwittingly falls for sweet elevator operator Fran Kubelik (MacMurray), the most recent social satire. 125m/B VHS, DVD. *D:* Randy Allred; *M:* James Clarke.

The Apartment ♂♂♂♂ *1960* Lowly insurance clerk C.C. Baxter (Lemmon) tries to climb the corporate ladder by "loaning" his apartment out to executives having affairs. Problems arise, however, when he unwittingly falls for sweet elevator operator Fran Kubelik (MacLaine), the boss' most recent girlfriend to the unfeeling boss J.D. Sheldrake (MacMurray). Highly acclaimed social satire. 125m/B VHS, DVD. Jack Lemmon, Shirley MacLaine, Fred MacMurray, Ray Walston, Shirley MacLaine, Joan Shawlee, Edie Adams, Hope Holiday, David Lewis; *D:* Billy Wilder; *W:* I.A.L. Diamond, Billy Wilder; *C:* Joseph LaShelle; *M:* Adolph Deutsch, Billy Wilder. "The Ape." 64m/B VHS, DVD. Henry Hall, Minerva Urecal, Wheeler Oakman, J. Farrell MacDonald, Wallace Ford, Beta Lugosi, Louise Currie; *D:* William Beaudine; *W:* Barney A. Sarecky; *C:* Mack Stengler.

Apartment 12 ♂♂1/2 *Low Rent; Liter Drawing 2006* (R) Artisan Alex (Ruffalo) is stunned when a gallery curator trashes his work and puts his show, causing his shallow bombshell of a girlfriend to lose interest. Dejected and homeless, he takes a pizza shop job and moves into more affordable digs where he meets several interesting characters, including goofy and loveable Lor (Ulrich). They start dating but Alex's cold feet mess things up, though the neighbors can't avoid one another. Solid work by leads Ruffalo and Ulrich keep this average romantic tale from getting evicted. 90m/C DVD. Mark Ruffalo, Alan Gelfant, Manuel Cabral, Beth Ulrich, Mary Colleston; *D:* Dan Bootzin; *W:* Dan Bootzin, Elizabeth Rivera Bootzin. **VIDEO**

Apartment Complex ♂♂1/2 *1988* (R) An assortment of Hollywood weirdos occupy Dr. Caligari's Wonder View Apartments where psych grad student Stan Warden (Lowe) has just taken a job as the building manager. There's a hot-to-trot psychic, a paranoid ex-government agent, and a recluse, among others and then Stan discovers the body of the previous super. Strange things begin happening (including the appearance of a giant snake), even as hapless Stan becomes the prime suspect and potential victim. Creepy and comic. 99m/C VHS. Chad Lowe, Fay Masterson, Obba Babatunde, Patrick Warburton, Ron Canada, Amanda Plummer, Miguel (Michael) Sandoval, Jon Polito, R. Lee Ermey, Charles Martin Smith; *D:* Tobe Hooper; *M:* Mark Adler. **CABLE**

Apartment Zero ♂♂♂1/2 *1988* (R) A decidedly weird, deranged psychological drama about the parasite/host-type relationship between two roommates in downtown Buenos Aires: one, an obsessive British movie nut, the other, a sexual, cold-blooded psycho. Although the movie comes fixated with the mission to real paralysis. Obviously distraught, he begins donning the hide of an escaped circus ape whose spinal fluid is the key to the serum. Hide-bedecked, he slays unknowing townspeople to tap them of their spinal fluid and cure his latest patient. 62m/B VHS, DVD via Android, Marikeva Monti; *D:* Martin Donovan; *W:* Martin Donovan, David Koepp; *M:* Elia Cmiral.

The Ape ♂♂ *1940* When his daughter dies of a crippling disease, Karloff becomes fixated with the mission to real paralysis. Obviously distraught, he begins donning the hide of an escaped circus ape whose spinal fluid is the key to the serum. Hide-bedecked, he slays unknowing townspeople to tap them of their spinal fluid and cure his latest patient. 62m/B VHS, DVD. Boris Karloff, Maris Wrixon, Henry Hall, Gertrude Hoffman; *D:* William Nigh.

A*P*E WOOF! *Attack of the Giant Horny Gorilla 1976* (PG) A*P*E* is 36 feet tall and ten tons of animal fury who destroys anything that comes between him and the actress he loves. Cheap rip-off of Kong. 87m/ C VHS, DVD. KR Rod Arrants, Joanna Kerns, Alex Nicol, Francis Lee; *D:* Paul Leder; *W:* Paul Leder, Reuben Leder.

The Ape ♂ *2005* In search of solitude as he struggles to write his first great novel, Harry (Franco, also debuting as writer and director) leaves his wife and chit for a studio apartment in NYC, where he is shocked to find that an ape already lives there—one that talks and wears a gaudy Hawaiian t-shirt. He somehow serves as Harry's inspiration despite stooping to lowbrow jokes and gags such as throwing poop. 93m/C DVD. James Franco, Brian Lally, Allison Bibicoff, Stacey Miller, Vince Merriwether, Williams. **VIDEO**

The Apocalypse ♂♂ *1996* (R) Coppola's $40 million epic vision of the Vietnam War was inspired by Joseph Conrad's novella "Heart of Darkness." Disillusioned Army captain Sheen travels upriver into Cambodia to assassinate overweight 'renegade colonel Brando. His trip is punctuated by surrealistic battles and a terrifying descent into a land where human rationality seems to have slipped away. Considered by some to be the definitive picture of war in its overall depiction of chaos and primal bloodletting; by others, over-wrought and unrealistic. May not translate as well to the small screen, yet worth seeing if for nothing more than Duvall's ten minutes of scenery chewing as a battle-obsessed major ("I love the smell of napalm in the morning!"), a study in manic machismo. Stunning photography by Vittorio Storaro, awe-inspiring battle scenes, and effective soundtrack montage. Both Sheen and Coppola suffered emotional breakdowns during the prolonged filming, and that's a very young Fishburne in his major film debut. Available now in a remastered version in letterbox on VHS with a remixed soundtrack that features Dolby Surround stereo. In 1991 a documentary detailing the making of the film, "Hearts of Darkness: A Filmmaker's Apocalypse," was released. 153m/C VHS, DVD. Francis Ford Coppola, Marlon Brando, Martin Sheen, Robert Duvall, Frederic Forrest, Sam Bottoms, Scott Glenn, Albert Hall, Laurence Fishburne, Harrison Ford, G.D. Spradlin, Dennis Hopper, Cynthia Wood, Colleen Camp, Linda Carpenter, Tom Mason, James Keane, Damien Leake, Jack Thibeau, R. Lee Ermey, Vittorio Storaro; *D:* Francis Ford Coppola; *W:* Francis Ford Coppola, John Milius, Michael Herr; *C:* Vittorio Storaro; *M:* Carmine Coppola. Oscars '79: Cinematog., Sound; AFI '98: Top 100; British Acad. '79: Director; Cannes '79: Film; Golden Globes '80: Director (Coppola), Support. Actor (Duvall), Score, Natl. Film Reg. '00; Natl. Soc. Film Critics '79: Support. Actor (Forrest).

The Apocalypse Watch ♂♂ *1997* CIA analyst Drew (Bergin) takes over his field agent brother's assignment when the latter is killed. Drew hooks up with his bro's girlfriend/partner (Madsen) and their spying leads to a neo-Nazi organization.

Apology ♂♂ *1986* A psychotic killer stalks Warren, an experimental artist, in Manhattan while a detective stalks the killer. Written by Medoff, author of "Children of a Lesser God." 98m/C VHS. Lesley Ann Warren, Peter Weller, John Glover, George Loros, Jimmie Ray Weeks, Christopher Noth, Harvey Firestein; *D:* Robert Bierman; *W:* Mark Medoff; *M:* Maurice Jarre. **CABLE**

The Apostate ♂♂ *Michael Angel 1998* (R) A young Jesuit priest, whose gay prostitute brother has been murdered by a serial killer heads home to Puerto Rico and offers his assistance to the police investigating the killer, who seems driven by religious torment. But the priest himself is torn by spiritual doubts about his calling and is plunged into a world of temptation and vengeance. 94m/C VHS, DVD. Richard Grieco, Dennis Hopper, Kristin

The Ape Man ♂♂ *Lock Your Doors 1943* With the aid of a secret potion, a scientist turns himself into a murderous ape. The only way to regain his human side is to ingest human spiral fluid. Undoubtedly inspired by Boris Karloff's 1940 film, "The Ape."

A.P.E.X. ♂♂ *1994* (R) Nicholas Sinclair (Keats), a researcher from 2073, time travels back to 1973 to retrieve a faulty robot probe called A.P.E.X. (Advanced Prototype Extermination Unit). Unwittingly he has been infected with a version virus and when he returns it's to a version of his own time where humans are dying from the virus and robots are sent to eradicate the few survivors. It also seems Sinclair, Yes, it sounds like "The Terminator" but the action moves and though the budget, with a confusing plot. 96m/C VHS, DVD. Sandra Bernhard, Laura San Giacomo, Hubert de la Bouillerie; *D:* Greg Gardiner.

Apollo 13 ♂♂♂1/2 *1995* (PG) Realistic big-budget reenactment of the 1970 Apollo lunar mission that ran into a "problem" 205,000 miles from home reunites Hanks and Sinese from "Splash." And an enjoyable reunion it is. Explosion in one of two oxygen tanks helping power the spacecraft leaves the three astronauts (led by Hanks) tumbling through space. With the electrical system kaput and oxygen running low, the men seek refuge in the Lunar Excursion Module. Since it's based on the real event and the outcome is known, director Howard concentrates on the personalities and the details of the seven-day adventure at Mission Control and in space, in the process delivering two dramatic payload. Weightless shots are welcoming the astronauts after their recovery ship, while Apollo 15 commander David Scott served as a consultant. 140m/ C VHS, DVD, HD DVD. Tom Hanks, Kevin Bacon, Bill Paxton, Gary Sinise, Ed Harris, Kathleen Quinlan, Brett Cullen, Emily Ann Lloyd, Miko Hughes, Max Elliott Slade, Jean Speegle Howard, Tracy Reiner, Michele Little, David Andrews, Mary Kate Schellhardt, Gabe Jarret, Chris Ellis, Joe Spano, Xander Berkeley, Marc McClure, Clint Howard, Loren Dean, Todd Louiso; *D:* Ron Howard; *W:* William Broyles Jr., Al Reinert; *C:* Dean Cundey; *M:* James Horner. Oscars '95: Film Editing, Sound; Directors Guild '95: Director (Howard); Screen Actors Guild '95: Support. Actor (Harris), Cast; Blockbuster '96: Drama Actor, T. (Hanks).

Apocalypto ♂♂♂ *2006* (R) Set during ancient times against a lavish, peaceful backdrop in the Yucatan Peninsula of the all-native cast) and his forest tribe are viciously rounded up by Mayan attackers as their rulers desperately attempt to save their decaying civilization by sacrificing Paw's people to the gods. As the graphic slaughter begins, Paw slips away and triggers an intense 45-minute jungle chase as he tries to outrun his captors and return to his pregnant wife and young son who he'd hidden in a village well. Gibson's talent at creating no-holds-barred action is on full display in the Mayan language of two hours. 137m/C DVD, Blu-ray Disc. LS Rudy Youngblood, Dalia Hernandez, Jonathan Brewer, Morris Birdyellowhead, Carlos Emilio Baez, Raoul Trujillo, Rodolfo Palacios; *D:* Mel Gibson; *M:* James Horner.

Apocalypto ♂♂♂ *2006* (R) Based on the novel by Lucium. 176m/C VHS, DVD. Patrick Bergin, Virginia Madsen, John Shea, Benedick Blythe, Christopher Neame, Malcolm Tierney; *D:* Kevin Connor; *W:* John Goldsmith, Christopher Canaan; *C:* Kevin Goldstein; *M:* Ken Thorne. **TV**

Minter, Frank Medrano, Michael Cole, Efrain Figueroa, Bridget Ann White; **D:** Bill Gove; **W:** Bill Gove; **C:** Reinhart Pesche; **M:** Thomas Morse. **VIDEO**

The Apostle ♪♪♪ **1997 (PG-13)** No-holds-barred look at one man's search for religious redemption. Euilis Dewey (Duvall) is a devout, middle-aged, Pentecostal preacher in Texas, with a true gift for inspiring his congregation. Unfortunately, he's not so inspiring to his wife Jessie (Fawcett), who's cheating on him with younger minister, Horace (Allen). When Euilis discovers the infidelity, he strikes Horace with a bat, sending the man into a coma. Eulis escapes and winds up in the predominantly black town of Bayou Boutte, Louisiana, having shed his old identity for that of E.F., "The Apostle" of God. He zealously starts up a new church, seeking salvation, but his past comes back to haunt him. **134m/C VHS, DVD.** Robert Duvall, Miranda Richardson, Farrah Fawcett, John Beasley, Todd Allen, June Carter Cash, Billy Joe Thornton, Rick Dial, Walton Goggins, Billy Joe Shaver; **D:** Robert Duvall; **W:** Robert Duvall; **C:** Barry Markowitz; **M:** David Mansfield. Ind. Spirit '98: Actor (Duvall), Director (Duvall); Film; L.A. Film Critics '97: Actor (Duvall); Natl. Soc. Film Critics '97: Actor (Duvall).

Appetite ♪♪ **1998 (R)** Try to stick with this slow-moving suspenser because it's got a wicked ending. A group of strangers, staying at the same hotel, play a game of cards where the loser must sleep in the reputedly haunted Room 207. **99m/C VHS, DVD.** Ute Lemper, Trevor Eve, Christien Anholt, Edward Hardwicke; **D:** George Milton; **W:** Dominik Scherrer; **C:** Peter Thwaites.

Applause ♪♪♪ **1929** Morgan plays a down-and-out burlesque star trying to protect her fresh from the convent daughter. Definitely dated, but a marvelous performance by Morgan. Film buffs will appreciate this early talkie. **78m/B VHS, DVD.** Helen Morgan, Joan Peers, Fuller Mellish Jr., Henry Wadsworth, Dorothy (Dorothy G. Cummings) Cumming; **D:** Rouben Mamoulian; **C:** George J. Folsey. Natl. Film Reg. '06.

The Apple Dumpling Gang ♪♪½ **1975 (G)** Three frisky kids strike it rich and trigger the wildest bank robbery in the gold-mad West. Unmistakably Disney, a familial subplot and a wacky duo are provided. Mediocre yet superior to its sequel, "The Apple Dumpling Gang Rides Again." **100m/C VHS, DVD.** Bill Bixby, Susan Clark, Don Knotts, Tim Conway, David Wayne, Slim Pickens, Harry (Henry) Morgan; **D:** Norman Tokar; **M:** Buddy (Norman Dale) Baker.

The Apple Dumpling Gang Rides Again ♪♪ **1979 (G)** Two lovable hombres terrorize the West in their bungling attempt to go straight. Fans of Conway or Knotts may appreciate this sequel to Disney's "The Apple Dumpling Gang." **88m/C VHS, DVD.** Tim Conway, Don Knotts, Tim Matheson, Kenneth Mars, Harry (Henry) Morgan, Jack Elam; **D:** Vincent McEveety; **M:** Buddy (Norman Dale) Baker.

The Applegates ♪♪½ *Meet the Applegates* **1989 (R)** Ecologically correct Amazonian beetles are more than a little miffed about the slash-and-burn tactics in their gentler habitat. Bug Begley and his brood transform themselves into average Americans, but then don't want to leave their decadent life: even insects aren't immune to the lure of sex, drugs, and cable shopping networks. Imaginative, often quite funny one-joke flick should've been shorter. Fits quite well as a double feature with Lehmann's earlier "Heathers." **90m/C VHS.** Ed Begley Jr., Stockard Channing, Dabney Coleman, Camille (Cam) Cooper, Bobby Jacoby, Glenn Shadix, Susan Barnes, Adam Blesk, Savannah Smith Boucher; **D:** Michael Lehmann; **W:** Michael Lehmann, Redbeard Simmons; **C:** Mitchell Dubin; **M:** David Newman.

The Appointment WOOF! **1982** A supernatural force enters the bodies and minds of people and suddenly everyone begins going crazy. **90m/C VHS.** Edward Woodward, Jane Merrow; **D:** Lindsey C. Vickers; **C:** Carlo Di Palma.

Appointment in Honduras ♪♪ **1953** An adventurer goes on a dangerous trek through the Central American jungles to deliver funds to the Honduran President. **79m/C VHS, DVD.** Glenn Ford, Ann Sheridan, Zachary Scott; **D:** Jacques Tourneur.

Appointment with Crime ♪♪½ **1945** After serving a prison sentence, an ex-con sets out to avenge himself against the colleagues who double crossed him. Well done, highlighted by superior characterizations. Based on the story by Michael Leighton. **91m/B VHS.** GB William Hartnell, Raymond Lovell, Robert Beatty, Herbert Lom, Joyce Howard, Alan Wheatley, Cyril Smith; **D:** John Harlow; **W:** John Harlow.

Appointment with Death ♪♪½ **1988 (PG)** Disappointing Agatha Christie mystery with Hercule Poirot solving the murder of a shrewish widow in 1937 Palestine. **103m/C VHS.** Peter Ustinov, Lauren Bacall, Carrie Fisher, John Gielgud, Piper Laurie, Hayley Mills, Jenny Seagrove, David Soul; **D:** Michael Winner; **C:** Anthony Shaffer, Peter Buckman, Michael Winner; **M:** Pino Donaggio.

Appointment with Fear ♪♪ **1985 (R)** A tough detective investigates a murder and all of the clues lead him mysteriously to a comatose asylum inmate. **95m/C VHS.** Michael Wyle, Michelle Little, Kerry Remsen, Douglas Rowe, Garrick Dowhen, Deborah Voorhees; **D:** Alan Smithee; **M:** Ralph L. (R.L.) Thomas; **W:** Allan Scott, Wesley Moore.

Apprentice to Murder ♪♪ **1988 (PG-13)** A small Pennsylvania Dutch town is shaken by a series of murders, thought to be associated with a bizarre local mystic and healer. Based on a true story, sort of. **97m/C VHS.** Donald Sutherland, Mia Sara, Chad Lowe, Eddie Jones; **D:** Ralph L. Thomas; **W:** Allan Scott, Wesley Moore.

The Apprenticeship of Duddy Kravitz ♪♪ **1974 (PG)** Young Jewish man in Montreal circa 1948 is driven by an insatiable need to be the "somebody" everyone has always told him he will be. A series of get-rich-quick schemes backfire in different ways, and he becomes most successful at driving people away. Young Dreyfuss is at his best. Made in Canada with thoughtful detail, and great cameo performances. Script by Richler, from his novel. **121m/C VHS, DVD.** CA Richard Dreyfuss, Randy Quaid, Denholm Elliott, Jack Warden, Micheline Lanctot, Joe Silver; **D:** Ted Kotcheff; **W:** Mordecai Richler, Lionel Chetwynd. Berlin Intl. Film Fest. '74: Adapt. Screenplay.

Apres-Vous ♪♪ *After You* **2003 (R)** Sometimes you should just mind your own business. Parisian maitre d' Antoine (Auteuil) saves depressive loser Louis (Garcia) from hanging himself in a park and then feels responsible for making the man happy. He gets Louis a wine steward job, though he has no abilities whatsoever, and seeks to reconcile the sad sack with ex-lover Blanche (Kiberlain), except that Antoine falls for her himself. Auteuil is so good he can make any character believable (even this overzealous nice guy), but this familiar farce doesn't do much to stretch his talents. French with subtitles. **110m/C DVD.** FR Daniel Auteuil, Jose Garcia, Sandrine Kiberlain, Marilyne Canto, Michele Moretti, Garance Clavel, Fabio Zenoni, Ange Ruzo; **D:** Pierre Salvadori; **W:** Pierre Salvadori, Benoit Graffin, David Colombo Leotard; **C:** Gilles Henry; **M:** Camille Bazbaz.

April Fool ♪♪½ **1926** A man makes a fortune in the umbrella business and then discovers his daughter has fallen in love with the son of a nouveaux riche neighbor, resulting in all sorts of complications. **63m/B VHS.** Alexander Carr, Mary Alden, Raymond Keane, Snitz Edwards; **D:** Nat Ross; **W:** Zion Myers.

April Fools ♪♪♪ **1969 (PG)** A bored stockbroker falls in love with a beautiful woman who turns out to be married to his boss. **95m/C VHS.** Jack Lemmon, Catherine Deneuve, Sally Kellerman, Peter Lawford, Harvey Korman, Melinda Dillon, Kenneth Mars; **D:** Stuart Rosenberg; **M:** Marvin Hamlisch.

April Fool's Day ♪♪½ **1986 (R)** Rich girl Muffy (Foreman) invites eight college friends to spend the April Fool's weekend with her at her family's isolated island mansion. Everyone is subjected to an endless series of practical jokes when things apparently turn deadly and several of the kids begin disappearing. Twist ending. Lame spoof of "Friday the 13th" and other teenagers-in-peril slasher films. **90m/C VHS, DVD.** Deborah Foreman, Jay Baker, Pat Barlow, Lloyd Berner, Deborah Goodrich, Ken Olandt, Griffin O'Neal, Tom Heaton, Mike Nomad, Leah K. Pinsent, Clayton Rohner, Amy Steel, Thomas F. Wilson; **D:** Fred Walton; **W:** Danilo Bach; **C:** Charles Minsky; **M:** Charles Bernstein.

April in Paris ♪♪ **1952** Dynamite Jackson (Day), a chorus girl accidentally sent by the State Department to perform in Paris, meets S. Winthrop Putnam (Bolger), a timid fellow trapped in an unpleasant marriage. They eventually sing and dance their way to warm feelings as they begin a lifelong romance and live happily ever after. **100m/C VHS.** Doris Day, Ray Bolger, Claude Dauphin, Eve Miller, George Givot, Paul Harvey; **D:** David Butler; **W:** Jack Rose, Melville Shavelson.

April's Shower ♪♪½ **2003 (R)** April's about to get married, but what few know is that April's been a lesbian most of her life. Her ex-lover, and now bridesmaid, has even kept it a secret. Until now. A slew of one-dimensional stereotypes parade across the screen, almost like they're one tired cliche. Tries too hard to be comedic and outrageous and oh, so culturally hip, assuming it can elude criticism by playing the indie card. Nope. Even the gay and lesbian crowds will find little amusement. **98m/C DVD.** US Maria Cina, Zack (Zach) Ward, Lara Harris, Molly Cheek, Trish Doolan, Frank Grillo, Randall Batinkoff, Arly Jover; **D:** Trish Doolan; **W:** Trish Doolan; **C:** Kristian Bernier, Rory King; **M:** Jeff Cardoni.

Apt Pupil ♪♪ **1997 (R)** In 1984, high school senior Todd Bowden (Renfro) becomes fascinated by the Holocaust during a school project and is able to discern from an old photo that neighbor Kurt Dussander (McKellen) was a Nazi concentration camp commander and is a war criminal. Todd agrees to keep quiet if the old man will tell exactly what he did during the war. But Dussander hasn't stayed quiet all these years he hasn't, so Todd gets an up close and personal lesson about the nature of evil. Very creepy adaptation of the Stephen King novella with a standout performance by McKellen. **111m/C VHS, DVD.** Ian McKellen, Brad Renfro, Jan Triska, Bruce Davison, Joe Morton, Elias Koteas, David Schwimmer, Michael Byrne, Heather McComb, Ann Dowd, Joshua Jackson, Michael Artura; **D:** Bryan Singer; **W:** Brandon Boyce; **C:** Newton Thomas (Tom) Sigel; **M:** John Ottman.

Aqua Teen Hunger Force Colon Movie Film for Theaters ♪♪½ **2007 (R)** As intentionally nonsensical as its title. This component of the Cartoon Network's "Adult Swim" feature has New Jersey roomies (and fast-food items) Frylock, Master Shake, and Meatwad going full-length and big screen, battling the Insane-O-Flex home exercise machine that's actually an alien (the outer space kind). Familiar characters like Carl, Dr. Weird, Err, and others make their appearances. Only for those who already know "Aqua Teen" or just can't stand to be out of the pop culture loop. **86m/C DVD.** US **D:** Matt Maiellaro, Dave Willis; **W:** Matt Maiellaro, Dave Willis; **V:** Bruce Campbell, Matt Maiellaro, Dave Willis, Dana Snyder, Carey Means, Mike Schatz, Andy Merrill, C. Martin Croker.

Aquamarine ♪♪ **2006 (PG)** Sweet tweener flick about best friends and a girl with a tail. Mermaid Aquamarine (Paxton) washes into a Florida beach club pool after a storm. She's discovered by 13-year-olds Claire (Roberts) and Hailey (Levesque) and the trio make a pact: Aqua needs to prove to her stern father that true love exists within three days or she will be forced to marry, and the girls want her to grant their wish to stop Hailey from moving away. Fortunately, Aqua is a blonde babe (her tail can conveniently vanish during daylight) who falls for cute lifeguard, Raymond (McDorman)—a romance the younger girls eagerly encourage. Generally comic calamities ensue. Based on the book by Alice Hoffman. **109m/C DVD.** US Sara Paxton, Emma Roberts, Arielle Kebbel, Claudia Karvan, Joanna "JoJo" Levesque, Jake McDorman, Bruce Spence, Roy Billing, Tammin Sursok, Julia Blake, Shaun Micallef; **D:** Elizabeth Allen; **W:** Jessica Bendinger, John Quaintance; **C:** Brian J. Breheny; **M:** David Hirschfelder.

The Arab Conspiracy ♪♪½ *The Next Man; Double Hit* **1976 (R)** Sharpe plays a hit-woman conspiring with assassins from all over the world to kill Arab leaders. One problem—she falls in love with Saudi Arabian ambassador Connery as he tries to gain peace with Palestine. **108m/C VHS, DVD.** Sean Connery, Cornelia Sharpe, Albert Paulsen, Adolfo Celi, Charles Cioffi; **D:** Richard Sarafian; **W:** Alan R. Trustman; **C:** Michael Chapman; **M:** Michael Kamen.

Arabesque ♪♪½ **1966** A college professor is drawn into international espionage by a beautiful woman and a plot to assassinate an Arab prince. Stylish and fast moving. From the novel "The Cipher" by Gordon Cotler. **105m/C VHS.** Gregory Peck, Sophia Loren, George Coulouris, Alan Badel, Kieron Moore; **D:** Stanley Donen; **M:** Henry Mancini.

Arabian Nights ♪♪ **1942** Two brothers fight for the throne of Turkey and the affection of the sultry dancing girl Scheherazade. Enchanting costumes and lavish sets augment the fantasy atmosphere. **87m/C VHS, DVD.** Jon Hall, Maria Montez, Sabu, Leif Erickson, Edgar Barrier, Richard Lane, Turhan Bey; **D:** John Rawlins; **W:** Michael Hogan; **C:** Milton Krasner.

Arabian Nights ♪♪♪ *Il Fiore delle Mille e Una Notte; Flower of the Arabian Nights; A Thousand and One Nights* **1974** The third of Pasolini's epic, explicit adaptations of classic portmanteau, featuring ten of the old Scheherazade favorites adorned by beautiful photography, explicit sex scenes and homoeroticism. In Italian with English subtitles; available dubbed. **130m/C VHS, DVD.** IT Ninetto Davoli, Franco Merli, Ines Pellegrini, Luigina Rocchi, Franco Citti; **D:** Pier Paolo Pasolini; **W:** Pier Paolo Pasolini; **C:** Giuseppe Ruzzolini; **M:** Ennio Morricone.

Arabian Nights ♪♪½ **2000** Lavish spectacle and good casting overcomes the somewhat sluggish storytelling that combines a number of familiar tales. Sultan Schahriar's (Scott) grip on reality is slim ever since his greedy brother (Frain) and his first (and now late) wife plotted to assassinate him. Although he agrees to marry lovely Scheherazade (Avital), he also plans to kill her the morning after. But she sooths her savage sultan with a number of stories involving genies, flying carpets, 40 thieves, and magic in order to stay alive until his sanity returns. Filmed on location in Turkey and Morocco. **175m/C VHS, DVD.** Mili Avital, Dougray Scott, James Frain, John Leguizamo, Rufus Sewell, Jason Scott Lee, Alan Bates, Tcheky Karyo; **D:** Steven Barron; **W:** Peter Barnes; **C:** Remi Adefarasin; **M:** Richard Harvey. TV

Arachnid ♪♪½ **2001 (R)** Plane carrying a rescue crew on a mission to find a downed pilot crashes on a tropical island that contains a gigantic, carnivorous alien spider. Nothing that hasn't been seen before. **95m/C VHS, DVD.** Chris Potter, Neus Asensi, Jose Sancho, Alex Reid; **D:** Jack Sholder; **W:** Mark Sevi; **C:** Carlos Gonzalez; **M:** Francesc Gener.

Arachnophobia 🦴🦴½ **1990 (PG-13)** Big-budget big-bug horror story has a few funny moments as lots and lots of spiders wreak havoc in a white picket-fence community somewhere off the beaten track. Lethal South American spider makes a trek to sunny California, meets up with local spiders, and rapidly multiplies. Utterly arachnophobic (read: totally scared of spiders) town doctor Daniels pairs with gung-ho exterminator Goodman to try and track down the culprits. The script's a bit yawn-inspiring but the cast and effects will keep you from dozing off. Directorial debut for Marshall, a longtime friend and producer for Spielberg. 109m/C VHS, DVD, Jeff Daniels, John Goodman, Harley Jane Kozak, Julian Sands, Roy Brocksmith, Stuart Pankin, Brian McNamara, Mark L. Taylor, Henry Jones, Peter Jason, James Handy; **D:** Frank Marshall; **W:** Wesley Strick, Don Jakoby; **C:** Mikael Salomon; **M:** Trevor Jones.

Ararat 🦴🦴🦴 **2002 (R)** The slaughter of more than one million Armenians by the Turks in 1915 is the difficult subject matter of Canadian/Armenian director Egoyan's historically-themed drama. Excellent ensemble cast portrays characters in modern-day Toronto who deal with pasts that have been affected by the event in different ways. A director (Aznavour) revisits his roots by making a movie about the Armenian genocide. An expert (Egoyan's wife Khanjian) on Armenian painter Gorky deals with her son (Alpay), whose father was killed after attempting to assassinate a Turkish diplomat, and stepdaughter (Croze), who's father committed suicide. Frequent Egoyan collaborator Greenwood turns up as an actor portraying a real-life U.S. doctor in Turkey during that era who published a book about the events. Stylistically intricate, which may leave some confused, but the heartfelt message is not lost in the crowd. 116m/C VHS, DVD, CA Charles Aznavour, Eric Bogosian, Brent Carver, David Alpay, Marie Josee Croze, Arsinee Khanjian, Bruce Greenwood, Elias Koteas, Christopher Plummer, Simon Abkarian; **D:** Atom Egoyan; **W:** Atom Egoyan; **C:** Paul Sarossy; **M:** Mychael Danna. Genie 02: Actress (Khanjian), Costume Des., Film, Support. Actor (Koteas), Score.

Arcade 🦴🦴½ **1993 (R)** All the kids in town are desperate to play the new virtual reality game Arcade, only the game is just a little too real. Seems it can transport you into another world with its stunning graphics and sound effects but you really put your life on the line. Only Alex (Ward) worries when kids start to disappear and she decides to battle the game for their lives. 85m/C V-VS, Megan Ward, Peter Billingsley, John de Lancie, Sharon Farrell, Seth Green, Humberto Ortiz, Jonathan Fuller, Norbert Weisser; **D:** Albert Pyun; **W:** David S. Goyer; **M:** Alan Howarth.

Arch of Triumph 🦴🦴🦴 **1948** In Paris, an Austrian refugee doctor falls in love with a mystery woman as the Nazis enter the city. Big-budget boxoffice loser featuring fine cast but sluggish pace. Based on the Erich Maria Remarque novel. 120m/B VHS, Ingrid Bergman, Charles Boyer, Charles Laughton, Louis Calhern, Ruth Warrick; **D:** Lewis Milestone. TV

Arch of Triumph 🦴🦴½ **1985** A refugee doctor falls in love with a mystery woman as the Nazis enter Paris. Remake of the 1948 film. 95m/C VHS, DVD, Anthony Hopkins, Lesley-Anne Down, Donald Pleasence, Frank Finlay; **D:** Waris Hussein; **W:** Charles Israel; **M:** Georges Delerue. TV

Archangel 🦴🦴½ **2005 (R)** Based on the novel by Robert Harris, this thriller follows British historian Kelso (Craig), an expert on the Stalin-era USSR, to a Moscow conference. He's approached by an elderly man (Chernvak) claiming to know the whereabouts of Stalin's lost diary and he's plausible enough to have Kelso harrying off to the port city of Archangel, accompanied by the man's daughter Zinaida (Rednikova) and reporter O'Brian (Macht). Only their search leads them to a dangerous underground movement to restore Stalinism to modern Russia. Originally broadcast as a BBC miniseries. 120m/C DVD, Daniel Craig, Yekaterina Rednikova, Gabriel Macht, Valery Chernvak; **D:** Jon Jones; **W:** Dick Clement, Ian La Frenais; **C:** Chris Seager; **M:** Rob-er (Rob) Lane. TV

Archer: The Fugitive from the Empire 🦴 **1981** A young warrior battles the forces of evil. Lots of strange names to learn even if you already know who's going to win the final battle. 97m/C VHS, Lane Caudell, Belinda Bauer, George Kennedy, Victor Campos, Kabir Bedi, George Innes, Marc Alaimo, Alan Rich, John Hancock, Priscilla Pointer, Sharon Barr; **D:** Nicholas J. Corea. TV

Archie: Return to Riverdale 🦴🦴½ **1990 (PG)** Archie, Reggie, Betty, Veronica, and Jughead return to Riverdale for their 15-year class reunion. Made for TV; based on the comic book. 85m/C VHS, Christopher Rich, Lauren Holly, Karen Kopins, Sam Whipple, Gary Kroeger, Matt McCoy, David Doyle, Fran Ryan; **D:** Dick Lowry; **C:** Frank Byers; **M:** Mark Snow. TV

The Architect 🦴🦴 **2006 (R)** Rickety construction undermines the cast. Affluent white architect Leo Waters (LaPaglia) lives with his dysfunctional family on Chicago's North Shore. Black activist Tonya Neely (Davis) is an occupant of a South Side housing tower that Leo designed, which in now gang-controlled and falling apart. Tonya, who has her own family issues, wants the towers torn down for new housing and thinks Leo's signature on her petition will help her efforts, but he's reluctant to participate. Based on a play by David Grieg. 82m/C DVD, Anthony LaPaglia, Viola Davis, Isabella Rossellini, Hayden Panettiere, Sebastian Stan, Paul James, Serena Reeder, Walton Goggins; **D:** Matt Tauber; **W:** Matt Tauber; **C:** Nancy Schreiber.

Arctic Blue 🦴🦴 **1993 (R)** Alaskan biologist Walsh gets stuck being the local lawman when he's the only one willing to escort Hauer, a homicidal trapper, to Fairbanks jail. But nothing's that easy—their plane crashes atop a glacier and the duo must battle each other and the elements to survive, while Hauer's brutal partners hunt Walsh. 95m/C VHS, DVD, Dylan Walsh, Rutger Hauer, Richard Bradford; **D:** Peter Masterson; **W:** Ross LaManna; **M:** Peter Melnick.

Arctic Tale 🦴🦴½ **2007 (G)** We love pretending animals are just like us, don't we? Just add some disco music ("We Are Family") and a narrator (Queen Latifah) and we all recognize and watch those wacky things animals do in the wild (like fart). Flick follows a polar bear and a walrus over six years, starting with their birth. The message is clear beyond our compulsion to humanize them, however, climate change, possibly caused by us, is dramatically effecting their habitat. Lush (if not chilly) backdrops and the directors' passion make this a fine family film. 86m/C DVD, HD DVD, US **D:** Adam Ravetch, Sarah Robertson; **W:** Linda Woolverton, Kristin Gore; **C:** Adam Ravetch; **M:** Joby Talbot; **Nar:** Queen Latifah.

Are Parents People? 🦴🦴 **1925** Lighthearted silent comedy about a young girl's successful attempts to reunite her feuding parents. It all begins as she runs away and spends the night in the office of a doctor she has grown to like. After a frantic night of searching, her parents are reunited through her love for her. 60m/B VHS, Betty Bronson, Adolphe Menjou, Florence Vidor, Andre Beranger, Lawrence Gray, Mary Beth Milford, Emily Fitzroy, William Courtwright; **D:** Malcolm St. Clair; **W:** Frances Agnew, Alice Duer Miller; **C:** Bert Glennon.

Archer's Adventure 🦴½ **1985** An Australian family film based on a true story. A horseraimer's young apprentice delivers a prize racehorse to Melbourne through 600 miles of tough frontier, devivious bush rangers, and disaster. 120m/C VHS, DVD, AU Brett Climo, Nicole Kidman; **D:** Denny Lawrence.

Are We There Yet? 🦴 **2005 (PG)** Ice Cube is Nick Persons, an easygoing, charming ladies' man with a self-professed hatred of kids, when in walks his dream woman in the form of Suzanne (Long), an event planner. Suzanne, unfortunately for Nick, is a divorcee with two children, 11-year-old Lindsey (Allen) and 8-year-old Kevin (Bolden). Nick reconsiders his anti-kid rule, and decides to court Suzanne anyway. However, the two kids, who stubbornly believe that their parents will get back together, have decided to thwart any of their mother's would-be boyfriends. As luck would have it, their mother is needed in Vancouver to plan a New Year's Eve party and needs Nick to bring the kids to her. While Ice Cube is certainly enjoyable to watch, the kids are so obnoxious that the obvious question is "is this movie done yet? 91m/C DVD, UMD, US Ice Cube, Nia Long, Jay Mohr, M.C. Gainey, Aleisha Allen, Philip Bolden, Tracy Morgan, Nichelle Nichols; **D:** Brian Levant; **W:** Steven Banks, Claudio Grazioso, J. David Stem, David N. Weiss; **C:** Thomas Ackerman; **M:** David Newman.

Are You in the House Alone? 🦴🦴 **1978** Adaptation of Richard Peck's award-winning novel. Story of a high school coed who becomes the target of a terror campaign. 100m/C VHS, Blythe Danner, Kathleen Beller, Tony Bill, Scott Colomby; **D:** Walter Grauman; **M:** Charles Bernstein. TV

Are You Lonesome Tonight 🦴🦴 **1992 (PG-13)** Suspense thriller casts Seymour as a wealthy socialite who discovers her husband is having an affair with a phone-sex girl. His sudden and mysterious disappearance forces her to hire a private detective (Stevenson) to track him down, with only the taped conversations as clues. Average made TV fare. 91m/C VHS, Jane Seymour, Parker Stevenson, Beth Broderick, Joel Brooks, Robert Pine; **D:** E.W. Swackhamer; **M:** Wesley Moore. TV CABLE

Are You Scared? WOOF! **2006** Scared only by this movie—a dire rip-off/combination of "Saw" and TV's "Fear Factor." Six young people wake up in an abandoned factory and learn they are contestants on the reality TV show of the title. They all have to face their worst fear—or die trying. 79m/C DVD, Aletha Kutscher, Erin Consolvi, Carlee Avers, Soren Bowie, Kariem Marbury, Brad Ashten, Caia Coley, Brent Fidler; **D:** Andy Hurst; **W:** Andy Hurst; **C:** Jeffrey Smith. VIDEO

Are We Done Yet? 🦴½ **2007 (PG)** Apparently this sequel to "Are We There Yet?" is based on the 1948 Cary Grant comedy "Mr. Blandings Builds His Dream House" but don't count on it. Nick's (Ice Cube) married to divorcee-with-kids Suzanne (Long) and she announces she's preggers. Nick decides the family needs larger digs and leaves city life for a decrepit country house sold to them by slick/crazy contractor/building inspector McGinley). Of course their new abode is actually a homeowner's worst nightmare. If you liked the first Ice Cube family flick, this is more of the same. 92m/C DVD, Blu-ray Disc, US Ice Cube, Nia Long, John C. McGinley, Aleisha Allen, Philip Bolden, Marc Alaimo; **D:** Steve Carr; **W:** Hank Nelken; **C:** Jack N. Green; **M:** Teddy Castellucci.

The Arena 🦴🦴 **1973** *Naked Warriors* Scantily-clad women capture beautiful women from around the world and force them to compete in gladiatorial games. New World exploitation gem featuring mostly Italian cast, including Bay, who starred in the previous year's "Lady Frankenstein." 75m/C VHS, DVD, Margaret Markov, Pam Grier, Lucretia Love, Paul Muller, Daniel Vargas, Marie Louise, Mary Count, Rosalba Neri; **D:** Steve Carver; **W:** John W. Corrington, Joyce H. Corrington; **C:** Joe D'Amato; **M:** Francesco De Masi.

Arena 🦴🦴 **1988 (PG-13)** Remember old boxing melodramas about good-natured palookas, slimy opponents, gangsters and a garish sci-fi setting with handsome Steve Armstrong battling ETs and the astro-mob to be the first human pugilistic champ in decades. A really cute idea (from the screenwriters of "The Rocketeer"), but it conks out at the halfway point. Worth a look for buffs. 97m/C VHS, Paul Satterfield, Claudia Christian, Hamilton Camp, Marc Alaimo, Armin Shimerman, Shari Shattuck, Jack Carter; **D:** Peter Manoogian; **W:** Danny Bilson, Paul DeMeo; **M:** Richard Band.

Aria 🦴🦴 **1987 (R)** Ten directors were given carte blanche to interpret ten arias from well-known operas. Henry and D'Angelo star in Julian Temple's rendition of Verdi's "Rigoletto." In Fonda's film debut, she and her lover travel to Las Vegas and eventually kill themselves in the bathtub, just like "Romeo & Juliet." Jarman's piece (a highlight) shows an aged operatic star at her last performance remembering an early love affair. "I Pagliacci" is the one aria in which the director took his interpretation in a straightforward manner. 89m/C VHS, DVD, GB Theresa Russell, Anita Morris, Bridget Fonda, Beverly D'Angelo, Buck Henry, John Hurt; **D:** Ken Russell, Charles Sturridge, Robert Altman, Bill Bryden, Jean-Luc Godard, Bruce Beresford, Nicolas Roeg, Franc Roddam, Derek Jarman, Julien Temple; **C:** Gale Tattersall.

Argentine Nights 🦴½ **1940** The Ritz Brothers arrive broke in Argentina with their all-girl band and try to save a local hotel from a con man. Debut of The Andrews Sisters. 75m/B VHS, A Ritz, The Andrews Sisters; George Reeves, Peggy Moran, Anne Nagel, Constance Moore, Harry Ritz, Jimmy Ritz; **D:** Albert Rogell; **W:** Ray Golden, Arthur T. Horman, Sid Kuller; **C:** Elwood "Woody" Bredell.

Ariel 🦴🦴🦴 **1989** Refreshing, offbeat comedy by highly praised newcomer Kaurismaki. Hoping to find work in Southern Finland, an out-of-work miner from Northern Finland (Pajala) jets off in his white Cadillac convertible given to him in a cafe by a friend, who promptly shoots himself. There's no linear progression toward a happy ending, although antiheroic subject does find employment and romances a meter maid. Mostly, though, he's one of those it's hell being me guys who wouldn't have any luck if it weren't for bad luck. Strange slice-of-life sporting film noir tendencies, an essentially anti-stylistic. 74m/C VHS, Fi Susanna Haavisto, Turo Pajala, Matti Pellonpaa; **D:** Aki Kaurismaki; **W:** Aki Kaurismaki; **C:** Timo Salminen. Natl. Soc. Film Critics '90: Foreign Film.

The Aristocrats 🦴🦴🦴½ **1999** True story of the scandalous 18th-century aristocratic Lennox family, including the four beautiful sisters whose elopements, illicit affairs, and intrigues provided ample English gossip. Based on the novel by Stella Tillyard. Three cassettes. 255m/C VHS, DVD, Jodhi May, Geraldine Somerville, Serena Gordon, Anne-Marie Duff, Alun Armstrong, Ben Daniels, Diane Fletcher, Clive Swift, Sian Phillips, Richard Dempsey; **D:** David Caffrey; **W:** Harriet C'Carroll. TV

The Aristocrats 🦴🦴½ **2005 (R)** "A family walks into a talent agency..." and so begins the raunchiest joke in cinematic history. It might seem odd to dedicate an entire documentary to one joke, but co-directors Provenza and Jillette excel at demonstrating how different comedians bring their own unique interpretations to the same material. The all-star interviewees (George Carlin, Chris Rock, and Robin Williams among many others) speak elegantly about the joys of working "blue," although the true joy of working "The Aristocrats" comes from Bob Saget, Gilbert Gottfried, and Sarah Silverman, who all give blisteringly filthy renditions of the titular joke that you'll be talking about for

The Aristocats 🦴🦴🦴 **1970** Typically entertaining Disney animated story about pampered pussy Duchess (Gabor) and her three kittens, who are left a fortune in their mistress' will. The fortune goes to the butler if the cats don't survive, so he dumps them in the country, hoping they won't find their way home. The cats are aided by tough alley denizen O'Malley (Harris)—it's kind of the feline version of "Lady and the Tramp." Maurice Chevalier sings the title tune. 78m/C VHS, DVD, **D:** Wolfgang Reitherman; **M:** George Bruns; **V:** Eva Gabor, Phil Harris, Sterling Holloway, Roddy Maude-Roxby, Bill Thompson, Hermione Baddeley, Carole Shelley, Pat Buttram, Nancy Kulp, Paul Winchell.

weeks to come. 87m/C **DVD.** *US* **D:** Paul Provenza; **M:** Gary Stockdale.

Arizona 🎬🎬½ **1940** Arthur is a hellion in wild 1860 Tucson who falls for the wandering Holden. He's headed for California and she can't keep him in town so Arthur throws herself into business by establishing a freight line. Only warring Apaches try to burn her out and Holden rides in to save the day (with the cavalry and a stampeding cattle herd). Holden's first romance is lively but long. 121m/B **VHS, DVD.** Jean Arthur, William Holden, Warren William, Porter Hall, Paul Harvey, George Chandler, Regis Toomey, Edgar Buchanan; **D:** Wesley Ruggles; **W:** Claude Binyon; **M:** Victor Young.

Arizona 🎬🎬½ **1986** A group of illegal aliens struggle for survival after they cross the border into the harsh desert. 94m/C **VHS.** *MX* Ana De Sade, Gilberto Trujillo, Roberto "Flaco" Guzman, Juan Valentin; **D:** Fernando Duran Rojas; **W:** Hector Kiev; **C:** Manuel Tejada; **M:** Gustavo Cesar Carrion.

Arizona Bound 🎬🎬 **1941** Mesa City is infested with a villain and our "Rough Rider" trio must rid the town of him. 57m/B **VHS, DVD.** Buck Jones, Tim McCoy, Raymond Hatton, Dennis Moore, Luana Walters; **D:** Spencer Gordon Bennet.

Arizona Bushwackers 🎬½ **1967** Routine western that has Confederate spy Keel taking job as sheriff in small Arizona town. Once there, he has to straighten out a few bad guys who have been selling weapons to the Apaches. Notable for presence of old western-movie veterans Ireland, Donlevy, Brady, and MacLane. Based on a story by Steve Fisher. 87m/C **VHS.** Howard Keel, Yvonne De Carlo, John Ireland, Marilyn Maxwell, Scott Brady, Brian Donlevy, Barton MacLane; **D:** Lesley Selander.

Arizona Cowboy 🎬 **1949** An ex-G.I., now the big attraction, gets involved in a robbery. 57m/B **VHS.** Rex Allen, Gordon Jones, Roy Barcroft; **D:** R.G. Springsteen.

Arizona Days 🎬½ **1937** Cowboys join a minstrel group and rescue the show when a group of toughs try to break it up. 56m/B **VHS.** Tex Ritter, Eleanor Stewart, Syd Saylor, Snub Pollard; **D:** John English.

Arizona Dream 🎬🎬 **1994 (R)** Alex (Depp) is a New York drifter who gets stuck working for his uncle's (Lewis) car dealership in a small Arizona town. He meets an eccentric older woman (Dunaway) with a homemade plane and some dreams of her own. Tends toward the surreal and confusing. 119m/C **VHS.** Johnny Depp, Faye Dunaway, Jerry Lewis, Lili Taylor, Paulina Porizkova, Tricia Leigh Fisher, Vincent Gallo; **D:** Emir Kusturica; **W:** Emir Kusturica, David Atkins; **C:** Vilko Filac.

Arizona Gangbusters 🎬 **1940** Below-average oater has real-life cowboy McCoy fighting city hall in order to fight other baddies. Newfield directed under the pseudonym "Peter Stewart." 57m/B **VHS.** Tim McCoy, Pauline Hadden, Forrest Taylor, Julian Rivero; **D:** Sam Newfield; **C:** Jack Greenhalgh.

Arizona Heat 🎬 **1987 (R)** A violent cop is teamed up with a tough, but tender female cop in this all-too-familiar tale of two cops chasing a cop killer. 91m/C **VHS.** Michael Parks, Denise Crosby, Hugh Farrington; **D:** John G. Thomas.

Arizona Kid 🎬 **1939** Another sagebrush saga featuring Roy in singin' and fightin' action. 54m/B **VHS, DVD.** Roy Rogers, George "Gabby" Hayes; **D:** Joseph Kane.

Arizona Mahoney 🎬 **1936** Weird mixture of circus adventure and serious western doesn't work too well. Confused film with farfetched reasons for having the paths of circus performers and cowboys cross. Based on a Zane Grey novel. 58m/B **VHS, DVD.** Joe Cook, Robert Cummings, June Martel, Marjorie Gateson, John Miljan; **D:** James Hogan; **W:** Robert Yost, Stuart Anthony.

Arizona Raiders 🎬🎬 **1965** Arizona rangers hunt down killers who have been terrorizing the territory. 88m/C **VHS.** Audie Murphy, Buster Crabbe, Gloria Talbott; **D:** William Witney.

Arizona Roundup 🎬½ **1942** Good vs. bad amid tumbleweed, bleached-white chaps, bloodless shootouts and happy endings. 54m/B **VHS.** Tom Keene, Sugar Dawn, Jack Ingram; **D:** Robert Emmett Tansey.

Arizona Stagecoach 🎬 **1942** The Range Busters set out to bust a notorious, guiltless, devil-may-care outlaw gang. 56m/B **VHS, DVD.** Ray Corrigan, Max Terhune, Kermit Maynard, Charles "Blackie" King, John "Dusty" King; **D:** S. Roy Luby.

Arizona Terror 🎬½ **1931** Our hero is on a quest for vengeance, seeking the posse that killed his partner. 64m/B **VHS.** Ken Maynard, Lena Basquette, Hooper Atchley, Michael Visaroff, Tom Lonson, Jack Nattelford; **D:** Phil Rosen; **W:** Jack Nattelford; **C:** Arthur Reed.

Arizona Whirlwind 🎬 **1944** Our intrepid heroes must battle torrents of gunfire in order to prevent a stage hold-up in this western saga. 59m/B **VHS.** Ken Maynard, Hood Gibson, Bob Steele; **D:** Robert Emmett Tansey.

Ark of the Sun God 🎬 **1982** Another adventurer battles the Nazis and nutsies for a 2000-year-old ark buried in the Sahara. 95m/C **VHS.** David Warbeck, John Steiner, Susie Sudlow, Alan Collins, Riccardo Palacio; **D:** Anthony M. Dawson.

Arlington Road 🎬🎬½ **1999 (R)** The tranquility of surburban life is shattered for college professor Faraday (Bridges) when he suspects the picket fence and overly friendliness of new neighbor Lang (Robbins) is a cover for his right-wing terrorism. As Faraday slowly uncovers Lang's true identity, it becomes harder for him to convince friends to believe the conspiracy. Impressive nail-biter with an interesting twist has a solid performance from Bridges as the paranoid professor, and an eerie one from the otherwise affable Robbins. Director Pellington, with the aide of Badalamenti's haunting score maintains the film's objective of showing how evil can come from the most unlikely place. 119m/C **VHS, DVD, Blu-ray Disc.** Jeff Bridges, Tim Robbins, Joan Cusack, Hope Davis, Mason Gamble, Stanley Anderson, Robert Gossett, Spencer (Treat) Clark; **D:** Mark Pellington; **W:** Ehren Kruger; **C:** Bobby Bukowski; **M:** Angelo Badalamenti, Tomandandy.

Armageddon 🎬🎬½ **1998 (PG-13)** A Texas-sized asteroid is hurtling towards earth, NASA gets nervous, and it's up to oil driller Harry Stamper (Willis) and his misfit crew to turn astronaut, blast off into space, land on that rock, and blow the sucker to kingdom come. Ya get a little romance as hotshot A.J. Frost (Affleck) smooches with babe Grace (Tyler), who's Harry's nubile daughter. Lots of action (naturally), some humor, and some sappy, heart-tugging moments for perfect put-your-brain-on-hold entertainment. The second "space rock hits earth" movie, following the somber "Deep Impact." 150m/C **VHS, DVD, Blu-ray Disc.** Bruce Willis, Ben Affleck, Billy Bob Thornton, Steve Buscemi, Liv Tyler, Will Patton, Peter Stormare, Keith David, Owen Wilson, William Fichtner, Jessica Steen, Grayson McCouch, Jason Isaacs, Michael Clarke Duncan, Erik Per Sullivan; **D:** (Jeffrey) Abrams; **C:** John Schwartzman; **M:** Trevor Rabin. MTV Movie Awards '99: Song ("I Don't Want to Miss a Thing"), Action Seq.; Golden Raspberries '98: Worst Actor (Willis).

Armageddon: The Final Challenge 🎬 **1994** After a nuclear holocaust, evil forces rule the Earth in the guise of "The Future Bank." They send out Fear-Permutator Clones to keep order and kill undesirables but naturally there's

a rebel ready to do battle. 85m/C **VHS.** Todd Jensen, Graham Clarke, Tony Caprari, Joanna Rowlands; **D:** Michael Garcia; **W:** George Garcia, Michael Garcia; **M:** Johan Lass.

Armed and Dangerous 🎬 **1986 (PG-13)** Candy and Levy are incompetent security guards assigned to a do-nothing job. Things get spiced up when a mobster tries to run a crime ring under their nose. Candy catches on and winds up in a full-fledged chase. Not as funny as it sounds, though occasionally has moments of genuine comedy. 88m/C **VHS, DVD.** John Candy, Eugene Levy, Kenneth McMillan, Brion James, Robert Loggia, Meg Ryan, Don Stroud, Jonathan Banks, Steve Railsback, Bruce Kirby, Tony Burton, Larry Hankin, Judy Landers, David Wohl; **D:** Mark L. Lester; **W:** Harold Ramis, Peter Torokvei, James Keach, Brian Grazer.

Armed for Action 🎬🎬 **1992** Routine action thriller casts Estevez as Sgt. Phil Towers who gets more than he bargained for when his prisoner, Mafia hitman David Montel, escapes while en route from New York to Los Angeles. When he finally catches up with them, Towers leads a small army of locals on a brutal assault. 88m/C **VHS.** Joe Estevez, Rocky Patterson, Barri Murphy, David Harrod, J. Scott Guy; **D:** Shane Spaulding.

Armed Response 🎬🎬 **1986 (R)** Carradine leads a group of mercenaries in a battle against Chinatown mobsters. They race to locate a priceless jade statue before it can fall into the wrong hands. 86m/C **VHS, DVD.** David Carradine, Lee Van Cleef, Mako, Lois Hamilton, Ross Hagen, Brent Huff; **D:** Fred Olen Ray; **C:** Paul Elliott.

Armistead Maupin's More Tales of the City 🎬🎬½ **1997** More risque and odd adventures for the inhabitants of Barbary Lane. Sequel picks up some six weeks after the first adventures. In 1977 San Francisco, Mary Ann (Linney) and Mouse (Hopkins) hunt for romance on a Mexican cruise. Mary Ann falls for handsome amnesiac Burke (Ferguson) and tries to help him regain his memory, while Mouse reunites with ex-lover, Dr. Jon (Campbell). Meanwhile, Mona (Siemszko) searches for her roots, which leads to revelations from Mrs. Madrigal (Dukakis). Brian (Hubley) becomes a voyeur and DeDe (Garrick) awaits the birth of twins—whose father is not her supercilious husband Beauchamp (Gibson). 330m/C **VHS, DVD.** Laura Linney, Olympia Dukakis, Colin Ferguson, Billy Campbell, Paul Hopkins, Nina Siemszko, Jackie Gibson, Barbara Garrick, Nina Siemszko, Jackie Burroughs, Swoosie Kurtz, Francoise Robertson, Dan E. Butler; **Cameos:** Parker Posey, Ed Asner, Paul Bartel, Brian Bedford, Sheila McCarthy, Scott Thompson; **D:** Pierre Gang; **W:** Nicholas Wright; **C:** Serge Ladouceur; **M:** Richard Gregoire.

Armistead Maupin's Tales of the City 🎬🎬🎬 **1993** *Tales of the City* is the setting for the interconnected stories of the inhabitants of 28 Barbary Lane. There's mysterious landlady Mrs. Madrigal (Dukakis); free-spirit Mona Ramsey (Webb); her gay roomie, Michael "Mouse" Tolliver (D'Amico); hetero lawyer-turned-waiter Brian (Gross); nerdy, secretive Norman (DeSantis); and the naively sweet Mary Ann Singleton (Linney). Definite time-warp factor in this pre-AIDS depiction of sex and drugs, but also the timeless search for love and happiness. Maupin first wrote the stories as an ongoing serial for the *San Francisco Chronicle* and they were later turned into six novels. Made for British TV. 360m/C **VHS, DVD.** *GB* Olympia Dukakis, Donald Moffat, Chloe Webb, Laura Linney, Marcus D'Amico, Billy Campbell, Thomas Gibson, Paul Gross, Barbara Garrick, Nina Foch, Edie Adams, Meagen Fay, Lou Liberatore, Country Joe McDonald, Mary Kay Place, Parker Posey, Kevin Sessums, McLean Stevenson, Stanley DeSantis, Cynda Williams, Karen Black, Michael Jeter, Paul Bartel, Lance Loud, Ian McKellen, Bob Mackie, Marissa Ribisi, Mother Love, Don Novello, Rod Steiger, Janeane Garofalo, Armistead Maupin; **D:** Alastair Reid; **W:** Richard Kramer; **M:** John Keane. TV

Armored Car Robbery 🎬🎬 **1950** Talman and his buddies plot to rob an armored car but are foiled by McGraw and his crimefighters. Surprisingly good B-

crime drama. 68m/B **VHS.** Charles McGraw, Adele Jergens, William Talman, Steve Brodie, Douglas Fowley, Don McGuire, James Flavin, Gene Evans; **D:** Richard Fleischer; **W:** Gerald Drayson Adams, Earl Felton; **C:** Guy Roe; **M:** Paul Sawtell.

Armored Command 🎬🎬½ **1961** A beautiful German spy infiltrates an American outpost during the Battle of the Bulge. Tepid WWII fare made too long after the fact. 105m/B **VHS.** Burt Reynolds, Tina Louise, Howard Keel, Earl Holliman, Warner Anderson, Carleton Young; **D:** Byron Haskin.

Army Brats 🎬½ **1984** In this Dutch film a military family goes bloodily and comically to war with itself. Even in a welfare state, parents can't control their wee ones. 105m/C **VHS.** *NL* Akkemay, Frank Schaafsma, Peter Faber; **D:** Ruud Van Hemert.

Army of Darkness 🎬🎬½ *Evil Dead 3: The Medieval Dead* **1992 (R)** Campbell returns for a third "Evil Dead" round as the square-jawed, none too bright hero, Ash in this comic book extravaganza. He finds himself hurled back to the 14th-century through the powers of an evil book. There he romances a babe, fights an army of skeletons, and generally causes all those Dark Age knights a lot of grief, as he tries to get back to his own time. Raimi's technical exuberance is apparent and, as usual, the horror is graphic but still tongue-in-cheek. 77m/C **VHS, DVD, HD DVD.** Bruce Campbell, Embeth Davidtz, Marcus Gilbert, Ian Abercrombie, Richard Grove, Michael Earl Reid, Tim Quill, Bridget Fonda, Patricia Tallman, Theodore (Ted) Raimi, Ivan Raimi, Donald Campbell, William Lustig, Josh Becker; **D:** Sam Raimi; **W:** Sam Raimi, Ivan Raimi; **C:** Bill Pope; **M:** Joseph LoDuca, Danny Elfman.

Army of One 🎬½ **1994 (R)** Santee (Lundgren) and his pal are hauling stolen cars across the desert when a cop pulls them over. Soon there's two dead bodies and Santee's in big trouble. An unrated version is also available. 102m/C **VHS, DVD.** Dolph Lundgren, George Segal, Kristian Alfonso, Geoffrey Lewis, Michelle Phillips; **D:** Vic Armstrong; **W:** Steven Pressfield, Joel Goldsmith.

Army of Shadows 🎬🎬🎬½ *L'Armee des Ombres; Army in the Shadows; The Shadow Army* **1969** Melville's stunning adaptation of the 1943 Joseph Kessel novel focuses on members of the French Resistance in 1942. They lead shadow lives under false identities, struggling to survive while living in fear of betrayal. The head of this cell is Luc Jardie (Meurisse) but the most necessary of its members is field commander Philippe Gerbier (Ventura), who metes out punishment for such betrayals. It's grim and dangerous and morally ambivalent and no one has time to be heroic (though they are) because there's too much at stake. You can't look away even if you want to. Melville himself was a member of the Resistance. French with subtitles. 140m/C **DVD.** *FR IT* Lino Ventura, Simone Signoret, Paul Meurisse, Jean-Pierre Cassel, Claude Mann, Paul Crauchet, Christian Barbier, Alain Libolt, Jean-Marie Robain; **D:** Jean-Pierre Melville; **W:** Jean-Pierre Melville; **C:** Pierre Lhomme; **M:** Eric Demarsan.

Arnold 🎬🎬½ **1973 (PG)** Outrageous black comedy involving a woman who marries a cadaver to gain his large inheritance. Lots of bizarre and creative deaths in this horror spoof. 96m/C **VHS.** Stella Stevens, Roddy McDowall, Elsa Lanchester, Victor Buono, Bernard Fox, Farley Granger, Shani Wallis, Jamie Farr, Patric Knowles, John McGiver, Norman Stuart; **D:** Georg Fenady; **W:** Jameson Brewer, John Fenton Murray; **C:** William B. Jurgensen; **M:** George Duning.

Around the Bend 🎬🎬 **2004 (R)** Dying patriarch Henry Lair (Caine) is being cared for by his grandson Jason (Lucas), who is also looking after his own young son, Zach (Bobo). Jason's black sheep father, Turner (Walken), abandoned him to Henry's care when he was a child. But Turner suddenly shows up, just in time to fulfill Henry's last request—he wants to be buried in a bizarre ritual that will mean a generational road trip from L.A. to Albuquerque. So does some male bonding occur? Boy, howdy, you betcha, but with Walken around the trip is never completely mundane. Feature debut of director/writer Roberts. **83m/C DVD. US** Christopher Walken, Joshua Lucas, Michael Caine, Glenne Headly, Jonah Bobo; **D:** Jordan Roberts; **W:** Jordan Roberts; **C:** Michael Grady; **M:** David Baerwald.

Around the Fire 🐾🐾 **1998 (R)** At boarding school, Simon (Sawa) tries to escape his emotional troubles by getting in with the school druggies, including Andrew (Mabius). He also begins a foray into the neo-hippie world of the Grateful Dead, where he falls for the free-spirited Jennifer (Reid). Simon does wind up in rehab, looking back on his life. **107m/C VHS, DVD.** Devon Sawa, Eric Mabius, Bil Smitrovich, Tara Reid, Charlaine Woodard, Michael McKeever; **D:** John Jacobson; **W:** John Comerford, Tommy Rosen; **M:** B.C. Smith. VIDEO

Around the World 🐾🐾 **1943** Kyser leads a USO-like tour to entertain troops. Interesting only in a historical sense. ♪"Doodle-Ee-Doo; He's Got a Secret Weapon; Candlelight and Wine; Great News in the Making; They Chopped Down the Old Apple Tree; A Moke from Shamokin. **80m/B VHS.** Kay Kyser, Ish Kabibble, Mischa Auer, Joan Davis, Marcy McGuire; **D:** Allan Dwan.

Around the World in 80 Days 🐾🐾 **1956 (G)** Niven is the unflappable Victorian Englishman who wagers that he can circumnavigate the earth in four-score days. With his faithful manservant Cantinflas they set off on a spectacular journey. A perpetual favorite providing ample entertainment. Star-gazers will particularly enjoy the more than 40 cameo appearances by many of Hollywood's biggest names. Adapted from the novel by Jules Verne. **178m/C VHS, DVD.** David Niven, Shirley MacLaine, Cantinflas, Robert Newton, Charles Boyer, Joe E. Brown, Martine Carol, John Carradine, Charles Coburn, Ronald Colman; **Cameos:** Melville Cooper, Noel Coward, Andy Devine, Reginald Denny, Fernandel, Marlene Dietrich, Hermione Gingold, Cedric Hardwicke, Trevor Howard, Glynis Johns, Buster Keaton, Evelyn Keyes, Peter Lorre, John Gielgud, Victor McLaglen, John Mills, Robert Morley, Jack Oakie, George Raft, Cesar Romero, Gilbert Roland, Red Skelton, Frank Sinatra, Beatrice Lillie, Ava Gardner; **D:** Michael Anderson Sr.; **W:** James Poe, John Farrow, S.J. Perelman; **C:** Lionel Lindon; **M:** Victor Young. Oscars '56: Adapt. Screenplay, Color Cinematog., Film Editing, Picture, Orig. Dramatic Score; Golden Globes '57: Actor—Mus./Comedy Film (Cantinflas), Film—Drama; N.Y. Film Critics '56.

Around the World in 80 Days 🐾🐾½ **1989** TV adaptation of the Jules Verne adventure novel that finds Victorian gentleman Phineas Fogg (Brosnan), Peter Ustinov, Eric Idle, Arielle Dombasle, Henry Gibson, John Hillerman, Jack Klugman, Christopher Lee, Patrick Macnee, Roddy McDowall, Darren McGavin, John Mills, Robert Morley, Lee Remick, Pernell Roberts, James B. Sikking, Jill St. John, Robert Wagner, Julia Nickson-Soul; **D:** Buzz Kulik.

Around the World in 80 Days 🐾🐾 **2004 (PG)** Fogg (Coogan) bets the London science community that he can circumnavigate the earth in 80 days, aided by assistant Passpartout (Chan). Surprising no one, a few people don't want him to make it. This time around Passpartout steals the show as a martial arts expert trying to return a stolen sacred heirloom to his village in China. In fact, Fogg's unworldly inventor seems at times like the sidekick. While departing wildly from the source material, it's a lightweight fun better suited to the lowered expectations of a rental. As in the previous version, entertaining cameos add to the humor. Schwarzenegger is especially silly as an over-the-top lusty Turkish prince. **125m/C DVD. GB IF GE** Steve Coogan, Jackie Chan, Cecile de France, Jim Broadbent, Kathy Bates, Arnold Schwarzenegger, John Cleese, Ian McNeice, Luke Wilson, Owen Wilson, Ewen Bremner, Rob Schneider, Mark Addy, Sammo Hung, Roger Hammond, David Ryall, Macy Gray, Daniel Wu, Will Forte, Robert Fyfe, Karen Joy Morris; Richard Branson; **D:** Frank Coraci; **W:** David Benullio, David Titcher, David Goldstein; **C:** Phil Meheux; **M:** Trevor Jones.

The Arousers 🐾🐾½ **1970 (R)** Sweet Kill; A Kiss from Eddie. Cult item starring hunk Hunter as a handsome California psycho. Tab travels the coast searching for a women he is able to make love to; those who fail to arouse him come to tragic, climactic ends. Definitely underground and moderately interesting. **85m/C VHS.** Tab Hunter, Nadyne Turney, Roberta Collins, Isabel Jewell, John Aprea, Angel Fox, Sandy Kenyon, Cherie Latimer; **D:** Curtis Hanson; **W:** Curtis Hanson; **M:** Charles Bernstein.

The Arrangement 🐾🐾½ **1969 (R)** Veteran advertising executive Douglas attempts suicide and then sets out to search for the meaning of life. Along the way he attempts to patch up his "arrangements" with his wife, his mistress and his father. Forced, slow, and self-conscious, though well acted. Adapted by Kazan from the director's own novel. **125m/C VHS, DVD.** Kirk Douglas, Faye Dunaway, Deborah Kerr, Richard Boone, Hume Cronyn; **D:** Elia Kazan; **W:** Elia Kazan; **M:** David Amram.

The Arrangement 🐾🐾 **1999 (R)** Jake (Keckhemnu) lives in Los Angeles. Luhann (James) is in New York. They're engaged until he admits to a one-night stand and invites her to experiment herself before the wedding. When she accepts, he is not pleased. Low-budget independent production is at obvious and slow moving in some respects, much more sophisticated in others. The details of everyday life are well observed and ring true. Editing is zippy and the characters are treated seriously. **90m/C DVD.** Billie James, GB Leslie Banks, Greta Gynt, Ian MacLean, Linda Lindan, Anthony Bushell, Esmond Knight; **D:** Thomas W. Shannon; **M:** Michael Bearden.

Arrest Bulldog Drummond 🐾🐾 **1938** Captain Drummond is accused of killing the inventor of a futuristic detonator machine and must track down the real killers. Part of the "Bulldog Drummond" series. **57m/B VHS, DVD.** John Howard, Heather Angel, George Zucco, H.B. Warner, E.E. Clive, Reginald Denny; **D:** James Hogan.

Around the World in a Daze 🐾🐾½ **1986 (R)** Sometimes clever, sometimes crude Australian comedy about an aging man rescued from a nursing home and taken on a phony trip around the world by his sons. Odd, but genuinely funny at times. **90m/C VHS. AU** Dingwall, Grosia Dobrowolska; **D:** Stephen MacLean; **W:** Stephen MacLean, Paul Leadon; **M:** Chris Neal.

Around the World Under the Sea 🐾🐾 **1965** Bunch of men and one woman scientist plunge under the ocean in an experiment to predict earthquakes. They plant earthquake detectors onto the ocean floor and discover the causes of tidal waves. They see big sea critters. **111m/C VHS.** Lloyd Bridges, Shirley Eaton, Gary Merrill, David McCallum, Keenan Wynn, Brian Kelly, Lloyd Bridges; **D:** Andrew Marton.

Aroused 🐾 **1966** Hollister is an apparently dedicated policeman who commits a number of blunders in the pursuit of a serial killer, including leaving his wife with the sociopath while he cavorts with the prostitute assigned to his protection. Director Holten's psycho-thriller was gorily ahead of its time. Includes heart-stopping castration sequence. **78m/B VHS, DVD.** Janine Lenon, Steve Hollister, Fleurette Carter, Joanna Mills, Tony Palladino, Ted Galanza; **D:** Anton Holden.

Around the World in 80 Days 🐾🐾 The Three Stooges Go Around the World in a Daze **1963** The Stooges are servants for Phileas Fogg's great-grandson, who has decided to repeat his ancestor's famous feat. Mayhem ensues when the three help out in their usual efficient, competent way. **93m/B VHS, DVD.** Moe Howard, Larry Fine, Joe DeRita, Jay Sheffield; **D:** Norman Maurer.

Arrivederci, Baby! 🐾🐾 **1966** An unfunny sex comedy with Curtis as a modern Bluebeard who weds rich women and kills them for their money. His last mate plans to turn the tables and kill him first. **100m/C VHS.** Tony Curtis, Rosanna Schiaffino, Lionel Jeffries, Zsa Zsa Gabor, Nancy Kwan, Fenella Fielding, Anna Quayle, Warren Mitchell, Mischa Auer; **D:** Ken Hughes.

Arrowhead 🐾🐾 **1953** A long-running argument between a tough Cavalry scout and an Apache chief pits the cowboys against the Indians in this western fantasy. The personal battles that become all-out wars turn back to fist-fights before the matter is finally settled. **105m/C VHS.** Charlton Heston, Jack Palance, Katy Jurado, Brian Keith, Milburn Stone; **D:** Charles Marquis Warren; **C:** Ray Rennahan.

Arrowsmith 🐾🐾 **1932** A small-town medical researcher battles his corrupt science as he juggles his selfish and unselfish motivations for the work he does. He travels to the West Indies to confront the facts of his life and come to terms with himself once and for all. A talented cast takes their time. Based on the classic Sinclair Lewis novel. Two edited versions available (99 and 89 minutes), both of which delete much of Loy. **95m/B VHS, DV2.** Ronald Colman, Helen Hayes, Myrna Loy; **D:** John Ford.

The Arrival 🐾🐾½ **1996** Shockwave 1996 Horror director Stuart Gordon cameos as a hairy biker. **107m/C VHS, DVD.** John Saxon, Joseph Culp, Robert Sampson, Michael J. Pollard; **W:** David Schmoeller; **M:** Richard Band.

The Arrival 🐾🐾½ **1996 (PG-13)** Radio astronomer Zane (Sheen) picks up a message from deep space and discovers a planned alien invasion. When he brings evidence of such to his boss Gordan (Silver) he finds himself on the run from both government operatives and morphing aliens. Starts off slow, but an intelligent script and premise makes this a grade above cheesy. The aliens, with their kooky flaps of skin and back bending knees, are fun to watch. Directorial debut for Twohy. **109m/C VHS, DVD.** Charlie Sheen, Ron Silver, Lindsay Crouse, Teri Polo; **D:** David N. Twohy; **W:** David N. Twohy; **C:** Hiro Narita; **M:** Arthur Kempel.

The Arrival 2 🐾🐾 **1998 (R)** The Second Arrival 1998 (R) Computer programmer Muldoon receives information describing an extraterrestrial conspiracy against earth. Dull story, dull cast. **101m/C VHS, DVD.** Patrick Muldoon, Michael Sarrazin, Jane Sibbett; **D:** Kevin S. Tenney; **W:** Mark David Perry; **C:** Bruno Philip; **M:** Nec Boukalissa. VIDEO

The Arsenal Stadium Mystery 🐾🐾 **1939** Inspector Banks of Scotland Yard tracks down the killer of a football star in this clever but unassuming murder mystery. **85m/B VHS.** GB Leslie Banks, Greta Gynt, Ian MacLean, Anthony Bushell, Esmond Knight; **D:** Thomas Bentley.

Arsenal 🐾🐾 **1929** Classic Russian propagandist drama about strikes affecting the Russian front during WWI, marking Dovzhenko's first great achievement in the realm of Eisenstein and Pudovkin. Silent. **70m/B VHS, DV2.** RU Semyon Svashenko, Luciano Albertini; **D:** Alexander Dovzhenko; **C:** Alexander Dovzhenko; **M:** Danil Demutsky.

Arsenic and Old Lace 🐾🐾🐾½ **1944** Set-bound but energetic adaptation of the classic Joseph Kesselring play. Easy-going drama critic Mortimer Brewster (Grant) is caught in a sticky situation when he learns of his aunts' favorite pastime. Apparently the kind, sweet, lonely spinsters lure gentlemen to the house and serve them elderberry wine with a touch of arsenic, then they bury the bodies in the cellar—a cellar which also serves as the Panama Canal for Mortimer's cousin (who thinks he's Theodore Roosevelt). Massey, as Brewster cousin Jonathan, and Lorre, as his sinister plastic surgeon, excel in their sinister roles. One of the best madcap comedies of all time—a must-see. Shot in 1941 and became a wee bit later. **118m/B VHS, DVD.** Cary Grant, Josephine Hull, Jean Adair, Raymond Massey, Jack Carson, Priscilla Lane, John Alexander, Edward Everett Horton, Peter Lorre, James Gleason, John Ridgely; **D:** Frank Capra; **W:** Julius J. Epstein, Philip G. Epstein; **C:** Sol Polito; **M:** Max Steiner.

The Arrival 🐾 **1990 (R)** An never-seen alien parasite turns an old man into a vampiric young stud after female blood. Plot and characterizations never do arrive. **98m/C VHS, DVD.** SP Ellen Pompeo, Jose Ferrer, Diana Fine, Evan Splichotoce; **C:** Jacques Haitkin. VIDEO

Art for Teachers of Children 🐾🐾 **1995** Autobiographical account of 14-year-old Jennifer (McDonnell) who becomes a model for married photographer Johr (Hannah), who's also well-known for his nude portraits of young women as well as his affairs with his modern dorm advisor (Hannah). He's cited by her emerging sexuality and exacted considering the provocative subject matter. Remarkably described, and John become lovers. Remarkably described considering the provocative subject matter. **82m/B VHS.** Caitlin Grace McDonnell, Duncan Hannah, Coles Burroughs, Bryan Kennell; **C:** Jennifer Montgomery; **W:** Jennifer Montgomery.

Art Heist 🐾🐾½ **2005 (R)** The theft of a precious painting from a Barcelona art gallery causes art expert Sandra (Pompeo) to leave New York to deal with Daniel (Folk), an old love interest, to investigate the crime. This comic elements are fit, only the most dedicated fans of low-budget (Baldwin), an NYPD cop, who tracks Sandra down, only to find her in over her head with the menacing Russian mafia. **98m/C VHS, DVD.** SP Ellen Pompeo, Dario D'Onahue, Chris Hardwick, Luisa Amodeo, Rebecca McFarland, Adam Carolla, Cheryl Pollak, Amy Weber; **D:** Leigh Slawner; **W:** Dan O'Donahue, Leigh Slawner; **C:** Billy Beard; **M:** Christopher Lennertz.

Art House 🐾½ **1998 (R)** Ray (O'Donahue) and his irritating pal Weston (irritating Hardwick) aspire to be filmmakers, but the road to success is blocked by rocky relationships, money problems, and lack of talent. The comic elements are fit, only the most dedicated fans of low-budget, fully funny but that image is so rough that get ($200,000 according to the director) independent productions will be willing to stick with it. Those hoping to see a lot of of Internet babe Weber will be disappointed. **89m/C DVD.** Dan O'Donahue, Chris Hardwick, Lui Cheryl Pollak, Amy Weber; **D:** Leigh Slawner; **W:** Dan O'Donahue, Leigh Slawner; **C:** Billy Beard; **M:** Christopher Lennertz.

The Art of Crime 🐾🐾 **1975** A gypsy/detective is drawn into a homicide case when one of his fellow antique dealers is charged with murder. Maintains an atmospheric edge over others of the crime art genre. A pilot for a prospective TV series based on the novel "Gypsy in Amber." **72m/C VHS.** Ron Leibman, Jose Ferrer, David Hedison, Jill Clayburgh; **D:** Richard Irving; **W:** Bill Davidson, Martin Smith. TV

The Art of Dying 🐾🐾 **1990** A loony videophile decides to start staging productions of his all-time favorite scenes. Trouble is, his idea of a fabulous film moment calls for lots of blood and bile as he lures teenage runaways to his casting couch. Director Hauser stars as the cop who's none too impressed with the cinematic remakes, while cult favorite Pollard is his partner. If you like a little atmosphere and psychological depth in your slashers, you'll find this to be the stuff that populates **90m/C VHS.** Wings Hauser, Michael J. Pollard, Kathleen Kinmont, Sydney Lassick, Mitch Hara, Gary Wertz; **D:** Wings Hauser.

The Art of Murder 🐾🐾 **1999 (R)** Married Elizabeth (Pacula) has a wealthy hubby (Moriarty) and a younger lover (Kesiner) to keep her motor running. But then sleazy Willie (Onorati) threatens to show her husband dirty pictures of the affair and blackmail is just the beginning. **97m/C VHS, DVD.** Joanna Pacula, Michael Moriarty, Boyd Kestner, Peter Onorati; **D:** Ruber Preuss; **W:** Shawn Smith, Anthony Stark; **C:** John Tarver. VIDEO

The Art of War 🐾🐾 **2000 (R)** Diplomatic thriller has Snipes starring as top-secret U.N. operative Neil Shaw, who is framed for the assassination of a Chinese ambassador (Hong). Also involved is his boss, Eleanor Hooks (Archer), Chinese power broker David Chan (Tagawa), and interpreter Julia (Matiko), whom Shaw kidnaps to help him prove his innocence. Plot is both convoluted and obvious (you can pretty much guess what's coming) and you learn so little about the players that you won't be very interested in what happens to them. **117m/C VHS, DVD.** Wesley Snipes, Marie Matiko, Cary-Hiroyuki Tagawa, Anne Archer, Maury Chaykin, Michael Biehn, Donald Sutherland, Liliana Komorowska, James Hong; *D:* Christian Duguay; *W:* Wayne Beach, Simon Davis Barry; *C:* Pierre Gill; *M:* Normand Corbeil.

Art School Confidential 🐾🐾
2006 (R) Underdeveloped and frequently flat satire about the art world. Idealistic Jerome (Minghella) wants to be the next Picasso when he enters art school. He soon learns it's not about art, it's about hype and commerce. Generic character types include pretentious professor Sandiford (Malkovich), no-talent filmmaker Vince (Suplee), shallow-but-beautiful artists' model Audrey (Myles), drunken failed artist Jimmy (Broadbent), and Jerome's own cynical guide Bardo (Moore). Jerome becomes disillusioned and desperate, and not just because a serial killer is working the neighborhood. Clowes adapted from his comic strip. Buscemi is uncredited as trendy restaurant owner Broadway Bob. **102m/C DVD.** *US* Max Minghella, Sophia Myles, John Malkovich, Jim Broadbent, Matt Keeslar, Ethan Suplee, Anjelica Huston, Joel David Moore, Nick Swardson, Steve Buscemi; *D:* Terry Zwigoff; *C:* Jamie Anderson; *M:* David Kitay.

Artemisia 🐾🐾
1997 (R) Artemisia (Cervi) is the teenaged daughter of well-known artist Orazio Gentileschi (Serrault) who encourages her artistic pursuits. He bullies the local art academy to admit Artemisia, a no-no in 17th-century Rome, and she even tries the forbidden territory of the male nude. Soon her artistic passion is matched by a sexual passion for fellow artist Agostino Tassi (Manojlovic), but this time her father isn't so understanding and Artemisia becomes the center of a rape trial. The real Artemisia is considered to be the first known female artist. French with subtitles. **95m/C VHS, DVD.** *FR* Valentina Cervi, Michel Serrault, Miki Manojlovic, Luca Zingaretti, Brigitte Catillon, Frederic Pierrot, Maurice Garrel, Yann Tregouet, Jacques Nolot; *D:* Agnes Merlet; *W:* Agnes Merlet; *C:* Benoit Delhomme; *M:* Krishna Levy.

Arthur 🐾🐾🐾
1981 (PG) Spoiled, alcoholic billionaire Moore stands to lose everything he owns when he falls in love with a waitress. He must choose between wealth and a planned marriage, or poverty and love. Surprisingly funny, with an Oscar for Gielgud as Moore's valet, and great performance from Minnelli. Arguably the best role Moore's ever had, and he makes the most of it, taking the one-joke premise to a Oscar nomination. 🎵*Arthur's Theme*; Blue Moon; If You Knew Susie; Santa Claus Is Coming to Town. **97m/C VHS, DVD.** Dudley Moore, Liza Minnelli, John Gielgud, Geraldine Fitzgerald, Stephen Elliott, Jill Eikenberry, Lou Jacobi, Ted Ross, Barney Martin; *D:* Steve Gordon; *W:* Steve Gordon; *C:* Fred Schuler; *M:* Burt Bacharach. Peter Allen, Peter Allen. Oscars '81: Song ("Arthur's Theme"); Support. Actor (Gielgud); Golden Globes '82: Actor—Mus./Comedy (Moore), Film—Mus./Comedy, Song ("Arthur's Theme"), Support. Actor (Gielgud); L.A. Film Critics '81: Support. Actor (Gielgud); N.Y. Film Critics '81: Support. Actor (Gielgud); Writers Guild '81: Orig. Screenplay.

Arthur 2: On the Rocks 🐾½
1988 (PG) When Arthur finally marries his sweetheart, it may not be "happily ever after" because the father of the girl he didn't marry is out for revenge. When Arthur discovers that he is suddenly penniless, a bit of laughter is the cure for the blues and also serves well when the liquor runs out. A disappointing sequel with few laughs. **113m/C VHS, DVD.** Dudley Moore, Liza Minnelli, John Gielgud, Geraldine Fitzgerald, Stephen Elliott, Ted Ross, Barney Martin, Jack Gilford; *D:* Bud Yorkin; *W:* Andy Breckman; *C:* Stephen Burum; *M:* Burt Bacharach. Golden Raspberries '87: Worst Actress (Minnelli).

Arthur and the Invisibles 🐾
Arthur et les Minimoys 2006 (PG) Maybe it makes sense to the French. Besson tackles kiddie fantasy in this mishmash combo of CGI and live-action. Arthur (Highmore) lives with his grandma (Farrow), who is about to lose their debt-ridden home. Arthur needs to follow clues left by grandpa to some rubies hidden in the land of the Minimoys, who look like fairies and happen to live in the backyard. A little hocus-pocus, and Arthur becomes mini, gets some help from the inhabitants, and goes after the gems, which are held by evil Maltazard (Bowie). Film's voices are frequently out of sync (it was dubbed from French) and since it's remarkably talky, this is a notable distraction (at least to adult eyes). **102m/C DVD.** *FR* Freddie Highmore, Mia Farrow, Adam LeFevre, Douglas Rand, Penny Balfour; *D:* Luc Besson; *W:* Luc Besson, Celine Garcia; *C:* Thierry Arbogast; *M:* Eric Serra; *V:* David Bowie, Madonna, Jimmy Fallon, Robert De Niro, Anthony Anderson, Chazz Palminteri, Snoop Dogg, Jason Bateman, Harvey Keitel, Emilio Estevez.

Arthur's Hallowed Ground 🐾
1984 A cricket field caretaker battles the board of directors over the fate of his favorite plot of sod. **75m/C VHS.** Jimmy Jewel, Jean Boht, Michael Elphick; *D:* Frederick A. (Freddie) Young.

Arthur's Quest 🐾🐾½
1999 (PG) In this switcheroo on Mark Twain's "A Connecticut Yankee in King Arthur's Court" a five-year-old Arthur is transported by Merlin from his medieval home to the modern age because the wizard fears for the boy's safety. Merlin doesn't reappear for 10 years, so Arthur has become a typical American teen. Now, how do you convince a 15-year-old that he's really a medieval monarch who must return to save Camelot? **91m/C VHS, DVD.** Kevin Elston, Zach Galligan, Arye Gross, Clint Howard, Brion James, Katie Johnston, Neil Mandt; *D:* Neil Mandt. **VIDEO**

Article 99 🐾🐾
1992 (R) Doctors in a Kansas City Veteran's Administration hospital try to heal patients while putting up with bureaucratic red tape and a stingy administrator. When rogue physician Sturgess (Liotta) is dismissed, the patients hold a siege. Sort of son of "M.A.S.H." (Big Daddy Sutherland did Hawkeye) that gets its title from a fictional rule that says veterans can be treated only for conditions related to military service. Erstwhile cast labors to combine comedic and dramatic intentions of script. **100m/C VHS, DVD.** Ray Liotta, Kiefer Sutherland, Forest Whitaker, Lea Thompson, John C. McGinley, John Mahoney, Keith David, Kathy Baker, Eli Wallach, Noble Willingham, Julie Bovasso, Troy Evans, Lynne Thigpen, Jeffrey Tambor, Rutanya Alda; *D:* Howard Deutch; *W:* Ron Cutler; *C:* Rick Bota; *M:* Danny Elfman.

Artists and Models 🐾🐾½
1955 Martin is a struggling comic book artist and Lewis his idiot roommate. The pair become mixed up in both romance and intrigue when Lewis begins talking in his sleep about spys and such. One of the duo's more pleasant cinematic outings. 🎵*Inamorata; Lucky Song; You Look So Familiar; Why You Pretend.* **109m/C VHS.** Dean Martin, Jerry Lewis, Shirley MacLaine, Dorothy Malone, Eddie Mayehoff, Eva Gabor, Anita Ekberg, George Winslow, Jack Elam, Herbert Rudley, Nick Castle; *D:* Frank Tashlin; *W:* Frank Tashlin, Hal Kanter, Herbert Baker; *C:* Daniel F. Fapp.

As Good as Dead 🐾🐾½
1995 (PG-13) A young woman allows her sick friend to assume her identity but when her friend is murdered, she realizes the killer was really after her. **88m/C VHS.** Crystal Bernard, Traci Lords, Judge Reinhold; *D:* Larry Cohen; *W:* Larry Cohen.

As Good As It Gets 🐾🐾🐾 *Old Friends* 1997 (PG-13) Entertaining and enjoyable outing from Brooks racked up an impressive list of Oscar noms (including Best Picture). Obsessive-compulsive romance novelist Melvin Udall (Nicholson) is also the meanest guy in New York, liked by nobody and hating all. The only exception is single-mother/waitress Carol (Hunt), who puts up with his annoying habits at the local restaurant where he dines.

Forced to look after gay neighbor Kinnear's fussy-but-cute dog, Udall falls into an improbable quest for love, friendship, and a life as "normal as it gets" in this sort of extended-sitcom universe. Snappy dialogue by Brooks and co-writer Andrus, and an easy-going non-stereotypical performance by Kinnear are highlights, although most overshadowing the script; but cast but delightful role (both of which won Oscars). **130m/C VHS, DVD.** Jack Nicholson, Helen Hunt, Greg Kinnear, Cuba Gooding Jr., Skeet Ulrich, Shirley Knight, Yeardley Smith, Lupe Ontiveros, Bibi Osterwald, Brian Doyle-Murray, Randall Batinkoff, Shane Black, Missi Pyle, Tara Subkoff, Danielle Brisebois, Harold Ramis, Jimmy Workman; *Cameos:* Lawrence Kasdan, Todd Solondz, Tom McGowan; *D:* James L. Brooks; *W:* Mark Andrus, James L. Brooks; *C:* John Bailey; *M:* Hans Zimmer. Oscars '97: Actor (Nicholson), Actress (Hunt); Golden Globes '98: Actor—Mus./Comedy (Nicholson), Actress—Mus./Comedy (Hunt), Film—Mus./Comedy; Natl. Bd. of Review '97: Actor (Nicholson), Support. Actor (Kinnear); Screen Actors Guild '97: Actor (Nicholson), Actress (Hunt); Writers Guild '97: Orig. Screenplay; Broadcast Film Critics '97: Actor (Nicholson).

As If It Were Raining 🐾🐾
1963 Constantine gets involved in an embezzlement scheme in Spain in this espionage thriller. **85m/C VHS.** *FR* Eddie Constantine, Henri Cogan, Elisa Montes, Jose Nieto, Silvia Solar; *D:* Jose Monter.

As Is 🐾½
1985 Two gay New Yorkers deal with a troubled romance and AIDS. Adapted from the William M. Hoffman play. **86m/C VHS.** Jonathan Hadary, Robert Carradine; *D:* Michael Lindsay-Hogg. **CABLE**

As Summers Die 🐾🐾
1986 Louisiana attorney Glenn fights in the late 1950s to protect the rights of a black family, against the wishes of a powerful local clan. Glenn finds support in surprising places, though. From Winston Groom's acclaimed novel. **100m/C VHS.** Scott Glenn, Jamie Lee Curtis, Penny Fuller, Bette Davis, John Randolph, Beah Richards, Ron O'Neal, John McIntire; *D:* Jean-Claude Tramont. **CABLE**

As You Desire Me 🐾🐾½
1932 Garbo plays an amnesia victim who returns to a husband she doesn't even remember after an abusive relationship with a novelist. An interesting, if not down-right bizarre movie, due to the pairing of the great Garbo and the intriguing von Stroheim. An adaption of Luigi Pirandello's play. **71m/B VHS.** Greta Garbo, Melvyn Douglas, Erich von Stroheim, Owen Moore, Hedda Hopper; *D:* George Fitzmaurice.

As You Like It 🐾🐾½
1936 A Duke's banished daughter poses as a man to win the attentions of one of her father's attendants in this highly stylized Shakespearean comedy adapted by J.M. Barrie and Robert Cullen. Early Shakespearean Olivier. **96m/B VHS, DVD.** *GB* Elisabeth Bergner, Laurence Olivier, Henry Ainley, Felix Aylmer; *D:* Paul Czinner; *W:* J.M. Barrie, Robert Cullen; *C:* Jack Cardiff, Harold Rosson; *M:* William Walton.

As You Like It 🐾🐾
2006 (PG) Branagh sets this version of Shakespeare's romantic fantasy in 18th-century Japan with a group of Europeans who live in a trade colony. Because of a family conflict, Rosalind (Howard) and her entourage are forced to flee into the enchanted forest of Arden. Disguising herself (fetchingly unconvincingly) as a boy, Rosalind then proceeds to confuse the heck out of would-be love interest Orlando (Oyelowo). Kline is along as the melancholy Jacques with the "all the world's a stage" speech. **135m/C DVD.** Bryce Dallas Howard, David Oyelowo, Kevin Kline, Alfred Molina, Adrian Lester, Brian Blessed, Janet McTeer, Romola Garai, Jade Jefferies; *D:* Kenneth Branagh; *W:* Kenneth Branagh; *C:* Roger Lanser; *M:* Patrick Doyle. **CABLE**

As You Were 🐾
1951 A girl with a photographic memory enlists in the Army, becoming both a nuisance and comedic victim to her sergeant. **57m/B VHS.** Joseph Vohs, Russell Hicks, John Ridgely; *D:* Bernard Girard; *W:* Edward E. Seabrook.

As Young As You Feel 🐾🐾🐾
1951 A 65-year-old man is forced to retire from his job. He poses as the head of the conglomerate and convinces them to repeal their retirement policy. He then gains national publicity when he makes a speech about the dignity of man. Watch for Monroe as the boss's secretary. Fine comic performances enhance the script; based on a story by Chayefsky. **77m/C VHS, DVD.** Monty Woolley, Thelma Ritter, David Wayne, Jean Peters, Constance Bennett, Marilyn Monroe, Allyn Joslyn, Albert Dekker, Clinton Sundberg, Minor Watson; *D:* Harmon Jones; *W:* Paddy Chayefsky.

The Ascent 🐾🐾🐾 *Voskhozhdeniye*
1976 During WWII, two Soviet partisans leave their comrades in order to obtain supplies from a nearby farm. Only the Germans have gotten there first, forcing the Soviets deeper into occupied territory, which leads to their eventual capture and interrogation. Russian with subtitles. **105m/ B VHS.** *RU* Boris Plotnikov, Vladimir Gostyukhin; *D:* Larisa Shepitko; *W:* Larisa Shepitko, Yuri Klepikov; *C:* Pavel Lebeshev, Vladimir Chukhnov; *M:* Alfred Schnittke.

The Ascent 🐾🐾½
1994 (PG) Based on the true story of Franco (Spano), a WWII Italian POW who's held in a camp in Africa. The prisoners enjoy making fun of the camp commander (Cross), who consistently fails at his attempts to climb the 15,500 peak of Mt. Kenya. Meanwhile, Franco decides to escape and climb the mountain himself—with the commander right behind. Beware if you suffer from vertigo. **96m/C VHS.** Vincent Spano, Ben Cross, Tony LoBianco, Rachel Ward; *D:* Donald Shebib; *C:* David Connell.

Ash Wednesday 🐾
1973 (R) Taylor endures the pain of cosmetic surgery in an effort to rescue her floundering union with Fonda. Another undistinguished performance by Liz. Fonda is especially slimy as the philandering husband, but only appears in the latter stages of the film. **99m/C VHS.** Elizabeth Taylor, Henry Fonda, Helmut Berger, Keith Baxter, Margaret Blye, Maurice Teynac, Monique Van Vooren; *D:* Larry Peerce; *M:* Maurice Jarre.

Ash Wednesday 🐾🐾
2002 (R) On Ash Wednesday, 1983, ex-Hell's Kitchen tough Francis Sullivan (Burns) is working in his bar when his younger brother Sean (Wood) suddenly turns up. Three years ago to the day, Sean killed some thugs after his bro and went into exile, allowing everyone to think he was dead, including his wife Grace (Dawson). In the intervening time, Grace and Francis have become more than just in-laws. Oh, and gangster Moran (Platt) still wants revenge on Sean for killing his goons. The penance references are all too obvious and Wood's an odd casting choice since he looks too young and innocent for his role. **98m/C VHS, DVD.** Edward Burns, Elijah Wood, Rosario Dawson, Oliver Platt, Pat McNamara, James Handy, Michael Mulherin, Malachy McCourt; *D:* Edward Burns; *W:* Edward Burns; *C:* Russell Fine; *M:* David Shire.

Ashanti, Land of No Mercy 🐾🐾🐾½
Ashanti 1979 Caine of the week movie with Michael portraying a doctor acting as a missionary in South Africa who finds himself alone in a battle to rescue his wife from a band of slave traders. The chase spans many Middle Eastern countries and begins to look bleak for our man. Talented cast and promising plot are undone by slow pace. Based on the novel "Ebano" by Alberto Vasquez-Figueroa. **117m/C VHS, DVD.** Michael Caine, Omar Sharif, Peter Ustinov, Rex Harrison, William Holden, Beverly Johnson; *D:* Richard Fleischer.

Ashes and Diamonds 🐾🐾🐾½
Popiol i Diament 1958 In the closing days of WWII, young Polish resistance fighter Maciek (Cybulski) is sent to a small town to assassinate a Communist Party official. Waiting around in a hotel, Maciek romances the beautiful barmaid, Krystyna (Krzyewska), and questions the meaning of struggle. A seminal Eastern European masterpiece that defined a generation of pre-solidarity Poles. The last installment of the trilogy that includes "A Generation"

Ashes and Embers ♂♂ 1982 A black Vietnam vet in Los Angeles has trouble fitting into society, eventually running afoul of the police. Ethiopian-born director Gerima endows vital subject matter with an evenly paced, alienated mood. 120m/C VHS. John Anderson, Evelyn Blackwell; **D:** Haile Gerima.

Ashik Kerib ♂♂♂ 1988 *strsi; The Hoax; Legends of the Caucasus* Ashik Kerib is a wandering minstrel who is rejected by a rich merchant as his daughter's suitor. He then journeys for 1,000 days trying to earn enough money to marry his beloved. Along the way he's imprisoned by an evil sultan and rides a flying horse, among other adventures. Wonderful use of exotic makeup and costumes highlight this Arabian Nights tale. Adapted from a story by Mikhail Lermontov. Paradjenov's last film. In Russian with English subtitles. 75m/C VHS, DVD. *RU* Yur Mgoyan, Veronika Metonidze, Levan Natroshvili, Sofiko Chiaureli, Dodo Abashidze, Sergei Paradjanov; **W:** Giya Badridze; **M:** Dzavashir Kuliev.

Ask Any Girl ♂♂½ 1959 Lighthearted fluff about a small-town girl who moves to Manhattan. MacLaine plays the bright Meg who gets a job at an ad agency and decides to set her sights on marrying her boss (Young). She asks his older brother's (Niven) help in her quest and the inevitable happens. 101m/C VHS. Shirley MacLaine, David Niven, Gig Young, Rod Taylor, Jim Backus, Claire Kelly, Elisabeth Fraser; **D:** Charles Walters. British Acad. '59: Actress (MacLaine).

Ask the Dust ♂♂ 2006 (R) Chasing an aspiring novelist's dream in 1930s Los Angeles, Arturo Bandini (Farrell)—the son of Italian immigrants but desperate to leave his heritage behind—collides into turbulent love/hate affair with Camilla (Hayek), a Latina waitress with her own agenda to quickly ascend the social ladder. When Arturo comes into money to write his book, their relationship oddly cools off, while later he struggles with what success has cost him. Taken from John Fante's 1939 novel of the same name and highlighted by brilliant desert scenery shot in South Africa. 117m/C DVD. *US* Colin Farrell, Salma Hayek, Donald Sutherland, Eileen Atkins, Idina Menzel, Justin Kirk, Jeremy Crutchley, Richard Schickel; **D:** Robert Towne; **W:** Robert Towne; **C:** Caleb Deschanel; **M:** Ramin Djawadi, Heitor Pereira.

Aspen Extreme ♂ 1993 (PG-13) Former Aspen ski instructor writes and directs a movie on (what else?) ski instructors in (where?) Aspen! Long on ski shots and short on plot, this movie never leaves the bunny hill. Two Detroiters leave Motown for Snowtown to pursue a life on the slopes. T.J. (Gross) soon has his hands full with two beautiful women (Polo and Hughes) who encourage his dream of becoming a writer. His friend Dexter (Berg), however, acquires a few bad habits, and the whole movie just goes downhill from there. 128m/C VHS, DVD. Paul Gross, Peter Berg, Finola Hughes, Teri Polo, Martin Kemp, Nicolette Scorsese, William Russ, Will MacMillan; **D:** Patrick Hasburgh; **W:** Patrick Hasburgh; **C:** Steven Fierberg; **M:** Michael Convertino.

The Asphalt Jungle ♂♂♂ 1950 An aging criminal emerges from his forced retirement (prison) and assembles a gang for one final heist. A very realistic story line and a superb cast make this one of the best crime films ever made. Highly acclaimed. 112m/B VHS, DVD, Sterling Hayden, Louis Calhern, Jean Hagen, James Whitmore, Sam Jaffe, John McIntire, Marc Lawrence, Barry Kelley, Anthony Caruso, Teresa Celli, Marilyn Monroe; **D:** John Huston; **W:** Ben Maddow; **M:** Miklos Rozsa. Natl. Bd. of Review '50: Actor (Hayden).

The Asphyx ♂♂½ 1972 (PG) Nineteenth century doctor Stephens is studying death when he discovers the Asphyx, an aura that surrounds a per-
son just before they die. Stephens delves deeper into his research and finds the keys to immortality. However, his irresponsibility in unleashing the obscure supernatural power on the world brings a swarm of unforeseen and irreversible troubles. High-class sci fi. 98m/C VHS. *GB* Robert Stephens, Robert Powell, Jane Lapotaire, Alex Scott, Ralph Arliss, Fiona Walker, John Lawrence, Paul Bacon, Terry Scully; **D:** Peter Newbrook; **W:** Brian Comfort; **C:** Frederick A. (Freddie) Young; **M:** Bill McGuffie.

Assassin ♂♂ 1986 (PG-13) Made for TV drama about a mad scientist who creates a bionic killer for a bizarre plot to take over the world. He programs the cyborg to assassinate the President and other key people to carry out his plan. A retired CIA operative emerges to stop the scientist by trying to destroy the robot. 94m/C VHS, DVD. Robert Conrad, Karen Austin, Richard Young, Jonathan Banks, Robert Webber; **D:** Sandor Stern; **W:** Sandor Stern; **C:** Chuck Arnold; **M:** Anthony Guefler.

Assassin of Youth ♂½ 1935 Fairy lame thriller about a CIA agent protecting a Senator who falls under suspicion when his charge is shot by an assassin. In investigating the killing the agent discovers the usual governmental conspiracy. 92m/C VHS. Steve Railsback, Nicholas Guest, Xander Berkley, Elpidia Carrillo; **D:** Jon Hess.

Assassin of Youth ♂½ 1935 Lame "Reefer Madness"-style melodrama. A serious threat has been made to First Lady Ireland and no one is taking it lightly. Secret Service agent Bronson has been called as the target of terrorist attacks. Strangely though, the attacks seem to be directed from inside the White House. Bronson as you've seen him many times before. 93m/C VHS, DVD. Charles Bronson, Jill Ireland, Stephen Elliot, Michael Ansara; **D:** Peter Hunt; **W:** Richard Sale; **C:** Hanania Baer.

The Assassination Bureau ♂♂♂ 1969 Set in Victorian era London, this amusing farce concerns a society of international assassins led by the charming Reed. Rigg is an intrepid reporter who pays Reed to have his own organization try to kill him. Reed in turn will try to get them first. A cross-European chase ends in a battle aboard a Zeppelin. Tongue-in-cheek whimsey with a fine cast. Based on a short story by Jack London. 106m/C VHS, DVD. *GB* Oliver Reed, Diana Rigg, Telly Savalas, Curt Jurgens, Philippe Noiret, Warren Mitchell, Beryl Reid, Clive Revill, Kenneth Griffith, Vernon Dobtcheff, Annabella Incontrera; **D:** Basil Dearden; **C:** Geoffrey Unsworth.

The Assassination File ♂♂ 1996 (R) FBI agent Lauren Jacobs (Fenn) quits the Bureau after the first African-American President (Winfield) is killed on her watch. But two years later, when she encounters former co-workers, there's talk of a conspiracy and things turn even more dangerous. 106m/C VHS. Sherilyn Fenn, Dan E. Butler, Tom Verica, Victor Love, Kevin Corrigan, Paul Winfield, Dietrich Bader; **D:** John Harrison; **W:** Bruce Miller; **C:** Rob Draper.

The Assassination Game ♂. 1992 (R) Rookie CIA agent teams up with a veteran KGB agent to prevent the assassination of a world leader. 90m/C VHS. Robert Rusler, Theodore Bikel, Doug Wert, Denise Bixler; **D:** Jonathan Winfrey.

Assassination in Rome ♂♂ // *Segreto del Vestito Rosso* 1965 American Shelley North (Charisse) and her husband are vacationing in Rome when he suddenly disappears. When she goes to the American embassy for help, Shelley is reunited with ex-lover, reporter Dick Sherman (O'Brian), who decides to help her out. A dead body in the Trevi fountain isn't the missing Mr. North but Dick thinks there's a connection and he and Shelley take their investigation to Venice. Available as a Drive-In Double Feature with "Espionage in Tangiers." 104m/C DVD. *IT* Cyd Charisse, Hugh O'Brian, Mario Feliciani, Juliette Mayniel, Alberto Closas; **D:** Silvio Amadio; **W:** Giovanni Simonelli, Silvio Amadio; **C:** Mario Pacheco; **M:** Armando Trovajoli.

The Assassination of Jesse James by the Coward Robert Ford ♂♂ 2007 (R) Calling this film a western is like calling a transcontinental railroad journey a trip to the coast. Tightly wound epic, brooding and dark yet visually spectacular. A true film lover's film, director Dominik brings a style and texture that transcends the genre. See it if you worship the craft of Pitt, or both. 152m/C DVD. *US* Brad Pitt, Casey Affleck, Sam Shepard, Mary-Louise Parker, Sam Rockwell, Paul Schneider, Jeremy Renner, Garret Dillahunt, Zooey Deschanel, Michael Parks, Ted Levine, Alison Elliott, James Carville, Tom Aldredge; **D:** Andrew Dominik; **W:** Andrew Dominik; **C:** Roger Deakins; **M:** Nick Cave, Warren Ellis; **Nar:** Hugh Ross.

The Assassination of Richard Nixon ♂♂½ 2005 (R) Sam Bicke (Penn), a hopeless loser who shoots himself in the foot at every turn, ends up blaming Nixon for his downfall and decides to hijack a jet and fly it into the White House. Based on the true story of a failed plot, film focuses on showing Bicke's gradual but certain descent, played by Penn with gut-wrenching nakedness. Incredibly dismal but revealing look at the making of a potential terrorist. 95m/C DVD. *US* Sean Penn, Don Cheadle, Naomi Watts, Jack Thompson, Michael Wincott, Mykelti Williamson, Nick Searcy, Brad William Henke, Lily Knight, Tracy Middendorf, April Grace, Eileen Ryan, Jared Dorrance and Burton, Alain Delon, Romy Schneider, Valentina Cortese, Jean Desailly; **D:** Joseph Losey; **C:** Emmanuel Lubezki; **M:** Steven Stern.

Assassination of Trotsky ♂♂ 1972 Middling attempt to dramatize the last days of the Russian Revolutionary leader in Mexico before he's done in with an ice pick. 113m/C VHS, DVD. *FR GB IT* Richard Burton, Alain Delon, Romy Schneider, Valentina Cortese, Jean Desailly; **D:** Joseph Losey; **C:** Pasquino De Santis.

The Assassination Run ♂ 1984 A retired British spy is involved against his will in an intricate plot of terrorism, counter-terrorism and espionage. 111m/C VHS. *GB* Malcolm Stoddard, Mary Tamm; **D:** Ken Hannam.

Assassination Tango ♂♂♂ 2003 (R) Aging Brooklyn hit man John J. (Duvall), who dotes on girlfriend Maggie (Beker), and her daughter Jenny (Miller), and likes to hang out at the local dance hall, is sent to Argentina to kill a general. When the hit is delayed, he meets and is enchanted by Tango instructor Manuela, as well as the dance she teaches to him. Deep character study, beautifully shown in slow, at times maddening pace. Duvall's performance redeems film's direction, while not perfect, makes the proceedings interesting to watch, but requires patience. 114m/C VHS, DVD. *US* Robert Duvall, Ruben Blades, Kathy Baker, Luciana Pedraza, Julio Oscar Mechoso, James Keane, Frank Gio, Katherine Micheaux Miller; **D:** Robert Duvall; **C:** Felix Monti; **M:** Luis Bacalov.

Assassins ♂½ 1995 (R) Stallone gets to play elder statesman in the very deadly rivalry between two contract killers. Richert Rath (Stallone) is the man—numbet one with a bullet—whose reputation has caught up with him. Hot-headed Miguel Bain (the ever-smoldering Banderas) wants to off Rath and assume the position of top hitman. Caught in the middle of this macho posturing is surveillance expert—Electra (Moore), and potential murderee—Electra (Moore). It's Stallone to the rescue but his character pays more attention to Pearl, Electra's pampered Persian cat than to the lovely lady herself. But then romance isn't what this film is about—and director Donner does know his action. 132m/C VHS, DVD. Sylvester Stallone, Antonio Banderas, Julianne Moore, Anatoly Davydov; **D:** Richard Donner; **W:** Richard Donner.

The Assault ♂♂♂½ // *De Aanslag* 1986 (PG) Powerful and disturbing drama about a Dutch boy who witnesses the arbitrary murder of his family by Nazis. The memory tortures him and leaves him empty as he matures. Years later he meets other victims and also the perpetrators of the incident, each of them changed forever by it. Thought-provoking consideration of WWII and the horrors of living in Nazi Germany from many points of view. Based on a novel by Harry Mulisch. Dutch language dubbed into English. 149m/C VHS. *NL* Derek de Lint, Marc Van Uchelen, Monique Van De Ven; **D:** Fons Rademakers, Oscars '86: Foreign Film; Golden Globes '87: Foreign Film.

Assault and Matrimony ♂½ 1987 Real-life married people Tucker and Eikenberry play a married couple fighting tooth and nail. Lots of slapstick and general nonsense. Based on the James Anderson's novel. 100m/C VHS. John Hillerman, Michelle Phillips, Joe Cortese, Michael Tucker, Jill Eikenberry; **D:** James Frawley; **C:** Dick Bush. TV

Assault at West Point: The Court-Martial of Johnson Whittaker ♂♂½ 1994 (PG-13) In 1880, Johnson C. Whittaker, a black West Point cadet, is found beaten, mutilated, and tied to his bed. Instead of seeking his attackers, the Academy sets up a court-martial to expel Whittaker, claiming he faked his own attack. Clashes also ignite between Whittaker's defense counsel—white abolitionist lawyer Chamberlain, whose own racism is thinly disguised, and black lawyer Greener, who originally encouraged Whittaker to enroll at the Point. Based on a true story and adapted from the book by John Marszalek. 98m/C VHS. Seth Gilliam, Samuel L. Jackson, Sam Waterston, John Glover, Al Freeman Jr.; **D:** Harry Moses; **W:** Harry Moses; **M:** Terence Blanchard. TV

Assault of the Killer Bimbos ♂½ 1988 (R) A show girl gets framed for the murder of her boss and takes off for the border with a couple of girlfriends. On its way they get pursued by the expected dumb cops and meet up with horny, clean-cut hunks. In Mexico they encounter the villain and extract comic vengeance. Watchable mainly due to the likable female leads and pleasant, lightly campy execution, although it might prove too tame for most of its target audience. 85m/C VHS, DVD. Patti Astor, Christina Whitaker, Elizabeth Kaitan, Griffin O'Neal, Nick Cassevetes, Clayton Landey, Eddie Deezen, Areli Blanton, David Marsh, Tammara Souza, Jamie Bozian, Joe Muscat, Jeffrey Osman, John Quenn, Jay O. Sanders; **D:** Anita Rosenberg; **W:** Ted Nicolaou; **C:** Thomas Callaway; **M:** Fred Lapides, Marc Ellis. VIDEO

Assault of the Party Nerds ♂ 1989 (R) Nerds throw a wild party to try and attract new members to their fraternity. 82m/C VHS, DVD. Michelle (McClellan) Bauer, Linnea Quigley, Troy Donahue, Richard Gabai; **C:** Paul Deenney, Marc Silverberg, Robert Mann, Richard Rifkin, Deborah Roust; **D:** Richard Gabai; **W:** Richard Gabai.

Assault of the Party Nerds 2: Heavy Petting Detective ♂ 1995 Detective tries to save a beauty from her scheming husband. 87m/C VHS, DVD. Linnea Quigley, Richard Gabai, Michelle (McClellan) Bauer, Arte Johnson, Burt Ward; **D:** Richard Gabai; **W:** Richard Gabai.

Assault of the Rebel Girls ♂½ *Cuban Rebel Girls; Attack of the Rebel Girls* 1959 A reporter gets involved with smuggling in Castro's Cuba. Flynn's last film, saving the worst for last. 66m/B VHS. Errol Flynn, Beverly Aadland, John McKay.

Jackie Jackier, Marie Edmund; *D:* Barry Mahon; *W:* Errol Flynn.

Assault on a Queen 1966
Stupid Sinatra vehicle about a group of con men who plot together to rob the Queen Mary on one of her trips. Their attack vessel is a renovated WWII German U-boat. The producers tried to capitalize on the popularity of "Ocean's Eleven," but they didn't even come close. Based on a novel by Jack Finney. 106m/C **VHS.** Frank Sinatra, Virna Lisi, Anthony (Tony) Franciosa, Richard Conte, Reginald Denny; *D:* Jack Donohue; *W:* Rod Serling; *C:* William H. Daniels.

Assault on Agathon 1975
(PG) Amid the scenic Greek Isles, an "executed" WWII guerilla leader returns to lead a revolution, and bloodshed and bombings ensue. 95m/C **VHS.** *GB IT* Nina Van Pallandt, Marianne Faithfull, John Woodvine, Nico Minardos; *D:* Laszlo Benedek.

Assault on Precinct 13 1976
Urban horror invades LA. Lt. Bishop (Stoker) is assigned to oversee the final shutdown of Precinct 13. Nearly abandoned, except for a couple of secretaries and a few officers, the phones and electricity have already been shut off. First problem: a busload of criminals and officers are forced to make a stop to look after a sick prisoner. Second problem: a father, who just witnessed his daughter's murder by a brutal street gang, stumbles in. Then said street gang surrounds the precinct to get the witness. Paranoia abounds as the police are attacked from all sides and can see no way out. Carpenter's musical score adds to the excitement of this low-budget police exploitation story. Semi-acclaimed cult feature and very gripping. 91m/C **VHS, DVD.** Austin Stoker, Darwin Joston, Martin West, Tony Burton, Nancy Loomis, Kim Richards, Henry (Kleinbach) Brandon, Laurie Zimmer, Charles Cyphers, Peter Bruni; *D:* John Carpenter; *W:* John Carpenter; *M:* John Carpenter.

Assault on Precinct 13 2005
(R) Richet's remake of the Carpenter cult classic has the cons and cops, led by burned-out Sgt. Roenick (Hawke) and criminal kingpin Bishop (Fishburne) holed up in a soon-to-be-closed Precinct 13 on a snowy New Year's Eve against a squad of corrupt cops intent on eliminating Bishop, their not-quite-silent-enough partner. Generally solid, if standard, updating loses much credibility by plopping a forest in the middle of a heavy industrial part of Detroit, where this one is set. Hawke and Fishburne are appropriately conflicted and heroic as it's called for, but it's the supporting cast that gives this rendition its zest. Slick around for the helpful plot-summarizing rap song that plays over the closing credits. 109m/C **VHS, DVD, UMD, HD DVD.** *US* Ethan Hawke, Laurence Fishburne, Brian Dennehy, Drea De Matteo, Maria Bello, Gabriel Byrne, Ja Rule, Matt Craven, John Leguizamo, Fulvio Cecere, Currie Graham, Dorian Harewood, Kim Coates, Hugh Dillon, Titus Welliver, Aisha Hinds; *D:* Jean-Francois Richet; *W:* James DeMonaco; *C:* Robert Gantz; *M:* Graeme Revell.

Assault with a Deadly Weapon 1982
When the police budget is cutback, crime runs rampant in an unnamed American city. 86m/C **VHS.** Sandra Foley, Richard Holliday, Lamont Jackson; *D:* Arthur Kennedy.

The Assignment 1978
The assassination of a high-ranking officer in an uneasy Latin American nation spurs violence and political instability. A Swedish diplomat is assigned the tremendous task of restoring peace and stability between the political factions. 92m/C **VHS, SW DVD.** *SW* Christopher Plummer, Thomas Hellberg, Carolyn Seymour, Fernando Rey; *D:* Mats Arehn.

The Assignment 1997 (R)
Workmanlike thriller is a case of deadly impersonation. Infamous terrorist Carlos the Jackal (Quinn) is shown plying his trade in Europe under the nose of CIA counterterrorism expert Jack Shaw (Sutherland). Later, in Israel, Mossad agent Amos (Kingsley) captures a man whom he thinks is Carlos, only it's his double—U.S. Navy officer Annibal Ramirez (Quinn again). So Shaw and Amos decide to turn the seaman into the terrorist, in an elaborate plot to have Carlos' Russian handlers think the terrorist has betrayed them. There's a very long setup for a somewhat lame payoff. 115m/C **VHS, DVD.** *CA* Aidan Quinn, Donald Sutherland, Ben Kingsley, Liliana Komorowska, Claudia Ferri, Celine Bonnier, Vlasta Vrana, Von Flores, Al Waxman; *D:* Christian Duguay; *W:* Don Gordon, Sabi H. Shabtai; *C:* David Franco; *M:* Normand Corbeil.

Assignment Outer Space
Space Men 1961 A giant spaceship with bytes for brains is on a collision course with Earth. A team of astronauts is sent to save the world from certain peril. Seems they take the task lightly, though, and their mission (and hence the plot) revolves more around saving sexy sultress Farinon from certain celibacy. If you're into stultifying Italian space operas with a gratuitous sex sub-plot then look up this gaseous entry, but don't say we didn't warn you. Director Margheriti is also known as Anthony Dawson, so to be confused with the actor of the same name. 79m/B **VHS, DVD.** *IT* Rik van Nutter, Gabriella Farinon, Archie Savage, Dave Montresor, Alan Dijon; *D:* Anthony M. Dawson; *Nar:* Jack Wallace.

The Assisi Underground 1984
True but boringly told story of how the Catholic Church helped to save several hundred Italian Jews from being executed by the Nazis during the 1948 German occupation of Italy. Edited from 178 minutes, a good-will gesture from the producers. 115m/C **VHS.** James Mason, Ben Cross, Maximilian Schell, Irene Papas; *D:* Alexander Ramati; *M:* Pino Donaggio.

The Assistant 1997
The Jewish Bober family have escaped the anti-Semitism of their homeland and emigrated to the U.S. where they are struggling to run a small grocery store during the depression. Drifter Frank (Bellows) hooks up with thief Ward (Woolvet) and they rob the store, with Ward attacking Morris Bober (Mueller-Stahl). A guilty Frank later returns. Morris doesn't know Frank was part of the robbery and agrees and Frank soons falls for the Bober's daughter, Helen (Greenhouse). Then Morris discovers the truth. Based on a novel by Bernard Malamud. 105m/C **VHS.** *CA* Gil Bellows, Armin Mueller-Stahl, Joan Plowright, Kate Greenhouse, Jaimz Woolvet; *D:* Daniel Petrie; *W:* Daniel Petrie; *C:* Philip Earnshaw.

The Associate 1979
L'Associe (R) French farce about penniless financial consultant Julien Pardot (Serrault) who invents a fictitious partner, Mr. Davis, in order to get his business rolling. When his clients, his wife, and even his mistress are all more intrigued by the partner than Julien, he becomes so jealous he decides to "murder" his creation. Based on the novel "My Partner, Mr. Davis" by Jenaro Prieto. French with subtitles; remade in 1996 with Whoopi Goldberg. 93m/C **VHS.** *FR* Michel Serrault, Claudine Auger, Catherine Alric, Matthieu Carriere; *D:* Rene Gainville; *W:* Jean-Claude Carriere.

The Associate 1996 (PG-13)
Whoopi drags a 20-minute premise over almost two hours when she invents an elderly, white, male business partner to give her fledgling financial consulting business some prestige. After having all her moneymaking ideas appropriated by male colleagues, Laurel Ayres (Goldberg) starts her own business, only to find that no one wants to hire her. She creates the genius and the money comes rolling in. Everyone clamors to meet the mystery man, so she goes undercover as the elusive Robert S. Cutty. The sight of Goldberg in old white guy garb and makeup is jarring, and the payoff doesn't merit the overlong build up. Based on the French film "L'Associe" and the Jenaro Prieto novel "El Socio." 113m/C **VHS, DVD.** Whoopi Goldberg, Timothy Daly, Bebe Neuwirth, Dianne Wiest, Eli Wallach; *D:* Donald Petrie; *W:* Nick Thiel; *C:* Alex Nepomniaschy; *M:* Christopher Tyng.

Asteroid 1997
Re-edited version of the NBC TV miniseries finds the special effects and action, which should help this routine disaster flick. Astronomer Lily McKee (Sciorra) discovers that several giant asteroids are on a collision course with Kansas City. She contacts FEMA and gets hotshot director Jack Wallach (Biehn) anxious to help out (and not just with the rock problem). Naturally, the citizens freak and one asteroid hits but there's an even bigger one on the way. 120m/C **VHS, DVD.** Michael Biehn, Annabella Sciorra, Don Franklin, Anne-Marie Johnson, Anthony Zerbe, Carlos Gomez, Jensen (Jennifer) Daggett, Michael Weatherly, Frank McRae, Denis Arndt; *D:* Bradford May; *W:* Robbyn Burger, Scott Sturgeon; *C:* David Hennings, Thomas Del Ruth; *M:* Shirley Walker. **TV**

Astoria 2000 (R)
The Astoria section of Queens is heavily Greek-American with all its ethnic traditions. Alex (Stear) is 28 and wants to escape his stagnant life by joining an archeological expedition to find the lost tomb of Alexander the Great. His father Demo (Setrakian) expects Alex to help with the family business. Alex isn't happy until Greek art restorer Elena (Turco) pays a visit and suddenly things look a lot brighter. 103m/C **DVD.** Rick Stear, Ed Setrakian, Paige Turco, Joseph (Joe) D'Onofrio; *D:* Nick Efteriades; *C:* Elia Lyssey; *M:* Nikos Papazoglou.

The Astounding She-Monster woof!
Mysterious Invader 1958 How can you not love a movie with a title like this? A bad script and snail-paced plot are a good start. A geologist wanting only to be left alone with his rocks survives a brush with the kidnappers of a wealthy heiress only to happen upon an alien spacecraft that's crashed nearby. At the helm is a very tall, high-heeled fem-alien in an obligatory skintight space outfit. Excellent, our rock jock thinks, but it seems she kills with the slightest touch. For connoisseurs of truly bad movies. 60m/B **VHS, DVD.** Robert Clarke, Kenne Duncan, Marilyn Harvey, Jeanne Tatum, Shirly Kilpatrick, Ewing Miles Brown; *D:* Ronnie Ashcroft; *W:* Frank Hall; *C:* William C. Thompson; *M:* Guenther Kauer.

The Astro-Zombies woof!
The Space Vampires 1967 A contender as one of the worst movies of all time. Carradine plays a mad scientist creating zombies who eat people's guts. Cult favorite Satanna stars. Co-written and co-produced by Rogers of "M*A*S*H" fame. 83m/C **VHS, DVD.** Tua Satana, Wendell Corey, John Carradine, Tom Pace, Joan Patrick, Rafael Campos, William Bagdad, Joseph Hoover, Victor Izay, Vincent Barbi, Rod Wilmoth; *D:* Ted V. Mikels; *W:* Ted V. Mikels, Wayne Rogers; *C:* Robert Maxwell; *M:* Nico Karaski.

The Astronaut Farmer 2007
(PG) NASA engineer Charlie Farmer (Thornton) left the space program for his family's failing Texas ranch but never gave up his dream of being an astronaut. He's got his very own shiny silver space suit and is building an actual rocket in his barn. His family and friends see Charlie as a larger-than-life eccentric but when he tries to buy rocket fuel the feds think Charlie's some kind of homegrown terrorist. Film treats Charlie and his dreams matter-of-factly as does Thornton, with Madsen luminous as his devoted wife and Simmons blustering as his fed nemesis. 104m/ C **DVD.** *US* Billy Bob Thornton, Virginia Madsen, Bruce Dern, J.K. Simmons, Tim Blake Nelson, Max Thieriot, Jon(athan) Gries, Mark Polish, Jasper Polish, Logan Polish; *Cameos:* Bruce Willis; *D:* Michael Polish; *W:* Mark Polish, Michael Polish; *C:* M. David Mullen; *M:* Stuart Matthewman.

The Astronaut's Wife 1999 (R)
Astronaut Spencer Armacost (Depp) just isn't the same guy after he returns from a nearly fatal space shuttle mission. He and his wife, Jillian (Theron), suddenly move to New York and she definitely notices some behavioral changes (he likes to listen to the test pattern on the TV screen). Oh, and then the little woman discovers she's pregnant and things get very "Rosemary's Baby." Theron's role is also very much like her beleaguered wife in "The Devil's Advocate," since everyone seems to think Jillian's nuts. Disappointingly formulaic; Depp's more believable in quirky roles in quirky movies. 109m/C **VHS, DVD.** Johnny Depp, Charlize Theron, Joe Morton, Tom Noonan, Blair Brown, Nick Cassavetes, Clea DuVall, Donna Murphy, Samantha Eggar; *D:* Rand Ravich; *W:* Rand Ravich; *C:* Allen Daviau; *M:* George S. Clinton.

Asunder 1999
Slick thriller with a familiar storyline. Michael (Beach) and wife Lauren (Morgan) are at the fairground with their best friends Chance (Underwood) and his pregnant wife Roberta (Hicks). Roberta is tragically killed in a fall while riding the Ferris wheel. Michael and Lauren invite Chance to stay with them and the viewer learns that Lauren and Chance once had an extramarital affair. Then Chance decides to wreck her marriage and get Lauren back. 102m/C **VHS, DVD.** Blair Underwood, Debbi (Deborah) Morgan, Michael Beach, Marva Hicks; *D:* Tim Reid; *W:* Eric Lee Bowers; *C:* Johnny (John W.) Simmons; *M:* Lionel Cole.

Asylum 1972 (PG)
Four strange and chilling stories weave together in this film. A murderer's victim seeks retribution. A tailor seems to be collecting his bills. A man who makes voodoo dolls...only to become one later on. A woman plagued by a double. A doctor visiting the asylum tells each tale. Horrifying and grotesque, not as humorless as American horror films. 100m/C **VHS, DVD.** *GB* Peter Cushing, Herbert Lom, Britt Ekland, Barbara Parkins, Patrick Magee, Barry Morse, Robert Powell, Richard Todd, Charlotte Rampling, Ann(e) Firbank, Sylvia Syms, James Villiers, Geoffrey Bayldon, Megs Jenkins; *D:* Roy Ward Baker; *W:* Robert Bloch; *C:* Denys Coop.

Asylum 1997 (R)
Unstable investigator Nick Tordone (Patrick) looks into his shrink's supposed suicide by become a patient at the doctor's mental hospital. By what he finds is serial killer Sullivan Rane (McDowell) and a doctor (Gibson) doing dangerous mind control experiments. Tension holds up well until the unfortunate finale. 92m/C **VHS.** Jason Schombing, Kevin Anthony Cole, Peter Brown, Robert Patrick, Malcolm McDowell, Henry Gibson, Sarah Douglas; *D:* James Seale; *W:* James Seale; *C:* David Rakoczy; *M:* Alan Williams.

Asylum 2005 (R)
Sex in the loony bin. In 1959, frustrated Stella Raphael (Richardson) accompanies her hubby Max (Bonneville) to the titular Victorian heap where he is the new superintendent. Stella meets hottie patient Edgar (Csokas), who helps out around the grounds, and the two are soon helping themselves to each other. Despite the fact that Edgar's locked up because he beat his wife to death in a jealous rage. Add to the mix Edgar's manipulative doctor, Peter Cleave (McKellen), and you've got a melodrama at high boil, just waiting to bubble over. As over-the-top as it sounds; adapted from the novel by Patrick McGrath. 99m/C **DVD.** *IR GB* Natasha Richardson, Ian McKellen, Marton Csokas, Hugh Bonneville, Judy Parfitt, Sean Harris, Gus Lewis, Wanda Ventham, Joss Ackland; *D:* David Mackenzie; *W:* Patrick Marber, Chrys Balls; *C:* Giles Nuttgens; *M:* Mark Mancina.

Asylum of Satan 1972
A beautiful concert pianist is savagely tortured by a madman in the Asylum of Satan. Filmed on location in Louisville, Kentucky. 87m/C **VHS, DVD.** Charles Kissinger, Carla Borelli, Nick Jolly, Sherry Steiner; *D:* William Girdler; *W:* William Girdler.

Asylum of the Damned
Hellborn 2003 (R) Naive psychologist believes he can tackle the worst offenders at the criminally insane asylum but isn't ready to deal with the hideous truth behind the high volume of vanishing inmates. 85m/C **VHS, DVD.** Bruce Payne, Tracy Scoggins, Matthew Tompkins (Tiny) Lister, Gregory Wagrowski, Bill McKinney, Randal England, Kyle T. Heffner, Michael Earl Reid, David Thomas, Matt Stasi, Julia Lee, Joe Sabatino, Deborah Flora, Stefan Marchand; *D:* Philip Jones; *W:* Matthew McCombs; *C:* Mark Melville; *M:* Valentine Leone, Steve Bauman.

VIDEO

At Any Cost 2000 (R)
Ah, the music business. Austin, Texas band Beyond Gravity has a shot at a major recording career in L.A. when they're signed by an indie label. Leader Lance (Mills) vows to wife/bandmember Chelsea (Flanigan) that they won't blow their big chance but problems arise quickly. Seems Lance's brother Mike (Franco) can't control his drug problem and ambitious pal

Ben (Quinn) wants to strike out on his own when the band starts to go south. Typical price-of-fame cable drama. **92m/C VHS.** Eddie Mills, James Franco, Glenn Quinn, Maureen Flannigan, Cyie Batem; **D:** Charles Winkler; **W:** Bruce Taylor; Roderick Taylor. **C:** Robert Steadman. **CABLE.**

At Close Range ⍟⍟⍟ 1986 (R) Based on the true story of Bruce Johnston Sr. and Jr. in Brandywine River Valley, Pennsylvania. Father, Walken, tempts his teenaged son, Penn, into pursuing criminal activities with talk of excitement and high living. Penn soon learns that his father is extremely dangerous and a bit unstable, but he's still fascinated by his wealth and power. Sometimes overbearing and depressing, but good acting and fancy camera work. A young cast of stars includes Masterson as the girl Penn tries to impress. Features Madonna's "Live to Tell." **115m/C VHS, DVD.** Sean Penn, Christopher Walken, Christopher Penn, Mary Stuart Masterson, Crispin Glover, Kiefer Sutherland, Candy Clark, Tracey Walter, Millie Perkins, Alan Autry, David Strathaim, Eileen Ryan; **D:** James Foley; **W:** Nicholas Kazan. **C:** Juan Ruiz-Anchia; **M:** Patrick Leonard.

At First Sight ⍟⍟½ 1998 (PG-13) *Two Guys Talkin' About Girls* 1995 (R) Yakky pedestrian comedy about schleppy Lenny (Silverman) and his best frie'd, macho Joey (Cortese), trying to help each other out with their romantic crises. Lenny meets cute when he picks up Rhonda (Smith) at the planetarium while she beds a string of girls, all of whom are named Cindy, in an effort to get over the first Cindy who broke his heart. It's been done before—and better. **90m/C VHS.** Jonatha'n Silverman, Dan Cortese, Allison Smith, Monte Markhiem, Kathlee'n Freeman; **D:** Steven Pearl; **W:** Ken Copel. **C:** Glenn Kershaw; **M:** Richard Gibbs.

At Gunpoint ⍟½ 1990 A no-account bank robber spends his six year stint in the slammer plotting his revenge. Having gone thoroughly stir-crazy, the vengeful criminal stalks the lawman who put him away, like so many revenge-seeking criminals before him. Run of the mill addition to big list of bad-guy-hunting-for-revenge flicks. **90m/C VHS.** Frank Kang, Tain Bodkin, Scott Claflin; **D:** Steven Harris; **W:** Steven Harris.

At Gunpoint ⍟⍟ *Gunpoint* 1955 A store owner becomes the town hero when, by accident, he shoots and kills a bank robber. **81m/C VHS.** Fred MacMurray, Dorothy Malone, John Queler, Walter Brennan; **D:** Alfred Werker. **C:** Ellsworth Fredericks.

At Home with the Webbers ⍟⍟ 1994 (R) Gerald, Emma, Johnny, and Miranda Webber win a contest to star in a cable TV series about their lives. What they don't expect is that the series will become a hit or that all the family idiosyncrasies will be exaggerated by stardom (the manipulative TV producer doesn't help). Over-the-top comedy requires tolerance but does have some amusing performances. **109m/C VHS.** Jeffrey Tambor, Rita Taggart, Jennifer Tilly, David Arquette, Robby Benson, Brian Bloom; Caroline Goodall; **D:** Brad (Sean) Marlowe; **W:** Brad (Sean) Marlowe.

At Midnight, I'll Take Your Soul ⍟ *A Meia-Noite Levarei Sua Alma* 1963 Brazilian import about sadistic gravedigger Coffin Joe (alter ego of director Jose Mojica Marins), who wanders the streets

---

of his hometown in order to meet a desirable woman. His mission is to sire a son to continue his legacy and wiggle his lips at screaming women. A study in psycho-sexual horror, this makes "Apocalypse Now" look like a beach party. Coffin Joe, or "Ze do Caixao," is a kind of South American Freddy or Jason; Mojica Marins' movies—which are graphically sadistic—were banned by the Brazilian government. In Portuguese with English subtitles. Followed by "Tonight I'll Be Incarnated in Your Corpse." **92m/B VHS, DVD, BR.**Jose Mojica Marins, Magda Mei, Nivaldo de Lima; **D:** Jose Mojica Marins; **W:** Jose Mojica Marins. **C:** Giorgio Attili.

At Play in the Fields of the Lord ⍟⍟ 1991 (R) A thoughtful epic that never quite lives up to its own self-importance—or length. Two yankee missionary couples try to evangelize a fearsome tribe of Brazilian rain-forest dwellers. One of the Christian families suffers a crisis of 'aith that's well-acted but not as powerful as a co-plot regarding a modern American Indian (Berenger) who joins the jungle natives with calamitous results. Based on the novel by Peter Matthiessen. **186m/C VHS, DVD, Blu-ray Disc, UMD, HD DVD.** Tom Berenger, Aidan Quinn, Kathy Bates, John Lithgow, Daryl Hannah, Tom Waits, Stenio Garcia, Nelson Xavier, Jose Dumont, Nilio Kivirinta; **D:** John Boorman; **W:** Jean-Claude Carriere, **M:** Zbigniew Preisner.

At Sword's Point ⍟⍟ *Sons of the Musketeers* 1951 Adventure tale based on characters from Alexandre Dumas's "The Three Musketeers," although the story is original. The French Queen (Cooper) is disturbed by sinister Duke Lavalle (Douglas) who wishes to marry Princess Henriette (Gates) and gain power to the throne. But the children of the four original musketeers come to her rescue, including swordswoman Claire (O'Hara). **81m/C VHS.** Cornel Wilde, Maureen O'Hara, Robert Douglas, Dan O'Herlihy, Alan Hale Jr., Blanche Yurka, Gladys Cooper, June Clayworth, Harpo Marx, Lewis Allen; **W:** Walter Ferris, Joseph Hoffman; **C:** Ray Rennahan; **M:** Roy Webb.

At the Circus ⍟⍟½ 1939 The Marx Brothers at the Circus 1939 Marx Brothers invade the circus to save it from bankruptcy and cause their usual comic insanity, though they've done it better before. Beginning of the end for the Marxes, a step down in quality from their classic work, though frequently quite funny. ♪Lydia the Tattooed Lady; Step Up and Take a Bow; Two Blind Loves; Blue Moon. **87m/B VHS, DVD.** Groucho Marx, Chico Marx, Harpo Marx, Margaret Dumont, Kenny L. Baker, Florence Rice, Eve Arden, Nat Pendleton, Fritz Feld, James Burke, Barnet Parker; **D:** Edward Buzzell; **W:** Irving Brecer. **C:** Leonard Smith; **M:** Harold Arlen.

At the Earth's Core ⍟⍟ 1976 (PG) A Victorian scientist invents a giant burrowing machine, which he and his crew use to dig deeply into the Earth. To their surprise, they discover a lost world of subhuman creatures and prehistoric monsters. Based on Edgar Rice Burroughs's novels. **90m/C VHS, DVD, GB** Doug McClure, Peter Cushing, Caroline Munro, Cy Grant, Godfrey James, Keith Barron; **D:** Kevin Connor; **W:** Milton Subotsky; **C:** Alan Hume; **M:** Michael Vickers.

At War with the Army ⍟⍟ 1950 Serviceable comedy from Martin and Lewis in their first starring appearance, as they recruits get mixed up in all kinds of wild situations at their army base. Based on the play by James Allardice. **93m/B VHS, DVD.** Dean Martin, Jerry Lewis, Polly Bergen, Mike Kellin; **D:** Ha Walker; **W:** Fred Finklehoffe; **C:** Stuart Thompson; **M:** Jerry Livingston.

Atalia ⍟⍟ 1985 Relates the love between Atalia, a war widow, and the younger man she loves. The problem stems from the fact that she lives in a Kibbutz, where all of her beliefs in love, forcing her to eventually make a momentous decision. **90m/C VHS.** Michal Bat-Adam, Yftach Katzur, Dan Toren; **D:** Akiva Tevet.

Athena ⍟⍟ 1954 Two sisters (Powell and Reynolds) from an eccentric, health-faddist family fall in love with their opposites. Purdom is the stuffy Boston lawyer who goes off with Powell and Reynolds entices a TV crooner (Damone).

---

able woman, who would become a star as a movie musclemar, appears in a brief role. ♪Love Can Change the Stars; The Girl Next Door; Imagine; Venezia; Chacun le Salt; I Never Felt Better; Vocalize. **96m/C VHS.** Jane Powell, Debbie Reynolds, Edmund Purdom, Vic Damone, Louis Calhem, Evelyn Varden, Linda Christian, Virginia Gibson, Nancy Kilgas, Dolores Starr, Jane Fischer, Cecile Rogers, Steve Reeves; **D:** Richard Thorpe; **W:** William Ludwig, Leonard Spigelgass; **M:** Hugh Martin, Ralph Blane.

ATL ⍟⍟ 2006 (PG-13) A pack of roller-skating Atlanta outsiders battle the streets and get their groove on to a bumpin' soundtrack (certain to be the perfect corporate tie-in). High-octane dazzle doesn't satisfy most looking for a safe urban-teen flick not loaded with the normally obligatory f-bomb. But the poor-boy-meets-rich-girl romance is too fluffy, and an evil drug-dealer conflict isn't given the bite it needs. Music-video director Chris Robinson makes his widely disobedient big-screen debut with bling and hoopla, but a lack of grit and coherence is all too apparent. **105m/C DVD, Blu-ray Disc, UMD, HD DVD.** Tip Harris, Lauren London, Evan Ross, Antwan Andre Patton, Jackie Long, Albert Daniels, Malika Khadijah, Tyree Simmons; **D:** Chris Robinson; **W:** Tina Gordon Chism, Antwone Fisher; **M:** Aaron Zigman.

Atlantic City ⍟⍟⍟½ *Atlantic City U.S.A.* 1981 (R) A small-time, aging Mafia hood falls in love with a young clam bar waitress, and they share the spoils of a big score against the backdrop of Atlantic City. Wonderful character study that becomes something more, a piercing declaration about a city's transformation and the effect on the people who live there. Lancaster, in a sterling performance, personifies the city, both of them fading with time. **104m/C VHS, DVD, FR** C.A Burt Lancaster, Susan Sarandon, Kate Reid, Michel Piccoli, Hollis McLaren, Robert Joy, Al Waxman; **D:** Louis Malle (Male); Genie '81: Support. Actress (Reid); L.A Film. Critics '81: Actor (Lancaster), Film, Screenplay, Nat. Film Reg. '03; N.Y. Film Critics '81: Actor (Lancaster), Screenplay; Nat. Soc. Film Critics '81: Actor (Lancaster), Director (Male), Film, Screenplay.

Atlantis, the Lost Continent ⍟ 1961 If anything could sink the fabled lost continent of Atlantis it's this cheap fantasy flick. A greek sailor saves a princess and takes her back to her Atlantis home where he's promptly enslaved by the island's evil ruler. But this hero won't put up with any nonsense so he leads his fellow slaves in a revolt and gains his freedom before sinking both evil ruler and island (using atomic power no less). **90m/C VHS.** Anthony Hall, Joyce Taylor, John Dall, William (Bill) Smith, Edward Platt, Frank De Kova; **D:** George Pal; **W:** Daniel Mainwaring. **C:** Harold E. Wellman; **M:** Russell Garcia; **Nar:** Paul Frees.

Atlantis: The Lost Empire ⍟⍟½ 2001 (PG) Fast-paced and action-packed animated Disney adventure about inexperienced explorer Milo Tratch (Fox) who uses his grandfather's secret journals to discover the whereabouts of the submerged city of Atlantis. Submarine Captain Rourke (Garner) leads the expedition, but the eccentric and multi-ethnic crew are not entirely who or what they seem to be. A love interest (Summer) for Milo holds a love interest (Summer) for Milo, and treasures to tempt the less benevolent members of the crew. The animation is old-fashioned and the plotting is reminiscent of adventure movies such as "Raiders of the Lost Ark" and "20,000 Leagues Under the Sea," but these should be considered merits instead of liabilities, especially if you're under 13 years old. **95m/C VHS, DVD. D:** Gary Trousdale, Kirk Wise; **W:** Tab Murphy; **M:** James Newton Howard; **V:** Michael J. Fox, James Garner, Claudia Christian, Cree Summer, John Mahoney, Leonard Nimoy, David Ogden Stiers, Jim Varney, Phil Morris, Don Novello, Florence Stanley, Corey Burton, Jacqueline Obradors.

Routine romance with routine songs. Reeves, who would become a star as a desirable woman.

Atlas ⍟ 1960 The mighty Atlas takes on massive armies, one of which includes director Corman, in a bid to win the hand of a princess. About as cheap as they come, although it's one of the few Sword & Sandal epics that isn't dubbed. **84m/C VHS, DVD.** Michael Forest, Frank Wolff, Barboura Morris, Walter Maslow, Christos Exarchos, Miranda Kounellaki, Theodore Dimitrou, Charles B. Griffith, Roger Corman; **D:** Roger Corman; **W:** Charles B. Griffith; **C:** Basil Marcos; **M:** Ronald Stein.

Atlas in the Land of the Cyclops WOOf! *Atlas Against the Cyclops; Maciste Nella Terra del Ciclopi* 1961 Atlas takes on a hideous one-eyed monster to save a baby from an evil queen. Not a divorce custody drama. **100m/C VHS.** Mitchell Gordon, Cheo Alonso, Vira (Vera) Silenti; **D:** Antonio Leonviola.

Atom Age Vampire WOOf! *Seddok, l'Erede di Satana* 1961 Mad scientist do-victims falls in love with a woman disfigured in an auto crash. To remove her scars, he treats her with a formula derived from the glands of freshly killed women. English dubbed. Not among the best of its kind (a low-rent district if ever there was one), but entertaining in a mischievous, boy-as-this-a-stup'd-film sort of way. **71m/B VHS, DVD. //**Alberto Lupo, Susanne Loret, Sergio Fantoni, Franca Franchel; **D:** Anton Giulio Majano; **W:** Anton Giulio Majano; **C:** Aldo Giordani.

Atom Man vs. Superman 1950 strostly 1964 An old woman hires a doctor to transplant her brain into the body of a beautiful young girl. Of the three girls who are abducted, two become homicidal zombies and the third starts to act catty when she is given a feline brain. A must-see for bad-brain movie fans. **72m/B VHS, DVD.** Frank Gerstle, Erika Peters, Judy Bamber, Marjorie Eaton, Frank Fowler, Margie Fisco; **D:** Joseph Mascelli; **W:** Jack Pollexfen, Vivian Russell, Dean Dillman Jr.; **M:** Sue Bernard.

The Atomic Brain WOOf! *Monstrosity* 1964 An old woman hires a doctor to transplant her brain into the body of a beautiful young girl.

The Atomic Cafe ⍟⍟⍟ 1982 A chillingly humorous compilation of newsreels and government films of the 1940s and '50s that show America's preoccupation with the A-Bomb. Some sequences are in black and white. Includes the infamous training film "Duck and Cover," which tells us what to do in the event of an actual bombing. **92m/C VHS, DVD. D:** Kevin Rafferty, Jayne Loader, Pierce Rafferty; **M:** Miklos Rozsa.

The Atomic City ⍟⍟½ 1952 Barry plays a nuclear physicist at Los Alamos whose son is kidnapped by terrorists who want his bomb-making formulas. As a result, he hir'self becomes radioactive and discovers that he has acquired some strange new powers which get him into what pass for hilarious predicaments. **86m/B VHS.** Mickey Rooney, Robert Strauss, Elaine

The Atomic Kid ⍟⍟½ 1954 A man survives an atomic blast because of a peanut butter sandwich he was eating. As

Atomic Dog ⍟⍟ 1998 (PG-13) The Yates family (Hugh-Kelly and Pickett) moves to a new town near a nuclear power plant. Soon, the sire turns out to be a radioactive hound who wants his offspring and he's a very determined doggie indeed. **86m/C VHS.** Daniel Hugh-Kelly, Isabella Hofmann, Cindy Pickett, Katie Stuart, Micah Gardener; **D:** Brian Trenchard-Smith; **W:** Miguel Tejada-Flores; **M:** Peter Bernstein. **CABLE.**

Davis, Bill Goodwin, Whit Bissell; **D:** Leslie Martinson; **W:** Blake Edwards; **M:** Van Alexander.

The Atomic Man 🦴½ *Timeslip* 1956 Owing to radioactive experimentation, a scientist exists for a short time in the future. Once there, both good and evil forces want to use him for their own purposes. 78m/B VHS. **GB** Gene Nelson, Faith Domergue, Joseph Tomelty, Peter Arne; **D:** Ken Hughes.

Atomic Submarine 🦴🦴 1959 Futuristic sci fi plots government agents against alien invaders. The battle, however, takes place in the ocean beneath the Arctic and is headed by an atomic-powered submarine clashing with a special alien underwater saucer. We all live on the atomic submarine: fun for devotees. 80m/C VHS, DVD. Arthur Franz, Dick Foran, Bob Steele, Brett Halsey, Joi Lansing, Tom Conway, Paul Dubov; **D:** Spencer Gordon Bennet; **W:** Orville H. Hampton; **C:** Gilbert Warrenton; **M:** Alexander Laszlo.

Atomic Train 🦴🦴 1999 (PG-13) Silly two-part TV mini about a runaway train that's packed with toxic waste and a nuclear bomb, which is headed straight for Denver. Lowe (who makes a surprisingly good action hero) is National Transportation Safety Board investigator John Seger, who must derail the disaster. Meanwhile the relentless media coverage has brought on widespread panic (those fiends!). 168m/C VHS, DVD. Rob Lowe, Kristen Davis, Esai Morales, John Finn, Mena Suvari, Sean Smith, Edward Herrmann, Erik King, Blu Mankuma; **D:** Dick Lowry, David S. Jackson; **C:** Steven Fierberg; **M:** Lee Holdridge. **TV**

Atonement 🦴🦴🦴 2007 (R) In 1935 England, 13-year-old Briony (Ronan) sees her sister Cecilia (Knightley) and their cook's son Robbie (McAvoy) together (literally) and, out of jealousy, accuses Robbie of a crime he didn't commit. The once beloved Robbie is sent to jail and the family, who had been paying for him to attend college, rejects him. Only Cecilia believes he is innocent, and cannot forgive her sister. Five years later, the now grown Briony (Garai) and Cecilia are nurses in London and Robbie has been released from prison to fight in the war. Desperate for forgiveness for ruining Robbie's life, Briony tries to find a way to fix her mistake, but it may be too late. Knightley and McAvoy shine as the long-lost lovers, and Ronan's Briony is stellar. Beautifully shot period film is faithful to McEwan's novel, and to the tone and style of 1930s and '40s-era melodramas. 122m/C DVD. **US GB** James McAvoy, Keira Knightley, Saoirse Ronan, Romola Garai, Vanessa Redgrave, Brenda Blethyn, Juno Temple, Patrick Kennedy, Benedict Cumberbatch, Harriet Walter, Gina McKee; **D:** Joe Wright; **W:** Christopher Hampton; **C:** Seamus McGarvey; **M:** Dario Marianelli. Oscars '07: Orig. Score; British Acad. '07: Film; Golden Globes '08: Film—Drama, Orig. Score.

The Atonement of Gosta Berling 🦴🦴🦴 *Gosta Berling's Saga; The Legend of Gosta Berling; The Story of Gosta Berling; The Saga of Gosta Berling* 1924 A priest, forced to leave the priesthood because of his drinking, falls in love with a young married woman. Garbo shines in the first role which brought her critical acclaim; Hanson's performance also makes this a memorable drama. Adapted from the novel by Selma Lagerlof. 91m/B VHS, DVD. **SW** Lars Hanson, Greta Garbo, Ellen Cederstrom, Mona Martenson, Jenny Hasselquist, Gerda Lundequist; **D:** Mauritz Stiller.

Ator the Fighting Eagle woof! 1983 (PG) Styled after "Conan The Barbarian" this mythical action fantasy stars O'Keeffe as Ator, son of Thorn. Ator must put an end to the tragic Dynasty of the Spiders, thereby fulfilling the legend of his family at the expense of the viewer. Goofy low-budget sword and sandal stuff. D'Amato used the pseudonym David Hills. Followed by "The Blade Master." 98m/C VHS, DVD. **IT** Miles O'Keeffe, Sabrina Siani, Ritza Brown, Edmund Purdom, Laura Gemser; **D:** Joe D'Amato.

Attack! 🦴🦴🦴 1956 Cowardly Captain Cooney (Albert) is order to move one of his platoons into a forward position in 1944 Belgium. They are slowly surrounded by the enemy as platoon leader, Lt. Costa (Palance), calls headquarters for reinforcements. But Cooney won't commit his reserves even as the platoon is decimated. Expert portrayals of men under pressure. 107m/B VHS, DVD. Eddie Albert, Jack Palance, Lee Marvin, Robert Strauss, Jack Jaeckel, Buddy Ebsen, William (Bill) Smithers, Strother Martin; **D:** Robert Aldrich; **W:** James Poe; **C:** Joseph Biroc; **M:** Frank DeVol.

Attack Force woof! 2006 (R) Even judging by the low standards set by Seagal movies, this dreck isn't worth the effort to figure out what might be going on. After Special Agent Marshall Lawson's strike team is wiped out by a super-strong, drugged-out prostie, he's determined to figure out how it happened. This leads to a military/political conspiracy to infect the water supply with a drug that turns its users ultra-violent. Even the dialogue over-dubbing is ludicrous, with someone else obviously substituting for Seagal in various scenes. 95m/C DVD. Steven Seagal, David Kennedy, Danny (Daniel) Webb, Andrew Bicknell, Lisa Lovbrand, Matthew Chambers; **D:** Michael Keusch; **W:** Steven Seagal, Joc Halpin; **C:** Sonja Rom; **M:** Barry Taylor. **VIDEO**

Attack Force Z 🦴🦴 1984 An elite corps of Australian military is Force Z. Volunteers are chosen for a dangerous mission: find the plane that crashed somewhere in the South Pacific and rescue the defecting Japanese government official on board, all before the end of WWII and the feature. Talented cast is effectively directed in low-key adventure featuring young Gibson. 84m/C VHS, DVD. **AU** Sam Neill, Chris Haywood, Mel Gibson, John Phillip Law, John Waters; **D:** Tim Burstall.

Attack from Mars 🦴🦴½ *Midnight Movie Massacre* 1988 Retro splatterama has really gross vampire alien land outside a Burbank movie theatre in 1956, and the really weird movie patrons try to terminate it. 86m/C VHS, DVD. Robert Clarke, Ann (Robin) Robinson; **D:** Mark Stock; **W:** Mark Stock, David Houston.

Attack of the Beast Creatures woof! 1985 The survivors of a wrecked ocean liner are stranded on a desert island overrun by savage creatures. This makes them anxious. 82m/C VHS. Robert Nolfi, Julia Rust, Lisa Pak; **D:** Michael Stanley.

Attack of the 50 Foot Woman 🦴🦴½ 1958 A beautiful, abused housewife has a frightening encounter with a giant alien, causing her to grow to an enormous height. Then she goes looking for hubby. Perhaps the all-time classic '50s sci fi, a truly fun movie highlighted by the sexy, 50-foot Hayes in a giant bikini. Has intriguing psychological depth and social commentary done in a suitably cheezy manner. 72m/B VHS. Allison Hayes, William (Bill) Hudson, Roy Gordon, Yvette Vickers, George Douglas, Ken Terrell, Michael Ross, Frank Chase, Eileen Stevens, Otto Waldis; **D:** Nathan "Jerry" Juran; **W:** Mark Hanna; **C:** Jacques "Jack" Marquette; **M:** Ronald Stein.

Attack of the 50 Ft. Woman 🦴🦴½ 1993 Campy remake of the 1958 sci-fi cult classic features the statuesque Hannah in the title role. Nancy's a put-upon hausfrau with zero self-esteem thanks to her domineering father (Windom) and loutish hubby (Baldwin). They should have been sweet to her because after an encounter with a flying saucer Nancy starts to grow...and grow...and grow. And then she decides to get some revenge. 90m/C VHS, DVD. Daryl Hannah, Daniel Baldwin, William Windom, Frances Fisher, Cristi Conaway, Paul Benedict, Lewis Arquette, Xander Berkeley, Hamilton Camp, Richard Edson, Victoria Haas, O'Neal Compton; **D:** Christopher Guest; **W:** Joseph Dougherty; **M:** Nicholas Pike. **TV**

Attack of the Giant Leeches 🦴 *The Giant Leeches; She Demons of the Swamp; Demons of the Swamp* 1959 Cheapo Corman fare about giant leeches in a murky swamp who suddenly decide to make human flesh their new food supply. Perturbed inn keeper plays along by forcing his wife and lover into the murk. Leeches frolic. Sometimes tedious, sometimes chilling, always low budget and silly. Although the special effects aren't top notch, this might be a fine choice for a late night scare/laugh. 62m/B VHS, DVD. Ken Clark, Yvette Vickers, Gene Roth, Bruno VeSota, Michael Emmet, Tyler McVey, Jan Shepard, George Cisar, Daniel White; **D:** Bernard L. Kowalski; **W:** Leo Gordon; **C:** John M. Nickolaus Jr.; **M:** Alexander Laszlo.

Attack of the Killer Tomatoes woof! 1977 (PG) Candidate for worst film ever made, deliberate category. Horror spoof that defined "low budget" stars several thousand ordinary tomatoes that suddenly turn savage and begin attacking people. No sci-fi cliche remains untouched in this dumb parody. A few musical numbers are performed in lieu of an actual plot. Followed by "Return of the Killer Tomatoes." Originally released at 87 minutes. 87m/C VHS, DVD, Georges Wilson, Jack Riley, Rock Peace, Eric Christmas, David Miller, Sharon Taylor; **D:** John DeBello; **W:** Costa Dillon, John DeBello; **C:** John K. Culley.

Attack of the Mayan Mummy woof! 1963 A greedy doctor gets his patient to channel her former self so that she can show him where to find an ancient tomb that is filled with treasure. Good idea. 77m/B VHS. **MX** Richard Webb, Nina Knight, Norman Burton, Steve Conte; **D:** Jerry Warren.

Attack of the Mushroom People 🦴🦴 *Matango; Fungus of Terror; Curse of the Mushroom People* 1963 Secluded island is the site where people eating mysterious mushrooms have been turning into oversized, killer 'shrooms' themselves. Trouble is, the only witness to this madness has gone insane. Will anyone believe him before it's too late? 70m/B VHS, DVD. **JP** Akira Kubo, Kenji Sahara, Yoshio Tsuchiya, Hiroshi Koizumi, Kumi Mizuno, Miki Yashiro, Eisei Amamoto, Hiroshi Tachikawa; **D:** Inoshiro Honda; **W:** Takeshi Kimura; **C:** Hajime Koizumi.

Attack of the Puppet People 🦴🦴 *Six Inches Tall* 1958 This alternative classic from the prolific Bert I. Gordon, a rival to Ed Wood Jr. in the schlock hall of fame, will not make anyone forget "The Incredible Shrinking Man." The insane dollmaker Dr. Franz (Hoyt) shrinks six people (including our heroes Agar and Kenny) to the size of Ken and Barbie. Can they escape the mad scientist? The rat? The effects are nostalgically charming. 79m/B DVD. John Agar, John Hoyt, June Kenney, Sally Reynolds, Susan Gordon, Laurie Mitchell; **C:** Ernest Laszlo; **M:** Albert Glasser.

Attack of the Robots 🦴🦴 *Cartes sur Table* 1966 Silly spy spoof about powerful government officials who are being killed off by a mad scientist's robots. Naturally they escape and maul and munch any human in reach. 88m/C DVD. **AU** Robert Carradine, Nicholas Bell, Billy Aaron Brown, Brian Wimmer, Stacy Haiduk, Natalie Avital, Amanda Stephens; **D:** George Miller; **W:** Tom Woosley, Chris Mankiewicz; **M:** Timothy S. (Tim) Jones. **CABLE**

Attack of the Sabretooth 🦴½ 2005 (R) Think cheap "Jurassic Park." Niles (Bell) invests his moolah in a combo tropical paradise resort and wildlife refuge that contains cloned sabretooth tigers. Grace wants to be Centerfold of the Year so badly that she gets a doctor to enhance her endowments even more through a mystery formula. Only there's a little complication. Cheesy, with pretty women and no discernable acting (and a spoof of that '58 gem "Attack of the 50 Ft. Woman"). 83m/C VHS, DVD. J.J. North, Tammy Parks, John Lazar, Russ Tamblyn, Tommy Kirk, Stanley Livingston, Michelle (McClellan) Bauer, George Stover, Forrest J. Ackerman, Ted Monte, Jim Wynorski, Raelyn Saalman, Tim Abell, Jay Richardson, Nikki Fritz; **D:** Fred Olen Ray; **W:** Steve Armogida; **C:** Gary Graver, Howard Wexler; **M:** Jeff Walton.

Attack of the Swamp Creature woof! *Blood Waters of Dr. Z; Zaat; The Legend of the Zaat Monster; Hydra* 1975 A deranged scientist transforms himself into a swamp critter and terrorizes a small town. 96m/C VHS. Marshall Grauer, Nancy Lien, Paul Galloway, Wade Popwell, Frank Crowell, David Robertson, Doug Thomas; **D:** Don Barton, Arnold Stevens; **W:** Lee Larew, Ron Kivett.

Attack Squadron 🦴½ *Kamakazi* 1963 Story of Japan's suicidal WWII pilots. 105m/C VHS. **JP** Toshiro Mifune, Yuzo Kayama, Takashi Shimura, Yosuke Natsuki, Makoto Sato; **D:** Shue Matsubayashi; **W:** Shinobu Hashimoto; **C:** Takao Saito; **M:** Ikuma Dan.

Attention Shoppers 🦴½ 1999 (R) Latin sitcom heartthrob Carbonell angers his wife and threatens his hunk status during a K-Mart publicity appearance in Houston that's taken over by his rival, soap star Perry. 87m/C VHS, DVD. Nestor Carbonell, Luke Perry, Martin Mull, Kathy Najimy, Michael Lerner, Cara Buono, Lin Shaye, Casey Affleck; **D:** Philip Charles MacKenzie; **W:** Nestor Carbonell. **VIDEO**

The Attic 🦴½ 1980 (R) Psychodrama about an overbearing invalid father and his insecure and unmarried daughter. The girl learns to escape her unhappy life by hiding in the attic. Not horrifying, but a clear analytical look into the game of control. 92m/C VHS, DVD. Carrie Snodgress, Ray Milland, Rosemary Murphy, Ruth Cox, Frances Bay, Marjorie Eaton; **D:** George Edwards.

The Attic 🦴🦴🦴 2006 (R) Not very scary horror flick that also suffers in the script and acting departments. Emma Callan (Moss) and her family move into what seems to be a perfect Victorian home. Only Emma begins to have visions of her twin, who's supposedly dead, evil, and hiding in the attic. 85m/C DVD. Elisabeth (Elizabeth, Liz) Moss, Jason Lewis, John Savage, Catherine Mary Stewart, Tom Malloy; **D:** Mary Lambert; **W:** Tom Malloy; **C:** James Callaway; **M:** Mario Grigorov. **VIDEO**

The Attic: The Hiding of Anne Frank 🦴🦴½ 1988 Steenburgen is wonderful in the true story of Miep Gies, the Dutch woman who hid Otto Frank, her employer, and his family from the Nazis. Unusual because it is told from Gies's perspective, rather than from the more familiar Anne Frank story. Based on Gies's book, "Anne Frank Remembered." 95m/C VHS, Mary Steenburgen, Paul Scofield, Huub Stapel, Eleanor Bron, Miriam Karlin, Lisa Jacobs, Ronald Pickup; **D:** John Erman; **W:** William Hanley; **M:** Richard Rodney Bennett. **TV**

Attica 🦴🦴🦴 1980 Tense depiction of the infamous Attica prison takeover in 1971 and the subsequent bloodbath as state troops were called in. Although edited due to the searing commentary by Nelson Rockefeller, it remains powerful and thought-provoking. Adapted from the Tom Wicker bestseller "A Time to Die." 97m/C VHS. George Grizzard, Charles Durning, Anthony Zerbe, Roger E. Mosley; **D:** Marvin J. Chomsky. **TV**

Attila 🦴🦴½ 2001 Epic miniseries takes on the life of Attila the Hun. Early years of Attila are swiftly dealt with as his family is slaughtered and the boy is raised by his uncle—with his cousin as his rival for leadership. The adult Attila (Butler) is tough, charismatic, and bloodthirsty enough to unite the Hun tribes and challenge the domination of the Roman empire, which leads to the politically savvy Roman general Flavius Aetius (Boothe) being dispatched to get Attila on Rome's side. Lots of big battles as this part of history is treacherous indeed. 177m/C VHS, DVD. Gerard Butler, Powers Boothe, Alice Krige, Simmone Jade MacKinnon, Tim Curry, Reg Rogers, Steven Berkoff, Tommy Flanagan, Pauline Lynch, Liam Cunningham, Jolyon Baker, Sian Phillips, Jonathan Hyde; **D:** Dick Lowry; **C:** Robert Cochran; **C:** Steven Fierberg; **M:** Nick Glennie-Smith. **CABLE**

Au Pair Girls 🦴🦴½ 1972 Four sexy young ladies leave their various homelands to embark on careers as au pair girls, making friends and love along the way. 86m/C VHS, DVD. **GB** Gabrielle Drake,

Au Revoir les Enfants 🎬🎬🎬 *Goodbye, Children* 1987 (PG) During the Nazi occupation of France in the 1940s, the headmaster of a Catholic boarding school hides three Jewish boys among the other students by altering their names and identities. Two of the students, Julien (Manesse) and Jean (Fejto), form a friendship that ends tragically when Jean and the other boys are discovered and taken away by the Gestapo. Compelling and emotionally wrenching coming of age tale based on an incident from director Malle's childhood, is considered to be his best film to date and quite possibly the best he will ever make. In French with English subtitles. Other themes are "Hope and Glory" and "Empire of the Sun." **110m/C VHS, DVD, FR GE** *C:* Gaspard Manesse, Raphael Fejto, Francine Racette, Stanislas Carre de Malberg, Philippe Morier-Genoud, François Berleand, Peter Fitz, François Negret, Irene Jacob, Pascal Rivet, Benoit Henriet, Richard Leboeuf, Xavier Legrand, Arnaud Henriet, Jean-Sebastien Chauvin, Luc Etienne; *D:* Louis Malle; *W:* Louis Malle; *C:* Renato Berta. British Acad. '88: Director (Malle); Cesar '88: Art Dir/Set Dec, Cinematog, Director (Malle), Film, Sound, Writing; L.A. Film Critics '87: Foreign Film; Venice Film Fest. '87: Film.

Audition 🎬🎬½ *Odishon* 1999 Director Miike successfully illustrates a middle-aged widower's worst nightmares about remarrying a younger woman. The benign Aoyama (Ishibashi) is persuaded by a producer friend to stage a fake movie audition in order to find a new bride, belies the gruesome turn of events revealed later. Seven years single, Aoyama wants a traditional, submissive young girl, which he finds in one of the actresses, Asami (Shiina). Aoyama's smitten, but buddy Yoshikawa (Kunimura) is decidedly less so, sensing something a tad askew in the girl's sadistic bent attest. Soon enough, Aoyama is on the business end o' Asami's macabre doings. Based on a story by Ryu Murakami, in Japanese with subtitles. **115m/C VHS, DVD, JP** *C:* Ryo Ishibashi, Eihi Shiina, Tetsu Sawaki, Jun Kunimura, Miyuki Matsuda; *D:* Takashi Miike; *W:* Daisuke Tengan; *C:* Hideo Yamamoto; *M:* Koji Endo.

The Audrey Hepburn Story 🎬🎬½ 2000 (PG) When you play a movie icon, expect the critical brickbats to fly. Sweet Hewitt does her best in the title role (Hepburn's her longtime idol) but it's at surface gloss. Bio covers 1935 to 1990 as Hepburn deals with family crises (dad's a two-timing Nazi sympathizer who abandons his family), war years in Nazi-occupied Holland, Hepburn's beginnings as a dancer in England and her first small roles. Then it's onto New York and the world of theatre and films. Along the way there's a little romance, a marriage to actor Mel Ferrer (McCormack), and various re-creations of some Hepburn movie roles. **133m/C VHS, DVD** *C:* Jennifer Love Hewitt, Eric McCormack, Frances Fisher, Peter Giles, Keir Dullea, Gabriel Macht, Marcel Jeannin, Sweede Svensson, Michael J. Burg, Ryan Hollyman; *D:* Steve Robman; *W:* Marsha Norman; *C:* Pierre Letarte; *M:* Lawrence Shragge. TV

Audrey Rose 🎬🎬 1977 (PG) Parents of a young girl are terrified when their darling daughter is having dreadful dreams. Mysterious friend Hopkins cements their fears when he declares that his dead daughter has been reincarnated in their child. The nightmares continue suggesting that none other than Lucifer could be at work. Good cast is hampered by slow-moving take-off on "The Exorcist" with a weak staged ending. Adapted by DeFelitta from his novel. **113m/C VHS, DVD** *C:* Anthony Hopkins, Marsha Mason, John Beck, John Hillerma , Susan Swift, Norman Lloyd; *D:* Robert Wise; *W:* Frank De Felitta; *C:* Victor Kemper.

Audrey's Rain 🎬🎬 2003 Audrey (Smart) is already caring for her younger, mentally challenged sister Marguerite (Wilhoite) when she must take in her orphaned niece and nephew after another sister commits suicide. No wonder Audrey is grateful for the attentions of old boy-friend Terry Lloyd (Smart's husband Gilliland). But can they overcome the trouble to take a second chance on love? Packs too much story into a too-short run time but Smart is always a pleasure to watch. **88m/C DVD** *C:* Jean Smart, Richard Gilliland, Kathleen Wilhoite, Angus T. Jones, Carol Kane; *D:* Sam Pillsbury; *W:* Jennifer Schwalbach Smith, Kate Smith; *C:* James W. Wrenn; *M:* Stephen (Steve) Edwards. C.A.B.L.E.

August 🎬🎬½ 1995 (PG) Yet another version of Chekov's "Uncle Vanya," this time transported to 1890s Wales. Hopkins (who makes his directorial debut and composed the score) stars as Ieuan Davies, a bitter drinker who manages the estate of brother-in-law Alexander Blathwaite (Phillips). Blathwaite arrives for his annual summer stay with unhappy, young second wife Helen (Burton), who's the object of desire for both Ieuan and the local doctor, Michael Loyd (Grainger). It's a perfectly adequate rendition but offers little that's new except a change of scenery. **93m/C VHS, GB** *C:* Anthony Hopkins, Kate Burton, Leslie Phillips, Gawn Grainger, Rhian Morgan, Hugh Lloyd, Rhoda Lewis, Menna Tusser; *D:* Anthony Hopkins; *W:* Julian Mitchell; *C:* Robin Vidgeon; *M:* Anthony Hopkins.

August Rush 🎬🎬 2007 (PG) Lyla (Russell) is a classical cellist who falls for club-banc musician Louis (Rhys Myers) and finds herself pregnant with his child. Her overbearing stage father tells her the baby has died and ships him off to an orphanage. Fast-forward 11 years and little orphan Evan (adorable Highmore) hears music in everything. He thinks if he learns how to play an instrument, his parents—who he knows are musicians—will find him. Through sheer force, a few side players, a healthy dose of appropriately sappy music, and a whole lotta far-fetched coincidences, the family is reunited. Utterly and unapologetically predictable, but it won't matter a it if your idea of a good film is one in which you need an entire box of tissues. **113m/C VHS, DVD** *C:* Freddie Highmore, Keri Russell, Jonathan Rhys Myers, Terrence Howard, Robin Williams, William Sadler, Leon G. Thomas III, Jamia Simone Nash; *D:* Kristen Sheridan; *W:* Nick Castle, James V. Hart; *C:* John Mathieson; *M:* Mark Mancina, Hans Zimmer.

Augustin 🎬🎬 1995 Very short comedy about aspiring actor Augustin (Silbertin-Blanc), who may just get his break when he hears about a part for a room-service waiter and prepares himself rigorously by actually getting a job in a Paris hotel. Pathetically earnest and dignified, his actual audition he bewilders actor Lhermitte, when instead of just reading the scene, Augustin proceeds to act it out in detail. Very slight but charming thanks to a deadpan performance by Silbertin-Blanc (who's also director Fontaine's brother in real life). In French with subtitles. **61m/C VHS, FP** *C:* Jean-Chretien Silbertin-Blanc, Thierry Lhermitte, Stephanie Zhang, Nora Habib, Guy Casabonne; *D:* Anne Fontaine; *W:* Anne Fontaine; *C:* Jean-Marie Dreujou.

Augustine of Hippo 🎬🎬🎬 *Agostino di Ippona* 1972 One of Rossellini's later historical epics, depicting the last years of St. Augustine and how they exemplify the growing conflicts between Church and State, Christian ethic and societal necessity. In Italian with subtitles. **120m/C VHS, IT** *D:* Roberto Rossellini.

Auntie WOOf! *Keep It Up, Jack* 1973 (R) Entertainer must dress and act like his madam aunt who has died, in order to fool her former employees in a house of prostitution. **85m/C VHS, GB** *C:* Mark Jones, Sue Longhurst, Frank Thornton, Linda Regan; *D:* Derek Ford; *W:* Derek Ford, Alan Selwyr; *C:* Geoff Glover; *M:* Terry Warr.

Auntie Lee's Meat Pies 🎬½ 1992 (R) Auntie Lee's meat pie business is booming, thanks to her five beautiful nieces. They help keep their aunt supplied with the secret ingredient—gorgeous young men! Four Playboy Playmates are featured in this cannibalistic horror comedy. **100m/C VHS** *C:* Karen Black, Noriyuki "Pat" Morita, Pat Paulsen, Huntz Hall, Michael Berryman, David Parry, Stephen Quadros, Ava Fabian, Teri Weigel; *D:* Joseph F. Robertson; *C:* Arledge Armenaki.

Auntie Mame 🎬🎬🎬 1958 A young boy is brought up by his only surviving relative—flamboyant and eccentric Auntie Mame. Mame is positive that "life is a banquet and most poor suckers are starving to death." Based on the Patrick Dennis novel about his life with "Auntie Mame." Part of the fun is with "A Night at the Movies" series, this tape simulates a 1958 movie evening, with a "Road Runner" cartoon, "Hook, Line and Stinker," a newsreel and coming attractions for "No Time for Sergeants" and "Chase a Crooked Shadow." **161m/C VHS, DVD** *C:* Rosalind Russell, Patric Knowles, Roger Smith, Peggy Cass, Forrest Tucker, Coral Browne; *D:* Morton DaCosta; *W:* Betty Comden, Adolph Green; *C:* Harry Stradling Sr. Golden Globes '59: Actress—Mus./Comedy (Russell).

The Aura 🎬🎬🎬 2005 To escape his bleak life in Buenos Aires, Esteban (Darin)—a quiet, reserved taxidermist—has fantasies of carrying out the perfect crime using a rea heist. He's able to convince Dietrich's wife and gang members that he's also in on the gig but much like his seizures the events that follow get out of control. Tense thriller was only the second movie directed by Bielinsky, who died of a heart attack after its completion. In Spanish with subtitles. **138m/C DVD, All FR SP** *C:* Ricardo Darin, Dolores Fonzi, Alejandro Awada, Pablo Cedron, Jorge d'Elia, Nahuel Perez, Walter Reyno, Manuel Rodal, Rafael Castejon; *D:* Fabian Bielinsky; *W:* Fabian Bielinsky; *C:* Checco Varese; *M:* Lucio Godoy.

Aurora 🎬🎬½ *Aurora by Night: Qualcosa di Biondo* 1984 Single mom Aurora (Loren) will do anything for her blind son Ciro (played by Loren's son Edoardo Ponti). When she discovers that there's a possible operation that could restore his sight, Aurora decides to call up all Ciro's possible fathers and get them to finance the surgery. This plan also reunites Aurora with the one man she truly loved. Made for Italian TV. **91m/C VHS, IT** *C:* Sophia Loren, Daniel J. Travanti, Ricky Tognazzi, Philippe Noiret, Anna Strasberg, Franco Fabrizi; *D:* Maurizio Ponzi; *M:* Georges Delerue. TV

Aurora Borealis 🎬🎬½ 2006 (R) Sutherland happily chews scenery as aged Ronald, whose increasingly ill health is proving too much for his wife Ruth (Fletcher) to handle. Fortunately, their slacker grandson Duncan (Jackson) gets a handyman's job at their apartment building to help out. Ruth also hires free-spirited home healthcare worker Kate (Lewis), whom Duncan immediately fancies. But Kate doesn't like to stay in one place for too long so Duncan may have to make a tough decision about where his future lies. Title refers to Ronald's belief that he can see the northern lights from his window. **110m/C DVD, US** *C:* Joshua Jackson, Donald Sutherland, Juliette Lewis, Louise Fletcher; *D:* James C.E. Burke; *W:* Brent Boyd; *C:* Alar Kivilo; *M:* Daniel Danna.

The Aurora Encounter 🎬🎬 1985 (PG) Alien is surreptitiously infiltrate a small town in 1897, and spread benevolence everywhere. Family fare. **90m/C VHS, DVD** *C:* Jack Elam, Peter Brown, Carol Bagdasarian, Dottie West, George "Spanky" McFarland; *D:* Jim McCullough

Austin Powers: International Man of Mystery 🎬🎬🎬 1997 (PG-13) Hilarious spoof of '60s spy babe movies. Groovy '60s spy Austin Powers (Myers) discovers that his arch-enemy, Dr. Evil (Myers again) has frozen himself in order to elude capture, so the

Austin Powers in Goldmember 🎬🎬½ 2002 (PG-13) Shag-happy superspy Austin Powers is back for the third installment of the spy-spoof franchise. Austin travels back to the 70's to find his secret agent dad Nigel (Caine), hook up with new love interest and fellow spy Foxxy Cleopatra (Knowles), and rescue the world. Myers again takes on numerous roles, this time adding new villain Goldmember, a disco-clad Dutchman with a gilded prosthetic and a penchant for world domination. Dr. Evil is in good form but soft newcomer Goldmember comes up short, and Myers is running out of funny ideas. Bond studio MGM raised a stink about the title (too close to "Goldfinger") but finally saw the light and allowed the parody to continue. **94m/C VHS, DVD, US** Mike Myers, Michael Caine, Seth Green, Beyonce Knowles, Verne Troyer, Michael York, Robert Wagner, Mindy Sterling, Fred Savage, Tommy (Tiny) Lister, Clint Howard, Nathan Lane; *Cameos:* Steven Spielberg, Gwyneth Paltrow, Tom Cruise, Kevin Spacey, Danny DeVito, John Travolta, Quincy Jones, Burt Bacharach, Britney Spears, Ozzy Osbourne, Donna D'Errico, Michael McCullers; *D:* Jay Roach; *W:* Mike Myers, Michael McCullers; *Cameos:* Peter Deming; *M:* George S. Clinton.

Author! Author! 🎬🎬½ 1982 (PG) Sweet, likable comedy about playwright Pacino who is about to taste success with his first big hit. Suddenly his wife walks out, leaving him to care for her four children and his own son. His views shift as he begins to worry about, among other things, who will watch the obnoxious kids on opening night. **100m/C VHS, DVD** *C:* Al Pacino, Dyan Cannon, Alan King, Andre Gregory; *D:* Arthur Hiller; *W:* Israel Horovitz; *M:* Dave Grusin.

Auto Focus 🎬🎬🎬 2002 (R) Paul Schrader examines the sordid life and death of "Hogan's Heroes" star Bob Crane (Kinnear). Kinnear's portrayal of Crane from the seemingly normal father

Austin Powers 2: The Spy Who Shagged Me 🎬🎬🎬 1999 (PG-13) Old snaggle-tooth (Myers) returns and time travels back to 1969 to foil his look-alike nemesis, Dr. Evil, who steals Powers' mojo. Myers wisely highlights the not-so-good Dr., along with some hilarious new characters, instead of the periodically wearisome Powers. Again plot takes a back seat to the great dialogue, characters including Rob Lowe as a dead-on Robert Wagner and a third Myers' incarnation, Fat Bastard, a kilted prosthetic that all still works because of Myers' winking good nature. **95m/C VHS, DVD, UMD, Mike Myers, Elizabeth Hurley, Seth Green, Heather Graham, Elizabeth Gia Carides, Clint Howard, Michael York, Will Ferrell, Mindy Sterling, Fred Willard, Jack Kehler; *Cameos:* Burt Bacharelson, Elvis Costello, Rebecca Romijn, Woody Harrelson, Willie Nelson, Jerry Springer; *D:* Jay Roach; *W:* Michael McCullers, Mike Myers, Verne Troyer; Steiger; *M:* George S. Clinton, MTV Movie Awards '00: On-Screen Duo (Mike Myers/Verne Troyer), Villain (Myers).

swingin' dentally challenged Brit decides to do the same. They awaken 30 years later in the same state: woefully out of touch. Dr. Evil is attempting to blackmail the British government and deal with his Gen-X son, Scott Evil (Green), who wants more quality time and less world conquest. Austin, on the other hand, is trying to stop the evil machinations and—well...Evil. A festival of crushed velvet, every once in a while, but he gets plenty of mileage out of the one-joke premise. **83m/C VHS, DVD, UMD** *C:* Mike Myers, Elizabeth Hurley, Fabiana Uderic, Paul Dillon, Charles Napier, Will Ferrell, Mindy Sterling, Robert Wagner, Seth Green, Clint Howard; *Cameos:* Tom Arnold, Carrie Fisher; *D:* Jay Roach; *W:* Mike Myers; *C:* Peter Deming; *M:* George S. Clinton. MTV Movie Awards '98: Villain (Myers), Dance Seq. (Mike Myers/Londoners).

Auto

and husband to the sexaholic who was found bludgeoned to death amongst his amateur pornography is startling. The trouble starts when he meets creepy pal (and possible murderer) Carpenter (Dafoe), who gets him drumming gigs in strip clubs. This easy access to women, along with his affable manner and Carpenter's array of video equipment lead to a torrent of carnal acts that the two obsessively commit to tape. Crane loses two wives (Wilson, Bello) and his wholesome image while remaining oblivious to the descent that his sex addiction is causing in his personal and professional life. The cast does a great job with difficult material, especially Kinnear and Ron Leibman as Crane's weary agent. **104m/C VHS, DVD.** *US* Greg Kinnear, Willem Dafoe, Rita Wilson, Maria Bello, Ron Leibman, Kurt Fuller, Ed Begley Jr., Michael E. Rodgers, Michael McKean, Bruce Solomon, Christopher Neiman, Lyle Kanouse; *D:* Paul Schrader; *W:* Michael Gerbosi; *C:* Fred Murphy; *M:* Angelo Badalamenti.

Autobiography of a Princess ✱✱ **1975** A brief character study shot by Merchant-Ivory in six days. An East Indian princess, living in self-enforced exile in London, invites her father's former tutor to tea. They watch old movie footage of royal India together and dream of a happier past. **59m/C VHS.** James Mason, Madhur Jaffrey; *D:* James Ivory; *W:* Ruth Prawer Jhabvala.

The Autobiography of Miss Jane Pittman ✱✱✱ **1974** The history of blacks in the South is seen through the eyes of a 110-year-old former slave. From the Civil War through the Civil Rights movement, Miss Pittman relates every piece of black history, allowing the viewer to experience the injustices. Tyson is spectacular in moving, highly acclaimed drama. Received nine Emmy awards; adapted by Tracy Keenan Wynn from the novel by Ernest J. Gaines. **110m/C VHS, DVD.** Cicely Tyson, Odetta, Joseph Tremice, Richard Dysart, Michael Murphy, Katherine Helmond; *D:* John Korty; *W:* Tracy Keenan Wynn; *C:* James A. Crabe; *M:* Fred Karlin. **TV**

Automatic ✱✱½ **1994 (R)** Renegade RoboGen Industries android Gruner saves Ashbrook from the loathsome sexual advances of the boss who kills the scum in the process. So the duo are targeted for death by company head Glover with killers, led by Kober, sent to do the mopping up. **90m/C VHS.** Olivier Gruner, Daphne Ashbrook, John Glover, Jeff Kober, Dennis Lipscomb; *D:* John Murdowski; *W:* Susan Lambert, Patrick Highsmith. **TV**

Autopsy ✱½ *Tarot* **1974 (R)** Forensic pathologist Farmer is working at a morgue compiling statistics concerning suicides and murders staged to look like suicides. Farmer begins to go nuts when it seems a stalker is killing people around her using the fake suicide method. Then there's the fact that the pathological pathologist is also sexually repressed and everything and everyone starts to scream sex to her and things get really kinky (and gory). **100m/C VHS, DVD.** *IT FR SP* Mimsy Farmer, Barry Primus, Angela Goodwin, Ray Lovelock; *D:* Armando Crispino, Lucio Battistrada; *C:* Carlo Carlini; *M:* Ennio Morricone.

Autopsy ✱ *Tarot* **1974** A young golddigger and a millionaire marry, and then cheat on each other, provoking blackmail and murder. **90m/C VHS, DVD.** *FR SP* Suzy Lyon, Fernando Rey, Gloria Grahame, Christian Hay; *D:* Jose Maria Forque; *W:* Rafael Azcona; *C:* Alejandro Ulloa; *M:* Michel Colombier.

Autopsy: A Love Story ✱✱½ **2002** Life is a cold, lonely place for morgue-worker Charlie, whose pushy boss has him knee-deep in the bootlegged organs business. Meanwhile, his cross, crippled girlfriend torments him. The arrival of a hot new amour at the office livens things up—even though when her (living) twin sister shows up. **90m/C VHS, DVD.** Joe Estevez, Paul DeGruccio, Dina Osmussen, Ginny Harman, Wendy Crawford, Robert McClure, Jill Seltz, Greg Hanson, Mike Watkis, Keith Arbo, Ashley Smith, John Scott Mills; *D:* Guy Crawford; *W:* Guy Crawford, Tamarie Hargrove. **VIDEO**

tionalized until her sister brought her home. Now the three women settle their scores, and balance the needs of their family. Excellent performance by Bergman in her last feature film. **97m/C VHS, DVD.** *SW* Ingrid Bergman, Liv Ullmann, Halvar Bjork, Lena Nyman, Gunnar Bjornstrand, Erland Josephson; *D:* Ingmar Bergman; *W:* Ingmar Bergman; *C:* Sven Nykvist. Golden Globes '79: Foreign Film; Natl. Bd. of Review '78: Actress (Bergman); Director (Bergman); N.Y. Film Critics '78: Actress (Bergman); Natl. Soc. Film Critics '78: Actress (Bergman).

An Autumn Afternoon ✱✱✱½ *Sanma No Aji* **1962** Ozu's last film is a beautiful expression of his talent. In postwar Tokyo, an aging widower loses his only daughter to marriage and begins a life of loneliness. A heart-wrenching tale of relationships and loss. In Japanese with English subtitles. **112m/C VHS.** *JP* Chishu Ryu, Shima Iwashita, Shin-Ichiro Mikami, Mariko Okada, Keiji Sada; *D:* Yasujiro Ozu; *W:* Yasujiro Ozu; *C:* Yuuharu Atsuta; *M:* Kojun Saito.

Autumn Born ✱½ **1979 (R)** Young heiress is abducted by her guardian and imprisoned while she's taught to obey his will. Ill-fated ex-Playmate Dorothy Stratton's first film. **76m/C VHS.** Dorothy Stratten, Dory Jackson, Gisselle Fredette, Nate Macintosh, Joanna McClelland Glass, Roberta Weiss, Roman Buchok, Sharon Elder; *D:* Lloyd A. Simandl; *W:* Sharon Christensen, Shannon Lee, Lloyd A. Simandl.

Autumn in New York ✱½ **2000 (PG-13)** Start with one clunky love story with no chemistry, then mix in cheesy melodrama and a dash of creepy Freudian undertones and what do you get? This recipe for disaster about a doomed May-December romance. Middle-aged Will Keane (Gere) leads a playboy's life as the owner of one of New York's most fashionable restaurants. He falls for much younger sensitive gal Charlotte (Ryder) after finding out that he dated her mother. Unfortunately, Charlotte is afflicted with a life-threatening disease whose symptoms include saying "Wow!" a lot and fainting at overly dramatic moments. Will's life is changed, and he rushes around trying to find some medical miracle or plot device which might be able to save her. Rent "Love Story" instead. Because love means never having to say you're sorry you wasted two hours of your life on this movie. **104m/C VHS, DVD.** Richard Gere, Winona Ryder, Anthony LaPaglia, Elaine Stritch, Vera Farmiga, Sherry Stringfield, Jill(ian) Hennessey; *D:* Joan Chen; *W:* Allison Burnett; *M:* Gabriel Yared.

Autumn Leaves ✱✱½ **1956** Crawford plays a middle-aged typist grasping at her last chance for love. She marries a younger man who's been romancing her, then finds him more and more unstable and violent. Weak story material that could turn melodramatic and tawdry, but doesn't because of Crawford's strength. **108m/B VHS.** Joan Crawford, Cliff Robertson, Vera Miles, Lorne Greene; *D:* Robert Aldrich; *W:* Robert Blees, Lewis Meltzer, Hugo Butler, Jean Rouveral; *C:* Charles B(ryant) Lang Jr. Berlin Intl. Film Fest. '56: Director (Aldrich).

Autumn Marathon ✱✱½ *Osenniy Maraton* **1979** To say that this is one of the better Russian movies of the past three decades is sort of faint praise, given the state of Soviet cinema. Written by playwright Volodin, it's just another paint-by-number version of the philandering man who's really an OK Joe who loves his kids comedy. In Russian with English subtitles. **100m/C VHS, DVD.** *RU* Oleg Basilashvili, Natalia Gundareva, Marina Neyolova; *D:* Georgi Daniela; *W:* Alexander Volodin.

Autumn Moon ✱✱ *Qiuyue* **1992** Young Japanese tourist (Nagase) travels to Hong Kong to enjoy some sexual fun but instead he befriends a 15-year-old girl (Wai), who's afraid of her family's impending emigration to Canada. Not much happens but the Hong Kong setting is eye-catching. English and Cantonese with subtitles. **108m/C VHS.** *HK* Masatoshi Nagase, Li Pui Wai; *D:* Clara Law; *C:* Tony Leung Siu Hung.

Autumn Sonata ✱✱✱ *Hostsonaten* **1978** Nordic family strife as famed concert pianist Bergman is reunited with a daughter she has not seen in years. Bergman's other daughter suffers from a degenerative nerve disease and had been institu-

Autumn Sun ✱✱✱ *Sol de Otono* **1998** This is a love story for appreciative adults. Clara (Aleandro) is a middleaged Buenos Aires accountant whose personal ad for a Jewish gentleman caller is answered by older widower (and non-Jew) Raul Ferraro (Luppi). Still, they're attracted to each other, and since Clara needs a man to pose as her admirer for a visit from her long-absent brother, Raul agrees to the ruse and undergoes a crash course in Jewish customs. This isn't actually played for laughs but as a reflection on expanding one's horizons and taking chances. Spanish with subtitles. **105m/C VHS, DVD.** *AR* Norma Aleandro, Federico Luppi, Jorge Luz, Cecilia Rossetto; *D:* Eduardo Mignogna; *W:* Eduardo Mignogna, Santiago Carlos Oves; *C:* Marcelo Camorino; *M:* Edgardo Rudnitzky.

Autumn Tale ✱✱½ *Conte d'Automne* **1998 (PG)** Middleaged, widowed winegrower Magali (Romand) is lonely now that her children are grown, so her best friend Isabelle (Riviere) secretly places a personal ad and decides to meet the respondents herself in order to find someone suitable for her friend. Isabelle decides saleman Gerald (Liboit) is a likely prospect and schemes to introduce them. Meanwhile, Rosine (Portal), the live-wire girlfriend of Magali's son Leo (Darmon), thinks that her older philosophy professor (and ex-lover), Etienne (Sandre), might be a match. Magali is simply mortified by the entire situation. The fourth film in Rohmer's "Tales of the Four Seasons." French with subtitles. **110m/C VHS, FR** Beatrice Romand, Marie Riviere, Alexia Portal, Alain Libolt, Didier Sandre, Stephane Darmon; *D:* Eric Rohmer; *W:* Eric Rohmer; *C:* Diane Baratier; *M:* Claude Marti. Natl. Soc. Film Critics '99: Foreign Film.

Avalanche ✱½ **1978 (PG)** Disaster-arama as vacationers at a new winter ski resort find themselves at the mercy of a monster avalanche leaving a so-called path of terror and destruction in its wake. Talented cast is buried by weak material, producing a snow-bound adventure yawn. **91m/C VHS, DVD.** Rock Hudson, Mia Farrow, Robert Forster, Rick Moses; *D:* Corey Allen; *W:* Corey Allen; *C:* Pierre William Glenn; *M:* William Kraft.

Avalanche ✱✱½ **1999 (PG-13)** Proto-typical cheesy disaster flic. Alaskan chopper pilot Neil (Griffith) helps out Lia (Feeney), the widow of an old pal, who works for the EPA. She believes the establishment of an oil company's overland pipeline through the mountains will trigger an avalanche that could destroy the city of Juneau. Naturally, no one believes her until there's an avalanche. (Considering the movie's title, you could have guessed this.) **105m/C VHS, DVD.** Thomas Ian Griffith, Caroleen Feeney, R. Lee Ermey, C. Thomas Howell, John Ashton, Hilary Shepard; *D:* Steve Kroschel; *W:* Steve Kroschel; *C:* Steve Kroschel, Richard Pepin; *M:* K. Alexander (Alex) Wilkinson.

Avalanche Express ✱ **1979 (PG)** Marvin is a CIA agent who uses a defector (Shaw) to lure a scientist (Schell), specializing in biological warfare, aboard a European train. Marvin wants to eliminate Schell but all plans go awry when the snow begins to fall. Ineffective thriller. Director Robson's and actor Shaw's last film—much of Shaw's dialogue was dubbed due to his death before the film's soundtrack was completed. Based on a novel by Colin Forbes. **89m/C VHS.** Lee Marvin, Robert Shaw, Maximilian Schell, Linda Evans, Mike Connors, Joe Namath, Horst Buchholz, David (Alexander) Hess; *D:* Mark Robson; *W:* Abraham Polonsky; *C:* Jack Cardiff.

Avalon ✱✱✱ **1990 (PG)** Powerful but quiet portrait of the break-up of the family unit as seen from the perspective of a Russian family settled in Baltimore at the close of WWII. Initially, the family is unified in their goals, ideologies, and social lives. Gradually, all of this disintegrates; members move to the suburbs and TV replaces conversation at holiday gatherings. Levinson based his film on experiences within his own family of Russian Jewish immigrants. **126m/C VHS, DVD.** Armin Mueller-Stahl, Aidan Quinn, Elizabeth Perkins, Joan Plowright, Lou Jacobi, Leo Fuchs, Eve Gordon, Kevin Pollak, Israel Rubinek, Elijah Wood, Grant Gelt, Bernard Hiller; *D:* Barry Levinson; *W:* Barry Levinson; *C:* Allen Daviau; *M:* Randy Newman. Writers Guild '90: Orig. Screenplay.

Avanti! ✱✱ **1972 (R)** Stuffy businessman Wendell Armbruster (Lemmon) heads to Italy to claim his father's body when the old man dies while on vacation. Then he discovers dad has been visiting his mistress to these many years. While trying to get through mountains of red tape, Wendell finds himself romancing the woman's daughter (Mills). Too long but still amusing. **144m/C VHS, DVD.** Jack Lemmon, Juliet Mills, Clive Revill, Edward Andrews, Gianfranco Barra, Franco Angrisano; *D:* Billy Wilder; *W:* I.A.L. Diamond, Billy Wilder.

Ava's Magical Adventure ✱✱½ **1994 (PG)** Ten-year-old Eddie decides to take Ava on a little adventure. Too bad she's a 2-ton elephant he's stolen from the circus. Based on the Mark Twain story "The Stolen White Elephant." **97m/C VHS.** Timothy Bottoms, Georg Stanford Brown, Patrick Dempsey, Priscilla Barnes, David Lander, Kaye Ballard, Remi Ryan; *D:* Patrick Dempsey, Rocky Parker; *W:* Susan D. Nimm; *M:* Mark Holden.

The Avenger ✱✱½ **1960** The story of a criminal who cuts off the heads of people and mails them off with makes for a shocker. Graphic violence will appeal to those who like a good mail-order gorefest and are not employed by the post office. **102m/B VHS, DVD.** *GE* Ingrid van Bergen, Heinz Drache, Ina Duscha, Mario Litto, Klaus Kinski; *D:* Karl Anton.

The Avenger ✱ *The Lost Glory of Troy* **1962** This time muscleman Reeves plays Aeneas and leads the Trojans in battle against the Greeks. It's supposedly an adaptation of "The Aeneid" by Virgil. **108m/C VHS, DVD.** *FRIT* Steve Reeves, Giacomo "Jack" Rossi-Stuart, Carla Marlier, Gianni "John" Garko, Liana Orfei; *D:* Giorgio Rivalta.

The Avengers ✱✱ **1998 (PG-13)** Based on the cultly '60s Brit TV series, this unfortunate big screen adaptation fails by choosing style over campy charm. Set in a surreal 1999 London, scientist (and leather-girl) Mrs. Emma Peel (Thurman) teams up with dapper secret agent John Steed (Fiennes) to defeat maximum baddie, Sir August de Wynter (Connery). Seems de Wynter has a machine that can manipulate the world's weather—and he's not intending to do good deeds. It's dull, the leads have no chemistry together (although they have their separate charms), and the creators have chosen to include some lesser aspects of the series, such as the boring character of Mother (Broadbent). Unforgiveably, Laurie Johnson's memorable TV theme is not used for the film's opening—replaced instead by generic music by McNeely. (Johnson's theme is heard later.) Original Steed, Patrick MacNee, does have an amusing cameo. **90m/C VHS, DVD.** Ralph Fiennes, Uma Thurman, Sean Connery, Jim Broadbent, Fiona Shaw, Eileen Atkins, John Wood, Eddie Izzard, Carmen Ejogo, Keeley Hawes; *Cameos:* Patrick Macnee; *D:* Jeremiah S. Chechik; *W:* Don MacPherson; *C:* Roger Pratt; *M:* Joel McNeely. Golden Raspberries '98: Worst Remake/Sequel.

The Avenging ✱✱ **1992 (PG)** Horse comes home from college to run the family ranch but has problems with his two resentful brothers. **90m/C VHS.** Michael Horse, Efrem Zimbalist Jr., Sherry Hursey, Joseph Runningfox, Taylor Lacher; *D:* Lyman Dayton; *W:* Lyman Dayton.

Avenging Angel Woof! 1985 (R) Law student Molly "Angel" Stewart is back on the streets to retaliate against the men who killed the policeman who saved her from a life of prostitution. Worthless sequel to 1984's "Angel," exploiting the original's exploitative intent. Followed listlessly by "Angel III: The Final Chapter." 94m/C VHS, DVD. Betsy Russell, Rory Calhoun, Susan Tyrell, Ossie Davis, Barry Pearl, Ross Hagen, Karin Mani, Robert Tessier; D: Robert Vincent O'Neil; W: Joseph M. Cala; C: Peter Lyons Collister; M: Paul Antonelli.

Avenging Angelo ⚔⚔½ 2002 (R) The Hound thinks this flick is supposed to be a mobster comedy with some romance and, well, it's such a mess who knows what was intended, except it's not gonna revive Stallone's career. He's bodyguard Frankie Delano. He works for mob boss Angelo Allighieri (Quinn), who gets whacked. Frankie then decides Angelo's daughter Jennifer (Stowe) is in danger, so he goes to protect her. Only Jennifer was adopted and doesn't know she's a mobster's daughter and thinks Frank is nuts—until she nearly gets whacked. Then she becomes him and wants revenge. 96m/C VHS, DVD. Sylvester Stallone, Madeleine Stowe, Harry Van Gorkum, Raoul Bova, Anthony Quinn; D: Martyn Burke; W: Will Aldis, Steve Mackall; C: Ousama Rawi; M: Bill Conti.

Avenging Conscience ⚔⚔ Thou Shall Not Kill 1914 An early eerie horror film, based on tales of Edgar Allan Poe. D.W. Griffith's first large-scale feature. Silent. 78m/B VHS. Henry B. Walthall, Blanche Sweet; D: D.W. Griffith.

Avenging Force ⚔⚔ 1986 (R) Okay actioner about retired CIA agent Dudikoff returning to the force to help colleague James run for political office. A group of right-wing terrorists called "Pentangle" threatens James, so Dudikoff adds his name to their wanted list. Conflict leads to a forest manhunt where the avenging force does its avenging. 104m/C VHS. Michael Dudikoff, Steve James, James Booth; D: Sam Firstenberg; W: Mercer Ellington, James Booth; M: George S. Clinton.

The Avenging Hand ⚔⚔ 1936 Leaden suspense story about a hotel filled with thieves all searching for stolen loot. 56m/B VHS. Noah Beery Jr., Kathleen Kelly, Louis Borell, James Harcourt, Charles Oliver, Reginald Long; D: Victor Hanbury.

Avenue Montaigne ⚔⚔½ 2006 (PG-13) Sweet, provincial gamine Jessica (De France) comes to Paris and gets a job at a cafe along the titular street. The cafe is particularly busy because three major events will be happening nearby: classical pianist Jean-Francois (Dupontel) is giving a concert, popular TV actress Catherine (Lemercier) is starring onstage, and aging businessman Jacques (Brasseur) is going to auction off his extensive art collection. Each are having personal difficulties, which come to a boil over a three-day period, with Jessica providing her commonsense reactions. French with subtitles. 100m/C DVD. FR Cecile de France, Valerie Lemercier, Albert Dupontel, Claude Brasseur, Dani, Laura Morante, Sydney Pollack, Annelise Hesme, Suzanne Flon; D: Daniele Thompson; W: Daniele Thompson; C: Jean-Marc Fabre; M: Nicola Piovani.

Avenging Disco Godfather ⚔½ Disco Godfather; Avenging Godfather 1976 (R) Moore parodies the "Godfather" and martial arts movies. 99m/C VHS, DVD. Rudy Ray Moore, Carol Speed, Jimmy Lynch, Jerry Jones, Lady Reeds, James H. Hawthorne, Frank Finn, Julius J. Carry III; D: J. Robert Wagoner; W: J. Robert Wagoner, Cliff Roquemore; C: Arledge Armenaki; M: Ernie Fields Jr.

The Aviator's Wife ⚔⚔⚔ La Femme de L'Aviateur 1980 The first in Rohmer's Comedies and Proverbs series is a whimsical romance in which a young postal worker (Marlaud) who believes that his older girlfriend (Riviere) is seeing another man, a pilot (Carriere). He enlists the aid of a young girl (Meury) to help him spy on his romantic obsession. French with subtitles. 104m/C VHS, DVD. FR Philippe Marlaud, Marie Riviere, Anne-Laure Meury, Matthieu Carriere; D: Eric Rohmer; W: Eric Rohmer; C: Bernard Lutic; M: Jean-Louis Valero.

Awake ⚔½ 2007 (R) Wealthy Clayton Beresford (Christensen), stricken with a heart defect, must undergo a transplant to save his life. Unfortunately, something goes wrong, and he experiences "anesthesia awareness," which means that he appears asleep but is actually awake and fully aware of everything going on during his operation. Rather than build suspense and tension from such an intense premise, the story's twists and surprises (including an absurd-even-by-horror-movie-standards plot for poor Clay to die on the operating table) pile on ad nauseum, and Christensen is expected to carry much of the movie while flat on his back. 78m/C DVD. US Hayden Christensen, Jessica Alba, Terrence Howard, Lena Olin, Arliss Howard, Christopher McDonald, Fisher Stevens, Sam Robards, Georgina Chapman; D: Joby Harold; M: Graeme Revell.

The Average Woman ⚔⚔ 1924 Gritty journalist consults plain Jane for "Modern Woman" story and finds a major rewrite in order when he falls with a thud for Miss Jane. 52m/B VHS. Pauline Garon, David Powell, Burr McIntosh, Harrison Ford, De Sacia Mooers; D: Christy Cabanne.

The Aviator ⚔⚔ 1985 (PG) Pilot Reeve, haunted by the memory of a fatal crash, tries to find a new line of work. Large sums of money persuade him to transport spoiled Arquette to Washington. When the biplane crashes in the mountain wilderness, the two fall in love while animals... From the director of "Man From Snowy River." 98m/C VHS, DVD. Christopher Reeve, Rosanna Arquette, Jack Warden, Tyne Daly, Marcia Strassman, Sam Wanamaker, Scott Wilson; D: George Miller; W: Marc Norman; C: David Connell; M: Dominic Frontiere.

The Aviator ⚔⚔⚔½ 2004 (PG-13) Scorsese's sweeping, rich biopic of eccentric movie producer/aviation pioneer Howard Hughes soars on many levels. The film follows Hughes from maverick producer taking Hollywood by storm in the '20s through his successes in aviation and the founding of TWA, and finally battling Pan Am and Congress in the '40s. DiCaprio, in full-on movie idol mode, captures the drive and intensity of Hughes, letting the audience see glimpses of the coming breakdown, but mostly keeping it bubbling below the surface (until a slightly over-the-top sequence about 90 minutes in). Blanchett also shines in a dazzling portrayal of Katharine Hepburn. Scorsese's eye for detail and love of Old Hollywood serve the proceedings well, providing fascinating peeks into the workings of the old studio system, the testing and building of experimental aircraft, and the wheeling and dealing of high-stakes politics. 166m/C VHS, DVD, Blu-ray Disc, HD DVD. US Leonardo DiCaprio, Cate Blanchett, Kate Beckinsale, John C. Reilly, Alec Baldwin, Alan Alda, Ian Holm, Danny Huston, Jude Law, Adam Scott, Matt Ross, Kelli Garner, Frances Conroy, Brent Spiner, Stanley DeSantis, Edward Hermann, Willem Dafoe, J.C. MacKenzie, Kenneth Welsh, Amy Sloan, Kevin O'Rourke, Lisa Bronwyn Moore, Gwen Stefani, Vincent Laresca, Josie Maran; D: Martin Scorsese; W: John Logan; C: Robert Richardson; M: Howard Shore. Oscars '04: Art Dir./Set Dec., Cinematography, Film Editing, Support. Actress (Blanchett); British Acad. '04: Film, Makeup, Support. Actress (Blanchett); Golden Globes '05: Actor—Drama (DiCaprio), Film—Drama, Orig. Score; Screen Actors Guild '04: Support. Actress (Blanchett).

Awakening of Candra Woof! 1981 Based on a 'real 1975 incident, a young couple honeymooning in the mountains is assaulted by a lunatic fisherman. The psycho kills the husband and rapes the girl, then he brainwashes poor Candra into thinking it was all an accident. Intense subject matter should be horrifying, but falls short of the mark in this flop. 96m/C VHS. Blanche Baker, Cliff DeYoung, Richard Jaeckel, Jeffrey Tambor, Paul Regina, Elizabeth Cheshire; D: Paul Wendkos; C: Richard C. Glouner; M: Billy Goldenberg. TV

Awakenings ⚔⚔⚔ 1990 (PG-13) Marshall's first dramatic effort is based on the true story of Dr. Oliver Sacks, from his book of the same title. It details his experimentation with the drug L-dopa which in 1969 "awakening" of a number of catatonic patients, some of whom had been "sleeping" for as long as 30 years. Occasionally over-sentimental, but still providing a poignant look at both the patients who find themselves confronted with lost opportunities and faded youth—and at Sacks, who must watch their exquisite suffering as they slip away. De Niro's performance as the youngest of the group is heart-rending, while Williams offers a subdued, moving performance as the doctor. 120m/C VHS, DVD. Robin Williams, Robert De Niro, John Heard, Julie Kavner, Penelope Ann Miller, Max von Sydow, Anne Meara, Dexter Gordon, Alice Drummond, Richard Libertini, Judith Malina, Barton Heyman, Bradley Whitford, Peter Stormare, Laura Esterman, Vincent Pastore, Vin Diesel; D: Penny Marshall; W: Steven Zaillian; M: Randy Newman; Natl. Bd. of Review '90: Actor (De Niro).

Awakenings of the Beast ⚔ Ritual dos Sadicos; Ritual of the Maniacs 1963 Documents the protracted sufferings of an LSD drug user who is beset with hallucinatory visions and is prone to fits of frenzied violence. Director Jose Mojica Marins (AKA Coffin Joe) steps out of his Ze do Caixao character in this disjointed mix of drugs and sex intercut with Mojica Marins himself on trial for his offensive movies, followed by a case study on drugs and sexual behavior. By the end of the movie, there is a point—that drugs aren't the cause of evil behavior—but it's very painful getting there. In Portuguese with English subtitles. 93m/B VHS, DVD. BR Jose Mojica Marins, Sergio Hingst, Andrea Bryan, Mario Lima; D: Jose Mojica Marins, Rubens Francisco Lucchetti; C: Giorgio Attili.

Away All Boats ⚔⚔½ 1956 The true story of one Captain Hawks, who led a crew of misfits to victory in WWII Pacific aboard transport USS Belinda. Battle scenes are well done; look for early (and brief) appearance by young Clint Eastwood. 114m/C VHS, DVD. Jeff Chandler, George Nader, Richard Boone, Julie Adams, Keith Andes, Lex Barker, Clint Eastwood; D: Joseph Pevney; W: Ted Sherdeman; C: William H. Daniels; M: Frank Skinner.

Away From Her ⚔⚔⚔ 2006 Polley makes her directorial debut with this adaptation of the Alice Munro story "The Bear Who Came Over the Mountain." Grant (Pinsent) and Fiona (Christie) have been married more than 40 years when she is diagnosed with Alzheimer's. As her mental acuity deteriorates, Fiona insists on entering a nursing home, where she befriends another married patient (Murphy), while Grant struggles to cope with the changes. Gracefully aging '60s British icon Christie is well-matched by, the actor Pinsent in a tender story about love and loss that shouldn't be seen by cynics. 110m/C DVD. CA Julie Christie, Gordon Pinsent, Olympia Dukakis, Michael Murphy, Wendy Crewson, Alberta Watson, Kristen Thomson; D: Sarah Polley; W: Sarah Polley; C: Luc Pompellier; M: Jonathan Goldsmith; Golden Globes '08: Actress—Drama (Christie); Screen Actors Guild '07: Actress (Christie).

The Awakening ⚔½ 1980 (R) An archeologist discovers the tomb of a murderous queen, but upon opening the coffin, the mummy's spirit is transferred to his baby daughter, born at that instant. They call that bad luck. 101m/C VHS, DVD. GB Charlton Heston, Susannah York, Stephanie Zimbalist, Patrick Drury, Ian McDiarmid, Bruce Myers, Nadim Sawalha, Jill Townsend; D: Mike Newell; W: Allan Scott, Chris Bryant, Clive Exton; C: Jack Cardiff; M: Claude Bolling.

Awesome! I F*in' Shot That!** ⚔⚔⚔ 2006 (R) Combination of professional and fans' footage of The Beastie Boys' October 9, 2004 show at Madison Square Garden. The band encouraged fans to film the concert and send them the results. Works as both a document of the show and as an experiment in cooperation and collaboration between the artists and their fans. 90m/C DVD. D: Adam "MCA" Yauch; C: Alexis Boling; M: Adam "MCA" Yauch, Adam Horovitz.

The Awful Dr. Orloff ⚔ Gritos en la Noche; The Demon Doctor 1962 Set in a bygone era, Dr. Orloff (Vernon) is a retired prison physician who needs unblemished skin to remedy his daughter Melissa (Lorys), ravaged by fire. He abducts promising young women and candidates with the help of his blind zombie henchman Morpho (Valle), who simply cannot be trusted with a scalpel. After several surgical mishaps, they kidnap the perfect specimen, a woman who bears an uncanny resemblance to Melissa. Unfortunately, she is engaged to suspicious police inspector Tanner (San Martin). French version with English subtitles that includes more explicit gore is also available. 86m/B VHS, DVD. SP FR Howard Vernon, Diana Lorys, Conrado San Martin, Ricardo Valle, Perla Cristal, Maria Silva, Mara Laso; D: Jess (Jesus) Franco; W: Jess (Jesus) Franco; C: Godofredo Pacheco; M: Jose Pagan, Antonio Ramirez Angel.

The Awful Truth ⚔⚔⚔ 1937 Lucy (Dunne) and Jerry (Grant) Warriner are a young couple who discard their marriage made in heaven and go their separate ways in search of happiness. Meticulously sabotaging each others' new relationships, they discover they really were made for each other. Grant is at his most charming with dead-on comic timing while Dunne is as brilliant as his needling ex. The scene where Dunne poses as Grant's prodigal fan-dancing sister who pays a surprise cocktail-hour visit to her stuffy, upper-class girlfriend (Lamont) is among the most memorable screwball victories of all time. And don't miss the custody battle they have over the family dog (Asta of "The Thin Man" fame). Based on Arthur Richman's '922 play. Preceded by as "Let's Do It Again" in 1925 and 1929 versions; remade in 1953 as "Let's Do It Again." 92m/B VHS, DVD. Irene Dunne, Cary Grant, Ralph Bellamy, Alexander D'Arcy, Cecil Cunningham, Molly Lamont, Esther Dale, Joyce Compton, Robert "Tex" Allen, Esther Warwick, Mary Forbes; D: Leo McCarey; W: Vina Delmar. Oscars '37: Director (McCarey); Natl. Film Reg. '96.

An Awfully Big Adventure ⚔⚔ 1994 (R) Coming-of-age saga set in postwar Liverpool around struck 16-year-old Stella (Cates) gets work as a company apprentice, immediately getting a crush on smarmy, callous theatre manager Meredith Potter (a deliciously nasty Grant), who enjoys degrading everyone around him. The company's chance for success rests on a production of "Peter Pan," with visiting actor P.L. O'Hara (dashing Rickman), who immediately seduces Stella and has more than a few secrets of his own. Theatrically exaggerated; based on the novel by Beryl Bainbridge. 113m/C VHS, DVD. GB Georgina Cates, Hugh Grant, Alan Rickman, Peter Firth, Alun Armstrong, Prunella Scales, Rita Tushingham, Alan Cox, Edward Petherbridge, Nicola Pagett, Carol Drinkwater, Clive Merrison, Gerard McSorley; D: Mike Newell; W: Charles Wood; C: Dick Pope; M: Richard Hartley.

Axe ⚔⚔½ Lisa, Lisa; California Axe Massacre 1974 (R) After a group of thugs kill a man (on an embarrassingly shoddy set), they flee to the country, where they take over a farmhouse. The only residents of this farmhouse are a young girl, Lisa (Lee), and her invalid grandfather. The criminals force Lisa to cook a chicken dinner (NO!) and then generally terrorize the girl and her grandfather. Eventually, Lisa (who is actively hallucinating throughout this episode) gets the titular axe and seeks her revenge. The film is slow and boring, and the sub-amateur acting doesn't help. The only positive aspect is the suspense that mounts over the course of the movie. Having seen films like this before, and given the fact that nothing else is happening, the audience knows that Lisa is going to strike back at some time. **68m/C DVD.** Leslie Lee, Jack Canon, Frederick Friedel, Frank Jones; **D:** Frederick Friedel; **W:** Frederick Friedel; **C:** Austin McKinney.

Axe WOOF! *Greed* 2006 Underwear acting. Babes Raven and Ashley (who spend a lot of time in their scanties) hit a desert bar after a rock-climbing expedition. After being harassed by a biker gang, they steal one of the bikes and wind up at a lonely motel with a satchel of cash. Oh, and there's an escaped con, Ivan the Axeman, on the loose as well. London has limited screen time as the bar owner in this incredibly stupid mishmash of genres. **92m/C DVD.** Tim Sitarz, Jason London, Joe Goodrich, Andrea Bogart, Darlena Tejeiro; **W:** Eyal Sher, Dred Ross; **C:** Moshe Levin, Scott Carithers; **M:** Erik Godal, Mark Fontana. **VIDEO**

Ay, Carmela! 1990 During the Spanish Civil War, two vaudevillians with strong anti-Franco views are captured by Franco forces and sentenced to execution. They are reprieved when a theatre-loving Lieutenant offers to spare their lives if they will entertain the troops. Clever and entertaining farce, with poignant undertones. **105m/C VHS.** *SP IT* Carmen Maura, Andres Pajares, Gabino Diego, Maurizio De Razza, Miguel Rellan, Edward Zentara, Jose Sancho, Antonio Fuentes; **D:** Carlos Saura; **W:** Rafael Azcona **C:** Jose Luis Alcaine.

B. Monkey 1997 (R) B—AKA Beatrice—(Argento) hopes she can escape her world of drugs and crime (she's a thief) with the romantic aid of schoolteacher Alan (Harris). But her past catches up with her when ex-partners Paul (Everett) and Bruno (Rhys Meyers) convince her to do one last job (she misses the rush). Based on the novel by Andrew Davies, this one is mainly cool Brit style over substance. **91m/C VHS, DVD.** *GB* Asia Argento, Jared Harris, Rupert Everett, Jonathan Rhys Meyers, Tim Woodward, Ian Hart; **D:** Michael Radford; **W:** Michael Thomas, Chloe King; **C:** Ashley Rowe; **M:** Jennie Muskett.

Baadasssss! *How to Get the Man's Foot Outta Your Asss!* 2003 (R) Mario Van Peebles' fictionalized biopic of his father Melvin's efforts to get his influential indie film "Sweet Sweetback's Baadasssss Song" (the forerunner of the blaxploitation genre) made. Melvin (Mario, who also directed, co-wrote, and produced) is plagued with money and health problems, union troubles and lack of studio interest. Well-made and highly entertaining film was adapted from Melvin's father's work without over-romaticizing the often-imperfect man behind it. **108m/C DVD.** *US* Mario Van Peebles, Nia Long, David Alan Grier, Ossie Davis, Terry Crews, Rainn Wilson, Joy Bryant, Saul Rubinek, T.K. Carter, Paul Rodriguez, Vincent Schiavelli, Khleo Thomas, Len Lesser, Sally Struthers, Adam West, Glenn Plummer, Khalil Kain, Pamela Gordon, Joseph Culp, Karimah Westbrook, Ralph Martin, Robert Peters, Wesley Jonathan, John Singleton; **D:** Mario Van Peebles; **W:** Mario Van Peebles; **C:** Robert Primes; **M:** Tyler Bates.

Baba *The Father* 1973 A poor boatman agrees to be the fall guy in a murder in exchange for the actual murderer supporting his family. But after 24 years in prison, the boatman finds all his sacrificing has been in vain. His daughter has become a prostitute and his son is working as one of the murderer's henchman. In Turkish with English subtitles. **95m/C VHS.** *TU* **D:** Yilmaz Guney.

Babar: The Movie 1988 (G) The lovable Babar, king of the elephants, must devise a plan to outwit an angry hoard of attacking rhinos. Based on the characters of Jean and Laurent de Brunhoff. **75m/C VHS, DVD.** *CA FR* **D:** Alan Bunce; **W:** Alan Bunce, John deKlein; **V:** Gavin Magrath, Gordon Pinsent, Sarah Polley, Chris Wiggins, Elizabeth Hanna.

Babe! 1975 A fine TV movie about the life of one of America's most famous woman athletes, Babe Didrickson. Adapted by Joanna Lee from Didrickson's autobiography "The Life I've Led." The movie was nominated for Outstanding Special of 1975-76 and Clark won an Emmy for her work. **120m/C VHS.** Susan Clark, Alex Karras, Slim Pickens, Jeanette Nolan, Ellen Geer, Ford Rainey; **D:** Buzz Kulik; **M:** Jerry Goldsmith. **TV**

The Babe 1992 (PG) Follows the life of legendary baseball player Babe Ruth, portrayed as a sloppy drunkard whose appetites for food, drink, and sex were as large as he was. Alvarado and McGillis do well as the Babe's first and second wives, but this is Goodman's show from start to finish. He's excellent as Ruth, and looks the part, but his fine performance can't make up for a lackluster script filled with holes. **115m/C VHS, DVD.** Michael (Mike) Papajohn, John Goodman, Kelly McGillis, Trini Alvarado, Bruce Boxleitner, Peter Donat, J.C. Quinn, Richard Tyson, James Cromwell, Joe Ragno, Bernard Kates, Michael McGrath; **D:** Arthur Hiller; **W:** John Fusco; **C:** Haskell Wexler; **M:** Elmer Bernstein.

Babe *Babe, the Gallant Pig* 1995 (G) Totally charming fable has intelligent piglet Babe being raised by matriarch sheepdog Fly, and learning the art of sheep herding along with his new canine brothers. Farmer Hoggett (Cromwell) enters Babe in a winning raffle ticket, sees that he's more than just a ham, and enters them in the world sheepdog herding championship. Whimsy that never crosses the line into treacle. Four different special effects houses were used to make the barnyard animals talk and walk. Filmed on location in Australia; based on Dick King-Smith's book "The Sheep-Pig." **91m/C VHS, DVD.** *AU* James Cromwell, Magda Szubanski; **D:** Chris Noonan; **W:** Chris Noonan, George Miller; **C:** Andrew Lesnie; **M:** Nigel Westlake; **V:** Christine Cavanaugh, Miriam Margolyes, Danny Mann, Hugo Weaving; **Nar:** Roscoe Lee Browne. Oscars '95: Visual FX; Golden Globes '96: Film—Mus/Comedy; Natl. Soc. Film Critics '95:

Babe: Pig in the City 1998 (PG) Miller takes over the director's chair for this trip. And he brings along more money, more effects, more animals, and more unsettling images, including Mickey Rooney in a creepy clown suit, than anyone who saw the original would expect. Babe returns home to a hero's welcome, but the joy doesn't last long. Farmer Hoggett (Cromwell) is injured, and with foreclosure imminent, Babe and Mrs. Hoggett (Szubanski) head out to turn Babe's fame into a little cash. Along the way, they miss their connecting flight in "the city" and are forced to stay at a hotel that caters to animals. There, they meet the aforementioned Rooney and his three chimp partners, along with various dogs and cats. Technically well-done, and sporting an imaginative story, but may be a little dark for the younger kiddies. **96m/C VHS, DVD.** James Cromwell, Magda Szubanski, Mickey Rooney, Mary Stein, Julie Godfrey; **D:** George Miller; **W:** Judy Morris, Mark Lamprell; **C:** Andrew Lesnie; **M:** Nigel Westlake; **V:** Elizabeth (E.G. Dailey) Daily, Danny Mann, Glenne Headly, Steven Wright, James Cosmo, Stanley Ralph Ross, Russi Taylor, Adam Goldberg, Nathan Kress, Myles Jeffrey; **Nar:** Roscoe Lee Browne.

Babe Ruth Story 1948 An overly sentimental biography about the famed baseball slugger. Bendix is miscast as the Bambino, but the actual film clips of the Babe are of interest. A movie to be watched during those infrequent bouts of sloppy baseball mysticism. **107m/B VHS, DVD.** William Bendix, Claire Trevor, Charles Bickford, Sam Levene, Gertrude Niesen; **D:** Roy Del Ruth.

Babel 2006 (R) A father in a Moroccan village allows his two young sons to shoot his hunting rifle and an international incident is sparked. The boys innocently aim at a tourist bus, never believing the bullets could actually hit someone. They do, of course, and this one foolish act leads to complications that will encompass a Mexican nanny and her Anglo charges back in California and an angry deaf-mute teenaged girl in Tokyo. Somehow director Gonzalez Inarritu manages to tie the stories together (with a certain amount of unbelievability). Pitt and Blanchett join an impressive international cast who live up to this gritty, realistic dramatic puzzle. **142m/C DVD, Blu-ray Disc, HD DVD.** *US* Brad Pitt, Cate Blanchett, Gael Garcia Bernal, Adriana Barraza, Elle Fanning, Koji Yakusho, Nathan Gamble, Rinko Kikuchi, Said Tarchani, Boubker Ait El Caid, Mustapha Rachidi, Abdelkader Bara; **D:** Alejandro Gonzalez Inarritu; **W:** Guillermo Arriaga; **C:** Rodrigo Prieto; **M:** Gustavo Santaolalla. Oscars '06: Orig. Score; British Acad. '06: Orig. Score; Golden Globes '07: Film—Drama.

Babes in Arms 1939 The children of several vaudeville performers team up to put on a show to raise money for their financially impoverished parents. Loosely adapted from the Rodgers and Hart Broadway musical of the same name, features some of their songs as well as new additions. ♪♪Babes in Arms; I Cried for You; Good Morning; You Are My Lucky Star; Broadway Rhythm; Where or When; Daddy Was a Minstrel Man; I'm Just Wild About Harry; God's Country. **91m/B VHS.** Judy Garland, Mickey Rooney, Charles Winninger, Guy Kibbee, June Preisser; **D:** Busby Berkeley; **M:** George Bassman, Richard Rodgers, Lorenz Hart.

Babes in Toyland 1961 A lavish Disney production of Victor Herbert's timeless operetta, with Toyland becoming menaced by the evil Barnaby and his Bogeymen. Yes, Annette had a life after Mickey Mouse and before the peanut butter commercials. Somewhat charming, although the roles of the lovers seem a stretch for both Funicello and Kirk. But the flick does sport an amusing turn by Wynn. **105m/C VHS, DVD.** Annette Funicello, Ray Bolger, Tommy Sands, Ed Wynn, Tommy Kirk; **D:** Jack Donohue; **C:** Edward Colman; **M:** George Bruns.

Babes in Toyland 1986 Young girl must save Toyland from the clutches of the evil Barnaby and his monster minions. Bland TV remake of the classic doesn't approach the original. **96m/C VHS.** Drew Barrymore, Noriyuki "Pat" Morita, Richard Mulligan, Eileen Brennan, Keanu Reeves, Jill Schoelen, Googy Gress; **D:** Clive Donner; **W:** Paul Zindel; **M:** Leslie Bricusse.

Babes on Broadway 1941 Mickey and Judy put on a show to raise money for a settlement house. Nearly the best of the Garland-Rooney series, with imaginative numbers staged by Berkeley. ♪♪Babes on Broadway; Anything Can Happen in New York; How About You?; Hoe Down; Chin Up! Cheerio! Carry On!; Mama Yo Quiero; F.D.R. Jones; Waiting for the Robert E. Lee. **118m/B VHS.** Mickey Rooney, Judy Garland, Fay Bainter, Richard Quine, Virginia Weidler, Ray Macdonald, Busby Berkeley; **D:** Busby Berkeley; **M:** George Bassman.

Babette's Feast *Babettes Gaestebud* 1987 A simple, moving pageant-of-life fable. Philippa (Kjer) and Martina (Federspiel) took over their late father's ministry in a small Danish coastal town. Widowed Frenchwoman Babette (Audran) has spent 14 years in their service and, after winning a lottery prize, decides she will prepare a lavish banquet in honor of their father's 100th birthday. The religiously conservative villagers don't know what to make of such bounty—or the pleasure it brings to their senses. Adapted from a tale by Isak Dinesen. French and Danish with subtitles. **102m/C VHS, DVD.** *DK FR* Stephane Audran, Bibi Andersson, Bodil Kjer, Birgitte Federspiel, Jean-Philippe LaFont, Ebbe Rode, Jarl Kulle; **D:** Gabriel Axel; **W:** Gabriel Axel; **C:** Henning Kristiansen; **M:** Per Norgard; **Nar:** Ghita Norby. Oscars '87: Foreign Film; British Acad. '88: Foreign Film.

The Baby 1972 (PG) Bizarre story of a social worker who resorts to swinging an ax to cut the apron strings of "baby," a retarded man-child, from his over-protective and insane mother (bad combination) mother and sisters. Low-budget production looks and feels like a low-budget production, but any movie featuring a grown man wandering around in diapers can't be all bad. **85m/C VHS, DVD.** Anjanette Comer, Ruth Roman, Marianna Hill, Suzanne Zenor, David Manzy, Michael Pataki, Erin O'Reilly, Virginia Vincent; **D:** Ted Post; **W:** Abe Polsky; **C:** Michael D. Margulies; **M:** Gerald Fried.

Baby 2000 John (Carradine) and Lily (Fawcett) Malone are unsuccessful in coping with their grief over the death of their infant son and in helping their 12-year-old daughter, Larkin (Pill), to deal with her own pain. Then a baby girl is abandoned on the Malone doorstep and Lily immediately wants to keep the child—much to the others' dismay. Formulaic weepie based on the novel by Patricia MacLachlan. **93m/C VHS.** Farrah Fawcett, Keith Carradine, Jean Stapleton, Alison Pill, Vincent Berry, Ann Dowd; **D:** Robert Allan Ackerman; **W:** Kerry Kennedy, Patricia MacLachlan, David Manson; **C:** Ron Garcia; **M:** Jeff Danna; **Nar:** Glenn Close. **CABLE**

The Baby and the Battleship 1956 The old baby out of (on the?) water plot. While on liberty in Italy, a sailor, after a series of complications, becomes custodian of a baby and attempts to hide the tyke aboard his battleship (hence the title). More complications ensue. Some funny moments. Great cast. **96m/C VHS.** *GB* John Mills, Richard Attenborough, Andre Morell, Bryan Forbes, Lisa Gastoni, Michael Hordern, Lionel Jeffries, Gordon Jackson, John Le Mesurier; **D:** Jay Lewis.

Baby Boom 1987 (PG) J.C. Wiatt (Keaton) is a hard-charging exec who becomes the reluctant mother to an orphaned baby girl (a gift from a long-lost relative). She adjusts with great difficulty to motherhood and life outside the rat race and New York City when J.C. decides she must make some radical changes to her routine. A fairly harmless collection of cliches bolstered by Keaton's usual nervous performance as a power-suited yuppie ad queen saddled with a noncareer-enhancing baby, who moves from manic career woman to jelly-packing Vermont store-owner/mom. Shepherd serves as her new, down-home, doctor beau. To best appreciate flick, see it with a bevy of five- and six-year-olds (a good age for applauding the havoc that a baby creates). **103m/C VHS, DVD.** Diane Keaton, Sam Shepard, Harold Ramis, Sam Wanamaker, James Spader, Pat Hingle, Mary Gross, Victoria Jackson, Paxton Whitehead, Annie Golden, Dori Brenner, Robin Bartlett, Christopher Noth, Britt Leach; **D:** Charles Shyer; **W:** Charles Shyer, Nancy Meyers; **C:** William A. Fraker; **M:** Bill Conti.

Baby Boy 2001 (R) Singleton's candid look at a culture that fosters and tolerates lack of emotional maturity in young African-American males. Jody (Gibson) is a 20-year-old manchild who still lives with his mother (Johnson), has two children with two different women, no job, and cheats on his current girl, Yvette. Jody's life changes when his mother's boyfriend moves in. Melvin (Rhames), an ex-con who's been down the road Jody is heading, shows no tolerance for his attitude. Real trouble starts when Rodney (Snoop Dogg), a street thug and Yvette's ex, is released from prison and refuses to leave her house. Singleton toys with two endings, but finishes the story with the message that the means to fix the problems he's described are within reach. **129m/C VHS, DVD, UMD.** *US* Tyrese Gibson, Omar Gooding, Taraji P. Henson, Adrienne-Joi (AJ) Johnson, Snoop Dogg, Tamara La Seon Bass, Ving Rhames, Angell Conwell; **D:** John Singleton; **W:** John Singleton; **C:** Charles Mills; **M:** David Arnold.

The Baby Dance 1998 Well-off, middleaged Hollywood marrieds Rachel (Channing) and Richard (Reigert) Luckman have unsuccessfully tried to have a baby for years. Finally they place an adoption ad and receive a response from poor Louisiana trailer park inhabitants Wanda (Dern) and Art (Lineback) LeFauvre, who have an unwanted fifth child on the way. A meeting between the couples soon points out monetary, religious, and cultural differences that may derail their bargain. The two leading ladies carry the picture, which is based on director Anderson's Off-Broadway play. **95m/C VHS, DVD.** Stockard Channing, Laura Dern, Peter

Baby Doll 🐶🐶🐶 1956 Suggestive sex at its best, revolving around this love of cotton in Mississippi. Nubile Baker is married to slow-witted Malden, who owns a cotton gin. His torching of Wallach's cotton gin begins a cycle of sexual innuendo and tension, brought to exhilarating life on screen, without a single filmed kiss. Performers and sets ooze during the steamy exhibition, which was considered highly erotic when released. Excellent performances from entire cast, with expert pacing by director Kazan. Screenplay is based on Tennessee Williams' "27 Wagons Full of Cotton." 115m/B VHS, DVD. Eli Wallach, Carol Baker, Karl Malden, Mildred Dunnock, Rip Torn; D: Elia Kazan; W: Tennessee Williams; C: Boris Kaufman; Golden Globes '57: Director (Kazan).

The Baby Doll Murders 🐶🐶 1992 (R) Someone in L.A. is killing beautiful young women and then leaving a broken baby doll at the scene of the crime. The gruesome murderer manages to elude everyone, until Detective Benz discovers a link between the victims and a pattern begins to form. He also discovers that his partner's wife is going to be the next victim, unless he can stop this ruthless serial killer from striking again. 95m/C VHS. Jeff Kober, Melanie Smith, John Saxen, Tom; (Thomas E.) Hodges, Bobby DiZicco; D: Paul Leder; W: Paul Leder.

Baby Face 🐶🐶 1933 A small town girl moves to the city when her father dies. There she gets a job at a bank and sleeps her way to the top of the business world, discarding used men left and right. The Hays Office was extremely upset with the then risque material and forced Warner to trim the first cut. 70m/B VHS, DVD. Barbara Stanwyck, George Brent, Donald Cook, John Wayne, Henry Kolker, Margaret Lindsay, Douglass Dumbrille, James Murray; D: Alfred E. Green; W: Gene Markey, Kathryn Scola; C: James Van Trees; M: Leo F. Forbstein. Natl. Film Reg. '05.

Baby Face Nelson 🐶🐶½ 1957 (R) Lame Depression-era gangster flick with George "Baby Face" Nelson (Rowell) and his moll Helen Womack (Zane) fighting rival Al Capone (Abraham) in Chicago. Rowell comes off well as gangster John Dillinger. 80m/C VHS. C: Thomas Howell, Lisa Zane, F. Murray Abraham, Doug Wert, Martin Kove; D: Scott Levy; M: Joseph Farruda, Craig J. Nevius; C: Christopher Bafia; M: Christopher Lennertz.

Baby Face Morgan 🐶🐶 1942 Poor comedy about gangsters who attempt to take advantage of the FBI's preoccupation with saboteurs and spies by muscling in on an insurance firm. 60m/B VHS, DVD. Mary Carlisle, Richard Cromwell, Robert Armstrong, Chick Chandler, Charles Judel; D: Arthur Dreifuss.

Baby Geniuses 🐶½ 1999 (PG) Steals the most irritating parts of "Look Who's Talking," "Home Alone" and that creepy dancing baby and pastes them onto a lame good kids vs. evil adults plot. Turner and Lloyd are evil scientists attempting to crack the secret language of babies, which they believe holds the secrets of the universe (such as how to enjoy drooling and making in your pants). Standing in their way are nursery school operators Cattrall and MacNichol and an array of babies that spout inane dialogue thanks to an abuse of computer morphing. The effect is more disturbing than cute, and an excellent supporting cast is wasted. More interesting things car be found inside a diaper. 94m/C VHS, DVD. Kathleen Turner, Christopher Lloyd, Kim Cattrall, Peter MacNichol, Dom DeLuise, Ruby Dee, Kyle Howard, Leo Fitzgerald, Wyes Fitzgerald, Gerry Fitzgerald; D: Bob (Benjamin) Clark; W: Bob (Benjamin) Clark, Steven Paul, Francesca Matos, Robert Grasmere, Greg Michael; C: Stephen M. Latz; M: Paul Zaza.

Baby Girl Scott 🐶🐶½ 1987 Hurt and Litti;ow play the parents of an extremely premature infant who is being kept alive by technology. They make a heartrending decision and then must battle doctors and the system to let their daughter die with dignity. 97m/C VHS. John Lithgow, Mary Beth Hurt, Linda Kelsey; D: John Korty. TV

Baby It's You 🐶🐶 1982 (R) In New Jersey in the '60s, the relationship between a smart, attractive Jewish girl who yearns to be an actress and a street-smart Catholic Italian boy puzzles their family and friends. It all works due to Arquette's strong acting and Sayles' script, which explores adolescent dreams, the transition to adulthood, class differences. Interesting period soundtrack (Woolly Bully and, for some reason, Bruce Springsteen) helps but is a commercial job which helped finance Sayles' more independent ventures. 105m/C VHS. Rosanna Arquette, Vincent Spano, Jack Davidson, Joanna Merlin, Nick Ferrari, Leora Dana, Robert Downey Jr., Tracy Pollan, Matthew Modine; D: John Sayles; W: John Sayles; C: Michael Balhaus.

Baby Love woof! 1969 (R) A softcore fluff-fest about a trollop seducing a doctor's family. The doctor may or may not be her father. Hayden tantalizes the doctor, the doctor's son, and the doctor's wife, as well as the neighbors, leaving only those in adjoining communities untouched. Based on the novel by Tina Chad Christian. 98m/C VHS. G8 Ann Lynn, Keith Barron, Linda Hayden, Derek Lamdan, Diana Dors, Patience Collier; D: Alastair Reid.

Baby Love woof! 1983 Lemon Popsicle v 1983 Nerds get revenge against the freshmen who run the local frat house. 80m/C VHS. IS Dolly, Dollar, Bea Fiedler, Jesse Katzur, Yftach Katzur, Dvora Kedar, Renata Langer, Zachi Noy, Jonathan Sagalle; D: Dan Wolman; C: Zion Rosenberg.

The Baby Maker 🐶🐶 1970 (R) A couple who cannot have children because the wife is sterile decides to hire a woman to have a child for them. However, the relationship between the husband and the surrogate progresses beyond what either of them wanted. Hershey stars as the free-love surrogate mama (just before she went into her directorial debut). Flick is interesting as a combo critique/exploitation of those wild and groovy 1960s. 109m/C VHS. Barbara Hershey, Collin Wilcox-Paxton, Sam Groom, Scott Glenn, Jeannie Berlin; D: James Bridges; W: James Bridges.

Baby Mama 🐶🐶½ 2008 (PG-13) Predictable mom com starring Fey and Poehler, who got comfortable doing skits together on SNL. Single, 37-year-old workaholic Kate Holbrook (Fey) determines she now has the time and resources to have a baby, but dang if her biological clock hasn't stopped ticking. So Kate goes the surrogacy route and chooses an unlikely candidate—South Philly good-time gal Angie (Poehler), who's unwilling to follow Kate's precise pregnancy plans when the duo wind up as roommates. Naturally, over the course of nine months and lots of preggo jokes, they bond. The leads sell the weak material and are backed up by such pros as Weaver, Kinnear, and Martin. 99m/C DVD. US Tina Fey, Amy Poehler, Greg Kinnear, Dax Shepard, Romany Malco, Holland Taylor, Sigourney Weaver, Maura Tierne; D: Michael McCullers; W: Michael McCullers; C: Daryn Okada; M: Jeff Richmond.

Baby Monitor: Sound of Fear 🐶🐶½ 1997 (R) Matt (Begrie) follow-up to "Children of the Bride" has McClanahan setting into wedded bliss with younger husband Shackleford when she discovers she's pregnant. Not only is she unsure about wanting to be a mom again at her age but then grown—and single—daughter McNichol announces she is also pregnant. The sheer silliness of this TV fare makes it fun to watch. 95m/C VHS. Rue McClanahan, Ted Shackleford, Kristy McNichol, John Wesley Shipp, Anne Bobby, Conor O'Farrell; D: Bill Bixby; W: Bart Baker. TV

Baby on Board 🐶🐶 1992 (PG) Kane plays the wife of a Mafia bookkeeper who is accidentally killed in a gangland murder. Out for revenge, she tracks her husband's killer to JFK airport with her four-year-old daughter in tow. Just as she pulls the loaded gun from her purse and takes aim, a pickpocket snatches her purse, accidentally firing the gun. Now she's on the run and jumps into the first cab she can find, driven by Reinhold. New York City is turned upside down as she tries to find him, the mob in this funny but predictable comedy. 90m/C VHS. Carol Kane, Judge Reinhold, Geza Kovacs, Errol Slue, Alex Stapley, Kelly Stapley; D: Francis Schaeffer.

The Baby-Sitters' Club 🐶🐶½ 1995 (PG) Centering on the summer vacation of seven enterprising Connecticut 13-year-olds and their teen trials with parents, boys, and babysitting, this film is sure to hit home with a crowd that is rarely featured, pre-teen girls. Director Mayron claims, "it's the 'Mystic Pizza' of their age." Young girls and girls young at heart should enjoy this touching look at the frag-ile years of our youth, leaving baby dolls behind and heading towards dating. Based on the best-selling book series by Ann Martin. Fisk, who plays club leader Kristy, is the daughter of actress Sissy Spacek and director Jack Fisk. 92m/C VHS, DVD. Schuyler Fisk, Bre Blair, Rachael Leigh Cook, Larisa Oleynik, Tricia Joe, Stacey Linn Ramsower, Zelda Harris, Brooke Adams, Peter Horton, Bruce Davison, Ellen Burstyn, Austin O'Brien, Aaron Michael Metchik, Ellen Burstyn, Marla-ene Young; W: Willy Kurant; M: David Michael Frank.

Baby... Secret of the Lost Legend 🐶🐶 1985 (PG) A sportswriter and his paleontologist wife risk their lives to reunite a hatching brontosaurus with its mother in the African jungle. Although this Disney film is not lewd in any sense, beware of several scenes displaying frontal nudity and some violence. 95m/C VHS. William Katt, Sean Young, Patrick McGoohan, Julian Fellowes; D: Bill W.L. Norton.

Baby, Take a Bow 🐶🐶 1934 (PG) Temple's first starring role. As a cheerful Pollyanna-type she helps her father, falsely accused of theft, by finding the true thief. 76m/B VHS, DVD. Shirley Temple, James Dunn, Claire Trevor, Alan Dinehart; D: Harry Lachman.

Baby, the Rain Must Fall 🐶🐶 1964 A rockabilly singer, paroled from prison after serving time for a knifing, returns home to his wife and daughter, but his outbursts of violence make the reunion difficult. Unsentimental with realistic performances, but script is weak (although written by Foote, based on his play). "Traveling Lady". Theme song was a Top 40 hit. 100m/B VHS, Steve McQueen, Lee Remick, Don Murray; D: Robert Mulligan; W: Horton Foote; C: Ernest Laszlo; M: Elmer Bernstein.

Babycakes 🐶🐶½ 1989 A marshmellow romance between an overweight mortuary attendant who decides to follow her heart when she falls for a hunky ice skater. Can she make him appreciate her inner beauty instead of just her not-thin-normal-beauty-standard outward appearance? (Happy ending guaranteed.) TV remake of the darker German film "Sugarbaby." 94m/C VHS, DVD. Ricki Lake, Craig Sheffer, Paul Benedict, Betty Buckley, John Karlen, Nada Despotovich; D: Paul Schneider. TV

Babyfever 🐶🐶½ 1994 (R) Women gather at a baby shower and tell stories about motherhood and related topics. May be viewed as a babblefest with video accompaniment or as an overdue cinematic exploration of a fairly important aspect of life (where would we be without mom?). That said, pace of the comedy drama is less than feverish, although director Jaglom captures the essence of the stories without disturbing their flow. Foyt, Jaglom's wife and co-screenwriter, makes her acting debut. 110m/C VHS, DVD. Matt Salinger, Eric Roberts, Frances Fisher, Victoria Foyt, Zack Norman, Dinah Lenney, Elaine Kagan; D: Henry Jaglom; W: Victoria Foyt, Henry Jaglom; C: Hanania Baer.

Babylon AD 🐶🐶 2008 (PG-13) The French Hughes formula using little tiny baby for original spin. Adorable Baby Bink crawls his way onto the city streets, much to his frantic mother's dismay, and unwittingly outsmarts his would-be kidnappers. As in "HA I and II," the bad guys fall victim to all sorts of cataclysmic Looney Tunes violence. Small kids will get a kick out of this one. Particular problem for the moviemakers was that the nine-month old Worton twins were past the year mark by the end of the shoot, a world of difference in infantdom. Blue screens and out-of-sequence shooting were used to overcome the developmental gap. 99m/C VHS, DVD. Adam Worton, Jacob Worton, Joe Mantegna, Lara Flynn Boyle, Joe Pantoliano, Fred Dalton Thompson, John Neville, Brian Haley, Matthew Glave; C: Pat-rick Reed Johnson; M: John Hughes; C: Thomas Ackerman; M: Bruce Broughton.

Baby's Day Out 🐶🐶½ 1994 (PG) Poor man's "Home Alone" refits tired Hughes formula using little tiny baby for original spin. Adorable Baby Bink crawls his way onto the city streets, much to his frantic mother's dismay, and unwittingly outsmarts his would-be kidnappers. As in "HA I and II," the bad guys fall victim to all sorts of cataclysmic Looney Tunes violence. Small kids will get a kick out of this one. Particular problem for the moviemakers was that the nine-month old Worton twins were past the year mark by the end of the shoot, a world of difference in infantdom. Blue screens and out-of-sequence shooting were used to overcome the developmental gap. 99m/C VHS. Joe Mantegna, Lara Flynn Boyle, Joe Pantoliano, Fred Dalton Thompson, John Neville, Brian Haley, Matthew Glave; C: Patrick Reed Johnson; M: John Hughes; C: Thomas Ackerman; M: Bruce Broughton.

The Babysitter 🐶🐶 1980 A family hires the mysterious but ingratiating Johanna (Zimbalist) as live-in help without checking on her references. (who'd all to all their problems—Mom's an alcoholic, Dad's a workaholic, and their daughter Jen-na's gained their trust (or, in Dad's case, just plain malad-justed—but once Johan-na's gained their trust (or, in Dad's case, lust)), she sets out to manipulate and exploit the family for her own psychotic purposes. Houseman plays the nosy neighbor who's on to her evil plan. Fair made-for-TV treatment of a common suspense plot. 96m/C VHS. William Shatner, Patty Duke, Stephanie Zimbalist, Quinn Cummings, John Houseman, David Wallace; D: Peter Medak.

The Babysitter 🐶🐶½ 1995 (R) All-American teen Jennifer (Silverstone) becomes the unexpected object of desire for family man -larry (Walsh), whose wife Dolly (Garlington) is fantasizing about having an affair with a neighbor (Segal). But then Jennifer's boyfriend (London) gets caught up in a malicious prank that turns bad for everyone involved. Based on a short story by Robert Coover. 90m/C VHS, DVD. Alicia Silverstone, Jeremy London, J.T. Walsh, Lee Garlington, Nicky Katt, Lois Chiles, George Segal; D: Guy Ferland; W: Guy Ferland; M: Loek Dikker.

The Bacchantes 🐶🐶 1963 Poorly dubbed account of a ballerina, her life and loves. Based on the play by Euripides. 100m/B VHS. IT Taina Elg, Pierre Brice, Alessandra Panaro, Alberto Lupo, Akim Tamiroff; D: Giorgio Ferroni.

The Bachelor 🐶🐶 1993 Beautiful, seductive period drama about a shy and solitary physician who is forced into a new life when a family tragedy changes everything he once took for granted. Richardson and Carradine give brilliant performances in this provocative story of a man's sexual awakening. Based on a novel by Arthur Schnitzler. 105m/C VHS. Keith Carradine, Miranda Richardson, Mari Torocsik, Max von Sydow, Kristin Scott Thomas, Sarah-Jane Fenton, Franco Interlenghi; D: Roberto Faenza, Ennio de Concini, Hugh Fleet-wood; M: Ennio Morricone.

The Bachelor 🐶🐶 1999 (PG-13) Exec producer/star Chris O'Donnell's remake of Buster Keaton's 1925 silent comedy "Seven Chances" falls short of bringing the story to a modern audience. Well, an audience that's aware of the discovery of talkies, feminism and plot holes anyway. O'Donnell plays Jimmy, who stands to inherit a fortune from his grandfather (Ustinov) if he marries before the age of 30. Unfortunately, he receives this news immediately after his odious proposal to girlfriend Anne (Zellweger) is rejected...and of course his 30th birthday happens to be 27 hours away. Madcap antics allegedly ensue as Jimmy trolls for a wife from the pool of his ex-girlfriends and flees the husband-hunting horde who respond to a front-page ad placed by his pal Marco (Lange). **101m/C VHS, DVD.** Chris O'Donnell, Renee Zellweger, Hal Holbrook, James Cromwell, Artie Lange, Ed Asner, Marley Shelton, Stacy Edwards, Rebeca Cross, Jennifer Esposito, Peter Ustinov, Mariah Carey, Brooke Shields; **D:** Gary Sinyor; **W:** Steve Cohen; **C:** Simon Archer; **M:** David A. Hughes, John Murphy.

The Bachelor and the Bobby-Soxer 🦴🦴🦴 *Bachelor Knight* 1947 Playboy Grant is brought before Judge Loy for disturbing the peace and sentenced to court her teenage sister Temple. Crue and unusual punishment? Maybe, but the wise Judge hopes that the dates will help Temple over her crush on handsome Grant. Instead, Loy and Grant fall for each other. **95m/B VHS, DVD.** Cary Grant, Myrna Loy, Shirley Temple, Rudy Vallee, Harry Davenport, Ray Collins, Veda Ann Borg; **D:** Irving Reis; **W:** Sidney Sheldon. **Oscars '47:** Orig. Screenplay.

Bachelor Apartment 🦴🦴½ 1931 Once at the leading edge of the bachelor on the loose genre, this one's hopelessly dated. The scandalous womanizing of a wealthy '30s Lothario just doesn't have the same impact on the "men just don't understand" generation. Nevertheless, as vintage if-the-walls-could-talk fluff, it's good for a giggle. **77m/B VHS.** Lowell Sherman, Irene Dunne, Norman Kerry, Claudia Dell, Noel Francis, Charles Coleman, Mae Murray, Claudia Dell, Ivan Lebedeff, Purnell Pratt, Kitty Kelly; **D:** Lowell Sherman; **W:** John Howard Lawson, J. Walter Ruben; **C:** Leo Tover; **M:** Max Steiner.

Bachelor Bait 🦴½ 1934 A marriage license clerk who's tired of just handing out licenses opens a matrimonial service for men. **75m/B VHS.** Stuart Erwin, Rochelle Hudson, Pert Kelton, Richard "Skeets" Gallagher, Berton Churchill, Grady Sutton, Clarence Wilson; **D:** George Stevens; **W:** Glenn Tryon; **C:** Dave Abel; **M:** Max Steiner.

Bachelor in Paradise 🦴🦴½ 1961 Silly tale where Hope as a writer of books to the lovelorn who decides to do firsthand research on the sexual goings-on of a suburban California community. All the married ladies find him charming (much to their husbands' disgust) and the lone single woman, Turner, isn't single by the end of the movie. **109m/C VHS.** Bob Hope, Lana Turner, Janis Paige, Jim Hutton, Paula Prentiss, Don Porter, Virginia Grey, Agnes Moorehead, John McGiver; **D:** Jack Arnold; **W:** Hal Kanter, Valentine Davies; **M:** Henry Mancini.

Bachelor Mother 🦴🦴🦴 1939 A single salesgirl causes a scandal when she finds an abandoned baby and is convinced by her boss to adopt the child. Smart, witty comedy with nice performance by Rogers. **82m/B VHS.** Ginger Rogers, David Niven, Charles Coburn; **D:** Garson Kanin.

Bachelor Party 🦴🦴 1984 (R) Rick (Hank) is silly, cute, and poor. Debbie (Kitaen) is intelligent, beautiful, and rich. It must be a marriage made in heaven, because no one in their right mind would put these two together. All is basically well, except that her parents hate him and his friends dislike her. Things are calm until right before the big event, when the bride-to-be objects to Rick's traditional pre-nuptial partying and with good reason. Light and semi-entertaining with scattered laughs. **105m/C VHS, DVD.** Tom Hanks, Tawny Kitaen, Adrian Zmed, George Grizzard, Robert Prescott, William Tepper, Wendie Jo Sperber, Barry Diamond, Michael Dudikoff, Deborah Harmon, John Bloom, Toni Alessandra, Monique Gabrielle, Angela Aames, Rosanne Katon, Bradford Bancroft; **D:** Neal Israel; **W:** Pat Proft; **C:** Hal Trussel; **M:** Robert Folk.

Bachelor Party 2: The Last Temptation 🦴 2008 Has, of course, nothing to do with the 1984 Tom Hanks comedy. Ron (Cooke) gets engaged to wealthy Melinda (Foster). Her scheming brother Todd (Christie) is convinced that the affable Ron will be anointed heir to the family business so he takes Ron and his buds to South Beach hoping some compromising situations will lead to the wedding being called off. An excuse for a lot of topless women to be on parade and men—and boys—to behave badly. **103m/C DVD.** *US* Ja Rule, Ving Rhames, Tatyana Ali, Giancarlo Esposito, Pam Grier, Joe Morton, Tia Carrere, Frank Langella, Debbi (Deborah) Morgan, AJ Sapienza, Lahmard Tate; **D:** James Hunter; **W:** James Hunter, Michael Raffaniello; **C:** Donald M. Morgan; **M:** Robert Folk. **VIDEO**

Bachelor Party Vegas woof! *Vegas, Baby* 2005 (R) Things go wrong for five friends when they head to Vegas and discover their bachelor party planner is a casino thief, which leads to all sorts of misunderstandings. Unbelievably crass and unfunny comedy that should have stayed in Vegas, preferably so the master print could have been shredded by one of Siegfried & Roy's white tigers. **90m/C DVD.** *US* Kal Penn, Jonathan Bennett, Donald Adeosun Faison, Charlie Talbert, Vincent Pastore, Jaime Pressly, Aaron Himelstein; **D:** Eric Bernt; **W:** Eric Bernt.

Back Door to Heaven 🦴🦴🦴 1939 Traces the path of a young boy who is born into a poor family and the reasons for his turning to a life of crime. A grim and powerful drama with many convincing performances. **85m/B VHS.** Wallace Ford, Aline MacMahon, Stuart Erwin, Patricia Ellis, Kent Smith, Van Heflin, Jimmy Lydon; **D:** William K. Howard.

Back from Eternity 🦴🦴½ 1956 Eleven survivors of a plane crash are stranded in a headhunter region of South America's jungle. Remake of "Five Came Back" (1939), which was also directed by Farrow. **97m/B VHS.** Robert Ryan, Rod Steiger, Anita Ekberg, Phyllis Kirk, Keith Andes, Gene Barry, Jon(athan) Provost, Beulah Bondi, Barbara Eden; **D:** John Farrow; **C:** William Mellor.

Back Home 🦴🦴½ 1990 A family reunion movie with pure Disney sentiment. A 12-year-old English girl, who has been living in America during WWII, is reunited with her family in postwar England. **103m/C VHS, DVD.** Hayley Carr, Hayley Mills, Jean Anderson, Rupert Frazer, Brenda Bruce, Adam Stevenson, George Clark; **D:** Piers Haggard. **CABLE**

Back in Action 🦴🦴 1994 (R) Veteran LA detective Rossi (Piper) is out to bust the ruthless drug gang who gunned down his partner. But he's got company—martial-arts expert Billy (Blanks) whose young sister has fallen prey to the same gang. So the two action junkies reluctantly team up to cause some major damage. **93m/C VHS, DVD.** Roddy Piper, Billy Blanks, Bobbie Phillips, Matt Birman, Nigel Bennett, Damon D'Oliveira, Kai Soremekun; **D:** Paul Ziller, Steve DiMarco; **W:** Karl Schiffman.

Back in Business 🦴🦴 1996 (R) Joe Elkhart's (Bosworth) life is down the drain. After failing to expose a fellow police officer as corrupt, he's kicked off the force, abandoned by his wife. Now working as a mechanic, Joe gets pulled back into the action when his ex-partner, Tony (Torry), goes undercover to bring down a major drug dealer and Joe discovers the corrupt cops that framed him are also behind the current heroin deal. **93m/C VHS.** Brian Bosworth, Joe Torry, Dara Tomanovich, Alan Scarfe, Brion James, Ron Glass; **D:** Philippe Mora; **W:** Ed Decatur, Ash Staley; **C:** Walter Bal.

Back in the Day 🦴🦴½ 2005 (R) Reggie Cooper (Ja Rule) is living with his successful, divorced father (Esposito) in an effort to stay away from the 'hood that nearly cost him his life. But when Reggie reconnects with gangster mentor J-Bone (Rhames) it can only mean trouble because J-Bone has some scores to settle. Reggie gets involved in the murder of a local preacher (Morton), but tries to keep his part a secret after he falls for the man's daughter (Ali). Now he must choose between old loyalties and new love. Decent effort with a familiar cast doing professional work. **103m/C DVD.** *US* Ja Rule, Ving Rhames, Tatyana Ali, Giancarlo Esposito, Pam Grier, Joe Morton, Tia Carrere, Frank Langella, Debbi (Deborah) Morgan, AJ Sapienza, Lahmard Tate; **D:** James Hunter; **W:** James Hunter, Michael Raffaniello; **C:** Donald M. Morgan; **M:** Robert Folk. **VIDEO**

Back in the Saddle 🦴½ 1941 Autry is a ranch foreman who discovers a nearby copper mine is poisoning his cattle. Gene manages to do a lot of singing in between the fist-fights. **71m/B VHS.** Gene Autry, Smiley Burnette, Mary Lee, Edward Norris; **D:** Lew Landers; **W:** Richard Murphy, Jesse Lasky Jr.; **C:** Ernest Miller.

Back in the USSR 🦴½ 1992 (R) Danger follows two lovers caught up in the Moscow underworld. When young American touring Russia unwittingly gets involved with a beautiful art thief. Lots of fast-paced action in an otherwise muddled film. The first American film shot entirely on location in Moscow. **87m/C VHS.** Frank Whaley, Natalia (Natalya) Negoda, Roman Polanski, Claudia Robinson, Dey Young, Andrew Divoff, Brian Blessed, Ravil Isyanov; **D:** Deran Sarafian; **C:** Yuri Neyman.

Back of Beyond 🦴🦴 1995 (R) Spectacular setting in the Australian outback can't make up for unfocused plot and characters with little impact. Tom (Mercurio) ran a remote desert gas station with his sister, Susan (Elmaloglou), before she was killed on his motorbike. When Connor's (Friels) car breaks down by the derelict station, he, girlfriend Charlie (Smart), and sidekick Nick (Polson) must wait while Tom tries to fix it. Only Connor is a diamond thief and patience isn't one of his virutes, especially when he notices the unhappy Charlie making friends with Tom. Mystical/supernatural elements involving ghosts and Aboriginal sites only add to the confusion. **84m/C VHS.** *AU* Paul Mercurio, Colin Friels, Dee Smart, John Polson, Rebekah Elmaloglou, Bob Maza, Terry Serio; **D:** Michael Robertson; **W:** Paul Leadon, A.M. Brosbank, Richard I. Sawyer; **C:** Stephen Dobson; **M:** Mark Moffatt, Wayne Goodwin.

Back Roads 🦴🦴 1981 (R) Southern hooker meets a down-on-his-luck boxer and both head out for a better life in California, finding love along the way. Ritt road trip lacks any comedic rhythm and survives on Field and Jones working to entertain. **94m/C VHS, DVD.** Sally Field, Tommy Lee Jones, David Keith; **D:** Martin Ritt; **W:** Gary De Vore; **C:** John A. Alonzo; **M:** Henry Mancini.

Back Street 🦴🦴½ 1941 Pretty Rae Stevens (Sullavan) falls in love with Walter Saxel (Boyer) but, thanks to a misunderstanding, they part company. They meet again five years later and, although Walter is married and has children, begin an affair. Over the years, Rae is to learn that the life of a mistress is a lonely one. Based on the novel by Fannie Hurst; also filmed in 1932 and 1961. **89m/B VHS.** Margaret Sullavan, Charles Boyer, Richard Carlson, Frank McHugh, Tim Holt, Frank Jenks, Esther Dale, Samuel S. Hinds; **D:** Robert Stevenson; **W:** Bruce Manning, Felix Jackson; **C:** William H. Daniels; **M:** Frank Skinner.

Back Street 🦴🦴 1961 The forbidden affair between a married man and a beautiful fashion designer carries on through many anxious years to a tragic end. The lavish third film version of the Fannie Hurst novel. **107m/C VHS.** Susan Hayward, John Gavin, Vera Miles; **D:** David Miller; **C:**

Back to Back 🦴 1990 (R) A beautiful young vigilante embarks on a rampage to clear her family's name and make her town's redneck crooks pay for their crimes. Never released in theatres. **95m/C VHS.** Bill Paxton, Todd Field, Apolonia, Luke Askew, Ben Johnson, David Michael-Standing, Susan Anspach, Sal Landi; **D:** John Kincade; **C:** James L. Carter.

Back to Back 🦴🦴½ 1996 (R) Ex-cop Malone (Rooker) must team up with hitman Koji (Ishibashi), who's holding Malone's daughter hostage, to double-cross a corrupt cop and stay alive while being hunted by the Mafia. **95m/C VHS, DVD.** Michael Rooker, Ryo Ishibashi, John Laughlin, Danielle Harris, Bob(cat) Goldthwait, Vincent Schiavelli; **D:** Roger Nygard; **M:** Lloyd Keith; **C:** Mark W. Gray; **M:** Walter Werzowa.

Back to Bataan 🦴🦴½ 1945 Colonel forms guerrilla army to raid Japanese in the Philippines and to help Americans landing on Leyte. Also available in a colorized version. **95m/B VHS, DVD.** John Wayne, Anthony Quinn, Beulah Bondi, Fely Franquelli, Richard Loo, Philip Ahn, Lawrence Tierney; **D:** Edward Dmytryk.

Back to Hannibal: The Return of Tom Sawyer and Huckleberry Finn 🦴🦴½ 1990 (PG-13) Mark Twain's characters Tom Sawyer and Huckleberry Finn are reunited as adults to solve a murder mystery. Tom is a lawyer, Finn a newspaper man, and it's Becky Thatcher's husband who's been murdered. Did a freed slave really commit the crime? **92m/C VHS.** Raphael Sbarge, Mitchell Anderson, Megan Follows, William Windom, Ned Beatty, Paul Krasny; **M:** Lee Holdridge. **TV**

Back to School 🦴🦴🦴½ 1986 (PG-13) Dangerfield plays an obnoxious millionaire who enrolls in college to help his wimpy son, Gordon, achieve campus stardom. His motto seems to be "if you can't buy it, can't be had." At first, his antics embarrass his shy son, but soon everyone is clamoring to be seen with the pair as Gordon develops his own self confidence. **96m/C VHS, DVD.** Rodney Dangerfield, Keith Gordon, Robert Downey Jr., Sally Kellerman, Burt Young, Paxton Whitehead, Adrienne Barbeau, M. Emmet Walsh, Sam Kinison, Kurt Vonnegut Jr., Robert Picardo, Terry Farrell, Edie McClurg, Jason Hervey, William Zabka; **D:** Alan Metter; **W:** Will Aldis, Steven Kampmann, Harold Ramis, Peter Torokvei; **C:** Thomas Ackerman; **M:** Danny Elfman.

Back to the Beach 🦴🦴 1987 (PG) Frankie and Annette return to the beach as self-parodying, middle-aged parents with rebellious kids, and the usual run of sun-bleached, lover's tiff comedy ensues. Plenty of songs and guest appearances from television past. Tries to bring back that surf, sun, and sand feel of the original "Beach Party" movies, but fails. ♪Absolute Perfection; California Sun; Catch a Ride; Jamaica Sky; Papa-Oom-Mow-Mow; Sign of Love; Sun, Sun, Sun, Sun; Surfin' Bird; Wooly Bully. **92m/C VHS, DVD.** Frankie Avalon, Annette Funicello, Connie Stevens, Lori Loughlin, Tommy Hinkley, Demian Slade, John Calvin, Joe Holland, David Bowe, Paul (Pee-wee Herman) Reubens, Don Adams, Bob Denver, Alan Hale Jr., Tony Dow, Jerry Mathers, Dick Dale, Stevie Ray Vaughan, Edd Byrnes, Barbara Billingsley; **D:** Lyndall Hobbs; **W:** James Komack, Bruce Surtees; **M:** Steve Dorff.

Back to the Future 🦴🦴🦴 1985 (PG) When neighborhood mad scientist Doc Brown (Lloyd) constructs a time machine from a DeLorean, his youthful companion Marty (Fox) accidentally transports himself to 1955. There, Marty must do everything he can to bring his high-school age parents together (so he can be born), elude the local bully, and get back...to the future. Solid fast-paced entertainment is even better due to Lloyd's inspired performance as the loony Doc while Fox is perfect as the boy completely out of his element. Soundtrack features Huey Lewis and the News. Followed by two sequels. **116m/C VHS, DVD.** Michael J. Fox, Christopher Lloyd, Lea Thompson, Crispin Glover, Wendie Jo Sperber, Marc McClure, Thomas F. Wilson, James Tolkan, Casey Siemaszko, Billy Zane, George Di-

Back to the Future, Part 2 🐾🐾½ 1989 (PG) Taking up exactly where Part 1 left off, Doc Brown and Marty time-hop into the future (2015 to be exact) to save Marty's kids, then find themselves returning to 1955 to retrieve a sports almanac that causes havoc for the McFly family. Clever editing allows for Marty Part 2 to see Marty Part 1 at the school dance. Most of the cast returns, although Glover appears only in cuts from the original and Shue steps in as girlfriend Jennifer. Not up to the original, but still satisfying. Bigger ending sets up Part 3, which was shot simultaneously with this. 107m/C VHS, DVD. *Cameos:* Huey Lewis; *W:* Robert Zemeckis, Bob Gale; *C:* Dean Cundey; *M:* Alan Silvestri. Michael J. Fox, Christopher Lloyd, Lea Thompson, Thomas F. Wilson, Harry Waters Jr., Charles Fleischer, Joe Flaherty, Elisabeth Shue, James Tolkan, Casey Siemaszko, Jeffrey Weissman, Flea, Billy Zane, J.J. (Jeffrey Jay) Cohen, Darlene Vogel, Jason Scott Lee, Crispin Glover, Ricky Dean Logan; *D:* Robert Zemeckis; *W:* Robert Zemeckis, Bob Gale; *C:* Dean Cundey; *M:* Alan Silvestri.

Back to the Future, Part 3 🐾🐾🐾 1990 (PG) Picks up where Part 2 climaxed à la California 1955, time-traveling hero Marty frantically searches for Doc Part 1 so he can return to 1985. Instead, he finds himself in the Wild West circa 1885, trying to save Doc's life. Plot is related to earlier BTTFs, so first time viewers might be confused. For those who've seen previous incarnations, they've clever interconnections are really nifty. Nearly matches the original for excitement and offers some snazzy new special effects. Supposedly the last installment, though don't be surprised if another sequel follows. The complete trilogy is available as a boxed set. 118m/C VHS, DVD. Michael J. Fox, Christopher Lloyd, Mary Steenburgen, Thomas F. Wilson, Lea Thompson, Elisabeth Shue, Matt Clark, Richard Dysart, Pat Buttram, Harry Carey Jr., Dub Taylor, Marc McClure, Wendie Jo Sperber, J.J. (Jeffrey Jay) Cohen, Ricky Dean Logan, Jeffrey Weissman; *D:* Robert Zemeckis; *W:* Robert Zemeckis, Bob Gale; *C:* Dean Cundey; *M:* Alan Silvestri.

Back to the Secret Garden 🐾🐾½ 2001 Well-meaning but dull sequel based on characters from the novel by Frances Hodgson Burnett. It's now the 1940s and sullen Mary has grown into the elegant Lady Mary (Lunghi), the wife of the ambassador to the U.S. Misterthwaite has turned into a severe English orphanage that is run by Martha (Plowright). Lady Mary arranges for Brooklyn-born orphan Lizzie (Buelle) to join their little band, and the young girl just happens to be a gardening whiz. Which is a good thing, since Mary's special garden has been badly neglected once again. 100m/C VHS, DVD. Camilla Belle, Cherie Lunghi, Joan Plowright, David Warner, Leigh Lawson, Florence Hoath; *D:* Michael Tuchner; *W:* Joe Wiesenfeld; *C:* Ian Wilson. *CABLE*

Back to the Wall 🐾🐾 1956 Moreau is an adulterous wife whose web of deceit results in a suspenseful tale of murder and blackmail. 94m/B VHS. FR Jeanne Moreau, Gerard Oury, Claire Maurier; *D:* Edouard Molinaro.

Backbeat 🐾🐾🐾 1994 (R) Backed by the beat of early Beatle tunes as rendered by some of today's top alternative musicians, the debut for director Softley explores the Fab Four's beginnings in Hamburg's underground music scene. Storyline is driven by the complications of a romantic triangle between John Lennon, Astrid Kirchherr (the photographer who came up with the bard's signature look) and Stu Sutcliffe, Lennon's best friend and the original bass player for the Beatles. Hart's dead-on as Lennon, playing him a second time (check out "The Hours and Times"). Energetic and enjoyable, particularly when the Was-produced music takes center stage. 100m/C VHS, DVD. *GB* Stephen Dorff, Sheryl Lee, Ian Hart, Gary Bakewell, Chris O'Neill, Scot Williams, Kai Wiesinger, Jennifer Ehle; *D:* Iain Softley; *W:* Michael Thomas, Stephen Ward, Iain Softley; *C:* Ian Wilson; *M:* Don Was.

Backdraft 🐾🐾½ 1991 (R) High action story of Chicago firemen has some of the most stupendous incendiary special effects ever filmed. But then there's that plot, B-movie hokum about a mystery arsonist torching strategic parts of the community with the finesse of an expert and a brother-against-brother conflict. Straightforward performances from most of the cast in spite of the weak storyline. Widen wrote from experience—he used to be a fireman; real-life Chicago firefighters were reportedly very happy with the realistic and intense fire scenes. Forget the plot and just watch the fires. Also available in a letterboxed version. 135m/C VHS, DVD, HD DVD. Kurt Russell, William Baldwin, Robert De Niro, Donald Sutherland, Jennifer Jason Leigh, Scott Glenn, Rebecca De Mornay, Jason Gedrick, J.T. Walsh, Tony Mockus Sr., Clint Howard, David Crosby; *D:* Ron Howard; *W:* Gregory Widen; *C:* Mikael Salomon; *M:* Hans Zimmer.

Backfield in Motion 🐾🐾 1991 Silly but harmless comedy about a widowed mom who tries to get closer to her high-schooler son by organizing a mother-son football game. But it's the boys' foot-ball coach who really wants to get close-to mom. TV movie debut of both Arnolds (past and present). 95m/C VHS, DVD. Roseanne, Tom Arnold, Colleen Camp, Conchata Ferrell, Johnny Galecki, Kevin Scannell; *D:* Richard Michaels. *TV*

Backfire 🐾🐾 1922 If you're gonna rob a bank, you shouldn't let anyone hear you plan it, and if you're not gonna rob a bank, you shouldn't let anyone hear you plan one. This vintage "Lightning" Carson crime western has Carson and friend suspected of bank robbery because someone heard their planning one. The sheriff follows their every footstep as they search for the rea perpetrators. 56m/B VHS. Jack Hoxie, George Sowards, Lew Meehan, Florence Gilbert; *D:* Alan James.

Backfire 🐾🐾 1988 (R) A mysterious stranger enters the lives of a disturbed 'Nam vet and his discontented wife, setting a pattern of murder and double-cross in motion. 90m/C VHS, DVD. Karen Allen, Keith Carradine, Jeff Fahey, Bernie Casey, Dinah Manoff, Dean Paul (Dino Martin Jr.) Martin; *D:* Gilbert Cates; *W:* Larry Brand; *M:* David Shire.

Backfire! 🐾½ 1994 (PG-13) Silly spoof finds Jeremy (Mosby) wanting to join New York City's all-female fire brigade who are trying to oust an arsonist from blowing up the city's toilets. Mitchum is the fire marshal and Ireland the mayor's charming assistant. 88m/C VHS, Shelley Winters; *D:* A. Dean Bell.

Backflash 🐾🐾 2001 (R) Ray (Patrick) runs a videostore and needs a little excitement in his life. He picks up pretty hitchhiker Harley (Esposito), who's just out of jail, and gets more than he's bargained for since Harley needs Ray to pretend to be her husband so she can get into a safety deposit box. But just who's conning who? 90m/C VHS, DVD. Robert Patrick, Jennifer Esposito, Melissa Joan Hart; *D:* Philip Jones; *W:* Philip Jones, Jennifer Farrell, Lillian Jackson; *C:* Maximo Munzi; *M:* Valentine Leone, Carl Wurtz.

Background to Danger 🐾🐾½ 1943 A suspenseful WWII actioner about American agent Raft who travels to Turkey to receive secret documents from the soon-to-be-murdered Massen. Greenstreet is the Nazi master spy who also wants the documents as do Russian spies Lorre and Marshall. Somewhat confusing p o t but fast-paced. Based on the thriller "Uncommon Danger" by Eric Ambler. This film was Warner Bros. follow-up to "Casablanca" with Raft in the Bogie role he had turned down in that cinema classic. 80m/B VHS. George Raft, Sydney Greenstreet, Peter Lorre, Brenda Marshall, Osa Massen, Turhan Bey, Kurt Katch; *D:* Raoul Walsh.

Backlash 🐾🐾½ 1986 (R) An aborigine barmaid is raped. When her assailant turns up dead, she's charged with murder and winds up in the custody of two police officers on a trip across the outback. Holes in the plot undermine this interest-ing, although graphic, drama with racial overtones. 88m/C VHS. *AU* David Argue, Gia Carides, Lydia Miller, Brian Syron, Anne Smith; *D:* Bill Bennett; *W:* Bill Bennett; *M:* Michael Spicer.

Backlash 🐾🐾 1999 (R) Federal prosecutor Gina Gallagher (Needham) has gotten on the wrong side of the Colombian drug cartel. After her partner is killed, Gina works with veteran homicide detective Moe Ryan (Durning) and uncovers a government conspiracy—so maybe trusting a convict (Belushi) to protect her isn't such a bad idea. 103m/C VHS, DVD. UMD: Tracey Needham, Charles Durning, James Plaine, Henry Silva, Warren Berlinger; *C:* Joakim (Jack) Ersgard; *M:* Patrick Ersgard. *VIDEO*

Backlash: Oblivion 2 🐾🐾½ *Oblivion 2* 1995 (PG-13) Galactic supervillainess. Lash stakes her claim to a rare decorium mine on the remote space outpost of Oblivion. Will cave monsters thwart her evil plan for total domination? 82m/C VHS, DVD. Andrew Divoff, Meg Foster, Isaac Hayes, Julie Newmar, Carel Struycken, George Takei, Musetta Vander, Jimmie F. Skaggs, Irwin Keyes, Maxwell Caulfield; *D:* Sam Irvin; *W:* Peter David; *M:* Pino Donaggio.

Backstab 🐾🐾 1990 (R) A spellbinding tale of work, lust, and murder. Architect Brolin finds himself unable to get over the death of his wife, until a seductive and mysterious woman helps him over his grief. They spend the night together, engulfed in passion, but in the morning he wakes to find himself sleeping with the corpse of his boss. Only the first twist in this intriguing thriller. 91m/C VHS. James Brolin, Meg Foster, Isabelle Truchon; *D:* Jim Kaufman.

Backstairs 🐾🐾 1921 An obscure German silent film about urban degradation and familial strife. 44m/B VHS. *GE* Henny Porten, Fritz Kortner, William Dieterle; *D:* Leopold Jessner.

Backstairs at the White House 🐾🐾🐾½ 1979 Drawn from Lillian Rogers Parks' 1961 novel "My Thirty Years Backstairs at the White House" and originally aired on NBC, recounts the head maid's real life as she works for eight presidents—from Taft through Eisenhower—and narrates a wide array of historical events during her 52 years of service. 540m/C VHS, DVD. Olivia Cole, Leslie Uggams, Louis Gossett Jr., Robert Hooks, Paul Winfield, Cloris Leachman, Hari Rhodes, Helen Carroll, Ruby Dee, Lee Grant, Larry Gates, Eileen Heckart, Claire Bloom, Celeste Holm, George Kennedy, Ed Flanders, Leslie Nielsen, Harry Morgan, Estelle Parsons, Jean Stapleton, Barbara Barrie, Andrew Duggan, Heather Angel, Marlyn Chris, Tom Carey, Ann Doran, BeBe Drake, Kevin Hooks, Nancy Morgan, Harrison Page, Woodrow Parfrey, Bill Quinn, Fonz Rainey, John Randolph, Noble William, Dana Wynter, Jean Wynter; *W:* Paul Dubov; *C:* Michael O'Reilly; *M:* Morton Stevens. *TV*

Backstreet Dreams 🐾🐾 1990 (R) The young parents of an autistic child find themselves torn apart due to their feelings of guilt. The father has an affair with a specialist hired to help the boy, causing further strife. Interesting story possibilities never get far. 104m/C VHS, Brooke Shields, Jason O'Malley, Sherilyn Fenn, Tony Fields, Burt Young, Anthony (Tony) Franciosa, Nick Cassavetes, Ray "Boom Boom" Mancini; *D:* Rupert Hitzig; *M:* Bill Conti.

Backstreet Justice 🐾🐾½ 1993 (R) Pittsburgh PI Keri Finnegan (Kozlowski) is investigating a series of murders in her neighborhood when she uncovers ties to police corruption dating back 30 years. This doesn't make her popular since it involves her nice dead cop father and a number of old friends (and enemies). Kozlowski is appropriately feisty and the plot twists will hold your attention. 91m/C VHS. Linda Kozlowski, Hector Elizondo, John Shea, Paul Sorvino, Viveca Lindfors, Tammy Grimes; *D:* Chris T. McIntyre; *W:* Chris T. McIntyre.

Backtrack 🐾🐾🐾 1989 (R) Catchfire 1989 (R) Federal agent Foster co-stars in this thriller about an artist who accidentally witnesses a mob hit. The mob puts a hitman (Hopper) on her trail, and after studying her background and listening to audio tapes she recorded, he finds himself falling in love. Originally intended for a theatrical release, it hit the European screens in a different cut as "Catchfire"; Hopper restored his original version and it was released on cable TV in the U.S. 102m/C VHS, DVD. Dennis Hopper, Jodie Foster, Dean Stockwell, Vincent Price, John Turturro, Fred Ward, Sy Richardson, Helena Kallianiotes, Bob Dylan; *Cameos:* Charlie Sheen, Joe Pesci; *D:* Dennis Hopper; *W:* Ann Louise Bardach; *M:* Michel Colombier.

Backwoods 🐾 1987 (R) Two campers wish they had never encountered a mountain man wr'en he begins to stalk them wth murder in mind. 90m/C VHS, DVD. Jack O'Hara, Dick Kreusser, Brad Armaoct; *D:* Dean Crow.

The Bad and the Beautiful 🐾🐾🐾½ 1952 The rise and fall of a Hollywood producer. Douglas stars as the ruthless, arrogant Jonathan Shields, who alienates actress Georgia (Turner), writer James Lee Bartlow (Powell), and director Fred Amiel (Sullivan) as he pursues his career. Much speculation at the time as to who the real-life models were. Winner of five Oscars; a splendid drama. 118m/B VHS, DVD. Kirk Douglas, Lana Turner, Dick Powell, Gloria Grahame, Barry Sullivan, Walter Pidgeon, Gilbert Roland, eo G. Carroll; *D:* Vincente Minnelli; *W:* Charles Schnee; *C:* Robert L. Surtees. *DVD.* Oscars '52: Art Dir/Set Dec, B&W, B&W Cinematog., Support. Actress (Grahame), Natl Film Reg. '02.

Bad Attitude 🐾🐾 1993 (R) Leon is a narcotics officer on a mission to restore his badge after his careless pistol work gets him bootiec cff the force. The quick-tempered cop relentlessly pursues drug-lord Finque with the help of an open-minded preacher (De Veaux) and his sexy, streetwise assistant (Lim). 87m/C VHS, DVD. Leon, Gina Lim, Nathaniel DeVeaux, Susan Firque; *D:* Bill Cummings.

Bad Behavior 🐾🐾½ 1992 (R) Unscripted character-driven drama. Gerry and Ellie McAllister are an Irish couple living in North London. He's tired of working for the local planning commission, and had the actors improvise their dialogue, in character, over a long rehearsal period to develop their roles. 103m/C VHS. DVD. *GB* Stephen Rea, Sinead Cusack, Philip Jackson, Clare Higgins, Phil Daniels, Sara Todd; *D:* Les Blair; *M:* John Altman.

Bad Blood 🐾🐾 1987 The true story of Stan Graham, who went on a killing spree in the New Zealand bush when his farm was foreclosed and his life ruined. 104m/C VHS. *NZ* Jack Thompson, Carol Burns, Dennis (Denis) Lill; *D:* Mike Newell.

Bad Blood 🐾½ 1994 (R) Travis Blackstone (Lamas) will use any methods to protect his brother Franklin, who's targeted for death by a ruthless drug lord. Lots of action and violence. 90m/C VHS. Lorenzo Lamas, Hank Cheyne, Frankie Thorn, Kimberley Kates, Joe Son; *D:* Tibor Takacs; *W:* Neil Ruttenberg; *C:* Bernard Salzmann.

Bad Boy 🐾½ *Branded* 1939 A country boy goes to the big city, and succumbs to urban evils and temptations, but is eventually saved by true mother love. 60m/B VHS. Johnny Downs, Frankie Thom, Kim-berley Kates, Helen MacKellar, Rosalind Keith, Holmes Herbert; *D:* Kurt Neumann.

Bad Boy Bubby 🐾🐾 1993 Bizarre black comedy about the extremely maladjusted Bubby (Hope), who becomes a pop culture phenomena. The 35-year-old childlike Bubby has been kept a virtual prisoner by his monstrous mom, who has told him the world outside is filled with poisonous gas. Bubby wraps it in plastic wrap and is puzzled when it dies. Still, this gives Bubby an idea—he wraps mom in plastic and escapes outside, where he's soon adopted by a struggling rock band that writes a cult song that he about his experiences. It's even stranger than it sounds. **114m/C VHS, DVD.** *IT AU* Nicholas Hope, Claire Benito, Carmel Johnson, Ralph Cotterill, Norman Kaye, Paul Philpot, Graham Duckett, Bridget Walters; **D:** Rolf de Heer; **W:** Rolf de Heer; **M:** Graham Tardif. Australian Film Inst. '94: Actor (Hope), Director (de Heer), Film Editing, Orig. Screenplay.

Bad Boys ✶✶✶ *1983* (R) When a gang member's little brother is killed in a rumble, the teen responsible (Penn, who else?) goes to a reformatory, where he quickly (though somewhat reluctantly) takes charge. Meanwhile, on the outside, his rival attacks Penn's girlfriend (Sheedy, in her feature film debut) in retaliation, is incarcerated, and ends up vying with Penn for control of the cell block. Backed into a corner by their mutual hatred and escalating peer pressure, the two are pushed over the brink into a final and shattering confrontation. Not as violent as it could be. To its credit, attempts to communicate a message. **104m/C VHS, DVD.** Sean Penn, Esai Morales, Reni Santoni, Jim Moody, Eric Gurry, Ally Sheedy, Clancy Brown; **D:** Rick Rosenthal; **W:** Richard Dilello; **C:** Donald E. Thorin; **M:** Bill Conti.

Bad Boys ✶✶✶½ *1995* (R) And you thought the old buddy-cop formula was played out. Well, Hollywood sticks with what works, and pairing the two TV personalities definitely works at the minimalist level required. Mike (Smith) and Marcus (Lawrence) are Miami cops who must track down $100 million worth of heroin stolen from their evidence room before internal affairs shuts down the precinct. The case leads them to a vicious thief and a beautiful female witness to his murderous handiwork. Plot lacks depth, but high energy and dazzling action sequences keep things moving. Loud adventure is made louder still by cranking soundtrack. Satisfying addition to the odd-couple cops genre with potential to spawn a "Lethal Weapon"-type franchise. Feature film debut for director Bay. **118m/C VHS, DVD.** Martin Lawrence, Will Smith, Tcheky Karyo, Tea Leoni, Theresa Randle, Marg Helgenberger, Joe Pantoliano, John Salley, Nestor Serrano, Michael Imperioli, Julio Oscar Mechoso; **D:** Michael Bay; **W:** Michael Barrie, Jim Mulholland; **C:** Howard Atherton; **M:** Mark Mancina. Blockbuster '96: Male Newcomer, T. (Smith).

Bad Boys 2 ✶✶ *2003* (R) Bombastic sequel finds Miami narcs Mike Lowrey (Smith) and Marcus Burnett (Lawrence) going after a violent network of Ecstasy dealers. The duo also has personal problems when Mike falls for Marcus' sister, Syd (Union), an undercover cop. Meanwhile, Marcus ponders whether he wants to remain partners with Mike, and whether, in classic Det. Murtaugh style, he's getting too old for this...stuff. Typical action-flick paper-thin plot doesn't stop Smith and Lawrence from clicking as a comedy-action team. Since this flick is basically the original, amped up to a ridiculous degree, your enjoyment will hinge on your opinion of that one, and your tolerance for the Bruckheimer-Bay "make-go-boom!" style. **146m/C VHS, DVD, UMD.** *US* Will Smith, Martin Lawrence, Gabrielle Union, Joe Pantoliano, Theresa Randle, Jordi Molla, Peter Stormare, Michael Shannon, Jon Seda, Yul Vazquez, Henry Rollins, Jason Manuel Olazabal, Otto Sanchez; **D:** Michael Bay; **W:** Ron Shelton, Jerry Stahl; **C:** Amit M. Mokri.

Bad Bunch ✶ *1976* A white liberal living in Watts tries to befriend a ruthless black street gang, but is unsuccessful. **82m/C VHS.** Greydon Clark, Tom Johnigam, Pamela Corbett, Jacqulin Cole, Aldo Ray, Jock Mahoney; **D:** Greydon Clark.

B.A.D. Cats ✶ *1980* Two members of a police burglary auto detail team chase after a group of car thieves who are planning a million-dollar gold heist. **74m/C VHS.** Asher Brauner, Michelle Pfeiffer, Vic Morrow, Jimmie Walker, Steve Hanks, LaWanda Page; **D:** Bernard L. Kowalski.

Bad Channels ✶✶ *1992* (R) Radio goes awry when female listeners of station KDUL are shrunk and put into specimen jars by an evil disc jockey and a visiting alien, who plans to take the women back to his planet. Mildly amusing comedy features ex-MTV VJ Quinn and score by Blue Oyster Cult. Also available with Spanish subtitles. **88m/C VHS.** Paul Hipp, Martha Quinn, Aaron Lustig, Ian Patrick Williams, Charlie Spradling, Tim Thomerson, Sonny Carl Davis, Robert Factor, Michael Huddleston; **D:** Ted Nicolaou; **W:** Jackson Barr; **C:** Adolfo Bartoli.

Bad Charleston Charlie Woof! *1973* (PG) Dud of a gangster comedy with terrible acting. A comedy? **91m/C VHS.** Ross Hagen, Kelly Thordsen, John Carradine, Hoke Howell, Carmen Zapata; **D:** Ivan Nagy; **W:** Ross Hagen, Ivan Nagy; **M:** Stan Kamber; **C:** Albert Aley; **M:** Luchi De Jesus.

Bad City ✶✶ *Dirty Work 2006* (R) Yes, gnomish Pendleton is playing a depraved Chicago crime lord named Julian Healy and he's scarily effective. Derek Manning (Reddick) is a tough detective with a gambling problem who is in debt to Healy, which makes investigating the murder of hooker Bridgette (McDonough) difficult. Then there's too-slick politico Frank Sullivan (McGlone) whose troublesome wife (Anglin) is also killed. **97m/C DVD.** Lance Reddick, Mike McGlone, Austin Pendleton, Nutsa Kukhianidze, Tim Decker, Meghan Maureen McDonough, Karin Anglin; **D:** Bruce Terris; **W:** Bruce Terris, Rick Rose; **C:** David Blood; **M:** Mark Messing.

Bad Company ✶✶✶ *1972* (PG) Thoughtful study of two very different Civil War draft dodgers roaming the Western frontier and eventually turning to a fruitless life of crime. Both the cast and script are wonderful in an entertaining film that hasn't been given the attention it's due. **94m/C VHS, DVD.** Jeff Bridges, Barry Brown, Jim Davis, John Savage; **D:** Robert Benton; **W:** Robert Benton, David Newman; **C:** Gordon Willis.

Bad Company ✶✶½ *1994* (R) Cynical thriller pits the bad against the worst. Vic Grimes (Langella) and Margaret Wells (Barkin) run a company of former secret agents who specialize in corporate dirty tricks. Nelson Crowe (Fishburne) is an ex-CIA agent who's their latest recruit. But maybe he's not so ex and maybe Margaret doesn't like sharing power and maybe the cold-blooded duo will get together to make some changes. Everything is stylish, including the leads, but there's a definite chill in the air. **118m/C VHS, DVD.** Ellen Barkin, Laurence Fishburne, Frank Langella, Michael Beach, Gia Carides, David Ogden Stiers, Spalding Gray, James Hong, Daniel Hugh-Kelly; **D:** Damian Harris; **W:** Ross Thomas; **C:** Jack N. Green; **M:** Carter Burwell.

Bad Company ✶✶½ *Mauvaises Frequentations 1999* Delphine (Forget) is a typically dissatisfied middle-class teen susceptible to her more-worldly peers, which include the attitudinal, punked-out Olivia (Dollon). Olivia takes Delphine clubbing and she meets requisite smoldering bad boy, Laurent (Stevenin). Delphine's hormones are soon out of control and she agrees to some very questionable suggestions to prove her "love." Frank and unsettling. French with subtitles. **98m/C VHS, DVD.** *FR* Maud Forget, Lou Doillon, Robinson Stevenin, Maxime Mansion, Delphine Rich, Rene Berleand, Micheline Presle, Cyril Cagnat; **D:** Jean-Pierre Ameris; **W:** Alain Layrac; **C:** Yves Vandermeeren; **M:** Lene Marlin, Giya Kanchell.

Bad Company ✶✶ *2002* (PG-13) Hustler Rock discovers his twin brother was a CIA operative who has just been murdered. He gets recruited by agency honcho Hopkins to take over his bro's assignment, which involves terrorists, bombs, and New York City. Considering these elements, it's no wonder this one got delayed. Rock deserves a better movie, but he almost salvages this one, anyway...almost. He's up against a standard-issue plot that merely serves to get to the next action set piece which, this being a Bruckheimer production, are done well, but done too often. Schumacher manages to (mostly) subdue his worst instincts (see "Batman & Robin" to watch him surrender to them completely), but it doesn't really help. **111m/C VHS, DVD.** *US* Chris Rock, Anthony Hopkins, Matthew Marsh, Garcelle Beauvais, Kerry Washington, Gabriel Macht, Peter Stormare, John Slattery, Adoni Maropis, Brooke Smith; **D:** Joel Schumacher; **W:** Michael Browning, Jason Richman; **C:** Darius Wolski; **M:** Trevor Rabin.

Bad Day at Black Rock ✶✶✶½ *1954* Story of a one-armed man uncovering a secret in a Western town. Wonderful performances from all concerned, especially Borgnine. Fine photography, shot using the new Cinemascope technique. Based on the novel by Howard Breslin. **81m/C VHS, DVD.** Spencer Tracy, Robert Ryan, Anne Francis, Dean Jagger, Walter Brennan, John Ericson, Ernest Borgnine, Lee Marvin; **D:** John Sturges; **C:** William Mellor; **M:** Andre Previn. Cannes '55: Actor (Tracy).

Bad Dreams ✶✶½ *1988* (R) The only surviving member of a suicidal religious cult from the '60s awakens in 1988 from a coma. She is pursued by the living-dead cult leader, who seeks to ensure that she lives up (so to speak) to the cult's pact. Blood begins flowing as her fellow therapy group members begin dying, but the only bad dreams you'd get from this flick would be over the money lost on the video rental. **84m/C VHS, DVD.** Bruce Abbott, Jennifer Rubin, Richard Lynch, Harris Yulin, Dean Cameron, Elizabeth (E.G. Dailey) Daily, Susan Ruttan, Charles Fleischer, Sy Richardson; **D:** Andrew Fleming; **W:** Andrew Fleming, Steven E. de Souza; **C:** Alexander Grusynski; **M:** Jay Ferguson.

Bad Education ✶✶✶ *La Mala Educacion 2004* Complicated film noir begins in 1980 Madrid where young movie director Enrique (Martinez) is seeking inspiration. It comes to him, literally, when old school friend Ignacio (Garcia Bernal) turns up and hands Enrique a story he's written about the sexual abuse he suffered at the hands of the principal of their Catholic boys' school. But something is wrong—and it's not just the fact that the wannabe actor returns demanding to play the part of transsexual prostitute Zahara (Garcia Bernal again—making quite a pretty woman) in the film, which plays out in Enrique's mind so you're watching two films at once. And if that's not confusing enough, the film has flashbacks to the boys' schooldays and a subsequent meeting in 1977. Somehow Almodovar makes it work. Spanish with subtitles. **104m/C DVD.** Fele Martinez, Gael Garcia Bernal, Lluis Homar, Javier Camara, Petra Martinez, Nacho Perez, Raul Garcia Forneiro, Juan Fernandez, Daniel Gimenez Cacho, Lluis Homar, Alberto Ferreiro, Francisco Boira; **D:** Pedro Almodovar; **W:** Pedro Almodovar; **C:** Jose Luis Alcaine; **M:** Alberto Iglesias.

Bad Georgia Road ✶✶½ *1977* (R) A New Yorker inherits a moonshine operation from her uncle, and fights off the syndicate for its profits. **85m/C VHS.** Gary Lockwood, Carol Lynley, Royal Dano, John Wheeler, John Kerry; **D:** John Broderick.

Bad Girls ✶✶½ *1994* (R) Latest in the current western craze turns the tables as women take their turns being the gunslingers. Four hooker chums hastily flee town after one kills a nasty customer—only to find the bank where their cash was stashed was robbed by baddies Loggia and Russo. Wearing stylish duds and with each hair perfectly in place the beauties manage to recover their loot. Unexciting script leaves a lot to be desired, but a strong performance from Stowe makes this nearly worthwhile. Lots of off-set drama with original director Tamra Davis fired, and the actresses reportedly having a less-than-bonding experience. **99m/C VHS, DVD.** Andie MacDowell, Madeleine Stowe, Mary Stuart Masterson, Drew Barrymore, James Russo, Dermot Mulroney, Robert Loggia, James LeGros, Nicholas Chinlund, Will MacMillan, Jim Beaver; **D:** Jonathan Kaplan; **W:** Ken Friedman, Yolande Finch; **M:** Jerry Goldsmith.

Bad Girls Do Cry Woof! *1954* Unbelievably bad exploitation film. Idiotic plot with long scenes of girls stripping down to their undies. Although an American film, the voice track was dubbed in later. **59m/B VHS, DVD.** Bill Page, Misty Ayers, Heather English, Ben Frommer; **D:** Sid Melton.

Bad Girls Dormitory ✶✶ *1984* (R) At the New York Female Juvenile Reformatory, suicide seems a painless and welcome escape. Utilizes standard genre identifiers, including rape, drugs, soapy showers, bad docs, and desperate young women trapped in a web of frustration and desire. Cheap and mindless titillation. **95m/C VHS, DVD.** Carey Zuris, Teresa Farley; **D:** Tim Kincaid.

Bad Girls from Mars Woof! *1990* (R) "B" movie sleaze-o-rama in which everyone is murdered, either before, after, or during sex, just like in real life. When the director of the film within this film hires an actress who is, shall we say, popular, to be the heroine of his latest sci-fier, the fun, slim as it is, begins. **86m/C VHS, DVD.** Edy Williams, Brinke Stevens, Jay Richardson, Oliver Darrow, Dana Bentley, Jeffrey Culver, Jasae; **D:** Fred Olen Ray; **W:** Sherman Scott, Mark Thomas McGee; **C:** Gary Graver; **M:** Chuck Cirino.

Bad Girls Go to Hell Woof! *1965* From the sultana of sleaze, Wishman, comes this winning entry into Joe Bob Briggs' "Sleaziest Movies in the History of the World" series. A ditsy-but-sexy housewife accidentally commits murder and what follows is a plethora of perversion involving hirsute men and gender-bending women who are hell-bent on showing her how hot it is where bad girls go. **98m/B VHS, DVD.** Gigi Darlene, George La Rocque, Sam Stewart, Sandee Norman, Marlene Starr, Harold Key; **D:** Doris Wishman; **W:** Doris Wishman, Dawn Whitman; **C:** C. Davis Smith.

Bad Guys ✶✶ *1979* A goulash western about the outlaw days of Hungary in the 1860s. A gang of bandits terrorizes the Transdanubian countryside. An Hungarian with English subtitles. For those seeking the Eastern European Wild West experience. **93m/C VHS.** *HU* Janos Derzsi, Djoko Rosic, Mari Kiss, Gyorgy Dorner, Laszlo Szabo, Miklos Benedek; **D:** Gyorgy Szomjas.

Bad Guys ✶✶ *1986* (PG) An inane comedy about two ridiculous policeman who decide to take the wrestling world by storm after being kicked off the police force. Featuring scenes with many of the world's most popular wrestlers. **86m/C VHS.** Adam Baldwin, Mike Jolly, Michelle Nicastro, Ruth Buzzi, James Booth, Gene LeBell, Norman Burton; **D:** Joel Silberg; **C:** Hanania Baer; **M:** William Goldstein.

Bad Influence ✶✶½ *1990* (R) A lackluster effort in the evil-doppelganger school of psychological mystery, where a befuddled young executive (Spader) is led into the seamier side of life by a mysterious stranger (Lowe). **99m/C VHS, DVD.** Rob Lowe, James Spader, Lisa Zane, Christian Clemenson, Kathleen Wilhoite; **D:** Curtis Hanson; **C:** Robert Elswit; **M:** Trevor Jones.

Bad Jim ✶✶½ *1989* (PG) A cowpoke buys Billy the Kid's horse and, upon riding it, becomes an incorrigible outlaw himself. First feature film for Hollywood legend Clark Gable's son. **110m/C VHS.** James Brolin, Richard Roundtree, John Clark Gable, Harry Carey Jr., Ty Hardin, Pepe Serna, Rory Calhoun; **D:** Clyde Ware.

Bad Lands ✶✶✶ *1939* A small cowboy posse finds themselves trapped by a band of Apache Indians in the Arizona desert. A remake of "The Lost Patrol." **70m/B VHS.** Robert Barrat, Guinn "Big Boy" Williams, Douglas Walton, Andy Clyde, Addison Richards, Robert Coote, Paul Hurst, Noah Beery Jr.; **D:** Lew Landers.

Bad Lieutenant ✶✶✶ *1992* (NC-17) Social chaos and degeneration characterize story as well as nameless loner lieutenant Keitel, who is as corrupt as they come. Assigned to a case involving a raped nun, he's confronted by his own lagging Catholic beliefs and the need for saving grace. From cult filmmaker Ferrara ("Ms. 45") and filled with violence, drugs, and grotesque sexual situations. Tense, over-the-top, urban drama is not intended for seekers of the subtle. Rent it with "Reservoir Dogs" and prepare yourself for a long tense evening of top-rated Keitel and screen-splitting violence. "R" rated version is also available at 91 minutes. **96m/C** VHS, DVD. Harvey Keitel, Brian McElroy, Frankie Acciarito, Peggy Gormley, Stella Keitel, Victor Argo, Paul Calderon, Leonard Thomas, Frankie Thorn; **C:** Ken Kelsch; **M:** Joe Lund, Abel Ferrara; **C:** Abel Ferrara; **M:** Zoe Lund; **Ind. Spirit '93:** Actor (Keitel).

The Bad News Bears 🐾🐾🐾🐾 1976 (PG) Family comedy about a misfit Little League team that gets whipped into shape by a cranky, sloppy, beer-drinking coach who recruits a female pitcher. O'Neal and Matthau are top-notch. Spawned two sequels and a TV series. **102m/C** VHS, DVD, Walter Matthau, Tatum O'Neal, Vic Morrow, Joyce Van Patten, Jackie Earle Haley, Chris Barnes, Erin Blunt, Jaime Escobedo, Scott Firestone, George Gonzales, Brett Marx, David Pollock, Gary Cavagnaro, Alfred Lutter, David Stambaugh, Brandon Cruz, Jaime Escobedo; **D:** Michael Ritchie; **W:** Bill Lancaster; **C:** John A. Alonzo; **M:** Jerry Fielding. Writers Guild '76; Orig. Screenplay.

The Bad News Bears 🐾🐾 2005 (PG-13) Here's some bad news: Indie darling Linklater hit a home run with his kid-friendly "School of Rock," but he couldn't squeeze any life out of this watered-down remake of the 1976 Walter Matthau classic. It's disturbing that the updated "Bears" is a million times less subversive, vulgar, and (let's face it) funny than the original, a film that was released almost thirty years ago. Isn't society supposed to be declining? Shouldn't Linklater's move be raunchier than a film released during the Carter administration? Casting Thornton in the lead was an inspired choice, but the toothless script just forces him to do the PG version of his "Bad Santa" routine. Do yourself a favor and rent the original. **111m/C** DVD, UMD, US Billy Bob Thornton, Greg Kinnear, Marcia Gay Harden, Tyler Patrick Jones, Sammi Kraft, Timmy Deters, Ridge Canipe, Brandon Craggs, Jeff Davies, Carter Jenkins, Jeffrey Tedmori, Troy Gentile, Carlos Estrada, Emmanuel Estrada, Kenneth Carlos Estrada; **D:** Richard Linklater; **W:** Glenn Ficarra, John Requa, Bill Lancaster; **C:** Rogier Stoffers; **M:** Ed Shearmur, Randall Poster.

The Bad News Bears Go to Japan 🐾 1978 (PG) The second sequel, in which the Little League team goes to Tokyo, Japan. Comic adventure features Curtis as a talent agent out to exploit the team's fame. **92m/C** VHS, DVD. Tony Curtis, Jackie Earle Haley, Tomisaburo Wakayama, George Wyner, Erin Blunt, George Gonzales, Brett Marx, David Pollock, David Stambaugh, Regis Phibini; **D:** John Berry; **W:** Bill Lancaster; **C:** Gene Polito; **M:** Paul Chihara.

The Bad News Bears in Breaking Training 🐾🐾 1977 (PG) The Bears get a chance to take on the Houston Toros for a shot at the little league baseball Japanese champs, the Bears devise a way to get to Texas to play at the famed Astrodome. Disappointing sequel to "The Bad News Bears"; followed by "The Bad News Bears Go to Japan" (1978). **99m/C** VHS, DVD, William Devane, Clifton James, Jackie Earle Haley, Jimmy Baio, Chris Barnes, Erin Blunt, George Gonzales, Jaime Escobedo, Jackie Earle Haley, Jimmy Baio; **D:** Michael Pressman; **W:** Paul Brickman; **C:** Fred W. Koenekamp; **M:** Craig Safan.

The Bad Pack 🐾1/2 1998 (R) Soldier of fortune puts together a team when he's hired to defend a town besieged by a sadistic militia. **93m/C** VHS, DVD. Robert Davi, Ralph (Raif) Moeller, Roddy Piper, Brent Huff, Larry B. Scott, Patrick Dollaghan, Marshall Teague; **D:** Brent Huff. **VIDEO**

Bad Reputation 🐾🐾🐾 2005 (R) Chillingly disturbing portrayal of victim's revenge. Michelle, though poor, attends an affluent school on scholarship. She chooses to keep buried in a book rather than mix with the shallow class populous. One night at a party, she is drugged and gang-raped. A metamorphosis follows, as the shy, smart, attractive girl becomes an avenging assassin, swiftly wiping out all who humiliated her. Excellent character development, smart script, and bright directing make for a very satisfying retaliation tale. **90m/C** DVD. Angelique Hennessy, Jerad Anderson, Danielle Noble, Mark Kunzman, Kristina Concer; **D:** Jim Hemphill; **W:** Jim Hemphill; **C:** Forrest Allison; **M:** John LeBoe, Eric Chronzy. **VIDEO**

Bad Ronald 🐾🐾🐾 1974 No, not a political biography of Ronald Reagan... Fascinating thriller about a disturbed teenager who kills a friend after being harassed repeatedly. The plot thickens after the boy's mother dies, and he is forced to hide out in a secret room when an unsuspecting family with three daughters moves into his house. The story is accurately recreated from the novel by John Holbrook Vance. **78m/C** VHS, Scott Jacoby, Pippa Scott, John Larch, Dabney Coleman, Kim Hunter, John Fiedler. **TV**

Bad Santa 🐾🐾1/2 2003 (R) This is not your grandparents' Christmas movie. Or your kids' for that matter. Thornton as the joke of the cuo, who berates Willie for letting his liquor-soaked ways interfere with the job. When they set up shop in Phoenix, things get complicated when a dough, outcast kid leeches onto Willie. Sentimentality is crushed beneath the g g to rob the store safe on Christmas Eve. His partner is sidekick/elf Marcus, the meek store manager. **91m/C** VHS, DVD. Billy Bob Thornton, Tony Cox, Lauren Graham, Brett Kelly, John Ritter, Bernie Mac, Lauren Tom, Cloris Leachman; **D:** Terry Zwigoff; **W:** Glenn Ficarra; **C:** John Requa; **M:** David Kitay.

Bad Seed 🐾🐾 1985 TV remake of the movie with the same name. Story about a sadistic little child who kills for her own evil purposes. Acting is not up to par with previous version. **100m/C VHS** Blair Brown, Lynn Redgrave, David Carradine, Richard Kiley, David Ogden Stiers, Carrie Wells, Chad Allen, Christa Denton, Anne Haney, Eve Smith; **D:** Paul Wendkos; **M:** Paul Chihara. **TV**

Bad Seed 🐾🐾1/2 1956 A mother makes the tortuous discovery that her chirpy eight-year-old daughter harbors an innate desire to kill. Based on Maxwell Anderson's powerful Broadway stage play. **129m/B** VHS, DVD, Patty McCormack, Nancy Kelly, Eileen Heckart, Henry Jones, Evelyn Varden, Paul Fix, Jesse White, Gage Clark, Joan Croyden, Paul Fix, Jesse White; **D:** Mervyn LeRoy; **W:** John Lee Mahin; **C:** Harold Rossom; **M:** Alex North. Golden Globes '57: Support. Actress (Heckart).

Bad Taste 🐾🐾🐾 1988 A definite pleaser 'or the person who enjoys watching starving aliens devour the average, everyday human being. Alien fast-food manufacturers come to earth in hopes of harvesting all of mankind. The earth's fate lies in the hands of the government who must stop these rampaging creatures before the world as seen through the eyes of humor tists. **90m/C VHS**, DVD, JP Toshiro Mifune, Masayuki Kato, Masayuki Mori, Takashi Shimura, Akira Nishimura; **D:** Akira Kurosawa; **W:** Akira Kurosawa, Shinobu Hashimoto, Ryuzo Kikushime, Hideo Oguni; **C:** Yuzuru Aizawa; **M:** Masaru Sato.

Baffled 🐾🐾1/2 1972 Nimoy is a race car driver who has visions of people in danger. He must convince an ESP expert (Hampshire) of t e credibility of his vision, and then try to save the lives of the people seen with his sixth sense. **90m/C VHS**, Leonard Nimoy, Susan Hampshire, Vera Miles, Rachel Roberts, Jewel Blanch, Christopher Benjamin; **D:** Philip Leacock. **TV**

Bagdad 🐾🐾 1949 Arabian nights story with the lovely O'Hara starring as Princess Marjan, the daughter of a sheik. She returns from England to find her father murdered and his sixth sense group known as The Black Riders. Turkish Pasha A. Nadim (Price) lurking sinisterly, as well. **83m/C** VHS, Maureen O'Hara, Paul (Price) lurking sinisterly; **M:** Russell Metty.

Bagdad Cafe 🐾🐾1/2 Out of Rosenheim 1988 (PG) A large German woman, played by Sagebrecht, finds herself stranded in the Mojave desert after her husband dumps her on the side of the highway. She encounters a rundown cafe where she becomes involved with the offbeat residents. A hilarious story in which their situations are treated kindly and not

---

Bad Love 🐾1/2 1995 (R) Un-lucky Eloise (Gidley) stays true to nature when she falls for loser Lenny (Sizemore), who decides the big score lies with robbing the fading movie star (O'Neill). Eloise works for. Naturally, things go badly. Slick production for anyone who likes fringe ro mances. **93m/C** VHS, DVD. Tom Sizemore, Pamela Gidley, Debi Mazar, Jennifer O'Neil, Margaux Hemingway, Richard Edson, Seymour Cassel, Joe Dallesandro; **D:** Jill Goldman; **C:** Gary Tieche; **M:** Rico Cox.

Bad Man of Deadwood 🐾 1941 A man-with-a-past joins a circus as a sharp-shooter, and is threatened with disclosure. **54m/B** VHS, DVD. Roy Rogers, George "Gabby" Hayes, Carol Adams, Henry (Kleinbach) Brandon, Herbert Rawlinson, Sally Payne, Wally Wales, Jay Novello, Horace Murphy, Monte Blue; **D:** Joseph Kane; **W:** James R. Webb; **C:** William Nobles; **M:** Cy Feuer.

Bad Manners 🐾 1984 (R) When an orphan is adopted by a wealthy but entirely selfish couple, a group of his orphan friends try to give a lecture and check in on his old girlfriend, brittle unhappy Nancy (Bedelia), and her prissy academic husband Wes (Strathairn). It's a weekend in hell for houseguests and hosts as they play not-so-adult games of truth-or-dare. Based on Gilman's play "Ghost in the Machine." **88m/C** VHS, DVD, David Strathairn, Bonnie Bedelia, Saul Rubinek, Caroleen Feeney, Julie Harris; **D:** Jonathan Kaufer; **W:** David Gilman; **C:** Denis Maloney; **M:** Ira Newborn.

Bad Manners 🐾🐾 1998 (R) Pompous musicologist Matt (Rubinek) returns to Boston with his razor-tongued girlfriend Kim (Feeney) to give a lecture and check in and visit her old flame from his new home and lifestyle. **85m/C** VHS. Martin Mull, Karen Black, Anne DeSalvo, Murphy Dunne, Pamela Segall, Edy Williams, Susan Ruttan, Richard Deacon; **D:** Bobby Houston; **C:** Jan De Bont.

Bad Man's River 🐾🐾 1972 A Mexican revolutionary leader hires a gang of outlaws to blow up an arsenal used by the Mexican Army. **92m/C** VHS, DVD. /T SP Lee Van Cleef, James Mason, Gina Lollobrigida; **D:** Eugenio (Gene) Martin; **W:** Philip Yordan; **C:** Alejandro Ulloa; **M:** Waldo de los Rios.

Bad Medicine WOOF! 1985 (PG-13) A youth who doesn't want to be a doctor is accepted by a highly questionable Latin American school of medicine. Remember that it was for medical students like this that the U.S. liberated Grenada. **97m/C** VHS, Steve Guttenberg, Alan Arkin, Julie Hagerty, Bill Macy, Curtis Armstrong, Joe Grifasi, Robert Romanus, Taylor Negron, Gilbert Gottfried; **D:** Harvey Miller; **W:** Harvey Miller.

Bad Men of the Border 🐾1/2 1945 Routine oater has Kirby posing as a bandit in order to infiltrate an outlaw band passing counterfeit money. He rounds up the bad guys and finds time to romance Armida too. **56m/B** VHS, Kirby Grant, Fuzzy Knight, Armida, John Eldridge, Francis McDonald; **D:** Wallace Fox; **W:** Adele Buffington.

Bad Moon 🐾🐾1/2 1996 (R) Let's put it this way the werewolf in this movie is not the only thing that bites. Shortest (merci-fully) studio release in recent history is a horror (in more ways than one) film with Pare leading the pack as Ted, a photo-journalist who comes back from the Amazon a different, more nocturnally hirsute man. Fleeing from the site of his nightly gore, Ted takes refuge with his loving sister (Janet (Hemingway) and her son Brett (Gamble). The real hero (and best actor) is a German shepherd named Thor (Primo) who discovers that Ted's a werewolf. Dog steals the show paws down (natural-ly). Decent special FX. Adapted from Wayne Smith's novel "Thor." **79m/C VHS**, DVD, Mariel Hemingway, Michael Pare, Mason Gamble, Ken Pogue; **D:** Eric Red; **W:** Eric Red; **C:** Jan Kiesser; **M:** Daniel Licht.

The Badge 🐾🐾 2002 (R) Small-town sheriff Darl (Thornton) must set aside his personal cistate to investigate the murder of a local transsexual, who was once married to stripper Scarlett (Ar-quette). But the deeper Darl digs, the more the powers that be want the incident covered up. Mediocre mystery despite the name cast. **103m/C** VHS, DVD, Billy Bob Thornton, Patricia Arquette, Sea e Ward, William Devane, Jena Malone, Tom Bower, Ray McKinnon, Julie Hagerty, Hill Harper; **D:** Robby Henson; **W:** Robby Henson; **C:** Irek Hartowicz; **M:** Robby Henson.

Badge 373 🐾1/2 1973 (R) In the vein of "The French Connection," a New York cop is suspended and decides to battle crime his own way. **116m/C** VHS, DVD, Robert Duvall, Verna Bloom, Eddie Egan; **D:** Howard W. Koch.

Badge of the Assassin 🐾🐾 1985 True story of a New York assistant DA who directed a campaign to catch a pair of cop-killers from the '73s. **96m/C VHS**, James Woods, Yaphet Kotto, Alex Rocco, David Harris, Pam Grier, Steven Keats, Richard Bradford, Rae Dawn Chong; **D:** Mel Damski. **TV**

The Badlanders 🐾🐾🐾 1958 A western remake of the crime drama "The Asphalt Jungle." Ladd and Borgnine plan a gold robbery against Smith, who cheated them out of their share in a gold mine. Cross and double-cross follow the partners as does romance. **85m/C VHS**, Alan Ladd, Ernest Borgnine, Kent Smith, Katy Jurado, Claire Kelly, Nehemiah Persoff, Adam Williams; **D:** Delmer Daves.

Badlands 🐾🐾🐾 1974 (PG) Based loosely on the Charlie Starkweather murders of the 1950s, this impressive debut by director Malick recounts a slow-thinking, unhinged misfit's killing spree across the midwestern plain's, accompanied by a starry-eyed 15-year-old schoolgirl. Sheen and Spacek are a disturbingly numb, apa-thetic, and icy duo. **94m/C VHS**, DVD, Martin Sheen, Sissy Spacek, Warren Oates, Ramon Bieri, Warren Oates, Charles Fitzpatrick, Howard Ragsdale, John Womack Jr., Dona Baldwin; **C:** Terrence Malick; **D:** Terrence Malick; **W:** Terrence Malick; **C:** Tak Fujimoto, Stevan Larner, Brian Probyn; **M:** Carl Orff. Natl. Film Reg. '93.

Badmen of Nevada 🐾🐾 The Worse You Are, the Better You Sleep; Warui Yatsu Hodo Yoku Nemuru 1960 Badmen roam Nevada in the early days before law and order. **57m/B** VHS, Kent Taylor, Lona Andre, Warren Hymer, Irving Pichel, Gail Patrick, Clarence Wilson, Nina Welch, Berton Churchill; **D:** Fred Allen; **C:** Robert N. Lee, Harvey Gates, Robert Niles; **C:** Archie Stout.

Badman's Territory 🐾🐾1/2 1946 A straight-shooting marshal has to cope with such notorious outlaws as the James and Dalton boys in a territory outside of government control. **79m/B** VHS, Randolph Scott, Ann Richards, George "Gabby" Hayes, Steve Brodie; **M:** Tim Whelan.

Bagdad

made to seem ridiculous. Spawned a short-lived TV series with Whoopi Goldberg. **91m/C VHS, DVD.** *GE* Marianne Saegebrecht, CCH Pounder, Jack Palance, Christine Kaufmann, Monica Calhoun, Darron Flagg; *D:* Percy Adlon; *W:* Percy Adlon, Eleonore Adlon; *C:* Bernd Heinl; *M:* Bob Telson. Cesar '89: Foreign Film.

Bahama Passage 🦴🦴½ **1942** Trite story of one lady's efforts to win the affection of a macho Bahamas stud. **83m/C VHS.** Madeleine Carroll, Sterling Hayden, Flora Robson, Leo G. Carroll, Dorothy Dandridge, Mary Anderson, Cecil Kellaway, Fred Kohler Jr.; *D:* Edward H. Griffith; *W:* Virginia Van Upp; *C:* Leo Tover.

Bail Jumper 🦴 **1989** A story of love and commitment against incredible odds; some of which happen to be a swarm of locusts, a tornado, and falling meteorites. Joe and Elaine are small-time hoods escaping their dreary lives in Murky Springs Missouri by heading for that great bastion of idyllism and idealism—New York City. But even as the world starts to crumble around them, get the message that love prevails. **96m/C VHS.** Esther Balint, B.J. Spalding, Tony Askin, Joie Lee; *D:* Christian Faber.

Bail Out 🦴 **1990 (R)** Three bounty hunters, armed to the teeth, run a car-trashing police gauntlet so they may capture a valuable crook. **88m/C VHS. DVD.** David Hasselhoff, Linda Blair, John Vernon, Tom Rosales, Charlie Brill; *D:* Max Kleven.

Bail Out at 43,000 🦴 **1957** Movie about the lifestyles and love affairs of your average, everyday parachutist. **80m/B VHS.** John Payne, Karen Steele, Paul Kelly; *D:* Francis D. Lyon; *W:* Paul Monash.

Bailey's Billion$ 🦴🦴½ **2005 (G)** Bailey (voiced by Lovitz) is a golden retriever who has been left a fortune by his late owner. Naturally, the woman's greedy nephew Caspar (Curry) and his scheming wife Dolores (Tilly) plot to get the money by kidnapping guardian Theodore (Cain), a geeky animal behaviorist who can speak dog, and animal-rights activist Marge (Holden) team up to do right by him. **93m/C DVD.** *CA* Dean Cain, Laurie Holden, Tim Curry, Jennifer Tilly, Jon Lovitz, Angela Vallee; *D:* David Devine; *W:* Heather Conkie, Mary Walsh; *C:* Gavin Finney; *M:* Lou Pomanti.

Baise Moi WOOf! *Rape Me* **2000** French porn dressed up for the arthouse crowd had critics spinning like tops to justify not calling the film what it is—exploitative trash, even if it is done by women. After Manu (Anderson) gets gang raped, she kills her boyfriend, steals his money, and hooks up with prostitute Nadine (Bach) to go on a sex and murder spree. Very, very graphic sex and violence and real rape. **77m/C VHS, DVD.** *FR* Raffaela Anderson, Karen Bach; *D:* Virginie Despentes, Coralie Trinh Thi; *W:* Virginie Despentes, Coralie Trinh Thi; *C:* Benoit Chamaillard; *M:* Varou Jan.

Bait 🦴 **2000 (R)** Bait is what you use to catch bigger fish, and hopefully star Foxx can use his performance in this otherwise by-the-book action-comedy to snag bigger and better roles. Petty thief Alvin (Foxx) winds up in the clink after a botched seafood robbery. His cellmate Jaster (Pastorelli) is the double-crossing partner of prancing archvillain Bristol (Hutchinson), who has stolen $40 million in gold. Unfortunately for Alvin, Jaster winds up in the Big House in the sky before he can tell anyone where the hidden loot is stashed. Head Fed Clenteen (Morse), thinking that Alvin knows where the gold is hidden, has him unwittingly equipped with surveillance devices and springs him from the pokey. Alvin, now followed by Bristol and the feds, tries to find the stashed loot by piecing together the cryptic clues that Jaster has left him. Lots of action on a minimal (for these types of movies) budget. **119m/C VHS, DVD.** Jamie Foxx, Doug Hutchison, David Morse, Jamie Kennedy, Robert Pastorelli, Kimberly Elise, David Paymer, Tia Texada, Mike Epps, Nestor Serrano, gan Dodds, Jeffrey Donovan, Kirk Acevedo; *D:* Antoine Fuqua; *W:* Tom Gilroy, Jeff Nathanson, Adam Scheinman, Andrew Scheinman; *C:* Tobias Schliessler; *M:* Mark Mancina.

Baja 🦴🦴 **1995 (R)** Bebe (Ringwald) hides out in Baja with her beau Alex (Logue) after a drug deal goes bad. They hold up in a sleazy motel while Bebe waits for dad, John (Bernsen), to bail her out. But instead, John persuades estranged hubby Michael (Nickles) to track down the runaways and hitman Tom (Henriksen) is hunting for Alex. Must be the desert heat causing all the ensuing commotion. **92m/C VHS, DVD.** Molly Ringwald, Lance Henriksen, Michael A. (M.A.) Nickles, Donal Logue, Corbin Bernsen; *D:* Kurt Voss; *W:* Kurt Voss; *C:* Denis Maloney; *M:* Reg Powell.

Baja Oklahoma 🦴 **1987** A country barmaid has dreams of being a country singer. Songs by Willie Nelson, Emmylou Harris, and Billy Vera. **97m/C VHS.** Lesley Ann Warren, Peter Coyote, Swoosie Kurtz, Willie Nelson, Julia Roberts; *D:* Bobby Roth; *W:* Bobby Roth; *C:* Michael Ballhaus. CABLE

Baker's Hawk 🦴🦴 **1976** A young boy befriends a red-tailed hawk and learns the meaning of family and caring. **98m/C VHS.** Clint Walker, Diane Baker, Burl Ives, Lee Montgomery, Alan Young, Danny Bonaduce; *D:* Lyman Dayton; *W:* Dan Greer, Hal Harrison Jr.; *C:* Bernie Abramson; *M:* Lex de Azevedo.

The Baker's Wife 🦴🦴🦴½ *La Femme du Boulanger* **1933** There's a new baker in town, and he brings with him to the small French village an array of tantalizing breads, as well as a discontented wife. When she runs off with a shepherd, her loyal and naive husband refuses to acknowledge her infidelity; however, in his loneliness, the baker can't bake, so the townspeople scheme to bring his wife back. Panned as overly cute Marcel Pagnol peasant glorification, and hailed as a visual poem full of wit, you decide. In French with subtitles. Also available for French students without subtitles; a French script booklet is also available. **101m/B VHS.** *FR* Raimu, Ginette LeClerc, Charles Moulton, Charpin, Robert Vattier; *D:* Marcel Pagnol; *W:* Marcel Pagnol; *C:* Georges Benoit; *M:* Vincent Scotto. N.Y. Film Critics '40: Foreign Film.

Balalaika 🦴🦴 **1939** Rather dull operetta about the Russian revolution with Eddy playing a Russian prince. Eddy masquerades as a member of the proletariat in order to romance Massey, who was expected to become the next Garbo. Didn't happen, though. Eddy's rendition of "Stille Nacht" ("Silent Night") is highlight of film. Based on the operetta by Eric Maschwitz, George Ponford, and Bernard Gruen. **102m/B VHS.** Nelson Eddy, Ilona Massey, Charlie Ruggles, Frank Morgan, Lionel Atwill, Sir C. Aubrey Smith, Joyce Compton; *D:* Reinhold Schunzel; *W:* Leon Gordon, Charles Bennett, Jacques Deval; *C:* Karl Freund.

Balance of Power 🦴🦴½ **1996 (R)** Martial arts master Matsumoto (Mako) prepares fighter Niko (Blanks) for a death match against a former student who's gone bad. **92m/C VHS.** Billy Blanks, Mako, James Lew; *D:* Rick Bennet; *W:* Phil Good, Rick Bennet; *C:* Gilles Corbeil.

Balboa WOOf! **1982** Set on sun-baked Balboa Island, this is a melodramatic tale of high-class power, jealousy, and intrigue. Never-aired pilot for a TV miniseries, in the night-time soap tradition (even features Steve Kanaly from TV's "Dallas"). Special appearance by Cassandra Peterson, also known as horror hostess Elvira; and, if that interests you, look for Sonny Bono, as well. **92m/C VHS.** Tony Curtis, Carol Lynley, Chuck Connors, Sonny Bono, Steve Kanaly, Jennifer Chase, Lupita Ferrer, Martine Beswick, Henry Jones, Cassandra Peterson; *D:* James Polakof. TV

The Balcony 🦴🦴🦴 **1963** A film version of the great Jean Genet play about a surreal brothel, located in an unnamed, revolution-torn city, where its powerful patrons act out their fantasies. Scathing and rude. **87m/B VHS, DVD.** Peter Falk, Shelley Winters, Lee Grant, Kent Smith, Peter Brocco, Ruby Dee, Jeff Corey, Leonard Nimoy, Joyce Jameson; *D:* Joseph Strick; *W:* Ben Maddow; *C:* George J. Folsey.

Ball & Chain 🦴🦴½ **2004 (PG-13)** Although raised in America, Ameet (Malhotra) and Saima (Ray) can't escape the customs of India when their respective parents arrange their marriage. They want to break their engagement, so Ameet decides that if he behaves outrageously enough, his prospective in-laws will be so dismayed that they will call things off. Only the more time Ameet and Saima spend together, the more they realize that their arrangement could actually work. **90m/C DVD.** Lisa Ray, Kal Penn, Purva Bedi, Suni Malhotra, Ismail Bagdadi; *W:* Shriaz Jafri; *W:* Thomas Mortimer; *C:* Peter Simonite; *M:* Deane Ogden.

Ball of Fire 🦴🦴🦴 **1941** A gang moll hides out with a group of mundane professors, trying to avoid her loathsome boyfriend. The professors are busy compiling an encyclopedia and Stanwyck helps them with their section on slang in the English language. Cooper has his hands full when he falls for this damsel in distress and must fight the gangsters to keep her. Stanwyck takes a personal liking to naive Cooper and resolves to teach him more than just slang. **111m/B VHS, DVD.** Gary Cooper, Barbara Stanwyck, Dana Andrews, Gene Krupa, Oscar Homolka, Dan Duryea, S.Z. Sakall, Henry Travers; *D:* Howard Hawks; *W:* Billy Wilder, Charles Brackett; *C:* Gregg Toland; *M:* Alfred Newman.

Ball of Wax 🦴½ **2003** Superstar baseball player Bret Packard (Mench) is a domination freak who plots the downfall of his teammates basically because he's a wealthy, arrogant sociopath and he can. Then manager Ingels (Morris) brings in motivational speaker Bob Tower (Tobias) to get the team back on track and Packard flips to find he's losing control of the situation. **90m/C DVD.** Larry Tobias, Mark Mench, Justin Smith, Traci Dinwiddie, Cullen Moss, Daniel Morris, Kevin Scanlon, Stephanie Wallace; *D:* Daniel Kraus; *W:* Daniel Kraus; *C:* Michael Caporale; *M:* Eric Bachman.

Ballad in Blue 🦴🦴 *Blues for Lovers* **1966** Real life story of Ray Charles and a blind child. Tearjerker also includes some of Charles' hit songs. ♪I Got a Woman; What'd I Say?. **89m/B VHS. GB** Ray Charles, Tom Bell, Mary Peach, Dawn Addams, Piers Bishop; *D:* Paul Henreid.

Ballad of a Gunfighter 🦴 **1964** A feud between two outlaws reaches the boiling point when they both fall in love with the same woman. **84m/C VHS.** Marty Robbins, Bob (Robert) Barron, Joyce Redd, Nestor Paiva, Laurette Luez, Michael Davis; *D:* Bill Ward; *W:* Bill Ward; *C:* Brydon Baker; *M:* Jaime Mendoza-Nava.

Ballad of a Soldier 🦴🦴🦴½ *Ballada o Soldate* **1960** As a reward for demolishing two German tanks, a 19-year-old Russian soldier receives a six-day pass so he can see his mother, however, he meets another woman. Well directed and photographed, while avoiding propaganda. Russian with subtitles. **88m/B VHS, DVD.** *RU* Vladimir Ivashov, Shanna Prokhorenko, Antonina Maximova, Nikolai Kryuchkov; *D:* Grigori Chukhraj; *W:* Grigori Chukhraj, Valentin Yezhov; *C:* Sergei Mukhin; *M:* Mikhail Ziv. British Acad. '61: Film.

The Ballad of Andy Crocker 🦴🦴½ **1969** Early TV movie take on vets returning home from Vietnam. Andy (Majors) comes home to find his girlfriend has married someone else, his small business is in ruins, and his friends and family haven't a clue as to what has happened or what to expected from the disillusioned ex-soldier. **80m/C VHS, DVD.** Lee Majors, Joey Heatherton, Jimmy Dean, Marvin Gaye, Agnes Moorehead, Pat Hingle, Jill Haworth, Peter Haskell, Bobby Hatfield; *D:* George McCowan; *W:* Stuart Margolin; *C:* Henry Croniager Jr.; *M:* Billy May. TV

Ballad of Cable Hogue 🦴🦴🦴 **1970 (R)** A prospector, who had been left to die in the desert by his double-crossing partners, finds a waterhole. A surprise awaits his former friends when they visit the remote well. Not the usual violent Peckinpah horse drama, but a tongue-in-cheek comedy romance mixed with tragedy. Obviously offbeat and worth a peek. **122m/C VHS, DVD.** Jason Robards Jr., Stella Stevens, David Warner, L.Q. Jones, Strother Martin, Slim Pickens; *D:* Sam Peckinpah; *C:* Lucien Ballard; *M:* Jerry Goldsmith.

Ballad of Gregorio Cortez 🦴🦴🦴 **1983 (PG)** Tragic story based on one of the most famous manhunts in Texas history. A Mexican cowhand kills a Texas sheriff in self-defense and tries to elude the law, all because of a misunderstanding of the Spanish language. Olmos turns in a fine performance as Cortez. **105m/C VHS.** Edward James Olmos, James Gammon, Tom Bower, Alan Vint, Barry Corbin, Rosanna Desoto, Bruce McGill, Brion James, Pepe Serna, William Sanderson; *D:* Robert M. Young; *W:* Robert M. Young; *C:* Reyraldo Villalobos; *M:* W. Michael Lewis.

The Ballad of Jack and Rose 🦴🦴🦴 **2005 (R)** Absorbing story about an idealistic father and daughter living on their own like the last two hippies on earth in an abandoned commune. Rose (Belle) loves her father, Jack (Day-Lewis). A lot. Actually, she's probably in love with him. This is a touchy subject (not literally, don't worry) for Jack. Jack knows his daughter is too attached, is going to lose him one day, and make it run to her own. After venturing into the real world for six months Jack begins dating a woman, mother to two boys, and asks her and the boys to move into the commune. Rose reacts with jealousy, trying to anger her father by seducing the sons. Writer/director Rebecca Miller, daughter of playwright Arthur Miller, sidesteps any cliches but piles on a few too many tricks at the end. **138m/C DVD.** *US* Daniel Day-Lewis, Catherine Keener, Camilla Belle, Beau Bridges, Jason Lee, Jena Malone, Paul Franklin Dano, Susanna Thompson, Ryan McDonald; *D:* Rebecca Miller; *W:* Rebecca Miller; *C:* Ellen Kuras; *M:* Michael Rohatyn. L.A. Film Critics '05: Actress (Keener).

The Ballad of Little Jo 🦴🦴½ **1993 (R)** Inspired by a true story set during the 1866 gold rush. Easterner Josephine Monaghan is cast out of her wealthy family after she has a baby out of wedlock. Heading west, she passes herself off as a man—Little Jo—in an attempt to forestall harrassment. Solemn and overly earnest attempt by Greenwald to demystify the old west and bring a feminist viewpoint to a familiar saga. **110m/C VHS, DVD.** Suzy Amis, Bo Hopkins, Ian McKellan, Carrie Snodgrass, David Chung, Rene Auberjonois, Heather Graham, Anthony Heald, Sam Robards, Ruth Maleczech; *D:* Maggie Greenwald; *W:* Maggie Greenwald; *C:* Declan Quinn; *M:* David Mansfield.

The Ballad of Narayama 🦴🦴🦴 *Narayama-Bushi-Ko* **1983** Director Imamura's subtle and vastly moving story takes place a vague century ago. In compliance with village law designed to control population among the poverty-stricken peasants, a healthy 70-year-old woman must submit to solitary starvation atop a nearby mountain. We follow her as she sets into motion the final influence she will have in the lives of her children and grandchildren, a situation described with detachment and without imposing a tragic perspective. In Japanese with English subtitles. **129m/C VHS.** *JP* Ken Ogata, Sumiko Sakamoto, Takejo Aki, Tonpei Hidari, Shoichi Ozawa; *D:* Shohei Imamura; *W:* Shohei Imamura; *C:* Maseo Tochizawa; *M:* Shinichiro Ikebe. Cannes '83: Film.

The Ballad of the Sad Cafe 🦴🦴½ **1991 (PG-13)** Unusual love story set in a small Southern town during the Depression. The everyday lives of its townspeople are suddenly transformed when a distant relation of the town's outcast (Redgrave) unexpectedly shows up. A moving story that tries to portray both sides of love and its power to enhance and destroy simultaneously. Emotion never seems to come to life in a movie that's nice to watch, but is ultimately disappointing. Adapted from the play by Edward Albee, which was based on the critically acclaimed novella by Carson McCullers. A British/U.S. co-production. 100m/C 1991. **DVD.** GB Vanessa, Redgrave, Keith Carradine, Cork Hubbert, Rod Steiger, Austin Pendleton, Beth Dixon, Lanny Flaherty, Mert Hatfield, Earl Hindman; **A:** Anne Pitchak; **D:** Simon Callow; **W:** Michael Hirst. Jr.

Ballet Russes 🐾🐾🐾 2005 Documentary covering the history of the various ballet companies who have used the Ballet Russes name, from its founding by impresario Serge Diaghilev in 1909 to the last performance in 1962, including its legendary choreographers, dancers, and designers. Although there's footage of various performances, the most appealing aspects are the interviews of dancers, who were in their 80s and 90s when reunited in 2000, recall ing their glory days on stage. 118m/C DVD. US **D:** Dan Geller, Dayna Goldfine; **C:** Dan Geller, Dayna Goldfine, Gary Weinberg; **M:** Todd Boekelheide, David Conte.

Ballistic: Ecks vs. Sever 🐾½
Ecks vs. Sever 2002 (R) Awkwardly titled action-er stars Banderas as Ecks, a disillusioned former FBI manhunter mourning his dead wife. Liu is code-name Sever, a former government-trained assassin. Ecks has been hired to track Sever for kidnapping the son of her former boss Giant (Henry), chief of the Defense Intelligence Agency. Both agents are also on the lookout for a supposedly dangerous and supremely ridiculous techno virus. Once the operatives find they have a lot in common, they join forces to gun down and blow up everything in sight. Superb, if overdone stunts take top billing, while dim lighting matches equally dim plot. Based on the far more entertaining video game. "The Matrix." Based on the far moves of "The Matrix." 95m/C VHS, DVD. US Antonio Banderas, Lucy Liu, Gregg Henry, Ray Park, Talisa Soto, Miguel (Michael) Sandoval, Terry Chen, Sandrine Holt, Roger R. Cross, Steve Bacic, Aidan Drummond; **D:** Kaos; **W:** Alan B. McElroy; **C:** Julie Macat; **M:** Don Davis.

Balloon Farm 🐾🐾½ 1997 Harvey Potter (Tom), using some magic, raises a crop of balloons on cornstalks. His drought-stricken fellow farmers see the miraculous crop as symbols of hope but grumpy farmer Wheezle (Blossom) is suspicious. And his suspicions begin to infect the rest of the community, except for spunky young Willow (Wilson). Based on Jerdine Nolen's children's book "Harvey Potter's Balloon Farm." 89m/C VHS, DVD. Rip Torn, Mara Wilson, Roberts Blossom, Laurie Metcalf, Neal McDonough, Frederic Lehne, Adam Wylie; **D:** William Dear; **W:** Steven M. Karczynski. TV

Balls of Fury 🐾🐾½ 2007 (PG-13) Former child prodigy ping-pong star Randy Daytona (Fogler) finds himself fat and washed up at the ripe old age of 32. He's approached by the feds (Lopez as FBI agent) to take on a dangerous mission—infiltrate an underground ping-pong tournament run by shifty Chinese crime boss Feng (Walken), who also happens to be responsible for Randy's father's murder, death. But Randy finds his mission has a dual purpose: avenge his father's comeback. Of course every would-be hero needs a little

---

help, and Randy's crackpot team includes blind restaurateur and ping-pong sage Master Wong (Hong) and his totally hot niece Maggie (Maggie Q.) Some funny moments intertwine with a backdrop of Def Leppard in this ode to '80s nostalgia and martial arts, but it never fully takes off. 90m/C DVD, HD DVD. US Dan Fogler, Christopher Walken, George Lopez, James Hong, Terry Crews, Robert Patrick, Diedrich Bader, Aisha Tyler, Thomas Lennon, Maggie Q.; **D:** Robert Ben Garant; **W:** Thomas Lennon, Robert Ben Garant; **C:** Thomas Ackerman; **M:** Randy Edelman.

Ballbuster 🐾🐾½ 1989 Cops take on gangs in an all-out high-stakes battle to win back the streets. 100m/C VHS. Ivan Rogers, Bonnie Paine, W. Randolph Gavin, Bill Shirk, Brenda Banet; **D:** Eddie Beverly Jr.; **W:** Eddie Beverly Jr.

Baltic Deputy 🐾🐾½ 1937 An early forerunner of Soviet historic realism, where an aging intellectual deals with post-revolution Soviet life. In Russian with subtitles. 95m/B VHS. RU Boris Livanov, Maria Domasheva, Oleg Zhakov, Nikolai Cherkasov; **D:** Iosif Kheifits, Alexander Zarkhi, Yosif Heifitz; **W:** Iosif Kheifits, Alexander Zarkhi; **C:** Edgar Shnyr-skoker; **M:** Nikolai Timofeyev.

The Baltimore Bullet 🐾🐾 1980 Two men make their living traveling through the country as pool hustlers, bilking would-be pool sharks. Features ten of the greatest pool players in the world, including Willie Mosconi. 103m/C VHS. James Coburn, Omar Sharif, Bruce Boxleitner, Ronee Blakley, Jack O'Halloran; **D:** Robert Ellis Miller; **W:** Robert Vincent O'Neil, John F. Brascia.

Balto 🐾🐾½ 1995 (G) Animated adventure, based on a true story, of a half-husky, half-wolf sled dog, Balto, who faces overwhelming odds to bring life-saving medicine to Nome, Alaska. It's 1925, there's a diptheria epidemic, and Balto is the lead team dog on the final leg of the race to get the serum to Nome in time. Balto and the rest of the team dogs became instant heroes and even journeyed to Hollywood to star in their own silent film "Balto's Race to Nome." 78m/C VHS, DVD. **D:** Simon Wells; **W:** Cliff Ruby, Elana Lesser; **V:** Kevin Bacon, Bob Hoskins, Bridget Fonda, Jim (Jonah) Cummings, Phil Collins, Juliette Erewer, Danny Mann, Miriam Margolyes.

Bambi 🐾🐾🐾 1942 (G) A true Disney classic, detailing the often harsh education of a newborn deer and his friends in the forest. Proves that Disney animation was—and still is—the best to be found. Thumper still steals the show and the music is delightful, including "Let's Sing a Gay Little Spring Song," "Love is a Song," "Little April Shower," "The Thumper Song," and "Twitterpated." Stands as one of the greatest children's films of all time; a genuine perennial from generation to generation. Based very loosely on the book by Felix Salten. 69m/C VHS, DVD, FR Aissa Maiga, Maimouna Helene Diarra, Tiecoura Traore, Habib Dembele; **D:** Abderrahmane Sissako; **W:** Abderrahmane Sissako; **C:** Jacques Besse.

Bambi II 🐾🐾½ 2006 (G) The sequel might not be up to the standards of the original but it will keep the tykes occupied. Bambi's dad, the Great Prince, takes over the raising of his fawn when mom gets killed but he's having a tough time. Still, Bambi tries his best to learn despite clumsiness and teasing with some help from his pals Thumper and Flower. 72m/C DVD. **D:** Brian Pimental; **W:** Alicia Kirk; **M:** Larry Morey; **V:** Patrick Stewart, Alexander Gould, Brendon Baerg, Nicky Jones, Andreana Weiner, Cammie King, Donnie Dunagan, Hardie Albright, John Sutherland, Tim Davis, Sam Edwards, Sterling Holloway, Ann Gillis, Perce Pearce.

Bamako 🐾🐾 The Court 2006 Didactic drama that pits African debt against the international Monetary Fund (IMF) and the World Bank. A makeshift courtroom is set up in the courtyard of Mele (Maiga) and Chaka's (Traore) home in a poor section of Barrako. Because of international monetary policies, African nations are in serious debt and cannot meet their obligations to their own people while paying exorbitant interest rates. Lawyers listen to witness testimony while life goes on around them. It's important, but most Westerners will probably go "huh?" French and Bambara with subtitles. 115m/C DVD. FR Aissa Maiga, Maimouna Helene Diarra, Tiecoura Traore, Habib Dembele; **D:** Abderrahmane Sissako; **W:** Abderrahmane Sissako; **C:** Jacques Besse.

Balzac: A Life of Passion 🐾🐾 1999 Bio of French writer Honore de Balzac (1799–1850)—a larger-than-life figure played by the larger-than-life Depardieu. He has mom problems (she never loved him) and tries to win women who encourage him as his writing consumes him. There are balls and duels and all sorts of high and low society life during the Napoleonic era to enjoy. French with subtitles. 210m/C VHS, DVD, FR Gerard Depardieu, Jeanne Moreau, Fanny Ardant, Virna Lisi, Katja Riemann, Claude Rich; **D:** Josee Dayan; **W:** Didier Decoin; **C:** Willy Stassen; **M:** Bruno Coulais. TV

Balzac and the Little Chinese Seamstress 🐾🐾🐾 Balzac et la petite tailleuse Chinois, Xiao cai feng 2002 Sijie dreamily adapts his own autobiographical novel depicting life in a remote Chinese mountain village in 1971. City boys Luo (Chen) and Ma (Liu) are sent to be re-educated under Mao's Cultural Revolution. The young watchful eyes of the village chief (Wang) and both become attracted to the nameless young woman (Zhou) in the title, reading to her from a secreted cache of Western books (including Balzac, Flaubert, and Dumas) and teaching her to read and write. There is eventual separation and loss and an abrupt epilogue that shows the men 20 years later wondering whatever happened to the girl they once knew. Mandarin and French with subtitles. 111m/C 2002. CH FR Liu Ye, Hongwei Wang, Zhou Xun, Chen Kun, Wang Shuangbao, Chung Zhixun; **D:** Dai Sijie; **W:** Dai Sijie, Nadine Perront; **C:** Jean-Marie Dreujou; **M:** Wang Pujian.

Bam Bam & Celeste 🐾🐾🐾 2005 Margaret Cho's screenplay features herself as Celeste, a social outcast on a quest to win a makeover on "Trading Faces," a popular show filmed in New York. On the road trip from Illinois to the Big Apple with her gay hairdresser, boy-friend/buddy Bam Bam (Daniels), the pair encounter offbeat characters and situations and a showdown with their high school rivals, while discovering beauty is

---

more than skin deep. Cheeky, loose, cry-while-you're-laughing entertainment. 85m/C DVD. Margaret Cho, Bruce Daniels, Alan Cumming, Elaine Hendrix, Jane Lynch, Jim Cho, Wilson Cruz, Kathy Najimi, Butch Klein; **D:** Lorene Machado; **W:** Margaret Cho; **C:** Matthew Clark; **M:** Pat Irwin.

Bamboozled 🐾🐾 2000 (R) Coming Course 1968 Russian and American sci-entists race to find a U.F.O. in Red China. 103m/C VHS. Dan Duryea, John Ericson, Lois Nettleton. Nan Leslie; **D:** Frank Telford.

The Bamboo Saucer 🐾½ 1968 VIDEO.

Lee aims for controversy once again as he criticizes Hollywood's portrayal of African-Americans as well as pointing the finger at the black community's complicity in the process. Fed-up black writer Pierre Delacroix (Wayans) comes up with a series idea for a fledgling TV network as a form of protest—a modern day minstrel show complete with performers in burnt cork blackface. Fully expecting the show to fail, he hires struggling street performers Manray (Glover) and Womack (Davidson), Sleep 'N Eat (a reference to '30s and '40s black actors Mantan Moreland and Stepin Fetchit). The show becomes a surprise hit but also riles a militant black group, resulting in chaos in the lives of Delacroix and his assistant Sloan (Pinkett). The feel of the movie sways toward melodrama halfway through, but the wry observations of the artistic treatment of African Americans ring eerily true. Don't say it couldn't happen these days 135m/C VHS, DVD. Damon Wayans, Jada Pinkett Smith, Savion Glover, Tommy Davidson, Michael Rapaport, Thomas Jefferson Byrd, Paul Mooney, Susan Batson, Mos Def, Sarah Jones, Gillian Iliana Waters; **D:** Spike Lee; **W:** Spike Lee; **C:** Ellen Kuras; **M:** Terence Blanchard.

Bananas 🐾🐾🐾 1971 (PG-13) Inter-mittently hilarious pre-"Annie Hall" Allen farce is full of the director's signature angst-ridden philosophical comedy. A frustrated product tester from New York runs off to South America, where he volunteers his support to the revolutionary force of a shaky Latin-American dictatorship and winds up the leader. Don't miss an early appearance by Stallone. Witty score contributes much. 82m/C VHS, DVD. Woody Allen, Louise Lasser, Carlos Montalban, Howard Cosell, Charlotte Rae, Conrad Bain, Allen (Goorwitz) Garfield, Sylvester Stallone; **D:** Woody Allen; **W:** Woody Allen; **C:** Andrew M. Costikyan; **M:** Marvin Hamlisch.

Bananas Boat Woof! What Charged Charley Farthing 1978 A captain takes a man and his daughter away from the collapsing government of their banana republic. The would-be comedy. 91m/C VHS. GB Doug McClure, Hayley Mills, Lionel Jeffries, Dilys Hamlett, Warren Mitchell; **D:** Sidney Hayers.

Band of Angels 🐾🐾½ 1957 Orphaned Amantha (De Carlo) learns she has African-American blood and since it's the pre-Civil War era she is promptly winds up on the auction block. She becomes both the property and the mistress of mysterious New Orleans landowner Hamish Bond (Gable). Then the Civil War comes along bringing threats and revelations. De Carlo looks properly sultry but this is a weak attempt at costume drama. Based on the novel by Robert Penn Warren. 127m/C VHS, DVD. Clark Gable, Yvonne De Carlo, Sidney Poitier, Efrem Zimbalist Jr., Rex Reason, Patric Knowles, Torin Thatcher, Andrea King, Ray Teal; **D:** Raoul Walsh; **W:** John Twist, Ivan Goff; **M:** Max Steiner.

Band of Brothers 🐾🐾🐾 2001 Steven Spielberg and Tom Hanks executive produced this excellent adaptation of Stephen Ambrose's epic tale of the 101 Airborne's Easy Company as they made their way from D-Day through Operation Market-Garden, The Battle of the Bulge, and finally, the capture of Hitler's "Eagle's Nest" compound. Although uniformly showing the influence of "Saving Private Ryan," each episode focuses on a separate sub-theme or character while not losing sight of the big-picture depth. Some characters are given short shrift, and sometimes it's hard to tell which characters lived or died during a battle, but that's a minor quibble with such a large and, in most cases, unknown, cast. Although they're young 3rd and mostly anonymous, they do give excellent, and in some cases, breakout performances (with the exception of one of the few "name" actors, Damian Lewis, Kirk Acevedo, Rick Gomez, Richard Speight Jr., Jimmy Fallon, Ian Virgo, Thomas (Tom) Hardy; **D:** David Frankel, Tom Hanks, Richard Loncraine, Phil Alden Robinson, Mikael Salomon, David Nutter, David Leland, Tony To; **W:** Tom Hanks, E. Max Frye, Erik Jendresen, Bruce McKenna, Graham Yost, Stephen E. Ambrose, Erik Bork, John Orloff; **C:** Remi Adefarasin; **M:** Michael Kamen. CABLE.

Band of Gold 🐾🐾🐾 1995 Unflinching British miniseries follows the lives of Yorkshire prostitutes Rosie (James), Carol (Tyson), and Gina (Gemmell) while they try to survive the streets of Bradford. On six cassettes 312m/C VHS, DVD. GB Geraldine James, Cathy Tyson, Ruth Gemmell, Barbara Dickson, David Schofield, Richard Moore, Rachel Davies, Samantha Morton; **D:** Richard Standeven, Richard Laxton; **W:** Kay Mellor; **C:** Peter Jessop; **M:** Hal Lindes.

Band of Outsiders 🐾🐾🐾 1964 Bande a Part; The Outsiders 1964 A woman hires a pair of petty criminals to rip off her aunt. Godard vehicle for exposing self-reflexive comments of modern film culture. In French with English subtitles. 97m/B VHS, DVD. FR Sami Frey, Anna Karina, Claude Brasseur, Louisa Colpeyn; **D:** Jean-Luc Godard; **W:** Jean-Luc Godard; **C:** Raoul Coutard; **M:** Michel Legrand.

Band of the Hand ⅋ **1986 (R)** A "Miami Vice" type melodrama about five convicts who are trained to become an unstoppable police unit. The first feature film by Glaser, last seen as Starsky in "Starsky & Hutch." **109m/C VHS, DVD.** Stephen Lang, Michael Carmine, Lauren Holly, Leon Robinson; **D:** Paul Michael Glaser; **W:** Jack Baran, Leo Garen.

The Band Wagon ⅋⅋ **1953** A Hollywood song-and-dance man finds trouble when he is persuaded to star in a Broadway musical. Charisse has been called Astaire's most perfect partner, perhaps by those who haven't seen Rogers. ♪That's Entertainment; Dancing in the Dark; By Myself; A Shine On Your Shoes; Something to Remember You By; High and Low; I Love Louisa; New Sun in the Sky; I Guess I'll Have to Change My Plan. **112m/C VHS, DVD.** Fred Astaire, Cyd Charisse, Oscar Levant, Nanette Fabray, Jack Buchanan, Bobby Watson; **D:** Vincente Minnelli; **W:** Betty Comden; **M:** Arthur Schwartz, Howard Dietz. Natl. Film Reg. '95.

Bandit King of Texas ⅋⅋½ **1949** A varmint is swindling unsuspecting settlers in a land scheme and then robbing and murdering them when they go to visit their supposed property. Rocky and friends come to the rescue. **60m/B VHS, DVD.** Allan "Rocky" Lane, Eddy (Eddie, Ed) Waller, Helene Stanley, Robert Bice, Harry Lauter, Jim Nolan, John Hamilton, Lane Bradford; **D:** Fred Brannon; **W:** Olive Cooper.

Bandit Queen ⅋⅋½ **1951** Spanish girl forms a band to stop seizure of Spanish possessions by lawless Californians. **71m/B VHS.** Barbara Britton, Willard Parker, Philip Reed, Jack Perrin; **D:** William Berke.

Bandit Queen ⅋⅋ **1994** Phoolan Devi (Biswas) is a female Robin Hood in modern-day India. A lower-caste woman, Devi is sold into marriage at 11, brutalized by her husband (and many others throughout the film), and eventually winds up with an equally brutal group of hill bandits. Only this time around, Devi takes action by aiding the group in robbing, kidnapping (and murdering) the rich and higher castes. Devi surrendered to authorities in 1983 and spent 11 years in jail. Based on screenwriter Sen's biography "India's Bandit Queen: The True Story of Phoolan Devi" and Devi's diaries in Hindi with subtitles. **119m/C VHS, DVD. GB IN** Seema Biswas, Nirmal Pandey, Manoj Bajpai, Raghuvir Yadav, Rajesh Vivek, Govind Namdeo; **D:** Shekhar Kapur; **W:** Mala Sen; **C:** Ashok Mehta; **M:** Nusrat Fateh Ali Khan, Roger White.

The Bandits ⅋⅋½ Crossfire **1967 (PG)** Three cowboys team up with a band of Mexican outlaws to find a traitor in the midst of the Mexican revolution. **83m/C VHS. MX** Robert Conrad, Jan-Michael Vincent, Roy Jenson, Manuel Lopez Ochoa; **D:** Alfredo Zacharias, Robert Conrad.

Bandits ⅋⅋½ **1986** Simon Verini (Yanne), a sophisticated fence, is given the loot from a $10 million Cartier heist to exchange for cash by Mozart (Bruel) the leader of the thieves. But two of Mozart's gang want to keep the jewels instead and kidnap Verini's wife as ransom. She's killed, even after he returns the goods, and Verini is then framed for the theft and spends 10 years in prison. He's sent his daughter Marie-Sophie to a Swiss boarding school and once in prison with her and to find those responsible for his wife's death. Director Lelouch's wife portrays the adult Marie-Sophie. In French with English subtitles. **98m/C VHS. FR** Jean Yanne, Marie-Sophie (Lelouch), Patrick Bruel, Charles Gerard, Corinne Marchand, Christine Barbelivien; **D:** Claude Lelouch; **W:** Pierre Uytterhoeven, Claude Lelouch.

Bandits ⅋⅋ **1999 (R)** Talk about your band on the run! Four young women form a prison rock-and-roll band called the Bandits. Their first gig on the outside is the policeman's ball, where they escape. They become folk heroes as they elude the police and a clandestine recording they sent to a music exec zooms up the charts. German with subtitles. **109m/C VHS, DVD. GE** Katja Riemann, Jutta Hoffmann, Jasmin Tabatabai, Nicolette Krebitz, Hannes Jaenicke, Werner Schreyer; **D:** Katja von Garnier; **W:** Katja von Garnier, Uwe Wilhelm; **C:** Torsten Breuer.

Bandits ⅋⅋½ **2001 (PG-13)** Willis and Thornton are Joe and Terry, quirky bank robbers known as the "sleepover bandits" for their unusual but non-violent heists. With Willis as the smirky brawn and Thornton as the neurotic brain, the two play the Butch-and-Sundance act until fate puts bored housewife Kate (Blanchett) in their path. She talks her way into their little gang, but can't decide which of the two she should fall for most. The plot then slams on the brakes, although Levinson adds enough padding to cushion the blow. Blanchett is excellent as the sultry, vulnerable Kate, but Thornton steals the show (and chomps on considerable scenery) as the omniphobic hypochondriac Terry (his fear of antique furniture is actually one of Thornton's well-documented quirks as well). **123m/C VHS, DVD. US** Bruce Willis, Billy Bob Thornton, Cate Blanchett, Troy Garity, Bobby Slayton, Brian F. O'Byrne, Azura Skye, Stacey Travis, William Converse-Roberts; **D:** Barry Levinson; **W:** Harley Peyton; **C:** Dante Spinotti; **M:** Christopher Young. Natl. Bd. of Review '01: Actor (Thornton).

Bandits of Orgosolo ⅋⅋½ Banditi a Orgosolo **1961** An acclaimed, patient drama about a Sardinian shepherd who shelters a band of thieves from the police. When one of the cops is killed the shepherd panics and flees into the hills for survival. Dubbed in English. **98m/B VHS. IT** Michele Cossu, Peppeddu Cuccu; **D:** Vittorio de Seta; **W:** Vittorio de Seta, Vera Gherarducci; **C:** Vittorio de Seta, Luciano Tovoli; **M:** Valentino Bucchi.

Bandolero! ⅋⅋½ **1968 (PG)** In Texas, Stewart and Martin are two fugitive brothers who run into trouble with their Mexican counterparts. **106m/C VHS, DVD.** James Stewart, Raquel Welch, Dean Martin, George Kennedy, Will Geer, Harry Carey Jr., Andrew V. McLaglen; **C:** William Clothier; **M:** Jerry Goldsmith.

The Band's Visit ⅋⅋⅋ Bikur Ha-Tizmoret **2007 (PG-13)** Eight members of an Egyptian police orchestra are accidentally stranded in the Israeli desert, far away from their intended destination. They end up in an Israeli town where they are anything but welcome. Through the culture clash, connections are made, and an unlikely attraction develops between band members and the beautiful restaurant owner who gives them a place to stay. Director Kolirin draws comedy out of the isolated, sad characters and their awkward situation without exploiting them. **89m/C DVD. FR IS US** Sasson Gabai, Ronit Elkabetz, Saleh Bakri, Shlomi Avraham, Khalifa Natour, Rubi Muscovich; **D:** Eran Kolirin; **W:** Eran Kolirin; **C:** Shai Goldman; **M:** Habib Shehadeh Hanna.

Bandwagon ⅋⅋½ **1995** Four unlikely twentysomething guys decide to form a band in Raleigh, NC. Tony Ridge (Holmes) is the lead singer-songwriter who's so shy he practices in a closet, chatty drummer Charlie Flagg (Hennessey) has the rehearsal space; Wynn Knapp (Corrigan) is the band's perpetually stoned guitarist; and bass player Eric Ellwood's (Parlavecchio) hot temper has him in big trouble with a local loan shark. They finally come up with a name (Circus Monkey), get a gig (a raucous frat party), and are on their way when they acquire Zenlike road manager Linus Tate (MacMillan) and a battered van. Of course, life on the road proves to be a challenge. **99m/C VHS.** Kevin Corrigan, Steve Parlavecchio, Lee Holmes, Matthew Hennessey, Doug MacMillan, Lisa Keller; **D:** John Schultz; **W:** John Schultz; **C:** Shawn Maurer; **M:** Greg Kendall.

Bang ⅋⅋ The Big Bang Theory **1995** This $20,000 indie concerns a nameless, powerless Asian-American would-be actress (Narita) in L.A. She gets kicked out of her apartment, accosted by a homeless crazy (Greene), and sexually propositioned by a sleazy producer (Graff). Finally, she's accused of causing a public disturbance by a cop (Newland), who'll let her off in exchange for sexual favors. Instead, she grabs his gun, forces him to strip, ties him to a tree, puts on the cop's uniform, and steals his motorcycle. In uniform, she's suddenly viewed with authority and decides to take some time to see what that's like. **98m/C VHS, DVD.** Darling Narita, Peter Greene, Michael Newland, David Allen Graff, Eric Schrody, Michael Arturo, James Sharpe, Luis Guizar, Art Cruz, Stanley Herman; **D:** Ash; **W:** Ash; **C:** Dave Gasperik.

Bang Bang Kid ⅋⅋ Bang Bang **1967 (G)** A western spoof about a klutzy gunfighter defending a town from outlaws. **78m/C VHS.** Tom Bosley, Guy Madison, Sandra Milo; **D:** Stanley Prager.

Bang Rajan ⅋⅋⅋½ **2000** Kind of a Thai version of the Alamo. The small village of Bang Rajan, circa 1765, finds itself geographically in the path of a very angry Burmese army on their way to the warring city of Ayudhya. With no outside help, the community must band together in hopes of protecting their land. One of the country's most legendary battles, told with Hollywood-like epic production helped the film become Thailand's biggest box office hit ever. One-upping "Braveheart," the film arguably contains the most violent images of warfare to date. Fan Oliver Stone helped secure U.S. release. **119m/C DVD. TH** Winai Kraibutr, Bin Bunluerit, Chumphorn Thepphithak, Jaran Ngamdee, Suntharee Maila-or; **D:** Thanit Jitnukul; **W:** Thanit Jitnukul, Kongkiat Khomsiri, Bunthin Thuaykaew, Patikam Phejmunee, Suttipong Muttanavee; **C:** Wichian Ruangwijchayakul; **M:** Chartachai Phongraphaphan.

Bang the Drum Slowly ⅋⅋ **1956** The original TV adaptation of a Mark Harris novel about baseball. A ball player stricken by a terminal illness strikes an unlikely friendship with a teammate. Interesting role for an actor (Newman) who claims to have been driven to acting by running away from the sporting goods business. **60m/B VHS.** Paul Newman, George Peppard, Albert Salmi; **D:** Daniel Petrie. TV

Bang the Drum Slowly ⅋⅋⅋ **1973 (PG)** The touching story of a major league catcher who discovers that he is dying of Hodgkins disease and wants to play just one more season. De Niro is the weakening baseball player and Moriarty is the friend who helps him see it through. Based on a novel by Mark Harris. **97m/C VHS, DVD.** Robert De Niro, Michael Moriarty, Vincent Gardenia, Phil Foster, Ann Wedgeworth, Heather MacRae, Selma Diamond, Danny Aiello; **D:** John Hancock. N.Y. Film Critics '73: Support. Actor (De Niro).

The Banger Sisters ⅋⅋ **2002 (R)** Fast forward "Almost Famous" thirty years and you'll find Kate Hudson has turned into her real-life mother, Hawn, who plays Suzette, a middle-aged former '60s/70s "band-aid" turned, well, not turned at all, still living the wild, free-spirit life. Her partner in rock n' roll groupie-dom, Vinnie (Sarandon), however, has grown up and uptight; now she's suburban mom Lavinia living in the 'burbs. When Suzette loses her job, she drifts back into Vinnie's life and helps her get back to her sleazy, but more honest, roots. Sanitized-for-your-protection version of groupie life rings false throughout. Characters are essentially modeled on groupie legends the Plaster Casters. Material isn't worthy of these A-listers and nostalgia appeal runs thin. Amurri is Sarandon's real-life daughter. **97m/C VHS, DVD. US** Goldie Hawn, Susan Sarandon, Geoffrey Rush, Erika Christensen, Robin Thomas, Eva Amurri, Matthew Carey; **D:** Bob Dolman; **W:** Bob Dolman; **C:** Karl Walter Lindenlaub; **M:** Trevor Rabin.

Bangkok Dangerous **2008 (R)** Hitman Joe (Cage) is on a job in Thailand, eliminating enemies of crime boss Surat. He hires street rat Kong (Yammarn) to run errands and provide local intel, which is how Joe learns one of his targets is a political assassination. Joe doesn't go for that and Surat decides his hitman needs to be eliminated. The Pang brothers remake their own 1999 Hong Kong pic. Not yet reviewed. **?m/C VHS, DVD. US** Nicolas Cage, Charlie Yeung, Shahkrit Yamnarm, Panward Hemmanee, James With, Dom Hetrakul, Philip Waley, Shaun Delaney; **D:** Danny Pang, Oxide Pang; **W:** Jason Richman; **C:** Decha Sirmantra; **M:** Brian Tyler.

Banjo Hackett ⅋⅋½ Banjo Hackett: Roamin' Free **1976** Banjo (Meredith) and his orphaned nephew (Eisenmann) travel the West in search of a rare Arabian horse that was stolen from the boy's mother before she died. Also in pursuit are a millionaire and a devious bounty hunter who will stop at nothing to capture the missing steed. Although the storyline is as rambling as the West, it's heartfelt all the same. **100m/C DVD.** Don Meredith, Ike Eisenmann, Carol Connors, Gloria De Haven, Jeff Corey, L.Q. Jones, Jan Murray, Dan O'Herlihy, Jennifer Warren, David Young, Richard Young, Anne Francis, Slim Pickens; **D:** Andrew V. McLaglen; **W:** Ken Trevey; **C:** Al Francis; **M:** Morton Stevens.

The Bank ⅋⅋½ **2001** Geeky mathematician/computer whiz Jim Doyle (Wenham) is offered a job by unscrupulous Centrabank CEO Simon O'Reilly (LaPaglia) to set up a computer program that will predict stock market fluctuations and increase the bank's profits. Victims of Centrabank's drive for profits are Wayne (Rodgers) and Diane (McElhinney) Davis, who are suing the bank as a cause of a family tragedy. The two stories come to overlap when O'Reilly pressures Doyle into questionable practices to resolve the various situations. **103m/C VHS, DVD, AU** David Wenham, Anthony LaPaglia, Steve Rodgers, Mandy McElhinney, Mitchell Butel, Sibylla Budd; **D:** Robert Connolly; **W:** Robert Connolly; **C:** Tristan Milani; **M:** Alan John.

The Bank Dick ⅋⅋⅋ The Bank Detective **1940** Fields wrote the screenplay (using an alias) and stars in this zany comedy about a man who accidentally trips a bank robber and winds up as a guard. Fields' last major role is a classic, a worthy end to his great career. **73m/B VHS, DVD.** W.C. Fields, Cora Witherspoon, Una Merkel, Evelyn Del Rio, Jack Norton, Jessie Ralph, Franklin Pangborn, Shemp Howard, Grady Sutton, Russell Hicks, Richard Purcell, Reed Hadley; **D:** Edward F. (Eddie) Cline; **W:** W.C. Fields; **C:** Milton Krasner. Natl. Film Reg. '92.

The Bank Job ⅋⅋ **2008 (R)** Terry (Statham) thinks his ex-lover Martine (Burrows) has recruited him to assemble a crew including his number two guy, porn king Kevin (Campbell Moore), for a straightforward cash heist. They end up involved in one of the greatest bank robberies in British history: the 1971 tunneled break in at the Baker Street branch of Lloyd's. The real-life investigation produced no arrests and recovered no loot, thus allowing writers Clement and La Frenais to construct an elaborate albeit fictionalized account that ties the crime to a conspiracy to retrieve sexually-compromising photos of a British royal from the safe deposit box of a black power operative (De Jersey). A near-perfect period heist-caper film that extracts terrific effect from the fashion and technology of the 70's. Particularly humorous are the giant walkie-talkies alleged to have played a role in the crime. **111m/C DVD. GB US** Jason Statham, Saffron Burrows, Daniel Mays, David Suchet, Richard Lintern, James Faulkner; **D:** Roger Donaldson; **W:** Dick Clement, Ian La Frenais; **C:** Michael Coulter; **M:** J. Peter Robinson.

Bank Robber ⅋⅋ **1993 (R)** Billy (Dempsey) is a thief who will retire after one final bank heist, if only he hadn't forgotten to beat that surveillance camera. Holed up in a New York hotel he's subjected to extortion schemes and finds himself a new outlaw celebrity to newshounds. Bonet is a sweet hooker who falls in love with him. Satire on crooks and fame is too mild-mannered for its own good but not without charm. Directorial debut of Mead. Unedited NC-17 version also available. **94m/C VHS.** Patrick Dempsey, Lisa Bonet, Olivia D'Abo, James Garde, Forest Whitaker, Judge Reinhold, Michael Jeter, Joe Alaskey, John Chapoulis; **D:** Nick Mead; **W:** Nick Mead; **M:** Stewart Copeland.

Bank Shot ⅋⅋⅋ **1974** Hilarious comedy about a criminal who plans to rob a bank by stealing the entire building. Based on the novel by Donald Westlake, and the sequel to "The Hot Rock." **83m/C VHS, DVD.** George C. Scott, Joanna Cassidy, Sorrell Booke, G(eorge) Wood, Clifton James Bob.

The Banker 🐾🐾 1989 (R) A cop, played by Forster, suspects a wealthy, highly influential banker of brutal serial killings. **90m/C VHS.** *D:* Harry Stradling Jr. *W:* Wendell Mayes. *C:* Robert Forster, Jeff Conaway, Leif Garrett, Duncan Regehr, Shanna Reed, Deborah Richter, Richard Roundtree, Teri Weigel, E.J. Peaker, Michael Fairman, Juan Garcia; *D:* William Webb; *C:* John Huneck; *M:* Reg Powell, Sam Winans.

Banzai Runner 🐾🐾 1986 A cop whose brother was killed in an exclusive desert-highway race decides to avenge by joining the race himself. **88m/C VHS, DVD.** *D:* Dean Stockwell, John Shepherd, Charles Dierkop; *C:* John G. Thomas; *W:* Phil Harnage. **VIDEO**

Baraka 🐾🐾🐾 1993 Time-lapse photography transforms a fascinating array of scenic panoramas into a thought-provoking experience. No dialogue, but the captivating visuals, shot in 24 countries, are a feast for the eyes. Points of interest include Iguazu Falls in Argentina, Ayers Rock in Australia, the temples of Angkor Wat in Cambodia, and the Grand Canyon. **96m/C VHS, DVD.** *D:* Ron Fricke; *W:* Ron Fricke, Mark Magidson, Bob Green; *C:* Ron Fricke; *M:* Michael Stearns.

B.A.P.'s 🐾1/2 1997 Ghetto to riches story about Georgia waitresses Nisi (Berry) and Mickey (Desselle) who dream about opening their own business—a combo restaurant and hair salon. An L.A. audition offering $10,000 gets them to the sunny coast and eventually into the Beverly Hills mansion of Mr. Blakemore (Landau), where Nisi's persuaded to pose as the granddaughter of his lost love by Blakemore's money-grubbing nephew, Isaac (Fried). Everybody bonds and butler Manley (Richardson) instructs the women in taste and etiquette. Good cast is wasted and the comedy's lame when not offensive. **91m/C VHS, DVD.** Halle Berry, Natalie Desselle, Martin Landau, Ian Richardson, Troy Beyer, Luigi Amodeo, Jonathan Fried, A.J. (Anthony) Johnson; *D:* Robert Townsend; *W:* Troy Beyer; *C:* Bill Dill; *M:* Stanley Clarke.

Bar-B-Q Woof! 2000 A pro-ball player turned actor needs a break and heads home to have a Bar-B-Q with his girl and old homies. When word gets out the entire neighborhood shows up for the party. A lot of music and a lot of crude jokes and infantile humor make this poorly made, horribly acted film practically unwatchable. The 102-minute running time includes nearly 15 minutes of credits and what the cast and crew apparently considered humorous outtakes. **102m/C VHS, DVD.** Layzie Bone, John West, Chanda Watts, Lea Griggs; *D:* Amanda Moss, John West; *W:* John West.

Bar Girls 🐾🐾 1995 (R) Mating ritual, set in L.A.'s watering hole "The Girl Bar," finds usually tough cookie Loretta (Wolfe) spotting new face Rachael (D'Agostino) and deciding she likes what she sees. There's various mind games which they chart a rocky course to true love—with jealousy, possessiveness, and past romance all playing their parts. Hoffman adapted from her play and the staginess remains; film debut for director Giovanni. **95m/C VHS, DVD.** Nancy Allison Wolfe, Liza D'Agostino, Justine Slater, Paula Sorge, Camila Griggs, Pam Raines; *D:* Marita Giovanni; *W:* Lauran Hoffman; *C:* Michael Ferris; *M:* Lenny Meyers.

Bar Hopping 🐾 2000 Disjointed series of vignettes about the singles scene in L.A. centered around a bar with Arnold as the bartender, narrating the action (or lack thereof). Lame. **88m/C VHS, DVD.** Tom Arnold, Nicole Sullivan, Scott Baio, John Henson, Sally Kellerman, Kevin Nealon, Kelly Preston, Roy Thinnes, Linda Favila, Anson Downes; *C:* Steve Cohen; *W:* Linda Favila, Anson Downes; *D:* Montgomery; *M:* Nick Loren. **CABLE**

Barabbas 🐾🐾🐾 1962 Barabbas, a thief and murderer, is freed by Pontius Pilate in place of Jesus. He is haunted by this event for the rest of his life. Excellent acting, little melodrama, lavish production make for fine viewing. Based on the novel by Lagerkvist. **144m/C VHS.** *D:* Anthony Quinn, Silvana Mangano, Arthur Kennedy, Jack Palance, Ernest Borgnine, Katy Jurado, Vittorio Gassman; *D:* Richard Fleischer; *W:* Diego Fabbri, Christopher Fry, Ivo Perilli, Nigel Balchin; *C:* Aldo Tonti; *M:* Mario Nascimbene.

Also tours Auschwitz and the streets of Calcutta, in an effort to warn the viewer of the planet's fragility. Filmed in 70mm. **96m/C VHS, DVD.** *D:* Ron Fricke; *W:* Ron Fricke, Mark Magidson, Bob Green; *C:* Ron Fricke; *M:* Michael Stearns.

Baran 🐾🐾1/2 **Rain** 2001 (PG) Latif (Abedini) works as a tea boy and cook on a construction site in Iran where many of the other laborers are illegal Afghan emigres. When one of his co-workers is injured, the man's young son, Baran (Bahrami), comes to take his place, although he's too frail to do the job. So Baran takes Latif's place and he must move to a more strenuous job, which he doesn't mind when he discovers that Baran is actually a girl, so Latif begins an awkward courtship while trying to keep her secret. Farsi with subtitles. **94m/C VHS, DVD.** *A:* Hossein Abedini, Zahra Bahrami, Mohammad Reza Naji, Hossein Rahimi; *D:* Majid Majidi; *W:* Majid Majidi; *C:* Mohammad Davudi; *M:* Ahmad Pejman.

Barb Wire 🐾1/2 1996 (R) "Don't call me babe!" That'll be difficult when the figure in question is Anderson Lee's bigscreen take on Dark Horse comic book heroine Barb Wire. Barb runs the sleazy Hammerhead Bar & Grille in Steel Harbor, the only neutral city in an America torn by a second civil war, and reluctantly agrees to aid hunky resistance leader Axel (Morrison) on a dangerous peace mission. Pambo gives Stallone a fight for the action title—fetching in high heels and black leather—with lots of fire power and a 'ake-no-prisoners' attitude. Plot's secondary to pulchritude but, unfortunately, the movie's just not a lotta fun. **98m/C VHS, DVD.** Pamela Anderson, Temuera Morrison, Jack Noseworthy, Victoria Rowell, Xander Berkeley, Udo Kier, Steve Railsback, Clint Howard, Tony Bill; *D:* David Hogan; *W:* Chuck Pfarrer, Ilene Chaiken; *C:* Rick Bota; *M:* Michel Colombier. Golden Raspberries '96: Worst New Star (Anderson).

Barbarella 🐾🐾1/2 Barbarella, Queen of the Galaxy 1968 (PG) Based on the popular French sci-fi comic strip drawn by Jean-Claude Forest, this cult classic details the bizarre adventures of a space nymphette (Fonda) encountering fantastic creatures and super beings. You'll see sides of Fonda you never saw before (not even in the workout videos). Notorious in its day; rather silly, dated camp now. Don't miss the elbow-sex scene. Southern contributed to the script. **98m/C VHS, DVD, FR IT.** Jane Fonda, John Phillip Law, David Hemmings, Marcel Marceau, Anita Pallenberg, Milo O'Shea, Ugo Tognazzi, Veronique Vendell, Giancarlo Cobelli, Serge Marquand; *D:* Roger Vadim; *W:* Roger Vadim, Terry Southern, Vittorio Bonicelli, Claude Brule, Tudor Gates, Clement Biddle Wood, Brian Degas, Jean-Claude Forest; *C:* Claude Renoir; *M:* Charles Fox.

Barbarian and the Geisha 🐾🐾 1958 The first U.S diplomat in Japan undergoes culture shock as well as a passionate love affair with a geisha, circa 1856. **104m/C VHS, DVD.** John Wayne, Eiko Ando, Sam Jaffe, So Yamamura; *D:* John Huston; *M:* Hugo Friedhofer.

The Barbarian Invasions 🐾🐾🐾 Les Invasions Barbares 2003 (R) Writer/director Arcand reunites characters from his 1986 film "The Decline of the American Empire" to capture the last days of lecherous, lustful divorced academic Remy (Girard), hospitalized with terminal cancer in his fifties. Through some pleading by his ex-wife (Berryman), estranged son Sebastian (Rousseau) reconnects with his father and deftly orchestrates his twilight days. He upgrades his medical care, persuades ex lovers and colleagues to come and see him off, and sneaks him heroin to ease the physical pain. Takes a few jabs at the Canadian health care system while showing how life and death can be celebrated. Sparkling performances by all, with clever writing that avoids being overly sentimental or maudlin, well deserving of its win in Cannes. **110m/C VHS, DVD, CA FR Remy Girard, Stephane Rousseau, Marie-Josee Croze, Marina Hands, Dorothee Berryman, Johanne-Marie Tremblay, Dominique Michel, Louise Portal, Yves Jacques, Pierre Curzi; *D:* Denys Arcand; *W:* Denys Arcand; *C:* Guy Dufaux; *M:* Pierre Aviat. Oscars '03: Foreign Film; British Acad. '03: Orig. Screenplay; Cannes '03: Actress (Croze), Screenplay; Natl. Bd. of Review '03: Foreign Film.

Barbarian Queen 🐾 1985 (R) Female warriors led by beauteous babe seek revenge for the capture of their men in this sword-and-sorcery epic. Low-budget rip-off "Conan the Barbarian" is laughable. Also available in an unrated version. Followed by "Barbarian Queen 2." **87m/C VHS, DVD.** *A:* Lana Clarkson, Frank Zagarino, Katt Shea, Dawn Dunlap, Susana Traverso; *D:* Hector Olivera; *W:* Howard R. Cohen; *C:* Rudy Donovan; *M:* Christopher Young.

Barbarian Queen 2: The Empress Strikes Back 🐾 1989 (R) Apparently one movie wasn't enough to tell the beautiful Princess Athalia's story. This time she fights her evil brother Ankaris. He throws her in prison, she escapes, joins a band of female rebels, and leads them into battle. No better than the first attempt. **87m/C VHS, DVD.** *A:* Lana Clarkson, Greg Wrangler, Rebecca Wood, Elizabeth Jaegen, Roger Cundy; *D:* Joe Finley; *W:* Howard R. Cohen; *C:* Francisco Bojorquez; *M:* Christopher Young.

The Barbarians 🐾 The Barbarians and Co 1987 (R) Two bodybuilder siblings in animal skins battle wizards and warlords in this dumb-budget low U.S./Italian co-production. **88m/C VHS, DVD.** *A:* David Paul, Peter Paul, Richard Lynch, Eva LaRue, Virginia Bryant, Sheeba Alahani, Michael Berryman; *D:* Ruggero Deodato; *M:* Pino Donaggio.

Barbarians at the Gate 🐾🐾1/2 1993 (R) In the "greed is good" financial climate of the '80s, this movie chronicles the $25 billion battle in 1988 for RJR Nabisco, which at the time was working on developing a "smokeless cigarette." Garner is CEO F. Ross Johnson, who is confident that their "smokeless cigarette" will boost the stock's value—until he gets the test-marketing results. Unwilling to risk the product's failure, Johnson decides to buy the company and is challenged by master dealer Kravis (Pryce). Fascinating social commentary on the nastiest mega-deal in history. Based on the book by Bryan Burrough and John Helyar. **107m/C VHS, DVD.** James Garner, Jonathan Pryce, Peter Riegert, Joanna Cassidy, Fred Dalton Thompson, Leilani Sarelle Ferrer, Matt Clark, Jeffrey DeMunn; *D:* Glenn Jordan; *W:* Larry Gelbart; *C:* Thomas Del Ruth, Nick Davis; *D:* Knowland; *M:* Richard Gibbs. **CABLE**

Barbarosa 🐾🐾🐾 1982 (PG) Offbeat western about an aging, legendary outlaw constantly on the lam who reluctantly befriends a naive farmboy and teaches him survival skills. Nelson and Busey are a great team, solidly directed. Lovely Rio Grande scenery. **90m/C VHS.** Willie Nelson, Gary Busey, Isela Vega; *D:* Fred Schepisi; *C:* Ian Baker; *M:* Bruce Smeaton.

Barbary Coast 🐾🐾🐾 1935 A ruthless club owner tries to win the love of a young girl by building her into a star attraction during San Francisco's gold rush days. **90m/B VHS, DVD.** Edward G. Robinson, Miriam Hopkins, Joel McCrea, Donald Meek, David Niven, Brian Donlevy, Walter Brennan; *D:* Howard Hawks.

The Barbary Coast 🐾🐾 1974 A turn-of-the-century detective sleuths the streets of San Francisco in this average TV movie. **100m/C VHS.** William Shatner, Dennis Cole, Lynda Day George, John Vernon, Charles Aidman, Michael Ansara, Neville Brand, Bill Bixby. **TV**

The Barber Shop 🐾🐾🐾 1933 Fields portrays the bumbling, carefree barber Cornelius O'Hare, purveyor of village gossip and problem solver. Havoc begins when a gangster enters the shop and demands that Cornelius change his appearance. **21m/B VHS, DVD.** W.C. Fields, Elise Cavanna, Harry Watson, Dagmar Oakland, Frank Yaconelli; *D:* Arthur Ripley.

Barbershop 🐾🐾🐾 2002 (PG-13) Ensemble comedy looks at the unique culture found in barbershops in the black male community. Cube plays Calvin, disinherited owner of a barbershop he inherited from his father. In debt, Calvin sells the shop to a loan shark, which

---

sends all the shop's regulars reeling, as their haven will be turned into a strip club. During the shop's final day, when the film takes place, Calvin must come to grips with his mistake and recognize the value of his father's legacy. Though two lesser subplots detract from the engrossing barbershop talk, a host of interesting characters mesh with an original and entertaining story. **102m/C VHS, DVD, UMD, US Ice Cube, Anthony Anderson, Cedric the Entertainer, Eve, Sean Patrick Thomas, Troy Garity, Michael Ealy, Leonard Earl Howze, Keith David, Lahmard Tate, Tom Wright, Jazsmin Lewis; *D:* Tim Story; *W:* Mark Brown; *C:* Tom Priestley; *M:* Terence Blanchard.

Barbershop 2: Back in Business 🐾🐾🐾 2004 (PG-13) Calvin and the rest of the crew are back. This time around, the shop faces a community crisis in the form of franchise cutters Nappy Cutz moving in across the street, threatening to put Calvin's shop out of business. Lacks the fresh charm of the first one, but the strong cast and crisp writing save the day. **106m/C VHS, DVD, US Ice Cube, Cedric the Entertainer, Sean Patrick Thomas, Troy Garity, Michael Ealy, Leonard Earl Howze, Harry J. Lennix, Robert Wisdom, Queen Latifah, Garcelle Beauvais; *D:* Kevin Rodney Sullivan; *W:* Don D. Scott; *C:* Tom Priestley; *M:* Richard Gibbs.

Barcelona 🐾🐾🐾 1994 (PG-13) Old-fashioned talkfest about two neurotic Americans experiencing sibling rivalry in Spain. Serious Tec (Nichols) is an American sales rep, posted to Barcelona, who can't quite get into the city's pleasure-loving rhythm. This is not a problem for Ted's cousin Fred (Eigeman), an obnoxious naval officer, with whom Ted has had a rivalry dating back to when they were little. With no cellular telephoning ability and an absence of large-ticket consumer goods to purchase, the two turn their reluctant sights on each other, focusing on the bare essentials, as I were. Great soul-searching scenes for the inarticulate. **102m/C VHS, DVD, US Taylor Nichols, Christopher Eigeman, Tushka Bergen, Mira Sorvino, Pep Munne, Francis Creighton, Thomas Gibson, Jack Gilpin, Nuria Badia, Hellena Schmied; *D:* Whit Stillman; *C:* John Thomas; *M:* Tom Judson, Mark Suozzo. Ind. Spirit '95: Cinematog.

The Barcelona Kill 🐾🐾1/2 1977 When a journalist and her boyfriend get in too deep with the Barcelona mob, their troubles begin. **86m/C VHS. Linda Hayden, John Astin, Simon Andreu, Maximo Valverde; *D:* Jose Antonio De La Loma.

Bare Essentials 🐾 1991 (PG) Made for TV yuppie Club Med nightmare in which a high-strung couple from New York find themselves marooned on a desert isle with only two other inhabitants. The quintessential flapper movie. **91m/C VHS. Gregory Harrison, Lisa Hartman Black, Mark Linn-Baker, Charlotte Lewis; *D:* Martha Coolidge. **TV**

Bare Knees 🐾 1928 A woman causes a scandal in her family when she arrives at her sister's birthday party with bare knees, cigarettes, and other flapper items. **61m/B VHS. Virginia Lee Corbin, Donald Keith, Jane Winton, Johnnie Walker, Forrest Stanley, Maude Fulton; *D:* Erle C. Kenton.

The Barefoot Contessa 🐾🐾🐾 1954 The story, told in flashback, of a Spanish dancer's rise to Hollywood stardom, as witnessed by a cynical director. Shallow Hollywood self-examination. **128m/C VHS. Ava Gardner, Humphrey Bogart, Edmond O'Brien, Valentina Cortese, Rossano Brazzi, Warren Stevens, Marius Goring; *D:* Joseph L. Mankiewicz; *W:* Joseph L. Mankiewicz; *C:* Jack Cardiff. Oscars '54: Support. Actor (O'Brien); Golden Globes '55: Support. Actor (O'Brien).

The Barefoot Executive 🐾🐾 1971 A mailroom boy who works for a national TV network finds a chimpanzee that can pick hit shows in this Disney family comedy. 92m/C VHS, DVD. Kurt Russell, John Ritter, (Henry) Morgan, Wally Cox, Heather North, Joe Flynn; **D:** Robert Butler; **M:** Robert F. Brunner.

Barefoot in Athens 🐾🐾 1966 TV presentation from "George Schaefer's Showcase Theatre" chronicles the last years of the philosopher Socrates who, barefoot and unkempt, an embarrassment to his wife, and a dangerous critic to the corrupt Athenian leaders, nevertheless believes that democracy and truth are all-important in his city. 76m/C VHS. Peter Ustinov, Geraldine Page, Anthony Quayle; **D:** George Schaefer. **TV**

Barefoot in the Park 🐾🐾🐾 1967 Neil Simon's Broadway hit translates well to screen. A newly wedded bride (Fonda) tries to get her husband (Redford, reprising his Broadway role) to loosen up and be as free-spirited as she is. 106m/C VHS, DVD. Robert Redford, Jane Fonda, Charles Boyer, Mildred Natwick, Herb Edelman, Mabel Albertson; **D:** Gene Saks; **W:** Neil Simon; **C:** Joseph LaShelle; **M:** Neal Hefti.

Barfly 🐾🐾🐾 1987 (R) Bukowski's semi-autobiographical screenplay is the story of a talented writer who chooses to spend his time as a lonely barfly, hiding his literary abilities behind glasses of liquor. Dunaway's character is right on target as the fellow alcoholic. 100m/C VHS, DVD. Mickey Rourke, Faye Dunaway, Alice Krige, Frank Stallone, J.C. Quinn, Jack Nance, Charles Bukowski, Pruitt Taylor Vince, Fritz Feld, Sandy Martin, Damon Hines; **D:** Barbet Schroeder; **W:** Charles Bukowski; **C:** Robby Muller; **M:** Jack Baran.

The Bargain 🐾🐾½ 1915 Hart's first feature, in which he portrays a bandit desperately trying to go straight. Original titles with musical score. 50m/B VHS. William S. Hart, J. Frank Burke, J. Barney Sherry, Clara Williams, Joseph J. Dowling, Roy Laidlaw, Herschel Mayall, Charles Swickard, Charles French; **D:** Reginald Barker; **W:** William H. Clifford, Thomas Ince; **C:** Joseph August.

Baritone 🐾🐾 1985 Concerned opera drama about a prominent opera singer who promises to deliver a grand concert upon returning to his small town, only to lose his voice just before the show is to start. Proof positive that the opera ain't over 'til the fat lady sings. 100m/C VHS. PL Zbigniew Zapasiewicz; **D:** Janusz Zaorski.

Barjo 🐾🐾 1993 In a bland and isolated French suburb lives willful housewife Fanfan (Bouchet) with her older businessman husband Charles (Bohringer) and her eccentric twin brother Barjo (Girardot). Barjo is obsessed with lists and extraterrestrials and his sister's affair with their next-door neighbor, which he likes to spy on. Her husband naturally begins to go crazy. Deadpan satire based on the novel "Confessions of a Crap Artist" by Philip K. Dick. The post-WWII American setting of the novel makes a decidedly uneasy transition to contemporary French life. In French with English subtitles. 85m/C VHS. FR Anne Brochet, Hippolyte Girardot, Richard Bohringer, Consuelo de Havilland, Renaud Danner, Nathalie Boutefeu; **D:** Jerome Boivin; **W:** Jerome Boivin, Jacques Audiard; **M:** Hugues LeBars.

Barkl 🐾½ 2002 (R) L.A. dog walker Lucy (Morgan) begins to overly-identify with her clients when she stops speaking and begins barking and displaying other canine behavior. Her baffled husband Peter (Tergesen) consults Lucy's equally odd parents as well as a vet (Kudrow) and a shrink (D'Onofrio) and decides to have his wife committed. But when Lucy becomes catatonic in the hospital, Peter decides to take her home and learn to adapt. He's a lot more understanding than the viewer will be. 100m/C VHS, DVD. US Lee Tergesen, Lisa Kudrow, Vincent D'Onofrio, Heather Morgan, Hank Azaria, Mary Jo Deschanel, Scott Wilson, Aimee Graham, Wade Andrew Williams; **D:** Kasia Adamik; **W:** Heather Morgan; **C:** Irek Hartowicz; **M:** Eric Colvin.

The Barkleys of Broadway 🐾🐾🐾 1949 The famous dancing team's last film together; they play a quarreling husband/wife showbiz team. ♪They Can't Take That Away From Me; The Sabre Dance; Swing Trot; Manhattan Downbeat; A Weekend in the Country; My One and Only Highland Fling; You'd Be Hard to Replace; Bouncin' the Blues; Shoes With Wings On. 109m/C VHS, DVD. Fred Astaire, Ginger Rogers, Gale Robbins, Oscar Levant, Jacques Francois, Billie Burke; **D:** Charles Walters; **W:** Adolph Green, Betty Comden; **C:** Harry Stradling Sr.; **M:** Ira Gershwin, Harry Warren.

Barn of the Naked Dead woof! Nightmare Circus; Terror Circus 1973 Prine plays a sicko who tortures women while his radioactive monster dad terrorizes the Nevada desert. Rudolph's first film, directed under the pseudonym Gerald Cormier. 86m/C VHS. Andrew Prine, Manuella Thiess, Sherry Alberoni, Gylian Roland, Al Cormier, Jennifer Ashley; **D:** Alan Rudolph; **W:** Alan Rudolph, Roman Valenti.

Barnaby and Me 🐾🐾 1977 Australian star Barnaby the Koala Bear joins an international con-man in this romantic adventure. The mob is chasing the conman when he meets and falls for a lovely young woman and her daughter. 90m/C VHS. AU Sid Caesar, Juliet Mills, Sally Boyden; **D:** Norman Panama.

Barney's Great Adventure 🐾🐾 1998 (G) First the bad news: that big purple dweebosaur made a movie and your three-year-old is going to make you buy the video. Now the good news: since it's on video you can cue it up for the young-uns and run screaming from the room. You see, they don't care what you think about Barney, who looks a little like a big lug in a purple felt suit, actually. In this extravaganza of not so special effects, Barney and two little girls chase a magical egg around town and encounter a parade, a circus and other allegedly wonderful things, all while trying to convince the older Kyle that Barney is "cool." In a surprise move, the egg hatches to reveal...that new stuffed animal you're going to have to buy! 75m/C VHS, DVD. George Hearn, Shirley Douglas, Kyla Pratt, Trevor Morgan, Diana Rice, Renee Madeleine Le Guerrier; **D:** Steve Gomer; **W:** Stephen White; **C:** Sandi Sissel; **V:** Bob West, Julie Johnson.

Barnum 🐾🐾½ 1986 P.T. Barnum's life is focused upon in this biography about the man who helped to form "The Greatest Show On Earth". 100m/C VHS. Burt Lancaster, Hanna Schygulla, Jenny Lind, John Roney; **D:** Lee Philips.

Barnyard 🐾🐾 2006 (PG) Young Otis the cow (James) is unconcerned about keeping the secret that animals can not only talk, but like to dance, sing, party, and play pranks. But when the farmer's away, Otis is given the unexpected responsibility of looking after things. Cute, but probably more enjoyable for younger kids. Some jokes click for older kids and adults, but not quite enough. 88m/C DVD. US D: Steve Oedekerk; **W:** Steve Oedekerk; **M:** John Debney; **V:** Kevin James, Courteney Cox, Sam Elliot, Danny Glover, Andie MacDowell, Wanda Sykes, David Koechner, Steve Oedekerk, Rob Paulsen, Dom Irrera, Maria Bamford, Laraine Newman, Maurice LaMarche, Jeff Garcia.

Barocco 🐾🐾 1976 Crook kills his lookalike and takes his place and his girlfriend. Together the duo try blackmail to get the money they need to start a new life. Self-conscious would-be film noir. 102m/C VHS, DVD. FR Gerard Depardieu, Isabelle Adjani, Marie-France Pisier, Jean-Claude Brialy; **D:** Andre Techine; **W:** Andre Techine, Marilyn Goldin; **C:** Bruno Nuytten; **M:** Philippe Sarde.

The Baron 🐾🐾½ 1988 Vengeance is the name of the game when an underworld boss gets stiffed on a deal. Fast-paced no-brainer street drama. 88m/C VHS, DVD. Calvin Lockhart, Charles McGregor, Joan Blondell, Richard Lynch, Marlene Clark; **D:** Philip Fenty.

The Baron and the Kid 🐾 1984 A pool shark finds out that his opponent at a charity exhibition game is his long-lost son. Based on Johnny Cash's song. Made for TV. 100m/C VHS, DVD. Johnny Cash, Darren McGavin, June Carter Cash, Richard Roundtree; **D:** Gary Nelson; **M:** Brad Fiedel. **TV**

Baron Munchausen 🐾🐾🐾 1943 The German film studio UFA celebrated its 25th anniversary with this lavish version of the Baron Munchausen legend, starring a cast of top-name German performers at the height of the Third Reich. Filmed in Agfacolor; available in English subtitled or dubbed versions. 120m/C VHS, DVD. GE Hans Albers, Kaethe Kaack, Hermann Speelmanns, Leo Slezak; **D:** Josef von Baky.

Baron of Arizona 🐾🐾🐾 1951 Land office clerk almost succeeds in convincing the U.S. that he owned the state of Arizona. 99m/B VHS, DVD. Vincent Price, Ellen Drew, Beulah Bondi, Reed Hadley, Vladimir Sokoloff; **D:** Samuel Fuller; **W:** Samuel Fuller; **C:** James Wong Howe.

Barracuda woof! The Lucifer Project 1978 (R) Lots of innocent swimmers are being eaten by crazed killer barracudas. 90m/C VHS. Wayne Crawford, Jason Evers, Roberta Leighton; **D:** Harry Kerwin.

The Barretts of Wimpole Street 🐾🐾🐾 Forbidden Alliance 1934 The moving, almost disturbing, account of poetess Elizabeth Barrett, an invalid confined to her bed, with only her poetry and her dog to keep her company. She is wooed by poet Robert Browning, in whose arms she finds true happiness and a miraculous recovery. Multi-faceted drama expertly played by all. 110m/B VHS. Fredric March, Norma Shearer, Charles Laughton, Maureen O'Sullivan, Katharine Alexander, Una O'Connor, Ian Wolfe; **D:** Sidney Franklin; **C:** William H. Daniels.

Barrio Wars 🐾½ 2002 (R) Hip hop Latino Romeo and Juliet staged on the mean streets of L.A. Plato and Angelina are the star-crossed lovers from rival gangs sparking violence and turmoil all over the city. Nice try, but the standard no-budget acting style and a rather jarring soft-core sex scene defeats any intended purpose. But really, what's the point? Leonardo DiCaprio and Claire Danes have already done modern-day Shakespeare much better. 90m/C VHS, DVD. Sevier Crespo, Luchana Gatica, Anthony Martins, Beny Mena, Chino XL; **D:** Paul Wynne; **W:** Paul Wynne. **VIDEO**

Barry Lyndon 🐾🐾🐾½ 1975 (PG) Ravishing adaptation of the classic Thackeray novel about the adventures of an Irish gambler moving from innocence to self-destructive arrogance in the aristocracy of 18th Century England. Visually opulent, Kubrick received excellent performances from all his actors, and a stunning display of history, but the end result still overwhelms. O'Neal has seldom been better. 185m/C VHS, DVD. Ryan O'Neal, Marisa Berenson, Patrick Magee, Hardy Kruger, Guy Hamilton; **D:** Stanley Kubrick; **W:** Stanley Kubrick; **C:** John Alcott. Oscars '75: Art Dir./Set Dec., Cinematog., Costume Des., Orig. Song Score and/or Adapt.; British Acad. '75: Director (Kubrick); L.A. Film Critics '75: Cinematog.; Natl. Bd. of Review '75: Director (Kubrick); Natl. Soc. Film Critics '75: Cinematog.

Barry McKenzie Holds His Own 🐾🐾½ 1974 In this sequel to "The Adventures of Barry McKenzie," we find that after a young man's aunt is mistaken for the Queen of England, two emissaries of Count Plasma of Transylvania kidnap her to use as a Plasma tourist attraction. Based on the 'Private Eye' comic strip, this crude Australian film is as disappointing as the first of the Barry McKenzie stories. 93m/C VHS. AU Barry Humphries, Barry Crocker, Donald Pleasence; **D:** Bruce Beresford; **W:** Barry Humphries, Bruce Beresford.

Bartleby 🐾🐾½ 1970 A new version of the classic Herman Melville short story. McEnery is Bartleby the clerk, who refuses to leave his job even after he's fired; Scofield is his frustrated boss. 79m/C VHS, DVD. Paul Scofield, John McEnery, Colin Jeavons, Thorley Walters; **D:** Anthony Friedman; **W:** Rodney Carr-Smith.

Bartleby 🐾🐾 2001 (PG-13) Contempo version of Herman Melville's 1856 novella "Bartleby the Scrivener." Eccentric Bartleby (Glover) is the model of efficiency when first hired to do clerical work in a nondescript records office. But gradually Bartleby begins to refuse tasks, then to do anything at all—even firing him has no effect to the consternation of his boss (Paymer) and the bewilderment of his co-workers. 83m/C VHS, DVD. US Crispin Glover, David Paymer, Glenne Headly, Joe Piscopo, Maury Chaykin, Seymour Cassel, Carrie Snodgress, Dick Martin; **D:** Jonathan Parker; **W:** Jonathan Parker, Catherine Di Napoli; **C:** Wah Ho Chan; **M:** Jonathan Parker, Seth Asarnow.

Barton Fink 🐾🐾🐾 1991 (R) This eerie comic nightmare comes laden with awards (including the Palme D'Or from Cannes) but only really works if you care about the time and place. Fink is a seedy New York playwright staying in a seedy Hollywood hotel in the 1940s, straining to write a simple B-movie script. Macabre events, both real and imagined, compound his writer's block. Superb set design from Dennis Gassner complements an unforgettable cast of grotesques. 116m/C VHS, DVD. John Turturro, John Goodman, Judy Davis, Michael Lerner, John Mahoney, Tony Shalhoub, Jon Polito, Steve Buscemi, David Warrilow, Richard Portnow, Christopher Murney; **D:** Joel Coen; **W:** Joel Coen, Ethan Coen; **C:** Roger Deakins; **M:** Carter Burwell. Cannes '91: Actor (Turturro), Director (Coen), Film; L.A. Film Critics '91: Cinematog., Support. Actor (Lerner); N.Y. Film Critics '91: Cinematog., Support. Actress (Davis); Natl. Soc. Film Critics '91: Cinematog.

The Base 🐾🐾½ 1999 (R) Army Intelligence officer Major John Murphy (Dacascos) is sent undercover to Fort Tilman to investigate the murder of an army operations officer. Murphy is assigned to a border patrol unit and discovers his fellow soldiers are muscling in on the Mexican/American drug trade. When he discovers who's behind the operation, Murphy's cover is blown and he's in for the fight of his life. 101m/C VHS, DVD. Mark Dacascos, Tim Abell, Paula Trickey, Noah Blake, Frederick Coffin; **D:** Mark L. Lester; **W:** Jeff Albert, William Martell; **C:** Jacques Haitkin; **M:** Paul Zaza. **VIDEO**

Based on an Untrue Story 🐾🐾½ 1993 Campy spoof of popular "true story" TV docudramas in which powerful Satin Chau (Fairchild), a perfume mogul, loses her sense of smell. Satin leaves her mentor Varda (Cannon) to discover herself but finds that only her two separated-at-birth sisters, Velour (Lake) and Corduroy (Jackson), hold the secrets to the past. It's hard to spoof a genre that's become a cliche but this TV movie does its best. 90m/C VHS. Morgan Fairchild, Dyan Cannon, Victoria Jackson, Ricki Lake, Harvey Korman, Robert Goulet, Dan Hedaya; **D:** Jim Drake.

BASEketball 🐾🐾 1998 (R) Dude! Three slacker buddies ("South Park"'s Parker and Stone plus Bachar) invent a new game in their driveway—a combo of basketball with baseball rules—and see it turn into big business. Parkere gets to romance Jenna Reed (Bleeth), a social worker who helps "health-challenged" kids. Stone and Parker's penchant for gross-out humor and having their characters say whatever's on their minds (no matter how offensive) mixes well with Zucker's talent for sight gags and physical humor to create an enjoyably guilty pleasure. Based on a game that Zucker invented with friends. 103m/C VHS, DVD. Trey Parker, Matt Stone, Yasmine Bleeth, Jenny McCarthy, Ernest Borgnine, Dian Bachar, Robert Vaughn, Bob Costas, Al Michaels, Reggie Jackson, Robert Stack, Steve Garvey, Kareem Abdul-Jabbar; **D:** David Zucker; **W:** David Zucker, Robert Locash, Jeffrey Wright, Lewis Friedman; **C:** Steve Mason; **M:** Ira Newborn.

The Bashful Bachelor 🐾🐾 1942 Yokel joker Abner trades his delivery car for a race horse, hoping to win a big race. 78m/B VHS, DVD. Chester Lauck, Norris Goff, Zasu Pitts, Grady Sutton, Louise Currie, Irving Bacon, Earle Hodgins, Benny Rubin; **D:** Malcolm St. Clair.

Basic ♂♂ 2003 (R) Travolta, swallowing scenery and his fellow actors in one gulp, is DEA agent and ex-Army Ranger Tom Hardy, brought in to investigate how a training mission ended in all but two soldiers being killed. Over the objections of the base's top cop, Capt. Julia Osborne (Nielsen, sporting an inconsistent Southern accent), he interrogates both survivors and gets two completely differing accounts. Sgt. West was universally hated, and the men were killed by each other, and the other one was killed in the flashback, Sgt. West was universally hated, and the men were killed by each other, and some been involved. Convoluted and confusing are two words you could use for this script, but both are woefully inadequate to describe how it messes with your head, and not in that good, "Wow, that was clever" way. It seems that the actors are as confused as the audience and decide to cover it's learned that the platoon's commander, Sgt. West was universally hated, and the men were killed by each other, and the other that with epidemic over-acting. 95m/C VHS, DVD. US John Travolta, Samuel L. Jackson, Connie Nielsen, Giovanni Ribisi, Brian Van Holt, Taye Diggs, Christian de la Fuente, Dash Mihok, Timothy Daly, Roselyn Sanchez, Harry Connick Jr.; D: John McTiernan; W: James Vanderbilt; C: Steve Mason; M: Klaus Badelt.

Basic Instinct ♂♂♂½ 1992 (R) Controversial thriller had tongues wagging months before its theatrical release. Burnt-out detective Douglas falls for beautiful, manipulative murder suspect Stone, perfectly cast as a bisexual ice queen who may or may not have done the deed. Noted for highly erotic sex scenes and an expensive (3 million bucks) script; ultimately the predictable plot is disappointing. Gay activists tried to interrupt filming because they objected to the depiction of Stone's character but only succeeded in generating more free publicity. The American release was edited to avoid an "NC-17" rating, but an uncut, unrated video version is also available. 123m/C VHS, Blu-ray Disc. Michae Douglas, Sharon Stone George Dzundza, Jeanne Tripplehorn, Denis Arndt, Leilani Sarelle Ferrer, Bruce A. Young, Chelcie Foss, Dorothy Malone, Wayne Knight, Stephen Tobolowsky; D: Paul Verhoeven; W: Joe Eszterhas; C: Jan De Bont; M: Jerry Goldsmith. AWARDS MTV Movie Awards '93: Female Perf. (Stone), Most Desirable Female (Stone).

Basic Instinct 2 ♂ 2006 (F) It took 14 years for a sequel and this glossy, laughably overwrought mess is what we get? Stone tries too hard reprising her role as cold-blooded vamp Catherine Tramell, who's now living in London. After a fatal car crash, suspicious Scotland Yard detective Washburn (Thewlis) asks criminologist Michael Glass (Morrissey) to evaluate Catherine 'cr possible criminal charges. His diagnosis is "risk addiction." Gee, doc, no kidding. Soon Michael is drawn into Catherine's possibly deadly web. Maybe this effort will become a midnight movie, just waiting to be mocked. 114m/C DVD, Blu-ray Disc. US Sharon Stone, David Morrissey, David Thewlis, Charlotte Rampling, Hugh Dancy, Flora Montgomery, Iain Robertson, Indira Varma, Anne Caillon, Stan Collymore, Heathcote Williams; D: Michael Caton-Jones; W: Leora Barish, Henry Bean; C: Gyula Pados; M: John Murphy. AWARDS Golden Raspberries '06: Worst Actress (Stone), Worst Picture, Worst Actress (Stone), Worst Screenplay, Worst Sequel/Prequel.

Basic Training WOOF! 1966 (R) Three sexy ladies wiggle into the Pentagon in their efforts to clean up the government. 85m/C VHS, DVD. Ann Dusenberry, Rhonda Shear, Angela Aames, Walter Gotell; D: Andrew Sugarman.

Basil ♂♂½ 1998 (R) Turn of the century English aristocrat Basil (Leto) strives for the approval of his overbearing father (Jacobi) while also trying to please the selfish woman he loves (Forlani). Based on the novel by Wilkie Collins. 113m/C VHS. Jared Leto, Claire Forlani, Christian Slater, Derek Jacobi; D: Radha Bharadwaj.

Basileus Quartet ♂♂♂ II Quartetto Basileus 1982 The replacement for a violinist in a well-established quartet creates emotional havoc. Beautiful music, excellent and evocative photography. 118m/C VHS. FR IT Pierre Malet, Hector Alterio, Omero Antonutti, Michel Vitold, Alain Cuny, Gabriele Ferzetti, Elisabeth (Lisa) Kreuzer; D: Fabio Carpi; W: Fabio Carpi; C: Dante Spinotti.

The Basket ♂♂½ 1999 (PG) There's a lot going on in a small Washington community, circa 1918. Martin Conlon (Coyote) is the new teacher (he's from Boston) at the one-room schoolhouse who introduces opera and basketball into the curriculum. Then German orphans Helmut and Brigitta (Willenborg) come to live with the local doctor and are persecuted for their nationality because of WWI. Mr. Emery (MacDonald) is especially hostile since his son was wounded in the war but Mrs. Emery (Allen) is willing to give the newcomers a chance. Helmut turns out to be a hoops natural and the team has a chance to compete in a national championship—if they can set their differences aside. 104m/C VHS, DVD. Karen Allen, Peter Coyote, Robert Karl Burke, Amber Willenborg, Jock MacDonald, Eric Dane, Casey Cowan, Brian Skala, Tony Lincoln, Patrick Treacway, Ellen Travolta; D: Rich Cowan; W: Rich Cowan, Frank Swoboda, Tessa Swoboda; C: Dan Heigh; M: Don Caron.

Basket Case ♂♂♂ 1982 A gory horror film about a pair of Siamese twins—one normal, the other grueosmely deformed. The pair is surgically separated at birth, and the evil disfigured twin is tossed in the garbage. Fraternal ties being what they are, the normal brother retrieves his twin—essentially a head atop shoulders—and totes him around in a basket (he ain't heavy). Together they begin twisted and deadly revenge, with the brother-in-a-basket in charge. Very entertaining, if you like this sort of thing. Followed by two sequels. 89m/C VHS. Kevin Van Hentenryck, Terri Susan Smith, Beverly Bonner, Robert Vogel, Diana Browne, Lloyd Pace, Elli Freeman, Joe Clarke, Ruth Neuman, Richard Pierce, Dorothy Strongin; D: Frank Henenlotter; W: Frank Henenlotter; C: Bruce Torbet; M: Gus Russo.

Basket Case 2 ♂♂½ 1990 (R) Surgically separated teenage mutant brothers Duane and Belial are back! This time they've found happiness in a "special" family—until they're plagued by the paparazzi. Higher production values make this sequel slicker than its low-budget predecessor, but it somehow lacks the same charm. 90m/C VHS, DVD. Kevin Van Hentenryck, Annie Ross, Kathryn Meisle, Heather Rattray, Jason Evers, Ted (Theodore) Sorel, Matt Miller, Ron Fazio, Leonard Jackson, Beverly Bonner; D: Frank Henenlotter; W: Frank Henenlotter and M. "Bob" Baldwin Jr.; M: Joe Renzetti.

Basket Case 3: The Progeny ♂♂ 1992 (R) In this sequel to the cult horror hits "Basket Case" and "Basket Case 2," Belial is back and this time he's about to discover the perils of parenthood as the mutant Mrs. Belial delivers a litter of bouncing mini-monsters. Everything is fine until the police kidnap the little creatures and chaos breaks out as Belial goes on a shocking rampage in his newly created mechanical body. Weird special effects make this a cult favorite for fans of the truly outrageous. 90m/C VHS, DVD. Annie Ross, Kevin Van Hentenryck, Gil Roper, Tina Louise Hilbert, Dan Biggers, Jim O'Doherty, Jackson Faw, Jim Grimshaw; D: Frank Henenlotter; W: Frank Henenlotter, Robert Martin; C: Bob Paone; M: Joe Renzetti.

The Basketball Diaries ♂♂ 1995 (R) Disappointing adaptation of underground writer/musician Jim Carroll's 1978 cult memoirs, with DiCaprio starring as the teen athlete whose life spirals into drug addiction and hustling on the New York streets. Carroll and friends Mickey (Wahlberg), Neutron (McGaw), and Pedro (Madio), form the heart of St. Vitus' hot hoopster team. But the defiant quartet really get their kicks from drugs, dares, and petty crime—leading to an ever-downward decade is, although DiCaprio (and Wahlberg) are particularly effective in a self-conscious first effort from Kalvert. 102m/C VHS, DVD. Leonardo DiCaprio, Mark Wahlberg, Patrick McGaw, James Madio, Bruno Kirby, Ernie Hudson, Lorraine Bracco, Juliette Lewis, Josh Mostel, Michael Rapaport, Michae Imperioli.

The Bat ♂♂♂ 1926 A bat-obsessed killer stalks the halls of a spooky mansion in this early film version of the Mary Roberts Rinehart novel. 81m/B VHS, DVD Andre de Beranger, Charles Herzinger, Emily Fitzroy, Louise Fazenda, Arthur Houseman, Robert McKim, Jack Pickford, Jewel Carmen; D: Roland West; W: Roland West.

The Bat ♂♂ 1959 A great plot centering around a murderer called the Bat, who kills hapless victims by ripping out their throats when he isn't busy searching for $1 million worth of securities stashed in the old house he is living in. Adapted from the novel by Mary Roberts Rinehart. 80m/B VHS, DVD. Vincent Price, Agnes Moorehead, Gavin Gordon, John Sutton, Lenita Lane, Darla Hood; D: Crane Wilbur; W: Crane Wilbur; C: Joseph Biroc; M: Louis Forbes.

Bastard out of Carolina ♂♂ 1996 (R) Huston's steeped-in-controversy directorial debut tells the story of young mom Anney (Leigh), who lives a hardscrabble life in Greenville, South Carolina. Anney's eager to find love and succumbs to the charms of laborer Glen (Eldard), despite his nasty temper. Eleven-year-old Bone and Glen are immediately at odds willing to face the truth, until a final horrific event. Based on the 1992 semiautobiographical novel by Dorothy Allison the film was originally made for Ted Turner's TNT network but was rejected as unsuitable because of its graphic depiction of child abuse. 97m/C VHS, DVD. Sonny Shroyer, Jennifer Jason Leigh, Jena Malone, Ron Eldard, Glenne Headly, Lyle Lovet, Dermot Mulroney, Christina Ricci, Michael Rooker, Diana Scarwid, Susan Traylor, Grace Zabriskie; D: Anjelica Huston; W: Anne Meredith; C: Anthony B. Richmond; M: Van Dyke Parks. TV

The Bastard ♂♂½ 1978 Dashing (but alas, illegitimate) nobleman roams Europe on futile "Roots"-like search, then settles for American during the Revolutionary War in this long-winded TV adaptation of John Jakes's equally cumbersome bestseller (part of his popular Bicentennial series). Stevens stars, along with many supporting performers merely keeping active. Followed by "The Rebels" and "The Seekers." 189m/C VHS, Andrew Stevens, Tom Bosley, Kim Cattrall, Buddy Ebsen, Lorne Greene, Olivia Hussey, Cameron Mitchell, Harry (Henry) Morgan, Patricia Neal, Eleanor Parker, Donald Pleasence, William Shatner, Barry Sullivan, Noah Beery Jr., James Gregory, Mark Neely, Ike Eisenmann, Charles Haid, Russell Johnson, James Whitmore Jr., Alan Napier, Stephen Furst, Philip Baker Hall; D: Lee H. Katzin; W: Guerdon (Gordon) Trueblood; C: Michael Hugo; M: John Addison; Nar: Raymond Burr. TV

Basquiat ♂♂♂ Build a Fort Set It on Fire 1996 (R) First-time writer/director and reknowned '80s pop artist Schnabel paints a celluloid portrait of African-American artist Jean Michel Basquiat, who went from graffiti artist to overnight sensation in the mid-1980s before dying of a drug overdose at 27. Schnabel's first-hand knowledge provides details of the painter's New York art scene of the time, using an all-star cast (no mean feat on a $3 million budget). Making the move from stage to screen, Wright is an aptly deep and elusive Basquiat and Bowie stands out in a marvelously conceived portrayal of Bas-quiat's pseudo-mentor, the equally sensational Warhol. Features authentic works of the artists portrayed and some very convincing Basquiat reproductions done by David Bowie, Dennis Hopper, Gary Oldman, Christopher Walken, Michael Wincott, Benicio Del Toro, Parker Posey, Elina Lowensohn, Courtney Love, Claire Forlani, Willem Dafoe, Paul Bartel, Tatum O'Neal, Chuck Pfeiffer; D: Julian Schnabel; W: Julian Schnabel; C: Ron Fortunato; M: John Cale. Ind. Spirit '97: Support. Actor (Del Toro). James Dennis (Jim) Carroll; D: Scot Kalvert; W: Bryan Goluboff; C: David Phillips; M: Graeme Revell.

Bataan ♂♂♂ 1943 A rugged wartime combat drama following the true story of a small platoon in the Philippines endeavoring to blow up a pivoral Japanese bridge. Also available in a colorized version. 115m/B VHS, DVD. Robert Taylor, George Murphy, Thomas Mitchell, Desi Arnaz Sr., Lee Bowman, Lloyd Nolan, Robert Walker, Barry Nelson, Phillip Terry, Tom Dugan, Roque Espiritu, Kenneth Spencer, Alex Havier, Donald Curtis, Lynne Carver, Bud Geary, Dorothy Morris; D: Tay Garnett; W: Robert D. (Robert Hardy) Andrews; C: Sidney Wagner; M: Bronislau Kaper, Eric Zeisl.

Bathing Beauty ♂♂½ 1944 This musical stars Skelton as a pop composer with the hots for college swim teacher Williams. Rathbone is a music executive who sees the romance as a threat to Skelton's career and to his own profit margin. Full of aquatic ballet, Skelton's shtick, and wonderful original melodies. The first film in which Williams received star billing. ♫ Cred for You; Bim, Bam, Boom; Tico-Tico; I'll Take the High Note; Loch Lomond; By the Waters of Minnetonka; Magic is the Moonlight; Trumpet Blues; Hora Staccato. 101m/C VHS, DVD. Red Skelton, Esther Williams, Basil Rathbone, Bill Goodwin, Jean Porter, Carlos Ramirez, Donald Meek, Ethel Smith Helen Forrest; D: George Sidney; C: Harry Stradling Sr.; M: Xavier Cugat.

The Bat People ♂ It Lives By Night 1974 (R) Less-than-gripping horror flick in which Dr. John Beck is bitten by a bat while on his honeymoon. He then begins to kill anyone who stumbles across his path. The gory special effects make for a great movie if you've ever been bitten by that sort of thing. 95m/C VHS. Stewart Moss, Marianne McAndrew, Michael Pataki, Paul Carr; D: Jerry Jameson; C: Matthew F. Leonetti; M: Artie Kane.

The Bat Whispers ♂♂♂½ 1930 A masked madman is stalking the residents of a large mansion; eerie tale that culminates in an appeal to the audience to keep the plot under wraps. Unusually crafted film for its early era. Comic mystery based on the novel and play by Mary Roberts Rinehart and Avery Hopwood. 82m/B VHS, DVD. Chester Morris, Chance West, Richard Tucker, Wilson Benge, DeWitt Jennings, Una Merkel, Spencer Charters; D: Roland West; W: Roland West; C: Ray June, Robert Planck.

Bat 21 ♂♂♂ 1988 (R) Hackman, an American officer, is stranded in the wilds of Vietnam alone after his plane is shot down. He must rely on himself and Glover, with whom he has radio contact, to get him out. Glover and Hackman give solid performances in this otherwise average film. 112m/C VHS, DVD. Gene Hackman, Danny Glover, Jerry Reed, David Marshall Grant, Clayton Rohner, Erich Anderson, Joe Dorsey; D: Peter Markle; W: William C. Anderson; C: Mark Irwin; M: Christopher Young.

Batman ♂♂♂½ 1966 Holy television camp, Batman! Will the caped crusader win the Bat-tle against the combined forces of the Joker, the Riddler, the Penguin, and Catwoman? Will Batman and Robin ever figure out that Russian journalist Council from dehydration? Will the Bat genius ever figure out that Russian journalist Miss Kitka and Catwoman are one and the same? Biff! Thwack! Socko! Not to be confused with the Michael Keaton version of the Dark Knight, this is the pot-bellied Adam West Batman, teeming with Bat satire and made especially for the big screen. Hollywood's faith in media blitzing. The Caped Crusader (Keaton) is back in Gotham City, where once the criminals are afraid to walk the streets alone. There's a new breed of criminal in Gotham, led by the infamous Joker (Nicholson). Their random attacks via acid-based make-up are just the beginning. Keaton is surprisingly good as the dual personality hero though Nicholson steals the show with his campy 104m/C VHS, DVD. Adam West, Burt Ward, Adam West, Burt Gorshin, Lee Meriwether, Alan Napier, Neil Hamilton, Stafford Repp, Madge Blake, Reginald Denny, Milton Frome; D: Leslie Martinson; W: Lorenzo Semple Jr.; C: Howard Schwartz; M: Nelson Riddle.

Batman ♂♂♂½ 1989 (PG-13) The blockbuster fantasy epic that renewed Hollywood's faith in media blitzing. The Caped Crusader (Keaton) is back in Gotham City, where once the criminals are afraid to walk the streets alone. There's a new breed of criminal in Gotham, led by the infamous Joker (Nicholson). Their random attacks via acid-based make-up are just the beginning...

performance. Basinger is blonde and feisty as photog Vicki Vale, who falls for mysterious millionaire Bruce Wayne (and the bat). Marvelously designed and shot. Followed by three sequels. **126m/C VHS, DVD, UMD.** Michael Keaton, Jack Nicholson, Kim Basinger, Robert Wuhl, Tracey Walter, Billy Dee Williams, Pat Hingle, Michael Gough, Jack Palance, Jerry Hall; *D:* Tim Burton; *W:* Sam Hamm, Warren Skaaren; *C:* Roger Pratt; *M:* Danny Elfman. Prince. Oscars '89. Art Dir./Set Dec.

Batman and Robin 🦴🦴 **1997 (PG-13)** Includes lots of flash but, as usual, not much substance in this fourth adventure, which features a less angst-ridden caped crusader in the charming persona of Clooney. O'Donnell, who apparently knows a good gig when he's got one, returns as Robin. They must battle evil industrialist, Mr. Freeze (an impressively costumed Schwarzenegger), and his partner-with-the-deadly-kiss (but what a way to go!), Poison Ivy (Thurman), who have plans to freeze Gotham City. Our heroes have some additional help in the person of Batgirl (Silverstone), who's now butler Alfred's (Gough) niece (she was Commissioner Gordon's daughter in the comics). Story's simplified but the secondary characters still get lost in the crowd. Director Schumacher's already agreed to helm a fifth film, but don't hold your breath since he succeeded in driving the impossible: killing the franchise. **125m/C VHS, DVD.** George Clooney, Chris O'Donnell, Arnold Schwarzenegger, Uma Thurman, Alicia Silverstone, Michael Gough, Pat Hingle, John Glover, Elle Macpherson, Vivica A. Fox, Vendela Thommesen, Jeep Swenson; *D:* Joel Schumacher; *W:* Akiva Goldsman; *C:* Stephen Goldblatt; *M:* Elliot Goldenthal. Golden Raspberries '97: Worst Support. Actress (Silverstone).

Batman Begins 🦴🦴🦴 **2005 (PG-13)** They got rid of the Bat-nipples? Joel Schumacher will be so disappointed. Fortunately for everyone else, Nolan rejects the other Bat-sequels' lame campiness and returns Batman to his gritty roots, showing us how a young Bruce Wayne (Bale) first became the Caped Crusader. After training abroad with the mysterious Ducard (Neeson) and Ra's Al Ghul (Watanabe), Wayne begins his one-man war on crime with the help of his butler Alfred (Caine), good cop Jim Gordon (Oldman), and tech-savvy Lucius Fox (Freeman). The cast is beyond stellar, and Nolan does an amazing job of making Batman's world seem almost plausible. There's a bit too much angsty pondering about the nature of fear, but you'll forget all that once you see the Lamborghini-inspired Batmobile. **141m/C DVD, Blu-ray Disc, UMD, HD DVD, US** Christian Bale, Michael Caine, Ken(saku) Watanabe, Liam Neeson, Katie Holmes, Gary Oldman, Morgan Freeman, Katie Holmes, Gary Oldman, Liam Neeson, Rutger Hauer, Mark Boone Jr., Linus Roache, Gus Lewis; *D:* Christopher Nolan; *W:* Christopher Nolan, David S. Goyer; *C:* Wally Pfister; *M:* Hans Zimmer, James Newton Howard.

Batman Forever 🦴🦴 **1995 (PG-13)** Holy franchise, Batman! Third-time actioner considerably lightens up Tim Burton's dark vision for a more family-oriented Caped Crusader (now played by Kilmer, who fills out lip requirement nicely). The Boy Wonder also makes a first-time appearance in the bulked-up form of O'Donnell, a street-smart Robin with revenge on his mind. Naturally, the villains still steal the show in the personas of maniacal Carrey (the Riddler) and the sartorially splendid Jones as Harvey "Two-Face" Dent. Rounding out this charismatic cast is Kidman's slinky psychologist Chase Meridian, who's eager to find the man inside the bat (and who can blame her). Lots of splashy toys for the boys and awe-inspiring sets to show you where the money went. A Gotham City gas that did $53 million at it's opening weekend boxoffice—breaking the "Jurassic Park" record, testimony to the power of aggressive marketing. **121m/C VHS, DVD.** Val Kilmer, Tommy Lee Jones, Jim Carrey, Chris O'Donnell, Nicole Kidman, Drew Barrymore, Debi Mazar, Michael Gough, Pat Hingle, John Favreau, George Wallace, Don "The Dragon" Wilson, Ed Begley Jr., Rene Auberjonois, Joe Grifasi, Jessica Tuck, Kimberly Scott; *D:* Joel Schumacher; *W:* Janet Scott Batchler, Akiva Goldsman, Lee Batchler; *C:* Stephen Goldblatt; *M:* Elliot Goldenthal. Blockbuster '96: Action Actress, T. (Kidman).

Batman: Mask of the Phantasm 🦴🦴1/2 *Batman: The Animated Movie* **1993 (PG)** Based on the animated Batman series with the Fox TV series with the animated Batman fending off old enemy the Joker, new enemy the Phantasm, and dreaming of his lost first love. Cartoon film noir set in the 1940s but filled with '90s sarcasm. Complicated storyline with a stylish dark look may be lost on the kiddies but adults will stay awake. **77m/C VHS, DVD.** *D:* Eric Radomski, Bruce W. Timm; *W:* Michael Reaves, Alan Burnett, Paul Dini, Martin Pakc; *M:* Shirley Walker; *V:* Kevin Conroy, Dana Delany, Mark Hamill, Stacy Keach, Hart Bochner, Abe Vigoda, Efrem Zimbalist Jr., Dick Miller.

Batman Returns 🦴🦴🦴1/2 **1992 (PG-13)** More of the same from director Burton, with Batman more of a supporting role overshadowed by provocative villains. DeVito is the cruely misshapen Penguin who seeks to rule over Gotham City; Pfeiffer is the exotic and dangerous Catwoman—who has more than a passing personal interest in Batman; Walken is the maniacal tycoon Max Shreck. Pfeiffer fares best in her wickedly sexy role and second-skin costume (complete with bull-whip). Plot is secondary to special effects and nightmarish settings. Despite a big budget, this grandiose sequel is of the love it or leave it variety. **126m/C VHS, DVD.** Michael Keaton, Danny DeVito, Michelle Pfeiffer, Christopher Walken, Michael Gough, Michael Murphy, Cristi Conaway, Pat Hingle, Vincent Schiavelli, Jan Hooks, Paul (Pee-wee Herman) Reubens, Andrew Bryniarski; *D:* Tim Burton; *W:* Daniel Waters; *C:* Stefan Czapsky; *M:* Danny Elfman.

Baton Rouge 🦴🦴 **1988** Gigolo Antonio (Banderas) gets together with psychiatrist Anao (Abril) in a scheme to seduce one of her patients, the wealthy Isabel (Maura), who suffers from terrible nightmares. They plan to kill her wealthy ex-husband and accuse her of the crime in order to get her fortune. But there's an elaborate double-cross and things go back for all concerned. The spanish trio, all veterans of director Pedro Almodovar's films, certainly know how to steam up the screen. Spanish with subtitles. **90m/C VHS.** *SP* Antonio Banderas, Victoria Abril, Carmen Maura; *D:* Rafael Moleon; *W:* Rafael Moleon, Agustin Diaz Yanes; *C:* Angel Luis Fernandez.

Bats 🦴1/2 **1999 (PG-13)** B-grade comedy/thriller proves that people with a warped vision can create something that'll suck the life right out of you. Unfortunately, they use dialogue and plot, and not the winged critters in the title. A mad scientist (Gunton) working for the military genetically engineers some extra-nasty super-intelligent bats. Mad scientists being notoriously bad at cage maintenance, they escape. They then rile up a bunch of normally docile bats, turning them into vicious killers through some type of rodent peer pressure. After several attacks on his small Texas town, Sheriff Kimsey (Phillips) summons the nearest beautiful female bat expert (Meyer) and comic relief sidekick (Leon) so the bats have someone to chase around until the finale. They decide to freeze the bats in their cave, at the risk of trudging through a lot of guano to reach the end. You'll know how they feel. **91m/C VHS, DVD.** Lou Diamond Phillips, Dina Meyer, Bob Gunton, Leon, Carlos Jacott, Oscar Rowland, David Shawn McConnell, Marcia Dangerfield; *D:* Louis Morneau; *W:* John Logan; *C:* George Mooradian; *M:* Graeme Revell.

*batteries not included 🦴🦴1/2 **1987 (PG)** As a real estate developer fights to demolish a New York tenement, the five remaining residents are aided by tiny metal visitors from outer space in their struggle to save their home. Each resident gains a renewed sense of life in this sentimental, wholesome family film produced by Spielberg. Cronyn and Tandy keep the schmaltz from getting out of hand. Neat little space critters. **107m/C VHS, DVD.** Hume Cronyn, Jessica Tandy, Frank McRae, Michael Carmine, Elizabeth Pena, Dennis Boutsikaris; *D:* Matthew Robbins; *W:* Matthew Robbins, Brad Bird, Brent Maddock, S.S. Wilson; *C:* John McPherson; *M:* James Horner.

Battle Beneath the Earth 🦴🦴 **1968** The commies try to undermine democracy once again when American scientists discover a Chinese plot to invade the U.S. via a series of underground tunnels. Perhaps a tad jingoistic. **112m/C VHS.** *GB* Kerwin Mathews, Peter Arne, Viviane Ventura, Robert Ayres; *D:* Montgomery Tully.

Battle Beyond the Stars 🦴🦴1/2 **1980 (PG)** The planet Akir must be defended against alien rapscallions in this intergalactic Corman creation. Sayles authored the screenplay and co-authored the story on which it was based. **105m/C VHS, DVD.** Richard Thomas, Robert Vaughn, George Peppard, Sybil Danning, Sam Jaffe, John Saxon, Darlanne Fluegel, Jeff Corey, Morgan Woodward, Marta Kristen, Ron Ross, Eric Morris; *D:* Jimmy T. Murakami; *W:* John Sayles; *C:* Daniel Lacambre; *M:* James Horner.

Battle Beyond the Sun 🦴🦴 **1963** Former Russian movie "Nebo Zowet" is Americanized. Everyone is trying to send a mission to Mars. Roger Corman was the producer, director Coppola used the pseudonym Thomas Colchart. **75m/C VHS, DVD.** Edd Perry, Arla Powell, Bruce Hunter, Andy Stewart; *D:* Francis Ford Coppola; *W:* Nicholas Colbert, Edwin Palmer; *M:* Les Baxter.

Battle Circus 🦴🦴1/2 **1953** Sappy drama casts Bogart as a surgeon at a M*A*S*H unit during the Korean War. Allyson is a combat nurse who finds love amongst the harsh reality of a war zone. Bogart was badly miscast and his performance proves it. Weak script and uninspired performances don't help this depressing story. **90m/B VHS.** Humphrey Bogart, June Allyson, Keenan Wynn, Robert Keith, William Campbell, Perry Sheehan, Patricia Tiernan, Adele Longmire, Jonathon Cott, Ann Morrison, Helen Winston, Sarah Selby, Danny Chang, Philip Ahn, Steve Forrest, Jeff Richards, Dick Simmons; *D:* Richard Brooks; *W:* Richard Brooks; *C:* John Alton; *M:* Lennie Hayton.

Battle Cry 🦴🦴🦴 **1955** A group of U.S. Marines train, romance, and enter battle in WWII. But it takes 'em a while to do it. Walsh's film focuses on the psychology of training men to fight, and to wait for the chance. Uris's script (from his own novel) also spends an inordinate amount of time on the love lives of the soldiers. **169m/C VHS, DVD.** Van Heflin, Aldo Ray, Mona Freeman, Tab Hunter, Dorothy Malone, Anne Francis, James Whitmore, Raymond Massey, William Campbell, John Lupton, L.Q. Jones, Perry Lopez, Fess Parker, Jonas Applegarth, Tommy Cook, Felix Noriego, Nancy Olson, Susan Morrow, Carleton Young, Rhys Williams, Gregory Walcott, Frank Ferguson, Sarah Selby, Willis Bouchey; *D:* Raoul Walsh; *W:* Leon Uris; *C:* Sid Hickox; *M:* Max Steiner.

Battle for the Planet of the Apes 🦴🦴 **1973 (G)** A tribe of human atomic bomb mutations are out to make life miserable for the peaceful ape tribe. The story is told primarily in flashback with the opening and closing sequences taking place in the year A.D. 2670. Final chapter in the five-movie simian saga. **96m/C VHS, DVD.** Roddy McDowall, Lew Ayres, John Huston, Paul Williams, Claude Akins, Severn Darden, Natalie Trundy, Austin Stoker, Noah Keen, Michael Stearns, John Landis; *D:* J. Lee Thompson; *W:* John W. Corrington, Joyce H. Corrington; *C:* Richard H. Kline; *M:* Leonard Rosenman.

Battle Hell 🦴🦴 *Yangtse Incident* **1956** The true story of how a British ship was attacked by the Chinese Peoples Liberation Army on the Yangtze River in 1949. **112m/B VHS.** *GB* Richard Todd, Akim Tamiroff, Keye Luke; *D:* Michael Anderson Sr.; *W:* Eric Ambler.

Battle Hymn 🦴🦴1/2 **1957** After accidentally bombing an orphanage as a WWII fighter pilot, Dean Hess (Hudson) becomes a minister. He returns to the Air Force in 1950 to train Korean pilots in Seoul and winds up building a home for the local orphans. True story on which the real Hess served as technical advisor. **109m/C VHS, DVD.** Rock Hudson, Dan Duryea, Martha Hyer, Anna Kashfi, Don DeFore, Jock Mahoney, Carl Benton Reid, Alan Hale Jr., Richard Loo, Philip Ahn; *D:* Douglas Sirk; *W:* Charles Grayson, Vincent B. Evans; *C:* Russell Metty; *M:* Frank Skinner.

Battle in Heaven 🦴 *Batalla En El Cielo* **2005** Set in Mexico, Marcos (Hernandez) is a general's chauffeur whose life collapses around him when the baby he and his wife kidnapped for ransom unexpectedly dies. He seeks out Ana (Mushkadiz)—the general's daughter and a prostitute in her spare time—to ease his pain. She in turn entrusts Marcos, her driver since she was a young child, with her secret life. For some, this is cutting edge art house material that lays bare the lives of Mexico's haves and have-nots; others may view the nonprofessional actors and blandly graphic sex scenes as a big yawn. **94m/C DVD.** Marcos Hernandez, Anapola Mushkadiz, Berta Ruiz, David Bornstein, Rosalinda Ramirez, El Abuelo; *D:* Carlos Reygadas; *W:* Carlos Reygadas; *C:* Diego Martinez Vignatti; *M:* John Tavener, Marcha Cordobesa.

The Battle of Algiers 🦴🦴🦴1/2 *La Bataglia d'Algeri; La Battaglia di Algeri* **1966** Famous, powerful, award-winning film depicting the uprisings against French Colonial rule in 1954 Algiers. A seminal documentary-style film which makes most political films seem ineffectual by comparison in its use of non-professional acto's, gritty photography, realistic violence, and a boldly propagandistic sense of social outrage. **123m/B VHS, DVD.** *AL IT* Yacef Saadi, Jean Martin, Brahim Haggiag, Tommaso Neri, Samia Kerbash, Fawzia el Kader, Michele Kerbash, Mohamed Ben Kassen; *D:* Gillo Pontecorvo; *W:* Gillo Pontecorvo, Franco Solinas; *C:* Marcello Gatti; *M:* Gillo Pontecorvo, Ennio Morricone. Venice Film Fest. '66: Film.

The Battle of Austerlitz 🦴🦴1/2 *Austerlitz* **1960 (PG)** Ambitious but numbling costume drama about the events leading up to the epic battle between Napoleon and the overwhelming forces of the Czar and the Austrian Emperor at Austerlitz. Napoleon won. Film has been drastically cut from original 166 minute release. Watch director Gance's silent version, "Napoleon," for a truly epic experience. **123m/C VHS.** *FR IT YU* Claudia Cardinale, Martine Carol, Rossano Brazzi, Vittorio De Sica, Jean Marais, Ettore Manni, Jack Palance, Orson Welles; *D:* Abel Gance.

The Battle of Blood Island 🦴 **1960** Two G.I.s, one Christian and one Jewish, face death at the hands of the Japanese during WWII. Still, they bicker incessantly before finally pulling together to save themselves. **64m/B VHS, DVD.** Richard Devon, Ron Kennedy; *D:* Joel Rapp.

Battle of Britain 🦴🦴1/2 **1969 (G)** A powerful retelling of the most dramatic aerial combat battle of WWII, showing how the understaffed Royal Air Force held off the might of the German Luftwaffe. **132m/C VHS, DVD.** Harry Andrews, Michael Caine, Laurence Olivier, Trevor Howard, Kenneth More, Christopher Plummer, Robert Shaw, Susannah York, Ralph Richardson, Curt Jurgens, Michael Redgrave, Nigel Patrick, Edward Fox, Ian McShane, Patrick Wymark; *D:* Guy Hamilton; *W:* James Kennaway, Wilfred Greatorex; *C:* Frederick A. (Freddie) Young; *M:* Malcolm Arnold, Ronald Goodwin, William Walton.

The Battle of El Alamein 🦴🦴 **1968** Action filled movie about the alliance of Italy and Germany in a war against the British, set in a North African desert in the year 1942. Ferroni used the pseudonym Calvin Jackson Padget. **105m/C VHS, DVD.** *IT FR* Frederick Stafford, Ettore Manni, Robert Hossein, Michael Rennie, George Hilton, Ira Furstenberg; *D:* Giorgio Ferroni.

Battle of Elderbush Gulch 🦴🦴1/2 **1913** An ancient pioneering western short famous for innocently employing the now-established cliches of bad guy, good guy, and helpless frontier heroine. One of Gish's first films. **22m/B VHS, DVD.** Mae Marsh, Alfred Paget, Robert "Bobbie" Harron, Lionel Barrymore, Leslie Loveridge, Lillian Gish; *D:* D.W. Griffith; *C:* Billy (G.W.) Bitzer.

Battle of Neretva 🦴🦴 **1969** During WWII, Yugoslav partisans are facing German and Italian troops and local Chetniks as they battle for freedom. Big budget war film lost continuity with U.S. cut. **106m/C VHS.** *YU* Yul Brynner, Curt Jurgens, Orson

The Battle of Shaker Heights ♂♂½ *Project Greenlights: The* pointing sophomore effort from the HBO series *Project Greenlight*, backed once again by producers Ben Affleck and Matt Damon. Kely Emswiler (LaBeouf) is a bright, middle-class Midwestern teen whose hobby is military re-enactment. He becomes best friends with Bart (Henson) after "saving his life" in a mock battle. He soon develops a crush on Bart's older sister Tabby, an engaged Yale grad student, much to the dismay of his coworker Sarah (Appleby). This only adds to Kelly's mounting problems, which include myriad family problems with ex-addict dad (Quinlan). LaBeouf's appealing, rising above the disjointed, uninspired mess. If there is another "Project" they should look for a director who will provide satisfying drama on the big screen as well as on the show. **89mℂ VHS, DVD.** *US* Shia LaBeouf, Elden (Raffi) Henson, Amy Smart, Billy Ray, Shirl Appleby, Kathleen Quinlan, William Sadler, Ray Wise, Anson Mount, Philip Baker Hall, Ilya Baruch; Efram Potelle; *M:* Richard (Rick) Marvin.

Battle of the Bulge ♂♂ 1965 A re-creation of the famous offensive by Nazi Panzer troops on the Belgian front during 1944-45, an assault that could have changed the course of WWII **141mℂ VHS, DVD, Blu-ray Disc, HD DVD.** Henry Fonda, Robert Shaw, Robert Ryan, Dana Andrews, Telly Savalas, Ty Hardin, Pier Angeli, George Montgomery, Charles Bronson, Barbara Werle, Hans-Christian Blech, James MacArthur, Karl Otto Alberty; *D:* Ken Annakin. *W:* Philip Yordan, John Nelson; *C:* Jack Hildyard; *M:* Benjamin Frankel.

Battle of the Commandos ♂ *Legion of the Damned* 1971 A tough Army colonel leads a group of convicts on a dangerous mission to destroy a German-built cannon before it's used against the Allied Forces. **94mℂ VHS.** *IT* Jack Palance, Curt Jurgens, Thomas Hunter, Robert Hunter; *D:* Umberto Lenzi.

Battle of the Eagles ♂½ 1979 Follows the true adventures of the "Partisan Squadron," the courageous airmen known as the "Knights of the Sky" during WWII in Yugoslavia. **102mℂ VHS, DVD.** Bekim Fehmiu, George Taylor, Gloria Samara; *D:* Tom Raymond.

The Battle of the Japan Sea ♂♂ 1970 (G) A Japanese epic, dubbed in English, centering around the historic WWII battle between Japan and Russia. **123mℂ VHS.** *JP* Tatsuya Nakadai, Yuzo Kayama, Chishu Ryu, Susumu Fujita, Mitsuko Kusabe, Toshiro Mifune; *C:* Masaru Sato; *M:* Seiji Maruyama; *W:* Toshio Yasumi; *D:* Seiji Maruyama.

Battle of the Rails ♂♂♂ *La Bataille du Rail* 1946 Docudrama based on actual events of French Resistance fighters who worked on the railways and, at great peril, stymied the Nazis efforts throughout World War II and aided the Allies during the D-Day invasion. Powerful debut feature film for French director Clement, who included real railroad workers in recreating events. ♂ French with subtitles. **85mB VHS.** *FR* Marcel Barnault, Jean Clarieux, Jean Daurand, Jacques Desagneaux, Francois Joux; *D:* Rene Clement. *W:* Rene Clement. **VIDEO**

The Battle of the Sexes ♂♂♂ 1928 Real estate tycoon Judson (Hersholt) abandons his wife (Bennett) and home for money-hungry flapper Marie (Haver). Based on the novel "The Single Standard" by Daniel Carson Goodman. Griffith's remake of his own 1913 film. **89mB VHS, DVD.** Jean Hersholt, Phyllis Haver, Belle Bennett, Don Alvarado, William "Billy" Batewell, Sally O'Neil; *D:* D.W. Griffith; *W:* Gerrit J. Lloyd; *C:* Billy (G.W.) Bitzer, Karl Struss.

The Battle of the Sexes ♂♂♂ 1960 Sophisticated British comedy has mild-mannered Sellers trying to prevent a business takeover by the brash American Cummings. A good supporting cast and the impeccable Sellers make this one unique. Adapted from the James Thurber short story "The Catbird Seat." **88mB VHS.**

Welles, Hardy Kruger, Franco Nero, Sergei Bondarchuk; *D:* Valko Bulajic.

Battle of Shaker Heights 2003 (PG-13). Disap-

GF Peter Sellers, Robert Morley, Constance Cummings, Jameson Clark, Ernest Thesiger, Donald Pleasence, Moultrie Kelsall, Alex Mackenzie, Roddy McMillan, Michael Goodliffe, Norman MacOwen, William Mervyn; *D:* Charles Crichton; *W:* Monja Danischewsky; *C:* Freddie Francis; *M:* Stanley Black; *Nar:* Sam Wanamaker.

Battle of the Worlds ♂ *Il Pianeta Degli Uomini Spenti; Planet of the Lifeless Men* 1961 Typical low-budget science fiction. A scientist tries to stop an alien planet from destroying the Earth. Even an aging Rains can't help this one. Poorly dubbed in English. **84mℂ VHS, DVD.** *IT* Claude Rains, Maya Brent, Bill Carter, Marina Orsini, Jacqueline Derval; *D:* Anthony M. Dawson.

Battle of Valiant ♂ 1963 Thundering hordes of invading barbarians trample the splendor of ancient Rome beneath their grimy sandals. **90mℂ VHS.** Gordon Mitchell, Ursula Davis, Massimo Serato; *D:* Giardon Genti.

Battle Queen 2020 ♂♂ 1999 (R) In a frozen post-apocalyptic future (eternal winter after asteroid crash), Gayle (Strain) leads the downtrodden masses in a revolution against the Elites who live above ground. She's a courtesan by day, freedom fighter by night...is one at least as good as "Battlefield Earth." It's certainly shorter and was made by people who were under no illusions about what they were doing. **80mℂ DVD, CA** Julie Strain, Jeff Wincott; *D:* Daniel D'Or. *W:* Michael B. Druxman, Mike Rule, Paul Henreid, Rosenda Monteros, Jose Ferrer, William D. Bostiance, Caron Nightengale; *C:* way, Yorge Stahl Jr.; *M:* Les Baxter.

Battle Shock 1956 Ex-GI painter is accused of murdering a cantina waitress while on his honeymoon in Mexico. Soon other women are turning up dead and he realizes he is having blackouts. Solid work all around. **88mℂ VHS.** Ralph Meeker, Janice Rule, Paul Henreid, Rosenda Monteros, Jose Torvay, Yerye Beirut; *D:* Paul Henreid; *W:* Robert J. Smith; *C:* Bert Haines, Devereaux Jennings.

Battle Shock *A Woman's Devotion; War Shock* 1956 *A Woman's Devotion* (reprised) **VIDEO**

Battlefield Earth woof! 2000 (PG-13) In the year 3000, the Earth has been decimated by 10-foot tall aliens known as "psychos who are stripping the planet of its natural resources. Only a few humans survive, including Pepper who becomes the leader of the bad aliens and is extremely evil-looking but in a strangely campy way. Based on a 1982 novel by Scientology founder L. Ron Hubbard. Film generated controversy for that reason and supposedly "subliminal" church messages but you'll simply be stunned into submission by how badly it blows. **117mℂ VHS, DVD.** John Travolta, Barry Pepper, Forest Whitaker, Kelly Preston, Kim Coates, Richard Tyson, Sabine Karsenti, Michael Byrne, Sean Hewitt, Michel Perron, Shaun Austin-Olsen, Marie Josee Croze; *D:* Roger Christian; *W:* J. David Shapiro, Corey Mandell; *C:* Giles Nuttgens; **'00:** Worst Picture, Worst Actor (Travolta), Worst Support. Actor (Pepper), Golden Raspberries **'00:** Worst Picture, Worst Actor (Travolta), Worst Support. Actress (Preston), Worst Director (Christian), Worst Screenplay.

Battlestar Galactica ♂♂½ 1978 (PG) Pilot episode of the sci-fi TV series which was later released in the theatres. The crew of the spaceship Galactica must battle their robot enemies in an attempt to reach Earth. Contains special effects designed by John "Star Wars" Dykstra. Individual episodes are also available. **125mℂ VHS, DVD.** Lorne Greene, Dirk Benedict, Maren Jensen, Jane Seymour, Patrick Macnee, Terry Carter, John Colicos, Richard A. Colla, Laurette Spang, Richard Hatch; *D:* Richard A. Colla; *W:* Glen Larson, Richard A. Colla; *C:* Ben Colman; *M:* Stu Phillips. **TV**

Battling Butler ♂♂½ 1926 Rich young Keaton tries to impress a young lady by impersonating a boxer. All goes well until he has to fight the real thing. Mostly charming if uneven; one of Keaton's more unusual efforts, thought to be somewhat autobiographical. Silent. **70mB VHS, DVD.** Buster Keaton, Sally O'Neil, Snitz Edwards, Francis McDonald, Mary O'Brien, Tom Wilson, Walter James; *D:* Buster Keaton.

Battling Bunyon ♂♂½ 1924 A somewhat dim-witted boxer becomes a comedy boxer battles the champ. Silent. **71mℂ VHS.** Chester Conklin, Wesley Barry, Mollie Malone, Jackie Fields, Paul Hurst, Frank Campeau, Johnny Relasco, Landers Stevens, Harry Mann, Pat Kemp; *D:* Paul Hurst.

Battling for Baby ♂♂ 1992 It's the war of the Grandmas. New mother Katherine decides to return to work and both her mother and mother-in-law want to look after the little tyke. Silly made-for-TV fluff **93mℂ VHS, DVD.** Courteney Cox, Suzanne Pleshette, Debbie Reynolds, John Terlesky, Doug McClure, Leigh Lawson, Mary Jo Catlett; *D:* Art Wolff; *W:* Walter Lockwood, Nancy Silvers.

Battling Marshal ♂½ 1948 Carson battles bad guys out to steal a family's gold-rich land. He foils a fake smallpox scare, thugs, and cheapo production values. **52mℂ/B VHS, DVD.** Sunset Carson, Lee Roberts; *D:* Oliver Drake.

Battling Orioles ♂♂½ 1924 The once scrappy baseball team is now a bunch of grumpy old men, that is until Glenn whips them into shape. Silent. **58mℂ/B VHS.** Glenn Tryon, Blanche Mehaffey, Noah Young; *D:* Ted Wilde, Fred Guiol.

Battling Outlaw ♂½ *Billy the Kid in Texas* 1940 Billy is made sheriff of a lawless Texas town after standing up to the local gang. Then he and his friend Fuzzy set out to retrieve money stolen by the gang. **64mℂ VHS.** Bob Steele, Al "Fuzzy" St. John, John Merton, Terry Walker, Carleton Young, Charles "Blackie" King, Charles "Slim" Whitaker, Frank LaRue; *D:* Sam Newfield; *W:* Joseph O'Donnell; *C:* Jack Greenhalgh.

Battling with Buffalo Bill ♂♂ 1931 Twelve episodes of the vintage serial concerning the exploits of the legendary Indian fighter. **180mℂ/B VHS.** Tom Tyler, Rex Bell, Franklyn Farnum, Lucille Browne, Francis Ford, William Desmond, Jim Thorpe, Yakima Canutt, Chief Thunderbird, Bud Osborne; *D:* Ray Taylor; *W:* Ella O'Neill, George Plympton.

Battleground ♂♂♂ 1949 A tightly conceived post-WWII character drama, following a platoon of American soldiers through the Battle of the Bulge. Available in a Colorized version. **118mℂ VHS, DVD.** Van Johnson, John Hodiak, James Whitmore, George Murphy, Ricardo Montalban, Marshall Thompson, Jerome Courtland, Don Taylor, Bruce Cowling, Leon Ames, Douglas Fowley, Richard Jaeckel, Scotty Beckett, Herbert Anderson, Thomas E. Breen, Denise Darcel, James Arness, Brett King; *D:* William A. Wellman; *W:* Robert Pirosh; *C:* Paul Vogel; *M:* Lennie Hayton. Oscars '49: **B&W Cinematog.**, Story & Screenplay; Golden Globes '50: Screenplay, Support. Actor (Whitmore).

Battleforce ♂♂ *The Battle of the Marath Line; The Greatest Battle* 1978 Exciting battle scenes lose their power in the confusion of this mixed-up WWII film about Rommel's last days. Dubbed sequences, news-reel vignettes and surprise performances by big name stars are incomprehensibly glued together. **97mℂ VHS, DVD.** *GE* Yul Henry Fonda, Stacy Keach, Helmut Berger, Samantha Eggar, Giuliano Gemma, John Huston; *D:* Umberto Lenzi; *Nar:* Orson Welles.

The Battleship Potemkin ♂♂♂ *Potemkin; Bronenosets Potemkin* 1925 Eisenstein's best work documents mutiny aboard the Russian battleship Potemkin in 1905 which led to a civilian uprising against the Czar in Odessa, and the resulting crackdown by troops loyal to the Czar. Beautiful cinematography, especially the use of montage sequences, charged filmmaking. In particular, a horrifying sequence depicting the slaughter of civilians on an Odessa beach to it is exceptional; many movies pay homage to this scene including "The Untouchables" and "Love and Death." Viewers should overlook obvious Marxist overtones and see this film for what it is: a masterpiece. Silent with music score available. **71mℂ/B VHS, DVD, RU** Alexander Antonov, Vladimir Barsky, Grigori Alexandrov, Mikhail Gomorov, Sergei Eisenstein, I. Brobov, Beatrice Vitoloi, N. Poltavseva, Alexandr Levshin, Repnikova, Korobei, Levchenko; *D:* Grigori Alexandrov, Sergei Eisenstein; *W:* Nina Agadzhanova Shutko, Sergei Eisenstein; *C:* Eduard Tisse.

The Bawdy Adventures of Tom Jones ♂½ 1976 (R) An expoitive extension of the Fielding novel about the philandering English lad with plenty of soft-core skin and lewdness. **89mℂ VHS.** *GB* Joan Collins, Trevor Howard, Terry-Thomas, Arthur Lowe, Murray Melvin; *D:* Cliff Owen.

The Baxter ♂♂ 2005 (PG-13) Elliot Sherman (Showalter) is so CPA meganerd even his sweet grandmother knows he's "the Baxter," the also-ran (the nice, safe, dull guy who never gets the girl) in the opening scene he's dumped at the altar by his beautiful fiancee Caroline (Banks) when her high school flame Brad (Theroux) reappears. You might learn to feel something for Elliot, but he's so unlikable that sympathy will be hard to find. Soon it becomes apparent that Elliot's office temp Cecil (Williams), who has been right there under his nose, is the perfect woman for him. **91mℂ VHS, DVD.** Michael Showalter, Elizabeth Banks, Michelle Williams, Justin Theroux, Zak Orth, Michael Ian Black, Catherine Lloyd Burns, Peter Dinklage, Paul Rudd; *D:* Michael Showalter; *W:* Michael Showalter; *C:* Theodore Shapiro, Craig (Shudder to Think) Wedren.

The Bay Boy ♂♂ ½ 1985 (R) Set in the 1930s in Nova Scotia, this period piece captures the coming-of-age of a rural teenage boy. Young Sutherland's adolescent angst becomes a more difficult struggle when he witnesses a murder, and is tormented by the need to study the latest search and rescue techniques from the state's premier lifeguard team. **107mℂ VHS, CA** Liv Ullmann, Kiefer Sutherland, Peter Donat, Matthieu Carriere, Jos MacPherson, Isabelle Mejias, Alan Scarfe, Chris Wiggins, Leah K. Pinsent; *D:* Daniel Petrie. *M:* Claude Bolling, Gene '85.

Bayou Romance ♂ 1986 Painter inherits a Louisiana plantation, moves in, and falls in love with a young gypsy. **90mℂ VHS.** Annie Potts, Michael Ansara, Barbara Horan, Paul Rossili; *D:* Alan Myerson.

Baywatch the Movie: Forbidden Paradise ♂♂½ 1995 (PG) The "Baywatch" babes and their fellow lifesaving "hunks-in-trunks head off to Hawaii to study the latest search and rescue techniques from the state's premier lifeguard team. **90mℂ VHS, UMD.** *US* John Travolta, Uma Thurman, Vince Vaughn, Cedric the Entertainer, Andre Benjamin, Robert Pastorelli, Christina Milian, Paul Adelstein, Debi Mazar, Gregory Alan-Williams, Harvey Keitel, Dwayne "The Rock" Johnson, Danny DeVito, James Woods; *D:* F. Gary Gray; *W:* Peter Steinfeld; *C:* Jeffrey L. Kimball; *M:* John Powell.

Be Cool ♂♂♂ 2005 (PG-13) Paging Dr. Tarantino STAT! This rightful sequel to "Get Shorty" proves that Travolta is in need of another new-career-ectomy. Jettisoning anything even mildly cool about the cuses on bombast and pointless cameos in the continuing adventures of Hollywood shylock Chili Palmer (Travolta). This time, Chili tries to break into the music business with the help of a widowed record producer (Thurman) and a young ingenue (Milian). Standing in their way are Russian mobsters, gangsta rap kingpins, and Vince Vaughn doing the tired white-guy-who-thinks-he's-black routine. Even The Rock as a flamboyantly gay bodyguard can't inject any life into such a flat unfunny mess. **112mℂ VHS, DVD, UMD.** *US* John Travolta, Uma Thurman, Vince Vaughn, Cedric the Entertainer, Andre Benjamin, Robert Pastorelli, Christina Milian, Paul Adelstein, Debi Mazar, Gregory Alan-Williams, Harvey Keitel, Dwayne "The Rock" Johnson, Danny DeVito, James Woods; *D:* F. Gary Gray; *W:* Peter Steinfeld; *C:* Jeffrey L. Kimball; *M:* John Powell.

Be Kind Rewind ♂♂½ 2008 (PG-13) Simple guy Jerry (Black) lives in a trailer, works at a junkyard, and likes to hang out at *Mr.* Fletcher's (Glover) titular video rental store, where his buddy Mike (Def) works. After a mishap at a local power plant magnetizes Jerry, accidentally erases all of the videotapes (the store is VHS only), so Jerry and Mike enlist the talents of the very cute Alma (Diaz) from the nearby dry cleaner to help them re-enact and re-record all of the movies for rental as usual. The oddball store regulars get wise to their shenanigans and everyone wants to play a part, which makes Jerry, Mike and the video store unlikely celebrities. Black is Black and the whole thing is often silly and obvious, but entertaining nonetheless. **100m/C DVD.** *US* Jack Black, Mos Def, Danny Glover, Mia Farrow, Melonie Diaz, Ajay Smith, Sigourney Weaver, Chandler Parker, Irv Gooch; *D:* Michel Gondry; *W:* Michel Gondry; *C:* Ellen Kuras; *M:* Jean-Michel Bernard.

Be Yourself 1930 Thin plot contrived for Ziegfeld Follies star Brice, who stars as nightclub entertainer Fanny Field. Fanny falls for a down-and-out-boxer (Armstrong) trying to make a comeback. Brice, who was married to impresario Billy Rose at the time, sings several songs co-written by Rose, including "Cookin' Breakfast for the One I Love." **65m/B VHS.** Fanny Brice, Robert Armstrong, Harry Green, Gertrude Astor, G. Pat Collins, Marjorie "Babe" Kane; *D:* Thornton Freeland; *W:* Thornton Freeland; *C:* Karl Struss, Robert Planck.

The Beach 2000 (R) DiCaprio's follow-up to the blockbuster "Titanic" is an uneven adaptation of the novel by Alex Garland concerning a group of hedonists trying to find paradise and destroying their ideal in the process. Cynical young journalist Richard (DiCaprio) meets the manic Daffy (Carlyle) in a Bangkok dive and is given a map to a supposedly unspoiled island off the Thai coast. Impulsively, Richard acquaintances Francoise (Ledoyen) and Etienne (Canet) to accompany him and they discover an odd settlement of Euro-trash, headed by Sal (Swinton), amidst a marijuana plantation guarded by gun-wielding thugs. Paradise turns out to be less than paradisical. **120m/C VHS, DVD.** Leonardo DiCaprio, Tilda Swinton, Virginie Ledoyen, Guillaume Canet, Robert Carlyle, Paterson Joseph, Peter Youngblood Hills, Jerry Swindall; *D:* Danny Boyle; *W:* John Hodge; *C:* Darius Khondji; *M:* Angelo Badalamenti.

Beach Babes 2: Cave Girl Island 1995 The babes crash land on a prehistoric planet populated by horny cavemen. **78m/C VHS, DVD.** Sara Bellomo, Stephanie Hudson, Rodrigo Botero; *D:* David DeCoteau. **VIDEO**

Beach Babes from Beyond 1993 (R) "HOT. TAN. ALIEN." Three words that would send shivers through the body of any red-blooded American boy. And as if alien silicone isn't enough to draw a crowd, this piece of fluff also features the relatives of big name stars hoping to cash in on the family name. Typical Hollywood cheese and sleaze should be fun for those who still can't get this kind of quality entertainment on cable. **78m/C VHS.** Joe Estevez, Don Swayze, Joey Travolta, Burt Ward, Jacqueline Stallone, Linnea Quigley, Sara Bellomo, Tamara Landry, Nicole Posey; *D:* David DeCoteau.

Beach Blanket Bingo 1965 Fifth entry in the "Beach Party" series (after "Pajama Party") is by far the best and has achieved near-cult status. Both Funicello and Avalon are back, but this time any young Evans catches Avalon's eye. Throw in a mermaid, some moon-doggies, skydiving, sizzling beach parties, and plenty of nostalgic golly-gee-whiz fun and you have the classic '60s beach movie. Totally implausible, but that's half the fun when the sun-worshiping teens become involved in a kidnapping and occasionally break into song. Followed by "How to Stuff a Wild Bikini." ♫Beach Blanket Bingo; The Cycle Set; Fly Boy; The Good Times; I Am My Ideal; I Think You Think; It Only Hurts When I Cry; New Love; You'll Never Change Him. **96m/C VHS, DVD.** Frankie Avalon, Annette Funicello, Linda Evans, Don Rickles, Buster Keaton, Paul Lynde, Harvey Lembeck, Deborah Walley, John Ashley, Jody McCrea, Marta Kristen, Timothy Carey, Earl Wilson, Bobbi Shaw, Brian Wilson; *M:* liam Asher, *W:* William Asher, Sher Townsend, Leo Townsend; *C:* Floyd Crosby; *M:* Les Baxter.

Beach Girls 1982 (R) Three voluptuous coeds intend to re-educate a bookish young man and the owner of a beach house. **91m/C VHS, DVD.** Debra Blee, Val Kline, Jeana Tomasina, Adam Roarke, Paul Richards; *D:* Patrice Townsend; *C:* Michael D. Murphy.

The Beach Girls and the Monster *Monster in the Surf; Monster from the Surf* 1965 Here's one on the cutting edge of genre bending; while it meticulously maintains the philosophical depth of '60s beach bimbo fare, it manages to graft successfully with the heinous critter from the sea genre to produce a hybrid horror with acres o' flesh. **70m/B VHS, DVD.** Jon Hall, Sue Casey, Walker Edmiston, Arnold Lessing, Elaine DuPont, Dale Davis; *D:* Jon Hall; *W:* Joan Gardner; *C:* Dale Davis; *M:* Frank Sinatra Jr.

Beach Hotel *Playa Azul; Blue Beach* 1992 Accused of fraud, a politican escapes to a remote and semi-abandoned hotel that he owns. He summons his family to decide what to do next, hoping his friends will also assist him. But his friends refuse their aid, and even his family eventually abandons him to his fate. Spanish with subtitles. **96m/C VHS, DVD.** *SP* Sergio Bustamante, Pilar Pellicer, Mercedes Olea; *D:* Alfredo Joskowicz; *W:* Alfredo Joskowicz; *C:* Rodolfo Sanchez; *M:* Amparo Rubin.

Beach House 1982 In this boring comedy, adolescents frolic on the beach, get inebriated, and listen to rock 'n' roll. **76m/C VHS.** Kathy McNeil, Richard Duggan, Ileana Seidel, John Cosola, Spence Waugh, Paul W.S. Gallagher, John A. Gallagher; *D:* John A. Gallagher; *W:* Marino Amaruso, John A. Gallagher.

Beach Party 1963 Started the "Beach Party" series with the classic Funicello/Avalon combo. Scientist Cummings studying the mating habits of teenagers intrudes on a group of surfers, beach bums, and bikers, to his lasting regret. Typical beach party bingo, with sand, swimsuits, singing, dancing, and bare minimum in way of a plot. Followed by "Muscle Beach Party." ♫Beach Party; Don't Stop Now; Promise Me Anything; Secret Surfin' Spot; Surfin' and a-Swingin'; Treat Him Nicely. **101m/C VHS, DVD.** Frankie Avalon, Annette Funicello, Harvey Lembeck, Robert Cummings, Dorothy Malone, Morey Amsterdam, Jody McCrea, John Ashley, Candy Johnson, Dolores Wells, Yvette Vickers, Eva Six, Brian Wilson, Vincent Price, Peter Falk, Dick Dale; *D:* William Asher; *W:* Lou Rusoff; *C:* Kay Norton; *M:* Les Baxter.

Beachcomber *Vessel of Wrath* 1938 Comedy set in the Dutch East Indies about a shiftless beachcomber (Laughton) who falls in love with a missionary's prim sister (Lanchester), as she attempts to reform him. The real-life couple of Laughton and Lanchester are their usual pleasure to watch. Remade in 1954. Story by W. Somerset Maugham. **88m/B VHS.** *GB* Charles Laughton, Elsa Lanchester, Robert Newton, Tyrone Guthrie; *D:* Erich Pommer.

Beaches 1988 (PG-13) Based on the novel by Iris Rainer Dart about two girls whose friendship survived the test of time. The friendship is renewed once more when one of the now middle-aged women learns that she is dying slowly. **123m/C VHS, DVD.** Bette Midler, Barbara Hershey, John Heard, Spalding Gray, Lainie Kazan, James Read, Mayim Bialik; *D:* Garry Marshall; *W:* Mary Agnes Donoghue; *C:* Dante Spinotti; *M:* Georges Delerue.

Beaks: The Movie WOOF! *Birds of Prey* 1987 (R) Two TV reporters try to figure out why birds of prey are suddenly attacking humans. Owes nothing to Hitchcock's "The Birds." **86m/C VHS, DVD.** Christopher Atkins, Michelle Johnson; *D:* Rene Cardona Jr.

Bean 1997 (PG-13) Big screen adaptation of rubber-faced Atkinson's Mr. Bean character finds disaster-magnet hero working as a guard in London's National Gallery. When a famous painting is purchased by a museum in L.A., the Gallery's curators jump at the chance to send Bean along with the painting as an "expert," although he is nearly mute and definitely not qualified. David (MacNicol), the American curator, invites him to stay at his house, much to the dismay of his wife and children. Bean, of course, wrecks the painting, ruins David's marriage and career, and generally makes an ass out of himself. He then resourcefully (and sometimes accidentally) puts things right. Atkinson proves himself a master of the almost lost art of slapstick comedy. **92m/C VHS, DVD.** *GB* Rowan Atkinson, Peter MacNichol, Pamela Reed, Harris Yulin, Burt Reynolds, Larry Drake, Johnny Galecki, Richard Gant, Tom McGowan, Dakin Matthews, Peter Capaldi, Sandra Oh, Tricia Vessey, Peter Egan; *D:* Mel Smith; *W:* Richard Curtis, Robin Driscoll; *C:* Francis Kenny; *M:* Howard Goodall.

Beanstalk 1994 (PG) Modern-day version of the fairytale finds young Jack Taylor (Daniels) scheming to make it big to help his hardworking single mom. He meets up with a wacky scientist (Kidder), who gives Jack some recently discovered seeds that naturally grow into an enormous beanstalk. And what does Jack find when he climbs the beanstalk—why an entire family of silly giants. **80m/C VHS.** J.D. Daniels, Margot Kidder, Richard Moll, Amy Stock-Poynton, Patrick Renna, Richard Paul, David Naughton, Stuart Pankin, Cathy McAuley; *D:* Michael Davis; *W:* Michael Davis; *M:* Kevin Bassinson.

The Bear *L'Ours* 1989 (PG) Breathtaking, effortlessly entertaining family film (from France) about an orphaned Kodiak bear cub tagging after a grown Kodiak male and dealing with hunters. The narrative is essentially from the cub's point of view, with very little dialogue. A huge money-maker in Europe; shot on location in the Dolomites and the Candian Arctic. Based on the 1917 novel "The Grizzly King" by James Oliver Curwood. **92m/C VHS, DVD.** *FR* Jack Wallace, Tcheky Karyo, Andre Lacombe; *D:* Jean-Jacques Annaud; *W:* Gerard Brach, Michael Kane; *C:* Philippe Rousselot; *M:* Bill Conti.

Bear Island 1980 (PG) Group of secret agents cleverly disguising themselves as U.N. weather researchers converge upon Bear Island in search of a Nazi U-Boat. Looks like rain. **118m/C VHS.** Donald Sutherland, Richard Widmark, Barbara Parkins, Vanessa Redgrave, Christopher Lee, Lloyd Bridges; *D:* Don Sharp.

Bear Ye One Another's Burden... *Einer Trage des Anderen Last* 1988 In the early 50s, communist police officer Josef Heilinger (Pose) is sent to a private sanitorium for consumptives. He's forced to share a room with a young Protestant curate, Hubertus Koschenz (Mock). Their ill health is the only thing they have in common, and they deliberately seem to annoy each other, but soon their situation has them grudgingly developing a mutual respect and even friendship. German with subtitles. **118m/C VHS.** *GE* Jorg Pose, Manfred Mock, Susanne Luning, Dieter Knaup; *D:* Lothar Warneke; *C:* Peter Ziesche; *M:* Gunther Fischer.

The Bears & I 1974 (G) A young Vietnam vet helps Indians regain their land rights while raising three bear cubs. Beautiful photography in this Disney production. **89m/C VHS, DVD.** Patrick Wayne, Chief Dan George, Andrew Duggan, Michael Ansara; *D:* Bernard McEveety; *W:* Jack Speirs, John Whedon; *C:* Ted D. Landon; *M:* Buddy Norman Dale Baker.

The Beast *La Bete* 1975 Long considered taboo due to its erotic subject matter, this 1975 French film from director Borowczyk arrives in its uncensored form for the first time in 2000. Young heiress Lucy Broadhurst (Hummel) arrives at the l'Esperance chateau, where she is to marry the young Mathurn de l'Esperance (Benedetti). After retiring to her room, Lucy finds herself dreaming of the 18th-century lady of the chateau, Romilda de l'Esperance (Lane), who according to legend, encountered a wild, sexual monster in the forest near the manor. Was this an isolated incident or does the Beast still roam the grounds? The once shocking sex scenes will be considered quite tame by today's audience, and some of them come across as quite silly. **94m/C DVD.** Sirpa Lane, Lisbeth Hummel, Elizabeth Kaza, Pierre Benedetti; Guy Trejan; *D:* Walerian Borowczyk; *W:* Walerian Borowczyk; *C:* Bernard Daillencourt; *M:* Marcel Grignon.

The Beast *The Beast of War* 1988 (R) Violent and cliche-driven war drama notable for its novel twist: wild Russian tank officer becomes lost in the Afghanistan wilderness while being tracked by Afghan rebels with revenge in mind. Filmed in the Israel desert and adapted by William Mastrosimone from his play. **93m/C VHS, DVD.** George Dzundza, Jason Patric, Steven Bauer, Stephen Baldwin, Don Harvey, Kabir Bedi, Erik Avari, Haim Gerafi; *D:* Kevin Reynolds; *W:* William Mastrosimone; *C:* Doug Milsome; *M:* Mark Isham.

The Beast *Peter Benchley's The Beast* 1996 (PG-13) Benchley once again terrorizes a small coastal community with a giant sea creature that preys on sailors and divers. When a poacher's attempts to capture the creature result in further disaster, a fishing boat captain, a Coast Guard officer, and a marine biologist set sail to to kill the critter. **116m/C VHS.** William L. Petersen, Karen Sillas, Charles Martin Smith, Ronald Guttman, Missy (Melissa) Crider, Sterling Macer, Denis Arndt, Larry Drake; *D:* Jeff Bleckner; *W:* J.B. White; *C:* Geoff Burton; *M:* Don Davis. **TV**

The Beast from Haunted Cave 1960 Gold thieves hicing in a wilderness cabin encounter a spiderlike monster. Surprisingly good performances from Sinatra (Frank's nephew) and Carol. Produced by Gene Corman, Roger's brother. **64m/B VHS, DVD.** Michael Forest, Sheila Carol, Frank Wolff, Richard Sinatra, Wally Campo; *D:* Monte Hellman; *W:* Charles B. Griffith; *C:* Andrew M. Costilyan.

The Beast from 20,000 Fathoms 1953 Atomic testing defrosts a giant dinosaur in the Arctic; the hungry monster proceeds onwards to its former breeding grounds, now New York City. Oft-imitated saurian-on-the-loose formula is still fun, brought to life by Ray Harryhausen special effects. Based loosely on the Ray Bradbury story "The Foghorn." **80m/B VHS, DVD.** Paul (Christian) Hubschmid, Paula Raymond, Cecil Kellaway, Kenneth Tobey, Donald Woods, Lee Van Cleef, Steve Brodie, Mary Hill, Jack Pennick, Ross Elliot; *D:* Eugene Lourie; *W:* Eugene Lourie, Fred Freiberger, Louis Morheim, Robert Smith; *C:* John L. "Jack" Russell; *M:* David Buttolph.

Beast in the Cellar 1970 (R) Every family has something to hide, and in the case of two spinster sisters, it's their murderous inhuman brother, whom they keep chained in the cellar. Like all brothers, however, the "beast" rebels against his sisters' bossiness and escapes to terrorize their peaceful English countryside. The sisters' (Reid and Robson) performances aren't bad, but rest of effort is fairly disappointing. **86m/C VHS, DVD.** *GB* Beryl Reid, Flora Robson, T.P. McKenna; *D:* James Kelly.

The Beast Must Die *Black Werewolf* 1975 (PG) A millionaire sportsman invites a group of men and women connected with bizarre deaths or the eating of human flesh to spend the cycle of a full moon at his isolated lodge. **93m/C VHS, DVD.** *GB* Peter Cushing, Calvin Lockhart, Charles Gray, Anton Diffring, Marlene Clark, Ciaran Madden, Tom Chadbon, Michael Gambon; *D:* Paul Annett; *W:* Michael Winder; *C:* Jack Hildyard; *M:* Douglas Gamley.

Beast of Morocco *Hand of Night* 1966 Interesting vampire film about a Morrocan vampire princess who sets her sights on seducing a noted archaeologist. Of course his girlfriend ends up being abducted by the vampire's servant. **88m/C VHS.** *GB* William Sylvester, Alizia Gur, Terence de Marney, Diane Clare, Edward Underdown, William Dexter, Sylvia Marriott; *D:* Frederick Goode; *W:* Bruce Stewart; *C:* William Jordan; *M:* John Shakespeare.

Beast of the Yellow Night WOOF! 1970 (R) A dying soldier sells his soul to Satan at the close of WWII. Years later, existing without aging, he periodically turns into a cannibal monster. Although the first half is tedious, the monster turns things around when he finally shows up. Decent gore effects. **87m/C**

The Beast of Yucca Flats WOOF! 1951 A really cheap, quasi-nuclear protest film. A Russian scientist is chased by communist agents into a nu-clear testing area and is caught in an atomic blast. As a result, he turns into a club-wielding monster. Voice over narration is used in lieu of dialogue as the process proved too expensive. 53m/B VHS, DVD. Tor Johnson, Douglas Mellor, Larry Aten, Barbara Francis Conrad Brooks, Anthony Cardoza, Bing Stafford, John Morrison; **D:** Coleman Francis; **W:** Coleman Francis; **C:** John Cagle; **M:** Irwin Nafshun, Al Remington.

The Beast That Killed Women ✓✓½ 1965 Colonists at a sunny Florida nudist camp have their beach party interrupted by an escaped gorilla. Director Mahon, in his first color effort, stretches this panicky moment into an hour of fleshy fun and games. 60m/C VHS, DVD. Darlene Bennett, Gigi Darlene, Jure Roberts; **D:** Barry Mahon; **W:** Barry Mahon; **C:** Barry Mahon.

The Beast with Five Fingers ✓✓½ 1946 After a pianist mysteriously dies and leaves his fortune to his private nurse, the occupants of his villa are terrorized by a creature that turns out to be the pianist's hand which was severed by his personal secretary (Lorre). Lorre is also terrorized by hallucinations of the hand, and no matter what he does to stop it (nail it to a desk, throw it in the fire, etc.), nothing can keep the hand from carrying out its mission. A creepy thriller with inventive shots of the severed hand. 88m/B VHS. Robert Alda, Andrea King, Peter Lorre, Victor Francen, J. Carrol Naish, Charles Dingle; **D:** Robert Florey; **W:** Curt Siodmak; **C:** Wesley Anderson; **M:** Max Steiner.

The Beast Within ✓✓ 1982 (R) Young woman has the misfortune of being raped by an unseen creature in a Mississippi swamp. Seventeen years later, her son conceived from that hellish union begins to act quite strange, developing a penchant for shedding his skin before turning into an insect-like critter with a cannibalistic appetite. First film to use the air "bladder" type of prosthetic make-up popularized in later, and generally better, horror films. Contains some choice cuts in photo editing: the juxtaposition of hamburger and human "dead meat" is witty. Based on Edward Levy's 1981 novel. 98m/C VHS, DVD. Ronny Cox, Bibi Besch, L.Q. Jones, Paul Clemens, Don Gordon, Katherine Moffat, John Dennis Johnston, R.G. Armstrong, Logan Ramsey, Ror Soble, Meshach Taylor; **D:** Philippe Mora; **W:** Tom Holland; **C:** Jack L. Richards; **M:** Les Baxter.

Beastmaster ✓✓ 1982 (PG) Adventure set in a wild and primitive world. The Beastmaster is involved in a life-and-death struggle with overwhelming forces of evil. Campy neanderthal flesh flick. 119m/C VHS, DVD. Marc Singer, Tanya Roberts, Rip Torn, John Amos, Josh Milrad, Billy Jacoby, Ben Hammer; **D:** Don A. Coscarelli; **W:** Paul Coscarelli, Paul Pepperman; **M:** Lee Holdridge.

Beastmaster 2: Through the Portal of Time ✓½ 1991 (PG-13) This time the laughs are intentional as the Beastmaster returns to modern-day L.A. where the shopping is better for both trendy clothes and weapons. Fun for genre fans, with a behind-the-scenes feature on the tape. 107m/C VHS. Marc Singer, Kari Wuhrer, Sarah Douglas, Wings Hauser, James Avery, Robert Fieldsteel, Arthur Malet, Robert Z'Dar, Michael Berryman; **D:** Sylvio Tabet; **M:** Robert Folk.

Beastmaster 3: The Eye of Braxus ✓✓½ 1995 (PG) Dar the Beastmaster (Singer) returns to battle evil. Lord Agon (Warner) needs to obtain a jeweled eye that will bring the demon Braxus back to life—and he'll stop at nothing, including kidnapping Dar's brother King Tal (Van Dien), to reach his terrifying goal. But Dar isn't alone—he's got the bewitching sorceress Morgana (Down), tempting warrioress Shada (Hess), and loyal advisor Seth (Todd) to help him out. 92m/C VHS. Marc Singer, David Warner, Lesley-Anne Down, Tony Todd, Casper Van Dien, Kaith Coulouris, Sandra Hess, Patrick Kilpatrick; **D:** Gabrielle Beaumont; **W:** David Wise; **C:** Barbara Claman; **M:** Jan Hammer.

Beasts ✓ 1983 A young couple's plans for a romantic weekend in the Rocky Four. Not the real Beatles, but impersonators who do a very inadequate job. Based on the equally disappointing stage show. 89m/C VHS. Mitch Weissman, Ralph Castelli, David Leon, Tom Teeley; **D:** Joseph Manduke.

The Beat ✓ 1988 Unrealistic film about a bookish new kid who intercedes in the tension between two rival street gangs, changing their lives in his literary way. 101m/C VHS. John Savage, Kara Glover, Paul Dillon, David Jacobson, William McNamara; **D:** Peter Mones; **W:** Peter Mones; **M:** Carter Burwell.

Beat ✓✓ 2000 Disappointing look at the events leading up to William S. Burroughs's shooting of his wife in Mexico in 1951. Tangled hetero- and homosexual relationships and unrequited longings between future literati Burroughs (Sutherland), his wife (Love), Allen Ginsberg (Livingston), Lucien Carr (Reedus), and Jack Kerouac (Martinez) should've provided more spark, but the indifferent direction and poor script give the actors little to work with. 88m/C VHS, DVD. Courtney Love, Kiefer Sutherland, Ron Livingston, Kyle Secor, Daniel Martinez, Sam Trammell; **D:** Gary Walkow; **C:** Ciro Cabello; **M:** Ernest Troost.

Beat Girl ✓✓ Wild for Kicks 1960 Poutty rebellious teen Jennifer (Hill) spends her days in art school and her nights at a London beat hangout. She's jealous when daddy (Farrar) marries sexy French Nichole (Adam) and plots to break them up. When Jennifer discovers Nichole's sordid past she winds up in a burlesque club, attracting the unsavory attentions of owner Kenny (Lee). Then Kenny winds up dead. Singer Adam Faith performs and Reed has a bit as a youthful tough. 85m/B VHS, DVD. GB Gillian Hills, David Farrar, Noelle Adam, Christopher Lee, Shirley Anne Field, Oliver Reed, Nada Beall, Adam Faith, Nigel Green, Claire Gordon; **D:** Edmond T. Greville; **W:** Dail Ambler; **C:** Walter Lassally; **M:** John Barry.

The Beat My Heart Skipped ✓✓✓ De batre mon coeur s'est arrete 2005 In adapting James Toback's 1978 "Fingers," French director Audiard changed the place (from New York to Paris), the pace (more somber and less high-strung), and the names—but the heart of the story stayed the same. Here Thomas Seyr (Duris, in Harvey Keitel's "Johnny Fingers" role) does his dad's dirty collections work in crooked real estate schemes though it repulses him. But when his long-discarded dreams of becoming a concert pianist reemerge, the pull between his two lives proves more than he can bear. 107m/C DVD, FR Romain Duris, Niels Arestrup, Linh Dan Pham, Emmanuelle Devos, Jonathan Zaccai, Gilles Cohen, Anton Yakovlev, Melanie Laurent; **D:** Jacques Audiard; **W:** Jacques Audiard, Tonino Benacquista; **C:** Stephane Fontaine. British Acad. '05: Foreign Film.

Beat Street ✓✓½ 1984 (PG) Intended as a quick cash-in on the break dancing trend, this essentially plotless musical features kids trying to break into local show biz with their rapping and dancing skills. Features the music of Afrika Bambaata and the Soul Sonic Force, Grand Master Melle Mel and the Furious Five, and others. 106m/C VHS, DVD. Rae Dawn Chong, Leon Grant, Saundra Santiago, Guy Davis, Jon Chardiet, Duane Jones, Kaceem Hardison; **D:** Stan Latham; **W:** Andrew Davis.

Beat the Devil ✓✓ 1953 Each person on a slow boat to Africa has a scheme to beat the other passengers to the uranium-rich land that they all hope to claim. An unusual black comedy which didn't fare well when re-eased, but over the years has come to be the epitome of spy-spoofs. 89m/C VHS, DVD. Humphrey Bogart, Gina Lollobrigida, Peter Lorre, Robert Morley, Jennifer Jones, Edward Underdown, Ivor Barnard, Bernard Lee, Marco Tulli; **D:** John Huston; **W:** John Huston, Truman Capote; **C:** Oswald Morris; **M:** Franco Mannino.

VideoHound's Golden Movie Retriever

Beatlemania! The Movie ✓ 1981 Boring look at the Fab

The Beatniks ✓ 1960 Story about the dark secrets of the beat generation in which a man is promised fame and fortune by an agent, but his dreams are cut short when he friend commits murder. A big waste of time. 78m/B VHS, DVD. Tony Travis, Peter Breck, Karen Kadler, Joyce Terry, Sam Edwards, Bob Wells; **D:** Paul Frees; **W:** Paul Frees; **C:** Murray Deatley; **M:** Stanley Wilson.

Beatrice ✓✓✓½ La Passion Beatrice 1988 (R) In France during the Middle Ages, a barbaric soldier of the Hundred Years' War returns to his estate that his daughter has maintained, only to brutalize and abuse her. In French with English subtitles. 132m/C VHS, FR Julie Delpy, Bernard Pierre Donnadieu, Nils (Niels) Tavernier; **D:** Bertrand Tavernier; **W:** Colo Tavernier O'Hagan; **C:** Bruno de Keyzer; **M:** Lili Boulanger, Cesar '88: Costume Des.

Beau Brummell ✓✓✓ 1924 The famous silent adaptation of the Clyde Fitch play about an ambitious English dandy's rise and fall. 80m/B VHS, John Barrymore, Mary Astor, Willard Louis, Irene Rich, Carmel Myers; **D:** Harry Beaumont.

Beau Brummell ✓✓½ 1954 Lavish production casts Granger in the rags-to-riches dandy and chief adviser to the Prince of Wales. Born into a life of poverty, George Bryan Brummel uses wit and intelligence to meet the vain Prince (George IV). He also manages to catch the eye of Taylor, who falls in love with him. Outstanding period piece cinematography, sets, and costumes. Shot on location in England's beautiful countryside, many of the interior shots are from a 15th-century mansion, Ockwell Manor, located near Windsor Castle. Remake of the 1924 silent film starring John Barrymore. Based on the play by Clyde Fitch. 113m/C VHS. Stewart Granger, Elizabeth Taylor, Peter Ustinov, Robert Morley, James Donald, James Hayter, Rosemary Harris, Paul Rogers, Noel Willman, Peter Dyneley, Charles Carson; **D:** Curtis Bernhardt; **W:** Karl Tunberg; **C:** Oswald Morris.

Beau Geste ✓✓✓½ 1939 The classic Hollywood adventure film based on the Percival Christopher Wren novel. To protect aging Lady Patricia (Thatcher), who raised the orphaned brothers, Beau Geste (Cooper) takes the blame for a jewel theft and decides to enlist in the Foreign Legion. He's followed by his brothers John (Milland) and Digby (Preston), and all face desert wars and despicable officers, including the psychotic Sgt. Markoff (Donlevy). A rousing, much-copied epic. 114m/B VHS, DVD. Gary Cooper, Ray Milland, Robert Preston, Brian Donlevy, Donald O'Connor, J. Carrol Naish, Susan Hayward, James Stephenson, Albert Dekker, Broderick Crawford, Charles T. Barton, Heather Thatcher, James Burke, G.P. (Tim) Huntley, Jr., Harold Huber, Harvey Stephens, Stanley Andrews, Harry Woods, Arthur Aylesworth, Henry Brandon, Nestor Paiva, George Chandler, George Regas; **D:** William A. Wellman; **W:** Robert Carson; **C:** Theodor Sparkuhl, Louis Owde Stouman, Archie Stout; **M:** Alfred Newman.

Beau Pere ✓✓✓ Stepfather 1981 Bittersweet satiric romp from Blier about the war zone of modern romance, wherein 14-year-old Besse pursues her 30-year-old responsible, widowed stepfather (Dewaere). Sharp-edged and daring. In French with subtitles. 125m/C VHS, DVD, FR Patrick Dewaere, Nathalie Baye, Ariel Besse, Maurice Ronet, Genevieve Mnich, Maurice Risch, Macha Meril, Rose Thiery; **D:** Bertrand Blier; **W:** Bertrand Blier; **C:** Sacha Vierny; **M:** Philippe Sarde.

Beau Revel ✓✓✓½ 1921 Critically acclaimed romantic drama of the silent era. A passionate dancing girl played by Victor, one of the '20s' more prolific roman-

Beau Travail ✓✓½ 1998 Very loose adaptation of Melville's "Billy Budd" is set in the French Foreign Legion. East through the eyes of soldiers who have lived their entire lives under the shadow of conflict. As the 18-year Israeli occupation of the medieval Lebanese castle the Beaufort comes to an end, the soldiers pray to survive random Hezbollah bombing attacks while waiting out the days until withdrawal. As the bombings increase, commander Liberti (Cohen) and his troops must hold on to hope while trying to manage the tedium of holding a castle for largely symbolic purposes. Film avoids political commentary and instead explores the minds of soldiers on the ground, to excellent effect. 125m/C DVD. IS

Beaufort ✓✓✓½ 2007 A fascinating, intense look at the strife in the Middle leads (and erstwhile wife of director King Vidor) is the object of romantic interest of a father and son, which leaves the threesome lovelorn, suicidal and emotionally scarred. You might recognize Stone from this later role as Judge Hardy in MGM's "Hardy Family" series. 70m/B VHS. Lewis Stone, Florenza Vidor, Lloyd Hughes, Katherine Kirkham, William Conklin, Griffith Wray.

Beaumarchais the Scoundrel ✓✓½ Beaumarchais L'insolent 1996 Adapted from an unpublished play by Sacha Guitry. Beautifully filmed romp of the social-climbing and political-spying gadfly Pierre Augustin Caron de Beaumarchais. Molinaro has simplified the fantastic life of the 18th-century dramatist, courtier, and watchmaker to Louis XV (and author of the comic masterpieces "The Barber of Seville" and "The Marriage of Figaro") but the result is still dizzying. 100m/C VHS, FR Fabrice Luchini, Jacques Weber, Michel Piccoli, Claire Nebout, Jean-Francois Balmer, Florence Thomassin, Michel Serrault, Dominique Besnehard, Jean-Claude Brialy, Manuel Blanc, Sandrine Kiberlain, Axelle Laffont; **D:** Edouard Molinaro; **W:** Edouard Molinaro, Jean-Claude Brisville; **C:** Michael Epp; **M:** Jean-Claude Petit.

The Beautician and the Beast ✓✓ 1997 (PG) Evita meets Lucille Ball when TV's "Nanny" enters Eastern Europe whining to conquer fictional Drescher as a beautician who becomes a local hero after a fire in her beauty class and is subsequently hired by a despotic dictator Pochenko (Dalton). Overriding well-known caricatures, loosely based on the fairy tale "Beauty and the Beast," as well as a host of old-time, culture clash movies ("The King and I," "Sound of Music"), where the humble nanny attempts to bring joy (get it?) into the life of a man who carries the weight of the world on his shoulders. Lensed in Prague inside a Gothic, 17th-century castle. Pleasant enough, if not original, time-killer. 105m/C VHS, DVD. Fran Drescher, Timothy Dalton, Ian McNeice, Patrick Malahide, Lisa Jakub, Michael Lerner, Phyllis Newman; **D:** Ken Kwapis; **W:** Todd Graff; **C:** Peter Lyons Collister; **M:** Cliff Eidelman.

Beauties of the Night ✓✓ Les Belles de Nuit 1952 Dreamy fantasy finds a shy music teacher (Philipe) escaping from his boring life into romantic adventures with beautiful women. But his dreams slowly turn nightmarish and he's forced to deal with reality—and real love. French with subtitles. 89m/B VHS, FR Gerard Philipe, Gina Lollobrigida, Martine Carol, Magali Vendeuil, Paolo Stoppa, Raymond Bussieres, Raymond Cordy; **D:** Rene Clair; **W:** Rene Clair; **C:** Armand Thirard; **M:** Georges Van Parys.

Beautiful ♪ 2000 (PG-13) Field's directorial debut is a cloying beauty pageant satire that wants you to like it. REALLY wants you to like it. Unfortunately, the jokes and characters are U-G-L-Y, and they ain't got no alibi. Minnie Driver is Mona, a bright girl from an abusive home who escapes her grim reality by trying to win beauty pageants. She's shown as a little ugly duckling who uses any means necessary to win her way up the escalating ladder of swimsuitability. Finally, she qualifies for the Holy Grail of beauty pageants, the Miss American Miss competition. Along the way, however, she has become a single mother, which automatically disqualifies her as a contestant. She comes up with a plan where her daughter Vanessa (Pepsi prodigy and demon-child Hallie Kate Eisenberg) is passed off as the child of her patient best friend Ruby (Adams). Mona then screeches complaints about the kid's behavior being a distraction to her goal (which is no way to treat your child, even if she is Satan's hand-puppet) while an ambitious reporter (Stefanson) tries to reveal her secret. Overly padded, and it doesn't even have a nice personality. **112m/C VHS, DVD.** Minnie Driver, Hallie Kate Eisenberg, Joey Lauren Adams, Kathleen Turner, Leslie Stefanson, Bridgette Wilson-Sampras, Kathleen Robertson, Michael McKean, Gary Collins, Brent Briscoe; **D:** Sally Field; **W:** Jon Bernstein; **C:** Robert Yeoman; **M:** John (Gianni) Frizzell.

Beautiful Beast ♪♪ XX Utsukushiki Gakuen; XX Beautiful Beast 1995 Mysterious Chinese warrior woman known as Black Orchid arrives in Japan and rubs out mob boss Ishizuka. Fleeing the scene, she hides out with bartender Yoichi Fujinami, who becomes torn between helping his old pal Yaguchi and the mystery girl that he's falling in love with. Foregoes a lot of empty soft-core sex in favor of providing more action. Director Toshihiru Ikeda is no John Woo, but at least Black Orchid's trunk full of high-powered weaponry provides a little fun. **87m/C DVD.** JP Kaori Shimamura, Takanori Kikuchi, Hakunyu, Minako Ogawa; **D:** Toshihiru Ikeda; **W:** Tamiya Takehashi, Hiroshi Takehashi; **C:** Seizo Sengen.

The Beautiful Blonde from Bashful Bend ♪♪½ 1949 Charming comedy-western gets better with age. Grable is the pistol packing mama mistaken for the new school teacher. Fun performances by all, especially Herbert. **77m/C VHS.** Betty Grable, Cesar Romero, Rudy Vallee, Olga San Juan, Hugh Herbert, Porter Hall, Sterling Holloway, El Brendel; **D:** Preston Sturges.

The Beautiful Country ♪♪½ 2004 (R) In 1990, 20-year-old Binh (Nguyen) lives with poverty and discrimination in Vietnam because of his mixed ancestry: his father was an American solider. Binh's dying mother sends him on an illegal journey to the U.S. in hopes of tracking down his dad in Houston. There's an extended sequence involving a Malaysian refugee camp (with Ling as a friendly prostitute) and a trip on a freighter (captained by Roth). Earnest, gentle, and sometimes harrowing (and rather too long). **137m/C DVD.** NO US Nick Nolte, Tim Roth, Ling Bai, Temuera Morrison, Damien Nguyen, Nguyen Thi Huong Dung, Chau Thi Kim Xuan, Anh Thu, Khong Duc Tuan, Chapman To, Vu Tang, Nguyen Than Kien, Bui Ti Hong, John Hussey; **D:** Hans Petter Moland; **W:** Larry Gross, Sabina Murray; **C:** Stuart Dryburgh; **M:** Zbigniew Preisner.

Beautiful Creatures ♪♪ 2000 (R) Fitful comedy/thriller follows the adventures of Petulia (Weisz) and Dorothy (Lynch), two Glasgow lasses with abusive boyfriends. Dorothy escapes a beating from her druggie boyfriend Tony (Glen), only to wind up aiding Petula, who is being attacked in the street by drunken Brian (Mannion). Unfortunately, Brian dies and the women decides to make it look like he's been kidnapped and ask a ransom from his equally violent brother Ronnie (Roeves) so they can get out of town.

Then a crooked detective (Norton) enters the scene and the women's plans turn a little complicated. **88m/C VHS, DVD.** GB Rachel Weisz, Susan Lynch, Alex Norton, Iain Glen; **W:** Maurice Roeves, Tom Mannion; **D:** Bill Eagles; **W:** Simon Donald; **C:** James Welland; **M:** Murray Gold.

Beautiful Dreamers ♪♪½ 1992 (PG-13) Maurice Bucke is a young Canadian physician who runs the London Insane Asylum. After a chance meeting with poet Walt Whitman, both men discover their mutual outrage for current treatment of the mentally ill. Bucke persuades Whitman to visit his asylum in order to try Whitman's theory of human compassion on the asylum's inmates. However, Bucke runs into opposition from the local townspeople, scandalized by Whitman's radical reputation. Fairly humdrum with a larger-than-life performance by Tom as Whitman. Based on Whitman's visit to Canada in 1880. **108m/C VHS.** CA Rip Torn, Colm Feore, Wendel Meldrum, Sheila McCarthy, Colin Fox; **D:** John Kent Harrison; **W:** John Kent Harrison.

Beautiful Girls ♪♪♪ 1996 (R) Slow but easy-going film highlights the differences between men, women, and relationships. A 10-year high school reunion brings together buddies Tommy (Dillon), Kev (Perlich), Paul (Rapaport), Mo (Emmerich), and Willie (Hutton). They icefish, drink, and talk about women (about whom they haven't a clue). All are smitten by Andera (Thurman), the gorgeous visiting cousin of another friend, and Willie becomes intrigued by Marty (Portman), his precociously tantalizing 13-year-old neighbor. The guys' whining gets annoying and the women are strictly secondary characters, but O'Donnell's tirade about fake femininity is just one of many amusing examples of smart dialogue. The Afghan Whigs are featured as the bar band. **110m/C VHS, DVD.** Matt Dillon, Timothy Hutton, Michael Rapaport, Max Perlich, Noah Emmerich, Lauren Holly, Uma Thurman, Natalie Portman, Mira Sorvino, Martha Plimpton, Rosie O'Donnell, Annabeth Gish, Pruitt Taylor Vince, Sam Robards, David Arquette, Anne Bobby, Richard Bright; **D:** Ted (Edward) Demme; **W:** Scott Rosenberg; **C:** Adam Kimmel; **M:** David A. Stewart.

Beautiful Hunter ♪♪ XX Beautiful Hunter 1994 Shion has been raised since birth to be the perfect assassin and executioner for the Magnificat crime family, a devoutly Catholic gang that do their criminal business in the vestments of priests and nuns. Blind Father Kano fully controls the life of his adopted daughter, until photographer Ito gets photos of her. The leathal yet naive heroine finds herself attracted to Ito, but Father Kano Sister Mitsuko and a squad of killers after them. Kuno looks—well, beautiful, in and out of a series of foxy outfits, but doesn't display any kind of martial arts to convince us of her master assassin status. **91m/C DVD.** JP Makiko Kuno, Koji Shimizu; **D:** Masaru Konuma.

Beautiful Joe ♪♪ 2000 (R) Joe (Connolly) decides to hit the road for adventure and discovers in Louisville, Kentucky when he meets Hush (Stone), an ex-stripper turned con artist. Then Joe gets in trouble when he tries to help Hush with her debt to crime boss George the Geek (Holm) and the twosome take off to Vegas with Geek's henchman (Bellows) on their trail. **98m/C VHS, DVD.** Billy Connolly, Sharon Stone, Gil Bellows, Ian Holm, Dann Florek, Barbara Tyson; **D:** Stephen Metcalfe; **W:** Stephen Metcalfe; **C:** Thomas Ackerman.

A Beautiful Mind ♪♪♪½ 2001 (PG-13) Loose adaptation of Sylvia Nasar's 1998 bio of John Forbes Nash Jr. An anti-social genius at Princeton University, Nash wrote his thesis on game theory at 21 and worked for the government in the 1950s before succumbing to paranoid schizophrenia, necessitating his confinement to a mental institution. (The treatment scenes are not for the faint-hearted.) His apparent recovery, after some 30 years, led to sharing a Nobel award in economics in 1994. Director Howard manages to keep the inherent sentimentality and sensationalism generally under control thanks to some powerful performances from Crowe (as Nash), Connelly (as wife Alicia), and Harris (as a sinister government official). The usual controversies swirled about the accuracy of the biopic and what was left out. Ignore the petty carping. **129m/C VHS, DVD.** US Russell Crowe, Jennifer Connelly, Ed Harris, Paul Bettany, Christopher Plummer, Judd Hirsch, Adam Goldberg, Josh(ua) Lucas, Anthony Rapp, Austin Pendleton, Vivien Cardone; **D:** Ron Howard; **W:** Akiva Goldsman; **C:** Roger Deakins; **M:** James Horner. Oscars '01: Adapt. Screenplay, Director (Howard), Film, Support. Actress (Connelly); British Acad. '01: Actor (Crowe), Support. Actress (Connelly); Directors Guild '01: Director (Howard); Golden Globes '02: Actor—Drama (Crowe), Film—Drama, Screenplay, Support. Actress (Connelly); Screen Actors Guild '01: Actor (Crowe); Writers Guild '01: Adapt. Screenplay; Broadcast Film Critics '01: Actor (Crowe), Director (Howard), Film, Support. Actress (Connelly).

Beautiful People ♪♪ 1999 (R) The war in Bosnia (circa 1993) comes to London when former neighbors-turned-enemies, one a Serbian and the other a Croatian, accidentally meet on a bus and one to kill each other. This chaos leads to a variety of intersecting situations: Portia (Coleman), a doctor and daughter of a snobby Tory MP, falls for a refugee; another doctor (Farrell) counsels a pregnant refugee who wants to abort her baby, who is the product of a rape; a druggy skinhead (Nussbaum) winds up experiencing battle firsthand, and on and on and on. **107m/C VHS, DVD.** GB Charlotte Coleman, Nicholas Farrell, Danny Nussbaum, Edin Dzandzanovic, Charles Kay, Rosalind Ayres, Heather Tobias, Siobhan Redmond, Gilbert Martin, Linda Bassett, Steve Sweeney; **D:** Jasmin Dizdar; **W:** Jasmin Dizdar; **C:** Barry Ackroyd; **M:** Gary Bell.

The Beautiful, the Bloody and the Bare ♪ 1964 Sordid screamer in the Herschell Gordon Lewis tradition. Set in New York City in the '60s, a depraved artist kills the nude models who pose for him. **2m/C VHS, DVD.** Adela Rogers St. John, Marlene Denes, Debra Page, Jack Lowe; **D:** Sande N. Johnsen; **W:** Sande N. Johnsen; **C:** Jerry Denby; **M:** Steve Karmen.

Beautiful Thing ♪♪♪ 1995 (R) Sweet, fairytalish, gay coming-of-age story set in a working-class southeast London council housing estate. Shy teenager Jamie (Berry) lives with his barmaid mum, Sandra (Henry), and her lover, Tony (Daniels). Next-door is his best mate, the stoic Ste (Neal), who's regularly abused by his father and brother. But when things get too bad, he sleeps over with Jamie. And one night, nature hesitantly takes its course. Their tart-tongued, Mama Cass fanatic, friend Leah (Empson) starts rumors about the twosome that lead to some uneasy (but ultimately conciliatory) confrontations. Fine performances; Harvey adapted from his play. **89m/C VHS, DVD.** GB Glen Berry, Scott Neal, Linda Henry, Tameka Empson, Ben Daniels; **D:** Hettie Macdonald; **W:** Jonathan Harvey; **C:** Chris Seager.

Beauty and the Beast ♪♪♪ 1983 From "Faerie Tale Theatre" comes the story of a Beauty who befriends a Beast and learns a lesson about physical appearance and true love. **60m/C VHS, DVD.** Susan Sarandon, Anjelica Huston, Klaus Kinski, Stephen Elliott; **D:** Roger Vadim. CABLE

Beauty and the Beast ♪♪♪ La Belle et la Bete 1946 The classic medieval fairy tale is brought to life on the big screen for the first time. Beauty takes the place of her father after he is sentenced to die by the horrible Beast and falls in love with him. Cocteau uses the story's themes and famous set-pieces to create a cohesive and captivating surreal hymn to romantic love that is still the definitive version of B&B. In French with subtitles. **90m/B VHS, DVD.** FR Jean Marais, Josette Day, Marcel Andre, Mila Parely, Nane Germon, Michel Auclair; **D:** Jean Cocteau; **W:** Jean Cocteau; **C:** Henri Alekan; **M:** Georges Auric.

Beauty and the Beast ♪♪♪ 1991 (G) Wonderful Disney musical combines superb animation, splendid characters, and lively songs about a beautiful girl, Belle, and the fearsome and disagreeable Beast. Supporting cast includes the castle servants (a delightful bunch of household objects). Notable as the first animated feature to be nominated for the Best Picture Oscar. Destined to become a classic. The deluxe video version features a work-in-progress rough film cut, a compact disc of the soundtrack, a lithograph depicting a scene from the film, and an illustrated book. ♫Beauty and the Beast; Belle; Something There; Be Our Guest. **84m/C VHS, DVD.** **D:** Kirk Wise, Gary Trousdale; **W:** Linda Woolverton; **M:** Alan Menken, Howard Ashman; **V:** Paige O'Hara, Robby Benson, Rex Everhart, Richard White, Jesse Corti, Angela Lansbury, Jerry Orbach, David Ogden Stiers, Bradley Michael Pierce, Jo Anne Worley, Kimmy Robertson. Oscars '91: Song ("Beauty and the Beast"), Orig. Score; Golden Globes '92: Film—Mus./Comedy, Natl. Film Reg. '02.

Beauty and the Devil ♪ 1939 La Beaute du Diable 1950 Ambitious retelling of the Faust legend finds old Faust (Simon) willing to sell his soul to the Devil, courtesy of his agent Mephistopheles (Philipe), in return for youth and beauty to pursue the beautiful woman he loves. Clair has his actors trade roles midway through as Faust makes his bargain. French with subtitles. **97m/B VHS.** FR Michel Simon, Gerard Philipe, Simone Valere, Raymond Cordy, Gaston Modot, Paolo Stoppa, Nicole Besnard; **D:** Rene Clair; **W:** Rene Clair, Armand Salacrou; **C:** Michel Kelber; **M:** Roman Vlad.

Beauty for the Asking ♪ 1939 It sounds like a workable Lucille Ball vehicle—a beautician develops a bestselling skin cream—and even the title sounds like something you'd like to love Lucy in. But somehow the numerous plot implausibilities managed to get by the story's five writers, and the idea of a jilted woman making millions while being financed by her ex's wife just doesn't fly (perhaps it was an idea ahead of its time). Die-hard Lucy fans may find this interesting. **68m/B VHS.** Lucille Ball, Patric Knowles, Donald Woods, Frieda Inescort, Frances Mercer; **D:** Glenn Tryon.

Beauty on the Beach ♪ 1961 A comedy about a mad psychologist, his bizarre experiments with women, and his eventual descent into insanity. In Italian with English subtitles. **90m/C VHS.** IT Ennio Girolami, Giulia Milland, Alberto Talegalli, Lorella De Luca, Valeria Fabrizi; **D:** Romolo Guerrieri; **C:** Tito Carpi, Fabio Dipas, Carlo Moscovini; **C:** Mario Fioretti; **M:** Carlo Savina.

Beauty School ♪ Sylvia Kristel's Beauty School 1993 (R) The promise of an advertising contract pits the owners of rival beauty schools against each other. **95m/C VHS.** Sylvia Kristel, Kevin Bernhardt, Kimberly Taylor, Jane (Veronica Hart) Hamilton; **D:** Ernest G. Sauer; **M:** Merrill Friedman; **M:** Jonathan Hannah.

Beauty Shop ♪♪♪ 2005 (PG-13) Spinning off from the "Barbershop" series, familiar tale of female empowerment succeeds, thanks to Queen Latifah's classy, charismatic lead performance. Beautician Gina moves to Atlanta, landing a job working for pretentious upscale salon owner Jorge (Bacon). Frustrated with Jorge's lack of respect, Gina opens her own beauty shop in a working-class black neighborhood, gathering a group of good-natured, eccentric stylists like outspoken Ms. Josephine (Woodard) and clueless white girl Lynn (Silverstone). All of the community pride themes from the "Barbershop" movies are touched on here, but "Beauty" distinguishes itself with genuine characters. Bacon and Suvari are exceptions, choosing instead to go ridiculously broad. **105m/C DVD, UMD.** US Queen Latifah, Alicia Silverstone, Andie MacDowell, Alfre Woodard, Mena Suvari, Della Reese, Golden Brooks, Paige Hurt, LisaRaye, Keisha Knight Pulliam, Bryce Wilson, Kevin Bacon, Djimon Hounsou, Adele Givens, Miss Laura Hayes, Little LJ, Sherri Shepherd, Kimora Lee Simmons, Sheryl Underwood; **D:** Bille Woodruff; **W:** Kate Lanier, Norman Vance, Jr; **C:** Theo van de Sande; **M:** Christopher Young.

Beavis and Butt-Head Do America ♪♪½ 1996 (PG-13) Moronic MTV metalheads go on the road in search of their stolen TV and are somehow mistaken for criminal masterminds. Okay, enough about plot. If you're thinking of renting this one, you don't care about that

...stuff anyway. Director/writer/voice of B&B Judge is smart enough not to change our "heroes" just because they're on a bigger screen. They're still stupid, obsessed with chicks. (Yeah! Chicks are cool!) and bliss-fully unaware of what's happening around them. The opening sequence, a parody of '70s cop shows, is hilarious (and cool). For those who like the show, and for people who just don't admit that they do, the boys' movie debut (he said "but") doesn't suck. **82m/C VHS, DVD.** *D:* Mike Judge; *W:* Joe Stillman, Mike Judge; *M:* John (Giani) Frizzell; *V:* Mike Judge, Robert Stack, Cloris Leachman, Demi Moore, Eric Bogosian, Richard Linklater, Pamela Blair, Tim Guinee, David Letterman, David Spade, Bruce Willis, Toby Huss.

Because of Winn-Dixie 🦴🦴½ **2005 (PG)** Based on the popular children's book by Kate DiCamillo of the same name about a lonely young girl who adopts a stray dog. India Opal Buloni (played by Robb) is a lonely 10 year-old who's just moved to Florida with her preacher father (Daniels). Without friends and missing her mother, who left her when she was three, Opal encounters a stray dog at the local grocery store. She adopts the dog as her own, naming him Winn-Dixie after the store. Slowly, the dog helps Opal ease her loneliness and she discovers some rare friendships in unusual places. While not perfect, the movie has more hits than misses and is helped along with a strong supporting cast, including Dave Matthews as a singing pet store clerk. **105m/C DVD.** *US* Jeff Daniels, Cicely Tyson, Eva Marie Saint, Courtney Jines, Elle Fanning, AnnaSophia Robb, Dave Matthews, Nick Price, Luke Benward; *D:* Wayne Wang; *W:* Joan Singleton; *C:* Karl Walter Lindenlaub; *M:* Rachel Portman.

Bebe's Kids 🦴🦴½ **1992 (PG-13)** When ladies' man Robin falls for the lovely Jamika, he gets some unexpected surprises when he takes her out on a first date to an amusement park—and she brings along four kids. Animated comedy takes some funny pot-shots at both black and white culture and Disneyland. The children are amusing, especially baby PeeWee, a tot with chronically dirty diapers and Tone Loc's gravelly voice. Based on characters created by the late comedian Robin Harris. The video includes the seven-minute animated short "Itsy Bitsy Spider." **74m/C VHS, DVD.** *D:* Bruce Smith; *W:* Reginald (Reggie) Hudlin; *M:* John Barnes; *V:* Faizon Love, Vanessa 3el Calloway, Wayne Collins, Jonell Green, Marques Houston, Tone Loc, Nell Carter, Myra J.

Because I Said So 🦴🦴 **2007 (PG-13)** Keaton stars as Daphne, a well-intentioned but overprotective and meddling mom to three beautiful daughters. Maggie (Graham) and Mae (Perabo) are safely married and successful, but youngest chick Milly (Moore) has terrible taste in men, so Daphne places a personal ad and screens the replies. Daphne approves of architect Jason (Scott) but Milly is drawn to musician and single dad Joe (Collins), whose own dad, Joe (Johnny) sparks with Daphne. Much over-the-top schtick follows but everything (and everyone) looks gorgeous. **102m/C DVD.** *US* Diane Keaton, Mandy Moore, Lauren Graham, Piper Perabo, Gabriel Macht, Tom Everett Scott, Stephen Collins, Ty Panitz, Colin Ferguson, Tony Hale, Matt Champagne; *D:* Michael Lehmann; *W:* Karen Leigh Hopkins, Jessie Nelson; *C:* Julio Macat; *M:* David Kitay.

Because of the Cats 🦴½ **1974** Police inspector uncovers an evil cult within his seaside village while investigating a bizarre rape and burglary. **90m/C VHS.** Bryan Marshall, Alexandra Stewart, Alex Van Rooyen, Sylvia Kriste, Sebastian Graham Jones; *D:* Fons Rademakers.

Because of Him 🦴🦴 **1945** Actress Kim Walker (Durbin) fakes a letter of introduction from famous thespian John Sheridan (Laughton) in order to impress Broadway producer Charles Gilbert (Ridges). It works and she's given the lead, much to the dismay of the playwright, Paul Taylor (Tone). Naturally, Kim turns out to be an opening night success and Paul comes around and realizes what a swell gal she is. Laughton is at his best as the hammy veteran performer. **88m/B VHS.** Deanna Durbin, Franchot Tone, Charles Laughton, Stanley Ridges, Helen Broderick, Donald Meek; *D:* Richard Wallace; *W:* Edmund Beloin; *C:* Hal Mohr; *M:* Miklos Rozsa.

Becket 🦴🦴🦴 **1964** Adaptation of Jean Anouilh's play about the tumultuous friendship between Henry II of England and the Archbishop of Canterbury, Thomas Becket. Becket views his position in the church of little relation to the sexual and emotional needs of a man, until he becomes archbishop. His growing concern for religion and his shrinking hold of Henry as friend and confidant eventually cause the demise of the friendship and the resulting tragedy. Flawless acting from every cast member, and finely detailed artistic direction make up for the occasional slow moment. **148m/C VHS, DVD.** Richard Burton, Peter O'Toole, John Gielgud, Donald Wolfit; *D:* Peter Glenville; *W:* Edward Anhalt; *C:* Geoffrey Unsworth. Oscars '64: Adapt. Screenplay; Golden Globes '65: Actor—Drama (O'Toole), Film—Drama.

Becky Sharp 🦴🦴 **1935** This premiere Technicolor film tells the story of Becky Sharp, a wicked woman who finally performs one good deed. **83m/C VHS, DVD.** Miriam Hopkins, Frances Dee, Cedric Hardwicke, Billie Burke, Nigel Bruce, Pat Nixon; *D:* Rouben Mamoulian; *C:* Ray Rennahan.

Becoming Colette 🦴🦴½ **1992 (R)** Tedious flashbacking bio of French writer Colette, from her innocent days in the country to her (bad) marriage to writer/publisher Willy and on and on to her own growing career as a writer. She begins writing stories, using an alter-ego character. Claudine, which detail her sexual escapades. Lots of naked flesh but little passion. A postscript notes that Colette wrote "Gigi" and was the first woman to receive the French Legion of Honor. **97m/C VHS.** Mathilda May, Klaus Maria Brandauer, Virginia Madsen, Paul Rhys, Jean-Pierre Aumont, John van Dreelen, Lucienne Hamon; *D:* Danny Huston; *W:* Ruth Graham; *M:* John Scott.

Because of You 🦴🦴 **1952 (PG-13)** Parolee Christine Carroll (Young) marries Steve Kimberly (Chandler) without revealing her sordid past. Then sad past bites her in the butt when her criminal associates find and involve her in another crime. Lots of tears. **95m/B VHS.** Loretta Young, Jeff Chandler, Alex Nicol, Frances Dee, Alexander Scourby, Lynne Roberts, Mae Clarke; *D:* Joseph Pevney; *W:* Ketti Frings; *C:* Russell Metty; *M:* Frank Skinner.

Because You're Mine 🦴🦴 **1952** Lanza plays an opera star who is drafted and falls in love with Morrow, his top sergeant's sister. Plenty of singing—maybe too much at times, but Lanza's fans will enjoy it nonetheless. ♫ All the Things You Are; Because You're Mine; Be My Love; Granada; Lee-Ah-Loo; The Lord's Prayer; The Song Angels Sing; You Do Something to Me. **103m/C VHS, DVD.** Mario Lanza, James Whitmore, Doretta Morrow, Dean Miller, Rita (Paula) Corday, Jeff Donnell, Spring Byington; *D:* Alexander Hall.

Because Why? 🦴🦴 **1993** After travelling abroad for five years, Alex (Riley) returns to Montreal with a back pack, a skateboard, and an old girlfriend's address. The address only leads to a new home and—longing to belong somewhere—a potentially new family and friends. **104m/C VHS, DVD.** *CA* Michael Riley, Marine Ricchio, Doru Bandol, Heather Mathieson; *D:* Arto Paragamian; *W:* Arto Paragamian; *C:* Anna Cawley.

Becoming Jane 🦴🦴½ **2007 (PG)** Jane Austen's writing has withstood the test of time, but films about the writer and her writings are still fledgling. This one's a love story—supposedly her own—and takes place before Jane (Hathaway) is well, Jane Austen as we know her. Penniless mom and dad (Walters and Cromwell) don't take the whole writing thing seriously and expect 20-year-old Jane to choose a wealthy suitor from among those that come calling. Then Thomas Lefroy (McAvoy) shows up, dashing and pushy, and Jane—after initial annoyance—enters a fantastic writer whom we love... **120m/C DVD, Blu-ray Disc, US GB** Anne Hathaway, James McAvoy, Julie Walters, James Cromwell, Laurence Fox, Maggie Smith, Ian Richardson, Anna Maxwell Martin, Joe Anderson, Helen McCrory, Lec Bill; *D:* Julian Jarrold; *W:* Kevin Hood, Sarah Williams; *C:* Eigil Bryld; *M:* Adrian Johnston.

Bed and Board 🦴🦴🦴 *Domicile Conjugal* **1970** The fourth film in the Antoine Doinel (Leaud) cycle finds him marrying Christine (Jade) and becoming a father. The responsibilities of adulthood upset him so much that Antoine leaves his new family and begins an affair. French with subtitles. **100m/C VHS, DVD.** *FR* Jean-Pierre Leaud, Claude Jade, Barbara Laage, Hiroko Berghauer, Daniel Boulanger, Pierre Fabre, Billy Kearns, Daniel Ceccaldi, Claude Girard, Claire Duhamel, Sylvana Blasi; *D:* Francois Truffaut; *W:* Francois Truffaut, Bernard Revon, Claude de Givray; *C:* Nestor Almendros; *M:* Antoine Duhamel.

Bed & Breakfast 🦴🦴½ **1992 (PG-13)** Three generations of women lead quiet lives while running a failing Nantucket bed and breakfast. When a mystery man washes up on their beach, he charms them all, but it seems that he has a past that could endanger everyone. Light-weight final role for Dewhurst, though she provides some sparks as the strong and loving matriarch. Gentle romantic comedy skims the surface, but is still enjoyable. **97m/C VHS.** Roger Moore, Talia Shire, Colleen Dewhurst, Nina Siemaszko, Ford Rainey, Stephen (Steve) Root, Jamie Walters, Victor Slezak; *D:* Robert Ellis Miller; *M:* Cindy Myers; *M:* David Shire.

Bed and Sofa 🦴🦴🦴 **1927** Adultery, abortion, and women's rights are brought about by a housing shortage which forces a man to move in with a married friend. Famous, ground-breaking Russian silent. **73m/B VHS, DVD, RU** Nikolai Batalov, Vladimar Fogel; *D:* Abram Room.

Bed of Roses 🦴🦴½ **1995 (PG)** Wistful romance finds workaholic investment banker Lisa Walker (Masterson) receiving lavish floral tributes from an unknown admirer. When Lisa tracks her giver down, it turns out to be lovestruck widowed florist Lewis Farrell (Slater), who noticed Lisa crying through her apartment window and sent the flowers to cheer her up. Best friend Kim (Segall) urges Lisa to go for Lewis but a problematic past has Lisa distrusting the emotions and their romantic path has a few bumps (easily overcome). Appealing leads, lots of cliches. Goldenberg's debut. **88m/C VHS, DVD.** Christian Slater, Mary Stuart Masterson, Pamela Segall, Josh Brolin, Ally Walker, Debra Monk; *D:* Michael Goldenberg; *W:* Michael Goldenberg; *C:* Adam Kimmel; *M:* Michael Convertino.

The Bed You Sleep In 🦴🦴 **1993** Ray (Blair) is a struggling lumber mill owner, living with his wife Jean (McLaughlin) in a small Oregon town. The couple are torn apart when they receive a letter from their daughter, who's away at college, accusing her father of sexual abuse. The secrets and lies of the family scon echo throughout their community. **117m/C VHS, DVD.** Tom Blair, Ellen McLaughlin, Kathryn Sannella; *D:* Jon Jost; *W:* Jon Jost; *C:* Jon Jost.

Bedazzled 🦴🦴🦴 **1968 (PG)** Short-order cook Stanley Moon (Moore) is saved from suicide by the devil, here known as George Spiggot (Cook), who makes Stanley an offer: seven wishes in exchange for his soul. What Stanley wants is waitress Margaret (Bron) but each of Stanley's wishes is granted with surprising consequences. Cult comedy is a sometimes uneven, but thoroughly entertaining and funny retelling of the Faustian story. **107m/C VHS, DVD. GB** Dudley Moore, Peter Cook, Eleanor Bron, Michael Bates, Raquel Welch, Bernard Spear, Parnell McGarry, Howard Goorney, Daniele Noel, Barry Humphries, Lockwood West, Robert Russell, Michael Trubshawe, Robin Hawdon, Evelyn Moore, Charles Lloyd-Pack; *D:* Stanley Donen; *W:* Dudley Moore, Peter Cook; *C:* Austin Dempster; *M:* Dudley Moore.

Bedazzled 🦴🦴 **2000 (PG-13)** Mortals have been falling for this scam for centuries: seven wishes in exchange for your eternal soul. Once again the Devil finds a taker; Elliot, a nice but hopeless geek who will do anything to improve his lowly stature in life and the girl of his dreams, O'Connor). The Devil (Hurley) misinterprets all of his requests result in Elliot becoming, among other things, a drug lord, an NBA star, and a much too sensitive bore. Will Elliot find a way out of his hellish obligation? Is there a lesson to be learned from his experiences? You probably know the answers. Ramis occasionally misfires, but the hits outnumber the misses. An updated remake of the Dudley Moore/Peter Cook film. **93m/C VHS, DVD.** Brendan Fraser, Elizabeth Hurley, Frances O'Connor, Rudolf Martin, Orlando Jones, Gabriel Casseus, Miriam Shor, Brian Doyle-Murray; *D:* Harold Ramis; *W:* Harold Ramis, Larry Gelbart, Peter Tolan; *C:* Bill Pope.

Bedelia 🦴🦴🦴 **1946** Lockwood well-plays a black widow. Bedelia is living happily in Monte Carlo with hubby Charlie (Hunter) until Ben Chaney (Barnes) shows up. Posing as an artist—but really a private eye—Ben has questions about Bedelia's past. Seems she poisoned three previous husbands for the insurance money and Charlie is a good bet to be her next victim. Based on the novel by Vera Caspary. **90m/B VHS.** Margaret Lockwood, Ian Hunter, Barry Barnes, Anne Crawford, Beatrice Varley, Jill Esmond, Julien Mitchell, Kynaston Reeves, Louise Hampton; *M:* sadone Goldsmith, Harry Victor; *C:* Frederick A. (Freddie) Young; *M:* Hans May.

Bedford Incident 🦴🦴🦴 **1965** The U.S.S. Bedford discovers an unidentified submarine in North Atlantic waters. The Bedford's commander drives his crew to the point of exhaustion as they find themselves the center of a fateful controversy. **102m/B VHS, DVD.** Richard Widmark, Sidney Poitier, James MacArthur, Martin Balsam, Wally Cox, Donald Sutherland, Eric Portman; James B. Harris.

Bedknobs and Broomsticks 🦴🦴½ **1971 (G)** A novice witch and three cockney waifs ride a magic bedstead and stop the Nazis from invading England during WWII. Celebrated for its animated art. **117m/C VHS, DVD.** Angela Lansbury, Roddy McDowall, David Tomlinson, Bruce Forsyth, Sam Jaffe; *D:* Robert Stevenson; *W:* Dor DaGradi, Bill Walsh; *C:* Frank Phillips; *M:* Richard M. Sherman, Robert B. Sherman. Oscars '71: Visual FX.

Bedlam 🦴🦴🦴 **1945** Creeper set in the famed asylum in 18th-century London. A woman, wrongfully committed, tries to stop the evil doings of the chief (Karloff) of Bedlam, and endangers herself. Fine horror film co-written by producer Lewton. **79m/B VHS, DVD.** Jason Robards Sr., Ian Wolfe, Glenn Vernon, Boris Karloff, Anna Lee, Billy House, Richard Fraser, Elizabeth Russell, Skelton Knaggs, Robert Clarke, Ellen Corby, Leyland Hodgson, Joan Newton; *D:* Mark Robson; *W:* Mark Robson, Val Lewton; *C:* Nicholas Musuraca; *M:* Roy Webb.

Bedroom Eyes 1986 (R) A successful businessman becomes a voyeur by returning nightly to a beautiful woman's window, until she is killed and he is the prime suspect. Part comic, part disappointing thriller. 90m/C VHS, DVD. Kenneth Gilman, Dayle Haddon, Christine Cattall; *D:* William Fruet.

Bedroom Eyes 2 1989 (R) After discovering his wife has had an affair, a stockbroker takes a lover. When she turns up dead, he and his wife become murder suspects. Provides some suspenseful moments. 85m/C VHS. Wings Hauser, Kathy Shower, Linda Blair, Jane (Veronica Hart) Hamilton, Jennifer Delora; *D:* Chuck Vincent.

The Bedroom Window 1987 (R) Guttenberg is having an illicit affair with his boss' wife (Huppert), who witnesses an assault on another woman (McGovern) from the bedroom window. To keep the affair secret Guttenberg reports the crime, but since it is secondhand, the account is flawed and he becomes a suspect. Semi-tight thriller reminiscent of Hitchcock mysteries isn't always believable, but is otherwise interesting. 113m/C VHS, DVD. Steve Guttenberg, Elizabeth McGovern, Isabelle Huppert, Wallace Shawn, Paul Shenar, Carl Lumbly, Frederick Coffin, Brad Greenquist; *D:* Curtis Hanson; *W:* Curtis Hanson; *C:* Gilbert Taylor; *M:* Patrick Gleeson, Michael Shrieve, Felix Mendelssohn.

Bedrooms and Hallways 1998 Single gay Leo (McKidd) is urged to join a new agey men's therapy group where, during one of their meetings, he expresses his interest in Brendan (Purefoy), who's breaking up with longtime lover, Sally (Ehle). After Leo and Brendan get together, Leo realizes that Sally is his old high school girlfriend and there's still a certain spark between them. And things just get more complicated. Zippy if glib humor, although the film tends to lose steam at the end. 96m/C VHS, DVD. *GB* Kevin McKidd, James Purefoy, Jennifer Ehle, Tom Hollander, Hugo Weaving, Simon Callow, Harriet Walter, Christopher Fulford, Julie Graham; *D:* Rose Troche; *W:* Robert Farrar; *C:* Ashley Rowe; *M:* Alfredo Troche.

Bedtime for Bonzo 1951 A professor adopts a chimp to prove that environment, not heredity, determines a child's future. Fun, lighthearted comedy that stars a future president. Followed by "Bonzo Goes to College." 83m/B VHS, DVD. Ronald Reagan, Diana Lynn, Walter Slezak, Jesse White, Bonzo the Chimp, Lucille Barkley, Herbert (Hayes) Heyes, Herb Vigran, Harry Tyler, Edward Clark; *D:* Fred de Cordova; *W:* Lou Breslow, Val Burton; *C:* Carl Guthrie; *M:* Frank Skinner.

Bedtime Story 1963 Two con artists attempt to fleece an apparently wealthy woman and each other on the French Riviera. Re-made in 1988 as "Dirty Rotten Scoundrels." One of Brando's thankfully few forays into comedy. 99m/C VHS, DVD. Marlon Brando, David Niven, Shirley Jones, Dody Goodman, Marie Windsor; *D:* Ralph Levy.

Bee Movie 2007 (PG) A bee named Barry B. Benson (Seinfeld) finds himself on a mission when he learns that humans have been profiting off bees forever. Wanting more out of life than his job at a honey-production company can offer, Barry goes out in search of adventure and meets florist Vanessa (Zellweger), a former lawyer wannabe. A budding legal eagle himself, Barry ends up taking on the honey industry with Vanessa's help, and by recruiting all sorts of folks to further his cause (Sting and Larry King, among others). The environmental tones are sound, but the big names behind this film (Seinfeld also co-wrote and co-produced) are the only real buzz. There are bursts of cuteness and the kids will enjoy it, but the frenetic pace and endless string of one-liners tend to come off as just too much business. 90m/C DVD. *US D:* Simon J. Smith, Steve Hickner; *V:* Jerry Seinfeld, Spike Feresten, Barry Marder, Andy Robin; *M:* Rupert Gregson-Williams; *V:* Jerry Seinfeld, Renée Zellweger, Matthew Broderick, John Goodman, Patrick Warburton, Chris Rock, Kathy Bates, Barry Levinson, Oprah Winfrey, Larry Miller, Megan Mullally, Rip Tom, Michael Richards, Larry King, Ray Liotta, Sting.

Bee Season 2005 (PG-13) Based on the bestselling novel by Myla Goldberg. Eleven-year-old Eliza (Cross), an average kid who lacks attention from her bright but aptly troubled parents, finds she's got a gift for spelling. Dad Saul (Gere), a religious studies professor and follower of Kabbalah mysticism, is at a loss as scientist wife Miriam (Binoche) teeters on the edge of instability. Meanwhile Eliza has fantastical visions of words she is to spell as she wins local spelling bees and heads toward the national competition in Washington, D.C. Dad becomes obsessed with Eliza's gift, ignoring Miriam and their other child, Aaron (Minghella). Viewers who didn't read the book may be set adrift in this somewhat pretentious, but earnest film. 104m/C DVD. *US* Richard Gere, Juliette Binoche, Flora Cross, Max Minghella, Kate (Catherine) Bosworth; *D:* Scott McGehee, David Siegel; *W:* Naomi Foner; *C:* Giles Nuttgens.

Beefcake 1999 Campy docudrama set in 1950s L.A. covers the muscle (or men's physique) magazine culture. Doting mama's boy Bob Mizer (MacIvor) found his talents as a still photographer and filmmaker, who also published Physique Pictorial, all of which featured chiseled studs. While Mizer insisted that his models were just clean-cut, all-American boys, he still fell afoul of pornography charges and operating a prostitution ring. The mock style turns harder-edged with Mizer's tribulations. To further confuse things, the film also includes present-day interviews with some of Mizer's one-time models and others familiar with the culture. 93m/C VHS, DVD. Daniel MacIvor, Josh Peace, Carroll Godsman; *D:* Thom Fitzgerald; *W:* Thom Fitzgerald; *C:* Thomas M. Harting; *M:* John Roby.

Beer 1985 (R) A female advertising executive devises a dangerous sexist campaign for a cheap beer, and both the beer and its nickname become nationwide obsessions. Not especially amusing. 83m/C VHS. Loretta Swit, Rip Torn, Dick Shawn, David Alan Grier, William Russ, Kenneth Mars, Peter Michael Goetz; *D:* Patrick Kelly; *C:* Bill Butler; *M:* Bill Conti.

Beer League 2006 (R) Howard Stern sidekick *Artie Lange's Beer League* sticks to his booze, smokes, and broads persona as Artie DeVanzo, the head of a lousy New Jersey softball team at war with their perennial winning cross-town rivals. The deadbeat team of losers can't win a game, but that's okay, they've got beer and brawls. Except that the local law is fed up and demands the team either win or be forced to disband. Oh, the horror. If you actually know how Lange is, you know what to expect, and criticism is beside the point. Sit back and have another beer. 86m/C DVD. *US* Artie Lange, Ralph Macchio, Anthony De Sando, Seymour Cassel, Cara Buona, Jimmy Palumbo, Joe Lo Truglio, Laurie Metcalf; *D:* Frank Sebastiano; *W:* Frank Sebastiano; *C:* David Phillips; *M:* B.C. Smith.

Beerfest 2006 (R) It's from those Broken Lizard boys, so don't go looking for sophistication. American brothers Todd and Jan Wolfhouse travel to Germany's Oktoberfest and stumble across a secret, long-standing beer competition. They also meet the arrogant German branch of the family who humiliate the brothers when they attempt to enter the contest and stand up for American males' ability to drink themselves stupid. "Strange Brew" meets "Fight Club" as this raucous comedy will probably have frat boys everywhere. 111m/C DVD. *US* Jay Chandrasekhar, Kevin Heffernan, Steve Lemme, Paul Soter, Erik Stolhanske, Eric Christian Olsen, Cloris Leachman, Donald Sutherland, Mo'Nique, Jürgen Prochnow, M.C. Gainey, Will Forte, Blanchard Ryan, Ralph (Ralf) Moeller; *D:* Jay Chandrasekhar; *W:* Jay Chandrasekhar, Kevin Heffernan, Steve Lemme, Paul Soter, Erik Stolhanske; *C:* Frank DeMarco; *M:* Nathan Barr.

The Bees WOOF! 1978 (PG) Sting of a poor movie is painful. A strain of bees have ransacked South America and are threatening the rest of the world. The buzz is that no one is safe. Cheap rip-off of "The Swarm," which is saying, something. 93m/C VHS, Jon Saxon, John Carradine, Angel Tompkins, Claudio Brook, Alicia Encinas; *D:* Alfredo Zacharias.

Beethoven 1992 (PG) Adorable St. Bernard puppy escapes from dognappers and wanders into the home of the Newtons, who, over dad's objections, adopt him. Beethoven grows into a huge, slobbering dog who sorely tries dad's patience. To make matters worse, two sets of villains also wreak havoc on the Newton's lives. Evil veterinarian Dr. Varnick plots to steal Beethoven for lab experiments, and yuppie couple Brad and Brie plot to take over the family business. Enjoyable cast, particularly Grodin as dad and Chris as Beethoven make this movie to please more than the milk and cookies set. Followed by "Beethoven's 2nd." 89m/C VHS, DVD. Charles Grodin, Bonnie Hunt, Dean Jones, Oliver Platt, Stanley Tucci, Nicholle Tom, Christopher Castile, Sarah Rose Karr, David Duchovny, Patricia Heaton, Laurel Cronin; *D:* Brian Levant; *W:* John Hughes, Amy Holden Jones; *C:* Victor Kemper; *M:* Randy Edelman.

Beethoven Lives Upstairs 1992 In 19th century Vienna 10 year-old Christoph's life is turned upside-down when the family's eccentric new tenant turns out to be composer Ludwig Van Beethoven. In time, Christoph comes to appreciate the beauty of the music and the tragedy of the composer's deafness. Features more than 25 excerpts of Beethoven's works. 52m/C VHS, DVD. Neil Munro, Ilya Woloshyn, Fiona Reid, Paul Soles, Sheila McCarthy, Albert Schultz; *D:* David Devine; *M:* Heather Conkie.

Beethoven's 2nd 1993 (PG) Sequel has awwww factor going for it as new daddy Beethoven slobbers over four adorable and appealing St. Bernard pups and his new love Missy. Same basic evil subplot as the first, with wicked kidnappers replacing evil vet. During the upheaval, the Newtons take care of the little yapping troublemakers, providing the backdrop for endless puppy mischief and exasperation on Grodin's part. Silly subplots and too many human moments tend to drag, but the kids will find the laughs (albeit stupid ones). 87m/C VHS, DVD. Charles Grodin, Bonnie Hunt, Nicholle Tom, Christopher Castile, Sarah Rose Karr, Debi Mazar, Christopher Penn, Ashley Hamilton; *D:* Rod Daniel; *W:* Len Blum; *C:* Bill Butler; *M:* Randy Edelman.

Beethoven's 3rd 2000 (PG) Dad Richard Newton (Reinhold) wants to take the family on vacation and, naturally, huge St. Bernard Beethoven is coming along. Suddenly, that rented luxury RV doesn't seem very big and dad's idea of fun is lame to the kids. Of course, it's not a typical vacation anyway, seems thieves Tommy (Ciccolini) and Bill (Marsh) need to retrieve a videotape that Richard has rented. Beethoven tries to protect his family while being blamed for every little mishap. A dog's life, indeed! 99m/C VHS, DVD. Judge Reinhold, Julia Sweeney, Joe Pichler, Michaela Gallo, Jamie Marsh, Michael Ciccolini, Frank Gorshin, Danielle Wiener; *D:* David Mickey Evans; *W:* Jeff Schechter; *C:* John Aronson; *M:* Philip Giffin. VIDEO

Beethoven's 4th 2001 Unruly Beethoven is sent to obedience school where he's accidentally switched with a well-behaved St. Bernard. Imagine the family's confusion. 94m/C VHS, DVD. Judge Reinhold, Julia Sweeney, Joe Pichler, Michaela Gallo, Matt McCoy, Veanne Cox, Mark Lindsay Chapman, Art LaFleur, Kaleigh Krish, Natalie Marston; *D:* David Mickey Evans; *W:* John Loy; *C:* John Aronson; *M:*

Beethoven's 5th 2003 Twelve-year-old Sara (Chase) and Beethoven spend the summer with eccentric Uncle Freddy (Thomas) in the old mining town of Quicksilver. Beethoven manages to dig up an old $10 bill that apparently comes from some loot buried by a couple of crooks in the 1920s and soon everyone in town is looking for the rest of the cash. 90m/C VHS, DVD. Daveigh Chase, Dave Thomas, Faith Ford, John Larroquette, Kathy Griffin, Tom Poston, Katherine Helmond, Clint Howard; *D:* Mark Griffiths; *W:* Elana Lesser, Cliff Ruby; *C:* Christopher Baffa; *M:* Adam Berry. VIDEO

Beethoven's Nephew 1988 A tepid pseudo-historical farce about Beethoven's strange obsession with his only nephew. Directed by erstwhile Warhol collaborator Morrissey. 103m/C VHS. *FR* Wolfgang Reichmann, Dittmar Prinz, Jane Birkin, Nathalie Baye; *D:* Paul Morrissey; *W:* Paul Morrissey, Matthieu Carrière. *Le Neveu de Beethoven*

Beetlejuice 1988 (PG) The after-life is confusing for a pair of ultra-nice novice ghosts Adam Maitland (Baldwin) and his wife Barbara (Davis), who are faced with chasing an obnoxious family of post-modern art lovers who move into their house. Then they hear of a poltergeist who promises to rid the house of all trespassers for a price. Things go from bad to impossible when the maniacal Keaton (as the demonic "Betelgeuse") works his magic. The calypso scene is priceless. A cheesy, funny, surreal farce of life after death with inventive set designs popping continual surprises. Ryder is striking as the misunderstood teen with a death complex, while O'Hara is hilarious as the yuppie art poseur. 92m/C VHS, DVD. Michael Keaton, Geena Davis, Alec Baldwin, Sylvia Sidney, Catherine O'Hara, Winona Ryder, Jeffrey Jones, Dick Cavett, Glenn Shadix, Robert Goulet; *D:* Tim Burton; *W:* Michael McDowell, Warren Skaaren; *C:* Thomas Ackerman; *M:* Danny Elfman. Oscars '88: Makeup; Natl. Soc. Film Critics '88: Actor (Keaton).

Before and After 1995 (PG-13) Disjointed drama depicts well-off suburban couple, Carolyn (Streep) and Ben (Neeson), who are thrown into chaos when their teenaged son Jacob (Furlong) is accused of murdering his girlfriend. Upon notification by the police that his son is the prime suspect and on the lam, Ben finds what seems to be bloody evide'nce in the family's car, which he destroys. The story loses steam from there. Based on the novel by Rosellen Brown, the focus is on the effect the death has on this picture book Massachusetts family. Neeson and Streep fall short of usually deliverable goods and director Schroeder takes the middle-of-the-road sentimental approach. 107m/C VHS, DVD. Meryl Streep, Liam Neeson, Edward Furlong, Alfred Molina, John Heard, Julia Weldon, Daniel von Bargen, Ann Magnuson, Alison Folland, Kaiulani Lee; *D:* Barbet Schroeder; *W:* Ted Tally; *C:* Luciano Tovoli; *M:* Howard Shore.

Before I Hang 1940 When a doctor invents a youth serum from the blood of a murderer, he'll stop at nothing to keep his secret. Karloff himself stands the test of time, and is satisfying as the mad scientist, giving this horror flick its appeal. 60m/B VHS, DVD. Boris Karloff, Evelyn Keyes, Bruce Bennett, Edward Van Sloan, Ben Taggart, Pedro de Cordoba, Wright Kramer, Bertram Marburgh, Don Beddoe, Robert (Fisk) Fiske; *D:* Nick Grinde; *W:* Robert D. (Robert Hardy) Andrews; *C:* Benjamin (Ben H.) Kline.

Before I Say Goodbye 2003 Political hopeful Nell's (Young) hubby faces accusations of crooked business deeds when he and his boat are blown to bits. But her desperate search for the truth might make her the next victim. A Mary Higgins Clark adaptation. 95m/C VHS, DVD. Sean Young, Lloyd Bochner, Peter DeLuise, Ursula Karven; *D:* Michael Storey; *W:* John Benjamin Martin, Jon Cooksey, Ali Matheson; *C:* David Pelletier. TV

Before Morning 1933 Police officer poses as a blackmailer to find out which of the two women in the murder victim's life are guilty. 68m/B VHS. Leo Carrillo, Lora Baxter, Taylor Holmes, Blaine Cordner, Louise Prussing, Russell Hicks, Louis Jean Heydt, Jules Epailly, Constance Bertrand, Terry Carroll; *D:* Arthur Hoerl; *C:* Walter Strenge.

Before Night Falls 🐾🐾🐾 2000 (R) Director Schnabel takes a quantum leap in skill in his second film (after "Basquiat"). This time his tortured artist is the literally tortured late Cuban poet Reinaldo Arenas (Bardem), who falls victim to Castro's repression against both his writings and his sexuality (he's gay). Arenas gets thrown into prison, eventually gets released after confessing his "crimes" and makes his escape as part of the 1980 Mariel boatlift. Ironically, freedom offers little solace to Arenas either in Miami or his last home in New York. Spanish actor Bardem is outstanding as the poet who only seeks to be true to himself and pays a tragic price. Based on the writer's autobiography. 134m/C VHS, DVD, Javier Bardem, Olivier Martinez, Andrea Di Stefano, Johnny Depp, Michael Wincott, Sean Penn, Hector Babenco, Najwa Nimri; *Cameos:* Cunningham O'Keefe, be, Lazaro Gomez Cariles, Cunningham O'Keefe; *C:* Xavier Perez Grobet, Guillermo Rosas; *M:* Carter Burwell. Ironically, Spirit '01: Actor (Bardem); Natl. Bd. of Review '00: Actor (Bardem).

Before Sunrise 🐾🐾🐾½ 1994 (R) Light, "getting-to-know-you," romance unfolds as two 20-somethings share an unlikely 14-hour date. Gen-Xer Jesse (Hawke) and French beauty (Delpy) meet on the Eurail and he convinces her to join him in exploring Vienna and their mutual attraction before he heads back to the States in the morning. The two exchange life experiences and philosophies in the typical Linklater conversational fashion, but the film strays from the comical accounts of earlier works "Slacker" and "Dazed and Confused." Cinematographer Daniel captures the Old World with finesse, especially in the inevitable "first kiss" atop the Ferris wheel made famous in Orson Welles' "The Third Man." 101m/C VHS, DVD, Ethan Hawke, Julie Delpy; *D:* Richard Linklater; *W:* Richard Linklater, Kim Krizan; *C:* Lee Daniel. Berlin Intl. Film Fest. '94: Director (Linklater).

Before Sunset 🐾🐾🐾½ 2004 (R) Sequel to Linklater's "Before Sunrise" reunites Jesse (Hawke) and Celine (Delpy), nine years after their Viennese fling. Now he's a writer promoting his book about their brief affair. She, a Parisian, shows up at a book signing. The two have only a few hours to catch up before Jesse has to fly back to America. In real time, they walk through Paris together - just talking. But what talking! They begin awkwardly polite and impersonal, but as the minutes slip away their questions and responses take on more urgency. Hawke and Delpy co-wrote the screenplay, (with Hawke using his real-life divorce as inspiration) and there's real chemistry between them. Movie veers cleverly back and forth between them and ends ambiguously. Great date film (Sorry, guys). 80m/C VHS, DVD. Ethan Hawke, Julie Delpy, Rodolphe Pauly; *D:* Richard Linklater; *W:* Ethan Hawke, Julie Delpy, Richard Linklater; *C:* Lee Daniel; *M:* Julie Delpy, Glen Gill.

Before the Devil Knows You're Dead 🐾🐾🐾 2007 (R) At 83, director Lumet shows he still has crime chops in this grubby tragedy about a botched heist. Calculating, fleshy Andy (Hoffman) has a drug problem and a trophy wife, Gina (Tomei), while his sadsack, skinny bro Hank (Hawke) who happens to be hitting the sheets with Gina, needs cash for his shrewish ex (Ryan). Andy plans a heist on their family's jewelry store but Hank manages to screw it up and things just get more complicated. Good performances by all concerned. 117m/C DVD. US Philip Seymour Hoffman, Ethan Hawke, Marisa Tomei, Amy Ryan, Rosemary Harris, Brian F. O'Byrne, Amy Ryan, Michael Shannon, Aleksa Palladino; *D:* Sidney Lumet. *W:* Kelly Masterson; *C:* Ron Fortunato; *M:* Carter Burwell.

Before the Fall 🐾🐾 NaPoLA 2004 In 1942, teenager Friedrich Weimer (Riemelt) goes against his father's wishes to enter an exclusive Berlin school designed to educate future Nazi leaders. Friedrich distinguishes himself with his boxing prowess but eventually begins to question his in-

Before the Rain Pc Dezju, Pred dozhdot 1994 War-torn Macedonia is the backdrop for Manchevski's first film (and first made in the newly declared republic of Macedonia). Powerful circular narrative joins three stories about the freedom of love and the pervasiveness of violence. "Words" finds young Macedonian monk Kiril (Colin) distracted from his spiritual duties by young Albanian Muslim Zamira (Mitevska), who takes refuge in his monastery. In "Faces," pregnant picture editor Anne (Cartlidge) is torn between her estranged husband and her lover, Aleksander (Serbedzija), a London-based war photographer who left his native Macedonia years before. "Pictures" finds Aleksandar returning to his old village—now torn by ethnic strife. In Macedonian, Albanian, and English, with subtitles. 129m/C VHS, DVD, GB/FR/MA Rade Serbedzija, Katrin Cartlidge, Gregoire Colin, Labina Mitevska, Phyllida Law; *C:* Manchevski; *W:* Milcho Manchevski; *C:* Manuel Teran; *M:* Anastasia. Ind. Spirit '96: Foreign Film; Venice Film Fest. '94: Golden Lion.

Before the Revolution 🐾🐾🐾½ Prima della Rivoluzione 1965 One of Bertolucci's first films. Love and politics are mixed when the young Fabrizio, who is dabbling in communism, is also flirting with his young aunt. Striking and powerful film that has yet to lose its effect despite the times. Italian with subtitles. 115m/C VHS, IT Frances-co Barilli, Adriana Asti, Alain Midgette, Morando Morandini, Domenico Alpi; *D:* Bernardo Bertolucci; *W:* Bernardo Bertolucci; *C:* Aldo Scavarda; *M:* Ennio Morricone, Gino Paoli.

Beggars of Life 🐾🐾 1928 In a panic, Nancy (Brooks) kills her abusive stepfather. She disguises herself as a boy and, with fellow runaway Jim (Arlen) serving as her protector, decides to hop a train to Canada. They wind up spending the night in a hobo camp, looked after by Oklahoma Red (Beery) who aids in their escape at great cost to himself. 100m/B VHS, Louise Brooks, Richard Arlen, Wallace Beery, Robert Perry, Roscoe Karns, Edgar "Blue" Washington; *D:* William A. Wellman; *W:* Benjamin Glazer, Jim Tully; *C:* Henry W. Gerrard; *M:* Karl Hajos.

Beggars in Ermine 🐾🐾 1934 A handicapped, impoverished man organizes all the beggars in the world into a successful corporation. Unusual performance from Atwill, Henry B. Walthall, Betty Furness, Jameson Thomas, James Bush, Astrid Allwyn, George "Gabby" Hayes; *D:* Phil Rosen.

Begin the Beguine See **Volver a Empezar**

Beginning of the End 🐾 1957 Produced the same year as "The Deadly Mantis," Gordon's effort adds to 1957's harvest of bugs on a rampage "B"-graders. Giant, radiation-spawned grasshoppers attack Chicago causing Graves to come to the rescue. Easily the best giant grasshopper movie ever made. 73m/B VHS, DVD, Peggy Castle, Peter Graves, Morris Ankrum, Richard Benedict, James Seay, Thomas B(rowne), Henry, Larry J. Blake, John Close, Frank Wilcox; *D:* Bert I. Gordon; *W:* Lester Gorr, Fred Freiberger; *C:* Jack Marta; *M:* Albert Glasser.

Behave Yourself! 🐾½ 1952 A married couple adopts a dog who may be the key for a million-dollar hijacking setup by a gang of hoodlums. 81m/B VHS, DVD. Shelley Winters, Farley Granger, William Demarest, Lon Chaney Jr., Hans Conried, Elisha Cook Jr., Francis L. Sullivan; *D:* George Beck.

The Beguiled 🐾🐾🐾 1970 (R) During the Civil War a wounded Union soldier is taken in by the women at a girl's school in the South. He manages to seduce both a student and a teacher, and jealousy and revenge ensue. Decidedly weird psychological melodrama from action vets Siegel and Eastwood. 109m/C VHS, Clint Eastwood, Geraldine Page, Elizabeth Hartman, Jo Ann Harris; *D:* Donald Siegel; *W:* Albert (John B. Sherry) Maltz, Irene (Grimes Grice) Kamp; *C:* Bruce Surtees; *M:* Lalo Schifrin.

Behind Enemy Lines 🐾🐾 2001 (PG-13) Balkan civil war is mere scenery, and soldiers only caricatures, in this cartoonish cat-and-mouse chase movie. Ace Navy navigator Lt. Burnett (Wilson), tired of flying peace missions, years for some real action. When a routine reconnaissance operation goes awry-his plane shot down over Serbian territory and his pilot ruthlessly executed—Burnett gets his wish. Crusty Admiral Reigart (Hackman) wants to rescue his flyboy, but a pesky international peace agreement gets in the way. First-time director Moore, best known for his action sequences do their duty. Despite a clear connection to the ordeal of real-life Air Force captain Scott O'Grady, this is so-so war story. 106m/C VHS, DVD, US Owen Wilson, Gene Hackman, Joaquim de Almeida, David Keith, Gabriel Macht, Charles Malik Whitfield, Olek Krupa, Vladimir Mashkov, Marko Ogonda; *C:* Brendan Galvin; *M:* Don Davis.

Behind Locked Doors 🐾🐾½ 1948 A journalist fakes mental illness to have himself committed to an asylum, where he believes a crooked judge is in hiding. A superior "B" mystery/suspense feature, with some tense moments. 61m/B VHS, DVD, Lucille Bremer, Richard Carlson, Tor Johnson, Douglas Fowley, Herbert (Hayes) Heyes, Ralf Harolde; *D:* Budd Boetticher; *W:* Eugene Ling, Malvin Wald; *C:* Guy Roe; *M:* Irving Friedman.

Behind Office Doors 🐾🐾 1931 Astor stars as the secretarial "power behind the throne" in this look at who really wields power in an office. Her boss takes her for granted until things go wrong. 82m/C VHS, DVD, Mary Astor, Robert Ames, Ricardo Cortez, Charles Sellon; *D:* Melville Brown; *W:* Carey Wilson.

Behind Prison Walls 🐾🐾 Youth Takes a Hand 1943 A steel tycoon and his son are sent to prison, and the son tries to convert his dad to socialism. A fun, light hearted film, the last for veteran Tully. 64m/B VHS, Alan Baxter, Gertrude Michael, Tully, Marshall, Edwin Maxwell, Jacqueline Dalya, Matt Willis; *D:* Steve Sekely.

Behind the Front 🐾🐾½ 1926 Two friends tumble in and out of trouble in this comic Army film. One of the most profitable films of the late '20s. 60m/B VHS, Wallace Beery, Raymond Hatton, Richard Arlen, Mary Brian, Chester Conklin; *D:* Edward Sutherland.

Behind the Lines 🐾🐾🐾 Regeneration 1997 (R) "focuses on the friendship between WWI soldier/poets Siegfried Sassoon (Wilby) and Wilfred Owen (Bunce), who receive a brief reprieve from the war when they're treated for shell shock at Edinburgh's Craiglockhart Hospital in 1917. Another patient is working-class soldier Billy Prior (Miller), made mute from the horrors he's witnessed. But their compassionate doctor, William Rivers (Pryce), is dutybound to return increasingly unstable over the ethical concerns his work engenders. If he can cure his patients, they go back to the front to fight again. The first book in Pat Barker's war trilogy. 96m/C VHS, DVD. GB CA Jonathan Pryce, James Wilby, Jonny Lee Miller, Stuart Bunce, Tanya Allen, John Neville, Dougray Scott, David Hayman, David Robb, Julian Fellowes, Kevin McKidd, Jeremy Child; *D:* Gilles Mackinnon; *W:* Allan Scott; *C:* Glen MacPherson; *M:* Mychael Danna.

Behold a Pale Horse 🐾🐾½ 1964 A Spanish police captain attempts to dupe Peck into believing that his mother is dying and he must visit her on her deathbed. Loyalist Spaniard Peck becomes privy to the plot against him, but goes to Spain anyway in this post Spanish Civil War film. 118m/B VHS, DVD, Gregory Peck, Anthony Quinn, Omar Sharif, Mildred Dunnock; *D:* Fred Zinnemann; *W:* (James) P(inckney) Miller; *M:* Maurice Jarre.

Beijing Bicycle 🐾🐾 Shiqisuide Danche 2001 (PG-13) Guei (Lin) leaves his provincial home and gets a job as a bike messenger in Beijing where most of his meager wages go to purchase his own bike. His bike is stolen and Guei loses his job. He finally discovers that petulant high schooler Jian (Bin), whose father wouldn't buy him a bike of his own, has purchased Guei's from a flea market and, because he can now join his friends riding after school, he refuses to let it go. Their

---

Behind Enemy Lines 🐾🐾½ 1985 (R) Special Forces soldier goes on a special mission to eliminate a possible Nazi spy. 83m/C VHS, Blu-ray Disc, UMD, Hal Holbrook, Ray Sharkey, David McCallum, Tom Skerritt, Ame Twomey, Robert Patrick; *D:* Sheldon Larry. TV

Behind Enemy Lines 🐾🐾½ 1996 (R) Ex-Marine Mike Weston (Griffith) believes he is responsible for the death of his friend Jones (Mulkey) during assignment in Vietnam. When Weston discovers Jones is actually being held hostage, he decides on a rescue mission. 89m/C VHS, DVD, Thomas Ian Griffith, Chris Mulkey, Courtney Dennis Cooley, C. Blake T. Evans; *M:* Andrew Osborne, Dennis Cooley, C. Blake T. Evans; *M:* Arthur Kempel.

Behind the Mask 🐾🐾½ 1946 Lamont Cranston, better known as dogooder "The Shadow," finds himself accused of murdering a blackmailing newspaper reporter. Based on the radio serial. 68m/C VHS, Kane Richmond, Barbara Read, George Chandler, Dorothea Kent, Robert Shayne, June Clyde; *D:* Phil Karlson.

Behind the Mask 🐾🐾½ 1999 Mentally challenged janitor James Jones (Fox) is employed at a hospital as doctor run by workaholic doctor Bob Shushan (Sutherland). When the doc suffers a heart attack, it's James who saves him. Shushan takes this as a wake-up call and decides to help James find the father who abandoned him while reconnecting with his own neglected adult son, Brian (Whitford). Based on a true story. 90m/C DVD Donald Sutherland, Matthew Fox, Bradley Whitford, Mary McDonnell, Sheila Larkin, Currie Graham, Lorena Gale, Ron Sauve; *D:* Tom McLoughlin; *W:* Gregory Goecell; *C:* Arthur Albert. TV

Behind the Red Door 🐾🐾 2002 (R) Natalie (Sedgwick) hasn't spoken to her arrogant older brother Roy (Sutherland) for 10 years. A New York photographer, Sales called by her friend and agent Julia (Channing) into accepting an assignment in Boston that turns out to be for her brother's company. Roy then bullies Natalie into staying for his birthday party—later revealing to her that he's dying. He wants to reconcile but a shaken Natalie (who blames Roy for some childhood traumas) insists she must return home. Good cast, but Sutherland's character is so secretive and obnoxious it's hard to drudge up any sympathy for him. And to cap it off with a plot device about some neglected childhood memories. 88m/C VHS, DVD, Kyra Sedgwick, Kiefer Sutherland, Stockard Channing, Jason Carter, Philip Craig; *D:* Matia Karrell; *W:* Matia Karrell; *C:* Robert Elswit; *M:* David Fleury. CABLE.

Behind the Rising Sun 🐾🐾 1943 A Japanese publisher's political views clash with those of his American-educated son in 1930s Japan. Well done despite pre-war propaganda themes. 88m/B VHS, Tom Neal, J. Carol Naish, Robert Ryan, Mike Mazurki, Margo, Gloria Holden, Don Douglas; *D:* Edward Dmytryk.

Behind the Sun 🐾🐾 Abril Despedacado: Broken April 2001 (PG-13) A blood feud between two families nearly destroys them both in Sales' adaptation of Ismail Kadare's novel, which the director relocated to Brazil in 1910. The Ferreiras and the Breves are both sugarcane planters determined to protect their honor if nothing else. Tonho Breves (Santoro) is expected to avenge the death of his older brother at the hands of the Ferreiras. Tonho's young brother (Lacerda) can't understand why the pointless violence continues and when Tonho falls in love with traveling circus performer Clara (Antonio), the boy becomes determined to stop his brother's safe and happy. Portuguese with subtitles. 91m/C VHS, DVD, BR FR Rodrigo Santoro, Ravi Ramos Lacerda, Luiz Carlos Vasconcelos, Cilton Bastos, Flavia Marco Antonio, Sergio Machado; *C:* Walter Carvalho; *M:* Antonio Pinto. British Acad. '01: Foreign Film.

Beijing

---
doctrination. German with subtitles. 110m/ C DVD, GE Tom Schilling, Max Riemelt, Michael Schenk, Jonas Jagermeyr, Leon A. Kersten, Thomas Drescher; *D:* Dennis Gansel; *W:* Dennis Gansel, Maggie Peren; *C:* Torsten Brewer; *M:* Angelo Badalamenti, Normand Corbeil.

confrontation turns violent as more and more people become involved. Chinese with subtitles. **113m/C VHS, DVD. TW FR** Cui Lin, Bin Li, Zhou Xun, Gao Yuanyuahn, Li Shuang, Zhao Yiwel, Pang Yan; **D:** Xiaoshuai Wang; **W:** Xiaoshuai Wang, Danian Tang, Peggy Chiao, Hsiang-Ming Hsu; **C:** Jie Liu; **M:** Wang Hsiao Feng.

The Being ☆ 1983 (R) People in Idaho are terrorized by a freak who became abnormal after radiation was disposed in the local dump. Another dull monster-created-by-nuclear-waste non-event. Of limited interest is Buzzi. However, you'd be more entertained (read: amused) by Troma's "The Toxic Avenger," which takes itself much (much!) less seriously. **82m/C VHS, DVD.** Ruth Buzzi, Martin Landau, Jose Ferrer; **D:** Jackie Kong.

Being at Home with Claude ☆☆ 1992 Yves (Dupuis) is a 22-year-old Montreal hustler being interrogated by a nameless inspector (Godin) for the murder of his lover, Claude (Pichette). Yves has admitted his guilt but the inspector wants to reconstruct the event and determine a motive. Lots of black-and-white flashbacks as Yves dwells on his work and his psychologically love-death relationship with Claude. Rather pretentious and long-winded. Based on the play by Rene-Daniel DuBois. In French with English subtitles. **86m/C VHS. CA** Roy Dupuis, Jacques Godin, Jean-Francois Pichette, Gaston Lepage; **D:** Johanne Boisvert; **W:** Jean Boudin. **G:** '92: Score.

Being Human ☆☆ 1994 (PG-13) Ambitious comedy drama promises more than it delivers, and shackles Williams in the process. Hector (Williams) is a regular guy continuously reincarnated throughout the millenia. He plays a caveman, a Roman slave, a Middle Ages nomad, a crew member on a 17th century new world voyage, and a modern New Yorker in separate vignettes that echo and/or extend the main themes of family, identity, and random fate. But he manages to emerge from each sketch as an unassuming everyman who never learns his lesson. One of Williams' periodic chancy ventures away from his comedic roots occasionally strikes gold, but often seems overly restrained. **122m/C VHS.** Robin Williams, John Turturro, Anna Galiena, Vincent D'Onofrio, Hector Elizondo, Lorraine Bracco, Lindsay Crouse, Kelly Hunter, William H. Macy, Grace Mahlaba, Theresa Russell, Charles Miller, Helen Miller, Robert Carlyle, Tony Curran, Bill Nighy, David Morrissey, Ewan McGregor, David Proval; **D:** Bill Forsyth; **W:** Bill Forsyth; **M:** Michael Gibbs.

Being John Malkovich ☆☆☆ 1999 (R) Very weird comedy is the debut feature for Jonze. High-strung street puppeteer Craig Schwartz (Cusack) is married to frumpy pet-store worker Lotte (an unrecognizable Diaz). Forced to take a job as an office clerk in a building on floor seven-and-a-half, Craig falls for office vixen, Maxine (Keener), but his big discovery is a sealed door that reveals a tunnel leading directly into actor John Malkovich's mind. Craig views the world through the actor's eyes for 15 minutes at a time and decides to profit on his findings. Things just get more surreal when both Lotte and Maxine get into the act. **112m/C VHS, DVD, HD DVD.** John Cusack, Cameron Diaz, Catherine Keener, John Malkovich, Orson Bean, Mary Kay Place, Charlie Sheen; **D:** Spike Jonze; **W:** Charlie Kaufman; **C:** Lance Acord; **M:** Carter Burwell. British Acad. '99: Orig. Screenplay; Ind. Spirit '00: First Feature, First Screenplay; L.A. Film Critics '99: Screenplay; MTV Movie Awards '00: New Filmmaker (Jonze); N.Y. Film Critics '99: Support. Actress (Keener); Natl. Soc. Film Critics '99: Film, Screenplay.

Being Julia ☆☆ 2004 (R) Bening triumphs in the title role as a larger-than-life stage actress suffering a midlife dip. But this delightful diva still has the deviousness to show a couple of whipper-snappers what it means to be a star. Swanning about in 1938 London, Julia has a strong support system, led by her unfaithful but loving manager/husband Michael (Irons). However, she's bored and ready for a little fling with Tom (Evans), a fawning young fan with an agenda of his own, involving his ambitious actress girlfriend

(Punch). When Julia discovers she's been used, she takes the opportunity not only to get revenge but as a step in revitalizing her life. Based on the novel "Theatre" by W. Somerset Maugham. **105m/C DVD. HU VHS.** CA GB Annette Bening, Jeremy Irons, Bruce Greenwood, Juliet Stevenson, Shaun Evans, Lucy Punch, Maury Chaykin, Sheila McCarthy, Michael Gambon, Leigh Lawson, Rosemary Harris, Rita Tushingham, Thomas Sturidge; **D:** Istvan Szabo; **W:** Ronald Harwood; **C:** Lajos Koltai; **M:** Mychael Danna. Golden Globes '05: Actress—Mus./Comedy (Bening).

Being There ☆☆☆½ 1979 (PG) A feeble-minded gardener, whose entire knowledge of life comes from watching TV, is sent out into the real world when his employer dies. Equipped with his prize possession, his remote control unit, the gardener unwittingly enters the world of politics and is welcomed as a mysterious sage. Sellers is wonderful in this satiric treat adapted by Jerzy Kosinski from his novel. **130m/C VHS, DVD.** Peter Sellers, Shirley MacLaine, Melvyn Douglas, Jack Warden, Richard Dysart, Richard Basehart; **D:** Hal Ashby; **W:** Jerzy Kosinski; **C:** Caleb Deschanel; **M:** Johnny Mandel. Oscars '79: Support. Actor (Douglas); Golden Globes '80: Actor—Mus./Comedy (Sellers), Support. Actor (Douglas); L.A. Film Critics '79: Support. Actor (Douglas); Natl. Bd. of Review '79: Actor (Sellers); N.Y. Film Critics '79: Support. Actor (Sellers); N.Y. Film Critics '79: Cinematog.; Writers Guild '79: Adapt. Screenplay.

Being Two Isn't Easy ☆☆½ 1962 Director Ichikawa shows the world through the eyes of a two-year-old as a young couple struggle to raise their son. In Japanese with English subtitles. **88m/C VHS. JP** Fujiko Yamamoto, Eiji Funakoshi; **D:** Kon Ichikawa.

Bela Lugosi Meets a Brooklyn Gorilla Woof! *The Boys from Brooklyn; The Monster Meets the Gorilla* 1952 Two men who look like Dean Martin and Jerry Lewis (but aren't) get lost in the jungle, where they meet mad scientist Lugosi. Worse than it sounds. Real Jerry sued for unflattering imitation. **74m/B VHS, DVD.** Bela Lugosi, Duke Mitchell, Sammy Petrillo, Charlita, Martin Garralaga, Al Kikume, Muriel Landers, Milton Newberger; **D:** William Beaudine; **W:** Tim Ryan; **C:** Charles Van Enger; **M:** Richard Hazard.

Belfast Assassin ☆ *Harry's Game* 1984 A British anti-terrorist agent goes undercover in Ireland to find an IRA assassin who shot a British cabinet minister. **130m/C VHS.** Derek Thompson, Ray Lonnen, Gil Brailey, Benjamin Whitrow; **D:** Lawrence Gordon-Clark.

Believe ☆☆½ 1999 (PG-13) Teen prankster Ben Stiles (Mabe) loves to scare people. In fact, his behavior gets him kicked out of prep school and sent to live with his no-nonsense grandfather (Rubes). But the fright's on him when Ben and his friend Katherine (Cuthbert) decide to turn the abandoned Wickwire House into a haunted mansion and a ghostly figure suddenly starts making appearances. **97m/C VHS, DVD.** Ricky Mabe, Elisha Cuthbert, Jan Rubes, Ben Gazzara, Andrea Martin, Jayne Heitmeyer; **D:** Robert Tinnell. **VIDEO**

Believe in Me ☆☆ 2006 (PG) Formulaic, standard "inspiring story" sports film plays like a distaff "Hoosiers" but occasionally conjures up an interesting twist. Clay Driscoll (Donovan) moves to small-town America to discover that his new job coaching a high school boy's team has been taken from him and he's been given the girl's team instead. At first offended, he takes the young women from zeros (giggling losers) to heroes (state finals) through hard work, dedication, inspiring locker room speeches, and other well-mined sports cliches. Based on a true story (of course). **108m/C DVD. US** Jeffrey Donovan, Samantha Mathis, Bruce Dern, Bob Gunton, Heather Matarazzo, Alicia Lagano; **D:** Robert Collector; **W:** Robert Collector; **C:** James L. Carter; **M:** David Tom.

The Believer ☆☆ 2001 Inspired by the true story of neo-Nazi Daniel Burros and the New York Times expose that revealed he was Jewish. In Bean's version, Danny Balint (Gosling) is a ferociously intelligent former yeshiva student whose personal identity crisis has led him to a

fascist movement led by Curtis Zampf (Zane) and to virulent anti-Semitism. But even while leading his own band of skinheads, Danny discovers he can't easily leave his Jewish heritage behind. **98m/C VHS, DVD.** Ryan Gosling, Summer Phoenix, Billy Zane, Theresa Russell, Glenn Fitzgerald; **D:** Henry Bean; **W:** Henry Bean; **C:** Jim Denault; **M:** Joel Diamond.

The Believers ☆☆½ 1987 (R) Tense horror mystery set in New York city about a series of gruesome, unexplained murders. A widowed police psychologist investigating the deaths unwittingly discovers a powerful Santeria cult with their lieves in the sacrifice of children. Without warning he is drawn into the circle of the "Believers" and must free himself before his own son is the next sacrifice. Gripping (and grim), unrelenting horror. **114m/C VHS, DVD.** Martin Sheen, Helen Shaver, Malick Bowens, Haris Yulin, Harley Cross, Elizabeth Wilson, Lee Richardson, Carla Pinza; **D:** John Schlesinger; **W:** Mark Frost; **C:** Robby Muller; **M:** J. Peter Robinson.

Believers ☆½ 2007 (R) Two paramedics (Messner, Huertas) are kidnapped by a doomsday cult that believes the end is at hand so they're going to commit mass suicide. Not quite sure why a suicidal cult wants paramedics in its midst, but it's a creepy story. **101m/C DVD.** Johnny Messner, Elizabeth Bogush, Daniel Benzali, Jon Huertas, John Farley, Deanna Russo; **D:** Daniel Myrick; **C:** Andrew Huebscher; **M:** Kays Al-Atrakchi. **VIDEO**

Belizaire the Cajun ☆☆½ 1986 (PG) 19th-century Louisiana love story. White prejudice against the Cajuns is rampant and violent, but that doesn't stop sexy faith healer Assante from falling in love with the inaccessible Cajun wife (Youngs) of a rich local. Made with care on a tight budget. Worthwhile, though uneven. **103m/C VHS, DVD.** Armand Assante, Gail Youngs, Will Patton, Stephen McHattie, Michael Schoeffling, Robert Duvall, Nancy Barrett; **D:** Glen Pitre; **W:** Glen Pitre; **C:** Richard Bowen; **M:** Michael Doucet, Howard Shore.

Bell, Book and Candle ☆☆½ 1958 Gillian Holroyd (Novak) is a beautiful modern-day witch (complete with a Siamese familiar) who has made up her mind to refrain from using her powers. That is until Shepherd Henderson (Stewart) moves into her building and she decides to enchant him with a love spell. But spells have a way of backfiring on those who cast them. Lanchester is romantic Aunt Queenie and Lemmon is a standout as Gillian's jazz-loving, bongo-playing brother, Nicky. **103m/C VHS, DVD.** James Stewart, Kim Novak, Jack Lemmon, Elsa Lanchester, Ernie Kovacs, Hermione Gingold, Janice Rule; **D:** Richard Quine; **C:** James Wong Howe; **M:** George Duning.

Bell from Hell ☆☆ 1974 A tale of insanity and revenge, wherein a young man, institutionalized since his mother's death, plots to kill his aunt and three cousins. **80m/C VHS, DVD.** Viveca Lindfors, Renaud Verley, Alfredo Mayo; **D:** Claudio Guerin Hill.

The Bell Jar ☆½ 1979 (R) Based on poet Sylvia Plath's acclaimed semi-autobiographical novel, this is the story of a young woman who becomes the victim of mental illness. Not for the easily depressed and a disjointed and disappointing adaptation of Plath's work. **113m/C VHS, DVD.** Marilyn Hassett, Julie Harris, Barbara Barrie, Anne Jackson, Robert Klein, Anne Jackson; **D:** Larry Peerce.

Bella Mafia ☆☆½ 1997 (R) Over-the-top trash and that's meant in the finest possible way. This lurid melodrama, originally a two-part miniseries, concerns the Sicilian mob family, the Lucianos, who have suffered the loss of father Roberto (Farina) and three sons. Widowed matriarch Graziella (Redgrave) decides to join with her three daughters-in-law, Sophia (Kinski), Teresa (Douglas), and Moyra (Tilly), and avenge their deaths. Oh yes, there's also Sophia's secret son Luca (Marsden), a killer who turns up to insinuates himself into family life. Adapted by La Plante from her novel. **117m/C VHS.** Vanessa

Redgrave, Nastassja Kinski, Illeana Douglas, Jennifer Tilly, James Marsden, Peter Bogdanovich, Dennis Farina, Gina Philips; **D:** David Greene; **W:** Lynda La Plante. **TV**

Bellamy ☆ 1980 Murderous madman massacres masseuses, and Bellamy is the cop out to get him. **92m/C VHS.** John Stanton, Timothy Elston, Sally Conabere; **D:** Colin Eggleston, Pino Amenta.

The Bellboy ☆☆½ 1960 Lewis makes his directorial debut in this plotless but clever outing. He also stars as the eponymous character, a bellboy at Miami's Fountainbleau Hotel. Cameos from Berle and Winchell are highlights. **72m/B VHS, DVD.** Jerry Lewis, Alex Gerry, Bob Clayton, Sonny Sands, Bill Richmond, Larry Best, Maxie "Slapsie" Rosenbloom; **Cameos:** Milton Berle, Walter Winchell; **D:** Jerry Lewis; **W:** Jerry Lewis; **C:** Haskell Boggs; **M:** Walter Scharf.

The Bellboy and the Playgirls Woof! *The Playgirls and the Bellboy; Mit Eva Fing Die Sunde An* 1962 Early Coppola effort adds new film footage to a 1958 German movie. Stars Playboy playmate June "The Body" Wilkinson, with other centerfolds of the time. **93m/C VHS, FR** Robert Dhery, Louis de Funes, Collette Brosset, Alfred Adam, Bernard Lavelette, Annie Ducaux; **D:** Robert Dhery; **W:** Robert Dhery, Alfred Adam, Pierre Tchernia; **C:** Ghislan Cloquet; **M:** Gerard Calvi.

Belle Americaine ☆☆ *What a Chassis!* 1961 Title refers to the Cadillac car young Parisian factory worker Dhery buys at a suspiciously bargain price. Naturally, his deal is too good to be true and trouble follows. Dubbed in English. **97m/C VHS, FR** Robert Dhery, Louis de Funes, Collette Brosset, Alfred Adam, Bernard Lavelette, Annie Ducaux; **D:** Robert Dhery; **W:** Robert Dhery, Alfred Adam, Pierre Tchernia; **C:** Ghislan Cloquet; **M:** Gerard Calvi.

Belle de Jour ☆☆☆½ 1967 (R) Based on Joseph Kessel's novel, one of director Bunuel's best movies has all his characteristic nuances: the hypocrisy of our society; eroticism; anti-religion. Deneuve plays Severine, a chic, frigid Parisian newlywed, who decides to become a daytime prostitute, unbeknownst to her husband. Bunuel blends reality with fantasy, and the viewer is never sure which is which in this finely crafted movie. French with subtitles. **100m/C VHS, DVD. FR** Catherine Deneuve, Jean Sorel, Genevieve Page, Michel Piccoli, Francisco Rabal, Pierre Clementi, Georges Marchal, Francoise Fabian; **D:** Luis Bunuel; **W:** Luis Bunuel, Jean-Claude Carriere; **C:** Sacha Vierny.

Belle Epoque ☆☆☆ *The Age of Beauty* 1992 (R) Young army deserter Fernando (Sanz) embarks on a personal voyage of discovery when he meets Manolo (Gomez), an eccentric old man, and father to four beautiful daughters. Fernando can't believe his luck—and the sisters share his interest, resulting in an amusing round of musical beds. Bittersweet tale set amidst the anarchy and war of 1930s Spain with a terrific screenplay that tastefully handles the material without stooping to the obvious leering possibilities. In addition to Oscar, won nine Spanish Goyas, including best picture, director, actress (Gil), and screenplay. Title ironically refers to the era at the end of the 19th century before the wars of the 20th century tore Europe apart. Spanish with English subtitles or dubbed. **108m/C VHS, DVD. SP** Jorge Sanz, Fernando Feman-Gomez, Ariadna Gil, Maribel Verdu, Penelope Cruz, Miriam Diaz-Aroca, Mary Carmen Ramirez, Michel Galabru, Gabino Diego; **D:** Fernando Trueba; **W:** Rafael Azcona; **C:** Jose Luis Alcaine; **M:** Antoine Duhamel. Oscars '93: Foreign Film.

The Belle of New York ☆☆ 1952 A turn-of-the-century bachelor falls in love with a Salvation Army missionary in this standard musical. ♫Naughty But Nice; Baby Doll; Oops; I Wanna Be a Dancin' Man; Seeing's Believing; When I'm Out With the Belle of New York; Let a Little Love Come In. **82m/C VHS.** Fred Astaire, Vera-Ellen, Marjorie Main, Keenan Wynn, Alice Pearce, Gale Robbins, Clinton Sundberg; **D:** Charles Walters.

Belle of the Nineties 🎬🎬 It singer who gets involved with a boxer. Her trademark sexual innuendos were already being censored but such lines were as "It's better to be looked over than overlooked." done in West style, get the point across. **73m/B** VHS, DVD. Mae West, Roger Pryor, John McRae West, Jonn Miljan, Katherine JeMille, Henry Woods, Edward (Ed) Gargan; **D:** Leo McCarey; **W:** Mae West; **C:** Karl Struss; **M:** Arthur Johnston.

The Belles of St. Trinian's 🎬🎬 1953 Sim is priceless in a dual role as the eccentric headmistress of a chaotic, bankrupt girls' school and her bookie twin brother who schemes the school into financial security. The first in a series of movies based on a popular British cartoon by Ronald Searles about a girls' school and its mischievous students. Followed by "Blue Murder at St. Trinian's," "The Pure Hell of St. Trinian's," and "The Great St. Trinian's Train Robbery." **86m/B** VHS. **GB** Alastair Sim, Joyce Grenfell, Hermione Baddeley, George Cole, Eric Pohlmann, Renee Houston, Beryl Reid, Babina, Jill Braidwood, Annabelle Covey, Betty Ann Davies, Diana Day, Jack Doyle, Irene Handl, Arthur Howard, Sidney James, Lloyd Lamble, Jean Langston, Belinda Lee, Vivian Martin, Andree Melly, Mary Merrall, Guy Middleton, Joan Sims, Jerry Verno, Richard Wattis; **D:** Frank Launder; **W:** Frank Launder, Sidney Gilliat, Val Valentine; **C:** Stanley Pavey; **M:** Malcolm Arnold.

Belles on Their Toes 🎬🎬 1952 Somewhat less charming sequel to 1950's 'Cheaper by the Dozen" is big on nostalgia. Now widowed, Lillian Gilbreth (Loy) is struggling to support her large family, having to overcome women in the workplace prejudice. Using her industrial engineering degree, Lillian finally gets a job training young engineers, but this means eldest daughter Ann (Cran) must pick up the domestic slack. Which puts a crimp in Ann's budding romance with young Dr. Bob (Hunter). Based on the memoir by Gilbreth children Frank and Ernestine. **89m/C DVD.** Myrna Loy, Jeanne Crain, Debra Page, Jeffrey Hunter, Edward Arnold, Hoagy Carmichael, Barbara Bates, Robert Arthur, Martin Milner, Verna Felton, Carole Kugert, Tommy "T.V." Ivo, Jimmy Hunt, Robert Easton, Cecil Weston; **D:** Henry Levin; **W:** Henry Ephron, Phoebe Ephron; **C:** Arthur E. Arling; **M:** Cyril Mockridge.

Bellissima 🎬🎬 1951 A woman living in an Italian tenement has unrealistic goals for her plain but endearing daughter when a famous director begins casting a role designed for a child. The mother's maternal fury and collision with reality highlight a poignant film. Italian with subtitles. **130m/B** VHS, DVD. **IT** Anna Magnani, Walter Chiari, Alessandro Blasetti, Tina Apicella, Gastone Renzelli; **D:** Luchino Visconti; **W:** Luchino Visconti; Cesare Zavattini, Francesco Rosi, Suso Cecchi D'Amico; **C:** Piero Portalupi, Paul Ronald.

Belle Starr 🎬🎬 1979 The career of Wild West outlaw Belle Starr is chronicled in this strange western pastiche about lawlessness and sexual aggression. Wertmuller directed under the pseudonym Nathan Wich. Dubbed in English. **90m/C** VHS. **IT** Elsa Martinell; George Eastman, Dan Harrison; **D:** Lina Wertmuller.

Belle Toujours 🎬🎬 2006 Thirty-nine years after "Belle de Jour" comes this sequel — or perhaps more of an homage — from Manoel de Oliveira. A chance meeting after so many years places Henri Husson (Piccoli) and Severine (Ogier) at a candlelit dinner table where they discuss the past, the intervening years, and thoughts of the future. Severine, now a widow worn down by years of carrying secrets and lies, seems to care little about reliving their sexually complicated past and in fact is prepared to retire to a convent. Henri, still feeling the dart of her rejection, wants to recount the sordid history they share. In the earlier film the young Severine supported herself and her disabled husband as a daytime prostitute, a secret she meticulously kept from her husband. Henri wants ec a relationship with her that never happened. Paris sparkles in this beautifully crafted work. **68m/C DVD, FR** PT Michel Piccoli, Bulle Ogier, Ricardo Trepa, Leonor Baldaque, Julia Buisel; **D:** Manoel de Oliveira; **C:** Sabine Lancelin.

Bells of Capistrano 🎬🎬 1942 The last film Autry made before serving in the Army finds the singing star wanted as a crowd-drawing attraction for two rival rodeo companies. Gene chooses the one owned by the pretty girl, which causes problems with the competition. **71m/B** VHS, DVD. Judy Holliday; Dean Martin, Fred Clark, Edie Foy Jr., Jean Stapleton; **D:** Vincente Minnelli; **W:** Betty Comden, Adolph Green; **C:** Milton Krasner; **M:** Andre Previn.

Bells of Coronado 🎬🎬 1950 Rogers and Evans team up to expose the murderer of the owner of a profitable uranium mine. A gang of smugglers trying to trade the ore to foreign powers is thwarted. The usual thin storyline, but filled with action and riding stunts. **67m/B** VHS, DVD. Roy Rogers, Dale Evans, Pat Brady, Grant Withers; **D:** William Witney.

Bells of Death 🎬🎬 1990 A young martial arts student infiltrates the gang that killed his family and kidnapped his sister, finishing them off one by one. **91m/C** VHS. Chun Ping, Chang Yi, Chao Hsin Yen; **D:** Yueh Fung.

Bells of Rosarita 🎬🎬 1945 Roy helps foil an evil plan to swindle Evans out of the circus she inherited. All-star western cast under the big top. **54m/B** VHS, DVD. Roy Rogers, Dale Evans George "Gabby" Hayes, Sunset Carson, Adele Mara, Grant Withers, Roy Barcroft, Addison Richards; **D:** Frank McDonald.

Bells of San Angelo 🎬🎬 1947 An easy-going priest finds himself in a subtle battle of wits with the Mother Superior over how the children of St. Mary's school should be raised. It's the sequel to "Going My Way." Songs include the title tune and "Aren't You Glad You're You?" Also available in a colorized version. **126m/B** VHS, DVD. Bing Crosby, Ingrid Bergman, Henry Travers; **D:** Leo McCarey; **W:** Dudley Nichols; **C:** George Barnes; **M:** Robert Emmett Dolan, Johnny Burke, James Van Heusen. Oscars '45: Sound; Golden Globes '46: Actress—Drama (Bergman); N.Y. Film Critics '46: Actress (Bergman).

Bells of San Fernando 🎬🎬 1947 An Irish seaman wanders into California during early Spanish rule and confronts a cruel overseer in this lackluster Western drama. Scripted by "Cisco Kid" Renaldo. **75m/B** VHS, DVD. Donald Woods, Gloria Warren,

The Bells of St. Mary's 🎬🎬½ 1945 Roy foils thieves' attempts to steal a girl's inherited ranch. **54m/C** VHS, DVD. Roy Rogers, Dale Evans; **D:** William Witney.

Bells Are Ringing 🎬🎬 1960 A girl who works for a telephone answering service can't help but take an interest in the lives of her clients, especially a playwright who can't get the pretty girl. Based on Adolph Green and Betty Comden's Broadway musical. **♪ Just in Time; The Party's Over; It's a Perfect Relationship; Do It Yourself; It's a Simple Little System; Better Than a Dream; I Met a Girl; Drop That Name; I'm Going Back; Long Before I Knew You. 126m/C** VHS, DVD, Lionel Barrymore, Boris Karloff, Gustav von Seyfertitz; **D:** James L. Young; **C:** L.W. O'Connell.

The Bells 🎬🎬🎬 1926 The mayor of an Alsatian village kills a wealthy merchant and steals his money. The murderer experiences pangs of guilt which are accentuated when a traveling mesmerist comes to town and claims to be able to discern a person's darkest secrets. Silent with music score. **67m/B** VHS, GB Bernard Hill, Kieran O'Brien, Richard Hope, Frances Tomelty, Derek Newark, Jorn Kavanagh, Ker Bones; **D:** Michael Lorcraine; **W:** Desmond Lowden; **C:** Ken Westbury; **M:** Colin Towns.

Bellman and True 🎬🎬½ 1988 (R) Rewarding, but sometimes tedious character study of a mild mannered computer whiz who teams with a gang of bank robbers. Fire performances, especially subtle dangerous gang characters. **112m/C** VHS. GB Bernard Hill, Kieran O'Brien, Richard Hope, Frances Tomelty, Derek Newark, Jorn Kavanagh, Ker Bones; **D:** Richard Loncraine; **W:** Desmond Lowden; **C:** Ken Westbury; **M:** Colin Towns.

Beloved 🎬🎬½ 1998 (R) Sethe (Winfrey) is a middle-aged former slave in rural Ohio years after her emancipation from a Kentucky plantation. She is haunted (literally) by the painful legacy of slavery in the form of a mud-covered feral child known as Beloved (Newton). Another reminder is Paul D (Glover), a former slave from the same Kentucky plantation, who stokes Sethe's embers. Metaphors abound as we wonder if Beloved really is the child Sethe killed years before. Oprah's pet project is a faithful adaptation of Toni Morrison's Pulitzer Prize-winning novel. Unfortunately, the long-awaited feature can't fulfill the huge expectations. While performances are excellent, pic suffers from a sense of self-indulgence, which is accentuated by the three-hour running time. At times powerful and moving, but also slow and occasionally confusing. **172m/C** VHS, DVD. Oprah Winfrey, Thandie Newton, Danny Glover, Kimberly Elise, Lisa Gay Hamilton, Beah Richards, Irma P. Hall, Albert Hall, Jason Robards Jr., Jude Ciccolella; **D:** Jonathan Demme; **W:** Akosua Busia, Richard LaGravenese, Adam Brooks; **C:** Tak Fujimoto; **M:** Rachel Portman.

Beloved Enemy 🎬🎬 1936 A romantic tragedy set in Civil War-torn Ireland in the 1920s. A rebel leader and a proper English lady struggle to overcome the war's interference with their burgeoning relationship. **86m/B** VHS. Merle Oberon, Brian Aherne, Karen Morley, Donald Crisp; **D:** H.C. Potter; **C:** Gregg Toland.

Beloved/Friend 🎬🎬 1999 Everybody wants something (or someone) they can't have. Jaume (Pou) is a middleaged gay college student who pines for his student David (Selvas), a coldhearted student who hustles to pay his tui-

Belly 🎬🎬 1998 (R) Inner-city crime tale preaches against crime, violence and drugs while it visually glorifies the opulent benefits of them. Childhood pals Tommy (Simmons) and Sincere (Jones) are successful criminals who head down different paths. Sincere dreams of turning legit and moving his family to Africa. Tommy gets deeper into the drug biz until he is caught by feds and forced to bring down innocent black leader Reverend Saviour (Muhammed). Although the movie ends with a plea for change, it may itself be part of the problem. **95m/C** VHS, DVD. Nas, DMX, Taral Hicks, Tionne "T-Boz" Watkins, Method Man, Tyrin Turner, Hassan Johnson, Power, Louie Rankin, Hype Williams, Anthony Bodden; **C:** Hype Williams; **W:** Nas, Hype Williams, Anthony Bodden; **C:** Malik Hassan Sayeed; **M:** Stephen Cullo.

Bellyfruit 🎬🎬 1999 Film, which refers to pregnancy, was inspired by the real-life stories of teen mothers in LA. 14-year-old Shanika is living in a home for troubled girls when she's taken in by the charms of Damon, equally young Christina when she was a teen) drug and party and decides to follow her example, while 16-year-old Aracely becomes pregnant by her boyfriend Oscar. Although he stands by her, Aracely's traditional Latin father kicks her out of the house. And when they have their babies the three lives just get more confused. **95m/C** VHS, DVD. Kelly Vint Tamara La Seon Bass, Toneizin Mondragon, T.E. Russell, Martita Pena, Bonnie Dickenson, Kimberly Scott, James Dumant; **D:** Kerri Green; **W:** Kerri Green, Mara Benward, Suzannah Blinkoff, Jane Boras; **C:** Peter Calvin.

The Belly of an Architect 🎬🎬🎬 1991 (R) A thespian feast for the larger-than-life Dennehy as a blustering American architect whose personal life and travail both crumble as he obsessively readies an exhibition in Rome. A multi-tiered, carefully composed tragicomedy from the idiosyncratic film-maker Greenaway, probably his most accessible work for general audiences. **119m/C** VHS, DVD. GB Brian Dennehy, Chloe Webb, Lambert Wilson, Sergio Fantoni, Geoffrey Copleston, Stefania Casini, Vanni Corbellini; **W:** Peter Greenaway; **C:** Sacha Vierny; **M:** Glenn Branca, Wim Mertens.

Below 🎬🎬½ 2002 (R) Nothing is certain in director David Twohy's creepy submarine thriller. The captain of a World War II torpedoed British hospital ship. When circumstances, and the crew is already on edge when they rescue three survivors of a torpedoed German sub. When one of these survivors is a woman (Williams), allegedly unlucky on a sub, tensions run even higher. With the Germans tracking the sub, strange events begin to occur, which could be vengeful actions of the captain's ghost a saboteur, hallucinations caused by lack of oxygen or some combination of the three. As the disasters pile up, the crew becomes divided between acting captain Brice (Greenwood) and rebellious ensign O'Dell (Davis), who has the strangely cutspoken calm on his side. Characters are a bit one-dimensional, but the effects and acting are above average for a B movie. **103m/C** VHS, DVD. US Bruce Greenwood, Matthew Davis, Olivia Williams, Holt McCallany, Scott Foley, Zach Galifianakis, Jason Flemyng, Dexter Fletcher, Nicholas Chinlund, Andrew Howard, Christopher Fairbank, Jonathan Hartman; **D:** David N. Twohy; **W:** David N. Twohy, Darren Aronofsky, Lucas Sussman; **C:** Ian Wilson; **M:** Graeme Revell.

Below the Belt 🎬🎬 1980 (R) Almost interesting tale of street-smart woman from New York City who becomes part of the blue-collar "circus" of lady wrestlers. Ex-wrestling champ Burke plays herself. **98m/C** VHS, DVD. Regina Baff, Mildred Burke, John C. Becker; **D:** Robert Fowler.

Below the Border 🎬🎬½ 1942 The Rough Riders go undercover to help break up some cattle rustlers. **57m/B** VHS, DVD. Buck Jones, Tim McCoy, Raymond Hatton, Linda Brent, Roy Barcroft, Charles "Blackie" King; **D:** Howard Bretherton.

Below the Deadline 🎬🎬 1929 A man framed for embezzlement is set free and allowed to clear his name by a sympathetic detective. **79m/B** VHS. Frank Leigh.

The Beloved Rogue 🎬🎬🎬 1927 Crosland—who gained a reputation for innovation, having directed "Don Juan" the previous year (noted for the debut of synchronized music) and "The Jazz Singer" the following year (noted for the first talkie bits)—mounted this well-designed and special effect-laden medieval costumer. Barrymore is in high profile as a swashbuckling caricature of French poet Francois Villon, who battles mightily (and verbally) with Louis XI (played by Veidt, in his first US film). Marred by the excesses typical of Barrymore's prestige days, it flouts history, taking generous poetic license when the facts ain't fab enough. In short, it's great entertainment for the debut of synthis. **99m/B** VHS, DVD. John Barrymore, Conrad Veidt, Marceline Day, Henry Victor, Mack Swain, Slim Summerville, Alan Crosland.

Beloved Infidel 🎬🎬½ 1959 Suddenly, lavish romance, based on the book by gossip queen Sheilah Graham, about her brief romance with novelist F. Scott Fitzgerald. Fitzgerald (a badly miscast Peck) was in Hollywood trying to write screenplays when he meets young English, aspiring writer Graham (an equally miscast Kerr). She becomes his mistress, putting up with Fitzgerald's drinking and insults, while he interferes with her career. Story is slanted towards Graham nobly trying to rescue Fitzgerald from himself (he did actually die from a heart attack while writing a novel). **123m/C** VHS. Gregory Peck, Deborah Kerr, Eddie Albert, Philip Ober Herbert Rudley, John Sutton, Karin (Keren, Katharine) Booth; **D:** Henry King; **W:** Sy Bartlett; **C:** Leon Shamroy; **M:** Franz Waxman.

tion. In fact, the only way Jaume can get attention from David is to buy his services (although David has something of a figure complex). Then, Jaume's best friend Pere (Gas) discovers that David has gotten his daughter, Alba (Montala), pregnant. David seems to be a catalyst for a lot of soul-searching but nothing much gets resolved. Spanish with subtitles. **90m/C** VHS, DVD. SP Jose Maria Pou, David Selvas, Mario Gas, Irene Montala, Rosa Maria Sardà; **C:** Ventura Pons; **W:** Josep Maria Benet i Jornet; **C:** Jesus Escosa; **M:** Carles Cases.

Barbara Worth, Arthur (L.) Rankin, Walter Merrill. **D:** J(ohn) (Paterson) McGowan.

The Belstone Fox ✓✓ 1973 Orphaned fox goes into hiding, and is hunted by the hound he has befriended and his former owner. **103m/C VHS.** Eric Porter, Rachel Roberts, Jeremy Kemp; **D:** James Hill.

Ben ✓½ 1972 (PG) Sequel to "Willard" finds police Detective Kirtland still on the hunt for a killer rat pack led by Ben, king of the rodents. Michael Jackson hit the top of the charts. **95m/C VHS.** Joseph Campanella, Lee Montgomery, Arthur O'Connell, Rosemary Murphy, Meredith Baxter, Norman Alden, Paul Carr, Kaz Garas, Kenneth Tobey, Richard Van Heet; **D:** Phil Karlson; **M:** Walter Scharf. Golden Globes '73: Song ("Ben").

Ben-Hur ✓✓✓ 1926 Second film version of the renowned story of Jewish and Christian divisiveness in the time of Jesus. Battle scenes and chariot races still look good, in spite of age. Problems lingered on the set and at a cost of over $4,000,000 it was the most expensive film of its time and took years to finish. A hit at the boxoffice, it still stands as the all-time silent classic. In 1931, a shortened version was released. Based on the novel by Lewis Wallace. **148m/B VHS, DVD.** Ramon Novarro, Francis X. Bushman, May McAvoy, Betty Bronson, Claire McDowell, Carmel Myers, Nigel de Bruiler, Ferdinand P. Earle; **D:** Fred Niblo; **C:** Clyde De Vinna. Natl. Film Reg. '97.

Ben-Hur ✓✓✓✓ 1959 The third film version of the Lew Wallace classic stars Heston in the role of a Palestinian Jew battling the Roman empire at the time of Christ. Won a record 11 Oscars. The breathtaking chariot race is still one of the best screen races today. Perhaps one of the greatest pictures of all time. Also available in letterbox format. **212m/C VHS, DVD.** Charlton Heston, Jack Hawkins, Stephen Boyd, Haya Harareet, Hugh Griffith, Martha Scott, Sam Jaffe, Cathy O'Donnell, Finlay Currie; **D:** William Wyler; **W:** Karl Tunberg; **C:** Robert L. Surtees; **M:** Miklos Rozsa. Oscars '59: Actor (Heston), Art Dir./Set Dec., Color, Color Cinematog., Costume Des (C), Director (Wyler), Film Editing, Picture, Sound, Support. Actor (Griffith), Orig. Dramatic Score; AFI '98: Top 100; British Acad. '59: Film; Directors Guild '59: Director (Wyler); Golden Globes '60: Director (Wyler), Film—Drama, Support. Actor (Boyd); Natl. Film Reg. '04; N.Y. Film Critics '59: Film.

The Benchwarmers ✓ 2006 (PG-13) Relentlessly stupid comedy with more than its share of gross-out moments. Gus (Schneider) was a bullied nerd in school, as were his two still-maladjusted pals, Richie (Spade) and Clark (Heder). Ex-bullied nerd-turned-billionaire Mel (a fun-loving Lovitz) offers a chance for sweet revenge by putting his trio of losers up against a Little League team of younger jokes follow, and Reggie Jackson offers baseball advice. **81m/C DVD, Blu-ray Disc, UMD.** US Rob Schneider, David Spade, Jon Heder, Jon Lovitz, Molly Sims, Craig Kilborn, Tim Meadows, Nick Swardson, Amaury Nolasco, Dennis Dugan, Erinn Bartlett, Max Prado, Brooke Langton, Lochlyn Munro, Mary Jo Catlett, Blake Clark, Terry Crews; **Cameos:** Reggie Jackson; **Cameo:** Dennis Dugan; **W:** Nick Swardson, Allen Covert; **C:** Thomas Ackerman; **M:** Waddy Wachtel; **V:** James Earl Jones.

Bend It Like Beckham ✓✓✓ 2002 (PG-13) Sweet family comedy has girl power galore. Jesminder (Nagra) is the teenaged daughter of East Indian parents, living in a middle-class London suburb. They wish Jess would be more like her older sister Pinky (Panjabi), who is anticipating her traditional wedding. But what shy Jess wants is to play professional soccer—her hero is superstar player David Beckham—and she secretly joins a local team after befriending fellow player Juliette (Knightley). She impresses (and develops a crush on) her coach Joe (Rhys-Meyers) while trying to keep her activities from her disapproving parents. Of course, there has to be a big game, which will showcase Jess's talents. **112m/C VHS, DVD.** GB GE Parminder K. Nagra, Keira Knightley, Jonathan Rhys Meyers, Shaheen Khan, Anupam Kher, Archie Panjabi, Juliet Stevenson, Frank Harper,

Shaznay Lewis; **D:** Gurinder Chadha; **W:** Gurinder Chadha, Paul Mayeda Berges, Guljit Bindra; **C:** Jong Lin; **M:** Craig Pruess.

Bend of the River ✓✓✓ 1952 (Where the River Bends) A haunted, hardened guide leads a wagon train through Oregon territory, pitting himself against Indians, the wilderness and a former comrade-turned-hijacker. **91m/C VHS, DVD.** James Stewart, Arthur Kennedy, Rock Hudson, Harry (Henry) Morgan, Royal Dano; **D:** Anthony Mann.

Beneath ✓ 2007 (R) Convoluted and plodding story about creepy, depressed people having visions usually followed by someone ending up dead. Initial suspense stems from in-laws' eerie house complete with mysterious hatches, weird holes, and a monster inside the walls. Although intriguing, its eccentricities never get fully explained as the darkness and drab lead only to an anti-climatic snore. **81m/C DVD.** Nora Zehetner, Matthew Settle, Gabrielle Rose, Carly Pope, Don S. Davis, Jessica Amlee; **D:** Dagen Merrill; **W:** Dagen Merrill, Kevin Burke; **C:** Mike Southon; **M:** John (Gianni) Frizzell, Frederik Wiedmann. **VIDEO**

Beneath Loch Ness ✓ 2001 Laughable adventure tale finds paleontologist Case Howell (Wimmer) carrying on the work of his mentor, Professor Egan, who believed that Loch Ness was a breeding ground for ancient marine reptiles. Unfortunately, the prof disappeared while conducting research at the loch. But that isn't stopping Howell from leading another expedition to find Nessie. **95m/C VHS, DVD.** Brian Wimmer, Patrick Bergin, Lysette Anthony, Vernon Wells; **D:** Chuck Comisky; **W:** Justin Stanley, Chuck Comisky, Shane Bitterling; **C:** Philip Timme; **M:** Richard John Baker. **VIDEO**

Beneath the Bermuda Triangle ✓✓ 1998 (R) Submarine commander Alan Deakins (Fahey) and his crew are cruising in dangerous waters that that transports them to the future. As usual, it's ugly—a repressive, military government is in control and Deakins decides to join a rebel organization, that happens to be lead by his grandson (Fahey again). No-brain actioner. **84m/C VHS.** Jeff Fahey, Richard Tyson, Linda Hoffman, Jack Coleman; **D:** Scott Levy. **VIDEO**

Beneath the Planet of the Apes ✓✓½ 1970 (G) In the first sequel, another Earth astronaut passes through the same warp and follows the same paths as Taylor, through Ape City and to the ruins of bomb-blasted New York's subway system, where warhead-worshipping human mutants are found. The strain of sequelling shows instantly, and gets worse through the next three films; followed by "Escape from the Planet of the Apes." **108m/C VHS, DVD.** James Franciscus, Kim Hunter, Maurice Evans, Charlton Heston, James Gregory, Natalie Trundy, Jeff Corey, Linda Harrison, Victor Buono, Paul (E.) Richards, David Watson, Thomas Gomez; **D:** Ted Post; **W:** Paul Dehn; **C:** Milton Krasner; **M:** Leonard Rosenman.

Beneath the 12-Mile Reef ✓✓ 1953 Two rival groups of divers compete for sponge beds off the Florida coast. Lightweight entertainment notable for underwater photography and early Cinemascope production, as well as More in a bathing suit. **102m/C VHS, DVD.** Angela (Clark) Clarke, Robert Wagner, Terry Moore, Gilbert Roland, Richard Boone, Peter Graves, J. Carrol Naish; **D:** Robert D. Webb; **W:** A(lbert) I(saac) Bezzerides; **C:** Edward Cronjager; **M:** Bernard Herrmann.

Beneath the Valley of the Ultra-Vixens ✓ 1979 Sex comedy retread directed by the man with an obsession for big. Scripted by Roger Ebert, who also scripted the cult classic "Beyond the Valley of the Dolls." Explicit nudity. **90m/C VHS, DVD.** Francesca "Kitten" Natividad, Ann Marie, Ken Kerr, Stuart Lancaster, Steve Tracy, Henry Rowland, DeForest Covan, Aram Katcher; Candy Samples, Robert Pearson; **D:** Russ Meyer; **W:** Roger Ebert, Russ Meyer; **C:** Russ Meyer.

Benedict Arnold: A Question of Honor ✓✓ 2003 By-the-numbers bio of Revolutionary War general turned British Loyalist, Benedict Arnold (Quinn). By 1776, Arnold was falling out of favor with Congress amidst accusations of incompetence, although he's still supported by his friend, George Washington (Grammer). But after meeting Margaret Shippen (Montgomery), the daughter of a loyalist sympathizer, the increasingly resentful Arnold, who also needs money to stave off bankruptcy, begins to sell information to turn over West Point to the redcoats. **100m/C VHS, DVD.** Aidan Quinn, Kelsey Grammer, Flora Montgomery; **W:** William Mastrosimone; **C:** Seamus Deasy; **M:** David Williams. **CABLE**

The Beneficiary ✓✓ 1997 (R) Widow Haiduk is the primary suspect in her wealthy husband's death until she gives her inheritance to charity, thus eliminating her motive for murder. But detective Ashby, a friend of the husband, still decides to keep his eye (and maybe more) on the lady. **97m/C VHS.** Suzy Amis, Ron Silver, Linden Ashby, Stacy Haiduk, Robert Davi; **D:** Marc Bienstock; **W:** Vladimir Nemirovsky; **C:** Sead Muhtarevic. **CABLE**

Benefit of the Doubt ✓✓ 1993 (R) Ex-con Sutherland, released from prison after 22 years, attempts to repaint his family a la Norman Rockwell. Grown-up daughter Irving, who testified against him in her mother's murder, wants to put a crimp in those plans since daddy's new vision of family fondness frankly makes her stomach turn. Aside from the sexual shenanigans, and the haunting Monument Valley backdrop, an extended chase scene would seem to be the film's only hope of salvation. Unfortunately, it fails to deliver, since it's both implausible and boring. Based on a story by Michael Lieber. **92m/C VHS.** Donald Sutherland, Amy Irving, Christopher McDonald, Rider Strong, Graham Greene, Theodore Bikel, Gisele Kovach, Ferdinand "Ferdy" Mayne; **D:** Jonathan Heap; **W:** Jeffrey Polman, Christopher Keyser; **M:** Hummie Mann.

The Beniker Gang ✓✓½ 1983 (G) Five orphans, supported by the eldest who writes a syndicated advice column, work together as a family. **87m/C VHS.** Andrew McCarthy, Jennifer (Jennie) Dundas Lowe, Danny Pintauro, Charlie (Charles) Fields; **D:** Ken Kwapis. **TV**

Benji ✓✓✓ 1974 (G) In the loveable mutt's first feature-length movie, he falls in love with a female named Tiffany, and saves two young children from kidnappers. Kiddie classic that was a boxoffice hit when first released. Followed by "For the Love of Benji." **87m/C VHS, DVD.** Benji, Peter Breck, Christopher Connelly, Patsy Garrett, Deborah Walley, Cynthia Smith; **D:** Joe Camp; **W:** Joe Camp; **C:** Don Reddy; **M:** Euel Box. Golden Globes '75: Song ("I Feel Love").

Benji: Off the Leash! ✓✓½ 2004 (PG) A generally amiable retro addition to the series that began in 1974. Colby's (Whitaker) nasty stepfather Hatchett (Kendrick) runs a puppy mill in their small Mississippi town. He plans to kill a mongrel pup, which Colby rescues and hides (and calls Puppy). Puppy (played by the latest version of Benji) befriends a smart stray named Lizard Tongue while avoiding a couple of inept dogcatchers (Newsome, Stephens) and trying to rescue his sickly mom from the mean breeder. The abuse themes (both animal and human) may scare the little ones but, of course, the dogs are cute and lovable. **97m/C VHS, DVD.** US Nick Whitaker, Nate Bynum, Chris Kendrick, Randall Newsome, Duane Stephens, Forrest Landis, Carleton Bluford, Neal Barth, Melinda Haynes, Kathleen Camp, Jeff Olson, Lincoln Hoppe, Joey Miyashima, Scott Wilkinson, Christy Summerhays; **D:** Joe Camp; **W:** Joe Camp; **C:** Don Reddy; **M:** Anthony DiLorenzo.

Benji the Hunted ✓✓½ 1987 (G) The heroic canine, shipwrecked off the Oregon coast, discovers a litter of orphaned cougar cubs, and battles terrain and predators to bring them to safety. **89m/C VHS, DVD.** Benji, Red Steagall, Frank Inn; **D:** Joe Camp; **W:** Joe Camp; **C:** Don Reddy; **M:** Euel Box.

Benny & Joon ✓✓½ 1993 (PG) Depending on your tolerance for cute eccentrics and whimsy this will either charm you with sweetness or send you into sugar shock. Masterson is Joon, a mentally disturbed young woman who paints and has a habit of setting fires. She lives with overprotective brother Benny (Quinn). Sam (Depp) is the outsider who charms Joon, a dyslexic loner who impersonates his heroes Charlie Chaplin and Buster Keaton with eery accuracy. Depp is particularly fine with the physical demands of his role, but the film's easy dismissal of Joon's mental illness is a serious flaw. **98m/C VHS, DVD.** Johnny Depp, Mary Stuart Masterson, Aidan Quinn, Julianne Moore, Oliver Platt, CCH Pounder, Dan Hedaya, Joe Grifasi, William H. Macy, Eileen Ryan; **D:** Jeremiah S. Chechik; **W:** Barry Berman; **M:** Rachel Portman.

The Benny Goodman Story ✓✓½ 1955 The life and music of Swing Era bandleader Benny Goodman is recounted in this popular bio-pic. Covering Benny's career from his child prodigy days to his monumental 1938 Carnegie Hall Jazz Concert, the movie's soggy plot machinations are redeemed by a non-stop music track featuring the real Benny and an all-star lineup. ♪ Don't Be That Way; Memories of You; Sing, Sing, Sing; Slipped Disc. **116m/C VHS, DVD.** Steve Allen, Donna Reed, Gene Krupa, Lionel Hampton, Kid Ory, Ben Pollack, Harry James, Stan Getz, Teddy Wilson, Martha Tilton; **D:** Valentine Davies; **M:** Henry Mancini.

Benny's Video ✓½ 1992 Teen Benny (Frisch) is obsessed with the violent videos he watches and makes, including the slaughter of a pig with a bolt gun, which Benny then uses in a very unfortunate manner. Heavy-handed message movie was Haneke's second feature. German with subtitles. **105m/C DVD.** GE Arno Frisch, Angela Winkler, Ulrich Muhe, Ingrid Strassner; **D:** Michael Haneke; **W:** Michael Haneke.

Bent ✓✓ 1997 (NC-17) Theatre director Mathias makes his film debut with Sherman's adaptation of his 1979 play. Gay playboy Max (Owen) is enjoying the nightlife in decadent Berlin—until the Nazi crackdown. Soon, Max is in a cattle car on his way to Dachau, where he passes himself off as Jewish, thinking he'll be treated better. However Horst (Bluteau), who befriended Max on the train, is openly part of the pink triangle prisoners. Still, Max gets Horst assigned to the same meaningless hard labor and the duo fall in love—without ever being allowed to touch. Good performances (with Jagger notable in a brief role as a drag star) but the lingering staginess is to the film's detriment. An R-rated version is also available. **104m/C VHS, DVD.** GB Clive Owen, Lothaire Bluteau, Ian McKellen, Brian Webber, Mick Jagger, Nikolaj Coster-Waldau, Paul Bettany; **Cameos:** Jude Law, Rupert Graves; **D:** Sean Mathias; **W:** Martin Sherman; **C:** Yorgos Arvanitis; **M:** Philip Glass.

Beowulf ✓½ 1998 (R) Cheesy retelling of the dark ages Saxon saga that has seemingly time travelled to a vague post-apocalypse time. Wandering knight Beowulf (Lambert) battles beast Grendel, who comes each night to feed on those who live in the Outpost. Cult icon Mitra was one of the models for Lara Croft of "Tomb Raider" game fame. **92m/C VHS, DVD.** Christopher Lambert, Rhona Mitra, Oliver Cotton, Patricia Velasquez, Goetz Otto, Layla Roberts, Brent J. Lowe; **D:** Graham Baker; **W:** Mark Leahy, David Chappe; **C:** Christopher Faloona; **M:** Ben Watkins.

Beowulf ✓✓✓ 2007 (PG-13) Not your father's epic poem! Director Zemeckis takes the Old English classic and turns it into both a highly stylized computer-generated swordfest and a satirical take on the lit class staple. Beowulf (Winstone) battles Grendel (Glover), gets sexy with Grendel's mom (Jolie), and fights a dragon on his way to eternal heroic glory. Purists may object to the liberties taken by writers Gaiman and Avery, but they do a good job of connecting and streamlining the source material's various storylines. While still resembling a video game, Zemeckis's second attempt at the "performance capture" digital style is a dramatic

Beowulf & Grendel 🎬🎬 2006 (R) Live-action adaptation of the 1000-year-old Scandinavian poem retells the story of Beowulf (Butler), the Norse warrior who helps his pal, Danish King Hrothgar (Skarsgard), 'rid his land of the murderous troll Grendel (Sigurdsson). Tries to appeal to modern audiences with flashy fighting, lots of blood and awkward comedic attempts, but succeeds only in showing how beautiful Iceland is (that's where it was filmed). 102m/C DVD, Blu-ray Disc, GE CA IC C: Gerard Butler, Stellan Skarsgard, Sarah Polley, Eddie Marsan, Ingvar Sigurdsson, Tony Curran, Rory McCann, Ronan Vibert, Martin Delaney, Ola-fur D: Sturla Gunnarsson; W: Andrew Rai Berzins; C: Jan Kiesser M: Hilmar Orn Hilmarsson.

Berkeley Square 🎬🎬½ 1998 In 1902 London, three young women become nannies and grow to be friends. Tough and experienced East Ender Matty (Wilkie) goes to work for the well-bred St. Johns; country-raised Hannah (Smurfit) has an illegitimate child by her previous employer's son—a fact she keeps hidden from the neglectful Hutchinsons; and farm girl Lydia (Wady) is hired by the avant-garde Lamson-Scribeners, who believe in education even for servants. Naturally, the threesome become very involved in each other's lives and loves. On five cassettes. 500m/C VHS, DVD, GB Victoria Smurfit, Tabitha Wady, Clare Wilkie, Rosemary Leach, Judy Perritt; D: Leslie Manning, Richard Signy, Martin Hutchings, Richard Holthouse. TV

The Berlin Affair 🎬🎬 1985 (R) A sordid tale from "The Night Porter" director about a Japanese woman seducing various parties in pre-WWII Germany. Melo-dramatic parable with biblical overtones considered by some to be a masterpiece. Based on the novel by Alfred Doblin; originally aired as a miniseries on German TV. 97m/C VHS, IT GE Mio Takaki, Gudrun Land-grebe, Kevin McNally; D: Liliana Cavani; M: Pino Donaggio.

Berlin Alexanderplatz 🎬🎬½ 1980 Fassbinder's 15 1/2-hour epic follows the life, death, and resurrection of Franz Biberkopf, a former transit worker who has just finished a lengthy prison term and must learn to adjust in the harsh social atmosphere of Berlin in the 1920s. Meanwhile, the Genie discovers the original. 930m/C VHS, GE Gunter Lamprecht, Hanna Schy-gulla, Barbara Sukowa, Gottfried John, Elisabeth Trissenaar, Brigitte Mira, Karin Baal, Ivan Desny, Margit Carstensen; D: Rainer Werner Fassbinder; W: Rainer Werner Fassbinder. C: Xaver Schwar-zenberger. M: Peer Raben. TV

Berlin Blues 1988 (PG-13) A nightclub singer is torn between two men. 90m/C VHS. Julia Migenes, Keith Baxter; D: Ricardo Franco.

The Berlin Conspiracy 🎬🎬½ 1991 (R) Espionage/action potboiler does an imaginative job of setting its action against the fall of the Berlin Wall and the end of the Cold War. A CIA agent forms a shaky alliance with his East German spy-master rival to prevent germ warfare technology from falling into terrorist hands. 83m/C VHS. Marc Singer, Mary Crosby, Stephen Davies, Richard Lepanmeier, Terence Henry; D: Terence H. Wi-kiess.

Berlin Express 🎬🎬½ 1948 Battle of wits ensues between the Allies and the Nazis who are seeking to keep Germans divided in post-WWII Germany. 86m/B VHS. Robert Ryan, Merle Oberon, Paul Lukas, Charles Korvin; D: Jacques Tourneur.

Berlin Tunnel 21 🎬½ 1981 Based on the novel by Donald Lindquist in which two American soldiers attempt a daring Cold War rescue of a beautiful German girl. The plan is to construct a tunnel under the Berlin Wall. Better-than-average. 150m/C VHS. Richard Thomas, Jose Ferrer, Horst Buchholz; D: Richard Michaels. TV

Berlinguer I Love You woof! Berlinguer Ti Voglio Bene 1977 Crude and disgustingly obnoxious comedy about a mama's-boy loser who is led to believe that his sweetish mother has died. When he returns home for the funeral, she is not happy to see him. Title refers to a popular politician of the era. Italian with subtitles. 95m/C DVD. IT Roberto Benigni, Alida Valli, Carlo Monni; D: Giuseppe Bertolucci; W: Sydney Penny, Frank Coletta.

Bernadette 🎬🎬 1990 A French-made version of the legend of St. Berna-diette, who endured persecution after claiming to have seen the Virgin Mary. Beautiful in its simplicity, but overly long. 120m/C VHS. FR Sydney Penny, Roland LeSaffre, Michele Simonet, M: Bernard Dheran, Arlette Didier; D: Jean Delannoy.

Bernard and Doris 🎬🎬½ 2008 (R) Doris (Sarandon) is eccentric, cynical, lonely, aging billionaire tobacco heiress Doris Duke. Bernard Lafferty (Fiennes) is her Irish, gay, alcoholic butler. They form a delightfully odd-couple partnership where the ever-more devoted Bernard protects Doris from hangers-on and herself)—so much so that Duke made Lafferty the executor of her will (and when he died, he left everything to her trusts). Gets the bones for the Sarandon/Fiennes combo alone as the ravaged Duke. 109m/C DVD. Susan Sarandon, Ralph Fiennes, James Rebhorn, Nick Rolfe; D: Bob Balaban; W: Hugh Costello; C: Mauricio Rubinstein; M: Alex Wurman. C.A.B.L.E

Bernard and the Genie 🎬🎬½ 1991 (G) It seems Bernard Bottle is not going to have a happy Christmas—he's been fired from his job and his girlfriend has left him. But things take a turn for the better when he discovers an antique lamp and its resident Genie. But with the Genie granting his every wish, Bernard's sudden wealth is causing some suspicions among police. Meanwhile, the Genie discovers the delights of modern-day England and poses as a department store Santa to truly fulfill a child's Christmas wish. Amusing family fare. 70m/C VHS. GB Alan Cumming, Lenny Henry, Fowan Atkinson; D: Paul Weiland.

Berserk! 🎬🎬½ 1967 A seedy traveling circus is beset by a series of murders. Not heralded as one of Crawford's best pieces. 95m/C VHS. Joan Crawford, Diana Dors, Judy Geeson, Ty Hardin; D: James O'Connolly.

Berserker 🎬 1987 (R) Six camping college students are attacked by a bloodthirsty psychotic out of a Nordic myth, who takes the shape of a bestial-than-the-average beast. 85m/C VHS. Joseph Alan Johnson, Valerie Sheldon, Greg Dawson; D: Jefferson Richard.

Bert Rigby, You're a Fool 🎬🎬½ 1989 (R) A starstruck British coal miner finds his way to Hollywood singing old showtunes, only to be rebuffed by a cynical industry. Available with Spanish subtitles. 94m/C VHS. Robert Lindsay, Robbie Coltrane, Jackie Gayle, Bruno Kirby, Cathryn Bradshaw, Corbin Bernsen, Anne Bancroft; D: Carl Reiner; W: Carl Reiner; C: Jan De Bont; M: Ralph Burns.

Beshkempir the Adopted Son 🎬🎬 1998 In a rural community in the Central Asian nation of Kyrgyzstan, a young teen lives a carefree existence getting into milic mischief with his buddies. Until one day, during an argument, he suddenly discovers he was adopted, which throws his world (at least temporarily) into rebellious turmoil. Kyrgyzstani with subtitles. 81m/B VHS, DVD. RU Mirlan Abdykalykov, Avtandil Adikulov, Marat Saruiu; C: Khasan Kydyralyev; M: Nurlan Nishanov.

The Best Intentions 🎬🎬🎬½ 1992 Ingmar Bergman wrote the screenplay chronicling the early years of the stormy relationship of his parents. Set in Sweden at the turn of the century, the film focuses on the class differences that divide his mother and father, while portrayal of little Bergy is limited to a bundle under his mother's maternity dress. Inspired performances and directing illuminates the emo-

Besieged 🎬🎬 1998 (R) Fans of Bertolucci will enjoy this airy quasi-love story, but the slow pace and meandering plot will frustrate other viewers. Shandurai (Newton) moves to Rome after her husband becomes a political prisoner in Kenya. In order to put herself through medical school, she takes a job as a maid for an eccentric British musician (Thewlis). He begins to fall for his beautiful housekeeper, but she ignores his advances. To prove his love, he begins selling off his personal belongings so he can bribe officials to release her husband. 94m/C VHS, DVD. IT David Thewlis Thandie Newton, Claudio Santamaria; D: Bernardo Bertolucci; W: Bernardo Bertolucci, Clare Peploe; C: Fabio Cianchetti; M: Alessio Vlad.

Best Defense 🎬 1984 (R) A U.S. Army tank operator is sent to Kuwait to test a new state-of-the-art tank in a combat situation. Although the cast is popular, the movie as a whole is not funny and the story frequency is hard to follow. 94m/C VHS, DVD. Dudley Moore, Kate Capshaw, George Dzundza, Helen Shaver, D: Willard Huyck; W: Willard Huyck, Gloria Katz

Best Enemies 🎬½ 1986 In English film about a man suffering the trials of the 1960s, including Vietnam, and how it affects his relationships with his friends and wife. 95m/C VHS. GB Sigrid Thornton, Paul Williams, Judy Morris, Brandon Burke; D: David Baker.

Best Foot Forward 🎬🎬 1943 Vintage musical about a movie star who agrees to accompany a young cadet to his military ball. Based on the popular Broadway show. The film debuts of Walker, Ally-son, and DeHaven. 93m/C VHS. June Allyson, Tommy Dix, Nancy Walker, Virginia Weidler, Gloria De Haven, William Gaxton, Harry James; D: Edward Buzzell; W: Irving Brecher; M: George Bassman.

Best Friends 🎬🎬 1982 (PG) A pair of screenwriters decide to marry after years of living and working together. Story concerns the lives of screenwriters Barry Levinson and Valerie Curtin. 109m/C VHS, DVD. Goldie Hawn, Burt Reynolds, Jessica Tandy, Barnard Hughes, Audra Lindley, Keenan Wynn, Ron Silver; D: Norman Jewison; W: Valerie Curtin, Barry Levinson; C: Jordan Cronenweth.

Best in Show 🎬🎬½ 2000 (PG-13) Director Christopher Guest follows the successful "Waiting for Guffman" with another faux-documentary mixing improvisation and unique characters. This time, the subject is the snooty world of show dogs and the freaky, neurotic pooch-owners hoping to claim its greatest prize: Best in Show at the Mayflower Kennel Club Dog Show. Jane's dog-lovers include Meg (Posey) and Hamilton (Hitchcock), whose kinky sex life is giving their Weimaraner angst; doting gay Shih-Tzu owners Scott (McKean) and Stefan (Higgins) and seemingly tame suburbanites Gerry (Levy) and Cookie (O'Hara). Fred Willard steals the spotlight as Buck Laughlin, a sports announcer who has no knowledge of the event he's broadcasting. Worth a rental just for the bizarre one-liners fired off by the clueless commentator on such subjects as the dogs' anatomy and edibility. 89m/C VHS, DVD. Christopher Guest, Michael McKean, Parker Posey, Eugene Levy, Catherine O'Hara, Fred Willard, Michael Hitchcock, John Michael Higgins, Jennifer Coolidge, Trevor Beckwith, Bob Balaban, Ed Begley Jr., Patrick Cranshaw, Don Lake, Larry Miller; D: Christopher Guest; W: Christopher Guest, Eugene Levy; C: Roberto Schaefer; M: C.J. Vanston.

The Best Man 🎬🎬🎬 1964 An incisive, darkly satiric political tract, based on Gore Vidal's play, about two presidential contenders who vie for the endorsement of the aging ex-president, and tramples political ethics in the process. 104m/B VHS. Henry Fonda, Cliff Robertson, Lee Tracy, Margaret Leighton, Edie Adams, Kevin McCarthy, Ann Sothern, Gene Raymond, Shelley Berman, Mahalia Jackson; D: Franklin J. Schaffner; W: Gore Vidal; C: Haskel Wexler.

The Best Man 🎬🎬½ II Testimone dello Sposo 1997 (PG) It's 1899 in a small northern Italian town and beautiful Francesca (Sastre) must marry the lascivious older Edgardo Osti (Cantarelli) in order to solve her father's business problems. Francesca is revolted but does become smitten by the best man—Angelo (Abatantuono), who's returned from America, apparently with a fortune. Marriage or no, Francesca becomes obsessed with getting Angelo. Italian with subtitles. 99m/C VHS, DVD. IT Ines Sastre, Diego Abatantuono, Dario Cantarelli, Valeria (Valerie Dobson) D'Obici, Mario Erpichini; D: Pupi Avati; W: Pupi Avati; C: Pasquale Rachini; M: Fiz Ortolani.

The Best Man 🎬🎬 1999 (R) Writer/director Malcom D. Lee, cousin of co-producer Spike Lee, makes an impressive debut in this ensemble piece that plays like a hipper "Big Chill." Novelist Harper (Diggs) heads to New York to attend the wedding of his best friend Lance (Chestnut) and the beautiful Mia (Calhoun). Unfortunately, his soon-to-be-released first novel is a thinly disguised autobiography which alludes to an affair between Harper and the bride-to-be. As oth-

Best Kept Secrets 🎬🎬½ 1988 A feisty woman discovers corruption and blackmail in the police department where her husband is an officer. 104m/C VHS. Patty Duke, Frederic Forrest, Peter Coyote; D: Jerrold Freedman.

Best Laid Plans 🎬🎬 1999 (R) Another contemporary noir where no one and nothing is as it seems (except the ordinary familiar plot). Nick (Nivola) and his bud, Bryce (Brolin), are bar hopping when Bryce picks up Lissa (Witherspoon). Later, a frantic Bryce calls Nick saying Lissa is underage and accusing him of rape. Nick offers to talk to Lissa and the story flashes back to the beginnings of an elaborate scam leading all concerned to a number of ill-considered decisions. 90m/C VHS, DVD. Alessandro Nivola, Josh Brolin, Reese Witherspoon, Rocky Carroll, Michael G. (Mike) Hagerty, Jamie Marsh; D: Mike Barker; W: Ted Griffin; C: Ben Seresin; M: Craig Armstrong.

The Best Little Girl in the World 🎬🎬 1981 Exceptional made-for-TV tale of an apparently perfect teenager (Leigh) suffering from anorexia. Slow starvation is her only cry for help. Fine performances from Durning and Saint. Look for Helen Hunt, and Ally Sheedy as classmates. 96m/C VHS. Charles Durning, Eva Marie Saint, Jennifer Jason Leigh, Melanie Mayron, Viveca Lindfors, Jason Miller, David Spielberg, Lisa Pelikan, Ally Sheedy, Helen Hunt; D: Sam O'Steen; M: Billy Goldenberg. TV

The Best Little Whorehouse in Texas 🎬🎬 1982 (R) Parton is the buxom owner of The Chicken Ranch, a house of ill-repute that may be closed down unless Sheriff-boyfriend Reynolds can think of a way out. Strong performances don't quite make up for the erratically comic script. Based on the long-running Broadway musical, in turn based on a story by Larry McMurtry. 115m/C VHS, DVD. Burt Reynolds, Dolly Parton, Dom DeLuise, Charles Durning, Jim Nabors, Lois Nettleton; Colin Higgins.

tionally complex relationship, revealing truths about the universal human condition along the way. Six-hour version was shot for TV in Europe and Japan. Director August and actress August met and married during filming. In Swedish with English subtitles. 182m/C VHS, SW Samuel Fro-lier, Pernilla August, Max von Sydow, Ghita Norby, Mona Malm, Lena Endre, Bjorn (Kjellman) D: Bille August; W: Ingmar Bergman; C: Jorgen Persson; M: Stefan Nilsson. Cannes '92: Actress (August), Film.

er college buddies and old flames show up for the nuptials, past issues and romantic tensions come bubbling back up to the surface. The cast gives good performances across the board, with Howard as the wisecracking and womanizing Quentin standing out in particular. **120m/C VHS, DVD.** Taye Diggs, Monica Calhoun, Morris Chestnut, Nia Long, Melissa De Sousa, Harold Perrineau Jr., Terrence Howard, Sanaa Lathan, Victoria Dillard; **D:** Malcolm Lee; **W:** Malcolm Lee; **C:** Frank Prinzi; **M:** Stanley Clarke.

Best Men ♪♪ ½ *Independence* 1998 (R) There's a wedding, there's a would-be bank heist, and there's five men caught in the siege at the bank of Independence in this kooky crime comedy/drama. Jesse (Wilson) is heading straight from prison to his wedding to Hope (Flanery) with his four tuxedo-clad buddies. Billy (Flanery) needs some cash before the big event and persuades the boys to stop at the bank—only his withdrawal so happens to be the local sheriff, is trying to contain the situation when the feds show up as does the bewildered bride-to-be. **89m/C VHS, DVD.** Sean Patrick Flanery, Dean Cain, Luke Wilson, Andy Dick, Mitchell Whitfield, Drew Barrymore, Fred Ward, Raymond J. Barry, Brad Dourif, Art Edler Brown, Tracy Fraim; **D:** Tamra Davis; **W:** Art Edler Brown, Tracy Fraim; **C:** James Glennon; **M:** Mark Mothersbaugh.

The Best of Everything ♪♪♪ 1959 Trashy sexist soap opera about women seeking success and love in the publishing world of N.Y.C. Several stories take place, the best being Crawford's hard-nosed editor who's having an affair with a married man. Look for Evans as a philandering playboy (he went on to become the producer of "Chinatown," among others.) Based on the novel by Rona Jaffe. **121m/C VHS, DVD.** Hope Lange, Stephen Boyd, Suzy Parker, Diane Baker, Martha Hyer, Joan Crawford, Brian Aherne, Robert Evans, Louis Jourdan; **D:** Jean Negulesco; **W:** Edith Sommer, Mann Rubin; **C:** William Mellor; **M:** Alfred Newman.

Best of the Badmen ♪♪½ 1950 A whole bunch of outlaws, although seemingly quite nice, are brought together by an ex-Union general who is being framed. Too much talk, not enough action. **84m/B VHS.** Robert Ryan, Claire Trevor, Jack Buetel, Robert Preston, Walter Brennan, Bruce Cabot, John Archer, Lawrence Tierney; **D:** William D. Russell.

Best of the Best 2 ♪½ 1993 (R) The Coliseum is a notorious martial-arts venue owned by the champion fighter Brackus and his manager Weldon. No rules death matches are the norm and when their friend is killed Tommy and Alex set up a grudge match with Brackus. **100m/C VHS, DVD.** Edward (Eddie) Bunker, Eric Roberts, Phillip Rhee, Christopher Penn, Ralph (Ralf) Moeller, Wayne Newton, Edan Gross, Sonny Landham, Meg Foster, Simon Rhee, Claire Stansfield, Betty Carvalho; **D:** Robert Radler; **W:** John Allen Nelson, Max Strom; **M:** Barry Goldberg.

Best of the Best 3: No Turning Back ♪♪ 1995 (R) Asian-American Tommy Lee (Rhee) discovers a band of racist vigilantes are trying to take over the rural community of Liberty, where his sister lives. But with the help of his brother-in-law Jack (McDonald), who's also the sheriff, and school teacher Margo (Gershon), Tommy is going to fight back. **102m/C VHS, DVD.** Phillip Rhee, Gina Gershon, Christopher McDonald, Mark Rolston, Peter Simmons, Dee Wallace Stone; **D:** Phillip Rhee; **W:** Deborah Scott; **C:** Jerry Watson; **M:** Barry Goldberg.

Best of the Best: Without Warning ♪½ 1998 (R) It's Russian mobsters, counterfeit money, and high tech gadgets this time around as LAPD martial arts consultant Tommy Lee (Rhee) goes after the gang who killed his best

friend's daughter. **90m/C VHS, DVD.** Phillip Rhee, Ernie Hudson, Tobin Bell, Thure Riefenstein, Chris Lemmon, Jessica Collins; **D:** Phillip Rhee; **C:** Michael D. Margulies; **M:** David Grant. **VIDEO**

The Best of Times ♪♪ 1986 (PG) Slim story of two grown men who attempt to redress the failures of the past by reenacting a football game they lost in high school due to a single flubbed pass. With this cast, it should have been better. **105m/C VHS, DVD.** Robin Williams, Kurt Russell, M. Emmet Walsh, Pamela Reed, Holly Palance, Donald Moffat, Margaret Whitton, Kirk Cameron; **D:** Roger Spottiswoode; **W:** Ron Shelton; **C:** Charles F. Wheeler; **M:** Arthur B. Rubinstein.

Best of Youth ♪♪♪ *La Meglio Gioventu* 2003 My Sprawling modern-times epic spanning 40 years of Italy's tumultuous history through the eyes of two brothers. At close to six hours the film encapsulates the entire relationship between Nicola (Lo Cascio), an optimistic med student, wooing women worldwide before settling into a successful career as a psychiatrist, and his brother Matteo (Boni), a world-weary, brooding idealist who eventually joins the Italian police in hopes of righting the wrongs of an unfair society. History is seen with human eyes and expressed in striking passion, somehow never overindulging itself. Originally an Italian television miniseries, it went on to win over the crowds and critics at Cannes. **383m/C DVD.** *IT* Luigi Lo Cascio, Adriana Asti, Alessio Boni, Jasmine Trinca, Sonia Bergamasco, Fabrizio Gifuni, Maya Sansa, Valentina Carnelutti, Andrea Tidona, Lidia Vitale, Claudio Filippi, Greta Cavuoti, Sara Pavoncello, Claudio Gioe; **D:** Marco Tullio Giordana; **W:** Sandro Petraglia, Stefano Rulli; **C:** Roberto Forza. **TV**

Best Revenge ♪♪ 1983 (R) Two aging hippies engage in a Moroccan drug deal in order to free a kidnapped friend from a sleazy gangster. They get caught by the police, but escape, searching for the engineers of the frame-up. **92m/C VHS.** John Heard, Levon Helm, Alberta Watson, John Rhys-Davies, Moses Znaimer; **D:** John Trent; **M:** Keith Emerson.

Best Seller ♪♪♪ 1987 (R) Interesting, subtext-laden thriller about a cop/bestselling author with writer's block, and the strange symbiotic relationship he forms with a slick hired killer, who wants his own story written. Dennehy is convincing as the jaded cop, and is paired well with the psychotic Woods. **112m/C VHS, DVD.** James Woods, Brian Dennehy, Victoria Tennant, Paul Shenar, Seymour Cassel, Allison Balson, George Coe, Anne Pitoniak; **D:** John Flynn; **W:** Larry Cohen; **C:** Fred Murphy; **M:** Jay Ferguson.

The Best Way ♪♪½ *The Best Way to Walk; La Meilleure Facon de Marcher* 1976 Two summer camp counselors discover they might be gay and desirous of each other. Miller's first film; in French with English subtitles. **85m/C VHS, DVD.** *FR* Patrick Dewaere, Patrick Bouchitey, Christine Pascal, Claude Pieplu; **D:** Claude Miller; **W:** Luc Beraud, Claude Miller; **C:** Bruno Nuytten; **M:** Alain Jomy.

The Best Years of Our Lives ♪♪♪♪ 1946 Three WWII vets return home to try to pick up the threads of their lives. A film that represented a large chunk of American society and helped it readjust to the American postwar ambience is now considered an American classic. Supporting actor Russell, an actual veteran, holds a record for winning two Oscars for a single role. In addition to his Best Supporting Actor award, Russell was given a special Oscar for bringing hope and courage to fellow veterans. Based on the novella by MacKinlay Kantor. Remade for TV as "Returning Home" in 1975. **170m/B VHS.** Fredric March, Myrna Loy, Teresa Wright, Dana Andrews, Virginia Mayo, Harold Russell, Hoagy Carmichael, Gladys George, Roman Bohnen, Steve Cochran, Charles Halton, Cathy O'Donnell, Ray Collins, Victor Cutler, Minna Gombell, Walter Baldwin, Dorothy Adams, Don Beddoe, Ray Teal, Howland Chamberlain; **D:** William Wyler; **W:** Robert Sherwood; **C:** Gregg Toland; **M:** Hugo Friedhofer. Oscars '46: Actor (March), Director (Wyler), Film Editing, Picture, Screenplay, Support. Actor (Russell), Orig. Dramatic Score; AFI '98: Top 100; British Acad. '47: Film; Golden Globes '47: Film—Drama; Natl. Bd. of Review '46: Director

(Wyler), Natl. Film Reg. '89; N.Y. Film Critics '46: Director (Wyler), Film.

Bethune ♪♪½ 1977 The life story of a Canadian doctor who started a practice in Communist China. **88m/C VHS.** Donald Sutherland, Kate Nelligan, David Gardner, James Hong; **D:** Eric Till.

Betrayal ♪ 1974 Psycho-thriller pits an unhappy widow against her seemingly innocent hired companion. Seems this girl has a boyfriend who has a plan to murder the lonely lady for her money. Routine and predictable. **78m/C VHS.** Amanda Blake, Dick Haymes, Tisha Sterling, Sam Groom; **D:** Gordon Hessler; **M:** Ernest Gold.

Betrayal ♪♪½ 1978 Telefilm based on the book by Lucy Freeman and Julie Roy about a historic malpractice case involving a psychiatrist and one of his female patients. The doctor convinced the female patient that sex with him would serve as therapy. **95m/C VHS, DVD.** Lesley Ann Warren, Rip Torn, Ron Silver, Richard Masur, Stephen Elliott, John Hillerman, Peggy Ann Garner; **D:** Paul Wendkos.

Betrayal ♪♪½ 1983 (R) An unusual adult drama, beginning at the end of a seven-year adulterous affair and working its way back in time to finally end at the start of the betrayal of a husband by his wife and his best friend. Kingsley and Irons make Pinter's adaptation of his own play work. **95m/C VHS, DVD.** *GB* Ben Kingsley, Patricia Hodge, Jeremy Irons; **D:** David Hugh Jones; **W:** Harold Pinter.

Betrayal from the East ♪♪ 1944 A carnival barker saves the Panama Canal from the vicious Japanese war machine in this rather silly wartime drama. **82m/B VHS.** Lee Tracy, Nancy Kelly, Richard Loo, Abner Biberman, Regis Toomey, Philip Ahn, Addison Richards, Victor Sen Yung, Drew Pearson; **D:** William Berke.

Betrayal of the Dove ♪♪ 1992 (R) Slater stars as a divorced woman set-up in this story by best friend Le Brock. Zane is the dashing doctor who sweeps Slater off her feet but things are never quite what they seem. He may not be Mr. Right and the best friend has her own hidden agenda. **93m/C VHS.** Helen Slater, Kelly Le Brock, Billy Zane, Alan Thicke, Harvey Korman, Stuart Pankin, David Lander; **D:** Strathford Hamilton; **W:** Robby Benson.

Betrayed ♪♪ 1954 Bombshell Turner and strongman Gable star in this story of WWII intrigue. Suspected of being a Nazi informer, Turner is sent back to Holland for a last chance at redemption. Her cover as a sultry nightclub performer has the Nazis drooling and ogling (can you spell h-o-t?), but her act may be blown by an informant. Can luscious Lana get by the police? **107m/C VHS.** Clark Gable, Lana Turner, Victor Mature, Louis Calhern, O.E. Hasse, Wilfrid Hyde-White, Ian Carmichael, Niall MacGinnis, Nora Swinburne, Roland Culver; **D:** Gottfried Reinhardt; **C:** Frederick A. (Freddie) Young.

Betrayed ♪♪ 1988 (R) A rabid political film, dealing with an implausible FBI agent infiltrating a white supremacist organization via her love affair with a handsome farmer who turns out to be a murderous racist. Winger is memorable in her role as the FBI agent, despite the film's limitations, and admirers of Costa-Gavras's directorial work will want to see how the director botched this one. **112m/C VHS, DVD.** Tom Berenger, Debra Winger, John Mahoney, John Heard, Albert Hall, Jeffrey DeMunn; **D:** Constantin Costa-Gavras; **W:** Joe Eszterhas; **C:** Patrick Blossier.

The Betsy ♪♪ 1978 (R) A story of romance, money, power, and mystery centering around the wealthy Hardeman family and their automobile manufacturing business. Loosely patterned after the life of Henry Ford as portrayed in the Harold Robbins' pulp-tome. Olivier is the redeeming feature. **132m/C VHS, DVD.** Laurence Olivier, Kathleen Beller, Robert Duvall, Lesley-Anne Down, Edward Hermann, Tommy Lee Jones, Katharine Ross, Jane Alexander; **D:** Daniel Petrie; **W:** William Bast, Walter Bernstein; **C:** Mario Tosi; **M:** John Barry.

Betsy's Wedding ♪♪ ½ 1990 (R) Betsy wants a simple wedding, but her father has other, grander ideas. Then there's the problem of paying for it, which Dad tries to take care of in a not-so-typical manner. Alda at his hilarious best. **94m/C VHS, DVD.** Alan Alda, Alan Alda, Joey Bishop, Madeline Kahn, Molly Ringwald, Catherine O'Hara, Joe Pesci, Ally Sheedy, Burt Young, Anthony LaPaglia, Julie Bovasso, Nicolas Coster, Bibi Besch, Dylan Walsh, Samuel L. Jackson, Frankie Faison; **D:** Alan Alda; **W:** Alan Alda; **C:** Kelvin Pike; **M:** Bruce Broughton.

Better Dayz ♪♪ 2002 High schooler Faye (Cargle) has her head turned by smoothie drug dealer Vaughn (Odel)—until she sees him kill a rival. When Vaughn threatens Faye, she turns to her hot-headed brother Johnny (Williams) to keep her safe. Technical flaws detract from what slowly becomes a dramatic story. **101m/C VHS, DVD.** Erik Williams, Shantel Cargle, Rich Odell; **D:** Norman C. Linton; **W:** Norman C. Linton; **C:** Brenden Flint. **VIDEO**

Better Late Than Never ♪♪ 1979 Fun TV tale of senior citizens in revolt at an old-age home. Fine characters portrayed by some of the best in the business. **100m/C VHS.** Harold Gould, Tyne Daly, Strother Martin, Harry (Henry) Morgan, Victor Buono, George Gobel, Lou Jacobi, Donald Pleasence, Larry Storch; **D:** Richard Crenna; **M:** Charles Fox. **TV**

Better Late Than Never ♪♪ 1983 Two penniless old fools vie for the acceptance of a bratty 10-year-old millionairess, who must choose one as her guardian. Niven's last film. **95m/C VHS.** David Niven, Art Carney, Maggie Smith, Kimberly Partridge, Catherine Hicks, Melissa Prophet; **D:** Bryan Forbes; **M:** Henry Mancini.

Better Luck Tomorrow ♪♪♪ 2002 (R) Controversial film about Asian-American teens gone wild. Overachieving students in a wealthy Orange County suburb, they outwardly conform to the stereotype of smart, well-behaved, ambitious kids. But their extracurricular activities involve drugs and criminal activities that escalate from the petty to the serious as events spin out of their control. **98m/C VHS, DVD.** *US* Parry Shen, Jason J. Tobin, Roger Fan, Sung Kang, John Cho, Karin Anna Cheung; **D:** Justin Lin; **W:** Justin Lin, Ernesto M. Foronda, Fabian Marquez; **C:** Patrice Lucien Cochet; **M:** Michael J. Gonzales.

Better Off Dead ♪♪½ 1985 (PG) A compulsive teenager's girlfriend leaves him and he decides to end it all. After several abortive attempts, he decides instead to out-ski his ex-girlfriend's obnoxious new boyfriend. Uneven but funny. **97m/C VHS, DVD.** John Cusack, Curtis Armstrong, Diane Franklin, Kim Darby, David Ogden Stiers, Dan Schneider, Amanda Wyss, Taylor Negron, Vincent Schiavelli, Demian Slade, Scooter Stevens, Elizabeth (E.G. Dailey) Daily, Yano Avana, Steven Williams; **D:** Savage Steve Holland; **W:** Savage Steve Holland; **C:** Isidore Mankofsky; **M:** Rupert Hine.

Better Than Chocolate ♪♪ 1999 (R) Sweetly touching romantic comedy follows college dropout Maggie (Dwyer), who's trying to establish her own identity, which isn't so easy when she hasn't told her flighty mother, Lila (Crewson), that she's a lesbian. But now mom's getting divorced and she and Maggie's brother Paul (Mundy) are temporarily moving in, with Maggie trying to pass off her lover Kim (Cox) as just a roommate. Meanwhile, naive Lila is confiding in Maggie's transsexual friend, singer Judy (a stellar Outerbridge), and discovering the joys of sex toys. **101m/C VHS, DVD.** *CA* Karyn Dwyer, Wendy Crewson, Christina Cox, Peter Outerbridge, Ann-Marie MacDonald, Kevin Mundy,

Better Than Sex ♂♂½ **2000 (R)** Cin (Porter) meets Josh (Wenham) at a party and taxis him home for the night. When things go exceptionally well, Cin agrees to Josh's staying on until he flies home to London in a couple of days. But amidst all the sex, little things like relationships, love, and commitment begin to creep in. Vc-oeevers from the twosome comment on the action and what they're really feeling rather than what they're telling each other. Porter and Wenham are attractive and charismatic, making the film really feeling rather than what they're telling each other. **83m/C VHS, DVD, AU FR** *D:* Jonathan Teplitzky; *W:* Jonathan Teplitzky; *C:* Garry Phillips; *M:* David Hirschfelder. Australian Film Inst. '00: Director, Film, Score (Hirschfelder).

A Better Tomorrow, Part 1 ♂♂♂½ **1986** Former hit men (Lung and Fat) team up to bring down the mob boss who double-crossed them and sent one to prison and the other to the streets. One of them also has to protect his younger brother, a cop, from the gang. Considered one of the best of Woo's Hong Kong efforts, there's plenty of Woo's hallmark balletic action and an interesting story. In Cantonese with English subtitles. **95m/C VHS, DVD, HK** *CH HK* Chow Yun-Fat, Waise Lee, John Woo; *C:* Wing-Hung Wong; *M:* Ka-Fai Koo.

A Better Tomorrow, Part 2 ♂♂½ **1989** A smooth-taking king gangster, who was killed in Part I, returns in Part II as the dead man's twin brother (unmentioned in Part I). He teams up with a cop and a reformed gangster to fight the forces of evil. In Cantonese with English subtitles. **100m/C VHS, DVD, HK** Chow Yun-Fat, Leslie Cheung, Ti Lung, Emily Chu, Waise Lee, John Woo; *D:* John Woo; *M:* Joseph Koo.

A Better Tomorrow, Part 3 ♂♂ *Love and Death in Saigon* **1989** Prequel set in 1974 finds detective Mark Gor (Fai) and his cousin (Leung) seeking to escape from Saigon. Unfortunately, they both fall for the same sultry babe (Mui), who's also a gangster's moll. Mandarin with English subtitles. **114m/C VHS, DVD, HK** Chow Yun-Fat, Tony Leung Ka-Fai, Anita Mui; *D:* Tsui Hark.

A Better Way to Die ♂♂ **2000 (R)** An ex-cop heads home to try to start a new life but is instead mistaken for a government agent who has had a contract put out on his life by a Chicago mob boss. So the cop tries to get the feds to assist him before the wiseguys get to him first. **101m/C VHS, DVD, FR** Marie Trintignant, Stephane Audran, Jean-Francoise Garreaud, Yves Lambrecht, Christiane Minazzoli, Pierre Vernier; *D:* Claude Chabrol; *W:* Claude Chabrol; *M:* Matthieu Chabrol.

Betty ♂♂ **1992** Sulky, drunken Betty (Trintignant) is doing her best to destroy her bourgeois life, escaping from her marriage into adultery and debasement. She meets the concerned middle-aged widow Laure (Audran), who inexplicably takes her to her hotel room, clears her up, and spends the remainder of the movie as Betty's sounding-board. Betty's passive personality offers little to explain her appeal to either Laure or the viewer. Based on the novel by Georges Simenon. French with subtitles. **103m/C VHS, DVD, FR** *D:* Claude Chabrol; *W:* Claude Chabrol; *C:* Bernard Zitzermann; *M:* Matthieu Chabrol.

Betty ♂♂½ **1997** Betty Monday (Pollak) is a well-known actress undergoing a breakdown. So she leaves Hollywood for Palm Springs and tries out a "normal" life—at least by movie star standards. Offbeat comedy has the potential to pleasantly surprise. **83m/C VHS, DVD** Cheryl Pollak, Holland Taylor, Ubü Kier, Ron Perlman, Stephen D. (R.D.) Murphy; *D:* Ric ard D. (R.D.) Murphy.

Better Than Sex ♂♂♂½ Maya Delver, Jay Brazeau, Tony Nappo; *D:* Anne Wheeler; *W:* Peggy Thompson; *C:* Gregory Middleton; *M:* Graeme Coleman.

Betty Blue ♂♂♂ **37.2 le Matin, 37.2 Degrees in the Morning 1986 (R)** A vivid, intensely erotic film about two young French lovers and their inordinately strong passion for each other destroys them, leading to poverty, violence, and insanity. English subtitles. From the director of "Diva." Based on the novel "37.2 Le Matin" by Philippe Djian. **121m/C VHS, DVD, FR** Jean-Hughes Anglade, Beatrice Dalle, Jean-Hughes Anglade, Gerard Darmon, Consuelo de Haviland, Clementine Celarie, Jacques Mathou, Vincent Lindon; *D:* Jean-Jacques Beineix; *W:* Jean-Jacques Beineix; *C:* Jean-Francois Robin; *M:* Gabriel Yared.

Between Friends ♂♂♂½ **1983** Two women with only their respective divorces in common, meet and become fast friends. The rapport between Burnett and Taylor makes for a touching drama. Adapted from the book "Nobody Makes Me Cry," by Shelley Last, one of the producers. **105m/C VHS, DVD** Elizabeth Taylor, Carol Burnett, Barbara Bush, Henry Ramer; *D:* Lou Antonio; *M:* James Horner. CABLE

Between God, the Devil & a Winchester ♂ **1972** Violent western with plenty of shooting and dust. Lots of cowboys are hot on the trail of some stolen loot from a church but apparently God isn't on their side since the majority bite the dust and become a snack for the vultures. **98m/C VHS** Gilbert Roland, Richard Harrison; *D:* Dario Silvestre.

Between Heaven and Earth ♂♂ **1993** Maria (Maura) is an ambitious TV journalist, prone to surreal dreams, who becomes pregnant after a one-night stand. After witnessing a violent protest, Maria becomes convinced that she can communicate with her unborn baby and that the child is unwilling to be born into such a violent world. So Maria must try to convince her baby otherwise. In French with English subtitles. **89m/C VHS, BE FR SP** Carmen Maura, Jean-Pierre Cassel, Didier Bezace, Samuel Mussen, Andre Delvaux; *D:* Marion Hansel; *W:* Marion Hansel.

Between Heaven and Hell ♂♂♂ **1956** Prejudiced Southern gentleman Wagner finds how wrong his misconceptions are, as he attempts to survive WWII on a Pacific Island. Epsen is exceptional, making this rather simplistic story a meaningful classic. **94m/C VHS, DVD.** Robert Wagner, Terry Moore, Broderick Crawford, Buddy Ebsen, Robert Keith, Brad Dexter, Mark Damon, Ken Clark, Harvey Lembeck, Frank Gorshin, Scatman Crothers, Carl "Alfalfa" Switzer, L.Q. Jones, Tod Andrews; *D:* Richard Fleischer; *W:* Harry Brown; *C:* Leo Tover; *M:* Hugo Friedhofer.

Between Men ♂♂ **1935** A father kills a man he believes killed his son and flees. Later in life, the son meets his father and son, this causes some major concern. **59m/B VHS.** Johnny Mack Brown, Beth Marion, William Farnum, Earl Dwire, Lloyd Ingraham, Milburn (Milt) Morante; *D:* Robert North Bradbury.

Between Strangers ♂♂ **2002 (R)** Three Toronto women suffer personal crises and contemplate changing their lives. Housewife Olivia (Loren) is debating whether to leave her abusive invalid husband (Postlethwaite); war photographer Natalia (Sorvino) is burned out trying to live up to her father's reputation and contemplates a career change; and cellist Catherine (Unger) is upset over her father's (McDowell) recent release from prison for a crime that has haunted her since childhood. Ponti's debut and his mom Loren's 100th film. **97m/C VHS, DVD, US CA IT** Sophia Loren, Mira Sorvino, Deborah Kara Unger, Pete Postlethwaite, Malcolm McDowell, Klaus Maria Brandauer, Gerard Depardieu, Wendy Crewson, Andrew Tarbet; *D:* Edoardo Ponti; *W:* Edoardo Ponti; *C:* Gregory Middleton; *M:* Zbigniew Preisner.

Betty Fighting Men ♂½ **1932** The orphaned daughter of a shepherd is adopted by the cowpoke who caused her father's death. The cowpoke's sons fall in love with, and compete for, the love of the girl. **62m/B VHS** Ken Maynard, Ruth Hall, Josephine Dunn, Wallace MacDonald; *D:* Forrest Sheldon.

Between Two Women ♂♂ **1986** A wife's relationship with her bossy mother-in-law is rocky until the latter has a stroke and needs care. Dewhurst won an Emmy for her portrayal of the mother-in-law. **95m/C VHS** Farrah Fawcett, Michael Nouri, Colleen Dewhurst, Steven Hill, Bridgette Andersen, Danny Corkill; *D:* Jon Avnet. TV

Between Wars ♂♂ **1974** Young doctor in Australia's Medical Corps encounters conflict when he tries to introduce Freud's principles into his work. **97m/C VHS, AU** Corin Redgrave, Arthur Dignam, Judy Morris, Patricia Leehy, Gunter Meisner; *D:* Michael Thornhill.

Between Your Legs ♂♂ *Entre las Piernas* **1999** Provocatively titled sexual thriller. Receptionist Miranda (Abril) meets writer Javier (Bardem) at a group therapy session for sex addicts. He's addicted to phone sex and the married Miranda likes to have sex with strangers. While they get to know each other a murder occurs and the investigation is assigned to detective Felix (Gomez), who happens to be Miranda's husband. Soon, suspicions begins to point in Javier's direction. The triangle is strong but subplots are undeveloped and the film sinks into implausibility. Spanish with subtitles. **120m/C VHS, DVD, SP** Victoria Abril, Javier Bardem, Carmelo Gomez, Juan Diego, Sergi Lopez, Javier Albalá; *D:* Manuel Gomez Pereira; *W:* Manuel Gomez Pereira, Joaquin Oristrell; *C:* Juan Amorós; *M:* Bernardo Bonezzi.

Beulah Land ♂½ **1980** Miniseries about 45 years in the lives of a Southern family, including the Civil War. Based on the novels "Beulah Land" and "Look Away, Beulah Land" by Lonnie Coleman. **267m/C VHS, DVD.** Lesley Ann Warren, Michael Sarrazin, Don Johnson, Meredith Baxter, Dorian Harewood, Eddie Albert, Hope Lange, Paul Rudd; *D:* Virgil W. Vogel. *Music:* Harry Fale. TV

The Beverly Hillbillies ♂♂½ **1993 (PG)** Big-screen transfer of the long-running TV show may appeal to fans. Ozark mountaineer Jed Clampett discovers oil, becomes an instant billionaire, and packs his backwoods clan off to the good life in California. Minimal plot finds dim-bulb nephew Jethro and daughter Elly May looking for a bride for Jed. Not that any of it matters. Everyone does fine by their impersonations, particularly Varney as the good-hearted Jed and Leachman as stubborn Granny. Ebsen, the original Jed, reprises another of his TV roles, detective Barnaby Jones. And yes, the familiar strains of the "Ballad of Jed Clampett" by Jerry Scoggins stars this one off, too. **93m/C VHS, DVD.** Jim Varney, Erika Eleniak, Diedrich Bader, Cloris Leachman, Dabney Coleman, Lily Tomlin, Lea Thompson, Rob Schneider, Linda Carlson, Penny Fuller, Kevin Connolly; *Cameo:* Dolly Parton, Buddy Ebsen, Zsa Zsa Gabor, Dolly Parton; *D:* Penelope Spheeris; *W:* Larry Konner, Mark Rosenthal, Jim Fisher, Jim Staahl; *C:* Robert Brinkmann; *M:* Lelo Schifrin.

Beverly Hills Bodysnatchers ♂½ **1989 (R)** A mad scientist and a greedy mortician plot to get rich, but their plan backfires when they bring a Mafia godfather back to life and he terrorizes Beverly Hills. **85m/C VHS.** Vic Tayback, Frank Gorshin, Brooke Bundy, Seth Jaffe, Art Metrano, Allison Barron, Rodney Eastman, Warren Selko, Keone Young; *D:* Jonathan Mostow.

Beverly Hills Brats ♂ **1989 (PG-13)** A spoiled, rich Hollywood brat hires a loser to kidnap him in order to gain his parents attention, only to have both of them kidnapped by real crooks. **90m/C VHS, DVD.** Martin Sheen, Burt Young, Peter Billingsley, Terry Moore; *D:* Dimitri Sotirakis; *M:* Barry Goldberg.

Beverly Hills Cop ♂♂♂ **1984 (R)** When a close friend of smooth-talking Detroit cop Axle Foley is brutally murdered, he traces the murderer to the posh streets of Beverly Hills. There he must stay on his toes to keep one step ahead of the law. Better than average Murphy vehicle. **105m/C VHS, DVD.** Eddie Murphy, Judge Reinhold, John Ashton, Lisa Eilbacher, Ronny Cox, Steven Berkoff, James Russo, Jonathan Banks, Stephen Elliott, Bronson Pinchot, Paul Reiser, Damon Wayans, Fick Overton; *D:* Martin Brest; *W:* Bach, Daniel Petrie Jr.; *C:* Bruce Surtees; *M:* Harold Faltermeyer.

Beverly Hills Cop 2 ♂♂½ **1987** The highly successful sequel to the first profitable comedy, with essentially the same plot, but this time deals with Foley infiltrating a band of international munitions smugglers. **103m/C VHS, DVD.** Eddie Murphy, Judge Reinhold, Jurgen Prochnow, Ronny Cox, John Ashton, Brigitte Nielsen, Allen (Goorwitz) Garfield, Paul Reiser, Dean Stockwell, Chris Rock, Gil Hill, Robert Ridgely, Gilbert Gottfried, Todd Susman, Robert Pastorelli, Tom (Tiny) Lister, Paul Guilfoyle, Hugh Hefner; *D:* Tony Scott; *W:* Larry Ferguson, Warren Skaaren; *C:* Jeffrey L. Kimball; *M:* Harold Faltermeyer. Golden Raspberry '87: Worst Song, "I Want Your Sex").

Beverly Hills Cop 3 ♂♂½ **1994 (R)** Yes, Detroit cop Axel Foley (Murphy) just happens to find another case that takes him back to his friends on the Beverly Hills PD. This time he uncovers a criminal network fronting WonderWorld, an amusement park with a squeaky-clean image. Fast-paced action, lots of gunplay, and Eddie wisecracks his way through the slow spots. Reinhold returns as the still briefly reprising his role as Serge of the undeterminable accent. Critically panned boxoffice disappointment relies too heavily on formula and is overdone and disappointing followup. **105m/C VHS, DVD.** Louis Lombardi, Timothy Carhart, Stephen McFaddie, Theresa Randle, John Saxon, Alan Young, Bronson Pinchot, Al Green, Gil Hill; *D:* John Landis; *W:* Steven E. de Souza; *C:* Mac Ahlberg; *M:* Nile Rodgers.

Beverly Hills Family Robinson ♂♂ **1997** Cooking show host Marsha Robinson decides to take her family on a yachting vacation in the South Seas. Naturally, they get hijacked by pirates and shipwrecked and must learn to survive on their not-quite-deserted island. And just how good is Marsha is at campfire cooking? **88m/C VHS, DVD.** Dyan Cannon, Martin Mull, Sarah Michelle Gellar, Josh Picker, Nique Needles, Ryan O'Donohue; *D:* Troy Miller. TV

Beverly Hills Madam ♂♂ **1986 (PG-13)** In this routine plot, a stable of elite call girls struggle with their lifestyle and their madam, played by Dunaway. **97m/C VHS.** Faye Dunaway, Louis Jourdan, Donna Dixon, Robin Givens, Marshall Colt, Melody Anderson, Terry Farrell; *D:* Harvey Hart. TV

Beverly Hills Ninja ♂½ **1996 (PG-13)** Farley plays Haru, a pathetically inept adopted son of a ninja, who is, nevertheless, sent to Beverly Hills on a rescue mission to break up an international counterfeiting ring. There, second-time spoof siren Sheridan hires the "great white ninja" to follow her "no-good" boyfriend and becomes the object of Haru's desire. Farley's extraordinary gift for physical comedy is exploited to the hilt, and the increase in Haru's tripping and stumbling (and in one harrowing scene, stripping) usually coincides with the tumbling of the plot. Rock's talents are squandered on a poorly conceived bellboy character. Farley's first feature sans fellow SNL alumni Spade suffers for his absence. Duggan, who also helmed Adam Sandler's "Happy Gilmore," might want to start screening his calls. **88m/C VHS, DVD.** Chris Farley, Chris Rock, Soon-Teck Oh, Francois Chau, Keith Cooke Hirabayashi; *D:* Dennis Dugan; *W:* Mark Feldberg, Mitch Klebanoff; *C:* Arthur Albert; *M:* George S. Clinton.

Beverly Hills Vamp ♂♂ **1988 (R)** A madame and her girls are really female vampires with a penchant for hot-blooded men. **88m/C VHS.** Britt Ekland, Eddie Deezen,

Debra Lamb, Michelle (McClellan) Bauer, Brigitte Burdine, Tim Conway Jr., Jillian Kesner, Tom Shell; **D:** Fred Olen Ray; **W:** Ernest Farino; **C:** Stephen Blake; **M:** Chuck Cirino.

Beware ✞½ 1946 A black singer saves a college from bankruptcy and makes off with the gym teacher. The photography may be a bit harsh, but the all-black cast made this a pioneering but impressive film. 64m/B VHS, DVD. Louis Jordan, Frank Wilson, Emory Richardson, Valerie Black, Milton Woods; **D:** Bud Pollard.

Beware! Children at Play WOOF! 1995 (R) Cult leader kidnaps kids and introduces them to cannibalism. Bleech! As if this didn't sound grim enough, there's also an unrated version. 90m/C VHS, DVD. Michael Robinson, Eric Tonken, Jamie Krause, Mik Cribben, Danny McClaughlin; **D:** Mik Cribben; **C:** Mik Cribben.

Beware, My Lovely ✞✞½ 1952 Taut chiller. Lonely widow Lupino hires a new handy-man. He's great with screen doors and storm windows, but has a problem with sharp tools. Intense and gripping with fine performances. 77m/B VHS. Ida Lupino, Robert Ryan, Taylor Holmes, O.Z. Whitehead, Barbara Whiting, Dee Pollock; **D:** Harry Horner.

Beware of a Holy Whore ✞✞ *Warnung Vor Einer Heiligen Nutte* 1970 German film crew sits around a Spanish resort—complaining, drinking, and making love—as they wait for financial support from Bonn. Provocative and self-indulgently honest look at filmmaking. Filmed on location in Sorrento, Italy; German with subtitles. 103m/C VHS, DVD. GE Lou Castel, Eddie Constantine, Hanna Schygulla, Marquard Bohm, Ulli Lommel, Margarethe von Trotta, Kurt Raab, Ingrid Caven, Werner Schroeter, Rainer Werner Fassbinder; **D:** Rainer Werner Fassbinder; **W:** Rainer Werner Fassbinder; **C:** Michael Ballhaus; **M:** Peer Raben.

Beware of Pity ✞✞½ 1946 A crippled baroness thinks she's found true love with a military officer, but it turns out his marriage proposal grew out of pity for her, not passion. A quality but somber British-made historical drama, based on a novel by Stefan Zweig. 129m/B VHS. Lilli Palmer, Albert Lieven, Cedric Hardwicke, Gladys Cooper, Ernest Thesiger, Freda Jackson, Linden Travers, Ralph Truman, Peter Cotes, Jenny Laird, Emrys Jones, Gerhard Kempinski, John Salew, Kenneth Warrington; **D:** Maurice Elvey; **W:** W.P. Lipscomb, Elizabeth Barron, Margaret Steen; **C:** Derick Williams.

Bewitched ✞✞ 2005 (PG-13) Instead of an actual remake of the 1964-72 hit TV show, the Ephron sisters opted for a behind-the-scenes parody. Down-and-out actor Jack Wyatt (Ferrell) hopes his new role as Darrin will magically revive his career. Not wanting to be upstaged, he picks (Kidman) for Samantha the witch, not knowing that she really IS one. Since she disavowed (sort of) her witchery to live a mortal life, she accepts and sees Jack as a potential worldly mate. Once his egomania becomes evident, she can't help but revert to a little voodoo to shake things up. Great cast but tale doesn't cast a spell. 100m/C DVD, UMD. US Nicole Kidman, Will Ferrell, Shirley MacLaine, Michael Caine, Jason Schwartzman, Heather Burns, Jim Turner, David Alan Grier, Steven Carell, Amy Sedaris, Richard Kind, Stephen Colbert, Kristin Chenoweth, Michael Badalucco, Carol(e) Shelley, Kate Walsh; **D:** Nora Ephron; **W:** Nora Ephron, Delia Ephron; **M:** George Fenton.

The Beyond ✞✞ *Seven Doors of Death; E Tu Vivrai Nel Terrore—L'aldilà* 1982 (R) A young woman inherits a possessed hotel. Meanwhile, hellish zombies try to check out. Chilling Italian horror flick that Fulci directed under the alias "Louis Fuller." 88m/C VHS, DVD. IT Al Cliver, Katherine MacColl, David Warbeck, Farah Keller, Tony St. John; **D:** Lucio Fulci; **W:** Lucio Fulci; Dardano Sacchetti, Giorgio Mariuzzo; **C:** Sergio Salvati.

Beyond a Reasonable Doubt ✞✞ 1956 In order to get a behind-the-scenes glimpse at the judicial system, a man plays the guilty party to a murder. Alas, when he tries to vindicate himself, he is the victim of his own folly. Not as interesting as it sounds on paper. 80m/B VHS. Dana Andrews, Joan Fontaine, Sidney Blackmer, Philip Bourneuf, Barbara Nichols, Shepperd Strudwick, Arthur Franz, Edward Binns; **D:** Fritz Lang; **W:** Douglas S. Morrow.

Beyond Atlantis WOOF! 1973 (PG) An ancient underwater tribe is discovered when it kidnaps land-lubbin' women with which to mate. 91m/C VHS, DVD. PH John Ashley, Patrick Wayne, George Nader; **D:** Eddie Romero; **C:** Charles Johnson; **C:** Justo Paulino.

Beyond Borders ✞½ 2003 (R) Decades-spanning romance between an over-zealous doctor and a lovely do-gooder suffers from a too-earnest presentation and romantic cliches. Dashing doctor Nick (Owen) inspires American socialite Sarah (Jolie) to leave her stuffy British hubby (Roache) and really get involved in international aid relief rather than just writing a check. She follows the doc to Ethiopia and later to Cambodia and Checknya (film goes from 1984-1995), where the trouble-prone Nick has apparently been kidnapped. At least the film inspired Jolie personally since she became a goodwill ambassador for the United Nations High Commissioner for Refugees and adopted her son from Cambodia. 127m/C VHS, DVD. US Angelina Jolie, Clive Owen, Teri Polo, Linus Roache, Yorick Van Wageningen, Noah Emmerich, Kate Ashfield, Jamie Bartlett, Timothy West, Kate Trotter, Burt Kwouk; **D:** Martin Campbell; **W:** Caspian Tredwell-Owen; **C:** Phil Meheux; **M:** James Horner.

Beyond Darkness ✞½ 1992 (R) When Peter and his family move into their New England home they are immediately beset by some unknown terror. With the help of Father George, Peter learns his house was built upon the graves of 20 witches burned for heresy. The witches have decided to seek revenge by kidnapping Peter's young son and sacrificing him to an evil demon. Can Peter destroy the evil spirits before they destroy his son? 111m/C VHS. Gene Le Brock, David Brandon, Barbara Bingham, Michael Stephenson, Stephen Brown; **D:** Clyde (Claudio Fragasso) Anderson.

Beyond Desire ✞✞½ 1994 (R) Elvis Ray (Forsythe) is released after 14 years in prison and gets picked up by corvette-driving prison groupie and Las Vegas prostitute Rita (Wuhrer) but more than sex is on both their minds. 87m/C VHS. William Forsythe, Kari Wuhrer, Leo Rossi, Sharon Farrell; **D:** Dominique Othenin-Girard; **W:** Dale Trevillion; **C:** Sven Kirsten; **M:** Mark Holden.

Beyond Dream's Door ✞✞ 1988 A young, All-American college student's childhood nightmares come back to haunt him, making dreams a horrifying reality. 86m/C VHS, DVD. Nick Baldasare, Rick Kesler, Susan Pinsky, Norm Singer; **D:** Jay Woelfel.

Beyond Erotica 1979 After being cut out of his father's will, a sadistic young man takes out his rage on his mother and a peasant girl. 90m/C VHS. David Hemmings, Alida Valli, Andrea Rau; **D:** Jose Maria Forque.

Beyond Evil WOOF! 1980 (R) Relatively dim-witted newlywed couple moves into an old island mansion despite rumors that the house is haunted. Sure enough, wife George becomes possessed by the vengeful spirit of a woman murdered 200 years earlier, and a reign of pointless terror begins. Poor rip-off of hybrid Amityville/Exorcist paranormality. 98m/C VHS, DVD. John Saxon, Lynda Day George, Michael Dante, Mario Milano; **D:** Herb Freed; **W:** Herb Freed; **M:** Pino Donaggio.

Beyond Fear ✞✞½ *Au-Delà de la Peur* 1975 Compelling drama about a man forced to aid a gang in robbery while they hold his wife and son captive. 92m/C VHS. FR IT Michael Boquet, Michel Constantin, Marilu Tolo, Paul Crauchet, Michel Creton, Moustache, Jean-Pierre Darras; **D:** Yannick Andrei; **W:** Yannick Andrei; **C:** Pierre Petit; **M:** Alain Goraguer.

Beyond Fear ✞✞ 1993 (R) Tipper Taylor (Lesseos) is a wilderness tour guide who's also a martial arts expert. This is going to come in handy when her tour group is stalked by two men who are after a videotape innocently filmed by someone in Tipper's group. It seems the tape shows the men committing a murder. 84m/C VHS, DVD. Mimi Lesseos; **D:** Robert F. Lyons; **W:** Robert F. Lyons, Mimi Lesseos; **C:** Bodo Holst; **M:** Miriam Cutler.

Beyond Forgiveness ✞✞½ 1994 (R) Basic maverick cop goes after his brother's killers and winds up involved in an international black market in transplantable human organs. 95m/C VHS. Thomas Ian Griffith, Rutger Hauer, John Rhys-Davies; **D:** Bob Misiorowski; **W:** Charles Cohen.

Beyond Innocence ✞ 1987 A 17-year-old lusts after a mature married woman. Ostensibly based on Raymond Radiguet's "Devil in the Flesh." 87m/C VHS. Keith Smith, Katia Caballero, John Morris; **D:** Scott Murray; **C:** Andrzej Bartkowiak.

Beyond Justice ✞✞ 1992 (PG-13) High action-adventure with the prolific Hauer starring as an ex-CIA agent who is hired to rescue the kidnapped son of a beautiful executive. 113m/C VHS, DVD. IT Rutger Hauer, Carol Alt, Omar Sharif, Elliott Gould, Kabir Bedi, David Flosi, Brett Halsey, Peter Sands; **D:** Duccio Tessari; **W:** Sergio Donati, Luigi Montefiore; **C:** Giorgio Di Battista; **M:** Ennio Morricone.

Beyond Justice 2001 New Zealand TV thriller with a modicum of action. Private detectives John Lawless (Smith) and Jodie Keane (Dotchin) are hired by widow Lana Vitale (Rubin) to investigate her husband's suspicious death. Lana's not exactly grieving since she's all too willing to get up close and personal with Lawless. Meanwhile, Jodie follows some clues that lead her to a porno ring. 95m/C VHS, DVD, NZ Kevin Smith, Jennifer Rubin, Angela Dotchin, Bruce Hopkins, Dean O'Gorman; **D:** Geoffrey Cawthorn; **W:** Gavin Strawhan. TV

Beyond Obsession ✞✞ *Oltre la Porta* 1982 The strange relationship between a political prisoner, his daughter, and her obsession with a mysterious American is provocatively explored. 116m/C VHS, DVD. IT Marcello Mastroianni, Eleonora Giorgi, Tom Berenger, Michel Piccoli; **D:** Liliana Cavani; **W:** Liliana Cavani.

Beyond Rangoon ✞✞½ 1995 (R) Sisters Laura (Arquette) and Andy (McDonnell) Bowman travel to Burma to unwind, only to have political unrest and a repressive regime spoil the holiday. Dr. Laura (yeah, right) loses her passport and must flee from trigger-happy soldiers with a political dissident (Ko, a real-life exiled Burmese activist) who befriends her. The search for her passport soon becomes a imperiled trek of survival and self-discovery. Tense, well-crafted action sequences hint at a potential for excitement and intrigue; too bad Arquette isn't the least bit convincing. Filmed in Malaysia. 100m/C VHS. Patricia Arquette, Frances McDormand, Spalding Gray, U Aung Ko, Victor Slezak; **D:** John Boorman; **W:** Alex Lasker, Bill Rubenstein; **C:** John Seale; **M:** Hans Zimmer.

Beyond Re-Animator ✞✞ 2003 (R) Mad scientist Herbert West (Combs) has been in a maximum security prison for 15 years but has continued his experiments (this time on the rats in his cell). When idealistic young Howard Phillips (Barry) becomes the new prison doctor, he wants to aid West with his re-animation experiments. Of course, things sell don't work out as planned and zombie mayhem ensues in this schlocky-but-fun third adventure. 95m/C DVD. US SP Jeffrey Combs, Jason Barry, Simon Andreu, Elsa Pataky; **D:** Brian Yuzna; **W:** Jose Manuel Gomez; **C:** Andreu Rebes; **M:** Xavier Capellas.

Beyond Reason ✞ 1977 A psychologist uses unorthodox methods by treating the criminally insane with dignity and respect. 88m/C VHS. Telly Savalas, Laura Johnson, Diana Muldaur, Marvin Laird, Priscilla Barnes; **D:** Telly Savalas; **C:** John A. Alonzo.

Beyond Reasonable Doubt ✞✞½ 1980 Chilling true-life murder mystery which shattered the peaceful quiet of a small New Zealand town and eventually divided the country. An innocent farmer (Hargreaves) was convicted of a grisly double murder based on evidence planted by a local cop (Hemmings, in a superb role). It wasn't until Yallop's book questioned the facts of the case that it was reopened. Yallop also wrote the screenplay. 127m/C VHS. NZ David Hemmings, John Hargreaves, Martyn Sanderson, Grant Tilly, Diana Rowan, Ian Watkin; **D:** John Laing; **W:** David Yallop.

Beyond Redemption ✞✞ 1999 (R) A serial killer goes after highly respected targets, crucifying his victims, and Detective Smith is in charge of catching the bad guy. It all hinges on faith—and whose is stronger. 97m/C VHS, DVD. CA Andrew McCarthy, Michael Ironside, Jayne Heitmeyer, Suzy Joachim; **D:** Chris Angel. VIDEO

Beyond Silence ✞✞½ *Jenseits der Stille* 1996 (PG-13) Lara (Trieb/Testud), the daughter of deaf parents, has been their guide to the outside world since childhood. When her Aunt Clarissa (Canonica) gives her a clarinet, it opens Lara's life to music and gives her the courage to move beyond the limits of her family. German with subtitles. 109m/C VHS, DVD. GE Sylvie Testud, Tatjana Trieb, Howie Seago, Emmanuelle Laborit, Sibylle Canonica; **D:** Caroline Link; **W:** Caroline Link; **C:** Gernot Roll; **M:** Niki Reiser.

Beyond Suspicion ✞½ *Auggie Rose* 2000 John C. Nolan Jr. (Goldblum) is an insurance bigshot, who stops by the neighborhood liquor store and gets caught up in an armed robbery. The store clerk, Auggie Rose (Coates), gets killed and Nolan feels responsible. He learns Auggie is fresh out of prison and is expecting to meet his prison pen pal, Lucy (Heche). John meets Lucy instead and doesn't correct her assumption that he's Auggie. In fact, John decides to just give up his old life and take up with Lucy. Film's got an intriguing premise that never develops. 108m/C VHS, DVD. Jeff Goldblum, Anne Heche, Timothy Olyphant, Nancy Travis, Richard T. Jones, Kim Coates, Joe Santos, Jack Kehler, Nicholas Chinlund; **D:** Matthew Tabak; **W:** Matthew Tabak; **C:** Adam Kimmel; **M:** Don Harper, Mark Mancina. VIDEO

Beyond the Bermuda Triangle ✞½ 1975 Unfortunate and flat TV flick. Businessman MacMurray, now retired, doesn't have enough to do. He begins an investigation of the mysterious geometric island area when his friends and fiancee disappear. Silly. 78m/C VHS. Fred MacMurray, Sam Groom, Donna Mills, Suzanne Reed, Dana Plato, Woody Woodbury; **D:** William A. Graham. TV

Beyond the Call ✞✞½ 1996 (R) Connecticut housewife Pam O'Brien (Spacek) learns from the paper that her high-school sweetheart Russell Cates (Strathairn) is on death row in South Carolina for killing a cop and his execution has been scheduled within weeks. Pam writes Russell and then hears from his sister Fran (Wright), who urges Pam to visit her brother and get him to apply for a clemency hearing. Husband John (Howard) becomes angry and alarmed as Pam gets more involved with Russell and his case, which hinges on Russell's Vietnam experiences and post-traumatic shock syndrome. 101m/C VHS, DVD. David Strathairn, Sissy Spacek, Arliss Howard, Janet Wright; **D:** Tony Bill; **W:** Doug Magee; **C:** Jean Lepine; **M:** George S. Clinton. CABLE

Beyond the Call of Duty ✞½ 1992 (R) Renegade U.S. Army Commander Len Jordan (Vincent) is after a particularly deadly Vietcong enemy. Aided by the head of a special forces naval unit he tracks this quarry through the notorious Mekong River Delta. But Jordan's mission may be hindered, both personally and pro-

---

Beyond the Clouds 🎬🎬½ 1995 *Par chila les Nuages* 1995 A wandering film director (Malkovich) muses on four stories of life and obsession, including uncertain mated relationships, romantic triangles, and even violence. Based on sketches from Antonioni's book "That Bowling Alley on the Tiber." English, French, and Italian with subtitles. 109m/C VHS, DVD. Jan John Malkovich, Marcello Mastroianni, Sophie Marceau, Fanny Ardant, Vincent Perez, Jean Reno, Jeanne Moreau, Irene Jacob, Peter Weller, Chiara Caselli, Ines Sastre, Kim Rossi-Stuart; **D:** Michelangelo Antonioni, Wim Wenders; **W:** Michelangelo Antonioni, Wim Wenders, Tonino Guerra; **C:** Robby Muller, Alfio Contini; **M:** Van Morrison, Lucio Dalla, Laurent Petitgand.

Beyond the Door 🎬½ *Beyond Obsession; Chi Sei; The Devil within Her* 1975 (R) San Francisco woman finds herself pregnant with a demonic child. One of the first disaster-movie rip-offs; skip this one and go right to the sequel, "Beyond the Door 2." In Italian; dubbed. 97m/C VHS, DVD. *IT* Juliet Mills, Richard Johnson, David Colin Jr.; **D:** Richard Barrett; **W:** Richard Barrett.

Beyond the Door 3 WOOF! 1991 (R) Fool American students in Yugoslavia board a hellish locomotive which speeds them toward a satanic ritual. Demonic disaster-movie stuff (with poor miniatures) isn't as effective as the on-location filming. Serbian scenery and crazed peasants impart an eerie pagan aura. What this has to do with earlier "Beyond the Door" movies only the marketing boys can say. Some titles. 94m/C VHS, Mary Kohnert, Sarah Conway Ciminera, William Geiger, Renee Rancourt, Alex Vitale, Victoria Zinny, Savina Gersak, Bo Svenson; **D:** Jeff Kwitny.

Beyond the Forest 🎬🎬½ 1949 Camp diva Davis, in her last role for Warner Bros., really turns on the histrionics as a big-city gal married to a small-town guy (Cotten) and bored out of her mind. Although the most memorable line, "What a dump," has become larger-than-life, the film itself is rather small and muddled (interestingly), Vidor directed "The Fountainhead" the same year.) A trashy melodrama full of ennui, envy, unwanted pregnancy, and murder; it's definitely high on camp and low on art. 96m/B VHS, Bette Davis, Joseph Cotten, David Bran, Ruth Roman, Minor Watson, Regis Toomey; **D:** King Vidor; **C:** Robert Burks; **M:** Max Steiner.

Beyond the Law 🎬🎬 *Bloodsilver; Firing the Shadow* 1992 (R) Ex-undercover cop Danny Saxon (Sheen) is recruited by the FBI to infiltrate a biker gang involved in drugs and gun smuggling. But Saxon finds himself drawn too close into the uncoventional biker lifestyle and into an uneasy friendship with leader Blood (Madsen). Clumsy and exploitative. 1c1m/C VHS, DVD. Michael Berry, Charlie Sheen, Michael Madsen, Linda Fiorentino, Courtney B. Vance, Leon Rippy, Rip Torn; **D:** Larry Ferguson; **W:** Larry Ferguson; **C:** Robert M. Stevens; **M:** Cory Lerios, John D'Andrea.

Beyond the Law 🎬🎬 1968 Spaghetti western with Van Cleef as the too smart bad guy. He becomes sheriff, picks up the stack of silver at the depot and disappears. Humorous and clever, with fine location photography. 91m/C VHS, DVD. *IT* Lee Van Cleef, Antonio (Tony) Sabato, Lionel Stander, Bud Spencer, Gordon Mitchell, Ann Smyrner; **D:** Giorgio Stegani.

Beyond the Limit 🎬🎬½ *The Honorary Consul* 1983 (R) The story of an intense and darkly ominous love triangle which takes place in the South American coastal city of Corrientes. Based on Graham Greene's novel "The Honorary Consul." 103m/C VHS. Michael Caine, Richard Gere, Bob Hoskins, Elpidia Carrillo, Joaquim de Almeida; **D:** John MacKenzie; **W:** Christopher Hampton; **C:** Phil Meheux.

Beyond the Time Barrier 🎬½ 1960 Air Force test pilot gets more than he bargained for when his high speed plane carries him into the future. He sees the ravages of an upcoming plague to which he must return. 75m/B VHS. Robert Clarke, Darlene Tompkins, Arianne Arden, Vladimir Sokoloff, D'Edgar G. Ulmer.

Beyond the Next Mountain 🎬 1987 (PG) A missionary in China attempts to convert all those he meets. Thin plot and marginal acting will likely make viewers fall asleep. 97m/C VHS. Alberto Isaac, Jon Lormer, Bennet Ohta, Richard Lineback, Edward Ashley, Barry Foster; **D:** James F. Collier, Rolf Forsberg.

Beyond the Poseidon Adventure 🎬 1979 (PG) A sequel to the 1972 film in which salvage teams and venture he must face Black Mike and his gang and rescue Mary from their clutches. Sinking ships should be abandoned. 115m/C VHS, DVD. Michael Caine, Sally Field, Telly Savalas, Peter Boyle, Jack Warden, Slim Pickens, Shirley Knight, Shirley Jones, Karl Malden, Mark Harmon; **D:** Irwin Allen; **C:** Joseph Biroc.

Beyond the Rockies 🎬🎬½ 1922 Sam Wood's 1922 silent film stars icons Rudolph Valentino and Gloria Swanson, and was until recently thought to have been lost forever. One surviving print was found in a Dutch archive, which has been given an impressive restoration and a new sound track. Zany rescues abound! Lord Bracondale (Valentino) rescues Theadora Fitzgerald (Swanson) after her rowboat capsizes off the British coast, and again later in the Swiss Alps after a mountaineering accident. Well worth seeing for the craft involved in creating early film. 81m/B DVD. *US* Gloria Swanson, Rudolph Valentino, Edythe Chapman, Alec B. Francis, Gertrude Astor, Mabel van Buren, June Elvidge, Robert Bolder, Helen Dunbar, Raymond Blathwayt, F.R. Butler; **D:** Sam Wood; **W:** Jack Cunningham; **C:** Alfred Giles.

Beyond the Sea 🎬🎬 2004 (PG-13) Energetic if superficial biography of Bobby Darin is the personal labor of love for director/star/producer Spacey—even if he's technically too old for the role (Darin died at 37 in 1973.) His conceit is showcasing the older Darin in his own fantasy autobiography, directing with his childhood self (Ullrich) and advancing confidently as Darin finds success crooning at the Copa. Spacey can really sing, and his Darin becomes a teen idol with the ditty "Splish Splash," and falls in love with teenaged golden girl actress Sandra Dee (Bosworth). This zoing showbiz, things eventually take a downward spiral for the insecure Darin as his smooth style becomes irrelevant in the hippie sixties before he attempts the inevitable comeback. It's Spacey's show (and he supplies his own more-than-adequate vocals) but supporting actors Hoskins, Blethyn, Aaron, and Goodman all run with their screen time. Title is taken from a 1960 Darin hit. 121m/C VHS, DVD. *US* Kevin Spacey, Kate (Catherine) Bosworth, John Goodman, Bob Hoskins, Brenda Blethyn, Greta Scacchi, Caroline Aaron, Peter Cincotti, William Ullrich, Tayfun Bademsoy; **D:** Kevin Spacey; **W:** Kevin Spacey, Lewis Colick; **C:** Eduardo Serra; **M:** Christopher Slaski.

Beyond the Silhouette 🎬 *Ultimate Desires* 1990 It starts out as another sleazy video sex thriller, as the lawyer heroine discovers her sensuality and poses as a "ghost" come back to help young lovers. Then in the third act it become a hyper-paranoid political-conspiracy assassination-o-rama. Pretty weird junk. 90m/C VHS. *CA* Tracy Scoggins, Marc Singer, Brion James; **D:** Lloyd A. Simandl.

Beyond the Stars 🎬 1989 A sci-fi adventure directed by the author of "Cocoon," wherein a whiz-kid investigates the NASA cover-up of a deadly accident that occurred on the moon during the Apollo 11 landing. Unfortunately, the interesting cast can't make up for the script. 94m/C VHS, DVD. Martin Sheen, Christian Slater, Olivia D'Abo, F. Murray Abraham, Robert Foxworth, Sharon Stone; **D:** David Saperstein.

Bhaji on the Beach 🎬🎬½ 1994 (R) Amusing comedy-drama about a group of Indian women who organize a bus outing from Birmingham to the seaside resort town of Blackpool. They range from sari-clad elders to feminist Gen Xers and a couple of teenagers looking for romance. There's bonding and gossiping and secrets galore before the story is tidily wrapped up. 100m/C VHS. *GB* Kim Vithana, Jimmi Harkishin, Sarita Khajuria, Mo Sesay, Lalita Ahmad, Shaheen Khan, Zohra Sehgal; **D:** Gurinder Chadha; **W:** Meera Syal, Gurinder Chadha; **C:** John Kenway; **M:** John Altman, Craig Pruess.

Bhowani Junction 🎬🎬 1956 A half-Indian, half-English woman is torn between her country and the British officer she loves in post-colonial India. Great cinematography. Based on a book by John Masters. 110m/C VHS. Ava Gardner, Stewart Granger, Bill Travers, Abraham Sofaer, Francis Matthews, Marne Maitland, Peter Illing, Edward Chapman, Freda Jackson, Lionel Jeffries; **D:** George Cukor; **W:** Ivan Moffat; **M:** Miklos Rozsa.

Beyond Therapy 🎬½ 1986 (R) A satire on modern psychotherapy, from the play by Christopher Durang, about a confused, crazily neurotic couple and their respective, and not any saner, analysts. Unfortunately, comes off as disjointed and confused. 93m/C VHS, DVD. Jeff Goldblum, Tom Conti, Julie Hagerty, Glenda Jackson, Christopher Guest; **D:** Robert Altman; **W:** Christopher Durang, Robert Altman.

Beyond the Walls 🎬🎬 *Mea chorai Hasragim* 1984 (R) The opposing factions of a hellish Israeli prison unite to beat the system. Brutal with good characterizations. Available in both subtitled and dubbed versions. 104m/C VHS. *IS* Arnon Zadok, Muhamad Bakri; **D:** Uri Barbash; **W:** Benny Barbash. Venice Film Fest. '85. Film.

Beyond the Wall of Sleep 🎬 *H.P. Lovecraft's Beyond the Wall of Sleep* 2006 (R) Ponderous, repetitive (and loose) adaptation of a Lovecraft story. In 1908, in New York's Catskill Mountains, deformed Joe Slaader (Sanderson) is institutionalized. The Ulster County Asylum after murdering his family. But with Joe's arrival come sinister forces that seemingly infect the inmates and they begin to take over the madhouse. 84m/C DVD. *US* William Sanderson, Tom Sevini, Rick Dial, Fountain Yount; **D:** Barrett J. Leigh, Tom Maurer; **W:** Barrett J. Leigh, Tom Maurer; **C:** Bill Burton; **M:** Kaveh Cohen.

VIDEO

Beyond the Valley of the Dolls 🎬🎬½ *Hollywood Vixens* 1970 (NC-17) Sleazy, spirited non-sequel to "Valley of the Dolls." Meyer ("Faster, Pussycat! Kill Kill!") directed this Hollywood parody ("BVD," as it came to be known) about an all-girl rock combo and their search for stardom. Labeled the first "exploitation horror camp musical"—how can you pass that up? Screenplay by film critic Ebert, from an original story by Ebert and Meyer. Mondo trasho. 109m/C VHS, DVD. Dolly Reed, Cynthia Myers, Marcia McBroom, Gavin, Edy Williams, Phyllis E. Davis, Harrison Page, Duncan McLeod, James Iglehart, Charles Napier, Haji, Pam Grier, Russ Meyer; **W:** Roger Ebert; **C:** Fred W. Koenekamp; **M:** The Strawberry Alarm Clock, Stu Phillips.

Beyond Tomorrow 🎬🎬 1940 Young romance is guided from the spirit world during the Christmas season, as two "ghosts" come back to help young lovers. 84m/B VHS, DVD. Richard Carlson, Sir C. Aubrey Smith, Jean Parker, Charles Winninger, Harry Carey Sr., Maria Ouspenskaya, Rod La Rocque; **D:** Edward Sutherland; **W:** Adele Comandini; **C:** Lester White.

Big 🎬🎬🎬½ 1988 (PG) 13-year-old Josh makes a wish at a carnival fortuneteller to be "big." When he wakes up the next morning he finds that he suddenly won't fit into his clothes and his mother doesn't recognize him. Until he finds a cure, he must learn to live in the adult world—complete with job (in a toy firm), world-class apartment, and romance. Perhaps it is wonderful as a cynical fellow employee who warms to the overgrown kid while Hanks is totally believable as the little boy inside a man's body. Marshal directs with authority and the whole thing clicks from the beginning. 98m/C VHS, DVD. Tom Hanks, Elizabeth Perkins, John Heard, Robert Loggia, Jared Rushton, David Moscow, Jon

Beyond the Trail 🎬🎬 1926 One of Bill Patton's most entertaining and funny films. In this comedic Western adventure he must face Black Mike and his gang and rescue Mary from their clutches. 50m/C VHS, Billy) (William Patton) Patton, Shelton Lewis, Stuart Holmes, Eric Wayne, Janet Dawn, Clare Horton, James F. Fulton; **D:** A(lbert) Herman.

The Bible and Gun Club 🎬🎬 1996 Four-mouthed look at the wasted lives of five middle age traveling salesmen who sell, you guessed it, bibles and guns. There's a turf war between the Anaheim, CA and the Las Vegas branches of the club; there's a sales convention, the salesmen try to sell their goods to the real-life denizens of a poor trailer park, there's a porn shoot. There's a number of shootouts and to say the least, the salesmen are not politically correct—they're racist, sexist losers. It's depressing and disturbing and highlighted by some spot-on acting. Harris' debut feature. 67m/B VHS. Andy Kalok, Don Yanan, Julian Ott, Al Schueman, Robert Blumenthal; **D:** Daniel J. Harris; **W:** Daniel J. Harris; **C:** Alex Vendler; **M:** Shawn Patterson.

Bicentennial Man 🎬🎬½ 1999 (PG) Robin Williams is Andrew, a domestic robot of the near-future. When he's purchased by the Martin family, they notice that he's different than most robots. He exhibits compassion, as well as other human qualities. Led by Sir, the father (Neill) they help to further Andrew's growth. As time goes on, Andrew continues to develop past his programming, and eventually seeks his freedom and the pursuit of a more human form. The first hour deals mostly with a very leisurely character development, with some amusing moments. The problems occur when the film turns to the serious question's of immortality, defining humanity, and the rights of artificial entities. Director Columbus opts for sentiment and empty platitudes instead of exploring the questions the film raises. 131m/C VHS, DVD. Robin Williams, Embeth Davidtz, Sam Neill, Wendy Crewson, Hallie Kate Eisenberg, Oliver Platt, Stephen (Steve) Root, Lynne Thigpen, Bradley Whitford, Kiersten Warren, John Michael Higgins, George D. Wallace; **D:** Chris Columbus; **W:** Nicholas Kazan; **C:** Phil Meheux; **M:** James Horner.

Bickford Shmeckler's Cool Ideas 🎬🎬 2006 (R) 80m/C DVD. Patrick Fugit, Olivia Wilde, John Cho, Matthew Lillard, Cheryl Hines; **D:** Scott Lew; **W:** Scott Lew; **C:** Lowell Peterson; **M:** John Swihart. **VIDEO**

The Bicycle Thief 🎬🎬🎬🎬 *Ladri di Biciclette* 1948 A world classic and indisputable masterpiece about an Italian workman who finds a job, only to have the bike he needs for work stolen; his and his son search Rome for it. A simple story that seems to contain the whole of human experience, and the masterpiece of Italian neo-realism. Based on the book by Luigi Bartolini. In Italian with English subtitles. 90m/B VHS, DVD. *IT* Lamberto Maggiorani, Lianella Carell, Enzo Staiola, Elena Altieri, Vittorio Antonucci, Gino Saltamerenda, Fausto Guerzoni; **D:** Vittorio De Sica; **W:** Vittorio De Sica, Cesare Zavattini; **C:** Carlo Montuori; **M:** Alessandro Cicognini. Oscars '49: Foreign Film; British Acad. '49: Film; Golden Globes '50: Foreign Film; Natl. Bd. of Review '49: Director (De Sica); N.Y. Film Critics '49: Foreign Film.

The Bible 🎬 1966 Bloated, even by religious epic standards, Huston's drama covers the first 22 chapters of Genesis. So you get the Creation, Adam and Eve, Noah and the ark, the flood, the Tower of Babel, and Abraham, among other would-be spectacles. 174m/C VHS, DVD. Michael Parks, Ulla Bergryd, Richard Harris, Stephen Boyd, George C. Scott, Ava Gardner, Peter O'Toole, Franco Nero, John Huston; **D:** John Huston; **W:** Christopher Fry, Vittorio Bonicelli; **C:** Giuseppe Rotunno; **M:** Toshiro Mayuzumi; **Nar:** John Huston.

Lovitz, Mercedes Ruehl; **D:** Penny Marshall; **W:** Gary Ross; **C:** Michael Ballhaus; *Golden Globes '88: Actor—Mus/Comedy (Hanks); L.A. Film Critics '88: Actor (Hanks).*

Big and Hairy 🐾🐾½ **1998** When Picasso Dewlap and his family move from Chicago to a small town, the kid has trouble making friends (no wonder with that name). Then he joins the school basketball team. However, Picasso sucks. But after he meets a teen bigfoot (nicknamed Ed) who just happens to be a natural at hoops, Picasso and his hairy friend become team heroes. Based on the book by Brian Daly. **94m/C VHS, DVD.** Richard Thomas, Donnelly Rhodes, Robert Karl Burke, Trevor Jones, Chilton Crane; **D:** Philip Spink; **C:** Peter Benison; **M:** Daryl Bennett, Jim Guttridge. **CABLE**

Big Bad John 🐾🐾½ **1990 (PG-13)** Some good ol' boys ride around in trucks as they get into a variety of shootouts. The soundtrack includes music by Willie Nelson, The Charlie Daniels Band, and others. **91m/C VHS, DVD.** Jimmy Dean, Ned Beatty, Jack Elam, Bo Hopkins, Romy Windsor, Doug English, John Dennis Johnston, Anne Lockhart, Jeffery Osterhage, Jerry Potter, Red Steagall; **D:** Burt Kennedy; **W:** Joseph Berry; **C:** Ken Lamkin; **M:** Ken Sutherland.

Big Bad Love 🐾🐾 **2002 (R)** Howard's ambitious directorial debut is an adaptation of the short stories of Larry Brown. Vietnam vet and would-be writer Leon Barlow's (Howard), obsession with writing about his constant melancholy and getting his stories published alienates him from everything around him, especially his family, which includes his terminally ill daughter. He seems to get away with his behavior through his wry wit and some past misfortunes. Howard gives in to his most poetic and literary impulses, which results in some breathtaking scenes alongside some annoyingly self-indulgent ones. Not surprisingly, film is uneven, with some quality performances lifting the proceedings. **111m/C VHS, DVD.** Arliss Howard, Debra Winger, Paul LeMat, Angie Dickinson, Rosanna Arquette, Michael Parks; **D:** Arliss Howard; **W:** Arliss Howard; **C:** Paul Ryan; **M:** Tom Waits; **V:** Sigourney Weaver.

Big Bad Mama 2 🐾🐾½ **1987** Belated Depression-era sequel to the 1974 Roger Corman gangster film, where the pistol-packin' matriarch battles a crooked politician with the help of her two daughters. **85m/C VHS, DVD.** Angie Dickinson, Robert Culp, Danielle Brisebois, Julie McCullough, Bruce Glover, Jeff Yagher, Jacque Lynn Colton, Ebbe Roe Smith, Charles Cyphers; **D:** Jim Wynorski; **W:** Jim Wynorski, R.J. Robertson; **C:** Robert New; **M:** Chuck Cirino.

The Big Bad Swim 🐾🐾½ **2006** Needing some stress relief from work and marital problems, Amy (Brewster) decides to join an adult swim class held at a local community center. In a mixed and quirky group, Amy befriends Jordan (Weixler), a croupier and part-time stripper who has the hots for their hunky-but-insecure instructor Noah (Branson). Sharp comedy that focuses on characters rather than situations. **93m/C VHS, DVD.** Paget Brewster, Joanna Adler, Jeff Branson, Jess Weixler, Grant Aleksander, Ricky Ullman, Avi Setton, Todd Sussman, Michael Mosley; **D:** Ishai Setton; **W:** Daniel Schechter; **C:** Josh Silfen; **M:** Chad Kelly. **VIDEO**

Big Bear 🐾🐾½ **1998** In the 1880s Chief Big Bear (Tootoosis) refuses to surrender Cree ancestral lands to settlers for fear of the many broken promises made by the government. So Canadian army

---

troops surround the Cree in order to starve them into submission. Cree warriors decide to stage an attack against the settlers that only brings the troops down on them. **190m/C VHS, DVD. CA** Tantoo Cardinal, Gordon Tootoosis, Ken Charlette; **D:** Gil Cardinal. **TV**

The Big Bet 🐾🐾 **1985 (R)** High school sex comedy about a guy who is challenged by the school bully to get the gorgeous new girl into bed. Energetic romp is for adults. **90m/C VHS.** Sylvia Kristel, Kimberly Evenson, Ron Thomas; **D:** Bert I. Gordon.

The Big Bird Cage 🐾🐾 *Women's Penitentiary 2* **1972 (R)** Prison spoof sequel to "The Big Doll House." Horny females incarcerated in a rural jail decide to defy their homosexual guards and plan an escape. They are aided by revolutionaries led by a Brooklynese expatriate and his lover. **93m/C VHS, DVD.** Pam Grier, Sid Haig, Anitra Ford, Candice Roman, Teda Bracci, Carol Speed, Karen McKevic, Vic Diaz; **D:** Jack Hill; **W:** Jack Hill; **C:** Felipe Sacdalan; **M:** William Allen Castleman, William Loose.

The Big Blue 🐾🐾½ *Le Grand Bleu* **1988 (PG)** Vapid, semi-true tale about competing free-divers, who makes friends love, but when she surprisingly recovers, her new husband decides to help her back along the path to death. Uneven and melodramatic. **70m/B VHS. SI** John Bromfield, Martha Vickers, Robert Hutton, Rosemary Bowe; **D:** W. Lee Wilder.

Big Bluff 🐾🐾 *Worthy Deceivers* **1955** Disappointing result from an interesting premise; fatally ill woman finds love, but when she surprisingly recovers, her new husband decides to help her back along the path to death. Uneven and melodramatic. **70m/B VHS. SI** John Bromfield, Martha Vickers, Robert Hutton, Rosemary Bowe; **D:** W. Lee Wilder.

Big Boss 🐾½ *Mr. Scarface* **1977 (R)** A hoodlum climbs to the top of a crime syndicate. An Italian film previously titled "Mr. Scarface." **90m/C DVD. IT** Jack Palance, Edmund Purdum, Al Cliver, Harry Baer, Gisela Hahn; **D:** Fernando Di Leo.

The Big Bounce 🐾🐾 **1969 (R)** First adaptation of Elmore Leonard's first crime novel after years of westerns is also Ryan O'Neal's first shot at leading man status. O'Neal shows his inexperience as well as glimpses of the boxoffice star he would become as Jack Ryan (not the CIA guy), a drifter who gets mixed up with dangerous woman Nancy (Taylor-Young, also very early in her career) and her plot to swindle her married lover, who happens to be his boss. Doesn't have the spark of Leonard's later crime capers, and the flat direction, disappointing finale, and overwhelming music don't help. But the obvious chemistry between O'Neal and Taylor-Young heats up the screen. **102m/C DVD.** Ryan O'Neal, Leigh Taylor-Young, Van Heflin, Lee Grant, James Daly, Robert Webber, Cynthia Elibacher, Noam Pitlik; **D:** Alex March; **W:** Robert Dozier; **C:** Howard Schwartz; **M:** Michael Curb.

The Big Bounce 🐾🐾 **2004 (PG-13)** Second adaptation of Elmore Leonard's first crime novel. Owen Wilson plays Jack Ryan, a small time hood who gets mixed up with Ray Ritchie, a crooked developer. Meanwhile, Ritchie's mistress Nancy (Foster) wants Ryan to steal $200,000 from Ritchie. Of course, double-crosses and deceptions ensue. Tends to meander about and lose focus, but it's somewhat enjoyable if you don't think too hard. Disappointing, considering the solid cast and the source material. **89m/C DVD. US** Owen Wilson, Morgan Freeman, Gary Sinise, Vinnie Jones, Sara Foster, Willie Nelson, Bebe Neuwirth, Charlie Sheen, Harry Dean Stanton, Andrew Wilmitage; **W:** Sebastian Gutierrez; **D:** George Armitage; **W:** George S. Clinton.

The Big Brass Ring 🐾🐾½ **1999 (R)** Murky political drama based on an unproduced screenplay by Orson Welles. Ambitious William Blake Pellarin (Hurt) is a candidate for governor of Mis-

---

souri but his ultimate goal is the presidency. However, an ugly scandal threatens his campaign, thanks to the appearance of Dr. Kimball Mennaker (Hawthorne), who's a little too close to the Pellarin family and knows about some skeletons even William isn't aware of. **104m/C VHS, DVD.** William Hurt, Nigel Hawthorne, Miranda Richardson, Irene Jacob, Jefferson Mays, Ewan Stewart, Ron Livingston, Gregg Henry; **D:** George Hickenlooper; **W:** George Hickenlooper, F.X. Feeney; **C:** Kramer Morgenthau; **M:** Thomas Morse.

The Big Brawl 🐾🐾½ **1980 (R)** Chicago gangster recruits a martial arts expert to fight in a free-for-all match in Texas. **95m/C VHS, DVD.** Jackie Chan, Jose Ferrer, Mako, Rosalind Chao; **D:** Robert Clouse; **W:** Robert Clouse; **M:** Lalo Schifrin.

The Big Broadcast of 1938 🐾½ **1938** Fields is the owner of an ocean liner which he enters in a race. Supposedly, the ship can convert the electricity from radio broadcasts into power for the propellers. No, it doesn't make sense, as it's just an excuse for various radio stars to show off their routines in the ship's entertainment room. Hope, in his first feature, gets to sing his Oscar-winning signature tune "Thanks for the Memories." **94m/B VHS, DVD.** W.C. Fields, Martha Raye, Dorothy Lamour, Shirley Ross, Russell Hicks, Bob Hope, Ben Blue, Leif Erickson; **D:** Mitchell Leisen; **W:** Walter DeLeon, Francis Martin; **C:** Harry Fischbeck; **M:** Boris Morros, Ralph Rainger, Leo Robin. *Oscars '38: Song ("Thanks for the Memories").*

Big Brother Trouble 🐾🐾½ **2000 (G)** Mitch (Suchenek) has always lived in the shadow of his big brother Sean (Hart), who's the star of the soccer team. But it's Mitch to the rescue when Sean is kidnapped to insure that his team loses the City Championship game. **88m/C VHS, DVD.** Michael Suchenek, Shad Hart, Lindsay Brooke, Mario Lopez, Bo Hopkins, Dick Van Patten; **D:** Ralph Portillo; **W:** Jeff Nimoy, Seth Walther; **C:** John Huneck; **M:** Steven Stern.

Big Brown Eyes 🐾🐾 **1936** Wisecracking hotel manicurist Eve (Bennett) is in love with detective Danny Barr (Grant). When Eve loses her job, she suddenly gets a new one working as a reporter and goes off to scope out a murder, which gets her in hot water. There's a lot of screwball complications, and the convoluted plot (which also involves a jewel heist) never does make much sense. **77m/B DVD.** Cary Grant, Joan Bennett, Walter Pidgeon, Lloyd Nolan, Alan Baxter, Marjorie Gateson, Isabel Jewell, Douglas Fowley, Henry (Kleinbach) Brandon; **D:** Raoul Walsh; **W:** Raoul Walsh, Bert Hanlon; **C:** George T. Clemens.

Big Bully 🐾🐾 **1995 (PG)** David Leary (Moranis) is an aspiring novelist who moves back to the town where he was picked on as a kid. His son immediately starts bullying a smaller child, whose father happens to be Roscoe "Fang" Bigger (Arnold), David's former tormentor. The timid hen-pecked Roscoe's sadistic streak is awakened with the reappearance of his old prey, leading to a barrage of wet willies and indian burns. The slapstick quickly escalates to danger before all is tied up in a syrupy sweet ending. With Moranis playing the nerdy bespectacled underdog and Arnold playing the loud obnoxious guy (although that might not be acting), it may be time to call the typecast acting cops. Don Knotts (looking very un-Barney-like) makes an appearance as the high school principal. **93m/C VHS, DVD.** Tom Arnold, Rick Moranis, Julianne Phillips, Don Knotts, Carol Kane, Jeffrey Tambor, Curtis Armstrong, Faith Prince, Tony Pierce, Blake Bashoff; **D:** Steve Miner; **W:** Mark Steven Johnson; **C:** Daryn Okada; **M:** David Newman. *Golden Raspberries '96: Worst Actor (Arnold).*

The Big Bus 🐾🐾 **1976 (PG)** The wild adventures of the world's first nuclear-powered bus as it makes its maiden voyage from New York to Denver. Clumsy disaster-movie parody. **88m/C VHS, DVD.** Joseph Bologna, Stockard Channing, Ned Beatty, Ruth Gordon, Larry Hagman, John Beck, Jose Ferrer, Lynn Redgrave, Sally Kellerman, Stuart Margolin, Richard Mulligan, Howard Hesseman, Richard B. Shull, Rene Auberjonois, Bob (Robert) Dishy, Vic Tayback, Murphy Dunne; **D:** James

---

Frawley; **W:** Lawrence J. Cohen, Fred Freeman; **C:** Harry Stradling Jr.; **M:** David Shire.

Big Business 🐾🐾 **1988 (PG)** Strained high-concept comedy about two sets of identical twins, each played by Tomlin and Midler, mismatched at birth by a near-sighted country nurse. The city set of twins intends to buy out the factory where the country set of twins work. So the country twins march up to the big city to stop the sale and destruction of their beloved home. Both set of twins stay in the Plaza Hotel and zany consequences ensue. Essentially a one-joke outing with some funny moments, but talented comediennes Midler and Tomlin are somewhat wasted. Great technical effects. **98m/C VHS, DVD.** Bette Midler, Lily Tomlin, Fred Ward, Edward Herrmann, Michele Placido, Barry Primus, Michael Gross, Mary Gross, Daniel Gerroll, Roy Brocksmith; **D:** Jim Abrahams; **C:** Dean Cundey.

Big Business Girl 🐾 **1931** Less than remarkable comedy starring Young as a corporate climber who must dodge her boss' advances and save her troubled marriage when her jazz singer husband is called away to perform in Paris. Based on a story by Patricia Reilly and Harold N. Swanson. **72m/B VHS.** Loretta Young, Frank Albertson, Ricardo Cortez, Joan Blondell, Dorothy Christy; **D:** William A. Seiter; **W:** Robert Lord.

The Big Bust Out WOOF! **1973 (R)** Several female convicts escape from prison only to be sold into slavery and face additional torture. Nothing redeeming about this exploitative film. **75m/C VHS.** Vonetta McGee, Monica Taylor, Linda Fox, Karen Carter, Gordon Mitchell; **D:** Karen Carter.

Big Calibre 🐾 **1935** A rancher is inches away from being lynched for his dad's murder before he is found to be innocent. **59m/B VHS.** Bob Steele, Bill Quinn, Earl Dwire, Peggy Campbell, John Elliott, Georgia O'Dell; **D:** Robert North Bradbury.

The Big Cat 🐾🐾 **1949** Mountain valley in Utah is ravaged by a cougar, while two ranchers fuss and feud. Big cat, bickering, help make okay adventure. **75m/C VHS, DVD.** Lon (Bud) McCallister, Peggy Ann Garner, Preston Foster, Forrest Tucker; **D:** Phil Karlson; **C:** William Howard Greene.

Big Chase 🐾 **1954** A rookie cop chases down a mob of payroll thieves in this early action film. **60m/B VHS.** Glenn Langan, Adele Jergens, Douglas Kennedy, Jim Davis, Jack Daly, Phil Arnold, Wheaton Chambers, Lon Chaney Jr.; **D:** Arthur Hilton; **W:** Fred Freiberger.

The Big Chill 🐾🐾🐾½ **1983 (R)** Seven former '60s radicals, now coming upon middle age and middle-class affluence, reunite following an eighth friend's suicide and use the occasion to re-examine their past relationships and commitments. A beautifully acted, immensely enjoyable ballad to both the counter-culture and its Yuppie descendants. Great period music. Kevin Costner is the dead man whose scenes never made it to the big screen. **108m/C VHS, DVD.** Tom Berenger, Glenn Close, Jeff Goldblum, William Hurt, Kevin Kline, Mary Kay Place, Meg Tilly, JoBeth Williams; **D:** Lawrence Kasdan; **W:** Lawrence Kasdan, Barbara Benedek; **C:** John Bailey. *Writers Guild '83: Orig. Screenplay.*

The Big City 🐾🐾 *Mahanagar* **1963** When debts threaten to overwhelm the Mazumdar family, Arati does the unthinkable and gets a job as a saleswoman. She soon begins to realize she not only likes to work but enjoys the freedom and respect her job brings. Bengali with subtitles. **131m/B VHS. IN** Anil Chatterjee, Madhabi Mukherjee, Vicky Redwood, Haren Chatterjee; **D:** Satyajit Ray; **W:** Satyajit Ray; **C:** Subrata Mitra; **M:** Satyajit Ray.

Big City Blues 🐾🐾 **1999 (R)** One long night in the lives of hit men Connor (Reynolds) and Hudson (Forsythe) as they get mixed up with the plans of a hooker (Cates). **94m/C VHS, DVD.** Burt Reynolds, William Forsythe, Georgina Cates, Giancarlo Esposito, Roger Floyd, Balthazar Getty, Arye Gross, Donovan Leitch, Roxana Zal, Amy Lyndon, Jad Mager; **D:** Clive Fleury; **W:** Clive Fleury; **C:** David Bridges; **M:** Tomas San Miguel.

The Big Clock 1948 George Stroud (Milland) is the editor of the successful Crimeways magazine, owned by tyrannical publisher Earl Janoth (Laughton). Forced to miss a vacation with his wife Georgette (O'Sullivan), George winds up spending time with lovely Pauline (Johnson) whom he inadvertently discovers is the boss' mistress. Pauline's murdered and George is quick to realize all the clues are deliberately pointed in his direction. Classic crime melodrama adapted from Kenneth Fearing's novel. Remade as "No Way Out" (1987). 95m/B VHS, DVD. Ray Milland, Charles Laughton, Maureen O'Sullivan, George Macready, Rita Johnson, Dan Tobin, Elsa Lanchester, Harry (Henry) Morgan; D: John Farrow; W: Jonathan Latimer; C: John Seitz; M: Victor Young.

Big Deadly Game 1954 A vacationing American gets caught up in a complicated wartime espionage plot by helping in a mysterious buddy. 63m/B VHS.

Big Combo 1955 A gangster's ex-girlfriend helps a cop to smash a crime syndicate. Focuses on the relationship between Wilde's cop and the gangster Conte in an effective film noir, with scenes of torture that were ahead of their time. 87m/B VHS, DVD. Cornel Wilde, Richard Conte, Jean Wallace, Brian Donlevy, Earl Holliman, Lee Van Cleef, Helen Walker; D: Joseph H. Lewis; W: Philip Yordan; C: John Alton; M: David Raksin.

The Big Country 1958 (R) Ex-sea captain Peck heads west to marry fiancée Baker and live on her father's (Bickford) ranch. Peck immediately clashes with ranch foreman Heston and finds out there's a vicious feud with neighbor Ives. Then Peck decides he and Baker aren't meant to be and he falls for schoolmarm Simmons instead. It's too long but if you like sprawling western sagas, this one has its moments. 166m/C VHS, DVD. Gregory Peck, Charlton Heston, Burl Ives, Jean Simmons, Carroll Baker, Chuck Connors, Charles Bickford; D: William Wyler; W: Jessamyn West, Robert Wilder; C: James R. Webb; M: Jerome Moross. Oscars '58: Support. Actor (Ives); Golden Globes '59: Support. Actor (Ives).

The Big Crimewave 1986 A cast of unknowns in a comedy about a loner who takes a bus to Kansas City (Kansas City?) to become a screenwriter, with comic adventures along the way. A feast of jabs at genre films. 80m/C V-IS, CA. John Paizs, Eva Covacs, Darrel Baran; D: John Paizs.

Big Daddy 1999 (PG-13) Critic-proof film for Sandler's fans—the rest won't find anything to tempt them. He's 32-year-old slacker law-school grad Sonny Koufax, who's got a big Peter Pan complex, since he's incapable of assuming any adult responsibility. However, he decides to go for the "awww" factor by becoming the guardian of his travelling-in-China roommate Kevin's (Stewart) heretofore unknown son, five-year-old Julian (Sprouse). He teaches the kid a number of disgusting traits and winds up bonding with the tyke (they have the same emotional IQ—how hard can it be?). 95m/C VHS, DVD, UMD. Adam Sandler, Joey Lauren Adams, Jon Stewart, Leslie Mann, Josh Mostel, Rob Schneider, Kristy Swanson, Joseph Bologna, Steve Buscemi; D: Dennis Dugan; W: Steve Franks, Tim Herlihy, Adam Sandler; C: Theo van de Sande, M: Teddy Castellucci. MTV Movie Awards '99: Comedic Perf. (Sandler); Golden Raspberries '99: Worst Actor (Sandler).

The Big Day 1999 (R) We Met on the Vineyard 1999 (R) Sara (Margulies) is supposed to be getting married. She shows up at the church but groom John (Sergei) is a no-show after his knucklehead brother Zack (Fohner) confesses to an indiscretion that leaves John "with big doubts about the marriage timing. So the family starts to panic and it's chaos everywhere you go. 86m/C VHS, DVD. Julianna Margulies, Ivan Sergei, Clayton Rohner, Dixie Carter, Kevin Tighe, Adrian Pasdar, Kathleen York, Andrew Buckley, Nancy Banks; D: Ian McCrudden; W: Andrew Buckley; C: Tony Cucchiari.

Lloyd Bridges, Simone Silva, Finlay Currie; D: Daniel Birt.

Big Deal on Madonna Street 1958 The Usual Unidentified Thieves / I Soliti ignoti; Persons Unknown 1958 Vittorio Gassman, Claudia Cardinale, Renato Salvatori, Memmo Carotenuto, Toto, Rosanna Rory; D: Mario Monicelli; W: Mario Monicelli, Furio Scarpelli, Suso Cecchi D'Amico; C: Gianni Di Venanzo; M: Pierro Umiliani.

The Big Dis 1989 An interracial comedy about a young black soldier on a weekend pass who's looking for a willing sexual partner. His confidence is shattered when 12 possibilities turn him down. Feature debut of Eriksen and O'Brien. 83m/B VHS, DVD. Gordon Eriksen, Heather Johnson, James Haig, Monica Sparrow; D: Gordon Eriksen, John O'Brien; W: Gordon Eriksen, John O'Brien; C: John O'Brien.

The Big Doll House 1971 (R) Women in Cages; Bamboo Dolls House 1971 (R) Roger Corman-produced prison drama about a group of tormented female convicts who decide to break out. Features vintage Grier, and a caliber of women's-prison sleaziness that isn't equalled in today's films. 93m/C VHS. Judy (Judith) Brown, Roberta Collins, Pam Grier, Brooke Mills, Patricia Woodell, Sid Haig, Christiane Schmidtmer, Kathryn Loder, Jerry Frank, Charles Davis; D: Les Baxter; W: Don Spencer; C: Fred Conde; M: Les Baxter.

VIDEO

The Big Fall 1996 (R) L.A. private investigator Blaize Rybeck (Howell) is hired by mystery babe Emma (Ward) to find her brother, Kenny, a pilot. Blaize meets some of Kenny's thrill-seeking friends at the airfield and draws the suspicious interest of FBI agent Wilcox (Applegate). Seems Kenny was mixed up in some shady dealings that get both his sister and her nosy P.I. into trouble. 94m/C VHS, DVD. C: Thomas Howell, Sophie Ward, Jeff Kober, Justin Lazard, Titus Welliver, William Applegate Jr.; C: Thomas Howell; W: William Applegate Jr.; M: Jurgen Baum.

Big Fat Liar 2002 (PG) The boy who cried wolf goes to Hollywood in search of Marty Wolf (Giamatti), the unscrupulous movie producer who stole his short story. As nobody believes his far-out tale of being ripped off by Hollywood, no-torious liar Jason Shepherd (Muniz) also makes sure to bring along a witness to his pursuit, in the form of his friend Kaylee (Bynes). Pulling an array of inspired pranks, the teens zestfully set about dismantling the sanity of Wolf, to the delight, and sometimes with the aid of, some of his many enemies. Talented small-screen star Muniz and his co-star Bynes make this a likeable, though not especially inspired, broad comedy with Giamatti mugging up a storm. Their romp through Universal Studios, especially, lets you know who's really behind this mostly entertaining movie for the pre-teen set. 87m/C VHS. US Frankie Muniz, Paul Giamatti, Amanda Bynes, Amanda Detmer, Donald Adeosun Faison, Lee Majors, Sandra Oh, Russell Hornsby, Chris French; D: Shawn Levy; W: Dan Schneider; C: Jonathan Brown.

man, Missi Pyle, Matthew McGrory, Loudon Wainwright III; D: Tim Burton; W: John August; C: Philippe Rousselot; M: Danny Elfman.

The Big Fix 1978 (PG) Private investigator Moses Wine himself in an ironic situation: searching for a fugitive alongside whom he'd protested in the 60s. Based on or a Roger Simon novel to include the horror. 108m/C VHS, Richard Dreyfuss, Susan Anspach, Bonnie Bedelia, John Lithgow, F. Murray Abraham, Fritz Weaver, Mandy Patinkin; D: Jeremy Paul Kagan; M: Bill Conti.

Big Foot 1972 WOOF! Even genre devotees will be disappointed with this one. Sasquatch, who has procreation on his mind, searches after another human mate. A horror flick that forgot to be scary. 92m/C VHS, Chris Mitchum, Joi Lansing, John Carradine, John Mitchell; D: Bob Slatzer.

The Big Easy 1987 (R) A terrific thriller. Slick New Orleans detective Remy McSwain (Quaid, oozing charm and a combal accent) uncovers a heroin-based mob war while romancing uptight assistant DA Anne Osborne (Barkin, all banked fire) who's investigating corruption on the police force. An easy, Cajun-flavored mystery, a fast-moving action-comedy, a very sexy romance, and a serious exploration of the dynamics of corruption. 101m/C VHS, DVD. Dennis Quaid, Ellen Barkin, Ned Beatty, John Goodman, Ebbe Roe Smith, Charles Ludlam, Lisa Jane Persky, Tom O'Brien, Grace Zabriskie, Marc Lawrence; D: Jim McBride; W: Daniel Petrie Jr.; C: Alfonso Beato; M: Brad Fiedel. Ind. Spirit '88: Actor (Quaid).

Big Eden 2000 (PG-13) Sweet-natured gay romance says you can go home again. Henry Hart (Gross) is an artist, living in New York, who returns to the small Montana town of Big Eden when his grandfather Sam (Coe) has a stroke. Henry has never admitted to anyone in his hometown that he's gay although it's pretty clear to his quirky neighbors, including the guys who hang out at the post office/general store, which is run by shy Native American Pike Dexter (Schweig), who will display some hidden talents on Henry's behalf. Henry is thrilled to discover his first crush, Dean (DeKay), is also back in town but he's looking for love in the wrong person. A happy ending is a comforting thing. 118m/C VHS, DVD. Arye Gross, Eric Schweig, George Coe, Tim DeKay, Louise Fletcher, Nan Martin, O'Neal Compton, Corinne Bohrer, Veanne Cox; D: Thomas Bezucha; W: Thomas Bezucha; C: Rob Sweeney; M: Joseph Conlan.

The Big Empty 1998 Lloyd Matthews (writer McManus) is a private eye who's burned out on divorce work when he's hired by a suspicious wife (Goldwasser) to find the truth about her too-good-to-be true husband (Bryant). Comparisons to Coppola's "The Conversation" are not out of place. This one's a solid sleeper. 93m/C VHS, DVD. Jon Favreau, Pablo Bryant, Ellen Goldwasser, H.M. Wynant; D: Jack Perez; W: Jack Perez; C: Shawn Maurer; M: Jean-Michael Michenaud.

The Big Empty 2004 (R) Struggling actor John Person accepts an offer to deliver a suitcase to a cowboy in a desert town for $25,000. Along the way he meets a wacky band of characters, including a bartender (Han-nah) and her nympho daughter (Cook), and space aliens. Solid cast who seem to be enjoying themselves, quirky and original story, and a great soundtrack add up to an entertaining time-waster. 94m/C VHS, DVD. Jon Favreau, Bud Cort, Daryl Hannah, Jon Gries, Kelsey Grammer, Rachael Leigh Cook, Joey Lauren Adams, Adam Beach, Melora Walters, Sean Bean, Danny Trejo, Gary Farmer, Brent Briscoe; D: Steve Anderson; W: Steve Anderson; M: Brian Tyler.

Big Fella 1937 Musical drama starring Robeson as Joe, a Marseilles dockworker (a familiar film occupation for the actor), who's asked by the police to help find a young boy (Grant) missing from an ocean liner. When Joe locates the boy, he discovers the child ran away from his wealthy family and doesn't want to return. Joe takes the boy to his cafe singer girlfriend, Miranda (Welch), and the two become his surrogate parents. Loose adaptation of the 1929 novel, "Banjo," by Claude McKay. Numbers: "Lazin'; Roll Up Sailorman; You Didn't Ought to Do Such Things; All God's Chillun Got a Robe; My Folks From Me. 73m/B VHS, DVD. GB Paul Robeson, Elisabeth Welch, Elton Grant; D: J. Elder Wills; W: Ingram D'Abbes, Fenn Sherie; C: Cyril Bristow; M: Eric Ansell.

Big Fish 2003 (PG-13) Burton's latest is right up his alley, as it's about a great storyteller prone to out-sized flights of fancy. Ed Bloom (Finney) is a man on his deathbed hoping to reconcile with the son (Crudup) he's alienated with the yarns he's spun about his life. When Will, who's become a journalist as a form of rebellion, returns and asks one last time for the truth, Ed again begins the familiar tall tale. This is where we learn of Ed's version of his courtship of wife Sandra, his battle with a huge catfish, his adventures with a giant in the circus, the Korean War, and an idyllic town where the residents seem content to walk around barefoot and happy. Burton is in his element with the flashback/yarn portion, but handles the delicate drama of the father-son scenes with aplomb as well. Cast is uniformly excellent, with Finney making the most of a largely sedentary role. Based on the novel by Daniel Wallace. 125m/C DVD, Blu-ray Disc. US Ewan McGregor, Albert Finney, Billy Crudup, Jessica Lange, Alison Lohman, Helena Bonham-Carter, Robert Guillaume, Steve Buscemi, Danny DeVito, Marion Cotillard, David Den-

Big Girls Don't Cry... They Get Even 1992 (PG) A teenage girl decides to run away from home after she's driven crazy by her eccentric new stepfamily. Comic confusion ensues as various family members set out to find her. Hackneyed script and annoying characters hinder this comedy. 96m/C VHS, DVD. Hillary Wolf, Griffin Dunne, Margaret Whitton, David Strathairn, Ben Savage, Adrienne Shelly, Patricia Kalember; D: Joan Micklin Silver.

The Big Green 1995 (PG) British teacher Anna Montgomery (D'Abo) blows into a small Texas town determined to give the deprived kiddies a boost of self-esteem. With help from the town sheriff (Guttenberg), Anna organizes a soccer team that's supposed to give the kids a reason to live. Problems abound when the star player disappears just before the face-off with the biggest, nastiest team in the league. Sound familiar? This is the soccer version of "The Bad News Bears," "The Little Giants," and "The Mighty Ducks." The formula is less successful in this case, but some mildly amusing moments and a few fresh performances from the kids offer mirror bright spots in this tired scenario. 100m/C VHS, DVD. Olivia D'Abo, Steve Guttenberg, Jay C. Sanders, John Terry, Chauncey Leopardi, Patrick Renna, David Hall; D: Holly Goldberg Sloan; C: Ralf Bode; M: Randy Edelman.

A Big Hand for the Little Lady 1966 Big Deal at Dodge City 1966 Fonda and Woodward, playing two West-headed country bumpkins, get involved in a card game in Laredo against high rollers Robards and McCarthy. Fonda risks their savings, finds himself stuck with a losing hand, and has a bit of heart trouble, that's where the little lady comes in. Fine performances and a nifty twist ending don't entirely compensate for the overly padded script (which evolved from a 48-minute TV play drafted by Sydney Carroll). 95m/C VHS. Henry Fonda, Joanne Woodward, Jason Robards Jr., Charles Bickford, Burgess Meredith, Kevin McCarthy; D: Fielder Cook; C: Lee Garmes.

The Big Hangover 1950 Odd story about a man whose allergy to alcohol makes him drunk at the most inopportune moments. Johnson stars as the attorney with the peculiar problem and Taylor plays the boss' daughter who helps him overcome the allergy. Good support-ing cast can't help its otherwise boring and predictable film. 82m/B VHS. Van Johnson, Elizabeth Taylor, Percy Waram, Fay Holden, Leon Ames, Edgar Buchanan, Selena Royle, Gene Lockhart; D: Norman Krasna; W: Norman Krasna; C: George J. Folsey.

The Big Heat 1953 When detective Ford's wife (played by Jocelyn Brando, sister of Marlon) is killed in an explosion meant for him, he pursues the gangsters behind it and uncovers a police scandal. His appetite is whetted after this discovery and he pursues the criminals even more vigorously with the help of gangster moll Grahame. Definitive film noir. 90m/B VHS, DVD. Glenn Ford, Lee

Marvin, Gloria Grahame, Jocelyn Brando, Alexander Scourby, Carolyn Jones; *D:* Fritz Lang; *W:* Sydney (Sidney) Boehm; *C:* Charles B(ryant) Larg Jr.

The Big Hit 1998 (R) Combustible mixture of extravagant stunts, cartoon violence, hip-hop soundtrack, and a colorful cast serve up an intermittently funny look at organized crime. When not executing their skills as ruthless hitmen, Melvin, Cisco, Vince, and Crunch (Wahlberg, Phillips, Sabato, Jr., and Woodbine) are regular working Joes with regular problems. For Melvin, financial and female problems force him to partner with Cisco in the kidnapping of a Chinese heiress. Said heiress turns out to be the goddaughter of their own crime boss. Much hilarity ensues. Phillips brings gusto to his flamboyant homeboy character and Wahlberg is his equal as the sappy gun for hire with a heart of gold. Big plot holes make you not care so much. American directorial debut of Hong Kong import Che-Kirk Wong. **91m/C VHS, DVD, Blu-ray Disc, UMD.** Mark Wahlberg, Lou Diamond Phillips, Bokeem Woodbine, Antonio Sabato Jr., Christina Applegate, Avery Brooks, China Chow, Lainie Kaza, Elliott Gould, Lela Rochon, Sab Shimono; *D:* Kirk Wong; *W:* Ben Ramsey; *C:* Danny Nowak; *M:* Graeme Revell.

The Big House 1930 Prison melodrama at its best follows top con Beery as he plans a big breakout—and s betrayed. Life in the pen is depicted as brutal and futile, with sadistic guards and a hapless warden. Spawned numerous imitators. **80m/B VHS.** Wallace Beery, Chester Morris, Robert Montgomery, Lewis Stone, Leila Hyams, George F. Marion Sr., Karl (Daen) Dana, DeWitt Jennings; *D:* George Hill; *W:* Frances Marion.

The Big Hurt 1987 (R) A reporter investigating a bizarre double murder discovers a secret government agency involved in torture and mind-control. **90m/C VHS.** AU David Bradshaw, Lian Lunson, Simon Chilvers, Nick Waters; *D:* Barry Peak.

Big Jake 1971 (PG) An aging Texas cattle man who has outlived his time swings into action when outlaws kidnap his grandson and wound his son. He returns to his estranged family to help them in the search for Little Jake. O'Hara is once again paired up with Wayne and the chemistry is still there. **90m/C VHS, DVD.** John Agar, John Wayne, Richard Boone, Maureen O'Hara, Patrick Wayne, Chris Mitchum, Bobby Vinton; *D:* George Sherman; *W:* William Clothier; *M:* Elmer Bernstein.

Big Jim McLain 1952 Wayne and Arness are federal agents working on behalf of the House Un-American Activities Committee to eliminate communist terrorism in Hawaii. And there's a suspicious psychiatrist, too: Wayne falls for a babe whose boss is a shrink who doesn't quite seem on the level. Definitely not a highpoint in the Duke's career. **90m/C VHS, DVD.** John Wayne, Nancy Olson, James Arness, Veda Ann Borg, *D:* Edward Ludwig; *C:* Archie Stout.

The Big Kahuna 2000 (R) Spacey produced and stars as Larry, a loudly cynical industrial lubricants salesman at a convention in Kansas. He's there with Phil (DeVito), his burned-out colleague who's going through a divorce and looking for spirituality; and Bob (Facinelli), a newlywed, devout Christian research engineer who's new to the company. They spend the night in a hospitality suite waiting for a potential client—the Big Kahuna—and discussing how work, religion, ethics, and personal life coexist. Adapted from Rueff's play "Hospitality Suite" and it feels like it. The dialogue and setting is very stagey, but the performances are excellent, especially DeVito's. **90m/C VHS, DVD.** Kevin Spacey, Danny DeVito, Peter Facinelli; *D:* John Swanbeck; *W:* Roger Rueff; *C:* Doug McKay.

The Big Knife 1955 Palance plays a Hollywood superstar who refuses to renew his studio contract, which enrages studio boss Steiger. It seems Steiger knows a very damaging secret about the star and is willing to go to any lengths to have Palance re-sign or wind up destroying himself. A ruthless, emotional look at fame and power, with excellent performances by all. Based on the play by Clifford Odets. **113m/B DVD.** Jack Palance, Rod Steiger, Ida Lupino, Shelley Winters, Wendell Corey, Jean Hagen, Ilka Chase, Everett Sloane, Wesley Addy, Paul Langton; *D:* Robert Aldrich; *C:* Ernest Laszlo.

The Big Lebowski 1997 (R) Jeff Lebowski (Bridges), a stuck-in-the-'70s stoner who insists on being called "the Dude" and loves to go bowling, is mistaken for a wheelchair-bound millionaire of the same name, and suffers a beating at the hands of thugs who are after money owed by the rich Lebowski's slutty wife. Dude is drawn into kidnapping, the attempted scamming of payoff money, and more bowling. While this may seem like plot-a-plenty, it's mainly a showcase for the Coen brothers' unique texturing of style and quirky-but-deep characters. Goodman is loud and funny as a Vietnam vet who takes any opportunity to pull a gun or explode into DI-like obscenities. Turturro steals his scenes as a pervert rival bowler who loves skintight lilac jumpsuits and polishing his ball. The showpiece is an amazing musical-bowling-fantasy sequence that would've made Busby Berkeley proud. **117m/C VHS, DVD, HD DVD.** Jack Kehler, Julianne Moore, John Goodman, Steve Buscemi, Julianne Moore, Peter Stormare, David Huddleston, Philip Seymour Hoffman, Flea, Leon Russom, Sam Elliott, John Turturro, David Thewlis, Ben Gazzara, Tara Reid; *D:* Joel Coen; *W:* Joel Coen, Ethan Coen; *C:* Roger Deakins; *M:* Carter Burwell.

The Big Lift 1950 Two G.I.s assigned to the Berlin airlift ally themselves in counter-intelligence when they discover that their mutual girlfriend is a spy. **119m/B VHS, DVD.** Montgomery Clift, Paul Douglas, Cornell Borchers, Bruni Lobel, O.E. Hasse; *D:* George Seaton.

The Big Man: Crossing the Line 1991 (R) *Crossing the Line* Neeson shines as a down on his luck Scottish miner who loses his job during a union strike. Desperate for cash and unable to resolve his bitterness at being unable to support his family, he's enticed by a Glasgow hood to fight in an illegal bare-knuckled boxing match. What follows is an overlong and extremely brutal fight. Good performances from a talented cast overcome a rather preachy script that doesn't disguise its contempt for the Thatcher government, but also allows a glimpse into the tough times that many Brits suffered during the '80s. Based on the novel by William McIlvanney. **93m/C VHS, DVD.** GB Liam Neeson, Joanne Whalley, Ian Bannen, Billy Connolly, Hugh Grant, Maurice Reeves, Rob Affleck; *D:* David Leland; *W:* Don MacPherson; *M:* Ennio Morricone.

Big Man on Campus 1989 (PG-13) A modern-day Quasimodo makes his home in an affluent university's belltower. Of course he falls in love with one of the pretty young co-eds and races out of his tower only to be captured by the psychology department. Really, really bad. **102m/C VHS,** Tom Skerritt, Corey Parker, Allan Katz, Cindy Williams, Melora Hardin, Jessica Harper, Gerrit Graham; *D:* Jeremy Paul Kagan; *W:* Allan Katz; *C:* Bojan Bazelli; *M:* Joseph Vitarelli.

Big Meat Eater 1985 A musical gore-comedy about extraterrestrials using radioactive butcher's discards for ship fuel. Deliberate camp that is so bad its funny! **81m/C VHS, DVD.** CA George Dawson, Big Miller, Andrew Gillies, Stephen Dimopoulos, Georgina Hegedos, Ida Carnevali, Sharon Wahl; *D:* Chris Windsor; *W:* Chris Windsor, Phil Savath, Laurence Keane; *C:* Doug McKay.

Big Mo 1973 (G) True story of the friendship that developed between Cincinnati Royals basketball stars Maurice Stokes and Jack Twyman after a strange paralysis hit Stokes. **110m/C VHS.** Bernie Casey, Bo Svenson, Stephanie Edwards, Janet MacLachlan; *D:* Daniel Mann.

Big Momma's House 2000 (PG-13) FBI agent Lawrence is sent to Georgia to protect single mom Long and her son from her escaped con ex. Since he's a master of disguise, Lawrence passes himself off as her grandma, who's known as "Big Momma." Lawrence, like his pal Eddie Murphy, has plenty of experience with costumes, disguises, and multiple roles. So it's kind of disappointing that this isn't a better movie. Sporadic laughs are too often mined from toilet humor, and the plot doesn't allow for many quiet moments, which Lawrence needs to balance out the slapstick. **98m/C VHS, DVD.** Martin Lawrence, Nia Long, Paul Giamatti, Terrence Howard, Anthony Anderson, Carl Wright, Ella Mitchell, Jascha Washington, Starletta DuPois, Cedric the Entertainer; *D:* Raja Gosnell; *W:* Darryl Quarles, Don Rhymer; *C:* Michael D. O'Shea; *M:* Richard Gibbs.

Big Momma's House 2 2006 (PG-13) Hey, if you liked seeing Lawrence in a fat suit and a dress the first time, you'll probably think the sequel is okay. The plot, such as it is, has FBI agent Malcolm Turner's alter ego Hattie Mae Pierce posing as a nanny (Moses), a computer expert who has created a worm that threatens national security. Long returns too, this time as Turner's suspicious pregnant missus. Be warned: the sight of Momma running along the beach in cornrows and a bright yellow bathing suit may scar the psyche for life. **98m/C DVD.** US Martin Lawrence, Nia Long, Emily Procter, Mark Moses, Kat Dennings, Chloe Grace Moretz, Marisol Nichols, Josh Flitter, Dan Lauria, Zachary Levi, Preston Shores, Trevor Shores, Lisa Arrindell Anderson; *D:* John Whitesell; *W:* Don Rhymer; *C:* Mark Irwin; *M:* George S. Clinton.

Big Mouth 1967 A dopey fisherman gets ahold of a treasure map and is pursued by cops and gangsters. Standard Lewis fare, with the requisite infantile histrionics; must be French to appreciate. **107m/C VHS,** Jerry Lewis, Jeannine Riley, Harold J. Stone, Charlie Callas, Buddy Lester, Susan Bay; *D:* Jerry Lewis; *W:* Jerry Lewis; *M:* Harry Betts.

Big News 1929 Based on the play "For Two Cents" by George S. Brooks, this early talkie uses sound to great advantage. Fired for going after a gangster who's a big advertiser (Hardy), reporter Armstrong nevertheless keeps after the crook. When the intrepid reporter pushes too far, murder enters the picture. **75m/B VHS.** Robert Armstrong, Carole Lombard, Tom Kennedy, Warner Richmond, Wade Boteler, Sam Hardy, Lew Ayres; *D:* Gregory La Cava.

Big Night 1995 (R) Set in '50s New Jersey, film provides an Old World/New World look at Italian brothers Primo (Shalhoub) and Secondo (Tucci) Pilaggi and their elegant but failing restaurant. Primo is the perfectionist chef who hates compromise while Secondo wants to Americanize the place in an effort to make it a success. (He knows the customer is always right even if they can't appreciate Primo's exquisitely authentic Italian dishes). In order to get attention, Secondo arranges a special night in honor of jazz great Louis Prima, with Primo out to cook the feast of a lifetime—if they can pull it off. Another food film guaranteed to make you hungry. **109m/C VHS, DVD.** Tony Shalhoub, Stanley Tucci, Ian Holm, Minnie Driver, Campbell Scott, Isabella Rossellini, Marc Anthony, Allison Janney, Gina Spybey; *D:* Stanley Tucci, Campbell Scott; *W:* Stanley Tucci, Joseph Tropiano; *C:* Ken Kelsch. Ind. Spirit '97: First Screenplay; Nat. Soc. Film Critics '96: Support. Actor (Shalhoub); Sundance '96: Screenplay.

Big Nothing 2006 Now there's a title just leaving it wide open. Well, it's more like "little nothing" anyway. Struggling writer Charlie (Schwimmer) takes a job at a call center. Co-worker Gus (Pegg) persuades Charlie to join him in blackmailing a preacher who likes kiddie-porn websites. They pick up a third partner in blonde babe Josie (Eve). **86m/C DVD.** GB David Schwimmer, Simon Pegg, Alice Eve, Mimi Rogers, Natascha (Natasha) McElhone, Jon Polito, Billy Asher, Mitchell Mullen; *D:* Jean-Baptiste Andrea; *W:* Jean-Baptiste Andrea, *C:* Richard Greatrex; *M:* Alan Anton. VIDEO

The Big One 1998 (PG-13) Moore once again takes his populist, CEO-baiting act on the road in search of corporate evil-doers, this time on Random House's dime. Documentary lovingly follows Moore on his 1996 book promo tour, as he highlights plant closings, verbally spars with Nike boss Phil Knight, plays pranks on his "handlers," and mugs for his adoring fans. His style is still the same as in "Roger & Me," but since he's joined the celebrity ranks, Moore isn't going to sneak up on anybody. To his credit, he doesn't try, but to his discredit, he ends up haranguing the very working people he claims to be standing up for, mostly exasperated receptionists and secretaries. Corporate greed and apathy are still squarely in Moore's crosshairs, but this time his own ego prevents him from getting a clear shot at his target. **90m/C VHS, DVD.** *D:* Michael Moore; *Nar:* Michael Moore.

The Big Parade 1925 Wonderful WWI silent, considered to be one of the best war flicks of all time. Gilbert and Adoree are exceptional as lovers torn apart by the conflict. Interesting and thoughtful picture of the trauma and trouble brought to men and their loved ones in wartime. Battle scenes are compelling and intense; Vidor's masterpiece. **141m/B VHS.** John Gilbert, Renee Adoree, Hobart Bosworth, Claire McDowell, Claire Adams, Karl (Daen) Dane, Robert Ober, Tom (Thomas E.) O'Brien, Rosita Marstini; *D:* King Vidor; *W:* Harry Behn; *C:* John Arnold; *M:* William Axt, David Mendoza. Natl. Film Reg. '92.

The Big Picture 1989 (PG-13) A hilarious, overlooked comedy by and starring a variety of Second City/National Lampoon alumni, about a young filmmaker who is contracted by a big studio, only to see his vision trampled by formula-minded producers, crazed agents, hungry starlets, and every other variety of Hollywood predator. **95m/C VHS, DVD.** Kevin Bacon, Jennifer Jason Leigh, Martin Short, Michael McKean, Emily Longstreth, J.T. Walsh, Eddie Albert, Richard Belzer, John Cleese, June Lockhart, Stephen Collins, Roddy McDowall, Kim Miyori, Teri Hatcher, Dan Schneider, Jason Gould, Tracy Brooks Swope; *D:* Christopher Guest; *W:* Michael Varhol, Michael McKean, Christopher Guest; *M:* David Nichtern.

The Big Push 1975 (PG) Motley bunch of Alaskan lumberjacks get together to save a poor widow's logging camp from a pair of greedy mill owners. **98m/C VHS.** Joseph Cotten, Claude Akins, Cesar Romero, Tab Hunter, Roosevelt 'Rosie' Grier, Leon Ames, Stubby Kaye, Patricia Medina; *D:* Tay Garnett.

Big Red 1962 Set amid the spectacular beauty of Canada's Quebec Province, an orphan boy protects a dog which later saves him from a mountain lion. **89m/C VHS, DVD.** Walter Pidgeon, Gilles Payant; *D:* Norman Tokar; *W:* Louis Pelletier; *C:* Edward Colman; *M:* Oliver Wallace, Richard M. Sherman, Robert B. Sherman.

The Big Red One 1980 (PG) Fuller's harrowing, intense semi-autobiographical account of the U.S. Army's famous First Infantry Division in WWII, the "Big Red One." A rifle squad composed of four very young men, led by the grizzled Marvin, cut a fiery path of conquest from the landing in North Africa to the liberation of the concentration camp at Falkenau, Czechoslovakia. In part a tale of lost innocence, the film scores highest by bringing the raw terror of war down to the individual level. New restored version adds about 47 minutes and sports an "R" rating. **113m/C VHS, DVD.** Lee Marvin, Robert Carradine, Mark Hamill, Stephane Audran, Bobby DiCicco, Perry Lang, Kelly Ward, Siegfried Rauch, Serge Marquand, Charles Macaulay, Alain Doutey, Maurice Marsac, Colin Gilbert, Joseph Clark, Ken Campbell, Doug Werner, Marthe Villalonga; *D:* Samuel Fuller; *W:* Samuel Fuller; *C:* Adam Greenberg; *M:* Dana Kaproff.

The Big Scam 1980 *A Nightingale Sang in Berkeley Square; The Mayfair Bank Caper* 1979 Criminal mastermind Niven recruits ex-con Jordan to pull off a massive bank heist. **102m/C DVD.** Richard Jordan, David Niven, Oliver Tobias, Elke Sommer, Gloria Grahame, Hugh Griffith, Richard Johnson, Joss Ackland, Al-

Big Score ⅃ 1983 (R) When a policeman is falsely accused and dismissed from the Chicago Police Department, he goes after the man who really stole the money from a drug bust. Script was originally intended to be a Dirty Harry flick, too bad it wasn't. **88m/C VHS, DVD.** Fred William-son, John Saxon, Richard Roundtree, Nancy Wilson, Ed Lauter, Ron Dean, D'Urville Martin, Michael Dante, Joe Spinell; **D:** Fred Williamson; **C:** Joao Fernandes.

Big Shot: Confessions of a Campus Bookie ⅃⅃½ 2002 (R) Based on the true story of Brooklyn-born Benny Silman (Krumholtz) who undergoes culture shock when he begins attending Arizona State University. He takes frequent trips to Vegas and is soon running his own campus bookmaking operation but wants more. Then Benny meets hoops star Stevin Smith (Kittles) who isn't adverse to making some money on the side. So Benny hooks up with a big-time Vegas gambler (Turturro) to shave points in ASU games. **83m/C VHS, DVD.** David Krumholtz, Robert Prosky, Alex Rocco, Kittles, Camira D. Giovinazzo, Nicholas Turturro, Jennifer Morrison, Tony James LeGros; **D:** Ernest R. Dickerson; **W:** Jason Keller; **C:** Steven Bernstein; **M:** Reinhold Heil, Johnny Klimek. **CABLE**

Big Shots ⅃ 1987 (PG-13) Two kids, one naive and white, the other black and streetwise, search for a stolen watch. **91m/C VHS.** Ricky Busker, Darius McCrary, Robert Joy, Paul Winfield, Robert Prosky, Jerzy Skolimowski; **D:** Robert Mandel; **W:** Joe Eszterhas; **M:** Bruce Broughton.

Big Shot's Funeral ⅃ Da Wan 2001 (PG) American director Don Tyler (Sutherland) is on location in Beijing when he suffers a serious health crisis and winds up in the hospital. He tells camera-man YoYo (Ge) that should he die, he wants a blow-out funeral, which YoYo promises to arrange. Since he has no money, YoYo auctions off advertising and sponsorships for the funeral but the humor begins to improve. Would-be comedy has very few laughs. English and Mandarin with subtitles. **100m/C VHS, DVD.** Donald Sutherland, Ge You, Rosamund Kwan, Daijinial Ying, Paul Mazursky; **D:** Feng Xiao Gang; **W:** Feng Xiao Gang; **C:** Li Zhang; **M:** San Bao.

Big Show ⅃⅃ Home in Oklahoma 1937 A western adventure about the making of a western movie. Autry jangles spurs aplenty in dual role. **5am/B VHS, DVD.** Gene Autry, Smiley Burnette; **D:** Mack V. Wright.

The Big Sky ⅃⅃⅃ 1952 It's 1830, and a rowdy band of fur trappers embark upon a back-breaking expedition up the uncharted Missouri River. Based on the A.B. Guthrie Jr. novel, it's an effortlessly enjoyable and level-headed Hawksian American myth, with a streak of gentle gallows humor. Also available colorized. **122m/C VHS.** Kirk Douglas, Dewey Martin, Arthur Hunnicutt, Elizabeth Threat, Buddy Baer, Steven Geray, Jim Davis; **D:** Howard Hawks.

The Big Sleep ⅃⅃⅃⅃ 1946 Private eye Philip Marlowe, hired to protect a young woman from her own indiscretions, falls in love with her older sister while unraveling murders galore. A dense, chaotic thriller that succeeded in defining and setting a standard for its genre. The very best Raymond Chandler on film combining a witty script with great performances, especially from Bogart and Bacall. **114m/B VHS, DVD.** Humphrey Bogart, Lauren Bacall, John Ridgely, Martha Vickers, Louis Jean Heydt, Regis Toomey, Peggy Knudsen, Dorothy Malone, Bob Steele, Elisha Cook Jr.; **D:** Howard Hawks; **W:** Jules Furthman, Leigh Brackett, William Faulkner; **C:** Sid Hickox; **M:** Max Steiner. **Natl. Film Reg. '97.**

The Big Sleep ⅃⅃ 1978 (R) A tired remake of the Raymond Chandler potboiler about exhausted Los Angeles private dick Marlowe and his problems in protecting a wild young heiress from her own decadence and mob connections. Mitchum appears to need a rest. **99m/C VHS, DVD.** Robert Mitchum, Sarah Miles, Richard Boone, Candy Clark, Edward Fox, Joan Collins, John Mills, James Stewart, Oliver Reed, Harry Andrews, James Donald, Colin Blakely, Richard Todd; **D:** Michael Winner.

The Big Slice ⅃½ 1990 (R) Two would-be crime novelists want to improve their fiction. One masquerades as a cop, the other as a crook, and they infiltrate the underworld from both ends. Clever comedy premise, but vaudeville-level jokes fall flat. **86m/C VHS, DVD.** Casey Siemaszki, Leslie Hope, Justin Louis, Heather Locklear, Kenneth Welsh, Nicholas (Nick) Campbell, Henry Ramer, el Danna, Jeff Janna.

The Big Sombrero ⅃⅃ 1949 Autry takes a stand against the marriage between an unsuspecting, wealthy Mexican girl and the fortune-seeking American who wants her land. **77m/C VHS.** Gene Autry, Elena Verdugo, Steve (Stephen) Dunne, George Lewis; **D:** Frank McDonald.

The Big Squeeze ⅃⅃½ 1996 (R) Married bartender Tanya (Boyle) is displeased to find out her born-again hubby Henry (Bercovici) has been holding out a large wad of cash from an insurance settlement, apparently about to donate it to a local Spanish mission. Enter Benny (Dobson), a cocky con man willing to help Tanya get her share of the dough for his own cut, sweet bartender Jesse (Tucci), who's secretly in love in Tanya, and fellow barmaid Cece (Dispina), who catches Benny's wandering eye. All get caught up in the frantic couple-dealing. **100m/C VHS, DVD.** Lara Flynn Boyle, Peter Dobson, Luca Bercovici, Danny Nucci, Teresa Dispina, Sam Vlanos, Valente Rodriguez; **D:** Marcus De Leon; **W:** Marcus De Leon; **C:** Jacques Haitkin; **M:** Mark Mothersbaugh.

Big Stakes ⅃ 1922 Extremely rare Western feature that has a Texas cowboy falling for a Mexican senorita. Plenty of action as complications ensue. **61m/B VHS.** H.B. Warner, Elinor Fair, Les Bates; **D:** Clifford S. Elfelt; **W:** Frank Howard Clark.

The Big Stampede ⅃⅃ 1932 Twenty-five-year-old Wayne stars in this action-packed Western that was a remake of "Land Beyond the Law" from Ken Maynard's silent. Based on a story by Marion Jackson. **63m/B VHS, DVD.** John Wayne, Noah Beery Sr., Luis Alberni, Berton Churchill, Paul Hurst, Late (Lafayette) McKee, Frank Ellis, Hank Bell; **D:** Tenny Wright; **W:** Kurt Kempler.

The Big Steal ⅃⅃ 1949 An Army officer recovers a missing payroll and captures the thieves after a tumultuous chase through Mexico. **72m/B VHS, DVD.** Robert Mitchum, William Bendix, Jane Greer, Ramon Novarro, Patric Knowles, Don Alvarado, John Qualen; **D:** Donald Siegel; **W:** Daniel Mainwaring, Gerald Drayson Adams; **C:** Harry Wild; **M:** Leigh Harline.

Big Store ⅃⅃ 1941 Late Marx Brothers in which they are detectives in a large metropolitan department store, foiling a hostile takeover and preventing a murder. Their last MGM effort, with some good moments between the Tony Martin song numbers which include the immortal "Tenement Symphony." Groucho also leads the "Sing While You Sell" number. **96m/B VHS, DVD.** Groucho Marx, Harpo Marx, Chico Marx, Tony Martin, Margaret Dumont, Virginia Grey, Virginia O'Brien, Douglass Dumbrille, Marion Martin, Henry Armetta; **D:** Charles Reisner; **W:** Hal Fimberg, Ray Golden, Sid Kuller; **C:** Charles Lawton Jr.; **M:** George Bassman.

Big Street ⅃⅃½ 1942 A timid busboy, in love with a disinterested nightclub singer, gets to prove his devotion when she is crippled in a fall. Based on a Damon Runyon story, "Little Pinks." **88m/B VHS, DVD.** Henry Fonda, Lucille Ball, Agnes Moorehead, Louise Beavers, Barton MacLane, Eugene Pallette, Ozzie Nelson; **D:** Irving Reis.

The Big Sweat ⅃⅃ 1990 Maybe you've heard this one before: a man who has been framed by the mob escapes from prison and heads for Mexico. But first, he's got to get past the mobsters and police who are hot on his trail. And maybe you've seen some of it before: some of the same stock footage appears in Lorrimel's "Cold Heat." Not surprisingly, this one bypassed theatres and went straight to video. **85m/C VHS.** Robert Z'Dar, Steve Malone, Ken McBride, William Roebuck, Cheri Caspari, David Rushing, Joanne Watkins, Ken Letner; **D:** Ulli Lommel; **C:** Max Bolt; **M:** Max Wassail. **VIDEO**

The Big Switch ⅃½ 1970 (R) Gambler is framed for murder and becomes embroiled in a plot to reinstate an old gangster kingpin. **68m/C VHS.** Sebastian Breaks, Virginia Wetherell, Erika Raffael; **D:** Pete Walker.

The Big Tease ⅃⅃ 1999 (R) Gay Glasgow hairdresser Crawford Mackenzie (Ferguson) thinks he's being asked to compete in the prestigious World Freestyle Hairdressing Championship being held in Los Angeles. So he heads to Hollywood and discovers he will not only find a way to enter but he will defeat his snippy Swedish rival, Stig (Rasche). Good-natured, campy fluff. **86m/C VHS, DVD.** Craig Ferguson, Frances Fisher, Chris Langham, Mary McCormack, Donal Logue, Larry Miller, Cathy Lee Crosby, Bruce Jenner, Isabella Aitken, David Rasche, Charles Napier, David Hasselhoff, Sacha Gervasi; **D:** Kevin Allen; **W:** Craig Ferguson, Sacha Gervasi; **C:** Seamus McGarvey; **M:** Mark Thomas.

Big Top Pee-wee ⅃⅃ 1988 (PG) Pee-wee's second feature film following the success of "Pee-wee's Big Adventure." This time Pee-wee owns a farm, has a girlfriend (!) and lives the good life until a weird storm blows a traveling circus onto his property. Cute, but not the manic hilarity the first one was. **86m/C VHS, DVD.** Paul (Pee-wee Herman) Reubens, Kris Kristofferson, Susan Tyrrell, Penelope Ann Miller; **D:** Randal Kleiser; **W:** Paul (Pee-wee Herman) Reubens; **C:** Steven Poster; **M:** Danny Elfman.

Big Town ⅃⅃ Guilty Assignment 1947 A newspaper is saved by a new editor who brings integrity to the once scandalous paper. The editor and his reporters also solve a series of murders. Some action, but weak dialogue and direction hold it back. Based on the radio program of the same name. **59m/B VHS.** Philip Reed, Hillary Brooke, Robert Lowery, Byron Barr, Veda Ann Borg, Nana Bryant, Charles Arnt, John Dehner; **D:** William C. Thomas; **W:** Daniel Mainwaring, Max Calker.

Big Town ⅃⅃⅃½ 1987 (R) A farm-boy, lucky with dice, hits Chicago to claim his fortune where he meets floozies, criminals, and other streetlife. Standard '50s period underworld drama is elevated by exceptional cast's fine ensemble work. Look for Lane's strip number. **109m/C VHS, DVD.** Matt Dillon, Diane Lane, Tommy Lee Jones, Bruce Dern, Tom Skerritt, Lee Grant, Suzy Amis, David Marshall Grant, Don Francis, Del Close, Cherry Jones, David James Elliot, Don Lake, Diego Matamoros, Gary Farmer, Sarah Polley, Lolita (David) Davidovich; **D:** Ben Bolt, Harold Becker; **W:** Robert Roy Pool; **C:** Ralf Bode; **M:** Michael Melvoin.

Big Town After Dark ⅃⅃ Underworld After Dark 1947 Daring journalists search for the bottom-line story on a gang of criminals. They find themselves caught behind the firing lines when the sun goes down. Slightly better than average thriller based on the radio show "Big Town." **69m/B VHS, DVD.** Philip Reed, Hillary Brooke, Richard Travis, Ann Gillis, Vince Barnett, Joseph (Joe) Sawyer, Robert Kent, Charles Arnt; **D:** William C. Thomas; **C:** Ellis W. Carter; **M:** Darrell Calker.

Big Trail ⅃⅃⅃ 1930 This pioneering effort in widescreen cinematography was Wayne's first feature film. A wagon train on the Oregon trail encounters civilization. Redwood Timberlands that are owned by a group of peaceful homesteaders. **89m/C VHS, DVD.** Kirk Douglas, Patrice Wymore, Eve Miller, Alan Hale Jr., Edgar Buchanan, Tyrone Power Sr., Ward Bond, Helen Parrish; **D:** Raoul Walsh. **Natl. Film Reg. '06.**

Big Trees ⅃⅃⅃ 1952 A ruthless lumberman attempts a takeover of the California Redwood Timberlands that are owned by a group of peaceful homesteaders. **89m/C VHS, DVD.** Kirk Douglas, Patrice Wymore, Eve Miller, Alan Hale Jr., Edgar Buchanan; **D:** Felix Feist.

Big Trouble ⅃⅃ 1986 (R) An insurance broker endeavors to sell his three sons to Yale by conspiring with a crazy couple in a fraud scheme that goes awry in every possible manner. Look for the cameo by screenwriter Bergman as Warren Bogle; **D:** John Cassavetes. **93m/C VHS, DVD.** Alan Arkin, Peter Falk, Beverly D'Angelo, Charles Durning, Robert Stack, Paul Dooley, Valerie Curtin, Richard Libertini; **Cameos:** Andrew Bergman; **D:** John Cassavetes; **W:** Andrew Bergman; **C:** Bill Butler; **M:** Bill Conti.

Big Trouble ⅃⅃ 2002 (PG-13) Fast-paced ensemble comedy based on the novel by Dave Barry packs a metric ton of narrative, not to mention characters, into a mere 84 minutes, most of which involve the clash of various characters tracking down a nuclear bomb in Miami. Suburban Anna (Russo) is trapped in a loveless marriage with unscrupulous businessman Arthur Herk (Tucci) who wants to buy a nuclear bomb, thus getting involved with some undesirable characters, most notably two hit men (Farina and Kehler). The plot kicks off when Matt (Foster), the son of divorced journalist Allen decides to snipe the Herk's daughter Jenny (Deschanel) with a high-powered squirt gun on the same night the real manic hilarity. **84m/C VHS, DVD.** Tim Allen, Rene Russo, Stanley Tucci, Tom Sizemore, Johnny Knoxville, Dennis Farina, Janeane Garofalo, Patrick Warburton, Ben Foster, Zooey Deschanel, Dwight "Heavy D" Myers, Omar Epps, Jason Lee, Andy Richter, Sofia Vergara; **D:** Barry Sonnenfeld; **W:** Robert Ramsey, Matthew Stone; **C:** Greg Gardiner; **M:** James Newton Howard.

The Big Turnaround ⅃ Turn-around 1988 Drug-dealing punks push their goods into Mexico via a truck from the early '60s get back together after the Vietnam war to reminisce about the good old days and take on the big wave. A doctor (Cranston), whose father, Joseph, serves as director and producer and a priest (Borgnine) boldly unite to save the day in this misguided effort. **93m/C VHS, DVD.** Jan-Michael Vincent, Gary Busey, William Katt, Lee Purcell, Patti D'Arbanville; **D:** John Milius; **W:** John Milius.

The Big Wheel ⅃⅃½ 1949 Old story retold fairly well. Rooney is young son determined to travel in his father's tracks as a race car driver, even when dad buys the farm on the oval. Good acting and direction keep this a cut above average. **92m/B VHS, DVD.** Mickey Rooney, Thomas Mitchell, Spring Byington, Mary Hatcher, Allen Jenkins, Michael O'Shea; **D:** Edward Ludwig.

The Big White ⅃½ 2005 (R) A waste of talent in a lame comedy. Alaska travel agent Paul Barnell (Williams) has money problems. Then he finds a frozen body in a dumpster. Paul hopes to pass the body off as his estranged brother Raymond (Harrelson) and collect the life insurance, but agent Ted (Ribisi) is suspicious. Add in Paul's troubled wife Margaret (Hunter), the sudden return of Raymond, and a couple of wannabe kidnapper/hitmen (Nelson, Brown) and Paul's got more complications than he can handle. **105m/C DVD. US CA NZ** Robin Williams, Holly Hunter, Woody Harrelson, Tim Blake Nelson, Giovanni Ribisi; **W:** Earl Brown, Alison Lohman; **D:** Mark Mylod; **M:** Collin Friesen; **C:** James Gleason; **M:** Gary Hope.

Big Wednesday ⅃⅃½ 1978 (PG) Three California surfers from the early '60s get back together after the Vietnam war to reminisce about the good old days and take on the big wave. **120m/C VHS, DVD.** Jan-Michael Vincent, Gary Busey, William Katt, Lee Purcell, Patti D'Arbanville; **D:** John Milius; **W:** John Milius. **VIDEO**

Big Trouble in Little China ⅃⅃½ 1986 (PG-13) A trucker plunges beneath the streets of San Francisco's Chinatown to battle an army of spirits. An uproarious comic-book-film parody with plenty of action and a keen sense of sophomoric sarcasm. **99m/C VHS, DVD. UMD.** Kurt Russell, Suzee Pai, Dennis Dun, Kim Cattrall, James Hong, Victor Wong, Kate Burton; **D:** John Carpenter; **W:** David Weinstein, Goldman, W.D. Richter; **C:** Dean Cundey; **M:** John Carpenter, Alan Howarth.

Big Zapper ⅃½ 1973 Violent P.I. Marlowe and masochistic assistant Rock work together in this British comic strip film. **94m/C VHS. GB** Linda Marlowe, Gary Hope, ersbaugh.

Sean Hewitt, Richard Monette, Penny Irving; **D:** Lindsay Shonteff.

The Bigamist 🦴🦴½ 1953 Have ycu heard the one about the traveling salesman in this movie? He has one wife in Los Angeles, another in San Francisco, and they inevitably find out about each other. A maudlin soap opera with a do-it-yourself ending, only shows why bigamy was done better as farce in the later "Micki and Maude." 79m/B VHS, DVD. Edmond O'Brien, Joan Fontaine, Ida Lupino, Edmund Gwenn, Jane Darwell, Kenneth Tobey; **D:** Ida Lupino.

Bigfoot: The Unforgettable Encounter 🦴🦴½ 1994 (PG) Young boy heads off into the woods, comes face to face with Bigfoot, and sets off a media frenzy and a band of ruthless bounty hunters determined to capture his hairy friend. 89m/C VHS, DVD. Zachery Ty Bryan, Matt McCoy, Barbara Willis Sweete, Clint Howard, Rance Howard, David Rasche; **D:** Corey Michael Eubanks; **W:** Corey Michael Eubanks; **M:** Shimon Arama.

Bigger Than the Sky 🦴🦴½ 2005 (PG-13) Recently-dumped Peter (Thomas), stuck in a lousy dead-end job, decides he needs something new. He tries out for the community theatre and fincs what he's looking for through company regulars Michael (Corbett) and Grace (Smart). A very mild romantic comedy that almost works. Anyone involve in small theatre will relish in the details. Features Patty Duke playing mother to her real-life son, Sean Astin. 106m/C VHS, DVD. Marcus Thomas, John Corbett, Amy Smart, Sean Astin, Clare Higgins, Patty Duke, Allan Cordurner, Matt Salinger, Greg Germann; **D:** Al Corley; **W:** Rodney Vaccaro; **C:** Christine Gentet; **M:** Rob Cairns. **VIDEO**

The Biggest Fan 🦴½ 2002 Silly teen romance about a fan and a boy band. Shy high school sophomore Debbie (Amariah) is the number one fan of Dream Street. Disappointed at missing their local concert, Debbie wakes up the next morning to a huge shock—she finds lead singer Chris Trousdale (playing himself) passed out in her room! Loopy from cold medicine, Chris missed the concert and stumbled around until he found a convenient place to crash. Debbie agrees to hide the dreamboat, who needs a timeout from all that squealing and screaming, but what if her parents find out? 95m/C DVD. US Marissa Tait, Richard Moll, Noryuki "Pat" Morita, Morgan Meyer, Kaila Amariah, Chris Trousdale, Morgan Brittany, Lesllie Easterbrook, Jesse McCartney, Shanelle Workman, Cindy Williams; **D:** Michael Criscione; **W:** Michael Criscione, LeeAnn Kemp, Liz Sinclair; **C:** Wes Llewellyn. **VIDEO**

Biggles 🦴🦴½ 1985 Biggles: Adventures in Time 1985 (PG) Time-travel fantasy in which a young businessman from present-day New York City is inexplicably transferred into the middle of a 1917 WWI flying ace. He suddenly finds himself aboard a fighter plane over Europe during WWI. 100m/C VHS, DVD. GB Neil Dickson, Alex Hyde-White, Peter Cushing; **D:** John Hough.

Biker Boyz 🦴🦴½ 2003 (PG-13) Kid (Luke) is the hotshot teenager biker who challenges Smoke (Fishburne) the longtime reigning "King of Cali." Often referred to as "The Fast and the Furious" on motorcycles, it doesn't achieve the same level of entertainment. Soap opera subplots and cliched dialogue don't help. Then again, "Furious" had the same problems and managed to make a boatload of cash. The actors, however, do a good job with a so-so script, and Luke is fast becoming an actor worth noticing. 111m/C VHS, DVD. US Laurence Fishburne, Derek Luke, Orlando Jones, Djimon Hounsou, Lisa Bonet, Brendan Fehr, Larenz Tate, Kid Rock, Rick Gonzalez, Meagan Good, Salli Richardson, Vanessa Bell Calloway, Eriq La Salle, Titus Welliver, Kadeem Hardison, Terrence Howard; Tyson Beckford; **D:** Reggie Rock Bythewood; **W:** Reggie Rock Bythewood, Craig Ferandez; **C:** Greg Gardiner; **M:** Cemara Kambon.

Bikini Beach 🦴🦴½ 1964 Surfing teenagers of the "Beach Party" series follow up "Muscle Beach Party" with a third fling at the beach and welcome a visitor, British recording star "Potato Bug" (Avalon in a campy dual role). But, golly gee, wealthy Wynn wants to turn their sandy, surfin' shores into a retirement community. What to do? Sing a few songs, dance in your bathing suits, and have fun. Classic early '60s nostalgia is better than the first two efforts; followed by "Pajama Party." ♫Because You're You; Love's a Secret Weapon; Bikini Drag. 100m/C VHS, DVD. Annette Funicello, Frankie Avalon, Martha Hyer, Harvey Lembeck, Don Rickles, Stevie Wonder, Jody Ashley, Keenan Wynn, Jody McCrea, Candy Johnson, Danielle Aubry, Meredith MacRae, Dolores Wells, Donna Loren, Timothy Carey, Boris Karloff; **D:** William Asher; **W:** William Asher, Leo Townsend, Robert Dillon; **C:** Floyd Crosby; **M:** Les Baxter.

Bikini Bistro 🦴 1994 (R) A boring vegetarian café gets turned into a gourmet restaurant but, faced with an eviction notice, the female owners decide to increase business by waitressing in bikinis. Also available in an unrated version at 84 minutes. 80m/C VHS, DVD. Marilyn Chambers, Amy Lynn Baxter, Joan Gerardi, Isabelle Fortea, John Altamura, Joseph Pallister; **D:** Ernest G. Sauer; **W:** Matt Unger.

The Bikini Car Wash Company WOOF! California Hot Wax 1990 (R) Babes in bikinis in Los Angeles. A young man is running his uncle's carwash when he meets a business major who persuades him to let her take over the business for a cut of the profits. She decides that a good gimmick would be to dress all the female employees in the tiniest bikinis possible. The story is of course secondary to the amount of flesh on display. Also available in an unrated version. 87m/C VHS, DVD. Joe Dusic, Neriah Napaul, Sara Suzanne Brown, Kristie Ducati; **D:** Ed Hansen.

The Bikini Car Wash Company 2 🦴🦴 1992 (R) Entrepreneur Melissa and the other lovely ladies of the Bikini Car Wash Co. find themselves a big success. Their new business adventure involves selling sexy lingerie which means the flesh quotient is as great as ever. An unrated version is also available. 94m/C VHS, DVD. Kristie Ducati, Sara Suzanne Brown, Neriah Napaul, Rikki Brando, Greg Raye, Larry De Russy; **D:** Gary Orona; **W:** Bart B. Gustis; **M:** Michael Smith.

Bikini Drive-In 🦴🦴½ 1994 (R) Babe (Rhey) inherits grandad's decrepit drive-in, which is wanted by a mall mogul, but she refuses to sell. So to raise some cash, Rhey stages a B-movie marathon with inperson, bikini-clad scream queens. 85m/C VHS, DVD. Ashlie Rhey, Richard Gabai, Ross Hagen, Sara Bellomo, Steve Barkett, Conrad Brooks; **D:** Fred Olen Ray.

Bikini House Calls 🦴 1996 The students of Bikini Med School love anatomy as much as they love to party. In fact, combining both activities is their idea of a perfect time. 87m/C VHS, DVD. Thomas Draper, Sean Abbananto, Kim (Kimberly Dawn) Dawson, Tamara Landry; **D:** Michael Paul Girard; **W:** Michael Paul Girard; **C:** Denis Maloney; **M:** Miriam Cutler. **VIDEO**

Bikini Island 🦴 1991 (R) Beautiful swimsuit models gather on a remote tropical island for a big photo shoot, each vying to be the next cover girl of the hottest swimsuit magazine. Before long, scantily clad lovelies are turning up dead and full out madness ensues. Will the mystery be solved before they run out of models, or will the magazine have no choice but to grace its cover with a bikinied cadaver? Low-budget trash that has few, if any, redeeming qualities. 85m/C VHS. Holly Floria, Alicia Anne, Jackson Robinson, Shannon Stiles, Cyndi Pass, Sherry Johnson; **D:** Anthony Markes; **W:** Emerson Bixby; **M:** Marc David Decker.

Bikini Med School 🦴 1998 So how do med students get rid of all that nasty tension? Why they party, of course! And practice playing doctor with all the nubile lovelies they can. 87m/C VHS, DVD. Kim (Kimberly Dawn) Dawson, Tamara Landry, Thomas Draper, Sean Abbananto; **D:** Michael Paul Girard; **W:** Michael Paul Girard; **C:** Denis Maloney; **M:** Miriam Cutler. **VIDEO**

Bikini Summer 🦴½ 1991 Laughs, music, and skin are the order of the day as two nutty guys and a few beautiful girls form an unlikely friendship on the beach. Konop was Julia Robert's "Pretty Woman" body double. Sort of the '90s version of the old '60s Frankie and Annette beach parties. 90m/C VHS, DVD. David Millbern, Melinda Armstrong, Jason Clow, Shelley Michelle, Alex Smith, Kent Lipham, Kelly Konop, Carmen Santa Maria; **D:** Robert Veze; **W:** Robert Veze, Nick Stone; **M:** John Gonzalez.

Bikini Summer 2 🦴 1992 (R) An eccentric family decides to stage a bikini contest to raise money to help the homeless. 94m/C VHS, DVD. Jeff Conaway, Jessica Hahn, Melinda Armstrong, Avalon Anders; **D:** Jeff Conaway; **M:** Jim Halfpenny.

Bikini Summer 3: South Beach Heat 🦴 1997 (R) Babes in bikinis frolic on Miami's fashionable South Beach for the chance to become the spokesmodel for Mermaid Body Splash. 84m/C VHS, DVD. Heather-Elizabeth Parkhurst, Tiffany Turner; **D:** Ken Blakey.

Bilitis 🦴½ 1977 (R) A young girl from a private girls' school is initiated into the pleasures of sex and the unexpected demands of love. One of director Hamilton's exploitative meditations on nudity. 95m/C VHS, DVD. FR Patti D'Arbanville, Bernard Giraudeau, Mona Kristensen; **D:** David Hamilton.

Bill 🦴🦴🦴 1981 Based on a true story about a mentally retarded man who sets out to live independently after 44 years in an institution. Rooney gives an affecting performance as Bill and Quaid is strong as the filmmaker who befriends him. Awarded Emmys for Rooney's performance and the well written script. Followed by "Bill: On His Own." 97m/C VHS. Mickey Rooney, Dennis Quaid, Largo Woodruff, Harry Goz; **D:** Anthony Page. **TV**

Bill & Ted's Bogus Journey 🦴🦴 1991 (PG) Big-budget sequel to B & T's first movie has better special effects but about the same quota of laughs. Slain by lookalike robot duplicates from the future, the airhead heroes pass through heaven and hell before tricking the Grim Reaper into bringing them back for a second duel with their heinous terminators. Most excellent closing-credit montage. Non-fans still won't think much of it. 98m/C VHS, DVD. Keanu Reeves, Alex Winter, William Sadler, Joss Ackland, Pam Grier, George Carlin, Amy Stock-Poynton, Hal Landon Jr., Annette Azcuy, Sarah Trigger, Taj Mahal, Roy Brocksmith, William Shatner, Chelcie Ross; **D:** Peter Hewitt; **W:** Chris Matheson, Edward Solomon; **C:** Oliver Wood; **M:** David Newman.

Bill & Ted's Excellent Adventure 🦴🦴½ 1989 (PG) Excellent premise: when the entire future of the world rests on whether or not two '80s dudes pass their history final, Rufus comes to the rescue in his time-travelling telephone booth. Bill and Ted share an adventure through time as they meet and get to know some of history's most important figures. Lightweight but fun. 105m/C VHS, DVD, UMD. Keanu Reeves, Alex Winter, George Carlin, Bernie Casey, Dan Shor, Robert V. Barron, Amy Stock-Poynton, Ted Steedman, Terry Camilleri, Rod Loomis, Al Leong, Tony Camilleri; **D:** Stephen Herek; **W:** Chris Matheson, Edward Solomon; **C:** Tim Suhrstedt; **M:** David Newman.

A Bill of Divorcement 🦴🦴½ 1932 Hepburn's screen debut, as the daughter of a shell-shocked WWI vet, who requires her care after her mother decides to divorce him. Creaky early talker. 76m/B VHS. John Barrymore, Katharine Hepburn, Billie Burke, Henry Stephenson, David Manners, Paul Cavanagh, Elizabeth Patterson; **D:** George Cukor; **M:** Max Steiner.

Bill: On His Own 🦴🦴🦴 1983 Rooney is again exceptional in this sequel to the Emmy-winning TV movie "Bill." After 44 years in an institution, a mentally retarded man copes more and more successfully with the outside world. Fine supporting cast and direction control the melodramatic potential. 100m/C VHS. Mickey Rooney, Helen Hunt, Teresa Wright, Dennis Quaid, Largo Woodruff, Paul Leiber, Harry Goz; **D:** Anthony Page.

Billboard Dad 🦴🦴½ 1998 (G) The Olsen twins decide it's time for their dad to remarry so they paint a personal ad on a billboard advertising his availability. Eventually, their Dad meets Brooke, who's a winner except for her bratty son who's the girls' rival. But nothing will stop the twins if it means making Dad happy. 90m/C VHS. Ashley (Fuller) Olsen, Mary-Kate Olsen, Tom Amandes, Jessica Tuck, Sam Selatta, Carl Banks; **D:** Alan Metter; **W:** Maria Jacquementon; **C:** Mauro Fiore; **M:** David Michael Frank. **VIDEO**

Billie 🦴🦴½ 1965 Duke stars as a tomboy athlete who puts the boys' track team to shame. Some amusing but very predictable situations, plus a few songs from Miss Duke. Based on Ronald Alexander's play "Time Out for Ginger." 86m/C VHS, DVD. Patty Duke, Jim Backus, Jane Greer, Warren Berlinger, Billy DeWolfe, Charles Lane, Dick Sargent, Susan Seaforth Hayes, Ted Bessell, Richard Deacon; **D:** Don Weis; **W:** Ronald Alexander.

The Billion Dollar Hobo 🦴🦴½ 1978 (G) Poor, unsuspecting heir of a multimillion dollar fortune must duplicate his benefactor's experience as a hobo during the Depression in order to collect his inheritance. Slow-moving family stuff. 96m/C VHS, DVD. Tim Conway, Will Geer, Eric Weston, Sydney Lassick; **D:** Stuart E. McGowan.

A Billion for Boris 🦴🦴½ 1990 Boris' TV gives a sneak preview of the future and Boris plans to make some money off of it. Zany comedy in the vein of "Let It Ride." 89m/C VHS, DVD. Lee Grant, Tim Kazurinsky; **D:** Alex Grasshof; **W:** Mary Rogers.

Billionaire Boys Club 🦴🦴½ 1987 Chilling look at greed in the '80s. Nelson plays Joe Hunt, who gets together with a group of rich, preppie friends to manipulate investments in the commodities markets. When a slick con man (Silver) gets in their way he's murdered to keep their schemes intact. Based on a true story and adapted from the book by Sue Horton. The video version is considerably pared down from the original TV broadcast. 94m/C VHS. Judd Nelson, Frederic Lehne, Brian McNamara, Raphael Sbarge, John Stockwell, Barry Tubb, Stan Shaw, Jill Schoelen, Ron Silver, James Sloyan, James Karen, Dale Dye; **D:** Marvin J. Chomsky. **TV**

Billy Bathgate 🦴🦴🦴½ 1991 (R) Uneven but well acted drama set in 1935 New York. A street-wise young man decides getting ahead during the Depression means gaining the attention of mobster Dutch Schultz and joining his gang. As Billy becomes the confidant of the racketeer he learns the criminal life is filled with suspicion and violence; in order to stay alive he must rely on every trick he's learned. Willis has a small role as a rival mobster who gets fitted for cement overshoes. Kidman does well as Dutch's girlfriend. Kid fine as the gang's number man. Based on the novel by E.L. Doctorow. 107m/C VHS, DVD. Dustin Hoffman, Nicole Kidman, Loren Dean, Bruce Willis, Steven Hill, Steve Buscemi, Stanley Tucci, Tim Jerome, Billy Jaye, Katharine Houghton, Mike Starr, John A. Costelloe, Moira Kelly; **D:** Robert Benton; **W:** Tom Stoppard; **C:** Nestor Almendros; **M:** Mark Isham.

Billy Budd 🦴🦴🦴 1962 The classic Melville good-evil allegory adapted to film, dealing with a British warship in the late 1700s, and its struggle between evil master-at-arms and innocent shipmate. Stamp's screen debut as the naive Billy who is tried for the murder of the sadistic first mate. Well directed and acted. 123m/B VHS, DVD. GB Terence Stamp, Peter Ustinov, Robert Ryan, Melvyn Douglas, Paul Rogers, John Neville, Ronald Lewis, David McCallum, John Meillon; **D:** Peter Ustinov; **W:** Peter Ustinov, Robert Rossen; **C:** Robert Krasker.

Billy Elliot 🦴🦴🦴 (Dancer 2000 (R) Eleven-year-old Billy (Bell) is trying to survive in a Durham County mining town during the 1984 miners' strike that is affecting his family. His widowed dad (Lewis) wants Billy to take boxing lessons but the boy is more interested in the ballet class taught at the same gym by hard-living Mrs. Wilkinson (Walters), whose daughter Debbie (Blackwell) taunts Billy into trying to dance. Billy's natural talent is so great that Mrs. Wilkinson encourages him to audition for the Royal Ballet School in London. Of course, when his dad finds out what's been going on, there's trouble. The unfortunate rating is due to language but the film has all-around appeal and some fine performances. Stage director: Daldry makes his film debut as does Bell. 111m/C VHS, DVD, GB Jamie Bell, Julie Walters, Gary Lewis, Jamie Driven, Nicola Blackwell, Jean Heywood, Stuart Wells, Adam Cooper; D: Stephen Daldry; W: Lee Hall; C: Brian Tufano; M: Stephen Warbeck, British Acad. '00: Actor (Bell), Film, Support. Actress (Walters).

Billy Galvin 🐾🐾½ **1986 (PG)** A bullheaded ironworker tries to straighten out the turbulent relationship he has with his rebellious son. 95m/C VHS, Karl Malden, Lenny Von Dohlen, Joyce Van Patten, Toni Kalem, Keith Szarabajka, Alan North, Paul Guilfoyle, Barton Heyman; D: John Gray; W: John Gray; M: Joel Rosenblum.

Billy Jack 🐾🐾 **1971 (PG)** On an Arizona Indian reservation, a half-breed ex-Green Beret tries to straighten out what's bad news and makes sure the Texans never forget... Laughlin. Parallels James Thurber's... undertaker's assistant. Parallels James Thurber's story... skills (Laughlin) stands between a rural town and a school for runaways. Laughlin stars with his real-life wife Taylor. Features the then-hit song "One Tin Soldier," sung by Coven. The movie sets the market-ing by Laughlin inspired a "Billy Jack" cult phenomenon. A Spanish-dubbed version of this film is also available. Followed by a sequel in 1974, "Trail of Billy Jack," which bombed. 112m/C VHS, DVD, Tom Laughlin, Delores Taylor, Clark Howat, Bert Freed, Julie Webb, Victor Izay, Teresa Kelly, Lynn Baker, Stan Rice, Howard Hesseman; D: Tom Laughlin; W: Tom Laughlin, Delores Taylor; C: Fred W. Koenekamp; M: Murdell Lowe.

Billy Liar 🐾🐾🐾 **1963** A young Englishman dreams of escaping from his working class family and dead-end job as an undertaker's assistant. Parallels James Thurber's story, "The Secret Life of Walter Mitty." 94m/B VHS, DVD, GB Tom Courtenay, Julie Christie, Finlay Currie; D: John Schlesinger; W: Willis Hall, Keith Waterhouse; C: Denys Coop; M: Richard Rodney Bennett.

Billy Madison 🐾🐾 **1994 (PG-13)** Wealthy slacker Billy (Sandler) must prove to Dad he is capable of running the family hotel business by undertaking the obvious challenge of repeating grades 1-12 in six months. Ponder a few bodily function gags, and you'll have exhausted the humor in this lame attempt at creating a feature-length movie out of what would barely pass as a Saturday Night Live sketch. For only the most diehard fans of Sandler's silly shtick. 90m/C VHS, DVD, HD DVD, Adam Sandler, Darren McGavin, Bridgette Wilson-Sampras, Bradley Whitford, Josh Mostel, Norm MacDonald, Mark Beltzman, Larry Hankin, Theresa Merritt, Chris Farley, Steve Buscemi; D: Tamra Davis; W: Adam Sandler; C: Victor Hammer; M: Randy Edelman.

Billy Rose's Jumbo 🐾🐾🐾 **1962** Better-than-average update of the circus picture. Durante and Raye are terrific, as are the Rodgers and Hart songs. Fun, with lively production numbers in the inimitable Berkeley style. 🎵Over and Over Again; Circus on Parade; Why Can't I?; That's Can't Be Love; The Most Beautiful Girl in the World; My Romance; Little Girl Blue; What Is a Circus; Sawdust, Spangles and Dreams. 125m/C VHS, DVD, Doris Day, Stephen Boyd, Jimmy Durante, Martha Raye, Dean Jagger; D: Charles Walters; W: Sidney Sheldon.

Billy the Kid 🐾🐾½ **1941** Billy Bonney joins up with a group of outlaws in a Southwest town where he bumps into his old friend Jim Sherwood, now the marshal. Attempting to change his ways, he falls back into the life of a bandit when an outlaw friend is murdered. Although an entertaining western, the story bears no resemblance to the actual last days of Billy the Kid. Based on a story by Howard Emmett Rogers and Bradbury Foote, suggested by the book "The Saga of Billy the Kid" by Walter Noble Burns. 94m/C VHS, Robert Taylor, Brian Donlevy, Ian Hunter, Mary Howard, Gene Lockhart, Lon Chaney Jr., Henry O'Neill, Ted Adams, Frank Puglia, Mitchell Lewis, Dick Curtis, Grant Withers, Joe Yule, Eddie Dunn, Kermit Maynard, Chill Wills, Cy Kendall, Guinn "Big Boy" Williams; D: David Miller; M: David Snell.

Billy the Kid in Texas 🐾½ **1940** The famed outlaw takes on trouble and makes sure the Texans never forget that he has been there. 52m/B VHS, Bob Steele, Al "Fuzzy" St. John, Carleton Young, John Merton; D: Sam Newfield; M: Joseph O'Donnell.

Billy the Kid Returns 🐾½ **1938** While trying to clean up a town of its criminal element, Rogers is mistaken for the legendary Billy. Complications ensue. 60m/C VHS, DVD, Roy Rogers, George "Gabby" Hayes, Smiley Burnette, Lynne Roberts; D: Joseph Kane.

Billy the Kid Trapped 🐾½ **1942** Billy and his partner are rescued from hanging by an outlaw band. To put the bite on a pretty lady ranch owner. Her fiance, the legendary outlaw Billy the Kid, steps in to save his girl from coming a vampire herself. A Carradine camp classic. 95m/C VHS, DVD, Chuck Courtney, John Carradine, Melinda Plowman, Walter Janovitz, Harry Carey Jr., Roy Barcroft, Virginia Christine, Bing (Neil) Russel, Olive Carey, William Challee, William Forrest; D: William Beaudine; W: Carl K. Hittleman; C: Lothrop Worth; M: Raoul Kraushaar.

Billy the Kid Versus Dracula 🐾🐾 **1966** The title says it all. Dracula travels to the Old West, anxious to put the bite on a pretty lady ranch owner. Her fiance, the legendary outlaw Billy the Kid, steps in to save his girl from becoming a vampire herself. A Carradine camp classic. 95m/C VHS, DVD, Chuck Courtney, John Carradine, Melinda Plowman, Walter Janovitz, Harry Carey Jr., Roy Barcroft, Virginia Christine, Bing (Neil) Russel, Olive Carey, William Challee, William Forrest; D: William Beaudine; W: Carl K. Hittleman; C: Lothrop Worth; M: Raoul Kraushaar.

Billy Two Hats 🐾🐾½ **1973** *The Lady and the Outlaw* **1974 (PG)** Grizzled Scottish bandit Deans (Peck) teams up with young half-breed Billy (Arnaz Jr.) to pull off a robbery that results in an accidental death and Billy's capture. Deans is shot while breaking the kid out of jail and must rely on Billy to get him through, while being pursued by the law. It ain't happy. Mainly notable as the first western shot in Israel. 99m/C VHS, Gregory Peck, Desi Arnaz Jr., Jack Warden, Sian Barbara Allen, David Huddleston; D: Ted Kotcheff; W: Alan Sharp; C: Brian West; M: John Scott.

Billy's Holiday 🐾🐾½ **1995 (R)** Excessively offbeat Australian musical lacks the "highly polished look of Hollywood's best, but given the setting and subject matter, it is probably not meant to have it. The subject is Billy Apples (Cullen), hangdog hardware operator by day, hangdog jazz musician at night. His audiences regularly fall asleep, but Kate (McQuade), owner of the beauty shop down the street, still loves him. Then one night, Billy magically receives the ability to sing just like his idol, Billie Holiday. The main attractions are the likeably middle-aged stars and a soundtrack filled with big band tunes. 92m/C DVD, AU Max Cullen, Kris McQuade, Tina Bursill, Drew Forsythe, Genevieve Lemon, Richard Roxburgh, Rachel Coopes; D: Richard Wherrett; W: Denis Whitburn; C: Roger Lanser.

Billy's Hollywood Screen Kiss 🐾🐾½ **1998 (R)** Very gay Billy (Hayes) is an aspiring arts photographer in L.A. who's looking for romance. He thinks he's got a hot prospect in hand-some-if-sexually-confused Gabriel (Rowe), a waiter/model. Billy's latest project is recreating great film romantic scenes with drag queens and he hires Gabriel to play the male lover. But it looks as if Billy is going to get his heart broken if he expects Gabriel to carry the role over into real life. Amusing feature debut for director O'Haver and a standout performance from the witty Hayes. 92m/C VHS, DVD, Sean P. Hayes, Brad Rowe, Richard Ganoung, Meredith Scott Lynn, Paul Bartel, Armando Valdes-Kennedy; D: Tommy O'Haver; W: Tommy O'Haver; C: Mark Mervis; M: Alan Ari Lazar.

Biohazard: The Alien Force 🐾½ **1995 (R)** Reptilian mutant, the result of a genetic experiment gone awry, must be hunted down before it can reproduce. Sounds like a rip-off of "Species." 86m/C VHS, DVD, Steve Zurk, Chris Mitchum, Susan Fronsoe, Tom Ferguson, Patrick Moran, John Maynard; D: Steve Latshaw.

The Bionic Woman 🐾🐾 **1975** Sky-diving accident leaves tennis pro Jaime Somers crippled and near death. Her bionic buddy, Steve Austin, gets his friends to rebuild her and make her better than she was before. Pilot for the TV series. 96m/C VHS, Lindsay Wagner, Lee Majors, Richard Anderson, Alan Oppenheimer; D: Richard (Dick) Moder. TV

Biozombie 🐾🐾½ **1998** Playing as a mixture of "Mallrats" and "Dawn of the Dead," this Hong Kong import is aimed squarely at a Generation-X audience. The film introduces us to Woody (Jordan Chan) and Bee (Sam Lee), two slackers who work at a video store. While on an errand to pick up their boss's car, they hit a strange pedestrian and take him back to the mall. This stranger turns out to be a zombie, and he soon infects several others. With the mall locked up for the night, Woody and Bee must fend for themselves to protect the few humans remaining...while doing the least amount of work possible. The two start with the comedic coaster ride, as we start into the action-horror, opening, then move into the action-horror, and then finally ending. 94m/C DVD, HK Jordan Chan, Sam Lee; D: Wilson (Wai Shun) Yip.

Bio-Dome 🐾 **1996 (PG-13)** Pauly Shore in a hermetically sealed environment. Shore is separated from the rest of society? Great! Where do I sign? Unfortunately, it's only a movie, and a typically useless one, at that. Shore brings his lame schtick to a buddy Doyle (Baldwin) mistake for a mall buddy Doyle (Baldwin) mistake for a mall and eventually destroy. In Bloom's notebook mesquerade as a script, while the supporting cast wanders aimlessly, perhaps pondering a switch in agents. 94m/C VHS, DVD, Jack Black, Kyle Gass, Pauly Shore, Stephen Baldwin, William Atherton, Henry Gibson, Joey Lauren Adams, Teresa Hill, Kylie Minogue, Kevin West, Denise Dowse, Dara Tomanovic; D: Jason Bloom; W: Kip Koenig, Scott Marcano; C: Phedon Papamichael; M: Andrew Gross. Golden Raspberries '96: Worst Actor (Shore).

Bird 🐾🐾🐾 **1988 (R)** The richly textured, though sadly one-sided biography of jazz sax great Charlie Parker, from his rise to stardom to his premature death via extended heroin use. A remarkably assured, deeply imagined film from Eastwood that never really shows the genius of creation. The soundtrack has Parker's own solos re-mastered from original recordings. 160m/C VHS, DVD, Forest Whitaker, Diane Venora, Michael Zelniker, Samuel E. Wright, Keith David, Michael McGuire, James Handy, Damon Whitaker, Morgan Nagler, Peter Crook; D: Clint Eastwood; W: Joel Oliansky; C: Jack N. Green; M: Lennie Niehaus. Oscars '88: Sound; Cannes '88: Actor (Whitaker); Golden Globes '89: Director (Eastwood); N.Y. Film Critics '88: Support. Actress (Venora).

Bird of Paradise 🐾🐾½ **1932** An exotic South Seas romance in which an adventurer is cast onto a remote Polyne-sian island when his yacht hazardly sails onto a coral reef. There he becomes enamored of an exotic island girl, and natives seems to disapprove. 80m/B VHS, DVD, Joel McCrea, Dolores Del Rio, Lon Chaney Jr.; D: King Vidor; M: Max Steiner.

Bird of Prey 🐾½ **1995 (R)** Nick Miley (Milushev) has just been released from a Bulgarian prison for attacking Jonathan Griffin (Chamberlain), the drugs-and-arms dealer who was responsible for the death of Miley's policeman father. But Miley still wants revenge, though matters get complicated by Mley (Tilly), Griffin's naive daughter, with whom he falls in love. Plot's so-so but the roughness. Filmed on location in Sofia, Bulgaria. 102m/C VHS, Boyan Milushev, Jennifer Tilly, Richard Chamberlain, Lenny Von Dohlen, Robert Carradine, Lesley Ann Warren; D: Temistocles Lopez; W: Robert Frimes; M: Hans Zimmer.

The Bird with the Crystal Plumage 🐾🐾½ **1970** *L'Uccello dalle Piume di Cristallo; The Phantom of Terror; The Bird with the Glass Feathers; The Gallery Murders* **1970 (PG)** An American writer living in Rome witnesses a murder. He becomes involved in the mystery when the alleged murderer is cleared because the woman believed to be his next victim is shown to be a psychopathic murderer. Vintage Argento mayhem. 98m/C VHS, Tony Musante, Suzy Kendall, Eva Renzi, Enrico Maria Salerno, Mario Adorf, Renato Romano, Reggie Nalder, Werner Peters, Umberto Raho, Dario Argento; D: Dario Argento; C: Vittorio Storaro; M: Ennio Morricone.

The Birdcage 🐾🐾🐾 **1996 (R)** Somewhat overlong but well-played remake of "La Cage aux Folles" features Williams suppressing his usual manic schtick to portray Armand, the subdued half of a longtime gay couple living in Miami. H's partner is the ever-hys-

Bimini Code 🐾 **1984** Two female adventurers accept a dangerous mission where they wind up on Bimini Island in a showdown with the mysterious Madame X. 95m/C VHS, Vickie Benson, Krista Richardson, Frank Alexander, Rosanna Simanaitis; D: Barry Clark.

Bingo 🐾🐾½ **1991 (PG)** Mediocre spoof of hero-dog movies. The heroic title mutt roams from Denver to Green Bay in search of his absent-minded master, with numerous absurd adventures en route. Some cute moments, but sometimes Bingo is just lame-o. Good family fare. 90m/C VHS, DVD, Cindy Williams, David Rasche, Robert J. Steinmiller Jr., David French, Kurt Fuller, Joe Guzzaldo, Glenn Shadix; D: Matthew Robbins; W: Jim Strain; M: Richard Gibbs.

Bingo Long Traveling All-Stars & Motor Kings 🐾🐾 **1976 (PG)** Set in 1939, this film follows the comedic adventures of a lively group of black ball players who have defected from the old Negro National League. The All-Stars travel the country challenging local white teams. 111m/C VHS, DVD, Billy Dee Williams, James Earl Jones, Richard Pryor, Stan Shaw; D: John Badham; W: Hal Barwood; C: Bill Butler; M: William Goldstein.

Bird on a Wire 🐾🐾 **1990 (PG-13)** Disappointing action-comedy finds Gibson forced to emerge from a prolonged period under the Witness Protection Program, whereupon he and ex-girlfriend Hawn are pursued by old enemies. Too little action and too little comedy add up to surprising-ly dull outing, considering the cast. 110m/C VHS, DVD, Mel Gibson, Goldie Hawn, David Carradine, Bill Duke, Stephen Tobolowsky, Clyde Kusatsu, Joan Severance, Harry Caesar, John Pyper-Ferguson, Jeff Corey; D: John Badham; W: David Seltzer; C: Robert Primes; M: Hans Zimmer.

The Birch Interval 🐾🐾½ **1978 (PG)** A chronicle of a young Amish girl growing up and experiencing adult passions and fears when she visits her kin in their isolated Pennsylvania community. 104m/C VHS, Eddie Albert, Rip Torn, Ann Wedgeworth; D: Delbert Mann; W: Joanna Crawford.

Biloxi Blues 🐾🐾🐾 **1988 (PG-13)** Eugene Morris Jerome has been drafted and sent to boot camp in Biloxi, Mississippi where he encounters a troubled drill sergeant, hostile recruits, and a skillful prostitute. Walken is the drill sergeant from hell. Some good laughs from the ever-wry Broderick. A sequel to Neil Simon's "Brighton Beach Memoirs" and adapted by Simon from his play. Followed by "Broadway Bound." 105m/C VHS, DVD, Matthew Broderick, Christopher Walken, Casey Siemaszko, Matt Mulhern, Corey Parker, Penelope Ann Miller, Michael Dolan, Park Overall; D: Mike Nichols; W: Neil Simon; C: Bill Butler; M: Georges Delerue.

terical-but-loving drag queen Albert (Lane), whose presence provides a distinct challenge when Armand's son Val (Futterman) announces his engagement to the daughter of family values, right-wing senator Kevin Keeley (Hackman). When the Senator and family arrive for dinner, Armand tries to play it straight while Albert opts for a matronly mom impersonation (think Barbara Bush). Highlights include Armand's initial attempts to teach Albert to be butch (walk like John Wayne) and Hackman congoing in drag. **120m/C VHS, DVD.** Robin Williams, Nathan Lane, Gene Hackman, Dianne Wiest, Hank Azaria, Dan Futterman, Christine Baranski, Calista Flockhart, Tom McGowan; *D:* Mike Nichols; *W:* Elaine May; *C:* Emmanuel Lubezki; *M:* Mark Mothersbaugh, Jonathan Tunick. Screen Actors Guild '96: Cast.

Birdman of Alcatraz 🦴🦴🦴 **1962** Robert Stroud, convicted of two murders and sentenced to life imprisonment on the Island, becomes an internationally accepted authority on birds. Lovingly told, with stunning performance from Lancaster. The confinement of Stroud's prison cell makes the film seem claustrophobic and tedious at times, just as the imprisonment must have been. Ritter played Stroud's mother, who never stops trying to get him out of prison. **143m/B VHS, DVD.** Burt Lancaster, Karl Malden, Thelma Ritter, Betty Field, Neville Brand, Edmond O'Brien, Hugh Marlowe, Telly Savalas; *D:* John Frankenheimer; *W:* Guy Trosper; *C:* Burnett Guffey, Robert Krasker; *M:* Elmer Bernstein. British Acad. '62: Actor (Lancaster).

The Birds 🦴🦴½ **1963 (PG-13)** Hitchcock attempted to top the success of "Psycho" with this terrifying tale of Man versus Nature, in which Nature alights, one by one, on the trees of Bodega Bay to stage a bloody act of revenge upon the civilized world. Only Hitchcock can twist the harmless into the horrific while avoiding the ridiculous; this is perhaps his most brutal film, and one of the cinema's purest, horrifying portraits of apocalypse. Based on a short story by Daphne Du Maurier; screenplay by novelist Evan Hunter (aka Ed McBain). **120m/C VHS, DVD.** Rod Taylor, Tippi Hedren, Jessica Tandy, Veronica Cartwright, Suzanne Pleshette, Ethel Griffies, Charles McGraw, Ruth McDevitt, Lonny (Lonnie) Chapman, Joe Mantell, Morgan Brittany, Alfred Hitchcock; *D:* Alfred Hitchcock; *W:* Evan Hunter; *C:* Robert Burks; *M:* Bernard Herrmann.

The Birds 2: Land's End woof! **1994 (R)** Unfortunate rip-off of the Hitchcock fright classic. Killer seagulls begin attacking the inhabitants of east coast Gull Island. Seems they're tired of being ol' slick victims. Hedren's the town shopkeeper in a role that's nothing like the one she played in the original. Definitely for the birds—even the director refuses to acknowledge it by officially using the film industry pseudonym "Alan Smithee." Made for TV. **87m/C VHS.** Brad Johnson, Chelsea Field, Tippi Hedren, James Naughton, Jan Rubes, Megan Gallagher; *D:* Rick Rosenthal; *W:* Jim Wheat, Ken Wheat. **TV**

Birds & the Bees 🦴🦴 **1956** A millionaire falls in love with an alluring card shark, and then calls it all off when he learns of her profession, only to fall in love with her again when she disguises herself. A remake—and poor shade—of Preston Sturge's 1941 classic "The Lady Eve." **94m/C VHS.** Mitzi Gaynor, David Niven, George Gobel, Reginald Gardiner, Hans Conried; *D:* Norman Taurog; *W:* Sidney Sheldon.

Birds of Prey 🦴🦴 **1972** Action film pits an ex-WWII army pilot against a group of kidnapping thieves in an airborne chopper chase. **81m/C VHS, DVD.** David Janssen, Ralph Meeker, Elayne Heilveil; *D:* William A. Graham; *C:* Jordan Cronenweth. **TV**

Birdy 🦴🦴½ **1984 (R)** An adaptation of the William Wharton novel about two Philadelphia youths, one with normal interests, the other obsessed with birds, and their eventual involvement in the Vietnam War, wrecking one physically and the other mentally. A hypnotic, evocative film, with a compelling Peter Gabriel soundtrack. **120m/C VHS, DVD.** Matthew Modine, Nicolas Cage, John Harkins, Sandy Baron, Karen

Young, Bruno Kirby; *D:* Alan Parker; *W:* Jack Behr, Sandy Kroopf; *M:* Peter Gabriel. Cannes '85: Grand Jury Prize.

Birgitt Haas Must Be Killed 🦴🦴½ **1983** A ruthless secret agent (Noiret) plots to murder a German female terrorist and make it appear that her boyfriend was the killer. Never quite hits the mark, despite novel premise and strong cast. **105m/C VHS.** Philippe Noiret, Jean Rochefort, Elisabeth (Lisa) Kreuzer; *D:* Laurent Heynemann.

Birth 🦴🦴 **2004 (R)** Creepy psychological thriller finds widowed Anna (Kidman) finally making a commitment to marry Joseph (Huston) ten years after her husband Sean's death. That is until a strange 10-year-old, also named Sean (Bright), turns up insisting that Anna cannot remarry because he is her spouse. Sean is impervious to any suggestion otherwise and his very insistence comes to convince the emotionally fragile woman. None of this goes over well with Anna's imperious mother (Bacall) in the form of angel Dudley (Grant), who's sent down to earth at Christmas to help work things out. Various explanations are offered and director Glazer elegantly camouflages plot holes. Kidman, with her severe pixie haircut, somewhat resembles Mia Farrow in "Rosemary's Baby," but one thing you can be certain of is here, the devil didn't do it. **100m/C DVD.** *US* Nicole Kidman, Cameron Bright, Danny Huston, Lauren Bacall, Arliss Howard, Alison Elliot, Anne Heche, Peter Stormare, Ted Levine, Cara Seymour, Zoe Caldwell, Milo Addica; *D:* Jonathan Glazer; *W:* Milo Addica, Jonathan Glazer, Jean-Claude Carriere; *C:* Harris Savides; *M:* Alexandre Desplat.

The Birth of a Nation 🦴🦴🦴🦴 *The Clansman* **1915** Lavish Civil War epic in which Griffith virtually invented the basics of film grammar. Gish and Walthall have some of the most moving scenes ever filmed and the masterful battle choreography brought the art of cinematography to new heights. Griffith's positive attitude toward the KKK notwithstanding, this was the first feature length silent, and it brought credibility to an entire industry. Based on the play "The Clansman" and the book "The Leopard's Spots" by Thomas Dixon, it is still a rouser, and of great historical interest. Silent with music score. Also available in a 124-minute version. **175m/B VHS, DVD.** Lillian Gish, Mae Marsh, Henry B. Walthall, Ralph Lewis, Miriam "Bobbie" Harron, George Siegmann, Joseph Henabery, Spottiswoode Aitken, George Beranger, Mary Alden, Josephine Crowell, Elmer Clifton, Walter Long, Howard Gaye, Miriam Cooper, John Ford, Sam De Grasse, Maxfield Stanley, Donald Crisp, Raoul Walsh, Erich von Stroheim, Eugene Pallette, Wallace Reid; *D:* D.W. Griffith; *W:* D.W. Griffith, Frank E. Woods; *C:* Billy (G.W.) Bitzer; *M:* D.W. Griffith. AFI '98: Top 100, Natl. Film Reg. '92.

Birth of the Blues 🦴🦴½ **1941** Songman Crosby starts a band in New Orleans in the midst of the jazz boom. Help from partner Martin and real-life trombonist Teagarden, with comic relief from Eddie "Rochester" Anderson, make for a fun-filled story. Plot is riddled with some unbelievable gangster scenes, but the music and laughs will keep you amused. In B&W with color segments. ♪St. Louis Blues; St. James Infirmary; Melancholy Baby; Birth of the Blues. **76m/B VHS, DVD.** Bing Crosby, Mary Martin, Brian Donlevy, Eddie Anderson, J. Carrol Naish, Cecil Kellaway, Warren Hymer, Horace McMahon, Carolyn Lee, Jack Teagarden; *D:* Victor Schertzinger; *W:* Harry Tugend, Walter Deleon; *C:* William Mellor; *M:* Robert Emmett Dolan.

Birthday Boy 🦴 **1985** A cable comedy about a buffoonish salesman's 30th birthday, on which he takes an ill-fated business trip. Written by Belushi. **33m/C VHS.** James Belushi; *D:* Claude Conrad; *W:* James Belushi. **CABLE**

Birthday Girl 🦴🦴 **2002 (R)** Love story cum actioner stars Chaplin as a timid London bank clerk, John, and Kidman as Nadia, his mysterious and sexy online Russian mail-order bride with a secret. Nadia doesn't speak English, but the two begin to speak the international language anyway. Afraid, intrigued, then tickled with his Soviet missus who brings some color

into his dull, drab life, John hardly has time to wallow in his newfound bliss when he's beset by Russian baddies (Frenchmen Kassovitz and Cassel) claiming to be Nadia's relatives, who show up on his doorstep one day. Kidman shows her range, however, and reportedly learned Russian for the film. Decent turn from the Butterworth clan, despite novel premise and the hip debut film "Mojo." **93m/C VHS, DVD.** *US GB* Nicole Kidman, Ben Chaplin, Vincent Cassel, Mathieu Kassovitz, Kate Evans; *D:* Jez Butterworth; *W:* Jez Butterworth, Tom Butterworth; *C:* Oliver Stapleton; *M:* Stephen Warbeck.

The Bishop's Wife 🦴🦴🦴 **1947** Episcopalian biship Henry (Niven) is praying to find the money to build a new church but his faith is shaky and his marriage to Julia (Young) even more so. But his prayers are answered (although Henry doesn't know it) in the form of angel Dudley (Grant), who's sent down to help this an entertaining outing. Based on the novel by Robert Nathan. **109m/B VHS, DVD.** Cary Grant, Loretta Young, David Niven, Monty Woolley, Elsa Lanchester, James Gleason, Gladys Cooper, Regis Toomey; *D:* Henry Koster; *W:* Leonardo Bercovici, Robert Sherwood; *C:* Gregg Toland; *M:* Hugo Friedhofer. Oscars '47: Sound.

The Bitch WOOF! **1978 (R)** High-camp follies and the rule in this lustful continuation of "The Stud" as it follows the erotic adventures of a beautiful divorcee playing sex games for high stakes on the international playgrounds of high society. A collaborative effort by the sisters Collins: written by Jackie, with sister Joan well cast in the title role. **90m/C VHS, DVD.** *GB* Joan Collins, Kenneth Haigh, Michael Coby, Ian Hendry, Carolyn Seymour, Sue Lloyd, John Ratzenberger; *D:* Gerry O'Hara.

Bite the Bullet 🦴🦴🦴½ **1975 (PG)** Moralistic western tells of a grueling 600-mile horse race where the participants reluctantly develop respect for one another. Unheralded upon release and shot in convincing epic style by Harry Stradling, Jr. Excellent cast. **131m/C VHS, DVD.** Gene Hackman, James Coburn, Candice Bergen, Dabney Coleman, Jan-Michael Vincent, Ben Johnson, Ian Bannen, Paul Stewart, Sally Kirkland, Mario Arteaga; *D:* Richard Brooks; *W:* Richard Brooks; *C:* Harry Stradling Jr.; *M:* Alex North.

Bitter Harvest 🦴🦴🦴 **1981** Emmy-nominated TV movie concerning a dairy farmer frantically trying to discover what is mysteriously killing off his herd. Howard is excellent as the farmer battling the bureaucracy to find the truth. Based on a true story. **98m/C VHS.** Ron Howard, Art Carney, Tarah Nutter, Richard Dysart, Barry Corbin, Jim Haynie, David Knell; *D:* Roger Young. **TV**

Bitter Harvest 🦴🦴 **1993 (R)** Rubin and Kensit are the femme fatales who turn their considerable wiles on the innocent Baldwin. He's more than happy to be their lover but does he want to be their victim as well? **98m/C VHS.** Stephen Baldwin, Patsy Kensit, Jennifer Rubin, Adam Baldwin, M. Emmet Walsh; *D:* Duane Clark; *W:* Randall Fontana; *C:* Remi Adefarasin.

Bitter Moon 🦴🦴 **1992 (R)** Polanski effort looks promising, but ultimately disappoints. Bored British couple (Grant and Scott Thomas) meet up with sexual deviants (Coyote and Seigner, aka Mrs. Polanski) on a cruise and learn that passion and cruelty often share the same path to destruction. Masquerades as high class art, but whenever substance is lacking expect a silly, kinky sex scene. Needless to say, there isn't much substance, so erotic mischief abounds. Scott Thomas manages to hold her own, but Coyote is almost embarrassingly over the top. Based on the Pascal Bruckner novel "Lunes de Fiel." **139m/C VHS, DVD.** Peter Coyote, Emmanuelle Seigner, Hugh Grant, Kristin Scott Thomas, Stockard Channing, Victor Banerjee, Sophie Patel; *D:* Roman Polanski; *W:* Roman Polanski, Gerard Brach, John Brownjohn; *C:* Tonino Delli Colli; *M:* Vangelis.

Bitter Rice 🦴🦴🦴 *Riso Amaro* **1949** Mangano became a star with her sultry performance about survival in postwar Italy. She scrapes by, working in the rice

fields of the Po Valley, loved by the down-to-earth Vallone, who provides her with little excitement. Gassman is the rotten-to-the-core thief who meets up with Mangano while he's running from the police. He mistreats her, she steals his money and betrays her friends, and both destroy each other. In Italian with English subtitles. **96m/C VHS.** *IT* Silvana Mangano, Vittorio Gassman, Raf Vallone, Doris Dowling; *D:* Giuseppe de Santis; *W:* Giuseppe de Santis, Carlo Lizzani, Gianni Puccini; *C:* Otello Martelli; *M:* Goffredo Petrassi.

Bitter Sugar 🦴🦴🦴 *Azucar Amarga* **1996** Young, idealistic communist Gustavo (Lavan) is a Havana university student who still believes that the Castro regime can make things better. His rock musician brother Bobby (Villanueva) is a radical, defying government policies, and his psychiatrist father Tomas (Gutierrez) makes more money playing piano at a tourist hotel than in his practice. But Gustavo's eyes are opened, not only by his family situation, but when he falls in love with cynical dancer Yolanda (Vilan), who longs to escape to Miami. Serious politics bolstered by excellent performances and sharp cinematography. Spanish with subtitles. **102m/B VHS, DVD.** *CU* René Lavan, Mayte Vilan, Miguel Gutierrez, Larry Villanueva; *D:* Leon Ichaso; *W:* Leon Ichaso, Orestes Matacena; *C:* Claudio Chea; *M:* Manuel Tejada.

Bitter Sweet 🦴🦴 **1933** Tragic tale of a woman who finally marries the man she loves, only to find that he is a compulsive gambler. Written by Coward, adapted from his operetta. **76m/B VHS.** *GB* Anna Neagle, Fernand Gravey, Esme Percy, Clifford Heatherley, Hugh Williams; *D:* Herbert Wilcox; *W:* Noel Coward.

Bitter Sweet 🦴🦴 **1940** The second version of the Noel Coward operetta, about young romance in 1875 Vienna. Creaky and overrated, but the lush Technicolor and Coward standards help to compensate. ♪Zigeuner; I'll See You Again. **94m/C VHS.** Jeanette MacDonald, Nelson Eddy, George Sanders, Felix Bressart, Ian Hunter, Sig Rumann, Herman Bing, Fay Holden, Curt Bois, Edward Ashley; *D:* Woodbridge S. Van Dyke; *W:* Lesser Samuels, Noel Coward.

Bitter Sweet 🦴🦴 **1998 (R)** Everhart spends four years in the big house after being tricked by her boyfriend into participating in a robbery. Just when she wants when she gets out is to get revenge on the lowlife and she gets the opportunity when approached by cop Russo, who's looking to bring down her ex-beau's gangster boss (Roberts). **96m/C VHS, DVD.** Angie Everhart, James Russo, Eric Roberts, Brian Wimmer; *D:* Luca Bercovici. **VIDEO**

The Bitter Tea of General Yen 🦴🦴🦴 **1933** Stanwyck arrives in Shanghai to marry a missionary (Gordon) during the threatening days of China's civil war. Unexpectedly swept into the arms of an infamous warlord (Asher), she becomes fascinated, although his enemies close in. Exotic and poetic, if melodramatic by today's standards. The interracial aspects were considered very daring for their time. Adapted from the book by Grace Zaring Stone. **89m/B VHS.** Barbara Stanwyck, Nils Asther, Gavin Gordon, Walter Connolly, Lucien Littlefield, Toshia Mori, Richard Loo, Clara Blandick; *D:* Frank Capra; *W:* Edward Paramore.

The Bitter Tears of Petra von Kant 🦴🦴½ *Die Bitteren Traenen der Petra von Kant* **1972** Dark German story of lesbian love, the fashion world, obsession and anger. Claustrophobic settings and slow pace may frustrate some viewers. In German with English subtitles. **124m/C VHS, DVD.** *GE* Margit Carstensen, Hanna Schygulla, Irm Hermann, Eva Mattes; *D:* Rainer Werner Fassbinder; *W:* Rainer Werner Fassbinder; *C:* Michael Ballhaus.

Bitter Vengeance 🦴🦴 **1994 (R)** Security guard Jack Westford (Greenwood) pulls off a bank heist with his lover Isabella (Hocking) and plans to frame his wife Annie (Madsen) for the crime. Only Annie finds out and sets out to get them before the police get her. **90m/C VHS.** Virginia Madsen, Bruce Greenwood, Kristen Dalton, Eddie Velez, Gordon Jump, Carlos Gomez, Tim Russ; **D:** Stuart Cooper; **W:** Pablo F. Fenjves; **M:** David Michael Frank. CABLE

Bittersweet Love ♂♂ 1976 (PG) Two young people fall in love and marry, only to have the bride's mother and the groom's father confess that the two newlyweds are actually half-siblings. 92m/C VHS. Lana Turner, Celeste Holm, Robert Alda, Meredith Baxter; **D:** David Miller.

Bix ♂♂ 1990 Based on the brief life of legendary Jazz Age cornetist Leon Bix Beiderbecke, who died at age 28. Story unfolds in flashbacks, through friend Joe Venuti memories of the dissipated genius and the music he created with fellow musicians. Pee Wee Russell, Paul White-michael, and others. 100m/C VHS. **IT** Bryant, Robert Egon Spechtenhauser, Sterano Sabelli. **D:** Giuliana Gamba.

Bizarre Bizarre ♂♂♂ *Drole de Drama* 1939 A mystery writer is accused of murder and disappears, only to return in disguise to try to clear his name. Along the way, a number of French comedians are introduced within a revue of comedy-farce sketches that include slapstick, burlesque, black humor, and comedy of the absurd. In French with English subtitles. 90m/B VHS, DVD. **FR** Louis Jouvet, Michel Simon, Françoise Rosay, Jean-Pierre Aumont, Nadine Vogel, Henri Guisol, Jacques Prevert; **C:** Eugen Shuftan; **W:** Maurice Jaubert.

Black & White ♂♂½ 1999 (R) Rookie coo Chris O'Brien (Cochrane) is partnered with tough veteran female officer Nora Hugosian (Gershon), who's known for her sexiness and her ruthless style. The two begin an affair while searching for a serial killer. And then the rookie comes across some evidence that seems to implicate his partner in the crimes. 97m/C VHS, DVD. Gina Gershon, Rory Cochrane, Ron Silver, Alison Eastwood, Marshall Bell; **D:** James Tobeck; **W:** James Tobeck; **C:** Phil Parmel.

Black Abbot, The ♂♂ 1963 A mysterious black-hooded figure is seen entering a ruined Abbey tower that leads to a country house with buried treasure. Based on an Edgar Wallace story. 95m/C VHS. GE Joachim Fuchsberger, Dieter Borsche, Grit Bottcher, Eva Scholtz, Franz Gottlieb; **D:** Franz Gottlieb.

Black and White ♂♂♂ 1999 (R) Director Toback attempts to investigate white kids' fascination with black hip-hop culture by creating an intriguing combination of pseudo-documentary and urban melodrama with cameos and performances by professional celebrities alongside professional actors. In the more effective part of the film, Mike Tyson (playing himself in one of the film's strongest scenes). The part that doesn't work as well is the more conventional storyline (which seems added to satisfy studio executives looking for straight narrative) involving an undercover cop, 'Stiller' bribing college basketball star Dean (Houston) to throw a game in an attempt to get at Dean's best friend Rich (Power), a drug kingpin turned rap mogul. While the parts don't add up to an entirely satisfying whole, the journey is worth the interesting ride. 98m/C VHS, DVD. Scott Caan, Robert Downey Jr., Stacy Edwards, Gaby Hoffman, Jared Leto, Marla Maples, Joe Pantoliano, Brooke Shields, Power, Claudia Schiffer, William Lee Scott, Ben Stiller, Eddie Kaye Thomas, Elliott Mooc, Mike Tyson, James Tobeck, Allan Houston, Kidada Jones, Bijou Phillips, Raekwon; **D:** James Tobeck; **W:** James Tobeck; **C:** David Ferrara.

Bizarre ♂ 1987 When a wife escapes her perverse, psychologically threatening marriage, she finds her husband still haunts her literally and figuratively, and plots psychological revenge. Dubbed. 93m/C VHS, DVD. **IT** Florence Guerin, Luciano Bartoli, Robert Egon Spechtenhauser, Sterano Sabelli. **D:** Giuliana Gamba.

Black Arrow, The ♂♂ 1934 Ex-iled bowman returns to England to avenge the injustices of a villainous nobleman. Cable version of the Robert Louis Stevenson medieval romp is not as well done as the 1948 adaptation. 93m/C VHS. Oliver Reed, Benedict Taylor, Georgia Slowe, Stephan Chase, Donald Pleasence. **D:** John Hough. CABLE

Black Beauty ♂♂ 1971 (G) International remake of the classic horse story has its shares of ups and downs. Timeless tale still captures children and adults to tears. Six-year-old quarterhorse named Justin gives a nuanced portrayal as the Black Beauty, recalling Olivier in "Hamlet." Directorial debut of "Secret Garden" screenwriter Thompson. 89m/C VHS, DVD. Mark Lester, Walter Slezak; **D:** James Hill; **C:** Chris Menges; **M:** Lionel Bart.

Black Beauty ♂♂ 1994 (G) Re-make of the classic Anna Sewell children's novel about an off-sold horse whose life is told by following a trail of clues from its owner by following a trail of clues of the first horse whose life has its shares of ups and downs. 88m/C VHS, DVD. Sean Bean, David Thewlis, Jim Carter, Alun Armstrong, Eleanor Bron, Pete Cook, Peter Davison, John McEnery, Nicholas Jones; **D:** Caroline Thompson; **C:** Alex Thomson.

Black Belly of the Tarantula, The ♂♂ *La Tarantula dal Ventre Nero* 1971 Inspector Tellini (Giannini) investigates a series of murders where the victims are first paralyzed with wasp venom before being cut open while they're still alive. And the connection between the victims seems to be a beauty spa. Italian with subtitles. 89m/C DVD. **IT** Giancarb Giannini, Claudine Auger, Barbara Bouchet, Stefania Sandrelli, Barbara Bach, Rossella Falk; **D:** Paolo Cavara; **M:** Ennio Morricone.

Black Angel ♂♂ 1946 Catherine Bennett (Vincent) tries to clear the name of estranged husband Kirk (Phillips), who's accused of murdering chanteuse Mavis Marlowe (Dowling). Catherine enlists the aid of another suspect in the crime by moonlighting as the club's new chanteuse, Mavis' husband, drunken songwriter Martin Blair (Duryea), whom she suspects actually did the deed. Another suspect is sleazy nightclub owner Marko (Lorre), where the duo get a job to check things out. Blair falls for Catherine and goes on the psychic ride as Kirk's execution day draws ever closer. Atmospheric noir is based on the novel by Cornell Woolrich. 80m/B VHS, DVD. June Vincent, Dan Duryea, Peter Lorre, Broderick Crawford, Hobart Cavanaugh, Constance Dowling, Wallace Ford; **D:** Roy William Neill; **M:** Frank Skinner.

Black Arrow ♂♂♂ 1948 Original adventure film of the famous Robert Louis Stevenson novel. Upon return from 16th century's War of the Roses, a young man must avenge his father's murder by following a trail of clues in the form of black arrows. Well made and fun. 76m/B VHS, DVD. Louis Hayward, Janet Blair, George Macready, Edgar Buchanan, Paul Cavanagh; **D:** Gordon Douglas.

Black Beauty ♂♂ 1946 In this adaptation of Anna Sewell's familiar novel, a young girl develops a kindred relationship with an extraordinary horse. 74m/B VHS. Mona Freeman, Richard Denning, Evelyn Ankers; **D:** Max Nosseck.

Black Box Affair ♂♂ 1966 An American secret agent must find a black box lost in a B-52 plane crash before it falls into the wrong hands. 95m/C VHS, SP Craig Hill, Teresa Gimpera, Luis Martin, Jorge (George) Rigaud; **D:** James B. Harris.

Black Brigade ♂♂ 1969 Pryor and Williams star in this low budget movie as leaders of an all-black outfit assigned to a suicide mission behind Nazi lines during WWII. Their force wreaks havoc and earns them the respect of their military higher-ups. Lots of action and climactic finish. 90m/C VHS, DVD. Stephen Boyd, Robert Hooks, Susan Oliver, Roosevelt "Rosie" Grier, Moses Gunn, Richard Pryor, Billy Dee Williams; **D:** George McCowan; **W:** Aaron Spelling; **M:** Fred Steiner.

Black Cadillac ♂♂ 2003 A night of partying goes awry when a bum car carrying three buddies in the frigid, lonely mountains. Their bad luck seems to change after a deputy sheriff rescues them, but relief turns to terror as they find a mysterious black Cadillac on their tail. Effective entry in the "mysterious spooky car" genre. 92m/C VHS, DVD. Randy Quaid, Kiersten Warren, Shane Johnson, Josh Hammond, Jason Dohring, Adam Verner; **D:** John Murlowski; **M:** Chris Bell. VIDEO

Black Caesar ♂♂ 1973 (R) A small-time hood climbs the ladder to the head of a Harlem crime syndicate. Music by James Brown. Followed by the sequel "Hell Up in Harlem." 92m/C VHS, DVD. Fred Williamson, Julius W. Harris, Val Avery, Art Lund, Gloria Hendry, James Dixon; **D:** Larry Cohen; **M:** Larry Cohen; **C:** Fenton Hamilton, James Brown.

Black and White in Color ♂♂♂ *La Victoire en Chantant* 1976 (PG) Award-winning satire about a French soldier at an African outpost, who, upon hearing the news of the beginning of WWI, takes it upon himself to attack a neighbor. In German fort. Calamity ensues. In French, with English subtitles. 100m/C VHS, DVD. **FR** Jean Carmet, Jacques Dufilho, Catherine Rouvel, Jacques Spiesser, Dora Doll, Jacques Perrin; **D:** Jean-Jacques Annaud; **M:** Georges Conchon, Jean-Jacques Annaud; **M:** Pierre Bachelet. Oscars '76: Foreign Film.

Black and White As Day and Night ♂♂ 1978 A man's talent for the game of chess becomes a destructive obsession, and he loses himself in the game. In German with English subtitles. 103m/C VHS. Bruno Ganz, Rene Deltgen, Ljuba Tadic, Gila von Weitershausen; **D:** Wolfgang Petersen; **W:** Jochen Wedegartner, Karl Heinz Willschrei; **C:** Jorg-Michael Baldenius; **M:** Klaus Doldinger.

Black Belt ♂♂ 1992 (R) A private detective is hired to protect a rock star from a fanatic Vietnam vet. 80m/C VHS, DVD. Don "The Dragon" Wilson, Richard Beymer, Alan Blumenfeld, Matthias Hues; **D:** Charles Philip Moore.

Black Belt Jones ♂♂ 1974 (R) Martial arts expert fights the mob to save a school of self-defense in Los Angeles' Watts district. 87m/C VHS. Jim Kelly, Gloria Hendry, Scatman Crothers; **D:** Robert Clouse.

Black Bikers from Hell ♂♂½ *Black Angels* 1970 (R) Black gang-members infiltrate and wreak havoc on their rivals. Who can stop these brutal young men? Cast: with real bikers and biker chicks. 87m/C VHS. John King III, Des Roberts, Linda Jackson, James Whitworth, James Young-El, Clancy Syrko, Beverly Gardner; **D:** Laurence Merrick.

Black Bird, The ♂½ 1975 (PG) In this satiric "sequel" to "The Maltese Falcon," detective Sam Spade, Jr. searches for the mysterious black falcon statuette that caused his father such trouble. Features appearances by Elisha Cook Jr. and Lee Patrick, who starred in the 1941 classic "The Maltese Falcon" with Humphrey Bogart. 98m/C VHS. George Segal, Stephane Audran, Lionel Stander, Lee Patrick, Elisha Cook Jr., Connie Kreski; **D:** David Giler.

Black Book ♂♂♂½ *Zwartboek* 2006 (R) Wow—Verhoeven directs his first film in his native Netherlands in 20 years and comes up with an unsentimental WWII thriller with a compelling lead performance by van Houten. In 1944, Jewish Rachel has been hiding out in the country until she joins a Dutch resistance unit. After some cosmetic changes, and now renamed Ellis, she's assigned to bed Gestapo chief Ludwig Muentze (Koch) and ferret out some Nazi secrets. What Rachel/Ellis doesn't mean to do is fall in love. The story twists and turns (eventually ending up in Israel in 1956) but is definitely worth the journey. English, Dutch, German, and Hebrew with subtitles. 145m/C VHS. Disc. GB GE DE NL Sebastian Koch, Thom Hoffman, Halina Rejn, Derek de Lint, Carice van Houten, Waldemar Kobus, Christian Berkel, Peter Blok; **D:** Paul Verhoeven; **W:** Paul Verhoeven, Gerard Soeteman; **C:** Karl Walter Lindenlaub; **M:** Anne Dudley.

Black Cat ♂½ 1990 Filmmakers find lots of action in a haunted house. Chock full of references to the works of spaghetti horror icons Mario Bava and Dario Argento. 122m/C VHS. **IT** Caroline Munro, Brett Halsey; **D:** Lewis (Luigi Cozzi) Coates; **W:** Lewis (Luigi Cozzi) Coates.

Black Cat, White Cat ♂♂♂ 1998 Emir Kusturica's rambling tale of scheming Gypsies who live on the banks of the Danube river is a mixture of slapstick humor, folk tales and music. The cheesily dressed and mostly nonprofessional actors light up a plot involving a cargo of fuel, an arranged marriage, and a corpse on ice. Non-political (and much lighter) follow-up to Kusturica's Palme d'Or-winning "Underground." Serbo-Croatian and Romany with subtitles. 129m/C VHS. Bajram Severdzan, Florijan Ajdini, Srdan Todorovic, Ljubica Adzovic, Miki (Predrag) Manojlovic; **D:** Emir Kusturica; **W:** Gordan Mihic; **C:** Thierry Arbogast; **M:** D. Nee Karajlic, Vaislav Aralica, Dejo Sparavalo.

Black Camel, The ♂♂ 1931 In the 2nd Charlie Chan mystery, set (and filmed) in Honolulu, the detective (Oland) investigates the murder of movie starlet Sheila Fane. Lugosi plays a psychic. Based on the Earl Derr Biggers' novel. 71m/B VHS. Warner Oland, Bela Lugosi, Robert Young, Victor Varconi, J.M. Kerrigan, Marjorie White, Sally Eilers, Dorothy Revier, Dwight Frye; **D:** Hamilton McFadden; **W:** Barry Connors, Philip Klein; **C:** Joseph August. Daniel B. Clark; **M:** Samuel Kaylin.

Black Castle, The ♂♂ 1952 Macabre tale of an 18th-century Austrian count whose guests tend to disappear after a visit. This happens to two of Greene's friends and he decides to investigate. Unhappy horror. Karloff doesn't have enough to do, and neither do the rest of a strong cast. 81m/B VHS. Richard Greene, Boris Karloff, Stephen McNally, Rita (Paula) Corday, Lon Chaney Jr., John "Hoyt"; **D:** Nathan "Jerry" Juran.

Black Cat, The ♂♂♂♂½ *House of Doom; Vanishing Body* 1934 The first of the many classic horror pairings stands up well years after release. Polished and taut, with fine sets and interesting acting. Con-frontation between architect and devil worshipper acts as pct, with strange twists. Worth a look. 65m/B VHS, strange twists. Bela Lugosi, David Manners, Julie Bishop, Lucille Lund, Henry Armetta, Egon Brecher, Albert Conti, Harry Cording, John Carradine; **D:** Edgar G. Ulmer, Peter Ruric; **C:** John Mescall; **M:** Heinz Roemheld.

Black Cat, The ♂♂½ 1941 Wealthy Henrietta Winslow (Loftus) has left her estate to her greedy grandchildren but known for his unabashed ripoffs of "Zombie" with some marbles loose (Magee) whose master calls up. The dreary English village setting and the downright myopic camera work add up to an oppressive viewing experience. 92m/C VHS, DVD. Hugh Herbert, Gale Sondergaard, Anne Gwynne, Basil Rathbone, Broderick Crawford, Bela Lugosi, Gladys Cooper, Alan Ladd, Cecilia Loftus, Clare Dodd, John Eldridge, Alan Ladd; **D:** Albert Rogell; **W:** Robert Lees, Frederic Rinaldo, Eric Taylor, Robert Neville; **C:** Stanley Cortez.

Black Cat Run ♂♂½ 1998 (R) Race car driver's girlfriend is abducted and then he gets involved with a psycho deputy. Lots of action. 89m/C VHS. Patrick Muldoon, Amelia Heinle, Russel Means, Kevin J. O'Connor, Peter Greene, Jake Busey; **D:** D.J. Caruso; **M:** Jeff Rona. CABLE

The Black Cauldron 🦴🦴🦴½ 1985 (PG) Disney's 25th full-length animated movie follows the adventures of pig-keeper Taran, who discovers his psychic pig Hen Wen is the key to keeping a magical cauldron out of the hands of the evil Horned King. Based on the "Chronicles of Prydain" novels by Lloyd Alexander. 82m/C VHS, DVD. D: Ted Berman, Richard Rich; W: Ted Berman, Richard Rich; M: Elmer Bernstein; V: Grant Bardsley, Susan Sheridan, John Hurt, Freddie Jones, Nigel Hawthorne, John Byner, Arthur Malet; Nar: John Huston.

Black Christmas 🦴🦴½ Silent Night, Evil Night; Stranger in the House 1975 (R) A college sorority is besieged by an axe-murderer over the holidays. 98m/C VHS, DVD. CA Andrea Martin, Art Hindle, Olivia Hussey, Keir Dullea, Margot Kidder, John Saxon; D: Bob (Benjamin) Clark; W: Roy Moore; C: Reginald Morris; M: Carl Zittrer.

Black Christmas 🦴 2006 (R) The 1974 original was an early entry in the slasher/dead teen genre. This weak remake, which takes itself way too seriously, ups the gore and adds lurid flashbacks for the killer, but so what? Sorority sisters (you may recognize a couple of faces) are stuck in their Alpha Kappa house at Christmas because of a blizzard, but the psycho killer (who lived in the sorority house when it was his family home) manages to escape the loony bin and hide out in the attic. He then terrorizes the gals before offing them, using handy holiday decorations for the most part. After seeing what he does with a cookie cutter, you may never eat Christmas cookies again. Writer/director Morgan deserves coal in his stocking. 84m/C DVD, HD DVD. US CA Michelle Trachtenberg, Lacey Chabert, Mary Elizabeth Winstead, Andrea Martin, Katie Cassidy, Robert Mann, Oliver Hudson, Crystal Lowe, Kristen Cloke, Jessica Harmon, Dean Friss; D: Glen Morgan; W: Glen Morgan; C: Robert McLachlan; M: Shirley Walker.

Black Circle Boys 🦴½ 1997 (R) Depressed high schooler Kyle (Bairstow) is still trying to fit in at his new school. He makes the mistake of getting involved with the "Black Circle Boys"—a clique of losers involved with drugs and the occult that's led by Shane (Mabius). The Boys enjoy malicious pranks and Kyle begins to have qualms about his participation but Shane doesn't want to let him go. Murky script gets increasingly silly as pic progresses. 100m/C VHS, DVD. Scott Bairstow, Eric Mabius, Heath Lourwood, Chad Lindberg, Tara Subkoff, Dee Wallace Stone, Donnie Wahlberg, John Doe; D: Matthew Carnahan; W: Matthew Carnahan; C: Geary McLeod.

Black Cloud 🦴🦴½ 2004 (PG-13) Schroder debuts as a writer/director in this formulaic but appealing drama about a Native American boxer. Black Cloud (Sparks) is an angry, out-of-control young boxer whose life outside the ring is marred by an alcoholic father, a dead mother, self-hatred, and racism. All he's got in his corner is his world-wise trainer Bud (Means) and his girlfriend Sammi (Jones). Black Cloud struggles with adversity in and out of the ring, but ultimately he's his own worst enemy. The story is strictly seen-it-before, but the strong performances (especially Sparks) balance out the predictability. 95m/C DVD. US Eddie Spears, Russell Means, Wayne Knight, Peter Greene, Julia Jones, Rick Schroder, Nathaniel Arcand, Tim McGraw, Branscombe Richmond; D: Rick Schroder; W: Rick Schroder; C: Steve Gainer; M: John E. Nordstrom.

The Black Cobra woof! 1983 (R) A lesbian exacts revenge for her lover's snakebite murder by trapping the guilty party with his own snakes. 97m/C VHS, DVD. IT Laura Gemser, Jack Palance; D: Joe D'Amato.

Black Cobra woof! Cobra Nero 1987 (R) After photographing a psychopath in the process of killing someone, a beautiful photographer seeks the help of a tough police sergeant to protect her. The leader of the Black Cobras gang gives chase. 90m/C VHS, DVD. IT Fred Williamson, Bruno Bilotta, Eva Grimaldi; D: Stelvio Massi.

Black Cobra 2 🦴🦴 1989 (R) A mismatched team of investigators tracks a notorious terrorist. They find him holding a school full of children as hostage. 95m/C VHS, DVD. IT Nicholas Hammond, Emma Hoagland, Najid Jadali, Fred Williamson; D: Stelvio Massi; C: Guglielmo Mancori; M: Aldo Salvi.

Black Cobra 3: The Manila Connection 🦴½ 1990 (R) Interpol turns to police lieutenant Robert Malone (Williamson) when a team of high-tech weapons thieves threatens the world. Malone attacks like a cyclone on the terrorists' jungle haven. They won't know what hit 'em! 92m/C VHS. Fred Williamson, Forry Smith, Debra Ward; D: Don Edwards.

The Black Dahlia 🦴🦴 2006 (R) Adaptation of James Ellroy's novel about the lurid unsolved murder features director De Palma's feverish eye for noir. Great-looking, over-stuffed, and ultimately unsatisfying production has Hollywood wannabe Elizabeth Short's (Kirshner) mutilated body discovered in a vacant lot in LA in 1947. Detective Lee Blanchard (Eckhart) becomes obsessed with the case—to the detriment of his life with blonde babe lover, Kay Lake (Johansson). Meanwhile, Lee's callow partner Buck (Hartnett) is investigating wealthy brunette Madeleine's (Swank) involvement with Short, which leads him to her lunatic clan. Fedoras, red lipstick, and cigarette smoke abound, but the glam hides plenty of dirt and corruption. 121m/C DVD. US Josh Hartnett, Scarlett Johansson, Aaron Eckhart, Hilary Swank, Mike Starr, Fiona Shaw, John Kavanagh, Rachel Miner, Mia Kirshner, Troy Evans, Gregg Henry, Rose McGowan, Jemima Shaw, Pepe Serna, Patrick Fischler; D: Brian De Palma; W: Josh Friedman; C: Vilmos Zsigmond; M: Mark Isham.

Black Day Blue Night 🦴🦴 1995 (R) Rinda (Forbes) and Hallie (Sara) take a road trip from Utah to Phoenix and pick up the handsome Dodge (Bellows). Turns out he's being pursued by cop John Quinn (Walsh) as a suspect in a murder/robbery. Women-in-peril-who-help-themselves type story. 99m/C VHS. Michelle Forbes, Mia Sara, Gil Bellows, J.T. Walsh, Tim Guinee, John Beck; D: J.S. Cardone; W: J.S. Cardone; M: Johnny Lee Schell, Joe Sublett.

Black Devil Doll from Hell 🦴 1984 This shot-on-video movie deals with a nasty little voodoo doll that likes to kill its owners. 70m/C VHS. Shirley Jones, Rickey Roach, Marie Sainvilvs; D: Chester Turner.

The Black Devils of Kali 🦴 Mystery of the Black Jungle 1955 Adventurers in the Indian jungle discover a lost race of idol-worshipping primitives. Racist garbage produced near the end of Republic Pictures' existence. Based on a novel by Emilio Salgari. 72m/B VHS. Lex Barker, Jane Maxwell, Luigi Tosi, Paul Muller; D: Ralph Murphy.

Black Dog 🦴 1998 (PG-13) Not since the '70s heyday of CBs and C.W. McCall have 18-wheelers been so lovingly portrayed. Too bad the rest of the characters weren't given the same attention. Swayze (resurrecting his sensitive bad-kicker persona from "Roadhouse") plays disgraced trucker Jack Crews, recently released from prison after a vehicular manslaughter rap. With no driver's license and an over-due mortgage, he agrees to an "off the books" run for his shady boss (Beckel). The cargo turns out to be guns, which attracts the attention of the FBI, ATF, and a scuzzy band of hijackers led by the Bible-quoting Red (Meatloaf). Of course, the harm's way, and gives him a soulful, country-croonin' ally (Travis). Avoid this mutt like three-day-old roadkill unless you're a big-rig fetishist. 88m/C VHS, DVD. Patrick Swayze, Randy Travis, Meat Loaf Aday, Gabriel Casseus, Graham Beckel, Stephen Tobolowsky, Charles S. Dutton, Brian Vincent, Brenda Strong, Erin Broderick; D: Kevin Hooks; W: William Mickelberry, Dan Vining; C: Buzz Feitshans IV; M: George S. Clinton.

The Black Doll 🦴🦴½ 1938 Shady mine owner Nicholas Rood is murdered as revenge for killing his business partner. While local officials have things utterly confused, Rood's daughter's fiance, who happens to be a private detective, eventually pieces the clues together. Low-caliber installment of the "Crime Club" series. 66m/B VHS. Donald Woods, Nan Grey, Edgar Kennedy, Doris Lloyd; D: Otis Garrett; W: Otis Buckley. VIDEO

The Black Dragons 🦴🦴 1942 Weird and fairly stupid war drama involving sabotage by the Japanese. Lugosi is the plastic surgeon who deftly cuts and pastes Japanese face parts to permit agents to pass as Americans. Also available colorized. 62m/B VHS, DVD. Bela Lugosi, Joan Barclay, George Pembroke, Clayton Moore; D: William Nigh.

Black Eagle 🦴🦴 1988 (R) Pre-Glasnost, anti-Soviet tale of two high-kicking spies. CIA and KGB agents race to recover innovative equipment in the Mediterranean. 93m/C VHS, DVD. Bruce Doran, Jean-Claude Van Damme, Sho Kosugi; D: Eric Karson; W: Shimon Arama; M: Terry Plumeri.

Black Eliminator 🦴 1978 A black cop struggles to stop a maniacal secret agent who plans to destroy the world. 84m/C VHS, DVD. Jim Kelly, George Lazenby, Harold Sakata, Bob Minor, Patch MacKenzie, Aldo Ray; D: Al Adamson.

Black Eyes 🦴🦴 1939 A lowly waiter, working in a Moscow restaurant, manages to overhear a number of stock tips from the wealthy patrons and makes a tidy pile of rubles to improve his daughter's life. The daughter already thinks he's a successful businessman and is disillusioned when she discovers dad's true profession. All comes out right in the end. 72m/B VHS. GB Otto Kruger, Mary Maguire, Walter Rilla, George L. Baxt, Marie Wright; D: Herbert Brenon.

Black Force 🦴🦴 1975 Brothers who fight crime with violent actions, are called for assistance in the recovery of an African artifact. Originally known as "Force Four." 82m/C VHS. Malachi Lee, Warhawk Tanzania, Owen Watson, Judie Soriano; D: Michael Fink.

Black Force 2 🦴🦴 1978 (R) The brothers are back on the scene in another violent, cartilage-shattering adventure. 90m/C VHS. Terry Carter, James B. Sikking, Gwen Mitchell; D: Edward Lakso.

Black Fox: Blood Horse 🦴 1994 Alan Johnson (Reeve) and Britt (Todd) try to maintain an uneasy peace with the local Kiowas until evil Ralph Holtz (Wiggins) tries to stir things up and have some vigilantes attack the tribe. The second episode in the three-part series. 90m/C VHS. Christopher Reeve, Raoul Trujillo, Tony Todd, Chris Wiggins; D: Steven Hilliard Stern; C: Frank Tidy; M: Eric N. Robertson.

Black Fox: Good Men and Bad 🦴🦴 1994 Britt (Todd) accepts a job as a federal marshall while Alan (Reeve) goes after desperado Carl Glenn (Fox) and his gang. During a stagecoach robbery, the outlaws take Hallie (Rowan) hostage, thinking she's the wife of a tycoon and Alan manages to use her to get to Glenn. The third episode in the sagebrush series. 90m/C VHS, DVD. Christopher Reeve, David Fox, Tony Todd, Kim Coates, Kelly Rowan; D: Steven Hilliard Stern; C: Frank Tidy; M: Eric N. Robertson.

Black Fox: The Price of Peace 🦴🦴 1994 Former plantation owner Alan Johnson (Reeve) and childhood friend Britt (Todd), whom he frees from slavery, try to forge a new life in 1860s Texas. But there's trouble when abusive bigot Ralph Holtz (Wiggins) threatens the peace between settlers and Indians when he goes after his wife delores (Holtz) who left him for a Kiowa warrior, Running Dog (Trujillo). Based on the novel by Matt Braun; made for TV. 90m/C VHS, DVD. Christopher Reeve, Raoul Trujillo, Tony Todd, Chris Wiggins, Cynthia (Cyndy Cindy) Preston; D: Steven Hilliard Stern; C: Frank Tidy; M: Eric N. Robertson. TV

Black Friday 🦴🦴½ 1940 Karloff is a surgeon who saves the life of his college professor friend (Ridges) by transplanting part of the brain of a gangster (involved in the same car crash) into the man's body. This results in a Jekyll/Hyde complex with the gangster's evil portion taking over and seeking revenge on rival mobster Lugosi. Horror stars Karloff and Lugosi never have any scenes together. 70m/B VHS, DVD. Boris Karloff, Stanley Ridges, Bela Lugosi, Anne Nagel, Anne Gwynne, Paul Fix, Virginia Brissac, James Craig; D: Arthur Lubin; W: Curt Siodmak, Eric Taylor; C: Elwood "Woody" Bredell.

Black Fury 🦴🦴🦴 1935 A coal miner's efforts to protest working conditions earn him a beating by the company goons who also kill his friend. He draws national attention to this brutal plight of the workers when he barricades himself inside the mine. Muni's carefully detailed performance adds authenticity to this powerful drama, but it proved too depressing to command a big boxoffice. 95m/B VHS. Paul Muni, Barton MacLane, Henry O'Neill, John Qualen, J. Carrol Naish; D: Michael Curtiz.

The Black Gate 🦴 The Darkening; Dark Encounters 1995 Psychic investigator Scott Griffin's (Rector) vacation to a seemingly pleasant cliff-top inn is interrupted by horrific visions that lead him to an ancient object of great evil that could wreak havoc on Earth unless he can destroy it. More frightening than the lame ghost story are the poor visual effects. 81m/C VHS, DVD. Jeff Rector, George Philip Saunders, Rebecca Kyler Downs, Red Montgomery, Brian Carlton; D: William Mesa; W: John G. Jones, Victoria Parker; C: William Mesa. VIDEO

Black Gestapo woof! 1975 (R) Black-exploitation film about a vigilante army taking over a Los Angeles ghetto, first to help residents, but later to abuse them. Extremely violent. 89m/C VHS, DVD. DVD. GB Alex Nicol, John Salew, Arthur Lane, Eleanor Summerfield, Paul Carpenter, Geoffrey Keen, Martin Boddey, Fred Johnson; D: Terence Fisher; W: Ernest Borneman; C: Walter J. (Jimmy W.) Harvey.

Black God, White Devil 🦴 Deus e o Diabo na Terra do Sol 1964 Another Brazilian socio-political commentary by Rocha, an oft-incendiary filmmaker whose left-leaning works are steeped in mysticism, obscure folklore, and powerful images. An impoverished man transforms from a religious zealot to a bandit, his tale underscored by conflict between poor masses and wealthy landowners. Portuguese with subtitles. 102m/C VHS. BR Yona Magalhaes, Geraldo Del Rey, Othon Bastos, Mauricio Do Vale, Lidio Silva; D: Glauce Rocha; W: Glauce Rocha; C: Waldemar Lima.

Black Godfather 🦴 1974 (R) The grueling story of a hood clawing his way to the top of a drug-selling mob. Features an all-black cast. 90m/C VHS, DVD. Rod Perry, Damu King, Don Chastain, Jimmy Witherspoon, Diane Summerfield; D: John Evans; W: John Evans; C: Jack Steely.

Black Gold 🦴 1936 Oil field suspense thriller by "B" movie king Hopton. 57m/B VHS, DVD. Frankie Darro, Leroy Mason; D: Russell Hopton.

The Black Hand 🦴🦴½ 1950 Kelly plays well against character in this atmospheric turn-of-the-century thriller. The evil society of the Black Hand murders his father, and he seeks revenge. Well-made drama. 93m/B VHS. Gene Kelly, J. Carrol Naish, Teresa Celli, Marc Lawrence, Frank Puglia; D: Richard Thorpe; C: Paul Vogel.

Black Hand 🦴½ 1973 Unemployed Italian immigrant is drawn into a web of murder and betrayal after he is attacked by an Irish gang. 90m/C VHS. IT Lionel Stander; D: Antonio Raccioppo; C: Riccardo (Pallton) Pallottini; M: Carlo Rustichelli.

Black Hawk Down 🦴🦴🦴 2001 (R) Producer Bruckheimer and director Scott faithfully re-create the Battle of Mogadishu of October, 1993. U.S. Army Rangers and Delta Force units are sent to apprehend Somali warlord Muhammad Farah Aidid's top staff in an Aidid-controlec section of the city. When two Black Hawk helicopters are shot down, the focus of the mission changes to rescue and defense. The usual introduction of the troops is dispensed with fairly quickly, in favor of background on the Somalian situation, and details of the impending operation. No-frills setup works perfectly with the following action, which is fierce, intense, and non-stop. Once the fighting begins, Scott's brilliance with visuals really kicks in, but nothing that happens, no matter how gruesome, seems forced or exploitative. Fine ensemble cast is nominally the focus, but no one really disappoints. Based on the book by Mark Bowden. **143m/C VHS, DVD, Blu-ray Disc, UMD.** *US* Josh Hartnett, Eric Bana, Ewan McGregor, Tom Sizemore, William Fichtner, Sam Shepard, Gabriel Casseus, Kim Coates, Hugh Dancy, Ron Eldard, Ioan Gruffudd, Tom Guiry, Charlie Hofheimer, Danny Hoch, Jason Isaacs, Zeljko Ivanek, Glenn Morshower, Jeremy Piven, Brendan Sexton III, Johnny Strong, Richard Tyson, Brian Van Holt, Steven Ford, Gregory Sporleder, Carmine D. Giovinazzo, Chris Beetem, George Harris, Ewen Bremner, Boyd Kestner, Nikolaj Coster-Waldau, Ian Virgo, Thomas (Tom) Hardy, Tac Fitzgerald, Matthew Marsden, Orlando Bloom, Kent Linville, Enrique Murciano, Michael Roof, Treva Etienne, Ty Burrell; *D:* Ridley Scott; *W:* Ken Nolan; *C:* Slawomir Idziak; *M:* Hans Zimmer. Oscars '01: Film Editing, Sound.

Black Horizon 🦴🦴½ (*Stranded; On Eagle's Wings Space Station*) 2001 (R) No matter what it's called, this flick is still a less-than-exciting space opera. A Russian space station is falling apart and an international team is sent aboard a space shuttle to rescue the inhabitants. While there, the station is struck by a meteor that knocks out all communication and causes an oxygen leak, which threatens the team and crew. And on Earth, a government agent discovers that some people don't want the team to ever return. **92m/C VHS, DVD.** Ice-T, Hannes Jaenicke, Michael Dudikoff, Yvette Nipar, Richard Gabai, Alex Veadov, Art Hindle, Larry Poindexter, Andrew Stevens; *D:* Fred Olen Ray; *W:* Steve Latshaw; *C:* Theo Angell. VIDEO

Black Ice 🦴🦴 1992 (R) After an affair with a popular politician ends violently, Vanessa (Paula) realizes her boss set up his death—and she's next in line. She finds the nearest taxi and offers the driver plenty of cash if he can quickly get her out of the country. It's going to be the ride of her life. Also available in an unrated version. **90m/C VHS.** Michael Nouri, Michael Ironside, Joanna Pacula; *D:* Neill Fearnley; *M:* Amin Bhatia.

Black Irish 🦴🦴½ 2007 (R) Familiar family drama buoyed by strong performances. Teenager Cole McKay (Angarano) is a promising high school baseball pitcher growing up in South Boston. His dad Desmond (Gleeson) is an unemployed drinker, his mother Margaret (Leo) holds to the illusion that they are a decent Catholic family, and his older sister Kathleen (Van Camp) is unmarried and pregnant. But the biggest problem for Cole is violent elder brother Terry (Guiry), who's drifted into drugs and crime and wants to drag Cole down with him. **95m/C VHS.** Michael Angarano, Brendan Gleeson, Tom Guiry, Melissa Leo, Emily Van Camp, Michael Rispoli, Francis Capra, Finn Curtin; *D:* Brad Gann; *W:* Brad Gann; *C:* Michael Fimognari; *M:* John (Gianni) Fizzelli.

Black Hills 🦴 1948 Dull oater with Dean and his sidekick Ates out to avenge the murder of a struggling ranch owner. **60m/B VHS, DVD.** Eddie Dean, Roscoe Ates, Shirley Patterson, Terry Frost, Nina Bara, William "Bill" Fawcett; *D:* Ray Taylor.

The Black Hole 🦴🦴½ 1979 (G) A high-tech, computerized Disney space adventure dealing with a mad genius who attempts to pilot his craft directly into a black hole. Except for the top quality special effects, a pretty creaky vehicle. **97m/C VHS, DVD.** Maximilian Schell, Anthony Perkins, Ernest Borgnine, Yvette Mimieux, Joseph Bottoms, Robert Forster; *D:* Gary Nelson; *W:* Gerry Day; *C:* Frank Phillips; *M:* John Barry.

Black Knight 🦴🦴 2001 (PG-13) The utterly unoriginal title should be a clue. Another remake of "A Connecticut Yankee in King Arthur's Court," and a particularly bad and formulaic one at that. Lazy, selfish Jamal (Lawrence) is transported from his minimum-wage job at theme park Medieval World to 14th century England, the real medieval world, where some silly lessons await. Obvious fish-out-of-water jokes ensue, as Jamal seeks to make sense of his new surroundings, knock boots with Nubian maidens and lead a revolution against an evil king. The film's few decent gags are swallowed by lots of inane humor, a tired script and Lawrence's desperate mugging. Ironically, the story's moral message about giving up selfishness for a cause is lost on its star, who acts as if he's the only person on screen. **95m/C VHS, DVD.** *US* Martin Lawrence, Tom Wilkinson, Vincent Regan, Marsha Thomason, Kevin Conway, Daryl (Chill) Mitchell, Jeannette Weegar, Michael Burgess, Isabell Monk, Helen Carey; *D:* Gil Junger; *W:* Darryl Quarles, Robert Gaulke, Gerry Swallow; *C:* Ueli Steiger; *M:* Randy Edelman.

The Black Klansman 🦴 (*I Crossed the Line*) 1966 A black man masquerades as a white extremist in order to infiltrate the KKK and avenge his daughter's murder. In the interest of racial harmony, he seduces the Klan leader's daughter. As bad as it sounds. **88m/B VHS, DVD.** Max Julien, Rima Kutner, Harry Lovejoy; *D:* Ted V. Mikels.

The Black King 🦴½ (*Harlem Hot Shot*) 1932 Prejudiced propaganda based on the life of Marcus Garvey, black leader of the '20s, who advocated black superiority and a return to Africa. A black con man takes advantage of fellow blacks by organizing a phony back-to-Africa movement, enriching himself in the process. When one man's girlfriend deserts him for the bogus leader, the jilted one blows the whistle. **70m/B VHS, DVD.** A.B. Comethiere, Vivianne Baber, Knolly Mitchell, Dan Michaels, Mike Jackson; *D:* Bud Pollard.

Black Jesus 🦴🦴 (*Seduta Alla Sua Destra; Seated At His Right*) 1968 Lalubi (Strode) is an African leader using passive resistance to save his people from a dictatorial regime that's supported by European colonialism. When he's betrayed by a follower, Lalubi's imprisoned and tortured, along with a thief who gains a greater understanding after contact with the leader. Film is a thinly disguised depiction of Zaire and its history. **100m/C VHS.** Woody Strode, Jean Servais; *D:* Valerio Zurlini.

Black Limelight 🦴🦴½ 1938 Massey plays a fugitive from justice and Marion of the murder of his mistress. Distracting lead performance by Marion who insists on shouting her lines. Based on the play by Gordon Sherry. **60m/B VHS.** *GB* Raymond Massey, Joan Marion, Mary Hinton, Henry Oscar, Dan Tobin; *D:* Paul Stein; *W:* Walter Summers.

Black Lizard 🦴🦴 (*Kurotokage*) 1968 A camp spectacle set in the Japanese underworld. The Lizard is the glamorous queen of Tokyo crime who plots to steal a famous diamond by female kidnapping the owner's daughter. Complications arise when she falls for a detective. The Lizard is played by female impersonator Maruyama and the screenplay, has a cameo as an embalmed corpse. Style is all. In Japanese with English subtitles. **112m/C VHS, JP** Akihiro Maruyama, Isao Kimura, Yukio Mishima, Kikko Matsuoka; *D:* Kinji Fukasaku; *W:* Yukio Mishima.

Black Magic 🦴🦴 1949 Cagliostro, the magician becomes involved in a plot to supply a double for Marie Antoinette. **105m/B VHS.** Orson Welles, Akim Tamiroff, Nancy Guild, Raymond Burr, Frank Latimore; *D:* Gregory Ratoff.

Black Magic 🦴🦴½ 1992 (PG-13) Insomniac Alex, haunted by the nightly appearances of his dead cousin Ross, goes to Ross's hometown to see if he can find a way to make the apparition disappear. On the way, he runs into his cousin's ex-girlfriend Lillian and falls in love. Problem is Lillian's a witch, maybe. Lightweight cable fare. **94m/C VHS.** Rachel Ward, Judge Reinhold, Brion James, Anthony LaPaglia; *D:* Daniel Taplitz. CABLE

Black Magic Terror 🦴🦴½ 1979 Jilted by her lover, the old queen of black magic has everybody under her spell. Trouble starts, however, when she turns her back on one of her subjects. **85m/C VHS.** *JP* Suzana, W.D. Mochtar, Alan Nuary; *D:* L. Sudio.

Black Magic Woman Woof! 1991 (R) An art gallery owner has an affair with a beautiful and exotic woman but starts to get cold feet when he's plagued by inexplicable phenomena. Seems that magic woman has put a voodoo spell on him. Listless companion to director Warren's "Blood Spell" that gives away the ending, has a wretched script, and poor acting. **91m/C VHS.** Mark Hamill, Amanda Wyss, Apollonia, Abadah Viera, Larry Hankin, Victor Rivers, Bonnie Ebson; *D:* Deryn Warren; *W:* Gerry Daly; *M:* Randy Miller.

Black Lemons 🦴 (*E venne il giorno dei limoni neri*) 1970 While in prison, a convict is stalked by the Mafia because of what he knows. He eventually spills the beans to the cops, putting himself in unavoidable jeopardy. **93m/C VHS.** *IT* Peter Carster, Antonio (Tony) Sabato, Florinda Bolkan; *D:* Camilo Bazzoni.

The Black Lash 🦴 1952 Two lawmen go undercover to break a silver hijacking gang. **55m/B VHS.** Lash LaRue, Al "Fuzzy" St. John, Peggy Stewart, Kermit Maynard; *D:* Ron Ormond.

The Black Legion 🦴🦴🦴 1937 Social drama isn't as dated as we'd like to think. Auto worker Frank Taylor (Bogart) is angry at being passed over for a promotion that goes to a Polish immigrant. So he's easy pickings for a Klan-like secret society that practices hatred and violence. His best pal, Ed (Foran), tries to get Frank out and one of tragedy follows. Very grim and one of Bogart's early unsympathetic starring roles. **83m/B VHS, DVD.** Humphrey Bogart, Dick Foran, Erin O'Brien-Moore, Helen Flint, Ann Sheridan, Henry (Kleinbach) Brandon, Robert Barrat, Joseph (Joe) Sawyer, Addison Richards, Samuel S. Hinds, John Litel, Eddie Acuff; *D:* Archie Mayo; *W:* Abem Finkel, William Wister Haines; *C:* George Barnes; *M:* Bernhard Kaun.

Black Like Me 🦴🦴½ 1964 Based on John Howard Griffin's successful book about how Griffin turned his skin black with a drug and traveled the South to experience prejudice firsthand. Neither the production nor the direction entrance the bloody 'or those not used to the material. **107m/B VHS, DVD.** James Whitmore, Roscoe Lee Browne, Will Geer, Walter Mason, John Marriott, Clifton James, Dan Priest; *D:* Carl Lerner; *W:* Carl Lerner, Gerda Lerner; *C:* Victor Lukens, Henry Mueller; *M:* Meyer Kupferman.

The Black Marble 🦴🦴🦴 1979 (PG) A beautiful policewoman is paired with a policeman who drinks too much, is divorced, and is ready to retire. Surrounded by urban craziness and corruption, they eventually fall in love. Based on the Joseph Wambaugh novel. **110m/C VHS, DVD.** Paula Prentiss, Harry Dean Stanton, Robert Foxworth, James Woods, Michael Dudikoff, Barbara Babcock, John Hancock, Judy Landers, Anne Ramsay, Christopher Lloyd; *D:* Harold Becker; *M:* Maurice Jarre.

Black Market Rusters 🦴🦴½ 1943 The Range Busters are at it again. This time they break up a cattle rustling syndicate. **60m/B VHS.** Ray Corrigan, Dennis Moore, Max Terhune; *D:* S. Roy Luby.

Black Mask 🦴🦴½ (*Hak Hap*) 1996 (R) Hong Kong action star Jet Li (second only to Jackie Chan in Hong Kong boxoffice success) is Tsui, a mild-mannered librarian who used to be a member of a secret, biogenetically enhanced squad of supersoldiers known as the "701 Squad." These commandos, who feel no fear or pain, are out to take over Hong Kong's underworld, and are killing the crime lords in grisly fashion. Tsui, aided by his detective buddy and dressed a lot like Kato from the "Green Hornet," goes into action to stop his ex-mates. Action may be a little bloody 'or those not used to the Hong Kong style, but Jet Li is an exciting performer who should break out big with this one after his impress've Stateside debut in 1996 Hong Kong release. **95m/C VHS, DVD. HK** Jet Li, Karen Mok, Francoise Yip, Lau Ching Wan; *D:* Daniel Lee; *M:* Tsui Hark, Teddy Chen; *C:* Cheung Tung Leung; *M:* Ben Vaughn, Tommy Robin.

Black Moon Rising 🦴🦴½ 1986 (R) Based on an idea by John Carpenter dealing with the theft of a new jet-powered car and its involvement in an FBI investigation. Solid performances and steady action enhance this routine effort. **100m/C VHS, DVD.** Tommy Lee Jones, Linda Hamilton, Richard Jaeckel, Robert Vaughn; *D:* Harley Cokliss; *W:* John Carpenter; *C:* Misha (Mikhail) Suslov; *M:* Lalo Schifrin.

Black Narcissus 🦴🦴🦴½ 1947 A group of Anglican nuns attempting to found a hospital and school in the Himalayas confront native distrust and frailties amid beautiful scenery. Adapted from the novel by Rumer Godden. Stunning cinematography. Crucial scenes were cut from the American release by censors. **101m/C VHS, DVD, GB** Deborah Kerr, David Farrar, Sabu, Jean Simmons, Kathleen Byron, Flora Robson, Esmond Knight, Jenny Laird, Judith Furse, May Hallatt, Nancy Roberts; *D:* Michael Powell, Emeric Pressburger; *W:* Michael Powell, Emeric Pressburger; *C:* Jack Cardiff; *M:* Brian Easdale. Oscars '47: Art Dir/Set Dec., Color, Color Cinematog; N.Y. Film Critics '47: Actress (Kerr).

Black Oak Conspiracy 🦴🦴 1977 (R) Based o' a true story, this film deals with a mining company conspiracy discovered by an inquisitive stuntman. **92m/C VHS.** Jesse Vint, Karen Carlson, Albert Salmi, Seymour Cassel, Robert F. Lyons; *D:* Bob Kelljan.

Black Orchid 🦴🦴½ 1959 A businessman and a crook's widow fall in love and try to persuade their children it can work out. **96m/B VHS, DVD.** Sophia Loren, Anthony Quinn, Ina Balin, Peter Mark Richman, Jimmy Baird; *D:* Martin Ritt; *W:* Joseph Stefano; *C:* Robert Burks.

Black Orpheus 🦴🦴🦴½ (*Orfeu Negro*) 1958 The legend of Orpheus and Eurydice unfolds against the colorful background of the carnival in Rio de Janeiro. Is a street-car conductor and Orpheus (Mello) a country girl fleeing from a stranger sworn to kill her. The man has followed her to Rio and disguised himself as the figure of Death. Dancing, incredible music, and black magic add to the beauty of this film. Based on the play "Orfeu da Conceica" by De Moraes. In Portuguese with English subtitles or dubbed. **103m/C VHS, DVD, BR FR PT** Breno Mello, Marpessa Dawn, Lea Garcia, Fausto Guerzoni, Lourdes De Oliveira, Ademar Da Silva, Alexandro Constantino, Waldetar De Souza, Jorge Dos Santos; *D:* Marcel Camus; *W:* Vinicius De Moraes, Jacques Viot; *C:* Jean (Yves Georges) Bourgoin; *M:* Antonio Carlos Jobim, Luis Bonfa. Oscars '59: Foreign Film; Cannes '59: Film; Golden Globes '60: Foreign Film.

Black Out 🦴 1996 (R) John Grey becomes desperate after a car crash, as he tries to remember his life and his wife (DuBois) is murdered. **98m/C VHS.** Brian Bosworth, Brad Dourif, Claire Yarlett, Marta DuBois; *D:* Allan Goldstein.

Black Panther 🦴½ 1977 True story of psycho-killer Donald Neilson, who murdered heiress Lesley Whittle in England in the 1970s. **90m/C VHS.** Donald (Don) Sumpter, Debbie Farrington; *D:* Ian Merrick; *M:* Michael Armstrong.

Black Peter 🦴🦴½ (*Cerny Petr, Peter and Pavla*) 1963 Director Forman's first feature offers a glimpse into the struggles of a young Czech man as he copes with an oppressive father, a menial grocery store job, and first-love jitters. In Czech, with subtitles. **85m/B VHS, DVD, CZ** Ladislav Jakim, Pavla Martinkova, Jan Vostril, Vladimir Pucholt, Pawel Sedlacek; *D:* Milos Forman; *W:* Milos Forman, Jaroslav Papousek; *C:* Jan Nemecek; *M:* Jiri Slitr.

The Black Pirate 🦴🦴🦴 (*Rage of the Buccaneers; The Black Buccaneer; Gordon II Pirata Nero*) 1926 A shipwrecked mariner vows revenge on the pirates who destroyed his father's ship. Quintessential Fairbanks, this film features astounding athletic feats and exciting swordplay. Silent film with music score. Also available in color. **122m/B VHS, DVD.** *IT* Douglas Fairbanks Sr., Donald Crisp, Billie Dove; **D:** Albert Parker; **C:** Henry Sharp; **M:** Mortimer Wilson. Natl. Film Reg. '93.

Black Pit of Dr. M ♂♂ *Misterios Gel Ultratumba* 1947 The ghost of a doctor who has been unjustly executed for murder seeks revenge on employees of an insane asylum. The horror is not just confined to the asylum. **90m/B VHS, DVD.** *MX* Gaston Santos, Rafael Bertrand, Mapita Cortes; **D:** Fernando Mendez; **W:** Ramon Obon.

Black Point ♂♂ 2001 (R) John Hawkins (Caruso) is a former Naval captain, down on his luck and living in the harbor town of Black Point. When he meets Natalie (Haskell), he thinks she's the woman of his dreams. He's wrong. **107m/C VHS, DVD.** *CA* David Caruso, Susan Haskell, Thomas Ian Griffith, Gordon Tootoosis, Alex Bruhanski; **D:** David Mackay; **W:** Thomas Ian Griffith, Greg Mellott; **C:** Stephen McNutt; **M:** Terry Frewer.

Black Rain ♂♂♂ *Kuroi Ame* 1988 Erstwhile Ozu assistant Imamura directs this powerful portrait of a post-Hiroshima family five years after the bombing. Tanaka plays a young woman who, having been caught in a shower of black rain (radioactive fallout) on an ill-timed visit to Hiroshima, returns to her village to find herself ostracized by her peers and no longer considered marriage-worthy. Winner of numerous awards (including five Japanese Academy Awards). In Japanese with English subtitles. **123m/B VHS, DVD.** *JP* Kazuo Kitamura, Yoshiko Tanaka, Etsuko Ichihara, Shoichi Ozawa, Norihei Miki, Keisuke Ishida; **D:** Shohei Imamura; **W:** Shohei Imamura, Toshiro Ishido; **C:** Takashi Kawamata; **M:** Toru Takemitsu.

Black Rain ♂♂♂½ 1989 (R) Douglas portrays a ruthless American cop chasing a Japanese murder suspect through gang-controlled Tokyo. Loads of action and stunning visuals from the man who brought you "Blade Runner." **125m/C VHS, DVD, Blu-ray Disc, HD DVD.** Stephen (Steve) Root, Michael Douglas, Andy Garcia, Kate Capshaw, Ken Takakura, Yusaku Matsuda, John Spencer, Shigeru Koyama; **D:** Ridley Scott; **W:** Craig Bolotin, Warren Lewis; **C:** Jan De Bont; **M:** Hans Zimmer.

The Black Rainbow ♂♂½ 1991 (R) Surprisingly good thriller that's relatively unknown, haunted by a menacing mood. Robards and Arquette are a father/daughter duo who perform clairvoyance scams at carnival sideshows. Suddenly, without warning, Arquette's former cons become real: she sees murder victims—before their demise. Quirky sleeper filmed on location in North Carolina. **103m/C VHS, DVD.** Rosanna Arquette, Jason Robards Jr., Tom Hulce, Ron Rosenthal, John Bennes, Linda Pierce, Mark Joy; **D:** Mike Hodges; **W:** Mike Hodges.

The Black Raven ♂♂♂½ 1943 An action film that combines several plots into one. The Black Raven is an inn that sees more excitement than any other—not the least of which is murder! **64m/B VHS, DVD.** George Zucco, Wanda McKay, Glenn Strange, I. Stanford Jolley; **D:** Sam Newfield; **W:** Fred Myton; **C:** Robert E. Cline.

Black Robe ♂♂♂½ 1991 (R) In 1634 young Jesuit priest Father Laforgue (Bluteau) journeys across the North American wilderness to bring the word of God to Canada's Huron Indians. The winter journey is brutal and perilous and he begins to question his mission after seeing the strength of the Indian's native ways. Stunning cinematography, a good script, and fine acting combine to make this superb. Portrays the Indians in a realistic manner, the only flaw being that Beresford portrays the white culture with very few redeeming qualities and as the only reason for the Indian's downfall. Moore adapted his own novel for the screen. **101m/C VHS, DVD.** *AU CA* Lothaire Bluteau, Aden Young, Sandrine Holt, August Schellenberg, Tantoo Cardinal, Billy Two Rivers, Lawrence Bayne, Harrison Liu, Marthe Turgeon; **D:** Bruce Beresford; **W:** Brian Moore; **C:** Peter James; **M:** Georges

---

Delerue. Australian Film Inst. '92: Cinematog.; Genie '91: Director (Beresford), Film.

The Black Room ♂♂♂ 1935 As an evil count lures victims into his castle of terror, the count's twin brother returns to fulfill an ancient prophecy. Karloff is wonderful in his dual role as the twin brothers. **70m/B DVD.** Boris Karloff, Marian Marsh, Robert "Tex" Allen, Katherine DeMille, John Buckler, Thurston Hall; **D:** Roy William Neill; **W:** Henry Myers, Arthur Strawn; **C:** Allen Siegler.

The Black Room ♂ 1982 (R) Couples are lured to a mysterious mansion where a brother and his sister promise to satisfy their sexual desires. Not much to recommend unless you're a fan of the vampire as psychology test case. **90m/C VHS, DVD.** Linnea Quigley, Stephen Knight, Cassandra Gaviola, Jim Stathis; **D:** Norman Thaddeus Vane.

The Black Rose ♂♂½ 1950 Technicolor action, set in the 13th century, as English Saxon Walter of Gurnie (Power) seeks to restore his fortunes by traveling in a caravan to the wilds of Cathay. Welles is the bizarre and brutal Tartan general Bayan, and pretty (and young) French actress Aubrey looks out of place as runaway concubine, Maryam, so the romance between her and Walter is sketchy at best. Based on the novel by Thomas B. Costain. **120m/C DVD.** Tyrone Power, Orson Welles, Cecile Aubry, Jack Hawkins, Finlay Currie, Herbert Lom, Michael Rennie, Robert (Bobby) Blake; **D:** Henry Hathaway; **W:** Talbot Jennings; **C:** Jack Cardiff; **M:** Richard Addinsell.

Black Roses ♂ 1988 (R) A disgusting band of rockers shows up in a small town, and the local kids start turning into monsters. Coincidence? **90m/C VHS.** Carmine Appice, Sal Viviano, Carla Ferrigno, Julie Adams, Ken Swofford, John Martin; **D:** John Fasano.

Black Sabbath ♂♂♂ *I Tre Volti della Paura; The Three Faces of Terror; The Three Faces of Fear; Les Trois Visages de la Peur* 1964 An omnibus horror film with three parts, climaxing with Karloff as a Wurdalak, a vampire who must kill those he loves. **99m/C VHS, DVD.** *IT FR* Boris Karloff, Jacqueline Pierreux, Michele Mercier, Lidia Alfonsi, Susy Andersen, Mark Damon, Rika Dialina, Glauco Onorato, Massimo Righi; **D:** Mario Bava; **W:** Mario Bava, Marcello Fondato, Alberto Bevilacqua; **C:** Ubaldo Terzano; **M:** Les Baxter.

Black Samurai ♂ 1977 (R) When his girlfriend is held hostage, a martial arts warrior will stop at nothing to destroy the organization that abducted her. **84m/C VHS, DVD.** Marilyn Joi, Biff Yeager, Bill Roy, Roberto Contreras, Jim Kelly; **D:** Al Adamson; **W:** B. Readick; **C:** Louis Horvath.

The Black Scorpion ♂♂½ 1957 Two geologists in Mexico unearth a nest of giant scorpions living in a dead volcano. Eventually one of the oversized arachnids escapes to wreak havoc on Mexico City. **85m/B VHS, DVD.** Richard Denning, Mara Corday, Carlos Rivas; **D:** Edward Ludwig; **W:** Robert Blees.

Black Scorpion ♂♂½ 1995 (R) Darcy Walker (Severance) is an ex-cop-turned-superhero (the scorpion is her symbol!), who dons a mask and fetching (and tight) black vinyl to fight crime and avenge her dad's death. She's got the prerequisite sidekick—an ex-chop shop operator (Morris)—and a supervillain—the asthmatic Breathtaker (Siemaszko) who threatens to annihilate the city with toxic gas. Campy, schlock fun. **92m/C VHS, DVD.** Joan Severance, Garrett Morris, Casey Siemaszko, Rick Rossovich; **D:** Jonathan Winfrey; **W:** Craig J. Nevius; **M:** Kevin Kiner. **CABLE**

Black Scorpion 2: Ground Zero ♂ *Black Scorpion 2: Aftershock* 1996 (R) Fetching crimefighter Darcy Walker (Severance) returns to battle villains Gangster Prankster (Jackson) and Aftershock (Rose), who are set on destroying the City of Angels by earthquake. **85m/C VHS, DVD.** Joan Severance, Whip Hubley, Stoney Jackson, Sherrie Rose, Garrett Morris, Laura Elena Harring; **D:** Jonathan Winfrey; **W:** Craig J. Nevius; **C:** Mark Kohl; **M:** Kevin Kiner. **CABLE**

Black Shampoo WOOF! 1976 A black hairdresser on the Sunset Strip fights the mob with a chainsaw. **90m/C VHS, DVD.** John Daniels, Tanya Boyd, Joe Ortiz; **D:** Greydon Clark.

Black Sheep ♂♂½ 1996 (PG-13) Isn't there a five-day waiting period for remakes? The previously viewed copies of "Tommy Boy" hadn't even hit the sale bin before Spade and Farley went in search of more property to destroy. The twist here? Spade is assigned to keep the oafish brother (not son) of a gubernatorial candidate (not auto parts dealer) out of trouble until after the election (not so he can save the family business). In an effort to provide humor, plot points, and character development, Farley falls out of, off of or onto every prop in sight while Spade smirks. **87m/C VHS, DVD.** Chris Farley, David Spade, Tim Matheson, Christine Ebersole, Gary Busey, Grant Heslov, Timothy Carhart, Bruce McGill, Fred Wolf; **D:** Penelope Spheeris; **W:** Fred Wolf; **C:** Daryn Okada; **M:** William Ross.

Black Sheep ♂♂ 2006 Cheery gorefest. Henry (Meister) returns to the family farm in rural New Zealand, hoping to cure his aversion to sheep and get a buy-out from older brother Angus (Feeney). Only Angus has been doing some genetic experimenting on the woollies that turns the placid creatures into blood-thirsty killers! **87m/C DVD.** *NZ* Nathan Meister, Peter Feeney, Tandi Wright, Oliver Driver, Danielle Mason, Tammy Davis; **D:** Jonathan King; **W:** Jonathan King; **C:** Richard Buck; **M:** Victoria Kelly.

The Black Shield of Falworth ♂♂½ 1954 Typically silly '50s Technicolor swashbuckler with Curtis (and his New York accent) as Myles, the son of a disgraced knight, who's out to thwart a conspiracy against King Henry IV (Keith) and win the hand of fair maiden, Lady Anne (Leigh, Curtis' wife at the time). Loosely based on the Howard Pyle novel, "Men of Iron." **98m/C VHS.** Tony Curtis, Janet Leigh, Ian Keith, David Farrar, Barbara Rush, Herbert Marshall, Dan O'Herlihy, Rhys Williams, Torin Thatcher, Patrick O'Neal, Craig Hill; **D:** Rudolph Mate; **W:** Oscar Brodney; **C:** Irving Glassberg; **M:** Joseph Gershenson.

Black Sister's Revenge ♂♂ *Emma Mae* 1976 Poorly selected video title mars this intelligent drama about a young black woman's struggle to adjust to the big city after growing up in the rural South. **100m/C VHS, DVD.** Jerri Hayes, Ernest Williams II, Charles D. Brook III, Eddie Allen; **D:** Jamaa Fanaka; **W:** Jamaa Fanaka.

The Black Six ♂ 1974 (R) Six black Vietnam veterans are out to punish the white gang who killed the brother of one of the black men. **91m/C VHS, DVD.** Gene Washington, Carl Eller, Lem Barney, Mercury Morris, Joe "Mean Joe" Greene, Willie Lanier, Rosalind Miles, John Isenbarger, Ben Davidson, Maury Wills, Mike Angel, Fred Scott; **D:** Matt Cimber, Maury Wills; **C:** Matt Cimber; **W:** George Theakos; **C:** William Swenning; **M:** David Moscoe.

The Black Sleep ♂ *Dr. Cadman's Secret* 1956 Mad scientist Dr. Cadman (Rathbone) invents a drug that causes a deathlike trance and uses it to perform brain surgery on unwilling patients. Needing an assistant, Cadman frames Dr. Ramsay (Rudley) for murder and uses the drug to rescue him from the gallows. Then some of Cadman's experiments get loose and want revenge. Over-the-top hokum that wastes a who's who of horror, including Lugosi (in nearly his last role) as a mute butler. **82m/B VHS.** Basil Rathbone, Herbert Rudley, Akim Tamiroff, Lon Chaney Jr., John Carradine, Bela Lugosi, Tor Johnson, Patricia Blake; **D:** Reginald LeBorg; **W:** John C. Higgins; **C:** Gordon Avil.

Black Snake Moan ♂♂ 2007 (R) Over-heated stew finds Jackson playing grizzled blues musician/farmer Lazarus, who's turned to religion to help him cope with his wife running off. So he's the one man ready to tackle the sex demons of abused white trash Rae (tiny Ricci in barely-there attire), even if it means chaining the nympho itch. Part sermon, part exploitation, wholly dull. **115m/C DVD, Blu-ray Disc, HD DVD.** *US* Samuel L. Jackson, Christina Ricci, Justin Timberlake, S. Epatha Merkerson, John

---

Cothran, Jr., Kim Richards; David Banner; **D:** Craig Brewer; **W:** Craig Brewer; **C:** Amy Vincent; **M:** Scott Bomar.

Black Snow ♂½ 1989 The mob is off on a violent search for 50 million bucks in cocaine. **90m/C VHS.** Jane Badler, Peter Sherayko, Julia Montgomery, Randy Brooks; **D:** Frank Patterson.

The Black Stallion ♂♂♂♂ 1979 (PG) A young boy and a wild Arabian Stallion are the only survivors of a shipwreck, and they develop a deep affection for each other. When rescued, they begin training for an important race. Exceptionally beautiful first half. Rooney plays a horse trainer, again. Great for adults and kids. **120m/C VHS, DVD.** Kelly Reno, Mickey Rooney, Teri Garr, Clarence Muse, Hoyt Axton; **D:** Carroll Ballard; **W:** William D. Wittliff, Melissa Mathison, Jeanne Rosenberg; **C:** Caleb Deschanel; **M:** Carmine Coppola. Oscars '79: Sound FX Editing; L.A. Film Critics '79: Cinematog.; Natl. Film Reg. '02;; Natl. Soc. Film Critics '79: Cinematog.

The Black Stallion Returns ♂♂½ 1983 (PG) Sequel to "The Black Stallion" follows the adventures of young Alec as he travels to the Sahara to search for his beautiful horse, which was stolen by an Arab chieftain. Unfortunately lacks much of the charm that was present in the first film. Adapted from the stories by Walt Farley. **103m/C VHS, DVD.** Kelly Reno, Teri Garr, Vincent Spano; **D:** Robert Dalva; **C:** Carlo Di Palma; **M:** Georges Delerue.

Black Starlet ♂♂ *Black Gauntlet* 1974 (R) A girl from the projects of Chicago travels to Hollywood in search of fame. She winds her way through a world of sleaze and drugs in order to make it to the top. **90m/C VHS.** Juanita Brown, Eric Mason, Rockine Tarkington, Damu King, Diane Holden; **D:** Chris Munger.

Black Sunday ♂♂♂ *La Maschera del Demonio; House of Fright; Revenge of the Vampire; Mask of Satan* 1960 In 1630, witch Asa (Steele) who also happens to be a vampire, is executed along with her lover Juvato (Dominici) by her own brother. Two hundred years later, they are accidentally resurrected and in revenge, Asa goes after her descendents, including her look-alike, Katia. A must see for horror fans; firsts for Steele as star and Bava as director. **83m/B VHS, DVD.** *IT* Barbara Steele, John Richardson, Ivo Garrani, Andrea Checchi, Arturo Dominici, Antonio Pierfederici, Tino Bianchi, Clara Bindi, Enrico Olivieri, Germana Dominici; **D:** Mario Bava; **W:** Mario Bava, Ennio de Concini, Mario Serandrei; **C:** Mario Bava, Ubaldo Terzano; **M:** Les Baxter.

Black Sunday ♂♂♂ 1977 (R) An Arab terrorist group, with the help of a disgruntled Vietnam vet, plots to steal the Goodyear Blimp and load it with explosives. Their intent is to explode it over a Miami Super Bowl game to assassinate the U.S. president and to kill all the fans. Based on Thomas Harris' novel. **143m/C VHS, DVD.** Robert Shaw, Bruce Dern, Marthe Keller, Fritz Weaver, Steven Keats, Michael V. Gazzo, William Daniels, Clyde Kusatsu; **D:** John Frankenheimer; **W:** Ernest Lehman; **C:** John A. Alonzo; **M:** John Williams.

The Black Swan ♂♂♂ 1942 Swashbuckling pirate film, based on the novel by Rafael Sabatini, stars Power as James Waring, compatriot of notorious buccaneer Henry Morgan (Cregar). Morgan is pardoned and sent to Jamaica as its new governor—if he can prevent his from associates from continuing their criminal ways. He enlists Waring to help him fight the renegades; meanwhile Waring falls in love with former governor's daughter Margaret (O'Hara). Lots of derring do. **85m/C VHS.** Tyrone Power, Maureen O'Hara, Laird Cregar, Thomas Mitchell, George Sanders, Anthony Quinn, George Zucco, Edward Ashley, Fortunio Bonanova; **D:** Henry King; **W:** Ben Hecht, Seton I. Miller; **C:** Leon Shamroy; **M:** Alfred Newman. Oscars '42: Color Cinematog.

Black Terrorist 1985 Terrorists take over a ranch and slay the inhabitants. They keep a young boy alive and the mother tries to rescue him. **81m/C VHS.** Allan Granville, Vera Jones; **D:** Neil Hetherington.

Black Thunder ♂️1/2 1998 (R) An Air Force stealth jet, nicknamed "Black Thunder," is hijacked by a Libyan agent during testing. A top gun, Vince Connors (Dudikoff), is paired with hotdog pilot Rick Jannick (Hudson) to retrieve the jet. A standard actioner. **85m/C VHS, DVD.** Michael Dudikoff, Gary Hudson, Richard Norton, Rob Maddid, Nancy Valen, Michael Cavanaugh, Robert Miranda, Frederic Forrest; **D:** Rick Jacobson; **W:** William Martell; **C:** Michael T. Michael Clark. **VIDEO**

Black Water Gold ♂️1/2 1969 TV movie about a search for sunken Spanish gold. **75m/C VHS.** Ricardo Montalban, Keir Dullea, Lana Wood, Bradford Dillman, France Nuyen; **M:** Rafael Mey.

Black Water ♂️ 2007 ♂️1/2 1994 Tennessee fishing trip turns into a nightmare for an innocent man accused of murder. Based on the novel "Minnie" by Hans Werner Kettenbach. **105m/C VHS.** Julian Sands, Stacey Dash, Ned Beatty, Ed Lauter, Denis Crosby, William McNamara, Rod Steiger; **D:** Nicolas Gessner; **W:** Nicolas Gessner, Laird Koenig; **M:** Gabriel Yared.

Black Venus ♂️1/2 1983 (R) A softcore epic, starring the former Miss Bahamas, Josephine Jacqueline Jones, about the 18th-century French aristocracy. Laughably based upon the stories of Balzac. European film dubbed in English. **80m/C VHS, DVD. SP** Josephine Jacqueline Jones, Emiliano Redondo, Jose Antonio Ceinos, Monique Gabrielle, Florence Guerin, Helga Line, Mandy Rice-Davies; **D:** Claude Mulot; **W:** Gregorio Garcia Segura, Harry Alan Towers; **C:** Jacques Assuerus, Julib Burgos.

Black Tower ♂️ 1950 An interesting murder mystery telling the story of a desperately impoverished medical student. **54m/B VHS, DVD, FR** Cyd Charisse, Peter Cookson, Warren William, Anne Gwynne, Charles Calvert.

A Black Veil for Lisa ♂️ 1968 A man attempts to exact revenge upon his unfaithful wife, but things go horribly awry. **87m/C VHS. IT GE** John Mills Luciana Paluzzi, Robert Hoffman; **D:** Massimo Dallamano.

Black Tights ♂️1/2 1960 Chevalier introduces four stories told in dance by Roland Petit's Ballet de Paris company: "The Diamond Crusher," "Cyrano de Bergerac," "A Merry Mourning," and "Carmen." A keeper for dance fans. Shearer's Roxanne in "Cyrano" was her last performance before retirement. **120m/C VHS, DVD.** JP Akira Kazayashi, Chieko Matsubara; **D:** Yasuhara Hasebe.

Black Tight Killers ♂️ Ore Ni Sawaru to Abunaze 1966 Imagine a Japanese Matt Helm movie with an Elvis impersonator in the lead. That's essentially what's going on in this gonzo adventure/comedy from the mid-'60s. Hondo (Kobayashi) is a combat photographer just back from Vietnam. He and his stewardess girlfriend (Matsubara) become involved with various gangsters in a fast-moving plot filled with such bizarre devices as Ninja chewing gum bullets. **84m/C DVD.** JP Akio Hasebe, Chieko Matsubara; **D:** Yasuhari Hasebe.

Black Tide ♂️1/2 Stormy Crossing 1958 Suspicions arise that a drowning may have actually been a murder. **69m/C VHS. GB** John Ireland, Derek Bond, Leslie Dwyer, Maureen Connell, Sheldon Lawrence, Jack Taylor, Joy Webster, Cameron Hall, Arthur Lowe, John Horsley; **D:** C.M. Pennington-Richards; **W:** Brock William; **C:** Geoffrey Faithfull; **M:** Stanley Black.

The Black Windmill ♂️1/2 1974 (PG) An English spy is caught between his service and the kidnapping of his family by rival spies. **102m/C VHS.** Michael Caine, Donald Pleasence, Delphine Seyrig, Clive Revill, Janet Suzman, John Vernon; **D:** Don Siegel.

Blackbeard the Pirate ♂️ 1952 The 18th-century buccaneer is given the full-blooded, Hollywood treatment. **99m/C VHS, DVD.** Robert Newton, Linda Darnell, Keith Andes, William Bendix, Richard Egan; **D:** Raoul Walsh.

Blackbeard's Ghost ♂️ 1967 Disney comedy in which the famed 18th-century pirate's spirit (Ustinov) is summoned to save a restaurant in order to prevent an old family home from being turned into a casino. **107m/C VHS, DVD.** Peter Ustinov, Dean Jones, Suzanne Pleshette, Elsa Lanchester, Richard Deacon, Joby Baker, Elliott Reid, Michael Conrad, Kelly Thordsen; **D:** Robert Stevenson; **W:** Bill Walsh, Don DaGradi; **C:** Edward Colman; **M:** Robert F. Brunner.

Blackbelt 2: Fatal Force ♂️1/2 Spyder 1993 (R) A man seeks to avenge his brother's murder by going after his killers. **83m/C VHS, DVD.** Blake Bahner, Roxanna Baird.

Blackboard Jungle ♂️♂️♂️1/2 1955 Well-remembered urban drama story follows the police investigation of some typical Hitchcock themes. The murder, and a detective's attempts to keep his girlfriend from being involved. Look for Hitchcock's screen cameo. Made to the community while Jared is filled with to decide where his loyalties lie. **100m/C VHS, DVD. AU** Laurence Breuls, Simon Lyndon, Linda Cropper, Rebecca Smart, David Field, Chris Haywood, Boyana Novakovich; **D:** Steven Vidler; **W:** Nick Enright; **C:** Martin McGrath, George Greenough; **M:** Steve Kilbey.

The Black Widow ♂️ Sombra, the Spider Woman 1947 A fortune-teller plots to steal scientific secrets and take over the world. Serial in 13 episodes. **164m/B VHS.** Bruce Edwards, Carol Forman, Anthony Warde; **D:** Spencer Gordon Bennet.

Black Widow ♂️♂️ 1954 Rogers gets cast against type as heartless Broadway diva Lottie, who's mixed-up in the death of secretive aspiring writer Nanny Peter's actress wife Iris (Tierney) too happy. **95m/C DVD.** Ginger Rogers, Van Heflin, Gene Tierney, George Raft, Peggy Ann Garner, Reginald Gardiner, Virginia Leith, Otto Kruger, Cathleen Nesbitt, Skip Homeier; **D:** Nunnally Johnson; **W:** Nunnally Johnson; **C:** Charles Clarke; **M:** Leigh Harline.

The Black Widow ♂️♂️ 1987 (R) A federal agent pursues a beautiful murderess who marries rich men and then kills them, making the deaths look natural. The agent herself becomes involved in the final seduction. The two women are enticing and the ocations picturesque. **101m/C VHS, DVD.** Debra Winger, Theresa Russell, Sami Frey, Nicol Williamson, Terry O'Quinn, Dennis Hopper, D.W. Moffett, Lois Smith, Mary Woronov, Rutanya Alda, James Hong, Diane Ladd; **Cameos:** David Mamet; **D:** Bob Rafelson; **W:** Ronald Bass; **C:** Conrad L. Hall; **M:** Michael Small.

Black Widow ♂️♂️ 1997 (R) A con artists have their scam down—the se-ductive Arnette (Alonso) picks up wealthy men, then Ray (Grieco) steps in, they team up, and takes their cash. Things get messy when they learn of a young woman (Loewi) who has yet to learn of an enormous inheritance, and Ray steps into the role of seducer. Although the film runs out of steam in the last 20 minutes, Grieco and Loewi are likeable in the lead roles. **95m/C VHS, DVD.** Mara Conchita Alonso, Richard Grieco, Fiona Loewi, Christopher Plummer; **D:** Dominic Shiach; **W:** Brock Simpson, Brad Simpson.

The Blackheath Poisonings ♂️♂️1/2 1992 The Collards and the Vandervents are toy-making families who share more than a profession—they share Albert Villa in the London suburb of Blackheath in 1894. Unhappily adults, an illicit affair, a scheming stranger—everyone has something to hide. But when a gruesome murder is committed the ensuing police inquiry will rattle both families skeletons. Based on the novel by Julian Symons. **150m/C VHS, DVD. GB** Christine Kavanagh, Ian McNeice, Zoe Wanamaker, Judy Parfitt, James Faulkner, Christien Anholt, Julia St. John, Nicholas Woodeson, Ronald Fraser, Donald (Don) Sumpter; **D:** Stuart Orme; **W:** Simon Raven; **C:** Dick Pope; **M:** Colin Towns. **TV**

Blackjack ♂️♂️ 1978 (R) Las Vegas is the scene for action and excitement as the mob puts the hit on tough guy William Smith. **104m/C VHS.** William Smith, Tony Burton, Pars Earl, Damu King, Diane Summerfield, Angela May; **D:** John Evans.

Blackjack ♂️♂️1/2 1997 (R) Former U.S. Marshal Jack Devlin (Lundgren), who has a pathological fear of the color white, becomes the bodyguard of a young super-model (Haskin) who's the target of a psycho killer (Mackenzie.) To highlight Devlin's phobia Woo uses one of his big action scenes in a dairy flooded with milk. **113m/C VHS, DVD. CA** Dolph Lundgren, Kam Haskin, Sau Rubinek, Fred Williamson, Phillip MacKenzie, Kate Vernon, Padraign Murphy, Philip Akin; **D:** John Woo; **W:** Peter Lance; **C:** Bill Wong; **M:** Micky Erbe. **VIDEO**

Blacklight ♂️♂️ 1998 Clairvoyant Sharon Avery (Welch) tried to help the police with a crash she found dead. In despair, Sharon gets into an auto accident and loses both her sight and, apparently her gift. She later tries to drown herself, but suddenly sees images of another child kidnapping. Inspector Frank Shumann (Ironside) is reluctant to accept her help until a little girl is found murdered. Now Sharon is on a collision course with a child killer. **91m/C VHS.** Tainee Welch, Michael Ironside, Billy Norton; **D:** Michael Storey; **C:** Walter Mills, Billy Norton; **M:** Ken Harrison. **VIDEO**

Blackmail ♂️♂️1/2 1929 This first sound film for Great Britain and director Hitchcock features an early visualization of some typical Hitchcock themes. The story follows the police investigation of a murder, and a detective's attempts to keep his girlfriend from being involved. Look for Hitchcock's screen cameo. Made as a silent, this was reworked to become a talkie. **86m/B VHS, DVD. GB** Anny Ondra, John Longden, Sara Allgood, Charles Paton, Cyril Ritchard, Donald Calthrop, Hannah Jones, Percy Parsons, Johnny Butt, Harvey Braban, Phyllis Monkman, Alfred Hitchcock; **D:** Alfred Hitchcock; **W:** Charles Bennett, Benn W. Levy, Garnett Weston; **C:** Jack Cox.

Blackmail ♂️♂️ 1991 (R) Familiar story is given new life in this suspenseful movie. Bakely is a lonely woman who succumbs to Mickiff's attentions. She doesn't suspect that he's conning her with the help of his lover, Toussaint. Engaging thriller adapted from a short story by Bill

Blackout ♂️♂️ 1978 (R) Four killers terrorize an office building during the 1977 New York electrical blackout. Soon the power goes out, confront them, and the police enter, confront them, and the fun starts. Comic touches provide some relief from the violence 'ere. **86m/C VHS.** Jim Mitchum, Robert Carradine, Ray Milland, June Allyson, Jean-Pierre Aumont, Belinda J. Montgomery; **D:** Eddy Matalon; **W:** Joseph Stefano.

Blackout ♂️♂️ 1988 (R) Strange memories from childhood come back to her past killings, in spite of the fact that he now leads a subdued family life. **95m/C VHS.** Richard Widmark, Keith Carradine, Kathleen Quinlan, Michael Beck, Gerald Hiken; **D:** Douglas Hickox; **W:** David Ambrose.

Blackout ♂️♂️ 1997 (R) Movie star Matty (Modine) has multiple addictions he indulges on a trip home to Miami. He proposes to pregnant girlfriend Annie (Dalle) but when he learns she's had an abortion, Matty goes on a binge and suffers a blackout. 16 months later in New York, Matty has kicked his addictions and compel him back to Miami and the possibility that he has committed murder. Sleazy and the symbolism is heavy-handed. **100m/C VHS, DVD.** Matthew Modine, Beatrice Dale, Claudia Schiffer, Dennis Hopper, Sarah Lassez; **D:** Abel Ferrara; **W:** Abel Ferrara, Chris Zois, Marla Hanson; **C:** Ken Kelsch; **M:** Joe Delia.

The Blackout ♂️♂️1/2 1985 Cable thriller in which an aging police chief suspects a disfigured amnesiac is responsible for a series of killings. **91m/C VHS.** Carol Lynley, Gail O'Grady, Michael Keys Hall, Joseph Gian, Joanna Miles; **D:** Doug Adams; **C:** Armledge Armenaki.

Blackheart ♂️♂️ 1998 (R) A pair of con artists have their scam down—the seductive Arnette (Alonso) picks up wealthy men and otherwise enjoys killing people and otherwise causing big trouble. Ripe blaxploitation. **87m/C VHS, DVD.** John Hart, Ivory Stone, Andrea King, Liz Renay, Joe DeSue, Roosevelt Jackson, Nick Solin; **C:** Robert Caramico; **M:** Frank R. Saletri; **C:** Cardella Demilo, Lou Frohman.

Blackmale ♂️♂️ 1999 (R) Small-time hustlers Jimmy (Woodbine) and Luther (Pierce) bet everything on a fixed fight and lose big. Now they owe $100,000 to a loan shark. So they decide to blackmail a coke dealer who they think would-be mark is actually more dangerous than they could have imagined. **85m/C VHS, DVD.** Bokeem Woodbine, Justin Pierce, Roger Fees, Sascha Knopf, Erik Todd Dellums; **D:** George Baluzy, Mike Baluzy; **W:** Harvey; **M:** Ivor Slaney.

The Blackout ♂️♂️1/2 1950 Blind man recovers his sight and finds the brother of his girlfriend, once thought dead, is actually alive and well and running a smuggling ring. Routine. **73m/B VHS, DVD.** Dinah Sheridan, Patric Doonan, Eric Pohlmann; **D:** Robert S. Baker.

Blackout ♂️♂️ Murder by Proxy 1954 A drunken private eye is offered a murder case, and is subsequently framed for the crime. **87m/B VHS.** Dane Clark, Belinda Lee, Betsy Ann Davies, Eleanor Summerfield, Andrew Osborn, Harold Lang, Alfie Bass; **D:** Terence Fisher; **W:** Richard H. Landau; **J.** (Jimmy W.) Harvey; **M:** Ivor Slaney.

Blacksnake! woof! Sweet Suzy; Duchess of Doom; Slaves 1973 (R) Overheated sex and race tale, set in 1835, finds a British lord travelling to a Caribbean island in search of his brother. What he finds is his sadistic sister-in-law and evil overseer using violence to keep the slaves in line. **82m/C VHS.** Milton McCollin, Anouska (Anoushka)

come "Blackenstein," a large African American with chip on hulking shoulder who enjoys killing people and otherwise... **D:** Ruben Preuss. **CABLE**

Crenshaw. **87m/C VHS.** Susan Blakely, Dale Midcliff, Beth Toussart, John Saxon, Mac Davis; **D:** Ruben Preuss. **CABLE**

Black Tice continued ...

Blackenstein woof! Black Frankenstein 1973 (R) Doctor into nouveau experimentation "restores a man's arms and legs. But a jealous assistant gives our man a bog's injection, causing him to become "Blackenstein," a large African American...

Hempel, David Warbeck, Percy Herbert, David Prowse; **D:** Russ Meyer; **W:** Russ Meyer, Leonard Neubauer; **C:** Arthur Ornitz; **M:** William Loose, Al Teeter.

Blackwater Trail 🦴🦴 **1995 (R)** Novelist Matt Curran (Nelson) travels from L.A. to Michelton, Australia, to attend the funeral of his best friend Andy, a cop who supposedly committed suicide. But Andy's sister (and Matt's former lover) Cathy (Smart) thinks he was murdered because of a case involving a serial killer. Matt decides to snoop around and finds out the killer likes to leave behind body parts and biblical quotations. Contrived plotting but some good performances and some spectacular scenery. **100m/C VHS.** *AU* Judd Nelson, Dee Smart, Peter Phelps, Mark Lee, Brett Climo; **D:** Ian Barry; **W:** Andrew Russell; **C:** John Stokes; **M:** Stephen Rae.

Blackwoods WOOF! **2002 (R)** It's just like a M. Night Shyamalan movie... only much, much worse. Uwe Boll, Germany's answer to Ed Wood, directs this pointless thriller that apes every third-act twist cliche in the book. Matt (Muldoon) and Dawn (Tracy) drive up to the "Blackwoods" to visit Dawn's hillbilly family, but after checking into a creepy motel (staffed by Clint Howard, no less), Dawn disappears and crazy axe-wielding psychos start attacking Matt. It's all leading up to one big twist that's telegraphed further than a ten-meter cattle prod. Honestly, if you can't figure out the whole movie in the first five minutes, you should put down the airplane glue and move your trailer away from the power lines. **90m/C VHS, DVD.** *GE CA* Patrick Muldoon, Keegan Connor Tracy, Michael Pare, Clint Howard, Will Sanderson, Matthew Walker, Anthony Harrison, Janet Wright, Sean Campbell, Ben Derrick; **D:** Uwe Boll; **W:** Robert Dean Klein, Uwe Boll; **C:** Mathias Neumann; **M:** Reinhard Besser.

Blacula 🦴🦴 **1972 (PG)** The African Prince Mamuwalde stalks the streets of Los Angeles trying to satisfy his insatiable desire for blood. Mildly successful melding of blaxploitation and horror that spawned a sequel, "Scream, Blacula, Scream." **92m/C VHS, DVD.** William Marshall, Thalmus Rasulala, Denise Nicholas, Vonetta McGee, Gordon Pinsent, Emily Yancy, Charles Macaulay, Ted Harris, Elisha Cook Jr., Lance Taylor; **D:** William Crain; **W:** Raymond Koenig, Joan Torres; **C:** John Stevens; **M:** Gene Page.

Blade 🦴🦴 **1998 (R)** Action-packed gore-fest that provides for high-octane escapist entertainment, with some eye-catching visuals and a pulsing techno soundtrack. Blade (Snipes) is a half-vampire/half-human, who's intent on preventing evil, ambitious Deacon Frost (Dorff) from unleashing a vampire apocalypse upon humanity so he can take over. Helping out Blade are his grizzled mentor, vampire hunter Abraham Whistler (Kristofferson), and Dr. Karen Janson (Wright), who's searching for a cure for vampirism. Adapted from the Marvel comic book character. **91m/C VHS, DVD, UMD.** Wesley Snipes, Stephen Dorff, Kris Kristofferson, N'Bushe Wright, Donal Logue, Udo Kier, Traci Lords, Tim Guinee, Arly Jover, Sanaa Lathan; **D:** Stephen Norrington; **W:** David S. Goyer; **C:** Theo van de Sande; **M:** Mark Isham. MTV Movie Awards '99: Villain (Dorff).

Blade 2 🦴🦴 **2002 (R)** Sequel takes the more, more, more approach—more vampires, more battles, more gore. Half-vampire, half-human daywalker Blade (Snipes at his coolest) first rescues mentor Whistler (Kristofferson) from the vamps who have been holding him prisoner. Then, he's offered a truce by vampire overlord Damaskinos (Kretschmann) who needs Blade to hunt an even more deadly enemy. The rat-like Reapers feed on both humans and vampires and their bite turns their victims into insatiable bloodsuckers themselves. Of course, as Blade goes a-huntin', he discovers the situation isn't as clear-cut as it seems. **116m/C VHS, DVD.** *US* Wesley Snipes, Kris Kristofferson, Ron Perlman, Leonor Varela, Norman Reedus, Thomas Kretschmann, Luke Goss, Matt Schulze, Donnie Yen, Dan-

ny John Jules, Daz Crawford, Karel Roden, Tony Curran, Santiago Segura, Marit Velle Kile; **D:** Guillermo del Toro; **W:** David S. Goyer; **C:** Gabriel Beristain; **M:** Marco Beltrami, Danny Saber.

Blade Boxer 🦴 **The Boxer 1997** Police detectives go undercover to expose an illegal fight ring that has its combatants battling to the death, and equipped with deadly steel talons. **91m/C VHS, DVD.** Kevin King, Todd McKee, Andrew Martino, Cass Magda, Dana Plato; **D:** Bruce Reisman.

Blade in Hong Kong 🦴🦴½ **1985** Investigator travels to Hong Kong, finds trouble and romance in the underbelly of the city. Pilot for un-sold series. **100m/C VHS.** Terry Lester, Keye Luke, Mike (Michael) Preston, Jean-Marie Hon, Leslie Nielsen, Nancy Kwan, Anthony Newley, Ellen Regan; **D:** Reza Badiyi. TV

A Blade in the Dark 🦴🦴 *La Casa con la Scala Nel Buio; House of the Dark Stairway* **1983** A young man composing a score for a horror film moves into a secluded villa and is inspired and haunted by the mysterious murder he witnesses. **104m/C VHS, DVD.** Michele (Michael) Soavi, Fabiola Toledo, Valeria Cavalli, Lara Naszinsky, Andrea Occhipinti, Anny Papa; **D:** Lamberto Bava; **W:** Dardano Sacchetti; **C:** Gianlorenzo Battaglia; **M:** Guido de Angelis, Maurizio de Angelis.

Blade Master 🦴½ **1984 (PG)** *Ator the Invincible* In this sequel to "Ator the Fighting Eagle," O'Keeffe as Ator is back as the Blade Master. Ator defends his people and his family name in a battle against the "Geometric Nucleus": a primitive bomb. His quest leads him and his small band of men to the castle of knowledge. D'Amato used the pseudonym David Hills. **92m/C VHS.** Miles O'Keeffe, Lisa Foster; **D:** Joe D'Amato.

Blade of the Ripper WOOF! **1970** *The Next Victim; Next!; Lo Strano Vizio della Signora Ward* A madman armed with a razor slashes his way through the lovelies of the international jet set. **90m/C VHS.** George Hilton, Edwige Fenech, Alberto De Mendoza, Ivan Rassimov; **D:** Sergio Martino; **W:** Ernesto Gastaldi, Eduardo Brochero.

Blade Runner 🦴🦴🦴🦴 **1982 (R)** Los Angeles, the 21st century. World-weary cop tracks down a handful of renegade "replicants" (synthetically produced human slaves who, with only days left of life, search madly for some way to extend their prescribed lifetimes). Moody, beautifully photographed, dark thriller with sets from an architect's dream. Based on "Do Androids Dream of Electric Sheep" by Philip K. Dick. Director's cut, released in 117 minutes, removes Ford's narration and the last scene of the film, which Scott considered too "up," and inserts several short scenes, including a dream sequence. **122m/C VHS, DVD, Blu-ray Disc, HD DVD.** Harrison Ford, Rutger Hauer, Sean Young, Daryl Hannah, M. Emmet Walsh, Edward James Olmos, Joe Turkel, Brion James, Joanna Cassidy, William Sanderson; **D:** Ridley Scott; **W:** Hampton Fancher, David Peoples; **C:** Jordan Cronenweth; **M:** Vangelis. L.A. Film Critics '82: Cinematog., Natl. Film Reg. '93.

Blade: Trinity 🦴🦴 **2004 (R)** The last of the "Blade" trilogy (at least with the stoic Snipes), bloody actioner sticks to what it does best, this time with writer Goyer also taking on directing chores. Bitchy bloodsucker Danica (a gleeful Posey), who leads the Vampire Nation, decides to wake up Dracula, aka Drake (Purcell)—whose blood will allow them to walk in the daylight. Blade is busy doing his slaying thing when he gets involved—along with a couple of mouthy youngsters, dishy Abigail (Biel), who happens to be Whistler's (Kristofferson) daughter, and wisecracking recovered vamp Hannibal King (Reynolds). There is, of course, a final mano a mano battle between Blade and Drac, uh, Drake. The ending also leaves wiggle room for the younger actors to continue the bloodletting. **105m/C VHS, DVD.** *US* Wesley Snipes, Kris Kristofferson, Jessica Biel, Ryan Reynolds, Parker Posey, Dominic Purcell, John Michael Higgins, James Remar, Eric Bogosian, Patton Oswalt, Callum Keith Rennie, Natasha Lyonne, Mark Berry, Francoise Yip, Chris Heyerdahl, Paul Anthony; **D:** David S. Goyer; **W:** David S. Goyer; **C:** Gabriel Beristain; **M:** The RZA, Ramin Djawadi.

Blades 🦴 **1989 (R)** Another junk heap from Troma, dealing with the efforts of three golfers who try to stop a maniacal power mower that's been grinding duffers with regularity. **101m/C VHS, DVD.** Robert North, Jeremy Whelan, Victoria Scott, Jon McBride; **D:** Thomas R. Rondinella; **W:** William R. Pace; **M:** James Hayman; **M:** John Hodian.

Blades of Courage 🦴🦴 *Skate!* **1988** Biography of Olympic skater Lori Larouche. Choreographed by Debbi Wilkes. **98m/C VHS.** *CA* Lynn Nightingale, Christianne Hirt, Colm Feore, Rosemary Dunsmore; **D:** Randy Bradshaw. TV

Blades of Glory 🦴🦴½ **2007 (PG-13)** Lumpy Ferrell gets a mullet and stuffs himself into spandex and sparkles to play bad boy ice skater Chazz Michael Michaels, whose only rival is wispy blonde peacock Jimmy MacElroy (Heder). After the two are banned from singles competition for public brawling, a loophole allows them to compete as the first male/male pairs skating team, much to the disgust of oh-so-close brother/sister skating champs, the Van Waldenbergs (real-life spouses Arnett and Poehler). The jokes are obvious, which doesn't necessarily mean they aren't funny. **93m/C DVD, Blu-ray Disc, HD DVD.** *US* Will Ferrell, Jon Heder, Amy Poehler, Will Arnett, Jenna Fischer, Craig T. Nelson, William Fichtner, Nick Swardson; **D:** Will Speck, Josh Gordon; **W:** Jeff Cox, Craig Cox, John Altschuler, Dave Krinsky; **C:** Stefan Czapsky; **M:** Theodore Shapiro.

The Blair Witch Project 🦴🦴 **1999 (R)** A Sundance Film Festival favorite, this low-budget horror film turned out to be the most successful indie ever, thanks to heavy (and savvy) market promotion. In 1994, a three-person film crew heads into the Black Hills region of Maryland to document a local legend about a year later their film footage is found and this amateurish, black and white footage makes up what the audience sees. Largely improvisational, the film manages a palpable sense of dread and claustrophobia, while being (deliberately) technically crude. However, the herky-jerky camera movements made a number of viewers physically sick and an equal number found the would-be theatrics boring. **87m/C VHS, DVD.** Michael Williams, Heather Donahue, Joshua Leonard; **D:** Eduardo Sanchez, Daniel Myrick; **W:** Eduardo Sanchez, Daniel Myrick; **C:** Neal Fredericks; **M:** Tony Cora. Golden Raspberries '99: Worst Actress (Donahue).

Blaise Pascal 🦴🦴🦴½ **1971** Another of Rossellini's later historical portraits, detailing the life and times of the 17th-century philosopher, seen as a man whose scientific ideas conflicted with his own religious beliefs. Italian with subtitles. **131m/C VHS.** *IT* Pierre Arditi, Giuseppe Addobati, Christian de Sica, Rita Forzano; **D:** Roberto Rossellini; **W:** Roberto Rossellini; **C:** Mario Fioretti; **M:** Mario Nascimbene. TV

Blake of Scotland Yard 🦴🦴½ **1936** Blake, the former Scotland Yard inspector, battles against a villain who has constructed a murderous death ray. Condensed version of the 15 episode serial (originally at 180 minutes). **70m/B VHS, DVD.** Ralph Byrd, Herbert Rawlinson, Joan Barclay, Lloyd Hughes; **D:** Robert F. "Bob" Hill.

Blame It on Fidel 🦴🦴🦴½ **2006** *La Faute a Fidel* Amusing and tender film told from the point of view of nine-year-old Anna (Kervel), who becomes increasingly upset when her bourgeois parents, Fernando (Accorsi) and Marie (Depardieu, daughter of Gerard), suddenly decide to devote their time and money to various political/activist causes (it's 1970 in Paris). She and her younger brother are moved from their comfortable home to a shabby apartment and are left in the care of oddball political refugees. Anna doesn't take well to all these changes and is confused about what she hears and is told to believe. Writer/director Gavras is the daughter of political filmmaker Costas-Gavras. French with subtitles. **100m/C DVD, FR IT** Julie Depardieu, Stefano Accorsi, Olivier Perrier, Nina Kremer, Benjamin Feuillet, Martine Chevallier, Marie Kremer, Marie-Noelle Bordeaux; **D:** Julie Gavras; **W:** Julie Gavras; **C:** Nathalie Durant; **M:** Armand Amar.

Blame It on Rio 🦴🦴 **1984 (R)** A middle-aged man has a ridiculous fling with his best friend's daughter while on vacation with them in Rio de Janeiro. Caine and Johnson are amusing, but the script is somewhat weak. Remake of the French film "One Wild Moment." **90m/C VHS, DVD.** Michael Caine, Joseph Bologna, Demi Moore, Michelle Johnson, Valerie Harper; **D:** Stanley Donen; **W:** Charlie Peters, Larry Gelbart; **C:** Reynaldo Villalobos; **M:** Kenneth Wannberg.

Blame It on the Bellboy 🦴🦴 **1992 (PG-13)** Wild farce set in Venice about a hotel bellboy who confuses three similarly named visitors—sending the wrong ones to meet corporate bigwigs, date women, or even kill. The brisk pace loses it towards the end and devolves into chase scenes. **79m/C VHS, DVD.** Dudley Moore, Bryan Brown, Richard Griffiths, Andreas Katsulas, Patsy Kensit, Alison Steadman, Bronson Pinchot, Lindsay Anderson, Penelope Wilton; **D:** Mark Herman; **W:** Mark Herman; **M:** Trevor Jones.

Blame It on the Night 🦴🦴 **1984 (PG-13)** A rock star gets to take care of the military cadet son he never knew after the boy's mother suddenly dies. Mick Jagger helped write the story. Available in VHS and Beta Hi-Fi. **85m/C VHS.** Nick Mancuso, Byron Thames, Leslie Ackerman, Billy Preston, Merry Clayton; **D:** Gene Taft.

Blanche Fury 🦴🦴½ **1948** Governess Blanche (Hobson) marries her wealthy widowed cousin but the man she truly desires is the illegitimate Philip Thorn (Granger), who manages the estate for her husband. So Blanche decides to get rid of the man she doesn't love. Based on England's 19th-century Rush murder and adapted from the novel by Joseph Shearing. **95m/C VHS.** *GB* Valerie Hobson, Stewart Granger, Walter Fitzgerald, Michael Gough, Maurice Denham, Sybilla Binder; **D:** Marc Allegret; **W:** Hugh Mills; **C:** Guy Green, Geoffrey Unsworth; **M:** Clifton Parker.

Blank Check 🦴 *Disney's Blank Check* **1993 (PG)** Parents may want to verify the whereabouts of their checkbooks after this one. Eleven-year-old Preston receives a blank check from a mobster on the run, cashes it for a million bucks, and goes on a spending orgy under an assumed name. Where are his parents? Apparently they don't have a problem with a shadowy benefactor taking their son under his wing. Sound familiar? And who thought it would be a good idea to have the little twerp mooning after a comely bank teller? Formula aside, this blatant rip-off of "Home Alone" tries to throw in an ending moral but probably won't fool the kids either. **93m/C VHS, DVD.** Brian Bonsall, Miguel Ferrer, Michael Lerner, Tone Loc, Ric(k) Ducommun, Karen Duffy; **D:** Rupert Wainwright; **W:** Colby Carr, Blake Snyder; **M:** Nicholas Pike.

Blankman 🦴🦴 **1994 (PG-13)** Self-appointed superhero (Wayans), who makes up in creativity what he lacks in superpowers, fights crime in his underwear and a cape made from his grandmother's bathrobe. Life is simple, until an ambitious TV reporter (Givens) finds out about him. Silly one-joke premise is carried a little too far; didn't similar "Meteor Man" crash? Gifted comedian Wayans tries, but can't make this guy fly. **96m/C VHS, DVD.** Damon Wayans, Robin Givens, David Alan Grier, Jason Alexander, Jon Polito, Nick(y) Corello; **D:** Mike Binder; **W:** J.F. Lawton, Damon Wayans; **C:** Newton Thomas (Tom) Sigel; **M:** Miles Goodman.

Blast 🦴🦴 **1996** Terrorists take a group of spectators hostage at the Atlanta Summer Olympics. **98m/C VHS.** Linden Ashby, Andrew Divoff, Rutger Hauer, Tim Thomerson; **D:** Albert Pyun.

Blast 🦴🦴½ **2004 (R)** Mercenaries try to detonate an electromagnetic bomb over the U.S using an oil rig. A tug boat captain (Griffin) teams with an FBI agent and computer expert in order to foil the plan. Griffin is surprisingly effective as an action hero, and the proceedings, while not breaking any new ground, provide the requisite excitement and wisecracks in the "Die Hard/Under Siege" mode. **91m/C DVD.** Eddie Griffin, Vinnie Jones, Breckin Meyer, Vivica A. Fox, Tommy (Tiny) Lister, Anthony Hickox; **D:** Anthony

Blast from the Past ✓✓1/2 1998 (PG-13) Mistaking a plane crash in his yard for an atomic bomb blast, paranoid scientist Calvin (Walken) and his pregnant wife Helen (Spacek) lock themselves in the shelter on a diet of canned goods. Fearful of radioactive fallout, they raise their son Adam (Fraser) in the shelter. After 35 years, Adam is sent out for supplies, just waiting for the right time. When Frank makes a mistake and tries to get out of the contract, he realizes that he'll be next on the hit parade. 106m/C VHS, DVD, Brendan Fraser, Alicia Silverstone, Christopher Walken, Sissy Spacek, Dave Foley, Joey Slotnick, Dale Raoul; *D:* Hugh Wilson; *W:* Hugh Wilson, Bill Kelly; *C:* Jose Luis Alcaine; *Nar:* Lionel Stander.

Blast of Silence ✓✓ 1961 Hardboiled crime. Frank Bono (Baron) comes to Manhattan at Christmas for a contract hit for the mob. He follows his target and decides on the best place to make his shot, just waiting for the right time. When the holidays get in the way of business and he meets a woman who offers him a low opinion of modern men. 77m/B DVD. Allen Baron, Molly McCarthy; *D:* Allen Baron; *W:* Allen Baron; *Nar:* Steve Dortl.

Blastfighter WOOF! 1985 (R) After local hoodlums kill his daughter, an ex-con cop goes on a spree of violence and revenge. Director Bava uses the pseudonym "John Old, Jr.," as his father Mario Bava occasionally credited himself as John Old. Italian film shot in Atlanta. 93m/C VHS. *IT* Michael Sopkiw, Valerie Blake, George Eastman; *D:* Lamberto Bava.

Blaze ✓✓1/2 1989 (R) The true story of Louisiana governor Earl Long who becomes involved with a stripper, Blaze Starr, causing a political scandal of major proportions. Roust, good-humored bio-pic featuring a fine character turn by Newman. 117m/C VHS, DVD. Paul Newman, Lolita Davidovich, Jerry Hardin, Robert Wuhl, Garland Bunting; *D:* Ron Shelton; *W:* Ron Shelton; *C:* Haskell Wexler.

Blazing Across the Pecos ✓✓ 1948 The Durango Kid (Starrett) is after Pecos Flats mayor Ace Brockaway (Wilson), who's secretly selling guns to the local Indian tribe so they'll attack the supply wagons of their business rivals. 54m/B VHS, DVD. Charles Starrett Smiley Burnette, Charles C. Wilson, Chief Thundercloud; *D:* Ray Nazarro.

Blazing Guns ✓ *Marshal of Heldorado* 1950 A marshal, masquerading inexplicably as a tenderfoot, enters a lawless town and is immediately hired as a deputy. 54m/B VHS. James Ellison, Russell Hayden, Raymond Hatton, Fuzzy Knight, Julie Adams; *D:* Thomas Carr.

Blazing Saddles ✓✓✓1/2 1974 (R) Wild, wacky spoof by Brooks of every cliche in the western film genre. Little is Black Bart, a convict offered a reprieve if he will become a sheriff and clean up a nasty frontier town. The previous recipients of this honor have all swiftly ended up in shallow graves. A crazy, silly film with a cast full of lovable loonies including comedy greats Wilder, Kahn, and Korman. Watch for the Count Basie Orchestra. A group writing effort, based on an original story by Bergman. Was the most-viewed movie in its first year of release on HBO cable. 90m/C VHS, DVD, Blu-ray Disc, HD DVD. Cleavon Little, Harvey Korman, Madeline Kahn, Gene Wilder, Liel Brooks, John Hillerman, Alex

Blazing Stewardesses WOOF! *Texas Layover* 1975 (R) The Hound salutes the distributor for truth in advertising, as they stamped this as one of the world's worst videos. Lusty, busty stewardesses relax at a western guest ranch under siege from hooded riders and the aging gags of the Ritz Brothers. 95m/C VHS, DVD. Yvonne De Carlo, Robert "Bob" Livingston, Donald "Red" Barry, Regina Carrol, Connie Hoff man; *Cameos:* Harry Ritz, Jimmy Ritz; *D:* Al Adamson.

Bleak House ✓✓1/2 1985 M Miniseries adaptation of the Charles Dickens tome about an interminable lawsuit and the decadent, criminal ruling class of 19th-century England. 391m/C VHS, DVD, GB Denholm Elliott, Diana Rigg, Philip Franks, Peter Vaughan, T.P. McKenna; *D:* Ross Devenish; *M:* Geoffrey Burgon. TV

Bleak Moments ✓✓ *Loving Moments* 1971 Bored secretary Sylvia (Raitt) tries to work her flirtatious charms on a repressed teacher (Allan) and an eccentric musician (Bradwell) in order to escape the pressures of caring for a mentally retarded sister. 110m/C VHS, DVD, GB Anne Raitt, Eric Allen, Mike Bradwell, Joolia Cappleman; *D:* Mike Leigh; *W:* Mike Leigh; *C:* Bahram Manoch-er; *M:* Mike Bradwell.

Bleeders WOOF! *Hemoglobin* 1997 (R) John Strauss (Dupuis), suffering from a hereditary blood disease, travels to a remote Atlantic island to research his ancestors and discovers the descendants are a grotesque clan of incestuous malformed creatures, who only emerge from their catacombs to satisfy their need for human blood and flesh. 89m/C VHS, DVD, CA Rutger Hauer, Roy Dupuis, Jackie Burroughs, Kristen Lehman, Joanna Noyes, John Dunn-Hill, Bronwyn Moore; *D:* Peter Svatek; *W:* Dan O'Bannon, Charles Adair, Ronald Shusett; *C:* Barry Gravelle; *M:* Alan Reeves. VIDEO

Bleeding Hearts ✓✓ 1994 A liberal white professor falls in love with the teenaged black student he's tutoring and then becomes aware of the vast differences between them. Their problems increase when the young woman becomes pregnant. 95m/C VHS, DVD. Gregory Hines, Mark Evan Jacobs, Renjit (Chaudry) Chowdhry, Elliott Gould, Robert Levine, Peter Riegert, Lorraine Toussaint; *D:* Gregory Hines.

Bless the Beasts and Children ✓✓1/2 1971 (PG) A group of six teenage boys at a summer camp attempt to save a herd of buffalo from slaughter at a national preserve. Treacly boredom as Maggie, aunt and caretaker to several men find themselves in captivity. Based on the novel by Glendon Swarthout. 109m/C VHS, DVD. Billy Mumy, Barry Robins, Miles Chapin, Darel Glaser, Bob Kramer, Ken Swofford, Jesse White; *D:* Stanley Kramer; *M:* Perry Botkin.

Bless the Child ✓ 2000 (R) Basinger doesn't even attempt to hide her boredom as Maggie, aunt and caretaker to her six-year-old with supernatural powers. Everyone drops the ball in this failed ripoff of "The Exorcist/Rosemary's Baby's Sixth Sense." Satanist and self-help guru Stark (Sewell) wants to recruit the gifted tyke to work for the Devil, while Maggie gets an occult-expert FBI agent (Smits, perhaps making a mortgage payment) and a bunch of expo-sition cameos on her side. This movie's idea of thrills is showing kids getting kidnapped and later turning up dead. Not ex-

Blessed Event ✓✓✓ 1932 Fast-moving, entertaining film about a Broadway gossip columnist with a poison pen. Tracy has the role of a lifetime as a Walter Winchell prototype who thinks no one is exempt from his juicy column. Powell makes film debut as a crooner after a brief career as a band singer. Based on a play by Manuel Seff and Forrest Wilson. 77m/B VHS. Lee Tracy, Mary Brian, Dick Powell, Allen Jenkins, Ruth Donnelly, Emma Dunn, Walter Miller, Tom Dugan, Isabel Jewell; *D:* Roy Del Ruth; *W:* Howard J. Green.

Blessing ✓✓ 1994 It's an unhappy time down on the Wisconsin dairy farm in this tale of family life. Embittered patriarch Jack (Griffis) can barely make a go of it and takes his frustrations out by beating his cows and climbing to the top of the silo. Despairing wife Arlene (Glynn) enters newspaper lotteries and collects religious statues while daughter Randi (Griffis) keeps delaying leaving the farm because of a nagging sense of responsibility. Claustrophobic atmosphere. 94m/C VHS. Melora Griffis, Gareth Williams, Clovis Siemon; *D:* Paul Zehrer; *W:* Paul Zehrer; *C:* Stephen Kazmierski; *M:* Joseph S. De-Beasi.

Blind Ambition ✓✓1/2 1979 Miniseries docudrama traces the career of John Dean, special counsel to President Richard M. Nixon. Focuses on his fractured personal life and touches on virtually all of the Watergate headlines. Violent scenes may be disturbing to some. 100m/C VHS, DVD. Joseph Bottoms, Kirstie Alley, Keir Dullea, James Clarkson, Marina Sirtis; *D:* Nico Mastorakis; *M:* Nico Mastorakis.

Blind Date ✓✓ 1984 (R) Blind man agrees to a visual computer implant-ed in his brain in order to help the police track down a psychopathic killer. 100m/C VHS, DVD. Joseph Bottoms, Kirstie Alley, Keir Dullea, James Clarkson, Marina Sirtis; *D:* Nico Mastorakis; *M:* Nico Mastorakis.

Blind Date ✓✓ 1987 (PG-13) A blind date between a workaholic yuppie and a beautiful blonde starts off well, but when she drinks too much at dinner, things get out of hand. In addition to embarrassing her date and destroying the restaurant, she has a jealous ex-boyfriend who must be dealt with. 95m/C VHS, DVD. Sab Shimono, Kim Basinger, Bruce Willis, John Larroquette, William Daniels, George Coe, Mark Blum, Phil Hartman, Stephanie Faracy, Alice Hirson, Brian Stark; *D:* Blake Edwards; *W:* Dale Launer; *C:* Harry Stradling Jr.; *M:* Henry Mancini.

Blind Dating ✓1/2 2006 (PG-13) Danny (Pine) is a young blind man, trying to decide if he should have experimental surgery that might allow him to see. Since he has no romantic experience, his sleazy brother (Kaye) has been setting him up on a series of really bad—uh—blind dates. But Danny falls for his doctor's reception-ist Leeza (Jay), an Indian woman who is in an arranged engagement. But neither can quite forget the other. 95m/C DVD. Chris Pine, Eddie Kaye Thomas, Jane Seymour, Anjali Jay; *D:* James Keach; *W:* Christopher Theo, Fay Wray; *D:* Erich von Stroheim.

Blind Faith ✓ 1989 (R) Action and adventure take a turn for the horrific when several men find themselves in a series of government silver from being stolen by bandits. 85m/C VHS, DVD. Eric Gunn, Kevin Yon, Lynne Browne; *D:* Dean Wilson; *W:* Dean Wilson.

Blind Faith ✓✓1/2 1998 (R) In 1957, John Williams (Vance) is a struggling new lawyer, living with elder sibling Charles (Dutton) and his family in a Bronx neighborhood. The first black NYPD sergeant, Charles has an uneasy relationship with his eldest son, Charlie (Whitt). The family's shocked when Charlie's accused

Blind Husbands ✓✓✓ 1919 An Austrian officer is attracted to the pretty wife of a dull surgeon. Controversial in its day, this lurid, sumptuous melodrama instigated many stubborn Hollywood myths, including the stereotype of the brusque, jodhpur-clad Prussian officer. This was von Stroheim's first outing as director. 98m/B VHS, DVD. Erich von Stroheim, Fay Wray; *D:* Erich von Stroheim.

Blind Justice ✓✓ 1986 An innocent man is identified as a rapist, and the accusation ruins his life. 94m/C VHS, DVD. Tim Matheson, Lisa Eichhorn, Mimi Kuzyk, Philip Charles MacKenzie, Tom Atkins; *D:* Rod Holcomb.

Blind Justice ✓✓1/2 1994 (R) Gunfighter gets blinded in battle and rides into a small town where he's nursed back to health by an attractive lady doctor. While he recovers, he learns the town is trying to protect a cache of government silver from being stolen by bandits. 85m/C VHS, DVD. Robert Davi, Armand Assante, Elisabeth Shue, Adam Baldwin; *C:* Jack Conroy; *M:* Miles Goodman. TV

Blind Man's Bluff ✓✓ 1991 (PG-13) A blind professor is accused of murdering his neighbor, but as he tries to solve the mystery, evidence points to his ex-girlfriend who may have framed him for

actly the feel-good movie of the year. 110m/C VHS, DVD. Kim Basinger, Jimmy Smits, Rufus Sewell, Holliston Coleman, Christina Ricci, Michael Gaston, Lumi Cavazos, Angela Bettis, Ian Holm, Eugene Lipinski, Anne Betancourt, Dimitra Arlys; *D:* Chuck Russell; *W:* Thomas (Tom) Rickman; *C:* Peter Menzies Jr.; *M:* Christopher Young.

Blind Fear ✓✓ 1989 (R) A blind woman is stalked by three killers in an abandoned country inn. 96m/C VHS, DVD. Courtney B. Vance, Charlette McKee, Karen Glave, Dan Lett; *D:* Ernest R. Dickerson; *M:* Frank Military; *C:* Rodney Charters; *M:* Ron Carter. C A B L E.

Blind Fools ✓1/2 1940 A scathing indictment of children neglected by ambitious parents. 66m/B VHS. Herbert Rawlinson, Claire Whitney, Russell Hicks, Miriam Battista, Vinton (Hayworth) Haworth, Wesley Barry, Robert Emmett Keane; *C:* William J. Miller.

Blind Fury ✓✓1/2 1990 (R) A blind Vietnam vet enlists the aid of a Zen master and a sharpshooter to tackle the Mafia. Hauer works well in the lead, but unfortunately, the movie doesn't. 86m/C VHS, DVD. Rutger Hauer, Terry O'Quinn, Brandon Call, Lisa Blount, Randall "Tex" Cobb, Noble Willingham, Meg Foster, Sho Kosugi, Nick Cassavetes, Charles Cooper, Rick Overton; *D:* Philip Noyce; *W:* Charles Robert Carner; *C:* Don Burgess; *M:* J. Keith Holland. VIDEO

Blind Heat ✓✓ 2000 (R) Unfaithful hubby Jeffrey Scott (Sapienza) takes wife Mercer (Alonso) on a business trip to Mexico where she gets kidnapped. Rather than pay the ransom, Scott hires negotia-tor Paul Burke (Fahey) to get his wife back to kill her when their plot turns sour. 90m/C VHS, DVD. Maria Conchita Alonso, Jeff Fahey, Eddie Peck, Al Sapienza; *D:* Adolfo Martinez Solares, Jeff O'Brien; *C:* Ivan Abramson; *C:* William J. Miller.

Blind Horizon ✓✓1/2 2004 (R) A head wound gives Frank Cavanaugh (Killmer) a case of amnesia but he can't shake ominous flashbacks of a presidential as-sassination attempt—especially when he hears the president is going to visit. But trying to convince a local New Mexico sheriff (Shepard) of the imminent danger isn't so easy since he's distracted by his reelection bid. And Frank can't be sure that his fiancee Chloe (Campbell) is really who she claims to be. Subplots are over-done and memory loss is nothing new. It works well enough though. Faye Duna-way gets a slick bit part. 99m/C VHS, DVD. Amy Smart, Gil Bellows, Giancarlo Esposito, Faye Dunaway; *D:* Michael Heussman; *W:* F. Paul Benz, Steve Tomlin; *C:* Max Malkin. VIDEO

of murdering a white boy during a robbery attempt, especially when he confesses. John thinks it's the cops but when the truth is told, there's a bigger sus-picious of the story. Charlie is telling him. 122m/C VHS, DVD. Courtney B. Vance, Charles S. Dutton, Garland Whitt, Kadeem Hardison, Lonette McKee, Karen Glave, Jack Langella, Kim Coates, Jan Rubes, Heidi von Palleske; *D:* Tom Berry; *W:* Sergio D. Altieri.

the murder. Surprisingly suspenseful cable movie in a stock Hollywood ending. **86m/C VHS.** Lisa Eilbacher, Patricia Clarkson, Ken Pogue, Ron Perlman; *D:* James Quinn; *W:* Joel Gross; *M:* Richard Bellis. **CABLE**

Blind Rage 🦴 **1978 (R)** When the United States government transports $15 million to the Philippines, five blind kung fu masters want a piece of the action. **81m/C VHS. PH** D'Urville Martin, Leo Fong, Tony Ferrer, Dick Adair, Darnell Garcia, Leila Hermosa, Fred Williamson; *D:* Efren C. Pinon.

Blind Side 🦴½ **1993 (R)** DeMornay and Silver are a married couple whose Mexican vacation turns into trouble when they get into a hit-and-run accident which they don't report. Back home, they're frightened by the sudden appearance of Hauer, who's also just back from Mexico. They think he's after blackmail but he's really just a run-of-the-mill psycho intrigued by DeMornay, who at least keeps her character in control. Silver and Hauer have a great time chewing scenery. Also available in a 98-minute unrated version. **92m/C VHS, DVD.** Rebecca De Mornay, Ron Silver, Rutger Hauer; *D:* Geoff Murphy; *W:* John Carlen.

Blind Spot 🦴🦴½ **1993** Okay family drama which works because of the performances and not the script. Woodward stars as Nell Harrington, a take-charge U.S. Representative long married to Simon (Weaver). Her troubled, pregnant daughter Phoebe (Linney) is married to Nell's aide Charlie (Diamond). Charlie is killed and Phoebe injured in a car crash but the real tragedy is when Nell discovers what caused the accident—drugs and that her daughter is a cocaine addict. Lots of suffering. **99m/C VHS.** Joanne Woodward, Laura Linney, Fritz Weaver, Reed Edward Diamond, Cynthia Martelis, Patti Yasutake, Patti D'Arbanville; *D:* Michael Toshiyuki Uno; *W:* Nina Shengold; *M:* Patrick Williams. **TV**

Blind Vengeance 🦴🦴½ **1990 (R)** A man whose son was murdered by white supremacists decides to take his own special revenge when they are acquitted by the local jury. But this isn't your usual bloodbath; instead, he plays psychological games with the men, waiting for them to break. **93m/C VHS.** Gerald McRaney, Marg Helgenberger, Thalmus Rasulala, Lane Smith, Don Hood, Grand L. Bush; *D:* Lee Philips; *W:* Henri Simoun, Curt Allen. **CABLE**

Blind Witness 🦴🦴½ **1989** Routine story about a blind woman who's the only witness to her husband's murder during a robbery. **92m/C VHS, DVD.** Victoria Principal, Paul LeMat, Stephen Macht, Matt Clark, Tim Choate; *D:* Richard A. Colla; *M:* Robert Alcivar. **TV**

Blinded by the Light 🦴🦴 **1982** Young woman tries to save her brother from attachment to a quasi-religious cult, The Light of Salvation. Real-life brother and sister McNichol team up in this drama. **90m/C VHS.** Kristy McNichol, Jimmy (James Vincent) McNichol, Anne Jackson, Michael McGuire; *D:* John A. Alonzo. **TV**

Blindfold: Acts of Obsession 🦴🦴 **1994 (R)** Madeline's (Doherty) marriage is boring so she consults therapist Jennings (Nelson). He suggests a number of sexual fantasies Madeline plays out with hubby Woods only to have murder enter the picture. Madeline's older sister Chris (Alfonso) is assigned to investigate and lets out lots of family secrets. Shannen in the buff, murd-

er, infidelity, deception, and sex. An unrated version is also available. **93m/C VHS.** Shannen Doherty, Judd Nelson, Michael Woods, Kristian Alfonso, Shell Danielson, Drew Snyder; *D:* Lawrence L. Simeone; *W:* Lawrence L. Simeone; *M:* Shuki Levy.

Blindside 🦴🦴 **1988 (R)** A surveillance hobbyist who owns a motel spies on his tenants until a murder involves him in a big-scale drug war. **98m/C VHS.** Harvey Keitel, Lori Hallier, Lolita (David) Davidovich, Alan Fawcett, Michael Rudder; *D:* Paul Lynch.

Blindsided 🦴🦴½ **1993 (PG-13)** A former police officer temporarily loses his sight when he plays the middle man in a bank robbery. Sight improving, he falls for a woman who draws him into another crime. **93m/C VHS.** Jeff Fahey, Mia Sara, Rudy Ramos, Jack Kehler, Ben Gazzara; *D:* Thomas Michael Donnelly.

Blink 🦴🦴½ **1993 (R)** Recent corneal transplants allow blind musician Emma (Stowe) to regain her sight, but until they "settle" what she sees may not register in her mind immediately, a phenomenon the script dubs "retroactive vision." This poses a problem for Chicago cop Quinn when he falls for Emma—the only one who can recognize a sadistic killer. Average thriller has been done better before, but adds two attractive leads, enough suspense, and a unique twist to the typical woman-in-jeopardy tale to keep things interesting. The distorted images in Stowe's blurry vision were created by computer. Stowe also learned fiddle for her role as the fictional member of the real-life Irish-American band, The Drovers. **106m/C VHS, DVD.** Madeleine Stowe, Aidan Quinn, Laurie Metcalf, James Remar, Bruce A. Young, Peter Friedman, Paul Dillon, Michael Kirkpatrick; *D:* Michael Apted; *W:* Dana Stevens; *C:* Dante Spinotti; *M:* Brad Fiedel.

Blink of an Eye 🦴🦴 *Blink of an Eye* **1992 (R)** Special agent Sam Browning (Pare) must use his psychic powers and military skills against the terrorists who have kidnapped the CIA director's daughter. **90m/C VHS.** Michael Pare, Janis Lee, Uri Gavriel, Amos Lavi, Sasson Gabai, Jack Widerker; *D:* Bob Misiorowski; *W:* Edward Kovach; *C:* David Gurfinkel; *M:* Vladimir Horunzhy.

Bliss 🦴🦴½ **1985 (R)** A savage, surreal Australian comedy about an advertising executive who dies suddenly for a few minutes, and upon his awakening he finds the world maniacally, bizarrely changed. Based on the Peter Carey novel, and one of the most inspired absurdist films of the decade. **112m/C VHS. AU** Barry Otto, Lynette Curran, Helen Jones; *D:* Ray Lawrence; *W:* Peter Carey, Australian Film Inst. '85. Film.

Bliss 🦴½ **1996 (R)** Creepy feature-length sex-ed lecture delves deeply into sexual problems in modern society. So deeply, in fact, that it could've been called "Ouch, You're on my Hair." Clueless yuppies Joseph (Sheffer) and Maria's (Lee) sexual dysfunctions lead her to seek aid from unconventional therapist Baltazar (Stamp), who does things like compare women to violins (hint: they're not really the same. Unless you REALLY like wood). Joseph has his doubts, but soon becomes a chanting tantric goofball. Too clinical to be sexy, but too sexy to be used as an Army training film. **103m/C VHS, DVD.** Sheryl Lee, Craig Sheffer, Terence Stamp, Casey Siemaszko, Spalding Gray, Leigh Taylor-Young, Lois Chiles, Blu Mankuma; *D:* Lance Young; *W:* Lance Young; *C:* Mike Molloy; *M:* Jan A.P. Kaczmarek.

The Bliss of Mrs. Blossom 🦴🦴🦴 **1968** Three's a crowd in this light-hearted romp through the machinations of a brassiere manufacturer (Attenborough) and his neglected wife (MacLaine). Mrs. Blossom finds sewing machine repairman Booth so appetizing that she hides him in the attic of the Blossom home. He reads books and redecorates, until, several plot twists later, Attenborough discovers the truth. Witty and wise, with fine supporting cast and excellent pacing. **93m/C GB** Shirley MacLaine, Richard Attenborough, James Booth, Freddie Jones, John Cleese; *D:* Joseph McGrath.

Blithe Spirit 🦴🦴🦴½ **1945** Charming and funny adaptation of Coward's famed stage play. A man re-marries and finds his long-dead wife is unhappy enough about it to come back and haunt him. Clever supporting cast, with Rutherford exceptional as the medium. Received Oscar for its Special Effects. **96m/C VHS, DVD. GB** Rex Harrison, Constance Cummings, Kay Hammond, Margaret Rutherford, Hugh Wakefield, Joyce Carey, Jacqueline Clarke; *D:* David Lean; *W:* Noel Coward, Anthony Havelock-Allan; *C:* Ronald Neame; *M:* Richard Addinsell.

Blitz 🦴½ **1993 (R)** A German car designer's pet project, a car that runs without gas, is halted by the influence of an Arab conglomerate. He nevertheless tries to complete it, and is hunted down. **104m/C VHS, DVD.** Jurgen Prochnow, Senta Berger, William Conrad, Agnes Sorai; *D:* Michael Verhoeven; *C:* Jacques Steyr; *M:* Michael Landau.

The Blob 🦴🦴½ **1958** Sci-fi thriller about a small town's fight against a slimy jello invader from space. Slightly rebellious McQueen (in his first starring role) redeems himself when he saves the town with quick action. Low-budget, horror/teen-fantasy became a camp classic. Other names considered included "The Glob," "The Glob that Girdled the Globe," "The Meteorite Monster," "The Molten Meteorite," and "The Night of the Creeping Dead." Followed by a worthless sequel in 1972, "Son of Blob," and a worthwhile remake in 1988. **83m/C VHS, DVD.** Steve McQueen, Aneta Corsaut, Olin Howlin, Earl Rowe, Alden "Steve" Chase, John Benson, Vincent Barbi; *D:* Irvin S. Yeaworth Jr.; *W:* Kate Phillips, Theodore Simonson; *C:* Thomas E. Spalding; *M:* Burt Bacharach, Hal David, Ralph Carmichael.

The Blob 🦴🦴 **1988 (R)** A hi-tech remake of the 1958 camp classic about a small town beset by a fast-growing, man-eating mound of glop shot into space by scientists, irradiated into an unnatural being, and then returned to earth. Well-developed characters make this an excellent tribute to the first film. **92m/C VHS, DVD.** Kevin Dillon, Candy Clark, Joe Seneca, Shawnee Smith, Donovan Leitch, Jeffrey DeMunn, Ricky Paull Goldin, Del Close; *D:* Chuck Russell; *W:* Chuck Russell, Frank Darabont; *C:* Mark Irwin.

Block-heads 🦴🦴🦴 **1938** Twenty years after the end of WWI, soldier Stan is found, still in his foxhole, and brought back to America, where he moves in with old pal Ollie. Also includes a 1934 Charley Chase short "I'll Take Vanilla." **75m/B VHS, DVD.** Stan Laurel, Oliver Hardy, Billy Gilbert, Patricia Ellis, James Finlayson, Charley Chase; *D:* John Blystone.

Blockhouse WOOF! **1973** Four men are entombed in a subterranean stronghold for six years after the D-Day invasion of Normandy. Encourages claustrophobic feeling in viewer. Based on Jean Paul Clements' novel. **88m/C VHS. GB** Peter Sellers, Charles Aznavour, Per Oscarsson, Peter Vaughan, Leon Lissek, Alfred Lynch, Jeremy Kemp; *D:* Clive Rees.

The Blonde 🦴🦴½ *La Bionda* **1992** Tommasso (Rubini) is driving through the Milan streets when he knocks down a young blonde woman (Kinski). She loses her memory (apparently due to shock) and Tommasso agrees to help her—soon falling in love. One day her memory returns and Christina remembers she's involved with a drug dealer and other shady characters. She leaves Tommasso to protect him but by luck gets other ideas. Italian with subtitles. **100m/C VHS, DVD. IT** Sergio Rubini, Nastassja Kinski, Ennio Fantastichini, Umberto Raho, Veronica Lazar, Giacomo Pipemo; *D:* Sergio Rubini; *W:* Sergio Rubini, Filippo Ascione, Umberto Marino; *C:* Alessio Gelsini Torresi; *M:* Jurgen Knieper.

Blonde 🦴🦴½ **2001** Montgomery may not be as curvy as the real Marilyn Monroe, but she does well in this routine biopic about the bombshell who suffered from life-long problems with self-esteem and men. Based on the novel by Joyce Carol Oates, the miniseries covers Marilyn from her disturbing childhood/teenage years to her transformation into a screen goddess, although it ends before her death. **240m/C DVD.** Poppy Montgomery, Skye McCole Bartusiak, Patricia Richardson, Ann-Margret, Kirstie Alley, Eric Bogosian, Wallace Shawn, Patrick Dempsey, Jensen Ackles, Titus Welliver, Griffin Dunne, Richard Roxburgh; *D:* Joyce Chopra; *W:* Joyce Eliason; *C:* James Glennon; *M:* Patrick Williams. **TV**

Blonde Ambition 🦴½ **2007 (PG-13)** Simpson plays a clueless blonde (how's that for typecasting?) in this would-be comedy that at least has a couple of supporting performances to save it. Naive Katie heads to NY to see her boyfriend, discovers him cheating, but bucks up when she suddenly gets a job working for a bigshot CEO (Larry Miller) and begins dating Ben (a befuddled Wilson) from the mailroom. The job is a set-up by a couple of sleazy co-workers (Penelope Ann Miller, Dick) looking for a corporate takeover and the blonde must save the day. **93m/C DVD.** Jessica Simpson, Luke Wilson, Larry Miller, Penelope Ann Miller, Andy Dick, Rachael Leigh Cook, Drew Fuller, Willie Nelson; *D:* Scott Marshall; *W:* John Cohen; *C:* Mark Irwin.

Blonde and Blonder 🦴 **2007 (PG-13)** The distaff "Dumb and Dumber" with lots of pink. Dee (Anderson) and Dawn (Richards) witness a mob hit done by pro Kat (Vaugier) and associate Kit (Ory) and then, somehow, get mistaken for the hired killers. They are offered a contract to take out Chinese gangster Mr. Wong (Mann), naturally believing that "take out" means something much less lethal, thus leading to more comic misadventure. Both blondes are getting too old to play ditzy dames even when they're in on the joke. **95m/C DVD.** Pamela Anderson, Denise Richards, Byron Mann, Emmanuelle Vaugier, Meaghan Ory, John Farley, Kevin Farley; *D:* Dean Hamilton; *W:* Dean Hamilton, Rolfe Kanefsky, Gerry Anderson; *C:* C. Kim Miles; *M:* William Goodrum. **VIDEO**

Blonde Blackmailer 🦴 **1958** Boring story about an innocent man who serves time for the murder of a female blackmailer. When he's released, he searches for the real killer. **66m/B VHS. GB** Richard Arlen, Susan Shaw, Vincent Ball, Constance Leigh; *D:* Charles Deane; *W:* Charles Deane.

Blonde Crazy 🦴🦴½ **1931** A charming grifter hooks up with a gorgeous blonde as he works the territory of a big wheel criminal. Escapist fare, with fun performances from Cagney and Blondell. **81m/B VHS.** James Cagney, Joan Blondell, Louis Calhern, Ray Milland, Nat Pendleton; *D:* Roy Del Ruth.

Blonde in Black Leather 🦴½ **1977** A bored Italian housewife takes up with a leather-clad lady biker, and together they cavort about. **88m/C VHS.** Claudia Cardinale, Monica Vitti; *D:* Carlo Di Palma.

Blonde Savage 🦴 **1947** Charting African territories, an adventurer encounters a white jungle queen swinging amongst the vines. Essentially a cheap, distaff "Tarzan." **62m/B VHS, DVD.** Leif Erickson, Gale Sherwood, Veda Ann Borg, Douglass Dumbrille, Frank Jenks, Matt Willis, Ernest Whitman; *D:* Steve Sekely.

Blonde Venus 🦴🦴½ **1932** A German cafe singer marries an Englishman, but their marriage hits the skids when he contracts radiation poisoning and she gets a nightclub job to pay the bills. Sternberg's and Dietrich's fourth film together, and characteristically beautiful, though terribly strange. Dietrich's cabaret number "Hot Voodoo," in a gorilla suit and blonde afro, attains new heights in early Hollywood surrealism. **94m/B VHS, DVD.** Marlene Dietrich, Herbert Marshall, Cary Grant, Dickie Moore, Hattie McDaniel, Sidney Toler; *D:* Josef von Sternberg.

Blondes Have More Guns 🦴🦴 **1995 (R)** Very dumb detective Harry Bates (McGaharin) is investigating a chainsaw murder and falls for the mysterious Montana (Key), who's possibly a serial killer, or maybe it's her half-sister, Dakota (Lusiak). Spoof of "Basic Instinct" and others of that ilk, done in the usual Troma fashion. **90m/C VHS, DVD.** Michael McGahern, Elizabeth Key, Gloria Lusiak, Richard Neil, Bennie Buttner, Romana Lisa, Andre Brazeau; *D:* George Merriweather; *W:* George Merri-

Blondie ♂♂½ 1938 Chic Young's famous comic strip debuted on the big screen with Singleton and Lake as the bumbling Dagwood and Blondie. Baby Dumpling (son Alexander, when he grows up). The couple are about to celebrate their 18th wedding anniversary when Dagwood loses his job and Blondie suspects him of infidelity. The series eventually contained 28 films. 63m/B VHS, DVD. Penny Singleton, Arthur Lake, Larry Simms, Gene Lockhart, Ann Doran, Jonathan Hale, Gordon Oliver, Stanley Andrews, Dorothy Moore; D: Frank Strayer; W: Richard Flournoy; C: Henry Freulich.

Blondie Brings Up Baby ♂♂ 1939 Baby Dumpling is enrolled in school but on his first day he plays hooky to find Daisy who's been caught by the dogcatcher. But Blondie and Dagwood think the tyke has been kidnapped! 67m/B VHS, DVD. Penny Singleton, Arthur Lake, Larry Simms, Jonathan Hale, Danny Mummert, Fay Helm, Peggy Ann Garner, Irving Bacon; D: Frank Strayer; W: Richard Flournoy, Gladys Lehman; C: Henry Freulich.

Blondie for Victory ♂½ 1942 As her personal contribution to the war effort, Blondie joins the Housewives of America who perform various home front cuties. Only their husbands aren't very happy since they're left home tending to the kids and the household chores. 68m/B VHS. Penny Singleton, Arthur Lake, Larry Simms, Jonathan Hale, Danny Mummert, Stuart Erwin, Irving Bacon; D: Frank Strayer; W: Karen De Wolf; C: Henry Freulich.

Blondie Goes Latin ♂♂ 1942 Mr. Dithers invites the Bumsteads on a South American cruise and Dagwood winds up the drummer in the shipboard band while Singleton gets to show off her Broadway background in some musical numbers. 70m/B VHS, DVD. Penny Singleton, Arthur Lake, Jonathan Hale, Larry Simms, Ruth Terry, Tito Guizar, Danny Mummert, Irving Bacon; D: Frank Strayer; W: Richard Flournoy, Karen De Wolf; C: Henry Freulich.

Blondie Goes to College ♂♂ 1942 Actually both Bumsteads enroll but decide to pass themselves off as single, which leads to complications. Blondie draws the attentions of the school's top athlete while Dagwood's joins the rowing team and turns the head of a pretty coed. 68m/B VHS, DVD. Penny Singleton, Arthur Lake, Jonathan Hale, Larry Parks, Lloyd Bridges; D: Frank Strayer; W: Lou Breslow; C: Henry Freulich.

Blondie Has Trouble ♂♂ 1940 Mr. Dithers has a property he just can't sell because of rumors that the house is haunted. So he offers to let the Bumsteads stay in it to prove that the rumors are false. The Bumsteads also find the creepy mansion comes complete with two equally creepy servants. 6th film in the series. 70m/B VHS, DVD. Penny Singleton, Arthur Lake, Larry Simms, Danny Mummert, Jonathan Hale, Arthur Hohl, Esther Dale, Irving Bacon; D: Frank Strayer; W: Richard Flournoy; C: Henry Freulich.

Blondie Hits the Jackpot ♂½ 1941 A weak entry (the ninth) in the comedic series. Dagwood is fired for the umpteenth time after he makes a mistake in a construction deal and tries frantically to get his job back. Meanwhile, Blondie wins the big prize on a radio quiz show. Then an important client of Dagwood's decides to enter the pooch in the local dog show. 66m/B VHS, DVD. Penny Singleton, Arthur Lake, Larry Simms, Marjorie Ann Mutchie, Jerome Cowan, Lloyd Corrigan, Danny Mummert, James Flavin; D: Edward L. Bernds; W: Vincent Farra; M: Mischa Bakaleinikoff.

Blondie in Society ♂½ 1941 A weak entry (the ninth) in the comedic series. Dagwood impersonates a pedigreed Great Dane and Blondie decides to enter the b dog. 66m/B VHS. Penny Singleton, Arthur Lake, Larry Simms, William Frawley, Edgar Kennedy, Jonathan Hale, Danny Mummert, C: Henry Freulich.

Blondie Knows Best ♂½ 1946 Dagwood impersonates his boss, Mr. Dithers, and causes all sorts of problems. Howard, one of the Three Stooges, has a cameo as a myopic process-server. The 18th film in the series. 66m/B VHS. Penny Singleton, Arthur Lake, Larry Simms, Shemp Howard, Danny Mummert; D: Abby Berlin; W: Edward L. Bernds, Al Martin.

Blondie Meets the Boss ♂♂ 1939 Dagwood goes on a fishing trip and manages to get into trouble with Blondie when a photograph puts him in a compromising pose with another woman. Then Blondie winds up at the office doing Dagwood's job. Whatever that may be). Second in the series. 75m/B VHS, DVD. Penny Singleton, Arthur Lake, Larry Simms, Jonathan Hale, Dorothy Moore, Don Beddoe, Stanley Brown, Danny Mummert, Irving Bacon; D: Frank Strayer; W: Richard Flournoy; C: Henry Freulich.

Blondie On a Budget ♂♂ 1940 Dagwood wins 200 bucks in a contest and enlists the aid of ex-girlfriend Joan (Hayworth) to buy Blondie the fur coat she's been wanting. But Blondie wants to use the money to get Dagwood into a fishing club and misinterprets the situation. 68m/B VHS, DVD. Penny Singleton, Arthur Lake, Larry Simms, Rita Hayworth, Danny Mummert, Don Beddoe, Fay Helm, John Qualen, Irving Bacon; D: Frank Strayer; W: Richard Flournoy; C: Henry Freulich.

Blondie Plays Cupid ♂♂ 1940 The Bumsteads are traveling to visit relatives in the country when they happen across a young couple (Ford and Walters) trying to elope. So Blondie decides to help the youngsters out. 68m/B VHS, DVD. Penny Singleton, Arthur Lake, Larry Simms, Jonathan Hale, Glenn Ford, Luana Walters, Danny Mummert, Irving Bacon; D: Frank Strayer; W: Richard Flournoy, Karen De Wolf; C: Henry Freulich.

Blondie Takes a Vacation ♂♂½ 1939 Third in the series of fluff films adapted from Chic Young's comic strip. After the Bumstead family is snubbed at a snobby mountain resort they move to a friendlier nearby hotel where they try to help out the owners who are in danger of losing their investment. Baby Dumpling does his bit by unleashing a skunk in the ventilation system of the competing hotel. 68m/B VHS, DVD. Penny Singleton, Arthur Lake, Larry Simms, Danny Mummert, Donald Meek, Donald MacBride, Thomas Ross, Robert Wilcox, Irving Bacon; D: Frank Strayer; W: Richard Flournoy; C: Henry Freulich.

Blondie's Blessed Event ♂♂½ 1942 Cookie is born, causing even more chaos in the Bumstead household. Meanwhile, Dagwood gets into trouble at work when he hires a cynical playwright to write an important speech for him. 11th entry in series. 69m/B VHS. Penny Singleton, Arthur Lake, Larry Simms, Norma Jean Wayne, Jonathan Hale, Danny Mummert, Hans Conried, Irving Bacon, Stanley Brown, Mary Wickes, Paul Harvey, Arthur O'Connell; D: Frank Strayer; W: Richard Flournoy, Karen De Wolf; C: Connie Lee; C: Henry Freulich.

Blood Alley ♂♂ 1955 A seasoned Merchant Marine captain takes on a cargo of refugee Chinese to smuggle through enemy territory. Midding, mid-career Wayne vehicle. 115m/C VHS, DVD. IT FR GE Cameron Mitchell, Eva Bartok, Mary Arden, Dante DiPaolo, Anita Ekberg; D: William A. Wellman; C: William Clothier.

Blood and Black Lace ♂♂ Fashion House of Death; Six Women for the Murderer; Sei Donne per l'Assassino 1964 Beautiful models are being brutally murdered and an inspector is assigned to the case, but not before more gruesome killings occur. Bava is, as usual, violent and suspenseful. Horror fans will enjoy this flick. 90m/C VHS, DVD. Mario Bava, Marcello Fondato, Joe Barilla; C: Ubaldo Terzano.

Blood and Sand ♂♂ 1922 Vintage romance based on Vicente Blasco Ibanez's novel about the tragic rise and fall of a matador, and the women in his life. The film that made Valentino a star. Remade in 1941. Silent. 87m/B VHS, DVD. Rudolph Valentino, Nita Naldi, Lila Lee, Walter Long; D: Fred Niblo; W: June Mathis; C: Alvin Wyckoff.

Blood and Sand ♂♂ 1941 Director Mamoulian "painted" this picture in the new technicolor technique, which makes it a veritable explosion of color and spectacle. Power is the matador who becomes famous and then falls when he is torn between two women, forsaking his first love, bullfighting. Based on the novel "Sangre y Arena" by Vicente Blasco Ibanez. This movie catapulted Hayworth to stardom, primarily for her dancing, but also for her sexiness and seductiveness (and of course, her acting). Remake of the 1922 silent classic; remade again in 1989. 123m/C VHS, DVD. Tyrone Power, Linda Darnell, Rita Hayworth, Alla Nazimova, Anthony Quinn, J. Carrol Naish, John Carradine, George Reeves; D: Rouben Mamoulian; W: Jo Swerling; C: Ernest Palmer, Ray Rennahan; M: Alfred Newman. Oscars '41: Color Cinematog.

Blood and Sand ♂♂ 1989 (R) A bullfighter on the verge of super-stardom risks it all when he falls under the spell of a sexy, seductive woman. Will she destroy his one opportunity for 'ame? Interesting for people who actually enjoy watching the "sport" of bullfighting. Originally made in 1922 and remade in 1941. 96m/C VHS, DVD. Christopher Rydell, Sharon Stone, Ana Torrent, Jose-Luis De Villalonga, Simon Andreu; D: Javier Elorrieta; W: Rafael Azzona, Ricardo Franco, Thomas Fucci; C: Antonio Rios; M: Jesus Gluck.

Blood and Steel ♂♂ 1925 The railroad tycoon's daughter and the construction foreman wind up together on an exciting train ride. Silent. 7m/B VHS, Helen Holmes, William Desmond; D: (John) Holmes; W: George Plympton; C: Roland Price.

Blood & Wine ♂♂½ 1996 (R) Miami wine merchant Alex (Nicholson) gets involved with terminally ill safecracker Victor (Caine) to steal a necklace worth a cool million. Meanwhile he must deal with his crumbling marriage to Suzanne (Davis) and the bitter relationship with his stepson Jason (Dorff), who has eyes for his Cuban mistress (Lopez). Characterizations and strong performances (particularly the sometimes lumbering plot to its violent conclusion. Promoted as the third part of a "dysfunctional family trilogy" with "Five Easy Pieces" and "The King of Marvin's Gardens." Seventh time Nicholson has worked with director Rafelson. 100m/C VHS, DVD. Jack Nicholson, Michael Caine, Judy Davis, Stephen Dorff, Jennifer Lopez, Harold Perrineau Jr.; D: Bob Rafelson; W: Nick Villars, Allison Cross; C: Newton Thomas (Tom) Sigel; M: Stephen Cohen.

Blood Angels ♂♂ Thralls 2005 (R) Ashley (Baruc) left her bad home life to live with her big sister—who just happens to be a vampire. When Ashley and her new friends visit, things get a little complicated. 92m/C VHS, DVD. Jodie Fisher, Leah Cairns, Fiona Scott, Lisa Marie Caruk, Monica Delain; D: Ron Oliver; W: Lisa Morton, Brett Thompson; C: David Pelletier. VIDEO

Blood at Sundown ♂½ 1988 Routine oater where man returns home to find his wife has kidnapped by a group of Mexican outlaws who have also taken over his village. 92m/C VHS. Giuliano Gemma, Nieves Navarro, Antonio Casas, Fernando San-cho, Pajarito, George Martin; D: Duccio Tessari.

Blood Beach woof! 1981 (R) A group of teenagers are devoured by menacing sand, which keeps people from getting to the water. Week parody with some humorous moments; more silly than scary. 92m/C VHS, David Huffman, Marianna Hill, John Saxon, Burt Young, Otis Young, Pamela McMyler, Bobby Bass, Darrell Fetty, Stefan Gierasch, Harriet Medin, Lynn(e) Marta; D: Jeffrey Bloom; W: Jeffrey Bloom; C: Steven Poster; M: Gil Melle.

Blood Beast Terror ♂½ The Vampire-Beast Craves Blood; Deathshead Vampire 1967 An entomologist transforms his own daughter into a Deathshead Moth and she proceeds to terrorize and drink innocent victims' blood. 81m/C VHS, DVD. Peter Cushing, Robert Flemyng, Wanda Ventin, Vanessa Howard; D: Vernon Sewell; W: Peter Bryan; C: Stanley Long; M: Paul Ferris.

Blood Bride ♂½ 1990 A lonely young woman finally finds happiness with her new husband but her world comes crashing about her with soul-mangling ferocity when she discovers he is actually a bloodthirsty maniac. 90m/C VHS. Ellen Barkin, Philip English; D: Robert J. Avrech.

Blood Brothers ♂♂ 1974 (R) A young man who dreams of becoming a lawyer is disturbed when he discovers that his family has mafia ties. 148m/C VHS. IT Claudia Cardinale, Franco Nero, Lina Polito; D: Pasquale Squitieri.

Blood Brothers ♂♂ 1997 Darryl has always looked up to older brother Sylvester. And then one day he witnesses a gang murder and Sylvester is one of the killers. The District Attorney senses Darryl knows more than he's saying and the gang bangers want to shut him up permanently, so each brother must look to his conscience and decide how best to be his

VideoHound's Golden Movie Retriever

Blood & Chocolate ♂½ 2007 (PG-13) Interspecies dating. American Vivian (Bruckner) works in a Bucharest chocolate shop when not turning furry at the full moon. She falls for cute human artist Aiden (Dancy), who's obsessed with werewolves, but has a problem since she's betrothed to hot pack leader Gabriel (Martinez). What's a shape-shifting gal to do? Tame story from von Garnier based on the novel by Annette Curtis Klause; the pic's ending goes for conventional romance as does the schmaltzy music. Special effects are minimal. 96m/C DVD, Blu-ray Disc. US GE RO Agnes Bruckner, Olivier Martinez, Hugh Dancy, Bryan Dick, Katja Riemann; D: Katja von Garnier; W: Ehren Kruger, Christopher Landon; C: Brendan Galvin; M: Johnny Klimek, Reinhold Heil.

Blood & Concrete: A Love Story ♂♂ 1990 (R) Bizarre, violent and stylish film-noir spoof, definitely not for all tastes. The innocent hero gets drawn into a maelstrom of intrigue over a killer aphrodisiac drug. Beals, an addicted punk rocker, gets to perform a few songs. 97m/C VHS, Billy Zane, Jennifer Beals, Darren McGavin, James LeGros, Nicholas Worth, Mark Pellegrino, Harry Shearer, Billy Bastiani; D: Jeff Reiner; W: Jeff Reiner, Richard LaBrie; C: Declan Quinn; M: Vinnie Golia.

Blood & Donuts ♂♂ 1995 (R) Hungry vampire Boya (Currie) is looking for a rat snack when he stumbles across an all-night donut shop where pretty cash-ier Molly (Clarkson) and friendly cabbie Earl (Louis) seek his aid in a local crime boss. Mild horror mixed with comedy and limited gore. 89m/C VHS, CA Gordon Currie, Justin Louis, Helene Clarkson, Fiona Reid, Frank Moore; Cameos: David Cronenberg; D: Holly Dale; W: Andrew Rai Berzins; C: Paul Sarossy.

Blood and Guns ♂♂ 1979 (R) Romance, revenge, and action abound in post-revolutionary Mexico. 96m/C VHS. Orson Welles, Tomas Milian, John Steiner; D: Giulio Petroni.

Blood and Roses ♂♂ El Mourir de Plaisir 1961 A girl who is obsessed with her family's vampire background becomes possessed by a vampire and commits numerous murders. The photography is good, but the plot is hazy and only effective in certain parts. Based on the story "Carmilla" by Sheridan Le Fanu. Later remade as "The Vampire Lovers" and "The Blood-Spattered Bride." 74m/C VHS, FR IT Mel Ferrer, Elsa Martinelli, Annette (Stroyberg) Vadim, Marc Allegret, Jacques-Rene Chauffard, Serge Marquand, Gabriella Farinon, Alberto Bonucci; Nathalie La Foret; D: Roger Vadim; W: Roger Vadim, Claude Martin, Roger Vailand, Claude Brule; C: Claude Renoir; M: Jean Prodromides.

brother's keeper. **91m/C VHS, DVD,** Clark Johnson, Richard Chevolleau, Mia Korf, Richard Yearwood, Ron White, Amir Williams, Ndehru Roberts, Timothy Stickney, Bill Nunn; **D:** Bruce Pittman; **W:** Paris Qualles; **M:** Harold Wheeler.

Blood Crime ♂♂½ **2002** No-brainer B movie. Seattle cop Daniel Pruitt (Schaech) and his wife Jessica (Lackey) take a camping trip into Oregon. While he's away, she gets attacked in the woods. When Jessica identifies her attacker, her husband beats him. Later, she changes her mind about who her assailant is but by then it's too late—the man, who turns out to be the no-good son of Sheriff McKenna (Caan)—has died. **128m/C VHS, DVD.** James Caan, Johnathon Schaech, Elizabeth Lackey, David Field; **D:** William A. Graham; **W:** Preston A. Whitmore II, Mark Lawrence Miller; **C:** Robert Steadman; **M:** Chris Boardman. **CABLE**

Blood Cult ♂ **1985 (R)** A bizarre series of murder-mutilations take place on a small midwestern campus. Contains graphic violence that is not for the squeamish. This film was created especially for the home video market. **89m/C VHS, DVD.** Chuck Ellis, Julie Andelman, Jim Vance, Joe Hardt; **D:** Christopher Lewis; **M:** Rod Slane. **VIDEO**

Blood Debts 1983 A father is out for revenge after he saves his daughter from some hunters who raped her and also killed her boyfriend. **91m/C VHS.** Richard Harrison, Mike Manty, Jim Gaines, Anne Milhench; **D:** Teddy Page.

Blood Diamond ♂♂½ **2006 (R)** Flawed, well-intentioned adventure-drama takes place in 1999, during the horrors of civil war in Sierra Leone. Rebels raid a village, committing mass murder and forcing the boys to become child soldiers while the men are slave labor in the diamond mines. These so-called "conflict stones" are then used to buy more weapons. Solomon Vandy (Hounsou) unearths and hides a valuable pink diamond in order to ransom his family after he escapes. But Vandy's find comes to the attention of the Afrikaner smuggler Danny Archer (DiCaprio), who is looking to use the diamond to his own advantage. American journalist Maddy (Connelly) happens to be around to prick Danny's nearly non-existent conscience. The actors do well and the story is harrowing but director Zwick has a tendency to be a scold. **143m/C DVD, Blu-ray Disc, HD DVD, US** Leonardo DiCaprio, Djimon Hounsou, Jennifer Connelly, Arnold Vosloo, Kagiso Kuypers, Michael Sheen, Jimi Mistry, Stephen Collins, David Harewood, Anthony Coleman, Benu Mabhena, Basil Wallace; **D:** Edward Zwick; **W:** Charles Leavitt; **C:** Eduardo Serra; **M:** James Newton Howard.

Blood Diner woof! **1987** Two spirit-possessed, diner-owning brothers kill countless young girls for demonic rituals, and serve their corpses as gourmet food in their restaurant. Dated, campy, and gross; reportedly shot in four days (it shows). **88m/C VHS.** Rick Burks, Carl Crew, Roger Dauer, Lisa Guggenheim, Roxanne Cybelle, Cynthia Baker; **D:** Jackie Kong; **W:** Michael Sonye; **C:** Jurg Walther; **M:** Don Preston.

Blood Feast ♂ *Feast of Flesh* **1963** The first of Lewis' gore-fests, in which a demented caterer butchers hapless young women to splice them together in order to bring back an Egyptian goddess. Dated, **C:** Herschell Gordon Lewis; **M:** Herschell Gordon Lewis.

Blood Feud ♂♂ *Revenge* **1979 (R)** In Italy preceding Europe's entry into WWII, a young widow is in mourning over the brutal murder of her husband by the Sicilian Mafia. In the meantime she must contend with the rivalry between Mastroianni as a lawyer and Giannini as a small-time crook both vying for her affections. Dubbed. **112m/C VHS. IT** Sophia Loren, Marcello Mastroianni, Giancarlo Giannini; **D:** Lina Wertmuller; **M:** Lina Wertmuller.

Blood for a Silver Dollar ♂½ *One Silver Dollar; Un Dollar Troue* **1966** Action-filled western, littered with murder, revenge and romance. **98m/C VHS. IT FR** Montgomery Wood, Evelyn Stewart, Pierre Cressoy; **D:** Giorgio Ferroni; **M:** Gianni Ferrio.

Blood for Blood ♂♂½ **1995 (R)** Cop must take up the martial arts skills he learned in childhood in order to protect his family from assassination. **93m/C VHS.** Lorenzo Lamas, James Lew, Mako, Eric Pierpoint, James Shigeta, James Callahan; **D:** John Weidner; **M:** Joel Goldsmith.

Blood Freak woof! *Blood Freaks* **1972** An absolutely insane anti-drug, Christian splatter film. A Floridian biker is introduced to drugs by a young woman and eventually turns into a poultry-monster who drinks the blood of junkies. Narrated by a chain smoker who has a coughing fit. Don't miss it. **86m/C VHS, DVD.** Steve Hawkes, Dana Cullivan, Randy Grinter Jr., Tina Anderson, Heather Hughes; **D:** Brad Grinter, Steve Hawkes.

Blood Frenzy ♂ **1987** Psychologist's patients take a therapeutic trip to the desert. The sun and heat take their toll, and everyone gets violent. This kind of therapy we don't need, and the movie's a waste, as well. Made for video. Loring was Wednesday on TV's "The Addams Family." **90m/C VHS.** Lisa Loring, Hank Garrett, Wendy MacDonald; **D:** Hal Freeman. **VIDEO**

Blood from the Mummy's Tomb ♂♂½ **1971** The immortal spirit of Tera, Egyptian queen of evil, haunts Margaret (Leon), the daughter of an archaeologist who discovered her tomb. As a long-prophesied conjunction of stars begins to occur, Margaret finds herself enthralled by Tera's power and finds herself becoming possessed by Tera's spirit. This adaptation of Bram Stoker's "The Jewel of Seven Stars" begins well, with a wonderfully mysterious and moody first half, but it loses steam in the somewhat muddled (and tedious) second half. Coulouris (without the old age makeup) looks exactly like his Thatcher character in "Citizen Kane." 30 years earlier, but sadly is given not much to do other than roll his eyes and scream. Leon is a likable heroine but that wig and false eyelashes have got to go! Remade in post-"Omen" fashion as "The Awakening." **94m/C VHS, DVD. GB** Andrew Keir, Valerie Leon, James Villiers, Hugh Burden, George Coulouris, Mark Edwards; **D:** Seth Holt; **W:** Christopher Wicking; **C:** Arthur Grant; **M:** Tristram Cary.

Blood Games woof! **1990 (R)** Buxom baseball team bats 1000 against the home team and the winning babes find out just how poor losers can be. Diamonds aren't always a girl's best friend. **90m/C VHS.** Gregory Cummings, Laura Albert, Shelly Abblett, Luke Shay, Ross Hagen; **D:** Tanya Rosenberg.

Blood Gnome ♂ **2002 (R)** Evil, hungry gnomes attack patrons of the local dominatrix, with a crime scene photographer as the sole spectator to the carnage. Grisly and made on the cheap, and looks it. **87m/C VHS, DVD.** Vincent Bilancio, Stephanie Beaton, Julie Strain, Massimo Avidano, Melissa Pursley; **D:** John Lechago; **W:** John Lechago. **VIDEO**

Blood, Guts, Bullets and Octane ♂♂ **1999 (R)** Used-car salesmen Sid (Carnahan) and Bob (Leis) are trying to keep their failing business afloat when a broker offers them a quarter million to let a 1963 Pontiac Le Mans convertible (burgundy) stay on their lot for 48 hours. The FBI are after the car and its owners, who've left a bloody cross-country trail. And the motor-mouth duo decide to renege on the deal. Desperate lowlifes and vicious crime winds up looking very familiar. **87m/C VHS, DVD.** Joe Carnahan, Dan Leis, Ken Rudolph, James Salter, Dan Harlan; **D:** Joe Carnahan; **W:** Joe Carnahan; **C:** John A. Jimenez; **M:** Mark Priolo, Martin Burke.

Blood Hook ♂½ **1986** A self-parodying teenage-slasher film about kids running into a backwoods fishing tournament while on vacation, complete with ghouls, cannibalism and grotesquerie. **85m/C VHS, DVD.** Mark Jacobs, Lisa Todd, Patrick Danz; **D:** James Mallon.

Blood In ... Blood Out: Bound by Honor ♂♂½ *Bound by Honor* **1993 (R)** Three-hour epic about Chicano gang culture focuses on three buddies whose lives evolve into a drug-addicted artist, a narc, and a prison regular. Written by acclaimed poet Baca, the film touches on issues such as poverty, racism, drugs, and violence as they pertain to Hispanic life. Unfortunately, the extreme violence (shootings, stabbings, and garrotings) completely overwhelms the rest of the story. Based on a story by Ross Thomas. **180m/C VHS, DVD.** Thomas F. Wilson, Damian Chapa, Jesse Borrego, Benjamin Bratt, Enrique Castillo, Victor Rivers, Delroy Lindo, Tom Towles; **D:** Taylor Hackford; **W:** Floyd Mutrux, Jimmy Santiago Baca, Jeremy Iacone; **C:** Gabriel Beristain; **M:** Bill Conti.

Blood Island ♂♂ *The Shuttered Room* **1968** A couple inherits an old house on a remote New England island where the woman grew up. They discover that this old house needs more than a paint job to make it livable; seems there's something evil in them there woods. Based on an H.P. Lovecraft story. Greene, who's best known for later directing "Godspell," and the solid cast fail to animate the inert script. **100m/C VHS. GB** Gig Young, Carol Lynley, Oliver Reed, Flora Robson; **D:** David Greene.

Blood Legacy ♂ *Legacy of Blood* **1973 (R)** Four heirs must survive a night in a lonely country estate to collect their money; what do you think happens? Average treatment of the haunted house theme. **77m/C VHS, DVD.** John Carradine, John Russell, Faith Domergue, Merry Anders, Richard (Dick) Davalos, Jeff Morrow, Roy Engle; **D:** Carl Monson; **W:** Eric Norden; **C:** Jack Beckett.

Blood Mania ♂ **1970 (R)** A retired surgeon's daughter decides to murder her father to collect her inheritance prematurely, but soon learns that crime doesn't pay as well as medicine. Low-budget, low-interest flick. **90m/C VHS, DVD.** Peter Carpenter, Maria de Aragon, Alex Rocco; **D:** Robert Vincent O'Neil.

Blood Money ♂½ **1980 (PG)** A dying ex-criminal returns to Australia to redeem his name and die with dignity. **64m/C VHS. AU** Bryan Brown, John Flaus, Chrissie James; **D:** Christopher Fitchett.

Blood Money ♂♂ **1988** Five dead bodies, $4 million, and one eye-witness, stripper Candy (Petty), are what remains of a drug deal gone south. Now, Detective Connor (Ironside) must protect his witness from Mob reprisals. **95m/C VHS, DVD.** Michael Ironside, Lori Petty, Currie Graham; **D:** Michael Ironside. **VIDEO**

Blood Money ♂♂ **1999 (R)** Tony Restrelli (Bloom) is the legit member of a mob family who made his money in the stock market. Now his financial knowledge is needed by his family to fend off would-be interlopers—and he can also avenge his brother's murder. **95m/C VHS, DVD.** Brian Bloom, Alan Arkin, Alicia Coppola, Jennifer Gatti, Bruce Kirby, Jonathan Scarfe, Gregory Sierra, Leonard Stone; **D:** Aaron Lipstadt. **CABLE**

Blood Money: The Story of Clinton and Nadine ♂♂½ *Clinton & Nadine* **1988** A confusing action/thriller with a good cast. Garcia is a small-time exotic bird smuggler whose gun-running brother has been murdered. He uses high-class hooker Barkin to get close to his brother's contacts, who turn out to be running guns to the Nicaraguan contras and involved in a dangerous government conspiracy. **95m/C VHS, DVD.** Andy Garcia, Ellen Barkin, Morgan Freeman; **D:** Jerry Schatzberg. **CABLE**

The Blood of a Poet ♂♂½ *Le Sang d'un Poete* **1930** Cocteau's first film, a practically formless piece of poetic cinema, detailing all manner of surreal events occurring in the instant of a chimney falls. In French with English subtitles. **55m/B VHS, DVD.** Enrique Rivero, Feral Benga, Jean Desbordes; **D:** Jean Cocteau; **W:** Jean Cocteau; **C:** Georges Perinal; **M:** Georges Auric.

Blood of Dracula ♂♂½ *Blood Is My Heritage; Blood of the Demon* **1957** They don't make 1950s rock 'n' roll girls' school vampire movies like this anymore, for which we may be grateful. Hypnotism, an amulet, and a greasepaint makeup job turn a shy female student into a bloodsucker. **71m/B VHS.** Sandra Harrison, Louise Lewis, Gail Ganley, Jerry Blaine, Heather Ames, Malcolm Atterbury, Richard Devor, Thomas B(rowne). Henry, Don Devlin, Edna Holland; **D:** Herbert L. Strock; **W:** Aben Kandel; **C:** Monroe Askins; **M:** Paul Dunlap.

Blood of Dracula's Castle ♂♂ *Dracula's Castle; Castle of Dracula* **1969** Couple inherits an allegedly deserted castle, but upon moving in discover Mr. and Mrs. Dracula have settled there. The vampires keep young women chained in the dungeon for continual blood supply. Also present are a hunchback and a werewolf. Awesome Adamson production is highlighted by the presence of the gorgeous Volante. Early cinematography effort by the renowned Laszlo Kovacs. **84m/C VHS, DVD.** John Carradine, Alexander D'Arcy, Paula Raymond, Ray Young, Vicki Volante, Robert Dix, John Cardos, Ken Osborne; **D:** Jean Hewitt, Al Adamson; **W:** Rex Carlton; **C:** Laszlo Kovacs.

Blood of Ghastly Horror woof! *The Fiend with the Atomic Brain; Psycho a Go Go!; The Love Maniac; The Man with the Synthetic Brain; The Fiend with the Electronic Brain* **1972** A young man thinks he has a new lease on life when he is the happy recipient of a brain transplant, but his dreams are destroyed when he evolves into a rampaging killer. This movie is so awful it hides behind numerous but rather creative aliases. **87m/C VHS, DVD.** John Carradine, Kent Taylor, Tommy Kirk, Regina Carrol, Roy Morton, Tracey Robbins; **D:** Al Adamson; **W:** Chris Martino, Dick Poston; **C:** Vilmos Zsigmond.

The Blood of Heroes ♂♂ *The Salute of the Jugger* **1989 (R)** A post-apocalyptic action flick detailing the adventures of a battered team of "juggers," warriors who challenge small village teams to a brutal sport (involving dogs' heads on sticks) that's a cross between jousting and football. **97m/C VHS, DVD.** Rutger Hauer, Joan Chen, Vincent D'Onofrio, Anna (Katerina) Katarina; **D:** David Peoples; **W:** David Peoples; **C:** David Eggby; **M:** Todd Boekelheide.

Blood of Jesus ♂ **1941** A sinful husband accidentally shoots his newly baptized wife, causing an uproar in their rural town. Williams later starred as Andy on the "Amos 'n' Andy" TV series. **50m/C VHS, DVD.** Spencer Williams Jr., Kathryn Craviness; **D:** Spencer Williams Jr.; **W:** Spencer Williams Jr. Natl. Film Reg. '91.

The Blood of Others ♂ **1984** A driveling adaptation of the Simone de Beauvoir novel about a young French woman at the outbreak of WWII torn between an at a kind, wealthy German. Made for French TV, it stars Jodie Foster and Michael Ontkean as the Gallic pair. **130m/C VHS. FR** Jodie Foster, Sam Neill, Michael Ontkean, Stephane Audran, Lambert Wilson, John Vernon, Kate Reid, Jean-Pierre Aumont; **D:** Claude Chabrol; **W:** Brian Moore. **TV**

Blood of the Hunter ♂♂½ **1994 (PG-13)** Psycho-killer holds postman's wife captive in a remote cabin in the Canadian wilderness. Turns out hubby and psycho share a mysterious past. **92m/C VHS.** Michael Biehn, Alexandra Vandernoot, Gabriel Arcand; **D:** Gilles Carle.

Blood of the Vampire ♂♂½ **1958** A Transylvanian doctor is executed for being a vampire and his hunchbacked assistant brings him back to life. **84m/C VHS, DVD. GB** Donald Wolfit, Vincent Ball, Barbara Shelley; Victor Madden; **W:** Jimmy Sangster.

The Blood on Satan's Claw 🎬🎬 **1971** Graphic tale centering on the Devil himself. Townspeople in an English village circa 1670 find the spirit of Satan taking over their children, who begin to practice witchcraft. Well made with lots of attention to period details. Not for the faint-hearted. **90m/C VHS, GB** Patrick Wymark, Linda Hayden, Barry Andrews; Michele Dotrice, James Hayter; Avice Landon; Simon Williams; Tamara Ustinov; **D:** Piers Haggard; **C:** Dick Bush; **M:** Marc Wilkinson.

Blood on the Badge 🎬½ **1992** Illegal arms have been stolen from a military arsenal and fall into the hands of Libyan Nationalists who begin a terrorist campaign. Detective Neal Farrow is assigned to stop them. **92m/C VHS** Remon Estevez, David Harrod, Rocky Patterson, Desiree Laforge, Dean Nolen, Melissa Dalton, Todd Everett; **D:** Bret McCormick.

Blood on the Moon 🎬🎬½ **1948** Well-acted film about a cowboy's involvement in a friend's underhanded schemes. Based on a Luke Short novel, this dark film revolves around a western land dispute between cattlemen and homesteaders. **88m/B VHS,** Robert Mitchum, Robert Preston, Walter Brennan, Barbara Bel Geddes; **D:** Robert Wise.

Blood on the Mountain 🎬🎬½ **1988** After escaping from prison, Jim plots revenge against his accomplice, only to kill an innocent man instead. **71m/C VHS,** Stracker Edwards, Tim Jones, Paula Preston, Cliff Turknett, Rich Jury; **D:** Donald W. Thompson.

Blood on the Sun 🎬🎬½ **1945** Newspaperman in Japan uncovers plans for world domination as propaganda, violence, and intrigue combine in this action-adventure. Also available colorized. **98m/B VHS, DVD,** James Cagney, Sylvia Sidney, Robert Armstrong, Wallace Ford; **D:** Frank Lloyd; **C:** Theodor Sparkuhl; **M:** Miklos Rozsa.

The Blood Oranges 🎬½ **1997** (R) Pretentious film is set in the anything-goes '70s in a tropical backwater village. Bohemian married couple Cyril (Dance) and Fiona (Lee) believe in fulfilling every sexual fantasy but their latest exchange of marital partners comes with unexpected complications. Fiona is attracted to photographer Hugh (Lane), who resists her charms for more deviant behavior, while Hugh's wife Catherine (Robins) is easily seduced by Cyril's courtship. Dialogue is laughable and the acting equally overblown. Based on the novel by John Fowles. **93m/C VHS, DVD,** Charles Dance, Sheryl Lee, Colin Lane, Laila Robins, Rachael Bella; **D:** Philip Haas; **W:** Belinda Haas, Philip Haas; **C:** Bernard Zitzermann; **M:** Angelo Badalamenti.

Blood Orgy of the She-Devils WOOf! **1974** (PG) Pretentious film is ... AKA: *Nightmare at Shadow Woods*. "Only for die-hard 'Mary Hartman' fans. **87m/C VHS, DVD** Louise Lasser, Mike Soper; **D:** John Grissmer; **M:** Richard Einhorn.

Blood Rage WOOf! **1988** (R) In 1835 Northern California, an Italian immigrant and his family give bloody battle to a powerful industrialist who wants their land in wine-growing country. Watch for the scenes involving veteran Roberts and his then-newcomer sister, pretty woman Julia. **91m/C VHS,** Eric Roberts, Dennis Hopper, Gian-carlo Giannini, Burt Young, Carlin Glynn, Lara Harris, Susan Anspach, Julia Roberts, Elias Koteas, Frank Campanella, Aldo Ray, Horton Foote Jr.; **D:** Peter Masterson; **W:** Ron Cutler.

Blood Red 🎬½ **1987** (R) A woman is introduced to her fiance's family only to find out that they, as well as her fiance, are murdering, perverted weirdos.

---

competing for an inheritance. **88m/C VHS, DVD,** CA Jan Rubes, Ray Walston, Lydia Denier, Kevin Hicks, Lynne Adams, Sam Malkin, Steven Saylor, Carrie Leigh; **D:** Graeme Campbell.

Blood Relatives 🎬 *Les Liens de Sang* **1977** Langlois admits she saw her brother kill her cousin, who she had been carrying on an incestuous relationship. But the discovery of the dead girl's diary by police inspector Sutherland reveals many more layers of intrigue than were initially evident. Based on a novel by Ed McBain. The French actors have been dubbed into English. **94m/C VHS, CA** Lisa Langlois, Donald Sutherland, Stephane Audran, Micheline Lanctot, Aude Landry; **D:** Claude Chabrol; **W:** Claude Chabrol.

Blood Relic 🎬½ **2005** (R) Pilot is turning the base into a museum when he discovers history buff Harry (Drago) is possessed by a mysterious talisman, commits mass murder on a naval base, and winds up in the loony bin for 22 years. Upon his release, he heads back to the scene of the crime and discovers history buff Harry (Drago) is turning the base into a museum with the help of a bunch of handy young people (hardy for slaughtering that is). Anyway, mayhem is likely since Campbell is determined to find his talisman again. **86m/C DVD,** John Christian, Billy Drago, Jennifer Grant, Debbie Rochon, Joshua Park, Kelly Ray; **D:** J. Christian Ingvordsen; **W:** J. Christian Ingvordsen.

Blood Ring 🎬½ **1993** When Sue's boxer husband goes missing she enlists old friend Max to help find him. They uncover a gambling ring run by drug lords where the kickboxing matches are to the death. Naturally, Max decides to use his expert kickboxing skills to get a violent revenge. **90m/C VHS,** Danny Nelson, Lori Birdsong, John Saxon, Ray Walston, Christian Hesler, Ralph Pruitt Vaughn, Laura Whyte, Evander Holyfield; **D:** Irvin Johnson; **W:** Ron Davies.

Blood Salvage 🎬 *Mad Jake* **1990** (R) A crazy junkman kidnaps beautiful girls, selling their organs to the highest bidder. He meets his match when a potential target refuses to cooperate. Interesting plot twists keep this Grade B thriller above average. **90m/C VHS,** Danny Nelson, Lori Birdsong, John Saxon, Ray Walston, Christian Hesler, Ralph Pruitt Vaughn, Laura Whyte, Evander Holyfield; **D:** Tucker Johnson; **W:** Ken Sanders; **C:** Michael Karp.

Blood Screams WOOf! **1988** (R) Nosy people drop in on an old town in Mexico and attempt to uncover the secrets hidden there, but bizarre entities throw out the unwelcome mat and terrorize them. Lots of blood and screaming. **75m/C VHS,** Ran Sands, James Garnett, Ralph Navarro, Mario Almada, Alfredo Gutierrez, Stacey Shaffer, Russ Tamblyn, Isela Vega; **D:** Glenn Gebhard.

Blood Simple 🎬🎬🎬½ **1985** (R) A jealous husband hires a sleazy private eye to murder his adulterous wife and her lover. A dark, intricate, morbid morality tale that deviates imaginatively from the standard murder mystery thriller. First film scripted by the Coen brothers. **96m/C VHS, DVD,** John Getz, M. Emmet Walsh, Dan Hedaya, Frances McDormand, Samm-Art Williams, Van Brooks, Lauren Bivens, Holly Hunter; **D:** Joel Coen; **W:** Joel Coen, Ethan Coer; **C:** Barry Sonnenfeld; **M:** Carter Burwell, Ind. Spirit '86: Actor (Walsh), Director (Coen); Sundance '85: Grand Jury Prize.

Blood Sisters WOOf! **1986** (R) Sorority babes intend to spend a giggle-strewn night in a haunted house but end up decapitated, butchered, and cannibalized. **85m/C VHS, DVD,** Amy Brentano, Maria MacHart, Brigete Cossu, Randy Mooers; **D:** Roberta Findlay.

Blood Song 🎬 *Dream Slayer* **1982** A patient (yester-decade teen throb Frankie Avalon) escapes into the night from a mental institution after murdering an attendant. He takes his only possession with him, a carved wooden flute. A young woman sees him burying his latest victim, and now he's on a hunt to play his "blood song" for her. Pretty bad, but fun to see Avalon play a less-than-squeaky-clean role. **90m/C VHS,** Frankie Avalon, Donna Wilkes.

Richard Jaeckel, Dane Clark, Antoinette Bower; **D:** Alan J. Levi.

The Blood Spattered Bride 🎬 *Blood Castle; La Novia Esangrentada; Bloody Fiancee; Till Death Us Do Part* **1972** Newlywed couple honeymoons in a remote castle in southern Spain. They are visited by a mysterious young woman who begins to influence the ways of lesbian bloodsucking. O.K. '70s Euro-eroti-horror based on Sheridan Le Fanu's "Carmilla." **101m/C VHS, DVD, SP** Simon Andreu, Maribel Martin, Alexandra Bastedo, Dean Selmier, Rosa Ma Rodriguez, Montserrat Julio, Angel Lombarte; **D:** Vicente Aranda; **W:** Vicente Aranda; **C:** Fernando Arribas.

Blood Surf 🎬 *Crocodile* **2000** (R) A filmmaker and her crew travel to Australia to do a documentary on the extreme sport of blood surfing where thrillseekers try to out surf sharks to shore. Only the sharks aren't the problem—a giant salt-water crocodile gets to the participants first. Very silly; your enjoyment will depend on your tolerance for the fake croc. **88m/C VHS, DVD,** Matt Borlenghi, Duncan Regehr, Kate Fischer, Taryn Reif, Joel West, Dax Miller; **D:** James D.R. Hickox; **W:** Sam Bernard, Robert L. Levy; **C:** Christopher Pearson; **M:** Jim Manzie. **VIDEO**

Blood Thirst 🎬🎬 **1965** Obscure horror film about a woman who stays young by indulging in ritual killings and strange experiments. **73m/B VHS, DVD, PH,** Robert Winston, Yvonne Nielson, Vic Diaz; **D:** Newton Arnold.

Blood Ties 🎬½ **1992** Reporter Harry Martin belongs to an unusual family—modern-day vampires (who prefer to be known as Carpathian-Americans). But they have an age-old problem with a band of fanatical vampire hunters. This time around you'll root for the bloodsuckers. **90m/C VHS, DVD,** Harley Venton, Patrick Bauchau, Kim Johnston-Ulrich, Michelle Johnson, Jason London, Bo Hopkins, Grace Zabriskie, Salvador Xuereb; **D:** Jim McBride; **W:** Richard Shapiro. **TV**

Blood Ties 🎬½ **1987** An American naval engineer in Sicily gets involved with the Mob in order to save his father's life. **98m/C VHS,** *Il Brad Davis*, Tony LoBianco, Vincent Spano, Barbara DeRossi, Maria Conchita Alonso; **D:** Giacomo Battiato.

Blood Tide 🎬 *The Red Tide* **1982** (R) A couple's vacation in the Greek isles. Beautiful scenery, good cast, bad movie, forgettable. **82m/C VHS, DVD,** James East, John Considine, James Earl Jones, Jose Ferrer; **D:** Richard Jeffries; **W:** Nico Mastorakis.

Blood Tracks 🎬 **1986** A woman kills her abusive husband, then hides out in the mountains with her kids until they become Cannibalistic savages. Years later, people show up to shoot a music video. **82m/C VHS,** Jeff Harding, Michael Fitzpatrick, Naomi Kaneda; **D:** Mike Jackson.

Blood Trails 🎬 **2006** (R) After a one-night stand with unstable bike cop Chris (Price), bike messenger Anne (Federick) takes off with boyfriend Michael (Frederick) for a weekend of mountain biking. Guess who appears to stalk Anne? Basically a chase on two wheels and not particularly frightening. **87m/C DVD,** Rebecca Palmer, Ben Price, Tom Frederick; **C:** Robert Krause; **W:** Robert Krause, Florian Puchert; **C:** Ralf Noack; **M:** Ben Bartlett. **VIDEO**

Blood Vows: The Story of a Mafia Wife 🎬🎬 **1987** TV's Laura Ingalls (Gilbert) leaps from the prairie to modern-day mafia in this warped Cinderella story. She meets the man of her dreams, whom she slowly finds is her worst nightmare as she becomes trapped within the confines of her new-found "family." TV soaper is way over the top in terms of melodrama. **100m/C VHS,** Melissa Gilbert, Joe Penny, Eileen Brennan, Talia Shire, Anthony (Tony) Franciosa; **D:** Paul Wendkos; **M:** William Goldstein. **TV**

Blood Voyage WOOf! **1977** (R) A crewman aboard a pleasure yacht must find out who is killing off his passengers one by one. **80m/C VHS,** Jonathan Lippe, Laurie Rose, Midori, Mara Modair; **D:** Frank Mitchell.

Bloodbrothers

Rosa, Midori, Mara Modair; **D:** Frank Mitchell.

Blood Warriors 🎬½ **1993** An ex-Marine finds out a old buddy is leading a private army of mercenaries. When he refuses to join up their friendship turns violent. **93m/C VHS,** David Bradley, Frank Zagarino; **D:** Sam Firstenberg; **W:** David Bradley.

Blood Wedding 🎬🎬🎬 *Bodas de Sangre* **1981** A wonderfully passionate dance film from Saura and choreographed by Gades, based on the play by famed author Federico Garcia Lorca. A young bride (Hoyos) runs off with her married lover (Gades) on her wedding day and her jilted husband (Jimenez) comes after them. The film is set-up at a dress rehearsal where the dancers, led by Gades, perform upon a bare stage. If you like flamenco, there are two more: "Carmen" and "El Amor Brujo." Spanish with subtitles. **71m/C VHS, SP** Antonio Gades, Cristina Hoyos, Marisol, Carmen Villena, Juan Antonio Jimenez; **D:** Carlos Saura; **W:** Carlos Saura, Antonio Gades; **C:** Teodoro Escamilla; **M:** Emilio De Diego.

Blood Work 🎬🎬½ **2002** (R) Retired FBI profiler Terry McCaleb (Eastwood) has just had a heart transplant. But while undergoing checkups, he's brought back to track a serial killer who apparently murdered the woman who became his donor. Clint can still do the loner detective to a T, the question is, should he? The evidence here points to "probably not." It's not that he's not good at it, it's that there's really nothing more he can do WITH it. The killer is easy to spot from a mile away, and thankfully McCaleb does, which leaves the how and when of catching him only suspense. Well done but ultimately forgettable. Based on the novel by Michael Connelly. **111m/C VHS, DVD, US** Clint Eastwood, Anjelica Huston, Jeff Daniels, Wanda De Jesus, Paul Rodriguez, Tina Lifford, Dylan Walsh, Mason Lucero, Rick Hoffman; **C:** Tom Stern; **M:** Lennie Niehaus.

Bloodbath 🎬 *Sky is Falling* **1976** Drugs, sex and terrorism—Hopper is typecast as an American degenerate who, along with his expatriate friends, is persecuted by local religious cults who need sacrifices. **89m/C VHS, DVD,** Dennis Hopper, Carroll Baker, Richard Todd, Faith Brook, Win Wells; **D:** Silvio Narizzano.

Bloodbath 🎬 **1998** Detectives Tony Martin and Maggie Donovan are investigating a series of murders whose victims are all starlets. As they dig into this world of underground filmmaking, they find a literal bloodbath involving a group of movie-happy vampires. **90m/C VHS,** Susannah Devereux, Kathryn Cleasby, Anthony Martin, Jan Bryant, Charles Currier, Dana Fredsti; **D:** Dan Speake; **M:** Arne Kimberly; **W:** Dana Fredsti; **C:** Joseph Raymond Garcia. **VIDEO**

Bloodbath at the House of Death 🎬🎬 **1985** Price and his compatriots fight a team of mad scientists in this parody of popular horror films. Fun to see Price spoofing his own genre; die-hard horror camp fans will be satisfied. Best line: "Wanna fork?" **92m/C VHS, GB** Kenny Everett, Pamela Stephenson, Vincent Price, Gareth Hunt, Sheila Steafel, John Fortune, Graham Stark, Cleo Rocos; **D:** Ray Cameron; **W:** Ray Cameron, Barry Cryer; **C:** Brian West, Dusty Miller; **M:** Mark London, Mike Moran.

Bloodbath in Psycho Town 🎬½ **1978** (R) A film crew is marked for death by a hooded man when it enters a remote little village. **87m/C VHS, DVD,** Ron Aragon, Donna Baltron, Dave Elliott; **D:** Alessandro DeGaetano.

Bloodbeat 🎬 **1985** A supernatural being terrorizes a family as they gather at their country home to celebrate Christmas. **84m/C VHS,** Helen Benton, Terry Brown, Claudia Peyton; **D:** Fabrice A. Zaphiratos.

Bloodbrothers 🎬🎬½ **1978** (R) Portrayal of working-class Italian men's lives—if that's possible with out the benefit of Italian writers, producers, or director. Still, lots of cussing and general intensity, as Gere's character struggles between staying in the family construction business and doing what he wants to do—work with children. Re-cut for TV and re-titled "A Father's Love." **120m/C VHS,** Richard Gere, Paul

Sorvino, Tony LoBianco, Kenneth McMillan, Marilu Henner, Danny Aiello, Leila Goldoni, Yvonne Wilder; **D:** Robert Mulligan; **C:** Robert L. Surtees; **M:** Elmer Bernstein.

Bloodfist 1989 (R) A kickboxer tears through Manila searching for his brother's killer. A Roger Corman production. 85m/C VHS, DVD. Don "The Dragon" Wilson, Rob Kaman, Billy Blanks, Kris Aguilar, Riley Bowman, Michael Shaner, Joe Mari Avellana, Marilyn Bautista; **D:** Terence H. Winkless; **W:** Robert King; **C:** Ricardo Jacques Gale. **M:** Sasha Matson.

Bloodfist 2 1990 (R) Six of the world's toughest martial artists find themselves kidnapped and forced to do the bidding of the evil Su. The mysterious recluse stages a series of incredible fights between the experts and his own army of drugged warriors. Better-than-average fight choreography. 90m/C VHS, DVD. Don "The Dragon" Wilson, Maurice Smith, James Warring, Timothy Baker, Richard (Rick) Hill, Rina Reyes, Kris Aguilar, Joe Mari Avellana; **D:** Andy Blumenthal; **W:** Catherine Cyran; **C:** Bruce Dorfman; **M:** Nigel Holton.

Bloodfist 3: Forced to Fight 1992 (R) Just as long as nobody's forced to watch, real-life world champion kickboxer Wilson thrashes his way through another showdown-at-the-arena plot. Better-than-average fight choreography. 90m/C VHS, DVD. Don "The Dragon" Wilson, Richard Roundtree, Laura Stockman, Richard Paul, Rick Dean, Peter "Sugarfoot" Cunningham; **D:** Oley Sassone; **W:** Allison Burnett; **C:** Rick Bota; **M:** Nigel Holton.

Bloodfist 4: Die Trying 1992 (R) To rescue his daughter, a fighter must do battle with the FBI, the CIA, and an international arms cartel. 86m/C VHS, DVD. Don "The Dragon" Wilson, Catya (Cat) Sassoon, Amanda Wyss, James Tolkan, Liz Torres; **D:** Paul Ziller.

Bloodfist 5: Human Target 1993 (R) When undercover FBI agent Jim Roth (Wilson) attempts to unravel an international arms deal he's found out and left for dead. He comes to with no memory only to find himself caught between the arms dealers and the FBI, who think he's turned double-agent. Both sides want Roth dead. 84m/C VHS, DVD. Don "The Dragon" Wilson, Denice Duff, Yuji Okumoto, Don Stark, Danny Lopez, Steve James, Michael Yama; **D:** Jeff Yonis; **W:** Jeff Yonis; **C:** Michael G. Wojciechowski; **M:** David Wurst, Eric Wurst.

Bloodfist 6: Ground Zero 1994 (R) Nick Corrigan (Wilson) must battle terrorists who have a nuclear missile aimed at New York City. 86m/C VHS, DVD. Don "The Dragon" Wilson, Cat Sasson, Steve Garvey; **D:** Rick Jacobson; **W:** Brendan Broderick, Rob Kerchner; **C:** Michael Gallagher; **M:** John Graham.

Bloodfist 7: Manhunt 1995 (R) Martial arts expert Jim Trudell is accused by corrupt cops of murder and is forced on the run while he tries to prove his innocence. 95m/C VHS, DVD. Don "The Dragon" Wilson, Jonathan Penner, Jillian McWhirter, Stephen Davies, Cyril O'Reilly, Eb Lottimer, Steven Williams; **D:** Jonathan Winfrey; **W:** Brendan Broderick, Rob Kerchner; **C:** Michael Gallagher; **M:** Elliot Anders, Mike Elliot. VIDEO

Bloodfist 8: Hard Way Out 1996 (R) Widowed teacher Hard Way Out 1996 (R) Widowed teacher Rick Cowan (Wilson) turns out to have a lurid past when he and teen son Chris (White) are targeted for death. Dull dad is ex-CIA and someone is afraid their dirty secrets will get out if he's not eliminated. 78m/C VHS, DVD. Don "The Dragon" Wilson, John Patrick White, Warren Burton, Richard Farrell; **D:** Barry Samson; **W:** Alex Simon; **C:** John Aronson; **M:** John Faulkner.

Bloodhounds 1996 (R) Detective Nikki Cruz (Harmos), who's skilled in the martial arts, reluctantly agrees to team up with writer Harrison Coyle (Bernsen), whose specialty is criminal cases, to catch escaped serial killer, Charles Veasey (Baltz). 86m/C VHS. Corbin Bernsen, Christina Harmos, Kirk Baltz, Gina Mastrogiacomo, James Pickens Jr., Marcus Flanagan; **D:** Michael Katleman; **W:** Pablo F. Fenjves; **C:** Fernando Arguelles. CABLE

Bloodhounds 2 1996 (PG-13) True-crime writer Harrison Coyle (Bernsen) teams up with PI Nikki Cruz (Peeples) to nab serial killer Matthew Standing (Tracey), who hunts down convicted rapists he thinks haven't been punished enough. Turns out the killer is also a fan of Coyle's and begins contacting him about them writing a book together. 89m/C VHS. Corbin Bernsen, Nia Peeples, Ian Tracey, Amy Yasbeck, Jim Byrnes, Suki Kaiser, Tom Cavanagh; **D:** Stuart Cooper; **W:** Pablo F. Fenjves; **C:** Curtis Petersen; **M:** Charles Bernstein. CABLE

Bloodhounds of Broadway 1952 New York bookie Numbers Foster (Brady) heads out of town to avoid a criminal investigation and winds up in backwoods Georgia where he meets talented Tessie (Gaynor), who convinces Numbers to take her back up north with him. She finds success on Broadway and finally persuades the bookie to turn himself in. Numbers does his time, and then gets his gal. Based on a story by Damon Runyon. 90m/C DVD. Mitzi Gaynor, Scott Brady, Mitzie Green, Marguerite Chapman, Michael O'Shea, Wally Vernon; **D:** Harmon Jones; **W:** Sy Gomberg; **C:** Edward Cronjager; **M:** Lionel Newman.

Bloodhounds of Broadway 1989 (PG) A musical tribute to Damon Runyon, detailing the clichéd adventures of an assortment of jazz-age crooks, flappers, chanteuses, and losers. 90m/C VHS, DVD. Madonna, Rutger Hauer, Randy Quaid, Matt Dillon, Jennifer Grey, Julie Hagerty, Esai Morales, Anita Morris, Josef Sommer, William S. Burroughs, Ethan Phillips, Stephen McHattie, Dinah Manoff, Googy Gress, Tony Azito, Tony Longo, Madeleine Potter; **D:** Howard Brookner; **W:** Howard Brookner, Colman DeKay; **C:** Elliot Davis; **M:** Jonathan Sheffer.

Bloodknot 1995 (R) The Reaves' are devastated when their son Martin is killed in a military accident. So they're an easy target when Kaye (Vernon) shows up, claiming to be Martin's girlfriend when Evelyn (Kidder) and brother Tom (Dempsey) are only too eager to welcome Kaye into the family but it wouldn't be a thriller if devious Kaye didn't have some deadly ulterior motives. 98m/C VHS. Patrick Dempsey, Kate Vernon, Margot Kidder, Craig Sheffer; **D:** Jorge Montesi; **W:** Randy Kornfield; **C:** Philip Linzey; **M:** Ian Thomas. CABLE

Bloodlines 2005 Policewoman Justine Hopkin (Pierson) finds her mother's dead body just after her dad James (McNally) is released from prison (he was in on a murder rap). She believes he's innocent and now has to prove it. 137m/C DVD. GB Kevin McNally, Robert Pugh, Kieran O'Brien, Jan Francis, Emma Pierson, Max Beesley; **D:** Philip Martin; **W:** Mike Cullen; **C:** Julian Court; **M:** Nicholas Hooper. TV

Bloodlink 1986 (R) A well-to-do doctor has a recurring nightmare about killing an elderly woman. This prompts him to explore his past, discovering that he was separated at birth from a twin brother. Naturally, only by searching frantically for his long-lost sibling can the good doctor hope to solve the mystery of the recurring nightmare. A somnolent tale indeed. 98m/C VHS. Michael Moriarty, Penelope Milford, Geraldine Fitzgerald, Cameron Mitchell, Sarah Langenfeld; **D:** Alberto De Martino.

Bloodlust 1959 More. teenagers fall prey to yet another mad scientist, who stores their dead bodies in glass tanks. Low-budget ripoff of "The Most Dangerous Game" and other such films. A must for Mike Brady (Robert Reed) fans though. 89m/B VHS, DVD. Wilton Graff, June Kenney, Robert Reed, Lilyan Chauvin; **D:** Ralph Brooke; **W:** Ralph Brooke.

Bloodlust: Subspecies 3 Subspecies 3 1993 (R) Equally gory followup to "Bloodstone: Subspecies 2." Sadistic vampire Radu is still battling for Michelle's soul, this time aided by his disgusting Mummy Becky, aided by his disgusting Mummy and the demonic Subspecies. Castle Vladislas is awash is blood and Becky discovers more than Michelle's fate is at risk. 83m/C VHS. Anders (Toting) Hove, Kevin Blair Spirtas, Denice Duff, Pamela Gordon, Ion Haiduc, Michael DellaFemina; **D:** Ted Nicolaou; **W:** Ted Nicolaou.

Bloodmatch 1991 (R) A whodunit, martial-arts-style: the "sleuth" kidnaps all the suspects in a corruption case and kickboxes each to death until somebody confesses. Not exactly Agatha Christie, and artsy camera moves fail to exploit the fancy footwork. 85m/C VHS. Thom Mathews, Michel Qissi, Benny "The Jet" Urquidez, Marianne Taylor, Hope Marie Carlton, Dale Jacoby, Thunder Wolf, Vincent Klyn, Peter "Sugarfoot" Cunningham, Hector Pena; **D:** Albert Pyun; **W:** K. Maanah; **M:** Tony Riparetti.

Bloodmoon WOOF! 1990 The setting is Australia but the sleazy story's all too familiar: an insane killer employs knives and other sharp objects to prevent sex-crazed students from getting past third base. 104m/C VHS, DVD. AU Leon Lissek, Christine Amor, Ian Patrick Williams, Helen Thomson, Hazel Howson, Craig Cronin, Anya Molina; **D:** Alec Mills; **W:** Richard Brennan; **M:** Brian May.

Bloodmoon 1997 A New York serial killer is quite a specialist—he only kills fighters, and he kills with his bare hands. So it's up to Ken O'Hara (Daniels), who specializes in tracking murderers, to find this guy before he kills again. A good display of martial arts skills keep this one interesting. 105m/C VHS, DVD. Gary Daniels, Chuck Jeffreys, Darren Shahlavi, Nina Repeta, Frank Gorshin, Jeffrey Pillars, Joe Hess; **D:** Derek M.K. Wan; **W:** Keith W. Strandberg; **C:** Derek M.K. Wan; **M:** Richard Yuen.

BloodRayne WOOF! 2006 There are moments in this painful period vampire "epic" where you honestly have to wonder if director Uwe Boll was aware that the camera was rolling. Whatever the excuse, Boll's latest video game movie proves that even sex, gore, and violence can be boring in the hands of the right director. Rayne (Loken) is a half-vampire, half-human warrior who's out to stop her illegitimate father, Kagin (Kingsley), the king of vampires, from... sigh, bored yet? You will be. Even the cast looks half-asleep. (Madsen and Kingsley take "phoning it in" to a new and scary level.) But nothing beats the barely rehearsed fight scenes. A community theatre production of "Braveheart" would have more convincing stage combat. 95m/C DVD. GE US Kristanna Loken, Michael Madsen, Matthew Davis, Michelle Rodriguez, Ben Kingsley, Will Sanderson, Udo Kier, Meat Loaf Aday, Michael Pare, Billy Zane, Geraldine Chaplin; **D:** Uwe Boll; **W:** Guinevere Turner; **C:** Mathias Neumann; **M:** Henning Lohner.

BloodRayne 2: Deliverance WOOF! 2007 (R) Probably the worst vampire western ever made, "BloodRayne" bombed, Boll somehow got financing to produce this direct-to-DVD sequel. Set in the Old West, the "plot" revolves around vampire Billy the Kid (played by Scut Farkus from "A Christmas Story"), and his plans to use the railroad to help his cowboy vamp posse to take over America. (Seriously.) Enter the sexually-ambiguous warrior-woman Rayne (Malthe), a half-human/half-vampire, who fights in the name of justice with her fangs and bare midriff. Unfortunately, vampire John Ford doesn't show up to punish Boll for his crimes against the western. 95m/C DVD. Natassia Malthe, Zack (Zach) Ward, Brendan Fletcher, Michael Pare, Christopher Coppola, Michael Eklund; **D:** Uwe Boll; **W:** Christopher Donelly, Neil Every; **M:** Jessica de Rooij. VIDEO

Bloodspell 1987 (R) A student with an evil power unleashes it on those who cross him. 87m/C VHS, DVD. Anthony Jenkins, Aaron Teich, Alexandra Kennedy, John Reno; **D:** Deryn Warren.

Bloodsport 1988 (R) American soldier Van Damme endeavors to win the deadly Kumite, an outlawed martial arts competition in Hong Kong. Lots of kickboxing action and the sound of bones cracking. 92m/C VHS, DVD. Jean-Claude Van Damme, Leah Ayres, Roy Chiao, Donald Gibb, Bolo Yeung, Norman Burton, Forest Whitaker; **D:** Newton Arnold; **M:** Christopher Cosby.

Bloodsport 2: The Next Kumite 1995 (R) Old-fashioned kickfest has Alex (Bernhardt) stealing antiquities in Thailand. He's left to take the fall by his partner in the theft of an ancient sword belonging to powerful businessman Leung (Morita) and is sent to a prison where sadistic head guard Demon (Han) takes an instant dislike to him. Alex learns about a sacred fighting competition, the Kumite, from wise prison sage Sun (Hong) and naturally, once Alex manages to get into the contest, his opponent is—you guessed it—Demon. 87m/C VHS. Daniel Bernhardt, Ong Soo Han, Nonyuki "Pat" Morita, James Hong; **D:** Alan Mehrez.

Bloodsport 3 1997 Alex (Bernhardt) must avenge the death of his mentor (Hong) and regain the Kumite sword. Enjoyable if a steady dose of kicks to the head is your idea of intricate plotting. 100m/C VHS, DVD. Daniel Bernhardt, Ivan Rhys-Davies, James Hong, Nonyuki "Pat" Morita; **D:** Alan Mehrez; **W:** James Williams; **M:** Stephen (Steve) Edwards.

Bloodsport 4: The Dark Kumite 1998 (R) Undercover agent infiltrates a prison to find out why prisoners are disappearing and ends up forced to participate in a to-the-death tournament. Enjoyable if a steady dose of kicks to the head is your idea of intricate plotting. 100m/C VHS, DVD. Daniel Bernhardt, Ivan Ivanov, Lisa Stothard, Elvis Restaino; **D:** Elvis Restaino; **M:** Alex Wurman. VIDEO

The Bloodstained Shadow Solamente Nero; Only Blackness 1978 Stefano (Capolicchio) decides to visit his priest brother Paolo (Hill), who lives on the island of Murano near Venice. He meets the mysterious Sandra (Casini) on his journey and then witnesses a midnight murder upon his arrival. More deaths follow as Paolo and Stefano investigate. Italian with subtitles. 109m/C DVD. IT Lino Capolicchio, Craig Hill, Stefania Casini, Massimo Serato, Juliette Mayniel; **D:** Antonio Bido; **W:** Antonio Bido, Marisa Andalo, Domenico Malan; **C:** Mario Vulpiani; **M:** Stelvio Cipriani, The Goblins.

Bloodstalkers WOOF! 1976 Two vacationers in Florida meet up with a band of slaughtering, swamp-based lunatics. 91m/C VHS. Kenny (Ken) Miller, Celea Ann Cole, Jerry Albert; **D:** Robert W. Morgan.

Bloodstone 1988 (PG-13) A couple honeymooning in the Middle East unexpectedly become involved in a jewel heist when they discover a valuable ruby amongst their luggage. Non-stop action and humor. 90m/C VHS, DVD. Charlie Brill, Christopher Neame, Jack Kehler, Brett Stimely, Anna Nicholas; **D:** Dwight Little; **W:** Nico Mastorakis, Curt Allen.

Bloodstone: Subspecies 2 1992 (R) A gory sequel to "Subspecies" finds Radu the vampire pursuing the luscious Michelle. Radu gets some help from his ghoulish mother and yucky demonic spawn. Filmed on location in Romania. 107m/C VHS. Anders (Toting) Hove, Denice Duff, Kevin Blair Spirtas, Michael Denish, Pamela Gordon, Ion Haiduc; **D:** Ted Nicolaou; **W:** Ted Nicolaou.

Bloodstorm: Subspecies 4 Subspecies 4: Bloodstorm—The Master's Revenge 1998 (R) Master vampire Radu Vladislas (Hove) has awakened with an agenda. He wants to reclaim his vast wealth and recapture fledgling vamp, Michelle (Duff). Meanwhile, Radu hangs around with former protege, Ash (Morris), and Michelle is taken in by a creepy doctor (Dinvale) who's after the bloodstone. If you liked the first three, this is just more of the same. 90m/C VHS, DVD. Anders (Toting) Hove, Denice Duff, Jonathan Morris, Mihai Dinvale, Floriela Grappini; **D:** Ted Nicolaou; **C:** Adolfo Bartoli; **M:** Richard Kosinski.

Bloodstream WOOF! 2000 Convoluted plot first involves a worker who smuggles a mystery vial out of a genetics lab and then gets murdered. Now we switch to Pamela (Mills), who's come to hear her sister sing at open-mic night, only sis has gone missing. And it turns out she's been taken by a serial killer but...oh, who cares. Low-budget crap. m/C VHS. Meredith Mills, Eric Bunton, Joe Decker, Joey Day; **D:** Dennis De-

The Bloodsuckers 🎬🎬 *Incense for the Damned; Doctors Wear Scarlet; The Freedom Seekers* 1970 British horror tale set on a Greek Island. An Oxford don is seduced into an ancient vampire cult. Director Michael Burrowes replaces Hartford-Davis in the credits due to a dispute over post-production editing. 90m/C VHS, DVD. GE Patrick Macnee, Peter Cushing, Patrick Mower, Edward Woodward, Alex Davion, Imogen Hassall, Madeline Hinde, Johnny Sekka; D: Robert Hartford-Davis; W: Julian Selke; D: Desmond Dickinson.

Bloodsuckers from Outer Space WOOF! 1983 Tourists are being brutally attacked and murdered during a small Spanish village's Festival of the Moon. 84m/C VHS. GE Olivia Pascal, Christopher Brugger, Ann-Beate Engelke, Antonia Garcia, Nadja Gerganoff, Corinna Gillwald, Jasmin Losensky, Maria Rubio, Alexander Waechter; D: Jess (Jesus) Franco; W: Jess (Jesus) Franco, Rayo Casablanca; C: Juan Soler.

Bloodsucking Freaks WOOF! *The Incredible Torture Show; The House of the Screaming Virgins* 1975 (R) Virtually plotless Troma gagfest full of torture, cannibalistic dwarfs, and similar debaucheries, all played out on a Scho Grand Guignol stage (horror shows that allegedly contained real torture and death). Features "The Caged Sexicids." If that tells you anything (a cage of naked cannibal women tended by a dwarf). Not to mention the woman who has her brain sucked out through a straw. Filmed in "Ghoulovision" and originally rated X. Intolerable for most. 89m/C VHS, DVD, Niles McMaster, Viju Krem, Alan Dekay, Dan Fauci; D: Joel M. Reed; W: Joel M. Reed; C: Gerry Toll; M: Michael Sahl.

Bloodsucking Pharoahs of Pittsburgh WOOF! *Picking up the Pieces* 1990 (R) Pittsburgh is plagued by crazed cannibals who think eternal life is in Pennsylvania. Two detectives on the case are mystified. 89m/C VHS, DVD. Jake Dengel, Joe Sharkey, Suzanna Fletcher, Beverly Penberthy, Shawn Elliott, Pat Logan, Jane (Veronica Hart) Hamilton; D: Dean "Schellenberger; W: Dean Tschetter; C: Peter Reniers; M: Michael Melvon.

Bloody Avenger 🎬 1980 A trio of detectives search for a murderer in the streets of Philadelphia. 100m/C VHS. Jack Palance, George Eastman, Jenny Tambur; D: Al (Alfonso Brescia) Bradley.

The Bloody Brood WOOF! 1959 Really bad flick about a drug-dealing beatnik gang who commit nasty crimes, like feeding messenger boys hamburgers filled with ground glass. 80m/C VHS, DVD. CA Jack Betts, Barbara Lord, Peter Falk, Robert Christie; D: Julian Hoffman.

Bloody Birthday 🎬½ *Creeps* 1980 (R) Three youngsters, bound together by their eerie birth during an eclipse (you know what that means), kill everyone around them that ever gave them problems. Typical 'and the fun continues' ending; standard fare. 92m/C VHS, DVD. Susan Strasberg, Jose Ferrer, Lori Lethin, Melinca Cordell, Joe Penny, Ellen Geer, Julie Brown, Michael Dudikoff, Billy Jacoby, Elizabeth Hoy, Andy Freeman; D: Ed(ward) Hunt; W: Ed(ward) Hunt, Barry Pearson.

Bloody Mama 🎬🎬 1970 (R) Corman's violent, trashy story of the infamous Barker Gang of the 30s, led by the bloodthirsty and sex-crazed Ma Barker (Winters, who also has a thing for Ma Barker). Winter's is a riot in this perverse stew of crime, violence, and, of course, sentimental blood bonding (the family that slays together stays together). First of the Corman-produced (and sometimes directed) mama movies, followed by "Big Bad Mama" and "Crazy Mama." 90m/C VHS. Shelley Winters, Robert De Niro, Don Stroud, Pat Hingle, Bruce Dern, Diane Varsi, Robert Walden, Clinton Kimbrough, Scatman Crothers, Pamela Dunlap, Michael Fox, Stacy Harris; D: Roger Corman; W: Robert Thom; C: John A. Alonzo; M: Don Randi.

Bloody Moon WOOF! *Die Saege des Todes* 1983 Tourists are being brutally attacked and murdered during a small Spanish village's Festival of the Moon. 91m/C VHS. W: Paul Harper, Rance Howard, John Mitchum; D: Richard Robinson.

Bloody Murder WOOF! 1999 (R) Stupid teen campers in peril from maniac movie. This time the creepoid wears a hockey mask (sound familiar?) and has a chainsaw in place of his left arm. Ick. 90m/C VHS, DVD. Michael Stone, Jessica Morris, Peter Guillemette, Patrick Cavanagh, Christelle Ford, Tracy Pacheco, Justin Martin; D: Ralph Portillo; W: John R. Stevenson; C: Keith Holland; M: Steven Stern. VIDEO

Bloody Murder 2 WOOF! 2003 (R) The sequel is no improvement over the first stinker, which was your basic teen slasher flick. Trevor Moorehorse returns to slaughter a new batch of teen camp counselors at Camp Placid Pines. 85m/C VHS, DVD. Katy Woodruff, Kelly Gunning, Amanda Magarian, Lane Anderson, Benjamin Schneider; D: Robert Spera; C: David Trulli; M: Steven Stern. VIDEO

Bloody New Year 🎬 *Time Warp Terror* 1987 (R) Corpses stalk the living as a group of teen's happen upon an impromptu New Year's Eve party on a deserted island. Auld acquaintance shouldn't be forgot, just this flick. 90m/C VHS, DVD. Suzy Aitchison, Nikki Brooks, Colin Haywood, Mark Powley, Catherine Roman, Julian Ronnie; D: Norman J. Warren; W: Frazer Pearce; C: John Shann; M: Nick Magnus.

The Bloody Pit of Horror 🎬½ *Crimson Executioner; The Red Hangman; Il Boia Scarlatto* 1965 While 'wife' Jayne Mansfield was in Italy filming "Primitive Love," bodybuilder Hargitlay starred in this sado-horror epic. He owns a castle that is visited by a group of models for a special shoot. While in the dungeon, Hargitlay becomes possessed by the castle's former owner, a sadist, and begins torturing the models. Supposedly based on the writings of the Marquis de Sade. 87m/B VHS, DVD. IT Mickey Hargitlay, Louise Barrett, Walter Brandi, Moa Thai, Ralph Zucker, Albert Gordon; D: Max (Massimo Pupillo) Hunter; W: Romano Miglionni, Roberto Natale; C: Luciano Trasatti; M: Gino Peguri.

Bloody Proof 🎬🎬 1999 A serial killer is stalking well-to-do women in Mexico. Detective Ibarra (Bauer) is assigned to the case. Rookie tabloid reporter Estela (Arizmendi) finds an important clue. The resolution of the stereotypical premise runs true to form, but the characters are treated seriously and the film is stylishly made with a few moments of abrupt, shocking violence. 95m/C VHS, DVD. Steven Bauer, Yareli Arizmendi, Olivia Hussey; D: Gabriel Beristain; W: M. Francesconi, Tim Hoy; C: Andres Leon Becker; M: Eduardo Gamboa.

Bloody Sunday 🎬🎬🎬 2001 (R) Docudrama covers the January 30, 1972 civil rights march through Derry, Northern Ireland to protest the policy of British internment without trial. Although the majority of the marchers are Catholic, they are led by the area's Protestant MP Ivan Cooper (Nesbitt), who believes the situation can be handled peacefully. Maj. Gen. Robert Ford (Piggott-Smith) reiterates that the British Army has banned all such marches and that participants are subject to arrest. As the march splinters into factions, the Army fires on the crowd—27 civilians are wounded and 14 died. The resolution of the event by director Greengrass is stunning at the very least. "Sunday Bloody Sunday" was eulogized in a song by U2. 110m/C VHS, DVD. IR GB James Nesbitt, Tim Piggott-Smith, Nicholas Farrell, Gerard McSorley, Kathy Kiera Clarke, Allan Gildea, Gerard Crossan, Mary Moulds, Carmel McCallion, Declan Duddy, Simon Mann; D: Paul Greengrass; W: Paul Greengrass; C: Ivan Strasburg; M: Dominic Muldowney; Berlin Intl. Film Fest. '02: Film.

Bloody Trail 🎬 1972 A Union soldier who chooses the recently pummeled South as the venue for postwar R-and-R is, for some reason, pursued by Confederates. And his good ol' boy pursuers don't have a sudden change of heart when he teams up with a former slave. Lots of violence and nudity; little plot and entertainment.

Blossoms in the Dust 🎬🎬 1941 The true story of Edna Gladney is told as she starts the Texas Children's Home and Aid Society of Fort Worth. Major league Garson tear-jerker. 100m/B VHS. Greer Garson, Walter Pidgeon, Felix Bressart, Marsha Hunt, Fay Holden, Samuel S. Hinds, Kathleen Howard; D: Mervyn LeRoy.

The Blot 🎬🎬 1921 A story about a poorly paid professor and his family, whose lifestyle contrasts with that of an affluent neighbor, a butcher. 55m/B VHS, DVD. Louis Calhern, Claire Windsor; D: Lois Weber.

Blossoms on Broadway 🎬 1937 Musical-comedy pre-World War II goofiness. A young con-woman (Ross) tries to bilk a mine owner out of his fortune, only he turns out to be short on funds as everyone else. She's got a love interest, of course, but he turns out to be a detective. 88m/B VHS. Edward Arnold, Shirley Ross, John Trent, William Frawley; D: Richard Wallace; W: Theodore Reeves.

Blow 🎬🎬½ 2001 (R) Memorable, visually stunning, true story of cocaine entrepreneur George Jung features, at its best, stellar performances (especially from Reubens, Cruz, and Depp) and at its worst, a "Goodfellas" meets "Traffic" familiarity. Epic follows Jung (Depp) from his humble New England beginnings through his California surfer-bum days, to his rise and fall as America's biggest cocaine pipeline of the 70s and '80s without judging him or his lifestyle, although it does tend to sympathize with his family issues with mom, dad and his own child. 124m/C VHS, DVD. US Johnny Depp, Penelope Cruz, Jordi Molla, Franka Potente, Rachel Griffiths, Ray Liotta, Ethan Suplee, Pau (Pee-wee Herman) Reubens, Max Perlich, Clifford Curtis, Miguel (Michael) Sandoval, Kevin Gage, Jesse James, Dan Ferro, Emma Roberts, Bob(cat) Goldthwait, Jaime (James) King; D: Ted (Edward) Demme; W: David McKenna, Nick Cassavetes; C: Ellen Kuras; M: Graeme Revell.

Blow Dry 🎬🎬 2000 (R) Comedic possibilities and family healing ensue when the National British Hairdressing Championships come to a sleepy English town. An odd assortment of Brits and Yanks populate this familiar tale, and even dependable Rickman can't save the film, whose destination is obvious from even the newspaper ads—take "The Full Monty," replace strippers with hairdressers, and, voila. "Blow Dry." Written by Simon Beaufoy, author of (you guessed it) "The Full Monty." Director Breathnach fared better with his previous film, the Irish comedy "I Went Down." 91m/C VHS, DVD. GB US Alan Rickman, Natashe Richardson, Rachel Griffiths, Rachael Leigh Cook, Josh Hartnett, Bill Nighy, Warren Clarke, Rosemary Harris, Hugh Bonneville, Peter McDonald, Heidi Klum, Michael McElhatton; D: Paddy Breathnach; W: Simon Beaufoy; C: Cian de Buitlear; M: Patrick Doyle.

Bloody Wednesday 🎬🎬½ 1987 It's sanity check-out time when a hotel caretaker is driven mad by tormentors. Or is he driving himself mad? What is it about vacant hotels that make men lose their minds? If you can remove "The Shining" from yours, this flick's worthwhile. 89m/C VHS, DVD. Raymond Elmendorf, Pamela Baker, Navarre Perry; D: Mark Gilhuis; W: Philip Yordan; M: Albert Sendrey.

Bloom 🎬🎬 Blm 2003 (R) Rookie director Walsh's drab take of James Joyce's revered 1922 "Ulysses" lays out the events of Leopold Bloom's (Rea) daylong journey on June 16th, 1904 in Dublin as he deals with his wife Molly's (Ball) affair and serves as young poet Stephen's (O'Conor) mentor. 100m/C VHS, DVD. Stephen Rea, Angeline Ball, Hugh O'Conor, Neili Conroy, Alan Lucches, Maria Hayden, Mark Huberman, Kenneth McDonnell, Andrew McGibney, Dan Colley, Des Braiden, Donncha Crowley, Hogan, Luke Hayden, Julie Hale, Caoileann Murphy, Ciaran O'Brian, Dermot Moore, Maurice Shana-han, Seamus Welsh, Adam Fox Clarke; D: Sean Walsh; W: Sean Walsh; C: Ciaran Tanham; M: David Kahne. VIDEO

Blowback 🎬🎬 1999 (R) Police officer Don Morell (Van Peebles) witnesses the execution of serial killer Claude Whitman (Remar)—or does ha? Former jury members are being murdered and Morell finds cryptic bible messages at the scenes—a Whitman hallmark. So has the killer come back from the grave or has someone conspired to keep Whitman alive for their own purposes? 93m/C VHS, DVD. Mario Van Peebles, James Remar, Stephen Caffrey, David Groh; D: Mark L. Lester; W: Jeffrey Goldenberg, Bob Held, Randall Frakes; C: Jacques Haitkin; M: Sean Callery. CABLE

Blow-Up 🎬🎬🎬½ 1966 A young London photographer takes some pictures of a couple in the park and finds out he may have recorded evidence of a murder. Though marred by badly dated 1960s mod/siness, this is Antonioni's most accessible film, a sophisticated treatise on perception and the film-consumer-as-voyeur, brilliantly assembled and wrought. An intricate mystery and homage to spiracy with the evidence he has gathered. 111m/C VHS, DVD. GB IT David Hemmings, Vanessa Redgrave, Sarah Miles, Jane Birkin, Veruschka, Peter Bowles, John Castle, Gillian Hills, Julian Chagrin, Harry Hutchinson, The Yardbirds; D: Michelangelo Antonioni; W: Michelangelo Antonioni, Tonino Guerra; C: Carlo Di Palma; M: Herbie Hancock; Cannes '67: Film; Natl. Soc. Film Critics '66: Director (Antonioni), Film.

Blow Out 🎬🎬 1981 (R) When a prominent governor and presidential candidate is killed in a car crash, a sound effects engineer becomes involved in politics as he tries to expose a con-spiracy with the evidence he has gathered. 108m/C VHS, DVD. John Travolta, Nancy Allen, John Lithgow, Dennis Franz; D: Brian De Palma; W: Brian De Palma; C: Vilmos Zsigmond; M: Pino Donaggio.

Blowin' Smoke 🎬🎬 *Freak Talks About Sex* 1999 (R) Goofball stoner Freak (Zahn) lives his life in the ultimate slacker. His best bud (besides the pot) is the equally unambitious Dave (Hamilton), who does at least have a job. Dave also has an ex-girlfriend who wants to see him again, a sweet high schooler who has a crush on him, and a family who wishes he would do something with his life. Well, at least Dave has Freak to turn to in times of stress. Based on the novel by co-writer Galvin. 88m/C VHS, DVD. Steve Zahn, Josh Hamilton, Heather McComb, Arabella Field, David Krimay; D: Paul Todisco; W: Paul Todisco, Michael M.B. Galvin, Peter Speek; man; C: Douglas W. Shannon; M: Pete Shel.

Blowing Wild 🎬🎬½ 1954 Filmed in Mexico, this Quinn-Stanwyck-Cooper love triangle, set in the early thirties, speaks of lust and vengeance, rashness and greed. Stanwyck, married to oil tycoon Quinn, lusts after one-time love wildcatter Cooper. 92m/B VHS. Gary Cooper, Barbara Stanwyck, Anthony Quinn, Ruth Roman, Ward Bond; D: Hugo Fregonese; W: Philip Yordan.

Blown Away 🎬 1993 (R) Haim and Feldman are brothers working at a ski resort where Haim falls for rich teenager Eggert. She's a young femme fatale who manages to get Haim all hot and bothered but she's actually using the unsuspecting dupe in a murder plot. Also available in an unrated version at 93 minutes. 91m/C VHS, DVD. CA Nicole Eggert, Corey Haim, Corey Feldman, Jean LeClerc, Kathleen Robertson, Gary Farmer; D: Brenton Spencer; M: Paul Zaza.

Blown Away 🎬🎬 1996 (R) A mafia wife goes up against her husband in order to retrieve her kidnapped pot. 92m/C VHS. Lori Anderson, John Haard, James Naughton; D: Michael Miller.

Blown Away 🎬🎬 1994 (R) Boston Irish bomb-squad cop Jimmy Dove (Bridges) is after former compatriot Ryan Gaerity (Jones), an Irish radical who's tracked him in his bombing expertise onto Jimmy's

"Full Monty." Director Breathnach fared

new turf. Meanwhile, Jimmy wants to keep his unsavory past from unsuspecting wife Amis. While Jones seems adequately obsessed with making things go boom and Bridges significantly concerned that they don't, thriller moves on predictable path toward explosive climax. Special effects create the suspense, as everyday objects become lethal in Gaerity's knowledgeable hands. The final explosion was more than even the special effects coordinator desired—windows were unintentionally blown out in nearby buildings. **121m/C VHS, DVD.** Jeff Bridges, Tommy Lee Jones, Suzy Amis, Lloyd Bridges, Forest Whitaker; *D:* Stephen Hopkins; *W:* Joe Batteer, John Rice; *C:* Gregory McClatchy; *M:* Alan Silvestri.

Blue 🦴 1968 A dull western about an American boy (Stamp) raised by Mexicans who doesn't trust another living soul until he finds himself face to face with his former gang, led by his adoptive father (Montalban). **113m/C VHS, DVD.** Terence Stamp, Joanna Pettet, Karl Malden, Ricardo Montalban, Joe De Santis, Sally Kirkland; *D:* Silvio Narizzano; *W:* Ronald M. Cohen; *M:* Manos Hadjidakis.

Blue 🦴 1993 (R) Meditation/memoir of director Jarman's deteriorating AIDS condition consists of narration and a soundtrack set against an unvaried blue screen. Jarman ponders the associations with the color blue (sky, ocean, blindness, heaven, eternity) and his own physical problems, alternately expressed with dreamy vagueness or incendiary contempt. Limited in appeal, depending highly on boredom tolerance and ability to suspend visual expectations. **76m/C VHS.** *GB D:* Derek Jarman; *W:* Derek Jarman; *M:* Simon Fisher Turner; *Nar:* John Quentin, Nigel Terry, Tilda Swinton, Derek Jarman.

The Blue and the Gray 🦴🦴🦴 1982 Epic miniseries about love and hate inflamed by the Civil War. Keach plays a Pinkerton's secret service agent in this loosely based historical romance. Available in uncut and 295-minute versions. **381m/C VHS, DVD.** Gregory Peck, Lloyd Bridges, Colleen Dewhurst, Stacy Keach, John Hammond, Sterling Hayden, Warren Oates; *D:* Andrew V. McLaglen; *M:* Bruce Broughton. TV

The Blue Angel 🦴🦴🦴🦴 *Der Blaue Engel* 1930 Tale of a man stripped of his dignity. A film classic filled with sensuality and decay, which made Dietrich a European star and led to her discovery in Hollywood. When a repressed professor (Jannings) goes to a nightclub hoping to catch some of his students in the wrong, he's taken by Lola, the sultry singer portrayed by Dietrich. After spending the night with her, losing his job, and then marrying her, he goes on tour with the troupe, peddling indiscreet photos of his wife. Versions were shot in both German and English, with the German version sporting English subtitles. ♪Falling in Love Again; They Call Me Wicked Lola. **90m/B VHS, DVD.** *GE* Marlene Dietrich, Emil Jannings, Kurt Gerron, Rosa Valetti, Hans Albers; *D:* Josef von Sternberg; *W:* Robert Liebmann, Carl Zuckmayer; *M:* Frederick "Friedrich" Hollander.

The Blue Bird 🦴🦴🦴 1940 (G) A weird, dark fantasy about two children who search for the blue bird of happiness in various fantasy lands, but find it eventually at home. Overlooked and impressively fatalistic. **98m/C VHS.** Shirley Temple, Gale Sondergaard, Jessie Ralph, Spring Byington, Sybil Jason; *D:* Walter Lang; *C:* Arthur C. Miller.

Blue Blazes Rawden 🦴🦴 1918 Hart plays a lumberjack who gains control of a local saloon after shooting its villainous proprietor. **65m/B VHS.** William S. Hart, Robert McKim, Maud(e) (Ford) George, Jack Hoxie; *D:* William S. Hart.

Blue Blood 🦴 1973 A demonic butler inflicts nightmares upon a family to gain possession of its mansion. **90m/C VHS.** *GB* Oliver Reed, Derek Jacobi, Fiona Lewis; *D:* Andrew Sinclair.

The Blue Butterfly 🦴🦴 2004 (PG) Based on a true story. Pete Carlton (Donato) is 10 and dying. His one wish is to capture the rare blue morpho butterfly. World-weary entomologist Alan Osborne (Hurt) is persuaded by Pete's mother, Teresa (Bussieres), to let them accompany his expedition into the rain forest of Costa Rica. Beautiful scenery but an overly-sappy saga. **97m/C DVD.** *CA* William Hurt, Marc Donato, Pascale Bussieres, Steve Adams; *D:* Lea Pool; *W:* Pete McCormack; *C:* Michel Arcand; *M:* Stephen Endelman.

Blue Canadian Rockies 🦴½ 1952 Autry's employer sends him to Canada to discourage his daughter from marrying a fortune hunter. The daughter has turned the place into a dude ranch and wild game preserve. When Autry arrives, he encounters some mysterious killings. **58m/B VHS, DVD.** Gene Autry, Pat Buttram, Gail Davis, Ross Ford, Tom London; *D:* George Archainbaud.

Blue Car 🦴🦴🦴 2003 (R) Impressive directorial debut by Moncrieff tells the story of troubled teen Meg (Bruckner) and her sad, beaten-down English teacher Mr. Auster (Strathairn). Meg's life has been turned upside down with the divorce of her parents. Her mother is distant and overworked, and her sister (Arnold, in an excellent performance) is self-destructive. When she finds solace in teacher, Auster recognizes and encourages her talent, which leads to an awkwardly closer relationship, skulkingly engineered by the teacher. Excellent script and direction, as well as stellar performances by Bruckner and Strathairn, allow the film to explore the situation without exploiting or judging. The characters are well-rounded and real, as is the dialogue, which makes the unfolding events that much more disturbing. **96m/C VHS, DVD.** *US* Agnes Bruckner, David Strathairn, Margaret Colin, Regan Arnold, Frances Fisher, A.J. Buckley, Sarah Beuhler; *D:* Karen Moncrieff; *W:* Karen Moncrieff; *C:* Rob Sweeney; *M:* Stuart Spencer-Nash.

Blue Chips 🦴🦴½ 1994 (PG-13) Nolte does Bobby Knight in this saga of Western U basketball coach Pete Bell, suffering through his first losing season. What follows is a tug of war between rich alumni who want to win at any cost and his ethics as he recruits for a new season. Larger than life hoopster O'Neal's film debut. McDonnell and Woodard are merely afterthoughts, but baller for cameos from many real life b-ballers, including Dick Vitale and Larry Bird. Average script is bolstered by exciting game footage, shot during real games for authenticity. **108m/C VHS, DVD.** Nick Nolte, Shaquille O'Neal, Mary McDonnell, Ed O'Neill, J.T. Walsh, Alfre Woodard; *Cameos:* Larry Bird, Bobby Knight, Rick Pitino; *D:* William Friedkin; *W:* Ron Shelton; *M:* Nile Rodgers, Jeff Beck, Jed Leiber.

Blue City 🦴½ 1986 (R) A young man returns to his Florida hometown to find his father murdered, and subsequently vows to solve and avenge the matter. Based on a Ross MacDonald thriller. **83m/C VHS.** Judd Nelson, Ally Sheedy, Paul Winfield, Anita Morris, David Caruso, Julie Carmen, Scott Wilson; *D:* Michelle Manning; *W:* Walter Hill, Lukas Heller; *M:* Ry Cooder.

Blue Collar 🦴🦴🦴 1978 (R) Funnyman Pryor (in one of his best film roles) offers most of the laughs in this very serious drama of how three Detroit auto assembly workers (Pryor, Kotto, and Keitel), feeling the strain of family life and inflation, hatch a plan to rob their corrupt union office only to stumble into a bigger crime that latter costs them dearly. Schrader makes his directorial debut in this searing study of the working class and the robbing of the human spirit, which is made memorable by the strong performances of its three leads. Filmed entirely in Detroit and Kalamazoo, Michigan. **114m/C VHS, DVD.** Richard Pryor, Harvey Keitel, Yaphet Kotto, Ed Begley Jr., Lane Smith, Cliff DeYoung; *D:* Paul Schrader; *W:* Paul Schrader, Leonard Schrader; *C:* Bobby Byrne; *M:* Jack Nitzsche.

Blue Country 🦴🦴🦴 *Le Pays Bleu* 1977 (PG) A joyful romantic comedy about a pair of free souls who leave their stagnant lives behind to seek out a more idyllic existence. Subtitled in English. **104m/C VHS.** *FR* Brigitte Fossey, Jacques Serres, Ginette Garcin, Armand Meffre, Ginette Mathieu, Roger Crouzet; *D:* Jean-Charles Tacchella; *W:* Jean-Charles Tacchella; *C:* Edmond Sechan; *M:* Gerard Antosso.

Blue Crush 🦴🦴🦴 2002 (PG-13) Director John Stockwell brings back the beach/surfing genre with a story about board riding women who would kick Gidget's narrow behind. Surfer girl Anne Marie (Bosworth) moves to Hawaii, determined to win the traditionally all-male Rip Masters competition. Aided by fellow surfers Eden (Rodriguez) and Lena (Lake), she tries to mentally recover from a near-fatal accident in time for the meet. Unfortunately, the distraction of new boyfriend Matt (Davis) may cause her dreams to wipe out. Both the ripped bodies and the surfing action seem a little enhanced by science, but both are very visually stimulating. **104m/C VHS, DVD.** *US* Kate (Catherine) Bosworth, Michelle Rodriguez, Matthew Davis, Sanoe Lake, Mika Boorem, Faizon Love, Chris Taloa, Kala Alexander; *D:* John Stockwell; *W:* John Stockwell, Elizabeth Weiss; *C:* David Hennings; *M:* Paul Haslinger.

The Blue Dahlia 🦴🦴🦴½ 1946 Classic film noir finds Navy vet Johnny Morrison (Ladd) returning home to discover his wife Helen (Dowling) has been keeping the home fires burning—with Eddie Harwood (Da Silva), owner of the Blue Dahlia nightclub. After a nasty fight, Johnny takes off and is picked up by sultry blonde Joyce (Lake). The next day Johnny discovers he's wanted by the cops for the murder of his wife and decides to hide out until he can find the real killer, with Joyce's help. Very stylish and fast-paced with excellent performances; Chandler's first original screenplay. **100m/B VHS.** Alan Ladd, Veronica Lake, William Bendix, Howard da Silva, Doris Dowling, Tom Powers, Hugh Beaumont, Howard Freeman, Don Costello; *D:* George Marshall; *W:* Raymond Chandler; *C:* Lionel London; *M:* Victor Young.

Blue De Ville 🦴🦴 1986 (PG) Two young women buy a '59 Cadillac and journey from St. Louis to New Mexico, having adventures on the way. The rambling, free-spirited movie was a pilot for a prospective series that never set sail—but when "Thelma & Louise" hit big this superficially similar item was hauled out on video. **96m/C VHS.** Jennifer Runyon, Kimberly Pistone, Mark Thomas Miller, Alan Autry, Robert Prescott; *D:* Jim Johnston. TV

Blue Desert 🦴🦴 1991 (R) Cox is strong in her performance as Lisa Roberts, a comic book artist who leaves New York City for small town Arizona life after surviving a traumatic rape. Once there, she's befriended by Sheffer and Sweeney, a local cop. Battersby does a good job of keeping the suspense level high (in his directorial debut) as Cox finds that there's danger in small towns, too. Fine performances keep this slightly above average. **98m/C VHS, DVD.** D.B. Sweeney, Courteney Cox, Craig Sheffer, Philip Baker Hall, Sandy Ward; *D:* Bradley Battersby; *W:* Bradley Battersby, Arthur Collis; *M:* Jerry Goldsmith.

Blue Fin 🦴🦴 1978 (PG) When their tuna boat is shipwrecked, and the crew disabled, a young boy and his father learn lessons of love and courage as the son tries to save the ship. **93m/C VHS, DVD.** *AU* Hardy Kruger, Greg Rowe; *D:* Carl Schultz; *C:* Geoff Burton.

Blue Fire Lady 🦴🦴 1978 The heartwarming story of a young girl and her love of horses which endures even her father's disapproval. Good family fare. **96m/C VHS.** *AU* Cathryn Harrison, Mark Holden, Peter Cummins, Marion Edward, Arne Sutherland, Garry Waddell, John Wood, John Ewart; *D:* Ross Dimsey; *C:* Vincent Monton; *M:* Mike Brady.

Blue Flame 🦴🦴 1993 (R) Vigilante cop is hired to track down two humanoid aliens who have escaped captivity in futuristic L.A. They evade him by time-traveling through alternate realities, infiltrating the cop's mind, and using his fantasies against him. **88m/C VHS, DVD.** Brian Wimmer, Ian Buchanan, Kerri Green, Cecilia Peck, Jad Mager; *D:* Cassian Elwes; *W:* Cassian Elwes.

The Blue Gardenia 🦴🦴🦴 1953 Seminal but rarely seen film noir. Norah Larkin (Baxter) wakes up one morning in the apartment of womanizing lout Harry Prebble (Burr). He's dead and she's labeled "The Blue Gardenia" murderess by newspaper columnist Casey Mayo (Conte). Required viewing for fans of vintage mysteries. **88m/B DVD.** Anne Baxter, Richard Conte, Ann Sothern, Raymond Burr, George Reeves, Nat King Cole, Jeff Donnell, Richard Erdman, Ray Walker, Ruth Storey; *D:* Fritz Lang; *W:* Charles Hoffman; *C:* Nicholas Musuraca; *M:* Raoul Kraushaar.

Blue Hawaii 🦴🦴 1962 (PG) A soldier, returning to his Hawaiian home, defies his parents by taking a job with a tourist agency. Presley sings "Can't Help Falling in Love." For Elvis fans. **101m/C VHS, DVD.** Pam(ela) Austin, Elvis Presley, Angela Lansbury, Joan Blackman, Roland Winters, Iris Adrian, John Archer, Steve Brodie; *D:* Norman Taurog; *W:* Hal Kanter.

Blue Heaven 🦴 1984 A couple struggles through problems with their marriage and alcohol abuse. **100m/C VHS.** Leslie Denniston, James Eckhouse; *D:* Kathleen Dowdey.

The Blue Hour 🦴🦴 1991 Theo is a Berlin hustler whose business is so good he can pick his clients. Marie, his next-door neighbor, lives with her boyfriend Paul until he just walks out one day. Marie is shattered and refuses to leave her apartment until Theo takes an interest in her plight. Just when it seems that the improbable couple could find true love, Paul comes back to Marie. In German with English subtitles. **87m/C VHS, DVD.** *GE* Andreas Herdler, Dina Leipzig, Cyrill Rey-Coquais; *D:* Marcel Gisler.

Blue Ice 🦴🦴½ 1992 (R) Harry Anders (Caine) is an ex-spy with an eye for the ladies and a loyalty to his friends. When his friends start winding up dead, Harry decides to investigate—a very dangerous decision, especially when a mysterious woman (Young) takes an interest. **96m/C VHS, DVD.** Michael Caine, Sean Young, Ian Bannen, Bob Hoskins; *D:* Russell Mulcahy; *W:* Ron Hutchinson; *M:* Michael Kamen. CABLE

Blue Iguana 🦴🦴 1988 (R) An inept bounty hunter travels south of the border to recover millions from a crooked South American bank, and meets up with sexy women, murderous thugs, and corruption. **88m/C VHS, DVD.** Dylan McDermott, Jessica Harper, James Russo, Dean Stockwell, Pamela Gidley, Tovah Feldshuh; *D:* John Lafia.

Blue in the Face 🦴🦴 1995 (R) Wang and Auster's immediate follow-up to "Smoke," shot in five days, recycles the same Brooklyn cigar shop setting and contains a dozen fast-paced, loosely scripted or wholly improvised scenes that they couldn't cram into "Smoke," led by 'Reed's deadpan riff on eyewear, New York, and smoking. The action again centers around Auggie (Keitel), the shop manager, who hangs out with the mostly eccentric, and sometimes famous clientele. Jarmusch idly waxes philosophic on smoking technique, while puffing on what he claims is his last. Scenes are woven together with videotaped interviews from actual Brooklyn residents, creating a tribute to life in the borough with a documentary feel. Improv lovers will enjoy watching what sometimes seems more like outtakes than finished performances. **83m/C VHS, DVD.** Harvey Keitel, Lou Reed, Michael J. Fox, Roseanne, Jim Jarmusch, Lily Tomlin, Mel Gorham, Jared Harris, Giancarlo Esposito, Victor Argo, Madonna, Keith David, Mira Sorvino, Malik Yoba, Michael Badalucco, Jose Zuniga, Stephen Gevedon, John Lurie, Sharif Rashed, RuPaul Charles; *D:* Wayne Wang, Paul Auster; *W:* Wayne Wang, Paul Auster.

Blue Jeans 🦴🦴½ 1978 A young French boy experiences sexual awakening and humiliation in a British school. In French with English subtitles. **80m/C VHS.** *FR* Gilles Budin, Michel Gibet, Daniel Very, Thierry Dolon; *D:* Hugues des Roziers; *W:* Hugues des Roziers; *C:* Jacques Assuerus; *M:* David MacNeil.

Blue Jeans and Dynamite 🦴🦴½ 1976 A stuntman is hired to lift the "Golden Mask of the Duct Tomb" and is followed on land, water, and air. Great chase scenes and action-filled finale. **90m/C VHS.** Robert Vaughn, Simon Andreu, Katia Kristine; *D:* Gordon Hessler; *W:* Jose

Maesso, Ricardo Ferrer. **C:** Julio Bragado; **M:** Adolfo Waitzran.

Blue Juice ♂♂½ 1995 (R) Early work from several young actors who've gone on to bigger things. Billed as Britain's first su♂f picture, this comedy follows the escapades of nearly 30 JC (Pertwee), a local hero of the Cornish surfing community who can't commit to his more practical girlfriend Chloe (Zeta-Jones). Then some of JC's London buddies, Dean (McGregor), Josh (Mackintosh), and Terry (Gunn), show up for a sort of last hurrah against the boredom of acting like adults. **90m/C VHS, DVD. GB** Sean Pertwee, Catherine Zeta-Jones, Ewan McGregor, Steven Mackintosh, Peter Gunn, Heathcote Williams; **D:** Carl Prechezer; **W:** Carl Prechezer, Peter Salmi; **C:** Richard Greatrex; **M:** Simon Davison.

The Blue Kite ♂♂♂ 1993 Fifteen years of political and cultural upheaval in China is shown through the eyes of young troublemaker Tietou, who certainly earns his nickname of "Iron Head" after his 1954 birth. Soon his father is sent to a labor reform camp and his mother remarries—only to be faced with more struggles as the years go by. As the kite is Tietou's cherished toy, which keeps getting lost or destroyed but is always being rebuilt, offering one token of hope. Chinese with subtitles. 138m/C VHS, DVD. **CH** Liping Lu, Zheng Wenyao, Pu Quanxin; **D:** Tian Zhuangzhuang; **W:** Xiao Mao; **C:** Yong Hou; **M:** Yoshihide Otomo.

The Blue Knight ♂♂½ 1975 Zhang with subtitles. Lan Fang comedic caper film about a wild, man, who gives birth to a huge insect larva.

The Blue Lagoon WOOF! 1980 (R) Useless remake of 1949 film of the same name. An adolescent boy and girl marooned on a desert isle discover love (read: sex) without the restraints of society. Not too explicit, but nonetheless intellectually offensive. Gorgeous photography of island paradise is wasted on this palatable offering. Led to the long-running sequel. 105m/C VHS, DVD. Brooke Shields, Christopher Atkins, Leo McKern, William Daniels; **D:** Randal Kleiser; **W:** Douglas Day Stewart; **C:** Nestor Almendros; **M:** Basil Poledouris. Golden Raspberries '80: Worst Actress (Shields).

The Blue Lamp ♂♂♂ 1949 Action-adventure fans familiar with the hoary plot where a cop must avenge the wrongful death of his partner will appreciate this suspenseful British detective effort. It's one of the very first in the genre to explore buddy cop revenge in a very British sort of way. Also sports a concluding chase scene which has stood the test of time. 84m/B VHS. **GB** Dirk Bogarde, Jimmy Hanley, Jack Warner, Bernard Lee, Robert Flemyng, Patric Doonan, Bruce Seton, Frederick Piper, Betty Ann Davies, Peggy Evans; **D:** Basil Dearden, British Acad. '50: Film.

The Blue Light ♂♂♂ 1932 Fairy-tale love story, based on an Italian table about a mysterious woman, thought to be a witch, and a painter. Riefenstahl's first film which brought her to the attention of Adolf Hitler, who requested she make films glorifying the Nazi Party. In German with English subtitles. 77m/B VHS. **GE** Leni Riefenstahl, Mathias Wieman, Max Holsboer; **D:** Leni Riefenstahl; **W:** Bela Balazs, Leni Riefenstahl; **C:** Hans Schneeberger; **M:** Giuseppe Becce.

The Blue Lightning ♂♂½ 1966 During WWI a young German, fresh out of aviation training school, competes for the coveted "Blue Max" flying award with other members of a squadron of seasoned flyers from aristocratic backgrounds.

Based on a novel by Jack D. Hunter. 155m/C VHS, DVD. George Peppard, James Mason, Ursula Andress, Jeremy Kemp, Karl Michael Vogler, Anton Diffring, Harry Towb, Peter Woodthorpe, Derek Newark, Derren Nesbitt, Loni von Friedl; **D:** John Guillermin; **W:** Ben Barzman, Basilio Franchina, David Pursall, Jack Seddon, Gerald Hanley; **C:** Douglas Slocombe; **M:** Jerry Goldsmith.

Blue Money ♂♂♂ 1984 A mystery-con alien plant impregnates a man who absconds with a briefcase packed with cash and is pursued by everyone, even the I.R.A. 82m/C VHS, **GB** Tim Curry, Debby Bishop, Billy Connolly, Frances Tomelty; **D:** Colin Bucksey; **TV**

Blue Monkey ♂ 1987 Green Monkey (R) A mysterious alien plant impregnates a man, who gives birth to a huge, man-eating insect larva. It subsequently grows up into a giant bug, and roams around in a quarantined hospital looking for patients to eat. What made you think if had anything to do with monkeys? 97m/C VHS. Steve Railsback, Susan Anspach, Gwynyth Walsh, John Vernon, Joe Flaherty; **D:** William Fruet.

Blue Movies WOOF! 1988 (R) A couple of jerks try their hand at making porn films with predictable results. 92m/C VHS. Larry Linville, Lucinda Crosby, Steve Levitt, Darien Calla, Russell Johnson; **D:** Paul Koval, Ed Fitzgerald.

Blue Moon ♂♂½ 2000 (PG-13) Married couple Gazzara and Moreno take a trip to the Catskills and wish on the blue moon which, according to legend, will grant them a wish. Of course, exactly how that wish will come true may not be what they expect. 90m/C VHS, DVD. Ben Gazzara, Rita Moreno, Alanna Ubach, Brian Vincent, Heather Matarazzo, Vincent Pastore, Burt Young, Victor Argo, Lillo Brancato; **D:** John A. Gallagher, **W:** John A. Gallagher, Steve Endelman.

Blue Murder at St. Trinian's ♂♂ 1956 The second of the madcap British comedy series (based on cartoons by Ronald Searle) about an incredibly ferocious pack of schoolgirls. This time they travel to the European continent and make life miserable for a jewel thief. Highlight: fantasy sequence in ancient Rome showing the girls thrown to the lions—and scaring the lions. 86m/B VHS. **GB** Joyce Grenfell, Terry-Thomas, George Cole, Alastair Sim, Lionel Jeffries, Thorley Walters; **D:** Frank Launder; **M:** Malcolm Arnold.

Blue Ridge Fall ♂♂ 1999 (R) In the small town of Jefferson Creek, North Carolina, Danny (Facinelli) is the star high school quarterback who can do no wrong. He's befriended simple-minded Aaron (Eastman), who is driven to violent desperation by his abusive father. Danny enlists his buddies to cover up Aaron's crime but their plans quickly go wrong and things just get more desperate for them all. 99m/C VHS, DVD. Peter Facinelli, Rodney Eastman, Will Estes, Jay R. Ferguson, Tom Arnold, Amy Irving, Chris Isaak, Brent Jennings, Heather Stephens, Gavin Funches; **D:** James Rowe; **W:** James Rowe; **C:** Chris Walling; **M:** Greg Edmonson.

Blue River ♂♂½ 1995 (PG-13) Flashbacks highlight this saga of a troubled family. Successful doctor Edward Sellers (McDonough) is dismayed when his derelict older brother Lawrence (O'Connell), whom he hasn't seen in 15 years, suddenly appears on his doorstep. A gifted teenager, Lawrence once built his world around science and logic after their father deserted the family but his only purpose turns out to be getting even with everyone he feels has betrayed him. Young Edward (Stahl) tried to the "good" son while Mom (Dey) retreated into religion and an affair with self-righteous, nasty school principal Henry Howland (Elliott). TV adaptation of the novel by Ethan Canin. 90m/C VHS, DVD. Jerry O'Connell, Nick Stahl, Susan Dey, Sam Elliott, Neal McDonough, Jean Marie Barnwell, Patrick Renna; **D:** Larry Elikann; **W:** Maria Nation; **C:** Eric Van Haren Noman; **M:** Lawrence Shragge.

Blue Skies ♂♂♂ 1946 Former dancer turned radio personality Astaire flashes back to his friendship with singer Crosby and the gal (Caulfield) that came

between them. Flimsy plot is just an excuse for some 20 Irving Berlin songs and Astaire's split-screen dance number, "Putin' on the Ritz." "All By Myself; Always; Any Bonds Today?; Blue Skies; A Couple of Song and Dance Men; Everybody Step; Getting Nowhere; Heat Wave; I'll See You in C-U-B-A. 104m/C VHS, DVD. Fred Astaire, Bing Crosby, Joan Caulfield, Billy DeWolfe, Olga San Juan, Frank Faylen; **D:** Stuart Heisler; **W:** Arthur Sheekman; **C:** Charles Lang Jr.

Blue Skies Again ♂♂♂ 1983 (PG) Spunky young woman determined to play major league baseball locks horns with the chauvinistic owner and the gruff manager of her favorite team. 91m/C VHS, Robyn Barto, Harry Hamlin, Mimi Rogers, Kenneth McMillan, Dana Elcar, Andy Garcia; **D:** Richard Michaels.

Blue Sky ♂♂♂ 1991 (PG-13) Carly Marshall (Lange) is an irrepressible beauty, long married to adoring but uptight military scientist Hank (Jones). Things are barely in control when they're stationed in Hawaii but after Hank's transfer to a backwater base in Alabama, Carly's emotional mood swings go wildly out of control. Hell breaks loose when Carly attracts the attention of the camp's commander (Boothe), who's only too willing to take advantage. Set in 1962, a nuclear radiation subplot (Hank's new project) proves a minor distraction. Exceptional performance by Lange along with Jones providing a quiet counterpoint as a man still deeply in love with his disturbed wife. Director Richardson's final film. Release date was delayed to 1994 due to studio Orion's financial problems. 101m/C VHS, DVD. Jessica Lange, Tommy Lee Jones, Powers Boothe, Carrie Snodgress, Amy Locane, Chris O'Donnell, Mitchell Ryan, Dale Dye, Richard Jenkins; **D:** Tony Richardson; **W:** Arlene Sarner, Jerry Leichtling, Rama Laurie Stagner; **C:** Steve Yaconelli; **M:** Jack Nitzsche. Oscars '94: Actress (Lange); Golden Globes '95: Actress—Drama (Lange); L.A. Film Critics '94: Actress (Lange).

Blue Smoke ♂♂½ Nora Roberts Blue Smoke 2007 After her family's pizzeria is destroyed by fire when she's 11, Reena grows up to become an arson investigator. A neighborhood reunion leads her to romance with carpenter Bo, but Reena soon discovers that the fire is following her. Seems an arsonist is targeting everything—and everyone—she holds dear. Lifetime original movie based on the novel by Nora Roberts. 90m/C DVD. Alicia Witt, Matthew Settle, Scott Bakula, Talia Shire, John Henry Reardon, Eric Keenleyside, Chris Fassbender, Ben Ayres; **D:** David Carson; **W:** Ronni Kern; **C:** Nikos Evdemon, Stuart M. Thomas.
CABLE

Blue State ♂ 2007 (R) Fervently liberal John (Meyer) drunkenly proclaims that he'll move to Canada if Dubya is elected POTUS and then feels he must follow through. He finds a green card marriage website and decides to travel to Winnipeg. Needing someone to share the driving, John meets secretive Chloe (Paquin) who has her own reasons for leaving the country. Tends toward one-sided diatribes and its views on Canadians vs. Americans are stereotypical and condescending. 99m/C DVD. Breckin Meyer, Anna Paquin, Richard Backburn, Adriana O'Neil, Joyce Krenz; **D:** Marshall Lewy; **W:** Marshall Lewy; **C:** Phil Parmet; **M:** Nathan Johnson.

Blue Steel ♂♂ 1934 A young Wayne saves a town from financial ruin by leading the citizens to a gold strike. 59m/B VHS, DVD. John Wayne, George "Gabby" Hayes; **D:** Robert North Bradbury.

Blue Steel ♂ 1990 (R) Director Bigelow's much-heralded, proto-feminist cop thriller. A serious female rookie's gun falls into the hands of a Wall Street psycho who begins a killing spree. Action film made silly with over-anxious sub-text and patriarchy-directed rage. 102m/C VHS, DVD. Jamie Lee Curtis, Ron Silver, Clancy Brown, Louise Fletcher, Philip Bosco, Elizabeth Pena, Tom Sizemore; **D:** Kathryn Bigelow; **W:** Kathryn Bigelow, Eric Red; **M:** Brad Fiedel.

Blue Streak ♂♂ 1999 (PG-13) Only hardcore Martin Lawrence fans will enjoy this formulaic buddy-cop-with-a-twist action comedy. Lawrence plays jewel thief

Miles Logan, who hides a gem from his latest heist at a construction site just before he's caught. Three years later and out of jail, Logan tries to retrieve his diamond only to discover the site is now a police station. While impersonating a detective in order to sneak in and grab the stash, he accidentally catches an escaping felon and is forced to continue the charade. Now he's saddled with rookie partner Carlson (Wilson) and begins using his criminal knowledge to catch other crooks, including old crony Tulley (Chappelle). Lawrence gives a good effort but all of his frantic mugging can't save the lame material he's forced to work with. "Beverly Hills Cop." feel like a poor man's. 94m/C VHS, DVD. Martin Lawrence, Luke Wilson, Peter Greene, Dave Chappelle, William Forsythe, Graham Beckel, Tamala Jones, Nicole Ari Parker, Olek Krupa, Anne Marie Howard; **D:** Les Mayfield; **W:** Stephen Carpenter, Michael Berry, John Blumenthal; **C:** David Eggby.

Blue Sunshine ♂♂½ 1978 (R) A certain brand of L.S.D. called Blue Sunshine starts to make its victims go insane when it starts to make its victims go insane. 94m/C VHS, DVD. Zalman King, Deborah Winters, Mark Goddard, Robert Walden, Charles Siebert, Ann Cooper, Ray Young, Alice Ghostley, Richard Crystal, Bill Adler, Stefan Gierasch, Brion James; **D:** Jeff Lieberman; **W:** Jeff Lieberman; **M:** Charles Gross.

Blue Thunder ♂♂½ 1983 (R) Police helicopter pilot Scheider is the test an experimental high-tech chopper that can see through walls, record a whisper, and level a city block. Seems anti-terrorist supercopter is needed to ensure security during 1984 Olympics. Bothered by Vietnam flashbacks Scheider then battles High-techy police drama with satisfying aerial combat scenes nearly crashes with story line. 110m/C VHS, DVD. Roy Scheider, Daniel Stern, Malcolm McDowell, Candy Clark, Warren Oates; **D:** John Badham; **W:** Dan O'Bannon, Don Jakoby; **C:** John A. Alonzo.

Blue Tiger ♂♂ 1994 (R) Gina Hayes is shopping with her young son when a masked gunman enters the store and opens fire. When Gina realizes her son has been killed she becomes obsessed with finding the assailant. Her one clue—a blue tiger tattoo. 88m/C VHS, DVD. Virginia Madsen, Toru Nakamura, Harry Dean Stanton, Ryo Ishibashi; **D:** Norberto Barba; **W:** Joel Soisson.

Blue Velvet ♂♂♂ 1986 (R) Disturbing, unique exploration of the dark side of American suburbia, involving an innocent college youth who discovers a severed ear in an empty lot, and is thrust into a turmoil of depravity, murder, and sexual deviance. Brutal, grotesque, and unmistakably Lynch; an immaculately made, fiercely imagined film that is unlike any other. Mood is enhanced by the Badalamenti soundtrack. Graced by splashes of Lynchian humor, most notably the movie's lumber theme. Hopper is riveting as the chief sadistic nutcase and Twin Peaks' MacLachlan is a study in loss of innocence. 121m/C VHS, DVD. Kyle MacLachlan, Isabella Rossellini, Dennis Hopper, Laura Dern, Hope Lange, Jack Nance, Dean Stockwell, George Dickerson, Brad Dourif, Priscilla Pointer, Angelo Badalamenti; **D:** David Lynch; **W:** David Lynch; **C:** Frederick Elmes; **M:** Angelo Badalamenti. Ind. Spirit '87: Actress (Rossellini); L.A. Film Critics '86: Director (Lynch), Support. Actor (Hopper); Montreal World Film Fest. '86: Support. Actor (Hopper); Nat. Soc. Film Critics '86: Cinematog., Director (Lynch); Film, Support. Actor (Hopper). *

Blue Tornado ♂ 1990 (PG-13) An eerie bright light, emitted from a mountain, makes supersonic jets disappear into thin air. A beautiful researcher and a cocky pilot set out to solve the mystery. Better-than-average aerial sequences don't make up for goofy story and ludicrous dialogue. 96m/C VHS. Dirk Benedict, Patsy Kensit, Ted McGinley, David Warner; **D:** Tony B. Dobb.

Blue, White and Perfect ♂ 1942 Shayne (Nolan) promises his marriage-minded girlfriend Merle (Hughes) that he'll leave the PI business behind and get a steady wartime job. Only the shamus soon finds himself mixed-up in the smuggling of industrial diamonds that has Shayne taking an ocean liner to Hawaii and discovering espionage and Nazis aboard ship. **74m/B DVD.** Lloyd Nolan; Mary Beth Hughes; George Reeves; Steven Geray; Helen Reynolds; Henry Victor; Curt Bois; Mae Marsh; Arthur Loft; **D:** Herbert I. Leeds; **W:** Samuel G. Engel; **C:** Glen MacWilliams.

The Blue Yonder 🐾🐾½ *Time Flyers* 1986 In this made-for-video feature, a young boy travels back in time to meet the grandfather he never knew, risking historical integrity. **88m/C VHS.** Art Carney, Peter Coyote, Huckleberry Fox; **D:** Mark Rosman.

Bluebeard 🐾🐾½ 1944 Tormented painter with a psychopathic urge to strangle his models is the basis for this effective, low-budget film. One of Carradine's best vehicles. **73m/B VHS, DVD.** John Carradine, Jean Parker, Nils Asther; **D:** Edgar G. Ulmer; **W:** Pierre Gendron; **C:** Jock Feindel.

Bluebeard 🐾🐾🐾 *Landru* 1963 French biography of Henri-Desire Landru, who seduced and murdered 11 women and was subsequently beheaded. Dubbed into English. **108m/C VHS.** *FR* Charles Denner, Danielle Darrieux, Michele Morgan, Hildegarde Knef; **D:** Claude Chabrol.

Bluebeard's Eighth Wife 🐾🐾 1938 Problematic comedy set on the French Riviera about a spoiled millionaire (Cooper) who's been married seven times and wants to go for eight with Colbert, the daughter of a destitute aristocrat. Good for a few laughs, but Coop seemed out of place in his role. Based on the play by Alfred Savoir. American version by Charlton Andrews. **86m/B VHS.** Claudette Colbert, Gary Cooper, David Niven, Edward Everett Horton, Elizabeth Patterson, Herman Bing, William Hymer, Franklin Pangborn; **D:** Ernst Lubitsch; **W:** Charles Brackett, Billy Wilder; **C:** Leo Tover; **M:** Werner R. Heymann, Frederick "Friedrich" Hollander.

Blueberry Hill 🐾🐾½ 1988 (R) While her mother struggles with the grief over husband's death, a young girl in a small town learns about life, music, and her late father from a jazz singer. Good soundtrack. **93m/C VHS.** Jennifer Rubin, Carrie Snodgress, Margaret Avery; **D:** Strathford Hamilton.

The Blues Brothers 🐾🐾🐾 1980 (R) As an excuse to run rampant on the city of Chicago, Jake (Belushi) and Elwood (Aykroyd) Blues attempt to raise $5,000 for their childhood orphanage by putting their old band back together. Good music, quotable dialogue, lots of wrecked cars, plenty of cameos. A classic. **133m/C VHS, DVD.** Murphy Dunne, John Belushi, Dan Aykroyd, James Brown, Cab Calloway, Ray Charles, Henry Gibson, Aretha Franklin, Carrie Fisher, John Candy, Kathleen Freeman, Steven Williams, Charles Napier, Stephen Bishop; **Cameos:** Frank Oz, Steven Spielberg, Twiggy, Paul (Pee-wee Herman) Reubens, Steve Lawrence, John Lee Hooker, John Landis, Chaka Khan; **D:** John Landis; **W:** John Landis, Dan Aykroyd; **C:** Stephen M. Katz; **M:** Ira Newborn, Elmer Bernstein.

Blues Brothers 2000 🐾🐾 1998 (PG-13) Eighteen years after the original caper, Landis, Aykroyd, and most of the original cast return to the scene of the crime. Jake's died but Elwood's (Aykroyd) still around. He gets the band back together, recruits a Blues cousin (Goodman), a half-foster-brother (Morton), and an orphan (Bonifant) in need of mentoring, and heads for a battle of the bands between New Orleans and Chicago. The music, performed by the original Blues Brothers Band as well as a rock and blues all-star lineup, is the highlight. As for the rest of the flick, watch the original instead. Did Aykroyd learn nothing from "Caddyshack 2"? **123m/C VHS, DVD.** Paul Shaffer, Murphy Dunne, Dan Aykroyd, John Goodman, Joe Morton, Evan Bonifant, Nia Peeples, Kathleen Freeman, Frank Oz, Steve Lawrence, Aretha Franklin, B.B. King, James Brown, Erykah Badu, Darrell Hammond; **D:** John Landis; **W:** John Landis, Dan Aykroyd; **C:** David Herrington; **M:** Paul Shaffer.

Blues Busters 🐾🐾½ 1950 Another entry in the "Bowery Boys" series. When Sach emerges from a tonsillectomy with the velvety voice of a crooner, Slip cashes in by turning Louie's Sweet Shop into a nightclub, the better to showcase his buddy's talents. Sach's singing voice provided by John Lorenz. **68m/B VHS.** Leo Gorcey, Huntz Hall, Adele Jergens, Gabriel Dell, Craig Stevens, Phyllis Coates, Bernard Gorcey, David Gorcey; **D:** William Beaudine.

Bluffing It 🐾🐾 1987 TV movie about an older man who has been disguising his illiteracy for years. **120m/C VHS.** Dennis Weaver, Janet Carroll, Michelle Little, Robert Sean Leonard, Cleavant Derricks, Victoria Wauchope; **D:** James Sadwith; **M:** Brad Fiedel. TV

The Blum Affair 🐾🐾 1948 In post-WWI Germany, a Jewish man is framed for the murder of an accountant and uncovers in his capture and prosecution a rat's nest of corruption and anti-Semitism. In German with English subtitles. **109m/B VHS.** *GE* Hans-Christian Blech, Gisela Trowe, Kurt Ehrhardt, Paul Bildt, Klaus Becker; **D:** Erich Engel.

Blume in Love 🐾🐾🐾 1973 (R) An ironic comedy/drama about a man who falls hopelessly in love with his ex-wife who divorced him for cheating on her while they were married. **115m/C VHS.** George Segal, Susan Anspach, Kris Kristofferson, Shelley Winters, Marsha Mason; **D:** Paul Mazursky; **W:** Paul Mazursky; **C:** Bruce Surtees; **M:** Bill Conti.

Blush 🐾🐾 *Hongfen* 1995 Shanghai prostitutes and friends Quiyi (Ji) and Xiao (Saifei) are stripped of their vocation by the communist takeover in 1949. Quiyi manages to take refuge with her favorite customer, wealthy Lao Pu (Zhiwen), while Xiao is re-educated and becomes a worker in a silk factory. Eventually thrown out of the house by Lao's disapproving mother, Quiyi learns to make her own way. Xiao meets Lao after his family has lost their money and winds up marrying him, unhappily since Lao continually pines for Quiyi. Based on the novel by Su Tong; Cantonese with subtitles. **119m/C VHS.** *CH* Wang Ji, Saifei He, Zhiwen Wang, Wang Rouli; **D:** Li Shaohong; **W:** Li Shaohong, Ni Zhen; **C:** Zeng Nianping; **M:** Guo Wenjing.

BMX Bandits 🐾🐾 1983 Three adventurous Aussie teens put their BMX skills to the test when they witness a crime and are pursued by the criminals. Much big air. **92m/C VHS.** Nicole Kidman, David Argue, John Ley, Angelo D'Angelo; **D:** Brian Trenchard-Smith; **W:** Patrick Edgeworth.

Boa 🐾🐾 2002 (R) A prehistoric snake, 100 feet in length, makes a reappearance beneath a maximum security prison located in Antarctic. Warden Ryan (Wasson) calls for a rescue team, which includes paleontologists Robert (Cain) and his wife Jessica (Lackey). A handful of survivors try to make it from the prison to the plane but that's one hungry snake. **96m/C VHS, DVD.** Dean Cain, Elizabeth Lackey, Grand L. Bush, Craig Wasson, Mark A. Seppard; **D:** Phillip J. Roth; **W:** Phillip J. Roth, Terry Neish; **C:** Todd Barron; **M:** Rich McHugh. VIDEO

Boarding House 🐾 1983 Residents of a boardinghouse discover sinister doings in the basement. It does not occur to any of them to move to another house. **90m/C VHS.** Hank Adly, Kalassu, Alexandra Day; **D:** John Wintergate.

Boarding School 🐾 *The Passion Flower Hotel* 1983 (R) Basic teen sex comedy about students at a proper Swiss boarding school for girls who devise a plan to seduce the boys at a nearby school by posing as prostitutes. Kinski stars as the American girl who masterminds the caper. **100m/C VHS, DVD.** *GE* Nastassja Kinski; **D:** Andre Farwagi.

Boardinghouse Blues 🐾🐾 1948 A showbiz musical centered around a boarding house with tenant troubles. It's an excuse for popular black entertainers of the day to perform, including Lucky Millinder, Bull Moose Jackson, Una Mae Carlisle, and Stumpy and Stumpy. **90m/C VHS, DVD.** Dusty Fletcher, Moms (Jackie) Mabley; **D:** Josh Binney.

The Boat Is Full 🐾🐾🐾 *Das Boot ist Voll* 1981 A group of refugees pose as a family in order to escape from Nazi Germany as they seek asylum in Switzerland. Available in German with English subtitles or dubbed into English. **104m/C VHS, DVD, SI** Tina Engel, Curt Bois, Renate Steiger, Mathias Gnaedinger, Hans Diehl, Martin Walz, Gerd David; **D:** Markus Imhoof; **W:** Markus Imhoof; **C:** Hans Liechti. Berlin Intl. Film Fest. '81: Director (Imhoof).

Boat Trip WOOF! 2003 (R) Isn't it about time for Gooding, Jr. to give back his Oscar? Or at least fire his agent? In this pathetic attempt at comedy, he's Jerry, a lovesick guy distraught over a failed relationship. To the rescue comes his buddy Nick (Sanz), a loud-mouth skirt chaser who suggests a singles cruise. When Nick insults the travel agent, they're sent on a gay cruise, where Jerry falls for the ship's choreographer Gabrielle (Sanchez) and must pretend to be gay to win her. Yep, it's a crappy as it sounds. Gooding, Jr. tries hard, but he can't bail out this floater, which is aimed straight at the rocks of a cliche-ridden and spectacularly unfunny script and direction that wouldn't make the cut on a third-rate sitcom. **95m/C VHS, DVD, UMD.** *US* Cuba Gooding Jr., Horatio Sanz, Roselyn Sanchez, Vivica A. Fox, Maurice Godin, Roger Moore, Lin Shaye, Victoria Silvstedt, Richard Roundtree, Will Ferrell, Artie Lange, Bob Gunton, Jennifer Gareis; **D:** Mort Nathan; **W:** Mort Nathan, William Bigelow; **C:** Shawn Maurer; **M:** Robert Folk.

The Boatniks 🐾🐾½ 1970 (G) An accident-prone Coast Guard ensign finds himself in charge of the "Times Square" of waterways: Newport Harbor. Adding to his already "titanic" problems is a gang of ocean-going jewel thieves who won't give up the ship! **99m/C VHS, DVD.** Robert Morse, Stefanie Powers, Phil Silvers, Norman Fell, Wally Cox, Don Ameche, Kelly Thordsen; **D:** Norman Tokar; **M:** Robert F. Brunner.

Bob & Carol & Ted & Alice 🐾🐾½ 1969 (R) Two California couples have attended a trendy therapy session and, in an attempt to be more in touch with sexuality, resort to applauding one another's extramarital affairs and swinging. Wacky and well-written, this is a farce on free love and psycho-speak. Mazursky's directorial debut. **104m/C VHS, DVD.** Natalie Wood, Robert Culp, Dyan Cannon, Elliott Gould; **D:** Paul Mazursky; **W:** Paul Mazursky, Larry Tucker; **C:** Charles B(ryant) Lang Jr.; **M:** Quincy Jones. N.Y. Film Critics '69: Screenplay, Support. Actress (Cannon); Natl. Soc. Film Critics '69: Screenplay; Writers Guild '69: Orig. Screenplay.

Bob le Flambeur 🐾🐾🐾 *Bob the Gambler* 1955 Aging Bob (Duchesne) is a down-on-his-luck gambler who visits the Deauville Casino with his friend Roger (Garret), who just happens to know croupier Jean (Cerval). Informed that the casino safe is bursting with cash, Bob decides to have a final fling by robbing the casino. Low-budget, bittersweet crime comedy. French with subtitles. **97m/B VHS, DVD.** *FR* Roger Duchesne, Isabel Corey, Daniel Cauchy, Howard Vernon, Gerard Buhr, Guy Decomble; **D:** Jean-Pierre Melville; **W:** Jean-Pierre Melville, Auguste Le Breton; **C:** Henri Decae; **M:** Jean Boyer, Eddie Barclay.

Bob Roberts 🐾🐾🐾 1992 (R) Excellent pseudo-documentary satire about a 1990 Pennsylvania senatorial race between Robbins' titular right-wing folk singer/entrepreneur versus Brickley Paiste's (Vidal) aging liberal incumbent. Roberts seems like a gee-whiz kinda guy but he'll stop at nothing to get elected and he knows a lot about political dirty tricks and, even more important, manipulating the media to get what he wants. Robbins directorial debut turned out to be very timely in view of the 1992 Clinton/Bush presidential campaign. Features a "vote first. Ask questions later." **105m/C VHS, DVD.** Jack Black, Tom Atkins, Helen Hunt, Peter Gallagher, Lynne Thigpen, Bingo O'Malley, Jeremy Piven, Matthew Faber, Matt McGrath, Gore Vidal, Alan Rickman, Giancarlo Esposito,

---

Ray Wise, Rebecca Jenkins, Harry J. Lennix, John Ottavino, Robert Stanton, Alan Rickman, Gore Vidal, Brian Murray, Anita Gillette, David Strathairn, Susan Sarandon, James Spader, John Cusack, Fred Ward, Pamela Reed; **D:** Tim Robbins; **W:** Tim Robbins; **C:** Jean Lepine; **M:** David Robbins.

Bob the Butler 🐾🐾 2005 (PG) Harmless fluff stars the usually obnoxious Green as perennial loser Bob Tree, who can't keep a job. His latest career attempt is attending butler school. His first placement is with neurotic Anne (Shields), who fired him when he was Bob the babysitter. Still, the single mom is desperate and hires Bob to look after her house and two exasperating children (Buechner, Smith), who decide the butler is better than mom's current boyfriend. **90m/C DVD.** *GB CA* Tom Green, Brooke Shields, Benjamin Smith, Simon Callow, Genevieve Buechner, Rob LaBelle; **D:** Gary Sinyor; **W:** Gary Sinyor, Jane Walker Wood, Steven Manners; **C:** Jason Lehel; **M:** David A. Hughes. VIDEO

Bobbie Jo and the Outlaw 🐾½ 1976 (R) Wonderwoman Carter is a bored carhop who yearns to be a country singer. She becomes involved with Marjoe, who fancies himself as a contemporary Billy the Kid. Together, they do their Bonnie and Clyde thing, to a significantly lesser dramatic effect than the original, though a glut of violence keeps the bodies dropping. **89m/C VHS.** Lynda Carter, Marjoe Gortner, Jesse Vint; **D:** Mark L. Lester.

Bobbie's Girl 🐾🐾 2002 Meandering drama long on theatrics and short on sense. American Bailey (Peters) and her lover, Englishwoman Bobbie (Ward) run a pub in a seaside town near Dublin, assisted by Bailey's brother David (Silverman). Bobbie is diagnosed with breast cancer at the same time she learns that her estranged brother and his wife have died and their 10-year-old son, Alan (Sangster), is orphaned into Bobbie's care. Bobbie and Alan are naturally struggling to cope with their situations while eccentrics (they're both ex-actors) Bailey and David try to provide encouragement. **100m/C VHS, DVD.** Bernadette Peters, Rachel Ward, Jonathan Silverman, Thomas Sangster; **D:** Jeremy Paul Kagan; **W:** Samuel Bernstein; **C:** Ciaran Tanham; **M:** Bruce Broughton. CABLE

Bobby 🐾🐾½ 2006 (R) Writer-director Emilio Estevez uses a star-studded cast to compare turbulent events of the '60s with modern conditions, with mixed results. This homage to Robert F. Kennedy uses multiple storylines and characters that revolve around L.A.'s Ambassador Hotel on the day leading up to RFK's assassination. Estevez liberally sprinkles the stories of no less than twenty-two characters surrounding the imminent tragedy, including the hotel beautician (Stone), her cheating husband (Macy) and a couple soon to be married (Lohan, Wood). The characters aren't allowed to achieve much depth, and the performances are hit and miss. The impact of the assassination drives home the trivialities of the characters and reinforces the loss of RFK, who only appears in archival footage. **119m/C DVD.** *US* Anthony Hopkins, Harry Belafonte, William H. Macy, Sharon Stone, Christian Slater, Freddy Rodriguez, Laurence Fishburne, Demi Moore, Martin Sheen, Helen Hunt, Lindsay Lohan, Elijah Wood, Nick Cannon, Heather Graham, Ashton Kutcher, Shia LaBeouf, Brian Geraghty, Joshua Jackson, David Krumholtz, Emilio Estevez, Mary Elizabeth Winstead, Jacob Vargas, Joy Bryant, Svetlana Metkina; **D:** Emilio Estevez; **W:** Emilio Estevez; **C:** Michael Barrett; **M:** Mark Isham.

Bobby Deerfield 🐾🐾 1977 (PG) Cold-blooded Grand Prix driver comes face to face with death each time he races, but finally learns the meaning of life when he falls in love with a critically ill woman. Even with race cars, soap opera stalls. **124m/C VHS.** Al Pacino, Marthe Keller, Anny (Annie Legras) Duperey, Romolo Valli; **D:** Sydney Pollack; **W:** Alvin Sargent; **C:** Henri Decae; **M:** Dave Grusin.

Bobby Jones: Stroke of Genius 🐾½ 2004 (PG) Bloated homage to the late great golfer of the title starring a red-hot post-"Passion" Caviezel. Practically a natural, Jones, who still reigns as the only golfer to win all four major tournaments in a single calendar year, had to overcome a number of personal demons to become one of the greatest golfers in the world. An extremely moral man. Jones suffered from depression battled and sported a legendary temper that he ct of golf world of the 1920s. After his Grand Slam coup, Jones was diagnosed with a spinal disorder and retired from golf at 28 to practice law and spend more time with wife Mary (Forlani). Historically faithful and elegant, but is hindered by sub-par script, for mulaic plot, and undeveloped supports. **125m/C** DVD James (Jim) Caviezel, Claire Forlani, Jeremy Northam, Malcolm McDowell, Connie Ray, Brett Rice, Dan Albright, Larry Thompson, Paul Freeman, John Curran, Aidan Quinn, Alistair Begg, Kenny Alfonso, Tom Arcuragi, Devon Gearhart, Thomas Lewis, Hilton McCrae; *D:* Rowdy Herrington; *W:* Rowdy Herrington, Tony Depaul, Bill Pryor; *C:* Tom Stern; *M:* Tim Jones.

The Bobo ♂️½ 1967 Lousy bullfighter tries to lure a gorgeous woman into romance. Filmed in Spain and Italy. **103m/C** VHS, GB Peter Sellers, Britt Ekland, Rossano Brazzi, Adolfo Celi; *D:* Robert Parrish; *M:* David R. Schwartz.

Boca ♂️ 1994 (R) American journalist t.J. (Chong) arrives in Rio during Carnival to investigate a story about random killings throughout the Brazilian streets. She gets stonewalled asking questions, until she meets an up-from-poverty crimelord named Boca De Ouro (Meira). Now, our noisy journalist may learn too much to keep her alive. Filmed in Rio de Janiero. **92m/C** VHS, Rae Dawn Chong, Martin Kemp, Tarcisio Meira, Martin Sheen; *W:* Walter Avancini; *W:* Ed Silverstein.

Boccaccio '70 ♂️♂️ 1962 Three short bawdy/comedy/pageant-of-life films inspired by "The Decameron," each pertaining to ironically twisted sexual politics in middle class life. A fourth story, "Renzo and Luciana," by Mario Monicelli, has been cut. Dubbed. **145m/C** VHS, DVD, /T Anita Ekberg, Romy Schneider, Tomas Millan, Sophia Loren, Peppino de Filippo, Luigi Giuliani; *D:* Vittorio De Sica, Luchino Visconti, Federico Fellini; *W:* Luchino Visconti, Federico Fellini, Tullio Pinelli, Ennio Flaiano, Cesare Zavattini; *C:* Otello Martelli, Giuseppe Rotunno; *M:* Nino Rota, Armano Trovajoli.

Bodies, Rest & Motion ♂️♂️ 1993 (R) Stagnant 20-something movie in which four young people basically do nothing in the sun-baked town of Enfield, Arizona. Similar to the movie "Singles," but without the Seattle grunge scene. The title's reference to Newton is fitting: "A body in rest or motion remains in that state unless acted upon by an outside force." Appealing cast is wasted in listless film that's content to just drift along. Based on the play by Roger Hedden. **94m/C** VHS, DVD, Phoebe Cates, Bridget Fonda, Tim Roth, Eric Stoltz, Scott Frederick, Scott Johnson, Alicia Witt, Rich Wheeler, Peter Fonda; *D:* Michael Steinberg; *W:* Roger Hedden; *C:* Bernd Heinl; *M:* Michael Convertino.

Bodily Harm ♂️♂️ 1995 (R) By-the-numbers neo-noir features Fiorentino as Vegas detective Rita Cates, who's investigating the murders of two women with ties to ex-cop Sam McKeon (Baldwin), not incidentally Rita's former lover. She reluctantly trusts Sam (Baldwin) and begins to have second thoughts about Sam's innocence. Unconvincing despite the expert cast. **91m/C**

Bobby Z ♂️♂️ 1994 (R) Let's Kill Bobby Z; The Life and Death of Bobby Z 2007 (R) Lots of action and limited acting required. Con Tim Kearney (Walker) agrees to DEA agent Tad Gruzsa's (Fishburne) plan to pass himself off as missing surfer/drug dealer Bobby Z in order to get paroled. Seems drug lords are holding Gruzsa's partner hostage and they'll trade for Bobby. Things go wrong and Kearney goes on the lam with Bobby's ex-lover (Wilce) and his young son (Villarreal) Based on "The Death and Life of Bobby Z" by Don Winslow. **97m/C** DVD Paul Walker, Laurence Fishburne, Olivia Wilde, Joaquim Almeida, J.R. Villarreal, Jason Lewis, Jacob Vargas, Jason Flemyng, Keith Carradine, Chuck Liddell; *D:* John Herzfeld; *W:* Bob Krakow, Allen Lawrence. *M:* Tim Jones.

The Body ♂️ 2001 (PG-13) Would-be religious thriller with wooden acting, laughable dialog, and clunky plot. In modern-day Jerusalem, Israeli archeologist Sharon Golban (Williams) checks out a tomb discovered beneath a shop and finds the skeleton of a crucified man. Could it be the remains of Jesus? When word reaches the Vatican, Cardinal Pesci (Wood) dispatches Father Matt Gutierrez (Banderas) to deal with the provocative situation. **108m/C** VHS, DVD, Antonio Banderas, Olivia Williams, John Shrapnel, Derek Jacobi, Jason Flemyng, Makram Khoury, Vernon Dobtch-eff, Ian McNeice; *D:* Jonas McCord; *C:* Vilmos Zsigmond; *M:* Serge Colbert.

Body and Soul ♂️♂️ 1924 The first screen appearance of Robeson has him cast in a dual role as a conniving preacher and his good brother. The preacher preys on the heroine, making her life a misery. (Goff). After becoming a champ, Charlie starts the inevitable downward slide. One-time pro-welterweight Lee plays boxing rival Ben. A vintage '40s boxing film that become worthy of the genre. Remade in 1981 with Leon Isaac Kennedy. **102m/B** VHS, Paul Robeson, Julia Theresa Russel, Mercedes Gilbert; *D:* Oscar Michaux.

Body and Soul ♂️♂️½ *An Affair of the Heart* 1947 Charlie Davis (Garfied) is a Jewish boxer whose parents want him to quit the ring and get an education. Instead, he rises quickly to the top, thanks in part to gangster "protector" Roberts (Goff). After becoming a champ, Charlie starts the inevitable downward slide. One-time pro-welterweight Lee plays boxing rival Ben. A vintage '40s boxing film that become worthy of the genre. Remade in 1981 with Leon Isaac Kennedy. **104m/B** VHS, DVD, John Garfield, Lilli Palmer, Hazel Brooks, Anne Revere, William Conrad, Canada Lee, Joseph Pevney, Lloyd Goff; *D:* Robert Rossen; *M:* Hugo Friedhofer. Oscars '47: Film Editing.

Body & Soul ♂️♂️½ 1981 (R) Interesting remake of 1947 gem about a boxer who loses his perspective in the world of fame, fast cars, and women. Anna is forced to deal with his pregnant widow (Redman) and two children and her family's failing Yorkshire mill. Anna suffers a crisis of faith as both the secular and the religious exert their strong influences and she's drawn as well to two very different men—younger Hal (Mavers), the mill's supervisor, and divorced bank manager Daniel Stern (Bowe). Based on the 1991 novel by Marcelle Bernstein; British TV miniseries. **312m/C** VHS, GB Kristin Scott Thomas, Amanda Redman, Gary Mavers, Anthony Valentine, Sandra Voe, John Bowe, Dorothy Tutin; *C:* Peter Middleton; *M:* Jim Parker.

Body and Soul ♂️♂️ 1998 (R) Clichéd remake of the familiar boxing saga that finds ambitious boxer Mancini and his manager Chiklis heading for a potential championship bout in Reno. Mancini might still have the boxing moves but he's certainly no amateur and his professionalism is actually a deterrent. **95m/C** VHS, DVD, Ray "Boom Boom" Mancini, Michael Chiklis, Rod Steiger, Joe Mantegna, Jennifer Beals, Tahnee Welch; *D:* Sam Henry Kass; *W:* Sam Henry Kass; *C:* Arturo Smith; *M:* David Waters. CABLE

Body Armor ♂️½ 1996 (R) Special agent Conway (McColm) is recruited by an ex-girlfriend (Schofield) to find a missing scientist. This leads our hero to nutball virologist Dr. Krago (Perlman) who's using germ warfare for personal gain. For the action junkie (who doesn't mind a little eye candy as well). **95m/C** VHS, DVD, Matt McColm, Ron Perlman, Annabel Schofield, Carol

---

Alt, Clint Howard, Morgan Brittany, Shaune O'Brien; *D:* Jack Gill; *W:* Jack Gill; *C:* Robert Hayes; *M:* Mark Holden. VIDEO

Body Bags ♂️♂️½ 1993 (R) *John Carpenter Presents Body Bags* Three gory, though humorous, stories hosted by horrormeister Carpenter as your friendly local coroner. "The Gas Station" finds the young female overnight attendant menaced by a psycho. "Hair" is about a bald-ng yuppie who'll do anything for a full head of hair. Then he meets the sinister Dr. Lock and his magical new-hair growth treatment. The grisly "Eye" concerns an appendage and finds that his transplanted eyeball, taken from an executed serial killer, is subject to ghastly visions. Several fellow horror directors have cameos. **95m/C** VHS, DVD, Alex Datcher, Robert Carradine, Stacy Keach, David Warner, Mark Hamill, Twiggy, John Agar, Deborah Harry, Sheena Easton, David Naughton, John Carpenter, Tobe Hooper; *D:* Tobe Hooper, John Carpenter; *W:* Billy Brown, Dan Angeleri; *M:* John Carpenter, Jim Lang. CABLE

Body Beat ♂️♂️ *Dance Academy* 1988 (PG) Wild jazz and rock dancers are integrated into a previously classical ballet academy. While the students become fast friends, the teachers loosen up with evil factions. **90m/C** VHS, Tony Fields, Galyn Gorg, Scott Grossman, Eliska Krupka, Virgil Frye, Steve La Chance, Leonora Leal, Julie Newmar, Paula Nichols, Serge Rodnunsky; *D:* Ted Mather.

The Body Beneath Woof! In Vampire's Thirst 1970 A living-dead ghoul survives on the blood of innocents and is still preying on victims today. **85m/C** VHS, DVD, Gavin Reed, Jackie Skarvellis, Susan Heard, Colin Gordon; *D:* Andy Milligan.

Body Chemistry ♂️ 1990 (R) A married sexual-behavior researcher starts up a passionate affair with his lab partner. When he tries to end the relationship, his female associate becomes psychotic. You've seen it all before in "Fatal Attraction." And you'll see it again in "Body Chemistry 2." **84m/C** VHS, DVD, Marc Singer, Mary Crosby, Lisa Pescia, Joseph Campanella, David Kagen; *D:* Kristine Peterson; *W:* Jackson Barr, Thom Babbes; *C:* Phedon Papamichael; *M:* Terry Plumeri.

Body Chemistry 2: Voice of a Stranger ♂️½ 1991 (R) An ex-cop (Harrison), obsessed with violent sex gets involved with a radio psychologist (Pescia) whose advice could prove deadly in this erotic sequel. **84m/C** VHS, DVD, Gregory Harrison, Lisa Pescia, Morton Downey Jr., Robin Riker, Jeremy Piven, John Landis; *D:* Adam Simon; *W:* Jackson Barr, Christopher Wooden; *C:* Richard Michalak; *M:* Nigel Holton.

Body Chemistry 3: Point of Seduction ♂️♂️ 1993 (R) TV producer Alan Clay (Stevens) finds himself caught in a business and sexual triangle when he okays the making of a movie about the life of a TV sex therapist (Shattuck). Seems the lady's lovers have a nasty habit of getting murdered which doesn't prevent Clay from getting personally involved. His ac-tress wife (Fairchild), who wants to star in the movie, is not pleased. Lives up to its title. **90m/C** VHS, DVD, Andrew Stevens, Morgan Fairchild, Shari Shattuck; *D:* Jim Wynorski; *M:* Jackson Barr; *C:* Don E. Fauntleroy; *M:* Chuck Cirino.

Body Chemistry 4: Full Exposure ♂️½ 1995 (R) When sex psychologist Claire Archer (Tweed) is accused of murder she hires Simon Mitchel (Poindexter), the best criminal defense attorney around. But Simon becomes just a little too closely involved with his possibly psycho client and it could cost him nct only his career and marriage but his life. Also available unrated. **88m/C** VHS, DVD, Shannon Tweed, Larry Poindexter, Andrew Stevens, Chick Vennera, Larry Manetti, Stella Stevens; *D:* Jim Wynorski; *W:* Karen Kelly; *C:* Zora Hochsatter; *M:* Paul Di Franco.

Body Count ♂️½ *The 11th Commandment* 1987 A weird and wealthy family will stoop at nothing, including murder and cannibalism, to enhance their fortune. Rather

---

than bodies, count: the minutes 'til the movie's over. **90m/C** VHS, Marilyn Hassett, Dick Sargent, Steve Ford, Greg Mullavey, Thomas Ryan, Bernie (Bernard) White; *D:* Paul Leder.

Body Count ♂️½ 1995 (R) Professional killer Makoto (Chiba) and his partner Sybil (Nielser) seek revenge on the New Orleans cops who set them up. Opposing them are special crime unit partners, Eddie Cook (Davi) and Vinnie Rizzo (Bauer). Lots of shootouts and macho bravado. **93m/C** VHS, DVD, Sonny Chiba, Brigitte Nielsen, Robert Davi, Steven Bauer, Jan-Michael Vincent, Talun Hsu; *D:* Talun Hsu; *W:* Henry Madden; *C:* Blake T. Evans; *M:* Curt Sobel.

Body Count ♂️♂️ 1997 (R) Fiorentino and Caruso are reteamed (after "Jade") in a crime saga about a heist gone bad. There is no honor among thieves as driver Hobbs (Caruso) learns when he plans a job with some unreliable associates and the Boston Museum of Fine Arts and things go very wrong. The gang decide to drive to Miami in order to sell their ill-gotten gains, squabbling all the way. Then mystery woman Natalie (Fiorentino) comes aboard, to cause more friction between the gun-happy boys. **84m/C** VHS, DVD, David Caruso, Linda Fiorentino, Ving Rhames, Donnie Wahlberg, Forest Whitaker; *D:* Robert Patton-Spruill; *W:* Theodore Witcher; *C:* Charles Mills; *M:* Curt Sobel. VIDEO

Body Double ♂️♂️♂️ 1984 (R) A voyeuristic unemployed actor peeps on a neighbor's nightly disrobing and sees more than he wants to. A grisly murder leads him into an obsessive quest through the world of pornographic films. **114m/C** VHS, DVD, Craig Wasson, Melanie Griffith, Gregg Henry, Deborah Shelton, Guy Boyd, Dennis Franz, David Haskell, Rebecca Stanley, Barbara Crampton, Mindi Miller; *D:* Brian De Palma; *W:* Brian De Palma, Robert J. Avrech; *C:* Stephen Burum; *M:* Pino Donaggio, Natl. Soc. Film Critics '84: Support. Actress (Griffith).

Body Heat ♂️♂️♂️½ 1981 (R) During a Florida heat wave, a none-too-bright lawyer becomes involved in a steamy love affair with a mysterious woman and then in a plot to kill her husband. Hurt and Turner (in her film debut) became stars under Kasdan's direction (the three would reunite for "The Accidental Tourist"). Hot love scenes supplement a twisting mystery with a suprise ending. Rourke's arsonist and Danson's soft shoe shouldn't be missed. **113m/C** VHS, DVD, William Hurt, Kathleen Turner, Richard Crenna, Ted Danson, Mickey Rourke, J.A. Preston, Kim Zimmer, Jane Hallaren; *D:* Lawrence Kasdan; *W:* Lawrence Kasdan; *C:* Richard H. Kline; *M:* John Barry.

The Body in the Library ♂️♂️½ 1984 *Agatha Christie's Miss Marple: The Body In the Library* 1984 A Miss Marple mystery, based on Agatha Christie's 1942 novel, involving the murder of a young woman in a wealthy British mansion. **155m/C** VHS, DVD, GB Gwen Watford, Valentine Dyall, Moray Watson, Frederick Jaeger, Raymond Francis, Joan Hickson; *D:* Silvio Narizzano; *W:* T.R. Bowen; *C:* John Walker; *M:* Alan Blakley. TV

Body Language ♂️♂️ 1992 (R) A successful businesswoman, with a man problem, hires a private secretary with answers to all life's questions—and a deadly agenda all her own. **93m/C** VHS, Heather Lockear, Linda Purl, Edward Albert, James Acheson; *D:* Arthur Allan Seidelman; *W:* Dan Gurskis; *C:* Hanania Baer.

Body Language 🦴🦴½ 1995 (R) Criminal defense attorney Gavin St. Claire (Berenger) falls for a topless dancer (Schanz), which leads him into all sorts of trouble, including murder. 95m/C VHS, DVD. Tom Berenger, Heidi Schanz, Nancy Travis; *D:* George Case.

Body Melt 🦴🦴½ 1993 When a crazed doctor unleashes an experimental drug on an unsuspecting town, the residents begin to literally melt away. 82m/C VHS, DVD. *AU* Gerard Kennedy, Andrew Daddo, Ian Smith, Vincent (Vince Gil) Gil, Regina Gaigalas; *D:* Philip Brophy; *W:* Philip Brophy, Rod Bishop; *M:* Philip Brophy.

Body Moves 🦴🦴 1990 (PG-13) Romantic entanglements heat up the competition when two couples enter a steamy dance contest. Not apt to move you. 98m/C VHS. *IT* Kirk Rivera, Steve Messina, Dianne Granger, Linsley Allen, Philip Spruce, Nicole Kolman, Susan Gardner; *D:* Gerry Lively; *W:* Daniel Steel.

Body of Evidence woof! 1992 (R) Bad movie with pretensions takes "Basic Instinct" a step further. Instead of an ice pick and sex, sex itself is used as the weapon in a murder trial featuring Madonna as the defendant, Dafoe as her lawyer, and Mantegna as the prosecutor. The plot is, of course, secondary to the S&M sex scenes with Dafoe which feature hot wax and broken glass. Madonna's lack of performance is the least of the film's problems since everyone seems to have forgotten any acting talent they possess. Director Edel fails to direct—the film even looks bad. "Body" was the subject of another NC-17 ratings flap but this film shouldn't be seen by anybody. An unrated version is also available. 99m/C VHS, DVD. Madonna, Willem Dafoe, Joe Mantegna, Anne Archer, Michael Forest, Charles Hallahan, Mark Rolston, Richard Riehle, Julianne Moore, Frank Langella, Jürgen Prochnow, Stan Shaw; *D:* Uli Edel; *W:* Brad Mirman; *C:* Doug Milsome; *M:* Graeme Revell. Golden Raspberries '93: Worst Actress (Madonna).

Body of Influence 2 🦴🦴 1996 (R) A Beverly Hills psychiatrist gets overly involved with a beautiful female patient. But she not only wants his love—she wants to play doctor with his latest patient, Leza (Fisher), whose seductive charms prove more than the doc can handle. The unrated version is 94 minutes. Also available in an unrated version. 96m/C VHS, DVD. Nick Cassavetes, Shannon Whirry, Sandahl Bergman, Don Swayze, Anna Karin, Catherine Parks, Diana Barton, Richard Roundtree; *D:* Andrew Garroni; *W:* David Schreiber.

Body Parts 🦴🦴 1991 (R) A crime psychologist loses his arm in an auto accident and receives a transplant from an executed murderer. Does the limb have an evil will of its own? Poorly paced horror goes off the deep end in gore with its third act. Based on the novel "Choice Cuts" by French writers Pierre Boileau and Thomas Narcejac, whose work inspired some of the greatest suspense films. 88m/C VHS, DVD. Jeff Fahey, Kim Delaney, Lindsay Duncan, Peter Murnik, Brad Dourif, Zakes Mokae, James Kidnie, Paul Ben-Victor; *D:* Eric Red; *W:* Eric Red, Norman Snider, Patricia Herskovic; *C:* Theo van de Sande; *M:* Loek Dikker.

Body Parts 🦴 1994 For fans of demented dismemberment niche. Body Parts, a sleazy skin club, loses some of its star talent when the strippers start turning up in cameo video appearances. Seems there's a psycho killer on the loose who videotapes the dismemberment of his stripper-victims. The police decide they've got to meet this guy when he sends them a sample of his work. 90m/C VHS, DVD. Teri Marlow, Clement von Franckenstein, Dick Monda, Johnny Mandel; *D:* Michael Paul Girard; *W:* Michael Paul Girard; *M:* Miriam Cutler.

Body Rock woof! 1984 (PG-13) Brooklyn breakdancer Lamas deserts his buddies to work at a chic Manhattan nightclub. Watching Lamas as the emcee/breakdancing fool is a hoot. ♫Body Rock; Why Do You Want to Break My Heart?; One Thing Leads to Another; Let Your Body, Rock; Vanishing Point; Sharpshooter; The Jungle, Deliver. 93m/C VHS. Lorenzo Lamas, Vicki Frederick, Cameron Dye, Michelle Nicastro, Ray Sharkey, Grace Zabriskie, Carole Ita White; *D:* Marcelo Epstein.

The Body Shop woof! *Doctor Gore* 1972 Unorthodox love story in which a man decides to patch up his relationship with his dead wife by piecing together her dismembered body. For lovers only. Under "Doctor Gore" title the film includes an intro by horror director Herschell Gordon Lewis. 91m/C VHS, DVD. Pat Patterson, Jenny Driggers, Roy Mehaffey, Linda Faile, Candy Furr; *D:* Pat Patterson.

Body Shot 🦴🦴½ 1993 (R) Celebrity shutterbug Mickey Dane (Patrick) is fingered in the murder of a rock star after it turns out he did a kinky layout for a look-alike. When police find out he had an obsession for the dead woman, he employs his photographic expertise in the search for the real killer. Effective tension-builder with fast-paced chases through the seamy side of Los Angeles. 98m/C VHS, DVD. Robert Patrick, Michelle Johnson, Ray Wise, Jonathan Banks, Kim Miyori, Kenneth Tobey, Charles Napier; *D:* Dimitri Logothetis; *W:* Robert Strauss; *C:* Nicholas Josef von Sternberg; *M:* Cliff Magness.

Body Shots 🦴🦴½ 1999 (R) An ensemble cast of twentysomethings explores sex and dating while traversing L.A.'s nightlife. Eight friends come to reflect on their hedonistic lifestyles when Sara (Reid) accuses macho football player Michael (O'Connell) of date rape. During the ultimate "he said/she said" battle, waferthin declarations on love in the '90s are made by characters who are as appealing as root canal surgery. 102m/C VHS, DVD. Sean Patrick Flanery, Jerry O'Connell, Amanda Peet, Tara Reid, Ron Livingston, Emily Procter, Brad Rowe, Sybil Temchen; *D:* Michael Cristofer; *W:* David McKenna; *C:* Rodrigo Garcia; *M:* Mark Isham.

Body Slam 🦴🦴½ 1987 (PG) A small-time talent monger hits it big with a rock and roll/ professional wrestling tour. Piper's debut; contains some violence and strong language. 100m/C VHS. Roddy Piper, Captain Lou Albano, Dirk Benedict, Tanya Roberts, Billy Barty, Charles Nelson Reilly, John Astin, Wild Samoan, Tonga Kid, Barry J. Gordon; *D:* Hal Needham; *W:* Steven H. Burkow; *M:* John D'Andrea.

The Body Snatcher 🦴🦴🦴½ 1945 Based on Robert Louis Stevenson's story about a grave robber who supplies corpses to research scientists. Set in Edinburgh in the 19th century, this Lewton production is superior. One of Karloff's best vehicles. 77m/B VHS, DVD. Boris Karloff, Bela Lugosi, Henry Daniell, Sharyn Moffett, Donna Lee; *D:* Robert Wise; *W:* Philip MacDonald, Val Lewton; *C:* Robert De Grasse.

Body Snatcher from Hell 🦴🦴½ *Goke, Body Snatcher from Hell; Goke the Vampire; Kyuketsuki Gokemidoro* 1969 An airliner passes through a mysterious cloud and crashes in a desert. One by one, the passengers are turned into vampires. Some interesting special effects. Set in 1969. 84m/C VHS. *JP* Hideo Ko, Teruo Yoshida, Tomomi Sato, Eizo Kitamura, Masaya Takahashi, Cathy Horlan, Kazuo Kato, Yuko Kusunoki; *D:* Hajime Sato.

Body Snatchers 🦴🦴🦴 1993 (R) Yet another version of "Invasion of the Body Snatchers." An innocent family arrive at an Army base which turns out to be infested with pod people. This time around the heroine is angst-ridden teenager Marti (Anwar) and the pods have something to do with a mysterious toxic spill. The 1978 remake was well done; this so-so version takes advantage of the advances in special effects particularly in Anwar's bathtub scene) and sound technology but is slow-paced with few jolts of terror. 87m/C VHS, DVD. Gabrielle Anwar, Meg Tilly, Terry Kinney, Forest Whitaker, Billy Wirth, R. Lee Ermey, Reilly Murphy; *D:* Abel Ferrara; *W:* Stuart Gordon, Dennis Paoli, Nicholas St. John; *C:* Bojan Bazelli; *M:* Joe Delia.

Body Strokes 🦴 *Siren's Kiss* 1995 Blocked artist Leo Kessler (Johnston) is aroused by the wild fantasies of his beautiful models Beth (Knittle) and Claire (Weber). But it's just fantasy and it also helps get Leo's marriage back on track when manager/wife Karen (Beck) gets jealous. Also available unrated. 99m/C VHS, DVD. Bobby Johnston, Dixie Beck, Kristen Knittle, Catherine Weber; *D:* Edward Holzman; *W:* April Moskowitz; *C:* Kim Haun; *M:* Richard Bronskill.

Body Trouble 🦴½ 1992 (R) After being attacked by sharks while vacationing in the Caribbean, a man washes ashore in Miami and then somehow makes his way to New York City. There he meets Vera Vin Rouge and her friends Cinnamon, Spice, Paprika, and Johnny Zero, a gangster. Zero decides he doesn't like the man, so he chases him back to the Caribbean. Supposedly this all happens in only one day. Hmmm... 98m/C VHS, DVD. Dick Van Patten, Priscilla Barnes, Frank Gorshin, James Hong, Marty Rackham, Michael Unger, Jonathan Soloman, Brit Helfer, Leigh Clark, Patricia Cardell, Richie Barathy; *D:* Bill Milling; *W:* Bill Milling.

The Body Vanished 🦴🦴 1939 Murder mystery featuring a corpse that disappears from the scene of the crime. 46m/B VHS, DVD. *GB* Anthony Hulme, Ernest Sefton, C. Denier Warren; *D:* Walter Tennyson.

Body Waves 🦴½ 1992 (R) Beach comedy starring Calvert as a teenager who bets his father that he can raise money on his own. In typical teen movie fashion, he invents a sex cream that drives boys and girls wild. Brain candy featuring lots of skimpy bikinis. 80m/C VHS. Bill Calvert, Leah Lail, Larry Linville, Dick Miller, Jim Wise; *D:* P.J. Pesce.

The Bodyguard 🦴🦴½ 1976 (R) The Yakuza's, Japan's mafia, and New York's big crime families face off in this martial arts extravaganza. 89m/C VHS, DVD. *JP* Etsuko (Sue) Shihomi, Sonny Chiba, Aaron Banks, Bill Louie, Judy Lee; *D:* Maurice Sarli.

The Bodyguard 🦴🦴 1992 (R) Buttoned-down, ex-Secret Service agent turned private bodyguard reluctantly takes on a wildly successful singer/actress as a client. Houston, in her acting debut as the over-indulged diva, doesn't have to stretch too far but acquits herself well. Costner has really bad hair day but easily portrays the tightly wound Frank. Critically trashed, a boxoffice smash, and too long. Originally scripted by producer Kasdan over a decade ago, with Steve McQueen in mind. Predictable romantic melodrama is kept moving by the occasional sharp dialog and a few action pieces. Songs include the smash hit "I Will Always Love You," written and originally performed by Dolly Parton. 130m/C VHS, DVD. Kevin Costner, Whitney Houston, Gary Kemp, Bill Cobbs, Ralph Waite, Tomas Arana, Michele Lamar Richards, Mike Starr, Christopher Birt, DeVaughn Nixon, Charles Keating, Robert Wuhl; *Cameos:* Debbie Reynolds; *D:* Mick Jackson; *W:* Lawrence Kasdan; *C:* Andrew Dunn; *M:* Alan Silvestri. MTV Movie Awards '93: Song ("I Will Always Love You").

The Bodyguard from Beijing 🦴🦴½ *The Defender; Zhong Nan Hai Bao Biao* 1994 Beijing bodyguard John Chang (Li) is hired to protect pampered rich girl Michelle (Chung), who's the witness to a murder. And John also has to deal with the revenge plans of an ex-soldier whose brother John has killed. Cantonese with subtitles. 90m/C VHS, DVD. *HK* Jet Li, Christy Chung, Kent Cheng, Collin Chou; *D:* Corey Yuen; *W:* Gordon Chan, Kin-Chung Chan; *C:* Tom Lau.

Bodywork 🦴🦴 1999 (R) Virgil Guppy (Matheson) buys a second-hand Jaguar that gives him nothing but trouble, especially when he finds a dead prostitute in the trunk of the car. Virgil goes on the run and hides out with a young woman (Colenese with subtitles) who's a professional car thief. British crime caper finally has too many twists for its own good. The Winslet who plays Virgil's girlfriend is the sister of actress Kate. 93m/C VHS, DVD. *GB* Hans Matheson, Charlotte Coleman, Clive Russell, Beth Winslet; *D:* Gareth Rhys Jones; *W:* Gareth Rhys Jones; *C:* Thomas Wuthvich; *M:* Dusan Kojic, Srdjan Kurpjel.

Boeing Boeing 🦴🦴½ 1965 A dated but still amusing sex farce about a bachelor newspaperman (Curtis) in Paris, his three stewardess girlfriends, and the elaborate plots he resorts to in trying to keep them from finding out about each other. When the new Boeing jet makes air travel faster all Curtis' schemes may come crashing down. Ritter is fun as the exasperated housekeeper and Lewis amazingly subdued as Curtis' business rival. 102m/C VHS. Tony Curtis, Jerry Lewis, Dany Saval, Christiane Schmidtner, Suzanna Leigh, Thelma Ritter; *D:* John Rich; *W:* Edward Anhalt.

Boesman & Lena 🦴🦴½ 2000 Adaptation of the apartheid-era play by Athol Fugard follows the travails of downtrodden couple, Boesman (Glover) and Lena (Bassett). Their shanty home in Cape Town has been bulldozed by the government so they take to the dusty road with their meager belongings, constantly bickering about their plight. The couple construct a makeshift abode for the night, which attracts the attention of an old man (Jonah) even lower on the economic ladder, whom Lena allows to stay to Boesman's displeasure. Performances are outstanding. Last film for director Berry. 86m/C VHS, DVD. *FR* Danny Glover, Angela Bassett, Willie Jonah; *D:* John Berry; *W:* John Berry; *C:* Alain Choquart; *M:* Wally Badarou.

Bog 🦴 1984 (PG) Boggy beast from the Arctic north awakens to eat people. Scientists mount an anti-monster offensive. 90m/C VHS, DVD. Gloria De Haven, Marshall Thompson, Leo Gordon, Aldo Ray, Glen Voros, Ed Clark, Carol Terry; *D:* Don Keeslar; *W:* Carl Kitt; *C:* Jack Willoughby; *M:* Bill Walker.

Boggy Creek II 🦴½ *The Barbaric Beast of Boggy Creek, Part II* 1983 (PG) The continuing saga of the eight-foot-tall, 300 pound monster from Texarkana. Third in a series of low-budget movies including "The Legend of Boggy Creek" and "Return to Boggy Creek." 93m/C VHS. Charles B. Pierce, Cindy Butler, Serene Hedin; *D:* Charles B. Pierce.

Bogie: The Last Hero 🦴🦴½ 1980 Biography of Humphrey Bogart, populated by almost-lookalikes who can almost act. 100m/C VHS. Kevin J. O'Connor, Kathryn Harrold, Ann Wedgeworth, Patricia Barry, Arthur Franz; *D:* Vincent Sherman; *M:* Charles Bernstein. TV

Bogus 🦴🦴 1996 (PG) Aptly named fantasy-comedy has orphan Albert (Osment) sent to foster aunt Harriet (Goldberg) after his magician's assistant mom (Travis) dies in a car accident. He brings along an imaginary friend, the eponymous Bogus (Depardieu) to ease the transition. Harriet is your typical workaholic easterner and isn't too thrilled with the arrangement. Goldberg and Depardieu are fine, but predictability drains most of the magic. 112m/C VHS, DVD. Whoopi Goldberg, Gerard Depardieu, Haley Joel Osment, Nancy Travis, Andrea Martin, Denis Mercier, Ute Lemper, Sheryl Lee Ralph, Al Waxman, Fiona Reid, Don Francks; *D:* Norman Jewison; *W:* Alvin Sargent; *C:* David Watkin; *M:* Marc Shaiman.

The Bogus Witch Project 🦴 2000 (R) In the long and ignoble history of cheap parodies, this is surely one of the cheapest. It's a series of short films—sketches and blackouts, really—that use the premise of the original "Blair Witch" film to poke fun at the movie biz. Here's the preface to one: "In August 1999, three out-of-work actors disappeared in the woods near Sherman Oaks, California, while looking for Blair Underwood to give him a script." Twenty-four hours later, their footage was found and turned into a vehicle for shameless self-promotion." The episode starring Pauly Shore is the weakest of the weak. Funnier bits appear between spoofs. 85m/C DVD. Pauly Shore, Michael Ian Black; *D:* Victor Kargan; *M:* Carvin Knowles.

Bohemian Girl 🦴🦴🦴 1936 The last of Laurel and Hardy's comic operettas finds them as guardians of a young orphan (Hood, famous for her roles in the

Our Gang comedies), whom no one realizes is actually a kidnapped princess. **74m/ B VHS.** Stan Laurel, Oliver Hardy, Mae Busch, Darla Hood, Julie Bishop, Thelma Todd, James Finlayson; **D:** James W. Home.

Boiler Room 🎬🎬🎬 **2000 (R)** Basic plot about a greedy naive young man caught up in a situation that's out of his control gets the high testosterone treatment. Seth (Ribisi) jumps at the chance to become a trainee at an up-and-coming brokerage firm filled with macho twenty-somethings greedy for success. But what he's allied himself with runs an illegal stock-trading operation that's under investigation. Well-cast and stylish, with Affleck effective in a small role as the firm's strutting recruiter **120m/C VHS, DVD.** Vin Diesel, Nicky Katt, Nia Long, Scott Caan, Ron Rifkin, Jamie Kennedy, Taylor Nichols, Tom Everett Scott, Ben Affleck; **D:** Ben Younger; **C:** Enrique Chediak.

Boiling Point 🎬🎬 **1932** Lewman proves once again that justice always triumphs. **67m/B VHS.** Hoot Gibson, Helen Foster, Wheeler Oakman, Skeeter Bill Robbins, Billy Bletcher, Lafe (Lafayette) McKee, Charles Bailey, George "Gabby" Hayes; **D:** George Melford; **W:** Donald W. Lee; **C:** Tom Galligan, Harry Naumann.

Boiling Point 🎬🎬 **3x Jugatsu 1990** Masaki (Ono) is a young, inarticulate, misfit, loser gas-station attendant who even lets down his local baseball team when he tries to play ball. Then he makes the mistake of slugging a yakuza member, so he heads to Okinawa to buy a gun to defend himself and meets up with the ultimate Mr. Cool—Uehara (Kitano). Uehara is such a bad ass ever the yakuza don't want anything to do with him, so who better than the master to teach Masaki how to survive. The Japanese title refers to a baseball score, which somehow seems more apt. Japanese with subtitles. **96m/C VHS, DVD.** **JP** Takeshi "Beat" Kitano, Masahiko Ono, Hisashi Igawa; **D:** Takeshi "Beat" Kitano; **C:** Katsumi Yanagishima.

Bojangles 🎬🎬 **2001** Made-for-cable biopic of Bill "Bojangles" Robinson strictly a by-the-numbers affair from the beginning at the funeral to the various characters who turn and address the camera era to explain what they thought of the contradictory man. Gregory Hines does his usual excellent job in the lead, and the film looks very good. **101m/C VHS, DVD.** Gregory Hines, Peter Riegert, Kimberly Elise, Savion Glover, Ma'a Ricossa; **D:** Joseph Sargent; **W:** Richard Wesley, Robert P. Johnson; **C:** Donald M. Morgan; **M:** Terence Blanchard. **CABLE**

The Bold Caballero 🎬½ **1936** Rebel chieftain Zorro overthrows oppressive Spanish rule in the days of early California. **69m/B VHS, DVD.** Robert "Bob" Livingston, Heather Angel, Sig Ruman, Robert Warwick; **D:** Wells Root.

The Boldest Job in the West 🎬 **El Más Fabuloso Golpe del Far West 1971** Italian western about bankrobbers who meet to divide their spoils. Problem is, the guys with the loot don't show. Dubbed in English. **200m/C VHS.** /T Mark Edwards, Frank Sancho, Carmen Sevilla; **D:** Jose Antonio De La Loma.

Bomb the System WOOF! **2005 (R)** A trio of young artists conduct world "bombings" in New York City, covering available spaces with their graffiti signatures. In sync with the subculture, their paint is always stolen, although they do pay for their drugs. One of the outlaws is continually nagged by his mother to take the art scholarship he was offered in San Francisco, but he's deaf to her pleadings. There are run-ins with the law, some girlfriend situations and self-righteous speeches thrown into the mix but one never feels much sympathy toward the rebel—they're just low-life druggie vandals. **99m/C DVD.** US Mark Webber, Gano Grills, Jade Yorker, Bonz Malone, Donna Mitchell, Al Sapienza, Kumar Pallana; **D:** Adam Bhala Lough; **W:** Adam Bhala Lough; **C:** Ben Kutchins; **M:** El-P.

Bomb at 10:10 🎬🎬 **1967** An American pilot escapes from a German POW camp and plots to assassinate a camp commandant. **87m/C VHS.** George Montgomery, Rada Popovic, Peter Banicevic; **D:** Charles Danic.

Bomb Squad 🎬🎬 **Cold Night Into Dawn 1997** Suicidal terrorist has a nuclear bomb small enough to fit into a suitcase and has decided to make Chicago his target. The Feds have 24-hours to find and defuse it. **91m/C VHS, DVD.** Anthony Michael Hall, Michael Ironside, Tony LoBianco; **D:** Serge Rodnunsky; **W:** Serge Rodnunsky. **VIDEO**

Bombay Talkie 🎬🎬½ **1970 (PG)** A bored British writer (Kendal) heads to India to gather "experiences" and be-see the Ponderosa is safe from an unscrupulous businessman. Lame update of the classic family western series. **96m/C VHS, DVD.** Edward James Olmos, Tony Nardi, Zachary Bennett, Philip Bosco, Claudia Ferri, Robert Logan; **D:** Martin Landau, Bruce Ramsay, Costas Mandylor, Edward James Olmos, Tony Nardi, Zachary Bennett, Philip Bosco, Claudia Ferri, Robert Logan; **W:** Thomas Michael Donnelly; **C:** Serge Ladouceur; **M:** Richard Gregoire. **CABLE**

Bonanza: The Return 🎬½ **1993 (PG)** In 1905, the children of various members of the Cartwright clan work to come true. A bored British writer (Kendal) heads to India to gather "experiences" and become involved with an Indian movie actor (Kapoor). Early clash-of-cultures film from Merchant Ivory has it's dull spots; the behind-the-scenes look at the Indian film industry is more interesting than the romance. **110m/C VHS, DVD.** IN Jennifer Kendal, Shashi Kapoor, Zia Mohyeddin, Aparna Sen; **D:** James Ivory; **W:** Ruth Prawer Jhabvala.

Bombs Away! 🎬 **1986** An atomic bomb is mistakenly shipped to a seedy war surplus store in Seattle, and causes much chicanery. **90m/C VHS.** Michael Huddleston, Pat McCormick; **D:** Bruce Wilson.

Bonanza Town 🎬½ **1951** Steve and sidekick Smiley (Burnette) are hired to locate the loot stolen in a Dodge City holdup. Marked money leads our heroes to corrupt officials. **56m/B VHS, DVD.** Charles Starrett, Smiley Burnette, Myron Healey, Fred F. Sears; **D:** Fred F. Sears; **C:** Henry Freulich.

Bolero 🎬🎬 **1982** Beginning in 1936, this international epic traces the lives of four families across three continents and five decades, highlighting the music and dance that is central to their lives. **173m/C VHS, DVD.** Jean Claudine Chaplin, Robert Hossein, Nicole Garcia, Jacques Villeret; **D:** Claude Lelouch; **W:** Claude Lelouch.

Bolero WOOF! **Bolero: An Adventure in Ecstasy 1984 (R)** What sounds like a wet dream come true is really just a good snooze: Bo Derek plays a beautiful young woman who goes on a trip around the world in 'ropes of losing her virginity; in Spain, she meets a bullfighter who's willing in perhaps the best performance of her good as she looks. Too bad Bo cannot act as good as she looks. Too bad Bo cannot act as good as she looks. **106m/C VHS, DVD.** Bo Derek, George Kennedy, Andrea Occhipinti, Anna (Ana Garcia) Obregon, Olivia D'Abo; **D:** John Derek; **W:** Peter Bernstein, Elmer Bernstein, Golden Raspberries '84: Worst Picture, Worst Actress (Derek), Worst Director (Derek), Worst Screenplay, Worst New Star (D'Abo).

Boltneck 🎬½ **Big Monster on Campus; Teen Monster 1998** When school outcast Karl turns into a series of a hazing by jocks, nerdy Frank Stein (get it?) decides to try an experiment in re-animating the dead. But unknown to Frank, the brain he's used (which he stole from his father's lab—how convenient) is that of a mass killer and the new Karl has developed quite an attitude. **92m/C VHS, DVD.** Justin Walker, Ryan Reynolds, Christine Lakin, Bianca Lawson, Kenny Blank, Matthew Lawrence, Richard Moll; **D:** Mitch Marcus; **W:** Dave Payne; **M:** Roger Neil. **VIDEO**

Bon Voyage! 🎬🎬½ **1962** A family's long-awaited European "dream" vacation turns into a series of comic misadventures for Walt Disney very family, very predictable comedy. **131m/C VHS, DVD.** Fred MacMurray, Jane Wyman, Deborah Walley, Michael Callan, Tommy Kirk, Jessie Royce Landis; **D:** James Neilson.

Bon Voyage 🎬🎬🎬 **2003 (PG-13)** Successful comedy-adventure mixes romance, espionage, murder, and melodrama amid the chaos of the Nazi occupation of France. In the role of a lifetime, Adjani is Viviane, an amoral movie star who's seeing government minister Beaufort (Depardieu) but gets humble former flame Frederic (Derangere) to do her bidding, including disposing of the body of a blackmailer (Vaude). Fred gets busted with the body, takes the rap, and winds up in jail only to escape with the help of resourceful criminal Raoul (Attal). Coyote does a turn as a spy posing as a journalist who also has a thing for the tres popular Viviane. The lives of all the characters intersect with interesting results in this not completely original but engaging and well-made romp. **114m/C DVD.** FR Isabelle Adjani, Gerard Depardieu, Virginie Ledoyen, Yvan Attal, Peter Coyote, Aurore Clement, Xavier De Guillebon, Edith Scob, Michel Vuillermoz, Gregori Derangere, Jean-Marc Stehle, Nicolas Pignon; **D:** Jean-Paul Rappeneau; **W:** Jean-Paul Rappeneau, Gilles Marchand, Patrick Modiano; **C:** Thierry Arbogast; **M:** Gabriel Yared.

Bonanno: A Godfather's Story 🎬🎬 **Youngest Godfather 1999** Old-fashioned storytelling seems to fit the story of an old-fashioned New York mobster—Joseph Bonanno (Landau)—who thought to be the inspiration for Mario Puzo's Don Vito Corleone. The elderly Bonanno reflects on his life and how he got into criminal activity back in the Prohibition days, drawing the attention of boss Salvatore Maranzano (Olmos). From there it's just a matter of time as Joe works his way up through the ranks. Based on the book written by his son Bill. **139m/C VHS, DVD.** Martin Landau, Bruce Ramsay, Costas Mandylor, Edward James Olmos, Tony Nardi, Zachary Bennett, Philip Bosco, Claudia Ferri, Robert Logan; **D:** Thomas Michael Donnelly; **C:** Serge Ladouceur; **M:** Richard Gregoire. **CABLE**

Bombardier 🎬🎬½ **1943** A group of cadet bombardiers discover the realities of war on raids over Japan during WWII. Also available colorized. **99m/B VHS.** Pat O'Brien, Randolph Scott, Robert Ryan, Eddie Albert, Anne Shirley, Barton MacLane; **D:** Richard Wallace.

Bombshell 🎬🎬 **Blonde Bombshell 1933** Wry insightful comedy into the Hollywood of the 1930s. Harlow plays a naive press agent. He thwarts her plans until she finally notices and begins to fall in love with him. Brilliant satire with Harlow turning in perhaps the best performance of her short career. **96m/B VHS.** Jean Harlow, Lee Tracy, Pat O'Brien, Una Merkel, Sir C. Aubrey Smith, Franchot Tone; **D:** Victor Fleming.

Bombshell 🎬🎬 **1997 (R)** Scientist Buck Hogan (Thomas) discovers a deadly flaw in the world's first cancer-killing drug, which he helps reveals, much to the dismay of the manufacturer's head honcho Donald (James). But then Hogan and his girlfriend Angeline (Amick) are abducted by a terrorist group, and Buck's implanted with a device that will kill him unless he does as they say. **95m/C VHS, DVD.** Henry Thomas, Frank Whaley, Madchen Amick, Bron James, Pamela Gidley, Shawnee Smith, Martin Hewitt; **D:** Paul Wynne; **W:** Paul Wynne.

The Bonfire of the Vanities 🎬🎬½ **1990 (R)** If you liked Tom Wolfe's viciously satirical novel, chances are you won't like this version. And you didn't read the book, you probably still won't like it. Miscast and stripped of the book's gutsy look inside its characters, the film's sole attribute is Vilmos Zsigmond's lush photography. Hanks is a young black panics and accidentally kills a young black kid. Willis' drunken journalist/narrator, Griffith's mistress, and Freeman's righteous judge are all awkward and thinly written. If you're still awake, look for F. Murray Abraham's cameo as the Bronx D.A. **126m/C VHS, DVD.** Tom Hanks, Melanie Griffith, Bruce Willis, Morgan Freeman, Alan King, Kim Cattrall, Saul Rubinek, Clifton James, Donald Moffat, Richard Liberni, Andre Gregory, Donald Stephens; **Cameos:** F. Murray Abraham; **D:** Brian De Palma; **W:** Michael Cristofer; **C:** Vilmos Zsigmond.

Bone Daddy 🎬🎬 **1997 (R)** Former chief medical examiner William Palmer (Hauer) turns his experiences into a best-selling novel and excites the rage of a psychopathic killer. The surgical killer, who's nicknamed "Bone Daddy" because he likes to extract the bones of his victims, is busy at work and Palmer teams up with a reluctant detective (Williams) to track the looney down. **90m/C VHS.** Rutger Hauer, Barbara Williams, R.H. Thomson, Joseph Kell, Robin Gammell, Daniel Kash, Christopher Heyerdahl; **D:** Mario Azzopardi; **W:** Thomas Szollosi; **C:** Danny Nowak; **M:** Christophe Beck.

The Bone Yard 🎬🎬 **1990 (R)** A weird medical mortuary is the setting for strange goings-on when a murder is investigated. **98m/C VHS, DVD.** Ed Nelson, Deborah Rose, Norman Fell, Jim Eisenmann, Denise Young, Willie Stratton Jr., Phyllis Diller; **D:** James Cummins; **W:** James Cummins; **C:** Irl Dixon; **M:** Kathleen Ann Porter, John Lee Whitener.

Bones 🎬🎬 **2001 (R)** Combining the best of blaxploitation and horror elements, Dickerson smartly reveals the story of benevolent pimp Jimmy Bones (Snoop Dogg) disappearance and subsequent resurrection 22 years later as a vengeful spirit. When an entrepreneurial buppie (Kain) decides to open a dance hall in Jimmy's former digs, walls begin oozing, animals become abundant and mean, and old secrets are revealed, most to the chagrin of the kid's rich father (Davis), a cop (Weiss). Grier shines as a neighborhood psychic, and Snoop adds miles of style and presence, keeping this one a notch above the standard-issue haunted house fare. **94m/C VHS, DVD.** Snoop Dogg, Pam Grier, Michael T. Weiss, Clifton Powell, Ricky Harris, Bianca Lawson, Khalil Kain, Katharine Isabelle, Merwin Mondesir, Sean Amsing; **D:** Ernest R. Dickerson; **W:** Adam Simon; **C:** Flavio Martinez Labiano; **M:** Elia Cmiral.

The Bone Collector 🎬🎬½ **1999 (R)** Lincoln Rhyme (Washington) is a brilliant NYPD detective and forensics expert who was left a quadriplegic after an on-the-job accident. His suicidal thoughts are distracted by the work of a serial killer with a gruesome MO and the admirable work of hotshot young policewoman, Amelia Donoghy (Jolie). Amelia soon becomes Rhyme's surrogate investigator. The situation comes to a climax in Rhyme's apartment as he lies helpless. Thriller turns out to be predictable but performance. Based on the 1997 novel by Jeffrey Deaver. **118m/C VHS, HD DVD.** Denzel Washington, Angelina Jolie, Queen Latifah, Ed O'Neill, Michael Rooker, Mike McGlone, Leland Orser, Luis Guzman, John Benjamin Hickey, Bobby Cannavale; **D:** Philip Noyce; **W:** Jeremy Iacone; **C:** Dean Semler; **M:** Craig Armstrong.

Bongwater 🎬🎬 **1998 (R)** David (Wilson) is a Portland pot dealer and aspiring artist who becomes roommates with Serena (Witt), although mixed signals prevents anything closer even if David is definitely lovesick. Thanks to a misunderstanding, Serena heads to New York, a bong ignites the house where David was living—burning it to the ground—and he is forced to rely on the kindness of his fellow pot buddies while Serena has her own problems in the Big Apple. However, you won't really care except Wilson is appealing in a goofy doper sort of way. **98m/C VHS, DVD.** Luke Wilson, Alicia Witt, Amy Locane, Brittany Murphy, Jack Black, Andy Dick, Jeremy Sisto, Jamie Kennedy, Scott Caan, Patricia Wettig; **C:** Richard Sears; **W:** Nora MacCoby, Eric Weiss; **C:** Richard Crudo; **M:** Mark Mothersbaugh, Josh Mancell.

Bonjour Monsieur Shlomi ♂♂♂

HaKochavim Shel Shlomi 2003 Light-hearted human comedy about sixteen-year-old, Shlomi, a mildly slow-witted Jewish boy juggling school, love, and the family circus at home. Willing to put his own interests aside, Shlomi dedicates most of his life to caring for his senile grandfather, cooking elaborate meals for the family, and falling behind in school. His secret joys come from poetry, snooping through his older brother's explicit diary, and daydreaming about the girl next door. A surprisingly warm Israeli film that manages to avoid the usual melodramatic pitfalls of most American coming-of-age flicks. **94m/C DVD.** Esti Zakheim, Aya Koren, Assi Cohen, Oshri Cohen, Arie Elias, Ygal Naor, Albert Illouz, Jonathan Rozen, Rotem Abuhav, Rotem Zisman, Nisso Khavia, Aya Steinovitz; **D:** Shemi Zarhin; **W:** Shemi Zarhin; **C:** Itzik Portal; **M:** Jonathan Bar-Giora.

Bonjour Tristesse ♂♂♂ 1957

An amoral French girl (Seberg) conspires to break up her playboy father's (Niven) upcoming marriage to her stuffy godmother (Kerr) in order to maintain her decadent freedom. Preminger attempted, unsuccessfully, to use this soaper to catapult Seberg to stardom. Based on the novel by Francoise Sagan. **94m/B VHS, DVD.** *FR* Deborah Kerr, David Niven, Jean Seberg, Mylene Demongeot, Geoffrey Horne, Walter Chiari, Jean Kent; **D:** Otto Preminger; **W:** Arthur Laurents; **C:** Georges Perinal.

Bonneville ♂♂ 2006 (PG)

On a mission to spread the ashes of a dead husband, three middle-aged women hit the open road in a 1966 Bonneville, driving from Idaho to California. Along the way they laugh about the good old days, cry about car trouble, and connect all the dots required of a formulaic road trip flick. Bates, Lange, and Allen are excellent, but ultimately wasted on a script that's lacking surprise and running on fumes from the start. **93m/C DVD.** *US* Jessica Lange, Kathy Bates, Joan Allen, Christine Baranski, Victor Rasuk, Tom Amandes, Tom Wopat, Tom Skerritt; **D:** Christopher Rowley; **W:** Daniel Davis; **C:** Jeffrey L. Kimball; **M:** Jeff Cardoni.

Bonnie & Clyde ♂♂♂♂½ 1967

Based on the biographies of the violent careers of Bonnie Parker (Dunaway) and Clyde Barrow (Beatty), who roamed the Southwest robbing banks. In the Depression era, when any job, even an illegal one, was cherished, money, greed, and power created an unending cycle of violence and fury. Highly controversial and influential, with pronounced bloodshed (particularly the pairs balletic and bullet-ridden end) that spurred mainstream cinematic proliferation. Established Dunaway as a star; produced by Beatty in one of his best performances. **111m/C VHS, DVD, Blu-ray Disc.** Warren Beatty, Faye Dunaway, Michael J. Pollard, Gene Hackman, Estelle Parsons, Denver Pyle, Gene Wilder; Dub Taylor, Evans Evans; **D:** Arthur Penn; **W:** David Newman, Robert Benton; **C:** Burnett Guffey; **M:** Charles Strouse. Oscars '67: Cinematog., Support. Actress (Parsons); AFI '98: Top 100, Natl. Film Reg. '92; N.Y. Film Critics '67: Screenplay, Support. Actor (Hackman); Writers Guild '67: Orig. Screenplay.

Bonnie Prince Charlie ♂♂♂½ 1948

Historical epic opening in 1745 and romanticizing the title pretender to the British throne, who united Scottish clans in a doomed campaign against King George. Talky and rather slow-moving except for stirring battle scenes. A notorious boxoffice flop in its native Britain, where the original running time was 140 minutes. **114m/C VHS.** *GB* David Niven, Margaret Leighton, Judy Campbell, Jack Hawkins, Morland Graham, Finlay

Currie, Elwyn Brook-Jones, John Laurie; **D:** Anthony Kimmins.

Bonnie Scotland ♂♂½ 1935

Laurel & Hardy accidentally join an India-bound Scottish regiment. Laughs aplenty. **81m/B VHS, DVD.** Stan Laurel, Oliver Hardy, James Finlayson, Daphne Pollard, June Lang; **D:** James W. Horne.

Bonnie's Kids ♂½ 1973 (R)

Two sisters become involved in murder, sex, and stolen money. **107m/C VHS.** Tiffany Bolling, Robin Mattson, Scott Brady, Alex Rocco; **D:** Arthur Marks.

Boo! ♂♂ 2005

Five college students decide to check out the abandoned Santa Mira Hospital on Halloween to see if rumors about it being haunted are true. They discover a vengeful spirit that wants to make sure no one gets out alive. Low-budget but inventive and sufficiently creepy for a dark and stormy night. **100m/C DVD.** Dee Wallace Stone, Trish Coren, M. Steven Felty, Josh Holt, Jilon Ghai, Nicole Rayburn, Michael Samluk, Dig Wayne; **D:** Anthony C. Ferrante; **W:** Anthony C. Ferrante; **C:** Carl F. Bartels. **VIDEO**

The Boogey Man ♂♂ 1980 (R)

Through the reflection in a mirror, a girl witnesses her brother murder their mother's lover. Twenty years later this memory still haunts her; the mirror is now broken, revealing its special powers. Who will be next? Murder menagerie; see footage from this flick mirrored in "The Boogey Man 2." **93m/C VHS, DVD.** John Carradine, Suzanna Love, Ron James; **D:** Ulli Lommel; **W:** Ulli Lommel, Suzanna Love; **C:** Jochen Breitenstein, David Sperling; **M:** Tim Krog.

Boogey Man 2 ♂ WOOF! 1983

The story continues; same footage, new director but with Lommel, the director of the original "Boogey Man," co-writing the script and appearing in the film. **90m/C VHS, DVD.** John Carradine, Suzanna Love, Shannah Hall, Ulli Lommel, Sholto Von Douglas; **D:** Bruce Starr.

Boogeyman ♂½ 2005 (PG-13)

Weak horror flick about monsters in the closet. Tim (Watson) returns to his hometown for his mother's (Lawless) funeral and revisits the childhood home where his father was apparently sucked into young Tim's bedroom closet by the boogeyman and killed. Naturally, Tim has an aversion to closets. He wants to prove the boogeyman is all in his imagination like his shrink says; the boogeyman has other ideas. **86m/C DVD, UMD.** *US* Barry Watson, Emily Deschanel, Skye McCole Bartusiak, Lucy Lawless, Philip Gordon, Aaron Murphy, Robyn Malcolm, Victoria (Tory) Mussett, Andrew Glover, Charles Mesure, Jennifer Rucker; **D:** Stephen Kay; **C:** Bobby Bukowski; **M:** Joseph LoDuca.

Boogeyman 2 ♂½ 2007

When Laura (Savre) and her brother (Cohen) were children, they watched their father get slaughtered by the boogeyman. Naturally, this caused a lot of trauma, so Laura decides to check herself into a local mental hospital in hopes of getting past her continuing fear. But when patients start dying, it becomes clear the creature is trolling the hospital for his next victims. **93m/C DVD.** Tobin Bell, Renee O'Connor, Danielle Sieve; **C:** Nelson Cragg. **VIDEO**

Boogie Boy ♂½ 1998 (R)

Recently released from prison, Jesse (Dacascos) gets involved as muscle for a drug deal involving his ex-cellmate, the drug-addicted Larry (Woolvett), in order to get some quick cash. Naturally, the deal goes sour and they wind up on the lam. **110m/C VHS, DVD.** Mark Dacascos, Emily Lloyd, Jaimz Woolvett, Traci Lords, Frederic Forrest, Joan Jett, Ben Browder, James Lew, Linnea Quigley; **D:** Craig Hamann; **M:** Tim Truman.

The Boogie Man Will Get You ♂♂½ 1942

Crazy scientist Nathaniel Billings (Karloff) has been working on creating a race of supermen in his basement. He sells his home to Bill (Parks) and Winnie (Donnell), who are turning the place into a bed and breakfast, thinking that he can use their guests as fresh subjects. Lorre plays multiple roles, including a fellow nutcase. Karloff was unavailable to reprise his role in the film ver-

sion of "Arsenic and Old Lace" so he did this similar comedy instead. **66m/B VHS.** Boris Karloff, Peter Lorre, Maxie "Slapsie" Rosenbloom, Larry Parks, Jeff Donnell, Maude Eburne; **D:** Lew Landers; **W:** Edwin Blum; **C:** Henry Freulich.

Boogie Nights ♂♂♂½ 1997 (R)

Epic tale covering the rise and fall of porn star Eddie Adams (Wahlberg). The protege of director Jack Horner (Reynolds), 17-year-old Eddie jumps in a hot tub at an industry bash, christens himself Dirk Diggler, and goes on to become the toast of the adult entertainment industry. Brilliantly spanning the decadent disco-era 70s and the excess of the 80s, 27-year-old writer/director Anderson boldly delves into fresh, albeit dangerous, territory most successfully in this lengthy sophomore outing. What Tarantino did for Travolta, Anderson does here for Reynolds, who plays the past-his-prime but touchingly ambitious auteur with a dream to make a legitimately legendary skin flick. Wahlberg proves himself a serious and seriously good actor in his turn, surrounded by equally fine performances of the ensemble cast. Details such as wardrobe, bits of dialogue, and music are deftly used, avoiding parody. Nonstop disco and early 80s music, often with a message, and energetic camera work, make you shake your booty. **155m/C VHS, DVD.** Michael Penn, Mark Wahlberg, Burt Reynolds, Julianne Moore, Don Cheadle, William H. Macy, Heather Graham, John C. Reilly, Luis Guzman, Philip Seymour Hoffman, Alfred Molina, Philip Baker Hall, Robert Ridgely, Joanna Gleason, Thomas Jane, Ricky Jay, Nicole Ari Parker, Melora Walters, Michael Jace, Nina Hartley, John Doe, Laurel Holloman, Robert Downey; **D:** Paul Thomas Anderson; **W:** Paul Thomas Anderson; **C:** Robert Elswit; **M:** Michael Penn. Golden Globes '98: Support. Actor (Reynolds); L.A. Film Critics '97: Support. Actor (Reynolds), Support. Actress (Moore); MTV Movie Awards '98: Breakthrough Perf. (Graham); N.Y. Film Critics '97: Support. Actor (Reynolds); Natl. Soc. Film Critics '97: Support. Actor (Reynolds), Support. Actress (Moore).

Book of Love ♂♂ 1991 (PG-13)

"Zany" hijinks as a teenager struggles with friendship, girls, and those all-important hormones when he moves to a new neighborhood in the mid-'50s. Average rehash of every '50s movie and TV show cliche in existence. Surprise! There's a classic rock 'n' roll soundtrack. Adapted by Kotzwinkle from his novel "Jack in the Box." **88m/C VHS, DVD.** Chris Young, Keith Coogan, Aeryk Egan, Josie Bissett, Tricia Leigh Fisher, Danny Nucci, Michael McKean, John Cameron Mitchell, Lewis Arquette; **D:** Robert Shaye; **W:** William Kotzwinkle; **M:** Stanley Clarke.

Book of Love ♂♂ 2004 (R)

David (Baker) and Elaine's (O'Connor) childless marriage hits a lull, so the couple befriends Chet (Smith)—David's 15-year-old student—to fill the void. Life for the happy wanna-be-family gets muddled up when David discovers that Chet and Elaine had a creepy and very illegal affair. **85m/C VHS, DVD.** Frances O'Connor, Simon Baker, Gregory Edward Smith, Bryce Dallas Howard, Joanna Adler, Ari Graynor; **D:** Alan Brown; **W:** Alan Brown; **C:** William Rexer. **VIDEO**

Book of Shadows: Blair Witch 2 ♂½ 2000 (R)

Blair Witch 2 Thankfully, they've gotten rid of the shaky-cam (which shook more than a few viewers' stomachs), that's one plus for this sequel that finds five followers of the Blair Witch myth heading back into the woods. Unfortunately, they've also gotten rid of the scares produced by mysterious offscreen witchy shenanigans and replaced them with buckets of fake blood. This group is led by Jeff (Donovan), a townie who's decided to cash in on the Blair Witch craze by organizing tours of the sites made famous in the first movie. Grad students Tristen (Skyler) and Stephen (Turner), practicing Wiccan Erica (Leerhsen) and goth-chick Kim (Director), have fun skewering the new movement and its internet movement while partying on the first night. The next day they realize they've lost five hours of their lives. They try to discover what happened, and if it has anything to do with another tour group getting disemboweled. Disappointing fictional debut

from documentary director Berlinger, who filmed the truly horrific (and true) "Paradise Lost: The Child Murders at Robin Hood Hills." The townspeople of Burkittsville, Maryland were so fed up with the first film that the second was filmed elsewhere. **90m/C VHS, DVD.** Jeffrey Donovan, Kim Director, Tristen Skylar, Stephen Barker Turner, Erica Leerhsen; **D:** Joe Berlinger; **W:** Joe Berlinger, Dick Beebe; **C:** Nancy Schreiber; **M:** Carter Burwell. Golden Raspberries '00: Worst Remake/Sequel.

The Book of Stars ♂♂½ 1999

Penny (Masterson) is the older sister and only support for teenaged Mary (Malone), who suffers from cystic fibrosis. Penny is a jaded, pill-popping hooker while Mary, however, refuses to give up her optimistic outlook on life. With the aid of cantankerous neighbor Professor (Lindo) and a couple of new friends, Mary is determined to change Penny's views as well. Manages to skirt the subject's inherent sentimentality with some winning performances. **98m/C VHS, DVD.** Mary Stuart Masterson, Jena Malone, Karl Geary, D.B. Sweeney, Delroy Lindo; **D:** Michael Miner; **W:** Tasca Shadix; **C:** James Whitaker; **M:** Richard Gibbs. **VIDEO**

Bookies ♂♂ 2003 (R)

Thinking they can strike it rich the easy way, three college pals set up shop as bookies. Naturally, their hot streak abruptly ends when the local syndicate takes issue with the amateurs cutting into their cash flow. **90m/C VHS, DVD.** Nick Stahl, Lukas Haas, Johnny Galecki, Rachael Leigh Cook, David Proval, John Diehl, Luis Guzman; **D:** Mark Illsley; **W:** Michael Bacall; **C:** Brendan Galvin; **M:** Christopher Tyng, Giuseppe Cristiano. **VIDEO**

Boom! ♂½ 1968 (PG)

Laughable adaptation of the Williams' play "The Milk Train Doesn't Stop Here Anymore" was a Hollywood star disaster. Flora Goforth (Taylor) is a dying millionairess living in isolated glory on an island near Sardinia. Chris Flanders (Burton) is a wandering poet, nicknamed the "Angel of Death," who shows up and becomes Flora's confidante. Does have pretty scenery. **113m/C VHS.** Elizabeth Taylor, Richard Burton, Noel Coward, Joanna Shimkus, Michael Dunn, Romolo Valli; **D:** Joseph Losey; **W:** Tennessee Williams; **C:** Douglas Slocombe; **M:** John Barry.

Boom in the Moon WOOF! A Modern Bluebeard 1946

Keaton fares poorly in this sci-fi comedy. He's trapped on a space ship to the moon. Poor production, with uneven direction and acting. **83m/C VHS.** Buster Keaton, Angel Garasa, Virginia Serret, Fernando Soto Mantequilla, Luis Barreiro; **D:** Jaime Salvador.

Boom Town ♂♂♂½ 1940

A lively vintage comedy/drama/romance about two oil-drilling buddies competing amid romantic mix-ups and fortunes gained and lost. **120m/B VHS, DVD.** Clark Gable, Spencer Tracy, Claudette Colbert, Hedy Lamarr, Frank Morgan, Lionel Atwill, Curt Bois; **D:** Jack Conway; **W:** John Lee Mahin; **C:** Harold Rosson, Elwood "Woody" Bredell; **M:** Franz Waxman.

Boomerang ♂♂♂ 1947

Film noir based on actual events features the murder of a Connecticut clergyman and the quick arrest of vagrant John Waldron (Kennedy). Prosecuting attorney Henry Harvey (Andrews) is told by his political bosses to get an equally quick conviction to stem public outrage. The evidence seems overwhelming but Harvey begins his own investigation and suddenly switches to the defense to prove Waldron's innocence in dramatic courtroom style. Kazan filmed on location in Bridgeport, CT in a successful semi-documentary style that heightened the tension. **88m/B VHS, DVD.** Dana Andrews, Arthur Kennedy, Lee J. Cobb, Jane Wyatt, Cara Williams, Sam Levene, Ed Begley Sr., Karl Malden, Taylor Holmes, Robert Keith; **D:** Elia Kazan; **W:** Richard Murphy; **C:** Norbert Brodine; **M:** David Buttolph.

Boomerang ♂♂ 1992 (R)

Successful, womanizing marketing exec for a cosmetics company (Murphy) meets his match when he falls for a colleague (Givens) who is as vain and sexually predatory as he is. She treats him the way the treats women (as a sex object), and he's shocked into the arms of a nice girl (Berry). Although it's refreshing to see this sexual role reversal, the typical Murphy-style humor is in play, with sexist jokes and a couple of vulgar female characters. Grier and Lawrence are great as Murphy's best friends. Blaustein and Sheffield are the same guys who wrote Murphy's "Coming to America." **118m/C VHS, DVD,** Eddie Murphy, Halle Berry, Robin Givens, David Alan Grier, Martin Lawrence, Grace Jones, Geoffrey Holder, Eartha Kitt, Chris Rock, Tisha Campbell, John Witherspoon, Melvin Van Peebles; **D:** Reginald (Reggie) Hudlin; **W:** Barry W. Blaustein, David Sheffield.

Boots Malone 🐾🐾½ **1952** An old down-on-his-luck gambling addict and a young, rich kid fascinated by the sordid atmosphere of the racetrack stumble upon one another and form a symbiotic relationship. All goes well for while, but there'd be...

Boots & Saddles 🐾🐾½ **1937** A young English lord wants to sell the ranch he has inherited but Autry is determined to make him a real Westerner. **54m/B VHS, DVD,** Gene Autry, Judith Allen, Smiley Burnette; **D:** Joseph Kane.

Boothill Brigade 🐾🐾 **1937** Former football star Brown rides to the rescue when criminals steal land from homesteaders. **58m/B VHS,** Johnny Mack Brown, Claire Rochelle, Dick Curtis, Horace Murphy, Frank Ball, Steve Clark; **D:** Sam Newfield.

Bootleg 🐾🐾 **1985** A detective is on a case that leads to crooked politics and espionage. **82m/C VHS,** John Flaus, Carmen Duncan, Ian Nimmo, Ray Meagher; **D:** John Prescott; **W:** John Prescott; **C:** Stephen Frost; **M:** Stephen Cronin.

Bootmen 🐾🐾 **2000 (R)** Young Sean must make his dance dreams come true despite a bitter, critical father and his working-class Australian surroundings. Director Dein Perry has turned his hit show "Tap Dogs" into a fictionalized and semi-autobiographical tale that combines some of the better qualities of "The Full Monty" and the standard twists and turns of so many other dance films. The "Let's put on a show" pic doesn't provide much sustenance to the viewer through to some of the excellent choreography. Features several players from the original Tap Dogs company. **95m/C VHS, DVD, AU** Adam Garcia, Sophie Lee, William Zappa, Sam Worthington, Susie Porter; **D:** Dein Perry; **W:** Steve Wo'and; **C:** Steve Mason; Australian Film Inst. '00: Cinematog., Costume Des., Score.

Bordello 🐾 **1979** Western spoof about cowboys and shady ladies. **90m/C VHS,** Chuck Connors, Michael Conrad, John Ireland, Isela Vega, Jorge (George) Rivero; **D:** Ray Fellows. **TV**

Boondock Saints 🐾🐾 **1999 (R)** Two Boston Irish-Catholic brothers, Connor (Flanery) and Murphy (Feedus) McManus, turn into unlikely local heroes after the self-defense killings of some Russian mobsters who were threatening to close down their local pub. They turn vigilante, believing they're doing God's work to rid the world of evil which leads to more slaughter. Investigating the crimes is gay FBI agent Paul Smecker (Dafoe), who is shown reconstructing the carnage in a series of flashbacks. **110m/C VHS, DVD, UMD** Sean Patrick Flanery, Norman Reedus, Willem Dafoe, David Della Rocco, Carlo Rota, Billy Connolly, David Ferry, Brian Mahoney; **D:** Troy Duffy; **W:** Troy Duffy; **C:** Adam Kane; **M:** Jeff Danna.

Boot Hill 🐾🐾 **1969 (PG)** Two guys in spaghetti oater. **97m/C VHS, DVD. /T** Terence Hill, Eud Spencer, Woody Strode, Victor Buono, Lionel Stander; **D:** Giuseppe Colizzi.

Boot Hill Bandits 🐾🐾½ **1942** "Crash" Corrigan fights on the side of right in this class c western as he helps corral Wells Fargo bandits. **58m/B VHS, DVD,** Ray Corrigan, John 'Dusty' King, Max Terhune, Jean Brooks, John Merton, Glenn Strange; **D:** S. Roy Luby.

Boots of Destiny 🐾 **1937** Cheap western with Maynard and his sidekick Barnett on the lam and coming to the aid of ranch owner Dell. Based on a story by Claudia Dell, Vince Barnett, Edward Cassidy, Martin Garralaga; **D:** Arthur Rosson; **W:** Arthur Rosson.

Booty Call 🐾🐾½ **1996 (R)** Reserved Rushon (Davidson) and conservative Nikki (Jones) have been dating for a couple of months and Rushon's decided they should consummate their relationship. Nikki's more ambivalent and first sets up a double date with her vivacious best friend Lysterine (Fox) and Rushon's bragging buddy Bunz (Foxx). The duos go their separate ways, but since the "no glove, no love" rule prevails, first the guys have to find some condoms. Raunch rules as might be expected but it's an appealing cast. **120m/C VHS, DVD,** Jamie Foxx, Tommy Davidson, Vivica A. Fox, Tamala Jones, Art Malik, Gedde Watanabe, Scott LaRose, Annie Sin, Bernie Mac, David Hemblen; **D:** Jeff Pollack; **W:** Takashi Bufford; **C:** Ronald Orieux; **M:** Robert Folk.

Bopha! 🐾🐾 **1993 (PG-13)** Father-son strife set against the anti-apartheid movement. In the Senior township police officer Mkali takes pride in his peaceful community, particularly in light of the growing unrest in the other townships. Son Zweli has become an activist and wife Rosie must be the family peacemaker. Then a prominent freedom movement member is arrested and two officers of the secret police make their sinister appearance. Well acted; directorial debut of Freeman. Adapted from the play by Percy Mtwa, although the hopeful ending has been changed in the movie. The title, a Zulu word, stands for arrest or detention. Filmed on location in Zimbabwe. **121m/C VHS, DVD,** Danny Glover, Maynard Ezeashi, Alfre Woodard, Malcolm McDowell, Marius Weyers, Malick Bowens, Robin Smith, Michael Chinyamurindi, Christopher John Hall, Grace Mahlaba; **D:** Morgan Freeman; **W:** Brian Bird, John Wierick; **M:** James Horner.

Borat: Cultural Learnings of America for Make Benefit Glorious Nation of Kazakhstan 🐾🐾🐾 **2006 (R)** British comic Sacha Baron Cohen is outrageously funny as Borat, the cheerfully ignorant and prejudiced "sixth best known reporter in Kazakhstan." The plot follows Borat's travels through America in order to bring back to his homeland two things the feels strongly about: lessons on America and Pamela Anderson. The plot is just a frame to prop up the real aim of the movie/film, which is to allow the American public to parody and incriminate itself. Viewers will simultaneously wince and laugh as Borat's seemingly innocent Third World anti-Semitism, homophobia and misogyny are reflected in unknowing victims from both jerkwater towns and cosmopolitan cities. Critically hailed upon its release, the film was dogged with numerous lawsuits and complaints from offended parties, particularly the Kazakh government. The humor is often crude (there is a credit for "Feces provided by") and disturbing (an extended scene of graphic "duddy" when Borat and producer Azamat (Davitian) wrestle over a magazine picture of Pamela) but genuinely funny and unsettling. **82m/C DVD, US** Sacha Baron Cohen, Pamela Anderson, Ken Davitian, Pat Haggerty, Alan Keyes, Luenell; **D:** Larry Charles; **W:** Sacha Baron Cohen, Peter Baynham, Dan Mazer, Anthony Hines; **C:** Luke Geissbuhler, Anthony Hardwick; **M:** Erran Baron Cohen; Golden Globes '07: Actor—Mus./Comedy (Cohen).

Border 🐾🐾 **1982 (R)** A border guard faces corruption and violence within his department and tests his own sense of decency when the infant of a poor Mexican girl is kidnapped. Excellent performance. **107m/C VHS, DVD,** Jack Nicholson, Harvey Keitel, Valerie Perrine, Warren Oates, Elpidia Carrillo; **D:** Tony Richardson; **W:** Deric Washburn, Walon Green; **M:** Ry Cooder.

Border Bandits 🐾 **1946** Plodding oater has Brown going after the bad guys. Not only is it a dirty job, but apparently pretty boring. **57m/B VHS,** Johnny Mack Brown, Raymond Hatton, John Merton, Frank LaRue, Steve Clark, Charles Stevens, Bud Osborne; **D:** Lambert Hillyer.

Border Badmen 🐾🐾½ **1945** It's just another tired old western, even if it does appropriate the classic mystery-thriller plot: following the reading of a silver baron's will, someone starts killing off the relatives. **59m/B VHS,** Buster Crabbe, Lorraine Miller, 'Blackie' King, Buster Crabbe, Ray Bennett, Arch (Archie) Hall; **D:** Sam Newfield.

Border Blues 🐾🐾½ **2003 (R)** Ex-Russian cop now tries to sneak a woman and her daughter across the U.S.-Mexico border as the primary suspect in connection with an L.A. mail-bomb scare. Painful to watch Busey and Estrada in their law enforcement roles. **86m/C VHS, DVD,** Eric Roberts, Gary Busey, Yekaterina Rednikova, Lisa Gerstein, Erik Estrada, Rodion Nakhapetov; **D:** Rodion Nakhapetov; **W:** Rodion Nakhapetov; **C:** Sergei Kozlov; **M:** David G. Russell. **VIDEO**

Border Caballero 🐾 **1936** Western star Maynard and lady enforcer McCoy and ... **60m/B VHS,** John Merton, Frank LaRue; **D:** Sam Newfield.

Border Devils 🐾 **1932** A boy is pursued by a ruthless gang of outlaws, until he is saved by the good guys, in this lackluster McCoy vehicle. Based on a story by Harry Carey Sr., Art Mix, George 'Gabby' Hayes, Norman S. Hall; **D:** William Nigh.

Border Feud 🐾 **1947** LaRue endeavors to prevent someone who, by instigating a family feud, will claim large goldmine rights. **54m/B VHS,** Lash LaRue, Al 'Fuzzy' St. John, Bob Duncan; **D:** Ray Taylor.

Border Incident 🐾🐾🐾 **1949** Average crime melodrama from director Mann in which federales on both sides of the border team up to prevent the exploitation and murder of illegal farm workers. Jack Bearnes (Murphy) has stolen work permits he's willing to sell to crooked rancher Owen Perkson (Da Silva) while Pablo Rodriguez (Montalban) poses as an illegal migrant, and both agents find themselves in grave danger. **94m/B DVD,** Ricardo Montalban, George Murphy, Howard da Silva, James Mitchell, Arnold Moss, Alfonso Bedoya, Teresa Celli, Charles McGraw, Jose Torvay, John Ridgely, Arthur Hunnicutt, Sig Ruman; **D:** Anthony Mann; **W:** John C. Higgins, George Zuckerman; **C:** John Alton.

Border Law 🐾🐾½ **1931** Jones plays a hero c Texas Ranger who goes undercover to find the man who killed his brother. One of Jones' finest outings and far better than most B westerns. **62m/B VHS,** Buck Jones, Lupita Tovar, James Mason, Frank Rice, Glenn Strange; **D:** Louis King; **W:** Stuart Anthony.

The Border Legion 🐾🐾½ **1931** *West of the Badlands* **1940** Sappy retelling of Grey's novel about an outlaw sacrificing himself for a pair of young lovers. This time Rogers is the outlaw with a heart of gold. Originally filmed in 1930 with Jack Holt, Richard Arlen, and Fay Wray. **58m/B VHS, DVD,** Roy Rogers, George "Gabby" Hayes, Carol Hughes, Joseph (Joe) Sawyer, Maude Eburne, Jay Novello; **D:** Joseph Kane; **W:** Olive Cooper, Louis Stevens.

Border Patrol 🐾🐾 **1943** Another installment in the Hopalong Cassidy series. This time there's a villainous owner of a silvermine to reckon with. A man so low he's abducting hapless Mexicans as they cross the border, forcing them to work his mines. Hoppy is saddled with the task of persuading him that the town ain't big enough for the both of them. Robert Mitchum makes his perfectly forgettable film debut as one of the bad guys. Not one of the best in the series, but plenty of action. **60m/B VHS, DVD,** William Boyd, Andy Clyde, Jay Kirby, Russell Simpson, Claudia Drake, George Reeves, Duncan Renaldo; **D:** Lesley Selander.

no movie unless a collection of obstacles suddenly threatens their success, friendship, and even their lives. A rather melodramatic buddy tale, but Holden and Stewart hold interest. **103m/C VHS,** William Holden, John Stewart, Ed Bagley Sr., Harry (Henry) Morgan, Whit Bissell; **D:** William Dieterle; **M:** Elmer Bernstein.

The Border 🐾🐾 **1982 (R)** A border...

Border Patrol 🐾🐾 **2001 (PG-13)** This Border Patrol is in charge of policing the realm of the dead, making sure sinners and the good get their proper punishment and rewards. Patrolman Numan is forced to break the rules and ask the help of a mortal Miami cop in order to stop vicious serial killer D. Helms from opening the gateway to other realms. **89m/C VHS,** Michael Delorenzo, Lewis Fitz-Gerald, Clayton Rohner, Kenny Ransom; **D:** Mark Haber; **M:** Miguel Tejada-Flores. **CABLE**

Border Phantom 🐾🐾 **1937** Steele (whom you might recognize as Canino in "The Big Sleep"), takes on a suave Chinese businessman who heads a mail order business; seems he's smuggling mail-order brides from Mexico in this vintage "B"-grade horse opera. **60m/B VHS, DVD,** Bob Steele, Harley Wood, Don Barclay, Karl Hackett, Horace Murphy; **D:** S. Roy Luby.

Border Radio 🐾🐾 **1988** A rock singer decides to steal a car and try to outrun some tough thugs not on his trail. **88m/B VHS,** Chris D, Luana Anders; **D:** Allison Anders, Kurt Voss; **W:** Allison Anders, Kurt Voss; **M:** Dave Alvin.

Border Rangers 🐾 **1950** A man joins the Rangers in order to avenge the murders of his brother and sister-in-law. **57m/B VHS,** Robert Lowery, Donald (Don "Red") Barry, Lyle Talbot, Pamela Blake; **D:** William Berke.

Border Romance 🐾🐾½ **1930** Three Americans have their horses stolen by bandits while riding through Mexico. Trouble with the locals follows in this early sound western. **58m/B VHS,** Don Terry, Armida, Marjorie Kane, Victor Potel, Nina Mae; **D:** Richard Thorpe; **W:** Jack Nattelford; **C:** Harry Zech; **M:** Al Short.

Border Roundup 🐾 **1941** The "Lone Rider" uncovers a gang of thieving crooks. **57m/B VHS,** George Houston, Al "Fuzzy" St. John, Dennis Moore; **D:** Sam Newfield.

Border Saddlemates 🐾🐾 **1952** U.S. government veterinarian Allen is asked to sub for the local doc in the Canadian border town of Pine Rock. But he learns that a gang is using silver fox pelts to smuggle illegal goods into the U.S. and it's up to Allen and the Rhythm Riders to stop them. **67m/B VHS,** Rex Allen, Mary Ellen Kay, Slim Pickens, Roy Barcroft, Forrest Taylor, Jimmy Moss, Zon Murray, Keith McConnell; **D:** William Witney; **M:** Stanley Wilson.

Border Shootout 🐾🐾 **1990 (PG)** A trigger-happy sheriff battles a rich young cattle rustler. **110m/C VHS, DVD,** Glenn Ford, Charlene Tilton, Jeff Kaake, Michael Horse, Russell Todd, Cody Glenn, Sergio Calderon, Michael Ansara; **D:** Chris T. McIntyre.

Border Vengeance 🐾🐾½ **1935** Reb is a member of a family of outlaws. He aims to improve himself and steer his family to the straight and narrow trail. **45m/B VHS, DVD,** Reb Russell, Mary Jane Carey, Kenneth MacDonald, Hank Bell, Glenn Strange, Norman Feusier, Charles "Slim" Whitaker; **D:** Ray Heinz.

Border Vigilantes 🐾🐾 **1941** Hopalong Cassidy rides to aid a town of outlaws that are being terrorized... **63m/B VHS,** William Boyd, Russell Hayden, Andy Clyde, Victor Jory, Morris Ankrum, Frances Gifford, Ethel Wales, Hal Taliaferro; **D:** Derwin Abrahams.

Borderline 🐾🐾 **1950** MacMurray and Trevor play undercover agents trying to infiltrate a Mexican drug ring. With their real identities hidden, they fall for each other and make a run for the border. Although the leads work well together, they're hindered by an occasionally confusing script. Unfortunately, director Seiter never decides whether the material is of a comedic or dramatic nature. **88m/B VHS, DVD,** Fred MacMurray, Claire Trevor, Raymond...

Burr, Roy Roberts, Jose Torvay, Morris Ankrum, Charles Lane, Don Diamond, Nacho Galindo, Pepe Hern, Richard Irving; *D:* William A. Seiter; *C:* Lucien N. Andriot; *M:* Hans J. Salter.

Borderline *♫♫* 1980 (PG) Bronson is a border patrol guard in pursuit of a murderer in this action flick. Meanwhile, he gets caught up in trying to help an illegal alien and her young child. 106m/C **VHS, DVD.** Charles Bronson, Wilford Brimley, Bruno Kirby, Benito Morales, Ed Harris, Kenneth McMillan; *D:* Jerrold Freedman.

Borderline *♫♫* 2002 (R) A good suspenser about obsession. Dr. Lila Colletti (Gershon) is a shrink for the criminally insane at the local prison, which may be why her ex got custody of their two daughters. Lily's troubles increase when one of her patients, Ed Baikman (Flanery), is released to a halfway house, despite his delusions that they are romantically involved. After murdering her ex on her behalf, Ed threatens Lily when she doesn't return his love and implicates her in his crime. Soon, even her detective boyfriend Macy Kobacek (Biehn) has doubts about Lily's innocence. 94m/C **VHS, DVD.** Gina Gershon, Sean Patrick Flanery, Michael Biehn; *D:* Evelyn Purcell; *W:* David Loucka; *C:* Michael Brierley; *M:* Anthony Marinelli. **CABLE**

Bordertown *♫1/2* 2006 (R) Generic thriller based on a true story. Ambitious Chicago journalist Lauren (Lopez) is assigned to write about a series of rape/murders that have happened to young women in Juarez, Mexico. She hooks up with former colleague Alfonso (Banderas), whose persistence on covering the crimes has him in trouble with authorities. Lauren meets Eva (Zapata), who is in hiding after surviving her attack, and it is implied that factories making goods for the U.S. market. The politics muddies a story that, unfortunately, hasn't been compellingly told. 112m/C **DVD.** Jennifer Lopez, Antonio Banderas, Maya Zapata, Sonia Braga, Martin Sheen; *D:* Gregory Nava; *W:* Gregory Nava; *C:* Reynaldo Villalobos; *M:* Graeme Revell.

Bordertown Gunfighters *♫1/2* 1943 A cowboy breaks up a vicious lottery racket and falls in love in the process. 56m/B **VHS.** William (Wild Bill) Elliot, Anne Jeffreys, George "Gabby" Hayes, Ian Keith, Harry Woods, Edward Earle, Karl Hackett, Roy Barcroft, Bud Geary, Carl Sepulveda; *D:* Howard Bretherton; *W:* Norman S. Hall; *C:* Jack Marta.

Boricua's Bond *♫♫* 2000 (R) First-time director Lik (at 21) debuts with an urban drama about Puerto Rican-born artist Tommy (Negron) who would rather paint than be an active part of the South Bronx street gangs that surround him. Then Anglo single mom Susan (Karp) and son Allen (played by Lik) move into the 'hood, where they are immediately hasseled. Tommy befriends Allen but there's a string of not entirely unexpected tragedies that change everyone's lives. 95m/C **VHS.** Val Lik, Frankie Negron, Robyn Karp, Marco Sorisio, Kirk "Sticky Fingaz" Jones; *D:* Val Lik; *W:* Val Lik; *C:* Brendan Flynt.

Boris and Natasha: The Movie *♫1/2* 1992 (PG) The two inept spies from the classic TV cartoon "The Adventures of Rocky and Bullwinkle" star in this mediocre live-action comedy. These nogoodniks are sent by "Fearless Leader" to America and encounter the usual misadventures. For true watch the original animated versions. Never released theatrically; it aired for the first time on cable TV. 88m/C **VHS.** Sally Kellerman, Dave Thomas, Andrea Martin, Alex Rocco, Larry Cedar, Arye Gross, Christopher Neame, Anthony Newley; **Cameos:** John Candy, John Travolta, Charles Martin Smith; *D:* Charles Martin Smith.

B.O.R.N. *♫1/2* 1988 (R) Hagen uncovers an underground network of doctors who kill people and sell the body parts and organs. 90m/C **VHS.** Ross Hagen, P.J. Soles, William (Bill) Smith, Hoke Howell, Russ Tamblyn, Amanda Blake, Clint Howard, Rance Howard, Debra Lamb; *D:* Ross Hagen.

Born Again *♫♫* 1978 Adaptation of Watergate criminal Charles Colson's biography of his becoming a born again Christian. Standard TV biopic stuff. 110m/C **VHS.** Dean Jones, Anne Francis, Dana Andrews, George Brent; *D:* Irving Rapper; *W:* Walter Bloch; *C:* Harry Stradling Jr.; *M:* Les Baxter.

Born American *♫* 1986 (R) Pre-Glasnost flick about teenagers vacationing in Finland who "accidentally" cross the Russian border. There they battle the Red Plague. Melodramatic and heavily politicized. Original release banned in Finland. 95m/C **VHS, DVD.** Mike Norris, Steve Durham, David Coburn, Thalmus Rasulala, Albert Salmi; *D:* Renny Harlin.

Born Bad *♫♫* 1997 (R) Teens bungle a bank robbery and hold up in the bank with hostages. The town sheriff wants to end the standoff calmly but the teens' hot-headed leader won't surrender. 84m/C **VHS, DVD.** James Remar, Corey Feldman, Taylor Nichols, Justin Walker, Heidi Noelle Lenhardt; *D:* Jeff Yonis. **VIDEO**

Born Beautiful *♫♫1/2* 1982 Made for TV. Beautiful young women come to New York, hoping to strike it rich in the world of modeling. At the same time, a still beautiful, but older and overexposed model comes to grips with a change in her career. Well-told, but sugar-coated. 100m/C **VHS.** Erin Gray, Ed Marinaro, Polly Bergen, Lori Singer, Ellen Barber, Judith Barcroft, Michael Higgins; *D:* Harvey Hart; *M:* Brad Fiedel. **TV**

Born for Hell *♫* *Naked Massacre* 1976 A maniac Vietnam vet kills nurses, leaving no clues for the police to follow. 90m/C **VHS, DVD.** Matthieu Carriere, Carole Laure; *D:* Denis Heroux.

Born Free *♫♫* 1966 The touching story of a game warden in Kenya and his wife raising Elsa the orphaned lion cub. When the cub reaches maturity, they work to return her to life in the wild. Great family entertainment based on Joy Adamson's book. Theme song became a hit. ♫Born Free. 95m/C **VHS, DVD.** Virginia McKenna, Bill Travers; *D:* James Hill; *W:* Lester Cole; *M:* John Barry. Oscars '66: Song ("Born Free"). Orig-Score.

Born in America *♫* *Dead Aim* 1990 A young orphan is adopted by an undertaker. The boy grows up enveloped by his guardian's business and, when things go slow, works to bring in business himself. 90m/C **VHS.** James Westerfield, Glen Lee, Virgil Frye, Venetia Vianello; *D:* Jose Antonio Bolanos.

Born in East L.A. *♫♫* 1987 (R) Marin brings his Bruce Springsteen-parody song to life as he plays a mistakenly deported illegal alien who struggles to return to the U.S. Suprisingly resolute effort by the usually self-exploiting Mexican-American. Stern is the American expatriate who helps him get back and Lopez is the love interest who stalks him. 85m/C **VHS, DVD.** Richard "Cheech" Marin, Daniel Stern, Paul Rodriguez, Jan-Michael Vincent, Kamala Lopez, Tony Plana, Vic Trevino, A. Martinez; *D:* Richard "Cheech" Marin; *W:* Richard "Cheech" Marin; *C:* Alex Phillips Jr.; *M:* Lee Holdridge.

Born in '45 *♫♫* *Jahrgang '45* 1965 Auto mechanic Alfred and maternity nurse Lisa are newlyweds. However, they might not be wed much longer as they find marital adjustment (especially in their tiny apartment) difficult to make. Alfred goes wandering around Berlin, hoping to make some decisions, but the film ends with their future uncertain. German with subtitles. 94m/B **DVD.** *GE* Monika Hildebrand, Rolf Romer, Paul Eichbaum, Holger Mahlich; *D:* Jurgen Bottcher; *W:* Jurgen Bottcher; *C:* Roland Graf; *M:* Klaus Poche.

Born Innocent *♫♫* 1974 As if "The Exorcist" weren't bad enough, Blair is back for more abuse-on-film, this time as a 14-year-old runaway from a dysfunctional family who lands in a reform school for girls. There, she must struggle to be as brutal as her peers in order to survive. Fairly tame by today's standards, but controversial at its made-for-TV premiere, chiefly due to a rape scene involving a broom handle. First trip up the river for Blair. 92m/C **VHS, DVD.** Linda Blair, Joanna Miles, Kim Hunter, Richard Jaeckel, Janit Baldwin, Mitch Vogel; *D:* Donald Wrye; *M:* Fred Karlin. **TV**

Born Into Brothels: Calcutta's Red Light Kids *♫♫1/2* 2004 (R) Photojournalist Zana Briski presents the world of Calcutta prostitution through the eyes and pictures of the children who live it. Not only does she give them photography instruction as a means to help lift them from their current situation, she goes a step further in trying to place them in boarding school—much to the chagrin of the opposing parents. The subject is nothing new but her drive to make a change in these doomed lives is commendable and may hopefully inspire others. 85m/C **DVD.** *US IN D:* Zana Briski, Ross Kauffman; *W:* Zana Briski, Ross Kauffman; *C:* Zana Briski, Ross Kauffman; *M:* John McDowell. Oscars '04: Feature Doc.

Born Killer *♫♫* 1989 Teenagers in the woods meet up with murderous escaped convicts. 90m/C **VHS, DVD.** Francine Lapensee, Fritz Matthews, Ted Prior, Adam Tucker; *D:* Kimberly Casey.

Born Losers *♫♫* 1967 (PG) The original "Billy Jack" film in which the Indian martial arts expert takes on a group of incorrigible bikers bothering some Californias babes and runs afoul of the law. Classic drive-in fare. 112m/C **VHS, DVD.** Tom Laughlin, Elizabeth James, Jeremy Slate, William Wellman Jr., Robert Tessier, Jane Russell, Stuart Lancaster, Edwin Cook, Jeff Cooper; *D:* Tom Laughlin; *W:* E. James Lloyd, Tom Laughlin; *C:* Gregory Sandor.

Born of Fire *♫1/2* 1987 (R) A flutist investigating his father's death seeks the Master Musician; his search leads him to the volcanic (and supernatural) mountains of Turkey. 84m/C **VHS.** Peter Firth, Susan Crowley, Stephan Kalipha; *D:* Jamil Dehlavi; *M:* Colin Towns.

Born on the Fourth of July *♫♫♫1/2* 1989 (R) A riveting meditation on American life affected by the Vietnam War, based on the real-life, best-selling experiences of Ron Kovic, though some facts are subtly changed. The film follows him as he develops from a naive recruit to an angry, wheelchair-bound paraplegic to an active antiwar protestor. Well-acted and generally lauded; Kovic co-wrote the screenplay and appears as a war veteran in the opening parade sequence. 145m/C **VHS, DVD, HD DVD.** Bill Allen, Tom Cruise, Kyra Sedgwick, Raymond J. Barry, Jerry Levine, Tom Berenger, Willem Dafoe, Frank Whaley, John Getz, Caroline Kava, Bryan Larkin, Abbie Hoffman, Stephen Baldwin, Josh Evans, Dale Dye, William Baldwin, Don "The Dragon" Wilson, Vivica A. Fox, Holly Marie Combs, Tom Sizemore, Daniel Baldwin, Ron Kovic; **Cameos:** Oliver Stone; *D:* Oliver Stone; *W:* Oliver Stone; *C:* Robert Richardson; *M:* John Williams. Oscars '89: Director (Stone), Film Editing; Directors Guild '89: Director (Stone); Golden Globes '90: Actor—Drama (Cruise), Director (Stone), Film—Drama, Screenplay.

Born Reckless *♫1/2* 1959 Van Doren plays a singer working the rodeo circuit who falls for aging rider Richards. Not bad enough to be funny, however, Van Doren shows an incredible lack of talent while singing several tunes. ♫Song of the Rodeo; Born Reckless; A Little Longer; Home Type Girl; Separate the Men from the Boys; Something to Dream About; You, Lovable You. 79m/B **VHS.** Mamie Van Doren, Jeff Richards, Arthur Hunnicutt, Carol Ohmart, Donald (Don "Red") Barry, Nacho Galindo; *D:* Howard W. Koch.

Born Romantic *♫♫* 2000 (R) Six lonely Londoners converge at a salsa club hoping to find a little romance. There's screwy Jocelyn (McCormack), no-nonsense Mo (Horrocks), uptight Eleanor (Williams), would-be Lothario Frank (Ferguson), awkward Eddie (Mistry), and Jim tom Fergus (Morrissey). Cabbie Jimmy (Lester) offers advice. Enjoyable (if predictable) romantic comedy. 97m/C **VHS, DVD.** *GB* Craig Ferguson, Adrian Lester, Catherine McCormack, Jimi Mistry, David Morrissey, Olivia Williams, Jane Horrocks, Hermione Norris, Ian Hart, Kenneth Cranham, Paddy Considine; *D:* David Kane; *W:* David Kane; *C:* Robert Alazraki; *M:* Simon Boswell.

Born to Be Bad *♫♫1/2* 1950 Fontaine, an opportunistic woman who marries a wealthy business man away from his wife while carrying on an affair with a novelist. Ray's direction (he's best known for "Rebel Without a Cause," filmed five years later) prevents the film from succumbing to standard Hollywood formula. 93m/B **VHS.** Joan Fontaine, Robert Ryan, Zachary Scott, Joan Leslie, Mel Ferrer; *D:* Nicholas Ray.

Born to Be Wild *♫♫* 1938 A pair of truck drivers are commissioned to deliver a shipment of dynamite. The dynamite will be used to destroy a dam, preventing the surrounding land from falling into the hands of unscrupulous land barons. Good action picture thanks to the cast. 66m/B **VHS, DVD.** Ralph Byrd, Doris Weston, Ward Bond, Robert Emmett Keane, Bentley Hewlett, Charles Williams; *D:* Joseph Kane.

Born to Be Wild *♫♫1/2* 1995 (PG) Rebellious teenager Rick (Homoff) befriends Katie, the three-year-old gorilla his behavioral scientist mom (Shaver) is studying. When Katie's owner (Boyle) decides she would make a better sideshow attraction than science project, Rick busts her out and they head for the Canadian border. Animal slapstick and bodily function jokes ensue as the chase continues. "Free Willy"-inspired plot and primate hijinks should keep young kids interested, but anyone over the age of nine probably won't be too impressed. 99m/C **VHS, DVD.** Thomas F. Wilson, Wil Horneff, Helen Shaver, Peter Boyle, Jean Marie Barnwell, John C. McGinley, Marvin J. McIntyre; *D:* John Gray; *W:* John Bunzel, Paul Young; *C:* Donald M. Morgan.

Born to Boogie *♫♫* *Marc Bolan and T-Rex: Born to Boogie* 1972 A concert, a chronicle, and a tribute, "Born To Boogie" is about Marc Bolan and his band T. Rex. The film, which features concert footage from a 1972 concert at the Wembley Empire Pool in London, chronicles the glitter rock era and the next wave of British rock and roll, and pays tribute to Bolan, who died in 1977 just as he was starting a comeback. Ringo Starr and Elton John join T. Rex in the studio for "Children of the Revolution" and "Tutti-Frutti" as well as a psychadelic soiree where Bolan plays acoustic versions of his hits. This film was never released in the United States. 75m/C **VHS, DVD.** Marc Bolan, Elton John, Ringo Starr; *D:* Ringo Starr.

Born to Dance *♫♫1/2* 1936 A quintessential MGM 1930s dance musical, wherein a beautiful dancer gets a sailor and a big break in a show. Great songs by Cole Porter sung in a less than great manner by a gangly Stewart. Powell's first star-ring vehicle. ♫Love Me Love My Pekinese; I've Got You Under My Skin; Hey Babe Hey; Easy to Love; Rolling Home; Rap Tap on Wood; Entrance of Lucy James; Swingin' the Jinx Away. 108m/B **VHS.** Eleanor Powell, James Stewart, Virginia Bruce, Una Merkel, Frances Langford, Sid Silvers, Raymond Walburn, Reginald Gardiner, Buddy Ebsen; *D:* Roy Del Ruth; *M:* Cole Porter, Cole Porter.

Born to Kill *♫♫♫* *Lady of Deceit* 1947 A ruthless killer marries a girl for her money. Minor tough-as-nails film noir exemplifying Tierney's stone-faced humandevil film persona. 92m/B **VHS, DVD.** Lawrence Tierney, Claire Trevor, Walter Slezak, Elisha Cook Jr.; *D:* Robert Wise.

Born to Lose *♫♫* 1999 The Spoilers are an L.A. punk back led by singer Stevie Monroe (Rye). They're an underground success but can't break out of the music ghetto until public relations gal Lisa (Ashton) takes an interest in Stevie. Too bad she's a junkie who pulls the singer into a downward spiral that effectively destroys the band as well. Filmed in a mockdocumentary style. 80m/C **VHS, DVD.** Joseph Rye, Elyse Ashton, Francis Fallon; *D:* Doug Cawker; *W:* Doug Cawker, Howard Roth; *C:* John Rhode; *M:* Greg Kuehn.

Born to Race *♫* 1988 (R) In the world of competitive auto racing, a beautiful engineer is kidnapped for her new controversial engine design. 95m/C **VHS.** George Kennedy, Marc Singer, Marfa Heasly; *D:* James Fargo.

Born to Ride *♫♫* 1991 (PG) A biker rebel joins the Army prior to WWII in order to escape a prison term after a good ol' boy brush with the law. He shuns Army.

discipline, but proves himself in action as the leader of a scout troup for the Army's motorcycle cavalry brigade. Available with Spanish subtitles. **88m/C VHS.** John Stockwell, Teri Polo, Kris Kamm; **D:** Graham Baker. **TV**

Born to Run ✫✫ **1993** Nicky Donatello (Grieco) is a Brooklyn street drag racer who gets mixed up with the mob while trying to rescue his no-account brother. But he's still has time to fall for an uptown model who also happens to be the mobster's girlfriend. **97m/C VHS.** Richard Grieco, Jay Acovone, Shelli Lether, Christian Campbell, Brent Stait, Martin Cummins, When Roberts, Joe Cortese; **D:** Albert Magnoli; **W:** Randall Badat. **TV**

Born Under Libra ✫✫✫ *Mahe Mehr* **2001** In Tehran, Daniel falls in love with fellow university student Mahtab, whose father is pushing for segregated classes. Daniel associates with the religious while Mahtab sides with the reformers. Despite their differences, the romance blossoms but trouble has them fleeing the city. Farsi with subtitles. **94m/C DVD.** IA Mohammad Reza Forutan, Mitra Hajjar; **D:** Ahmad Reza Darvish; **W:** Ahmad Reza Darvish; **C:** Adam Herschman; **M:** Mohammad Reza Aligholi.

Born Wild ✫✫½ **1995 (PG)** Documentary filmmaker Christine Shaye (Shields) has just gotten her first important assignment from overbearing boss Dan Walker (Sheen), which is to capture the beauty of Africa. Christine arrives at the South African game preserve of Londolozi where she meets passionate conservationist John Varty (who plays himself). Varty has filmed one leopard family for 12 years but when the mother leopard is killed, he violates his own ethical code when he rescues her two orphaned cubs. She retaliates against him and gets to deliver that now-famous line: 'Do me a favor, drop dead.' **99m/C VHS.** Brooke Shields, Martin Sheen, John Varty, David Keith; **D:** Duncan McLachlan, Andrea Buck.

Born Yesterday ✫✫✫½ **1950** Ambitious junk dealer Harry Brock (Crawford) is in love with smart but uneducated Billie Dawn 'Holliday'. He hires newspaperman Paul Verrall (Holden) to teach her the finer points of etiquette. During their sessions, they fall in love and Billie realizes how she has been used by Brock. She retaliates against him and gets to do deliver that now-famous line: 'Do me a favor, drop dead.' Holliday is a solid gold clamor as the not-so-dumb blonde, in the role she originated in Garson Kanin's Broadway play. Remade in 1993. **103m/B VHS, DVD.** Judy Holliday, Broderick Crawford, William Holden, Howard St. John, Frank Otto, Larry Oliver, Barbara Brown; **D:** George Cukor; **W:** Albert Mannheimer; **C:** Joseph Walker; **M:** Frederick 'Friedrich' Hollander. Oscars '50: Actress (Holliday); Golden Globes '51: Actress—Mus./Comedy (Holliday).

Born Yesterday ✫✫ **1993 (PG)** Remake of the 1950 classic suffers in comparison, particularly Griffith, who has the thankless task of supassing (or even meeting) Judy Holliday's Oscar-winning mark as not-so-dumb blonde Billie Dawn. Her intellectual inadequacies are glaring when she hits the political world of D.C. with obnoxious tycoon boyfriend Goodman. To save face, he hooks her up with a journalist (Johnson) willing to coach her in Savvy 101, a la Eliza Doolittle. What worked well in post-WWII America seems sadly outdated today; stick with the original. **102m/C VHS, DVD.** Melanie Griffith, John Goodman, Don Johnson, Edward Herrmann, Max Perlich, Fred Dalton Thompson, Nora Dunn, Benjamin C. Bradley, Sally Quinn, Michael Ensign, William Frankfather, Celeste Yarnall, Meg Wittner; **D:** Luis Mandoki; **W:** Douglas McGrath; **C:** Lajos Koltai; **M:** George Fenton.

Borough of Kings ✫✫ **1998 (R)** Jimmy O'Conner (Stanek) is trying to get away from a life of crime in Brooklyn but the ties are hard to cut. Similar stories have been told dozens of times before. This little independent production has a strong spirit and commitment to its characters on its side, which outweigh its predictability, but never develops behind the basic grossout situation. **97m/C VHS.** Patrick Newall, Olympia Dukakis; **D:** Elyse Lewin; **W:** Patrick Newall; **C:** Nils Kenaston; **M:** Alan El-liott.

Borsalino ✫✫✫ **1970 (R)** Delon and Belmondo are partners in crime in this seriocomic film about gang warfare in 1930s Marseilles. The costumes, settings, and music perfectly capture the mood of the period. Followed by a sequel 'Borsalino and Co.' Based on 'The Bandits of Marseilles' by Eugene Saccomano. **124m/C VHS.** FR Jean-Paul Belmondo, Alain Delon, Michel Bouquet, Catherine Rouvel, Françoise Christophe, Corinne Marchand; **D:** Jacques Deray; **W:** Jacques Deray, Jean Cau, Claude Sautet, Jean-Claude Carriere; **C:** Jean-Jacques Tarbes; **M:** Claude Bolling.

Borstal Boy ✫✫½ **2000** Irish teen, IRA partisan, (and future writer) Brendan Behan (Hatosy) is caught smuggling dynamite into Britain and sent to reform school, known as a 'borstal,' in East England in 1939. Naturally, he learns that all Brits aren't the devil incarnate as he befriends gay Cockney sailor Charlie (Millwall) and falls in love with fair-but-tough Warden Joyce's (York) daughter, Liz (Birthistle). Inspired by Behan's 1958 memoirs. **91m/C VHS, DVD.** IR GB Shawn Hatosy, Danny Dyer, Eva Birthistle, Michael York, Lee Ingleby, Robin Laing; **D:** Peter Sheridan; **W:** Peter Sheridan, Nye Heron; **C:** Ciaran Tanham; **M:** Stephen McKeon.

Boss ✫✫½ *The Black Bounty Killer, Boss Nigger, The Black Bounty Hunter* **1974 (PG)** Blaxploitation western parody with Williamson and Martin as a couple of bounty hunters tearing apart a town to find a fugitive. Relatively non-violent. **87m/C VHS.** Fred William-

Boss' Son ✫✫✫ **1978** Worthwhile coming-of-age tale about a young man who learns more than he bargained for about life when he goes to work for his father in the family carpet business. Dad feels he should work his way up through the ranks and makes him a delivery man. The young man meets reality head on and must deal with the injustices of the world around him. Independently filmed by director/writer Roth. **97m/C VHS.** Rita Moreno, James Darren, Asher Brauner, Rudy Solari, Henry Sanders, Richie Havers, Piper Laurie, Elena Verdugo; **D:** Bobby Roth; **W:** Bobby Roth; **C:** Alfonso Beato.

The Boss' Wife ✫✫ **1986 (R)** A young stockbroker attempts to fix what's wrong with his life by maneuvering sexually with the boss' wife, and complications set in. **83m/C VHS.** Daniel Stern, Arielle Domba-

The Borrower ✫✫ **1989 (R)** An exiled unstable mutant insect alien serial killer (you know the type) must switch heads with human beings regularly to survive. This colorful, garish gorefest has humor and attitude, but never develops behind the basic grossout situation. **97m/C VHS.** Rae Dawn Chong, Don Gordon, Antonio Fargas, Tom Towles; **D:** John McNaughton.

The Borrowers ✫✫✫ **1993** Excellent TV adaptation of the May Norton children's classics 'The Borrowers' and 'The Borrowers Afield.' This miniature family (about mouse-size) live beneath the floorboards of an English house and borrow what they need to survive from the normal-sized human inhabitants. Problems come when the teeny family are discovered and must make their way to a new home. Sweet and humorous. **199m/C VHS.** GB Ian Holm, Penelope Wilton, Rebecca Callard, Paul Cross, Sian Phillips, Tony Haygarth; **D:** John Henderson; **W:** Richard Carpenter; **C:** Clive Tickner. **TV**

The Borrowers ✫✫½ **1997 (PG)** Charming, big-screen, big-budget tale about the little people who live under the floor. The British, elfin, and about four inch tall Clock family, headed by papa Pod (Broadbent) lives hidden in the walls of the home of the normal-sized American Lenders and exist by 'borrowing' objects from their human's household. When an evil lawyer (Goodman), also American, threatens their happiness, the Borrowers bond with young Peter Lender (Pierce) who 'discovers' them and volunteers to help them save their way of life. This remake focuses mainly on the impressive special effects, lending a modern look and appeal. Goodman is lovably evil in that wonderful 'Snidely Whiplash' way. Based on the children's books of Mary Norton. **86m/C VHS, DVD.** GB Ian Goodman, Hugh Laurie, Jim Broadbent, Mark Williams, Celia Imrie, Bradley Michael Pierce, Raymond Pickard, Aden (John) Gillet, Ruby Wax, Flora Newbigin, Tom Felton, Doon Mackichan; **D:** Peter Hewitt; **W:** John Kamps, Gavin Scott; **C:** John Fenner, Trevor Brooker; **M:** Harry Gregson-Williams.

Boss of Rawhide ✫ **1944** The Texas Rangers fight for law and order in the old west despite odds against them. **60m/B VHS.** Dave O'Brien, James Newill, Guy Wilkerson, Nell O'Day, Edward Cassidy, Jack Ingram, Billy Bletcher, Charles 'Blackie' King, George O'Brien; **D:** Elmer Clifton; **W:** Elmer Clifton; **C:** Robert E. Cline; **M:** Lee Zahler, Oliver Drake, Herbert Myers, Dave O'Brien, James Ne-will.

The Boss of It All ✫✫ *Direktoren for Det Hele* **2006** Von Trier trades in polemics for a corporate comedy. Ravn (Gantzler), the director of an IT firm, decides to hire actor Kristoffer (Albinus) to portray the non-existent president of his company so he can sell out to a larger organization. But thanks to Kristoffer's overacting, the deal gets put on hold for a week and they must keep up the charade. The film was shot by Von Trier's experimental Automavision, a computer-controlled camera, and looks fairly awful. Danish with subtitles. **99m/C DVD.** CZ FR IT SW Peter Gantzler, Jens Albinus, Frank Thor Fridriksson, Iben Hjejle, Sofie Graabol, Benedikt Erlingsson; **D:** Lars von Trier, Lars von Trier.

Boss of Bullion City ✫✫½ **1941** A crooked sheriff is exposed by Brown and sidekick Knight in this sagebrush saga. Based on a story by Arthur St. Clair. **61m/B VHS, DVD.** Johnny Mack Brown, Fuzzy Knight, Maria Montez, Earle Hodgins, Harry Woods; **D:** Ray Taylor; **W:** Victor McLeod, Arthur St. Claire.

Boss of Big Town ✫✫ **1943** Gangsters try to infiltrate the milk industry in this standard crime drama. **66m/B VHS, DVD.** Chaaz Palminteri, Daniel Benzali, Jay O. Sancers, Clancy Brown, Al Ruscio, Steven Bauer, Angela Alvarado, Sonny Marinelli; **D:** Dwight Little; **M:** Jere P. Cunningham; **C:** Brian Reynolds; **M:** Arthur Dreifuss.

Boss of Bosses ✫✫½ **1999** Yet another in a long line of Mafia portrayals and betrayals but this one is flat and uninspired. Paul Castellano (Palminteri) takes organized crime into the white-collar level from the streets into legit businesses but the world is still violent, plagued by internal feuds and the feds sniffing around. Castellano wound up being the last public Mafia hit (arranged by John Gotti) outside a New York steak house. **94m/C VHS, DVD.** Chaaz Palminteri, Daniel Benzali, Jay O. Sancers, Clancy Brown, Al Ruscio, Steven Bauer, Angela Alvarado, Sonny Marinelli; **C:** Brian Reynolds; **M:**

The Boss Is Served ✫✫ *La Patrona e Servita* **1976** A mother (Berger) and three daughters, racked with debt, are forced to take in boarders. The lascivious mar and teenage son want to be more than just boarders to the lovely Berger. In Italian with English subtitles. **96m/C VHS.** IT Senta Berger, Maurizio Arena, Bruno Zanin, Erika Blanc, Pina Cei, Angiolina Quinterno, Patrizia de Clara; **D:** Mario Lanfranchi; **W:** Mario Lanfranchi, Pupi Avati; **C:** Pasquale Fanetti; **M:** Stelvio Cipriani.

Boss Cowboy ✫ **1935** A cowboy shows who wears the chaps in his family when he kidnaps his girlfriend to prevent her from moving East. **51m/B VHS.** Buddy Roosevelt, Frances Morris, Sam Pierce, Fay McKenzie, Lafe (Lafayette) McKee; **D:** Victor Adamson.

Bossa Nova ✫✫½ **1999 (R)** Sexy romantic comedy set to the beat of sultry Brazil. Middleaged American widow Mary (Irving) teaches English in Rio and catches the romantic eye of Pedro (Fagundes), an attorney who has been dumped by his wife. Meanwhile, Mary's soccer-playing pupil Acacio (Borges) is trying to become a teacher's pet before trying to become a teacher's pet before involved with Pedro's half-brother (Cardoso). And the romantic complications just keep building. Soundtrack is filled with the songs of bossa 'cria composer Antonio Carlos Jobim. Based on the novel "Miss Simpson" by Sergio Sant'Anna. **95m/C VHS, DVD.** BR Amy Irving, Antonio Fagundes, Alexandre Borges, Debora Bloch, Pedro Cardoso, Alberto De Mendoza, Stephen Tobolowsky, Drica Moraes, Giovanna Antonelli, Rogerio Cardoso; **D:** Bruno Barreto; **W:** Alexandre Machado, Fernanda Young; **C:** Pascal Rabaud; **M:** Eumir Deodato.

Boston Kickout ✫✫ **1995** A quartet of teenaged friends/losers struggle to grow up in a bleak concrete town outside London. There are neglected girlfriends, dysfunctional families, menial jobs, petty crime, emotional disasters—and some faint glimmer of hope for at least a couple of the lads. Title refers to a destructive game the boys play. **105m/C VHS, DVD.** GB John Simm, Andrew Lincoln, Richard Hanson, Nathan Valente, Emer McCourt, Marc Warren, Derek Martin, Vincent Phillips, Natalie Davies; **D:** Paul Hills; **W:** Paul Hills, Diane Whitley, Roberto Troni; **C:** Roger Bonnici; **M:** Robert Hartshorne.

The Boston Strangler ✫✫½ **1968** Based on Gerold Frank's bestselling factual book about the deranged killer who terrorized Boston for about a year and a half. Traces events from first killing to prosecution. Curtis, going against type, is compelling in title role, is based on Henry James' classic novel. **120m/C VHS, DVD.** Christopher Reeve, Vanessa Redgrave, Madeleine Potter, Jessica Tandy, Nancy Marchand, Wesley Addy, Linda Hunt, Wallace Shawn; **D:** James Ivory; **W:** Ruth Prawer Jhabvala; **C:** Walter Lassally, Natl. Soc. Film Critics '84: Actress (Redgrave).

The Bostonians ✫✫✫ **1984 (PG)** A faith healer's daughter is forced to choose between the affections of a militant suffragette and a young lawyer in 19th Century Boston. Based on Henry James' classic novel. **120m/C VHS, DVD.** Christopher Reeve, Vanessa Redgrave, Madeleine Potter, Jessica Tandy, Nancy Marchand, Wesley Addy, Linda Hunt, Wallace Shawn; **D:** James Ivory; **W:** Ruth Prawer Jhabvala; **C:** Walter Lassally, Natl. Soc. Film Critics '84: Actress (Redgrave).

Botany Bay ✫✫ **1953** A rousing costumer about a convict ship in the 1700s that, after a trying voyage, lands in Australia, wherein a framed doctor conquers the local plague. From the novel by Charles Nordoff. **89m/C VHS.** Alan Ladd, James Mason, Patricia Medina, Cedric Hardwicke; **D:** John Farrow.

Botched ✫✫ **2007** Odd and not particularly successful mix of horror, comedy, and crime. American Ritchie (Dorff) must steal an antique cross that's kept in a bank building and is given a couple of inept locals for back-up. Naturally they get away gets screwed and they wind up with hostages and are diverted to the building's unused 13th floor. They find out it's been abandoned for a very good reason. **94m/C DVD.** Stephen Dorff, Sean Pertwee, Jamie Foreman, Russell Smith, Jaime Murray, Bronagh Gallagher, Edward Baker-Duly; **D:** Kit Ryan; **W:** Derek Boyle, Eamon Friel, Raymond Friel; **C:** Bryan Loftus. **M:** Tom Green. **VIDEO**

Bottle Rocket ✫✫½ **1995 (R)** A genial tric of inexperienced but aspiring criminals attempt to make their mark on the world in suburban Dallas. Newcomers Wilson, who plays the group's ambitious leader Dignan, and Anderson penned this smart ensemble piece first as a 13-minute black and white short. A subsequent showing at the Sundance Film Festival got the attention of producer James L. Brooks ('Broadcast News"). Film got the backing to go

son, D'Urville Martin, R.G. Armstrong, William (Bill Smith, Carmen Hayworth, Barbara Leigh; **D:** Jack Arnold; **W:** Fred Williamson.

Bottle

feature length with Anderson directing, and deservedly so, with its fresh dialogue and surprising warmth. **91m/C VHS, DVD.** Ned Dowd, Owen Wilson, Luke Wilson, Robert Musgrave, Lumi Cavazos, James Caan, Andrew Wilson, Jim Ponds; **D:** Wes Anderson; **W:** Wes Anderson, Owen Wilson; **C:** Robert Yeoman; **M:** Mark Mothersbaugh. MTV Movie Awards '96: New Filmmaker (Anderson).

The Bottom of the Sea ♂♂♂
2003 Dark comedic thriller has an obsessively jealous young architect stalking his girlfriend's secret lover on one fateful night. An unexpected climax and easy-on-the-eyes actors make this Argentinean endeavor cinematically satisfying. Subtitled. **95m/C DVD. AR** Dolores Fonzi, Daniel Hendler, Gustavo Garzon, Ramiro Aguero; **D:** Damien Szifron; **W:** Damien Szifron. **VIDEO**

Bottoms Up WOOf! 2006 (R) Bottom of the barrel is more like it. Owen (Mewes) heads to L.A. to enter a bartending contest in hopes of using the winnings to save his dad's restaurant. Things don't exactly work out and Owen's uncle (Keith) gets him a job with actor Hayden (Hallisay) and his vapid girlfriend, Lisa (a typecast Hilton). When Owen learns a few tabloid-worthy secrets, he has to decide whether to sell out to this even newer pals for the much-needed cash. Even Mewes can't work up much enthusiasm for this mess. **89m/C DVD.** Jason Mewes, Paris Hilton, David Keith, Phil Morris, Brian Hallisay, Jon Abrahams, Tim Thomerson; **D:** Erik MacArthur; **W:** Erik MacArthur, Nick Ballo; **C:** Massimo Zeri. **VIDEO**

Boudu Saved from Drowning ♂♂♂♂½
Eaux 1932 A suicidal tramp completely disrupts the wealthy household of the man that saves him from drowning. A gentle but sardonic farce from the master filmmaker. Remade in 1986 as "Down and Out in Beverly Hills." **87m/B VHS, DVD, FR** Michel Simon, Charles Granval, Jean Daste, Marcelle Hainia, Severine Lerczinska, Jacques Becker; **D:** Jean Renoir; **W:** Jean Renoir; **C:** Marcel Lucien.

Bought and Sold ♂♂ 2003
Coming of age tale set in Jersey City. Ray Ray Morales (Sardina) is working for minimum wage at a shoe store but really wants to buy some pawnshop turntables so he can be a DJ. So he gets a second job with local loan shark Chunks (Grifasi) who wants him to keep an eye on elderly pawnshop owner Kutty (Margulies) who owes Chunks money. Soon Ray Ray is falling for Kutty's niece, Ruby (Neshat), and getting too involved. When Kutty can't meet his payments, Ray Ray has to make some decisions about what's really important to him. **92m/C DVD.** Margulies, Joe Grifasi, Rafael Sardina, Marjan Neshat, Frank Harts, Christina Ablaza, Anthony Chisholm; **D:** Michael Tolajian; **W:** Michael Tolajian; **C:** Kip Bogdahn; **M:** Joe Delia.

Boulevard ♂½ 1994 (R) Jennefer (Wuhrer) is forced to give her baby up for adoption, after escaping from an abusive husband, and make her way on the city's mean streets. She meets prostitute Ola (Chong), who decides to look after the naif and protect Jennefer from violent pimp Hassan (Phillips). But Ola gets into trouble with tough cop Claren (Henriksen) and soon Jennefer must survive on her own—against both Hassan and her vengeful husband. Woman empowerment, complete with standard cliches. **96m/C VHS.** Kari Wuhrer, Rae Dawn Chong, Lou Diamond Phillips, Lance Henriksen, Joel Bissonnette, Penelope Buitenhuis; **W:** Rae Dawn Chong; **M:** Ian Thomas.

Boulevard Nights ♂♂ 1979 (R) A young Latino man tries to escape his neighborhood's streetgang violence, while his older brother is sucked into it. Music by Schifrin, known for the "Mission: Impossible" theme. **102m/C VHS.** Richard Yniguez, Danny De La Paz, Marta DuBois, Carmen Zapata, Victor Millan; **D:** Michael Pressman; **C:** John Bailey; **M:** Lalo Schifrin.

Boulevard of Broken Dreams ♂♂ 1988 (PG-13) Successful Hollywood screenwriter Tom Garfield (Waters) returns to his native Australia to figure out how his life got so screwed up. His estranged wife is living with someone

else and his daughter barely remembers him. Affecting look at personal priorities versus success. **95m/C VHS. AU** John Waters, Kim Gyngell, Penelope Stewart; **D:** Pino Amenta.

Bounce ♂♂½ 2000 (PG-13) Ad exec Affleck swaps his airline ticket with a stranger who's anxious to get home to his wife. But since no good deed goes unpunished, the plane crashes and the man is killed. The guilt-stricken Affleck visits the stranger's widow (Paltrow) and winds up falling in love with her, only she doesn't know about their unfortunate connection. Okay, the plot is contrived, predictable, and a little schmaltzy, but it somehow avoids maudlin, and takes pains to make the emotions real. In this, director Roos is aided greatly by Affleck, who turns in some of his best work to date, and Paltrow, who seems less actress-y in an understated, smart performance. The two leads were said to be an item during filming. **105m/C VHS, DVD.** Gwyneth Paltrow, Ben Affleck, Natasha Henstridge, Jennifer Grey, Tony Goldwyn, Joe Morton, David Paymer, Johnny Galecki, Alex D. Linz, Juan Garcia, Sam Robards, Julia Campbell, Michael Laskin, John Levin, David Dorfman; **D:** Don Roos; **W:** Don Roos; **C:** Robert Elswit; **M:** Mychael Danna.

Bound ♂♂ 1996 (R) Ex-con Corky (Gershon) is busy fixing up her new apartment after serving five years for robbery. Her next-door neighbors are Caesar (Pantoliano), a neurotic, money-laundering mobster, and his sexy girlfriend, a seemingly dumb brunette named Violet (Tilly). The femme twosome hook up (in and out of bed) and hatch a plan to steal two million freshly laundered dollars from Caesar, who goes ballistic when he discovers the money gone. It's a flashy—but not substantive—thriller. Directorial debut for the brothers Wachowski. **107m/C VHS, DVD.** Gina Gershon, Jennifer Tilly, Joe Pantoliano, John P. Ryan, Barry Kivel, Christopher Meloni, Peter Spellos, Richard Sarafian, Mary Mara, Susie Bright, Ivan Kane, Kevin M. Richardson, Gene Borkan; **D:** Andy Wachowski, Larry Wachowski; **W:** Andy Wachowski, Larry Wachowski; **C:** Bill Pope; **M:** Don Davis.

Bound and Gagged: A Love Story ♂ 1993 (R) For some reason, Elizabeth (Saltarelli), who is desperate for a husband, thinks that she might increase her chances of finding one if she kidnaps her friend Leslie (Allen) and goes on a weird wild goose chase through Minnesota with the hostage and her hopeless partner-in-crime, Cliff (Denton). Go figure. **96m/C VHS, DVD.** Ginger Lynn Allen, Karen Black, Chris Denton, Elizabeth Saltarelli, Mary Ella Ross, Chris Mulkey; **D:** Daniel Appleby; **W:** Daniel Appleby; **D:** Dean Lent; **M:** William Murphy.

Bound by Lies ♂½ 2005 Detectives Max Garrett (Baldwin) and Eddie Fulton (Whitfield) are assigned to protect Laura (Swanson)—a sexy photographer of erotic images—when a rash of serial murders linked to her work is uncovered. But Garrett puts himself in danger by falling for her. **85m/C VHS, DVD.** Kristy Swanson, Stephen Baldwin, Charles Malik Whitfield, Natassia Malthe, Kevin Chamberlin, Joel Brooks, Tracy Howe; **D:** Valerie Landsburg; **W:** D. Alvelo, Leland Zaitz; **C:** Maximo Munzi. **VIDEO**

Bound for Glory ♂♂♂ 1976 (PG) The award-winning biography of American folk singer Woody Guthrie set against the backdrop of the Depression. Superb portrayal of the spirit and feelings of the period featuring many of his songs encased in the incidents that inspired them. Haskell Wexler's award-winning camera work is superbly expressive. **149m/C VHS, DVD.** David Carradine, Ronny Cox, Melinda Dillon, Randy Quaid; **D:** Hal Ashby; **W:** Robert Getchell; **C:** Haskell Wexler. Oscars '76: Cinematog., Orig. Song Score and/or Adapt.; L.A. Film Critics '76: Cinematog.; Natl. Bd. of Review '76: Actor (Carradine); Natl. Soc. Film Critics '76: Cinematog.

The Bounty ♂♂½ 1984 (PG) A new version of "Mutiny on the Bounty," with emphasis on a more realistic relationship between Fletcher Christian and Captain Bligh—and a more sympathetic portrayal of the captain, too. The sensuality of Christian's relationship with a Tahitian beauty also receives greater importance.

130m/C VHS, DVD, Mel Gibson, Anthony Hopkins, Laurence Olivier, Edward Fox, Daniel Day-Lewis, Bernard Hill, Philip Davis, Liam Neeson; **D:** Roger Donaldson; **W:** Robert Bolt; **C:** Arthur Ibbetson; **M:** Vangelis.

Bounty Hunter 2002 ♂♂ 2002:
The Rape of Eden 1994 A rogue virus kills most of the world's population and few of those remaining are completely immune. Slave trading in the capture and sale of immune survivors is a lucrative business and a bounty hunter's last assignment is to bring in a beautiful but deadly woman. **90m/C VHS.** Phil Nordell, Francine Lapensee, Vernon Wells, Jeff Conaway; **D:** Sam Auster; **W:** Sam Auster.

Bounty Hunters ♂♂½ 1989 (R) A man hunts down his friend's killer. **91m/C VHS.** Robert Ginty, Bo Hopkins, Loeta Waterdown; **D:** Robert Ginty.

Bounty Hunters ♂♂ 1996 (R) Rival bounty hunters (and ex-lovers) Jersey Bellini (Dudikoff) and B.B. Mitchell (Howard) join forces to capture bail-jumping, stolen-car king Delmos (Ratner), who's also the target of mob hitmen. Gunplay and car chases. **98m/C VHS, DVD.** Michael Dudikoff, Lisa Howard, Benjamin Ratner; **D:** George Erschbamer; **W:** George Erschbamer; **C:** A.J. Vesak; **M:** Norman Orenstein.

Bounty Hunters 2: Hardball ♂♂ *Hardball* 1997 (R) A bounty hunter and his female partner tick off the mob by foiling a heist and now must fend off hired killers looking for revenge. **97m/C VHS, DVD.** Michael Dudikoff, Lisa Howard, Steve Bacic, Tony Curtis; **D:** George Erschbamer; **W:** George Erschbamer, Jeff Barmash, Michael Ellis; **C:** Brian Pearson; **M:** Leon Aronson. **VIDEO**

The Bounty Man ♂♂ 1972 A bounty hunter brings an outlaw in, robbing him of his freedom and his girlfriend. **74m/C VHS.** Clint Walker, Richard Basehart, Margot Kidder, Arthur Hunnicutt, John Ericson, Gene Evans; **D:** John Llewellyn Moxey.

Bounty Tracker ♂½ 1993 (R) Johnny Damone (Lamas) is a bounty-hunter in pursuit of the killer-for-hire who murdered his brother. This personal vendetta leads to an action-packed martial arts showdown between Johnny and his cold-blooded prey. **90m/C VHS.** Lorenzo Lamas, Matthias Hues, Eugene Robert Glazer, Cyndi Pass, Eric Mansker, Judd Omen, Eddie Frias, George Perez; **D:** Kurt Anderson.

Bouquet of Barbed Wire ♂♂½
1976 Overlong soaper revolves around a wealthy family and their hidden secrets: incest and infidelity. On three tapes. **330m/C VHS.** Frank Finlay, Susan Penhaligon, Deborah Grant, Sheila Allen, James Aubrey; **D:** Tom Wharmby.

The Bourne Identity ♂♂½ 1988 Chamberlain stars as an amnesiac trying to piece together the fragments of his memory. Is he U.S. espionage agent Jason Bourne or an international terrorist? Aided by Smith (the kidnap victim who falls in love with her captor), the two traverse Europe trying to escape the spy network out to assassinate the mystery man who knows too little. Exciting miniseries adaptation of the Robert Ludlum thriller. **185m/C VHS, DVD.** Richard Chamberlain, Jaclyn Smith, Denholm Elliott, Anthony Quayle, Donald Moffat, Yorgo Voyagis; **D:** Roger Young; **W:** Carol Sobieski. **TV**

The Bourne Identity ♂♂♂½
2002 (PG-13) First-rate international espionage thriller loosely based on the first book (published in 1981) of Robert Ludlum's trilogy, previously filmed as a 1988 TV miniseries starring Richard Chamberlain. A young man (Damon) gets fished out of the ocean with a couple of bullet holes and amnesia—his only clue a numbered Swiss account. This reveals that he has multiple identities, including that of Jason Bourne, who has an apartment in Paris. Marie (Potente) for a ride. As Bourne tries to piece his past together, he learns he's a highly efficient assassin for a covert CIA operation and his boss (Cooper) considers him a rogue operative and is trying to kill him. **118m/C VHS, DVD, UMD, HD DVD. US** Matt Damon, Franka Potente, Chris Cooper, Brian

Cox, Clive Owen, Julia Stiles, Gabriel Mann, Adewale Akinnuoye-Agbaje, Walton Goggins, Josh Hamilton, Tim Dutton; **D:** Doug Liman; **W:** Tony Gilroy, W(illiam) Blake Herron; **C:** Oliver Wood; **M:** John Powell.

The Bourne Supremacy ♂♂♂
2004 (PG-13) Warning! The easily-queasy should be wary of the hand-held camerawork and quick edits of the action sequences. Amnesiac CIA-trained assassin Jason Bourne (Damon) is now living quietly with girlfriend Marie (Potente) when he's targeted for death by Russian bad guys and made the patsy for a Berlin hit on a couple of agents. CIA officer Landy (Allen) and her boss (Cox) try to reel Bourne in while he tries to figure out just who wants him dead this time (and why). The non-stop action moves from India to Berlin to Amsterdam to Moscow, and while the plot eventually turns out to be simple enough, the chases are not. Damon once again proves adept as an action man while making Bourne an intelligent and oddly sympathetic character. Loosely adapted from the second book of Robert Ludlum's Bourne trilogy. **109m/C VHS, DVD, UMD, HD DVD. US** Matt Damon, Franka Potente, Joan Allen, Brian Cox, Marton Csokas, Gabriel Mann, Karel Roden, Julia Stiles, Karl Urban, Tomas Arana, Tim Griffin, Michelle Monaghan, Tom Gallop, John Bedford Lloyd, Ethan Sandler, Oksana Akinshina; **D:** Paul Greengrass; **W:** Tony Gilroy; **C:** Oliver Wood; **M:** John Powell.

The Bourne Ultimatum ♂♂♂½ 2007 (PG-13) In this third (and final?) chapter Jason Bourne (Damon) continues his search for clues to to his past with Treadstone, the mothballed facility where he was trained him. Now CIA official Vosen (Strathairn) wants to revive the project, and assigns agent Lundy (Allen) to eliminate Bourne. Meanwhile, Bourne is outmaneuvering cops, feds, spooks, and Interpol agents in Moscow, Paris, Madrid, Tangier, London, and New York. Smart, tense, and frenetic, with excellent performances from all involved. The only drawback is the confusion- and nausea-inducing camera work during the action sequences. **111m/C DVD, HD DVD.** US Matt Damon, Julia Stiles, Joan Allen, David Strathairn, Paddy Considine, Edgar Ramirez, Scott Glenn, Albert Finney, Tom Gallop, Corey Johnson, Daniel Bruhl, Colin Stinton, Joey Ansah; **D:** Paul Greengrass; **W:** Tony Gilroy, Scott Burns, George Nolfi; **C:** Oliver Wood; **M:** John Powell. Oscars '07: Film Editing, Sound, Sound FX Editing; British Acad. '07: Film Editing, Sound.

Boutique ♂♂♂½ 2004 Window dresser at a chic boutique in Tehran steals a pair of jeans for a girl he's interested in after she says she can't afford anything at the establishment. This is the beginning of a downward spiral in his life. Thoughtfully moving film makes startling observations of Iranian society. In Farsi with English subtitles. **113m/C DVD.** Mohammad Reza Golzar, Golshifteh Farahani, Reza Rooygari; **D:** Hamid Nematollah; **W:** Hamid Nematollah; **C:** Mahmoud Kalari; **M:** Fariborz Lachini. **VIDEO**

The Bowery ♂♂♂ 1933 Chuck Connors (Beery) owns a saloon on New York's Bowery in the 1890s and is a friendly rival to daredevil gambler Steve Brodie (Raft). Only things aren't so friendly when the men both fall for hard-luck dame Lucy (Wray). Connors proposes that Brodie jump off the Brooklyn Bridge (a feat he allegedly accomplished before) to impress Lucy and offers ownership of his saloon as added incentive. Cooper, who starred opposite Beery in 1931's "The Champ," plays streetwise orphan Swipes McGurk. **92m/B VHS.** Wallace Beery, George Raft, Fay Wray, Jackie Cooper, Pert Kelton; **D:** Raoul Walsh; **W:** Howard Estabrook; **C:** Barney McGill; **M:** Alfred Newman.

Bowery at Midnight ♂½ 1942 Lugosi plays a man who recycles criminals into zombies that commit crimes for his benefit. Bela and an intense mood can't quite save this pic. **60m/B VHS, DVD.** Bela Lugosi, Tom Neal, Dave O'Brien, Wanda McKay; **D:** Wallace Fox; **W:** Gerald Schnitzer; **C:** Mack Stengler; **M:** Edward Kay.

Bowery Blitzkrieg 🐾 *Stand and Deliver* 1941 This lesser "East Side Kids" entry has Gorcey opting to enter the boxing ring rather than turn to crime. Needs more hijinks in this comedy in which they confront a group of transplant-happy scientists. **62m/C VHS, DVD.** *Cast:* Leo Gorcey, Huntz Hall, Bobby Jordan, Warren Hull, Charlotte Henry, Kaye Luke; *D:* Wallace Fox.

Bowery Buckaroos 1947 The Bowery Boys take their act West in search of gold, meeting up with the usual hoots with an anti-establishment train robber. Based on the book "Sister of the Road" by Boxcar Bertha Thompson. **90m/C VHS, DVD.** Barbara Hershey, David Carradine, Barry Primus, Bernie Casey, Victor Argo, Martin Scorsese, Joyce H. Corrington; *C:* John Stephens; *M:* Gib Guilbeau.

Bowery Boys Meet the Monsters 🐾🐾 1954. The infamous Bowery Boys display their usual hilarious hijinks in this comedy in which they confront a group of transplant-happy scientists and misunderstandings. **66m/B VHS.** Leo Gorcey, Huntz Hall, Bobby Jordan, Gabriel Dell, William Benedict, David Gorcey, Julie Briggs, Bernard Gorcey, Chief Yowlachie, Ilon Eyes Cody; *D:* Edward L. Bernds.

Bowfinger 🐾🐾🐾 1999 (PG-13). Martin stars as wannabe Hollywood player Bobby Bowfinger, who is desperate to break into the big time. His one hope is to convince action star Kit Ramsey (Murphy) to be in a cheesy sci-fi scare flick entitled "Chubby Rain." But Ramsey and his tyrannical New Age advisor Stricter (Stamp) want nothing to do with the movie. After his 'antics send Ramsey to the "relaxation home," Bowfinger hires geeky lookalike Jiff (also Murphy) to take his place. The pairing of Martin and Murphy works well, and Frank Oz is an expert at directing off-beat comedies such as this. **96m/C VHS, DVD.** Steve Martin, Eddie Murphy, Christine Baranski, Heather Graham, Terence Stamp, Jamie Kennedy, Robert Downey Jr., Barry Newman; *D:* Frank Oz; *W:* Steve Martin; *C:* Ueli Steiger; *M:* David Newman.

Bowling for Columbine 🐾🐾🐾 2002 (R) Moore takes on the trigger-happy American gun culture, as well as the media, the NRA and Littleton, Colorado—the site of the Columbine High School killings—with his usual blend of satire and chutzpah. **122m/C VHS, DVD.** *D:* Michael Moore. Oscars '02: Feature Doc.; Ind. Spirit '03: Feature Doc.; Writers Guild '02: Orig. Screenplay.

The Box 🐾🐾 1/2 2003 (R) Ah, it must be true love when an ex-con and an ex-stripper hook up at the local diner. But problems plague the happy pair's future like his mob connections, her psycho ex-husband, and the thugs who want their big bag of loot. **95m/C VHS, DVD.** James Russo, Theresa Russel, Brad Dourif, Steve Railsback, Jon Polito, Michael Rooker, Joe Palese, Lee Weaver; *D:* Richard Pepin; *W:* James Russo; *C:* Chris Anderson. **VIDEO**

The Box 🐾🐾 2007 (R) Two homicide detectives question a thief and a victim of a robbery gone wrong. One detective has to face past mistakes, while the other gets an offer from the criminal behind the botched heist. **96m/C DVD.** Gabrielle Union, Giancarlo Esposito, A.J. Buckley, Jason George, Mia Maestro, James Madio, Yul Vazquez, Brett Donowho; *D:* A.J. Kparr; *C:* Sion Michel; *M:* James T. Sale.

Box of Moonlight 🐾🐾 1996 (R) Hardworking, by-the-book electrical systems engineer Al Fountain (Turturo) feels mysteriously compelled to play hockey from his family and career while on an out-of-town business trip. Lost and confused, Al meets up with the Kid, a quirky recluse played with energy and appeal by Rockwell. Through a series of mix-ups, the nice-but-stuffy Al and the wild-but-well-meaning Kid end up spending the fourth of July weekend together. Lost and confused, the point of his journey long after the audience probably has makes the film a bit predictable and stale. DeCillo's third feature was six years in the making and financed by the success the film has garnered by his second feature. "Living in Oblivion." **111m/C VHS, DVD.** John Turturro, Sam Rockwell, Catherine Keener, Lisa Blount, Annie Corley, Dermot Mulroney, Alexander Goodwin; *D:* Tom DiCillo; *W:* Tom DiCillo; *C:* Paul Ryan; *M:* Jim Farmer.

Boxcar Bertha 🐾🐾 1/2 1972 (R) Scorsese's vivid portrayal of the South during the 1930s Depression casts Hershey as a woman who winds up in cahoots with an anti-establishment train robber. Based on the book "Sister of the Road" by Boxcar Bertha Thompson. **90m/C VHS, DVD.** Barbara Hershey, David Carradine, John Carradine, Barry Primus, Bernie Casey, Victor Argo, Martin Scorsese, Joyce H. Corrington; *C:* John Stephens; *M:* Gib Guilbeau.

Boxcar Blues 🐾 1990 Bird (Couros) is a down and out fighter who decides to fight "The Man" (Ventura), a bare knuckle fighter who enjoys beating his opponents to death. On the way to the fight, he meets up with his girl Casey (Langrick), along with some other shady characters, including a truck driving preacher. **96m/C VHS.** Paul Coufos, Margaret Langrick, Jesse Ventura, M. Emmet Walsh, Donny Lalonde; *D:* Damian Lee.

The Boxer 🐾🐾 1997 (R) Affecting, if predicable, romance set in Ulster, Northern Ireland. Having served 14 years in prison Danny Flynn (Day-Lewis) wants nothing more to do with politics and violence. But his return to his old neighborhood—where he hopes to get back to his boxing career—finds him in the thick of both. Danny manages to persuade his ex-trainer, the alcoholic Ike (Stott), to help reopen the local gym but resentment is high. Particularly from hard-liner Harry (McSorley), who doesn't like Danny's live-and-let-live attitude and is incensed that he's interested in rekindling his lost-but-never-forgotten love for Maggie (Watson), the daughter of local IRA boss Joe (Cox), and the wife of another IRA prisoner. Things quickly turn ugly but the emotionally fragile Danny and Maggie continue to fight to be together against formidable odds. **113m/C VHS, DVD, GB IP** Daniel Day-Lewis, Emily Watson, Brian Cox, Gerard McSorley, Ken Stott, Ciaran Fitzgerald, Kenneth Cranham; *Cameos:* Tom Bell; *D:* Jim Sheridan; *W:* Jim Sheridan, Terry George; *C:* Chris Menges; *M:* Gavin Friday, Maurice Seezer.

The Boxer and Death 🐾🐾🐾 1963 A new-wave Czech film about a boxer in a Nazi concentration camp who interests the boxing-obsessed commandant in a match. In Czech with subtitles. **120m/B VHS.** Manfred Krug, Josef Kondrat, Valentina Thielova, Edwin Marian, Gerhard Rachold, Stefan Kvietik; *D:* Peter Solan; *C:* Tibor Biath; *M:* William Bukovy.

Boxing Helena 🐾🐾 1993 (R) Highly publicized as the film that cost Basinger almost $9 million in damages, the directorial debut of director/writer Jennifer Lynch (daughter of David) explores the dark side of relationships between men and women. Sands is Dr. Nick Cavanaugh, a surgeon who becomes dangerously obsessed with the beautiful, yet unattainable Helena (Fenn). When she is hit by a car near his home, he performs emergency surgery and amputates her arms and legs, forcing her to be dependent on him. Metaphorically a situation, albeit an extreme one, that mirrors the power struggle in any sexual relationship. Problematic in some aspects, although equally fascinating as it is disturbing. **107m/C VHS, DVD.** Julian Sands, Sherilyn Fenn, Bill Paxton, Kurwood Smith, Betsy Clark, Nicolette Scorsese, Art Garfunkel, Meg Register, Bryan Smith; *C:* Bojan Bazelli; *M:* Graeme Revell, Goden Raspberries '93: Worst Director (Lynch).

A Boy and His Dog 🐾🐾 1/2 1975 (R) In the post-holocaust world of 2024, a young man (Johnson) and his telepathic canine (McIntire supplies narration of the dog's thoughts) cohort search for food and sex. They happen upon a community that drafts Johnson to repopulate their largely impotent race. Johnson discovers the mechanical methods they mean to employ. Based on a short story by Harlan Ellison. The dog was played by Tiger on "The Brady Bunch." **87m/C VHS, DVD.** Don Johnson, Susanne Benton, Jason Robards Jr., Charles McGraw, Alvy Moore, Helene Winston, Hal Baylor, L.Q. Jones; *D:* L.Q. Jones; *W:* L.Q. Jones; *C:* John Morrill; *M:* Tim McIntire.

A Boy Called Hate 🐾🐾 1995 (R) Troubled teen Steve (Caan)—whose nickname is "Hate" after his tattoo—lives with his divorced dad in an L.A. suburb. Steve's on a latenight motorcycle ride, taking potshots at billboards with his trusty handgun, when he stumbles onto what he thinks is an attempted rape. So Steve shoots at the rapist, Richard (Gould), and takes off with would-be victim Cindy (Crider). Turns out Richard is the assistant D.A. and he tells the cops he's been robbed, so the teen duo are now on the run. Familiar tale with some good twists and believable performances. Caan is the son of James (seen in a cameo as the dad). Debut for director Marcus. **96m/C VHS.** Scott Caan, Missy (Melissa) Crider, Elliott Gould, Adam Beach; *Cameos:* James Caan; *D:* Mitch Marcus; *W:* Mitch Marcus; *C:* Paul Holahan.

Boy Culture 🐾🐾 2006 Money, desire, and emotional denial. X (Magyar) is a cynical hustler with a high-end and limited clientele of older men. His newest client, the urbane Gregory (Bachau), confuses X by paying for his company but refusing his sexual favors unless X is also emotionally involved. X can't even admit this attraction to his roommate Andrew (Stevens), who's unsure of his own sexuality, while their other roommate, twink Joey (Trent), openly lusts after X. Based on the novel by Matthew Rettenmund. **90m/C DVD, Derek Magyar, Patrick Bauchau, Darryl Stephens, John Trent; *D:* Q. Allan Brocka; *W:* Q. Allan Brocka; *C:* Jerusha Hess; *M:* Ryan Beveridge.

Boy, Did I Get a Wrong Number! 🐾 1966 A real estate agent gets more than he bargained for when he accidentally dials a wrong number. Zany comedy persists as Hope gets entangled in the life of sexy starlet Sommer. **100m/C VHS.** Bob Hope, Phyllis Diller, Marjorie Lord, Elke Sommer, Cesare Danova, Kelly Thordsen; *D:* George Marshall; *W:* Albert Lewin, Burt Styler; *C:* Lionel Lindon; *M:* Richard LaSalle.

The Boy Friend 🐾🐾🐾 1971 (G) Russell pays tribute to the Busby Berkeley Hollywood musical. Lots of charming dance numbers and clever parody of plot-lines in this adaptation of Sandy Wilson's stage play. Fun! 🎵 The Boy Friend: I Could Be Happy; Won't You Charleston With Me?; Fancy Forgetting; Sur La Plage; A Room in Bloomsbury; Safety in Numbers; It's Never Too Late to Fall in Love; Poor Little Pierette. **135m/C VHS, GB** Twiggy, Christopher Gable, Moyra Fraser, Max Adrian, Vladek Sheybal, Georgina Hale, Tommy Tune; *D:* Ken Russell; *W:* Ken Russell; *C:* David Watkin. Golden Globes '72: Actress—Mus./Comedy (Twiggy).

Boy in Blue 🐾🐾 1/2 1986 (R) A speed-rower Ned Hanlan, who set aside lackluster pursuits to turn to rowing. **97m/C VHS, DVD.** CA Nicolas Cage, Christopher Plummer, David Naughton, Cynthia Dale, Melody Anderson, James B. Douglas; *D:* Charles Jarrott; *W:* Douglas Bowie; *C:* Pierre Mignot; *M:* Roger Webb.

The Boy in the Plastic Bubble 🐾🐾 1/2 1976 Well-made, sensitive drama about a young man born with immunity deficiencies who must grow up in a specially controlled plastic environment. Travolta is endearing as the boy who meets every film is a variation on the boy meets girl theme. Trouble is they're running out of ideas and their scripts get increasingly outlandish. A fading cowboy actor is supposed to star in the duo's next film—if they can ever settle down to work. Then they get the idea to feature their friend Wilson's baby in the movie—and guess who becomes a new star. Good satire on movie-making and movie moguls, which made fine use of the Warner studio back lots, sound stages, and offices. **86m/B VHS.** Alan Marcus, Emily Watson, Mark Snow. **TV**

Boy Meets Girl 🐾🐾 1938 Cagney and O'Brien play screenwriters whose every film is a variation on the boy meets girl theme. Trouble is they're running out of ideas and their scripts get increasingly outlandish. A fading cowboy actor is supposed to star in the duo's next film—if they can ever settle down to work. Then they get the idea to feature their friend Wilson's baby in the movie—and guess who becomes a new star. Good satire on movie-making and movie moguls, which made fine use of the Warner studio back lots, sound stages, and offices. Screenplay by Bella and Samuel Spewack who also wrote the screenplay. **86m/B VHS.** James Cagney, Pat O'Brien, Ralph Bellamy, Dick Foran, Marie Wilson, Frank McHugh, Bruce Lester, Ronald Reagan, Penny Singleton, James Stephenson; *D:* Lloyd Bacon; *W:* Bella Spewack, Samuel Spewack.

Boy Meets Girl 🐾🐾 1984 Alex (Lavant), a French "Holden Caulfield type character, cruises the seamier side of Paris in this acclaimed film. Carax's directorial debut at age 22. Alex will return in Carax films "Bad Blood" (1986) and "The Lovers on the Bridge" (1991). French with subtitles. **100m/B VHS, DVD, FR** Denis Lavant, Mireille Perrier, Carroll Brooks, Anna Baldaccini; *D:* Leos Carax; *W:* Leos Carax; *C:* Jean-Yves Escoffier; *M:* Jacques Pinault.

Boy of Two Worlds 🐾 1/2 1970 **96m/C VHS, DVD.** Tim Moore, Duke Williams, Sheila Guyse, Beth Mays, Elwood Smith; *D:* Arthur Leonard.

Boy Takes Girl 🐾🐾 1983 A little girl finds it hard adjusting to life on a farm, and is fought over by a couple of suitors. **93m/C VHS, Gabi Elbo; Hillel Neeman, Dina Limon; *D:* Michal Bat-Adam.

Boy! What a Girl 🐾🐾 1945 Moore (in drag) is mistaken for a woman, and is fought over by a couple of suitors, in this late father's town, a boy is exiled to the life of a junior Robinson Crusoe. **103m/C VHS, Jimmy Stenman, Edwin Adolphson; *D:* Astrid Henning Jensen.

The Boy Who Could Fly 🐾🐾🐾 1986 (PG) After a plane crash kills his parents, a boy withdraws into a fantasy land where he can fly. The only problem is Ofeoti only has a day to live, and Paul must find a way to save him. Aired on PBS as part of the "Wonderworks" series. **120m/C VHS, DVD.** Lucy Deakins, Jay Underwood, Bonnie Bedelia, Colleen Dewhurst, Fred Savage, Fred Gwynne, Louise Fletcher, Jason Priestley; *D:* Nick Castle; *W:* Nick Castle; *C:* Steven Poster; *M:* Bruce Broughton.

The Boy Who Left Home to Find Out About the Shivers 🐾🐾 1981 From "Faerie Tale Theatre" comes this tale about a boy who learns about fear. **60m/C VHS, DVD.** Peter MacNichol, Christopher Lee, David Warner, Dana Hill, Frank Zappa; *D:* Graeme Clifford; *V:* Vincent Price. **CABLE**

The Boy with the Green Hair 🐾🐾🐾 1948 When he hears that his parents were killed in an air raid, a boy's hair turns green. The narrow-minded members of his community suddenly want nothing to do with him and he becomes an outcast. Thought-provoking social commentary. **82m/C VHS, DVD.** Pat O'Brien, Robert Ryan, Barbara Hale, Dean Stockwell; *D:* Joseph Losey.

Boycott 🐾🐾🐾 1/2 2002 Superb HBO docudrama re-creates the Civil Rights movement's early days, from Rosa Parks's (Little-Thomas) refusal to give up her seat to a white man on a segregated bus, through the narrow-minded Montgomery, Alabama, bus, through the subsequent boycott of the bus system by the city's black population, to the success of the boycott and the rise to prominence of Dr. Martin Luther King Jr. (Wright) as its leader. Through the use and mix of many different visual styles, director Johnson uses artful touches to tell the story fantastic as King, with other outstanding performances turned in by Howard as organizer Jo Anne Robinson. **112m/C VHS.**

DVD. Jeffrey Wright, Terrence Howard, CCH Pounder, Carmen Ejogo, Reg E. Cathey, Brent Jennings, Shawn Michael Howard, Erik Todd Dellums, Iris Little-Thomas, Whitman Mayo, E. Roger Mitchell, Mike Hodge, Clark Johnson; **D:** Clark Johnson; **W:** Timothy J. Sexton, Herman Daniel Farrell III; **C:** David Hennings; **M:** Stephen James Taylor. **CABLE**

Boyfriends 🦴🦴 **1996** Gay sexual roundelay that takes place over a weekend spent in the English countryside. Paul (Dreyfus) and Ben (Sands) are on the verge of splitting up after five years, orderly Matt's (Urwin) in love with philandering Owen (Ableson), and social worker Will (Coffey) wants more than a one-nighter with working-class pickup Adam (Petrucci). They all head to social games begin. Low budget first feature from Hunter and Hunsinger. **82m/C VHS, DVD.** *GB* James Dreyfus, Mark Sands, Andrew Ableson, Michael Urwin, David Coffey, Darren Petrucci, Michael McGrath, Russell Higgs; **D:** Neil Hunter, Tom Hunsinger; **W:** Neil Hunter, Tom Hunsinger; **C:** Richard Tisdall.

Boyfriends & Girlfriends 🦴🦴½ *My Girlfriend's Boyfriend; L'Ami de Mon Ami* **1988 (PG)** Another one of Rohmer's "Comedies and Proverbs," in which two girls with boyfriends fade in and out of interest with each, casually reshuffling their relationships. Typical, endless-talks-at-cafes Rohmer, the most happily refreshing setting for a romantic comedy. In French with subtitles. **102m/C VHS, DVD.** *FR* Emmanuelle Chaulet, Sophie Renoir, Eric Viellard, Francois-Eric Gendron, Anne-Laure Meury; **D:** Eric Rohmer; **W:** Eric Rohmer; **C:** Bernard Lutic; **M:** Jean-Louis Valero.

The Boynton Beach Club 🦴🦴½ *The Boynton Beach Bereavement Club* **2005 (R)** Aged lonely hearts find support and possibly love as members of a Florida "active adult" community—an unlikely but surprisingly refreshing setting for a romantic comedy. Newly widowed Marilyn (Vaccaro) joins the group after a car backs over her husband. There she meets a range of characters more interested in romance and life beyond blue hair and early-bird specials. Hotties-of-a-certain-age Cannon and Kellerman mix with master casanova Cariou and Bologna and his reluctant teenager. Plays a little sit-com-y at times, but manages to keep things dignified and unpatronizing. Director Seidelman got the idea for the movie from her mother Florence, who received a producer's credit. **105m/C DVD.** *US* Dyan Cannon, Brenda Vaccaro, Sally Kellerman, Joseph Bologna, Len Cariou, Michael Nouri, Renee Taylor; **D:** Susan Seidelman; **W:** Susan Seidelman, Shelly Gitlow; **C:** Eric Moynier; **M:** Marcelo Zarvos.

Boys 🦴🦴½ *The Girl You Want* **1995 (PG-13)** Seems like only yesterday we saw Haas as that big-eared, doe-eyed Amish kid from "Witness," but now, in this dry love story, he has grown into a big-eared, doe-eyed teenager lusting after older woman Ryder. John (Haas) saves Patty (Ryder) after a riding accident leaves her unconscious near his New England prep school. Immediately taken by her beauty and mystery, John decides to hide her in his dorm room and a romance blossoms between the unlikely pair. But John isn't the only one hiding something. Patty has a terrible secret from her past (gasp!), but when it's finally revealed, you'll be too bored to care. Based on the short story "Twenty Minutes" by James Salter. **86m/C VHS, DVD.** Winona Ryder, Lukas Haas, John C. Reilly, William Sage, Skeet Ulrich; **D:** Stacy Cochran; **W:** Stacy Cochran; **C:** Robert Elswit; **M:** Stewart Copeland.

The Boys 🦴🦴½ *Les Boys* **1997** Popular, simply plotted French-Canadian comedy about a group of ordinary guys who play in an amateur hockey league. "Les Boys" are sponsored by local tavern-owner Stan (Girard), who's got a gambling problem and is in debt to small-time mobster Meo (Lebeau). Meo strikes a deal pitting Stan's ragtag hockey players against his own team of thugs. If Stan's team is defeated, he loses his bar. Dirty tricks abound on both sides. French with subtitles. **107m/C VHS, DVD.** *CA* Remy Girard, Marc Messier, Patrick Huard, Serge Theriault, Yvan Ponton, Dominic Philie, Patrick Labbe, Roc Lafortune, Pierre Lebeau, Paul Houde; **D:** Louis Saia; **W:** Christian Fournier; **C:** Sylvain Brault; **M:** Normand Corbeil.

The Boys 🦴🦴🦴 **1998 (R)** After his release from prison on an assault charge, psychopathic Brett (Wenham), heads to the home of his mother Sandra (Curran) and younger brother Stevie (Hayes). His other brother Glenn (Polson) is now married to Jackie (Cronin) who wants him to stay out of trouble. As greeting Brett is girlfriend Michelle (Collette) but the volatile duo are soon arguing furiously. As Brett gets drunker and more stoned, he also becomes more enraged, leading to a brutal crime. Chilling story with powerful performances; adapted from the 1991 play by Gordon Graham. **84m/C VHS.** *AU* David Wenham, Toni Collette, John Polson, Lynette Curran, Anthony Hayes, Jeanette Cronin, Anna Lise, Pete Smith; **D:** Rowan Woods; **W:** Stephen Sewell; **C:** Tristan Milani; Australian Film Inst. '98: Adapt. Screenplay, Director (Woods), Support. Actor (Polson), Support. Actress (Collette).

The Boys and Girl From County Clare 🦴🦴½ *The Boys From County Clare* **2003** Set in the 1960s, Liverpool businessman Jimmy (Meaney) returns to his home in Ireland after 24 years to compete in the annual Celli music festival, which brings him into direct conflict with his long-estranged older brother John Joe (Hill). Soon enough the brothers are fighting about music and Maisie (Bradley), who Jimmy deserted for life in Liverpool. Meanwhile their bands are doing everything they can to sabotage each other, and Jimmy's flutist (Evans) is falling for John Joe's fiddler (Corr). Lighthearted comedy/drama uses traditional Irish music as a backdrop for an appealing but routine sibling rivalry story. **90m/C DVD.** *GB IR GE* Bernard Hill, Colm Meaney, Charlotte Bradley, Stephen Brennan, Andrea Corr, Eamon Owens, Shaun Evans, Phil Barantini, Patrick Bergin; **D:** John Irvin; **W:** Nicholas Adams; **C:** Thomas Burstyn; **M:** Fiachra Trench.

Boys and Girls 🦴🦴 **2000 (PG-13)** Nondescript teen romance has lifelong acquaintances and most-time friends Ryan (Prinze Jr.) and Jennifer (Forlani) trying to decide if they love each other after their hormones get the better of them one night. And get this! They're complete opposites! She's carefree and live-for-the-moment. He's button-down, plan-every-second-precise. Biggs and Donahue, as the respective sidekicks, steal the movie from the leads whenever they show up. Sort of a young, poor man's "When Harry Met Sally," without the wit and insight. **94m/C VHS, DVD.** Freddie Prinze Jr., Claire Forlani, Jason Biggs, Heather Donahue, Alyson Hannigan, Amanda Detmer, Lisa Eichhorn; **D:** Robert Iscove; **W:** Andrew Lowery, Andrew Miller; **C:** Ralf Bode; **M:** Stewart Copeland.

The Boys Club 🦴🦴 **1996 (R)** Teens-in-trouble film is given a tough core by first time director Fawcett. Excitement-craving 14-year-olds Kyle (Zamprogna), Eric (Sawa), and Brad (Stone) spend all their free time at an abandoned shack at the outskirts of their small town. Only one day they discover it occupied by gun-pointing criminal Luke Cooper (Penn), who tells the boys he's actually a good cop who's been shot and is on the run from some bad cops. The boys are willing to buy into the story at first but Cooper is quick to show his psycho colors, taking Eric hostage, and precipitating a violent finale. **92m/C VHS, DVD.** *CA* Christopher Penn, Stuart Stone, Devon Sawa, Dominic Zamprogna, Nicholas (Nick) Campbell, Jarred Blanchard; **D:** John Fawcett; **W:** Peter Wellington; **C:** Thom Best; **M:** Michael Timmins.

Boys Don't Cry 🦴🦴🦴 **1999 (R)** Falls under the truth is stranger than fiction category. Brandon Teena (heavily awarded Swank) moves from Lincoln, Nebraska, to the small town of Falls City hoping to start over and keep his past a secret. Brandon gets a girlfriend, Lana (Sevigny), and runs afoul of the reckless John (Sarsgaard). And then Brandon's secret is discovered—he is actually a girl and the gender revelation leads to tragic consequences. Based on a true story, which is also the subject of the documentary, "The Brandon Teena Story." Pierce's version, not unexpectedly, was subjected to the charges of dramatic license, but the story is still forceful. **116m/C VHS, DVD.** Hilary Swank, Chloe Sevigny, Peter Sarsgaard, Brendan Sexton III, Alison Folland, Alicia (Leoy) Goranson, Matt McGrath, Rob Campbell, Jeanetta Arnette; **D:** Kimberly Peirce; **W:** Kimberly Peirce, Andy Bienen; **C:** Jim Denault; **M:** Nathan Larson. Oscars '99: Actress (Swank); Golden Globes '00: Actress Drama (Swank); Ind. Spirit '00: Actress (Swank), Support. Actress (Sevigny); N.Y. Critics '99: Actress (Swank); L.A. Film Critics '99: Actress (Swank), Support. Actress (Sevigny); Natl. Soc. Film Critics '99: Actress (Swank); Broadcast Film Critics '99: Actress (Swank).

The Boys from Brazil 🦴🦴½ **1978 (R)** Based on Ira Levin's novel, a thriller about Dr. Josef Mengele endeavoring to reconstitute the Nazi movement from his Brazilian sanctuary by cloning a brood of boys from Hitler's genes. **123m/C VHS, DVD.** Gregory Peck, James Mason, Laurence Olivier, Uta Hagen, Steve Guttenberg, Denholm Elliott, Lilli Palmer; **D:** Franklin J. Schaffner; **W:** Heywood Gould; **C:** Henri Decae; **M:** Jerry Goldsmith. Natl. Bd. of Review '78: Actor (Olivier).

The Boys in Company C 🦴🦴 **1977 (R)** A frank, hard-hitting drama about five naive young men involved in the Vietnam War. **127m/C VHS.** Stan Shaw, Andrew Stevens, James Canning, Michael Lembeck, Craig Wasson, R. Lee Ermey, James Whitmore Jr., Scott Hylands, Noble Willingham, Santos Morales, Claude Wilson, Drew Michaels, Karen Hilger, Peggy O'Neal, Stan Johns; Cameos: Rick Natkin; **D:** Sidney J. Furie; **W:** Sidney J. Furie, Rick Natkin; **C:** Godfret A. Godar; **M:** Jaime Mendoza-Nava.

Boys in Love 🦴🦴 **1995** Four gay shorts about young men in love. "Death in Venice, CA" finds a repressed academic drawn to his landlady's stepson. The animated "Achilles" features the Greek heros Achilles and Petroclus at the battle of Troy. A young man becomes determined to conquer "My Polish Waiter" and a rejected Latin lover finds love again (with some help from a dog) in "Miguel, Ma Belle." **83m/C VHS.** **D:** Barry Purves, P. David Ebersole.

The Boys in the Band 🦴🦴½ **1970 (R)** A group of gay friends get together one night for a birthday party. A simple premise with a compelling depiction of friendship, expectations, and lifestyle. One of the first serious cinematic presentations to deal with the subject of homosexuality. The film was adapted from Mart Crowley's play using the original cast. **120m/C VHS, DVD.** Frederick Combs, Cliff Gorman, Laurence Luckinbill, Kenneth Nelson, Leonard Frey; **D:** William Friedkin; **W:** Matt Crowley.

Boys Life 🦴🦴 **1994** Three shorts about gay teenagers coming of age. "Pool Days" has 17-year-old Justin (Weinstein) taking a summer job as a lifeguard at a health spa. Still clueless as to his sexual preferences, Justin is flustered when cruised by a charming male swimmer but it does get him to thinking. "A Friend of Dorothy" finds NYU student Winston (O'Connell) seeking freedom in Greenwich Village as he looks for like-minded friends (and a little romance). "The Disco Years" takes place in California during the Nixon era as casually gay-bashing high-schooler Tom (Nolan) gradually realizes his true nature. **90m/C VHS, DVD.** Josh Weinstein, Nick Poletti, Kimberly Flynn, Richard Salamanca, Raoul O'Connell, Kevin McClatchy, Greg Lauren, Anne Zupa, Matt Nolan, Russell Scott Lewis, Gwen Welles, Dennis Christopher; **D:** Robert Lee King, Brian Sloan, Raoul O'Connell; **W:** R. Mott Hupfel III, Jonathan Schell, Greg Gardiner.

The Boys Next Door 🦴🦴½ **1985 (R)** Two California lads kill and go nuts during a weekend in Los Angeles. Sheen overacts as a budding psychotic, not an easy thing to do. Apparently trying to show what a particular lifestyle can lead to. Violent. **90m/C VHS, DVD.** Maxwell Caulfield, Charlie Sheen, Christopher McDonald, Hank Garrett, Patti D'Arbanville, Moon Zappa; **D:** Penelope Spheeris; **W:** Glen Morgan, James Wong; **C:** Arthur Albert; **M:** George S. Clinton.

The Boys Next Door 🦴🦴½ **1996 (PG)** Gentle comedy/drama, based on Tom Griffin's play, about four mentally disabled men—Norman (Lane), Barry (Leonard), Arnold (Jeter), and Lucien (Vance)—who share a house under the supervision of too-dedicated social worker Jack (Goldwyn). In fact, Jack's devotion is causing enough problems in his marriage to have him consider changing careers, even as each of "the boys" struggle with their daily lives. TV movie is overly sweet but the performances are very good. **99m/C VHS.** Nathan Lane, Tony Goldwyn, Robert Sean Leonard, Michael Jeter, Courtney B. Vance, Mare Winningham, Jenny Robertson, Elizabeth Wilson, Richard Jenkins, Lynne Thigpen; **D:** John Erman; **W:** William Blinn; **C:** Frank Tidy; **M:** John Kander. **TV**

Boys' Night Out 🦴🦴🦴 **1962** Amusing comedy about four businessmen who desperately want to escape the suburban doldrums by setting up an apartment equipped with plaything Novak. Little do they know, but Novak is a sociology student studying the American male, and they are merely her guinea pigs in an experiment beyond their control. Blair, Page, and Gabor provide comic relief. Based on a story by Marvin Worth and Arne Sultan. **113m/C VHS.** Kim Novak, James Garner, Tony Randall, Howard Duff, Janet Blair, Patti Page, Jessie Royce Landis, Oscar Homolka, Zsa Zsa Gabor; **D:** Michael Gordon; **W:** Ira Wallach.

The Boys of Baraka 🦴🦴½ **2005** Directors Ewing and Grady inform us that 76 percent of Baltimore's black male students do not graduate from high school. So, in 2002, 20 at-risk students are given scholarships to attend the progressive Baraka boarding school—in Kenya—which is run by American volunteers. They are supposed to stay two years, but a transformation is begun that cannot be completed when terrorists attack Nairobi and the school is forced to close. The film may not have the "feel good" ending viewers are expecting, although it seems the lives of several boys are changed for the better. **84m/C US**

The Boys of St. Vincent 🦴🦴🦴 **1993** Outstanding, and heartbreaking, story of sexual abuse by Catholic clergy that was inspired by actual events. Divided into two segments, the drama begins in 1975 with 10-year-old Kevin Reevey (Morina) living at the St. Vincent orphanage in an eastern Canadian town. The orphanage is run by charismatic and terrifying Brother Lavin (Czerny), who it turns out is a special fondness for "his boy" Kevin. Nor is Brother Lavin alone—a fact eventually revealed by a police investigation, although the matter is hushed up by both the church and the government. Until 15 years later. In 1990, the case is reopened and Lavin, having married and fathered two sons, is returned to face charges. Now the young men must open wounds that have never truly healed and confront their tormentors in a court of law, amidst a blaze of publicity. Czerny gives a truly inspired performance as the self-loathing monster. The emotional agony is excruciating to watch and be forwarned that the depiction of the sexual abuse is unflinching. Made for Canadian TV; on two cassettes. **186m/C VHS, DVD.** *CA* Henry Czerny, Johnny Morina, Sebastian Spence, Brian Dodd, David Hewlett, Jonathan Lewis, Jeremy Keefe, Phillip Dinn, Brian Dooley, Greg Thomey, Michael Wade, Lise Roy, Timothy Webber, Kristine Demers, Ashley Billard, Sam Grana; **D:** John N. Smith; **W:** Sam Grana, John N. Smith, Des Walsh; **C:** Pierre Letarte; **M:** Neil Smolar. **TV**

The Boys of 2nd Street Park 🦴🦴🦴 **2003 (R)** Drawn together for this compelling documentary, childhood buddies frankly recount the life-changing events they've confronted over the years while pining for the simpler times growing up in Brighton Beach, NY, in the 1950s. **91m/C VHS, DVD.** **D:** Dan Klores, Ron Berger; **C:** Buddy Squires. **VIDEO**

Boys of the City 🐾 *The Ghost Creeps* 1940 The East Side Kids run amuck in an eerie mansion while trying to solve the murder of a judge. **63m/B VHS, DVD.** Leo Gorcey, Bobby Jordan; *M:* Joseph H. Lewis.

Boys on the Side 🐾🐾½ 1994 It's "Thelma & Louise" come to "Terms of Endearment" by way of "Philadelphia." Goldberg is Jane, an unemployed lesbian singer, who connects with Very Brady Sequel." **88m/C VHS, DVD.** Shelley Long, Gary Cole, Marcia Wallace, Christine Taylor, Paul Sutera, Jennifer Elise Cox, Jesse Lee, Olivia Hack, Cory the frosty pursed lips. Look for neat-o cameos from some original Bradys and most of the Monkees. Followed by *A* **C:** Donald E. Thorin; *M:* David Newman.

Boys Town 🐾🐾½ 1938 Righteous portrayal of Father Flanagan and the creation of Boys Town, home for juvenile delinquents. Expect chaos when the boys discover that their father's business rival has something going around to defeat him. **89m/C VHS, DVD.** Randy Travis, Julie Hagerty, Jon Voight, Michael DeLuise, Catherine Oxenberg, Mickey Rooney, Ruth Buzzi, Dom DeLuise, Charles Nelson Reilly, James Williams, Drew Winger; *L:* Dom DeLuise; *M:* Gregory Poppen, Mark Dubis; *C:* Leonard Schwartz. **VIDEO**

Boyz N the Hood 🐾🐾🐾🐾½ 1991 (R) Singleton's debut as a writer and director is an astonishing picture of young black men, four high school students with different backgrounds, aims, and abilities trying to survive L.A. gangs and bigotry. Excellent acting throughout, with special nods to Fishburne and Gooding Jr. Violent outbreaks outside the theatres where this ran only proves the urgency of this passionately nonviolent, pro-family message. Hopefully those viewers scared off at the time will give this a chance in the safety of their VCRs. Singleton was the youngest director ever nominated for an Oscar. **112m/C VHS, DVD, UMD.** Laurence Fishburne, Ice Cube, Cuba Gooding Jr., Nia Long, Morris Chestnut, Tyra Ferrell, Angela Bassett, Whitman Mayo, Dedrick D. Gobert; *W:* John Singleton; *D:* John Singleton. **MTV Movie Awards '92: New Filmmaker (Singleton). Natl. Film Reg. '02.**

Braddock: Missing in Action 3 🐾 1988 (R) The battle-scarred, high-kicking 'Nam vet battles his way into the jungles once more, this time to rescue his long-lost Vietnamese family. A family effort. Chuck co-wrote the script; his brother directed. **104m/C VHS, DVD.** Chuck Norris, Aki Aleong, Roland Harrah III; *D:* Aaron Norris; *W:* Chuck Norris, James Bruner; *C:* Joao Fernandes.

The Brady Bunch Movie 🐾🐾 1995 (PG-13) Grunge and CDs may be the norm in the '90s, but the Bradys still live in the eight-track world of the '70s, where Davy Jones rocks and every day is a sunshine day. Then greedy developer McKean schemes to cash in on Mike and Carol's financial woes. (Hawaii) The Grand Canyon! What were they thinking?

Boy's Reformatory 🐾 1939 Brothers are framed. One takes the rap, goes to the title institution, breaks out, and hunts the real bad guys. Creaky and antiquated. **62m/B VHS, DVD.** Frankie Darro, Grant Withers, David Durand, Warren McCollum; *D:* Howard Bretherton.

Brady's Escape 🐾🐾 1984 *Le Ceveau* 1969 *The Long Ride* 1984 American WWII pilot is shot down in the Hungarian countryside and befriended by the Hungarian csikos (cowboys). **92m/C VHS, HU John Savage, Kelly Reno; D:** Pal Gabor. **CABLE**

The Brain 🐾🐾½ 1962 *A* scientist earns that a mind isn't always a terrible thing to waste when he finds himself being manipulated by the brain of a dead man he's trying to keep alive. Remake of "Donovan's Brain" (1953). **83m/B VHS, GB** GE Anne Heywood, Peter Van Eyck, Bernard Lee, Cecil Parker, Jack MacGowran; *D:* Freddie Francis.

The Brain 🐾½ 1988 (R) Dr. Blake, host of a popular TV talk-show is in train. The caper begins when lots of other crooks decide to rob the same train. The cast holds this one together. **100m/C VHS.** David Niven, Jean-Paul Belmondo, Andre Bourvil, Eli Wallach, Silvia Monti, Fernand Valois; *D:* Gerard Oury; *M:* Georges Delerue.

Brain Damage 🐾🐾 1988 (R) A tongue-in-bloody-cheek farce about a brain-sucking parasite. The parasite in question, Aylmer, addicts our dubious hero to the euphoria induced by the blue liquid he injects into his brain, paving the way for the bloody mayhem that follows. Expect spoofs of Henenlotter's far-superior "Basket Case." In fact, it even includes an inside-joke cameo by Van Hentenryck, reprising his "Basket Case" character; look for him on the subway. **89m/C VHS, DVD.** Rick Herbst, Gordon MacDonald, Jennifer Lowry, Theo Barnes, Lucille Saint Peter; *W:* Kevin Van Hentenryck, Brian DeFrank-Henenlotter, Beverly Bonner; *D:* Bruce Torbat; *M:* Gus Russo, Clutch Reiser; *V:* John Zacherie.

Brain Dead 🐾🐾🐾 1989 (R) Low-budget but brilliantly assembled puzzle-film about a brain surgeon who agrees to perform experimental surgery on a psychotic to 'retrieve some corporately valuable data—his first mistake, which begins a seemingly endless cycle of nightmares and identity alterations. A mind-bending sci-fi feast from ex-"Twilight Zone" writer Charles Beaumont. **85m/C VHS, DVD.** Bill Pullman, Bill Paxton, Bud Cort, Patricia Charbonneau, Nicholas Pryor, George Kennedy, Brian Brophy, Lee Arenberg, Andy Wood; *D:* Adam Simon; *W:* Adam Simon, Charles Beaumont; *M:* Peter Rotter.

Brain Donors 🐾🐾½ 1992 (PG) Goofy, uneven film starring Turturro as a sleazy lawyer trying to take over the Oglethorpe Ballet Company by sweet-talking its aged patroness. He is helped by two eccentric friends, and together the three crack a lot of bad but witty jokes. The film culminates into a hilarious ballet scene featuring someone giving CPR to the ballerina playing the dying swan, an actor in a duck suit, duck hunters, and a pack of hounds. This trio reminds us of second-rate Marx Brothers (or the Three Stooges)

inc'?) Great ensemble cast capably fills the white platform shoes of the originals—Ccle sounds just like Mr. Brady, Cox hilariously channels Jan's tormented middle child angst, and Taylor's self-absorbed Marcia, Marcia, Marcia is dead-on, right Very Brady Sequel." **88m/C VHS, DVD.** Shelley Long, Gary Cole, Marcia Wallace, Jean Smart, Henriette Mantel, Christopher Daniel Barnes, Christine Taylor, Paul Sutera, Jennifer Elise Cox, Jesse Lee, Olivia Hack, Cory Noseworthy, Shane Conrad, RuPaul Charles; *Cameos:* Ann B. Davis, Florence Henderson, Davy Jones, Barry Williams, Christopher Knight, Tori; *D:* Betty Thomas; *W:* Bonnie Turner, Terry Turner, Laurice Elehwany, Rick Copp; *C:* Mac Ahlberg; *M:* Guy Moon.

The Brain from Planet Arous 🐾 1957 Lassie meets Alien when an evil alien brain appropriates the body of a scientist in order to take over planet Earth. His plans are thwarted, however, by a good alien brain that likewise inhabits the body of the scientist's dog. High camp and misdemeanors. **80m/B VHS, DVD.** John Agar, Joyce Meadows, Robert Fuller, Henry Travis, Bill Giorgio, Tim Graham, Thomas Browne, Henry, Ken Terrell; *D:* Nathan "Jerry" Juran; *W:* Fay Burton; *C:* Jacques "Jack" Marquetta; *M:* Joe Van Haastrecht.

Brain of Blood Woof! 1971 *The Creature's Revenge; Brain Damage* 1971 Deals with a scientist who transplants the brain of a politician into the body of a deformed idiot. The change is minimal. **107m/C VHS, DVD.** Kent Taylor, John Bloom, Regina Carrol, Angelo Rossitto, Grant Williams, Reed Hadley, Vicki Volante, Zandor Vorkov, Richard Smedley; *D:* Al Adamson; *W:* Joe Van Rodgers, David Louis Horvath.

Brain Smasher... A Love Story 🐾 1993 (PG-13) A bouncer and a super model become the targets of a gang of killer ninjas who want the mysterious blood-red lotus the model's been given. Of course they do. What's the lovely Faitcher doing in such a stupid movie? **88m/C VHS, DVD.** Andrew (Dice Clay) Silverstein, Teri Hatcher, Deanna (Dee) Booher, Deborah Van Valkenburgh, Brion James, Yuji Okumoto, Tim Thomerson, Charles Rocket, Nicholas Guest, Lin Shaye; *D:* Albert Pyun; *W:* Albert Pyun; *C:* George Mooradian; *M:* Tony Riparetti.

The Brain that Wouldn't Die 🐾½ 1963 *The Head that Wouldn't Die* Love is a many-splattered thing when a brilliant surgeon keeps the decapitated head of his fiancee alive after an auto accident while he searches for a suitably stacked body onto which to transplant the head. Absurd and satiric (head tanks so much that Doc tapes her/its mouth shut) adding up to major entry in trash film genre; much of the gore was slashed for the video, however. **92m/B VHS, DVD.** Herb Evers, Virginia Leith, Acele Lamont, Leslie Daniel, Bruce Brighton, Paula Maurice; *D:* Joseph Green; *W:* Joseph Green; *D:* Stephen Hajnal; *M:* Tony Restano.

The Brain 🐾🐾½ 1969 (G) Run of the mill comedy caper has Niven planning to heist millions from a NATO train. The caper begins when lots of other crooks decide to rob the same train.

The Brain Eaters 🐾🐾 1958 A strange ship from inside the Earth invades a small town, and hairy monsters promptly attach themselves to people's necks in a daring bid to control the planet. **60m/B VHS.** Edwin Nelson, Alan Frost, Jack Hill, Joanna Lee, Jody Fair, Leonard Nimoy; *D:* Bruno VeSota.

Brain Drain 🐾🐾 1998 Young Argentine street kids are thieves who specialize in car radios. Their dreams of a better life are at odds with their surroundings. Things go wrong when they make false accusations against a cop and he comes after them. **92m/C VHS, DVD.** Nicolas Cabre, Luis Quiroz, Enrique Liporace; *D:* Fernando Musa; *W:* Fernando Musa, Branko Anidic; *C:* Carlos Torlaschi.

Brainscan 🐾🐾½ 1994 (R) Teenage loner takes a trip in virtual reality and finds that murder is the first stop. Furlong ("Terminator 2") is the troubled youth whose voyage is led by Smith as Trickster, the Freddy Krueger meets David Bowie tour guide from virtual hell. Langella turns in a straight performance as a local cop hot on the trail. Hard-core horror fans will be dis-

The Brainiac 🐾🐾 1961 *El Baron de Terror, Baron of Terror* 1961 Sorcerer sentenced for black magic returns to strike dark deeds upon the descendants of those who judged him. He turns himself into a hideous monster, feeding on his victims' brains and blood. Yuck. **75m/B VHS, DVD, MX** Abel Salazar, Ariadne Welter, Mauricio Garces, Rosa Maria Gallardo, Ruben Rojo, German Robles; *D:* Chano Urueta; *W:* Frederick Curiel, Antonio Torres Portillo; *C:* Jose Ortiz Ramos; *M:* Gustavc Cesar Carrion.

but the movie has enough funny moments to be worth a watch. **79m/C VHS, DVD.** John Turturro, Bob Nelson, Mel Smith, Nancy Marchand, John Savident, George de la Pena, Juli Donald, Spike Alexander, Teri Copley; *D:* Dennis Dugan; *W:* Pat Proft; *M:* Ira Newborn.

The Brain Eaters 🐾🐾 1958

Brainwaves 🐾🐾 1982 (R) A young woman has disturbing flashbacks after her brain is electrically revived following a car accident. Curtis is the demented doctor who jump-starts her. **83m/C VHS, DVD.** Suzanna Love, Tony Curtis, Keir Dullea, Vera Miles, Percy Rodriguez, Paul Willson; *D:* Ulli Lommel; *W:* Ulli Lommel; *C:* Ulli Lommel, Jon Kranhouse; *M:* Robert O. Ragland.

Bram Stoker's Dracula 🐾🐾 1992 (R) Coppola's highly charged view of the vampire classic is visually stunning, heavy on eroticism and violence, and weak in plot and performance. Oldman, in a number of amazing transformations, portrays the deadly bloodsucker as a lonely soul determined to reunite with his lost love, the innocent Ryder. Hopkins cheerfully chews the scenery as nemesis Van Helsing, newcomer Frost is fetching, Reeves is lightweight, and Ryder goes way over the top. Musician Waits is great as bug-eating madman Renfield. Filmed entirely on soundstages with beautiful costumes and some amazing visual effects and sets. **128m/C VHS, DVD, Blu-ray Disc.** Monica Bellucci, Christina (Kristina) Fulton, Gary Oldman, Winona Ryder, Anthony Hopkins, Keanu Reeves, Richard E. Grant, Cary Elwes, Billy Campbell, Sadie Frost, Tom Waits; *D:* Francis Ford Coppola; *W:* James V. Hart; *C:* Michael Ballhaus. Oscars '92: Costume Des., Makeup, Sound FX Editing.

Bram Stoker's Shadowbuilder 🐾🐾 1998 (R) Silly update that apparently takes the title of the Bram Stoker short story but not much else. Shadowbuilder (Jackson) is a demonic creature that wants to unleash hell's power upon the unsuspecting town of Grand River. But he needs a 12-year-old Chris (Zegers) for your basic satanic ritual, which doesn't go over well with the local priest (Rooker) and sheriff (Thompson). **101m/C VHS, DVD.** Michael Rooker, Leslie Hope, Andrew Jackson, Kevin Zegers, Shawn Thompson, Tony Todd, Richard McMillan; *D:* Jamie Dixon; *W:* Michael Stokes; *C:* David Pelletier; *M:* Eckart Seeber. **VIDEO**

Bram Stoker's The Mummy 🐾 *The Mummy: Legend of the Mummy* 1997 (R) Modern retelling of a horror tale focuses on the savage incident that left Egyptologist Abel Trelawny (Bochner) in a coma. Now his daughter, Margaret (Locane), seeks the help of her ex-lover, Robert (Lutes), to uncover the connection between Trewlawny and an Egyp-

Brainstorm 🐾🐾½ 1983 (PG) Husband-and-wife scientist team invents headphones that can record dreams, thoughts, and fantasies (VCR-style) and then allow other people to experience them by playing back the tape. Their marriage begins to crumble as the husband becomes more and more obsessed with pushing the limits of the technology; things get worse when the government wants to exploit their discovery. Special effects and interesting camera work punctuate this sci-fi flick. Wood's last film; in fact, she died before production was completed. **106m/C VHS, DVD.** Natalie Wood, Christopher Walken, Cliff Robertson, Louise Fletcher; *D:* Douglas Trumbull; *W:* Bruce Joel Rubin; *M:* James Horner.

Brainwashed 🐾🐾 *Die Schachnovelle; The Royal Game; Three Moves to Freedom* 1960 Austrian aristocrat Werner von Basil (Jurgens) is captured by the Nazis and interrogated to uncover military intentions in order to keep his sanity, the prisoner concentrates on a chess book he keeps hidden in his cell. Based on the novel by Stefan Zweig. German with subtitles. **127m/C VHS.** GE Curt Jurgens, Claire Bloom, Hansjorg Felmy, Mario Adorf, Albert Lieven, Alan Gifford, Karel Stepanek; *D:* Gerd Oswald; *W:* Gerd Oswald, Harold Medford; *C:* Gunther Senftleben; *M:* Hans-Martin Majewski.

appointed by the lack of on-screen violence, and special effects buffs won't see anything new; Lame effort tries to appeal to a wide audience and is bland as a result. The end is left wide open, so expect a sequel or two or three. **96m/C VHS, DVD.** Edward Furlong, Frank Langella, T. Ryder Smith, David Hemblen, Amy Hargreaves, Jamie Marsh, Victor Ertmanis; *D:* John Flynn; *W:* Andrew Kevin Walker; *M:* George S. Clinton.

tian ritual to raise a queen from her tomb. Based on Stoker's book "The Jewel of the Seven Stars." **100m/C VHS, DVD.** Mary Jo Catlett, Amy Locane, Eric Lutes, Louis Gossett Jr., Victoria Tennant, Lloyd Bochner, Mark Lindsay Chapman, Richard Karn; **C:** Jeffrey Obrow; **W:** Jeffrey Obrow; **C:** Antonio Soriano; **M:** Rick Cox. **VIDEO**

Bram Stoker's Way of the Vampire ⊘ **2005 (R)** Has absolutely nothing to do with Stoker's writings. Van Helsing (Giles) goes after Dracula (Logan), leaving his wife in the care of colleague Sebastian (Beckett). Only Sebastian is actually a blood-drinker, so no more missus. Van Helsing makes a deal with God to gain immortality until the last of Dracula's kin are dead. Which leads to a showdown in present-day LA between Van Helsing and Sebastian. **81m/C DVD.** Denise Boutte, Paul Logan, Rhett Giles, Brent Falco; **D:** Sara Nean Bruce, Eduardo Durao; **W:** Karrie Melendrez, Sherri Strain; **C:** Andreas Beckett, Zack Richard; **M:** Ralph Rieckermann.

The Bramble Bush ⊘⊘½ **1960** Guy (Burton) is a doctor who returns to his New England hometown to care for a dying friend, Larry (Drake). Unfortunately, Guy falls for Larry's wife Mar (Rush) and they have an affair. When Guy pulls the plug on his friend's suffering, suspicious townspeople (who of course know what's going on) wonder just how "merciful" the doctor was really being and he's tried for murder. Tawdry "Peyton Place"-ish soap opera based on the novel by Charles Mergendahl. **104m/C VHS.** Richard Burton, Barbara Rush, Tom Drake, Jack Carson, Angie Dickinson, James Dunn, Henry Jones, Frank Conroy, Carl Benton Reid; **D:** Daniel Petrie; **W:** Philip Yordan.

Brand New Life ⊘ **1972** A childless couple in their 40s are unexpectedly confronted by the wife's first pregnancy. Both have careers and well-ordered lives that promise to be disrupted. **74m/C VHS, DVD.** Cloris Leachman, Martin Balsam, Wilfrid Hyde-White, Mildred Dunnock; **D:** Sam O'Steen; **M:** Billy Goldenberg. **TV**

Brand of Fear ⊘½ **1949** Crooning cowpoke Wakely puts down his guitar long enough to chase rustlers off the land of an innocent lady in this average oater. **56m/B VHS.** Jimmy Wakely, Dub Taylor, Gail Davis, Tom London; **D:** Oliver Drake; **W:** Basil Dickey.

Brand of Hate ⊘ **1934** A good cowboy rustles up a gang of rustlers. **61m/ B VHS, DVD.** Bob Steele, George "Gabby" Hayes, Lucille Browne, James Flavin; **D:** Lewis D. Collins.

Brand of the Outlaws ⊘ **1936** A cowboy becomes an unwitting aid to rustlers in this early western. **56m/B VHS.** Bob Steele, Margaret Marquis, Virginia True Boardman, Jack Rockwell; **D:** Robert North Bradbury.

Brand Upon the Brain! ⊘⊘⊘ **2006 (R)** Like most of writer/director Guy Maddin's work, this requires a deliberate viewing. A silent film in black and white sets up primarily as a flashback, possibly to the director's youth, set on an island with a lighthouse that has served as an orphanage in the past. Film moves freely through images and recollections, revealing secret longings within an utterly absurd plot for which the film is not the least diminished. Make no mistake, this is a grandly indulgent art film. But what did you expect? Most enjoyable with the narration by Isabella Rossellini. **95m/C DVD.** **CA US** Erik Steffen Maahs, Sullivan Brown, Gretchen Krich, Maya Lawson, Todd Jefferson Moore, Katherine E. Scharhon; **D:** Guy Maddin; **W:** Guy Maddin, George Toles; **C:** Benjamin Kasulke; **M:** Jason Staczek; **Nar:** Isabella Rossellini.

Branded ⊘⊘½ **1950** Ladd (pre-"Shane") impersonates the long-gone son of rich rancher Bickford, with unusual results. Nicely balanced action and love scenes makes this story a better-than-average western. Filmed in Technicolor. Based on the novel "Montana Rides" by Max Brand. **95m/C VHS, DVD.** Alan Ladd, Mona Freeman, Charles Bickford, Joseph Calleia, Milburn Stone; **D:** Rudolph Mate.

Branded a Bandit ⊘⊘ **1924** Yakima must avoid the sheriff while tracking down the killers of an old miner so that he can clear himself of the crime. **58m/B VHS.** Yakima Canutt; **D:** Paul Hurst.

Branded a Coward ⊘ **1935** A man whose parents were killed seeks revenge via his trusty six-shooters. **56m/B VHS, DVD.** Johnny Mack Brown, Billie Seward; Yakima Canutt; **D:** Sam Newfield.

Branded Men ⊘⊘ **1931** A couple of oddballs become mixed up in a number of zany, western-type adventures. **60m/B VHS.** Ken Maynard, June Clyde, Irving Bacon, Billy Bletcher, Charles "Blackie" King, Donald Keith; **D:** Phil Rosen.

Branded to Kill ⊘⊘ *Koroshi no Rakuin* **1967** Visual tricks, including animated graphics, and a blues score highlight this gangster story, which follows No. 3 Killer, who's bungled his last hit. Now he's the target of No. 1 Killer. Japanese with subtitles. **91m/B VHS, DVD.** **JP** Joe Shishido, Mari Annu, Koji Nanbara, Isao Tamagawa, Mariko Ogawa; **D:** Seijun Suzuki; **W:** Hachiro Guryu; **C:** Kazue Nagatsuka; **M:** Naozumi Yamamoto.

Brannigan ⊘⊘½ **1975 (PG)** The Duke stars in the somewhat unfamiliar role of a rough and tumble Chicago police officer. He travels across the Atlantic to arrest a racketeer who has fled the States rather than face a grand jury indictment. Humor and action abound. **111m/C VHS, DVD.** John Wayne, John Vernon, Mel Ferrer, Daniel Pilon, James Booth, Ralph Meeker, Lesley-Anne Down, Richard Attenborough; **D:** Douglas Hickox; **W:** Michael Butler, William W. Norton Sr.; **C:** Gerry Fisher; **M:** Dominic Frontiere.

Brass ⊘⊘½ **1985 (PG)** First post-Archie Bunker role for O'Connor, who plods through this average police drama at a snail's pace, dragging everything else down with him. Made-for-TV pilot for a series that never aired. **94m/C VHS.** Carroll O'Connor, Lois Nettleton, Jimmy Baio, Paul Shenar, Vincent Gardenia, Anita Gillette; **D:** Corey Allen. **TV**

The Brass Bottle ⊘⊘½ **1963** Silly but amusing comedy that served as the inspiration for the TV series "I Dream of Jeannie," although Eden plays the girlfriend in this movie. Ives stars as jovial genie Fakrash, whose antique bottle is bought by architect Harold Ventimore (Randall). Fakrash wants nothing more than to make his new master happy but his efforts cause constant crises for the bewildered man, who'd prefer his life return to normal. Based on the novel by F. Anstey. **90m/C VHS.** Tony Randall, Burl Ives, Barbara Eden, Edward Andrews, Ann Doran, Kamala Devi, Howard Smith, Parley Baer; **D:** Harry Keller; **W:** Oscar Brodney; **C:** Clifford Stine; **M:** Bernard Green.

Brass Target ⊘⊘½ **1978 (PG)** Hypothetical thriller about a plot to kill George Patton in the closing days of WWII for the sake of $250 million in Nazi gold stolen by his staff. Interesting cast can't find story. **111m/C VHS.** Sophia Loren, George Kennedy, Max von Sydow, John Cassavetes, Patrick McGoohan, Robert Vaughn, Bruce Davison, Edward Herrmann, Ed Bishop; **D:** John Hough; **W:** Alvin Boretz.

Brassed Off ⊘⊘½ **1996 (R)** Bittersweet tale of despair and hope in the fictional coal mining town of Grimly in Yorkshire, England. Set in 1992, when sweeping closures of British coal mines devastated the area, the sole respite of these workers is playing in the pit's brass band. Secretly suffering from black lung disease, the band's leader (Postlethwaite) dreams of winning a competition in Albert Hall. Fitzgerald plays the flugelhorn-tooting vixen who returns to the small town, inspiring the music (and virility) of the formerly all male band. She resumes her relationship with former flame MacGregor, but all is on shaky ground with the imminent closure of the mine. Fine performances brighten the generally gloomy proceedings. The band is played by the real-life Grimethorpe Colliery Brass Band. **106m/C VHS, DVD.** **GB** Pete Postlethwaite, Ewan McGregor, Tara Fitzgerald, Jim Carter, Philip Jackson, Peter Martin, Stephen Tompkinson; **D:** Mark Herman; **W:** Mark Herman; **C:** Andy Collins; **M:** Trevor Jones; **M:** Foreign Film.

Bratz woof! **2007 (PG)** Four high school freshmen and best friends (Ramos, Browning, Parrish, and Shayne) find themselves at odds with the bossy student body president, who aims to split them up into (gasp!) separate social cliques. There's singing and dancing (like a big, long, pink, fluffy music video), and how sweetly cliche is it that these real-life Bratz are all from different ethnicities and socioeconomic classes, yet still BFFs? At least these girls are (somewhat) real humans and not the creepy-faced, bubble-headed dolls (and animated characters) the movie is based on, but even your lip gloss-wearing 'tweener will roll her eyes at the mere suggestion of this film, which is cloying at best, intolerable at worst. **100m/C DVD.** **US** Skyler Shaye, Anneliese van der Pol, Jon Voight, Lainie Kazan, Nathalia Ramos, Janel Parrish, Logan Browning, Chelsea Staub, Stephen Lunsford, Ian Nelson; **D:** Sean McNamara; **W:** Susan Estelle Jansen; **C:** Christian Sebaldt; **M:** John Coda.

The Bravados ⊘⊘⊘ **1958** A rough, distressing Western revenge tale, wherein a man is driven to find the four men who murdered his wife. In tracking the perpetrators, Peck realizes that he has been corrupted by his vengeance. **98m/C VHS, DVD.** Gregory Peck, Stephen Boyd, Joan Collins, Albert Salmi, Henry Silva, Lee Van Cleef, George Voskovec, Barry Coe; **D:** Henry King; **W:** Philip Yordan; **C:** Leon Shamroy. Natl. Bd. of Review '58: Support. Actor (Salmi).

The Brave Bunch ⊘½ **1970** A courageous Greek soldier tries to save his men and country during WWII. **110m/C VHS.** **GR** Peter Funk, Giannis Voglis; **D:** Costa Carayiannis.

Brave New Girl ⊘⊘½ **2004 (PG-13)** Holly's got what it takes to get into the big-time music school and her poor-yet-resourceful mom won't let her lack of money stand in the way of her daughter's dream. But getting there is only half the ditty. Generically inspiring tale. Based on the novel "A Mother's Gift," by co-executive producers Britney and Lynne Spears. **90m/C VHS, DVD.** Virginia Madsen, Barbara Mamabolo, Aaron Ashmore, Lindsey Haun, Jackie Rosenbaum, Joanne Boland, Nick Roth; **D:** Bobby Roth; **W:** Britney Spears, Lynne Spears, Amy Talkington; **C:** Eric Van Haren Noman; **M:** Asher Ettinger. **TV**

The Brave One ⊘⊘⊘ **1956** A love story between a Spanish boy and the bull who saves his life. The animal is later carted off to the bullring. Award-winning screenplay by the then-blacklisted Trumbo, credited as "Robert Rich." **100m/C VHS, DVD.** Michel Ray, Rodolfo Hoyos, Joi Lansing; **D:** Irving Rapper; **W:** Dalton Trumbo; **C:** Jack Cardiff; **M:** Victor Young. Oscars '56: Story.

The Brave One ⊘⊘½ **2007 (R)** Erica Bain (Foster), the host of a radio show called "City Walk," has spent years gushing about the wonders of life in her beloved New York City. She encounters a trio of thugs while walking with fiance David (Andrews) in Central Park. The two suffer a gruesome beating, which proves lethal for David and barely survivable for Erica, who, after months of recovery and in the throes of post-traumatic stress, acquires a hand gun. Erica suddenly and routinely witnesses violent criminal acts and begins to mete out street justice while forming a platonic relationship with Detective Mercer (Howard), who is investigating the series of vigilante-style slayings. Their interactions are a bright spot in an otherwise brutal story line. It may sound a bit (okay, a lot) like "Death Wish" but the distinction is Erica's inner turmoil, skillfully played out by Foster. Still, the overwhelming violence outweighs the attempt to humanize her character, and ultimately it fails as both an insightful psycho-thriller and as a vigilante shoot-'em-up. **119m/C DVD, HD DVD, DVD.** **US** Jodie Foster, Terrence Howard, Naveen Andrews, Carmen Ejogo, Nicky Katt, Mary Steenburgen, Lenny Venito, Lenny Kravitz; **D:** Neil Jordan; **W:** Roderick Taylor, Bruce Taylor, Cynthia Mort; **C:** Philippe Rousselot; **M:** Dario Marianelli.

Braveheart ⊘⊘ **1925** When a Native American adapts to the white man's world, he alienates his own people. He eventually chooses to renounce his love for a white woman, and returns to lead his people. Silent. **62m/B VHS.** Lillian Rich, Robert Edeson, Tyrone Power, Sally Rand, Arthur Housman, Rod La Rocque; **D:** Alan Hale; **W:** Mary O'Hara; **C:** Faxon M. Dean.

Braveheart ⊘⊘⊘½ **1995 (R)** Producer-director-star Gibson does it all in this bold, ferocious, reasonably accurate epic about the passion and cost of freedom. Charismatic 13th century Scottish folk hero William Wallace leads his desperate and outnumbered clansmen in revolt against British oppression. Sweeping, meticulous battle scenes fit surpisingly well with moments of stirring romance and snappy wit. Among the mostly unknown (in the States, anyway) cast, Marceau and McCormack are elegant as Wallace's lady loves, and McGoohan is positively hateful as King Edward I. Gory and excessively violent (as medieval warfare tends to be) and a bit too long (as historical epics tend to be), but rewarding entertainment for those who stick it out—where else can you see the king's army get mooned en masse? Script was based on 300 pages of rhyming verse attributed to a blind poet known as Blind Harry. Gibson put up $15 million of his own money to complete the film. **178m/C VHS, DVD.** Mel Gibson, Sophie Marceau, Patrick McGoohan, Catherine McCormack, Brendan Gleeson, James Cosmo, David O'Hara, Angus MacFadyen, Peter Hanly, Ian Bannen, Sean McGinley, Brian Cox, Stephen Billington, Barry McGovern, Alun Armstrong, Tommy Flanagan; **D:** Mel Gibson; **W:** Randall Wallace; **C:** John Toll; **M:** James Horner. Oscars '95: Cinematog., Director (Gibson), Makeup, Picture; British Acad. '95: Cinematog.; Golden Globes '96: Director (Gibson); MTV Movie Awards '96: Action Seq.; Writers Guild '95: Orig. Screenplay; Broadcast Film Critics '95: Director (Gibson).

Brazil ⊘⊘⊘½ **1985 (R)** The acclaimed nightmare comedy about an Everyman trying to survive in a surreal paper-choked bureaucratic society. There are copious references to "1984" and "The Trial," fantastic mergings of glorious fantasy and stark reality, and astounding visual design. The DVD version has a 142-minute director's cut as well as a documentary. **131m/C VHS, DVD.** **GB** Jonathan Pryce, Robert De Niro, Michael Palin, Katherine Helmond, Kim Greist, Bob Hoskins, Ian Holm, Peter Vaughan, Ian Richardson; **D:** Terry Gilliam; **W:** Charles McKeown, Terry Gilliam, Tom Stoppard; **C:** Roger Pratt; **M:** Michael Kamen. L.A. Film Critics '85: Director (Gilliam), Film, Screenplay.

Breach ⊘⊘⊘½ **2007 (PG-13)** Somber true story follows ambitious FBI agent Eric O'Neill (Phillippe), who's planted by tough boss Kate Burroughs (Linney) as the new assistant to veteran agent Robert Hanssen (Cooper). She says the perv is worried because Hanssen is a perv, but he's actually been selling info to the Russians and the feds won't catch him in the act. Hanssen starts getting suspicious, which ratchets up the tension, but there's never any clear idea of why he turned traitor, although Cooper is a creepily effective enigma. **110m/C DVD. HD DVD, DVD. US** Chris Cooper, Ryan Phillippe, Laura Linney, Dennis Haysbert, Caroline Dhavernas, Gary Cole, Bruce Davison, Kathleen Quinlan; **D:** Billy Ray, Adam Mazer, William Rotko; **C:** Tak Fujimoto; **M:** Mychael Danna.

Breach of Conduct ⊘⊘½ **1994 (PG-13)** Col. Bill Case (Coyote) is the commander of the Fort Benton, Utah, Army base where Helen Lutz's (Thorne-Smith) husband Tom (Verica) has just been transferred. At first there's a mutual attraction between Helen and Case, but then hubby is assigned a mission off base and, when Helen refuses Case's overtures, things turn very nasty. **93m/C VHS.** Peter Coyote, Courtney Thorne-Smith, Tom Verica, Beth Toussaint; **D:** Tim Matheson; **W:** Scott Abbott; **C:** Gideon Porath. **CABLE**

Breach of Trust ⊘⊘½ **1995 (R)** Smalltime crook Casey (Biehn) winds up in big trouble when he steals a computer disc with access codes to millions in drug cartel money. He goes on the lam and

Bread and Chocolate 🦴🦴🦴 *Pane e Cioccolata* 1973 Uneducated Italian immigrant Manfredi works a series of odd jobs in Italy, then tries desperately to fit in and better himself (which he fails utterly to do). Culture clash satire, with an engaging everyman lead. Italian with subtitles. **110m/C VHS, DVD.** *IT* Nino Manfredi, Anna Karina, Johnny Dorelli, Paolo Turco; *D:* Franco Brusati; *W:* Nino Manfredi, Franco Brusati, Iaia Fiastri; *C:* Luciano Tovoli; *M:* Daniele Patrucchi. N.Y. Film Critics '78: Foreign Film.

The Break 🦴🦴 1995 (R) Disillusioned IRA gunman Dowd (Rea) breaks out of prison and escapes to New York to give up his dreams even after his befriends (and falls in love with one of) a group of Guatemalan refugees who plan to kill the dictator who persecuted them. Appalled by their inability, he agrees to help them. This is definitely Rea's film (it's...)

The Break 🦴🦴 1995 (PG-13) Clumsy teen tennis hopeful Ben (Jorgensen) refuses to give up his dreams even after his bookie (Sheen) hires washed-up player Nick Irons (Van Patten) as a coach to show Ben the error of his game. **104m/C VHS, DVD.** Vincent Van Patten, Martin Sheen, Ben Jorgensen, Rae Dawn Chong, Valerie Perrine, Betsy Russell; *D:* Lee H. Katzin; *W:* Dan Jenkins, Vincent Van Patten. Scott Baio, Kristin Minter, Rosemary Prinz, John Seitz, Billy Mott, Snuller Hensley; *C:* Melissa Martin; *D:* Mark Krolik; *M:* Susan Hartford.

Bread and Roses 🦴🦴 2000 (R) Typical Loach political polemic—this time about union organizing of janitors (many of them illegals) in Los Angeles. Maya (Padilla) is an illegal immigrant from Mexico who's working for an office cleaning company. She meets union organizer Sam (Brody) who convinces Maya to join with him, even though she not only risks her job but deportation. Things go from bad to worse for Maya but Loach never takes the easy road and his characters are flawed human beings rather than mere symbols. English and Spanish with subtitles. **106m/C VHS, DVD.** *GB* Adrien Brody, Elpidia Carrillo, Pilar Padilla, George Lopez, Jack McGee, Alonso Chavez; *D:* Ken Loach; *W:* Paul Laverty; *C:* Barry Ackroyd; *M:* George Fenton.

The Bread, My Sweet 🦴🦴½ 2001 (PG-13) A *Wedding* for *Bela* 2001 Corporate exec Dominic (Baio) also helps his brothers, Eddie (Mott) and Pinio (Hensley), run a bakery in an old Italian neighborhood in Pittsburgh. Their landlords, (and surrogate parents) are old-fashioned immigrants Massimo (Seitz) and Bela (Prinz), who confides to Dominic that she's dying. So Dominic impulsively decides to marry their free-spirited daughter Lucca (Mintan), who goes along so her marriage-minded mother can die in peace. Naturally (and unsurprisingly) the cutie twosome develop real feelings for one another. **105m/C DVD. US** Scott Baio, Kristin Minter, Rosemary Prinz, John...

Bread and Tulips 🦴🦴 2000 (PG-13) Sweet Rosalba (Maglietta) is a much-neglected wife and mother who is accidentally left behind at a rest stop while on vacation. Rosalba doesn't get her back to her old life but events don't work out as expected. Italian with subtitles. **105m/C VHS, DVD.** *IT* Licia Maglietta, Bruno Ganz, Marina Massironi, Giuseppe Battiston, Antonio Catania, Felice Andreasi, Vitalba Andrea; *D:* Silvio Soldini; *W:* Silvio Soldini, Doriana Leondeff; *C:* Luca Bigazzi; *M:* Giovanni Venosta.

Break a Leg 🦴🦴½ 2003 (R) Struggling actor Max (John Cassini) has talent but keeps losing roles to bigger names and crosses into the U.S. to take his family... So he decides to literally cripple the competition, only to find out that an undercover cop (Rivera) is taking an interest in the case. **98m/C DVD.** John Kennedy, Jorge Sanz, Zachary Seymour, Sean McGinley, Paul Giamatti; *D:* Robert Dornhelm, Alfred Molina; *W:* Ronan Bennett; *C:* Andrzej Sekula; *M:* John Keane.

Break of Dawn 🦴🦴 1988 Pedro J. Gonzalez (Chavez) is a veteran of Pancho Villa's army who takes his family and crosses into the U.S. Despite the Depression, he finds work at a radio station in L.A. and soon becomes a popular personality in the Latino community. But Gonzalez never leaves politics very far behind and his radical civil rights views lead to a political witchhunt that sends him to prison. **105m/C VHS, DVD.** Oscar Chavez, Maria Rojo, Tony Plana, Peter Henry Schroeder, Pepe Serna, Kamala Lopez-Dawson; *D:* Isaac Artenstein; *W:* Isaac Artenstein; *C:* Stephen Lighthill; *M:* Mark Adler. TV

Break of Hearts 🦴🦴½ 1935 Hepburn marries Boyer, who becomes an alcoholic, and then more troubles arise. Very soapy, but well-made. **78m/B VHS.** Katharine Hepburn, Charles Boyer, Jean Hersholt, John Beal, Sam Hardy; *D:* Phillip Moeller; *W:* Victor Heerman; *M:* Max Steiner.

The Break Up 🦴🦴½ 1958 (R) Predictable thriller finds Jimmy Dade (Fonda) awakening in the hospital to discover her abusive husband (Bochner) is dead and she is the prime suspect. **101m/C VHS, DVD.** Bridget Fonda, Kiefer Sutherland, Penelope Ann Miller, Steven Weber, Hart Bochner, Tippi Hedren; *D:* Paul Marcus; *W:* Anne Amanda Opotowsky.

The Break-Up 🦴🦴 2006 (PG-13) Gary (Vaughn) and Brooke (Aniston) are a completely incompatible couple (he's boorish, she's high-strung) who own a Chicago condo that comes into bitter dispute when they split. Since neither will willingly leave, they decide to drive the other crazy enough so they'll bail...as everyone else must watch and suffer. There's not much romance or comedy to be seen and it's definitely NOT a date movie—unless you're planning a break-up of your own. **106m/C DVD, HD DVD.** *US* Jennifer Aniston, Vince Vaughn, Joey Lauren Adams, Judy Davis, Cole Hauser, Jon Favreau, Ann-Margret, Justin Long, Vincent D'Onofrio, Jason Bateman, Peter Billingsley, John Michael Higgins, Ivan Sergei; *D:* Peyton Reed; *W:* Jeremy Garelick, Jay Lavender; *C:* Eric Alan Edwards; *M:* Jon Brion.

Breakaway 🦴 1995 (R) Myra (Thompson) decides to get away from her drop-woman job with $300,000 of mob money. Naturally, she's pursued by a hit man (Estevez) and then betrayed by a boyfriend (De Rosa), who steals the cash and hides in the apartment of the other woman he's seeing (Harding). Thompson does fine but to describe Harding's debut performance as wooden is to be very, very kind. **94m/C VHS.** Teri Thompson, Joe Estevez, Chris De Rosa, Tonya Harding, Tony Noakes, Rick Beatty, Michael Gargarssee; *D:* Sean Dash; *W:* Gwynne Sheldon Leonard, Wally Cassell; *C:* Carlos Montaner; *M:* Robert Wait.

Breakdown 🦴🦴 1953 A boxer is set up by his girlfriend's father to take the rap for a murder. Lackluster effort. **76m/B VHS.** Ann Richards, William Bishop, Anne Gwynne, Sheldon Leonard, Wally Cassell, Richard Benedict; *D:* Edmond Angelo.

Breakdown 🦴🦴🦴 1996 (R) Jeff (Russell) and Amy (Quinlan) are high-flootin' Easterners on their way to San Diego when their car breaks down somewhere in the vast Southwest. When a trucker (Walsh) stops and offers to take Amy to the next stop while Jeff guards their yuppie treasure trove, they accept willingly. Inconvenience soon turns to terror when Jeff gets the car started, drives to meet his wife and finds her nowhere in sight. Spotting the truck by the side of the road, he confronts the trucker with the cops only to have him deny ever having seen them before. Thus begins the frantic hunt. Russell's descent from dismay to panic is grippingly played. You may know where it's going, but the fun is in getting there. **93m/C VHS, DVD. US** Kurt Russell, Kathleen Quinlan, J.T. Walsh, M.C. Gainey, Jack Noseworthy, Rex Linn, Ritch Brinkley, Kim Robillard; *D:* Jonathan Mostow; *W:* Jonathan Mostow; *C:* Doug Milsome; *M:* Basil Poledouris.

Breaker! Breaker! 🦴 1977 (PG) Convoy of angry truck drivers launch an assault on the corrupt and sadistic locals of a small Texas town. Goofy entry in the "mad or sex-crazed trucker armed with a CB radio" genre. **86m/C VHS, DVD.** Chuck Norris, George Murdock, Terry O'Connor, Don Gentry, Jack Nance; *D:* Don Hulette; *W:* Terry Chambers; *C:* Mario Cilleo; *M:* Don Hulette.

Breaker Morant 🦴🦴🦴½ 1980 (PG) In 1901 South Africa, three Australian soldiers are put on trial for avenging the murder of several prisoners. Based on a true story which was then turned into a play by Kenneth Ross, this riveting, popular antiwar statement and courtroom drama heralded Australia's film renaissance. Rich performances by Woodward and Brown. **107m/C VHS, DVD, Blu-ray Disc.** *AU* Edward Woodward, Jack Thompson, John Waters, Bryan Brown, Charles "Bud" Tingwell, Terence Donovan, Vincent Ball, Ray Meagher, Chris Haywood, Lewis Fitz-Gerald, Rod Mullinar, Alan Cassell, Rob Steele; *D:* Bruce Beresford; *W:* Bruce Beresford, Jonathan Hardy, David Stevens; *C:* Donald McAlpine; *M:* Phil Cunneen. Australian Film Inst. '80: Actor (Thompson), Film.

Breakfast at Tiffany's 🦴🦴🦴½ 1961 Truman Capote's amusing story of an endearingly eccentric New York City playgirl and her snaky romance with a young writer. Hepburn lends Holly Golightly just the right combination of naivete and worldly wisdom with a dash of melancholy. A wonderfully offbeat romance. ♫Moon River. **114m/C VHS, DVD.** Audrey Hepburn, George Peppard, Patricia Neal, Buddy Ebsen, Mickey Rooney, Martin Balsam, John McGiver, Blake Edwards; *W:* George Axelrod; *C:* Franz Planer; *M:* Henry Mancini. Oscars '61: Song ("Moon River"), Orig. Dramatic Score.

The Breakfast Club 🦴🦴 1985 (R) Five students from different cliques at a Chicago suburban high school spend a day "together" in detention. Rather well done teenage culture study; these characters delve a little deeper than the standard adult view of adolescent stereotypes. One of John Hughes's best movies. Soundtrack features Simple Minds and Wang Chung. **97m/C VHS, DVD, HD DVD.** Ally Sheedy, Molly Ringwald, Judd Nelson, Emilio Estevez, Anthony Michael Hall, Paul Gleason, John Kapelos; *D:* John Hughes; *C:* Thomas Del Ruth; *M:* Gary Chang, Keith Forsey.

Breakfast in Hollywood 🦴🦴½ 1946 Movie about the popular morning radio show of the 1940s hosted by Tom Breneman, a coast-to-coast coffee klatch. **93m/B VHS, DVD.** Tom Breneman, Bonita Granville, Eddie Ryan, Beulah Bondi, Billie Burke, Zasu Pitts, Hedda Hopper, Spike Jones; *D:* Harold Schuster.

Breakfast in Paris 🦴½ 1981 Two American professionals in Paris, both crushed from past failures in the love department, find each other. **85m/C VHS. AU** Rod Mullinar, Barbara Parkins, Jack Lenoir; *D:* John Lamond.

Breakfast of Champions 🦴½ 1999 (R) Messy adaptation of Kurt Vonnegut's 1973 satire on American greed and commercialism. Relentlessly upbeat salesman Dwayne Hoover (Willis) runs the most successful car dealership in middle...

Breakin' 🦴🦴 1984 (PG) Dance phenomenon break dancing along with the hit songs that accompanied the fad. ♫Tibetan Jam; Heart of the Beat. **87m/C VHS, DVD. US** Lucinda Dickey, Adolfo "Shabba Doo" Quinones, Michael "Boogaloo Shrimp" Chambers, Ben Lokey, Christopher McDonald, Phineas Newborn III; *D:* Joel Silberg; *W:* Allen N. DeBevoise; *C:* Hanania Baer; *M:* Michael Boyd.

Breakin' 2: Electric Boogaloo 🦴🦴 1984 (PG) *Breakdance 2: Electric Boogaloo; Breakin' 2* Breakdancers hold a benefit concert to preserve an urban community center. ♫Electric Boogaloo; Radiotron; Action; When I.C.U. **94m/C VHS, DVD.** Lucinda Dickey, Adolfo "Shabba Doo" Quinones, Michael "Boogaloo Shrimp" Chambers, Susie Bono; *D:* Sam Firstenberg; *C:* Hanania Baer.

Breakin' All The Rules 🦴🦴½ 2004 (PG-13) Predictable romantic comedy stars Foxx as L.A. men's magazine exec Quincy Watson, who gets dumped by his fiancee Helen (Lawson) the same day his timid boss Phillip (MacNicol) wants Quincy to lay off 15% of the mag's staff. Instead, Quincy axes himself and takes his frustrations and rejections out on paper, writing what turns out to be the best-selling "Breakup Handbook." Suddenly, Quincy is Mr. Advice for Phillip, who wants to know how to avoid the gold-digging Rita (Esposito), and Quincy's playa cousin Evan (Chestnut), who wants to dump his girlfriend Nicky (Union) before she dumps him. Complications ensue when Quincy unwittingly falls for Nicky and Rita goes after Evan thinking he's Quincy. It's confusing for the characters, but likeably and convincingly done. **85m/C VHS, DVD. US** Jamie Foxx, Gabrielle Union, Morris Chestnut, Peter MacNicol, Jennifer Esposito, Bianca Lawson, Jill Ritchie; *Cameos:* Heather Headley; *D:* Daniel Taplitz; *W:* Daniel Taplitz; *C:* David Hennings; *M:* Marcus Miller.

Breakin' Through 🦴🦴 1984 The choreographer of a troubled Broadway-bound musical decides to energize his shows with a troupe of street dancers. **73m/C VHS.** Ben Vereen, Donna McKechnie, Reid Shelton; *D:* Peter Medak.

Breakheart Pass 🦴🦴 1976 (PG) A governor, his female companion, a band of cavalrymen, and a mysterious man travel on a train through the mountains of Idaho in 1870. The mystery man turns out to be a murderer. Based on a novel by Alistair MacLean. **92m/C VHS, DVD.** Charles Bronson, Ben Johnson, Richard Crenna, Jill Ireland, Charles Durning, Ed Lauter, Archie Moore, Sally Kirkland; *D:* Tom Gries; *W:* Alistair MacLean; *C:* Lucien Ballard; *M:* Jerry Goldsmith.

Breaking All the Rules 🦴½ 1985 (R) Comedy about two teenage lovers who find themselves embroiled in a slapstick jewel robbery at an amusement park during the last day of summer break. **91m/C VHS. CA** Carolyn Dunn, Carl Marotte, Thor Bishopric, Rachel Hayward; *D:* James Orr; *W:* James Orr, Jim Cruickshank.

Breaking and Entering 🦴🦴 2006 (R) Landscape architect Will (Law) and his partner Sandy (Freeman) are pioneers in the urban renewal of the crime-ridden King's Cross area in North London. However, after their office is repeatedly broken into, Will finally manages to chase the young thief ung enough to discover...

Breakdown America's Midland City. A leading citizen, who stars in his own garish TV commercials, Dwayne has estranged from his own wife, Celia (Hershey), and his aspiring lounge singer son, Bunny (Haas). Dwayne also thinks he's going nuts and loses this one hope for salvation lies with Kilgore Trout (Finney), an eccentric hack sci fi writer/philosopher. Oh yeah, and Nolte is around as Dwayne's sales manager Harr, who likes to wear women's lacy lingerie beneath his suits. **110m/C VHS, DVD.** Bruce Willis, Albert Finney, Nick Nolte, Barbara Hershey, Glenne Headly, Lukas Haas, Omar Epps, Buck Henry, Vicki Lewis, Ken H. Campbell, Will Patton, Chip Zien, Owen Wilson, Alison Eastwood, Shawnee Smith, Kurt Vonnegut Jr.; *D:* Alan Rudolph; *W:* Alan Rudolph; *C:* Elliot Davis; *M:* Mark Isham.

where he lives. The thief, Miro (Gavron), is a teenaged Bosnian refugee, living with his widowed seamstress mother, Amira (Binoche). Instead of immediately ratting Miro out, Will cozies up to his attractive mum since his own home life is lacking. Law's character is a polite cipher and the dicey situations resolve themselves a little too neatly in Minghella's slice of life drama. **116m/C DVD.** *GB* Jude Law, Juliette Binoche, Robin Wright Penn, Martin Freeman, Ray Winstone, Vera Farmiga, Juliet Stevenson, Rafi Gavron, Poppy Rogers; *D:* Anthony Minghella; *W:* Anthony Minghella; *C:* Benoit Delhomme; *M:* Gabriel Yared.

Breaking Away 𝄞𝄞𝄞½ **1979 (PG)** A lighthearted coming-of-age drama about a high school graduate's addiction to bicycle racing, whose dreams are tested against the realities of a crucial race. An honest, open look at present Americana with tremendous insight into the minds of average youth; shot on location at Indiana University. Great bike-racing photography. Quaid, Barrie, and Christopher give exceptional performances. Basis for a TV series. **100m/C VHS, DVD.** Dennis Christopher, Dennis Quaid, Daniel Stern, Jackie Earle Haley, Barbara Barrie, Paul Dooley, Amy Wright; *D:* Peter Yates; *W:* Steve Tesich; *C:* Matthew F. Leonetti; *M:* Patrick Williams. Oscars '79: Orig. Screenplay; Golden Globes '80: Film—Mus./Comedy; Natl. Bd. of Review '79: Support. Actor (Dooley); N.Y. Film Critics '79: Screenplay; Natl. Soc. Film Critics '79: Film, Screenplay; Writers Guild '79: Orig. Screenplay.

Breaking Free 𝄞𝄞½ **1995 (PG)** Teenaged loser Rick Chilton (London) forms an unlikely friendship with bitter gymnast Lindsay (Phillips) who's been blinded and forced to give up her dreams. Mostly avoids the stickiness inherent in such stories thanks to some fine performances. **106m/C VHS.** Jeremy London, Gina Philips, Christine Taylor, Megan Gallagher, Nicolas Surovy, Adam Wylie, Brian Krause, Scott Coffey; *D:* David Mackay; *C:* Christopher Faloona; *M:* Steve Dorff.

Breaking Glass 𝄞𝄞 **1980 (PG)** A "New Wave" musical that gives an insight into the punk record business and at the same time tells of the rags-to-riches life of a punk rock star. **94m/C VHS, DVD.** *GB* Hazel O'Connor, Phil Daniels, Jon Finch, Jonathan Pryce; *D:* Brian Gibson.

Breaking Home Ties 𝄞𝄞½ **1987** Norman Rockwell's *Breaking Home Ties* illustration is the basis for this coming-of-age story set in a small Texas town. A young man is eager to be off to college and lessen his family ties but his mother's serious illness may prevent both. Good performances help overcome the sentimentality. **95m/C VHS.** Jason Robards Jr., Eva Marie Saint, Doug McKeon, Claire Trevor, Erin Gray; *D:* John Wilder. *W:* John Wilder. **TV**

Breaking In 𝄞𝄞𝄞 **1989 (R)** A semi-acclaimed comedy about a professional thief who takes a young amateur under his wing and shows him the ropes. Under-estimated Reynolds is especially charming, and he's a great straight man to the energetic Siemaszko. Witty and innovative script, with intelligent direction from Forsyth. **95m/C VHS, DVD.** Burt Reynolds, Casey Siemaszko, Sheila Kelley, Lorraine Toussaint, Albert Salmi, Harry Carey Jr., Maury Chaykin, Stephen Tobolowsky, David Frishberg; *D:* Bill Forsyth; *W:* John Sayles; *C:* Michael Coulter; *M:* Michael Gibbs.

Breaking Loose 𝄞½ **1990 (R)** A surfer is on the run from a vicious motorcycle gang that kidnapped his girlfriend, but turns to fight eventually, board in hand. **88m/C VHS.** Peter Phelps, Vince Martin, Abigail, David Ngoombujara; *D:* Rod Hay.

Breaking Point 𝄞𝄞½ **1994** Ex-cop Dwight Meadows (Busey), retired from the force when he was nearly killed by a scalpel-wielding mass murderer known as "The Surgeon." Now the psycho is back and Meadows returns to active duty, paired with relentless officer Dana Preston (Fluegel), who wants the killer caught—at any cost. Vancouver, British Columbia fills in for the Seattle, Washington setting. **95m/C VHS.** Gary Busey, Darlanne Fluegel, Jeff Griggs, Kim Cattrall; *D:* Paul Ziller; *M:* Graeme Coleman.

Breaking the Code 𝄞𝄞½ **1995** Alan Turing (Jacobi) is a British mathematical genius whose work leads to the birth of the digital computer and who is instrumental in enabling the allies to crack the German WWII Enigma code. An active homosexual when homosexuality was illegal, Turing's personal behavior was tolerated because of the importance of his war work but after the gay spy scare of the '50s, Turing was regarded as a security risk and his life increasingly restricted. British TV adaptation based on the play by Hugh Whitemore (Jacobi also played the role on stage) and the book "Alan Turing: The Enigma" by Andrew Hodges. **90m/C VHS.** *GB* Derek Jacobi, Amanda Root, Prunella Scales, Harold Pinter, Julian Kerridge, Richard Johnson; *D:* Herbert Wise; *W:* Hugh Whitemore.

Breaking the Ice 𝄞𝄞 **1938** Unlikely mixture of Mennonites and a big city ice skating show. Young man leaves the farm to get a job singing at the rink. Musical numbers abound with backing by Victor Young and his Orchestra. **79m/B VHS.** Bobby Breen, Charlie Ruggles, Dolores Costello, Billy Gilbert, Margaret Hamilton, Jonathan Hale; *D:* Edward F. (Eddie) Cline; *W:* Mary C. McCall, Bernard Schubert, Manuel Seff; *C:* Jack MacKenzie; *M:* Victor Young.

Breaking the Rules 𝄞𝄞 **1992 (PG-13)** Predicatable buddy-road movie with a tearjerking premise and comedic overtones. Rob, Gene, and Phil were best buds growing up in Cleveland but young adulthood has separated them. They are reunited by Phil, who is dying of leukemia, and whose last wish is a cross-country road trip to California so he can appear as a contestant on "Jeopardy." Along the way they meet brassy waitress Mary, who impulsively decides to join them and winds up bringing the trio's shaky friendship back together. Potts does a good job as the big-haired, big-hearted Mary but the actors must work hard to maintain any dignity given the story's melodrama. **100m/C VHS.** Jason Bateman, C. Thomas Howell, Jonathan Silverman, Annie Potts, Kent Bateman, Shawn (Michael) Phelan; *D:* Neal Israel; *W:* Paul Shapiro; *M:* David Kitay.

Breaking the Surface: The Greg Louganis Story 𝄞𝄞½ **1996** Trials and tribulations of the gold-medal winning Olympic diver, including his overbearing father, abusive lover, and his own HIV-positive status. Based on Louganis' autobiography; made for TV. **95m/C VHS, DVD.** Mario Lopez, Michael Murphy, Jeffrey Meek, Bruce Weitz, Rosemary Dunsmore; *D:* Steven Hilliard Stern; *W:* Alan Hines. **CABLE**

Breaking the Waves 𝄞𝄞𝄞 **1995 (R)** Sacrificial journey of shy, religious Bess (Watson), who's living in an austere northern Scotland coastal village in the '70s. Bess, who regularly talks to God, marries Jan (Skarsgard), an adventurer working on a North Sea oil rig. It must be a case of opposites attracting but the couple are happy until Jan is paralyzed from the neck down in a rig accident. Bess, who blames herself, begins sleeping around, believing her actions can somehow help Jan, and slides ever deeper into mental instability. Powerful story is divided into seven chapters and an epilogue. **152m/C VHS, DVD.** *DK FR* Emily Watson, Stellan Skarsgard, Katrin Cartlidge, Adrian Rawlins, Jean-Marc Barr, Sandra Voe, Udo Kier, Mikkel Gaup; *D:* Lars von Trier; *W:* Lars von Trier; *C:* Robby Muller; *M:* Joachim Holbek. Cannes '96: Grand Jury Prize; Cesar '97: Foreign Film; N.Y. Film Critics '96: Actress (Watson), Cinematog., Director (von Trier); Natl. Soc. Film Critics '96: Actress (Watson), Cinematog., Director (von Trier). Film.

Breaking Up 𝄞𝄞½ **1978** A woman fights to rediscover her personal identity after her 15-year marriage crumbles in this Emmy-nominated movie. **90m/C VHS.** Lee Remick, Granville Van Dusen, David Stambaugh; *D:* Delbert Mann. **TV**

Breaking Up 𝄞𝄞 **1997 (R)** What steamy sheet action brings together, dreary day to day living easily pulls apart. That is the basic message of this bland romantic comedy that brings nothing new to the tired genre. Typical opposites attract but can't stay together (yet can't stay apart)

plot finds photographer Crowe and teacher Hayek madly in lust and impulsively marrying. Hayek had more to work with when she played this role in "Fools Rush In," and Crowe seems uncomfortable as the lackluster boyfriend. Told in a chatty style with frequent asides to the audience by the main characters and a string of flashback sequences, director Greenwald's theatre background is apparent here. Clever camera work and editing are highlights. Adapted from Michael Cristofer's Pulitzer Prize-winning play. **90m/C VHS, DVD.** Salma Hayek, Russell Crowe; *D:* Robert Greenwald; *W:* Michael Cristofer; *M:* Mark Mothersbaugh.

Breaking Up Is Hard to Do 𝄞 **1979** Six men leave their wives and shack up together on Malibu for a summer of partying and introspection. Made for television; edited down from its original 201 minute length. **96m/C VHS.** Billy Crystal, Bonnie Franklin, Ted Bessell, Jeff Conaway, Tony Musante, Robert Conrad, Trish Stewart, David Ogden Stiers, George Gaynes; *D:* Lou Antonio; *M:* Richard Bellis. **TV**

Breakout 𝄞𝄞 **1975 (PG)** The wife of a man imprisoned in Mexico hires a Texas bush pilot (Bronson) to help her husband (Duvall) escape. **96m/C VHS, DVD.** Charles Bronson, Jill Ireland, Randy Quaid; *D:* Tom Gries; *W:* Sheree North, Howard B. Kreitsek, Marc Norman, Elliott Baker; *C:* Lucien Ballard; *M:* Jerry Goldsmith.

Breakout 𝄞𝄞 **1998** Zack (Carradine) has invented an environmentally friendly alternative energy source that makes him the scourge of the oil cartels. So the bad guys decide to kidnap Zack's son Joe (Bonifant) as a bargaining chip, only the kid turns out to be as smart as his old man. **86m/C VHS, UMD.** Robert Carradine, Evan Bonifant, James Hong, Chris Chinchilla; *D:* John Bradshaw; *W:* Naomi Jantzen; *C:* Edgar Egger; *M:* Gary Kotinoff. **VIDEO**

The Breaks 𝄞𝄞 **1999 (R)** White Irish kid gets adopted by a black family in South Central L.A. and naturally grows up to think of himself as a homeboy. But his adoptive mom is tired of his shenanigans and gives him one simple task to do—bring home a carton of milk by supper—or else. Why isn't this as easy as it sounds ('cause it certainly is as dumb). **86m/C VHS, DVD.** Mitch Mullany, Carl Anthony Payne II, Paula Jai Parker, Clifton Powell, Loretta Devine; *D:* Eric Meza; *W:* Mitch Mullany; *C:* Carlos Gonzalez; *M:* Adam Hirsh. **VIDEO**

Breakthrough 𝄞𝄞 *Sergeant Steiner* **1978 (PG)** German soldier, broken at the end of WWII, sets out to negotiate with the Allies. Based at best. **96m/C VHS.** Richard Burton, Robert Mitchum, Rod Steiger, Michael Parks, Curt Jurgens; *D:* Andrew V. McLaglen.

The Breakup Artist 𝄞𝄞½ **2004 (R)** A rom-com from the male point of view. Jim (Taylor) is looking for love in the Big Apple, except he can't stay focused on just one girl (hence the title). Meanwhile, sweet co-worker Teresa (Devica) is engaged to a jerk. Of course, they're made for each other—if only Jim and Teresa can figure it out. **86m/C DVD.** Joseph Lyle Taylor, Paula DeVicq, Sarita Choudhury, Sabrina Lloyd, Ron Mongeluzzo; *Cameos:* Edward Burns, Regis Philbin, Bobby Cannavale; *D:* Vincent Rubino; *W:* Vincent Rubino; *C:* Nicholas Baratta; *M:* Thomas DeRenzo, Paul Conte.

Breast Men 𝄞𝄞½ **1997 (R)** A campy fictional look into the lives and careers of the two doctors who invented the silicone breast implant in 1960s Texas. Struggling Kevin Saunders (Schwimmer) is an ambitious geek who works with grumpy plastic surgeon mentor, Dr. William Larson (Cooper), to develop a prosthetic breast, made from Dow-Corning's silicone gel. It's an immediate success, and the doctors become rich, successful, and ever more obnoxious. Then come the lawsuits and life is suddenly no longer so sweet. And yes, you will see a lot of naked breasts. **90m/C VHS, DVD.** John Stockwell, Terry O'Quinn, Kathleen Wilhoite, Lisa Marie, David Schwimmer, Chris Cooper, Louise Fletcher, Emily Procter, Matt Frewer; *D:* Lawrence O'Neil; *W:* John Stockwell; *C:* Robert M. Stevens; *M:* Dennis McCarthy. **CABLE**

Breath of Scandal 𝄞𝄞 **1960** An American diplomat in Vienna rescues a princess when she is thrown off a horse; he falls for her like a ton o' bricks. Viennese politics complicate things. Based on a play by Molnar. **98m/C VHS, DVD.** Sophia Loren, John Gavin, Maurice Chevalier, Angela Lansbury; *D:* Michael Curtiz.

Breathing Fire 𝄞𝄞 **1991 (R)** A Vietnamese teenager and his American brother find out their ex-GI father is behind an armed bank robbery and murder. They join together to protect the only eyewitness—a young girl—against their own father. Lots of kickboxing action for martial arts fans. **86m/C VHS, DVD.** Bolo Yeung, Jonathan Ke Quan, Jerry Trimble; *D:* Lou Kennedy.

Breathing Lessons 𝄞𝄞 **1994 (PG)** Sweet look at a long-term marriage that renews itself on a road trip. Flighty Maggie and pragmatic Ira have been married for 28 squabbling years. They're driving from their Baltimore home to a funeral in Pennsylvania and the road stops provide some small adventures and a great deal of conversation. Drama rests easily on the capable shoulders of the veteran performers. Based on the novel by Anne Tyler. Made for TV. **98m/C VHS.** James Garner, Joanne Woodward, Paul Winfield, Kathryn Erbe, Joyce Van Patten, Eileen Heckart, Tim Guinee, Henry Jones, Stephi Lineburg, Jean (Louisa) Kelly, Joan Considine; *D:* John Erman; *W:* Robert W. Lenski. **TV**

Breathing Room 𝄞𝄞 *'Til Christmas* **1996 (R)** New Yorker David (Futterman) has trouble with commitment to girlfriend Kathy (Floyd) and the duo break up again at Thanksgiving when he won't tell her he loves her. Kathy decides they need a break and refuses to see David until Christmas. She plays at seeing her boss, both get too much advice from friends and family, they attend the same holiday party—and the inevitable happens. Nothing new here. **90m/C VHS.** Dan Futterman, Susan Floyd, David Thornton; *D:* Jon Sherman; *W:* Jon Sherman, Tom Hughes; *C:* Jim Denault; *M:* Pat Irwin.

Breathless 𝄞𝄞𝄞 **1959** *A Bout de Souffle* Godard's first feature catapulted him to the vanguard of French filmmakers. Carefree Parisian crook, Michel (Belmondo), who emulates Humphrey Bogart, falls in love with gamine American student Patricia (Seberg) with tragic results. Wonderful scenes of Parisian life. Established Godard's Brechtian, experimental style. Belmondo's film debut. Mistitled "Breathless" for American release, the film's French title actually means "Out of Breath"; however, the fast-paced, erratic musical score leaves you breathless. French with English subtitles. Remade with Richard Gere in 1983 with far less intensity. **90m/B VHS, DVD.** *FR* Jean-Paul Belmondo, Jean Seberg, Daniel Boulanger, Jean-Pierre Melville, Liliane Robin; *D:* Jean-Luc Godard; *W:* Jean-Luc Godard; *C:* Raoul Coutard; *M:* Martial Solal. Berlin Intl. Film Fest. '60: Director (Godard).

Breathless 𝄞𝄞 **1983 (R)** Car thief turned cop killer has a torrid love affair with a French student studying in Los Angeles as the police slowly close in. Glossy, smarmy remake of the Godard classic that concentrates on the thin plot rather than any attempt at revitalizing the film syntax. **105m/C VHS, DVD.** Richard Gere, Valerie Kaprisky, Art Metrano, John P. Ryan, Lisa Jane Persky; *D:* Jim McBride; *W:* Jim McBride, L.M. Kit Carson; *M:* Jack Nitzsche.

Breathtaking 𝄞𝄞 **2000** Workaholic Dr. Caroline Henshaw (Whalley) is a psychologist with many mental problems of her own, stemming from her own past sexual abuse. But Caroline has managed to keep it together until she meets a new patient (Maitland)—a self-destructive masseuse who's being battered by her sicko hubby (Foreman). **105m/C VHS.** *GB* Joanne Whalley, Neil Dudgeon, Sandra Maitland, Jamie Foreman; *D:* David Green; *W:* Nicky Cowan; *C:* Gavin Finney; *M:* Robert (Rob) Lane.

The Breed 𝄞𝄞 **2001 (R)** Set in a noir-ish anytime, this horror film tells the story of an FBI agent Grant (a very stiff Woodbine), who starts out searching for a serial killer and ends up teamed with Aaron Grey (Paul), who turns out to be a vampire. Seems that the vampires who walk among us are ready to come out of the closet and join society, but a political dissident in the vampire ranks is trying to start a war...or is he? Could there be crosses afoot? Grant, a black man, is less than thrilled at being teamed with a vampire, which results in some subtle moral banter about racism and the humans' fear of the vamps' fear of the Nazis to explain the vamps' fear of the promise, but the poor acting and choppy editing and direction make everyone look uncomfortable amid the atmospheric scenery. **91m/C VHS, DVD, Adrian Paul, Bai Ling, Bokeem Woodbine, Zen Gesner, Jake Busche; D:** Michael Oblowitz; **W:** Christos N. Gage, Ruth Fletcher. **VIDEO**

The Breed ◻ 2006 (R) Bad doggie flick! Two brothers inherit their uncle's remote island and decide to fly three friends to join them in a party weekend. Too bad they didn't know their uncle rented part of the island to a special canine research unit and that the genetically-enhanced dogs have gone wild. Lots of plot holes, lots of genre cliches. **87m/C DVD, Oliver Hudson, Hill Harper, Eric Livialy, Michelle Rodriguez, Taryn Manning; D:** Nick Mastandrea. **M:** Tom Mesmer. **VIDEO**

A Breed Apart ◻◻ 1984 (R) An on-going battle over a rare eagle's eggs strikes sparks between a reclusive conservationist and a scheming adventurer hired by a billionaire collector. **95m/C VHS, Kathleen Turner, Rutger Hauer, Powers Boothe, Donald Pleasence, Brion James, John Dennis Johnson; D:** Philippe Mora.

Breeders ◻◻½ 1986 (R) Ridiculous foam rubber monster attacks and impregnates women in New York. **77m/C VHS, DVD, Teresa Farley, Frances Raines, Amy Brenta; C:** Lance Lewman Natalie O'Connell; **D:** Tim Kincaid; **C:** Arthur Marks.

Breeders woof! 1997 (R) Alien on a mating mission so terrorizes a Boston women's college. Doesn't deliver on its exploitation premise, so don't bother. **92m/C VHS, DVD, Todd Jensen, Samantha Janus, Kadamba Simmons, Oliver Tobias; D:** Paul Matthews; **W:** Paul Matthews; **M:** Ben Heneghan.

Brenda Starr ◻½ 1986 (PG) Amateurish adaptation of the comic strip by Dale Messick. Shields stars as girl reporter Brenda Starr, who is once again risking her life to get the scoop. She finds herself in the jungles of South America searching for a mad scientist who is creating a rocket fuel that could destroy the world. The most entertaining thing about this film is the costumes designed by Bob Mackie. **94m/C VHS, DVD, Brooke Shields, Timothy Dalton, Tony Peck, Diana Scarwid, Nestor Serrano Jeffrey Tambor, June Gable, Charles Durning, Eddie Albert, Henry Gibson, Ed Nelson; D:** Robert Ellis Miller; **W:** James David Buchanan; **C:** Freddie Francis; **M:** Johnny Mandel.

The Brets ◻◻◻ 1988 Amusing two-part British miniseries follows the egos and eccentricities of the British theatrical dynasty, the Brets. Part 1 is set in the '20s and introduces the family heads, Charles (Rodway) and Lydia (Murray), who enjoy performing off-stage almost as well as they enjoy performing on. Also introduced are their five children and loyal (if opinionated) servants. Part 2 follows the family into the '30s with son Edwin (Yelland) having become a film star, actress daughter Martha (Lang) falling for a politician, and son Tom (Winter) continuing to write his gloomy social dramas. Each part is on six cassettes. **600m/C VHS, DVD, GB Barbara Murray, Norman Rodway, David Yelland, Belinda Lang, George Winter, Janet Maw, Tim Wylton, Bert Famaly, ysette Anthony, Clive Francis, Frank Middlemass, John Castle, Hugh Fraser, Patrick Ryecart, Sally Cookson, Billy Boyle; W:** Rosemary Anne Sisson.

Brewster McCloud ◻◻◻½ 1970 (R) Altman's first picture after M*A*S*H reunites much of the cast and combines fantasy, black comedy, and satire in the story of a young man whose head is in the clouds (or at least in the upper reaches of the Houston Astrodome). Brewster (Cort) lives covertly in the Dome and dreams of flying. He also has a guardian angel (Kellerman) who watches over him and may actually be killing people who give him a hard time. Murphy is a cop obsessed with catching the killer. And there's a circus allegory as well. Hard to figure what it all means and offbeat as they come, but for certain tastes, exquisite. **101m/C VHS, Bud Cort, Sally Kellerman, Shelley Duvall, Michael Murphy, William Windom, Rene Auberjonois, Stacy Keach, John Schuck, Margaret Hamilton; D:** Robert Altman; **W:** Doran William Cannon; **C:** Lamar Boren, Jordan Cronenweth; **M:** Gene Page.

Brewster's Millions ◻◻½ 1945 If Brewster, an ex-G.I., can spend $1 million in one year, he will inherit a substantially greater fortune. Originally a 1902 novel, this is the fifth of seven film adaptations. **79m/B VHS, Dennis O'Keefe, June Havoc, Eddie Anderson, Helen Walker, Gail Patrick, Mischa Auer; D:** Allan Dwan.

Brewster's Millions ◻◻½ 1985 (PG) An aging minor league baseball player must spend $30 million in order to collect an inheritance of a substantially greater fortune. If he can spend that money can't buy happiness. Seventh remake of the story. **101m/C VHS, DVD, Richard Pryor, John Candy, Lonette McKee, Stephen Collins, Jerry Orbach, Pat Hingle, Tovah Feldshuh, Hume Cronyn, Rick Moranis; D:** Walter Hill; **W:** Timothy Harris, Herschel Weingrod; **C:** Ric Waite; **M:** Ry Cooder.

Brian's Song ◻◻◻ 1971 (G) The story of the unique relationship between Gale Sayers, the Chicago Bears' star running back, and his teammate Brian Piccolo. The friendship between the Bears' first interracial roommates ended suddenly when Brian Piccolo lost his life to cancer. Incredibly well received in its time, a moving, sentimental favorite. Made-for-TV. **74m/C VHS, DVD, James Caan, Billy Dee Williams, Jack Warden, Shelley Fabares, Judy Pace, Bernie Casey; D:** Buzz Kulik; **W:** William Blinn; **C:** Joseph Biroc; **M:** Michel Legrand. **TV**

Brian's Song ◻◻ 2001 Unnecessary remake of the 1971 made-for-TV classic dealing with the friendship between Gale Sayers and Brian Piccolo, and Piccolo's fight against cancer heads right for the disease-of-the-week cliches with depth. Phifer, as Sayers, and Cale as Joy Piccolo, along with a deeper understanding of the wives' point of view, are the main reasons to check it out. But it still can't compare to the original. **89m/C VHS, DVD, Mekhi Phifer, Sean Maher, Paula Cale, Elise Neal, Ben Gazzara, Aidan Devine, Dean McDermott; D:** John Gray; **W:** Allen Clare William Blinn; **C:** James Chressanthis; **M:** Richard (Rick) Marvin.

Brick ◻◻◻ 2006 (R) Ever wonder what it would look like if Raymond Chandler wrote for the "Sweet Valley High" series? In his debut film, writer/director Johnson delivers one of the most impressive examples of hard-boiled noir in years, set strangely enough, in a California high school. Gordon-Levitt brilliantly channels Humphrey Bogart as Brendan, a tough-as-nails teenaged shamus who's trying to locate his missing ex-girlfriend (de Ravin) in the seamy underbelly of drug-dealing jocks and cheerleader femme fatales. The mystery's a twisty one, peppered with Johnson's own brand of tough guy slang that will either delight or confound you. But you can't ignore the ambition of this "Mallet's Crossing" meets "Breakfast Club" hybrid. **110m/C DVD, US Joseph Gordon-Levitt, Lukas Haas, Noah Fleiss, Matt O'Leary, Nora Zehetner, Noah Segan, Meagan Good, Emile de Ravin, Brian White, Richard Roundtree, Lucas Babin; D:** Rian Johnson; **W:** Rian Johnson; **C:** Steve Yedlin; **M:** Nathan Johnson.

The Bride ◻◻ 1985 (PG-13) Re-telling of "The Bride of Frankenstein." Sting's Dr. Frankenstein has much more success in creating his second monster and he may

---

even be falling in love with her. When she begins to gain too much independence, though, the awful truth about her origins comes out. Fans of the two leads will want to see this one, but for a true classic see Elsa Lanchester's bride. **118m/C VHS, DVD GB Sting, Jennifer Beals, Anthony (Corlan) Higgins, David Rappaport, Geraldine Page, Clancy Brown, Phil Daniels, Veruschka, Quentin Crisp, Cary Elwes; D:** Franc Roddam; **W:** Lloyd Fonvielle; **C:** Stephen Burum; **M:** Maurice Jarre.

Bride & Prejudice ◻◻ 2004 (PG-13) Bollywood meets Jane Austen in Chandra's brightly-colored confection. Will Darcy (Henderson) and chum Balraj (Andrews) arrive in Amritsar for a friend's wedding. A stuffy but wealthy businessman, Will finds himself drawn to the strikingly beautiful and headstrong Lalita (Rai) who's irritated by his arrogance. That they are meant for each other is obvious but the film must travel from India to London and L.A. and back again before it all plays out, amidst various musical numbers and family trials. **110m/C DVD, US Aishwarya Rai, Martin Henderson, Anupam Kher, Naveen Andrews, Daniel Gillies, Indira Varma, Marsha Mason, Nadira Babbar, Nimrala Shirodkar, Meghna Peeya Rai Choudhury; D:** Gurinder Chadha; **W:** Edward D. Wood Gurinder Chadha, Paul Mayeda Berges; **C:** Santosh Sivan.

The Bride & the Beast woof! 1958 Queen of the Gorillas 1958 While on an African safari honeymoon, a big game hunter's new bride is carried off by a gorilla. Ludicrous, jungle tale. **78m/B VHS, DVD, Charlotte Austin, Lance Fuller, William Justine, Johnny Roth, Jeanne Gerson, Gilbert Frye, Slick Slavin, Bhogwan Singh; D:** Adrian Weiss; **W:** Edward D. Wood Jr.; **C:** Roland Price; **M:** Les Baxter.

The Bride Came C.O.D. ◻◻ 1941 Rough/tough pilot Cagney is hired by a rich Texas oil man to prevent his daughter (the one with the Bette Davis eyes) from marrying cheesy bandleader Carson. The payoff: $10 per pound if she's delivered unwed. What a surprise when Cagney faces the timeworn dilemma of having to choose between love and money. A contemporary issue of "Time" magazine trumpeted: "Screen's most talented tough guy rough-houses one of screen's best dramatic actresses." That tells you right there it's a romantic comedy. Cagney and Davis—a likely pairing—you'd think—are essentially fish out of water, bothered and bewildered by a weak script. **92m/B VHS, DVD, James Cagney, Bette Davis, Jack Carson, George Tobias, Eugene Pallette, William Frawley; D:** William Keighley; **W:** Julius J. Epstein, Philip G. Epstein; **M:** Max Steiner.

The Bride Is Much Too Beautiful ◻◻½ 1958 Her Bridal Night; La Mariee Est Trop Belle 1958 French farm girl Bardot becomes a model with the help of some fashion magazine employees and then winces up posing as the bride in a fake marriage. Dubbed. **90m/C VHS, FR Brigitte Bardot Louis Jourdan, Micheline Presle, Marcel Amont; D:** Pierre Gaspard-Huit; **W:** Odette Joyeux, Philippe Agostini; **C:** Louis Page; **M:** Norbert Glanzberg.

Bride of Chucky ◻◻½ 1998 (R) Just when you thought you had seen the last of that creepy little doll, "Chucky" returns. This fourth installment of the "Child's Play" franchise finds Chucky back on the lam after being sprung from the pen by the ex-girlfriend of his former human incarnation, serial killer Charles Lee Ray. After killing her off (she's Tiffany (Tilly)), Chucky transforms her soul into an equally creepy girl doll. Together, they must make their way to the very spot where he was gunned down by police in order to transfer from Chucky and both incarnations of Tiffany, the rest of the characters are undeveloped and rather useless. Fortunately, the filmmakers knew not to take themselves too seriously, and managed a few funny moments. But its really only Tilly's excellent camp-vampy performance and an occasional clever jab from the Chuckster that lift this one above a woof. **89m/C VHS, DVD Jennifer Tilly, Katherine Heigl, Nick Stabile, John Ritter, Alexis Arquette, Gordon Michael Woolvett, Lawrence Dane, Michael Johnson,**

Bride of the Monster woof! 1956 Newlywed crisis: a woman with rich taste learns how to adjust to living on her husband's poor salary, but not before she samples the life of the wealthy. Interesting in a sociological sort of way. **81m/B VHS, Barbara Stanwyck, Gene Raymond, Hattie McDaniel; D:** Leigh Jason.

The Bride Walks Out ◻◻ 1936 Newlywed crisis: a woman with rich taste learns how to adjust to living on her husband's poor salary, but not before she samples the life of the wealthy. Interesting in a sociological sort of way. **81m/B VHS, Barbara Stanwyck, Gene Raymond, Robert Young, Ned Sparks, Willie Best, Helen Broderick, Hattie McDaniel; D:** Leigh Jason.

Kathy Najimy; **D:** Ronny Yu; **W:** Don Mancini; **C:** Peter Pau; **M:** Graeme Revell; **V:** Brad Dourif.

The Bride of Frank ◻◻ 1996 Former homeless man Frank has a tamper and he's not afraid to use it on the belittling ladies who make the ill-fated gaffe of responding to his personals ad, which leads to their horrific, over-the-top, brutal demises. But, hey, he still has a sense of humor about it all. The viewer, however, might not. **89m/C VHS, DVD, Frank Meyer, Johnny Honzor, Steve Ballot; D:** Steve Ballot; **C:** Steve Ballot. **VIDEO**

The Bride of Frankenstein ◻◻◻◻ 1935 The classic sequel to the classic original in which Dr. F. seeks to build a mate for his monster. More humor than the first, but also more pathos, including the monster's famous but short-lived friendship with a blind hermit. Lanchester plays both the bride and Mary Shelley in the opening sequence. **75m/B VHS, DVD, Boris Karloff, Elsa Lanchester, Ernest Thesiger, Colin, Una O'Connor, Valerie Hobson, Dwight Frye, John Carradine, E.E. Clive, O.P. Heggie, Gavin Gordon, Douglas Walton, Billy Barty, Walter Brennan; D:** James Whale; **W:** John Lloyd Balderston, William Hurlbut; **C:** John Mescall; **M:** Franz Waxman. Natl. Film Reg. '98.

Bride of Killer Nerd ◻ 1991 Harold Kunkel, left over from the original "Killer Nerd," finds his opposite sex nirvana in the person of Thelma, also a nerd in mind, body, and soul. They relentlessly pursue revenge on the rockers who humiliate them at a campus beer bash. **75m/C VHS, DVD, Toby Radloff, Wayna A. Harold, Heidi Lohr; D:** Mark Steven Bosko.

Bride of Re-Animator ◻◻½ 1989 Herbert West is back, and this time he not only re-animates life but creates life—sexy female live-in sequel to the immensely popular "Re-Animator." High camp and blood curdling gore make this a standout in the sequel parade. Available in an R-rated version as well. **99m/C VHS, DVD, Bruce Abbott, Claude Earl Jones, Fabiana Udenio, Jeffrey Combs, Kathleen Kinmont, David Gale, Mel Stewart, Irene Forrest; D:** Brian Yuzna; **W:** Brian Yuzna, Rick Fry, Woody Keith; **C:** Rick Fichter; **M:** Richard Band.

Bride of the Gorilla ◻◻ 1951 Burr travels to the jungle where he finds a wife, a plantation, and a curse in this African twist on the werewolf legend. Chaney is the local policeman on his trail. Burr's physical changes are fun to watch. **76m/B VHS, DVD, Raymond Burr, Barbara Payton, Lon Chaney Jr., Tom Conway, Paul Cavanagh; D:** Curt Siodmak; **W:** Curt Siodmak.

Bride of the Wind ◻◻½ 2001 (R) Dull biopic of Alma Mahler (Wynter), a 20th-century femme who put her own musical career aside to marry composer Gustav Mahler (Pryce) in old Vienna. Alma in turn trigues a number of famous men, including architect Oskar Kokoschka (Perez), and artist Oskar Kokoschka (Perez) and others while her marriage to the stoic Gustav suffers. Unfortunately, it's neither titillating nor interesting despite the players. **99m/C VHS, DVD, Sarah Wynter, Jonathan Pryce, Vincent Perez, Simon Verhoeven, August Schmolzer, Gregor Seberg, Dagmar Schwarz, Wolfgang Hubsch, Johannes Silberschneider; D:** Bruce Beresford; **W:** Marilyn Levy; **C:** Peter James; **M:** Stephen Endelman.

Bride

The Bride with White Hair 🦴🦴 *Jiang-Hu: Between Love and Glory* 1993 Operatic martial arts fable based on a novel by Leung Yu-Sang. A young warrior revives a beautiful witch (also a champion warrior) who was killed by jealous Siamese twins. Now the duo, who have fallen in love, must battle the evil twins who rule the corrupt Mo Dynasty. Available dubbed or in Chinese with subtitles. 92m/C VHS, DVD. HK Leslie Cheung, Brigitte Lin, Nam Kilying, Frances Ng, Elaine Lui; D: Ronny Yu; W: Ronny Yu, David Wu, Lan Kei-Tou, Tseng Pik-Yin; C: Peter Pau; M: Richard Yuen.

The Bride with White Hair 2 🦴🦴 *Jiang-Hu: Between Love and Glory 2* 1993 The magic saga continues with the massacre of the followers of the Eight Lineages. Powerful and obsessed with vengeance, the Bride can only be stopped by the one man who loves her. Chinese with subtitles or dubbed. 80m/C VHS, DVD. HK Brigitte Lin, Leslie Cheung, Christy Chung; D: David Wu, Ronny Yu; W: David Wu.

The Bride Wore Black 🦴🦴🦴 *La Mariee Etait en Noir* 1968 Truffaut's homage to Hitchcock, complete with Bernard Herrmann score. Young bride Julie (Moreau) exacts brutal revenge on the five men who accidentally killed her husband on the steps of the church on their wedding day. Adapted from a novel by Cornell Woolrich. 107m/C VHS, DVD. FR Jeanne Moreau, Claude Rich, Jean-Claude Brialy, Michel Bouquet, Michael (Michel) Lonsdale, Charles Denner, Daniel Boulanger; D: Francois Truffaut; W: Francois Truffaut, Jean-Louis Richard; C: Raoul Coutard; M: Bernard Herrmann.

The Bride Wore Red 🦴🦴 1937 Crawford stars as a cabaret singer who masquerades as a socialite in an attempt to break into the upper crust. When a wealthy aristocrat invites her to spend two weeks at a posh resort in Tyrol, Crawford plays her part to the hilt, managing to charm both a rich gentleman and the village postman. Typical "love conquers all" melodrama. 103m/B VHS. Joan Crawford, Franchot Tone, Robert Young, Billie Burke, Reginald Owen, Lynne Carver, George Zucco; D: Dorothy Arzner; M: George J. Folsey.

Brides of Christ 🦴🦴🦴½ 1991 Set in the Australian Santo Spirito Convent during the Vatican II upheaval of the 1960s. Explores the tensions between old and new religious ideas by focusing on novices, older nuns, and the Reverend Mother of the convent as they try to cope with a changing world. TV miniseries. 300m/C VHS, DVD. Brenda Fricker, Sandy Gore, Josephine Byrnes, Lisa Hensley, Naomi Watts, Kym Wilson, Melissa Thomas; D: Ken Cameron; W: John Alsop, Sue Smith.

Brides of the Beast woof! *Brides of Blood; Grave Desires; Island of the Living Horror* 1968 Filipino radiation monsters get their jollies by eating beautiful young naked women. Newly arrived research scientist and his bride oppose this custom. First in a series of "Blood Island" horrors. 85m/B VHS, DVD. PH John Ashley, Kent Taylor, Beverly (Hills) Powers, Eva Darren, Mario Montenegro; D: Eddie Romero, Gerardo (Gerry) De Leon.

Brideshead Revisited 🦴🦴🦴 1981 The acclaimed British miniseries based on the Evelyn Waugh classic about an Edwardian young man who falls under the spell of a wealthy aristocratic family and struggles to retain his integrity and values. On six tapes. 540m/C VHS, DVD. GB Jeremy Irons, Anthony Andrews, Diana Quick, Laurence Olivier, John Gielgud, Claire Bloom, Stephane Audran, Mona Washbourne, John Le Mesurier, Charles Keating; D: Charles Sturridge, Michael Lindsay-Hogg; M: Geoffrey Burgon. TV

The Bridesmaid 🦴🦴 *La Demoiselle d'Honneur* 2004 Creepy thriller based on a novel by Ruth Rendell. Hard-working Philippe (Magimel) lives with his flirtatious mother Christine (Clement) and his two younger siblings. At his sister's wedding, he meets sultry bridesmaid Senta (Smet), who likes a lot of drama in her life. She easily seduces the uptight Philippe, who turns out to have some dark inner urges and continually tests the limits of his love. Then Senta asks, would he kill for her? French with subtitles. 111m/C DVD. FR Benoit Magimel, Laura Smet, Aurore Clement, Bernard Le Coq, Solene Bouten, Anna Mihalcea, Michel Duchaussoy, Eric Seigne, Pierre-Francois Dumeniaud; D: Claude Chabrol; W: Claude Chabrol, Pierre Leccia; C: Eduardo Serra; M: Matthieu Chabrol.

The Bridge 🦴🦴 *Die Brucke* 1959 In 1945, two days before the end of WWII, seven German schoolboys are drafted to defend an unimportant bridge from American tanks. Emotional anti-war film based on the autobiographical novel of Manfred Gregor. German with subtitles. 102m/B VHS, DVD. GE Fritz Wepper, Volker Bohnet, Franz Glaubrecht, Karl Michael Balzer, Gunther Hoffman, Michael Hinz, Cordula Trantow, Wolfgang Stumpf, Volker Lechtenbrink, Gunter Pfitzmann, Edith Schultze-Westrum, Ruth Hausmeister, Eva Vaitl; D: Bernhard Wicki; W: Bernhard Wicki, Michael Mansfield, Karl-Wilhelm Vivier; C: Gerd Von Bonen; M: Hans-Martin Majewski.

The Bridge 🦴🦴🦴 2000 In 1963, Mira (Bouquet) loves to go to the movies to watch "Jules et Jim" and "West Side Story." She has a 15-year-old son, but that doesn't stop her from entering into an affair with a visiting engineer (Berling) who's in her little town to build a bridge. Director Depardieu plays her husband, a builder who's working on the bridge. It's precisely the sort of material that the French handle so deftly and Depardieu proves that he's a competent craftsman behind the camera. 92m/C DVD. FR Carole Bouquet, Gerard Depardieu, Charles Berling; D: Frederic Auburtin, Gerard Depardieu; W: Francois Bupeyron; C: Pascal Ridao; M: Frederic Auburtin.

The Bridge at Remagen 🦴🦴½ 1969 (PG) Based on the true story of allied attempts to capture a vital bridge before retreating German troops destroy it. For war-film buffs. 115m/C VHS, DVD. George Segal, Robert Vaughn, Ben Gazzara, Bradford Dillman, E.G. Marshall; D: John Guillermin; W: William Roberts; C: Stanley Cortez; M: Elmer Bernstein. VIDEO

Bridge of Dragons 🦴🦴 1999 (R) Dictator Tagawa, having murdered the kingdom's rightful ruler, plots to marry the country's princess (Shane) to consolidate his power. But when the princess escapes to join the rebel forces, human killing machine Lundgren is sent to retrieve her. Only he decides to fight with her instead. Lots of explosions and high-tech gadgets. 91m/C VHS, DVD. Dolph Lundgren, Cary-Hiroyuki Tagawa, Gary Hudson, Scott Schwartz, Rachel Shane; D: Isaac Florentine; W: Carlton Holder; C: Yossi Wein; M: Stephen (Steve) Edwards.

The Bridge of San Luis Rey 🦴🦴🦴 1944 A priest investigates the famous bridge collapse in Lima, Peru that left five people dead. Based upon the novel by Thornton Wilder. 89m/B VHS, DVD. Lynn Bari, Francis Lederer, Louis Calhern, Akim Tamiroff, Donald Woods, Alla Nazimova, Blanche Yurka; D: Rowland V. Lee; W: Howard Estabrook, Herman Weissman; C: John Boyle; M: Dimitri Tiomkin.

The Bridge of San Luis Rey 🦴🦴 2005 (PG) Thornton Wilder's moving, Pulitzer Prize-winning 1928 novel is disastrously adapted by director McGluckian, with stellar actors generally miscast in a stuffy costume drama. In colonial Peru in the early 18th century, Franciscan missionary Brother Juniper (Byrne) has been investigating five travelers who plunged to their deaths when the titular bridge collapsed. He's trying to determine if there's some common denominator to their fate and delivers his conclusions to a church court presided over by the Archbishop of Lima (De Niro). Flashbacks depict the lives of the victims and their survivors and the abrupt shifts in scene and character make for confusion. 120m/C DVD. SP GB FR Robert De Niro, Kathy Bates, Gabriel Byrne, Geraldine Chaplin, Emilie Dequenne, Adriana Dominguez, Harvey Keitel, Pilar Lopez de Ayala, Jim Lynch, Mark Polish, Michael Polish; D: Mary McGuckian; C: Javier Aguirresarobe; M: Lalo Schifrin.

The Bridge on the River Kwai 🦴🦴🦴🦴 1957 Award-winning adaptation of the Pierre Bouelle novel about the battle of wills between a Japanese POW camp commander and a British colonel over the construction of a rail bridge, and the parallel efforts to destroy it. Holden's role was originally cast for Cary Grant. Memorable too for whistling "Colonel Bogey March." Because the writers were blacklisted, Bouelle (who spoke no English) was originally credited as the screenwriter. 161m/C VHS, DVD, Blu-ray Disc. GB William Holden, Alec Guinness, Jack Hawkins, Sessue Hayakawa, James Donald, Geoffrey Horne, Andre Morell, Ann Sears, Peter Williams, John Boxer, Percy Herbert, Harold Goodwin, Henry Okawa, Keiichiro Katsumoto, M.R.B. Chakrabandhu; D: David Lean; W: Carl Foreman, Michael Wilson; C: Jack Hildyard; M: Malcolm Arnold. Oscars '57: Actor (Guinness), Adapt. Screenplay, Cinematog., Director (Lean), Film Editing, Picture, Orig. Song Score and/or Adapt.; AFI '98: Top 100; British Acad. '57: Actor (Guinness), Film, Screenplay; Directors Guild '57: Director (Lean); Golden Globes '58: Actor—Drama (Guinness), Director (Lean), Film—Drama; Natl. Bd. of Review '57: Actor (Guinness), Director (Lean), Support. Actor (Hayakawa), Natl. Film Reg. '97:; N.Y. Film Critics '57: Actor (Guinness), Director (Lean), Film.

Bridge to Hell 🦴½ 1987 A group of allied P.O.W.s try to make their way to the American front during WWII in Yugoslavia. A heavily guarded bridge occupied by Nazi troops stands between them and freedom. A special introduction by Michael Dudikoff doing martial arts. 94m/C VHS. Jeff Connors, Francis Ferre, Andy Forrest, Paky Valente; D: Umberto Lenzi.

The Bridge to Nowhere 🦴🦴 1986 Five city kids go hunting and backpacking in the New Zealand wilderness, only to be hunted by a maniacal backwoodsman. 82m/C VHS. NZ Bruno Lawrence, Alison Routledge, Margaret Umbers, Philip Gordon; D: Ian Mune.

Bridge to Silence 🦴🦴 1989 A young hearing-impaired mother's life begins to crumble following the death of her husband in a car crash. Her mother tries to get custody of her daughter and a friend applies romantic pressure. Melodrama features Matlin in her first TV speaking role. 95m/C VHS. Marlee Matlin, Lee Remick, Josef Sommer, Michael O'Keefe, Allison Silva, Candice Becker; D: Karen Arthur. TV

Bridge to Terabithia 🦴🦴½ 2007 (PG) Katherine Paterson's popular 1977 novel isn't so much about a fantasy world (the film's CGI is limited) as it is about friendship and imagination. Jess (Hutcherson) is a bullied 10-year-old misfit with four sisters and a stern dad (Patrick). Adventurous new neighbor Leslie (Robb) turns out to be Jess' imaginative kindred soul and, between his drawings and her stories, they populate the nearby woods with their own world. For those not familiar with the book, beware—there's tragedy looming that will affect both kids and adults. 94m/C DVD, Blu-ray Disc. US Josh Hutcherson, AnnaSophia Robb, Robert Patrick, Zooey Deschanel, Bailey Madison, Kate Butler, Lauren Clinton; D: Gabor Csupo; W: Jeff Stockwell, David Paterson; C: Michael Chapman; M: Aaron Zigman.

A Bridge Too Far 🦴🦴 1977 (PG) A meticulous re-creation of one of the most disastrous battles of WWII, the Allied defeat at Arnhem in 1944. Misinformation, adverse conditions, and overconfidence combined to prevent the Allies from capturing six German border towns that connected Holland to the German border. 175m/C VHS, DVD. GB Sean Connery, Robert Redford, James Caan, Michael Caine, Elliott Gould, Gene Hackman, Laurence Olivier, Ryan O'Neal, Liv Ullmann, Dirk Bogarde, Hardy Kruger, Arthur Hill, Edward Fox, Anthony Hopkins, Maximilian Schell, Denholm Elliott, Wolfgang Preiss, Nicholas (Nick) Campbell, Christopher Good, John Ratzenberger, Colin Farrell; D: Richard Attenborough; W: William Goldman; C: Geoffrey Unsworth; M: John Addison. British Acad. '77: Support. Actor (Fox); Natl. Soc. Film Critics '77: Support. Actor (Fox).

The Bridges at Toko-Ri 🦴🦴🦴½ 1955 Based on the James A. Michener novel, the rousing war-epic about a lawyer being summoned by the Navy to fly bombing missions during the Korean War. A powerful anti-war statement. 103m/C VHS, DVD. William Holden, Grace Kelly, Fredric March, Mickey Rooney, Robert Strauss, Earl Holliman, Keiko Awaji, Charles McGraw, Richard Shannon, Willis Bouchey; D: Mark Robson; W: Valentine Davies; C: Loyal Griggs; M: Lyn Murray.

The Bridges of Madison County 🦴🦴🦴 1995 (PG-13) Robert Kincaid (Eastwood) is on assignment in 1965 Iowa to photograph Madison County's scenic covered bridges. Only problem is he gets lost and stops for directions at Francesca Johnson's (Streep) farmhouse. There's an immediate attraction between the repressed Italian war-bride-turned-farm-wife and the charismatic world traveler, which they act on in four short days. Much of the treacle from Robert James Waller's novel has been fortunately abandoned but the mature romance remains. 64-year-old Eastwood exudes low-key sexiness while Streep (with a light Italian accent) is all earthy warmth. Fans of both book and stars should be pleased, though the leisurely paced film takes too long to get started. 135m/C VHS, DVD. Clint Eastwood, Meryl Streep, Victor Slezak, Annie Corley, Jim Haynie; D: Clint Eastwood; W: Richard LaGravenese; C: Jack N. Green; M: Lennie Niehaus.

Bridget Jones: The Edge of Reason 🦴🦴½ 2004 (R) The film sequel (loosely based on Fielding's book sequel) tries too hard to be endearingly kooky, but can't go that far wrong with Zellweger, who once again packed on the pounds to play the plumpish London singleton. When we last saw Bridget, she had finally chosen steady lawyer Mark Darcy (Firth), but her insecurities get the better of her. She trashes their relationship and is soon once-again with sly cad Daniel (Grant), now the host of a TV travel show. This leads Bridget and Daniel to Thailand where, in an unfortunate plot contrivance, Bridget is thrown into a Thai jail. This only serves to teach Bridget that she really loves Mark. Zellweger is subjected to many pratfalls, which she handles with good spirit, and all the supporting roles are on the money. 108m/C VHS, DVD. US Renee Zellweger, Hugh Grant, Colin Firth, Jim Broadbent, Gemma Jones, Jacinda Barrett, James Callis, Shirley Henderson, Sally Phillips, Neil Pearson, Jessica Stevenson, Paul Nicholls; D: Beeban Kidron; W: Andrew Davies, Helen Fielding, Richard Curtis, Adam Brooks; C: Adrian Biddle; M: Harry Gregson-Williams.

Bridget Jones's Diary 🦴🦴🦴 2001 (R) So you've got this petite, sunny-faced Texan playing a "singleton" Brit who drinks and smokes and consumes too many calories and has man trouble and is the beloved heroine of Helen Fielding's novel. No wonder the English got a little upset—not, as it turns out, for any good reason since Zellweger is fab as Bridget tries to take control of her chaotic life. Of course having a romp with your caddish, clever boss Daniel Cleaver (Grant) and ignoring the handsome but apparently stuffy Mark Darcy (Firth) isn't a good start but Bridget—bless her—does try. The movie is truncated (to the detriment of Bridget's friendships) but it still works. 115m/C VHS, DVD. Renee Zellweger, Hugh Grant, Colin Firth, Gemma Jones, Jim Broadbent, Embeth Davidtz, Shirley Henderson, James Callis, Sally Phillips, Lisa Barbuscia; D: Sharon Maguire; W: Richard Curtis, Andrew Davies, Helen Fielding; C: Stuart Dryburgh; M: Patrick Doyle.

Brief Encounter 🦴🦴🦴 1946 Based on Noel Coward's "Still Life" from "Tonight at 8:30," two middle-aged, middle-class people become involved in a short and bittersweet romance in WWII England. Intensely romantic, underscored with Rachmaninoff's Second Piano Concerto. 86m/B VHS, DVD. GB Celia Johnson, Trevor Howard, Stanley Holloway, Cyril Raymond, Joyce Carey, Everley Gregg, Margaret Barton,

Dennis Harkin, Valentine Dyall, Marjorie Mars, Irene Handl; **D:** David Lean; **W:** Noel Coward, David Lean, Ronald Neame, Anthony Havelock-Allan; **C:** Robert Krasker. N.Y. Film Critics '46: Actress (Johnson).

A Brief History of Time 1992 (G) A stunning documentary about physicist Stephen Hawking, the author of the popular book "Brief History of Time." Crippled by Lou Gehrig's Disease, Hawking narrates the film in the computer-synthesized voice he uses to speak. Interviews with family, friends, and colleagues bring Hawking's scientific theories to light. 85m/C VHS. Stephen Hawking; **C:** Errol Morris; **W:** Stephen Hawking; **C:** John Bailey; **M:** Philip Glass. Sundance '92: Filmmakers Trophy.

The Brig 1964 A film by Jonas Mekas documenting the Living Theatre's infamous performance of Kenneth H. Brown's experimental play. Designed 65m/B VHS. Adolfas Mekas, Jim Anderson, Warren Finnerty, Henry Howard, Tom Lillard, James Tiroff, Gene Lipton; **D:** John Mekas.

Brigadoon 1954 The story of a magical, 18th century Scottish village which awakens once every 100 years and the two modern-day vacationers who stumble upon it. Main highlight is the Lerner and Loewe score. I'll Go Home With Bonnie Jean; Wedding Dance; From This Day On; Heather on the Hill; Waitin' For My Dearie; Once in the Highlands. 108m/C VHS, DVD. Gene Kelly, Van Johnson, Cyd Charisse; **D:** Vincente Minnelli; **W:** Alan Jay Lerner; **C:** Joseph Ruttenberg; **M:** Alan Jay Lerner, Frederick Loewe.

Brigham City 2001 (PG-13) Skillful murder-mystery set in the fictitious Brigham City, Utah. The townspeople mostly know each other and most are also members of the Mormon Church. Sheriff Wes Clayton (Dutcher) and his deputy Terry's (Brown) duties are usually mundane—until they discover the mutilated body of a young female tourist at an abandoned homestead. Clayton is willing to defer to the FBI but then a second body is discovered and the media vultures descend on the formerly quiet community as their faith is all put to an unexpected test. 115m/C VHS, DVD. Richard Dutcher, Wilford Brimley, Matthew A. Brown, Carrie Morgan, John Enos, Tayva Patch; **D:** Richard Dutcher; **W:** Richard Dutcher.

Brigham Young: Frontiersman 1940 Somewhat interesting story about the pioneering Mormons and their founding of Salt Lake City. Under the leadership of Brigham Young (Jagger), Brian Donlevy, John Carradine, Jane Darwell, Mary Astor, Vincent Price, Willard Robertson, Moroni Olsen, Marc Lawrence, Selmer Jackson, Stanley Andrews; **D:** Henry Hathaway; **W:** Lamar Trotti, Ann E. Todd; **C:** Arthur C. Miller; **M:** Cyril Mockridge, Alfred Newman.

Bright Angel 1991 (R) Road movie pairs an unconventional team: George wants to visit his aunt to see if she's heard from his mother who ran off with another man; Lucy is a free-spirit trying to free her brother from jail. Good performances by Mulroney, Taylor, & Pullman. Ford adapted two of his short stories, "Children" and "Great Falls" for the gritty and uncompromising script of this modern west. 94m/C VHS. Dermot Mulroney, Lili Taylor, Sam Shepard, Valerie Perrine, Burt Young, Bill Pullman, Benjamin Bratt, Mary Kay Place, Delroy Lindo, Kevin Tighe, Sheila McCarthy; **D:** Michael Fields; **W:** Richard Ford; **M:** Christopher Young.

Bright Eyes 1934 (PG) Shirley (Temple) lives with her widowed mother Mary (Wilson), who works as a maid for the snobbish Smythe family, where only wealthy, crotchety Uncle Ned (Sellon) befriends the cutie. His niece Adele (Allen) is engaged to Shirley's godfather, flyboy Loop Merritt (Dunn), who wants the tyke to live with him when her mom is killed. But Uncle Ned also wants to adopt her and there's a battle over custody. Shirley warbles "On the Good Ship Lollipop" in her usual winsome way. 84m/B VHS. Shirley Temple, James Dunn, Lois Wilson, Jane Withers, Judith Allen, Jane Darwell, Charles Sellon; **D:** David Butler; **W:** David Butler, Edwin Burke, William Conselman; **C:** Arthur C. Miller.

Bright Future 2003 Mamoru and Yuji are best friends, co-workers, and roommates in an existential... **C:** Tatsuya Fuji, Joe Odagiri, Marumi Shiraishi; **D:** Kiyoshi Kurosawa; **W:** Kiyoshi Kurosawa; **C:** Takahide Shibanushi; **M:** Pacific 231.

Bright Lights, Big City 1988 (R) Based on Jay McInerney's popular novel. Fox plays a contemporary yuppie working in Manhattan as a magazine journalist. As his world begins to fall apart, he embarks on an endless cycle of drugs and nightlife. Fox is poorly cast, and his character is hard to care for as he becomes more and more dissolute. Although McInerney wrote his own screenplay, the intellectual abstractness of the novel can't be captured on film. 110m/C VHS, DVD. Michael J. Fox, Kiefer Sutherland, Phoebe Cates, Frances Sternhagen, Swoosie Kurtz, Tracy Pollan, Jason Robards Jr., John Houseman, Dianne Wiest, Charlie Schlatter, William Hickey; **D:** James Bridges; **C:** Gordon Willis.

A Bright Shining Lie 1998 (R) Based on Neil Sheehan's 1988 Pulitzer Prize-winning book, which chronicles the Vietnam War as seen through the eyes of Lt. Col. John Paul Vann (Paxton). The brash Vann arrived as a military advisor to the Vietnamese Army in 1962 and eventually left that post to become part of the State Department's Civilian Aid Program, where he exposed falsified battle reports and other deceptions to newsmen and other officers. The complex and controversial Vann was killed in a chopper crash in 1972. 118m/C VHS, DVD. Bill Paxton, Amy Madigan, Vivian Wu, Robert John Burke, James Rebhorn, Ed Lauter, Harve Presnell; **D:** Terry George; **W:** Terry George; **C:** Jack Conroy; **M:** Gary Chang. CABLE

Bright Young Things 2003 (R) Actor/director/writer Stephen Fry tackles literary satire with his adaptation of Evelyn Waugh's 1930 novel, "Vile Bodies." And if not precisely vile, those bodies are wicked indeed as seen through the everyman eyes of Adam (Moore), a poor aspiring novelist-turned-gossip columnist who wishes to marry superficial party girl Nina (Mortimer). Fry breezily tackles the jaded, flapper milieu of upper-class London between the wars that lends itself to glitter and eccentricity, embodied by feckless social butterflies (Woolgar) and drug-taking peers (the gentlemanly 94-year-old Sir John Mills doing a little coke in a can-can. 106m/C DVD. Emily Mortimer, James McAvoy, Michael Sheen, David Tennant, Fenella Woolgar, Dan Aykroyd, Jim Broadbent, Simon Callow, Julia McKenzie, Peter O'Toole, Stephen Campbell Moore; **D:** Stephen Fry; **W:** Stephen Fry; **C:** Henry Braham; **M:** Anne Dudley.

Brimstone & Treacle 1982 (R) Weird, obsessive psychodrama in which a young rogue (who may or may not be an actual agent of the Devil) infiltrates the home of a staid British family caring for their comatose adult daughter. 85m/C VHS, DVD. GB Sting, Denholm Elliott, Joan Plowright, Suzanna Hamilton; **D:** Richard Loncraine; **W:** Dennis Potter. Montreal World Film Fest. '82: Film.

Brighton Beach Memoirs 1986 (PG-13) The film adaptation of the popular (and semiautobiographical) Neil Simon play. Poignant comedy/drama about a young Jewish boy's coming of age in Depression-era Brooklyn. Followed by "Biloxi Blues" and "Broadway Bound." 108m/C VHS. Blythe Danner, Bob (Robert) Disty, Judith Ivey, Jonathan Silverman, Brian Dillinger, Stacey Glick, Lisa Waltz, Jason Alexander; **D:** Gene Saks; **W:** Neil Simon; **C:** John Bailey; **M:** Michael Small.

Brighton Rock Young Scarface 1947 Sterling performances highlight this seamy look at the British underworld. Attenborough is Pinkie Brown, a small-time hood who ends up committing murder. He manipulates a waitress to get himself off the hook, but things don't go exactly as he plans. Based on the novel by Graham Greene. 92m/B VHS. Richard Attenborough, Hermione Baddeley, William Hartnell, Carol Marsh, Nigel Stock, Wylie Watson, Alan Wheatley, George Carney, Reginald Purdell; **D:** John Boulting; **W:** Graham Greene.

Brighton Strangler 1945 An actor who plays a murderer assumes the role of the strangler after suffering from a concussion. Decent psychodrama. 67m/B VHS. John Loder, June Duprez, Miles Mander; **D:** Max Nossek.

Brighty of the Grand Canyon 1967 The spunky donkey Brighty roams across the Grand Canyon in search of adventure. He finds friendship with a gold-digging old prospector. 89m/C VHS, DVD. Joseph Cotten, Pat Conway, Dick Foran, Karl Swenson; **D:** Norman Foster.

A Brilliant Disguise 1993 (R) Sportswriter gets involved with an artist who turns out to have multiple personality disorder and a sinister psychiatrist. Then his friends start to turn up dead but things aren't exactly what they seem. 97m/C VHS. Lysette Anthony, Anthony John (Tony) Denison, Corbin Bernsen, Gregory McKinney, Robert (Bobby Ray) Shafer; **D:** Nick Vallelonga.

Brilliant Lies 1996 Susy Connor (Gia Carides) has brought an official complaint of sexual harassment against former boss Gary Fitzgerald (LaPaglia), who denies the charge. She claims her sister Katie (Zoe Carides) will substantiate her story, which she will even though Katie knows it's a lie. As a matter of fact, Susy's a consummate liar telling the truth. Fine performances from the Carides sisters, as well as LaPaglia (who's married to Gia) and Barrett, who plays the self-pitying Connor patriarch. Adapted from the play by David Williamson. 93m/C VHS. AU Gia Carides, Anthony LaPaglia, Zoe Carides, Ray Barrett, Michael Veitch, Catherine Wilkin, Grant Tilly; **D:** Richard Franklin; **W:** Richard Franklin, Peter Fitzpatrick; **C:** Geoff Burton; **M:** Nerida Tyson-Chew.

Bring It On 2000 (PG-13) Bring on the guilty pleasure. Equal parts satire, exploitation and earnest (if not totally successful) teen flick, the film follows squeaky-clean, peppy cheerleader Torrance (Dunst) as she becomes captain of the Rancho Carne High Toros cheer squad, who soon after discovers her squad's championship moves have been lifted from another source, the East Compton High Clovers. All of this culminates in a showdown between the two squads, while interspersed throughout are standard teenage goings-on. No gem, by any means, but fun if you're in the mood (or spirit). But be advised: probably too raunchy for its intended young adult audience. 98m/C VHS, DVD. Kirsten Dunst, Eliza Dushku, Jesse Bradford, Gabrielle Union, Clare Kramer, Nicole Bilderback, Tsianina Joelson, Riri Bell, Ian Roberts, Richard Hillman, Lindsay Sloane, Cody McManis; **D:** Peyton Reed; **W:** Jessica Bendinger; **C:** Shawn Maurer; **M:** Christophe Beck.

Bring It On Again 2003 (PG-13) College freshman Whittier (Judson-Yager) proves to be a cheerleading rival that head pom-girl Tina (Turner) won't tolerate. So when Whittier is cut from the squad, she decides to form a new team and challenge the national... 90m/C VHS, DVD. Anne Judson-Yager, Bree Turner, Richard Lee Jackson, Faune A. Chambers, Kevin Cooney, Bryce Johnson; **D:** Damon Santostefano; **W:** Claudio Graziosi; **C:** Richard Crudo; **M:** Paul Haslinger. VIDEO

Bring It On: All or Nothing 2006 (PG-13) The plot hardly matters as long as the cheer routines astonish (which they do). Britney (Panettiere) was the cheer captain at her rich "burb school but is just another wannabe after a move to a more urban setting. But she wins over leader Camille (Knowles-Smith) with some new routines and they're determined to get back into the finals. 90m/C DVD. Hayden Panettiere, Jake McClernan, Solange Knowles-Smith, Gus Carr, Marcy Rylan; **D:** Steve Rash; **W:** Alyson Fouse. VIDEO

Bring It On: In It to Win 2007 (PG-13) It's the battle of the coastal babes as SoCal Carson (Benson) and Big Apple Brooke (Scerbo) and their cheer squads meet up at the national championships. Carson falls for Penn (Copon), who happens to be a brawl team, and Brooke challenges Carson to a cheer-off. This leads to a brawl and both teams are disqualified. 112m/C VHS, DVD. Ashley Benson, Cassie Scerbo, Michael Copon, Jennifer Tisdale, Kierstin Koppel, Noe Arciniega; **D:** Steve Rash; **W:** Alyson Fouse. VIDEO

Bring Me the Head of Alfredo Garcia 1974 (R) Peckinpah faters... 112m/C VHS, DVD. Warren Oates, Isela Vega, Gig Young, Robert Webber, Helmut Dantine, Emilio Fernandez, Kris Kristofferson; **D:** Sam Peckinpah; **W:** Gordon Dawson, Sam Peckinpah; **C:** Alex Phillips Jr.; **M:** Jerry Fielding.

Bringing Down the House 2003 (PG-13) Straitlaced divorced lawyer Martin makes an online date and winds up with parolee Queen Latifah, who proceeds to turn his life upside-down in her quest to get him to help her prove her innocence. Moments of inspired comedy have everything to do with the talents of Martin and Latifah and little to do with script or direction. Levy makes the most of this sidekick role. May play better on the small screen. 105m/C VHS, DVD. US Steve Martin, Queen Latifah, Eugene Levy, Jean Smart, Angus T. Jones, Kimberly J. Brown, Joan Plowright, Missi Pyle, Steve Harris, Michael Rosenbaum, Betty White; **D:** Adam Shankman; **W:** Jason Filardi; **C:** Julio Macat; **M:** Lalo Schifrin.

Bringing Out the Dead 1999 (R) Cage hasn't looked this haggard since his boozehound role in "Leaving Las Vegas," which could be considered a dress rehearsal for his turn as burnt-out New York City paramedic Frank Pierce. Aided by Scorsese's kinetic filmmaking style, Schrader's on-tempo script, and revved up performances by Rhames and Sizemore as Pierce's partners, movie successfully conveys the day-to-day stress of emergency units. Unfortunately, Cage's sleepwalking character is a bore, and a lack of chemistry with real-life spouse Arquette as Pierce's singular ray of hope only makes you yearn for Scorsese's similarly themed masterpiece "Taxi Driver." Based on the novel by Joe Connelly. 120m/C VHS, DVD. Jon Arzalluns, Nicolas Cage, John Goodman, Tom Sizemore, Ving Rhames, Patricia Arquette, Marc Anthony, Mary Beth Hurt, Clifford Curtis, Nestor Serrano, Aida Turturro, Afemo Omilami, Arthur J. Nascarelli, Cynthia Roman, Cullen Oliver Johnson; **D:** Martin Scorsese; **W:** Paul Schrader; **C:** Robert Richardson; **M:** Elmer Bernstein.

Bringing Up Baby 1938 The quintessential screwball comedy, featuring Hepburn as a giddy socialite on the unwitting object of her affections. One ridiculous situation after another adds up to high speed fun. Hepburn looks lovely, the supporting actors are fine in form, and director Hawks manages the perfect balance of control and mayhem. From a story by Hagar Wilde, who helped Nichols with the screenplay. Also available in a colorized version. **103m/B VHS, DVD.** Katharine Hepburn, Cary Grant, May Robson, Charlie Ruggles, Walter Catlett, Fritz Feld, Jonathan Hale, Barry Fitzgerald, Ward Bond; **D:** Howard Hawks; **W:** Dudley Nichols; **C:** Russell Metty. AFI '98: Top 100, Natl. Film Reg. '90.

Brink ♫♫½ **1998** Andy Brinker leads of group of in-line skaters who are dedicated to the sport. But Andy also needs money to help out his family and when a rival team offers him cash to join them on the circuit, Andy's forced into a hard choice. **88m/C VHS.** CABLE

Brink of Life ♫♫½ *Nara Livet* **1957** Three pregnant women in a hospital maternity ward await the impending births with mixed feelings. Early Bergman; in Swedish with English subtitles. **82m/B VHS.** *SW* Eva Dahlbeck, Bibi Andersson, Ingrid Thulin, Barbo Ornas, Max von Sydow, Erland Josephson, Gunnar Sjöberg; **D:** Ingmar Bergman. Cannes '58: Actress (Andersson), Actress (Thulin), Director (Bergman).

Brink's Job ♫♫♫ **1978 (PG)** Recreates the "crime of the century," Tony Pino's heist of $2.7 million from a Brink's truck. The action picks up five days before the statute of limitations is about to run out. **103m/C VHS.** Peter Falk, Peter Boyle, Warren Oates, Gena Rowlands, Paul Sorvino, Sheldon Leonard, Allen (Goorwitz) Garfield; **D:** William Friedkin; **W:** Walon Green; **M:** Richard Rodney Bennett.

Britannia Hospital ♫♫½ **1982** (R) This is a portrait of a hospital at its most chaotic: the staff threatens to strike, demonstrators surround the hospital, a nosey BBC reporter pursues an anxious professor, and the eagerly anticipated royal visit degenerates into a total shambles. **111m/C VHS, DVD.** *GB* Malcolm McDowell, Leonard Rossiter, Graham Crowden, Joan Plowright, Mark Hamill, Alan Bates, Dave Atkins, Marsha A. Hunt; **D:** Lindsay Anderson; **W:** David Sherwin; **C:** Mike Flash; **M:** Alan Price.

Britannic ♫♫ **1999** The Britannic, the Titanic's sister ship, was built as a luxury liner but when WWI began the ship was turned into a hospital transport after its launch in 1914. The ship did sink off the Greek coast in 1916 (probably due to a torpedo or mine) but the filmmakers haven't let any other facts of the story stand in the way of this poor man's "Titanic" with its class difference romance and other cliches. **96m/C VHS, DVD.** Edward Atterton, Jacqueline Bisset, John Rhys-Davies, Bruce Payne, Amanda Ryan, Ben Daniels; **D:** Brian Trenchard-Smith; **W:** Brian Trenchard-Smith, Brett Thompson, Dennis A. Pratt; **C:** Ivan Strasburg; **M:** Alan Parker. CABLE

British Intelligence ♫½ **1940** Silly American-made film about British espionage. Boris Karloff plays a butler (who is also a spy) trapped by an agent who visits the home of a British bureaucrat. Half-baked story that doesn't hold up. **62m/B VHS, DVD.** Boris Karloff, Margaret Lindsay, Maris Wrixon, Holmes Herbert, Leonard Mudie, Bruce Lester; **D:** Terry Morse.

Brittanic ♫♫♫ **2000** Talk about your lousy luck! The Britannic is the sister ocean liner to the infamous Titanic and guess what happens? Yes, indeedy, it sinks as well. But this one was being used as a hospital ship in WWI. **96m/C VHS, DVD.** Jacqueline Bisset, Edward Atterton, Amanda Ryan, Bruce Payne, John Rhys-Davies; **D:** Brian Trenchard-Smith. CABLE

A Brivele der Mamen ♫♫♫ *A Letter to Mother; A Letter to Mama* **1938** A Jewish mother does her best to hold her fragile family together, in spite of the ravages of war and poverty. Her travails take her and her family from the Polish Ukraine to New York City. In Yiddish with English subtitles. **90m/C VHS.** *PL* Berta Gersten, Lucy Gehrman, Misha Gehrman, Edmund Zayenda; **D:** Joseph Green.

Broadcast Bombshells ♫♫ **1995 (R)** TV station WSEX has a station manager who'll do anything to improve ratings, an ambitious associate producer after the weather girl's job, a sexaholic sportscaster, and lots of chaos involving a mad bomber. The barely there plot is just the excuse for a considerable display of T&A anyway. Also available unrated. **80m/C VHS, DVD.** Amy Lynn Baxter, Debbie Rochon, John Richardson, Elizabeth Heyman, Joseph Pallister; **D:** Ernest G. Sauer.

Broadcast News ♫♫♫½ **1987** (R) The acclaimed, witty analysis of network news shows, dealing with the three-way romance between a driven career-woman romance, an ace nebbish reporter and a brainless, popular on-screen anchorman. Incisive and funny, though often simply idealistic. **132m/C VHS, DVD.** William Hurt, Albert Brooks, Holly Hunter, Jack Nicholson, Joan Cusack, Robert Prosky, Lois Chiles, John Cusack, Gennie James; **D:** James L. Brooks; **W:** James L. Brooks; **C:** Michael Ballhaus; **M:** Bill Conti, Michael Gore. L.A. Film Critics '87: Actress (Hunter); Natl. Bd. of Review '87: Actress (Hunter); N.Y. Film Critics '87: Actress (Hunter), Director (Brooks), Film, Screenplay.

Broadway Bill ♫♫♫ *Strictly Confidential* **1934** A man decides to abandon his nagging wife and his in-laws, whose business for the questionable pleasures of owning a racehorse known as Broadway Bill. This racetrack comedy was also remade by Frank Capra in 1951 as "Riding High." **90m/C VHS, DVD.** Warner Baxter, Myrna Loy, Walter Connolly, Helen Vinson, Margaret Hamilton, Frankie Darro; **D:** Frank Capra.

Broadway Bound ♫♫½ *Neil Simon's Broadway Bound* **1992** The final film in Simon's trilogy (preceded by "Brighton Beach Memoirs" and "Biloxi Blues"), this playwright's after ego, Eugene Morris Jerome, is ready to leave Brooklyn for good, hoping to make it as a comedy writer for a radio show. Meanwhile, his mother decides what to do about his unfaithful father. **90m/C VHS.** Jonathan Silverman, Anne Bancroft, Jerry Orbach, Corey Parker, Hume Cronyn, Michele Lee; **D:** Paul Bogart; **W:** Neil Simon. TV

Broadway Damage ♫♫½ **1998** Amateurish gay comedy whose best asset is the shopaholic (and only female) character played by Hobel, as the typical overweight fag hag roomie of aspiring New York actor Marc (Lucas). Beyond-shallow Marc is looking for a lover and only a perfect 10 will do, which means he gets dumped a lot by narcissistic manipulators. All in all, Danny Rose is pathetically lovable. **85m/B VHS, DVD.** Woody Allen, Mia Farrow, Nick Apollo Forte, Sandy Baron, Milton Berle, Howard Cosell; **D:** Woody Allen; **W:** Woody Allen; **C:** Gordon Willis. British Acad. '84: Orig. Screenplay; Writers Guild '84: Orig. Screenplay.

The Broadway Drifter ♫♫ **1927** A silent Jazz Age drama about a playboy who repents his decadent ways by opening a girls' health school. Complications ensue. **90m/B VHS.** George Walsh, Dorothy Hall, Bigelow Cooper, Arthur Donaldson; **D:** Bernard McEveety Sr.

Broadway Danny Rose ♫♫♫½ **1984 (PG)** One of Woody Allen's best films, a hilarious, heart-rending anecdotal comedy about a third-rate talent agent involved in one of his client's infidelities. The film magically unfolds as show business veterans swap Danny Rose stories at a delicatessen. Allen's Danny Rose is pathetically lovable. **85m/B VHS, DVD.** Woody Allen, Mia Farrow, Nick Apollo Forte, Sandy Baron, Milton Berle, Howard Cosell; **D:** Woody Allen; **W:** Woody Allen; **C:** Gordon Willis. British Acad. '84: Orig. Screenplay; Writers Guild '84: Orig. Screenplay.

Broadway Limited ♫♫ *The Baby Vanishes* **1941** Three aspiring actors head for the Great White Way with a baby to use as a prop. Thinking the baby kidnapped, the police make things tough for the trio. McLaglen was wasted on this one, which was apparently made to show off the considerable assets of Woodworth. **75m/B VHS.** Victor McLaglen, Marjorie Woodworth, Dennis O'Keefe, Patsy Kelly, Zasu

---

Pitts, Leonid Kinskey, George E. Stone; **D:** Gordon Douglas.

Broadway Melody ♫♫½ **1929** Early musical in which two sisters hope for fame on Broadway, and encounter a wily song and dance man who traps both their hearts. Dated, but still charming, with a lovely score. Considered the great grand-daddy of all MGM musicals; followed by three more melodies in 1935, 1937, and 1940. ♫Broadway Melody; Give My Regards to Broadway; Truthful Parson Brown; The Wedding of the Painted Doll; The Boy Friend; You Were Meant For Me; Love Boat; Broadway Babies. **104m/B VHS, DVD.** Bessie Love, Anita Page, Charles King, Jed Prouty, Kenneth Thomson, Edward Dillon, Mary Doran; **D:** Harry Beaumont; **M:** Nacio Herb Brown, Arthur Freed. Oscars '29: Picture.

Broadway Melody of 1936 ♫♫♫ **1935** Exceptional musical comedy with delightful performances from Taylor and Powell. Benny is a headline-hungry columnist who tries to entrap Taylor by using Powell. ♫Broadway Melody; Broadway Rhythm; You Are My Lucky Star; I've Got a Feeling You're Fooling; All I Do Is Dream of You; Sing Before Breakfast; On a Sunday Afternoon. **110m/B VHS.** Jack Benny, Eleanor Powell, Robert Taylor, Una Merkel, Sid Silvers, Buddy Ebsen; **D:** Roy Del Ruth; **C:** Charles Rosher; **M:** Nacio Herb Brown, Arthur Freed.

Broadway Melody of 1938 ♫♫½ **1937** Third entry in the melody series lacks the sparkle of "Broadway Melody of 1936" despite the all-star cast. Lots of singing and dancing without much charm. Two bright spots: a young Garland singing the now famous "Dear Mr. Gable" and the always lovely Powell's dance numbers. ♫Broadway Rhythm; Dear Mr. Gable (You Made Me Love You); A New Pair of Shoes; Yours and Mine; I'm Feeling Like a Million; Everybody Sing; Follow in My Footsteps; Your Broadway and My Broadway; Sun Showers. **110m/B VHS.** Eleanor Powell, Robert Taylor, George Murphy, Judy Garland, Sophie Tucker, Buddy Ebsen, Binnie Barnes; **D:** Roy Del Ruth; **C:** William H. Daniels; **M:** Nacio Herb Brown, Arthur Freed.

Broadway Melody of 1940 ♫♫½ **1940** The last entry in the melody series features the only screen teaming of Astaire and Powell. The flimsy plot is just an excuse for a potent series of Cole Porter musical numbers. ♫I Concentrate on You; I've Got My Eye on You; Begin the Beguine; I am the Captain; Please Don't Monkey With Broadway; Between You and Me; Il Bacio. **103m/B VHS, DVD.** Fred Astaire, Eleanor Powell, George Murphy, Frank Morgan, Ian Hunter; **D:** Norman Taurog.

Broadway Rhythm ♫♫½ **1944** A too-long look at Broadway behind-the-scenes. Murphy plays a Broadway producer who hopes to land a Hollywood star for his new show. She rejects his offer in favor of a show being produced by his father. Just a chance to showcase a number of popular vaudeville acts, songs, and the music of Tommy Dorsey and his orchestra. ♫All the Things You Are; That Lucky Fellow; In Other Words; Seventeen; All In Fun; Brazilian Boogie; What Do You Think I Am?; Somebody Loves Me; Milkman Keep Those Bottles Quiet. **111m/C VHS.** George Murphy, Ginny Simms, Charles Winninger, Gloria De Haven, Nancy Walker, Ben Blue, Lena Horne, Eddie Anderson; **D:** Roy Del Ruth; **M:** Dorothy Kingsley, Harry Clork.

Broadway Serenade ♫♫½ **1939** Melodramatic musical in which a songwriter (Ayres) and his wife, singer MacDonald, make career choices that destroy their marriage. ♫Broadway Serenade for the Lonely Heart; High Flyin'; One Look at You; Time Changes Everything; Un Bel Di; No Time to Argue; Italian Street Song; Les Filles de Cadiz; Musical Contract. **114m/B VHS, DVD.** Jeanette MacDonald, Lew Ayres, Ian Hunter, Frank Morgan, Wally Vernon, Rita Johnson, Virginia Grey, William Gargan; **D:** Robert Z. Leonard; **C:** Charles Lederer.

Broadway to Cheyenne ♫ *From Broadway to Cheyenne* **1932** A group of big city gangsters try to take over a small western town but are opposed by heroic cowboys. **53m/B VHS, DVD.** Rex Bell, George "Gabby" Hayes, Marceline Day, Robert Ellis, Alan Bridge, Matthew Betz; **D:** Harry Fraser.

Brokeback Mountain ♫♫♫½ **2005 (R)** Yes, it's primarily known as the movie that inspired a million "gay cowboy" jokes, but Lee's heartbreaking drama deserves so much better. In 1963, cowhands Ennis (Ledger) and Jack (Gyllenhaal) spend the summer watching over a herd of sheep on a Wyoming mountain range and falling deeply and inexplicably in love. Terrified to admit their feelings to the outside world, Ennis and Jack try to ignore their passions by getting married to aloof women (Williams and Hathaway) and only meeting for semi-annual fishing trips. The script blends the powerful western themes of "Lonesome Dove" with a classic tragic love tale, and Ledger's outstanding lead performance carries the picture. **134m/C DVD, HD DVD.** *US* Heath Ledger, Jake Gyllenhaal, Linda Cardellini, Anna Faris, Anne Hathaway, Michelle Williams, Randy Quaid, Graham Beckel, Scott Michael Campbell, Kate Mara, Roberta Maxwell, Peter McRobbie, David Harbour; **D:** Ang Lee; **W:** Larry McMurtry, Diana Ossana; **C:** Rodrigo Prieto; **M:** Gustavo Santaolalla. Oscars '05: Adapt. Screenplay, Director (Lee), Orig. Score; British Acad. '05: Adapt. Screenplay, Film—Drama, Screenplay, Song ('A Love That Will Never Grow Old"); Ind. Spirit '06: Director (Lee), Film; L.A. Film Critics '05: Director (Lee), Film; Natl. Bd. of Review '05: Director (Lee), Film; N.Y. Film Critics '05: Actor (Ledger), Director (Lee), Film; Writers Guild '05: Adapt. Screenplay.

Brokedown Palace ♫♫½ **1999 (PG-13)** Danes and Beckinsale take a trip to Thailand following their high school graduation and are targeted by a smooth-talking Australian drug dealer. After he invites the pair to Hong Kong, he hides heroin in their luggage and gets them busted at the airport. Accused of drug trafficking, they are sentenced to 33 years in a Thai prison. Phillips is an unfriendly DEA official, while Pullman is the expatriate American lawyer who comes to their aid. The story focuses more on the girls' relationship as friends than on the legal nightmare, however. Nevertheless, the government of Thailand was none too pleased by the script, so most of the Thai scenes were actually shot in the Phillipines. **100m/C VHS, DVD.** Claire Danes, Kate Beckinsale, Bill Pullman, Daniel Lapaine, Lou Diamond Phillips, Jacqueline Kim, Tom Amandes, Aimee Graham, John Doe; **D:** Jonathan Kaplan; **W:** David Arata; **C:** Newton Thomas (Tom) Sigel; **M:** David Newman.

Broken Angel ♫♫½ **1988** Jamie seemed to be such a nice girl, with good looks and great grades—and membership in a notorious street gang. When Jamie disappears, her family discovers her secret activities and dad tries to find his wayward little girl. Melodramatic TV goo. **94m/C VHS.** William Shatner, Susan Blakely, Erika Eleniak, Roxann Biggs-Dawson; **D:** Richard T. Heffron. TV

Broken Arrow ♫♫♫ **1950** A U.S. scout befriends Cochise and the Apaches, and helps settlers and Indians live in peace together in the 1870s. Acclaimed as the first Hollywood film to side with the Indians, and for Chandler's portrayal of Cochise. Based on the novel "Blood Brother" by Elliot Arnold. **93m/C VHS, DVD.** James Stewart, Jeff Chandler, Will Geer, Debra Paget, Basil Ruysdael, Arthur Hunnicutt, Jay Silverheels; **D:** Delmer Daves; **W:** Albert (John B. Sherry) Maltz; **C:** Ernest Palmer.

Broken Arrow ♫♫½ **1995 (R)** Air Force pilot Vic Deakins (Travolta) rips off a couple of nuclear weapons during a routine exercise over the Utah desert. Deakins' ex-co-pilot Riley Hale (Slater), with help from spunky park ranger Terry Carmichael (Mathis), sets out to find and retrieve the warheads before the big bang. Hong Kong action king Woo once again tries his hand at the big-budget Hollywood action extravaganza, with mixed results. Triple script whammy of cheesy dialogue,

continuity problems, and predictability undercuts, but doesn't obscure, his talent for
choreographing mayhem. Travolta plays
the All-American Boy as creepily charming
psychotic to great effect. **108m/C VHS, DVD,
Blu-ray Disc** *C:* John Travolta, Christian Slater, Samantha Mathis, Delroy Lindo, Bob Gunton, Frank
Whaley, Howie Long; *D:* John Woo; *W:* Graham
Yost. *C:* Pete' Levy; *M:* Hans Zimmer.

Broken Badge *185* Crenna stars as a macho,
chauvinistic cop whose attitude towards
rape victims changes dramatically after he
himself is raped by a couple of thugs. Excellent TV movie. **100m/C VHS, DVD.** Richard
Crenna, Meredith Baxter, Pat Hingle, Frances Lee
McCain, Cotter Smith, George Dzundza, Joanna
Kerns; *D:* Karen Arthur; *W:* James G. Hirsch; *M:*
Peter Banister.

Broken Blossoms ⅍⅍⅍ 1919
One of Griffith's most widely acclaimed
films, about a young Chinese man in London's squalid Limehouse district hoping to
spread the peaceful philosophy of his
Eastern religion. He befriends a pitiful
street waif who is mistreated by her brutal
father, resulting in tragedy. Silent. Revised
edition contains introduction from Gish
and a newly recorded score. **89m/B VHS,
DVD.** Lillian Gish, Richard Barthelmess, Donald
Crisp; *D:* D.W. Griffith; *W:* D.W. Griffith. *C:* Billy
(G.W.) Bitzer; *M:* Louis F. Gottschalk. Natl. Film
Reg. '96.

The Broken Chain ⅍⅍½ 1993
In the mid-18th-century Joseph Brant
(Schweig), a member of the Mohawk tribe,
is sent away to be educated by the British.
When he returns, his loyalties are divided
between his Native American roots and
his English mentor, Sir William Johnson
(Brosnan). He is boyhood friend Lohahleo
(White Shirt) disdains Joseph's white man
ways, leading to tragic consequences.
Historical background features the French
and Indian Wars, the splintering of the Iro-
quois Confederacy, and the coming of the
American Revolution. Filmed on location
in Virginia. **95m/C VHS.** Eric Schweig, Wes Stu-
di, Buffy Saint-Marie, Pierce Brosnan, J.C. White
Shirt, Floyd "Red Crow" Westerman, Graham
Greene, Elaina Bilstad, Kim Snyder; *D:* Lamont
Johnson. *W:* Earl W. Wallace; *M:* Charles Fox.
TV

Broken English ⅍⅍½ 2007
(NC-17) Ethically diverse New Zealand is
the setting for this story of young lovers
and the parents who don't understand
them. Croatian refugee Nina (Vujcic) and
Maori cook Eddie (Arahanga) meet in the
Chinese restaurant where they both work
and quickly fall in love. Nina's menacing
father Ivan Serbedzija) objects to their
passion, sometimes with a baseball bat.
Film deals honestly with immigration and
racial issues. Engaging debut for Vujcic, a
Croatian refugee director Nicholas met in
a bar. Also available in an R-rated version.
92m/C VHS. NZ Aleksandra Vujcic, Julian (Sonny)
Arahanga, Rade Serbedzija, Marton Csokas, Jing
Zhao, Yang Li, Madeline McNamara; *D:* Gregor
Nicholas; *W:* Gregor Nicholas, Johanna Pigott, Jim
Salter. *C:* John Toon.

Broken English ⅍⅍½ 1996
(NC-17) Nora (Posey) is a single, moderately neurotic New Yorker working a job
for which she's over-qualified, while both
she and her mother wonder why she's so
unlucky at love. Enter charming and perfect Julien, who seems to look past Nora's
insecurities and fears in exchange for a
(mostly) perfect weekend. Posey shines
and Cassavetes (daughter of legendary
director John) shows insight into her characters, but it's not enough to completely
transcend the well-worn lonely-hearts story. **97m/C DVD.** US Parker Posey, Melvil Poupaud, Drea De Matteo, Gena Rowlands, Justin
Theroux, Tim Guinee, Josh Hamilton, Michael
Panes; *D:* Zoe Cassavetes; *W:* Zoe Cassavetes;
C: John Pirozzi; *M:* Scratch Massive.

Broken Flowers ⅍⅍⅍ 2005 (R)
Quirky, if forlorn, comedy from Jarmusch.
Murray does minimalism in his portrayal of
confirmed, middle-aged bachelor Don
Johnston whose orderly life becomes dis-
arrayed when he learns he fathered a
son from a long-ago liaison. Only there
are four potential moms (a fifth has died),
so Don reluctantly goes on a road trip to

re-acquaint himself with Laura (Stone),
Dora (Conroy), Carmen (Lange), and Pen-
ny (Swinton). His welcome varies—not
much really happens—and Murray is more
Don Quixote (with Wright as his stay-at-
home Sancho Panza) than Don Juan.
105m/C DVD. FR US Bill Murray, Jeffrey Wright,
Sharon Stone, Frances Conroy, Jessica Lange,
Tilda Swinton, Julie Delpy, Mark Webber, Chloe
Sevigny, Christopher McDonald, Alexis Dziena,
Larry Fessenden, Chris Bauer, Pell James, Heath-
er Jim Jarmusch, Brea Frazier; *D:* Jim Jarmusch;
W: Jim Jarmusch. *C:* Frederick Elmes.

Broken Glass ⅍⅍½ 1996 Set in
Brooklyn in 1938 and adapted from a play
by Arthur Miller. Jewish housewife, Sylvia
Gellberg (Leicester), has been stricken by
a mysterious paralysis and Dr. Harry Hyman (Patinkin) is called in to treat her. Her
illness is apparently psychosomatic and
Sylvia gradually reveals her anxiety about
her unhappy marriage and her obsessive
fears with newspaper reports concerning
Jewish persecution in Germany. Hyman
could have imagined. Made for TV. **120m/C
VHS.** Mandy Patinkin, Margot Leicester, Henry
Goodman, Elizabeth McGovern; *D:* David Thacker;
W: David Thacker, David Holman. TV

Broken Harvest ⅍⅍½ 1994 Jimmy O'Leary remembers his youth in rural
1950s Ireland when a poor wheat harvest
led to his family's financial demise and a
feud between his father (Lane) and neighbor Josie McCarthy (O'Brien) threatened
to destroy their lives. The man fought side
by side for Ireland's independence but the
friendship dissolved when they took different sides during the ensuing civil war, and
fought over Jimmy's mother. Strong performances and the beautiful West Cork
and Wicklow location shots provide a nice
balance to the uneven narrative. The
black and white scenes were actually
filmed in the mid-'80s when the independently financed project was begun. Adapted from O'Callaghan's own story "The
Shilling." **101m/C VHS, DVD.** IR Colin Lane,
Niall O'Brien, Marian Quinn, Darren McHugh, Joy
Florish, Joe Jeffers, Pete O'Reilly, Michael Crowley. *D:* Maurice O'Callaghan; *W:* Maurice
O'Callaghan; *C:* Jack Conroy; *M:* Patrick Cassidy.

**Broken Hearts of
Broadway** ⅍⅍ 1923 Stories of he-
artbreak and success along the Great
White Way. **85m/B VHS.** Colleen Moore, John-
nie Walker, Alice Lake, Tully Marshall, Creighton
Hale; *D:* Irving Cummings.

**The Broken Hearts
Club** ⅍⅍⅍ 2000 (R) Talk can be
cheap, but it's also what sustains the relationships in the lives of a group of gay
friends in this chatty, likable film set in
West Hollywood. Despite their mostly superficial (sex) conversations, the boys
suspect there's more to life, and aim, hesitantly, to move beyond this dead-end family. Witty and confident in its characters,
writer/director Berlanti (co-creator of
"Dawson's Creek") has put together a film
about gay men that thankfully moves beyond the staleness of many of its predecessors. Good cast with notable performances by Cain (Superman in TV's "Lois
and Clark") and Mahoney as the fatherly
proprietor of the Broken Hearts restaurant.
94m/C VHS, DVD. Dean Cain, John Mahoney,
Timothy Olyphant, Andrew Keegan, Nia Long,
Zach Braff, Matt McGrath, Billy Porter, Justin Theroux, Mary McCormack; *D:* Greg Berlanti; *W:* Greg
Berlanti; *C:* Paul Elliot; *M:* Christophe Beck.

Broken Lance ⅍⅍⅍ 1954
Western remake of "House of Strangers"
that details the dissolution of a despotic
cattle baron's family. Beautifully photo-
graphed. **96m/C VHS, DVD.** Spencer Tracy,
Richard Widmark, Robert Wagner, Jean Peters,
Katy Jurado, Earl Holliman, Hugh O'Brien, E.G.
Marshall; *D:* Edward Dmytryk; *W:* Philip Yordan; *C:*
Joe MacDonald; *M:* Leigh Harline Oscars '54: Sto-
ry.

The Broken Mask ⅍⅍ 1928 A
doctor performs remarkable plastic surgery on a patient, but when the patient
becomes attracted to his sweetheart, he
throws their relationship to the wind,
and his patient's spiffy new look has got to
go. A ground-breaker amid plastic sur-

gery-gone-amok pieces. **58m/B VHS.** Cullen
Landis, Barbara Bedford, Wheeler Oakman,
James A. Marcus; *D:* James Hogan.

Broken Mirrors ⅍⅍½ 1987 *Gebroken
Spiegels* 1985 A disturbing film which inter-
wines two stories of violence against
women: prostitutes go about their daily
business in Amsterdam, while a twisted
serial killer who imprisons, photographs,
and ultimately destroys his victims, draws
near. An independently made chiller with
staunch feminist agenda. **110m/C VHS, NL.**
Lineke Rijpman, Henriette Tol, Edda Barends, Eddie Brugman, Coby Stunnenberg; *D:* Marleen Gorris; *M:* Marleen Gorris.

Broken Silence ⅍⅍⅍
2001 Director Armendáriz's engaging production is set in 1944 when a 21-year-old
Lucia (Jimenez) goes back to her homeland only to witness the dramatic and violent impact that the Spanish Civil War has
had upon the rustic village.
Still, she finds love with Manuel (Botto), a
blacksmith who is part of the resistance
group, the Maquis. An uprising swells and
Franco's fascist army shows up to squash
it, forcing the young lovers to face the cruel realities inherent to the hostilities. In
Spanish with subtitles. **110m/C VHS, DVD.**
SP Juan Diego Botto, Mercedes Sampietro, Lucia
Jimenez, Maria Botto, Andoni Erburu, Alvaro de
Luna; *D:* Montxo Armendáriz; *M:* Pascal Gaigne.
VIDEO

Broken Strings ⅍ 1940 All-black
musical in which a concert violinist must
come to terms with himself after an auto
accident limits the use of his left hand.
50m/B VHS. Clarence Muse, Sybil Lewis, William
Washington, Matthew "Stymie" Beard; *D:* Bernard
B. Ray.

Broken Trail ⅍⅍⅍ 2006 In 1898,
aging cowpoke Print Ritter (Duvall) is
herding 500 horses from Oregon to
Wyoming, with the help of his estranged
nephew Tom Harte (Church). During the
trip they hire on Heck (Cooper) and rescue
five Chinese girls who were sold to be
prostitutes in a mining camp. But this puts
the horse traders at odds with madam Big
Rump Kate (Mulkey) after her property,
distic Big Ears (Mulkey) after her property.
Not having enough to deal with, Print also
protects good-hearted whore Nola (Scacchi) on that long, dusty trail. But everyone's in very good company. But this puts
US Robert Duvall, Thomas Haden Church, Greta
Scacchi, Chris Mulkey, Rusty Schwimmer, James
Russo, Scott Cooper, Gwendoline Yeo, Van Dyke
Parks; *D:* Walter Hill; *W:* Alan Geoffrion; *C:* Lloyd
Ahern II; *M:* David Mansfield. C.A.B.L.E.

Bronco Billy ⅍⅍⅍ 1980 (PG)
Eastwood stars as a New Jersey shoe
clerk who decides to fulfill his dream of
being a cowboy hero by becoming the
proprietor of a rag-tag wild west show.
Locke's one-note performance as a
spoiled rich girl who joins up is a problem
and the film's charm is as ragged as the
acts. Good if you want to see Eastwood in
something other than a shoot-'em-up.
117m/C VHS, DVD. Clint Eastwood, Sondra
Locke, Bill McKinney, Scatman Crothers, Sam Bottoms, Geoffrey Lewis, Dan Vadis, Sierra Pecheur;
D: Clint Eastwood; *W:* Dennis Hackin; *C:* David
Worth; *M:* Steve Dorf.

Bronson's Revenge ⅍½ *Conde-
nados a Vivir: Cut-Throats Nine* 1972 (R) Two
frontier soldiers face constant danger as
they attempt to transport death row prisoners, a large quantity of gold, and a stranded woman across the Rocky Mountains
territory. **90m/C VHS.** SP Claudio Undari, Emma
Cohen, Alberto Dalbes Antonio Iranzo; *D:* Joaquin
Luis Romero Marchent; *W:* Joaquin Luis Romero
Marchent; *C:* Luis Cuadrado; *M:* Carmelo A. Ber-
nabla.

Broken Melody ⅍½ *Vagabond Violinist* 1934 An opera singer sent to prison by
mistake must escape in return to the
the woman of his dreams. **62m/B VHS, DVD.**
GB John Garrick, Margot Grahame, Merle Oberon,
Austin Trevor, Charles Carson, Harry Terry; *D:*
Bernard Vorhaus.

Broken Vows ⅍⅍⅍ 1987 Thriller
with Jones as ghetto priest Father Joseph,
who has doubts about his calling. When
he gives last rites to a murder victim, he
decides to help the victim's girlfriend find
his killers. Based on the novel "Where the
Dark Secrets Go" by Dorothy Salisbury
Davis. **95m/C VHS, DVD.** Tommy Lee Jones, Annette O'Toole, M. Emmet Walsh, Milo O'Shea, De-
vid Groh, Madeline Sherwood, Jean De Baer, David Strathairn; *D:* Jud Taylor; *C:* Thomas Burstyn.
TV

**Broken
Wings** ⅍⅍⅍ *Knafayim
Shvurot* 2002 (R) Writer/director Bergman's
touching feature debut about an Israeli
family's inability to cope with the recent
loss of patriarch David. Widow Dafna Ul-
man (Zilbershatz-Banai) takes up working odd shifts as a midwife for a local hospital, forcing 17-year-old daughter Maya
(Maron) to put her music career on hold to
care for younger siblings Ido (Daniel Magon) and Bahr (Eliana Magon). Faring little
better is 16-year-old son Yair (Gvitza), who
has thrown away a potential basketball career by dropping out of school and now
passes out leaflets in the subway dressed
in a mouse costume. Things suddenly go
from bad to worse, forcing the Ulmans into
crisis mode. Simply told but very effective
human drama. In Hebrew with subtitles.
83m/C DVD. *IS* Orly Silbersatz Banai, Maya Maron, Nirai Gavirtaz, Vladimir Friedman, Dana Ivgi,
Danny Niv, Daniel Magon, Eliana Magon; *D:* Nir
Bergman; *W:* Nir Bergman; *C:* Valentin Belonogov;
M: Avi Belilili.

Broken Vessels ⅍⅍⅍ 1998 (R)
Rent this with "Bringing Out the Dead"
and you'll have a double-feature that will
make you take 911 off the speed dial.
Both movies were released in the same
year but Scorsese's movie depicts a paramedic demented by caring too much.
The ambulance drivers in "Broken Vessels" become unhinged by a cold, drug-
induced indifference. Tom (London) is
pulled into a downward spiral by his
crazed partner Jimmy (Field), who smokes
heroin and feels up unconscious girls
while on break from saving lives. Clearly,
things are not destined to go well for the
pair, not to mention those who end up in
the back of their meat wagon. Excellent
debut from producer-director Scott Ziehl.
90m/C VHS, DVD. Todd Field, Jason London,
Roxana Zal, Susan Traylor, James Hong, Patrick
Cranshaw, William (Bill) Smith, Dave Baer; *D:*
Scott Ziehl; *W:* Scott Ziehl, Dave Baer, John
McMahon; *C:* Antonio Calvache.

**The Brontes of
Haworth** ⅍⅍½ 1973 The bleak
moorlands and the village of Haworth are
the setting for a dramatic look at the lives
of writers Charlotte, Emily, and Anne
Bronte, their wastrel brother Branwell, and
the tragedies that haunted them all. On 4
cassettes. **270m/C VHS, DVD, GB** Ann Penfold,
Michael Kitchen, Vickery Turner, Rosemary McHale, Alfred Burke; *D:* Marc Miller; *W:* Christopher
Fry. TV

The Bronx Executioner ✗ 1986 Android, robot, and human interests clash in futuristic Manhattan and all martial arts hell breaks loose. Special introduction by martial arts star Michael Dudikoff. **88m/C VHS, DVD.** Rob Robinson, Margie Newton, Chuck Valenti, Gabriel Gori; **D:** Bob Collins.

The Bronx Is Burning ✗✗½ 2007 In 1977, New York City was paralyzed by a citywide blackout, political strife, and the Son of Sam killing spree. And then there were the New York Yankees, owned by bombastic George Steinbrenner (Platt), managed by volatile, hard-drinking Billy Martin (Turturro), and with egotistical Reggie Jackson (Sunjata) as their star hitter. Nostalgic miniseries shows how the city came together as the Yanks made their bid for the World Series. **360m/C DVD.** John Turturro, Oliver Platt, Daniel Sunjata, Erik Jensen, Michael Rispoli, Dan Lauria, Kevin Conway, Loren Dean, Charles S. Dutton, Alex Cranmer, Leonard Robinson; **D:** Jeremiah S. Chechik; **W:** James Solomon, Gordon Greisman; **C:** Douglas Koch; **M:** Tree Adams. **CABLE**

A Bronx Tale ✗✗✗ 1993 (R) Vivid snapshot of a young Italian-American boy growing up in the '60s among neighborhood small-time wiseguys. As a nine-year-old Calogero witnesses mobster Sonny kill a man but doesn't rat to the police, so Sonny takes the kid under his wing. His upright bus-driving father Lorenzo doesn't approve but the kid is drawn to Sonny's apparent glamor and power. At 17, he's gotten both an education in school and on the streets but he needs to make a choice. Good period detail and excellent performances. Palminteri shows both Sonny's charisma and violence and De Niro handles the less-showy father role with finesse. Based on Palminteri's one-man play; De Niro's directorial debut. **122m/C VHS, DVD.** Robert De Niro, Chazz Palminteri, Lillo Brancato, Francis Capra, Taral Hicks, Kathrine Narducci, Clem Caserta, Alfred Sauchelli Jr., Frank Pietrangolare, Joseph (Joe) D'Onofrio; **Cameos:** Joe Pesci; **D:** Robert De Niro; **W:** Chazz Palminteri; **C:** Reynaldo Villalobos; **M:** Butch Barbella.

The Bronx War ✗✗ 1990 (R) Rival gangs take to the streets in this film from the director of "Hangin'" with the Homeboys." A malicious gang leader tricks his gang into going to war over a girl he wants. Very violent; an unrated version available. **91m/C VHS, DVD.** Joseph B. Vasquez, Fabio Urena, Charmaine Cruz, Andre Brown, Marlene Forte, Francis Colon, Miguel Sierra, Kim West; **D:** Joseph B. Vasquez.

Bronze Buckaroo ✗✗ 1939 Horse opera in which a cowpoke seeks revenge for his pa's death. Commendable performances from the all-black cast and crew. **57m/B VHS, DVD.** Herbert Jeffries, Artie Young, Rellie Hardin, Spencer Williams Jr., Clarence Brooks, F.E. (Flourney) Miller; **D:** Richard C. Kahn; **W:** Richard C. Kahn.

The Brood ✗✗½ 1979 (R) Cronenberg's inimitable biological nightmares, involving an experimentally malformed woman who gives birth to murderous demon-children that kill every time she gets angry. Extremely graphic. Not for all tastes. **92m/C VHS, DVD.** CA Samantha Eggar, Oliver Reed, Art Hindle, Susan Hogan, Nuala Fitzgerald, Cindy Hinds; **D:** David Cronenberg; **W:** David Cronenberg; **C:** Mark Irwin; **M:** Howard Shore.

Brooklyn Lobster ✗✗ 2005 Frank Giorgio (Aiello) is a hard-headed Sheepshead Bay lobster wholesaler whose business is about to be auctioned off and whose wife, Maureen (Curtin), has walked out on him. Son Michael (Sauli) comes home for the Christmas holidays to lend a hand, accompanied by his girlfriend Kerry (Burns), but her presence creates more problems. Aiello is especially impressive in a slice of life drama that was inspired by writer/director Jordan's own family. **90m/C DVD.** US Danny Aiello, Jane Curtin, Marisa Ryan, Heather Burns, Sam Freed, Daniel Serafini Sauli, Ian Kahn, Tom Mason, Barbara Garrick, John Rothman, Rick Aiello; **D:** Kevin Jordan; **W:** Kevin Jordan; **C:** David Tumblety; **M:** Craig Maher.

Brooklyn Rules ✗✗ 2007 (R) Mild coming of age pic about three lifelong buddies, set in 1985 Brooklyn. Michael (Prinze) leaves the 'hood behind to go to law school and date an uptown girl (Suvari). Easy-going Bobby (Ferrara) plans to get married and have a steady straight job. But slickster Carmine (Caan) wants to be part of local wiseguy Cesar's (Baldwin) crew. Naturally these differing aims pull the guys apart. **99m/C DVD.** Freddie Prinze Jr., Scott Caan, Mena Suvari, Alec Baldwin, Jerry Ferrara, Monica Keena, Robert Turano, Phyllis Kay; **D:** Michael Corrente; **W:** Terence Winter; **C:** Richard Crudo; **M:** Benny Rietveld.

A Brooklyn State of Mind ✗✗ 1997 (R) Al (Spano) works for shady real estate developer Frank Parente (Aiello) in Brooklyn. When his Aunt Rose (King) rents a room to beautiful Gabriella (Cucinotta), who says she's working on a documentary about the neighborhood, Al is quick to succumb to her charms. But he's also suspicious—and when he finds a dossier on Frank in Gabriella's room, Al learns her father's murder is tied to his own father's death and both involve Frank. **90m/C VHS.** Vincent Spano, Danny Aiello, Maria Grazia Cucinotta, Tony Danza, Morgana King, Abe Vigoda; **D:** Frank Rainone; **W:** Frank Rainone, Fred Stroppel; **C:** Ken Kelsch; **M:** Paul Zaza.

Broth of a Boy ✗✗½ 1959 A hungry British producer decides to film a birthday party of the oldest man in the world. The old Irishman wants a portion of the profits. Well made and thought provoking. **77m/B VHS.** IR Barry Fitzgerald, Harry Brogan, Tony Wright, June Thorburn, Eddie Golden; **D:** George Pollock.

Brother ✗✗ Brat 1997 Danila (Bodrov Jr.) has just gotten out of the army and needs a job so he decides to visit big brother Viktor (Sukhoroukov) in St. Petersburg. He discovers his bro is a contract killer for the Russian mob and hires on as Viktor's assistant. Danila successfully accomplishes his first assignment—the murder of a mob rival—but then has the other gangsters out for revenge. Fast-paced and gritty, with casual violence and crime the easiest options in a brokendown society. Russian with subtitles. **96m/C VHS.** RU Sergei Bodrov Jr., Viktor Sukhorukov, Svetlana Pismitchenko, Maria Joukova, Yuri Kouznetzov; **C:** Sergei Astakhov; **M:** Viatcheslav Boutoussov.

Brother ✗✗✗ 2000 (R) Kitano's films are something of an acquired taste. He mixes abrupt graphic (and usually brief) violence with prolonged scenes of introspection, and when it comes to expressing emotion, he seldom does more than twitch or take off his sunglasses. But then also transcends the cliches. English and Japanese dialog with subtitles. **118m/C VHS, DVD.** JP Takeshi "Beat" Kitano, Omar Epps, Kuroudo Maki, Masaya Kato, Susumu Terajima, James Shigeta; **D:** Takeshi "Beat" Kitano; **W:** Takeshi "Beat" Kitano; **C:** Katsumi Yanagishima; **M:** Joe Hisaishi.

Brother Bear ✗✗½ 2003 (G) Rather grim but ultimately heartwarming coming-of-ager invoking the far superior "The Lion King," and "Bambi." Kenai (Phoenix) is a brash Native American youth living with his two brothers in the Pacific Northwest during the end of the Ice Age. After a bear attacks and kills his brother Sitka (Sweeney), Kenai is magically transformed into a bear himself. In his new hirsute form, Kenai learns some important lessons about nature with the help of orphaned bear cub Koda (Suarez). Much needed but underdeveloped comic relief comes from Thomas and Moranis as a pair of bickering moose. Largely hand-drawn animation is lushly beautiful but overshadowed by derivative plot and heavy-handed message. Lackluster score by soft pop-meister Phil Collins. **85m/C VHS, DVD.**

US **D:** Aaron Blaise, Robert Walker; **W:** Tab Murphy, Lorne Cameron, David Hoselton, Steve Bencich, Ron J. Friedman; **M:** Phil Collins, Mark Mancini; **V:** Joaquin Rafael (Leaf) Phoenix, Jeremy Suarez, Jason Raize, Rick Moranis, Dave Thomas, D.B. Sweeney, Joan Copeland, Michael Clarke Duncan, Harold Gould, Estelle Harris.

Brother Bear 2 ✗✗½ 2006 (G) Animated Disney sequel based on the 2003 release. Nita had a strong bond with Kenai when they were children (before he was turned into a bear). But if she wants to marry, Nita has to break that bond. She is told by the shaman that she and Kenai must perform a certain ritual but Kenai thinks maybe he should ask the Great Spirit if he can become human again (which he refused to do in the first film). For pure comic relief, moose buddies Rutt and Tuke are back and chasing after some moosettes. **74m/C DVD.** US **D:** Ben Gluck; **W:** Rich Burns; **M:** Matthew Gerrard, Dave Metzger, Robbie Nevil; **V:** Patrick Dempsey, Mandy Moore, Jeremy Suarez, Rick Moranis, Dave Thomas, Wanda Sykes, Andrea Martin, Catherine O'Hara. **VIDEO**

The Brother from Another Planet ✗✗✗ 1984 A black alien escapes from his home planet and winds up in Harlem, where he's pursued by two alien bounty hunters. Independently made morality fable by John Sayles before he hit the big time; features Sayles in a cameo as an alien bounty hunter. **109m/C VHS, DVD.** Joe Morton, Dee Dee Bridgewater, Ren Woods, Steve James, Maggie Renzi, David Strathairn; **Cameos:** John Sayles; **D:** John Sayles; **W:** John Sayles; **M:** Mason Daring.

Brother Future ✗✗✗ 1991 T.J., a black, streetsmart city kid who thinks school and helping others is all a waste of time gets knocked out in a car accident. As he's lying unconscious, he is transported back in time to a slave auction block in the Old South. There the displaced urbanite is forced to work on a cotton plantation, and watch the stirrings of a slave revolt. T.J. sees the light and realizes how much opportunity he's been wasting in his own life. He comes to just a few moments later, but worlds away from who he was before. Part of the "Wonderworks" series. **110m/C VHS.** Phill Lewis, Frank Converse, Carl Lumbly, Vonetta McGee; **D:** Roy Campanella; **W:** Roy Campanella.

Brother John ✗✗✗ 1970 (PG-13) An early look at racial tensions and labor problems. An angel goes back to his hometown in Alabama to see how things are going. **94m/C VHS, DVD.** Sidney Poitier, Will Geer, Bradford Dillman, Beverly Todd, Paul Winfield; **D:** James Goldstone; **M:** Quincy Jones.

Brother of Sleep ✗✗ Schlafes Bruder 1995 (R) Elias (Eisermann), the illegitimate son of the local priest, is discovered to have perfect pitch, a beautiful voice, and a special symbiosis with nature. Which does nothing to endear him to the superstitious inhabitants of his 19th-century Austrian mountain village. Elias doesn't know whether his gift is a blessing or a curse but he'd give it up if he could win the love of his cousin Elspeth (Vavrova). Schneider scripted from his 1992 novel, which has previously been adapted as a ballet and opera. German with subtitles. **133m/C VHS, DVD.** GE Andre Eisermann, Dana Vavrova, Ben Becker; **D:** Joseph Vilsmaier; **W:** Robert Schneider; **C:** Joseph Vilsmaier; **M:** Norbert J. Schneider.

Brother Orchid ✗✗✗ 1940 Mobster puts a henchman in charge of his gang while he vacations in Europe. Upon his return, he is deposed and wounded in an assassination attempt. Hiding out in a monastery, he plots to regain control of the gang, leading to fish outta water episodes and a change in his outlook on life. Fine cast fans through farce intelligently. **87m/B VHS.** Edward G. Robinson, Humphrey Bogart, Ann Sothern, Donald Crisp, Ralph Bellamy, Allen Jenkins, Charles D. Brown, Cecil Kellaway; **D:** Lloyd Bacon; **C:** Gaetano Antonio "Tony" Gaudio.

Brother Sun, Sister Moon ✗✗½ 1973 (PG) Post-'60s costume epic depicting the trials of St. Francis of Assisi as he evaluates his beliefs in Catholicism. **120m/C VHS, DVD.** Graham Faulkner, Judi Bowker, Alec Guinness, Leigh Lawson, Kenneth Cranham, Lee Montague, Valentina Cortese; **D:** Franco Zeffirelli; **M:** Donovan.

Brother to Brother ✗✗½ 2004 Ambitious debut effort ties the personal plight of a modern African-American painter to the artistic turmoil of the Harlem Renaissance. Perry (Mackie) is thrown out of his house once his father discovers that he is homosexual. Embittered, Perry rails against the anti-gay hostility within the black community and his college classrooms. After he meets a homeless man, Bruce Nugent (Robinson), in a local shelter, Perry realizes that Bruce was once a noted poet during the Harlem Renaissance. We then flash back to the 1930s to witness Bruce interacting with such luminaries as Langston Hughes and Zora Neale Hurston. Evans effectively shows how issues of politics and sexuality transcend time, but the film lapses into didacticism once too often. **94m/C DVD.** US Anthony Mackie, Roger Robinson, Larry (Lawrence) Gilliard Jr., Aunjanue Ellis, Duane Boutte, Daniel Sunjata, Alex Burns; **D:** Rodney Evans; **W:** Rodney Evans; **C:** Harlan Bosmajian; **M:** Marc Anthony Thompson, Bill Coleman.

The Brotherhood ✗✗ 1968 Two hot-headed brothers in a Mafia syndicate clash over old vs. new methods and the changing of the Family's guard. **96m/C VHS, DVD.** Kirk Douglas, Alex Cord, Irene Papas, Luther Adler, Susan Strasberg, Murray Hamilton; **D:** Martin Ritt; **W:** Lewis John Carlino; **C:** Boris Kaufman; **M:** Lalo Schifrin.

Brotherhood 2: The Young Warlocks WOOF! 2001 Luke is a new kid at a private school who decides to recruit a group of fellow outcast kids for a coven he's starting. Laughably bad in all regards except that some of the cast are hotties. **85m/C DVD.** Sean Faris, Forrest Cochran, Stacey Scowley, Noah Frank, Julie Briggs, Justin Allen, C.J. Thomason; **D:** David DeCoteau. **VIDEO**

The Brotherhood 3: The Young Demons WOOF! 2002 Teenagers heavily into a role-playing wizard and warriors game gather every Friday to perform faux ceremonies complete with costumes and weaponry. When they find a real book of magic, they can't resist chanting a few spells, which conjures up some medieval horrors. **82m/C VHS, DVD.** Kristopher Turner, Paul Andrich, Ellen Wieser, Julie Pedersen; **D:** David DeCoteau. **VIDEO**

Brotherhood of Death ✗✗ 1976 (R) Three black Vietnam veterans return to their southern hometown to get even with the Klansmen who slaughtered people in the townspeople. **85m/C VHS, DVD.** Roy Jefferson, Larry Jones, Mike Bass, Le Tari, Haskell V. Anderson; **D:** Bill Berry.

Brotherhood of Justice ✗✗ 1986 Young men form a secret organization to rid their neighborhood of drug dealers and violence. As their power grows, their propriety weakens, until all are afraid of the "Brotherhood of Justice." **97m/C VHS, DVD.** Keanu Reeves, Kiefer Sutherland, Billy Zane, Joe Spano, Darren Dalton, Evan Mirand, Don Michael Paul; **D:** Charles Braverman; **M:** Brad Fiedel. **TV**

Brotherhood of Murder ✗✗ 1999 Based on the book by Thomas Martinez and John Gunther that depicts the rise and fall of the white supremacist group known as "The Order." Martinez (Baldwin) is a struggling family man who falls in with charismatic Bob Mathews (Gallagher) and his hate group—until William Baldwin, Peter Gallagher, Kelly Lynch, Joel S. Keller, Zack (Zach) Ward, Vincent Gale; **D:** Martin Bell; **W:** Robert J. Avrech; **C:** James R. Bagdonas; **M:** Laura Karpman. **CABLE**

The Brotherhood of Satan ✗✗ 1971 (PG) In an isolated southern town, a satanic coven persuades children to join in their devil-may-care attitude. Worthwhile. **92m/C VHS, DVD.** Strother Martin, L.Q. Jones, Charles Bateman, Anna Capri, Charles Robinson, Alvy Moore, Geri Reischl, Helene Winston; **D:** Bernard McEveety; **W:** William Welch; **C:** John Morrill.

The Brotherhood of the Rose 🐾½ 1989 (PG-13) Too many twists and turns mar the otherwise mediocre plot of this import of Gilliam's adaption of a book by David (First Blood) Morrell, Strauss and Morse are the C.I.A. agents marked for death and running for their lives after uncovering their boss's (Mitchum) plot of world domination. Though almost every scene takes place in a different country, the movie was in fact filmed entirely in New Zealand. Convoluted and frustrating, it's difficult to follow. 103m/C VHS, Robert Mitchum, Peter Strauss, Connie Sellecca, James B. Sikking, David Morse, M: Emmet Walsh, James Hong; **D:** Marvin J. Chomsky.

Brotherhood of the Wolf 🐾🐾 Le Pacte des Loups 2001 (R) French legend Gregoire de Fronsac (Le Bihan) and his Iroquois blood brother Mani (Dacascos) are sent by King Louis XV to kill and stuff the beast for posterity. But what they finally discover is quite unexpected. Flamboyant-ly entertaining adventure. French, with subtitles. 143m/C VHS, DVD, FR Samuel Le Bihan, Mark Dacascos, Vincent Cassel, Emilie Dequenne, Jeremie Renier, Monica Bellucci, Jean Yanne, Edith Scob, Jean-Francois Stevenin, Hans Meyer, Jacques Perrin, Philippe Nahon, Eric Prat, Johan Leysen, Bernard Fresson, Bernard Farcy, Virginie Darmon; **D:** Christophe Gans; M: Christophe Gans, Stephane Cabel; **C:** Dan Laustsen; M: Joseph LoDuca.

Brotherly Love 🐾½ 1985 Good twin/bad twin made-for-TV mystery about an escaped psychopath who's out to get his businessman twin brother (Hirsch in both roles). 94m/C VHS, Judd Hirsch, Karen Carlson, George Dzundza, Barry Primus, Lori Lethin; **D:** Jeff Bleckner.

Brothers 🐾🐾🐾 2001 (R) A chain reaction of male introspection is set off as four successful, young African-American man navigate the tricky waters of serious relationships in modern Los Angeles. All the bases are covered: there is the womanizing lawyer, Brian (Bellamy); the one night stand-weary physician, Jackson (Chestnut); the just-engaged Terry (Sherman) and the unhappily married Derrick (Hughley). Not quite as strong as its female counterpart, the much-praised "Waiting to Exhale," but novelist Hardwick's first film is well managed and funny, and he never lets his capable comic actors veer too far away from the exploration of modern sexual politics. 101m/C VHS, DVD, Morris Chestnut, D.L. Hughley, Bill Bellamy, Shemar Moore, Gabrielle Union, Tamala Jones, Susan Dalian, Angela Brooks, Jenifer Lewis, Clifton Powell, Marla Gibbs, Tatyana Ali, Julie Benz; **D:** Gary Hardwick; **W:** Gary Hardwick; **C:** Alexander Gruszynski.

Brothers 🐾🐾🐾 Brodre 2005 (R) Michael is a husband and father in the Danish military deployed to Afghanistan. When his helicopter crashes he is presumed dead. In his absence his younger "screw-up" brother steps up to the plate to help Michael's wife and children cope with life in his absence. However, Michael was not dead, but captured by guerrilla fighters and forced to commit a barbaric act. When he finally returns home he is a different man. Great narrative drive, emotionally explosive and brutally honest. In Danish with English subtitles. 110m/C DVD, Connie Nielsen, Ulrich Thomsen, Nikolaj Lie Kaas; **D:** Susanne (Susanne) Bier; **W:** Anders Thomas Jensen; **C:** Morten Soborg; M: Johan Soderqvist.

The Brothers Grimm 🐾🐾 2005 (PG-13) Rather grim indeed is this ill-conceived fairytale from Gilliam that had a rocky and delayed production (it was filmed in 2003). Wilhelm (Damon) and Jacob (Ledger) are 18th century German con men fleecing credulous country folk who believe in the supernatural. But in order to save their own skins, the brothers must investigate the disappearance of a number of young women who have vanished into a truly enchanted forest that is

the domain of the Mirror Queen (Bellucci). The film looks good but it's really all an illusion. 118m/C DVD, Blu-ray Disc, UMD, US director Rosenfeld. 92m/C VHS, DVD, US C2 Matt Damon, Heath Ledger, Monica Bellucci, Jonathan Pryce, Lena Headey, Peter Stormare, Jan Unger; **D:** Terry Gilliam; **W:** Ehren Kruger; **C:** Newton Thomas (Tom) Sigel; M: Dario Marianelli.

A Brother's Kiss 🐾🐾 1997 (R) Growing up in an East Harlem neighborhood with an alcoholic mother (Moriarty), two brothers are set on different paths that fishing boat and start drinking. Ex-partner/lover Travis (Orser) shows up when his current homicide case turns out to be identical to the incident that ended Lucinda's career. She unofficially agrees to help but solving the case may lead her close to home and her crazy brother Ellis (Nemec). 86m/C VHS, DVD, Jeanne Tripplehorn, Corin Nemec, Leland Orser, Evan Dexter Parker; **D:** John Badham; **W:** Steven Baigelman, Glen Gers; **C:** Ron Stannett; M: John Ottman, John Willett. CABLE.

The Brothers Karamazov 🐾🐾🐾 Karamazov; The Murderer Dmitri Karamazov; Der Mörder Dmitri Karamasoff 1958 Hollywood adaptation of the classic novel by Dostoyevsky, in which four 19th-Century Russian brothers struggle with their desires for the same beautiful woman and with the father who brutalizes them. Incredible performances from every cast member, especially Cobb. Long and extremely intense, with fine direction from Brooks. Marilyn Monroe tried desperately to get Schell's part. 147m/C VHS, Yul Brynner, Claire Bloom, Lee J. Cobb, William Shatner, Maria Schell, Richard Basehart; **D:** Richard Brooks; **W:** Richard Brooks; **C:** John Alton.

Brother's Keeper 🐾🐾🐾 1992 Filmmakers Berlinger and Sinofsky document the story of the eccentric and reclusive Ward brothers, four bachelor dairy farmers who shared the same two-room shack for more than 60 years in rural New York. When Bill Ward dies, brother Delbert is accused of murder and goes to trial. The film covers a year's span in preparation for the trial and how the media attention changed the Ward's lives. 104m/C VHS, DVD, D: Joe Berlinger, Bruce Sinofsky; **C:** Douglas Cooper; Directors Guild '92: Feature Doc. (Berlinger), "Feature Doc. (Sinofsky); Natl. Bd. of Review '92: Feature Doc.; Sundance '92: Aud. Award; N.Y. Film Critics '92:

Brother's Keeper 🐾🐾 My Brother's Keeper 2002 (R) After police detective Lucinda Pond (Tripplehorn) screwed up and let a killer get away, she left the force to run a

The Brothers Solomon 🐾½ 2007 (R) Dean (Forte) and and John (Arnett) decide to grant their father's (Majors) last wish before he be slipped into a coma: a grandchild. Unfortunately, they were raised in the Arctic, have no social skills, and are, well, idiots. Along comes surrogate Janine (Wiig), who is willing to bear the child for a price. Mostly, though, it's just a set up for an endless series of gags based on how stupid and out of touch the brothers are. Arnett and Forte's "even dumber than dumberer" act, as directed by Odenkirk, is exhausting and the occasional splashes of sweetness don't make up for what is basically a one-joke extended sketch comedy skit. 93m/C DVD, US Will Arnett, Will Forte, Chi McBride, Jenna Fischer, Kristen Wiig, Malin Akerman, David Koechner, Lee Majors; **D:** Bob Odenkirk; **W:** Will Forte; **C:** Tim Suhrstedt; M: John Swihart.

Brothers Three 🐾 2007 (R) Dysfunctional family 101. College-educated businessman Peter (Wilson) receives an urgent message from his hot-tempered

strong but runs out of energy by the second half. Expanded from a one-act play by director Rosenfeld. 92m/C VHS, DVD.

Brothers in Arms 🐾🐾 1988 (R) Savage mountainmen have developed a weird religion that requires them to hunt down and mercilessly massacre human prey. 95m/C VHS, Todd Allen, Jack Starrett, Dee Pfeiffer, Mitch Pileggi; **D:** George J. Bloom III; **W:** Steve(n) Fisher.

Brothers in Law 🐾🐾 1957 Wry British humor in this tale of a rookie lawyer up against a veteran judge who forces him to sink or swim. 94m/B VHS, GB Richard Attenborough, Ian Carmichael, Terry-Thomas, Miles Malleson, John Le Mesurier; **D:** Roy Boulting; **W:** Roy Boulting.

Brothers in Trouble 🐾🐾 1995 Illegal Pakistani immigrants occupy a squalid boardinghouse in '60s Yorkshire, including newly arrived Amir (Malhotra). He settles in, befriending young student Satib (Kumar), and learning the ropes from house leader Hossein Shah (Puri). But Shah brings unexpected problems to the group when his pregnant, white English girlfriend Mary (Ball) comes to stay and his nephew Irshad (Bhatti) arranges a paper marriage with the young woman. Based on the novel "Return Journey" by Abdullah Hussein. 104m/C VHS, GB Om Puri, Pavan Malhotra, Pravesh Kumar, Angeline Ball, Ahsan Bhatti; **D:** Udayan Prasad; **W:** Robert Buckler; **C:** Alan Almond; M: Stephen Warbeck.

Brothers of the Head 🐾🐾 2006 (R) Bizarre mockumentary a la "This Is Spinal Tap," only without the humor, tells the fictional story of British conjoined twins who are sold by their father to an unsavory music promoter who turns them into a freak-show punk band. The flashback-documentary style shows the rapid rise and fall of the band due to the usual rock and roll excesses. Pic gets a half bone for recreating an authentic 1970s British art/rock scene that makes an otherwise creepy flick watchable. Based on the 1977 illustrated novel by Brian Aldiss. 120m/C DVD, GB Sean Harris, Jonathan Pryce, John Simm, Jane Horrocks, Harry Treadway, Luke Treadway, Bryan Dick, Elizabeth Rider, Howard Attfield, Luke Wagner, Anna Nygh, Ed Hogg, Thomas Shuridge, Barbara Ewing; Cameos: Ken Russell; **D:** Keith Fulton, Louis Pepe; **W:** Tony Grisoni; **C:** Anthony Dod Mantle; M: Clive Langer.

Brothers of the West 🐾½ 1937 Cowboy saves his brothers from being lynched by proving the guilt of the real outlaws. 56m/B VHS, Tom Tyler, Bob Terry, Lois Wilde, Dorothy Short, Late (Lafayette) McKee, Dave O'Brien, Roger Williams; **D:** Sam Katzman; **W:** Basil Dickey; **C:** William (Bill) Hyer.

Brothers O'Toole 🐾🐾 1973 (G) The misadventures of a pair of slick drifters who, by chance, ride into a broken-down mining town in the 1890s. 94m/C VHS, DVD, John Astin, Steve Carlson, Pat Carroll, Hans Conried, Lee Meriwether; **D:** Richard Erdman.

ond half. Expanded from a one-act play by

Brothers Lionheart 🐾🐾½ 1977 (G) The Lion brothers fight for life, love and liberty during the Middle Ages. Based on a novel by Astrid Lindgren. 120m/C VHS, SW Staffan Gotestam, Lars Soderdahl, Allan Edwall; **D:** Olle Hellbom.

The Brothers McMullen 🐾🐾🐾 1994 (R) Slice of life drama finds three Irish-American brothers suddenly living under the same Long Island roof for the first time since childhood. Eldest brother Jack (Mulcahy) is a stolid high-school basketball coach married to teacher Molly (Britton) who's pressing him to have children. Cynical middle brother Barry (Burns), a writer, has just broken up with free-spirited Ann (McKay), and earnest young Patrick (McGlone) is engaged to Jewish girlfriend Susan (Albert). All three find their romantic relationships, as well as their belief in each other, tested. Generally good performances and dialogue, with Burns proving himself a triple threat as actor/writer/director. 98m/C VHS, DVD, Edward Burns, Jack Mulcahy, Mike McGlone, Connie Britton, Shari Albert, Elizabeth P. McKay, Maxine Bahns, Jennifer Jostyn, Catharine Bolt, Peter Johansen; **D:** Edward Burns; **W:** Edward Burns; **C:** Dick Fisher; M: Seamus Egan. Ind. Spirit '96: First Feature; Sundance '95: Grand Jury Prize.

Brown Sugar 🐾🐾 2002 (PG-13) Using the world of hip-hop music as its background, this romantic comedy succeeds in breathing life into a rather tired formula. Record producer Dre (Diggs) and music journalist Sidney (Lathan) are childhood friends who are drawn together by their shared love of the music. Although they think that romance is out of the question for them, everyone else knows that they're wrong, especially Sidney's friend Francine (Latifah). Unfortunately, Sidney doesn't figure it out until Dre becomes engaged to lovely lawyer Reese (Parker). She rebounds with suave basketball player Kelby (Kodjoe). Mos Def steals scenes as the shy, rapping cabbie who has a crush on Francine. 109m/C VHS, DVD, US Taye Diggs, Sanaa Lathan, Mos Def, Nicole Ari Parker, Queen Latifah, Wendell Pierce, Boris Kodjoe, Erik Weiner, Reggi Wynns; **D:** Rick Famuyiwa; **W:** Rick Famuyiwa, Michael Elliot; **C:** Enrique Chediak; M: Robert Hurst.

The Browning Version 🐾🐾🐾½ 1951 A lonely, unemotional classics instructor at a British boarding school realizes his failure as a teacher and as a husband. From the play by Terrence Rattigan. 89m/B VHS, DVD, GB Michael Redgrave, Jean Kent, Nigel Patrick, Wilfrid Hyde-White, Bill Travers; **D:** Anthony Asquith.

The Browning Version 🐾🐾½ 1994 (R) Mediocre remake of the Terence Rattigan play, previously filmed in 1951. Austere classics professor (Finney) at prestigious British boys school is disillusioned with both his floundering career and marriage. His emotional chill drives his younger wife (Scacchi) into an affair with a visiting American science teacher (Modine). Unfortunately updated to contemporary times, which can't hide apparent mustiness. Worth seeing for Finney's superb work as the out-of-touch prof. 97m/C VHS, DVD, Albert Finney, Greta Scacchi, Matthew Modine, Michael Gambon, Julian Sands, Ben Silverstone, Maryam D'Abo; **D:** Mike Figgis; **W:** Ronald Harwood; M: Mark Isham.

Brown's Requiem 🐾🐾½ 1998 (R) Ex-cop and ex-drunk Fritz Brown (Rooker) is a sometime L.A. private eye and repo man. He's hired by the aptly named Freddie "Fat Dog" Baker (Sasso) to locate his kid sister Jane (Blair) is living. Solly's involved with ex-cop Cathcart (James), with whom Fritz has a long-standing beef, and the P.I. uncovers various lowlifes and a scam. Based on James Ellroy's Chandleresque detailed and dialogue-heavy first novel, which was published in 1981. 97m/C VHS, DVD, Michael Rooker, Brion James, Harold Gould, Selma Blair, Kevin Corrigan, Tobin Bell, Jack Conley, Brad Dourif, Will Sasso, Valerie Perrine, Barry Newman;

outdoorsman brother Rick (McDonough) to join him and their mentally-challenged younger brother Norman (Campbell) at the family's remote, run-down cabin. Once there, Peter learns that their shifty father (Heard) has recently died a violent death. The brothers then spend their time drinking and offering up confessions that reveal dark secrets (through some confusing flashbacks), and their sins. 102m/C DVD, Patrick Wilson, Neal McDonough, Scott Michael Campbell, John Heard, Melora Walters; **D:** Paul Kampf; **W:** Paul Kampf; **C:** Henryk Cymerman.

The Brown Bunny 🐾🐾½ 2003 After this film's trashing as the worst movie in the history of the Cannes Film Festival, director/writer/star Gallo slashed nearly a half-hour from this story of a forlorn motorcycle racer's long, lonely coast-to-coast journey from a New Hampshire competition to his home in L.A. where he eventually meets up with love Daisy (Sevigny). An infamously graphic oral sex scene ensues, which leads to a funky final plot twist. Curiosity, about the Cannes hubbub and the sex scene, will be rewarded by an interesting, sometimes poignant, homage to the maverick filmmaking of the 1970s. 93m/C DVD, Vincent Gallo, Chloe Sevigny, Cheryl Tiegs, Elizabeth Blake, Anna Vareschi, Mary Morasky; **D:** Vincent Gallo; **W:** Vincent Gallo; **C:** Vincent Gallo.

D: Jason Freedland; **W:** Jason Freedland; **C:** Cynthia Millar.

Brubaker 🦴🦴🦴 **1980 (R)** A sanctimonious drama about a reform warden who risks his life to replace brutality and corruption with humanity and integrity in a state prison farm. Powerful prison drama. **131m/C VHS, DVD.** Robert Redford, Jane Alexander, Yaphet Kotto, Murray Hamilton, David Keith, Morgan Freeman, Matt Clark, M. Emmet Walsh, Everett McGill; **D:** Stuart Rosenberg; **W:** W.D. Richter, Arthur Ross; **M:** Lalo Schifrin.

The Bruce 🦴🦴1/2 **1996** Based on the story of Scottish king, Robert the Bruce (Welch) and the battle at Bannockburn against English King Edward 1's (Blessed) forces. Not blessed with the biggest budget and the actors tend to chew the scenery but not a bad bit of history. Robert the Bruce may also be familiar from the film "Braveheart." **110m/C VHS. GB** Sandy Welch, Oliver Reed, Brian Blessed, Michael Van Wijk, Pavel Douglas; **D:** Bob Carruthers, David McWhinnie; **M:** Paul Farrer.

Bruce Almighty 🦴🦴1/2 **2003 (PG-13)** No, it's not a Springsteen documentary, it's an enjoyable, if slight, Jim Carrey comedy. Carrey is Bruce Nolan, a TV reporter stuck with the fluff stories and longing to be taken seriously. He gets his chance when God (Freeman) decides to turn over the reins for a day and gives Bruce his divine powers. The comedy set-pieces are well done, and Carrey can do a lot with a little (at least in his comedies), but the overall effect is less laugh-out-loud funny than fans of the earlier Carrey/Shadyac pairings would expect. Aniston's not given much to do, but Carrell and Freeman stand out among the supporting cast. **101m/C VHS, DVD, HD DVD. US** Jim Carrey, Jennifer Aniston, Morgan Freeman, Lisa Ann Walter, Philip Baker Hall, Catherine Bell, Nora Dunn, Steven Carell; **D:** Tom Shadyac; **W:** Steve Oedekerk, Steve Koren, Mark O'Keefe; **C:** Dean Semler; **M:** John Debney.

Bruce Lee: Curse of the Dragon 🦴🦴 **1993** *The Curse of the Dragon* A behind the scenes look at the life and continuing mystery surrounding the life and untimely death of the martial arts superstar who died in 1973 at the age of 32. Highlights the spectacular fight sequences from Lee's movies as well as footage from his funeral and an interview with his son Brandon Lee, whose own death in 1993 raised further comment about a Lee family curse. **90m/C VHS. D:** Tom Kuhn, Fred Weintraub; **Nar:** George Takei.

Bruce Lee Fights Back from the Grave 🦴 **1976 (R)** Bruce Lee returns from the grave to fight the Black Angel of Death with his feet and to wreak vengeance on the evil ones who brought about his untimely demise. **84m/C VHS, DVD.** Bruce Le, Deborah Chaplin, Anthony Bronson; **D:** Umberto Lenzi.

Bruiser 🦴1/2 **2000** First film from horror icon Romero in more than seven years offers a great central premise, but little else. Henry Creedlow (Flemyng) is a nice guy who gets used by everyone around him, his cheating wife, his overbearing boss, and his dishonest stock broker all push Henry around, but he never stands up for himself. That is, until the day that he wakes up to find that his face has been replaced by a blank white mask. Being "faceless" allows Henry to assert himself and get revenge. The film is boring and filled with many unlikable characters, the worst of which is Henry. The last act is simply absurd and one can't help but wonder what has happened to the once great Romero. **99m/C VHS, DVD.** Jason Flemyng, Peter Stormare, Leslie Hope, Nina Garbiras, Tom Atkins, Jeff Monahan; **D:** George A. Romero; **W:** George A. Romero; **C:** Adam Swica; **M:** Donald Rubinstein.

Brush with Fate 🦴🦴 **2003** Mousy teacher Cornelia (Close) in possession of a 300-year-old Dutch painting called "Girl in Hyacinth Blue." It's possibly a Vermeer but Cornelia is afraid to find out since she may not be the legal owner. Still Cornelia would like new art professor Richard (Gibson) to give her his opinion. But the painting's history (told in flash-

backs) has caused its previous owners trouble as well. Based on the novel by Susan Vreeland. **100m/C VHS, DVD.** Glenn Close, Thomas Gibson, Ellen Burstyn, Phyllida Law, Kelly Macdonald, Patrick Bergin; **D:** Brent Shields; **W:** Richard Russo; **C:** Eric Van Haren Noman; **M:** Lawrence Shragge. **TV**

Brutal Fury 🦴🦴 **1992** Detective Molly Griffin goes undercover at a local high school and discovers a secret female vigilante group, called the "Fury," which goes after the drug dealers and rapists preying on the school's students. Teenagers with an attitude. **97m/C VHS.** Tom Campbell, Lisa-Gabrielle Greene, Annette Gerbon, Karen Eppers, Jennifer Winder, Allen Arkus; **D:** Frederick P. Watkins.

Brutal Glory 🦴🦴 **1989** Set in New York City in 1918 and based on the true story of the boxer known as "The Real McCoy." Fascinating and detailed history of a period, a champion, and the man who made it happen. **96m/C VHS.** Robert Vaughn, Timothy Brantley, Leah K. Pinsent; **D:** Koos Roets.

The Brutal Truth 🦴🦴 **1999 (R)** Group of high school friends get together for a 10-year reunion at a secluded mountain cabin for a weekend of fun, but then learn that one of the gang, Emily (Applegate), has committed suicide. This leads to arguments and secrets revealed. **89m/C VHS, DVD.** Christina Applegate, Justin Lazard, Johnathon Schaech, Moon Zappa, Paul Gleason, Molly Ringwald, Leslie Horan; **D:** Cameron Thor.

Brute 🦴1/2 **1997** Schweiger is doing humanitarian work in Eastern Europe when he discovers a group of orphans who are being abused by institute director Postlethwaite. So he tries to come to their rescue. Based on a true story. English and Polish with subtitles. **90m/C DVD. GE PL** Til Schweiger, Pete Postlethwaite, John Hurt, Polly Walker, Ida Joblonska; **D:** Maciej Dejczer; **W:** Cezary Harasimowicz; **C:** Paul Prokop, Arthur Reinhart; **M:** Michael Lorenc.

Brute Force 🦴🦴🦴1/2 **1947** Lancaster (in a star-making turn) is Joe, an inmate in an overcrowded prison lorded over by sadistic guard Munsey (Cronyn). When Munsey pushes the prisoners too far, Joe leads a daring prison break attempt. While some see this intense drama as heavy-handed (all of the inmates are victims of circumstance), the portrayals are compelling, and the story is first-rate noir. **102m/B DVD.** Burt Lancaster, Ann Blyth, Ella Raines, Yvonne De Carlo, Hume Cronyn, Charles Bickford, Whit Bissell, Howard Duff, Jeff Corey; **D:** Jules Dassin; **W:** Richard Brooks; **C:** William H. Daniels; **M:** Miklos Rozsa.

The Brute Man 🦴🦴 **1946** A young man who had been disfigured by his school mates goes out on a trail of revenge. Hatton is convincing in the title role, as in real life he was afflicted with acromegaly, an ailment that produces an enlargement of the bones in the face, hands, and feet. **62m/B VHS, DVD.** Rondo Hatton, Tom Neal, Jane Adams, Donald McBride, Peter Whitney; **D:** Jean Yarbrough; **W:** George Brickert, er, M. Coates Webster; **C:** Maury Gertsman; **M:** Hans J. Salter.

The Brylcreem Boys 🦴🦴 **1996 (PG-13)** In September, 1941, Canadian pilot Miles Keogh (Campbell) and his crew are forced to bail out of their plane. They land in neutral southern Ireland, where they're interned in the local POW camp run by Sean O'Brien (Byrne). The camp holds both Allies and Germans—separated only by a thin wire fence. Keogh figures it's his patriotic duty to try to escape as does German officer Rudolph von Stegenbeck (Macfadyen), and problems compound when both soldiers are let out on day-release passes and, naturally, fall for the same lovely local colleen, Mattie (Butler). **105m/C VHS, DVD. GB** Billy Campbell, Angus Macfadyen, William McNamara, Gabriel Byrne, Jean Butler, Joe McGann, Oliver Tobias, Gordon John Sinclair; **D:** Terence Ryan; **W:** Terence Ryan, Jamie Brown; **C:** Gerry Lively; **M:** Richard Hartley.

BTK Killer WOOF! **2006 (R)** Nonsensical and loathsome flick purportedly about Dennis Rader, the Wichita serial killer who wasn't caught for 30 years. The initials stand for Rader's methods: Bind,

Torture. Kill. For some unknown reason, hack director Lommel pads things out by including non-related animal slaughter scenes. **82m/C DVD.** Gerard Griesbaum; **D:** Ulli Lommel; **W:** Ulli Lommel; **C:** Blanco Pacelli; **M:** Robert Walsh. **VIDEO**

Bubba Ho-Tep 🦴🦴🦴 **2003 (R)** Elvis and JFK team up to battle the dark forces of Egypt, who threaten the residents of their East Texas convalescent home. Believable plot aside, director Coscarelli's delightfully wacky cult-concept comedy still manages to take the whole thing seriously, especially with an inspired performance from Campbell, playing it totally straight. In addition to the presumed-dead celebrities and world leaders, the small town of Mud Creek also attracts an Egyptian mummy known as Bubba Ho-Tep, who terrorizes the aged Texans. The feisty King and former Prez gleefully open a king-sized can of whoop-ass on the ancient terror. While flawed, it's still solid campy fun. Adapted from a short story by Joe Lansdale. **92m/C VHS, DVD. US** Bruce Campbell, Ossie Davis, Ella Joyce, Reggie Bannister, Bob Ivy, Larry Pennell, Heidi Marhout; **D:** Don A. Coscarelli; **W:** Don A. Coscarelli; **C:** Adam Janeiro; **M:** Brian Tyler.

Bubble 🦴🦴 **2006 (R)** Soderbergh's uneven, low-budget experiment features a nonprofessional cast portraying blue-collar workers at a small Midwestern doll factory. Overweight, middle-aged Martha's (Doebereiner) life consists of caring for her sick, elderly father and hanging over young, shy co-worker Kyle (Ashley). The boring predictability of their lives is shaken when Rose asks Kyle out on a date. Then one of the three is murdered and there's an investigation. It's all as minimalist and banal as the lives it depicts. Besides directing, Soderbergh shot the film under the pseudonym Peter Andrews. **73m/C DVD. US** Debbie Doebereiner, Dustin Ashley, Misty Wilkins, K. Smith; **D:** Steven Soderbergh; **W:** Coleman Hough; **C:** Steven Soderbergh; **M:** Robert Pollard.

The Bubble 🦴🦴 **2006** *Ha Buah* The westernized district of Sheikin St. in Tel Aviv seems far removed from the racial and religious conflicts plaguing the area. Lulu (Wircer) shares her apartment (and life) with two gay men: Yali (Friedmann) and Noam (Knoller), who is in love with Palestinian Ashraf (Sweid). Ashraf is living and working in the city illegally and his abrupt return to his home in Nablus leads to a last act that strains credibility. Hebrew and Arabic with subtitles. **117m/C DVD. IS** Ohad Knoller, Yousef (Joe) Sweid, Alon Friedmann, Daniela Wircer, Roba Blal, Shredy Jabarin; **D:** Eytan Fox; **W:** Eytan Fox, Gal Uchovsky; **C:** Yaron Sharf; **M:** Ivri Lider.

Bubble Boy 🦴🦴 **2001 (PG-13)** Disney has finally jumped on the crude and offensive humor bandwagon, with a simplistic storyline involving the journey of Jimmy (Gyllenhaal), a naive guy born with an immune system deficiency that requires him to live in a germ-free environment, as he races across the country to stop his sweetheart (Shelton) from marrying a jerk. Jimmy constructs a mobile bubble and hits the road. Along the way, the alleged jokes manage to offend Christians, Hindus, Jews, Republicans, Latinos, Asians and circus freaks while still wallowing in boner humor. That'd be almost forgivable if the "humor" was actually funny. **84m/C VHS, DVD. US** Jake Gyllenhaal, Swoosie Kurtz, Marley Shelton, Danny Trejo, John Carroll Lynch, Stephen Spinella, Verne Troyer, Dave Sheridan, Brian George, Patrick Cranshaw, Fabio; **D:** Blair Hayes; **W:** Ken Daurio, Cinco Paul; **C:** Jerzy Zielinski; **M:** John Ottman.

The Buccaneer 🦴🦴 **1958** A swashbuckling version of the adventures of pirate Jean LaFitte and his association with President Andrew Jackson during the War of 1812. Remake of Cecille B. DeMille's 1938 production. **121m/C VHS, DVD.** Yul Brynner, Charlton Heston, Claire Bloom, Inger Stevens, Charles Boyer, Henry Hull, E.G. Marshall, Lorne Greene; **D:** Anthony Quinn; **C:** Loyal Griggs; **M:** Elmer Bernstein.

The Buccaneers 🦴🦴🦴 **1995** Lavish adaptation of the Edith Wharton novel follows the adventures of four American girls in 1870s society. Nouveaux riche, the young ladies are unable to crack New York snobbery and, after vivacious Brazilian Conchita (Sorvino) manages to snag Lord Richard (Vibert), the others are encouraged by English governess Laura Testvalley (Lunghi) to try their luck in London. There, Virginia (Elliott), sister Nan (Gugino), their friend Lizzy (Kinlstedt), and Conchita all find hope and heartbreak among the English aristocracy. Wharton's novel was unfinished at her death and, though she left story notes, scripter Wadey concedes to changes. Made for TV. **288m/C VHS, DVD. GB** Carla Gugino, Mira Sorvino, Alison Elliott, Rya Kihlstedt, Cherie Lunghi, Connie Booth, Mark Tandy, Ronan Vibert, Jenny Agutter, Richard Huw, Greg Wise, James Frain, Michael Kitchen, Sheila Hancock, Rosemary Leach, Elizabeth Ashley, Conchata Ferrell, Peter Michael Goetz, James Rebhorn, E. Katherine Kerr; **D:** Philip Saville; **W:** Maggie Wadey; **C:** Maggie Wadey; **M:** Colin Towns. **TV**

Buccaneer's Girl 🦴🦴1/2 **1950** Charming swashbuckler. Pirate Frederick Baptiste (Friend) only attacks the ships of evil Narbonne (Douglas) as revenge for his father's death. During one of his raids, New Orleans entertainer Deborah (De Carlo) stows away and falls for the seafaring Robin Hood. However, hoping to marry into money, Deborah sets her sights on an aristocrat, only to figure out that Baptiste has been leading a double life. **77m/C DVD.** Yvonne De Carlo, Philip Friend, Robert Douglas, Elsa Lanchester, Andrea King, Norman Lloyd, Jay C. Flippen; **D:** Fred de Cordova; **W:** Joseph Hoffman, Harold Shumate; **C:** Russell Metty; **M:** Walter Scharf.

Buck and the Magic Bracelet 🦴🦴1/2 **1997 (PG-13)** In the old west a teen and his dog escape an attack on their prospecting camp. They're aided in bringing the bad guys to justice by a shaman's magic bracelet. **99m/C VHS.** Matt McCoy, Abby Dalton, Felton Perry, Conrad Nichols; **D:** Tonino Ricci; **W:** Fabio Campi; **C:** Giovanni Bergami; **M:** Stefano Curti.

Buck and the Preacher 🦴🦴1/2 **1972 (PG)** A trail guide and a con man preacher join forces to help a wagon train of former slaves who are seeking to homestead out West. Poitier's debut as a director. Poitier had a few great success, and the film that established the formula for each subsequent film. **102m/C VHS, DVD.** Sidney Poitier, Harry Belafonte, Ruby Dee, Cameron Mitchell, Denny Miller; **D:** Sidney Poitier.

Buck Privates 🦴🦴🦴 **1941** *Rookies* Abbott and Costello star as two dim-witted tie salesmen, running from the law, who become buck privates during WWII. The duo's first great success, and the film that also try to help a French girl sneak into the United States. Funny antics culminate into a wild chase scene. **77m/B VHS, DVD.** Bud Abbott, Lou Costello, Tom Brown, Joan Shawlee, Nat Pendleton, Beverly Simmons, Don Beddoe, Don Porter, Donald MacBride; **D:** Arthur Lubin; **W:** Arthur T. Horman, John Grant; **C:** Milton Krasner; **M:** Charles Previn.

Buck Privates Come Home 🦴🦴🦴 **1947** *Rookies Come Home* The story of Buck Privates return to their "Buck Privates" roles as two soldiers trying to adjust to civilian life after the war. They also try to help a French girl sneak into the United States. Many of the "inventions" seen in this movie have actually come into existence—space-ships, ray guns (lasers), anti-gravity belts—a testament to Nolan's almost psychic farsightedness. **91m/B VHS.** Buster Crabbe, Constance Moore, Jackie Moran; **D:** Ford Beebe, Saul Goodkind.

Buck Rogers Conquers the Universe 🦴🦴 **1939** The story of Buck Rogers, written by Phil Nolan in 1928, was the first science-fiction story done in the modern superhero space genre. Many of the "inventions" seen in this movie have actually come into existence—space-ships, ray guns (lasers), anti-gravity belts—a testament to Nolan's almost psychic farsightedness. **91m/B VHS.** Buster Crabbe, Constance Moore, Jackie Moran; **D:** Ford Beebe, Saul Goodkind.

Buck Rogers in the 25th Century 🐾🐾 1979 (PG) An American astronaut, preserved in space for 500 years, is brought back to life by a passing scene. TV miniseries adapted by Kureishi from his novel. **220m/C VHS. GB** Naveen Andrews, Roshan Seth, Susan Fleetwood, Steven Mackintosh, Brenda Blethyn, John McEnery, Janet Dale, David Bamber, Donald (Don) Sumpter, Jemma Redgrave, Brad Bradley; **D:** Roger Michell; **W:** Hanif Kureishi, Roger Michell; **C:** John McGlashan; **M:** David Bowie. **TV**

spy from Earth. Based on the classic movie serial, TV movie that began the popular series. Additional series episodes are available. **90m/C VHS, DVD.** Gil Gerard, Pamela Hensley, Erin Gray, Henry Silva; **D:** Daniel Haller; **V:** Mel Blanc. **TV**

The Bucket List 🐾½ 2007 (PG-13) Yes, that's as in "kick the bucket." Clichéd sitcom finds cancer patients Edward Cole (Nicholson) and Carter Chambers (Freeman) getting the bad news that their time is very limited. Since Edward is a self-satisfied gazillionaire estranged from his family, he decides to indulge his every last whim and takes fellow patient Carter, a working-class married father, on their own buddy road trip 'round the world. Nicholson's crazy-wealthy serious, and the scenery seems to be all computer-generated. **97m/C DVD. US** Jack Nicholson, Morgan Freeman, Sean P. Hayes, Beverly Todd, Alfonso Freeman, Rowena Kroy, Rob Morrow; **D:** Rob Reiner; **W:** Justin Zackham; **C:** John Schwartzman; **M:** Marc Shaiman.

A Bucket of Blood 🐾🐾🐾 1959 Cult favorite Dick Miller stars as a sculptor with a peculiar "talent" for lifelike artwork. Corman stars will see thematic similarities to his subsequent work, "Little Shop of Horrors" (1960). "Bucket of Blood" was made in just five days, while "Little Shop of Horrors" was made in a record breaking two days. Corman horror/spoof noted for its excellent beatnik atmosphere. **66m/B VHS, DVD.** Dick Miller, Barboura Morris, Antony Carbone, Julian Burton, Ed Nelson, Bert Convy, Judy Bamber, John Brinkley, Myrtle Domerel, John Herman Shaner, Bruno VeSota; **D:** Roger Corman; **W:** Charles B. Griffith; **C:** John Marquette; **M:** Fred Katz.

Buckeye and Blue 🐾½ 1987 (PG) A hero turned outlaw, his 14-year-old female sidekick, and a gang known as the McCoys are all on the lam from the law in this western adventure. **94m/C VHS.** Robin (Robyn) Lively, Jeffery Osterhage, Rick Gibbs, Will Hannah, Kenneth Jensen, Patrick Johnston, Stuart Rogers, Michael Horse; **D:** J.C. Compton.

Buckskin 🐾½ 1968 Slow-moving western about a marshal protecting townspeople from a greedy, land-grabbing cattle baron. **99m/C VHS.** Barry Sullivan, Wendell Corey, Joan Caulfield, Lon Chaney Jr., John Russell, Barbara Hale, Barton MacLane, Bill Williams; **D:** Michael D. Moore.

Buckskin Frontier 🐾½ 1943 Story is built around Western railroad construction and cattle empires in the 1860s. Cobb tries to stop the railroad from coming through by hiring Jory to do his dirty work. **75m/B VHS, DVD.** Richard Dix, Jane Wyatt, Lee J. Cobb, Albert Dekker, Victor Jory, Lola Lane, Max Baer Sr.; **D:** Lesley Selander.

Bucktown 🐾½ 1975 (R) A black drama recounts Abbott & Costello's rise in Hollywood. While the story, based on the book by Bob Thomas, is interesting, the two funnymen in the leads can't pull off the old classic skits. **96m/C VHS.** Harvey Korman, Williamson, Pam Grier, Bernie Hamilton, Thalmus Rasulala, Art Lund, Robert (Skip) Burton, Carl Weathers; **D:** Arthur Marks; **W:** Bob Ellison; **C:** Robert Birchl; **M:** Johnny Pate.

Bud and Lou 🐾½ 1978 Comedy/drama recounts Abbott & Costello's rise in Hollywood. While the story, based on the book by Bob Thomas, is interesting, the two funnymen in the leads can't pull off the old classic skits. **98m/C VHS.** Harvey Korman, Buddy Hackett, Michele Lee, Arte Johnson, Robert Reed; **D:** Robert C. Thompson.

The Buddha of Suburbia 🐾🐾🐾 1992 Satire set in late '70s suburban London follows the coming of age adventures of Karim (Andrews), the handsome son of an Indian father and English mother. His gleeful father Haroon (Seth) exploits the vogue for eastern philosophies he knows nothing about with lectures to the upper-middle classes while he carries on with devotee Eva (Fleetwood). When his mother finds out, Karim and his father move into central London with Eva, where Karim decides to take up acting in fringe theatre and sex while his friend, Eva's son Charlie (Macintosh), experiments with the punk music scene. TV miniseries adapted by Kureishi from his novel. **220m/C VHS. GB** Naveen Andrews, Roshan Seth, Susan Fleetwood, Steven Mackintosh, Brenda Blethyn, John McEnery, Janet Dale, David Bamber, Donald (Don) Sumpter, Jemma Redgrave, Brad Bradley; **D:** Roger Michell; **W:** Hanif Kureishi, Roger Michell; **C:** John McGlashan; **M:** David Bowie. **TV**

Buddy 🐾½ 1997 (PG) Animals run amok in the Lintz household. Mother hen Gertrude Lintz (Russo) raises just about everything from mischievous chimps to impressionable parrots on her estate. A baby gorilla (named Buddy, short for Buddha) becomes part of the family, but as he grows in size, so does the difficulty in caring for him. Amiable tale of one woman's motherly bond with a gorilla includes convincing performances by Russo and an animatronic gorilla courtesy of Jim Henson's Creature Shop. Well-paced and very touching at moments, children will definitely enjoy the zany animal antics, and adults should be moved by the unusual relationship. Based on the book by Lintz. **84m/C VHS, DVD.** Rene Russo, Robbie Coltrane, Irma P. Hall, Alan Cumming, Paul (Pee-wee Herman) Reubens; **D:** Caroline Thompson; **W:** Caroline Thompson; **M:** Elmer Bernstein.

Buddy Boy 🐾½ 1999 (R) Isolated by the need to care for his ailing mother (Tyrrell), shy Francis (Gillen) begins a voyeuristic relationship with his sexy neighbor (Seigner). Strange but captivating film provides some gothic creepiness as well as commentary on the toll of enforced isolation. **105m/C DVD.** Aidan Gillen, Emmanuelle Seigner, Susan Tyrrell, Mark Boone Jr., Hector Elias, Harry Groener; **D:** Mark Hanlon; **W:** Mark Hanlon; **C:** Hubert Taczanowski; **M:** Graeme Revel, Brian Eno, Michael Brook.

Buddy Buddy 🐾½ 1981 (R) A professional hitman's well-ordered arrangement to knock off a state's witness keeps being interrupted by the suicidal attempts of a man in the next hotel room. **96m/C VHS.** Jack Lemmon, Walter Matthau, Paula Prentiss, Klaus Kinski; **D:** Billy Wilder; **W:** Billy Wilder, I.A.L. Diamond; **C:** Harry Stradling Jr.; **M:** Lalo Schifrin.

The Buddy Holly Story 🐾🐾🐾½ 1978 (PG) An acclaimed biography of the famed 1950s pop star, spanning the years from his meteoric career's beginnings to his tragic, early death in the now famous plane crash of February 3, 1959. Busey performs Holly's hits himself. ♫Rock Around the Ollie Vee; That'll Be the Day. Oh, Boy; It's So Easy; Well All Right; Chantilly Lace; Peggy Sue. **113m/C VHS, DVD.** Gary Busey, Don Stroud, Charles Martin Smith, Conrad Janis, William Jordan, Albert "Poppy" Popwell; **D:** Steve Rash; **W:** Robert Gittler; **C:** Steven Larner; **M:** Joe Renzetti. *Oscars '78: Orig. Song Score and/or Adapt.; Natl. Soc. Film Critics '78: Actor (Busey).*

The Buddy System 🐾🐾 1983 (PG) A tale of contemporary love and the modern myths that outline the boundaries between lovers and friends. **110m/C VHS.** Richard Dreyfuss, Susan Sarandon, Jean Stapleton, Nancy Allen, Wil Wheaton, Edward Winter, Keene Curtis; **D:** Glenn Jordan; **W:** Mary Agnes Donohue.

Buddy's Song 🐾🐾 1991 (R) A '60s coming of age tale, only in this case it's the father and not the son who needs to grow up. Dad (Daltrey) is more interested in hanging out with his no-account musician friends than in looking after his family. Although he's not above meddling in his teenage son's musical career, which could be the success his father's never was. Based on the novel by Nigel Hinton and also did the screenplay. British teen idol Hawkes (in his film debut) had a top ten hit song from the film with "The Ore and Only." **106m/C VHS. GB** Roger Daltrey, Chesney Hawkes, Sharon Duce, Michael Elphick, Douglas Hodge, Lee Ross, James Aubrey, Liza Walker; **D:** Claude Whatham; **W:** Nigel Hinton; **C:** John Hooper; **M:** John Grover, Roger Daltrey.

Buffalo Bill 🐾🐾 1944 A light, fictionalized account of the life and career of Bill Cody, from frontier hunter to showman. **89m/C VHS, DVD.** Joel McCrea, Maureen O'Hara, Linda Darnell, Thomas Mitchell, Edgar Buchanan, Anthony Quinn, Moroni Olsen, Sidney Blackmer; **D:** William A. Wellman; **C:** Leon Shamroy.

Buffalo Bill & the Indians 🐾🐾🐾 1976 (PG) A perennially underrated Robert Altman historical pastiche, portraying the famous Wild West character as a charlatan and shameless exemplar of encroaching imperialism. Great all-star cast chaos. **135m/C VHS, DVD.** Paul Newman, Geraldine Chaplin, Joel Grey, Will Sampson, Harvey Keitel, Burt Lancaster, Kevin McCarthy; **D:** Robert Altman; **W:** Robert Altman, Alan Rudolph; **M:** Richard Baskin.

Buffalo Bill Rides Again 🐾½ 1947 With an Indian uprising on the horizon, Buffalo Bill is called in. Mr. Bill finds there's a land swindle going on. **66m/B VHS.** Richard Arlen, Jennifer Holt, Edward Cassidy, Edmund Cobb Charles Stevens; **D:** Robert E. Cline.

Buffalo Boy 🐾🐾 *Mua Len Treu* 2004. Coming-of-age story set in 1940s Vietnam. Teenaged Kim is sent by his ill father Dinh to herd their two starving water buffalo to new pasture. Kim falls in with a tough group of buffalo herders, winds up with one buffalo, and tries to mend the rift with his father before the old man dies. Vietnamese with subtitles. **102m/C DVD. VT BE FFLe** the L.I. Nguyen Hu Thanj, Vo Hoang Nhan, **D:** Minh Nguyen-Vo; **W:** Minh Nguyen-Vo; **C:** Yves Cape; **M:** Ton That Tiet.

Buffalo Girls 🐾½ 1995 Western saga, set in the 1870s, tells of the lifelong friendship between hard-drinking, hard-living Calamity Jane (Huston—who's not exactly any plain Jane) and buxom, softhearted madam Dora DuFran (Griffith). Dora's in love (but refuses to marry) with rancher Teddy Blue (Byrne) while Calamity has a daughter by Wild Bill Hickok (Elliott) that she gives up for adoption. There's lots of rambling and commisserating over the changing and civilizing of the west and various man troubles. Based on the novel by Larry McMurty, originally a two-part TV miniseries. **180m/C VHS, DVD.** Anjelica Huston, Melanie Griffith, Gabriel Byrne, Peter Coyote, Jack Palance, Sam Elliott, Reba McEntire, Floyd "Red Crow" Westerman, Tracey Walter, Russell Means, Charlaine Woodard, Jean Diehl, Liev Schreiber, Andrew Bicknell, Kathryn Witt; **D:** Rod Hardy; **W:** Cynthia Whitcomb; **C:** David O'Connell; **M:** Lee Holdridge.

Buffalo Jump 🐾🐾🐾 *Getting Married in Buffalo Jump* 1990 An independent woman, working as a lounge singer in Toronto, returns to her home in Alberta when her father dies. To her surprise he has left her the family ranch and, to the surprise of everyone else, she decides to stay and run it. She hires a good-looking local man to help her out and they both discover that they want more than a working relationship. However, the fireworks really start when he proposes a marriage of convenience. Engaging performances and beautiful scenery help raise this romantic tale of opposites above the average. **97m/C VHS, DVD.** ♫A Wendy Crewson, Paul Gross, Marion Gilsenan, Kyra Harper, Victoria Snow; **D:** Eric Till.

Buffet Froid 🐾🐾🐾½ 1979 Surreal black comedy about a group of bungling murderers. First rate acting and directing makes this film a hilarious treat. From the director of "Menage." In French with English subtitles. **95m/C VHS, DVD. FR** Gerard Depardieu, Bernard Blier, Jean Carmet, Genevieve Page, Denise Gence, Carole Bouquet, Jean-Benguigui, Michel Serrault; **D:** Bertrand Blier; **W:** Bertrand Blier; **C:** Jean Penzer; **M:** Philippe Sarde. Cesar '80: Writing.

Buena Vista Social Club 🐾🐾🐾 1999 (G) American musician Ry Cooder assembled a number of aging Cuban musicians and singers, informally known as the Buena Vista Social Club, to record an album in Havana. The success of that 1997 venture led director Wenders to record this documentary as Wenders reunites for a concert tour that culminates in a 1998 performance at Carnegie Hall. **105m/C VHS, DVD.** Ry Cooder, Wim Wenders, L.A. Film Critics '99: Feature Doc.; N.Y. Film Critics '99: Feature Doc.; Natl. Bd. of Review '99: Feature Doc.; Natl. Soc. Film Critics '99: Feature Doc.

Buffalo Rider 🐾½ 1978 An adventure film depicting the real-life experiences of C.J. "Buffalo" Jones who worked to save the American buffalo from extinction. **90m/C VHS.** Rick Quinn, John Freeman, Priscilla Laurie, George Sager, Rich Scheeland; **D:** George Laurie.

Buffalo 66 🐾🐾🐾 1997 Billy Brown (Gallo) is a loser of epic proportions. He's named after the Buffalo Bills, notorious losers of Super Bowls. After he loses $10,000 on of these Super Bowls, he turns to a life of crime and promptly lands in prison. Stumbling into a dance studio, Billy kidnaps the nubile Layla (Ricci) and forces her to pose as his wife for a visit to his parents. He had explained his five-year absence to them by saying that he was working for the CIA overseas with his new bride. His father Jimmy (Gazzara), a bitter ex-lounge singer, barely hides his disdain for Billy, and mother Janet (Huston) is so too obsessed with the Bills to interact with him. They both like Layla instantly, and she seems to take unexpected glee in playing her part. Former artist and rock musician Gallo also directed, cowrote and composed the music for the-book Army man, Sgt. Washington Wyatt (Glover) leads the chase for Apache warrior Victorio (Lowe) across the New Mexico Territory while trying to deal with the common degradation suffered by his troops at the hands of white officers. Lots of cruelty and explicit violence. **112m/C VHS, DVD.** Vincent Gallo, Christina Ricci, Anjelica Huston, Ben Gazzara, Kevin Corrigan, Mickey Rourke, Rosanna Arquette, Jan-Michael Vincent; **D:** Vincent Gallo; **W:** Alison Bagnall, Vincent Gallo; **C:** Lance Acord; **M:** Vincent Gallo. Natl. Bd. of Review '98: Support. Actress (Ricci).

Buffalo Soldiers 🐾🐾🐾 1997 Post-Civil War western concerns the all-black Cavalry troops, created by Congress in 1866 to patrol the west. They received their nickname from the Indians, who thought the black soldiers on horseback looked like buffalo. A former slave and byfilm. **112m/C VHS, DVD.** Vincent Gallo, Christina Ricci, Anjelica Huston, Ben Gazzara, Kevin Corrigan, Mickey Rourke, Rosanna Arquette, Jan-Michael Vincent; **D:** Vincent Gallo; **W:** Alison Bagnall, Vincent Gallo; **C:** Lance Acord; **M:** Vincent Gallo. **CABLE**

Buffalo Soldiers 🐾🐾🐾 2001 (R) Darkly satiric look at the military revolves around a supply unit of an American Army base in 1989 Germany. Leader of the pack is the bored, amoral Elwood (Phoenix) who gets his kicks and a few extra bucks by dabbling in the black market, dealing in heroin and illegal weapons, and other equally illicit activities. Soon, the newly prosperous Elwood's basically running things at the base until a new Top Sergeant (Glenn) cracks down. Elwood retaliates by dating Sarge's daughter (Paquin) but finds he's actually falling for her. Premiered at the Toronto Film Festival in 2001, then waited for a more appropriate release date, which never actually came (it's not exactly complimentary to the military). Based on a novel by Robert O'Connor. **98m/C VHS, DVD. US GB GE** Joaquin Phoenix, Scott Glenn, Anna Paquin, Ed Harris, Leon Robinson, Dean Stockwell, Elizabeth McGovern, Gabriel Mann, Shiek Mahmud-Bey, Michael Pena, Glenn Fitzgerald, Brian Delate, Jimmie Ray Weeks; **D:** Gregor Jordan; **W:** Gregor Jordan, Eric Weiss, Nora MacCoby; **C:** Oliver Stapleton; **M:** David Holmes.

Buffalo Stampede 🐾 1933 Our heroes are involved in a plot to round up buffalo to sell for meat. **60m/B VHS, DVD.** Randolph Scott, Buster Crabbe, Harry Carey Sr., Noah Beery Sr., Raymond Hatton, Judith Allen, Blanche Frederici; **D:** Henry Hathaway.

Buffy the Vampire Slayer ✓✓✓ 1992 (PG-13) Funny, near-camp teen genre spoof. Buffy is a typical mall gal concerned with shopping and cheerleading, until the mysterious Sutherland proclaims it her destiny to slay the vampires who have suddenly infested Los Angeles. Like, really. Buffy requires some convincing, but eventually takes up the challenge, fighting off the vamps and their seductive leader Hauer, aided by perpetual guy-in-distress Perry. "Pee-wee" Reubens is unrecognizable and terribly amusing in one of the longer death scenes of film history. Check out Cassandra (Wagner), Natalie Wood's daughter. **98m/C VHS, DVD.** D: Stephen (Steve) Root, Ben Affleck, Mark DeCarlo, Thomas Jane, Ricki Lake, Kristy Swanson, Donald Sutherland, Luke Perry, Paul (Pee-wee Herman) Reubens, Rutger Hauer, Michele Abrams, Randall Batinkoff, Hilary Swank, Paris Vaughan, David Arquette, Candy Clark, Natasha Gregson Wagner; D: Fran Rubel Kuzui; W: Joss Whedon; C: James Hayman; M: Carter Burwell.

Bug WOOF! *The Bug* 1975 (PG) The city of Riverside is threatened with destruction after a massive earth tremor unleashes a super-race of ten-inch mega-cockroaches that belch fire, eat raw meat, and are virtually impervious to Raid. Produced by gimmick-king William Castle, who wanted to install windshield wiper-like devices under theatre seats that would brush against the patrons' feet as the cockroaches crawled across the screen; unfortunately, the idea was squashed flat. **100m/C VHS, DVD.** Bradford Dillman, Joanna Miles, Richard Gilliland, Jamie Smith-Jackson, Alan Fudge, Jesse Vint, Patty McCormack, Brendan Dillon Jr., Frederic Downs, William Castle; D: Jeannot Szwarc; W: Thomas Page, William Castle; C: Michael Hugo; M: Charles Fox.

Buford's Beach Bunnies ✓ 1992 (R) Harry Buford has made a fortune selling barbecued rabbit sandwiches served by the sexiest waitresses around. Harry wants to leave the business to his son Jeeter—if Jeeter can overcome his overwhelming fear of women. So three of Harry's waitresses decide to show Jeeter a very good time. Lots of pretty girls in not much clothing. **90m/C VHS, DVD.** Rikki Brando, Monique Parent, Amy Page, Barrett Cooper, Ina Rogers, Charley Rossman, David Robinson; D: Mark Pirro; W: Mark Pirro.

Bug Buster ✓✓ 1999 (R) The Griffins, dad (Kopell), mom (Lockhart) and daughter Shannon (Heigl) move to scenic Mountainview to flee the stress of city life. But they didn't bargain for the giant creature "unknown to science" that's attacking people and leaving giant bug larvae in 'em. Mutant insects overrun the town, leaving the survivors one last hope, in the form of ex-military man-turned-uberexterminator General George (Quaid). Plenty of gore and over-the-top acting, plus Scotty and Mr. Sulu, give this one late-night cult potential. **93m/C VHS, DVD.** Randy Quaid, Katherine Heigl, Meredith Salenger, Bernie Kopell, Anne Lockhart, George Takei, James Doohan, Ty O'Neal, Downtown Julie Brown, Brenda Doumani, David Lipper; D: Lorenzo Doumani; W: Malik Khoury; C: Hanania Baer; M: Sidney James.

Bugged! ✓ 1996 (PG-13) Flesh-eating insects attack a beautiful homemaker and her only hope: a group of bumbling exterminators are her

---

Ronald K. Armstrong; C: S. Toriano Berry; M: Boris Elkis.

Bugles in the Afternoon ✓✓ 1952 Life in the army during Custer's last days, with a love triangle, revenge and the Little Big Horn for added spice. **85m/C VHS.** Ray Milland, Hugh Marlowe, Helena Carter, Forrest Tucker, Barton MacLane, George Reeves, James Millican, Gertrude Michael, Hugh Beaumont, Sheb Wooley; D: Roy Rowland; W: Daniel Mainwaring, Harry Brown; C: Wilfrid M. Cline; M: Dimitri Tiomkin.

A Bug's Life ✓✓✓ 1998 (G) Computer animated feature by Pixar, the makers of "Toy Story," takes a cutesy look into the world of insects. Flik (Foley) is an ant who must help defend his colony after he messes up a tribute to a bullying group of grasshoppers led by Hopper (Spacey). He recruits a crew of misfits from a flea circus, including a male ladybug with gender issues (Leary), a prissy stick bug (Pierce), and an obese caterpillar (Ranft). Together they form a plan to keep the grasshoppers away, but still must confront Hopper in order to ensure lasting peace. Amazing animation, from the blades of grass down to the facial expressions of the bugs, along with dozens of sight gags keep this family feature flying. Competed with fellow computer animated insect feature "Antz" on its release. **94m/C VHS, DVD.** D: John Lasseter, Andrew Stanton; W: Donald McEnery, Bob Shaw, Andrew Stanton, Joe Ranft; C: Sharon Calahan; M: Randy Newman; V: Dave Foley, Kevin Spacey, Julia Louis-Dreyfus, Phyllis Diller, Richard Kind, David Hyde Pierce, Joe Ranft, Denis Leary, Jonathan Harris, Madeline Kahn, Bonnie Hunt, Michael McShane, John Ratzenberger, Brad Garrett, Roddy McDowall, Edie McClurg, Hayden Panettiere, Alex Rocco, David Ossman.

Bugsy ✓✓✓½ 1991 (R) Beatty is Benjamin "Bugsy" Siegel, the 40s gangster who built the Flamingo Hotel in Las Vegas when it was still a virtual desert, before it became a gambling mecca. Bening is perfect as Bugsy's moll, Virginia Hill, who inspired him to carry out his dream of building the Flamingo (which was her nickname). Beatty and Bening heat up the screen and their off-screen relationship was no different. Fans anticipated their seemingly imminent marriage almost as much as the release of this movie. Almost nothing mars this film which Toback adapted from a novel by Dean Jennings, "We Only Kill Each Other: The Life and Bad Times of Bugsy Siegel." **135m/C VHS, DVD.** Warren Beatty, Annette Bening, Harvey Keitel, Ben Kingsley, Elliott Gould, Joe Mantegna, Richard Sarafian, Bebe Neuwirth, Wendy Phillips, Robert Beltran, Bill Graham, Lewis Van Bergen, Debrah Farentino; D: Barry Levinson; W: James Toback; C: Allen Daviau; M: Ennio Morricone. Oscars '91: Art Dir./Set Dec., Costume Des.; Golden Globes '92: Film—Drama; L.A. Film Critics '91: Director (Levinson), Film, Screenplay; Natl. Bd. of Review '91: Actor (Beatty).

Bugsy Malone ✓✓✓½ 1976 (R) Delightful musical features an all-children's cast highlighting this spoof of 1930s' gangster movies. **94m/C VHS, DVD.** Jodie Foster, Scott Baio, Florrie Augger, John Cassisi, Martin Lev; C: Peter Biziou; M: Paul Williams. British Acad. '76: Screenplay.

Bull Durham ✓✓✓½ 1988 (R) Lovable American romantic comedy, dealing with a very minor minor-league team and three of its current constituents: aging baseball groupie Annie Savoy (Sarandon) who beds one player each season; cocky, foolish new pitcher, Ebby Calvin "Nuke" LaLoosh (Robbins); and older, weary catcher Crash Davis (Costner), who's assigned to wise the rookie up. The scene in which Annie tries poetry out on the banal rookie (who has more earthly pleasures in mind) is a hoot. Highly acclaimed, this the film sears with Sarandon and Costner's love scenes and some clever dialogue. **107m/C VHS, DVD.** Kevin Costner, Susan Sarandon, Tim Robbins, Trey Wilson, Robert Wuhl, Jenny Robertson; D: Ron Shelton; W: Ron Shelton; C: Bobby Byrne; M: Michael Convertino. L.A. Film Critics '88: Screenplay; N.Y. Film Critics '88: Screenplay; Natl. Soc. Film Critics '88: Screenplay; Writers Guild '88: Orig. Screenplay.

Bull of the West ✓✓½ 1971 Cattlemen battle for land in the wide open spaces of the old West. **90m/C VHS.** Charles Bronson, Lee J. Cobb, Brian Keith, George Kennedy, DeForest Kelley, Doug McClure, James Drury, Geraldine Brooks, Lois Nettleton, Ben Johnson, Gary Clarke; D: Jerry Hopper; W: Don Ingalls; C: Benjamin (Ben H.) Kline; M: Hal Mooney.

Buldance ✓ *Forbidden Son* 1988 At a gymnastic school in Crete, a girl's obsession with Greek mythological ritual leads to murder. **105m/C VHS, DVD.** Lauren Hutton, Cliff DeYoung, Renee Estevez; D: Zelda Barron.

Bulldog Courage ✓✓ 1935 Young man is out to avenge his father's murder. **66m/B VHS, DVD.** Tim McCoy, Lois January, Joan Woodbury, John Elliott; D: Sam Newfield.

Bulldog Drummond ✓✓½ 1929 The Bulldog Drummond character, created by "Sapper" (Herman Cyril McNeile), underwent a number of different incarnations from 20s silents through the 40s, and even occasionally in the 50s and 60s. A suave ex-British officer (a precursor to the glib shaken-not-stirred gentleman-spy variety), Bulldog has been played by the likes of Colman, Ralph Richardson, and Tom Conway, among others. In this, the first installment in the long-standing series, a WWI vet, bored with civilian life, is enlisted by a beautiful woman to help her father in various adventures. **85m/B VHS.** Ronald Colman, Joan Bennett, Montagu Love, Lilyan Tashman, Lawrence Grant, Wilson Benge, Claud Allister, Adolph Millar, Charles Sellon, Tetsu Komai, Donald Novis; D: F. Richard Jones; W: Sidney Howard, Wallace Smith; C: George Barnes, Gregg Toland.

Bulldog Drummond at Bay ✓ 1937 Drummond searches for a group of foreign agents who are trying to steal the plans for a top-secret warplane. Poor British entry to the "Bulldog Drummond" series. **63m/B VHS, DVD.** GB John Lodge. Dorothy Mackaill, Victor Jory, Claud Allister, Hugh Miller; D: Norman Lee.

Bulldog Drummond Comes Back ✓✓ 1937 Drummond, aided by Colonel Nielson, rescues his fiancee from the hands of desperate kidnappers. **119m/B VHS, DVD.** John Howard, John Barrymore, Louise Campbell, Reginald Denny, Guy Standing; D: Louis King.

Bulldog Drummond Escapes ✓✓ 1937 Drummond, aided by his side-kick and valet, rescues a beautiful girl from spies. He then falls in love with her. **67m/B VHS, DVD.** Ray Milland, Heather Angel, Reginald Denny, Guy Standing, Porter Hall, E.E. Clive; D: James Hogan; W: Edward T. Lowe; C: Victor Milner.

Bulldog Drummond's Bride ✓✓ 1939 Ace detective Bulldog Drummond has to interrupt his honeymoon in order to pursue a gang of bank robbers across France and England. The last of the Bulldog Drummond film series. **69m/B VHS, DVD.** John Howard, Heather Angel, H.B. Warner, E.E. Clive, Reginald Denny, Eduardo Ciannelli, Elizabeth Patterson, John Sutton; D: James Hogan; W: Garnett Weston; C: Harry Fischbeck.

Bulldog Drummond's Peril ✓ 1938 Murder and robbery drag the adventurous Drummond away from his wedding and he pursues the villains surrounding his crime in the character of Inspector Neilson of Scotland Yard. Barrymore revels in the characterization and Denny is stalwart. In this typically fast-paced installment, suave sleuth Drummond stalks the master criminal responsible for stealing the formula to an explosive. **55m/B VHS, DVD.** John Howard, John Barrymore, Reginald Denny, Louise Campbell, Frank Puglia, Nydia Westman, Lucien Littlefield; D: Louis King.

Bulldog Drummond's Revenge ✓✓½ 1937 Bulldog's "Revenge" was made during the series' heyday and was the second to star Howard as Drummond; the bulk of the Bulldog Drummond film series

---

Bulldog Drummond's Secret Police ✓✓ 1939 The 15th Drummond film, adapted from Herman Cyril McNeile's famed detective novels featuring a millionpound treasure stashed in the Drummond manor and the murderous endeavors to retrieve it. **54m/B VHS, DVD.** John Howard, Heather Angel, H.B. Warner, Reginald Denny, E.E. Clive, Leo G. Carroll; D: James Hogan; W: Garnett Weston; C: Merritt B. Gerstad.

Bulldog Edition ✓✓ 1936 Two newspapers engage in an all-out feud to be number one in the city, even going so far as to employ gangsters for purposes of sabotage. **57m/B VHS.** Ray Walker, Evelyn Knapp, Regis Toomey, Cy Kendall, William "Billy" Newell, Oscar Apfel, Betty Compson, Robert Warwick; D: Charles Lamont.

Bulldog Jack ✓✓✓ *Alias Bulldog Drummond* 1935 Fine entry in the series has Drummond's colleague battling it out with Richardson, the leader of gang of jewel thieves. **62m/B VHS.** GB Fay Wray, Jack Hulbert, Claude Hulbert, Ralph Richardson, Paul Graetz, Gibb McLaughlin; D: Walter Forde.

Bullet ✓½ 1994 (R) Butch (Rourke) gets released from prison and immediately returns to his old drug and burglary ways on New York's mean streets. And he's got a score to settle with crazy drug kingpin Tank (Shakur). Has little to recommend it, except to those who like violence, with lackluster performances and a dull script. **96m/C VHS.** Mickey Rourke, Tupac Shakur, Ted Levine, Adrien Brody, John Enos; D: Julien Temple; W: Bruce Rubenstein; C: Crescenzo G.P. Notarile.

Bullet Code ✓✓ 1940 It's quick-shooting shenanigans when O'Brien chases a pack of angry rustlers off his neighbor's land. **56m/B VHS.** George O'Brien, Virginia Vale, Howard Hickman, Harry Woods, Charles "Slim" Whitaker; D: David Howard; W: Doris Schroeder.

Bullet Down Under ✓ *Signal One* 1994 (R) Cop Atkins joins Australian police and gets involved with a crime syndicate and a female killer. **?m/C VHS.** AU Christopher Atkins, Mark "Jacko" Jackson, Virginia Hey; D: Rob Stewart; W: Karl Schiffman; C: Martin McGrath; M: Art Phillips.

A Bullet for Joey ✓½ 1955 Fifties red scare flick. American physicist Carl Macklin (Dolenz) is teaching in Montreal. Gangster Joey Victor (Raft) has been hired to kidnap Macklin, unaware that the commies are behind the snatch. A couple of murders bring Inspector Raoul Leduc (Robinson) onto the scene and he soon tags Joey, who turns patriotic when he discovers he's being used by reds. **85m/B DVD.** Edward G. Robinson, George Raft, Peter Van Eyck, Joseph (Joe) Vitale, George Dolenz, Audrey Trotter, Bill Bryant, John Cliff; D: Lewis Allen; W: Daniel Mainwaring, A(lbert) (Isaac) Bezzerides; C: Harry Neuman; M: Harry Sukman.

Bullet for Sandoval ✓ 1970 (PG) An ex-Confederate renegade loots and pillages the north Mexican countryside on his way to murder the grandfather of the woman he loves. **96m/C VHS, DVD. SP** IT Ernest Borgnine, George Hilton; D: Julio Buchs.

A Bullet for the General ✓✓✓ *Quien Sabe?* 1968 An American mercenary joins with rebel forces during the Mexican Revolution. **95m/C VHS, DVD.** IT Martine Beswick, Lou Castel, Gian Marie Volonte, Klaus Kinski; D: Damiano Damiani; W: Salvatore Laurani, Franco Solinas; C: Antonio Secchi; M: Luis Bacalov.

A Bullet in the Head ✓✓✓ *Die Xue Jie Tou* 1990 Violent (no surprise there) tale of friendship finds Frank (Cheung), Ben (Leung), and Paul (Lee) heading out of 1967 Hong Kong for Saigon, where they hope to make money selling contraband goods in the city. They wind up on the wrong side of the Vietnamese Army, steal a fortune in gold from a local crime lord, and end up the prisoners of the Viet Cong. There's betrayal and death and a final moral reckoning and—did we mention lots and lots of (over-the-top) violence? Chinese with subtitles. **85m/C VHS, DVD.** HK Tony Leung Chiu-Wai, Jacky Cheung, Waise Lee, Simon Yam, Fennie Yuen, Yolinda Yam, John Woo; W: Janet Chun, Patrick Leung, John Woo; C: Wilson Chan, Ardy

---

A Bullet is Waiting 🐾🐾 1954. A diligent sheriff finally catches his man only to be trapped in a blinding snowstorm with the hardened criminal. 82m/C VHS. Jean Simmons, Rory Calhoun, Stephen McNally, Brian Aherne; **D:** John Farrow.

Bullet to Beijing 🐾🐾½ Len Deighton's Bullet to Beijing 1995 (R) After some 30 years, Caine returns to his role as intelligence agent Harry Palmer. Forced into retirement, Harry finds himself privately recruited by Russian businessman Alex (Gambon) to retrieve a stolen chemical weapon being transported on a train headed for China. Harry gets a little local help from Nicolai and Natasha (Conney and Sara) but treachery is all around. Follows "The Ipcress File," "Funeral in Berlin," and "Billion Dollar Brain," based on the novel by Len Deighton. 105m/C VHS. GE Michael Caine, Michael Gambon, Jason Connery, Mia Sara, Patrick Allen, Burt Kwouk, Michael Sarrazin, Sue Lloyd; **D:** George Mihalka; **W:** Harry Alan Towers; **C:** Terence Cole; **M:** Rick Wakeman.

Bulletproof 🐾 1988 (R) An unstoppable ex-CIA agent battles to retrieve a hightech nuclear tank from terrorist hands. 93m/C VHS, DVD. Gary Busey, Darlanne Fluegel, Henry Silva, Thalmus Rasulala, L.Q. Jones, R.G. Armstrong, Rene Enriquez; **D:** Steve Carver; **W:** Steve Carver.

Bulletproof 🐾 1996 (R) Desperately trying to be a male buddy bonding movie, "Bulletproof" fails miserably in every respect. Keats (Wayans) and Moses (Sandler) are an equally unlikely pair of car thieves with an equally unlikely bond to each other. Turns out Keats is really undercover cop Jack Carter, who is trying to infiltrate a drug cartel via his pal Moses. When the bust goes bad, Carter must bring Moses in unharmed to testify. Meanwhile the two rejuvenate their tainted relationship amid many homoerotic innuendoes. It's an embarrassment all around, especially for ex-Spike Lee cinematographer Dickerson on his first directing outing. 85m/C VHS, DVD, HD DVD. Damon Wayans, Adam Sandler, James Caan, Kristen Wilson, James Farentino, Bill Nunn, Mark Roberts, Xander Berkeley, Allen Covert, Larry McCoy; **D:** Ernest R. Dickerson; **W:** Joe Gayton, Lewis Colick; **C:** Steven Bernstein; **M:** Elmer Bernstein.

Bulletproof Heart 🐾🐾🐾 Killer 1995 (R) Mick (LaPaglia, a hit man with a severe case of burnout, is assigned to kill Fiona (Rogers), a beautiful socialite who, conveniently, wants to die. Despite being warned by his boss (Boyle) that Fiona has a habit of making men weak, he falls in love and can't bring himself to kill her. First-time director Malone takes great care to establish the tension level. LaPaglia and Rogers turn in riveting performances, but can't stop the film from losing momentum when it becomes self-consciously melodramatic near the end. 95m/C VHS. Anthony LaPaglia, Mimi Rogers, Peter Boyle, Matt Craven, Monica Schnarre, Joseph Maher; **D:** Mark Malone; **W:** Gordon Melbourne, Mark Malone; **C:** Tobias Schliessler; **M:** Graeme Coleman.

Bulletproof Monk 🐾🐾½ 2003 (PG-13) Chow-Yun Fat is the monk with no name, chosen to protect The Scroll of the Ultimate, which gives the power to shape the world to the person who reads it aloud. Each monk can only protect the scroll for 60 years, so the new chosen one must be found. An unlikely candidate emerges in a New York pickpocket named Kar, after a chance meeting between the two. Adding a definite "Indiana Jones" vibe are Jade, a mysterious "bad girl" who catches Kar's eye, and the villains, a Nazi who tried to steal the scroll years earlier, and his icy granddaughter. Plot holes abound if you look too closely, but the action sequences are nicely timed to distract you from them, and Chow-Yun Fat's cool persona adds a touch of grace. Scott makes a nice first step from teen comedy doofus 'o action hero. 103m/C VHS, DVD, Blu-ray Disc. US (James) King, Karel Roden, Victoria Smurfit, Mako, Chow, Yun-Fat, Seann William Scott, Jaime

Lam, Chai Kinkum Sam, Wing-Hung Wong; **M:** Romeo Diaz, James Wong.

Bullets over Broadway 🐾🐾🐾½ 1994 (R) Mediocre playwright David Shayne (Cusack, in the Allen role) talks up the virtues of artistic integrity to his pretentious hothouse contemporaries, then sells out to a gangster who agrees to finance his stage play provided he gets a part. And it's her hit-man body guard's (Palminteri) unexpected artistic touches that redeem Shayne's otherwise lousy work. Wiest as the eccentric diva Ullman gets a little ingenue, Reiner as the Greenwich Village sage, and Broadbent as the increasingly plump matinee idol lead a collection of delicious, over-the-top performances in this smart and howlingly funny tribute to Jazz Age New York City that showcases Woody at his self-conscious best. 106m/C VHS, DVD. Dianne Wiest, John Cusack, Jennifer Tilly, Rob Reiner, Chazz Palminteri, Tracey Ullman, Mary-Louise Parker, Joe (Johnny) Viterelli, Jack Warden, Jim Broadbent, Harvey Fierstein, Annie-Joe Edwards; **D:** Woody Allen; **W:** Woody Allen, Douglas McGrath; **C:** Carlo Di Palma. Oscars '94: Support. Actress (Wiest); Golden Globes '95: Support. Actress (Wiest); Ind. Spirit '95: Support. Actor (Palminteri) Support. Actress (Wiest); L.A. Film Critics '94: Support. Actress (Wiest); N.Y. Film Critics '94: Support. Actress (Wiest); Natl. Soc. Film Critics '94: Support. Actress (Wiest); Screen Actors Guild '94: Support. Actress (Wiest).

Bullets or Ballots 🐾🐾🐾 1938 Tough New York cop goes undercover to join the mob in order to get the goods on the crime lords. Old-fashioned danger and intrigue follow, making for some action-packed thrills. 82m/B VHS, DVD. Edward G. Robinson, Humphrey Bogart, Barton MacLane, Joan Blondell, Frank McHugh, Louise Beavers; **D:** William Keighley; **W:** Seton I. Miller; **C:** Hal Mohr.

Bullfighter & the Lady 🐾🐾½ 1950 An American goes to Mexico to learn the fine art of bullfighting in order to impress a beautiful woman. 87m/B VHS. Robert Stack, Gilbert Roland, Virginia Grey, Katy Jurado; **D:** Budd Boetticher.

Bullfighters 🐾🐾 1945 Stan and Ollie are in hot pursuit of a dangerous criminal which leads them to Mexico where Stan winds up in a bull ring. 61m/B VHS. Stan Laurel, Oliver Hardy, Margo Woode, Richard Lane; **D:** Malcolm St. Clair.

Bullies woof! 1986 (R) A woodland-transplanted young man decides to fight back against an ornery mountain clan who have raised his mother, tortured his father, and beat up his girlfriend. Brutal and unpalatable. 96m/C VHS, DVD, CA Janet-Laine Green, Deni Beriti, Stephen Hunter, Jonathan Crombie, Olivia D'Arc; **D:** Paul Lynch.

Bullitt 🐾🐾🐾 1968 (PG) A detective is assigned to protect a star witness for 48 hours senses danger; his worst fears are confirmed when his charge is murdered. Based on the novel, "Mute Witness" by Robert L. Pike, and featuring one of film-dom's most famous car chases. 105m/C VHS, Blu-ray Disc, HD DVD, Steve McQueen, Robert Vaughn, Jacqueline Bisset, Don Gordon, Robert Duvall, Norman Fell, Simon Oakland; **D:** Peter Yates; **W:** Alan R. Trusman; **C:** William A. Fraker; **M:** Lalo Schifrin. Oscars '68: Film Editing; Natl. Film Reg. '07; Natl. Soc. Film Critics '68: Cinematog.

Bullshot 🐾🐾½ 1983 (PG) Zany English satire sends up the legendary Bulldog Drummond. In the face of med profes.sors, hapless heroines, devilish Huns and deadly enemies, our intrepid hero remains distinctly British. 84m/C VHS, DVD. GB Alan

Bullseye! 🐾½ 1990 (PG-13) Knockabout farce is a letdown considering the talents involved. Shady scientists and Caine/ Caine, pursue/are pursued by looa-like con-artists (Caine and Mocre), who are pursued in turn by international agents. Full of inside jokes and celebrity cameos, but nothing exceptional. 95m/C VHS. Michael Caine, Roger Moore, Sally Kirkland, Deborah Leng, Alexandra Pigg. **Cameos:** Lynn Nesbitt, Stefanie Pitt; **D:** Michael Winner; **W:** Michael Winner; **M:** John Du Prez.

Bummer woof! 1973 (R) Rock band's wild party turns into tragedy when the bass player goes too far with two groupies. It's a bad scene, man. 90m/C VHS, DVD. Kipp Whitman, Dennis Burkley, Carol Speed, Connie Strickland; **D:** William Allen Castleman; **W:** Alvin L. Fast.

Bums 🐾🐾 1993 Sergeant Andrew Holloman is a military officer in search of his long lost brother. It turns out his brother was homeless and is now dead at the hands of a skid row killer. Holloman recruits a platoon of other homeless people to help him track the killer but what he

Roger Yuan, Marcus Jean Pirae; **D:** Paul Hunter; **W:** Ethan Reiff, Cyrus Voris; **C:** Stefan Czapsky; **M:** Eric Serra.

Bully 🐾 2001 Director Clark continues his cinematic theme (announced in "Kids") of amoral and hedonistic young adults with his adaptation of the true story of a 1993 murder by a group of teens in Florida. Bobby (Stahl) is a dominating scumbag who pushes his best friend Marty (Renfro) around and pressures him into unwanted sexual and narcotic experimentation. When Marty meets and begins dating Lisa (Miner), Bobby forces himself into their sexual encounters. After Bobby rapes Lisa's friend Ali (Phillips), Lisa decides that the only solution is to kill Bobby. A dull posse gets some advice from a hit man (Fitzpatrick) who's barely older than they are. Filling the screen with graphic scenes of drug use and joyless sex, Clark doesn't seem to have any message other than "Look how bad these kids are. Now look at them naked." No psychological depth is given to the characters, although the actors do their best with what they've got. Also available in an R-rated version at 107 minutes. 113m/C VHS, DVD. US Brad Renfro, Nick Stahl, Bijou Phillips, Rachel Miner, Michael Pitt, Kelli Garner, Daniel Franzese, Leo Fitzpatrick. **Cameos:** Larry Clark; **D:** Larry Clark; **W:** Zachary Long, Roger Pullis; **C:** Steve Gainer.

Bulworth 🐾🐾🐾 1998 (R) No-holds-barred look at the political process. Senator John Jay Bulworth (Beatty), bored and disillusioned by the banality of his own political career, hires a hitman to take him out. During his last days on earth fulfilling re-election duties, and with nothing to loose, he starts spewing the truth about politics and big business, much to the dismay of his constituents and assistants. Morphing into a hip-hop political prophet, he becomes entranced and invigorated by beautiful South Central resident Nina (Berry). Beatty (in an engaging and funny performance) tackles his fiery subject matter of dwindling racial harmony and corporate deceit with a brazen and winning sense of humor lost in contemporary films. Fire script and enjoyable supporting performances by Platt as Bulworth's panic-stricken aide and Cheadle as an enterprising thug lord. 107m/C VHS, DVD. Warren Beatty, Halle Berry, Oliver Platt, Paul Sorvino, Don Cheadle, Jack Warden, Christine Baranski, Isaiah Washington, Jr., Joshua Malina, Graham Beckel, Nora Dunn, Jackie Gayle; **D:** Warren Beatty; **W:** Jeremy Pikser, Warren Beatty; **C:** Vittorio Storaro; **M:** Ennio Morricone. L.A. Film Critics '98: Screenplay.

The Bumblebee Files Anyway 🐾🐾½ 1998 (PG-13) Amnesiac Barney Snow (Wood) is residing at a facility where all the other youths are terminally ill. As the doctors try to help Barney remember his past, Barney and the other patients go through the usual bonding rituals. Ordinary story at least has some winning performers to get past the maudlin aspects. Based on the novel by Robert Cormier. 95m/C VHS, DVD. Elijah Wood, Janeane Garofalo, Rachael Leigh Cook, Roger Rees, Joe Perrino, George Gore III, Chris Patrizzo; **D:** Martin Duffy; **W:** Jennifer Sarja; **C:** Stephen Kazmierski; **M:** Christopher Tyng.

Shearman, Diz White, Ron House, Frances Tomelty, Michael Aldridge, Ron Pember, Christopher Good; **D:** Dick Clement; **M:** John Du Prez.

Bullwhip 🐾🐾 1958 A man falsely accused of murder saves himself from the hangman's noose by agreeing to a shotgun wedding. 80m/C VHS, Guy Madison, Rhonda Fleming, James J. Griffith, Peter Adams; **D:** Harmon Jones.

Bunco 🐾 1977 Two policemen working for the Los Angeles Police Department's Bunco Squad discover a college for con artists complete with tape-recorded lessons and on-the-job training. 60m/C VHS. Tom Selleck, Robert Urich, Donna Mills, Will Geer, Arte Johnson, Alan Feinstein, James Hampton, Michael Sacks, Bobby Van, Diana Scarwid, Kenneth Mars; **D:** Alexander Singer.

Bundle of Joy 🐾🐾½ 1956 Salesgirl who saves an infant from falling off the steps of a founding home is mistaken for the child's mother; Remake of 1939's "Bachelor Mother." ♪ "Bundle of Joy"; Never Felt This Way Before"; "Lullaby in Blue; Worry About Tomorrow; All About Love; Someday Soon; What's So Good About Morning?; You're Perfect in Every Way. 98m/C VHS. Debbie Reynolds, Eddie Fisher, Adolphe Menjou; **D:** Norman Taurog.

Bunny Whipped 🐾 2006 (R) Where's a killer rabbit when you need one? Bob (Powell) is looking to change his one? but as it seems Bob's suspect, rival rapper Kenny Kent (Alonso), doesn't want this goof poking into his business. Just all-around lame-but gets a bone for having Corey Adams (as "The Whip") and the cartoonish vigilante ("The Whip") and the media attention gets Bob a call from ex-girlfriend Ann (Adams), an animal rights activist, who wants Bob's help in saving some lab rabbits. But his rapper case does't go away as it seems Bob's suspect, her dedication as a feminist. Based on the book by Steinem. 97m/C VHS. Kirstie Alley, Cotter Smith, Deborah Van Valkenburgh, Joanna Kerns, Delta Burke, Diana Scarwid; **D:** Karen Arthur.

A Bunny's Tale 🐾 1985 The story of Gloria Steinem's undercover journey into the Playboy Club as a fledgling journalist. It is here that she discovered her dedication as a feminist. Based on the book by Steinem. 97m/C VHS. Kirstie Alley, Cotter Smith, Deborah Van Valkenburgh, Joanna Kerns, Delta Burke, Diana Scarwid; **D:** Karen Arthur.

Buona Sera, Mrs. Campbell 🐾🐾½ 1968 The lovely Lollobrigida and some fast-paced plot moves are the main highlights of this comedy. Mrs. Campbell convinced her three American WWII lovers that each of them had fathered her daughter. All three have supported mother and child through the years, unbeknowns to each other and their wives. When their 20-year reunion brings them back to Italy, Mrs. Campbell must do some fast-thinking and some quick-stepping to keep everyone happy. 113m/C VHS. Gina Lollobrigida, Shelley Winters, Phil Silvers, Peter Lawford, Telly Savalas, Lee Grant, Janet Margolin, Marian Moses; **D:** Melvin Frank.

The 'Burbs 🐾½ 1989 (PG) A rapid satire about suburbanites suspecting their creepy new neighbors of murderous activities. Well-designed and sharp, but light on story. 101m/C VHS, DVD. Tom Hanks, Carrie Fisher, Rick Ducommun, Corey Feldman, Brother Theodore, Bruce Dern, Gale Gordon, Courtney Gains; **D:** Joe Dante; **W:** Dana Olsen; **C:** Robert M. Stevens; **M:** Jerry Goldsmith.

Burden of Dreams 🐾🐾🐾½ 1982 The landmark documentary chronicling the berserk circumstances behind the scenes of Werner Herzog's epic "Fitzcarraldo." Stuck in the Peruvian jungles, the film crew was subjected to every disaster imaginable while executing Herzog's vision, including disease, horrendous accident, warring local tribes and the megalomaniacal director himself. Considered better than "Fitzcarraldo," although both films discuss a man's obsession. 94m/C VHS, DVD. Klaus Kinski, Mick Jagger, Jason Robards, Jr., Werner Herzog, Jeanne Moreau; **D:** Les Blank.

Bureau of Missing Persons 🐾🐾½ 1933 Comedy-drama about big-city bureau of missing persons, in which the hardened Stone is in charge. O'Brien plays a tough cop who is transferred to the bureau and Davis stars as the mystery woman with whom he gets involved. Although fast-paced and intriguing, the film is somewhat confusing and never stays in one direction for very long. **75m/B VHS.** Bette Davis, Lewis Stone, Pat O'Brien, Glenda Farrell, Allen Jenkins, Ruth Donnelly, Hugh Herbert; **D:** Roy Del Ruth; **W:** Robert Presnel Sr.; **C:** Barney McGill; **M:** Bernhard Kaun.

Burglar *1987 (R)* A cat burglar moves to the right side of the law when she tries to solve a murder case. Whoopi's always a treat, but this movie's best forgotten; Goldberg's fans should watch "Jumpin' Jack Flash" again instead. Costar Goldthwait elevates the comedic level a bit. **103m/C VHS, DVD.** Whoopi Goldberg, Bob(cat) Goldthwait, G.W. Bailey, James Handy, Anne DeSalvo; **D:** Hugh Wilson; **W:** Hugh Wilson; **C:** William A. Fraker; **M:** Sylvester Levay, Bernard Edwards.

Burglar *1987 Vzlomschik* Not to be confused with the Whoopi Goldberg vehicle, this Russian film relates a story no less American than apple pie and teenage angst. Senka and would-be punk star Kostya are two neglected and disaffected brothers whose father is a drunken womanizer best known for absentee paternalism. When Howmuch, a serious heavy metalloid, pressures Kostya to steal a synthesizer, brother Senka steps in to steal the Community Center's property himself. In Russian with English subtitles, the solid performances hold their own against the heavy musical content. **89m/C VHS, DVD.** *RU* Konstantin Kinchev, Oleg Yelykomov; **D:** Valery Orgorodnikov.

Burial Ground *1985* A classically grisly splatter film in which the hungry dead rise and proceed to kill the weekend denizens of an isolated aristocratic mansion. **85m/C VHS, DVD.** Karen Well, Peter Bark; **D:** Andrea Bianchi.

Burial of the Rats *1/2 Roger Corman Presents Burial of the Rats; Bram Stoker's Burial of the Rats 1995 (R)* Based on a short story by Bram Stoker, this cable campiness features young Bram (Alber) himself being kidnapped while traveling in Eastern Europe. He's taken to the "Queen of Vermin" (Barbeau), who heads a bloodthirsty cult that hate men, worship rats, and live by violence. Fortunately, the Queen decides to spare Bram so he can write of their exploits and he falls for the fleshy charms of rat-woman Madeleine (Ford). **85m/C VHS, DVD.** Adrienne Barbeau, Maria Ford, Kevin Alber; **D:** Dan Golden.

Buried Alive *1939* A man is sent to prison on trumped up charges. Only the prison nurse believes he is innocent as a crooked politician strives to keep him behind bars. **74m/B VHS.** Beverly Roberts, Robert Wilcox, George Pembroke, Ted Osborn, Paul McVey, Alden Chase; **D:** Victor Halperin.

Buried Alive *1981* Director d'Amato reaps his finest gore-fest to date, incorporating the well-established taxidermist gone loony motif in his repertoire of appalling bad taste. Not for the squeamish, this bloodier-than-thou spaghetti spooker is chock full of necrophilia, cannibalism, and more. **90m/C VHS.** **D:** Joe D'Amato.

Buried Alive *1989 (R)* Once Ravenscroft Hall was an asylum for the incurably insane. Now, the isolated mansion is a school for troubled teenage girls, run by a charismatic psychiatrist. Captivated by his charm, a young woman joins the staff. Soon, she is tormented by nightmare visions of the long-dead victims of a nameless killer. When the students begin to disappear, she realizes she still lives...and she may be his next victim. Carradine's last role. **97m/C VHS, DVD.** Robert Vaughn, Donald Pleasence, Karen Witter, John Carradine, Ginger Lynn Allen; **D:** Gerard Kikoine.

Buried Alive *1/2 1990 (PG-13)* One of the many horror flicks entitled "Buried Alive," this one is not bad, injecting a bit of levity into the time-worn genre. Schemestress Leigh and her paramour poison her husband. Or so they think, only to discover that he's not quite dead. **93m/C VHS.** Tim Matheson, Jennifer Jason Leigh, William Atherton, Hoyt Axton; **D:** Frank Darabont; **W:** Mark Patrick Carducci, Jake Ciesi; **M:** Michel Colombier. **CABLE**

Buried Alive 2 *1997 (PG-13)* Randy (Caffrey) wants to get rid of rich wife Laura (Sheedy) so he and girlfriend Roxanne (Needham) can enjoy her cash. So he slips some blowfish venom into her wine and buries her. But the venom only simulated death and after clawing her way out of the grave, Laura is one angry gal. Clint Goodman (Matheson), who was buried in the first movie, shows up to help out the wronged wife. **92m/C VHS.** Ally Sheedy, Stephen Caffrey, Tracey Needham, Tim Matheson; **D:** Tim Matheson; **W:** Walter Klenhard. **CABLE**

Burke & Wills *1985 (PG-13)* A lush, big-budgeted true story of the two men who first crossed Australia on foot, and explored its central region. Popular Australian film. **120m/C VHS.** *AU* Jack Thompson, Nigel Havers, Greta Scacchi, Ralph Cotterill, Drew Forsythe, Chris Haywood, Matthew Fargher; **D:** Graeme Clifford; **W:** Michael Thomas; **C:** Russell Boyd; **M:** Peter Sculthorpe.

Burlesque on Carmen *1916* A silent pastiche of the Bizet opera, with Charlie as Don Schmose. Interesting early work. **30m/B VHS, DVD.** Charlie Chaplin, Ben Turpin, Edna Purviance; **D:** Charlie Chaplin; **W:** Charlie Chaplin.

Burma Convoy *1941* A truck driver on the Burma Road—a dangerous stretch of roadway in Asia used to hall munitions during World War II—sets out to uncover the mystery of his younger brother's death. **72m/B VHS.** Charles Bickford, Evelyn Ankers, Frank Albertson, Cecil Kellaway, Willie Fung, Keye Luke; **D:** Noel Mason Smith; **W:** Roy Chansler, Stanley Rubin.

The Burmese Harp *Harp of Burma; Birumano Tategoto 1956* At the end of WWII, a Japanese soldier is spiritually traumatized and becomes obsessed with burying the masses of war casualties. A searing, acclaimed anti-war statement, in Japanese with English subtitles. Remade by Ichikawa in 1985. **115m/B VHS, DVD.** *JP* Shoji Yasui, Rentaro Mikuni, Tatsuya Mihashi, Tanie Kitabayashi, Yunosuke Ito; **D:** Kon Ichikawa; **W:** Natto Wada; **C:** Minoru Yokoyama; **M:** Akira Ifukube.

Burn! *Quemaimai! 1970 (PG)* An Italian-made indictment of imperialist control by guerrilla-filmmaker Pontecorvo, depicting the efforts of a 19th century British ambassador to put down a slave revolt on a Portuguese-run Caribbean island. Great Brando vehicle. **112m/C VHS, DVD.** *FR IT* Marlon Brando, Evarist Marquez, Renato Salvatori, Norman Hill, Dana Ghia, Giampiero Albertini, Tom Lyons; **D:** Gillo Pontecorvo; **W:** Giorgio Arlorio, Franco Solinas; **C:** Marcello Gatti; **M:** Ennio Morricone.

Burn Witch, Burn! *Night of the Eagle 1962* A college professor proudly finds himself rapidly rising in his profession. His pride turns to horror though when he discovers that his success is not due to his own abilities, but to the efforts of his witchcraft practicing wife. Excellent, atmospheric horror with a genuinely suspenseful climax. **87m/B VHS.** *GB* Peter Wyngarde, Janet Blair, Margaret Johnston, Anthony Nichols, Colin Gordon, Kathleen Byron, Reginald Beckwith, Jessica Dunning, Norman Bird, Judith Scott; **D:** Sidney Hayers; **W:** Richard Matheson, Charles Beaumont, George L. Baxt; **C:** Reg Wyer.

Burndown *1989 (R)* Victims of a serial killer in a town with a large nuclear reactor are themselves radioactive, which leads the Police Chief and a beautiful reporter to the truth and the hidden conspiracy. **97m/C VHS.** Cathy Moriarty, Peter Firth; **D:** James Allen.

The Burning *1982 (R)* Story of macabre revenge set in the dark woods of a seemingly innocent summer camp. **90m/C VHS.** Brian Matthews, Leah Ayres, Brian Backer, Larry Joshua, Jason Alexander, Ned Eisenberg, Garrick Glenn, Carolyn Houlihan, Fisher Stevens, Lou David, Holly Hunter; **D:** Tony Maylam; **W:** Bob Weinstein, Peter Lawrence; **C:** Harvey Harrison; **M:** Rick Wakeman.

The Burning Bed *1985* Dramatic expose based on a true story about wife-beating. Fawcett garnered accolades for her performance as the battered wife who couldn't take it anymore. Highly acclaimed and Emmy-nominated. **95m/C VHS, DVD.** Farrah Fawcett, Paul LeMat, Penelope Milford, Richard Masur; **D:** Robert Greenwald. **TV**

The Burning Court *La Chambre Ardente 1962* Unusual horror film involving occultism, possession, and family curses. Dubbed into English. Based on a story by John Dickson Carr. **102m/C VHS.** *IT FR* Nadja Tiller, Jean-Claude Brialy, Edith Scob, Perette Pradier, Claude Rich; **D:** Julien Duvivier.

Burning Daylight *1928* Alaskan real estate baron loses everything to a group of San Francisco sharpies. Based on the story by Jack London. **72m/B VHS.** Milton Sills, Arthur Stone, Doris Kenyon, Guinn "Big Boy" Williams; **D:** Richard A. Rowland.

Burning Down the House *2001 (R)* Desperate director Jake Selling (Savage) has his next story all lined up but no money to pursue his ambitions until he crosses paths with B-movie producer Arnie Green (Wilder). They figure out the only way to raise money is to burn down Jake's house for the insurance. Only Jake's ex—actress Brenda Goodman (Baron)—catches the scam on film and demands to be in the movie. And the insurance investigator turns out to be a wannabe actor as well whom they may also have to placate. **84m/C VHS, DVD.** John Savage, James Wilder, Joanne Baron, William Atherton, Arye Gross, Rene Auberjonois, Orson Bean, John Ales, C. Thomas Howell, Luca Bercovici, David Keith; **Cameos:** Mick Fleetwood; **D:** Philippe Mora; **W:** Michael Cole Dinelli; **C:** Dan Gillham; **M:** Jeff Marsh.

The Burning Hills *1/2 1956* Unexpectional cow flick based on a Louis L'Amour novel. Hunter hides from cattle thieves in a barn and, eventually, in the arms of a half-breed Mexican girl (Wood). Tedious and unsurprising. **94m/C VHS.** Tab Hunter, Natalie Wood, Skip Homeier, Eduard Franz; **D:** Stuart Heisler.

Burning Rage *1984* A blazing, abandoned coal mine threatens to wreak havoc on the Appalachians. The government sends geologist Mandrell to help prevent a disaster. **100m/C VHS, DVD.** Barbara Mandrell, Tom Wopat, Bert Remsen, John Pleshette, Carol Kane, Eddie Albert; **D:** Gilbert Cates. **TV**

The Burning Season *1994* In one of his last performances, Julia inspires as Chico Mendes, a socialist union leader who fought to protect the homes and land of Brazilian peasants in the western Amazon rain forest. With Mendes' help the peasants form a union and struggle to prevent the building of a road that will provide easy access to forest land for speculators and cattlemen. Naturally, they are violently opposed by corruption-ridden capitalist powers in the government. Julia provides a haunting portrayal of the heroic figure who was assassinated in 1990. Based in part on the book by Andrew Revkin. Filmed on location in Mexico. **123m/C VHS.** Raul Julia, Edward James Olmos, Sonia Braga, Luis Guzman, Nigel Havers, Kamala Dawson, Tomas Milian, Esai Morales, Tony Plana, Carmen Argenziano; **D:** John Frankenheimer; **W:** William Mastrosimone, Michael Tolkin, Ron Hutchinson; **M:** Gary Chang. **CABLE**

Burnt by the Sun *Outomilomnye Solntsem 1994 (R)* Masterful evocation of '30s Stalinist Russia, covering a day in the life of Soviet revolutionary hero Serguei (Mikhalkov) and his family, far from the purges and gulags. Enjoying a country existence with wife Moroussia (Dapkounaite) and daughter Nadia (played by Mikhalkov's daughter), his idyll is disturbed by mystery man Dimitri (Menchikov), and Serguei realizes their fates are bound by the difference between their Communist dreams and reality. Symbolism is a little heavy but film delivers emotionally. Russian with subtitles. **134m/C VHS, DVD.** *RU FR* Nikita Mikhalkov, Ingeborga Dapkounaite, Oleg Menshikov, Nadia Mikhalkov, Andre Oumansky, Viatcheslav Tikhonov, Svetlana Krioutchkova, Vladimir Ilyine; **D:** Nikita Mikhalkov; **W:** Nikita Mikhalkov, Rustam Ibragimbekov; **C:** Vilen Kalyuta; **M:** Eduard Artemyev. Oscars '94: Foreign Film; Cannes '94: Grand Jury Prize.

Burnt Money *Plata Quemada 2000* Based on a 1965 true crime story set in Argentina and Uruguay. Twentysomething lovers Nene (Sbaraglia) and the unstable Angel (Noriega), nicknamed the Twins, are stickup men hired by veteran criminal Fontana (Bartis) for a big money heist in Buenos Aires. They're paired with young, pill-popping getaway driver Cuervo (Echarri) but things go wrong when the Twins become cop killers. The foursome flee with the money to a squalid apartment in Montevideo where they wait for new identity papers. The young trio begin to unravel amidst a lot of drinking, drugs (who knew cocaine was so popular in the '60s?), and boredom, leading to a lethal confrontation with authorities. Title refers to what happens to the heist cash. Spanish with subtitles. **125m/C VHS, DVD.** *AR* Leonardo Sbaraglia, Eduardo Noriega, Ricardo Bartis, Pablo Echarri, Leticia Bredice, Dolores Fonzi; **D:** Marcelo Pineyro; **W:** Marcelo Figueras; **C:** Alfredo Mayo; **M:** Osvaldo Montes.

Burnt Offerings *1976 (PG)* A family rents an old mansion for the summer and they become affected by evil forces that possess the house. Based on the novel by Robert Marasco. **116m/C VHS, DVD.** Oliver Reed, Karen Black, Bette Davis, Burgess Meredith; **D:** Dan Curtis; **W:** Dan Curtis.

Burnzy's Last Call *1995* Sal (McCaffrey) tends bar at Eppy's, a Manhattan joint where Burnzy (Gray), a retired newspaperman, is a regular. The film is an ensemble piece that focuses on the various colorful characters who drift in and out of the place. **88m/C VHS, DVD.** Sam Gray, David Johansen, James McCaffrey, Christopher Noth, Sherry Stringfield, Roger Robinson, Tony Todd; **D:** Michael de Avila; **W:** George Gilmore; **C:** Scott St. John.

Bury Me an Angel *1971* A female biker sets out to seek revenge against the men who killed her brother. **85m/C VHS.** Dixie Peabody, Terry Mace, Clyde Ventura, Dan Haggerty, Stephen Whittaker, Gary Littlejohn, Dave Atkins, Marie Denn, Alan DeWitt; **D:** Barbara Peeters; **C:** Sven Walnum; **M:** Richard Hieronymous.

Bury Me Not on the Lone Prairie *1941* When his brother is murdered in cold blood by claim jumpers, mining engineer Brown goes to avenge the dead. Based on a story by Sherman Lowe. **57m/B VHS, DVD.** Johnny Mack Brown, Fuzzy Knight, Nell O'Day, Frank O'Connor, Kermit Maynard; **D:** Ray Taylor; **W:** Sherman Lowe, Victor McLeod.

Bury My Heart at Wounded Knee *2007* Loose adaptation of the 1970 Dee Brown book. This over-simplified version concentrates on the experiences of the Sioux from Little Big Horn to the Wounded Knee massacre. It follows Charles Eastman (Beach)—who's not in Brown's book, by the way—who grew up among the Sioux (he's a quarter white on his mother's side) until his Christianized father claims him. Eastman is educated in the East and becomes a doctor at Pine Ridge, aided by his white wife (Paquin). The story is given over to various confrontations and philosophical differences. **7m/C DVD.** Adam Beach, Aidan Quinn, Anna Paquin, August Schellenberg, J.K. Simmons, Shawn Johnston, Gordon Tootoosis, Wes Studi, Eric Schweig, Colm Feore, Fred Dalton Thompson; **D:** Yves Simoneau; **W:** Daniel Giat; **C:** David Franco; **M:** George S. Clinton. **CABLE**

Bus Stop *The Wrong Kind of Girl 1956* Murray plays a naive cowboy who falls in love with Monroe, a barroom singer, and decides to marry her without her permission. Considered by many to be the finest performance by Marilyn Monroe; she sings "That Old Black Magic" in this one. Very funny with good performances by all. Based on the William Inge play. **96m/C VHS, DVD.** Marilyn Monroe, Arthur O'Connell, Hope Lange, Don Murray, Betty Field,

Bush *1/2* 1947 Red North (Willis) has "his own small business as a bush pilot in the Canadian north. Then his vindictive half-brother Paul (La Rue) decides to muscle in and steal Red's routes (and maybe his girl as well). 60m/C VHS, DVD, CA Austin Willis, Jack La Rue Jr., Rochelle Hudson; *D:* Sterling Campbell; *W:* Scott Darling.

The Bushbaby *1/2* 1970 The young Brooks is given a tiny bushbaby while visiting Africa with her father. Because of her pet she misses her ship home and finds herself with former servant Gossett, who agrees to take her to a family friend. Unfortunately, the authorities think he's kidnapped the girl and the two, along with the trouble-causing pet, are pursued by the police. Simple-minded kiddie fare. 100m/C VHS, Margaret Brooks, Louis Gossett Jr., Donald Houston, Laurence Naismith, Marne Maitland, Geoffrey Bayldon, Jack (Gwyllam) Gwillim; *D:* John Trent.

Bush's Brain *1/2* 2004 Election year investigation of the role Karl Rove played in crafting Dubyah into a president. Yet another volley in the political documentary war of 2004. Interesting exploration of behind-the-scenes political dirty work. Though based largely on hearsay, film will surely outrage democrats everywhere. 80m/C VHS, DVD, *D:* Michael Shoob, Joseph Mealey; *C:* Joseph Mealey; *M:* David Friedman, Michelle Shocked.

The Busher *1/2* 1919 1970. The pitcher's romance is interrupted by a gratuitous Mr. Moneybags. Minor-league conflict with little real hardball. 54m/B VHS, Charles Ray, Colleen Moore, John Gilbert Margaret Livingston; *D:* Jerome Storm.

The Bushido Blade *1/2* 1980 All-American samurai thriller of adventure and betrayal set in medieval Japan. 92m/C VHS, DVD, JP Richard Boone, James Earl Jones, Frank Converse; *D:* Tom Kotani.

The Bushwackers *1/2* 1952 Ireland plays a veteran of the Confederate army who wishes only to put his violent past behind him. He is forced to retaken for the leader of a group of Cub Scouts out on their maiden camping trip and soon finds himself in an unlikely partnership with the boys. Together they encounter everything from grizzly bears to whitewater rapids. Light-hearted goofy comedy continues Stern's tendency toward kid-intensive, family-oriented fare in the "Rookie of the Year" vein. 85m/C VHS, DVD, Daniel Stern, Jon Polito, Brad Sullivan, Ann Dowd, Anthony Heald, Tom Wood; *D:* Greg Beeman; *W:* Tommy Swerdlow, Michael Goldberg, John Jordan, Danny Byers; *M:* Bill Conti.

A Business Affair *1/2* 1993 Kate Swallow (the ravishing Bouquet), the neglected wife of temperamental author Alex Bolton (Pryce), begins an affair with his flamboyant American publisher Vanni Corso (Walken). While the men posture between themselves for her affections, Kate, who has literary aspirations, decides to strike out on her own. Based on the romantic triangle of British writers Barbara Skelton and Cyril Connolly and his publisher George Weidenfeld and taken from Skelton's memoirs "Tears Before Bedtime" and "Weep No More." 102m/C VHS, DVD, Carole Bouquet, Jonathan Pryce, Christopher Walken, Sheila Hancock; *D:* Charlotte Brandstrom; *W:* William Stadiem; *C:* Willy Kurant; *M:* Didier Vasseur.

Bushwhacked *1/2* 1995 (PG-13) Crude, rude, dim-witted, kid-hating Max Grabelski (Stern) is falsely accused of murder and forced to become a fugitive. While not to be confused with Harrison Ford, he is mistaken...

The Bushido Blade ...

Max (Casey Adams) Showalter, Eileen Heckart; *D:* Joshua Logan; *W:* George Axelrod; *M:* Cyril Mockridge, Alfred Newman.

The Business of Fancydancing *1/2* 2002 Seymour (Adams) is a gay Native American who has left the reservation, gone to college, and now uses his heritage to achieve literary fame as a poet. He hasn't been back to the rez in years but returns for the funeral of onetime friend Mouse (Xanim). Seymour's return is awkward as it triggers the frustrated resentment of another boyhood pal Aristotle (Tagaban) as well as a confrontation with his college girlfriend Agnes (St. John) who is now Aristotle's lover. 103m/C VHS, DVD, US Evan Adams, Michelle St. John, Gene Tagaban, Swil Kanim, Rebecca Carroll, Cynthia Geary, Leo Rossi, Kevin Phillip, Elaine Miles; *D:* Sherman Alexie; *W:* Sherman Alexie; *C:* Holly Taylor.

The Business of Strangers *1/2* 2001 (R) Julie Styron (Channing) is a tough, mid-leaguer executive for a software company who is having a bad day as an out-of-town meeting. She worries she's about to be fired and then fires her young assistant Paula (Stiles) for missing the meeting and ruining Julie's presentation. Instead, Julie gets a promotion and decides to rehire Paula after they diss men over drinks at the hotel bar. When Paula spots corporate headhunter Nick (Weller), she tells Julie that he raped a friend of hers and it's payback time. But since the two women have been playing mind games, is this the truth or not? 83m/C VHS, DVD, US Stockard Channing, Julia Stiles, Frederick Weller, Marcus Giamatti; *C:* Patrick Stettner; *W:* Patrick Stettner; *C:* Teodoro Maniaci; *M:* Alexander Lasarenko.

Business As Usual *1/2* 1988 (PG) A meek boutique manager in Liverpool defends a sexually harassed employee; is fired, fights back, and creates a national furor over her rights as a woman. 93m/C VHS, CA national crimelords. Collins makes her screen debut as one of Britain's most infamous criminals. Collins also performs on the film's soundtrack, spawning two hit singles, "Two Hearts" and "Groovy Kind of Love." 102m/C VHS, DVD, GB Phil Collins, Julie Walters, Larry Lamb, Stephanie Lawrence, Ellen Beaven, Michael Atwell, Ralph Brown, Christopher Ellison, Sheila Hancock, Martin Jarvis, Anthony Quayle; *D:* David Green; *M:* Anne Dudley.

Business for Pleasure 1996 Wealthy tycoon orchestrates a sexual tryst between himself, his closest assistant, and a beautiful exec in order to explore the wilder side of sex and fantasy. 97m/C VHS, Glenda Jackson, Cathy Tyson, John Thaw, Craig Charles, Eamon Boland; *D:* Lezli-Ann Barrett; *W:* Lezli-Ann Barrett; *C:* Ernest Vincze.

Business is Business *1/2* Diary of a Hooker Any Special Way 1971 Verhoeven's first feature film (after his television work) is a sex comedy about a couple of prostitutes who are apartment neighbors in Amsterdam. Nel's got an abusive boyfriend she just can't shake despite the efforts of her friend Blonde Greet. BG decides they should become partners (she's put out when Nel finds a nice, boring guy who wants to marry her and take her out of the life. Especially since Blonde Greet's special guy is already hitched. A slight and surprisingly timid story considering Verhoeven's later work but everyone's gotta start somewhere. Dutch with subtitles. 89m/C DVD, NL Ronnie Bierman, Sylvia De Leur, Piet Romer, Jules Hamel, Bernard Droog, Henk Molenberg, Albert Mol; *D:* Paul Verhoeven; *W:* Gerard Soeteman; *C:* Jan De Bont; *M:* Marius Steffaro.

Buster *1/2* 1988 (R) The story of Buster Edwards, the one suspect in the 1963 Great Train Robbery who evaded being captured by police.

Buster and Billie *1/2* 1974 (R) Tragedy ensues when a popular high school student falls in love with the class load of misplaced kids and their keeper tramp in rural Georgia in 1948. Serious, decently appointed period teen drama. 100m/C VHS, Jan-Michael Vincent, Joan Goodfellow, Clifton James, Pamela Sue Martin, Robert England; *C:* Daniel Petrie.

Bustin' Loose *1/2* 1981 (R) A fast-talking ex-con reluctantly drives a busload of misplaced kids and their keeper cross-country. 94m/C VHS, DVD, Richard Pryor, Cicely Tyson, Robert Christian, George Coe, Bill Quinn; *D:* Oz Scott; *W:* Lonnie Elder III, Richard Pryor; *C:* Dennis Dalzell; *M:* Roberta Flack, Mark Davis.

Busting *1/2* 1974 (R) Gould and Blake play a pair of slightly off-the-wall L.A. cops. The pair are forced "to bust" local addicts and prostitutes instead of the real crime bosses because much of the police department is on the take. Plenty of comedy and action as well as highly realistic drama. 92m/C VHS, Elliott Gould, Robert (Bobby) Blake, Allen (Goorwitz) Garfield, Antonio Fargas, Michael Lerner, Sid Haig, Cornelia Sharpe; *D:* Peter Hyams; *W:* Peter Hyams; *M:* Billy Goldenberg.

But I'm a Cheerleader *1/2* 1999 (R) Broad satire falls flat. Megan (Lyonne) is a peppy high school cheerleader who is suspected of being a lesbian by her rigid parents, who send her off to a rehabilitation camp designed to turn adolescent homosexuals into straight members of society. Megan (who's only naively unaware of her true nature) goes along with the program until she befriends rebellious Graham (DuVall) and discovers that golly, she really does like girls. 81m/C VHS, DVD, Natasha Lyonne, Clea DuVall, Cathy Moriarty, RuPaul Charles, Bud Cort, Mink Stole, Julie Delpy, Eddie Cibrian; *D:* Jamie Babbit, Brian Wayne Peterson; *C:* Jules Labarthe; *M:* Pat Irwin.

But Not for Me *1/2* 1959 Gable stars as a middled-aged entertainment executive who can forestall maturity by carrying on with his youthful secretary. 105m/B VHS, Clark Gable, Carroll Baker, Lilli Palmer, Lee J. Cobb, Barry Coe, Thomas Gomez, Charles Lane; *D:* Walter Lang; *W:* John Michael Hayes; *C:* Robert Burks.

But Where Is Daniel Wax? *1/2* 1974 At a class reunion, a doctor and a popular singing star reminisce about their youth and Daniel Wax, their one-time hero. Hebrew with English subtitles. 95m/C VHS, Lior Yaeni, Michael Lipkin, Esther Zewko; *D:* Avram Heffner.

Busted Up *1/2* 1986 (R) A young, hardluck urban street-fighter battles for the sake of his family and neighborhood against local crimelords. 93m/C VHS, CA Irene Cara, Paul Coufos, Tony Rosato, Stan Shaw, Gordon Judges; *D:* Conrad Palmisano; *M:* Charles P. Barnett.

Butch and Sundance: The Early Days *1/2* 1979 (PG) Traces the origins of the famous outlaw duo. It contains the requisite shoot-outs, hold-ups, and escapes. A "prequel" to "Butch Cassidy and the Sundance Kid." 111m/C VHS, DVD, Tom Berenger, William Katt, John Schuck, Jeff Corey, Jill Eikenberry, Brian Dennehy, Peter Weller; *D:* Richard Lester; *W:* Allan Burns.

Butch Cassidy and the Sundance Kid *1/2* 1969 (PG) Two legendary outlaws at the turn of the century take it on the lam with a beautiful, willing ex-school teacher. With a clever script, humanly fallible characters, and witty dialogue, this film was destined to become a classic. Featured on the hit song "Raindrops Keep Falling on My Head" and renewed the buddy film industry, as Newman and Redford trade insult for insult. Look for the great scene where Newman takes on giant Ted Cassidy in a fist fight. *♫* "Raindrops Keep Fallin' on My Head; On a Bicycle Built for Joy. 110m/C VHS, DVD, Paul Newman, Robert Redford, Katharine Ross, Jeff Corey, Strother Martin, Cloris Leachman, Kenneth Mars, Ted Cassidy, Henry Jones, George Furth, Sam Elliott; *D:* George Roy Hill; *W:* William Goldman; *C:* Conrad L. Hall; *M:* Burt Bacharach. Oscars '69: Cinematog., Song ("Raindrops Keep Fallin' on My Head"), Story & Screenplay, Orig. Score; AFI '98: Top 100; British Acad. '70: Actor (Redford), Actress (Ross), Director (Hill), Film, Screenplay; Golden Globes '70: Score, Natl. Film Reg. '03; Writers Guild '69: Orig. Screenplay.

The Butcher Boy *1/2* 1997 (R) Offbeat, black comedy takes a disturbing look into the madness of 12-year old Francie Brady (Owens) is electrifying as the red-haired dynamo whose lost childhood turns him into a monster and Stephen Rea (a regular in any Jordan film) provides stern support as Francie's loser father and film's narrator. The rural Irish town is recreated with stunning detail, with some light touches of kitsch that may put off some looking for a serious treatment of main character's plight. Still a daring movie, with pop star O'Connor as the Virgin Mary. Based on the novel by Patrick McCabe. 105m/C VHS, DVD, Eamon Owens, Stephen Rea, Fiona Shaw, Sinead O'Connor, Aisling O'Sullivan, Alan Boyle, Ian Hart, Andrew Fullerton, Patrick McCabe, Sean McGinley, Brendan Gleeson, Milo O'Shea; *D:* Neil Jordan; *W:* Neil Jordan, Patrick McCabe; *C:* Adrian Biddle; *M:* Elliot Goldenthal. L.A. Film Critics '98: Score.

The Butcher's Wife *1/2* 1991 (PG-13) Charming tale of a young psychic (Moore) who brings romance to a Greenwich Village neighborhood that never quite gets off the ground. Moore stars as the clairvoyant whose mystical powers bring magic into the lives of everyone around her, including the local psychiatrist (Daniels), who falls under her spell. Talented cast is virtually washed with a script that is lightweight; excepting Steenburgen and Dzundza who shine. 107m/C VHS, DVD, Demi Moore, Jeff Daniels, George Dzundza, Frances McDormand, Margaret Colin, Mary Steenburgen, Max Perlich, Miriam Margolyes, Christopher Durang, Diane Salinger; *D:* Terry Hughes; *W:* Ezra Litwack, Marjorie Schwartz; *C:* Frank Tidy; *M:* ...

Butler's Dilemma *1/2* 1943 A jewel thief and a playboy both claim the identity of a butler who never existed, with humorous results. 75m/B VHS, GB Richard Hearne, Francis L. Sullivan, Hermione Gingold, Ian Fleming, Alf Goddard, Judy Kelly, Henry Kendall, Wally Patch, Frank Pettingell, Andre Randall, Marjorie Rhodes, Ronald Shiner, Ralph Truman; *D:* Leslie Hiscott; *W:* Michael Barringer; *C:* Erwin Hillier.

Butterfield 8 *1/2* 1960 A seedy prostitute that wants to go straight and settle down. Taylor won an Oscar, perhaps because she was ill and had lost in the two previous years in more deserving roles. 109m/C VHS, DVD, Elizabeth Taylor, Laurence Harvey, Eddie Fisher, Dina Merrill, Mildred Dunnock, Betty Field, Susan Oliver, Kay Medford; *D:* Daniel Mann; *W:* John Michael Hayes, Charles Schnee; *C:* Joseph Ruttenberg. Oscars '60: Actress (Taylor).

Butterflies Are Free *1/2* 1972 (PG) Fast-paced humor surrounds the Broadway play adapted to the big screen. Blind youth Albert is determined to be self-sufficient. A next-door-neighbor actress helps him gain independence from his over-protective mother. 109m/C VHS, DVD, Goldie Hawn, Edward Albert, Eileen Heckart, Michael Glaser; *D:* Milton Katselas; *C:* Charles B(ryant) Lang Jr.; *M:* Robert Alcivar. Oscars '72: Support. Actress (Heckart).

Butterfly 1982 (R) Based on James M. Cain's novel about an amoral young woman (Pia, who'd you thought) uses her beauty and sensual appetite to manipulate the men in her life, including her father. Set in Nevada of the 1930s, father and daughter are drawn into a daring and forbidden love affair by their lust and desperation. 105m/C VHS. Pia Zadora, Stacy Keach, Orson Welles, Edward Albert, James Franciscus, Lois Nettleton, Stuart Whitman, June Lockhart, Ed McMahon; **D:** Matt Cimber; **W:** Matt Cimber; **M:** Ennio Morricone. Golden Raspberries '82: Worst Actress (Zadora), Worst Support. Actor (McMahon), Worst New Star (Zadora).

Butterfly La Lengua de las Mariposas; Butterfly's Tongue 1998 (R) Young Moncho (Lozano) grows up in 1935 Galicia, Spain and is guided by his leftist teacher Don Gregorio (Gomez). But their lives are soon torn apart by the gathering of the Spanish Civil War. This kind of languidly paced coming-of-age story is almost never found in American theatrical releases these days. Europeans tend to treat the material with more seriousness. Director Jose Cuerda's work is solidly in the tradition of Fellini and Truffaut. Based on the stories of Manuel Riva; Spanish with subtitles. 94m/C VHS, DVD. *SP* Fernando Fernan-Gomez, Manuel Lozano, Uxia Blanco; **D:** Jose Luis Cuerda; **W:** Rafael Azcona; **C:** Javier Salmones; **M:** Alejandro Amenabar.

The Butterfly Le Papillon 2002 Likeable tale of Julien—a lonely, grumpy old guy in Paris—who can't resist his spunky yet equally lonely eight-year-old neighbor, Elsa, who's working, single mom doesn't have time for her. When he sets off to the mountains in a quest to snag a rare butterfly, Elsa slyly tags along and the two connect amid the stunning scenery. Her unwitting mother notices she's missing, becomes despondent, and triggers an APB for her. In French with subtitles. 80m/C VHS, DVD. Michel Serrault, Francoise Michaud, Dominique Marcas, Idwig Stephane, Francis Frappat, Francoise Dubois, Dominic Gould, Auriele Meriel, Claire Bouanich, Nade Dieu, Helene Hilly, Pierre Poirot, Jacky Nercessian, Jacques Bouanich, Catherine Cyler, Jerry Lucas, Laurent Adrien, Gabrielle Arger, Fabien Behar, Alain Bert, Alain Blazquez, Magali Bonat, Christiane Bopp, Armand Chagot, Laurent Chouteau, Jerome Foucher, Philippe LeDem, Gerard Maillet, Esther Perez-Pajares, Fabien Traverci; **D:** Philippe Muyl; **W:** Philippe Muyl; **C:** Nicolas Herdt; **M:** Nicolas Errera. VIDEO

Butterfly Affair 1971 (PG) Beautiful singer, involved in a scheme to smuggle $2 million worth of gems, plots to double-cross her partners in crime. 75m/C VHS. Claudia Cardinale, Henri Charriere, Stanley Baker; **D:** Jean Herman.

Butterfly Ball 1976 Retelling of the 19th century classic combines the rock music of Roger Glover, live action and animation by Halas and Batchelor. Only for the brain-cell depressed. 85m/C VHS, DVD. *GB* Twiggy, Ian Gillian, David Coverdale; **D:** Tony Klinger; **Nar:** Vincent Price.

Butterfly Collectors 1999 While investigating a murder, DI John McKeown (Postlethwaite) develops an unlikely friendship with 17-year-old suspect Dex (Draven), who is raising his younger siblings. But as McKeown gets closer to the family, his suspicions grow, and not just about Dex's involvement in the original crime. 150m/C DVD. *GB* Pete Postlethwaite, Crissy Rock, Jamie Draven, Alison Newman; **D:** Jean Stewart; **W:** Paul Abbott; **C:** Cinders Forshaw; **M:** Philip Appleby, Jocelyn Pook. TV

The Butterfly Effect 2004 (R) Kutcher takes time out from his usual dumb pretty-boy roles and tries his hand at a thriller. He plays Evan Trebom, a college psych major with a troubled past. He discovers that he can go back in time and change childhood events, which he does, to save himself and a group of friends from childhood traumas. Unfortunately, when he returns to the present, he finds his actions have changed everything that has happened since then, and not always for the better. There's a strong "ick" factor, touching on several rather disturbing topics. Kutcher acquits himself admirably, but not enough to save this jumbled mess. 113m/C DVD, UMD. *US* Ashton Kutcher, Amy Smart, Eric Stoltz, William Lee Scott, Elden (Ratliff) Henson, Logan Lerman, Irene Gorovaia, Jesse James, Melora Walters, Ethan Suplee, John Patrick Amedori, Kevin G. Schmidt; **D:** Eric Bress, J. Mackye Gruber; **W:** Eric Bress, J. Mackye Gruber; **C:** Matthew F. Leonetti; **M:** Michael Suby.

The Butterfly Effect 2 2006 (R) Nick (Lively) loses control of his car, resulting in an accident that kills his girlfriend Julie (Durance) and two friends. Still traumatized after a year, Nick realizes that he feels a power whenever he looks at the photos of their last trip and can actually travel back in time to that particular moment. But when Nick returns to the present, he doesn't always like the changes that occurred as he tries to save Julie's life. An overly-complicated execution ruins the suspense factor. 92m/C DVD. Eric Lively, Gina Holden, J.R. Bourne, Erica Durance, Dustin Milligan; **D:** John R. Leonetti; **W:** Michael D. Weiss; **C:** Brian Pearson; **M:** Michael Suby. VIDEO

Butterfly Kiss 1994 Strange psychodrama/road tale finds drifter Eunice (Plummer) wandering the motorways of northern England. At one service station she meets Miriam (Reeves)—the two, immediately drawn together, make love at Miriam's that night. When Eunice hitches a ride with a trucker next morning, Miriam decides to follow and discovers Eunice with the truck and the driver's dead body. It's soon not the only dead body Miriam encounters as she discovers Eunice is a serial killer—not that this seems to worry Miriam a great deal as she herself gets into the spirit of their crimes. Grim all the way 'round. 90m/C VHS, DVD. *GB* Amanda Plummer, Saskia Reeves, Paul Bown, Des McAleer, Ricky Tomlinson; **D:** Michael Winterbottom; **W:** Frank Cottrell-Boyce; **C:** Seamus McGarvey; **M:** John Harle.

Butterfly Wings Alas de Mariposa 1991 The tragedy of a dysfunctional family. Pregnant Carmen longs for a boy to carry on her husband's name but she's afraid to tell her shy six-year-old daughter Ami about the baby. Maybe with reason, since the child's birth triggers a series of nightmarish events. Spanish with subtitles. 105m/C VHS. *SP* Silvia Munt, Susan Garcia, Fernando Valverde; **D:** Juanma Bajo Ulloa; **W:** Juanma Bajo Ulloa; **C:** Aiter Mantxola; **M:** Bingen Mendizabal.

Buy & Cell 1989 (R) A stockbroker attempts to set up a business while serving a prison sentence. An assortment of amusing inmates doesn't help matters much. Fans of Malcolm McDowell will enjoy his performance as the shady warden. 95m/C VHS. Robert Carradine, Malcolm Winslow, Malcolm McDowell, Ben Vereen, Lise Cutter, Randall "Tex" Cobb, Roddy Piper; **D:** Robert Boris.

Buying the Cow 2002 (R) Commitment-phobe David (O'Connell) is being pressured by long-time girlfriend Sarah (Wilson) to get married. Clichéd romantic comedy. 88m/C VHS, DVD. Jerry O'Connell, Bridgette Wilson-Sampras, Ryan Reynolds, Bill Bellamy, Annabeth Gish, Ron Livingston; **D:** Walt Becker; **W:** Walt Becker; **M:** Andrew Gross.

Buying Time 1989 (R) Two teenagers are arrested when they try to pry their money away from a dishonest bookie, and the police use their connections to solve a drug-related murder. 97m/C VHS. Dean Stockwell, Jeff Schultz, Michael Rudder, Tony De Santis, Leslie Toth, Laura Cruickshank; **D:** Mitchell Gabourie.

Buzzy Rides the Range 1940 Average "B" western with a kid sawing the day. 60m/C VHS. Robert "Buzzy" Henry, Dave O'Brien, George Eldredge, Frank Mario, George Morrell, Claire Rochelle; **D:** Richard C. Kahn.

By Dawn's Early Light 1989 Thriller about two Air Force pilots who must decide whether or not to drop the bombs that would begin WWIII. 100m/C VHS, DVD. Powers Boothe, Rebecca De Mornay, James Earl Jones, Martin Landau, Rip Torn, Darren McGavin; **D:** Jack Sholder; **M:** Trevor Jones. CABLE

By Dawn's Early Light 2000 Aging Colorado cowboy Ben (Crenna) is pleased when his grandson Mike (Olivero) comes to stay for the summer. Until he realizes that Mike is a sullen teen given to pranks that backfire. After one such episode, Ben decides Mike needs some discipline and decides they should go on an 800-mile trip—by horseback. 105m/C VHS, DVD. Richard Crenna, Chris Olivero, David Carradine, Stella Stevens, Ben Cardinal; **D:** Arthur Allan Seidelman; **W:** Jacqueline Feather, David Seidler. CABLE

By Design 1982 (R) Two cohabiting women want to have a baby, so they embark on a search for the perfect stud. Not one of Astin's better performances. 90m/C VHS. *CA* Patty Duke, Sara Botsford; **D:** Claude Jutra.

By Love Possessed 1961 Can a seemingly typical, quiet, New England town stay quiet when Lana Turner is your neighbor? Vintage romantic melodrama about an attorney who is drawn into an affair when he realizes his home life is not all it could be. 115m/C VHS. Lana Turner, Efrem Zimbalist Jr., Jason Robards Jr., George Hamilton, Thomas Mitchell; **D:** John Sturges; **C:** Russell Metty; **M:** Elmer Bernstein.

By the Blood of Others 1973 In a small French town, a psycho holds two women hostage in a farmhouse, and the townspeople try to figure out a solution without getting anyone killed. In French with English subtitles. 90m/C VHS. *FR* Yves Beneyton, Francis Blanche, Bernard Blier, Robert Castel, Mariangela Melato; **D:** Marc Simenon; **W:** Jean Max; **C:** Rene Verzier; **M:** Francis Lai.

By the Light of the Silvery Moon 1953 The equally old-fashioned sequel to "On Moonlight Bay" finds Day engaged to MacRae, who's just returned from Army service in WWI. He wants to postpone their marriage until he gets financially secure and the waiting causes some jealous misunderstandings (naturally enough by movie's end). Based on Booth Tarkington's "Penrod" stories. ♪By the Light of the Silvery Moon; I'll Forget You; Your Eyes Have Told Me So; Be My Little Baby Bumble Bee; If You Were the Only Girl in the World; Ain't We Got Fun; King Chanticleer. 101m/C VHS, DVD. Doris Day, Gordon MacRae, Leon Ames, Billy Gray, Rosemary DeCamp, Mary Wickes, Russell Arms, Maria Palmer; **D:** David Butler; **W:** Robert O'Brien, Irving Elinson; **M:** Max Steiner.

By the Sword 1993 (R) Maximilian Suba (Abraham) is a one-time fencing whiz who has spent the last 25 years in prison for the murder of his mentor during a fencing match. Upon his release, Suba heads back to his old fencing grounds to see what's become of the murdered man's now-grown son and discovers Alexander (Roberts) as ruthless and ambitious as Suba once was. Incoherent plot leaves both actors and viewers in the dark. 91m/C VHS. F. Murray Abraham, Eric Roberts, Mia Sara, Christopher Rydell; **D:** Jeremy Paul Kagan; **W:** John McDonald, James Donadio; **C:** Arthur Albert; **M:** Bill Conti.

By Way of the Stars 1992 (PG) Young man is pursued by a killer while he searches for his father on the 19th-century Canadian frontier. Made for TV. 150m/C VHS. *CA* Zachary Bennett, Tantoo Cardinal, Gema Zamprogna, Jan Rubes, Michael Mahonen; **D:** Allan King. TV

Bye-Bye 1996 Ismael (Bouajila), 25, and his 14-year-old brother Mouloud (Embarek) are French-born Arabs whose parents have abruptly returned to their Tunisian homeland after a family tragedy. The brothers have travelled from Paris to stay with their uncle (Ahourai) and his family in the port city of Marseilles. Their cousin Rhida (Mammeri), a petty criminal involved with drugs, takes the innocent Mauloud under his wing and hides him away so the boy won't be sent back to his parents. Ismael desperately roams the city trying to find his brother while he also struggles to make a fresh start amidst much societal hostility. French and Arabic with subtitles. 105m/C VHS, DVD. *FR* Sami Bouajila, Ouassini Embarek, Benhaissa Ahourari, Sofiane Mammeri, Jamila Darwich-Farah, Nozha Khouadra; **D:** Karim Dridi; **W:** Karim Dridi; **C:** John Mathieson; **M:** Jimmy Oihid, Steve Shehan.

Bye Bye Baby 1988 (R) Two luscious young women cavort amid lusty Italian men on various Mediterranean beaches. 80m/C VHS, DVD. *IT* Carol Alt, Brigitte Nielsen, Jason Connery, Luca Barbareschi; **D:** Enrico Oldoini; **M:** Manuel De Sica.

Bye, Bye, Birdie 1963 Energized and sweet film version of the Broadway musical about a teen rock and roll idol (Pearson doing Elvis) coming to a small town to see one of his fans before he leaves for the army. The film that made Ann-Margret a star. ♪Bye Bye Birdie; The Telephone Hour; How Lovely to be a Woman; Honestly Sincere; One Boy; Put on a Happy Face; Kids; One Last Kiss; A Lot of Livin' to Do. 112m/C VHS, DVD. Dick Van Dyke, Janet Leigh, Ann-Margret, Paul Lynde, Bobby Rydell, Maureen Stapleton, Ed Sullivan, Trudi Ames, Jesse Pearson; **D:** George Sidney; **W:** Irving Brecher; **C:** Joseph Biroc; **M:** Johnny Green.

Bye Bye Birdie 1995 (G) TV adaptation of the Broadway musical (previously filmed in 1963) about an Elvis-like singer, about to be inducted into the Army, who causes havoc when he visits fans in a small town. 135m/C VHS, DVD. Jason Alexander, Vanessa (Lynne) Williams, Chynna Phillips, George Wendt, Tyne Daly, Marc Kudisch; **D:** Gene Saks. TV

Bye Bye Blues 1989 (PG) The lives of the Cooper family are disrupted when the husband is called to service during WWII and is then taken prisoner by the Japanese. In need of money, wife Daisy (Jenkins) joins a local swing band and begins charming all who watch her, especially the band's trombone player (Reilly). A sweet-spirited tale of love, loyalty, and the search for inner strength. Jenkins gives a strong performance as the shy wife who becomes an independent woman during her husband's absence. 110m/C VHS. *CA* Rebecca Jenkins, Michael Ontkean, Luke Reilly, Stuart Margolin, Robyn Stevan, Kate Reid, Wayne Robson, Sheila Moore, Leon Pownall, Vincent Gale, Susan Sneath; **D:** Anne Wheeler; **W:** Anne Wheeler; **C:** Vic Sarin; **M:** George Blondheim. Genie '90: Actress (Jenkins), Support. Actress (Stevan).

Bye Bye Brazil 1979 A changing Brazil is seen through the eyes of four wandering gypsy minstrels participating in a tent show traveling throughout the country. Lots of Brazilian charm. In Portuguese with English subtitles. 115m/C VHS. *BR* Jose Wilker, Betty Faria, Fabio Junior, Zaira Zambelli; **D:** Carlos Diegues; **W:** Carlos Diegues; **M:** Chico Buarque.

Bye Bye, Love 1994 (PG-13) Forty-eight hours in the lives of three divorced buddies starts at the local Mickey D's for the biweekly exchange of their kids. The dads don't offer any surprises: Donny (Reiser) still loves his ex, Vic (Quaid) hates his, and Dave (Modine) loves anything in a skirt. Sometimes witty, but just as often sadly poignant, the plot is as shallow as a TV sitcom, with an easy answer for every difficult question about divorce. The three leads are likeable enough, but Garofalo is the gem in an otherwise dull flick. She looks like she's having a blast, stealing scenes with abandon as Vic's blind date from hell. 107m/C VHS, DVD. Matthew Modine, Randy Quaid, Paul Reiser, Rob Reiner, Janeane Garofalo, Ed Flanders, Lindsay Crouse, Johnny Whitworth, Maria Pitillo, Amy Brenneman, Ross Malinger, Eliza Dushku, Wendell Pierce, Cameron Boyd, Mae Whitman, Jayne Brook, Dana Wheeler-Nicholson, Amber Benson, Stephen (Steve) Root, Danny Masterson, Brad Hall, Jack Black; **D:** Sam Weisman; **W:** Gary David Goldberg, Brad Hall; **M:** J.A.C. Redford.

Byron 2003 Byron as poet comes in second to Byron as scandalous lover in this BBC production that depicts the price of fame. Byron's (Miller) romantic style includes radical politics and adventure after the aristocrat becomes famous in 1812. His marriage to the pious Anna-bella (Cox) is a disaster and he's forced into exile when Byron's alleged love affair with half-sister Augusta (Little) becomes society gossip. Miller is both sympathetic and self-aware in the title role. 150m/C DVD.

The C-Man 🐾🐾 1949 Customs agent Jagger finds work isn't so dull after all. Murder and theft on an international scale make for a busy week as he follows jewel smugglers from Paris to New York. Docu-style though routine crime story. 75m/B VHS, DVD. Dean Jagger, John Carradine, Harry Landers, Rene Paul; D: Joseph Lerner.

Cabaret 🐾🐾🐾½ 1972 (PG) Hitler is rising to power, racism and anti-Semitism are growing, and the best place to hide from it all is the Berlin cabaret. Witt dancing girls, an androgynous master of ceremonies (Grey), and American expatriate singer Sally Bowles (Minnelli), you can laugh and drink and pretend tomorrow will never come. Sally does just that. Face to face with the increasing horrors of Nazism, she persists in the belief that the "show must go on." Along for the ride is Englishman Brian Roberts (York, in a role based on Christopher Isherwood's own experiences, who serves both as participant and observer. Based on the John Kander's hit Broadway musical (and Isherwood's stories), the film is impressive, with excellent direction and cinematography. 🎵Cabaret; Willkommen; Mein Herr; Maybe This Time; Two Ladies; Money, Money, Money; Tomorrow Belongs to Me; If You Could See Her. 119m/C VHS, DVD. Joel Grey, Michael York, Marisa Berenson, Helmut Griem, Fritz Wepper, Elisabeth Neumann-Viertel; D: Bob Fosse; W: Jay Presson Allen; C: Geoffrey Unsworth; M: Ralph Burns. Oscars '72: Actress (Minnelli), Art Dir./Set Dec., Cinematog., Director (Fosse), Film Editing, Sound, Support. Actor (Grey); Orig. Song Score and/or Adapt.; British Acad. '72: Actress (Minnelli), Director (Fosse), Film; Golden Globes '73: Actress—Mus./Comedy (Minnelli), Film—Mus./Comedy, Support. Actor (Grey); Natl. Bd. of Review '72: Director (Fosse), Support. Actor (Grey), Support. Actress (Berenson); Natl. Film Reg. '95; Natl. Soc. Film Critics '72: Support. Actor (Grey); Writers Guild '72: Adapt. Screenplay.

Cabeza de Vaca 🐾🐾🐾 1990 (R) In 1528, a Spanish expedition shipwrecks in unknown territory off the Florida coast. Only survivor Cabeza de Vaca is captured by the Iguase Indian tribe and made a slave to their shaman. He's later freed, but leaves with respect for their culture. Spanish soldiers find him and want his help in capturing the natives, but he is outraged by their cruelty and must confront his own people. Strong visual style easily brings the audience deeply into this uncharted world. Based on Cabeza de Vaca's book "Naufragios." Director Echevarria's feature film debut. Spanish and Indian with subtitles. 111m/C VHS, DVD. MX SP Juan Diego, Daniel Gimenez Cacho, Roberto Sosa, Carlos Castanon, Gerardo Villareal, Roberto Cobo, Jose Flores, Ramon Barragan; D: Nicolas Echevarria; W: Guillermo Sheridan, Nicolas Echevarria; C: Guillermo Navarro; M: Mario Lavista.

Cabaret Balkan 🐾🐾 The Powder Keg; Bure Baruta 1998 (R) Acerbicly cruel and frequently physically brutal comedy is set in Belgrade one winter night and features characters whose stories turn out to be inter-related and are bookended by the comments of sneering nightclub M.C. Boris (Ristanovski). There are betrayals, frauds, random acts of violence, and various absurdities set in a war-torn country where the veneer of civilization has long since disappeared. Based on the play "Bure Barura" by Dukovski. Serbo-Croatian with subtitles. 102m/C VHS. YU Miki (Predrag) Manojlovic, Nikola Ristanovski, Nebojsa Glogovac, Marko Urosevic, Bogdan Diklic; D: Goran Paskaljevic; W: Goran Paskaljevic, Dejan Dukovski; C: Milan Spasic; M: Zoran Simjanovic.

Cabin Boy WOOF! 1994 (PG-13) Obnoxious "fancy lad" Elliot mistakenly boards the wrong boat and becomes the new cabin boy for a ridiculous bunch of mean, smelly sailors. Fish out of water saga is so bad it's—bad, a blundering attempt at parody that's just plain stupid. Surprisingly produced by Tim Burton, but even diehard fans will disappoint. Look for Chris' real life dad Bob as the effort.

Cabin by the Lake 🐾🐾 2000 Screenwriter Stanley (Nelson) takes his work a little too seriously when he does research on a story about a serial killer who kidnaps and drowns his female victims. Stanley has his own garden of victims until one young woman escapes and is laid for the killer. 91m/C VHS, DVD. Judd Nelson, Hedy Burress, Michael Weatherly, Bernie Coulson, Susan Gibney; D: Po-Chih Leung; W:C: David Stephens; C: Philip Linzey; M: Frankie Blue, Daniel Licht.

Cabin Fever 🐾🐾 2003 (R) Scattershot horror/comedy with a twist has five teenagers rent a cabin in the woods for a week contend with a very deadly and very gross virus. A bloody man who appears in the woods is the harbinger of doom for the appropriately sex- and booze-crazed archetypical horror movie teens. They are soon knee-deep in local weirdos and red necks as well as appropriate amounts of blood and gore. Though nor outstanding, pic boasts enough gore to satisfy the most hard-core horror fans. 94m/C VHS, DVD, UMD. US Jordan Ladd, Rider Strong, James De Bello, Cerna Vincent, Joey Kerr, Arie Verveen, Giuseppe Andrews, Eli Roth; D: Eli Roth; W: Eli Roth, Randy Pearlstein; C: Scott Kevan; M: Nathan Barr.

The Cabin in the Cotton 🐾🐾½ 1932 Davis stars as a rich, ruthless Southern belle in this dated melodrama about sharecroppers. Bar chetyplcal cast as a poor sharecropper who is almost brought to ruin when he falls for the sexy Southern vamp. Contains Davis's most famous line, "Ah'd love t'kiss you, but ah jes washed mah hair." 77m/B VHS. Bette Davis, Richard Barthelmess, Dorothy Jordan, Henry B. Walthall, Tully Marshall; D: Michael Curtiz; W: Paul Green.

Cabin in the Sky 🐾🐾🐾 1943 A poor woman fights to keep her husband's soul out of the devil's clutches. Based on a Broadway show and featuring an all-Black cast. Lively dance numbers and a musical score with contributions from Duke Ellington. 🎵Happiness Is Just a Thing Called Joe; Taking a Chance on Love; Life's Full of Consequence; Li'l Black Sheep; Shine. Honey in the Honeycomb. 99m/C VHS, DVD. Ethel Waters, Eddie Anderson, Lena Horne, Rex Ingram, Louis Armstrong, Duke Ellington; D: Vincente Minnelli; M: Duke Ellington, Harold Arlen, E.Y. Harburg, George Bassman.

The Cabinet of Dr. Caligari 🐾🐾🐾 Das Cabinet des Doktor Caligari 1919 A pioneering film in the most extreme expressionistic style about a hypnotist in a carnival and a girl-snatching somnambulist. Highly influential in its approach to lighting, composition, design and acting. Much imitated. Silent. 92m/B VHS, DVD. GE Conrad Veidt, Werner Krauss, Li Dagover, Hans von Twardowski, Rudolf Klein-Rogge, Friedrich Feher, Rudolf Lettinger; D: Robert Wiene; W: Carl Mayer, Hans Janowitz; C: Willy Hameister.

The Cable Guy 🐾🐾 1996 (PG-13) Carrey's first $20 million paycheck finds cable subscriber Broderick in for a comedic nightmare when he accepts the offer of free movie channels. The overeager installer (Carrey, naturally) turns his life upside down. A little darker humor than usual, the acerbic Letterman gets the best line, "Man, oh, man do I hate them fancy lads." "We know how you feel, Dave. 96m/C VHS, DVD, Ancy Richter, Chris Elliott, Ann Magnuson, Ben Stiller, James Gannon, Brian Doyle-Murray, Russ Tamblyn, Bron James, Ricki Lake, Bob Elliott; Cameos: David Letterman; D: Ben Stiller; W: Adam Resnick; C: Amy Barrett; M: Steve Bartek.

lad's dad; good friend Letterman appears briefly as nasty "Old Salt," but uses the alias Earl Hofert in the final credits. As usual the acerbic Letterman gets the best line. "Man, oh, man do I hate them fancy lads." "We know how you feel, Dave. 96m/C VHS, DVD, Ancy Richter, Chris Elliott, Ann Magnuson, Ben Stiller, James Gannon, Brian Doyle-Murray, Russ Tamblyn, Bron James, Ricki Lake, Bob Elliott; Cameos: David Letterman; D: Ben Stiller; W: Adam Resnick; C: Amy Barrett; M: Steve Bartek.

Cabiria 🐾🐾🐾½ 1914 The pioneering Italian epic about a Roman and a slave girl having a love affair in Rome during the Second Punic War. Immense sets and set-pieces; an important influence on Griffith and DeMille. Silent. 123m/B VHS, DVD. IT Lidia Quaranta, Bartolomeo Pagano, Umberto Mozzato; D: Giovanni Pastrone; W: Giovanni Pastrone, Gabriele D'Annunzio; C: Segundo de Chomon.

The Caddy 🐾🐾 1953 Lewis plays frantic caddie prone to slapstick against Martin's smooth professional golfer with a bent toward singing. Mostly a series of Martin and Lewis sketches that frequently land in the rough. Introduces several songs, including a classic Martin and Lewis rendition of "That's Amore." Look for cameos by a host of professional golfers. 95m/C VHS. Dean Martin, Jerry Lewis, Donna Reed, Barbara Bates, Joseph Calleia, Marshall Thompson, Fred Clark; Cameos: Ben Hogan, Sam Snead, Byron Nelson, Julius Boros, Jimmy Thomson. 🎵M: Patrick Flynn.

Cabo Blanco 🐾🐾 1981 (R) A bartender and a variety of other characters, including an ex-Nazi and a French woman searching for her lover, assemble in Peru after WWII. Nazi Robards controls police chief Rey, while American Bronson runs the local watering hole and eyes French woman Sanda. Hey, this sounds familiar. Everyone shares a common interest: finding a missing treasure of gold, lost in a ship wreck. Remaking "Casablanca" via "The Treasure of Sierra Madre" is never easy. 87m/C VHS, DVD. Charles Bronson, Jason Robards Jr., Dominique Sanda, Fernando Rey, Gilbert Roland, Simon MacCorkindale, D: J. Lee Thompson; W: Morton S. Fine, Milton S. Gelman; C: Alex Phillips Jr.; M: Jerry Goldsmith.

Cactus 🐾🐾½ 1986 Melodrama about a young French woman, separated from her husband, who faces the reality of losing her sight after a car accident. She experiences a growing relationship with a blind man and contemplates the thought of risky surgery which may improve her eyesight or cause complete blindness. Countering all that blindness and tangled romance is a camera that pans lush Australian landscapes and humorously focuses on the small telling details of daily life. 95m/C VHS, DVD. AU Isabelle Huppert, Robert Menzies, Monica Maughan, Sheila Florance, Norman Kaye, Paul Cox, Bob Ellis; C: Yuri Sokol; M: Giovanni Pergolese, Yannis Markopolous, Elise Davis.

Cactus Flower 🐾🐾 1969 (PG) Good cast doesn't quite suffice to make this adaptation of a Broadway hit work. A middle-aged bachelor dentist gets involved with a kookie mistress, refusing to admit his real love for his prim and proper receptionist. Hawn's big leap to stardom. 103m/C VHS, DVD. Walter Matthau, Goldie Hawn, Ingrid Bergman, Jack Weston, Rick Lenz; D: Gene Saks; W: I.A.L. Diamond; C: Charles Bryan] Lang Jr.; M: Quincy Jones. Oscars '69: Support. Actress (Hawn); Golden Globes '70: Support. Actress (Hawn).

Cactus in the Snow 🐾½ 1972 A virginal Army private serving during the Vietnam War era tries to find sex on a 72-hour leave and instead discovers love. Some guys have all the luck. Melodrama never grabs where it ought to. 90m/C VHS. Richard Thomas, Mary Layne, Lucille Benson; D: Martin Zweiback.

Caddie 🐾🐾½ 1976 Based on an autobiographical story of a woman who leaves her unfaithful husband in 1930s Australia. Struggling to raise her two children, she works as a waitress in a bar where she finds romance with one of the regulars. Average script bolstered by Morse's performance. 107m/C VHS. AU Helen Morse, Jack Thompson, Takis Emmanuel, Jacki Weaver; D: Donald Crombie; W: Joan Long; C: Peter James; M: Patrick Flynn.

Cadence 🐾🐾 1989 (PG-13) The directorial debut of actor Martin Sheen, this fit ful melodrama stars son Charlie as an unruly trooper on a 1950s army base. Placed in an all-black stockade for punishment, he bonds with his brother prisoners by defying the hardcase sergeant (played by Sheen the elder). Characters and situations are intriguing but not rendered effectively. Based on the novel "Count a Lonely Cadence" by Gordon Weaver. 97m/C VHS, DVD. Charlie Sheen, Martin Sheen, Laurence Fishburne, Michael Beach, Ramon Estevez; D: Martin Sheen; M: Georges Delerue.

Cadillac Girls 🐾½ 1993 Page is a self-destructive teenager who is arrested for car theft. To avoid jail, Page is placed in her single mom's custody and moves to her family's straitlaced hometown in Nova Scotia. Mom isn't exactly good at parenting and Page's adolescent anger extends to putting the moves on mom's potential new beau. 90m/C VHS. Jennifer Dale, Gregory Harrison, Mia Kirshner, Adam Beach; D: Nicholas (Nick) Kendall. Gene '93: Score.

Cadillac Man 🐾🐾 1990 (R) Williams is the quintessential low-life car salesman in this rather disjointed comedy. A lesser comedic talent might have stalled and been abandoned, but Williams manages to drive away despite the flat script and direction. One storyline follows his attempt to sell 12 cars in 12 days or lose his job while another follows his confrontation with a gun-toting, mad-as-hell cuckolded husband. Williams and Robbins are often close to being funny in a hyperkinetic way, but the situations are dumb enough to rob most of the scenes of their comedy. Watch for a movie-stealing bit by the spunky waitress at the local Chinese restaurant. 95m/C VHS. Robin Williams, Tim Robbins, Pamela Reed, Fran Drescher, Zack Norman, Annabella Sciorra, Lori Petty, Paul Guilfoyle, Tristen Skylar; D: Roger Donaldson; W: Ken Friedman; C: David Gribble; M: J. Peter Robinson.

Carrey fans may be used to, and don't expect any bodily ventriloquism. Carrey (did we mention he's in it?) gets to act with the acerbic Letterman ... Director Stiller does a nice job of reining in his more manic impulses when necessary. Broderick holds his own as the reluctant pal. Original scripter Holtz won a Writer's Guild arbitration for sole writing credit from producer-writer Judd Apatow. 96m/C VHS, DVD, Jim Carrey, Matthew Broderick, Leslie Mann, George Segal, Diane Baker, Jack Black, Janeane Garofalo, Andy Dick, Charles Napier, Ben Stiller, Bob Odenkirk, David Cross, Owen Wilson, Joel Murray, Kathy Griffin, Sean M. Whalen, Annabelle Gurwitch, Conrad Janis, Alex D. Linz; D: Ben Stiller; W: Judd Apatow, Lou Holtz Jr.; C: Robert Brinkmann; M: John Ottman. MTV Movie Awards '97: Villain (Carrey), Comedic Perf. (Carrey).

Caddyshack 🐾🐾🐾 1980 (R) Inspired performances by Murray and Dangerfield drive this sublimely moronic comedy, onto the green. The action takes place at Bushwood Country Club, where caddy Danny (O'Keefe) is bucking to win the club's college scholarship. Characters involved in various sophomoric set pieces include obnoxious club president Judge Smalls (Knight), playboy Ty Webb (Chase), who is too laid back to keep his score, loud, vulgar, and extremely rich Al Czernik (Dangerfield), and filthy gopher-hunting groundskeeper Carl (Murray). Occasional dry moments are followed by scenes of pure (and tasteless) anarchy, so watch with someone immature. Does for golf what "Major League" tried to do for baseball. 99m/C VHS, DVD. HD DVD. Chevy Chase, Rodney Dangerfield, Ted (Edward) Knight, Michael O'Keefe, Bill Murray, Sarah Holcomb, Brian Doyle-Murray; C: Steven Lamer; M: Johnny Mandel.

Caddyshack 2 🐾½ 1988 (PG) Obligatory sequel to "Caddyshack," minus Bill Murray, who wisely avoided further encroachment of gopher holes, and director Ramis who opted for. the screenwriting chore. Mason is the star of the show as a crude self-made millionaire who tangles with the snobs at the country club. Although the original, proving once again that funny guys are always undone by lousy scripts and weak direction. "Shack 2" has significantly fewer guffaws than the original. 103m/C VHS, DVD. Jackie Mason, Chevy Chase, Dan Aykroyd, Dyan Cannon, Robert Stack, Dina Merrill, Randy Quaid, Jessica Lundy, Jonathan Silverman, Chynna Phillips; D: Allan Arkush; W: Harold Ramis, Peter Torokvei; C: Harry Stradling Jr.; M: Ira Newborn. Golden Raspberries '88: Worst Support. Actor (Aykroyd), Worst Song ("Jack Fresh").

son, Harry E. Cooper; D: Norman Taurog; W: Danny Arnold.

Cadillac Ranch 🐾🐾½ 1996 (R) Three squabbling Texas sisters who have reunited to celebrate Mary K.'s upcoming marriage. Katharine (Humphrey) Crowley are three Frances (Feeney), and Mary C: David Gribble; M: ...

riage. CJ works in a strip club owned by greedy ex-Texas Ranger Wood (Lloyd), who sent their long-gone daddy, Travis (Metzler), to prison for a heist Wood was involved in. When CJ gets fired, the three-some steal a key from Wood that will supposedly access money from the heist and the vengeful Wood goes after them. **104m/ C VHS, DVD.** Suzy Amis, Renee Humphrey, Kathleen Feeney, Christopher Lloyd, Jim Metzler, Linden Ashby; **D:** Lisa Gottlieb; **W:** Jennifer Cecil; **C:** Bruce Douglas Johnson; **M:** Christopher Tyng.

Caesar and Cleopatra 🦴🦴½ **1946** Based on the classic George Bernard Shaw play. Caesar meets the beautiful Cleopatra in ancient Egypt and helps her gain control of her life. Remains surprisingly true to Shaw's adaptation, unlike many other historical films of the same era. **135m/C VHS, DVD.** *GB* Claude Rains, Vivien Leigh, Stewart Granger, Flora Robson, Francis L. Sullivan, Cecil Parker; **D:** Gabriel Pascal; **C:** Robert Krasker.

Cafe au Lait 🦴🦴🦴 *Metisse* **1994** Actor/director/writer Kassovitz scores in his debut feature about an interracial menage a trois. Beautiful mulatto Lola (Mauduech) is pregnant but she's not sure by which of her two contrasting lovers (who don't yet know about each other). It could be white, Jewish, easy-going bicycle messenger Felix (Kassovitz) or stuffy, wealthy, black Moslem student Jamal (Kounde). Both men desire the fatherhood role and both move in with Lola to share responsibility. This is not without complications. Generally light and frothy without ignoring racial tensions. French with subtitles. **94m/ C VHS, DVD.** *FR* Mathieu Kassovitz, Julie Mauduech, Hubert Kounde, Vincent Cassel, Tadek Lokcinski, Jany Holt; **D:** Mathieu Kassovitz; **W:** Mathieu Kassovitz; **C:** Pierre Aim; **M:** Marie Daune, Jean-Louis Daulne.

Cafe Express 🦴🦴½ **1983** A con artist (he sells coffee illegally aboard an Italian train) stays one step ahead of the law as he raises money to help his ailing son. As in "Bread and Chocolate," Manfredi is again the put-upon working class hero comedically attempting to find a better way of life in this bittersweet tale. **90m/C VHS, DVD.** *IT* Nino Manfredi, Gigi Reder, Adolfo Celi, Vittorio Mezzogiorno; **D:** Nanni Loy.

Cafe Lumiere 🦴½ *Kohi jikou* **2005** Taiwanese director Hou dedicates his homage to Japanese director Yasujiro Ozu with a narrative about loneliness, isolation, and modern urban life. In Tokyo, Yoko (pop star Hitoto in her debut) announces to her father and stepmother that she's pregnant but has no intention of marrying. She is doing research on composer Jiang Wen-Ye (whose work is used on the soundtrack); he's doing a computer art project about the city's commuter trains, which mean you see a lot of the subway system. It's understated to the point of inertia. Japanese with subtitles. **104m/C DVD.** **D:** Hou Hsiao-Hsien; **W:** Chu Tien-Wen; **C:** Lee Ping-Bing; **M:** Jiang Wen.

Cafe Ole 🦴🦴½ **2000** Malcolm lives a happy, if somewhat lonely, existence in his Montreal neighborhood, working at a video store and passing time with neighbors at the local cafe. After a string of unsuccessful dates, mostly engineered by his matchmaker brother, Malcolm meets Alicia. He realizes she's the one for him, but she has a secret that will disrupt his heretofore uneventful life. Charming little romantic comedy, with the kick of some steamy love scenes. **97m/C VHS.** Andrew Tarbet, Laia Marull, Macha Grenon, Dino Tavarone, Stephanie Morgenstern; **D:** Richard Roy; **W:** Emil Sher. **VIDEO**

Cafe Romeo 🦴 **1991** Tale of 20-something friendships forged in the neighborhood coffeehouse of a heavily Italian community. Lia (Stewart) is a waitress who dreams of becoming a fashion designer, but her marriage to a small time hood holds her back. Crombie, her cousin by marriage, is a dental student confused about his future, but's helped along by strong performances. Originally broadcast on Canadi-an TV. **93m/C VHS.** *CA* Catherine Mary Stewart, Jonathan Crombie; **D:** Rex Bromfield.

Cafe Society 🦴🦴½ **1997 (R)** The fictional nightclub El Casbah is the setting for director De Felitta's debut take on a 1952 New York prostitution scandal. Wealthy young playboy Mickey Jelke (Whaley) prefers to mix with lowlifes rather than high society. Newcomer Jack Kale (Gallagher) is working the scene and turns out to be an undercover cop investigating a prostitution ring operating out of the clubs. Jack befriends both Mickey and his latest girlfriend, in-the-know Patricia Ward (Boyle), who's not above selling her favors. Then patsy Jelke gets indicted as a pimp and all cafe society's tawdriness is exposed. **104m/C VHS.** Peter Gallagher, Frank Whaley, Lara Flynn Boyle, John Spencer, Anna Thomson, David Patrick Kelly, Paul Guilfoyle; **D:** Raymond De Felitta; **W:** Raymond De Felitta; **C:** Mike Mayers; **M:** Chris Guardino.

The Cage 🦴 **1989 (R)** Gangsters enlist a brain-damaged Vietnam vet played by Ferrigno to participate in illegal "cage fights," enclosed wrestling matches fought to the death. Crude and annoying. **101m/C VHS, DVD.** Lou Ferrigno, Reb Brown, Michael Dante, Mike Moroff, Marilyn Tokuda, James Shigeta, Al Ruscio; **D:** Hugh Kelley.

The Cage 🦴🦴 **1990** Sent to prison for murdering his girlfriend, Jive has no idea what the pen has in store for him. The inmates stage a mock trial, the defendant is found guilty and the sentence is too horrible to imagine. From a stage play by the San Quentin Drama Workshop and co-starring Hayes, author of "Midnight Express." **90m/C VHS, DVD.** Rick Cluchey, William Hayes; **D:** Rick Cluchey; **W:** Rick Cluchey.

Cage 2: The Arena of Death 🦴½ **1994 (R)** Billy Thomas (Ferrigno) is kidnapped by a vicious mobster and forced to battle martial arts experts in a steel cage battle to the death. But his best friend (Brown) plans to infiltrate the show and put a stop to the carnage. **94m/C VHS.** Lou Ferrigno, Reb Brown; **D:** Lang Elliott.

Caged 🦴🦴🦴 **1950** Innocent Marie Allen (Parker) is sent to prison as an accomplice to her husband's fatal armed robbery attempt because she was in the car. Once inside, the frightened, pregnant widow encounters reform-minded warden Benton (Moorehead) and vicious matron Harper (Emerson), who fight for her soul, along with a varied cast of fellow inmates. Harper's vicious treatment of the inmates eventually turns Allen into a hardened con. A classic, which shouldn't be lumped in with later exploitation examples of the genre. Excellent performances and scripting make it a fine representation of noir. **96m/B DVD.** Eleanor Parker, Agnes Moorehead, Hope Emerson, Ellen Corby, Betty Garde, Jan Sterling, Lee Patrick, Olive Deering, Sheila MacRae, Jane Darwell, Gertrude Michael, Don Beddoe, Edith Evanson, Gertrude Hoffman; **D:** John Cromwell; **W:** Bernard C. Schoenfeld, Virginia Kellogg; **C:** Carl Guthrie; **M:** Max Steiner.

Caged Fear 🦴½ **1992 (R)** Young Krissie (Cloke) is mistakenly put behind bars in a brutal, high-security prison for a shootout caused by her outlaw husband Tommy (Keith) during their honeymoon. Tommy comes up with an outrageous scheme to rescue her. Not quite as bad as it sounds, but close. **94m/C VHS.** David Keith, Deborah May, Ray Sharkey, Loretta Devine, Karen Black, Kristen Cloke, Stanley DeSantis; **D:** Bobby Houston; **W:** Bobby Houston; **C:** Alan Caso.

Caged Fury 🦴 **1980 (R)** American women being held captive in Southeast Asia are brainwashed into becoming walking time bombs. Yes, that dame's gonna blow. Made in the Philippines with the best of intentions. **90m/C VHS.** *PH* Bernadette Williams, Taaffe O'Connell, Jennifer Laine; **D:** Cirio H. Santiago.

Caged Fury 🦴 **1990** Two Los Angeles women allegedly commit sexual crimes and are sent to prison. Cheap, exploitive women's prison rehash. **85m/C VHS.** Erik Estrada, Richie Barathy, Roxanna Michaels, Paul Smith, James Hong, Greg Cummins, Mindi Miller; **D:** Bill Milling.

Caged Hearts 🦴 **1995 (R)** Chicks-behind-bars flick finds Kate (Genzel) and Sharon (McClure) framed for murder by a shady organization called "The Shield." Cliches abound. **87m/C VHS, DVD.** Tane McClure, Carrie Genzel, Taylor Leigh, Nick Wilder; **D:** Henri Charr.

Caged Heat 🦴🦴 *Renegade Girls; Caged Females* **1974 (R)** Low-budget babes-behind-bars film touted as the best sexploitation film of the day. Demme's directorial debut is a genre-altering installment in Roger Corman's formulaic cellblock Cinderella cycle. Recycled plot—innocent woman is put behind bars, where she loses some of her innocence—boasts an updated treatment. These babes may wear hot pants and gratuitously bare their midriffs, but they're not brainless bimbos. They're strong individuals who work together to liberate themselves. Reached cult status. Cult diva Steele returned to the big screen after six years to play the wheelchair-ridden prison warden, written specifically for her. **83m/C VHS, DVD.** Juanita Brown, Erica Gavin, Roberta Collins, Barbara Steele, Ella Reid, Cheryl "Rainbeaux" Smith, Ann Aprea, Amy Barrett, Gary Goetzman; **D:** Jonathan Demme; **W:** Jonathan Demme; **C:** Tak Fujimoto; **M:** John Cale.

Caged Heat 2: Stripped of Freedom 🦴½ **1994 (R)** Women-in-prison formula with a princess thrown into the pen following a political coup. CIA agent is sent undercover as an inmate to bust her out. Usual sadistic guards, rape, and revenge scenes. From Roger Corman's direct-to-video factory. **84m/C VHS.** Jewel Shepard, Chanel Akiko Hirai, Pamella D'Pella, Vic Diaz; **D:** Cirio H. Santiago.

Caged Heat 3000 🦴 **1995 (R)** Yes, it's a sci-fi chicks-in-prison movie! Innocent Kira Murphy (Leigh) is wrongly condemned to an underground prison located 45 lightyears from Earth where there are 45 of racial tensions and evil prison officials. Prerequisite shower scenes and sadistic guards also add to the standard exploitation. **84m/C VHS.** Cassandra Leigh, Kena Land, Debra Beatty; **D:** Cirio H. Santiago; **W:** Paul Ziller.

Caged in Paradiso 🦴½ **1989 (R)** A convicted criminal and his wife are dumped onto a remote prisoner's isle to live out their lives. When Cara loses contact with her husband, she must fend for herself. Survival tale boringly told. **90m/C VHS.** Irene Cara; **D:** Michael Snyder.

Caged Terror WOOF! **1972** Two urbanites hit the countryside for a weekend and meet a band of crazy rapists who ravage the wife and set the husband raging with bloodthirsty revenge. Squalid stroll through the ruins. **76m/C VHS, DVD.** Percy Harkness, Elizabeth Suzuki, Leon Morenzie; **D:** Barry McLean.

Caged Women 🦴 *Women's Penitentiary 4* **1984 (R)** Undercover journalist enters a women's prison and gets the usual eyeful. Mattei used the pseudonym Vincent Dawn. **97m/C VHS, DVD.** *FR IT* Laura Gemser, Gabriele Tinti, Lorraine (De Selle) De Selle, Maria Romano; **D:** Bruno Mattei.

Cahill: United States Marshal 🦴🦴 **1973 (PG)** The aging Duke in one of his lesser moments, portraying a marshal who comes to the aid of his sons. The boys are mixed up with a gang of outlaws, proving that no matter how good a parent you are, sometimes the kids just lean toward the wayward. Turns out, though, that the boys harbor a grudge against the old man due to years of workaholic neglect. Will Duke see the error of his ways and reconcile with the delinquent boys? Will he catch the outlaw leader? Will he go on to star in other Duke vehicles? **103m/C VHS, DVD.** John Wayne, Gary Grimes, George Kennedy, Neville Brand, Marie Windsor, Harry Carey Jr., Clay O'Brien; **D:** Andrew V. McLaglen; **M:** Elmer Bernstein.

The Caine Mutiny 🦴🦴🦴 **1954** A group of naval officers revolt against a captain they consider mentally unfit. Bogart is masterful as Captain Queeg, obsessed with cleanliness while onboard and later a study in mental meltdown during the court-martial of a crew member who participated in the mutiny. Based on the Pulitzer-winning novel by Herman Wouk, the drama takes a close look at the pressure-filled life aboard ship during WWII. **125m/C VHS, DVD.** Humphrey Bogart, Jose Ferrer, Van Johnson, Fred MacMurray, Lee Marvin, Claude Akins, E.G. Marshall, Robert Francis, May Wynn, Tom Tully, Arthur Franz, Warner Anderson, Katherine Warren, Jerry Paris, Steve Brodie, Whit Bissell, Robert Bray, Ted Cooper; **D:** Edward Dmytryk; **W:** Stanley Roberts, Michael Blankfort; **C:** Franz Planer; **M:** Max Steiner.

The Caine Mutiny Court Martial 🦴🦴🦴 **1988 (PG)** A young lieutenant is up for a court-martial after taking control of the USS Caine in the midst of a typhoon. In order to save him, his lawyer must discredit the paranoid Commander Queeg. As the events of the mutiny unfold, it becomes clear that Queeg's obsession with discipline had become a threat to everyone aboard. Good performances, particularly by Bogosian as the lawyer. Based on the novel by Pulitzer prize-winner Herman Wouk. **100m/C VHS.** Jeff Daniels, Eric Bogosian, Brad Davis, Peter Gallagher, Michael Murphy, Kevin J. O'Connor, Daniel H. Jenkins; **D:** Robert Altman. **TV**

Cain's Cutthroats 🦴 *Cain's Way; The Blood Seekers; Justice Cain* **1971 (R)** A former Confederate army captain and a bounty hunting preacher team up to settle the score with soldiers on a gang-raping, murdering spree. **87m/C VHS.** Scott Brady, John Carradine, Robert Dix, Don Epperson, Adair Jamison, Darwin Joston, Bruce (Kemp) Kimball, Russ McCubbin, Valda Hansen; **D:** Kent Osborne; **W:** Wilton Denmark; **C:** Ralph Waldo; **M:** Harley Hatcher.

Cairo 🦴🦴 **1942** War correspondent Young lands in Cairo where he is supposed to pass along classified information to a Nazi spy posing as a Brit. He meets and falls in love with American movie queen thought to be enemy agent (MacDonald) and a race across the desert follows when Young is trapped in a pyramid. Catchy tunes can't save this cheesy WWII spy spoof that marked the end of MacDonald's MGM contract. **101m/B VHS.** Jeanette MacDonald, Robert Young, Ethel Waters, Reginald Owen, Grant Mitchell, Lionel Atwill, Eduardo Ciannelli, Mitchell Lewis; **D:** Woodbridge S. Van Dyke; **M:** Herbert Stothart.

Cake 🦴🦴 **2005 (R)** Happily single with no interest in married life, travel writer Pippa (Graham) is thrown for a loop when her publisher father puts her in charge of his wedding publication. As her day-to-day work causes her to face her marital phobias, her fling with her usual study-type guy (Diggs) is complicated by her feelings for her more grounded mentor (Sutcliffe)at the magazine. **94m/C DVD.** Heather Graham, David Sutcliffe, Taye Diggs, Sandra Oh, Cheryl Hines, Sarah Chalke, Reagan Pasternak, Kate Kelton, Bruce Grey, Sabrina Grdevich, Suzanne Cyr; **D:** Nisha Ganatra; **W:** Tassie Cameron; **C:** Gregory Middleton; **M:** Andrew Lockington. **VIDEO**

Cal 🦴🦴🦴 **1984 (R)** Cal (Lynch), a young Catholic man, is reluctantly recruited into the Irish Republican Army. He falls in love with the older Marcella (Mirren), the widow of a Protestant policeman whom he helped kill while acting as the get-away driver for his fellow Republicans. Thoughtful and tragic, with excellent performances; set in Northern Ireland. **104m/C VHS.** *IR* Helen Mirren, John Lynch, Donal McCann, Kitty Gibson, Ray McAnally, John Kavanagh; **D:** Pat O'Connor; **W:** Bernard MacLaverty; **M:** Mark Knopfler. Cannes '84: Actress (Mirren).

Calamity Jane 🦴🦴🦴 **1953** In one of her best Warner musicals, Day stars as the rip-snortin', gun-totin' Calamity Jane of Western lore, in an on-again, off-again romance with Wild Bill Hickok. ♪Secret Love; Just Blew in From the Windy City; The Black Hills of Dakota; The Deadwood Stage (Whip-Crack-Away); The Windy City. **101m/C VHS, DVD.** Doris Day, Howard Keel, Allyn Ann McLerie, Dick Wesson; **D:** David Butler; **M:** James O'Hanlon; **C:** Wilfrid M. Cline; **M:** Sammy Fain, Paul Francis Webster. Oscars '53: Song ("Secret Love").

Calamity Jane 🐾🐾½ 1982 A bi-ography of the famous lady crack shot. Alexander is cast as the tough-as-nails woman who considered herself on a par with any man. 96m/C VHS. **D:** James Goldstone. **TV** Frederic Forrest, Ken Kercheval, Talia Balsam, David Hemmings. **C:** Jane Alexander, Patti D'Arbanville, Sam Freed, Boyd Gaines, Stephen McIntire; **D:** Sollace Mitchell.

Calendar 🐾🐾½ 1993 A Canadian photographer (Egoyan) is hired to take pictures of ancient Armenian churches for a calendar. His wife (Egoyan's real-life spouse Khanjian) accompanies him, serving as a translator, and they hire a driver (Adamian) who turns out to be an architectural expert. Told in flashback, the film gradually reveals a romantic triangle—with the photographer becoming so caught up in his work that he fails to realize his wife, increasingly drawn to the ethnic heritage, and their driver are having an affair. This romantic puzzle also includes the photographer, having returned to Canada and apparently seeking a replacement, having dinner with a series of women he's meet through the personals. In English and Armenian. 73m/C VHS, DVD. **CA** Atom Egoyan, Arsinee Khanjian, Ashot Adamian; **D:** Atom Egoyan; **W:** Atom Egoyan; **C:** Norayr Kasper.

Calendar Girl 🐾🐾½ 1993 *(PG-13)* In 1962 three high-school best friends borrow a convertible and travel from their Nevada home to Hollywood to meet their pinup idol, Marilyn Monroe. Roy's (Priestley) a rebel, Ned's (Olds, in his film debut) sensitive, and Scott's (O'Connell) just a nice guy. They stay with Roy's Uncle Harvey (Pantoliano), an aspiring actor, and work to meet their dream girl. Which they finally do in a notably weak sequence which fits in with this notably unispired film. The three actors at least have enough cockery to make a realistic buddies—one of the few true touches in the film. 86m/C VHS. Jason Priestley, Gabriel Olds, Jerry O'Connell, Joe Pantoliano, Stephen Tobolowsky, Kurt Fuller, Steve Railsback, Emily Warfield, Stephanie Anderson; **Cameos:** Chubby Checker; **D:** John Whitesell; **W:** Paul Shapiro; **M:** Hans Zimmer.

Calendar Girl Murders 🐾🐾½ 1984 Minor mystery about the murder of some girlie magazine pin-ups. 104m/C VHS, DVD. Robert Culp, Tom Skerritt, Barbara Parkins, Sharon Stone; **D:** William A. Graham; **M:** Brad Fiedel. **TV**

Calendar Girls 🐾🐾 2003 *(PG-13)* The local members of the Women's Institute club in Yorkshire decide to pose nude for a calendar in order to raise money for leukemia research. The calendar, surprisingly, is a hit, even though the models are a little older than your usual calendar pinup girls. Enjoyable for the right audience (read: fans of veddy understated British humor that's secondary to the drama), but starts losing cohesiveness near the end. Loosely based on a true story. 108m/C VHS, DVD. **GB** Helen Mirren, Julie Walters, John Alderton, Linda Basset, Annette Crosbie, Philip Glenister, Ciaran Hinds, Celia Imrie, Geraldine James, Penelope Wilton, George Costigan, Graham Crowden; **D:** Nigel Cole; **W:** Juliette Towhidi, Tim Firth; **C:** Ashley Rowe; **M:** Patrick Doyle.

Califomia Casanova Woof! 1989 *(R)* Lirthless, semi-musical farce about a nerdy stagehand learning to be a great lover to win a beautiful singer's heart who's being blackmailed by a cruel gangster. Nice cast; nobody's home. 94m/C VHS. Jerry Orbach, Audrey Landers, Tyrone Power Jr., Bryan Genesse, Ken Kercheval, Ted Davis, Joyce Blair; **D:** Nathaniel Christian; **W:** Nathaniel Christian.

Califom a Dreaming 🐾🐾 1979 *(PG)* Nerdy young man heads west to California where he tries to fit in with the local beach crowd. Reminiscent of the popular beach movies of the '60s. 93m/C VHS. Dennis Christopher, Tanya Roberts, Glynnis O'Connor, John Calvin, Seymour Cassel; **D:** John Hancock.

California a Dreaming 2007 *(R)* See *Out of Omaha*. (Thompson) Gainer seem like the typical married suburban couple: they have jobs, they have a house, they have two kids and a dog. Control freak Ginger thinks it would be fun to rent an RV and take a family vacation from their Omaha home to California. Naturally, it's the road trip from heck (the pic is rated PG after all). 2m/C DVD. Dave Foley, Lea Thompson, Patricia Richardson, Ethan Phillips, Vicki Lewis, Lindsay Seim, David Kals, Melissa Jaracke, Nicholas Fackler, Ethan Phillips; **D:** Linda Voorhees; **W:** Linda Voorhees; **C:** James Bartle.

California Girls 🐾 1984 Radio station stages a beauty contest and three sexy ladies drive to be tough competition. Features women in little swimsuits, minimal plot, and a soundtrack by the Police, Kool & the Gang, Blondie, Queen, and 10cc. 83m/C VHS, DVD. Al Music, Mary McKinley, Alicia Allen, Lantz Douglas, Barbara Parks; **D:** Rick Wallace; **C:** Gil Hubbs.

California Gold Rush 🐾🐾 1981 Hays portrays young aspiring writer, Bret Harte, who, in search of adventure in 1849, arrives in Sutter's Fort and takes on a job at the local sawmill. When gold is found, Sutter's Fort is soon overrun with fortune hunters whose greed, violence, and corruption threaten to tear apart the peaceful community. 100m/C VHS, Robert Hays, John Dehner, Dan Haggerty, Ken Curtis; **D:** Johanna Harwood.

California Joe 🐾 1943 California is being eyed by Confederate sympathizers and also by their leader, who wants it for his own plans. Enter California Joe, a Union officer in disguise, who will save the day. Standard western. 55m/B VHS. Donald "Red" Barry, Lynn Merrick, Helen Talbot, Wally Vernon, Twinkle Watts, Brian O'Hara, Terry Frost, Leroy Mason, Edward Earle, Charles "Blackie" King; **D:** Spencer Gordon Bennet; **W:** Norman S. Hall; **C:** Ernest Miller.

California Straight Ahead 🐾🐾 1925 Denny—whose niche in the 20s was silent action comedies, and who had teamed with director Pollard earlier in the decade to produce "The Leatherpushers" series—stars in this silent actioner which features a cross-country road trip, zoo animals-on-a-rampage, and a car-racing conclusion (sounds like an action formula ahead of its time). Audiences didn't realize until the talkies that the All-American man—ly man was in fact played by a Brit. For those who revel in trivia, Denny appeared in the 1966 "Batman." 77m/B VHS. Reginald Denny, Gertrude (Olmstead) Olmsted, Tom Wilson, Lucille Ward, John Steppling; **D:** Harry A. Pollard.

California Suite 🐾🐾🐾 1978 *(PG)* The posh Beverly Hills Hotel is the setting for four unrelated Neil Simon skits, ranging from a battling husband and wife to feuding friends. Smith is notable as a neurotic English actress in town for the Oscar awards while Caine is effectively low-key in the role of her bisexual husband. Simon's dialogue is crisp and funny. 103m/C VHS, DVD. Alan Alda, Michael Caine, Bill Cosby, Jane Fonda, Walter Matthau, Richard Pryor, Maggie Smith, Elaine May; **D:** Herbert Ross; **W:** Neil Simon; **C:** David M. Walsh; **M:** Claude Bolling. Oscars '78: Support. Actress (Smith); Golden Globes '79: Support. Actress (Smith)/Comedy (Smith).

Caligula Woof! 1980 Infamous, expensive, extremely graphic, and sexually explicit adaptation of the life of the mad Roman emperor, Caligula. Scenes of decapitation, necrophilia, rape, bestiality, and sadomasochism abound. Biggest question is why Gielgud, O'Toole, and McDowell lent their talents to this monumentally abhorred film (not to mention Gore Vidal on the writing end, who didn't want the credit). Adult magazine publisher Bob Guccione coproduced and didn't particularly want to release it. Also available in a censored, "R" rated version. 143m/C VHS, DVD. **IT** Malcolm McDowell, John Gielgud, Peter O'Toole, Helen Mirren, Theresa-Ann Savoy, John Steiner, Paolo Bonacelli, Adriana Asti; **D:** Tinto Brass, Silvano Ippoliti; **M:** Paul Clemente.

Call Him Mr. Shatter 🐾 1974 *(R)* A hired killer stalks a tottering Third World president and becomes embroiled in international political intrigue. 90m/C VHS, DVD. **GB** Stuart Whitman, Peter Cushing, Anton Diffring; **D:** Michael Carreras.

Call Me 🐾🐾 1988 *(R)* Psycho-drama about a lusty young woman who responds positively to an obscene telephone caller until she witnesses him murder another person. Doubt creeps into the relationship comes to life. Filmed in Finland. 105m/C DVD. Patricia Charbonneau, Patti D'Arbanville, Sam Freed, Boyd Gaines, Stephen McIntire; **D:** Sollace Mitchell.

Call Me Claus 🐾🐾 2001 Goldberg mugs her way through her role as a TV shopping network producer with Scrooge-like tendencies. Hawthorne is the good-natured St. Nick who wants to retire and have her replace him at the yuletide gig. Might rate a few chuckles if you've seen all the good Christmas movies twice already. 90m/C VHS, DVD. Whoopi Goldberg, Nigel Hawthorne, Taylor Negron, Brian Stokes Mitchell, Victor Garber, Gregory Bernstein; **D:** Peter Werner; **W:** Sarah Bernstein; **M:** Garth Brooks. **TV**

Call Me: The Rise and Fall of Heidi Fleiss 🐾🐾½ 2004 Stale made-for-TV flick follows the real story of Heidi Fleiss (DiScala) as she leaves behind her posh family life to take over a call-girl business for the rich and famous Hollywood crowd. Her time to revel in the excess is cut short, and Tinseltown's movers-and-shakers fear exposure from the publicity of Heidi's little black book. Interestingly, DiScala is said to have shunned most of the sex scenes. 84m/C VHS, DVD. Jamie-Lynn Sigler, Saul Rubinek, Emmanuelle Vaugier, Ian Tracey, Natassia Malthe, Corbin Bernsen, Brenda Fricker, Robert Davi, Lisa Marie Caruk, Missy Peregrym; **D:** Charles McDougall; **W:** Norman Snider; **C:** David Franco; **M:** Ryan Shore. **VIDEO**

Call Northside 777 🐾🐾🐾½ Calling *Northside 777* 1948 Hard-boiled Chicago reporter McNeal (Stewart) finds himself in the crux of a decade-old murder investigation when he follows up a newspaper ad offering $5,000 for any information leading to the arrest and conviction of a police killer. The cunning reporter discovers police coverups and missing evidence pointing to an imprisoned man's innocence. Powerful performance from Stewart directs this docu-drama based on the real-life story of Chicago's Joe Majczek, unjustly imprisoned for 11 years, and the Pulitzer Prize winning reporter Jim McGuire who, through a clever investigation, found enough evidence to have his case re-opened. 111m/B VHS, DVD. James Stewart, Richard Conte, Lee J. Cobb, Helen Walker, Betty Garde, Moroni Olsen, E.G. Marshall, Howard Smith, John Mclntire, Paul Harvey, George Tyne, Michael Chapin, Addison Richards, Richard Rober, Eddie Dunn, Charles Lane, Walter Greaza, William Post Jr., George Melford, Charles F. Miller, Lionel Stander, Jonathan Hale, Freddie (Fred) Steele; **D:** Henry Hathaway; **W:** Jerome Cady, Jay Dratler; **C:** Joe MacDonald; **M:** Alfred Newman.

Call of the Canyon 🐾🐾½ 1942 A crooked agent for a local meat packer won't pay a fair price, so Gene goes off to talk to the head man. It gets him straight. 71m/B VHS, DVD. Gene Autry, Smiley Burnette, Ruth Terry, Thurston Hall, Pat Brady; **D:** Joseph Santley.

Call of the Forest 🐾🐾 1949 Bobby makes friends with a beautiful wild black stallion which is captured and tamed by his father. The father has found a goldmine, also desired by an villain, and Bobby and his horse must come to his father's aid. Black Diamond (the horse) has the best role. 74m/B VHS, Robert Lowery, Ken Curtis, Martha Sherrill, Chief Thundercloud, Charles Hughes; **D:** John F. Link.

Call of the Rockies 🐾🐾 1944 Action-packed oater in which Carson and Burnette ride across country to save Placer City's mine from crooked townsmen. 54m/B VHS, Sunset Carson, Smiley Burnette; **D:** Lesley Selander.

Call of the Wild 🐾🐾½ 1972 *(PG)* Another of Jack London's famous story about a man whose survival depends upon his knowledge of the Alaskan wilderness almost edge of the Alaskan wilderness almost comes to life. Filmed in Finland. 105m/C VHS, DVD. Charlton Heston, Michele Mercier, George Eastman; **D:** Ken Annakin; **W:** Harry Alan Towers, Hubert Frank; **C:** John Cabrera; **M:** Carlo Rustichelli.

Call Out the Marines 🐾🐾 1942 A group of army buddies re-enlist to break up a spy ring. Two of the guys fall in love with the same girl, not realizing that she's one of the spies. McLaglen and Lowe's last comedy outing. Mediocre musical numbers. 67m/B VHS. Beware Hards Across the Border, 67m/B VHS. Edmund Lowe, Victor McLaglen, Binnie Barnes, Paul Kelly, Dorothy Lovett, Franklin Pangborn; **D:** Frank Ryan; **W:** Frank Ryan, William Hamilton; **C:** J. Roy Hunt, Nicholas Musuraca.

Call to Glory 🐾🐾½ 1984 Pilot for the critically praised TV series. An Air Force pilot and his family face turbulent times during the Cuban missile crisis. 96m/C VHS. Craig T. Nelson, Cindy Pickett, Gabriel Damon, Keenan Wynn, Elisabeth Shue, G.D. Spradlin, David Hollander, Kathleen Lloyd; **D:** Thomas Carter. **TV**

A Call to Remember 🐾🐾½ 1997 *(R)* Paula Rubinek (Danner) and David Tobias (Mantegna) are concentration camp survivors who both had their spouses and children killed by the Nazis. They've married, moved to America, and are living in the suburbs with their two sons and trying to forget the past, which causes problems for their children. But Paula's quiet world explodes when she receives a phone call notifying her that a son she thought died in the war has in fact survived. Writer Eisenberg based this drama on his parents' history. 105m/C VHS. Blythe Danner, Joe Mantegna, David Lascher, Kevin Zegers, Joe Spano, Bill McNulty, Blu Mankuma; **D:** Jack Bender; **W:** Max Eisenberg; **C:** David Geddes.

Callas Forever 🐾🐾 2002 Cinematic tribute by Zeffirelli to his longtime friend, opera diva Maria Callas who died in 1977. His own alter ego is British impresario Larry Kelly (Irons), Callas's former manager. Callas (Ardant) is living in isolation in her Paris apartment, mourning the loss of both her voice and her great love, Aristotle Onassis. Kelly and journalist friend Sarah Onassis. Kelly and journalist friend Sarah (Plowright) persuade the singer to come out of retirement to lip-synch in a film version of "Carmen," one of her best roles. She agrees and the film shoot reveals that Ardant may not resemble the real Callas but she has a commanding presence that enhances her portrayal. 108m/C DVD. Fanny Ardant, Jeremy Irons, Joan Plowright, Jay Rodan, Gabriel Garko; **D:** Franco Zeffirelli; **W:** Franco Zeffirelli, Martin Sherman; **C:** Ennio Guarnieri; **M:** Alessio Vlad.

The Caller 🐾 1987 *(R)* A strange man enters the house of a lone woman and sets off a long night of suspense and an almost longer evening of inept movie-making. 90m/C V-S. Malcolm McDowell, Madolyn Smith; **D:** Arthur Allan Seidelman.

Callie and Son 🐾🐾 1981 Rags to Riches 1981 Details the sordid story of a waitress who works her way up to become a Dallas socialite and her obsessive relationship

VideoHound's Golden Movie Retriever · **173** · Callie

with her illegitimate son. **97m/C VHS, VHS, DVD.** Lindsay Wagner, Dabney Coleman, Jameson Parker, Andrew Prine, James Sloyan, Michelle Pfeiffer; **D:** Waris Hussein; **M:** Billy Goldenberg.

Calling Paul Temple 🦴🦴½ **1948** The wealthy patients of a nerve doctor have been dying and a detective is called in to investigate. **92m/B VHS. GB** John Bentley, Dinah Sheridan, Margaretta Scott, Abraham Sofaer, Celia Lipton, Alan Wheatley, Wally Patch; **D:** Maclean Rogers.

Calling Wild Bill Elliott 🦴🦴½ **1943** The crooked territorial governor is exposed by hero Elliott and sidekick Hayes in this typical B-western. Elliott's first film for Republic; he went on to star in 16 Red Ryder films as well as other westerns for the studio. **55m/B VHS.** William (Wild Bill) Elliott, George "Gabby" Hayes, Herbert (Hayes) Hayes, Anne Jeffreys, Fred Kohler Jr., Roy Barcroft, Yakima Canutt; **D:** Spencer Gordon Bennet.

Calm at Sunset 🦴🦴½ **1996 (PG)** James Pfeiffer (Facinelli) drops out of college to pursue his dream of becoming a commercial fisherman, much to the dismay of his parents (Moriarty, Nelligan) who already know how rough that life can be. But James gets his chance when he rescues seaman Kelly Dobbs (Conway) and the two become partners. Still, James must deal with secrets, a tragedy, and some hard decisions. TV drama with some solid performances. Based on the novel "Calm at Sunset, Calm at Dawn" by Paul Watkins. **98m/C VHS.** Peter Facinelli, Michael Moriarty, Kate Nelligan, Kevin Conway, Gretchen Mol, Melvin Van Peebles; **D:** Daniel Petrie; **W:** Pamela Gray, John Kent Harrison, David Young; **C:** Glen MacPherson; **M:** Ernest Troost. **TV**

Cambridge Spies 🦴🦴½ **2003** Semi-fictional and romanticized account of the friendship of longtime British spies Harold Philby (Stephens), Guy Burgess (Hollander), Anthony Blunt (West), and Donald Maclean (Penry-Jones), which began in the 1930s while the quartet was at Cambridge University and continued for more than 30 years (Philby defected to Moscow in 1964). **240m/C DVD. GB** Toby Stephens, Samuel West, Tom Hollander, Rupert Penry-Jones, Anthony Andrews, Imelda Staunton, Stuart Laing, Patrick Kennedy, James Fox, Anna-Louise Plowman, John Light; **D:** Tim Fywell; **W:** Peter Moffatt; **M:** John Lunn. **TV**

Came a Hot Friday 🦴🦴 **1985 (PG)** Two cheap conmen arrive in a 1949 southern New Zealand town, run various scams and pursue women. **101m/C VHS. NZ** Peter Bland, Philip Gordon, Billy T. James; **D:** Ian Mune; **C:** Alun Bollinger.

Camel Boy 🦴½ **1984** True story of a young Arabian duo who befriends a camel and their treacherous trek across the desert. **78m/C VHS. AU D:** Yoram Gross; **V:** Michael Pate, Ron Haddrick, John Meillon.

Camelot 🦴🦴 **1967** The long-running Lerner and Loewe Broadway musical about King Arthur, Guinevere, and Lancelot was adapted from T.H. White's book, "The Once and Future King." Redgrave and Nero have chemistry as the illicit lovers, Harris is strong as the king struggling to hold together his dream, but muddled direction undermines the effort. ♪ Wonder What the King is Doing Tonight; The Simple Joys of Maidenhood; Camelot; C'est Moi; The Lusty Month of May; Follow Me; How To Handle a Woman; Then You May Take Me to the Fair; If Ever I Would Leave You. **150m/C VHS, DVD.** Richard Harris, Vanessa Redgrave, David Hemmings, Franco Nero, Lionel Jeffries; **D:** Joshua Logan; **W:** Alan Jay Lerner; **C:** Richard H. Kline; **M:** Frederick Loewe, Alan Jay Lerner. Oscars '67: Adapt. Score, Art Dir./Set Dec., Costume Des.; Golden Globes '68: Actor--Mus./Comedy (Harris), Song ("If Ever I Should Leave You"), Score.

Camera Buff 🦴🦴 **1979** Satire on bureaucracy finds a factory worker buying a home-movie camera to film his new baby but becoming obsessed with his new toy. So he begins recording everything he sees--even things the authorities don't want shown. Polish with subtitles. **108m/C VHS, DVD. PL** Jerzy Stuhr, Malgorzata Zajaczkowska, Ewa Pokas, Krzysztof Zanussi; Krzysztof Kieslowski; **W:** Jerzy Stuhr, Krzysztof Kieslowski; **M:** Krzysztof Knittel.

The Cameraman 🦴🦴🦴 **1928** After moving to MGM, Keaton made his first feature with a major studio, giving up the artistic control he had enjoyed in his previous films. Spared from the vilification of studio politics (not the case with later Keaton films) "The Cameraman" enjoyed both critical and popular success. Keaton's inept tintype portrait-maker has a heart that pitter-patters for an MGM office girl. He hopes to impress her by joining the ranks of the newsreel photographers. Fortuitously poised to grab a photo scoop on a Chinese tong war, he is forced to return empty-handed when an organ-grinder's monkey absconds with his first-hand footage. Silent with a musical score. **78m/B VHS, DVD.** Buster Keaton, Marceline Day, Harold Goodwin, Harry Gribbon, Sidney Bracy, Edward Brophy, Vernon Dent, William Irving; **D:** Edward Sedgwick. Natl. Film Reg. '05.

Cameron's Closet 🦴½ **1989 (R)** Every family's nightmare comes true. A young boy is convinced that a monster lives in his closet due to his perverse father's psychological tortures. Only this time the monster is real! **86m/C VHS, DVD.** Cotter Smith, Mel Harris, Scott Curtis, Chuck McCann, Leigh McCloskey, Kim Lankford, Tab Hunter; **D:** Armand Mastroianni; **W:** Gary Brandner; **C:** Russell Carpenter.

Camila 🦴🦴🦴 **1984** The true story of the tragic romance between an Argentine-an socialite and a Jesuit priest in 1847. The two lovers escape to a small provincial village where they live together as man and wife. Eventually they are recognized and condemned to death. Available in Spanish with English subtitles or dubbed into English. **105m/C VHS, DVD. AR SP** Susu Pecoraro, Imanol Arias, Hector Alterio, Elena Tasisto; **D:** Maria-Luisa Bemberg.

Camilla 🦴🦴½ **1994 (PG-13)** Tandy is delightful in her last starring role as a former violinist on the run with frustrated musician Fonda. Oafish son (Chaykin) and insensitive husband (Koteas) just don't understand, so its time to head to Toronto, site of a fondly, if perhaps incorrectly, remembered triumph. Sort of a May-December female-bonding roadtrip with lots of conversation and comic asides. An inevitably poignant pairing of Tandy and real-life husband Cronyn offers the chance to experience one of America's greatest acting teams one last time. Lack of stereotyping and fairly novel twist on the road movie keep this one on the highway. **91m/C VHS, DVD.** Jessica Tandy, Bridget Fonda, Hume Cronyn, Elias Koteas, Maury Chaykin, Graham Greene; **D:** Deepa Mehta; **W:** Paul Quarrington; **M:** Daniel Lanois.

Camille 🦴🦴 **1921** Dying courtesan falls in love with innocent young man in the Dumas classic. Valentino in his prime. **55m/B VHS.** Rudolph Valentino, Alla Nazimova; **D:** Fred Niblo.

Camille 🦴🦴🦴½ **1936** Marguerite (Garbo) has found success as Parisian courtesan "La Dame aux Camille" but has never found love. Until she unwisely falls for a handsome but innocent, young aristocrat, Armand (Taylor). Still, Camille agrees to give him up, realizing her scandalous past will jeopardize his future. Oh yes, then she contracts TB and fades away beautifully in gowns by Adrian. This classic Alexandre Dumas story somehow manages to escape the cliches and stands as one of the most telling monuments to Garbo's unique magic and presence on film. **108m/B VHS, DVD.** Greta Garbo, Robert Taylor, Lionel Barrymore, Henry Daniell, Elizabeth Allan, Rex O'Malley, Lenore Ulric, Laura Hope Crews; **D:** George Cukor; **W:** Frances Marion, James Hilton, Zoe Akins; **C:** William H. Daniels; **M:** Herbert Stothart. N.Y. Film Critics '37: Actress (Garbo).

Camille Claudel 🦴🦴🦴 **1989 (R)** A lushly romantic version of the art world in the late 19th century, when art was exploding in new forms and independence for women was unheard of. Young sculptor Claudel's (Adjani) tragic love for art, Auguste Rodin (the larger-than-life Depardieu), and independence clash, costing her sanity and her confinement to an institution for the last 30 years of her life. Very long, it requires an attentive and thoughtful viewing. In French with English subtitles. **149m/C VHS, DVD. FR** Isabelle Adjani, Gerard Depardieu, Laurent Grevill, Alain Cuny, Madeleine Robinson, Katrine Booman, Daniele Lebrun; **D:** Bruno Nuytten; **W:** Bruno Nuytten, Marilyn Goldin; **C:** Pierre Lhomme; **M:** Gabriel Yared. Cesar '89: Actress (Adjani), Art Dir./Set Dec., Cinematog., Costume Des., Film.

Camille 2000 🦴½ **1969** Dumas meets Debbie Does Rome in this artier than thou mess. Unreasonably well endowed Marguerite (Gaubert) spends much horizontal time with Rome's decadent society denizens while pining pitifully for tru luv Armand (Castelnuovo). She dies a horrible death in the end, but her disease's highs aren't it TB. **115m/C VHS, DVD.** Silvana Venturelli, Massimo Serato, Daniele Gaubert, Nino Castelnuovo, Eleanora Rossi-Drago; **D:** Radley Metzger; **W:** Michael DeForrest; **C:** Ennio Guarnieri; **M:** Piero Piccioni.

The Camomile Lawn 🦴🦴½ **1992** In August 1939, various young cousins gather at their uncle's house on the Cornish coast for a last holiday before the inevitable war changes all their lives. Thirteen years later, they return to the house for a funeral and the chance to look back on their frequently risque behavior. Naughty adaptation of the novel by Mary Wesley. **264m/C DVD. GB** Jennifer Ehle, Tara Fitzgerald, Toby Stephens, Felicity Kendal, Rebecca Hall, Paul Eddington, Oliver Cotton, Claire Bloom, Rosemary Harris, Richard Johnson, Virginia McKenna, Nicholas Le Prevost; **D:** Peter Hall; **W:** Kenneth Taylor; **C:** Ernest Vincze; **M:** Stephen (Steve) Edwards. **TV**

Camorra: The Naples Connection 🦴🦴½ (Un Complicato Intrigo Di Donne, Vicoli E Delitti) **1985 (R)** A prostitute and an American drug dealer find themselves embroiled in the murders of Neapolitan Mafia heads. Violent, overblown, minor Wertmuller. **106m/C VHS. IT** Harvey Keitel, Angela Molina, Lorraine Bracco, Francesco Rabal; **D:** Lina Wertmuller; **W:** Lina Wertmuller. **VIDEO**

Camouflage 🦴🦴½ **2000 (R)** Dumb, blond but likeable actor Marty Mackenzie (Munro) wants to perfect his tough-guy persona so he decides to apprentice with old-timer PI Jack Potter (Nielsen). But the routine surveillance case that Jack assigns Marty to turns out to be the tip of a deadly iceberg. It's a goof but don't expect "Naked Gun" type humor. **98m/C VHS, DVD.** Leslie Nielsen, Lochlyn Munro, Vanessa Angel, William Forsythe; **D:** James Keach; **W:** Tom Epperson, Billy Bob Thornton; **C:** Glen MacPherson.

Camp 🦴🦴½ **2003 (PG-13)** Wanna-be teenage thesps flock to Camp Ovation-the summertime equivalent of the "Fame" school--where they can sing, dance and generally be nerdy to their heart's content. First-time director/writer Graff, who in real life was a counselor at a performing arts camp, assembles a cast of typical misfit kids drawn to the stage: budding transvestite Michael (de Jesus), tomboy Ellen (Chilcoat), and the good-looking, seemingly straight Vlad (Letterle), shepherded into adult theaterhood by the cynical, alcoholic musical-theater pro (Dixon). Story follows the ups and downs of these hopefuls, as well as other fringe characters but especially focuses on the sexual preference of Vlad. Despite uneven acting and stereotypical scenarios, flick is an indie that works. Also features some rousing musical numbers. **114m/C VHS, DVD. US** Daniel Letterle, Joanna Chilcoat, Robin De Jesus, Tiffany Taylor, Sasha Allen, Alana Allen, Anna Kendrick, Don Dixon; **D:** Todd Graff; **W:** Todd Graff; **C:** Kip Bogdahn; **M:** Stephen Trask.

Camp Cucamonga: How I Spent My Summer Vacation 🦴 **1990** Zany antics at summer camp abound when Camp Cucamonga's owner mistakes the new handyman for the camp inspector. Well-known stars from TV's "Cheers," "The Jeffersons," "The Wonder Years," and "The Love Boat" are featured in this silly flick. **100m/C VHS, DVD.** John Ratzenberger, Sherman Hemsley, Josh Saviano, Danica McKellar, Chad Allen, Dorothy Lyman, Lauren Tewes; G. Gordon Liddy; **D:** Roger Duchowny. **TV**

Camp Nowhere 🦴🦴 **1994 (PG)** Video fodder for the juniors in the household as kids turn tables on parents. Instead of trudging off to summer camp for the umpteenth time, a group of laid-off drama teacher Lloyd, who must first con their parents into believing that Camp Nowhere is legit. What follows is that very special summer camp in the Hollywood tradition with lots of junk food, video games galore, and of course, no rules. Camp beserko formula good for a few laughs. **106m/C VHS, DVD.** Christopher Lloyd, Wendy Makkena, M. Emmet Walsh, Peter Scolari, Peter Onorati, Ray Baker, Kate Mulgrew, Jonathan Jackson, Romy Walthall, Maryedith Burrell, Thomas F. Wilson, Nathan Cavaleri, Andrew Keegan, Melody Kay, Joshua Gibran Mayweather; **D:** Jonathan Prince; **W:** Andrew Kurtzman, Eliot Wald; **C:** Sandi Sissel.

Campfire Tales 🦴🦴 **1998 (R)** Four teens get lost in the woods and are terrorized by a maniac. **103m/C VHS, DVD.** James Marsden, Kim Murphy, Christine Taylor, Jay R. Ferguson, Christopher K. Masterson, Ron Livingston, Jennifer MacDonald, Hawthorne James, Alex McKenna, Glenn Quinn, Erick Fleeks, Amy Smart, Rick Lawrence, Suzanne Goddard; **D:** David Semel, Martin Kunert, Matt Cooper; **W:** Martin Kunert, Matt Cooper, Eric Manes; **C:** John Peters; **M:** Andrew Rose.

Campus Confessions 🦴🦴 **1938** Son of the college dean, Wayne Atterbury (Henry) struggles to be an ace student and top jock in this campus-set romantic comedy so that Joyce (Grable) will notice him. So he joins the basketball team, hoping to win the championship game (teammates include All-American star player Hank Luisetti). **67m/B VHS.** William Henry, Betty Grable, Richard Denning, Fritz Feld, Thurston Hall, Roy Gordon, Eleanore Whitney, John Arledge; **D:** George Archainbaud; **W:** Lloyd Corrigan; **C:** Henry Sharp; **M:** John Leipold, Stephan Pasternacki.

The Campus Corpse 🦴 **1977 (PG)** Young man stumbles into deadly college frat hazing and discovers he and rest of cast are utterly devoid of acting ability. **92m/C VHS.** Charles Martin Smith, Jeff East, Brad Davis; **D:** Douglas Curtis.

Campus Knights 🦴 **1929** If you're a serious student of the campus caper film, this is one of the earliest (though not one of the best) of the genre (if such a distinction can be made). The story involves twin brothers--one a tweedy high-browed professor, the other a bon vivant man about town--who wreak fraternal chaos on the quads. **70m/B VHS.** Raymond (Ray) McKee, Shirley Palmer, Marie Quillen, Jean Laverty, Sybil Grove; **D:** Albert Kelley.

Campus Man 🦴 **1987 (PG)** An entrepreneurial college student markets a beefcake calendar featuring his best friend, until the calendar's sales threaten his friend's amateur athletic status. **94m/C VHS, DVD.** John Dye, Steve Lyon, Kim Delaney, Miles O'Keeffe, Morgan Fairchild, Kathleen Wilhoite; **D:** Ron Casden; **W:** Geoffrey Baere; **M:** James Newton Howard.

Can-Can 🦴🦴 **1960** Lackluster screen adaptation of the Cole Porter musical bears little resemblance to the stage version. MacLaine is a cafe owner who goes to court to try and get the "Can-Can," a dance considered risque in gay Paree at the end of the 19th century, made legal. Love interest Sinatra happens to be a lawyer. ♪ C'est Manifique; Let's Do It; I Love Paris; You Do Something to Me; It's All Right With Me; Live and Let Live; Come Along With Me; Just One of Those Things. **131m/C VHS, DVD.** Frank Sinatra, Shirley MacLaine, Maurice Chevalier, Louis Jourdan, Juliet Prowse, Marcel Dalio, Leon Belasco; **D:** Walter Lang; **C:** William H. Daniels.

Can I Do It... Till I Need Glasses? 🦴 **1977** More to the point, can you stay awake till the end? Prurient juvenile junk. Brief Williams footage was grafted to this mess during 15 minutes of Mork fame. **72m/C VHS.** Robin Williams, Roger Behr, Debra Klose, Moose Carlson, Walter Olkewicz; **D:** I. Robert Levy.

Can of Worms 🐾🐾½ 2000 When young Mike Pillsbury's science project goes wrong, he sends a message into outer space to be rescued from his dismal life on Earth. But he certainly isn't expecting aliens to hear his plea and come to his aid. 88m/C VHS, DVD, Malcolm McDowell, Adam Wylie, Michael Shulman, Erika Christensen, Lee Garlington, Brighton Hertford, Terry David Mulligan. D: Paul Schneider. CABLE

Can She Bake a Cherry Pie? 🐾🐾½ 1983 Two offbeat characters meet and fall in love in an odd sort of way. Slow-moving and talky but somewhat rewarding. One of Black's better performances. 90m/C VHS, DVD, Karen Black, Michael Emil, Michael Margotta, Frances Fisher, Martin Frydberg. D: Henry Jaglom; W: Henry Jaglom; M: Karen Black.

Can You Feel Me Dancing? 🐾🐾 1985 Family-happy lightweight entertainment coproduced by Kent Bateman and starring Bateman progeny Jason and Justine as brother and sister, a novel premise that only a father could love. A blind independence-impaired teenager tries to liberate herself from her overbearing family, and finds the secret to conquering her fears and to standing up for herself when she falls in love. Written by spouse-team Steven and L. Miyoko Hensley. 95m/C VHS, Jason Bateman, Justine Bateman; D: Michael Miller; W: Steven Hensley, L. Miyoko Hensley.

Can You Hear the Laughter? The Story of Freddie Prinze 🐾🐾 1979 Heartstring-tugging biography of the late Puerto Rican comedian whose troubled life lead to suicide in spite of his apparent success. He was most noted for his starring role in "Chico and the Man." 100m/C VHS, Ira Angustain, Kevin Hooks, Randee Heller, Devon Ericson, Julie Carmen, Stephen Elliott. D: Burt Brinckerhoff.

Canada's Sweetheart: The Saga of Hal C. Banks 🐾🐾 1954 (PG) Sweetheart! 1985 True story of Banks, hired by the Canadian government to break up a strike among the communist-led seaman's union which had put a stranglehold on Canadian commerce, and who was eventually convicted of strong-arm tactics. 115m/C VHS, CA Maury Chaykin, Colin Fox, R.H. Thomson, Sean McCann; D: Donald Brittain; W: Donald Brittain; C: Andreas Poulsson; M: Eldon Rathburn. Near: Donald Brittain. Toronto-City '85: Canadian Feature Film.

Canadian Bacon 🐾🐾 1994 (PG) Regrettably amateurish satire (with some sharp observations) serves as the feature film debut for Moore, who irritated many with "Roger & Me." Title refers to the military code name for a campaign to whip up anti-Canadian hysteria and justify a U.S. invasion of its neighbor to the north. Evil political advisor Pollak convinces well-meaning but inept President Alda that it's just the thing to get the presidential popularity up and those defense industries humming. Ugly Americans abound, at expense of polite Canadians, eh? Filmed in Toronto, which is shown to good advantage. Candy in one of last roles in the superpatriotic sheriff of Niagara Falls, New York. 110m/C VHS, DVD, Alan Alda, Kevin Pollak, John Candy, Rhea Perlman, Rip Torn, Bill Nunn, Kevin J. O'Connor, Steven Wright, G.D. Spradlin, James Belushi, Wallace Shawn, Dan Aykroyd; Cameos: Michael Moore; C: Haskell Wexler; M: Elmer Bernstein, Peter Bernstein.

Cancel My Reservation 🐾 1972 (G) New York talk show host Hope sets out for a vacation on an Arizona ranch, but winds up in trouble due to a mysterious corpse, a rich rancher, and an enigmatic mystic. Even more muddled than it sounds. Based on the novel "Broken Gun" by Louis L'Amour, with pointless cameos by Crosby, Wayne, and Wilson. 99m/C VHS, Bob Hope, Eva Marie Saint, Ralph Bellamy, Anne Archer, Forrest Tucker, Keenan Wynn, Flip Wilson, Noriyuki "Pat" Morita, Chief Dan George; Cameos: John Wayne, Bing Crosby, Doodles Weaver; D: Paul Bogart; W: Arthur Marx; C: Russell Metty.

The Candidate 🐾🐾 1972 (PG) Realistic, satirical look at politics and political campaigning. Bill McKay (Redford) is a telegenic, idealistic lawyer whose father (Douglas) was once governor of California. Uninterested in politics, Bill is eventually persuaded to run for the Senate against tight incumbent Jarman (Porter). Bill refuses to follow the party line but discovers the lure of political power when he begins to gain in the polls. Director Ritchie also worked with Redford on "Downhill Racer." 105m/C VHS, DVD, Robert Redford, Peter Boyle, Don Porter, Allen (Goorwitz) Garfield, Karen Carlson, Melvyn Douglas, Michael Lerner; D: Michael Ritchie; W: Jeremy Larner; C: John Korty, Victor Kemper; M: John Rubinstein. Oscars '72: Story & Screenplay; Writers Guild '72: Orig. Screenplay.

Candles at Nine 🐾🐾½ 1944 An innocent showgirl must spend a month in her late uncle's creepy mansion in order to inherit it, much to the malevolent chagrin of the rest of the family who want the place and the loot for themselves. Uninspired. 84m/B VHS, GB Jessie Matthews, John Stuart, Reginald Purdell; D: John Harlow.

Candleshoe 🐾🐾 1978 (G) A Los Angeles street urchin poses as an English matron's long lost granddaughter in order to steal a fortune hidden in Candleshoe, her country estate, where Niven butlers. Somewhat slapschticky Disney fare. 101m/C VHS, DVD, Vivian Pickles, Helen Hayes, David Niven, Jodie Foster, Leo McKern; D: Norman Tokar; W: Rosemary Anne Sisson, David Swift; C: Paul Beeson; M: Ronald Goodwin.

Candy 🐾🐾 1968 (R) Sexual satire, based on the book by Terry Southern and Mason Hoffenberg, can't sustain its simple premise. The teenaged nubile, blonde, and naive title character (Aulin) sets out to discover her sexual awakening and gets chased by every kook she meets, including Brando, alcoholic poet Burton, gardener Starr, general Matthau, hunchback Aznavour, surgeon Coburn, and even her psychedelic age. Very much of part of its psychedelic age. 124m/C VHS, DVD, FR IT Ewa Aulin, Marlon Brando, Charles Aznavour, Richard Burton, Ringo Starr, James Coburn, Walter Matthau, John Huston, John Astin, Elsa Martinelli, Anita Pallenberg, "Sugar Ray" Robinson; D: Christian Marquand; W: Buck Henry; C: Giuseppe Rotunno.

Candy 🐾🐾 2006 (R) Heroin chic. Handsome Dan (Ledger) is a would-be poet wooing lovely artist Candy (Cornish). He's already shooting heroin and Candy (who sniffs the stuff) demands to try the needle up. A near-overdose doesn't dim Candy's enthusiasm, especially when their fatherly dealer Casper (Rush) is such a reliable supplier. Pic naturally descents into druggie hell as the two turn to crime to help pay for their habits, with intermittent efforts to get clean. Typical junkie fare, although much less harrowing than a lot of addiction flicks. 108m/C VHS, DVD, AU Heath Ledger, Abbie Cornish, Geoffrey Rush, Tony (Anthony) Martin, Noni Hazlehurst; W: Neil Armfield, Luke Davies; C: Garry Phillips; M: Paul Charlier.

Candy Mountain 🐾🐾 1987 (R) Guitar playin' O'Connor roadtrips across America and Canada in search of a legendary guitar maker Yulin. Occasional interest derives from musician cameos from the likes of Buster Poindexter, Dr. John, and Redbone. 90m/C VHS, FR SI CA Kevin J. O'Connor, Harris Yulin, Tom Waits, Eulie Ogier, David Johansen, Leon Redbone, Joe Strummer, Roberts Blossom; Cameos: Rita MacNeil, Laurie Metcalf; D: Robert Frank; W: Rudy Wurlitzer.

Candy Stripe Nurses 🐾 1974 (R) Sweet Candy, 1974 (R) Even hard-core Roger Corman fans might find his final installment in the nursing comedy pentad to be a lethargic exercise in gratuitous "sexual situations." Bet those uniforms don't meet hospital standards. The previous films in the series are: "The Student Nurses," "Private Duty Nurses," "Night Call Nurses," and "The Young Nurses." 80m/C VHS, DVD, Candice Rialson, Robin Mattson, Maria Rojo, Kimberly Hyde, Dick Miller, Stanley Ralph Ross, Monte Landis, Tom Baker, Don Keeler, Sally Kirkland. D: Allan Holleb.

Cannery Row 🐾🐾 1982 (PG) Baseball has-been Nolte lives anonymously among the downtrodden in a cannery/screenwriter Frank Rhinoslavsky (Quinn) a star, all while being schmoozed at Cannes by stars who want to be in his latest story, with the ties to find backers for his unwritten script, 96m/C VHS, DVD, Tony Todd, Donna D'Errico, Jsu Garcia, Lupe Ontiveros; D: Turi Meyer; W: Turi Meyer, Al Septien; C: Michael G. Wojciechowski. VIDEO

Cannes Man 🐾🐾 1996 (R) Features legendary Hollywood producer Sy Lerner (Cassel), who vows to make unknown cable/screenwriter Frank Rhinoslavsky (Quinn) a star, all while being schmoozed at Cannes by stars who want to be in his latest story, with the ties to find backers for his unwritten script, 96m/C VHS, DVD, IT Seymour Cassel, Francesco Quinn, Rebecca Broussard; D: Richard Martini.

Cannibal Apocalypse WOOF! Cannibals in the Streets; Savage Apocalypse; The Slaughterers; Cannibals in the City; Virus; Invasion of the Flesh Hunters 1980 Group of tortured Vietnam veterans returns home carrying a cannibalistic curse with them. Smorgasbord of gore and sensationalism at best—indiscriminating tastes. 96m/C VHS, DVD, IT John Saxon, Elizabeth Turner, Giovanni Lombardo Radice, Tony King; D: Anthony M. Dawson; W: Anthony M. Dawson, Dardano Sacchetti, Jimmy Gould; C: Fernando Arribas; M: Alexander Blonksteiner.

Cannibal Campout 🐾 1988 Crazed orphans with eating disorders make square meal of coed babes getting back to nature. 85m/C VHS, DVD, Carrie Lindell, Richard Marcus, Amy Chludzinski, Jon McBride; D: Jon McBride, Tom Fisher.

Cannibal Man 🐾🐾 The Apartment on the 13 Floor; La Semana del Asesino; Week of the Killer 1971 Slaughterhouse worker Marcos (Parra) accidentally kills a man in a fight and then covers up the incident with more killings. Then he's got to get rid of all those dead bodies and what better place than at the butcher's where he works. 98m/C VHS, DVD, SP Vicente Parra, Emma Cohen, Eusebio Poncela; D: Eloy De La Iglesia; W: Eloy De La Iglesia.

Candy Tangerine Man 🐾 1975 Respectable businessman leads a double life as loving father and LA pimp. 88m/C VHS, John Daniels, Tom Hankerson, Eli Haines, Marva Farner, George "Buck" Flower; D: Matt Cimber.

Candyman 🐾🐾 1992 (R) Terrifying tale from horror maven Clive Barker is an effective combination of American gothic, urban myth of Candyman, the son of a former slave who was lynched and is now back with a hook and a vendetta. Filled with the appropriate amount of yucky stuff, yet successfully employs subtle scare tactics and plausible characters. 99m/C VHS, DVD, Virginia Madsen, Tony Todd, Xander Berkeley, Kasi Lemmons, Vanessa Williams, DeJuan Guy, Michael Culkin, Gilbert Lewis, Stanley DeSantis, Mark Daniels; D: Bernard Rose; W: Bernard Rose; C: Anthony B. Richmond; M: Philip Glass.

Candyman 2: Farewell to the Flesh 🐾 1994 (R) Explains the origins of the urban bogeyman called Candyman—the man, the hook, and the bees. Rehashes the same old scare tactics from previous and better horror movies and uses cheesy special effects. The sensual background of New Orleans during Mardi Gras can't help this stale sequel. Embrace this "Farewell" from a distance. Based on stories by Clive Barker. 99m/C VHS, DVD, Tony Todd, Kelly Rowan, Veronica Cartwright, Timothy Carhart, William O'Leary, Bill Nunn, Fay Hauser, Joshua Gibran Mayweather, Bill Conti; D: Bill Condon; W: Rand Ravich, Mark Kruger; C: Tobias Schliessler; M: Philip Glass.

Candyman 3: Day of the Dead 🐾 1998 (R) The Candyman (Todd), haunts an L.A. descendant hopes that life will join him. 93m/C VHS, DVD, Tony Todd, Donna D'Errico, Jsu Garcia, Lupe Ontiveros; D: Turi Meyer; W: Turi Meyer, Al Septien; C: Michael G. Wojciechowski. VIDEO

Cannonball 🐾🐾 1976 (PG) Assorted ruthless people leave patches of rubber across the country competing for grand prize in less than legal auto race. Not top drawer New World but nonetheless a cult fave. Inferior to Bartel's previous cult classic, "Death Race 2000." Most interesting for plethora of cult cameos, including Scorsese, Dante, and grandmas. 93m/C VHS, DVD, HK Martin, Scorsese, Roger Corman, Joe Dante, Paul Bartel, David Carradine, Bill McKinney, Veronica Hamel, Gerrit Graham, Robert Carradine, Jonathan Kaplan, Belinda Balaski, Judy Canova, Carl Gottlieb, Archie Hahn, Sylvester Stallone, Dick Miller, Mary Woronov; D: Paul Bartel; W: Paul Bartel, Donald Stewart; C: Tak Fujimoto; M: David A. Axelrod.

Cannibal! The Musical 🐾 1996 (R) Only those wacky people at Troma could offer a horror/musical about a group of 1883 gold miners who get lost in the Colorado Rockies, leave some strange and ghastly musical numbers, leac up to the reporter while in prison). Seven rather the body musical numbers, leac up to the "South Park." 105m/C VHS, DVD, UMD, Ian Hardin, Jason McHugh, Matt Stone, Trey Parker, Juan Schwartz; D: Trey Parker; W: Trey Parker.

Cannibal Women in the Avocado Jungle of Death 🐾🐾½ 1989 (PG-13) Tongue-in-cheek cult classic features erstwhile playmate Tweed as feminist anthropologist who searches with dizzy student and mucho macho male guide for lost tribe of cannibal women who dine on their mates. Lawton directed under the alias "J.D. Athens." 90m/C VHS, DVD, Shannon Tweed, Adrienne Barbeau, Karen Mistal, Barry Primus, Bill Maher, Jim MacKrell, Brett Stimely, Paul Ross; D: J.F. Lawton, J.D. Athens; W: J.F. Lawton; C: Robert Knox33; M: Carl Dante.

Cannonball Run 🐾 1981 (PG) So many stars, so little plot. Reynolds and sidekick DeLuise disguise themselves as paramedics to foil cops while they compete in cross-country Cannonball race. Shows no sign of having been directed by an ex-stuntman. One of 1981's top grossers—go figure. Followed by equally lamentable sequel "Cannonball Run II." 95m/C VHS, DVD, Burt Reynolds, Farrah Fawcett, Roger Moore, Dom DeLuise, Dean Martin, Sammy Davis Jr., Jack Elam, Adrienne Barbeau, Peter Fonda, Molly Picon, Bert Convy, Jamie Farr; C: Michael C. Butler; M: Al Capps.

Cannonball Run 2 🐾 1984 (PG) More mindless cross-country wheel spinning with gratuitous star cameos. Director Needham apparently subscribes to the two wrongs make a right school of sequel making. 108m/C VHS, DVD, Burt Reynolds, Dom DeLuise, Jamie Farr, Marilu Henner, Shirley MacLaine, Jim Nabors, Frank Sinatra, Sammy Davis Jr., Dean Martin, Telly Savalas, Susan Anton, Catherine Bach, Jack Elam, Sid Caesar, Ricardo Montalban, Charles Nelson Reilly, Tim Conway, Don Knotts, Molly Picon, Jackie Chan; D: Hal Needham; W: Harvey Miller; C: Nick McLean; M: Steve Dorff.

Can't Buy Me Love 🐾🐾 1987 (PG-13) Unpopular high school nerd Dempsey buys a month of dates with teen babe Peterson for $1000 in order to win friends and influence people. Semi-amusing and earnest. 94m/C VHS, DVD, Patrick Dempsey, Amanda Peterson, Dennis Dugan, Courtney Gains, Seth Green, Katrina Caspary, Sharon Farrell, Darcy Demoss, Devin Devasquez, Eric Bruskotter, Gerardo Mejia, Ami Dolenz, Max Perlich; D: Steve Rash; W: Michael Swerdlick; C: Peter Lyons Collister; M: Robert Folk.

Can't Hardly Wait 🐾🐾 The Party 1998 (PG-13) Writer-directors Kaplan and Elfont attempt to reheat the 80s teen-party-end-angst casserole for the kids of the 90s. Unfortunately, it's lost its flavor. All of your favorite high school cardboard cut-ups are here. Jock-jerk

Mike (Facinelli) dumps teen queen Amanda (Hewitt) on the eve of a graduation blowout. Shy, sensitive Preston (Embry), who believes himself linked to Amanda by fate and their mutual love of toaster pastry, decides this is his opportunity to finally tell her how he feels. Frolicking in the background are your stereotypical foreign exchange students, stoners, geeks, metal heads, jocks and bimbos herded around by the ever-present Girl Whose Party It Is. Wavers between (unsuccessfully) trying to be thoughtful like "American Graffiti" and thoughtless like "Animal House." **101m/C VHS, DVD.** Ethan (Randall) Embry, Jennifer Love Hewitt, Peter Facinelli, Charlie Korsmo, Seth Green, Jerry O'Connell, Lauren Ambrose, Jenna Elfman, Michelle Brookhurst, Erik Palladino, Steve Monroe; **D:** Harry Elfont, Deborah Kaplan; **W:** Harry Elfont, Deborah Kaplan; **C:** Lloyd Ahern II; **M:** David Kitay, Matthew Sweet.

Can't Help Singing 🎵🎵½ **1945** In 1849, willful heiress Caroline (Durbin) ignores her senator father's (Collins) wishes and heads west to marry her Army sweetheart (Bruce). But on the wagon train she falls for wagon master Lawlor (Paige), who's a better guy anyway. Durbin's first color musical. **90m/C VHS, DVD.** Deanna Durbin, Robert Paige, David Bruce, Akim Tamiroff, Leonid Kinskey, Ray Collins, June Vincent, Thomas Gomez; **D:** Frank Ryan; **W:** Frank Ryan, Lewis R. Foster; **C:** Elwood "Woody" Bredell, William Howard Greene; **M:** Hans J. Salter, Jerome Kern, E.Y. Harburg.

Can't Stop the Music woof! **1980 (PG)** Retired model invites friends from Greenwich Village to a party to help the career of her roommate, an aspiring composer. Disco inferno that nearly reaches heights of surreal ineptness. Put it in a time capsule and let the people of the future decide what the heck was going on in the '70s. Features two of the top hits by the Village People. 🎵Y.M.C.A.; Macho Man; Give Me a Break; The Sound of the City; Samantha; I'm a Singing Juggler; Sophistication; Liberation; I Love You to Death. **120m/C VHS, DVD.** Valerie Perrine, Bruce Jenner, Steve Guttenberg, Paul Sand, Leigh Taylor-Young, Village People; **D:** Nancy Walker; **W:** Bronte Woodard, Allan Carr; **C:** Bill Butler; **M:** Jacques Morali. Golden Raspberries '80: Worst Picture, Worst Screenplay.

A Canterbury Tale 🐶🐶🐶 **1944** Writer-director team Powell and Pressburger have loosely modeled a retelling of Chaucer's famous tale of a pilgrimage to the cathedral in Canterbury. Set in Nazi-threatened Britain in 1944, the story follows the pilgrimage of three Brits and an American GI to the eponymous cathedral. Strange, effective, worth looking at. The 95-minute American version, with added footage of Kim Hunter, is inferior to the 124-minute original. **124m/B VHS, DVD.** *GB* Eric Portman, Sheila Sim, Dennis Price, Esmond Knight, Charles Hawtrey, Hay Petrie; **D:** Michael Powell, Emeric Pressburger.

The Canterbury Tales 🐶🐶 **1971** *Racconti di Canterbury* Four Chaucer tales, most notably "The Merchant's Tale" and "The Wife of Bath," are recounted by travelers, with director Pasolini as the bawdy poet. Deemed obscene by the Italian courts, it's the second entry in Pasolini's medieval "Trilogy of Life," preceded by "The Decameron" and followed by "The Arabian Nights." In Italian with English subtitles. **109m/C VHS, DVD.** *IT* Laura Betti, Ninetto Davoli, Pier Paolo Pasolini, Hugh Griffith, Josephine Chaplin, Michael Balfour, Jenny Runacre; **D:** Pier Paolo Pasolini; **W:** Pier Paolo Pasolini; **C:** Tonino Delli Colli; **M:** Ennio Morricone. Berlin Intl. Film Fest. '72: Golden Berlin Bear.

The Canterville Ghost 🐶🐶 **1944** Laughton, a 300-year-old ghost with a yellow streak, is sentenced to spook a castle until he proves he's not afraid of his own shadow. American troops stay at the castle during WWII, and, as luck would have it, soldier Young is distantly related to spunky young keeper of the castle O'Brien, ghost Laughton's descendant. Once Young is acquainted with his cowardly ancestor, he begins to fear a congenital yellow streak, and both struggle to be brave despite themselves. Vaguely derived from an Oscar Wilde tale. **95m/B VHS.** Charles Laughton, Robert Young, Margaret O'Brien, William Gargan, Reginald Owen, Rags Ragland, Una O'Connor, Peter Lawford, Mike Mazurki; **D:** Jules Dassin; **W:** Edwin Blum; **M:** George Bassman.

The Canterville Ghost **1991** During a family's vacation in an old English manor, they run into a ghost who is doomed to haunt the place until he can overcome his fears. Problems start when the family tries to scare him away. From the "Wonderworks" family movie series. **58m/C VHS, DVD.** Richard Kiley, Mary Wickes, Shelley Fabares; **D:** William Claxton.

The Canterville Ghost 🐶🐶½ **1996 (PG)** Stewart is the highlight of this updated TV version of the Oscar Wilde short story. He's the cursed Elizabethan spirit of Sir Simon de Canterville, doomed to haunt the family mansion until a prophecy is fulfilled. But he's not happy with a family of American intruders, until teenager Virginia (Campbell) discovers Sir Simon and realizes she may hold the key to freeing the unhappy ghost. **91m/C VHS, DVD.** Patrick Stewart, Neve Campbell, Ed Wiley, Cherie Lunghi, Donald Sinden, Joan Sims, Leslie Phillips, Ciaran Fitzgerald, Daniel Betts, Raymond Pickard; **D:** Syd Macartney; **W:** Robert Benedetti; **C:** Denis Lewiston; **M:** Ernest Troost.

The Cantor's Son 🐶🐶½ *Dem Khann's Zindl* **1937** Real-life story based on Moishe Oysher's life, vaguely influenced by Jolson's "Jazz Singer." Runaway Oysher joins troupe of performers as a youth, travels to the shores of America, and finds fame once his beautiful voice is discovered. Returning to his mother country to celebrate his parents' golden anniversary, he encounters his childhood sweetheart and falls in love, but another woman is written into the plot to complicate matters. Poorly acted, laughable staging. In Yiddish with English subtitles. **90m/B VHS.** Judith Abarbanel, Florence Weiss, Moishe Oysher, Isadore Cashier; **D:** Ilya Motyleff.

Canvas 🐶🐶½ **2006 (PG-13)** Convincing performances round out a somewhat familiar plot about mental illness. Ten-year-old Chris (Gearhart) returns home after a stay with relatives. His mom, Mary (Harden), was hospitalized for schizophrenia and her sanity is still in question, despite the best efforts of hard-working hubby John (Pantoliano). Countless problems inundate their lives as Mary becomes more disruptive and an embarrassment Chris finds hard to bear. **101m/C DVD.** William Morrissey, Marcia Gay Harden, Joe Pantoliano, Devon Gearhart, Marcus Johns, Sophia Bairley; **D:** Joseph Greco; **W:** Joseph Greco; **C:** Rob Sweeney; **M:** Joel Goodman.

Canvas; The Fine Art of Crime 🐶🐶 **1992 (R)** A ruthless, underhanded art gallery owner recruits a desperate young artist into his art of stealing schemes. The artist learns how to steal, but decides he wants out after his burglary partner has a brush with death. The gallery owner, however, wants one last job completed. **94m/C VHS.** Gary Busey, John Rhys-Davies, Vittorio Rossi, Nick Cavaiola, Cary Lawrence; **D:** Alain Zaloum.

Canyon Passage 🐶🐶🐶 **1946** Rip-roarin' western set in the Oregon Territory in 1856. Stuart (Andrews) is a former scout turned store owner who falls for Lucy (Hayward), who happens to be the fiancee of banker/gambler Camrose (Donlevy). Camrose gets into money troubles, there's a villain named Bragg (Bond), and a pretty spectacular Indian attack. Carmichael serves as the wandering minstrel to the action, singing four songs. Director Tourneur was best known for his horror films. **92m/C VHS, DVD.** Dana Andrews, Brian Donlevy, Susan Hayward, Ward Bond, Hoagy Carmichael, Lloyd Bridges, Andy Devine, Patricia Roc; **D:** Jacques Tourneur; **W:** Ernest Pascal; **C:** Edward Cronjager; **M:** Frank Skinner.

Cape Fear 🐶🐶🐶½ **1961** Former prosecutor turned small-town lawyer Peck and his family are plagued by the sadistic attentions of criminal Mitchum, who just finished a six year sabbatical at the state pen courtesy of prosecutor Peck. Taut and creepy; Mitchum's a consummate psychopath. Based on (and far superior to) John MacDonald's "The Executioners." Don't pass this one up in favor of the Scorsese remake. **106m/B VHS, DVD.** Gregory Peck, Robert Mitchum, Polly Bergen, Martin Balsam, Telly Savalas, Jack Kruschen, Lori Martin; **D:** J. Lee Thompson; **C:** Sam Leavitt; **M:** Bernard Herrmann.

Cape Fear 🐶🐶🐶 **1991 (R)** Scorsese takes on this terrifying tale of brutality and manipulation (previously filmed in 1961) and cranks it up a notch as a paroled convict haunts the lawyer who put him away. From Great cast, a rollercoaster of suspense. Note the cameos by Mitchum, Peck, and Balsam, stars of the first version. Original source material was "The Executioners" by John D. MacDonald. Breath-taking rollercoaster of a film. Elmer Bernstein adapted the original score by Bernard Herrmann. **128m/C VHS, DVD.** Robert Mitchum, Gregory Peck, Martin Balsam, Robert De Niro, Nick Nolte, Jessica Lange, Juliette Lewis, Joe Don Baker, Illeana Douglas, Fred Dalton Thompson; **D:** Martin Scorsese; **W:** Wesley Strick; **C:** Freddie Francis; **M:** Elmer Bernstein.

Cape of Good Hope 🐶🐶½ **2004 (PG-13)** A Cape Town animal rescue shelter is the link for numerous characters and their stories. Kate (Brown) runs the shelter and is the object of attraction for a shy vet (Visser). She befriends young Thabo (Masilo), whose widowed mother, Lindiwe (Moshesh), is being pressured to marry an elderly, wealthy minister, but refugee Jean Claude (Ebouaney), who works at the shelter, loves her. Meanwhile, Kate's friend and co-worker Sharifa (Adams) is having marital trouble. Director Bamford doesn't ignore poverty and racism in a post-apartheid South Africa but his focus remains on how this group deals with ordinary, everyday life. **107m/C DVD.** *US* Eriq Ebouaney, Nthati Moshesh, David Isaacs, Nick Boraine, Debbie Brown, Morne Visser, Quanita Adams, Kamo Masilo; **D:** Mark Bamford; **W:** Mark Bamford, Suzanne Kay; **C:** Larry Fong; **M:** J.B. Ecki.

Caper of the Golden Bulls 🐶 *Carnival of Thieves* **1967** Former bank robber Boyd is blackmailed into joining a group of safecrackers who plan to assault the Royal Bank of Spain during the annual Santa Maria bull run. More like siesta of the golden bulls. **104m/C VHS.** Stephen Boyd, Yvette Mimieux, Giovanna Ralli, Walter Slezak, Vito Scotti; **D:** Russell Rouse.

Capitaine Conan 🐶🐶🐶 *Captain Conan* **1996** On the Bulgarian border in 1918, during the last clashes of WWI, Conan (Torreton) is a fearless, impulsive warrior, reserving his respect only for his men. Although armistice is finally declared, the troops stationed in the Balkans are not demobilized and become increasingly fractious. This causes a rift between Conan and his educated friend Norbert (Le Bihan), who's been appointed a military legal representative. They are warily reunited in defense of a soldier (Val) charged with desertion, while still dealing with the ravages of the long conflict. Adapted from the book by Roger Vercel; French with subtitles. **129m/C VHS, DVD.** *FR* Philippe Torreton, Samuel Le Bihan, Bernard Le Coq, Francois Berleand, Claude Rich, Catherine Rich, Pierre Val; **D:** Bertrand Tavernier; **W:** Bertrand Tavernier, Jean Cosmos; **C:** Alain Choquart; **M:** Oswald D'Andrea. Cesar '97: Actor (Torreton), Director (Tavernier), Film.

Capital Punishment 🐶½ **1996** Martial arts expert James Thayer (Daniels) is recruited by the DEA to go undercover and stop Nakata (Yamashita), the supplier of a new illegal drug. His operation turns up a corrupt police chief (Carradine), who frames him for murder, and lots of action. **90m/C VHS, DVD.** Gary Daniels, Tadashi Yamashita, David Carradine, Mel Novak, Ian Jacklin, Ava Fabian; **D:** David Hue; **W:** David Hue; **C:** David Swett.

The Capitol Conspiracy 🐶½ **1999 (R)** CIA agents Jarrid Maddox (Wilson) and Vicki Taylor (Keith) uncover evidence that links government officials with illegal mind-control experiments. As they become targets of a hit squad determined to keep the information secret. Very familiar actioner. **83m/C VHS, DVD.** Don "The Dragon" Wilson, Alexander Keith, Paul Michael Robinson, Arthur Roberts, Barbara Steele; **D:** Fred Olen Ray; **C:** Gary Graver. **VIDEO**

Capone 🐶🐶½ *The Revenge of Al Capone* **1989 (R)** Story of the gangster after Elliot Ness put him in a Chicago jail. That didn't stop Capone from running his crime empire until a single FBI agent worked to sent the crime boss to Alcatraz, where his power would be useless. Exuberant performances from Sharkey and Carradine. **96m/C VHS, DVD.** Ray Sharkey, Keith Carradine, Debrah Farentino, Jayne Atkinson, Bradford English, Marc Figueroa, Neil Giuntoli, Charles Haid, Nicholas Mele, Scott Paulin, Alan Rosenberg; **D:** Michael Pressman; **W:** Tracy Keenan Wynn; **C:** Tim Suhrstedt; **M:** Craig Safan. **TV**

Capote 🐶🐶🐶 **2005 (R)** Based on the book "Capote" by Gerald Clark. Enigmatic Truman Capote (an outstanding Hoffman) was a celebrated author and a member of elite New York society. Biopic sheds light on Capote's obsessive research into the killers behind the startling murders of a Kansas family, which formed the groundwork for his "In Cold Blood," an obsession that ultimately led to Capote's own demise, spiraling into obesity, alcoholism and ouster from the intellectual elite. Hoffman nails his portrayal of the self-absorbed man at his manipulative best. **114m/C DVD.** *US* Philip Seymour Hoffman, Catherine Keener, Chris Cooper, Bruce Greenwood, Bob Balaban, Amy Ryan, Mark Pellegrino, Clifton (Gonzalez) Collins Jr.; **D:** Bennett Miller; **W:** Dan Futterman; **C:** Adam Kimmel; **M:** Mychael Danna. Oscars '05: Actor (Hoffman); British Acad. '05: Actor (Hoffman); Ind. Spirit '06: Actor (Hoffman), Screenplay; L.A. Film Critics '05: Actor (Hoffman), Screenplay, Support. Actress (Keener); Natl. Bd. of Review '05: Actor (Hoffman); N.Y. Film Critics '05: First Feature; Natl. Soc. Film Critics '05: Actor (Hoffman); Film; Screen Actors Guild '05: Actor (Hoffman); Broadcast Film Critics '05: Actor (Hoffman).

Caprice 🐶 **1967** Truly awful comedy, best left to Day fans only. The middle-aged actress is still playing wide-eyed and primly sunny, even as industrial spy Patricia Fowler. Pat is trying to get something on a rival cosmetics company, which leads her to mystery man Christopher White (Harris), her would-be rescuer and love interest. Actually, the only interesting thing is how Day's costumes are frequently coordinated to their settings. With material like this, no wonder she retired from movies in 1968. **98m/C DVD.** Doris Day, Richard Harris, Ray Walston, Jack Kruschen, Edward Mulhare, Lilia Skala, Michael J. Pollard, Irene Tsu; **D:** Frank Tashlin; **W:** Frank Tashlin; **C:** Leon Shamroy; **M:** Frank DeVol.

Capricorn One 🐶🐶🐶 **1978 (R)** As astronauts Brolin, Simpson and Waterston follow Mission Controller Holbrook's instructions to fake a Mars landing on a soundstage when their ship is discovered to be defective. When they find out they're supposed to expire in outer space so that the NASA scam won't become public knowledge, they flee to the desert, while reporter Gould sniffs out the cover up. Based on a pseudonymous novel by Ken Follett. **123m/C VHS, DVD.** Elliott Gould, James Brolin, Brenda Vaccaro, O.J. Simpson, Hal Holbrook, Sam Waterston, Karen Black, Telly Savalas; **D:** Peter Hyams; **W:** Peter Hyams; **C:** Bill Butler; **M:** Jerry Goldsmith.

Captain America 🐶🐶 **1944** Captain America battles a mad scientist in this 15-episode serial based on the comic book character. **240m/B VHS.** Dick Purcell, Adrian Booth, Lionel Atwill; **D:** John English; **W:** Elmer Clifton.

Captain America 🐶½ **1979** Marvel Comic character steps into feature film and flounders. The patriotic superhero son of WWII hero fights bad guy with contraband nuclear weapon. **98m/C VHS.** Reb Brown, Len Birman, Heather Menzies, Steve Forrest, Robin Mattson, Joseph Ruskin, Michael McManus; **D:** Rod Holcomb. **TV**

Captain America 🐶🐶🐶 **1989 (PG-13)** Based on the Marvel Comics superhero. It's 1941 and Steve Rogers has just been recruited to join a top secret experimental government program after flunking his army physical. Injected with a serum, Steve becomes super strong, fast, and smart but is matched in all three by an evil Nazi counterpart, Red Skull. The two battle in a WWII standstill and while Red Skull goes on an evil rampage, the next 40 years finds Captain America fast frozen in the Alaskan tundra. Finally, our hero is thawed in time to do a final battle with his evil nemesis. This one is ridiculous even by comic book standards, but it may amuse the kids. 103m/C VHS. Matt Salinger, Scott Paulin, Ronny Cox, Ned Beatty, Darren McGavin, Melinda Dillon; **D:** Albert Pyun; **W:** Stephen Tolkin.

Captain America 2: Death Too Soon 1979 Terrorists hit America where it hurts, threatening to use age accelerating drug. Sequelized superhero fights chronic crow lines and series dies slow, painful death. 98m/C VHS. Reb Brown, Connie Sellecca, Len Birman, Christopher Lee, Katherine Justice, Lana Wood, Christopher Cary; **D:** Ivan Nagy. **TV**

Captain Apache 1971 Union intelligence officer Van Cleef investigates murder of Indian war commissioner and discovers fake Indian war landscam. As clever as the title. 95m/C VHS, DVD. Lee Van Cleef, Carroll Baker, Stuart Whitman; **D:** Alexander Singer; **W:** Philip Yordan.

Captain Blackjack 1951 All-star cast craps out in wanna-be thriller about drug smuggling on the French Riviera. Social butterfly Moorehead directs drug traffic, detective Marshall undercovers as doctor, and Sanders looks bored in a British sort of way. 90m/B VHS. *FR* George Sanders, Herbert Marshall, Agnes Moorehead, Patricia Roc, Marcel Dalio; **D:** Julien Duvivier.

Captain Blood 1935 Sabatini adventure story launched then unknown 26-year-old Flynn and 19-year-old De Havilland to fame in perhaps the best pirate story ever. Exiled into slavery by a tyrannical governor, Irish physician Peter Blood is forced into piracy but ultimately earns a pardon for his swashbuckling ways. Love interest De Havilland would go on to appear in seven more features with Flynn, who took the part Robert Donat declined for health reasons. Cleverly budgeted using ship shots from silents, and miniature sets when possible. First original film score by composer Korngold. Also available colorized. 120m/B VHS, DVD. Errol Flynn, Olivia de Havilland, Basil Rathbone, J. Carrol Naish, Guy Kibbee, Lionel Atwill, Ross Alexander; **D:** Michael Curtiz; **W:** Casey Robinson; **C:** Hal Mohr; **M:** Erich Wolfgang Korngold.

Captain Boycott 1947 In 1880 Ireland, Boycott (Parker) is the despised rent collector for an aristocratic English landlord. When the poor tenant farmers can't pay, he's quick to throw them off the land. The farmers then band together to get rid of Boycott. Granger and Ryan are the prerequisite young lovers. Adapted from the novel by Philip Rooney. 94m/B VHS. *GB* Cecil Parker, Stewart Granger, Kathleen Ryan, Niall MacGinnis, Robert Donat, Mervyn Johns, Alastair Sim, Noel Purcell, Maurice Denham; **D:** Frank Launder; **W:** Frank Launder, Wolfgang Wilhelm; **C:** Wilkie Cooper, Oswald Morris.

Captain Caution 1940 Young girl throws caution to the wind when dad dies during the War of 1812, assisting young Mature to take over the old man's ship to do battle with the British. Watch for the unknown sailor Ladd. 84m/B VHS. Victor Mature, Louise Platt, Bruce Cabot, Alan Ladd, Robert Barrat, Vivienne Osborne; **D:** Richard Wallace.

Captain Corelli's Mandolin 2001 (R) Based on the novel by Louis de Bernieres, the film is set on the Greek island of Cephallonia during the early days of WWII. After numerous scenes of hearty Greek peasant life, the island is occupied by green Italian army troop, led by mandolin-strumming Captain Corelli (Cage). He moves quickly falls for his daughter Pelagia (Cruz). The problem is that she's engaged to fisherman Mandras (Bale), a Greek partisan. Cage's over-done accent makes him sound like he's trying to sell you a

pizza, but it matches the overwrought tone. Director Madden was signed late in pre-production after scheduled director Roger Michell suffered a heart attack. Much guilt and agonizing, with comic relief courtesy of Curtis. Peck is sub par; the direction flounders and there's something unsetting about quicksilver shifts from pathos to parody. 127m/C VHS, DVD, *GB US* Nicolas Cage, Penelope Cruz, Christian Bale, John Hurt, David Morrissey, Irene Papas, Patrick Malahide; **D:** John Madden; **W:** Shawn Slovo; **C:** John Toll; **M:** Stephen Warbeck.

Captain from Castile 1947 Exciting saga finds 16th-century Spanish nobleman Pedro De Vargas (Power) forced to flee the wrath of Inquisition chief De Silva (Sutton). He takes peasant girl Cantana (Peters), who's helped him, and joins Cortez's expedition to Mexico and the search for Aztec riches. Lots of adventures and old-fashioned pageantry. Peters' screen debut. 141m/C VHS, DVD. Tyrone Power, Jean Peters, Cesar Romero, Lee J. Cobb, John Sutton, Antonio Moreno, Thomas Gomez, Alan Mowbray; **D:** Henry King; **W:** Lamar Trotti; **C:** Charles Clarke, Arthur E. Arling; **M:** Alfred Newman.

Captain Horatio Hornblower 1951 A colorful drama about the life and loves of the British sea captain during the Napoleonic wars. Peck is rather out of his element in the courageous, swashbuckling hero (Errol Flynn was originally cast) but there's enough fast-paced derring-do to make this a satisfying saga. Based on the novel by C.S. Forester. 117m/C VHS, DVD. *G3* Gregory Peck, Virginia Mayo, Robert Beatty, Denis O'Dea, Christopher Lee; **D:** Raoul Walsh; **W:** Ivan Goff; **C:** Guy Green.

Captain Jack 1998 *An Inch Over the Horizon* 1998 Sentimental, old-fashioned story about eccentric sea captain Jack (Hoskins) who dreams of sailing the same journey as Captain Scoresby made in 1791—from Whitby in northern England to the Arctic. But his misfit crew is a group of novices and his vessel is deemed unseaworthy by authorities. Nevertheless, Jack and his group set sail. 96m/C VHS, DVD, *GB* Bob Hoskins, Peter McDonald, Sadie Frost, Gemma Jones, Anna Massey, Maureen Lipman, Jack Rosenthal; **C:** John McGlashan; **M:** Richard Harvey.

The Captain from Koepenick *Der Hauptmann von Koepenick* 1956 Popular true life comedy about a Berlin shoemaker who's stumped against a military bureaucracy by impersonating a Prussian officer and capturing soldiers, only to enjoy folk herodom when his ruse is discovered. Remake of Richard Oswald's 1931 classic. 93m/B VHS. *GE* Heinz Ruhmann, Hannelore Schroth, Martin Held, Erich Schellow; **D:** Helmut Kautner.

Captain Kidd 1945 Laughton huffs and puffs and searches for treasure on the high seas, finds himself 'neath captive with rest of cast in anemic swashbuckler. 83m/B VHS, DVD. Charles Laughton, Randolph Scott, Reginald Owen, Gilbert Roland, Barbara Britton, John Qualen, Sheldon Leonard; **D:** Rowland V. Lee; **W:** Norman Reilly Raine; **C:** Archie Stout.

Captain Kronos: Vampire Hunter 1974 Captain Kronos fences thirsty foes in Hammer horror hybrid. Artsy, atmospheric and atypical, it's written and directed with tongue firmly in cheek by Clemens, who penned many an "Avengers" episode. 91m/C VHS, DVD. *GB* Horst Janson, John Carson, Caroline Munro, Ian Hendry, Shane Briant, Wanda Ventham, John Cater, Lois Daine, William Hobbs, Robert James, Elizabeth Dear; **D:** Brian Clemens; **W:** Brian Clemens; **M:** Laurie Johnson.

Captain Nuke and the Bomber Boys 1995 (PG) Three teenagers, who've stumbled across an atomic bomb, decide to use the device to get school called off. Instead, they wind up with the FBI and a couple of crooks after them. 90m/C VHS. Joe Mantegna, Martin Sheen, Joe Piscopo, Joanna Pacula, Rod Steiger, Kate Mulgrew; **D:** Charles Gale; **W:** Charles Gale.

Captain Ron 1992 (PG-13) Harried couple Short and Place inherit a large boat and, with their two smart-mouthed kids, go to the Caribbean to sail the boat back to the U.S. Of course they know nothing about sailing, so they hire Captain Ron (Russell), a one-eyed, long-haired, rum-talking boat captain. From there, numerous mishaps occur. Amusing, courtesy of Amar. Most novel aspect of the production is that the post-Napoleon French terrain has that vaguely south of the border feel. 75m/C VHS, DVD. Kurt Russell, Martin Short, Mary Kay Place, Meadow Sisto, Benjamin Salisbury, Dan E. Butler; **D:** Thom Eberhardt; **W:** Thom Eberhardt.

Captain Scarlett 1953 Formulaic swashbuckler has nobleman Greene and highway guy Young fighting nasty French Royalists who've been putting the pressure on impecunious peasants. Runaway Spanish damsel in distress courtesy of Amar. 75m/C VHS, DVD. Richard Greene, Leonora Amar, Isobel Del Puerto, Nedrick Young, Manolo Fabregas; **D:** Thomas Carr.

Captain Sinbad 1963 Captain Sinbad must tackle a many-headed ogre, man-eating fish and crocodiles, a large fist clad in a spiked glove, an invisible monster, and more. To kill the villain, Sinbad must destroy his heart, which is kept in a tower with no entrance. A huge, witty, epic production with lots of special effects. This one is fun. 85m/C VHS. Guy Williams, Heidi Bruhl, Pedro Armendariz Sr., Abraham Sofaer, Bernie Hamilton, Helmuth Schneider; **D:** Byron Haskin; **W:** Ian McLellan Hunter, Guy Endore.

Captain Newman, M.D. 1963 Three army guys visit stiff shrink Peck during the final months of WWII in VA ward for the mentally disturbed. Much guilt and agonizing, with comic relief courtesy of Curtis. Peck is sub par; the direction flounders and there's something unsetting about quicksilver shifts from pathos to parody. Nonetheless touching with fine performance from Darin and a slight den hero. Based on the novel by Leo Rosten. 126m/C VHS. Gregory Peck, Bobby Darin, Tony Curtis, Angie Dickinson, Eddie Albert, James Gregory, Jane Withers, Larry Storch, Robert Duvall; **D:** David Miller.

Captain Swagger 1925 A man on the brink of thievery experiences some changes that keep him on the right side of the law. 50m/B VHS. Rod La Rocque, Sue Carol, Richard Tucker, Victor Potel, Ullrich Haupt; **D:** Edward H. Griffith.

Captains Courageous 1937 Rich brat Bartholomew takes a clip over the side of the law. When spoiled brat Bartholomew takes a clip, sans life jacket while leaning over an ocean liner railing to relieve himself of the half dozen ice cream sodas impudently consumed and is saved by a Portuguese fisher-man, he at first treats his mandatory three month voyage as an unscheduled cab ride, but eventually, through a deepening friendship with crewman Tracy, develops a hitherto unheard-ed work ethic. The boy's filial bond with Tracy, of course, requires that the seaman meet with watery disaster. Based on the Rudyard Kipling novel. Director Fleming went on to "Gone With the Wind" and "The Wizard of Oz." 116m/B VHS, DVD. Spencer Tracy, Lionel Barrymore, Freddie Bartholomew, Mickey Rooney, Melvyn Douglas, Charley Grapewin, John Carradine, Bobby Watson, Jack La Rue; **D:** Victor Fleming; Oscars '37: Actor (Tracy).

Captains Courageous 1995 TV adaptation of the 1897 novel by Rudyard Kipling finds pampered rich kid Vadas learning to become a man at the hands of stalwart sea captain Ulrich. 93m/C VHS, DVD. Robert Urich, Kenny Vadas, Kai-Erik Eriksen, Robert Wisden, Duncan Fraser; **D:** Michael Anderson Jr.; **W:** John McSweeney; **C:** Glen MacPherson; **M:** Eric N. Robertson, Claude Desjardins.

Captains of the Clouds 1942 Unabashedly patriotic film starring Cagney as a daredevil, independent Canadian bush pilot who makes his own flying rules. When WWII begins he joins the Royal Canadian Air Force but washes out when he can't follow orders. However, he finds a way to prove himself a hero as a civilian pilot ferrying a bomber to England. Cagney's first Technicolor film. 113m/C VHS, DVD. James Cagney, Dennis Morgan, Brenda Marshall, Alan Hale, George Tobias, Reginald Denny, Russell Arms, Paul Cavanagh, Charles Halton; **D:** Michael Curtiz; **M:** Max Steiner.

Captain's Paradise 1953 Golden Fleece captain Guinness chugs between wives in Gibraltar and North Africa, much to the acclaim of chief officer Goldner. While Gibraltar's little woman de Carlo's a homegrown homebody, little woman de Carlo's paint the town red type, allowing Guinness to have cake and eat it too, it seems, except that he's doing. 89m/B VHS, DVD, *GB* Alec Guinness, Yvonne De Carlo, Celia Johnson, Miles Malleson, Nicholas Phipps, Ferdinand "Ferdy" Mayne, Sebastian Cabot; **D:** Anthony Kimmins; **W:** Alec Coppel, Nicholas Phipps; **C:** Edward Scaife; **M:** Malcolm Arnold.

The Captain's Table 1960 Former cargo vessel captain Gregson is given luxury liner to command, and fails to revise his cargo captain style to fit new crew and clientele. British cast saves unremarkable script from mediocrity. 90m/C VHS. *GB* John Gregson, Peggy Cummins, Donald Sinden, Nadia Gray; **D:** Jack Lee.

Captive 1987 (R) Spoiled heiress is kidnapped by terrorist trio and brainwashed into anti-establishment Hearst-like creature. 98m/C VHS. Oliver Reed, Irina Brook, Xavier Deluc, Hiroshi Arai; **D:** Paul Mayersberg.

Captive 1997 New bride Samantha Hoffman's husband is murdered on their wedding night. Blaming herself, Samantha attempts suicide and then voluntarily commits herself to a mental institution at her brother-in-law's suggestion. But Samantha soon discovers she can't leave. What's worse is she finds that she's the pawn in a plot involving her husband's death. 93m/C VHS. *CA* Erika Eleniak, Michael Ironside, Catherine Colvey, Stewart Bick; **D:** Rodney Gibbons; **W:** Forney Gibbons, Richard Stanford; **C:** Bruno Philip; **M:** David Findlay. **VIDEO**

Captive Heart 1947 Czech soldier Redgrave assumes the identity of a dead British officer in order to evade Nazis in WWII. Captured and imprisoned in camp reserved for British POWs, his stratagems think they smell a spy, but he manages to convince them he's an OK Joe. Meanwhile, he's been writing letters home to the little missus, which means he's got a little explaining to do when he's released from prison. Especially fine Redgrave performance. 86m/B VHS. *GB* Michael Redgrave, Basil Radford, Jack Warner, Jimmy Hanley, Rachel Kempson, Mervyn Johns; **D:** Basil Dearden.

Captive Hearts 1987 (PG) Well frayed story holds cast captive in sushi romance. Two American flyers are shot down and taken prisoner in isolated Japanese mountain village, and one is shot by Cupid's arrow. 97m/C VHS. Noriyuki "Pat" Morita, Michael Sarrazin, Chris Makepeace; **D:** Paul Almond; **M:** David Benoit.

A Captive in the Land 1991 (PG) Routina survival pic pits two strangers against the frozen Arctic tundra. Potapov is a Soviet airman who's too injured to walk when he's discovered by American meteorologist Waterston. When a rescue seems unlikely, the two are forced to try for a trek to civilization. Based on the novel by James Aldridge. **96m/C VHS.** Sam Waterston, Alexander Potapov; **D:** John Berry; **M:** Bill Conti, Lee Gold.

Captive Planet ⅃ **1978** Bargain basement FX and really atrocious acting hold audience captive in routine earth on the verge of obliteration yarn. **95m/C VHS, DVD.** Sharon Baker, Chris Auram, Anthony Newcastle; **D:** Al (Alfonso Brescia) Bradley.

Captive Rage ⅃ **1988 (R)** South American general Reed hijacks planeful of girlies to encourage US to release his son, who's in trouble because he swaps money for white powder. Violence lives up to title, all else disappoints. **99m/C VHS.** Oliver Reed, Robert Vaughn, Claudia Udy; **D:** Cedric Sundstrom.

The Captive: The Longest Drive 2 ⅃⅃ *The Quest* **1976 (PG-13)** Matheson and Russell play two recently reunited brothers in search of their sister, whom they believe is still a captive of the Cheyenne Indians who also raised Russell. Along the way the two come to the aid of a pioneer woman and her young son. This western was actually a pilot for a TV series known as "The Quest," and is a continuation of the pilot episode released on video as "The Longest Drive." **80m/C VHS.** Kurt Russell, Tim Matheson; **D:** Lee H. Katzin. **TV**

Captive Wild Woman ⅃⅃½ **1943** Mad scientist Dr. Sigmund Walters (Carradine) transforms an ape into the beautiful Paula Depress (Aquanetta), who promptly joins the circus as a mysterious animal trainer. Unfortunately, she falls in love with fellow trainer Fred (Stone), who already has a gal, making back the beast in the pretty Paula. Sequelled by "Jungle Captive" and "Jungle Woman." **61m/B VHS.** Acquanetta, John Carradine, Milburn Stone, Evelyn Ankers, Lloyd Corrigan, Vince Barnet, Paul Fix; **D:** Edward Dmytryk; **W:** Griffin Jay, Henry Sucher.

Captives ⅃⅃½ **1994 (R)** The kazillionth contribution to the relatively new subgenre known as torture-porn. Yeah, they keep coming—only by now anything shocking, original, or smart has been milked. Generic fashion model Jennifer (Cuthbert) has been drugged and abducted for the purpose of sporting torture and mutilation. Forced by her captor to endure one indignity after another as she pleads for her life, Jennifer somehow strikes up an unlikely romance with dungeon mate and hot guy Gillies. Way too grisly to sit through, not even the pretty people can save it. **85m/C DVD. US RU** Elisha Cuthbert, Daniel Gillies, Laz Alonso, Pruitt Taylor Vince, Michael Harney; **D:** Roland Joffe; **W:** Larry Cohen, Joseph Tura; **C:** Daniel Pearl; **M:** Marco Beltrami.

The Capture ⅃⅃⅃ **1950** Above-average story told in flashback has Ayres hiding out in Mexico because he thought he killed an innocent man. He seeks out the widow to question her about him and they wind up marrying. When he finds the real culprit, the man is killed and the evidence points to Ayres. Ayres and Wright are great, as is the native Mexican musical score. **67m/B VHS, DVD.** Lew Ayres, Teresa Wright, Victor Jory, Jacqueline White, Jimmy Hunt, Duncan Renaldo, William "Billy" Bakewell; **D:** John Sturges.

The Capture of Bigfoot ⅃ **1979(PG)** Barefoot monster tracks footprints around town after 25 years of peace, and evil businessman attempts to capture creature for personal gain. **92m/C VHS.** Stafford Morgan, Katherine Hopkins, Richard Kennedy, Otis Young, George "Buck" Flower, John Goff; **D:** Bill Rebane.

The Capture of Grizzly Adams ⅃½ **1982** South Adams and his ever-faithful companion Ben the bear must not only clear his name but outwit a band of outlaws who are holding his young daughter captive. **96m/C VHS.** Dan Haggerty, Chuck Connors, June Lockhart, Kim Darby, Noah Beery Jr., Keenan Wynn, Sydney Penny, G.W. Bailey, Todd Everett; **D:** Don Keeslar. **TV**

Captured ⅃ **1999 (R)** Car thief picks the wrong auto to boost when he gets locked inside a special high-tech Porsche, which is maneuvered by a remote control in the hands of its sadistic owner. Who decides the thief needs to be taught a lesson. **95m/C VHS, DVD.** Andrew Divoff, Nick Mancuso, Linda Hoffman, Michael Mahonen; **D:** Peter Paul Liapis. **VIDEO**

Captured in Chinatown ⅃ **1935** Dog chases bad guys in Chinatown. Bow wow. **53m/B VHS.** Marion Shilling, Charles Delaney, Philo (Philip, P.H., P.M.) McCullough, Robert Ellis; **D:** Elmer Clifton.

Capturing the Friedmans ⅃⅃⅃ **2003** Disturbing documentary follows the lives of the Friedman family of Great Neck, Long Island. On Thanksgiving of 1987, police raid the Friedman home and find child pornography belonging to father Arthur, who's a high school science and computer teacher. The police allege that Arthur and youngest son, Jesse (then 18), molested dozens of boys. There is a rash of conflicting testimony as the case goes to trial (both are convicted, though Jesse's guilt is called into question). Shows excerpts from some 50 hours of home movies, much of which eldest son David filmed, and which the family permitted director Jarecki to use. He also conducted present-day interviews with a number of figures involved in the case. **107m/C DVD. US D:** Andrew Jarecki; **C:** Adolfo Doring; **M:** Andrea Morricone. Sundance '03: Feature Doc.

The Car ⅃⅃ **1977 (PG)** Driverless black sedan appears out of nowhere to terrorize the residents of a small New Mexico town. And it's up to Sheriff Wade Parent (Brolin) to stop the demonic auto. **96m/C VHS, DVD.** James Brolin, Kathleen Lloyd, John Marley, Ronny Cox, John Rubinstein, R.G. Armstrong, Elizabeth Thompson, Roy Jenson, Robert Phillips; **D:** Elliot Silverstein; **W:** Dennis Shryack, Michael Butler; **C:** Gerald Hirschfeld; **M:** Leonard Rosenman.

Car Crash ⅃ **1980** Organized crime hits stock car racing head on to produce crashing bore. **103m/C VHS.** Joey Travolta, Anna (Ana Garcia) Obregon, Vittorio Mezzogiorno; **D:** Antonio Margheriti; **W:** Massimo De Rita, Mario Giordano; **C:** Hans Burman; **M:** Giosy Capuano, Mario Cupuano.

Car 54, Where Are You? ⅃ **1994 (PG-13)** Exceedingly lame remake of the exceedingly lame TV series, which ran for only two seasons, 1961-63. This time, Toody (Johansen) and Muldoon (McGinley) are protecting a mafia stool pigeon (Piven), while vampy Velma Velour (Drescher) sets her sights on Muldoon. Sad cast. Sat on the shelf at Orion for three years (with good reason). **89m/C VHS, DVD.** David Johansen, Fran Drescher, Rosie O'Donnell, John C. McGinley, Nipsey Russell, Al Lewis, Daniel Baldwin, Jeremy Piven; **D:** Bill Fishman; **W:** Ebbe Roe Smith, Erik Tarloff, Peter McCarthy, Peter Crabbe; **M:** Bernie Worrell, Pray for Rain. Golden Raspberries '94: Worst Support. Actress (O'Donnell).

Car Trouble ⅃⅃½ **1986 (R)** Young English husband buys new Jaguar and wife's not so minor car trouble causes major marital trouble. Funnybone-tickling pairing of Walters and Charleson. **93m/C VHS. GB** Julie Walters, Ian Charleson; **D:** David Green; **M:** Meat Loaf Aday.

Car Wash ⅃⅃½ **1976 (PG)** L.A. carwash provides a soap-opera setting for disjointed comic bits about owners of dirty cars and people who hose them down for a living. Econo budget and lite plot, but serious comic talent. A sort of disco carwash version of "Grand Hotel." **97m/C VHS, DVD.** Franklin Ajaye, Sully Boyar, Richard Brestoff, George Carlin, Richard Pryor, Melanie Mayron, Ivan Dixon, Antonio Fargas; **D:** Michael A. Schultz; **W:** Joel Schumacher; **C:** Frank Stanley; **M:** Norman Whitfield.

Caracara ⅃⅃ *The Last Witness* **2000 (R)** Ornithologist Rachel Sutherland (Henstridge) agrees to allow the FBI to use her apartment for a stakeout and falls for agent David MacMillan (Schaech). Then she learns she's been duped—her "guests" are actually assassins planning to kill Nelson Mandela. **93m/C VHS, DVD.** Natasha Henstridge, Johnathon Schaech, David McIlwraith, Lauren Hutton; **D:** Graeme Clifford; **W:** Craig Smith; **C:** Bill Wong. **CABLE**

Caramel ⅃⅃ *Sukkar Banat* **2007 (PG)** Modernity collides with custom as five women, portrayed mostly by local nonprofessionals, lament on issues involving sex, religion, and family at a beauty salon in Beirut, Lebanon (where apparently the titular sticky-sweet treat is used to remove unwanted hair). Even when it gets a bit soapy, actor/writer/director Labaki (a stunner both in front of and behind the camera) deftly winds the personal and cultural impact of each woman's dilemma into a story of universal sisterhood. The result is a cut above most Western chick-flickery, with a refreshing lack of Hollywood gloss. **95m/C DVD. FR** Nadine Labaki, Yasmine Al Masri, Joanna Moukarzel, Gisele Aouad, Sihame Haddad, Aziza Semaan; **D:** Nadine Labaki; **W:** Nadine Labaki, Jihad Hojeily, Rodney Al Haddad; **C:** Yves Schnaoui; **M:** Khaled Mouzanar.

Carandiru ⅃⅃ **2003 (R)** Hellish fact-based prison drama based on events leading up to the 1992 San Paolo massacre in which 111 inmates died. A nameless doctor (Vasconcelos) arrives at the city's infamous House of Detention because of an AIDS epidemic. As he tests and treats the inmates of the severely overcrowded facility, he learns about their lives on the outside (shown in flashbacks) and about the prison's codes, which are enforced by the inmates and not the guards or warden. Viewers are lulled into a false sense of normalcy before the horror begins. Based on "Carandiru Station," the fictionalized account of Dr. Drauzio Varella's experiences. Portuguese with subtitles. **148m/C DVD. BR** Luiz Carlos Vasconcelos, Milhem Cortaz, Milton Goncalves, Ivan de Almeida, Ailton Graca, Maria Luisa Mendonca, Aida Lerner, Rodrigo Santoro, Gero Camilo, Caio Blat, Wagner Moura; **D:** Hector Babenco; **W:** Hector Babenco, Victor Nava, Fernando Bonassi; **C:** Walter Carvalho; **M:** Andre Abujarura.

Caravaggio ⅃⅃⅃ **1986** Controversial biography of late Renaissance painter Caravaggio (Terry), famous for his bisexuality, fondness for prostitute models, violence and depravity. The painter divides his time between two street models, Ranuccio (Bean) and his lover Lena (Swinton), the decadent cardinals who commission his religious works, and Caravaggio's young assistant (Leigh), who cares for the artist as he's dying. Photography by Gabriel Beristain reproduces the artist's visual style. **97m/C VHS, DVD. GB** Spencer Leigh, Michael Gough, Nigel Davenport, Robbie Coltrane, Jack Birkett, Nigel Terry, Sean Bean, Tilda Swinton; **D:** Derek Jarman; **W:** Derek Jarman; **C:** Gabriel Beristain; **M:** Simon Fisher.

Caravan to Vaccares ⅃⅃ **1974 (PG)** French Duke hires young American to sneak Eastern European scientist into the States, and little suspense ensues. Based on Alistair MacLean novel. **98m/C VHS.** David Birney, Charlotte Rampling; **D:** Geoffrey Reeve.

The Caravan Trail ⅃⅃ **1946** A cowboy becomes marshal in order to bring to justice those who have stolen land and murdered his friend. This was shot in color, which was rare for the 1940s. **53m/C VHS.** Eddie Dean, Lash LaRue, Emmett Lynn, Jean Carlin, Charles "Blackie" King, Bob (Robert) Barron, Lloyd Ingraham, Bud Osborne; **D:** Robert Emmett Tansey.

Carbide and Sorrel ⅃½ *Karbid und Sauerampfer* **1963** To rebuild a Dresden cigarette factory destroyed by bombing in WWII, workers need carbide for welding torches. So Kalle travels to Wittenberg to buy seven barrels of the rationed material and then must find a way to get them home while dodging Soviet soldiers, mines, and other various hazards. German with subtitles. **80m/B DVD. GE** Erwin Geschonneck, Marita Bohme, Kurt Rackelmann, Margot Busse; **D:** Frank Beyer; **W:** Frank Beyer, Hans Oliva; **C:** Gunter Marzinkowski; **M:** Joachim Werzlau.

Carbon Copy ⅃⅃ *Time of the Wolves; The Last Shot; The Heist; Le Temps des Loups; Dillinger 70* **1969** A criminal with a split personality (Hossein) has renamed himself Dillinger because he patterns his crimes after the legendary gangster. As he and his gang strike, an Inspector (Aznavour) tries to bring him down. Dubbed. **105m/C VHS, DVD. FR IT** Robert Hossein, Charles Aznavour, Virna Lisi, Marcel Bozzuffi; **D:** Sergio Gobbi; **W:** Andre Tabet, Sergio Gobbi; **C:** Daniel Diot; **M:** Georges Garvarentz.

Carbon Copy ⅃⅃ **1981 (PG)** Successful white executive has life turned inside out when his 17-year-old illegitimate son, who happens to be black, decides it's time to look up dear old dad. Typical comedy-with-a-moral. **92m/C VHS, DVD.** George Segal, Susan St. James, Jack Warden, Paul Winfield, Dick Martin, Vicky Dawson, Tom Poston, Denzel Washington; **D:** Michael A. Schultz; **W:** Stanley Shapiro; **M:** Bill Conti.

Cardiac Arrest ⅃ **1974 (PG)** Lunatic eviscerates victims in trolley town. They left their hearts in San Francisco. **95m/C VHS, DVD.** Garry Goodrow, Mike Chan, Max Gail; **D:** Murray Mintz.

The Cardinal ⅃⅃½ **1963** Priestly young Tryon rises through ecclesiastical ranks to become Cardinal, struggling through a plethora of tests of faith, none so taxing as the test of the audience's patience. Had Preminger excised some 60 minutes of footage, he might have had a compelling portrait of faith under fire, but as it stands, the cleric's life is epic confusion. Fine acting, even from Tryon, who later went on to bookish fame, and from Huston who's normally on the other side of the camera. McNamara's final performance. Based on the Henry Morton Robinson novel. **175m/C VHS, DVD.** Tom Tryon, Carol Lynley, Dorothy Gish, Maggie McNamara, Cecil Kellaway, John Huston, John Saxon, Burgess Meredith; **D:** Otto Preminger; **C:** Leon Shamroy. Golden Globes '64: Film—Drama, Support. Actor (Huston).

Career ⅃⅃⅃ **1959** An overwrought, depressing drama about the trials and tribulations of an actor trying to make it on Broadway. He'll try anything to succeed. Good direction, but so-so acting. **105m/B VHS.** Dean Martin, Anthony (Tony) Franciosa, Shirley MacLaine, Carolyn Jones, Joan Blackman, Robert Middleton, Donna Douglas; **D:** Joseph Anthony; **C:** Joseph LaShelle. Golden Globes 60: Actor—Drama (Franciosa).

Career Girls ⅃⅃⅃ **1997 (R)** Two young women, the caustic acid-tongued Hannah (Cartlidge) and shy eczema-scarred Annie (Steadman), are introduced in a flashback sequence as they meet and become college roommates. They reunite for a weekend visit six years after they graduate. Both have become career women and have smoothed out their rough edges. In their wanders around London, they coincidentally run into people they knew back in the day, including a smarmy real estate agent (Tucker) who dated them both and a despondent schizophrenic (Benton) who pursued Annie. Excellent performances from a largely unknown cast. **87m/C VHS, DVD.** Katrin Cartlidge, Lynda Steadman, Kate Byers, Mark Benton, Andy Serkis, Joe Tucker, Margo Stanley, Michael Healy; **D:** Mike Leigh; **W:** Mike Leigh; **C:** Dick Pope; **M:** Marianne Jean-Baptiste, Tony Remy.

Career Opportunities ⅃½ **1991 (PG-13)** "Home Alone" clone for teenagers from John Hughes' factory. Whaley is an unsuccessful con-artist who finally gets a job as the night janitor of the local department store. He focuses around at company expense until he fincs the town's beauty (Connelly) asleep in a dressing room. The pair then play make-believe until its time to thwart some small-time thieves. Unexciting and unrealistic in the worst way; no wonder Candy isn't billed—he probably didn't want to be. **83m/C VHS, DVD.** *M:* John Forsythe; *D:* Bryan Gordon; *W:* John Hughes. *C:* Donald McAlpine; *M:* Thomas Newman.

Carefree 🐾🐾🐾 1938 Dizzy radio singer Rogers can't make up her mind about beau Bellamy, so he sends her to analyst Astaire. Seems she can't even dream a little dream until shrink Astaire prescribes that she ingest some funny food, which causes her to dream she's in love with the Freudian thing, and he hypnotically suggests that she really loves Bellamy. The two line up to march down the aisle together, and Fred stops dancing just long enough to realize he's in love with Ginger. A screwball comedy with music. ♫ Used to be Colorblind; The Night is ... Filled With Music; Change Partners; The Night is ... **83m/B VHS, DVD.** Fred Astaire, Ginger Rogers, Ralph Bellamy, Jack Carson, Franklin Pangborn, Hattie McDaniel; *D:* Mark Sandrich; *M:* Irving Berlin.

Careful 🐾🐾 1992 Butler-in-training Neale courts Neville in an alpine mountain village where silence is golden, or at least being quiet will lessen the chance of an avalanche. Dig a little deeper and you find incest, repression and other nasty things. Highly individualistic black comedy parodies German Expressionism and Freudian psychology to the point of absurdity, dealing with snow, sex, sleep, spirits, and obsessive/compulsive personality disorders. Third film from Canadian cult director Maddin is awash in vivid primary colors when it suits the scene's mood and employs between-scenes titles in a homage to cinematic antiquity. **100m/C VHS, DVD.** Kyle McCulloch, Gosia Dobrowolska, Jackie Burroughs, Sarah Neville, Brent Neale, Paul Cox Victor Cowie, Michael O'Sullivan, Vince Rimmer, Katya Gardner; *D:* Guy Maddin; *W:* Guy Maddin; *M:* John McCulloch.

Careful, He Might Hear You 🐾🐾 1984 (PG) Abandoned by his father, six-year-old P.S. becomes a pawn between his dead mother's two sisters, one working class and the other wealthy, and his worldview is further overturned by the sudden reappearance of his prodigal father. Set in Depression-era Australia, Schultz's vision is touching and keenly observed, and manages a sort of child's eye sense of proportion. Based on a novel by Sumner Locke Elliot. **113m/C VHS, DVD.** AU Nicholas Gledhill, Wendy Hughes, Robyn Nevin, John Hargreaves; *D:* Carl Schultz; *W:* Michael Jenkins; '83: Actress (Hughes), Film. Australian Film Inst.

Caresses 🐾🐾 1997 Eleven short scenes confront the lack of tenderness in the restless lives of a big city's inhabitants over the course of one night, until the film circles back to where it began—with the domestic argument between a young man and woman who no longer love each other. Adaptation of Belbel's play. Spanish with subtitles. **94m/C VHS, DVD.** SP Julieta Serrano, Augustin Gonzalez, Sergi Lopez, David Selvas, Laura Conejero, Montserrat Salvador, Naim Thomas, Merce Pons, Jordi Dauder, Roger Coma, Rosa Maria Sarda; *D:* Ventura Pons; *W:* Ventura Pons, Sergi Belbel; *C:* Jesus Escosa; *M:* Carles Cases.

Caribe 🐾½ 1987 Caribbean travelogue masquerades as spy thriller. Arms smuggling goes awry, and neither voodoo nor bikinied blondes can prevent release from dozing. Never released theatrically. **96m/C VHS, DVD.** John Savage, Kara Glover, Stephen McHattie, Sam Malkin; *D:* Michael Kennedy.

The Cariboo Trail 🐾🐾 1950 Two prospecting men seek their fortune in British Columbia, the golden West of Canada in the 1890s. But they find themselves opposed by a ruthless rancher and claim jumpers. Actually filmed in Colorado with excellent cinematography and solid performances from some big names, it's still a run-of-the-mill entry. Made the same year that the Gabby Hayes show first aired. **80m/C VHS.** Randolph Scott, George 'Gabby' Hayes, Bill Williams, Victor Jory; *D:* Edwin L. Marin.

Carla's Song 🐾🐾 1997 Left-leaning director Loach sets his sometimes gripping, sometimes over-bearing political love story in war torn Nicaragua in the late 1980s. George (Carlyle) is a Glasgow bus driver who helps out passenger Carla (Cabezas), a Nicaraguan emigre who raises money for the Sandanista cause. George falls in love with Carla and decides that the only way she can get on with her life is to confront her former lover Antonio, who was maimed by the contras and has disappeared. The two lovers go to Nicaragua, where George is totally out of his element. Shot (with great difficulty) on location in Nicaragua. **127m/C VHS, DVD.** Robert Carlyle, Oyanka Cabezas, Gary Lewis, Scot Glenn, Subash Singh Pall; *D:* Ken Loach; *W:* Paul Laverty; *C:* Barry Ackroyd; *M:* George Fenton.

Carlito's Way 🐾🐾🐾 1993 (R) Puerto Rican crime czar Carlito Brigante (Pacino) has just gotten out of jail and wants to go straight. But his drug underworld cohorts don't believe he can do it. Penn (barely recognizable) is great as a sleazy coked-out lawyer who's way out of his league. Remarkably subdued violence given DePalma's previous rep—It's effective without being gratuitous, especially the final shootout set in Grand Central Station. Pacino's performance is equally subdued, with controlled tension and lots of eye contact rather than grandiose emotions. Based on the novels "Carlito's Way" and "After Hours" by Edwin Torres. Pacino and DePalma previously teamed up for "Scarface." **145m/C VHS, DVD, HD DVD.** Al Pacino, Sean Penn, Penelope Ann Miller, Luis Guzman, John Leguizamo, Ingrid Rogers, James Rebhorn, Viggo Mortensen, Jorge Porcel, Joseph Siravo, Adrian Pasdar, Jon Seda, Vincent Pastore; *D:* Brian De Palma; *W:* David Koepp; *C:* Stephen Burum; *M:* Patrick Doyle.

Carlito's Way: Rise to Power 🐾 2005 (R) Depicts the early years of Puerto Rican drug dealer Carlito Brigante (Hernandez), who wants to become the crime kingpin of New York's Spanish Harlem in the '70s. Carlito is drawn into an alliance with numbers runner Earl (Van Peebles) and mobster Rocco (Kelly) despite Harlem boss Hollywood Nicky (Combs) and various crooked cops. Hernandez does what he can with Pacino's shadow looming over him but this is familiar territory. Adapted from a book by Edwin Torres. **100m/C DVD, UMD, HD DVD.** Jay Hernandez, Mario Van Peebles, Sean (Puffy, Puff Daddy, P. Diddy) Combs, Michael Kelly, Luis Guzman, Jaclyn DeSantis, Gancaric Esposito, Burt Young, Domenick Lombardozzi, Juan Carlos Hernandez, Ntume Gant, Tony Cucci; *D:* Michael Scott Bregman; *W:* Michael Scott Bregman; *C:* Scott Bregman.

Carlton Browne of the F.O. 🐾🐾½ 1959 *Man in a Cocked Hat* VIDEO Bumbling Brit diplomat Thomas visits tiny Pacific island of Gallardia, so long the mother country for some 50 years, to insure tenuous international agreement after the island's king dies. Not starring Sellers but some shining moments. **88m/C VHS, DVD.** GB Peter Sellers, Terry-Thomas, Luciana Paluzzi, Ian Bannen; *D:* Roy Boulting, Jeffrey Dell; *W:* Roy Boulting; *M:* Joe Della.

Carmen 🐾🐾🐾 1983 (R) Choreographer casts Carmen and finds life imitates art when he falls under the spell of the hotblooded Latin siren. Bizet's opera lends itself to erotically charged flamenco context. Well acted, impressive scenes including cigarette girls' dance fight and romance between Carmen and Don Jose. In Spanish with English subtitles. **99m/C VHS.** SP Antonio Gades, Laura Del Sol, Paco de Lucia, Cristina Hoyos; *D:* Carlos Saura; *W:* Antonic Gades, Carlos Saura; *C:* Teodoro Escamilla, British Acad. '84: Foreign Film.

Carmen: A Hip Hopera 🐾🐾½ 2001 (PG-13) Modernized and urban set version of Bizet's tragic opera, originally made for MTV. Carmen (Knowles) is the femme fatale who seduces straight-laced cop Derek Hill (Phfer) to keep herself out of jail. He abandons everything to follow her to California, where, naturally, Carmen wants to break into show biz. But she tires of Derek's devotion and becomes interested in an up-and-coming rapper. Surprisingly effective and the cast does a fine job. **88m/C VHS, DVD.** Beyonce Knowles, Mekhi Phifer, Mos Def, Reh Digga, Rah Digga, Neius Wyclef Jean, Troy Winbush; *D:* Robert Kevin Townsend; *W:* Michael Elliot; *C:* Seary McLeod; *M:* Kip Collins; *Nar:* Da 3rat; CABLE.

Carmen, Baby 🐾🐾 1966 Metzger's erotic modern update of Bizet's opera "Carmen." Spanish prostitute Carmen (Levka) becomes the object of obsession for a local cop (Ringer) and things wind up badly because of his jealousy. **90m/C VHS, DVD.** Uta Levka, Claus Ringer, Barbara Valentin; *D:* Radley Metzger; *W:* Jesse Vogel; *C:* Hans Jura; *M:* Daniel Hart.

Carmen Jones 🐾🐾🐾 1954 Bizet's tale of fickle femme fatale Carmen heads South with an all-black cast and new lyrics by Hammerstein I. Soldier Belafonte falls big time for factory working belle Dandridge during the war, and runs off with miss tharg after he kills his C.O. and quits the army. Then if prettyboy Belafonte, Dandridge's eye wanders upon prize pugilist Escambio, inspiring ex-soldier beau to wring her throaty little neck. Film debuts of Carroll and Peters. More than a little racist undertone to the direction. Actors' singing is dubbed. ♫That's Love; Dere's a Cafe on de Corner; Beat Out Dat Rhythm on a Drum; You Talk Just Like My Maw; Stand Up and Fight; Dis Flower; My Joe. **105m/C VHS, DVD.** Dorothy Dandridge, Harry Belafonte, Pearl Bailey, Roy Glenn, Diahann Carroll, Brock Peters; *D:* Otto Preminger; *W:* Harry Kleiner; *C:* Sam Leavitt; *M:* Oscar Hammerstein, Georges Bizet. Golden Globes '55: Film—Mus./Comedy, Natl. Film Reg. '92.

Carnage 🐾 1984 Hungry house consumes inhabitants. **91m/C VHS.** Leslie Den Dooven, Michael Chiodo, Deeann Veeder; *D:* Andy Milligan.

Carnage 🐾🐾 2002 Okay, this film s about a dead bull and its various bociy parts. Said bull gores a matador during a bullfight and is subsequently killed ard butchered. It's various parts go to various people throughout Spain and France, including a young girl named Winnie who gets a bull bone for her Great Dane, a taxidermist who gets the animal's horns, steaks that wind up in a restaurant, etc. There's a lot of obscure symbolism about how life and death are connected. You may not care. Spanish and French with subtitles. **130m/C VHS, DVD.** FR SP SB St Chiara Mastroianni, Angela Molina, Lucia Sanchez, Bernard Sens, Esther Gorintin, Jacques Gamblin, Raphaële Molinier, Lio; *D:* Delphine Gleize; *W:* Delphine Gleize; *C:* Crystal Fournier; *M:* Eric Neveux.

Carnal Crimes 🐾½ 1991 (R) Well-acted upscale softcore trash about a sensuous woman, ignored by her middle-aged lawyer husband and drawn to a young stud photographer with a shady past and S&M tendencies. Available in a sexy unrated version also. **103m/C VHS, DVD.** Martin Hewitt, Linda Carol, Rich Crater, Alex Kubik, Yvette Stefens, Paula Trickey; *D:* Alexander Gregory (Gregory Dark) Hippolyte; *M:* Jon Robert Fishman.

Carnal Knowledge 🐾🐾🐾 1971 Chronicles the sex-saturated lives of college buddies Nicholson and Garfunkel, chronicled through girlfriends, affairs, and marriages. Controversial upon release, it's not a flattering anatomy of Y-chromosome carriers. Originally written as a play. Kane's debut. **96m/C VHS, DVD.** Jack Nicholson, Candice Bergen, Art Garfunkel, Ann-Margret, Rita Moreno, Carol Kane; *D:* Mike Nichols; *W:* Jules Feifer; *C:* Giuseppe Rotunno, Golden Globes '72: Support. Actress (Ann-Margret).

Carnival of Souls 🐾🐾🐾 1962 Cult-followed zero budget zombie opera has young Hilligoss and girlfriends take a wrong turn off bridge into river. Mysteriously unscathed, Hilligoss rents room and keeps running into dancing dead people, led by director. Harvey. Spooky, very spooky. **72m/B VHS, DVD.** Candace Hilligoss, Sidney Berger, Frances Feist, Stan Levitt, Art Ellison, Bill de Jarnete, Steve Boozer, Pamela Ballard (Harvey); *D:* Harold (Herk) Harvey; *W:* John Clifford; *C:* Maurice Prather; *M:* Gene Moore.

Carnival of Souls WOOF! *Wes Craven Presents Carnival of Souls* 1998 (R) A young girl witnesses the brutal murder of her mother by a circus clown. As an adult she has nightmares about the circus, which intensify when the carnival hits town. Craven's "remake" has nothing much in common with the original except the title. Boring, disjointed waste of time. **87m/C VHS, DVD.** Bobbie Phillips, Larry Miller, Paul Johansson, Cleavant Derricks, Sidney Berger, Shawnee Smith. *D:* Adam Grossman; *W:* Adam Grossman; *M:* Andrew Rose.

Carnival Rock 🐾½ 1957 Story of love triangle in seedy nightclub. Club owner Stewart loves chanteuse Cabot who loves card playin' Hutton. Who cares? Maybe hard-core Corman devotees. Good tunes from the Platters, the Blockbusters, Bob Luman, and David Houston. **80m/B VHS.** Susan Cabot, Brian Hutton, David J. Stewart Dick Miller, Iris Adrian, Jonathan Haze, Ed Nelson, Bob Luman, Frankie Ray, Bruno VeSota; *D:* Roger Corman; *W:* Leo Lieberman; *C:* Floyd Crosby; *M:* Buck Ram.

Carnival of Blood 🐾 *Death Rides a Carousel* 1971 (PG) Boring talky scenes punctuated by Coney Island murder mayhem, followed by more boring talky scenes. Young's debut, not released for five years. The question's not why they delayed release but why they bothered at all. A carnival of cliches. **80m/C VHS, DVD.** Earle Edgerton, Judith Resnick, Martin Barosky, John Harris, Burt Young, Kaly Mills, Gloria Spivak; *D:* Leonard Kirman; *W:* Leonard Kirman; *C:* David Howe.

Carnival in Flanders 🐾🐾🐾½ 1935 *La Kermesse Heroique* 1935 When Spanish invaders enter a small 17th century Flemish village they discover all the men have disappeared. So it's up to the women to save the town from destruction—and they decide to do it by seducing the invaders. Classic French costume farce with a witty script and fine performances. In French with English subtitles. **90m/B VHS, FR** Françoise Rosay, Louis Jouvet, Jean Murat, Andre Aleme, Micheline Cheirel; *D:* Jacques Feyder; *C:* Harry Stradling Sr.; *M:* Louis Beydts. N.Y. Film Critics '36: Foreign Film; Venice Film Fest. '36: Director (Feyder).

Carnival Lady 🐾 1933 Silver spooner Vincent is scheduled to tie the knot until little lady-to-be discovers he's a bit out of pocket after the stock market takes a wee dip...jilted and impecunious, he heads to the big top, where he horns in on the high diver's turf, and it's all downhill from there. **80m/C DVD.** Boots Mallory, Allen Vincent Gertrude Astor, Kit Guard, Donald (Don) Kerr, Follo Lloyd, Jason Richards Sr.; *D:* Howard Higgin; *W:* Harold Tarshis; *C:* Edward Kull.

Carnegie Hall 🐾🐾½ 1947 Widowed Irish-American Nora (Hunt) gets a job at Carnegie Hall and raises her son Tony (Prince) deve ops an interest in jazz and popular music that his ma despises. They have a rift, Tony goes on the road as a band...marries singer Ruth (O'Drsicoll), and becomes a famous jazz pianist. After years pass, Ruth decides it's time to reunite mother and son and Carnegie Hall plays a big part in her scheme. Schmatzy story showcases a number of big musical stars of the day. **134m/B VHS, DVD.** Marsha Hunt, William Prince, Martha O'Driscoll, Frank McHugh; *D:* Edgar G. Ulmer; *C:* William J. Miller.

Carnival Story ♪♪½ 1954 Yet another melodramatic cliche about love triangular under the big top. German girl joins American-owned carnival and two guys start acting out unbecoming territorial behavior. Filmed in Germany. **94m/C VHS, DVD.** Anne Baxter, Steve Cochran, Lyle Betger, George Nader; **D:** Kurt Neumann.

Carnosaur ♪♪ 1993 (R) Straight from the Corman film factory, this exploitive quickie about dinosaurs harkens back to "50s-style monster epics. Predictable plot with extremely cheap effects. Genetic scientist Dr. Jane Tiptree (Ladd) is hatching diabolic experiments with chickens when things go awry. The experiments result in a bunch of lethal prehistoric creatures wrecking havoc among the community. **82m/C VHS, DVD.** Diane Ladd, Raphael Sbarge, Jennifer Runyon, Harrison Page, Clint Howard, Ned Bellamy; **D:** Adam Simon; **W:** Adam Simon; **C:** Keith Holland; **M:** Nigel Holton.

Carnosaur 2 ♪♪½ 1994 (R) Technicians investigating a power shortage at a secret military mining facility encounter deadly dinos. Entertaining schlock. **90m/C VHS, DVD.** John Savage, Cliff DeYoung, Arabella Holzbog, Ryan Thomas Johnson; **D:** Louis Morneau; **C:** John Aronson; **M:** Ed Tomney, Michael Palmer.

Carnosaur 3: Primal Species ♪♪ 1996 Terrorists get big surprise when the cargo they hijack turns out to be three very hungry dinos who make snacks of them all. Then it's up to commando Valentine, scientist Gunn, and some soldiers to get rid of the beasts. **82m/C VHS, DVD.** Scott Valentine, Janet Gunn, Rick Dean, Rodger Halston, Tony Peck; **D:** Jonathan Winfrey; **C:** Andrea V. Rossotto; **M:** Kevin Kiner.

Carny ♪♪ 1980 (R) Hothead carnival bozo Busey and peacemaker Robertson experience friendship difficulties when runaway Foster rolls in hay with one and then other. Originally conceived as a documentary by "Derby" filmmaker Kaylor, it's a candid, unsavory, behind-the-scenes anatomy. Co-written by "The Band" member Robertson. **102m/C VHS, DVD.** Gary Busey, Robbie Robertson, Jodie Foster, Meg Foster, Kenneth McMillan, Elisha Cook Jr., Craig Wasson; **D:** Robert Kaylor; **W:** Robbie Robertson, Thomas Baum; **C:** Harry Stradling Jr.; **M:** Alex North.

Carolina Cannonball ♪♪½ 1955 Slapstick comedy stars yodeling singer Canova as herself. Judy and Grandpa Canova run a trolley between a train depot and a Nevada ghost town. Meanwhile, three spies are tracking a stray atomic missile, which has crashed nearby. When the trolley breaks down, Judy and Grandpa unwittingly use the engine from the missile to make repairs. Much lowbrow hilarity ensues. **73m/B VHS.** Judy Canova, Andy Clyde, Ross Elliott, Emil Sitka, Sig Rumann, Jack Kruschen, Frank Wilcox, Leon Askin; **D:** Charles Lamont, Charles Lamont; **W:** Barry Shipman; **C:** Reggie Lanning; **M:** Donald Kahn.

Carolina Moon ♪♪½ Nora Roberts' Carolina Moon 2007 Psychic Tory returns to her hometown to confront the terrible memories of her past—the night her friend Hope was murdered. But Tory discovers death was only the first in a series of deaths and that the killer has been waiting patiently for Tory's return. Can Hope's old-time original movie based on the novel by Nora Roberts. **90m/C DVD.** Claire Forlani, Oliver Hudson, Jacqueline Bisset, Jonathan Scarfe,

Josie Davis, Chad Willet, Greg Lawson; **D:** Stephen Tolkin; **W:** Stephen Tolkin; **C:** Derick Underschutz; **M:** Steve Porcaro. **CABLE**

Carolina Skeletons ♪♪ 1992 (R) As a child in a small southern town, Gossett watched his brother was accused of a vicious double murder and quickly tried and executed. Thirty years later, the ex-Green Beret returns home to find the real killer and clear his brother's name. But there are those in the town who will do anything to stop their secrets from being revealed. **94m/C VHS, DVD.** Louis Gossett Jr., Bruce Dern, Melissa Leo, Paul Roebling, G.D. Spradlin, Bill Cobbs, Henderson Forsythe, Clifton James; **D:** John Erman; **W:** Tracy Keenan Wynn; **C:** Tony Imi; **M:** John Morris.

Caroline? ♪♪ 1990 (PG) A wealthy young woman is presumed dead in a plane crash. Now 15 years later a stranger appears at the family home claiming to be Caroline—and wanting her inheritance. Is it possible that what she says is true or is it all an elaborate ruse? An especially good performance by Zimbalist. A a "Hallmark Hall of Fame" presentation. Based on the novel "Father's Arcane Daughter" by E.L. Konigsburg. **100m/C VHS, DVD.** Stephanie Zimbalist, Pamela Reed, George Grizzard, Dorothy McGuire, Patricia Neal, Shawn (Michael) Phelan, Jenny Jacobs; **D:** Joseph Sargent; **M:** Charles Bernstein. **TV**

Caroline at Midnight ♪♪ 1993 (R) After a reporter's former girlfriend, Caroline, dies in a mysterious auto accident he winds up falling for her girlfriend Victoria. Then he discovers both women are connected to drug-dealing cops. Good cast in this atmospheric erotic thriller with plenty of puzzles. **92m/C VHS.** Clayton Rohner, Mia Sara, Timothy Daly, Judd Nelson, Virginia Madsen, Zach Galligan, Thomas F. Wilson, Stacey Travis; **D:** Scott McGinnis.

Carousel ♪♪♪ 1956 Much-loved Rodgers & Hammerstein musical based on Ferenc Molnar's play "Liliom" (filmed by Fritz Lang in 1935) about a swaggering carnival barker (MacRae) who tries to change his life after he falls in love with a good woman. Killed while attempting to foil a robbery he was supposed to help commit, he begs his heavenly hosts to return to the mortal realm just long enough to set things straight with his teenage daughter. Now indisputably a classic, the film lost $2 million when it was released. ♪If I Loved You; Soliloquy; You'll Never Walk Alone; What's the Use of Wond'rin; When I Marry Mister Snow; When the Children Are Asleep; A Real Nice Clambake; Carousel Ballet; Carousel Waltz. **128m/C VHS, DVD.** Gordon MacRae, Shirley Jones, Cameron Mitchell, Gene Lockhart, Barbara Ruick, Robert Rounseville, Richard Deacon, Tor Johnson; **D:** Henry King; **W:** Henry Ephron, Phoebe Ephron; **C:** Charles Clarke; **M:** Richard Rodgers, Oscar Hammerstein.

The Carpathian Eagle ♪ 1981 Police wonder why murdered victims have hearts ripped out while audience wonders what weird title has to do with anything. Routine evisceration fest, part of Elvira's Thriller Video. **60m/C VHS, DVD.** Suzanne Danielle, Sian Phillips, Pierce Brosnan, Anthony Valentine; **D:** Francis Megahy.

The Carpenter ♪ 1989 (R) Post-nervous breakdown woman receives nightly visits from guy who builds stuff with wood. Very scary stuff. Also available in slightly longer unrated version. **85m/C VHS.** CA Wings Hauser, Lynne Adams, Pierce Lenoir, Barbara Ann Jones, Beverly Murray; **D:** David Wellington; **W:** Doug Taylor; **C:** David Franco.

Carpet of Horror ♪♪ 1964 The city of London is terrorized by a small band emitting poison gas in this schlock horror film. Death results when the ball is rolled into the living rooms of intended victims. **93m/C VHS.** GE Joachim Fuchsberger, Carl Lange, Karin Dor; **D:** Harald Reinl.

The Carpetbaggers ♪♪ 1964 (PG) Uncannily Howard Hughesian Peppard wallows in wealth and women in Hollywood in the 1920s and 1930s. Spayed version of the Harold Robbins novel. Ladd's final appearance. Followed by the prequel "Nevada Smith." Introduced by Joan Collins. **150m/C VHS, DVD.**

George Peppard, Carroll Baker, Alan Ladd, Elizabeth Ashley, Lew Ayres, Martha Hyer, Martin Balsam, Robert Cummings, Archie Moore, Audrey Totter, Leif Erickson, Tom Lowell; **D:** Edward Dmytryk; **W:** John Michael Hayes; **C:** Joe MacDonald; **M:** Elmer Bernstein. Natl. Bd. of Review '64: Support. Actor (Balsam).

Carpool ♪♪ 1996 (PG) Dumb but amiable comedy finds harried dad Daniel Miller stuck driving a minivan filled with kids to school. Too bad he gets sidetracked and hijacked by bumbling would-be bank robber Franklin Laszlo (Arnold) who takes them hostage and on a really wild ride through the streets and shopping malls of Seattle (except it's filmed in Vancouver). **92m/C VHS, DVD.** Tom Arnold, David Paymer, Rhea Perlman, Rod Steiger, Kim Coates, Rachael Leigh Cook, Mikey Kovar, Micah Gardener, Blake Warkol; **D:** Arthur Hiller; **W:** Don Rhymer; **C:** David M. Walsh; **M:** John Debney. Golden Raspberries '96: Worst Actor (Arnold).

Carrie ♪♪ 1952 In a part turned down by Cary Grant, Olivier plays a married American who self destructs as the woman he loves scales the heights to fame and fortune. The manager of a posh epicurean mecca, Olivier deserts wife Hopkins and steals big bucks from his boss to head east with paramour Jones, a country bumpkin transplanted to Chicago. Once en route to thespian fame in the Big Apple, Jones abandons her erstwhile beau, who crumbles pathetically. Adapted from Theodore Dreiser's "Sister Carrie," it's mega melodrama, but the performances are above reproach. **118m/B VHS, DVD.** Laurence Olivier, Jennifer Jones, Miriam Hopkins, Eddie Albert, Basil Ruysdael, Ray Teal, Barry Kelley, Sara Berner, William Reynolds, Mary Murphy, Charles Halton; **D:** William Wyler; **C:** Victor Milner.

Carrie ♪♪♪ 1976 (R) Overprotected by religious fanatic mother Laurie and mocked by the in-crowd, shy, withdrawn high school girl Carrie White is asked to the prom. Realizing she's been made the butt of a joke, she unleashes her considerable telekinetic talents. Travolta, Allen, and Irving are teenagers who get what they deserve. Based on the Stephen King novel. **98m/C VHS, DVD.** Sissy Spacek, Piper Laurie, John Travolta, William Katt, Amy Irving, Nancy Allen, Edie McClurg, Betty Buckley, P.J. Soles, Sydney Lassick, Stefan Gierasch; **D:** Brian De Palma; **W:** Lawrence D. Cohen; **C:** Mario Tosi; **M:** Pino Donaggio. Natl. Soc. Film Critics '76: Actress (Spacek).

Carrie ♪½ 2002 This remake (broadcast on NBC) of King's first novel was stretched to three hours (with commercials) by introducing new characters and using flashbacks. Face it, what you want to see is the outcast Carrie (Bettis) getting her telekinetic revenge on all her tormentors at the high school prom. That's about the last half-hour, so just fast-forward to the good stuff. **132m/C VHS, DVD.** Angela Bettis, Patricia Clarkson, Rena Sofer, Tobias Mehler, Kandyse McClure, Emilie de Ravin, Katharine Isabelle, David Keith, Jasmine Guy; **D:** David Carson; **W:** Bryan Fuller; **C:** Victor Goss; **M:** Laura Karpman. **TV**

Carried Away ♪♪½ Acts of Love 1995 (R) Exposing his middle-aged bod, as well as the myth that he can play only psycho toughs, Hopper, as the Midwestern teacher Joseph, is seduced by a 17-year-old student (Locane) in their small conservative town. Based on Harrison's novel "Farmer," this is a sexually active slice of life with the injured Joseph limping through the care of his dying mother, the fate of the small country school where he teaches and his relationship with longtime lover Rosealee (Amy Irving). Hopper's not the only one playing against type, as Irving turns in a fine performance as the widowed schoolmarm. Director Barreto (and Irving's husband) pushes the envelope with full frontal nudity. **107m/C VHS, DVD.** Dennis Hopper, Amy Irving, Amy Locane, Gary Busey, Julie Harris, Hal Holbrook, Christopher Pettiet, Priscilla Pointer, Gail Cronauer; **D:** Bruno Barreto; **W:** Ed Jones; **C:** Declan Quinn; **M:** Bruce Broughton.

The Carrier ♪♪ 1987 (R) Smalltown Sleepy Rock is ideal family-raising turf until plague mysteriously blights inhabitants, and townspeople are out to exterminate all potential carriers. Silverman is standout as local spiritual leader; well-orchestrated crowd scenes. Best park your IQ before watching. Filmed on location in Manchester, Michigan. **99m/C VHS.** Gregory Fortescue, Steve Dixon, Paul Silverman, Paul Urbanski, Patrick Butler; **D:** Nathan J. White; **W:** Nathan J. White; **C:** Peter Deming; **M:** Joseph LoDuca.

Carrie's War ♪♪½ 2004 14-year-old Carrie (Fawcett) and her younger brother Nick (Stanley) are sent to live in the country to escape the London bombings during WWII. Naturally, they must cope with a variety of characters both pleasant and strict. Based on the Nina Bawden novel. **90m/C DVD.** GB Jack Stanley, Lesley Sharp, Alun Armstrong, Geraldine McEwan, Keeley Fawcett, Pauline Quirke, Eddie Cooper, Jamie Boddard; **D:** Coky Giedroyc; **W:** Michael Crompton; **C:** Julian Court; **M:** Nick Bicat. **TV**

Carrington ♪♪♪ 1995 (R) England's artistic Bloomsbury group is examined through the eccentric relationship of artist Dora Carrington (Thompson) and her love for homosexual Lytton Strachey (Pryce), celebrated author of "Eminent Victorians." There's many a menage as the duo live together with Carrington's husband (Waddington), on whom Strachey has a crush, and both their various amours (though Carrington's heart is reserved for Lytton). Film is distractingly divided into titled segments (from 1915 to 1932) and, while Pryce gives a bravura performance, Thompson is merely enigmatic. Based on Michael Holroyd's biography "Lytton Strachey." Hampton's directorial debut. **120m/C VHS, DVD.** FR GB Emma Thompson, Jonathan Pryce, Steven Waddington, Samuel West, Rufus Sewell, Penelope Wilton, Jeremy Northam, Peter Blythe, Janet McTeer, Alex Kingston, Sebastian Harcombe, Richard Clifford; **D:** Christopher Hampton; **W:** Christopher Hampton; **C:** Denis Lenoir; **M:** Michael Nyman. Cannes '95: Special Jury Prize, Actor (Pryce); Natl. Bd. of Review '95: Actress (Thompson).

Carrington, V.C. ♪♪♪ Court Martial 1954 British army major Niven is brought up for a court-martial on embezzlement charges because he arranges, without official permission, to be reimbursed for money owed to him. A former war hero, he decides to defend himself in court, and, once an affair comes to light, his vindictive wife joins the opposition. Good cast, superlative Niven performance. **100m/B VHS.** GB David Niven, Margaret Leighton, Noelle Middleton, Laurence Naismith; **D:** Anthony Asquith.

Carry Me Back ♪♪ 1982 Two brothers carry dead dad back to Australian ranch in order to inherit mucho dinero. **93m/C VHS.** NZ Grant Tilly, Kelly Johnson, Dorothy McKegg, Derek Hardwick, Joanne Mildenhall, Alex Trousdell, Frank Edwards; **D:** John Reid; **W:** John Reid, Keith Aberdein, Derek Morton; **C:** Graeme Cowley; **M:** James Hall.

Carry Me Home ♪♪ 2004 (PG-13) As Harriet (Miller) suffers through the loss of her husband from his WWII tour of duty, her tomboy daughter Carrie (Orr) deals with the pain by angrily shutting her mom out, particularly when Harriet moves on with the highbrow Bernard (Basche) causing Carrie to seek comfort from Charlie (Anderson), a mentally-challenged and troubled local farmhand. Showtime cable coming-of-age drama feels more like a tearjerker-of-the-week Lifetime channel show. **97m/C VHS, DVD.** Penelope Ann Miller, Kevin Anderson, David Alan Basche, Ashley Rose Orr, Jane Alexander, Leo Burmester, Nicholas Braun; **D:** Jace Alexander; **W:** Christopher Fay; **C:** David Herrington; **M:** Bill Elliott. **CABLE**

Carry On Admiral ♪♪½ The Ship was Loaded 1957 Weak British comedy about two friends who get drunk and decide it would be fun to switch identities. One has an easy job as a public relations exec but the other is supposedly the captain of a ship. His lack of sea knowledge causes wacky catastrophes. Unrelated to the "Carry On" series of comedies. **85m/B VHS.** GB David Tomlinson, Brian Reece, Peggy

Carry On at Your Convenience ♂½ *Carry On* the *Bend* 1971 Williams, who played in the original ("Carry On Sergeant"), and Carry On regulars ("chapel-mugged James and ever-zaftig Jacques) go 'round the bend in yet another installment of the British spoof in and around a toilet factory. **86m/C VHS. GB** Sidney James, Kenneth Williams, Charles Hawtrey, Joan Sims, Kenneth Cope, Hattie Jacques; **D:** Gerald Thomas.

Carry On Behind ♂♂ 1975 "Carry On" crew heads for archeological dig and find themselves sharing site with holiday caravan. **95m/C VHS. GB** Sidney James, Kenneth Williams, Elke Sommer, Joan Sims; **D:** Gerald Thomas.

Carry On Camping ♂½ 1971 Another entry in the silly series finds James and Bresslaw trying to persuade their girlfriends to go on a camping trip to what the men hope is a nudist colony. They don't find nudists but they do find a group of sex-starved schoolgirls. **88m/C VHS. GB** Sidney James, Bernard Bresslaw, Kenneth Williams, Joan Sims, Jim Dale, Charles Hawtrey, Joan Sims; **D:** Gerald Thomas.

Carry On Cowboy ♂♂ 1966 *Rumpo Kid* "Carry On" Western parody of "High Noon." **91m/C VHS, DVD. GB** Sidney James, Kenneth Williams, Jim Dale, Joan Sims, Charles Hawtrey, Angela Douglas, Peter Butterworth, Bernard Bresslaw, Percy Herbert, Davy Kaye; **C:** Gerald Thomas; **W:** Talbot Rothwell; **C:** Alan Hume; **M:** Eric Rogers.

Carry On Cruising ♂ 1962 "Carry On" gang attacks sailing world with low humor and raunchiness. **89m/C VHS, DVD.** Sidney James, Kenneth Williams, Liz Fraser; **D:** Gerald Thomas.

Carry On Dick ♂♂ 1975 *What* made the seemingly endless "Carry On" series of super-low-budget British farces such a hit is a mystery not to be solved. Low production values, scripts that peter out midway, and manifest humor don't normally a classic make; and yet the gang has its following. "Dick," a spoof on highwayman Dick Turpin, was preceded by some 20-odd carryings on; suffice it to say that the series, which began in 1958 with "Carry on Sergeant," has not improved with age in subsequent incarnations. **95m/C VHS. GB** Sidney James, Joan Sims; **D:** Gerald Thomas.

Carry On Doctor ♂♂ 1968 British series continues as characters of questionable competence join the medical profession. **95m/C VHS, DVD. GB** Frankie Howerd, Kenneth Williams, Jim Dale, Barbara Windsor; **D:** Gerald Thomas.

Carry On Emmanuelle ♂ 1978 Emmanuelle, the wife of the French Ambassador to England, uses bedroom diplomacy to foster international relations. Part of the British "Carry On" series. **104m/C VHS. GB** Suzanne Danielle, Kenneth O'Connor, Kenneth Williams, Beryl Reid; **D:** Gerald Thomas.

Carry On England ♂ 1976 Mercifully, the gang didn't carry on much beyond this entry, in which a WWII anti-aircraft gun battery crew bumbles through the usual pranks and imbroglios. **89m/C VHS. GB** Kenneth Connor, Patrick Mower, Judy Geeson; **D:** Gerald Thomas.

Carry On Henry VIII ♂½ 1971 Slapstick sex humor with Henry marrying the French Marie of Normandie and having to deal with both her addiction to garlic and the fact that she's pregnant by her lover. **88m/C VHS. GB** Sidney James, Kenneth Williams, Kenneth Connor, Julian Holloway; **D:** Gerald Thomas; **W:** Talbot Rothwell.

Cummins, Eunice Gayson, A.E. Matthews, Lionel Murton, Joan Sims; D: Val Guest; W: Val Guest.

Carry On Cleo ♂½ 1965 "Carry On" spoof of Shakespeare's "Antony and Cleopatra "The film used some of the sets from the budget-busting 1963 disaster "Cleopatra." **91m/C VHS, DVD. GB** Sidney James, Amanda Barrie, Kenneth Williams, Kenneth Connor, Jim Dale, Charles Hawtrey, Joan Sims; **D:** Gerald Thomas.

Carry On Nurse ♂♂ 1959 Men's ward in a British hospital declares war on nurses and the rest of the hospital. The second of the "Carry On" series. **86m/B VHS, DVD. GB** Shirley Eaton, Kenneth Connor, Hattie Jacques, Wilfrid Hyde-White; **D:** Gerald Thomas.

The Cars That Ate Paris ♂♂ *The Cars That Eat People* 1974 (PG) Parasitic town in the Parisian (Australia) outback preys on car and body parts generated by deliberate accidents inflicted by wreck-driving wreckless youths. Weir's first film released internationally, economically via deliberately contriving car accidents and selling the wrecks; scrap parts. A broad, bitter black comedy with some horror touches. **91m/C VHS, DVD.** AU Terry Camilleri, Kevin Miles, John Meillon, Melissa Jaffer; **D:** Peter Weir; **W:** Peter Weir; **M:** Bruce Smeaton.

Carson City Kid ♂½ 1940 Typical western which has Rogers trying to exact revenge on the man who killed his brother. **54m/B VHS, DVD.** Roy Rogers, George "Gabby" Hayes, Bob Steele, Noah Beery Jr., Pauline Moore, Francis McDonald, Wally Wales, Arthur Loft, George Rosener, Chester Gan; **D:** Joseph Kane; **W:** Gerald Geraghty, Robert Yost; **C:** William Nobles; **M:** Cy Feuer, Peter Tinturin.

Certel Woof! 1990 (R) O'Keeffe, "B" actor extraordinaire, plays the wrong man to pick up in this rancid dope opera. Hounded by drug lord Stroud and framed for murder, pilot O'Keeffe decides the syndicate has gone too doggone far when they kill his sister. Exploitive and otherwise very bad. **106m/C VHS, DVD.** Miles O'Keeffe, Don Stroud, Crystal Carson, William Smith; **D:** John Stewart; **W:** Moshe Hedar; **C:** Thomas Callaway; **M:** Rick Krizman.

Carthage in Flames ♂♂ *Cartagine in Flamme; Carthage en Fammes* 1960 A graphic portrayal of the destruction of ancient Carthage in a blood and guts battle for domination of the known world. A tender love story is a welcome aside in this colorful Italian-made epic. **96m/C VHS.** IT Anne Heywood, Jose Suarez, Pierre Brasseur; **C:** Carmine Gallone.

Cartier Affair ♂ 1984 A beautiful TV actress unwittingly falls in love with the man who wants to steal her jewels. Collins designed her own wardrobe. **120m/C VHS, DVD.** Joan Collins, David Hasselhoff, Telly Savalas, Ed Lauter, Joe La Due; **D:** Rod Holcomb; **C:** Hanania Baer. **TV**

Cartouche ♂♂♂ *Swords of Blood* 1962 A swashbuckling action-comedy set in 18th-century France. Belmondo plays a charming thief who takes over a Paris gang, aided by the lovely Cardinale. When the gang is captured, he sacrifices his life to save him and Belmondo and his cohorts vow to have their revenge. Based on the

---

Carry On Screaming ♂♂ 1966 "Carry On" does horror. A pair of goofy detectives track monsters suspected in kidnapping. **97m/C VHS, DVD. GB** Harry H. Corbett, Kenneth Williams, Fenella Fielding, Jim Sims, Charles Hawtrey, Jim Dale, Angela Douglas, Jon Pertwee; **D:** Gerald Thomas.

Cars ♂♂♂ 2006 (G) Brightly-colored animated adventure from those Pixar folks about automobiles. Arrogant rookie racecar Lightning McQueen (Wilson) is detoured to the sleepy town of Radiator Springs on his way to a big race. Forced to perform community service, Lightning gets a lesson in humility and figures out their fame isn't everything, thanks to new friends as Sally Carrera (Hunt, in a 20:2 Porsche 911; gruff Doc (Newman), the 1951 Hudson Hornet, and Mater (Larry the Cable Guy), a goofy, good-natured tow truck. Just as heartwarming and funny as you'd expect a Pixar feature to be. **118m/C DVD, Blu-ray Disc.** US Larry the Cable Guy; **D:** John Lasseter; **V:** Owen Wilson, Paul Newman, Bonnie Hunt, Paul Dooley, Joe Ranft, George Carlin, Katherine Helmond, Michael Keaton, Richard Petty, John Ratzenberger, Tony Shalhoub, Cheech Marin, Jenifer Lewis, Michael Wallis; **Golden Globes '07:** Animated Film.

Casa de los Babys ♂♂♂ 2003 (R) Sayles's quiet, insightful look at adoption, poverty, politics and international trade as five diverse American women wait (and wait at a local motel nicknamed Casa de Los Babys to adopt children in an unnamed South American country. Each has a particular reason for adoption: Fitness freak Skipper (Hannah) has had three miscarriages while Jennifer (Gyllenhaal) hopes adoption will help her ailing marriage. Rounding out the gang of expectant mothers are the hardened single-alcoholic Gayle; and the extremely disagreeable Nan (Harden). Memorably poignant scene as the Irish Eileen and the Latina Asuncion (Lynch and Martinez, respectively bond over heartfelt exchanges in a language that neither can understand. **95m/C VHS, DVD.** US Maggie Gyllenhaal, Marcia Gay Harden, Daryl Hannah, Susan Lynch, Mary Steenburgen, Lili Taylor, Rita Moreno, Vanessa Martinez; **D:** John Sayles; **W:** John Sayles; **C:** Mauricio Rubinstein; **M:** Mason Daring.

Casablanca ♂♂♂♂ 1942 (PG) Can you see George Raft as Rick? Jack Warner did, but producer Hal Wallis wanted Bogart. Considered by many to be the best film ever made and one of the most quoted movies of all time, it rocketed Bogart from gangster roles to romantic leads as he and Bergman (who never looked lovelier) sizzle on screen. Bogart runs a gin joint in Morocco during the Nazi occupation, and meets up with Bergman, an old flame, but romance and politics do not mix especially in Nazi-occupied French Morocco. Greenstreet, Lorre, and Rains all create memorable characters, as does Wilson, the piano player to whom Bergman says the oft-misquoted, "Play it Sam." Without a doubt, the best closing scene ever written; it was scripted on the fly during the set shooting, and actually shot several ways. Written from an unproduced play. See it in the original black and white. 50th Anniversary Edition contains a restored print, the original 1942 theatrical trailer, a film documentary narrated by Lauren Bacall, and a booklet **102m/B VHS, DVD, Blu-ray Disc, HD DVD.** Hum-

---

Carve Her Name with Pride ♂♂½ 1958 The true story of Violette Szabo who at age 19 became a secret agent with the French Resistance in WWII. **119m/B VHS. GB** Virginia McKenna, Paul Scofield, Jack Warner, Denise Grey, Alan Saury, Maurice Ronet, Anne Leon, Nicole Stephane, Sydney Tafler, Avice Landone; **D:** Lewis Gilbert; **W:** Lewis Gilbert, Vernon Harris; **C:** John Wilcox; **M:** William Alwyn.

Carved ♂♂ *Kuchisake-onna; Slit-Mouthed Woman* 2007 Urban legend has the spirit of a woman grotesquely disfigured by her jealous husband roaming the streets of a suburban town terrorizing young victims. Children are coming up missing, but as teachers and officials desperately investigate, panic rises and dark secrets are revealed. Remake does not add any depth or height to an already well used premise. Japanese with subtitles. **90m/C DVD.** JP Eric Sato, Haruhiko Kato, Miki Mizuno, Chiharu Kawai, Rie Kuwana, Kazuyuki Matsuzawa, Saaya Irie; **D:** Koji Shiraishi; **W:** Kohi Fujino Chika, Wano Gen.

Carver's Gate ♂♂ 1996 Thanks to an environmental disaster, earth is in big trouble and its inhabitants take refuge in a virtual reality game called Afterlife. But when an engineer tries to improve the game by heightening its reality, the game's computer-generated demons get loose and it's up to cybercop Pare to stop them by traveling between virtual reality and the actual world. **97m/C VHS, DVD.** Michael Pare, Kevin Stapleton, Marian Skretas, Tara Maria Manuel, Peter Wylde, Pamela Keyes; **D:** Sheldon Inkol; **W:** Sheldon Inkol; **C:** Jonathan Freeman; **M:** Donald Quan.

Casablanca Express ♂ 1989 Nazi commandos hijack Churchill's train in this action-adventure drama. **90m/C VHS, DVD.** Glenn Ford, Donald Pleasence, Jason Connery; **D:** Sergio Marina.

Casanova ♂♂ 1987 (PG-13) A comedic romp through the bedrooms of 18th-century Europe with Chamberlain as the legendary lover Lots of lovely ladies and hammy performances. **122m/C VHS.** Richard Chamberlain, Faye Dunaway, Sylvia Kristel, Ornella Muti, Hanne Schygulla, Sophie Ward, Frank Finlay, Roman Colley; **D:** Simon Langton; **W:** George MacDonald Fraser; **C:** Giuseppe Rotunno. **TV**

Casanova ♂ 2005 (R) Set in Venice and loosely based on the legendary life of the 18th century womanizer. Casanova (Ledger) is running from the Roman Inquisitor Pucci (Irons) who wants to try him for heresy, which sets up an excuse for dramatic costume comedies set in Venice and you're house-bound for the weekend, you could do worse. **108m/C DVD.** US Heath Ledger, Sienna Miller, Jeremy Irons, Oliver Platt, Lena Olin, Omid Djalili, Stephen Greif, Ken Stott, Charlie Cox, Tim (McInnerny McInnery, Phil Davies, Paddy Ward, Helen McCrory, Leigh Lawson, Natalie Dormer; **D:** Lasse Hallstrom; **W:** Jeffrey Hatcher, Kimberly Sim; **C:** Oliver Stapleton; **M:** Alexandre Desplat.

Casanova Brown ♂♂½ 1944 Lighthearted comedy about a shy English professor (Cooper) who learns that his recent ex-wife (Wright) has had a baby (guess whose). When Cooper learns Wright has decided to give their daughter up for adoption he kidnaps the tyke and attempts fatherhood in a hotel room. When Wright finds out where he is, the twosome (who have really been in love all along) decide to remarry and be a family. Cooper, with baby and surrounded by diapers, makes a comedic sight. Based on the play "The Little Accident" by Floyd Dell and Thomas Mitchell. **94m/B VHS, DVD.** Gary Cooper, Teresa Wright, Frank Morgan, Anita Louise, Patricia Collinge, Edmund Breon, Jill Esmond, Emory Parnell, Isobel Elsom, Mary Treen, Halliwell Hobbes; **D:** Sam Wood; **W:** Nunnally Johnson; **M:** Arthur Lange.

Casanova '70 ♂♂½ 1965 Mastroianni plays a handsome soldier who has a knack for enticing liberated women has a knack for enticing the much-cine-matized legendary yarn. Trouble is, he's in the mood only when he believes that he's in imminent danger. In Italian with English subtitles. **113m/C VHS.** IT Marcello Mastroianni, Virna Lisi, Michele Mercier, Guido Alberti, Margaret Lee, Bernard Blier, Lara Ortei; **D:** Mario Monicelli; **W:** Tonino Guerra.

---

phrey Bogart, Ingrid Bergman, Paul Henreid, Claude Rains, Peter Lorre, Sydney Greenstreet, Conrad Veidt, S.Z. Sakall, Dooley Wilson, Marcel Dalio, John Qualen, Helmut Dantine, Madeleine LeBeau, Joy Page, Leonid Kinskey, Curt Bois, Gruning, Ludwig Stosse, Frank Puglia, Dan Seymour, Oliver Blake, Monte Blue, Martin Garralaga, Ilka Curtiz; **W:** Julius J. Epstein, Philip G. Epstein, Howard Koch; **C:** Arthur Edeson; **M:** Max Steiner; Oscars '43: Director (Curtiz), Picture, Screenplay; AFI '98; Top 100; Natl. Film Reg. '89.

Casanova's Big Night 1954 Classic slapstick comedy stars Hope masquerading as Casanova to test Fontaine's virtue before her marriage to a duke. The all-star cast provides one hilarious scene after another in this dated film. Price has a cameo as the "real" Casanova. Based on a story by Aubrey Wisberg. 85m/C VHS, DVD. Bob Hope, Joan Fontaine, Audrey Dalton, Basil Rathbone, Hugh Marlowe, Vincent Price, John Carradine, Raymond Burr; D: Norman Z. McLeod; W: Hal Kanter, Edmund Hartmann; C: Lionel Lindon.

Casbah 1948 Fine musical remake of the 1937 French film "Pepe Le Moko" and its American counterpart, 1938's "Algiers." Criminal Pepe (Martin) is safe as long as he hides out in the Casbah—outside lurks patient policeman Slimmane (Lorre), who's determined to capture him. Of course, it's l'amour that trips Pepe up when he falls for tourist Gaby (Toren), who's leaving Algiers. Pepe had many brains, he would have stuck with hot local number, Inez (De Carlo), instead. 94m/B VHS. Tony Martin, Peter Lorre, Yvonne De Carlo, Marta Toren, Douglas Dick, Hugo Haas, Thomas Gomez, Katherine Dunham; D: John Berry; W: Arnold Manoff; C: Irving Glassberg; M: Walter Scharf.

A Case for Murder 1993 (R) Jack Hammett has just become the youngest full partner ever at his Chicago law firm, with a knack for winning impossible cases. His next one's a beaut. Seems an envious colleague has gotten himself murdered and his estranged wife is the prime suspect. Jack decides to work with newly arrived lawyer Kate Weldon but the two become personally involved, and Kate begins to question Jack's ethics. Seems the evidence is more than a little shady and Jack isn't telling all. 94m/C VHS. Peter Berg, Jennifer Grey, Belinda Bauer; D: Duncan Gibbins; W: Duncan Gibbins, Pablo F. Fenjves.

A Case of Deadly Force 1986 Based on the true story of a black man wrongfully killed by Boston's Tactical Police Force who mistook him for a robber. The police investigation calls it self-defense but the family and the attorney they hire fight to change the verdict. Excellent cast, great dramatic story. 95m/C VHS. Richard Crenna, John Shea, Lorraine Toussaint, Francis X. (Frank) McCarthy, Tom Isbell; D: Michael Miller. TV

A Case of Libel 1983 Dramatization based on attorney Louis Nizer's account of Quentin Reynolds's libel suit against columnist Westbrook Pegler. 90m/C VHS. Daniel J. Travanti, Ed Asner; D: Eric Till. TV

The Case of the Bloody Iris Perche Quelle Strane Gocce di Sangre sul Corpo di Jennifer; Where Are Those Strange Drops of Blood on the Body of Jennifer? 1972 Models and friends Jennifer (French) and Marilyn (Quatrini) move into an apartment building where two women have already been killed. The police suspect Andrea Barto (Hilton), who not only owns the apartment building but a modeling agency, and who knew both women. Soon, Jennifer realizes she is being stalked but there are several candidates, including her estranged husband who belongs to a weird sex cult. Italian with subtitles. 94m/C DVD. IT Edwige Fenech, George Hilton, Giampiero Albertini, Paola Quattrini, Jorge (George) Rigaud; C: Giuliano Carnimeo; W: Ernesto Gastaldi; C: Stelvio Massi; M: Bruno Nicolai.

The Case of the Frightened Lady The Frightened Lady 1939 A homicidal family does its collective best to keep its dark past a secret in order to collect some inheritance money. Watch, if you're still awake, for the surprise ending. 80m/B VHS, DVD. GB Marius Goring, Helen Haye, Penelope Dudley Ward, Felix Aylmer, Patrick Barr; D: George King.

The Case of the Lucky Legs 1935 Yes, there was a Perry Mason before Raymond Burr. Erle Stanley Gardner's sleuthing litigator's first appearance was 1934's "The Case of the Howling Dog," which initiated Warner Bros' "A"-grade (but soon-to-be "B"-grade) series. More akin to Nick Charles than to Gardner's character or to his later TV incarnation, the "Lucky Legs" Perry is a high-living, interminably hungover tippler who winces and wisecracks as he unravels the case of the corpse of a crooked con man. William, who left shortly after the series was downgraded to "B" status, plays the esquire; Tobin plays his smart-mouthed secretary, and Ellis is the tomato suspected of murder. 76m/B VHS. Warren William, Genevieve Tobin, Patricia Ellis, Lyle Talbot, Allen Jenkins, Barton MacLane, Peggy Shannon, Porter Hall; D: Archie Mayo.

The Case of the Scorpion's Tail La Coda dello Scorpione 1971 A series of murders follows a million-dollar insurance settlement, which brings investigator Peter Lynch (Hilton) looking into the situation. Reporter Cleo Dupont (Strindberg) helps out and becomes a potential victim. Set in Athens. Italian with subtitles. 90m/C VHS, DVD. IT George Hilton, Anita Strindberg, Alberto De Mendoza, Ida Galli, Janine Reynaud, Luigi Pistilli; D: Sergio Martino; W: Ernesto Gastaldi, Sauro Scavolini, Eduardo Brochero; C: Emilio Foriscot; M: Bruno Nicolai.

Casey's Shadow 1978 (PG) The eight-year-old son of an impoverished horse trainer raises a quarter horse and enters it in the world's richest horse race. 116m/C VHS, DVD. Walter Matthau, Alexis Smith, Robert Webber, Murray Hamilton; D: Martin Ritt; C: John A. Alonzo.

Cash Crop Harvest 2001 (R) Kids try to protect their farmer parents who decided to grow marijuana in order to pay off big debts. The DEA shows up, coming into conflict with the local sheriff, who's sympathetic to the farmers' plight. Fairly even-handed treatment, confounding expectations of an easy stoner comedy. 96m/C VHS, DVD. Mary McCormack, John Slattery, James Van Der Beek, Jeffrey DeMunn, Will Horneff, Frederick Weller, Paula Garces, Julianne Nicholson, Lisa Emery, Josh(ua) Lucas, Evan Handler; D: Stuart Burkin; W: Stuart Burkin, James Biederman, David A. Kom; C: Oliver Bokelberg; M: Paul Rabjohns. VIDEO

Cash McCall 1960 McCall (Garner) is a corporate raider who just loves making money. But problems come in when he falls for the lovely daughter (Wood) of his latest takeover target, failing businessman Jagger. Based on the novel by Cameron Hawley. 116m/C VHS. James Garner, Natalie Wood, Dean Jagger, Nina Foch, E.G. Marshall, Henry Jones, Otto Kruger, Roland Winters, Parley Baer, Dabbs Greer; D: Joseph Pevney; W: Lenore Coffee, Marion Hargrove; C: George J. Folsey; M: Max Steiner.

Cashback 2006 (R) After a painful break-up, art student Ben Willis develops insomnia. So he decides to get a job working the late night shift at the supermarket. Ben can freeze time—so he does, and wanders around the store, mostly stripping down unsuspecting women, drawing them, and then re-dressing them. It sounds sleazier than it actually is, but still. Ick. 90m/C DVD. GB Sean Biggerstaff, Emilia Fox, Shaun Evans, Michael Dixon, Michelle Ryan, Stuart Goodman, Marc Pickering, Michael Lambourne; D: Sean Ellis; W: Sean Ellis; C: Angus Hudson; M: Guy Farley.

Casino 1980 Thriller about backstabbings and ritzy romance aboard a high-priced gambling liner. 100m/C VHS. Mike Connors, Lynda Day George, Bo Hopkins, Gary Burghoff, Lynda Carter, Joseph Cotten, Robert Reed, Barry Sullivan; D: Don Chaffey. TV

Casino 1995 (R) Final part of the Scorsese underworld crime trilogy that began with "Mean Streets" and continued in "GoodFellas." Casino boss Sam "Ace" Rothstein (De Niro), his ex-hustler wife Ginger (Stone), and his loose-cannon enforcer pal Nicky (Pesci) are the principals in this lengthy, fictionalized account of how the mob lost Las Vegas in a haze of drugs, sex, coincidence, and betrayal. Flashy, intricate, and unflinchingly violent account of mob-run '70s Vegas clicks when exploring the inner workings of a major casino and its hierarchy. Although Stone shines as a hedonistic money chaser, visuals are great and the soundtrack is a killer, storyline suffers from deja vu. Pileggi again adapted the screenplay from his own book. 177m/C VHS, DVD, HD DVD. Robert De Niro, Joe Pesci, Sharon Stone, James Woods, Don Rickles, Alan King, Kevin Pollak, L.Q. Jones, Dick Smothers, John (Joe Bob Briggs) Bloom, Frankie Avalon, Steve Allen, Jayne Meadows, Jerry Vale; D: Martin Scorsese; W: Nicholas Pileggi, Martin Scorsese; C: Robert Richardson. Golden Globes '96: Actress—Drama (Stone).

Casino Royale 1967 The product of five directors, three writers and a mismatched cast of dozens, this virtually plotless spoof of James Bond films can stand as one of the low-water marks for 1960s comedy. And yet, there are some marvelous bits within, scenes of bizarre hilarity. Welles and Sellers literally couldn't stand the sight of one another, and their scenes together were filmed separately, with stand-ins. 130m/C VHS, DVD. David Niven, Woody Allen, Peter Sellers, Ursula Andress, Orson Welles, Jean-Paul Belmondo, Charles Boyer, Joanna Pettet, John Huston, William Holden, George Raft, Kurt Kasznar, Terence Cooper, Barbara Bouchet, Anna Quayle, Geoffrey Bayldon, Caroline Munro; D: John Huston, Ken Hughes, Robert Parrish, Val Guest, Joseph McGrath; W: Wolf Mankowitz, John Law, Michael Sayers; C: Jack Hildyard; M: Burt Bacharach.

Casino Royale 2006 (PG-13) Bond is back and Craig does not destroy the franchise as the whiners would have you believe. Based on Fleming's first (1953) novel, Bond has just achieved 007 status and is still learning his way. He may be blond(ish) but he's brutal, ruthless, and arrogant (and he bleeds). Story revolves around a high-stakes poker game with a Eurotrash banker (Mikkelsen) to terrorists and the Bond babe is Vesper Lynd (Green), a sexy, cool accountant. Dench returns as M, and she and and Dench share some of the best moments as she tries to keep her "blunt instrument" in line. It's a little too long but Craig proves he can wear a tux, say "Bond...James Bond," and kill, which is what true aficionados require. 144m/C DVD, Blu-ray Disc. GB US CZ GE Daniel Craig, Eva Green, Mads Mikkelsen, Judi Dench, Jeffrey Wright, Giancarlo Giannini, Caterina Murino, Isaach de Bankole, Simon Abkarian, Ivana Milicevic, Tobias Menzies, Claudio Santamaria, Jesper Christensen, Sebastien Foucan; D: Martin Campbell; W: Paul Haggis, Neal Purvis, Robert Wade; C: Phil Meheux; M: David Arnold. British Acad. '06: Sound.

Casper 1995 (PG) World's friendliest ghost appears on the big screen with outstanding visual trickery (from Industrial Light and Magic) and a lively, if hokey, story. Evilish Carrigan Crittenden (Moriarty) inherits ghost-infested Whipstaff Manor and hires scatterbrained "ghost therapist" Dr. Harvey (Pullman) to get rid of its unwanted occupants. His daughter Kat (Ricci) is soon the object of Casper's friendly attention while the good doc must contend with Casper's mischievous uncles—Stinkie, Fatso, and Stretch. Exec producer Spielberg shows his influence with numerous topical gags and screen references that help amuse the adults while the ghosts work their magic on the kiddies. Silberling's directorial debut; based on the comic-book and TV cartoon character created more than 30 years ago. 95m/C VHS, DVD. Christina Ricci, Bill Pullman, Cathy Moriarty, Eric Idle, Amy Brenneman, Ben Stein; Cameos: Don Novello, Rodney Dangerfield, Clint Eastwood, Mel Gibson, Dan Aykroyd; D: Brad Silberling; W: Sherri Stoner, Deanna Oliver; C: Dean Cundey; M: James Horner; V: Malachi Pearson, Joe Nipote, Joe Alaskey, Brad Garrett.

Casque d'Or Golden Marie 1952 Crime passionnel in turn-of-the-century Paris as an honest carpenter (Reggiani) gets drawn into the netherworld of pimps and thieves. He's finally driven to murder—all for love of gangster's moll Marie (a very sultry Signoret). French with subtitles. 96m/B VHS, DVD. FR Serge Reggiani, Simone Signoret, Claude Dauphin, Raymond Bussieres, Gaston Modot; D: Jacques Becker, Jacques Companeez; C: Robert Lefebvre; M: Georges Van Parys.

Cass 1978 Disenchanted filmmaker returns home to Australia to experiment with alternative lifestyles. 90m/C VHS. AU Michelle Fawden, John Waters, Judy Morris, Peter Carroll, Peter Whitford; D: Chris Noonan; W: Laura Jones; C: Mick von Bornemann; M: Rory O'Donoghue.

Cass Timberlane 1947 Scandalous story of a May-December romance set in a small Midwestern town. Tracy stars as Cass Timberlane, a widowed judge who falls for a voluptuous young girl from the wrong side of the tracks (Turner). They marry and experience problems when she is shunned by his snobbish friends. Good performances, especially from the supporting cast, dominate this fairly predictable film. Based on the novel by Sinclair Lewis. 119m/B VHS. Spencer Tracy, Lana Turner, Zachary Scott, Tom Drake, Mary Astor, Albert Dekker, Margaret Lindsay, John Litel, Mona Barrie, Josephine Hutchinson, Rose Hobart, Selena Royle; Cameos: Walter Pidgeon; D: George Sidney; W: Donald Ogden Stewart.

Cassandra 1987 (R) A fragile young woman has dreams that foretell the future—specifically, a series of grisly murders. 94m/C VHS. Shane Briant, Briony Behets, Tessa Humphries, Kit Taylor, Lee James; D: Colin Eggleston.

The Cassandra Crossing 1976 (R) A terrorist with the plague causes havoc on a transcontinental luxury train. Turgid adventure filmed in France and Italy. 129m/C VHS, DVD. GB Sophia Loren, Richard Harris, Ava Gardner, Burt Lancaster, Martin Sheen, Ingrid Thulin, Lee Strasberg, John Phillip Law, Lionel Stander, O.J. Simpson, Ann Turkel, Alida Valli; D: George P. Cosmatos; W: George P. Cosmatos, Tom Mankiewicz; C: Ennio Guarnieri; M: Jerry Goldsmith.

Cassandra's Dream 2007 (PG-13) Not a comedy and not in New York? Woody Allen fortunately breaks form again with this decidedly unfunny crime drama set in London. A tale of two brothers, ambitious Ian (McGregor) is stuck in the family restaurant; Terry (Farrell) is a mechanic, gambler, and addict. On a winning streak at the dog races, the pair buy a yacht and name it "Cassandra's Dream," the name of the winning pooch. Things are looking up, but Ian finds love in a dangerous woman and Terry's gambling luck dries up. They both turn to elusive and wealthy Uncle Howard (Wilkinson), and their already tenuous lives really begin to unravel. Turns out Uncle Howard is in his own trouble, and his help will come at a cost. Like many of Allen's serious films, moral ties are far-reaching and devastating consequences, and the characters are smart and multilayered. 108m/C DVD. FR US Ewan McGregor, Colin Farrell, Hayley Atwell, Sally Hawkins, Tom Wilkinson, John Benfield, Clare Higgins, Tom Fisher; D: Woody Allen; W: Woody Allen; C: Vilmos Zsigmond; M: Philip Glass.

Cassie Up 'n Coming 1983 (R) Follows the rise of Cassie, a successful country and western singer, and documents all her trials along the way. 75m/C VHS. Lisa De Leeux, Herschel Savage, Richard Pacheco, Marilyn Chambers; D: Stu Segall; C: Jacques Remy; M: Mike Lyman.

Cast a Dark Shadow 1955 Bogarde is the charmer who decides to reap his reward by marrying and murdering elderly women for their fortunes. But Bogarde meets his match when he plots against his latest intended (Lockwood). Tidy thriller with effective performances. Based on the play "Murder Mistaken" by Janet Green. 82m/B VHS, DVD. GB Dirk Bogarde, Margaret Lockwood, Mona Washbourne, Kay Walsh, Kathleen Harrison, Robert Flemyng, Walter Hudd; D: Lewis Gilbert; W: John Cresswell.

Cast a Deadly Spell 1991 (R) A bubbly, flavorful witch's brew of private-eye and horror cliches, set in a fantasy version of 1948 Los Angeles where sorcery and voodoo abound, but gumshoe Harry P. Lovecraft uses street smarts instead of magic to track down a stolen Necronomicon—and if you know what that is you'll want to watch. Wild creatures and f/x wizardry complement this cabler-TV trick and treat. **93m/C VHS.** *D:* Fred Ward, David Warner, Julianne Moore, Clancy Brown, Alexandra Powers; *D:* Martin Campbell; *W:* Joseph Dougherty, Dave Edison. **CABLE**

Cast a Giant Shadow 🐾🐾 1966 Follows the career of Col. David "Mickey" Marcus, an American Jew and WWII hero who helped turn Israel's army into a formidable fighting force during the 1947-48 struggle for independence. **138m/C VHS, DVD.** Kirk Douglas, Senta Berger, Angie Dickinson, John Wayne, James Donald, Chaim Topol, Frank Sinatra, Yul Brynner; *D:* Melville Shavelson; *C:* Aldo Tonti; *M:* Elmer Bernstein.

The Castle 🐾🐾 1997 (R) The Kerrigans are a working class clan who happily live directly adjacent to Melbourne's Tullamarine airport. But when the airport decides to expand, their house is subject to a compulsory acquisition order. However, Daryl Kerrigan (Caton) decides to fight back and takes their case all the way to the High Court in Canberra. It's a David vs. Goliath comedy with an Aussie disdain for authority figures. Cultural references may not travel overseas but the film was a hit on its home turf. **93m/C VHS, DVD, AU** Michael Caton, Charles "Bud" Tingwell, Sophie Lee, Anne Tenney, Eric Bana, Stephen Curry, Anthony Simcoe, Wayne Hope, Tiriel Mora; *D:* Rob Sitch; *W:* Rob Sitch, Santo Cilauro, Tom Gleisner, Jane Kennedy; *C:* Miriana Marusic; *M:* Craig Harnath. Australian Film Inst. '97. Orig. Screenplay.

Cast Away 🐾🐾½ 2000 (PG-13) Hanks first gained, and then lost, 40 pounds for his role as FedEx employee Chuck Noland, who gets marooned on a South Pacific island for four years. He does an excellent job of showing Chuck's desperation, isolation, and finally, resignation, and for a good chunk of the movie, does it without saying a single word (although later he makes a "pal" to a volleyball named Wilson). Zemeckis does his part with amazing visuals a nd a restrained approach to the score, which he uses sparingly. **143m/C VHS, DVD, Blu-ray, Disc.** Tom Hanks, Helen Hunt, Nick Searcy, Michael Forest, Viveka Davis, Christopher Noth, Geoffrey Blake, Jenifer Lewis, David Allan Brooks, Nan Martin, Steve Monroe; *D:* Robert Zemeckis; *W:* William Broyles Jr.; *C:* Don Burgess; *M:* Alan Silvestri.

Castaway 🐾🐾 1987 (R) Based on the factual account by Lucy Irvine. The story of Michael Wilmington, who placed an ad for a young woman to spend a year on a Pacific atoll with him, and the battle of the sexes that followed. **118m/C VHS, GB** Oliver Reed, Amanda Donohoe, Tony Rickards, Georgina Hale, Frances Barber, Todd Rippon; *D:* Nicolas Roeg; *W:* Allan Scott; *M:* Stanley Myers.

The Castaway Cowboy 🐾🐾 1974 (G) Shanghaied Texas cowboy Lincoln Constan (Garner) jumps ship in Hawaii and becomes partners with widowed Henrietta MacAvoy (Miles) when she turns her potato farm into a cattle ranch. That means turning the islanders into cowpokes and dealing with both a loca witch doctor and Henrietta's suitor. **91m/C VHS, DVD.** James Garner, Robert Culp, Vera Miles; *D:* Vincent McEveety; *M:* Robert F. Brunner.

The Castilian 🐾½ *Valley of the Swords* 1963 Some very odd casting in this historical tale of heroism and swordplay about a Spanish nobleman who leads his followers against the invading Moors and their evil King (Crawford). Based on a 13th century poem. **128m/C VHS.** Cesar Romero, Broderick Crawford, Alida Valli, Frankie Avalon, Espartaco (Spartaco) Santoni, Fernando Rey, Jorge (George) Rigaud; *D:* Javier Seto; *W:* W. Pink.

The Castle 🐾🐾🐾 *Das Schloss* 1968 A man is summoned by the seemingly-invisible occupants of a castle to their village. All his efforts to meet with those inhabiting the castle are futile and the task gradually becomes his obsession. Both wonderfully acted and shot, this is a well-executed adaptation of Franz Kafka's novel. **90m/C VHS, GE** S/ Maximilian Schell, Cordula T antow, Trudik Daniel, Helmut Qualtinger; *D:* Rudolf Noelte.

Cast the First Stone 🐾🐾 1989 Made for TV soaper based on the true story of a former nun who becomes a small town schoolteacher. After being raped, Diane Martin discovers she's pregnant and when she decides to keep the baby the school board dismisses her. The plot centers around her fight to regain her job and dignity—while trying to convince everybody that she doesn't deserve to lose her job simply because she doesn't deserve it. Eikenberry gives a strong performance, but it can't carry this lackluster film. **94m/C VHS, jill Eikenberry, Richard Masur, Joe Spano, Lew Ayres, Holly Palance; *D:* John Korty; *M:* Ira Newborn. **TV**

Castle of Blood 🐾🐾 *Castle of Terror; Coffin of Terror; Danza Macabra; Dimensions in Death; Terrore* 1964 Staying overnight in a haunted castle, a poet is forced to deal with a number of creepy encounters. Cult favorite Steele enhances this atmospheric chiller. Dubbed in English. **85m/B VHS, DVD.** *IT FR* Barbara Steele, George Riviere, Margrete Robsahm, Henry Kruger, Silvano Tranquilli, Sylvia Sorente; *D:* Anthony M. Dawson; *W:* Jean (Giovanni Grimaldi) Grimaud; *C:* Riccardo (Pallini) Pallottini; *M:* Riz Ortolani.

Castle of Cagliostro 🐾🐾 1980 Animated Japanese adventure tale featuring a hero named Wolf, who's a thief. Wolf infiltrates the suspicious country of Cagliostro, whose one industry is counterfeiting money, and winds up rescuing a princess. Lots of violence to go with some fun. In Japanese with English subtitles. **100m/C VHS, DVD, JP D:** Hayao Miyazaki; *V:* David Hayter, Bridget Hoffman, Dorothy Elias-Fahn. Kirk Thornton.

The Castle of Evil WOOF! 1966 Group of heirs gathers on a deserted isle to hear the reading of the will of your basic mad scientist. One by one, they fall victim to a humanoid created by the loony doc in his own image. Inspired moments of unintentional fun. **81m/C VHS.** Scott Brady, Virginia Mayo, Lisa Gaye, David Brian, Hugh Marlowe, William Thourby, Shelley Morrison; *D:* Francis D. Lyon.

The Castle of Fu Manchu 🐾 *Assignment: Istanbul; Die Folterkammer des Dr. Fu Manchu* 1968 (PG) The final chapter in a series starring Lee as the wicked doctor. This time, Lee has developed a gadget which will put the earth into a deep freeze, and at his mercy. To fine tune this con-

Castle Freak 🐾🐾 1995 (R) Italian countess leaves her creepy haunted castle to her American nephew and his family. They find an unwelcome surprise lurking in the cellar. **96m/C VHS, DVD.** Jeffrey Combs, Barbara Crampton, Jonathan Fuller, Jessica Dollarhide; *D:* Stuart Gordon; *W:* Dennis Paoli; *C:* Mario Vulpiani; *M:* Richard Band.

Castle in the Desert 🐾🐾½ 1942 Charlie Chan investigates murder and other strange goings-on in a spooky old castle. One of the last in the series. **62m/B VHS.** Sidney Toler, Arleen Whelan, Richard Derr, Douglass Dumbrille, Henry Daniel, Victor Sen Yung; *D:* Harry Lachman.

Castle Keep 🐾🐾🐾 1969 One of the most bizarre war films ever made. Eight battle-weary American soldiers, led by a randy one-eyed major (Lancaster), make a defiant last stand in a fairytale medieval castle against the German assault on the Ardennes in WWII. Loopy surreal and parable pushes past every boundary of good taste and makes it as enjoyable to the end. Full of great memorable characters and silly over-the-top moments that almost always work, such as an incompetent count (Aumont) pimping out his wife to German and American alike to keep the dynasty going, and a soldier (Falk) who takes over the local village bakery, waxing poetically about the superiority of bread to war. The whole film is absurdly done up in full sixties regalia and topped off with a loungy camp treasure. A forgotten Michel Legrand soundtrack. **105m/C VHS, DVD.** Burt Lancaster, Patrick O'Neal, Jean-Pierre Aumont, Peter Falk, Astrid Heeren, Scott Wilson, Tony Bill, Bruce Dern, Al Freeman Jr., James Patterson, Michael Conrad, Caterina Boratto, Olga Bisera, Harry Baird, Ernest Clark; *D:* Sydney Pollack; *W:* Daniel Taradash; *C:* Henri Decae; *M:* Michel Legrand.

Casualties 🐾🐾 1997 (R) Annie's (Goodall) got very unfortunate luck with men. Her abusive husband Bill's (Gries) a cop and she can't safely get away from home. Then she meets a seemingly nice guy, Tommy (Harmon), at her cooking class, who offers to help Annie out. But when Tommy's behavior becomes erratic (turns out he's a hitman), Annie figures she just has to rely on herself. **88m/C VHS, DVD.** Caroline Goodall, Michael Beach, Mark Harmon, Caroline Goodall; *W:* Jonathan) Gries, John Diehl; *D:* Alex Graves; *W:* Alex Graves.

Casualties of Love: The "Long Island Lolita" Story 🐾🐾 1993 (PG-13) Told from the Buttafuoco's point of view. Amy Fisher was nothing but a wacko fatally attracted teenager who misunderstood Joey's harmless flirtations and deliberately went after his wife with a gun. The Buttafuocos received $300,000 from CBS to tell their side of the story which features Milano, who resembles Army not in the least, as the lead. One of three competing network TV versions of the sordid story. See also: "The Amy Fisher Story" and "Lethal Lolita—Amy Fisher: My Story." **94m/C VHS.** Jack Scalia, Alyssa Milano, Phyllis Lyons, Jack Kehler, Michael Bowen, J.E. Freeman, Nicky) Corello, Lawrence Tierney, Peter Van Norden, Anne DeSalvo, Leo Rossi; *D:* John Herzfeld; *M:* Michael Herzfeld, *C:* Karl Walter Lindenlaub; *M:* David Michael Frank. **TV**

Casualties of War 🐾🐾🐾 1989 (R) A Vietnam war morality play about army private Fox's in the bush who refuses to let his fellow soldiers and commanding sergeant (Penn) skirt responsibility for the rape and murder of a native woman Fox achieves his dramatic breakthrough. Based on the true story by Daniel Lang. **120m/C VHS, DVD.** Sean Penn, Michael J. Fox, Don Harvey, Thuy Thu Le, John Leguizamo, Sam Robards, John C. Reilly, Erik King, Dale Dye; *D:* Brian De Palma; *W:* David Rabe; *C:* Stephen Burum; *M:* Ennio Morricone.

Castle of the Creeping Flesh WOOF! 1968 A surgeon's daughter is brutally murdered. Vowing to bring her back he begins ripping out the organs of innocent people and transplanting them into her body. Has the dubious honor of being one of the few movies to sport actual open heart surgery footage. So bad it's...just bad. **85m/C VHS.** Adrian Hoven, Janine Reynaud, Howard Vernon; *D:* Percy G. Parker.

Castle of the Living Dead 🐾🐾 *Il Castello de Morti Vivi* 1964 Evil Count Drago's hobbies include mummifying a traveling circus group visiting his castle. Lee is as evil as ever, but be sure to look for Sutherland's screen debut. In a dual role, he plays a witch, in drag. **90m/B VHS, DVD.** *IT FR* Christopher Lee, Gaia Germani, Philippe LeRoy, Jacques Stanislawsky, Donald Sutherland; *D:* Herbert Wise.

Casual Sex? 🐾½ 1988 (R) Two young women, looking for love and commitment, take a vacation at a posh resort where they are confronted by men with nothing or their minds but sex, be it casual or the more formal black-tie variety. Supposedly an examination of safe sex in a lightly comedic vein, though the comic is too light and the morality too limp. Adapted from the play by Wendy Goldman and Judy Toll. **87m/C VHS, DVD.** Lea Thompson, Victoria Jackson, Stephen Shellen, Jerry Levine, Mary Gross, Andrew (Dice Clay) Silverstein; *W:* William Goldman, Judy Toll; *C:* Rolf Kestermann; *M:* Van Dyke Parks.

Castle of the Creeping Flesh — *see above*

Cat and Mouse 🐾🐾½ 1990 *Le Chat et la Souris* (R) Made-for-TV adaptation of Frederick Forsyth's thriller about modern-day arms smuggling (Libya to Ireland) and espionage. Well-acted, with the exception of Hack. **96m/C VHS.** Sreley Hack, David Threlfall, Richard Hope, Alan Howard, Clarke Peters; *D:* Tom Clegg; *W:* Frederick Forsyth.

The Cat 🐾 1966 A boy and a tamed mountain lion become friends on the run from a murderous poacher. **95m/C VHS.** Peggy Ann Garner, Roger Perry, Barry Coe; *D:* Ellis Kadison.

The Cat and the Canary 🐾🐾 1927 A group of greedy relatives gather on a stormy night to hear the reading of a will. A very unorthodox police inspector is assigned to investigate a millionaire's mysterious death. Who done it? French dialogue with English subtitles. **107m/C VHS, FR** Michele Morgan, Serge Reggiani, Jean-Pierre Aumont, Philippe Leotard, Valerie Lagrange, Michel Perelon, Chris tine Laurent; *D:* Claude Lelouch; *W:* Claude Leiouch; *C:* Andre Perisfelr; *M:* Francis Lai.

The Cat and the Canary 🐾🐾½ 1927 A group of greedy relatives gather on a stormy night to hear the reading of a will. A very unorthodox police inspector is assigned to investigate a millionaire's mysterious death. Who done it? **96m/C VHS, DVD, GB** Carol Lynley, Michael Callan, Wendy Hiller, Olivia Hussey, Daniel Massey, Honor Blackman, Edward Fox, Wilfrid Hyde-White, Beatrix Lehmann, Peter McEnery; *D:* Radley Metzger; *W:* Radley Metzger; *C:* Alex Thomson.

The Cat and the Fiddle 🐾🐾🐾 1934 Lovely Jerome Kern-Oscar Hammerstein operetta in which Novarro plays a struggling composer who forces his affections on MacDonald. She sings in response to his romantic proposals. The film sequence is in color. 🐾 The Night Was Made for Love; She Didn't Say 'Yes'; A New Love is Old; Try to Forget; One Moment Alone; Don't Ask Us Not To Sing; I Watch the Love Parade; The Breeze Kissed Your Hair; Impressions in a Harlem Flat. **90m/B VHS.** Ramon Novarro, Jeanette MacDonald, Frank Morgan, Charles Butterworth, Jean Hersholt, Vivienne Segal, Frank Conroy, Henry Armetta, Adrienne D'Ambricourt, Joseph Cawthorn; *D:* William K. Howard; *W:* Bella Spewack, Samuel Spewack, Jerome Kern; *C:* Charles Clarke, Ray Rennahan, Harold Rosson; *M:* Herbert Stothart, Jerome Kern.

Cat Ballou 🐾🐾🐾½ 1965 At the turn of the century, a schoolmarm turns outlaw with the help of a drunken gunman. Marvin played Kid Shelleen and his silver-nosed evil twin Tim Strawn in this cheery spoof of westerns. Cole and Kaye sing the narration in a one of a kind Greek chorus. **96m/C VHS, DVD.** Jane Fonda, Lee Marvin, Michael Callan, Dwayne Hickman, Reginald Denny, Nat King Cole, Stubby Kaye, Robert Phillips; *D:* Elliot Silverstein; *W:* Frank Pierson; *C:* Jack Marta; *M:* Frank DeVol. Oscars '65: Actor (Marvin); Berlin Intl. Film Fest. '65: Actor (Marvin); British Acad. '65: Actor (Marvin); Golden Globes '66: Actor (Marvin); Natl. Bd. of Review '65: Actor (Marvin).

Cat Chaser 🐾🐾 1990 Weller walks listlessly through the role of an ex-soldier in Miami who has an affair with the wife of an exiled—but still lethal—military dictator. Surprisingly low-key, sometimes effective thriller that saves its energy for sex scenes, also available in a less steamy, 90-minute "R" rated version. Based on an Elmore Leonard novel. **97m/C VHS, DVD.** Kelly McGillis, Peter Weller, Charles Durning, Frederic Forrest, Tomas Milian, Juan Fernandez; *D:* Abel Ferrara; *W:* Elmore Leonard; *M:* Chick Corea.

The Cat from Outer Space 🐾🐾 1973 (G) An extraterrestrial cat named Jake crashes his spaceship on Earth and leads a group of people on

A Casualty of War 🐾🐾½ 1990 *Le Chat...*

Cat and Mouse 🐾🐾½ 1990

endless escapades. Enjoyable Disney fare. **103m/C VHS, DVD.** Ken Berry, Sandy Duncan, Harry (Henry) Morgan, Roddy McDowall, McLean Stevenson; **D:** Norman Tokar; **W:** Ted Key; **C:** Charles F. Wheeler; **M:** Lalo Schifrin.

Cat Girl 𝒲 1957 A young bride on her honeymoon finds she has inherited the family curse—she has a psychic link to a ferocious leopard. Numerous murders ensue. Poor production value and a weak script, despite Shelley's fine acting, add up to an unworthy film. **69m/B VHS.** Barbara Shelley, Robert Ayres, Kay Callard, Paddy Webster, Ernest Milton; **D:** Alfred Shaughnessy; **W:** Lou Rusoff; **C:** Peter Hennessy.

Cat in the Cage 𝒲1/2 1968 A young man finds many things have changed when he was in a mental institution. Dad has remarried, the housekeeper is practicing witchcraft, the chauffeur is after his mistress, and the cat is gone. So where'd that cat go? **96m/C VHS, DVD.** Colleen Camp, Sybil Danning, Mel Novak, Frank De Kova; **D:** Tony Zarin Dast.

The Cat o' Nine Tails 𝒲 1971 (PG) A blind detective and a newsman team up to find a sadistic killer. A gory murder mystery. **112m/C VHS, DVD. GE FR IT** Karl Malden, James Franciscus, Catherine Spaak, Cinzia de Carolis, Carlo Alighiero; **D:** Dario Argento; **C:** Erico Menczer; **M:** Ennio Morricone.

Cat on a Hot Tin Roof 𝒲𝒲1/2 1958 Tennessee Williams' powerful play about greed and deception in a patriarchal Southern family. Big Daddy (Ives) is dying. Members of the family greedily attempt to capture his inheritance, tearing the family apart. Taylor is a sensual wonder as Maggie the Cat, though the more controversial elements of the play were toned down for the film version. Intense, believable performances from Ives and Newman. **108m/C VHS, DVD.** Paul Newman, Burl Ives, Elizabeth Taylor, Jack Carson, Judith Anderson; **D:** Richard Brooks; **W:** Richard Brooks, James Poe; **C:** William H. Daniels.

Cat on a Hot Tin Roof 𝒲𝒲1/2 1984 Showtime/PBS co-production of the Tennessee Williams classic about alcoholic ex-jock Brick (Jones) and his sultry wife Maggie (Lange) and their desires. This version uses a script revised by Williams to revive some of the sexual frankness watered down in other productions. **122m/C VHS, DVD.** Tommy Lee Jones, Jessica Lange, Rip Tom, Kim Stanley, David Dukes, Penny Fuller; **D:** Jack Hofsiss; **W:** Tennessee Williams. TV

Cat People 𝒲𝒲𝒲 1942 Irena (Simon) is an immigrant from the Balkans who believes in a curse that will change her into a deadly panther who must kill to survive. So she won't consummate her marriage to Oliver (Smith). When he confides her troubles to co-worker Alice (Randolph), Irena's jealousy precipitates her transformation as she stalks Alice. A classic among the horror genre with unrelenting terror from beginning to end, especially since the metamorphosis only suggested. First horror film from RKO producer Val Lewton. **73m/B VHS, DVD.** Simone Simon, Kent Smith, Jane Randolph, Jack Holt, Elizabeth Russell, Alan Napier, Tom Conway; **D:** Jacques Tourneur; **W:** DeWitt Bodeen; **C:** Nicholas Musuraca; **M:** Roy Webb. Natl. Film Reg. '93. TV

Cat People 𝒲𝒲1/2 1982 (R) A beautiful young woman learns that she has inherited a strange family trait—she turns into a vicious panther when sexually aroused. The only person with whom she can safely mate is her brother, a victim of the same genetic heritage. Kinski is mesmerizing as the innocent, sensual woman. Remake of the 1942 film. **118m/C VHS, DVD, HD DVD.** Nastassja Kinski, Malcolm McDowell, John Heard, Annette O'Toole, Ruby Dee, Ed Begley Jr., John Larroquette; **D:** Paul Schrader; **W:** Alan Ormsby; **C:** John Bailey; **M:** Giorgio Moroder.

Cat Women of the Moon 𝒲𝒲 1953 Scientists land on the moon and encounter an Amazon-like force of skimpily attired female chauvinists. Remade as "Missile to the Moon." Featuring the Hollywood Cover Girls as various cat women. Available in its original 3-D format. **65m/B VHS, DVD.** Sonny Tufts, Victor Jory, Marie Windsor, Bill Phipps, Douglas Fowley, Carol Brewster, Suzanne Alexander, Susan Morrow, Ellye Marshall, Bette Arlen, Judy W. Roxann Delman; **D:** Arthur Hilton; **W:** Roy Hamilton; **C:** William F. Whitley; **M:** Elmer Bernstein.

Cataclysm 𝒲𝒲1/2 *Satan's Supper* 1981 (R) A swell flick about a sadistic demon who spends his time either finding people willing to join him or killing the people who won't. **94m/C VHS, DVD.** Cameron Mitchell, Marc Lawrence, Faith Clift, Charles Moll; **D:** Tom McGowan, Gregg Tallas, Philip Marshak.

Catacombs 𝒲 1989 (R) An investigative monk and a beautiful photographer stumble across a mysterious, centuries-old evil power. **112m/C VHS.** Timothy Van Patten, Laura Schaefer, Ian Abercrombie, Jeremy West; **D:** David Schmoeller; **W:** C. Courtney Joyner; **M:** Pino Donaggio.

Catacombs 𝒲 2007 The running and screaming turns out to be remarkably boring. Nervous Victoria (Sossamon) heads to Paris to visit her naughty sister Caroline (Moore) who insists on taking her to a secret rave held in the catacombs, the limestone tunnels that run for miles under the city and that house the bones of the dead. Carolyn's friends scare Victoria with a legend about a satanic cult and a flesh-eating beast and when she's convinced something is stalking her. **92m/C DVD.** Shannyn Sossamon, Alicia Moore, Emil Hostina, Mihai Stanescu, Sandi Dragoi, Cabral Ibacka, Cain Manoli; **D:** Tomm Coker; **M:** Yoshiki Hayashi. VIDEO

The Catamount Killing 𝒲1/2 1974 (PG) The story of a small town bank manager and his lover. They decide to rob the bank and run for greener pastures only to find their escape befuddled at every turn. **82m/C VHS. GE** Horst Buchholz, Ann Wedgeworth; **D:** Krzysztof Zanussi.

Catch a Fire 𝒲𝒲1/2 2006 (PG-13) Fierce political drama centering on the Apartheid-era terrorism in South Africa during the early '80s. Patrick Chamusso (Luke) is an unassuming oil refinery foreman wrongly accused, imprisoned, and tortured for a plant bombing. The injustice transforms the apolitical worker into a radicalized insurgent, who then carries out his own successful sabotage mission. Robbins plays the Security Branch Colonel on Chamusso's case. A decent script and good performances, but the dated material lacks a sense of urgency and importance. **101m/C DVD, US GB SA** Derek Luke, Tim Robbins, Bonnie Henna, Mncedisi Shabangu, Malcolm Purkey, Phillip Noyce; **W:** Shawn Slovo; **C:** Ron Fortunato, Garry Phillips; **M:** Philip Miller.

Catch and Release 𝒲 2007 (PG-13) Kevin Smith is cuddly. But fortunately, he's not the rebound romance for the ever-appealing Garner because that would really make heads spin. Garner plays Gray, a one-of-the-guys kinda gal whose fiance Grady died before the wedding. Crushed, Gray (who seems to have no family or girlfriends) becomes roomies with his buds Sam (Smith) and Dennis (Jaeger), who was also Grady's partner in a fly-fishing venture. Frisky Fritz (Olyphant), will eventually console Gray, who finds out some secrets about Grady that involve a ditzy single mom, played too weirdly by Lewis. Grant's directorial debut veers uncertainly between tragedy and comedy. **110m/C DVD, Blu-ray Disc. US** Jennifer Garner, Timothy Olyphant, Kevin Smith, Juliette Lewis, Sam Jaeger, Fiona Shaw, Joshua Friesen; **D:** Susannah Grant; **W:** Susannah Grant; **C:** John Lindley; **M:** BT (Brian Transeau), Tommy Stinson.

Catch as Catch Can 𝒲 *Lo Scatenato* 1968 An Italian male model is comically besieged by animals of every type, making a mess of his life and career. Dubbed. **95m/C VHS. IT** Vittorio Gassman, Martha Hyer, Gila Golan; **D:** Franco Indovina; **M:** Luis Bacalov.

Catch Me a Spy 𝒲1/2 *To Catch a Spy* 1971 A foreign agent attempts to lure an innocent man into becoming part of a swap for an imprisoned Russian spy. **94m/C VHS, DVD. GB FR** Kirk Douglas, Tom Courtenay, Trevor Howard, Marlene Jobert, Bernard Blier, Patrick Mower, Bernadette LaFont; **D:** Dick Clement; **W:** Dick Clement, Ian La Frenais; **M:** Claude Bolling.

Catch Me... If You Can 𝒲𝒲 1989 (PG) High school class president Melissa doesn't want to see the school torn down. To raise fast cash, she teams up with a drag racer and the fun begins. **105m/C VHS.** Matt Lattanzi, Loryn Locklin, M. Emmet Walsh, Geoffrey Lewis; **D:** Stephen Sommers.

Catch Me If You Can 𝒲𝒲1/2 2002 (PG-13) Spielberg's lightweight, entertaining, but overly lengthy flick follows the exploits of Frank Abagnale Jr. (DiCaprio) who, starting at age 16, eluded the FBI (in the person of Carl Hanratty, played by Hanks) while passing bad checks in the guise of airline pilot, doctor, lawyer, and college professor in the early 60s. Frank's journey starts when his perfect suburban life is turned upside-down by the divorce of his parents and his dad's (Walken) troubles with the IRS. DiCaprio is chameleon-like in his portrayal of Frank, as befits the role, but takes it further by looking every age he's supposed to be. Hanks make the most of what could've been a thankless role as Frank's workaholic pursuer/father figure, but Walken stands out as the broken father who, with more chutzpah and luck, might've been what Junior became. Based on the real Frank Abagnale, Jr's memoirs. **140m/C VHS, DVD. US** Leonardo DiCaprio, Tom Hanks, Christopher Walken, Nathalie Baye, Martin Sheen, Amy Adams, James Brolin, Jennifer Garner, Frank John Hughes, Steve Eastin, Chris Ellis, John Finn, Brian Howe; **D:** Steven Spielberg; **W:** Jeff Nathanson; **C:** Janusz Kaminski; **M:** John Williams. British Acad. '02: Support. Actor (Walken); Natl. Soc. Film Critics '02: Support. Actor (Walken); Screen Actors Guild '02: Support. Actor (Walken).

Catch That Kid 𝒲𝒲 2004 (PG) One part kid caper to one part heist movie, equals a real klunky movie. Maddy (Stewart), a 12-year-old adventurous (and apparently morally flexible) tomboy, decides to pull off a $250,000 bank robbery so the family can afford an operation for her father (Robards), who is paralyzed. The worst crime here is the lackluster writing and uninspired direction. Adapted from the Danish film "Klatretosen." **92m/C VHS, DVD. US** Kristen Stewart, Corbin Bleu, Max Thieriot, Jennifer Beals, Sam Robards, John Carroll Lynch, James LeGros, Michael Des Barres, Kevin G. Schmidt, Stark Sands, Grant Hayden Scott, Shane Avery Scott; **D:** Bart Freundlich; **W:** Michael Brandt, Derek Haas; **C:** Julio Macat; **M:** George S. Clinton.

Catch the Heat 𝒲 *Feel the Heat* 1987 (R) Alexandra is an undercover narcotics agent sent to infiltrate Steiger's South American drug operation. **90m/C VHS, DVD.** Tiana Alexandra, David Dukes, Rod Steiger; **D:** Joel Silberg; **W:** Stirling Silliphant; **M:** Tom Chase, Steve Rucker.

Catch-22 𝒲𝒲𝒲 1970 (R) Buck Henry's adaptation of Joseph Heller's black comedy about a group of fliers in the Mediterranean during WWII. A biting anti-war satire portraying the insanity of the situation in both a humorous and disturbing manner. Perhaps too literal to structure, causing occasional problems in the "are you following along department?" Arkin heads a fine and colorful cast. **121m/C VHS, DVD.** Alan Arkin, Martin Balsam, Art Garfunkel, Jon Voight, Richard Benjamin, Buck Henry, Bob Newhart, Paula Prentiss, Martin Sheen, Charles Grodin, Anthony Perkins, Orson Welles, Jack Gilford, Bob Balaban, Susanne Benton, Norman Fell, Austin Pendleton, Peter Bonerz, Jon Korkes, Collin Wilcox-Paxton, John Brent; **D:** Mike Nichols; **W:** Buck Henry; **C:** David Watkin.

The Catcher 𝒲1/2 1998 After being released from an insane asylum, a man returns to the ballfield where he murdered his father and begins hanging around the minor-league stadium in order to finish off various players and managers. **90m/C VHS.** David Dillenger; **M:** Monique Parent, Joe Estevez, Sean Dillinger; **D:** Guy Crawford, Yvette Hoffman. VIDEO

Category 7 : The End of the World 𝒲1/2 2005 Delightfully inept disaster pic finds FEMA head Judith Carr (sexy Gershon) trying to pinpoint the cause of deadly weather that's causing worldwide havoc. She turns to ex-beau and discredited scientist Ross (Daddo) for answers while fighting the bureaucrats. Meanwhile, scientist Faith (Doherty) teams up with Tornado Tommy (Quaid) to track the storms up close and personal. The subplots are especially lame, although Brolin as an evangelist is a hoot. **169m/C DVD. US** Gina Gershon, Cameron Daddo, Shannen Doherty, Randy Quaid, James Brolin, Swoosie Kurtz, Robert Wagner, Sebastian Spence, Nicholas Lea, Tom Skerritt; **D:** Dick Lowry; **W:** Christian Ford, Roger Soffer; **C:** Neil Roach; **M:** Joseph Williams. TV

Category 6 : Day of Destruction 𝒲𝒲𝒲 2004 Amusingly cheesy disaster flick with lots of predictable subplots and bad CGI. Hackers shut down the Chicago power company's computers during a heatwave, just as a super tornado is heading to that toddlin' town to make one major headache for all involved. Followed by "Category 7: The End of the World." **174m/C DVD.** Thomas Gibson, Nancy McKeon, Chandra West, Brian Markinson, Nancy Sakovich, Randy Quaid, Dianne Wiest, Brian Dennehy, Andrew Jackson, Christopher Shyer, Ari Cohen; **D:** Dick Lowry; **W:** Matt Dorff; **C:** Neil Roach; **M:** Jeff Rona, Joseph Williams. TV

The Catered Affair 𝒲𝒲𝒲 *Wedding Breakfast* 1956 Davis, anti-typecast as a Bronx housewife, and Borgnine, as her taxi-driving husband, play the determined parents of soon-to-be-wed Reynolds set on giving her away in a style to which she is not accustomed. Based on Paddy Chayefsky's teleplay, the catered affair turns into a familial trial, sharing the true-to-life poignancy that marked "Marty," the Oscar-winning Chayefsky drama of the previous year. **92m/B VHS.** Bette Davis, Ernest Borgnine, Debbie Reynolds, Barry Fitzgerald, Rod Taylor, Robert F. Simon; **D:** Richard Brooks; **W:** Gore Vidal; **C:** John Alton; **M:** Andre Previn.

Caterina in the Big City 𝒲𝒲 *Caterina va in citta* 2003 Caterina (Teghil) is a small town teenager who experiences a nasty case of culture shock when her family moves to Rome. Frustrated, ambitious school teacher dad Giancarlo (Castellitto) is glad to be out of the sticks and back to the big city but Caterina is soon pulled between two high school cliques—lead by rebellious bohemian Margherita (Iaquaniello) and spoiled debutante Daniela (Sbrenna). Meant to be seen (in a cynical comedic way) as a microcosm of Italian society with the middle-class caught between the strident, communist left and the elitist, conservative right. Italian with subtitles. **106m/C DVD. IT** Alice Teghil, Sergio Castellitto, Margherita Buy, Carolina Iaquaniello, Federica Sbrenna, Claudio Amendola; **D:** Paolo Virzi; **W:** Paolo Virzi, Francesco Bruni; **C:** Arnaldo Catinari; **M:** Paolo Virzi.

Catfish in Black Bean Sauce 𝒲𝒲1/2 2000 (PG-13) While serving in Vietnam, African-American Harold Williams (Winfield) saved the lives of Vietnamese Mai (Tom) and her young brother Dwayne (Lo) and he and wife Dolores (Alice) adopted the duo. Dwayne acts black and has a black girlfriend, Nina (Lathan), but married Mai has never forgotten her roots and announces to the stunned family that she has located her birth mother, Thanh (Chinh), and the woman is coming not only to visit but to live with her. But Thanh turns out to be a critical schemer, unreasonably jealous of the Williams', and determined to reclaim her grown children, no matter what the cost. **111m/C VHS, DVD.** Chi Muoi Lo, Lauren Tom, Kieu Chinh, Paul Winfield, Mary Alice, Sanaa Lathan, Tzi Ma, Tyler Christopher; **D:** Chi Muoi Lo; **W:** Chi Muoi Lo; **C:** Dean Lent; **M:** Stanley A. Smith.

Catherine & Co. 𝒲1/2 1976 (R) Lonely, penniless girl arrives in Paris and "opens shop" on the streets of Paris. As business booms, she takes a cue from the big corporations and sells stock in herself. **91m/C VHS. FR IT** Jane Birkin, Patrick Dewaere, Jean-Pierre Aumont, Jean-Claude Brialy; **D:** Michel Boisrond.

Catherine Cookson's Colour Blind 𝒲𝒲1/2 *Colour Blind* 1998 In post-WWI England, Bridget McQueen comes to stay with her sprawling, poor family with

Catherine Cookson's The Black Candle 🐾🐾½ 1952 Mill owner is caught up in a murder case that involves the father of her child, her husband (not the same guy), her husband's brother, and many aristocratic machinations. Well-done story boasts an excellent cast. Based on the novel by Catherine Cookson; made for British TV. 103m/C VHS, DVD. *GB* Nathanie Parker, James Gaddas, Bob Smeaton, Brian Hogg, Cathy Sandford, Samantha Bond, Tara Fitzgerald, Denholm Elliott; *D:* Roy Battersby; *W:* Gordon Hann; *C:* Ken Morgar; *M:* Dominic Muldowney. TV

Catherine Cookson's The Black Velvet Gown 🐾🐾½ 1992 *The Black Velvet Gown.* Rlah Millican (McTeer) is a poor miner's widow living in rural 1834 England with her three children. She finds work as a housekeeper in the reclusive Miller (Peck), who agrees to educate her children and even gives Rlah the titular gown, which was once hers. Now educated out of their working-er's. The Millican's lives provide unexpected love and tragedy for all concerned. Based on the novel by Catherine Cookson; made for British TV. 103m/C VHS, DVD. *GB* Janet McTeer, Bob Peck, Geraldine Somerville; *D:* Norman Stone; *W:* Alan Seymour; *M:* Carl Davis. TV

Catherine Cookson's The Cinder Path 🐾🐾½ 1994 Coming-of-age story begins in 1913 with unassuring Charlie MacFell (Owen) forced to take over the family farm. Charlie (who needs a spine transplant) also goes along with an arranged marriage to local lovely Victoria (Zeta-Jones), a disaster since she's little more than a well-bred tart and it's her younger sister Nellie (Miles) who's really in love with Charlie anyway. As if Charlie didn't have enough to cope with, he's soon an army soldier as WWI begins and up up against vindictive Ginger (Byrne), a former farmhand who resents the monied classes Charlie represents. Based on the novel by Catherine Cookson. 145m/C VHS, DVD. *GB* Lloyd Owen, Catherine Zeta-Jones, Maria Miles, Antony Byrne, Tom Bell; *D:* Simon Langton; *W:* Alan Seymour; *M:* Barrington Pheloung. TV

Catherine Cookson's The Dwelling Place 🐾🐾½ *The Dwelling Place* 1994 Sixteen-year-old Cissie (Whitwell) struggles to hold her family together after the death of their parents in 1830's England. But her situation turns tragic when she's raped and left pregnant but drunken young aristocrat Clive 'Rawle-Hicks), eventually giving the baby to be raised by Clive's father (Fox). Based on a novel by Catherine Cookson. 145m/C VHS, DVD. *GB* Gavin Miller, James Fox, Edward Rawle-Hicks; *D:* Gavin Millar; *W:* Gordon Hann; *C:* John Hooper; *M:* Colin Towns. TV

Catherine Cookson's The Fifteen Streets 🐾🐾½ *The Fifteen Streets* 1990 Kind-hearted dock worker John O'Brien (Teale) is the quiet one in a boozing, brawling Irish family living in near poverty in late-Victorian England. He meets well-bred schoolteacher Mary Llewellyn (Holman) and the two fall in love but bigotry, scandal, and tragedy challenge their chances at happiness. Based on a novel by Catherine Cookson. 108m/C VHS, DVD. *GB* Owen Teale, Clare Holman, Sean Bean, Billie Whitelaw, Ian Bannan, Jane Horrocks, Amy Tobin, Leslie Schofield; *D:* David Wheatley; *W:* Rob Betinson. *C:* Ken Morgan; *M:* Colin Towns. TV

Catherine Cookson's The Gambling Man 🐾🐾½ *The Gambling Man* 1998 Rent collector Rory O'Connor is ambitious to escape his humble past and his talent at gambling leads him to winning a fortune. But a lie and a tragedy return to haunt him. Based on a book by Catherine Cookson. 150m/C VHS

her new husband and their baby daughter. But Bridget has neglected to tell her family that her husband is black. This not only stirs up a lot of trouble but more tribulations follow as Bridget's mixed-race daughter grows up. On two cassettes. 150m/C VHS. *GB* Niamh Cusack, Carmen Ejogo, Art Malik, Tony Armatrading; *D:* Alan Grint; *W:* Gordon Hann. TV

Catherine Cookson's The Girl 🐾🐾½ *The Girl* 1996 Illegitimate Hannah Boyle is simply called "The Girl" by her jealous stepmother, who forces her into a disastrous marriage. But Hannah is willing to fight to regain her freedom and the man she truly loves. TV adaptation of the novel by Catherine Cookson. 150m/C VHS, DVD. *GB* Siobhan Flynn, Malcolm Stoddard, Jonathan Cake, Jill Baker, Mark Benton; *D:* David Wheatley; *W:* Gordon Hann; *C:* Doug Hallows; *M:* Colin Towns. TV

Catherine Cookson's The Glass Virgin 🐾🐾½ *The Glass Virgin* 1995 In 1859, young Annabella Lagrange (Mortimer) discovers on her spendthrift father, Edmund (Haver), has been hiding the secrets surrounding her birth. These revelations force Annabella to find her own way in a new life. Based on a novel by Catherine Cookson. 150m/C VHS, DVD. *GB* Emily Mortimer, Nigel Havers, Brendan Coyle, Christine Kavanagh, Sylvia Syms, Samantha Glenn, Jan Graveson; *D:* Sarah Hellings; *W:* Alan Seymour; *C:* Doug Hallows; *M:* Christopher Gunning. TV

Catherine Cookson's The Man Who Cried 🐾🐾½ *The Man Who Cried* 1993 Abel Mason (Hinds) is an unhappily married man with a vindictive wife (Walsh) and a young son he's desperate to provide for. When an affair with a married woman ends in murder, Mason and his son travel in search of a new life. Desperate for a home, Mason enters into a bigamous marriage with a widow—only to find himself falling in love with her sister. Based on the novel by Catherine Cookson. Set in the years between England's depression and WW2. 156m/C VHS, DVD. *GB* Ciaran Hinds, Amanda Root, Kate Buffery, Angela Walsh, Daniel Massey; *D:* Michael Whyte; *W:* Gordon Hann; *C:* Fred Tammes; *M:* Richard Hartley. TV

Catherine Cookson's The Moth 🐾🐾½ *The Moth* 1996 Robert Bradley leaves the shipyards to work in his uncle's furniture business but soon finds himself at odds with the old man. So he becomes a servant for the destructive Thormans, and falls for the lady of the house, Sarah. But in 1913 this upstairs/downstairs romance can only lead to disaster. TV movie based on the novel by Catherine Cookson. 150m/C VHS, DVD. *GB* Jack Davenport, Juliet Aubrey, David Bradley, Justine Waddell; *D:* Roy Battersby; *W:* Gordon Hann; *C:* Alec Mills; *M:* Colin Towns. TV

Catherine Cookson's The Rag Nymph 🐾🐾½ *The Rag Nymph* 1996 Aggie Winkowski finds 10-year-old Millie Forrester abandoned on the streets. Knowing how dangerous the child's life could become, Aggie decides to take Millie in. TV movie based on the novel by Catherine Cookson. 150m/C VHS, DVD. *GB* Honeysuckle Weeks, Val McLane, Percita Weeks, Barron, Jean Harvey, Ben Miles, Denis Lawson; *D:* Alan Grint; *W:* T.R. Bowen; *C:* Alec Mills; *M:* Colin Towns. TV

Catherine Cookson's The Round Tower 🐾🐾½ *The Round Tower* 1998 Post-WWII Britain finds 17-year-old Vanessa Radcliffe pregnant. Her wealthy, socially conscious parents are appalled, especially when they think the father is the son of their housekeeper, Angus Cotten. He's not but winds up marrying Vanessa anyway—this unlikely circumstance putting Angus on the road to success. 150m/C VHS. *GB* Emilia Fox, Keith McGann, Ian Richardson, Jeanne Moreau, Mark McGann, Hannes Jaenicke, Mel Ferrer, Omar Sharif, John Rhys-Davies, Brian Blessed; *D:* Marvin J. Chomsky; *W:* John Goldsmith; *C:* Elemer Ragalyi; *M:* Laurence Rosenthal. TV

Catherine's Grove 🐾🐾½ 1998 (R) Miami detective Jack Doyle (Fahey) is tracking down a serial killer while moonlighting as a P.I. Along with girlfriend Charley (Alonso), Jack's investigating the disappearance of rich girl Catherine, who may be involved with her creepy Uncle Joe (Madsen). So, do you think Doyle's two cases could possibly be connected? 91m/C VHS. Michael Madsen, Jeff Fahey, Maria Conchita Alonso, Priscilla Barnes, Jeffrey Donovan, Rick King; *W:* Tony DiTocco; *C:* Bart Tau; *M:* Harry Manfredini. VIDEO

Catholics 🐾🐾🐾 *The Conflict* 1973 A sensitive exploration of contemporary mores and changing attitudes within the Roman Catholic church. Anonymous letters, diamonds, and the like are involved. Stephen Moyer, Hannah Yelland, Clare Higgins; *D:* van Der Plicht has to work through secrets hidden in his own past as a runner and messenger for criminals. Anonymous letters, diamonds, and the like are involved. Based on the novel by Catherine Cookson. 156m/C VHS

Catherine the Great 🐾🐾½ 1934 Slow but lavish and engrossing British dramatization of the tortured and doomed love affair between Catherine, Empress of Russia, and her irrational, drunken husband Peter. 88m/B VHS, DVD. *GB* Douglas Fairbanks Jr., Elisabeth Bergner, Flora Robson; *D:* Paul Czinner; *C:* Georges Perinal.

Catherine the Great 🐾🐾½ 1995 Teenaged German princess Sophia (Zeta-Jones) marries into Russian royalty in 1744 when she weds Peter (Jaenicke), nephew of the Empress Elizabeth (Moreau), and has a name change when she's crowned Catherine II. The marriage is a disaster and with the help of her lover Gregory Orlov (McGann), Catherine eventually gets rid of Peter and is crowned Empress and Czarina of all the Russias as she struggles to drag her medieval empire into the modern world. Typically lavish and simplistic historical retelling. Originally released as a two-part miniseries. 100m/C VHS, DVD. *GB* Catherine Zeta-Jones, Paul McGann, Ian Richardson, Jeanne Moreau, Mark McGann, Hannes Jaenicke, Mel Ferrer, Omar Sharif, John Rhys-Davies, Brian Blessed; *D:* Marvin J. Chomsky; *W:* John Goldsmith; *C:* Elemer Ragalyi; *M:* Laurence Rosenthal. TV

Catherine Cookson's The Tide of Life 🐾 1996 TV adaptation of Catherine Cookson's novel finds young Emily Kennedy entering service as a maid to the McGilby family and weathering various tragedies, romantic and otherwise. 156m/C VHS, DVD. *GB* Gillian Kearney, Ray Stevenson, James Purefoy, Diana Hardcastle; *D:* David Wheatley; *W:* Gordon Hann; *C:* Doug Hallows; *M:* Colin Towns.

Catherine Cookson's The Wingless Bird 🐾🐾½ *The Wingless Bird* 1997 Agnes Conway (Skinner) is a strong-minded daughter of a Newcastle shop-owner in class-conscious England in December, 1913. Managing her unhappy father's store, Clare waits on two members of the wealthy Farrier family and is soon drawn into their lives when the younger Farrier son, Charles (Atterton), falls in love with her, despite their class differences. But the Conway's have their own class problems—Agnes' younger sister Jessie becomes pregnant by a lower-class lad and her father's fury is murderous. Still Jessie is Agnes' love for Charlie grows, she must also deal with the outbreak of WWI, which will bring changes for all concerned. 156m/C VHS, DVD. *GB* Claire Skinner, Edward Atterton, Julian Wadham, Frank Grimes, Moira Redmond, Elspet Gray, Dinsdale Landen, Anne Reic; *D:* David Wheatley; *W:* Alan Seymour; *M:* Colin Towns. TV

Catherine Cookson's Tilly Trotter 🐾🐾½ *Tilly Trotter* 1999 Tilly lives in rural England in the 1830s where the young woman is envied for her beauty by the local ladies and lusted after by the gentlemen. Accused of witchcraft, Tilly is rescued by a married farmer but there's another romance on the horizon as well. 210m/C VHS. *GB* Carli Norris, Simon Shepherd, Gavin Abbott, Madelaine Newton, Rosemary Leach, Basil Moss, Amelia Bullmore, Richard Dempsey; *D:* Alan Grint; *W:* Ray Marshall; *C:* Robin Vidgeon; *M:* Colin Towns. TV

Cathy's Curse 🐾 *Cauchemares* 1977 The spirit of an aunt, who died as a child, possesses a young girl in this Canadian-French collaboration. The film tries to capitalize on the popularity of "The Exorcist," but falls seriously short. 90m/C VHS, DVD. *FR CA* Alan Scarfe, Beverly Murray; *D:* Eddy Matalon.

Catlow 🐾🐾½ 1971 (PG-13) A comedic western with Brynner aiming to steal $2 million in gold from under the nose of his friend, lawman Crenna. Based on the novel by Louis L'Amour. 103m/C VHS, DVD. Yul Brynner, Richard Crenna, Leonard Nimoy, JoAnn Pflug, Daliah Lavi, Jeff Corey, Michael Delano, Bessie Love; *D:* Sam Wanamaker; *M:* Roy Budd.

Cats & Dogs 🐾🐾 2001 (PG) Mix of live-action and animatronics as the secret war between cats and dogs is exposed in your neighborhood. It seems the latest cat plot is to destroy a vaccine that would prevent all human allergies to dogs and the dogs, of course, must keep that from happening. The human actors are upstaged at every turn (naturally) and the plot shows he only gets parts playing animals. He gets into trouble with bratty human star Darla Dimple (Peldon) and nearly sees his chance at a career vanish. Combines "Singin' in the Rain" and "Who Framed Roger Rabbit," with some optimistic cynicism from "The Player" to create a cartoon that will most likely sail over the heads of its target audience. Most of the time, as in the old Warner Bros. classics, that's a good thing. Not in this case, however. 77m/C VHS, DVD. *D:* Mark Dindal; *W:* Cliff Ruby, Roberts Garraway, Elana Lesser, Theresa Pettengill; *M:* Steve Goldstein; *V:* Scott Bakula, Jasmine Guy, Ashley Peldon, Kathy Najimy, John Rhys-Davies, George Kennedy, Rene Auberjonois, Hal Holbrook, Don Knotts, Frank Welker, David Johansen, Natalie Cole.

Cats Don't Dance 🐾🐾 1997 (G) Animated musical comedy finds Danny (Bakula), a hoofer wanna-be trying to break into '30s Hollywood. Only problem is that he's a cat and can't understand why.

Cat's Eye 🐾🐾 *Stephen King's Cat's Eye* 1985 (PG-13) An anthology of three Stephen King short stories connected by a stray cat who wanders through each tale. 94m/C VHS, DVD. Drew Barrymore, James Woods, Alan King, Robert Hays, Candy Clark, Kenneth McMillan, James Naughton, Charles S. Durton; *D:* Lewis Teague; *W:* Stephen King; *C:* Jack Cardiff; *M:* Alan Silvestri.

The Cat's Meow 🐾🐾½ 2001 (PG-13) Bogdanovich takes on an old Hollywood scandal in this period drama, in 1924 publishing tycoon William Randolph Hearst (Herrmann) and his much-younger mistress, actress Marion Davies (Dunst), invite a group of partygoers aboard Hearst's yacht for a weekend. Producer/director Thomas Ince (Elwes) dies—but how is in question (heart attack? murder?)—and there's a coverup. Did Hearst mistakenly kill Ince while aiming for guest Charlie Chaplin (Izzard), whom Hearst suspected of carrying on with Davies? Film looks terrific, has a talented cast, and the story shows that little has changed in Hollywood regarding sex, scandal, ambition, and power. 112m/C VHS, DVD. *GB GE* Edward Herrmann, Kirsten Dunst, Cary Elwes, Eddie Izzard, Joanna Lumley, Jennifer Tilly, Victor Slezak, James Laurenson, Ronan Vibert, Claudia Harrison; *D:* Peter Bogdanovich; *W:* Steven Peros; *C:* Bruno Delbonnel.

Cat's Play 🐾🐾 *Macskajáték* 1974 A widowed music teacher makes a ceremonial occasion of a weekly dinner with an old flame. Then an old friend from her youth suddenly reappears and begins an

Catherine's Grove continued... [Alan Grint; *W:* T.R. Bowen; *C:* Allan Pyrah; *M:* Eddy Matalon.] *DVD.* *GB* Robson Green, Sylvestra Le Touzel, Bernard Hill, Stephanie Pulson, Anne Kent; *D:* Norman Stone; *W:* T.R. Bowen; *C:* Doug Hallows; *M:* David Ferguson. TV ... 86m/C VHS, DVD; Martin Sheen, Trevor Howard; *D:* Jack Gold; *M:* Carl Davis. TV affair with the gentleman, causing self-destructive passions to explode. In Hungarian with English subtitles. 115m/C VHS, DVD. *HU* Margit Dayka, Margit Makay, Elma Bulla; *D:* Karoly Makk.

Cattle Queen of Montana 🎬🎬 ½ 1954

Reagan stars as an undercover federal agent investigating livestock rustlings and Indian uprisings. 88m/C VHS, DVD. Ronald Reagan, Barbara Stanwyck, Jack Elam, Gene Evans, Lance Fuller, Anthony Caruso; *D:* Allan Dwan; *W:* Robert Blees.

Catwoman 🎬 2004 (PG-13)

Halle Berry is Patience Phillips, an artist in the ad department of a cosmetics company who overhears a discussion about side effects of their newest product. Soon she and the scientist who discovered the problem are disposed of. Luckily, a few cats are around to revive our heroine and dress her in a tight leather catsuit to take her revenge. Unfortunately, Berry's talents and wardrobe are not enough to carry a movie that, while it will undoubtedly have an extended shelf-life as a camp classic, is a mess. Director Pitof saturates every frame with his presence and revels in drawing attention to flamboyant visuals and frenetic editing rather than focusing on characterization or good, old-fashioned storytelling. Wooden characters and a laughable storyline make this arguably one of the worst comic book adaptations ever made. 91m/C VHS, DVD. Halle Berry, Sharon Stone, Benjamin Bratt, Lambert Wilson, Alex Borstein, John Cassini, Frances Conroy, Byron Mann, Michael Massee, Kim Smith, Chris Heyerdahl, Peter Wingfield; *D:* Pitof; *W:* John Brancato, Michael Ferris, John Rogers; *C:* Thierry Arbogast; *M:* Klaus Badelt. Golden Raspberries '04: Worst Picture, Worst Actress (Berry), Worst Director (Pitof), Worst Screenplay.

Caught 🎬🎬🎬 1949

A woman marries for wealth and security and is desperately unhappy. She runs away and takes a job with a struggling physician, and falls in love with him. Her husband finds her, forcing her to decide between a life of security or love. 90m/B VHS. James Mason, Barbara Bel Geddes, Robert Ryan, Curt Bois, Natalie Schafer, Art Smith; *D:* Max Ophuls; *C:* Lee Garmes.

Caught 🎬🎬🎬 1996 (R)

Homeless Irishman Nick (Verveen) winds up in the New Jersey fish shop run by Joe (Olmos) and his wife Betty (Alonso). Betty takes a liking to the good-looking young man and encourages Joe to offer him a job and even invites Nick to stay with them in departed son Danny's (Schub) old room. Soon, room and board isn't all the spicy Betty is offering and Nick's wife is ready to please, especially since Joe turns a blind eye. Too bad cocaine-addicted Danny, a failed comedian, returns home and immediately becomes jealous of the interloper. He's also too willing to drag secrets out into the open, whatever the cost. Based on Pomerantz's novel "Into It." 109m/C VHS, DVD. Edward James Olmos, Maria Conchita Alonso, Arie Verveen, Steven Schub, Bitty Schram, Shawn Elliot; *D:* Robert M. Young; *W:* Edward Pomerantz; *C:* Michael Barrow; *M:* Chris Botti.

Caught in the Act 🎬🎬 ½ 1993

(PG-13) Scott McNally (Harrison) is an out-of-work actor who teaches acting classes to make a buck. Into one of his classes walks the sultry Rachel (Hope) and they start a hot affair. Then Rachel calls Scott, claiming to be kidnapped, he suddenly finds $10 million in his bank account, and his landlord is murdered. Scott finds himself the pawn in an embezzlement scheme and framed for murder. But this is one role Scott doesn't want and he intends to work with a new script of his own devise. 93m/C VHS. Gregory Harrison, Leslie Hope, Patricia Clarkson, Kevin Tighe; *D:* Deborah Reinisch; *W:* Ken Hixon. CABLE

Caught in the Draft 🎬🎬🎬 1941

Hope's funniest role has him as a Hollywood star trying to evade the draft in WW II, but he ends up accidentally enlisting himself. Lamour plays the daughter of a colonel in the Army whom Hope plans to marry, thinking it will get him out of the service. Very funny military comedy and one of Hope's best. Based on a story by

Harry Tugend. 82m/B VHS, DVD. Bob Hope, Dorothy Lamour, Lynne Overman, Eddie Bracken, Clarence (William) Kolb, Paul Hurst, Ferike Boros, Irving Bacon; *D:* David Butler; *W:* Harry Tugend.

Caught Up 🎬🎬 1998 (R)

Directorial debut for Darin Scott follows the luckless path of ex-con Daryl (Woodbine). After serving five years as an unwitting accomplice to a bank robbery, he meets Vanessa (Williams) who is a dead ringer for his ex-girlfriend. She gets him a job as a limo driver that caters to thugs and gangsters. Unfortunately for Daryl, Vanessa has stolen some diamonds from a Rastafarian, so Daryl gets tangled up violence and deceit. He is also tangled in a plot that twists and turns a little too much for its own good. Director Scott tries a few too many fancy tricks, although some of them work reasonably well. Cameos from Snoop Doggy Dog and LL Cool J. 95m/C VHS, DVD. Bokeem Woodbine, Cynda Williams, Snoop Dogg, Joseph Lindsey, Clifton Powell, Basil Wallace, Tony Todd, LL Cool J, Jeffrey Combs, Damon Saleem, Shedric Hunter Jr.; *D:* Darin Scott; *W:* Darin Scott; *C:* Thomas Callaway; *M:* Marc Bonilla.

Cauldron of Blood 🎬🎬 ½ Blind

Man's Bluff; El Coleccionista de Cadaveres 1967 (PG) Blind sculptor Karloff unwittingly uses human skeletons supplied by his crazed wife Lindfors as the framework of his art pieces. 95m/C VHS. *SP* Boris Karloff, Viveca Lindfors, Jean-Pierre Aumont, Rosenda Monteros, Ruben Rojo, Dianik Zurakowska; *D:* Edward Andrew (Santos Alcocer) Mann; *W:* Edward Andrew (Santos Alcocer) Mann.

Cause Celebre 🎬🎬🎬 1987

Absorbing true crime drama set in Britain during the '30s. Alma Rattenbury (Mirren) is in a dull marriage to an aging and ill husband (Andrews) and is beset by financial and domestic difficulties. Then Alma hires 18-year-old George Bowman (Morrissey) as a family servant/chauffeur and, despite their age difference, the two are soon lovers. When her husband is bludgeoned to death, both Alma and George are swiftly arrested and on trial. But just who committed the crime and who is covering up? 105m/C VHS, DVD. *GB* Helen Mirren, David Morrissey, David Suchet, Harry Andrews, Norma West, Oliver Ford Davies, Geoffrey Bayldon, Gillian Martell; *D:* John Gorrie; *W:* Kenneth Taylor; *C:* Malcolm Harrison, Trevor Vaisey; *M:* Richard Harvey. TV

Cause for Alarm 🎬🎬 ½ 1951

A jealous husband recovering from a heart attack begins to lose his mind. He wrongly accuses his wife of having an affair and attempts to frame her for his own murder. A fast-paced thriller with a nifty surprise ending. 74m/B VHS, DVD. Loretta Young, Barry Sullivan, Bruce Cowling, Margalo Gillmore, Irving Bacon, Carl "Alfalfa" Switzer; *D:* Tay Garnett; *M:* Andre Previn.

Cause of Death 🎬🎬 1990 (R)

After the accidental death of his brother, Colombian drug lord Manuel Ramirez is lured to L.A. to collect his millions in blood money. 90m/C VHS, DVD. Michael Barak, Sydney Coale Phillips, Daniel Martine; *D:* Philip Jones.

Cause of Death 🎬 2000 (R)

Taylor Lewis (Bergin) is a prosecutor in Baltimore, who is assigned to a seemingly open-and-shut murder in which Angela Carter (Severance) has murdered her corrupt businessman husband to collect on his large insurance policy. But Lewis is cautious because of a past mistake and then he starts getting very close to the beautiful widow. Is Angela guilty or is someone in power pulling the strings? 95m/C VHS, DVD. Patrick Bergin, Joan Severance, Maxim Roy, Michael Ironside, Larry Day; *D:* Marc S. Grenier; *W:* Les Weldon; *C:* Yves Belanger. VIDEO

Cavalcade 🎬🎬🎬 1933

Traces the lives of the British Marryot family from the death of Queen Victoria, through WWI, the Jazz Age, and the Depression. A wistful adaptation of the hit play by Noel Coward with its touching portrayal of one family trying to weather good times and bad together. 110m/B VHS. Diana Wynyard, Clive Brook, Herbert Mundin, Una O'Connor, Ursula Jeans, Beryl Mercer, Merle Tottenham, Frank Lawton, John Warburton, Margaret Lindsay, Billy Be-

van; *D:* Frank Lloyd; *C:* Ernest Palmer. Oscars '33: Director (Lloyd), Picture.

Cavalcade of the West 🎬 1936

Typical western with two brothers, separated by a kidnapping, growing up on opposite sides of the law. Much later they meet, and the question is: will the outlaw be reformed and reunited with his happy family? 70m/B VHS, DVD. Hoot Gibson, Rex Lease, Marion Shilling, Earl Dwire; *D:* Harry Fraser.

Cavalier of the West 🎬 1931

An Army captain is the only negotiating force between the white man and a primitive Indian tribe. 66m/B VHS. Harry Carey Sr., Kane Richmond, George "Gabby" Hayes; *D:* John P. McCarthy.

Cavalry 🎬🎬 ½ 1936

A Union Army Lieutenant is reunited with his family after the Civil War, bringing them happiness and joy. 60m/B VHS. Bob Steele, Frances Grant, Karl Hackett, Hal Price; *D:* Robert North Bradbury.

Cavalry Charge 🎬🎬 ½ The Last

Outpost 1951 Vance Britton (Reagan) is the captain of a brigade of Confederate troops wreaking havoc on Union outposts. His brother Jeb (Bennett) is a Union soldier sent to the western frontier to take care of the Confederate problem. Vance's former fiance Julie (Fleming) is also living in the territories with her new husband. All three converge when the Union fort, where Julie is living and Jeb is defending, is attacked by Apaches. Brother Vance rides to the rescue. Lots of action. 72m/C VHS, DVD. Ronald Reagan, Bruce Bennett, Rhonda Fleming, Noah Beery Jr., Bill Williams, Peter Hansen, Hugh Beaumont, John Ridgely, Lloyd Corrigan, James Burke, Richard Crane, Ewing Mitchell; *D:* Lewis R. Foster; *W:* Daniel Mainwaring, George Worthing Yates, Winston Miller; *C:* Loyal Griggs.

Cavalry Command 🎬🎬 ½ Cavalleria

Commandos 1963 Good will and integrity characterize the U.S. soldiers called into a small village to quiet a guerrilla rebellion. 77m/C VHS, DVD. John Agar, Richard Arlen, Myron Healey, Alicia Vergel, William Phipps, Eddie Infante; *D:* Eddie Romero; *W:* Eddie Romero.

The Cave 🎬 2005 (PG-13)

Cut from the same cloth as the hundred or so other films you've seen that were called "The (insert scary place or thing here)." All of the essential stereotypes are present, so everyone gets a character to relate to, hate, or both. Explorers Jack (Hauser) and Tyler (Cibrian) assemble a team of cavers, divers and scientists to explore a massive network of caves beneath a medieval Romanian church. As they descend into the cave it becomes clear that they have completely run out of hideous flying monsters. 97m/C DVD, UMD. *US* Cole Hauser, Morris Chestnut, Eddie Cibrian, Marcel Iures, Daniel Dae Kim, Lena Headey, Piper Perabo, Rick Ravanello, Kieran Darcy-Smith; *D:* Bruce Hunt; *W:* Michael Steinberg, Tegan West; *C:* Emery Ross; *M:* Johnny Klimek, Reinhold Heil.

Cave Girl woof! Cavegirl 1985 (R)

After falling through a time-warp during a high-school field trip, a social pariah makes a hit with a pre-historic honey. Sexist teen exploitation film, with few original ideas and a not-so-hot cast. 85m/C VHS, DVD. Daniel Roebuck, Cindy Ann Thompson, Saba Moor, Jeff Chayette; *D:* David Oliver; *W:* David Oliver; *C:* David Oliver; *M:* Jon St. James.

Cave of the Living Dead woof! Der Fluch Der Gruenen Augen; Night of the Vampire; The Curse of Green

Eyes 1965 Mad professor with a past is up to something in a cave under castle. Villagers summon Inspector Doren of Interpol to solve a rash of nasty murders that they've blamed on green-eyed, cave-dwelling vampires. A challenge to watch till the end. Filmed in Sepiatone. 87m/B VHS, DVD. *GE* YU Adrian Hoven, Erika Remberg, Carl Mohner, Wolfgang Preiss, Karin (Karen) Field, John Kitzmiller, Akos Von Rathony; *D:* Akos Von Rathony; *W:* C.V. Rock; *C:* Hrvoje Saric.

Caveman 🎬🎬 1981 (PG)

Starr stars in this prehistoric spoof about a group of cavemen banished from different tribes who band together to form a tribe called "The Misfits." 92m/C VHS, DVD. Ringo Starr, Barbara Bach, John Matuszak, Dennis Quaid, Jack Gilford, Shelley Long, Cork Hubbert, Avery

Schreiber; *D:* Carl Gottlieb; *W:* Carl Gottlieb, Rudy DeLuca; *C:* Alan Hume; *M:* Lalo Schifrin.

The Caveman's Valentine 🎬🎬 ½

2001 (R) Jackson plays a homeless schizophrenic who finds a dead body outside his cave in Central Park and must pull his faltering mental faculties together enough to play Sherlock Holmes and solve the who-done-it. Plot points stretch well beyond the bounds of believability and venture into the territory of the ridiculous as the Caveman conveniently infiltrates every realm of society he wishes in order to follow up on his suspicions. Granted, he used to be a master pianist before his mental downfall, but come on. Director Lemmons's second feature film, the first being "Eve's Bayou." Based on the Edgar Award-winning 1994 novel by George Dawes Green. 105m/C VHS, DVD. Samuel L. Jackson, Aunjanue Ellis, Colm Feore, Ann Magnuson, Rodney Eastman, Tamara Tunie, Anthony Michael Hall, Jay Rodan; *D:* Kasi Lemmons; *W:* George Dawes Green; *C:* Amy Vincent; *M:* Terence Blanchard.

The Cavern 🎬🎬 ½ Within 2005 (R)

An eight-person team exploring a newly discovered cavern in Kyzl Kum Desert in Central Asia run into big trouble when they find themselves trapped. Too familiar story and not very frightening. 81m/C DVD. *AU* Sybil Temtchine, Mustafa Shakir, Ogy Durham, Andrew Caple-Shaw, Danny A. Jacobs, Andres Saenz-Hudson, Johnnie Colter, Neno Pervan; *D:* Olatunde Osunsanmi; *W:* Olatunde Osunsanmi; *C:* Yasu Tanida; *M:* Bryan Galvez.

Cavite 🎬🎬 ½ 2005 No-budget thriller

set and filmed in the Philippines. Adam (Gamazon) is summoned to Manila to attend his father's funeral but his mother and sister aren't at the airport to meet him. Instead, Adam gets a cell phone call informing him that they have been kidnapped and he must not only retrieve money his father had stashed but also carry out a terrorist mission if Adam wants to keep his family alive. All the while, the jeering caller sends Adam running throughout the poor city of Cavite, doing his bidding. English and Tagalog with subtitles. 80m/C DVD. Ian Gamazon, Dominique Gonzalez, Jeffrey Lagna; *D:* Ian Gamazon, Neill Dela Llana; *W:* Ian Gamazon, Neill Dela Llana; *C:* Neill Dela Llana.

CB4: The Movie 🎬 ½ 1993 (R)

Falling somewhere between a serious attempt and parody, CB4 tries to do both and succeeds at neither. Written in the key of "Wayne's World" by "Saturday Night Live's" Rock, it starts out as a "rockumentary" (please refer to "This is Spinal Tap"), but quickly turns into a sitcom after two gangsta rap friends assume the identity of a local club owner when he is in jail. Hartman, also of SNL, appears as a right-wing city councilman. Chock full of violence, sexism, and profanity tucked into a wandering plot. 83m/C VHS, DVD. Chris Rock, Allen Payne, Deezer D, Phil Hartman, Charlie (Charles Q.) Murphy, Khandi Alexander, Art Evans, Chris Elliott, Willard Pugh, Theresa Randle; *D:* Tamra Davis; *W:* Chris Rock, Nelson George, Robert Locash; *M:* John Barnes.

C.C. & Company 🎬 Chrome Hearts

1970 (R) Rebel biker rescues a buxom gal from a fate worse than death, than vies for control of the gang. Laughable, with Namath hopeless in his film debut. Redeemed only by Ann-Margret in continual disarray. 91m/C VHS, DVD. Joe Namath, Ann-Margret, William (Bill) Smith, Jennifer Billingsley, Teda Bracci, Greg Mullavey, Sid Haig, Bruce Glover; *D:* Seymour Robbie; *W:* Roger Smith; *C:* Charles F. Wheeler; *M:* Lenny Stack.

Cease Fire 🎬🎬 ½ 1985 (R)

The story of a troubled Vietnam vet who finds solace in a veterans' therapy group. Adapted from the play by George Fernandez. 97m/C VHS. Don Johnson, Robert F. Lyons, Lisa Blount; *D:* David Nutter; *M:* Gary Fry.

Cecil B. Demented 🎬🎬 ½ 2000

(R) Waters returns to a more hard-edged satire with this indictment against the studio system. Dorff is Cecil B. Demented, indie auteur who, along with his band of cinema terrorists, wreack havoc on Hollywood. They kidnap A-list actress Honey Whitlock (Griffith) and force her to appear in their film—in doing so, making her the

Ceiling Zero 🎬 1935 Cagney is an irrepressible pilot who does as he pleases and loves to aggravate his soft-hearted boss O'Brien. He falls for aviatrix Travis and neglects his duties to woo her, which leads to tragedy. Naturally, it's so-bers Cagney up and he volunteers for a dangerous test flight. Lots of fast-paced action and camaraderie. Cagney is at his swaggering best. Based on the screenplay. Remade in 1941 as "International Squadron." **95m/B VHS.** James Cagney, Pat O'Brien, June Travis, Stuart Erwin, Henry Wadsworth, Isabel Jewell, Barton MacLane; **D:** Howard Hawks; **W:** Frank Wead.

The Celebration 🎬🎬 *Festen* 1998 (R) Danish patriarch Helge (Moritzen) is turning 60 and a black-tie bash is being given to celebrate the event. But the celebration turns into a rancid display when all the family skeletons coming rattling out of the family's closets. Everyone's got a score to settle and is more than happy to air the family's dirty linen. Danish with subtitles. The film was shot with a hand-held video-camera in available light and sound according to the tenets of Dogma 95—a Danish filmmaking collective Vinterberg belongs to. **105m/C VHS, DVD, DK** Henning Moritzen, Ulrich Thomsen, Thomas Bo Larsen, Paprika Steen, Lena Laub Olsen, Helle Dolleris, Gbatokai Dakinah; **D:** Thomas Vinterberg; **W:** Thomas Vinterberg, Mogens Rukov; **C:** Anthony Dod Mantle. Ind. Spirit '99. Foreign Film; L.A. Film Critics '98; Foreign Film; N.Y. Film Critics '98. Foreign Film.

Celebrity 🎬🎬 1998 (R) Woody examines the phenomenon of celebrity with his usual sarcastic and semi-autobiographical perspective. Lee Simon (Branagh) is a 'lack celebrity' journalist who attempts to enter the glitz and glam world of the famous people he follows and writes about. In true Allen fashion, bitter irony abounds as Simon loses sight of his pathetic reality while those around him acquire what he so desperately seeks. DiCaprio steals his 15 minutes of screen time playing a hedonistic, hotel-trashing, spoiled young film star with amazing ease and conviction. (Coincidence? Perhaps...) The writing is among Allen's best, but watching Branagh and Judy Davis as Lee's estranged wife, do their best Woody Allen impressions grates on the nerves. Although it's redundant, nobody plays Woody like Woody. **113m/B VHS, DVD.** Kenneth Branagh, Judy Davis, Hank Azaria, Leonardo DiCaprio, Joe Mantegna, Famke Janssen, Winona Ryder, Bebe Neuwirth, Dylan Baker, Patti D'Arbanville, Kate Burton, Gretchen Mol, Allison Janney, Aida Turturro, Jeffrey Wright, J.K. Simmons, Polly Adams; **Cameos:** Greg Mottola, Isaac Mizrahi, Andre Gregory, Donald Trump; **D:** Woody Allen; **W:** Woody Allen; **C:** Sven Nykvist.

Celeste 🎬🎬 1981 Action (who later made the offbeat comedy "Sugarbaby") directed this longish but finely detailed and beautifully photographed period look at French writer Marcel (Remembrance of Things Past) Proust. Based on the memoirs of Proust's housekeeper, Celeste Albaret, an uneducated farmgirl, portraying the woman's devoted relationship with the middle-aged death did them part) with the (celibate and homosexual author. It does so with wit, poignancy, and insight, but is not entirely successful in its attempt to render Proust's verbal literary style into a visual medium. In German with English subtitles. **107m/C VHS, GE** Eva Mattes, Jürgen Arndt, Norbert Wartha, Wolf Euba; **D:** Percy Adlon; **W:** Percy Adlon.

Celestial Clockwork 🎬🎬½ *Mecaniques Celestes* 1994 Runaway Venezuelan bride Ana (Gil), an aspiring opera singer, takes off for Paris clutching her Maria Callas poster. God must protect the innocent because she meets a friendly cabbie, immediately finds a place to live, and gets the perfect singing teacher, a cranky Russian émigré named Grigorieff (Debrane). In fact, the only problem in this Cinderella's life is jealous would-be star Celeste (Dombasle), who wants the same lead theatrical role that Ana is also interested in. French with subtitles. **85m/C VHS, DVD, FR** Ariadna Gil, Arielle Dombasle, Evelyne Didi, Frédéric Longbois, Lluis Homar, Michel Debrane; **D:** Fina Torres; **W:** Fina Torres; **C:** Ricardo Aronovich; **M:** Michel Musseau, François Farrugia.

The Celestine Prophecy 🎬 2006 (PG) Pure hokum and clumsy n narrative, dialog, and character development. John Woodson (Settle) impulsively travels to Peru after a friend alerts him to the discovery of ancient scrolls said to reveal universal life truths. But when John arrives he discovers that both the church and the government want to suppress the find and stop those involved from talking. Based on the metaphysical novel by James Redfield, who co-scripted. **99m/C DVD.** Matthew Settle, Thomas Kretschmann, Annabeth Gish, Hector Elizondo, Sarah Wayne Callies, Jürgen Prochnow, Obba Babatunde, Joaquim Almeida; **D:** Armand Mastroianni; **W:** Dan Gordon, James Redfield, Barnet Bain; **C:** R. Michael Givens; **M:** Nuno Malo.

Cella: Child of Terror 🎬🎬 1989 Set in the 1950s, this film deals with the awful results of a young girl's inability to handle disappointment. **110m/C VHS, AU** Rebecca Smart, Nicholas Eadie, Victoria Longley, Mary-Anne Fahey; **D:** Ann Turner; **C:** Geoffrey Simpson.

Celine and Julie Go Boating 🎬🎬 1974 Strange fantasy follows magician Céline (Berto) and her librarian friend, Julie (Labourier). Céline sometimes works as a governess for a little girl who lives with her widowed father in a possibly haunted house. Two women are in love with the father but her prom-ised his wife never to remarry as long as their invalid daughter was still alive. Celine and Julie become worried for the little girl and decide to rescue her. An adaptation of the Henry James story "A Romance of Certain Old Clothes." French with subtitles. **193m/C VHS.** Juliet Berto, Dominique Labourier, Bulle Ogier, Marie-France Pisier, Barbet Schroeder, Philippe Clévenot, Nathalie Asnor; **D:** Jacques Rivette; **W:** Jacques Rivette, Eduardo Di Gregorio; **C:** Jacques Renard; **M:** Jean-Marie Senia.

The Cell 🎬🎬½ 2000 (R) Psychotherapist Catherine (Lopez) is involved in breakthrough research that allows her access into a patient's mind. Desperate FBI agent Novak (Vaughn) asks her to invade the mind of a comatose serial killer (D'Onofrio) in order to save his latest victim. She's not an exactly pleasant place to be, and Catherine (and the audience) encounters some pretty creepy and disturbing stuff. Feature debut of music video director Tarsem (REM's "Losing My Religion") is going on dazzling visual effects, trippy images, and style, but short on real suspense and cohesive plotting. Narrative is not the main focus here, however, so the faint of heart and the plot-dependent are forewarned. **110m/C VHS, DVD.** Jennifer Lopez, Vince Vaughn, Vincent D'Onofrio, Marianne Jean-Baptiste, Dylan Baker, Jake Weber, Patrick Bauchau, James Gammon, Tara Subkoff, Gareth Williams, Colton James, Catherine Sutherland, Dean Norris, Pruitt Taylor Vince; **D:** Tarsem; **W:** Mark Protosevich; **C:** Paul Laufer; **M:** Howard Shore.

The Cellar 🎬½ 1990 (PG-13) A young boy finds an ancient Comanche monster spirit in the basement of his home. His parents, as usual, don't believe him, so he must battle the monster alone. **90m/C VHS.** Patrick Kilpatrick, Suzanne Savoy, Chris Miller, Ford Rainey; **D:** Kevin S. Tenney.

Cellar Dweller Woof! 1987 A cartoonist moves into an old house and soon discovers it's haunted by a demonic cartoonist who killed himself 30 years earlier. What a coincidence. Low-budget scare-'em-up. **78m/C VHS, DVD.** Debrah Mullowney, Brian Robbins, Vince Edwards, Jeffrey Combs, Yvonne De Carlo; **D:** John Carl Buechler.

Cellblock Sisters: Banished Behind Bars 🎬½ 1995 (R) Biker babe Harris reunites with college girl sis Wood to off their disgusting stepfather who separately sold them to adoptive families after killing their junkie mom. Harris does the crime but Wood does the time—until her guilty sibling deliberately gets thrown behind bars in order to protect her. Has all the standard jail chicks elements. **95m/C VHS, DVD.** Gail Harris, Annie Wood, Ace Ross; **D:** Henri Charr.

Cello 🎬½ 2005 (R) Confusing Korean ghost story—or maybe the main character is just nuts. Cello teacher Mi-Ju (Seong) barely survived a car accident that ruined her professional career and acted her best friend. Now Mi-Ju is being threatened by one of her students and thinks she's haunted by a ghost. Korean with subtitles. **93m/C DVD.** KN Heyon-a Seong, Ho-bin Jeong, Da-an Park; **D:** Woo-cheol Lee; **W:** Woo-cheol Lee.

Cellular 🎬🎬 2004 (PG-13) Efficient little thriller wastes no time. Science teacher Jessica Martin (Basinger) is kidnapped and locked in a grungy attic. Head bad guy Ethan (Statham) smashes the wall phone but Jessica hears a dial tone and manages to connect the wires and randomly gets the cell phone of beach bum Ryan (Evans), who naturally thinks it's a prank. Finally convinced, Ryan also figures out if he loses the call, the lady is lost, which leads to a number of realistic obstacles as he races to warn her husband and son, who are also targets. Veteran actor Macy plays veteran LAPD desk sergeant Mooney, who's about to retire when this case lands in his lap. The story is by Larry Cohen, who was also into phones as the screenwriter of 2002's "Phone Booth." **94m/C VHS, DVD.** Kim Basinger, Chris Evans, Jason Statham, Eric Christian Olsen, Matt McCoin, Noah Emmerich, William H. Macy, Brendan Kelly, Caroline Aaron, Richard Burgi, Rick Hoffman, Eric Etebari, Adam Taylor Gordon, Jessica Biel; **D:** David R. Ellis; **W:** Larry Cohen, Chris Morgan; **C:** Gary Capo; **M:** John Ottman.

The Celluloid Closet 🎬🎬🎬½ 1995 (R) Terrific documentary on how Hollywood films have depicted homosexual characters, subliminally and otherwise. Working chronologically and in an historical context, beginning with silent films, there are clips from more than 100 films, along with interviews from writers and actors. (Notable is writer Gore Vidal's comments on the gay subtext in 1959's "Ben-Hur"). Based on Vito Russo's 1981 book. **102m/C VHS, DVD.** D: Robert Epstein, Jeffrey Friedman; **W:** Armistead Maupin; **C:** Nancy Schreiber; **Nar:** Lily Tomlin.

Celtic Pride 🎬 1996 (PG-13) Mike O'Hara (Stern) and Jimmy Flaherty (Aykroyd) are the worst kind of crazy. They're sports nuts. They are so consumed with passion for their beloved Celtics that they kidnap foul-mouthed superstar Lewis Scott (Wayans) of the Utah Jazz before game seven of the NBA finals. If this sounds far fetched, well...it is, unless you have an ESPN junkie in your life. There's not as much court action as you would expect, since most of the story revolves around intermittent trash-talking and escape attempts. If you're a Celtic hater, stick around for the end, when the Boston Garden is demolished using special effects. **90m/C VHS, DVD.** Damon Wayans, Daniel Stern, Dan Aykroyd, Gail O'Grady, Adam Hendershott, Paul Guilfoyle, Deion Sanders, Christopher McDonald, Gus Williams, Ted Rooney, Vladimir Cuk; **Cameos:** Bill Walton, Larry Bird; **D:** Tom De-man.

Cement 🎬🎬 1999 (R) Intense performances in a nasty crime story told via flashbacks. Hollywood vice detectives Holt (Penn) and Nin (Wright) have crossed the line between the cops and the criminals. When violent Holt catches 'his gal (Fenn) with a vice wiseguy (DeSardo), he buries him in a cement freeway and the mob is out for revenge. Pascar's directorial debut. **100m/C VHS, DVD.** Christopher Penn, Jeffrey Wright, Sherilyn Fenn, Anthony De Sardo, Henry Czerny; **D:** Adrian Pasdar; **W:** Justin Monjo; **C:** Geary McLeod; **M:** Doug Caldwell.

The Cement Garden 🎬🎬 1993 Fatherless 15-year-old Jack (Robertson) and 15-year-old sister Julie (Gainsbourg) are afraid that they and their two younger siblings Sue (Courtnard) and Tom (Birkin) will be taken into foster care after their mother dies at home. So to keep their secret, they bury her in the basement and try to assume a normal family life. Not that this works for long—Jack and Julie give into an incestuous fascination and the household slowly sinks into chaotic squalor around them. Gainsbourg is the director's niece and the young Birkin is his son. Based on Ian McEwan's 1978 novel. **105m/C VHS, DVD, FR GE GB** Charlotte Gainsbourg, Andrew Robertson, Alice Coulthard, Ned Birkin, Sinead Cusack, Hanns Zischler, Jochen Horst; **D:** Andrew Birkin; **W:** Andrew Birkin; **C:** Stephen Blackman; **M:** Ed Shearmur.

The Cemetery Club 🎬🎬½ 1993 (PG-13) Story of three Jewish widows who make weekly visits to their husband's graves while attempting to cope with their lives. Doris (Dukakis) is loyal to the memory of her husband and acts as the moral conscience of the trio. Lucille (Ladd) is the merry widow who wears clothes more suitable for younger women but she also harbors a painful secret. Esther (Burstyn) struggles with her loneliness until a widowed cab driver begins to woo her. Commendably the characters are given more dimension than Hollywood usually grants women 'of a certain age. Based on the play "The Cemetary Club" by Menchell, who also wrote the screenplay. **114m/C VHS, DVD.** Ellen Burstyn, Olympia Dukakis, Diane Ladd, Danny Aiello, Lainie Kazan, Christina Ricci, Bernie Casey, Alan Mason, Sam Schwartz, Jeff Howell, Robert Costanzo, Wallace Shawn, Louis Guss; **D:** Bill Duke; **W:** Ivan Menchell; **C:** Steven Poster; **M:** Elmer Bernstein.

Cemetery High 🎬 1989 Beautiful high school girls decide to lure the local boys into a trap and kill them. **80m/C VHS, DVD.** Debi Thibeault, Karen Nielsen, Lisa Schmidt, Ruth (Coreen) Collins Simone, Tony Kruk, David Coughlin, Frank Stewart; **D:** Gorman Bechard; **W:** Gorman Bechard, Carmine Capobianco.

Cemetery Man 🎬🎬🎬 *Dellamorte Dellamore: Of Death of Love* 1995 (R) Grotesque more: set in a small Italian cemetery. Thanks to a weird post-death plague the corpses refuse to stay quietly in their graves, forcing watchman Francisco Dellamorte (Everett) and mute gravedigger Gnaghi (Hadji-Lazaro) to split their hands open. But when Francisco's dead sweetheart (Falchi) rises from her grave, he's a little slow to rebury the still-active corpse. Based on the Italian graphic novel "Dellamorte Dellamore," from the "Dylan Dog" series by Tiziano Sclavi. **100m/C VHS, DVD, IT** Rupert Everett, Anna Falchi, François Hadji-Lazaro, Mickey Knox; **D:** Michele (Michael) Soavi; **W:** Gianni Romoli; **C:** Mauro Marchetti; **M:** Manuel De Sica.

Centennial 🎬🎬🎬 1978 Epic 12-cart TV miniseries, based on the 1974 novel by James Michener, about the building of the Rocky Mountain town of Centennial, Colorado, from 1795 to the present. There are trappers and I'cians, immigrants and cattlemen, soldiers, conservationists, and politicians all with their own stories to tell. **1258m/C VHS** Robert Conrad, Richard Chamberlain, Raymond Burr, Sally Kellerman, Barbara Carrera, Michael Ansara, Gregory Harrison, Stephanie Zimbalist, Christina Raines, Stephen McHattie, Karo Salem, Chad Everett, Alex Karras, Mark Harmon, Dennis Weaver, Timothy Dalton, Richard Crenna, Cliff DeYoung, Glynn Turman, Brian Keith, Les Lannom, Rafael Campos, Anthony

Centennial

Zerbe, Doug McKeon, Lynn Redgrave, William Atherton, A. Martinez, Lois Nettleton, David Janssen, Robert Vaughn, Andy Griffith, Sharon Gless; *D:* Virgil W. Vogel, Harry Falk, Paul Krasny, Bernard McEveety; *W:* John Wilder.

Center of the Web 🐶🐶 **1992 (R)** John Phillips is a victim of mistaken identity—someone thinks he's a professional hit man. After surviving an apparent mob attempt on his life, Phillips is persuaded by a CIA operative to go along with the deception in order to capture a potential political assassin. At least that's what Phillips is told, but he soon realizes that the deeper he gets into his new role, the deadlier the plot becomes. Davi is one of the best bad guys around and the fast-paced stunts and plot twists make this watchable. **88m/C VHS.** Ted Prior, Robert Davi, Tony Curtis, Charlene Tilton, Bo Hopkins, Charles Napier; *D:* David A. Prior.

The Center of the World 🐶🐶 **2001** Put this one strongly in the love it or hate it category. Richard (Sarsgaard) is a wealthy dot.com geek who offers stripper Florence (Parker) a lot of dough to spend a few days with him in Vegas. She makes some strict rules about what she will and won't do for him—which she promptly breaks. They're both immature and vulnerable and inclined to play humiliating mind games with each other. The sex show turns out to be nothing but hot and bothered about and the leads give as credible performances as the narrowness of their characters allow. Shot in digital video; the screenwriters used the pseud. "Ellen Benjamin Wong." **66m/C VHS, DVD.** Peter Sarsgaard, Molly Parker, Carla Gugino, Balthazar Getty, Mel Gorham; *D:* Wayne Wang; *W:* Wayne Wang; *C:* Mauro Fiore.

Center Stage 🐶🐶 **2000 (PG-13)** How familiar does this sound? Newcomers enrolled at the American Ballet Academy vie for places in the professional company. Meanwhile, former dancer/company director Jonathan (Gallagher) has to contend with his insolent star dancer Cooper (Stiefel), whose ambitions are growing by leaps and bounds. There's also the usual love connections to be made (and unmade). The professional dancers in the cast have limited acting ability and aren't served particularly well by most of the choreography. **116m/C VHS, DVD.** Peter Gallagher, Ethan Stiefel, Amanda Schull, Sascha Radetsky, Susan May Pratt, Ilia Kulik, Donna Murphy, Zoe Saldana, Debra Monk, Julie Kent, Eion Bailey, Shakiem Evans, Victor Anthony, Elizabeth Hubbard, Priscilla Lopez; *D:* Nicholas Hytner; *W:* Carol Heikkinen; *C:* Geoffrey Simpson; *M:* George Fenton.

The Centerfold Girls woof! **1974 (R)** Microscopic story line involves a deranged man who is determined to kill all the voluptuous young women who have posed nude for a centerfold. **93m/C VHS.** Andrew Prine, Tiffany Bolling, Aldo Ray, Jeremy Slate, Ray Danton, Francine York; *D:* John Peyser.

Centipede woof! **2005 (PG-13)** A party of spelunkers encounter, yup, you guessed it, killer centipedes. But the caves are so dark that the actors and centipedes are rarely seen. When the creatures go show up, they look like killer sock-puppets. Too goofy and takes itself too seriously. **90m/C DVD.** George Foster, Larry Casey, Margaret Cash, Trevor Murphy, Matthew Pohlson, Danielle Kirlin, Steve Herd; *D:* Gregory Gieras; *W:* Gregory Gieras; *C:* Ajavan Vincent; *M:* Tom Batoy, Franco Tortora. **CABLE**

Central Station 🐶🐶🐶 *Central Do Brasil* 1998 (R) Dora (Montenegro) is a bitter, aging woman who makes a living writing letters for the illiterate at a stand located in Rio de Janeiro's central railway station. One of her customers sends letters to her 9-year-old son Josue's (de Oliveira) father, who lives in northern Brazil and who has never seen the boy. When Josue's mother is killed in an accident, Dora reluctantly takes the homeless boy in and reluctantly decides they must locate his father. Their road trip turns out to have some unexpected consequences. Portuguese with subtitles. **110m/C VHS, DVD.** *BR* Fernanda Montenegro, Vinicius de Oliveira, Marilia Pera, Othon Bastos; *D:* Walter Salles; *W:* Joao Emmanuel Carneiro, Marcos Bernstein, Mi-

Cavalho; *M:* Antonio Pinto, Jaques Morelembaum. British Acad. '98: Foreign Film; Golden Globes '99: Foreign Film; L.A. Film Critics '98: Actress (Montenegro); Natl. Bd. of Review '98: Actress (Montenegro); Foreign Film.

Century 🐶🐶 **1994 (R)** Ambitious young doctor Paul Reisner (Owen), the son of a prosperous Jewish father (Stephens), gets a position at a London research hospital headed by the charismatic Professor Mandry (Dance). Paul manages to disgrace himself by provoking Mandry and is dismissed but finds out some disturbing information and is determined to discredit his former mentor. Anti-Semitism lurks as does the change from Victorian mores to the challenging dawn of the 20th century. Complex performances are somewhat undermined by the static direction. **112m/C VHS.** *GB* Clive Owen, Charles Dance, Miranda Richardson, Robert Stephens, Joan Hickson, Lena Headey, Neil Stuke; *D:* Stephen Poliakoff; *W:* Stephen Poliakoff; *C:* Witold Stok; *M:* Michael Gibbs.

Certain Fury 🐶 **1985 (R)** Two timid women go on the lam when they are mistaken for escaped prostitutes who shot up a courthouse. The sooner they get caught, the better. **88m/C VHS.** Tatum O'Neal, Irene Cara, Peter Fonda, Nicholas (Nick) Campbell, Moses Gunn; *D:* Stephen Gyllenhaal.

A Certain Justice 🐶🐶½ **1999** Adam Dalgleish's (Marsden) latest case of murder involves barrister Venetia Aldridge (Downie), who is found bizarrely costumed and stabbed to death in her chambers. It turns out a number of people had a reason to dislike Venetia and prying the truth from a group of lawyers proves to be a challenge even for Scotland Yard's eminent Commander. **150m/C VHS, DVD.** *GB* Roy Marsden, Penny Downie, Ricci Harnett, Flora Montgomery, Frederick Treves, Matthew Marsh, Ian McNeice, Sarah Winman, Richard Huw, Ken Jones, Britta Smith, Miles Anderson, Philip Stone; *D:* Ross Devenish; *W:* Michael Russell. **TV**

Certain Sacrifice 🐶 **1980** Nineteen-year-old Madonna expresses herself in her film debut. Seeking revenge on the man who raped her, she murders him in a strange ritualistic manner underneath the Brooklyn Bridge. Poor is the man whose pleasures depend on the permission of another? **60m/C VHS.** Madonna, Jeremy Pattnosh, Charles Kurtz; *D:* Stephen Lewicki.

Cesar 🐶🐶🐶 **1936** This is the third and most bittersweet part of Pagnol's famed trilogy based on his play depicting the lives and loves of the people of Provence, France. Marius returns after a 20-year absence to his beloved Fanny and his now-grown son, Cesariot. The first two parts of the trilogy are "Marius" and "Fanny" and were directed by Alexander Korda and Marc Allegret respectively. In French with English subtitles. **117m/B VHS, DVD.** *FR* Raimu, Pierre Fresnay, Orane Demazis, Charpin, Andre Fouche, Alida Rouffe; *D:* Marcel Pagnol; *W:* Marcel Pagnol; *M:* Vincent Scotto.

Cesar & Rosalie 🐶🐶🐶 **1972 (PG)** Acclaimed French comedy depicts the love triangle between a beautiful divorcee, her aging live-in companion and a younger man. Engaging portrait of how their relationship evolves over time. In French with English subtitles. **110m/C VHS, DVD.** *FR* Romy Schneider, Yves Montand, Sami Frey, Umberto Orsini; *D:* Claude Sautet; *W:* Jean-Loup Dabadie, Claude Neron, Claude Sautet; *C:* Jean Boffety; *M:* Philippe Sarde.

Cesare Borgia 🐶🐶 **1923** Veidt stars in this bloodthirsty saga as the ruthless son of Pope Alexander VI who'll let nothing come between him and his desires. **83m/B VHS.** *GE* Conrad Veidt; *D:* Richard Oswald.

Chain Gang Killings 🐶 **1980** Pair of shackled prisoners, one black, the other white, escape from a truck transporting them to prison. **99m/C VHS.** Ian Yule, Ken Gampu; *D:* Clive Harding; *W:* Ian Yule; *C:* Vincent Cox; *M:* Paul Nissen.

Chain Gang Women woof! **1972 (R)** Sordid violence. Two escaped convicts plunder, rob, and rape until a victim's husband comes looking for revenge. **85m/C VHS, DVD.** Robert Lott, Barbara Mills, Mi-

chael Stearns, Linda York, Wes Bishop, Phil Hoover, Chuck Wells; *D:* Lee Frost.

Chain Lightning 🐶🐶 **1950** Bogart stars as a bomber pilot who falls in love with a Red Cross worker (Parker) while fighting in Europe in 1943. They lose touch after the war until Bogie goes to work as a test pilot for the same shady airplane manufacturer (Massey) where Parker works. He is given the chance to test a new plane, which has already cost the life of one of his friends. Bogart has more success, along with rekindling the flames of romance. Average script but the flying sequences are well-done. **94m/B VHS.** Humphrey Bogart, Eleanor Parker, Raymond Massey, Richard Whorf; *D:* Stuart Heisler; *W:* Liam O'Brien, Vincent B. Evans.

Chain of Command 🐶🐶 **1995 (R)** Anti-terrorist agent Merrill Ross (Dudikoff) goes up against hired mercenaries trying to overthrow the government of the oil-rich Republic of Qumir. Then Ross realizes he's being manipulated and it could be by any number of players. **97m/C VHS, DVD.** Todd Curtis, Keren Tishman, Michael Dudikoff, R. Lee Ermey; *D:* David Worth; *W:* Christopher Applegate, Ben Jonson Handy; *C:* Avi Koren; *M:* Gregory King.

Chain of Command 🐶🐶 **2000 (R)** Agent Mike Connelly (Muldoon) must protect the President's (Scheider) briefcase-sized computer that holds the nuclear codes. But when one of Connelly's colleagues betrays them, a nuclear winter could be as close as a madman's command. **96m/C VHS, DVD.** Patrick Muldoon, Roy Scheider, Michael Biehn, Maria Conchita Alonso, Ric Young, William R. Moses, Michael Mantell, Pat Skipper; *D:* John Terlesky. **VIDEO**

Chain of Desire 🐶🐶 **1993** Nightclub inside Manhattan's Chrysler Building is the spot for numerous folk to have a lot of meaningless sexual encounters and look at the emptiness of their lives. **107m/C VHS.** Linda Fiorentino, Elias Koteas, Malcolm McDowell, Grace Zabriskie, Tim Guinee, Assumpta Serna, Patrick Bauchau, Seymour Cassel, Kevin Conroy, Angel Aviles, Holly Marie Combs, Jamie Harrold, Dewey Weber, Suzzanne Douglass; *D:* Temistocles Lopez; *C:* Temistocles Lopez; *M:* Nathan Birnbaum.

Chain of Fools 🐶🐶½ **2000 (R)** Suicidal barber Zahn comes into possession of a stolen treasure and falls for detective Hayek, who's assigned to the case. Director Traktor is actually a six-person Swedish filmmaking collective. **98m/C DVD.** Steve Zahn, Salma Hayek, Jeff Goldblum, Elijah Wood, David Cross, Tom Wilkinson, Orlando Jones, Kevin Corrigan, David Hyde Pierce, Lara Flynn Boyle, Michael Rapaport, Craig Ferguson, John Cassini; *D:* Traktor.

Chain of Souls woof! **2000** Cult finds self-fulfillment through murder, luring wannabe actresses to fake auditions. One victim has a sister who worries when she doesn't hear from her sibling so she hightails it to Hollywood to find out what happened. Sound familiar? **105m/C VHS, DVD.** Joe Decker, Eric Chaikin, Denise Gossett, Suzanne Talhouk, Deborah Joy Vinall, Stephanie Kane; *D:* Steve Jarvis; *W:* Dennis Devine; *C:* Dennis Devine; *M:* Michael Kelley. **VIDEO**

Chain Reaction 🐶🐶½ *Nuclear Run* 1996 (PG-13) Government/scientific conspiracy chase story finds Chicago lab tech Eddie Kasalivich (Reeves) a member of a research team that's discovered the formula for cheap, pollution-free energy. This doesn't sit well with someone since the team's leader is murdered and the lab destroyed in an explosion. Eddie and scientist Lily Sinclair (Weisz) become prime suspects and are pursued by the feds as they try to find the real culprits. Old pro Freeman, as money man Paul Shannon, is the best reason to watch (as usual). Davis did "The Fugitive," so he knows his tension-filled chases but this is just more same old-same old. **107m/C VHS, DVD.** Blu-

ray Disc, **UMD.** Keanu Reeves, Morgan Freeman, Rachel Weisz, Fred Ward, Brian Cox, Kevin Dunn, Joanna Cassidy, Chelcie Ross, Tzi Ma, Nicholas Rudall, Peter J. D'Noto; *D:* Andrew Davis; *W:* J.F. Lawton, Michael Bortman; *C:* Frank Tidy; *M:* Jerry Goldsmith.

Chained 🐶🐶½ **1934** Crawford and Gable star in this love triangle that somehow never sizzles. Crawford, in love with married businessman Kruger, takes a South American cruise to get away from it all, meets Gable, and of course falls in love. Seems simple enough, but wait! Crawford goes back to New York City and marries Kruger (his wife grants him a divorce) and is miserable. But then Gable shows up, further complicating matters. Choices, choices. Predictable script was not helped by half-hearted performances. **73m/B VHS.** Joan Crawford, Clark Gable, Otto Kruger, Stuart Erwin, Una O'Connor; *D:* Clarence Brown; *C:* George J. Folsey.

Chained for Life woof! **1951** Daisy and Violet Hilton, real life Siamese twins, star in this old-fashioned "freak" show. When a gigolo deserts one twin on their wedding night, the other twin shoots him dead. The twins go on trial and the judge asks the viewer to hand down the verdict. Exploitative and embarrassing to watch. **81m/B VHS, DVD.** Daisy Hilton, Violet Hilton, Allen Jenkins, Sheldon Leonard; *D:* Harry Fraser; *W:* Nat Tanchuck.

Chained Heat 🐶🐶 **1983 (R)** Seamy tale of the vicious reality of life for women behind bars. Naive Blair is imprisoned again (after another bad jailhouse gig in "Born Innocent") and has usual assortment of negative experiences with domineering prisoners, degenerate guards, and the creepy warden who maintains a prison bachelor pad equipped with hot tub. Needless to say, she grows up in a hurry. Trashifying, archetypal women-in-prison effort that aims to satisfy full range of low-quality audience demands. Sequel to 1982 "Concrete Jungle." **97m/C VHS, DVD.** *GE* Linda Blair, Stella Stevens, Sybil Danning, Tamara Dobson, Henry Silva, John Vernon, Nita Talbot, Louisa Moritz, Sharon Hughes, Robert Miano, Kendal Kaldwell; *D:* Paul Nicholas; *W:* Paul Nicholas, Vincent Mongol; *C:* Mac Ahlberg; *M:* Joseph Conlan. Golden Raspberries '83: Worst Support. Actress (Danning).

Chained Heat 2 🐶🐶½ **1992 (R)** Another sordid tale of women behind bars. Nielsen stars as the psychotic stiletto-heeled warden of an infamous prison, complete with sadistic heroin-smuggling guards. This drug ring also deals in prostitution, which results in two imprisoned sisters (innocent, naturally) being separated from one another. One sister is determined to find true justice. **98m/C VHS, DVD.** Brigitte Nielsen, Paul Koslo, Kari Whitman, Kimberley Kates; *D:* Lloyd A. Simandl; *W:* Chris Hyde.

Chained Heat 3: Hell Mountain 🐶🐶½ *Chained Heat 3: The Horror of Hell Mountain; Chained Heat 3* 1998 (R) Future Earth is a barren wasteland where survivors are forced to work in the mines of overlord Stryker. Each year, young women are taken to the mines on Hell Mountain but this time Kal is determined to save his girlfriend and destroy Stryker. **97m/C VHS, DVD.** Bentley Mitchum, Kate Rodger, Christopher Clarke, Karel Augusta, Noelle Balfour, Jack Scalia, Sarah Douglas; *D:* Mike Rohl; *W:* Chris Hyde; *C:* David Frazee; *M:* Peter Allen. **VIDEO**

Chains 🐶🐶 **1989 (R)** A Chicago gangland feud entraps two couples in its web, and the innocents must take care of themselves when the situation goes from bad to worse. **93m/C VHS.** Jimi Jourdan, Michael Dixon, John L. Eves; *D:* Roger J. Barski.

Chains of Gold 🐶🐶 **1992 (R)** Kind social worker (Travolta) befriends teen who wants to get out of the crack-dealing gang in which he's involved. He infiltrates the gang and risks his life helping the boy get out. **95m/C VHS, DVD.** John Travolta, Marilu Henner, Bernie Casey, Hector Elizondo, Joey Lawrence; *D:* Rod Holcomb; *M:* Trevor Jones. **CABLE**

The Chair 🐾🐾 *Hot Seat* 1987 (R) The penitentiary where an evil superintendent was fried in his own electric chair during an inmate uprising is reopened after two decades. The new warden (Benedict), a man who used to be a subordinate to th dead man, believes in rigid control of the inmates and locks horns with the big-house shrink (Coco), who on the surface is an intelligent humanitarian, but may have a darker side. This acrimonious dispute takes a back seat, when it appears that the spirit of the late warden has come back to make the inmates pay for his untimely death. 90m/C VHS. James Coco, Paul Benedict, Stephen Geoffreys, Trini Alvarado, Gary McCleery, Paul Calderon; D: Waldemar Korzeniowsky; C: Steven J. Ross.

Chairman of the Board Woof! 1997 (PG-13) Some studio executive decided to take a bad prop comic named after a vegetable and give him a major motion picture. If this movie accomplishes one thing, it may be the abolition of Friday afternoon 12-martini lunches in Hollywood. Carrot Top plays Edison, a wacky surfer/inventor who befriends an old eccentric man. After the old guy heads for the big wave in the sky, it turns out that he was fabulously wealthy and left his company to Edison. This doesn't sit well with the conniving Bradford (Miller). Courtney Thorne-Smith plays Natalie (although this does not stop Mr. Top from calling her Courtney in one scene) as the standard love interest. Also appearing are Jack Warden, Raquel Welch and M. Emmet Walsh. Why? That's what they're asking their agents. Rent it only if every single video, including the instructional mime section, is already out. 95m/C VHS, DVD, Carrot Top, Larry Miller, Raquel Welch, Jack Warden, Estelle Harris, Bill Erwin, M. Emmet Walsh, Jack McGee, Glenn Shadix, Fred Stoller, Mystro Clark, Jack Plotnick; D: Alex Zamm; W: Al Septien, Turi Meyer, Alex Zamm; M: Chris Hajian.

Chalk 🐾🐾½ 2006 (PG-13) Dark ccmedic look at the frustrations endured by a group of high school teachers over a typical school year. Assistant principal Reddell (Haragan) finds administrative duties are even worse than teaching. Vain Mr. Stroope (Mass) is determined to be popular with his students so he can be named teacher of the year, tough gym coach Ms. Webb (J. Schrenmer) is tired of everyone assuming she's a lesbian, and shy rookie Mr. Lowrey (T. Schrenmer) can't manage his unruly students. 84m/C DVD. C ris Mass, Shannon Haragan, Janelle Schremmer, Troy Schremmer; D: Mike Akel; W: Chris Mass, Mike Akel; C: Steven Schaefer; M: Chris Jagich.

The Chalk Garden 🐾🐾🐾 1964 A woman with a mysterious past takes on the job of governess for an unruly 14-year-old girl, with unforseen consequences. An excellent adaptation of the Enid Bagnold play although not as suspenseful as the stage production. 106m/C VHS. GB Deborah Kerr, Hayley Mills, Edith Evans, John Mills, Elizabeth Sellars, Felix Aylmer; D: Ronald Neame; W: John Michael Hayes; M: Malcolm Arnold. Natl. Bd. of Review '64. Support. Actress (Evans).

Challenge Woof! 1974 (PG) When his entire family is killed, dad decides to seek revenge with his shotgun. Very bloody and violent and very nearly plotless. 90m/C VHS. Earl Owensby, William T. Hicks, Katheyn Thompson, Johnny Popwell; D: Martin Beck.

The Challenge 🐾🐾 1938 Story of the courageous party of explorers who conquered the Matterhorn. Incredible avalanche scenes. 77m/B VHS. GB Luis Trenker, Robert Douglas, Joan Gardner, Mary Clare, Frank Birch, Geoffrey Wardwell, Lyonel (Lionel) Watts, Fred Groves, Lawrence (Lawrence) Baskcomb, Ralph Truman; D: Milton Rosmer; C: Albert Benitz, Georges Perinal; M: Allan Gray, Muir Mathieson.

The Challenge 🐾🐾½ 1982 (R) A contemporary action spectacle which combines modern swordplay with mysticism and fantasy of ancient Samurai legends. 108m/C VHS. Scott Glenn, Toshiro Mifune; D: John Frankenheimer; W: John Sayles; Richard Maxwell; M: Jerry Goldsmith.

A Challenge for Robin Hood 🐾½ 1968 Innocuous and poorly done children's adventure tale about the daring 12th-century nobleman-turned-bandit, Robin Hood (Ingham), and his usual gang in Sherwood Forest. This time Robin has been framed for murder by his evil cousin, Roger (Blythe), and must prove his innocence. 96m/C VHS. GB Barrie Ingham, Peter Blythe, James Hayter, John Arnatt, Leon Greene, Gay Hamilton; D: C.M. Pennington-Richards; W: Peter Bryan; C: Arthur Grant; M: Gary Hughes.

Challenge of a Lifetime 🐾🐾½ 1985 Marshall stars as a divorcee whose dream is to compete in the Hawaiian Ironman Triathlon. Cult favorite; Woronov has a substantial supporting role. 100m/C VHS. Penny Marshall, Richard Gilliland, Jonathan Silverman, Mary Woronov, Paul Gleason, Mark Spitz, Cathy Rigby; D: Russ Mayberry.

Challenge of McKenna 🐾🐾 1970 Run-of-the-prairie horse opera has drifter Ireland stumble upon danger and intrigue when he enters a mysterious town. 90m/C VHS. IT SP Annabella Incontrera, Roberto Camardiel, John Ireland, Robert Woods; D: Leon Klimovsky; W: Leon Klimovsky; C: Francisco Sanchez; M: Francesco De Masi.

Challenge of the Masters 🐾 1989 A young Kung-Fu artist wins a new tutor in a contest. Soon he's fighting for a friend to protect his family's honor. 97m/C VHS. Liu Chia Hui, Liu Chia-Yung, Chen Kuan-Tai, Chiang Yang; D: Liu Chia-Lang.

Challenge To Be Free 🐾🐾 1976 (G) Mad Trapper of the Yukon 1976 (G) Action adventure geared toward a young audience depicting the struggles of a man being pursued by 12 men and 100 dogs across a thousand miles of frozen wilderness. The original hero was a Skye Terrier; remake cameo as Marshal McGee. Produced in 1972, the release wasn't until 1976. 90m/C VHS, DVD. Mike Mazurki, Jimmy Kane; Cameos: Tay Garnett; D: Tay Garnett.

Challenge to Lassie 🐾🐾½ 1949 (G) When Lassie's Scottish master dies, the faithful pup remains at his grave. An unsympathetic policeman orders Lassie to leave the premises, inspiring a debate among the townsfolk as to the dog's fate. Based on a true story (although the original hero was a "Greyfriar's Bobby"). 76m/C VHS. Edmund Gwenn, Donald Crisp, Geraldine Brooks, Reginald Owen, Alan Webb, Henry Stephenson, Alan Napier, Sara Allgood; D: Richard Thorpe; M: Andre Previn.

Challenge to White Fang 🐾½ 1986 (PG) A courageous dog prevents a scheming businessman from taking over an old man's gold mine. 89m/C VHS. Harry Carey Jr., Franco Nero; D: Lucio Fulci.

The Challengers 🐾🐾½ 1989 Young Mackie wants to join local rock band The Challengers, only to discover their main rule is no girls. So Mackie disguises herself as her male cousin Mac—getting ever more confused as she tries to juggle her dual identities. Then she gets found out. 97m/C VHS. Gena Zamprogna, Gwynyth Walsh, Eric Christmas, Eric Till; W: Clive Endersby.

The Chamber 🐾🐾 1996 (R) Dull retelling of yet another John Grisham legal thriller fails to engross. White supremacist Sam Cahall (Hackman) is on Mississippi's death row for killing two Jewish boys in a 1967 bombing. Young Chicago lawyer Adam Hall (O'Donnell), looking to find out more about his family's odious past, volunteers to work on his grandfather's case and win a stay of execution. Sam's an unrepentant racist but there's some question about whether he was the only culprit. Michigan to impersonate a lawyer for the daughter) are their usual professional selves while the charming O'Donnell seems out of his depth. Co-screenwriter Robinson used the pen name Chris Reese. 113m/C VHS, DVD. Gene Hackman, Chris O'Donnell, Faye Dunaway, Lela Rochon, Robert Prosky, Raymond J. Barry, Bo Jackson, David Marshall Grant, Millie Perkins; D: James Foley; W: Phil Alden Robinson, William Goldran; C: Ian Baker; M: Carter Burwell.

Chamber of Horrors 🐾🐾½ 1940 A family is brought together at an English castle to claim a fortune left by an aristocrat. However, there's a catch—seven keys may open the vault with the fortune, or leave the key turner dead. Based on the novel by Edgar Wallace. 80m/B VHS, DVD. GB Leslie Banks, Lilli Palmer; D: Norman Lee.

The Chambermaid on the Titanic 🐾🐾🐾½ La Femme de Chambre du Titanic, The Chambermaid 1997 French foundry worker Horty (Martinez) wins a strongman contest and his prize is a trip to Southampton to see the launch of the Titanic. There he (platonically) shares a hotel room with maid Maria (Sanchez-Gijon), who says she has a job aboard the ship. After returning home and learning about the Titanic's sinking, Horty regales his friends with stories of his night with Maria—gradually beginning to believe his own lies about his passionate escapade. Based on the novel by Didier Decoin. French with subtitles. 96m/C VHS, FR SP Olivier Martinez, Aitana Sanchez-Gijon, Romane Bohringer, Didier Bezace Aldo Maccione; D: Bigas Luna; W: Bigas Luna, Cuca Canals; C: Patrick Blossier; M: Alberto Iglesias.

Chameleon 🐾🐾 1995 (R) Undercover agent, and master of disguise, Willie Serling (LaPaglia), had his wife and daughter murdered by drug smuggler Alberto Cortese (Mandola) and he has naturally wants revenge. Willie poses as a bank auditor to learn if Cortese is behind a money-laundering scheme and things get increasingly complex. Talky thriller with lots of cliches. 108m/C VHS. Anthony LaPaglia, Kevin Pollak, Melora Hardin, Wayne Knight, Tony Lo Bianco, Derek McGrath, Andy Romano, Robin Thomas, Richard Brooks; D: Michael Pavone; W: Michael Pavone; C: Ross Berryman; M: John Debney.

Chameleon 🐾🐾 1998 (R) Phillips is a genetically engineered hit woman who can literally blend into any background (hence the title). Her evil creator/employers send her to dispose of a ragtag band of malcontent scientists whose leader has developed a dangerous microchip. But she develops unexpected maternal feelings towards the group's leader and vows to protect him. 90m/C VHS. Bobbie Phillips, Eric Lloyd, Philip Casnoff; D: Stuart Cooper. TV

Chameleon 2: Death Match 🐾🐾 1999 Kam (Phillips), the genetically engineered ultimate hunter, returns and her assignment is to infiltrate an exclusive nightclub where a terrorist is holding a bunch of execs hostage. 90m/C VHS. Bobbie Phillips, Casey Siemaszko, Tasha Smith, Kara Zediker, Simon Westaway, Mark Lee; D: Russell King; W: Bennett Cohen; C: David Connell; M: Roger Neill. TV

Chameleon 3: Dark Angel 🐾🐾 2000 Genetically engineered Kam (Phillips), who's working for the International Bureau of Investigation, is called upon to protect a sullen, suspicious young woman who knows how to control an energy matter device that was stolen from a government facility. But Kam's assignment is threatened by her evil counterpart—her own genetically engineered brother, Kane (Kuzelicki). 87m/C VHS. Bobbie Phillips, Suzi Dougherty, Alex Kuzelicki, Teal Redmann, Doug Penty; D: John Lafia; W: Ronnie Christensen; C: David Foreman; M: Joel Goldsmith. TV

Chameleon Street 🐾🐾🐾 1989 (R) Entertaining fact-based account of William Douglas Street, a Detroit man who successfully impersonated, among others, a Time magazine reporter and a surgeon until he was caught and sent to prison. He escaped and went to Yale, faked his identity as a student, and then returned to Detroit's Human Rights Commission. Harris wrote and directed this insightful look into the man who fooled many people, including the mayor of Detroit. Coleman A. Young, who appears briefly as himself. 95m/C VHS. Wendell B. Harris Jr., Angela Leslie, Amina Fakir; Paula McGee, Mano Breckenridge; on: D: Addison Randall; Charles Kanganis.

Champagne 🐾🐾 1928 A socialite's father fakes bankruptcy to teach his irresponsible daughter a lesson. Early, silent endeavor from Hitchcock is brilliantly photographed. 93m/B VHS. DVD, GB Betty Balfour, Gordon Harker, Ferdinand von Alten, Clifford Heatherley, Jack Trevor; D: Alfred Hitchcock; W: Alfred Hitchcock.

Champagne for Breakfast 🐾 1935 (R) Sex comedy follows the fun-filled adventures of "Champagne," a free-spirited beauty living life to the fullest. 69m/B VHS. Mary Carlisle, Hardie Albright, Joan Marsh, Lila Lee, Sidney Toler, Bradley Page, Emerson Treacy; D: Melville Brown.

Champagne for Caesar 🐾🐾🐾 1950 The laughs keep coming in this comedy about a self-proclaimed genius-on-everythingy subject who goes on a TV quiz show and proceeds to win everything in sight. The program's sponsor, in desperation, hires a femme fatale to distract the contestant before the final program. Wonderful spoof of the game-show industry. 99m/B VHS, DVD. Ronald Colman, Celeste Holm, Vincent Price, Art Linkletter, Barbara Britton; D: Richard Whorf.

Champion 🐾🐾🐾 1949 An ambitious prizefighter alienates the people around him as he desperately fights his way to the top. When he finally reaches his goal, he is forcec to question the cost of his success. From a story by Ring Lardner. Certainly one of the best films ever made about boxing, with less sentiment than "Rocky" but concerned with sociological correctness. 99m/B VHS, DVD. Kirk Douglas, Marilyn Maxwell, Ruth Roman, Lola Albright, Paul Stewart; D: Mark Robson; C: Franz Planer; M: Dimitri Tiomkin. Oscars '49: Film Editing.

Champions 🐾🐾 1984 Moving but cliched story of Bob Champion, a leading jockey who overcame cancer to win England's Grand National Steeplechase. A true story, no less. 113m/C VHS, DVD. GB John Hurt, Gregory Jones, Mick Dillon, Ann Bell, Jan Francis, Peter Barkworth, Edward Woodward, Ben Johnson, Kirstie Alley, Alison Steadman; D: John Irvin; W: Evan Jones; M: Carl Davis.

Chan Is Missing 🐾🐾🐾 1982 Two cab drivers try to find the man who stole their life savings. Wry, low-budget comedy filmed in San Francisco's Chinatown was an art-house smash. The first full-length American film produced exclusively by an Asian-American cast and crew. 80m/B VHS, DVD. Wood Moy, Marc Hayashi, Laureen Chew, Judy Mihei, Peter Wang, Presco Tabios, Frankie Allarcon, Virginia Cerenio, Roy Chan, George Woo, Emily Yamasaki, Ellen Yeung; D: Wayne Wang; W: Wayne Wang, Terrel Seltzer, Isaac Cronin; C: Michael J. Chin; M: Robert Kikuchi-Yngojo. Natl. Film Reg. '95.

Chance 🐾½ 1989 With over $1 million in diamonds missing, Haggerty and Jacobs throw out all the stops to recover them in this action thriller. 90m/C VHS, DVD. Dan Haggerty, Lawrence-Hilton Jacobs, Addison Randall, Roger Rudd, Charles Gries, Pamela Dixon; D: Addison Randall; Charles Kanganis.

The Champ 🐾🐾🐾 1932 A washed up boxer dreams of making a comeback and receives support from no one but his devoted son. Minor classic most notorious for jerking the tears and ladling the hankie; this was the first of three Beery/Cooper screen teamings. Remade per screen teamings. 87m/B VHS, DVD. Wallace Beery, Jackie Cooper, Irene Rich, Roscoe Ates, Edward Brophy, Hale Hamilton, Jesse Scott, Marcia Mae Jones; D: King Vidor; W: Frances Marion. Oscars '32: Actor (Beery), Story.

The Champ 🐾🐾 1979 (PG) An ex-fighter with a weakness for gambling and drinking is forced to return to the ring in an attempt to keep custody of his son. Excessive sentiment may cause cringing. Remake of the 1931 classic. 121m/C VHS. Jon Voight, Faye Dunaway, Rick Schroder, Jack Warden, Arthur Hill, Strother Martin, Joan Blondell, Elisha Cook Jr.; D: Franco Zeffirelli; C: Fred W. Koenekamp; M: Dave Grusin.

Chamber of Horrors — Young; D: Wendell B. Harris Jr.; W: Wendell B. Harris Jr.; C: Daniel S. Noga; M: Peter S. Moore. Sundance '90: Grand Jury Prize.

Chances Are 🐾🐾 1989 (PG) After her loving husband dies in a chance accident, a pregnant woman remains unmarried, keeping her husband's best friend as her only close male companion. Years later, her now teenage daughter brings a friend home for dinner, but due to an error in heaven, the young man begins to realize that this may not be the first time he and this family have met. A wonderful love-story hampered only minimally by the unbelievable plot. 108m/C VHS, DVD. Cybill Shepherd, Robert Downey Jr., Ryan O'Neal, Mary Stuart Masterson, Josef Sommer, Christopher McDonald, Joe Grifasi, James Noble, Susan Ruttan, Fran Ryan; D: Emile Ardolino; W: Randy Howze, Perry Howze; C: William A. Fraker; M: Maurice Jarre.

Chandu on the Magic Island 🐾🐾 1934 Chandu the Magician takes his powers of the occult to the mysterious lost island of Lemuria to battle the evil cult of Ubasti. Sequel to "Chandu the Magician" and just as campy. 67m/B VHS, DVD. Bela Lugosi, Maria Alba, Clara Kimball Young; D: Ray Taylor.

Chandu the Magician 🐾🐾 1932 Bad guy searches desperately for the secret of a powerful death ray so he can (surprise!) destroy civilization. Not well received in its day, but makes for great high-camp fun now. One of Lugosi's most melodramatic performances. 70m/B VHS. Edmund Lowe, Bela Lugosi, Irene Ware, Henry B. Walthall; D: William Cameron Menzies, Marcel Varnel; C: James Wong Howe.

Chanel Solitaire 🐾🐾 1981 (R) Uninspiring biography follows the fabulous (simply fabulous) career of dress designer Gabrielle "Coco" Chanel. Ah, go sew something. 124m/C VHS, DVD. D: Marie-France Pisier, Rutger Hauer, Timothy Dalton, Karen Black, Brigitte Fossey; D: George Kaczender.

Chang: A Drama of the Wilderness 🐾🐾🐾½ 1927 A farmer and his family has settled a small patch of ground on the edge of the jungle and must struggle for survival against numerous wild animals. The climactic elephant stampede is still thrilling. Shot on location in Siam. 67m/B VHS, DVD. D: Merian C. Cooper, Ernest B. Schoedsack; W: Merian C. Cooper, Ernest B. Schoedsack; C: Ernest B. Schoedsack.

Change of Habit 🐾🐾 1969 (G) Three novitiates undertake to learn about the world before becoming full-fledged nuns. While working at a ghetto clinic a young doctor forms a strong, affectionate relationship with one of them. Presley's last feature film. 🎵Change of Habit; Let Us Pray; Rubberneckin'. 93m/C VHS, DVD. Elvis Presley, Mary Tyler Moore, Barbara McNair, Ed Asner, Ruth McDevitt, Regis Toomey, Jane Elliot, Leora Dana, Robert Emhardt, Richard Carlson, William (Bill) Elliott; D: William A. Graham; W: Eric Bercovici, John Joseph; C: Russell Metty; M: Billy Goldenberg.

Change of Heart 🐾🐾½ 1998 Smart is always good in wronged woman roles and she's got a doozy in this weepie. Elaine Marshall (Smart) thinks she and husband Jim (Terry) are doing okay marriage-wise. They've been together 20 years, have a couple of kids, two good careers, and apparent happiness. Then Elaine realizes Jim's having an affair. The real shocker for Elaine comes when she finds out her husband's lover is another man. 7m/C VHS. Jean Smart, John Terry, Gretchen Corbett, Phillip Geoffrey Hough, Shawna Waldron, Dorian Harewood; D: Arvin Brown; W: Aaron Mendelsohn; C: John Campbell; M: Patrick Williams. CABLE

A Change of Seasons 🐾🐾 1980 (R) One of them so-called sophisticated comedies that look at the contemporary relationships and values of middle-class, middle-aged people who should know better. The wife of a college professor learns of her husband's affair with a seductive student and decides to have a fling with a younger man. The situation reaches absurdity when the couples decide to vacation together. 102m/C VHS, DVD. Shirley MacLaine, Bo Derek, Anthony Hopkins, Michael Brandon, Mary Beth Hurt; D: Richard Lang; W: Erich Segal; M: Henry Mancini.

The Changeling 🐾🐾½ 1980 (R) A music teacher moves into an old house and discovers that a young boy's ghostly spirit is his housemate. The ghost wants revenge against the family that replaced him upon his death. Scary ghost story with some less than logical leaps of script. 114m/C VHS, DVD. CA George C. Scott, Trish Van Devere, John Russell, Melvyn Douglas, Jean Marsh, John Colicos, Barry Morse, Roberta Maxwell, James B. Douglas; D: Peter Medak; W: William Gray, Diana Maddox; C: John Coquillon. Genie '80: Film.

Changes 🐾 1969 (PG) A young man leaves home and thumbs across the California coast in order to find himself. On the road again. 103m/C VHS. Kent Lane, Michele Carey, Jack Albertson, Marcia Strassman; D: Hall Bartlett.

Changing Habits 🐾🐾 1996 (R) Starving artist Soosh (Kelly) moves into a nunnery, in exchange for doing chores, in order to save money. She's so broke, she's taken to stealing art supplies, but salesman Felix (Walsh) is more interested in romancing Soosh than turning her in. Dull, dull, and a waste of a talented cast. 92m/C VHS, DVD. Moira Kelly, Christopher Lloyd, Teri Garr, Shelley Duvall, Dylan Walsh, Marissa Ribisi, Frances Bay, Bob Gunton, Anne Haney, Eileen Brennan; D: Lynn Roth; W: Scott Davis Jones; C: Mike Mayers; M: David McHugh.

Changing Lanes 🐾🐾🐾 2002 (R) A fender-bender on the FDR pits two harried New Yorkers in an escalating battle of revenge. Banek (Affleck), a privileged Wall Street lawyer, and Gipson (Jackson), a recovering-alcoholic insurance man, both need to get to court on time. Banek to file documents crucial to his firm's success, and Gipson to prove he's fit to retain joint custody of his two kids. Because of the accident, neither gets quite what he wants. When Gipson finds that he has the the vital document, after having been stranded by Banek (and subsequently late to the custody hearing), he begins the battle. Throughout the back and forth, the plot (and many of its excesses), gives way to a fully realized character study and thoughtful pondering of motivations, corruption, and desperation, powered by dialogue not usually seen in a "revenge" flick. Michell deftly brings out the best in every member of a talented cast. 98m/C VHS, DVD. US Ben Affleck, Samuel L. Jackson, Toni Collette, Sydney Pollack, William Hurt, Amanda Peet, Richard Jenkins, Kim Staunton, John Benjamin Hickey, Jennifer (Jennie) Dundas Lowe, Dylan Baker, Matt Malloy, Pamela Hart; D: Roger Michell; W: Michael Tolkin, Chap Taylor; C: Salvatore Totino; M: David Arnold.

Changing Times 🐾🐾 Les Temps Qui Changent 2004 Sucessful engineer Antoine (Depardieu) has spent the last three decades pining for Cecile (Deneuve), the love of his life, who left France for Morocco more than 30 years ago, and has since moved on with her life. Antoine volunteers for a job in Tangiers and promptly tracks down Cecile (and her much younger documentary filmmaker son. Layers of heady complications follow, including the appearance of Cecile's son, who drops by with his girlfriend despite his being gay, Cecile's own deteriorating marriage, and cultural clashes between French and Moroccan characters and their values. Pic is a reunion of French legends Deneuve, Depardieu and director Andre Techine and will appeal to Francophiles and probably few. 90m/C VHS, DVD. FR Catherine Deneuve, Gerard Depardieu, Gilbert Melki, Malik Zidi, Lubna Azabal, Tanya Lopert, Nabila Baraka, Idir Elomri, Nadem Rachati, Jabir Elomri; D: Andre Techine; W: Andre Techine, Pascal Bonitzer, Laurent Guyot; C: Julien Hirsch; M: Juliette Garrigues.

The Channeler 🐾 1989 The traditional dopey students probe an old Colorado mine and encounter black-robed, demon whazzits. A spunky cast and nice scenery didn't stop the Hound from switching channels on this one. 90m/C VHS. Dan Haggerty, Richard Harrison, Jay Richardson, David Homb, Oliver Darrow, Robin Sims, Charles Solomon; D: Grant Austin Waldman.

The Chant of Jimmie Blacksmith 🐾🐾🐾 1978 (R) Intense, ultraviolent true story set in 19th century Australia follows aborigine Jimmie as he is brutalized by white civilization and responds in kind. Shocking violence perpetrated by and to Jimmie is not for the faint of heart, and is not softened in the least by the superb performances by the excellent cast. 120m/C VHS. AU Tommy (Tom E.) Lewis, Bryan Brown, Ray Barrett, Elizabeth (Liz) Alexander, Jack Thompson, Peter Carroll, Liddy Clark, Ruth Cracknell, Arthur Dignam, Ian Gilmour, John Jarratt, Ray Meagher, Kevin Miles, Robyn Nevin, Angela Punch McGregor, Peter Sumner; D: Fred Schepisi; W: Fred Schepisi; C: Ian Baker; M: Bruce Smeaton.

Chantilly Lace 🐾🐾½ 1993 (R) Ensemble cast tries hard in this story of modern American women and friendship in the '90s. Val (Eikenberry) gathers a group of seven close friends at her new house in Sundance. Turns out trying to "have it all" is causing some emotional crises to surface, which are explored over the course of a year. Actresses improvised their dialogue from basic character information. Lots of weeping and bonding. 102m/C VHS. Jill Eikenberry, Ally Sheedy, Helen Slater, Lindsay Crouse, JoBeth Williams, Martha Plimpton, Talia Shire; D: Linda Yellen; W: Linda Yellen, Rosanne Ehrlich; M: Patrick Seymour. CABLE

Chaos 🐾🐾 2001 Workaholic Parisian businessman Paul (Lindon) and his wife Helene (Frot) are on their way to dinner when a frantic young Algerian immigrant, Noemie (Brakni), begs them to let her in as thugs grab and beat her before their eyes. Paul refuses to get involved and abandons the girl, which sets in motion a domestic crisis for Helene. Guilt-ridden and disgusted by her husband's indifference, Helene tracks the severly-injured Noemie to a hospital and abandons her family to assume responsibility for Noemie and her rehabilitation, which includes protecting from her abusers. French with subtitles. 109m/C VHS, DVD. FR Catherine Frot, Vincent Lindon, Rachida Brakni, Line Renaud, Wojciech Pszoniak, Aurelien Wiik; D: Coline Serreau; W: Coline Serreau; C: Jean-Francois Robin; M: Ludovic Navarre.

Chaos WOOF! 2005 (NC-17) Repulsive, exploitative horror flick features a group of psycho-sickos, led by the Manson-like Chaos (Gage), who torture and finally murder two female college students. Atrocious in every imaginable way. 78m/C DVD. US Kevin Gage, Sage Stallone, Kelly K. C. Quann, Stephen Wozniak; D: David DeFalco; W: David DeFalco; C: Brandon Trost. VIDEO

Chaos & Cadavers 🐾🐾½ 2003 Newlyweds Edward (Moran) and Samantha (Hawes) have their honeymoon at a remote hotel disrupted by rowdy conventioneers attending an undertakers' conference. But when the head of American director's association is found dead under suspicious circumstances, they decide to find out whodunit. 90m/C DVD. GB Nick Moran, Keeley Hawes, Steve Huison, John Bennett, Ian McNeice, Hugh Fraser, Rick Mayall; D: Niklaus Hilber; W: Niklaus Hilber, Drew Bird; C: Tony Imi; M: Warren Bennett.

Chaos Factor 🐾🐾 2000 (R) Jack Poynt (Sabato Jr.) is an Army Intelligence officer working in Cambodia. He discovers evidence linking the death of American soldiers to high-ranking officials and becomes the target of a deadly coverup by the Defense Department. 102m/C VHS, DVD. Antonio Sabato Jr., Fred Ward, Kelly Rutherford, Sean Kanan, R. Lee Ermey; D: Terry Cunningham.

Chaos Theory 🐾🐾 2008 (PG-13) Motivational speaker and efficiency expert Frank Allen (Reynolds) has driven wife Susan (Mortimer) nuts with their micromanaged lifestyle. (Frank really lives what he preaches.) Susan resets their clocks, making Frank late for a conference and throwing his organized world into chaos, which he decides to embrace when he can't seem to get it back under control. But his new attitude leads to Frank and Susan splitting up and just causing a whole different set of problems. Reynolds is likeable (Mortimer less so) but it's a rather odd rom-com entry until it heads into happy ending territory. 86m/C DVD. US Ryan Reynolds, Emily Mortimer, Stuart Townsend, Sarah Chalke, Mike Erwin, Constance Zimmer, Elisabeth Harnois, Damon, Jocelyne Loewen; D: Marcos Siega; W: Daniel Taplitz; C: Ramsay Nickell; M: Gilad Benamram.

Chapayev 🐾🐾🐾 1934 Striking propagandist drama dealing with the exploits of a legendary Red Army commander during the 1919 battle with the White Russians. Stunning, and carefully choreographed, battle scenes. Adapted from a biographical novel by Dmitri Furmanov. In Russian with English subtitles. 101m/B VHS. RU Boris Babochkin, Leonid Kmit, Boris Chirkov, Varvara Myasnikova, Illarian Pevzov, Stephan Shkurat, Boris Blinov, Vyacheslav Volkov, Nikolai Simonov, Georgi Zhzhenov; D: Sergei Vassiliev, Georgy Vassiliev; W: Sergei Vassiliev, Georgy Vassiliev; C: Aleksander Sigayev, Alexander Xenofontov; M: Gavriil Popov.

Chaplin 🐾🐾🐾 1992 (PG-13) The life and career of "The Little Tramp" is chronicled by director Attenborough and brilliantly portrayed by Downey, Jr., as Chaplin. A flashback format traces his life from its poverty-stricken Dickensian origins in the London slums through his directing and acting career, to his honorary Oscar in 1972. Slow-moving at parts, but captures Chaplin's devotion to his art and also his penchant towards jailbait. In a clever casting choice, Chaplin's own daughter from his fourth marriage to Oona O'Neill, Geraldine Chaplin, plays her own grandmother who goes mad. 135m/C VHS, DVD. GB Robert Downey Jr., Dan Aykroyd, Geraldine Chaplin, Kevin Dunn, Anthony Hopkins, Milla Jovovich, Moira Kelly, Kevin Kline, Diane Lane, Penelope Ann Miller, Paul Rhys, John Thaw, Marisa Tomei, Nancy Travis, James Woods, David Duchovny, Deborah Maria Moore, Bill Paterson, John Standing, Robert Stephens, Peter Crook; D: Richard Attenborough; W: Bryan Forbes, William Boyd, William Goldman; C: Sven Nykvist; M: John Barry. British Acad. '92: Actor (Downey).

The Chaplin Revue 🐾🐾½ 1958 The "Revue," put together by Chaplin in 1958, consists of three of his best shorts: "A Dog's Life" (1918), "Shoulder Arms" (1918), and "The Pilgrim," in which a convict hides out in a clerical guise (1922). Chaplin added self-composed score, narration, and some documentary on-the-set material. 121m/B VHS, DVD. Charlie Chaplin, Edna Purviance, Sydney Chaplin, Mack Swain; D: Charlie Chaplin.

Chapter Two 🐾🐾 1979 (PG) Loosely based on Neil Simon's marriage to Mason and his Broadway hit of the same name. A writer, grief-stricken over the death of his first wife, meets the woman who will become his second. Witty dialogue in first half deteriorates when guilt strikes. 124m/C VHS. James Caan, Marsha Mason, Valerie Harper, Joseph Bologna; D: Robert Moore; W: Neil Simon.

Character 🐾🐾 Karakter 1997 (R) Based on the 1938 novel by F. Bordewijk, which follows the troubled relationship of young lawyer Jacob Willem Katadreuffe (van Huet) and his overbearing father in 1920s Rotterdam. Dreverhaven (Decleir) is a powerful bailiff who has an illegitimate son with his servant, Joba (Schuurman), who turns down his marriage proposal. Still, Dreverhaven is determined to control his son's life, even if it means ruining him first. No wonder the old man gets murdered. Dark and unsentimental. Dutch with subtitles. 114m/C VHS, DVD. NL Fedja Van Huet, Jan Decleir, Betty Schuurman, Victor Low, Tamar van Den Dop, Hans Kesting; D: Mike van Diem; W: Mike van Diem; C: Rogier Stoffers; M: Paleis Van Boem. Oscars '97: Foreign Film.

Charade 🐾🐾 1953 Mason and wife Pamela star in this trilogy of love and violence. "Portrait of a Murderer" has a young artist sketching the picture of the man who—unknown to her—has just murdered her girlfriend. "Duel at Dawn" concerns an 1880s Austrian officer who steals a woman from another officer and is then challenged to a duel. "The Midas Touch" revolves around a successful but dissatisfied man who abandons his riches to find the meaning of life. Mason himself had said he hoped "this curiosity" would disap-

Charade 🐾🐾🐾 1963 After her husband is murdered, a young woman finds herself on the run from crooks and double agents who want the $250,000 her husband stole during WWII. Hepburn and Grant are charming and sophisticated as usual in this stylish intrigue filmed in Paris. Based on the story "The Unsuspecting Wife" by Marc Behm and Peter Stone. 113m/C VHS, DVD, Cary Grant, Audrey Hepburn, Walter Matthau, James Coburn, George Kennedy; D: Stanley Donen; W: Peter Stone; C: Charles Lang Jr.; M: Henry Mancini. British Acad. '64: Actress (Hepburn).

The Charge of the Light Brigade 🐾🐾🐾 1936 (PG-13) A British army officer stationed in India deliberately starts the Balaclava charge to even an old score with Surat Khan, who's on the other side. Still an exciting film, though it's hardly historically accurate. De Havilland is along to provide the requisite romance with Flynn. Also available colorized. 115m/ B VHS, DVD, Errol Flynn, Olivia de Havilland, David Niven, Nigel Bruce, Patric Knowles, Donald Crisp, C. Henry Gordon, J. Carrol Naish, Henry Stephenson, E.E. Clive, Scotty Beckett, G.P. (Tim) Huntley Jr., Robert Barrat, Spring Byington, George Regas; D: Michael Curtiz, J.G. Jacoby; C: Sol Polito; M: Max Steiner.

The Charge of the Light Brigade 🐾🐾½ 1968 (PG-13) A British indictment of imperialistic England in this revisionist retelling of the notorious British defeat by the Russians at Balaclava. Battle scenes are secondary to this look at the stupidity of war. Fine cast; notable animation sequences by Richard Williams. 130m/C VHS, DVD, GB Trevor Howard, John Gielgud, David Hemmings, Vanessa Redgrave, Harry Andrews, Jill Bennett, Peter Bowles, Mark Burns, Alan Dobie, T.P. McKenna, Corin Redgrave, Norman Rossington, Rachel Kempson, Donald Wolfit, Howard Marion-Crawford, Mark Dignam, Ben Aris, Peter Woodthorpe, Roger Mutton, Joely "Richard-son; D: Tony Richardson; W: Charles Wood; C: David Watkin; M: John Addison.

Charge of the Model T's 🐾½ 1981 (PG) Comedy about a WWI German spy who tries to infiltrate the U.S. army. 90m/C VHS, Louis Nye, John David Carson, Herb Edelman, Carl Bagdasarian, Arte Johnson; D: Jim McCullough.

Chariots of Fire 🐾🐾🐾 1981 A lush telling of the parallel stories of Harold Abraham and Eric Liddell, English runners who competed in the 1924 Paris Olympics. One was consumed by a hatred of anti-Semitism, the other by the love of God. Outstanding performances by the entire cast. 123m/C VHS, DVD, GB Ben Cross, Ian Charleson, Nigel Havers, Ian Holm, Alice Krige, Brad Davis, Dennis Christopher, Patrick Magee, Cheryl Campbell, John Gielgud, Lindsay Anderson, Nigel Davenport; D: Hugh Hudson; W: Colin Welland; C: David Watkin; M: Vangelis. Oscars '81: Costume Des., Orig. Screenplay, Picture, Orig. Score; British Acad. '81: Film, Support, Actor (Holm); Golden Globes '82: Foreign Film; N.Y. Film Critics '81: Cinematog.

Charlemagne 🐾🐾½ 1995 British miniseries follows the life of the royal conqueror who civilized western Europe and ruled as emperor from 800-814. On five cassettes. 250m/C VHS, DVD.

Charles & Diana: A Palace Divided 🐾🐾 1993 Trashy scandalous tale of the disintegration of the fairytale romance and marriage of Prince Charles and Princess Diana. Oxenberg stars as Princess Di, a role she played a decade ago in "The Royal Romance of Charles and Diana," a fine job playing the conservative Prince Charles. Although the film covers all of the couple's highly publicized troubles, it's such a quick superficial treatment that it's often hard to follow. Nonetheless, it's a flashingly inviting look into the privileged House of Windsor. 92m/C VHS, DVD, Roger Rees, Catherine Oxenberg, Benedict Taylor, Tracy Brabin, Amanda Walker; D: John Power.

Charles: Dead or Alive 🐾🐾 *Charles: Mort ou Vif* 1969 Aging Charles De (Simon) has always lead an ordinary life when he suddenly drops out and reemerges as a madman, who lives only on his own terms. His family becomes so upset by his bizarre behavior that they commit him to an asylum. First feature film by Tanner. French with subtitles. 93m/B VHS; SI Francois Simon; D: Alain Tanner; W: Alain Tanner.

Charles et Lucie 🐾🐾🐾 1979 A has-been couple are ripped off, pursued, persecuted, and saddled with very bad luck in the South of France. Essentially a character study, semi-acclaimed. In French with subtitles. 96m/C VHS, FR Daniel Ceccaldi, Ginette Garcin, Jean-Marie Proslier, Samson Fainsilber; D: Nelly Kaplan.

Charleston 🐾🐾 1926 Renoir's third film, a simple erotic dance fantasy that caused much controversy in its day. Silent, with jazz score and historical introduction. 30m/B VHS, Catherine Hessling; D: Jean Renoir.

Charley and the Angel 🐾🐾½ 1973 (G) Touching story of a man who changes his cold ways with his family when informed by an angel that he hasn't much time to live. Amusing Disney movie set in the Great Depression. 93m/C VHS, DVD, Walter Matthau, Joe Don Baker, Fred MacMurray, Cloris Leachman, Harry Morgan, Kurt Russell, Vincent Van Patten, Kathleen (Kathy) Cody, Kelly Thordsen; D: Vincent McEveety.

Charley Varrick 🐾🐾🐾 1973 (PG) Matthau, a small-town hood, robs a bank only to find out that one of its depositors is the Mob. Baker's the vicious hit-man assigned the job of getting the loot back. A well-paced, on-the-mark thriller. 111m/C VHS, DVD, Walter Matthau, Joe Don Baker, Felicia Farr, John Vernon, Sheree North, Norman Fell, Andrew (Andy) Robinson, Jacqueline Scott, Albert "Poppy" Popwell; D: Donald Siegel; M: Dean Riesner; M: Lalo Schifrin.

Charley's Aunt 🐾🐾🐾 1941 Benny's at his comedic best in this amusing farce. Based on the play by Brandon Thomas. 81m/B VHS, Jack Benny, Kay Francis, James Ellison, Richard Haydn, Arleen Whelan, Anne Baxter, Laird Cregar, Edmund Gwenn, Reginald Owen; D: Archie Mayo; W: George Seaton; C: J. Peverell Marley; M: Alfred Newman.

Charley's Aunt 🐾🐾½ 1925 Amusing Victorian farce in which two young male students convince a co-fellow student to dress up as their female chaperon so they can pitch woo to two local lovelies. Fun performances and well-paced direction by Sidney. Based on the farce, the movie was remade in 1930, starring Charles Ruggles, and again in 1941, with Jack Benny. 75m/B VHS, Sydney Chaplin, Ethel Shannon, Lucien Littlefield, Alec B. Francis, Mary Akin, Priscilla Bonner, Jimmy Harrison, David James, Eulalie Jensen, James E. Page, Phillips Smalley; D: Scott Sidney; W: F. McGrew Willis, Joe Farnham; C: Gus Peterson, Paul Garnett.

Charlie 🐾🐾 2004 (R) Based on the actual events of South London's "Torture Gang" leader Charlie Richardson's (Goss) barbaric 1960s underworld reign. Dramatizes the gang's 1966 trial after Richardson is caught going shady deals with a South African diamond baron. Director Needs' dizzying flashbacks are intense but also question whether the group was really to blame. 94m/C VHS, DVD, Luke Goss, Steven Berkoff, Marcus Weyers, Anita Dobson, Leslie Grantham; D: Malcolm Needs; M: Alfred.

Charlie Chan at Monte Carlo 🐾🐾 1937 Chan (Oland) is gambling in Monaco when two murders occur. One is a two-bit gangster working as a hotel bartender and the other is a casino messenger who was traveling to Paris with a million bucks in bonds that has disappeared. Now Chan has to tie the cases together to solve the crimes. A good portion of the dialog is in French and much is made of the language difficulties of Chan and company. This was Oland's last appearance as the sleuth; he died in 1938. 16th in the series. 71m/B DVD, Warner Oland, Keye Luke, Virginia Field, Sidney Blackmer, Harold Huber, Kay Linaker, Robert Kent; D: Eugene Forde; W: Jerome Cady, Charles Belden; C: Daniel B. Clark; M: Samuel Kaylin.

Charlie Chan at the Circus 🐾🐾 1936 On vacation, Chan takes his wife and 12 (!) children to the circus. When one of the owners is murdered, Chan investigates with the help of some of the performers. Filmed at the Al G. Barnes Circus. 11th in the series. 72m/B DVD, Warner Oland, Keye Luke, Shirley Deane, John McGuire, Francis Ford, J. Carrol Naish, George Brasno, Olive Brasno, Maxine Reiner, Drue Leyton; D: Harry Lachman; W: Robert Ellis, Helen Logan; C: Daniel B. Clark; M: Samuel Kaylin.

Charlie Chan and the Curse of the Dragon Queen 🐾½ 1981 (PG) The famed Oriental sleuth confronts his old enemy the Dragon Queen, and reveals the true identity of a killer. 97m/C VHS, DVD, Peter Ustinov, Lee Grant, Angie Dickinson, Richard Hatch, Brian Keith, Roddy McDowall, Michelle Pfeiffer, Rachel Roberts; D: Clive Donner; W: David Axelrod, Stanley Burns.

Charlie Boy 🐾½ 1981 The new owner of an ancient African idol enters the world of the supernatural when he casts a death spell on six people. 60m/C VHS, DVD, FR Bruno Pradal, Karen Verlier, Jean-François; C: Poxon; D: Rene Demourin.

Charlie Bravo 🐾 1980 (R) A commando group is commanded to rescue a captured nurse in Vietnam. Dubbed. 94m/C VHS, Jean Vincent, Angela Bruce, Marius Goring; D: Robert M. Young.

Charlie Bartlett 🐾🐾 2007 (R) Troubled rich kid Charlie (Yelchin) got kicked out of his private school after doing whatever he could to make himself accepted and popular. Now the new kid at a public high school, Charlie decides the way to ingratiate himself is to become his fellow students' shrink and pharmaceutical supplier. Not yet reviewed. ?m/C US Anton Yelchin, Robert Downey Jr., Hope Davis, Tyler Hilton, Kat Dennings, Jonathan Meen, Jake Epstein, Megan Park, Ishan Dave, Anton Yelchin, Kat Dennings, Robert Downey Jr., Hope Davis, Tyler Hilton, Mark Rendall; D: Jon Poll, Jon Poll; W: Gustin Nash, Gustin Nash; C: Paul Sarossy, Paul Sarossy; M: Christophe Beck.

Charlie and the Great Balloon Chase 🐾🐾 1982 When a grandfather takes his grandson on a cross-country balloon trip, they are hotly pursued by the boy's mother, her stuffy fiance (who wants the boy in military school), the FBI, a reporter, and Adrienne Barbeau, Slim Pickens, Mosie Drier; D: Larry Elikann. TV

Charlie Chan at the Opera 🐾🐾🐾 1936 The great detective investigates an amnesiac opera star (Karloff) who may have committed murder. Considered one of the best of the series. Interesting even to those not familiar with Charlie Chan. 66m/B VHS, DVD, Warner Oland, Boris Karloff, Keye Luke, Charlotte Henry, Thomas Beck, Nedda Harrigan, William Demarest; D: H. Bruce Humberstone; C: Harry Jackson.

Charlie Chan at the Race Track 🐾🐾 1936 Chan (Oland) is traveling by ship from Honolulu to L.A. with some racehorses after his friend, the owner of a champion, is murdered. He and Charlie figures out that gamblers have substituted a nag for a winning horse in order to cash in on the betting action. 12th in the series. 70m/B DVD, Warner Oland, Keye Luke, Helen Wood, Thomas Beck, Alan Dinehart, Gavin Muir; D: H. Bruce Humberstone; W: Robert Ellis, Helen Logan, Edward T. Lowe; C: Harry Jackson.

Charlie Chan at Treasure Island 🐾🐾 1939 Chan (Toler) investigates the alleged suicide of a writer friend, aided by Fred Racini (Romero), an illusionist at the Treasure Island theater at the San Francisco International Exposition. The trail leads them to phony mystic Dr. Zodiac (Mohr), whose predictions somehow involve blackmail. 19th entry in series. 72m/B DVD, Sidney Toler, Victor Sen Yung, Cesar Romero, Gerald Mohr, Pauline Moore, Douglas Fowley, June Gale, Douglass Dumbrille, Sally Blane, Louis Jean Heydt, Donald MacBride; D: Norman Foster; W: John Larkin; C: Virgil Miller; M: Samuel Kaylin.

Charlie Chan at the Wax Museum 🐾🐾½ 1940 Charlie and number one son must find a criminal hiding out in a wax museum. Chills abound when the fugitive heads for the chamber of horrors. 63m/B VHS, Sidney Toler, Victor Sen Yung, C. Henry Gordon, Marc Lawrence, Joan Valerie, Marguerite Chapman, Ted Osborn, Michael Visaroff; D: Lynn Shores.

Charlie Chan in City of Darkness 🐾½ 1939 Chan (Toler) travels to Paris for a reunion of his WWI buddies and finds himself investigating the murder of a munitions manufacturer (Dumbrille) with unsavory clients. Notably preachy entry that reflects the distrust of appeasement and the Munich pact. 20th entry in series. 75m/B DVD, Sidney Toler, Lynn Bari, Richard Clarke, Harold Huber, Leo G. Carroll, Lon Chaney Jr., Henry Gordon, Dorothy Tree, Noel Madison, Pedro de Cordoba; D: Herbert I. Leeds; W: Robert Ellis; C: Virgil Miller.

Charlie Chan in Egypt 🐾🐾 1938 Toler makes his first appearance as Chan, who discovers a murder aboard a cruise ship docked at Honolulu and refuses to let the liner leave until the case is... 1935 Charlie Chan (Oland) is at a dig in Egypt where an archeologist has disappeared. An X-ray reveals that the body in a pharaoh's sarcophagus is that of the missing man. Is there a curse on them for desecrating the ruler's tomb? 8th in the series. 72m/B DVD, Warner Oland, Thomas Beck, Rita Hayworth, Stepin Fetchit, Pat Paterson, Frank M. Thomas Sr., Stepin Fetchit; D: Louis King; W: Robert Ellis, Helen Logan; C: Daniel B. Clark; M: Samuel Kaylin.

Charlie Chan in Honolulu 🐾🐾 ...

Oompa Loompas still sing. And Burton does a more faithful adaptation of the 1964 book by Roald Dahl. Poor boy Charlie Bucket (Highmore) is one of five winners of a golden ticket that allows him to tour the mysterious Willy Wonka's (Depp) chocolate factory. Fans of the original may have qualms, but this one has a little more depth and heart, great visuals, and the co-operation of Dahl's widow, an exec producer. Deep so brilliantly quirky and Highmore shines. 115m/C DVD, Blu-ray Disc, UMD, HD DVD US GB Johnny Depp, Freddie Highmore, David Kelly, AnnaSophia Robb, Deep Roy, Christopher Lee, Helena Bonham-Carter, Noah Taylor, James Fox, Missi Pyle, Julia Winter, Jordan Fry, Philip Wiegratz, Franziska Troegner, Harry Taylor, Adam Godley, Eileen Essell, Liz Smith, David Morris; D: Tim Burton; W: John August; C: Philippe Rousselot; M: Danny Elfman; Nar: Geoffrey Holder.

Charlie Chan at the Olympics 🐾🐾½ 1937 Chan's (Oland) son Lee (Luke) is a member of the American swim team at the Berlin Olympics. When an experimental auto pilot device is stolen, Chan is called in (arriving by blimp) and suspects German spies. Since Lee is busy training, Charlie Chan Jr. (Tom Jr.) steps in to help his pop, but when Lee is kidnapped they may have to stop their investigation to save his life. Newsreel shots of the actual 1936 Olympics add to the atmosphere. 14th in the series. 71m/B DVD, Warner Oland, Keye Luke, Katherine DeMille, Pauline Moore, Layne Tom Jr., Allan "Rocky" Lane, C. Henry Gordon; D: H. Bruce Humberstone.

solved. Sons Jimmy (Yung) and Willie (Tom Jr.) try to help out. 17th entry in the series. **67m/B DVD.** Sidney Toler, Phyllis Brooks, Victor Young, Layne York, Eddie Collins, John "Dusty" King, Claire Dodd, George Zucco, Robert Barrat; **D:** H. Bruce Humberstone; **W:** Charles Belden; **C:** Charles Clarke.

Charlie Chan in London ♪♪ **1934** Pamela (Leyton) pleads with Chan (Oland) to help her brother Paul (Walton) who is about to be hanged for murder. Chan follows Pamela to the country home of Geoffrey Richmond (Mowbray) and tries to reconstruct the crime, nearly getting himself killed in the process. 6th in the series. **72m/B DVD.** Warner Oland, Alan Mowbray, Douglas Walton, Ray Milland, Drue Leyton, Mona Barrie; **D:** Eugene Forde; **W:** Philip MacDonald; **C:** L.W. O'Connell; **M:** Samuel Kaylin.

Charlie Chan in Paris ♪♪½ **1935** Chan scours the city of lights to track down a trio of counterfeiters. Top-notch plot and plenty of suspense will please all. **72m/B VHS.** Warner Oland, Mary Brian, Thomas Beck, Erik Rhodes, John Miljan, Minor Watson, John Qualen, Keye Luke, Henry Kolker; **D:** Lewis Seiler.

Charlie Chan in Rio ♪♪ **1941** Local police call on Chan to help solve a double murder. One of the series' weaker entries but with fine setting and music. **60m/B VHS.** Sidney Toler, Mary Beth Hughes, Cobina Wright Jr., Ted North, Victor Jory, Harold Huber, Victor Sen Yung; **D:** Harry Lachman.

Charlie Chan in Shanghai ♪♪ **1935** Chan (Oland) is called in by the Chinese government to investigate a murder that is tied to an opium ring and he's aided by number one son Lee (Luke). Pretty standard fare is ninth in the series. **70m/B DVD.** Warner Oland, Keye Luke, Irene Hervey, Jon Hall, Russell Hicks, Halliwell Hobbes; **D:** James Tinling; **W:** Edward T. Lowe, Gerald Fairlie; **C:** Barney McGill; **M:** Samuel Kaylin.

Charlie Chan in the Secret Service ♪½ **1944** Toler's Chan is now a government agent who is assigned to find the killer of an inventor. Moreland joins up as Chan's taxi-driving, constantly terrified sidekick. The series moved from 20th-century Fox to low-budget Monogram Pictures with this entry, with an ensuing drop in production quality. **64m/B VHS, DVD.** Sidney Toler, Mantan Moreland, Gwen Kenyon, Arthur Loft, Marianne Quon, Lela Tyler, Benson Fong; **D:** Phil Rosen.

Charlie Chan on Broadway ♪♪ **1937** Fellow ocean liner passenger Billie Bronson (Henry) hides her diary in Chan's (Oland) luggage for safekeeping. Seems Billie is wanted as a material witness in a gangster scandal (the diary names names) and upon her return to New York, she's soon murdered. The diary disappears and Chan has to hit the city's nightspots to investigate. 15th entry in the series. **68m/B DVD.** Warner Oland, Keye Luke, Joan Marsh, J. Edward Bromberg, Louise Henry, Douglas Fowley, Harold Huber, Leon Ames, Joan Woodbury, Jerome Cady; **D:** Eugene Forde; **C:** Charles Belden; **M:** Samuel Kaylin.

Charlie Chan's Secret ♪♪ **1935** Chan must solve the murder of the heir to a huge fortune. A good, logical script with plenty of suspects to keep you guessing. **72m/B VHS.** Warner Oland, Rosina Lawrence, Charles Quigley, Henrietta Crosman, Edward Trevor, Astrid Allwyn; **D:** Gordon Wiles.

Charlie Chaplin: Night at the Show ♪♪ **1915** Chaplin plays two different mugs, both out for a night on the town. Mr. Pest, a sharp-dressed upper-cruster, clings to his disgusting habits, and Mr. Rowdy is his working-class doppelganger. Both obnoxious Chaplins-in-disguise collaborate to wreak havoc on a local theatre. Contains original organ score. **7m/B VHS.** Charlie Chaplin, Edna Purviance; **D:** Charlie Chaplin; **W:** Charlie Chaplin.

Charlie Chaplin .... Our Hero! ♪♪♪ **1915** Two shorts from 1915 written and directed by Chaplin, "Night at the Show" and "In the Park," as well as a 1914 film, "Hot Finish," in which Charlie plays the villain. **58m/B VHS.** Charlie Chaplin, Edna Purviance, Lloyd Bacon, Mabel Nor-

mand, Chester Conklin, Mack Sennett; **D:** Charlie Chaplin.

Charlie Grant's War ♪♪ **1980** The true story of a Canadian businessman who hears of Nazi brutality and determines to save European Jews from persecution during the Holocaust. Not among the more distinguished works of its kind. **130m/C VHS.** GB Jan Rubes, R.H. Thomson, Joan Orenstein; **D:** Martin Lavut.

Charlie McCarthy, Detective woof! **1939** Crooked newspaper editor with mob ties is murdered, and Charlie McCarthy shows up to not really help solve much of anything. Doesn't really work as a mystery or a comedy. **65m/B VHS.** Edgar Bergen, Robert Cummings, Constance Moore, John Sutton, Louis Calhern, Edgar Kennedy, Samuel S. Hinds; **D:** Frank Tuttle; **W:** Harold Shumate, Edward Eliscu, Richard Mack; **C:** George Robinson. **VIDEO**

Charlie Muffin ♪♪ *A Deadly Game* **1979** East-West intrigue prior to the fall of the Berlin Wall finds a Western operative returning from a dangerous mission, only to walk into a trap set by his own side. **104m/C VHS.** GB David Hemmings, Sam Wanamaker, Jennie Linden, Pinkas Braun, Ian Richardson, Ralph Richardson, Shane Rimmer, Donald Churchill, Clive Revill, Frederick Treves; **D:** Jack Gold; **W:** Keith Waterhouse; **M:** Christopher Gunning.

Charlie, the Lonesome Cougar ♪♪ **1967** (G) Life for a rugged logger will never be the same after he adopts an orphaned cougar. From the Disney factory. **75m/C VHS.** Ron Brown, Brian Russell, Clifford Peterson; **D:** Winston Hibler; **W:** Jack Speirs; **C:** William W. Bacon III, Lloyd Beebe; **Nar:** Rex Allen.

Charlie White woof! **2004** Charlie White is a self-destructive party boy with more money than brains, trying to get noticed on the London scene. Charlie takes it badly when someone else steals the limelight but you won't care at all about **DVD.** GB Alex McGettigan, Danny George, Alex Besley, Lucy McCall, Hamish Jenkinson; **D:** Samuel P. Abrahams; **W:** Samuel P. Abrahams; **C:** Samuel P. Abrahams, Oliver Campbell; **M:** Philip Zikking.

Charlie Wilson's War ♪♪ **2007** (R) In the "truth is stranger than fiction" category, Charlie Wilson (Hanks) is a hard-drinking, pleasure-loving Democratic congressman from East Texas who's also resourceful and interested in foreign affairs. Houston socialite Joanne Herring (Roberts in big hair) is a power broker who convinces Charlie that they can help end the cold war by arming the Afghan mujahideen so they can defeat the invading Russkies. (It's set in the 1980s.) Charlie heads off to Afghanistan to check things out and is given assistance by renegade CIA op Gust Avrakotos (Hoffman), which leads back to some D.C. maneuvering. A big story (based on the bestseller by George Crile) that's packed into a brief running time, so things seem just a little hurried, with Hanks and Hoffman vying to see who can steal the picture. **97m/C DVD.** US Tom Hanks, Julia Roberts, Philip Seymour Hoffman, Amy Adams, Ned Beatty, Emily Blunt, Om Puri, Ken Stott, John Slattery, Denis O'Hare, Peter Gerety, Brian Markinson; **D:** Mike Nichols; **W:** Aaron Sorkin; **C:** Stephen Goldblatt; **M:** James Newton Howard.

Charlie's Angels ♪♪½ **2000** (PG-13) Seventies TV jigglefest finally gets a belated big screen treatment that has the trio (Barrymore, Diaz, Liu) saving Charlie (Forsythe reprises his voice role) from assassination and thwarting bad guy Roger Corwin (Curry). Merchant-Ivory it ain't (yay!), but it's everything a summer movie's supposed to be: loud, flashy, and fun. Matt LeBlanc, Tom Green, and Luke Wilson are around as nominal romantic interests but it's the women who run the show. Everyone seems to be having a good time, especially Murray as Bosley and Diaz as "perky" angel Natalie. **99m/C VHS, DVD, UMD.** Drew Barrymore, Cameron Diaz, Lucy Liu, Bill Murray, Tim Curry, Sam Rockwell, Kelly Lynch, Crispin Glover, Matt LeBlanc, LL Cool J, Tom Green, Luke Wilson, Sean M. Whalen, Alex

Trebek, Michael (Mike) Papajohn; **D:** McG; **W:** John August, Ryan Rowe, Ed Solomon; **C:** Russell Carpenter; **M:** Ed Shearmur; **V:** John Forsythe.

Charlie's Angels: Full Throttle ♪♪ **2003** (PG-13) The Angels investigate murders linked to the theft of a Witness Protection database. Enough about plot. Murray's been replaced by Bernie Mac, Demi Moore returns to the screen as a former Angel gone bad, and a good time is still had by all. McG and the girls amp up the "boom" quotient, but some of the breezy fun of the original feels a bit forced this time around. **105m/C VHS, DVD.** US Drew Barrymore, Cameron Diaz, Lucy Liu, Bernie Mac, Demi Moore, Luke Wilson, Matt LeBlanc, Crispin Glover, Robert Patrick, John Cleese, Shia LaBeouf, Jaclyn Smith, Justin Theroux, Rodrigo Santoro, Ja'net DuBois, Robert Forster, Eric Bogosian, Carrie Fisher; **Cameos:** Pink, Ashley (Fuller) Olsen, Mary-Kate Olsen; **D:** McG; **W:** John August, Marianne S. Wibberley, Cormac Wibberley; **C:** Russell Carpenter; **M:** Ed Shearmur; **V:** John Forsythe. Golden Raspberries '03: Worst Remake/Sequel, Worst Support. Actress (Moore).

Charlie's Ghost: The Secret of Coronado ♪♪½ *Charlie's Ghost Story* **1994** (PG) Kid who has trouble fitting in is befriended by the ghost of a Spanish conquistador. **92m/C VHS, DVD.** Richard "Cheech" Marin, Trenton Knight, Anthony Edwards, Linda Fiorentino, Daphne Zuniga; **D:** Anthony Edwards.

Charlotte Forten's Mission: Experiment in Freedom ♪♪♪ *Half Slave, Half Free 2* **1985** Fact-based story, set during the Civil War. A wealthy, educated black woman, determined to prove to President Lincoln that blacks are equal to whites, journeys to a remote island off the coast of Georgia. There she teaches freed slaves to read and write. Part of the "American Playhouse" series on PBS. Preceded by "Solomon Northrup's Odyssey." **120m/C VHS.** Melba Moore, Mary Alice, Ned Beatty, Carla Borelli, Micki Grant, Moses Gunn, Anna Maria Horsford, Bruce McGill, Glynn Turman, Roderick Wimberly; **D:** Barry Crane; **W:** Samm-Art Williams.

Charlotte Gray ♪♪ **2001** (PG-13) Uninvolving WWII romantic drama based on the 1998 novel by Sebastian Faulks. Scottish Charlotte (Blanchett) is living in London when she meets dashing RAF pilot Peter Gregory (Penry-Jones). After learning that Peter has been shot down over France, Charlotte (who speaks perfect French) volunteers for British Special Operations and is sent to work with the Resistance in Vichy. Charlotte's contacts are Levade (Gambon) and his handsome son Julian (Crudup). Naturally, there are supposed to be sparks between the two but the romance fizzles rather than sizzles as does the film itself. Chameleon Blanchett and gruff Gambon are the main reasons to watch. **118m/C VHS, DVD.** GB AU Cate Blanchett, Billy Crudup, Michael Gambon, Rupert Penry-Jones, Anton Lesser, James Fleet, Ron Cook, Jack Shepherd, Nicholas Farrell, Helen McCrory, Abigail Cruttenden, Charlie Condou, David Birkin; **D:** Gillian Armstrong; **W:** Jeremy Brock; **C:** Dion Beebe; **M:** Stephen Warbeck.

Charlotte Sometimes ♪♪ **2002** (R) Michael manages his Aunt Margie's (Hoshi) duplex and runs the family auto repair business. He has a crush on tenant Lori (Yuan), who has a boyfriend, Justin (Westmore), although she frequently turns to the diffident Michael for friendly companionship. Then Michael meets the mysterious Darcy (Kim) at the local bar. She is sexually aggresive, while insisting that she's only in town for a few days. But Darcy seems overly interested in the relationship between Michael and Lori and it turns out the two women have a history than neither wants Michael to discover. **85m/C VHS, DVD.** Michael Idemoto, Jacqueline Kim, Eugenia Yuan, Matt Westmore, Shizuko Hoshi, Kimberly Rose; **D:** Eric Byler; **W:** Eric Byler; **C:** Robert Humphreys; **M:** Michael Brook.

Charlotte's Web ♪♪ **1973** (G) E.B. White's classic story of a friendship between a spider and a pig is handled only adequately by Hanna-Barbera studios. Some okay songs. **94m/C VHS, DVD.** **D:** Charles A. Nichols, Iwao Takamoto; **W:** Earl Hamner; **V:** Pamelyn Ferdin, Dan-

ny Bonaduce, Debbie Reynolds, Agnes Moorehead, Paul Lynde, Henry Gibson; **Nar:** Rex Allan.

Charlotte's Web ♪♪ **2006** (G) Faithful to E.B. White's timeless 1952 children's novel about a young girl, Fern (played graciously by Fanning, just barely young enough for the role), who rescues runt pig Wilbur from the smokehouse. Wilbur is later aided by Charlotte, a sophisticated spider (Roberts) whose "some pig" artwork awes the masses. Though the animals' mouths move thanks to CG effects, the animals and action are the real deal, as are the appealing gaggle of celebrities. Sticks to the book's gentle nature, but things get a bit sluggish at times. **96m/C DVD.** US Dakota Fanning, Kevin Anderson, Essie Davis, Gary Basaraba, Siobhan Fallon, Beau Bridges; **D:** Gary Winick; **M:** Danny Elfman; **V:** Julia Roberts, Steve Buscemi, John Cleese, Dominic Scott Kay, Oprah Winfrey, Cedric the Entertainer, Kathy Bates, Reba McEntire, Robert Redford, Thomas Haden Church, Andre Benjamin, Sam Shepard, Abraham Benrubi.

Charly ♪♪♪ **1968** A retarded man becomes intelligent after brain surgery, then romances a kindly caseworker before slipping back into retardation. Moving account is well served by leads Robertson and Bloom. Adapted from the Daniel Keyes novel "Flowers for Algernon." **103m/C VHS, DVD.** Cliff Robertson, Claire Bloom, Lilia Skala, Leon Janney, Dick Van Patten, William Dwyer; **D:** Ralph Nelson; **W:** Stirling Silliphant. Oscars '68: Actor (Robertson); Golden Globes '69: Actor (Robertson); Natl. Bd. of Review '68: Actor (Robertson).

Charm of La Boheme ♪♪ **1936** A vintage German musical based on the Puccini opera. With English subtitles. **90m/B VHS, DVD.** GE Jan Kiepura, Martha Eggerth, Paul Kemp; **D:** Geza von Bolvary.

The Charmer ♪♪♪ **1987** Havers stars as Ralph Gorse, a charming but amoral con man who uses any means to get what he wants. This includes using the affection (and money) of an older woman, blackmail, and even murder. Set in the late '30s. Made for British TV miniseries. **312m/C VHS, DVD.** GB Nigel Havers, Rosemary Leach, Bernard Hepton, Fiona Fullerton, Abigail McKern, George Baker, Judy Parfitt; **D:** Alan Gibson; **W:** Allan Prior. **TV**

Charming Billy ♪♪ **1998** Living a life of quiet desperation finally proves to be too much for Billy Starkman (Hayden) and he goes postal—sniping at passersby from the top of a rural water tower. Flashbacks show how Billy got to that desperate point in his life. **80m/C VHS, DVD.** Michael Hayden, Sally Murphy, Tony Mockus Sr., Chelcie Ross; **D:** William R. Pace; **W:** William R. Pace; **C:** William Newell; **M:** David Barkley.

Charms for the Easy Life ♪♪½ **2002** Southern matriarch and holistic healer, Miss Charlie Kate (Rowlands) has a generally low opinion of men since her husband ran off but the more fragile Sophie is pleased to have a suitor (Johnson) and teen Margaret also finds a boy (Mitchell) who thinks she's neat. Set in the mid-1940s; based on Kaye Gibbon's 1993 novel. Graceful and sentimental and all three actresses keep the sentimental excess to a minimum. **111m/C VHS, DVD.** Gena Rowlands, Mimi Rogers, Susan May Pratt, Geordie Johnson, Kenneth Mitchell; **D:** Joan Micklin Silver; **W:** Angela Shelton; **C:** Jean Lepine; **M:** Van Dyke Parks. **CABLE**

Charro! ♪ **1969** (G) Presley in a straight role as a reformed bandit hounded by former gang members. Western falls on nearly all accounts, with Presley hopelessly acting outside the bounds of his talent. Furthermore, he sings only one song. **98m/C VHS, DVD.** Elvis Presley, Ina Balin, Victor French, Lynn Kellogg, Barbara Werle, Paul Brinegar, James B. Sikking; **D:** Charles Marquis Warren; **W:** Charles Marquis Warren; **M:** Hugo Montenegro.

Charulata *The Lonely Wife* 1964 — Charulata is a loyal and dutiful wife taken for granted by her husband. But when his young cousin Amal comes to live with them, Charulata glimpses what true love could be. Adapted from the novella by Rabindranath Tagore. Bengali with subtitles. **117m/B VHS, DVD.** *IN* Shailen Mukherjee, Madhabi Mukherjee, Shyamal Ghosal, Gitali Roy, Bholanath Koyal, Suku Mukherjee, Dilip Bose, Joydeb, Jankim Ghosh, Subrata Sensharma, Madhabi Mukherjee, Scumitra Chatterjee; **C:** Subrata Mitra; **M:** Satyajit Ray; **D:** Satyajit Ray; **W:** Satyajit Ray, Rabindranath Tagore.

Chasers 1994 (R) — Gruff Navy petty officer Rock Reilly (Berenger) and his conniving partner Eddie Devane (McNamara) are suck escorting maximum security prisoner Toni Johnson (Eleniak) to a Charleston naval base. Imagine their surprise when Toni turns out to be a beautiful blonde whose one purpose is to escape her jail-sentence for going AWOL. Consider how dumb her jailers are this shouldn't be too difficult. Lots of sneering, leering, and macho posturing. **100m/C VHS, DVD.** Tom Berenger, William McNamara, Erika Eleniak, Gary Busey, Crispin Glover, Dean Stockwell, Seymour Cassel, Frederic Forrest, Marilu Henner, Dennis Hopper; **D:** Dennis Hopper; **W:** Joe Batteer, John Rice, Dan Gilroy; **C:** Ueli Steiger; **M:** Dwight Yoakam, Pete Anderson.

The Chase 1946 — Not realizing that his boss-to-be is a mobster, Cummings takes a job as a chauffeur. Naturally, he falls in love with the gangster's wife (Morgan), and the two plan to elope. Somewhat miffed, the cuckolded mafioso sends his bodyguard (Lorre) pursue the eloping couple as they head for Havana. The performances are up to snuff, but the story's as unimaginative as the title, with intermittent bouts of suspense. **86m/B VHS, DVD.** Robert Cummings, Michele Morgan, Peter Lorre, Steve Cochran, Lloyd Corrigan, Jack Holt, Don Wilson; **D:** Arthur Ripley; **W:** Philip Yordan.

The Chase 1966 — Southern community is undone when rumors circulate of a former member's prison escape and return home. Excellent cast only partially shines. Brando is outstanding as the beleaguered, honorable sheriff, and Duvall makes a splash in the more showy role of a cuckold who fears the escapee is returning home to avenge a childhood incident. Reliable Dickinson also makes the most of her role as Brando's loving wife. Fonda, however, was not yet capable of fashioning complex characterizations, and Redford is under-utilized as the escapee. Adapted from the play by Horton Foote. Notorious conflicts among producer, director, and writer kept it from being a winner. Routine drama. **135m/C VHS, DVD.** Marlon Brando, Robert Redford, Angie Dickinson, E.G. Marshall, Jane Fonda, James Fox, Janice Rule, Robert Duvall, Miriam Hopkins, Martha Hyer; **D:** Arthur Penn; **W:** Lillian Hellman, Horton Foote; **M:** John Barry.

Chase 1985 — A big-city lawyer returns to her small hometown to defend a killer and ends up at odds with the town, including an ex-lover. Loosely based on a true story. **93m/C VHS.** Jennifer O'Neill, Robert Woods, Richard Farnsworth, Michael Parks; **D:** Rod Holcomb. **M:** Charles Bernstein. TV

The Chase 1991 (PG-13) — Routine actioner in which an ex-con killer leads a ruthless cop and a TV news team on a wild chase. Loosely based on a true story. **93m/C VHS, DVD.** Ben Johnson, Casey Siemaszko, Gerry Bamman, Robert Beltran, Barry Corbin, Ricki Lake, Megan Follows, Sheila Kelley, Galard Sartain; **D:** Paul Wendkos; **W:** Guerdon Trueblood; **C:** Chuck (Charles C.) Arnold.

The Chase 1994 (PG-13) — Heiress Natalie Voss (Swanson) is in the wrong place at the wrong time when she's carjacked by escaped con Jack Hammond (Sheen) who uses a Butterfinger for his weapon. Frantic chases ensues as it turns out that Daddy Voss is a media hungry millionaire and he's followed by not only the cops but the media as well. One-dimensional characters aren't helped by a one-dimensional script, but slick film-making and a little charm helps. Skewers the media hype that surrounds crime, taking on news programs and reality based shows with glee. **87m/C VHS, DVD.** Joao Fernandes, Kristy Swanson, Charlie Sheen, Josh Mostel, Ray Wise, Henry Rollins, Flea; **D:** Adam Rifkin; **W:** Adam Rifkin; **M:** Richard Gibbs.

Chasing Amy 1997 (R) — Holden (Affleck) and best friend Banky (Lee), New Jersey comic book artists, attend a convention in New York where Holden is immediately attracted to fellow artist Alyssa (Adams). His ego is quickly deflated when Alyssa lets him know she's a lesbian. They try for friendship, head into a rocky romance, and then Holden discovers Alyssa's had a wild (and heterosexual) past, which pushes all his emotional buttons. Writer/director Smith supplies his trademark sharp dialogue, and the leads all contribute fine performances. Jay (Mewes) and Silent Bob (Smith), from Smith's earlier pics, make another appearance and supply the story that gives the film its title. **113m/C VHS, DVD.** Ben Affleck, Joey Lauren Adams, Jason Lee, Dwight Ewell, Jason Mewes, Kevin Smith, Matt Damon, Carmen (Lee) Llywelyn, Ethan Suplee, Brian O'Halloran, Guinevere Turner; **D:** Kevin Smith; **W:** Kevin Smith; **C:** David Klein; **M:** David Pirner, Ind. Spirit '97; Screenplay, Support. Actor (Lee).

Chasing Butterflies *La Chasse aux Papillons* 1994 — Society's decline is represented by a once-grand, now-decaying chateau, located in a small French village, and its equally decaying inhabitants. Marie-Agnes, confined to a wheelchair, is attended to by her cousin Solange and sullen maid Valerie. When Marie-Agnes suddenly dies, the greedy relatives descend, as well as untrustworthy antiques dealers, and Japanese businessmen interested in acquiring foreign real estate. The film is also an acquired taste. French with subtitles. **115m/C VHS.** *FR* Thamar Tarassachvili, Narda Blanchet, Pierrette Pompom Bailhache, Alexandre Tcherkassoff; **D:** Otar Iosseliani; **W:** Otar Iosseliani.

Chasing Christmas 2005 (PG) — Bah-humbug. Bitter divorcee Jack Cameron (Arnold) is a holiday Scrooge who comes to the attention of the "Bureau of Yuletide Affairs. It's decided to "Dickens" him with the ghosts of Christmas Past, Present, and Future, only when peevish Past (Jordan) takes Jack back to his 1965 boyhood, he decides to take a sudden vacation and leaves Jack stranded. This means Present (Roth) has to fix the timeline and get Jack to see the error of his ways. Lame holiday humor, although seeing Arnold tied to a chair with Christmas lights is kinda funny. **90m/C DVD.** Tom Arnold, Andrea Roth, Leslie Jordan, Jed Rees, Brittney Wilson; **D:** Ron Oliver; **W:** Todd Berger; **C:** C. Kim Miles; **M:** John Sereda. CABLE

Chasing Destiny 2000 (PG-13) — Once famous as a '60s rock 'n' roller, Jet James (Lloyd) is in debt and has a collector (Van Dien) and his door. But when his pretty daughter (Graham) comes to visit, Jet thinks getting the two young people together could be his way out of financial crisis. **90m/C VHS, DVD.** Christopher Lloyd, Casper Van Dien, Lauren Graham, Roger Daltrey, Justin Henry, Stuart Pankin, Deborah Van Valkenburgh; **D:** Tim Boxell. VIDEO

Chasing Dreams 1981 (PG) — Sticky melodrama about a farmboy who finds fulfillment as a baseball player. Lame film promoted as Costner baseball vehicle, but the star of "Bull Durham" and "Field of Dreams" appears only briefly in a secondary role. **96m/C VHS.** David G. Brown, John Fife, Jim Shane, Lisa Kingston, Matt Clark, Kevin Costner; **D:** Sean Roche, Therese Conte.

Chasing Freedom 2004 — After escaping the brutal Taliban rule in Afghanistan in 2004, Meena (Alizada) must battle to remain in the United States or face death in her native country if deported. Pro bono lawyer Libby (Lewis), a cocky corporate counselor is been ordered to take on her case. An original drama by cable channel Court TV. **89m/C VHS, DVD.** Juliette Lewis, Brian Markinson, Bruce Gray, Layla Alizada Gail Hanahan; **D:** Don McBearty; **W:** Barbara Samuels. CABLE

Chasing Ghosts 2005 — Derivative cop caper. Kevin Harrison (Madsen) is about to retire and is trying to get through a complicated murder case while breaking in new partner Davies (Large). But Harrison is also guilt-ridden over the death of cop Mark Spencer (Rooker), which happened because Harrison has been bought and paid for by mobster Aifiri (Busey). Soon the investigation is leading in directions Harrison doesn't want it to go. **114m/C DVD.** Michael Madsen, Michael Rooker, Meat Loaf Aday, Gary Busey, Corey Large, Shannyn Sossamon, Lochlyn Munro, Sean Michael Walsh; **D:** Kyle Dean Jackson; **W:** Scott Glasgow. VIDEO

Chasing Holden 2001 (R) — Cliched teen angst comedy/drama does refer to Holden Caulfield of "Catcher in the Rye." 19-year-old Neal (Qualls) is back at prep school after a two-year stay in a mental hospital. His English teacher Alex (Kanan) assigns his students an essay on what happened to Holden after the end of the Salinger novel. Neal decides the best way to find out is to visit the reclusive author T.J. (Blanchard). **101m/C VHS, DVD.** D.J. Qualls, Rachel Blanchard, Sean Kanan; **D:** Malcolm Clarke. VIDEO

Chasing Liberty 2004 (PG-13) — Singer Moore is restless and rebellious First Daughter Anna, who chafes under the scrutiny of the Secret Service. Mayhem and romance ensues when Anna tags along on a friend's travels across Europe and meets up with a cutie Brit (Goode). While Moore has better acting chops than your average pop singer turned movie actor, this isn't much more than a decaffeinated version of "Roman Holiday." Even so, it should please its target audience of pre-adolescent girls. **110m/C DVD.** *US* Mandy Moore, Matthew Goode, Mark Harmon, Caroline Goodall, Jeremy Piven, Annabella Sciorra, Stark Sands, Beatrice Rosen(blatt); **D:** Andy Cadiff; **W:** Derek Guiley, David Schneiderman; **C:** Ashley Rowe; **M:**

Chasing Papi 2003 (PG-13) — Hottie L.A. ad exec Tomas Fuentes (Verastegui) travels a lot for his work and makes friends wherever he goes—girlfriends, that is. There's dancer Cici (Vergara) in Miami, attorney Lorena (Sanchez) in Chicago, and heiress Patricia in New York (Velasquez). But the pressure is getting to this lothario and his doctor (Gomez) prescribes tranquilizers and abstinence. Then, Tomas's three ladies all decide to pay him surprise visits. Naturally, the surprise is on them. There's an odd subplot about stolen money and an FBI agent (Vidal) but it's what the threesome discover about themselves—girl power—that's important. Everyone involved is very, very attractive. **92m/C VHS, DVD.** *US* Eduardo Verastegui, Roselyn Sanchez, Sofia Vergara, Jaci Velasquez, Lisa Vidal, Freddy Rodriguez, D.L. Hughley, Maria Conchita Alonso, Ian Gomez; **D:** Linda Mendoza; **W:** Steve Antin, Laura Angelica Simon, Alison Balian, Elizabeth Sarnoff; **C:** Xavier Perez Grobet; **M:** Emilio Estefan Jr.

Chasing Sleep 2000 (R) — College prof. Ed Saxon (Daniels) worries when his wife doesn't return from work. The cops find her car but that's all. Meanwhile, pill-popping insomniac Ed discovers having an affair with a neighbor. Then he keeps having to deal with strange household plumbing problems. Ed becomes increasingly disoriented, so is he hallucinating the whole thing or has something terrible really happened? Daniels gives an effective off-center performance but the story loses its momentum. **104m/C VHS, DVD.** Jeff Daniels, Emily Bergl, Gil Bellows, Zach Grenier; **D:** Michael Walker; **W:** Michael Walker; **C:** Jim Denault.

Chasing the Deer 1994 — In 1745, Scotland's Bonnie Prince Charlie (Carrara) has returned from France intent on resurrecting the Jacobite cause and regaining the English throne. Reluctant Alistair Campbell (Zajac) joins the army only to protect his son Euan (Rae), who's supposedly being held prisoner for shooting a Highlander. Euan's actually fallen into the hands of a sympathetic Englishman, Major Elliot (Blessed), advisor to the government's troops. The Jacobites begin their march south until the fateful day on Culloden Moor, which will determine all their futures. **92m/C VHS.** *GB* Brian Blessed, Matthew Zajac, Iain Cuthbertson, Lewis Rae, Dominique Carrara, Fish; **D:** Graham Holloway; **W:** Jerome Vincent, Bob Carruthers, Steve Gillham; **C:** Alan M. Trow; **M:** John Wetton.

The Chatterley Affair 2006 — In October of 1950, D.H. Lawrence's scandalous novel "Lady Chatterley's Lover" is brought before a British jury in a famous (and landmark) obscenity trial. But jurors Keith (Spall) and Helena (Delamere) soon find themselves more enthralled with each other than the court proceedings. **90m/C DVD.** *GB* Rafe Spall, Louise Delamere, Karl Johnson, Kenneth Cranham, Mary Healey, Claire Bloom; **D:** James Hawes; **W:** Andrew Davies; **C:** James Aspinall; **M:** Nicholas Hooper. TV

The Chateau 2001 (R) — Naif geek Graham (Rudd) and his black entrepreneurial adoptive brother Allen (Malco) unexpectedly inherit a crumbling chateau in the French countryside. The servants seemed surprised by their arrival and even more shocked when the brothers say they intend to sell the property. They conspire to make the sale as difficult as possible until they can outsmart (which isn't hard) these uncouth Americans and save their home and jobs. English and French with subtitles. **92m/C VHS, DVD.** *US* Paul Rudd, Romany Malco, Sylvie Testud, Didier Flamand, Philippe Nahon, Maria Verdi, Nathalie Jouen, Donal Logue; **D:** Jesse Peretz; **W:** Jesse Peretz, Thomas Bidegain; **C:** Tom Richmond; **M:** Nathan Larson, Patrik Bartosch, Nina Persson.

Chato's Land 1971 (PG) — An Indian is tracked by a posse eager to revenge a lawman's death. Conventional revenge Western that is bolstered by presence of masterful Palance. **100m/C VHS, DVD.** Charles Bronson, Jack Palance, Richard Basehart, James Whitmore, Simon Oakland, Richard Jordan, Ralph Waite, Victor French, Lee Patterson; **D:** Michael Winner; **W:** Gerald Wilson; **C:** Robert Paynter; **M:** Jerry Fielding.

Chattahoochee 1989 — A man suffering from post-combat syndrome lands in a horrifying institution. Strong cast, with Oldman fine in the lead, and Hopper memorable in extended cameo. Fact-based film is, unfortunately, rather conventionally rendered. **97m/C VHS, DVD.** Gary Oldman, Dennis Hopper, Frances McDormand, Pamela Reed, Ned Beatty, M. Emmet Walsh, William De Acutis, Lee Wilkof, Matt Craven, Gary Klar; **D:** Mick Jackson; **W:** James Cresson.

Chattanooga Choo Choo 1984 (PG) — A football team owner must reinstate the Chattanooga Choo Choo and make a 24-hour run from Chattanooga to New York in order to collect $1 million left to him in a will. The train never leaves the station. **102m/C VHS, DVD.** Barbara Eden, George Kennedy, Melissa Sue Anderson, Joe Namath, Bridget Hanley, Christopher McDonald, Clu Gulager; **D:** Bruce Bilson.

Chatterbox 1976 — A starlet's life and career are severely altered when her sex organs begin speaking. So why didn't they warn her about movies like this? Plenty of B-queen Rialson on view. Good double bill with "Me and Him". **73m/C VHS.** Candice Rialson, Larry Gelman, Jean Kean, Perry Bullington; **D:** Tom De Simone.

The Cheap Detective 1978 (PG) — Neil Simon's parody of the "Maltese Falcon" gloriously exploits the genre. Peter Falk in a Bogart-like role. Vast sourceful cast—notable Brennan, De Luise, and Kahn—equally game for fun in this consistently amusing venture. **92m/C VHS, DVD.** Peter Falk, Ann-Margret, Eileen Brennan, Sid Caesar, Stockard Channing, James Coco, Dom DeLuise, Louise Fletcher, John Houseman, Madeline Kahn, Fernando Lamas, Marsha Mason, Phil Silvers, Vic Tayback, Abe Vigoda, Paul Williams, Nicol Williamson; **D:** Robert Moore; **W:** Neil Simon; **C:** John A. Alonzo.

Cheap Shots ♪½ 1991 (PG-13) Cheap best describes this. Two guys running a sleazy New York State resort motel plot to videotape patrons having sex, but capture an apparent mob murder instead. Unsurprisingly they get more than they bargained for and learn some valuable lessons about what's really important in life. Great family classic. 90m/C VHS. Louis Zorich, David Patrick Kelly, Mary Louise Wilson, Michael Twaine, Patience Moore; **D:** Jeff Ureles; **W:** Jeff Ureles, Jerry Stoelfhaas; **M:** Jeff Beal.

Cheaper by the Dozen ♪♪♪ 1950 Turn-of-the-century family comedy based on the book by Frank B. Gilbreth Jr., and Ernestine Gilbreth Carey, which chronicled life in the expansive Gilbreth household—12 children, efficiency expert father Frank (Webb), and psychologist mother Lillian (Loy). Stern dad likes to test his theories on the family (and have everything his own way) while nurturing mom easily manages him as well as their large household. There are various family crises (times 12) but it's all very heartwarming. Followed by "Belles on Their Toes." 85m/C VHS, DVD. Clifton Webb, Myrna Loy, Jeanne Crain, Edgar Buchanan, Mildred Natwick, Sara Allgood, Betty Lynn, Barbara Bates, Norman Ollestad; **D:** Walter Lang; **W:** Lamar Trotti; **C:** Leon Shamroy; **M:** Cyril Mockridge.

Cheaper by the Dozen 2 ♪♪ 2003 (PG) Has little in common with the 1950 original, except the title and the number of kids. Mom (Hunt) and Dad (Martin) and the 12 kids have to cope with moving to Chicago while Mom goes on a book tour and Dad ponders a higher-profile coaching gig. A rather perky, old-fashioned lot, this is a brood for which the term "family values" was presumably invented. Cute in a harmless, antiseptic kind of way. Martin adds his usual bemused charm, and the kids should enjoy the sibling-induced highjinks. 98m/C VHS, DVD, UMD. US Steve Martin, Bonnie Hunt, Piper Perabo, Tom Welling, Hilary Duff, Ashton Kutcher, Kevin J. Edelman, Alyson Stoner, Jacob Smith, Liliana Mumy, Paula Marshall, Alan Ruck, Richard Jenkins, Holmes Osborne, Vanessa Bell Calloway, Rex Linn, Amy Hill, Morgan York, Forrest Landis, Blake Woodruff, Brent Kinsman, Shane Kinsman, Steven Anthony Lawrence; **Cameos:** Regis Philbin, Kelly Ripa; **D:** Adam Shankman; **W:** Sam Harper, Joel Cohen, Alec Sokolow; **C:** Jonathan Brown; **M:** Christophe Beck.

Cheaper to Keep Her WOOF! 1980 (PG) Alleged comedy about a private detective hired to track likely alimony dodgers. Loathsome, repellent fare, with Davis hopeless in the lead. 92m/C VHS. Mac Davis, Tovah Feldshuh, Jack Gilford, Rose Marie; **D:** Ken Annakin; **W:** Herschel Weingrod, Timothy Harris.

The Cheat ♪♪♪ 1915 Ward plays a frivolous socialite heavily indebted to Hayakawa as the Japanese money lender. Hayakawa makes Ward pay with her honor and her flesh by branding her. A dark and captivating drama. Silent with piano score. 55m/B VHS, DVD. Jack Dean, James Neill, Dana Ong, Hazel Childers, Fannie Ward, Sessue Hayakawa; **D:** Cecil B. DeMille; **W:** Alvin Wyckoff, Hector Turnbull. Natl. Film Reg. '93.

The Cheaters ♪♪♪ 1945 A well-to-do family has a fabulous idea to impress their friends for the holidays, they take in a down-and-out actor who has recently tried to commit suicide. Unsurprisingly they get more than they bargained for and learn some valuable lessons about what's really important in life. Great family classic. 87m/B VHS. Joseph Schildkraut, Billie Burke, Eugene Pallette, Robert "Bob" Livingston; **D:** Joseph Kane; **W:** Frances Hyland. VIDEO

The Cheaters ♪ 1976 (R) A young gambler runs away with his boss's son's girlfriend, and is pursued therein. 91m/C VHS, DVD. IT Dayle Haddon, Luc Merenda, Lino Troisi, Enrico Maria Salerno; **D:** Sergio Martino.

Cheaters ♪♪½ 1984 Two middle class couples are having affairs with each other's spouses. Complications arise when their respective children decide to marry each other. 103m/C VHS, DVD. Peggy Cass, Jack Kruschen.

Cheaters ♪♪½ 2000 (R) Students at Chicago's run-down Steinmetz High School don't have a prayer of winning the state Academic Decathalon championship until they stumble across a copy of the test and decide that winning is everything—encouraged by their teacher/coach Gerald Plecki (Daniels), who helps them cheat, believing his intentions are good. Based on a true story. 106m/C VHS, DVD. Jeff Daniels, Jena Malone, Paul Sorvino, Luke Edwards, Blake Heron; **D:** John Stockwell; **W:** John Stockwell; **C:** David Hennings; **M:** Paul Haslinger. CABLE

Cheatin' Hearts ♪♪½ 1993 (R) Kirkland is a woman beset by woe: she's about to lose her house, her philandering husband (Brolin) wanders back to town with his latest bimbo in tow, and her daughter's getting married. This should be a good thing, except hubby makes a fool of himself at the wedding and nearly ruins everything. Well, at least local rancher Kristofferson is around to lift a woman's spirits. And yes, there's a (predictably) happy ending. 88m/C VHS, DVD. Sally Kirkland, James Brolin, Kris Kristofferson, Pamela Gidley, Laura Johnson; **D:** Rod McCall.

Check & Double Check ♪ 1930 Radio's original Amos 'n' Andy (a couple of black-faced white guys) help solve a lover's triangle in this film version of the popular radio series. Interesting only as a novelty. Duke Ellington's band plays "Old Man Blues" and "Three Little Words." 85m/B VHS, DVD. Freeman Gosden, Charles Correll, Duke Ellington; **D:** Melville Brown; **M:** Max Steiner.

Check Is in the Mail ♪♪½ 1985 (R) Lame comedy about a financier determined to make his home entirely independent from the rat-race of capitalist society. Dependables Dennehy and Archer are wasted. 83m/C VHS. Brian Dennehy, Anne Archer, Dick Shawn; **D:** Joan Darling.

Check Your Guns ♪♪ 1948 A crooked judge and a gang of outlaws team up to prey on law-abiding folk and cause headaches for the new sheriff, who's pushing an unsuccessful Old West version of gun control. Nothing really noteworthy here. 55m/B VHS. Eddie Dean, Roscoe Ates, Nancy Gates, George Chesebro, I. Stanford Jolley, Mikel Conrad, William "Bill" Fawcett; **D:** Ray Taylor.

The Checkered Flag ♪ 1963 Lame auto-racing drama about an aging, millionaire race car driver with an alcoholic wife who would like nothing more than to see him dead. She talks a young rookie into helping her dispose of hubby. Plans go awry—with horrifying results. Racing scenes overshadow incredibly weak script and performances. 110m/C VHS. "Miami" Joe Morrison, Evelyn King, Charles G. Martin, Peggy Vendig; **D:** William Grefe; **W:** William Grefe.

Checking Out ♪♪½ 1989 (R) Black comedy about a manic hypochondriac who is convinced that his demise will soon occur. You'll pray that he's right. Daniels can't make it work, and supporters Mayron and Magnuson also have little chance in poorly conceived roles. 95m/C VHS, DVD. Jeff Daniels, Melanie Mayron, Michael Tucker, Kathleen York, Ann Magnuson, Allan Havey, Jo

Harvey Allen, Felton Perry, Alan Wolfe; **D:** David Leland; **M:** Carter Burwell.

Cheech & Chong: Still Smokin' ♪½ 1983 (R) Not really. More like still trying to make a buck. Veteran marijuana-dazed comedy duo travel to Amsterdam to raise funds for a bankrupt film festival group by hosting a dope-a-thon. Lots of concert footage used in an attempt to hold the slim boat together. Only for serious fans of the dopin' duo. 91m/C VHS, DVD. Richard "Cheech" Marin, Thomas Chong; **D:** Thomas Chong; **W:** Richard "Cheech" Marin, Thomas Chong; **C:** Harvey Harrison; **M:** George S. Clinton.

Cheech and Chong: Things Are Tough All Over ♪♪ 1982 (R) Stoner comedy team are hired by two rich Arab brothers (also played by Cheech and Chong in acting stretch) and unwittingly drive a car loaded with money from Chicago to Las Vegas. Tired fourth in the series. 87m/C VHS, DVD. Richard "Cheech" Marin, Thomas Chong, Shelby Fiddis, Rikki Marin, Evelyn Guerrero, Rip Taylor; **D:** Tom Avildsen; **W:** Richard "Cheech" Marin, Thomas Chong.

Cheech and Chong's Next Movie ♪♪ 1980 (R) A pair of messed-up bumblers adventure into a welfare office, massage parlor, nightclub, and flying saucer, while always living in fear of the cops. Kinda funny, like. Sequel to "Up in Smoke." 95m/C VHS, DVD. Richard "Cheech" Marin, Thomas Chong, Evelyn Guerrero, Edie McClurg, Paul (Pee-wee Herman) Reubens, Phil Hartman; **D:** Thomas Chong; **W:** Richard "Cheech" Marin, Thomas Chong.

Cheech and Chong's Nice Dreams ♪♪ 1981 (R) The spaced-out duo are selling their own "specially mixed" ice cream to make cash and realize their dreams. Third in the series. 97m/C VHS, DVD. Sab Shimono, Sandra Bernhard, Linnea Quigley, Michael Winslow, Richard "Cheech" Marin, Thomas Chong, Evelyn Guerrero, Stacy Keach, Paul (Pee-wee Herman) Reubens; **Cameos:** Timothy Leary; **D:** Thomas Chong; **W:** Richard "Cheech" Marin, Thomas Chong; **C:** Charles Correll; **M:** Harry Betts.

Cheech and Chong's The Corsican Brothers WOOF! 1984 (PG) Wretched swashbuckler features the minimally talented duo in a variety of worthless roles. Dumas would vomit in his casket if he knew about this. Fifth in the series. 91m/C VHS, DVD. Richard "Cheech" Marin, Thomas Chong, Roy Dotrice, Rae Dawn Chong, Shelby Fiddis, Rikki Marin, Edie McClurg; **D:** Thomas Chong; **W:** Richard "Cheech" Marin, Thomas Chong; **C:** Harvey Harrison.

Cheech and Chong's Up in Smoke ♪♪½ Up in Smoke 1979 (R) A pair of free-spirited bum-outs team up for a tongue-in-cheek spoof of sex, drugs, and rock and roll. First and probably the best of the dopey duo's cinematic adventures. A boxoffice bonanza when released and still a cult favorite. 87m/C VHS, DVD. Richard "Cheech" Marin, Thomas Chong, Stacy Keach, Tom Skerritt, Edie Adams, Strother Martin, Cheryl "Rainbeaux" Smith; **D:** Lou Adler; **W:** Richard "Cheech" Marin, Thomas Chong; **C:** Gene Polito.

The Cheerful Fraud ♪♪½ 1927 Denny, who appeared in some two hundred-odd films in his career, masquerades as a butler to be near the girl he loves. A fool for love is a cheerful fraud. A zanily romantic silent comedy. 64m/B VHS. Reginald Denny, Gertrude (Olmstead) Olmsted, Emily Fitzroy, Gertrude Astor; **D:** William A. Seiter.

Cheering Section WOOF! 1973 (R) High school football teams compete for the grand prize—the privilege of ravishing the losing school's cheerleaders. Rah, rah, rah. 84m/C VHS. Rhonda Foxx, Tom Leindecker, Gregg D'Jah, Patricia Michelle, Jeff Laine; **D:** Harry Kerwin.

Cheerleader Camp WOOF! Bloody Pom Poms 1988 (R) Nubile gals are stalked by a psychopath while they cavort semi-clad at summer camp. 89m/C VHS, DVD. Betsy Russell, Leif Garrett, Lucinda Dickey, Lorie Griffin, George "Buck" Flower, Teri Weigel, Rebecca Ferratti, Travis McKenna, Kathryn Litton; **D:** John Quinn; **W:** David Lee Fein, R.L. O'Keefe; **C:** Bryan England; **M:** Joel Hamilton, Muriel Hodler-Hamilton.

The Cheerleaders WOOF! 1972 (R) Dim-witted exploitation effort has the usual suspects—moronic jocks and lamebrained gals—cavorting exuberantly. Followed by "Revenge of the Cheerleaders." 84m/C VHS, DVD. Stephanie Fondue, Denise Dillaway, Jovita Bush, Debbie Lowe, Sandy Evans; **D:** Paul Glickler.

Cheerleaders' Wild Weekend WOOF! 1985 (R) Group of cheerleaders are held captive by a disgruntled former football star. Pom poms wave. 87m/C VHS, DVD. Jason Williams, Kristine DeBell; **D:** Jeff Werner.

Cheers for Miss Bishop ♪♪½ 1941 The story of a woman who graduates from college then teaches at the same institution for the next 50 years. Somewhat moving. Based on Bess Streeter Aldrich's novel. 95m/B VHS, DVD. Martha Scott, William Gargan, Edmund Gwenn, Sterling Holloway, Rosemary DeCamp; **D:** Tay Garnett; **M:** Edward Ward.

Cheetah ♪♪ 1989 (G) Two California kids visiting their parents in Kenya embark on the adventure of their lives when, with the help of a young Masai, they adopt and care for an orphaned cheetah. Usual Disney kids and animals story. 80m/C VHS, DVD. Keith Coogan, Lucy Deakins, Collin Mothupi; **D:** Jeff Blyth; **W:** John Cotter; **C:** Thomas Burstyn.

A Chef in Love ♪♪♪ Les Mille et Une Recettes du Cuisinier Amoureux; The Cook in Love 1996 (PG-13) In 1920, Parisian Pascal Ishac (Richard) meets Georgian Princess Cecilia (Kirtadze) while travelling and decides to stay and open a French restaurant in the capital of Tbilisi. When the capital is invaded by the Red Army in 1921, communist leader Zigmund (Kahmhadze) forces Cecilia to marry him and shuts down Pascal's eatery. With his great love gone, Pascal writes a master cookbook and memoir that is later discovered and translated by Cecilia's son Anton (Gautier), who also discovers that Pascal is his father. French, Russian and Georgian with subtitles. 95m/C VHS, DVD. FR Pierre Richard, Nino Kirtadze, Temur Kahmhadze, Jean-Yves Gautier, Micheline Presle; **D:** Nana Dzhordzadze; **W:** Irakli Kvirikadze; **C:** Georgi Beridze; **M:** Goran Bregovic.

Chelsea Walls ♪½ 2001 (R) Hawke's directorial debut features wife Thurman as one of the would-be artists living at the legendary (and seedy) Chelsea Hotel. There's a variety of struggling writers, musicians, and artists who all have romantic dilemmas and substance abuse problems as well. Lots of chatter and atmosphere but the characters are all walking cliches. 108m/C VHS, DVD. US Kris Kristofferson, Uma Thurman, Vincent D'Onofrio, Natasha Richardson, Tuesday Weld, Rosario Dawson, Mark Webber, Kevin Corrigan, Robert Sean Leonard, Steve Zahn, Frank Whaley; **D:** Ethan Hawke; **W:** Nicole Burdette; **C:** Tom Richmond; **M:** Jeff Tweedy.

Cherish ♪♪ 2002 (R) Zoe (Tunney) is a nervous San Francisco dot.commer who, under convoluted circumstances, winds up accused of vehicular manslaughter while driving under the influence. She winds up under house arrest wearing an electronic surveillance anklet with deputy Daly (Blake) to check up on her. She gets to make friends with her neighbors and convinces Daly to help her find the stalker who's the cause of all her misery. Confusing blend of genres with a good soundtrack. 99m/C VHS, DVD. US Robin Tunney, Tim Blake Nelson, Jason Priestley, Nora Dunn, Brad Hunt, Liz Phair, Lindsay Crouse, Stephen Polk, Ricardo Gil, Kenny Kwong; **D:** Finn Taylor; **W:** Finn Taylor; **C:** Barry Stone; **M:** Mark De Gil Antoni.

The Cherokee Kid ♪♪½ 1996 (PG-13) Western/comedy about a novice gunslinger (Sinbad) avenging his family. There's a corrupt banker (Coburn), a bounty hunter (Hines), a Mexican freedom fighter (Martinez), and a gang of bankrobbing nuns to keep things interesting while the Kid learns his outlaw ways. 91m/C VHS, DVD. Sinbad, James Coburn, Burt Reynolds, Gregory Hines, A. Martinez, Ernie Hudson; **D:** Paris Barclay; **W:** Tim Kazurinsky, Denise DeClue; **M:** Stanley Clarke. CABLE

Cherry Crush ⚼½ 2007 (R) Dull noir wannabe. Prep school student Jordan Wells (Tucker) is expelled after taking naughty pics of female classmates. Now enrolled in public school, Jordan is putty for wrong side of the tracks Shay (Reed), even more petulant than provocative. 89m/C DVD. Jonathan Tucker, Nikki Reed, Frank Whaley, Michael O'Keefe, Julie Gonzalo, Dennis Boutsikaris; D: Nicholas DiBella; W: Nicholas DiBella, Paul Root; C: Tim Wainwright; M: Joe Kaltenbach. **VIDEO**

Cherry Falls ⚼½ 2000 (R) The small town of Cherry Falls is plagued by a serial killer who only kills teenaged virgins, so naturally every teen there is out to do it and save themselves. However Sheriff Marken (Biehn) has no intention of letting daughter Jody (Murphy) go to such ex-tremes. This one is an amusing parody of slasher flicks, teen sex comedies, and suburban nightmares. 100m/C VHS, DVD. Jay Mohr, Michael Biehn, Brittany Murphy, Candy Clark, Gabriel Mann, Keram Malicki-Sanchez, Jesse Bradford; D: Geoffrey Wright; W: Ken Selden; C: Anthony B. Richmond; M: Walter Werzowa.

Cherry Hill High WOOF! 1976 (R) Five teen girls compete for former-virgin status. Pass on this one. 82m/C VHS. Linda McInerney, Gloria Upson, Stephanie Lawlor, Dawn Golten.

Cherry 2000 ⚼⚼ 1988 (PG-13) Futuristic flick concerns a man who's not-circuits his sex-toy robots and embarks on a search for replacement parts across treacherous territory, only to meet a real female—Griffith. Offbeat, occasionally funny. 94m/C VHS, DVD. Melanie Griffith, David Andrews, Ben Johnson, Tim Thomerson, Michael C. Gwynne, Pamela Gidley; D: Steve DeJarnatt; W: Michael Almereyda; C: Jacques Haitkin; M: Basil Poledouris.

The Chess Player ⚼⚼ Le Joueur d'Echecs 1927 Polish nobleman Boleslas Vorowski heads a secret movement to free his country from Russian control. When Vorowski is wounded in battle, his mentor, inventor Baron von Kempelen, constructs a chess-playing automation named Turk that conceals Vorowski in order to smuggle him to safety. When Catherine the Great learns of Turk's chess prowess, she commands the automation be brought to Russia for a royal match. From the novel by Henri Dupuy-Mazuel, which is based on the real 18th-century machine. 123m/B VHS, DVD. FR Pierre Blanchar, Edith Jehanne, Charles Dullin, Camille Bert, Pierre Batcheff; D: Raymond Bernard; W: Raymond Bernard; C: Joseph-Louis Mundwiler, Willy, Marc Bujard; M: Henri Rabaud.

Chesty Anderson USN ⚼ Anderson's Angels 1976 Ultra-lame sexploitation about female naval recruits. Minimal nudity. 90m/C VHS, DVD. Shari Eubank, Dori Thompson, Rosanne Katon, Marcie Barkin, Scatman Crothers, Frank Campanella, Fred Willard; D: Ed Forsyth.

Cheyenne Autumn ⚼⚼½ 1964 The newly restored version of the ambitious, ultimately hit-and-miss western epic about three hundred Cheyenne Indians who migrate from Oklahoma to their Wyoming homeland in 1878. The cavalry, for once, are not the good guys. Widmark is strong in the lead. Stewart is memorable in his comic cameo as Wyatt Earp. Last film from genre master Ford, capturing the usual rugged panoramas. Based on a true story as told in the Mari Sandoz novel. 156m/C VHS, DVD. Richard Widmark, Carroll Baker, Karl Malden, Dolores Del Rio, Sal Mineo, Edward G. Robinson, Ricardo Montalban, Gilbert Roland, Arthur Kennedy, John Carradine, Victor Jory, Mike Mazurki; George O'Brien, John Qualen; Cameos: James Stewart; D: John Ford; C: William Clothier; M: Alex North.

Cheyenne Kid ⚼½ 1933 Determined bronco buster is up against a gang of bad guys. 40m/B VHS. Tom Keene, Mary Mason, Roscoe Ates, Alan Bridge, Otto Hoffman, Anderson Lawler, Alan Roscoe; D: Robert F. "Bob" Hill; W: Jack Curtis; C: Nicholas Musuraca; M: Max Steiner.

Cheyenne Rides Again ⚼½ 1938 Cheyenne poses as an outlaw to hunt a gang of rustlers. 60m/B VHS. Tom Tyler, Lucille Browne, Lon Chaney Jr., Roger Williams, Charles "Slim" Whitaker; D: Robert F. "Bob" Hill.

The Cheyenne Social Club ⚼⚼ 1970 (PG) Stewart inherits a brothel and Fonda helps him operate it. Kelly directs, sort of. Some laughs, but this effort is beneath this trio. 103m/C VHS, DVD. Henry Fonda, James Stewart, Shirley Jones, Sue Ane Langdon, Elaine Devry, Arch Johnson, Dabbs Greer, Jackie Joseph; Richard Collier, Charles Tyner, Robert J. Wilke, Warren Kemmerling; C: William Clothier; M: Walter Scharf.

Cheyenne Takes Over ⚼ 1947 Lash sniffs out the bad guy in the case of a murdered ranch heir. 56m/B VHS. Lash La Rue, Al "Fuzzy" St. John, George Chesebro; D: Ray Taylor.

Cheyenne Warrior ⚼⚼½ 1994 Pregnant young bride Rebecca heads west with a husband who soons winds up dead, leaving her stranded at an isolated trading post. She takes in a wounded Cheyenne warrior, nurses him back to health, and he tries to convince her to let his tribe care for her. Respectable performances all around. 90m/C VHS, DVD. Kelly Preston, Pato Hoffmann, Bo Hopkins, Dan Haggerty, Charles Powell, Rick Dean, Clint Howard; D: Mark Griffiths; W: Michael B. Druxman.

Chicago ⚼⚼⚼½ 2002 (R) The first Oscar-winning musical since the 1970s celebrates the unlikely themes of murder, adultery and greed with winning results. Heroine Roxie Hart (Zellweger) in jail for offing her two-timing boyfriend, finally finds the career she craved. Ditto for Zeta-Jones' Velma Kelly, who's also in stir for popping her old man. The hot-headed beauties share the same slick lawyer, Billy Flynn (Gere). Reilly is Zellweger's simpleton husband, the sole spot of earnestness in an otherwise cynical film. Deftly directed, with musical numbers done as fantasy segments. Zeta-Jones and Latifah are the ones with the pipes for the genre, while lesser singer/dancers Gere and Zellweger score with appealing performances. Big screen version of the award-winning musical by John Kander, Fred Ebb, and Bob Fosse. 113m/C VHS, DVD. US Renee Zellweger, Catherine Zeta-Jones, Richard Gere, Queen Latifah, John C. Reilly, Christine Baranski, Lucy Liu, Taye Diggs, Colm Feore, Dominic West, Mya; D: Rob Marshall; W: Bill Condon; C: Dion Beebe; M: Danny Elfman, John Kander, Fred Ebb; Oscars '02: Art Dir/Set Dec, Costume Des., Film, Film Editing, Sound, Support. Actress (Zeta-Jones); British Acad. '02: Sound; Directors Guild '02: Director (Marshall); Golden Globes '03: Actor—Mus./Comedy (Gere), Actress—Mus./Comedy (Zellweger), Film—Mus./Comedy; Screen Actors Guild '02: Actress (Zellweger), Support. Actress (Zeta-Jones), Cast.

Chicago Cab ⚼⚼ Hellcab 1998 (R) This checkered sketch piece about a cab driver (Dillon) and the assorted passengers he picks up during a "normal" day never really pulls away from the curb. Despite cameos from actors such as John Cusack, Gillian Anderson and Laurie Metcalf, the passengers are nasty obnoxious stereotypes drawn to prove the point that other people are irritating. Will Kern adapted the screenplay from his original play "Hellcab." 96m/C VHS. Paul Dillon, Gillian Anderson, John Cusack, Julianne Moore, Michael Ironside, John C. Reilly, Laurie Metcalf, Matt Roth, Shulie Cowen, Philip Van Lear, Michael Shannon; D: Mary Cybulski, John Tintori; W: Will Kern; C: Hubert Taczanowski; M: Page Hamilton.

Chicago Joe & the Showgirl ⚼⚼ 1990 (R) A London-based GI befriends a loopy showgirl and helps her in various crimes during WWII. Appealing Lloyd overwhelms Sutherland, who shows only limited acting ability here. Based on a true story and set in smaller roles, but provides otherwise conventional entertainment. 100m/C VHS, DVD. GB Emily Lloyd, Kiefer Sutherland, Patsy Kensit, Keith Allen, Liz Fraser, Alexandra Pigg, Ralph Nossek, Colin Bruce; D: Bernard Rose; M: Hans Zimmer.

Chicago 10 ⚼⚼½ 2007 (R) A unique blend of archival footage, vocal reenactment, and rotoscope animation recounts the infamous trial of eight anti-war protesters following the 1968 Democratic National Convention, along with the chaos surrounding the case. An unconventional and fresh take on the documentary form, almost as radical as its subjects. Rather than being sad to the music of the heroes of the day, like Dylan or CSN, contemporary artists provide the soundtrack, going as far as having "Rage Against the Machine covering "Kick Out the Jams" during footage of the MC5 performing the original live during the protests. 103m/C VHS, DVD. Hank Azaria, Dylan Baker, Nick Nolte, Mark Ruffalo, Roy Scheider, Liev Schreiber, Jeffrey Wright.

The Chicken Chronicles ⚼ 1977 (PG) An affluent high school dude longs to get horizontal with his dream girl. Set in the 1960s. First feature film appearance for Gutenberg. 94m/C VHS, Phil Silvers, Ed Lauter, Steve Guttenberg, Lisa Reeves, Meridith Baer; D: Francis Simon.

Chicken Little ⚼⚼½ 2005 (G) Disney's first solo (without Pixar) foray into CG animation won't please everyone, but the intended audience of grade-schoolers probably won't notice. Chicken Little (Braff) causes a panic and big trouble for himself when he thinks the sky is falling when an alien kid gets stranded in town, and sounds the alarm. He spends most of his time trying to live the incident down and build a good relationship with his pop (Marshall), a former athletic hero. When a piece of the "sky" falls on him again, it's up to him and his pals to convince everyone that it really happened, especially one that it really happened, especially when an alien kid gets stranded in town. Lacks the originality, verve, and adult-pleasing in not a bad first try. 82m/C DVD, Blu-ray Disc. US D: Mark Dindal; W: Steve Bencich, Ron J. Friedman, Ron Anderson; M: John Debney; V: Zach Braff, Garry Marshall, Joan Cusack, Steve Zahn, Amy Sedaris, Don Knotts, Harry Shearer, Patrick Stewart, Wallace Shawn, Fred Willard, Catherine O'Hara, Adam West, Patrick Warburton.

Chicken Run ⚼⚼½ 2000 (G) It's a prisoner-of-war escape movie with chickens. This Claymation wonder is a comedy set on a falling 1950s Yorkshire chicken farm, where the hens realize their necks are literally on the chopping block when greedy farm wife, Mrs. Tweedy (Richardson), decides to go into the chicken pie business. So chicken leader, Ginger (Sawalha), tries to find a workable mass escape plan. And then daredevil Yankee rooster Rocky (Gibson) literally drops into the barnyard and Ginger believes he can teach all the hens to fly out. Chickens are just funny and you'll be amazed at what the animators have managed to make them do and how expressive they are. 86m/C VHS, DVD, GB D: Nick Park, Peter Lord; W: Karey Kirkpatrick; M: John Powell, Harry Gregson-Williams; V: Mel Gibson, Julia Sawalha, Miranda Richardson, Jane Horrocks, Tony Haygarth, Timothy Spall, Imelda Staunton, Phil Daniels, Benjamin Whitrow, Lynn Ferguson.

Chicks, Man ⚼ 1999 Boring, man. Rod and Jack are a couple of clueless, mopey Gen-Xers who don't understand the ladies. Jack gets dumped and then tries rebound dating while Rod macks on Heather at a party and is later beaten up by Heather's boyfriend for taking liberties. There's much whining—not least by unwary viewers of this tedious pic. 93m/C DVD. Aaron Priest, Robia LaMorte, Krista Ganci, Nick Wechsler, Scott Roberts, Renee Humphrey; D: Jeremy Wagener; W: Jeremy Wagener; C: Michael J. Bruggemeyer; M: David Stout.

Chiefs ⚼⚼ 1983 A police chief in a Southern town discovers a series of murders concealed by town big wigs. Made for TV film boasts a surprisingly strong cast, sure from the Civil War. A Disney made for TV movie. 93m/C VHS, Charlton Heston, Paul Sorvino, Keith Carradine, Brad Davis, Billy Dee Williams, Wayne Rogers, Stephen Collins, Tess Harper, Victoria Tennant; D: Jerry London. TV

The Child ⚼ L'Enfant 2005 (R) Amoral 20-year-old petty criminal Bruno (Renier) and his younger girlfriend Sonia (Francois) have just had a baby boy. Unprepared for fatherhood, he casually sells the child to a black market adoption ring. Shrugging off his thoughtless actions have no consequences when Sonia becomes hysterical and wants her son back. This turns out to be less easy than the original transaction. French with subtitles. 95m/C DVD. BE FR Jeremie Renier, Fabrizio Rongione, Olivier Gourmet, Deborah Francois, Jeremie Segard, Samuel de Ryck, Mireille Bailly; D: Jean-Pierre Dardenne, Luc Dardenne; W: Jean-Pierre Dardenne, Luc Dardenne; C: Alain Marcoen.

The Child ⚼ Kill and Go Hide 1976 (R) Low-budget horror-cuckle combining elements of "The Bad Seed", "The Omen", and "Night of the Living Dead," that attempts to cash in on the fright-film craze of the early '70s. What we get is a poorly dubbed film that makes little sense. A young woman returns to her hometown to be the nanny for a disturbed girl, Rosalie (Cole), who has a bad habit of killing neighbors and talking to zombies in the local graveyard, all the way harping on her mother's mysterious death. This is one of those movies where everyone acts very eccentric, but said behavior doesn't add anything to the plot. The finale offers some excitement, but overall the film is more of a curiosity than a "must-see." 95m/C VHS, DVD. Laurel Barnett, Rosalie Cole, Frank Janson, Richard Hanners, Ruth Ballan; D: Robert Voskanian; W: Ralph Lucas; C: Mori Alavi; M: Rob Wallace.

Child Bride of Short Creek ⚼⚼ 1981 (R) A young Korean war veteran returns to his community where polygamy is allowed, to find that his father intends to marry again, this time to a 15-year-old. Conflict ensues. Based on an actual event that occurred in the 1950s. 100m/C VHS, DVD. Diane Lane, Conrad Bain, Christopher Atkins, Kel Martin, Helen Hunt; D: Robert Lewis. TV

Child in the Night ⚼⚼ 1990 (R) A shaken eight-year-old boy is a witness to murder in his family, and a psychologist with plenty of her own problems must get him to testify. First film for Wood. Middling TV-movie suspense. 93m/C VHS. Tom Skerritt, JoBeth Williams, Darren McGavin, Season Hubley, Elijah Wood; D: Mike Robe.

A Child Is Waiting ⚼⚼⚼ 1963 Poignant and provocative story of teachers in an institution for the mentally retarded. Fine performances include Lancaster as the institution's administrator and Garland as a teacher who cares too much for everyone's good. Cassavetes incorporates footage using handicapped children providing a sensitive and candid edge. 105m/B VHS. Burt Lancaster, Judy Garland, Gena Rowlands, Steven Hill, Bruce Ritchey; D: John Cassavetes; W: Abby Mann; M: Ernest Gold.

Child of Darkness, Child of Light ⚼½ 1991 (PG-13) A priest is sent to investigate two virgin pregnancies and discovers that one child will be a savior and the other the Anti-Christ. Totally mindless brain candy resembling the "Omen" movies and "Rosemary's Baby." Adapted from James Patterson's book "Virgin." 88m/C VHS. Anthony John (Tony) Denison, Brad Davis, Paxton Whitehead, Claudette Nevins, Sydney Penny, Kristin Dattilo-Hayward, Viveca Lindfors, Sela Ward, Alan Oppenheimer, Eric Christmas; D: Marina Sargenti; W: Brian Taggert. CABLE

Child of Glass ⚼⚼ 1978 (G) A young boy's family moves into a huge New Orleans mansion, and soon after encounters a young girl's ghost and lost treasure from the Civil War. A Disney made for TV movie. 93m/C VHS, Barbara Barrie, Biff McGuire, Anthony Zerbe, Nina Foch, Steven Shaw, Katy Kurtzman, Olivia Barash; D: John Erman. TV

Child of the Prairie ⚼ 1918 An early Mix film about a young cowboy and his city-loving wife out in the wild, wild western town. Silent with music score. 63m/B VHS. Tom Mix; D: Tom Mix; W: Tom Mix.

Child Star: The Shirley Temple Story ⅋⅋½ 2001 TV biopic that charts the rise to Depression-era fame of little Shirley Temple (with an entertaining performance by Orr). Shirley's mom Gertrude (Britton) is around to see that big bad studio mogul Darryl Zanuck (Vidler) doesn't take advantage of her little darling. The best parts are the faithful re-creations of some of Temple's most famous song-and-dance numbers, including those with Bill (Bojangles) Robinson, here played by Battle. **88m/C VHS, DVD.** Ashley Rose Orr, Connie Britton, Steven Vidler, Colin Friels, Emily Anne Hart, Hinton Battle; **D:** Nadia Tass; **W:** Joe Wiesenfeld; **C:** David Parker; **M:** Bill Elliot. **TV**

The Children WOOF (R) Familiar nuclear leak leads to monster mutants done to a novel (though extremely low-budget) turn: after a school bus passes through radioactive fog, the kiddies inside assume the ability to incinerate whoever they hug. They also assume a certain zombie-like demeanor and sport black fingernails. None of this is noted by their uncaring and less-than-observant parents, many of whom are enticed into a very warm hug. This may be intended as social satire. Not only are the little microwaves extremely dangerous, the only way to kill them is to chop off their hands, leading to a wild limbless finale. **89m/C VHS, DVD.** Martin Shaker, Gale Garnett, Gil Rogers; **D:** Max Kalmanowicz.

The Children ⅋⅋½ 1990 Kingsley stars as a middle-aged engineer who finds himself caring for seven children in this touching love story from novelist Edith Wharton. Shot on location in Venice, the old boy drifts unloved by his suicidal father and by his mother, who's only interested in her own love life. Worthy example of Italian neo-realism marks the first collaboration between Zavattini and De Sica. In Italian with subtitles. **92m/B VHS, DVD.** *IT* Luciano de Ambrosis, Isa Pola, Emilio Cigoli; **D:** Vittorio De Sica; **W:** Cesare Zavattini, Vittorio De Sica.

Children in the Crossfire ⅋⅋½ 1984 When youngsters from war-torn Northern Ireland spend a summer in America with children from the Republic of Ireland, both sides find their nationalistic prejudices falling away. But a great challenge awaits them when they return home from their summer of fun. Nicely done drama. **96m/C VHS, DVD.** Charles Haid, Karen Valentine, Julia Duffy, David Huffman; **D:** George Schaefer; **M:** Brad Fiedel. **TV**

The Children Are Watching Us ⅋⅋⅋ *The Little Martyr; I Bambini Ci Guardano* 1944 Sobering drama of a family dissolution as seen by a child. A four-year-old boy drifts unloved by his suicidal father and by his mother, who's only interested in her own love life. Worthy example of Italian neo-realism marks the first collaboration between Zavattini and De Sica. In Italian with subtitles. **92m/B VHS, DVD.** *IT* Luciano de Ambrosis, Isa Pola, Emilio Cigoli; **D:** Vittorio De Sica; **W:** Cesare Zavattini, Vittorio De Sica.

Children of a Lesser God ⅋⅋⅋½ 1986 (R) Based upon the play by Mark Medoff, this sensitive, intelligent film deals with an unorthodox speech teacher at a school for the deaf, who falls in love with a beautiful and rebellious ex-student. Inarguably romantic; the original stage production won the Best Play Tony in 1980. Hurt and Matlin reportedly continued their romance off-screen as well. **119m/C VHS, DVD.** William Hurt, Marlee Matlin, Piper Laurie, Philip Bosco, E. Katherine Kerr; **D:** Randa Haines; **W:** Hesper Anderson, Mark Medoff; **C:** John Seale; **M:** Michael Convertino. Oscars '86: Actress (Matlin); Golden Globes '87: Actress—Drama (Matlin).

The Children of An Lac ⅋⅋½ 1980 Three women attempt to rescue hundreds of Vietnamese orphans before Saigon falls to the communists. The film derives from actress Balin's actual wartime experience. **100m/C VHS.** Shirley Jones, Ina Balin, Beulah Quo, Alan Fudge, Ben Piazza, Lee Paul, Kieu Chinh, Vic Diaz; **D:** John Llewellyn Moxey; **M:** Paul Chihara. **TV**

Children of Divorce ⅋⅋½ 1980 TV drama shows divorce from the children's point of view. Standard fare. **96m/C VHS.** Barbara Feldon, Lance Kerwin, Stacey Nelkin, Billy Dee Williams; **D:** Joanna Lee. **M:** Minette Alton. **TV**

Children of Dune ⅋⅋ 2003 The continuation of the 2000 miniseries "Dune" is based on the second and third novels of Frank Herbert's series and may be confusing to the uninitiated. It's now 12 years since Paul Atreides (Newman) has become emperor of Arrakis, which has a monopoly on the precious commodity Spice, but his ascension to the throne has caused a holy war across the universe. It has also caused rivalry with the deposed royal family led by scheming Princess Wensicia (Sarandon). Paul's children, Leto (McAvoy) and Ghanima (Brooks), who are being groomed to rule, soon come to realize they must destroy their father's legacy in order to save their world. **266m/C VHS, DVD.** Alec Newman, Susan Sarandon, James McAvoy, Jessica Brooks, Alice Krige, Edward Atterton, Steven Berkoff, Julie Cox, Barbara Kodetova, Ian McNeice, P. H. Moriarty; **D:** Greg Yaitanes; **W:** John Harrison; **C:** Arthur Reinhart; **M:** Brian Tyler. **CABLE**

Children of Fury ⅋⅋ *In the Line of Duty: Siege at Marion* 1994 (PG-13) Fact-based TV movie covers the death (at police hands) of self-proclaimed prophet, Utah polygamist John Singer (Weisser), whose wife Vickie (Harper) and children vow revenge. When fundamentalist Addam Swapp (Secor) joins their group, he soon begins intimidating the locals and bombs a building in the town of Marion. Authorities call in the FBI and chief agent Bill Bryant (Franz) sets up a siege of the property. **85m/C VHS.** Dennis Franz, Ed Begley Jr., Paul LeMat, Norbert Weisser, William H. Macy, Rex Linn; **D:** Charles Haid; **W:** Rich Husky; **C:** William Wages; **M:** Gary Chang. **TV**

Children of Hannibal ⅋⅋ *Figli di Annibale* 1998 Unemployed sad-sack Domenico (Orlando) decides to rob a Turin bank and head north to Switzerland, but he bungles the job and winds up with businessman Tommaso (Abatantuono) as a hostage. However, Tommaso has his own money troubles—nearly bankrupt, he persuades Domenico to head south with the loot and get help from Tommaso's friend, Orfeo (Insinni), who just happens to be a cop and Tommaso's lover. Then, Tommaso's daughter Rita (Cervi) decides to join their strange road trip. Italian with subtitles. **93m/C VHS, DVD.** *IT* Diego Abatantuono, Silvio Orlando, Valentina Cervi, Flavio Insinna, Ugo Conti; **D:** Davide Ferrario; **W:** Davide Ferrario; **C:** Giovanni Cavallini; **M:** Damiano Rota.

Children of Heaven ⅋⅋⅋½ 1998 (PG) When nine-year-old Ali (Hashemian) discovers that his younger sister Zahra's (Seddiqi) shoes have somehow been lost, he keeps the information from his parents who are already desperately struggling to provide for them. They share the knowledge so that both children can still go to school. Then Ali learns of a race where one of the prizes is a pair of running shoes and he becomes determined to win them. Story is simple enough that kids may enjoy watching other kids even in a foreign film. Farsi with subtitles. **88m/C VHS, DVD.** *IR* Mir Farrokh Hashemian, Bahareh Seddiqi, Amir Naji; **D:** Majid Majidi; **W:** Majid Majidi; **C:** Parviz Malek-zadeh; **M:** Keivan Jahanshahi.

Children of Men ⅋⅋⅋ 2006 (R) The future's never fun. It's 2027 and there's global infertility and worldwide chaos, which doesn't matter much to British bureaucratic drone Theo Faron (Owen), until he's pulled into an activist group headed by his ex, Julian (Moore). Seems they need Faron to take illegal refugee Kee (Ashitay), who's pregnant with the first child conceived in 18 years, to safety. This involves a long, strange, and dangerous trip—and a stop at Theo's pot-head friend Jasper's (a raucous Caine) cottage. Dark and dreary yet oddly fascinating. Loosely based on the 1993 novel by P.D. James. **108m/C DVD, HD DVD, US**

Children of Nature ⅋⅋½ *Born Natturunnar* 1991 A 78-year-old man unwillingly enters a nursing home where he meets a long-ago sweetheart. The two fall in love again and decide to escape from the home and return to their childhood village. Sweet love story about late-blooming passions laced with fantasy and humor. Iceland's first Academy Award nomination. In Icelandic with English subtitles. **85m/C VHS.** *IC* Gisli Halldorsson, Sigridur Hagalin, Bruno Ganz; **D:** Fridrik Thor Fridriksson; **W:** Fridrik Thor Fridriksson, Einar Mar Gudmundsson; **M:** Hilmar Orn Hilmarsson.

The Children of Noisy Village ⅋⅋½ *The Children of Bullerby Village; Alla vi barn i Bullerby* 1986 Noisy Village is a small town in the Swedish countryside consisting of three red frame houses. In the town, a group of adventurous children discover a multitude of fantasy lands right in their own backyard—their backyard being the beautiful pastures, ponds, and fields of Sweden. Based on the stories of Astrid "Pippi Longstocking" Lindgren. **88m/C VHS.** *SW* Linda Bergstrom, Anna Sahlin, Ellem Demerus, Harsald Lonnbro; **D:** Lasse Hallstrom.

Children of Paradise ⅋⅋⅋⅋ *Les Enfants du Paradis* 1944 Considered by many to be the greatest film ever made, certainly one of the most beautiful, in the Parisian theatre district of the 1800s an actor falls in love with a seemingly unattainable woman. Although circumstances keep them apart, their love never dies. Produced in France during WWII right under the noses of Nazi occupiers; many of the talent (including the writer, poet Jacques Prevert) were active resistance fighters. In French with English subtitles. **188m/C B VHS, DVD.** *FR* Jean-Louis Barrault, Arletty, Pierre Brasseur, Maria Casares, Albert Remy, Leon Larive, Marcel Herrand, Pierre Renoir, Gaston Modot, Jane (Jeanne) Marken, Louis Salou; **D:** Marcel Carne; **W:** Jacques Prevert; **C:** Roger Hubert; **M:** Maurice Thiriet, Joseph Kosma.

Children of Rage ⅋⅋ 1975 (PG) High-minded and long-winded drama dealing with the Israeli/Palestinian war and terrorism from the viewpoint of an Israeli doctor yearning for peace. **106m/C VHS.** *GB IS* Simon Ward, Cyril Cusack, Helmut Griem, Olga Georges-Picot; **D:** Arthur Allan Seidelman; **W:** Richard Alfieri.

Children of Sanchez ⅋⅋ 1979 (PG) Mexican man attempts to provide for his family with very little except faith and love. U.S./Mexican production based on Oscar Lewis' novel. **103m/C VHS, DVD.** *MX* Anthony Quinn, Dolores Del Rio, Katy Jurado, Lupita Ferrer; **D:** Hall Bartlett; **W:** Hall Bartlett; **M:** Chuck Mangione.

Children of the Century ⅋⅋ *Les Enfants du Siecle* 1999 Attenuated costumer depicting the volatile affair between the Baroness Dudevant, soon to be known as writer George Sand (Binoche), and the younger (and dissolute) poet, Alfred de Musset (Magimel). To escape his wealthy family's disapproval, the lovers travel to Venice where Alfred's continued dissipation leads to illness and the services of Dr. Pagello (Dionisi), with whom a fed-up Sands soon begins a romance. Musset returns to Paris and when Sands follow later, the duo try to rekindle their romantic ardor. Musset's fictionalized version of their affair was entitled "Confessions of a Child of the Century." French with subtitles. **137m/C VHS, DVD.** *FR* Juliette Binoche, Benoit Magimel, Stefano Dionisi, Robin Renucci, Karin Viard, Isabelle Carre, Denis Podalydes; **D:** Diane Kurys; **W:** Diane Kurys, Murray Head, Francois Olivier Rousseau; **C:** Vilko Filac; **M:** Luis Bacalov.

Children of the Corn ⅋⅋½ 1984 (R) Young couple lands in a small Iowa town where children appease a demon by murderously sacrificing adults. Time to move or dispense with some major spankings. Infrequently scary. Another feeble attempt to translate the horror of a Stephen King book to film. **93m/C VHS, DVD, UMD.** Peter Horton, Linda Hamilton, R.G. Armstrong, John Franklin, Courtney Gains, Robbie Kiger; **D:** Fritz Kiersch; **W:** George Goldsmith; **C:** Raoul Lomas; **M:** Jonathan Elias.

Children of the Corn 2: The Final Sacrifice ⅋⅋½ 1992 (R) Reporter working for a tabloid paper gets more than he bargained for when he decides to do a story on the adults murdered in the town of Gatlin, Nebraska. Gatlin's surviving children, who killed their parents in the first film, are now living in a neighboring town and free to kill again. This youthful satanic cult does in authority figures in a number of sacrificial ways, working ever more smartly to create the prime attraction—blood flow. Not based on anything written by Stephen King. **93m/C VHS.** Terence Knox, Paul Scherrer, Rosalind Allen, Christie Clark, Ned Romero, Ryan Bollman, Ted Travelstead; **D:** David F. Price; **W:** Gilbert Adler, A.L. Katz.

Children of the Corn 3: Urban Harvest ⅋⅋ 1995 (R) Joshua (Melendez) and younger brother Eli (Cerny) are adopted by a wealthy couple and transplanted from Nebraska to Chicago's suburbia. But when Eli grows a corn patch that resurrects an evil force, only Joshua can stop his reign of terror. Contrived premise but lots of nifty special effects. **103m/C VHS, DVD.** Daniel Cerny, Ron Melendez, Mari Morrow, Duke Stroud, Jim Metzler, Nancy Lee Grahn; **D:** James D.R. Hickox; **W:** Dode Levenson; **M:** Daniel Licht.

Children of the Corn 4: The Gathering ⅋ *Deadly Harvest* 1996 (R) Medical student Grace Rhodes (Watts) seeks to free the children of her Nebraska hometown from a mysterious plague and a shadowy figure. **85m/C VHS, DVD.** Naomi Watts, Brent Jennings, Jamie Renee Smith, William Windom, Karen Black; **D:** Greg Spence; **W:** Stephen Berger, Greg Spence; **C:** Richard Clabaugh; **M:** David Williams.

Children of the Corn 5: Fields of Terror ⅋⅋ 1998 (R) Allison (Galina), Greg (Arquette), Tyrus (Vaughan), and Kir (Mendez) have traveled to Divinity Falls to bury the cremated remains of Kir's recently deceased boyfriend. That's when they run into the local cult of murderous children and Alison realizes that her long-lost brother, Jacob (Buzzotta), is one of them. She's determined to get him away but the evil force that leads the children has other ideas. **85m/C VHS, DVD.** Alexis Arquette, Greg Vaughan, Stacy Galina, Eva Mendes, Adam Wylie, Dave Buzzotta, David Carradine, Fred Williamson; **D:** Ethan Wiley; **W:** Ethan Wiley; **C:** David Lewis; **M:** Paul Rabjohns. **VIDEO**

Children of the Corn: Revelation ⅋⅋ 2001 Jamie (Mink) is looking for her missing grandma at the condemned Hampton Arms where the remaining residents are meeting grisly fates. She and detective Armbrister (Cassie) are informed by a mysterious priest (Ironside) that the condos were built on the site of a tent revival fire that killed a number of children. Of course the kids turn out to be the Gatlin killer-kiddie cult and they return to reclaim their land. Some decent shockers in this 7th installment of the series. **81m/C VHS, DVD.** Claudette Mink, Michael Ironside, Troy Yorke, Sean Smith, Kyle Cassie, Michael Rogers, Taylor Hobbs, Jeffrey) Ballard, Crystal Lowe; **D:** Guy Magar. **VIDEO**

Children of the Corn 666: Isaac's Return ⅋⅋½ 1999 (R) Hannah Martin (Ramsey) is traveling to Nebraska in search of her birth mother but when she arrives in the small town of Gatlin, she finds the residents want to keep their secrets. **82m/C VHS, DVD.** Natalie Ramsey, John Franklin, Stacy Keach, Alix Koromzay, Nancy Allen; **D:** Keri Skogland. **VIDEO**

Children of the Damned ⅋⅋½ 1963 Six children, who are a sample of what man will evolve to in a million years, are born all around the world with genius IQs, ray-gun eyes, and murderous dispositions. Two investigators bring the children together, and while they are being examined by scientists they escape. The children hide out in a church, but they are doomed because their destiny is to be destroyed because their destiny is to be de-

Children of the Full Moon 🐾
1984 A young couple find themselves lost in a forest that is the home of werewolves. Earns praise only for brevity. Even bad movie aficionados will want to skip this howler. 60m/C VHS, DVD, GB Christopher Cazenove, Celia Gregory, Diana Dors, Jacqueline Rex, Franchesca Lee, Harold Goldblatt, Ralph Michael, Martin Miller, Lee Yoke-Moon; D: Tom Clegg.

Children of the Living Dead WOOF!
2000 (R) Standard "...of the Living Dead" fare has only producer John Russo as a connection to the original. One of the worst of these seemingly endless low-budget horrors. The voice dubbing sounds exceptionally unnatural, lighting is amateurish with the odd flash when someone behind the camera mishandles a mirror; acting is poor. Story is the same old same old. 90m/C DVD. Tom Savini, A. Barret Woland, Jamie McCoy; D: Tor Ramsey. W: Karen Wolf.

Children of the Night 🐾½
1992 (R) Allburg seems like a typically quiet small town far removed from any danger—until a vampire is released from an underground crypt and decides to make the town his bloodthirsty target. When a teacher, whose girlfriend is visiting Allburg, learns of the supernatural goings on he decides to investigate, which may be a deadly mistake. 92m/C VHS, DVD. Peter DeLuisa, Karen Black, Ami Dolenz, Maya McLaughlin, Evan Mackenzie, David Sawyer, Garret Morris; D: Tony Randel; W: Nicolas Falacci; C: Richard Michalak.

Children of the Revolution 🐾🐾
1995 (R) Mockumentary covering 45 years of Australian history and politics, beginning in 1951 when the conservative Prime Minister attempts to ban the Australian Communist Party. Party member (and Stalin admirer) Joan Fraser (Davis) helps to prevent the ban, bringing her to the Russian leader's attention, and she's invited to Moscow. There, Joan winds up in bed with Stalin (Abraham), son Joe (Rush) makes an entry into the Australian political scene, resulting in chaos. There's almost too much more for the film to handle, although the actors don't seem to have any problems. 101m/C VHS, DVD. AU Judy Davis, Sam Neill, Richard Roxburgh, Rachel Griffiths, Geoffrey Rush, F. Murray Abraham; D: Peter Duncan; W: Peter Duncan; C: Martin McGrath; M: Nigel Westlake. Australian Film Inst. '96: Actress (Davis), Art Dir./Set Dec., Costume Des.

Children of the Wild 🐾🐾½
Killers of the Wild 1937 Adventure story about a pack of dogs surviving in the Rocky Mountain wilderness. Splendid scenery and some interesting sequences. 65m/B VHS. Joan Valerie, James Bush, Leroy Mason, Patsy Moran; D: Charles (Hutchinson) Hutchinson.

The Children of Theatre Street 🐾🐾🐾
1977 Absorbing documentary follows three children attending the renowned Kirov Ballet School. A show for all ages that may be especially enjoyed by kids who are interested in ballet. Kelly's last film appearance. 92m/C VHS, DVD, RU Angelina Armeiskaya, Alec Timoushin, Lena Voronzova, Michaela Cerna, Galina Messenzeva, Konstantin Zaklinsky; D: Robert Dornhelm; W: Beth Gutcheon; C: Karl Kofler; Nar: Grace Kelly.

The Children of Times Square 🐾🐾
1986 A mother pursues her son who has fled home and joined a gang of drug dealers in N.Y.C.'s seedy Times Square. Ordinary film despite strong casting of Cassidy and Rollins. 95m/C VHS. Joanna Cassidy, Howard E. Rollins Jr., Brandon Douglas, David Ackroyd, Griffin O'Neal, Danny Nucci, Larry B. Scott, Jacob Vargas, Devoreaux White, Joe Spinell, Jasor Bernard.

Child's Play 🐾🐾½
1988 (R) A boy discovers that his new doll named Chucky is actually the embodiment of a deranged killer. His initially skeptical mom and a police officer come around after various killings. Exciting, if somewhat moronic, fare, with fine special effects. Followed by "Child's Play 2." 95m/C VHS, DVD. Catherine Hicks, Alex Vincent, Chris Sarandon, Dinah Manoff, Brad Dourif, Tommy Swerdlow, Jack Colvin; D: Tom Holland; W: Tom Holland, Don Mancini, John Lafia; C: Bill Butler; M: Joe Renzetti.

Child's Play 2 🐾🐾
1990 (R) Chucky lives. Basic doll-on-a-rampage story, a metaphor for the Reagan years, lives on in the sequel (you remember: somehow guy-doll Chucky made it past the quality control people with a highly inflammable temper). A little dotty from playing with dolls, young Vincent finds himself fostered by two new parents, and plagued by an obnoxious and very animated doll that fosters ill will toward all. What's worse is the doll is transmigratory, craving the boy's body as his next address. Chef d'effects Kevin Yagher's new toy is bad, real bad, and so are the other part two FX. Little Chucky's saga, however grows a tad tiresome. A bad example for small children. 84m/C VHS, DVD. Alex Vincent, Jenny Agutter, Gerrit Graham, Christine Elise, Grace Zabriskie; D: John Lafia; W: Don Mancini; C: Stefan Czapsky; M: Graeme Revell; V: Brad Dourif.

Child's Play 3 WOOF!
1991 (R) Possessed doll Chucky returns to life again in search of a new child to control, and luckily finds his old pal (Whalin) at a military school filled with the usual stereotypes. Gory sequel in a mostly awful series. "Don't F— with the Chuck" was its catch

Children On Their Birthdays 🐾🐾½
2002 (PG) Based on a short story by Truman Capote and set in small Medda, Alabama in 1947, which is where 13-year-old Billy Bob Murphy (Pichler) lives with his widowed mother (Plemons) but the two are soon vying for the affections of the new girl in town—Lily Jane Bobbit (Raymonde). Meanwhile, romantic mechanic Speedy (McDonald) to Billy Bob's dismay. And there's even more excitement over the shady dealings of smooth-talking Lionel Quince (Arnold). 102m/C VHS, DVD. Joe Pichler, Jesse Plemons, Sheryl Lee, Tania Raymonde, Phyllis Frelich, Christopher McDonald, Tom Arnold; D: Mark Medoff; W: Douglas J. Sloan; C: Steve (Steven) Shaw; M: James D. Hinton, Ross Vannelli.

Children Shouldn't Play with Dead Things 🐾🐾½
Revenge of the Living Dead 1972 A band of foolhardy hippie filmmakers on an island cemetery skimp on special effects by using witchcraft to revive the dead. The plan works. Soon the crew has an island full of hungry ghouls to contend with. Film strives for yucks, frequently succeeds. A late night fave, sporting some excellent dead rising from their grave scenes as well as a selection of groovy fashions. Screenwriter/star "Ormsby" went on to write the remake of "Cat People," while director Clark would eventually helm "Porky's." 85m/C VHS, DVD. Alan Ormsby, Valerie Manches, Jeff Gillen, Anya Ormsby, Paul Cronin, Jane Daly, Roy Engleman, Robert Philip, Bruce Solomon, Alec Baird, Seth Sklarey; D: Bob (Benjamin) Clark; W: Bob Clark, Alan Ormsby; C: Jack McGowan; M: Carl Zittrer.

The Children's Hour 🐾🐾
The Loudest Whisper 1961 The teaching careers of two women are ruined when girls begin circulating vicious rumors. Only an occasionally taut drama despite forceful handling of a lesbian theme. Updated version of Lillian Hellman's play (adapted by Hellman) is more explicit, but less suspenseful in spite of excellent performances from the talented cast. Remake of Wyler's own "These Three." 107m/C VHS, DVD. Shirley MacLaine, Audrey Hepburn, James Garner, Miriam Hopkins, Veronica Cartwright, Fay Bainter; D: William Wyler; W: John Michael Hayes; M: Alex North.

Chilly Dogs WOOF!
Kevin of the North 2001 (PG-13) A woofer that deserves to be buried. Slacker Kevin Manley (Ulrich) learns he's inherited land in Alaska from his grandfather. But in order to collect he must compete in the 1,000 mile dog sled race between Anchorage and Nome, Alaska. Babe Bonnie (Nestridge) is willing to help the tenderfoot out while sneaky lawyer Thornton (Nielsen) is among those trying to undermine Kevin's every chance. At least the similarly themed "Snow Dogs" had a certain amount of kiddie humor to sustain it 102m/C VHS, DVD, CA Skeet Ulrich, Natasha Henstridge, Leslie Nielsen, Rik Mayal, Lochlyn Munro, Jay Brazeau; D: Bob Spiers; W: William Osborne; M: Harvey Summers.

Chilly Scenes of Winter 🐾🐾½
Head Over Heels 1979 (PG) Quirky comedy with a cult following about a man obsessed with regaining the love of a former girlfriend who is now married. He must also deal with an insane mom and various other problems. Strong, subtle performances from Heard and Rieger. Hurt is somewhat less satisfying as the supposedly fascinating woman. Released with a different, inferior ending as "Head Over Heels." Adapted by Joan Micklin Silver from Ann Beattie's first novel. Watch for Beattie's cameo as a waitress. 96m/C VHS. John Heard, Mary Beth Hurt, Peter Riegert, Kenneth McMillan, Gloria Grahame, Nora Heflin, Griffin Dunne; Cameos: Ann Beattie; D: Joan Micklin Silver; W: Joan Micklin Silver; M: Harvey Summers.

Chillers 🐾
1986 Travellers waiting for a bus are besieged by carnivorous zombies and voracious vampires. How this is different from the standard bus trip is unclear. 90m/C VHS, DVD. Jesse Emery, Marjorie Fitzsimmons, Laurie Pennington, Jim Wolfe, David Wohl; D: Daniel Boyt; W: Daniel Boyd.

The Chilling WOOF!
Gamma 693 1988 (R) Corpses preserved in a deep freeze come alive and plague Kansas City as flesh-chomping zombies. Utterly worthless film doesn't even provide convincing effects. 91m/C VHS. Linda Blair, Dan Haggerty, Troy Donahue, Jack A. De Rieux, Ron Vincent; D: Deland Nuse, Jack A. Sunseri.

Chimes at Midnight 🐾🐾🐾🐾
Falstaff; Campanadas a Medianoche 1967 Classic tragedy—derived by a corpulent Shakespeare plays—about a prince. Meanwhile his friendship with a prince. Crammed with classic sequences, including a battle that is both realistic and funny.

The love scene between massive Welles also and a nonetheless willing Moreau also manages to be both sad and amusing. Great performances all around, but Welles understandably dominates. The film's few flaws (due to budget problems) are inconsequential before considerable strengths. This one ranks among Welles's very best. 115m/B VHS. SP Sir Orson Welles, Jeanne Moreau, Margaret Rutherford, John Gielgud, Marina Vlady, Keith Baxter, Fernando Rey, Norman Rodway; D: Orson Welles; W: Orson Welles; C: Edmond Richard; M: Angelo Francesco Lavagnino; Nar: Ralph Richardson.

phrase; that should indicate the level of this junk. 89m/C VHS, DVD, Justin Whalin, Patrick Gleeson. TV.

R.D. Call, John Capodice, Ami Dolenz, Courtney Gains; D: Curtis Hanson; W: Curtis Hanson; M: ...rey Reeves, Jeremy Sylvers, Peter Haskell, Dakin Matthews, Travis Fine, Dean Jacobson, Matthew Bender; W: Don Mancini; M: Cory Lerios, John D'Andrea; V: Brad Dourif.

Chill Factor 🐾🐾
1990 (R) A TV reporter for an investigative news show uncovers evidence of an international conspiracy. Plot twists abound. 95m/C VHS, DVD. Paul Williams, Patrick Macnee, Andrew Prine, Carrie Snodgress, Patrick Wayne, Gary Crosby; D: David L. Stanton.

Chill Factor 🐾🐾½
1999 (R) Stealing every plot device and cliché in the action thriller genre, this is indeed one unoriginal cold turkey. After accidentally blowing up a platoon of soldiers while testing a chemical weapon codenamed "Elvis" and pinning the blame on clumsy general Brynner (Firth), scientist Dr. Long (Paymer) moves to Montana to take up fly-fishing while continuing his research. He befriends diner clerk Tim (Ulrich), but only until the general is released from prison with a grudge to settle. The general has plans to sell the weapon to the highest bidder, but Long manages to get Elvis out of the building. The canister can't get hotter than 50 degrees, or Elvis will blow a hunka hunka burnin' Armageddon. Tim hijacks an ice cream truck and its driver Arlo (Gooding), and the pair are chased and shot at until the movie is mercifully over. 102m/C VHS, DVD. Skeet Ulrich, Cuba Gooding Jr., Peter Firth, David Paymer, Daniel Hugh-Kelly, Kevin J. O'Connor, Judson Mills, Hudson (Heidi) Leick, Jim Grimshaw; D: Hugh Johnson; W: Drew Gitlin, Mike Cheda; C: David Gribble; M: Hans Zimmer, John Powell.

China Beach 🐾🐾🐾
1988 TV movie/pilot launched the acclaimed series about American military women behind the lines during the chaos of the Vietnam War. Nurse McMurphy has only seven days left on her first tour of duty, and in spite of her hate of the brutality of the war, she has mixed feelings about leaving her friends and her work. A USO singer on a one week tour finds her reason for men brings the war too close for comfort. Cheri, a new Red Cross volunteer, shows up at the Beach. Skillfully introduces the characters, their problems and joys, without melodrama or redundancy. 89m/C VHS, DVD, Dana Delany, Chloe Webb, Robert Picardo, Nan Woods, Michael Boatman, Marg Helgenberger, Tim Ryan, Concetta Tomei, Jeff Kober, Brian Wimmer; D: Rod Holcomb; W: John Sacret Young. TV.

China Cry 🐾🐾½
1991 (PG-13) Based on the true story of Sung Negn Yee who escaped from Communist China to the freedom of Hong Kong in the early '60s. Fine portrayal of the young woman and joys, without melodrama or redundancy. 103m/C VHS, DVD. Julia Nickson-Soul, Russell Wong, James Shigeta, France Nuyen; D: James F. Collier.

China Gate 🐾🐾½
1957 A band of multi-national troops follows a French officer against a communist stronghold in Indochina. Conventional fare bolstered considerably by director Fuller's flair for action. Weak male leads, but Dickinson shines. 97m/B VHS Gene Barry, Angie Dickinson, Nat King Cole, Paul Dubov, Lee Van Cleef, George Givot, Marcel Dalio, Gerald Milton, Neyle Morrow, Maurice Mersac, Warren Hsieh, Paul Busch, Sasha Hardin, James Hong, Walter Soo Hoo, Weaver Levy; D: Samuel Fuller; W: Samuel Fuller; C: Joseph Biroc; M: Max Steiner; Young.

China Girl 🐾🐾½
1987 (R) An Italian-American boy and a Chinese-American girl romance despite a war between gangs in their respective NYC communities. This often violent drama is enriched by director Ferrara's slick, high-energy approach. 90m/C VHS. Richard Panebianco, James Russo, Sari Chang, Russell Wong, David Caruso, Joey Chin; D: Abel Ferrara; M: Joe Delia.

The China Lake Murders 🐾🐾½
1990 (PG-13) Crazy cop-on-the-loose fable in which a serial killer disguised as a highway patrolman practices population control on the inhabitants of a small town in the Mojave desert. Meanwhile the local sheriff (Skerritt, unwittingly befriends the killer-patrolman. 100m/C VHS. Tom Skerritt, Michael Parks, Nancy Everhard, Lauren Tewes, Bill McKinney, Lonnie (Lonnie) Chapman; D: Alan Metzger; W: Nevin Schreiner. CABLE.

China Moon ✓✓½ 1991 (R) Convoluted police thriller, set in Florida, about beautiful Rachel (Stowe), who's married to rich-but-abusive Rupert (Dance). Kyle (Harris) is the lonely homicide detective who's besotted by Rachel and conveniently helps her dispose of her murdered husband's body. Kyle's problems increase when his rookie partner (Del Toro) turns out to be smarter than anyone thinks. Good performances but the suspense is only average. 99m/C VHS, DVD. Ed Harris, Madeleine Stowe, Benicio Del Toro, Charles Dance; D: John Bailey; W: Roy Carlson; C: Willy Kurant; M: George Fenton.

China, My Sorrow ✓✓½ Chine, Ma Douleur 1989 Thirteen-year-old "Little Four Eyes" is sent to a Chinese re-education camp for the crime of playing a love song to a girl. There he befriends another enemy of the revolution and a Buddhist monk who help him maintain his familial traditions and identity. Tragi-comic look at how freedom's spirit survived the Cultural Revolution. Mandarin with subtitles. 86m/C VHS. CH Guo Yiang Yi, Tieu Quan Nghieu, Vong Han Lai, Chi-Viy Sam, Chang Cheung Siang; D: Dai Sijie; W: Dai Sijie, Shan Yuan Zhu; M: Chen Qi Gang.

China O'Brien ✓✓½ 1988 (R) Gorgeous police officer with martial arts expertise returns home for a little R&R, but finds she has to kick some major butt instead. Violent, dim-witted action drama proves only that cleavage can be macho too. 90m/C VHS, DVD. Cynthia Rothrock, Richard Norton, Patrick Adamson, David Blackwell, Steven Kerby, Robert Tiller, Lainie Watts, Keith Cooke; D: Robert Clouse; W: Robert Clouse; C: Kent Wakeford; M: Paul Antonelli

China O'Brien 2 ✓½ 1989 (R) The unbreakable China, now a sheriff, battles the standard-issue Vietnam-vet druglord who invades her little town. Made back-to-back with the first film (note that both pics' bad guys have the same gang of henchman), and in both films Rothrock is basically invincible, so there's no suspense. 85m/C VHS. Cynthia Rothrock, Richard Norton, Keith Cooke; D: Robert Clouse.

China Seas ✓✓✓ 1935 The captain of a commercial steamship on the China route has to fight off murderous Malay pirates, a spumed woman, and a ragging typhoon to reach port safely. Fast-moving romantic action taken from Crosbie Garstin's novel. 89m/B VHS, DVD. Clark Gable, Jean Harlow, Wallace Beery, Rosalind Russell, Lewis Stone, Sir C. Aubrey Smith, Dudley Digges, Robert Benchley, William Henry, Lillian Bond, Edward Brophy, Hattie McDaniel, Akim Tamiroff; D: Tay Garnett; W: Jules Furthman, James Kevin McGuinness; C: Ray June; M: Herbert Stothart.

The China Syndrome ✓✓✓½ 1979 (PG) A somewhat unstable executive at a nuclear plant uncovers evidence of a concealed accident and takes drastic steps to publicize the incident. Lemmon is excellent as the anxious exec, and Fonda and Douglas are scarcely less distinguished as a sympathetic TV journalist and camera operator, respectively. Tense, prophetic thriller that ironically preceded the Three Mile Island accident by just a few months. Produced by Douglas. 123m/C VHS, DVD. Jane Fonda, Jack Lemmon, Michael Douglas, Scott Brady, James Hampton, Peter Donat, Wilford Brimley, James Karen; D: James Bridges; W: James Bridges, Mike Gray, T.S. Cook; C: James A. Crabe. British Acad. '79: Actor (Lemmon), Actress (Fonda); N.Y. Film Critics '79: Actor (Lemmon); Writers Guild '79: Orig. Screenplay.

China White 1991 (R) Violence erupts in the streets of Paris, Amsterdam, and Bangkok, when international drug cartels battle over the ownership of China White—premium heroin, its sources and its outlets. Rousing, realistic action. 99m/C VHS. Billy Drago, Russell Wong, Lisa Schrage, Steven Leigh; D: Ronny Yu.

Chinatown ✓✓✓✓ 1974 (R) Private detective Jake Gittes (Nicholson) finds himself overwhelmed in a scandalous case involving the rich and powerful of Los Angeles. Gripping, atmospheric mystery excels in virtually every aspect, with strong narrative drive and outstanding performances from Nicholson, Dunaway, and Huston. Director Polanski also appears in a suitable unsettling cameo. Fabulous. A sneaky, snaking delight filled with seedy characters and plots-within-plots. Followed more than 15 years later by "The Two Jakes." 131m/C VHS, DVD. Roman Polanski, Jack Nicholson, Faye Dunaway, John Huston, Diane Ladd, John Hillerman, Burt Young, Perry Lopez, Darrell Zwerling, Joe Mantell; D: Roman Polanski; W: Robert Towne; C: John A. Alonzo; M: Jerry Goldsmith. Oscars '74: Orig. Screenplay; AFI '98: Top 100; British Acad. '74: Actor (Nicholson), Director (Polanski), Screenplay; Golden Globes '75: Actor—Drama (Nicholson), Director (Polanski); Film—Drama, Screenplay, Natl. Film Reg. '91; N.Y. Film Critics '74: Actor (Nicholson); Natl. Soc. Film Critics '74: Actor (Nicholson); Writers Guild '74: Orig. Screenplay.

Chinatown After Dark ✓ 1931 Ludicrous, inane melodrama about a white girl raised by the Chinese. 50m/B VHS, DVD. Rex Lease, Barbara Kent, Carmel Myers; D: Stuart Paton.

Chinatown Connection ✓ 1990 (R) For some inexplicable reason, local drug dealers start selling poisoned cocaine. Two renegade cops discover the super-secret organization doing the poisoning, arm themselves heavily, and kill lots of people while putting an end to the poisonings. Violent, foolish film with dull performances. 94m/C VHS. Bruce Ly, Lee Majors, Pat McCormick, Art Camacho, Susan Fralley, Scott Richards; D: Jean-Paul Ouellette.

The Chinatown Kid ✓ 1978 Tan Tung escapes from Red China on a ship bound for San Francisco. There he becomes involved in a local extortion racket and he'll need all his martial arts skills to overcome the two gangs fighting for power. 115m/C VHS, DVD. Alexander Fu Sheng, Sun Chien, Shirley Yu, Shaw Yin-Yin; D: Chen Chen.

The Chinatown Murders: Man against the Mob ✓✓ Man Against the Mob: The Chinatown Murders 1989 (R) A tough cop is up against the Chinese mafia and his own corrupt police force as he tries to stay alive and find some justice. 96m/C VHS, DVD. George Peppard, Charles Haid, Richard Bradford, Ursula Andress, Jason Beghe, Julia Nickson-Soul, James Pax, Sandy Ward; D: Michael Pressman; C: Ray June.

Chinese Box ✓✓½ 1997 Hong Kong's return to Chinese rule is the backdrop for Wang's story of a dying British journalist (Irons) and a former bar girl turned nightclub owner (Li). In the months before the 1997 handover, business writer John learns he is dying of leukemia and decides to pursue Vivian, the woman he has secretly loved for some time. He also sets out to discover the "meaning" of Hong Kong itself. This quest is personified by Jean (Cheung), a street hustler with stories to tell. Metaphors abound as Wang tries to convey the everyday chaos and impenetrability of Hong Kong life. Striking visuals provide cues and clues to the not-always-subtle symbolism. Mandarin and English dialogue. 109m/C VHS, DVD. FR JP Jeremy Irons, Gong Li, Maggie Cheung, Ruben Blades, Michael Hui; D: Wayne Wang; W: Wayne Wang, Jean-Claude Carriere, Larry Gross, Paul Theroux; C: Vilko Filac; M: Graeme Revell.

Chinese Boxes ✓✓½ 1984 An American man in Berlin is framed in a murder and becomes caught in an international web of crime and intrigue. Low budget but interesting thriller. 87m/C VHS. GE GB Will Patton, Adelheid Arndt, Robbie Coltrane; D: Christopher Petit; W: L.M. Kit Carson.

The Chinese Cat ✓ 1944 Poorly scripted formula mystery has the younger Chan smitten with a girl who needs the elder Chan's detective skills in finding her father's killer. 65m/B VHS, DVD. Sidney Toler, Benson Fong, Mantan Moreland, Weldon Heyburn, Joan Woodbury, Ian Keith, Sam Flint; D: Phil Rosen.

Chinese Connection ✓✓✓ Fist of Fury; The Iron Hand; Jing Wu Men 1973 (R) A martial arts expert tracks sadistic brutes who slew his instructor. Wild action sequences provide a breathtaking view of Lee's skill. Dubbed. 90m/C VHS, DVD. HK Bruce Lee, James Tien, Robert Baker; D: Lo Wei; W: Lo Wei; C: Chen Ching Chu; M: Fu-ling Wang.

Chinese Connection 2 ✓ Fistful of the Dragon; Fists of Fury 2; Jie Quan Ying Zhao Gorb 1977 (R) A martial-arts expert learns that the school where he trained is now run by an unappealing master. Conflict ensues. Bruce Li is not Bruce Lee (who, to make things more confusing, is shown in flashbacks since he started in the first film), but he is fairly good in action portions of this otherwise dull, sloppy venture. 96m/C VHS, DVD. HK Bruce Li, Bruce Lee, Lieh Lo, Quin Lee; D: Tso Nam Lee.

Chinese Roulette ✓✓½ 1986 A host of unappealing characters convene at a country house for sexual shenanigans and a cruel game masterminded by a sadistic crippled girl. Cold effort from German master Fassbinder. In German with English subtitles. 82m/C VHS, DVD. GE Anna Karina, Margit Carstensen, Ulli Lommel, Brigitte Mira, Macha Meril, Andrea Schober, Volker Spengler; D: Rainer Werner Fassbinder; W: Rainer Werner Fassbinder; C: Michael Ballhaus.

Chinese Web ✓ 1978 Spiderman adventure in which Spidey becomes entwined in international intrigue and corrupt officials. 95m/C VHS. Nicholas Hammond, Robert F. Simon, Rosalind Chao, Ted Danson; D: Donald McDougall.

Chino ✓✓ Valdez the Half-Breed; The Valdez Horses 1975 (PG) A half-Indian horse rancher struggles to maintain his livelihood in this spaghetti western. Not among Bronson's stronger—that is, more viscerally effective—films. Adapted from Lee Hoffman's novel. 97m/C VHS, DVD. IT Charles Bronson, Jill Ireland, Vincent Van Patten; D: John Sturges; W: Massimo De Rita, Clair Huffaker, Arduino (Dino) Maiuri; C: Armando Nannuzzi; M: Guido de Angelis, Maurizio de Angelis.

Chips, the War Dog ✓✓½ 1990 A WWII Army recruit, who's scared of dogs, is assigned to train a German shepherd for duty. 90m/C VHS. Brandon Douglas, Ned Vaughn, Paxton Whitehead, Ellie Cornell, Robert Miranda, William Devane; D: Ed Kaplan. CABLE.

The Chisholms ✓✓½ 1979 If you're into oaters, here's a high fiber six-hour serial: Chisolm (Preston) leads the family as they head west and find trouble with a capital "T" en route from Virginia to Californ-i-a. Originally a network miniseries, it's now a two-cassette rentable, adapted by Evan Hunter from his novel. 300m/C VHS. Robert Preston, Rosemary Harris, Brian Keith, Ben Murphy, Charles Frank; D: Mel Stuart; M: Elmer Bernstein.

Chisum ✓✓ 1970 (G) Cattle baron faces various conflicts, including a confrontation with Billy the Kid. Lame Wayne vehicle contributes nothing to exhausted western genre. 111m/C VHS, DVD. John Agar, John Wayne, Forrest Tucker, Geoffrey Deuel, Christopher George, Ben Johnson, Bruce Cabot, Patric Knowles, Richard Jaeckel, Glenn Corbett; D: Andrew V. McLaglen; W: Andrew J. Fenady; C: William Clothier.

Chitty Chitty Bang Bang ✓✓ 1968 (G) An eccentric inventor spruces up an old car and, in fantasy, takes his children to a land where the evil rulers have forbidden children. Poor special effects and forgettable score stall effort. Loosely adapted by Roald Dahl and Hughes from an Ian Fleming story. ♫Chitty Chitty Bang Bang; Hushabye Mountain; Truly Scrumptious; Toot Sweet; Me Ol' Bamboo; Lovely Lonely Man; Posh; The Roses of Success. 142m/C VHS, DVD. GB Dick Van Dyke, Sally Ann Howes, Lionel Jeffries, Gert Frobe, Anna Quayle, Benny Hill; D: Ken Hughes; W: Ken Hughes, Roald Dahl; C: Christopher Challis; M: Richard M. Sherman, Robert B. Sherman.

Chloe in the Afternoon ✓✓ L'Amour l'Apres-midi 1972 (R) A married man finds himself inexplicably drawn to an ungainly young woman. Sixth of the "Moral Tales" series is typical of director Rohmer's talky approach. Not for all tastes, but rewarding for those who are drawn to this sort of thing. In French with English subtitles. 97m/C VHS, DVD. FR Bernard Verley, Zouzou, Francoise Verley, Daniel Ceccaldi, Malvina Penne, Babette Ferrier, Suze Randall, Marie-Christine Barrault; D: Eric Rohmer; W: Eric Rohmer; C: Nestor Almendros; M: Arie Dzierlatka.

Chocolat ✓✓✓ 1988 (PG-13) A woman recalls her childhood spent in French West Africa and the unfulfilled sexual tension between her mother and black servant. Vivid film provides a host of intriguing characters and offers splendid panoramas of rugged desert landscapes. Profound, if somewhat personal filmmaking from novice director Denis. In French with English subtitles. 105m/C VHS, DVD. Mireille Perrier, Emmet Judson Williamson, Cecile Ducasse, Giulia Boschi, Francois Cluzet, Isaach de Bankole, Kenneth Cranham; D: Claire Denis; W: Claire Denis, Jean-Pol Fargeau.

Chocolat ✓✓✓ 2000 (PG-13) Freespirited Vianne (Binoche) and her young daughter Anouk (Thivisol) are literally blown into the dull French town of Lansquenet in the late 1950s. Before the scandalized eyes of the Comte de Reynaud (Molina), the community's moral arbitrator, the unmarried hussy opens a chocolaterie—during Lent! While the Comte tries to rally the residents to boycott the establishment, Vianne's delicacies are setting the townspeople's pulses racing, as she becomes intrigued by gypsy vagabond Roux (Depp). Sweetly predictable if overly chastising against religion and conventional morality. Binoche is radiant as usual (and have some chocolate handy when you watch). Based on the novel by Joanne Harris. 121m/C VHS, DVD. FR Juliette Binoche, Victoire Thivisol, Johnny Depp, Alfred Molina, Judi Dench, Lena Olin, Peter Stormare, Carrie-Anne Moss, John Wood, Hugh O'Conor, Leslie Caron, Aurelien Parent Koenig; D: Lasse Hallstrom; W: Robert Nelson Jacobs; C: Roger Pratt; M: Rachel Portman. Screen Actors Guild '00: Support. Actress (Dench).

The Chocolate Soldier ✓ 1941 Dull musical in which an opera star tests his wife's fidelity. Lovers of the musical genre will find that this one has too much talking, not enough singing. Lovers of fine films will realize that more singing would hardly improve things. Based loosely on Molnar's play "The Guardsman." 102m/B VHS. Nelson Eddy, Rise Stevens, Nigel Bruce, Florence Bates, Dorothy Gilmore, Nydia Westman; D: Roy Del Ruth; C: Karl Freund.

The Chocolate War ✓✓✓ 1988 (R) An idealistic student and a hardline headmaster butt heads at a Catholic boys' school over an unofficial candy business in this tense, unsettling drama. Glover is notable in his familiar villain role, and Gordon is effective in his first effort as director. Based on the Robert Cormier novel. 95m/C VHS, DVD. John Glover, Ilan Mitchell-Smith, Wally Ward, Adam Baldwin; D: Keith Gordon; W: Keith Gordon.

The Choice ✓✓ 1981 A young woman must make the choice between aborting or keeping her baby in this fairly insipid drama. 96m/C VHS. Susan Clark, Jennifer Warren, Mitchell Ryan, Largo Woodruff; D: David Greene. TV

Choice of Arms ✓✓½ 1983 A gangster's rural retirement is undone by a dim-witted criminal in this sometimes-gripping drama. Montand and Deneuve are serviceable in undemanding roles of the gangster and his glamorous wife; Depardieu is more impressive as the trouble-making punk. In French with English subtitles. 114m/C VHS. FR Gerard Depardieu, Catherine Deneuve, Yves Montand; D: Alain Corneau.

Choice of Weapons ✓✓ A Dirty Knight's Work; Trial by Combat 1976 Ex-cop trying to solve murders focuses on a curious group of 20th-century men who live within a 12th-century fantasy—jousting for sport and chivalrous honor. Offbeat lance

Choices 🎬🎬 1981 A hearing-impaired athlete suffers alienation when banned from the football squad. What? Controversial covergirl Moore is a supporting player in this, her first film. **90m/C VHS, DVD.** Paul Carafotes, Victor French, Leila Goldoni, Val Avery, Dennis Patrick, Demi Moore; **D:** Rami Alon; **W:** Rami Alon; **C:** Hanania Baer; **M:** Christopher Stone.

Choices 🎬🎬½ 1986 David Birney, Peter Cushing, Donald Pleasence, Barbara Hershey, John Mills, Margaret Leighton; **D:** Kevin Connor; **W:** Julian Bond.

The Choir 🎬🎬🎬 1995 Crisis has overtaken Aldminster Cathedral and its famed boys' choir, which was begun more than 400 years before. Expensive repairs are needed on the building and ambitious dean Hugh Cavendish (Fox), is ready to sacrifice the choir if it will get funding and some Simon Lyndon. **D:** David War... blunt city council criticism about what cace see as an expensive frill. Opposing are King's School headmaster Alexander Troy (Warner) and music master Leo Beckford (Farrell)—who just happens to be having an affair with his top choirster's mother (Harrison). Religion, politics, music, and sex all provide for some interesting drama. Based on the novel by Joanna Trollope. **?m/C VHS.** **GB** James Fox, David Warner, Nicholas Farrell, Cathryn Harrison, Jane Asher, Anthony Way, Peter Vaughan, Richenda Carey, Oliver Milburn, Claire Cox, John Standing, Robert Fleming; **D:** Ferdinand Fairfax; **W:** Ian Curteis. **TV**

The Choirboys 🎬 1977 (R) Thoroughly mediocre production about overbearing L.A. cops and their off-hours handling of job stress. Few of the strong cast emerge unscathed. Based on the Joseph Wambaugh novel. **120m/C VHS.** Charles Durning, Louis Gossett Jr., Perry King, Clyde Kusatsu, Stephen Macht, Tim McIntire, Randy Quaid, Chuck Sacci, Don Stroud, James Woods, Burt Young, Robert Webber, Barbara Rhoades, Vic Tayback, Blair Brown, Charles Haid, Jim Davis; **D:** Robert Aldrich; **C:** Joseph Biroc.

Choke 🎬½ 2000 (R) Weak thriller with dumb dialogue. Shady businessman Harry (Hopper) is trying to cover up his daughter's deadly drunken hit-and-run accident when he's threatened by a con man who knows about the crime. Then Harry just makes the situation worse by accepting the help of a killer (Madsen) who knows how to get rid of troublesome bodies. **95m/C VHS, DVD.** Dennis Hopper, Michael Madsen, L.P. Brown III, Chelsy Reynolds, Ray Tate; **D:** John Skogen.

Choke Canyon 🎬🎬 1986 (PG) An environmentalist thwarts the henchmen of an industrialist eager to coverup a nuclear dump in a picturesque canyon. Good intentions do not necessarily make for a good movie. **95m/C VHS.** Stephen Collins, Bo Svenson, Lance Henriksen; **D:** Charles "Chuck" Bail.

Choose Me 🎬🎬½ 1984 (R) Comedy-drama about sad, lonely, and offbeat quirky characters linked to an unlikely L.A. radio sex therapist. Moody, memorable fare features especially strong playing from Bujold as a sexually inexperienced sex therapist and Warren as one of her regular listeners. Typically eccentric fare from director Rudolph. **106m/C VHS, DVD.** Genevieve Bujold, Lesley Ann Warren, Rae Dawn Chong, John Larroquette, Keith Carradine...

C.H.O.M.P.S. 🎬🎬 1979 (PG) Comedy in which a youthful inventor and a popular robot guard cog become the target of a business takeover. Harmless but unfunny and unfun. **90m/C VHS, DVD.** Jim Backus, Valerie Bertinelli, Wesley Eure, Conrad Bain, Chuck McCann, Red Buttons; **D:** Don Chaffey.

Chopper Chicks in Zombietown 🎬🎬 1991 (R) Tough but sexy Chopper Chicks show up in that American vacation mecca, Zombietown, for a little rest and relaxation. Little do they know that a mad mortician has designs on turning our hot heroines into mindless zombie slaves. Can the buxom biker babes thwart the evil embalmer before it's too late, or will they abandon their Harleys to shuffle about in search of human flesh? From the Troma Team, featuring "Oscar"-winner Billy Bob Thornton as "Donny." **86m/C VHS, DVD.** Jamie Rose, Catherine Carlen, Lycia Naff, Vicki Frederick, Kristina Loggia, Gretchen Palmer, Whitney Reis, Nina Peterson, Ed Gale, David Knell, Billy Bob Thornton, Don Calfa, Martha Quinn; **D:** Dan Hoskins; **W:** Dan Hoskins; **C:** Tom Fraser; **M:** Daniel May.

The Choppers 🎬 1961 Naw not a fable about false teeth. Teen punk Hall operates a car theft ring made up of fellow punksters. Rock'n'roll tunes by the Hall-meister include the much-overcooked "Monkey in my Hatband." **66m/B VHS, DVD.** Arch Hall Jr., Marianne Gaba, Robert Paget, Tom Brown, Rex Holman, Bruno Ve Sota; **D:** Leigh Jason; **M:** Al Pellegrini.

Chopping Mall 🎬🎬 1986 (R) A freak electric storm unleashes killer security robots on a band of teens trapped inside the mall. Nobody shops. Premise undone by obscure humor, lack of flair, action, or horror. Updated imitation of the 1973 TV movie "Trapped." **77m/C VHS, DVD.** Kelli Maroney, Tony O'Dell, Suzee Slater, Russell Todd, Paul Bartel, Mary Woronov, Dick Miller, Karrie Emerson, Barbara Crampton, Nick Segal, John Terlesky, Gerrit Graham, Mel Welles; **D:** Jim Wynorski; **W:** Jim Wynorski, Steve Mitchell; **C:** Tom Richmond; **M:** Chuck Cirino.

The Chorus 🎬🎬 Les Choristes 2004 (PG-13) Two childhood friends, drawn together again by personal tragedy, reflect on the role of an old mentor who elevated their lives through song. Story of saintly teacher is told in flashback from his point of view. Very schmaltzy retread that has been made so many times before. Tired and predictably inspiring. **95m/C VHS, DVD, DVD.** **FR** Gerard Jugnot, Francois Berleand, Jacques Perrin, Marie Bunel, Kad Merad, Jean-Baptiste Maunier, Didier Flamand, Jean-Paul Bonnaire, Philippe Du Janerand, Maxence Perrin; **D:** Christophe Barratier; **W:** Christophe Barratier, Philippe Lopes-Curval; **C:** Carlo Varini; **M:** Bruno Coulais.

A Chorus Line 🎬🎬 1985 (PG-13) A range of performers reveal their insecurities and aspirations while auditioning before a hardnosed director in this adaptation of the popular, overblown Broadway musical. Singing and dancing is rarely rousing. Director Attenborough probably wasn't the right choice for this one. **118m/C VHS, DVD.** Michael Douglas, Audrey Landers, Gregg Burge, Alyson Reed, Janet Jones, Michael Blevins, Terrence Mann, Cameron English, Vicki Frederick, Nicole Fosse, Michelle Johnson; **D:** Richard Attenborough; **W:** Arnold Schulman; **M:** Marvin Hamlisch, Ralph Burns.

Christ Stopped at Eboli 🎬🎬🎬 *Eboli; Cristo si è fermato a Eboli* 1979 Subdued work about an anti-Fascist writer exiled to rural Italy in the 1930s. Excellent performances from the lead Volonte and supporting players Papas and Cuny. Slow, contemplative film is probably director Rosi's masterpiece. Adapted from Carlo Levi's book. In Italian with English subtitles. **118m/C VHS, DVD.** **IT** Gian Marie Volonte, Irene Papas, Paolo Bonacelli, Francois Simon, Alain Cuny, Lea Massari; **D:** Francesco Rosi; **C:** Pasqualino De Santis, **M:** Stanley Myers. **TV**

Christabel 🎬🎬 1989 Condensed version of the BBC miniseries based on the true-life WWII exploits of Christabel Bielenberg, a British woman who battled to save her German husband from the horrors of the Ravensbruck concentration camp. **148m/C VHS.** **GB** Elizabeth Hurley, Stephen (Dillon) Dillane, Nigelle Vaillant, Geoffrey Palmer; **D:** Adrian Shergold; **W:** Dennis Potter; **C:** Remi Adefarasin; **M:** Stanley Myers. **TV**

Christian the Lion 🎬🎬½ 1976 (G) The true story of Christian, a lion cub raised in a London zoo, who is transported to Africa to learn to live with other lions. With the principals from "Born Free." **87m/C VHS, DVD.** **GB** Virginia McKenna, Bill Travers, George Adamson, James Hill; **D:** Bill Travers.

Christiane F. 🎬🎬🎬 1982 (R) Gripping, visually impressive story of a bored German girl's decline into drug use and prostitution. Based on a West German magazine article. Sobering and dismal look at a milieu in which innocence and youth have run amok. The film's impact is only somewhat undermined by poor dubbing. Bowie appears in a concert sequence. **120m/C VHS, DVD.** **GE** Natja Brunk-

---

Chopper 🎬🎬½ 2000 Biopic of famous Aussie criminal Mark "Chopper" Read is highlighted by Bana's extraordinary performance in the title role. Domi-nik's directorial debut follows Read's career from prison, where he murders one inmate, forces another to cut off his ears, and generally makes hardened criminal fear for their lives. To this old haunts, Full of gore and ultraviolence, it's not for the squeamish but it does make its point about society's preoccupation with the "celebrity criminal." Read didn't participate in the production, but it was based on his nine bestsellers, and he did suggest Bana for the lead. **54m/C DVD, AU** Eric Bana, Vince Colosimo, Simon Lyndon, David Field, Daniel Wyllie, Bill Young, Garry Waddell, Kate Beahan, Kenny Graham; **D:** Andrew Dominik; **W:** Andrew Dominik, Support. Inst. '00: Actor (Bana), Director (Dominik), Actor (Lyndon).

The Chosen 🎬🎬🎬 1981 Set in 1940s Brooklyn about the friendship between two teenagers—Benson, the Hassidic son of a rabbi, and Miller, whose father is a Zionist professor. Based on the novel by Chaim Potok. **108m/C VHS, DVD.** Robby Benson, Barry Miller, Maximilian Schell, Rod Steiger, Hildy Brooks, Ron Rifkin, Val Avery; **D:** Jeremy Paul Kagan; **M:** Elmer Bernstein.

The Chosen One: Legend of the Raven 🎬½ 1998 (R) McKenna Ray ("Baywatch" babe Electra) wants payback after her sister is murdered and is transformed into a superheroine avenger (guided by her shaman father) so she can rid the world of scum. Electra has a provocative costume but the nude scenes are courtesy of a body-double. **105m/C VHS, DVD.** Carmen Electra, Michael Stadvec, Dave Oliver, Shaura Sand; **D:** Lawrence Lanoff; **W:** Sam Rappaport, Khara Bromiley; **C:** Robert New; **M:** Keith Arem.

A Chorus of Disapproval 🎬½ 1989 (PG) Adaptation of prolific Alan Ayckbourn's play about a withdrawn, somewhat dim-witted British widower who attempts social interaction by joining community theatre, then finds himself embroiled in romantic shenanigans and theatrical intrigue. Irons is fine in the lead, but Hopkins sparkles in the more spectacular role of the musical production's tedious director. Seagrove is impressive as an amoral sexpot. Sharper focus from director Winner would have improved this one, but the film is fun even when it isn't particularly funny. **105m/C VHS.** **GB** Jeremy Irons, Anthony Hopkins, Jenny Seagrove, Lionel Jeffries, Patsy Kensit, Gareth Hunt, Prunella Scales, Sylvia Syms, Richard Briers, Barbara Ferris; **D:** Michael Winner; **M:** Michael Winner.

The Chosen WOOF! *Holocaust 2000* 1977 (R) Executive of a nuclear power facility located in the Sahara Desert realizes that his son is the Anti-Christ bent on the world's destruction. This truly horrible film provides nothing in terms of entertainment. It's rarely even laughably bad. **102m/C VHS.** Kirk Douglas, Simon Ward, Agostina Belli, Anthony Quayle, Virginia McKenna, Alexander Knox; **D:** Alberto De Martino; **M:** Ennio Morricone.

A Christmas of Disapproval

Christina 🎬🎬 1974 (PG) Gloomy suspense fare in which a beautiful woman pays a forlorn fellow $25,000 to marry her, then disappears as he begins to actually fall in love with her. His search takes him to various gothic settings. Intriguing, but not really fulfilling. Parkins, however, is appropriately mysterious in the lead. **95m/C VHS.** **CA** Barbara Parkins, Peter Haskell; **D:** Paul Krasny.

Christine's House 🎬🎬 1999 Teen learns she's likely to be the next victim of a murderous stalker who's being hunted by police. Then it's within her own home. **97m/C VHS, DVD.** **CA** Brendan Fehr, Brad Rowe, John Savage, Allison Lange, Lorne Stewart; **D:** Gavin Wilding.

Christine 🎬🎬 1984 (R) Unassuming teen gains possession of a classic auto equipped with a murderous will. Then it's the car doing the possessing. The car-more than the average treatment ation its owner provides. It are your listenation is about to be demolished, thanks to one of her father's development projects. Leila and her friend Tre discover some of the teens can sing and they decide to hold a fund-raising concert that's helped by some heavenly influence. **87m/C DVD.** Keisha Knight Pulliam, Richard Lawson, Tom Bosley, Earl Billings, Pooch Hall, Ray J, Norston, Mike Watts. **CABLE**

Christmas at Water's Edge 🎬🎬½ 2004 Leila Turner is from a wealthy family but she helps out at a home for troubled teens. However, the building is about to be demolished, thanks to one of her father's development projects. Leila and her friend Tre discover some of the teens can sing and they decide to hold a fund-raising concert that's helped by some heavenly influence. **87m/C DVD.** Keisha Knight Pulliam, Richard Lawson, Tom Bosley, Earl Billings, Pooch Hall, Ray J, Norston, Mike Watts. **CABLE**

The Christmas Blessing 🎬🎬½ 2005 Weepy, heartfelt sequel to "The Christmas Shoes." The Teerjerking Christmas drama based on Richard Paul Evans' surprising 1992 bestseller, which started out as a story for the author's children. Richard (Thomas) and Keri (O'Toole) Evans have money troubles so they and their five-year-old daughter Jenna (Mulrooney) move into the mansion of elderly widow Mary Parkin (O'Hara) as caretakers. Richard keeps seeing an angel in a recurring dream and hears a familiar tune—all of which leads to a music box hidden in the attic, a series of love notes, and Mary's unhappy past. **92m/C VHS, DVD.** Maureen O'Hara, Richard Thomas, Annette O'Toole, Kelsey Mulrooney; **D:** Marcus Cole; **W:** Greg Taylor; **C:** John Newby.

The Christmas Card 🎬🎬½ 2006 Career soldier Cody Cullen (Newton) is touched by the strangers who have sent Christmas cards to his unit in Afghanistan. He saves one special card from Faith Spelman (Evans) and when Cody gets leave, he impulsively decides to visit her small hometown. Faith and her father (Asner) welcome Cody and he soon feels part of their family but as Cody and Faith get closer, he needs to decide where his future lies. **84m/C DVD.** Alice Evans, Ed Asner, Lois Nettleton, Peter Jason, Ben Weber, **D:** Steph-zi, John Newton; **M:** Roger Bellon, Brian Robinson. **CABLE**

Christmas

A Christmas Carol 1938 An early version of Dickens' classic tale about miser Scrooge, who is instilled with the Christmas spirit after a grim evening with some ghosts. Good playing from Owen as Scrooge and Lockhart as the hapless Bob Cratchit. Scary graveyard sequence too. **70m/B VHS, DVD.** Reginald Owen, Gene Lockhart; Terence (Terry) Kilburn, Leo G. Carroll, Lynne Carver, Ann Rutherford; **D:** Edwin L. Marin.

A Christmas Carol 1951 *Scrooge* 1951 A fine retelling of the classic tale about a penny-pinching holiday hater who learns appreciation of Christmas following a frightful, revealing evening with supernatural visitors. Perhaps the best rendering of the Dickens classic. "And God bless Tiny Tim!" **86m/B VHS, DVD.** *GB* Alastair Sim, Kathleen Harrison, Jack Warner, Michael Hordern, Patrick Macnee, Mervyn Johns, Hermione Baddeley, Clifford Mollison, George Cole, Carol Marsh, Miles Malleson, Ernest Thesiger, Hattie Jacques, Peter Bull, Hugh Dempster; **D:** Brian Desmond Hurst; **W:** Noel Langley; **C:** C.M. Pennington-Richards; **M:** Richard Addinsell.

A Christmas Carol 1954 Musical version of the Dickens' classic about a stingy old man who is visited by three ghosts on Christmas Eve. **54m/B VHS.** Fredric March, Basil Rathbone, Ray Middleton, Bob Sweeney, Christopher Cook; **D:** Ralph Levy; **W:** Maxwell Anderson; **M:** Bernard Herrmann.

A Christmas Carol 1984 (PG) Excellent TV adaptation of the Dickens Christmas classic features a memorable Scott as miserly misanthrope Ebenezer Scrooge, who gets a scary look at his life thanks to a Christmas Eve visit from the ghosts of Christmas Past, Present, and Future. Terrific supporting cast; filmed on location in Shrewsbury, England. **100m/C VHS, DVD.** George C. Scott, Nigel Davenport, Edward Woodward, Frank Finlay, Lucy Gutteridge, Angela Pleasence, Roger Rees, David Warner, Susannah York; **D:** Clive Donner; **W:** Roger O. Hirson; **C:** Tony Imi; **M:** Nick Bicat.

A Christmas Carol 1999 Oft-told tale does have the advantage of Stewart (who has a one-man stage production of the Dickens saga as well as recording an audiobook) in the lead role. It also has a strong supporting cast and special effects that enhance but don't overwhelm. **120m/C VHS, DVD.** Patrick Stewart, Richard E. Grant, Joel Grey, Saskia Reeves, Desmond Barrit, Bernard Lloyd, Tim Potter, Ben Tibber, Dominic West, Trevor Peacock, Liz Smith, Elizabeth Spriggs, Laura Fraser, Celia Imrie; **D:** David Hugh Jones; **W:** Peter Barnes; **C:** Ian Wilson; **M:** Stephen Warbeck. **CABLE**

The Christmas Coal Mine Miracle *Christmas Miracle in Caulfield, U.S.A* 1977 Syrupy story about miners struggling for survival in a collapsed mine on Christmas Eve. **96m/C VHS.** Mitchell Ryan, Kurt Russell, Andrew Prine, John Carradine, Barbara Babcock, Melissa Gilbert, Don Porter, Shelby Leverington; **D:** Jud Taylor. **TV**

Christmas Comes to Willow Creek 1987 Mutually antagonistic brothers are enlisted to deliver Christmas gifts to an isolated Alaskan community. Can brotherly love be far off? Two leads played together in the rowdy TV series "Dukes of Hazzard." This is hardly an improvement. **96m/C VHS, DVD.** John Schneider, Tom Wopat, Hoyt Axton, Zachary Ansley, Kim Delaney; **D:** Richard Lang; **M:** Charles Fox.

Christmas Do-Over 2006 Think "Groundhog Day" only at Christmas. Grumpy Kevin (Mohr) isn't happy to be spending the holiday with his ex-wife Jill (Zuniga) and his in-laws but he does want to see his cute-as-a-button son Ben (Grove). Ben wishes to keep Christmas every day and Kevin is stuck reliving the holiday until he understands this is his last chance to get his old life back. Except Kevin is such a selfish whiner you know why Jill dumped him, which spoils the whole fantasy. **90m/C DVD.** Jay Mohr, Daphne Zuniga, Adrienne Barbeau, Logan Grove, Tim Thomerson, David Millbern, Ruta Lee; **D:** Catherine Cyran; **W:** Trevor Reed Cristow, Jacqueline David; **C:** Ken Blakey; **M:** Andrew Gross. **CABLE**

Christmas Eve 1947 When a conniving nephew tries to deem his spinster aunt unfit so he can control her estate, she rallies together her three adopted sons, a globe-trotting playboy, a shady criminal type and a wayward cowboy to help. Involves some cute adventures but rather poor acting. Story culminates on Christmas Eve, but it's not a holiday tale. **90m/B VHS.** George Raft, George Brent, Randolph Scott, Joan Blondell, Virginia Field; **D:** Edwin L. Marin; **W:** Laurence Stallings. **VIDEO**

Christmas Evil *Terror in Toyland; You Better Watch Out* 1980 (R) Once again a knife-wielding lunatic dresses as Santa Claus to strike terror and death into the hearts of children. **92m/C VHS, DVD.** Brandon Maggart, Jeffrey DeMunn, Dianne Hull, Scott McKay, Peter Friedman, Joe Jamrog, Rutanya Alda, Raymond J. Barry, Andy Fenwick, Sam Gray, Patricia Richardson; **D:** Lewis Jackson; **W:** Lewis Jackson; **C:** Ricardo Aronovich.

Christmas in Connecticut *Indiscretion* 1945 Lightweight comedy about a housekeeping magazine's successful columnist who isn't quite the expert homemaker she presents herself to be. When a war veteran is invited to her home as part of a publicity gimmick, she must master the ways of housekeeping or reveal her incompetence. Stanwyck is winning in the lead role. Also available in a colorized version. **101m/B VHS, DVD.** Barbara Stanwyck, Reginald Gardiner, Sydney Greenstreet, Dennis Morgan, S.Z. Sakall, Una O'Connor, Robert Shayne, Joyce Compton; **D:** Peter Godfrey.

Christmas in Connecticut 1992 Cannon hosts a weekly TV show as America's favorite homemaker/hostess. A local forest ranger (Kristofferson) becomes a hero by saving a little boy's life and her network stages a media event by inviting him to her home for a traditional Christmas dinner. There's only one problem: she can't cook. Schwarzenegger's directorial debut lacks challenge in this fluffy remake. See the original instead. **93m/C VHS, DVD.** Dyan Cannon, Kris Kristofferson, Tony Curtis, Richard Roundtree, Kelly Cinnante, Gene Lithgow, Vivian Bonnell; **D:** Arnold Schwarzenegger; **W:** Janet Brownell.

Christmas in July 1940 A young man goes on a spending spree when he thinks he's won a sweepstakes. Things take a turn for the worse when he finds out that it was all a practical joke. Powell provides a winning performance in this second film from comic master Sturges. **67m/B VHS.** Dick Powell, Ellen Drew, Raymond Walburn, William Demarest, Franklin Pangborn; **D:** Preston Sturges.

Christmas in the Clouds 2001 (PG) Fun, screwball comedy set in a very upscale Native-American owned resort. The main characters all seem to bring a peculiar little twist to the story line. A writer from a prestigious travel guide publication is expected to make a surprise visit. Joe Clouds on Fire (Vhos) has secretly been writing love letters to a pen pal, Tina (Tosca), who shows up to spy on her suitor only to be mistaken for the hotel critic. The actual critic, Stu O'Malley (Walsh), is a disheveled half-drunk grouch, and is shuffled to a small, cramped room. Very funny farce filmed in Utah's Sundance Resort. **97m/C DVD.** *US* Sam Vlahos, M. Emmet Walsh, Graham Greene, Sheila Tousey, Rosalind Ayres, Tim Vahle, MariAna Tosca, Jonathan Joss; **D:** Kate Montgomery; **W:** Kate Montgomery; **C:** Steven Bernstein; **M:** Rita Coolidge.

The Christmas Kid 1968 A desperado struggles to determine his true identity while stopping in a frontier town. Gunplay ensues. Don't bother with this one. **87m/C VHS.** *SP* Jeffrey Hunter, Louis Hayward, Gustavo Rojo, Perla Cristal, Luis Prendes; **D:** Sidney W. Pink.

Christmas Lilies of the Field 1984 Sequel to "Lilies of the Field" follows an ex-soldier who returns to the church he helped build. This time he sets out to build an orphanage. **98m/C VHS.** Billy Dee Williams, Maria Schell, Fay Hauser, Judith Piquet; **D:** Ralph Nelson. **TV**

The Christmas Miracle of Jonathan Toomey 2007 Reclusive woodcarver Jonathan Toomey (Berenger) is hired by widowed Susan McDowell (Richardson) to carve a replica of a nativity set (now lost) that was given to her son Thomas (Ward-Wilkinson) by his late father. But the work and the approaching holiday bring up painful memories for everyone that they must overcome in order to find hope in the season. **97m/C DVD.** *GB* Tom Berenger, Joely Richardson, Ronald Pickup, Saoirse Ronan, Luke Ward-Wilinson; **D:** Bill Clark; **W:** Bill Clark; **C:** Emmanuel (Manu) Kadosh; **M:** Guy Farley. **VIDEO**

A Christmas Reunion 1993 (PG) Young boy, still trying to adjust to his parents' death, runs away from his grandfather's house. But they're reunited thanks to street corner Santa and an enchanted book. **92m/C VHS,** James Coburn, Edward Woodward, Meredith Edwards; **D:** David Hemmings.

The Christmas Shoes 2002 Lawyer Robert Layton (Lowe) isn't feeling any Christmas cheer as his work commitments keep him from his family, including daughter Lily's (Marshall) choir concerts. Choir director Maggie Andrews (Williams) is terminally ill and her son Nathan (Morrow) wants to buy his mother a special pair of red shoes. Naturally, Robert and Nathan's lives will overlap to make the spirit of the season meaningful for them all. Still, this is a flick about a dying mom so it may be too sad for the youngest members of the family to view. Based on the novel by Donna Van Lieve. **100m/C DVD.** Rob Lowe, Kimberly Williams, Max Morrow, Maria Del Mar, Hugh Thompson, Dorian Harewood, Shirley Douglas, Amber Marshall; **D:** Andy Wolk; **W:** Wesley Bishop; **C:** John Berrie; **M:** Lawrence Shragge. **TV**

A Christmas Story 1983 (PG) Unlikely but winning comedy of Ralphie's (Billingsley) single-minded obsession to acquire a Red Ryder BB-gun for Christmas, and the obstacles that everyday life in 1940s Indiana can throw his way. Particularly great sequence involving an impatient department-store Santa. Fun for everyone. Based on "In God We Trust, All Others Pay Cash," an autobiographical story by Shepherd. Followed by "My Summer Story" in 1994, also from Shepherd's book. **95m/C VHS, DVD, Blu-ray Disc, HD DVD.** *CA US* Peter Billingsley, Darren McGavin, Melinda Dillon, Ian Petrella, Bob (Benjamin) Clark, Zack (Zach) Ward, Leslie (Les) Carlson, Scott Schwartz, R.D. Robb, Tedde Moore, Yano Ayana; *Cameos:* Jean Shepherd; **D:** Bob (Benjamin) Clark; **W:** Bob (Benjamin) Clark, Leigh Brown, Jean Shepherd; **C:** Reginald Morris; **M:** Paul Zaza, Carl Zittrer; *Narr:* Jean Shepherd. Genie '84: Director (Clark).

The Christmas That Almost Wasn't *Il Natale Che Quasi Non Fu* 1966 (G) Loathsome humbug decides to destroy Christmas forever by removing Santa Claus from the North Pole. Crude Italian-made children's film nonetheless remembered fondly by a generation of kids. ...The Christmas That Almost Wasn't; Christmas is Coming; Hustle Bustle; I'm Bad; Kids Get All the Breaks; The Name of the Song is Prune; Nothing to do But Wait; Santa Claus; Time For Christmas. **95m/C VHS, DVD.** *IT* Rossano Brazzi, Paul Tripp, Lidia Brazzi, Sonny Fox, Mischa Auer; **D:** Rossano Brazzi.

A Christmas to Remember 1978 (G) Depression-era Minnesota farmer who has lost his son in WWI brings his city-bred grandson to the farm for a holiday visit. Somber, occasionally poignant film buoyed by Robards presence, and Saint's as well. **96m/C VHS.** Jason Robards Jr., Eva Marie Saint, Joanne Woodward; **D:** George Englund. **TV**

The Christmas Wife 1988 A lonely man pays a woman to be his holiday companion at a mountain retreat. Sturdy performances by Robards and Harris manage to keep this one from going to the dogs. Based on a story by Helen Norris. **73m/C VHS, DVD.** Jason Robards Jr., Julie Harris, Don Francks, Patricia Hamilton, Deborah Grover, James Eckhouse; **D:** David Hugh Jones. **CABLE**

Christmas With the Kranks 2004 (PG) After the two "Santa Clause" movies, Allen sticks with the holiday in this crass, slapstick comedy based on John Grisham's 2001 novel "Skipping Christmas." That is what "Luther (a game Allen) and wife Nora (the ill-used Curtis) intend to do when their only daughter, Blair (Gonzalo), announces she won't be coming home to suburban Chicago for the holiday. Mr. Krank decides a nice Caribbean cruise is in order, but the duo find themselves the recipients of neighborhood scorn when they refuse to get in the seasonal spirit. That changes when Blair suddenly decides to return, accompanied by her brand-new fiance, and the Kranks cave in to Christmas commercialism with zealous glee. Pic is dedicated to the late Alan King, who was cast in a small role as Allen's boss. **99m/C VHS, DVD, UMD.** *US* Tim Allen, Jamie Lee Curtis, Dan Aykroyd, Erik Per Sullivan, Jake Busey, M. Emmet Walsh, Elizabeth Franz, Rene Lavan, Austin Pendleton, Patrick Breen, Felicity Huffman, Julie Gonzalo, Richard "Cheech" Marin, Kevin Chamberlain, Caroline Rhea, Arden Myrin; **D:** Joe Roth; **W:** Chris Columbus; **C:** Don Burgess; **M:** John Debney.

A Christmas Without Snow 1980 A lonely divorced woman finds communal happiness within a local church choir led by a crusty choir master. **96m/C VHS, DVD.** Michael Learned, John Houseman, Ramon Bieri, James Cromwell, Valerie Curtin, Ruth Nelson, Beah Richards, Calvin Levels; **D:** John Korty; **M:** Ed Bogas. **TV**

Christopher Columbus 1949 Step-by-step biography of the 15th-century explorer, his discovery of America, the fame that first greeted him, and his last days. **103m/C VHS.** *GB* Fredric March, Florence Eldridge, Francis L. Sullivan; **D:** David MacDonald.

Christopher Columbus 1985 The man who explored the New World is shown in all his flawed complexity in this film that takes a contemporary approach to the discoveries and character of Christopher Columbus. Shot on location in Spain, Malta, and the Dominican Republic, the film features an exact replica of Columbus's flagship, the Santa Maria. Originally aired as a six-hour TV miniseries. **128m/C VHS.** Gabriel Byrne, Faye Dunaway, Oliver Reed, Max von Sydow, Eli Wallach, Nicol Williamson, Jose Ferrer, Virna Lisi, Raf Vallone; **D:** Alberto Lattuada. **TV**

Christopher Columbus: The Discovery 1992 (PG-13) The 500th anniversary of Columbus' voyage brought this lame excursion in historical biography to the screen briefly. Columbus is portrayed as a swashbuckling adventurer who finally gets the Queen of Spain to agree to finance his voyage of discovery (which primarily consists of discovering a lot of bare-breasted native women). Story is secondary to the banality of the entire production, including the acting. Brando is briefly seen as Torquemada—another film in which he took his substantial paycheck and ran. **120m/C VHS.** Georges Corraface, Rachel Ward, Tom Selleck, Marlon Brando, Robert Davi, Oliver Cotton, Benicio Del Toro, Catherine Zeta-Jones, Matthieu Carriere, Nigel Terry, Branscombe Richmond; **D:** John Glen; **W:** John Briley, Mario Puzo, Cary Bates; **M:** Cliff Eidelman. Golden Raspberries '92: Worst Support. Actor (Selleck).

Christopher Strong 1933 Interesting Hepburn turn as a daredevil aviatrix who falls in love with a married British statesman. **77m/B VHS.** Katharine Hepburn, Billie Burke, Colin Clive, Helen Chandler; **D:** Dorothy Arzner; **M:** Max Steiner.

Christy 1994 Pilot movie for the TV series finds 19-year-old Christy Huddleston (Martin) leaving her privileged Southern life to teach school in the Great Smoky Mountains. It's 1912 in Cutter Gap, Tennessee, and her students are literally dirt poor, with ignorance and superstition the norm. Christy's inspiration in Miss Alice (Daly), a middle-aged Quaker who runs the mission school. And Christy needs encouragement as she struggles to cope with her new life and responsibilities. Based on the novel by Catherine Marshall, which is a fictional biography of her mother. **90m/C VHS.** Kellie Martin, Tyne Daly, Tess

Chrome and Hot Leather 1971 (PG) A Green Beret is out for revenge after vicious bikers kill his fiance. Conventional, tasteless genre fare notable only as Marvin Gaye's first film. 91m/C VHS, DVD. William (Bill) Smith, Tony Young, Michael Haynes, Peter Brown, Marvin Gaye, Michael Stearns, Kathrine Baumann, Wes Bishop, Herbert Jeffries; D: Lee Frost.

The Chronicles of Narnia: Prince Caspian 2008 (PG) In this sequel to "The Lion, the Witch, and the Wardrobe," the four Pevensie siblings are once again transported to the fantasy world of Narnia. Although only a year has passed in 1940s England, its been 1,300 years in Narnia, which has been conquered by the Telmarines and now ruled by ruthless King Miraz. It's up to the exiled rightful heir, Prince Caspian, in claiming the throne from his evil uncle. Based on the book by C.S. Lewis. Not yet reviewed. 7m/C. Georgie Henley, Skandar Keynes, William Moseley, Anna Popplewell, Sergio Castellito, Pierfrancesco Favino, Peter Dinklage, Warwick Davis, Ben Barnes; D: Andrew Adamson; W: Andrew Adamson, Christopher Markus, Stephen McFeely; C: Ka'l Walter Lindenlaub; M: Harry Gregson-Williams; V: Liam Neeson, Eddie Izzard.

The Chronicles of Narnia 1989 Exceptional EBC production of the C.S. Lewis fantasy about four brave children who battle evil in a mythical land where the animals talk and strange creatures roam the countryside. In three volumes; aired on PBS as part of the "Wonderworks" family movie series. 180m/C VHS, DVD. GB Barbara Kellerman, Jeffrey S. (Jeff) Perry, Richard Dempsey, Sophie Cook, Jonathan Scott, Sophie Wilcox, David Thwaites, Tom Baker; D: Alex Kirby.

Chrome Soldiers 1992 Five Vietnam veterans come together to avenge a friend's murder in a town controlled by drug dealers. Busey, as the murdered man's brother, leads the "Chrome Soldiers" in their battle to expose the killers and local corruption. 92m/C VHS. Gary Busey, Ray Sharkey, William Atherton, Yaphet Kotto, Nicholas Guest, Kim Robillard, Norman Skaggs, D. Davd Monte; C: Billy Dickson.

Chronically Unfeasible 2000 Social satire takes on the Brazilian middleclass as six disparate characters meet in a restaurant in Sao Paulo, struggling with political, class, sexual, and economic issues. Portuguese with subtitles. 101m/C VHS, DVD, BR Patrick Alenear, Leonardo Vieira, Umberto Magnani, Betty Gofman, Daniel Dantas, Dira Paes, Dan Stulbach, Cecil Thire; D: Sergio Bianchi; W: Sergio Bianchi, Gustavo Steinberg; C: Marcelo Coutinho, Antonio Penido.

Chronicle of a Boy Alone 1964 Eleven-year-old Polin is abandoned by his family and sent to live in a state-run orphanage where well-meaning administrators succeed in destroying the childrens' lives. Spanish with subtitles. 86m/C VHS, AR Oscar Espindola, Beto Gianola, Victoriano Moreira, Leonardo Favio; D: Leonardo Favio; W: Leonardo Favio; C: Ignacio Souto.

Chronicle of a Disappearance 1996 Born in Nazareth in 1960, Suleiman has been living in New York in self-imposed exile for 12 years. He finally decides to return to the Middle East and explore his roots as a Palestinian and the problems that political instability have caused his people and their identity. Arabic with subtitles. 88m/C VHS, DVD. Elia Suleiman; D: Elia Suleiman; W: Elia Suleiman; C: Marc Andre Batigne.

Chronicle of the Raven 2004 (R) Fairly atmospheric horror flick finds Jennifer (Phillips) traveling to Buenos Aires after she inherits the house of her recently deceased twin. Her sinister grandmother Mary Ellen (a theatrical Dunaway), who also lives there, doesn't want Jennifer to sell the place. Suddenly, Jennifer begins having nightmares about being attacked by flesh-eating ravens and discovers strange wounds when she wakes up. Seems Granny isn't above killing her kin to get her way. 90m/C DVD. US AR Gi'a Phillips, Faye Dunaway, Dullo Marzio, Hilde Benard, Nicolas Pauls; D: Daniel De La Vega, Pablo Pares; C: Mony Rowan, Robin Melnush; M: Micra Liberman.

The Chronicles of Narnia: The Lion, the Witch and the Wardrobe 2005 (PG) "Shrek" director Adamson turns C.S. Lewis children's classic into a "Lord of the Rings" meets "Veggie Tales" adventure-allegory for kids. The four Pevensie siblings stumble into a magical wardrobe that transports them to the wonderful world of Narnia, a fairy tale kingdom torn between the evil White Witch (Swinton, in the film's best role) and the messianic lion Aslan (Neeson). Adamson stays faithful to the book, but bolsters the eye candy factor with lots of PG-friendly battles between fauns, unicorns, and giants. Fun stuff for seven-year-olds, but if you're a grown-up, you'll be rolling your eyes at the heavy-handed religious allusions and cut-rate CGI effects. 139m/C DVD, UMD, US Tilda Swinton, Anna Popplewell, James McAvoy, Jim Broadbent, James Cosmo, Judy McIntosh, Elizabeth Hawthorne, Georgie Henley, Skandar Keynes, William Moseley, Kiran Shah; D: Andrew Adamson; W: Andrew Adamson, Christopher Markus, Stephen McFeely; C: Donald McAlpine; M: Harry Gregson-Williams; V: Liam Neeson, Ray Winstone, Dawn French, Rupert Everett, Sim Evan-Jones, Cameron Rhodes, Philip Steuer, Jim May. Oscars '05: Makeup; British Acad. '05: Makeup.

The Chronicles of Riddick 2004 (PG-13) Riddick 2004 Riddick (of "Pitch Black" fame) is back in this overstuffed compilation of cliched space shenanigans. The fascist Necromongers, led by Lord Marshall (Feore), have one edict: join us or we destroy your planet. Dame Judi Dench goes slumming as an ethereal prophetess named Aereon, who predicts that Riddick (Diesel again) will once again (if reluctantly) be a big hero. Diesel scowls a lot and then goes about saving the galaxy with a lot of big battles that not much gore given the MPAA rating. All acting is subordinate to the action anyway, but Newton swans about nicely as a devious wife who thinks her hubby (Urban) should be head creep. 119m/C VHS, DVD, UMD, HD DVD. US Vin Diesel, Judi Dench, Thandie Newton, Colm Feore, Karl Urban, Linus Roache, Nicholas Chinlund, Keith David, Alexa Davalos, Yorick Van Wageningen; D: David N. Twohy; W: David N. Twohy; C: Hugh Johnson; M: Graeme Revell.

Chu Chu & the Philly Flash 1981 (PG) A has-been baseball player and a lame dance teacher meet while hustling the same corner, he sells hot watches, she's a one-woman band. A briefcase full of government secrets soon involves them with the feds the mob, and a motley collection of back-alley bums. Insipid comedy is actually worse than its title, with Burnett and Arkin both trying too hard. Supporters Warden, Aiello, and Glover don't help either. 102m/C VHS. Alan Arkin, Carol Burnett, Jack Warden, Danny Aiello, Ruth Buzzi, Danny Glover, Lou Jacobi; D: David Lowell Rich; W: Barbara Dana.

Chuck & Buck 2000 (R) In stalking homosexual idiot man-child? Buck (White), the childhood friend from hell, attempts to latch back onto former pal Chuck (Chris Weitz) after a reunion at the funeral of Buck's mother. Apparently, Chuck and Buck shared a furtive moment of experimental sexuality as kids, and Buck never advanced emotionally beyond this point. So when Chuck (who, being an adult, prefers being called Charles) and his fiancee Carlyn (Coft) casually invite Buck to their home in L.A., he drops everything in order to rekindle the imagined affair with the poor guy. After Chuck tells him to stay away, Buck writes and produces an uncomfortably transparent play titled "Hank & Frank" about their relation-

---

C.H.U.D. 2: Bud the Chud 1989 (R) Asinine teens steal a corpse that is actually a zombie cannibal capable of passing the trait to anyone it bites (but doesn't eat entirely). Graham excels as the kidnapped corpse, but this horror-comedy is consistently repellent. Contains one of Jagger's few film appearances, a situation of no despair. 84m/C VHS. Brian Robbins, Bill Calvert, Gerrit Graham, Tricia Leigh Fisher, Bianca Jagger, Robert Vaughn, Larry Ceder; D: David Irving.

Chuka 1967 A gunfighter tries to resolve a conflict between Indians and unlikeable troops while simultaneously romancing the fort's beautiful occupant. Pedestrian western features convincing playing from the always reliable Taylor. 105m/C VHS, DVD, Rod Taylor, Ernest Borgnine, John Mills, Luciana Paluzzi, James Whitmore, Angela Dorian, Louis Hayward, Michael Cole, Hugh Reilly, Oliver Hardy, James Finlayson, Wilfrid Lucas, Peter Cushing, Charlie Hall; D: Gordon Douglas.

A Chump at Oxford 1940 Two street cleaners foil a bank robbery and receive an all-expenses-paid education at Oxford as their reward. This loopy Laurel and Hardy vehicle provides regular amusement in detailing the duo's exploits in Britain. 63m/B VHS, Stan Laurel, Oliver Hardy, James Finlayson, Wilfrid Lucas, Peter Cushing, Charlie Hall; D: Alfred Goulding.

The Chumscrubber 2005 (R) The unfortunate title refers to a videogame avenger who appears a la the creepy rabbit in "Donnie Darko," throughout this smug satire. Brooding SoCal teen Dean (Bell)—yes, think James—fails to tell anyone that his best friend, Troy (Janowicz), has hung himself in his bedroom. Problem is, Troy was the local drug supplier and when word does get out, his fellow high school scuzzballs expect Dean to find Troy's stash or else. Depiction of self-satisfied suburbia and teen angst has been better told elsewhere. 102m/C DVD. US Jamie Bell, Camilla Belle, Justin Chatwin, Glenn Close, Ralph Fiennes, Caroline Goodall, John Heard, Lauren Holly, Jason Isaacs, Allison Janney, Carrie-Anne Moss, Lou Taylor Pucci, Rita Wilson, Thomas Curtis, Richard Gleason, Josh Janowicz; D: Arie Posin; W: Zac Stanford; C: Lawrence Sher; M: James Horner.

Chungking Express 1995 (PG-13) Kong Express Chongqing Senlin 1995 (PG-13) Director Kar-wai presents two quirky tales of loneliness and love, loosely linked by a

---

Chuck Berry: Hail! Hail! Rock 'n' Roll 1987 (PG) Engaging, energetic portrait of one of rock's founding fathers, via interviews, behind-the-scenes footage and performance clips of Berry at 60. Songs featured: "Johnny B. Goode," "Roll Over Beethoven," "Maybelline," and more. Appearances by Eric Clapton, Etta James, John and Julian Lennon, Roy Orbison, Linda Ronstadt, Bo Diddley, Bruce Springsteen among others. 121m/C VHS, DVD, Chuck Berry, Eric Clapton, Etta James, Robert Cray, Julian Lennon, Keith Richards, Linda Ronstadt, John Lennon, Roy Orbison, Bo Diddley, Jerry Lee Lewis, Bruce Springsteen, Kareem Abdul-Jabbar; D: Taylor Hackford.

The Church 2005 (R) La Chiesa 2005 (R) Chiacabra: Dark Seas 2005 (R) A mythical beast, the Chupacabra, is caught in the Caribbean by cryptozoologist Dr. Pena, who happens to stand or the site of a gruesome mass murder is renovated, and kirk-cleaning turns into a special-effects loaded demonic epiphany. It'll have you muttering your pater noster. Unrated, it's also available in an R-rated version. 102m/C VHS, DVD. It Tomas Arana, Hugh Quarshie, Feodor Chaliapin Jr., Barbara Cupisti, Antonella Vitale, Asia Argento; D: Michele (Michael) Soavi; W: Dario Argento, Michele (Michael) Soavi, Franco Ferrini; C: Renato Tafuri; M: Keith Emerson.

Chunhyang 2000 Romance based on a 13th-century folktale of forbidden love. Chunhyang (Lee) is the educated daughter of a courtesan who is expected to be a plaything for wealthy gentlemen. Instead, she falls in love and secretly marries the higher-caste Mongryong (Cho), who leaves his bride to complete his studies in Seoul. Chunhyang is soon beset by advances from the new governor and, when she refuses, he sentences her to death. Korean with subtitles. 120m/C VHS, DVD, KN Hyo Jung Lee, Seung Woo Cho, Jung Hun Lee, Sung Nyu Kim, D: Kwon Taek Im; W: Myoung Kon Kim; C: Il Sung Jung; M: Jung Gil Kim.

Chupacabra Terror 2005 (R) Based on a 13th-century folktale of forbidden love. Chunhyang (Lee) is the educated daughter of a courtesan who is expected to be a plaything for wealthy gentlemen. Instead, she falls in love and secretly marries the higher-caste Mongryong (Cho), who leaves his bride to complete his studies in Seoul. Chunhyang is soon beset by advances from the new governor and, when she refuses, he sentences her to death. Korean with subtitles. VIDEO

Churchill and the Generals 1981 The true story of how Winston Churchill led England away from the bleak Dunkirk battle and rallied the Allied generals to a D-Day victory. Based upon Churchill's memoirs. 180m/C VHS, Timothy West, Joseph Cotten, Arthur Hill, Eric Porter, Richard Dysart; D: Alan Gibson; Nar: Eric Sevareid.

Chutney Popcorn 1999 Amusing and touching comedy about family ties and cultural differences. Reena (Ganatra) is a New York photographer from a very traditional East Indian immigrant family. Her mother Meenu (Jaffrey) is already upset because her daughter is a lesbian but Reena has a chance to get in her good graces when she impulsively agrees to act as a surrogate for her married older sister Sarita (Jaffrey), who is infertile. But the plan upsets Reena's girlfriend Lisa (Hennessy) and then Sarita has her own change of heart, even though Reena is now pregnant. 93m/C VHS, DVD. Nisha Ganatra, Jill(ian) Hennessey, Madhur Jaffrey, Sakina Jaffrey, Nicroas Chinlund, Cara Buono, Ajay Naidu, Priscilla Lopez; D: Nisha Ganatra; W: Susan Carnival, Nisra Ganatra; C: Erin King; M: Karsh Kale.

ship, hiring a Chuck look-alike (Paul Kong. Cops and drugs are still a part of the storyline, but this is no chop-socky action movie. Both male protagonists are cops, identified only by their badge numbers, who have recently been dumped by their girlfriends. One has a fixation for canned pineapple and expiration dates, the other talks to the inanimate objects in his apartment. The high energy is reflected in the pacing and acting performances. Chosen by Quentin Tarantino as the first release of his Miramax-backed Rolling Thunder imprint. 102m/C VHS, HK Brigitte Lin, Takeshi Kaneshiro, Tony Leung Chiu-Wai, Faye Wong, Valerie Chow, Peggy Chan; D: Wong Kar-Wai; W: Wong Kar-Wai; C: Christopher Doyle, Lau Wai-Keung; M: Frankie Chan, Roel A. Garcia.

snack bar in the tourist section of Hong Kong.

C.I.A.: Code Name Alexa 1992 (R) Alexa is the beautiful and deadly protege of Victor, who heads an international crime ring. A CIA agent decides the best way to stop Victor is to turn Alexa against her boss. Lots of action and violence. 93m/C VHS, DVD. Kathleen Kinmont, Lorenzo Lamas, Alex Cord, O.J. Simpson, Stephen Quadros, Pamela Dixon, Michael Smith; D: Joseph Merhi.

C.I.A. 2: Target Alexa 1994 When a nuclear guidance system is stolen from a government facility CIA agent Mark Graver (Lamas) reteams with former terrorist Alexa (Kinmont) to retrieve the system from international terrorist Franz Klug (Savage). Complicating things are ex-CIA agent Straker (Ryan), who now heads his own commando army and wants to sell the device to the highest bidder. 90m/C VHS, DVD. Lorenzo Lamas, Kathleen Kinmont, John Savage, John P. Ryan, Pamela Dixon, Larry Manetti; D: Lorenzo Lamas; W: Michael January.

Ciao Federico! Fellini Directs Satyricon 1969 A documentary of Frederico Fellini's filming of Petronius' "Satyricon." Portrays the Italian filmmaker's larger-than-life directorial approach and relationship with his actors. In English and Italian, with English subtitles. 60m/C VHS. Federico Fellini, Martin Potter, Hiram Keller, Roman Polanski, Sharon Tate; D: Gideon Bachmann.

Ciao, Professore! 1994 (R) Io Speriamo Che Me La Cavo comedy about conventional teacher Marco Sperelli (Villaggio), from northern Italy, who is mistakenly sent to a ramshackle village school in Naples, populated by poor, wily, unruly students. Both, of course, manage to learn from each other. Humor derived from northern vs. southern Italian culture clash may bypass most viewers although the cast of amateur kid actors provide charm. Italian with subtitles. 91m/C VHS, DVD. IT Paolo Villaggio, Isa Danieli, Ciro Esposito; D: Lina Wertmuller; W: Leonardo Benvenuti, Piero De Bernardi, Alessandro Bencivenni, Domenico Saverni, Lina Wertmuller.

The Cider House Rules 1999 (PG-13) Homer Wells (Maguire) grows up in the St. Clouds, Maine orphanage, with his mentor, Dr. Larch (Caine), teaching Homer everything about caring for the children, delivering babies, and performing (illegal) abortions (which Homer refuses to do). But, in 1943, when flyboy Wally (Rudd) shows up with girlfriend Candy (Theron), Homer gets his chance to see something of the world. He winds up as an apple picker and, when Wally returns to the war, Candy's new beau. But Homer has a lot of lessons to learn about making—and living by—your own rules. Irving wrote his first screenplay from his novel. Old-fashioned, coming of age story with excellent performances. 125m/C VHS, DVD. Evan Dexter Parke, Tobey Maguire, Charlize Theron, Michael Caine, Delroy Lindo, Paul Rudd, Erykah Badu, Kathy Baker, Jane Alexander, Kieran Culkin, Kate Nelligan, K. Todd Freeman, Dwight "Heavy D" Myers, J.K. Simmons, Erik Per Sullivan; Cameos: John Irving; C: Oliver Stapleton; M: Rachel Portman. Oscars '99: Adapt. Screenplay, Support. Actor (Caine); Screen Actors Guild '99: Support. Actor (Caine).

Cider with Rosie 1999 Adaptation of Laurie Lee's 1959 story about his childhood. Set in 1918, in the Slad Valley, disorganized Annie Lee (Stevenson) has been left to raise nine children on her own. Laurie's childhood consists of school, church, village festivals, eccentric relations and neighbors, and the usual childhood tribulations. Lee himself provided narration before his death at 82 in 1997. 120m/C VHS, DVD. GB Juliet Stevenson, Emily Mortimer, Joe Roberts, Dashiell Reece, David Troughton, Robert Lang, Hugh Lloyd; D: Charles Beeson; W: John Mortimer; C: Rex Maidment; M: Geoffrey Burgon. TV

The Cigarette Girl of Mosselprom 1924 A lowly cigarette girl is thrust into the world of moviemaking in this sharp Russian satire. Silent with orchestral score. 78m/B VHS. RU Yulia Solntseva, Igor Ilyinsky, Nikolai Tseretelli, Anna Dmokhovskaya, Leonid Baratov, M. Tsybulsky; D: Yuri Zhelyabuzhsky; W: Aleksey Fajko, Fyodor Otsep; C: Yuri Zhelyabuzhsky.

Cimarron 1931 (R) Hopelessly overblown saga of an American frontier family from 1890 to 1915. Hokey, cliched, with only sporadic liveliness. How did this one win an Oscar? An adaptation of Edna Ferber's novel, featuring Dunne in an early major role. Remade in 1960. 130m/B VHS, DVD. Richard Dix, Irene Dunne, Estelle Taylor, Nance O'Neil, William "Buster" Collier Jr., Roscoe Ates, George E. Stone, Stanley Fields, Edna May Oliver, Dennis O'Keefe; D: Wesley Ruggles; M: Max Steiner. Oscars '31: Adapt. Screenplay, Picture.

Cimarron 1960 Director Mann's remake of the 1931 Academy Award-winning film about frontier life in Oklahoma. This version features Ford as a carefree survivor of the Old West with an extreme case of wanderlust. Schell plays his civilizing wife. Based on Edna Ferber's novel. 140m/C VHS. Glenn Ford, Maria Schell, Anne Baxter, Arthur O'Connell, Russ Tamblyn, Mercedes McCambridge, Vic Morrow, Robert Keith, Charles McGraw; D: Anthony Mann; W: Arnold Schulman; M: Franz Waxman.

The Cincinnati Kid 1965 Gambler "The Cincinnati Kid" (McQueen) is hustling card games in New Orleans when he comes up against the veteran cardshark Lancey Howard (Robinson). During a marathon card game, Kid notices dealer Shooter (Malden) is throwing the game his way but he only wants to win fair and square. Conventional fare, with Ann-Margaret around for some conventional romance, helped along by serviceable performances and some stunning cinematography. 104m/C VHS, DVD. Steve McQueen, Edward G. Robinson, Ann-Margret, Tuesday Weld, Karl Malden, Joan Blondell, Rip Torn, Jack Weston, Cab Calloway; D: Norman Jewison; M: Lalo Schifrin. Natl. Bd. of Review 65: Support. Actress (Blondell).

Cinderella 1950 Classic Disney animated fairytale about the slighted beauty who outshines her evil stepsisters at a royal ball, then returns to her grim existence before the handsome prince finds her again. Engaging film, with a wicked stepmother, kindly fairy godmother, and singing mice. ♪Cinderella; Bibbidy-Bobbidi-Boo; So This Is Love; A Dream Is a Wish Your Heart Makes; The Work Song; Oh Sing, Sweet Nightingale. 76m/C VHS, DVD. D: Wilfred Jackson; V: Ilene Woods, William Phipps, Verna Felton, James MacDonald, Mike Douglas. Venice Film Fest. '50: Special Jury Prize.

Cinderella 1964 Charming musical version of the fairy tale as scored by Rodgers and Hammerstein. Warren is lovely as Cinderella, Damon is a handsome prince, and Holm is a perfect fairy godmother. 83m/C VHS, DVD. Lesley Ann Warren, Ginger Rogers, Walter Pidgeon, Stuart Damon, Celeste Holm; D: Charles S. Dubin; W: Joseph Schrank; M: Richard Rodgers. TV

Cinderella 1984 From the "Faerie Tale Theatre" comes the classic tale of a poor girl who goes to a ball to meet the man of her dreams, despite her nasty stepmother and stepsisters. 60m/C VHS, DVD. Jennifer Beals, Jean Stapleton, Matthew Broderick, Eve Arden; D: Mark Cullingham. CABLE

Cinderella 1997 Disney does some multiracial casting in this lavish, latest TV version of the fairytale. Norwood is sweet, if sincere in the title role, with Houston as her diva-like Fairy Godmother. Peters camps as wicked stepmama, Goldberg's the Prince's mother, and the Prince is handsome newcomer Montalban. And Alexander gets the role of comic relief as the princely confidante, Lionel. The Rodgers and Hammerstein score, written for the 1957 TV version, has been augmented with other Richard Rodgers tunes. ♪The Sweetest Sounds; Impossible; Do I Love You Because You're Beautiful?; Falling in Love with Love. 92m/C VHS, DVD. Brandy Norwood, Whitney Houston, Paolo Montalban, Jason Alexander, Bernadette Peters, Whoopi Goldberg, Victor Garber; D: Robert Iscove; W: Robert Freedman. TV

Cinderella Liberty 1973 (R) Bittersweet romance in which a kindly sailor falls for a brash hooker with a son. Sometimes funny, sometimes moving, with sometimes crude direction overcome by truly compelling performances from Caan and Mason. Story written by Darryl Ponicsan from his novel. 117m/C VHS, DVD. James Caan, Marsha Mason, Eli Wallach, Kirk Calloway, Burt Young, Bruce Kirby, Dabney Coleman, Sally Kirkland; D: Mark Rydell; W: Darryl Ponicsan; C: Vilmos Zsigmond; M: John Williams. Golden Globes '74: Actress—Drama (Mason).

Cinderella Man 2005 (PG-13) Taken from the true story of heavyweight boxer Jim Braddock (Crowe) whose promising career was stalled by an injury, winless streak, and a revoked license. Despite his fall from glory, wife Mae (Zellweger) and their children remain unwavering in their devotion while Braddock labors on the Jersey docks during the Depression. Out of shape after a year, he finds himself back in the ring and winning again, which leads to a title bout in 1935 against the (fictitiously) vicious Max Baer (well-played by Bierko). Just as in the Oscar-winning "A Beautiful Mind," Crowe and Howard connect, with Crowe pounding out another stellar portrayal while Howard easily blends the fierceness of the boxing ring with the plain-spoken goodness of family-man Braddock. 144m/C DVD, HD DVD. US Russell Crowe, Renee Zellweger, Paul Giamatti, Craig Bierko, Paddy Considine, Bruce McGill, Ron Canada, David Huband, Connor Price, Ariel Waller, Patrick Louis, Rosemarie DeWitt, Linda Kash, Nicholas (Nick) Campbell, Gene Pyrz; D: Ron Howard; W: Cliff Hollingsworth, Akiva Goldsman; C: Salvatore Totino; M: Thomas Newman. Screen Actors Guild '05: Support. Actor (Giamatti); Broadcast Film Critics '05: Support. Actor (Giamatti).

A Cinderella Story 2004 (PG) A movie designed for tweenies who worship the chirpy Duff. This trifle finds Valley teen Samantha (Duff) bereft after the death of her father and stuck slaving for pea-brained stepmom Fiona (Coolidge) and her vicious twin daughters. Sam's only consolation is an email flirtation with poetic soul who's actually the school's hottie football star Austin (Murray). Thanks to fairy godmother Rhonda (King), the cute twosome hook up at the Halloween dance but, alas, Sam slips out before revealing her true identity to hunk boy (although she does leave behind her cell phone). Of course, it's all so sugary that anyone who's not a 12-and-under girl will probably gag. 96m/C VHS, DVD. US Hilary Duff, Jennifer Coolidge, Chad Michael Murray, Dan Byrd, Regina King, Julie Gonzalo, Lin Shaye, Madeline Zima, Andrea Avery, Mary Pat Gleason, Paul Rodriguez, Whip Hubley, Kevin Kilner, Erica Hubbard, Simon Helberg, Brad Bufanda, J.D. Pardo, Kady Kole, Hannah Robinson; D: Mark Rosman; W: Leigh Dunlap; C: Anthony B. Richmond; M: Christophe Beck.

Cinderella 2000 1978 (R) Softcore musical version of the classic fairy tale. It's the year 2047 and sex is outlawed, except by computer. Strains of Sugarman's score, including "Doin' Without" and "We All Need Love," set the stage for Erhardt's Cinderella to meet her Prince Charming at that conventional single prince romance venue, a sex orgy. Trouble is, it wasn't a shoe Cinderella lost before she fled, and the charming one must interface, as it were, with the local pretenders to the throne in order to find his lost princess. Touching. 86m/C VHS, DVD. Catharine Erhardt, Jay B. Larson, Vaughn Armstrong; D: Al Adamson; M: Sparky Sugarman.

Cinderella 1960 This twist on the classic children's fairy tale features Lewis as the hapless buffoon guided by his fairy godfather. Somewhat overdone, with extended talking sequences and gratuitous musical interludes. Lewis, though, mugs effectively. 88m/C VHS, DVD. Jerry Lewis, Ed Wynn, Judith Anderson, Anna Maria Alberghetti, Henry Silva, Count Basie, Robert Hutton; D: Frank Tashlin; W: Frank Tashlin.

Cinema Paradiso 1988 Nuovo Cinema Paradiso Memoir of a boy's life working at a movie theatre in small-town Italy after WWII. Film aspires to both majestic sweep and stirring poignancy, but only occasionally hits its target. Still manages to move the viewer, and it features a suitably low-key performance by the masterful Noiret. Autobiographically inspired script written by Tornatore. The version shown in America is approximately a half-hour shorter than the original Italian form. 123m/C VHS, DVD. IT Philippe Noiret, Jacques Perrin, Salvatore Cascio, Marco Leonardi, Agnes Nano, Leopoldo Trieste; D: Giuseppe Tornatore; W: Giuseppe Tornatore; C: Blasco Giurato; M: Ennio Morricone. Oscars '89: Foreign Film; British Acad. '90: Actor (Noiret), Foreign Film, Orig. Screenplay, Support. Actor (Cascio); Cannes '89: Grand Jury Prize; Golden Globes '90: Foreign Film.

The Circle Dayereh 2000 Arezou (Almani) and Nargess (Mamizadeh) have just been released from an Iranian prison. Arezou apparently prostitutes herself (you don't see anything) in order to get the money for Nargess to travel back to her village, only because of Iranian law the girl can't travel without permission from a male. Nargess leads to two other former inmates who suffer because of their female identity and eventually everything circles back to the prison again. The film was banned in Iran because it makes the ceaseless difficulties of being born female in such a society very clear. Farsi with subtitles. 91m/C VHS, DVD. IA Mariam Palvin Almani, Nargess Mamizadeh, Fereshteh Sadr Orfani, Fatemeh Naghavi, Monir Arab, Elham Saboktakin, Mojhan Faramarzi; D: Jafar Panahi; W: Kambuzia Partovi; C: Bahram Badakhshami. Venice Film Fest. '00: Film.

Circle Canyon 1933 In a remote canyon two opposing outlaw gangs battle to the death. 48m/B VHS. Buddy Roosevelt, Allen Holbrook, Clyde McClary, Ernest Scott, John Tyke, Bob Williamson; D: Victor Adamson; W: Burt R. Tuttle.

Circle Man Last Man Standing 1987 A made-for-video action drama about the underground sporting phenomenon, bareknuckle fighting. 90m/C VHS. Vernon Wells, Michael Copeman, Real Andrews, Franco (Columbo) Columbu, William Sanderson; D: Damian Lee; W: Damian Lee, David Mitchell; C: Ludek Bogner; M: Charles P. Barnett.

Circle of Death 1936 Average formula western about a white boy who is raised as an Indian. Later he falls in love with a white girl and leaves the tribe. 55m/B VHS. Monte Montana, Yakima Canutt, Henry Hall, Ben (Benny) Corbett; D: J. Frank Glendon; W: Roy Claire; C: James Diamond.

Circle of Deceit 1994 SAS officer John Neil (Waterman) is called back into service in Belfast two years after his wife and child were killed by terrorists. His assignment is to assume the identity of recently deceased IRA soldier Jackie O'Connell and learn about an arms shipment headed for Northern Ireland. But can his disguise hold against local IRA commander Liam McAuley (Vaughan)? Made for British TV. 103m/C VHS, DVD. GB Dennis Waterman, Peter Vaughan, Derek Jacobi, Clare Higgins; W: Jean-Claude Carriere. TV

Circle of Fear 1989 (R) An ex-hitman who is on the run from the Mob upends the black market for sex and drugs in the Philippines while looking for his daughter who was sold into a sex slave ring. El cheapo exploiter. 90m/C VHS, DVD. PH Patrick Dollaghan, Welsey Pfenning, Joey Aresco, Vernon Wells; D: Clark Henderson.

Circle of Friends 1994 (PG-13) Nostalgic Irish coming-of-ager focuses on three friends and the trials and tribulations they face when hearts and hormones conflict with a strict Catholic upbringing. Small-town teenager Benny (Driver), overweight and slightly awkward, reunites with her friends at university in Dublin. Benny begins a romance with gentle, doe-eyed Jack Foley (O'Donnell) and endures the humorous but sometimes painful passage from adolescence to womanhood. Sentimental moments can be too sticky-sweet at times, but humor, disappointment, and small triumphs are convincingly portrayed, offering a universal appeal. Adapted from the Maeve Binchy novel. 96m/C VHS, DVD. Chris O'Donnell, Minnie Driver, Geraldine O'Rawe, Sal-

Circle of Iron 🐾🐾½ *The Silent Flute* 1978 (R) Plenty of action and martial arts combat abound in this story of one man's eternal quest for truth. Originally co-written by and intended for Bruce Lee as a rib-crunching vehicle, until he died before production began and was replaced by Kung-Fu Carradine. A cut above most crop-socky actioners. Filmed in Israel. **102m/C VHS, DVD.** *GB* Jeff Cooper, David Carradine, Roddy McDowall, Eli Wallach, Christopher Lee; *D:* Richard Moore; *W:* Bruce Lee, James Coburn, Stirling Silliphant; *M:* Michael Kamen.

Circle of Love 🐾🐾 1964 Episodic melodrama drifts from romance to romance in contemporary Paris. A somewhat pretentious remake of Ophuls classic "La Ronde," which was in turn adapted from Arthur Schnitzler's play. Credible performers are undone by Vadim's strained direction. **111m/C VHS, DVD.** *FR* Jane Fonda, Francine Berge, Marie DuBois, Jean-Claude Brialy, Catherine Spaak, Claude Giraud; *D:* Roger Vadim; *W:* Jean Anouilh.

Circle of Passion 🐾🐾 1997 (R) Devoted hubby Thomas Murray (Finch) works for his father-in-law at a London bank. But when Thomas is transferred to Paris and his socialite wife (March) refuses to go with him, devotion falls by the wayside when he falls in love with the free-spirited Katherine (Bonnaire). Now Thomas has to choose between money and love. **94m/C VHS.** Charles Finch, Sandrine Bonnaire, Jane March, Julian Sands, James Fox; *D:* Charles Finch.

Circle of Power 🐾🐾½ *Brainwash; Mystique* 1983 (R) Mimieux must cure various business men of their problems (homosexuality, alcoholism and the like) to help them become better executives. Intriguing and somewhat disturbing, supposedly based on a true story. **103m/C VHS.** *EB* Yvette Mimieux, John Considine, Terence Knox, Cindy Pickett, Christopher Allport; *D:* Bobby Roth; *W:* Stephen F. Belio; *C:* Alfonso Beato.

Circle of Two 🐾🐾½ 1980 (PG) A platonic friendship between an aging artist and a young girl is misunderstood by others. Well, of course they do meet in a porno theatre. Pedestrian fare adapted from a story by Marie Therese Baird. **90m/C VHS, DVD.** *C4* Richard Burton, Tatum O'Neal, Kate Reid; *D:* Jules Dassin.

Circuit 🐾🐾 2002 Sexual hedonism is alive and well in West Hollywood in this would-be cautionary tale of a small town Midwesterner who comes to the big, bad city. John (Draskó) gets introduced to the party circuit of casual gay sex and lots of drugs but vows to keep his distance. This doesn't last and John sinks ever deeper into the self-destructive pursuit of pleasure. **90m/C VHS, DVD.** Jonathan Wade Draskó, Daniel Kucan, Andre Khabbazi, Brian Lane Green, Kiersten Warren, William Katt; *D:* Dirk Shafer; *W:* Dirk Shafer, Gregory Hinton; *C:* Joaquin Sedillo; *M:* Tony Moran.

Circuitry Man 🐾🐾½ 1990 (R) Post-apocalyptic saga of future American life as a woman tries to deliver a briefcase full of computer chips to the underground Big Apple. Along the way she runs into Plughead, a humanoid with electrical outlets that allow him to "plug in" to other people's fantasies. Intelligent retelling of a standard tale with an inspired soundtrack by Deborah Holland. Witty and original. **85m/C VHS, DVD.** Jim Metzler, Dana Wheeler-Nicholson, Lu Leonard, Vernon Wells, Barbara Alyn Woods, Dennis Christopher; *D:* Steven Lovy; *W:* Robert Lovy, Steven Lovy; *C:* Jamie Thompson; *M:* Deborah Holland.

Circumstances Attenuantes 🐾🐾½ *Extenuating Circumstances* 1939 French classic about a retired judge who moves to the outskirts of Paris with his wife and attempts to convert the locals from disreputable to law-abiding citizens. Also available dubbed. **90m/B VHS.** *FR* Michel Simon, Arletty; *D:* Jean Boyer.

Circus 🐾🐾 2000 (R) British gambler/con man Leo Garfield (Hannah) is being pressured by gang boss Bruno (Conley) to manage his Brighton casino. But Leo and his equally shady American wife Lily (Janssen) have some double-crossing ideas of their own, involving Bruno's brother Caspar (Burfield), his accountant Julius (Stormare), Julius' unfaithful wife Gloria (Donohue), and, well, things get even more complicated but the film doesn't have the flair to pull off all the plots. It does make an interesting attempt, though. **95m/C VHS, DVD.** *GB* John Hannah, Famke Janssen, Peter Stormare, Brian Conley, Eddie Izzard, Fred Ward, Amanda Donohoe, Ian Burfield, Tommy (Tiny) Lister, Neil Stuke; *D:* Rob Walker; *W:* David Logan; *C:* Ben Seresin; *M:* Simon Boswell.

Circus Angel 🐾🐾🐾 1965 The renowned director of "The Red Balloon" creates a fantasy about a klutzy burglar transformed by a found nightgown into an angel. He begins to serve the dreams and actions of an odd lot of characters. Subtitled in English. **80m/B VHS.** *FR* Philippe Avron, Mireille Negre; *D:* Albert Lamorisse.

Circus of Fear 🐾🐾 *Psycho-Circus* 1967 A travelling troupe is stalked by a murderer. The unedited version is occasionally scary. **92m/C VHS, DVD.** *GB* Christopher Lee, Leo Genn, Anthony Newlands, Heinz Drache, Eddi Arent, Klaus Kinski, Margaret Lee, Suzy Kendall; *D:* John Llewellyn Moxey.

Circus of Horrors 🐾🐾 1960 Nip 'n' tuck horror about a plastic surgeon who takes over a circus to escape a disfigured patient bent on revenge. The circus is staffed by former patients with new faces who, one by one, fall victim in fine circus style. A bloody one-ring extravaganza. **92m/C VHS, DVD.** *GB* Donald Pleasence, Anton Diffring, Erika Remberg, Yvonne Monlaur, Jane Hylton, Kenneth Griffith, Colette Wilde, Charla Challoner; *D:* Sidney Hayers; *W:* George L. Baxt; *C:* Douglas Slocombe; *M:* Muir Mathieson.

Circus World 🐾🐾 *The Magnificent Showman* 1964 A circus boss tries to navigate a reckless, romancing crew through a European tour while searching for an aerialist he loved 15 years before and whose daughter he has reared. Too long and too familiar, but nonetheless well done with an excellent finale. **132m/C VHS, DVD.** John Wayne, Rita Hayworth, Claudia Cardinale, Lloyd Nolan, Richard Conte; *D:* Henry Hathaway; *W:* Ben Hecht, James Edward Grant, Julian Zimet; *C:* Jack Hildyard. Golden Globes '65: Song ("Circus World").

Circumstances Unknown 🐾🐾½ 1995 (R) Paul Kinsey (Nelson) is a serial killer who drowns his victims, including a woman who happens to be the fiance of his friend Tim (Moses). Years later, Tim has married and Paul decides to stalk him and wife Deena (Glasser). Too many loose ends since you never know why Paul kills. Based on the novel by Jonellen Heckler. **91m/C VHS, DVD.** Judd Nelson, Isabel Glasser, William R. Moses; *D:* Robert Lewis; *W:* Thomas Hood, Emily Shoemaker; *C:* Bruce Worrall.

Circumstantial Evidence 🐾🐾 1935 Newspaper reporter (Chandler) goes to extremes for a story and nearly dies as a result. Chandler sets it up to look like he's murdered a colleague, and he's tried and convicted on, you guessed it, circumstantial evidence. The colleague's then supposed to come forward but there's a problem. **69m/B VHS, DVD.** Chick Chandler, Shirley Grey, Dorothy Revier, Arthur Vinton; *D:* Charles Lamont; *W:* Ewart Adamson.

The Circus 🐾🐾🐾½ 1919 Classic comedy silent details the tramp's exploits as a member of a traveling circus, including a romance with the bareback rider. Hilarious, less sentimental than most of Chaplin's feature films. Chaplin won a special Academy Award for "versatility and genius in writing, acting, directing and producing" for this one. Outrageous final scenes. **105m/B VHS, DVD.** Charlie Chaplin, Merna Kennedy, Allan Garcia; *D:* Charlie Chaplin; *W:* Charlie Chaplin; *C:* Roland H. Totheroh; *M:* Charlie Chaplin.

Citizen Cohn 🐾🐾 1992 (R) An appallingly fascinating look at a human monster. Told in hallucinatory flashbacks, as he lays dying from AIDS, Roy Cohn is brought to life in virtual life. Adapted from the biography by Nicholas von Hoffman. **112m/C VHS, DVD.** James Woods, Joe Don Baker, Joseph Bologna, Ed Flanders, Frederic Forrest, Lee Grant, Pat Hingle; *D:* Frank Pierson; *W:* David Franzoni; *C:* Paul Elliott. **CABLE**

Citizen Kane 🐾🐾🐾🐾 1941 Extraordinary film is an American tragedy of a newspaper tycoon (based loosely on William Randolph Hearst) from his humble beginnings to the solitude of his final years. One of the greatest films ever made—a stunning tour-de-force in virtually every aspect, from the fragmented narration to breathtaking, deep-focus cinematography; from a vivid soundtrack to fabulous ensemble acting. Welles was only 25 when he co-wrote, directed, and starred in this masterpiece. Watch for Ladd and O'Connell as reporters. **119m/B VHS, DVD.** Orson Welles, Joseph Cotten, Everett Sloane, Dorothy Comingore, Ruth Warrick, George Coulouris, Ray Collins, William Alland, Paul Stewart, Erskine Sanford, Agnes Moorehead, Alan Ladd, Gus Schilling, Philip Van Zandt, Harry Shannon, Sonny Bupp, Arthur O'Connell; *D:* Orson Welles; *W:* Orson Welles, Herman J. Mankiewicz; *C:* Gregg Toland; *M:* Bernard Herrmann. Oscars '41: Orig. Screenplay; AFI '98: Top 100, Natl. Film Reg. '89...; N.Y. Film Critics '41: Film.

Citizen Ruth 🐾🐾🐾½ *Precious; Meet Ruth Stoops* 1996 (R) Glue-sniffing, pregnant Ruth Stoops (Dern) has already borne four children and been declared an unfit mother. In trouble again, Ruth's quietly told it's in her best interests to get an abortion but a couple (Smith and Place) from the pro-life community bail her out and give her a place to stay, while the group uses her as a propaganda symbol. Added to the commotion is a smarmy televangelist (Reynolds) and tough pro-choice Diane (Kurtz), who manages to get Ruth to stay with her while Ruth ineffectually tries to get some control over her wayward life. Doesn't take sides—both the pro-choice and pro-life camps are tweaked, with neither willing to compromise. **104m/C VHS, DVD.** Laura Dern, Swoosie Kurtz, Mary Kay Place, Kurtwood Smith, Kelly Preston, Burt Reynolds, M.C. Gainey, Kenneth Mars, Kathleen Noone, David Graf, Tippi Hedren, Alicia Witt, Diane Ladd; *D:* Alexander Payne; *W:* Alexander Payne, Jim Taylor; *C:* James Glennon; *M:* Rolfe Kent. Montreal World Film Fest. '95: Actress (Dern).

The Cisco Kid 🐾🐾½ 1994 The Cisco Kid and his sidekick Pancho went from O. Henry's short story, to silent movies, talkies, a '50s TV series, and now this made for TV movie. Benito Juarez is leading an uprising to overthrow the French-backed Emperor Maximilian in 1867 Mexico. Cisco's (Smits) supplying the rebels with guns while carrying on romantic escapades (watch for the tango). Meanwhile, true-believer Pancho tries to convince his friend to become a revolutionary. Light-hearted with pedestrian action shots. Filmed on location in Mexico. **96m/C VHS, DVD.** Jimmy Smits, Cheech Marin, Sadie Frost, Tim Thomerson, Bruce Payne; *D:* Luis Valdez; *M:* Michael Kane, Luis Valdez. **TV**

The Citadel 🐾🐾🐾 1938 From the A.J. Cronin novel, the intelligent and honest Hollywood drama about a young British doctor who is morally corrupted by the move from a poor mining village to a well-off practice treating wealthy hypochondriacs. Somewhat hokey but still consistently entertaining, with Donat fine in the lead. Filmed on location in England. **114m/C VHS.** *GB* Robert Donat, Rosalind Russell, Rex Harrison, Ralph Richardson, Emlyn Williams, Penelope Dudley Ward; *D:* King Vidor; *C:* Harry Stradling Sr. N.Y. Film Critics '38: Film.

Citizen X 🐾🐾🐾 1995 (R) Based on the true story of '80s Russian serial killer Andrei Chikatilo (DeMunn) and his 52 victims. Viktor Burakov (Rea) is a beleaguered rural forensics expert who is blatantly told by party officials that the Soviet state does not have serial killers—in spite of a rising body count. His only ally's Col. Fetisov (Sutherland), who's adept at political maneuvering, but it takes the duo eight frustrating years to bring the grisly killer to justice. Fine performances highlight a literate script from Robert Cullen's book "The Killer Department." Filmed on location in Budapest, Hungary. **105m/C VHS, DVD.** Stephen Rea, Donald Sutherland, Jeffrey DeMunn, John Wood, Joss Ackland, Max von Sydow, Ralph Nossek, Imelda Staunton, Radu Amzulescu, Czeslaw Grochoklski, Ion Caramitru, Andras Balint, Tusse Silberg; *D:* Chris Gerolmo; *W:* Chris Gerolmo; *M:* Randy Edelman. **CABLE**

Citizens Band 🐾🐾🐾 *Handle With Care* 1977 (PG) Episodic, low-key comedy about people united by their CB use in a midwestern community. Notable performance from Clark as a soft-voiced guide for truckers passing through. Demme's first comedy is characteristically idiosyncratic. **98m/C VHS.** Paul LeMat, Candy Clark, Ann Wedgeworth, Roberts Blossom, Charles Napier, Marcia Rodd, Bruce McGill, Ed Begley Jr., Alix Elias; *D:* Jonathan Demme; *W:* Paul Brickman; *C:* Jordan Cronenweth; *M:* Bill Conti. Natl. Soc. Film Critics '77: Support. Actress (Wedgeworth).

Citizen Toxie: The Toxic Avenger 4 WOOF! 2001 As gleefully offensive as always, this sequel comes 12 years after part 3. An explosion in Tromaville creates a parallel universe in which Toxie and his evil twin, Noxie AKA Noxious Offender (both of whom live in Amortville), change places. Noxie promptly terrorizes the community while Toxie goes on with his good deeds in his new dimension. Meanwhile, a coalition of other superheroes try to eliminate the evil Noxie from their midst. **109m/C DVD.** David Mattei, Heidi Sjursen, Paul Kyrmse, Dan Snow; *D:* Lloyd Kaufman; *W:* Lloyd Kaufman, Gabriel Friedman, Trent Haaga; *C:* Brendan Flynt; *M:* Wesly Nagy.

The City 🐾🐾 1976 Police desperately search for a psychotic determined to kill a country singer. He shouldn't be too hard to find. **78m/C VHS.** Cor Johnson, Robert Forster, Ward (Edward) Costello, Jimmy Dean, Mark Hamill; *D:* Harvey Hart. **TV**

The City and the Dogs 🐾🐾🐾 *La Ciudad y los Perros* 1985 A brutal, cynical adaptation of Mario Vargas Llosa's novel. A young military recruit rebels against the authority establishments around him. In Spanish with English subtitles. **135m/C VHS.** *SP* Pablo Serra, Gustavo Bueno, Juan Manuel Ochoa, Pilí Flores-Guerra, Eduardo Adrianzen; *D:* Francisco J. Lombardi; *Perf:* W: Jose Watanabe; *C:* Enrique Iturraga.

City Boy 🐾🐾 1993 At the turn of the century the orphaned Nick makes his way from Chicago to the Pacific Northwest in search of his natural father. He takes a job guarding Limberfoot, a valuable old-growth forest, from thieves and is torn between the ideals of two new friends. His mentor Tom sees the forest as timber that will build homes and provide jobs, while Angelica sees the forest as an irreplaceable sanctuary. Filmed on location in Vancouver, British Columbia. Adaptation of "Freckles" by Gene Stratton Porter. **120m/C VHS, DVD.** *C4* Christian Campbell, James Brolin, Sarah Chalke, Wendel Meldrum, Christopher Bolton; *D:* John Kent Harrison; *W:* John Kent Harrison.

City by the Sea 🐾🐾½ 2002 (R) Pitch-black drama starring De Niro as NYC homicide detective La Marca, an absentee father trying to find his lost son Joey (Franco), a junkie on the lam for murder. Though he's not exactly a model son La Marco is convinced Joey is set to the perp, down Long Island city, where he must confront his bitter ex (LuPone) and the fate 14 years ago. McDormand appears as La Marca's troubled past-he fled 14 years ago. McDormand appears as La Marca's sometime-girlfriend. Suffers from over-wrought, lengthy exposition, mostly via De

203

Niro (not exactly his specialty). Overacting only exposes a depressing, overcooked script. Loosely based on a true story. 108m/C VHS, DVD. *US* Robert De Niro, James Franco, Frances McDormand, Eliza Dushku, William Forsythe, George Dzundza, Patti LuPone, Anson Mount, John Doman, Brian Tarantina, Nestor Serrano, Leo Burmester; *D:* Michael Caton-Jones; *W:* Ken Hixon; *C:* Karl Walter Lindenlaub; *M:* John Murphy.

City for Conquest 🦴🦴🦴 1940
Two lovers go their separate ways to pursue individual careers. He attempts to become a boxing champ, but is blinded in the ring and ends up selling newspapers. She takes a shot at a dancing career but hooks up with an unscrupulous partner. Will the ill-fated pair find happiness again? 101m/B VHS, DVD. James Cagney, Ann Sheridan, Frank Craven, Donald Crisp, Arthur Kennedy, Frank McHugh, George Tobias, Anthony Quinn, Blanche Yurka, Elia Kazan, Bob Steele; *D:* Anatole Litvak; *W:* John Wexley; *C:* James Wong Howe; *M:* Max Steiner.

City Girl 🦴🦴½ *Our Daily Bread* 1930
Friedrich Murnau, who directed the silent vampire classic "Nosferatu," was removed from the director's chair before "City Girl" was completed and it shows. But so do the marks of his inimitable camera direction. The story concerns a Minnesota grain grower who visits the Windy City and returns with a waitress as his wife. Frustratingly inconsistent, leading you to wonder what could have been had Murnau remained behind the camera (he died the following year). Silent. 90m/B VHS. Charles Farrell, Mary Duncan; *D:* F.W. Murnau.

City Hall 🦴🦴🦴 1995 (R)
Investigating the deaths of a heroic cop, a drug dealer, and six-year old boy in a shootout, idealistic deputy mayor Cusack uncovers a web of corruption and deceit in the Big Apple. Pacino excels as charismatic mayor John Pappas by showing the crafty string-puller behind the glossy image of the modern politico. Supporting cast is also strong, including Aiello as a Rodgers and Hammerstein-loving Brooklyn boss and Fonda as the police union lawyer and standard issue love interest. Screenplay was conceived by Ken Lipper, who was once deputy mayor under Ed Koch, but the involvement of three other scripters causes confusion over what type of picture it's aiming to be. Cash-strapped New York rented its actual city hall out for filming at a price of $50,000. 111m/C VHS, DVD. Al Pacino, John Cusack, Bridget Fonda, Danny Aiello, David Paymer, Martin Landau, Anthony (Tony) Franciosa, Lindsay Duncan, Nestor Serrano. Mel Winkler, Richard Schiff; *D:* Harold Becker; *W:* Paul Schrader, Nicholas Pileggi, Bo Goldman, Ken Lipper; *C:* Michael Seresin; *M:* Jerry Goldsmith.

City Heat 🦴🦴½ 1984 (PG)
A hard-nosed cop and a plucky private eye berate each other while opposing the mob in this overdone caper. Both Eastwood and Reynolds spoof their screen personas, but the results are only slightly satisfactory. Good back-up, though, from Alexander and Kahn as the dames. Screenplay written by Blake Edwards under the pseudonym Sam O. Brown. 98m/C VHS, DVD. Clint Eastwood, Burt Reynolds, Jane Alexander, Irene Cara, Madeline Kahn, Richard Roundtree, Rip Torn, Tony LoBianco, William Sanderson; *D:* Richard Benjamin; *W:* Blake Edwards; *M:* Lennie Niehaus.

City in Fear 🦴🦴½ 1980
Stellar cast lights up a drama about a tired newspaper columnist (Janssen) who communicates directly with a murdering psychotic (Rourke), as publisher Vaughn applauds and hypes. Rourke's first role, Janssen's last, and Smithee is actually Jud Taylor. 135m/C VHS. David Janssen, William Daniels, Perry King, Susan Sullivan, William Prince; *D:* Alan Smithee. TV

City in Panic 🦴 1986
A detective and radio talk show host try to catch a psychotic mass murderer busy offing homosexuals throughout the city. Violent with no redeeming social qualities. 85m/C VHS. Dave Adamson, Ed Chester, Leeann Westergard; *D:* Robert Bouvier.

City Killer 🦴 1987
A lunatic tries to blackmail the girl he loves into going out on a few dates by committing huge destructive acts of inner-city terrorism (flowers won't do). 120m/C VHS. Heather Locklear, Gerald McRaney, Terence Knox, Peter Mark Richman, John Harkins; *D:* Robert Lewis. TV

City Lights 🦴🦴🦴🦴 1931
Masterpiece that was Chaplin's last silent film. The "Little Tramp" falls in love with a blind flower seller. A series of lucky accidents permits him to get the money she needs for a sight-restoring surgery. One of the most eloquent movies ever filmed, due to Chaplin's keen balance between comedy and tragedy. 86m/B VHS, DVD. Charlie Chaplin, Virginia Cherrill, Florence Lee, Hank Mann, Harry C. (Henry) Myers, Henry Bergman, Jean Harlow; *D:* Charlie Chaplin; *C:* Roland H. Totheroh, Gordon Pollock; *M:* Alfred Newman, Charlie Chaplin. AFI '98: Top 100, Natl. Film Reg. '91.

City Limits 🦴 1985 (PG-13)
In a post-apocalyptic city, gangs of young people on choppers clash. 85m/C VHS. John Stockwell, Kim Cattrall, Darrell Larson, Rae Dawn Chong, Robby Benson, James Earl Jones, Jennifer Balgobin; *D:* Aaron Lipstadt.

City of Angels 🦴🦴½ 1998 (PG-13)
Weepy American remake of Wim Wenders' "Wings of Desire" finds guardian angel Seth (Cage) falling in love with heart surgeon Maggie (Ryan) and then trying to decide whether he wants to become mortal in order to join her. Subtle, it is not. Cage does his doe-eyed best to convey Seth's longing and innocence to earthly ways, and the chemistry with Ryan really clicks. Overly sappy and sentimental, especially near the end, but that won't stop the intended audience from loving it. Big Hollywood flick that wears its arthouse pedigree on its sleeve. 117m/C VHS, DVD. Nicolas Cage, Meg Ryan, Andre Braugher, Dennis Franz, Colm Feore, Robin Bartlett, Joanna Merlin; *D:* Brad Silberling; *W:* Dana Stevens; *C:* John Seale; *M:* Gabriel Yared.

City of Blood 🦴🦴 1988 (R)
A South African doctor is embroiled in mystery with racial overtones when prostitutes are being killed with a spiked club. Packaged as a horror film, this movie actually deals with the questions of South African racial tensions in a sophisticated, ultimately tragic manner. 96m/C VHS. Joe Stewardson, Ian Yule, Susan Coetzer; *D:* Darrell Roodt.

City of Ghosts 🦴🦴½ 2003 (R)
Dillon makes his directorial debut (as well as starring and co-writing the screenplay) with this overly-ambitious effort. Jimmy Creemins (Dillon) works for a shady New York insurance agency. His boss (and Jimmy's mentor), Marvin (Caan), has cleaned out the firm's offshore accounts and the feds think Jimmy was in on the scam. Jimmy discovers Marvin is holed up in Phnom Penh and he heads to Cambodia to join him at the Belleville Hotel, the usual sort of seedy Euro-dive, which is run by Frenchman Emile (Depardieu). Soon Jimmy is caught up in further unsavory activities, with various unsavory characters, a damsel-in-distress (McElhone), and more sideline plots. 117m/C VHS, DVD. *US* Matt Dillon, James Caan, Natascha (Natasha) McElhone, Gerard Depardieu, Sereyvuth Kem, Chalee Sankhavesa, Stellan Skarsgard, Rose Byrne, Christopher Curry, Shawn Andrews; *D:* Matt Dillon; *W:* Matt Dillon, Barry Gifford; *C:* Jim Denault; *M:* Tyler Bates.

City of God 🦴🦴🦴½ *Cidade de Deus* 2002 (R)
A long and generally lively chronicle (covering the late sixties to the early eighties) of the drug trade and gang warfare in the slums of Rio. Taken from Paulo Lins novel, the narrator is budding photographer Rocket (Rodrigues), a kid from the projects observing the violence and trying to stay out of its grip. He observes the rise to gang power of the ruthless Little Ze (da Hora), who will eventually go up against his rival, amateur boxer Knockout Ned (Jorge), who has a professional grudge. Portuguese with subtitles. 130m/C DVD. *BR* Alexandre Rodrigues, Leandro Firmino da Hora, Phelipe Haagensen, Matheus Nachtergaele, Seu Jorge, Johnathan Haagensen; *D:* Fernando Meirelles, Katia Lund; *W:* Braulio Mantovani; *C:* Cesar Charlone; *M:* Antonio Pinto, Ed Cortes. N.Y. Film Critics '03: Foreign Film.

City of Hope 🦴🦴🦴 1991 (R)
The picture that "Bonfire of the Vanities" wanted to be, an eventful few days in the fictional metropolis of Hudson: an ugly racial incident threatens to snowball, the corrupt mayor pushes a shady real-estate deal, and a botched robbery has profound implications. Some of the subplots resolve too easily, but this cynical, crazy-quilt of urban life is worthy of comparison with "American Graffiti" and "Nashville" as pure Americana. 132m/C VHS. Vincent Spano, Tony LoBianco, Joe Morton, Todd Graff, David Strathairn, Anthony John (Tony) Denison, Barbara Williams, Angela Bassett, Gloria Foster, Lawrence Tierney, John Sayles, Maggie Renzi, Kevin Tighe, Chris Cooper, Jace Alexander, Frankie Faison, Michael Mantell, Josh Mostel, Joe Grifasi, Louis Zorich, Gina Gershon, Rose Gregorio, Bill Raymond, Maeve Kinkead, Ray Aranha; *D:* John Sayles; *W:* John Sayles; *C:* Robert Richardson; *M:* Mason Daring. Ind. Spirit '92: Support. Actor (Strathairn).

City of Industry 🦴🦴 1996 (R)
Efficient contemporary noir that doesn't also live up to its promise. Old pro thief Roy Egan (Keitel), now retired, is drawn into the final jewel heist of his younger brother, Lee (Hutton), who's also vowed to get out of the game. Unfortunately for him, Lee's picked one wrong partner in volatile wheelman Skip Kovich (Dorff). When the violent Skip decides he doesn't want to share the goods it starts an elaborate cat-and-mouse hunt through the seedier sides of L.A. 97m/C VHS, DVD. Harvey Keitel, Stephen Dorff, Famke Janssen, Timothy Hutton, Michael Jai White, Wade Dominguez, Reno Wilson, Lucy Liu, Dana Barron, Elliott Gould; *D:* John Irvin; *W:* Ken Solarz; *C:* Thomas Burstyn; *M:* Stephen Endelman.

City of Joy 🦴🦴 1992 (PG-13)
Disillusioned American heart surgeon Swayze flees to India after losing a patient. In Calcutta he is beaten by a street gang and loses his money and passport, but finds help from a farmer (Puri) who takes him to a nearby clinic in the City of Joy, one of Calcutta's poorest areas. Collins runs the clinic and recruits the reluctant doctor, who undergoes a life-changing transformation. The squalor of Calcutta is shown, but the city's portrayal as a magical place where problems miraculously disappear is unrealistic. Swayze lacks the emotional range for his part, but Collins and Puri are excellent in their roles. Adapted from the book by Dominique Lapierre. 134m/C VHS, DVD. *GB FR* Patrick Swayze, Pauline Collins, Om Puri, Shabana Azmi, Art Malik, Ayesha Dharker, Santu Chowdhury, Imran Badsah Khan, Shyamanand Jalan; *Cameos: W:* Mark Medoff; *C:* Peter Biziou; *M:* Ennio Morricone.

The City of Lost Children 🦴🦴🦴 *La Cite des Enfants Perdus* 1995 (R)
Weird not-for-the-kiddies fairy-tale finds crazed inventor Krank (Emilfork) getting his evil one-eyed minions, the appropriately named Cyclops, to kidnap local children so that he can steal their dreams (because Krank himself is incapable of dreaming). The latest victim is young Denree (Lucien), the adopted brother of sideshow strongman One (Perlman), who single-mindedly pursues a way to get Denree back—aided by nine-year-old feral child Miette (Vittel) and a band of orphan thieves. Freaks galore with avant-garde designer Jean-Paul Gaultier in charge of costumes. French with subtitles or dubbed. 114m/C VHS, DVD. *FR* Marc Caro, Ron Perlman, Daniel Emilfork, Joseph Lucien, Judith Vittet, Dominique Pinon, Jean-Claude Dreyfus, Odile Mallet, Genevieve Brunet, Mireille Mosse; *D:* Jean-Pierre Jeunet, Marc Caro; *C:* Darius Khondji; *M:* Angelo Badalamenti; *V:* Jean-Louis Trintignant. Cesar '96: Art Dir./Set Dec.

City of M 🦴🦴 *Ciudad de M* 2001
M (Magill) lives on the streets and has no job prospects, but he's happy enough since he can still party with his girlfriend and the guys. Then, he's offered the chance to become a drug courier to Miami. It's the only opportunity he's got but is the risk worth his future? Spanish with subtitles. 102m/C VHS, DVD. *PV* Santiago Magill, Christian Meier, Vanessa Robbiano; *D:* Felipe Degregori; *W:* Giovanna Pollarolo; *C:* Micaela Cajhuaringa.

City of Men 🦴🦴🦴 *Cidade des Homens* 2007 (R)
Two teenage friends, Ace and Wallace, struggle to grow up in a gang-ridden Brazilian shantytown, where much of their thoughts drift to the idea of fatherhood. Ace's father was gunned down at an early age, and he's now become a new father himself. Wallace, about to turn 18 and needing an ID card, must track down his long-lost deadbeat dad to get a necessary signature. The fight to connect with his father is touching and plagued with danger as the two friends scurry from the neighborhood to neighborhood, dodging gang warfare along the way. Based on the Brazilian television series of the same name, and loosely follows Meirelles' earlier gangster epic "City of God," using some of the same actors, but taking a more emotional and mature approach to the themes. 110m/C DVD. *BR* Douglas Silva, Darlan Cunha, Johnathan Haagensen, Camila Monteiro, Rodrigo dos Santos, Eduardo BR Piranha; *D:* Paulo Morelli; *W:* Elena Soarez; *C:* Adriano Goldman; *M:* Antonio Pinto.

City of Shadows 🦴🦴 1986 (R)
Twins separated at birth are reunited by a criminal mind with evil intentions. Double trouble? 97m/C VHS. John P. Ryan, Paul Coufos, Tony Rosato; *D:* David Mitchell; *M:* Tangerine Dream.

City of the Walking Dead 🦴 *Nightmare City; Nightmare; Incubo Sulla Citta Contaminata* 1980
Eco-misery as a community must contend with prowling, radiation-zapped zombies who enjoy chewing through human flesh. 92m/C VHS, DVD. *IT SP* Mel Ferrer, Hugo Stiglitz, Laura Trotter, Francesco Rabal; *D:* Umberto Lenzi; *W:* Antonio Corti, Luis Maria Delgado, Piero Regnoli; *C:* Hans Burman; *M:* Stelvio Cipriani.

City of Women 🦴🦴 *La Citta delle Donne* 1981 (R)
Visually stunning, but otherwise thin fantasy/drama about a man smothered with women. A journalist wanders through a feminist theme park replete with a roller rink and screening room. Some worthwhile adventures are mixed in with rather dull stretches. Not among the best from either Mastroianni, who is under utilized, or Fellini, who here seems incapable of separating good ideas from bad. Plenty of buxom babes, but otherwise undistinguished. In Italian with English subtitles. 140m/C VHS, DVD. *IT* Marcello Mastroianni, Ettore Manni, Anna Prucnal, Bernice Stegers; *D:* Federico Fellini; *W:* Federico Fellini; *C:* Giuseppe Rotunno; *M:* Luis Bacalov.

City on Fire 🦴🦴 *woof!* 1978 (R)
Arguably the worst of Hollywood's disaster epics, this stinker came at the end of the cycle. The plot borrows heavily from such boxoffice heavyweights as "The Towering Inferno" and "The Poseidon Adventure." A cast of second-magnitude stars (with the exception of Henry Fonda) deals with civic corruption, an enraged pyromaniac, political ambitions, blackmail, and assorted hanky-panky. Several stuntmen are set afire, but the titular blaze is handled with unimpressive effects. The rest is choppy editing, cliched situations, and flat characters. 101m/C VHS. *CA* Barry Newman, Susan Clark, Shelley Winters, Leslie Nielsen, Henry Fonda, Ava Gardner; *D:* Alvin Rakoff.

City on Fire 🦴🦴½ 1987
Ko Chow (Chow Yun-Fat) is an undercover cop who just wants out so he can marry his girl and forget about his past. He agrees to do one more job for his uncle, an aging inspector being forced out by an ambitious newcomer. He infiltrates a violent crew (one that's already killed a cop who had gotten in with them) that's planning a jewel heist. Like most Hong Kong cops-and-gangs flicks, it goes heavy on the action, but it also delves into Chow's character, sometimes to the detriment of the pacing. Most people know this as the inspiration for Tarantino's "Reservoir Dogs". 98m/C VHS, DVD. *HK* Chow Yun-Fat, Sun Yueh, Danny Lee, Carrie Ng, Roy Cheung; *D:* Ringo Lam; *W:* Ringo Lam, Tommy Sham; *C:* Wai Keung (Andrew) Lau; *M:* Teddy Robin Kwan.

City Slickers 🐾🐾🐾 1991 (PG-13) Three men with mid-life crises leave New York City for a cattle-ranch vacation that turns into an arduous, character-building stint. Many funny moments supplied by leads Crystal, Stern, and Kirby, but Palance steals the film as a salty, wise cowpoke. Slater is fetching as the lone gal vacationer on the cattle drive. Boxoffice winner notable for a realistic calf birthing scene, one of few in cinema history. From an idea by Crystal, who also produced. Palance stole the show from Oscar ceremonies host Crystal a second time when he accepted his award and suddenly started doing one-arm pushups, starting the audience into laughter. **114m/C VHS, DVD.** Billy Crystal, Daniel Stern, Jack Palance, Bruno Kirby, Patricia Wettig, Helen Slater, Jack Palance, Noble Willingham, Tracey Walter, Josh Mostel, David Paymer, Bill Henderson, Jeffrey Tambor, Phill Lewis, Kyle Secor, Yeardley Smith, Jayne Meadows; **D:** Ron Underwood. **W:** Lowell Ganz, Babaloo Mandel; **C:** Dean Semler; **M:** Marc Shaiman. Oscars '91: Support. Actor (Palance); Golden Globes '92: Support. Actor (Palance); MTV Movie Awards '92: Comedic Perf. (Crystal).

City Slickers 2: The Legend of Curly's Gold 🐾🐾 1994 (PG-13) Mid-life crisis meets the wild urban part deux. Crystal and his fellow urban dudes discover a treasure map in the hat of departed trail boss Curly and decide to go a-huntin'. Palance is back as Curly's saddlehart (equally cantankerous twin brother, Lovitz occupies the screen as Crystal's ne'er-do-well brother, replacing sidekick Bruno Kirby. A bit of a rehash, formulaic and occasionally straining for a punchline, it's still pretty darn funny, especially when the boys star to improvise. **116m/C VHS, DVD.** Billy Crystal, Daniel Stern, Jon Lovitz, Jack Palance, Patricia Wettig, Pruit Taylor Vince, Bill McKinney, Lindsay Crystal, Noble Willingham; **D:** Paul Weiland; **W:** Billy Crystal, Lowell Ganz, Babaloo Mandel; **M:** Marc Shaiman.

City That Never Sleeps 🐾🐾½ 1953 A Chicago cop must decide whether or not to run off with an entertainer, or continue his life with his family. Decisions, decisions. Moody but dated melodrama that's finely acted and indecisively directed, with good use of dim city lights. Nothing new here. **90m/B VHS.** Gig Young, Mala Powers, Edward Arnold, Paula Raymond, Chill Wills, Marie Windsor; **D:** John H. Auer.

City Unplugged 🐾🐾½ 1943 Me-*Darkness in Tallinn* 1995 Heist film with some twists. $970 million in gold, in Paris for safekeeping since WWII, has been returned to the Russian mob, plan to cut all electricity in the capital city of Tallinn, break into the bank, and move the gold to a nearby cigarette factory where it can be melted down and repackaged as cigarettes. The mob's use of local electrician Toivo proves to be their undoing in a comedy of errors. Estonian with subtitles. **95m/C VHS.** Peter Oja, Ivo Uukkivi, Milena Gulbe, Monika Mager; **D:** Ilkka Harviluovi; **W:** Paul Kolsby; **C:** Rain Kotov.

City Without Men 🐾🐾½ 1943 Melodramatic story about a boarding house near a prison where the women tenants await the release of their imprisoned men. Little plot, no suspense. **75m/B VHS.** Linda Darnell, Sara Allgood, Michael Duane, Edgar Buchanan, Leslie Brooks, Glenda Farrell, Margaret Hamilton, Sheldon Leonard; **D:** Sidney Salkow.

The City's Edge 🐾½ 1983 A young man becomes involved with the mysterious residents of a boarding house on the edge of the ocean. **86m/C VHS, AU Mark Lee; **D:** Ken Quinnell.

Civic Duty 🐾🐾 2006 (R) Terry Allen (Krause) has lost his job, and now spends his days at home while his wife goes to work. Eventually he begins obsessing over a middle-eastern looking neighbor who he begins to believe is a terrorist. Soon he's driving off his wife, annoying the FBI, and watching media hype about the 'terrorist threat' to our country. And stalking his neighbor, who may or may not be what he seems. Take it seriously and you may begin to wonder what those gophers in your yard are up to... **98m/C DVD.** US Peter Krause, Richard Schiff, Kari Matchett, Ian Tracey, Khaled Abol Naga, Mark Brandon, Val Cole, Brenda Crichlow, Agam Darshi; **P:** Lynn Johnson; **D:** Jeff Renfroe; **W:** Andrew Joiner; **C:** Dylan MacLeod; **M:** Terry Huud, Eli Krantzberg.

Civil Brand 🐾🐾½ 2002 (R) Minority inmates stage a bloody revolt against abuse and exploitation. Melodrama quickly boils over the top and doesn't cast its charge. Notable performances by rappers MC Lite, Da Brat, and Mos Def. Neema Barnette makes good use of her low-budget but scrimps on attention to pertinent civil issues. **95m/C VHS, DVD.** US LisaRaye, Mos Def, N'Bushe Wright, Monica Calhoun, Da Brat, MC Lite, Clifton Powell, Lark Voorhies, Tichina Arnold, Reed McCarris; **D:** Neema Barrette; **W:** Joyce Renee Lewis, Preston A. Whitmore II; **C:** Yuri Neyman; **M:** Mandrill.

Civil War Diary 🐾🐾🐾 Across Five Aprils 1990 Too young to go to war, a young amish man struggles for the survival of his family amidst harsh winters, the devastation of the Civil War and his own personal nightmares. Winner of the International Heritage Award in 1990. Based on the Newberry Award winning young people's novel "Across Five Aprils." **89m/C VHS.** Miriam Byrd-Nethery, Todd Duffey, Hollis McCarthy; **D:** Kevin Meyer; **W:** Kevin Meyer.

Civilization 🐾🐾🐾 1916 A silent epic envisioned by the horrors and immorality of war as pioneer Ince, who was later murdered. Famous scene involves Christ walking through body-ridden battlefields. **80m/B VHS.** Howard Hickman, Enid Markey, Lola May; **D:** Thomas Ince, Reginald Barker, Raymond B. West. Natl. Film Reg. '99.

The Claim 🐾🐾½ 2000 (R) Winterbottom, who already adapted Thomas Hardy's "Jude the Obscure," takes on Hardy's "The Mayor of Casterbridge," transporting the tale to California during the gold rush. Miner Dillon (Mullan) sells his wife Elena (Kinski) and baby daughter for gold and uses the money to establish his own town. But his sins come back to haunt him when his dying wife and grown daughter Hope (Polley) arrive, as does railway surveyor Dalglish (Bentley). Now Dillon's very future is threatened. There's more than the winter weather that's chilly about the film, which never reaches the tragic dimensions it should. **120m/C VHS, DVD.** GB Peter Mullan, Nastassja Kinski, Sarah Polley, Wes Bentley, Milla Jovovich, Sean McGinley, Julian Richings; **D:** Michael Winterbottom; **W:** Frank Cottrell-Boyce; **C:** Alwin Kuchler; **M:** Michael Nyman.

Claire Dolan 🐾🐾 1997 Irish immigrant Claire (Cartlidge), a hooker, decides to relocate after her mother dies and she leaves town owing her pimp. Roland (Meaney), a lot of money. She moves to Newark, gets a job as a beautician, and begins a romance with Elton (D'Onofrio). Then Roland finds her and forces Claire back into business to pay off her debt. Bleak but well-acted. **95m/C VHS.** Katrin Cartlidge, Vincent D'Onofrio, Colm Meaney; **D:** Lodge Kerrigan; **W:** Lodge Kerrigan; **C:** Teodoro Maniaci; **M:** Simon Fisher Turner.

Clarence, the Cross-eyed Lion 🐾🐾 1965 Follows the many adventures of a cross-eyed lion and his human companions. Great family viewing from the creator of "Flipper." **98m/C VHS.** Marshall Thompson, Betsy Drake, Richard Haydn, Cheryl Miller, Rockne Tarkington, Maurice Marsac; **D:** Andrew Marton; **W:** Alan Caillou.

Clarissa 🐾🐾½ 1991 Clarissa Harlowe (Wickham) is a wealthy heiress famed for her virtue who is badgered by her family to marry a nobleman, which leads her to rebellion and into the arms of the handsome rake Lovelace (Bean). His seductive tactics are foiled by Clarissa's strength of character and his own heart, leading him down a path of self-destruction. Fabulous period costumes, gorgeous settings and stellar acting. **156m/C DVD.** Saskia Wickham, Sean Bean, Lynsey Baxter, Sean Pertwee, Jonathan Phillips, Jeffrey Wickham, Cathryn Harrison, Shirley Henderson; **D:** Robert Bierman; **W:** Janet Baron, David Nokes; **C:** Colin Towns. VIDEO

A Civil Action 🐾🐾½ 1998 (PG-13) Low-key courtroom thriller doesn't contain many thrills. Travolta is Jan Schlichtmann, a flashy lawyer who freely admits that he's an ambulance chasing weasel. When a grieving mother (Quinlan) approaches him with a case accusing two corporate conglomerates of causing an outbreak of leukemia among children, Jan smells a big payoff. As the case drags on (and his firm falls deeper into debt pursuing it), his perspective changes and he begins to seek justice for the lost children. Robert Duvall steals the show as the homespun Harvard lawyer representing one of the companies. Based on a true story. **115m/C VHS, DVD.** James Gandolfini, John Travolta, Robert Duvall, Kathleen Quinlan, Tony Shalhoub, Zeljko Ivanek, John Lithgow, William H. Macy, Bruce Norris, Sydney Pollack, Peter Jacobson; **D:** Steven Zaillian; **W:** Steven Zaillian; **C:** Conrad L. Hall; **M:** Danny Elfman. Screen Actor's Guild '98: Support. Actor (Duvall).

Claire of the Moon 🐾🐾 1992 Famous satirist Claire goes to a women writers' retreat in the Pacific Northwest where she's assigned a room with Noel, a solemn sex therapist. Noel's recovering from a disastrous love affair while Claire is promiscuous and unwilling to commit. In spite of their differences, the two women find themselves drawn together. Too many philosophical debates slow the story down but the gentle romance works well. **102m/C VHS, DVD.** Trisha Todd, Karen Trumbo, Nicole Conn; **D:** Nicole Conn; **W:** Faith McDevit, Damon Craig; **D:** Nicole Conn.

Claire's Knee 🐾🐾🐾½ Le Genou de Claire 1971 A grown man about to be married goes on a holiday and develops a fixation on a young girl's knee. Another of Rohmer's Moral Tales, exploring sexual and erotic obsessions. Lots of talk, little action, lovely visions of summer on Lake Geneva. In French with English subtitles. **105m/C VHS, DVD.** FR Jean-Claude Brialy, Aurora Cornu, Beatrice Romand, Laurence de Monaghan, Gerard Falconetti; **D:** Eric Rohmer; **W:** Eric Rohmer; **C:** Nestor Almendros. Natl. Soc. Film Critics '71: Film.

Clambake 🐾 1967 Noxious Elvis vehicle about a rich man's son who wants success on his own terms, so he trades places with a water-skiing teacher. Inane, even to other Elvis ventures. ♪Clambake; The Girl I Never Loved; Hey, Hey, Hey; Confidence; Who Needs Money?; A House That Has Everything. **98m/C VHS, DVD.** Elvis Presley, Shelley Fabares, Bill Bixby, James Gregory, Gary Merrill, Will Hutchins, Harold (Hal) Peary, Suzie Kaye, Angelique Pettyjohn; **D:** Arthur Nadel; **M:** Jeff Alexander.

The Clan of the Cave Bear 🐾½ 1986 (R) A scrawny cavegirl is taken in by Neanderthals after her own parents are killed. Hannah is lifeless as a DOA. Porderous and only unintentionally funny. Based on the popular novel by Jean M. Auel. **100m/C VHS, DVD.** Daryl Hannah, James Remar, Pamela Reed, John Doolittle, Thomas G. Waites; **D:** Michael Chapman; **W:** John Sayles; **C:** Jan De Bont; **M:** Alan Silvestri.

Clancy Street Boys 🐾🐾 1943 Muggs McGinnis (Gorcey) recruits his pals to pose as his siblings to fool wealthy Pete, a visiting friend of his late father's aid under the mistaken impression the thug hears about the scam and tries to horn in. Part of the "East Side Kids" series. **89m/B DVD.** Leo Gorcey, Huntz Hall, Bobby Jordan, Amelita Ward, Noah Beery Sr., Martha Wentworth, Bernie Bartlett; **D:** William Beaudine; **W:** Harvey Gates; **C:** Mack Stengler.

Clara's Heart 🐾🐾 1988 (PG-13) A Jamaican maid enriches the lives of her insufferable, bourgeois employers and their particularly repellent son. A kinder, gentler waste of film and Goldberg; sentimental clap-trap with occasionally lapses into comedy. **108m/C VHS.** Whoopi Goldberg, Michael Ontkean, Kathleen Quinlan, Neil Patrick Harris, Spalding Gray, Beverly Todd, Hattie Winston; **D:** Robert Mulligan; **W:** Mark Medoff; **M:** Dave Grusin.

Clarence 🐾🐾½ 1991 (G) Clarence, the benevolent angel from the classic "It's a Wonderful Life" is back, risking his wings for a beautiful young woman. **92m/C VHS.** Robert Carradine, Kate Trotter; **D:** Eric Till; **W:** Lorne Cameron. CABLE.

Clash by Night 🐾🐾½ 1952 A wayward woman marries a fisherman, then beds his best friend. Steamy story line is exploited to the hilt by master filmmaker Lang. An utterly unflinching melodrama too. Based on the Clifford Odets play. Early Monroe shines in a supporting role too. **105m/B VHS, DVD.** Barbara Stanwyck, Paul Douglas, Marilyn Monroe, Robert Ryan, J. Carrol Naish; **D:** Fritz Lang.

Clash of the Ninja 🐾🐾🐾½ 1986 Evil Occidental ninja runs medical smuggling operation. Interpol ninja sets out to stop him. Wild ninja nonsense includes ninja with rotating head and exploding ninja. Dubbed poorly. **90m/C VHS, HK Paul Tornel, Kaus Mutter, Eddie Chan, Max Kwan, Tom Allen, Stanley Tong; **D:** Wallace Chan; **W:** Kurt Spielberg.

Clash of the Titans WOOF! 1981 (PG) Mind-numbing fantasy derived from Greek legends about heroic Perseus, who slays the snake-haired Medusa and rescues a semi-clad maiden from the monstrous Kraken. Wooden Hamlin plays Perseus and fares better than more accomplished Olivier and Smith, who seem in need of enemas as they lurch about Mt. Olympus. Only Bloom seems truly godlike in a supporting role. Some good, some wretched special effects from pioneer Harryhausen. **118m/C VHS, DVD, GB Laurence Olivier, Maggie Smith, Claire Bloom, Ursula Andress, Burgess Meredith, Harry Hamlin, Sian Phillips, Judi Bowker; **D:** Desmond Davis; **W:** Beverley Cross; **C:** Ted Moore.

Class 🐾🐾 1983 (R) A prep school student discovers that his mother is the lover whom his roommate has bragged about. Lowe is serviceable as the stunned son of sexy Bisset, who woos McCarthy, even in an elevator. Too ludicrous to be enjoyed, but you may watch just to see what happens next. **98m/C VHS, DVD.** Jacqueline Bisset, Rob Lowe, Andrew McCarthy, Cliff Robertson, John Cusack, Stuart Margolin, Casey Siemaszko; **D:** Lewis John Carlino; **W:** Jim Kout, David Greenwalt; **C:** Ric Waite; **M:** Elmer Bernstein.

Class Act 🐾🐾½ 1991 (PG-13) Rappers Kid 'N Play team up once again in this role reversal comedy. A straight-laced brain and a partying, macho bully find their identities switched when they enroll in a new high school. This turns out to be good for the character of both young men, as the egghead learns to loosen up and the bully learns what it feels like to be respected for his ideas rather than a fierce reputation. Comedy is very uneven but the duo are energetic and likable. **98m/C VHS.** Christopher Reid, Christopher Martin, Meshach Taylor, Karyn Parsons, Doug E. Doug, Rick) Ducommun, Rhea Perlman; **D:** Randall Miller; **M:** Vassal Benford.

Class of Fear 🐾🐾 1991 (R) Monday Morning 1960s versus 1990s ethics clash when a father and daughter, both lawyers, wind up on opposing sides of a litigation against an auto manufacturer. Hackman and Mastrantonio give intense, exciting performances, almost surmounting the melodramatic script. **110m/C VHS, DVD.** Mary Elizabeth Mastrantonio, Gene Hackman, Joanna Merlin, Colin Friels, Laurence Fishburne, Donald Moffat, Jan Rubes, Matt Clark, Fred Dalton Thompson, Jonathan Silverman, Dan Hicks; **D:** Michael Apted; **M:** Samantha Shad, Christopher Ames; **M:** James Horner.

Class of '44 1973 (PG) The sequel to "Summer of '42" finds insufferable boys becoming insufferable men at military school. Worse than its predecessor, and notable only in that it is Candy's film debut. 95m/C VHS. Gary Grimes, Jerry Houser, Oliver Conant, Deborah Winters, William Atherton, Sam Bottoms, John Candy; D: Paul Bogart; M: David Shire.

The Class of Miss MacMichael 1978 (R) A dedicated instructor inherits and ultimately inspires a class of high school misfits and malcontents. Derivative venture is beneath considerable talents of Jackson. Based on a novel by Sandy Hutson. 95m/C VHS. GB Glenda Jackson, Oliver Reed, Michael Murphy, Rosalind Cash; D: Silvio Narizzano; W: Judd Bernard.

Class of 1984 WOOF! 1982 (R) Teacher King must face a motley crew of teenagers in the classroom. Ring leader and student psychopath Van Patten leads his groupies on a reign of terror through the high school halls, stopping to gang rape King's wife. Teacher attempts to revenge. Bloody and thoughtless update of "Blackboard Jungle." Early Fox appearance. Followed by "Class of 1999." 93m/C VHS, DVD. CA Perry King, Roddy McDowall, Timothy Van Patten, Michael J. Fox, Merrie Lynn Ross, Stefan Arngrim, Al Waxman, Lisa Langlois; D: Mark L. Lester; W: Mark L. Lester, Tom Holland; C: Albert J. Dunk; M: Lalo Schifrin.

Class of 1999 1990 (R) Freewheeling sci-fi set in the near future where teen gangs terrorize seemingly the entire country. A high school principal determines to enforce law and order by installing human-like robots with rocket launchers for arms. Violent, crude entertainment. Sequel to "Class of 1984" and available in an unrated version. 98m/C VHS. Bradley Gregg, Traci Lind, Malcolm McDowell, Stacy Keach, Patrick Kilpatrick, Pam Grier, John P. Ryan, Darren E. Burrows, Joshua John Miller; D: Mark L. Lester; W: C. Courtney Joyner.

Class of 1999 2: The Substitute 1993 (R) High school in 1999 is filled with violent gangs who murder at random. Enter substitute teacher John Bolen, who has his own ideas of discipline—leading to an even higher body count. John just doesn't seem human and when a CIA agent starts investigating, school may never be the same. 90m/C VHS. Sasha Mitchell, Nick Cassavetes, Caitlin Dulany, Jack Knight, Gregory West, Richard (Rick) Hill; D: Spiro Razatos; W: Mark Sevi.

Class of Nuke 'Em High 1986 (R) Team Troma once again experiments with the chemicals, with violent results. Jersey high school becomes a hotbed of mutants and maniacs after a nuclear spill occurs. Good teens Chrissy and Warren succumb, the school blows, life goes on. High camp, low budget, heavy gore. Followed by "Class of Nuke 'Em High Part 2." 84m/C VHS, DVD. Janelle Brady, Gilbert Brenton, Robert Prichard, R.L. Ryan, Theo Cohan, Diana De Vries, Brad Dunker, Gary Schneider; D: Richard W. Haines, Lloyd Kaufman; W: Richard W. Haines, Lloyd Kaufman, Mark Rudnitsky, Stuart Strutin.

Class of Nuke 'Em High 2: Subhumanoid Meltdown 1991 (R) The Troma team brings us back into the world of the strange. In this adventure, the evil Nukamama Corporation holds secret experiments at their "college" and create sub-humanoids as slave labor, swelling unemployment and wrecking the economy. This does not fare too well with the rest of society, including our heroes Roger the reporter, Professor Holt, and the scantily clad sub-humanoid Victoria. 96m/C VHS, DVD. Lisa Gaye, Brick Bronsky, Leesa Rowland, Michael Kurtz, Scott Resnick; D: Eric Louzil; W: Eric Louzil, Lloyd Kaufman; C: Ron Chapman; M: Bob Mithoff.

Class of Nuke 'Em High 3: The Good, the Bad and the Subhumanoid WOOF! 1994 (R) Revisit Tromie the nuclear rodent and the other disaster-prone denizens of Tromaville, USA. Admire the classic good twin vs. evil subhumanoid twin plot as they battle against each other, aided by chicks with guns and tin undergarments. Supposedly inspired by Shakespeare's "Comedy of Errors." Tip: stick to the BBC production for your senior thesis. 95m/C VHS, DVD. Brick Bronsky, Lisa Gaye, Lisa Star, John Tallman, Albert Rear, Phil Rivo; D: Eric Louzil; W: Lloyd Kaufman; C: Ron Chapman; M: Bob Mithoff.

Class of '61 1992 1861, that is, as this class of West Point cadets prepares for the outbreak of war. Three close friends find themselves on opposing sides and find romantic entanglements, as well. Illustrated history, complete with voiceover passages from soldiers' letters, tend to slow the action, although the battles scenes are well done. 95m/C VHS. Dan Futterman, Clive Owen, Josh(ua) Lucas, Sophie Ward, Laura Linney, Andre Braugher, Len Cariou, Dana Ivey, Scott Burkholder, Niall O'Brien, Christien Anholt, Paul Guilfoyle, Beverly Todd, Ed Wiley, Sue-Ann Leeds; D: Gregory Hoblit; W: Jonas McCord; C: Janusz Kaminski. TV

Class of '63 1973 An unfulfilled woman finally discovers the lover she lost nearly ten years ago at her college reunion. Nearly average. 74m/C VHS. James Brolin, Joan Hackett, Cliff Gorman, Ed Lauter; D: John Korty. TV

Class Reunion WOOF! 1972 Sexual highjinks are the order of the day at a 10-year high school reunion. Insipid softcore effort. It's cheaper just to cut out heads from yearbooks and paste 'em to skin mags torsos. Not to be confused with "National Lampoon's Class Reunion," equally bad but nonetheless distinct. 90m/C VHS. Marsha Jordan, Renee Bond, Terry Johnson; D: Stephen C. Apostolof; W: Edward D. Wood Jr.; C: Allen Stone.

Class Reunion Massacre WOOF! The Redeemer 1977 (R) Typically lame-brained horror about the mysterious deaths of former school jerks who've reconvened for the 10-year reunion. Worthless flick stars someone named Finkbinder. Contains graphic violence that is not for the squeamish. 87m/C VHS. T.K. Finkbinder, Damien Knight, Nick Carter, Jeanetta Arnette, Christopher Flint; D: Constantine S. Gochis; W: William Vernick.

Claudia 1985 (R) A wealthy woman who's part of London's high society falls for a lowly musician while trying to escape her dominating husband. Melodramatic meanderings not likely to move you. 88m/C VHS. Deborah Raffin, Nicholas Ball; D: Anwar Kawadri.

The Claw 1927 A young British profligate goes to Africa to prove his manhood to the woman who rejected him. Silent. 54m/B VHS. Claire Windsor, Norman Kerry; D: Sidney Olcott; W: John Stumar.

Clawed: The Legend of Sasquatch The Unknown 2005 (R) A group of bear poachers are found brutally mauled on Echo Mountain and many in the nearby town of Pine Creek believe a grizzly was to blame—or maybe the mountain's lurid legend has resurfaced. A Native American forest ranger sets out to investigate and so do four teen campers. 90m/C DVD. Miles O'Keeffe, Nathaniel Arcand, Jack Conley, Chelsea Hobbs, Dylan Purcell, Brandon Henschell, David "Shark" Fralick, Casey LaBow; C: Victor Lou; W: Karl Kozak, Don J. Rearden. VIDEO

Claws 1977 (PG) A woodsman, a game commissioner, and an Indian band together to stop a grizzly bear who is killing residents of a small Alaskan town. 100m/C VHS. Leon Ames, Jason Evers, Anthony Caruso, Glenn Sipes, Carla Layton, Myron Healey; D: Richard Bansbach, R.E. Pierson.

Claws WOOF! 1985 A lone farmboy is subjected to repeated attacks by feline mutants. Meow, baby. 84m/C VHS. Jason Roberts, Brian O'Shaughnessy, Sandra Prinsloo; D: Alan Nathanson.

The Clay Bird Matir Moina 2002 Anu (Bablu) is sent to a strict Islamic religious school where he befriends outcast Rokon (Farazi). Times are troubled in East Pakistan (it's the late 1960s) as the residents wish to create an independent state, which is causing problems with the Muslim rulers in West Pakistan. As Anu's family gets more politically involved, life becomes more dangerous. (Bangladesh was formed in 1971.) Bengali with subtitles. 98m/C DVD. Nurul Islam Bablu, Russell Farazi, Jayanto Chattopadhyay, Rokeya Prachy, Soaeb Islam; D: Tareque Masud; W: Tareque Masud, Catherine Masud; C: Sudhir Palsane; M: Moushumi Bhowmik.

The Clay Pigeon 1949 Seaman comes to in the hospital after a long coma and discovers he's about to be court-martialed for treason and murder. Effective suspense as he goes after the man who incriminated him. 63m/B VHS. Bill Williams, Barbara Hale, Richard Loo, Richard Quine, Frank Fenton, Frank Wilcox, Robert Bray, Martha Hyer, Ann Doran, Mary(a) Marco; D: Richard Fleischer; W: Carl Foreman; C: Robert De Grasse; M: Paul Sawtell.

Clay Pigeons 1998 (R) Bodies are mysteriously piling up in a sleepy Montana town after strange cowboy trucker Lester (Vaughn) shows up. Clay Bidwell (Phoenix) finds himself a prime suspect after a series of bizarre twists stemming from his affair with his best friend's wife. After crossing paths, Clay and Lester quickly become best buddies. When they discover a body while fishing, Clay begins to link unsolved murders elsewhere in the state to his new pal. Problem is, the FBI has just shown up to investigate the disappearance of Clay's best friend and his wife, while Lester has disappeared, leaving Clay to take the heat. Features outstanding performances by Phoenix and Vaughn. Vaughn is given free reign, and goes near, but never over, the top. Second half is slower and less fun than the first half. Still, the original story and clever twists keep it interesting. 104m/C VHS, DVD. Vince Vaughn, Joaquin Rafael (Leaf) Phoenix, Janeane Garofalo, Scott Wilson, Georgina Cates, Phil Morris, Vince Vieluf, Nikki Arlyn, Monica Moench, Joseph D. Reitman, Gregory Sporleder; D: David Dobkin; W: Matthew Healy; C: Eric Alan Edwards; M: John Lurie.

Clayton County Line 1978 Plucky buddies decide to end a cruel sheriff's reign of terror. Derivative and unredeeming. 80m/C VHS. Kelly Bradish, Vince Casapos, Michael Heinz, Donald Kenney, Kathy Kenney, Gregg Schultz, Dean Quine, Steve Szilagyi, Dean Wilson.

Clean 2004 (R) Emily (Cheung) and her common-law husband Lee Hauser (Johnston) are heroin addicts who abandoned their young son to Lee's parents. Lee, a faded 80s rocker, dies of an overdose, and Emily is sent to jail, where she tries to get clean. After her release, Emily wants to reconnect with her son, but grandma Rosemary (Henny) hates her, and grandpa Albrecht (Nolte) is more willing to give Emily a chance. Emily struggles to keep off drugs while attempting to find work and mend fences but the character is so prickly and self-centered that she garners little sympathy. 110m/C VHS, DVD. CA GB FR Maggie Cheung, Nick Nolte, Beatrice Dalle, Jeanne Balibar, Don McKellar, Martha Henry, James Johnston, Remi Martin, James Dennis, Laetitia Spigarelli; Cameos: David Roback; D: Olivier Assayas; W: Olivier Assayas; C: Eric Gautier; M: David Roback, Brian Eno.

Clean and Sober 1988 (R) A drug addict hides out at a rehabilitation clinic and undergoes treatment. A serious, subtle, and realistic look at the physical/emotional detoxification of an obnoxious, substance-abusing real estate broker; unpredictable and powerful without moralizing. Keaton is in unsympathetic lead, with both Baker and Freeman excelling in lesser roles. Not for all tastes, but it's certainly a worthwhile work. Caron, creator of TV's "Moonlighting," debuts here as director. 124m/C VHS, DVD. Michael Keaton, Kathy Baker, Morgan Freeman, M. Emmet Walsh, Claudia Christian, Pat Quinn, Ben Piazza, Brian Benben, Luca Bercovici, Tate Donovan, Henry Judd Baker, Mary Catherine Martin; D: Glenn Gordon Caron; W: Tod Carroll; C: Jan Kiesser; M: Gabriel Yared. Natl. Soc. Film Critics '88: Actor (Keaton).

Clean, Shaven 1993 Schizophrenic Peter Winter (Greene in a stunning performance) is searching bleak Miscou Island, off the New Brunswick coast, for the young daughter his mother put up for adoption after Peter was institutionalized and his wife died. Peter's being tailed by Detective McNally (Albert), who suspects him of a child's murder, and his tenuous hold on reality slowly disintegrates into torment and self-mutilation. Debut for director/writer Kerrigan. 80m/C VHS, DVD. Peter Greene, Robert Albert, Jennifer MacDonald, Megan Owen, Molly Castelloe; D: Lodge Kerrigan; W: Lodge Kerrigan; C: Teodoro Maniaci; M: Hahn Rowe.

Clean Slate 1994 (PG-13) Private-eye Maurice Pogue (Carvey) sustains injuries that cause a rare type of amnesia making every day seem like the first day of his life. As the only witness to a crime, he bumbles through mix-ups with the mob and his job as a bodyguard. Lightweight comedy fare is good for a few yuks but doesn't work as well as the similar "Groundhog Day." Barkley the sight-impaired dog steals nearly every scene he's in. 106m/C VHS, DVD. Bob Odenkirk, Dana Carvey, Valeria Golino, James Earl Jones, Kevin Pollak, Michael Murphy, Michael Gambon, Jayne Brook, Vyto Ruginis, Olivia D'Abo, Peter Crook; D: Mick Jackson; W: Robert King; M: Alan Silvestri.

Cleaner 2007 (R) Disappointingly lackluster thriller. Former New Jersey cop Tom Carver (Jackson) now makes his living cleaning up crime scenes. But Tom is shocked to discover that his recent clean-up of a shooting has erased evidence, which points to a cover-up and maybe Tom becoming the fall guy for murder. 91m/C DVD. Samuel L. Jackson, Ed Harris, Robert Forster, Luis Guzman, Marc Macaulay, Eva Mendes, Keke Palmer, Jose Pablo Cantillo, Maggie Lawson; D: Renny Harlin; W: Matthew Aldrich; C: Scott Kevan; M: Richard Gibbs. VIDEO

Clear and Present Danger

Clear and Present Danger 1994 (PG-13) Ford returns for a second go at CIA agent Jack Ryan in the third installment of Tom Clancy's bestselling adventures. With the Cold War over, the U.S. government is the bad guy as Ryan discovers a link between a South American drug cartel and a Presidential advisor. Viewers will also finally get an answer to that nagging question at the end of "Patriot Games": is it a boy or a girl? Archer's back as Ryan's annoying wife, and Birch and Jones also return. Keep alert for complex plot twists in lieu of tons of action, though there's enough to keep action fans happy. 141m/C VHS, DVD. Harrison Ford, Anne Archer, James Earl Jones, Willem Dafoe, Thora Birch, Henry Czerny, Harris Yulin, Raymond Cruz, Joaquim de Almeida, Miguel (Michael) Sandoval, Donald Moffat, Theodore (Ted) Raimi, Dean Jones; D: Phillip Noyce; W: John Milius, Donald Stewart, Steven Zaillian; C: Donald McAlpine; M: James Horner. Blockbuster '95: Action Actor, T. (Ford); Blockbuster '96: Action Actor, V. (Ford).

Clearcut 1992 (R) Progressive lawyer finds his liberalism and his survival skills tested among modern Canadian Indians, when a militant native resorts to kidnapping the businessman who threatens their land. Well-acted, brutal drama that asks tough questions; it includes what purports to be the first authentic sweat-lodge ceremony ever filmed. 98m/C VHS. CA Graham Greene, Ron Lea, Michael Hogan, Floyd "Red Crow" Westerman, Rebecca Jenkins; D: Richard Bugajski.

The Clearing 2004 (R) Rich businessman Redford is kidnapped from his driveway by frustrated former employee Dafoe. As Dafoe leads Redford through the woods towards an appointed meeting spot with the other kidnappers, Redford tries to talk Dafoe into letting him go free. His wife (Mirren), meanwhile, finally notices his prolonged absence and calls in family and FBI. Redford talks to Dafoe about his wife; Mirren talks to an understanding agent about her husband. As the tension builds around them, the two reflect upon their importance to one another. Quietly suspenseful and full of interesting, fully fleshed characters, with a deliberate pace, beautiful acting, and a rewarding twist at the end. 91m/C DVD. US Robert Redford, Willem Dafoe, Helen Mirren, Matt Craven, Alessandro Nivola, Melissa Sagemiller, Wendy Crewson, Larry Pine, Diana Scarwid, Eliza-

Clearing the Range ⚐½ 1931 Hoot wants the bad guy who knocked off his brother so he poses as a cringing coward in the hopes of uncovering the villain. Ellers is the love interest as well as his real-life wife. **64m/B** VHS. Hoot Gibson, Sally Eilers, Hooper Atchley; **D:** Otto Brower.

Cleo from 5 to 7 ⚐⚐⚐½ Cleo de 5 à 7 1961 A singer strolls through Paris for 90 minutes, while awaiting the results of medical tests for cancer. Typical documentary-like effort from innovative filmmaker Varda, who constructed the film in real time. Look for a brief appearance of master director Jean-Luc Godard. In French with English subtitles. **90m/B** VHS, DVD. **FR** Corinne Marchand, Antoine Bourseiller, Dorothee Blanck, Michel Legrand, Jean-Claude Brialy, Jean-Luc Godard, Anna Karina, Eddie Constantine, Sami Frey; **D:** Agnes Varda. **W:** Agnes Varda. **C:** Jean Rabier; **M:** Michel Legrand.

Cleo/Leo ⚐ 1989 (R) Crude and sexist jerk Leo gets chased into the East River by a gun-toting feminist. Reincarnated, Leo returns as Cleo and endures the same Neanderthal remarks and attitudes that "he" used to dish out. Tasteless, expletive comedy only cynically explores the sex reversal theme. **94m/C** VHS. Jane (Vernonica Hart) Hamilton, Scott Thompson Baker, Kevin Thomas, Alan Naggar, Ginger Lynn Allen, Chuck Vincent.

Cleopatra ⚐ 1963 And we thought the death of Julius Caesar. Cleopatra, Queen of Egypt, becomes infatuated with Mark Antony. Costly four-hour epic functions like a blimp-sized multi-colored sleeping tablet. Historical characters are utterly dwarfed by the film's massive scope, and audiences are benumbed by a spectacle of crowd scenes and opulent, grotesque interiors. Taylor looks and often acts like a sex bomb ruler, while Harrison has some fiction of Caesar's majesty. Burton, however, is hopelessly wooden. Hard to believe this came from director Mankiewicz. **246m/C** VHS, DVD. Elizabeth Taylor, Richard Burton, Rex Harrison, Roddy McDowall, Martin Landau, Pamela Brown, Michael Hordern, Kenneth Haigh, Andrew Keir, Hume Cronyn, Carroll O'Connor; **D:** Joseph L. Mankiewicz. **W:** Joseph L. Mankiewicz; **C:** Leon Shamroy; **M:** Alex North. Oscars '63: Art Dir (Set Dec), Color, Color Cinematog, Costume Des, (C), Visual FX; Natl. Bd. of Review '63: Actor (Harrison).

Cleopatra ⚐⚐ 1934 Early Hollywood DeMille's version was extravagant. After Caesar's lust for Marc Antony after Julius Caesar's death. Intermittently interesting extravaganza. Colbert seems to be enjoying herself in the lead role in this hokey, overdone epic. Includes the original theatrical trailer on laser-track 2. Remade in 1963. **100m/B** VHS, DVD. Claudette Colbert, Warren William, Gertrude Michael, Joseph Schildkraut Sir C. Aubrey Smith; **D:** Cecil B. DeMille; **C:** Victor Milner. Oscars '34: Cinematog.

Cleopatra Jones ⚐⚐ 1973 (PG) Lean and lethal government agent with considerable martial arts prowess takes on loathsome drug lords. Dobson's fetching as the lead performer in this fast-paced, violent flick. Followed by "Cleopatra Jones and the Casino of Gold." **89m/C** VHS, DVD. Tamara Dobson, Shelley Winters, Bernie Casey, Brenda Sykes, Albert "Poppy" Popwell,

Cleopatra Jones & the Casino of Gold ⚐⚐ 1975 (R) Dobson returns as the lethal, physically imposing federal agent to Hong Kong to take on a powerful druglord in this sequel to "Cleopatra Jones." Watch for sexy Stevens as the Dragon Lady. **96m/C** VHS. Tamara Dobson, Stella Stevens, Norman Fell, Albert "Poppy" Popwell; **D:** Charles "Chuck" Bail.

Cleopatra's Second Husband ⚐⚐ 2000 (R) Let's play master and servant. Whiny, selfish yuppie couple Robert (Hipp) and Hallie (Schram) go on vacation and need houseseaters for their fabulous L.A. pad. They accept a recommendation and Sophie (Mitchell). Some friends—when the Marrs return early, their housesitters ask to stay on a little longer and proceed to take over. Hallie takes off after Robert gets in on with Sophie but the sexual/mind games are just beginning. **92m/C** VHS, DVD. Paul Hipp, Boyd Kestner, Radha Mitchell, Bitty Schram, Alexis Arquette, Jonathan Penner; **D:** Jonathan Reiss. **W:** Jonathan Reiss. **C:** Matt Faw; **M:** Gary Barger.

Clerks ⚐⚐⚐ 1994 (R) "What kind of convenience store do you run here? Day in the life of a convenience store clerk is an often hilarious lesson in the profane from first time writer/director Smith (who has a cameo as Silent Bob). Twenty-two-year-old Dante Hicks (O'Halloran) is a disaffected New Jersey Quick Stop employee who spends most of his time bored and dealing with borderline crazies. The next-door video store is clerked by his best friend Randal (Anderson), who derives equal delight from tormenting his customers and debating absolutely anything (especially anything sexual). Nothing much actually happens but the very low-budget ($27,575) production has a decidedly scuzzy charm and a cult following. Based on the director's four years of clerking at the Quick Stop and shot on location. **89m/B** VHS, DVD. UMD. Brian O'Halloran, Jeff Anderson, Marilyn Ghigliotti, Lisa Spoonhauer, Jason Mewes; **Cameos:** Kevin Smith; **D:** Kevin Smith; **W:** Kevin Smith; **C:** David Klein; **M:** Scott Angley. Sundance '94: Filmmakers Trophy.

Clerks 2 ⚐⚐⚐ 2006 (R) Writer/director/actor Kevin Smith revisits the New Jersey suburban landscape that put him and his recurring characters on the map 12 years ago. Little has changed in the lives or ambitions of clerks Dante (Brian O'Halloran) and Randal (Jeff Anerson)—they still pass the time with Smith's signature debates and diatribes on such topics as beastiality, "The Man," and the virtues of "Star Wars" vs. "Lord of the Rings"—while harassing the occasional, unfortunate customer. The same semi-professional, low-budget charm of its predecessor makes for a strong follow-up. Simply put, if you liked "Clerks," you'll like "Clerks II"; if you were offended by the first, you'll be horrified by this one. **96m/C** DVD, HD DVD. US US Brian O'Halloran, Jeff Anderson, Jason Mewes, Rosario Dawson, Kevin Smith, Jennifer Schwalbach Smith, Jason Lee, Ethan Suplee, Trevor Fehrman, Kevin Weisman, Wanda Sykes; **Cameos:** Ben Affleck; **D:** Kevin Smith; **W:** Kevin Smith; **M:** James L. Venable.

Click ⚐⚐ 2006 (PG-13) Workaholic family man Michael Newman (Sandler) needs a universal remote to simplify at all. Based on the thing in his life. Seinscle's Morty (Walken) hands over a special device that allows Michael to pause, mute, fast-forward, and rewind his actual life. Naturally, this is not the blessing that Michael first imagines it to be. Sandler does some more of his disgruntled man-child shtick, Walken is benignly crazy, and Beckinsale is nagging and hot. **98m/C** DVD, Blu-ray Disc. US Adam Sandler, Kate Beckinsale, Christopher Walken, Sean Astin, David Hasselhoff, Henry Winkler, Julie Kavner, Jennifer Coolidge; **D:** Frank Coraci; **W:** Mark O'Keefe, Steve Koren; **C:** Dean Semler; **M:** Rupert Gregson-Williams.

The Client ⚐⚐½ 1994 (PG-13) Another legal thriller from the Grisham factory. Reggie Love (Sarandon) is a troubled attorney hired by 11-year-old Mark (Renfro),

A Climate for Killing ⚐⚐½ 1991 (R) Arizona police are baffled when a woman murdered 16 years earlier is again found dead. Case open? Hunks Bauer and Beck are earnest in leads, and Ross and Sara are foxy. Passable entertainment. **104m/C** VHS. Steven Bauer, John Beck, Katharine Ross, Mia Sara, John Diehl, Phil Brock.

Clifford woof! 1992 (PG) Short plays a 10-year-old in an effort delayed by Orion's financial crisis. Creepy little Clifford's uncle Martin (Grodin) rues the day he volunteered to babysit his nephew to prove to his girlfriend (Steenburgen) how much he likes kids. Clifford terrorizes Grodin in fashion that raises questions about who was controlling the bodies of the producers. To create the effect of Short really being short, other actors stood on boxes and sets were built slightly larger. **90m/C** VHS, DVD. Martin Short, Charles Grodin, Mary Steenburgen, Dabney Coleman, Sonia Jackson Rock, Steven Kampmann, Will Aldis; **C:** John A Alonzo; **M:** Richard Gibbs.

Clifford's Really Big Movie ⚐⚐½ 2004 (G) Animated tale of TV's lovably oversized canine hero Clifford (Ritter), and normal-sized friends Cleo the poodle (Summer) and T-Bone the mutt (McHale), who take to the road after the Big Red Dog mistakenly thinks his large appetite is causing his owners to go broke. The trio join up with a traveling carnival populated by plenty of child-delighting characters. Clifford revives the Bowery Boys are at their best as they invade a star, all in the hope that the act will help him win a lifetime supply of his fave snack Tummy Yummies. Mildly evil doggie-treat tycoon (Goodman) has other plans for Clifford, however, and plots to kidnap the dog. Extremely gentle story and nice message especially suitable for younger viewers, older watchers won't find much here. **73m/C** VHS, DVD. **D:** Robert Ramirez; **W:** Robert Ramirez, Rhett Reese; **M:** Jody Gray; **V:** John Ritter, Wayne Brady, Jenna Elfman, John Goodman, Kel Mitchell, Judge Reinhold, Kath Soucie, Cree Summer, Grey DeLisle, Wilmer Valderrama, Earl Boen, Teresa Ganzel, Jess Harnell, Ernie Hudson, Oren Williams, Cam(eron) Clarke.

Clipped Wings ⚐⚐½ 1953 The Bowery Boys are at their best as they invade the army while visiting a friend, in the process of their usual bumblings, they uncover a Nazi plot. **62m/B** VHS. Leo Gorcey, Huntz Hall, Bernard Gorcey, David Condon, Bennie Bartlett, June Vincent, Mary Treen, Philip Van Zandt, Elaine Riley, Jeanne Dean, Lyle Talbot; **D:** Edward L. Bernds.

Cloak and Dagger ⚐⚐½ 1946 An American physicist joins the secret service during WWII and infiltrates Nazi territory to release a kidnapped scientist who is forced to build a nuclear bomb. Disappointing spy show with muted anti-nuclear tone. **106m/B** VHS, DVD. Gary Cooper, Lilli Palmer, Robert Alda, James Flavin, Vladimir Sokoloff, J. Edward Bromberg, Marc Lawrence, Ludwig Stossel; **D:** Fritz Lang; **W:** Ring Lardner Jr., (John B. Sherry) Maltz; **M:** Max Steiner.

Cloak & Dagger ⚐⚐ 1984 (PG) A young boy, last seen befriending E.T., depends upon his imaginary super-friend to help him out when some real-life agents are after his video game. Coleman is particularly fun as both dad and fantasy hero.

ro), who witnessed the suicide of a Mafia attorney and now knows more than he should. Ambitious federal prosecutor Foltrigg's (Jones) willing to risk the boy's life in exchange for career advancement. Lacks the "mega-big Hollywood names of "The Firm" and "The Pelican Brief" but gains solid acting in return with Renfro's film debut. No frills, near-faithful adaptation by Schumacher basically traveling down the path of least resistance. Filmed on location in Memphis. **121m/C** VHS, DVD. Susan Sarandon, Tommy Lee Jones, Brad Renfro, Mary-Louise Parker, Anthony LaPaglia, Bradley Whitford, Anthony Edwards, Ossie Davis, Walter Olkewicz, J.T. Walsh, Will Patton, Anthony Heald, William H. Macy; **D:** Joel Schumacher; **W:** Robert Getchell, Akira Goldsman; **C:** Tony Pierce-Roberts; **M:** Howard Shore. British Acad. '94: Actress (Sarandon).

Cliffhanger ⚐⚐⚐ 1993 (R) Action-packed thriller. Expert climber Gabe Walker (Stallone) faces his greatest challenge when criminal mastermind Lithgow and his henchman appear on the scene. Turner plays fellow climber and love interest. Lithgow makes a particularly convincing, if not downright chilling, murderous thief. Filmed in the Italian Alps with a budget of $70 million-plus; boasts stunning cinematography and breathtaking footage of the Dolomite mountain range. Harlin's expert pacing and direction combine to produce maximum thrills and suspense. The hit Stallone's been waiting for, placing eighth on the list of top 1993 boxoffice grossers. **113m/C** VHS, DVD. Sylvester Stallone, John Lithgow, Michael Rooker, Janine Turner, Rex Linn, Caroline Goodall, Leon, Paul Winfield, Ralph Waite, Craig Fairbrass, Michelle Joyner, Max Perlich; **D:** Renny Harlin; **W:** Sylvester Stallone, Michael France; **C:** Alex Thomson; **M:** Trevor Jones.

The Climb ⚐⚐½ 1997 (PG-13) In late '50s Baltimore, 12-year-old Danny (Smith) is the target of bullies and humiliated by the fact that his dad Earl (Strathairn) is accused of cowardice before his own courage by climbing the local, soon-to-be-demolished 203-foot radio tower. Danny is unexpected aided by his crotchety neighbor, Chuck Langer (Hurt), a hard-drinking grump dying of cancer. But when Danny gets into trouble, it's his dad who comes to the rescue. Nostalgic family fare. **94m/C** VHS, DVD, **FR FZ** Gregory Edward Smith, John Hurt, David Strathairn, Stephen McHattie, Seth Smith, Sarah Buxton; **D:** Bob Swaim; **W:** Vince McKewin; **C:** Allen Guilford; **M:** Greco Casadeus.

The Climb ⚐⚐½ 1987 (PG) German mountain climbers attempt to conquer the Himalayan Nanga Parbat, the world's fifth highest peak. Sometimes compelling film based on 1953 expedition in which only one member succeeded in reaching the summit. **90m/C** VHS. Bruce Greenwood, James Hurdle, Kenneth Welsh; **D:** Donald Shebib; **W:** Donald Shebib; **M:** Peter Jer-myn.

The Climax ⚐⚐½ 1944 Technicolor highlights this horror saga of obsession. House physician for Vienna's Royal Theatre, Dr. Hohner (Karloff) kills opera singer Marcellina (Vincent) when she rehears the beautiful voice of Angela (Foster). Twenty years later, Hohner tries to prevent her singing. Now, it's up to Angela's composer friend Franz (Bey) to overcome the doctor's evil influence. Adapted from a play by Edward Locke. Waggner directed this "The Phantom of the Opera" clone using the 1943 "Phantom" remake sets as the 1943 "Phantom" remake. **86m/C** VHS, DVD. Boris Karloff, Susanna Foster, Turhan Bey, Gale Sondergaard, Thomas Gomez, June Vincent, Jane Farrar, Scotty Beckett; **D:** George Waggner; **C:** Curt Siodmak, Lynn Starling; **C:** Hal Mohr, William Howard Greene; **M:** Edward Ward.

Climates ⚐⚐⚐ Iklimler 2006 A Turkish couple's decision to call things off spans not only their native countryside but also several seasons. Beginning in summer, the distant 40ish professor Isa and his much-younger TV art director girlfriend Bahar break up, through the reasons are never given. In fact, not much is said throughout, though their feelings are usually obvious. Moving along to fall Isa has a manic sex encounter with Serap (Kesal)—a possible culprit in Isa and Bahar's troubles—even though, in winter, Serap tells Isa where to find Bahar. Writer-director-lead actor Nuri Bilge Ceylan (Isa) is the real-life husband of Ebru Ceylan (Bahar). In Turkish with subtitles. **97m/C** DVD. **FR TU** Nuri Bilge Ceylan, Ebru Ceylan, Nazan Kirilmis, Mehmet Eryilmaz, Arif Asci, Can Ozbatur; **D:** Nuri Bilge Ceylan; **W:** Nuri Bilge Ceylan; **C:** Gokhan Tiryaki.

Dedee Pfeiffer, Lu Leonard, Jack Dodson, Eloy Casados; **D:** J.S. Cardone; **W:** J.S. Cardone; **M:** Robert Folk.

in an interesting family adventure. 101m/C VHS, DVD. Dabney Coleman, Henry Thomas, Michael Murphy, John McIntire, Jeanette Nolan; D: Richard Franklin; M: Brian May.

The Clock 🦴🦴🦴 *Under the Clock* 1945 Appealing romance about an office worker who meets and falls in love with a soldier on two-day leave in NYC. Charismatic Walker and likeable Garland make a fine screen couple, and Wynn is memorable as the drunk. 91m/B VHS, DVD. Judy Garland, Robert Walker, James Gleason, Marshall Thompson, Keenan Wynn; D: Vincente Minnelli; C: George J. Folsey; M: George Bassman.

Clockers 🦴🦴🦴 1995 (R) Strike (Phifer), leader of a group of bottom-feeding drug dealers ("clockers"), engages in a power struggle with his boss (Lindo), his do-the-right-thing brother Victor (Washington), and his own conscience. Wynn is suspected of murder by relentless narcotics cop Rocco Klein (Keitel). Supported by an excellent cast, first-timer Phifer surprises with a fierce and powerful performance. Lindo, in particular, stands out as the paternally evil Rodney. Aggressively edited, with Turturro's performance mostly lost on the cutting room floor. Critically lauded cinematography is marred by the occasional boom shot. Poignant and compelling street drama is based on the Richard Price novel. Lee took over after Scorsese and De Niro dropped out to make "Casino." 128m/C VHS, DVD. Mekhi Phifer, Harvey Keitel, John Turturro, Delroy Lindo, Keith David, Isaiah Washington IV, Lisa Arrindell Anderson, Kirk "Sticky Fingaz" Jones; D: Spike Lee; W: Spike Lee, Richard Price; C: Malik Hassan Sayeed; M: Terence Blanchard.

The Clockmaker 🦴🦴🦴½ *L'Horloger de Saint-Paul* 1973 Contemplative drama about a clockmaker whose life is shattered when his son is arrested as a political assassin. Tavernier regular Noiret excels in the lead. In French with English subtitles. 105m/C VHS, DVD. FR Philippe Noiret, Jean Rochefort, Jacques Denis, William Sabatier, Christine Pascal; D: Bertrand Tavernier; W: Bertrand Tavernier, Jean Aurenche, Pierre Bost; C: Sylvain Rougerie; M: Philippe Sarde.

Clockstoppers 🦴🦴½ 2002 (PG) Amusing kid fare has heroes Zak (Bradford) and Venezuelan exchange student Francesca (Garces) zipping around in speeded-up "hypertime" to rescue Zak's scientists dad Dr. Gibbs (Thomas) from time-traveling baddies, headed by corporate bigwig Henry Gates (Biehn). It seems the wristwatch/time machine Gibbs invented needs tweaking, so Gibbs and top grad student Dopler (Stewart) are kidnaped to fix the snag by the evil QT corporation, which wants to use the device to, what else, conquer the world. The teen duo must do their rescuing, however, before they all prematurely age in hypertime (one of the sleep gags). No stranger to sci-fi, director Frakes (Riker on "Star Trek: Next Generation") makes the most of the inherent FX. 94m/C VHS, DVD. US Jesse Bradford, French Stewart, Michael Biehn, Paula Garces, Robin Thomas, Julia Sweeney, Linda Kim, Garikayi Mutambirwa; D: Jonathan Frakes; W: Rob Hedden, J. David Stem, David N. Weiss; C: Tim Suhrstedt; M: Jamshied Sharifi.

Clockwatchers 🦴🦴½ 1997 (PG-13) Decent cast gets wasted in a slice of life story that goes nowhere. Meek temp Iris's (Collette) new assignment is at a big, faceless credit company. Iris is taken in hand by fellow temps Margaret (Posey), Paula (Kudrow), and Jane (Ubach), who like to complain about how badly they're treated when the company makes an announcement about a rash of petty thefts and the temps get blamed. That's it. 105m/C VHS, DVD. Toni Collette, Parker Posey, Lisa Kudrow, Alanna Ubach, Stanley DeSantis, Jamie Kennedy, Paul Dooley; D: Jill Sprecher; W: Jill Sprecher, Karen Sprecher; C: Jim Denault.

Clockwise 🦴🦴½ 1986 (PG) Monty Python regular Cleese is a teacher preoccupied by punctuality. His neurosis proves his undoing when he falls victim to misadventure while traveling to deliver a speech. Cleese is acceptable, dialogue and story is less so, though sprinkled with a fair amount of humor. 96m/C VHS, DVD. GB John Cleese, Penelope Wilton, Alison Steadman, Stephen Moore, Sharon Maiden; D: Christopher Morahan; W: Michael Frayn; C: John Coquillon; M: George Fenton.

A Clockwork Orange 🦴🦴🦴🦴 1971 (R) In the Britain of the near future, a sadistic punk leads a gang on nightly rape and murder sprees, then is captured and becomes the subject of a grim experiment to eradicate his violent tendencies in this extraordinary adaptation of Anthony Burgess's controversial novel. The film is an exhilarating experience, with an outstanding performance by McDowell as the funny, fierce psychopath. Many memorable, disturbing sequences, including a rape conducted while assailant McDowell belts "Singing in the Rain." Truly outstanding, provocative work from master filmmaker Kubrick. 137m/C VHS, DVD, Blu-ray Disc, HD DVD. Malcolm McDowell, Patrick Magee, Adrienne Corri, Michael Bates, Warren Clarke, Aubrey Morris, James Marcus, Steven Berkoff, David Prowse, John Clive, Carl Duering, Miriam Karlin; D: Stanley Kubrick; W: Stanley Kubrick; C: John Alcott; M: Walter (Wendy) Carlos. AFI '98: Top 100; N.Y. Film Critics '71: Director (Kubrick), Film.

Clodhopper 🦴🦴 1917 A farmboy decides to head out for New York where he achieves fame on Broadway for his dance number, the "Clophooper Glide." He stays true to his hometown girl, however, and returns to save his father's farm from financial ruin. 47m/B VHS. Charles Ray, Margery Wilson; D: Victor Schertzinger.

The Clones 🦴🦴 1973 (PG) A doctor discovers a government experiment engineered to murder him with a perfect clone. 90m/C VHS. Michael Greene, Gregory Sierra; D: Paul Hunt, Lamar Card.

Clones of Bruce Lee 🦴🦴 1980 (R) It's a martial arts free-for-all as bold masters from throughout the world duel for supremacy in the realm of self defense. If you like martial arts movies, you'll probably like this one. If you don't know if you like martial arts movies, head out with one of the actual Bruce Lee's flicks. 87m/C VHS, DVD. Dragon Lee, Bruce Le, Bruce Lai, Bruce Thai; D: Joseph Kong.

The Clonus Horror 🦴🦴½ 1979 *The Clonus Horror* 1979 A scientist discovers a government plot to clone the population by freezing bodies alive and using their parts in surgery. 90m/C VHS, DVD. Tim Donnelly, Keenan Wynn, Peter Graves, Dick Sargent, Paulette Breen; D: Robert S. Fiveson.

Close Encounters of the Third Kind 🦴🦴🦴🦴 1977 (PG) Middle-American strangers become involved in the attempts of benevolent aliens to contact earthlings. Despite the sometimes mundane nature of the characters, this Spielberg epic is a stirring achievement. Studded with classic sequences; the ending is an exhilarating experience of special effects and peace-on-earth feelings. Dreyfuss and Dillon excel as friends who are at once bewildered and obsessed by the alien presence, and French filmmaker Truffaut is also strong as the stern, ultimately benign scientist. 152m/C VHS, DVD, Blu-ray Disc. Richard Dreyfuss, Teri Garr, Melinda Dillon, Francois Truffaut, Bob Balaban, Cary Guffey, J. Patrick McNamara; D: Steven Spielberg; W: Steven Spielberg; C: Vilmos Zsigmond; M: John Williams. Oscars '77: Cinematog., Sound FX Editing; AFI '98: Top 100. Natl. Film Reg. '07.

Close My Eyes 🦴🦴 1991 (R) Insecure Natalie (Reeves) is newly married to wealthy and garrulous entrepreneur Sinclair (Rickman) when she reunites with her long-estranged younger brother, Richard (Owen). Richard has just taken a job as a city planner in London and is suddenly Natalie's confidante and soon much more. The simmering sexual tension between the two finally explodes into a volatile relationship that becomes an obsession for Richard. And when Natalie decides to break off their affair, he's determined to stop her. Reeves's character is somewhat whiny and unappealing so it's up to the men to carry the movie, which they do with aplomb. 105m/C VHS, DVD. GB Alan Rickman, Clive Owen, Saskia Reeves, Karl Johnson, Lesley Sharp; D: Stephen Poliakoff; W: Stephen Poliakoff; C: Witold Stok; M: Michael Gibbs.

Close to Eden 🦴🦴 *Urga* 1990 (PG) A peasant couple living in inner Mongolia with their three children are prevented by strict Chinese law from having a fourth. The husband sets out from his village to obtain birth control from the nearby town. While on his way, the farmer (Bayaertu) saves a Russian truck driver (Gostukhin) after he drives into a lake. Sergei is introduced to another way of life when he's taken home by his rescuer to meet the family and becomes accustomed to the tranquility of farm life in the rural Mongolian steppe. Essentially a story about the changes modern civilization can bring to a rural way of life. Filmed in Mongolia. In Russian with English subtitles. 109m/C VHS. RU Baoyinhexige, Badema, Nikita Mikhalkov; D: Nikita Mikhalkov; W: Rustam Ibragimbekov; M: Eduard Artemyev. Venice Film Fest. '91: Film.

Close to Home 🦴🦴 1986 A runaway fleeing a home life of abuse and neglect befriends a TV journalist doing a story on similar girls. She turns to him for support after she is arrested and returned home. Merely mediocre. 93m/C VHS. CA Daniel Allman, Jillian Fargey, Anne Petrie; D: Rick Beairsto.

Close to Leo 🦴🦴 *Tout Contre Leo* 2002 Uneven-but-intimate family drama finds 20-year-old Leo (Mignard), the eldest of four sons, revealing to his family that their youngest, 12-year-old Marcel (Lespert), is too young to hear the news, although the kid is bright enough to realize something serious is going on and resentful that he is being left out. Honore adapted and directed from his own 1996 novel. French with subtitles. 90m/C DVD. FR Pierre Mignard, Yannis Lespert, Marie Bunel, Dominic Gould, Rodolphe Pauly, Jeremie Lippmann; D: Christophe Honore; W: Christophe Honore, Dias teme; C: Remy Chevrin; M: Alexandre Beaupain. TV

Close Your Eyes 🦴½ *Hypnotic; Dr. Sleep* 2002 (R) Psychic hypnotist Michael Strother (Visnjic) has limited himself to curing smokers after an unsavory event in the U.S. caused him to flee to the UK. When Janet (Henderson), who also happens to be a British cop, comes to Michael hoping to kick her cigarette habit, Michael has a involvement in the highly publicized "tattoo murderer" case and the serial killer's only living victim, Heather. After hypnotizing the now-mute Heather to find some answers, Michael is knee deep in the case against the serial killer. As the end approaches, the film boasts interesting locales, suitably moody climate, and good performances. 108m/C DVD. GB Goran Visnjic, Shirley Henderson, Miranda Otto, Paddy Considine, Claire Rushbrook, Fiona Shaw, Corin Redgrave, Sophie Stuckey; D: Nick Willing; W: Nick Willing, William Brookfield; C: Peter Sova; M: Simon Boswell.

Closely Watched Trains 🦴🦴🦴½ *Ostre Sledovane Vlaky* 1966 A novice train dispatcher attempts to gain sexual experience in German-occupied Czechoslovakia during WWII. Many funny scenes in this film regarded by some as a classic. Based upon the Czech novel by Bohumil Hrabal. In Czech with English subtitles. 89m/B VHS, DVD. CZ Vaclav Neckar, Jitka Bendova, Vladimir Valenta, Josef Somr; D: Jiri Menzel; W: Jiri Menzel; C: Jaromir Sofr; M: Jiri Sust. Oscars '67: Foreign Film.

The Closer 🦴🦴½ 1991 (R) Aiello is "The Closer," a high-powered salesman whose world is falling apart. Somewhere between the money and the power, he's lost touch with his family and the truly important things in life. Is it too late to get them back? 87m/C VHS. Danny Aiello, Michael Pare, Joe Cortese, Justine Bateman, Diane Baker, James Karen, Rick Aiello, Michael Lerner; D: Dimitri Logothetis; W: Robert Keats, Louis LaRusso II; C: Al Kasha.

Closer 🦴🦴🦴 2004 (R) Love stinks. Especially in this caustic adaptation by Marber of his 1997 drama. Waifish stripper Alice (Portman) enchants writer Dan (Law) after they meet cute in London. Dan later writes a novel about his life with Alice and indulges in a flirtation with successful photographer Anna (Roberts). Dan then decides to impersonate Anna during an Internet sex chat and arranges to meet dermatologist Larry (a ferocious performance by Owen), who does meet, and eventually marries, the real Anna. Dan has an affair with Anna, which Larry finds out about (in a laceratingly brutal verbal scene), and Larry meets the abandoned Alice without knowing about their second-hand connection. Marber changed Alice's fate from his play and made both female characters American to accommodate his leads. Owen played the role of Dan in the original National Theatre production. 101m/C DVD, HD DVD, DVD. US Julia Roberts, Jude Law, Natalie Portman, Clive Owen; D: Mike Nichols; W: Patrick Marber; C: Stephen Goldblatt; M: Steven Patrick Morrissey. British Acad. '04: Support. Actor (Owen); Golden Globes '05: Support. Actor (Owen), Support. Actress (Portman).

Closer and Closer 🦴🦴½ 1996 Cable thriller finds author Kate Sander (Delaney) paralyzed after being stalked by someone resembling the stalker character in her last book "Gargoyle." Kate works with wheelchair-bound personal trainer B.J. Connors (York) to regain her strength, which she'll need as she writes "Gargoyle 2." This time Kate's decided to kill off her stalker/serial killer and soon real murders begin to occur. 93m/C VHS, DVD. Kim Delaney, John J. York, Peter Outerbridge, Peter MacNeill, Scott Craft, Anthony Sherwood; D: Fred Gerber; W: Matt Dorff. CABLE

The Closet 🦴🦴½ *Le Placard* 2000 (R) Francois Pignon (Auteuil) is a dull everyguy accountant who learns he's about to be fired after 20 years (from his job at a condom factory). His new (gay) neighbor Belone (Aumont) makes a unique suggestion—he will send doctored photos, showing Pignon at a gay bar, to Pignon's company and they will be forced to back down or be accused of sexual discrimination. Francois protests he can't pass as gay but he doesn't have to—his bosses and coworkers believe the rumors and make their own assumptions, including the homophobic personnel director Felix (Depardieu) who fears for his own job if he's not especially nice to Francois. Balances neatly between slapstick and sentiment. French with subtitles. 86m/C VHS, DVD. FR Daniel Auteuil, Gerard Depardieu, Thierry Lhermitte, Michel Aumont, Michele Laroque, Jean Rochefort, Alexandra Vandernoot; D: Francis Veber; W: Francis Veber; C: Luciano Tovoli; M: Vladimir Cosma.

Closet Land 🦴½ 1990 (R) Severe, stylized political allegory aims high but fails to convincingly distill totalitarian repression into just two characters—a government inquisitor and his captive, a woman subjected to hideous mental and physical torture. Child-molesting emerges as an ill-advised subtheme. A better video on the same subject: "Interrogation," from Poland. 95m/C VHS. Madeleine Stowe, Alan Rickman; D: Radha Bharadwaj; W: Radha Bharadwaj; C: Bill Pope; M: Richard Einhorn.

Closure woof! *Straightheads* 2007 (R) Cheap, violent and nasty. Alice and Adam are brutally attacked by a group of hunters while driving home from a country party. A chance meeting leads Alice to the identity of the attackers and she forces the guilt-ridden Adam to go along with her plan for revenge. 80m/C DVD. GB Gillian Anderson, Danny Dyer, Ralph Brown; D: Dan Reed; W: Dan Reed; C: Chris Seager; M: Ilan Eshkeri.

Cloud Dancer 🦴🦴 1980 (PG) A self-absorbed acrobat uses and abuses those around him, including his girlfriend. Carradine and O'Neill fail to distinguish themselves in this mediocre film. 107m/C VHS. David Carradine, Jennifer O'Neill, Joseph Bottoms, Colleen Camp; D: Barry Brown; W: William Goodhart.

The Clouded Yellow ♂♂½ 1951 Young, lovely, and a little unstable, Sophie Malraux (Simmons) is accused of murdering the handyman who worked for her guardians (Jones and Dresdel). Ex-British Secret Service agent David Somers (Howard), who's in love with Sophie, helps her escape from jail and the two head for Liverpool and a ship to Mexico. But the police (hoping to find the real killer) are hot on their trail. Romantic suspense with good lead pairing. 95m/B VHS. *GB* Jean Simmons, Trevor Howard, Sonia Dresdel, Barry Jones, Maxwell Reed, Kenneth More, Andre Morell, Geoffrey Keen; *D:* Ralph Thomas; *W:* Eric Ambler; *C:* Geoffrey Unsworth.

Clouds over Europe ♂♂ → *Q Planes* 1939 A test pilot and a man from Scotland Yard team up to find out why new bomber planes are disappearing. 82m/B VHS. Laurence Olivier, Valerie Hobson, Ralph Richardson, George Curzon, George Merritt, Gus McNaughton, David Tree, Sandra Storme, Hay Petrie, Frank Fox, Gordon McLeod, John Longden, Reginald Purcell, John Laurie, Pat Aherne; *D:* Tim Whelan; *W:* Ian Dalrymple; *C:* Harry Stradling Sr.

Clown ♂♂½ 1953 A broken-down funny man with a worshipful son obtains one last career opportunity. This "Champ"-derived tearjerker features credible playing from Skelton and Considine as father and son, respectively. 91m/B VHS. Red Skelton, Jane Greer, Tim Considine, Steve Forrest; *D:* Robert Z. Leonard; *C:* Paul Vogel.

Clown House ♂ 1988 (R) Young brothers are stalked in their home by three demonic clowns. 95m/C VHS, DVD. Nathan Forrest Winters, Brian McHugh, Sam Rockwell, Viletta Skillman, Timothy Enos, Tree; *D:* Victor Salva.

Clown Murders ♂ 1983 Posh Halloween party is undone when a cruel group fakes a kidnapping to ruin a too-prosperous pal's business deal. Awkward thriller boasts little suspense. Candy plays it straight, mostly, in this one. 94m/C VHS. John Candy, Al Waxman, Susan Keller, Lawrence Dane; *D:* Martyn Burke.

Clowning Around ♂♂½ 1992 Simon, who has lived in foster homes all his life, dreams of becoming a famous circus clown. When he's sent to a new home, his new foster parents think his idea is silly, so he runs away and joins the circus. There he meets Anatole, a European clown has-been who can no longer perform because of injuries. Simon believes Anatole can teach him how to make his dream come true. Part of the

Clowning Around 2 ♂♂½ 1993 The continuing story of Sim, whose dream is to become a world-famous clown. Now a member of the Winter Circus in Paris, he is still training with his mentor Anatole. But Sim is dissatisfied and when he befriends Eve, another young clown, he learns an experimental style of clowning which gets them both fired. He first follows Eve to her own home in Australia where he has been left the co-owner of a less-than-successful circus by a former employer. Filmed on location in Paris, France and Perth, Australia. 125m/C VHS. *AU* Clayton Williamson, Jean-Michel Dagory, Ernie Dingo, Frederique Fouche; *D:* George Whaley.

Clowning Around → "Wonderworks" series. 165m/C VHS. *AU* Clayton Williamson, Jean-Michel Dagory, Ernie Dingo; *D:* George Whaley.

The Clowns ♂♂♂½ 1971 (G) An idiosyncratic documentary about circus clowns. Director Fellini has fashioned an homage that is sincere, entertaining, and personal. Contains some truly poignant sequences. Made for Italian TV with English subtitles. 90m/C VHS. *IT* D: Federico Fellini; *W:* Federico Fellini, Bernardino Zapponi; *C:* Dario Di Palma; *M:* Nino Rota. TV

The Club ♂♂♂ 1994 (R) Typical teens-soccer coach tries to train and motivate a mediocre squad into one winning playing for—and perhaps even winning—the league cup. Conventional sports story is significantly improved by Thompson's rendering of the coach. 99m/C VHS. *AU* Jack Thompson, Graham Kennedy, John Howard, Alan Cassell; *D:* Bruce Beresford; *W:* David Williamson.

The Club ♂♂½ 1981 (PG) A soccer coach tries to train and motivate a top some night life. Somewhat disappointing with Williams largely playing the straight man. Most laughs provided by Martin, particularly when she is assaulted by a snowball, and Moranis, who gets lost while windsurfing. 96m/C VHS, DVD. Robin Williams, Peter O'Toole, Rick Moranis, Andrea Martin, Jimmy Cliff, Brian Doyle-Murray, Twiggy, Eugene Levy, Adolph Caesar, Joanna Cassidy, Mary Gross, Carey Lowell, Robin Duke, Simon Jones; *D:* Harold Ramis; *M:* David Mansfield, Van Dyke Parks.

Club Dread ♂ → *Broken Lizard's Club Dread* 2004 (R) Fresh off spoofing highway patrolmen in Super Troopers, the Broken Lizard crew takes on beach vacation slasher movies. Typical teens-a killer on the loose at an island resort run by Jimmy Buffet wanna-be Coconut Pete (Paxton), interrupting the party. Stupidity ensues. Plot takes a backseat to lame gags, nudity, and slasher pic gore. Vacation elsewhere, because this club is a waste of time. 103m/C VHS, DVD. Bill Paxton, Jay Chandrasekhar, Kevin Heffernan, M.C. Gainey, Jordan Ladd, Lindsay Price, Michael Weaver, Samm Levine, Dan Montgomery Jr., Steve Lemme, Paul Soter, Erik Stolhanske, Brittany Daniel, Nat Faxon, Elena Lyons, Tanja (Tanya) Reichert; *D:* Jay Chandrasekhar; *W:* Jay Chandrasekhar, Kevin Heffernan, Steve Lemme, Paul Soter, Erik Stolhanske; *C:* Lawrence Sher; *M:* Nathan Barr.

Club Extinction ♂♂½ → *Docteur M* 1989 (R) A near-future thriller in which Berlin is plagued by a wave of suicides. An investigator suspects a spa representative and a media tycoon of being involved. Features a fine international cast, but the film is a lesser venture from prolific master Chabrol. 105m/C VHS. *GE* Alan Bates, Andrew McCarthy, Jennifer Beals, Jan Niklas, Hanns Zischler, Benoit Regent, Peter Fitz, Wolfgang Preiss, Isolde Barth; *D:* Claude Chabrol.

Club Fed ♂½ 1990 (PG-13) A rigid prison warden's plot to impose greater discipline is undone by inmate highjinks. Crude laughs and one-dimensional play from a cast of recognizable names and faces. 93m/C VHS, DVD. Judy Landers, Sherman Hemsley, Karen Black, Burt Young, Rick Schmidt, Allen (Goorwitz) Garfield, Joseph Campanella, Lyle Alzado, Mary Woronov, Debbie Lee Carrington; *D:* Nathaniel Christian; *C:* Arledge Armenaki.

Club Havana ♂½ 1946 A benevolent nightclub owner tries to save one of his singers from the depths of despair by reuniting her with her boyfriend. Minor musical with minor musical numbers. ♫ *Be-same Mucho*; *Tico Tico*. 62m/B VHS. Tom Neal, Margaret Lindsay, Don Douglas, Isabelita, Dorothy Morris, Ernest Truex; *D:* Edgar G. Ulmer.

Cloverfield ♂♂½ 2008 (PG-13) Rob (Stahl-David) and friends are enjoying his going-away party in Manhattan on the night before he is to leave for Japan. Pal Hud (Miller) is filming the party, complete with mushy goodbyes and confessions of things undone—and one night get drowsy here if not for the dizzying effect of Hud's camerawork—when there's a terrifying rattle. Thinking an earthquake hit, the friends rush to the roof only to realize it's no earthquake and the city's in total chaos, evidenced by screams and fire-balls and Lady Liberty's head (yes, the statue) rolling down a city street. Not to spoil the fun, but it's an old-fashioned monster movie. The "Blair Witch" generation will be nonplussed by the jumpy, hyperactive filming (the unfolding tragedy is all captured courtesy of Hud's digital video cam), and others will appreciate the nod to a scary monster and a little love story tossed in—mix it up and enjoy. 90m/C VHS, DVD. *US* Lizzy Caplan, Jessica Lucas, Michael Stahl-David, Mike Vogel, T.J. Miller, Odette Yustman; *D:* Matt Reeves; *W:* Drew Goddard; *C:* Michael Bonvillain.

Clue ♂♂ 1985 (PG) The popular boardgame's characters must unravel a night of murder at a spooky Victorian mansion. The entire cast seems to be subsisting on sugar, with wild eyes and frantic movements. One of three endings was shown in theaters—three theatrical version played with three alternate endings, and the video version shows all three successively. 96m/C VHS, DVD. Lesley Ann Warren, Tim Curry, Martin Mull, Madeline Kahn, Michael McKean, Christopher Lloyd, Eileen Brennan, Howard Hesseman, Lee Ving, Jane Wiedlin, Colleen Camp, Bill Henderson; *D:* Jonathan Lynn; *W:* John Landis, Jonathan Lynn; *C:* Victor Kemper; *M:* John Morris.

Clubhouse Detectives ♂½ 1995 (PG) When Billy witnesses a crime at a neighbor's no one believes him—except his friends, so the clubhouse detectives decide to investigate. 85m/C VHS, DVD. Michael Galeota, Jimmy Galeota, Suzanne Barnes; *D:* Eric Hendershot.

Club Vampire ♂ 1998 (R) Vampire Zero (Savage) wants to bite stripper Corri Zero (Andreff) but Laura (Parris) gets there first, and Corri starts to transform. Vampire leader Aiko (Parris) doesn't want any new converts and sends Zero to kill her. But Zero has other plans. A bore. 77m/C VHS, DVD. John Savage, Starr Andreeff, Diana Frank, Michael J. Anderson, Marriam Parris, Ross Malinger; *D:* Andy Ruben; *W:* Andy Ruben; *C:* Steve Gainer; *M:* David Mansfield. **VIDEO**

Club Paradise ♂♂ 1986 (PG-13) A Chicago fireman flees the big city for a faltering tropical resort and tries to develop some night life. Somewhat disappointing with Williams largely playing the Coolidge together. 60m/C VHS, DVD, Alan Thicke, Jim Carrey, Jean-Claude Kelly, Rita Coolidge, Ronnie Hawkins; *D:* David Mitchell, Bob Giraldi; *M:* Peter Bernstein.

Club Med ♂♂ 1983 (PG) An insecure comedian and his goofy friend try to make the most of a ski vacation. Perhaps your only chance to catch Thicke, Killy, and Coolidge together. 60m/C VHS, Alan Thicke, Jim Carrey, Jean-Claude Killy, Rita Coolidge, Ronnie Hawkins; *D:* David Mitchell.

Club Life ♂♂ 1986 (R) A hardened biker finds sex, drugs, and violence on the mean streets. What did he expect? 93m/C VHS. Tony Curtis, Dee Wallace Stone, Tom Parsekian, Michael Parks, Jamie Barrett; *D:* Norman Thaddeus Vane.

Club Land ♂♂½ 2001 (R) Stuey Waters (Weber) is an unhappy talent agent, working for his hard-driving, abrasive father Willie (Alda) in the 1950s. When their biggest client, comic Lou Montane (Garrett) fires Willie, Stuey doesn't know how to break it to his old man that he doesn't want to continue in the business. Now, with Steven Weber, Alan Alda, Brad Garrett, Jenna Byrne, Louise Lasser, David Deblinger, Eugene Levy; *D:* Saul Rubinek; *M:* Steven Weber; *C:* Rene Ohashi. **C A B L E**

Clueless ♂♂♂ 1995 (PG-13) Watch out "Beverly Hills 90210," here comes Cher. No, not the singer Cher, but ultra-filthy-rich brat Cher, who's out to make over her classmates and teachers, specifically financial-not-shirted transfer student Tai (Murphy). Aerosmith's vamp Silverstone stars as the teenage manipulator who knows all too well how to get what she wits and directs a bright, surprisingly satirical romp 113m/C VHS, DVD. Alicia Silverstone, Stacey Dash, Paul Rudd, Brittany Murphy, Donald Faison, Julie Brown, Jeremy Sisto, Dan Hedaya, Wallace Shawn, Breckin Meyer, Elisa Donovan, Aida Linares; *D:* Amy Heckerling; *W:* Amy

Heckerling; *C:* Bill Pope; *M:* David Kitay, MTV Movie Awards '96: Female Perf. (Silverstone); Most Desirable Female (Silverstone); Natl. Soc. Film Critics '95: Screenplay; Blockbuster '96: Female Newcomer, T. (Silverstone).

The Clutching Hand ♂ 1936 The Clutching Hand seeks a formula that will turn metal into gold and detective Craig Kennedy is out to prevent him from doing so. A serial in 15 chapters on three cassettes. 268m/B VHS, DVD. Jack Mulhall, Rex Lease, Mae Busch, William Farnum, Robert Frazer, Reed Howes, Marion Shilling; *D:* Albert Herman.

Coach ♂♂½ 1978 (PG) Sexy woman is unintentionally hired to coach a high school basketball team and mold rookies into lusty young champions. Low-grade roundball fever. 100m/C VHS, DVD. Cathy Lee Crosby, Michael Biehn, Keenan Wynn, Sidney Wicks; *D:* Bud Townsend.

Coach Carter ♂♂♂ 2005 (PG-13) Based on a true story of a coach who benched his entire 'team until their grades improved. Coach Carter (Jackson) is perfect in the lead, as the even provides acceptable rendering of Lynn's tunes. Band drummer Helm shines as Lynn's father, and Jones is strong as Lynn's down-home husband. Uneven melodrama toward the end, but the film is still a good one. 137m/C DVD, UMD. *US* Samuel L. Jackson, Robert Richard, Debbi (Deborah) Morgan, Rick Gonzalez, Antwon Tanner, Denise Dowse, Rob Brown, Ashanti, Nana Gbewonyo, Channing Tatum, Texas Battle; *D:* Thomas Carter; *M:* Trevor Rabin.

Coal Miner's Daughter ♂♂♂ 1980 (PG) A strong bio of country singer Loretta Lynn, who rose from Appalachian poverty to Nashville riches. Spacek is perfect in the lead, as she even provides the 'familiar plot of inspirational teacher making a difference, the movie rises above due to a good supporting cast and a great performance by Jackson, making excellent use of his commanding screen presence. 125m/C VHS, DVD. Sissy Spacek, Tommy Lee Jones, Levon Helm, Beverly D'Angelo, D: Michael Apted; *C:* Ralf Bode. Academy Awards '80: Actress (Spacek); Golden Globes '81: Actress—Mus./Comedy (Spacek); Film—Mus./Comedy; L.A. Film Critics '80: Actress (Spacek); Natl. Bd. of Review '80: Actress (Spacek); N.Y. Film Critics '80: Actress (Spacek); Natl. Soc. Film Critics '80: Actress (Spacek).

The Coast Patrol ♂♂ 1925 B. Reeves Eason, responsible for the chariot scene in the silent "Ben Hur" and the action scenes in "The Charge of the Light Brigade," directed Fay in one of her earliest parts, eight years before the role that prompted her to say "I didn't realize that King Kong and I were going to be together for the rest of our lives, and longer..." 63m/B VHS. Kenneth McDonald, Claire De Lorez, Fay Wray; *D:* Bud Barsky.

Coast to Coast ♂♂ 2004 (R) An older married couple isn't sure they want to stay together anymore but luckily they have loads of time to figure things out cruising from Connecticut to L.A. to see their son tie the knot. 107m/C VHS, DVD. Richard Dreyfuss, Judy Davis, Selma Blair, Maximilian Schell, Jason Isaacs, Frederick Weller, Robert Wisdom; *D:* Paul Mazursky; *W:* Frederic Raphael; *C:* David J. Miller; *M:* Cliff Eidelman.

millan Schell, Fred Ward, Saul Rubinek, John Salley, Paul Mazursky, Kate Lynch, Richard Fitzpatrick, Clare Coulter, Catherine Disher, James Kee, Nancy Sakovich, David Julian Hirsh, Owen Rothamel, Rick Mota, Angela Asher, Catherine Burdon, Lyssa J. Caster, Laura Catalano, Paul Essiembre, Dominic Fung, Paula Garrido, Chris Gillett, Carolyn Goff, Lindsay Leese, Richard Partington, Les Porter, Krista Sutton, Joreen Todd; **D:** Paul Mazursky; **W:** Frederic Raphael; **C:** Jean Lepine; **M:** Bill Conti. **TV**

Coastlines ♂♂ **2002 (R)** Pulp noir in the Florida panhandle. Sonny (Olyphant) took the fall for his drug partners Fred (Forsythe) and Eddie (Lucas) Vance. Out of prison, he wants the $200K they owe him and to be left alone. The Vances would like Sonny gone permanently, which brings in Sonny's best bud, Dave (Brolin), who's the local sheriff, and his unsatisfied wife Ann (Wynter), immediately leading to a familiar and not very exciting triangle. Unfortunately, this is a mix of crime and sex, that never successfully meshes together. **110m/C DVD.** *US* Timothy Olyphant, Josh Brolin, Sarah Wynter, Scott Wilson, Angela Bettis, Josh(ua) Lucas, Robert Wisdom, Daniel von Bargen, Blake Lindsley, Bob Glaudini, Edwin Hodge, Abigail Mavity, Elizabeth Caity; **D:** Victor Nunez; **W:** Victor Nunez; **C:** Virgil Marcus Mirano; **M:** Charles Engstrom.

Cobb ♂♂♂ **1994 (R)** Biography of Ty Cobb (Jones), the universally acknowledged "most hated man in baseball" who, near the end of his life, realizes he doesn't want to be remembered in that way. So he hires sportswriter Al Stump (Wuhl) to ghostwrite (read: sugarcoat) his life story. As seen through Stump's eyes, Cobb is an unrelenting, petty, bigoted, hateful, paranoid, drunken, and yet compelling man. They form an uneasy bond as Stump duly records the fiction Cobb is feeding him, secretly deciding to write the truth after the legend's death. Jones is at his scene-chewing, antagonistic best, while Wuhl seems both overwhelmed and overshadowed as the embattled Stump. Shelton has something to say about American hero worship and a celebrity's desire for posterity, but with the focus intent on portraying Cobb's meanness, it's hard to say what. Surprisingly little baseball action for a baseball bio. Based on "Cobb: A Biography." **128m/C VHS, DVD.** Tommy Lee Jones, Robert Wuhl, Lolita (David) Davidovich; **D:** Ron Shelton; **W:** Ron Shelton; **C:** Russell Boyd.

Cobra ♂ **1925** To pay off the debts incurred by his profligate playboyance, Valentino takes a job with an antique dealer, falls for the dealer's secretary and arranges an assignment with the dealer's wife, who is inconveniently killed at the designated rendezvous. Complications abound as Valentino finds himself Sheik out of luck. Lease Valentino effort was released a year before the famous heartthrob's untimely death and enjoyed a rather acrid critical reception. Which isn't to say the public didn't flock to see the Italian stallion flare his nostrils. **75m/B VHS, DVD.** Rudolph Valentino, Nita Naldi, Casson Ferguson, Gertrude (Olmstead) Olmsted; **D:** Joseph Henabery.

The Cobra ♂ *Il Cobra; El Cobra* **1968** A tightlipped U.S. agent ogles a voluptuous siren when not fighting opium smugglers from the Middle East. A must for all admirers of Ekberg. **93m/C VHS.** Dana Andrews, Anita Ekberg; **D:** Mario Sequi.

Cobra ♂♂½ *Le Sant de l'Ange* **1971** A hired killer destroys most of a mob family and becomes the target of revenge for the lone survivor. Moody thriller boasts an international cast. **93m/C VHS.** *FR* IT Sterling Hayden, Senta Berger, Jean Yanne; **D:** Yves Boisset.

Cobra ♂ **1986 (R)** A cold-blooded cop protects a model from a gang of deranged killers. Low-brow, manipulative action fare void of feeling. Truly explotive, with little expression from the leads. Highlight is the extended chase sequence. Based on the Paula Gosling novel "Fair Game," which was remade under the book's title (and a more faithful adaptation) in 1995. **87m/C VHS, DVD.** Sylvester Stallone, Reni Santoni, Brigitte Nielsen, Andy (Andy) Robinson; **D:** George

P. Cosmatos; **W:** Sylvester Stallone; **C:** Ric Waite; **M:** Sylvester Levay.

The Cobra Strikes ♂½ **1948** Nosey thief gets more than he bargained for when he works his way through an inventor's studio. Low-budget and unexceptional. **62m/B VHS.** Sheila Ryan, Richard Fraser, Leslie Brooks, Herbert (Hayes) Heyes; **D:** Charles Reisner.

Cobra Verde ♂♂ *Slave Coast* **1988** Even by Herzog/Kinski standards, their last collaboration is one wild trip. Kinski is a 19th-century Brazilian bandit, known as Cobra Verde, who finds work as a slave overseer on a sugar plantation. When he impregnates all three of the owner's daughters, he's sent on an impossible mission to re-open the slave trade with a mad African king. Discovering he's being cheated, Cobra Verde trains an army of women to overthrow the king, so he can control the slave trade himself. Based on the novel "The Viceroy of Ouidah" by Bruce Chatwin. German with subtitles. **110m/C VHS, DVD.** *GE* Klaus Kinski, Peter Berling, Jose Lewgoy, Salvatore Basile; **D:** Werner Herzog; **W:** Werner Herzog; **C:** Viktor Ruzicka; **M:** Popul Vuh.

Cobra Woman ♂♂½ **1944** Technicolor adventure fantasy about the jungle queen (Montez) of a cobra-worshipping cult and her evil twin sister who wants the throne for herself. **70m/C VHS.** Maria Montez, Jon Hall, Sabu, Edgar Barrier, Lois Collier, Lon Chaney Jr., Mary Nash, Samuel S. Hinds, Moroni Olsen; **D:** Robert Siodmak; **W:** Richard Brooks, Gene Lewis; **C:** William Howard Greene; **M:** Edward Ward.

The Cobweb ♂♂ **1955** Shady goings on are uncovered at a psychiatric ward run by a bunch of neurotic administrators. A strong cast, director and producer do not add much to this dull outing. **125m/C VHS.** Lauren Bacall, Richard Widmark, Gloria Grahame, Charles Boyer, Lillian Gish, John Kerr, Susan Strasberg, Oscar Levant, Tommy Rettig, Paul Stewart, Adele Jergens, Bert Freed, Sandy Descher, Fay Wray, Virginia Christine; **D:** Vincente Minnelli; **C:** George J. Folsey.

The Coca-Cola Kid ♂♂♂½ **1984 (R)** Smug U.S. sales exec Becker (Roberts) treks to Australia to improve regional sales and becomes embroiled in sexual and professional shenanigans. He gets involved with free-spirited secretary Terri (sexy Scacchi) and discovers that a soft drink locally brewed by eccentric McDowall (Kerr) is his determined competition. Roberts is strong in the difficult lead role, and Scacchi is compelling in an awkwardly constructed part. Ambitious satire is somewhat scattershot, with more storylines than it needs. Still, filmmaker Makavejev is usually capable of juggling the entire enterprise. **94m/C VHS, DVD.** *AU* Eric Roberts, Greta Scacchi, Bill Kerr, Chris Haywood, Kris McQuade, Max Gillies; **D:** Dusan Makavejev; **W:** Frank Moorhouse; **C:** Dean Semler; **M:** William Motzing.

Cocaine Cowboys ♂½ **1979 (R)** Lame rockers support themselves between gigs by peddling drugs then find out they've run afoul of the mob. Palance is the only worthwhile aspect of this rambling venture produced at Andy Warhol's home. **90m/C VHS, DVD.** Jack Palance, Andy Warhol, Tom Sullivan, Suzanna Love, Richard Young; **D:** Ulli Lommel; **W:** Ulli Lommel, Victor Bockris, Tom Sullivan; **C:** Jochen Breitenstein; **M:** Elliot Goldenthal.

Cocaine Fiends ♂♂ *The Pace That Kills* **1936** Drug use leads siblings into a squalid life of addiction, crime, prostitution, and eventually suicide. Ostensibly straight morality tale functions better as loopy camp. Features memorable slang. **74m/B VHS, DVD.** Lois January, Noel Madison, Willy Castello, Dean Benton, Lois Lindsay, Sheila (Manors) Mannors; **D:** William A. O'Connor.

Cocaine: One Man's Seduction ♂♂½ **1983** Documents one man's degeneration into drug addiction. Weaver snorts convincingly in a well-made TV film. **97m/C VHS.** Dennis Weaver, David Ackroyd; **D:** Paul Wendkos; **M:** Brad Fiedel. **TV**

Cocaine Wars ♂ **1986 (R)** An undercover U.S. agent kills dozens while trying to rescue his kidnapped girlfriend from an evil South American drug tycoon. Violent, but otherwise unaffecting. **82m/C VHS.** John Schneider, Kathryn Witt, Royal Dano; **D:** Hector Olivera.

Cock & Bull Story ♂♂ *Southside* **2003** Gritty examination of the machismo world of boxing and homophobia in a depressed working-class environment. Up-and-coming boxer Travis (Roberts) is the last hope for aging manager/trainer Pascoe (Mullavey). Pascoe (and everyone else) disapproves of the inseparable friendship between Travis and unemployed screw-up Jacko (Green). Rumors begin to circulate about Travis's sexuality and Jacko's own volatility makes matters worse. Of course, on the night of Travis's biggest fight, matters come to a head between the two men. Adapted from the play by Richard Crowe and Richard Zajdlic. **102m/C DVD.** Bret Roberts, Brian A(ustin) Green, Greg Mullavey, Wendy Fowler, Darin Heames; **D:** Billy Hayes; **W:** Billy Hayes; **C:** Ben Kufrin; **M:** Pierpaolo Tiano.

Cockeyed Cavaliers ♂♂ **1934** Wheeler and Woolsey are stockaded for stealing the Duke's horses and carriage. To escape jail they swap clothes with some drunken royalty. **70m/B VHS.** Bert Wheeler, Robert Woolsey, Dorothy Lee, Thelma Todd; **D:** Mark Sandrich.

Cockfighter ♂♂♂ *Gamblin', Man; Born to Kill; Wild Drifters* **1974 (R)** A unique, grim portrait of a cockfighting trainer. Oates, in the lead, provides voiceover narrations, but the film otherwise remains silent until the end. Strong support from Stanton. Interesting, violent fare. **84m/C VHS, DVD.** Warren Oates, Harry Dean Stanton, Richard B. Shull, Troy Donahue, Millie Perkins, Robert Earl Jones, Warren Finnerty, Ed Begley Jr., Charles Willeford; **D:** Monte Hellman; **W:** Charles Willeford; **C:** Nestor Almendros; **M:** Michael Franks.

Cocktail ♂½ **1988 (R)** A smug young man finds fame and fortune as a proficient, flashy bartender, charming the ladies with his bottle and glass juggling act. Slick, superficial film boasts a busy soundtrack and serviceable exchanges between male leads Cruise and Brown. There's less chemistry between Cruise and love interest Shue. Filmed in a high-tech rock video style. **103m/C VHS, DVD.** Tom Cruise, Bryan Brown, Elisabeth Shue, Lisa Banes, Laurence Luckinbill, Kelly Lynch, Gina Gershon, Ron Dean, Paul Benedict; **D:** Roger Donaldson; **W:** Heywood Gould; **C:** Dean Semler; **M:** J. Peter Robinson. Golden Raspberries '88: Worst Picture, Worst Screenplay.

The Cocoanuts ♂♂½ **1929** In their film debut, the Marx Brothers create their trademark, indescribable mayhem. Stagey, technically crude comedy nonetheless delights with zany, free-for-all exchanges, antics. Includes famous "viaduct" exchange. **96m/B VHS, DVD.** Groucho Marx, Chico Marx, Harpo Marx, Zeppo Marx, Margaret Dumont, Kay Francis, Oscar Shaw, Mary Eaton, Cyril Ring, Basil Ruysdael; **D:** Robert Florey, Joseph Santley; **W:** George S. Kaufman, Morrie Ryskind; **C:** George J. Folsey; **M:** Irving Berlin.

Cocoon ♂♂♂ **1985 (PG-13)** Humanist fantasy in which senior citizens discover their fountain of youth is actually a breeding ground for aliens. Heartwarming, one-of-a kind drama showcases elderly greats Ameche, Brimley, Gilford, Cronyn, and Tandy. A commendable, recommendable venture. Based on David Saperstein's novel and followed by "Cocoon: The Return." **117m/C VHS, DVD.** Wilford Brimley, Brian Dennehy, Steve Guttenberg, Don Ameche, Tahnee Welch, Jack Gilford, Hume Cronyn, Jessica Tandy, Gwen Verdon, Maureen Stapleton, Tyrone Power Jr., Barret Oliver, Linda Harrison, Herta Ware, Clint Howard; **D:** Ron Howard; **C:** Dan Benedek; **M:** James Horner. Oscars '85: Support. Actor (Ameche), Visual FX.

Cocoon: The Return ♂♂ **1988 (PG)** Old timers who left with aliens in "Cocoon" return to earth and face grave problems. Less compelling sequel misses guiding hand of earlier film's director, Ron Howard. Still, most of cast from the original is on board here, and the film has its

moments. **116m/C VHS, DVD.** Don Ameche, Wilford Brimley, Steve Guttenberg, Maureen Stapleton, Hume Cronyn, Jessica Tandy, Gwen Verdon, Jack Gilford, Tahnee Welch, Courteney Cox, Brian Dennehy, Barret Oliver; **D:** Daniel Petrie; **C:** Tak Fujimoto; **M:** James Horner.

C.O.D. ♂ **1983 (PG)** Bosom buddies must develop advertising campaign for brassiere producer or find their careers are bust. Premise milked for all its worth, so you may want to keep abreast of this one. On the other hand, you may not give a hoot. Oh well, tit for tat. **96m/C VHS.** Chris Lemmon, Olivia Pascal, Jennifer Richards, Corinne Alphen, Teresa Ganzel, Carole (Raphaelle) Davis; **D:** Chuck Vincent; **W:** R.J. Marx.

Code 46 ♂♂½ **2003 (R)** Stylish, sci-fi noir explores the not-too-distant future where, in order to travel from city to cloistered city, people need "papelles," a combination visa, passport and genetic ID code. Evidently, excessive cloning has led to DNA protected zones that require strict policing. Robbins is William Geld, an investigator who has been infected with an empathy virus that enables him to read minds. Geld is tracking forged papelles, which leads him to Shanghai and the suspect Maria (Morton), a Shanghai factory worker. Geld, however falls for Maria and they enter into an intense love affair. Some provocative ideas and good premise are compromised by lack of chemistry between Robbins and Morton. **92m/C DVD.** *GB* Tim Robbins, Samantha Morton, Jeanne Balibar, Om Puri, Essie Davis, Shelley King, David Fahm; **D:** Michael Winterbottom; **W:** Frank Cottrell-Boyce; **C:** Alwin Kuchler, Marcel Zyskind; **M:** David Holmes.

Code Name Alpha ♂♂ *Red Dragon; A-009 Missione Hong Kong* **1967** You don't have to have a federal case of intelligence to figure out where this FBI story's going and how it's going to get there. Some one's smuggling sophisticated electrical components to the communists, and a team of intelligence agents, including Granger and Schiaffino, hike over to Hong Kong to break up the party. Based on the story "Le Riviere des Trois Jonques" by Georges Godefroy. **89m/C VHS.** *IT GE* Stewart Granger, Rosanna Schiaffino, Harald Juhnke, Paul Klinger, Helga Sommerfield, Horst Frank; **D:** Ernest Hofbauer.

Code Name: Chaos ♂♂ *Spies, Lies, and Alibis* **1990 (R)** A political spoof featuring a group of renegade spies trying to come up with a get-rich-quick scheme. It involves inventing a global crisis in a small Asian country but the plan comes under the scrutiny of a CIA agent who's not in on the scheme. **96m/C VHS.** Robert Loggia, Diane Ladd, David Warner, Alice Krige, Brian Kerwin; **D:** Antony Thomas.

Code Name: Dancer ♂♂ *Her Secret Life* **1987** A retired spy leaves her peaceful life, husband, and family to take care of business in Cuba. **93m/C VHS, DVD.** Kate Capshaw, Jeroen Krabbe, Gregory Sierra, Cliff DeYoung, Valerie Mahaffey, James Sloyan; **D:** Buzz Kulik; **M:** Georges Deleue. **TV**

Code Name: Diamond Head ♂ **1977** In Hawaii, a secret agent is assigned to retrieve a deadly chemical that has been hidden by a master of disguises. **78m/C VHS.** Roy Thinnes, France Nuyen, Zulu, Ian McShane; **D:** Jeannot Szwarc. **TV**

Code Name: Emerald ♂ **1985 (PG)** WWII drama in which an American agent must stop an enemy spy with knowledge of impending D-Day invasion. Conventional TV fare boasts a fine performance by von Sydow, but Stolz is hopelessly miscast as an adult. Perhaps the only film featuring both Buchholz and Berger. First feature film by NBC-TV network. **95m/C VHS.** Ed Harris, Max von Sydow, Eric Stoltz, Horst Buchholz, Helmut Berger, Cyrielle Claire, Patrick Stewart, Graham Crowden; Jonathan Sanger; **W:** Ronald Bass; **M:** John Addison.

Code Name: The Cleaner ♂½ **2007 (PG-13)** Low-brow action-comedy for Mr. The Entertainer's fans. Jake wakes up in a hotel room with no memory, next to a dead FBI agent and a lot of cash. Vavoomish Diane (Sheridan) picks him up, says they're married, and takes Jake to a grandiose mansion. Jake has flashbacks

Code Name: Zebra 🐾½ 1984
The Zebra Force helps the cops put bad guys away. When the bad guys get out, they want revenge. The result: lots of violence and action. Wasn't released theatrically. **96m/C VHS, DVD.** Mike Lane, Timothy Brown, Joe Dante, Deana Jurgens, Frank Sinatra Jr., Robert Z'Dar; **D:** Joe Tornatore.

Code Name: Kyril 🐾🐾½ 1991 (R)
Woodward plays a British spy, pitted against Soviet assassin Kyril (Charleson) who's been sent to England by the KGB to root out a double agent. Turns out there's more to it than Kyril knows, and nobody loves to it than Kyril knows, and nobody loves it more than he is Kyril a bad guy or a good guy? **91m/C DVD.** Edward Woodward, Ian Charleson, Denholm Elliott, Joss Ackland, Richard E. Grant, Sven-Bertil Taube, Catherine Nielson, John McEnery, Peter Vaughan, James Laurenson; **D:** Ian Sharp; **W:** John Hopkins. **CABLE**

Code of Honor 🐾 Kill Squad 1982
Prominent businessman embarks on mission of revenge when police fail to apprehend his wife's rapist. No surprise here. You either enjoy this sort of thing or you don't. **90m/C VHS.**

Code of Silence 🐾🐾 1985 (R) A police loner must contend with both a gang war and police department corruption. Hectic, violent action-drama with some wild stunts. **100m/C VHS, DVD, Chuck Norris, Henry Silva, Bert Remsen, Molly Hagen, Nathan Davis, Dennis Farina; D: Andrew Davis; W: Michael Butler, Mike Gray.**

Code of the Fearless 🐾 1939 A cowboy wins the heart of a beautiful maiden while bringing evildoers to justice. **56m/B&W VHS.**

Code Unknown 🐾🐾 Code Unknown: Incomplete Tales of Several Journeys; Code Inconnu: Recit Incomplet De Divers Voyages 2000 Teenager Jean (Hamidi) has run away from the farm work his father (Bierbichler) expects from him. He goes to see his brother Georges (Neuvic), a war photographer, in Paris. Although Georges is frequently away, Jean stays with Georges' lover Anne (Binoche) in their apartment. On the street, Jean insults Romanian beggar Maria (Gheorghiu) and gets into a scuffle with young black teacher Amadou (Yenke) over Jean's lack of respect. The characters' lives continue to interact in random ways. French and Romanian with subtitles. **118m/C VHS, DVD.** Juliette Binoche, Thierry Neuvic, Sepp Bierbichler, Ona Lu Yenke, Luminita Gheorghiu; **D:** Michael Haneke; **W:** Michael Haneke. **—urges; M:** Gina Conceives.

Codename: Vengeance 🐾 1987 (R) A macho fellow tries to stop a killer holding the shah's wife and son hostage. Dated. **97m/C VHS, Robert Ginty, Cameron Mitchell, Shannon Tweed; D: David Winters.**

Codename: Wildgeese 🐾½ Geheimecode Wildgänse 1984 (R) The big-name cast of this meandering mercenary macho-rama probably wish they'd been credited under code names; solid historionics cannot a silly script save. A troop of commandos-for-hire are engaged by the Drug Enforcement Administration to obliterate an opium operation in Asia's infamous Golden Triangle, and much mindless agitation ensues. **101m/C VHS, DVD, IT GE Lewis Collins, Lee Van Cleef, Ernest Borgnine, Klaus Kinski, Mimsy Farmer; D: Anthony M. Dawson.**

Codename: Terminate 🐾½ 1990 Title says it all in this tender exploration of the human condition. Jungle-trained mercenaries grab their guns and go after an American pilot shot down behind enemy lines. **84m/C VHS, Robert Mason, Jim Gaines.**

Cody 🐾 1977 A former bronco buster wants his son to "take it like a man" when the boy's dog dies. Then a mystical goose arrives to mellow the old man. That's real-ly the plot. **82m/C VHS, Tony Becker, Terry Evans; D: William D. Blackburn.**

Coffee and Cigarettes 🐾🐾🐾 2003 (R) Director/writer Jarmusch returns after a five-year absence with these 11 short films inspired by or having to do with the two addictions of the title. Shot in black and white, the short vignettes feature a wide range of talent from Cate Blanchett to Steven Wright. Jarmusch filmed the shorts over a period of 17 years between projects, and while some of the episodes are better than others there are more hits than misses. The highlight is "Somewhere in California," featuring Tom Waits and Iggy Pop. Jarmusch again demonstrates why he is the king of independent filmmakers today. **96m/B DVD, US Iggy Pop, Tom Waits, Cate Blanchett, Steve Buscemi, Alfred Molina, The RZA, Steve Coogan, Jack White, Roberto Benigni, Joie Lee, Steven Wright, Cinque Lee, Alex Descas, Isaach de Bankole, Michael Hogan, Meg White, Joe Rigano, Vinnie Vella, Vinnie Vella Jr., Renee French, E.J. Rodríguez, Bill Rice, Taylor Mead, Katy Hansz; Cameos: Bill Murray; D: Jim Jarmusch; W: Jim Jarmusch; C: Tom DiCillo, Frederick Elmes, Ellen Kuras, Robby Muller.**

Coffee Date 🐾🐾 2006 Generally sweet romantic comedy has straight-laced Todd's (Bray) loser brother Barry (Silverman) decides to hook him up with an online date. Only Barry places the ad in the "men seeking men" section. Todd chats with Kelly (Cruz) online, they arrange to meet for coffee, and—whoops—Kelly's a guy! The two become friends and everyone assumes divorced Todd is gay—and maybe Todd isn't quite as upset as he thinks he should be. **93m/C DVD, Wilson Cruz, Jonathan Silverman, Sally Kirkland, Leigh Taylor-Young, Deborah Gibson; D: Stuart Wade; W: Stuart Wade; C: Howard Wexler; M: Eban Schletter.**

Coffy 🐾🐾 1973 (R) A beautiful woman feigns drug addiction to discover and destroy the evil dealers responsible for her sister's death. Grier is everything in this exploitative flick full of violence and nudity.

Codename: Jaguar 🐾🐾½ 2000 (R) Innocent Stuart Dempsey (Nucci) has just moved to New York when he is mistaken for an international assassin, code-named Jaguar, is in town to kill the visiting Russian prez. But is innocent Stuart really that innocent after all? **93m/C VHS, DVD.** Danny Nucci, David Carradine, Victoria Sanchez, Jack Langellc; **D:** Bert Tougas. **VIDEO**

Codename: Foxfire 🐾 Slay It Again, Sam 1985 An attractive secret agent is framed for wrongdoing and must clear her name by tracking the enemy spy lurking within the intelligence network. Always interesting Cassidy is an asset, but this by-the-numbers TV film is otherwise a misappropriation of the term "intelligence" in relation to espionage. **99m/C VHS. Joanna Cassidy, John McCook, Sheryl Lee Ralph, Henry Jones, Luke Andreas; D: Corey Allen.**

Codename: Icarus 🐾🐾½ 1985 A young mathematical genius, enrolled at a special school for accelerated study, uncovers evil government plots to use the students for espionage. **106m/C VHS, DVD. TV**

Codename Kyril 🐾🐾½ 1991 (R)
(duplicate/cross column) — see Code Name: Kyril.

Cold

Cohen and Tate 🐾🐾 1988 (R)
Two antagonistic mob hitmen kidnap a nine-year-old who witnessed his parent's recent murder by the mob, in order to survive, the boy begins to play one psycho off the other. **113m/C VHS, Roy Scheider, Adam Baldwin, Harley Cross, Cooper Huckabee; D: Eric Red; W: Eric Red; M: Bill Conti.**

Cold and Dark 🐾½ 2005 Mud-dled Brit frightener finds young copper John Dark (Goss) being mentored by experienced detective Mortimer Shade (Howarth) as they investigate a series of strange murders. Dark eventually realizes that his partner is committing the crimes; having been taken over by an alien parasite, Shade needs fresh blood to survive. But Dark worries (as well he should!) when he realizes that Shade is becoming more monster and less human each time he kills. **94m/C DVD, Malcolm Culkin, Matt Lucas, Carly Jane Turnbull, Steven Elder; D: Andrew Goth; W: Joanne Reay; C: Sam McCurdy; M: Lauren Yason.**

Cold Around the Heart 🐾🐾 1997 (R) Familiar crime/road movie finds sensitive jewel thief Ned (Caruso) partnering up (both in and out of the sack) with tough cookie Jude (Lynch). Only in their latest heist, Jude takes off with the diamonds and Ned's in pursuit across the southwest but never by an alien hitchhiker Bec (Dash). If you don't expect much, you won't be disappointed. **96m/C VHS, DVD. David Caruso, Kelly Lynch, Stacey Dash, Christopher Noth, John Spencer; D: John Ridley; C: Malik Hassan Sayeed; M: Mason Daring.**

Cold Blood 🐾½ Das Amulett des Todes 1975 (R) A pair of kidnap victims turn the tables on their captors. **90m/C VHS, DVD. GE Rüdiger Hauer, Vera Tschechowa, Horst Frank, Gunther Stoll; D: Ralf Gregan, Gunter Vaessen; W: Gunter Vaessen; C: Michael Ballhaus; M: Rolf Bauer.**

Cold Blooded 🐾🐾 2000 (R) Reporter suspects a cover-up when the porter dismiss the death of a young woman as a suicide. He thinks she's another victim of a serial killer who has already killed 12 and isn't done yet. **94m/C VHS, DVD, Michael Moriarty, Patti LuPone, John Kapelos, Gloria Reuben; D: Randy Bradshaw; M: Ian Adams; C: Dean Bennett; M: Tim McCauley. VIDEO**

Cold Comfort 🐾½ 1990 (R) A father arranges his teen daughter's romance, but finds his plans going awry in this Canadian thriller. Nominated for several Canadian TV awards, including Best Actress, Best Actor, Best Picture and Best Musical Score. **90m/C VHS, CA Margaret Langrick, Maury Chaykin, Paul Gross; D: Vic Sarin; W: Richard Beattie, Elliot L. Sims; C: Vic Sarin. TV**

Cold Comfort Farm 🐾🐾½ 1971 The original BBC production of Stella Gibbon's satiric novel. Orphaned London sophisticate Flora Poste (Badel) is forced to rely on the kindness of her dotty country cousins, the Starkadders, when she needs somewhere to live. But Flora is determined to set things right with the peculiar clan. **135m/C VHS, GB Sarah Badel, Brian Blessed, Fay Compton, Rosalie Crutchley, Alastair Sim; Peter Egan, Fionnula Flanagan, Freddie Jones, Sharon Gurney; D: Peter Hammond; W: C: Bryan Duggan; M: Tom Bahler.**

Cold Comfort Farm 🐾🐾🐾 1994 (PG) Stella Gibbons classic 1932 comedic novel is brought to life in this TV adaptation, which finds orphaned London lass Flora Poste (Beckinsdale) trying to take charge of the lives of her very odd country cousins, the Starkadders. The rowdy family and their dilapidated farm are putty in ly and their dilapidated farm are putty in practical Flora's hands as she works to make everybody happy (including herself). Terrific ensemble cast, with a fast pace and wicked humor. **104m/C VHS, DVD, GB Kate Beckinsale, Eileen Atkins, Ian McKellen, Sheila Burrell, Rufus Sewell, Maria Miles, Freddie Jones, Ivar Kaye, Miriam Margolyes, Joanna Lumley, Stephen Fry, Christopher Bower; D: John Schlesinger; W: Malcolm Bradbury; C: Chris Seager; M: Robert Lockhart.**

Cold Creek Manor 🐾🐾½ 2003 (R) How is it that Michael Douglas isn't involved with this? This is just the kind of yuppie nightmare thriller for which he was the go-to guy for much of the '90s. Quaid does an admirable job filling his shoes, however, as an NYC-based documentary filmmaker who, along with his business hotshot wife (Stone), decides to chuck the rat race of the city for a nice, quiet life in the country. Oops. They buy a big, creepy house "for a steal" and it comes with some secrets, and a redneck caretaker (Dorff) who strangely attracts the missus, but creeps out the kids, especially daughter Kristen. Not much that is truly creepy moments, and Figgis does some much-needed subtle satire. Top-notch cast helps, as well. **118m/C VHS, DVD, US Dennis Quaid, Sharon Stone, Stephen Dorff, Juliette Lewis, Kristen Stewart, Christopher Plummer, Ryan Wilson, Dana Eskelson; D: Mike Figgis; W: Andras Kovacs; C: Declan Quinn; M: Mike Figgis.**

Cold Days 🐾🐾½ 1966 Four men await execution for their part in the WWII massacres of Jews and Serbs. Their reminiscences and justifications, if any, are examined. Stunning cinematography and unusual theme for 1960s Hungarian political cinema. **102m/C VHS, HU Zoltan Latinovits, Ivan Darvas, Tibor Szígeligy, Adam Szirtes; D: Andras Kovacs; W: Andras Kovacs; C: Ferenc Szecsenyi.**

Cold Eyes of Fear 🐾½ 1970 A man and his girlfriend are besieged by a raving convict whom his uncle, a judge, had put away years before. Shades of through a break-up herself. **96m/C VHS, Giffin Dunne, Marissa Chibas, Blanche Baker, Mark Cronogue; D: Bruce Van Dusen.**

Cold Feet 🐾🐾 1989 (R) Light romantic comedy about a TV director just recovering from a failed marriage and his fall for a lab researcher who just went through a break-up herself.

Cold Feet 🐾🐾½ 1989 (R) Modernday western in which a trio of loopy desperados smuggle jewels inside a racehorse's stomach. Quirky comedy offers wild performances from Waits and sexbomb Kirkland, but could use a few more laughs. Filmed largely on McGuane's ranch. **94m/C VHS, DVD, Keith Carradine, Tom Waits, Sally Kirkland, Rip Torn, Kathleen York, Bill Pullman, Vincent Schiavelli, Jeff Bridges; D: Robert Dornhelm; W: Thomas McGuane, Jim Harrison; C: Bryan Duggan; M: Tom Bahler.**

Cold Fever 🐾🐾 1995 Japanese yuppie Atsushi Hirata (Nagase) is expecting to vacation in the tropical paradise of Hawaii but the frozen reaches of Iceland. But instead he must perform a memorial ritual on the remote Icelandic spot where his parents died some time before. He arrives in a blizzard and things just go downhill from there. Some quirky characters but the film loses focus. **85m/C VHS, IC Masatoshi Nagase, Gisli Halldorsson, Lili Taylor, Fisher Stevens; D: Fridrik Thor Fridriksson; W: Fridrik Thor Fridriksson, Jim Stark; M: Hilmar Orn Hilmarsson.**

Cold Front 🐾½ 1989 (R) A hired assassin turned serial killer is hunted by two dedicated cops. **94m/C VHS, CA Martin Sheen, Michael Ontkean, Beverly D'Angelo, Kim Coates; D: Allan Goldstein; C: Thomas Burstyn.**

Cold Harvest 🐾🐾 1998 (R) A comet strikes the earth, killing a great portion of the population and then disaster strikes again when a deadly disease runs unchecked, killing t'cse who become infected. A bounty hunter and his partner seek to find one of the seven people who carry the antibody for the disease. **93m/C DVD, Gary Daniels, Barbara Crampton, Bryan Genesse; D: Isaac Florentine; W: Frank Dietz; C: David Varod; M: Stephen (Steve) Edwards. VIDEO**

Codename: Terminate *(additional notes)* ...
named Jaguar, is in town to kill the visiting Russian prez. But is innocent Stuart really that innocent after all? **93m/C VHS, DVD.** Danny Nucci, David Carradine, Victoria Sanchez, Jack Langellc; **D:** Bert Tougas. **VIDEO**

Cold

Codename: Jaguar *(see above)*

Cold Creek Manor 🐾🐾½ 2003 (R) *(see above)*

91m/C VHS, DVD, William (Bill) Elliott, Sid Haig, Pam Grier, Booker Bradshaw, Robert DoQui, Allan Arbus; **D:** Jack Hill; **W:** Jack Hill; **C:** Paul Lohmann; **M:** Roy Ayers.

(footer, left) **VideoHound's Golden Movie Retriever** | **211**

Cold Hearts ♂♂½ 1999 Charles is the head of a group of young vampires who take over a small New Jersey town. But best friends Viktoria and Alicia want to escape from Charles' influence and turn to a stranger for help. Low-budget vamp flick is surprisingly professional and watchable. **88m/C VHS, DVD.** Marisa Ryan, Amy Jo Johnson, Christopher Wiehl, Robert Floyd; **D:** Robert Masciantonio. **VIDEO**

Cold Heat ♂♂ 1990 When a custody battle rocks a crime boss' world, he pulls out all the stops in the war against his wife. **85m/C VHS.** John Phillip Law, Britt Ekland, Robert Sacchi, Roy Summerset, Joanne Watkins, Chance Michael Corbitt; **D:** Ulli Lommel.

Cold Heaven ♂½ 1992 (R) Alex and Marie Davenport are on vacation when an accident occurs and Alex dies—or does he? The next day his body disappears and his unfaithful wife begins to have paranoid delusions that he is returning to exact retribution for her affair. But these aren't her only visions, for during the past year Marie has also had religious visions she believes are part of a personal battle with God. Harmon does what he can with his role as the alleged corpse but Russell is uncharacteristically whiny and bland. Convoluted story of marriage, death, and spirituality; doesn't pan out on any accounts. Based on a novel by Brian Moore. **103m/C VHS.** Theresa Russell, Mark Harmon, James Russo, Talia Shire, Will Patton, Richard Bradford; **D:** Nicolas Roeg; **W:** Allan Scott.

Cold Justice ♂♂ 1989 (R) An ex-prizefighter (Daltrey) and his friends welcome an English priest into their tough southside Chicago neighborhood. The good father seems too good to be true as he befriends the locals—even raising funds for the children's hospital. When the funds never make it to the hospital and the neighborhood begins to experience a number of violent tragedies, the residents decide to take their own revenge. **106m/C VHS.** Dennis Waterman, Roger Daltrey, Penelope Milford, Ron Dean, Bert Rosario; **D:** Terry Green; **W:** Terry Green.

Cold Light of Day ♂♂ 1995 Police officer Victor Marek (Grant) is hunting a serial killer of young children in the English countryside—and he'll do anything, including using a young girl as bait. Marek seduces single mother Milena (Baxter) to use her young daughter to set a trap for the killer but can he catch the madman before it's too late? **101m/C VHS.** *GB* Richard E. Grant, Lynsey Baxter, Simon Cadell, Perdita Weeks, James Laurenson, Heathcote Williams; **D:** Rudolf Van Den Berg; **W:** Doug Magee.

Cold Mountain ♂♂♂½ 2003 (R) Minghella's excellent adaptation of Charles Frazier's dense and challenging novel has Inman (Law) attempting to return home, "Odyssey"-style, to North Carolina after his friends are all killed in the disastrous battle at Petersburg, Virginia in 1864. Inman sees no point in continuing the fight and begins his journey so he can continue the brief, chaste, tentative courtship he had begun with the sophisticated Ada (Kidman) before the war. Ada has also seen hardship during their separation. Her father has died, leaving her unprepared to tend the farm until neighbor Ruby (Zellweger) is sent to help. All the actors are superb, with Zellweger stealing every scene she's in, and Minghella strikes the perfect balance between the two stories, thanks to some expert editing. **155m/C DVD.** *GB RO IT* Jude Law, Nicole Kidman, Renee Zellweger, Donald Sutherland, Eileen Atkins, Brendan Gleeson, Philip Seymour Hoffman, Natalie Portman, Giovanni Ribisi, Ray Winstone, Kathy Baker, Ethan Suplee, Jena Malone, Melora Walters, Lucas Black, Taryn Manning, Tom Aldredge, James Rebhorn; **D:** Anthony Minghella; **W:** Anthony Minghella; **C:** John Seale; **M:** Gabriel Yared. Oscars '03: Support. Actress (Zellweger); British Acad. '03: Support. Actress (Zellweger); Golden Globes '04: Support. Actress (Zellweger); Screen Actors Guild '03: Support. Actress (Zellweger).

Cold River ♂♂½ 1981 (PG) An experienced guide takes his two children on an extended trip through the Adirondacks. For the children, it's a fantasy vacation un-

til their father succumbs to a heart attack in the chilly mountains. "Cold River" is a journey of survival, and an exploration of human relationships. **94m/C VHS, DVD.** Robert Earl Jones, Pat Petersen, Richard Jaeckel, Suzanne Weber, Brad Sullivan, Elizabeth Hubbard, Augusta Dabney; **D:** Fred G. Sullivan.

Cold Room ♂♂ *The Prisoner* 1984 College student on vacation with her father in East Berlin discovers the horrors hidden in an antiquated hotel room next to hers. From the novel by Jeffrey Caine. **95m/C VHS.** George Segal, Renee Soutendijk, Amanda Pays, Warren Clarke, Anthony (Corian) Higgins; **D:** James Dearden; **M:** Michael Nyman. **CABLE**

Cold Sassy Tree ♂♂♂½ 1989 Endearing romance of a scandalous May-December marriage as experienced by the younger woman's teenage son. Dunaway and Widmark shine, and small-town pettiness is vividly rendered. Adapted from the books by Olive Ann Burns. A superior made-for-cable production. **95m/C VHS.** Faye Dunaway, Richard Widmark, Neil Patrick Harris, Frances Fisher, Lee Garlington, John M. Jackson; **D:** Joan Tewkesbury; **W:** Joan Tewkesbury; **M:** Brad Fiedel. **CABLE**

Cold Showers ♂♂ *Douches Froides* 2005 Mickael (Libereau) is 17 and proud of his judo skills and hot squeeze Vanessa (Stevenin). He becomes friends with judoclub member Clement (Perrier) and the trio briefly become a menage although Mickael's jealousy soon surfaces. Slight story includes nudity and sex scenes (remember it's French). French with subtitles. **102m/C DVD.** *FR* Salome Stevenin, Florence Thomassin, Jean-Philippe Ecoffey, Johan Libereau, Pierre Perrier; **D:** Anthony Cordier; **W:** Anthony Cordier; **C:** Nicolas Gaurin; **M:** Nicolas Lemercier.

Cold Steel ♂½ 1987 (R) Standard revenge drama about a mercenary rescuing his woman and his gold from an evil governor. Dubbed. **95m/C VHS.** *IT* Guy Madison, Rick (Rik) Battaglia, Ingeborg (Inge) Schoener; **D:** Luigi Capuano.

Cold Steel for Tortuga ♂ 1965 An Italian epic about a mercenary rescuing his woman and his gold from an evil governor. Dubbed. **95m/C VHS.** *IT* Charles Bronson, Jill Ireland, Liv Ullmann, James Mason; **D:** Terence Young; **W:** Albert Simonin, Shimon Winceleberg; **C:** Jean Rabier; **M:** Michel Magne.

Cold Sweat ♂♂ *L'Uomo Dalle Due Ombre; De la Part des Copains* 1971 (R) A brutal drug trader takes his ultra-violent revenge after his wife is captured by a drug boss' moronic henchmen. Typical Bronson flick boasts superior supporting cast of Ullmann and Mason. Writing and direction, however, are mediocre. **94m/C VHS, DVD.** *IT FR* Charles Bronson, Jill Ireland, Liv Ullmann, James Mason; **D:** Terence Young; **W:** Albert Simonin, Shimon Winceleberg; **C:** Jean Rabier; **M:** Michel Magne.

Cold Sweat ♂♂ 1993 (R) A professional hit man (Cross) is literally haunted by the ghost of his last victim (who happens to be female and usually appears naked), so he decides his next assignment will be his last. A ruthless businessman suspects his very sexy wife (Tweed) has been unfaithful but she has lots of others' secrets to hide. **93m/C VHS.** Ben Cross, Shannon Tweed, Adam Baldwin, Dave Thomas; **D:** Gail Harvey; **W:** Richard Beattie.

Cold Turkey ♂♂½ 1971 (PG) Often witty satire about what happens when an entire town tries to stop smoking for a contest. Van Dyke is fine as the anti-smoking minister; newscasters Bob and Ray are riotous; oldtimer Horton's swansong. Wholesome, somewhat tame fare. **99m/C VHS.** Dick Van Dyke, Pippa Scott, Tom Poston, Bob Newhart, Vincent Gardenia, Barnard Hughes, Jean Stapleton, Graham Jarvis, Edward Everett Horton; **D:** Norman Lear; **W:** Norman Lear; **M:** Randy Newman.

Cold War Killers ♂♂ 1986 (PG) Soviet and British agents vie for control of prized cargo plane recently retrieved from the sea floor. **85m/C VHS, DVD.** *GB* Mike Lane, Robin Sachs, Peter Ivatts, Martin Dale, Terence Stamp; **D:** William Brayne; **W:** Murray Smith; **C:** Mike Blakely.

Coldblooded ♂½ 1994 (R) Minor mob flunky (and dim bulb) Cosmo (Priestley) is unwillingly promoted to the position of hit man by his mobster boss. He's tutored by the organization's primo professional (Riegert) and finds out he has a real knack for murder. More sophomoric than satiric and a waste of Riegert's talents; Williams is attractive as Priestley's clueless girlfriend. Directorial debut of Wolodarsky. **92m/C VHS.** Jason Priestley, Peter Riegert, Kimberly Williams, Robert Loggia, Janeane Garofalo, Josh Charles, David Anthony Higgens, Doris Grau; **Cameos:** Talia Balsam, Michael J. Fox; **D:** M. Wallace Wolodarsky; **W:** M. Wallace Wolodarsky; **C:** Robert Yeoman; **M:** Steve Bartek.

Coldfire ♂♂½ 1990 Two rookie cops work to undo the havoc unleashed on the streets of LA because of a deadly new drug sought for its powerful high. Not many surprises here. **90m/C VHS, DVD.** Wings Hauser, Kamar De Los Reyes, Robert Viharo, Gary Swanson; **D:** Wings Hauser.

The Colditz Story ♂♂½ 1955 Prisoners of war from the Allied countries join together in an attempt to escape from Colditz, an allegedly escape-proof castle-prison deep within the Third Reich. **93m/B VHS, DVD.** John Mills, Eric Portman, Lionel Jeffries, Bryan Forbes, Ian Carmichael, Anton Diffring; **D:** Guy Hamilton.

Cole Justice ♂½ 1989 An older man, haunted by the memory of his girlfriend's rape and murder 35 years earlier, takes to the streets to protect innocent citizens from lowlife criminals. Somewhat unusual revenge pic filmed in and around Tulsa, Oklahoma. **90m/C VHS.** Carl Bartholomew, Keith Andrews, Mike Wiles, Nick Zickefoose; **D:** Carl Bartholomew.

Collateral ♂♂♂ 2004 (R) Vincent (Cruise) is a contract killer as cool and sleek as his gray-haired, gray-suited appearance suggests. He's got a busy schedule to keep in nighttime LA—five hits and out on the 6 A.M. flight. Fortunately, he's got the perfect cabbie, 12-year veteran Max (Foxx), who can get anywhere in the least possible time. Naturally, there's time to talk, and as Vincent shares his advice on how to adapt and improvise, Max gets some ideas on how he's going to survive. It's basically a two-handed drama and both actors give nuanced performances; Mann is also at the top of his game. Also notable is the high-def digital video of cinematographers Beebe and Cameron that makes the city another character in the drama. **119m/C DVD.** *US* Tom Cruise, Jamie Foxx, Mark Ruffalo, Irma P. Hall, Jada Pinkett Smith, Bruce McGill, Barry (Shabaka) Henley, Debi Mazar; **D:** Michael Mann; **W:** Stuart Beattie; **C:** Dion Beebe, Paul Cameron; **M:** James Newton Howard, Antonio Pinto, Tom Rothrock. British Acad. '04: Cinematog.

Collateral Damage ♂♂ 2002 (R) Revenge drama pits Ah-nuld against the Columbian terrorists whose actions caused the death of his wife and child. When investigators come up short, nothing-left-to-lose fireman Gordy Brewer (Schwarzenegger) takes matters into his own hands and sets out to catch "The Wolf," the rebel leader of Columbia's civil war and the one responsible for his family's demise. In Columbia, he meets Selena (Neri) and her son Mauro (Posey) and his instinct to protect and serve them kicks into action, giving him renewed purpose. Highlights are Leguizamo as Felix, the Columbian drug producer, and Turturro as an exiled Canadian working as a mechanic. Mexico subs for Columbia in this unbelievable and formulaic actioner for genre and Arnold fans only. **109m/C VHS, DVD.** *US* Arnold Schwarzenegger, Elias Koteas, Francesca Neri, Clifford Curtis, John Leguizamo, John Turturro, Miguel (Michael) Sandoval, Harry J. Lennix, Lindsay Frost, Jisu Garcia; **D:** Andrew Davis; **W:** David Griffiths, Peter Griffiths; **C:** Adam Greenberg; **M:** Graeme Revell.

Collected Stories ♂♂♂ 2002 Fine two-character study based on the 1997 play by Margulies, who adapted for this PBS presentation. Ruth Steiner (Lanvin) is a respected writer and teacher in her mid-50s who lives comfortably in her Greenwich Village apartment. It's there

that Ruth agrees that ambitious graduate student and aspiring writer Lisa Morrison (Mathis) will become her assistant. Over six years, their relationship evolves into a friendship, and Lisa betrays when she turns the scandalous details of Ruth's life into a best-selling novel. **120m/C VHS.** Linda Lavin, Samantha Mathis; **D:** Gilbert Cates; **W:** Donald Margulies; **C:** Johnny (John W.) Simmons; **M:** Charles Fox. **TV**

The Collector ♂♂♂½ 1965 Compelling adaptation of the John Fowles novel about a withdrawn butterfly collector who decides to add to his collection by kidnapping a beautiful girl he admires. He locks her in his cellar hoping she will fall in love with him. Chilling, unsettling drama with Stamp unnerving, yet sympathetic in lead. **119m/C VHS, DVD.** *GB* Terence Stamp, Samantha Eggar, Maurice Dallimore, Mona Washbourne; **D:** William Wyler; **W:** John Kohn, Stanley Mann; **C:** Robert Krasker, Robert L. Surtees; **M:** Maurice Jarre. Cannes '65: Actor (Stamp), Actress (Eggar); Golden Globes '66: Actress–Drama (Eggar).

The Collectors ♂♂ 1999 (R) Mob boss sends hit men Ray (Van Dien) and A.K. (Fox) to collect a big debt that's owed but they would rather take the payoff and get out of New York—preferably alive. **97m/C VHS, DVD.** Casper Van Dien, Rick Fox, Catherine Oxenberg, Daniel Pilon; **D:** Sidney J. Furie. **VIDEO**

Collector's Item ♂♂♂ 1989 Two lovers reunite after 16 years and a flurry of memories temporarily rekindles their passion, which comes dangerously close to obsession. Casting of the physically bountiful Antonelli helps this effective erotic drama. **99m/C VHS, DVD.** *IT* Tony Musante, Laura Antonelli, Florinda Bolkan; **D:** Giuseppe Patroni-Griffi.

College ♂♂♂½ 1927 A high school valedictorian tries out for every sport in college, hoping to win the girl. Vintage Keaton antics, including disaster as a soda jerk, an attempt to be a track star, and the pole vault through a window to rescue the damsel in distress. **60m/B VHS, DVD.** Buster Keaton, Anne Cornwall, Harold Goodwin; **D:** James W. Horne; **W:** Brian Foy, Carl Harbaugh; **C:** Bert Haines; **M:** John Muri.

College Humor ♂♂½ 1933 Early musical comedy for Crosby finds him a college prof, Frederick Danvers, who attracts the attentions of pretty coed Barbara (Carlisle). Only Barbara's crush is leaving her football star boyfriend Mondrake (Arlen) in a jealous rage just before the big game. Fortunately, Barbara's brother Barney (Oakie) fills in. Burns and Allen appear as caterers. **80m/B VHS.** Bing Crosby, Jack Oakie, Richard Arlen, Mary Carlisle, Mary Kornman, Joseph (Joe) Sawyer, George Burns; **D:** Wesley Ruggles; **W:** Claude Binyon, Frank Butler; **C:** Leo Tover; **M:** Arthur Johnston, Sam Coslow.

College Swing ♂♂ *Swing, Teacher, Swing* 1938 Lightweight, lackluster musical about Allen inheriting a small town college which she turns into a hangout for her vaudeville pals. Top cast is basically wasted performing many forgettable songs and performing routines. Based on an adaptation by Frederick Hazlitt Brennan from a story by Ted Lesser. ♪College Swing; What Did Romeo Say to Juliet?; I Fall In Love With You Every Day; You're a Natural; The Old School Bell; Moments Like This; How D'ja Like to Love Me?; What a Rumba Does to Romance. **86m/B VHS, DVD.** George Burns, Gracie Allen, Martha Raye, Bob Hope, Edward Everett Horton, Ben Blue, Betty Grable, Jackie Coogan, John Payne; **D:** Raoul Walsh; **W:** Walter DeLeon, Francis Martin; **C:** Victor Milner; **M:** Boris Morros, Hoagy Carmichael, Burton Lane, Frank Loesser.

Collier & Co.: Hot Pursuit ♂♂½ 2006 (PG). Down-on-his-luck J.R. Collier (Schneider) wants to go legit and start his own car dealership to win back his estranged wife and daughter. He decides to sell the cars he wins street racing but a Dodge Charger has something in its glovebox that some goofy bad guys want back. Harmless family fun and a family affair since Schneider cast his own wife and daughter as his onscreen family too. He also cast The General Lee

Collision Course ♂ 1989 (PG) A wise-cracking cop from Detroit teams up with Japan's best detective to nail a ruthless gang leader. Release was delayed until 1992 due to a lawsuit, but it was resolved in time to coordinate the release with Leno's debut as the host of "The Tonight Show." Pretty marginal, but diehard fans of Leno may appreciate it. **107m/C DVD.** Jay Leno, Chris Sarandon, A. Waxman; **D:** Lewis Teague.

The Colombian ♂ 1991 America's best undercover agent battles a powerful cocaine empire deep in the jungles of the Amazon, where slave labor and political corruption abound. **90m/C VHS.** Miles O'Keeffe, Henry Silva; **D:** Michael Lemick.

Colombian Love ♂♂½ 1994 Light-hearted Israeli romantic comedy about three buddies coping with adulthood and amore. Womanizing Zydane is surprised when he begins obsessing over his Colombian ex-girlfriend; Omer is newly married and already having problems handling it; and Uri is caught between his independent girlfriend Tali and his domineering father. Hebrew with subtitles. **96m/C DVD. IS** Assi Cohen, Mili Avital, Nir Levy, Italy Barnea, Eli Shai Kaimot; **W:** Regev Levy, Reshef Levy; **C:** Ofer Harari; **M:** Asaf Amdurski.

Colonel Chabert ♂♂ 1994 In the 1307 Battle of Eylau, French officer Chabert (Depardieu) is thought dead and stripped of all he possesses. After 10 years of imprisonment, a man shows up in the office of Paris lawyer Derville (Luchini), claiming to be the dead Chabert. His remarried wife (Ardant), now the Countess Ferraud, has used his fortune to bolster the political aspirations of her second husband (Dussolier) and refuses to acknowledge this stranger's claims. Is Chabert a fraud? And what exactly are the motives of all the players? Based on the novel by Honore de Balzac. Directorial debut of Angelo. French with subtitles. **111m/C VHS, FR** Gerard Depardieu, Fanny Ardant, Fabrice Luchini, Andre Dussollier; **D:** Yves Angelo; **W:** Yves Angelo, Jean Cosmos, Veronique Lagrange; **C:** Bernard Lutic.

Colonel Effingham's Raid ♂♂½ 1945 A retired army colonel uses military tactics to keep an old historical courthouse open, while defeating some crooked politicians in the process. **70m/B VHS, DVD.** Joan Bennett, Charles Coburn, William Eythe, Donald Meek, Allyn Joslyn, Elizabeth Patterson, Frank Craven, Thurston Hall, Cora Witherspoon, Emory Parnell, Henry Armetta, Steve (Stephen) Dunne, Foy Roberts, Charles Trowbridge; **D:** Irving Pichel; **W:** Kathryn Scola; **C:** Edward Cronjager.

Colonel Redl ♂♂♂ 1984 (R) Absorbing, intricately rendered psychological study of an ambitious officer's rise and fall in pre-WWI Austria. Brandauer is excellent in the vain, insecure homosexual ultimately undone by his own ambition and is superior officer's smug loathing. Mahler-Stahl and Landgrebe are particularly distinguished among the supporting players. The second in the Szabo/Brandauer trilogy, after "Mephisto" and before "Hanussen." In German with English subtitles. **142m/C VHS, DVD. GE HU** Klaus Maria Brandauer, Armin Mueller-Stahl, Gudrun Landgrebe, Jan Niklas, Hans-Christian Blech, Laszlo Mensaros, Andras Balint; **D:** Laszlo Szabo; **W:** Laszlo Szabo, Peter Dobai; **C:** Lajos Koltai; **M:** Zdenko Tamassy; British Acad. '85: Foreign Film; Cannes '85: Special Jury Prize.

Colonel Wolodyjowski ♂♂♂½ 1969 An adaptation of the monumental novels by Henryk Sinkiewicz chronicling the attack on Poland's eastern border by the Turks in 1668. In Polish with English subtitles. **160m/C VHS, DVD. PL** Tadeusz Lomnicki, Magdalena Zawadzka, Daniel Olbrychski; **D:** Jerzy Hoffman.

The Colony ♂♂ 1998 (R) Aliens planning an earth invasion decide to test humankind by abducting four people and observing their survival skills. **94m/C VHS, DVD.** Isabella Hofmann, Michael Weatherly, Cristi Conway, Eric Allen Kramer, Jeff Kober, James Avery, Clare Salstrom; **D:** Peter Geiger; **W:** Peter Geiger, Richard Kletter; **C:** Zoltan David; **M:** Paul Rabjohns. C.A.B.L.E.

Color Me Blood Red Woof! 1964 Artist decides that the red in his paintings is best rendered with human blood. He even manages to continue his art career—when not busy stabbing and mutilating the unsuspecting citizenry. Short and shoddy. **74m/C VHS, DVD.** Don Joseph, Candi Conder, Elyn Warner, Scott H. Hall, Jerome (Jerry Stallon) Eden, Patricia Lee, James Jackel; **D:** Herschell Gordon Lewis; **W:** Herschell Gordon Lewis; **C:** Herschell Gordon Lewis.

Color Me Dead ♂ 1969 (R) A victim of an extremely slow-acting poison frantically spends his final days trying to uncover his killer. Another inferior remake of B-thriller "D.O.A." Rent that one instead. **97m/C VHS.** Au Tom Tryon, Carolyn Jones, Rick Jason, Patricia Connolly, Tony Ward; **D:** Eddie Davis.

Color Me Kubrick ♂½ 2005 Malkovich swans about in outrageous attire and attitude as con man Alan Conway, who made his way to London in the early 1990s and passed himself off as reclusive director Stanley Kubrick despite knowing nothing about filmmaking. The con man was after money and sex, which he was given by the flattered and gullible who were too embarrassed to press charges when they'd discovered they'd been had (much to the real Kubrick's frustration). A bit of silly fluff. **86m/C DVD, GB FR** John Malkovich, Jim Davidson, Richard E. Grant, Luke Mably, Terence Rigby, James Dreyfus, Peter Bowles, Leslie Phillips, William Hootkins; **D:** Brian Cook; **W:** Anthony Frewin; **C:** Howard Atherton; **M:** Bryan Adams.

Color of a Brisk and Leaping Day ♂ 1995 While living in L.A. at the end of WWII, Chinese-American John Lee (Alexander) learns that the Yosemite Valley Railroad is being scrapped and he becomes determined to save it—in part as a homage to his grandfather who emigrated to work as a railroad laborer. A romantic train fanatic himself, Lee arranges financing from wealthy businessman Pinchot (Diehl) but must make the automobile rapidly takes over as preferred transportation. Well-captures a '40s atmosphere but pacing and dialogue are uneven. **87m/B VHS, DVD.** Peter Alexander, Jeri Arredondo, Henry Gibson, Michael Stipe, John Diehl, David Chung, Diana Larkin, Bok Yun Chon; **C:** Christopher Munch; **W:** Christopher Munch; **C:** Rob Sweeney; Sundance '96: Cinematog.

The Color of Courage ♂♂ 1998 (PG) Anna Sipes (Hamilton) is pleased to welcome Minnie McGhee (Whitfield) to her Detroit neighborhood in 1944. But not every one feels the same, since the McGhees are black. The community (including Anna's husband) wants to force an eviction but since Anna and Minnie have become friends, they are equally determined that the McGhees will remain where they are. Based on the landmark civil rights case, Sipes vs. McGhee. **92m/C VHS.** Linda Hamilton, Lynn Whitfield, Bruce Greenwood, Roger Guenveur Smith; **D:** Lee Rose; **W:** Kathleen McGhee-Anderson; **C:** Eric Van Haren Noman; **M:** Terence Blanchard.

Color of Night ♂½ 1994 (R) Psychologist Dr. Bill Capa (Willis) takes over a murdered colleague's therapy group hoping to find out the killer's identity. Then he meets temptress Rose (March) and gets involved in a hot affair, but she's not what she seems—nor is anyone else. Preposterous thriller fails to deliver necessary suspense although the eroticism could spark some interest, particularly in the director's cut, which puts the sex back in the sex scenes between Willis and March (and is 15 minutes longer than the theatrical release). **135m/C VHS, DVD.** Bruce Willis, Jane March, Scott Bakula, Ruben Blades, Lesley Ann Warren, Lance Henriksen, Kevin J. O'Connor, Andrew Lowery, Brad Dourif, Eriq La Salle, Jeff Corey, Shirley Knight, Kathleen Wilhoite; **D:** Richard Rush; **W:** Matthew Chapman, Billy Ray, Richard Rush; **C:** Dietrich Lohmann; **M:** Dominic Frontiere; Golden Raspberries '94: Worst Picture.

The Color of Paradise ♂♂ 1999 (PG) Mohammad is an eight-year-old blind boy who is regarded as a burden by his recently widowed and hardworking father. His father hopes to remarry but thinks his son will be an obstacle and sends him to live with a carpenter who is also blind, so that the boy can learn a trade. Of course, it is the father who must truly learn to see, since Mohammad already appreciates everything surrounding him. Farsi with subtitles. **90m/C DVD. IA** Mohsen Ramezani, Hossein Mahjoub; **D:** Majid Majidi; **W:** Majid Majidi; **C:** Mohammad Davudi; **M:** Alireza Kohandairy.

The Colony ♂♂½ 1995 (PG-13) "The Colony" is a luxurious and exclusive gated community owned by secretive billionaire developer Phillip Denning (Linden). Newest residents, security expert Rick Knowlton (Ritter), wife Leslie (Keller) and their two children, find out things are just too good to be true—and that trying to leave could be the very last thing they'll ever do. **93m/C VHS, DVD.** John Ritter, Hal Linden, Mary Page Keller, Marshall Teague, Frank Bonner, Michelle Scarabelli, June Lockhart, Todd Jeffries, Alexandra Picatti, Cody Dorkin; **D:** Rob Hedden; **W:** Rob Hedden; **C:** David Geddes. C.A.B.L.E.

The Color of Freedom ♂♂ 2007 (PG-13) Celie is a poor black girl who fights for her self-esteem when she is separated from her sister and forced into a brutal marriage. Spanning 1909 to 1947 in a small Georgia town, the movie chronicles the joys, pains, and people in her life. Adaptation of Alice Walker's acclaimed book features strong lead from Goldberg (her screen debut). Gover, Avery, and talk-show host Winfrey (also her film debut). It's hard to see director Spielberg as the most suited for this one, but he acquits himself nicely, avoiding the facelessness that sometimes flaws his pics. Brilliant photography by Allen Daviau and musical score by Jones (who co-produced) compliment this strong film. **154m/C VHS, DVD.** Whoopi Goldberg, Danny Glover, Oprah Winfrey, Margaret Avery, Adolph Caesar, Rae Dawn Chong, Willard Pugh, Akosua Busia; **D:** Steven Spielberg; **W:** Menno Meyjes; **C:** Aler Daviau; **M:** Chris Boardman, Quincy Jones; Directors Guild '85: Director; Golden Globes '86: Actress—Drama (Goldberg); Natl. Bd. of Review '85: Actress (Goldberg).

Colorado ♂½ 1940 Roy tries to find his brother, a Union deserter, during the Civil War. **54m/B VHS, DVD.** Roy Rogers, George "Gabby" Hayes, Milburn Stone; **D:** Joseph Kane.

Colorado Serenade ♂½ 1946 Standard oater has Dean, Sharpe and Ates trying to prevent a young outlaw from bullying the local citizenry. Sharpe shows off his athletic prowess, and King provides many assets in this controversial, unsettling depiction of deadly streetlife. Colorful, freewheeling direction from the underrated Hopper. Rattling rap soundtrack too. Additional footage has been added for video release. **120m/C VHS, DVD.** Glenn Plummer, Sy Richardson, Damon Wayans, Fred Asparagus, Sherman Augustus, R.D. Call, Seymour Cassel, Nicky Corello, Virgil Frye, Courtney Gains, Clark Johnson, Leon, Tina Lifford, Micole Mercurio, Jack Nance, Tony Todd, Gerardo Mejia, Sean Penn, Robert Duvall, Maria Conchita Alonso, Trinidad Silva, Randi Brooks, Grand L. Bush, Don Cheadle, Rudy Ramos; **D:** Dennis Hopper; **W:** Michael Schifter; **C:** Haskell Wexler; **M:** Herbie Hancock.

Colors ♂♂♂½ 1988 (R) Vivid, realistic cop drama pairs sympathetic veteran Duvall and trigger-tempered rookie Penn on the gang-infested streets of East Los Angeles. Fine play from each is one of the many assets in this controversial, unsettling depiction of deadly streetlife. Colorful, freewheeling direction from the underrated Hopper. Rattling rap soundtrack too. Additional footage has been added for video release. **120m/C VHS, DVD.** Glenn Plummer, Sy Richardson, Damon Wayans, Fred Asparagus, Sherman Augustus, R.D. Call, Seymour Cassel, Nicky Corello, Virgil Frye, Courtney Gains, Clark Johnson, Leon, Tina Lifford, Micole Mercurio, Jack Nance, Tony Todd, Gerardo Mejia, Sean Penn, Robert Duvall, Maria Conchita Alonso, Trinidad Silva, Randi Brooks, Grand L. Bush, Don Cheadle, Rudy Ramos; **D:** Dennis Hopper; **W:** Michael Schifter; **C:** Haskell Wexler; **M:** Herbie Hancock.

Colorz of Rage ♂♂½ 1997 Story of an interracial relationship between Tony (Resteghini) and Debbie (Richards) cov-ers familiar ground, but the New York locations have a gritty feel that's accentuated by the rough production values. **91m/C DVD.** Dale Resteghini, Nicki Richards, Cheryl "Pepsii" Riley, Don Wallace; **D:** Dale Resteghini; **W:** Dale Resteghini; **C:** Martin Ahlgren; **M:** Tony Prendatt.

Colossus and the Amazon Queen ♂½ La Regina delle Amazzoni 1964 Colossus and the Amazons are unwilling recruited for service to Amazons. Doesn't seem like the worst way to make a living. But lead actor Taylor—so notable in comedies, thrillers, and action flicks—is too good for this sort of thing. **84m/C VHS, DVD. IT** Rod Tay-

The Color of Evening ♂♂ 1995 Aging painter Landau tries to regain his youth by pursuing his young model Skye, but it's the older Eurstyn who really inspires his imagination. **90m/C VHS.** Kyle Chandler, Bill Erwin, Roddy McDowall, Martin Landau, Ellen Burstyn, Ione Skye; **D:** Stephen Stafford; **W:** Tamara Lynn Roth; **C:** Bernard Salzmann; **M:** Leonard Roseman.

The Color of Money ♂♂♂½ 1986 (R) Flashy, gripping drama about former pool hustler Fast Eddie Felson (Newman) who, after an absence of 25 years, takes a brilliant but immature pool shark (Cruise) under his wing. Strong performances by Newman as the grizzled veteran, Cruise as the showboating youth, and Mastrantonio and Shaver as the men's worldly girlfriends. Worthy sequel to "The Hustler," 25 years later. **119m/C VHS, DVD.** Paul Newman, Tom Cruise, Mary Elizabeth Mastrantonio, Helen Shaver, John Turturro, Forest Whitaker; **D:** Martin Scorsese; **W:** Richard Price; **C:** Michael Ballhaus; **M:** Robbie Robertson; Oscars '86: Actor (Newman); Natl. Bd. of Review '86: Actor (Newman). C.A.B.L.E.

Color of Justice ♂♂ 1997 A political circus ensues after a suburban white woman is killed by four black teens. Betty Gainer (Pelikan) is forced to stop behind a death seems to be forgotten. **95m/C VHS. F,** Murray Abraham, Judd Hirsch, Gregory Hines, Bruce Davison, Lisa Pelikan, Saul Rubinek, Mark L. Taylor, Gloria Carlin, Mia Korf, Dule Hill, Eugene Byrd, Malcolm Goodwin; **D:** Jeremy Paul Kagan; **W:** Lionel Chetwynd; **C:** Steven Foster; **M:** Michael Kane.

Colorado Sundown ♂ 1952 A conniving brother and sister attempt to cheat a man out of his inheritance. **67m/B VHS, DVD.** Rex Allen, Mary Ellen Kay, Slim Pickens, June Vincent, Koko; **D:** William Witney.

The Color Purple ♂♂♂½ 1985 (PG-13) Celie is a poor black girl who fights for her self-esteem when she is separated from her sister and forced into a brutal marriage. Spanning 1909 to 1947 in a small Georgia town, the movie chronicles the joys, pains, and people in her life. Adaptation of Alice Walker's acclaimed book features strong lead from Goldberg (her screen debut). Gover, Avery, and talk-show host Winfrey (also her film debut). It's hard to see director Spielberg as the most suited for this one, but he acquits himself nicely, avoiding the facelessness that sometimes flaws his pics. Brilliant photography by Allen Daviau and musical score by Jones (who co-produced) compliment this strong film. **154m/C VHS, DVD.** Whoopi Goldberg, Danny Glover, Oprah Winfrey, Margaret Avery, Adolph Caesar, Rae Dawn Chong, Willard Pugh, Akosua Busia; **D:** Steven Spielberg; **W:** Menno Meyjes; **C:** Aler Daviau; **M:** Chris Boardman, Quincy Jones; Directors Guild '85: Director; Golden Globes '86: Actress—Drama (Goldberg); Natl. Bd. of Review '85: Actress (Goldberg).

The Color of Pomegranates ♂♂♂½ 1985 Sayat Nova; Tsvet Granata 1969 Paradjanov's depiction of the life of Armenian poet Arutiun Sayadin, known as Sayat Nova, who rises from cantor to court minstrel to archbishop. Eloquent imagery and symbols are derived from Armenian paintings, poetry and history; in Armenian with English subtitles. Also includes "Hagop Hovnatanian," a 12-minute short on the artist. **80m/C VHS, DVD. RU** Sofiko Chiaureli, M. Aleksanian, V. Galstian; **D:** Sergei Paradjanov; **W:** Sergei Paradjanov; **C:** A. Samvelyan.

lor, Dorian Gray, Ed Fury, Gianna Maria Canale; **D:** Vittorio Sala.

Colossus of the Arena 🦴🦴
Maciste, Il Gladiatore piu Forte del Monte 1962 In 4th century Rome, Forest plays a mighty gladiator who uncovers a plot to imprison a beautiful princess. Through an incredible series of feats and combats, he exposes an evil duke as a traitor. 98m/C VHS. *IT* Mark Forest, Scilla Gabel; **D:** Michele Lupo; **W:** Lionello De Felice, Ernesto Guida; **M:** Francesco De Masi.

Colossus: The Forbin Project 🦴🦴🦴
The Forbin Project 1970 A computer designed to manage U.S. defense systems teams instead with its Soviet equal and they attempt world domination. Wire-tight, suspenseful film seems at once dated yet timely. Based on the novel by D.F. Jones. 100m/C VHS, DVD. Eric (Hans Gudegast) Braeden, Susan Clark, Gordon Pinsent, William Schallert, Georg Stanford Brown; **D:** Joseph Sargent; **W:** James Bridges; **C:** Gene Polito; **M:** Michel Colombier.

Colt Comrades 🦴🦴 1943 A bad guy's monopoly on water rights is jeopardized when Boyd and Clyde strike water while drilling for oil. Nothing really notable here, except for Bob (Robert) Mitchum and George ("Superman") Reeves in minor roles. 67m/B VHS, DVD. William Boyd, Andy Clyde, Jay Kirby, George Reeves, Gayle Lord, Earle Hodgins, Victor Jory, Douglas Fowley, Herbert Rawlinson, Robert Mitchum; **D:** Lesley Selander.

Columbo: Murder by the Book 🦴🦴½ 1971 The rumpled, cigar-smoking TV detective investigates the killing of a mystery writer. Scripted by Bochco of "Hill Street Blues" and "L.A. Law" fame. 79m/C VHS, DVD. Peter Falk, Jack Cassidy, Rosemary Forsyth, Martin Milner; **D:** Steven Spielberg; **W:** Steven Bochco.

Columbo: Prescription Murder 🦴🦴🦴 1967 Falk's debut as the raincoat-clad lieutenant who always has just one more question. In the TV series pilot he investigates the death of a psychiatrist's wife. Rich with subplots. Good mystery fare. 99m/C VHS. Peter Falk, Gene Barry, Katherine Justice, William Windom, Nina Foch, Anthony James, Virginia Gregg; **D:** Richard Irving; **W:** Richard Levinson, William Link. **TV**

Coma 🦴🦴🦴 (PG) 1978 A doctor discovers murder and corpse-napping at her Boston hospital, defies her male bosses, and determines to find out what's going on before more patients die. Exciting, suspenseful fare, with Bujold impressive in lead. Based on the novel by Robin Cook. 113m/C VHS, DVD. Genevieve Bujold, Michael Douglas, Elizabeth Ashley, Rip Torn, Richard Widmark, Lois Chiles, Hari Rhodes, Tom Selleck, Ed Harris; **D:** Michael Crichton; **W:** Michael Crichton; **C:** Victor Kemper, Gerald Hirschfeld; **M:** Jerry Goldsmith.

Comanche Moon 🦴½ 2008 Disappointing adaptation of McMurtry's 1997 novel, which falls second in terms of "The Lonesome Dove" timeframe, set mostly in the 1850s. Best friends Gus (Zahn) and Call (Urban) are Texas Rangers hunting Comanches, including leader Buffalo Hump (Studi). When their eccentric captain, Inish Scully (Kilmer), goes after a horse thief, they are left in charge. Kilmer spends a lot of time stuck in a pit and going crazy after Inish is captured by a Mexican bandito (Lopez). Back in town, Gus pines for Clara (Cardellini) while Call struggles with his feelings for Maggie (Banks), and Inish's wife Inez (Griffiths) spreads her charms amongst the Rangers. Oh yeah, and the Comanches attack. Disjointed storyline, stilted dialogue, and poor (miscast) performances doom this effort. 284m/C DVD. Steve Zahn, Karl Urban, Val Kilmer, Linda Cardellini, Elizabeth Banks, Rachel Griffiths, Wes Studi, Sal Lopez, Ryan Merriman, Adam Beach, James Rebhorn, Jake Busey, Melanie Lynskey, Floyd "Red Crow" Westerman; **D:** Simon Wincer; **W:** Larry McMurtry, Diana Ossana; **C:** Alan Caso; **M:** Lennie Niehaus. **TV**

Comanche Station 🦴🦴½ 1960 Loner Jefferson Cody (Scott) agrees to rescue Mrs. Lowe (Gates) from the Comanches. After Cody achieves her rescue, they fall in with outlaw Ben Lane (Akins) and his two young proteges, who insist on accompanying them back to the Lowe homestead, saying that they'll need additional protection. But Cody soon realizes that Lane is after the reward money and is planning an ambush. 73m/C VHS. Randolph Scott, Nancy Gates, Claude Akins, Skip Homeier, Richard Rust, Rand Brooks; **D:** Budd Boetticher; **W:** Burt Kennedy; **C:** Charles Lawton Jr.

Comanche Territory 🦴🦴 1950 Western frontiersman Jim Bowie travels to Comanche country and helps the Indians save their land from settlers. Routine oater. Based on a story by Meltzer. 76m/C VHS. Maureen O'Hara, MacDonald Carey, Will Geer, Charles Drake; **D:** George Sherman; **W:** Oscar Brodney, Lewis Meltzer.

The Comancheros 🦴🦴🦴 1961 Texas Ranger Wayne and his prisoner fight with the Comancheros, an outlaw gang who is supplying guns and liquor to the dreaded Comanche Indians. Musical score adds flavor. Last film by Curtiz. 108m/C VHS, DVD. John Wayne, Ina Balin, Stuart Whitman, Nehemiah Persoff, Lee Marvin, Bruce Cabot; **D:** Michael Curtiz; **C:** William Clothier; **M:** Elmer Bernstein.

Combat Academy 🦴 1986 Weak comedy about two goofballs sent to a military academy to straighten out, but instead turn the academy on its ear with their antics. Unremarkable. 96m/C VHS. Keith Gordon, Jamie Farr, Sherman Hemsley, John Ratzenberger, Bernie Kopell, Charles Moll; **D:** Neal Israel.

Combat Killers 🦴 1980 A WWII Army captain grabs for individual glory on the battlefield and jeopardizes the lives of his platoon. 96m/C VHS. Paul Edwards, Marlene Dauden, Claude Wilson; **D:** Ken Loring.

Combat Shock 🦴 *American Nightmares* 1984 (R) A Vietnam veteran returns home and can't cope with the stresses of modern life, including the lowlifes who have been taking over the streets. So he goes after some scum who have been trying to kill him, succeeds, but things don't end well. Familiar plot handled in a conventional manner. 85m/C VHS, DVD. Ricky Giovinazzo, Nick Nasta, Veronica Stork, Mitch Maglio, Aspah Livni; **D:** Buddy Giovinazzo; **W:** Buddy Giovinazzo; **C:** Stella Varveris; **M:** Ricky Giovinazzo.

Combination Platter 🦴🦴½ 1993 Anxious young immigrant Robert (Lau), newly arrived from Hong Kong, becomes a waiter at the Szechuan Inn in Queens, New York, where he gets a crash course in American culture and romance as well as tipping. Gentle comedy works best with little details that ring true: overheard customer conversations, staff banter, the kitchen scenes. Lau's earnest, but effort feels like a complete story. Still, a worthy first effort for the then 24-year-old Chan, who directed on a $250,000 budget, using his parents' restaurant after hours for a set. 84m/C VHS, DVD. Jeff Lau, Coleen O'Brien, Lester Chan, Thomas S. Hsiung, David Chung, Colin Mitchell, Kenneth Lu, Eleonara Khliberg, James DuMont; **D:** Tony Chan; **W:** Tony Chan, Edwin Baker; **C:** Yoshifumi Hosoya; **M:** Brian Tibbs. Sundance '93: Screenplay.

Come Along with Me 🦴🦴½ 1984 TV adaptation of Shirley Jackson's unfinished novel about a woman who sells all and leaves her hometown when her husband dies, determined to start a new career as a seer. 60m/C VHS, DVD. Estelle Parsons, Barbara Baxley, Sylvia Sidney; **D:** Joanne Woodward. **TV**

Come and Get It 🦴🦴🦴 *Roaring Timber* 1936 A classic adaptation of the Edna Ferber novel about a lumber king battling against his son for the love of a woman. Farmer's most important Hollywood role. 99m/B VHS, DVD. Frances Farmer, Edward Arnold, Joel McCrea, Walter Brennan, Andrea Leeds, Mady Christians; **D:** William Wyler, Howard Hawks; **W:** Jules Furthman, Jane Murfin; **C:** Rudolph Mate, Gregg Toland; **M:** Alfred Newman. Oscars '36: Support. Actor (Brennan).

Come and See 🦴🦴🦴 *Idi i Smotri; Go and See* 1985 Harrowing, unnerving epic which depicts the horrors of war as a boy soldier roams the Russian countryside during the Nazi invasion. Some overwhelming sequences, including tracer-bullets flashing across an open field. War has rarely been rendered in such a vivid, utterly grim manner. Outstanding achievement from Soviet director Klimov. In Russian with English subtitles. 137m/C VHS, DVD. *RU* Alexei Kravchenko, Olga Mironova, Lubomiras Lauciavicus, Vladas Bagdonas, Viktor Lorents, Juris Lumiste, Kazimir Rabetsky, Yevgeni Tilicheyev; **D:** Elem Klimov; **W:** Elem Klimov, Alex Adamovich; **C:** Alexei Rodionov; **M:** Oleg Yanchenko.

Come as You Are 🦴🦴½ 2005 Quickly sinking dotcom entrepreneur Craig (Sterling) hosts a reunion for his old college chums so they can meet Kellie (Fixx), his knockout fiancee. Little do they know, their buddy is desperately launching a new business. After a series of contrived events occur, a hostile porn director, crew, and cast show up to the rental house to start filming a sex video, causing Craig to fess up to his new smut-meister gig. Mostly unknown cast plays out matters of the heart and groin commendably. 83m/C DVD. Maury Sterling, James Russo, Michelle Harrison, Janet Marshall, Barbara Fixx; **D:** Chuck Rose; **W:** Chuck Rose; **C:** Lawrence Schweich; **M:** Nathan Wang, John Abella. **VIDEO**

Come Back, Little Sheba 🦴🦴½ 1952 Unsettling drama about a worn-out housewife, her abusive, alcoholic husband and a comely boarder who causes further marital tension. The title refers to the housewife's despairing search for her lost dog. Booth, Lancaster, and Moore are all excellent. Based on the play by William Inge, this film still packs an emotional wallop. 99m/B VHS, DVD. Burt Lancaster, Shirley Booth, Terry Moore, Richard Jaeckel, Philip Ober, Lisa Golm, Walter Kelley; **D:** Daniel Mann; **C:** James Wong Howe. Oscars '52: Actress (Booth); Cannes '53: Actress (Booth); Golden Globes '53: Actress—Drama (Booth); N.Y. Film Critics '52: Actress (Booth).

Come Back to the Five & Dime Jimmy Dean, Jimmy Dean 🦴🦴🦴 1982 (PG) Five women convene at a run-down Texas drugstore for a 20-year reunion of a local James Dean fan club. The women recall earlier times and make some stunning revelations. Altman's filming of Ed Graczyk's sometimes funny, sometimes wrenching play proves fine vehicle for the actresses. Cher is probably the most impressive, but Dennis and Black are also memorable. 109m/C VHS. Sandy Dennis, Cher, Karen Black, Kathy Bates, Sudie Bond, Marta Heflin; **D:** Robert Altman.

Come Blow Your Horn 🦴🦴½ 1963 Neil Simon's first major Broadway success is a little less successful in its celluloid wrapper, suffering a bit from a familiar script. Sinatra's a playboy who blows his horn all over town, causing his closeknit New York Jewish family to warp a bit. Dad's not keen on his son's pledge of allegiance to the good life, and kid brother Bill would like to be his sibling's understudy in playboyhood. 115m/C VHS. Frank Sinatra, Lee J. Cobb, Tony Bill, Molly Picon, Barbara Rush, Jill St. John; **D:** Bud Yorkin; **W:** Norman Lear; **C:** William H. Daniels.

Come Early Morning 🦴🦴🦴 2006 (R) Lucy Fowler (Judd) lives two lives in her Arkansas community: she's very efficient at her day contractor job while raising hell as a hard-drinking, one-nightstand kinda gal in the evening. Maybe she's just emulating her womanizing, alcoholic dad (Wilson). Courtly newcomer Cal (Donovan) refuses to let her see him and leave, but even Cal may not be able to overcome Lucy's self-destructiveness. Adams does well with her slice-of-life tale—her writing/directing debut—as does surrogate Judd (Adams once intended to play the lead herself). 97m/C DVD. *US* Ashley Judd, Jeffrey Donovan, Tim Blake Nelson, Laura Prepon, Stacy Keach, Scott Wilson, Diane Ladd, Pat Corley; **D:** Joey Lauren Adams; **W:** Joey Lauren Adams; **C:** Tim Orr; **M:** Alan Brewer.

Come on, Cowboys 🦴🦴½ 1937 The Three Mesquiteers rescue an old circus friend from certain death. Part of "The Three Mesquiteers" series. 54m/B VHS. Robert "Bob" Livingston, Ray Corrigan, Max Ter-

Come On Danger! 🦴🦴½ 1932 Keene makes his "B" Western debut, out to avenge the death of his brother and battle an outlaw gang. Haydon is forced into a life of crime in order to save her ranch from villain Ellis and only Texas Ranger Keene can set her free. 60m/B VHS. Tom Keene, Julie Haydon, Roscoe Ates, Robert Ellis, Wade Boteler; **D:** Robert F. "Bob" Hill; **W:** Bennett Cohen.

Come on Rangers 🦴 *Come On Ranger* 1938 Rogers and his friends go to Texas to save the death of a comrade. 54m/B VHS, Roy Rogers, George "Gabby" Hayes, Lynne Roberts, Raymond Hatton, J. Farrell MacDonald, Purnell Pratt, Harry Woods; **D:** Joseph Kane; **W:** Gerald Geraghty, Jack Natteford; **C:** Al Wilson; **M:** Cy Feuer.

Come on Tarzan 🦴🦴½ 1932 Maynard and his trusty horse Tarzan save wild horses from the bad guys who want to turn them into dog food. 60m/B VHS. Ken Maynard, Kate Campbell, Robert F. (Bob) Kortman, Nelson McDowell, Jack Rockwell; **D:** Alan James; **W:** Alan James.

Come See the Paradise 🦴🦴🦴 1990 (R) Jack McGurn (Quaid) takes a job at a movie theatre in Los Angeles' Little Tokyo and falls for owner's daughter Lily (Tomita). They marry, but after the bombing of Pearl Harbor all Japanese-Americans are interned. Told in flashback, the story offers a candid look at the racism implicit in the relocations and the hypocrisy that often lurks beneath the surface of the pursuit of liberty and justice for all. Sometimes melodramatic script indulges a bit too much in the obvious, but the subject is worthwhile, one that has not yet been cast into the vast bin of Hollywood clichés. The cast, apart from Quaid's misguided attempt at seriousness, is excellent. 135m/C VHS, DVD. Dennis Quaid, Tamlyn Tomita, Sab Shimono, Shizuko Hoshi, Stan(ford) Egi, Ronald Yamamoto, Akemi Nishino, Naomi Nakano, Brady Tsurutani, Pruitt Taylor Vince, Joe Lisi; **D:** Alan Parker; **W:** Alan Parker; **M:** Randy Edelman.

Come September 🦴🦴🦴 1961 American business tycoon Robert Talbot (Hudson) maintains a holiday villa on the Italian Riviera. But the only time he uses the place is the month of September, so when Talbot arrives in July he discovers his enterprising major domo Maurice (Slezak) has been managing the place as a hotel the rest of the year. Talbot finds his home filled with tourists and, to make matters worse, discovers his Italian lover Lisa (Lollobrigida) about to get married. Darin and Dee are the film's romantic ingenues and wound up getting married after filming wrapped; his screen debut. 114m/C VHS, DVD. Rock Hudson, Gina Lollobrigida, Sandra Dee, Bobby Darin, Walter Slezak, Joel Grey, Brenda de Banzie; **D:** Robert Mulligan; **W:** Stanley Shapiro, Maurice Richlin; **C:** William H. Daniels; **M:** Hans J. Salter.

Come to the Stable 🦴🦴🦴 1949 Warm, delightful story about two French nuns, Young and Holm, who arrive in New England and set about building a children's hospital. Although Catholic in intent, pic demonstrates that faith and tenacity can move mountains. (This film must have been Fox's response to Paramount's "Going My Way" and "The Bells of Saint Mary's.") Based on a story by Clare Boothe Luce. 94m/B VHS. Loretta Young, Celeste Holm, Hugh Marlowe, Elsa Lanchester, Regis Toomey, Mike Mazurki; **D:** Henry Koster; **W:** Oscar Millard, Sally Benson; **C:** Joseph LaShelle; **M:** Cyril Mockridge.

Come Undone 🦴🦴 *Presque Rien* 2000 A matter of fact coming of age tale about a French teenager, Mathieu (Elkaim), who acknowledges his sexuality when he falls in love with the slightly older Cedric (Rideau). Mathieu and his younger sister Sarah (Legrix) are stuck at their summer house in a coastal resort town with their depressed mother (Reymond) and their aunt (Matheron) who's serving as a nurse/housekeeper. The emotional Mathieu finds sex and solace with the vol-

The Comeback 🎬 *The Lay, the Screening Stopped* 1977 A singer attempting a comeback in England finds his wife murdered. Film is non-linear and the viewer must piece together what has happened from the various scenes, which can be confusing. French with subtitles. 98mC VHS, DVD, FR Jeremie Elkaim, Stephane Rideau, Marie Matheron, Laetitia Legrix, Dominique Reymond, Nils Ohlund, Rejana Kerdaffrec, Guy Houssier; D: Sebastian Lifshitz; W: Sebastian Lifshitz, Stephane Bouquet; C: Pascal Pacquot; M: Perry Bake.

Comeback 🎬🎬½ 1983 The story of Eurdon (the lead singer of the Animals), a disillusioned rock star, played by Eric Burdon, who gives up his life in the fast lane and tries to go back to his roots. 105mC VHS, DVD. Eric Burdon; D: Christel Bushmann; M: Eric Burdon.

Comeback Kid 🎬 1980 An ex-big league baseball player is conned into coaching an urban team of smarmy street youths, and falls for their playground supervisor. 97mC VHS. John Ritter, Susan Dey; C: Peter Levin. TV

The Comebacks 🎬 2007 (PG-13) Truly lame spoof of sports flicks. Losing football coach Lambeau Fields gets a last chance when he's hired at Heartland State U. So he moves his family, including limber hottie daughter Michelle (Nevin), to Texas to whip a bunch of losers into shape. The climactic game is called the Toilet Bowl—yee, those are the jokes, folks, in another "spoof everything and something might be funny" outing. 84mC DVD. US David Koechner, Matthew Lawrence, Brooke Nevin, Carl Weathers, Matthew Lawrence, Nick Searcy, Jermaine Williams, Jesse Garcia, George Back, Eric Christian Olsen, Will Arnett, Bradley Cooper, Dax Shepard, Jackie Long, Robert Richard, Martin Spanjers, Jonathan Gries, Andy Dick, Kerri Kenney, Dennis Rodman, Frank Caliendo, Finesse Mitchell, Noureen DeWulf. Cameos: John Salley, Lawrence Taylor, Eric Dickerson, Michael Irvin; D: Tom Brady; W: Ed Yeager, Joey Gutierrez; C: Anthony B. Richmond; M: Christopher Lennertz.

Comedy of Innocence 🎬🎬 *Comedie de L'Innocence* 2000 Nine-year-old Camille (Hugon) is addicted to videotaping everything that happens in his life. During a visit to the park, Camille insists that Ariane (Huppert) isn't his real mother and gives her an address that she says is his real home. When they visit, Ariane learns that the owner, Isabelle (Balibar) had a son Camille's age who drowned. Isabelle is later institutionalized, but escapes and Camille also runs away. Ariane watches Camille's videotapes to get clues to what's happened to her son. Adapted from the novel "Il Figlio di Due Madre" by Massimo Bontempelli. French with subtitles. 98mC DVD. FR Isabelle Huppert, Jeanne Balibar, Charles Berling, Nils Hugon, Edith Scob, Denis Podalydes; D: Raul Ruiz; W: Raul Ruiz, Françoise Dumas; C: Jacques Bouquin; M: Jorge Arriagada.

Comedy of Power 🎬🎬 *L'Ivresse du Pouvoir* 2006 This comedy comes from the self-important behavior of the characters. Huppert grimaces her way through her seventh collaboration with Chabrol, playing zealous, incorruptible examining magistrate Jeanne Charmant-Killman. She's looking into a corporate embezzlement scandal (based on a true incident)

that has serious political implications for the government. Meanwhile, her neglected hubby (Renucci), becomes even more unhappy when the case brings Jeanne a lot of attention. But she's breaking unspoken social codes among what is still a very male-dominated world. French with subtitles. 110mC DVD, FR Isabelle Huppert, François Berleand, Robin Renucci, Patrick Bruel, Marilyne Canto, Jean-Francois Balmer; D: Claude Chabrol; W: Claude Chabrol, Odile Barski; C: Eduardo Serra;

The Comedy of Terrors 🎬🎬🎬 *The Graveside Story* 1964 Comedy in which some deranged undertakers take a hands-on approach to insuring their continued employment. Much fun is supplied by the quartet of Price, Lorre, Karloff, and Rathbone, all veterans of the horror genre. 84mC VHS, DVD. Vincent Price, Peter Lorre, Boris Karloff, Basil Rathbone, Joe E. Brown, Joyce Jameson, Beverly (Hills) Powers, Buddy Mason; D: Jacques Tourneur; W: Richard Matheson; C: Floyd Crosby; M: Les Baxter.

Comes a Horseman 🎬🎬½ 1978 (PG) Robards is a cattle baron, attempting to gobble up all the oil-rich land his neighbor owns. Neighbor Fonda has the courage to stand up to him, with the help of a WWII veteran and the local old timer Farnsworth, in this slow-moving but intriguing western drama. 119mC VHS, DVD. James Caan, Jane Fonda, Jason Robards Jr., George Grizzard, Richard Farnsworth, Jim Davis, Mark Harmon; D: Alan J. Pakula; W: Dennis Lynton Clark; C: Gordon Willis; M: Michael Small. Natl. Bd. of Review 78: Support. Actor (Farnsworth); Natl. Soc. Film Critics 78: Support. Actor (Farnsworth).

Comfort and Joy 🎬🎬½ 1984 (PG) After his kleptomaniac girlfriend deserts him, a Scottish disc jockey is forced to reevaluate his life. He becomes involved in an underworld battle between two mob-owned local ice cream companies. Another odd comedy gem from Forsyth, who did "Gregory's Girl" and "Local Hero." Music by Dire Straits guitarist Knopfler. 93mC VHS. GB Bill Paterson, Eleanor David, Clare Grogan, Alex Norton, Patrick Malahide, Rikki Fulton, Roberto Bernardi; D: Bill Forsyth; W: Bill Forsyth; C: Chris Menges; M: Mark Knopfler. Natl. Soc. Film Critics '84: Cinematog.

The Comfort of Strangers 🎬🎬🎬 1991 (R) Atmospheric psychological thriller. Mary and Colin (Richardson and Everett), a handsome young British couple, take a Venetian holiday to rediscover the passion in their relationship. Lost in the city, they chance, it seems, upon Robert (Walken), a sort of Virgil in an Italian suit. He later reappears, and, abetted by his wife Caroline (Mirren), gradually leads the couple on an eerie tour of urbane decadence that hints at danger. Psychologically tantalizing and horrifyingly erotic, the movie's based on Ian McEwan's novel. 102mC VHS, DVD. Christopher Walken, Natasha Richardson, Rupert Everett, Helen Mirren; D: Paul Schrader; W: Harold Pinter; C: Dante Spinotti; M: Angelo Badalamenti.

The Comic 🎬🎬🎬 1969 (PG) Van Dyke is terrific as a silent screen comedian (a composite of several real-life screen comics) whose ego destroys his career. Recreations of silent films, and the blend of comedy and pathos, are especially effective. 96mC VHS. Dick Van Dyke, Mickey Rooney, Michele Lee, Cornel Wilde, Nina Wayne, Pert Kelton, Jeannine Riley; D: Carl Reiner; W: Carl Reiner, Aaron Ruben.

The Comic 🎬 1985 In a future police state, a young comedian kills the star and takes his place in the show. His future rises, but who cares? 90mC VHS. Steve Munroe, Bernard Padden, Jeff Pirie; D: Richard Driscoll.

Comic Act 🎬🎬🎬 1998 The world of London stand-up comedy is the setting for a surprisingly sexy look at life beyond the microphone. Gus (Schneider) and Jay (MullarKey) are struggling until Alex (Webster) joins their act. Her combination of intelligence and unembarrassed sexuality makes them a hit with audiences, and with great. Dern's character suffers from weak cliches of show business. Yes, the same

that come all the temptations (and all the cliches) of show business.

Comic Book: The Movie 🎬🎬🎬 2004 (PG-13) Donald Swan (director Hamill) is a teacher and comic book fan who has been hired as a technical consultant by a Hollywood studio that's adapting his favorite character into a big-budget movie. He soon learns that the studio plans on transforming the character from a wholesome WWII-era Nazi-fighter into a vengeful anti-terrorist vigilante, and begins a crusade to prevent the change. Hamill has a deep well of knowledge and affection for the comics industry and its fans, not to mention the rhythms of the fan convention. He uses it all to good effect here, capturing, but not making fun of, the attitudes of everyone involved. Much of the dialogue seems ad-libbed, and that also works to the movie's advantage. 106mC DVD. Mark Hamill, Scott LaRose, Roger Rose, Arlen (Arlene) Sorkin, Tom Kenny, Billy West, Debi Derryberry, Donna D'Errico, Jonathan Winters, Sid Caesar, Lori Alan. Cameos: Jim (Jonah) Cummings, Stan Lee, Peter David, Kevin Smith, Ray Harryhausen, Bruce Campbell, Phil Morris, Chase Masterson, J.J. (Jeffrey) Abrams, Paul Dini, Billy Mumy, Ron Perlman, Peter Mayhew, David Prowse, Hugh Hefner, Mark Hamill; C: Jason Cooley; M: Billy West. VIDEO

Comic Book Villains 🎬🎬 2002 (R) Raymond (Logue) owns a comic book store for the love of the genre while Norman (Rapaport) and his wife Judy (Lyonne) are in it for the money. Both learn that a local collector has just died but refuses to sell his valuable collection. This doesn't stop either Raymond or Norman from planning ways to acquire the goods—although both decides he'll just steal Carter (Elwes) decides he'll just steal them. 93mC VHS, DVD. Donal Logue, Michael Rapaport, Natasha -lyonne, DJ Qualls, Cary Elwes, James Duval, Danny Masterson, Monet Mazur; D: James Dale Robinson; W: James Dale Robinson; C: Blake T. Evans; M: Joseph (Joey) Altura.

Comin' Round the Mountain 🎬🎬 1951 The duo are caught in a Kentucky family feud while seeking a fortune in gold. Funniest bit has backwoods witch Hamilton squaring off with Costello when he refuses to pay for the love potion she's made him. 77mB VHS, DVD. Bud Abbott, Lou Costello, Dorothy Shay, Kirby Grant, Joseph (Joe) Sawyer, Margaret Hamilton, Glenn Strange, Joan Giant, Robert Lees, Frederic Rinaldo.

Coming Apart 🎬🎬 1969 Free-love was never really very free as shrink Tom Herman, an outstanding American athlete who worked in Russia in the 1930s. He falls in love with a Vietnam vet, paralyzed from war injuries. His attitudes, pain, and first-hand knowledge of the war force her to re-examine her previously automatic responses. Honest look at the everyday life of disabled veterans, unusual vision of the possibilities of simple friendship between men and women. Fonda and Voight are great. Dern's character suffers from weak scriptwriting late in the film. Critically acclaimed. Compelling score from late '60s

story has been told countless times, but this version is fresh and energetic. 107mC VHS, DVD. Stephen Moyer, Neil Mullarkey, David Schneider, Suki Webster, Magnus Hastings; C: Jack Hazan; W: Jack Hazan; M: Patrick Gowers.

Comic Book Kids 🎬½ 1982 (G) Two youngsters enjoy visiting their friend's comic strip studio, since they have the power to project themselves into the cartoon stories. Viewers will be less impressed. 90mC VHS. Joseph Campanella, Billy Barty, Robyn Finn, Jim Engelhardt, Fay De Witt, Anjelica Huston; D: Gene Nash; W: Jim Engelhardt.

Coming Home 🎬🎬🎬 *Rosamunde Pilcher's Coming Home* 1998 It's 1935, and Judith (Dunbar) is left behind in a British boarding school when her mother and sister travel to Singapore to join Judith's father. A school friendship with Loveday Carey-Lewis introduces Judith to the eccentric world of British aristocracy but the coming of WWII proves to be her coming of age. Based on the book by Rosamunde Pilcher. Made for German TV. 205mC VHS, DVD. GE Peter O'Toole, Joanna Lumley, David McCallum, Emily Mortimer, Kate Ryder, Richard son, Paul Bettany, Susan Hampshire, Penelope Keith, Patrick Ryecart, Malcolm Stoddard; D: Giles Foster; W: John Goldsmith. TV

The Coming of Amos 🎬🎬½ 1925 A wonderful send-up of all those Fairbanks-style melodramas, with La Rocque as an Aussie on vacation on the French Riviera falling for and eventually rescuing Goudal, as the Russian princess held captive by the lustful Beery. 60mB VHS. Rod La Rocque, Jetta Goudal, Noah Beery Sr., Florence Vidor; D: Paul Sloane.

Coming Out 🎬🎬 1989 The first film produced by East Germany to deal with homosexuality. Ambivalent Philip (Freihof) is a popular high school educator, who has been involved with another teacher, Tanja (Manzel), who has just learned she's pregnant. But Philip has just admitted to himself that his attraction to the younger Matthias (Kummer) is more erotic than friendly. Philip, however, is an emotional coward—he's worried about prejudice and can't be honest with either lover, leading to a painful confrontation. German with subtitles. 113mC VHS, DVD. GE Matthias Freihof, Dagmar Manzel, Dirk Kummer; D: Heiner Carow; W: Wolfram Witt; C: Martin Schlesinger; M: Stefan Carow.

Coming Out Alive 🎬🎬 1984 Tense thriller about a woman and her hired mercenary who try to rescue her kidnapped son from his estranged father—a radical is involved in an assassination plot. Hylands is especially compelling. 73mC VHS. CA Helen Shaver, Scott Hylands, Michael Ironside, Monica Parker; D: Don McBrearty.

Coming Out of the Ice 🎬🎬 1984 1982 (PG) Engrossing true story of Victor (Root), and Jenny (Hoffman) discuss orgasms and try to find just the right guy. The unrated version clocks in at 96 minutes. 90mC VHS, DVD. Gaby Hoffman, Tricia Vessey, Ryan Reynolds, Bonnie Root, James Foxley, Spalding Gray, Mia Farrow, Peter Bogdanovich, Leslie Lyles, Yasmine Bleeth; D: Colette Burson; W: Colette Burson, Kate Robin; C: Wars Hussein; M: Maurice Jarre. TV

Coming Soon 🎬🎬½ 1999 (R) Three Manhattan prep school seniors deal with their sexual coming of age as well as college admission. Nell (Vessey), Stream

Coming Through 🎬🎬½ 1985 Writer D.H. Lawrence meets the married Frieda von Richt-rcfer and begins a scandalous affair which interviews with his own writings, and the life of a young man in the present day. British TV production. 78mC VHS. Kenneth Branagh, Helen Mirren, Alison Steadman, Philip Martin Brown, Norman Rodway; D: Peter Barber-Fleming; W: Alan Plater. TV

Coming to America 🎬🎬🎬 1988 (R) An African prince (Murphy) decides to come to America in search of a suitable bride. He lands in Queens, and quickly finds American women to be more confusing than he imagined. Sometimes overly cute entertainment relieved by clever costume cameos by Murphy and Hall. Later lawsuit resulted in columnist Art Buchwald being given credit for story. **116m/C VHS, DVD, Blu-ray Disc, HD DVD.** Eddie Murphy, Arsenio Hall, James Earl Jones, John Amos, Madge Sinclair, Shari Headley, Don Ameche, Louie Anderson, Paul Bates, Allison Dean, Eriq La Salle, Calvin Lockhart, Samuel L. Jackson, Cuba Gooding Jr., Vanessa Bell Calloway, Frankie Faison, Vondie Curtis-Hall; **D:** John Landis; **W:** David Sheffield, Barry W. Blaustein; **C:** Woody Omens; **M:** Nile Rodgers.

Coming Up Roses *Rhosyn A Rhith* 1987 (PG) Pleasant comedy about the residents of a small mining village in the South of Wales who fight to keep their local movie house from being shut down. In Welsh with English subtitles. **95m/C VHS.** *GB* Dafydd Hywel, Iola Gregory, Olive Michael, Mari Emlyn, Bill Paterson; **D:** Stephen Bayly; **W:** Ruth Carter; **M:** Michael Storey.

Command Decision 1948 Upon realizing he must send his men on missions-of-no-return to destroy German jet production, Gable's WWII flight commander becomes tactically at odds with his political superior, Pidgeon (who's not keen to have his precision bombing plans placed in an unflattering light). Based on the stage hit by William Wister Haines, it's a late war pic by Wood, who earlier directed such diverse efforts as "A Night at the Opera," "The Devil and Miss Jones," and "Our Town." Vintage war-is-hell actioner. **112m/B VHS, DVD.** Clark Gable, Walter Pidgeon, Van Johnson, Brian Donlevy, Charles Bickford, John Hodiak, Ray Collins, Edward Earle, Sam Flint, Warner Anderson, Don Haggerty, Henry Hall, Alvin Hammer, Holmes Herbert; **D:** Sam Wood; **W:** George Froeschel, William Wister Haines, William R. Laidlaw; **C:** Harold Rosson; **M:** Miklos Rozsa.

Commandments 1996 (R) When Seth Warner (Quinn) loses his wife (Going), job, and even his dog, he finds no solace in faith and decides to test why God would make a good man suffer by breaking every one of the 10 commandments. Rachel (Cox), his wife's sister, persuades him to move in with her and her jerk husband Harry (LaPaglia), who can't really be bothered by Seth's problems. The three leads certainly have presence but given the ambivalence of the material, the movie doesn't hang together. **92m/C VHS, DVD.** Aidan Quinn, Courteney Cox, Anthony LaPaglia, Louis Zorich, Pat McNamara, Tom Aldredge, Pamela Gray, Alice Drummond, Jack Gilpin; *Cameos:* Joanna Going; **D:** Daniel Taplitz; **W:** Daniel Taplitz; **C:** Slawomir Idziak; **M:** Joseph Vitarelli.

Commando 1985 (R) An excommando leader's daughter is kidnapped in a blackmail scheme to make him depose a South American president. He fights instead, and proceeds to rescue his daughter amid a torrential flow of falling bodies. Violent action spiced with throwaway comic lines. **90m/C VHS, DVD, Blu-ray Disc.** Arnold Schwarzenegger, Rae Dawn Chong, Dan Hedaya, Vernon Wells, James Olson, David Patrick Kelly, Alyssa Milano, Bill Duke; **D:** Mark L. Lester; **W:** Steven E. de Souza; **C:** Matthew F. Leonetti; **M:** James Horner.

Commando Attack 1967 A tough sergeant leads a group of misfit soldiers to blow up a German radio transmitter the day before D-Day. **90m/C VHS.** Michael James, Monica Randall, Bob Sullivan; **D:** Leon Klimovsky.

Commando Invasion 1987 When an army captain is accused of murder, he hunts down the man he knows is responsible for the crime. Jungle revenge mayhem is confusing. Set in Vietnam. **90m/C VHS.** Jim Gaines, Michael James, Gordon Mitchell, Carol Roberts, Pat Vance, Ken(saku) Watanabe; **D:** John Gale.

Commando Squad 1976 (R) During WWII, soldiers go to battle to prevent the development of a device that reanimates flesh. The script stays dead. **82m/C VHS.** Chuck Alford, Peter Owen, April Adams; **D:** Charles Nizet.

Commando Squad 1987 (R) Story of drug agents undercover in Mexico, and a female agent who rescues her kidnapped lover. Firepower is wasted, but Shower is a former "Playboy" Playmate of the Year. **90m/C VHS.** Brian Thompson, William (Bill) Smith, Kathy Shower, Sid Haig, Robert Quarry, Ross Hagen, Mel Welles, Marie Windsor, Russ Tamblyn; **D:** Fred Olen Ray.

Commandos *Sullivan's Marauders* 1973 (PG) Commando operation against Rommel's forces in North Africa during WWII. Too much said, not enough action. **100m/C VHS, DVD.** *GE IT* Lee Van Cleef, Jack Kelly, Giampiero Albertini, Marilu Tolo; **D:** Armando Crispino; **W:** Armando Crispino, Lucio Battistrada, Dario Argento, Stefano Strucchi; **C:** Benito Frattari; **M:** Mario Nascimbene.

Commandos Strike at Dawn 1943 Norwegian villagers, including Muni, fight the invading Nazis, and eventually help the British Navy battle them over an Arctic supply line. Okay script helped along by veteran actors Muni and Gish. Based on a C.S. Forester story. **100m/B VHS, DVD.** Paul Muni, Lillian Gish, Cedric Hardwicke, Anna Lee, Ray Collins, Robert Coote, Alexander Knox, Rosemary DeCamp; **D:** John Farrow; **W:** Irwin Shaw; **C:** William Mellor.

Comment Ca Va? *How Is It Going?* 1976 The boss and workers in a Communist publishing house decide to make a simple film about how information is manufactured. But Odette, one of the workers, has some strange ideas about filmmaking. In French with English subtitles. **76m/C VHS.** *FR* Michel Marot, Anne-Marie Mieville; **D:** Anne-Marie Mieville, Jean-Luc Godard; **W:** Anne-Marie Mieville, Jean-Luc Godard; **C:** William Lubtchansky; **M:** Jean Schwarz.

The Commies Are Coming, the Commies Are Coming *Red Nightmare* 1957 Cult classic will leave viewers red from laughing in disbelief. Webb narrates this anticommunist movie about the Russians taking over the United States. Filmed in a documentary style, it captures the paranoia of the times. Re-released in 1984, just before the Evil Empire collapsed. **60m/B VHS.** Jack Webb, Jack Kelly, Jeanne Cooper, Peter Brown, Pat(ricia) Woodell, Andrew Duggan, Peter Breck, Robert Conrad; **D:** George Waggner; **W:** Vincent Fotre; **C:** Robert Hoffman; **M:** William Lara.

Commissar *Komissar* 1968 Before the Soviet Union ended up in the ashcan of history, this film was labeled as "treason" and shelved in Red Russia. Now, even Americans can view the story of a female Soviet soldier who becomes pregnant during the civil war of 1922. The Soviet military has no policy regarding pregnancy, so the woman is dumped on a family of outcast Jews to complete her pregnancy. This film makes the strong statement that women were just as discriminated against in the U.S.S.R. as were many races or creeds, especially Jews. In Russian with English subtitles. Released in the U.S. in 1988. **105m/B VHS, DVD.** *RU* Nonna Mordyukova, Rolan Bykov, Raisa Nedashkovskaya, Vasily Shukshin, Pavlik Levin, Ludmila Volinskaya; **D:** Alexander Askoldov; **W:** Alexander Askoldov; **C:** Valery Ginsberg; **M:** Alfred Schnittke.

The Commitments 1991 (R) Convinced that they can bring soul music to Dublin, a group of working-class youth form a band. High-energy production paints an interesting, unromanticized picture of modern Ireland and refuses to follow standard showbiz cliches, even though its lack of resolution hurts. Honest, whimsical dialogue laced with poetic obscenities, delivered by a cast of mostly unknowns. Very successful soundtrack features the music of Wilson Pickett, James Brown, Otis Redding, Aretha Franklin, Percy Sledge, and others, and received a Grammy nomination. Based on the book "The Commitments" by Roddy Doyle, part of a trilogy which includes "The Snapper" and "The Van." **116m/C VHS, DVD.** *IR* Andrew Strong, Bronagh Gallagher, Glen Hansard, Michael Aherne, Dick Massey, Ken McCluskey, Robert Arkins, Dave Finnegan, Johnny Murphy, Angeline Ball, Felim Gormley, Maria Doyle Kennedy, Colm Meaney; **D:** Alan Parker; **W:** Dick Clement, Roddy Doyle, Ian La Frenais; **C:** Gale Tattersall; **M:** Paul Bushnell. British Acad. '91: Adapt. Screenplay, Director (Parker), Film.

Committed 1991 (R) Schlockmeister Levey's latest directorial effort is a step above his earlier "Slumber Party" and "Happy Hooker Goes to Washington," a statement ringing with the faintest of praise. Thinking she's applying for a job at an asylum, a nurse discovers she has committed herself. Try as she may, not even a committed nurse can snake her way out of the pit of madness they call "The Institute." **93m/C VHS.** Jennifer O'Neill, William Windom, Robert Forster, Ron Palillo, Sydney Lassick; **D:** William A. Levey.

Committed 1999 (R) Joline (Graham) is the madly devoted wife of Carl (Wilson) who, two years after their marriage, decides he should leave their New York home to take a job in the Southwest—alone. Joline soon decides to track him down and heads out on the usual misadventurous road trip, accompanied by her brother (Affleck) and a handsome neighbor (Visnjic). Of course, when she does find Carl there's quite a lot that needs to be resolved. **98m/C VHS, DVD.** Heather Graham, Luke Wilson, Casey Affleck, Goran Visnjic, Patricia Velasquez, Alfonso Arau, Mark Ruffalo, Kim Dickens, Clea Duvall; **D:** Lisa Krueger; **W:** Lisa Krueger; **C:** Tom Krueger. Sundance '00: Cinematog.

Common Bonds 1991 (PG) After being put together in an experimental outreach program, two mismatched partners struggle to break free from a system that threatens to destroy them both. **109m/C VHS.** Rae Dawn Chong, Michael Ironside, Brad Dourif; **D:** Allan Goldstein; **M:** Graeme Coleman.

Common Ground 2000 Three stories dealing with homosexuality in America from the 1950s to the present in the same small town of Homer, Connecticut. Vogel's "A Friend of Dorothy" finds Dorothy (Murphy) returning home after being dishonorably discharged from the Navy after being caught at a gay bar. McNally's "Mr. Roberts" focuses on the 70s and confused high school senior Toby Anderson (Thomas). Toby reaches out for some understanding from his closeted French teacher (Weber), only to be rejected. Fierstein's "Andy and Amos" takes place in 2000, with Amos (Le Gros) having the jitters before his commitment ceremony to lover Andy (Airlie). But it's his conservative dad Ira (Asner) who turns out to be an unexpected booster. **105m/C VHS.** Brittany Murphy, Margot Kidder, Brian Kerwin, Mimi Rogers, Jason Priestley, Joanne Vannicola, Helen Shaver, Jonathan Taylor Thomas, Steven Weber, Dan Lauria, Ed Asner, James LeGros, Andrew Airlie, Harvey Fierstein, Beau Bridges, Eric Stoltz; **D:** Donna Deitch; **W:** Harvey Fierstein, Terrance McNally, Paula Vogel; **C:** Jacek Laskus. CABLE

Common Law Wife 1963 (R) Made-for-the-drive-in flick about a man whose common law marriage is threatened by his niece, who wants his money. Murder and mayhem abound when the man's moonshine is poisoned. Cheap and hard to swallow. **81m/B VHS, DVD.** Lacy Kelly, Shugfoot Rainey, Annabelle Lee, Jody Works, Anne MacAdams, George Edgely; **D:** Eric Sayers.

Communion 1989 (R) A serious adaptation of the purportedly nonfictional bestseller by Whitley Strieber about his family's abduction by extraterrestrials. Spacey new age story is overlong and exploitative. **103m/C VHS, DVD.** Christopher Walken, Lindsay Crouse, Frances Sternhagen, Joel Carlson, Andreas Katsulas, Basil Hoffman; **D:** Philippe Mora; **M:** Eric Clapton.

Companeros 1970 (R) The Mexican revolution. Shoeshine boy Vasco (Milian) kills a federale officer and is made a lieutenant by General Mongo (Bodalo), one of many warring revolutionary warlords. Vasco and Swedish gun salesman Yodlof Pederson (Nero) become unlikely companions when MonMongo sends them to Yuma, to liberate authentic revolutionary Xantos (Rey), a pre-Gandhi preacher of nonviolence imprisoned by American oil interests in the process of extorting oil leases from him. The conflict is a simple one between virtuous Communists and oppressive generals and capitalists. Director Corbucci's mood is less cynical, and more inclined toward comedy. The comedy direction is broader than broad, and obvious to the point of playing to juveniles. There is plenty of action in the film, guaranteeing a shootout or stunt every few minutes. **118m/C DVD. IT SP GE** Franco Nero, Tomas Milian, Jack Palance, Fernando Rey, Iris Berben, Francisco Bodalo; **D:** Sergio Corbucci; **W:** Sergio Corbucci, Massimo De Rita, Arduino (Dino) Maiuri, Fritz Ebert; **C:** Alejandro Ulloa; **M:** Ennio Morricone.

The Companion 1994 (R) In 2015 romance novelist Gillian Tanner (Harrold) decides to hide out at a remote mountain cabin to get over a broken love affair. For safety's sake, Gillian takes along custom-designed android companion Geoffrey (Greenwood). But then Gillian decides to tinker with Geoffrey's programming, turning him from domestic guardian to devoted lover. Unfortunately, Geoffrey doesn't understand the difference between fantasy and reality (especially since he's getting his ideas from Gillian's romance novels) and becomes lethally obsessed. **94m/C VHS, DVD.** Kathryn Harrold, Bruce Greenwood, Talia Balsam, Brion James, Bryan Cranston, Joely Fisher; **D:** Gary Fleder; **W:** Ian Seeberg, Valerie Bennett; **C:** Rick Bota; **M:** David Shire. VIDEO

The Company 2003 (PG-13) Altman delivers another fine ensemble work, this time dealing with the inner workings of the Joffrey Ballet of Chicago. Campbell stars as Ry, an up and coming ballerina struggling to establish herself. But even her story takes a backseat to the dancing and the behind-the-scenes business of creating a ballet. Strong cast, most of whom are dancers and not actors, makes for compelling viewing. Campbell, who once studied ballet before turning to acting, collaborated on the story as a personal project. **112m/C DVD. US GE** Neve Campbell, Malcolm McDowell, James Franco, Barbara Robertson, Susie Cusack, William Dick, Marilyn Dodds Frank; **D:** Robert Altman; **W:** Barbara Turner; **C:** Andrew Dunn; **M:** Van Dyke Parks.

The Company 2007 Miniseries about the Cold War and the CIA based on the Robert Littell novel. Jack McAuliffe (O'Connell) is recruited to join the Agency fresh out of Yale, mentored by cynical expert Harry Torriti (Molina). In postwar Berlin, it's spy vs. spy with the KGB as the CIA tries to find a mole in their midst. McAuliffe is on hand for the 1956 Hungarian uprising—and gets involved with local freedom fighter Elizabet (McElhone)—and eventually is drawn into the fiasco that was the Bay of Pigs. Overstuffs a plot that spans decades and has to rush to tie up its loose ends. **286m/C DVD, Blu-ray Disc.** Chris O'Donnell, Alfred Molina, Michael Keaton, Rory Cochrane, Alessandro Nivola, Ulrich Thomsen, Natascha (Natasha) McElhone, Tom Hollander, Alexandra Maria Lara, Raoul Bova, Ted Atherton; **D:** Mikael Salomon; **W:** Ken Nolan; **C:** Ben Nott; **M:** Jeff Beal. CABLE

Company Business 1991 (PG-13) Sam Boyd is a retired CIA agent who's brought back to swap Pyiotr Grushenko (Baryshnikov), a Russian mole in the State Department, for a U-2 pilot being held in Moscow. The swap is to be made in Berlin and also involves $2 million of what turns out to be Colombian drug money. When things inevitably go wrong (both intelligence agencies would like these two men out of the way permanently) the two men find they must depend on each other if they want to stay alive. An unimaginative plot wastes a stalwart cast in this old-fashioned spy drama. **104m/C VHS, DVD.** Gene Hackman, Mikhail Baryshnikov, Kurtwood Smith, Terry O'Quinn; **D:** Nicholas Meyer; **W:** Nicholas Meyer.

Company Man 2000 (PG-13) Goofy satire about the Bay of Pigs invasion co-written and co-directed by McGrath, who also stars as a wimpy grammar teacher who, through some bizarre coincidences, manages, unwittingly, to cause the Cold War debacle. Though the big name cast seems to be having fun, absurdity abounds and eventually topples

The Company of Wolves 🐾🐾🐾 1985 (R) Allen makes an appearance as a CIA veteran in Cuba. 81m/C VHS, DVD, Douglas McGrath, Sigourney Weaver, John Turturro, Anthony LaPaglia, Ryan Phillippe, Denis Leary, Alan Cumming, Woody Allen, Heather Matarazzo, Jeffrey Jones; **D:** Douglas McGrath, Peter Askin; **W:** Douglas McGrath, Peter Askin; **C:** Russell Boyd; **M:** David Lawrence.

this romping, madcap throwback, Woody on the verge of womanhood listens to her grandmother (Lansbury) tell fairy tales and dreams of a medieval fantasy world inhabited by men who turn into wolves. An adult "Little Red Riding Hood" that's heavy on dreamy visuals and Freudian symbolism. 95m/C VHS, DVD, Angela Lansbury, David Warner, Stephen Rea, Tusse Silberg, Sarah Patterson, Brian Glover, Danielle Dax, Graham Crowden, Micha Bergese, Kathryn Pogson, Georgia Slowe; **D:** Neil Jordan; **W:** Neil Jordan, Angela Carter; **C:** Bryan Loftus; **M:** George Fenton.

Compromising Positions 🐾🐾 1985 (R) A philandering dentist is killed on Long Island, and a bored housewife begins to investigate, uncovering scandal after scandal. Black comedy mixed unevenly with mystery makes for unsatisfying brew. However, Ivey is a standout as Sarandon's best friend. Screenplay was written by Susan Isaacs, based on her novel of the same title. 99m/C VHS, Susan Sarandon, Raul Julia, Edward Herrmann, Judith Ivey, Mary Beth Hurt, Josh Mostel, Anne DeSalvo; **D:** Frank Perry; **M:** Brad Fiedel.

Compulsion 🐾🐾🐾½ 1959 Artie Strauss (Dillman) is a mother-dominated sadist who, along with submissive friend Judd Steiner (Stockwell), plan and execute a cold-blooded murder. Flamboyant lawyer Jonathan Wilk (brilliantly portrayed by Welles) knows he has no defense so he attacks the system and establishment, seeking to at least save his clients from death. A suspenseful shocker with taut direction and a tight script. Based on the notorious 1924 Leopold and Loeb murder trial; also filmed as "Rope" and "Swoon." 103m/B VHS, DVD, Orson Welles, Bradford Dillman, Dean Stockwell, Diane Varsi, E.G. Marshall, Martin Milner, Richard Anderson, Robert F. Simon, Edward Binns, Robert Burton, Wilton Graff, Gavin MacLeod, Wendell Holmes; **D:** Richard Fleischer; **W:** Richard Murphy; **C:** William Mellor.

Computer Beach Party 🐾 1988 A couple of surf-head college computer hackers foil their mayor's plans to develop their favorite beach. The title, at least, is original. 97m/C VHS, Hank Amigo, Stacey Nemour, Andre C~imere; **D:** Gary A. Troy.

Computer Wizard 🐾🐾 1977 (G) Boy genius builds a powerful electronic device. His intentions are good, but the invention disrupts the town and lands him in big

trouble. Not the "Thomas Edison Story." 91m/C VHS, Henry Darrow, Kate Woodville, Guy Madison, Marc Gilpin; **D:** John Florea.

The Computer Wore Tennis Shoes 🐾½ 1969 (G) Disney comedy (strictly for the kids) about a slow-witted college student who turns into a genius after a "shocking" encounter with the campus computer. His new brains give the local gangster headaches. Sequel: "Now You See Him, Now You Don't." 87m/C VHS, DVD, Kurt Russell, Cesar Romero, Joe Flynn, William Schallert, Alan Hewitt, Richard Bakalyan; **D:** Robert Butler; **M:** Robert F. Brunner.

Comrade X 🐾🐾½ 1940 Gable is an American correspondent in Moscow who is blackmailed into marrying die-hard Communist Lamarr in this comedic spinoff of "Ninotchka." The two stars failed to create any sparks as a love duo, although their previous film "Boom Town" was a hit. Based on a story by Walter Reisch. 87m/B VHS, Clark Gable, Hedy Lamarr, Oscar Homolka, Felix Bressart, Eve Arden, Sig Rumann, Natasha Lytess, Vladimir Sokoloff; **D:** King Vidor; **W:** Ben Hecht, Charles Lederer.

Comrades in Arms 🐾½ 1991 (R) When an international drug cartel threatens to take over the world, the United States and Russia must set their differences aside and team up to stop them. 90m/C VHS, Lyle Alzado, Rick Washburne, John Christian, Lance Henriksen; **D:** J. Christian Ingvordsen.

The Comrades of Summer 🐾🐾 1992 (R) Mantegna plays big-league baseball coach Sparky Smith, whose fiery temper gets him into big trouble. Out of a job, he discovers the only team willing to take a chance on him happens to be Russian. Sparky finds the players of the Russian National team need a lot of help—and not just with their English. 90m/C VHS, Joe Mantegna, Natalia (Natalya) Negoda, Mark Rolston, John Fleck, Eric Allen Kramer, Michael Lerner, Ian Tracey; **D:** Tommy Lee Wallace; **W:** Robert Rodat; **M:** William Olvis. **CABLE**

The Con 🐾🐾½ 1998 (PG-13) Barbara (De Mornay) is willing to do anything to get the money to pay off her loanshark, including marry small town mechanic Bobby Sommersdinger (Macy), who doesn't know he's a standout in a lot of money. But Bobby isn't quite the dim-wit he first appears to be, even as he succumbs to Barbara's charms. 92m/C VHS, Rebecca De Mornay, William H. Macy, Frances Steinhagen, Angela Paton, Don Harvey; **D:** Steven Schachter; **W:** William H. Macy, Steven Schachter; **C:** Peter Stein; **M:** Peter Manning Robinson. **CABLE**

Con Air 🐾🐾🐾 1997 (R) Producer Bruckheimer flies solo for the first time, and has a very successful flight. Cage reups as former Ranger Cameron Poe, jailed for manslaughter, who gets paroled just in time to catch a ride home aboard a plane filled with the worst of America's criminals. Led by Cyrus "The Virus" Grissom (Malkovich), the first-class psycho passengers take over the plane, and Cameron must save the day. Among the snappy one-liners, chases, shoot-outs, and stuff blowin' up real good, comes Federal Marsha Larkin (Cusack) to help Poe from the ground. Cusack can't shake his indie-film, quirky-kid image enough to really pass as an action hero, but he gives it his all. Flick supplies everything you'd expect from a summer blockbuster actioner, but it's best seen on a big-screen with surround sound to get the full effect. 105m/C VHS, DVD, Blu-ray Disc, Nicolas Cage, John Malkovich, John Cusack, Mykelti Williamson, Ving Rhames, Steve Buscemi, Colm Meaney, Rachel Ticotin, Dave Chappelle, M.C. Gainey, Danny Trejo, Nicholas Chinlund, Jesse Borrego, Angela Featherstone, Monica Potter, Jose Zuniga; **D:** Simon West; **W:** Scott Rosenberg; **C:** David Tattersall; **M:** Mark Mancina, Trevor Rabin.

The Con Artists 🐾½ 1980 After con man Quinn is sprung from prison, he and his protege set up a sting operation against the beautiful Capucine. Not clever or witty enough for the caper to capture interest. 86m/C VHS, DVD, Anthony

Quinn, Adriano Celentano, Capucine, Corinne Clery; **D:** Sergio Corbucci.

Con Games 🐾🐾 2002 (R) John Woodrow (Thomas) goes undercover in a maximum security California prison to investigate the murder of a senator's grandson. The prison is ruled by corrupt guard Hopkins (Roberts) and Woodrow's life expectancy takes a nosedive when Hopkins learns his true identity. 90m/C VHS, DVD, Eric Roberts, Martin Kove, Tommy Lee Thomas, Jody Nolan; **D:** Jefferson Edward Donald; **W:** Tommy Lee Thomas, Jefferson Edward Donald; **C:** John Lazear. **VIDEO**

Conagher 🐾🐾½ 1991 Louis L'Amour's Conagher 1991 A lyrical, if poorly plotted Western about a veteran cowboy who takes the whole movie to decide to end up in the arms of Louis L'Amour's novel doesn't capation of Louis L'Amour's novel doesn't create much intensity, though Elliott captures his character well. 94m/C VHS, DVD, Sam Elliott, Katharine Ross, Barry Corbin, Buck Taylor, Dub Taylor, Daniel Quinn, Anndi McAfee, Billy Green Bush, Ken Curtis; **D:** Reynaldo Villalobos. **C·A·B·L·E**

Conan the Barbarian 🐾🐾🐾 1982 (R) A fine sword and sorcery tale featuring brutality, excellent production values, and a rousing score. Conan's (Arnie, as always, this time as bad guy Thulsa Doom. Based on the character created by Robert E. Howard. Sequel: "Conan the Destroyer." 115m/C VHS, DVD, Arnold Schwarzenegger, James Earl Jones, Max von Sydow, Sandahl Bergman, Mako, Ben Davidson, Valerie Quennessen, Cassandra Gaviola, William (Bill) Smith; **D:** John Milius; **W:** John Milius, Oliver Stone; **C:** Duke Callaghan, John Cabrera; **M:** Basil Poledouris.

Conan the Destroyer 🐾🐾½ 1984 (PG) Conan is manipulated by Queen Tarami's into searching for a treasure. In return she'll bring Conan's love Valeria back to life. On his trip he meets Jones and Chamberlain, who later give him a hand. Excellent special effects, good humor, camp fun, somewhat silly finale. Sequel to the better "Conan the Barbarian." 101m/C VHS, DVD, Arnold Schwarzenegger, Grace Jones, Wilt Chamberlain, Sarah Douglas, Mako, Jeff Corey, Olivia D'Abo, Tracey Walter; **D:** Richard Fleischer; **W:** Stanley Mann; **C:** Jack Cardiff; **M:** Basil Poledouris. Golden Raspberres '84: Worst New Star (D'Abo).

Concealed Weapon 🐾½ 1994 (R) A struggling actor gets the part of a lifetime but then becomes the prime suspect in a brutal crime. 80m/C VHS, DVD, Sam Haney, Suzanne Wouk, Monica Simpson, Mark Driscoll, Karen Stone; **D:** Dave Payne, Milan Zirkovich.

Conceiving Ada 🐾🐾 1997 Experimental film is a homage to Lady Ada Lovelace (Swinton), daughter of Lord Byron, a 19th-century mathematician who developed what is now considered the first computer programming language. Ada is regarded by contemporary computer scientist Amy Coer (Fandang) as her spiritual mentor and Amy becomes obsessed with devising a method to actually communicate with the long-deceased Ada, whose life uncannily parallels her own. 85m/C VHS, DVD, Tilda Swinton, Francesca Faridany, Karen Black, John E. O'Keefe, J.D. Wolfe, Timothy Leary, John Perry Barlow, Owen Murphy; **D:** Lynn Hershman Leeson; **W:** Lynn Hershman Leeson, Eileen Jones; **C:** Hiro Narita.

The Concentratin' Kid 🐾🐾 1930 An unusual horse opera sans gunshot. Hoot's fiancee is kidnapped and taken to the range so that the renegade cowpokes can, uh, benefit from a female perspective on home decorating. Despite being outnumbered, Hoot concentrates and sets the rescue in motion, taking on the gang of rustlers without firing a shot. 54m/B VHS, Hoot Gibson, Kathryn Crawford, Duke Lee, Robert E. Homans, James Mason; **D:** Arthur Rosson.

The Concorde: Airport '79 🐾 1979 (PG) A supersonic film in the "Airport" tradition has the Concorde chased by missiles and fighter aircraft before it crashes in the Alps. Incredibly far-fetched nonsense with an all-star cast doesn't fly. 103m/C VHS, DVD, Alain Delon, Susan Blakely, Robert Wagner, Sylvia Kristel, John Davidson, Charo, Sylva Danning, Jimmie Walker, Eddie Albert, Bibi Andersson, Monica Lewis, Andrea Marcovicci, Martha Raye, Cicely Tyson, Mercedes McCambridge, George Kennedy, David Warner; **D:** David Lowell Rich; **W:** Eric Roth; **M:** Lalo Schifrin.

Concrete Angels 🐾 1987 (R) A poignant glimpse at the influence of rock music in its infancy. A group of deprived teens in Toronto form a band and audition to open for the Beatles. Lack of nostalgia is refreshing, but too much of this is amateurish. 97m/C VHS, CA Joseph Dimambro, Luke McKeehan, Ornie Craden, Dean Bosacki; **D:** Carlo Licomi.

Concrete Beat 🐾🐾 1984 A newspaper reporter simultaneously searches for a murderer, tries to win his ex-wife back, and writes front page stories for his editor/ex-father-in-law. Tough assignment. 74m/C VHS, Kenneth McMillan, John Getz, Darlanne Fluegel, Rhoda Gemignani; **D:** Robert Butler. **TV**

The Concrete Cowboys 🐾½ 1979 Two bumbling cowboys from Montana come to the metropolis of Nashville and promptly turn detective to foil a blackmail scheme and locate a missing singer. Barbara Mandrell and Roy Acuff play themselves. Silly made-for-TV pilot of short-lived series. 100m/C VHS, DVD, Jerry Reed, Tom Selleck, Morgan Fairchild, Claude Akins, Gene Evans, Roy Acuff, Barbara Mandrell; **D:** Burt Kennedy. **TV**

The Concrete Jungle 🐾🐾 The Criminal 1982 (R) After being set up by her no-good boyfriend, Bregman is sent to a correctional facility for drug smuggling. There she must learn to fend for herself (or else). Typical prison for gals fare with cute babes in revealing outfits, a topless riot, the bad warden, and a concerned social worker. Followed by "Chained Heat." 106m/C VHS, Tracy Bregman, Jill St. John, Barbara Luna, Peter Brown, Aimee (Amy) Eccles, Nita Talbot, Sondra Currie; **D:** Tom De Simone; **M:** Alan J. Adler.

Condemned 🐾🐾🐾 1929 Colman's second talkie fincs his character, Michel, sent to Devil's Island for theft. Michel makes life easier for himself by getting into the heart of the warden's unhappy wife (Harding). Adapted from the novel "Condemned to Devil's Island" by Blair Niles. 86m/B VHS, Ronald Colman, Ann Harding, Dudley Digges, Louis Wolheim; **D:** Wesley Ruggles; **W:** Sidney Howard; **C:** George Barnes, Gregg Toland; **M:** Jack Meskill, Pete Wendling.

Condemned 🐾 2007 (R) Violent grade-D actioner does exactly what it's supposed to and no more. Media slime Ian (Mammone) hits on a new reality concept: drop ten death-row inmates onto a remote island and tell them that the last survivor earns freedom and a paycheck while Internet subscribers pay to watch a live feed. Probably the only recognizable faces are former WWE wrestler Austin (Tony) Mussett, Masa Yamaguchi, Manu Bennett, Marcus Johnson, Christopher Baker, Rick Hoffman, Luke Pegler, Samantha Healy, Madeleine West, Emelia Burns, Nathan Jones, Angie Milliken; **D:** Scott Wiper; **W:** Scott Wiper, Rob Hedden; **C:** Ross Emery.

Condemned to Hell woof! Atrapados 1984 A tough-as-iron street punk gets thrown into a women's prison, where she must fight for her existence. Low-brow violence galore. 97m/C VHS, AR Camila Perisse, Betiana Blum, Cristina Murta, ..eonor Benedeto; **D:** Anibal Di Salvo; **W:** Anibal Di Salvo; **C:** Carlos Torlaschi; **M:** Luis Maria Serra.

Complex World 🐾½ 1992 (R) The Heartbreak Hotel is a notorious rock club which may not be around much longer. It seems the young owner's father is an ex-CIA redneck who is running for President and his son's profession is a political liability. Meanwhile, the town's mayor wants to replace the club with a shopping mall. A bomb is planted in the club's basement, spoiling for a fight but the crowd at the Heartbreak just rocks on. 90m/C VHS, Dan Welch, Bob Owczarek, Jay Charbonneau Tilman, Gandy Jr., David P.B. Stephens, Captain Lou Albano, Stanley Matis; **D:** James Wolpaw; **W:** James Wolpaw.

The Competition 🐾🐾🐾 1980 (PG) Two virtuoso pianists meet at an international competition and fall in love. Will they stay together if one of them wins? Can they have a performance career and love too? Is he trying to distract her with sex, so he can win? Dreyfuss and Irving are fine (they practiced for four months to look like they were actually playing the pianos), and Remick's character has some interesting insights into the world of art. 125m/C VHS, Richard Dreyfuss, Amy Irving, Lee Remick, Sam Wanamaker, Joseph Cali, Ty Henderson, Priscilla Pointer, James B. Sikking; **D:** Joel Oliansky; **M:** Lalo Schifrin.

Condemned to Live ♂♂ *1935*
Mild-mannered doctor Ralph Morgan and his fiancee Maxine Doyle seem like your average early 20th Century Middle-European couple...but the doctor's hunchbacked servant Mischa Auer is a tipoff that this is a horror movie of some sort. Like many men, the doctor has suffered from a vampire curse all his life. And, like many men, he is unaware of his blood-sucking habit, thanks to the concealment efforts of his loyal (hunchback) servant. Doyle discovers her fiance's sanguine secret, but not before she finds out she really loves Gleason, anyway. Answers the question: just how do you jilt a vampire? **68m/B VHS, DVD;** Ralph Morgan, Maxine Doyle, Russell Gleason, Pedro de Cordoba, Mischa Auer, Lucy Beaumont, Carl Stockdale; **D:** Frank Strayer.

Condition Red ♂♂ *1995 (R)* Philadelphia prison guard Dan Capelli's (Russo) illicit involvement with inmate Gidell (Williams) turns into big trouble and double-crosses thanks to her drug-dealing boyfriend Angel (Calderon). **85m/C VHS;** James Russo, Cynda Williams, Paul Calderon; **D:** Mika Kaurismaki; **W:** Andre Degas; **C:** Ken Kelsch; **M:** Mauri Sumen.

Condorman ♂♂ *1981 (PG)* Woody Wilkins, an inventive comic book writer, adopts the identity of his own character, Condorman, in order to help a beautiful Russian spy defect. A Disney film, strictly for the small fry. **90m/C VHS, DVD;** Michael Crawford, Oliver Reed, Barbara Carrera, James Hampton, Jean-Pierre Kalfon, Dana Elcar; **D:** Charles Jarrott; **W:** Glenn Gordon Caron; **C:** Charles F. Wheeler; **M:** Henry Mancini.

Conduct Unbecoming ♂♂½ *1975 (PG)* Late 19th-century India is the setting for a trial involving the possible assault of a British officer's wife. Ambitious production based on a British stage play suffers from claustrophobic atmosphere but is greatly redeemed by the first rate cast. **107m/C VHS, DVD, GB** Michael York, Richard Attenborough, Trevor Howard, Stacy Keach, Christopher Plummer, Susannah York, James Faulkner, Michael Culver, Persis Khambatta; **D:** Michael Anderson Sr.

The Conductor ♂♂ *Dyrygent 1980* A famous Polish-born conductor (Gielgud) returns to his birthplace after 50 years of living in the U.S. A dying man, he decides to work with a struggling provincial orchestra, much to the dismay of their own conductor. But the conductor finds himself being used in government schemes to take advantage of his return. In English and Polish with subtitles. **101m/C VHS, PL** John Gielgud, Krystyna Janda, Andrzej Seweryn, Jan Ciercierski, Tadeusz Czechowski; **D:** Andrzej Wajda; **W:** Andrzej Kijowski.

Coneheads ♂♂½ *1993 (PG)* Comedy inspired by once popular characters from "Saturday Night Live" coasts in on the coattails of "Wayne's World." Aykroyd and Curtin reprise their roles as Beldar Remulak who are just trying to fit in on Earth. Newman, who created the role of teenage daughter Connie, appears as Beldar's sister, while Thomas takes over as Connie (toddler Connie is Aykroyd's daughter, in her film debut). One-joke premise is a decade late and a dime short, though cast of comedy all-stars provides a lift. **86m/C VHS, DVD;** Dan Aykroyd, Jane Curtin, Laraine Newman, Jason Alexander, Michelle Rene Thomas, Chris Farley, Michael Richards, Lisa Jane Persky, Sinbad, Shishir Kurup, Michael McKean, Phil Hartman, David Spade, Dave Thomas, Jan Hooks, Chris Rook, Adam Sandler, Julia Sweeney, Danielle Aykroyd; **D:** Steven Barron; **W:** Tom Davis, Bonnie Turner, Terry Turner, Dan Aykroyd; **C:** Francis Kenny; **M:** David Newman.

Confess ♂♂ *2005 (R)* Former hacker Terell (Byrd) is ticked off when the surveillance technology he developed is stolen, so he takes compromising footage (via spy-cams) of those who slighted him and puts it on the Internet. Then Terrell decides to go big-time and he and accomplice Olivia (Larter) start targeting CEOs, politicians, and others of the power elite. He becomes a front-page anti-hero but the feds are calling Terrell a cyber-terrorist and want him brought to justice. Terrell's got bigger problems when imitators take his idea to a violent extreme. **87m/C DVD;** Eugene Byrd, Ali Larter, William Sadler, Melissa Leo, Glenn Fitzgerald; **D:** Stefan C. Schaefer; **W:** Stefan C. Schaefer; **C:** Leland Krane; **M:** Scott Jacoby. **VIDEO**

Confessing to Laura ♂♂ *Confesion a Laura 1990* Set in Colombia after the 1948 assassination of liberal leader Jorge Elieser Gaitain, which begets a violent civil war. Two people are trapped at Laura's house by the riots—setting up a spate of volatile emotion. Spanish with subtitles. **90m/C VHS, CL D:** Jaime Osorio Gomez.

The Confession ♂♂½ *1920* A priest hears a killer's confession and must protect the oath of confidentiality, even as his own brother is being convicted of the murder. **78m/B VHS,** Henry B. Walthall, Francis McDonald, William H. Clifford, Margaret McWade, Margaret Landis; **D:** Bertram Bracken.

The Confession ♂♂½ *1998 (R)* Slick lawyer Roy Bleakie (Baldwin) suffers a crisis of conscience with his latest case—the one he expects will hand him the District Attorney's office. Harry Fertig (Kingsley) has killed the three people he regards as responsible for the death of his young son. He's confessed to the crime and wants to plead guilty and accept responsibility—for his own ambitions Roy wants Harry to plead temporary insanity. But it turns out there's more to the case than even Roy knows. Good performances in what could be just another courtroom melodrama. **114m/C VHS, DVD;** Alec Baldwin, Ben Kingsley, Amy Irving, Jay O. Sanders, Kevin Conway, Anne Twomey, Christopher Lawford, Boyd Gaines, Christopher Noth; **D:** David Hugh Jones; **W:** David Black; **C:** Mike Fash; **M:** Mychael Danna.

The Confessional ♂ *House of Mortal Sin 1975 (R)* A mad priest unleashes a monster from his confessional to wreak havoc upon the world. Pray for your VCR. **108m/C VHS, DVD, GB** Anthony Sharp, Susan Penhaligon, Stephanie Beacham, Norman Eshley, Sheila Keith; **D:** Pete Walker.

The Confessional ♂♂♂ *Le Confessional 1995* Ambiguous psychological drama that's, in part, a homage to Alfred Hitchcock's 1952 film "I Confess," which was filmed in the same Quebec City locations. Pierre (Bluteau) returns to Quebec in 1989 for his father's funeral and to reunite with his adoptive brother Marc (Goyette). Marc's mother Rachel (who committed suicide shortly after his birth) refused to name his father, thought to be a priest, perhaps at the church where Hitchcock filmed his movie. Flashbacks depict the rotund director (Burrage) and his assistant (self Thomas) and their production. Lots of intriguing visuals, thanks to director Lepage's innovative stage background. French with subtitles. **100m/C VHS, CA FR GB** Lothaire Bluteau, Patrick Goyette, Jean-Louis Millette, Kristin Scott Thomas, Ron Burrage, Richard-Fraser Goyette, Francois Papineau, Marie Gignac, Anne-Marie Cadieux, Normand Daneau, Suzanne Clement, Lynda Lepage-Beaulieu; **D:** Robert Lepage; **W:** Robert Lepage; **C:** Alan Dostie; **M:** Sacha Putnam. Genie '95: Art Dir/Set Dec., Director (Lepage), Film.

Confessions of a Dangerous Mind ♂♂♂½ *2002 (R)* Clooney makes his directorial debut in this uneven but ultimately enjoyable biopic of TV game show producer Chuck Barris (Rockwell), who claimed in his "unauthorized" biography to be a CIA assassin during the height of his success. Clooney sometimes gets a little self-consciously "arty," but doesn't go overboard, and it actually fits with the absurdist tone of Kaufman's script. It's Rockwell who stands out here, with a breakout performance that showcases his range. **113m/C VHS, DVD, US** Sam Rockwell, Drew Barrymore, Rutger Hauer, George Clooney, Julia Roberts, Maggie Gyllenhaal, Kristen Wilson, Jennifer Hall; *Cameos:* Chuck Barris, Brad Pitt, Matt Damon, Jaye P. Morgan; **D:** George Clooney; **W:** Charlie Kaufman; **C:** Newton Thomas (Tom) Sigel; **M:** Alex Wurman. Natl. Bd. of Review '02: Screenplay.

Confessions of a Hit Man ♂♂ *1994 (R)* Nephew who stole millions from his mobster uncle must amend his sordid past. **93m/C VHS,** James Remar, Michael Wright, Emily Longstreth; **D:** Larry Leahy; **W:** Tony Cincripini, Larry Leahy; **M:** Billy Talbot.

Confessions of a Police Captain ♂♂ *1972 (PG)* A dedicated police captain tries to wipe out the bureaucratic corruption that is infecting his city. Balsam gives a fine performance in a heavy-going tale. **104m/C VHS, DVD, IT** Martin Balsam, Franco Nero, Marilu Tolo; **D:** Damiano Damiani; **W:** Damiano Damiani, Salvatore Laurani; **C:** Claudio Ragona; **M:** Riz Ortolani.

Confessions of a Serial Killer ♂♂ *1987* True story based on the life of Henry Lee Lucas, one of the nation's most vicious killers. Burns plays Lucas in this grisly account of his most violent murders. Shocking realistic look inside the mind of a serial killer. **85m/C VHS,** Robert A. Burns, Dennis Hill; **D:** Mark Blair.

Confessions of a Sociopathic Social Climber ♂♂ *2005 (R)* Katya Livingston (Hewitt) is a bad girl—a bitchy, self-serving but successful ad exec who is desperate to be invited to the San Francisco social event of the year. Unfortunately for her, Katya previously insulted the hostess. But that won't stop her angling for an invite, even if it causes problems for her dreamboat beau, Charles (Ferguson). **85m/C DVD;** Jennifer Love Hewitt, Colin Ferguson, Natasha Malthe, Daniel Roebuck, Joseph Lawrence; **D:** Dana Lustig; **W:** Eric Charnelo, Nicole Snyder; **C:** Luc Montpellier; **M:** Phil Marshall. **CABLE**

Confessions of a Teenage Drama Queen ♂ *2004 (PG)* Hip 15-year-old Lola (Lohan)—who decides her real name, Mary, isn't cool enough—is totally bumming when her divorced mom (Headly) grows weary of Manhattan's big city lifestyle and banishes her to a quaint New Jersey suburb. To make matters worse she is snubbed by the popular set at her new high school and decides to take action, which includes vying against ultra-popular Carla (Fox) for the lead in the school play. Along the way there's ample opportunity to witness the self-absorbed, shallow, and materialistic behaviors that drown out any positive messages for the 'tweener target group. Mediocre Disney production is based on Dyan Sheldon's successful book. **89m/C VHS, DVD, US** Lindsay Lohan, Adam Garcia, Glenne Headly, Alison Pill, Carol Kane, Eli Marienthal, Sheila McCarthy, Tom McCamus, Megan Fox, Richard Fitzpatrick; **D:** Sara Sugarman; **W:** Gail Parent; **C:** Stephen Burum; **M:** Mark Mothersbaugh.

Confessions of a Vice Baron ♂ *1942* Vice Baron Lombardo makes it big as a drug dealer and flesh peddler, then loses it all when he falls in love. Sleazy exploitation. **70m/B VHS, DVD,** Willy Castello; **D:** John Melville.

Confessions of Sorority Girls ♂♂½ *1994 (PG-13)* Sometime in the early '60s, sweet Sabrina (Luner) shows up at college and takes it by storm. Will she steal Rita's (Milano) beau? That's the least of her schemes. The villainy is played strictly for campy laughs and the film is never as trashy as its title suggests. Originally made as part of Showtime's "Rebel Highway" series and a remake of Roger Corman's 1957 "Sorority Girl." **83m/ C VHS,** Jamie Luner, Alyssa Milano, Bette Rae, Brian Bloom, Natalija Nogulich; **D:** Uli Edel; **C:** Jean De Segonzac. **CABLE**

Confessions of Tom Harris ♂ *Tale of the Cock; Childish Things 1972 (PG)* Somewhere between all the prize-fighting, leg-breaking for the mob, and jail terms for rape, Tom Harris finds time for a life-changing encounter with Don. Based on true story. **90m/C VHS,** Don Murray, Linda Evans, David Brian, Gary Clarke, Logan Ramsey, Angelique Pettyjohn; **D:** John Derek, David Nelson; **W:** Don Murray.

The Confessor ♂♂½ *The Good Shepherd 2004 (PG-13)* Worldly Father Daniel Clemens (Slater) is shocked when a parish priest (Flores) is arrested for the murder of a young street hustler and apparently commits suicide in jail. Clemens is convinced the priest was innocent and sets out to find out whodunit with the aid of journalist (and ex-flame) Madeline (Parker). Predictable story with huge plot holes. **90m/C DVD, CA** Christian Slater, Molly Parker, Stephen Rea, Gordon Pinsent, Von Flores, Nancy Beatty; **D:** Lewin Webb; **W:** Brad Mirman; **C:** Curtis Petersen; **M:** Gary Koffnoff. **VIDEO**

Confetti ♂♂ *2006 (R)* Over the top Brit romantic comedy about three would-be weddings. Bridal magazine Confetti is sponsoring a contest for the year's most original wedding. The three finalists are: competitive yuppies Josef (Mangan) and Isabelle (MacNeill) who choose a tennis theme; Matt (Freeman) and Sam (Stevenson) who want a musical extravaganza, though neither of them can sing or dance; and nudists Michael (Webb) and Joanna (Colman) who want a clothes-free ceremony, to the consternation of Confetti editor Vivien (Montagu). Meltdowns occur as the big finale approaches for one overwhelmed couple. **100m/C DVD, GB** Martin Freeman, Jessica Stevenson, Robert Webb, Stephen Mangan, Meredith MacNeill, Olivia Colman, Marc Wootton, Vincent Franklin, Jason Watkins; **D:** Debbie Isitt; **C:** Dewald Aukema; **M:** Paul Englishby.

Confidence ♂♂♂½ *2003 (R)* That would be "confidence" as in manner and game. Jake Vig (Burns) and his cronies are smalltime con artists who scam the wrong man—an accountant for L.A. crime boss King (Hoffman). To forestall any further unpleasantness, Jake goes to King and agrees to repayment by performing an elaborate con on King's rival. Let's just say that there's always another scam and things are hardly ever what they seem. Hoffman, with king-sized tics and quirks, veers into territory usually reserved for Walken or Pacino, but at least he's having fun. The movie could use a little more of that. Gritty and dark at times, this one's still an enjoyable entry in the scam/heist genre. **98m/C VHS, DVD, US** Edward Burns, Dustin Hoffman, Rachel Weisz, Andy Garcia, Paul Giamatti, Donal Logue, Luis Guzman, Brian Van Holt, Franky G., Morris Chestnut, Robert Forster, Leland Orser, Louis Lombardi, Tommy (Tiny) Lister, John Carroll Lynch; **D:** James Foley; **W:** Doug Jung; **C:** Juan Ruiz-Anchia.

Confidential *woof! 1986 (R)* A '40s detective tries to solve a decades-old axe murder, only to disappear himself. Horrible fare from our friends north of the border. **95m/C VHS, CA** Neil Munro, August Schellenberg, Chapelle Jaffe, Tom Butler; **D:** Bruce Pittman.

Confidentially Yours ♂♂♂ *Vivement Dimanche; Finally, Sunday 1983* Truffaut's homage to Hitchcock, based on Charles Williams' "The Long Saturday Night." A hapless small-town real estate agent is framed for a rash of murders and his secretary, who is secretly in love with him, tries to clear his name. Truffaut's last film is stylish and entertaining. In French with English subtitles. **110m/B VHS, DVD, FR** Fanny Ardant, Jean-Louis Trintignant, Philippe Morier-Genoud, Philippe Laudenbach, Caroline Sihol; **D:** Francois Truffaut; **W:** Francois Truffaut, Suzanne Schiffman, Jean Aurel; **C:** Nestor Almendros; **M:** Georges Delerue.

Conflict ♂♂♂ *1945* Bogart falls for his sister-in-law and asks his wife for a divorce. She refuses, he plots her murder, and thinks up the alibi. When the police fail to notify him of her death, Bogart is forced to report his wife missing. But is she dead? Her guilty husband smells her perfume, sees her walking down the street, and discovers the body is missing from the scene of the crime. Suspenseful thriller also features Greenstreet as a psychologist/family friend who suspects Bogart knows more than he's telling. **86m/B VHS,** Humphrey Bogart, Alexis Smith, Sydney Greenstreet, Rose Hobart, Charles Drake, Grant Mitchell; **D:** Curtis Bernhardt.

Conflict of Interest 𝒹𝒹½ 1992 (R) Gideon (Nelson) is a thug who runs stolen cars, drugs, and women from his heavy-metal club on the wrong side of town. Mickey Flannery (McDonald) is the new cop determined to get Gideon behind bars, especially after Gideon kills Mickey's wife, sets up his son on a phony murder rap, and kidnaps his son's girlfriend. Now it's personal and Mickey will stop at nothing to get his revenge. Over-the-top performance by Nelson will have the viewer hoping he gets it soon and puts the film out of its misery. **88m/C VHS.** Judd Nelson, Christopher McDonald, Alyssa Milano, Dey Young, Gregory Alan Harris; **D:** Gary Davis; **W:** Gregory Miller, Michael Angeli, **C:** Bryan England.

The Conformist 𝒹𝒹𝒹 1971 Character study of young Italian fascist, plagued by homosexual feelings, who must prove his loyalty by killing his old professor. Decadent and engrossing story is brilliantly acted. Based on the novel by Alberto Moravia. **108m/C VHS, DVD.** **IT FR GE** Jean-Louis Trintignant, Stefania Sandrelli, Dominique Sanda, Pierre Clementi, Gastone Moschin, Pasquale Fortunato; **D:** Bernardo Bertolucci; **W:** Bernardo Bertolucci; **C:** Vittorio Storaro; **M:** Georges Delerue. Natl. Soc. Film Critics '71: Cinematog (Storaro), Director (Bertolucci).

Confusion of Genders 𝒹𝒹 2000 Bisexual fortyish lawyer Alain (Gregory) wallows in various sexual relationships without committing emotionally to anyone in this provocative but ultimately tiresome farce, whose characters are all slick surface. The narcissist has a vague interest in having a family and has reluctantly agreed to marry long-time law partner Laurence (Richard), who is pregnant by him. Meanwhile, there's the lustful teenage brother, Christophe (Thouvenin), of one of Alain's ex-girlfriends and Alain's own interest in one of his incarcerated clients, Marc (Martinez). Marc is willing to trade sex with Alain for a jailhouse meeting with his girlfriend Babette (Gayet), whom Alain also gets involved with. And so it continues. French with subtitles. **94m/C DVD.** **FR** Pascal Greggory, Nathalie Richard, Julie Gayet, Vincent Martinez, Cyrille Thouvenin, Alain Bashung; **D:** Ilan Duran Cohen; **W:** Ilan Duran Cohen, Philippe Lasry; **C:** Jeanne Lapoirie; **M:** Jay-Jay Johanson.

Congo 𝒹𝒹 1995 (PG-13) Communications company supervisor jets off to the African jungle along with a primatologist to search for a lost city's priceless diamonds, the thrills or fun of other Crichton adaptations. **109m/C VHS, DVD.** Mary Ellen Trainor, Dylan Walsh, Laura Linney, Ernie Hudson, Tim Curry, Grant Heslov, Joe Don Baker; **D:** Frank Marshall; **W:** John Patrick Shanley; **C:** Allen Daviau; **M:** Jerry Goldsmith.

Congress Dances 𝒹𝒹 Der Kongress Tanzt 1931 A rare German musical about a romance in old Vienna. Popular in its day, it was subsequently banned by the Nazis in 1937. In German with English subtitles. **92m/B VHS. GE** Lilian Harvey, Conrad Veidt, Willy Fritsch; **D:** Erik Charell.

A Connecticut Yankee 𝒹𝒹𝒹 1931 A charming, if somewhat dated, version of the popular Mark Twain story, "A Connecticut Yankee in King Arthur's Court." Rogers is a radio shop owner who dreams his way back to the Knights of the Round Table. Story rewritten to fit Rogers' amiable style and overcomes weak points in the script. **96m/B VHS.** Will Rogers, Myrna Loy, Maureen O'Sullivan, William Farnum, Frank Albertson; **D:** David Butler.

A Connecticut Yankee in King Arthur's Court 𝒹𝒹½ A Yankee in King Arthur's Court 1949 A pleasant version of the famous Mark Twain story about a 20th century man transported to Camelot and mistaken for a dangerous wizard. This was the third film version of the classic, which was later remade as "Unidentified Flying Oddball," a TV movie, and an animated feature. **T** "Once and For Always; Busy Doin' Nothin'; If You Stub Your Toe on the Moon; When Is Sometime?; Twixt Myself and Me. **106m/C VHS, DVD.** Bing Crosby, Rhonda Fleming, William Bendix, Cedric Hardwicke, Henry Wilcoxon, Murvyn Vye, Virginia Field; **D:** Tay Garnett; **C:** Ray Rennahan.

A Connecticut Yankee in King Arthur's Court 𝒹𝒹½ 1989 The Mark Twain classic has had a gender switch in this TV version, with Pulliam as the time-travelling heroine who winds up in the royal court. **100m/C VHS.** Keshia Knight Pulliam, Jean Marsh, Rene Auberjonois, Emma Samms, Whip Hubley, Michael Gross; **D:** Mel Damski; **W:** Paul Zindel. TV

The Connection 𝒹𝒹𝒹 1961 The Living Theatre's ground-breaking performance of Jack Gelber's play about heroin addicts waiting for their connection to arrive, while a documentary filmmaker hovers nearby with his camera. **105m/B VHS, DVD.** Warren Finnerty, Carl Lee, William Redfield, Roscoe Lee Browne, Garry Goodrow, James Anderson, Jackie McLean; **D:** Shirley Clarke.

Connie and Carla 𝒹𝒹½ 2004 (PG-13) "Victor/Victoria" meets "Some Like It Hot" in this train wreck. Writer Vardalos and Collette are Connie and Carla, who have been a singing team since childhood and who perform medleys in an airport lounge where, despite being has-beens that never were, the two still dream of stardom. In an unlikely turn of events, they go to witness a mob hit and are forced to go on the lam to L.A. where they pretend to be female impersonators. The girls' act is a surprise hit, allowing minor celebrity and close calls with the mob to ensue. Duchovney is the interior sub-plot love interest who adds nothing to this unfunny, forced comedy filled with extremely cliched, stereotypical gay humor. **98m/C DVD. US** Nia Vardalos, Toni Collette, David Duchovny, Stephen Spinella, Ian Gomez, Nick Sandow, Dash Mihok, Robert John Burke, Alec Mapa, Christopher] Logan, Robert Kaiser, Boris McGivern; **D:** Babz Chula, Linda Darlow; **Cameos:** Debbie Reynolds; **D:** Michael Lembeck; **W:** Nia Vardalos; **C:** Richard Greatrex; **M:** Randy Edelman.

Connor's War 𝒹½ 2006 (R) After CIA special agent Connors (Treach) is blinded during a mission, he asks hot doctor Amanda (Peeples) to help him out while he tracks down his former boss, Brooks (Markuma), who's gone rogue. Treach does well in his routine actioner. **90m/C DVD.** Treach, Nia Peeples, Blu Markuma, **D:** Nick Castle; **W:** D. Kyle Johnson; **C:** Suki Medencevic. VIDEO

The Conqueror WOOF! Conqueror of the Desert 1956 Wayne in pointed helmet and goatee as Genghis Khan is convincingly miscast as the kidnapped daughter of a powerful enemy. Rife with stilted, unintentionally funny dialogue, Oriental western was very expensive to make (with backing by Howard Hughes), and is now listed in the "Fifty Worst Films of All Time." No matter, it's surreal enough to enable viewer to approximate an out-of-body experience. Even those on the set suffered; filming took place near a nuclear test site in Utah and many members of the cast and crew eventually developed cancer. **111m/C VHS, DVD.** John Wayne, Susan Hayward, Pedro Armendariz Sr., Thomas Gomez, John Hoyt, Ted de Corsia, Leslie Bradley, Peter Mamakos; **D:** Dick Powell; **W:** Oscar Millard; **C:** Joseph LaShelle, Harry Wild; **M:** Victor Young.

The Conqueror Worm 𝒹𝒹𝒹 Witchfinder General; Edgar Allan Poe's Conqueror Worm 1968 Price turns in a fine performance portraying the sinister Matthew Hopkins, a real-life 17th-century witchhunter. No "ham" in this low-budget, unbilled thriller, based on Ronald Bassett's novel. The last of three films from director Reeves, who died from an accidental overdose in 1969. **95m/C VHS, DVD.** Vincent Price, Ian Ogilvy, Hilary Dwyer, Rupert Davies, Robert Russell, Patrick Wymark, Wilfrid Brambell, Nicky Henson, Bernard Kay, Tony Selby; **D:** Michael Reeves; **W:** Michael Reeves, Louis M. Heyward, Tom Baker; **C:** John Coquillon; **M:** Paul Ferris.

Conquest 𝒹𝒹𝒹 Marie Walewska 1937 Garbo, as the Polish countess Marie Walewska, tries to persuade Napoleon (Boyer) to free her native Poland from the Russian czar. Garbo, Boyer, and Ouspenskaya are outstanding, while the beautiful costumes and lavish production help, but the script is occasionally weak. A boxoffice flop at the time, which ended up costing MGM more than any movie it had made up until that time. **115m/B VHS.** Greta Garbo, Charles Boyer, Reginald Owen, Alan Marshall, Henry Stephenson, Leif Erickson, May Whitty, Maria Ouspenskaya, Vladimir Sokoloff, Scotty Beckett; **D:** Clarence Brown; **C:** Karl Freund.

Conquest 𝒹½ 1983 (R) Sword and sorcery tale of two mighty warriors against an evil sorceress who seeks world domination. Excellent score. **92m/C VHS, DVD. IT SP MX** Jorge (George) Rivero, Andrea Occhipinti, Violeta Cela, Sabrina Siani; **D:** Lucio Fulci; **M:** Claudio Simonetti.

Conquest 𝒹𝒹 1998 Pincer Bedier moves back to Conquest, the dying prairie town of his childhood, to run the local bank. Most of the town's aging citizens think he's crazy for trying to revitalize its boarded-up businesses. But Pincer's unexpectedly aided in his mission by Daisy MacDonald, a determined English lass who doesn't have the money to repair the ear that stranded her in Conquest. She agrees to help out Bedier and they wind up falling in love. And then the town's other residents begin to believe in Bedier's maybe not-so-impossible dream. **90m/C VHS, CA GB** Lothaire Bluteau, Tara Fitzgerald, Monique Mercure, David Fox; **D:** Piers Haggard; **W:** Rob Forsyth; **C:** Gerald Packer; **M:** Ron Sures.

Conquest of Cochise 𝒹𝒹 1953 Mediocre oater about a cavalry officer who must stop the war between the Apache and Comanche tribes and a group of Mexicans in the Southwest of the 1850s. **70m/C VHS.** John Hodiak, Robert Stack, Joy Page; **D:** William Castle.

Conquest of Mycene 𝒹½ Ercole Contro Molock; Hercules vs. the Moloch 1963 The Prince of Mycene (who becomes Hercules thanks to dubbing) battles evil queen Neri and her equally evil son, Moloch. Typical musclemen fodder. **102m/C VHS, DVD. IT FR** Gordon Scott, Rosalba Neri, Jany Clair, Alessandra Panaro, Michel Lemoine; **D:** Giorgio Ferroni; **W:** Giorgio Ferroni, Remigio del Grosso; **C:** Augusto Tiezzi; **M:** Carlo Rustichelli.

Conquest of Space 𝒹½ 1955 A spaceship sets off to explore Mars in spite of the commander's attempts to sabotage the voyage. He believes the flight is an heretical attempt to reach God. An uneasy mixture of religion and space exploration detracts from the nifty special effects which are the only reason to watch. **81m/C VHS, DVD.** Walter Brooke, Eric Fleming, Mickey Shaughnessy, Phil Foster, William Redfield, William Hopper, Benson Fong, Ross Martin; **D:** Byron Haskin; **C:** Lionel Lindon.

Conquest of the Normans 𝒹 Normanni, I: Attack of the Normans 1962 During the Norman invasion of England, Oliver is accused of kidnapping the King. To save his life, Oliver must find the true identity of the abductors. With so much plot, there should have been some suspense. **83m/C DVD. IT** Cameron Mitchell; **D:** Giuseppe Vari; **W:** Nino Stresa.

Conquest of the Planet of the Apes 𝒹𝒹½ 1972 (PG) The apes are pushed to the human Earth population when they lead a revolt against their cruel masters in the distant year of 1990. Sure, there's plenty of cliches—but the story drags you along. The 4th film in the series. Followed by "Battle for the Planet of the Apes." **87m/C VHS, DVD.** Roddy McDowall, Don Murray, Ricardo Montalban, Natalie Trundy, Severn Darden, Hari Rhodes, Asa Maynor, Gordon Jump, John Randolph, H.M. Wynant; **D:** J. Lee Thompson; **W:** Paul Dehn; **C:** Bruce Surtees; **M:** Tom Scott.

Conrack 𝒹𝒹𝒹 1974 (PG) The true story of Pat Conroy, who tried to teach a group of illiterate Black children in South Carolina by using common-sense teaching techniques to inspire their interest. Voight is convincing as the earnest teacher. Based on Conroy's novel "The Water Is Wide." **111m/C VHS.** Jon Voight, Paul Winfield, Madge Sinclair, Hume Cronyn, Martin Ritt; **D:** Martin Ritt; **W:** Harriet Frank Jr., Irving Ravetch; **C:** John A. Alonzo; **M:** John Williams.

The Conrad Boys 𝒹𝒹 2006 After his mother dies, 19-year-old Charlie Conrad (Lo) must put off his own plans in order to care for his young brother Ben (Stewart). Their alcoholic father (Shay) has been out of the picture for years but suddenly re-enters their lives, sober and wanting to make amends. Charlie has more troubles than just that—he's also succumbed to drifter Jordan (Barizen), who has charmed his way into the Conrad home and Charlie's bed. Lo's ambitious and the gay aspects are taken matter-of-factly but the film seems overly familiar. **111m/C VHS. FR** Johnny Hallyday, Remi Martin, Fanny Ardant, Guy Marchand; **C:** Constantin Costa-Gavras; **D:** Constantin Costa-Gavras; **W:** Constantin Costa-Gavras.

Conseil de Famille 𝒹𝒹 1986 Halyday returns to his family from a five-year prison stint, ready to resume his safe-cracking career. Then he discovers the real talent lies with his son Francois (Martin), whose expertise raises the family to middleclass prosperity. But just as dad decides to affiliate with a bigger crime organization, Francois decides to get a straight job because he's fallen in love. Based on a novel by Francis Ryck, French with subtitles. **130m/C VHS, FR** Johnny Hallyday, Remi Martin, Fanny Ardant, Guy Marchand; **D:** Costa-Gavras; **M:** Georges Delerue.

Consenting Adult 𝒹𝒹½ 1985 A distressed family comes to terms with a favorite son's homosexuality. Restrained exploration of the controversial subject. Based on Laura Z. Hobson's novel. **100m/C VHS.** Mario Thomas, Martin Sheen, Barry Tubb, Talia Balsam, Ben Piazza, Corinne Michaels; **D:** Gilbert Cates; **W:** John McGreevey. TV

Consenting Adults 𝒹𝒹 1992 (R) Cookie-cutter thriller capitalizes on popular "psycho-destroys-your-normal-life" theme. Average yuppie couple (Kline and Mastrantonio) are startled and then seduced by the couple moving in next door (Spacey and Miller), who conduct a considerably less-restrained lifestyle. Wife-swapping leads to murder and an innocent man is framed. Plot and characters are underdeveloped yet manage to hold interest through decent performances. **100m/C VHS, DVD.** Kevin Kline, Mary Elizabeth Mastrantonio, Kevin Spacey, Rebecca Miller, Forest Whitaker, E.G. Marshall, Billie Neal; **D:** Alan J. Pakula; **W:** Matthew Chapman.

Consolation Marriage 𝒹𝒹½ Married in Haste 1931 A couple meet and marry after being jilted by others, then must make a choice when their old flames return. Dunne and O'Brien make a charming couple in this early talkie. One of Dunne's early starring roles. **82m/B VHS.** Irene Dunne, Pat O'Brien, John Halliday, Matt Moore, Myrna Loy, Lester Vail; **D:** Paul Sloane.

Conspiracy 𝒹𝒹 1989 (R) Defense Secretary William Baine is haunted by a past sexual encounter, and a top secret team moves in to avert any hint of what

The Conqueror & the Empress WOOF! Sandokan alla Riscossa 1964 Low-budget tale of English explorers who roust an island prince from his throne, motivating him to engage in inspired blood-letting. **89m/C VHS. IT** Guy Madison, Ray Danton, Mario Petri, Alberto Farley; **D:** Luigi Capuano; **W:** Luigi Capuano.

could become a "sex scandal." Based on a true story. 87m/C VHS. James Wilby, Kate Hardie, Glyn Houston; **D:** Christopher Barnard.

Conspiracy 🦴🦴½ 2001 (R) Another in HBO's long line of excellent movies based on real-life events. This one covers the January, 1942 meeting of high-ranking Nazi SS and civilian government leaders to decide what to do about "the Jewish question." Led by SS Genneal Reinhard Heydrich (Branagh), in a riveting performance) and set up by SS Col. Adolf Eichmann (Tucci), this conference was conducted like a board meeting, and that's where the power of the movie comes from, because the outcome of the conference was implementation of the "final solution," the attempted extermination of the Jewish population of Europe. While every man in the room is a villain, they aren't the kind of Nazi villain we're used to. They are bureaucrats who offer administrative and/or logistical objections, but only token moral dissent (which is dispensed with rather quickly and completely). 96m/C VHS, DVD. Stanley Tucci, Kenneth Branagh, Colin Firth, Barnaby Kay, Ben Daniels, David Threlfall, Jonathan Coy, Brendan Coyle, Ian McNeice, Owen Teale, Nicholas Woodeson, Ewan Stewart, Kevin McNally, Brian Pettifer; **D:** Frank Pierson; **W:** Loring Mandel; **C:** Stephen Goldblatt. **CABLE**

Conspiracy 🦴🦴 2008 (R) William Macpherson was forced to retire as a sniper after an injury. Bored with civilian life, he's eager to help out fellow Iraq War vet Miguel Silva with his new ranch in Lukeville, Arizona. Except when Macpherson arrives, Silva has disappeared and no one in town will admit to knowing anything. Macpherson discovers the town is controlled by ruthless John Rhodes, but Rhodes learns that Macpherson can't be intimidated. 90m/C DVD. Val Kilmer, Gary Cole, Jennifer Esposito, Greg Serano, Bob Rumnock, Adam Marcus, Jay Jablonski; **D:** Debra Sullivan; **W:** Debra Sullivan; **M:** Ben Weinstein; Nam. **VIDEO**

Conspiracy of Fear 🦴🦴 1996 (R) After his father's strange death, Chris discovers he's being followed by a sadistic stalker and double agents who believe he has a package that everybody wants. Chris teams with a thief to solve both the mystery of the package and his father's death. 112m/C VHS. Christopher Plummer, Geraint Wyn Davies, Leslie Hope, Andrew Lowery, Ken Walsh, Don Francks; **D:** John Eyres; **W:** Roy Sallows; **C:** Peter Benison; **M:** Stephen (Steve) Edwards.

Conspiracy of Hearts 🦴🦴🦴 1960 A convent of nuns hide Jewish children in 1943 Italy despite threats to their personal safety. Suspenseful tale despite the familiar plot. 113m/B VHS. **GB** Lilli Palmer, Yvonne Mitchell, Sylvia Syms, Ronald Lewis; **D:** Ralph Thomas; **W:** Robert Presnell Jr.

A Conspiracy of Love 🦴 1987 Three generations of a divorce-torn family try to pull itself back together. Sugary domestic tale tries to be uplifting, succeeds in being cliche-ridden. 93m/C VHS. Robert Young, Drew Barrymore, Glynnis O'Connor, Elizabeth Wilson, Mitchell Laurance, John Fujioka, Alan Fawcett; **D:** Noel Black. **TV**

Conspiracy of Silence 🦴🦴½ 2003 A desperately unbiased Irish drama about the troubles arising from priests required to take the vow of celibacy. Director John Deery is very obviously claiming that these otherwise good men are forced into a life of quiet lust and despair, leading to suicide and disturbing homosexual relations. Although well-acted, Deery's characters are presented in such sharp black or white, good or bad, friend or enemy, that it's kind of like watching a man argue with himself. 84m/C DVD. **GB** Jason Barry, Brenda Fricker, Hugh Bonneville, John Lynch, Jim Norton, Sean McGinley, James Ellis, Hugh Quarshie, Fintan Mckeown, Jonathan Forbes, Catherine Cusack, Catherine Walker, Patrick Casey, Owen McDonnell; **Cameos:** Gay Byrne; **D:** John Deery; **W:** John Deery; **C:** Jason Lehel; **M:** Stephen Deery, Francis Haines.

Conspiracy of Terror 🦴🦴 1975 Married detectives investigate a series of murders and unearth a grisly cult in a quiet suburb. Standard fare with a few too cute lines concerning the leads' mixed-faith marriage. 78m/C VHS. Michael Constantine, Barbara Rhoades, Mariclare Costello, Roger Perry, David Opatoshu, Logan Ramsey; **D:** John Llewellyn Moxey. **TV**

Conspiracy Eight: The Trial of the Chicago Eight 🦴🦴🦴 1987 Courtroom drama focuses on the rambunctious trial of the Chicago Eight radicals, charged with inciting a riot at the Democratic National Convention of 1968. Dramatized footage mixed with interviews with the defendants. Imaginative reconstruction of history. 118m/C VHS, DVD. Peter Boyle, Elliott Gould, Robert Carradine, Martin Sheen, David Clennon, David Kagen, Michael Lembeck, Robert Loggia; **D:** Jeremy Paul Kagan.

Conspiracy Theory 🦴🦴🦴 1997 (R) Whacked-out New York cabbie Jerry Fletcher (Gibson) writes a newsletter on conspiracy theories, which he finds in every possible place and situation. Naturally, he doesn't keep his thoughts to himself and exasperated Justice Department attorney Alice Sutton (Roberts) is stuck listening to the love-struck fool. But as the saying goes just because you're paranoid doesn't mean they're not out to get you. Sure enough, one of Jerry's conspiracies turns out to be true and suddenly he and Alice are being pursued by CIA shrink Dr. Jonas (Stewart), who's not what he seems to be either. Gibson's more geek than hero but appealing regardless, as is heroine Roberts. Another successful, enjoyable, and highly profitable, teaming of Donner, Gibson and producer Joel Silver. 135m/C VHS, DVD. Terry Alexander, Mel Gibson, Julia Roberts, Patrick Stewart, Cylk Cozart; **D:** Richard Donner; **W:** Brian Helgeland; **C:** John Schwartzman; **M:** Carter Burwell.

Conspirator 🦴🦴½ 1949 Somewhat engrossing drama about a beautiful young girl who discovers that her new husband, a British army officer, is working with the Communists. Elizabeth Taylor stars as the naive American wife and Robert Taylor plays her Russkie agent husband. Although madly in love with his wife, he is given orders to kill her. Picture falls apart at end due to weak script. Based on the novel by Humphrey Slater. 85m/B VHS. **GB** Robert Taylor, Elizabeth Taylor, Robert Flemyng, Harold Warrender, Honor Blackman, Marjorie Fielding, Thora Hird; **D:** Victor Saville; **W:** Sally Benson, Gerald Fairlie; **C:** Frederick A. (Freddie) Young.

The Constant Gardener 🦴🦴🦴 2005 (R) Multi-faceted, multi-layered tale hits all the buttons of a great thriller: sex, love, murder, intrigue, exotic (if underprivileged) locale, and international politics, all mixed with a topical bent ripped from today's headlines. Justin (Fiennes) and Tessa (Weisz) plunge headfirst from passion into marriage, hardly knowing a thing about each other. He's an official in the British government; she's an activist; together they end up in Kenya where she witnesses foul play by drug companies who use the locals as guinea pigs for drug testing. The film starts with Tessa's brutal murder, and we follow along with Justin as he uncovers the mysteries of her life and death. Adapted from the 2001 novel by John le Carre. 129m/C DVD. **GB** Ralph Fiennes, Rachel Weisz, Danny Huston, Bill Nighy, Pete Postlethwaite, Richard McCabe, Donald (Don) Sumpter, Juliet Aubrey, Hubert Kounde, Archie Panjabi; Gerard McSorley; **D:** Fernando Meirelles; **W:** Jeffrey Caine; **C:** Cesar Charlone; **M:** Alberto Iglesias. Oscars '05: Support. Actress (Weisz); British Acad. '05: Film Editing; Golden Globes '06: Support. Actress (Weisz); Screen Actors Guild '05: Support. Actress (Weisz).

Constantine 🦴🦴½ 2005 (R) Freelance exorcist and all-around surly loner John Constantine (Reeves) stalks the divide between good and evil, playing the forces of Heaven and Hell against themselves, all for his own benefit. When a pol-chain-smoking ghostbuster to help solve her twin sister's mysterious suicide, Constantine acts as her guide into LA's supernatural underworld, revealing a plot involving the Spear of Destiny, rogue angels, and a scheme to unleash Hell on earth. Director Lawrence creates a nifty neo-noir atmosphere, but confusing exposition and an over-reliance on CGI scares hurts the final product. Based on DC's "Hellblazer" comic. 120m/C VHS, DVD, Blu-ray Disc, UMD, HD DVD. **US** Keanu Reeves, Rachel Weisz, Tilda Swinton, Peter Stormare, Shia LaBeouf, Gavin Rossdale, Jose Zuniga, Larry Cedar; **D:** Francis Lawrence; **W:** Kevin Brodbin, Frank Cappello; **C:** Philippe Rousselot; **M:** Brian Tyler, Klaus Badelt.

Consuming Passions 🦴½ 1988 (R) A ribald, food-obsessed English comedy about a young idiot who rises within the hierarchy of a chocolate company via murder. You'll never guess what the secret ingredient in his wonderful chocolate is. Based on a play by Michael Palin and Terry Jones (better known as part of the Monty Python troupe), the film is sometimes funny, more often gross, and takes a single joke far beyond its limit. 95m/C VHS. **GB** Vanessa Redgrave, Jonathan Pryce, Tyler Butterworth, Freddie Jones, Prunella Scales, Sammi Davis, Thora Hird, John Wells, William Rushton, Timothy West; **D:** Giles Foster; **W:** Michael Palin, Andrew Davies, Paul Zimmerman.

Contact 🦴🦴½ 1997 (PG) Thought-provoking (if overlong) drama rather than sci-fi spectacular (though it has its fair share of special effects). Radio astronomer Dr. Ellie Arroway (Foster) discovers signals being transmitted from the distant star Vega. When they're deciphered, the signals turn out to be blueprints for a craft that will take its occupant into space and a first meeting with aliens. Ellie fights to become that first spokesperson for Earth's inhabitants. More philosophical than the usual sci-fi alien encounter epic, but the excellent cast, led by Foster, pulls it off nicely. Based on the novel by Carl Sagan. 150m/C VHS, DVD. Jodie Foster, Matthew McConaughey, James Woods, Tom Skerritt, Angela Bassett, John Hurt, David Morse, Rob Lowe, Jake Busey, William Fichtner, Geoffrey Blake, Jena Malone; **D:** Robert Zemeckis; **W:** Michael Goldenberg; **C:** Don Burgess; **M:** Alan Silvestri.

Contagion 🦴🦴½ 1987 Innocent real estate agent meets a reclusive, eccentric millionaire who offers him unlimited wealth and beautiful women, but only if he kills someone. Interesting ethical premise loses its philosophic purity. 90m/C VHS. **AU** John (Roy Slaven) Doyle, Nicola Bartlett, Roy Barrett, Nathy Gaffney; Pamela Hawksford; **D:** Karl Zwicky.

Contagious 🦴🦴½ 1996 (PG-13) Epidemiologist Hanna (Wagner) discovers that passengers aboard a flight from Latin American have been exposed to cholera and could cause an epidemic. She teams with Detective Lou (Pena), who's tracking an infected drug smuggler, to find the source of the disease. 90m/C VHS. Lindsay Wagner, Elizabeth Pena, Tom Wopat, Alexandra Purvis, Matt Hill, Brendan Fletcher; **D:** Joe Napolitano; **W:** Sandy Kroopf; **C:** Andreas Poulsson; **M:** Stephen Graziano. **CABLE**

The Contaminated Man 🦴 2001 (R) An infectious disease expert (Hurt) loses his family to an unknown disease. Now some years later an an "infectious disease laboratory" in a vaguely defined Russia, disgruntled security guard Muller (Weller) has been infected with a deadly pathogen, where one drop of his blood will now kill a person in matter of seconds. The disease expert is called in to investigate and teams up with an American reporter, as Muller is determined to get home to see his wife and son, even if it means infecting the entire Russian population. TV movie dull beyond belief, Peter Weller getting to do an Eastern-accented, bald Muller is the only fun in the whole film. 98m/C DVD. William Hurt, Natascha (Natasha) McElhone, Peter Weller, Katja Woywood, Michael Brandon; **D:** Anthony Hickox; **W:** John Penney; **C:** Bruce Douglas Johnson; **M:** Michael Hoenig. **TV**

Contempt 🦴🦴🦴½ *Le Mepris; Il Disprezzo* 1964 A film about the filming of a new version of "The Odyssey," and the rival visions of how to tell the story. Amusing look at the film business features Fritz Lang playing himself, Godard as his assistant. Bardot is pleasant scenery. Adapted from Moravia's "A Ghost at Noon." 102m/C VHS, DVD. **IT FR** Brigitte Bardot, Jack Palance, Fritz Lang, Georgia Moll, Michel Piccoli, Jean-Luc Godard, Linda Veras; **D:** Jean-Luc Godard; **W:** Jean-Luc Godard; **C:** Raoul Coutard; **M:** Georges Delerue.

The Contender 🦴🦴🦴½ 2000 (R) An excellent cast propels this political potboiler, although the plot contains some hot air. After the sitting Veep dies, downhome Prez Evans (Bridges) nominates Sen. Laine Hanson (Allen) for the post. Although principled and experienced, she also happens to be a woman with a past. Runyon (Oldman) takes advantage by digging up photos of the senator doing the life of a college fraternity party. Hanson refuses to answer questions about her youthful indiscretions, arguing that her sexual history is nobody's business. As in real politics, much speechifying ensues and not much is accomplished. Allen shines in a role that was written expressly for her. Reports filtered out after the film's release that executive producer Oldman, a conservative himself, was unhappy about the editing and portrayal of his character, who he thought was the hero of the movie. 127m/C VHS, DVD. Joan Allen, Gary Oldman, Jeff Bridges, Sam Elliott, Christian Slater, William L. Petersen, Philip Baker Hall, Saul Rubinek; **D:** Rod Lurie; **W:** Rod Lurie; **C:** Denis Maloney; **M:** Lawrence Nash Groupe.

Continental Divide 🦴🦴 1981 (PG) A hard-nosed political columnist takes off for the Colorado Rockies on an "easy assignment"—interviewing a reclusive ornithologist, with whom he instantly falls in love. A city slicker, he first alienates her, but she eventually falls for him, too. But it's not exactly a match made in heaven. Story meanders to a conclusion of sorts. Probably the most normal Belushi ever was on screen. 103m/C VHS, DVD. John Belushi, Blair Brown, Allen (Goorwitz) Garfield, Carlin Glynn, Val Avery, Tony Ganios, Tim Kazurinsky; **D:** Michael Apted; **W:** Lawrence Kasdan; **C:** John Bailey.

Contraband 🦴🦴½ *Blackout* 1940 Danish sea captain Andersen (Veidt) and the mysterious Mrs. Sorenson (Hobson) are kidnapped by a cell of Nazi spies operating in London in the early days of WWII. They manage to turn the tables on the bad guys. Story takes place under blackout conditions lending a lot of atmosphere to this early thriller. 88m/B VHS, DVD. **GB** Conrad Veidt, Valerie Hobson, Esmond Knight, Hay Petrie, Raymond Lovell, Harold Warrender, Charles Victor; **D:** Michael Powell; **W:** Michael Powell; **C:** Frederick A. (Freddie) Young.

Contraband 🦴½ 1986 The leader of a smuggling gang escapes from an ambush in which his brother was murdered. He searches for a haven of safety while his cronies seek brutal revenge. Average crime yarn lacks much excitement. Dubbed into English. 95m/C VHS, DVD. **IT** Fabio Testi, Ivana Monti; **D:** Lucio Fulci.

Contract 🦴🦴🦴½ 1980 A marriage ceremony between the children of two important families gets disrupted when the friends and relatives in attendance can't get along, and the bride can't seem to commit. Provides a biting social commentary against dirty politicians and unethical entrepreneurs. Polish with subtitles. 111m/C VHS. **PL** Maja Komorowska, Tadeusz Lomnicki, Magda Jaroszowna, Leslie Caron, Ignacy Machowski; **C:** Krzysztof Zanussi; **W:** Krzysztof Zanussi; **C:** Slawomir Idziak; **M:** Wojciech Kilar.

The Contract 🦴🦴 1998 (R) Former black ops specialist Luc (Imbault) is now making a living as a pro assassin and is teaching the trade to daughter Hannah (Black). When dad gets killed in a set-up, Hannah wants revenge against the man behind the deed. It's Presidential candidate J. Harmon (Williams), who wants his own black ops past to stay hidden—but Hannah has other ideas. 90m/C VHS, DVD. Billy Dee Williams, Johanna Black, Laurent Imbault; **D:** K.C. Bascombe. **VIDEO**

The Contract 🦴🦴 2007 (R) Frank Carden (Freeman) is a freelance hitman who gets arrested by some Washington state cops and is turned over to the feds for transport. Carden escapes into the woods with the help of some cronies, only to be re-captured by Ray Keene (Cusack), a former cop who is hiking with his teenaged son Chris (Anderson). Keene forces Carden to face towards the authorities while his gun-toting associates come searching. **96m/C DVD, HD DVD,** Morgan Freeman, John Cusack, Jamie Anderson, Alice Krige, Megan Dodds, Corey Johnson, Jonathan Hyde, Bill Smitrovich, Ned Bellamy; **D:** Bruce Beresford; **W:** Stephen Katz, John Darrouzet; **C:** Dante Spinotti; **M:** Normand Corbeil. **VIDEO**

The Convent 2000 (R) In 1960, a young woman enters a church, shoots several nuns and a priest, and then torches the place. Jump ahead to the present, as a group of college kids enter the now-condemned convent to perform a fraternity prank. Elsewhere in the dilapidated convent, amateur Satanists perform a ritual, releasing the evil spirits held captive in the sanctuary. From this point on,

The Convent 1995 idiosyncratic saga of Paris-based American scholar Michael Padovic (Malkovich) and his French wife Helene (Deneuve) who travel to an ancient Portuguese monastery so Michael may do research at their library. The convent's guardian is the charming and sinister Baltar (Cintra), who flirts with neglected Helene, while playing Mephistopheles to Michael's Faust. Lots of mysticism, French, and English dialogue. **90m/C VHS, DVD, PT FR** John Malkovich, Catherine Deneuve, Luis Miguel Cintra, Leonor Silveira; **D:** Manoel de Oliveira; **C:** Marc Barroso.

Control 1987 Tedious tale of 15 volunteers for a 20-day fallout shelter habitation experiment who become trapped when a real nuclear emergency occurs. Filmed in Rome. **83m/C VHS, IT** Burt Lancaster, Kate Nelligan, Ben Gazzara, Andrea Ferreol, Lavinia Segurini, Andrea Occhipinti, Cyrelia Clare, Jean Benguigui, Kate Reid, Erland Josephson, Ingrid Thulin; **D:** Giuliano Montaldo. **VIDEO**

Control 2007 (R) Corbijn makes his directorial debut in this compelling B&W bio of Ian Curtis (Riley), frontman for British post-punk band "Joy Division." Epileptic and suffering from depression, Curtis is torn between a conventional life—a teenage marriage, child, and steady job—and the excitement and temptations of the music world. Although Curtis committed suicide in 1980 at the age of 23 this isn't the typical live-fast/die-young rock fantasy, but a thoughtful depiction of a young man who couldn't reconcile competing impulses. Based on the memoir "Touching from the Distance" by Deborah Curtis. **121m/B DVD, GB AU JP** Samantha Morton, Alexandra Maria Lara, Joe Anderson, James Anthony Pearson, Sam Riley, Craig Parkinson, Toby Kebbell, Harry Treadway, Andrew Sheridan, Robert Shelly; **D:** Anton Corbijn; **W:** Matt Greenhalgh, Deborah Curtis; **C:** Martin Ruhe; **M:** New Order.

Control Room 2004 Shot days prior to the Iraqi War, director Noujaim provides a fly on the wall account of the goings on at Al Jazeera, the leading news service for Arab-speaking viewers and also at Centcom, a makeshift media village set up by the U.S. military for the purpose of holding and briefing journalists from around the world. Your certainties will be scrambled and your assumptions shaken, if you think you can believe everything you hear on your news broadcasts. Presented in a surprisingly unbiased manner, provocative critique strongly questions the notion of journalistic objectivity. **84m/C VHS, DVD,** **D:** Jehane Noujaim; **W:** Jehane Noujaim; **C:** Jehane Noujaim, Julia Bacha; **C:** Jehane Noujaim; **M:** Hani Salama, Thomas DeRanzo.

The Contractor 2007 (R) Routine would-be thriller has retired CIA assassin James Dial (Snipes) called in for one last job. Suddenly he's on the lam when the killing of a terrorist mastermind is befriended by 12-year-old Emma (Bennett), a witness who wants to help him prove his innocence. **105m/C DVD,** Wesley Snipes, Lena Headey, Eliza Bennett, Charles Dance, Ralph Brown, Gemma Jones; **D:** Josef Rusnak; **W:** Roger Foster, Joshua Michael Stern; **C:** Wendigo von Schulzendorff; **M:** Nicholas Pike. **VIDEO**

the movie becomes a monster mash, as each character is either possessed, killed, or both. The only hope for the trapped youngsters is the now-grown girl who started all of this in 1960. The film isn't as horrible as it sounds, but has some nice touches. **79m/C VHS,** Adrienne Barbeau, Coolio, Bill Moseley, Joanna Canton, Megahn Perry, Dax Miller, David Gunn; **D:** Mike Mendez; **W:** Chad Anderson; **C:** Jason Lowe; **M:** Joseph Bishara.

The Conversation 1974 (PG) Freelance surveillance expert Harry Caul (Hackman) is becoming increasingly uneasy about his current job for a powerful businessman (Duvall). He and assistant Stan (Cazale) are watching a young couple (Williams, Forrest) when Harry begins to suspect that they are murder targets. Powerful statement about privacy, responsibility and guilt. One of the best movies of the '70s. **113m/C VHS, DVD,** Gene Hackman, John Cazale, Frederic Forrest, Allen Garfield, Cindy Williams, Robert Duvall, Teri Garr, Michael Higgins, Elizabeth McRae, Harrison Ford; **D:** Francis Ford Coppola; **W:** Francis Ford Coppola; **C:** Bill Butler; **M:** David Shire. Cannes '74: Film; Natl. Bd. of Review '74: Actor (Hackman), Director (Coppola), Natl. Film Reg. '95; Natl. Soc. Film Critics '74: Director (Coppola).

Conversation Piece Violence et Passion; Gruppo di Famiglia in un Interno 1975 (R) An aging art historian's life is turned upside down when a Countess and her daughters rent out the penthouse in her estate. Sometimes-talky examination of scholarly pretensions. **112m/C VHS, IT FR** Burt Lancaster, Silvana Mangano, Helmut Berger, Claudia Cardinale, Claudia Marsani; **D:** Luchino Visconti; **W:** Luchino Visconti, Suso Cecchi D'Amico, Enrico Medioli; **C:** Pasqualino De Santis; **M:** Franco Mannino.

Conversations with Other Women 2005 (R) Arty romantic-suspenser in which a man (Eckhart) and a woman (Bonham Carter) meet at a wedding reception and end up in bed, but as the night progresses it's revealed that they are possibly not strangers. Clever split-screen style shows each character separately navigating their encounter over the course of the evening, a technique that provides both emotional weight and insight to the film's theme of perception-is-reality. Chemistry and fine acting turn a he said/she said one-night stand story into an examination of the passage of time, regret, and knowing better. **84m/C DVD, US** Helena Bonham-Carter, Aaron Eckhart, Brian Geraghty, Olivia Wilde, Brianne Brown, Thomas Lennon, Nora Zehetner; **D:** Hans Canosa; **W:** Gabrielle Zevin; **C:** Steve Yedlin; **M:** Starr Parodi, Jeff Eden Fair.

Convict Cowboy 1995 (R) Hardbitten professional rodeo cowboy Ry Weston (Voight) killed a man and now works the Montana prison rodeo circuit. Newcomer greenhorn Clay Treyton (Chandler) wants to get out of kitchen duty and decides Ry is the perfect ridin' and ropin' teacher. Only Ry isn't interested in wasting his time (at first). It's a predictable bonding experience in a melodramatic movie. **106m/C VHS,** Jon Voight, Kyle Chandler, Ben Gazzara, Marcia Gay Harden, Glenn Plummer, Stephen McHattie; **D:** Rod Holcomb; **C:** James L. Carter. **CABLE**

Convict 762 1998 (R) Zagarino and Drago are survivors of a remote penal colony who are rescued by the all-female crew of a cargo ship. But it turns out one of the duo is a murderer who begins to kill again. **100m/C VHS, DVD,** Frank Zagarino, Billy Drago, Shannon Sturges; **D:** Luca Bercovici; **W:** J. Reifel; **C:** Steven Wacks. **VIDEO**

Convicted 1932 Lean thriller about a woman cleared of a murder charge, but only when a second, identical murder occurs while she is jailed. **57m/B VHS,** Aileen Pringle, Jameson Thomas, Harry C. (Henry) Myers, Dorothy Christy, Richard Tucker; **D:** Christy Cabanne.

Convicted 1986 Solid story of innocent man imprisoned for rape, and his wife's determined efforts to free him. Larroquette does well in unexpected role. Based on a true story. **94m/C VHS,** John Larroquette, Carroll O'Connor, Lindsay Wagner; **D:** David Lowell Rich; **M:** Steve Dorff. **TV**

Convicted 2004 (R) A deceitful former attorney (Quinn) makes some quick bucks selling off his letters with death row prisoners until he falls for convicted child killer Charlotte (Nielsen) and struggles to help clear her name but stoops to stale action-message movie but stoops to stale action movie-type twists toward the end. **100m/C VHS, DVD,** Aidan Quinn, Timothy Daly, Mark Holton; **D:** Billie August; **M:** David Shire. **VIDEO**

Convicted: A Mother's Story 1987 Jillian embezzles cash from her employer, and for the sake of a boyfriend, and goes to jail. Odd casting hinders a ho-hum plot. **95m/C VHS,** Christa Denton; **D:** Richard T. Heffron; **M:** David Shire. **TV**

Conviction 2002 (R) Philadelphia-born Carl Upchurch (Epps) drops out of school at nine and into a life of crime that leads to various prison sentences. A man with a violent temper, he's no one to mess with but he also wants more from his life. This leads to his mentoring by Quaker prison instructor Martha (Delany) and Carl's goal to save other inner-city youth from a life of violence and imprisonment. Based on Upchurch's autobiography. **100m/C VHS, DVD,** Omar Epps, Dana Delany, Charles S. Dutton, Treach, Bentley Mitchum; **D:** Kevin Rodney Sullivan; **W:** Jon Huffman, Carl Upchurch; **C:** Miroslaw Baszak; **M:** Jeff Beal. **CABLE**

Convicts at Large 1938 An escaped convict steals the clothes of a inept architect. Left with only prison duds, the architect stumbles into the bad side of town and gets involved with the mob. Info. **58m/B VHS, DVD,** Ralph Forbes, Paula Stone; **D:** Scott E. Beal; **W:** Scott E. Beal.

Convoy 1940 Life aboard a convoy ship in the North Sea during WWII. The small cruiser is picked on by a German U-Boat. Will a rescuer appear? Noted for technical production values. **95m/B VHS,** Clive Brook, John Clements, Edward Chapman, Judy Campbell, Edward Rigby, Stewart Granger, Michael Wilding, George Benson; **D:** Pen Tennyson.

Convoy 1978 (R) A defiant trucker leads an indestructible truck convoy to Mexico to protect high gasoline prices. Lightweight stuff was inspired by the song "Convoy" by C.W. McCall. **106m/C VHS, DVD,** Kris Kristofferson, Ali MacGraw, Ernest Borgnine, Burt Young, Madge Sinclair, Franklin Ajaye, Cassie Yates; **D:** Sam Peckinpah; **C:** Harry Stradling Sr.

Coogan's Bluff 1968 (PG) An Arizona deputy sheriff (Eastwood) travels to New York in order to track down a killer on the loose. First Eastwood/Siegel teaming is tense actioner. The TV series "McCloud" was based on this film. **100m/C VHS, DVD,** Clint Eastwood, Lee J. Cobb, Tisha Sterling, Don Stroud, Betty Field, Susan Clark, Tom Tully, Albert "Poppy" Popwell; **D:** Donald Siegel; **W:** Dean Riesner; **M:** Lalo Schifrin.

The Cook, the Thief, His Wife & Her Lover 1990 (R) An exclusive restaurant houses four disturbing characters. Greenaway's powerful vision of greed, love, and violence may be too strong for some tastes. Available in several different versions: the unrated theatrical release, and an R-rated cut which runs half an hour shorter. **123m/C VHS, DVD, GB** Richard Bohringer, Michael Gambon, Helen Mirren, Alan Howard, Tim Roth; **D:** Peter Greenaway; **W:** Peter Greenaway; **C:** Sacha Vierny; **M:** Michael Nyman.

Cookie 1989 (R) Light comedy about a Mafia don's daughter trying to smart mouth her way into the mob's good graces. A character-driven vehicle, this plot takes a backseat to casting. Wiest is superb as Falk's moll. **93m/C VHS,** Emily Lloyd, Peter Falk, Dianne Wiest, Brenda Vaccaro, Ricki Lake, Jerry Lewis, Lionel Stander, Michael V. Gazzo, Adrian Pasdar, Bob Gunton, Ricki Lake; Recdjere, G. Anthony "Tony" Sirico; **D:** Susan Seidelman; **W:** Alice Arlen, Nora Ephron; **M:** Thomas Newman.

The Cookout 2004 (PG-13) Low-brow, slack-paced comedy debut from Rivera is filled with stereotypes. Todd Anderson (Storm P) takes advantage of being the NBA's No. 1 draft pick by letting his greedy girlfriend Brittany (Good) talk him into buying an ostentatious mansion in a distrustful mom (Lewis) insists he keep to his down-home ways by hosting the big annual cookout for family and friends, which brings all the hangers-on into the backyard. Queen Latifah has what's basically an extended cameo as a zealous community security guard. **88m/C VHS, DVD, US** Tim Meadows, Jenifer Lewis, Meagan Good, Jonathan Silverman, Ja Rule, Storm P; Farrah Fawcett, Frankie Faison, Eve, Danny Glover, Rita Owens, Marci Reed, Ruperto Vanderpool, Queen Latifah; **Cameos:** Marv Albert, Elton Brand, Baron Davis, Mark Cuban; **D:** Lance Rivera; **W:** Laurie B. Tuner, Ramsay Gbelawoe, Jeffrey Brian Holmes; **C:** Tom Houghton; **M:** Camara Kambon.

Cooking Up Trouble Three of a Kind 1944 The crazy trio become foster dads in this "Stooge" type comedy. **60m/B VHS,** Shemp Howard, Billy Gilbert, Maxie "Slapsie" Rosenbloom; **D:** David Ross Lederman; **W:** Earle Snell.

Cookie's Fortune 1999 (PG-13) Neal is Jewel Mae "Cookie" Orcutt, the matriarch of a Mississippi family with its share of female eccentrics. When Cookie offs herself to join her deceased husband, her officious, scandal-fearing spinster niece Camille (Close) destroys the suicide note, setting up the family's loyal, good-natured handyman (Dutton) for the fall. At the same time, she's directing practically the whole town in a church performance of "Salome." Excellent script by Rapp allows more characterization than usual for Altman, as well as a pleasantly leisurely pace. Flawless ensemble work (another Altman hallmark) is highlighted by the performances of Neal, Close, and Dutton. **118m/C VHS, DVD,** Charles S. Dutton, Glenn Close, Patricia Neal, Liv Tyler, Chris O'Donnell, Julianne Moore, Ned Beatty, Courtney B. Vance, Donald Moffat, Lyle Lovett, Matt Malloy, Rufus Thomas, Danny Darst, Randle Mel, Niecy Nash, Ruby Wilson, Preston Strobel; **D:** Robert Altman; **W:** Anne Rapp; **C:** Toyomichi Kurita; **M:** David A. Stewart, Neil; Bd. of Review '99: Support. Actress (Moore).

Cool and the Crazy 1994 (R) High school sweethearts Michael (Leto) and Roslyn (Silverstone) are now in a troubled marriage. Apparently dissatisfied by hubby's sexual performance, Roslyn decides to take a walk on the wide side with hoodlum Joey (Flint). Michael finds out and decides to have his own extramarital fling with a beatnik co-worker (Silverstone) in the 50s set. But there's even more trouble ahead. Rather than "cool" and "crazy," it's amateurish and nonsensical. **90m/C VHS, DVD,** Alicia Silverstone, Jared Leto, Jennifer Blanc, Matthew Flint, Bradford Tatum, Christina Harnos, Tuesday Knight; **D:** Ralph Bakshi; **C:** Roberto Schaefer; **M:** Hummie Mann. **CABLE**

Cool As Ice 1991 (PG) "Rapper" Vanilla Ice makes his feature film debut as a rebel with an eye for the ladies, who motors into a small, conservative town. Several so-so musical segments. For teenage girls only. **92m/C VHS,** Vanilla Ice, Kristin Minter, Michael Gross, Sydney Lassick, Dody Goodman, Naomi Campbell, Candy Clark, Deezer D. Clark; **D:** David Kellogg; **C:** Janusz Kaminski; **M:** Stanley Clarke. Golden Raspberries '91: Worst New Star (Vanilla Ice).

Cool Blue 1988 (R) An unsuccessful painter meets the woman of his dreams, has a brief affair, then tries to locate her in the greater Los Angeles metro area. Good luck. Watch for Penn's cameo. **93m/C VHS,** Woody Harrelson, Hank Azaria, Ely Pouget, John Diehl; **Cameos:** Sean Penn; **D:** Mark Mullin, Richard Shepard.

A Cool, Dry Place 🦴🦴½ 1998 (PG-13) Basically a variation on "Kramer vs. Kramer," Russ Durrell (Vaughn) was a hotshot Chicago lawyer with a five-year old son, Calvin (Moat), when wife Kate (Potter) took a hike. So Russ moves to small town Kansas to make a go of single fatherhood in a slower-paced world. Eventually, he begins dating Beth (Adams) and when things start to get serious, guess who turns up and decides she wants back into her son's life? Vaughn does fine as the dad but Potter is stuck with a dopey, inarticulate character. 97m/C VHS, DVD. Vince Vaughn, Monica Potter, Joey Lauren Adams, Bobby Moat, Devon Sawa; D: John N. Smith; W: Matthew McDuffie; C: Jean Lepine; M: Curt Sobel.

Cool Hand Luke 🦴🦴½ 1967 One of the last great men-in-chains films. A man (Newman) sentenced to sweat out a term on a prison farm refuses to compromise with authority. Martin shines in his supporting role as the oily warden, uttering that now-famous phrase, "What we have here is a failure to communicate." Kennedy's performance as leader of the chain gang won him an Oscar. Based on the novel by Donn Pearce. 126m/C VHS, DVD. Paul Newman, George Kennedy, J.D. Cannon, Strother Martin, Dennis Hopper, Anthony Zerbe, Lou Antonio, Wayne Rogers, Harry Dean Stanton, Ralph Waite, Joe Don Baker, Richard (Dick) Davalos, Jo Van Fleet, Robert Drivas, Clifton James, Morgan Woodward, Luke Askew, Robert Donner, Warren Finnerty, James Gammon, Rance Howard, Buck Kartalian, John McLiam, Charles Tyner, Donn Pearce, Marc Cavell, Charles Hicks, James Jeter, Robert Luster, John Pearce, Eddie Rosson; D: Stuart Rosenberg; W: Frank Pierson, Donn Pearce; C: Conrad L. Hall; M: Lalo Schifrin. Oscars '67: Support. Actor (Kennedy); Natl. Film Reg. '05.

Cool Mikado 🦴🦴 1963 A jazzy modernization of the Gilbert-Sullivan operetta, in which an American soldier is kidnapped by the gangster fiance of the Japanese girl he loves. 81m/C VHS. GB Stubby Kaye, Frankie Howerd, Dennis Price; D: Michael Winner.

Cool Runnings 🦴🦴½ 1993 (PG) Bright, slapstick comedy based on the true story of the Jamaican bobsled team's quest to enter the 1988 Winter Olympics in Calgary. Candy is recruited to coach four unlikely athletes who don't quite exemplify the spirit of the Games. He accepts the challenge not only because of its inherent difficulty but because he needs to reconcile himself to past failures as a former sledder. When our heroes leave their sunny training ground for Calgary, their mettle is tested by serious sledders from more frigid climes who pursue the competition with a stern sense of mission. An upbeat story which will appeal to children, its target audience. 98m/C VHS, DVD. Leon, Doug E. Doug, John Candy, Marco Brambilla, Malik Yoba, Rawle Lewis, Raymond J. Barry, Peter Outerbridge, Larry Gilman, Paul Coeur; D: Jon Turteltaub; W: Tommy Swerdlow, Lynn Siefert, Michael Goldberg; C: Phedon Papamichael; M: Hans Zimmer.

The Cool Surface 🦴🦴 1992 (R) Sex and ambition, Hollywood style. Dani, a wanabe actress, and Jarvis, an aspiring screenwriter become lovers. Jarvis turns their hot affair into a sizzling novel and then a script. Dani may have inspired the lead role but that doesn't mean she'll get the part. But it won't be for lack of trying (anything). 88m/C VHS, DVD. Robert Patrick, Teri Hatcher, Matt McCoy, Cyril O'Reilly, Jan Buchanan; D: Erik Anjou; W: Erik Anjou; M: Dave Kopplin.

The Cool World 🦴🦴½ 1963 Tough-talking docudrama, set on the streets of Harlem, focuses on a 15-year-old black youth whose one ambition in life is to own a gun and lead his gang. 107m/B VHS. Gloria Foster, Hampton Clanton, Carl Lee; D: Shirley Clarke. Natl. Film Reg. '94.

Cool World 🦴🦴 1992 (PG-13) Underground cartoonist Jack Deebs enters his own adult cartoon "Cool World," lured by his sex-kitten character "Holli Would," who needs him to leave her animated world and become human. Holli's plan is opposed by the only other human to occupy Cool World, a slick detective whose main job is to prevent noids (humans) and doodles (cartoons) from having sex and destroying the balance between the two existences. A mixture of live-action and wild animation. Director Bakshi's creations are not intended for children but this is less explicit than usual, which may be one of the problems. Little humor and a flat script leave this film too uninvolving. 101m/C VHS, DVD. Gabriel Byrne, Kim Basinger, Brad Pitt, Michele Abrams, Deirdre O'Connell, Carrie Hamilton, Frank Sinatra Jr., Michael David Lally, William Frankfather; D: Ralph Bakshi; W: Michael Grais, Mark Victor; C: John A. Alonzo; M: Mark Isham.

The Cooler 🦴🦴🦴 2003 (R) Bernie Lootz (Macy) is a Las Vegas gambler with a nasty losing streak. After getting into debt to casino manager Shelly Kaplow (Baldwin), Bernie finds himself indentured as a "cooler," a walking bad luck charm sent to cool off the winning streaks simply by sitting next to the gamblers. Bernie's luck begins to change about a week before he's finished paying off. He meets and falls for Natalie (Bello), a casino waitress, and it seems his perennial bad luck begins to disappear (but of course, there are complications). Great cast provides sterling performances all around. Most notable is Macy, who hits the jackpot playing a loser. 101m/C VHS, DVD. US William H. Macy, Alec Baldwin, Maria Bello, Shawn Hatosy, Ron Livingston, Paul Sorvino, Estella Warren, Arthur J. Nascarelli, M.C. Gainey, Ellen Greene, Joey Fatone, Tony Longo; D: Wayne Kramer; W: Wayne Kramer, Frank Hannah; C: James Whitaker; M: Mark Isham. Natl. Bd. of Review '03: Support. Actor (Baldwin).

A Cooler Climate 🦴🦴½ 1999 (R) Iris (Fields) is a middleaged married woman who divorces her husband (refusing any settlement) after she falls in love with another man. When her lover leaves her, Iris has no money and no job skills except to become the live-in housekeeper for the wealthy Tanners. But brittle Paula Tanner (Davis) soon finds herself on the rocky road to divorce and unable to cope while Iris discovers her self-esteem in her independence. The men are strictly cardboard but Fields and Davis are worth a watch. Based on a novel by Zena Collier. 100m/C VHS. Sally Field, Judy Davis, Winston Rekert, Jerry Wasserman, Jessalyn Gilsig, Gerard Plunkett, Carly Pope, Peter Yunker; D: Susan Seidelman; W: Marsha Norman; C: John Bartley; M: Patrick Williams. CABLE.

Cooley High 🦴🦴🦴 1975 (PG) Black high school students in Chicago go through the rites of passage in their senior year during the '60s. Film is funny, smart, and much acclaimed. Great soundtrack featuring Motown hits of the era, is highlight. Basis for the TV series "What's Happening." 107m/C VHS, DVD. Glynn Turman, Lawrence-Hilton Jacobs, Garrett Morris, Cynthia Davis; D: Michael A. Schultz; W: Eric Monte.

Cooperstown 🦴🦴½ 1993 Harry (Arkin) is a former major-league pitcher who now works as a baseball scout in Florida. He's been angry for 30 years over giving up a home-run pitch that kept his team (the fictional Chicago Barons) out of the World Series. Harry's feels this error cost him his chance at induction into the Baseball Hall of Fame in Cooperstown, New York, and he's always blamed ex-friend and former catcher Raymond (Greene), who's just had the gall to be elected. Only Raymond's just died—but his ghostly figure visits Harry and urges him to take a road trip not only to the baseball shrine but into his past. 100m/C VHS. Alan Arkin, Graham Greene, Hope Lange, Josh Charles, Ed Begley Jr., Maria Pitillo, Ann Wedgeworth, Paul Dooley, Joanna Miles, Charles Haid; D: Charles Haid; W: Lee Blessing. CABLE.

Cop 🦴🦴½ 1988 (R) Left by his wife and child, a ruthless and work-obsessed detective goes after a twisted serial killer. Woods' exceptional ability to play sympathetic weirdos is diluted by a script—based on James Ellroys's novel "Blood on the Moon"—that warps the feminist theme, is violent, and depends too heavily on coincidence. 110m/C VHS, DVD. James Woods, Lesley Ann Warren, Charles Durning, Charles Haid, Raymond J. Barry, Randi Brooks, Annie McEnroe, Victoria Wauchope; D: James B. Harris; W: James B. Harris; M: Michel Colombier.

Cop and a Half 🦴½ 1993 (PG) Streetwise eight-year-old (Golden) accidentally witnesses a murder and then bullies police into letting him join the force (for a day) when he withholds key information. Enter his partner for the day—hard-edged detective Reynolds, who claims to hate kids, but who we know will learn to love them. Meanwhile, the outlaw (Sharkey) knows Devon saw him and is trying to silence him permanently. Predictable fantasy may appeal to kids, but will make most adults yawn. One of Sharkey's last roles. 87m/C VHS, DVD. Norman D. Golden II, Burt Reynolds, Ruby Dee, Ray Sharkey, Holland Taylor, Frank Sivero, Marc Macaulay, Rocky Giordani, Sammy Hernandez; D: Henry Winkler; W: Arne Olsen; C: Bill Butler; M: Alan Silvestri. Golden Raspberries '93: Worst Actor (Reynolds).

The Cop & the Girl 🦴 1986 A cop falls for a teenage runaway, ends up on the lam. Confused story overpowered by camera work. Lots of violence and strong language. Dubbed. 94m/C VHS. GE Jurgen Prochnow, Annette Von Kler; D: Peter Keglevic.

Cop in Blue Jeans 🦴 1978 Undercover cop goes after a mob kingpin in this violent, badly dubbed crime yarn. 92m/C VHS, DVD. Tomas Milian, Jack Palance, Maria Rosaria Omaggio, Guido Mannari; D: Bruno Corbucci.

Cop Killers WOOF! 1973 (R) Two men desperate for an easy way to make money embark on a murderous shooting spree. Mostly blanks. 93m/C VHS, DVD. Jason Williams, Bill Osco; D: Walter R. Cichy; W: Walter R. Cichy; C: Howard Ziehm; M: Hal Yoergler.

Cop Land 🦴🦴🦴 Copland 1997 (R) Partially deaf sheriff (Stallone), whose small New Jersey town is home to a number of New York cops, has divided loyalties when a criminal investigation could implicate his department and the cops he idolizes. Stallone wanted to put "actor" back on his resume, and made the ultimate sacrifice of his physique for the role by gaining some 35 pounds and letting his muscles go. Writer-director Mangold, who grew up in an upstate New York town populated by NYC cops and firemen, pairs his earnest morality tale with a Western feel to provide the excellent cast a chance to do what they do best. Welcome departure from the usual summer bombast. 105m/C VHS, DVD. Sylvester Stallone, Robert De Niro, Annabella Sciorra, Harvey Keitel, Peter Berg, Janeane Garofalo, Michael Rapaport, Ray Liotta, Cathy Moriarty, Robert Patrick, Noah Emmerich, John Spencer, Malik Yoba, Frank Vincent, Arthur J. Nascarelli, Edie Falco, Deborah Harry; D: James Mangold; W: James Mangold; C: Eric Alan Edwards; M: Howard Shore.

Cop-Out 🦴🦴 Stranger in the House 1967 John Sawyer (Mason) is an alcoholic retired attorney who has lived in seclusion since his wife left him. His estranged daughter, Angela (Chaplin), runs with a swinging crowd and her boyfriend, Jo (Bertoya), is accused of killing another member of their group. So daddy comes to the rescue to defend him and expose the real killer. Mason is the only reason to watch this mishmash. "Stranger in the House" and previously filmed in 1942. 95m/C VHS. GB James Mason, Geraldine Chaplin, Paul Bertoya, Bobby Darin, Ian Ogilvy, Clive Morton, James Hayter, Moira Lister; D: Pierre Rouve; W: Pierre Rouve; C: Ken Higgins; M: Patrick John Scott.

Cop-Out 🦴🦴 1991 A cop is framed. His brother is mad. Teamed up with a sexy-lawyer, he exposes the filth that is corrupting the city. Okay melodrama. 102m/C VHS. David Buff, Kathryn Luster, Dan Ranger, Reggie DeMorton, Lawrence L. Simeone; D: Lawrence L. Simeone; W: Lawrence L. Simeone.

Copacabana 🦴🦴 1947 A shady theatrical agent (Groucho) books a nightclub singer in two shows at the same time at New York's ritzy nightclub. Lots of energy spent trying to enliven a routine script. Also available colorized. ♪Tico Tico; Stranger Things Have Happened; Je Vous Amie; My Heart Was Doing a Bolero; Let's Do the Copacabana; I Haven't Got a Thing to Sell; We've Come to Copa. 91m/B VHS, DVD. Groucho Marx, Carmen Miranda, Steve Cochran, Gloria Jean, Andy Russell; Cameos: Earl Wilson; D: Alfred E. Green; W: Allen Boretz, Laszlo Vadnay; C: Bert Glennon.

Copper Canyon 🦴🦴½ 1950 Milland plays a Confederate Army officer who heads West after the Civil War, meets up with Lamarr, and sparks a romance. Good chemistry between the leads in this otherwise standard western. 84m/B VHS, DVD. Ray Milland, Hedy Lamarr, MacDonald Carey, Mona Freeman, Harry Carey Jr., Frank Faylen, Taylor Holmes, Peggy Knudsen; D: John Farrow.

Copperhead 🦴 1984 (R) A group of copperhead snakes attack a family who possess a stolen Incan gold necklace. This one bites. 90m/C VHS. Jack Renner, Gretta Ratliff, David Fritts, Cheryl Nickerson; D: Leland Payton; W: Leland Payton.

Cops and Robbers 🦴🦴½ 1973 (PG) Two cops use a Wall Street parade for returning astronauts as a cover for a multi-million dollar heist. Exceptional caper film thanks to the likable leads and genuine suspense. 89m/C VHS, DVD. Joseph Bologna, Dick Ward, Shepperd Strudwick, John P. Ryan, Ellen Holly, Dolph Sweet, Joe Spinell, Cliff Gorman; D: Aram Avakian; W: Donald E. Westlake.

Cops and Robbersons 🦴 1994 (PG) Bored, dim-witted dad Chase, a TV cop-show junkie, wishes his life had a little more danger and excitement. How lucky for him when hard-nosed cop Palance sets up a command post in his house to stake out the mobster living next door (Davi). Predictable plot isn't funny and drags Chase's bumbling idiot persona on for too long; Wiest and Davi are two bright spots, but their talents are wasted, while Palance does little more than reincarnate his "City Slickers" character. Poor effort for otherwise notable director Ritchie. 93m/C VHS, DVD. Jack Kehler, Chevy Chase, Jack Palance, Dianne Wiest, Robert Davi, Jason James Richter, Fay Masterson, Miko Hughes, Richard Romanus, David Barry Gray; D: Michael Ritchie; W: Bernie Somers; C: Gerry Fisher; M: William Ross.

Copycat 🦴🦴🦴 1995 (R) Crowded serial killer genre yields crooner Connick as southern psychopath stuck on murder. Soon he's in jail, advising the police who imitates the murders of other infamous serial killers. Agoraphobic, boozing criminal psychologist Helen Hudson (Weaver), still suffering the after effects of an attack by sicko subject Darryl Lee Cullum (Connick), is enlisted to help detective M.J. Monahan (Hunter) catch the homage specialist. Weaver and Hunter bring sparks to the usually testosterone-laden formula, helping mask the preponderance of serial killer cliches and giant holes in the script. Connick's turn as a nut-job killer won't make you forget Anthony Hopkins, or even Frank Sinatra. Exploitative and imitative, and always faithful to the formula. 124m/C VHS, DVD. Sigourney Weaver, Holly Hunter, Dermot Mulroney, Harry Connick Jr., William McNamara, Will Patton, John Rothman, David Michael Silverman; D: Jon Amiel; W: Ann Biderman, David Madsen; C: Laszlo Kovacs; M: Christopher Young.

Coquette 🦴🦴½ 1929 Pickford's first talkie portrays her as a flirtatious flapper from a well-to-do family who falls in love with a poor man her father despises. So much in fact that daddy kills the young daughter and then commits suicide, leaving his daughter to face the world alone. Pickford and Brown get to share a melodramatic death scene and audiences flocked to hear "America's Sweetheart" speak on screen. Based on a play by George Abbott and Anne Preston. 75m/B VHS. Mary Pickford, Johnny Mack Brown, Matt Moore, John St. Polis, Henry Kolker, George Irving, Louise Beavers, William Janney; D: Sam Taylor; C: Karl Struss. Oscars '29: Actress (Pickford).

Cora Unashamed 🦴🦴½ 2000 Adaptation of the Langston Hughes short story that finds racism and tragedy in a small Iowa town in the 1930s. Cora Jenkirs (Taylor) and her mother (Pounder) are the only blacks in the community. Cora works as a housekeeper for the Stuyvesant family and becomes strongly attached to the family's daughter, Jessie (Graham). This bond is resented by Jessie's mother, selfish and cold. Lizbeth (Graham), whose exaggerated sense of propriety brings about disaster. **95m/C VHS, DVD.** Regina Taylor, Cherry Jones, CCH Pounder, Michael Gaston, Aren Dean Snyder, Molly Graham, Ellen Muth, Kohl Sudduth; **D:** Deborah Pratt; **W:** Ann Peacock; **C:** Ernest Holzman; **M:** Patrice Rushen. **TV.**

The Core ♂♂½ 2003 (PG-13) The molten-hot magma goo at the Earth's core has stopped spinning (?!), bringing about the end of the world...unless a team of scientists and pilots can drill to the center of the planet and detonate an atomic device to get it going again in this unabashedly silly popcorn flick. Led by scruffy geophysicist Josh Keyes (Eckard), the assigned crew members set off on their preposterous mission, knowing full-well that the whole thing is ridiculous. This self knowledge, agreeing that it's all absurd, and not taking itself to seriously is what gets this disaster flick by. Everybody has a good time playing their characters' assigned quirks, especially Tucci as a smug, smarmy geophysicist. **DVD. US**/Aaron Eckhart, Hilary Swank, Delroy Lindo, Stanley Tucci, DJ Qualls, Richard Jenkins, Tcheky Kayo, Bruce Greenwood, Alfre Woodard; **D:** Jon Amiel; **W:** John Rogers, Cooper Layne; **C: D:** Jon Lindley; **M:** Christopher Young.

Corky Romano ♂ 2001 (PG-3) Remember when ex-SNL cast members made good movies? Yeah, neither do they. Kattan is the title character—a spastic, twitchy veterinary assistant, estranged from his mob family, who's so nave, he thinks his Pops (Falk) is actually a landscaping mogul. He is talked into infiltrating the FBI to retrieve evidence against the family by gruff henchman Leo (Ward), the actual stool pigeon talking to the feds. His frantic bumbling is mistaken for genius by his FBI superior Schuster (Roundtree) and hottie special agent Kate (Shaw). The plot is just dressing for Kattan's "funny-looking rubbery guy knocks everything over" routine, and he plays it like Jerry Lewis without the subtlety. First, "Night at the Roxbury," then "Monkeybone" and now this? Can someone get Kattan a script consultant? Please? **85m/C VHS, DVD. US** Chris Kattan, Vinessa Shaw, Peter Falk, Peter Berg, Christopher Penn, Fred Ward, Richard Roundtree, Matthew Glave, Dave Sheridan, Roger Fan; **M:** Randy Edelman. (German)

Corleone ♂ 1979 (R) Limp tale about two boyhood friends who grow up to fight the evil landowners who dominate Italy. To accomplish this, one becomes a mobster, the other a politician. **95m/C VHS. IT** Claudia Cardinale, Giuliano Gemma; **D:** Pasquale Squitieri. Montreal World Film Fest. '79: Actor (Gemma).

Corn 2002 (PG) The locals don't put much stock in Emily's word when the unmarried, pregnant college dropout starts carrying on about the dangers of "genetically enhanced" corn crops even though a bunch of folks suddenly aren't feeling so good. What is it about corn that makes small towns go all crazy in the movies, anyway? **97m/C VHS, DVD.** Jena Malone, Pamela Gray, Peter McRobbie, Jim Haynie, Harrold, Libby Langdon, Don Harvey, John Hartmann, Brian Dykstra, David Matthew Feldman, Denise Grayson, Joan Quincy Lee, Rick-yon, Adam Martinez; **D:** Dave Silver; **W:** Dave Silver; **C:** H. Michael Otano; **M:** Craig Snyder. **VIDEO**

The Corn Is Green ♂♂♂ 1945 Touching story of a school teacher in a poor Welsh village who eventually sends her pet student to Oxford. Davis makes a fine teacher, though a little young, while the on-site photography provides atmosphere. Based on the play by Emlyn Williams. Remade in 1979. **115m/B VHS.** Bette Davis, John Dall, Nigel Bruce, Joan Lorring, Arthur Shields, Mildred Dunnock, Rhys Williams, Rosalind Ivan; **D:** Irving Rapper; **M:** Max Steiner.

The Corn Is Green ♂♂♂ 1979 Excellent TV adaptation of the Emlyn Williams play has Hepburn as dedicated teacher Lilly Moffat, determined to bring education to a small Welsh mining village. She finds and mentors a student she believes can escape only through the power of his intellect. Cukor overcomes the limitations of television in his last collaboration with Hepburn. **93m/C VHS, DVD.** Katharine Hepburn, Bill Fraser, Anna Massey, Patricia Hayes, Dorothy Phillips; **D:** George Cukor; **W:** Ivan Davis; **M:** John Barry. **TV.**

Cornbread, Earl & Me ♂♂ 1975 (R) A high school basketball star from the ghetto is mistaken for a murderer by cops and shot, causing a subsequent furor of protest and racial hatred. Superficial melodrama. **95m/C VHS, DVD.** Moses Gunn, Rosalind Cash, Bernie Casey, Tierre Turner, Madge Sinclair, Keith Wilkes, Antonio Fargas, Laurence Fishburne; **D:** Joseph Manduke; **W:** Leonard Lamensdorf; **C:** Jules Brenner; **M:** Donald Byrd.

The Corner ♂♂½ 2000 This HBO miniseries was adapted from reporter David Simon's book "The Corner: A Year in the Life of an Inner-City Neighborhood" being Fayette Street in Baltimore. This corner is the local hub of drug activity that draws in members of the same family: Fran Boyd (Alexander) and Gary McCullough (Carter), who are both addicts, as well as their 15-year-old son DeAndre (Nelson). His parents are using drugs, gangs, and other trouble but when Fran learns that DeAndre's equally young girlfriend is pregnant, it spurs her into rehab and the hope of making something right. **376m/C DVD.** Khandi Alexander, T.K. Carter, Sean Nelson, Glenn Plummer, Clarke Peters, Tyra Ferrell, Tasha Smith, Toy Connor, **D.** Charles S. Dutton; **W:** David Mills; **C:** Ivan Strasburg; **M:** Henry Butler, Corey Harris. **CABLE**

Cornered ♂ 1932 McCoy is a sheriff, chasing bad guys, whose life is saved by Welch. Basically boring. **62m/B VHS.** Tim McCoy, Niles Welch, Raymond Hatton, Noah Beery Sr., Shirley Grey, Walter Long; **D:** B. Reeves Eason.

Cornered ♂♂ 1945 Tough Powell plays an airman released from a German prison camp who pursues a Nazi war criminal to avenge the death of his wife and child. **102m/B VHS.** Dick Powell, Walter Slezak, Micheline Cheirel, Luther Adler; **D:** Edward Dmytryk.

The Coroner ♂♂ 1998 (R) Dr. Leon Urasky (St. Louis) is a coroner and a serial killer. He chooses lawyer Emma Santiago (Longenecker) as a victim, but she is no pushover. Horror/thriller has some humor, a few nice moments, but mostly tedious. **75m/C DVD.** Jane Longenecker, Dean St. Louis, Rebeca Gray; **D:** Juan A. Mas; **W:** Geralyn Ruane; **C:** Charles "Chip" Schneer.

Coroner Creek ♂♂½ 1948 Chris Danning's (Scott) fiancee commits suicide after being held hostage during an Indian attack on her stagecoach and a payroll robbery. Danning sets out to trace the loot and exact his revenge. A superior production, notable for being one of the first westerns with an adult theme. **89m/B VHS.** Randolph Scott, Marguerite Chapman, George McCready, Sally Eilers, Edgar Buchanan, Wallace Ford, Forrest Tucker, William Bishop, Joe Dellva, Joseph (Joe) Sawyer, Russell Simpson; **D:** Ray Enright; **W:** Kenneth Gamet; **C:** Fred H. Jackman Jr.; **M:** Rudolph (Rudy) Schrager.

Corporate Affairs ♂ 1990 (R) A ruthless business woman climbing her way to the top literally seduces her boss to death. **92m/C VHS, DVD.** Peter Scolari, Mary Crosby, Chris Lemmon, Ken Kercheval, Terence H. Winkless, Geoffrey Baere.

Corporate Affairs ♂ 2007 (R) Lame flick that can't make up its mind whether to be a morality tale or an office sex comedy. Ted (Meyer) is married to Cassie (Harris) and they live in the 'burbs with their kids. Ted enjoys being a computer programmer for a software company but can't turn down a big promotion to management because the pay is too good, but unfortunately Ted's a techno geek, not a schmoozer of clients. He starts to question a lot for business and soon realizes that managers employ hookers as perks (for themselves and the clients), and Ted isn't man enough to resist. **99m/C DVD.** Irving Rapper; **M:** ...

The Corporate Ladder ♂ 1997 (R) Matt Taylor is looking for the perfect executive and his choice is Nicole—she's beautiful, bright, and devoted. It's no wonder that soon Matt and Nicole are having an affair. Too bad that Nicole would much rather run the company than take dictation—and she has a lethal way of implementing her business plan. Unfortunately, everything about this film is boringly predictable. **112m/C VHS,** Anthony John Denison, Kathleen Kinmont, Talisa Soto, Jennifer O'Neill, Ben Cross; **D:** Nick Vallelonga; **M:** Jan Hammer.

The Corporation ♂♂½ 1997 Seduction; Roger Corman Presents Subliminal Seduction 1996 (R) Darrin Danver (Ziering), the new exec at a computer game company, discovers the games are controlling their users with powerful subliminal messages. So he tries to expose his company's lethal manipulations before they can kill him. Standard-issue made-for-TV movie doesn't bring anything new to the "evil company" genre. Shot on location in L.A. and Las Vegas. **82m/C VHS,** Ian Ziering, Andrew Stevens, Katherine Kelly Lang, Dee Wallace Stone, Larry Manetti, Kim Morgan Greene, Kin Shriner, Stella Stevens; **D:** Andrew Stevens; **W:** Karen Kelly; **C:** Gary Graver; **M:** Terry Plumeri. **VIDEO**

The Corpse Grinders woof! 1971 (R) Low-budget bad movie classic in which a cardboard corpse-grinding machine makes nasty cat food that makes cats nasty. Sets are cheap, gore effects silly and cat attacks ridiculous. **73m/C VHS, DVD.** Sean Kenney, Monika Kelly, Sanford Mitchell, Byron J. Foster, Warren Ball, Ann Noble; **D:** Ted V. Mikels; **W:** Ted V. Mikels, Arch Hall Jr., Joseph L. Cranston; **C:** Bill Anneman.

The Corpse Vanishes ♂♂½ 1942 Lugosi at his chilling best as a diabolical scientist who snatches young brides and drains their blood in an effort to keep his 70-year-old wife eternally youthful. Not for newlyweds! **64m/B VHS, DVD.** Bela Lugosi, Luana Walters, Tristram Coffin, Elizabeth Russell, Vince Barnett, Joan Barclay, Angelo Rossitto; **D:** Wallace Fox.

Corregidor ♂♂ 1943 A love triangle develops between doctors treating the wounded during the WWII battle. A poor propaganda piece which contains only shaky stock footage for its "action" sequences. **73m/B VHS, DVD.** Otto Kruger, Elissa Landi, Donald Woods, Rick Vallin, Frank Jenks, Wanda McKay, Ian Keith; **D:** William Nigh.

Corridors of Blood ♂♂½ 1958 Karloff is a doctor, in search of a viable anesthetic, who accidentally becomes addicted to drugs, then turns to grave robbers to support his habit. Karloff plays usual threatening role to perfection. **86m/C VHS, DVD, GB** Boris Karloff, Betta St. John, Finlay Currie, Christopher Lee, Francis Matthews, Adrienne Corri, Nigel Green; **D:** Robert Day; **W:** Jean Scott Rogers; **C:** Geoffrey Faithfull; **M:** Buxton Orr.

Corrina, Corrina ♂♂½ 1994 (PG) Newly widowed jingle-writer Liotta needs someone to care for his withdrawn eight-year-old daughter. Enter Whoopi, as housekeeper and eventual love interest. Sweet, nostalgic romance set in the 1950s. Goldberg also found off-screen romance (again), this time with the film's union organizer Lyle Trachtenberg. Last role for Ameche. **115m/C VHS, DVD.** Whoopi Goldberg, Ray Liotta, Don Ameche, Tina Majorino, Wendy Crewson, Jennifer Lewis, Larry Miller, Erica Yohn, Anita Baker; **D:** Jessie Nelson; **W:** Jessie Nelson; **C:** Bruce Surtees; **M:** Rick Cox, Thomas Newman.

Corrupt ♂♂ Order of Death; Cop Killers 1984 (PG) Bad narcotics cop goes after murderer, but mysterious Lydon gets in the way. An acquired taste, best if you appreciate Lydon, better known as Johnny Rotten of the Sex Pistols. **95m/C VHS, DVD.** Harvey Keitel, John (Johnny Rotten) Lydon, Sylvia Sidney, Nicole Garcia, Leonard Mann; **D:** Roberto Faenza; **W:** Roberto Faenza, Ennio de Concini, Hugh Fleetwood; **C:** Giuseppe Pinori; **M:** Ennio Morricone.

Corrupt ♂♂½ 1999 (R) Corrupt (Ice-T) is the drug lord who holds the South Bronx but he has would-be competition from some up-and-coming homeboys. However, one ex-gang banger (Silkk the Shocker) wants out of the 'hood to make a new life for himself and his girl. Only Corrupt and his posse stand in the way. **72m/C VHS, DVD,** Ice-T, Ernie Hudson, silkk the Shocker, Karen Dyer; **D:** Albert Pyun. **VIDEO**

The Corrupt Ones ♂♂½ 1999 (R) Il Sigillo di Pechino; Die Hölle von Macao; Les Corrompus, The Peking Medallion; Hell to Macao 1967 A medallion that will lead to buried treasure in China. Great characters hampered by pedestrian script. **87m/C VHS,** Robert Stack, Elke Sommer, Nancy Kwan, Christian Marquand, Werner Peters; **D:** James Hill; **W:** Brian Clemens.

The Corruptor ♂♂♂ 1999 (R) Mostly soft-porn. Sweet Trash 1970 (R) Slick crime thriller starring Wahlberg as Danny, a young Caucasian cop assigned to New York's Chinatown precinct and partnered with shrewd veteran Chen (Chow Yun-Fat). The two men are drawn into a web of deception and betrayal as they try to stop a war between rival underworld factions. Chow finally receives a Hollywood role that showcases the talents that made him an international star in Asia, although the action segments suffer in comparison to his work with John Woo. The plot and performances are excellent, and there's enough shoot-'em-up to satisfy the average appetite for destruction. **110m/C VHS.** Chow Yun-Fat, Mark Wahlberg, Ric Young, Paul Ben-Victor, Brian Cox, Byron Mann, Kim Chan, Tovah Feldshuh, Ken Leung, Andrew Pang, Elizabeth Lindsey, Bill MacDonald, Susie Trinh; **D:** James Foley; **W:** Robert Pucci; **C:** Juan Ruiz-Anchia; **M:** Carter Burwell.

Corsair ♂♂ 1931 Actioner about a gorgeous debutante and a handsome gangster who find themselves caught up with a gang of bootlegging pirates. Todd is always worth watching. **75m/B VHS, DVD.** Chester Morris, Thelma Todd, Frank McHugh, Ned Sparks, Mayo Methot; **D:** Roland West.

The Corsican Brothers ♂♂♂½ 1942 Siamese-twins Mario and Lucien are separated by Dr. Paoli (Warner) shortly before their parents are murdered by evil Colonna (Tamiroff). One boy is sent to Paris and the other grows up in the Corsican mountains. Reunited as adults (and dashingly played by Fairbanks Jr.), the twins plot revenge. Entertaining swashbuckler based on a novel by Alexandre Dumas. **111m/B VHS, DVD.** Douglas Fairbanks Jr., Akim Tamiroff, Ruth Warrick, J. Carol Naish, H.B. Warner, Henry Wilcoxon, Veda Ann Borg; **D:** Gregory Ratoff; **W:** George Bruce; **C:** Harry Stradling Sr.; **M:** Dimitri Tiomkin.

Corvette Summer ♂ 1978 (PG) The Hot One After spending a semester restoring a Corvette n his high school shop class, an L.A. student must journey to Las Vegas to recover the car when it is stolen. There he meets a prostitute, falls in love, and steps into the "real world" for the first time. Potts is intriguing as the low-life love interest, but she can't save this one. **104m/C VHS, DVD.** Mark Hamill, Annie Potts, Eugene Roche, Kim Milford, Richard McKenzie, William (Bill) Bryant; **D:** Matthew Robbins; **W:** Matthew Robbins, Hal Barwood.

Cosh Boy woof! The Slasher 1961 Vicious male youths stalk women on the streets of London in this low-budget Jack the Ripper rip-off. **90m/B VHS.** Joan Collins.

James Kennedy, Hermione Baddeley; **D:** Lewis Gilbert; **W:** Lewis Gilbert.

Cosi *Caught in the Act* 1995 (R) Amiable Lewis (Mendelsohn) is hired to help with drama therapy at the local Sydney mental institution. Pressured by long-term patient Roy (Otto), Lewis finds himself agreeing to stage a production of Mozart's opera 'Cosi Fan Tutte' though none of the patients can speak Italian or sing. Rehearsals prove a challenge, there are numerous setbacks, and then it's show time. Fine ensemble cast delivers; adapted from Nowra's play. Friels stepped into the role of security guard Errol when Bruno Lawrence died before filming was completed; pic is dedicated to Lawrence. 100m/C VHS, DVD. *AU* Ben Mendelsohn, Barry Otto, Aden Young, Toni Collette, Rachel Griffiths, Colin Friels, Paul Chubb, Pamela Rabe, Jacki Weaver, David Wenham, Colin Hay, Tony Llewellyn-Jones, Kerry Walker; **Cameos:** Greta Scacchi, Paul Mercurio; **D:** Mark Joffe; **W:** Louis Nowra; **C:** Ellery Ryan; **M:** Stephen Endelman. Australian Film Inst. '96: Adapt. Screenplay, Support. Actress (Collette).

The Cosmic Eye 1971 Animated tale of three musicians from outer space who come to earth to spread the message of worldwide peace and harmony. A variety of cultural perspectives about the origins and destiny of the Earth are offered. Rather moralizing but the animation is impressive. 71m/C VHS, DVD. **D:** Faith Hubley; **V:** Dizzy Gillespie, Maureen Stapleton, Benny Carter.

The Cosmic Man 1959 An alien arrives on Earth with a message of peace and restraint. He is regarded with suspicion by our nasty Earthlings. Essentially "The Day the Earth Stood Still" without the budget, but interesting nonetheless. 72m/B VHS, DVD. Bruce Bennett, John Carradine, Angela Greene, Paul Langton, Scotty Morrow; **D:** Herbert Greene; **W:** Arthur C. Pierce; **C:** John F. Warren; **M:** Paul Sawtell, Bert Shefter.

The Cosmic Monsters *The Strange World of Planet X* 1958 Scientist accidentally pops a hole in the ionosphere during a magnetism experiment. Then huge, mean insects arrive to plague mankind. Coincidence? You figure it out. 75m/B VHS. Forrest Tucker, Gaby Andre, Alec Mango, Hugh Latimer, Martin Benson; **D:** Gilbert Gunn.

Cosmic Slop 1994 (R) Three-part anthology. "Space Traders," based on a story by Derrick Bell, finds a fleet of aliens offering to solve all of U.S. society's most pressing social ills if they can have the entire black population in return (for what purpose is never explained). "The First Commandment" features a Catholic priest in a Latino parish who comes up against Santeria. "Tang," based on a story by Chester Himes, finds a poor, desperately unhappy married couple dreaming about what they'll do with the rifle mysteriously delivered in a flower carton to their door. 87m/C VHS. Robert Guillaume, Jason Bernard, Nicholas Turturro, Richard Herd, Paula Jai Parker, Chi McBride; **D:** Reginald (Reggie) Hudlin, Warrington Hudlin, Kevin Sullivan; **W:** Trey Ellis, Kyle Baker; **C:** Peter Deming.

Cosmos: War of the Planets WOOF! *Cosmo 2000: Planet Without a Name; War of the Planets* 1980 (PG) The ultimate battle for survival is fought in outer space, though not very well and on a small budget. Special effects especially laughable. 90m/C VHS, DVD. *IT* Katia Christine, West Buchanan, John Richardson, Yanti Somer; **D:** Al (Alfonso Brescia) Bradley.

Cote d'Azur *Crustaces et Coquillages; Cockles and Muscles* 2005 Silly sex farce set on the sunny French Riviera. Marrieds Beatrix and Marc take their daughter Laura and Marc's best pal Martin for a summer beach holiday. Laura promptly disappears with a new beau and Charly has his own reasons for not correcting his parents' misconception that he and the openly gay Martin are sexually involved. Meanwhile, Beatrix's city lover shows up to surprise her and Marc has a secret involving boyhood friend Didier. French with subtitles. 93m/C DVD. *FR* Valeria Bruni-Tedeschi, Gilbert Melki, Jean-Marc Barr, Jacques Bonnaffe, Romain, Edouard Collin, Sabrina Seyvecou; **D:** Olivier Ducastel, Jacques Martineau; **W:** Olivier Ducastel, Jacques Martineau; **C:** Mathieu Poirot-Delpech; **M:** Philippe Miller.

Cottage to Let *Bombsight Stolen* 1941 Propaganda thriller about a Nazi plot to kidnap the inventor of a new bombsight. Focused cast struggles with lackluster script. 90m/B VHS. *GB* Leslie Banks, Alastair Sim, John Mills, Jeanne de Casalis, Carla Lehmann, George Cole, Michael Wilding, Frank Cellier, Wally Patch, Catherine Lacey; **D:** Anthony Asquith.

Cotter 1972 A Native American rodeo clown feels responsible for a cowboy's death, returns home to reflect on his life. Fair story, best at the small town feeling. 94m/C VHS. Don Murray, Carol Lynley, Rip Torn, Sherry Jackson, Christopher Knight; **D:** Paul Stanley; **W:** William D. Gordon; **C:** Alan Stensvold.

Cotton Candy 1982 Follows the faintly interesting trials and tribulations of a high school senior who tries to form a rock band. At first he meets failure, but is ultimately successful with the band and romance. Joint script-writing venture by brothers Clint and Ron Howard. 97m/C VHS. Charles Martin Smith, Clint Howard, Leslie King; **D:** Ron Howard; **W:** Clint Howard, Ron Howard. **TV**

The Cotton Club 1984 (R) With $50 million in his pocket, Francis reaches for an epic and delivers: handsome production, lots of dance, bit of singing, confused plot, uneven performances. tad too long. A musician playing at The Cotton Club falls in love with gangster Dutch Schultz's girlfriend. A black tap dancer falls in love with a member of the chorus line who can pass for white. These two love stories are told against a background of mob violence and music. Excellent performances by Hoskins and Gwynne. ♪Minnie the Moocher; Ill Wind; The Mooch; Ring Dem Bells; Drop Me Off in Harlem; Cotton Club Stomp; Truckin'; Mood Indigo; Copper Colored Gal. 121m/C VHS, DVD. Diane Lane, Richard Gere, Gregory Hines, Lonette McKee, Bob Hoskins, Fred Gwynne, James Remar, Nicolas Cage, Lisa Jane Persky, Allen (Goorwitz) Garfield, Gwen Verdon, Joe Dallesandro, Jennifer Grey, Tom Waits, Diane Venora, Robert Earl Jones; **D:** Francis Ford Coppola; **W:** Francis Ford Coppola, William Kennedy, Mario Puzo; **C:** Stephen Goldblatt; **M:** John Barry.

Cotton Comes to Harlem 1970 (R) Cambridge and St. Jacques star as Harlem plainclothes detectives Grave Digger Jones and Coffin Ed Johnson in this successful mix of crime and comedy. They're investigating a suspicious preacher's back-to-Africa scheme which they suspect is a swindle. Directorial debut of Davis. Filmed on location in Harlem, New York. Based on the novel by Chester Himes. Followed by a weak sequel, "Come Back, Charleston Blue." 97m/C VHS, DVD. Godfrey Cambridge, Raymond St. Jacques, Calvin Lockhart, Judy Pace, Redd Foxx, John Anderson, Emily Yancy, J.D. Cannon, Teddy Wilson, Eugene Roche, Cleavon Little, Lou Jacobi; **D:** Ossie Davis; **W:** Ossie Davis; **C:** Gerald Hirschfeld; **M:** Galt MacDermot.

Cotton Mary 1999 (R) Lily (Scacchi) is the lonely wife of reporter John (Wilby), living in India in 1954. She cannot nurse her newborn daughter and turns to the ministrations of bossy Anglo-Indian nurse Mary (Jaffrey), who is soon living in their household and having the child fed by her own sister, Blossom (Gupta). Meanwhile, the philandering John eyes Mary's niece, Rosie (Sakina Jaffrey), while Lily sinks into depression, and an increasingly mad Mary ruthlessly takes over their home. 124m/C VHS, DVD. *GB* Madhur Jaffrey, Greta Scacchi, James Wilby, Neena Gupta, Joanna David, Riyu Daijo, Prayag Raj; **D:** Ismail Merchant; **W:** Alexandra Viets; **C:** Pierre Lhomme; **M:** Richard Robbins.

Cotton Queen *Crying Out Loud* 1937 Romance and light intrigue plague the children of two rival textile mill owners. 80m/B VHS. Will Fyffe, Stanley Holloway; **D:** Bernard Vorhaus.

A Couch in New York *Un Divan a New York* 1995 (R) Limp romantic comedy features that old standby—opposites attracting. French dancer Beatrice (Binoche) responds to an ad for a temporary Paris-New York apartment switch placed by a stuffy psychoanalyst, Henry Harriston (Hurt). Henry's patients presume Beatrice is his replacement (he works at home) and the free-spirit begins giving them ad hoc advice. Meanwhile in Paris, Henry's plagued by all Beatrice's heartsick boyfriends and decides to come back early. When he arrives unannounced, she assumes he's a new patient and he's intrigued enough to go along. Lots of yakking, not too many sparks, and a strained artificiality make for a dull mix. 104m/C VHS, DVD. *FR BE GE* William Hurt, Juliette Binoche, Paul Guilfoyle, Stephanie Buttle, Richard Jenkins, Kent Broadhurst, Henry Bean, Barbara Garrick; **D:** Chantal Akerman; **W:** Chantal Akerman, Jean-Louis Benoit; **C:** Dietrich Lohmann; **M:** Paolo Conte, Sonia Atherton.

The Couch Trip 1987 (R) Aykroyd is an escapee from a mental institution who passes himself off as a radio psychologist and becomes a media sensation. There are a few laughs and some funny characters but for the most part this one falls flat. 98m/C VHS, DVD. Dan Aykroyd, Walter Matthau, Charles Grodin, Donna Dixon, Richard Romanus, Arye Gross, David Clennon, Mary Gross; **D:** Michael Ritchie; **W:** Will Aldis, Steven Kampmann; **M:** Michel Colombier.

Cougar Club 2007 Usual sex comedy about horny guys. Two recent college grads are dismayed to find that their dream jobs at an upscale law firm consist of menial and demeaning tasks. So they decide to open an exclusive dating club for young men like themselves who are interested in fulfilling their fantasies with experienced older women. Soon their day jobs and their nighttime escapades are overlapping. 99m/C DVD. Joe Mantegna, Kaley Cuoco, Izabela Scorupco, Joanie Laurer, Jason Jurman, Warren Kole, Jon Polito, Loretta Devine; **Cameos:** Faye Dunaway, Carrie Fisher; **D:** Christopher Duddy; **W:** Chris Mancuso; **C:** Dennis Laine; **M:** Steve Porcaro.

Could It Happen Here? *Italia ultimo atto* 1977 A lurid Italian spectacle about a metropolis thrown into a state of chaotic martial law by terrorism. Dubbed. 90m/C VHS. *IT* Luc Merenda, Marcella Michelangeli; **D:** Massimo Pirri.

Counsellor-at-Law 1933 One of Barrymore's best. He stars as Jewish lawyer George Simon, who has climbed to the top of his profession in New York from a poverty-stricken past that continues to haunt him. His constant struggles in the elitist law community are taking their toll and his personal life is no better when George discovers that his gentile wife Cora (Kenyon) has been unfaithful. But his secretary Regina (Daniels), who has always loved him, remains loyal. Rice adapted from his own play. Director Wyler dumped the musical score except for what's heard over the opening and closing credits. 80m/B VHS, DVD. John Barrymore, Bebe Daniels, Doris Kenyon, Onslow Stevens, Isabel Jewell, Melvyn Douglas, Thelma Todd, Mayo Methot; **D:** William Wyler; **W:** Elmer Rice; **C:** Norbert Brodine.

The Count 1916 Chaplin pretends to be the secretary of his boss, who in turn is posing as a count. Silent with musical soundtrack added. 20m/B VHS, DVD. Charlie Chaplin; **D:** Charlie Chaplin.

Count Dracula *Bram Stoker's Count Dracula; Il Conte Dracula; Dracula 71; Nachts wenn Dracula Erwacht; The Nights of Dracula* 1971 (R) Passable version of the Dracula legend (based on the novel by Bram Stoker) has Lee as the thirsty count on the prowl for fresh blood. Starts out as one of the most faithful adaptations, but loses momentum because Franco was running out of money. 90m/C VHS, DVD. *SP GE IT* Christopher Lee, Herbert Lom, Klaus Kinski, Frederick Williams, Maria Rohm, Soledad Miranda, Paul Muller; **D:** Jess (Jesus) Franco; **W:** Jess (Jesus) Franco, Augusto Finochi, Harry Alan Towers, Milo G. Cuccia, Carlo Fadda; **C:** Manuel Merino.

The Count of Monte Cristo 1912 One of the first full-length features starring popular stage stars of the day. The first truly American feature, it was based on the classic tale of revenge by Alexander Dumas. Silent. Remade many times. Lead actor O'Neill was the father of famed American playwright, Eugene O'Neill, who covered his father's success in this role in his own family drama "Long Day's Journey Into Night". 90m/B VHS. James O'Neill; **D:** Edwin S. Porter.

The Count of Monte Cristo 1934 A true swashbuckling revenge tale about Edmond Dantes (Donat), who unjustly spends years in prison. After escaping and retrieving a pirate treasure from the island of Monte Cristo, he gains ever so sweet and served quite cold revenge. Adaptation of the Alexandre Dumas classic. 114m/B VHS. Robert Donat, Elissa Landi, Louis Calhern, Sidney Blackmer, Irene Hervey, Raymond Walbum, O.P. Heggie; **D:** Rowland V. Lee; **W:** Rowland V. Lee, Philip Dunne; **C:** J. Peverell Marley; **M:** Alfred Newman.

The Count of Monte Cristo 1974 The Alexander Dumas classic about an innocent man (Chamberlain) who is imprisoned, escapes, and finds the treasure of Monte Cristo, which he uses to bring down those who wronged him. Good version of the historical costumer. Originally shown in theatres in Europe, but broadcast on TV in the U.S. 104m/C VHS. *GB* Richard Chamberlain, Kate Nelligan, Donald Pleasence, Alessio Orano, Tony Curtis, Louis Jourdan, Trevor Howard, Taryn Power; **D:** David Greene.

The Count of Monte Cristo *Le Comte de Monte Cristo* 1999 It seems only fitting that French TV produced this zestful miniseries version of the 1844 novel by Dumas pere. Depardieu obviously is enjoying himself in the lead role of Edmond Dantes, who is unjustly imprisoned for 20 years. After his escape, he discovers a fortune and uses it to get revenge as he adopts a fictional identity as the Count of Monte Cristo. Overwrought, over-the-top and lots of fun. Depardieu's daughter Julie and son Guillaume both have roles. French with subtitles. 480m/C VHS, DVD. *FR* Gerard Depardieu, Ornella Muti, Sergio Rubini, Guillaume Depardieu, Pierre Arditti, Jean Rochefort, Florence Darel, Julie Depardieu, Naike Rivelli, Jean-Claude Brialy, Ines Sastre, Helene Vincent, Christopher Thompson, Stanislas Merhar, Constanze Engelbrecht, Georges Moustaki; **D:** Josee Dayan; **W:** Didier Decoin; **C:** Willy Stassen; **M:** Bruno Coulais. **TV**

The Count of Monte Cristo 2002 (PG-13) Yet another remake of the Dumas classic revenge tale with some beautiful cinematography by Dunn to distinguish it. Hero Edmond Dantes (Caviezel) is betrayed by best friend Fernand Mondego (Pearce), who wants his girlfriend Mercedes (Dominczyk) among other things, and unjustly imprisoned. Dantes learns of a great treasure from fellow inmate Abbe Faria (Harris), eventually escapes, finds said treasure, and seeks his revenge under the disguise of—well, you know, Pearce has fun as the foppish villain and Caviezel is suitably heroic. 131m/C VHS, DVD. *US* James (Jim) Caviezel, Guy Pearce, Richard Harris, Dagmara Dominczyk, Luis Guzman, James Frain, Albie Woodington, Henry Cavill, Michael Wincott, Alex Norton, Freddie Jones; **D:** Kevin Reynolds; **W:** Jay Wolpert; **C:** Andrew Dunn; **M:** Ed Shearmur.

The Count of the Old Town *Munkbrogreven* 1934 Feisty townsfolk settle the score after a gang of booze smugglers trick them out of their money. Bergman's film debut as a maid swept off her feet by a mysterious young stranger. Adapted from the play "Greven fran Gamla Sta'n" by Arthur and Sigfried Fischer. In Swedish with English subtitles. 90m/B VHS. *SW* Edvin Adolphson, Ingrid Bergman, Sigurd Wallen, Valdemar Dahlquist; **D:** Edvin Adolphson, Sigurd Wallen; **W:** Gosta Stevens.

Count Yorga, Vampire *The Loves of Count Yorga, Vampire* 1970 (PG-13) The vampire Count Yorga is practicing his trade in Los Angeles, setting up a coven and conducting seances. Good update of the traditional character, with Quarry suitably solemn and menacing. Followed by "The Return of Count Yorga." **93m/C VHS, DVD.** Robert Quarry, Roger Perry, Michael Murphy, Michael Macready, Donna Anders, Judith Lang, Marsha Jordan, Julie Conners, Paul Hansen; **D:** Bob Kelljan; **W:** Bob Kelljan; **C:** Arch Archambault; **M:** Bill Marx.

Countdown ✗✗✗✗½ **1968** Documentary-type fictional look at the first moon mission and its toll on the astronauts and their families. Timely because the U.S. was trying to send a man to the moon in 1968. Interesting as a look at the developing Altman style. **102m/C VHS, DVD.** Robert Duvall, Michael Murphy, Ted (Edward) Knight, Joanna Moore, Barbara Baxley, Charles Aidman, Steve Ihnat, Robert Altman; **D:** Robert Altman.

Counter Attack ✗✗½ **1968** Story of murder and insurance fraud takes place on the back lots of the Hong Kong film industry. As good as these get. **105m/C VHS, DVD.** Bruce Li, Dan Inosanto, John Ladalski, Young Kong; **D:** Bruce Li.

Counter Measures ✗ **1985** A helicopter pilot stumbles on to a bizarre chain of crimes and disasters. **98m/C VHS.** Norman Forsey, Martin Howells, David Weatherley, Monte Merkham; **D:** Gerban Ceth.

Counter Measures ✗✗ **1999 (R)** Zach Silver (Dudikoff) and the USS Springfield are deployed to hunt the Odessa, a Russian nuclear submarine that's been hijacked by terrorists. **93m/C VHS, DVD.** *IT* Robert (Bobby) Blake, Alexander Keith, Scott Marlowa, Tracy Brooks Swope, Cliff (Potter) Potts, Robert F. Lyons; **D:** Fred Ray Olen; **W:** Steve Latsawar; **C:** Thomas Callaway; **M:** Eric Wurst, David Wurst. **VIDEO**

Counter Punch ✗✗ ½ **1971 (R) Ripped Off.** *The Boxer; Uomo Dalla Pelle Dura; Murder in the Ring; Tough Guy.* **1971 (R)** Blake is a boxer framed for the murder of his manager who begins when he refuses to carry out an order to execute a pretty young assistant. Fair rendition of a familiar plot. **72m/C VHS, DVD.** Gabriele Ferzetti, Catherine Speak, Tomas Milian; **D:** Franco Prosperi.

Counterblast ✗✗ **1948** A Nazi spy assumes the role of a British scientist in order to gain classified information for the Fatherland. The trouble begins when he refuses to carry out an assignment. Based on the true adventures of Eric Erickson, the top Allied spy of WW II, who was captured by the Gestapo but escaped. **140m/C VHS, DVD.** William Holden, Lilli Palmer, Hugh Griffith, Werner Peters, Eva Dahlbeck; **D:** George Seaton; **W:** George Seaton; **C:** Jean (Yves, Georges) Bourgoin.

The Counterfeit Traitor ✗✗✗ **1962** Suspense thriller with Holden playing a double agent in Europe during WWII. Based on the true adventures of Eric Erickson, the top Allied spy of WW II, who was captured by the Gestapo but escaped. **140m/C VHS, DVD.** William Holden, Lilli Palmer, Hugh Griffith, Werner Peters, Eva Dahlbeck; **D:** George Seaton; **W:** George Seaton; **C:** Jean (Yves, Georges) Bourgoin.

The Counterfeiters ✗✗✗½ **2007 (R)** *Die Falscher.* **2007 (R)** Russian-Jewish counterfeiter Salomon "Sally" Sorowitsch (Markovics) is arrested and winds up in a concentration camp in 1944 Berlin, where he's not only marked as Jewish, but designated as a habitual criminal, alienating him from the general prisoner population. There he's placed in charge of a secret counterfeiting unit with other prisoners, all of whom are afforded special privileges like clean sheets and cigarettes. Even with the "luxuries," there's no doubt about where they are—the screams penetrate the walls and their new clothes are from the victims. Sally and the others are forced to confront the morality of their situation (aid those who imprison them or rebel at the ultimate cost) as well as confronting their individual demons. Darkly provocative alternative to the more common heroic stories of camp survivorship. In German, with subtitles. **98m/C DVD.** *AT* GE Karl Markovics, August Diehl, August Zirner, Marie Baumer, Dolores Chaplin, David Striesow, Martin Zirner; **D:** Stefan Ruzowitzky; **W:** Stefan Ruzowitzky; **C:** Benedict Neuenfels; **M:** Marius Ruhland.

Counterforce ✗ *Escuadron* **1987 (R)** A rough group of mercenaries is hired to guard a Mideastern leader being chased by his country's ruling despot. Mild action with predictable story. **98m/C VHS, DVD.** Jorge (George) Rivero, George Kennedy, Andrew Stevens, Isaac Hayes, Louis Jourdan, Kevin Bernhardt, Hugo Stiglitz, Robert Forster, Susana Dosamantes; **D:** Jose Antonio De La Loma.

Counterstrike ✗ **2003 (PG-13)** Typical escapist cable fare finds a couple of secret service-type brothers (Estes, Joe Lando, Marie Matiko, Carmen Dunbar). **96m/C DVD.** Rob Estes, Joe Lando, Marie Matiko, Carmen Dunbar, Rachel Blakely, Christopher Lawford, Ron Lee; **D:** Jerry London; **W:** J.B. White; **C:** Ben Nott. **CABLE**

A Countess from Hong Kong ✗ **1967 (G)** Very bad romantic comedy features impoverished Russian countess Natasha (would you believe Loren is Russian?) stowing away in the luxury liner suite of stuffy American diplomat Ogden to escape her. Chaplin's final film. **108m/C VHS, DVD.** Marlon Brando, Sophia Loren, Sydney Chaplin, Tippi Hedren, Patrick Cargill, Michael Medwin, Oliver Johnston, Margaret Rutherford; **D:** Charlie Chaplin; **W:** Charlie Chaplin; **C:** Arthur Ibbetson; **M:** Charlie Chaplin.

Country ✗✗ **1984 (PG)** Strong story of a farm family in crisis when the government attempts to foreclose on their land. Good performances all around and an excellent portrayal of the wife by Lange. "The River" and "Places in the Heart," both released in 1984, also dramatized the plight of many American farm families in the early 1980s. **109m/C VHS, DVD.** Jessica Lange, Sam Shepard, Wilford Brimley, Matt Clark, Therese Graham, Levi L. Knebel; **D:** Richard Pearce; **W:** William D. Wittliff.

The Country Bears ✗✗ **2002 (G)** Fresh out of new ideas, Disney apparently saw gold in a few of their amusement park rides and decided to make movies out of them. This tale of talking, singing bears is the first installment. When Beary (voice of Osment) finds out that he's adopted, and not actually part of the human family that raised him, he decides to take a journey to visit Country Bear Hall in order to find his roots. Unfortunately, the hall is slated for demolition by evil banker Reed Thimple (Walken). Beary attempts to reunite the Country Bears, the legendary band that made the hall famous, in order to save it. Standard Disney fare, which means nothing objectionable except the attempt to make you buy more of their toys. **88m/C VHS, DVD.** *US* Christopher Walken, Daryl (Chill) Mitchell, Diedrich Bader, Alex Rocco, Stephen Tobolowsky; **M:C.** Gainey, Meagan Fay, Eli Marienthal, Queen Latifah; **D:** Peter Hastings; **W:** Mark Perez; **C:** C. Mitchell Anderson; **M:** Christopher Young, John Hiatt; **V:** Diedrich Bader, Haley Joel Osment, James Gammon, Brad Garrett, Candy Ford, Toby Huss, Kevin M. Richardson, Stephen (Steve) Root.

Country Gentlemen ✗✗ **1936** Vaudeville team, Olsen and Johnson, play fast-talking conmen who sell shares in a worthless oil field to a bunch of WWI veterans. What a surprise when oil is actually found there. Not one of the duo's better performances. **54m/B VHS, DVD.** Ole Olsen, Chic Johnson, Joyce Compton, Lila Lee, Ray Corrigan, Donald Kirke, Pierre Watkin; **D:** Ralph Staub.

Country Girl ✗✗✗✗ **1954** In the role that completely de-glamorized her (and won her an Oscar), Kelly plays the wife of alcoholic singer Crosby who tries to make a comeback with the help of director Holden. One of Crosby's four dramatic parts, undoubtedly one of his best. Seaton won an Oscar for his adaptation of the Clifford Odets play. Remade in 1982. **The Search is Through; Dissertation on**

---

the State of Bliss; It's Mine, It's Yours; The Land Around Us. **104m/B VHS, DVD.** Bing Crosby, Grace Kelly, William Holden, Gene Reynolds, Anthony Ross; **D:** George Seaton; **W:** George Seaton. Oscars '54: Actress (Kelly); Screenplay; Golden Globes '55: Actress—Drama (Kelly); Natl. Bd. of Review '54: Actress (Kelly); N.Y. Film Critics '54: Actress (Kelly).

Country Girl ✗ **1982** Aging, alcoholic actor is desperate for a comeback. His director blames his fiercely loving wife for the downfall. Poor cable TV remake of 1954 version with Bing Crosby. **137m/C VHS.** Dick Van Dyke, Faye Dunaway, Ken Howard; **D:** Gary Halvorson. **CABLE**

The Country Kid ✗✗ **1923** A freckle-faced teenager and his two brothers are beset by a wicked uncle out to steal their inheritance. One of Barry's best-remembered films. **60m/B VHS.** Wesley Barry, "Spec" (Walter) O'Donnell, Bruce Guerin, Kate Toncray, Helen Jerome Eddy, George Nicholls Jr.; **D:** William Beaudine.

Country Life ✗✗ **1995 (PG-13)** Down Under adaptation of Chekov's "Uncle Vanya" has Blakemore returning to his Aussie farm roots after 22-year stint as unsuccessful London theatre critic. His bored young wife (Scacchi) upsets the business-as-usual life of her husband's doned daughter, Sally (Fox), who is also jealous of the attention paid the beautiful Deborah by both her uncle and her crush, Dr. Askey (Neill). Exchanges Chekov's emotional exploration for a light comedy of manners and a message of Australian independence from England. **107m/C VHS, DVD.** *AU* Sam Neill, Greta Scacchi, Kerry Fox, John Hargreaves, Google Withers, Patricia Kennedy, Michael Blakemore; **C:** Michael Blakemore; **W:** Peter Best.

Countryman ✗✗ **1983 (R)** A dope-smuggling woman crashes her plane in Jamaica and is rescued by Countryman, a rasta super hero. Not very good, but at least there's great music by Bob Marley. **103m/C VHS, DVD.** Hiram Keller, Kristine Sinclair; **D:** Dickie Jobson.

County Fair ✗✗ **1920** This early silent film is an adaptation of Neil Burgess' play about life in New England. **60m/B VHS.** Helen Jerome Eddy, David Butler; **D:** Edmund Mortimer, Maurice Tourneur; **W:** J. Grubb Alexander.

Coup de Grace ✗✗½ **1978** Engaging political satire about a wealthy aristocratic woman in Latvia during the 1919–20 Civil War, and how she attempts to maintain her lifestyle as German soldiers are housed on her estate. Her unrequited love for a German officer adds to her troubles. In German with English subtitles. Co-written by von Trotta and based on the novel by Marguerite Yourcenar. **96m/B DVD. GE FR** Marguerite von Trotta, Matthias Habich, Rudiger Kirschstein, Mathieu Carriere; **D:** Volker Schlondorff; **W:** Margarethe von Trotta.

Coup de Torchon ✗✗✗½ **1981** *Clean Slate.* **1981** Set in 1938 French West Africa, Noiret plays corrupt police chief Lucien Cordier who is consistently harrassed by his community, particularly by the town pimp. He usually overlooks the pimp's crimes, but when Cordier catches him and a friend shooting at plague victims' bodies floating down the river he decides to "murder" them in cold blood. Based on the novel "POP 1280" by Jim Thompson. In French with English subtitles. **128m/C VHS, DVD. FR** Philippe Noiret, Isabelle Huppert, Guy Marchand, Stephane Audran, Eddy Mitchell, Pierre Marielle, Irene Skobline; **D:** Bertrand Tavernier; **C:** Pierre William Glenn; **M:** Philippe Sarde.

Coupe de Ville ✗✗½ **1990 (PG-13)** Three brothers are forced by their father to drive mom's birthday present from Detroit to Florida in the summer of '63. Period concerns and music keep it interesting. **99m/C VHS, DVD.** Patrick Dempsey, Daniel Stern, Arye Gross, Joseph Bologna, Alan Arkin, Rita Taggart, James Gammon; **D:** Joe Roth; **W:** Mike Binder; **M:** James Newton Howard.

Courage ✗✗✗ **1986** Based on fact, about a Hispanic mother in NYC who, motivated by her drug-troubled children, goes undercover and exposes a multimillion-dollar drug ring. Loren is great in a decidedly non-glamorous role. **141m/C VHS, DVD.** Sophia Loren, Billy Dee Williams, Hector Elizondo, Val Avery, Dan Hedaya, Ron Rifkin, Jose Perez; **D:** Jeremy Paul Kagan. **TV**

Courage Mountain ✗ **1989 (PG)** If you're looking for a good sequel to Johanna Spyri's classic "Heidi," this isn't it. Europe is on the brink of WWI when teenage Heidi leaves her beloved mountain for an exclusive boarding school in Italy. Not surprisingly for a war zone, the military takes over and the kids are sent to an orphanage run by nasties (see also "Oliver!"). The girls escape to the mountains and are saved by none other than Sheen as a twenty-something Peter (who cast the 20-something Sheen as a teenager? Bad mistake). Ridiculous sequel to the classic tale will appeal to kids despite what the critics say. **92m/C VHS, DVD.** Juliette Caton, Joanna Clarke, Nicola Stapleton, Charlie Sheen, Jan Rubes, Leslie Caron, Jade Magri, Kathryn Ludlow, Yoav agii, Laura Betti; **D:** Christopher Leitch; **W:** Weaver Levy.

Courage of Black Beauty ✗✗½ **1957** Another version of the perennial heart warmer about a boy and his horse. **80m/C VHS.** Johnny Crawford, Mimi Gibson, John Bryant, Diane Brewster, J. Pat O'Malley; **D:** Harold Schuster.

Courage of Lassie ✗✗½ **1946 (G)** Fourteen-year-old Taylor is looking for her dog tale. In this case, the dog is actually called Bill, not Lassie, in spite of the film's title. Bill is found wounded by Taylor and she nurses him back to health. He proves to be loving, loyal, and useful, so much so that, through a complicated plotline, he winds up in the Army's K-9 division and returns home with the doggie version of shell-shock. Taylor's still there to nurse him back to his old kind self again. **93m/C VHS, DVD.** Elizabeth Taylor, Frank Morgan, Tom Drake, Selena Royle, Harry Davenport, Arthur Walsh; **D:** Fred M. Wilcox.

Courage of Rin Tin Tin ✗✗½ **1957** Rusty and his faithful dog Rin Tin Tin help the cavalry ring with the help of Captain Dog and Dynamite Horse. Bound to set your hair on end. **55m/B VHS.** John Preston, June Love, William Desmond, Tom London, Jimmy Aubrey; **D:** Robert Emmet Tansey.

Courage of the North ✗✗½ **1935** The Mounties break up a fur-stealing ring with the help of Captain Dog and Dynamite Horse. Bound to set your hair on end. **55m/B VHS.** John Preston, June Love, William Desmond, Tom London, Jimmy Aubrey; **D:** Robert Emmet Tansey.

The Courage to Love ✗✗½ **2000 (PG-13)** Real-life portrayal of Henriette DeLille who, as the product of an affair between a white plantation owner and an African-American woman, shunned family and societal pressures to devote her life to caring for the underprivileged through her group the Sisters of the Holy Family in 19th-century New Orleans. **90m/C VHS, DVD.** Vanessa Lngme Williams, Gil Bellows, Lisa Bronwyn Moore, David La Haye, Cynda Williams, Diahann Carroll, Stacy Keach, Eddie Bo Smith Jr., Kevin Jubinville, Jean-Louis Roux, Lise Roy, Mariah Inger, Paul-Antoine Taillefer, Christopher Heyerdahl, Karen Williams, Graeme Somerville, Susannah Hoffman, Raven Dauda, Sylvia Stewart; **C:** Jonathan Freeman; **M:** Christopher Dedrick.

Courage Under Fire ✗✗✗ **1996 (R)** Army Lt. Col. Nat Serling (Washington) is unexpectedly assigned to review the candidacy of Capt. Karen Emma Walden (Ryan, seen only in flashbacks) to receive the posthumous Medal of Honor for bravery in combat. A Gulf War Medevac pilot, Walden would be the first woman awarded the honor if Serling can figure out the truth from her surviving crew's wildly conflicting reports. Ironically, she's dealing with a guilt complex since four members of his tank unit died in the war

---

under friendly fire. Stellar performances, including a frightening one by Phillips. Based on the novel by Duncan, who also did the screenplay; Washington and director Zwick previously worked together on "Glory." **120m/C VHS, DVD, Blu-ray Disc.** Denzel Washington, Meg Ryan, Matt Damon, Lou Diamond Phillips, Michael Moriarty, Scott Glenn, Bronson Pinchot, Seth Gilliam, Sean Astin, Regina Taylor, Tim Guinee, Ken Jenkins, Kathleen Widdoes, Zeljko Ivanek, Tim Ransom, Ned Vaughn; *D:* Edward Zwick; *W:* Patrick Sheane Duncan; *C:* Roger Deakins; *M:* James Horner.

Courageous Avenger 1935 A sheriff brings a treacherous one mine foreman to justice. **55m/B VHS.** Johnny Mack Brown; *D:* Robert North Bradbury; *W:* Charles Francis Royal.

Courageous Dr. Christian 1940 Dr. Christian is faced with an epidemic of meningitis among the inhabitants of a shanty town. Typical entry in the "Dr. Christian" series. **66m/B VHS, DVD.** Jean Hersholt, Dorothy Lovett, Tom Neal, Robert Baldwin, Maude Eburne; *D:* Bernard Vorhaus; *C:* John Alton.

The Courageous Mr. Penn *Penn of Pennsylvania* 1941 Slow-moving British film, outlining the achievements of William Penn, the Quaker founder of Pennsylvania. **79m/B VHS.** *GB* Clifford Evans, Deborah Kerr, Dennis Arundell, Aubrey Mallalieu, D.J. Williams, O.B. Clarence, Charles Carson, Henry Oscar, J.H. Roberts; *D:* Lance Comfort.

The Courier 1988 (R) A former drug addict seeks revenge on the dealers who killed his friend. Only thing that saves it are the songs by U2, The Pogues, and Hothouse Flowers. Musical score by Elvis Costello. **85m/C VHS.** *IR* Gabriel Byrne, Ian Bannen, Padraig O'Loingsigh, Cait O'Riordan, Patrick Bergin; *D:* Frank Deasy, Joe Lee; *M:* Elvis Costello.

Courier of Death 1984 A courier is embroiled in a mob war/struggle over a locked briefcase with mysterious contents. **77m/C VHS.** Joey Johnson, Barbara Garrison; *D:* Tom Shaw.

Court Jester 1956 Swashbuckling comedy stars Danny Kaye as a former circus clown who teams up with a band of outlaws trying to dethrone a tyrant king. Kaye poses as the court jester so he can learn of the evil king's intentions. Filled with more color, more song, and more truly funny lines than any three comedies put together; this is Kaye's best performance. ♪They'll Never Outfox the Fox; Baby, Let Me Take You Dreaming; My Heart Knows a Lovely Song; The Maladjusted Jester. **101m/C VHS, DVD.** Danny Kaye, Glynis Johns, Basil Rathbone, Angela Lansbury, Cecil Parker, John Carradine, Mildred Natwick, Robert Middleton; *D:* Melvin Frank, Norman Panama; *W:* Norman Panama; *C:* Ray June; *M:* Sammy Cahn, Sylvia Fine, Vic Schoen. Natl. Film Reg. '04.

The Court Martial of Billy Mitchell *One-Man Mutiny* 1955 Terrific courtroom drama depicts the secret trial of Billy Mitchell, head of the Army Air Service in the 1920s, who predicted the role of airpower in subsequent warfare and the danger of war with Japan. Mitchell incurred the wrath of the military by publicly faulting the lack of U.S. preparedness for invasion. Steiger is outstanding as the attorney; Cooper is great as Mitchell. Debut for Montgomery. **100m/C VHS, DVD.** Gary Cooper, Charles Bickford, Ralph Bellamy, Rod Steiger, Elizabeth Montgomery, Fred Clark, James Daly, Jack Lord, Peter Graves, Darren McGavin, Robert F. Simon, Jack Perrin, Charles Dingle; *D:* Otto Preminger; *C:* Sam Leavitt.

The Court Martial of Jackie Robinson 1990 (R) True story of a little-known chapter in the life of the famous athlete. During this stint in the Army, Robinson refused to take a back seat on a bus and subsequently faced the possibility of court martial. **94m/C VHS.** Andre Braugher, Daniel Stern, Ruby Dee, Stan Shaw, Paul Dooley, Bruce Dern, Dale Dye; *D:* Larry Peerce; *W:* Dennis Lynton Clark; *C:* Don Burgess. CABLE

The Courtesans of Bombay 1985 Gritty docudrama, set in Pavanpul, the poverty-stricken brothel section of Bombay, looks at how the impoverished women support themselves through a combination of prostitution and performing. **74m/C VHS, DVD.** *GB* Kareem Samar, Zohra Sehgal, Saeed Jaffrey; *D:* Ismail Merchant, James Ivory; *W:* Ruth Prawer Jhabvala. TV

Courtin' Wildcats 1929 Early Gibson programmer in which he plays a frail eastern college boy who was sent west by his father to toughen up. Once there, he meets Gilbert and ends up marrying her. **56m/B VHS.** Hoot Gibson, Eugenia Gilbert, Monte Montague; *D:* Jerome Storm.

The Courtney Affair *The Courtneys of Curzon Street* 1947 An aristocratic young Britisher causes a stir when he marries an Irish maid. As a result, the couple must face terrific social ostracism. Classy soap opera family saga was a big money maker in England. **112m/B VHS.** *GB* Anna Neagle, Michael Wilding, Gladys Young, Michael Medwin, Coral Browne, Jack Watling, Bernard Lee; *D:* Herbert Wilcox.

The Courtship of Eddie's Father 1962 A clever nine-year-old boy plays matchmaker for his widowed dad in this rewarding family comedy-drama (the inspiration for the TV series). Some plot elements are outdated, but young Howard's performance is terrific; he would later excel at direction. Based on the novel by Mark Toby. **117m/C VHS. DVD.** Glenn Ford, Shirley Jones, Stella Stevens, Dina Merrill, Ron Howard, Jerry Van Dyke, Roberta Sherwood; *D:* Vincente Minnelli; *W:* John Gay; *C:* Milton Krasner.

The Courtyard 1995 (R) Jonathan (McCarthy) seems to have the perfect life—a great job, great girl, great California apartment. But then his own downfall, a series of sinister crimes and Jonathan becomes the prime suspect. **103m/C VHS.** Andrew McCarthy, Madchen Amick, Richard "Cheech" Marin, Vincent Schiavelli; *D:* Fred Walton; *W:* Christopher Hawthorne.

Cousin Bette 1997 (R) Lange plays a mean game of Old Maid in this adaptation of Honore Balzac's novel, set in 1840s Paris. Always outshone by her more beautiful cousin Adeline (Chaplin), Bette is considered plain and not very bright by her aristocratic family. When Adeline's husband Hector (Laurie) asks her to become his housekeeper instead of his wife after Adeline dies, there is no doubt what she means when she hisses she will "take care of everyone." She uses her family's own baser instincts to bring about their downfall. Lange's performance as the cold and manipulative Bette is worth the price of a rental by itself. Big screen debut for theatrical director McAnuff. **112m/C VHS, DVD.** Jessica Lange, Elisabeth Shue, Aden Young, Bob Hoskins, Kelly Macdonald, Hugh Laurie, Geraldine Chaplin, Toby Stephens, John Sessions; *D:* Des McAnuff; *W:* Lynn Siefert, Susan Tarr; *C:* Andrzej Sekula; *M:* Simon Boswell.

Cousin, Cousine 1976 (R) Pleasant French comedy about pleasant cousins who meet at a round of family parties, funerals, and weddings and become friends, but their relationship soon becomes more than platonic. Remade in the U.S. as "Cousins." In French with English subtitles. **95m/C VHS, DVD.** *FR* Marie-Christine Barrault, Marie-France Pisier, Victor Lanoux, Guy Marchand, Ginette Garcin, Sybil Maas; *D:* Jean-Charles Tacchella; *W:* Jean-Charles Tacchella; *C:* Georges Lendi; *M:* Gerard Anfosso. Cesar '76: Support. Actress (Pisier).

The Cousins *Les Cousins* 1959 Set against the backdrop of Parisian student life, two very different cousins (one twisted, the other saintly) vie for the hand of Mayniel. This country mouse, city mouse adult tale ultimately depicts the survival of the fittest. Chabrol's lovely but sad second directorial effort. **112m/B VHS.** *FR* Jean-Claude Brialy, Gerard Blain, Juliette Mayniel, Claude Cerval, Genevieve Cluny; *D:* Claude Chabrol; *W:* Claude Chabrol.

Cousins 1989 (PG-13) An American remake of "Cousin, Cousine," in which two distant cousins-by-marriage meet at a wedding and, due to their respective spouses' infidelities, fall into each other's arms. A gentle love story with a humorous and biting look at the foibles of extended families. **110m/C VHS, DVD.** Isabella Rossellini, Sean Young, Ted Danson, William L. Petersen, Norma Aleandro, Lloyd Bridges, Keith Coogan; *D:* Joel Schumacher; *W:* Stephen Metcalfe; *C:* Ralf Bode; *M:* Angelo Badalamenti.

The Covenant 2006 (PG-13) Dull and dopey horror story focuses on the sons of Ipswich, four young studs who attend private Spenser Academy and have inherited supernatural powers from their spooky Massachusetts ancestors. Caleb (Strait) will come into his full powers on his 18th birthday but the more he uses them, the faster he'll age. This will be a problem since new transfer student Chase (Stan) is challenging Caleb for top warlock status. Can't even be considered cheesy fun, although the spider scene is pretty nasty. **97m/C DVD, Blu-ray Disc.** *US* Steven Strait, Laura Ramsey, Wendy Crewson, Sebastian Stan, Taylor Kitsch, Toby Hemingway, Jessica Lucas, Chace Crawford; *D:* Renny Harlin; *W:* J.S. Cardone; *C:* Pierre Gill; *M:* Tomandandy.

Cover 2008 (PG-13) Screechy and simplistic morality tale. Church-going wife and mother Valerie (Ellis) is outraged when she's questioned about a murder. The problem stems from her family's recent move to Philly and distant hubby Dutch's (Adoti) taking up with some old college friends. Shady goings-on and infidelity turn out to be the least of the problems. **98m/C DVD.** Aunjanue Ellis, Louis Gossett Jr., Raz Adoti, Paula Jai Parker, Vivica A. Fox, Mya, Patti LaBelle, Obba Babatunde; *D:* Bill Duke; *W:* Aaron Rashaan Thomas; *C:* Francis Kenny; *M:* Kurt Farquhar.

Cover Girl 1944 A vintage wartime musical about a girl who must decide between a nightclub career and a future as a cover model. Hayworth is beautiful, Kelly dances like a dream, and Silvers and Arden are hilarious. ♪Cover Girl; Sure Thing; Make Way For Tomorrow; Put Me to the Test; Long Ago and Far Away; That's the Best of All; The Show Must Go On; Who's Complaining?; Cover John. **107m/C VHS, DVD.** Rita Hayworth, Gene Kelly, Phil Silvers, Otto Kruger, Lee Bowman, Jinx Falkenberg, Eve Arden, Edward Brophy, Anita Colby; *D:* Charles Vidor; *C:* Rudolph Mate; *M:* Ira Gershwin, Jerome Kern. Oscars '44: Orig. Dramatic Score.

Cover Girl Models 1975 An action-packed '70s adventure in which beautiful models are forced to fight for survival. **82m/C VHS, DVD.** Lindsay Bloom, Pat Anderson, John Kramer, Rhonda Leigh Hopkins, Mary Woronov; *D:* Cirio H. Santiago.

The Cover Girl Murders 1993 (PG-13) Six beautiful models have been brought together on a remote island to shoot a magazine's popular swimsuit issue. Each one wants to be the cover model—but someone is willing to kill to get the job. **87m/C VHS.** Lee Majors, Jennifer O'Neill, Adrian Paul, Beverly Johnson, Vanessa Angel; *D:* James A. Contner; *W:* Douglas Barr, Bernard Maybeck; *M:* Rick Marotta.

Cover Me 1995 (R) When beautiful models turn up dead, L.A. detectives Bobby Colter (Rossovich) and J.J. Davis (Sorvino) discover they are all on the cover of L.A. Erotica magazine. So detective Holly Jacobsen, Colter's girlfriend, (Taylor) goes undercover as the magazine and learns more about the seamy sex underworld than she wants her to know. **94m/C VHS.** Courtney Taylor, Rick Rossovich, Paul Sorvino, Elliott Gould, Corbin Bernsen; *D:* Michael Schroeder; *W:* Steve Johnson.

Cover Story 1993 Journalist Matt McKendree falls in love with a mystery woman whose story he's investigating. Too bad she's dead—or is she. **93m/C VHS.** William Wallace, Tuesday Knight, Robert Forster, Christopher McDonald; *D:* Gregg Smith; *W:* Gregg Smith.

Cover-Up 1991 (R) Terrorist attacks on U.S. military bases in Israel are just a smokescreen for a greater threat. The below-par actioner stands out only for the hokey religious symbolism in its Good Friday climax. **89m/C VHS, DVD.** Dolph Lundgren, Louis Gossett Jr., John Finn; *D:* Manny Coto.

The Covered Wagon 1923 Prototypical silent Western began the genre. Wagon train moves cross-country, battling weather and wild Indians. By today's standards, somewhat bucolic and uneventful, but the location photography holds up quite well. Big budget film in its day, and enormously popular. **98m/B VHS.** Warren Kerigan, Lois Wilson, Alan Hale, Ernest Torrence; *D:* James Cruze.

Covered Wagon Days 1940 The Three Mesquiteers set out after silver smugglers who have framed Rico's brother for murder. **54m/B VHS.** Robert "Bob" Livingston, Raymond Hatton, Duncan Renaldo, John Merton, Reed Howes; *D:* George Sherman.

Covered Wagon Trails 1940 Substandard Western has good guy Randall dealing with the shifty cattleman's association and making the West safe for the hardworking locals. Future Frankenstein monster Strange plays the hired muscle. **52m/B VHS.** Addison "Jack" Randall, Sally Cairns, David Sharpe, Late (Lafayette) McKee, Budd Buster, Glenn Strange; *D:* Bernard B. Ray; *W:* Tom Gibson.

Covergirl *Dreamworld* 1983 (R) Wealthy man decides to relieve his boredom by molding a young woman into a supermodel. She finds the glamorous life isn't always what it's cracked up to be. TV-type melodrama. **98m/C VHS.** *CA* Jeff Conaway, Irena Ferris, Cathie Shirriff, Roberta Leighton, Deborah Wakeham; *D:* Jean-Claude Lord.

Covert Action 1988 A drug kingpin who desires to protect his business tries to frame a captain for a crime he did not commit. **85m/C VHS.** Rick Washburne, John Christian, Jimmy Stumper; *D:* J. Christian Ingvordsen.

Covert Assassin 1994 (R) Anti-terrorist specialist is hired by wealthy widow to avenge her husband's murder. Adapted from the novel "Wild Justice" by Wilbur Smith. **114m/C VHS, DVD.** Roy Scheider, Sam Wanamaker, Ted McGinley, Christopher Bucholiz; *D:* Tony Whamby.

The Cow 1993 Adam (Holub) is the simple-minded son of the local prostitute in a remote mountain village. With his mother dying, Adam sells his beloved cow to pay for her morphine but after her death he sinks into further poverty and despair until the beautiful Rosa (Mihulova) takes pity on him. Bleak but powerful; Czech with subtitles. **86m/C VHS.** *CZ* Radek Holub, Alena Mihulova; *D:* Karel Kachyna; *W:* Karel Cabradek, Karel Kachyna.

Cow Town 1950 A range war results when ranchers begin fencing in their land to prevent cattle rustling. Autry's 72nd film has some good songs and a dependable cast. **70m/B VHS, DVD.** Gene Autry, Gail Davis, Jock Mahoney, Harry Shannon; *D:* John English.

The Coward 1962 A schoolteacher and his wife are living in a remote Slovak village during the last days of WWII. The wife supports the anti-Nazi partisans while her husband collaborates with the Germans that occupy the village. Eventually, he finds the courage to save some innocent victims of the Nazi purge. Czech with subtitles. **113m/C VHS.** *CZ* Daniel Smutna, Ladislav Chudik, Oleg Strizhenov, Willem Koch-Hooge; *D:* Jiri Weiss; *W:* Jiri Weiss; *C:* Josef Strecha; *M:* Jiri Smka.

Coward of the County 1981 A devout pacifist is put to the test when his girlfriend is raped. Good performances by all concerned. Based on the lyrics of Kenny Rogers's hit song of the same name. 115m/C VHS. Kenny Rogers, Frederic Lehne, Largo Woodruff, Maricara Costello, Ana Alicia, Noble Willingham; *D*: Dick Lowry. **TV**

Cowboy ✍✍✍ 1958 Western round-up based on the memoirs of tenderfoot-turned-cowpoke Frank Harris, (Lemmon) is a Chicago hotel clerk who meets cattle boss Tom Reece (Ford) who's in the city on business. Losing his money in a poker game, Reece reluctantly accepts a loan from Harris in exchange for a piece of his cattle business. So Harris and Reece hit the dusty trail on a cattle drive that takes them into Mexico where Harris falls in love with Maria (Kashfi), the daughter of a wealthy rancher, and gradually turns from city slicker into hardened trail boss. "Reminiscences As a Cowboy" by book. 92m/C VHS, DVD. Jack Lemmon, Glenn Ford, Anna Kashfi, Brian Donlevy, Dick Vick; *C*: Manuel Mendoza, Richard Jaeckel, King Donovan; *D*: Delmar Daves; *M*: George Duning.

The Cowboy and the Ballerina ✍✍ 1984 An aging rodeo star falls in love with a petite ballerina defecting from a Russian Dance Company. Good cast makes it watchable. 96m/C VHS. Lee Majors, Leslie Wing, Christopher Lloyd, Anjelica Huston, George de la Pena; *D*: Jerry Jameson. **TV**

Cowboy & the Bandit ✍ 1935 A cowboy comes to the aid of a widow being victimized by outlaws. 58m/B VHS. Rex Lease, Bobby Nelson, William Desmond; *D*: Charles Lawton Jr.; *M*: Al(bert) Herman.

The Cowboy and the Lady ✍✍ 1938 Oberon plays a madcap heiress who is deposited by her politician father on their Florida estate to keep her out of trouble while he seeks the Presidential nomination. She is bored and decides to go to a local rodeo where she meets cowboy Cooper. Both are instantly smitten and marry on impulse. Cooper doesn't know about her wealth and when he's appalled that his daughter has married beneath her. Since this is a comedy all comes out right in the end. Good cast. 91m/B VHS. Gary Cooper, Merle Oberon, Patsy Kelly, Walter Brennan, Fuzzy Knight, Mabel Todd, Henry Kolker, Harry Davenport; *D*: H.C. Potter; *C*: Gregg Toland Oscars '38: Sound.

Cowboy & the Senorita ✍✍ 1944 A cowboy solves the mystery of a missing girl and wins her lovely cousin. The first "Im that paired Rogers and Evans, who went on to become a winning team, on and offscreen. 58m/B VHS, DVD. Roy Rogers, Dale Evans! **W:** Joseph Kane; **W:** Gordon Kahn.

Cowboy Commandos ✍½ 1943 Improbable plot has cowboys riding out after Nazi spies, who want to steal valuable ore. 55m/B VHS. Ray Corrigan, Dennis Moore, Max Terhune, Budd Buster, John Merton. Moore; *D*: S. Roy Luby.

Cowboy Counselor ✍ 1933 Cowboy Hoot Gibson helps an enchanting girl clear her innocent brother's name. 60m/B VHS. Hoot Gibson, Sheila (Manors) Mannors, Skeeter Bill Robbins, Alan Bridge, Bobby Nelson, Merrill McCormick. *D*: George Melford; **W:** Jack Natteford.

Cowboy Millionaire ✍✍ 1935 An Englishwoman comes to an American dude ranch and falls in love with one of the ranch hands. Entertaining Western comedy. 65m/B VHS. George O'Brien, Evalyn Bostock, Edgar Kennedy, Aiden Chase; *D*: Edward F. (Eddie) Cline.

Cowboy Up ✍✍ *Ring of Fire* 2000 (PG-13) Hank (Sutherland) is a rodeo clown while younger brother Ely (Thomas) is a bullrider. They clash when barrel rider Celia (Hannah) comes into the picture, which causes Ely to take some dangerous chances to win a bullriding championship. The film's original title, which was changed for the video release, comes from the Johnny Cash song. 105m/C VHS. Kiefer Sutherland, Marcus Thomas, Daryl Hannah, Melinda Dillon, Molly Ringwald, Russell Means, Bo Hopkins, Pete Postlethwaite, Al Corley;

D: Xavier Koller; **W:** James Redford; *C*: Andrew Dintenfass; *M*: Daniel Licht.

The Cowboy Way ✍½ 1994 A mess from start to finish made somewhat watchable by complete charm of the leads and one good horse chase. Two rodeo stars (Harrelson and Sutherland) from New Mexico ride into New York City to avenge a buddy's death, with Hud-son as a mounted NYC cop who always yearned to be a cowboy. Great premise is overcome by tasteless humor and a patched-up plot shot full of holes. Good for a gander is the 90-foot Times Square billboard of Harrelson's character as a Calvin Klein underwear model, which stopped traffic even in jaded New York. 106m/C VHS, DVD. Woody Harrelson, Kiefer Sutherland, Dylan McDermott, Ernie Hudson, Cara Buono, Marg Helgenberger, Tomas Milian, Joaquin Martinez. *Cameos:* Travis Tritt; *D*: Gregg Champion; **W:** William D. Wittliff, Rob Thompson; *C*: Dean Semler; *M*: David Newman.

The Cowboys ✍✍✍ 1972 (PG) Wayne stars as a cattle rancher who is forced to hire 11 schoolboys to help him drive his cattle 400 miles to market. Clever script makes this one of Wayne's better Westerns. Carradine's film debut. Inspired the TV series. 128m/C VHS, DVD, Blu-ray, Disc, HD DVD. John Wayne, Roscoe Lee Browne, A. Martinez, Bruce Dern, Colleen Dewhurst, Slim Pickens, Robert Carradine, Clay O'Brien, Nicolas Beauvy; *D*: Mark Rydell; **W:** Harriet Frank Jr., Irving Ravetch; *C*: Robert L. Surtees; *M*: John Williams.

Cowboys and Angels ✍✍½ 2000 (PG) Danny (Trese) gets dumped by his fiancee on the eve of their wedding (in favor of his best friend) and isn't sure he'll ever love again. So Danny decides to make some changes—he'll follow his dream of becoming a cowboy. Then, the bubbly Jo Jo (Mitchell) comes into his life. However, Jo Jo has a secret (let's put it this way—she's the second half of the title), and tries to steer Danny's affections in the direction of the receptive Candace (Kirshner). 97m/C VHS, DVD. Adam Trese, Radha Mitchell, Lilia Kirshner, Hamilton von Watts, Carmen (Lee) Llywelyn; *D*: Gregory C. Haynes; **W:** Gregory C. Haynes; *C*: Kramer Morgenthau; *M*: Stephen Edwards.

Cowboys & Angels ✍✍✍ 2004 (PG) Shane (Legge), a straight-laced 20-year-old decides to break away from his family and move to the city on his own. He takes an apartment with Vincent (Leech), a charismatic, gay art student. They strike up a friendship, and Shane develops the confidence to create a new life for himself, with its fresh possibilities and dangers. When the film's director, Paul finds a great, unknown cast. Notable for its portrait of a healthy gay/straight friendship. 90m/C DVD. Michael Legge, Alan Leech, Frank Kelly, David Murray, Amy Shiels; *D*: David Gleeson; **W:** David Gleeson; *C*: Volker Tittel; *M*: Stephen McKeon.

Cowboys Don't Cry ✍✍ 1988 When a modern cowboy's wife is killed in an automobile accident, he must change his immature ways and build a solid future with his teenage son or perish in loneliness. 96m/C VHS. Rebecca Jenkins, Ron White, Janet-Laine Green; *D*: Anne Wheeler.

Cowboys from Texas ✍½ 1939 The Three Mesquiteers bring about a peaceful settlement to a fight between cattlemen and homesteaders. Part of "The Three Mesquiteers" series. 54m/B VHS. Robert "Bob" Livingston, Raymond Hatton, Duncan Renaldo, Carole Landis; *D*: George Sherman; **W:** Oliver Drake; *C*: Ernest Miller.

Coyote Summer 1996 (G) Troubled teen girl tries to help an untamed horse. 93m/C VHS. Cindy Pickett, Ed Lauter, Gordon Tootoosis, Michelle St. John, Vinessa Shaw, Adam Beach; Bruce Weitz; *D*: Matias Alvarez; **W:** Karen Krenis; *C*: Bran Sullivan; *M*: Steve Dorff.

Coyote Trails ✍½ 1935 Standard western adventure has cowboy Tyler helping a damsel in distress. 60m/B VHS. Tom Tyler, Ben (Benny Corbett); *D*: Bernard E. Ray; **W:** Ross Gordon.

Coyote Ugly ✍ 2000 (PG-13) Producer Bruckheimer revisits the "Flash-dance" formula for this tale of a young innocent songwriter (Perabo) who ends up slingin' drinks and barin' her navel in the eponymous bar while seeking fame and fortune in New York. The main character, and wide-eyed as the naive John Goodman as the concerned dad and leaving no room for surprise twists, but also a discovery in Aussie Garcia as the love interest. The rest of the cast consists of jiggly window dressing, but the PG-13 rating guarantees disappointment for a large segment of the audience. It's bad, but not a career-destroying "Showgirls" kind of way. 94m/C VHS, DVD, UMD, Piper Perabo, Maria Bello, Tyra Banks, John Goodman, Melanie Lynskey, Ellen Cleghorne, Bud Cort, Izabella Miko, Bridget Moynahan, Adam Garcia, Del Pentacost, Michael Weston; *D*: David McNally; **W:** Todd Graff, Kevin Smith, Gina Wendkos; *C*: Amir M. Mokri; *M*: Trevor Horn.

Coyote Waits ✍✍½ 2003 Another adaptation of a Tony Hillerman novel, following "Skinwalker" about Navajo policemen Jim Chee (Beach) and Joe Leaphorn (Studi). Chee discovers the dead body of a fellow officer near some caves and finds drunken suspect Ashie Pinto (Herman) wandering the roads with a bottle and a gun. Since Leaphorn's wife Emma (Tousey) and Pinto are kin, she requests her husband investigate, while legends involving Butch Cassidy to a local professor, who believed the outlaw survived Bolivia, only to die on the Navaho reservation. A Vietnamese immigrant with ties to the CIA and Native American mysticism all play their part but the slow-paced story is sometimes confusing. 105m/C VHS, DVD. Wes Studi, Adam Beach, Sheila Tousey, Jimmy Herman, Keith Carradine, Graham Greene, Alex Rice, Bodhi (Pine) Elfman, Long Nguyen; *D*: Jan Egleson; **W:** Lucky Gold; *C*: Roy Wagner; *M*: B.C. Smith. **TV**

CQ ✍✍½ 2001 (R) It's 1969 and film editor Paul (Davies) is in Paris working on an arty futuristic thriller for egotistical director Andrezej (Depardieu) while filming his own black and white personal documentary. When the film's director, Enzo (Giannini), fires the director, Paul winds up with the slam-bang ending Enzo is demanding. Also demanding is leading lady Valentine (Lindvall), who is paying extra attention to the new director, which distracts Paul from the film and his French girlfriend Marlene (Bouchez). Paul's a dull character and the film suffers for it but it's not bad for a first effort from Coppola (son of Francis and brother of Sofia). 92m/C VHS, DVD. *US* Jeremy Davies, Elodie Bouchez, Angela Lindvall, Gerard Depardieu, Giancarlo Giannini, Massimo Ghini, Jason Schwarzman, Billy Zane, John Phillip Law, Dean Stockwell; *D*: Roman Coppola; **W:** Roman Coppola; *C*: Robert Yeoman.

Crack House ✍✍ 1989 (R) A man seeks revenge for the murder of a relative by drug dealers. Average exploitation flick. 91m/C VHS, DVD. Jim Brown, Richard Roundtree, Anthony Geary, Angel Tompkins, Greg Gomez Thomson, Clyde Jones, Cheryl Kay; *D*: Michael Fischa; *C*: Arledge Armenaki.

A Crack in the Floor ✍½ 2000 (R) Three couples go on a weekend hiking trip in the mountains and run into the deranged local folk. But their nightmare really begins when they make camp in a seemingly abandoned cabin that's not so empty after all. 90m/C VHS, DVD. Gary Busey, David Naughton, Mario Lopez, Tracy Scoggins, Bo Hopkins, Rance Howard, Justine Priest-Stanek; *D*: Sean Stanek, Corbin Timbrook; **W:** Sean Stanek. **VIDEO**

Crack Shadow Boxers ✍ 1979 Through a series of misadventures, Wu Lung and Chu San battle to protect the inhabitants of a small village from the onslaught of relentless bandits. 91m/C VHS, DVD. Hsi Ki Feng, Chou Li Lung, Han Guo Gai; *D*: Weng Yao Hai.

Crack-Up ✍✍½ 1946 Largely ignored at the time of its release, this tense film noir. An art expert suffers a blackout while investigating a possible forgery and must piece together the missing hours to uncover a criminal conspiracy. 70m/B VHS. Pat O'Brien, Claire Trevor, Herbert Marshall, Ray Collins, Wallace Ford, Damian O'Flynn, Erskine Sanford; *D*: Irving Reis.

Crack Up ✍✍ 1997 Three buddies hit a losing streak and decide they can improve their lives by ripping off a drug house. They wind up with more than he'll million in cash without the dealers having a clue as to who committed the crime. That is, until two newscasters decide to focus on the story—each tidbit of information leading the drug dealers closer to the guys' hideout and a deadly confrontation. 90m/C VHS. John Sayre, Mike Temer, Steven Saucedo, Guiliano Bela, Gregg Madsen, Jenny Royer; *D*: Jeff Leroy; **W:** Jeff Leroy, Marc Lutz; *M*: Jeffrey Alan Jones. **VIDEO**

Cracked Nuts ✍½ 1941 Small town young man (Erwin) wins some dough and heads to New York to propose to his gal (Merkel). However, he gets mixed up with a shyster lawyer and a couple of con men with a fake robot. 61m/B VHS. Stuart Erwin, Una Merkel, Mischa Auer, William Frawley, Shemp Howard, Mantan Moreland, Astrid Allwyn; *D*: Edward F. (Eddie) Cline; **W:** Scott Darling, Ernst Lazarus; *C*: Charles Van Enger.

Cracker: Best Boys ✍✍½ 1995 Typically involving psycho-mystery actually finds Fitz (Coltrane) on the wrong track. A murder precipitates a crime spree and knows repressed factory foreman Grady (Cunningham) has befriended troubled teenaged apprentice Bill (Simm) who's turned shockingly violent. Meanwhile, Judith (Flynn) has gone into an emotional tailspin, leaving Fitz to cope with the new baby. 7m/C VHS. *GB* Robbie Coltrane, Liam Cunningham, John Simm, Ricky Tomlinson, Geraldine Somerville, Barbara Flynn; *D*: Tim Fywell; **W:** Paul Abbott.

Cracker: Brotherly Love ✍✍✍ 1995 Everyone carries lots of emotional baggage in this entry of the British series. Detective Jane Penhaligon (Somerville) is still suffering from the aftereffects of rape, which she believes was by colleague Jimmy Beck (Cranitch); who's just returned to duty following a breakdown. Meanwhile, Fitz's (Coltrane) mother has died bringing him into contact with his stodgy brother Danny (Russell). And yes, there are murders to investigate—a killer who likes prostitutes to dress up as little girls. 150m/C VHS. *GB* Robbie Coltrane, Geraldine Somerville, Lorcan Cranitch, Kieran O'Brien, Tessa Thompson, Brid Brennan, David Calder, Mark Lambert; *D*: Roy Battersby; **W:** Jimmy McGovern. **TV**

The Cracker Factory ✍✍½ 1979 Wood is impressive as a woman committed to a mental institution who attempts to charm her way out of treatment. 90m/C VHS. Natalie Wood, Perry King, Shelley Long, Vivian Blaine, Juliet Mills, Peter Haskell; *D*: Burt Brinckerhoff; *M*: Billy Goldenberg. **TV**

Cracker: Men Should Weep ✍✍½ 1994 Fitz's skills are called into play when he must deal with a serial rapist (Aggr'e?). However, things become personal when Detective Jane Penhaligon (Somerville) is raped. 150m/C VHS, DVD, UMD. *GB* Robbie Coltrane, Geraldine Somerville, Lorcan Cranitch, Graham Aggrey; *D*: Jean Stewart; **W:** Jimmy McGovern. **TV**

Cracker: To Be a Somebody ✍✍ 1994 The leader of a Christian fundamentalist sect has an affair with a schoolgirl and plots her murder to avoid a scandal. But what he can't avoid is Fitz (Coltrane). 150m/C VHS, DVD. *GB* Robbie Coltrane, Geraldine Somerville. Lorcan Cranitch, Jim Carter, Samantha Morton, James Fleet, Cheritih Mellor; *D*: Julian Jarrold. **TV**

Cracker: The Big Crunch ✍✍ 1994 The murder of an Asian shopkeeper first prompts the Manchester police to look 'on their suspect in the violent world of skinheads. But when the professor is helping to profile the killer is murdered, the cops are forced to call in irascible forensic psychologist "Fitz" Fitzgerald (Coltrane) to aid in their investigation. Made for TV. **150m/C VHS, DVD. GB** Robbie Coltrane, Robert Carlyle, Barbara Flynn, Christopher Eccleston, Geraldine Somerville, Lorcan Cranitch; **D:** Tim Fywell; **W:** Jimmy McGovern. **TV**

Cracker: True Romance 🦴🦴🦴 **1995** Fitz (Coltrane) becomes the target of obsessive romantic Janice (Joyce) who sends him love letters and begins killing young men to get his attention. But when his son Mark (O'Brien) is placed in danger it will take all Fitz's psychological skills to discover the truth before it's too late. Meanwhile, Judith (Flynn) finds a good listener in Fitz's brother Danny (Russell) and the two edge towards more than friendship. **?m/C VHS. GB** Robbie Coltrane, Ricky Tomlinson, Geraldine Somerville, Barbara Flynn, Kieran O'Brien, Robert Cavanah, Wilbert Johnson, Rosemary Martin, Clive Russell, Emily Joyce; **D:** Tim Fywell; **M:** Paul Abbott.

Crackerjack 🦴🦴 **1994 (R)** Chicago cop Jack Wild (Griffith) agrees to join his brother's family at a vacation resort in Rocky Mountains. Coincidentally, a team of mercenaries are determined to hijack $50 million in diamonds from the resort and it's up to Jack to stop them. **96m/C VHS.** Thomas Ian Griffith, Nastassja Kinski, Christopher Plummer; **D:** Michael Mazo; **W:** Jonas Quastel, Michael Bafaro; **C:** Danny Nowak; **M:** Peter Allen.

Crackerjack 2 🦴½ *Hostage Train; Crackerjack 2: Hostage Train* **1997 (R)** Cop Jack Wild (Reinhold) discovers that the train carrying his girlfriend, financial analyst Dana Townsend (Alt), and several of the wealthy clients has been hijacked by terrorists. The train is trapped by an explosion in a tunnel in the Rockies and Jack must rescue the passengers before the rest of the terrorists' plan goes into motion. **98m/C VHS.** Karel Roden, Judge Reinhold, Carol Alt, Michael Sarrazin; **D:** Robert Lee; **W:** Chris Hyde; **C:** John Herzog; **M:** Peter Allen. **VIDEO**

Crackerjack 3 🦴🦴 **2000 (PG-13)** Jack Thorn (Svenson) is an ex-Navy S.E.A.L. and the current director of the CIA's covert ops. He's planning to retire when he discovers his would-be replacement, Marcus Clay (Gruner), wants to cause a worldwide economic catastrophe. So Jack gathers together some fellow oldtimers and tries to cope with high tech in order to save the world. **97m/C VHS, DVD.** Bo Svenson, Olivier Gruner, Leo Rossi, Amy Weber; **D:** Lloyd A. Simandl; **M:** Peter Allen. **VIDEO**

Cracking Up 🦴½ *Smorgasbord* **1983 (PG)** Accident-prone misfit's mishaps on the road to recovery create chaos for everyone he meets. Lewis plays a dozen characters in this overboard comedy with few laughs. **91m/C VHS.** Jerry Lewis, Herb Edelman, Foster Brooks, Milton Berle, Sammy Davis Jr., Zane Buzby, Dick Butkus, Buddy Lester; **D:** Jerry Lewis.

Cradle 2 the Grave 🦴½ **2003 (R)** Jewel thief Fait (DMX) steals some black diamonds that draw attention from many factions, including Li's Taiwanese government agent Su and some oily, world-domination types led by Su's former partner and friend Ling (Dacascos), who isn't above kidnapping Fait's daughter to get what he wants. DMX is pretty good at looking all cool and bad-ass, but runs into trouble when acting is called for. Li, the only real reason to bother with this flick, provides all the martial arts action you'd expect, but looks kinda bored doing it. Anderson and Arnold are around for comic relief (take that info as warning or praise, depending on your tolerance for both). **100m/C VHS, DVD, US** Jet Li, DMX, Anthony Anderson, Kelly Hu, Tom Arnold, Mark Dacascos, Gabrielle Union, Michael Jace, Chi McBride, Paolo Seganti, Drag-On, Paige Hurd; **D:** Andrzej Bart-kowiak; **W:** John O'Brien; **C:** Daryn Okada; **M:** John (Gianni) Frizzell, Damon Blackman.

The Cradle Will Fall WOOf! **1983** Adaptation of the pulpy bestselling mystery by Mary Higgins Clark about a woman who cannot convince anyone she witnessed a murder. The cast of "The Guiding Light" appear. Poor script and poor direction do not a thriller make. **103m/C VHS.** Lauren Hutton, Ben Murphy, James Farentino, Charita Bauer, Peter Simon; **D:** John Llewellyn Moxey. **TV**

The Cradle Will Rock 🦴🦴½ **1999 (R)** An exuberant if not always successful attempt by Robbins to capture the artistic/political fervor of New York in the '30s. Theatrical collaborators Orson Welles (Macfadyen) and John Houseman (Elwes) agree to produce Marc Blitzstein's (Azaria) new political musical "The Cradle Will Rock" for their Federal Theater pany in 1937. Right-wing political interference closes the theater on opening night but Welles leads his company to another venue in Manhattan where the actors (because of their union) must perform the piece from the audience—the dramatic circumstances offering a unique success and a place in theatre history. **133m/C VHS, DVD.** Angus MacFadyen, Cary Elwes, Hank Azaria, Cherry Jones, Ruben Blades, Joan Cusack, John Cusack, Philip Baker Hall, Bill Murray, Vanessa Redgrave, Susan Sarandon, Jamey Sheridan, John Turturro, Emily Watson, Bob Balaban, Paul Giamatti, Barnard Hughes, Barbara Sukowa, John Carpenter, Gretchen Mol, Harris Yulin, Dominic Chianese, Jack Black, Kyle Gass, Lee Arenberg, Daniel H. Jenkins, Peter Jacobson; **D:** Tim Robbins; **W:** Tim Robbins; **C:** Jean-Yves Escoffier; **M:** David Robbins.

The Craft 🦴🦴½ **1996 (R)** Call it "Heathers" with hexes. Troubled 17-year-old Sarah (Tunney) moves to L.A. and begins her senior year at St. Benedict's Academy. She takes up with three rebels—Nancy (Balk), Bonnie (Campbell) and Rochelle (True)—who like to dabble in witchcraft. Now, with the addition of would-be witch Sarah, these black magic women start slinging spells at their uppity classmates. Works best when concentrating on the girls and their problems, but degenerates into a special effects barrage toward the end. Alas, no one is turned into a newt. **100m/C VHS, DVD.** Robin Tunney, Fairuza Balk, Neve Campbell, Rachel True, Skeet Ulrich, Helen Shaver, Cliff DeYoung, Christine Taylor, Assumpta Serna; **D:** Andrew Fleming; **W:** Andrew Fleming, Peter Filardi; **C:** Alexander Grusynski; **M:** Graeme Revell. MTV Movie Awards '97: Fight (Fairuza Balk/Robin Tunney).

Craig's Wife 🦴🦴🦴 **1936** A classic soap opera about a pitiful woman driven to total ruin by her desire for social acceptance and material wealth. Russell makes her surprisingly sympathetic. Based on a Pulitzer Prize-winning George Kelly play. Remake of a silent film, was also remade as "Harriet Craig." **75m/B VHS.** Rosalind Russell, John Boles, Alma Kruger, Jane Darwell, Billie Burke; **D:** Dorothy Arzner.

Crainquebille 🦴🦴🦴 **1923** The classic satire based on the Anatole France story about a simple merchant in Paris unfairly imprisoned and eventually surviving peacefully as a tramp. Silent. **50m/B VHS, DVD. FR** Maurice Feraudy; **D:** Jacques Feyder.

The Cranes Are Flying 🦴🦴🦴½ *Letyat Zhuravli* **1957** When her lover goes off to fight during WWII, a girl is seduced by his cousin. Touching love story is free of politics. Filmed in Russia; English subtitles. **91m/B VHS, DVD. RU** Tatyana Samoilova, Alexei Batalov, Vasily Merkuryev, A. Shvorin; **D:** Mikhail Kalatozov; **W:** Viktor Rozov; **C:** Sergei Urusevsky; **M:** Moisej Vajnberg. Cannes '58: Film.

Crank 🦴🦴🦴 **2006 (R)** Mindlessly enjoyable "B" pic and proud of it. Freelance assassin Chev Chelios (Statham) learns his rival Ricky (Cantillo) has injected him with a toxin that kills if his heart rate drops too low. The only way Chev can fight the toxin is to continuously pump up his adrenaline, which leads him to rampage through LA in search of revenge, an antidote, and thrills of any kind. The premise is a variation on the 1950 noir "D.O.A." and it actually works if you don't think about it. **87m/C DVD, Blu-ray Disc. US** Jose Pablo Cantillo, Jason Statham, Amy Smart, Efren Ramirez, Dwight Yoakam, Carlos Sanz, Reno Wilson; **D:** Mark Neveldine, Brian Taylor; **W:** Mark Neveldine, Brian Taylor; **C:** Adam Biddle; **M:** Paul Haslinger.

Crash 🦴🦴 **1995 (NC-17)** You can always expect surreal kinkiness from Cronenberg and this film, awarded a Special Jury Prize at Cannes for 'daring, originality, and audacity,' won't prove the exception. It's "auto" erotica taken to the max, with car crashes and bodily injury turned into fetishes. James (Spader) lands in the hospital after an accident, which injured Helen (Hunter), a passenger in the other car. Helen and James' shared experience soon leads to a sexual relationship, which doesn't bother James' wife, Catherine (Unger). Then there's Vaughan (Koteas) and his group, who like to reenact famous auto crashes (like those of James Dean and Jayne Mansfield). Oh yes, there's lots more sex in (various combinations). Based on J.G. Ballard's 1973 cult novel. An R-rated version clocks in at 90 minutes. **98m/C VHS, DVD. CA** James Spader, Holly Hunter, Elias Koteas, Deborah Kara Unger, Rosanna Arquette, Peter MacNeill; **D:** David Cronenberg; **W:** David Cronenberg; **C:** Peter Suschitzky; **M:** Howard Shore. Cannes '96: Special Jury Prize; Genie '96: Adapt. Screenplay, Cinematog., Director (Cronenberg), Film Editing.

Crash 🦴🦴🦴½ **2005 (R)** From the writer of "Million Dollar Baby" comes this racially charged ensemble piece, which follows numerous lives intersecting over a 36-hour period in the volatile melting pot of L.A. Opening with a car-jacking, a central event that connects most of the characters, Haggis's drama meditates on the levels of class conflict between cops, criminals, showbiz types, and various ethnic and racial groups. A bit preachy at times, but the cast is so uniformly strong and the characters so multi-layered, you won't care. Cheadle, as always, stands out, but even the ensemble's typically bland Hollywood actors (Bullock, Fraser, Phillippe) acquit themselves nicely. **100m/C DVD, Blu-ray Disc, UMD. US** Ludacris, Sandra Bullock, Don Cheadle, Matt Dillon, Jennifer Esposito, William Fichtner, Brendan Fraser, Terrence Howard, Thandie Newton, Ryan Phillippe, Larenz Tate, Nona Gaye, Michael Pena, Beverly Todd, Keith David, Shaun Toub, Loretta Devine; **D:** Paul Haggis; **W:** Paul Haggis, Robert Moresco; **C:** J.(James) Michael Muro; **M:** Mark Isham. Oscars '05: Film Editing, Orig. Screenplay; British Acad. '05: Orig. Screenplay, Support. Actress (Newton); Ind. Spirit '06: First Feature, Support. Actor (Dillon); Natl. Bd. of Review '05: Breakthrough Perf. (Howard); Screen Actors Guild '05: Cast; Writers Guild '05: Orig. Screenplay.

Crash and Burn 🦴🦴 **1990 (R)** Rebels in a repressive future police state reactivate a huge, long-dormant robot to battle the establishment's army of powerful androids. Special effects by David Allen make the mayhem interesting. **85m/C VHS, DVD.** Ralph Waite, Paul Ganus, Eva LaRue, Bill Moseley, Jack McGee; **D:** Charles Band; **W:** J.S. Cardone; **M:** Richard Band.

Crash & Byrnes 🦴🦴½ **1999** Jack "Crash" Riley (Larson) is a retired CIA agent who is reluctantly called back into service to bring down a bioterrorist. A by-the-book kinda guy, Crash is, of course, paired with loose cannon DEA agent Roman Byrnes (Ellis). If the two can ever figure out a way to work together, they may just accomplish their mission. Standard fare in the wannabe "Lethal Weapon" mold. **92m/C VHS, DVD. CA** Wolf Larson, Joanna Pacula, Steven Williams, Sandra Lindquist, Terry Chen, Melanie Angel; **D:** Jon Hess; **W:** Wolf Larson; **C:** Anthony C. Metchie; **M:** Ken Williams.

Crash Course 🦴🦴½ *A Mother's Fight for Justice* **2000** Terry Stone's (Baxter) college student son Terry (Lively) is critically injured in a car crash and suffers from severe brain trauma. Since the accident was caused by a drunk driver, Terry seeks justice while Andrew struggles to regain his life. Based on a true story. **91m/C VHS, DVD.** Meredith Baxter, Alan Rosenberg, Eric Lively; **D:** Thomas (Tom) Rickman. **CABLE**

Crash Dive 🦴🦴🦴½ **1943** WWII glory film provides comic relief in the form of romance. Second-in-command Power falls hopelessly in love with school teacher Baxter, only to find out later that she is Lt. Commander Andrews' fiance. Once this little tidbit of information is disclosed, the two officers embark on a mission to destroy a Nazi U-Boat responsible for laying mines in the North Atlantic. Fantastic special effects and sound. Based on the story by W.R. Burnett. **105m/B VHS, DVD.** Tyrone Power, Anne Baxter, Dana Andrews, James Gleason, May Whitty, Harry (Henry) Morgan, Ben Carter, Frank Conroy, Florence Lake, John Archer, Minor Watson, Kathleen Howard, Stanley Andrews, Thurston Hall, Trudy Marshall, Charles Tannen, Chester Gan; **D:** Archie Mayo; **W:** Jo Swerling; **C:** Leon Shamroy; **M:** David Buttolph. **VIDEO**

Crash Dive 🦴🦴 **1996 (R)** An atomic submarine is taken hostage by Richter (Schone) and his band of terrorists, who demand $1 billion in gold or Washington D.C. will become a nuclear disaster. Naturally, there's one hero—sub designer James Carter (Dudikoff)—who manages to sneak aboard and plots to save the day. Fast pace and top special effects make this one watchable. **90m/C VHS, DVD.** Michael Dudikoff, Reiner Schone, Frederic Forrest, Jay Acovone; **D:** Andrew Stevens; **W:** William Martell; **C:** Michael Slovis; **M:** Eric Wurst, David Wurst. **VIDEO**

The Crash of Flight 401 🦴🦴 **1978** A plane, full of recognizable TV stars, crashes in the Florida Everglades. "Airport" for a smaller screen. Based on a real event. **97m/C VHS.** William Shatner, Adrienne Barbeau, Eddie Albert, Brooke Bundy, Christopher Connelly, Lorraine Gary, Ron Glass, Sharon Gless, Brett Halsey, George Maharis, Gerald S. O'Loughlin; **D:** Barry Shear. **TV**

Crashout 🦴🦴½ **1955** Six men break out of prison in this entertaining melodrama. Bendix plays the gang's leader to nasty perfection. **88m/B VHS.** William Bendix, Gene Evans, Arthur Kennedy, Luther Adler, William Talman, Marshall Thompson, Beverly Michaels, Gloria Talbott, Adam Williams, Percy Helton, Melinda Markey, Morris Ankrum; **D:** Lewis R. Foster; **W:** Hal E. Chester; **C:** Russell Metty; **M:** Leith Stevens.

The Crater Lake Monster WOOf! **1977 (PG)** The dormant egg of a prehistoric creature hatches after a meteor rudely awakens the dozing dino. He's understandably miffed and begins a revenge campaign. Prehistoric yawner. **85m/C VHS, DVD.** Richard Cardella, Glenn Roberts, Mark Siegel, Bob Hyman, Kacey Cobb; **D:** William R. Stromberg; **W:** Richard Cardella; **C:** Paul Gentry.

The Craving 🦴🦴 *Return of the Wolfman; El Retorno del Hombre-Lobo* **1980 (R)** Naschy (AKA Jacinto Molina) returns as El Hombre Lobo for the umpteenth time and once again battles a female vampire (see "Werewolf vs. the Vampire Woman"). Although continental Europe's biggest horror star, this film was such a boxoffice disaster that Naschy went bankrupt. He was then forced to turn to Japan for financing (see "The Human Beasts"). Naschy/Molina directed under the pseudonym "Jack" Molina. **93m/C VHS. SP** Paul Naschy, Julie Saly, Silvia Aguilar, Azucena Hernandez, Beatriz Elorrieta, Pilar Alcon; **D:** Paul Naschy.

The Crawlers 🦴 **1993 (R)** Illegal radioactive dumping has caused a living, lethal organism to invade in a small western town. Seems the local sheriff and the nuclear plant manager were partners in a toxic dumping scheme that went awry and two teenagers are the only ones willing to expose the truth. More to the point—scary monster attacks woman with artistically enhanced cleavage. Laurenti used an assumed pseudonym Martin Newlin. **94m/C VHS.** Jason Saucier, Mary Sellers; **D:** Fabrizio Laurenti; **W:** Dan Price, Fabrizio Laurenti.

The Crawling Eye 🦴🦴 *The Trollenberg Terror* **1958** Hidden in a radioactive fog on a mountaintop, the crawling eye decapitates its victims and threatens mankind. Average acting, but particularly awful special effects. Based on a British TV series. **87m/B VHS, DVD. GB** Forrest Tucker, Laurence Payne, Janet Munro, Jennifer Jayne, Warren Mitchell; **D:**

The Crawling Hand woof! 1963 An astronaut's hand takes off without him on an unearthly spree of stranglings. Silly stuff is a hands-down loser. 98m/B VHS, DVD. Kent Taylor, Peter Breck, Rod Lauren, Sirry Steffen, Alan Hale Jr., Richard Arlen, Allison Hayes, Arline Judge; D: Herbert L. Strock; W: Herbert L. Strock; C: Willard Van der Veer.

Crawlspace ✗ 1986 (R) Beautiful girls lease rooms from a murdering, perverted doctor whc spies on them, then kills. You may find Kinski amusing but not terrifying. 86m/C VHS, DVD. Klaus Kinski, Talia Balsam, Joyce Van Patten, Sally Brown, Barbara Whinnery; D: Devic Schmoeller; W: David Schmoeller; M: Piro Donaggio.

Craze ✗✗ 1974 (R) The internal Boi; Demon Master Tongue-in-cheek tale of a crazed antique dealer who slays a number of women as sacrifices to an African idol named Chuku. 96m/C VHS, DVD. Jack Palance, Diana Dors, Julie Ege, Suzy Kendall, Michael Jayston, Edith Evans, Hugh Griffith, Trevor Howard; D: Freddie Francis.

Crazed Cop ✗ One Way Out 1988 A man's mind snaps when his wife is found raped and murdered and nothing will stop him on his quest for revenge. Low budget and violent. 85m/C VHS, Ivan Rogers, Sandy Brooke, Rich Sutherin, Doug Ilk, Abdulah the Great; D: Paul Kyriazi.

The Crazies ✗✗ 1973 (R) Code Name: Trixie A poisoned water supply makes the residents of a small town go on a chaotic, murderous rampage. When the army is called in:o to quel the anarchy in a small war breaks out. 'Message film about the military is muddled and derivative. 103m/C VHS, DVD. Lane Carroll, Will MacMillan, Harold W. Jones, Lloyd Hollar, Lynn Lowry, Richard France, Richard Liberly, Will Disney, Harry Spillman; D: George A. Romero; W: George A. Romero; C: Bill Hinzman; M: Bruce Roberts.

Crazy as Hell ✗✗½ 2002 (R) Eriq La Salle makes his feature directorial debut in this unever swirl of psychiatric and metaphysical themes. Renowned psychiatrist Dr. Adams (Beach) arrives at a mental hospital to treat a group of patients using his controversial methods. Fueling his already robust superiority complex, his efforts are being filmed by weaselly documentary mraker Parker (McGinley). When patients and his own sanity. Worthwhile for La Salle's performance but seems to drag when he's not on screen. 113m/C VHS, DVD. Eriq La Salle, Michael Beach, Ronny Cox, John C. McGinley, Ta Texada, Sinbad, Tracy Pettit; D: Eriq La Salle; W: Erik Jendresen, Jeremy Leven, Butch Robinson; C: George Mooradian; M: Billy Childs.

crazy/beautiful ✗✗½ 2001 (PG-13) Cultural clash and teen 'relationship troubles all set in the affluent neighborhood of Pacific Palisades. Latino Carlos (Hernandez), from the wrong-side-of-the tracks in East L.A., is going to the rich high school in order to better himself. Nicole (Dunst) is the self-destructive wealthy chick (and congressman's daughter) who shows him that money doesn't buy happiness because she's got troubles, man. Familiar teen flick redeemed somewhat by the lead performances with handsome newcomer Hernandez appealing as a decent guy who's intrigued by willful, misunderstood hottie Dunst. 99m/C VHS, DVD. US Kirsten Dunst, Jay Hernandez, Taryn Manning, Rolando Molina, Bruce Davison, Lucinda Jenney, Soledad St. Hilaire; D: John Stockwell; W: Phil Hay, Matt Manfredi; C: Shane Hurlbut; M: Paul Haslinger.

Crazy Eights ✗ 2006 (R) You don't expect Oscar-caliber work in a cheap horror flick but it would be nice if the plot was at least semi-coherent. Six childhood friends reunite after 20 years for a friend's funeral. In his will said friend requests that

they open the trunk they buried as kids. In the trunk, they find the decayed corpse of a young girl. Somehow the group then becomes trapped in an abandoned psychiatric hospital where the girl's ghost starts killing them off. So they have to figure out their past connection to the dead girl. 80m/C DVD. Traci Lords, Dina Meyer, Gabrielle Anwar, Frank Whaley, George Newbern, Dan DeLuca; D: James Koya Jones; W: Dan DeLuca, James Koya Jones; C: Stephen M. Lyons; M: Piro Donaggio.

Crazy Fat Ethel II woof! 1985 A fat, hungry, homicidal female psychopath gets released from the asylum and goes on a cannabalistic rampage. Offensive junk. Sequel to "Criminally Insane." 90m/C VHS. Priscilla Alden, Michael Flood, Robert Copple; D: Nick (Steve Millard) Phillips.

Crazy for Love ✗✗ Le Trou Normand 1952 A village idiot stands to inherit the town inn if he can get a diploma within a year. With English subtitles. 80m/B VHS. FR Brigitte Bardot, André Bourvil, Jane (Jeanne) Marken, Nadine Basile; D: Jean Boyer; W: Arlette de Pitray; M: Paul Misraki.

Crazy Horse ✗✗✗ 1996 TV bio of the Oglala Sioux warrior (Greyeyes) whose home in the Black Hills of South Dakota was threatened by western expansion and the constant breaking of government treaties. As war chief, Crazy Horse, along with Teton Sioux leader Sitting Bull (Schellenberg), lead the Cheyenne and Sioux against Custer (Horton) at the battle of Little Bighorn. They elude capture by constant harassment by troops lead to 1877, betrayed by both the writies and some of his own people. Gripping story with a fine cast. 120m/C VHS. Michael Greyeyes, Jimmy Herman, Wes Studi, Irene Bedard, Peter Horton, John Finn, Steve Reevis, Gordon Tootoosis, August Schellenberg, Sheldon Peters Wolfchild, Ned Beatty; D: John Irvin; W: Robert Schenkkan; C: Thomas Burstyn; M: Lennie Niehaus.

Crazy Horse and Custer: "The Untold Story" ✗✗ 1990 (R) Long before Little Big Horn, two legendary enemies find themselves trapped together in deadly Blackfoot territory. George Armstrong Custer and Crazy Horse are forced to form a volatile alliance in their life-or-death struggle against the murderous Blackfoot Tribe. History takes a back seat to Hollywood scriptwriting. 120m/C VHS, DVD. Slim Pickens, Wayne Maunder, Mary Ann Mobley, Michael Dante; D: Norman Foster; C: Harold E. Stine; M: Leith Stevens.

Crazy House ✗✗½ 1943 Olsen and Johnson have a fabulous time at their 'Hellzapoppin' feature but get refused by every studio in town, leading them to try and shoot the picture themselves. Much slapstick and great cameos ensue, including Shemp Howard, Count Basie, plus Basil Rathbone and Nigel Bruce as their famous sleuths. 80m/B VHS. Ole Olsen, Chic Johnson, Martha O'Driscoll, Cass Daley; D: Edward F. (Eddie) Cline, Frédéric Rinaldo; W: Robert Lees. VIDEO

Crazy in Alabama ✗½ 1999 If they greenlighted this southern fried mess, they're crazy in Hollywood, too. Lucille (Griffith) is an unbalanced aspiring southern belle who decapitates her husband and heads off to fulfill her dream of becoming a Hollywood star. She also takes his severed noggin with her, al-

though it is a little talkative. Woven through this bizarre storyline is another that focuses on Lucille's nephew Peejoe back home in Alabama as he stands up to a bigoted sheriff. helps protest for civil rights and meets Martin Luther King. Banderas directoral debut is fine technically, but veers wildly all over the road as he can't content goes. 111m/C VHS, DVD. Melanie Griffith, David Morse, Lucas Black, Cathy Moriarty, Meat Loaf Aday, Rod Steiger, Richard Schiff, John Beasley, Robert Wagner, Noah Emmerich, Sandra Seacat, Paul Ben-Victor, Brad Beyer, Fannie Flagg, Elizabeth Perkins, Linda Hart, Paul Mazursky, William Converse-Roberts, Holmes Osborne, David Speck; D: Antonio Banderas; W: Mark Childress; C: Julio Macat; M: Mark Snow.

Crazy in Love ✗✗½ 1992 Three generations of women live on an island in the home that has been in their family for years. Hunter is wildly in love with her husband, but misses (and doesn't quite trust) him when he is away on business. Enter Sands, who showers her with affection and fills the void in her life. The supporting cast fleshes out the story nicely and illustrates the reasons behind Hunter's insecurity. Enjoyable romantic comedy doesn't throw out anything heavy. Adapted from the novel by Luanne Rice. 94m/C VHS. Holly Hunter, Gena Rowlands, Bill Pullman, Julian Sands, Frances McDormand, Herta Ware, Joanna Baron; D: Martha Coolidge; M: Gerald Ayres. TV

Crazy Like a Fox ✗✗ 2004 (PG-13) No, just crazy. Irresponsible Nat Banks (Rees) is the 8th generation to live on his now-impoverished family farm in a cave, and practising some guerila warfare. Probably plays best south of the Mason-Dixon line. 99m/C DVD. Roger Rees, Mary McDonnell, Robert Wisdom, Mark Joy, Paul Fitzgerald, Christina Rouner; D: Richard Squires; W: Richard Squires; C: Gary Grieg; M: David Kane, Richard Squires.

Crazy Little Thing ✗✗½ The Perfect You 2002 (R) That 'thing' would be love, of course. But reporter Whitney (McCarthy), newly arrived in New York, tells her friend Dee (de Matteo) that she's only looking for sex. So Dee sends her to a certain bar where Whitney can hire a male escort for the evening. Meanwhile, walter Jimmy (Eigeman) is also hoping to get lucky and happens to turn up at the same bar. Whitney thinks Jimmy knows the score but after a night of wild sex, Jimmy turns out to want more than a one-night stand. 90m/C VHS, DVD. Christopher Eigeman, Jenny McCarthy, Drea De Matteo, Paul Dooley, Aanna Ubach; D: Matthew Miller; W: Matthew Miller; C: Michael Barrett; M: Adam Dorn.

Crazy Love ✗✗ 2007 (PG-13) Documentary tells of the bizarre romance of Bronx-born ambulance-chasing attorney Bur. Pugach and a stunning younger woman, Linda Riss, who breaks things off when she discovers he is married. Her departure pushes the obsessive Pugach over the edge, and he contracts three wiseguys to throw acid in her face, disfiguring and partially blinding her. Somehow the strength of attraction wins out, unthinkably bringing Burt and Linda together again. The film includes interviews with the couple, old friends, and reporters who covered the case as well as news footage and photographs. This is way too weird to be made up. 92m/C DVD. US Burt Pugach, Linda Riss Pugach; D: Dan Klores; C: Wolfgang Held; M: Douglas J. Cuomo. Ind. Spirit '08: Feature Doc.

Crazy Mama ✗✗½ 1975 (PG) Three women go on a crime spree from California to Arkansas, picking up men and having a hoot. Crime and comedy in a campy romp. Set in the 1950s and loaded with period kitsch. 81m/C VHS, DVD. Cloris Leachman, Stuart Whitman, Ann Sothern, Jim Backus, Linda Purl, Donny Most, Sally Kirkland, Dick Miller, Bill Paxton; D: Jonathan Demme; W: Robert Thom; C: Bruce Logan.

Creation of Adam ✗✗ 1993 Weirdly mystical Russian drama finds Andrey's marriage in trouble because his wife thinks he's gay. She may be right because during a business meeting, Andrey is drawn to the charasmatic Philip, who, it turns out, is some sort of angelic messenger whose mission seems to be to give Andrey confidence in his love. Good performances although the plot lacks coherence and is not helped by the poor subtitling. Russian with subtitles. 93m/C VHS, FU Alex-

Crazy Moon ✗✗½ Huggers 1987 (PG-13) A rich high school nerd falls in love with a deaf girl, and must struggle against his commeering 'father's and older brother's prejudices. The viewer must struggle against the romantic cliches and heavy-handed message to enjoy a basically tender tale of romance. 89m/C VHS. Kiefer Sutherland, Vanessa Vaughan, Peter Spence, Ken Pogue, Eve Napier; D: Allan Eastman; W: Tom Berry, Stefan Wodoslawsky; M: Lou Forestieri.

Crazy People ✗✗ 1990 (R) Advertising exec Emory Leeston (Moore) writes commercials that describe products with complete honesty, and is committed to a mental hospital as a result. He meets a variety of characters and in the hospital, including Hannah, with whom he falls in love. Tepid boxoffice blunder sounds funnier than it is. We give half a bone for the ad slogans, the funniest part of the movie. Our favorite: "Most of our passengers arrive alive," for an airline. 91m/C VHS, DVD. Dudley Moore, Daryl Hannah, Paul Reiser, Mercedes Ruehl, J.T. Walsh, Ben Hammer, Richard (Dick) Cusack, Alan North, David Paymer, Danton Stone, Doug Yasuda, Bill Smitrovich, Paul Bates, Floyd Vivino; D: Tony Bill; W: Mitch Markowitz; C: Cliff Eidelman.

The Crazy Ray ✗✗✗ Paris Qui Dort 1923 The classic silent fantasy about a mad scientist who endeavors to put the whole population of Paris in a trance. Vintage Clair nonsense. 60m/B VHS. FR Henri Rollan, Albert Préjean, Marcel Vallee, Madeleine Rodrigue; D: Rene Clair.

The Crazy Stranger ✗✗✗ Gadjo Dilo 1998 The third film in director Gatlif's Gypsy trilogy following "Latcho Drom" and "Mondo." In order to honor his late father, Parisian Stephane (Duris) travels to Romania to track down and record the music of his father's favorite Gypsy singer. He's taken in by village headman, Isidor (Serban), whose own son has just been sent to prison. Isidor and the villagers make their living as musicians and Stephane is drawn ever deeper into their lives until tragedy forces him to make a choice. In French and Romany with subtitles. 97m/C VHS, DVD. FR Romain Duris, Isidor Serban, Rona Hartner, Florin Moldovan; D: Tony Gatlif; W: Tony Gatlif; C: Eric Guichard; M: Tony Gatlif.

Crazylove ✗✗ 2005 (R) Letty Mayer is happy with her teaching job, happy with her attorney boyfriend, and happy about her sister's upcoming wedding. But stress and her need for perfection drive Letty into a nervous breakdown and a stay in a mental institution. There she meets charming schizophrenic Michael. They decide to pursue their newfound passion when both are released, although Letty seems purposefully unaware of the severity of Michael's condition, especially when he's off his meds. 99m/C DVD. Reiko Aylesworth, Bruno Campos, Maria Schclofi, Meat Loaf Aday, JoBeth Williams, David Alan Basche, Greg Germann, K. Callan; D: Ellie Kanner; W: Carol Watson; C: Matthew Heckerling; M: Brad Segal.

Crazy Six ✗✗½ 1998 (R) In a futuristic Europe, organized crime families vie for control of the underground arms trade and the black market. 94m/C VHS, DVD. Rob Lowe, Burt Reynolds, Ice-T, Mario Van Peebles, Ivana Milicevic; D: Albert Pyun.

The Crazysitter ✗✗ 1994 (PG-13) Edie (D'Angelo), a petty thief recently released from jail, is hired as a sitter to the twins-from-hell. So, she decides to sell the little monsters. 92m/C VHS, DVD. Beverly D'Angelo, Ed Begley Jr., Carol Kane, Phil Hartman, Brady Bluhm, Rachel Duncan, Nell Carter, Steve Landesberg; D: Michael James McDonald; W: Michael James McDonald; C: Christopher Baffa; M: David Wurst, Eric Wurst.

ander Strizhenov, Anzhelika Nevolina, Saulius Ba-landis, Serghei Vinogradov, Irina Metlitskaya; **D:** Yuri Pavlov.

The Creation of the Humanoids

WOOF! **1962** Set in the familiar post-holocaust future, this is a tale of humans outnumbered by androids and the resulting struggle for survival. Slow and silly low-budget sets. For some reason, Andy Warhol was reported to love this film. **84m/C VHS, DVD.** Don Megowan, Frances McCann, Erica Elliot, Don Doolittle, Dudley Manlowe; **D:** Wesley Barry.

Creator

♂♂ **1985 (R)** A Frankenstein-like scientist plans to clone a being based on his wife, who died 30 years ago. As his experiments begin to show positive results, his romantic attention turns towards his beautiful lab assistant. O'Toole as the deranged scientist almost saves this one. Based on a novel by Jeremy Leven. **108m/C VHS, DVD.** Peter O'Toole, Mariel Hemingway, Vincent Spano, Virginia Madsen, David Ogden Stiers, John Dehner, Karen Kopins, Jeff Corey; **D:** Ivan Passer; **W:** Jeremy Leven; **C:** Robbie Greenberg; **M:** Sylvester Levay.

Creature

♂ *Titan Find* **1985 (R)** A two thousand-year-old alien life form is killing off astronauts exploring the planet Titan. "Alien" rip-off as its moments, but not enough of them. Kinski provides some laughs. **97m/C VHS, DVD.** Klaus Kinski, Stan Ivar, Wendy Schaal, Lyman Ward, Annette McCarthy, Diane Salinger; **D:** William Malone; **M:** Tom Chase, Steve Rucker.

Creature from Black Lake

♂♂ **1976 (PG)** Two anthropology students from Chicago travel to the Louisiana swamps searching for the creature from Black Lake. Predictably, they find him. McClenny, incidentally, is Morgan Fairchild's sister. **95m/C VHS, DVD.** Jack Elam, Dub Taylor, Dennis Fimple, John David Carson, Bill (Billy) Thurman, Catherine McClenny; **D:** Joy Houck Jr.

Creature from the Black Lagoon

♂♂♂ **1954** An anthropological expedition in the Amazon stumbles upon the Gill-Man, a prehistoric humanoid fish monster who takes a fancy to fetching Adams, a coed majoring in "science," but the humans will have none of it. Originally filmed in 3-D, this was one of the first movies to sport top-of-the-line underwater photography and remains one of the most enjoyable monster movies ever made. Sequels: "Revenge of the Creature" and "The Creature Walks Among Us." **79m/B VHS, DVD.** Richard Carlson, Julie Adams, Richard Denning, Antonio Moreno, Whit Bissell, Nestor Paiva, Ricou Browning, Ben Chapman, Bernie Gozier; **D:** Jack Arnold; **W:** Arthur Ross, Harry Essex; **C:** William E. Snyder, Charles S. Welbourne; **M:** Hans J. Salter, Henry Mancini.

Creature from the Haunted Sea

♂♂ **1960** Monster movie satire set in Cuba shortly after the revolution and centering around an elaborate plan to loot the Treasury and put the blame on a strange sea monster. Corman comedy is predictably low budget but entertaining. "Wain" is really Robert Towne, winner of an Oscar for screenwriting. Remake of "Naked Paradise." **76m/B VHS, DVD.** Antony Carbone, Betsy Jones-Moreland, Beach Dickerson, Edward (Robert Towne) Wain, Edmundo Rivera Alvarez, Robert Bean, Sonya Noemi Gonzalez; *Cameos:* Roger Corman; **D:** Roger Corman; **W:** Charles B. Griffith; **C:** Jacques "Jack" Marquette; **M:** Fred Katz.

Creature of Destruction

♂ **1967** A beautiful young woman is hypnotized and inadvertently reverted to her past life as a hideous sea monster. Buchanan's remake of his own 1956 production, "The She Creature." **80m/B VHS.** Les Tremayne, Aron Kincaid, Pat Delaney, Neil Fletcher, Ann McAdams, Scott McKay; **D:** Larry Buchanan; **C:** Robert C. Jessup.

Creature of the Walking Dead

♂½ *La Marca del Muerto* **1960** Scientist brings his grandfather back to life with horrifying results for the cast and the audience. Made cheaply and quickly in Mexico in 1960, then released with added footage directed by Warren. **74m/B VHS. MX** Ann Wells, George Todd, Willard Gross, Bruno Ve-Sota, Rosa Maria Gallardo, Katherine Victor; **D:** Fernando Cortes, Jerry Warren; **W:** Fernando Cortes, Alfredo Varela; **C:** Jose Ortiz Ramos.

The Creature Walks among Us

♂½ **1956** Sequel to "Revenge of the Creature" has the Gill-Man once again being captured by scientists for studying purposes. Through an accidental lab fire, the creature's gills are burned off and he undergoes surgery in an attempt to live out of water. Final entry in the Creature series has little magic of the original. Also shot in 3-D. **79m/B VHS, DVD.** Jeff Morrow, Rex Reason, Leigh Snowden, Gregg (Hunter) Palmer, Ricou Browning, Don Megowan, Maurice Manson, Frank Chase, Larry Hudson, Paul Fierro; **D:** John Sherwood; **W:** Arthur Ross; **C:** Maury Gertsman; **M:** Henry Mancini, Joseph Gershenson.

The Creature Wasn't Nice

♂ *Spaceship; Naked Space* **1981 (PG)** Spacecraft Vertigo ventures into outer space to an uncharted planet where a fast-growing, human-eating, song-singing creature snacks on the ship's crew. Nielsen stars in another genre spoof. **88m/C VHS, DVD.** Cindy Williams, Leslie Nielsen, Bruce Kimmel, Gerrit Graham, Patrick Macnee, Paul Brinegar, Cherie(?) Anderson, Ron Kurowski; **D:** Bruce Kimmel; **W:** Bruce Kimmel; **C:** Denny Lavil; **M:** Bruce Kimmel, David Spear. **VIDEO**

Creature with the Blue Hand

♂♂½ **1970** A German horror film about a passable Edgar Wallace story actually convicted of murders actually committed by a lunatic. Dubbed. **92m/C VHS, DVD. GE** Klaus Kinski, Harald Leopold, Hermann Leschau, Diana Kerner, Carl Lange, Ilse Page; **D:** Alfred Vohrer.

Creatures from the Abyss

♂♂½ *Plankton* **1994** After being stranded on a raft, five young people board an abandoned yacht, which is actually an oceanographic research vessel where very strange fish were being studied. The youngsters decide to make the yacht their party-place, but things get running wild on board the ship. As if that weren't bad enough, exposure to these aquatic nasties causes humans to mutate into monsters! On the surface (?!), this looks like the average Italian thriller, with bad acting, atrocious dubbing, and lackluster pacing, but the odd plot concerning mutant plankton and the fact that the movie consistently crosses the line with its disturbing special effects make it stand out. The timid will find the last act revolting, but those looking for a throwback to the gore-soaked '80s will love it. **86m/C DVD.** *IT*

Creatures from the Pink Lagoon

♂♂ **2007** B-movie spoof that sets-up "50s monsters and gay stereotypes. A group of gay friends gather at a beach cottage for a birthday party in 1967. They learn a nearby lagoon is overrun with zombies, who are man-eaters in more ways than one. **71m/B DVD.** Phillip Clarke, Nick Garrison, Lowell Deo, Evan Mosher, Vincent Kovar; **D:** Chris Diani; **W:** Chris Diani; **C:** Peter Torr; **M:** David Moddux. **VIDEO**

Creatures the World Forgot

WOOF! **1970** A British-made bomb about two tribes of cavemen warring over power and a cavewoman. No special effects, dinosaurs, or dialogue. **96m/C VHS.** Julie Ege, Robert John, Tony Bonner, Rosalie Crutchley, Sue Wilson; **D:** Don Chaffey; **W:** Michael Carreras.

The Creeper

♂♂ **1948** After experimenting with a variety of serums, a doctor turns into a murderous monster with feline paws. **65m/B VHS.** Eduardo Ciannelli, Onslow Stevens, June Vincent, Ralph Morgan; **D:** Jean Yarbrough.

Creepers

♂♂½ *Phenomena* **1985 (R)** A young girl talks to bugs and gets them to follow her instructions, which comes in handy when she battles the lunatic who is killing her school chums. Argento weirdness—and graphic gore—may not be for all tastes. **82m/C VHS, DVD.** *IT.* Jennifer Connelly, Donald Pleasence, Daria Nicolodi, Elenora Giorgi, Dalla di Lazzaro, Patrick Bauchau, Fiore Argento, Federica Mastroianni, Michele (Michael) Soavi, Gavin Friday; **D:** Dario Argento; **W:** Dario Argento, Franco Ferrini; **C:** Romano Albani; **M:** Simon Boswell.

The Creeping Flesh

♂♂ **1972 (PG)** A scientist decides he can cure evil by injecting his patients with a serum derived from the blood of an ancient corpse. Some truly chilling moments will get your flesh creeping. **89m/C VHS, DVD.** *GB* Peter Cushing, Christopher Lee, Lorna Heilbron, George Benson, Kenneth J. Warren, Duncan Lamont, Harry Locke, Hedger Wallace, Michael Ripper, Jenny Runacre; **D:** Freddie Francis; **W:** Peter Spenceley, Jonathan Rumbold; **C:** Norman Warwick.

Creeping Terror

WOOF! *The Crawling Monster; Dangerous Charter* **1964** Gigantic alien carpet monster (look for the tennis shoes sticking out underneath) devours slow-moving teenagers. Partially narrated because some of the original soundtrack was lost, with lots of bad acting, a worse script, laughable sets, and a ridiculous monster. Beware of the thermometer scene. **81m/B VHS.** Vic Savage, Shannon O'Neal, William Thourlby, Louise Lawson, Robin James, Byrd Holland, Jack King, Art J. Nelson; **D:** Art J. Nelson; **W:** Robert Silliphant; **C:** Andrew Janczak.

Creepozoids

♂ **1987** In the near future, a monster at an abandoned science complex stalks army deserters hiding out there. Violent nonsense done better by others. **72m/C DVD.** Linnea Quigley, Ken Abraham, Michael Aranda; **D:** David DeCoteau.

The Creeps

♂♂ **1997 (PG-13)** A horror-film obsessed scientist, Dr. Winston Berber, steals the original manuscript of Mary Shelley's "Frankenstein" and librarian Anna (Griffin) hires detective David Rawley (Lauer) to get it back. Then Berber returns to steal Bram Stoker's original "Dracula" and kidnaps Anna to use in his wacky experiment as well. He decides to reanimate his four favorite movie monsters but when David rescues Anna before the experiment is complete, Dracula (Fondacaro), the Mummy (Smith), the Wolfman (Simanton), and Frankenstein's Monster (Wellington) wind up only three feet tall. Not pleased by their diminutive size, the creeps work to restore themselves to the proper height (and cause a little mayhem as well). **80m/C VHS, DVD.** Phil Fondacaro, Rhonda Griffin, Justin Lauer, Bill Moynihan, Kristin Norton, Jon Simanton, Joe Smith, Thomas Wellington; **D:** Charles Band; **W:** Benjamin Carr; **C:** Adolfo Bartoli; **M:** Carl Dante. **VIDEO**

Creepshow

♂♂♂ **1982 (R)** Stephen King's tribute to E.C. Comics, those pulp horror comic books of the 1950s that delighted and horrified young horror tales, and morbid humor. The film tells five horror tales, and features King himself in one segment, as a none-too-bright farmer who unknowingly cultivates a strange, alien-origin moss. With despicable heroes and gory monsters, this is sure to delight all fans of the horror vein. Those easily repulsed by cockroaches beware! **120m/C VHS, DVD.** Hal Holbrook, Adrienne Barbeau, Viveca Lindfors, E.G. Marshall, Stephen King, Leslie Nielsen, Carrie Nye, Fritz Weaver, Ted Danson, Ed Harris, John Amplas, Tom Savini; **D:** George A. Romero; **W:** Stephen King; **C:** Michael Gornick; **M:** John Harrison.

Creepshow 2

♂♂½ **1987 (R)** Romero adapted three Stephen King stories for this horror anthology which presents gruesome looks at a hit-and-run driver, a wooden Indian, and a vacation gone wrong. Gory and childish stuff from two masters of the genre. Look for King as a truck driver. **92m/C VHS, DVD.** Lois Chiles, George Kennedy, Dorothy Lamour, Tom Savini, Domenick Jhon, Frank S. Salsedo, Holt McCallany, David Holbrook, Page Hannah, Daniel Beer, Stephen King, Paul Satterfield, Jeremy Green, Tom Wright; **D:** Michael Gornick; **W:** George A. Romero; **C:** Richard Hart, Tom Hurwitz; **M:** Les Reed, Rick Wakeman.

Cremains

♂♂♂ **2000** Anthology centers on a mortician (Chester Delacruz) who is being investigated for cremating two bodies at once. As he is questioned by an unseen panel of inquisitors, he relates three stories. In the first, a young woman (Plimmer) makes the mistake of driving through a small town famous for its ritual sacrifices. In the next story, a serial killer (Williams) captures a hitchhiker and then the mind-games begin. The third sto-

ry features a woman (Cole) who seeks out the help of a horror author (Smith), as she's convinced that a female vampire is after her. The final segment returns to the mortician and the macabre results of his double-cremation. The stories are good; while they aren't incredibly original, they all have that "urban legend" feel, which makes them more accessible. Howeverm the film is way too long, and all of the segments feel padded. Not perfect, but actually better than some studio horror films released lately. **107m/C DVD.** Chester Delacruz, Wanda Plimmer, Chris(topher) Williams, Kimberly Lynn Cole, R.W. Smith; **D:** Steve Sessions; **W:** Steve Sessions. **VIDEO**

The Cremators

WOOF! **1972** A meteorite carrying an alien lands at a seaside resort and everyone begins bursting into flames. Low budget effort from the scripter of "It Came from Outer Space." **90m/C VHS, DVD.** Marvin Howard, Maria de Aragon; **D:** Harry Essex.

The Crew

♂♂ **1995 (R)** Sometimes it doesn't pay to be a good samaritan—as when they rescue two psychopaths from a burning boat in the Bahamas. **99m/C VHS.** Viggo Mortensen, Jeremy Sisto, Pamela Gidley, Donal Logue, Laura Del Sol, Grace Zabriskie, John Philbin; **D:** Carl Colpaert; **W:** Carl Colpaert.

The Crew

♂♂ **2000 (PG-13)** Dreyfuss, Hedaya, Reynolds, and Cassel are a quartet of retired wiseguys who hatch a plan to save their South Beach Miami retirement home with a fake mob hit. Complications arise when the body turns out to be a South American druglord's missing father. Occasionally funny but overly plotted script was written by former "Golden Girls' writer Fanaro, and the sitcom lineage is obvious. **88m/C VHS, DVD.** Richard Dreyfuss, Burt Reynolds, Dan Hedaya, Seymour Cassel, Carrie-Anne Moss, Jennifer Tilly, Lainie Kazan, Miguel (Michael) Sandoval, Jeremy Piven, Casey Siemaszko, Matt Borlenghi, Jeremy Ratchford, Mike Moroff, Billy Jayne Young, Jose Zuniga, Louis Lombardi, Allan Nichols, Ron Karabatsos, Frank Vincent, Fyvush Finkel; **D:** Michael Dinner; **W:** Barry Fanaro; **C:** Juan Ruiz-Anchia; **M:** Steve Bartek.

Cria

♂♂♂ *Cria Cuervos; Raise Ravens* **1976 (PG)** The award-winning story of a nine-year-old girl's struggle for maturity in a hostile adult world. In Spanish with English subtitles. **115m/C VHS.** *SP* Geraldine Chaplin, Ana Torrent, Conchita Perez, Maite Sanchez; **D:** Carlos Saura; **W:** Carlos Saura; **C:** Teodoro Escamilla; **M:** Federico Mompoll. Cannes '76: Grand Jury Prize.

Cria Cuervos

♂♂♂ **1976** Movling freely between reality and fantasy, Saura portrays the complexities of childhood emotions through the grief of 8-year-old Ana (Torrent), who lives in Madrid and conjures her mother's ghost (Chaplin), as well as the struggles of Spain's middle class under fascist rule. Well-scripted, beautifully written and acted, the title is derived from the Spanish proverb: "Raise ravens and they'll peck out your eyes." Spanish with subtitles. **109m/C DVD.** *SP* Sydney Chaplin, Monica Randall, Ana Torrent, Florinda Chico, Hector Alterio, German Cobos, Mirta Miller; **D:** Carlos Saura; **W:** Carlos Saura; **C:** Teodoro Escamilla; **M:** Federico Mompou.

Cricket on the Hearth

♂♂ **1923** An adaptation of Charles Dickens' short story about a mail carrier and his bride, who find the symbol of good luck, a cricket on the hearth, when they enter their new home. Silent with organ score. **66m/B VHS.** Paul Gerson, Virginia Brown Faire, Paul Moore, Joan Standing, Lorimer Johnston; **D:** Lorimer Johnston; **W:** Caroline Francis Cooke.

Cries and Whispers

♂♂♂ **1972 (R)** As a woman dies slowly of tuberculosis, three women care for her: her two sisters, one sexually repressed, the other promiscuous, and her servant. The sisters remember family love and closeness, but are too afraid to look death in the face to aid their sister. Only the servant can touch her in her dying and will. Beautiful imagery, focused through a nervous camera, which lingers on the meaningless and whisks away from the meaningful. Absolute mastery of cinematic art by Bergman. **91m/C VHS, DVD.** SW Harriet Andersson, Ingrid Thulin, Liv Ullmann, Kari Sylwan, Erland Josephson, Henning Moritzen; **D:** Ingmar Bergman; **W:** Ingmar Bergman; **C:** Sven Nykvist. Oscars '73: Cinematog.; Natl. Bd. of Review '73: Director (Bergman), Film; N.Y. Film Critics '72: Cinematog. Screenplay.

Cries of Silence ✦✦ **1997** In 1969 a teenaged girl (Buchanan) is found along a remote Mississippi island shore in the aftermath of Hurricane Camille. Young doctor Dorrie Walsh (York) brings the girl to her mother's (Black) home after the locals swear they don't know who she is and the girl herself is mute from trauma. Dorrie calls her Camille and struggles to communicate with her in the face of community opposition. It seems learning Camille's identity could reveal the truth behind more than one local secret. **109m/C VHS.** Kathleen York, Karen Black, Erin Buchanan, Ed Nelson, Ellen Crawford, Guy Boyd; **D:** Avery Crounse; **W:** Avery Crounse; **C:** Michael Hol...

Crime & Passion ✦½ **1975 (R)** Two scheming lover's plan to get rich by having the woman marry a multimillionaire and sue for a quick divorce. The multimillionaire is no patsy, however, and seeks a deadly revenge. Three scripts by six writers were combined to create this story. That explains the many problems. **92m/C VHS, DVD.** Omar Sharif, Karen Black, Joseph Bottoms, Bernard Vicki; **D:** Ivan Passer.

Crime and Punishment ✦✦✦ *Crime et Chatiment* **1935** Original French production (preceding the American version by just one week) of Dostoyevski's novel, the tale of a young murderer, his crime, and ultimately, his confession. Generally considered better than the American version, tho French throw out all that is not cinematic, keeping the psychology and suspense. Remade in 1958. French with subtitles. **110m/B VHS.** Harry Baur, Pierre Blanchar, Madeleine Ozeray, Marcelle Geniat, Lucienne Lemarchant; **D:** Pierre Chenal; **W:** Marcel Ayme, Chenal, Christian Stengel; **M:** Arthur Honegger.

Crime and Punishment ✦✦✦ **1935** Pared down but well-executed version of the Dostoyevski novel. Lorre is superb as Raskolnikov, who robs and murders an elderly pawnbroker. Believing he has committed the perfect murder, he accepts the invitation of police inspector Porfiry (Arnold) to observe the investigation. Gradually Raskolnikov's conscience begins to overwhelm him as Porfiry slowly works to wring a confession from the killer. Von Sternberg's subdued directorial approach worked well to explore the psychological aspects of guilt, although the melodramatic French film version (released at the same time) scored better with the critics. **88m/B VHS.** Peter Lorre, Edward Arnold, Marian Marsh, Tala Birell, Elisabeth Risdon, Robert "Tex" Allen, Douglass Dumbrille, Gene Lockhart; **D:** Josef von Sternberg; **W:** S.K. Lauren, Joseph Anthony.

Crime and Punishment in Suburbia ✦½ **2000 (R)** Dostoyevsky heads to the mall in this suburban gloomfest very loosely based on the classic Russian novel. Roseanne (Keena)'s a pretty, popular teen whose family life is screwed up beyond repair. Her father Fred (Ironside) is an abusive monster and her mother Maggie (Barkin) is a drunken floozy. She hopes that she can endure the situation until she graduates, but Fred's reaction to an affair by Maggie (the contempt killing her father. With the help of her boyfriend Jimmy (DeBello), Roseanne murders her old man. When her mother is arrested for the crime and she becomes an outcast at school, she

turns to mysterious classmate Vincent (Kartheiser) for solace, not knowing he's been lurking in the shadows and observing everything. The themes explored in this grim view of suburbia are better served up in "American Beauty." **98m/C VHS, DVD.** Michael Ironside, Jeffrey Wright, Ellen Barkin, Monica Keena, Vincent Kartheiser, Ellen DeBello, Conchata Ferrell, Marshall Teague, Brad Greenquist, Lucinda Jenney; **D:** Rob Schmidt; **W:** Larry Gross; **C:** Bobby Bukowski; **M:** Michael Brook.

Crime Broker ✦✦ **1994** A respected judge (Bisset) decides to experience life on the other side of the bench for a change. So she hooks up with a handsome partner to execute a series of high-profile robberies of bank vaults and museums..implied sex so don't look for this under erotic thrillers. **93m/C VHS, DVD.** Jacqueline Bisset, Masaya Kato, Gary Day; **D:** Ian Barry; **W:** Tony Morphett; **C:** Dan Burstall; **M:** Roger Mason.

Crime Busters ✦½ **1978 (PG)** Two guys attempt to pull of a bank heist but accidentally join the Miami police force instead. Hill and Spencer are enjoyable as usual but the hijinks get tiresome long before the finale of "Two Supercops." **114m/C VHS.** ITTerence Hill, Bud Spencer, Laura Gemser, Luciano Catenacci, David Huddleston; **D:** E.B. Clucher.

Crime Killer ✦ **1985** Confusing shenanigans about an explosive ex-CIA agent enlisted by the FBI to battle a brutal crime syndicate shipping guns to nasty Arabs. **90m/C VHS.** George Pan-Andreas, Leo Morrell, Althan Karras; **D:** George Pan-Andreas. **C:** Aikledge Armenak.

Crime Lords ✦✦ **1991 (R)** When a pair of cops are suspended from the force for committing a blunder, they travel to Hong Kong to continue their investigation. Little do they know their sleuthing has drawn them into a confrontation with one of largest crime syndicates in the world. Lots of action, beautiful women, and exotic locations keep this basic buddy plot moving well. **96m/C VHS.** Wayne Crawford, Martin Hewitt, Susan Byun, Mel Castelo, James Hong; **D:** Wayne Crawford.

The Crime of Dr. Crespi ✦✦ **1935** A doctor takes his revenge on a man who is after his girlfriend by injecting him with suspended animation serum. Extremely campy performance from von Stroheim; Frye's biggest role in terms of screen time. **64m/B VHS.** Erich von Stroheim, Dwight Frye, Paul Guilfoyle, Harriett Russell, John Bohm; **D:** John H. Auer.

The Crime of Father Amaro ✦✦ **2002 (R)** *El Crimen del Padre Amaro* Eca de Queiroz's 1875 Portuguese novel is transplanted to modern-day Mexico, confronting a number of controversies surrounding the Catholic Church, including abortion, celibacy, and corruption. Young cleric Padre Amaro (Bernal) is the protege of Bishop Ernesto (Gomez Cruz) who sends him to the provinces to learn church politics from the seasoned Padre Benito (Grecia). Benito has had a longtime affair with Sanjuanera (ArAmelia (Talancon) becomes infatuated with the handsome young priest. Amaro is soon learning to justify his less than priestly behavior with Amelia, which leads him down increasingly precarious moral paths. Spanish with subtitles. **120m/C VHS, DVD.** MX Gael Garcia Bernal, Sancho Grace, Ana Claudia Taancon, Damian Alcazar, Angelica Aragon, Pedro Armendariz Jr., Luisa Huertas, Ernesto Gomez Cruz; **D:** Carlos Carrera; **W:** Vicente Lenero; **C:** Guillermo Granillo; **M:** Rosino Serrano.

Crime of Honor ✦✦ **1985** A European executive goes public with his company's corruption, and his family suffers predictable ruin as a result. Based on a true story. **95m/C VHS.** Maria Schneider, David Suchet; **D:** John Goldschmidt.

The Crime of Monsieur Lange ✦✦✦ *Le Crime de Monsieur Lange* **1936** Charming French socialist fantasy where workers at a publishing company turn the business into a thriving cooperative while their evil boss is gone. When he returns, worker plots to

kill him. Rather talky, but humorous. In French with subtitles. French script booklet also available. **90m/B VHS.** FR Rene Lefevre, Jules Berry, Florelle, Sylvia Bataille, Jean Daste, Nadia Sibirskaia, Henri Guisol; **D:** Jean Renoir. **W:** Jean Renoir, Jacques Prevert; **C:** Jean Bachelet; **M:** Jean Wiener, Joseph Kosma.

Crime of Passion ✦✦½ **1957** Stanwyck plays a femme fatale whose ambitions for detective hubby lead to murder. Good performances from Stanwyck, Hayden, and Burr make this an above-average, although outlandish, crime-drama. **85m/B VHS, DVD.** Barbara Stanwyck, Sterling Hayden, Raymond Burr, Fay Wray, Royal Dano, Virginia Grey, Dennis Cross, Robert E. (Bob) Griffin, Jay Adler, Malcolm Atterbury, S. John Launer, Brad Trumbull, Skipper McNally, Peg La Centra, Nancy Reynolds, Marjorie Owens, Robert Quarry, Joe Conley, Stuart Whitman; **D:** Gerd Oswald; **W:** Jo Eisinger; **C:** Joseph LaShelle; **M:** Paul Dunlap.

Crime of the Century ✦✦½ *Wanted* **2003 (R)** After bungling a Paris heist, Daniel (Depardieu), Julien (Freiss), and Raymond (Dray) are sent by their boss, Laurent (Bohringer), to Chicago for a diamond heist. Joined by Marcel (Hallyday), Zero (Renaud), and Sami (Taghmaoui), the group manages to rob the wrong house that of Chicago hood Frankie Zammeti (Keitel). Frankie has been staked out by the FBI, who want an audio cassette the French hoods have also taken, which incriminates his boss Giancarlo (Vigoda). Equal opportunity stereotypes abound with the bad guys—French, Italian, Latino, and blacks—but this aging buddy cast is so self-confident that they can carry this caper a long way. English and some French with subtitles. **99m/C VHS, DVD.** CA GB Gerard Depardieu, Johnny Hallyday, Harvey Keitel, Richard Bohringer, Said Taghmaoui, Stephane Freiss, Albert Dray, Abe Vigoda; **D:** Brad Mirman; **W:** Brad Mirman; **C:** Derek Rogers; **M:** Rupert Gregson-Williams.

Crime Story ✦✦ *Hard to Die* **1993 (R)** Police Inspector Eddie Chan (Chan) tries to crack a kidnapping case and discovers his partner, Detective Hung (Cheng), is not on the up-and-up. Usual acrobatic stunts from Chan and company. Cantonese with subtitles. **104m/C VHS, DVD.** HK Jackie Chan, Kent Cheng, Law Hang Kang, Christine Ng; **D:** Kirk Wong; **C:** Law Wong Ngok Tai, Ardy Lam.

Crime Wave ✦✦ **1954** Cons break out of San Q and then botch a gas-station robbery. They head for the home of excellmate Steve Lacey (Nelson), who's married Ellen (Kirk), gone straight, and doesn't want the trouble landing at his door. Steve's willing to cooperate with hard-boiled detective Sims (Hayden) but Penny (de Corsia) and Hastings (Bronson) take Ellen hostage and threaten Steve unless he helps them in a bank job. Nelson was better known as a song-and-dance man, but he's good in this noir role, and the toothpick-chewing Hayden can snarl with the best of them. **73m/B DVD.** Sterling Hayden, Gene Nelson, Phyllis Kirk, Ted de Corsia, Charles Bronson, Jay Novello, Nedrick Young, Timothy Carey; **D:** Andre de Toth; **W:** Bert Glennon; **M:** David Buttolph.

Crime Zone ✦✦½ **1988 (R)** In a totalitarian, repressive, future society, two young lovers try to beat the system and make it on their own. A well-made, if occasionally muddled, low-budget film shot in Peru, of all places. **96m/C VHS.** David Carradine, Peter Nelson, Sherilyn Fenn, Orlando Sacha.

kill him, Michael Shaner; **D:** Luis Llose; **W:** Daryl Haney; **M:** Rick Conrad.

Crimebroker ✦✦ **1993 (R)** Australian judge Holly McPhee (Bisset) has a sideline—she devises criminal blueprints and then anonymously hires the rabbies that come before the bench to carry out the crime. But things get complicated when a Japanese criminologist Jim Okazaki (Kato) figures out what's going on. **93m/C DVD.** AU JP Jacqueline Bisset, Masaya Kato, John Bach, Ralph Cotterill; **D:** Ian Barry; **W:** Tony Morphett; **C:** Dan Burstall; **M:** Roger Mason.

Crimebusters ✦½ **1979 (PG)** A man exacts revenge against a a government conspiracy that kidnapped his loved ones. **90m/C VHS, DVD.** Henry Silva, Antonio (Tony) Sabato; **D:** Michael Tarantini.

Crimes & Misdemeanors ✦✦✦ **1989 (PG-13)** One of Allen's most mature films, exploring a whole range of moral ambiguities through the parallel and eventually interlocking stories of a nebbish filmmaker—who agrees to make a profile of a smug Hollywood TV comic and then sabotages it—and an esteemed ophthalmologist who is being threatened with exposure by his neurotic mistress. Intriguing mix of drama and comedy few directors could pull off. Look for Daryl Hannah in an unbilled cameo. **104m/C VHS, DVD.** Martin Landau, Woody Allen, Alan Alda, Mia Farrow, Joanna Gleason, Angelica Huston, Jerry Orbach, Sam Waterston, Hannah, Nora Ephron, Jerry Zaks; **D:** Woody Allen; **W:** Woody Allen; **C:** Sven Nykvist; Natl. Bd. of Review '89: Support. Actor (Alda); N.Y. Film Critics '89: Support. Actor (Alda); Writers Guild '89: Orig. Screenplay.

Crimes at the Dark House ✦✦ **1939** In this campy, melodramatic adaptation of Wilkie Collins's novel "The Woman in White," a man kills the book's rich wife and puts a disguised mental patient in her place. Later remade using the book's title. **69m/B VHS, DVD.** GB Tod Slaughter, Hilary Eaves, Sylvia Marriott, Hay Petrie, Geoffrey Wardwell; **D:** George King.

Crimes of Dr. Mabuse ✦✦ **1932** *The Testament of Dr. Mabuse, The Last Will of Dr. Mabuse* Supernatural horror classic about the evil Dr. Mabuse controlling an underworld empire while confined to an insane asylum. Empire third, and only sound. Mabuse film by Lang. German with subtitles. **120m/B VHS, DVD.** GE Rudolf Klein-Rogge, Otto Wernicke, Gustav Diessl, Karl Meixner; **D:** Fritz Lang.

Crimes of Passion ✦✦✦ **1984** Vintage whacked-out Russell, not intended for the kiddies. A business-like fashion designer becomes a kinky prostitute at night. A disturbed street preacher makes her the heroine of his erotic fantasies. A dark terrifying vision of the underground sex world and moral hypocrisy. Sexually explicit and violent, with an extremely honest and believable, until he nearly gets a nosebleed, but it's all for good effect. Cut for "R" rating to get it in the theatres; this version restores some excised footage. Also available in rated version. **101m/C VHS, DVD.** Kathleen Turner, Anthony Perkins, Annie Potts, John Laughlin, Bruce Davison, Norman Burton, Ian Petrella, Gerald S. O'Loughlin; **D:** Ken Russell; **W:** Barry Sandler; **C:** Dick Bush; **M:** Rick Wakeman; L.A. Film Critics '84: Actress (Turner).

The Crimes of Stephen Hawke ✦✦ *Strangler's Morgue* **1936** The world knows Stephen Hawke as a bighearted money lender. What they don't know is his favorite hobby is breaking people's spines. An entertaining thriller set in the 1800s. **65m/B VHS.** GB Tod Slaughter, Marjorie Taylor, D.J. Williams, Eric Portman, Ben Soutten; **D:** George King.

Crimes of the Heart ✦✦½ **1986 (PG-13)** Based on Beth Henley's acclaimed play. A few days in the lives of three very strange Southern sisters, one of whom has just been arrested for calmly shooting her husband after he chased her black lover out of town. Spacek as the suicidal sister is a lark. A tart, black comedy that works better as a play than a film.

105m/C VHS, DVD. Sissy Spacek, Diane Keaton, Jessica Lange, Sam Shepard, Tess Harper, Hurd Hatfield; **D:** Bruce Beresford; **M:** Georges Delerue. **C:** Dante Spinotti; **M:** Georges Delerue. Golden Globes '87: Actress—Mus./Comedy (Spacek); N.Y. Film Critics '86: Actress (Spacek).

Crimetime ♂♂½ **1996 (R)** Silly thriller has actor Bobby (Baldwin) finding unexpected success portraying a serial killer in a crime re-enactment TV show called "Crimetime." Meanwhile, Sydney (Postlethwaite), who's the real killer Bobby's character is based on, becomes seduced by the media frenzy surrounding the crimes and seeing them re-enacted on television. He goes on killing, so the show can literally go on. **118m/C VHS, DVD.** Stephen Baldwin, Pete Postlethwaite, Sadie Frost, Geraldine Chaplin, Karen Black, James Faulkner. **Cameos:** Marianne Faithfull; **D:** George Sluizer; **W:** Brendan Somers; **C:** Jules Van Den Steenhoven.

Crimewave ♂♂ *The XYZ Murders; Broken Hearts and Noses* **1985 (PG-13)** Zany spoof about serial killers set in Detroit (director Raimi's hometown). A rhapsody to comic book style, short on plot and long on style. With such credentials you expect more. **83m/C VHS.** Louise Lasser, Paul Smith, Brion James, Bruce Campbell, Reed Birney, Sheree J. Wilson, Edward R. Pressman, Julius W. Harris, Antonio Fargas, Sean Farley, Frances McDormand, Theodore (Ted) Raimi; **D:** Sam Raimi; **C:** Robert Primes; **M:** Joseph LoDuca, Arlon Ober.

The Criminal ♂♂ **2000 (R)** Unemployed musician Jasper (Mackintosh) thinks he's gotten lucky when he meets sultry Sarah (Little) at the pub and she agrees to go home with him. But before anything intimate happens, Sarah's killed by intruders in Jasper's flat. A grumpy detective (Hill) and his smart woman partner (Aird) are certain of Jasper's guilt while Jasper tries to elude both the cops and Sarah's killers. **96m/C VHS, DVD. GB** Steven Mackintosh, Natasha Little, Bernard Hill, Holly Aird, Eddie Izzard, Yvan Attal, Andrew Tiernan; **D:** Julian Simpson; **W:** Julian Simpson; **C:** Nic Morris; **M:** Tolga Kashif, Mark Sayer-Wade.

Criminal Act ♂½ *Tunnels* **1988** A newspaper editor hits the street to prove she's still a tough reporter, but uncovers a dangerous scandal in the process. **94m/C VHS, DVD.** Catherine Bach, Charlene Dallas, Nicholas Guest, John Saxon, Vic Tayback; **D:** Mark Byers.

Criminal ♂♂ **2004 (R)** Experienced con man takes a novice under his wing to help bilk a rich collector. But like most con/heist flicks, everything is not what it seems. Complex and enjoyable remake of Argentine filmmaker Fabian Bielinski's "Nine Queens." Reilly and Luna give great performances, as do Gyllenhaal and Mullan. Fun in the vein of "Matchstick Men," full of twists and turns with a terrific payoff. **87m/C DVD. US** John C. Reilly, Diego Luna, Maggie Gyllenhaal, Jonathan Tucker, Peter Mullan; **D:** Gregory Jacobs; **W:** Gregory Jacobs, Steven Soderbergh; **C:** Chris Menges; **M:** Alex Wurman.

Criminal Code ♂♂½ **1931** Aging melodrama about a young man who's jailed for killing in self-defense. His life worsens at the hands of a prison warden when the head guy's daughter falls for him. Remade as "Penitentiary" and "Convicted." **98m/B VHS.** Walter Huston, Phillips Holmes, Boris Karloff, Constance Cummings, Mary Doran, DeWitt Jennings, John Sheehan; **D:** Howard Hawks.

Criminal Court ♂♂ **1946** A man accused of murdering his blackmailer hires the real killer as his attorney. Hard to follow, with an interesting premise that turns flat. **63m/B VHS.** Tom Conway, Martha O'Driscoll, Robert Armstrong, Addison Richards, June Clayworth, Pat Gleason, Steve Brodie; **D:** Robert Wise.

Criminal Hearts ♂♂ **1995 (R)** Keli (Locane) is driving to Phoenix when she picks up the hitchhiking Rafe (Dillon), who's just robbed a gas station. Turns out the stations are laundering mob drug money and when the store owners are killed, Rafe gets the blame for the murders as well. The killers are actually corrupt FBI agents Martin (Walsh) and Tierney (Mc-

Donald) who are soon of the trail of the twosome. **92m/C VHS.** Kevin Dillon, Amy Locane, Morgan Fairchild, M. Emmet Walsh, Michael Ironside, Mal McDonald, Don Stroud; **D:** Dave Payne; **W:** Dave Payne; **C:** Christopher Baffa.

Criminal Justice ♂♂♂ **1990 (R)** A black man is accused of a crime by a woman with whom he was involved. Is it justice or revenge? Strong cast in important story. **92m/C VHS.** Forest Whitaker, Jennifer Grey, Rosie Perez, Anthony LaPaglia, Tony Todd; **D:** Andy Wolk; **W:** Andy Wolk; **C:** Steven Fierberg. **CABLE**

Criminal Law ♂♂ **1989 (R)** An ambitious young Boston lawyer gets a man acquitted for murder, only to find out after the trial that the man is guilty and renewing his killing spree. Realizing he's the only one privy to the killer's trust, the lawyer decides to stop him himself. A whiteknuckled thriller burdened by a weak script. **113m/C VHS.** Kevin Bacon, Gary Oldman, Karen Young, Joe Don Baker, Tess Harper; **D:** Martin Campbell; **W:** Mark Kassen; **C:** Phil Meheux; **M:** Jerry Goldsmith.

The Criminal Life of Archibaldo de la Cruz ♂♂♂ *Ensayo de un Crimen; Rehearsal for a Crime* **1955** Seeing the death of his governess has a lasting effect on a boy. He grows up to be a demented cretin whose failure with women leads him to conspire to kill every one he meets, a task at which he also fails. Hilarious, bitter Bunuelian diatribe. In Spanish with English subtitles. **95m/B VHS. MX SP** Ernesto Alonso, Ariadne Welter, Rita Macedo, Rodolfo Landa, Andrea Palma, Miroslava Stern; **D:** Luis Bunuel; **W:** Luis Bunuel; **C:** Augustin Jimenez; **M:** Jorge Perez.

Criminal Lovers ♂♂♂ *Les Amants Criminels* **1999** Aggressive 17-year-old Alice (Regnier) persuades her ambivalent boyfriend Luc (Renier) to kill their classmate Said, after telling Luc that Said got his friends to rape her. They drive the body into the woods to bury it but then become lost and seek refuge in a ramshackle cottage that happens to belong to a hermit (Manojlovic) who witnessed the burial. He tosses them in his cellar but soon releases Luc to satisfy his own pleasures (and those of the sexually confused boy). Eventually the duo escape, only to find the police on their trail. French with subtitles. **96m/C VHS, DVD. FR** Natacha Regnier, Jeremie Renier, Miki (Predrag) Manojlovic, Salim Kechiouche; **D:** Francois Ozon; **W:** Francois Ozon; **C:** Pierre Stoeber; **M:** Philippe Rombi.

The Criminal Mind ♂♂ **1993 (R)** L.A. District Attorney Nick August (Rossi) reunites with his long-lost brother (Cross), whom he discovers is very familiar with the other side of the law. Tied up with the mob, Cross forces his bro to watch a hit and then Rossi winds up the next target for a group of assassins and some corrupt cops. **93m/C VHS.** Ben Cross, Frank Rossi, Tahnee Welch, Lance Henriksen, Joseph Ruskin, Lynn-Holly Johnson; **D:** Joseph Vittorie; **W:** Sam A. Scribner.

Criminally Insane ♂ **1975** Authorities release 250 pounds of cleaver-wielding maniacal fury from the loony bin. She seeks food and human blood. They should have known better. Followed by "Crazy Fat Ethel II." **61m/C VHS, DVD.** Priscilla Alden, Michael Flood; **D:** Nick (Steve Millard) Phillips.

The Crimson Code ♂½ **1999 (R)** FBI agents Chandler (Muldoon) and Dobson (Moriarty) discover a serial killer who goes after other serial killers. Then Chandler is offered a chance to circumvent that pesky legal thing by joining a covert ops that takes retribution as it sees fit. Just one cliche after another. **90m/C VHS, DVD.** Patrick Muldoon, Cathy Moriarty, C. Thomas Howell, Fred Ward, Tim Thomerson; **D:** Jeremy Haft; **W:** Alex Metcalf; **C:** Ian Elkin; **M:** Ken Williams. **VIDEO**

The Crimson Cult ♂ *The Crimson Altar; Curse of the Crimson Altar* **1968 (PG)** Eden and his girlfriend are invited to a mysterious mansion. They discover that Lee is out to enact revenge as his ancestor was burned for witchcraft by Eden's. An all-star horror disaster. Karloff was 80 and confined to a wheelchair. Despite ads claiming this as his last film, he made four more in Mexico. Highlights include the scantily clad Steele in sado-masochistic sequences and a psychedelic party with strippers and body painters. **87m/C VHS. GB** Boris Karloff, Christopher Lee, Mark Eden, Barbara Steele, Virginia Wetherell, Michael Gough, Rupert Davies; **D:** Vernon Sewell.

Crimson Gold ♂♂½ *Talaye Sorgh* **2003** Hussein (Emadeddin) is a simple, war-veteran-turned-pizza-deliveryman, but the opening sequence shows him in the midst of a botched jewelry-store robbery that ends abruptly and grimly—resulting in tragedy. What follows are flashbacks (compelling yet often slow-paced) that attempt to define his behavior and the social rejection that led him down his destructive path. Set in Tehran and based on a true story, this has—like other Panahi films—been banned in Iran. Farsi with subtitles. **95m/C DVD. IA** Hossain Emadeddin, Kamyar Sheisi, Azita Rayeji, Shahram Vaziri, Ehsan Amani, Pourang Nakhael, Kaveh Najmabadi, Saber Safaei; **D:** Jafar Panahi; **W:** Abbas Kiarostami; **C:** Hossain Djafarian; **M:** Peyman Yazdanian.

Crimson Pirate ♂♂♂½ **1952** An 18th-century buccaneer pits his wits and brawn against the might of a ruthless Spanish nobleman. Considered by many to be one of the best swashbucklers, laced with humor and enthusiastically paced. Showcase for Lancaster and Cravat's acrobatic talents. **104m/C VHS, DVD. GB** Charles Farrell, Burt Lancaster, Eva Bartok, Torin Thatcher, Christopher Lee, Nick Cravat; **D:** Robert Siodmak.

The Crimson Rivers ♂♂ *Les Rivieres Pourpres* **2001 (R)** Audacious and gruesome thriller set in the French Alps. A librarian from the local private university is found horribly mutilated on a mountain slope and Parisian investigator Pierre Niemans (Reno) is called in. Before long, there's another murder, one more victim, all of whom have ties to the university, and Niemans has a young, aggressive partner in provincial policeman Max Kerkerian (Cassel). French with subtitles or dubbed. **105m/C VHS, DVD. FR** Jean Reno, Vincent Cassel, Nadia Fares, Dominique Sanda, Laurent Avare, Jean-Pierre Cassel, Didier Flamand; **D:** Mathieu Kassovitz; **W:** Mathieu Kassovitz, Jean-Christophe Grange; **C:** Thierry Arbogast; **M:** Bruno Coulais.

Crimson Rivers 2: Angels of the Apocalypse ♂♂ *Les Rivieres Pourpres II: Les Anges de L'apocalypse* **2005** A series of religious-related murders puts Parisian detective Pierre Niemans (Reno) on the case. He's paired with police captain Reda (Magimel)—who has stumbled upon a man resembling Jesus Christ—to solve the mystery and contend with a dark, deadly organization bent on razing Europe. Fans of the original should be pleased, though the story needs an oar and compass to find its way to shore. In French, with English subtitles or dubbed. **99m/C VHS, DVD. FR GB IT** Jean Reno, Benoit Magimel, Christopher Lee, Johnny Halliday, Camille Natta, Augustin Legrand; **D:** Olivier Dahan; **W:** Jean-Christophe Grange, Luc Besson; **C:** Alex Lamarque; **M:** Colin Towns. **VIDEO**

Crimson Romance ♂♂ **1934** Two unemployed American pilots in Europe decide to join the German airforce for want of anything better to do. Conflicts revolve around a warmongering Commandant and his pilot. **70m/B VHS, DVD.** Ben Lyon, Sari Maritza, James Bush, Erich von Stroheim, Jason Robards Sr., Herman Bing, Vince Barnett; **D:** David Howard.

Crimson Tide ♂♂♂ **1995 (R)** Mutiny erupts aboard the submarine USS Alabama as Captain Ramsey (Hackman) and his Executive Officer Hunter (Washington) clash over the validity of orders to launch the sub's missiles. Ramsey, who wants to fire the missiles, and Hunter, who refuses to comply until the message is verified,

battle for control of the sub. Suspenseful and well-paced thriller lets Hackman and Washington show off their considerable screen presence, while Bruckheimer, Simpson, and Scott show that they haven't lost any of their trademark big-budget, testosterone-laden flash. Original screenplay went under the knife of a number of script doctors, most notably Quentin Tarantino. **116m/C VHS, DVD, Blu-ray Disc, UMD.** Gene Hackman, Denzel Washington, George Dzundza, Viggo Mortensen, James Gandolfini, Matt Craven, Lillo Brancato, Danny Nucci, Steve Zahn, Rick Schroder, Vanessa Bell Calloway, Rocky Carroll; **Cameos:** Jason Robards Jr.; **D:** Tony Scott; **W:** Michael Schiffer, Richard P. Henick; **C:** Darius Wolski; **M:** Hans Zimmer.

The Crimson Trail ♂♂½ **1935** Buck believes his uncle may be involved in cattle rustling. Lots of action, minimal plot. **56m/B VHS.** Buck Jones, Polly Ann Young, Carl Stockdale, Charles French, Ward Bond, Robert F. (Bob) Kortman, Bud Osborne, Charles Brinley, Robert Walker; **D:** Al Raboch; **W:** Jack Natteford.

The Crippled Masters ♂♂ **1982 (R)** After Li Ho's (Shum) arms are cut off by an evil warlord, he wanders the countryside facing ridicule until he teams up with disfigured Dax Oh Jen (Conn). Helped by an elderly yoga master, the duo unite to seek revenge. Features kung-fu masters with real-life disabilities. **90m/C VHS, DVD.** Frankie Shum, Jack Conn; **D:** Joe Law.

Crisis at Central High ♂♂♂ **1980** A dramatic re-creation of the events leading up to the 1957 integration of Central High in Little Rock, Arkansas. Based on teacher Elizabeth Huckaby's journal. Emmy-nominated performance by Woodward as Huckaby. **120m/C VHS.** Joanne Woodward, Charles Durning, William Ross, Henderson Forsythe; **D:** Lamont Johnson; **M:** Billy Goldenberg. **TV**

Criss Cross ♂♂♂ **1948** A classic grade-B film noir, in which an armored car driver is suckered into a burglary by his ex-wife and her hoodlum husband. Multiple back-stabbings and double-crossings ensue. **98m/B VHS, DVD.** Burt Lancaster, Yvonne De Carlo, Dan Duryea, Stephen McNally, Richard Long, Tony Curtis, Alan Napier; **D:** Robert Siodmak; **W:** Daniel Fuchs; **C:** Franz Planer; **M:** Miklos Rozsa.

Crisscross ♂♂½ *Alone Together* **1992 (R)** It's 1969 and Tracy Cross is a divorced mom whose ex-husband is a traumatized Vietnam vet who has left her alone to raise their 12 year-old son Chris during some hard times. She works two jobs, as a waitress and, unbeknownst to her son, as a stripper in a local club. When Chris sneaks into the club and sees her act he takes drastic measures to help out—by selling drugs. Film is sluggish and relies too much on voice-overs to explain thoughts but Hawn gives a convincing and restrained performance as the mother. **107m/C VHS, DVD.** Goldie Hawn, David Arnott, Arliss Howard, James Gammon, Keith Carradine, J.C. Quinn, Steve Buscemi, Paul Calderon; **D:** Chris Menges; **M:** Trevor Jones.

Critical Care ♂♂½ **1997 (R)** Spader is a doctor in a high-tech intensive care unit dealing with the ethics of modern health care, such as insurance scams, euthanasia, and a drunken administrator (Brooks) whose only concern is the hospital's profits. Two sisters (Sedgwick and Martindale) fight over the fate of their terminally ill, near-vegetable father. Spader finds his career on the line after bedding Sedgwick and backing her attempts to pull the plug. Given the meatiness of the subject, director Lumet could have made a much more scathing satire. Schwartz's script is lame even for a first-time effort, and the usually interesting Shawn falls horribly flat with an embarrassing bit of dialogue. Occasional laughs (this was supposed to be a dark comedy) and good performances from Brooks and Mirren can't keep this one from flatlining. Watch an episode of "ER" instead. **105m/C VHS, DVD.** James Spader, Albert Brooks, Kyra Sedgwick, Helen Mirren, Margo Martindale, Jeffrey Wright, Wallace Shawn, Anne Bancroft, Philip Bosco, Edward Herrmann, Colm Feore, James Lally, Al Waxman, Harvey Atkin; **D:** Sidney Lumet; **W:** Steven S

Critical Choices 🐶🐶 1997 (R) The Women's Health Clinic in Milwaukee, Wisconsin, provides safe and legal abortions. Run by Dr. Margaret Ludlow (Buckley) and her pro-choice supporter, Diana Johnson (Scarwid), the clinic becomes the focal point for right-wing evangelists Bobby Ray Flood (Kerwin) and his supporters, including Arlene Dickens (Reed). Tensions mount and violence erupts as everyone believes they're doing the right thing. 88m/C VHS, DVD. Terry Kinney, Brian Kerwin; D: Claudia Weill. W: Susan Cuscuna, Robin Green, Mitchell Burgess; M: Patrick Seymour. CABLE

Critical Condition 🐶 1986 (R) During a blackout, a criminal masquerades as a doctor in a city hospital. Limp comedy embarrassing for Pryo. 95m/C VHS, DVD. Richard Pryor, Rachel Ticotin, Ruben Blades, Joe Mantegna, Kate MacGregor-Stewart; D: Michael Apted. C: Ralf Bode; M: Alan Silvestri.

Critical Mass 🐶🐶 2000 (R) This one will seam very familiar. Terrorist Samson (Kier) and his crew steal nuclear material and retreat to a deserted nuclear power plant in southern California in order to build a bomb. Only the power plant isn't so deserted and security guard Mike (Williams), aided by babe Janine (Loughlin), work to thwart Samson's nefarious plan. 95m/C VHS, DVD. Treat Williams, Udo Kier, Lori Loughlin, Blake Clark, Andrew Prine; D: Fred Olen Ray. C: Theo Angel; M: Neal Acree. VIDEO

Critic's Choice 🐶🐶 1963 Tedious adaptation of Ira Levin's insider play that's likely to only be appreciated by Ball and/or Hope fans. Angela Ballantine (Ball) is an aspiring playwright whose first effort is about to open on Broadway. And it's going to be reviewed by her theater critic husband, Parker (Hope), who would rather be doing anything else. Like having a few drinks with his consoling ex-wife Ivy (Maxwell). Parker stumbles into the theater, drunk and the center of unwelcome attention, especially from the current Mrs. Ballantine, who's not pleased. Edith Head did the costumes. 100m/C DVD. Bob Hope, Lucille Ball, Marilyn Maxwell, Rip Torn, Jessie Royce Landis, John Dehner, Jim Backus, Rick Keenan, Marie Windsor, Joseph (Joe) Gallison, Richard Deacon, Jerome Cowan. Donald Losby, Stanley Adams; D: Don Weis; W: Jack Sher; C: Charles Bryant/Lang Jr.; M: George Duning.

Critters 🐶🐶 1986 (PG-13) A gang of furry, razor-toothed aliens escapes from its prison ship to Earth with their bounty hunters right behind them. They make it to a small town in Kansas where they begin to attack anything that moves. Not just a thrill-kill epic, but a sarcastic off-er-worldly thrill-kill epic. Like having a few drinks with his consoling ex-wife Ivy. 86m/C VHS, DVD. Dee Wallace Stone, M. Emmet Walsh, Billy Green Bush, Scott Grimes, Nadine Van Der Velde, Terrence Mann, Billy Zane, Don Opper; D: Stephen Herek. W: Stephen Herek, Domnic Muir; D: Tim Sunstedt; M: David Newman.

Critters 2: The Main Course 🐶🐶 1988 (PG-13) Sequel to the hit horror-comedy, wherein the voracious alien furtballs return in full force to Grovers Bend, Kansas, from eggs planted two years before. Occasionally inspired "Gremlins" rip. 93m/C VHS, DVD. Scott Grimes, Liane (Alexandra) Curtis, Don Opper, Barry Corbin, Terrence Mann; D: Mick Garris; W: Mick Garris, David N. Twohy; C: Russell Carpenter.

Critters 3 🐶🐶 1991 (PG-13) The not-so-loveeble critters are back, terrorizing the occupants of a tenement building. 86m/C VHS, DVD. Frances Bay, Aimee Brooks, Leonardo DiCaprio, Don Opper; D: Kristine Peterson; M:

Critters 4 🐶🐶 1991 (R) Giant crocodile attacks a beach town, killing and devouring dozens of people. The locals sit around trying to figure out a way to stop the

Crocodile Woof! 1981 (R) Giant crocodile attacks a beach town, killing and devouring dozens of people. The locals sit around trying to figure out a way to stop the

Schwartz. C: David Watkin; M: Michael Converti.

critter. Special effects include rear-projected croc. Lots of blood but lacking humor of "Alligator." Filmed in Thailand and Korea. 95m/C VHS, DVD. Kirk Nat Puvanai, Tany Tim, Angela Wells, Kirk Warren; D: Sompote Sands.

Crocodile 🐶🐶 2000 (R) Cheesy special effects doom this low-budget horror. College students spend spring break on a houseboat and are terrorized by a giant crocodile who regards them as a humor. Simon becomes a huge success but can he live with the consequences? Outrageous if heavy-handed. 84m/C VHS, DVD. Ted Sod, William Salyers, Dan Savage, Jeanne L. Klein; D: Ann Coppel; M: Ted Sod, Rockett. VIDEO

Crocodile Dundee 🐶🐶🐶½ 1986 (PG-13) New York reporter Sue Charlton (Kozlowski) is assigned to the Outback to interview living legend Mike Dundee (Hogan). When she finally locates the man, she is so taken with him that she brings him back to New York with her. There, the naive Aussie wanders about, amazed at the wonders of the city and unwittingly charming everyone he comes in contact with, from high-society tax-swelties to street hookers. One of the surprise hits of 1986. 98m/C VHS, DVD. AU Paul Hogan, Linda Kozlowski, John Meillon, David Gulpilil, Mark Blum; D: Peter Faiman; W: Paul Hogan, Ken Cornell, Russell Boyd; M: Peter Best. Goden Globes '87: Actor—Mus./Comedy (Hogan).

Crocodile Dundee 2 🐶🐶½ 1988 (PG) In this sequel Mike Dundee, the loveable rube, returns to his native Australia looking for new adventure, having "conquered" New York City. He finds trouble when Colombian drug lords kidnap the couple to the Australian Outback. Lacks the charm and freshness of the first film. 110m/C VHS, DVD. Stephen (Steve) Root, Jace Alexander, Luis Guzman, Colin Quinn, Paul Hogan, Linda Kozlowski, Kenneth Welsh, John Meillon, Ernie Dingo, Juan Fernandez, Charles S. Dutton; D: John Cornell; W: Paul Hogan; C: Russell Boyd; M: Peter Best.

Crocodile Dundee in Los Angeles 🐶½ 2001 (PG) Mick is back, for no good reason other than Hogan and Kozlowski probably needed the dough. The happy couple return to the States so Sue (Kozlowski) can investigate a movie studio that may be involved in a smuggling ring and, even worse, keeps cranking out dumb sequels. Where DO they come up with these ideas? Meanwhile, Dundee introduces their son (Cockburn) to life in the big city while working as an extra on the suspicious studio lot. It looks and feels like a real movie, but something's missing. What is it? Hmmmmm....Oh, yeah! A point! Unless the previous two install-ments left too many unanswered questions, you can probably skip this one. 95m/C VHS, DVD. Paul Hogan, Linda Kozlowski, Jere Burns, Jonathan Banks, Paul Rodriguez, Alec Wilson, Serge Cockburn, Aida Turturro, Kaitlin Hopkins, Camrose; Mike Tyson; D: Simon Wincer; W: Matthew Berry, Eric Abrams; C: David Burr; M: Basil Poledouris.

The Crocodile Hunter: Collision Course 🐶🐶½ 2002 (PG) Nature show hosts Steve Irwin and his wife Terri take their "The Crocodile Hunter" TV shtick to the big screen in this far-fetched story about a croc who swallows a top secret U.S. satellite beacon. Irwin attempts to protect the animal from a gun-toting farmer and some secret agents he mistakes for poachers. The story is just an excuse for Irwin to round up and irritate some of the world's most dangerous animals, presumably while Terri is checking the early lives of Generation X to date file of an African-American middle-class family growing up in 1970s Brooklyn. 89m/C VHS, DVD. AU US Steve Irwin, Terri Irwin, Magda Szubanski; David Wenham, Aden Young, Kenny Ransom, Lachy Hulme, Kate Beahan, Steven Vidler.

Crooked Trail 🐶 1936 A lawman and bad guy become friends. 58m/B VHS. Johnny Mack Brown, John Merton, Lucille Browne; D: S. Roy Luby; M: George Plympton.

Crooklyn 🐶🐶🐶 1994 (PG-13) Director Lee turns from the life of Malcolm X to the early lives of Generation X in this file of an African-American middle-class family growing up in 1970s Brooklyn. Based on a novel by Robert Boswell. 113m/C VHS, DVD. Peter Coyote, Jennifer Jason Leigh, Peter Berg, Cindy Pickett, Vincent D'Onofrio, Noah Wyle, Juliette Lewis, Wendy Gazelle, Marg Helgenberger; D: Michael Bortman; C: Tak Fujimoto; M: Mark Isham.

Crooked Hearts 🐶🐶 1991 (R) Dysfunctional family drama means well but lays it on too thick, as a father/son rivalry threatens to sunder the tight-knit Warrens. Based on a novel by Robert Boswell. 113m/C VHS, DVD. Peter Coyote, Jennifer Jason Leigh, Peter Berg, Cindy Pickett, Vincent D'Onofrio, Noah Wyle, Juliette Lewis, Wendy Gazelle, Marg Helgenberger; D: Michael Bortman; C: Tak Fujimoto; M: Mark Isham.

The Crooked Circle 🐶½ 1932 More comedy than mystery as slapstick policeman Gleason goes under cover as a swami. Not helped at all by a weak script and poor photography. 68m/B VHS, DVD. Ben Lyon, Zasu Pitts, James Gleason, C. Henry Gordon, Raymond Hatton, Roscoe Karns; D: H Bruce Humberstone.

Cronica 🐶🐶 2004 (R) Manolo Bonilla (Leguizamo) is an ambitious Miami TV tabloid reporter who heads to an Ecuadorrian village that has been targeted by a serial child rapist and killer. Bible sales-man Vinicio (Alcazar) accidentally runs over a victim's brother, is set upon by a mob, and saved by Bonilla. In return, Vinicio claims they met on his travels. But is just how far will Manolo go to get his story? Runs out of steam but Leguizamo gives an intense performance. 111m/C DVD. MX John Leguizamo, Leonor Watling, Damian Alcazar, Alfred Molina, Jose Maria Yazpik; D: Sebastian Cordero; W: Sebastian Cordero; C: Enrique Chediak; M: Antonio Pinto.

Cronos 🐶🐶 Chronos 1994 (R) Stylish Mexican variation on the vampire tale. Aged antiques dealer Jesus Gris (Luppi) comes across the mysterious title object—a 14th century golden egg possessing magical powers to grant eternal life. But can its possessor stand the consequences, which include a developing taste for blood? Another problem is Gris isn't the only one to know about the device. First feature for writer/director del Toro. Spanish with subtitles. 92m/C VHS, DVD. MX Federico Luppi, Ron Perlman, Claudio Brook, Tamara Shanath, Margarita Isabel; D: Guillermo del Toro; W: Guillermo del Toro; C: Guillermo Navarro; M: Javier Alvarez.

Crocodiles in Amsterdam 🐶🐶 *Krokodillen in Amsterdam* 1989 Lunatic girl-meets-girl movie about flighty Gino and would-be terrorist Nina who team up to rob the country estate of an eccentric British dowager. 106m/C VHS. Joan Nederlof, Yolanda Entius; D: Annette Apon; M: Yolanda Entius, Annette Apon.

Cromwell 🐶🐶½ 1970 (G) A lavish British-made spectacle about the conflict between Oliver Cromwell and Charles I, as Cromwell becomes the liberator of the oppressed. Harris gives a commanding performance and the battle scenes are stunners. 139m/C VHS, DVD. GB Richard Harris, Alec Guinness, Robert Morley, Frank Finlay, Patrick Magee, Timothy Dalton; D: Ken Hughes; W: Ken Hughes; C: Geoffrey Unsworth. Oscars '70: Costume Des.

Crocodile Tears 🐶🐶 1998 Gay art teacher Simon (Sco) makes a devil's bargain (literally) when he learns he's HIV-positive. Sinister Mr. Cheseboro (Salyers) offers the gift of health if Simon will be humor. Simon becomes a huge success but can he live with the consequences? Outrageous if heavy-handed. 84m/C VHS, DVD. Ted Sod, William Salyers, Dan Savage, Jeanne L. Klein; D: Ann Coppel; M: Ted Sod, Rockett. VIDEO

Crocodile 2: Death Swamp Woof! 2001 (R) Airliner crashes into a Mexican swamp and the survivors get picked off by big hungry crocodile. This one is too boring to even be bad fun. 90m/C VHS, DVD. Heidi Lenhart, Steve Moreno, Joe Shkaroff, Martin Kove, Darryl Theirse; D: Gary Jones; W: Jace Anderson, Adam Gierasch. C: Rasool Ellore; M: Bill Wandel. VIDEO

Steve Bastoni; D: John Stainton; W: Holly Goldberg Sloan. C: David Burr; M: Mark McDuff.

and Cinque, and profiles the only girl in a family of five children coming of age. Tender and real performances from all, especially newcomer Harris, propel the sometimes messy, music-laden trip to nostalgia land. 112m/C VHS, DVD. Alfre Woodard, Delroy Lindo, Zelda Harris, David Patrick Kelly, Carlton Williams, Sharif Rashed, Tse-Mach Washington, Christopher Knowings, Jose Zuniga, Isaiah Washington IV, Ivelka Reyes, N. Jeremi Duru, Frances Foster, Norman Matlock, Patrice Nelson, Joie Lee, Vondie Curtis-Hall, Tiasha Reyes, Spike Lee, RuPaul Charles; D: Spike Lee; W: Joie Lee, Cinque Lee; C: Arthur Jafta; M: Terence Blanchard.

Crooks & Coronets 🐶½ 1969 (PG) Two-bit crooks plot to rob the country estate of an eccentric British dowager. 106m/C VHS. Telly Savalas, Warren Oates, Edith Evans; D: James O'Connolly.

The Cross & the Switchblade 🐶🐶 1972 (PG) An idealistic priest tries to bring the message of religion to the members of a vicious street gang. They don't wanna listen. Spanish language version available. 106m/C VHS, DVD. Pat Boone, Erik Estrada, Jackie Giroux, Jo-Ann Robinson; D: Don Murray.

Cross Country 🐶🐶½ 1983 (R) Action revolves around the brutal murder of a call girl with initial suspicion falling on a woman. The story twists and turns from the suspect to investigating detective Ironside without becoming particularly interesting. 95m/C VHS, CA Richard Beymer, Nina Axelrod, Michael Ironside; D: Paul Lynch; W: Logan N. Danforth.

Cross Creek 🐶🐶½ 1983 (PG) Based on the life of Marjorie Kinnan Rawlings, author of "The Yearling" who, after 10 years as a frustrated reporter/writer, moves to the remote and untamed Everglades. There she meets colorful local characters and receives the inspiration to write numerous bestsellers. Well acted though overtly sentimental at times. 120m/C VHS, DVD. Mary Steenburgen, Rip Torn, Peter Coyote, Dana Hill, Alfre Woodard, Malcolm McDowell; D: Martin Ritt; W: Dalene Young; C: John A. Alonzo; M: Leonard Rosenman.

Cross Examination 🐶½ 1932 A boy is charged with his father's murder, and a defense attorney struggles to acquit him. 61m/B VHS. H.B. Warner, Sally Blane, Sarah Padden; D: Richard Thorpe; W: Arthur Hoerl; C: M.A. Anderson.

Cross Mission 🐶 1989 (R) Predictable actioner about a photographer and a soldier who are captured by the enemy. Packed with a bit of ninja, ammo, and occult. 90m/C VHS. Richard Randall; D: Al (Alfonso Brescia) Bradley.

Cross My Heart 🐶🐶 1988 (R) Light comedy about two single people with complicated, post-divorce lives who go on a date and suffer accordingly. Will true love prevail? 91m/C VHS, DVD. Martin Short, Annette O'Toole, Paul Reiser, Joanna Kerns; D: Armyan Bernstein; W: Armyan Bernstein; M: Bruce Broughton.

Cross My Heart 🐶🐶🐶 *La Fracture du Myocarde* 1991 A group of school children conspire to hide the death of their fellow student Martin's mother. This will prevent his placement in the state orphanage. Interesting premise is blandly treated by Fansten. Child actors don't seem realistic, photography is without flair. In French with English subtitles. 105m/C VHS. FR Sylvain Copans, Nicolas Parodi, Cecilia Rouaud, Delphine Goutman, Lucie Bossier; D: Jacques Fansten. W: Jacques Fansten; C: Jean-Claude Saillier; M:

Cross My Heart and Hope to Die 🐶 *Ti Kniver I Hjertet* 1994 Young Otto (Garfalk) is an average misfit kid until he comes to the attention of the mischief-making Frank (Kornstad), who is the catalyst for Otto to get into all kinds of trouble. Based on the novel by Lars Saaby Christensen. Norwegian with subtitles. 96m/C VHS, DVD. NO Martin Dahl Garfalk, Jan Devo Kornstad; D: Marius Holst; C: Philip Ogaard; M: Kjetil Bjerkestrand, Megne Furuholmen.

Cross of Iron ♂♂½ *Steiner—Das Eiserne Kreuz* 1976 (R) During WWII, two antagonistic German officers clash over personal ideals as well as strategy in combatting the relentless Russian attack. Followed by "Breakthrough." 120m/C VHS, DVD. GB GE James Coburn, Maximilian Schell, James Mason, David Warner, Senta Berger, Klaus Lowitsch, Vadim Glowna, Roger Fritz, Dieter Schidor, Burkhard Driest, Fred Stillkrauth, Michael Nowka, Veronique Vendell, Arthur Brauss; D: Sam Peckinpah; W: Julius J. Epstein, Walter Kelley, James Hamilton; C: John Coquillon; M: Ernest Gold.

Crossbar ♂♂ 1979 Aaron Kornylo is determined to reach Olympic qualifications in the high jump despite having only one leg. Inspired by a true story, this program dramatically shows how far determination and work can take a person. 77m/C VHS. John Ireland, Brent Carver, Kate Reid; D: John Trent.

Crosscut ♂♂ 1995 (R) Mob hitman Martin Niconi (Mandylor) makes a mistake that could cost him his life when a barroom brawl leads him to shooting the son of a Mafia don. He escapes to a small California logging town, changes his identity, and falls for single mom Anna (Gallagher) but the mob manages to track him down. Big shootout. 90m/C VHS. Costas Mandylor, Megan Gallagher, Casey Sander, Allen (Cutter) Cutler, Zack Norman, George Murdock; D: Paul Raimondi; W: Paul Masiel, Scott Phillips; C: David Bridges; M: Christopher Tyng.

Crossfire ♂♂♂½ 1947 A Jewish hotel guest is murdered and three soldiers just back from Europe are suspected of the crime. The first Hollywood film that explored racial bigotry. Due to the radical nature of its plot, the director and the producer were eventually black-listed for promoting "un-American" themes. Loosely based on Richard Brooks' "The Brick Foxhole." 86m/B VHS, DVD. Robert Young, Robert Mitchum, Robert Ryan, Gloria Grahame, Paul Kelly; D: Edward Dmytryk.

Crossfire ♂♂ 1989 (R) A rescue team heads to Vietnam to pick up their MIA comrades. With no help from the government and the enemy at every turn, can they possibly succeed? 99m/C VHS. Richard Norton, Michael Meyer, Daniel Dietrich, Don Pemrick, Eric Hahn, Wren Brown, Steve Young; D: Anthony Maharaj; W: Noah Blough.

Crossfire ♂♂ 1998 (R) Dekova wants revenge for the accidental death of his family and decides to use his wealth to hire terrorists to destroy the Statue of Liberty. Assassin Pike is visiting the site for professional reasons when he figures out something's going on and he might be in for a change of plans. 90m/C VHS. Andrew Divoff, Mitchell Cox, Tim Thomerson, Yancey Arias; D: Gary S. Lipsky, Joe Zimmerman; W: Gary S. Lipsky, Joe Zimmerman; C: Ronald Vidor; M: Jose J. Herring. VIDEO

Crossfire Trail ♂♂♂ 2001 Cowboy Rafe Covington (Selleck) promises his dying friend that he will look out for the man's wife, Ann (Madsen), and their Wyoming spread. Rafe heads to town with his sidekicks (Brimley, O'Hara, Kane) and discovers the widow is already being courted by ruthless Bruce Barkow (Harmon), who wants the ranch since there's oil on the land. Naturally, Barkow has a hired gun (Johnson) and the sheriff (Corbin) in his pocket. Accomplished cast, straight forward direction, lush scenery (it's Calgary, Alberta), and a little humor. Based on Louis L'Amour's 1954 novel. 100m/C VHS, DVD. Tom Selleck, Virginia Madsen, Mark Harmon, Wilford Brimley, David O'Hara, Christian Kane, Barry Corbin, Brad Johnson, William Sanderson, Joanna Miles, Ken Pogue, Rex Linn; D: Simon Wincer; W: Charles Robert Carner; C: David Egby; M: Eric Colvin. CABLE

The Crossing ♂♂ 1992 (R) Powerful coming-of-age story in which Meg, a sheltered young woman, falls in love with an ambitious artist named Sam. When he decides to leave their small town to pursue his career, she turns to his best friend for comfort and companionship. However, when Sam unexpectedly returns, Meg is forced to make a choice that could drastically change all of their lives. 92m/C VHS. AU Russell Crowe, Danielle Spencer, Robert Mammone; D: George Ogilvie; W: Ranald Allan; C: Jeff Darling; M: Martin Armiger.

The Crossing ♂♂½ 2000 No, General George Washington did not cross the Delaware river standing in his boat as Emanuel Leutze's famous painting shows. But this historical story is still pretty darn exciting. On Christmas Day in 1776, it seems the American Revolution is still tined for failure. Washington (Daniels) has only 2000 troops left and the Continental Army has continually been defeated by the British. But Washington wants to make a final push—a surprise attack on the Hessian garrison at Trenton. Adapted by Howard Fast from his novel. 100m/C VHS, DVD. Jeff Daniels, Roger Rees, Sebastian Roche, Steven McCarthy, John Henry Canavan, Ned Vukovic; D: Robert Harmon; W: Howard Fast. CABLE

Crossing Delancey ♂♂♂ 1988 (PG) Jewish woman (Bozyk), in old world style, plays matchmaker to her independent 30-something granddaughter. Charming modern-day New York City fairy tale deftly manipulates cliches and stereotypes. Lovely performance from Irving as the woman whose heart surprises her. Riegert is swell playing the gentle but newer wimpy suitor. Perfectly cast Bozyk was a star on the Yiddish vaudeville stage; this is her film debut. Appealing music by the Roches, with Suzzy Roche giving a credible performance as Irving's friend. Adapted for the big screen by Sandler from her play of the same name. 97m/C VHS, DVD. Amy Irving, Reizl Bozyk, Peter Riegert, Jeroen Krabbe, Sylvia Miles, Suzzy Roche, George Martin, John Bedford Lloyd, Rosemary Harris, Amy Wright, Claudia Silver, David Hyde Pierce; D: Joan Micklin Silver; W: Susan Sandler.

The Crossing Guard ♂♂♂ 1994 (R) Nicholson headlines as Freddy Gale, a revenge-minded father who hunts down a drunk driver (Morse), who killed his daughter five years previous. Story focuses on dual emotions of the two men: Gale seeks an end to his grief and rage; Booth attempts to deal with guilt and regret. Writer Penn pairs one-time lovers Nicholson and Huston (playing exspouses here) in his sophomore directorial effort with explosive results. Focus is, accordingly, on emotional performances while narrative and directorial finesse take a back seat. Dedicated to the late chronicler of the curbside, Charles Bukowski. 111m/C VHS, DVD. Jack Nicholson, Anjelica Huston, David Morse, Robin Wright Penn, Robbie Robertson, Piper Laurie, Richard Bradford, John Savage, Priscilla Barnes, Kari Wuhrer, Jennifer Leigh Warren, Richard Sarafian, Jeff Morris, Joe (Johnny) Viterelli, Eileen Ryan, Ryo Ishibashi, Michael Ryan, Nicky Blair; D: Sean Penn; W: Sean Penn; C: Vilmos Zsigmond; M: Jack Nitzsche.

Crossing Over ♂♂ 2008 That would be crossing over the border, which in L.A. is a precarious position, whether it's legal or otherwise. A clash of cultures, counter-terrorism, document fraud, lawyers, green cards, counter-terrorism, and other hot button topics are explored. Ford, Penn, and Liotta in the same flick? Who's the hot-head and who's the voice of reason? Not yet reviewed. ?m/C. Harrison Ford, Clifford Curtis, Ashley Judd, Sean Penn, Ray Liotta, Alice Braga, Alice Eve, Jim Sturgess, Summer Bishil; D: Wayne Kramer; W: Wayne Kramer; C: James Whitaker; M: Mark Isham.

Crossing the Bridge ♂♂ 1992 (R) An after-high-school tale of three buddies and their restless lives as they take their uncertain steps towards adulthood. It's 1975 in Detroit and Mort, Danny, and Tim cling to high-school memories as they pass time on petty jobs, drinking, and cruising across the Ambassador Bridge to check out the Canadian strip joints. Their big moment—for better or worse—comes when they are offered the chance to make a lot of quick cash if they'll smuggle hash from Toronto to Detroit. Directorial debut of Binder. 105m/C VHS, DVD. Josh Charles, Jason Gedrick, Stephen Baldwin, Cheryl Pollak, Jeffrey Tambor; D: Mike Binder; W: Mike Binder.

Crossing the Line ♂ 1990 (R) Two motocross racers battle it out for the championship. 90m/C VHS, DVD. Jon Stafford, Rick Hearst, Paul Smith, Cameron Mitchell, Vernon Wells, Colleen Morris, John Saxon; D: Gary Graver.

Crossover ♂½ 1982 (R) A devoted male nurse works the graveyard shift in the psychiatric ward and neglects his personal life. 96m/C VHS. James Coburn, Kate Nelligan; D: John Guillermin.

Crossover ♂ 2006 (PG-13) So why are streetballers playing their game in an abandoned Detroit train station? Too cold outside? Not enough grunge atmosphere? A dopey and cliched sports soap opera, with very few actual basketball sequences, which has studious Cruise (Johnathan) getting a b-ball scholarship to an LA college while his best bud, dropout Tech (Mackie), just wants to beat local rival Jewelz (Champion). There's also a slick wannabe sports agent (Brady) and a couple of hotties (one good and one a gold-digger). This amateur night don't got game. 95m/C DVD. US Anthony Mackie, Wesley Jonathan, Wayne Brady, Kristen Wilson, Lil' J.J., Phillip Champion, Eva Pigford, Alecia Fears; D: Preston A. Whitmore II; W: Preston A. Whitmore II; C: Christian Sebaldt; M: Matthias Weber.

Crossover Dreams ♂♂½ 1985 Actor and musician Blades moves this old story along. Sure that he has at last made the international Big Time, a salsa artist becomes a self-important back-stabber after cutting an album. Great music. Blades's first film. ♪Good For Baby; Liz's Theme; Sin Fe; Todos Vuelven; Libra Merecumbe; Merecumbe; Judy, Part 2; Yiri Yiri Bon. 86m/C VHS, DVD. Ruben Blades, Shawn Elliott, Elizabeth Pena, Virgilio Marti, Tom Signorelli, Frank Robles, Joel Diamond, Amanda Barber, John Hammil; D: Leon Ichaso; W: Leon Ichaso, Manuel Arce; M: Mauricio Smith.

Crossroads ♂♂½ 1986 (R) A blues-loving young white man, classically trained at Juilliard, befriends an aging black blues-master. After helping the old man escape from the nursing home, the two hop trains to the South where it's literally a duel with the devil. Fine performances by Macchio, Gertz, Seneca, and Morton. Wonderful score by Ry Cooder, with some help from Steve Vai in the final showdown. 100m/C VHS, DVD. Ralph Macchio, Joe Seneca, Jami Gertz, Joe Morton, Robert Judd, Harry Carey Jr., Steve Vai; D: Walter Hill; W: John Fusco; C: John Bailey; M: Ry Cooder, Steve Vai.

Crossroads ♂♂½ 2002 (PG-13) Underwhelming teen buddy road pic has pop tart Spears' debut as Lucy, a virginal, small-town high school senior who hits the road to L.A. with childhood buds Kit (Saldana) and Mimi (Manning), with depressing results. Lucy's searching for her real mom (Cattrall); Kit, a no-good boyfriend; and Mimi trying to get to an open audition as a singer. Convenient cute love interest for Lucy is driver Ben (Mount), who may harbor a dangerous secret. Most laughable scene features Lucy scribbling "poetry" (actually lyrics to one of her soundtrack songs) which Ben "composes" the music for it. Spears is likeable and harmless while Manning is the real stand-out. One notch up from "Glitter," quality competed with quantity (of wardrobe) as lowest priority. 94m/C VHS, DVD. US Britney Spears, Taryn Manning, Zoe Saldana, Anson Mount, Kim Cattrall, Dan Aykroyd, Justin Long, Beverly Johnson, Kool Moe Dee, Richard Voll; D: Tamra Davis; W: Shonda Rhimes; C: Eric Alan Edwards; M: Trevor Jones. Golden Raspberries '02: Worst Actress (Spears), Worst Song ("I'm Not a Girl, Not Yet a Woman").

Crossworlds ♂♂ 1996 (PG-13) All dimensions of the universe collide in the mystical valley of Crossworlds. When alien night riders attack Joe Talbolt (Charles), he escapes with girlfriend Laura (Roth) and they meet up with mercenary A.T. (Hauer). Turns out the crystal pendant Joe's father left him is one of the keys that unlock the boundaries between the worlds. Along with a scepter, they give the owner unlimited power. So the trio enter Crossworlds to fight a battle between good and evil. 91m/C VHS, DVD. Jack Black, Rutger Hauer, Josh Charles, Andrea Roth, Stuart Wilson; D: Krishna Rao; W: Raman Rao, Krishna Rao; C: Chris Walling; M: Christophe Beck. CABLE

Crouching Tiger, Hidden Dragon ♂♂♂½ 2000 Two veteran Wudan fighters (Yun-Fat and Yeoh) in 19th-century China recognize their passion for each other while tracking down a vengeful master criminal (Pei-Pei) and her protege (the exciting Ziyi). A martial arts love story that satisfies on both accounts. The emotional impact of the romance is as real and true as the choreographed fight scenes are spectacular and graceful. The film's overt feminism flies (literally) in the face of its patriarchal setting, yet doesn't seem a bit out of place. The extraordinary battle scenes were choreographed by Yuen Wo-Ping, who performed the same duties for "The Matrix." Mandarin with subtitles. 120m/C VHS, DVD, UMD. Chow Yun-Fat, Michelle Yeoh, Zhang Ziyi, Chang Chen, Cheng Pei-Pei, Sihung Lung; D: Ang Lee; W: James Schamus, Wang Hui Ling, Tsai Kuo Jung; C: Peter Pau; M: Tan Dun. Oscars '00: Art Dir.-Set Dec., Cinematog., Foreign Film, Orig. Score; Australian Film Inst. '01: Foreign Film; British Acad. '00: Director (Lee), Foreign Film, Score; Directors Guild '00: Director (Lee); Golden Globes '01: Director (Lee), Foreign Film; Ind. Spirit '01: Director (Lee), Film, Support. Actress (Ziyi); L.A. Film Critics '00: Cinematog., Film, Score; Natl. Bd. of Review '00: Foreign Film; N.Y. Film Critics '00: Cinematog.; Broadcast Film Critics '00: Foreign Film.

Croupier ♂♂♂ 1997 Director Hodges scored a hit with the 1971 British crime thriller "Get Carter." And after some rocky followups, he scores another with this cool casino neo-noir. A cynical South African, now living in London, Jack Manfred (Owen) is trying to escape the reach of his own dad. The would-be writer (his detective character Jake does the film's narrative) takes a job as a casino dealer where he can observe life at his preferred distance—that is until a fellow South African, sultry gambling beauty Jani (Kingston), talks him into a shady scheme that provides fodder for Jack's writing. Owen is especially watchable in the title role. 91m/C VHS, DVD. GB Clive Owen, Alex Kingston, Kate Hardie, Gina McKee, Nicholas Ball, Nick Reding; D: Mike Hodges; W: Paul Mayersberg; C: Mike Garfath; M: Simon Fisher Turner.

The Crow ♂♂½ 1993 (R) Revenge-fantasy finds Eric Draven (Lee) resurrected on Devil's Night, a year after his death, in order to avenge his own murder and that of his girlfriend. 90% of the scenes are at night, in the rain, or both, and it's not easy to tell what's going on (a blessing considering the violence level). Very dark, but with good performances, particularly from Lee, in his last role before an unfortunate on set accident caused his death. That footage has been destroyed, but use of a stunt double and camera trickery allowed for the movie's completion. Film was dedicated to Lee and his fiance Eliza. Based on the comic strip by James O'Barr. The video release includes Brandon Lee's final interview. 100m/C VHS, DVD, UMD. Brandon Lee, Ernie Hudson, Michael Wincott, David Patrick Kelly, Rochelle Davis, Angel David, Michael Massee, Bai Ling, Laurence Mason, Bill Raymond, Marco Rodriguez, Anna Thomson, Sofia Shinas, Jon Polito, Tony Todd; D: Alex Proyas; W: David J. Schow, John Shirley; C: Dariusz Wolski; M: Graeme Revell. MTV Movie Awards '95: Song ("Big Empty").

The Crow 2: City of Angels ♂♂½ 1996 (R) James O'Barr's cult graphic-novel "hero" returns in a new incarnation. It's eight years later (in film time) and the setting's changed from Detroit to L.A. but the horror remains. Ashe (Perez) and his young son witness a murder and are killed themselves by scumbags working for drug lord Judah (Brooks). So the Crow brings back Ashe to get revenge. Also involved is Sarah narrator but is now a grown-up tattoo artist who falls in love with Ashe. Lots of kink as well. The eerie sepia-toned look is created with sodium lighting. 93m/C VHS,

Crow Hollow 🐾🐾 1952 A Victorian mansion inhabited by three whacko sisters is the site of a murder committed in an attempt to cash in on an inheritance. When a young woman investigates, eyebrows are raised. 69m/B VHS. GB Donald Houston, Natasha Parry, Nora Nicholson, Esma Cannon, Melissa Stribling. D: Michael McCarthy. W: Bryan Edgar Wallace. C: Jean-Yves Escoffier; M: Graeme S. Goyer. C: Jean-Yves Escoffier; M:

The Crow Road 🐾🐾 1996 Prentice Hogan comes back to his hometown for his grandmother's funeral. Old conflicts surface and Prentice becomes determined to solve the disappearance of his Uncle Rory, who's been missing seven years. As he reads his uncle's unpublished novel, Prentice discovers some very disturbing family secrets. Based on the novel by Iain Banks. 210m/C DVD. GB Joseph McFadden, Peter Capaldi, Dougray Scott, Bill Paterson, Stella Gonet, Valerie Edmond, David Robb. D: Gavin Millar; W: Bryan Elsley. C: John Else; M: Colin Towns. TV

The Crow: Salvation 🐾🐾 2000 (R) Third in the series of films based on James O'Barr's comic book finds Alex Corvis (Mabius) wrongly convicted of murdering girlfriend Lauren Randall (O'Keefe). He's executed on his 21st birthday but returns as the Crow to seek revenge on those who wronged him. Alex convinces Erin (Dunst), Lauren's teenaged sister, of his innocence and they team up. Rather than revitalizing the franchise, this one basically got dumped by the studio, although the performances and the production are worth your time. 102m/C VHS, DVD. Eric Mabius, Kirsten Dunst, Fred Ward, Jodi Lyn O'Keefe, William Atherton, Dale Midkiff, Grant Shaud; D: Bharat Nalluri; W: Chip Johannessen; C: Carolyn Chen; M: Marco Beltrami.

The Crow: Wicked Prayer 🐾🐾 2005 (R) A satanic gang murders a juvenile delinquent (Furlong) and his mystical girlfriend (Chriqui) so that their leader (Boreanaz) can become a powerful demon. Instead, the kid becomes The Crow and returns for vengeance against the gang. Not a whole lot to recommend in this one of the franchise, although Hopper scores in his campy cameo. 104m/B VHS. Edward Furlong, Emmanuelle Chriqui, David Boreanaz, Tara Reid, Dennis Hopper, Macy Gray, Danny Trejo, Marcus Chong, Yuji Okumoto; D: Lance Mungia; W: Lance Mungia, Sean Hood; C: Kurt Brabbee; M: Jason Christopherson. VIDEO

The Crowd 🐾🐾🐾 1928 A look at the day-to-day trials of a working-class family set against the backdrop of wealthy society. True-to-life, it's peppered with some happy moments, too. One of the best silent films. 104m/B VHS. Eleanor Boardman, James Murray, Bert Roach, Daniel G. Tomlinson, Dell Henderson, Lucy Beaumont; D: King Vidor. Natl. Film Reg. '89.

Crown Heights 🐾🐾½ 2002 (R) An orthodox Rabbi and an African-American community leader join forces to save their racially-fractured neighborhood from more violence. Inspired by real-life events after the 1991 Brooklyn riots that were triggered by a Jewish man accidentally running down a back child. 93m/C VHS, DVD. Jeremy Piven, Mpho Koaho, Michael Yarmush, Kash, Judah Katz, Howard Jerome, Daniel Kash; D: Jeremy Paul Kagan; W: Michael D'Antonio, Toni Johnson; C: Rudolf Blahacek; M: Aaron Zigman. TV

The Crown Prince 🐾🐾½ 2006 Kronprinz Rudolf 2006 In the late 1880s, Crown Prince Rudolf, heir to the Austro-Hungarian Empire, enters into an unhappy marriage of convenience to try to please his controlling father, Emperor Franz-Joseph. Progressive for his time, Rudolf finds his suggestions for political alliances and reforms shunned and as he seemingly has nothing better to co than fall obsessively in love with the beautiful Baroness Mary Vetsera, whom he takes to co prove. things don't end well. Based on a true story that has been filmed before, notably as 1969's "Mayerling." 181m/C DVD. AT GE Omar Sharif, Christian Clavier, Klaus Maria Brandauer, Sandra Ceccarelli, Max von Thun, Vittoria Puccini, Alexandra Vandernoot, Birgit Minichmayr; D: Robert Dornhelm; W: Didier Decoin, Klaus Lintschinger; C: Michael Riebi; M: Ludwig Eckmann, Joerg Magnus Pfeil. TV

Crows 🐾🐾🐾 Wrony 1994 Emotionally neglected by her single, known scornfully year-old nameless girl, known scornfully as The Crow (Ostrzyna), desperately wants a family of her own. So she kidnaps a three-year-old to serve as her make-believe daughter and convinces the young child that they are going on a fairytale adventure to the end of the world. Polish with subtitles. 66m/C VHS. PL Karolina Ostrzyna, Kasia Szczepanik, Malgorzata Hajewska, Dorota Kedzierzawska; W: Dorota Kedzierzawska. C: Arthur Reinhart. M: Wlodek Pawlik.

Crows and Sparrows 🐾🐾🐾 Wuya Yu Maque 1949 Poor tenants of a Shanghai boardinghouse are about to lose their home when their greedy landlord decides to sell and move to Taiwan. But the advancing Red Army causes a change in plans and they're saved! Sounds politically turgid but isn't, thanks to naturalistic acting and dialog. Completed just before the revolution, the film was censored by the Nationalist Kuomintang government but cuts were restored when the Communists came to power. Mandarin with subtitles. 108m/B VHS. CH Zhao Dan, Wu Yin, Wei Heling, Daolin Sun, Li Tianji, Ouyang Yunzhu; D: Zheng Junli; W: Zhao Dan, Zheng Junli; C: Miao Zhenhua, Hu Zhenhua; M: Wang Yunjie.

The Crucible 🐾🐾🐾 Les Sorcières de Salem 1957 The Witches of Salem, Les Sorcières de Salem 1957 Signoret is outstanding, in this version of Arthur Miller's play about the Salem witch trials in 17th-century New England. Miller's depiction of witch hunts was written as a searing commentary on McCarthyism and the anti-communist panic that swept America because Miller was blacklisted in America and blackballed by Hollywood at the time. In French with English subtitles. 135m/B VHS. FR Raymond Rouleau, Simone Signoret, Yves Montand, Mylene Demongeot, Jean Debucourt, Jean Gaven, Jeanne Fusier-Gir; D: Raymond Rouleau; W: Jean-Paul Sartre; C: Claude Renoir; M: Georges Auric.

The Crucible 🐾🐾🐾 1996 (PG-13) Mass hysteria reigns in 17th century Salem, Mass., when a group of teenaged girls, caught performing heathen rituals in the woods concoct an elaborate story to exonerate themselves by whipping the town into a witch-hunting frenzy. Chief liar is Abigail Williams (Ryder), who was cast aside by married farmer John Proctor (Day-Lewis), for whom she still lusts. The deranged lass puts her dubious talents into getting Proctor's wife (Allen) out of the picture. Director Hytner demanded authentic period reproduction, down to the finest detail. Impressive cast does justice to the story, especially Scofield's delightfully odious Judge Danforth. Based on Miller's 1953 play which, not so coincidentally, opened during the communist witch hunts of the early 1950s. Screenwriter Miller willingly slashed dialogue from his original work for cinematic purposes. Filmed at the remote wildlife sanctuary of Hog Island, Massachusetts. 123m/C VHS, DVD. Daniel Day-Lewis, Winona Ryder, Paul Scofield, Joan Allen, Bruce Davison, Jeffrey Jones, Rob Campbell, Peter Vaughan, Karron Graves, Charlaine Woodard, Frances Conroy, Elizabeth Lawrence, George Gaynes; D: Nicholas Hytner; W: Arthur Miller; C: Andrew Dunn; M: George Fenton. British Acad. '96: Support. Actress (Scofield); Broadcast Film Critics '96: Support. Actress (Allen).

Crucible of Horror 🐾🐾 Velvet House; The Corpse 1969 Chilling story of a terrorized wife, who, along with her daughter, plots to murder her sadistic husband to end his abusive treatment of them. However, he isn't yet ready to die and comes back to drive them mad. 91m/C VHS, DVD. GB Michael Gough, Yvonne Mitchell, Sharon Gurney, Simon Gough, Nicholas Jones, Olaf Pooley, Mary Hignett; D: Viktors Ritelis; W: Olaf Pooley; C: John Mackey.

Crucible of Terror WOOF! 1972 Mad sculptor covers beautiful models with hot wax, then imprisons them in a mold of bronze. 95m/C VHS, DVD. GB Mike Raven, Mary Maude, James Bolam, John Arnatt, Ronald Lacey, Judy Matheson, Me Me Lai, Melissa Stribling, Beth Morris; D: Ted Hooker; Tom Parkinson; D: Ted Hooker, Tom Parkinson.

The Crucifer of Blood 🐾½ 1991 A disappointing Sherlock Holmes yarn. Heston is adequate as the Baker Street sleuth, but the mystery—about two retired British soldiers who share an accursed secret and a vengeful comrade—unreels clumsily in the form of flashbacks that give away most of the puzzle from the start. Interesting only in that Dr. Watson has a love affair, more or less. Adapted from a play and looking like it by Paul Giovanni, inspired by Arthur Conan Doyle's "The Sign of Four." 105m/C VHS. Charlton Heston, Richard Johnson, Susannah Harker, John Castle, Clive Wood, Simon Callow, Edward Fox; D: Fraser Heston. CABLE

The Crucified Lovers 🐾🐾🐾½ Chikamatsu Monogatari 1954 A shy scrollmaker falls in love with his master's wife. Excellent Japanese tragedy with fine performances all around. 100m/B VHS. JP Kazuo Hasegawa, Kyoko Kagawa, Yoko Minamida, Eitaro Shindo, Shigehiro (Sakae) Ozawa; D: Kenji Mizoguchi.

The Crude Oasis 🐾🐾½ 1995 (R) Shot in 14 days on a $25,000 budget, producer/writer/director Graves' debut is an aggressively moody character. Karen (Taylor)'s a neglected, suicidal Kansas housewife who is haunted by dreams of a mystery man. He turns up in the form of Harley (Runyan) O'Connor whose father and Mika (Runyan) O'Connor whose father begins following him, leading to situations paralleling her dream. Adept at setting up an atmosphere of small-town menace and constructing a plot with surprising twists and turns, Graves can't quite deliver the payoff required. 82m/C VHS, DVD. Jennifer Taylor, Aaron Shields, Robert Peterson, Mussel Sibay, Lynn Bieler, Roberta Eaton; D: Alex Graves; W: Alex Graves; C: Steven Quale.

Cruel and Unusual 🐾🐾 Watchtower 2001 (R) Adam Turrell (Berenger) comes to stay in a quiet Oregon fishing town, introducing himself as an English professor working on a first novel. He befriends sister and brother Kate (Hayward) and Mike (Runyan), whose friendship takes a terrifying turn since Adam isn't at all what he seems. 100m/C VHS, DVD. Tom Berenger, Rachel Hayward, Tygh Runyan, Mitchell Kosterman; D: George Mihalka; W: Robert Geoffrion, Rod Browning, Dan Witt; C: Peter Benison. VIDEO

Cruel Intentions 🐾🐾½ 1998 (R) Fourth film adaptation of Choderlos de Laclos's 1782 novel "Les Liaisons Dangereuses" takes the tale of seduction and intrigue from the 18th century French court to a modern Manhattan prep school. Think "I Know Who You Did Last Summer." Gellar plays teen vamp Kathryn, who bets her stepbrother Sebastian (Phillipe) a night of passion against his car that he can't deflower the virginal Annette (Witherspoon). The overall effect is like the characters' lives: full of guilty pleasures. 95m/C VHS, DVD, Blu-ray Disc, UMD. Sarah Michelle Gellar, Ryan Phillippe, Reese Witherspoon, Selma Blair, Joshua Jackson, Eric Mabius, Louise Fletcher, Swoosie Kurtz, Christine Baranski, Sean Patrick Thomas; D: Roger Kumble; W: Roger Kumble; C: Theo van de Sande; M: Ed Shearmur. MTV Movie Awards '00: Female Perf. (Gellar), Kiss (Sara Michelle Gellar/Selma Blair).

Cruel Intentions 2 🐾🐾 Manchester Prep 1999 (R) A prequel to the 1998 release, plots a rather precocious 16-year-old Sebastian deciding to become a one-woman guy—in this case to naive Danielle, the high school headmaster's daughter. However, his new stepsister Katherine intended as the pilot to a TV series (based on the film) that was cancelled before it aired. 87m/C VHS, DVD. Amy Adams, Mimi Rogers, Robin Dunne, Sarah Thompson, Keri Lynn Pratt, David McIlwraith; D: Roger Kumble; W: Robert Kumble; C: James R. Bagdonas, Mary Frat, David McIlwraith; D: Roger Kumble; W: Robert Kumble; C: James R. Bagdonas, Mary

Cruel Intentions 3 🐾½ 2004 (R) Gratuitous, rehashed third version in which the scene has shifted to an exclusive southern California college. All-new fiendish players Cassidy (Anapau), Jason (Smith), and Patrick (Wetherington) use their considerable free time plotting and pursuing sexual conquests with others and among themselves. 85m/C VHS, DVD. Kerr Smith, Natalie Ramsey, Tom Parker, Kristina Anapau, Nathan Wetherington, Melissa Yvonne Lewis; D: Scott Ziehl; W: Rhett Reese; C: Thomas Callaway; M: David Reynolds. VIDEO

Cruel Sea 🐾🐾🐾 1953 Well-made documentary-like account of a Royal Navy corvette on convoy duty in the Atlantic during WWII. 121m/B VHS, DVD. GB Jack Hawkins, Stanley Baker, Denholm Elliot, Virginia McKenna; D: Charles Frend; W: Eric Ambler.

The Cruel Story of Youth 🐾🐾🐾 Seishun Zankoku Monogatari; Naked Youth; A Story of the Cruelties of Youth 1960 A teenage girl and her criminal boyfriend use sex to get money out of rich, middle-aged men in this controversial look at the disillusionment of youth and the breaking of old values and traditions in Japan after WWII. In Japanese with English subtitles. 96m/C VHS, DVD. JP Yusuke Kawazu, Miyuki Kuwano, Yoshiko Kuga; D: Nagisa Oshima.

Cruel World WOOF! 2005 (R) Grubby and stupid, Philip (Furlong) goes psycho over being dumped by Catherine (Pressly) on the Love Boat. 100m/C VHS. Raj Milland, Hugh O'Brian, John Forsythe, Christopher George, Dick Benedict, Frank Converse, Lynda Day George, Stella Stevens; D: Bruce Kessler.

Cruise Missile 🐾 1978 Unique task force is on a mission to keep the world from nuclear holocaust. 100m/C VHS. Peter Graves, Curt Jurgens, Michael Dante; D: Ted V. Mikels.

Cruise into Terror WOOF! 1978 A sarcophagus brought aboard a pleasure cruise ship unleashes an evil force that slowly starts to kill off the ship's passengers, most of whom likely thought they were on the Love Boat. 100m/C VHS. Ray Milland, Hugh O'Brian, John Forsythe, Christopher George, Dirk Benedict, Frank Converse, Lynda Day George, Stella Stevens; D: Bruce Kessler.

Cruisin' High 🐾 Cat Murkil and the Silks 1975 (R) Two city street gangs battle it out. 100m/C VHS, David Kyle, Kelly Yaegermann, Rhodes Reason; D: John Bushelman; W: William C. Thomas.

Cruising 🐾🐾 1980 (R) Rookie cop Pacino is deep undercover investigating the bizarre murders of homosexuals in New York's West Village. Sexually explicit but less than suspenseful mystery. Released, re-released with many gay rights groups voicing loud disapproval of the sordid gay characterization, while others feared copy-cat crimes. Excellent NYC cinematography. 102m/C VHS, DVD. Al Pacino, Paul Sorvino, Karen Allen, Powers Boothe, Richard Cox, Don Scardino, Joe Spinell, Ed O'Neill, James Remar, William Russ, Barton Heyman, Mike Starr; D: William Friedkin; W: William Friedkin; C: James A. Contner; M: Jack Nitzsche.

Crumb 🐾🐾🐾 1994 (R) Countercultural documentary looking at the life of underground cartoonist Robert Crumb—'60s satirist and social misfit who created such drug and sex characters as Fritz the Cat and Mr. Natural. Crumb's extraordinary, dysfunctional family play a significant role, with his mother and two brothers, elder brother Charles and younger brother Max, also interviewed as well as Crumb's friends and current and former wives. The dead abusive father also plays a part. Director Zwigoff spent six years filming his work after taking the Grand Jury prize at Sundance. 119m/C VHS, DVD. Robert Crumb; D: Terry Zwigoff; C: Maryse Alberti. Directors Guild '95: Feature Doc. (Zwigoff); Natl. Soc.

Film Critics '95; Feature Doc.; Sundance '95: Cinematog., Grand Jury Prize.

The Crusades 🦴🦴½ 1935 Typical DeMille extravaganza, loosely based on the Third Crusade, which finds Richard the Lionheart (Wilcoxon) and the armies of Europe battling Saladin and the Mahammedan horde in order to reclaim Jerusalem. Meanwhile, Richard marries by proxy in order to gain supplies for his army—something that enrages his bride Berengaria (Young). Once he realizes how beautiful she is, Richard tries to win her love. Obviously, not historically accurate and it's all secondary to the battle scenes, anyway. Based on the Harold Lamb book "The Crusade: Iron Men and Saints." 126m/B VHS, DVD. Henry Wilcoxon, Loretta Young, Sir C. Aubrey Smith, Ian Keith, Katherine DeMille, Joseph Schildkraut, Alan Hale, C. Henry Gordon, George Barbier, Lumsden Hare, William Farnum, Hobart Bosworth, Montagu Love, Pedro de Cordoba, Mischa Auer; D: Cecil B. DeMille; W: Waldemar Young, Dudley Nichols, Harold Lamb; C: Victor Milner; M: Rudolph Kopp.

Crush 🦴🦴 1993 Christina is a local New Zealand literary critic on her way to interview Colin, a reclusive novelist. Along for the ride is her seductive American friend Lane who manages to crash the car but walk away with hardly a scratch. Christina appears to be dead and Lane abandons her, finding her way to the home Colin shares with his teenage daughter Angela. Lane promptly sets out to seduce Colin, making Angela jealous, (oh, and Christina's not dead after all). Poor script finds the characters' actions baffling and why Lane is so wildly attractive is never apparent. 97m/C VHS, DVD. NZ Marcia Gay Harden, Donogh Rees, William Zappa, Caitlin Bossley; D: Alison Maclean; W: Alison Maclean, Anne Kennedy; C: Dion Beebe.

The Crush 🦴½ 1993 (R) Wealthy 14-year-old temptress Silverstone (in her debut) develops an obsessive crush on handsome 28-year-old Elwes, who rents her family's guest house. In an attempt to win his heart, she rewrites his poorly composed magazine articles. This doesn't convince him they should mate for life, so she sabotages his apartment to vent her rage. Sound familiar? The plot's lifted right out of "Fatal Attraction" and Shapiro doesn't offer viewers anything inventively different. He does manage to substitute new methods for the spurned lover to snare her prey. Limp plot would have been exciting if we hadn't seen it so many times before. 89m/C VHS, DVD. Cary Elwes, Alicia Silverstone, Jennifer Rubin, Kurtwood Smith, Gwynth Walsh, Amber Benson; D: Alan Shapiro; W: Alan Shapiro; C: Bruce Surtees; M: Graeme Revell. MTV Movie Awards '94: Breakthrough Perf. (Silverstone), Villain (Silverstone).

Crush 🦴🦴 2002 (R) A "with friends like these, who needs enemies" movie that leaves a sour aftertaste. Kate (MacDowell), Janine (Staunton), and Molly (Chancellor) are three professional women in their 40s who live in a small English town and meet weekly to drink and commiserate about their lousy love lives. That is, until sexily repressed American headmistress Kate sets off sparks with hottie twentysomething Jed (Doughty), an organist and former pupil. Her friends are outraged and turn distinctly nasty trying to break up the happy twosome. Maybe they're jealous that Kate is having great sex and they're not. 115m/C VHS, DVD, GB Andie MacDowell, Imelda Staunton, Anna Chancellor, Kenny Doughty, Bill Paterson; D: John McKay; W: John McKay; C: Henry Braham; M: Kevin Sargent.

Crusoe 🦴🦴½ 1989 (PG-13) A lushly photographed version of the Daniel Defoe classic. Crusoe is an arrogant slave trader stranded on a desert island populated by unfriendly natives. Themes of prejudice, fear, and choice appear in this never-padded, thoughtful film. Quinn gives an excellent performance as the stranded slave-trader. 94m/C VHS. Aidan Quinn, Ade Sapara, Jimmy Nail, Timothy Spall, Colin Bruce, Michael Higgins, Shane Rimmer, Hepburn Grahame; D: Caleb Deschanel; W: Walon Green, Christopher Logue; M: Michael Kamen.

Crutch 🦴½ 2004 (R) Sixteen-year-old David (Gordon) must deal with his alcoholic mom Katie (Walsh), who's forced into rehab after an accident. This leaves David vulnerable to the predatory desires of his 30-something drama teacher, Kenny (Moretti), who also introduces the impulsive, lonely teen to drugs. Unsettling story based on Moretti's own experiences. 88m/C DVD. Rob Moretti, Eben Gordon, Juanita Walsh, James Earley; D: Rob Moretti; W: Rob Moretti; Paul Jacks; C: Brian Fass; M: Ben Goldberg.

Cry-Baby 🦴🦴 1990 (PG-13) An homage and spoof of '50s teen-rock melodramas by the doyen of cinematic Bad Taste, involving a terminal bad-boy high schooler who goes with a square blond and starts an inter-class rumble. Musical numbers, throwaway gags and plenty of knee-bending to Elvis, with a weak story supported by offbeat celeb appearances. 85m/C VHS, DVD. Johnny Depp, Amy Locane, Polly Bergen, Traci Lords, Ricki Lake, Iggy Pop, Susan Tyrrell, Patty (Patricia Campbell) Hearst, Kim McGuire, Darren E. Burrows, Troy Donahue, Willem Dafoe, David Nelson, Mink Stole, Joe Dallesandro, Joey Heatherton, Robert Walsh, Mary Vivian Pearce; D: John Waters; W: John Waters; C: David Insley; M: Patrick Williams.

Cry Blood, Apache 🦴🦴 1970 (R) An old man (Joel McCrae) remembers when, as a young man (Jody McCrae), he and his sadistic friends massacred a group of Apaches and were hunted by the husband of one of their victims. It's violent but not as sadistic as some. 90m/C VHS. Joel McCrea, Jody McCrea, Robert Tessier, Marie Gahva, Don Henley; D: Jack Starrett; W: Sean McGregor; C: Bruce Scott; M: Elliot Kaplan.

Cry Danger 🦴🦴🦴 1951 A falsely imprisoned man is released from jail, and he searches for those who framed him. 80m/B VHS. Dick Powell, Rhonda Fleming, William Conrad, Richard Erdman; D: Robert Parrish; C: Joseph Biroc.

A Cry for Love 🦴🦴 1980 An amphetamine addict and an alcoholic meet, fall in love, and help each other recover. Based on the best seller by Jill Schary Robinson, "Bedtime Story." 96m/C VHS. Susan Blakely, Powers Boothe, Gene Barry, Charles Siebert, Herb Edelman, Fern Fitzgerald, Lainie Kazan; D: Paul Wendkos.

Cry Freedom 🦴🦴½ 1987 (PG) A romantic look at the short life of South African activist Steven Biko, and his friendship with the white news editor, Donald Woods. The film focuses on Woods' escape from Africa while struggling to bring Biko's message to the world. Based on a true story. 157m/C VHS, DVD. Kevin Kline, Denzel Washington, Penelope Wilton, Kevin McNally, John Thaw, Timothy West, John Hargreaves, Alec McCowen, Zakes Mokae, Ian Richardson, Juanita Waterman; D: Richard Attenborough; W: John Briley; C: Ronnie Taylor; M: George Fenton, Jonas Gwangwa.

A Cry from the Mountain 🦴 1985 (PG) Heavily religious film about a father and son who go on a kayak trip through Alaska's wilderness so the father can break the news of his impending divorce. A series of events occurs that change their lives, and they meet a mysterious mountain man who relies on his faith in God to get by in the wilderness. Features an appearance by Rev. Billy Graham. 78m/C VHS. James Cavan, Wes Parker, Rita Walter, Chris Kidd, Coleen Gray, Jerry Ballew, Allison Argo, Glen Ailsworth, Myrna Kidd; D: James F. Collier.

A Cry from the Streets 🦴🦴 1957 Drama about the plight of orphan children and dedicated social workers in England. 100m/C VHS. GB Max Bygraves, Barbara Murray, Kathleen Harrison, Colin Petersen; D: Lewis Gilbert; M: Larry Adler.

A Cry in the Dark 🦴🦴🦴½ 1988 (PG-13) Tight film story of the infamous Australian murder trial of Lindy Chamberlain (Streep), who was accused of killing her own baby, mostly because of the intensely adverse public opinion, aroused by vicious press, that surrounded the case. Chamberlain blamed the death on a wild dingo dog, which dragged off the baby from where the family was camped. Near-documentary style, with Streep excellent as the religious, unknowable mother. Based on the book "Evil Angels" by John Bryson. This case was also detailed in the film "Who Killed Baby Azaria?" 120m/C VHS, DVD. AU Meryl Streep, Sam Neill, Bruce Myles, Charles "Bud" Tingwell, Nick (Nicholas) Tate, Neil Fitzpatrick, Maurice Fields, Lewis Fitz-Gerald, Tony (Anthony) Martin; D: Fred Schepisi; W: Fred Schepisi, Robert Caswell; C: Ian Baker; M: Bruce Smeaton. Australian Film Inst. '89: Actor (Neill), Actress (Streep), Film; Cannes '89: Actress (Streep); N.Y. Film Critics '88: Actress (Streep).

A Cry in the Night 🦴🦴½ 1993 (PG-13) After Jenny (Higgins Clark) marries an internationally acclaimed artist, she thinks her life is complete. However, once she and her two daughters move into his country estate, her life takes a tragic turn as she's haunted by the mysterious deaths of her ex-husband and newborn child. King plays the new husband who turns out to have a few psychological quirks of his own. Actress Higgins Clark is the daughter of bestselling novelist Mary Higgins Clark, upon whose work the story is based. 99m/C VHS. Perry King, Carol Higgins Clark; D: Robin Spry; W: Robin Spry. TV

A Cry in the Wild 🦴🦴 1990 (PG) A 14-year-old boy must find his way back to civilization when he's the lone survivor of an airplane crash. Strong acting from Rushton, excellent nature photography make this well used story work again. 93m/C VHS, DVD. Jared Rushton, Ned Beatty, Pamela Sue Martin, Stephen Meadows; D: Mark Griffiths; W: Catherine Cyran; C: Gregg Heschong; M: Arthur Kempel.

Cry of a Prostitute: Love Kills 🦴🦴 1972 (R) Former prostitute joins with a professional assassin in an effort to pacify rival gangsters in Italy. 86m/C VHS. Henry Silva, Barbara Bouchet; D: Andrea Bianchi.

Cry of Battle 🦴🦴 (To Be a Man) 1963 Anxious for the challenges of manhood, a well-heeled young man joins a guerrilla militia in the Philippines. 99m/B VHS, DVD. Van Heflin, Rita Moreno, James MacArthur; D: Irving Lerner.

Cry of the Banshee 🦴🦴½ 1970 (PG) Witch-hunter Price and family are tormented by Satanic powers seeking revenge. Superior horror period piece. 87m/C VHS, DVD. GB Vincent Price, Elisabeth Bergner, Essy Persson, Hugh Griffith, Hilary Dwyer, Sally Geeson, Patrick Mower, Marshall Jones, Michael Elphick, Pamela Fairbrother, Robert Hutton; D: Gordon Hessler; W: Christopher Wicking, Tim Kelly; C: John Coquillon; M: Les Baxter.

Cry of the Innocent 🦴🦴 1980 An action-packed thriller about a Vietnam veteran who is out to find a group of Irish terrorists that killed his family. 93m/C VHS, DVD. Cyril Cusack, Alexander Knox, Rod Taylor, Joanna Pettet, Nigel Davenport; D: Michael O'Herlihy.

The Cry of the Owl 🦴🦴 (Le Cri du Hibou) 1987 Robert (Malavoy) has divorced the dreadful Veronique (Thevenet) and struck up a friendship with Juliette (May). He admires the way her life seems so satisfied and orderly but Juliette decides she doesn't like this idea of herself and impulsively drops her swinish fiance Patrick (Penot) and pursues Robert instead. But Robert is only interested in friendship, leading to some very twisted revenge plots. Suspenseful look at what obsessions can drive people to do. Adapted from the novel by Patricia Highsmith. In French with English subtitles. 102m/C VHS, DVD. FR IT Christophe Malavoy, Mathilda May, Virginie Thevenet, Jacques Penot, Jean-Pierre Kalfon, Patrice Kerbrat; D: Claude Chabrol; W: Claude Chabrol, Odile Barski; C: Jean Rabier; M: Matthieu Chabrol.

Cry of the Penguins 🦴🦴 (Mr. Forbush and the Penguins) 1971 Womanizing biologist Forbush (Hurt) heads off on an Antartic expedition to study penguins when his would-be romance with Tara (Mills) comes to naught. Beautiful photography, shallow story. Adapted from the novel "Mr. Forbush and the Penguins" by Graham Billing. Note the similarities with "Never Cry Wolf." 105m/C VHS, DVD. GB John Hurt, Hayley Mills, Dudley Sutton, Tony Britton, Thorley Walters, Judy Campbell, Joss Ackland, Nicholas Pennell; D: Albert T. Viola; W: Anthony Shaffer; M: John Addison.

Cry of the Werewolf 🦴🦴 1944 A beautiful New Orleans gypsy protects her mother's mummified remains by periodically turning into a werewolf and killing people. 63m/B VHS. Nina Foch, Stephen Crane, Osa Massen, Blanche Yurka, Barton MacLane, Ivan Triesault, John Abbott, Fritz Leiber; D: Henry Levin; W: Charles "Blackie" O'Neal.

Cry Panic 🦴🦴 1974 A man is thrown into a strange series of events after accidentally running down a man on a highway. 74m/C VHS, DVD. John Forsythe, Anne Francis, Earl Holliman, Claudia McNeil, Ralph Meeker; D: James Goldstone. TV

Cry Terror 🦴🦴 (Kill Two Birds; Thriller: Kill Two Birds) 1976 Two escaped convicts take two beautiful women hostage hoping to gain their own freedom. Only a quick-thinking undercover police officer can save the girls. 71m/C VHS. GB Bob Hoskins, Susan Hampshire, Gabrielle Drake; D: Robert Tronson; M: Brian Clemens. TV

Cry, the Beloved Country 🦴🦴½ African Fury 1951 A black country minister travels to Johannesberg to be with his son after the youth is accused of killing a white man. Through the events of the trial, the horror, oppression, and destruction of South Africa's apartheid system are exposed. Startling and moving, the first international feature set against the backdrop of apartheid. Still trenchant; based on the novel by Alan Paton. 111m/B VHS. GB Canada Lee, Charles Carson, Sidney Poitier, Joyce Carey, Geoffrey Keen; D: Zoltan Korda; W: John Howard Lawson, Alan Paton; C: Robert Krasker.

Cry, the Beloved Country 🦴🦴🦴 1995 (PG-13) Alan Paton's classic South African apartheid novel (first filmed in 1951) depicts a Zulu Christian pastor and a wealthy white farmer finding common ground through personal loss—both of their sons were killed in regional violence. Rural black minister Stephen Kumalo (Jones), travels to Johannesburg only to discover his sister (Kente) is a prostitute, his younger brother John (Dutton) no longer believes in Christianity and his son is in prison for the murder of a white man. That man turns out to be the son of rich farmer James Jarvis (Harris), from Kumalo's own village. Both Jones and Harris turn in wonderfully understated performances in this hopeful tale of potential racial harmony. 120m/C VHS, DVD. SA James Earl Jones, Richard Harris, Charles S. Dutton, Leleti Khumalo, Dambisa Kente, Vusi Kunene, Eric Mlyeni, Ian Robers; D: Darrell Roodt; W: Ronald Atwood; C: Paul Gilpin; M: John Barry.

Cry Uncle 🦴½ 1971 (R) Comic account of a private eye who investigates a blackmailing case involving a film of orgies in which, much to his chagrin, he participated. 85m/C VHS, DVD. Allen (Goorwitz) Garfield, Paul Sorvino, Devin Goldenberg, Madeleine Le Roux; D: John G. Avildsen; W: David Odell; C: John G. Avildsen; M: Harper McKay.

Cry Vengeance 🦴🦴 1954 A falsely imprisoned detective gets out of jail and searches for the people who framed him and killed his family. 83m/B VHS. Mark Stevens, Joan Vohs, Martha Hyer, Skip Homeier; D: Mark Stevens.

Cry Wolf 🦴🦴 1947 Weak mystery thriller places Stanwyck in creepy environs when she goes to claim her inheritance from her late husband's estate. 83m/B VHS. Errol Flynn, Barbara Stanwyck, Richard Basehart, Geraldine Brooks, Jerome Cowan, John Ridgely, Patricia Barry; D: Peter Godfrey; W: Catherine Turney.

The Crying Child 🦴½ 1996 (PG-13) Madeline Jeffreys (Hemingway) and her husband Ran (DelHoyo) retreat to their 19th-century island vacation cottage after the stillbirth of their first child. Madeline begins to hear a child crying in the house and sees a ghostly apparition—now she has to discover what the spirit wants (and convince everyone she's not just going crazy). TV movie based on the novel by Barbara Michaels. 93m/C VHS. Mariel Hemingway, George DelHoyo, Finola

The Crying Game 🦴🦴🦴½ **1992 (R)** PR lesson in how to launch a small movie into the hypersphere and en- sure critical silence on salient character- ization. Jordan's gritty drama is on par with his best, a complex blend of violence, love, betrayal, guilt, and redemption and is not about what it seems to be about most of the time. Wonderful performances by all, including Rea as the appealing, con- science-stricken Fergus; Richardson as the cold, violent IRA moll Jude; and David- son, in that hit debut, as the needy charis- matic Dil. Whitaker is terrific in his 15 min- utes of intense screen time. Filled with definite surprises and unexpected plea- sures. Title is based on a top-5 British hit of 1964, three versions of which are heard. **112m/C VHS, DVD, /R** Stephen Rea, Jaye Davidson, Miranda Richardson, Forest Whitaker, Adrian Dunbar, Jim Broadbent, Ralph Brown, Bref- fini McKenna, Joe Savino, Birdy Sweeney, Andre Bernard; **D:** Neil Jordan; **W:** Neil Jordan; **C:** Ian Wilson; **M:** Anne Dudley; Oscar '92: Orig. Screen- play; Australian Film Inst. '93: Foreign Film; Ind. Spirit '93: Foreign Film; L.A. Film Critics '92: For- eign Film; N.Y. Film Critics '92: Screenplay, Sup- port. Actress (Richardson); Natl. Soc. Film Critics '92: Screenplay, Writers Guild '92: Orig. Screen- play.

Crypt of Dark Secrets 🦴 **1976 (R)** Vietnam veteran recovering from wounds in the Louisiana swamps encoun- ters a friendly Indian spirit who saves him from death. **100m/C VHS, DVD,** Maureen Chan, Ronald Tanet, Wayne Mack, Herbert G. Jahncke; **D:** Jack Weis.

Crypt of the Living Dead WOOf! **1973 (PG)** An undead woman from the 13th century makes life miserable for visitors on Vampire Island. **75m/C VHS,** Andrew Prine, Mark Damon, Teresa Gimpera, Patty (Patti) Shepard, Francisco (Frank) Brana; **D:** Ray Danton.

Crystal Heart 🦴 **1987 (R)** A medi- cally isolated songwriter with an incurable disease falls in love with a lovely rock singer. **103m/C VHS,** Lee Curreri, Tawny Kitaen, Lloyd Bochner; **D:** Gil Bettman; **M:** Joel Goldsmith.

Crystal's Diary 🦴 **1999** Small town Emmanuel Crystal moves to Hollywood and winds up sharing a place with free- spirited Tabetha. The twosome make their cash lap dancing until Emmanuel makes the mistake of falling for a client and things just go downhill from there. **90m/C VHS,** Shelly Guretz, Monique Albers, David Alan, Vin- cent Bilancio, John Sayre; **D:** Jeff Leroy; **W:** Jeff Leroy; **M:** Larry Washington.

Crystalstone 🦴🦴 **1988 (PG)** A wooden cross leads a pair of orphans on a dangerous search for the legendary Crys- talstone. **103m/C VHS,** Frank Grimes, Kamleish Gupta, Laura Jane Goodwin, Sydney Bromley; **D:** Antonio Pelaez.

CryWolf 🦴🦴 **2005 (PG-13)** Bored trust-funders at a boarding school start up an internet game of spreading stories and rumors. The game turns serious when someone makes up a story about a serial killer and people start turning up dead. Twisty plot goes for sleight-of-hand and visceral thrills, and doesn't completely fail. But it's all only mildly effective. Typical slasher fare might not keep you entertained but won't register past the final credits. **90m/C DVD. US** Lindy Booth, Jared Padalecki, Kristy Wu, Paul James, Julian Morris, Sandra McCoy, Jon Bon Jovi, Gary Cole, Jesse Janzen, Anna Deavere Smith; **D:** Jeff Wadlow; **W:** Jeff Wadlow, Beau Bauman; **C:** Romeo Tirone; **M:** Mi- chael Wandmacher.

CSA: The Confederate States of America 🦴🦴½ **2004** Mocku- mentary ponders the history of the past 150 years had the Confederacy won the Civil War and slavery endured. Told via a faux British public network Ken Burns-type series and presented by Spike Lee. Pur- posely unsettling, with images like a black- faced Lincoln in hiding as Harriet Tubman helps him to escape to Canada, the picky attention to historical details falls short by presuming such modern events as JFK's presidency and assassination, and the... Vietnam War would have really took place in such a world. **89m/C DVD. US** Charles Frank, Evamarii Johnson, Rupert Pate, Larry J. Pe- terson; **C:** Matthew Jacobson; **M:** Kelly Werts.

Cthulhu Mansion WOOf! **1991 (R)** The oldest-looking juvenile delinquents you've ever seen release evil spirits when they take over a magician's estate. Not very special effects and an abominable dia- logue, it claims to be based on H.P. Love- craft stories, but that's a load of dung. **95m/C VHS,** Frank Finlay, Marcia Layton, Brad Fisher, Melanie Shatner, Luis Fernando Alves, Kaethe Cheney, Paul Birchard; **D:** Juan Piquer Simon; **D:** Juan) Piquer Simon; **M:** Patrick Williams.

Cuba 🦴🦴🦴 **1979 (R)** Cynical, satirical adventure/love story. Mercenary soldier rekindles an old affair during the Castro revolution. Charismatic cast and good di- rection make for an entertaining, if over- looked, Connery vehicle. **121m/C VHS, DVD,** Sean Connery, Brooke Adams, Jack Weston, Hec- tor Elizondo, Denholm Elliott, Chris Sarandon, Lon- ette McKee; **D:** Richard Lester; **W:** Charles Wood; **C:** David Watkin; **M:** Patrick Williams.

Cuban Blood 🦴🦴½ **Dreaming of Ju- lia 2003 (PG-13)** Director Gerard's nostalgic semi-autobiographical tale centers around young, nympho wife (Dorleac) who has some unexpected ties to his grandfather, Che (Keitel). **105m/C DVD.** Harvey Keitel, Iban Hjejle, Gael Garcia Bernal, Andhy Mendez, Diana Bracho; **D:** Juan Gerard; **W:** Juan Gerard, Latvia Arza-Goderich; **C:** Kramer Morgenthau; **M:** Jose Padilla, Edesio Alejandro; **V:** Tony Plena.

Cube 🦴🦴½ **1998 (R)** Claustrophobic sci-fi thriller about six people who inexpli- cably wake up chained together in a bare room attached to other bare rooms that are fiendishly booby-trapped. They are forced to work together in order to escape. The fact that the bizarro force holding these people hostage is never explained may escape you; since your senses will be dulled by the bad acting and lack of plot. Not as much fun as spending an hour and a half in a refrigerator box. **90m/C VHS, DVD, CA** Maurice Dean Wint, Nikki de Boer, David Hew- lett, Wayne Robson, Andrew Miller, Nicky Guadag- ni, Julian Richings; **D:** Vincenzo Natali; **W:** Graeme Manson, Vincenzo Natali, Andre Bijelic; **C:** Derek Rogers; **M:** Mark Korven.

Cube 2: Hypercube 🦴½ **2004 (R)** Hyper- cube 2002 (R) The sequel's basically a car- bon copy of the first film with a couple more hostages. This time eight people find themselves trapped in a paranormal cube made up of deadly chambers. They strug- gle to escape and discover their would-be leader, Kate (Matchett), has her own agenda. Yawn. **94m/C VHS, DVD, CA** Kari Matchett, Geraint Wyn Davies, Matthew Ferguson, Neil Crone, Barbara Gordon, Lindsey Connell, Grace Lynn King, Greer Kent; **D:** Andrzej Sekula; **W:** Sean Hood; **M:** Norman Orenstein.

Cube: Zero 🦴🦴½ **2004 (R)** Third flick in the series is actually a story prequel that stays pretty close to the formula. Cube tech Wynn (Bennett) falls for Rain (Moore), an unwilling prisoner of the maze. Since Wynn has some idea of what's happening—and is a rebel—he en- ters the cube to try and rescue her. **94m/C DVD, CA** Zachary Bennett, Stephanie Moore, Da- vid Huband, Martin Roach, Michael Riley, Richard McMillan; **D:** Ernie Barbarash; **W:** Ernie Barba- rash; **C:** Francois Dagenais; **M:** Norman Orenstein.

The Cuckoo 🦴🦴½ **Kukushka 2002 (PG-13)** It's not a joke but the film does have its humorous moments; a Russian, a Finn, and a Lapp are drawn together in 1944. That was the year the Nazis, who occupied Finland, pulled out, leaving be- hind Finns who had been pressed into service against the advancing Russians. One of these Finns is reluctant sniper Veiko (Bychkov), wounded and found by the Lapp—young war widow Anni (Juuso)— who is caring for him in her hut. Veiko also stumbles upon the hut. None speak the other's language, which doesn't prevent a lot of conversation and misunderstandings as well as desire. In Finnish, Russian, and Sami (the Lapp language) with subtitles. **104m/C DVD, RU** Willie Haapasalo, Anni-Kristina Yuso, Viktar Bychkov; **D:** Alexander Rogozhkin; **W:** Alexander Rogozhkin; **M:** Dmitri Pavlov.

Cujo 🦴🦴 **1983 (R)** Bad doggie!! A ra- bid St. Bernard goes berserk and attacks mom Donna (Wallace Stone) and her five- year-old son Tad (Pintauro), who are trapped inside a broken-down Pinto. Frighteningly realistic film is based on Stephen King's bestseller. **94m/C VHS, DVD,** Dee Wallace Stone, Daniel Hugh-Kelly, Danny Pin- tauro, Ed Lauter, Christopher Stone, Kaiulani Lee, Mills Watson, Jerry Hardin, Billy Jacoby, Sandy Ward; **D:** Lewis Teague; **W:** Lauren Currier, Don Carlos Dunaway; **C:** Jan De Bont; **M:** Charles Bernstein.

Cul de Sac 🦴🦴🦴 **1966** A maca- bre, psychological thriller set in a dreary castle on a small island off the British coast. Pleasance is an eccentric, middle- aged hermit living acrimoniously with his young, nympho wife (Dorleac) when their home is invaded by two wounded gang- sters (Stander and MacGowran), who pro- ceed to hold the couple hostage. MacGowran soon dies of his wounds, leaving Stander and Pleasence to fight it out, encouraged by the luscious Dorleac, who finds her fun where she can. A bleak, sinister film considered one of Polanski's best. **111m/C VHS, GB** Donald Pleasence, Fran- cose Dorleac, Lionel Stander, Jack MacGowran, Jacqueline Bisset; **D:** Roman Polanski; **W:** Roman Polanski, Gerard Brach.

Culpepper Cattle Co. 🦴🦴½ **1972 (PG)** A young, starry-eyed yokel wants to be a cowboy and gets himself enlisted in a cattle drive, where he learns the harsh reality of the West. **92m/C VHS, DVD,** Gary Grimes, Billy Green Bush, Bo Hopkins, Charles Martin Smith, Geoffrey Lewis; **D:** Dick Richards; **M:** Jerry Goldsmith.

Cult of the Cobra 🦴🦴 **1955** Mysterious horror film that became minor camp classic. It seems ex-servicemen are being killed by exotic snake-lady Do- mergue. Cheesy film that can be fun. Based on a story by Jerry Davis. **75m/B VHS,** Faith Domergue, Richard Long, Marshall Thompson, William Reynolds, Jack Kelly, Kathleen Hughes; **D:** Franco S. D. Lyon; **W:** Jerry Davis.

Cult 🦴½ **2007** Dumb college horror. While researching a class project, co-ed Mindy (Milner) becomes obsessed with a Chinese legend about a murdered young girl who took a magical jade amulet to her grave. The amulet has been recovered by a cult leader who is using ritual sacrifice to harness its power. **90m/C DVD,** Rachel Miner, Taryn Manning, Joel Michaely, Glenn Dunk, M;ke Michaels; **D:** Joe Knee; **W:** Benjamin Oren; **C:** Dave McFarland; **M:** Tung Thanh Tran. VIDEO

The Cup 🦴🦴½ **Phorpa 1999 (G)** Ti- betan teenager Orgyen arrives at a mon- astery in the Himalayan foothills where he is to join the religious life. But Orgyen is soccer-mad and obsessed with the World Cup (he wears a soccer shirt under his robes) and sneaks out to watch the games. Eventually, the monastery's ab- bot agrees to allow the monks to have a satellite dish to watch the finals—if they can raise the money to do it. Bhuta- nese with subtitles. **94m/C VHS, DVD, AU** Jamyang Lodro, Orgyen Tobgyal, Lama Chonjor, **D:** Khyentse Norbu; **W:** Khyentse Norbu; **C:** Paul Warren; **M:** Douglas Mills.

Cup Final 🦴🦴½ **G'mar Givya 1992** The similarities and contradictions in war and sports, where passions and competi- tion run high, are depicted in this emotion- al drama. Set in 1982 during Israel's inva- sion of Lebanon. Cohen is an Israeli sol- dier passionately interested in the World Cup soccer tournament. When he is taken prisoner by the PLO he discovers his cap- tor Ziad shares his interest in the Italian national team. This common interest brings the two antagonists reluctantly to- gether. In Hebrew and Arabic with English subtitles. **107m/C VHS, DVD, /S** Moshe Ivg, Mu- hamad Bakri, Suheil Haddad; **D:** Eran Riklis; **W:** Eyal Halfon; **M:** Raviv Gazit.

Cupid 🦴½ **1996 (R)** Eric (Galligan) develops a deadly obsession for beautiful Jennifer (Laurence), who discovers that Jack and his equally crazy sister Dana (Crosby) have a nasty habit of killing the women that don't measure up to Jack's fantasies. **94m/C VHS,** Zach Galligan, Ashley Laurence, Mary Crosby, Joseph Kell, Michael Bowen; **D:** Doug Campbell; **W:** David Mullen.

Cupid & Cate 🦴🦴½ **2000** Cate De Angelo (Parker) is the quirky owner of a failing D.C. vintage clothing store. The youngest in a large Italian/Irish American family, Cate is still trying to deal with her alcoholic mother's death and an ongoing feud with her overbearing father, Dominic (Bosco). She has a reliable relationship with dull Phillip (Lansbury) but doesn't real- ize the passion she's been missing until she meets handsome Harry (Gallagher)... 96m/C Mary-Louise Parker, Peter Gallagher, Philip Bosco, David Lansbury, Bebe Neuwirth, Joanna Going, Brenda Fricker, Kurt McKinney, Rebecca Lucier; **D:** Brent Shields; **W:** Jennifer Miller, Ron Raley; **C:** Rees Van Oostrum; **M:** Mark Adler. TV

Curdled 🦴🦴½ **1995 (R)** And you thought your job sucked. Tarantino-funded dark comedy arouses interest with that tag line alone. Gore-obsessed Gabriela (Jones) gets her dream job cleaning up blood and guts with the Post-Forensic Cle- aning Service and becomes obsessed with serial killer (Baldwin), who is keeping her company hopping with one beheading after another. Cultishly vio- lent pic culminates in a tango by the grue- some twosome around a murder scene. Tarantino spotted Jones, starring in Brad- dock's original student short, while touring with "Reservoir Dogs" and borrowed her for "Pulp Fiction", only to return the favor by exec producing this interesting feature debut. Soundtrack adds spice to the form- ulaic flavor. **87m/C VHS, DVD,** Angela Jones, William Baldwin, Mel Gorham, Barry Cor- bin, Bruce Ramsay, Daisy Fuentes, Lois Chiles, Carmen Lopez; **D:** Reb Braddock; **W:** John Maass, Reb Braddock; **C:** Steven Bernstein; **M:** Joseph Julian Gonzalez.

The Cure 🦴🦴 **1917** Chaplin arrives at a spa to take a rest cure, accompanied by a trunk full of liquor that somehow gets dumped into the water at the resort. Silent with music track. **20m/B VHS, DVD,** Charlie Chaplin, Edna Purviance, Eric Campbell, Albert Austin; **D:** Charlie Chaplin.

The Cure 🦴🦴½ **1995 (PG-13)** Erik (Renfro), the neighborhood bad kid, be- friends Dexter (Mazzello), a boy with AIDS. As Dexter's health weakens, Erik decides they must go on a quest for a cure. Huck Finn style, by floating along the Mississippi River to New Orleans. Despite film's preposterous plot, the performances of the two young leads do inspire a level of sentiment. **99m/C VHS, DVD,** Renee Humphrey, Brad Renfro, Joseph Mazzello, Annabella Sciorra, Diana Scarwid, Bruce Davison; **D:** Peter Horton, **W:** Robert Kuhn; **C:** Andrew Dintenfass; **M:** Dave Grusin.

The Curfew Breakers 🦴🦴 **1957** Teen-exploitation/message-movie finds a pair of community workers investi- gating the murder of a gas station atten- dent by a drug-crazed youth. **78m/B VHS, DVD,** Regis Toomey, Paul Kelly, Cathy Downs, Marilyn Madison, Sheila Urban; **D:** Alex Wells.

Curfew 🦴🦴 **1988 (R)** A young woman rushes home so she doesn't break her curfew, only to find two killers with time on their hands waiting for her. Violent. **86m/C VHS, DVD,** John Putch, Kyle Richards, William Wellman Jr., Bert Remsen; **D:** Gary Winick.

Curiosity Kills 🦴🦴 **1990 (R)** Young people find more than they bar- gained for when they begin to investigate the death of a fellow tenant. Tense made- for-cable thriller. **86m/C VHS,** Rae Dawn Chong, C. Thomas Howell, Courteney Cox, Paul Guilfoyle, Jeff Fahey; **D:** Colin Bucksey; **W:** Joe Batteer, John Rice; **C:** Bojan Bazelli. CABLE

The Curious Dr. Humpp ✗ 1970 A mad scientist (Barbero) kidnaps exotic dancers and extracts their libidos to preserve his youth. Under the guise of research, he encourages his victims to engage in trysts so that their carnal energies will increase. Everything is hunky dory until a reporter (Bauleo) starts snooping around the laboratory, discovering Dr. Humpp observing multiple couplings via closed-circuit TV. Boldly exploitative, the American distributor added about 10 minutes of raunchy hard-core footage of exotic dance routines. 87m/B VHS, DVD. AR Gloria Prat, Susan Beltran, Ricardo Bauleo, Aldo Barbero; D: Emilio Vieyra; W: Emilio Vieyra, Raul Zorrilla; C: Anibal Gonzalez Paz; M: Victor Buchino.

Curious George ✗✗½ 2006 (G) The cute, mischievous chimp and The Man in the Yellow Hat (Ferrell) take a pleasant trip to the big screen. The New York museum where TMitYH works is having financial trouble, so he ventures to Africa to find a lost idol that will bring in the crowds. Along the way he meets George, who has been having fun with his jungle playmates. George takes a liking to The Man after a game of peek-a-boo and manages to follow him back to NYC. George's playful and curious nature gets The Man in trouble with the museum owner's son, who wants to close the museum and build a parking garage. The animation and story are simplistic, but that's just fine with the target audience of pre-schoolers and elementary-agers. The adults will find a few chuckle-worthy gags here and there, as well. 86m/C DVD. US D: Matthew O'Callaghan; W: Ken Kaufman; C: Julie Rogers; M: Heitor Pereira; V: Will Ferrell, Drew Barrymore, David Cross, Eugene Levy, Dick Van Dyke, Frank Welker, Joan Plowright, Clint Howard, Ed O'Ross.

Curley ✗✗ 1947 High-spirited youngsters play pranks on their schoolteacher. A part of the Hal Roach Comedy Carnival. 53m/C VHS. Larry Olsen, Frances Rafferty, Eilene Janssen, Walter Abel; D: Bernard Carr.

Curly Sue ✗✗½ 1991 (PG) Adorable, homeless waif Porter and her scheming, adoptive father Belushi plot to rip off single, career-minded female attorney Lynch in order to take in some extra cash. Trouble is, all three heartstrings are tugged, and the trio develop a warm, caring relationship. A throwback to the Depression era's Shirley Temple formula films met with mixed reviews. Undiscriminating younger audiences should have a good time, though. 102m/C VHS, DVD. James Belushi, Kelly Lynch, Alison Porter, John Getz, Fred Dalton Thompson; D: John Hughes; W: John Hughes; M: Georges Delerue.

Curly Top ✗✗½ 1935 (G) Orphan Temple finds a husband for her beautiful sister. Along the way, she sings "Animal Crackers in My Soup." Remake of the silent "Daddy Long Legs," which was remade again in 1955. 74m/B VHS, DVD. Shirley Temple, John Boles, Rochelle Hudson, Jane Darwell, Esther Dale, Arthur Treacher, Rafaela (Rafael, Raphaella) Ottiano; D: Irving Cummings.

The Curse ✗ The Farm 1987 (R) After a meteorite lands near a small farming community and contaminates the area, a young boy tries to prevent residents from turning into slime-oozing mutants. Remake of "Die, Monster, Die." 92m/C VHS. Wil Wheaton, Claude Akins, Malcolm Danare, Cooper Huckabee, John Schneider, David Keith, Amy Wheaton, David Chaskin, Kathleen Jordan Gregory; D: David Keith; W: David Chaskin; C: Robert D. Forges.

Curse 2: The Bite ✗ 1988 (R) Radiation affected snakes are transformed into deadly vipers whose bites change their unsuspecting victims into horrible creatures. 97m/C VHS. Jill Schoelen, J. Eddie Peck, Jamie Farr, Savina Gersak, Bo Svenson, Sydney Lassick, Marianne Muellerleile, Terrence Evans; D: Fred Goodwin; W: Fred Goodwin, Susan Zelouf; C: Roberto D'Ettorre Piazzoli.

Curse 3: Blood Sacrifice ✗½ Panga 1990 (R) An African sugar cane plantation becomes host to a horrible nightmare when a voodoo curse is placed on the owners. The monstrous God of the Sea is summoned to avenge the accidental death of a baby, and the hellish journey into insanity begins. 91m/C VHS. Christopher Lee, Jenilee Harrison, Henry Cele; D: Sean Barton.

Curse 4: The Ultimate Sacrifice ✗½ Catacombs 1990 (R) Beneath the monastery at San Pietro lies buried the beast of the Apocalypse. For 400 years the secret has been kept and then an American priest and a lovely school teacher unwittingly break the seal and unleash the cursed beast upon an unsuspecting world. 84m/C VHS. Timothy Van Patten, Laura Schaefer, Jeremy West, Ian Abercrombie; D: David Schmoeller.

The Curse of Frankenstein ✗✗½ 1957 Young Victor Frankenstein reenacts his father's experiments with creating life from the dead resulting in a terrifying, hideous creature. The first in Hammer's Frankenstein series and followed by "Revenge of Frankenstein." From the "Shelley story. Make-up by Jack Pierce, who also created the famous make-up for Universal's Frankenstein monster. 83m/C VHS, DVD. GB Peter Cushing, Christopher Lee, Hazel Court, Robert Urquhart, Valerie Gaunt, Noel Hood; D: Terence Fisher; W: Jimmy Sangster; C: Jack Asher; M: James Bernard.

The Curse of Inferno ✗½ 1996 (R) Dumb-as-posts bankrobbers Shore and Perlich get mixed up in a sting operation to flush out the head of a money-laundering operation. 87m/C VHS. Pauly Shore, Max Perlich, Janine Turner, Ned Beatty, John Pleshette, Stephen Tobolowsky, Edward "Blue" Deckert; D: John Warren; W: John Warren; C: Nancy Schreiber.

The Curse of King Tut's Tomb ✗½ 1980 In 1922, archaeologists have just opened Tutankhamen's tomb. The curse of the boy king is unleashed as tragic events bring the adventurers uncommon gloom. Oh boy. 98m/C VHS. Robin Ellis, Harry Andrews, Eva Marie Saint, Raymond Burr, Wendy Hiller; D: Philip Leacock; Nar: Paul Scofield. TV

Curse of Nostradamus ✗✗ The Monster Demolisher; Genie of Darkness 1960 The descendent of Nostradamus is a vampire, thus causing havoc for many townsfolk. Edited from a Mexican serial. 77m/B VHS, DVD. MX German Robles; D: Frederick Curiel.

The Curse of the Aztec Mummy WOOF! La Maldicion de la Momia Azteca 1959 A mad scientist schemes to rob a Mayan pyramid of its treasure but the resident mummy will have none of it. Sequels are "Robot vs. the Aztec Mummy" and "Wrestling Women vs. the Aztec Mummy." 65m/B VHS, DVD. MX Ramon Gay, Rosita (Rosa) Arenas, Crox Alvarado; D: Rafael Portillo.

Curse of the Black Widow ✗✗ Love Trap 1977 An investigator follows a trail of brutal murders to the lair of a supernatural gigantic spider in the middle of Los Angeles. 100m/C VHS. Patty Duke, Anthony (Tony) Franciosa, Donna Mills, June Lockhart, Sid Caesar, Vic Morrow, June Allyson, Roz Kelly, Jeff Corey; D: Dan Curtis. TV

Curse of the Blue Lights WOOF! 1988 (R) Mysterious lights begin appearing at the local romantic spot. Little do the young lovers know, it hails the arrival of a ghoul, intent on raising the dead. Also available in a colorized version. 70m/B VHS, DVD. Brent Ritter, Bettina Julius, Kent E. Fritzell, Willard Hall; D: John H. Johnson; W: John H. Johnson.

Curse of the Cat People ✗✗✗ 1944 A young sensitive girl is guided by the vision of her dead mother. Sequel to "Cat People." Available on laserdisc. 70m/B VHS, DVD. Simone Simon, Kent Smith, Jane Randolph, Elizabeth Russell, Ann Carter; D: Robert Wise, Gunther Von Fritsch.

The Curse of the Crying Woman ✗½ La Maldicion de la Llorona; La Casa Embrujada 1961 Unknowing descendant of a witch is lured to her aunt's home to perform the act that will revive the monstrous crying woman and renew a reign of evil. 74m/B VHS. AR Rosita (Rosa) Arenas, Abel Salazar, Rita Macedo; D: Rafael Baledon Sr.; W: Rafael Baledon Sr., Fernando Galiana; C: Jose Ortiz Ramos.

Curse of the Crystal Eye ✗✗ 1993 (PG-13) A gunrunner tries to get the treasure of Ali Baba aided by the requisite lovely lady and opposed by your usual bad guys. 90m/C VHS. Jameson Parker, Cynthia Rhodes, Mike Lane, David Sherwood, Andre Jacobs; D: Joe Tornatore.

Curse of the Demon ✗✗✗½ Night of the Demon; The Haunted 1957 A famous psychologist investigates a colleague's mysterious death and enters a world of demonology and the occult, climaxing in a confrontation with a cult's patron demon. Superb thriller based upon the story "Casting the Runes" by M.R. James. 81m/B VHS, DVD. GB Dana Andrews, Peggy Cummins, Niall MacGinnis, Maurice Denham, Athene Seyler, Liam Redmond, Reginald Beckwith, Ewan Roberts, Peter Elliott, Brian Wilde, Rosamund Greenwood; D: Jacques Tourneur; W: Charles Bennett, Hal E. Chester; C: Edward Scaife; M: Clifton Parker.

Curse of the Devil ✗½ El Retorno de la Walpurgis 1973 (R) This time Naschy is turned into a werewolf by annoyed gypsies whose ancestors were slain by his. 73m/C VHS, DVD. MX SP Paul Naschy, Maria Silva, Patty (Patti) Shepard, Fay Falcon, Fabiola Falva, Mariano Vidal Molina, Ines Morales; D: Carlos Aured; W: Paul Naschy; C: Francisco Sanchez.

Curse of the Golden Flower ✗✗ Man Cheng Jin Dai Huang Jin Jia 2006 (R) Zhang's tale, set in the 10th-century Tang Dynasty, is a sumptuous, convoluted saga of family mayhem. The Emperor (Chow) has returned home from a long battle, just before the annual chrysanthemum festival (the flower of the title). The emperor is having the royal doctor poison his unloved empress (Gong), who is having an affair with Crown Prince Wan, her stepson, who is actually in love with the doctor's daughter, Chan. The doctor's wife warns the empress about the poison; she turns out to be the emperor's ex-wife, and the mother of Wan (who thought she was dead) and Chan. There's some martial arts stuff between the imperial factions and it's all very operatic, including the elaborate corseted, bosom-lifting costumes the empress wears. Mandarin with subtitles. 114m/C DVD, Blu-ray Disc. CH Gong Li, Liu Ye, Chow Yun-Fat, Jay Chou, Qin Junjie, Man Li, Ni Dahong, Chen Jin; D: Yimou Zhang; W: Yimou Zhang, Wu Nan, Bian Zhihong; C: Xiaoding Zhao; M: Shingeru Umebayashi.

Curse of the Headless Horseman 1972 The headless horseman rides again, bringing terror to all who cross his path! 80m/C VHS, DVD. Don Carrara, Claudia Dean, B.G. Fisher, Margo Dean, Lee Byers, Joe Cody; D: John Kirkland.

The Curse of the Jade Scorpion ✗✗½ 2001 (PG-13) Where can a 65-year-old guy with looks like Woody Allen bag a babe like Helen Hunt? In a Woody Allen movie, that's where. Hunt plays efficiency expert Betty Ann Fitzgerald, who's hired to update the offices of a Manhattan insurance agency where C.W. Briggs (Allen) is the chief investigator, so he and "Fitz" develop an immediate mutual dislike. After several increasingly tedious games of verbal darts, the two are mesmerized by nightclub hypnotist Voltan (Stiers) into believing that they're in love. He also uses hypnotic cues to have C.W. unknowingly pull off jewel heists of his own clients. After a mystery woman (Theron) shows up, C.W. begins to question where he's been and who he's been with late at night and enlists the help of the Coopersmith Brothers (Mulheren and Linari) to help crack the case. Lighter and shallower than most of Allen's work, it's still mostly fun to watch. Soundtrack is chock full of Allen's beloved 40s era jazz and Big Band tunes. 103m/C VHS, DVD. US Woody Allen, Helen Hunt, Dan Aykroyd, Elizabeth Berkley, Charlize Theron, Wallace Shawn, David Ogden Stiers, John Schuck, Brian Markinson, Michael Mulheren, Peter Linari, Prof. Irwin Corey, Peter Gerety; D: Woody Allen; W: Woody Allen; C: Fei Zhao.

Curse of the Living Corpse ✗ 1964 A millionaire comes back to rotting life to kill his negligent relatives. Schneider's first film. 84m/C VHS, DVD. Candace Hilligoss, Roy Scheider, Helen Warren, Margot Hartman; D: Del Tenney.

Curse of the Pink Panther ✗✗ 1983 (PG) Clifton Sleigh, an inept New York City detective played by Wass, is assigned to find the missing Inspector Clouseau. His efforts are complicated by an assortment of gangsters and aristocrats who cross paths with the detective. So-so attempt to keep popular series going after Seller's death. Niven's last film. 110m/C VHS, DVD. Ed Parker, Ted Wass, David Niven, Robert Wagner, Herbert Lom, Joanna Lumley, Capucine, Robert Loggia, Harvey Korman, Leslie Ash, Denise Crosby; D: Blake Edwards; W: Blake Edwards; C: Dick Bush; M: Henry Mancini.

Curse of the Puppet Master: The Human Experiment ✗½ 1998 (R) The little guys have been taking a break since 1994's "Puppet Master 5" but they're baaaack. This time they're trying to prevent their new master, evil Dr. Magrew, from transforming more victims into living dolls. The director, "Victoria Sloan," is actually DeCoteau. 90m/C VHS, DVD. George Peck, Emily Harrison, Michael Guerin, Robert Donovan; D: David DeCoteau; W: Benjamin Carr; C: Howard Wexler; M: Richard Band. VIDEO

Curse of the Queerwolf ✗✗ 1987 A man is bitten on the butt by gay werewolf and transforms into the title character. Filmed in Santa Barbara in 8mm; some funny moments. From the director of "A Polish Vampire in Burbank." 90m/C VHS, DVD. Michael Palazzolo, Kent Butler, Taylor Whitney, Danwyn Carson, Sergio Bandera, Mark Pirro, Forrest J Ackerman, Conrad Brooks; D: Mark Pirro; W: Mark Pirro; M: Gregg Gross.

Curse of the Starving Class ✗✗ 1994 (R) Ineffective adaptation of Sam Shepard's 1977 play exploring family disintegration. Weston (Woods) is the alcoholic, irresponsible patriarch of a decaying farm. His unhappy wife, Ella (Bates), wants to sell out to land speculator Taylor (Quaid) and move to Paris while rebellious teenager Emma (Fiorella) plans to run off to Mexico and sullen older brother Wesley (Thomas) desires to stay and make a go of things. One-dimensional characterizations don't translate well from stage to screen. 102m/C VHS. James Woods, Kathy Bates, Henry Thomas, Kristin Fiorella, Randy Quaid, Louis Gossett Jr.; D: Michael McClary; W: Bruce Beresford; C: Dick Quinlan.

Curse of the Stone Hand WOOF! 1964 A pair of stone hands causes folks to do suicidal things. A mutation of a Mexican and a Chilean horror film, each purchased and monster-mashed into one by Warren. 72m/B VHS. MX John Carradine, Ernest Walch, Sheila Bon, Katherine Victor, Lloyd Nelson; D: Jerry Warren.

Curse of the Swamp Creature ✗ 1966 A mad scientist in the Everglades attempts to create half human/half alligator monsters. In turn, a geologic expeditionary force attempts to stop his experimentation. Low budget thrills courtesy of Larry Buchanan. 80m/C VHS, DVD. John Agar, Francine York, Shirley McLine, Bill (Billy) Thurman, Jeff Alexander; D: Larry Buchanan.

Curse of the Undead ✗✗½ 1966 A western finds a small town suffering from the deaths of several young women—all with small wounds in the neck. Suspicions fall on gunslinger Drake Robey (Pate) and it's up to preacher Dan Young (Fleming) to take care of the blood-sucking miscreant. 89m/B VHS. Eric Fleming, Michael Pate, Kathleen Crowley, John Hoyt, Bruce Gordon, Edward Binns, Jimmy Murphy, Jay Adler; D: Edward Dein; W: Edward Dein, Mildred Dein; C: Ellis W. Carter; M: Irving Gertz.

The Curse of the Werewolf ✗✗½ Alfairs of the Vampire; Mark of the West; Mark of the Beast; The Invisible Killer; Le Teur Invisible; Les Griffes du Vampire 1959 Mediocre vampire western finds a small 1961 Horror film about a 19th-century European werewolf that is renowned for its ferocious departure from the stereotypical portrait of the beast. **91m/C VHS, DVD, GB** Oliver Reed, Clifford Evans, Yvonne Romain, Catherine Feller, Anthony Dawson; Michael Ripper, Peter Sallis; An: (Batinkoff), and Chris (Vartan) learn that student myth is true at their small university. Should a roomie commit suicide, the survivors receive an automatic 4.0 for the semester. So Tim offs Rand and has Chris help him cover things up. Naturally this doesn't work out entirely as expected. Not nearly as clever as it tries to be. **90m/C VHS, DVD**, Matthew Lillard, Michael Vartan, Randall Batinkoff, Ken Russell, Dana Delany, Tamara Craig Thomas, Anthony Griffin, Bo Dietla, Kevin Huff, Henry Strozier; **D:** Dan Rosen; **W:** Dan Rosen; **C:** Joey Forsyte.

Curse of the Yellow Snake 🐍🐍 1963 Voluminous yarn features a running battle over an ancient Chinese artifact, with crazed Chinese cultists running through foggy London streets. **98m/C VHS, GE** Joachim Fuchsberger, Werner Peters; **D:** Franz Gottlieb.

The Cursed Mountain 🐍🐍 1993 (R) Two petty thieves steal a legendary precious gem rumored to cursed. The immortal warrior by the ghosts of bickering theatrical marrieds Max (Caine) and Lily (Smith). Unfortunately for him, Stevenson is the only one who can see the duo, so his girlfriend Julia (Walken) thinks he's nuts. She has a problem with her commitment-phobe beau anyway and it's up to Max and Lily to see the duo stay together. **94m/C VHS, DVD**, James Garner, Polly Walker, Michael Caine, Maggie Smith, Buck Henry, Sam Shepard, Todd Alcott; Susan Berman, Marcia Gay Harden, Valerie Perrine, Frances Sternhagen, Frank Whaley; **D:** Peter Yates; **W:** Todd Alcott. **C:** Sven Nykvist; **M:** Richard Hartley. **VIDEO**

Curtis's Charm 🐍 1996 Thanks to his drug paranoia, crack addict Curtis (Wint) believes his wife Cookie (Crawford) and mother-in-law (Barnes-Hopkins) have put a voodoo spell on him. His friend Jim (Callum Rennie), a former addict, tries to help Curtis by coming up with some magic of his own, intended to convince the addled druggie that it will protect him. Lots of wonder why director Richard C. Lupka hides behind pseudonym Stryker. Based on a short story by Jim Carroll. **90m/C VHS, CA** John Vernon, Samantha Eggar; **D:** Jonathan Stryker; **W:** Robert Guza Jr.

Curtains woof! 1933 (R) Director has a clash of wills with a film star that spells "Curtains" for a group of aspiring actresses gathered together at a haunted house for an audition. Hamfest with no thrills, chills, gore, or gratuitous skin. No narration does little to make the character's friendship convincing. **74m/B VHS, CA** Maurice Dean Wint, Callum Keith Rennie, Rachael Crawford, Barbara Barnes-Hopkins; **D:** John L'Ecuyer; **W:** James Dennis (Jim) Carroll, John L'Ecuyer; **C:** Harald Bachmann; **M:** Mark Korven. Genie '96: Score.

The Curve 🐍🐍 *Dead Man's Curve* 1997 (R) Think "Dead Man on Campus" since you've got basically the same premise. College roomies Tim (Lillard), Rand

Cured 🐍🐍 2004 (PG-13) Writer Wil-liamson and director Craven were much more successful with their "Scream" franchise than with this obvious werewolf horror. Los Angeleno Ellie (Ricci) and her geeky brother Jimmy (Eisenberg) encounter a nasty beastie after a car accident. They get bitten and start developing were-wolf-like tendencies. Ellie doesn't want to accept the truth as her girlfriend dies becoming beastie fodder. Rick Baker did better (when he doesn't know what else to do) but Davis' exuberance for her pirate creation of the original production pamphlet. **50m/B VHS. D:** Francis Ford.

Custer's Last Fight 🐍🐍 1912 Contains the earliest surviving film of Custer's last stand. This 1925 re-release version of the original 1912 Thomas Ince production, filmed on location at the original battlefield, hosts a cast of real American Indians who claim to have taken part in the actual battle. Provides an authentic recreation of the original battle. Comes with a copy of the original production pamphlet.

Custer's Last Stand 🐍1/2 1936 Feature-length version of the Mascot serial recounting the last days of the famous General. **70m/B VHS, DVD,** Frank McGlynn, Rex Lease, Nancy Caseell, Lona Andre, William Farnum, Reed Howes, Jack Mulhall, Jose Swickard, Ruth Mix; **D:** Elmer Clifton.

The Custodian 🐍🐍 1994 (R) Honest cop must battle corruption of Australian police precinct while dealing with numerous personal problems. Good cast goes a long way in routine story. **110m/C VHS, AU** Anthony LaPaglia, Hugo Weaving, Barry Otto, Bill Hunter, Kelly Dingwall, Gosia Dobrowolska; **D:** John Dingwall.

Cut 🐍🐍 2000 (R) In this instance the title can be taken literally since a killer is knocking off those involved in a low-budget horror film. It seems that a group of film students want to finish a film that was shut down 15 years earlier after it's female director (Minogue) was murdered on the set. The students manage to get Vanessa (Ringwald), the star of the original, to re-prise her role but is the film cursed or is someone giving their efforts a critical thumbs down? **82m/C VHS, DVD, AU** Molly Ringwald, Jessica Napier, Simon Bossell, Sarah Kants, Stephen Curry, Geoff Revell, Frank Roberts, Sam Lewis; **Cameos:** Kylie Minogue; **D:** Kimble Rendall; **W:** Dave Warner; **C:** David Foreman; **M:** Guy Gross. **VIDEO**

Cut and Run 🐍 *Inferno in Diretta; Straight 'o Hell* 1985 (R) Two journalists follow a lead to the former South American home of Jim Jones, and are instantly captured by local guerrillas. **91m/C VHS, DVD,** /f Lisa Blount, Leonard Mann, Willie Aames, Richard Lynch, Michael Berryman, Karen Black, Eriq La Salle; **D:** Ruggero Deodato; **W:** Cesare Frugoni; **C:** Alberto Spagnoli; **M:** Claudio Simonetti.

The Cut Throats 🐍 *She Devils of the S.S* 1969 (R) Americans stumble upon an isolated Nazi outpost stocked with gold and beautiful women. Exploitation at its worst. **80m/C VHS,** Jay Scott, Joanne Douglas, Jeff Letham, Pat Michaels, Barbara Lane; **D:** John Hayes; **W:** John Hayes.

Cutaway 🐍🐍 2000 (R) Vic Cooper (Baldwin) is a customs agent who goes under-cover to infiltrate a group of drug dealers who deliver their goods via skydiving. He discovers the sport gives him a bigger adrenaline rush than his job, so which one will he choose? **104m/C VHS,** DVD, Tom Berenger, Stephen Baldwin, Dennis Rodman, Maxine Bahns, Casper Van Dien, Ron Silver; **D:** Guy Manos; **W:** Guy Manos, Greg Manos; **C:** Gerry Lively. **VIDEO**

Cutter's Way 🐍🐍1/2 *Cutter and Bone* 1981 (R) An embittered and alcoholic disabled Vietnam vet and his small-time crook/gigolo friend wrestle with justice and morality when the drifter uncovers a murder. An unusually cynical mystery from the novel by Newton Thorburg. **105m/C VHS, DVD,** Jeff Bridges, John Heard, Lisa Eichhorn, Ann Dusenberry, Stephen Elliott, Nina Van Pallandt, George

---

Dickerson; **D:** Ivan Passer; **W:** Jeffrey Alladin Fiskin; **C:** Jordan Cronenweth; **M:** Jack Nitzsche.

Cutthroat Island 🐍🐍1/2 1995 (PG-13) Big-budget swashbuckling adventure—long on action and short on plot and character. Female pirate captain Morgan Adams (Davis) is left part of a treasure map by her father and "persuades" educated slave/thief William Shaw (Modine), who has lots of charm and no morals, to assist her. Her scurvy Uncle Dawg (despicably well-played by Langella) also has a portion of the map and is willing to let Morgan find the treasure—on Cutthroat Island—before taking it for himself. Directors Harlin likes lots of big, noisy explosions but Davis' exuberance for her pirate queen role is appealing. **123m/C VHS, DVD,** Geena Davis, Matthew Modine, Frank Langella, Patrick Malahide, Stan Shaw, Maury Chaykin, Harris Yulin, Roger Murcell; **D:** Renny Harlin; **W:** Robert King, Marc Norman; **C:** Peter Levy; **M:** John Debney.

Cutting Class 🐍🐍 1989 (R) Murders proliferate in a high school, where a student with a history of mental illness is number one on the suspect list. Tongue-in-cheek mayhem. **91m/C VHS, DVD,** Roddy McDowall, Donovan Leitch, Martin Mull, Brad Pitt; **D:** Rospo Pallenberg.

The Cutting Edge 🐍🐍1/2 1992 Spoiled figure skater's lifelong quest for Olympic gold is seriously hampered by her inability to snag the medal she teams up with a cocky guy who thinks the only sport on ice is hockey, but whose own dreams of NHL stardom were cut short by an injury. Saddled with a predictable and thin plot, it sometimes looks and feels like a TV movie. So why bother? Because the chemistry between photogenic leads Kelly and Sweeney is terrific. Add half a bone for the flying sparks and snappy dialogue. Sit back, and enjoy. **101m/C VHS, DVD,** D.B. Sweeney, Moira Kelly, Roy Dotrice, Terry O'Quinn, Dwier Brown, Rachelle Ottley, Jo Jo Starbuck; **D:** Paul Michael Glaser; **W:** Tony Gilroy; **C:** Elliot Davis; **M:** Patrick Williams.

The Cutting Edge: Going for the Gold 🐍1/2 2005 (PG-13) Kate (Kramer) and Doug (Thompson) got married and their bratty girl Jackie (Romano) is now a teenager following in their skate tracks as a promising figure skater who decided to skip it. **99m/C VHS, DVD,** Christy Carlson Romano, Ross Thomas, Scott Thompson Baker, Stephane Kramer, Kim Kindrick; **D:** Sean McNamara; **W:** Tony Gilroy, Daniel Berendsen. **VIDEO**

Cyber Bandits 🐍1/2 1994 (R) In a future society, navigator Jack Morris (Kemp) has just sailed a pleasure craft to the island city of Pacifica. His passengers included wealthy Morgan Wells (Hays), whose scientists have developed a deadly virtual reality weapon, and Wells' mistress Rebecca (Paul). Rebecca steals the plans for the weapon and seduces Jack into having the data digitally transferred onto his back in the form of a tattoo. Then Rebecca disappears and Jack finds himself in big trouble. **86m/C VHS, DVD,** Martin Kemp, Alexandra Paul, Robert Hays, Adam Ant, Grace Jones; **D:** Erik Fleming; **W:** James Robinson, Winston Beard; **M:** Steve Hunter.

Cyber Ninja 🐍🐍1/2 *Mirai Ninja; Future Ninja; Robo Ninja* 1994 Warrior princess Saki is captured by the Dark Overlord, who plans to sacrifice her. It's up to a mercenary to come to her rescue. Lightweight, action-oriented Japanese mix of samurai and science fiction. Dubbed. **80m/C VHS, JF** Hanbei Kawai, Hiroki Ida; **D:** Keito Amamiya; **W:** Keito Amamiya.

Cyber-Tracker 🐍 1993 (R) In the judicial system of the future androids hunt down vicious criminals and execute them immediately. When secret service agent Eric Phillips is framed for murder, he's

---

also marked for death. His only chance is to link up with rebels fighting the mechanized monsters. **91m/C VHS, DVD, Don** "The Dragon" Wilson, Richard Norton, Joseph Ruskin, Abby Dalton, John Aprea; **D:** Richard Pepin; **W:** Jacobsen Hart; **C:** Ken Blakey; **M:** Bill Montei, Lisa Pepei.

Cyber-Tracker 2 🐍🐍 1995 (R) An international weapons dealer has gotten control of the cybertracker technology and created cyborg lookalikes of secret agent Eric Phillips (Wilson) and his newscaster wife Connie (Foster). When the cyborgs commit murder on live TV the human duo become fugitives who must expose the real killers. **97m/C VHS, DVD, Don** "The Dragon" Wilson, Stacie Foster, Steve (Stephen) Burton; **D:** Richard Pepin; **W:** Richard Preston Jr.

Cybercity 🐍🐍1/2 1999 (R) When mercenary Howell's family is murdered by virtual prophet Piper, who's trying to take over the world, Howell tries for revenge with the aid of assassin von Palleske. **86m/C VHS, DVD, C:** Thomas Howell, Roddy Piper, Heidi von Palleske, David Carradine; **D:** Peter Hay-man; **W:** Nehu Ghiran; **C:** Graeme Means; **M:** Don ad Quan. **VIDEO**

Cybermutt 🐍🐍 *Rex: Le cyber chien* 2002 (PG) Eccentric scientist Nelson implants a computer chip into the dog that saved him from a car accident. The chip enables the dog to communicate with other computers and draws the attention of techno-spies who naturally want to use the bionic pup for their own nefarious purposes. Of course a boy who has befriended the dog is imperiled long the way. Adults won't find much worth sitting through, but kids will enjoy the feats of this canine star. **86m/C VHS, DVD, CA** Judd Nelson, Michelle Nolden, Ryan Cooley, Paulina Malecki, Tonio Arango; **D:** George Miller; **W:** Kevin Commins, Gerald Santoff; **C:** Gerald R. Goozie, TV

Cyberstalker 🐍1/2 *The Digital Prophet* 1996 Detective twosome must track down a serial killer who uses the Internet to stalk his victims. **96m/C VHS, DVD,** Blake Bahner, Jeffrey Combs, Annie Biggs, Schnele Wilson; **D:** Christopher Romero; **W:** Tony Brownrigg, Annie Biggs.

Cyberzone 🐍1/2 *Droid Gunner* 1995 (R) Intergalactic investigator pursues four dangerous androids who are hiding on earth. **95m/C VHS,** Marc Singer, Matthias Hues, Rochelle Swanson, Robin Clarke, Kin Shriner, Brinke Stevens; **D:** Fred Oen Ray; **W:** William Mertel.

Cyborg 🐍 1989 (R) In a deathly, dirty, post-holocaust urban world, an able cyborg battles a horde of evil mutant thugs. Poorly made action flick. **85m/C VHS, DVD,** Jean-Claude Van Damme, Deborah Richter, Vincent Klyn, Dayle Haddon, Alex Daniels, Terrie Batson, Janice Graser, Jackson "Rock" Pinckney; **D:** Albert Pyun; **W:** Kitty Chalmers; **C:** Philip Alan Waters; **M:** Kevin Bassinson.

Cyborg 2 🐍🐍 *Cyborg 2: Glass Shadow* 1993 (R) In the year 2074 cyborgs have replaced humans at all levels. A devious company which manufactures cyborgs decides to get rid of its chief competition by literally killing them off. They plan to inject cyborg Cash Reese (Jolie) with a liquid explosive that will detonate her and everything else in sight. Tech-master Mercy (Palance) clues Cash in and she escapes with the help of the human Colton (Koteas) but they've become prey to a group of ruthless hunters. **99m/C VHS, DVD,** Angelina Jolie, Elias Koteas, Jack Palance, Billy Drago; **D:** Michael Schroeder; **W:** Michael Schroeder, Ron Yanover; **C:** Jamie Thompson; **M:** Peter Allen.

Cyborg Cop 🐍🐍 1993 (R) DEA agent Phillip (Jenson) is captured during a foreign drug raid and is turned into a half-man, half-machine by mad scientist Kessel (Rhys-Davies), who wants to sell his brother Jack (Bradley) tries to come to his rescue. Lots of stunts and car chases and

---

VideoHound's Golden Movie Retriever | 239

Cyborg

even a minor romantic subplot with Jack and a tough reporter (Shaw). **97m/C VHS**. David Bradley, John Rhys-Davies, Todd Jensen, Alonna Shaw; **D:** Sam Firstenberg; **W:** Glenn A. Bruce, Greg Latter; **C:** Yossi Wein.

Cyborg Soldier ♂♂½ *Cyborg Cop 2* 1994 (R) Loose cannon cop Jack Ryan (Bradley) is up against psycho killer Starkraven (Hunter) who gets turned into a new-model cyborg by your basic suspicious government agency. But when the cyborg decides to go on an unplanned human killing spree, Ryan gets to break out the heavy artillery to mow him down. Also available in an unrated version. **96m/C VHS**. David Bradley, Morgan Hunter, Jill Pierce; **D:** Sam Firstenberg; **W:** Jon Stevens.

Cycle Psycho WOOf! *Numbered Days; Savage Abduction* 1972 (R) Serial killer blackmails the businessman whose wife he was contracted to kill into bringing him young girls to slaughter. The businessman hires out the job to sleazy motorcycle gang. **80m/C VHS**. Joe Turkel, Tom Drake, Stephen Oliver; **D:** John Lawrence; **W:** John Lawrence.

Cycle Vixens WOOf! *The Young Cycle Girls* 1979 (R) Three girls jump on their hogs and head from Colorado to California. Much leather, motor revving and other obligatory motorcycle-trash trimmings. **90m/C VHS**. Loraine Ferris, Daphne Lawrence, Deborah Marcus, Lonnie Pense, Kevin O'Neill, Bee Lechat, Billy Bullet; **D:** Peter Perry.

Cyclo ♂♂ *Xich Lo* 1995 An orphaned 18-year-old (Van Loc), known only by by his profession of cyclo (pedal-taxi) driver, struggles on the streets of Ho Chi Minh City. When his vehicle is stolen, he's forced by his boss to repay its value and takes small-time jobs from local crime boss, The Poet (Leung), who, unbeknownst to the cyclo, is also his sister's (Yen-Khe) pimp. The deeper the young man gets into the criminal world, the closer he also gets to tragedy. Vietnamese with subtitles. **123m/C VHS, DVD**. *VT* Le Van Loc, Tran Nu Yen-Khe, Tony Leung Chiu-Wai, Nguyen Nhu Quynh; **D:** Tran Anh Hung; **W:** Tran Anh Hung; **C:** Benoit Delhomme; **M:** Ton That Tiet.

Cyclone ♂♂ 1987 (R) The girlfriend of a murdered scientist must deliver a secretly devised motorcycle into righteous government hands, much to the dismay of evil agents and corrupt officials. Good fun, sparked by a stellar "B" cast. **89m/C VHS, DVD**. Heather Thomas, Jeffrey Combs, Ashley Ferrare, Dar Robinson, Martine Beswick, Robert Quarry, Martin Landau, Huntz Hall, Troy Donahue, Michael Reagan, Dawn Wildsmith, Bruce Fairbairn, Russ Tamblyn; **D:** Fred Olen Ray; **C:** Paul Elliott.

Cyclone Cavalier 1925 A dauntless hero travels through Central America on an adventurous ride. **58m/B VHS**. Carmelita Geraghty, Wilfrid Lucas, Jack Mower, Eric Mayne, Reed Howes; **D:** Albert Rogell; **W:** Burke Jenkins, Krag Johnson; **C:** H. Lyman Broening.

Cyclone of the Saddle ♂ 1935 Typical Western about a range war. **53m/B VHS**. Rex Lease, Bobby Nelson, William Desmond, Yakima Canutt; **D:** Elmer Clifton.

Cyclops ♂ 1956 When an expedition party searches throughout Mexico for a woman's long lost fiance, they are shocked when they find out that radiation has turned him into a one-eyed monster. **72m/B VHS, DVD**. Tom Drake, Gloria Talbott, Lon Chaney Jr., James Craig; **D:** Bert I. Gordon.

Cyclotrode "X" ♂½ *The Crimson Ghost* 1946 The Crimson Ghost attempts to kidnap the inventor of the title machine, which would enable him to rule the world. Moore (The Lone Ranger) plays a bad guy, and it's also his sister's. Serial in 12 episodes. Also available in a 93-minute colorized edition. **100m/B VHS**. Charles Quigley, Linda Stirling, I. Stanford Jolley, Clayton Moore, Kenne Duncan; **D:** William Witney, Fred Brannon; **W:** Albert DeMond.

Cypher ♂♂♂ 2002 (R) Somewhat convoluted but intriguing sci-fi thriller. Milquetoast businessman Morgan Sullivan (Northam) hopes for a more exciting life when he applies for a job at multinational Digicorp. He's put to work as a corporate spy under the alias Jack Thursby and sent to a number of conventions to record the speeches that are made. Morgan/Jack doesn't understand the purpose of this un-

til he meets mystery femme Rita (Liu), who informs Morgan that he has been brainwashed. She convinces him to turn double-agent and work for rival Sunway Systems but this only makes his life more confusing until a final assignment and a shocking revelation. **96m/C DVD**. Jeremy Northam, Lucy Liu, Nigel Bennett, Timothy Webber, David Hewlett, Kari Matchett; **D:** Vincenzo Natali; **W:** Brian King; **C:** Derek Rogers; **M:** Michael Andrews.

Cypress Edge ♂♂½ 1999 (R) The murder of Louisiana Senator Woodrow McCammon's (Steiger) daughter brings her estranged family back together. The motive is clear—an $18 million estate—and the benefactors are the usual suspects. **90m/C VHS, DVD**. Rod Steiger, Damian Chapa, Brad Dourif, Ashley Laurence, Charles Napier; **D:** Serge Rodnunsky; **W:** Serge Rodnunsky; **M:** Carl Dante.

Cyrano de Bergerac ♂♂♂ 1925 Silent version of Edmond Rostand's novel about romantic Cyrano who fears to reveal his love to Roxanne because he feels his enormous nose makes him unattractive. So, he serves as a surrogate lover by encouraging another man's attention to her and a secret that has been protected by the Catholic Church. Color-tinted. **114m/C VHS, DVD**. *IT* Pierre Magnier, Linda Moglia, Angelo Ferrari; **D:** Augusto Genina; **M:** Carlo Moser.

Cyrano de Bergerac ♂♂♂ 1950 Edmund Rostand's famous story of a large-nosed yet poetic cavalier, who finds himself too ugly to be loved. He bears the pain of his devotion to Roxanne from afar, and helps the handsome but tongue-tied Christian to romance her. Ferrer became famous for this role, which won him an Oscar. Based on Brian Hooke's translation of the play. Also available colorized. **113m/B VHS, DVD**. Jose Ferrer, Mala Powers, William Prince, Elena Verdugo, Morris Carnovsky; **C:** Carl Foreman; **C:** Franz Planer; **M:** Dimitri Tiomkin. Oscars '50: Actor (Ferrer); Golden Globes '51: Actor—Drama (Ferrer).

Cyrano de Bergerac ♂♂♂½ 1985 Edmund Rostand's gallant poet and swordsman, with the extraordinary nose, is well-portrayed by Jacobi in this Royal Shakespeare Company production. Translated and adapted by Anthony Burgess. **177m/C VHS**. *GB* Derek Jacobi, Sinead Cusack; **D:** Michael A. Simpson, Terry Hands; **W:** Anthony Burgess.

Cyrano de Bergerac ♂♂♂ 1990 (PG) Depardieu brings to exhilarating life Rostand's well-loved play about the brilliant but grotesque-looking swordsman/poet, afraid of nothing—except declaring his love to the beautiful Roxanne (Brochet). But Cyrano expresses his own feelings by helping handsome (but tongue-tied) fellow soldier Christian (Perez) woo Roxanne instead. One of France's costliest modern productions, a multi-award winner for its cast, costumes, music and sets. English subtitles (by Anthony Burgess) are designed to capture the intricate rhymes of the original French dialogue. **135m/C VHS, DVD**. *FR* Gerard Depardieu, Jacques Weber, Anne Brochet, Vincent Perez, Roland Bertin, Josiane Stoleru, Philippe Volter, Philippe Morier-Genoud, Pierre Maguelon; **D:** Jean-Paul Rappeneau; **W:** Jean-Claude Carriere, Jean-Paul Rappeneau; **C:** Pierre Lhomme; **M:** Jean-Claude Petit. Oscars '90: Costume Des.; Cannes '90: Actor (Depardieu); Cesar '91: Actor (Depardieu), Art Dir./Set Dec., Cinematog., Costume Des., Director (Rappeneau), Film, Sound, Support. Actor (Weber), Score; Golden Globes '91: Foreign Film.

D-Day on Mars ♂ 1945 Alien invader the Purple Monster is bent on taking over Earth. Originally a 15-part Republic serial titled "The Purple Monster Strikes." **100m/B VHS**. Dennis Moore, Linda Stirling, Roy Barcroft, James Craven, Bud Geary, Mary Moore; **D:** Spencer Gordon Bennet, Fred Brannon.

D-Day, the Sixth of June ♂♂♂ *The Sixth of June* 1956 An American soldier has an affair with a Englishwoman weeks before D-Day, where he unhappily finds himself fighting side by side with her husband. Based on the novel by Lionel Shapiro. **106m/C VHS, DVD**. Richard Todd, Dana Wynter, Robert Taylor, Edmond O'Brien, John Williams, Jerry Paris, Richard Stapley; **D:** Henry Koster; **C:** Lee Garmes.

Da ♂♂ 1988 (PG) A middle-aged man returns to Ireland for his father's funeral. As he sorts out his father's belongings, his father returns as a ghostly presence to chat with him about life, death, and their own relationship. Based on the Hugh Leonard play with Hughes recreating his Tony-award winning role. **102m/C VHS**. Barnard Hughes, Martin Sheen, William Hickey, Hugh O'Conor; **D:** Matt Clark; **W:** Hugh Leonard; **M:** Elmer Bernstein.

Da Hip Hop Witch ♂ 2000 (R) Not so much a parody of "Blair Witch Project" as a collection of rap artists' unscripted monologues about a woman who is doing terrible things to them. It also marks the return to the screen of Vanilla Ice, last seen in the abominable "Cool As Ice." **93m/C VHS, DVD**. Stacii Jae Johnson, Dale Resteghini, Pras, Killah Priest, Spliff Star, Mobb Deep, Eminem, Rock, Colleen (Ann) Fitzpatrick; **D:** Dale Resteghini; **W:** Dale Resteghini.

The Da Vinci Code ♂♂♂ 2006 (PG-13) Dan Brown's controversial megabestseller hits the big screen with Howard and Hanks reuniting for their first feature since "Apollo 13." The murder of a Louvre curator leads to a conspiracy and a secret that has been protected by the Catholic Church since its beginnings. Cryptologist Sophie Neveu (Tautou) and Harvard symbiologist Robert Langdon (Hanks) team up to puzzle out the clues that are hidden in the works of Leonardo Da Vinci. Naturally, there are those who will protect the secret from being revealed at any cost. Solid performances by great cast generally overcomes Howard's faithful re-creation of the novel's talkiness, which doesn't always make for an abundance of thrills. **149m/C DVD**. *US* Tom Hanks, Audrey Tautou, Ian McKellen, Alfred Molina, Paul Bettany, Jean Reno, Jurgen Prochnow, Etienne Chicot, Jean-Pierre Marielle; **D:** Ron Howard; **W:** Akiva Goldsman; **C:** Salvatore Totino; **M:** Hans Zimmer.

Dad ♂♂½ 1989 (PG) Hoping to make up for lost time, a busy executive rushes home to take care of his father who has just had a heart attack. What could have easily become sappy is made bittersweet by the convincing performances of Lemmon and Danson. Based on the novel by William Wharton. **117m/C VHS, DVD**. Jack Lemmon, Ted Danson, Ethan Hawke, Olympia Dukakis, Kathy Baker, Chris Lemmon; **D:** Gary David Goldberg; **W:** Gary David Goldberg; **M:** James Horner.

Dad On the Run ♂♂ *Cours Toujours* 2000 In the summer of 1997, the Pope's visit to Paris has the city in an uproar, which makes things even more chaotic for new Jewish father Jonas (Sibony). Custom demands that after their son's bris, Jonas bury the foreskin within three days. He suffers a series of complications in his task, involving religious pilgrims and a truck filled with fish. French with subtitles. **92m/C VHS, DVD**. *FR* Clement Sibony, Rona Hartner, Isaac Sharry, Marie Desgranges, Emmanuelle Devos, Gilbert Levy, Francois Chattot, Francoise Bertin; **D:** Dante Desarthe; **W:** Dante Desarthe, Agnes Desarthe, Fabrice Guez; **C:** Laurent Machuel; **M:** Krishna Levy.

Dad Savage ♂♂ 1997 (R) Strange British crime pic told in flashbacks. Dad Savage (Stewart) is an East Anglia gangster who grows tulips and has a fondness for country music and dressing like a cowboy. His son Sav (Wood) works for him but tells fellow criminals Vic (Warren) and Bob (McFadden) that Dad has a stash of cash buried in a deserted house in the nearby woods. Dad finds out his workers are double-crossing him and there's hell to pay for everyone concerned. **104m/C VHS, DVD**. *GB* Patrick Stewart, Kevin McKidd, Joseph McFadden, Jake Wood, Marc Warren, Helen McCrory; **D:** Betsan Morris-Evans; **W:** Steven Williams; **C:** Gavin Finney; **M:** Simon Boswell.

Daddy & Them ♂♂ 1999 (R) Part romance, part dysfunctional family comedy, Thornton's followup to "Sling Blade" is set in Little Rock, Arkansas. Claude (Thornton) and wife Ruby (Dern) decide to head back home after they learn that Claude's Uncle Hazel (Varney) is in jail,

convicted of a petty crime. But the homecoming with Claude's extended family is chaotic to say the least. The constant family bickering gets annoying and the film's minimal charm tires quickly. **101m/C VHS, DVD**. Billy Bob Thornton, Laura Dern, Ben Affleck, Jamie Lee Curtis, Kelly Preston, Diane Ladd, Brenda Blethyn, Andy Griffith, Jim Varney, Walton Goggins; **D:** Billy Bob Thornton; **W:** Billy Bob Thornton; **C:** Barry Markowitz; **M:** Marty Stuart.

Daddy Day Camp ♂ 2007 (PG) Is it still a sequel if the cast is nearly all new? In this sequel to "Daddy Day Care," Charlie Hinton (Gooding, Jr.) and buddy Phil (Rae) have finished their second year as owners of Daddy Day Care. Charlie's son Ben (Bridges) is about to attend summer day camp, but Charlie's trauma from his own childhood camp experience makes him put the kibosh or Ben's plans for uber-cool Camp Canola. Yep, Ben will relive his dad's past at scrappy Camp Driftwood—except the long-neglected Driftwood is about to be put to rest. It's daddies to the rescue as Camp Driftwood is resurrected (sort-of) and the bumbling pops try not to make a flop of their kids' summers (trying equally hard not to kill anyone in the process). Embarrassing and dreadfully predictable. **53m/C DVD, Blu-ray Disc, UMD**. Cuba Gooding Jr., ..ochlyn Munro, Richard Gant, Spencir Bridges, Paul Rae, Josh McLerran, Tamala Jones, Brian Doyle-Murray, Talon G. Ackerman; **D:** Fred Savage; **W:** David N. Weiss, Geoff Rodkey, J. David Stem; **C:** Geno Salvatori; **M:** James Dooley. Golden Raspberries '07: Worst Sequel/Prequel.

Daddy Day Care ♂♂ 2003 (PG) Laid-off coworkers (Murphy, Garlin) become stay-at-home dads and caregivers and come up with the idea of opening their own unconventional day-care center. This puts them in direct competition with the director (Huston) of the expensive Chapman Academy. The new Murphy's Law seems to be that for every success, he'll have four disasters. This one is definitely one of the latter, as even in his usually-successful family-friendly mode, he merely mugs amid the chaos. The script is ridiculous and unfunny, and the talented adult cast is wasted as foils for the ankle-biter inmates running the asylum. Sure they're cute, but it shouldn't be that hard to carry an Eddie Murphy vehicle. Pre-school set may be amused by the antics of their on-screen peers, but their parents won't enjoy anything but the 93 minutes of quiet while their progeny zone out. **92m/C VHS, DVD, UMD**. *US* Eddie Murphy, Steve Zahn, Jeff Garlin, Regina King, Anjelica Huston, Lacey Chabert, Sloane Momsen, Kevin Nealon, Jonathan Katz, Khamani Griffin; **D:** Steve Carr; **W:** Geoff Rodkey; **C:** Steven Poster; **M:** David Newman.

Daddy Long Legs ♂♂½ 1919 Judy (Pickford), the eldest inhabitant of a dreary orphanage, comes to the attention of a mysterious benefactor who sends her to college. She eventually discovers the identity of her guardian, falls in love, and marries him. Based on a play by Jean Webster. **94m/B VHS, DVD**. Mary Pickford, Milla Davenport, Mahlon Hamilton, Lillian Langdon, Marshall Neilan; **D:** Marshall Neilan; **W:** Agnes Christine Johnston; **C:** Charles Ros'er, Henry Croniag-.

Daddy Long Legs ♂♂♂ 1955 Far from the great musicals, but enjoyable. An eccentric millionaire glimpses a French orphan and becomes her anonymous benefactor. Her musing over his identity spawns some surreal (often inexplicable) dance numbers, but love conquers all, even lesser Johnny Mercer songs. From a story by Jean Webster, also done in 1919 with Mary Pickford, 1931 with Janet Gaynor and 1935 with Shirley Temple as "Curly Top." ♪Daddy Long Legs; Something's Got To Give; Sluefoot; Dream; History of the Beat; C-A-T Spells Cat; Welcome Egghead. **126m/C VHS, DVD**. Fred Astaire, Leslie Caron, Terry Moore, Thelma Ritter, Fred Clark, Charlotte Austin, Larry Keating; **D:** Jean Negulesco; **C:** Leon Shamroy; **M:** Alex North.

Daddy Nostalgia ♂♂♂ *These Foolish Things; Daddy Nostalgie* 1990 Birkin plays the estranged daughter of Bogarde, who rushes from her home in England to

France to be with her seriously ill father. She must come to terms with her feelings for him just as Bogarde must deal with his own mortaliy. Wonderful performances, with Bogarde a charming and dominating presence. In French with English subtitles. **105m/C VHS, DVD, FR BR** Dirk Bogarde, Jane Birkin, Odette Laure; *D:* Bertrand Tavernier; *M:* Antoine Duhamel.

Daddy-O ♂ *Out on Probation* 1959 Drag racer Daddy-O traps the killers of his best friend and lands the blonde bombshell ..ana. It might seem bad since it's dated, but, hey, it may have been bad in 1959, too! **74m/B VHS,** Dick Contino, Sandra Giles; *D:* Lou Place; *W:* David Moessinger.

Daddy's Boys ♂½ 1987 (R) Since farming during the Depression is a rather low-paying endeavor, this family turns to thieving instead. But all-for-one and one-for-all is not the credo for one of the sons who decides to branch out on his own. Produced by Roger Corman. **90m/C VHS,** Daryl Haney, Laura Burkett, Raymond J. Barry, Dan Shor, Richart V. Barron; *D:* Joe Minion; *W:* Daryl Haney; *C:* David G. Stump; *M:* Sasha Matson.

Daddy's Dyin'... Who's Got the Will? ♂♂♂ 1990 (PG-13) Based on the critically acclaimed play, th s bitter-sweet comedy stars Bridges and D'Angelo as two members of the spiteful Turnover clan. When Daddy is on his death.ed, the entire family uses the opportunity to stab each other in the back. Non-stop humor and deep-hearted honesty carries this de... to end. **95m/C VHS, DVD,** Beau Bridges, Beverly D'Angelo, Tess Harper, Judge Reinhold, Amy Wright, Keir Carradine, Patrika Darco, Molly McClure, Bert Remsen; *D:* Jack Fisk; *W:* Del Shores; *C:* Paul Elliott; *M:* David McHugh.

Daddy's Girl ♂♂½ 1996 (R) When adopted Jcdy's new family is threatened she'll stop at nothing to protect herself and them. **95m/C VHS,** William Katt, Michele Greene, Roxana Zal, Mimi (Meyer) Craven, Whp p Hubley, Gabrielle Boni; *D:* Martin Kitrosser; *W:* Steve Pesce.

Daddy's Gone A-Hunting ♂♂♂ 1959 (PG) It's an eye for an eye, a baby for a baby in this well-done psychological thriller. A happily married woman is stalked by her deranged ex-boyfriend, whose baby she aborted years before. Now he wants the life of her child as just compensation 'or the loss of his. **108m/C VHS,** Carol White, Paul Burke Scott Hylands, Rachel Ames, Mala Powers, James B. Sikking; *D:* Mark Robson; *W:* Larry Cohen; *C:* Ernest Laszlo; *M:* John Williams.

Daddy's Little Girls 2007 (PG-13) *Tyler Perry's Daddy's Little Girls* ♂♂½ This isn't really about the little girls as much as it is about Monty (Elba) overcoming all obstacles to be a good father. He's a hard-working mechanic who loses custody to his greedy ex (Smith), thanks to some problems in his own past. This also leads to trouble in his growing relationship with his uptown lawyer, Julia (Union). Perry's characters tend to be two-dimensional but he's never less than sincere, and it's an uplifting story. **95m/C DVD, Blu-ray Disc. US** Idris Elba, Gabrielle Union, Louis Gossett Jr., Tasha Smith, Malinda Williams, Tracee Ellis Ross, Gary Sturgis, Sierra McClain, China McClain, Lauryn McClair; *D:* Tyler Perry, *W:* Tyler Perry. *C:* Toyomichi Kurita; *M:* Brian McKnight.

Daens ♂♂½ 1992 Looks at the disparity between rich and poor at the turn of the century. Daens, a priest, returns home to Flanders to find desperate poverty among the Flemish-speaking workers of the local textile mill. The French-speaking mill owners are supported by the local Catholic church while Daens believes in the rights of the workers. Declair makes his priest a complex and troubled man, who must choose between his conscience and social reform and the dictates of his church. Married by somewhat cardboard villains and a complex political/social situation that isn't adequately explained. Based on the novel by Louis Paul Boon. Flemish and French with English subtitles. **134m/C VHS, FR BE NL** Jan Decleir, Gerard De- sarthe, Antje Le Boeck, Michael Pas, Johan Leysen, Idwig Stephane, Linda Van Dijck, Wim Meuwissen; *D:* Stin Coninx; *W:* Francois Chevallier, Stijn Coninx; *M:* Dirk Brosse.

Dagger Eyes ♂½ *Mystery: Murder Near Perfect* 1983 A political assassin at work is inadvertently captured on film by a photographer. The assassin's mob employers will go to any lengths to destroy the film. Say cheeeeeese! **84m/C VHS,** Carlo Bouquet, Philip Coccioletti, John Steiner; *D:* Carlo Varzina.

The Dagger of Kamui ♂♂♂ *Kamui No Ken; Revenge of the Ninja Warrior* 1985 The only family Jiro has ever known is killed and he is accused of the crime. The real killer, the evil Tenkai, promises to take him to the real killer later, how cruelly he has been tricked. Then Jiro goes on a quest to find his past, all the while being manipulated by a vast and complex political machine. Watching this and Jiro's reactions make this anime more than a simple adventure or coming of age story. Whatever their motivations, Jiro's travels take him as far as America and into the paths of some characters as familiar to Western viewers as the historical figures in his homeland are to anyone knowledgeable of Japanese history. Based on the novels by Tetsu Yano; **132m/C VHS, DVD, JP** Michio Hazama; *D:* Taro Rin.

Dagora, the Space Monster WOOf! *Dagora, Space Monster* 1965 Giant slimy, pulsating mess from space lands on Earth and begins eating everything in its path. Scientists join together in a massive effort to destroy the creature. Believe it or not, it's sillier than most of the Japanese sci-fi genre. **80m/C VHS, DVD, JP** Yosuke Natsuki, Yoko Fujiyama, Akiko Wakabayashi; *D:* Inoshiro Honda; *W:* Shinichi Sekizawa; *C:* Hajime Koizumi.

Dahmer ♂♂ 2002 (R) That would be Dahmer as in serial killer Jeffrey who murdered, dismembered, and even munched on some 15 young men whom he killed in his Milwaukee, Wisconsin apartment. Although the story is sensationalistic, the film is surprisingly restrained and Renner gives a spooky performance as a psycho whose psychosis can never be explained. **101m/C VHS, DVD,** Jeremy Renner, Artel Kayaru, Bruce Davison, Matt Newton; *D:* David Jacobson; *C:* Chris Manley.

The Dain Curse ♂♂½ 1978 *Dashiell Hammett's The Dain Curse* in 1928, private eye Hamilton Nash must recover stolen diamonds, solve a millionaire's suicide, avoid being murdered, and end a family whose ... based on the novel by Dashiell Hammett. **138m/C VHS, DVD,** James Coburn, Jason Miller, Jean Simmons, Beatrice Straight, Hector Elizondo, Nancy Addison; *D:* E.W. Swackhamer. TV

Daisy Kenyon ♂♂½ 1947 Daisy (Crawford) finally gets fed up when married lover Dan (Andrews) keeps breaking his promises. She decides to move on with kind war vet Peter (Fonda) and they get married. Despite this, Dan starts Daisy finally figures things out and gets a divorce. Now a free man, Dan wants Daisy for himself but does she go to him or stay with the decent guy? Crawford can suffer with the best of 'em but Andrews character is pretty much a heel. **99m/C DVD,** Joan Crawford, Dana Andrews, Henry Fonda, Peggy Ann Garner, Ruth Warwick, Martha Stewart, Connie Marshall, Nicholas Joy; *D:* Otto Preminger; *W:* David Hertz; *C:* Leon Shamroy; *M:* David Raskin.

Daisy Miller ♂♂½ 1974 (G) Shepherd portrays the title character in this adaptation of the Henry James novella about a naive young American woman travelling through Europe and getting a taste of the Continent during the late 19th century. Though it is intelligently written and has a good supporting cast, the film seems strangely flat, due in large part to Shepherd's hollow performance. **93m/C VHS, DVD,** Cybill Shepherd, Eileen Brennan, Coris Leachman, Mildred Natwick; *D:* Peter Bogdanovich; *W:* Frederic Raphael.

Daltry Calhoun ♂ 2005 (PG-13) Debut feature from Bronson stars Knoxville as the slick sod salesman of the title. Dal- ... try highballed it out of Ducktown, Tennessee, leaving behind his teenaged girlfriend May (Banks) is dying of some mystery illness and needs Daltry to take responsibility for June (Traub). There are quirky townsfolk and quirky situations and quirky, annoying narration from June. And an intrusive soundtrack. **100m/C DVD, US** Johnny Knoxville, Juliette Lewis, Elizabeth Banks, Kick (Christopher) Gurry, David Koechner, Sophie Traub, Andrew Prine; *D:* Katrina Holden Bronson; *W:* Katrina Holden Bronson; *C:* Matthew Irving; *M:* John Swihart.

The Dallas Connection ♂ 1994 (R) Three of the four scientists working on a satellite weapons system are assassinated by a trio of sexy but lethal females. Now the remaining scientist is under federal protection in Dallas while he continues his work. Lots of T&A. **90m/C VHS, DVD,** Julie Strain, Samantha (Sam) Phillips, Julie K. Smith, Wendy Hamilton; *D:* Andy Sidaris.

Dalva ♂½ 1995 Dull TV movie fin ds restless Dalva Northridge (Fawcett) de-cding to search for the son she was forced to give up for adoption some 20 years before. But she gets sidetracked juggling two love affairs—with Sam Creek-mouth (Boothe), whose Indian heritage is tied to Dalva's family, and alcoholic University professor Michael (Coyote) who wants the the Northridge family diaries for his research on the Great Plains. Based on the novel by Jim Harrison. **96m/C VHS, DVD,** Farrah Fawcett, Powers Boothe, Peter Coyote, Fod Steiger, Carroll Baker; *D:* Ken Cameron; *W:* Jim Harrison; *C:* Tony Imi. TV.

Dam Busters ♂♂♂½ 1955 Well-done and exciting film details the efforts of British scientists trying to devise a method of destroying a strategic dam in Nazi Germany during WWII. Definitely one of the better in the war movie genre. **119m/B VHS,** Michael Redgrave, Richard Todd, Ursula Jeans, Basil Sydney, Frank Phillips; *D:* Michael Anderson Sr.

Dakota ♂♂ 1945 Fine cast becomes embroiled in railroad land dispute. In the meantime, love strikes The Duke. Standard Wayne western saga where quite ... gets on track. **82m/B DVD,** John Wayne, Vera Hruba Ralston, Walter Brennan, Ward Bond, One Munson; *D:* Joseph Kane.

Dakota ♂♂ 1988 (PG) A troubled half-breed teenager works for a rancher, romances his daughter, and befriends his crippled 12-year-old son. A well-meaning but predictable drama. **96m/C VHS, DVD,** Lou Diamond Phillips, Dee Dee Norton, Eli Cummins, Herta Ware, Jordan Burton; *D:* Fred Holmes; *C:* James W. Wrenn.

Dakota Incident ♂♂ 1956 Decent western about stagecoach passengers travelling through Dakota Territory who must defend themselves against an Indian attack. **88m/C VHS,** Dale Robertson, Ward Bonc, Linda Darnell, John Lund, Ward Bond, Chill Wills; *D:* Lewis R. Foster.

Daleks—Invasion Earth 2150 A.D. ♂♂½ *Invasion Earth 2150 A.D* 1965 A sequel to "Dr. Who and the Daleks," wherein the popular British character embarks on the second ... saga. **81m/C VHS, DVD, GB** Peter Cushing, Andrew Keir, Jill Curzon, Ray Brooks; *D:* Gordon Flemyng.

Dallas 362 ♂♂ 2003 (R) Rusty (Hatosy) and Dallas (Caan) waste away their lives in a cycle of drinking, bar fights, and minor arrests—always to be bailed out by Rusty's mother Mary (Lynch). Mary puts her son in therapy and through uncoventional methods he starts to see a better life for himself, though Dallas hurtles further toward the dark side. The subplot romance between the mother and therapist (Goldblum) is engaging but lacks depth. Conclusion provides a surprise emotional tug. **100m/C DVD, US** Scott Caan, Jeff Goldblum, Shawn Hatosy, Kelly Lynch, Dwight "Heavy D" Myers, Bob Gunton, Marley Shelton, Selma Blair, Isla Fisher, Freddy Rodriguez, James Caan; *D:* Scott Caan; *W:* Scott Caan; *C:* Phil Parmet.

Damien: Omen 2 ♂♂ 1978 (R) Sequel to "The Omen" about Damien, a young boy possessed with mysterious demonic powers, who kills those people who anger him. Followed by "The Final Conflict." **110m/C VHS, DVD,** William Holden, Lee Grant, Lew Ayres, Robert Foxworth, Sylvia Sidney, Lance Henriksen, Jonathan Scott-Taylor, Nicholas Pryor, Allan Arbus, Meshach Taylor; *D:* Don Taylor; *W:* Mike Hodges; *C:* Bill Butler; *M:* Jerry Goldsmith.

Damien: The Leper Priest ♂♂ 1980 (R) *Father Damien: The Leper Priest* The story of a Roman Catholic priest who doomed himself by voluntarily serving on a leper colony 100 years ago. Somewhat disappointing considering the dramatic material. Originally a vehicle for David Janssen, who died prior to filming. **100m/C VHS,** Ken Howard, Mike Farrell, Wilfrid Hyde-White, William Daniels, David Ogden Stiers; *D:* Steven Gethe's. TV

Dames ♂♂♂ 1934 A millionaire with fanatically religious beliefs tries to stop the opening of a Broadway show. In the last of the grand budget-breaking spectacles before the "product.on code" came into being, distinguished choreographer Busby Berkeley took his imagination to the limit. Watch for the dancing clothes on an ironing board and dancing girls with puzzle pieces on their backs which form the real You; When You Were a Twinkle in Your Father's Eye; Try To See It My Way; The Girl at the Ironing Board. **95m/B VHS, DVD,** Dick Powell, Joan Blondell, Ruby Keeler, Zasu Pitts, Guy Kibbee, Busby Berkeley; *D:* Ray Enright; *W:* Delmer Daves; *C:* George Barnes.

Dames Ahoy ♂ 1930 Three sailors on shore leave try to find the blonde who tricked one of them out of his pay. This is the original silent version with a piano score. **52m/B VHS,** Glenn Tryon, Otis Harlan, Eddie Gribbon, Helen Wright, Gertrude Astor; *D:* William James Craft.

Damage ♂♂♂ 1992 (R) The elegant Irons portrays Stephen, a middle-aged, married British politician who has always been completely in control of his life, especially where his feelings are concerned. Then he meets Anna (Binoche), his son's less-than-innocent fiance, and immediately begins an obsessive, wildly sexual affair with her. Stephen should have listened to Anna's warning about herself "Damaged people are dangerous, they know they can survive," because their passion leads to betrayal and tragedy. Binoche is more icon than human being but the film still hypnotizes as an exploration of passion. Based on the novel by Josephine Hart. An unrated version is also available. **111m/C VHS, DVD, GB FR** Jeremy Irons, Juliette Binoche, Rupert Graves, Miranda Richardson, Ian Bannen, Leslie Caron, Peter Stormare, Gemma Clark, Julian Fellowes; *D:* Louis Malle; *W:* David Hare; *C:* Peter Bizlou; *M:* Zbigniew Preisner. *British Academy '92: Support. Actress (Richardson); L.A. Film Critics '92: Score.*

Damn the Defiant! ♂♂♂ 1962 Adventure abounds when Guinness, as captain of the HMS Defiant during the Napoleonic wars, finds himself up against not only the French but his own mutinous crew as well. In the end, both a second-in-command (Bogarde) and a fleet-wide mutiny and a French invasion of England are avoided. Much attention is paid to period detail in this well-crafted film. **101m/C VHS, DVD, GB** Alec Guinness, Dirk Bogarde, Maurice Denham, Anthony Quayle; *D:* Lewis Gilbert; *W:* Nigel Kneale, Edmund H. North; *C:* Christopher Challis; *M:* Clifton Parker.

Damn Yankees ♂♂♂ *What Lola Wants* 1958 Musical feature adapted from the Broadway hit. A baseball fan frustrated by his team's lack of success makes a pact with the devil to become the team's new star. Vercon is dynamite as the devil's accomplice. Great Bob Fosse choreography. ♪Whatever Lola Wants; (You Gotta Have) Heart; Shoeless Joe From Hannibal Mo; Goodbye, Old Girl; A Little Brains, a Little Talent; Who's Got the Pain; Two Lost Souls; There's Something About an Empty Chair; Those Were the Good

Old Days. 110m/C VHS, DVD. Gwen Verdon, Ray Walston, Tab Hunter, Jean Stapleton, Russ Brown; D: George Abbott, Stanley Donen.

Damnation Alley ♪♪½ 1977 (PG) A warrior, an artist, and a biker jump in tank and set off in search of civilization after Armageddon. They go to Albany instead. So-so attempt to revive the post-nuclear holocaust genre which was more successfully accomplished by the "Mad Max" series. Adapted from Roger Zelazny's novel. 87m/C VHS, DVD. George Peppard, Jan-Michael Vincent, Paul Winfield, Dominique Sanda, Jackie Earle Haley; D: Jack Smight; W: Alan Sharp, Lukas Heller; C: Harry Stradling Jr.; M: Jerry Goldsmith.

The Damned ♪♪½ 1969 (R) Depicts the Nazi takeover of a German industrialist family and their descent into greed, lust, and madness. Comes in dubbed or subtitled formats. 146m/C VHS, DVD. IT GE Dirk Bogarde, Ingrid Thulin, Helmut Griem, Charlotte Rampling, Helmut Berger; D: Luchino Visconti; M: Maurice Jarre.

The Damned Don't Cry ♪♪½ 1950 Crawford is a small-town girl who leaves her family to climb the social ladder to the top of organized crime as a boss's moll by using her looks and guile. Melodrama, in the vein of Crawford's "Mildred Pierce," mixes with a noirish atmosphere to create an interesting crime drama/character study. 103m/C DVD. Joan Crawford, David Brian, Steve Cochran, Kent Smith, Hugh Sanders, Selena Royle, Jacqueline DeWit, Morris Ankrum, Edith Evanson, Richard Egan, Jimmy Moss, Eddie Marr; D: Vincent Sherman; W: Harold Medford; C: Ted D. McCord; M: Daniele Amfitheatrof.

Damned River ♪♪½ 1989 (R) Four friends take a guided tour down Zimbabwe's Zambezi River, only to find midway down that their guide is a murderous psycho. Survival becomes a priority. 93m/C VHS. Stephen Shellen, Lisa Aliff, John Terlesky, Marc Poppel, Bradford Bancroft; D: Michael Schroeder; W: John Crowther.

A Damsel in Distress ♪♪½ 1937 Astaire falls for an upper-class British girl, whose family wants her to have nothing to do with him. Features memorable songs from the Gershwins. ♫A Foggy Day in Londontown; Nice Work If You Can Get It; Stiff Upper Lip; Put Me to the Test; I Can't Be Bothered Now; The Jolly Tar and the Milkmaid; Things Are Looking Up; Sing of Spring; Ah Che a Voi Perdoni Iddio. 101m/B VHS. Fred Astaire, Joan Fontaine, George Burns, Gracie Allen, Ray Noble, Montagu Love, Reginald Gardiner; D: George Stevens; M: George Gershwin, Ira Gershwin.

Dan Candy's Law ♪♪½ Alien Thunder 1973 A Canadian mountie becomes a driven hunter, and then desperate prey, when he tries to track down the Indian who killed his partner. 90m/C VHS. DVD. CA Donald Sutherland, Gordon Tootoosis, Chief Dan George, Kevin McCarthy; D: Claude Fournier; M: Georges Delerue.

Dan in Real Life ♪♪½ 2007 (PG-13) Gee, a romantic comedy that features age-appropriate adults who actually act like grown-ups! Who knew? Likeable (if baffled) widower Dan (Carell) is trying to raise three daughters and write his family advice newspaper column (of course none of his advice works for him). Dan's not even thinking about dating until he takes his brood to a family reunion and meets beautiful, friendly Marie (Binoche), who happens to be his younger bro Mitch's (Cook) new love. Dan tries to suppress his feelings, which results in a number of amusing moments for Carell that don't go over the top. Engaging if predictable. 98m/C DVD. US Steve Carell, Juliette Binoche, Dane Cook, Dianne Wiest, John Mahoney, Emily Blunt, Alison Pill, Brittany Robertson, Marlene Lawston, Norbert Lee Butz, Amy Ryan; D: Peter Hedges; W: Peter Hedges, Pierce Gardner; C: Lawrence Sher; M: Sondre Lerche.

Dance ♪♪½ 1990 Two ballet dancers struggle to find love amidst the backstage treacheries and demanding schedules of their profession. 90m/C VHS. John Revill, Ellen Troy, Carlton Wilborn, Charlene Campbell; D: Robin Murray.

Dance Fools Dance ♪♪♪ 1931 Fast-paced drama has Crawford and Bakewell as a pair of spoiled rich kids who are forced to face poverty when the stock market crashes. He meets up with Gable, who's producing liquor illegally, while she gets a job at a newspaper. When Gable arranges something akin to the St. Valentine's Day Massacre, Bakewell's investigative reporting of the situation produces fatal results. The Hays Office had a problem with Crawford and friends appearing in their underwear. Cast notes: Gable was just starting out at MGM, which is why he was billed sixth; the William Holden here is not THE William Holden, and Edwards went on to provide the voice of Jiminy Cricket in "Pinocchio." 82m/B VHS. Joan Crawford, Lester Vail, Cliff Edwards, William "Billy" Bakewell, Clark Gable; D: Harry Beaumont; C: Charles Rosher.

Dance, Girl, Dance ♪♪ 1940 The private lives and romances of a wartime nightclub dance troupe. Standard Hollywood potpourri of dance, drama, comedy. ♫Mother, What Do I Do Now?; Jitterbug Bite; Morning Star. 88m/B VHS, DVD. Maureen O'Hara, Louis Hayward, Lucille Ball, Virginia Field, Ralph Bellamy, Maria Ouspenskaya, Mary Carlisle, Katharine Alexander, Edward Brophy, Walter Abel, Harold Huber; D: Dorothy Arzner; W: Frank Davis, Tess Slesinger; C: Russell Metty; M: Edward Ward. Natl. Film Reg. '07.

The Dance Goes On ♪♪ 1992 After the death of an uncle, Keach and his estranged son Almond reunite at the old Quebec family farm left to them. The father is country-bred and appreciates the property but his Los Angeles-reared son wants to sell for a quick profit. Director Almond cast his own son in the starring role as well as ex-wife Bujold, who plays the ambitious showbiz mother. 104m/C VHS. James Keach, Matt Almond, Genevieve Bujold, Cary Lawrence; D: Paul Almond; W: Paul Almond.

Dance Hall ♪♪½ 1941 A Pennsylvania dance hall owner is propelled into romantic confusion with the introduction of a sultry blond dancer into his club. 73m/B VHS. Cesar Romero, Carole Landis, William Henry, June Storey, Charles Halton; D: Irving Pichel.

Dance Hall Racket ♪♪ 1958 A sleazy, stilted expose of dance hall vice featuring a brief appearance by Bruce and his wife, Harlow. 60m/B VHS, DVD. Lenny Bruce, Honey Harlow; D: Phil Tucker.

Dance Macabre ♪ 1991 (R) Englund takes on a dual role as a man with a split personality—one of whom is deadly. Jessica, an American ballerina, enrolls in a Russian dance academy and meets mesmerizing choreographer, Anthony. Unfortunately for Jessica she happens to look exactly like Anthony's long-dead lover and he becomes obsessed with her. Also, her fellow dancers are being brutally murdered. Are the events connected? 97m/C VHS. Robert Englund, Michelle Zeitlin, Marianna Moen, Alexander Sergeyev; D: Greydon Clark; W: Greydon Clark.

Dance Me Outside ♪♪½ 1995 (R) Native Canadian teens look for some excitement on their Northern Ontario reservation and find themselves cut off from their tradition-bound parents in this slice of life drama. Friends Silas and Blackie plot revenge against a white who murdered a native girl while Silas' sister Illianna comes to visit from Toronto, just as her ex-boyfriend returns from a prison stint. Based on the novel by W.P. Kinsella. 91m/C VHS. CA Ryan Black, Adam Beach, Michael Greyeyes, Lisa Lacroix; D: Bruce McDonald; W: Bruce McDonald, Don McKellar, John Frizzell. Genie '95: Film Editing.

Dance Me to My Song ♪♪ 1998 Very difficult movie to watch provides its own rewards thanks to the skills of filmmaker de Heer and lead Rose. Julia (Rose) suffers from severe cerebral palsy, is wheelchair-bound, and can only speak through a voice synthesizer. Although she lives alone, she is dependent on the daily caregivers supplied by the health department. Her latest is the short-tempered Madelaine (Kennedy), who is neglectful and

ill-suited to her demanding work. What makes the situation more difficult is Julia's amiable friend Eddie (Brumpton), whom Madelaine jealously decides is the ideal man. 103m/C VHS. AU Heather Rose, Joey Kennedy, John Brumpton, Rena Owen; D: Rolf de Heer; W: Rolf de Heer, Frederick Stahl, Heather Rose; C: Tony Clark; M: Graham Tardif.

Dance of Death WOOF! House of Evil; Macabre Serenade 1968 Just before his death, Karloff agreed to appear in footage for four Mexican cheapies that were practically thrown together (Karloff actually filmed his scenes in Los Angeles). If they had mixed the footage instead of matched it, the flicks couldn't be any worse. This one concerns a lunatic toy-maker whose toys kill and maim his heirs. 89m/C VHS, DVD. MX Boris Karloff, Julissa, Andres Garcia, Jack Hill; D: Juan Ibanez.

Dance of Life ♪♪½ 1929 A look at the backstage goings-on at a burlesque theatre. A successful entertainer's life goes down the tubes when he hits the bottle. His wife leaves him because of his philandering, but returns when she sees how much he really needs her. One scene of the Ziegfeld Follies uses two-tone Technicolor technology. This was re-made twice: as "Swing High, Swing Low" in 1937 and as "When My Baby Smiles at Me" in 1948. Carroll replaced the stage lead, who was said to have no "name recognition"—Barbara Stanwyck. ♫True Blue Lou; King of Jazzmania; Cuddlesome Baby; Flippity Flop; Ladies of the Dance; The Mightiest Matador; Sweet Rosie O'Grady; In the Gloaming; Sam, the Accordion Man. 115m/B VHS. Nancy Carroll, Hal Skelly, Ralph Theadore, Charles D. Brown, Dorothy Revier, Al "Fuzzy" St. John, Oscar Levant; D: John Cromwell.

Dance of the Damned ♪♪ 1988 (R) A case where low-budget isn't synonymous with bomb. Fascinating noirish plot concerning a vampire who wants to learn more about the life of his next victim, a deep-thinking stripper, who has lost the will to live it. Surprisingly well-done and acted; above-par for this genre. 83m/C VHS. Cyril O'Reilly, Starr Andreeff, Deborah Ann Nassar, Maria Ford; D: Katt Shea; W: Katt Shea, Andy Ruben; C: Phedon Papamichael; M: Gary Stockdale.

Dance or Die ♪ 1987 Just goes to show that in Las Vegas you can't have your dance and drugs too, because if the Mob doesn't get you, the Feds will. Made for video (though maybe it shouldn't have been made at all). In HIFI Stereo. 90m/C VHS. Ray Kieffer, Rebecca Barrington; D: Richard W. Munchkin. VIDEO

A Dance to the Music of Time ♪♪½ 1997 Explores the social, political, and artistic fortunes and foibles of upper-class Brits from the 1920s through the '60s from the viewpoint of everyman Nicholas Jenkins (D'Arcy and Purefoy) and his journey from schooldays to old age. Richardson is sexy man-eater Pamela Flitton and Beale is the unremarkable but ambitious and lucky Widmerpool among a cast of hundreds. Based on Anthony Powell's 12-volume series. 480m/C DVD. GB James Purefoy, Miranda Richardson, Simon Russell Beale, James D'Arcy, Paul Rhys, Jonathan Cake, Claire Skinner, Alan Bennett, John Gielgud, Zoe Wanamaker, Edward Fox, Michael Williams, Eileen Atkins; D: Alvin Rakoff, Christopher Morhan; W: Hugh Whitemore; C: Chris Seager; M: Carl Davis. TV

Dance with a Stranger ♪♪♪½ 1985 (R) The engrossing and factual story of Ruth Ellis (Richardson) who gained notoriety as the last woman hanged in Great Britain in 1955. This emotional and sometimes violent film mirrors the sensationalism and class conflicts of 1950s British society. The film follows single mom Ellis's pre-trial life as a tawdry nightclub hostess, struggling to maintain her independence, while becoming obsessively involved with immature cas/upper-class playboy David Blakely (Everett) whom she murders when he finally rejects her. 101m/C VHS, DVD. GB Miranda Richardson, Rupert Everett, Ian Holm, Joanne Whalley, Matthew Carroll, Tom Chadbon, Jane Bertish, David Troughton, Paul Mooney,

Stratford Johns, Susan Kyd Leslie Manville, Sallie-Anne Field, Martin Murphy, Michael Jenn, Daniel Massey; D: Mike Newell; W: Shelagh Delaney; C: Peter Hannan; M: Richard Hartley. Cannes '85: Film.

Dance with Death ♪ 1991 (R) When strippers turn up brutally murdered, a young journalist goes undercover to solve the case. 90m/C VHS, DVD. Maxwell Caulfield, Barbara Alyn Jones, Martin Mull, Drew Snyder, Catya (Cat) Sassoon; D: Charles Philip Moore.

Dance with Me ♪♪♪½ Shut Up and Dance 1998 (PG) Cuban emigre Rafael (Chayanne) winds up in Houston, teaching at the fading Excelsior Dance Studio, which is owned by a friend of his late mother's, John Burnett (Kristofferson). Instructor (and single mom) Ruby (Williams) is looking for a partner who can help her enter the competitive ballroom dance world but she's not looking for love. But at the World Open Dance Championships in Las Vegas, she may find both. Hot salsa music and dancing, as well as the charm watching for any dance fever fan. 126m/C VHS, DVD. Vanessa Lynné Williams, Chayanne, Kris Kristofferson, Joan Plowright, Jane Krakowski, Beth Grant; D: Randa Haines; W: Daryl Matthews; C: Fred Murphy; M: Michael Convertino.

Dance with Me, Henry ♪½ 1956 When Lou becomes involved with Bud's gambling debts and the local district attorney turns up dead, Lou's not only wanted by the law, bu' by the mafia as well. This was the great comedy duo's last picture together and it's clear the pair are not happy about working with each other, even on this mediocre effort. 90m/B VHS, DVD. Bud Abbott, Lou Costello, Gigi Perreau, Rusty Hamer, Mary Wickes, Ted de Corsia; D: Charles T. Barton.

Dance with the Devil ♪ Perdita Durango 1997 (R) Prostitute Perdita (Perez) and witch doctor/drug dealer Romeo (Bardem) meet at the Mexican border and soon become lovers and criminal partners. They get a kinky job hijacking human fetuses for a Vegas mob boss and, since Romeo believes in human sacrifice before starting a new endeavor, they kidnap a cute teen couple as the victims. Then Romeo discovers his ex-partner, Shorty (Segura), isn't so ex—and there's lots more that's very weird and bloody. Based on the novel "59 and Raining: The Story of Perdita Durango" by Barry Gifford. 126m/C VHS, DVD. MX SP Rosie Perez, Javier Bardem, Harley Cross, Aimee Graham, Don Stroud, James Gandolfini, Santiago Segura, Screamin' Jay Hawkins, Alex Cox, Carlos Bardem; D: Alex de la Iglesia; W: Alex de la Iglesia, Barry Gifford, Jorge Guerricaechevarria, David Trueba; C: Flavio Martinez Labiano; M: Simon Boswell.

Dancer in the Dark ♪♪ 1999 (R) A love it or hate it production from Danish provocateur Von Trier. Czech immigrant Selma (Bjork) is a single mom working in a small factory, where her zest friend is another immigrant, Kathy (Deneuve). Selma is also close to her landlords Bill and Jean (Morse, Seymour) but tells no one that she's going blind, a fate her son will also suffer unless he gets an expensive operation. Then the money Selma has been saving is stolen and she accuses the bankrupt Bill, leading to tragedy. It sounds clear enough but mixed up in the story is Selma's participation in an amateur production of "The Sound of Music" and her numerous musical fantasies. Exteriors were filmed in Sweden and interiors in a Danish studio, although it's set in rural America. 141m/C VHS, DVD. DK SW FR Bjork, Catherine Deneuve, David Morse, Peter Stormare, Cara Seymour, Joel Grey, Vincent Paterson, Vladica Kostic, Jean-Marc Barr, Udo Kier, Zeljko Ivanek; D: Lars von Trier; W: Lars von Trier; C: Robby Muller; M: Bjork. Cannes '00: Actress (Bjork), Film; Ind. Spirit '01: Foreign Film.

Dancer, Texas—Pop. 81 ♪♪♪ 1998 (PG) Four buddies have to decide if they're going to fulfill the pact they made when they were 11 to leave the eponymous town upon graduating from high school. Each one has a reason to consider sticking around: Keller (Meyer) tkaes care of his widowed grandfather; Terrell

The Dancer Upstairs 🐾🐾🐾½

2002 (R) Politics and romance once again make strange bedfellows in this adaptation of Shakespeare's 1995 novel. In an unidentified Latin American country (filmed in Ecuador), idealistic lawyer Agustin Rejas (Bardem) abandons the law to pursue justice by joining the police. He's been assigned to track down Ezequiel (Folk), a terrorist who's behind a series of executions of government leaders. Rejas ballet lessons from the lovely Yolanda (Morante), with whom he becomes infatuated. But his interest leads to him learning of a connection between the teacher and his quarry. Malkovich's directorial debut. **128m/C VHS, DVD.** *US SP* Javier Bardem, Laura Morante, Juan Diego Botto, Elvira Minguez, Oliver Cotton, Luis Miguel Cintra, Abel Folk, Alexandra Lencastre; *D:* John Malkovich; *W:* Nicholas Shakespeare. *C:* Jose Luis Alcaine; *M:* Alberto Iglesias.

Dancers 🐾🐾½

1987 (PG) During the filming of the ballet "Giselle" in Italy, a famous, almost-over-the-hill dancer (Baryshnikov, ten years after his role in "The Turning Point") coaches a young, inexperienced starlet. He hopes to revitalize his life and his dancing. Features dancers from the Baryshnikov-led American Ballet Theatre. **95m/C VHS.** Mikhail Baryshnikov, Leslie Browne, Julie Kent, Mariangela Melato, Alessandra Ferri, Lynn Seymour, Victor Barbee, Tommy Rall; *D:* Herbert Ross; *M:* Pino Donaggio.

Dances with Wolves 🐾🐾🐾½

1990 (PG-13) The story of a U.S. Army soldier, circa 1870, whose heroism in battle allows him his pick of posts. His choice, to see the West before it disappears, changes his life. He meets, understands, and eventually becomes a member of a Lakota Sioux tribe in the Dakotas. Costner's first directorial attempt proves him a talent of vision and intelligence: his sometimes too objective character, unconvincing performances, and interesting perspective on the plight of Native Americans. Lovely music and epic proportions. Adapted by Blake from his novel. **181m/C VHS, DVD.** Kevin Costner, Mary McDonnell, Graham Greene, Rodney A. Grant, Floyd "Red Crow" Westerman, Tantoo Cardinal, Robert Pastorelli, Charles Rocket, Maury Chaykin, Jimmy Herman, Nathan Lee Chasing, Wes Studi; *D:* Kevin Costner; *W:* Michael Blake; *C:* Dean Semler, John Barry. *Oscars '90:* Adapt. Screenplay, Cinematog., Director (Costner), Film Editing, Picture, Sound, Orig. Score; *AFI '98:* Top 100; *Directors Guild '90:* Director (Costner); *Golden Globes '91:* Director (Costner), Film—Drama, Screenplay; *Natl. Bd. of Review '90:* Director (Costner), *Natl. Film Reg. '07'; Writers Guild '90:* Adapt. Screenplay.

Dancing at Lughnasa 🐾🐾

1998 (PG-13) Kate (Streep) is the eldest of five lonely unwed sisters living together on a farm in 1930s Ireland. Their brother Father Jack (Gambon) returns home, fresh from a stint as a missionary in Africa, and Gerry (Ifans), who fathered a son with sister Christina, turns up as well. The reunion stirs up emotions and resurrects memories in this anecdotal tale, but unfortunately most of the episodes are lacking energy and fun. Streep gives her usual impeccably accented performance. McCormack is sensual as Christina, but it's Ifans who delivers the only gusto as he readies to go to war in Spain. Adapted from the Tony Award-winning stage play by Brian Friel. The refers to a pagan ritual with accompanying musical score. **95m/C VHS.** Meryl Streep, Michael Gambon, Catherine McCormack, Rhys Ifans, Brid Brennan, Kathy Burke, Sophie Thompson, Lorcan Cranitch, Darrell Johnston, Peter Gowen, Dawn Bradfield, Marie Mullen; *D:* Pat O'Connor; *W:* Frank McGuinness; *C:* Kenneth Macmillan; *M:* Bill Whelan.

Dancing at the Blue Iguana 🐾🐾½

2000 (R) These "dancers" are strippers at the titular San Fernando Valley club and their interwoven stories comprise the plot. Stormy (Kelley) is the tough veteran with the questionable past; Angel (Hannah) is sweet but dumb; Jo (Tilley) must deal with an unplanned pregnancy; Jasmine (Oh) is an aspiring poet; and Jesse (Ayanna) is an over-eager newcomer. Eddie (Wisdom) presides over the establishment and has his own demons. Much of the film was improvised in workshops and rehearsals. **123m/C VHS, DVD.** Sheila Kelley, Daryl Hannah, Sandra Oh, Jennifer Tilly, Charlotte Ayanna, Rober Wisdom, Elias Koteas, Vladimir Mashkov, W. Earl Brown, Chris Hogan, Rodney Rowland, Kristin Bauer; *D:* Michael Radford; *W:* David Linter, Michael Radford. *C:* Ericson Core; *M:* Tal Bergman, Renato Neto.

Dancing in September 🐾🐾½

2000 (R) Black writer Tomasina "Tommy" Crawford (Parker) has just lost her job at a sitcom and she has nothing to lose by pitching a black issues comedy to George (Washington), a slick exec looking to make a name for himself at a start-up network. Tommy also discovers the show's lead—former gangbanger and single dad James (Shannon). The three gain success but come under the bar for the black community for being sellouts as they re-evaluate their personal and professional aspirations. **106m/C VHS, DVD.** Nicole Ari Parker, Isaiah Washington IV, Vicellous Shannon, Malinda Williams, Jay Underwood, Michael Cavanaugh, Chi McBride, James Avery, LeVar Burton, Peter Onorati, Kaoeem Hardison, Jenifer Lewis, Anna Maria Horsford; *D:* Reggie Rock Bythewood; *W:* Reggie Rock Bythewood; *C:* Bill Dill. **CABLE.**

Dancing in the Dark 🐾🐾½

1986 (PG-13) An interesting but slow-moving Canadian film about the perfect housewife who learns that after 20 years of faithful, Realizing how her life has been wasted she murders her husband and, in the end, suffers a mental breakdown. **93m/C VHS, DVD.** *CA* Martha Henry, Neil Munro, Rosemary Dunsmore, Richard Monette; *D:* Leon Marr.

Dancing in Twilight 🐾

2005 (PG-13) Houston businessman Madhav Singh (Evan) can barely function after the unexpected death of his wife (Patel). His loneliness is amplified when his estranged son Sam (Penn) comes home for a visit, accompanied by his girlfriend (Sheth). Now Madhav realizes he must make a decision about moving on with his life. **90m/C VHS, DVD.** Erik Avari, Kal Penn, Mimi Rogers, Louise Fletcher, Sheetal Sheth, Antee Patel; *D:* Bob Rose; *W:* Rishi Wij; *C:* Robert Steadman; *M:* Scott Szabo.

Dancing Lady 🐾🐾

1933 Rarely seen film is MGM's answer to "42nd Street," with Crawford as a small-time hoofer trying to break into Broadway. Her screen debuts of Astaire and Eddy. Look for none other than the Three Stooges as stage hands. Everything I Have Is Yours; Heigh-Ho! The Gang's All Here; Hold Your Man; That's the Rhythm of the Day; My Dancing Lady; Let's Go Bavarian! Hey Young Fella. **93m/B VHS, DVD.** Clark Gable, Joan Crawford, Fred Astaire, Franchot Tone, Nelson Eddy, Ted Healy, Moe Howard, Larry Fine, May Robson, Robert Benchley, Eve Arden; *D:* Robert Z. Leonard; *W:* F.L. Wolfson, Allen Rivkin, Zelda Sears; *C:* Oliver Marsh; *M:* Richard Rodgers, Burton Lane, Jimmy McHugh.

Dancing Man 🐾½

1933 A gigolo romances both mother and daughter and winds up implicated in murder as a result. Dismissable. **65m/B VHS.** Judith Allen, Reginald Denny, Natalie Moorhead; *D:* Albert Ray.

Dancing Mothers 🐾🐾½

1926 A fast-living woman becomes involved with her mother's roguish boyfriend in this silent film with accompanying musical score. **85m/B VHS.** Clara Bow, Alice Joyce, Conway Tearle, Donald Keith; *D:* Herbert Brenon; *W:* Forrest Halsey; *C:* J. Roy Hunt.

Dancing Pirate 🐾🐾

1936 A Boston dance instructor is kidnapped by pirates and jumps ship in Mexico, where he romances a mayor's daughter. The silly story boasts some Rodgers and Hart tunes, plus the early use of Technicolor, exploited here for all it was worth and then some. Are You My Love?; When You're Dancing the Waltz. **83m/C VHS.** Charles Collins, Frank Morgan, Steffi Duna, Luis Alberni, Victor Varconi, Jack La Rue; *D:* Lloyd Corrigan.

The Dancing Princesses 🐾🐾🐾

1984 When five naughty princesses wear the soles of their slippers out every night, their father the King must foot the bill. He soon tires of this expense and offers a reward to the person who can discover how this happens. A handsome prince becomes invisible to follow the lovely ladies and discover their secret. From the "Faerie Tale Theatre" series. **60m/C VHS, DVD.** Lesley Ann Warren, Peter Weller, Sachi (Maclaine) Parker, Roy Dotrice; *D:* Peter Medak. **CABLE. TV.**

Dancing with Danger 🐾🐾½

1993 (PG-13) A private investigator is hired to find out why a taxi dancer's customers all end up dead. Soon the PI's employer is the next victim of a serial killer whose ultimate target is the dancer herself. **90m/C VHS.** Cheryl Ladd, Ed Marinaro, Miguel (Michael) Sandoval, Pat Skipper; *D:* Stuart Cooper; *W:* Elisa Bell. TV.

Dandelions 🐾

1974 German softcore flick starring Frauer in an early role as a man jilted by his wife. To make himself feel better he decides to explore the sleazier side of life. Meaningless film evokes no sympathy. Not recommended. Dubbed. **92m/C VHS.** *GE* Rutger Hauer, Dagmar Lassander; *D:* Adrian Hoven.

Dandy in Aspic 🐾½

1968 (R) A double-agent is asked to kill himself in this hard-to-follow British spy drama. The film is based on Derek Marlowe's novel. Mann died midway through shooting and Harvey finished direction. **107m/C VHS, GB** Laurence Harvey, Tom Courtenay, Lionel Stander, Mia Farrow, Harry Andrews, Peter Cook, Per Oscarsson; *D:* Anthony Mann; *M:* Quincy Jones.

Dandy, the All American Line

1940 Newill stars again as Renfrew of the Mounties—this time he tries to rid the north woods of fur baddies who are trying to take over. **57m/B VHS.** James Newill, Dorothea Kent, Guy Usher, Dave O'Brien, Bob Terry; *D:* Ralph Staub.

Danger Beneath the Sea 🐾🐾

2002 What appears to be a made-for-TV adventure trots out every known submarine movie cliche. The massively jawed Van Dien is Capt. Sheffield, who's been given command of the Lansing, much to the dismay of many of the boat's officers. A nuclear incident occurs while the sub is in the China Sea, and he must deal with uncertainties about a possible war and a mutinous crew. The pace moves along nicely and production values are on the high side. **93m/C VHS, DVD.** Casper Van Dien, Gerald McRaney, Shane Daly, Stewart Bick; *D:* Jon Cassar; *W:* Lucian K. Truscott IV; *C:* Derick Underschultz; *M:* Norman Orenstein.

Danger: Diabolik 🐾🐾

2002 (PG-13) A superthief called Diabolik (Law) continuously evades the law while performing his criminal antics. **99m/C VHS, DVD.** *IT* John Phillip Law, Marisa Mell, Michel Piccoli, Terry-Thomas, Adolfo Celi; *D:* Mario Bava; *W:* Mario Bava, Adriano Baracco, Brian Degas, Tudor Gates; *C:* Antonio Rinaldi; *M:* Ennio Morricone.

Danger in the Skies 🐾½

The Pilot 1979 (PG) An alcoholic airline pilot tries to straighten out his life while he nearly loses everything while drinking on the job. **99m/C VHS.** Cliff Robertson, Diane Baker, Frank Converse, Edward Binns; *D:* Cliff Robertson; *C:* Walter Lassally. **CABLE.**

Danger Lights 🐾½

1930 Depicts the railroads and the railroad men's dedication to each other and their trains. **73m/B VHS.** Jean Arthur, Louis Wolheim, Robert Armstrong, Andrews, Gordon MacRae, Milo O'Shea, Frank Andrews; *D:* George B. Seitz.

Danger on the Air 🐾½

1938 A radio program sponsor—a much-despised misogynist—is murdered, and the sound engineer attempts to solve the mystery. Features Cobb in one of his earliest roles. Garrett also directed "Lady in the Morgue" that year. **70m/B VHS.** Donald Woods, Nan Grey, Berton Churchill, Jed Prouty, William Lundigan, Richard "Skeets" Gallagher, Edward Van Sloan, George Meeker, Lee J. Cobb, Edward Arnhur, Linda Hayes, Louise Stanley; *D:* Otis Garrett.

Danger Trails 🐾½

1935 Rehashed western programmer. Features the hero who must save the rancher's honor as well as the ranch, while fighting detestable hombres with the traditional fare as an arsenal. **55m/B VHS.** Guinn "Big Boy" Williams, Marjorie Gordon, Wally Wales, John Elliott, Ace Can, Edmund Cobb; *D:* Robert F. "Bob" Hill.

Danger UXB 🐾🐾½

1981 During the 1940 London blitz, "Danger UXB" was scrawled wherever there was—or thought to be—an unexploded German bomb. This miniseries covers the exploits of the Royal Engineers whose job it was, with little training and lots of nerve, to defuse the bombs. Based on the memoirs of Major A.B. Hartley of the Royal Engineers. Jeremy Summers. TV.

Danger Zone 🐾🐾

1951 A man is hired to bid for a saxophone at an auction and then has the instrument stolen from him. He discovers it contained stolen jewelry and tries to recover it. **56m/B VHS.** Hugh Beaumont, Tom Neal, Richard Travis, Virginia Dale; *D:* William Burke; *W:* Julian Harmon; *C:* Jack Greenhalgh.

Danger Zone 🐾🐾

1987 (R) A low-budget, low-brow flick about an all-female rock band whose bus breaks down in the middle of the desert, leaving the girls to defend themselves against a merciless motorcycle gang. You'll wish this one was never made. **90m/C VHS.** Robert Canada, Jason Williams, Kriss Braxton, Dana Dowell, Jamie Ferreira; *D:* Henry Vernon.

Danger Zone 2 🐾

1989 (R) Americcan mining expert Rick Morgan (Zane) uncovers a worldwide nuclear plot when he's lured to East Africa to supposedly contain a toxic spill. Instead, he's being used to recover a load of plutonium. **92m/C VHS, Billy** Zane, Ron Silver, Robert Downey Jr., Cary-Hiroyuki Tagawa; *D:* Allan Eastman; *W:* Jeff Albert; *C:* Yossi Wein.

Danger Zone 3: Steel Horse War 🐾

1990 (R) The "Danger Zone" dude is back and this time he's taken on a bevy of biker-types in a most gruesome battle to make our deserts safe. **91m/C VHS.** Jason Williams, Robert Random, Robert Random; *D:* Geoffrey G. Bowers; *W:* Duany Ross Clements.

Dangerous 🐾🐾🐾

1935 Davis won her first Oscar for her rather overdone portrayal of a has-been alcoholic actress recognizes her from her days as a star. **72m/B VHS.** Bette Davis, Franchot Tone, Margaret Lindsay, Alison Skipworth, John Eldridge, Dick Foran; *D:* Alfred E. Green. *Oscars '35:* Actress (Davis).

Danger of Love 🐾½

1995 (R) Married teacher Michael Carlin (Penny) has an affair with seductive colleague Carolyn Warmus (Robertson) but when he's about to end it, his wife is murdered. The detective (Bologna) thinks Michael is guilty but it's Carolyn who's hiding all the seecrets. Based on a true story; made for TV. **95m/C VHS.** Joe Penny, Jenny Robertson, Joseph Bologna, Richard Lewis, Fairuza Balk, Deborah Benson, Sydney Walsh; *D:* Joyce Chopra. TV.

Lee (Facinelli) is expected to join the family's failing oil business; Squirrel (Embry) thinks he should care for his alcoholic father; and John (Mills) is a natural at cattle ranching. Coming-of-age comedy deals in honest emotion and humor, and doesn't resort to syrupy sentiment or small-town stereotyping. Texas-born writer-director McCanlies' feature debut. **95m/C VHS, DVD.** Michael O'Neill, Eddie Jones, Alexandre Holden; *D:* Tim McCanlies; *W:* Tim McCanlies; *C:* Andrew Dintenfass; *M:* Steve Dorff.

The Dangerous 🎬½ (R) 1995 New Orleans' seamy underworld is the setting for a hot-headed cop (Pare), a mystery man (Davi), and the beauty (Barbien) they're both interested in. Also available unrated. **96m/C VHS.** Robert Davi, Michael Pare, Paula Barbieri, Elliott Gould, John Savage, Joel Grey; **D:** Maria Dante, Rod Hewitt; **W:** Rod Hewitt.

A Dangerous Age 🎬½ 1957 A young girl, hoping to marry her lover, runs away from boarding school. **70m/C VHS.** Ben Piazza, Ann Pearson; **D:** Sidney J. Furie; **W:** Sidney J. Furie; **C:** Herbert S. Alpert.

Dangerous Appointment 🎬🎬
One in a Million 1934 Story of an innocent store clerk accused of theft and attempted murder. **66m/B VHS.** Charles Starrett, Dorothy Wilson, Guinn "Big Boy" Williams, Holmes Herbert; **D:** Frank Strayer; **W:** Karl Brown, Robert Ellis; **C:** M.A. Anderson.

Dangerous Beauty 🎬🎬🎬 *The Honest Courtesan; Indiscretion; Venice; Courtesan* 1998 (R) In 16th-century Venice, poor but beautiful Veronica (McCormack) gains wealth and power by becoming a sought after courtesan. The bewigged, bewitched and bewildered heads of state fall as hard for the comely courtesan as victims to the plague that strikes Venice later in the film. The one man she wants, however, Marco Venier (Sewell), comes from a wealthy family that looks down on the common Veronica. Director Herskovitz mixes the strong feminist messages with humor and a modern sensibility that sometimes make you forget you're watching a period film. Based on the biography of the real Veronica Franco by Margaret Rosenthal. **112m/C VHS, DVD.** Catherine McCormack, Rufus Sewell, Moira Kelly, Jacqueline Bisset, Oliver Platt, Fred Ward, Naomi Watts, Jeroen Krabbe, Joanna Cassidy, Daniel Lapaine, Jake Weber, Simon Dutton, Michael Culkin, Peter Eyre; **D:** Marshall Herskovitz; **W:** Jeannine Dominy; **C:** Bojan Bazelli; **M:** George Fenton.

Dangerous Charter 🎬🎬½ 1962 A group of fishermen discover a deserted yacht and man its helm. But their good fortune takes a decided turn for the worst as they become caught in mob-propelled danger. **76m/C VHS.** Chris Warfield, Sally Fraser, Richard Foote, Peter Foster, Wright King; **D:** Robert Gottschalk.

Dangerous Child 🎬🎬½ 2001 Sixteen-year-old Jack Cambridge (Merriman) is one angry kid. He lives with his divorced mom Sally (Burke), who tries to make allowances for his temper, even when he starts hitting her, because she doesn't want Jack taken away from her. But it's only a matter of time before the situation gets worse. Scarily good performance by Merriman. **95m/C VHS, DVD.** Delta Burke, Ryan Merriman, Marc Donato; **D:** Graeme Campbell; **W:** Karen Stillman; **C:** Nikos Evdemon. **CABLE**

Dangerous Corner 🎬🎬🎬 1934 Adaptation of J.B. Priestley's play captures a seance after the suicide of the prime suspect in a theft of government bonds. Those closest to the deceased share inner secrets that reveal truths about the heist. Great twists, well cast, a film much ahead of its time. **66m/B VHS.** Virginia Bruce, Conrad Nagel, Melvyn Douglas; **D:** Phil Rosen; **W:** J.B. Priestley, Anne Morrison Chapman, Madeleine Ruthman. **VIDEO**

Dangerous Crossing 🎬🎬 1953 Crain's lovely but this is a B-list film noir. Ruth Bowman (Crain) is enjoying her transatlantic honeymoon cruise until her new spouse John (Betz) disappears. The only problem is the passenger list says Ruth is traveling alone and no one admits to seeing the doctor Paul Manning (Rennie) is willing to help out the bewildered bride. **75m/B DVD.** Jeanne Crain, Michael Rennie, Carl Betz, Max (Casey Adams) Showalter, Mary Anderson, Willis Bouchey, Yvonne Peattie, Marjorie Hoshelle; **D:** Joseph M. Newman; **W:** Leo Townsend; **C:** Joseph LaShelle; **M:** Lionel Newman.

Dangerous Curves 🎬½ 1988 (PG) Two friends are assigned to deliver a new Porsche to a billionaire's daughter—one of them talks the other into taking a little detour, and the trouble begins. **93m/C VHS.** Robert Stack, Tate Donovan, Danielle von Zerneck, Robert Klein, Elizabeth Ashley, Leslie Nielsen; **D:** David Lewis. **VIDEO**

Dangerous Curves 🎬🎬 1999 (R) Handsome attorney decides to track down a former lover. This is always a mistake. **85m/C VHS, DVD.** Robert Carradine, David Carradine, Maxine Bahns, Marina Carradine; **D:** Jeremiah Cullinane; **W:** Christopher Wood; **C:** Laurence Manly; **M:** Siobhan Cleary. **VIDEO**

Dangerous Evidence: The Lori Jackson Story 🎬🎬½ 1999 Whitfield stars in this true story as Lori Jackson, a 1980s civil rights activist who takes on the case of Marine Corporal Lindsay Scott (Yearwood), the only black in the battalion, who is falsely accused of raping a white officer's wife. When he is convicted on circumstantial evidence, Jackson secures a new trial, which exacts a high price on her own life. Based on the book "Dangerous Evidence" by Ellis A. Cohen. **90m/C VHS, DVD.** Lynn Whitfield, Richard Lineback, Richard Yearwood, Peter MacNeill, Erica Luttrell, Barbara Mamabolo, Geordie Johnson, Bruce Gray; **D:** Sturla Gunnarsson; **W:** Sterling Anderson; **M:** Jonathan Goldsmith. **CABLE**

Dangerous Game 🎬½ 1990 (R) A computer hacker leads his friends through a department store's security system, only to find they can't get out until morning. They soon discover they are not alone when one of the group turns up dead. **102m/C VHS, DVD.** Miles Buchanan, Sandy Lillington, Kathryn Walker, John Polson; **D:** Stephen Hopkins.

Dangerous Game 🎬🎬 *Snake Eyes* 1993 (R) Abrasive filmmaker Eddie Israel's (Keitel) new movie is about a couple's disintegrating marriage turning violent. Stars Sarah (Madonna) and Francis (Russo) find the on-camera violence spilling over into their tangled private lives while Eddie finds his personal traumas intruding more and more into the fictional material. Very raw movie within a movie features volatile Keitel (who also worked with Ferrara on "Bad Lieutenant") and suitably histrionic Russo; Madonna manages to hold her own in the least showy role, a cinematic first. Eddie's betrayed and bewildered wife is sympathetically portrayed by Ferrara, director Abel's wife. Also available in an unrated version. **107m/C VHS, DVD.** Harvey Keitel, James Russo, Madonna, Nancy Ferrara; **D:** Abel Ferrara; **W:** Nicholas St. John.

Dangerous Ground 🎬🎬 1996 (R) Hackneyed thriller has expatriate South African Vusi (Cube) returning to his homeland to find his younger brother Steven, who has double-crossed the head of a drug cartel. Since Vusi's departure 12 years ago, apartheid's been replaced by gangs and drugs, and while combing the dangerous streets of Johannesburg, the graduate student implausibly turns into a gun-wielding hero. Rhames's sinister drug lord Muki is pic's best character. Lead Cube shows just how limited his acting ability is while Hurley displays the rest of her showy role. Interracial relationships are as sociological problems are used as plot devices and then ignored. Filmed on location in South Africa, this shoot-em-up's locale could easily be Anytown, USA. **92m/C VHS, DVD.** Ice Cube, Elizabeth Hurley, Ving Rhames, Eric Miyeni, Sechaba Morojele; **D:** Darrell Roodt; **W:** Darrell Roodt, Greg Latter; **C:** Paul Gilpin; **M:** Stanley Clarke.

Dangerous Heart 🎬🎬 1993 (R) A crooked undercover cop steals a bundle from a drug dealer and gets himself killed for his troubles. Only the dealer doesn't know where the money is. So he decides to befriend the cop's widow, get romantically involved, and see what she knows. **93m/C VHS.** Timothy Daly, Lauren Holly, Jeffrey Nordling, Alice Carter, Joe Pantoliano; **D:** Michael Scott; **W:** Patrick Cirillo.

Dangerous Holiday 🎬🎬 1937 A young violin prodigy would rather be just "one of the boys" than be forced to practice all the time. He decides to run away but has everyone in an uproar thinking he's been kidnapped. **54m/B VHS.** Hedda Hopper, Guinn "Big Boy" Williams, Jack La Rue,

Franklin Pangborn, Grady Sutton; **D:** Nicholas T. Barrows; **W:** Nicholas T. Barrows; **C:** William Nobles; **M:** Alberto Colombo.

Dangerous Hours 🎬🎬 1919 An anti-communist propaganda film with Hughes as the innocent young college boy who gets duped by the evil Marxists until he realizes the truth of his all-American upbringing. Silent with original organ score. **88m/B VHS.** Lloyd Hughes; **D:** Fred Niblo; **C:** George Barnes.

Dangerous Indiscretion 🎬🎬 1994 (R) Ad exec finds his girlfriend is actually a woman married to a very powerful man, who's not going to be happy to find out about their liaison. **81m/C VHS.** Joan Severance, C. Thomas Howell, Malcolm McDowell; **D:** Richard Kletter; **W:** Richard Kletter, Jack Tarpon; **M:** Richard Gibbs.

Dangerous Liaisons 🎬🎬 *Les Liaisons Dangereuses; Dangerous Love Affairs* 1960 A couple take each other to the brink of destruction via their insatiable desire for extra-marital affairs. Vadim attempted to repeat his success with Brigitte Bardot by featuring wife Annette as a new sex goddess, but lightning didn't strike twice. **111m/B VHS, DVD.** *FR FT* Gerard Philipe, Jeanne Moreau, Jeanne Valerie, Annette (Stroyberg) Vadim, Simone Renant, Jean-Louis Trintignant, Nicolas Vogel; **D:** Roger Vadim; **W:** Roger Vadim; **C:** Marcel Grignon.

Dangerous Liaisons 🎬🎬🎬 1988 (R) Stylish and absorbing, this adaptation of the Laclos novel and the Christopher Hampton play centers around the relationship of two decadent members of 18th-century French nobility. The Marquise de Merteuil (Close) and the Vicomte de Valmont (Malkovich) spend their time testing and manipulating the loves of others. Merteuil wishes Valmont to deflower teenager Cecile (Thurman) while Valmont himself is after the virtuous married Madame de Tourvel (Pfeiffer). They find love often has a will of its own. Interesting to comparison-view with director Milos Forman's version of this story, 1989's "Valmont". **120m/C VHS, DVD.** John Malkovich, Glenn Close, Michelle Pfeiffer, Uma Thurman, Keanu Reeves, Swoosie Kurtz, Mildred Natwick, Peter Capaldi; **D:** Stephen Frears; **W:** Christopher Hampton; **C:** Philippe Rousselot; **M:** George Fenton. Oscars '88: Adapt. Screenplay, Art Dir./Set Dec., Costume Des.; British Acad. '89: Adapt. Screenplay, Support. Actress (Pfeiffer); Cesar '90: Foreign Film; Writers Guild '88: Adapt. Screenplay. **TV**

Dangerous Life 🎬🎬 1989 Explosive drama brings to the screen the story of the Philippine uprising. It shows the horrible events that lead to the fall of Marcos and permitted the rise of Corazon Aquino. **163m/C VHS.** Gary Busey, Ruben Rustia, Cris Vertido; **D:** Robert Markowitz; **W:** David Williamson.

The Dangerous Lives of Altar Boys 🎬🎬🎬 2002 (R) Don't let the title keep you away from this innovative coming-of-ager set in the '70s. Rebellious Catholic schoolmates Francis (Hirsch) and Tim (Culkin) seek love and chaos, respectively, while attending St. Agatha Parochial school, run by iron-fisted, wooden-legged nun Foster and hard-drinking priest D'Onofrio. While Francis falls for a girl with a secret past (Malone), Tim fantasizes about staging a coup against the sadistic Sister. The boys channel their boredom into increasingly dangerous pranks and a sacrilegious comic book called "The Atomic Trinity," which stars motorcycle-riding witch Nunzilla (Foster's nun rides a moped). Inventive directorial debut by Care with animated fantasy segments deftly directed by Spawn creator Todd McFarlane. Based on the 1994 novel by

Chris Fuhrman. **105m/C VHS, DVD.** *US* Kieran Culkin, Emile Hirsch, Jena Malone, Jodie Foster, Vincent D'Onofrio, Jake Richardson, Tyler Long; **D:** Peter Care; **W:** Jeff Stockwell, Michael Petroni; **C:** Lance Acord; **M:** Marco Beltrami, Joshua Homme. Ind. Spirit '03: First Feature.

Dangerous Love WOOF! 1987 Advice to the lovelorn: Avoid this one. Female members of a video dating service are being filmed in a death scene—their own. **87m/C VHS.** Lawrence Monoson, Brenda Bakke, Peter Marc, Elliott Gould, Anthony Geary; **D:** Marty Ollstein.

A Dangerous Man: Lawrence after Arabia 🎬🎬🎬 1991 At the 1919 Paris Peace Conference, T.E. Lawrence serves as the liaison to the Hashemite delegation in an effort to have the Allies agree to Arab independence. He finds the diplomatic fields more treacherous than anything he encountered during WWI. Fiennes does well in the difficult role of the reluctant, ambivalent hero. **104m/C VHS, DVD.** *GB* Ralph Fiennes, Denis Quilley, Alexander Siddig, Nicholas Jones, Roger Hammond, Peter Copley, Paul Freeman, Polly Walker; **D:** Christopher Menaul; **W:** Tim Rose Price. **TV**

Dangerous Minds 🎬🎬½ *My Posse Don't Do Homework* 1995 (R) Based on the autobiography of LouAnne Johnson (Pfeiffer), a 10-year Marine turned inspirational inner-city high school English teacher. Naturally, Johnson has to take on the establishment educational system to fight for her kids. If you can buy Pfeiffer as an ex-jarhead, a tough teacher should be no problem. A subplot romance involving Pfeiffer and Andy Garcia was cut from the film to focus on the teacher/student byplay (which seems a real shame); Elaine May did a uncredited script rewrite. Kinda squishy and surprisingly successful. **99m/C VHS, DVD.** Michelle Pfeiffer, George Dzundza, Courtney B. Vance, Robin Bartlett, Renoly Santiago, Lorraine Toussaint, John Neville; **D:** John N. Smith; **W:** Ronald Bass; **C:** Pierre Letarte. Blockbuster '96: Drama Actress, T. (Pfeiffer).

Dangerous Mission 🎬🎬½ 1954 A young woman witnesses a mob murder in New York and flees to the Midwest, pursued by killers and the police. Good cast couldn't do much with this one. **75m/D VHS.** Victor Mature, Piper Laurie, Vincent Price, William Bendix; **D:** Louis King; **W:** W.R. Burnett, Charles Bennett.

Dangerous Moonlight 🎬🎬🎬 *La Dialgonale du Fou* 1984 (PG) A drama built around the World Chess championship competition between a renowned Russian master and a young, rebellious dissident. The chess game serves as both metaphor and background for the social and political tensions it produces. With English subtitles. **96m/C VHS, DVD.** *SI* Liv Ullmann, Michel Piccoli, Leslie Caron, Alexandre Arbatt; **D:** Richard Dembo; **C:** Raoul Coutard. Oscars '84: Foreign Film.

Dangerous Obsession 🎬 *Divine Obsession; Mortal Sins* 1988 (R) A woman kidnaps the doctor she blames for her boyfriend's death and instead of exacting revenge, she makes him her personal sex slave. In the case of this flick, it's really a fate worse than death. **81m/C VHS.** *IT* Corinne Clery, Brett Halsey; **D:** Lucio Fulci; **M:** Simon Boswell.

Dangerous Orphans 🎬🎬½ 1986 (R) Not completely awful tale of three brothers, orphaned as boys when their father is murdered before their very eyes, and the vendetta they have against the killer. **90m/C VHS, DVD.** *NZ* Peter Stevens, Peter Bland, Ian Mune, Ross Girven, Jennifer Ward-Lealand; **D:** John Laing.

Dangerous Passage ∂∂ 1944 A ne'er-do-well inherits 200 grand but gets in trouble before he can collect it. He ends up falling in with assorted misfits aboard a tramp steamer. 60m/B VHS, DVD, Robert Lowery, Phyllis Brooks, Jack La Rue, Victor Kilian, Charles Arnt, John Eldridge. **D:** William Berke. **W:** Daniel Mainwaring. **C:** Fred H. Jackman Jr.; **M:** Alexander Laszlo.

A Dangerous Woman ∂∂ 1993 (R) No, not the femme fatale romance the word "dangerous" suggests. Instead, the eponymous character is a mildly retarded woman, Martha (Winger), whose simplistic view on life places her in ethically compromising positions. When a hunky Irish handyman (Byrne) comes on the scene and seduces both her and the aunt with whom she lives (Hershey), Martha awakens to feelings she has never experienced. Winger's performance is both sensitive and provocative, but is wasted in a film filled with two-dimensional characters, and rarely, not too much of a point. Adapted from a novel by Mary McGarry Morris. Screenplay by Foner, wife of director Gyllenhaal. 101m/C VHS, Debra Winger, Barbara Hershey, Gabriel Byrne, David Strathairn, Chloe Webb, John Terry, Jan Hooks, Paul Dooley, Viveka Davis, Richard Riehle, Laurie Metcalf; **D:** Stephen Gyllenhaal; **W:** Naomi Foner; **C:** Robert Elswit; **M:** Carter Burwell.

Dangerous Youth ∂ These Dangerous Years 1958 Would-be Liverpool rocker Vaughan is drafted into the army where he becomes a man. He gets into trouble, goes AWOL, but manages to set things right. The Brit version of the troubled-teen exploitation flick. 97m/B VHS, GB Frankie Vaughan, George Baker, Carole Lesley, Jackie Lane, Eddie Byrne, Thora Hird; **D:** Herbert Wilcox. **W:** Jack Trevor Story.

Dangerously Close ∂½ 1986 (R) A group of anti-crime high school students organize a hall monitoring gang that becomes a group of neo-fascist disciplinarians. The Brit version of the troubled-teen... well, J. Eddie Peck; **D:** Albert Pyun; **C:** Walt Lloyd.

Daniel ∂∂½ 1983 (R) The children of a couple who were executed for espionage (patterned after the Rosenbergs) struggle with their past in the 1960s. So-so adaptation of E.L. Doctorow's "The Book of Daniel." 130m/C VHS, Timothy Hutton, Amanda Plummer, Mandy Patinkin, Lindsay Crouse, Ed Asner, Ellen Barkin; **D:** Sidney Lumet; **C:** Andrzej Bartkowiak.

Daniel Boone ∂∂½ 1934 Daniel Boone guides a party of settlers from North Carolina to the fertile valleys of Kentucky, facing Indians, food shortages and bad weather along the way. O'Brien turns in a fine performance as the early American frontier hero. 75m/B VHS, DVD, George O'Brien, Heather Angel, John Carradine; **D:** David Howard.

Daniel Boone: Trail Blazer ∂∂½ 1956 Low-budget, though surprisingly well-acted rendition of the frontiersman's heroics, filmed in Mexico. 75m/B VHS, DVD, Bruce Bennett, Lon Chaney Jr., Faron Young, Damian O'Flynn, Fred Kohler Jr., Claudio Brook, Kem Dibbs; **D:** Ismael Rodriguez, Albert C. Gannaway; **W:** Tom Hubbard, John Patric; **C:** Jack Draper; **M:** Raul Lavista.

Daniel Deronda ∂∂½ 2002 Daniel Deronda (Dancy) is the handsome, idealistic young ward of Sir Hugo Malinger (Fox), who dreams of doing something with his life in 1875 Victorian England. Two women will influence his decisions. The first is the headstrong Gwendolen Harleth (Garai), who will make a devil's bargain when she agrees to marry the wealthy and possessive Henleigh Grandcourt (Bonneville) to rescue her family from penury. The second is Jewess Vira Lapidoth (Mary), whom Daniel saves from drowning. He aids her singing career and helps her search for her family—a search that will lead to revelations about Daniel's own past. Last novel by George Eliot. 210m/C VHS, DVD, GB Hugh Dancy, Romola Garai, Hugh Bonneville, Jodhi May, Edward Fox, Barbara Hershey, Amanda Root, Greta Scacchi, Celia Imrie, David Bamber, Daniel Evans, Alan Corduner, Jamie Bamber; **D:** Tom Hooper; **W:** Andrew Davies; **M:** Robert (Rob) Lane. TV

Daniel Takes a Train ∂∂ Szerencses Daniel 1983 Daniel (Rudolf) and his friend Gyuri (Zsoter) take a train to a small town on the Austrian border, seeking to escape Hungary after the 1956 uprising. Gyuri is a soldier who has deserted and is anxious to get away, but Daniel refuses to leave his missing girlfriend Mariann (Szeri) behind. Hungarian with subtitles. 92m/C VHS, HU Mari Torocsik, Peter Rudolf, Sandor Zsoter, Kati Szerb, Dezso Garas; **D:** Pal Sandor; **W:** Zsuzsa Toth; **C:** Elemer Ragalyi; **M:** Gyorgy Selmeczi.

Daniella by Night ∂∂ 1961 French model Daniella (Sommer) gets a contract to work for an Italian fashion house in Rome and she's soon attracting a lot of attention, including some that involves a spy plot. This leads to a chase through a Paris cabaret and a nude scene of Sommer, so how much does the story really matter, anyway. French with subtitles. 83m/B VHS, FR Elke Sommer, Ivan Desny, D: Max Pecas; M: Grisha Dabat, Wolfgang Steinhardt; D: Andre Germain; M: Charles Aznavour, Georges Garvarentz.

Danielle Steel's Changes ∂∂½ Changes 1991 Ladd is a successful, divorced New York TV anchorwoman who turns her life upside-down when she marries an equally successful, widowed Los Angeles surgeon (Nouri). Can they overcome their bicoastal careers to make things work? What do you think? 96m/C VHS, DVD, Cheryl Ladd, Michael Nouri, Christopher Gartin, Randee Heller, Charles Frank, James Sloyan, Cynthia Bain; D: Charles Jarrott. TV

Danielle Steel's Daddy ∂∂½ Daddy 1991 Ad exec Oliver Watson (Duffy) is happily married to Sarah (Mulgrew) and living the good life with their three kids—so he thinks. Then Sarah announces she's leaving and Oliver's left to cope with family crisis as a single parent. A move to a new job in LA finds Oliver falling for an actress (Carter) and wondering if his family can ever be put back together again. 95m/C VHS, DVD, Patrick Duffy, Lynda Carter, Kate Mulgrew; D: Michael Miller. TV

Danielle Steel's Fine Things ∂∂ Fine Things 1990 Bernie Fine thinks everything will be dandy now that he has a beautiful new bride and a cute stepdaughter. Then his wife dies and his stepdaughter's unreliable father wants sole custody. What's a nice guy to do? Based on the novel by Danielle Steel. 145m/C VHS, DVD, D.W. Moffett, Tracy Pollan, Judith Hoag, Cloris Leachman, Noley Thornton; D: Tom (Thomas R.) Moore; M: Peter Lefcourt. TV

Danielle Steel's Heartbeat ∂∂½ Heartbeat 1993 Shameless soap opera with Draper as Adrian Townsend, an L.A. TV-news producer with a self-involved ad-exec hubby (Kilner) who never wants children because of his own lousy childhood. When Adrian gets preggers the louse dumps her and she's left to weep prettily. That is until lovable divorced dad Bill Grant (Ritter) comes along to dry her eyes. Predictable and glossy adaptation of the Steel best-seller. 95m/C VHS, DVD, Polly Draper, John Ritter, Kevin Kilner, Michael Lembeck, Nancy Morgan, Victor Dimattia, Christian Cousins; D: Michael Miller; W: Jan Worthington. TV

Danielle Steel's Kaleidoscope ∂∂½ Kaleidoscope 1990 Three sisters are separated in childhood, after the mysterious deaths of their parents. Then a detective is hired to reunite the adult siblings. But Hilary, the eldest, has secrets she doesn't want her sisters to share. 96m/C VHS, DVD, Jaclyn Smith, Perry King, Colleen Dewhurst, Donald Moffat; D: Jud Taylor. TV

Danielle Steel's Palomino ∂∂½ Palomino 1991 Bittersweet romance with Frost as an ambitious photojournalist who gets involved with a headstrong cowboy (Horsley). Their differences drive them apart and tragedy strikes when Frost becomes a paraplegic after a horse-riding accident. This leads her to new goals and the eventual return of her old flame. Between the career and the equally impressive blond locks of Frost, there's a lot of streaming in the wind hair shots. Horsley's merely tall, dark, and handsome. 96m/C VHS, DVD, Lindsay Frost, Lee Horsley, Eva Marie Saint, Rod Taylor, Michele Greene, Beau Gravitte; D: Michael Miller; W: Karol Ann Hoeffner; C: Lloyd Ahern II; M: Dominic Frontiere. TV

Danielle Steel's Star ∂∂½ Star 1993 Garth is the country girl with big dreams of a singing career but an unhappy love life. She falls for an idealist lawyer (Bierko) but their romance is put on hold by career ambitions. She goes to Hollywood and gets discovered, becoming a singing/acting sensation who's under the thumb of her increasingly obsessed manager. Wass. Meanwhile, Bierko's trapped in a miserable marriage to the wealthy, influential Farrell. Do the true lovers get together? (Take a guess.) Although the story spans 15 years and lots of tribulations the young Garth never ages a day. 90m/C VHS, Jennie Garth, Craig Bierko, Ted Wass, Terry Farrell, Penny Fuller, Mitchell Ryan, Jim Haynie; D: Michael Miller; W: Claire Labine. TV

Danny ∂∂½ 1979 (G) Charming story of a lonely young girl who receives an injured horse that was no longer fit for the spoiled daughter of the rich owners. 90m/C VHS, Rebecca Page, Janet Zarish, Barbara Jean Earhardt, Gloria Maddox, George Luce; D: Gene Feldman.

Danny Boy ∂∂½ Angel 1982 (R) Takes place in Ireland where a young saxophonist witnesses a murder and, in an effort to understand it, sets out to find the killer. Thought-provoking film is meant to highlight the continuing struggles in Ireland. 92m/C VHS, IR Stephen Rea, Veronica Quilligan, Honor Heffernan, Alan Devlin, Peter Caffrey, Ray McAnally; D: Neil Jordan; W: Neil Jordan; C: Chris Menges.

Danny Boy ∂∂∂ 1946 Veteran dog, returning from the war, has difficulty adjusting to life back home. Things get worse for him and his young master when Danny Boy is assumed to be shell-shocked dog stories ever filmed. Danny Boy is assumed to be shell-shocked and dangerous. One of the few shell-shocked dog stories ever filmed. 67m/B VHS, Robert "Buzzy" Henry, Ralph Lewis, Sybil Merritt; D: Terry Morse; W: Raymond L. Schrock; C: Jack Greenhalgh; M: Walter Greene.

Danny Deckchair ∂∂∂ 2003 Danny Morgan (Rhys) an eccentric dreamer and cement-truck driver, has just discovered his realtor girlfriend Trudy (Clarke) is dating one of her clients. Well, as any young man faced with this knowledge would do, he attaches giant helium balloons to a lawn chair and flies away. Faster than you can say "'99 Luftballoons" he crashes in the backyard of Glenda (Otto), a small town parking cop who is lonely and frustrated with love. Typical of such premises, it'y fall in love in an endearing fashion. Despite uncritical script and enormous plot holes, Aussie comedy is mainly watchable due to its two romantic leads. 99m/C VHS, DVD, AU Rhys Ifans, Miranda Otto, Justine Clarke, Rhys Muldoon, Rod Zuanic, Maggie Dence, Jeanette Cronin, Frank Magree, Andrew Fielan, Andrew Batchelor, Jules Sobotta, Alex Mann; D: Jeff Balsmeyer; W: Jeff Balsmeyer, Martin McGrath; M: David Donaldson, Janet Roddick, Steve Roche.

Danny Roane: First Time Director ∂½ 2006 (R) One-time sitcom star Danny Roane (Dick) has been blacklisted in Hollywood because of his infamous partying. After sobering up, Danny tries to make a comeback by directing his own autobiographical movie. But after Danny goes on a bender, he decides to suddenly turn his production into a musical and winds up in deep trouble. Your tolerance for Dick's antics will determine if you enjoy the flick. 83m/C DVD, Andy Dick, Michael Hitchcock, Bob Odenkirk, Anthony Rapp, James Van Der Beek, Maura Tierney, Jack Black, Mo Collins, Danny Trejo, Sara Rue, Kevin Farley, Paul Henderson; Cameos: Ben Stiller; D: Andy Dick; W: Andy Dick; C: Ben Gamble; M: Jason Miller. CABLE

Dante's Inferno ∂∂∂ 1924 Abandon all hope you who watch this film. A one-time friend sends his capitalist nemesis a copy of Dante's "Inferno," and the man reads the book and dreams he's gone to hell (would that be the dress circle?) A silent film that was controversial in its day: the body-stockinged actors were believed to be nude (which would have made it the first nudie comedy). 54m/B VHS, Lawson Butt, Howard Gaye, Ralph Lewis, Pauline Starke, Josef Swickard; D: Henry Otto.

Dante's Inferno: Life of Dante Gabriel Rossetti ∂∂ 1969 The flamboyant life of mid-19th century English Pre-Raphaelite artist/poet Dante Gabriel Rossetti is depicted with the usual womanizing Rossetti was part of the lead-womanizing Rossetti was part of the lead-intellectual group of his age, which in...

cluded Swinburne, Morris, Ruskin, and Rossetti's sister, the poet Christina Rossetti. **90m/B VHS. GB** Oliver Reed; **D:** Ken Russell.

Dante's Peak 1997 (PG-13) Northwest volcano serves up a smorgasbord of molten disaster in the second most desirable town in the U.S.—the titular Dante's Peak. Brosnan is the intuitive scientist who comes to Washington to match wits with the conical adversary and joins forces with the town's tres femme mayor Wando (Hamilton). Ashes fall like snow in January, computer generated lava flows profusely, poisonous gases leak out and water turns to acid, all with desired nail-biting effect. Wando's two kids, dog and grandma lend folksy charm and the requisite loved-ones-flick is not exactly for the whole family. Clichéd and predictable, flick runs the Disaster Movie Playbook page by page as plot takes a backseat to nonstop action. **112m/C VHS, DVD, HD DVD.** Pierce Brosnan, Linda Hamilton, Charles Hallahan, Grant Heslov, Elizabeth Hoffman, Jamie Renee Smith, Arabella Field, Tzi Ma, Jeremy Foley, Brian Reddy, Kirk Trutner; **C:** Andrzej Bartkowiak; **D:** Roger Donaldson; **W:** Leslie Bohem; **M:** John (Gianni) Frizzell.

Danton 1982 (PG) A sweeping account of the reign of terror following the French Revolution. Focuses on the title character (wonderfully portrayed by Depardieu) and is directed with searching parallels to modern-day Poland by that country's premier filmmaker, Andrzej Wajda. Well-done period sets round out a memorable film. In French with English subtitles. **136m/C VHS, DVD. FR** Gerard Depardieu, Wojciech Pszoniak, Patrice Chereau, Angela Winkler, Boguslaw Linda; **D:** Andrzej Wajda; **W:** Jean-Claude Carriere, Agnieszka Holland, Boleslaw Michalek, Jacek Gasiorowski, Andrzej Wajda. '83: Foreign Film; Cesar '83: Director (Wajda). Montreal World Film Fest. '83: Actor (Depardieu).

Danzon 1991 (PG) Julia (Rojo), a single, working-class mom escapes the drudgery of her simple existence by going to a Mexico City dance hall every Wednesday. There she loses herself to the movement of the danzon, a dance with Haitian roots, popular in Mexico for over 100 years. When her partner of six years, Carmelo (Rergis), doesn't show up one night, her life is turned upside down. So begins a search for Carmelo—and herself. Quiet and restrained, like the ballroom-style danzon at the center of the plot. Applauded at Cannes. In Spanish with English subtitles. **103m/C VHS. SP** Maria Rojo, Carmen Salinas, Blanca Guerra, Tito Vasconcelos, Victor Carpinteiro, Victor Vasconcelos; **D:** Maria Novaro; **W:** Maria Novaro, Beatriz Novaro.

Darby O'Gill & the Little People 1959 (G) Set in Ireland, roguish old story teller Darby O'Gill (Sharpe), tumbles into a well and visits the land of leprechauns who give him three wishes in order to rearrange his life. When he tries to tell his friends what happened, they think that it is only another one of his stories. Connery plays the young man who takes Darby's job and courts his daughter (Munro) as well. A wonderful Disney production (despite its disappointing boxoffice performance) with wit, charm and an ounce or two of terror. **93m/C VHS, DVD.** Albert Sharpe, Janet Munro, Sean O'Connery, Estelle Winwood, Kieron Moore, Jimmy O'Dea; **D:** Robert Stevenson; **W:** Lawrence Edward Watkin; **C:** Winton C. Hoch.

Darby's Rangers 1958 WWII pot-boiler with Garner as the leader of a commando team put together for covert operations in North Africa and Italy. Slow-paced battle sequences combine with lots of romantic scenes as the soldiers chase women when not chasing the enemy. **122m/B VHS.** James Garner, Jack Warden, Edd Byrnes, Peter Brown, Stuart Whitman, David Janssen, Etchika Choureau, Venetia Stevenson, Torin Thatcher, Joan Elan, Corey Allen, Murray Hamilton; **D:** William A. Wellman; **W:** Guy Trosper; **C:** William Clothier; **M:** Max Steiner.

Daredevil 2003 (PG-13) Daredevil made his appearance in Marvel Comics in 1964. Having lost his sight in an industrial accident when he was a kid, his remaining senses are enhanced but he's basically still human. Too bad the movie isn't. It's flashy and loud but uninvolving. Lawyer Matt Murdock (Affleck) turns vigilante and dons red leather and a goofy mask when one too many criminals goes free. The big (literally) bad guy is Kingpin (an avuncular Duncan) who keeps flashy assassin Bullseye (Farrell) on the payroll. Meanwhile, Matt is trying to make time with heiress Elektra (Garner) who thinks Daredevil killed her father—putting a crimp in the potential romance. Garner looks great in leather and refines the butt-kicking skills she uses in her TV series "Alias" to good effect. Affleck's sorta lightweight since Daredevil has lots of issues; he's better at sarcasm than angst. **114m/C VHS, DVD. US** Ben Affleck, Jennifer Garner, Michael Clarke Duncan, Colin Farrell, Joe Pantoliano, Jon Favreau, David Keith, Erik Avari, Paul Ben-Victor, Derrick O'Connor, Leland Orser, Scott Terra, Kevin Smith; **Cameos:** Stan Lee; **D:** Mark Steven Johnson; **W:** Mark Steven Johnson; **C:** Ericson Core; **M:** Graeme Revell. Golden Raspberries '03: Worst Actor (Affleck).

Daredevils of the Red Circle 1938 Three young men set out to free a man held prisoner by an escaped convict. A serial in 12 chapters. **195m/B VHS.** Charles Quigley, Bruce Bennett, Carole Landis; **D:** John English, William Witney.

Darfur Now 2007 (PG) Documentary attempts to bring the complex, tribal-based Darfur (Sudan) conflict and its accompanying genocide to American audiences. Director Braun focuses on six individuals—three in the midst of the horror (a refugee camp leader, a mother who joins a guerilla group after the death of her son, and a food aid worker), and three trying to affect change from the outside (an activist advocating divestment of Sudanese stock, the UN prosecutor preparing a case against those responsible for the genocide, and actor Cheadle, who is committed to raising awareness about the conflict). Cheadle and fellow American Sterling are noble, but their stories are significantly less interesting than the others, especially Argentinian-born prosecutor Moreno-Ocampo, who has already lived through a brutal dictatorship in his homeland, and is committed to bringing justice to Darfur. **99m/C DVD. US D:** Theodore Braun; **W:** Theodore Braun; **C:** Kirsten Johnson; **M:** Graeme Revell.

Daring Danger 1932 McCoy is nearly killed in a fight with the villainous Alexander. When he recovers he finds Alexander has joined forces with a rustler (Ellis), so McCoy battles both of them—while his horse goes for help. **58m/B VHS.** Tim McCoy, Richard Alexander, Robert Ellis, Alberta Vaughn, Wallace MacDonald, Murdock MacQuarrie, Max Davidson; **D:** David Ross Lederman.

Daring Dobermans 1973 (PG) In this sequel to "The Doberman Gang," the barking bank-robbers get a new set of crime-planning masters. A young Indian boy who loves the dogs enters the picture and adds a new twist to their perfect crime. **88m/C VHS.** Charles Robinson, Tim Considine, David Moses, Claudio Martinez, Joan Caulfield; **D:** Byron Ross Chudnow.

Daring Game 1968 A group of scuba divers nicknamed the Flying Fish attempt to rescue a woman's husband and daughter from an island dictatorship. Failed series pilot by producer Ivan Tors, better known for "Sea Hunt" and "Flipper." **100m/C VHS.** Lloyd Bridges, Brock Peters, Michael Ansara, Joan Blackman, Michael Walker; **D:** Laslo Benedek; **M:** George Bruns. **TV**

Dario Argento's Trauma Trauma 1993 (R) When a teenage girl's parents are decapitated, she and an artist friend start following the clues to a psychotic killer known as "The Headhunter." Trademark horror work for Italian cult director Argento with high suspense quotient and equally high gore. An unrated version is also available. **106m/C VHS, DVD.** Christopher Rydell, Asia Argento, Laura Johnson, James Russo, Brad Dourif, Frederic Forrest, Piper Laurie; **D:** Dario Argento; **W:** T.E.D. Klein, Dario Argento.

The Darjeeling Limited 2007 (R) Brothers Francis (Wilson), Peter (Brody), and Jack (Schwartzman) seek spiritual healing after their father's death on a cross-Asia trip aboard the Darjeeling Limited. Along the way, the three men struggle with each other and their own problems, including a (possibly intentional) accident that's left Francis's head in bandages, Peter's desertion of his pregnant wife, and Jack's recent breakup (chronicled in the companion short film "Hotel Chevalier"), until Francis reveals that their trip is taking them to their estranged mother (Huston), now a nun living in India. Anderson manages to capture the absurdity and humanity of the crises while exploring the individual struggles for meaning and purpose, while infusing the film with his traditional detail-obsessed style. He and co-screenwriters Schwartzman and Coppola penned the film while traveling across India by, of course, train. **91m/C DVD. GB** Owen Wilson, Adrien Brody, Jason Schwartzman, Amara Karan, Wally Wolodarsky, Anjelica Huston; **D:** Wes Anderson; **W:** Jason Schwartzman, Wes Anderson, Roman Coppola; **C:** Robert Yeoman.

The Dark The Mutilator 1979 (R) A supernatural beast commits a string of gruesome murders. **92m/C VHS, DVD.** William Devane, Cathy Lee Crosby, Richard Jaeckel, Keenan Wynn, Vivian Blaine, Biff (Elliott) Elliot, Warren Kemmerling, Casey Kasem, John Bloom; **D:** John Cardos; **W:** Stanford Whitmore; **C:** John Morrill.

The Dark 1994 (R) Cop and scientist seek a mysterious graveyard creature who holds both the power to heal and destroy. One man wants to kill it, one man wants to save it, and they race to be the first to find it. **90m/C VHS.** Bron James, Jaimz Woolvett, Cynthia Belliveau, Stephen McHattie, Dennis O'Connor, Neve Campbell, Christopher Bondy, William Lynn; **D:** Craig Pryce; **W:** Robert Cooper.

A Dark Adapted Eye 1993 Sinister TV mystery adapted from the psychological thriller by Ruth Rendell (writing as Barbara Vine). In 1951 Vera Hillyard (Imrie) is hung for murdering her younger sister Eden (Ward)—an act that including young niece Faith (Bonham Carter). Long haunted by the "why" of the crime, Faith later begins an investigation into her family's past—and discovers very dark and disturbing secrets dating back to WWII. Title refers to a vision problem caused by remaining in darkness too long. **150m/C VHS. GB** Helena Bonham-Carter, Celia Imrie, Sophie Ward, Robin Ellis, Ciaran Hinds, Pip Torrens, William Gaminara, Polly Adams, Bernice Stegers, Steven Mackintosh, Jason Durr; **D:** Tim Fywell; **W:** Sandy Welch; **C:** Rex Maidment; **M:** David Ferguson.

Dark Age 1988 (R) An Australian conservationist must track down a rampaging, giant, semi-mythical alligator before it is killed by bounty hunters. Based on the novel (and Aboriginal legend) "Numunwari." **90m/C VHS. AU** John Jarratt, David Gulpilil, Max Phipps, Ray Meagher, Nikki Coghill, Burnam Burnam; **D:** Arch Nicholson.

The Dark Angel 1935 Kitty Vane (Oberon) loves both Alan Trent (March) and her best friend Gerald Shannon (Marshall) who are going off to fight in WWI. However, Kitty accepts Alan's marriage proposal. A misunderstanding leads to trouble and Alan is presumed dead. Actually, he's been blinded and decides not to return to Kitty after the war, so Alan changes his name and tries to make a new life. Meanwhile, Kitty has agreed to marry Gerald, although he knows she's still pining. Naturally, everyone finds out the truth in this sentimental weepie that got Oberon an Oscar nomination. **108m/B VHS.** Merle Oberon, Fredric March, Herbert Marshall, Janet Beecher, John Halliday, Claud Allister, Henrietta Crosman, Frieda Inescort; **D:** Sidney Franklin; **W:** Lillian Hellman, Mordaunt Sharp; **C:** Gregg Toland; **M:** Alfred Newman. Oscars '36: Art Dir./Set Dec.

The Dark Angel 1991 Maud is the young and innocent heiress to a fortune in this gothic romance of creeping unease. She is intrigued by the romantic portrait of her youthful and unknown Uncle Silas. But her mysterious uncle is no longer the Byronic hero. What secret wickedness does his ravaged face hide? And what about Maud's drug-addicted governess and the brutish young man in the cemetery? Does Uncle Silas just want Maud's fortune or Maud herself? Excellent performances by O'Toole as the decadent uncle and Edney as the innocent-but-not-stupid Maud. Based on the novel "Uncle Silas" by Sheridan Le Fanu. Made for British TV. **150m/C VHS. GB** Peter O'Toole, Beatie Edney, Jane Lapotaire, Tim Woodward, Alan MacNaughton, Barbara Shelley, Guy Rolfe; **D:** Peter Hammond. **TV**

Dark Angel: The Ascent 1994 (R) She-devil gets tired of hell and decides to get a look at the world upstairs. She also decides to turn vigilante and dispatch some bad guy souls to her former home. **80m/C VHS.** Charlotte Stewart, Daniel Markel, Michael C. Mahon, Nicholas Worth, Milton James, Angela Featherstone; **D:** Linda Hassani; **M:** Matthew Bright; **M:** Fuzzbee Morse.

Dark Asylum 2001 (R) Shrink Maggie Bleham (Porizkova) is called on to examined a serial killer (Drake) who's so dangerous that authorities have brought him to an abandoned asylum to be evaluated. Naturally, the nutball gets loose and kills his guards with the doc next on his list. Only she's got other ideas. **96m/C VHS, DVD.** Paulina Porizkova, Larry Drake, Judd Nelson, Jurgen Prochnow; **D:** Gregory Gieras; **W:** Gregory Gieras; **C:** Viorel Sergovici Jr. **VIDEO**

Dark August 1976 (PG) A New Yorker drops out and transplants to rural Vermont, where he accidentally kills a young girl and then suffers numerous horrors as a result of a curse put on him by the girl's grandfather. **87m/C VHS.** J.J. Barry, Carole Shelyne, Kim Hunter, William Robertson; **D:** Martin Goldman.

The Dark Backward 1991 (R) A dark, subversive comedy about a garbage man who dreams of making it big in show biz as a stand-up comedian. He's terrible until a third arm starts growing out of his back and the sheer grotesqueness of his situation makes him a temporary star. Caan and Newton are interestingly cast, but young, first-time director Rifkin's foray into David Lynch territory was not well received by critics. **97m/C VHS, DVD.** Judd Nelson, Bill Paxton, Wayne Newton, Lara Flynn Boyle, James Caan, Rob Lowe, Claudia Christian, King Moody, Adam Rifkin; **D:** Adam Rifkin; **W:** Adam Rifkin; **C:** Joey Forsyte; **M:** Marc David Decker.

Dark Before Dawn 1989 (R) American farmers and Vietnam veterans team up against corrupt government officials and ruthless businessmen in this violent film about the plight of the underdog. **95m/C VHS.** Doug McClure, Sonny Gibson, Ben Johnson, Billy Drago, Rance Howard, Morgan Woodward, Buck Henry, Jeffery Osterhage, Red Steagall, John Martin, Gary Cooper; **D:** Robert Totten.

Dark Blue 2003 (R) Another James Ellroy L.A. cop novel comes to life in this powerful tale of deep-seated corruption set against the Rodney King verdict and its aftermath. Veteran cop Eldon Perry (Russell) is part of the elite Special Investigations Squad, a brutal, corrupt, and racist unit run by Jack Van Meter (Gleeson). Partnered with Van Meter's green nephew Bobby (Speedman), Eldon is assigned to steer a homicide investigation away from the two snitches who did it. Standing in his way is the black deputy chief (Rhames) who has vowed to shut down the SIS. Russell's outstanding performance anchors the proceedings, which gets somewhat muddied by the 1965 Watts riots, and Ayers wrote "Training Day" at about the same time he was adapting "Blue." **116m/C VHS, DVD. US** Kurt Russell, Ving Rhames, Scott Speedman, Brendan Gleeson, Mi-

Dark Blue Almost Black 🐾½ *Azul Oscuro Casi Negro* 2006 Overstuffed debut drama about personal ambition vs. responsibility and family obligation. Jorge is forced to put his life on hold after his father suffers a severe stroke. He takes over his father's janitorial job while continuing his studies at night and coping with other personal issues, including an imprisoned brother and a gay best friend. Spanish with subtitles. 105m/C **DVD.** *SP* Quim Gutierrez, Antonio de la Torre, Hector Colomo, Marta Etura, Raúl Arévalo, Eva Pallares; *D:* Daniel Sanchez Arevalo. *W:* Daniel Sanchez Arevalo. *C:* Juan Carlos Gomez. *M:* Pascal Gaigne.

Dark Breed 🐾🐾 1996 (R) Ewww, yuck, it's sci-fi infestation time once again as Nick Saxon (Scalia) is assigned to find the bodies of six astronauts whose top secret space craft has mysteriously crashed. He discovers that the bodies are playing host to reptilian parasites with designs on world domination. 104m/C **VHS, DVD.** Jack Scalia, Jonathan Banks, Robin Curtis, Donna W. Scott; *D:* Richard Pepin.

Dark City 🐾🐾 1997 Brooding city of gloom floats in a sunless world, with skylines nightmarishly changing as its residents sleep. The city seems to belong to no era, looking at others like a work of German expressionism. Sometimes it looks like '60s Cleveland. Director Proyas seems to have wanted to make a futuristic film noir like "Blade Runner," but gets lost somewhere along the way. He does however, keep the style. Disfigured Dr. Schreber (Sutherland) is forced by a dying race of pasty-faced long-coated aliens to use humans as guinea pigs in an attempt to find out what makes them tick. John Murdoch (Sewell) wakes up in a hotel room with a dead body and no memory of his life. Searching for his past, he wanders through one incredible set after another, but is it real or is it hypodermically injected? Hurt is a detective who only wants to stop the grisly murders. Garbled story rewards persistence at the end. 103m/C **VHS, DVD.** Kiefer Sutherland, William Hurt, Rufus Sewell, Richard O'Brien, Jennifer Connelly, Ian Richardson, Colin Friels, Frank Gallacher, Bruce Spence, John Bluthal, Mitchell Butel, Melissa George; *D:* Alex Proyas; *W:* Alex Proyas, Lem Dobbs, David S. Goyer; *C:* Darius Wolski; *M:* Trevor Jones.

Dark Command 🐾🐾🐾 1940 The story of Quantrell's Raiders who terrorized the Kansas territory during the Civil War until one man came along to put a stop to it. Colorful and talented cast add depth to the script. Also available colorized. 95m/B **VHS.** John Wayne, Walter Pidgeon, Claire Trevor, Roy Rogers, Marjorie Main, George "Gabby" Hayes; *D:* Raoul Walsh.

Dark Corner 🐾🐾🐾 1946 Private detective Bradford Galt (Stevens) is framed and suspects his ex-partner during the winds up dead. Then there's a guy in a white suit (Bendix) who keeps dogging him, and sinister wealthy art dealer Hardy Cathcart (Webb) seems to be pulling everyone's strings. It's a good thing Kathleen (Ball) believes in

chael Michele, Lolita (David) Davidovich, Dash Mihok, Kurupt, Khandi Alexander, Master P; *D:* Ron Shelton; *W:* David Ayer; *C:* Berry Peterson; *M:* Terence Blanchard.

Dark Blue World 🐾🐾½ *Tmavo-modry Svet* 2001 (R) Told in flashbacks, this is an old-fashioned WWII epic about heroism and romance in 1950 in Czechoslovakia, Franta (Veichy) is imprisoned by the Communists who fear the war hero's previous contacts with democracy. After the Nazis invaded his country in 1939, Franta fled to England, where he joins the RAF and befriends younger Czech pilot Karel (Hadek). But the duo have a falling out over a local woman, Susan (Fitzgerald), who favors the mature Franta. Czech, German, and English dialogue. 115m/C **VHS, DVD.** *CZ GB* Ondrej Veichy, Tara Fitzgerald, Krysztof Hadek, Oldrich Kaiser, Charles Dance, Linda Rybova, Hans-Jorg Assmann, Anna Massey; *D:* Jan Sverak; *W:* Zdenek Sverak; *C:* Vladimir Smutny; *M:* Ondrej Soukup.

Dark Corners 🐾 2006 Writer/director Ray Gower plays mind games with his audience and then leaves us confused and dissatisfied. Karen Clark (Birch), a suburban housewife undergoing fertility treatments, begins having horrific nightmares. Disturbed mortuary assistant Susan Hamilton (yep, Birch again) has a few backouts. Both women learn that people they know are victims of a serial killer. Ah, if only the plot were actually that simple. 92m/C **DVD.** *GB* Thora Birch, Christien Anholt, Toby Stephens, Oliver Price, Ray Charleson, Joanna Hole; *D:* Ray Gower; *W:* Ray Gower; *C:* Paul Sadourian; *M:* Andrew Pearce. **VIDEO**

The Dark Crystal 🐾🐾🐾 1982 (PG) Jen and Kira, two of the last surviving Gelflings, attempt to return a crystal shard (discovered with the help of a sorceress) to the castle where the Dark Crystal lies, guarded by the cruel and evil Skeksis. Designed by Brian Froud and the creators of the Muppets. 93m/C **VHS, DVD, UMD.** *D:* Jim Henson, Frank Oz; *W:* Jim Henson, David Odell; *C:* Oswald Morris; *M:* Trevor Jones; *V:* Jim Henson, Frank Oz, Kathryn Mullen, Dave Goelz.

The Dark Dancer 🐾½ 1995 (R) Psychology prof Maggie (Tweed), who authors books on feminine sexual behavior, gets her experience first-hand by working in a strip club. Now, she's also the target of a police investigation. Also available unrated. 98m/C **VHS.** Shannon Tweed, Jason Carter, Lisa Pescia, Francesco Quinn; *D:* Robert Burge; *W:* Robert Burge, Terry Chambers; *C:* Eric Scott; *M:* David Connor.

The Dark Dealer 🐾🐾 1995 Three terror tales find the Devil's assistant dealing a deadly game of blackjack to a trio in limbo, with the cards propelling each man into a horrific adventure. Provides some real scares along with effective (if low-budget) special effects. 85m/C **VHS.** Mark Fickert, Richard Hull, Vincent Gaskins, Rocky Patterson, Gordon Fox; *D:* Tom Alexander.

Dark Eyes 🐾🐾½ *Les Yeux Noirs; Oci Ciornie* 1987 An acclaimed Italian film based on a several short stories by Anton Chekov. Mastroianni is a weak-willed Italian, trapped in a marriage of convenience, who falls in love with a mysterious, also married, Russian beauty he meets in a health spa. He embarks on a journey to find her and, perhaps, his lost ideals. Hailed as Mastroianni's consummate performance in Italian with English subtitles. 118m/C **VHS.** *IT* Marcello Mastroianni, Silvana Mangano, Elena Sofonova, Marthe Keller, Pina Cei; *C:* Franco Di Giacomo, Carlo Di Palma; *M:* Mastroianni.

Dark Forces 🐾🐾 *Harlequin* 1983 (PG) A faith-healer promises to help a senator's dying son and finds the politician's wife also desires his assistance. This Australian film is uneven and predictable. Though rated "PG," beware of two rather brief, but explicit, nudity scenes. 96m/C **VHS, DVD.** *AU* Robert Powell, David Hemmings, Broderick Crawford, Carmen Duncan; *D:* Simon Wincer.

the lug. Gripping, intricate film noir. 99m/B **VHS, DVD.** Mark Stevens, Clifton Webb, William Bendix, Lucille Ball, Cathy Downs, Reed Hadley, Constance Collier, Kurt Kreuger; *D:* Henry Hathaway; *W:* Jay Dratler, Bernard C. Schoenfeld, Leo Rosten; *C:* Joe MacDonald; *M:* Cyril Mockridge.

The Dark Half 🐾🐾 1991 (R) Flawed chiller based on a Stephen King novel. Thad Beaumont's serious novels have been failures, but writing as George Stark, he's had phenomenal success with grisly horror stories. In a publicity stunt Thad kills off and publicly buries George (who doesn't want to stay dead). Soon everyone who's crossed Thad is brutally murdered. Hutton acquits himself well in a dual role. Otherwise, the psychological thrills are few and the gore is plentiful. Pittsburgh serves as location for King's usual New England territory. Film's release was delayed due to Orion's bankruptcy problems. 122m/C **VHS, DVD.** Timothy Hutton, Amy Madigan, Michael Rooker, Julie Harris, Robert Joy, Kent Broadhurst, Beth Grant, Rutanya Alda, Tom Mardirosian, Chelsea Field, Royal Dano; *D:* George A. Romero; *W:* George A. Romero; *C:* Tony Pierce-Roberts; *M:* Christopher Young.

Dark Habits 🐾🐾½ *Entre Tinieblas* 1984 An early Almodovar farce about already-demented nuns in a failing convent trying to raise funds with the help of a nightclub singer who is on the run. Although certainly irreverent, it doesn't quite have the zing of his later work. In Spanish with subtitles. 116m/C **VHS, DVD.** *SP* Carmen Maura, Christina Pascual, Julieta Serrano, Marisa Paredes; *D:* Pedro Almodovar; *W:* Pedro Almodovar; *C:* Angel Luis Fernandez.

Dark Harbor 🐾🐾 1998 (R) A wealthy married couple, traveling to their vacation home off the coast of Maine, stop to help an injured young man. A series of coincidences leads the threesome to spend the weekend together in the couple's isolated retreat, where sexual attraction makes the situation very volatile. 89m/C **VHS, DVD.** Alan Rickman, Polly Walker, Norman Coleman Howard, Justin Lazard; *C:* Walt Lloyd; *M:* Adam Gorgoni.

Dark Horse 🐾½ 1992 (PG) Meyers is a young woman distraught over the death of her mother. She gets into trouble and is assigned to do community service work at a horse farm where she finds herself caring for a prize-winning horse. 98m/C **VHS.** Ari Meyers, Mimi Rogers, Ed Begley Jr., Donovan Leitch, Samantha Eggar; *D:* David Hemmings.

Dark Hour, The 🐾½ 1936 Two detectives team up to solve a murder in which multiple suspects are involved. Clever, sophisticated production; Leigh's best role. 72m/B **VHS, DVD.** Ray Walker, Irene Ware, Benton Churchill, Hedda Hopper, Hobart Bosworth, E.E. Olive; *D:* Charles Lamont.

Dark Journey 🐾🐾 1937 WWI Stockholm is the setting for a love story between a double agent and the head of German intelligence. Based on Sinclair Gluck's "The Last Trap." 82m/B **VHS, DVD.** *GB* Vivien Leigh, Conrad Veidt, Joan Gardner, Anthony Bushell, Ursula Jeans; *D:* Victor Saville.

change of pace dual role. Otherwise, the psychological thrills are few and the gore is plentiful. Pittsburgh serves as location for King's usual New England territory...

Dark Justice 🐾🐾 1991 Judge by day, avenger by night, in this actioner created from three episodes of the late-night TV series. Judge Nicholas Marshall is disgusted by the criminals sprung on legal loopholes and backroom deals, so he decides to take justice into his own hands. 95m/C **VHS, DVD.** Ramy Zada, Dick O'Neill, Clayton Prince, Begona Plaza. **TV**

Dark Justice 🐾🐾 *Yup-Yup Men* 2000 Thirty years after Robert (Bumiller) sees his homeless dad murdered on the LA streets, he's still traumatized—wandering around and muttering to himself (hence the alternate film title). Robert's personal hero is vigilante comic book star Dark Justice, in fact, he decides to emulate his hero by taking on real street criminals, except Robert kills them instead of turning them in to the cops. 89m/C **DVD.** William Bumiller, David Bowe, Jocelyn Seagrave, Matt Gallini, Chase Mackenzie Bebak; *D:* Glenn Kinker; *W:* Glenn Kinker; *C:* Yoram Astrakhan; *M:* Sharon Farber.

The Dark Knight 2008 (PG-13) The brooding Bat (Bale) is back (after 2005's "Batman Begins") and has been making headway battling criminals in Gotham City. At least until super-freaky evil mastermind The Joker (Ledger in his last completed role before his untimely death) enters the picture. And if our hero didn't have enough trouble, good guy District Attorney Harvey Dent (Eckhart) is also having some personality issues. Caine, Freeman, and Oldman lend their talents again (as coos director Nolan). Fortunately, boring Katie Holmes has been replaced by the more lively Gyllenhaal as Bruce Wayne's friend, ADA Rachel Dawes. Not yet reviewed. 7m/C **DVD.** Christian Bale, Heath Ledger, Aaron Eckhart, Maggie Gyllenhaal, Gary Oldman, Michael Caine, Morgan Freeman, Eric Roberts, Anthony Michael Hall, Christian Bale, Maggie Gyllenhaal, Gary Oldman, Michael Caine, Eric Roberts, Cillian Murphy, Morgan Freeman, Anthony Michael Hall, Monique Gabriela Curnen, Nestor Carbonell, Michael Jai White, Melinda McGraw, William Fichtner, Joshua Harto, Colin McFarlane; *D:* Christopher Nolan; *W:* Christopher Nolan, Jonathan Nolan.

Dark of the Night 🐾🐾 *Mr. Wrong* 1985 A young woman, new to the city, purchases a used Jaguar and finds she must share it with the car's former owner—a woman murdered inside the Jag. Decent psycho-thriller with some suspenseful and amusing moments. 88m/C **VHS, DVD.** *NZ* Heather Bolton, Gary Stalker, Michael Haigh, Danny Mulheron, Kate Harcourt; *D:* Gaylene Preston; *W:* Gaylene Preston, Geoff Murphy, Graham Tetley; *C:* Thomas Burstyn; *M:* Jonathan Crawford.

Dark of the Sun 🐾🐾½ 1947 Bogart plays a convict who escapes from San Quentin to prove he was framed for the murder of his wife. He undergoes plastic surgery and is hidden and aided by Bacall as he tries to find the real killer. Stars can't quite compensate for a far-fetched script and so-so direction. 107m/B **VHS, DVD.** Humphrey Bogart, Lauren Bacall, Agnes Moorehead, Bruce Bennett, Tom D'Andrea; *D:* Delmer Daves.

The Dark Past 🐾🐾½ 1949 A

than Nolan, Christopher Nolan, Jonathan Nolan; *C:* Hans Zimmer, Wally Pfister, Wally Pfister, Hans Zimmer, James Newton Howard.

Dark Mirror 🐾🐾 1946 A psychologist and a detective struggle to determine which twin sister murdered a prominent physician. Good and evil siblings finely acted by de Havilland. 85m/B **VHS, DVD.** Olivia de Havilland, Lew Ayres, Thomas Mitchell, Garry Owen; *D:* Robert Siodmak; *C:* Milton Krasner.

Dark Mountain 🐾½ 1944 A forest ranger rescues his gal from the clutches of a hardened criminal. 56m/B **VHS, DVD.** Robert Lowery, Ellen Drew, Regis Toomey, Eddie Quillan, Elisha Cook Jr.; *D:* William Berke, William C. Thomas; *W:* Maxwell Shane; *C:* Fred H. Jackman Jr.; *M:* Willy Stahl.

Dark Night of the Scarecrow 🐾🐾½ 1981 Thriller with a moral. Prejudiced townspeople execute a retarded man who was innocently befriended by a young girl. After his death, unusual things begin to happen. Slow to start but effective. 100m/C **VHS.** Charles Durning, Tanya Crowe, Larry Drake; *D:* Frank De Felitta. **TV**

Dark Obsession 🐾🐾 *Diamond Skulls* 1990 (R) Byrne portrays a husband who lives out his dark erotic fantasies with his wife (Donohoe), and is involved in a hit-and-run accident. Driven by guilt, madness slowly begins to take him. Ugly and depressing. Based on a true scandal. Available in an "NC-17" rated version. 87m/C **VHS, DVD.** Peter Allen, Gabriel Byrne, Amanda Donohoe, Michael Hordern, Judy Parfitt, Douglas Hodge, Sadie Frost, Ian Carmichael; *D:* Nick Broomfield; *W:* Tim Rose Price; *C:* Michael Coulter; *M:* Hans Zimmer.

Dark Odyssey 🐾🐾 1957 Metzger's first feature tells the tragic tale of a young Greek seaman who jumps ship in New York in order to avenge his sister's rape. He finds himself confronted between his masculine sense of family honor and love when he falls for a Greek-American woman. Director's cut includes the original theatrical trailer. 85m/B **VHS, DVD.** David Hooks, Edward Brazier, Jeanne Jerrams; *D:* William Kyriakis, Radley Metzger; *W:* William Kyriakis, Radley Metzger; *C:* Peter Erik Winkler; *M:* Laurence Rosenthal.

Dark Places ⚫⚫ 1973 (PG) Masquerading as a hospital administrator, a former mental patient inherits the ruined mansion of a man who had killed his wife and children and died insane. As he lives in the house, the spirit of its former owner seems to overcome him with a need to repeat the crime. Meanwhile, Collins, and Lom think the nut is hiding money they would like to get their collective hands on. Low-budget but fairly effective. **91m/C VHS**. *GB* Joan Collins, Christopher Lee, Robert Hardy; *D:* Don Sharp.

Dark Planet ⚫⚫ 1997 (R) In the year 2636 Earth is in the middle of WW6 and it's up to rebel commander Hawke (Mercurio) to search for the Dark Planet and complete a secret assignment that's humanity's last hope. **99m/C VHS, DVD**. Paul Mercurio, Harley Jane Kozak, Michael York, Maria Ford, Ed O'Ross; *D:* Albert Magnoli; *W:* S.O. Lee; *C:* William MacCollum.

The Dark Power ⚫ 1985 Ex-cowboy LaRue and his trusty whip provide this flick with its only excitement. As sheriff, he must deal with the dead Mexican warriors who rise to wreak havoc when a house is built on their burial ground. **87m/C VHS, DVD**. Lash LaRue, Anna Lane Tatum; *D:* Phil Smoot.

Dark Remains ⚫⚫ 2005 Scary little indie horror flick. Allen and Julie are devastated when their young daughter Emma is murdered in her bed. They rent a remote mountain cabin hoping the distance will help them heal, but photographer Julie sees Emma's ghostly image in the pictures she's taking. Seems the cabin has been the spot of numerous suicides and Emma is trying to warn her parents to get out. **91m/C VHS, DVD**. Greg Thompson, Cheri Christian, Rachel Jordan, Jeff Evans, Scott Hodges; *D:* Brian Avenet-Bradley; *W:* Brian Avenet-Bradley; *C:* Laurence Avenet-Bradley; *M:* Benedikt Bryden.

The Dark Ride ⚫⚫½ 1984 Lunatic picks up women with the intention of raping and killing them. Ugly thriller based on the evil deeds of serial murderer Ted Bundy. **83m/C VHS**. James Luisi, Susan Sullivan, Martin Speer; *D:* Jeremy Hoenack.

Dark Rider 1991 Dark Rider is a mysterious, motorcycle riding hero who comes to the rescue of a small town. Besieged by a gangster who buys up all their land, the townspeople must abandon their homes and indeed, their very dreams. That is until Dark Rider rolls into to town to enact his own unique brand of vengeance. **94m/C VHS**. Joe Estevez, Doug Shanklin, Alicia Kowalski, David "Shark" Fralick, Chuck Williams; *D:* Bob Ivy; *W:* Bob Ivy, Chuck Williams; *C:* Mark W. Gray; *M:* Brad Scott Gish.

Dark River: A Father's Revenge ⚫⚫ 1990 When his daughter is killed in a toxic waste dump accident, a man begins revenge on the company and its managers. Tense, with important message. **95m/C VHS**. Helen Hunt, Mike Farrell, Tess Harper, Philip Baker Hall; *D:* Michael Pressman. **TV**

Dark Sanity Woof! 1982 Uninvolving attempt at horror has a recently de-institutionalized woman confront a pagan cult in the New England town into which they've moved. Based upon the Thomas Tryon novel. **118m/C VHS**. Betta Davis, Rosanna Arquette, David Ackroyd, Rene Auberjonois, Michael O'Keefe, Joanna Miles; *D:* Lee Penn; *W:* Jennifer Miller, Jack Guss; *Nar:* Donald Pleasence. **TV**

Dark Secrets ⚫ 1995 (R) Reporter Claire (Parent) wants to get a hot story on sex club mogul Justin DeVille (Carroll) and winds up falling prey to his charms. But Justin's not the trusting kind and sets up some loyalty tests for Claire. The unrated version is 99 minutes. **90m/C VHS, DVD**. Monique Parent, Julie Strain, Justin Carroll; *D:*

The Dark Secret of Harvest Home ⚫⚫½ 1978 An urban couple confront a pagan cult in the New England town into which they've moved. Something you'll wish the film would do) while everyone else just thinks she's losing her marbles. Problem is we don't really care. **89m/C VHS**. Aldo Ray, Kory Clark, Andy Gwyn, Bobby Holt; *D:* Martin Greene.

Bowen; *W:* Steve Tymon; *C:* Keith Holland); *M:* Erfem Bergman.

Dark Side ⚫⚫ *Darkness Falling* 2002 (R) While investigating the suicide of her twin sister Jane, corporate lawyer Megan (Kidder) discovers that Jane was involved with the lurid underworld of kinky sex and a mysterious lover. **85m/C VHS, DVD**. *CA GB* Janet Kidder, Jason Priestley, Patsy Kensit, Paul Johansson; *D:* Dominic Shiach; *W:* Sheldon Inkol; *C:* Harry Makin.

Dark Side of Genius ⚫⚫ 1994 (R) Jennifer Cole (Hughes), a reporter for an L.A. arts weekly, tries to get the story on artist Julian Jons (Fraser), who's just been paroled after being imprisoned for the murder of his model. Now his lurid new paintings of a sultry nude model hint at some obsessive behavior and Jennifer's reporter instincts may be the death of her. **86m/C VHS**. Finola Hughes, Brendan Fraser, Glenn Shadix, Moon Zappa, Patrick Richwood, Seymour Cassel; *D:* Phedon Papamichael; *W:* Fred Stroppel; *C:* Phedon Papamichael; *M:* Tom Hiel.

The Dark Side of Love ⚫⚫½ 1979 A young girl gets involved with the rougher side of New Orleans society, gets pregnant, and realizes how she's been degraded. **94m/C VHS**. James Stacy, Glynnis O'Connor, Jan Sterling, Mickey Rooney; *D:* Sam Wanamaker; *C:* Michael D. Margulies. **TV**

Dark Side of Midnight ⚫⚫½ *The Creeper* 1986 (R) A super-detective tracks down a psychopathic killer. **108m/C VHS, DVD**. James Moore, Wes Olsen, Sandy Schemmel, Dave Bowling; *D:* Wes Olsen; *W:* Wes Olsen; *C:* Wes Olsen.

The Dark Side of the Heart ⚫⚫ *El Lado Oscuro del Corazon* 1992 Magic realism features in this story of struggling Buenos Aires poet Oliverio (Grandinetti) who falls in love with prostitute Ana (Ballesteros). She wants to keep things businesslike but when a man finds a woman whose lovemaking causes them to actually levitate, he's not about to make stable planets. During their journey, they battle their alien mascot (who closely resembles a walking beach ball), as well as a "sensitive" and intelligent bombing device which starts to question the meaning of its existence. Enjoyable early feature from John "Halloween" Carpenter and Dan "Aliens" O'Bannon. Fun, weird, and unpredictable. **95m/C VHS, DVD**. Dan O'Bannon, Brian Narelle, Dre Panich, Cal Duniholm; *D:* John Carpenter; *W:* John Carpenter, Dan O'Bannon; *C:* Douglas Knapp; *M:* John Carpenter.

Dark Tide ⚫⚫ 1993 (R) Erotic action thriller about a pair of deep sea divers whose love life is disturbed when their boat captain becomes sexually fixated on the woman. Also available in an uncut, unrated version. **92m/C VHS**. Brigitte Bako, Richard Tyson, Chris Sarandon; *D:* Luca Bercovici.

Dark Tower ⚫⚫ 1987 (R) Decent cast is wasted in yet another inept attempt at horror. An architect is dismayed to learn that an evil force is inhabiting her building and it might just be the ghost of her dearly departed husband. **91m/C VHS**. Michael Moriarty, Jenny Agutter, Theodore Bikel, Carol Lynley, Anne Lockhart, Kevin McCarthy; *D:* Ken Barnett,

---

Freddie Francis, Ken Wiederhorn; *W:* Robert J. Avrech, Kenneth G. Blackwell.

Dark Universe ⚫⚫½ 1993 (R) An alien terror wants to conquer the Earth and make its inhabitants their new food source. **83m/C VHS, DVD**. Blake Pickett, Cherie Scott, Bently Tittle, John Maynard, Paul Austin Saunders, Tom Ferguson, Steve Barkett, Joe Estevez, Patrick Moran; *D:* Steve Latshaw; *W:* Patrick Moran.

Dark Victory ⚫⚫⚫½ 1939 A spoiled young heiress discovers she is dying from a brain tumor. She attempts to pack a lifetime of parties into a few months, but is rescued by her doctor, with whom she falls in love. Classic final scene with Davis at the top of her form. Bogart plays an Irish stable hand, but not especially well. Also available in a colorized version. **106m/B VHS, DVD**. Bette Davis, George Brent, Geraldine Fitzgerald, Humphrey Bogart, Ronald Reagan, Henry Travers; *D:* Edmund Goulding; *W:* Casey Robinson; *C:* Ernest Haller; *M:* Max Steiner.

Dark Water ⚫⚫ 2005 (PG-13) Dahlia Williams' (Connelly) soon-to-be ex-husband tells her she's nuts and she wonders if he might be right when she moves with her five-year-old daughter Ceci (Gabe) into a dilapidated and perhaps, yes, haunted Roosevelt Island apartment that is plagued by creepy noises from a supposedly vacant flat upstairs. Then there's that little-but-quickly-expanding water stain on the ceiling that seems a little...alive. Tries to be spooky but is just all wet. Based on Hideo Nakata's 2002 Japanese horror film of the same name. **120m/C DVD, Blu-ray Disc, UMD**. *US* Ariel Gade, Jennifer Connelly, John C. Reilly, Tim Roth, Pete Postlethwaite, Dougray Scott, Camryn Manheim, Perla Haney-Jardine, Debra Monk, Elina Lowensohn, Jennifer Baxter; *D:* Walter Salles; *W:* Rafael Yglesias; *C:* Alfonso Beato; *M:* Angelo Badalamenti.

Dark Waters ⚫⚫ 1944 The drowning death of her parents has left a young woman mentally unstable. She returns to her family home in the backwaters of Louisiana with her peculiar aunt and uncle to serve as guardians. It eventually becomes apparent that someone is trying to drive her insane. This one tends to be rather murky and it's not simply due to the plentiful scenes of misty swampland. **93m/B VHS, DVD**. Merle Oberon, Franchot Tone, Thomas Mitchell, Fay Bainter, Elisha Cook Jr., John Qualen, Rex Ingram; *D:* Andre de Toth; *W:* Joan Harrison, Marian Cockrell; *C:* Archie Stout, John Mescall; *M:* Miklos Rozsa.

The Dark Wind ⚫⚫½ 1991 (R) The first of Tony Hillerman's popular Native American mysteries comes to the screen in a lame adaptation. Phillips stars as the Navaho cop investigating a murder on a New Mexico Indian reservation. Since the Navaho believe a "dark wind" enters a man's soul when he does evil, expect some "spirited" goings-on as well. **111m/C VHS, DVD**. Lou Diamond Phillips; *D:* Errol Morris; *W:* Eric Bergren.

Darkdrive ⚫⚫½ 1998 (R) In the near future, the Zircon Corporation has created a virtual prison where the minds of criminals are held in isolation. Naturally, something's gone wrong and it's up to special operations officer Steven Falcon (Olandt) to risk his mind and solve the problem. **100m/C VHS, DVD**. Ken Olandt, Julie Benz, Claire Stansfield, Carlo Scandiuzzi; *D:* Phillip J. Roth; *W:* Alec Carlin; *C:* Andres Garreton; *M:* Jim Goodwin. **VIDEO**

Darker than Amber ⚫⚫ 1970 (R) John D. MacDonald's houseboat-dwelling detective Travis McGee (Taylor) rescues a girl (Kendall) he's fallen for, and soon discovers that the mugs who thugged her were part of a collection racket. A violent action melodrama upgraded from its original "R" rating. **96m/C VHS**. Rod Taylor, Suzy Kendall, Theodore Bikel, Jane Russell, James Booth, Janet MacLachlan, William (Bill) Smith, Anna Capri, Chris Robinson; *D:* Robert Clouse.

Darkest Africa ⚫⚫ *Batmen of Africa; King of the Jungleand* 1936 Legendary animal trainer Beatty is the hero of this 15 episode cliffhanger serial as he vies with beasts—both animal and human. **270m/B VHS**. Edmund Cobb, Clyde Beatty, Manuel King,

---

Elaine Shepard; *D:* Joseph Kane; *W:* Barney A. Sarecky.

Darkman ⚫⚫½ 1990 (R) Raimi's disfigured-man-seeks-revenge suspenser is comicbook kitsch cross-pollinated with a strain of gothic horror. Neeson plays a scientist who's on the verge of discovering the key to cloning body parts; brutally attacked by the henchmen of a crooked politico, his lab is destroyed and he's left for dead. Turns out he's not dead—just horribly disfigured and a wee bit chafed—and he stalks his deserving victims from the shadows, using his lab know-how to disguise his rugged bad looks. Exquisitely violent. Montage by Pablo Ferro. **96m/C VHS, DVD, HD DVD**. Liam Neeson, Frances McDormand, Larry Drake, Colin Friels, Nelson Mashita, Jenny Agutter, Rafael H. Robledo, Nicholas Worth, Theodore (Ted) Raimi, John Landis, William Lustig, Scott Spiegel, Bruce Campbell; *D:* Sam Raimi; *W:* Sam Raimi, Ivan Raimi, Daniel Goldin, Joshua Goldin, Chuck Pfarrer; *C:* Bill Pope; *M:* Danny Elfman.

Darkman 2: The Return of Durant ⚫⚫½ 1994 (R) The first in a series of direct-to-video adventures about disfigured scientist Peyton "Darkman" Westlake (now played by Vosloo), who's continuing his liquid skin research in the hopes of transforming his grotesque appearance. He finds an ally in scientist David Brinkman but Westlake's nemesis, crime boss Robert G. Durant (Drake), wants the property where Brinkman's lab is located. And what Durant wants, he takes. Sam Raimi, who directed the original film, is one of the series producers. **93m/C VHS, DVD**. Arnold Vosloo, Larry Drake, Kim Delaney, Renee O'Connor, Rod Wilson; *D:* Bradford May; *W:* Steven McKay, Chuck Pfarrer; *C:* Bradford May; *M:* Randy Miller. **VIDEO**

Darkman 3: Die Darkman Die ⚫⚫½ 1995 (R) The second direct-to-video Darkman saga finds Dr. Peyton Westlake (Vosloo) disrupting the drug-dealing activities of underworld boss Peter Rooker (Fahey). The obsessed Rooker is determined to figure out the secret to Darkman's enormous strength, employing the feminine wiles of his mistress, Dr. Bridget Thorne (Fluegel). Then Westlake/Darkman finds himself drawn to Rooker's neglected wife and young daughter. Our hero suffers a lot (as usual) and there's lots of action (as usual). **87m/C VHS**. Arnold Vosloo, Jeff Fahey, Darlanne Fluegel, Nigel Bennett, Roxann Biggs-Dawson; *D:* Bradford May; *W:* Mike Werb, Michael Colleary; *C:* Bradford May; *M:* Randy Miller.

Darkness ⚫ 2002 (PG-13) Spanish director Balaguero follows up his debut feature, "The Nameless," with a haunted house chiller that fails its fright quotient. Americans Mark (Glen), his wife Maria (Olin), and their kids Regina (Paquin) and Paul (Enquist) relocate to a rural house somewhere in Spain. Various paranormal experiences begin to occur, which Regina's parents ignore. Her little brother develops unexplained bruises and becomes afraid of the dark. Regina finds out the house has a disturbing history involving children who disappeared. Should have been more scary. **102m/C DVD**. *US* Lena Olin, Iain Glen, Giancarlo Giannini, Fele Martinez, Anna Paquin, Fermi Rexach, Stephen Enquist; *D:* Jaume Balaguero; *W:* Jaume Balaguero, Fernando de Felipe; *C:* Xavi Gimenez; *M:* Carles Cases.

Darkness Falls ⚫⚫½ 1998 (R) John Barrett (Winstone) is looking for revenge. His adulterous wife Jane (McCaffrey) was critically injured in a car crash from which her lover escaped. So John goes to the Driscoll home and decides to terrorize Jane's boyfriend Mark (Dutton) and his unsuspecting wife Sally (Fenn). Filmed on the Isle of Man, which may be the most interesting thing about this routine thriller. **91m/C VHS, DVD**. Sherilyn Fenn, Ray Winstone, Tim Dutton, Bob Hoskins, Oliver Tobias, Michael Praed; *D:* Gerry Lively; *W:* John Howlett; *C:* Adam Santelli; *M:* Guy Farley.

Darkness Falls ⚫⚫½ 2003 (PG-13) In the small New England town of Darkness Falls (aren't you asking for trouble when you name a town that?), young Kyle Walsh witnesses his mother's murder by a ghost who was wrongfully hanged

150 years earlier. Known as the Tooth Fairy, the spirit takes her revenge on the children of the town after they lose the last of their baby teeth. Twelve years later, Kyle is living in Las Vegas, psychologically scarred and paranoid from his encounter. Knowing that the ghost only comes in the dark, he surrounds himself with light. Caitlin (Caulfield), his childhood girlfriend, asks him to come back and help her younger brother, who's starting to have the same nightmares that Kye use to have. Genuinely scary moments overcome some obvious 3dot devices. Wisally, the movie is restrained and delivers in some spooky atmosphere. **88**mC VHS, DVD, US *C:* Chaney Kiley, Emma Caulfield, Lee Cormie, Grant Piro, Sullivan Stapleton, Steve Mouzakis, Peter Curtin; *D:* Jonathan Liebesman; *M:* James Vander-bilt, Joe Harris; *C:* Dan Laustsen; *M:* Brian Tyler.

Darkroom 🐾½ *1990* An unstable young man devises a scheme to photograph his father in bed with his mistress, and then use the pics to blackmail dear ol' dad. **90**mC VHS, DVD, Jill Pierce, Jeffrey Allen Arbaugh, Sara Lee Wade, Aaron Teich; *D:* Terence O'Hara. **VIDEO**

The Darkside 🐾½ *1987* (R) In this frightening drama, a young prostitute and an innocent cabbie attempt to escape the clutches of a man acal film producer who's secret he won't let them reveal. **95**mC VHS, DVD. Tony Galati, Cynthia (Cyndy, Cindy) Preston; *D:* Constanto Magnatta.

Darktown Strutters 🐾 *and Boogie 1974* (PG) Effort to satirize racial stereotypes is humorless and ineffective. Black female motorcycle gang searches for the kidnapped mother of one of the members. **85**mC VHS. Trina Parks Roger E. Mosley, Shirley Washington; *D:* William Witney.

Darkwolf 🐾½ *2003* (R) A werewolf (Hodder) is stalking Los Angeles in search of newbie Jos e (Armstrong) so they can mate and perpetuate the species. Detective Steve Turley (Alosio) wants to protect her from the big bad beast. Limited special effects and an overly confusing plot for the genre. **94**mC VHS, DVD. Samaire Armstrong, Kane Hodder, Ryan A osio, Tippi Hedren, Steven Williams, Jaime Bergman, Alexis Cruz; *D:* Richard Friedman; *W:* Geoffrey Alan Holliday; *C:* Stuart Asbjornsen; *M:* Geof Levin. **VIDEO**

Darling 🐾🐾🐾 *1965* Amoral young model Diana Scott (Christie) tries to hold boredom at bay by having a number of love affairs. She moves from intellectual Robert (Bogarde) to playboy Miles (Harvey) and eventually joins the international jet set and manages to reach the top of European society by marrying a prince. Diana then learns what an empty life she has. Christie won an Oscar for her portrayal of the disillusioned, cynical young woman. **122**mB VHS, DVD, GB Julie Christie, Dirk Bogarde, Laurence Harvey, Jose-Luis De Villalonga, Roland Curram; *D:* John Schlesinger; *W:* Frederic Raphael; *C:* Ken Higgins; *M:* John Dankworth. *Oscars '65:* Actress (Christie), Costume Des. (B&W), Story & Screenplay; *British Acad. '65:* Actor (Bogarde), Actress (Christie), Screenplay; *Golden Globes '66:* Foreign Film; *Natl. Bd. of Review '65:* Actress (Christie), Director (Schlesinger). **N.Y. Film Critics '65** Actress (Christie), Director (Schlesinger). **Film**

Darling Lili 🐾🐾½ *1970* Big-budget WWI spy comedy/musical with Andrews as a German agent posing as an English music hall performer, who falls in love with squadron leader Hudson and finds she can't betray him. A critical flop when first released, film has its charms though directror Edwards did much better for Andrews in "Victor/Victoria." *Whistling Away the Dark, The Girl in No Man's Land; Smile Away Each Rainy Day; I'll Give You Three Guesses; Your Good Will Ambassador; Darling Lili; The Little Birds.* **136**mC VHS, DVD. Julie Andrews, Rock Hudson, Jeremy Kemp, Jacques Marin, Michael Witney, Vernon Dobtcheff, Lance Percival; *D:* Blake Edwards, William Peter Blatty; *M:* Henry Mancini, Johnny Mercer. *Golden Globes '71:* Song ("Whistling Away the Dark").

Darlings of the Gods 🐾🐾🐾 *1990* The glittering marriage of actors Sir Laurence Olivier and Vivien Leigh is just as dramatic as anything on stage or screen as Olivier's devotion to work and

---

Leigh's fragile mental and physical health plagued by ill health. Meanwhile, playwright Hellman has her own trials which she's blacklisted in the '50s during the Red Scare. **180**mC VHS, GB Anthony (Corfan) Higgins, Mel Martin, Jerome Ehlers, Rhys McCorrnochie, Lindy Davies, Shane Briant, Anthony Hawkins, Jackie Kelleher; *D:* Catherine Millar; *W:* Roger Simpson, Graeme Farmer; *M:* Brian May. **TV**

The Darwin Awards 🐾½ *2006* (R) Lumpy, leaden comedy. The Darwin Awards are given (posthumously) to those who die in the most stupid and preventable ways. Michael (Fiennes), a former San Francisco forensic detective-turned-insurance profiler, is paired up with claims investigator Siri (Ryder) and a film student are plagued by pushers and assorted other bad guys. There's death by pay-outs). There's also a serial killer (Nelson), who previously escaped Michael, that figures in the insurance firm lots of pay-outs). There's also a serial killer (Nelson), who previously escaped Michael, that figures in the plot. Last role for Chris Penn. **90**mC DVD. Joseph Fiennes, Winona Ryder, Winner Valderrama, Tim Blake Nelson, David Arquette, Ty Burrel, Alessandro Nivola, Tom Hollander, Julianna Margulies, Christopher Penn, David Penfich; *D:* Finn Taylor; *W:* Finn Taylor; *C:* Hiro Narita; *M:* David Kitay.

Darwin's Nightmare 🐾🐾½ *2004* Compelling documentary probing the traumatic economic and social effects on the people of Tanzania by the 1950s introduction of the non-native Nile perch into Lake Victoria, which has since depleted the lake of over 200 natural species. With out the guidance of voiceovers, director/writer Sauper depicts the local citizens' poor living conditions, as they don't benefit from the country's Nile perch industry—in fact, most struggle to survive on little food (the fish are too costly) and small wages (even with the highly hazardous nature of fishing on Victoria) despite the great profit that perch shipments to Europe and Russia bring to the government. **107**mC DVD. *D:* Hubert Sauper; *W:* Hubert Sauper; *C:* Hubert Sauper.

D.A.R.Y.L. 🐾🐾 *1985* (PG) The little boy found by the side of the road is too polite, too honest and too smart. His friend explains to him the necessity of imperfection. (If you don't want the grown-ups to bother you too much) and he begins to become more like a real little boy. But the American military has a top-secret interest in this child, since he is in fact the combination of a cloned body and a computer brain. More interesting when it's involved with the human beings and less so when it focuses on science. Standard good guys/bad guys story—with the human beings as the bad. Excellent performances, especially from Prochnow. In German with subtitles. From the novel by Lothar-Guenther Buccheim. Originally a six-hour special made for German TV. **210**mC VHS, DVD. GE Jurgen Prochnow, Herbert Gronemeyer, Klaus Wennemann, Hubertus Bengson, Martin Semmelrogge, Bernd Tauber, Erwin Leder, Martin Mary, Heinz Hong, Uwe Ochsenknecht, Claude-Oliver Rudolph , Jan Fedder, Ralph Richter, Joachim Bernhard, Olver Stritzel, Konrad Becker, Lutz Schnell, Martin Hemme, Rita Cadillac; *D:* Jost Vacano; *M:* Klaus Dottinger. **TV**

Das Boot 🐾🐾🐾 *1981* (R) Superb detailing of life in a German U-boat during WWII. Intense, claustrophobic atmosphere complemented by nail-biting action provides a realistic portrait of the stressful conditions that were endured on these submarines. Excellent performances, especially from Prochnow. In German with subtitles. From the novel by Lothar-Guenther Buccheim. Originally a six-hour special made for German TV. **210**mC VHS, DVD. GE Jurgen Prochnow, Herbert Gronemeyer, Klaus Wennemann, Hubertus Bengson, Martin Semmelrogge, Bernd Tauber, Erwin Leder, Martin Mary, Heinz Hong, Uwe Ochsenknecht, Claude-Oliver Rudolph , Jan Fedder, Ralph Richter, Joachim Bernhard, Olver Stritzel, Konrad Becker, Lutz Schnell, Martin Hemme, Rita Cadillac; *D:* Jost Vacano; *M:* Klaus Dottinger. **TV**

Dash and Lilly 🐾🐾½ *1999* Depicts the 30-year love affair between hard-drinking, promiscuous writer's Dashiell Hammett (Shepard) and Lillian Hellman (Davis). Meeting in the 1930s, the successful Hammett becomes the up-and-coming Hellman's mentor. Though both are married, they also begin an affair. Eventually, their positions are reversed and, after serv-

---

The Darwin Conspiracy 🐾 *1999* (PG) Scientist uncovers a plot to conduct radical experiments in human intelligence. **90**mC VHS. Kevin Tighe, Jason Brooks, Jennifer Floyd, Stacy Halduk; *D:* Winnich (Rich) Kolbe; *W:* Glen Larson; *C:* Mark Melville; *M:* Rob Walsh.

A Date with Judy 🐾🐾 *1948* Standard post-war musical dealing with teenage mix-ups in and around a high school dance. Choreography by Stanley Donen. *Cuanto La Gusto; Strictly on the Corny Side; It's a Most Unusual Day; Judaline; I've Got a Date with Judy; I'm Gonna Meet My Mary; Temptation; Mulligatawny.* **114**mC VHS, Jane Powell, Elizabeth Taylor, Carmen Miranda, Wallace Beery, Robert Stack, Xavier Cugat, Selena Royle, Leon Ames; *D:* Richard Thorpe; *C:* Robert L. Surtees.

Dating the Enemy 🐾🐾 *1995* War between the sexes comedy about two instantaneous lovers who have nothing in common. Tash (Karvan) is a serious journalist who falls for easy-going Brett (Pearce). After a year of togetherness, Tash wishes macho Brett could understand what it's like to be a woman. Surprise! The duo mysteriously switch bodies and find their new sexual (and job) roles aren't easy. **104**mC VHS, AU Claudia Karvan, Guy Pearce, Matthew Day, Lisa Hensley, Pippa Grandison, John Howard; *D:* Megan Simpson; *W:* Megan Simpson; *M:* David Hirschfelder.

Daughter of Darkness 🐾🐾½ *1989* (R) A young woman goes to Hungary in search of her family tree, only to discover vampires nestled there. **93**mC VHS, Mia Sara, Anthony Perkins, Robert Reynolds, Jack Coleman; *D:* Stuart Gordon.

Daughter of Death 🐾 *Julie Darling 1982* (R) A little mentally off-center since she witnessed the gruesome rape and murder of her mother, a teenage girl doesn't bond well with her new mom when dad remarries. **100**mC VHS, DVD, C4 GE Anthony (Tony) Franciosa, Isabelle Mejias, Sybil Danning, Cindy Girling, Paul Hubbard, Benjamin Schmidt; *D:* Paul Nicholas.

Daughters of Darkness 🐾🐾🐾 *Le Rouge aux Levres; Blut an den Lippen; Erzsebeth; The Promise of Red Lips; The Red Lips 1971* (R) Newlyweds on their way to England stop at a posh French hotel. There they meet a beautiful woman whom they has been there 40 years ago, ever though she hasn't aged a bit. When she introduces herself as Countess of Bathory (the woman who bathed in the blood of virgins to stay young) folks begin to wonder. A really superb erotic vampire film charged with sensuality and a sense of dread. **87**mC VHS, DVD, BE GE IT FR Delphine Seyrig, John Karlen, Daniele Ouimet, Andrea Rau, Paul Esser, Georges Jamin, Joris Collet, Fons Rademakers; *D:* Parry Kumel; *W:* Harry Kumel, Pierre Drouot, Jean Ferry; *C:* Eddy van der Enden; *M:* Francois de Roubaix.

Daughters of Satan 🐾🐾 *1972* (R) Selleck, in an early role as a virile museum buyer, antagonizes a coven of witches when he purchases a painting. His wife, played by Grant, becomes a target of the witches' revenge and salacious shenanigans ensue. **96**mC VHS, DVD, Tom

---

The Darwin Conspiracy 🐾 *1999*

Date Bait 🐾 *1960* When a teen couple decides—much to their parents' chagrin—to elope, they find themselves on a date with danger when their post-nuptuals are plagued by pushers and assorted others, including Sin (Valderrama) who's taping their investigation as they try to justify possible victims and prevent their demise (thus saving the insurance firm lots of pay-outs). **80**mC VHS. Gary Clarke, Marlo Ryan, Richard Gering, Danny Logan; *D:* O'Dale Ireland.

Date Movie 🐾½ *2006* (PG-13) Shameless mockery of romantic movies such as "My Big Fat Greek Wedding" and "Meet the Fockers" can't make it to first base. Obese Julia (Hannigan) is looking for love and freedom from her overbearing African-American "Greek" dad (Griffin) when she meets handsome Brit Grant Funckyerdoder and seeks the aid of a "Hitch"-like date doctor (Cox) to shape up. Penned by two of the "Scary Movie" series writers. **83**mC DVD, UMD. US Alyson Hannigan, Eddie Griffin, Fred Willard, Jennifer Coolidge, Adam Campbell, Sophie Monk, Meera Simhan, Marie Matiko, Judah Friedlander, Carmen Electra, Tony Cox, Valery Ortiz; *D:* Aaron Seltzer; *W:* Aaron Seltzer, Jason Friedberg; *C:* Shawn Maurer; *M:* David Kitay. *Golden Raspberries '06:* Worst Support. Actress (Electra).

Date with an Angel 🐾🐾 *1987* (PG) When aspiring musician Knight fishes a beautiful angel out of the swimming pool, he is just trying to rescue her. But the beauty of the angel overwhelms him and he finds himself questioning his upcoming wedding to Cates, a cosmetic mogul's daughter. Sickeningly cute and way too sentimental, though Beart's beauty is other-worldly. **105**mC VHS, DVD, Charles Lane, Emmanuelle Beart, Michael E. Knight, Phoebe Cates, David Dukes, Bibi Besch, Albert Macklin, David Hunt, Michael Goodwin; *D:* Tom McLoughlin; *C:* Alex Thomson; *M:* Randy Kerber.

Daughter of Don Q 🐾🐾½ *1946* Delores' father is very rich with a huge real estate empire and she is his only heir. Greedy cousin Carlos would like to change that—by killing Delores. Delores must dodge speeding cars, hurling harpoons, and more to escape Carlos' evil plot. Part of "The Cliffhanger Serials" series. **166**mB VHS. Adrian Booth, Kirk Alyn, Leroy Mason; *D:* Fred Brannon, Spencer Gordon Bennett; *W:* Albert DeMond, Basil Dickey, Jesse Duffy, Lynn Perkins.

Daughter of Horror 🐾🐾 *Dementia 1955* A young woman finds herself involved with a porno mobster who resembles her abusive father. Trouble is, Dad's dead, and daughter dearest abetted his departure. Obscure venture into expressionism that was initially banned by the New York State Board of Censors. Shot on a low budget (how low was it? So Low that McMahon narrated because shooting with sound was too expensive). The 55 minutes tend to lag, although the film should be intriguing to genre enthusiasts and to fans of things pseudo-Freudian. **60**mB VHS. Adrienne Barrett, Ben Roseman, Richard Barron, Ed Hinkle, Lucille Howland, Angelo Rossitto, Bruno Vesota; *D:* John Parker; *W:* John Parker; *C:* William C. Thompson; *M:* George Antheil; *V:* Marni Nixon; *Nar:* Ed McMahon.

Daughter of Keltoum 🐾🐾 *2001* Rallia is 19 and has been raised by adoptive parents in Switzerland. She returns to her birthplace, a remote Berber settlement in Algeria, in order to learn from her mother and son Rallia's mother, accompanied by her Aunt Nedjma. This road trip opens Rallia's eyes to the harshness of Algerian life and finally meeting her mother leads to other revelations. French and Arabic with subtitles. **101**mC DVD. FR TU Cylia Malki, Beyra Charef; *M:* Mehdi Charef; *C:* Alain Levent; *M:* Bernardo Sandoval.

Daughter of the Dragon 🐾🐾 *1931* Fu Manchu is again on the prowl. His time sending his daughter to murder Fletcher to avenge the death of his wife and son during China's Boxer Rebellion. Based on a Sax Rohmer story. **70**mB VHS. Anna May Wong, Warner Oland, Sessue Hayakawa, Bramwell Fletcher, Holmes Herbert; *D:* Lloyd Corrigan.

Daughter of the Tong 🐾 *1939* FBI agent gets long twisted when he tries to put a lid on a smuggling ring headed by a woman (who's beautiful, of course). Something that "resembles acting is west in a mess of a movie. **56**mB VHS, DVD. Evelyn Brent, Grant Withers, Dorothy Short, Dave O'Brien; *D:* Bernard B. Ray.

Selleck, Barra Grant, Paralaman, Tani Phelps Guthrie; *D:* Hollingsworth Morse.

Daughters of the Dust 🐾🐾½ 1991 Five women of a Gullah family living on the Sea Islands off the Georgia coast in 1902 contemplate moving to the mainland in this emotional tale of change. The Gullah are descendants of West African slaves and their isolation has kept their superstitions and native dialect (a mixture of Western African, Creole, and English) intact. Family bonds and memories are celebrated with a quiet narrative and beautiful cinematography in Dash's feature-film directorial debut. 113m/ **C VHS, DVD.** Cora Lee Day, Barbara O, Alva Angerson, Kaycee Moore, Cheryl Lynn Bruce, Adisa Anderson, Eartha D. Robinson, Bahni Turpin, Tommy Redmond Hicks, Malik Farrakhan, Cornell (Kofi) Royal, Vertamae Crosvenor, Umar Abdurrahman, Sherry Jackson, Rev. Ervin Green; *D:* Julie Dash; *W:* Julie Dash; *C:* A. Jafa Fielder; *M:* John Barnes. Natl. Film Reg. '04; Sundance '91: Cinematog.

Daughters of the Sun 🐾🐾 2000 Amanagol (Taghani) is the eldest of six daughters from a poor rural family. In order to get money to support them and help her ill mother, Amanago'l father cuts her hair and disguises her as a boy named Aman, sending her to a distant village as an apprentice weaver. But her employer is dishonest—keeping her earnings instead of sending them to Aman's family. Then Aman learns her mother has died because of her employer's deception. Persian with subtitles. 92m/ **C VHS, DVD.** *A* Altinay Ghelich Taghani; *D:* Mariam Shahriar; *C:* Mariam Shahriar; *C:* Homayun Paynar; *M:* Hosein Ali-Zadeh.

Dave 🐾🐾🐾 1993 **(PG-13)** Regular guy Dave Kovic (Kline) is a dead ringer for the President, launching him into the White House after the prez suffers a stroke in embarrassing circumstances. Seamless comedy prompts lots of hearty laughs and the feel-good fun that despite the overwhelming odds, everything will turn out just fine. Political cameos abound: look for real-life Senators Alan Simpson, Paul Simon, Howard Metzenbaum, Tom Harkin, and Christopher Dodd as well as the commentators from TV's "The McLaughlin Group," and Stone, poking fun at himself on "'Larry King Live," as he tries to convince the public there's a conspiracy going on. 110m/**C VHS, DVD.** Stephen (Steve) Root, Dan E. Butler, Bonnie Bartlett, Kevin Kline, Sigourney Weaver, Frank Langella, Kevin Dunn, Ving Rhames, Ben Kingsley, Charles Grodin, Faith Prince, Laura Linney, Bonnie Hunt, Parley Baer, Stefan Gierasch, Anna Deavere Smith, Bonnie Bartlett, Ben Stein; *Cameos:* Jay Leno, Larry King, Oliver Stone, Arnold Schwarzenegger; *D:* Ivan Reitman; *W:* Gary Ross; *C:* Adam Greenberg; *M:* James Newton Howard.

Dave Chappelle's Block Party 🐾🐾🐾 2006 **(R)** Comedian Chappelle is followed from his Ohio home to the free all-day concert he stages on a Brooklyn street on September 18, 2004. He impulsively hands out tickets and buses to the concertgoers while keeping the lineup a secret until such performers as Kanye West, Mos Def, the reunited Fugees, Dead Prez, Erykah Badu, Jill Scott, and Ohio's Central State University marching band take the stage. 100m/**C DVD.** *US* Dave Chappelle; *D:* Michel Gondry; *C:* Ellen Kuras.

David 🐾🐾½ 1979 A haunting portrait of the survival of a Jewish teenager in Berlin during the Nazi reign of terror, based on the novel by Joel Koenig. Universally acclaimed, this was the first film about the Holocaust made in Germany by a German Jew. In German with English subtitles. 106m/**C VHS.** *GE* Mario Fischel, Walter Taub, Irene Vrklan, Torsten Hentes, Eva Mattes; *D:* Peter Lilienthal. Berlin Intl. Film Fest. '79: Gold.

David 🐾🐾½ 1997 TNT's Old Testament biblical series continues with the story of shepherd boy David (Turner) who succeeds Saul (Pryce) to become king over the tribes of Israel. When King David (Parker) becomes smitten with the married Bathsheba (Lee), he sends her husband into battle, soon leaving her a comely widow (although not for long). And there's also subplots involving three of David's

children: Absalom (Rowan), Amnon (Hall), and Tamar (Bellar). Lots of action. 190m/**C VHS, DVD.** Nathaniel Parker, Sheryl Lee, Jonathan Pryce, Leonard Nimoy, Dominic Rowan, Edward Hall, Clara Bellar, Marco Leonardi, Franco Nero, Ben Daniels, Maurice Roeves, Gina Bellman, Gideon Turner; *D:* Robert Markowitz; *W:* Larry Gross; *C:* Raffaele Mertes; *M:* Carlo Siliotto. **CABLE**

David and Bathsheba 🐾🐾🐾 1951 The Bible story comes alive in this lush and colorful Fox production. Peck and Hayward are great together and Peck is properly concerned about the wrath of God over his transgressions. Terrific costumes and special effects, lovely music and a fine supporting cast keep this a notch above other Biblical epics. 116m/ **C VHS, DVD.** Gregory Peck, Susan Hayward, Raymond Massey, Kieron Moore, James Robertson Justice, Jayne Meadows, John Sutton, Dennis Hoey, Francis X. Bushman, George Zucco; *D:* Henry King; *W:* Philip Dunne; *C:* Leon Shamroy.

David and Lisa 🐾🐾🐾 1962 Director Perry was given an Oscar for this sensitive independently produced film. Adapted from Theodore Isaac Rubin's true case history novel concerning a young man and woman who fall in love while institutionalized for mental illness. Dulllea and Margolin are excellent in the title roles of this sleeper. 94m/**B VHS, DVD.** Keir Dullea, Janet Margolin, Howard da Silva, Neva Patterson, Clifton James; *D:* Frank Perry; *W:* Eleanor Perry; *C:* Leonard Hirschfield; *M:* Mark Laurence.

David Copperfield 🐾🐾🐾🐾 1935 Superior adaptation of Charles Dickens' great novel. An orphan grows to manhood in Victorian England with a wide variety of help and harm. Terrific acting by Bartholomew, Fields, Rathbone, and all the rest. Lavish production, lovingly filmed. 132m/**B VHS, DVD.** Lionel Barrymore, W.C. Fields, Freddie Bartholomew, Basil Rathbone, Lewis Stone, Frank Lawton, Madge Evans, Roland Young, Edna May Oliver, Lennox Pawle, Elsa Lanchester, Una O'Connor, Arthur Treacher; *D:* George Cukor; *W:* Howard Estabrook, Hugh Walpole; *M:* Herbert Stothart.

David Copperfield 🐾🐾½ 1970 This British made-for-TV production is more faithful to the Dickens classic than any of its predecessors. The added material, however, fails to highlight any one character as had the successful 1935 MGM version. Still, the exceptional (and largely stage-trained) cast do much to redeem the production. 118m/**C VHS, DVD.** Richard Attenborough, Cyril Cusack, Edith Evans, Pamela Franklin, Susan Hampshire, Wendy Hiller, Ron Moody, Laurence Olivier, Robin Phillips; *D:* Delbert Mann; *M:* Malcolm Arnold. **TV**

David Copperfield 🐾🐾½ 1999 Lavish and traditional retelling of the Dickens saga, which concerns the hard-knock life, from birth to maturity, of the title character. Hoskins' Mr. Micawber and Smith's Aunt Betsey Trotwood are particular standouts in a large cast. 210m/**C VHS, DVD.** *GB* Daniel Radcliffe, Ciaran McMenamin, Bob Hoskins, Maggie Smith, Ian McKellen, Nicholas Lyndhurst, Pauline Quirke, Emilia Fox, Trevor Eve, Zoe Wanamaker, Alun Armstrong, Imelda Staunton, Amanda Ryan, Ian McNeice, Joanna Page; *D:* Simon Curtis; *W:* Adrian Hodges; *C:* Andy Collins; *M:* Robert (Rob) Lane; *Nar:* Tom Wilkinson. **TV**

David Harum 🐾🐾½ 1934 Rogers plays the philosophical title character, a small-town banker, confirmed bachelor, and horse trader in the 1890s. Young bank teller John (Taylor) places a large bet on a horse so he can afford to marry rich girl Ann (Venable) and Harum provides encouragement. 83m/**B DVD.** Will Rogers, Louise Dresser, Kent Taylor, Evelyn Venable, Stepin Fetchit, Noah Beery Sr., Roger Imhof, Charles Middleton, Frank Melton; *D:* James Cruze; *W:* Walter Woods; *C:* Hal Mohr.

David Holzman's Diary 🐾🐾🐾 1967 Director McBride helmed this fake underground movie, a legendary put-on focusing on film student pretensions. Holzman is a sincere geek who seeks the meaning of life by filming his own existence in oh-so-chic grainy black-and-white verite. He learns reality is more important than film. Drolly captures the state of the art in late '60s America. 71m/**B VHS.** L.M. Kit

Carson; *D:* Jim McBride; *W:* L.M. Kit Carson, Jim McBride. Natl. Film Reg. '91.

David Searching 🐾🐾 1997 Aspiring documentary filmmaker David (Rapp) is broke and boyfriendless in his two-bedroom apartment. He needs a roomie to help with the rent and comes up with newly separated Gwen (Mannheim). She's equally in search of romance (or sex, as the case may be). Oh, and David still needs to find that elusive job. Series of vignettes do feature some talented actors but the film never goes anywhere. 103m/**C VHS.** Anthony Rapp, Camryn Mannheim, Joseph Fuqua, Julie Halston, Stephen Spinella, John Cameron Mitchell, David Drake, Kathleen Chalfant, David Courier; *D:* Leslie L. Smith; *W:* Leslie L. Smith; *D:* John P. Scholz.

DaVinci's War 🐾🐾 1992 **(R)** Frank DaVinci's sister is murdered and he wants revenge. So he hooks up with a professional killer and a bunch of Vietnam vets and gets the firepower he needs to blow the bad guys away. 94m/**C VHS, DVD.** Joey Travolta, Michael Nouri, Vanity, Richard Foronjy, Branscombe Richmond, Sam Jones, Jack Bannon, Brian Robbins, James Russo, Kamar De Los Reyes; *D:* Raymond Martino; *W:* Raymond Martino; *M:* Jeff Lass.

Davy Crockett and the River Pirates 🐾🐾 1956 **(G)** Another Disney splice and dice of two episodes from the TV series, chronicling the further adventures of our frontier hero. Davy meets up with Mike Fink, the King of the Ohio River, and the two engage in a furious keelboat race, and then unite to track down a group of thieves masquerading as Indians and threatening the peace. 81m/**C VHS, DVD.** Fess Parker, Buddy Ebsen, Jeff York; *D:* Norman Foster; *M:* George Bruns.

Davy Crockett, King of the Wild Frontier 🐾🐾🐾 1955 **(PG)** Three episodes of the popular Disney TV series are blended together here to present the life and some of the adventures of Davy Crockett, including his days as an Indian fighter and his gallant stand in defense of the Alamo. Well-done by a splendid cast, the film helped to spread Davy-mania among the children of the 1950s. 93m/**C VHS, DVD.** Fess Parker, Buddy Ebsen, Hans Conried, Ray Whiteside, Pat Hogan, William "Billy" Bakewell, Basil Ruysdael, Kenneth Tobey; *D:* Norman Foster; *M:* George Bruns. **TV**

Dawg 🐾🐾 *Bad Boy* 2002 **(R)** Following 2001's "Double Whammy," Leary and Hurley also teamed up for this romantic comedy. The aptly named Doug "Dawg" Munford (Leary) stands to inherit a fortune but only if the love 'em and leave 'em lothario finds and apologizes to the many women he's used and dumped. And they have to forgive him. Estate attorney Anna Lockheart (Hurley) will tag along to make sure Dawg doesn't make a mess. 83m/**C VHS, DVD.** Denis Leary, Elizabeth Hurley, Vanessa Bell Calloway, Alex Borstein, Mia Cottet; *D:* Victoria Hochberg; *W:* Ken Hastings; *C:* Steven Finestone; *M:* Jason Frederick.

Dawn! 🐾🐾 1983 True story of Dawn Fraser, an Olympic champion swimmer and an unfulfilled woman willing to fight for her happiness. 114m/**C VHS.** Bronwyn Mackay-Payne, Tom Richards, Bunny Brooke, Ron Haddrick; *D:* Ken Hannam; *W:* Joy Cavill; *C:* Russell Boyd.

Dawn Express 🐾½ 1942 Nazi spies infiltrate the U.S. in search of a secret formula designed to enhance the power of gasoline. Another film made to contribute to the war effort that doesn't make much sense. 63m/**B VHS.** Michael Whalen, Anne Nagel, William "Billy" Bakewell, Constance Worth, Hans von Twardowski, Jack Mulhall, George Pembroke, Kenneth Harlan, Robert Frazer; *D:* Al(bert) Herman.

Dawn of the Dead 🐾🐾🐾 1978 *Zombi; Zombie; Zombies* 1978 Romero's gruesome sequel to his "Night of the Living Dead." A mysterious plague causes the recently dead to rise from their graves and scour the countryside for living flesh. Very violent, gory, graphic, and shocking, yet not without humor. Gives interesting consideration to the violence created by the living humans in their efforts to save themselves. 126m/**C VHS, DVD, Blu-ray Disc.** David

Emge, Ken Foree, Gaylen Ross, Scott H. Reiniger, David Crawford, David Early, Daniel Dietrich, Richard France, Tom Savini, Howard K. Smith, George A. Romero; *D:* George A. Romero; *W:* George A. Romero; *C:* Michael Gornick; *M:* Dario Argento, The Goblins.

Dawn of the Dead 🐾🐾🐾 2004 **(R)** The dead are rising from their graves yet again in this remake of the 1978 classic, except now the zombies move around much faster (no waddling allowed!). To level the playing field, Snyder (making his feature film directorial debut) includes more survivors to fight 'em off. The result is still lots of gory fun, but the biting humor so vital to the original is lacking. 100m/**C DVD, UMD, HD DVD.** *US* Sarah Polley, Ving Rhames, Jake Weber, Mekhi Phifer, Ty Burrell, Michael Kelly, Kevin Zegers, Michael Barry, Lindy Booth, Jayne (Jane) Eastwood, Boyd Banks, Matt Frewer, R.D. Reid, Justin Louis, Kim Poirier, Tom Savini; *D:* Zack Snyder; *W:* James Gunn; *C:* Matthew F. Leonetti; *M:* Tyler Bates.

Dawn of the Mummy *woof!* 1982 Lousy plot and bad acting—not to mention gore galore—do this one in. A photographer and a bevy of young fashion models travel to Egypt for a special shoot. They unwittingly stumble upon an ancient tomb, teeming with vengeance-minded mummies. 93m/**C VHS, DVD.** Brenda King, Barry Sattels, George Peck, Joan Levy; *D:* Frank Agrama.

Dawn on the Great Divide 🐾🐾½ 1942 Jones' last film before his tragic and untimely death trying to save people from a fire at the Coconut Grove in Boston. Wagon train has to battle not only Indians, but bad guys as well. Plot provides more depth than the usual western fare. 57m/**B VHS, DVD.** Buck Jones, Tim McCoy, Raymond Hatton, Mona Barrie, Robert Lowery, Betty Blythe, Jan Wiley, Harry Woods, Roy Barcroft; *D:* Howard Bretherton.

Dawn Patrol 🐾🐾🐾 1938 Flynn plays a flight commander whose nerves are shot in this story of the British Royal Flying Corps during WWI. The focus is on the effects that the pressures and deaths have on all those concerned. Fine performances from all in this well-done remake of the 1930 film. 103m/**B VHS, DVD.** Errol Flynn, David Niven, Basil Rathbone, Donald Crisp, Barry Fitzgerald, Melville Cooper, Carl Esmond, Peter Willes, Morton Lowry, Michael Brooke, James Burke, Stuart Hall; *D:* Edmund Goulding; *W:* Seton I. Miller, Dan Totheroh; *C:* Gaetano Antonio "Tony" Gaudio; *M:* Max Steiner.

Dawn Rider 🐾🐾 1935 Formula western has all the right ingredients: Wayne as a cowboy out to get revenge on the gang that murdered his father. Features stuntman Canutt in rare acting role. 60m/**B VHS, DVD.** John Wayne, Marion Burns, Yakima Canutt; *D:* Robert North Bradbury.

The Dawning 🐾🐾½ 1988 An Irish revolutionary in the 1920s draws a young woman into his dangerous world of romance, intrigue, and death. Howard's last film. Based on the novel "Old Jest" by Jennifer Johnston. 97m/**C VHS, DVD.** *GB* Anthony Hopkins, Jean Simmons, Trevor Howard, Rebecca Pidgeon, Hugh Grant, Tara MacGowran; *D:* Robert Knights.

The Dawson Patrol 🐾🐾🐾 1978 Royal Canadian Mountie dog-sled race turns into a dramatic battle for survival. 75m/**C VHS.** George R. Robinson, Tim Henry, Neil Dainard; *D:* James B. Douglas; *D:* Peter Kelly.

The Day After 🐾🐾🐾 1983 Powerful drama graphically depicts the nuclear bombing of a midwestern city and its aftereffects on the survivors. Made for TV, and very controversial when first shown, gathering huge ratings and vast media coverage. 122m/**C VHS, DVD.** Jason Robards Jr., Jobeth Williams, John Lithgow, Steve Guttenberg, John Cullum; *D:* Nicholas Meyer. **TV**

The Day After Tomorrow 🐾🐾½ 2004 **(PG-13)** It was more fun watching the good guys battle aliens in Emmerich's "Independence Day" than this bunch of mopes who try to survive global warming. Paleoclimatologist Jack Hall (Quaid) predicts a new ice age and, sure enough, there's suddenly softball-sized hail blanketing Tokyo, L.A. gets leveled by tornadoes, New York is buried

...under ice and snow, and most of the northern hemisphere is wiped out just for fun. Jack's intrepid son Sam (Gyllenhaal) is trapped in Manhattan, riding out the weather with some friends in the New York Public Library. Meanwhile, Dad decides to snowshoe it from D.C. to NYC to rescue his boy. If you like watching familiar monuments destroyed (poor Lady Liberty), this special effects melodrama is for you. **123m/C DVD, Blu-ray Disc, UMD,** *US* Rossum, Ian Holm, Dash Mihok, Arjay Smith, Kenneth Welsh, Glenn Plummer, Nestor Serrano, Adrian Lester, Sheila McCarthy, Perry King; **D:** Roland Emmerich; **W:** Roland Emmerich, Jeffrey Nachmanoff. **C:** Ueli Steiger **M:** Harald Kloser. British Acad. '04: Visual FX.

The Day and the Hour 🐾🐾½ **1963**
Today We Live; Le Jour et l'Heure; Il Giorno e L'Ora; Viviano Oggi A woman becomes accidentally involved in the resistance movement during the Nazi occupation of France in WWII. **110m/C VHS, FR JP IT** Simone Signoret, Stuart Whitman, Genevieve Page, Michel Piccoli, Regga Nalder, Pierre Dux, Billy Kearns; **D:** Rene Clement; **M:** Claude Bolling.

Day at the Beach 🐾🐾 **1998**
Jimmy (Veronis) works in a mob-fronted New York ravioli factory where Jimmy's dealt with and numerous other problems—all eventually leading to the palatial home of wealthy (and connected) Antonio Gintolini (Ragno). **93m/C VHS, DVD,** Nick Veronis, Patrick Fitzgerald, Neal Jones, Robert Maisonett, Catherine Kellner, Jane Adams, Joe Ragno, Ed Setrakian; **D:** Nick Veronis; **W:** Nick Veronis; **C:** Nils Kenaston; **M:** Tony Seracene.

A Day at the Races 🐾🐾🐾½ **1937**
Though it seems labored at times, the brilliance of the brothers Marx still comes through in this rather weak tale of a patient in a sanitorium who convinces horse doctor Groucho to take on running the place. ♫ A Message from the Man in the Moon. On Blue Venetian Waters; Tomorrow is Another Day; All God's Chillun Got Rhythm. **111m/B VHS, DVD,** Groucho Marx, Harpo Marx, Chico Marx, Sig Rumann, Margaret Dumont, Allan Jones, Maureen O'Sullivan, Leonard Ceeley, Esther Muir; **D:** Sam Wood; **W:** Robert Pirosh, George Seaton, George Oppenheimer. **C:** Joseph Ruttenberg; **M:** George Bassman, Bronislau Kaper, Walter Jurmann.

Day for Night 🐾🐾🐾 **1973 (PG)**
La Nuit Americaine Director Ferrand (Truffaut) is working on a mediocre romantic melodrama with sullen actor Alphonse (Leaud) who "falls for his married co-star Julie (Bisset) in just one of the off-screen stories that's more interesting than what's being filmed. A wryly affectionate look at the profession of moviemaking—its craft, character, and the personalities that interact against the performances commanded by the camera. In French with English subtitles. **116m/C VHS, DVD, FR** Francois Truffaut, Jean-Pierre Leaud, Jacqueline Bisset, Jean-Pierre Aumont, Valentina Cortese, Alexandra Stewart, Dani, Nathalie Baye; **D:** Francois Truffaut; **W:** Suzanne Schiffman, Jean-Louis Richard, Francois Truffaut. Oscars '73: Foreign Film; British Acad. '73: Director; N.Y. Film Critics '73: Director (Truffaut), Film, Support. Actress (Cortese); Natl. Soc. Film Critics '73: Director (Truffaut), Film, Support. Actress (Cortese).

A Day for Thanks on Walton's Mountain 🐾🐾 **1982**
Many of the original television-show cast members, returned for this sentimental Thanksgiving reunion on Walton's Mountain. **97m/C VHS,** Ralph Waite, Ellen Corby, Judy Norton-Taylor, Eric Scott, Jon Walmsley, Robert Wightman, Mary (Elizabeth) McDonough, David W. Harper, Kami Cotler, Joe Conley, Ronnie Claire Edwards, Richard Gilliland, Melinda Naud; **D:** Harry Harris; **Nar:** Earl Hamner. **TV**

A Day in October 🐾🐾½ **1992**
Copenhagen, Denmark. There are signs the Jewish population is in danger from occupying Nazi officials and the resistance movement is active. Wounded resistance fighter Sweeney is rescued by young woman Sara (Wolf), and their relationship deepens as the realities of WWII change their lives. Based on historical fact, but there's little explanation of the politics or the fierce nationalism and intense loyalty most Danes felt towards their fellow countrymen, a loyalty that ultimately saved most of the Danish Jews from the Holocaust. Good performances, particularly Benzali as Sara's father, help overcome the script weaknesses. Filmed on location in Denmark. **96m/C VHS,** D.B. Sweeney, Kelly Wolf, Tovah Feldshuh, Daniel Benzali, Ole Lemmeke, Kim Romer, Anders Peter Bro, Lars Oluf Larsen; **D:** Kenneth Madsen; **W:** Damian F. Slattery; **M:** Jens Lysdal.

A Day in the Country 🐾🐾🐾½ **1946**
Une Partie de Campagne The son of the famed painter gives us the moving tale of a young woman's sudden and intense love for a man she meets while on a picnic with her family. Beautifully adapted from a story by Guy de Maupassant. Renowned photographer Henri Cartier-Bresson contributed to the wonderful cinematography. Subtitled. **40m/B VHS, FR** Sylvie Bataille, Georges Darnoux, Jane (Jeanne) Marken, Paul Temps; **D:** Jean Renoir. **C:** Henri Cartier-Bresson.

A Day in the Death of Joe Egg 🐾🐾🐾 **1971 (R)**
Based on the Peter Nichols play, an unlikely black comedy about a British couple which plots to care for their retarded/autistic child, nearly destroying their marriage in the process. They begin to contemplate euthanasia as a solution. Well-acted, but potentially offensive to some. **106m/C VHS, GB** Alan Bates, Janet Suzman, Elizabeth Robillard, Peter Bowles, Joan Hickson, Sheila Gish; **D:** Peter Medak; **W:** David Deutsch.

The Day It Came to Earth WOOF! **1977 (PG)**
Completely silly and unbelievable sci-fi flick has meteor crashing in the watery grave of a mobster. The decomposed corpse is revived by the radiation and plots to take revenge on those who fitted him with cement shoes. **89m/C VHS, DVD,** Roger Manning, Wink Roberts, Bob Ginnaven, Rita Wilson, Delight de Bruine; **D:** Harry Z. Thomason.

The Day My Parents Ran Away 🐾🐾½ **1993 (PG)**
Rebellious 16-year-old gets a tough lesson in responsibility when his parents get tired of his antics and decide to leave home in search of a new life. He finds out things aren't so easy on your own. **95m/C VHS, DVD,** Matt Frewer, Bobby Jacoby, Brigid Brannah, Blair Brown, Martin Mull; **D:** Martin Nicholson; **W:** Handel Glassberg; **M:** J. Peter Robinson.

Day Night Day Night 🐾🐾🐾 **2006**
Luisa Williams plays a nameless young woman who at the story's outset is holed up in a shabby motel receiving instruction from black-hooded men. While few clues are given about her motivation, her intention is clearly to become a suicide bomber in Times Square. Once on the streets of New York, her scenes are filmed with handheld cameras in daylight amid the unwitting masses of Manhattan. The film raises many issues, leaving most unresolved and leaving viewers to contemplate the very real possibility of terrorism close to home. **94m/C DVD,** *US GE* Luisa Williams; **D:** Julia Loktev; **W:** Julia Loktev; **C:** Benoit Debie.

Day of Atonement 🐾🐾½ **1993 (R)**
It's a war for power between rival drug lords when Hanin is released from prison and finds out his son and cousin are battling over turf. Then Walken is dragged into the fracas. Beals is the government agent trying to regain some control of the dangerous situation. Told from the view of a cynical art director wise to the ways of Hollywood. **127m/C VHS, DVD, US GE** Luisa Williams, Richard Berry; **D:** Alexandre Arcady; **W:** Alexandre Arcady, Daniel Saint Hamont; **C:** Willy Kurant.

The Day of the Jackal 🐾🐾🐾½ **1973 (PG)**
Frederick Forsyth's best-selling novel of political intrigue is splendidly brought to the screen by Zinnemann. A brilliant and ruthless assassin hired to kill Charles de Gaulle skirts the international intelligence pool, while intuitive police work try to stop him. Terse, suspenseful, beautiful location photography. Excellent acting by Fox, Cusack and Britton. **142m/C VHS, DVD,** Edward Fox, Alan Badel, Tony Britton, Derek Jacobi, Cyril Cusack, Olga Georges-Picot, Michael (Michel) Lonsdale; **D:** Fred Zinnemann; **W:** Kenneth Ross; **C:** Jean Tournier; **M:** Georges Delerue.

The Day of the Locust 🐾🐾🐾½ **1975 (R)**
Compelling adaptation of Nathanael West's novel concerning the dark side of 1930's Hollywood. A no-talent amoral actress's affair with a meek accountant leads to tragedy and destruction. Chronicles the two year top-secret efforts of the Manhattan Project, with General Leslie Groves (Dennehy) having to supervise the project and contain the scientific rivalries. Outstanding cast, with Strathairn notable as physicist J. Robert Oppenheimer. Adapted from "Day One: Before Hiroshima and After by Peter Wyden. **110m/B VHS, DVD, DK** Thorkild Roose, Sigrid Neiiendam, Lisbeth Movin, Preben Lerdorff, Anna Svierkier; **D:** Carl Theodor Dreyer; **W:** Carl Theodor Dreyer; **C:** Karl Andersson; **M:** Poul Schierbeck.

Day of Judgment 🐾½ **1981 (R)**
A mysterious stranger arrives in a town to slaughter those people who violate the Ten Commandments. **101m/C VHS,** William T. Hicks, Harris Bloodworth, Brownlee Davis; **D:** C.D.H. Reynolds.

Day of the Animals 🐾 **1977 (R)**
Something Is Out There Nature gone wild. It seems a depleted ozone layer has exposed the animals to the sun's radiation, turning them into brutal killers. A group of backpackers trek in the Sierras, unaware of the transformation. Far-fetched gore (all we hope), **95m/C VHS,** Day George, Richard Jaeckel, Michael Ansara, Ruth Roman, Leslie Nielsen, Lynda Day George, Christopher George, Susan Backlinie, Andrew Stevens, Gil Lamb; **D:** William Girdler; **W:** William W. Norton Sr.; **C:** Robert Sorrentino; **M:** Lalo Schifrin.

The Day of the Beast 🐾🐾 **1995 (R)**
Lurid horror/melodrama concerns Father Angel (Angulo), whose study of the Apocrypha has convinced him that the Antichrist will be born in Madrid on Christmas, which is only a few hours away. He enlists a couple of unlikely companions in his search for the infant. There's a lot of mayhem for all involved. Spanish with subtitles. **104m/C VHS, SP** Alex Angulo, Armando de Razza, Santiago Segura, Nathalie Sesena; **D:** Alex de la Iglesia; **C:** Flavio Martinez Labiano; **M:** Battista Lena.

Day of the Cobra 🐾½ **1984**
A corrupt narcotics bureau official hires an ex-cop to find a heroin kingpin on the back streets of Genoa, Italy. **95m/C VHS, DVD, IT** Franco Nero, Sybil Danning, Mario Maranzana, Licinia Lentini, William Berger; **D:** Enzo G. Castellari.

Day of the Dead 🐾🐾 **1985**
The third in Romero's trilogy of films about flesh-eating zombies, taking over the world. Romero hasn't thought up anything new for the ghouls to do, and the humans are too nasty to care about this time around. For adult audiences. **91m/C VHS, DVD, Blu-ray Disc,** Lori Cardille, Terry Alexander, Joe Pilato, Jarlath Conroy, Richard Liberty; **D:** George A. Romero; **W:** George A. Romero; **C:** Michael Gornick; **M:** John Harrison.

The Day of the Dolphin 🐾🐾 **1973 (PG)**
Research scientist, after successfully working out a means of teaching dolphins to talk, finds his animals kidnapped for a military espionage and assassination are involved. Dolphin voices by Henry, who also wrote the screenplay. **104m/C VHS, DVD,** George C. Scott, Trish Van Devere, Paul Sorvino, Fritz Weaver, Jon Korkes, John Dehner, Edward Herrmann, Severn Darden; **D:** Mike Nichols; **W:** Buck Henry; **M:** Georges Delerue; **V:** Buck Henry.

Day of Triumph 🐾½ **1954**
A dynamic version of the life of Christ as seen through the eyes of the apostles Andrew and Zadok, the leaders of the Zealot underground. **110m/C VHS,** Lee J. Cobb, Robert Wilson, Ralph Freud; **D:** Irving Pichel.

Day of Wrath 🐾🐾🐾 **1943**
Vredens Dag An involving psychological thriller based on records of the WWII race to build the atomic bomb. Set in the early 1600's, Young Anne (Movin) is married to the much older and puritanical widower, Absalon (Roose), but falls in love with his son Martin (Lerdorff). She wishes aloud for her husband's death and when he does dies, Anne is accused of witchcraft. Grim and unrelentingly pessimistic, moving from one horrific scene to another, director Dreyer creates a masterpiece of witch-terror. Based on a play by Hans Wiers Jenssen. In Danish with English subtitles. **110m/B VHS, DVD, DK**

Day of the Outlaw 🐾🐾½ **1959**
Bleak wintry western. Wounded Jack Bruhn (Ives) and his gang take over the remote town of Bitter, Wyoming. Cattleman Blaise Starrett (Ryan) ignores the town's plight since he's upset that the settlers are stringing up barbed wire and his young love Helen (Louise) has married another. But finally Starrett's decency gets the better of him and he decides to take a stand against Bruhn. **92m/B DVD,** Robert Ryan, Burl Ives, Tina Louise, Alan Marshall, Nehemiah Persoff, Jack Lambert, Venetia Stevenson, David Nelson, Elisha Cook Jr., Dabbs Greer; **D:** Andre de Toth; **W:** Philip Yordan; **C:** Russell Harlan; **M:** Alexander Courage.

Day of the Maniac 🐾🐾½ **1977 (R)**
Psychotic drug addict will stop at nothing to support his growing habit. **89m/C VHS, DVD,** George Hilton, Nieves Navarro; **D:** Sergio Martino. **Page: D:** John Schlesinger; **C:** Conrad L. Hall; **M:** John Barry.

Day of the Panther 🐾½ **1988**
The world's most formidable martial artists—are mighty torqued when panther-Linda is pitched, and they're not known to turn the other cheek. Much chop-socky kicking and shrilling. **86m/C VHS, DVD,** John Stanton, Eddie Stazak; **D:** Brian Trenchard-Smith.

The Day of the Triffids 🐾🐾🐾 **1963**
The majority of Earth's population is blinded by a meteor shower which also causes plant spores to mutate into giant carnivores. Well-done adaptation of John Wyndham's science fiction classic; Philip Yordan acknowledged "fronting" for blacklisted screenwriter Gordon, who finally received credit in 1996. **94m/C VHS, DVD, GB** Howard Keel, Janette Scott, Nicole Maurey, Kieron Moore, Mervyn Johns, Alison Leggatt, Ewan Roberts, Janina Faye, Gilgi Hauser, Carol Ann Ford; **D:** Steve Sekely, Freddie Francis; **W:** Bernard Gordon, Philip Yordan; **C:** Ted Moore.

Day of the Warrior 🐾🐾 **1996 (R)**
Babes who belong to a paramilitary law-and-order group infiltrate crime lord, the Warrior's, smuggling operations, strip joints and porn palaces. **96m/C VHS, DVD,** Julie Strain, Marcus Bagwell; **D:** Andy Sidaris.

Day One 🐾🐾🐾 **1989**
Vivid recreation of one of the most turbulent periods of American history—the WWII race to build the atomic bomb. Chronicles the two year top-secret efforts of the Manhattan Project, with General Leslie Groves (Dennehy) having to supervise the project and contain the scientific rivalries. Outstanding cast, with Strathairn notable as physicist J. Robert Oppenheimer. Adapted from "Day One: Before Hiroshima and After by Peter Wyden. **140m/C VHS,** Brian Dennehy, David Strathairn, Michael Tucker, Hume Cronyn, Richard Dysart, Barry Bostwick; **D:** Joseph Sargent. **VIDEO**

ter Wyden. **141m/C VHS.** Brian Dennehy, David Strathairn, Michael Tucker, Hume Cronyn, Richard Dysart, Barnard Hughes, Hal Holbrook, David Ogden Stiers, John McMartin; *D:* Joseph Sargent; *W:* David W. Rintels. **TV**

The Day Reagan Was Shot ♂♂ 2001 (R)
Recalls March 30, 1981 when President Reagan (Crenna) lay critically wounded in George Washington University hospital after having been shot by John W. Hinckley Jr. The administration is in chaos and power struggles break out between Secretary of State Alexander Haig (Dreyfuss) and Secretary of Defense Caspar Weinberger (Feore). Cable drama seems to be more satire than fact. **95m/C VHS, DVD.** Richard Crenna, Richard Dreyfuss, Colm Feore, Holland Taylor, Kenneth Welsh, Leon Pownall, Michael Murphy, Jack Jessop; *D:* Cyrus Nowrasteh; *W:* Cyrus Nowrasteh; *C:* Michael McMurray. **CABLE**

The Day Silence Died ♂♂
Dia Que Murio el Silencio 1998 Into the sleepy, provincial town of Villaserena, Bolivia, comes Abelardo. This charismatic stranger calls himself a "radio operator" and he installs four public loudspeakers in the town square where he plays music and broadcasts the news. He also offers to sell airtime to the local residents, which results in the airing of much private and dirty laundry, causing a good deal of turmoil within the community. And just who are they going to blame? Spanish with subtitles. **108m/C VHS.** Dario Grandinetti, Gustavo Angarita, Elias Serrano, Guillermo Granda, Maria Laura Garcia, Blanca Morisson; *D:* Paolo Agazzi; *W:* Paolo Agazzi, Guillermo Aguirre; *C:* Livio Delgado, Guillermo Medrano.

The Day That Shook the World ♂♂ 1978 (R)
Slow-moving but intriguing account of events surrounding the assassination of Archduke Ferdinand of Austria that triggered WWI. Garnered an R-rating due to some disturbingly graphic scenes. **111m/C VHS.** Christopher Plummer, Florinda Bolkan, Maximilian Schell; *D:* Veljko Bulajic.

Day the Bookies Wept ♂♂ 1939
Decent yarn about cabbies tricked into buying a "racehorse." Turns out she's old as the hills and hooked on alcohol to boot, but they enter her in the big race anyway. **50m/B VHS.** Betty Grable, Joe Penner, Tom Kennedy, Richard Lane; *D:* Leslie Goodwins.

The Day the Earth Caught Fire ♂♂♂½ 1961
The earth is knocked out of orbit and sent hurtling toward the sun when nuclear testing is done simultaneously at both the North and South Poles. Realistic and suspenseful, this is one of the best of the sci-fi genre. **95m/B VHS, DVD.** Janet Munro, Edward Judd, Leo McKern; *D:* Val Guest; *W:* Wolf Mankowitz, Val Guest; *C:* Harry Waxman; *M:* Stanley Black. British Acad. '61: Screenplay.

The Day the Earth Froze ♂♂ 1959
Witch steals the sun because she couldn't have a magical mill that produced grain, salt, and gold. Everything on Earth freezes. Based on a Finnish epic poem. **67m/B VHS, DVD.** *FI:* RU Nina Anderson, Jon Powers, Ingrid Elhardt, Paul Sorenson; *D:* Gregg Sebelious; *Nar:* Marvin Miller.

The Day the Earth Stood Still ♂♂♂♂ 1951
A gentle alien lands on Earth to deliver a message of peace and a warning against experimenting with nuclear power. He finds his views echoed by a majority of the population, but not the ones who are in control. In this account based loosely on the story of Christ, Rennie is the visitor backed by the mighty robot Gort. One of the greatest science fiction films of all time. **92m/B VHS, DVD.** Michael Rennie, Patricia Neal, Hugh Marlowe, Sam Jaffe, Frances Bavier, Lock Martin, Billy Gray, Edith Evanson, Frank Conroy, Drew Pearson; *D:* Robert Wise; *W:* Edmund H. North; *C:* Leo Tover; *M:* Bernard Herrmann. Natl. Film Reg. '95.

The Day the Sky Exploded ♂½ 1957
Death From Outer Space; La Morte Viene Dalla Spazio; Le Danger Vient de l'Escape Sci-fi disaster drama doesn't live up to the grandiose title, but it's still Italian. A runaway rocket ship hits the sun, unleashing an asteroid shower that threatens Earth with tidal waves, earthquakes, heat

---

waves and terrible dialogue. The highlight of this Franco-Italian effort is the cinematography of horror director Mario Bava. **80m/B VHS, DVD.** *FR IT* Paul (Christian) Hubschmid, Madeleine Fischer, Fiorella Mari, Ivo Garrani, Dario Michaelis; *D:* Richard Benson; *C:* Mario Bava.

The Day the Sun Turned Cold ♂♂ 1994
Tianguo Niezi In an apparent crisis of conscience a young man (Zhong Hua) tries to convince a weary captain (Hu) that his mother (Gowa) murdered his cruel father (Jingwu) 10 years before in order to marry another man. The detective eventually concludes he should investigate the supposed crime, which happened in a remote village, but Zhong Hua's accusations naturally stir up a great deal of resentment and anger. There's lots of questions about guilt, innocence, and motives—on everybody's part. Mandarin with subtitles. **99m/C VHS.** *HK* Siqin Gaowa, Tuo Zhong Hua, Wai Zhi, Ma Jingwu, Li Hu; *D:* Yim Ho; *W:* Yim Ho; *C:* Hou Yong; *M:* Yoshihide Otomo.

The Day the Women Got Even ♂♂½ 1980
Four suburban homemakers take up the life of vigilantes to save unsuspecting actresses from a talent agent's blackmail scheme. **98m/C VHS.** JoAnn Pflug, Tina Louise, Georgia Engel, Barbara Rhoades, Julie Hagerty, Ed O'Neill; *D:* Burt Brinckerhoff; *M:* Brad Fiedel. **TV**

Day the World Ended ♂ 1955
The first science-fiction film of exploitation director Roger Corman. Five survivors of nuclear holocaust discover a desert ranch house fortress owned by a survivalist (Birch) and his daughter (Nelson). With relatively abundant supplies, they fatuously wallow in false misery until a disfigured visitor, wasting away from radiation, stumbles into their paradise. His mutation into an alien...being confronts them with the horror that lurks outside. **79m/B VHS, DVD.** Paul Birch, Lori Nelson, Adele Jergens, Raymond Hatton, Paul Dubow, Richard Denning, Mike Connors, Paul Blaisdell, Jonathan Haze; *D:* Roger Corman; *W:* Lou Rusoff; *C:* Jockey A. Feindel; *M:* Ronald Stein.

The Day, the World Ended ♂♂½ 2001 (R)
Shrink Dr. Jennifer Stillman (Kinski) leaves New York for a small town as the school district's new therapist. Her first patient, Ben (Edner), is a young outsider whose adoptive father is hiding something about his mother's mysterious death, which involves a coverup by the town. When several locals are brutally murdered, Jennifer becomes a suspect but Ben blames his biological father—a space alien. This cable remake has nothing to do with the 1955 original and even the title seems off. **90m/C VHS, DVD.** Nastassja Kinski, Randy Quaid, Debra Christofferson, Bobby Edner, Stephen Tobolowsky, Lee DeBroux, David Getz, Alexander Gould; *D:* Terence Gross; *W:* Annie de Young, Max Enscoe; *C:* Mark Vargo; *M:* Charles Bernstein. **CABLE**

Day Time Ended ♂♂ 1980
Vortex; Timewarp A pair of glowing UFO's streaking across the sky and an alien mechanical device with long menacing appendages are only two of the bizarre phenomena witnessed from a lone house in the desert. Good special effects. Also released as "Time Warp" (1978). **80m/C VHS, DVD.** Chris Mitchum, Jim Davis, Dorothy Malone; *D:* John Cardos; *W:* David Schmoeller, J. Larry Carroll; *M:* Richard Band.

Day Watch ♂♂♂ 2006 (R)
Sudbi Vampires, chases, explosions, "Matrix"-style fight scenes, and just a touch of post-Communist allegory make this an incoherent but fun ride. Two factions of Moscow vampires ("Darks" and "Lights") struggle to manage an uneasy truce as an inevitable conflict rises. Good-guy vamp Anton (Khabensky) is torn between two rising powers: his lover Svetlana (Poroshina) on one side and his increasingly evil son Yegor (Martynov) on the other. Non-stop action sequences make up for the thin plot but what really stands out is the creative characterization and innovative direction. Sequel to 2004's "Night Watch." **132m/C DVD.** RU Konstantin

---

Khabensky, Maria Poroshina, Vladimir Menshov, Viktor Verzhbitsky, Galina Tyunina, Alexei Chadov, Dima Martinov, Valery Zolotukhin; *D:* Timur Bekmambetov; *W:* Timur Bekmambetov, Sergei Lukyanenko, Aleksandr Talal; *C:* Sergei Trofimov; *M:* Yuri Potyeyenko.

The Day Will Dawn ♂♂♂
Avengers 1942 Suspenseful British-made WWII thriller about a reporter and a young Norwegian girl who plot to sabotage a secret Nazi U-boat base near the girl's town. **100m/B VHS.** *GB* Deborah Kerr, Hugh Williams, Niall MacGinnis, Ralph Richardson, Francis L. Sullivan, Roland Culver, Finlay Currie, Patricia Medina; *D:* Harold French; *W:* Terence Rattigan.

A Day Without a Mexican ♂♂½ 2004 (R)
Un dia sin mexicanos One morning, the state of California wakes up to find the entire Latino population has disappeared. The consequences are huge. Fields remain unharvested, cars are abandoned, schools are closed and the poor Anglos are left holding the bag. Without cheap laborers and migrant workers, the economy falls into a hopeless shambles. The lone Latino survivor is Lila Rodriguez (Arizmendi, who also co-scripted), a reporter who becomes the center of intense scrutiny. Amusingly shot as a mockumentary, but what could have been a biting critique suffers from lack of focus and overly broad scope. **97m/C VHS, DVD.** *US MX* Yareli Arizmendi, John Getz, Maureen Flanigan, Muse Watson, Caroline Aaron, Melinda Allen, Eduardo Palomo, Bru Muller; *D:* Sergio Arau; *W:* Yareli Arizmendi, Sergio Arau, Sergio Guerrero; *C:* Alan Caudillo; *M:* Juan J. Colomer.

Day Zero ♂½ 2007 (R)
In this slightly futuristic fare, the U.S. military draft has been reinstated because of increasing terrorist acts. Three New York friends are called up and react to the news in different ways: lawyer George (Klein) asks his wealthy dad to help him wriggle out; insecure writer Aaron (Wood) thinks the military can make him a man; and cabdriver James (Bernthal) is patriotic and willing to serve. Overly self-important and formulaic. **96m/C DVD.** Chris Klein, Elijah Wood, Ginnifer Goodwin, Elissabeth (Elisabeth, Elizabeth, Liz) Moss, Jon Bernthal, Ally Sheedy, Sofia Vassilieva; *D:* Bryan Gunnar Cole; *W:* Rob Makani; *C:* Matthew Clark; *M:* Erin O'Hara.

Daybreak ♂♂♂ 1993 (R)
In the near future America has been decimated by a nameless, sexually transmitted disease (read AIDS parable) and public policy is to quarantine the infected in concentration camp-like prisons. This leads to a quasi-official group of green-shirted thugs roaming the streets and imprisoning or killing anyone they suspect has the disease. A small resistance movement is lead by Torch (Gooding Jr.), who happens to fall in love with Blue (Kelly), the sister of one of the fascist leaders. Based on Alan Bowne's play "Beirut, Daybreak." **91m/C VHS, DVD.** Cuba Gooding Jr., Moira Kelly, Omar Epps, Martha Plimpton, Alice Drummond, David Eigenberg, John Savage; *Cameos:* Phil Hartman; *D:* Stephen Tolkin; *W:* Stephen Tolkin. **CABLE**

Daybreak ♂♂ 2001 (R)
A throwback to the cheesy disaster flicks of the '70s, which isn't necessarily a bad thing. An L.A. subway train is stuck in a tunnel after an earthquake and it's up to subway supervisor Dillan Johansen (McGinley) to find a way to save himself and the passengers from fire, water, and toxic chemicals. **93m/C VHS, DVD.** Ted McGinley, Roy Scheider, Adam Wylie, Ursula Brooks, Jaime Bergman; *D:* Jean Pellerin. **VIDEO**

The Daydreamer ♂♂½ 1975 (PG-13)
Absent Minded; Le Distrait Actor/director/writer Richard stars as a bumbling fool let loose in the French corporate world with comical results. In French with subtitles. **90m/C VHS.** *FR* Pierre Richard, Bernard Blier, Maria Pacome, Marie-Christine Barrault; *D:* Pierre Richard; *W:* Pierre Richard; *M:* Vladimir Cosma.

Daylight ♂♂ 1996 (PG-13)
After a massive explosion seals both ends of New York's Holland Tunnel (The Tunneling Inferno?), a small band of stock disaster flick survivors are trapped under the waters of the Hudson River. Fortunately, a cab driver with a really square jaw who, conveniently, is an ex-emergency rescue worker

---

AND who knows the entire layout of the tunnel happens to be driving toward the tunnel at the exact moment of the disaster. Coincidence? Nope, just Hollywood. Kit Latura (Stallone) leads the survivors through cave-ins, floods, fire, rats, and poison gas (The Poison-Hiding Adventure!) only to discover to their dismay that they have emerged in New Jersey. Long on special effects but short on character development, this nod to the catastrophe movies of the '70s is still enjoyable for those who like to watch things go boom. **109m/C VHS, DVD, HD DVD, DVD.** Sylvester Stallone, Viggo Mortensen, Amy Brenneman, Stan Shaw, Claire Bloom, Renoly Santiago, Sage Stallone, Dan Hedaya, Jay O. Sanders, Karen Young, Vanessa Bell Calloway, Colin Fox, Danielle Harris, Jo Anderson, Mark Rolston, Rosemary Forsyth, Barry Newman; *D:* Rob Cohen; *W:* Leslie Bohem; *C:* David Eggby; *M:* Randy Edelman.

Days ♂♂½ 1989
Giorni Caludio (Trabacchi) is a workaholic mid-30s bank exec in Rome. HIV-positive, he's stayed healthy with a rigid regime of drugs and exercise. Claudio also has a longtime lover, Andrea (Salerno), and they are supposed to be moving to Milan together. Except Claudio is suddenly reluctant—could this have anything to do with his encounter with handsome young waiter Dario (Bechini)? (What do you think.) Suddenly, uptight Claudio is acting very recklessly. He begins an affair with Dario, goes off his meds, sloughs off his job, and can't make up his mind about either man. Claudio's not the most likeable guy around but he's very, very real and you'll even understand why both his lovers still around to see what happens next. Italian with subtitles. **90m/C VHS, DVD.** *IT* Thomas Trabacchi, Riccardo Salerno, Davide Bechini; *D:* Laura Muscardin; *W:* Laura Muscardin, Francesco Mohli, David Oserio, Jane Ruhm; *C:* Sabrina Varani; *M:* Ivan Iusco.

Days and Nights in the Forest ♂♂½ 1970
Aranyer Din Ratri Four men living in Calcutta decide to leave the city for a brief vacation. Each 'has a different emotional experience which will change him forever, including a brief love affair and finding true romance. In Bengali with English subtitles. **120m/C VHS.** *IN* Soumitra Chatterjee, Shamila Tagore, Shubhendu Chatterjee, Samit Bhanja; *D:* Satyajit Ray; *W:* Satyajit Ray; *C:* Soumendu Roy; *M:* Satyajit Ray.

Days of Glory ♂♂½ 1943
Peck's screen debut finds him as a Russian peasant bravely fighting the Nazi blitzkrieg almost single-handedly. **86m/B VHS.** Tamara Toumanova, Gregory Peck, Alan Reed, Maria Palmer, Lowell Gilmore, Hugo Haas; *D:* Jacques Tourneur; *C:* Gaetano Antonio "Tony" Gaudio.

Days of Glory ♂♂½ 2006 (R)
Issue-based WWII drama caused a furor as it brought up the shabby treatment received by North African colonial recruits who fought for France as second-class citizens. Poorly trained, they bravely battle on while being unjustly treated and degraded by their superior officers. The Moroccans are more mouthpieces than individuals but the actors work well as an ensemble, and director Bouchareb keeps his drama to human scale. French and Arabic with subtitles. **123m/C DVD.** *AL BE FR* Jamel Debbouze, Roschdy Zem, Sami Bouajila, Mathieu Simonel, Samy Naceri, Bernard Blancan, Benoit Giros; *D:* Rachid Bouchareb; *W:* Rachid Bouchareb, Olivier Morelle; *C:* Patrick Blossier; *M:* Armand Amar.

Days of Heaven ♂♂♂½ 1978 (PG)
Drifter Gere, his younger sister, and a woman he claims is his sister become involved with a Texas sharecropper. Told through the eyes of the younger girl, this is a sweeping vision of the U.S. before WWI. Loss and loneliness, deception, frustration, and anger haunt these people as they struggle to make the land their own. Deservedly awarded an Oscar for breathtaking cinematography. **95m/C VHS, DVD.** Richard Gere, Brooke Adams, Sam Shepard, Linda Manz, Stuart Margolin; *D:* Terrence Malick; *W:* Terrence Malick; *C:* Nestor Almendros; *M:* Ennio Morricone. Oscars '78: Cinematog.; Cannes '79: Director (Malick); L.A. Film Critics '78: Cinematog., Natl. Film Reg. '07; N.Y. Film Critics '78: Director (Malick); Natl. Soc. Film Critics '78: Cinematog., Director (Malick), Film

Days of Hell ♂ / *Giorni Dell'inferno* 1984 Forgettable tale of four mercenaries who are hired to rescue a doctor and his daughter held captive by guerrillas somewhere in Afghanistan only to find out they're pawns in an even bigger scheme. **90m/C** VHS. **C:** Conrad Nichols, Ottaviano Dell'Acqua, Stephen Elliot, Kiwako Harada. **D:** Anthony Richmond.

Days of Jesse James ♂♂ 1939 Roy is a member of a detective agency who joins the James gang incognito in order to prove that they didn't rob the Northfield bank. Roy figures out that bank officials actually planned the whole scheme. **63m/B** VHS. **C:** Buster Keaton, Charlie Chaplin, Harold Lloyd, Stan Laurel, Oliver Hardy; **D:** Anthony Richmond.

Days of Thrills and Laughter ♂♂♂½ 1961 Delightful compilation of clips from the era of silent films, showcasing the talents of the great comics as well as daring stuntman. **93m/B** VHS. **C:** Roy Rogers, George "Gabby" Hayes, Donald (Don "Red") Barry, Harry Woods, Pauline Moore, Mike Worth, Glenn Strange; **D:** Joseph Kane. **W:** Earle Snell. **C:** Reggie Lanning.

Days of Thunder ♂♂ 1990 "Top Gun" in race cars! Cruise follows the same formula he has followed for several years now (with the notable exception of "Born on the Fourth of July") Cruise and Towne co-wrote the screenplay concerning a young kid bursting with talent and raw energy who must learn to deal with his mentor, his girlfriend, and eventually the bad guy. First film that featured cameras that were actually on the race cars. If you like Cruise or race cars then this is the movie for you. **108m/C** VHS. DVD. **C:** Tom Cruise, Robert Duvall, Randy Quaid, Nicole Kidman, Cary Elwes, Michael Rooker, Fred Dalton Thompson, John C. Reilly; **D:** Tony Scott; **W:** Tom Cruise, Robert Towne; **C:** Ward Russell; **M:** Hans Zimmer.

Days of Wine and Roses ♂♂♂½ 1962 A harrowing tale of an alcoholic advertising man who gradually drags his wife down with him into a life of booze. Big screen adaptation of the play originally shown on TV. *27* Days of Wine and Roses. **138m/B** VHS. DVD. **C:** Jack Lemmon, Lee Remick, Charles Bickford, Jack Klugman, Jack Albertson; **D:** Blake Edwards; **W:** J.P. Miller) Pinckney) Miller; **M:** Henry Mancini. Johnny Mercer. Oscars '62: Song ("Days of Wine and Roses").

Days of Wine and Roses ♂♂♂½ 1958 The original "Playhouse 90" TV version of J.P. Miller's story which was adapted for the big screen in 1962. An executive on the fast track and his young wife, initially only social drinkers, find themselves degenerating into alcoholism. A well-acted, stirring drama. **89m/B** VHS. DVD. Cliff Robertson, Piper Laurie; **D:** John Frankenheimer. TV

The Daytrippers ♂♂½ 1996 Happily married Eliza D'Amico is living on Long Island while husband Louis (Tucci) goes to work in Manhattan. That is she's happy until she finds what appears to be a love letter addressed to her husband. Frantic, Eliza runs to aggressive mom Rita (Meara), who decides that her daughter should immediately confront her possibly erring husband at his office. So Eliza, her mom and dad (McNamara), sarcastic younger sister Jo (Posey), and Jo's pretentious boyfriend Carl (Schreiber) all pile into the family station wagon and head into the city. Only Louis isn't at his office and they scour Manhattan to track him down. **83m/C** VHS. DVD. Hope Davis, Anne Meara, Stanley Tucci, Campbell Scott, Marcia Gay Harden, Andy Brown; **D:** Greg Mottola. **C:** John Inwood.

Dayton's Devils ♂♂ 1968 Nielsen is the leader of a motley crew of losers who plan to rob a military base bank in this action-packed heist flick. **107m/C** VHS. Rory Calhoun, Leslie Nielsen, Lainie Kazan, Eric (Hans Gudegast) Braeden, Georg Stanford Brown, Rigg Kennedy; **D:** Jack Shea.

De Mayerling a Sarajevo ♂♂½ 1940 Looks at the romance and marriage, as well as royal pomp and circumstance, of the Countess Sophie (Feuillere) and the Archduke Franz-Ferdinand (Lodge). The assassination of these innocuous rulers at Sarajevo would lead to the outbreak of WWI. French with subtitles. **89m/B** VHS. FR Edwige Feuillere, John Lodge, Aime Clariond, Gabrielle Dorziat; **D:** Max Ophuls; **W:** Kurt Alexander; **C:** Curt Courant, Otto Heller; **M:** Oscar Straus.

Deacon Brodie ♂♂ 1998 William Deacon Brodie (Connolly) is one of Edinburgh's most respected citizens in 1788. So his trial and conviction for defrauding the city is doubly shocking—until his secret life of gambling, drinking, and wenching is exposed. **90m/C** VHS. DVD. GB Billy Connolly, Patrick Malahide, Catherine McCormack, Lorcan Cranitch; **D:** Philip Saville; **W:** Simon Donald; **C:** Ivan Strasburg; **M:** Simon Boswell. TV

Dazed and Confused ♂♂♂ 1993 (R) A day in the life of a bunch of high schoolers should prove to be a trip back in time for those coming of age in the '70s. Eight seniors facing life as they have one last year long hurrah, as they search for themselves. Keen characterization by writer/director Linklater captures the spirit of a generation shaped by Watergate, the Vietnam War, feminism, and marijuana. Groovy soundtrack features Alice Cooper, Deep Purple, KISS, and Foghat. **97m/C** VHS. DVD. DVD. Jason London, Roy Cochrane, Sasha Jenson, Wiley Wiggins, Michelle Rene Thomas, Adam Goldberg, Anthony Rapp, Marissa Ribisi, Parker Posey, Joey Lauren Adams, Ben Affleck, Milla Jovovich, Cole Hauser, Matthew McConaughey, Kirstin Hinojosa. **D:** Richard Linklater; **W:** Richard Linklater; **C:** Lee Daniel.

DC 9/11: Time of Crisis ♂♂ *The Big Dance* 2004 (R) Retelling of the horrific terrorist attacks in New York City and Washington D.C. while providing a supposed behind-the-scenes view of the reaction of President Bush (played by Bottoms) and his administration. Undoubtedly will cause debates between those who see this as a vehicle to inflate the president's image and combat Michael Moore's flogging in "Fahrenheit 9/11" and others who consider it as fact. Let's remember it's a made for TV flick. **127m/C** VHS. DVD. Timothy Bottoms, John Cunningham, James Carroll, Greg Elward, Lawrence Pressman, Stephen Macht, Gregory Itzin, Penny Johnson, Myron Natwick, Andrew Gillies, Bobby Johnston, Debra McGrath, David McIlwraith, Brian Rhodes, Allen Barnes, Geoffrey Bowes, Domenico) Fiore, Chris Gillet, Thomas Hauff, Howard Jerome, Doug Lennox, Gerry Mendicino, Mary Gordon Murray, David Wolos-Fonteno; **D:** Brian Trenchard-Smith; **W:** Lionel Chetwynd; **C:** Oussana Rawi; **M:** Lawrence Shragge. TV

D.C. Cab ♂♂ 1984 (R) A rag-tag group of Washington, D.C. cabbies learn a lesson in self-respect in this endearing comedy. Though not without flaws, it's charming all the same. **100m/C** VHS. DVD. Mr. T, Leif Erickson, Adam Baldwin, Charlie Barnett, Irene Cara, Anne DeSalvo, Max Gail, Gloria Gifford, Gary Busey, Jill Schoelen, Marsha Warfield; **D:** Joel Schumacher; **W:** Joel Schumacher; **C:** Dean Cundey.

De-Lovely ♂♂ *She's De Lovely* 2004 (PG-13) Biopic of songwriter Cole Porter (Kline) is played as if Porter himself were directing a musical about his life. Focuses on his adultery-ridden marriage to put-upon wife Linda (Judd), who puts up with everything for as long she can. Dreary film is brightened by oddly updated covers of his tunes done by contemporary pop stars such as Elvis Costello, Alanis Morissette, and Sheryl Crow, but the story contains no real nods to Porter's artistic genius or creative struggles. Contrived staging is stolen from better films like "All That Jazz" and "Cabaret." Solid cast is very good, especially Judd, but story is deadly dull and glum. **125m/C** VHS. Kevin Kline, Ashley Judd, Jonathan Pryce, Keith Allen, Natalie Cole, Elvis Costello, Kevin McNally, Allan Corduner, Sandra Nelson, James Wilby, Kevin McKidd, Richard Dillane, Peter Polycarpou, Edward Baker-Duly; **D:** Irwin Winkler; **W:** Jay Cocks; **C:** Tony Pierce-Roberts.

Dead Ahead: The Exxon Valdez Disaster ♂♂ at *Valdez* 1992 (PG-13) Focuses on the first crucial days after the March 24, 1989, oil spill when the Exxon Valdez ran aground off Alaska in Prince William Sound. Portrays the inadequate precautions, incompetence, greed, and petty bureaucracy that made an appalling situation even worse. Lloyd stars as Exxon official Frank Iarossi, in charge of the official cleanup, caught between onsite confusion and corporate bungling while Heard is outraged environmentalist Dan Lawn. News and home videotapes of the actual spill are used to enhance the dramatization. Filmed in Vancouver, British Columbia. **90m/C** VHS. Christopher Lloyd, John Heard, Rip Torn, Michael Murphy, Don S. Davies, Kenneth Welsh, Bob Gunton, Mark Metcalf, Paul Guilfoyle, David Morse, Jackson Davies; **D:** Paul Seed; **W:** Michael Baker; **M:** Paul Ferguson. CABLE

Dead Aim woof! 1987 (R) A dud about Soviet spies who introduce even more drugs into New York City, ostensibly to bring about the downfall of the U.S. Obviously a completely far-fetched plot. **91m/C** VHS, Ed Marinaro, Isaac Hayes, Corbin Bernsen; **D:** William Vanderkloot.

Dead Air ♂♂ 1994 (PG-13) Atmospheric murder mystery finds radio deejay Hines getting calls from a mystery woman who says she knows him well and has kidnapped his new girlfriend. Meanwhile, a woman claiming to be a reporter wants to interview him and things around the radio station start looking decidedly sinister. **91m/C** VHS. Gregory Hines, Debrah Farentino, Gloria Reuben, Beau Starr, Laura Harrington, Michael (M.K.) Harris, W. Earl Brown, Veronica Cartwright; **D:** Fred Walton; **W:** David Amann; **M:** Dana Kaproff.

Dead Alive ♂♂ *Braindead* 1993 This outrageously over-the-top horror flick from New Zealand is a gore aficionado's delight (think "Evil Dead" movies for comparison).

The Dead ♂♂♂½ 1987 (PG) The poignant final film by Huston, based on James Joyce's short story from "Dubliners." At a Christmas dinner party in 1904 Dublin, Gabriel Conroy (McCann) discovers how little he knows about his wife Gretta (Angelica Huston) when a song reminds her of a cherished lost love. Beautifully captures the spirit of the story while providing Huston an opportunity to create a last lament on the fickle nature of time and life. **82m/C** VHS. DVD. GB Anjelica Huston, Donal McCann, Marie Kean, Donal Donnelly, Dan O'Herlihy, Helen Carroll, Frank Patterson; **D:** John Huston; **W:** Tony Huston (Walter Anthony) Huston; **C:** Fred Murphy; **M:** Alex North. Ind. Spirit '88: Director (Huston), Support. Actress (Huston); Natl. Soc. Film Critics '87; Film.

Dead Again ♂♂♂½ 1991 (R) Branagh's first film since his brilliant debut as the director/star of "Henry V" again proves him a visionary force on and off camera. Smart, cynical L.A. detective Mike Church (Branagh) is hired to discover the identity of a beautiful but mute woman (Thompson) whom he calls Grace. With the help of hypnotist Franklyn Madson (Jacobi) Mike finds that he's apparently trapped in a nightmarish cycle of murder begun years before, involving a jealous conductor and his concert pianist wife, Liz erate, lovely to lock at, suspenseful, with a sense of humor to match its high style. **107m/C** VHS. DVD. Kenneth Branagh, Emma Thompson, Andy Garcia, Lois Hall, Richard Easton, Derek Jacobi, Hanna Schygulla, Campbell Scott, Wayne Knight, Christine Ebersole; *Cameos:* Robin Williams; **D:** Kenneth Branagh; **W:** Scott Frank; **C:** Matthew F. Leonetti; **M:** Patrick Doyle.

Dead Ahead ♂♂ 1996 (PG-13) Skilled archer Maura Loch (Zimbalist) is enjoying a camping trip with her family until four bankrobbers on the lam stumble across them and take Maura's son hostage. Armed with her bow, Maura tracks the criminals to save her child. **92m/C** VHS. Stephanie Zimbalist, Sarah Chalke, Tom Butler, Brendan Fletcher, Peter Onorati, John Tench, Michael Tayles, Douglas Arthurs; **D:** Stuart Cooper; **W:** David Alexander; **C:** Curtis Petersen; **M:** Charles Bernstein. CABLE

Dead and Buried ♂♂♂½ 1981 (R) Set in 1957 and satirizing the bland times "the plot" has the mom of a nerdy son getting bitten by an exotic monkey, which promptly turns her into a particularly nasty ghoul. This condition is apparently contagious, (except for her son who tries to hide the fact mom is literally a monster) and calls for lots of spurting blood and body parts which take on lives of their own. For those with strong stomachs and senses of humor. Also available in an 85-minute R-rated version. **97m/C** VHS. DVD. NZ Timothy Balme, Elizabeth Moody, Diana Penaver, Ian Watkin, Brenda Kendall, Stuart Devenie, Peter Jackson; **D:** Peter Jackson; **W:** Peter Jackson, Stephen Sinclair, Fran Walsh, Stephen Sinclair; **C:** Murray Milne; **M:** Peter Dasent.

Dead Are Alive ♂♂ 1972 Alcoholic archaeologist Jason (Cord) hes come to Italy to search for Etruscan ruins near the home of orchestral conductor Nicos (John Marley) and his wife Myra (Samantha Eggar), Jason's ex-lover. Soon after he opens an Etruscan tomb, a series of violent murders begin. The above-average giallo shocker and is much better than director Crispino's more popular "Autopsy." **103m/C** DVD. // Alex Cord, Samantha Eggar, John Marley, Nadia Tiller, Horst Frank, Enzo Tarascio; **D:** Armando Crispino; **C:** Erico Menczer; **M:** Riz Ortolani.

Dead As a Doorman ♂½ 1985 A young writer takes a part-time post as a doorman and becomes the target of a murderous lunatic. **83m/C** VHS. Bradley Whitford, Sharon Schlarth, Bruce Taylor; **D:** Gary Youngman.

Dead Badge ♂♂½ 1994 (R) An honest cop is reassigned to a corrupt precinct and becomes targeted for death. Somewhat conventional cop plot into an effective vehicle "or Johnson. **95m/C** VHS. Brian Wimmer, Olympia Dukakis, Yaphet Kotto, M. Emmet Walsh, James B. Sikking, Marta DuBois; **D:** Douglas Barr.

Dead Bang ♂♂½ 1989 (R) A frustrated cop uncovers a murderous white supremacist conspiracy in L.A. Frankenheimer's deft directorial hand shapes a somewhat conventional cop plot into an effective vehicle "or Johnson. **102m/C** VHS. DVD. Don Johnson, Bob Balaban, William Forsythe, Penelope Ann Miller, Tim Reid, Frank William Higgins, Michael Jeter, Evans Evans, Tate Donovan; **D:** John Frankenheimer; **W:** Robert Foster; **C:** Gerry Fisher; **M:** Gary Chang, Michael Kamen.

Dead Beat ♂♂½ 1994 (R) Teen love and lust—and murder—all set in Albuquerque, New Mexico, circa 1965. Womanizer Kit (Ramsey) will use any tale to score with his dates—and is happy to pass on tips to adoring disciple Rudy (Getty). When Kit meets up with rebellious rich girl Kirsten (Wagner), she demands proof of his love and he confides he once murdered a girl. Kirsten tries to tighten her stranglehold on Kit with this info and force Rudy from his life but Kit's dark side doesn't stay hidden either. **94m/C** VHS. Bruce Ramsay, Natasha Gregson Wagner, Balthazar Getty, Meredith Salenger, Sara Gilbert, Deborah Ramsay, Max Perlich, Alex Cox; **D:** Adam Dubov; **W:** Adam Dubov.

Dead Birds ♂♂ 2004 (R) In 1863 Alabama, a group of Confederate soldiers, led by William (Thomas), rob a bank of its gold bullion—leaving a lot of dead bodies behind—and plan to head to Mexico. But first, they spend the night in an abandoned plantation house that apparently isn't so abandoned. They hear noises and strange creatures, and start to get very spooked indeed. **91m/C** DVD. Henry Thomas, Patrick Fugit, Nicki Aycox, Michael Shannon, Muse Watson, Mark Boone Jr., Isaiah Washington; **D:** Alex Turner; **W:** Simon Barrett; **M:** Peter Lopez.

Dead Bodies ⅆ½ 2003 Premise strains credulity. After an argument, slacker Tommy (Scott) discovers that whiny ex-girlfriend Jean (Davis) has accidentally died. So Tommy decides to bury the body in the woods, only to find the one patch of dirt that already contains a dead body—a woman missing for 8 years. So the police find 2 dead bodies and Tommy is in deep muck. **84m/C** DVD. *IR* Andrew Scott, Kelly Reilly, Sean McGinley, Gerard McSorley, Darren Healy, Katy Davis; *D:* Robert Quinn; *W:* Derek Landy; *C:* Donal Gilligan; *M:* Ray Harman.

Dead Boyz Can't Fly ⅆⅆ 1993 (R) Disturbing look at urban violence. Dysfunctional punk leads his equally amoral cohorts on a looting spree in a near-empty highrise in revenge against a patronizing businessman. The unrated version contains 10 more minutes of violence. **92m/C** VHS. Della Sheppard, Sheila Kennedy, Ruth (Coreen) Collins, Mark McCulley, Brad Friedman; *D:* Howard Winters.

Dead Broke ⅆⅆ 1999 (R) Lying witnesses make it hard for detective Sam (Glover) to solve a murder that happens outside a Brooklyn debt collection agency, whose employees are all suspicious characters. Hits all the film noir clichés but you're never quite sure if this is intended as a spoof or not. **98m/C** DVD. John Glover, Paul Sorvino, Jillian) Hennessey, Tony Roberts, Justin Theroux, Patricia Scanlon, Nela Wagman, Cheryl Rogers; *D:* Edward Vilga; *W:* Edward Vilga; *C:* Joaquin Baca-Asay; *M:* Edward Bilous.

A Dead Calling ⅆ½ 2006 (R) Familiar horror storyline has a few frights. Reporter Rachel (Holden) has returned home after a personal tragedy and joined the local TV station. She's given a fluff assignment to investigate the town's historic homes but runs into trouble with the Frank Sullivan place. That's where Frank Sullivan (Oman) butchered his family and escaped custody. And when Rachel enters the house, the ghosts of the slain family plead for her help to find their eternal rest. Except Frank has other ideas. **90m/C** DVD. Alexandra Holden, Bill Moseley, Sid Haig, Leslie Easterbrook, Timothy Oman, John Burke, Caia Coley; *D:* Michael Feifer; *W:* Michael Feifer; *C:* Hank Baumert Jr.; *M:* Glenn Morrisette. VIDEO

Dead Calm ⅆⅆⅆ 1989 (R) A taut Australian thriller based on a novel by Charles Williams. A young married couple is yachting on the open seas when they happen upon the lone survivor of a sinking ship. They take him on board only to discover he's a homicidal maniac. Makes for some pretty suspenseful moments that somewhat make up for the weak ending. **97m/C** VHS, DVD. *AU* Sam Neill, Billy Zane, Nicole Kidman, Rod Mullinar; *D:* Phillip Noyce; *W:* Terry Hayes; *C:* Dean Semler; *M:* Graeme Revell.

Dead Center ⅆⅆ *Crazy Joe* 1994 (R) Street punk gets trained as assassin by secret government agency that frames him for the murder of a U.S. senator. So now he has to stay alive long enough to prove his innocence. **90m/C** VHS. Justin Lazard, Ed Lottimer, Rachel York; *D:* Steve Carver.

Dead Certain ⅆ 1992 (R) A "Silence of the Lambs" rip-off. Dourif (again specializing in weirdos) is the jailed serial killer providing tantalizing clues to the identity of a new killer on the loose. **93m/C** VHS. Brad Dourif, Francesco Quinn, Karen Russell, Joel Kaiser; *D:* Anders Palm; *W:* Anders Palm.

Dead Cold ⅆ½ 1996 (R) Screenwriter Eric Thornsen (Mulkey) decides he and wife Alicia (Anthony) need a second honeymoon at a remote cabin. But their privacy is disturbed by homicidal fugitive Kale (Dobson), who drugs and dumps Eric's body down a ravine. But of course Eric's not really dead. Decent thriller is slow to start but picks up speed in the second half. **91m/C** VHS. Lysette Anthony, Chris Mulkey, Peter Dobson, Alina Thompson; *D:* Kurt Anderson; *M:* Richard Bowers.

Dead Connection ⅆ 1994 (R) Beautiful reporter Bonet is in cahoots with cop Madsen to see justice brought the "phone sex killer" who is terrorizing Los Angeles. **93m/C** VHS. Michael Madsen, Lisa Bonet, Gary Stretch; *D:* Nigel Dick; *W:* Larry Grolin; *M:* Rolfe Kent.

Dead Creatures ⅆ 2001 A close-knit group of British twentysomething women travels around the dingy areas outside of London satiating their need for human flesh with saran-wrapped body parts they carry in their luggage. The girls are all suffering from a kind of zombie-disease that is inflicted by a bite and eventually results in the victim's literal decomposition. The dreary tone of the film echoes that of lower-class British TV dramas: heavy grainy images, squalid locations with minimal lighting and makeup. Parkinson directs this low-key horror drama without the usual female nudity prevalent in today's micro-budgeted horror films, but the lack of a thriller element or traditional genre structure works against it. Without anywhere to go with the story, this one peters out around the halfway mark. The gore effects, though used minimally, are repugnant and truly nauseating. **89m/C** DVD. Beverly Wilson, Antonia Beamish, Brendan Gregory; *D:* Andrew Parkinson; *W:* Andrew Parkinson; *C:* Jack Shepherd; *M:* Andrew Parkinson.

Dead Dog ⅆⅆ 2000 Tom and Perri's dog gets mowed down by a hit-and-run driver on the streets of NYC. Tormented, Tom's life unravels causing Perri to worry about the possible fallout from his urge for vengeance. **90m/C** VHS, DVD. Jeremy Sisto, Paige Turco, Emily Cline, Julianne Nicholson, Lisa Bowman, Christopher Cousins, Jay O. Sanders, Adrienne Shelly, David Thornton; *D:* Christopher Goode; *W:* Grant Morris; *C:* Eric Schmidt; *M:* John M. Davis. VIDEO

The Dead Don't Die ⅆ 1975 Unbelievable plot set in the 1930s has Hamilton as a detective trying to prove his brother was wrongly executed for murder. He ultimately clashes with the madman who wants to rule the world with an army of zombies. Perhaps if they had cast Hamilton as Master of the Zombies. **74m/C** VHS. George Hamilton, Ray Milland, Linda Cristal, Ralph Meeker, Joan Blondell, James McEachin; *D:* Curtis Harrington. TV

Dead Easy ⅆ 1982 Livin' ain't easy for a Sydney sleaze-club owner, his working-girl girlfriend, and a slandered cop when they're caught between machete-wielding enemy gangs (it seems some body made the crime boss REALLY mad). **92m/C** VHS. *AU* Scott Burgess, Rosemary Paul; *D:* Bert Deling.

Dead End ⅆⅆ½ *Cradle of Crime* 1937 Sidney Kingsley play, adapted for the big screen by Lillian Hellman, traces the lives of various inhabitants of the slums on New York's Lower East Side as they try to overcome their surroundings. Gritty drama saved from melodrama status by some genuinely funny moments. Film launched the Dead End Kids. **92m/B** VHS, DVD. Sylvia Sidney, Joel McCrea, Humphrey Bogart, Wendy Barrie, Claire Trevor, Allen Jenkins, Marjorie Main, Billy Halop, Huntz Hall, Bobby Jordan, Gabriel Dell, Leo Gorcey, Charles Halton, Bernard Punsley, Minor Watson, James Burke; *D:* William Wyler; *W:* Lillian Hellman; *C:* Gregg Toland; *M:* Alfred Newman.

Dead End ⅆ½ 1998 (R) Police sergeant Henry Smolenski (Roberts) gains custody of his troubled 16-year-old son Adam (Tierney) after his ex-wife's death. Then he learns that the death is being investigated as a murder and Adam is the primary suspect. When Adam takes off, Henry searches for him and winds up becoming a suspect himself. Soon the estranged father and son are teaming up to discover who's out to frame them. Roberts gets to play a likable, caring character for a change of pace. **93m/C** VHS, DVD. *CA* Eric Roberts, Jacob Tierney, Jayne Heitmeyer, Eliza Roberts, Jacob Tierney, Jayne Heitmeyer, Eliza Douglas Jackson; *W:* Karl Schiffman; *C:* Georges Archambault; *M:* Milan Kymlicka. VIDEO

Dead End City ⅆ½ 1988 Street-wise resident of L.A. organizes fellow citizens into a vigilante force to fight the gangs for control of the city. **88m/C** VHS. Dennis Cole, Gregory Scott Cummins, Christine Lunde, Robert Z'Dar, Darrell Nelson, Alena Downs; *D:* Peter Yuval; *W:* Michael Bogert.

Dead End Drive-In ⅆⅆ 1986 (R) In a surreal, grim future a man is trapped at a drive-in theatre-cum-government-run concentration camp, where those considered to be less than desirable members of society are incarcerated. **92m/C** VHS, DVD. *AU* Ned Manning, Natalie McCurry, Peter Whitford; *D:* Brian Trenchard-Smith.

Dead End Street ⅆⅆ½ *Kwish L'Lo Motzah* 1983 Young prostitute attempts to change her self-destructive lifestyle. It's not easy. **86m/C** VHS, DVD. *IS* Anat Atzmon, Yehoram Gaon; *D:* Yaky Yosha; *W:* Yaky Yosha, Eli Tavor.

Dead Evidence ⅆ½ *Lawless: Dead Evidence* 2000 (R) Young P.I. Jodie Keane (Dotchin) teams up with ex-cop John Lawless (Smith) to track a serial killer by offering herself as the next potential victim. **94m/C** VHS, DVD. *NZ* Kevin Smith, Angela Dotchin, C. Thomas Howell, Bruce Hopkins, Geoff Dolan, Andrew Binns; *D:* Charlie Haskell; *W:* Gavin Strawhan; *C:* Mark Olsen; *M:* Peter Blake. TV

Dead Eyes of London ⅆⅆ½ *Dark Eyes of London; Die Toten Augen von London* 1961 Blind old German men are dying to lower their premiums in this geriatric thriller: someone (perhaps the director of the home for the blind?) is killing off the clientele for their insurance money, and a Scotland Yard inspector aims to expose the scam. Relatively early vintage Kinski, it's a remake of the eerie 1939 Lugosi vehicle, "The Human Monster" (originally titled "Dark Eyes of London"), adapted from Edgar Wallace's "The Testament of Gordon Stuart." **95m/B** VHS, DVD. *GE* Joachim Fuchsberger, Karin Baal, Dieter Borsche, Ady Berber, Klaus Kinski, Eddi Arent, Wolfgang Lukschy; *D:* Alfred Vohrer.

Dead Fire ⅆⅆ 1998 A space sub-station has been in orbit around earth for the past 50 years trying to regenerate the planet's poisoned atmosphere. But now a shipboard traitor is trying to destroy the operation. **105m/C** VHS. Matt Frewer, C. Thomas Howell, Monica Schnarre; *D:* Robert Lee; *M:* Peter Allen. VIDEO

Dead Fish ⅆⅆ 2004 (R) Despite the cast, it stinks like week-old dead fish too. Contract killer Lynch (Oldman) runs into trouble when he helps out Abe (Potts) and his pregnant girlfriend Mimi (Anaya) with a would-be thief. His and Abe's cell phones accidentally get switched and Lynch falls inexplicably and instantly in love with Mimi despite the fact that he's on the way to his next hit. **94m/C** DVD. *GB* Gary Oldman, Elena Anaya, Robert Carlyle, Karel Roden, Terence Stamp, Andrew Lee Potts, Billy Zane, Jimi Mistry; *D:* Charley Stadler; *W:* David Mitchell, Adam Kreutner; *C:* Fraser Taggart; *M:* Andrew Cato.

Dead for a Dollar ⅆ½ *Tammazzol Raccomandati a Dio* 1970 A Colonel, a con man, and a mysterious woman team up in the Old West to search for the $200,000 they stole from a local bank. **92m/C** VHS. John Ireland, George Hilton, Piero Vida, Sandra Milo; *D:* Osvaldo Civirani.

Dead Funny ⅆⅆ 1994 (R) Vivian (Pena) returns to her Manhattan walk-up to find boyfriend Reggie (McCarthy) dead on her kitchen table, skewered by a Samurai sword. Instead of calling the police, Viv gets gal pal Louise (Turco) to come over to figure out who did Reg in. Instead, they get drunk and discuss Reggie's who seen in flashbacks) immaturity and penchant for practical jokes. Good performances, twist ending, but situation runs out of steam. **91m/C** VHS. Elizabeth Pena, Andrew McCarthy, Paige Turco, Blanche Baker, Lisa Jane Persky, Michael Mantell; *D:* John Feldman; *W:* John Feldman; *M:* Sheila Silver.

The Dead Girl ⅆⅆ 2006 (R) Moncrieff's troubling drama showcases one victim of a serial killer from five female perspectives. The title character is runaway druggie hooker Krista (Murphy), whose body is found by downtrodden Arlene (Collette). Forensic student Leah (Byrne) first thinks the body is that of her missing sister, while enabling wife Ruth (Hurt) suspects her husband (Searcy) is the killer. Then Melora (Harden) rounds out the story when Krista is identified and the grieving mom is forced to confront how her daughter was living. **93m/C** DVD. US Toni

---

Collette, Rose Byrne, Mary, Beth Hurt, Marcia Gay Harden, Brittany Murphy, Kerry Washington, Giovanni Ribisi, Nick Searcy, Piper Laurie, Josh Brolin, James Franco, Mary Steenburgen, Bruce Davison; *D:* Karen Moncrieff; *W:* Karen Moncrieff; *C:* Michael Grady; *M:* Adam Gorgoni.

Dead Girls ⅆ 1990 (R) A rock group whose lyrics focus on suicide goes on vacation. The members find themselves stalked by a serial killer who decides to take matters out of the musicians' hands and into his own. Graphic violence. **105m/C** VHS. Diana Karanikas, Angela Eads; *D:* Dennis Devine; *W:* Steve Jarvis; *C:* Aaron Schneider.

Dead Gorgeous ⅆⅆ½ 2002 Antonia Ashton (McCrory) is a brazen hussy and a consummate schemer. She's married to boring business tycoon Hector (Cook) while carrying on with hunky professor Vic (Owen). She wants out of her marriage—by murder if necessary. Mousy Rose Bell (Ripley) wishes she could get rid of her drunken, philandering spouse as well. Antonia and Rose—old friends from the war—meet again in a gray 1946 London. Antonia has a plan—she'll see that Rose's husband has an "accident" and Rose will do the same with Hector. Antonia carries through but a grateful Rose is more cautious. Some unexpected twists in this variation of "Strangers on a Train." From the 1989 novel, "On the Edge," by Peter Lovesey. **100m/C** VHS, DVD. *GB* Fay Ripley, Helen McCrory, Ron Cook, Lloyd Owen, Jonathan Phillips, Dermot Crowley, Michael Mueler; *D:* Sarah Harding; *W:* Andrew Payne; *C:* Simon Kossoff; *M:* Jennie Muskett. TV

The Dead Hate the Living ⅆⅆ 1999 (R) Young filmmakers sneak into an abandoned medical research facility to make a low-budget horror feature about a scientist who raises the dead to be his zombie slaves. Little do they know that the facility was abandoned after a scientist's experiments to revive the dead through alchemical means went horribly wrong. When they discover the scientist's body, they decide to go use what they've found to add to the film's production value and accidentally manage to open a rift into the dimension of the dead. The script is a patchwork of influences. Effects are impressive, with many spectacular (and gruesome) zombies. **90m/C** DVD. Eric Clawson, Jamie Donahue, Brett Beardslee, Wendy Speake; *D:* Dave Parker; *W:* Dave Parker; *C:* Tom Calloway; *M:* Jared DePasquale.

Dead Heart ⅆⅆ 1996 Culture clash story set in the 1930s is highlighted by a terrific lead performance by Brown. He's cop Ray Lorkin, whose territory is the tiny community of Wala Wala in Australia's outback. This remote spot just happens to be a focal point for the local aboriginals, who regard the area as a spiritual place. Trouble erupts when an aboriginal prisoner (Pederson), who just happened to be having an affair with the schoolteacher's white wife (Mikkiken) is found hanged in his cell. Tradition demands revenge—from there every other situation in the community just gets worse. First-timer Parsons directs from his stage play. **106m/C** VHS, DVD. *AU* Bryan Brown, Ernie Dingo, Angie Milliken, Aaaron Pedersen, Lewis Fitz-Gerald, John Jarratt, Anne Tenney, Gnamayarahe Waitaire, Late Charlton; *D:* Nick Parsons; *W:* Nick Parsons; *C:* James Bartle; *M:* Stephen Rae.

Dead Heat ⅆⅆ½ 1988 (R) Some acting talent and a few funny moments unfortunately don't add up to a fine film, though they do save it from being a complete woofer. In this one even the cops are zombies when one of them is resurrected from the dead to help his partner solve his murder and rid the city of the rest of the undead. **86m/C** VHS, DVD. Joe Piscopo, Treat Williams, Lindsay Frost, Darren McGavin, Vincent Price, Keye Luke, Clare Kirkconnell; *D:* Mark Goldblatt; *W:* Terry Black; *C:* Robert Yeoman; *M:* Ernest Troost.

Dead Heat ⅆⅆ½ 2001 (R) *I Fought the Law* 2001 (R) Pally Lamarr (Sutherland) is a suicidal ex-cop with a drinking problem. His shady stepbrother Ray (LaPaglia) persuades Pally to purchase a long-shot racehorse with a jockey (Bluteau) who's an ex-con gambling addict. Things get even

Dead Heat on a Merry-Go-Round 🐾🐾🐾 1966 (R) Coburn turns in a great performance as the ex-con who masterminds the heist of an airport safe. Intricately woven plot provides suspense and surprises. The film is also notable for the debut of Ford in a bit part (he has one line as a hotel messenger). 107m/C VHS, DVD. James Coburn, Camilla Sparv, Aldo Ray, Nina Wayne, Robert Webber, Rose Marie, Todd Armstrong, Marian Moses, Severn Darden, Harrison Ford, Vic Tayback; D: Bernard Girard; W: Bernard Girard. C: Lionel Lindon. M: Stu Phillips.

Dead Heist 🐾🐾 2007 199E (PG-13) Four friends pick the wrong night for a bank heist and get trapped by vampire zombie towns-folk. Were it not for Hunter (Kane), a mysteriously shady bloke familiar with creature extermination, they might never get away with their loot or their lives. A giddy attempt, seriously lacking in horror. 80m/C DVD. Big Daddy Kane, D.J. Naylor, E-40, Bone Crusher; D: Bo Webb; W: Angelus Houvouras, Eric Tomousas; C: Mark Melone; M: Patrick Borowiac; M: Jim McKeever. VIDEO

Dead Husbands 🐾🐾 1998 (PG-13) Alex (Sheridan) is the beautiful wife of slick Dr. Carter Elston (Ritter), the best-selling author of relationship books. When Carter decides he wants to give everything up for smalltown life, horrified pampered spouse Alex meets a group of wives who offer her a unique solution (much more permanent than divorce). You see, the wives have a list of husbands to be gotten rid of—Alex kills the hubby at the top of the list and then adds Carter's name. Eventually, a fellow member will return the favor and off her annoying mate. But what happen when Dr. Elston finds the list? 90m/C VHS, Nicolette Sheridan, John Ritter, Amy Yasbeck, Donna Pescow, Wendii Malick. D: Paul Shapiro. CABLE

Dead in a Heartbeat 🐾🐾 2002 Veteran bomb squad cop Royko (Reinhold) teams up with heart surgeon Dr. Hayes (Miller) to find the mad bomber who's blowing people up via their pacemakers. Mediocre TV movie features a cliched p•t that telegraphs all the twists. The leads do what they can with what they're given. 91m/C VHS, DVD, CA Judge Reinhold, Penelope Ann Miller, Fulvio Cecere, Timothy Busfield, Matthew (Matt) Walker, Jeffrey Ballard, Sarah Jane Redmond; D: Paul Antier; M: Mark Rosman, Richard Adea; C: Danny Nowak. M: Louis Febre. TV

Dead in the Water 🐾🐾 1991 Wealthy not babe Gloria (Swain) takes her boyfriend (Bairstow), their buddy (Thomas), and Marcos, the son of her father's business partner on the family cabin cruiser for a day of fun. Only tensions rise and violence erupts when Gloria gets too involved with the wrong guy. 89m/C VHS, DVD. Dominique Swain, Henry Thomas, Scott Bairstow, Renata Fronzi, Sebastian DeVincente; D: Gustavo Lipzstein. VIDEO

Dead in the Water 🐾🐾 2006 (R) Arriving for a weekend retreat at the family cabin, Tiffany, Jen and her boyfriends find the cabin void of parents, cell phone reception, or a running vehicle. As night falls, zombies begin their attack. Instead of running like deer through the woods, the foursome decides to seek refuge in a boat out on the lake. Bad move, fairly decent movie. 78m/C DVD, Alissa Bailey, Megan Renne Burgess, Mike Parrish, Bill Zesadil; D:

worse when a mobster (Benzali), who also wanted the horse, gets involved. Plot has too many holes but the two leads are worth watching. 97m/C VHS, DVD, CA Kiefer Sutherland, Anthony LaPaglia, Radha Mitchell, Le-thaire Bluteau Daniel Benzali; D: Mark Malone; W: Mark Malone; M: Patric Caird.

Dead Leaves 🐾½ 1998 After a young girl falls to her death her unstable boyfriend steals the body and embarks on a trip from New York to West Virginia, stopping along the way to perform strange rituals to preserve her beauty. As she increasingly decays physically, so the mad love. Not much in the way of dialogue, as the conversations tend to be a little one-sided. 80m/C DVD, UMD, Haim Abransky, Beth Gondek; D: Constantin Werner; W: Constantin Werner; C: Mindaugas Blaudziunes. VIDEO

Dead Lenny 🐾½ 2006 Low-level LA mobster Lenny Long (Bauer) goes missing along with the five million bucks he was supposed to deliver to NY wiseguy Tony Thick (Assante). Thick sends associate Shady (Baker) to straighten things out, only he finds a lot of crazy people who want a cut of any cash that turns up. Unsatisfying mob comedy. 89m/C DVD, Armand Assante, Nicole Eggert, Stephen Baker, Steven Bauer, John Heard, Joe Piscopo, Whitney Able; D: Serge Rodnunsky; C: Serge Rodnunsky; M: Greg Manning. VIDEO

Dead Letter Office 🐾🐾 1998 Lonely Alice (Otto) gets a job at the dead letter office of the postal system. Her boss is Frank (DelHoyo), a political refugee from Chile who lost his family to the junta. Frank and Alice seem destined to hit it off but not before a few obstacles get in their path. Otto's father Barry has a brief scene as Alice's irresponsible dad. More distinctive than the story might indicate, thanks to the performances and tart comedy. 95m/C VHS, AU Miranda Otto, Georgia Del-borye, Nicholas Bell, Syd Brisbane, Georgina Naidu, Vanessa Steele, Barry Otto; D: John Ruane. W: Deb Cox; C: Ellery Ryan; M: Roger Mason.

Dead Lucky 🐾🐾 1960 A novice tries gambling and wins a fortune, but his luck leads him into an entanglement with an assassin, a scam artist, and a beautiful woman. Based on the novel "Lake of Darkness." 91m/B VHS, GB Vincent Ball, Betty McDowall, John Le Mesurier, Alfred Burke, Michael Ripper. D: Montgomery Tully.

Dead Man 🐾🐾 1995 (R) Depp wanders through the 19th-century American west as William Blake, an Ohio accountant who runs afoul of the law, hooking up with a Native American named Nobody (Farmer), who envisions Blake as the famous English poet, the two try to stay one step ahead of the hired guns and lawmen out to get them. Action is sporadic and pace is all over the road in this offbeat and long-winded western, while Farmer's performance and Jarmusch's polished visuals are high points. 121m/B VHS, DVD, Johnny Depp, Gary Farmer, Lance Henriksen, Michael Wincott, Mili Avital, Crispin Glover, Gabriel Byrne, Iggy Pop, Billy Bob Thornton, Jared Harris, Jimmie Ray Weeks, Mark Bringelson, John Hurt, Alfred Molina, Robert Mitchum; D: Jim Jarmusch; W: Jim Jarmusch; C: Robby Muller; M: Neil Young, N.Y. Film Critics '96: Cinematog.; Natl. Soc. Film Critics '96. Cinematog.

Dead Man on Campus 🐾🐾 1997 (R) Failing college freshmen Scott and Gosselaar learn that if your roomie commits suicide, you get a straight-A average to honor the year. So they decide to find a new roommate who's on the edge and make certain to push him over. Anyone who's ever done time in the dorms has heard this rumor, so it was only a matter of time before someone turned it into a screenplay. The wait wasn't long enough. One-joke premise can't sustain a whole movie, and Gosselaar goes a long way toward duplicating "Saved By the Bell" costar Elizabeth Berkley's "Showgirls" unsuccess. 94m/C VHS, DVD, Tom Everett Scott, Mark Paul Gosselaar, Alyson Hannigan, Poppy Montgomery, Lochlyn Munro, Randy Pearlstein, Corey Page, Dave Ruby, Linda Cardellini, Mari Morrow; D: Alan Cohn; W: Michael Traeger, Mike White; M: Mark Mothersbaugh.

Bunman; W: David Moore; C: Fred Miller; M: Piernicola Di Muro.

Dead Man's Revenge 🐾½ 1993 (PG-13) Ruthless railroad mogul Payton McCay (Dern) doesn't let anyone stand in his way—even if it means framing innocent homesteader Hatcher (Ironside) in order to get his land. Hatcher escapes from jail and goes after McCay, trailed by bounty hunter Bodeen (Couloris). But Bodeen's not what he seems and has his own plans on getting even with the villainous McCay. 92m/C VHS, Bruce Dern, Michael Ironside, Keith Coulouris, Randy Travis; D: Alan J. Levi; W: Jim Byrnes, David Chisholm.

Dead Mate 🐾 1988 A woman marries a mortician after a whirlwind romance only to discover that, to her husband, being an undertaker is not just a job, it's a way of life. 93m/C VHS, Elizabeth Mannino David Gregory, Lawrence Bockus, Adam Wahl; D: Straw Weisman.

Dead Man's Shoes 🐾🐾½ 2004 Grungy revenge thriller has disturbed ex-soldier Richard (Considine) returning to his hometown in England's Midlands to get payback on the yabbos who tormented his mentally retarded younger brother Anthony (Kebbell). Things get quite bloody. 86m/C DVD, GB Paddy Considine, Gary Stretch, Toby Kebbell; D: Shane Meadows; W: Shane Meadows; C: Danny Cohen.

Dead Men Can't Dance 🐾🐾 1997 (R) CIA agent Victoria Ellis (York) gets sent to South Korea to train with a women-only group of Army Rangers. Meanwhile, Vic's boyfriend Hart (Biehn) and his buddy Shooter (Paul) are in the demilitarized zone where Hart learns Shooter is out to steal nuclear detonators on behalf of a crazy Senator Fowler (Ermey), who wants to revive the Cold War. Things go bad and the women are forced to take things into their own more than capable hands. Lots of action. 97m/C VHS, Kathleen York, Michael Biehn, Adrian Paul R. Lee Ermey, Grace Zabriskie; D: Steve (Stephen M.) Anderson; W: Mark Sevi, Bill Kerby; Paul Sinor; C: Levie Issacks; M: Richard (Rick) Marvin.

Dead of Night 🐾 1977 This trilogy features Richard Matheson's tales of the Supernatural. "Second Chance," "No Such Thing As a Vampire," and "Bobby," all served up by your hostess, Elvira. 76m/C VHS, Joan Hackett, Ed Begley Jr., Patrick Macnee, Anjanette Comer; D: Dan Curtis.

Dead of Night 🐾 Lighthouse 1999 (R) Leo Rook (Adamson) is a psycho who collects the severed heads of his victim's as trophies. He's aboard the prison ship Hyperion, which is transporting criminals to a remote island off the northern English coast. Leo steals a lifeboat and escapes to desolate Gehenna Rocks just before the ship runs aground. Then the few survivors are subjected to Leo's stalking and slashing. Crude and gory. 95m/C VHS, DVD, GB Christopher) Adamson, James Purefoy, Rachel Shelley, Paul Brooke, Don Warrington, Chris Dunne, Bob Goody, Pat Kelman; D: Simon Hunter; W: Simon Hunter; M: Debbie Wiseman.

Dead Man Out 🐾🐾🐾 1989 Both Glover and Blades turn in exceptional performances in this thought-provoking drama. A convict on Death Row (Blades) goes insane and therefore cannot be executed. The state calls in a psychiatrist (Glover) to review the case and determine whether he can be cured so that the sentence can be carried out. Powerful and riveting morality check. 87m/C VHS, Danny Glover, Ruben Blades, Tom Atkins, Larry Block, Samuel L. Jackson, Maria Ricossa; D: Richard Pearce; M: Cliff Eidelman.

Dead Man Walking 🐾🐾 1988 (R) True story of a nun whose anti-death penalty beliefs put her in moral crisis with grieving victims when she becomes the spiritual advisor to a death-row murderer. Based on the book by Sister Helen Prejean, Sarandon stars as the nun who develops a relationship of understanding with inmate Poncelet (Penn), unwavering in her Christian beliefs even though Penn's character shows little or no remorse for the two young lovers he was accused of murdering (but worst hair-dos) the best performances (but worst hair-dos) of his career, while writer/director Robbins presents both sides of the death-penalty issue mingled with simple human compassion. 122m/C VHS, DVD, Jon Abrahams, Jack Black, Susan Sarandon, Sean Penn, Robert Prosky, Raymond J. Barry, R. Lee Ermey, Celia Weston, Lois Smith, Scott Wilson, Roberta Maxwell, Margo Martindale, Barton Heyman, Larry Pine; Dekins; Tim Robbins; W: Tim Robbins; C: Roger Deakins; M: David Robbins. Oscars '95: Actress (Sarandon); Ind. Spirit '96: Actress (Sarandon); Screen Actors Guild '95: Actress (Sarandon).

Dead Man Walking 🐾🐾½ 1995 (R) The Devil 1943 In a post-holocaust future, half the population has been stricken, with a deadly plague. Hauser is a mercenary, dying from the disease, who is hired to rescue a young woman who was kidnapped and is being held in the plague zone. 90m/C VHS, Wings Hauser, Brion James, Pamela Ludwig, Sy Richardson, Leland Crooke, Jeffrey Combs; D: Gregory Brown; W: RJ. Marx.

Dead of Night 🐾🐾🐾 1945 The template for episodic horror films, this suspense classic, set in a remote country house, follows the individual nightmares of five houseguests. Redgrave turns in a chillingly convincing performance as a demonic dummy. Not recommended for light-sleepers. Truly spine-tingling. 84m/C VHS, DVD, GB Michael Redgrave, Mervyn Johns, Sally Ann Howes, Basil Radford, Naunton Wayne, Roland Culver, Googie Withers, Frederick Valk, Antony Baird, Judy Kelly, Miles Malleson, Ralph Michael, Mary Merrall, Renee Gadd, Michael Allan, Robert Wyndham, Esme Percy, Peggy Bryan, Hartley Power, Elisabeth Welch, Magda Kun, Garry Marsh; D: Alberto Cavalcanti, Charles Crichton, Basil Dearden, Robert Hamer; W: T.E.B. Clarke, John Baines, Angus MacPhail; C: Stanley Pavey, Douglas Slocombe; M: Georges Auric.

Dead Man Don't Die 🐾🐾 1991 An anchorman is slain by criminals but resurrected as a shambling voodoo zombie. Few viewers notice the difference in this inoffensive but repetitious farce. The living-dead Gould appears to be having a lot of fun. 94m/C VHS, DVD, Elliott Gould, Melissa Anderson, Mark Moses, Philip Bruns, Jack Betts, Mabel King; D: Malcolm Marmorstein.

Dead Men Don't Wear Plaid 🐾🐾½ 1982 (PG) Martin is hilarious as a private detective who encounters a bizarre assortment of suspects while trying to find out the truth about a scientist's death. Ingeniously interspliced with clips from old Warner Bros. films. Features Humphrey Bogart, Betta Davis, Alan Ladd, Burt Lancaster, Ava Gardner, Barbara Stanwyck, Ray Milland, and others. Its only flaw is that the joke loses momentum by the end of the film. 89m/B VHS, DVD, Steve Martin, Rachel Ward, Reni Santoni, George Gaynes, Francis X. (Frank) McCarthy, Carl Reiner; D: Carl Reiner; W: Steve Martin, Carl Reiner; C: Michael Chapman; M: Miklos Rozsa.

Dead Man Walk 🐾🐾 Creatures of the Devil 1943 A decent, albeit low budget, chiller about twin brothers (Zucco in a dual role); one a nice, well-adjusted member of society, the other a vampire who wants to suck his bro's blood. Sibling rivalry with a bite. 65m/B VHS, George Zucco, Mary Carlisle, Dwight Frye, Nedrick Young, Al "Fuzzy" St. John, Fern Emmett, Robert Strange; D: Sam Newfield; C: Jack Greenhalgh; M: Leo Erdody.

The Dead Next Door 🐾 1989 Eerily reminiscent of "Night of the Living Dead." A scientist manufactures a virus which inhabits corpses and multiplies while replacing the former cells with its own. But the newly living corpses need human flesh to survive. In response, the government creates "The Zombie Squad" who do heroic battle with the stiffs. When a bizarre cult whose goal is the eradication of the human race befriend the dead, the battle gets ugly. 84m/C VHS, DVD, Pete Ferry, Bogdan Pecic, Michael Grossi, Len Kowalewich, Jolie Jackunas, Robert Kokai, Scott Spiegel, J.R. Bookwalter; D: J.R. Bookwalter; W: J.R. Bookwalter. M: J.R. Bookwalter.

Dead of Winter ✓✓✓ **1987 (R)** A young actress is suckered into a private screen test for a crippled old director, only to find she is actually being remodeled in the guise of a murdered woman. Edge-of-your-seat suspense as the plot twists. **100m/C VHS, DVD.** Mary Steenburgen, Roddy McDowall, Jan Rubes, Ken Pogue, William Russ; **D:** Arthur Penn; **W:** Mark Shmuger, Mark Malone; **M:** Richard Einhorn.

Dead On ✓✓1/2 **1994 (R)** A college student dreams of a masked man, a knife, a bound woman, and other terrors. Too bad her nightmares match the actions of a serial killer. **96m/C VHS.** Jennifer Beals, Daniel Baldwin, Kurtwood Smith, William H. Macy; **D:** Ruben Preuss; **W:** Lewis Green; **M:** Harry Manfredini.

Dead on the Money ✓✓1/2 **1991** Adequate made for TV suspenser about a woman who believes her lover plots a dire fate for her cousin. His restless spirit becomes a slave to the rest is what it seems here. Confusing, droopy in spots, but fun. **92m/C VHS.** Corbin Bernsen, Amanda Pays, John Glover, Eleanor Parker, Kevin McCarthy; **D:** Mark Cullingham; **W:** Gavin Lambert. **TV**

The Dead One ✓✓ **2007 (PG-13)** Diego (Valderrama) outfits himself in a zombie mariachi costume for the Mexican Day of the Dead parties but he's killed before he gets to do any celebrating. His restless spirit becomes a slave to the god of death, who has captured his soul. Diego is returned to the living to battle the death god for the soul of his girlfriend Maria (Cepeda) among others. Flashy-looking and fairly mild horror (note the rating) based on the comic book, "El Muerto." **88m/C DVD.** Wilmer Valderrama, Joel David Moore, Tony Plana, Maria Conchita Alonso, Angie Cepeda, Michael Parks, Tony Amendola, Billy Drago; **D:** Brian Cox; **W:** Brian Cox; **C:** Steve Yedlin; **M:** Tony Humecke. **VIDEO**

Dead or Alive ✓1/2 **1944** Tex and the Texas Rangers pretend to be outlaws in order to join a gang terrorizing a town. **54m/B VHS, DVD.** Tex Ritter, Dave O'Brien, Guy Wilkerson, Charles "Blackie" King, Bud Osborne, Reed Howes; **D:** Elmer Clifton.

Dead Pet ✓✓1/2 **2001** Kevin Coetteler follows in the footsteps of Adam Sandler as a likeable, slightly geeky nice guy. He plays Jake Thompson who comes home from college to find that his repulsive parents have forgotten to pick him up at the airport and they've spent the rest of his education fund on an operation for their beloved poodle. From there, the comedy is nicely deadpan and inventive. **93m/C DVD.** Kevin Coetteler, Gina Doctor, Brian Sostek; **D:** Kevin Coetteler; **W:** Kevin Coetteler; **C:** Dan Ming.

Dead Pigeon on Beethoven Street ✓✓1/2 **1972 (PG)** Sandy (Corbett) is a detective whose partner gets murdered while investigating blackmailers who take compromising pictures of international big-wigs. So Sandy goes undercover and joins the gang. Cheeky paranoia from Fuller. **92m/C VHS, DVD.** GE Glenn Corbett, Christa Lang, Anton Diffring, Alexander D'Arcy; **D:** Samuel Fuller; **W:** Samuel Fuller; **C:** Jerzy Lipman.

Dead Pit woof! **1989 (R)** Leave this one in the pit it crawled out of. Twenty years ago a mad scientist was killed as a result of horrible experiments he was conducting on mentally ill patients at an asylum. A young woman stumbles across his experiments, awakening him from the dead. **90m/C VHS.** Jeremy Slate, Steffen Gregory Foster; **D:** Brett Leonard.

Dead Poets Society ✓✓✓1/2 **1989 (PG)** An idealistic English teacher inspires a group of boys in a 1950s' prep school to pursue individuality and creative endeavor, resulting in clashes with school and parental authorities. Williams shows he can master the serious roles as well as the comic with his portrayal of the unorthodox educator. Big boxoffice hit occasionally scripted with a heavy hand in order to elevate the message. The ensemble cast is excellent. **128m/C VHS, DVD.** Robin Williams, Ethan Hawke, Robert Sean Leonard, Josh Charles, Gale Hansen, Kurtwood Smith, James Waterson, Dylan Kussman, Lara Flynn Boyle, Melora Hardin, Alexandria Powers; **D:** Peter Weir, **W:** Tom Schulman; **C:** John Seale; **M:** Maurice Jarre. Oscars '89; Orig. Screenplay; British Acad. '89; Film; Cesar '91: Foreign Film.

The Dead Pool ✓✓1/2 **1988 (R)** Dirty Harry Number Five features a new twist on the sports pool: a list of celebrities is distributed and bets are placed on who will be first to cross the finish line, literally. Unfortunately someone seems to be hedging their bet by offing the celebs themselves. When Harry's name appears on the list, he decides to throw the game. **92m/C VHS, DVD.** Clint Eastwood, Liam Neeson, Patricia Clarkson, Evan C. Kim, David Hunt, Michael Currie, Michael Goodwin, Jim Carrey; **D:** Buddy Van Horn; **M:** Lalo Schifrin.

Dead Presidents ✓✓1/2 **1995 (R)** Sophomore release for the Hughes brothers falls short of impact of "Menace II Society," but not for lack of ambition. Combination coming of age tale, war story, period piece and caper film follows Anthony ("Menace" veteran Tate) from his Bronx neighborhood in 1968 to Vietnam (for "Platoon" adventures in the wilds of Florida) and then back to the 'hood, where his life continues to spiral downward. Desperate to escape, he becomes involved in an armoured car heist to grab some cash (the "dead presidents"). Supported by hard-edged and effective acting, the Hughes continue to develop their control of cinematic imagery, displaying genius for staging violent, confrontational scenes. But the script, based on a story by the brothers, fails to live up to the vision, with characterization and dialogue lagging. Pounding period soundtrack with contributions by Curtis Mayfield, James Brown, and Marvin Gaye keeps things humming. **120m/C VHS, DVD.** Larenz Tate, Keith David, Chris Tucker, Freddy Rodriguez, N'Bushe Wright, Bokeem Woodbine, Rose Jackson, Clifton Powell, Kirk "Sticky Fingaz" Jones; **D:** Albert Hughes, Allen Hughes; **W:** Michael Henry Brown; **C:** Lisa Rinzler; **M:** Danny Elfman.

Dead Reckoning ✓✓✓ **1947** Bogart and Prince are two WWII veterans en route to Washington when Prince disappears. Bogart trails Prince to his Southern hometown and discovers he's been murdered. Blackmail and more murders follow as Bogie tries to uncover the truth. Suspenseful with good performances from all, especially Bogart. **100m/B VHS, DVD.** Malthew "Stymie" Beard, William Forrest, Humphrey Bogart, Lizabeth Scott, Morris Carnovsky, Charles Cane, Wallace Ford, William Prince, Marvin Miller; **D:** John Cromwell; **W:** Steve Fisher, Allen Rivkin, Oliver H.P. Garrett; **C:** Leo Tover; **M:** Martin Skiles, Hugo Friedhofer.

Dead Reckoning ✓✓1/2 **1989 (R)** A plastic surgeon and his lovely wife embark on a cruise aboard his new luxury yacht. The intrigue begins with a storm, an isolated island, and the discovery that the captain is the wife's former lover. **95m/C VHS.** Cliff Robertson, Susan Blakely, Rick Springfield; **D:** Robert Lewis.

Dead Right ✓1/2 *If He Hollers, Let Him Go* **1968** A black man is unjustly put into prison in the Deep South. He manages to escape in order to try and prove his innocence. **111m/C VHS.** Raymond St. Jacques, Dana Wynter, Kevin McCarthy, Barbara McNair; **D:** Charles Martin.

Dead Ringer ✓✓✓1/2 **1964** Bette Davis plays twins: Margaret, who's rich and recently widowed, and Edith, who's poor and feels that Margaret won her husband by unfairly (they were rivals for his affection). Edith kills Margaret and takes over her life, only to discover that the grass isn't always greener. Solid thriller showcases Davis in one of the better of her mystery/suspense roles of the 1960s. **115m/B VHS, DVD.** Bette Davis, Karl Malden, Peter Lawford, Phil Carey, Jean Hagen, George Macready, Estelle Winwood, George Chandler, Cyril Delevanti, Bert Remsen, Monika Henreid; **D:** Paul Henreid; **W:** Albert Beich, Oscar Millard; **C:** Ernest Haller; **M:** Andre Previn.

Dead Ringers ✓✓✓ **1988 (R)** A stunning, unsettling chiller, based loosely on a real case and the bestseller by Bari Wood and Jack Geasland. Irons, in an excellent dual role, is effectively disturbing as the twin gynecologists who descend into madness when they can no longer handle the fame, fortune, drugs, and women in their lives. Bujold is the actress/patient bedded by both brothers but jealously loved by Beverly. Acutely upsetting film made all the more so due to its graphic images and basis in fact. **117m/C VHS, DVD.** CA Jeremy Irons, Genevieve Bujold, Heidi von Palleske, Barbara Gordon, Shirley Douglas, Stephen Lack, Nick Nichols; **D:** David Cronenberg; **W:** David Cronenberg, Norman Snider; **C:** Peter Suschitzky; **M:** Howard Shore. Genie '89: Actor (Irons), Director (Cronenberg), Film; L.A. Film Critics '88: Director (Cronenberg), Support. Actress (Bujold); N.Y. Film Critics '88: Actor (Irons).

Dead Sexy ✓✓1/2 **2001 (R)** Detective Kate McBain (Tweed) is investigating the murders of four L.A. high-price hookers. Of course, she becomes more than a little interested in one of her suspects, charming Blue (Enos), but is Kate willing to die to find out the truth? **89m/C VHS, DVD.** Shannon Tweed, John Enos, Kenneth White, Sam Jones, Eric Keith; **D:** Robert Angelo; **W:** Anthony Laurence Greene, Elroy Canton; **C:** Kazuo Minami; **M:** Nicholas Rivera. **VIDEO**

Dead Silence **1990 (R)** Screenwriter Cliff Morgan has written a classic film noir screenplay... with the money, it seems all of Cliff's problems are solved... or are they? **92m/C VHS.** Clete Keith, Doris Anne Soyka, Johnny Scott, Craig Fleming; **D:** Harrison Ellenshaw.

Dead Silence ✓✓1/2 **1996 (R)** Three escaped convicts, including ruthless Ted Handy (Coates), have hijacked a busload of deaf children and their teacher (Matlin) and are holding them hostage in an abandoned slaughterhouse. Veteran FBI agent John Cooper (Garner) is called in but he not only has to deal with a tense and possibly tragic situation but who's criticizing his every action, the last-minute arrival of another hostage negotiator (Davidovich). Based on the novel "A Maiden's Grave" by Jeffery Deaver. **105m/C VHS, DVD.** Gary Basaraba, Vanessa Vaughan, Blu Mankuma, Mimi Kuzyk, Scott Speedman, John Bourgeois, Barry Pepper, James Garner, Kim Coates, Marlee Matlin, Charles Martin Smith, Lolita (David) Davidovich, Kenneth Welsh, James Villemaire; **D:** Daniel Petrie Jr.; **W:** Donald Stewart; **C:** Thomas Burstyn; **M:** Jonathan Goldsmith. **CABLE**

Dead Silence ✓1/2 *Wilbur Falls* **1998** Renata (Edwards) decides on a simple plan of revenge against Jeff (Newmark) who humiliated her at their junior-high prom five years before. Only her plans backfire and he accidentally dies. That should be the plot but it's surrounded by so many other storylines that it gets lost in the telling, which is a shame since Edwards does a good job. **95m/C VHS, DVD.** Shanee Edwards, Danny Aiello, Sally Kirkland, Suzanne Stapleton; **D:** Juliane Glantz; **W:** Juliane Glantz; **C:** Kurt Brabbee; **M:** Jim Halfpenny.

Dead Silence ✓1/2 **2007 (R)** Did you know that automatonophobia is the fear of ventriloquist dummies? Well, they're usually pretty creepy even though this retro-looking flick isn't. Jamie (Kwanten) receives a vintage wooden dummy in the mail and then his wife gets murdered. He actually realizes that there's a connection between the two events and travels to his hometown of Ravens Fair, where ventriloquist Mary Shaw (Roberts) was murdered and her dummies buried with her. Except they're not staying in the ground and Mary's using them to get her revenge. **90m/C DVD, HD DVD.** US Ryan Kwanten, Donnie Wahlberg, Amber Valletta, Michael Fairman, Bob Gunton, Judith Roberts, Laura Regan, Joan Heney; **D:** James Wan; **W:** Leigh Whannell; **C:** John R. Leonetti; **M:** Charlie Clouser.

Dead Silent ✓1/2 **1999 (R)** Doctor Julia Kerrbridge (Stewart) must care for her traumatized young niece whose parents were killed by the mob. But the girl, who has become mute, also has information that the bad guys will do anything to keep secret. Then there's Julia's new neighbor Kevin Finney (Lowe)—is he really a nice guy? Or a potential killer? **95m/C VHS, DVD.** Catherine Mary Stewart, Rob Lowe, Peter Colvey, Larry Day, Sean Devine, Allen Altman, Mark Camacho; **D:** Roger Cardinal; **W:** Ed Fitzgerald, Paul Koval; **C:** Bruno Philip; **M:** David Findlay. **VIDEO**

Dead Simple ✓✓ **2001 (R)** Frank Jacobs (Stern) and his nagging wife Helen (Richardson) owe a failing motel in dusty nowhere Kansas. Frank dreams of being a C&W singer and he hooks up with lounge performer Julie (Kohl), who has an abusive manager, has-been Roy Baker (Caan). Then there's Helen's twin sister Wanda (Richardson again), barmaid Marguerite (Stringfield), and the motel's garden, which gets a lot of unexpected fertilizer. Black comedy can't sustain its edge. **95m/C VHS, DVD.** Daniel Stern, James Caan, Patricia Richardson, Sherry Stringfield, Lacey Kohl, Tim Abell; **D:** Jason Bloom; **W:** Richard Uhlig, Steve Seltz; **C:** James Glennon; **M:** Andrew Gross.

Dead Sleep ✓✓ **1991 (R)** A nurse discovers that comatose patients at a private clinic have been used as guinea pigs by an overzealous doctor. This minor-league chiller from Down Under is said to have been inspired by an actual medical scandal. **95m/C VHS.** DVD. Linda Blair, Tony Bonner; **D:** Alec Mills.

Dead Solid Perfect ✓✓ **1988** Quaid stars a golf pro whose life on the PGA tour is handicapped by his taste for scotch and his eye for the ladies. Based on the book by Dan Jenkins. **97m/C VHS.** Randy Quaid, Kathryn Harrold, Jack Warden, Larry Riley, Brett Cullen, Corinne Bohrer; **D:** Bobby Roth; **W:** Dan Jenkins, Bobby Roth.

Dead Space ✓ **1990 (R)** Dead space lay between the ears of whoever thought we needed this remake of 1982's "Forbidden World." At a lab on a hostile planet an experimental vaccine mutates into a prickly puppet monster who menaces the medicos. Needed: a vaccine against cheapo "Alien" ripoffs. **72m/C VHS.** Marc Singer, Laura Tate, Bryan Cranston, Judith Chapman; **D:** Fred Gallo.

Dead Tides ✓ **1997 (R)** Former Navy SEAL Mick (Piper) is hired by Nola (Kitaen) to pilot a sailboat from California to Mexico. But Mick soon realizes that Nola's the wife of a powerful drug dealer and he's in more trouble than he can imagine. **100m/C VHS.** Roddy Piper, Tawny Kitaen, Trevor Goddard, Miles O'Keeffe, Juan Fernandez; **D:** Serge Rodnunsky; **W:** Serge Rodnunsky. **VIDEO**

Dead to Rights ✓✓1/2 *Donato and Daughter* **1993 (R)** TV movie finds veteran LAPD cop Donato (Bronson) on the trail of a serial killer along with his new partner—who's not only his daughter but his superior officer. Based on the novel by Jack Early. **90m/C VHS.** Charles Bronson, Dana Delany, Xander Berkeley, Bonnie Bartlett, Jenette Goldstein, Louis Giambalvo; **D:** Rod Holcomb; **W:** Robert Roy Pool; **C:** Thomas Del Ruth; **M:** Sylvester Levay.

Dead Waters ✓✓1/2 *Dark Waters* **1994** Elizabeth (Salter) travels to a remote Russian island to visit her sister, Theresa (Phipps), who resides at the convent there. But Theresa is murdered after witnessing an occult ritual and Elizabeth finds strange references to "The Beast" in the convent library and realizes the nuns are trying to raise the demonic creature. **94m/C VHS, DVD.** IT RU GB Louise Salter, Venera Simmons, Maria Kapnist, Anna Rose Phipps; **D:** Mariano Baino; **W:** Mariano Baino, Andrew Bark; **C:** Alex Howe; **M:** Igor Clark.

Dead Weekend ✓✓ **1995 (R)** Lt. Weed (Baldwin) is given the task of finding and destroying a seductively dangerous female alien. Turns out she has the ability to physically change into a number of different women—all of whom attract the willing-and-eager soldier. **82m/C VHS.** Richard Speight Jr., Stephen Baldwin, David Rasche, Alexis Arquette, Bai Ling, Tom Kenny, Jennifer MacDonald, Barbara Alyn Woods; **D:** Amos Poe;

Dead Women in Lingerie woof! 1990 (R) When a beautiful models are turning up dead, a detective is called in to solve the mystery. Perhaps they picture any longer than necessary. Title sounds like the next episode of "Geraldo." *&mc* VHS, DVD. *W:* Joel Rose; *C:* Gary Tieche; *M:* Steve Hunter. CABLE.

Dead Wrong 1990 (R) Undercover agent falls in love with the drug smuggler she's supposed to bring to justice. 93m/C VHS. *D:* Len Kowalewich.

The Dead Zone 1983 Pilot film for the cable series, which is based on the characters and story from the Stephen King novel. Johnny Smith (Hall) was in a coma for six years after a car crash. When he regains consciousness he has psychic abilities that allow him to see into the lives of those he touches. And when he shakes the hand of presidential candidate Greg Stillson (Sheen), he foresees a holocaust. So Johnny decides to use his "gift" to save mankind from impending evil. A good adaptation of the Stephen King thriller. 104m/C VHS, DVD. *C:* Christopher Walken, Brooke Adams, Tom Skerritt, Martin Sheen, Herbert Lom, Anthony Zerbe, Colleen Dewhurst; *D:* David Cronenberg; *W:* Jeffrey Boam; *C:* Mark Irwin; *M:* Michael Kamen.

Dead Zone 1983 (R) Diffident teacher Johnny Smith (Walken) gains extraordinary psychic powers following a near-fatal car accident and a five-year coma. He is developed the ability to foresee a person's future by touching their hands—and when he shakes the hand of presidential candidate Greg Stillson (Sheen), he foresees a holocaust. So Johnny decides to use his "gift" to save mankind. 113m/C VHS, DVD. *C:* Dashne Khoury, Brandon Dixon, Jennifer Wetter, Nicole Cook, Jason Magee; *M:* Philip Kappaz.

The Deadbeat Club 2004 Misfit teens in a small Texas town try to help a man whose family died in a fire. The actors look too old for their teen roles and virtue turns out to be really boring. 89m/C VHS, DVD. *W:* Israel Luna; *C:* Brad Walker; *M:* Philip Kappaz.

Deadbolt 1992 (R) Divorced med student Marty Hillier (Bateman) desperately needs a roommate and Alec Danz (Baldwin) seems perfect. Soon they're sharing more than the rent, until Danz kills her friends and imprisons her in the apartment (equipped of course with soundproof walls and bulletproof glass—one wonders why she doesn't bang on the floor to gain attention.) Predictable and silly would-be thriller attempts to capitalize on the roommate-from-hell theme that started with "Single White Female," but isn't nearly as effective. Went straight to video and showed up on network TV several months later. 95m/C VHS. *C:* Justine Bateman, Adam Baldwin, Michelle Scarabelli, Chris Mulkey, Cyndi Pass, Isabelle Truchon. *D:* Douglas Jackson. VIDEO

Deadfall 1993 (R) Father/son grifters plan an elaborate scam that goes wrong when son Joe (Biehn) inadvertently kills dear old dad (Coburn). When Joe is going through his father's effects he finds out about an unknown twin uncle, who also turns out to be a racketeer. Along with Uncle Lou's mistrustful henchman Eddie (Cage), they plan another con but swindles and vendettas abound. 99m/C VHS, DVD. Michael Biehn, Sarah Trigger, Nicolas Cage, James Coburn, Charlie Sheen, Peter Fonda. *D:* Christopher Coppola. *W:* Christopher Coppola, David Peoples; *C:* Maryse Alberti; *M:* Jim Fox.

Deadlier Than the Male 1967 In his swinging '60s update on the '20s British hero, Bulldog Drummond (Johnson) is now a suave London insurance investigator after industrialist Carl Petersen (Green) uses his own sexy assassins, Irma (Sommer) and Penelope (Koscina), to get rid of business partners and the competition. Gadgetry, exotic locations, and bikinied babes in a James Bond knockoff. 95m/C VHS, DVD. *C:* Richard Johnson, Nigel Green, Elke Sommer, Sylva Koscina, Suzanna Leigh, Steve Carlson; *D:* Ralph Thomas; *W:* Jimmy Sangster, Liz Charles-Williams, David Osborn; *C:* Ernest Steward; *M:* Malcolm Lockyer.

Deadline 1981 Journalist must find out the truth behind a minor earthquake in Australia. 94m/C VHS. Barry Newman, Trisha Noble, Bill Kerr; *D:* Arch Nicholson; *W:* Walter Halsey Davis.

Deadline 1982 Eerie tale of horror writer's life as it begins to reflect his latest story in this play on the "truth is stranger than fiction" adage. 85m/C VHS. Stephen Young, Sharon Masters, Cindy Hinds, Phillip Leonard; *D:* Mario Azzopardi.

Deadline 1987 (R) Walken is a cynical American journalist assigned to cover the warring factions in Beirut. He finds himself becoming more and more involved in the events he's supposed to report when he falls in love with a German nurse who is aiding the rebel forces. Tense, though sometimes murky drama. 110m/C VHS, DVD. *C:* Christopher Walken, Hywel Bennett, Marita Marschall; *D:* Nathaniel Gutman.

Deadline 2000 (R) The publisher of a leading Chicago newspaper is murdered following his hostile takeover of the paper and the leading suspect is the paper's editor (but he's the wrong guy). Formulaic thriller. 94m/C VHS, DVD. Patrick Bergin, Bruce Dinsmore, Annie Dufresne, Alex Ivanovic, Edward Yankie; *D:* Robbie Ditchburn; *W:* Ron Base, Michael Stokes; *C:* Daniel Vadeilleneuve. VIDEO

Deadline Assault 1990 (R) Kate McSweeny is a beautiful young reporter who is brutally attacked and raped by a gang of savage youths. Kate must now face the unsettling facts; they're still on the streets and stalking her again. 90m/C VHS. Elizabeth Montgomery, James Sloyan, Sean Frye, Biff McGuire, Michael Goodwin, Linden Chiles; *D:* Paul Wendkos.

Deadline at Dawn 1946 Hayward is an aspiring actress who tries to help a sailor (Williams) prove that he is innocent of murder. Based on a novel by Cornell Woolrich. 82m/B VHS, Bill Williams, Susan Hayward, Lola Lane, Paul Lukas, Joseph Calleia. *D:* Harold Clurman; *W:* Clifford Odets.

Deadline Auto Theft 1983 A fun lovin' guy drives fast cars and meets beautiful women. Nudge, nudge, wink, wink. 90m/C VHS, H.B. Halicki, Hoyt Axton, Marion Busia, George Cole, Judi Gibbs, Lang Jeffries; *D:* H.B. Halicki.

Deadlock 1991 (R) Hauer and Rogers star as inmates in a prison of the future. This prison has no walls, no fences and no guards—and no one EVER escapes. Each prisoner wears an explosive collar that is tuned to the same frequency as one of the other prisoner's. Should the two separate by more than 100 yards, the collars explode. When Rogers convinces Hauer that they are inmates in a violent correctional facility. Inmates wear electronic collars programmed to explode if they venture too far. 90m/C VHS, DVD. Rutger Hauer, Mimi Rogers, Joan Chen, James Remar, Stephen Tobolowsky, Basil Wallace; *D:* Lewis Teague. CABLE

Deadlock 2 1994 (R) Same basic plot as in the first TV movie, Tony Archer (Morales) and Allie Thompson (Peeples), two strangers who have been set up by the same corrupt businessman, are being held in a violent correctional facility. Inmates wear electronic collars programmed to explode if they venture too far. But Tony figures a way around this well. Can the two find the freedom they are looking for—without losing their heads? 103m/C VHS, DVD. Rutger Hauer, Nia Peeples, Stephen McHattie, Jon Cuthbert. *D:* Graeme Campbell.

Deadlocked (Jonz) 2000 Demond Doyle (Jonz) is convicted of rape and murder and prosecutor Ned Stark (Caruso) wants the death penalty. Demond's father, Jacob (Dutton), is convinced that his son is innocent, so he takes the jury hostage. He tells Stark that he has 24 hours to find the evidence that will clear his son or the captives start dying. Compelling. 100m/C VHS, DVD. David Caruso, Charles S. Dutton, John Finn, Jo D. Jonz, Malcolm Stewart, Tom Butler, Diego Wallraff, Erik Jandresen; *C:* Thomas Burstyn; *M:* B.C. Smith. CABLE

Deadly Advice 1993 (R) Meek bookseller Jodie (Horrocks) and her sister are constantly humiliated by their overbearing mother (Fricker), who also objects to Jodie's romance with the local doctor (Pryce). As life becomes increasingly unbearable, Jodie discovers a book on infamous killers and is visited by their ghosts, including Jack the Ripper, who is happy to suggest ways to get rid of mom. 91m/C VHS, DVD. Jane Horrocks, Imelda Staunton, Brenda Fricker, Jonathan Pryce; *D:* Mandie Fletcher.

Deadly Alliance 1978 Two impecunious filmmakers (who happen to be hunks) and a babe (for good measure) poke their noses in where they're not wanted for the shady business of an international oil cartel; "Deadly Dull" would be a more appropriate moniker. 90m/C VHS, DVD. Kathleen Aro, Tony de Fonte, Michele Marsh, Walter Prince; *D:* Paul S. Parco.

The Deadly and the Beautiful (Wonder Women 1973) (PG) Dr. Tsu sends her "deadly but beautiful" task force to kidnap the world's prime male athletes for use in her private business enterprise. 82m/C VHS, Nancy Kwan, Ross Hagen, Maria de Aragon, Roberta Collins, Tony Lorca, Sid Haig, Vic Diaz, Shirley Washington, Gale Hansen; *D:* Robert Vincent O'Neil.

Deadly Bet 1991 (R) A made-for-video saga of a kickboxer who loses his money and his girl when he loses the big match. Lots of fight sequences as he works to regain his career. 93m/C VHS. Jeff Wincott, Charlene Tilton, Steven Leigh; *D:* Richard W. Munchkin.

Deadly Blessing 1981 (R) A young, recently widowed woman is visited in her rural Pennsylvania home by some friends from the city. Something's not quite right about this country life and they become especially suspicious after meeting their friend's very religious in-laws. 104m/C VHS. Maren Jensen, Susan Buckner, Sharon Stone, Ernest Borgnine, Jeff East, Lisa Hartman Black, Lois Nettleton, Colleen Riley, Douglas Barr, Michael Berryman; *D:* Wes Craven, Glenn Benest, Matthew F. Barr; *C:* Robert C. Jessup; *M:* James Horner.

Deadly Breed 1989 Beware your friendly neighborhood cop. A band of white supremacists has infiltrated the local police force, intent on causing violence, not keeping the peace. 90m/C VHS, DVD. William (Bill) Smith, Addison Randall, Blake Bahner, Joe Vance; *C:* Charles Kanganis.

Deadly Business 1986 The true story of a man who turned from crime to become a government informant. As a garbage man, he works to stop the illegal dumping of chemicals in New Jersey. An interesting made-for-television drama. 100m/C VHS, Alan Arkin, Armand Assante, Michael Learned, Jon Polito, George Morfogen, James Rebhorn; *D:* Zale Dalen; *W:* Zale Dalen.

Deadly Business 1977 Hard-nosed collection man for a loan shark finds he is the one with the debt to pay as he's stalked through the city street by hit men. 95m/C VHS, David Peterson, John Lazarus; *D:* John Korty.

Deadly Companions 1961 Keith is an ex-gunslinger who agrees to escort O'Hara through Apache territory in order to make up for inadvertently killing her son. Director Peckinpah's first feature film. 90m/C VHS, DVD. Maureen O'Hara, Brian Keith, Chill Wills, Steve Cochran, Strother Martin; *C:* William Clothier.

Deadly Conspiracy 1991 (R) Scott plays a former sea captain who owns a bar on the island of Curacao who enjoys regaling his patrons with his seagoing tales. Petersen is the exiled CIA agent stuck as the security officer of the American consulate. The dangerous past of both men can catch them up and find them caught in a web of international intrigue. Based on the novel "The Prince of Malta" by James David Buchanan. 93m/C VHS. Wings Hauser, John Saxon, Frances Fisher, Patti D'Arbanville, Margaux Hemingway, Greg Mullavey; *D:* Paul Leder.

Deadly Currents 1993 (R) Gory story of the hitchhiker Cindy is beaten and raped by the hoofers in LA. 88m/C VHS, Adolfo "Shabba Doo" Quinones, Smith Wordes, Walter W. Cox, Steve Jonson; *D:* Kimberly Casey; *W:* David A. Prior.

Deadly Dancer 1990 It's up to a lone cop to find out who's been offing the hoofers in L.A. 86m/C VHS. Adolfo "Shabba Doo" Quinones, Smith Wordes, Walter W. Cox, Steve Jonson; *D:* Kimberly Casey; *W:* David A. Prior.

Deadly Daphne's Revenge 1993 Gory story of rape and revenge from the Troma Team. Charlie Johnson, when she seeks justice via the local police, Johnson makes plans to have her snuffed out. Meantime, another of his victims escapes from the asylum. 91m/C VHS, Fonda Lynn, Warren Chan, Bernard Tsui, Cheryl Kwok. *D:* Karen Young.

Deadly Darling 1985 Muddied, completely awful tale centering on two different rapes with no discernible attempt made to link the two or establish a plot. 91m/C VHS. *D:* John Eanning.

Deadly Desire 1991 (R) Seduced by the beautiful Harrold, security guard Scalia finds himself putting his life on the line when Harrold asks him to help cheat her husband out of millions in insurance scam. Trouble ensues when they try to outsmart Harrold's powerful entrepreneurial husband. 90m/C VHS. Jack Scalia, Kathryn Harrold, Will Patton, Joe Santos; *D:* Charles Correll.

Deadly Diamonds 1991 Cop is on the trail of diamond smugglers who leave a trail of death in their wake. 99m/C VHS. Dan Haggerty, Troy Donahue, Ell Rich, Kathleen Kane, Kenna Grob, Nicholas Mercer; *D:* Thomas Atcheson; *W:* Ron Herbst.

Deadly Dreams 1988 (R) A young boy's parents are killed by a maniac who then commits suicide. Years later, he dreams that the killer is being stalked anew by the same killer. Nightmares turn into reality in this decent horror/suspense flick. 79m/C VHS. Mitchel Anderson, Xander Berceley, Thom Babbes, Juliette Cummins; *D:* Kristine Peterson; *W:* Thom Babbes.

Deadly Embrace woof! 1988 (R) Sordid tale of wealthy man (Vincent) who wants to get rid of his wife—permanently. He enlists the aid of a beautiful young coed. Soft-core sleaze with nary a redeemable quality. 80m/C VHS. Jan-Michael Vincent, Jack Carter, Mindi Miller, Linnea Quigley, Michelle (McClellan) Bauer, Ken Abraham; *D:* David DeCoteau.

Deadly Encounter woof! 1972 Thrilling actioner in which Hagmar portrays a helicopter pilot—a former war ace—who allows an old flame to talk him into helping her escape from the mobsters on her trail. Terrific edge-of-your-seat aerial action. 90m/C VHS, DVD. Larry Hagman, Susan Anspach, James Gammon; *D:* William A. Graham.

Deadly Exposure 🎬 1993 (R) Benson stars as a burned-out journalist doing his own investigation of the right-wing extremist group that killed his father. Aspiring reporter Johnson helps out and turns up a conspiracy between the extremists, the government, and a plot to assassinate a U.S. senator. Also available in an unrated version. 100m/C VHS. Robby Benson, Laura Johnson, Paul Hampton, Andrew Prine, Bentley Mitchum, Isaac Hayes; *D:* Lawrence Mortoff; *W:* Asher Brauner.

Deadly Eyes 🎬½ 1982 (R) *The Rats.* After eating grain laced with steroids a group of rats grows to mammoth proportions (dachshunds in rat drag were used). Their appetites grow accordingly—now they crave humans. Amid the nibbling by the giant rat-dogs, romance blooms. Silly adaptation by Charles Eglee of Frank Herbert's "The Rats." 93m/C VHS. Sam Groom, Sara Botsford, Scatman Crothers, Lisa Langlois, Cec Linder; *D:* Robert Clouse.

Deadly Fieldtrip 🎬½ 1974 Four female students and their teacher are abducted by a biker gang and held hostage on a deserted farm. 91m/C VHS. Zalman King, Brenda Fogarty, Robert Porter; *D:* Earl Barton.

Deadly Force 🎬½ 1983 (R) Ex-cop turned private detective stalks a killer in Los Angeles who has left an "X" carved in the forehead of each of his 17 victims. If he had just signed his name, things could have been tidied up much earlier. 95m/C VHS. Wings Hauser, Joyce Ingalls, Paul Shenar, Al Ruscio, Arlen Dean Snyder, Lincoln Kilpatrick; *D:* Paul Aaron; *W:* Robert Vincent O'Neil, Barry Schneider.

Deadly Friend 🎬🎬 1986 (R) A well-meaning horror flick? That's what Wes Craven has promised to provide for us. When the girlfriend of a lonely teenage genius is accidentally killed, he decides to insert his robot's "brain" in her body, though the results aren't entirely successful. The same can be said for the film which was based on Diana Henstell's more effective novel "Friend." 91m/C VHS. Matthew Laborteaux, Kristy Swanson, Michael Sharrett, Anne Twomey, Richard Marcus, Anne Ramsey; *D:* Wes Craven; *W:* Bruce Joel Rubin; *C:* Philip Lathrop; *M:* Charles Bernstein.

Deadly Game 🎬🎬 1982 (R) A reunion at a remote hotel leads to an ordeal of psychological terror and murderous intrigue. 108m/C VHS. George Segal, Robert Morley, Trevor Howard, Emlyn Williams, Alan Webb; *D:* George Schaefer.

Deadly Game 🎬½ 1983 Much-maligned and preyed-upon witness is protected by a weary cop, who speaks with the use of English subtitles. 90m/C VHS. *GE* Mel Ferrer, Helmut Berger, Barbara Sukowa; *D:* Karoly Makk, Dieter Geissler.

Deadly Game 1991 (R) Horribly burned, a vengeful millionaire invites seven people he believes have wronged him to spend the weekend on his isolated island. He has promised them each a reward for their good deeds, but instead plans to have a big-game hunt with his "guests" as the prey. 89m/C VHS. Roddy McDowall, Jenny Seagrove, Marc Singer, Michael Beck; *D:* Thomas J. Wright; *W:* Wes Claridge.

Deadly Lessons 🎬🎬 1994 Misfit Ann gets shunned by the college "in" crowd but then a childhood friend comes to her aid and decides to take revenge on the nasty students. 90m/C VHS. Andrea Gail, Mat McGinnis, Diana Wise; *D:* Leslie Delano.

Deadly Games 🎬½ 1980 Ineffective plot involving a series of murders in a small town is seemingly played out by the principal characters in a horror board game. Film is saved from being a complete waste by Groom's good performance as the local cop. 94m/C VHS. Sam Groom, Jo Ann Harris, Steve Railsback, Dick Butkus, June Lockhart, Colleen Camp; *D:* Scott Mansfield.

Deadly Harvest 🎬 1972 (PG) Scientists' worst fears have been realized—due to ecological abuse and over-development of the land, food has become extremely scarce. This in turn has caused people to become a bit savage. They are particularly nasty to a farmer and his family. Not a bad plot, but a poorly acted film. 86m/C VHS. DVD. Clint Walker, Nehemiah Persoff, Kim Cattrall, David G. Brown, Gary Davies; *D:* Timothy Bond.

Deadly Hero 🎬🎬 1975 (R) Gripping tale of a young woman who becomes the prey of a New York City cop after questioning the brutal methods he employed while saving her from being assaulted, ultimately killing her attacker. Williams makes film debut in this chilling suspenser. 102m/C VHS. Don Murray, James Earl Jones, Diahn Williams, Lilia Skala, Conchata Ferrell, George S. Irving, Treat Williams, Josh Mostel; *D:* Ivan Nagy; *C:* Andrzej Bartkowiak; *M:* Brad Fiedel.

Deadly Heroes 🎬🎬 1996 (R) Terrorists highjack an American plane at Athens International Airport with the demand that their leader, Carlos (Drago), who's jailed in Miami, be delivered to them. CIA agent and ex-Navy SEAL, Captain Cody Grant (Vincent), is forced to take Carlos to Athens but when he has captured Carlos once, Grant is determined that the terrorist and his associates won't be free for long. 104m/ C VHS. Jan-Michael Vincent, Billy Drago, Michael Pare, Claudette Mink; *D:* Menahem Golan; *M:* Damian Lee, Gregory Lee. VIDEO

Deadly Illusion 🎬🎬 *Love You to Death* 1987 (R) Williams is a private detective who manages to get himself tangled in a complex web of intrigue and winds up framed for murder. Decent outing for all. 95m/C VHS. Billy Dee Williams, Morgan Fairchild, Vanity, John Beck, Joe Cortese; *D:* William (Bill) Tannen, Larry Cohen; *W:* Larry Cohen; *M:* Patrick Gleeson.

Deadly Impact 🎬½ 1984 Las Vegas casinos are targeted for rip-off by means of a computer. Svenson and Williamson give good performances, but that's not enough to save this one. *D:* Angelis used the pseudonym Larry Ludman. 90m/C VHS. *IT* Bo Svenson, Fred Williamson, Marcia Clingan, Giovanni Lombardo Radice, Vincent Conti; *D:* Fabrizio de Angelis.

Deadly Innocence 🎬½ 1988 (R) A shy, lonely girl works at an isolated gas station. After her father's death, she takes in a boarder—a mysterious woman being chased by her past. 90m/C VHS. Mary Crosby, Andrew Stevens, Amanda Wyss; *D:* John D. Patterson, Hugh Parks.

Deadly Intent 🎬🎬 1988 The widow of a murdered archeologist becomes the target of fortune hunters when they try to get their hands on the priceless jewel her husband brought back from a dig. 83m/C VHS. Lisa Eilbacher, Steve Railsback, Maud Adams, Lance Henriksen, Fred Williamson, Persis Khambatta; *D:* Nigel Dick.

Deadly Intruder 🎬½ 1984 Quiet vacation spot is being terrorized by an escapee from a mental institution. So much for a little R and R. 86m/C VHS. Chris Holder, Molly Creek, Tony Crupi; *D:* John McCauley; *W:* Tony Crupi.

The Deadly Mantis 🎬½ 1957 A gigantic praying mantis lies in a million-year-old sleep in the frozen reaches of the Arctic. The volcanic eruption releases the critter and the flying beastie does it's destructive best on Washington, D.C., and New York City until the military can gas it into oblivion. Typically silly '50s sci-fi with decent special effects. 79m/B VHS. Craig Stevens, William Hopper, Alix Talton, Pat Conway, Donald Randolph; *D:* Nathan "Jerry" Juran; *W:* Martin Berkeley.

Deadly Mission 🎬½ *Quel Maledetto Treno Blindato* 1978 (R) Five soldiers in WWII France are convicted of crimes against the Army, only to escape from lock-up and become focal points in a decisive battle. 99m/ C VHS. *IT* Bo Svenson, Peter Hooten, Fred Williamson; *D:* Enzo G. Castellari; *W:* Alessandro Continenza, Sergio Grieco, Romano Migliorini, Laura Toscano, Franco Marotta.

Deadly Neighbor 🎬🎬 1991 New neighbor moves in, dead neighborhood housewives move out. Another neighbor becomes suspicious and investigates. 90m/C VHS. DVD. Don Leifert, George Stover, Lydia Laurans; *D:* Donald M. Dohler.

Deadly Obsession 🎬½ 1988 (R) A disfigured lunatic stalks a young co-ed hoping to extort $1 million from the wealthy dean of the school. 93m/C VHS. Jeffrey R. Iorio; *D:* Jeno Hodi; *W:* Brian Cox.

Deadly Outbreak 🎬🎬 1996 (R) A chemical weapons facility is taken over by a renegade colonel who threatens to unleash a deadly plague. Now it's up to one man (Speakman) to free the hostage scientist who knows the formula for the antidote. 94m/C VHS. Jeff Speakman, Ron Silver, Rochelle Swanson, Jonathan Sagalle; *D:* Rick Avery; *M:* Harvey W. Mason.

Deadly Passion 🎬½ 1985 (R) A private eye getting carnally involved with a beautiful and treacherous woman who is manipulating her late husband's estate through murder and double-crossing. 100m/C VHS. *SA* Brent Huff, Ingrid Boulting, Harrison Coburn, Lynn Maree; *D:* Larry Larson.

Deadly Past 🎬½ 1995 (R) Predictable story finds dumb ex-con bartender (Marquette) making the mistake of getting involved with a femme fatale (Alt) from his past. Also available in an unrated version. 90m/C VHS. Ron Marquette, Carol Alt, Dedee Pfeiffer, Mark Dacascos; *D:* Tibor Takacs; *W:* Steven Iyama; *C:* Bernard Salzmann; *M:* K. Alexander (Alex) Wilkinson.

Deadly Possession 🎬🎬 1988 A college student plays amateur detective when she tries to clear her ex-husband's name after he is accused of the horrible murder of a fellow student. 99m/C VHS. *AU* Penny Cook, Anna-Maria Winchester, Liddy Clark, Olivia Hamnett; *D:* Craig Lahiff.

Deadly Prey WOOF! 1987 (R) Prior is up against a fully outfitted army of bloodthirsty mercenaries who are using innocent people as "live targets" at their secret bootcamp. Plot lifted from "The Most Dangerous Game" has more than its share of gruesome violence. 87m/C VHS. Cameron Mitchell, Troy Donahue, Ted Prior, Fritz Matthews; *D:* David A. Prior; *W:* David A. Prior.

Deadly Reactor 🎬🎬 1989 In a post-nuclear future a lone preacher turns into an armed vigilante to protect the people of a town being terrorized by a vicious motorcycle gang. 88m/C VHS. David Heavener, Stuart Whitman, Darwyn Swalve, Allyson Davis; *D:* David Heavener.

Deadly Recruits 🎬½ 1986 The Russians did it! The Russians did it! Stamp is convinced that the downfall of several top students at Oxford, amid scandal and rumor, is due to a KGB conspiracy. 92m/C VHS, DVD. *GB* Terence Stamp, Michael Culver, Carmen (De Sautoy) Du Sautoy, Robin Sachs; *D:* Roger Tucker.

Deadly Revenge 🎬🎬 1983 (R) Action-adventure pic with not much adventure and even less action. Small-town reporter finds himself up against a mob boss when he takes over the nightclub business of a friend killed by the mobsters. Dubbed. 90m/C VHS. *IT* Rodolfo Ranni, Julio de Grazia, Silvia Montanari, Fred Commoner; *D:* Juan Carlos Sesanzo.

Deadly Rivals 🎬🎬 1992 (R) Stevens plays a laser specialist in Miami for a top-secret weapons conference. A beauty takes a interest in him but then she's first accused of being a spy and then mistaken for a courier in the pay of a ruthless crime boss. Can Stevens find the truth? 93m/C VHS. Andrew Stevens, Cela Wise, Joseph Bologna, Margaux Hemingway, Richard Roundtree, Francesco Quinn, Randi Ingerman; *D:* James Dodson; *W:* Redge Mahaffey; *M:* Ashley Irwin.

Deadly Sanctuary WOOF! 1968 Censors stopped production of this film several times. The Marquis de Sade's writings provided the inspiration (though there's nothing inspired about it) for this tale of two recently orphaned young women who get caught up in prostitution, an S&M club, and murder. 92m/C VHS. DVD. Jack Palance, Mercedes McCambridge, Sylva Koscina, Klaus Kinski, Akim Tamiroff, Romina Power; *D:* Jess (Jesus) Franco.

The Deadly Secret 🎬 1994 Randall Parks is a successful real estate agent with a past he has managed to hide for 20 years. When he is blackmailed, he decides to take matters into his own hands and track down his accusers. 96m/C VHS. Joe Estevez, Tracy Spaulding, Reggie Cale, Douglas Stalgren; *D:* Jason Hammond; *W:* Douglas Stalgren; *M:* Erik Hansen.

Deadly Sins 🎬🎬½ 1995 (R) Deputy sheriff Jack Gates (Keith) hooks up with P.I. Christina Herrera (Milano) to investigate a murder in a Catholic girls school. Christina poses as a student and uncovers sinister secrets. 96m/C VHS. David Keith, Alyssa Milano, Terry David Mulligan, Corrie Clark; *D:* Michael Robison; *W:* John Langley, Malcolm Barbour.

Deadly Spygames 1989 A special agent for the United States Special Operations Bureau finds himself in deep trouble. 86m/C VHS. Troy Donahue, Tippi Hedren; *D:* Jack M. Sell; *W:* Jack M. Sell.

Deadly Sting 🎬½ 1982 Silva devises an intricate scheme to gain revenge on the men who cheated him out of his share of a gold bullion heist. 90m/C VHS. *FR* Henry Silva, Philip Clay, Andre Pousse; *D:* Jean-Claude Roy.

Deadly Stranger 🎬 *Border Heat* 1988 Fluegel's talents could have been put to much better use than as the selfish mistress of a plantation owner who is taking advantage of the migrant workers toiling on his land. Moore is a drifter and hired hand who rallies the workers to stand up to the owner. 93m/C VHS. Darlanne Fluegel, Michael J. Moore, John Vernon, Ted White; *D:* Max Kleven.

Deadly Strangers 🎬🎬 1982 Two people meet up on the road and decide to share a ride. We discover that one of them is an insane killer who's escaped from a mental institution. Suspense builds nicely, but the ending is flawed. 89m/C VHS. *GB* Hayley Mills, Simon Ward, Sterling Hayden, Ken Hutchison; *D:* Sidney Hayers.

Deadly Sunday 🎬½ 1994 A family's weekly Sunday drive turns terrifying when desperate jewel thieves detour them and hold them hostage. 85m/C VHS. Dennis Ely, Henry Sanders, Gyllian Roland, Douglas Alexander; *D:* Donald M. Jones.

Deadly Surveillance 🎬🎬 1991 (R) Two tough policemen investigate a series of drug-related murders and stake out a possible suspect—a beautiful woman who's the lover of one of the lawmen. Tension in this Canadian-made cop opera evaporates in the third act for a standard buddy-buddy action finale. 92m/C VHS. Michael Ironside, Christopher Bondy, Susan Almgren, Vlasta Vrana, David Carradine; *D:* Paul Ziller. TV

Deadly Target 🎬½ 1994 (R) Detective Charles Prince (Daniels) is sent to L.A. to return a notorious Chinese gangster to Hong Kong for trial. But Prince finds out his would-be prisoner's escaped and soon he's involved in martial arts mayhem. 90m/C VHS, DVD. Gary Daniels, Kenneth McLeod, Max Gail, Susan Byun; *D:* Charla Driver; *W:* Michael January, James Adelstein; *C:* Richard Pepin; *M:* Michael Lewis.

The Deadly Trackers 🎬 1973 (PG) If gorey oaters are your thing, this one's definitely for you; if not, make tracks. Harris plays a spiteful sheriff who heads south of the border to get his pound of flesh from the outlaws who slew his family in a bank robbery. Overlong revenge-o-rama based on Samuel Fuller's short story, "Riata"; might have been bearable if Fuller hadn't been bumped from the director's chair (as it is, he and other contributors refused to be listed in the credits). 104m/C VHS, Richard Harris, Rod Taylor, Al Lettieri, Neville Brand, William (Bill) Smith, Paul Benjamin, Pedro Armendariz Jr.; D: Earry Shear.

The Deadly Trap ✗ *Death Scream* **1971 (PG)** Confusing thriller that couldn't. Dunaway is the mentally unstable wife of an ex-spy. His former employers have targeted him with plans to use her and her fragile state-of-mind to their advantage. 95m/C VHS. FF/T Faye Dunaway, Frank Langella, Barbara Parkins, Maurice Ronet; D: Fene Clement.

Deadly Twins WOOF! **1985** After being beaten and gang-raped, twin sisters are out to get revenge. Nothing new here; don't waste your time. 87m/C VHS. Audrey Landers, Judy Landers, Ellie Rossell, Wayne Allison; D: Joe Oaks.

Deadly Vengeance ✗ **1981** It's strictly low budget as the mob kills Jones's boyfriend, forcing her to mount a vengeful, inexpensive offensive against the crime syndicate's bigwigs. 84m/C VHS. Grace Jones, Alan Marlowe, Arthur Roberts; D: Joe Oaks.

Deadly Voyage ✗✗½ **1996 (R)** In 1992, nine Ghanaian dockworkers are discovered hiding aboard a Ukrainian freighter bound for New York. Since each stowaway would cost the shipping company a hefty fine, sadistic first officer Ion (Pertwee) orders them killed. Only one, Kingsley (Epps), manages to survive and reveal the truth. 92m/C VHS, Omar Epps, Sean Pertwee, Joss Ackland, David Suchet, Jean LaMarre; D: John Mackenzie; W: Michael Thomas; C: Stuart Urban; M: John Scott. CABLE.

Deadly Weapon ✗✗ **1988 (PG-13)** It's a bit of nerdish wish fulfillment when 15-year-old geek Eastman finds a secret anti-matter weapon conveniently lost by the military in an Arizona stream. You won't like the kid any more than you'll like the bullies. 89m/C VHS, Rodney Eastman, Gary Frank, Michael Horse, Ed Nelson, Kim Walker; D: Michael Miner; W: Michael Miner; C: James L. Carter.

Deadly Weapons ✗ **1970 (R)** Chesty Morgan, she of the 73-inch busline, takes on the mob using only her God-given abilities. One of Joe Bob Brigg's "Sleaziest Movies in the History of the World" series, and he is welcome to it. 90m/C VHS, DVD, Chesty Morgan, Harry (Herbert Sincher) Reems, Greg Reynolds, Saul Meth, Philip Stahl; D: Doris Wishman; W: J.J. Kendall; C: Juan Fernandez.

Deadtime Stories ✗ **1986** Mother Goose it's not. Fairy tales "Little Red Riding Hood" and "Goldilocks and the Three Bears" among others, are presented like you've never before seen them—as low-budget horror tales. 93m/C VHS, DVD, Michael Mesmer, Brian DePersia, Scott Valentine, Phyllis Craig, Melissa Leo, Nicole Picard; D: Jeffrey Delman.

Deadman's Curve ✗✗ **1978** Decent bio pic detailing the lives of Jan Berry and Dean Torrence, who, as Jan and Dean, started the surf music wave only to wipe out after an almost-fatal car wreck. Shows how they deal with and recover from the tragedy. 100m/C VHS, Richard Hatch, Bruce Davison, Pamela Bellwood, Susan Sullivan, Dick Clark, Wolfman Jack; D: Richard Compton. TV

Deadwood ✗✗½ **1965** In the untamed West, a young cowboy is mistaken for the notorious Billy the Kid. 100m/C VHS, DVD, Arch Hall Jr., Jack Lester, Liz Renay, Robert Dix; D: James Landis; C: Vilmos Zsigmond.

Deadwood Pass ✗ **1933** Below-standard fare has Tyler rescuing Monti more times than seems reasonable. Monti was once an all-around helper to W.C. Fields. 62m/B VHS, DVD, Tom Tyler, Alice Dahl, Wally Wales, Buffalo Bill Jr., Lafe (Lafayette) McKee, Bud Osborne, Charles "Slim" Whitaker.

Charlotte (Charlotta) Monti; D: (John) Paterson McGowan.

The Deal ✗✗ **2005 (R)** It's the near future, the U.S. is at war with the "Confederation of Arab States" and gas is $6 a gallon and rising. A Wall Street hotshot, Tom Grover (Slater), is called in to help seal a $20-billion deal with a Russian oil conglomerate called Black Star which is most likely a Russian Mafia "oil-laundering" operation. Young Harvard grad, and new hire (Blair) acts as Grover's investigative partner and lust interest. Early portions of Epstein's script contain copious amounts of intriguing industrial data but once Angie Harmon enters the scene with her laughable Russian accent it becomes a corporate espionage thriller spoof. 107m/C DVD, US Christian Slater, Selma Blair, John Heard, Angie Harmon, Kevin Tighe, Francoise Yip, Colm Feore, Robert Loggia, Philip Granger, Jim Thorburn, Ruth Epstein; D: Harvey Kahn; C: Adam Sliwinski; W: Ruth Epstein. VIDEO

Deal of a Lifetime ✗✗ **1999 (PG)** It's a deal that's too good to be true, of course. Loser teen Henry (Gocrijian) is tempted to sell his soul to the Devil's agent, Jerry (Pollak), in order to get a date with the school's most popular babe (Appleby). 95m/C VHS, DVD, Kevin Pollak, Michael Goorjian, Shiri Appleby, Jennifer Rubin; D: Paul Levine; M: Katharine V. Sloan; C: Denise Brassard; W: William Friedkin. VIDEO

Deal of the Century ✗✗ **1983 (PG)** A first-rate hustler and his cohorts sell second-rate weapons to third-word nations, unfortunately, their latest deal threatens to blow up in their faces—literally. 99m/C VHS, DVD, Chevy Chase, Sigourney Weaver, Gregory Hines, Richard Libertini, Wallace Shawn; D: William Friedkin; W: Paul Erickman; C: Peter Sinclair.

Dealers ✗½ **1989 (R)** Two money-hungry stock traders mix business and pleasure, then set their sights on one final all or nothing score. 92m/C VHS, DVD, GB Paul Guilfoyle, Rebecca De Mornay, Paul McGann, Derrick O'Connor; D: Colin Bucksey; W: Andrew Maclear; C: Peter Sinclair.

Dean Koontz's Black River ✗✗ *Black River* **2001 (PG)** Novelist/screenwriter Bo Aikens (Mohr) is in need of a little creative inspiration and leaves Hollywood for the bucolic friendliness of the small town of Black River. Then Bo discovers the town is monitored by video cameras and he begins to get weird phone calls and notices an SUV tailing him. He can't escape unless he figures out the community's sinister secrets (which unfortunately turn out to be lame-o). 87m/C VHS, DVD, Jay Mohr, Lisa Edelstein, Ann Cusack, Ron Canada, Stephen Tobolowsky; D: Jeff Bleckner; W: Daniel Taplitz; C: John Eartley. TV

Dean Koontz's Mr. Murder ✗✗ *Mr. Murder* **1993 (R)** Marty Stillwater (Baldwin) is a successful mystery writer and family man who discovers that he has a killer clone. Seems industrialist Drew Oslett Jr. (Church) managed to screwup in the biotech lab and now there's a bloodthirsty Marty lookalike named Alfie, who decides he wants Marty's life. Meanwhile, everyone thinks Marty is going crazy. 132m/C VHS, DVD, Stephen Baldwin, Thomas Haden Church, Julia Warner, Bill Smitrovick; James Coburn, Don Hood, Dan Lauria; D: Dick Lowry; W: Stephen Tolkin; C: Greg Gardiner; M: Louis Febre. TV

Dear Boys ✗✗ **1980** A stylized film of sexual fantasies and romance between a moody writer and a carefree young man who relentlessly pursues excitement. Based on the novel by Gerald Reve. 90m/C VHS, NL Hugo Nelsers, Hans Dagelet, Bill Van Dijk, Albert Mol; D: Paul de Lussanet.

Dear Brigitte ✗✗ **1965** A young American kid ("Lost in Space"-tyke Mumy) writes a love letter to Brigitte Bardot and travels to Paris to meet her in person. Based on the novel "Erasmus with Freckles" by John Haase. 100m/C VHS, James Stewart, Billy Mumy, Glynis Johns, Fabian, Cindy Caro, John Williams, Jack Kruschen, Brigitte Bardot, Ed Wynn, Alice Pearce; D: Henry Koster; W: Hal Kanter.

Dear Wendy ✗½ **2005** A misfit gang of teens form, call themselves the Dandies, meet in a dingy mine with their guns and profess their vows of non-violence. Dick thinks Wendy is a toy gun at first, but she's not—and she's got some kind of hold on him. As if things aren't odd enough from the start, the only African American member of the Dandies has a thing for Wendy, making Dick jealous. Um. Sure. It all leads to pacifist misfit teens brandishing their beloved handguns. Artsy, unraveling presentation of bizarre images and lost messages. 100m/C DVD, DK FR GE GB Jamie Bell, Bill Pullman, Michael Angarano, Novella Nelson, Chris Owen, Alison Pill, Mark Webber, Danso Gordon; D: Thomas Vinterberg; W: Lars von Trier; C: Anthony Dod Mante; M: Benjamin Wallfisch.

Dear Murderer ✗✗ **1947** A husband suspects his wife of having an affair, and devises an ingenious, if complicated, trap for her. Inspired performances from the leads, but the plot is grim and confusing. 94m/B VHS, GB Eric Portman, Greta Gynt, Dennis Price, Jack Warner, Maxwell Reed, Hazel Court, Andrew Crawford, Jane Hylton; D: Arthur Crabtree.

Dear Dead Delilah ✗½ **1972** Mooorehead is Delilah, the matriarch of a southern family, who is on her deathbed. Her heirs are fighting to the bitter—and bloody—end to be first to find Delilah's money, buried somewhere on her land. 90m/C VHS, DVD, Agnes Moorehead, Will Geer, Michael Ansara, Patricia Carmichael, Dennis Patrick; D: John Farris.

Dear Detective ✗✗ *Dear Inspector* *Tendre Poulet* **1977** Comedy/thriller/romance finds female police commissioner (Girardot) investigating a murder while romancing a somewhat pompous professor of Greek (Noiret). French with subtitles. 105m/C VHS, Annie Girardot, Philippe Noiret, Catherine Alric, Guy Marchand, Simone Renant; D: Philippe de Broca; W: Philippe de Broca, Michel Audiard; M: Georges Delerue.

Dear Frankie ✗✗ **2004 (PG-13)** Scottish tearjerker about a woman, her deaf son, and the guy she pays to pretend to be Dad. Lizzie (McElhone) has raised 9-year-old Frankie (McElhone) to believe that the father he doesn't remember is a member of a cargo ship crew, when in reality he was an abusive jerk that Lizzie left years ago. Of course, this means that she has to come up with a fake father on the spot, and finds a stranger (Butler) to fill the role, with the ensuing fake-dad-learns-to-like-his-fake-family results. Solid performances by all fail to make up for a bland, manipulative story. 102m/C DVD, GB Emily Mortimer, Jack McElhone, Gerard Butler; D: Shona Auerbach; W: Andrea Gibb; M: Alex Heffes.

Dear God ✗ **1996 (PG)** TV vets Marshall (director) and Kinnear team up for a sappy and predictable "Miracle on Mel-rose," a little piece of Capra-corn that feels like it lodged in your tooth. Cynical con man Tom (Kinnear) goes to work for the post office and gets stuck with a group of misfits at the Dead Letter Office, sorting mail for the likes of Elvis, Santa, and God. Even though he's merely working the ultimate angle for easy cash, the oddball team of postal workers think he's on a mission from the Lord and joins him in aiding the needy. Most unbelievable is the premise that single mom and love interest Gloria (Pirillo) can give the hardened criminal an instant psychological makeover. Broadly characterized supporting cast, including Conway and Metcalf, smooth over the hardened criminal. 112m/C VHS, Greg Kinnear, Laurie Metcalf, Maria Pitillo, Hector Elizondo, Tim Conway, Roscoe Lee Browne, Jon Seda, Anna Maria Horsford, Donal Logue, Nancy Marchand, Larry Miller, Rue McClanahan, Toby Huss, Jack Klugman; Cameos: Gary Marshall; D: Garry Marshall; W: Ed Kaplan, Warren Leight; C: Charles Minsky.

Death and Desire ✗✗ *Illicit Dreams 2* **1997 (R)** Former political prisoner and torture victim (Weaver) turns the tables on the man she believes was her tormentor in 1953's "House of Wax." 79m/C VHS, Andrew Stevens, Joan Severance, Shadoe Stevens, Paul Bartel, Mink Stole; D: Michael James McDonald; W: Michael James McDonald, Brendan Broderick; C: Christopher Baffa; M: David Wurst, Eric Wurst.

The Death Artist ✗✗✗ **1995 (R)** Struggling busboy and fine artist Walter Paisley (Hall) finds fame creating sculptures from dead bodies. Gruesome plot is a remake of Corman's 1960 "A Bucket of Blood" but the same premise was done much better with Vincent Price in 1953's "House of Wax." 79m/C VHS, Anthony Michael Hall, Darcy Demoss, Shadoe Stevens, Paul Bartel, Mink Stole; D: Michael James McDonald. TV

Death at a Funeral ✗✗ **2007 (R)** Ridiculous situations arise at the funeral of the patriarch of a dysfunctional British family, which brings about a reunion of estranged brothers Daniel (Macfayden) and Robert (Graves). They are also confronted by a blackmailer who's determined to give the family's dirty laundry a good airing, unless they can find a way to stop him. Not yet reviewed. 90m/C DVD, US NL GE Rupert Graves, Peter Dinklage, Alan Tudyk, Daisy Donovan, Matthew Macfadyen, Ewen Bremner, Peter Vaughan, Keeley Hawes, Andy Nyman, Jane Asher, Kris Marshall, Peter Egan; D: Frank Oz; W: Dean Craig; C: Oliver Curtis; M: Murray Gold.

Death at Love House ✗½ **1975** A screenwriter becomes obsessed when he is hired to write the life story of a long dead silent movie queen. Filmed at the Harold Lloyd estate. 74m/C VHS, DVD, Robert Wagner, Kate Jackson, Sylvia Sidney, Joan Blondell, John Carradine, Dorothy Lamour. TV

Death Be Not Proud ✗✗✗ **1975** Based on the book by John Gunther detailing the valiant battle fought by his son against the brain tumor that took his life at the age of 17. Wonderfully acted by the three principals, especially Alexander, this film leaves us feeling hopeful despite its subject. 74m/C VHS, Arthur Hill, Robby Benson, Jane Alexander, Lincon Chiles, Wendy Phillips; D: Donald Wrye. TV

Dear Wife ✗✗ **1949** Comedy about those ties that bind. Even though Jeff Reed isn't tempted by the beautiful models he shoots because she's beautiful married. But when his wife is killed in an accident, the vulnerable Jeff becomes the target of fashion mag editor, Lynn, who desperately wants to offer him comfort. Too desperately. Soon Lynn's obsessed son runs 88 minutes. 84m/C VHS, DVD, Sigourney Weaver, Ben Kingsley, Stuart Wilson; D: Roman Polanski; W: Rafael Yglesias, Ariel Dorfman; C: Tonino Delli Colli; M: Wojciech Kilar.

Death and the Maiden ✗✗✗ **1994 (R)** Fashion photographer Jeff Reed isn't tempted by the beautiful models he shoots because she's beautifully married. But when his wife is killed in an accident, the vulnerable Jeff becomes the target of fashion mag editor, Lynn, who desperately wants to offer him comfort. Too desperately. Soon Lynn's obsessed son runs 88 minutes. 84m/C VHS, DVD, Sigourney Weaver, Ben Kingsley, Stuart Wilson; D: Roman Polanski; W: Rafael Yglesias, Ariel Dorfman; C: Tonino Delli Colli; M: Wojciech Kilar. From the Ariel Dorfman play. 103m/C VHS, DVD. Billy DeWolfe, William Holden, Joan Caulfield, Edward Arnold, Mona Freeman; D: Richard Haydn.

Death Becomes Her 1992 (PG-13) Aging actress Streep will do anything to stay young and beautiful, especially when childhood rival Hawn shows up, 200 pounds lighter and out to revenge the loss of her fiance, Streep's henpecked hubby. Doing anything arrives in the form of a potion that stops the aging process (and keeps her alive forever). Watch for the hilarious party filled with dead celebrities who all look as good as the day they died. Great special effects and fun performances by Streep and Hawn playing their glamour-girl roles to the hilt add merit to this biting commentary on Hollywood's obsession with beauty and youth. **105m/C VHS, DVD.** Meryl Streep, Bruce Willis, Goldie Hawn, Isabella Rossellini; Sydney Pollack, Michael Caine, Ian Ogilvy, Adam Storke, Nancy Fish, Alaina Reed Hall, Michelle Johnson, Mimi Kennedy, Jonathan Silverman, Mary Ellen Trainor; *Cameos:* Fabio,; **D:** Robert Zemeckis; **W:** Martin Donovan, David Koepp; **C:** Dean Cundey; **M:** Alan Silvestri. Oscars '92: Visual FX.

Death Before Dishonor 1987 (R) Formula actioner stars Dryer as a tough Marine sergeant who battles ruthless Middle Eastern terrorists after they slaughter his men and kidnap his commanding officer (Keith). **95m/C VHS, DVD.** Fred (John F.) Dryer, Brian Keith, Joanna Pacula, Paul Winfield; **D:** Terry J. Leonard; **W:** John Gatliff; **C:** Don Burgess; **M:** Brian May.

Death Benefit 1996 (PG-13) Corporate attorney Steven Keeney (Horton) takes on the case of Lou Anne Wilkins (Ruscio), who's having trouble getting her insurance company to cover the funeral expenses for her teenaged daughter Melissa, who died in a fall. The more Steven investigates, the more suspicious Melissa's death becomes—and he discovers money is the root of all evil. Based on the book "Death Benefit" by David Heilbroner. **89m/C VHS.** Jack Kehler, Peter Horton, Carrie Snodgress, Wendy Makkena, Elizabeth Ruscio, Belita Morena, Lee DeBroux; **D:** Mark Piznarski; **W:** Philip Rosenberg; **C:** Christopher Taylor. **CABLE**

Death Blow 1987 (R) The victims of a violent rapist team together to stop the criminal after he repeatedly skirts conviction. **90m/C VHS.** Laura Albert, Ken Sagoes; **D:** Tom Dewier.

Death Challenge 1980 Gangs battle without weapons, motive or discretion in this kung fu extravaganza. **94m/C VHS.** Steve Leving, Susan Wong.

Death Chase 1987 An average Joe, just jogging down the street, is thrown into a desperate game of cat-and-mouse when a body lands at his feet. **86m/C VHS.** William Zipp, Paul Smith, Jack Starrett, Bainbridge Scott; **D:** David A. Prior.

Death Collector 1989 (R) In the future when insurance companies run the world, if you don't pay your premium, you die. **90m/C VHS.** Daniel Chapman, Ruth (Coreen) Collins; **D:** Tom Gniazdowski.

Death Cruise 1974 The six winners of a free cruise find that there is a fatal catch to the prize in this made-for-TV movie. **74m/C VHS.** Kate Jackson, Celeste Holm, Tom Bosley, Edward Albert, Polly Bergen, Michael Constantine, Richard Long; **D:** Ralph Senensky.

The Death Curse of Tartu WOOf! 1966 Another aspiring cult classic. (Read: A low-budget flick so bad it's funny). Students accidentally disturb the burial ground of an Indian medicine man who comes to zombie-like life with a deadly prescription. **84m/C VHS, DVD.** Fred Pinero, Doug Hobart, Babette Sherrill, Mayra Christine, Bill Marcos, Sherman Hayes, Gary Holtz, Frank Weed; **D:** William Grefe; **W:** William Grefe; **C:** Julio Chavez; **M:** Al Greene, Al Jacobs.

Death Dreams 1992 Crista thinks she has a perfect life with her wealth, beautiful daughter Jennie, and handsome new husband George. Then Jennie tragically drowns. It appears to be an accident until Jennie contacts her mother from beyond the grave to tell what really happened. Is the tragedy turning Crista's mind or is there truly something sinister going on—something that involves George? Based on the novel by William Katz. **94m/C VHS.** Marg Helgenberger, Christopher Reeve, Fionnula Flanagan; **D:** Martin Donovan; **W:** Robert Glass. **CABLE**

Death Driver 1978 In order to make a comeback, a stuntman attempts to do a stunt that was responsible for ending his career ten years earlier. Obviously brave but none too smart. **93m/C VHS.** Earl Owensby, Mike Allen, Patty Shaw, Mary Ann Hearn; **D:** Jimmy Huston.

Death Drug 1983 Cliched alarmist film about a talented musician ruining his career by becoming addicted to the drug angel dust. **73m/C VHS.** Philip Michael Thomas, Vernee Watson-Johnson, Rosalind Cash; **D:** Oscar Williams.

Death Feud 1989 A man tries to save the woman he loves from the man who would destroy her and her former pimp. **98m/C VHS.** Karen Mayo-Chandler, Chris Mitchum, Frank Stallone; **D:** Carl Monson.

Death Force 1978 (R) When a Vietnam veteran comes to New York City, he becomes a hitman for the Mafia. **90m/C VHS, DVD.** Jayne Kennedy, Leon Isaac Kennedy, James Iglehart, Carmen Argenziano; **D:** Cirio H. Santiago.

Death from a Distance 1936 A reporter and a detective put the moves on a group of astronomers who may be responsible for a murder. **73m/B VHS, DVD.** Russell Hopton, Lola Lane, George F. Marion Sr., John St. Polis, Lee Kohlmar, Lew Kelly, Wheeler Oakman, Robert Frazer, Cornelius Keefe; **D:** Frank Strayer.

Death Games *Final Cut* 1980 Two young men shooting a documentary about an influential music promoter ask too many wrong questions, causing the powers-that-be to want them out of the picture for good. **78m/C VHS.** Lou Brown, David Clendenning, Jennifer Cluff; **D:** Ross Dimsey; **W:** Ross Dimsey; **C:** Ron Johanson; **M:** Howard J. Davidson.

Death Goes to School 1953 A strangler is loose in a girl's school, and the music teacher has a hunch as to who it is. **65m/B VHS.** GB Barbara Murray, Gordon Jackson, Pamela Allan, Jane Aird, Beatrice Varley; **D:** Stephen Clarkson.

Death House 1988 Derek Keillor is on Death Row at Townsend State Prison when he discovers a plot to use inmates for scientific experiments in biological warfare. He decides the best way to get out is to volunteer, which means convincing the man who put him in prison that they're now on the same side. **92m/C VHS, DVD.** Dennis Cole, Anthony (Tony) Franciosa, Michael Pataki, John Saxon; **D:** John Saxon.

Death in Deep Water 1974 A sensuous woman lures a man into a plot to kill her incredibly rich husband. **71m/C VHS.** Bradford Dillman, Suzan Farmer; **D:** James Ormerod; **W:** Brian Clemens. **TV**

A Death in the Family 2002 Adaptation of James Agee's Pulitzer Prize-winning novel, set in Knoxville in 1915. Title tells you the tragedy that's about the befall the loving family of May (Gish) and Jay (Slattery) Follet when Jay is killed in an auto accident. It's up to the grieving May to cope and to tell their 7-year-old son Rufus (Wolff) that his father is dead. **90m/C VHS, DVD.** Annabeth Gish, John Slattery, James Cromwell, Austin Wolff, Kathleen Chalfant, Bill Raymond, David Alford, Christopher Strand; **D:** Gilbert Cates; **W:** Robert W. Lenski; **C:** Stephen M. Katz; **M:** Charles Fox. **TV**

Death in the Garden 1956 *La Mort en Ce Jardin; Evil Eden* Surreal film, filled with symbolism, about a group of French people, living in a South American settlement, who must flee a riot between soldiers and striking miners. Local adventurer, Chark (Marchal), agrees to lead them to safety but their trek through the jungle is fraught with peril (and not just from the animal life). French with subtitles. **90m/C VHS.** MX FR Georges Marchal, Simone Signoret, Charles Vanel, Michele Girardon, Michel Piccoli; Tito Junco; **D:** Luis Buñuel; **W:** Luis Buñuel, Luis Alcoriza, Raymond Queneau; **C:** Jorge Stahl Jr.; **M:** Paul Misraki.

Death in Venice 1971 (PG) *Morte a Venezia* A lush, decadent adaptation of the Thomas Mann novella about a aging, jaded, and dying composer Gustav von Aschenbach (Bogarde)—here suggested to be Gustav Mahler—who is plagued by fears that he can no longer feel anything. Instead, he becomes tragically obsessed with ideal beauty as personified in the young boy, Tadzio (Andresen). Visconti uses Mahler's 3rd and 5th symphonies to haunting effect. **124m/C VHS, DVD.** IT Dirk Bogarde, Mark Burns, Bjorn Andresen, Marisa Berenson, Silvana Mangano; **D:** Luchino Visconti; **W:** Luchino Visconti, Nicola Badalucco; **C:** Pasqualino De Santis.

Death Is Called Engelchen 1963 *Not Forgive* An influential, important work of the Czech new wave. A survivor of WWII remembers his experiences with the SS leader Engelchen in a series of flashbacks. In Czech with subtitles. **111m/B VHS.** CZ Jan Kacer, Eva Polakova, Martin Ruzek, Blazena Holisova, Otto Lackovic q; **D:** Jan Kadar, Elmar Klos; **W:** Milos Faber; **C:** Rudolf Milic; **M:** Zdenek Liska.

Death Journey 1976 (R) Producer and director Williamson portrays private eye Jesse Crowder, hired by the New York D.A. to escort a key witness crosscountry. A regular Williamsonfest. **90m/C VHS, DVD.** Fred Williamson, D'Urville Martin, Bernie Kuby, Heidi Dobbs, Stephanie Faulkner; **D:** Fred Williamson.

The Death Kiss 1933 Creepy thriller about eerie doings at a major Hollywood film studio where a sinister killer does away with his victims while a cast-of-thousands movie spectacular is in production. **72m/B VHS, DVD.** Bela Lugosi, David Manners, Adrienne Ames, Edward Van Sloan, Vince Barnett; **D:** Edwin L. Marin.

Death Kiss 1974 (R) When a man hires a psychopath to murder his wife, his plan doesn't proceed exactly as expected. **90m/C VHS.** GR Larry Daniels, Dorothy Moore; **D:** Costas Karagiannis.

Death Machine 1995 (R) New company exec Hayden Cale (Pouget) uncovers questionable scientific project at weapons technology company and scientist in charge Jack Dante (Dourif) decides which works by sensing fear, in corporate headquarters. **99m/C VHS, DVD.** Brad Dourif, Ely Pouget, William Hootkins; **D:** Stephen Norrington; **W:** Stephen Norrington; **C:** John de Borman.

Death Machines 1976 (R) Young karate student must face the "Death Machines," a team of deadly assassins who are trained to kill on command. **93m/C VHS, DVD.** Ron Marchini, Michael Chong, Joshua Johnson; **D:** Paul Kyriazi.

Death Magic 1992 A group of five ceremonial magicians performs a spell to bring someone back from the dead, but the man they bring back, a soldier from the Civil War, decides to go on a vicious murdering spree to kill the descendants of the people who convicted him of murder in 1875. A suspenseful first entry from director Clinco. **93m/C VHS.** Anne Coffrey, Keith DeGreen, Jack Dunlap, Danielle Frons, Norman Stone; **D:** Paul E. Clinco; **W:** Paul E. Clinco.

Death Mask 1998 Screenwriter, executive producer, and star James Best plays Wilbur Johnson, a vengeful carnival worker who was abused and disfigured as a child. He becomes friends with Angel (Linnea Quigley), a sideshow dancer. After hearing Wilbur's story, she takes him to the swamp, where he meets a witch (Brigitte Hill), who gives him the titular "Death Mask." It causes violent and painful death to Wilbur's enemies when he dons the mask, so Wilbur goes on a killing spree. Then it's up to Angel to convince him to stop. Best hams it up in every scene and Quigley proves that she's still willing to take her clothes off whenever necessary. The film doesn't aim to be anything more than campy fun, and on that point, it delivers. **97m/C DVD.** James Best, Linnea Quigley, Brigitte Hill; **D:** Steve Latshaw; **W:** James Best.

Death Match 1994 (R) John Larson gives up kickboxing after a tragedy but when his friend disappears, John is forced into a fighting bout with no rules and only one outcome. **90m/C VHS.** Matthias Hues, Martin Kove, Ian Jacklin, Nick (Nicholas, Niko) Hill, Renee Griffin; **D:** Joe Coppoletta.

The Death Merchant 1991 Foundering attempt at a nuclear thriller. A modern mad man hopes to sell a computer chip to third world countries but is thwarted by a secret agent. Confusing, illogical plot highlighted by mediocre performances. **90m/C VHS.** Lawrence Tierney, Martina Castle, Melody Munyan, Monica Schnarre; **D:** James R. Winburn; **W:** Kari Holman.

Death Nurse 1987 Fresh from "Crazy Fat Ethel II," aspiring Queen of Camp Alden takes takes up residence in a health care establishment, much to the dismay of the patients who give up their lives in exchange for their money. **80m/C VHS.** Priscilla Alden, Michael Flood; **D:** Nick (Steve Millard) Phillips.

Death of a Bureaucrat *La Muerte de un Burocrata* 1966 A Cuban hero dies, and in tribute, the Communist government buries him with his union card. His widow, however, needs the card in order to collect a pension, and she enlists her nephew's help to retrieve it. The nephew soon finds himself buried in red tape, and digs himself in ever-deeper as he seeks to disinter his late uncle. A wry satire of the communist bureaucracy in Cuba, brimming with comedic tributes to Harold Lloyd, Buster Keaton and Laurel & Hardy. Alea's film was only briefly released in 1966 and was promptly banned, eventually finding its way to the U.S. in 1979. In Spanish with English subtitles. **87m/B VHS.** CU Salvador Wood, Silvia Planas, Manuel Estanillo, Gaspar de Santelices, Carlos Ruiz de la Tejera, Omar Alfonso, Ricardo Suarez, Luis Romay, Elsa Montero; **D:** Tomas Gutierrez Alea; **W:** Tomas Gutierrez Alea, Ramon Suarez; **C:** Ramon Suarez; **M:** Leo Brouwer.

Death of a Centerfold 1981 Drama based on the life and tragic death of Playboy model and actress Dorothy Stratten. More effectively handled in Bob Fosse's "Star 80." **96m/C VHS.** Jamie Lee Curtis, Bruce Weitz, Robert Reed, Mitchell Ryan, Bibi Besch; **D:** Gabrielle Beaumont.

Death of a Gunfighter 1969 (PG) A western town courting eastern investors and bankers seeks a way to kill their ex-gunslinger sheriff. **94m/C VHS.** Richard Widmark, Lena Horne, Carroll O'Connor, John Saxon, Larry Gates, David Opatoshu, Kent Smith, Dub Taylor, Jacqueline Scott, Darlene Carr, Morgan Woodward, Michael McGreevey, Royal Dano, Kathleen Freeman, Harry Carey Jr., Victor French; **D:** Robert Totten, Donald Siegel; **W:** Joseph Calvelli; **C:** Andrew Jackson.

Death of a Salesman ✍✍✍ 1951 Screen adaptation of Arthur Miller's Pulitzer Prize-winning play has Fredric March superbly playing the failure and lament of Loman along with a first-rate supporting cast. Classic must-see cinema. 115m/B VHS, DVD. Fredric March, Mildred Dunnock, Kevin McCarthy, Cameron Mitchell, Cari lo Benedek; **W:** Stanley Roberts; **C:** Franz Planer. **M:** Alex North. **VIDEO**

Death of a Salesman ✍✍✍½ 1986 A powerful adaptation of the famous Arthur Miller play. Hoffman won an Emmy (as did Malkovich) for his stirring portrayal of Willy Loman, the aging salesman who realizes he's past his prime and tries to come to grips with the life he's wasted and the family he's neglected. Reid also turns in a fine performance as his long-suffering wife. 135m/C VHS, DVD. Dustin Hoffman, John Malkovich, Charles Durning, Stephen Lang, Kate Reid, Louis Zorich; **D:** Volker Schlondorff. **C:** Michael Ballhaus; **M:** Alex North. **VIDEO**

Death of a Scoundrel ✍✍½ 1956 A womanizing entrepreneur is murdered and the culprit could be any one of his many jealous lovers. The lawyer hired to defend him has to fight political as well as legal influences. Based on a true story. 119m/B VHS. George Sanders, Zsa Zsa Gabor, Yvonne De Carlo, Victor Joy; **D:** Charles Martin; **M:** Max Steiner.

Death of a Soldier ✍✍ 1985 (R) During WWII, the uneasy U.S.-Australian alliance explodes when a psychotic American soldier murders three Melbourne women. The lawyer hired to defend him has to fight the life he's wasted and the news of the fall of the Third Reich. While the film avoids cliche, it lacks emotional depth. 107m/C VHS, GB Frank Finlay, Caroline Mortimer; **D:** Rex Firkin. **TV**

The Death of Adolf Hitler ✍✍½ 1984 Depicts Hitler's last ten days in an underground bunker. Drug-addicted, suicidal, and Eva Braun-haunted, he receives the news of the fall of the Third Reich. While the film avoids cliche, it lacks emotional depth. 107m/C VHS, GB Frank Finlay, Caroline Mortimer; **D:** Rex Firkin. **TV**

Death of an Angel ✍✍ 1986 When her crippled daughter runs away to join a cult in Mexico, a recently ordained priest (Bedelia) follows her, only to become caught up herself with the leader of the group. 95m/C VHS. Bonnie Bedelia, Nick Mancuso, Pamela Ludwig, Alex Colon; **D:** Petru Popescu.

The Death of Mr. Lazarescu ✍✍ Moartea Comnului Lazarescu 2005 (R) The title character (F-scutenau) is a grubby 62-year-old widower living in a shabby apartment with a lot of cats. After suffering head and stomach pains all day, he finally calls for help. Medic Mioara (Gheorghiu) and the ambulance driver eventually arrive and the dying man is trundled from one over-crowded hospital to another to be seen by one overworked and/or indifferent doctor after another. He gets sicker and weaker until someone finally pays attention. This all takes a very, very long time and the message seems to be to don't get seriously sick in Bucharest. Inspired by an actual 1997 incident. Romanian with subtitles. 154m/C DVD. RO Lumnita Gheorghiu, Ion Fiscuteanu, Gabriel Spahiu, Doru Ana, Dana Dogaru, Florin Zamfirescu; **D:** Cristi Puiu; **W:** Cristi Puiu, Razvan Radulescu; **C:** Oleg Mutu; **M:** Andrea Paduraru.

The Death of Richie ✍✍ 1976 Gazzara does a fine job as a father driven to kill his drug-addicted teenage son, portrayed by Benson. Occasionally lapses into melodrama, but all-in-all a decent adaptation of Thomas Thompson's book "Richie," which was based on a true story. 97m/C VHS, DVD. Ben Gazzara, Robby Benson, Eileen Brennan, Clint Howard; **D:** Paul Wendkos. **TV**

Death of the Incredible Hulk ✍½ 1990 Scientist David Banner's new job just may provide the clues for stopping his transformation into the monstrous Incredible Hulk. But first there are terrorists after the Hulk, who need to be defeated and Banner's new romance to contend with. 96m/C VHS, DVD. Bill Bixby, Lou Ferrigno, Elizabeth Gracen, Philip Sterling; **D:** Bill Bixby. **TV**

Death on the Nile ✍✍½ 1978 (PG) Agatha Christie's fictional detective, Hercule Poirot, is called upon to interrupt his vacation to uncover who killed an heiress aboard a steamer cruising down the Nile. Ustinov's first stint as the Belgian sleuth. Anthony Powell's costume design won an Oscar. 135m/C VHS, DVD. GB Peter Ustinov, Jane Birkin, Lois Chiles, Bette Davis, Mia Farrow, David Niven, Olivia Hussey, Angela Lansbury, Jack Warden, Maggie Smith, George Kennedy, Simon MacCorkindale, Harry Andrews, Jon Finch; **D:** John Guillermin; **W:** Anthony Shaffer; **C:** Jack Cardiff; **M:** Nino Rota. Oscars '78: Costume Des.; Natl. Bd. of Review '78: Support. Actress (Lansbury).

Death Proof ✍✍½ Quentin Tarantino's Death Proof, Grindhouse: Death Proof 2007 Tarantino's half of the "Grindhouse" double bill features the best and worst of his creative impulses. Q creepily indulges foot and cheerleader fetishes, and overdoses on the dialogue-heavy scenes that have become his stock-in-trade, but in this instance just delay the action that everyone came to see. He pays homage to the slasher drive-in flicks of his youth with this souped-up and reinforced muscle cars. The extended, and exciting chase scene that closes the film comes obscuring digressions that led up to it. It is, in 'act, one of the best car chase sequences put to film. 120m/C DVD. US Kurt Russell, Rosario Dawson, Vanessa Ferlito, Sydney Tamiia Poitier, Zoe Bell, Tracie Thoms, Rose McGowan, Jordan Ladd, Mary Elizabeth Winstead, Eli Roth, Omar Doom, Michael Bacall, Jonathan Loughran, Melissa Arcaro, Michael Parks, James Parks, Marley Shelton, Nicky Katt, Quentin Tarantino; **D:** Quentin Tarantino; **W:** Quentin Tarantino; **C:** Quentin Tarantino.

Death Race 2000 ✍✍½ 1975 (R) In the 21st century, five racing car contenders challenge the national champion of a cross country race in which drivers score points by killing pedestrians. Gory fun. Based on the 1956 story by Ib Melchior, and followed by "Deathsport." 80m/C VHS, DVD, UMD. David Carradine, Simone Griffeith, Sylvester Stallone, Mary Woronov, Roberta Collins, Martin Kove, Louisa Moritz, John Landis, Don Steele; **D:** Paul Bartel; **W:** Paul Chihara, Robert Thom; **C:** Tak Fujimoto; **M:** Paul Chihara.

Death Rage ✍✍ 1977 (R) A hitman comes out of retirement to handle the toughest assignment he has ever faced: search for and kill the man who murdered his brother. He finds out he's the victim of a Mafia doublecross. 92m/C VHS, DVD. IT Yul Brynner, Martin Balsam; **D:** Anthony M. Dawson.

Death Ray 2000 ✍½ 1981 Bondian superspy T.R. Sloane must search out the whereabouts of a stolen military device that could kill all life on Earth. TV pilot for the series "A Man Called Sloane." 100m/C VHS, DVD. Robert F. Logan, Ann Turkel, Maggie Cooper, Dan O'Herlihy; **D:** Lee H. Katzin. **TV**

Death Ray WOOF! 1967 It's a race to the finish as terrorists threaten to unleash the world's most powerful weapon. A very poor James Bond rip-off. Batcanello used the pseudonym Frank G. Carroll. 93m/C VHS. IT SP Massimo Righi, Maureen Delphy, Nello Pazzafini, Gordon Scott; **D:** Gianfranco Baldanello; **W:** Juan Antonio Cabezas; **C:** Manuel Hernandez Sanjuan; **M:** James Anderson.

Death Rides the Plains ✍✍ 1944 Western with a twist. A man lures prospective buyers to his ranch, kills them, and steals their money. It's up to our heroes to ride to the rescue. 53m/B VHS, DVD. Robert "Bob" Livingston, Al "Fuzzy" St. John, Nica Doret, Ray Bennett; **D:** Sam Newfield.

Death Rides the Range ✍½ 1940 Russian spies start a range war as a cover for an operation to pipe helium off a ranch and over the border. Maynard, an undercover FBI agent posing as a cowboy, is out to stop them. 58m/B VHS, DVD. Ken Maynard, Fay McKenzie, Ralph Peters, Julian Rivero, Charles "Blackie" King, John Elliott, Bud Osborne; **D:** Sam Newfield.

Death Ring ✍ 1993 (R) Basic action' martial arts tale about three men who must battle the bad guys to ensure their own survival. 91m/C VHS. Mike Norris, Chad McQueen, Don Swayze, Billy Drago, Isabel Glasser; **D:** Robert J. Kizer; **W:** George T. LeBrun.

Death Row Diner ✍½ 1988 A movie mogul, executed for a crime he didn't commit, is brought back to life by a freak electrical storm. Nothing will stop him from exacting revenge. 90m/C VHS. Charles Bonet; **D:** Robert Warmflash; **W:** Norbert Albertson Jr.

Death Scream ✍✍ Street Kill 1975 Drama based on the New York murder of Kitty Genovese, whose cries for help while being assaulted went ignored by her neighbors. Good casting but the pacing deteriorates. 100m/C VHS. Raul Julia, John Ryan, Lucie Arnaz, Ed Asner, Art Carney, Diahann Carroll, Kate Jackson, Cloris Leachman, Tina Louise, Nancy Walker, Eric (Hans Gudegast) Braeden, Allyn Ann McLerie, Tony Dow, Sally Kirkland, Helen Hunt; **D:** Richard T. Heffron; **W:** Stirling Silliphant. **TV**

Death Screams ✍ 1983 (R) Attractive college coeds have a party and get hacked to pieces for their troubles by a machete-wielding maniac. 88m/C VHS. Susen Kiger, Jennifer Chase, Jody Kay, William T. Nick Nolte, William Schallert; **D:** David Nelson; **W:** Paul Elliot. **M:** Laurence Rosenthal. **TV**

Death Sentence ✍½ 2007 (R) Nick Hume (Bacon) is a suited exec with a seemingly picture-perfect life: beautiful wife (Preston), two sons, comfortable suburban digs. Out for an evening hockey game, Nick and oldest son Brendan (Lafferty) stop for gas in a seedy neighborhood and in the blink of an eye, find themselves part of a gang initiation that ends in Brendan's brutal murder at the hands of gangbanger wannabe Joe Darly (O'Leary). Joe's caught, but Nick has his own idea of justice for Joe and his gang, and it doesn't involve a jail cell. Unfortunately the film can't decide if it wants to be a thoughtful melodrama or an overly-violent action thriller, so it misses both targets. Missed opportunities for redemption and social commentary make this just another vigilante shoot-em-up. 105m/C DVD. US Kevin Bacon, Garrett Hedlund, Kelly Preston, Aisha 'Yier, John Goodman, Matt O'Leary, Jordan Garrett, Stuart Lafferty; **D:** James Wan; **W:** Ian Mackenzie Jeffers; **C:** John R. Leonetti; **M:** Charlie Clouser.

Death Ship ✍ 1980 (R) A luxury liner is destroyed by an ancient, mysterious freighter on open seas, leaving the survivors 'o confront the ghost ship's inherent evil in this slow-going horror flick. 91m/C VHS. GB CA George Kennedy, Richard Crenna, Nick Mancuso, Sally Ann Howes, Saul Rubinek, Kate Reid, Victoria Burgoyne, Danny Higham, Jennifer Mackinnon; **D:** Alvin Rakoff; **W:** John Robins; **C:** Rene Verzier; **M:** Ivor Slaney.

Death Shot ✍ 1973 Two plainclothes detectives (who seem just as sleazy as the criminals they're trying to bust) try to break up a drug ring and find that, with a little coercion, their best sources of information are the pimps and junkies they want to stop. Senseless attempt to make an action pic. 90m/C VHS. Richard C. Watt, Frank Himes; **D:** Mitch Brown.

Death Spa WOOF! 1987 (R) A health club is possessed by the spirit of a vengeful woman. The fitness craze takes on a campy new twist. 87m/C VHS. William Bumiller, Brenda Bakke, Merritt Buttrick; **D:** Michael Fischa.

Death Sport ✍½ 1978 (R) Another offering from Corman and Carradine follows, but isn't really a sequel of "Death Race 2000." Carradine is Kaz Oshay, leading a band of rebels against organized society. Upon capture Kaz participates in Death Sport, resulting in a show of fighting to the cult hit, but it seems to fit into the genre. 83m/C VHS, DVD. David Carradine, Claudia Jennings, Richard Lynch, William (Bill) Smith, Will Walker, David McLean, Jesse Vint; **D:** Allan Arkush, Nicholas Niciphor; **C:** Gary Graver; **M:** Andrew Stein.

The Death Squad ✍✍ 1973 A police commissioner hires an ex-cop 'o find a series of gangland-style executions. Good cast, though that's about all this flick has got going for it. 74m/C VHS. Robert Forster, Melvyn Douglas, Michelle Phillips, Mark Goddard, Bert Remsen, Claude Akins; **D:** Harry Falk. **TV**

Death Stalk ✍½ 1974 Dream vacation turns nightmarish for two couples when the wives are taken hostage by several escaped convicts. 90m/C VHS. Vince Edwards, Vic Morrow, Anjanette Comer, Robert Webber, Carol Lynley, Neville Brand, Norman Fell; **D:** Robert Day. **TV**

Death Takes a Holiday ✍✍✍ 1934 Death (March) is bored and wonders why humans fear him so much. He takes on human form, pretending to be a handsome Prince Sirki, and become as a guest of Italian nobleman. Duke Lambert (Standing). He bewilders most, except the lovely Grazia (Venable), who falls in love with him. And when she does, nothing dies because Death is also in love and not attending to business. But Death is also afraid to reveal his true self for fear of repelling her. Based on Alberto Casela's play and the inspiration for the bloated 1998 "Meet Joe Black." 79m/B VHS. Fredric March, Evelyn Venable, Guy Standing, Katherine Alexander, Gail Patrick, Helen Westley, Kent Taylor, Edward Van Sloan; **D:** Mitchell Leisen; **W:** Maxwell Anderson, Gladys Lehman, Walter Ferris; **C:** Charles Biryani; Lang Jr.

Death Target ✍½ 1983 Three former mercenaries team up for one last mission that gets sidetracked when one of the soldiers-of-fortune falls for a worker with a habit. 72m/C VHS, Jorge Montesi, Elaine Lakeman; **D:** Peter Hyams.

Death Tide ✍ 1958 Hoodlums pirate a ship full of diamonds in this story of death and crime on the high seas. *m/B VHS. Frank Silvera, Joan Alexander; **D:** Victor Komorow.

Death to Smoochy ✍ 2002 (F) DeVito-directed dark comedy follows a clash of the clowns: one good and one evil. Rainbow Randolph (Williams), is the corrupt, alcoholic star of a kiddie show fired over a bribery scandal and replaced by his polar opposite: Barney-esque purple rhino good-guy, Smoochy (Norton). Keener is the ruthless Kidsnet exec who takes orders from her fetid network boss (Stewart). Director DeVito doubles as a loathsome agent. Although Norton is proficient as the cloying, wide-eyed kiddie magnet and Williams clearly revels in ranting, this over-the-top to the point of ugliness revenge comedy's one note joke wears thin and behind the scenes kiddie show satire is way less subtle than t needs to be. 109m/C VHS, DVD. US Robin Williams, Edward Norton, Catherine Keener, Danny DeVito, Jon Stewart, Harvey Fierstein, Michael Rispoli, Pam Ferris, Danny Woodburn, Vincent Schiavelli; **D:** Danny DeVito; **W:** Adam Resnick; **C:** Anastas Michos; **M:** David Newman.

Death Train ✍½ 1979 Dead man seems to have been struck by a trar', but seems wrong for the women when they are trapped inside a deserted—and haunted—asylum with the only route to safety being an underground tunnel through

Death Tunnel ✍½ 2005 (R) A college freshman initiation gag goes 'c terribly wrong for five women when they are trapped inside a deserted—and haunted—asylum with the only route to safety being an underground tunnel through which scores of deceased patients had once traveled. Filmed at the actual site of the Waverly Hills Sanatorium, which was built in the early 1900s and housed patients suffering from tuberculosis; many local residents were offended by the content of the film. **97m/C DVD.** Steffany Huckaby, Melanie Lewis, Yolanda Pecoraro, Kristin Novak, Annie Burgstede; *D:* Philip Adrian Booth; *W:* Philip Adrian Booth, Christopher Saint Booth. **VIDEO**

Death Valley 🐾🐾½ **1946** Greed turns gold prospectors in Death Valley against each other. **70m/C VHS.** Robert Lowery, Helen Gilbert, Sterling Holloway; *D:* Lew Landers.

Death Valley 🐾🐾½ **1981 (R)** Good cast, lousy plot. Youngster (Billingsley) gets caught with a psycho cowpoke while visiting mom in Arizona. **90m/C VHS, DVD.** Paul LeMat, Catherine Hicks, Peter Billingsley, Wilford Brimley, Edward Hermann, Stephen McHattie; *D:* Dick Richards; *C:* Stephen Burum.

Death Valley Manhunt 🐾🐾 **1943** A marshal hired to protect a man's oil wells discovers that the company manager is keeping the profits for himself. **55m/B VHS.** William (Wild Bill) Elliott, George "Gabby" Hayes, Anne Jeffreys; *D:* John English.

Death Valley Rangers 🐾🐾½ **1944** The hero pretends to be an outlaw to expose a gang robbing gold-laden stagecoaches. **55m/B VHS.** Ken Maynard, Hoot Gibson, Bob Steele, Linda Brent, Kenneth Harlan; *D:* Robert Emmett Tansey.

Death Valley: The Revenge of Bloody Bill 🐾 **2004** Several college students on a road trip are carjacked by drug dealer Earl (Bastien) who takes them to the ghost town of Sunset Valley in search of his missing partner. Seems the town is haunted by the spirit of vengeful Confederate soldier "Bloody Bill" Anderson (Bouvet), who uses zombies to make his guests feel at home. **88m/C DVD.** Scott Carson, Chrissa Jean, Jeremy Bouvet, Gregory Bastien, Denise Boutte, Matt Marraccini, Steven Glinn, Kandis Erickson; *D:* Byron Werner; *W:* John Yuan, Matt Yuan; *C:* Byron Werner; *M:* Ralph Rieckermann.

Death Warmed Up 🐾🐾½ **1985** A crazed brain surgeon turns ordinary people into bloodthirsty mutants, and a small group of young people travel to his secluded island to try to stop him. **83m/C VHS.** Michael Hurst, Margaret Umbers, David Letch; *D:* David Blyth.

Death Warrant 🐾🐾 **1990 (R)** Van Damme whams and barns a little less than usual in this cop-undercover-in-prison testosterone fest. As a Royal Canadian Mountie undercover in a prison—where inmates are perishing under mysterious circumstances—the pectoral-perfect Muscles from Brussels on the brink of addling two plus two when an inmate transferee threatens his cover. Contains the requisite gratuitous violence, prison bromide, and miscellaneous other Van Dammeages. **111m/C VHS, DVD.** Jean-Claude Van Damme, Robert Guillaume, Cynthia Gibb, George Dickerson, Patrick Kilpatrick; *D:* Deran Sarafian; *W:* David S. Goyer; *C:* Russell Carpenter; *M:* Gary Chang.

Death Watch 🐾🐾🐾 **1980 (R)** In the future, media abuse is taken to an all time high as a terminally ill woman's last days are secretly filmed by a man with a camera in his head. Intelligent, adult science fiction with an excellent cast. **128m/C VHS.** *FR GE* Romy Schneider, Harvey Keitel, Harry Dean Stanton, Max von Sydow; *D:* Bertrand Tavernier; *W:* Bertrand Tavernier, David Rayfiel.

Death Weekend 🐾🐾½ *House by the Lake* **1976** A woman is stalked by a trio of murderous, drunken hoodlums who seek to spoil her weekend. **89m/C VHS.** *CA* Brenda Vaccaro, Don Stroud, Chuck Shamata, Richard Ayres, Kyle Edwards; *D:* William Fruet.

Death Wish 🐾🐾🐾½ **1974 (R)** Paul Kersey (Bronson) is a middle-aged businessman who turns vigilante after his wife and daughter are raped and left for dead by a gang of hoodlums (one is Goldblum in his film debut). He stalks the streets of New York seeking revenge on other muggers, pimps, and crooks, making the neighborhood safer for those less macho. Brosnan's his usual stoic self and the violence could be deemed excessive—certainly Brian Garfield, whose novel the film is based on, thought so. **93m/C VHS, DVD.** Charles Bronson, Vincent Gardenia, William Redfield, Hope Lange, Jeff Goldblum, Stuart Margolin, Olympia Dukakis; *D:* Michael Winner; *W:* Wendell Mayes; *C:* Arthur Ornitz; *M:* Herbie Hancock.

Death Wish 2 WOOF! **1982 (R)** Bronson re-creates the role of Paul Kersey, an architect who takes the law into his own hands when his family is victimized once again. Extremely violent sequel to the successful 1974 movie. Followed by "Death Wish 3" (1985) and 4 (1987) in which Bronson continues to torture the street scum and the viewers as well. **89m/C VHS.** Charles Bronson, J.D. Cannon, Jill Ireland, Vincent Gardenia, Anthony (Tony) Franciosa, Laurence Fishburne; *D:* Michael Winner; *C:* Richard H. Kline; *M:* Jimmy Page.

Death Wish 3 🐾🐾½ **1985 (R)** Once again, Charles Bronson blows away the low lifes who have killed those who were dear to him and were spared in the first two films. **100m/C VHS, DVD.** Charles Bronson, Martin Balsam, Deborah Raffin, Ed Lauter, Alex Winter, Marina Sirtis; *D:* Michael Winner; *M:* Jimmy Page.

Death Wish 4: The Crackdown 🐾🐾 **1987 (R)** The four-times-weary urban vigilante (Bronson) gets involved in a club with an unusual mission—suicide. **100m/C VHS, DVD.** Charles Bronson, John P. Ryan, Kay Lenz, Danny (Daniel) Webb; *D:* J. Lee Thompson.

Death Wish 5: The Face of Death WOOF! **1994 (R)** Paul Kersey (Bronson) returns to vigilantism when his clothing manufacturer fiancee Olivia (Downs) has her business threatened by mobsters, one of whom turns out to be her sadistic ex (Parks). Bronson looks bored with the rehashed material. Lots of explicit and grisly violence. **95m/C VHS, DVD.** Charles Bronson, Lesley-Anne Down, Michael Parks, Kenneth Welsh; *D:* Allan Goldstein; *W:* Allan Goldstein; *C:* Curtis Petersen; *M:* Terry Plumeri.

Death Wish Club 🐾½ *Carnival of Fools* **1983** Young woman gets involved in a club with an unusual mission—suicide. **93m/C VHS.** Meridith Haze, Rick Barnis, J. Martin Sellers, Ann Fairchild; *D:* John Carr.

Deathcheaters 🐾🐾½ **1976 (G)** Australian Secret Service offers two stuntmen a top secret mission in the Philippines. **96m/C VHS.** John Hargreaves, Grant Page, Noel Ferrer; *D:* Brian Trenchard-Smith; *W:* Michael Cove.

Deathdream 🐾🐾🐾 *Dead of Night; Night Walk; The Veteran; The Night Andy Came Home* **1972** In this reworking of the "Monkey's Paw" tale, a mother wishes her dead son would return from Vietnam. He does, but he's not quite the person he used to be. Gripping plot gives new meaning to the saying, "Be careful what you wish for—it might come true." One of Tom Savini's earliest F/X assignments. **98m/C VHS, DVD.** *CA* John Marley, Richard Backus, Lynn Carlin, Alan Ormsby; *D:* Bob (Benjamin) Clark; *W:* Alan Ormsby; *C:* Jack McGowan; *M:* Carl Zittrer.

Deathfight 🐾🐾½ **1993 (R)** Let's face it, no one watches these movies because they have a plot. This is a fast-paced B-grade martial arts flick with numerous butts getting kicked. Oh, all right, if you insist on a plot—Norton's evil half-brother (Guerrero) is trying to turn their legitimate family business into a criminal front by framing Norton for murder. **92m/C VHS.** Richard Norton, Franco Guerrero, Karen Moncrieff, Chuck Jeffreys, Ron Vreeken, Tetchie Agbayani, Joe Mari Avellana; *D:* Anthony Maharaj; *W:* Tom Huckabee.

Deathhead Virgin 🐾½ **1974 (R)** An evil virgin spirit is waiting to possess one of two men eager to find a sunken fortune. The fate of the fortunate one is only death! **94m/C VHS.** Jock Gaynor, Larry Ward, Diane McBain, Vic Diaz; *D:* Norman Foster; *W:* Jock Gaynor, Larry Ward; *C:* Fred Conde; *M:* Richard LaSalle.

Deathmask 🐾🐾 **1969** A four-year-old boy's corpse is found buried in a cardboard box, and a medical examiner—whose daughter met a similar fate—investigates the murder. Could've been done more tastefully. **102m/C VHS.** Farley Granger, Ruth Warrick, Danny Aiello; *D:* Richard Friedman.

Deathmoon 🐾🐾½ **1978** A businessman plagued by recurring werewolf nightmares goes on a Hawaiian vacation to try to forget his troubles. Made for television. **90m/C VHS.** Robert Foxworth, Joe Penny, Debralee Scott, Dolph Sweet, Charles Haid; *D:* Bruce Kessler. **TV**

Deathrow Gameshow 🐾🐾½ **1988** Condemned criminals can either win their freedom or die in front of millions on a new TV show that doesn't win the host many friends. **78m/C VHS.** John McCafferty, Robin Blythe, Beano, Mark Lasky; *D:* Mark Pirro; *W:* Mark Pirro.

Deathstalker WOOF! *El Cazador de la Muerte* **1983 (R)** Deathstalker sets his sights on seizing the evil wizard Munkar's magic amulet so he can take over Munkar's castle. The only excuse for making such an idiotic film seems to have been to fill it with half-naked women. Filmed in Argentina and followed by two sequels that were an improvement. **80m/C VHS, DVD.** Richard (Rick) Hill, Barbi Benton, Richard Brooker, Victor Bo, Lana Clarkson; *D:* John Watson; *W:* Howard R. Cohen; *C:* Leonardo Solis; *M:* Oscar Cardozo Ocampo.

Deathstalker 2: Duel of the Titans 🐾 **1987 (R)** Campy fantasy comically pits the lead character against an evil wizard. Sword-and-sorcery spoof doesn't take itself too seriously. **85m/C VHS, DVD.** John Terlesky, Monique Gabrielle, John Lazar, Toni Naples, Maria Socas, Deanna (Dee) Booher; *D:* Jim Wynorski; *W:* Jim Wynorski; *C:* Leonardo Solis; *M:* Chuck Cirino.

Deathstalker 3 🐾½ *Deathstalker 3: The Warriors From Hell* **1989 (R)** Another humorous entry in the Deathstalker saga. This time there's action, romance, magic and the Warriors From Hell. **85m/C VHS.** John Allen Nelson, Carla Herd, Terri Treas, Thom Christopher; *D:* Alfonso Corona; *W:* Howard R. Cohen.

Deathstalker 4: Match of Titans 🐾 **1992 (R)** The sword and sorcery epic continues, with our hero revealing yet more musculature in his efforts to defeat an evil queen and her legion of stone warriors. **85m/C VHS, DVD.** Richard (Rick) Hill, Maria Ford, Michelle Moffett, Brett (Baxter) Clark; *D:* Howard R. Cohen.

Deathtrap 🐾🐾🐾 **1982 (PG)** A creatively blocked playwright, his ailing rich wife, and a former student who has written a surefire hit worth killing for, are the principals in this compelling comedy-mystery. Cross and double-cross are explored in this film based on the Broadway hit by Ira Levin. **116m/C VHS, DVD.** Henry Jones, Michael Caine, Christopher Reeve, Dyan Cannon, Irene Worth; *D:* Sidney Lumet; *W:* Jay Presson Allen; *C:* Andrzej Bartkowiak; *M:* Johnny Mandel.

Deathwatch 🐾🐾½ **2002 (R)** After an intensely bloody World War I battle, nine soldiers get off-track inside a massive labyrinth of deserted German trenches filled with mounds of the deceased and packed with a mother lode of rats. Further complicating matters is a deadly unearthly force that pits the men against one another for the uninspired dialogue. **95m/C VHS, DVD.** Jamie Bell, Ruaidhri Conroy, Laurence Fox, Dean Lennox Kelly, Kris Marshall, Hans Matheson, Hugh O'Conor, Matthew Rhys, Andy Serkis, Hugo Speer, Mike Downey, Roman Horak; *D:* Michael J. Bassett; *W:* Michael J. Bassett; *C:* Hubert Taczanowski; *M:* Curt Cress. **VIDEO**

D.E.B.S. 🐾🐾 **2004 (PG-13)** Low-budget riot grrl send-up of "Charlie's Angels" begs the question "Why parody something that never took itself seriously in the first place?" A secret government agency known as the D.E.B.S. recruits nubile teenage girls through trick questions in the S.A.T. that identify their willingness to lie, cheat, and kill. After the team monitors supervillian Lucy Diamond (Brewster) during her blind date with assassin Ninotchka (Cauffiel), leader Amy (Foster) gets a crush on Lucy, which jeopardizes the whole team. Even with the lesbianism added for extra taste, Robinson can't elevate her material beyond its one-joke premise. Pretty anemic comedy, but plenty for schoolgirl fetishists to be happy about. **91m/C DVD.** *US* Sara Foster, Jordana Brewster, Meagan Good, Devon Aoki, Jill Ritchie, Holland Taylor, Michael Clarke Duncan, Jimmi Simpson, Jessica Cauffiel, Geoff Stults; *D:* Angela Robinson; *W:* Angela Robinson; *C:* M. David Mullen; *M:* Steven Stern.

The Debt 🐾🐾 *Back to Even* **1998 (R)** Printing press operator Mitch's (Lamas) gambling problems get him deeply in debt to local wiseguy Danny Boyle (Pare) who gets Mitch to help him in a counterfeiting operation. Usual gangster cliches but the action moves along. **92m/C VHS, DVD.** Lorenzo Lamas, Michael Pare, Heidi Thomas, Angela Jones, Herb Mitchell; *D:* Rod Hewitt; *W:* Rod Hewitt; *C:* Garrett Fisher. **VIDEO**

The Debt 🐾🐾½ **2003** Safecracker Geoff Dresner (Clarke) has left his criminal past behind until his stupid son-in-law Terry (Freeman) fails to repay a dangerous loan shark. In order to protect his family, Geoff agrees to do one last job, which goes horribly wrong. **110m/C DVD.** Warren Clarke, Martin Freeman, Hugo Speer, Lee Williams, Orla Brady, Barbara Marten, Amanda Abbington; *D:* Jon Jones; *W:* Richard McBrien; *C:* John Pardue; *M:* Martin Phipps. **TV**

A Decade Under the Influence 🐾🐾🐾½ **2002 (R)** Filmmakers LaGravenese and Demme chronicle the rise of new, independent filmmakers from the ashes of the old Hollywood studio system, beginning in 1967 with such films as "The Graduate" and "Bonnie & Clyde" and ending in 1977 with "Star Wars." Contains extensive film clips and interviews with diretors, actors, writers, and producers. Originally a three-part series shown on the Independent Film Channel; a theatrical version was released at 108 minutes. **180m/C DVD.** *US D:* Richard LaGravenese, Ted (Edward) Demme; *C:* Clyde Smith, Anthony Janelli; *M:* John Kimbrough.

The Decalogue 🐾🐾🐾🐾½ **1988** Originally produced for Polish TV, Kieslowski's 10-hour epic offers moments from the lives of residents of a late-Communist era Warsaw apartment complex. Each of the segments is a modern retelling of the Ten Commandments as the individuals confront morality, ethics, betrayal, and a variety of human frailities and crises. Polish with subtitles. **584m/C VHS, DVD.** *PL* Krystyna Janda, Aleksander Bardini, Maja Komorowska, Daniel Olbrychski, Janusz Gajos, Maria Pakulnis, Jerzy Stuhr, Zbigniew Zamachowski, Boguslaw Linda, Artur Barcis, Henryk Baranowski; *D:* Krzysztof Kieslowski; *C:* Wieslaw Zdort, Edward Klosinski, Krzysztof Pakulski, Slawomir Idziak, Witold Adamek, Dariusz Kuc, Andrzej Jaroszewicz, Piotr Sobocinski, Jacek Blawut; *M:* Zbigniew Preisner. **TV**

The Decameron 🐾🐾🐾½ *Il Decameron* **1970 (R)** Pasolini's first epic pageant in his "Trilogy of Life" series. An acclaimed, sexually explicit adaptation of a handful of the Boccaccio tales. In Italian with English subtitles. **111m/C VHS, DVD.** *FR IT GE* Franco Citti, Ninetto Davoli, Angela Luce, Patrizia Capparelli, Jovan Jovanovich, Silvana Mangano, Pier Paolo Pasolini; *D:* Pier Paolo Pasolini; *M:* Ennio Morricone. Berlin Intl. Film Fest. '71: Silver Prize.

Decameron Nights 🐾🐾½ **1953** Story of Boccaccio's pursuit of a recently widowed young women is interwoven amongst the three of the 14th century Italian writer's bawdy tales. **87m/C VHS.** *GB* Louis Jourdan, Joan Fontaine, Binnie Barnes, Joan Collins, Marjorie Rhodes; *D:* Hugo Fregonese.

Decay WOOF! **1998** Katherine (Davies) is bored by dentist hubby Richard (Brock) and takes up with sleazy nightclub owner Ronnie (Storli), who offers to set up a hit on her spouse. But the hit man turns out to be a serial killer who specializes in strippers and—unbeknownst to his wife—the dentist has mob ties. The plot's actually more convoluted and not worth your time and effort. **86m/C VHS.** Tamara Davies, Raymond Storli, Robert Z'Dar, Brian Brock, Ron von Gober; *D:* Jason Robert Stephens; *W:* Jason Robertson.

et Stephens; **C:** Dennis Devine; **M:** Jonathan Price.

December Boys ☆☆½ 2007 (PG-13) The four "December Boys"—named so because they were all born in December—Sparks (Byers), Spit (Fraser), Misty (Cormie) and Maps (Radcliffe—yep, Harry Potter) are tight friends, and all orphans in Australia in the 60s. The 'teens get to leave the orphanage for a seaside holiday

December ☆☆ 1991 (PG) Four prep-school students in New Hampshire must confront the reality of war when the Japanese bomb Pearl Harbor. A touching story of courage and friendship that takes place in one night during the surprise-attack. 92m/C VHS, DVD. Wil Wheaton, Chris Young, Brian Krause, Balthazar Getty, Jason London; **D:** Gabe Torres.

The Deceivers ☆☆ 1988 (PG-13) Brosnan stars as a British officer sent on a dangerous undercover mission in 1820s India. He's to infiltrate the notorious Thuggee cult, known for robbing and murdering unwary travelers. Interesting premise falters due to slow pacing and Brosnan's lack of believability. 112m/C VHS, DVD. IN GB Pierce Brosnan, Saeed Jaffrey, Shashi Kapoor, Keith Michell; **D:** Nicholas Meyer; **C:** Walter Lassally.

Deceit ☆☆ 1989 (R) A sci-fi sex comedy with an environmental premise. Bailey and Brick are two aliens working for their planet's Environmental Protection Agency, whose idea of protection is to vaporize polluter planets. Guess which planet is next on their hit list. But before they get down to business, our two alien studs want to do the horizontal bop with two moments on earth. It has a happy ending. 92m/C VHS, Scott Paulin, Norbert Weisser, Samantha (Sam) Phillips; **D:** Albert Pyun; **M:** Kitty Chalmers.

Deceived ☆☆½ 1991 (PG-13) A successful career woman with a husband and a young daughter feels she has it all until her husband is apparently killed in a bizarre tragedy. But just how well did she know the man she married? Who was he really and what secrets are hidden in his past? As she struggles to solve these mysteries, her own life becomes endangered in this psychological thriller. 115m/C VHS, DVD. Goldie Hawn, John Heard, Ashley Peldon, Jan Rubes, Amy Wright, Maia Filar, Kate Reid; **D:** Damian Harris; **W:** Mary Agnes Donoghue, Derek Saunders; **C:** Jack N. Green; **M:** Thomas Newman.

Deceiver ☆☆ *Liar* 1997 (R) Contrived psychological thriller starts out with the requisite dead prostitute (Zellweger, in a questionable career move) and the rounding up of the usual suspects, settling on disturbed but brainy Princeton grad Wayland (in the film con Roth). Twin directors Jonas and Joshua Pate's convoluted spin on a noirish murder mystery follows up their 1996 debut, "Grave." 102m/C VHS, DVD. Renee Zellweger, Tim Roth, Christopher Penn, Michael Rooker, Ellen Burstyn, Rosanna Arquette; **D:** Jonas Pate, Josh Pate; **W:** Jonas Pate, Josh Pate; **C:** Bill Butler; **M:** Harry Gregson-Williams.

Deception ☆½ *Ruby Cairo* 1992 (PG-13) Talented cast is wasted in an old-fashioned mystery that lacks a coherent script. MacDowell is married to Mortensen, the owner of an aircraft salvage company. He's supposedly killed in a plane crash but she thinks he's just pulled a fast one and sets off to find him. tracking her hubby's secret bank accounts takes her all over the world, and finally to Cairo, Egypt where she meets Neeson. Together they discover Mortensen's scam involves smuggling poison gas and the duo then try to outwit the hoods on their trail. Film was originally released at 110 minutes. 90m/C VHS. Andie MacDowell, Liam Neeson, Viggo Mortensen, Jack Thompson, Jeff Corey, Miriam Reed, Luis Cortes, Paco Mauri; **D:** Graeme Clifford; **W:** Robert Dillon, Michael Thomas; **M:** John Barry.

Deception ☆☆ 1946 Davis is a pianist torn between two loves: her intensely jealous sponsor (Rains) and her cellist boyfriend (Henreid). Plot in danger of going over the melodramatic edge is saved by the very effective performances of the stars. 112m/B VHS. Bette Davis, Paul Henreid, Claude Rains, John Abbott, Benson Fong; **D:** Irving Rapper.

Deception ☆½ 2008 (R) McGregor is a milquetoast accountant, Jackman is a silky snake, and Williams is a bionce sexductress. If you can buy the leads in these roles you may possibly find some enjoyment in this transparent thriller. Corporate numbers-cruncher Jonathan (McGregor) is led on a journey into NYC's anonymous sex underground by lawyer Wyatt ("Jack"-man). Among the women Jonathan meets is the mysterious S (Williams), who soon disappears. The sex is all a set-up for something much more dangerous but—as

December Bride ☆☆½ 1991 Determined young woman (Reeves) becomes the housekeeper to two taciturn Irish farmer/brothers (Hinds and McCann) and proceeds to bully them into prosperity in early 20th century rural Ireland. She also scandalizes the community by sleeping with both men and refusing to marry either—even after she becomes pregnant. Based on the novel by Sam Hanna Bell. 88m/C VHS. IR Saskia Reeves, Donal McCann, Patrick Malahide, Brenda Bruce, Ciaran Hinds, David Ruckin; **D:** Thaddeus O'Sullivan; **M:** Richard Hartley.

December Flower ☆☆½ 1984 A young woman arrives at her aunt's estate so she can nurse her back to health, but she finds her aunt a bit down in the mouth; seems someone is trying to kill her, and she could be next in line. 65m/C VHS. Jean Simmons, Mona Washbourne, Bryan Forbes; **D:** Stephen Frears; **M:** Carlo Giaco.

December 7th: The Movie ☆☆ 1991 Banned for 50 years by the U.S. Government, this planned Hollywood explanation to wartime audiences of the Pearl Harbor debacle offers such "offensive" images as blacks fighting heroically alongside whites, loyal Japanese-Americans, and Uncle Sam asleep on the morning of the attack. The Chief of Naval Operations comes off as an original film, claiming it condemned the Navy. The battle scenes were so realistic they fooled even documentarians. This isn't the most incisive video on the event—just an unforgettable snapshot. 82m/B VHS, DVD. Walter Huston, Harry Davenport. **D:** John Ford; **M:** Alfred Newman.

Deck the Halls ☆½ 2006 (PG) Joyless holiday fare pumped out by the studio to scrooge a few dollars from its Christmas mall crowd. Steven (Broderick) is the smug, self-appointed "Christmas guy" of a sleepy New England town, making sure the holidays are celebrated tastefully. His crass neighbor Buddy (DeVito) wants to put enough lights on his house so that it can be seen from space. A war of childish pranks erupts between the two until a forced lesson on the "true meaning of Christmas" is tacked onto the ending. File this one in the Bastard Children of "Christmas Vacation" folder. 93m/C DVD. US Danny DeVito, Matthew Broderick, Kristen Davis, Kristin Chenoweth, Alia Shawkat, Jorge Garcia, Dylan Blue, Kelly Aldridge, Sabrina Aldridge; **D:** John Whitesell; **W:** Don Rhymer, Matt Corman, Chris Ord; **C:** Mark Irwin; **M:** George S. Clinton.

The Decline of the American Empire ☆☆☆½ *Le Déclin De L'Empire Américain* 1986 (R) The critically acclaimed French-Canadian film about eight academic intellectuals who spend a weekend shedding their sophistication and engaging in interwining sexual affairs. Examines the differing attitudes of men and women in regards to sex and sexuality. In French with English subtitles. 102m/C VHS, DVD. CA Dominique Michel, Dorothee Berryman, Louise Portal, Genevieve Rioux; **D:** Denys Arcand; **W:** Denys Arcand, Genevieve Rioux; **C:** Guy Dufaux. AWARDS: Cannes '86; Genie '87; Director (Arcand), Support. Actor (Arcand), Support. Actress (Portal). N.Y. Film Critics '86: Foreign Film; Toronto-City '86: Canadian Feature Film.

Decline of Western Civilization ☆☆☆ 1981 The L.A. hard core punk scene. Music by X, Circle Jerks, Black Flag, Fear and more. 100m/C VHS. **D:** Penelope Spheeris.

Decline of Western Civilization 2: The Metal Years ☆☆½ 1988 (R) Following Spheeris's first documentary about hardcore punk, she in turn delves into the world of heavy metal rock. We are given a look at some of the early rockers, as well as some of the smaller bands still playing L.A. clubs. Features appearances by Alice Cooper, Ozzy Osbourne, Poison, Gene Simmons, and Megadeth. 90m/C VHS. Alice Cooper, Ozzy Osbourne, Gene Simmons, Lizzie Borden; **D:** Penelope Spheeris.

Deconstructing Harry ☆☆☆½ 1997 (R) Interesting idea has Allen as a successful author, Harry Block, whose thinly veiled autobiographical fiction spills the beans on his ex-wives, lovers, friends, and family, thereby pissing them all off. Toggles back and forth between Harry's "real life and scenes from his books, giving character's and situations two versions: one slanted to suit Harry and a more real than Harry wants or knows how to deal with. Infidelity, divorce, and art all get their usual treatment. Another art bad, but not great project by Allen that may be too self-absorbed for most. Features an elaborate, star-studded cast, mostly, delegated to minor roles. 96m/C VHS, DVD. Woody Allen, Billy Crystal, Judy Davis, Elisabeth Shue, Kirstie Alley, Caroline Aaron, Bob Balaban, Richard Benjamin, Eric Bogosian, Mariel Hemming-

the title blatantly proclaims—nothing is what it seems. 108m/C DVD. US Ewan McGregor, Hugh Jackman, Michelle Williams, Maggie Q, Rachael Taylor, Natasha Henstridge, Lisa Gay Hamilton, Charlotte Rampling, Margaret Colin, Paz de la Huerta; **D:** Marcel Langenegger; **W:** Mark Bomback; **C:** Dante Spinotti; **M:** Ramin Djawadi.

Deceptions ☆☆ 1990 (R) A risque, semi-erotic thriller about a wealthy society woman (Sheridan) who kills her husband. Sheridan claims that she acted in self-defense, but macho cop Hamlin has a different view. He interrogates her, grows increasingly attracted, and is drawn into her web of seduction. 105m/C VHS, Harry Hamlin, Nicolette Sheridan; **D:** Ruben Preuss; **W:** Richard G. Taylor.

Deceptions 2: Edge of Deception ☆½ 1994 (R) Voyeur detective becomes obsessed with his comely neighbor, leading to unpleasant consequences. 100m/C VHS, Mariel Hemingway, Jennifer Rubin, Stephen Shellen; **D:** George Mihalka.

way; Amy Irving, Julie Kavner, Eric Lloyd, Julia Louis-Dreyfus, Tobey Maguire, Demi Moore, Stanley Tucci, Robin Williams, Philip Bosco, Gene Saks, Hazelle Goodman; **D:** Woody Allen; **W:** Woody Allen; **C:** Carlo Di Palma; **M:** Woody Allen.

Deconstructing Sarah ☆☆ 1994 (R) Sarah Vincent (Ticotin) is a high-powered but bored ad exec who assumes an alter-ego, Ruth, when she heads for the wrong side of the tracks in her pursuit of casual sex. Her secret life is discovered when Sarah is murdered and best friend Elizabeth (Kelley) begins to turn up some unlikely suspects. Fast-paced whodunit with good cast work. 120m/C VHS, Rachel Ticotin, Sheila Kelley, A. Martinez, David Andrews, John Vickery, Jennifer Lewis, Dwier Brown, Peter Jason; **D:** Craig R. Baxley; **W:** Lee Rose; **C:** Joao Fernandes; **M:** Tim Scott. TV.

Decoration Day ☆☆☆ 1990 (PG) Garner plays reclusive retired Southern judge Albert Sidney Finch who aids an angry black childhood friend, Gee (Cobbs), who has refused to accept his long-overdue Medal of Honor. Investigating the tragic secret that has repercussions for everyone involved. Based on the novel by John William Corrington. A Hallmark Hall of Fame presentation. 99m/C VHS, DVD. James Garner, Bill Cobbs, Judith Ivey, Ruby Dee, Laurence Fishburne, Jo Anderson, Peter Jason; **D:** Robert Markowitz; **W:** Robert W. Lenski. TV.

Decoy ☆☆½ 1946 Oooooh—bad girl flick! Margot (Gillie) is the heartless moll of death row gangster Olins (Armstrong) who won't reveal where he hid $400K. So Margot gets rival gangster Vincent (Norris) to agree to help her remove Olin's body from the gas chamber and 'force prison doc Craig (Rudley) to revive him with a special drug. The plan works—sorta—Olin revives, hands Margot a map, Vincent kills him for real, and they take the doc hostage as they go 'for the dough. But Margot doesn't want to split the loot, see, so she just happens to run over Vincent several times. There's also a prime detective cross as Margot relates her 'crime doesn't pay' tale to a cop (Leonard). 76m/B DVD. Edward Norris, Herbert Rudley, Robert Armstrong, Sheldon Leonard, Jean Gillie, Philip Van Zandt; **D:** Jack Bernhard; **W:** Nedrick Young; **C:** L.W. O'Connell; **M:** Edward Kay.

Decoy ☆☆ 1995 (R) Two ex-government operatives, Baxter (Weller) and Travis (Patrick), are hired by their former commanding officer, Wellington (Breck), to protect his daughter Diana (Vogel) from a grudge against dad. But then it turns out the job's a set-up, and Wellington and Jensen have their own deadly agenda. 98m/C VHS. Peter Weller, Robert Patrick, Darlene Vogel, Charlotte Lewis, Peter Breck, Scott Hylands; **D:** Victor Rambaldi; **W:** Robert Sarno; **C:** Jon Kranhouse; **M:** Mark Adler.

Dédée d'Anvers ☆☆☆½ *Woman of Antwerp* 1949 A gritty dockside melodrama about a drunken prostitute abused by her pimp. A sailor and a local barkeep don't like it. In French with subtitles. 95m/B VHS. Simone Signoret, Marcel Dalio, Bernard Blier, Marcel Pagliero, Jane (Jeanne) Marken; **D:** Yves Allegret; **C:** Jean (Yves Georges) Bourgoin.

A Dedicated Man ☆☆ 1986 A lonely businessman agrees to act as a wife for a businessman to lend him credibility. A British "Romance Theater" presentation. 60m/C VHS. GB Alec McCowen, Joan Plowright; **D:** Robert Knights.

Dedication ☆ 2007 (R) Henry Roth (Crudup), the most neurotic, compulsive children's book writer on the planet, finds himself without an illustrator after his collaborator Rudy (Wilkinson) dies suddenly. Henry and Rudy have had one big success together entitled "Marty the Beaver" and now Henry's editor forces a new illustrator, Lucy Reilly (Moore), on him to complete a "Marty" follow-up. Not easily accommodating change, Henry hates her, which isn't a surprise since he hates nearly everything. But wait, this is a romantic comedy, so of course his tune changes. Complications ensue in the forms of Rudy's ghost and Lucy's ex-lover, as well as her kooky mother. Worth a whirl if you can't get enough of the rom-com formula. **111m/C DVD. US** Billy Crudup, Mandy Moore, Tom Wilkinson, Bob Balaban, Dianne Wiest, Bobby Cannavale, Christine Taylor, Peter Bogdanovich, Martin Freeman; **D:** Justin Theroux; **W:** David Bromberg; **M:** Stephen Kazmierski; **M:** Ed Shearmur.

Dee Snider's Strangeland WOOF! *Strangeland* 1998 (R) Former Twisted Sister singer Dee Snider proves than he can fail at movie-making worse than he can fail as a musician. He wrote, produced and starred in this dud that proves it's possible to be stupid, disgusting and boring at the same time. Snider plays Captain Howdy, an internet chat room sicko who lures young girls into a dungeon and tortures them by involuntarily piercing them and trying to turn them into one of them. Gage plays the dim detective trying to find the hair-sculpting madman. Only proves that Snider with a movie camera is more dangerous than the internet. **90m/C VHS, DVD.** Dee Snider, Kevin Gage, Brett Harrelson, Elizabeth Pena, Robert Englund, Amy Smart, Linda Cardellini; **D:** John Pieplow; **W:** Dee Snider; **C:** Goran Pavicevic; **M:** Anton Sanko.

The Deep ✓✓ 1977 (PG) An innocent couple get involved in an underwater search for a shipwreck, and they quickly find themselves in over their heads. Gorgeous photography manages to keep this slow mover afloat. Famous for Bisset's wet T-shirt scene. Based on the novel by Peter Benchley. **123m/C VHS, DVD.** Nick Nolte, Jacqueline Bisset, Robert Shaw, Louis Gossett Jr., Eli Wallach; **D:** Peter Yates; **W:** Peter Benchley, Tracy Keenan Wynn; **C:** Christopher Challis; **M:** John Barry.

Deep Blue ✓✓✓½ 2003 (G) British documentary from the creators of the BBC TV series "The Blue Planet" about (what else) ocean life, which was shot in some 250 locations worldwide. Killer whales, gray whales, dolphins, sea lions, sharks, penguins, jellyfish, and a variety of other strange deep sea dwellers are shown going about their daily struggle to survive. All accompanied by some stunning cinematography and a lush score. **90m/C DVD. GB D:** Alastair Fothergill; **W:** Alastair Fothergill, Andy Byatt, Tim Ecott; **C:** Doug Allan, Peter Scoones; **M:** George Fenton; **Nar:** Michael Gambon.

Deep Blue Sea ✓✓½ 1999 (R) It's no longer safe to go back in the water. Marine biologist Susan McAlester (Burrows) is obsessed with finding a cure for Alzheimer's and has genetically enhanced the brains of a group of test sharks at a floating research facility off the Baja coast. Oh, and she didn't bother to tell anyone else in her group about these smarter-than-the-average sharks. But they soon learn, when the research facility suffers several accidents, begins to flood, and the sharks get loose—and looking for snacks. It's not a bomb but it's also nothing that you haven't seen before. And the fake sharks look, well, fake (and hokey). **105m/ C VHS, DVD.** Saffron Burrows, Samuel L. Jackson, Thomas Jane, LL Cool J, Jacqueline McKenzie, Michael Rapaport, Stellan Skarsgard, Aida Turturro; **D:** Renny Harlin; **W:** Duncan Kennedy, Donna Powers, Wayne Powers; **C:** Stephen Windon; **M:** Trevor Rabin.

Deep Core ✓✓ 2000 (PG-13) A rupture deep in the Earth's core causes a chain of natural disasters and could destroy the planet unless scientist Brian Goodman (Sheffer) can find a way to stop the geological threat. **90m/C VHS, DVD.** Craig Sheffer, James Russo, Terry Farrell, James Lew, Wil Wheaton, Bruce McGill; **D:** Rodney McDonald; **W:** Martin Lazarus; **C:** Richard Clabaugh. **VIDEO**

Deep Cover ✓✓½ 1992 (R) Fishburne plays Russell Stevens Jr., a straight-arrow cop who goes undercover to infiltrate a Latin American cocaine cartel. While undercover, he becomes partners with drug dealer David Jason (Goldblum), and undergoes an inner transformation until he realizes he is betraying his cause. Confusing and commercial, yet marked with a moral rage. **107m/C VHS, DVD.** Laurence Fishburne, Jeff Goldblum, Victoria Dillard, Charles Martin Smith, Sydney Lassick, Clarence Williams III, Gregory Sierra, Roger Guenveur Smith, Cory Curtis, Glynn Turman, Def Jef; **D:** Bill Duke; **W:** Michael Tolkin, Henry Bean; **C:** Bojan Bazelli; **M:** Michel Colombier.

Deep Crimson ✓✓ *Profundo Carmesi* 1996 In 1949 Mexico, overweight nurse and willful romantic Coral (Orozco), impulsively answers a lonely hearts ad placed by Nicolas (Gimenez Cacho), who turns out to be a seedy con man. Coral, however, is certain she's found her true love and is obsessive in her devotion. So much so that she decides to help him with his swindling of vulnerable widows. But Coral's uncontrolled jealousy leads to murder. Based on the same true crime story that inspired the 1969 film, "The Honeymoon Killers." Spanish with subtitles. **109m/C VHS. MX SP** Regina Orozco, Daniel Gimenez Cacho, Marisa Paredes; **D:** Arturo Ripstein; **W:** Paz Alicia Garciadiego; **C:** Guillermo Granillo; **M:** David Mansfield.

Deep Down ✓✓½ 1994 (R) When young Andy (Young) moves into a new apartment, he discovers his neighbor (Roberts) is a gorgeous married woman just looking for a little fun on the side. Too bad her husband (Segal) is a violent psychopath, totally suspicious of his wife's fidelity. Just how far will everyone go to get what they want? Also available in an unrated version. **86m/C VHS.** Tanya Roberts, Chris Young, George Segal; **D:** John Travers; **W:** John Travers, Alice Horrigan.

Deep End ✓✓✓ *Na Samym Dnie* 1970 A 15-year-old boy working as an attendant in a bath house falls in love with a 20-year-old woman in this tragic tale of a young man obsessed. Good British cast and music by Cat Stevens. **88m/C VHS. GB GE** Jane Asher, John Moulder-Brown, Diana Dors, Karl Michael Vogler, Christopher Sandorf; **D:** Jerzy Skolimowski; **W:** Jerzy Skolimowski, Jerry Gruza, Bloeslaw Sulik; **C:** Charly Steinberger; **M:** Cat Stevens.

The Deep End ✓✓✓ 2001 (R) Moms are used to cleaning up their kids' messes and Margaret Hall (Swinton) is no different, even if her situation is. Margaret lives with her three kids and cranky father-in-law in a quiet Lake Tahoe community. Her naval base is away, which means when Margaret learns that teenaged son Beau (Tucker) is gay and involved with sleazy older bar owner, Darby (Lucas), she has no one to turn to. Things get tricky when Darby turns up dead on the beach and mom thinks son did the deed. She gets rid of the body but is soon being blackmailed by slick stranger Alek (Visnjic). Swinton is amazing as the woman who has no limits when it comes to maternal care. Based on Elizabeth Sanxay Holding's 1947 novel "The Blank Wall," which was previously filmed by Max Ophuls in 1949 as "The Reckless Moment." **99m/C VHS, DVD. US** Tilda Swinton, Goran Visnjic, Jonathan Tucker, Raymond J. Barry, Josh(ua) Lucas, Peter Donat, Tamara Hope, Jordan Dorrance; **D:** Scott McGehee, David Siegel; **W:** Scott McGehee, David Siegel; **C:** Giles Nuttgens; **M:** Peter Nashel. Sundance '01: Cinematog. (Nutgens).

The Deep End of the Ocean ✓✓✓ 1998 (PG-13) Beth (Pfeiffer) and husband Pat (Williams) live the ideal life in the suburbs, with a nice home and three beautiful kids. All of that is shattered when three-year-old Ben is abducted while Beth is distracted at a hotel. Shows the tortuous road of depression that Beth travels, and the effect it has on her family. Suddenly, nine years later Ben shows up at her doorstep, now named Sam, and offers to cut the lawn. Beth and detective Candy (Goldberg) determine that he is the lost boy, and painful choices must be made by all. Glosses over the story behind the child's abduction and wraps everything up a bit too easily. **105m/C VHS, DVD.** Michelle Pfeiffer, Treat Williams, John Kapelos, Jonathan Jackson, Ryan Merriman, Whoopi Goldberg, Michael McGrady, Brenda Strong, Alexa Vega, Tony Musante; **D:** Ulu Grosbard; **W:** Stephen Schiff; **C:** Stephen Goldblatt; **M:** Elmer Bernstein.

Deep Impact ✓✓½ 1998 (PG-13) Poor Morgan Freeman. He gets a chance to play the President of the United States only to have his term shortened by a dastardly comet the size of the Grand Canyon. Although his presidency would have been more interesting, the destruction's the star of this show, as well as the touchy-feely interaction of various two-dimensional characters. There's the astronauts (led by Duvall) sent into space to nuke the thing; ordinary teenager Leo (Wood) who initially discovered the rock; and career-conscious news anchor (Leoni), who first breaks the story. The all-star cast is underused, but lend the film a sense of gravity by their presence. The remaining stick figure characters evoke more yawns than tears. Good thing the comet comes along to, ironically, inject a little life into the flick. The special effects are the best in recent film history, and worth the price, laborious wait. **120m/C VHS, DVD.** Morgan Freeman, Robert Duvall, Tea Leoni, Elijah Wood, Vanessa Redgrave, Maximilian Schell, James Cromwell, Blair Underwood, Ron Eldard, Jon Favreau, Leelee Sobieski, Mary McCormack, Dougray Scott, Alexander Baluyev, Charles Martin Smith, Richard Schiff, Gary Werntz, Bruce Weitz, Betsy Brantley, O'Neal Compton, Rya Kihlstedt, Denise Crosby, Laura Innes; **D:** Mimi Leder; **W:** Michael Tolkin, Bruce Joel Rubin; **C:** Dietrich Lohmann; **M:** James Horner.

Deep in My Heart ✓✓✓ 1954 A musical biography of the life and times of composer Sigmund Romberg, with guest appearances by many MGM stars. ♪Leg of Mutton; You Will Remember Vienna; Softly, as in a Morning Sunrise; Mr. & Mrs.; I Love to Go Swimmin' with Wimmin; The Road to Paradise; Will You Remember; It; Serenade. **132m/C VHS.** Jose Ferrer, Merle Oberon, Paul Henreid, Walter Pidgeon, Helen Traubel, Rosemary Clooney, Jane Powell, Howard Keel, Cyd Charisse, Gene Kelly, Ann Miller; **D:** Stanley Donen; **C:** George J. Folsey.

Deep in the Heart ✓✓ *Handgun* 1983 (R) When a young teacher is raped at gunpoint on a second date, she takes the law into her own hands. Just-off-the-target film tries to take a stand against the proliferation of guns in the U.S. Thought-provoking all the same. **99m/C VHS, DVD. GB** Karen Young, Clayton Day, Ben Jones, Suzie Humphreys; **D:** Tony Garnett; **W:** Tony Garnett.

Deep in the Heart (of Texas) ✓✓ 1998 Two British documentary filmmakers, Robert (Cranham) and his wife Kate (Root), take an assignment for British TV to interview Texans. They choose the capital of Austin and the eccentric locals provide the requisite color but the couple are undergoing their own personal crisis that keeps interfering with their work. **90m/C VHS, DVD.** Kenneth Cranham, Amanda Root; **D:** Stephen Purvis; **W:** Tom Huckabee, Stephen Purvis, Jesse Sublett; **C:** Thomas Flores Alcala; **M:** Joe Ellen Doering, George Doering.

Deep in the Woods ✓✓ *Promenons Nous dans les Bois* 2000 (R) Isolated castle, mute little boy, and a psycho-rapist on the loose as five actors are hired to give a performance of "Little Red Riding Hood." Then they begin to die at the paws of someone wearing the wolf costume. Gruesome creeper; French with subtitles. **88m/ C VHS, DVD. FR** Clotilde Courau, Clement Sibony, Vincent Lecoeur, Alexia Stresi, Maud Buquet; **D:** Lionel Delplanque; **W:** Annabelle Perrichon; **C:** Denis Rouden; **M:** Jerome Coullet.

Deep Red ✓✓ 1994 (R) When a young girl has an encounter with an extraterrestrial spacecraft her blood chemistry is mysteriously altered. Now the proteins her body manufactures can lead to immortality and ruthless scientist Newmeyer wants to take advantage of the fact—any way he can. **85m/C VHS, DVD.** Michael Biehn, Joanna Pacula, John de Lancie; **D:** Craig R. Baxley; **W:** D. Brent Mote.

Deep Red: Hatchet Murders ✓✓ *The Hatchet Murders; Profundo Rosso; Dripping Deep Red; The Sabre Tooth Tiger; Deep Red* 1975 A stylish but gruesome rock music-driven tale of a composer who reads a book on the occult which happens to relate to the sadistic, sangfroid murder of his neighbor. When he visits the book's author, he discovers that she has been horribly murdered as well. **100m/C VHS, DVD. IT** David Hemmings, Daria Nicolodi, Gabriele Lavia, Macha Meril, Eros Pagni, Giuliana Calandra, Erykah Badu, Clara Calamai, Nicoletta Elmi, Glauco Mauri; **D:** Dario Argento; **W:** Dario Argento, Bernardino Zapponi; **C:** Luigi Kuveiller; **M:** Giorgio Gaslini, The Goblins.

Deep Rising ✓✓½ 1998 (R) Huge sea serpents cause massive destruction to the cruise ship Argonautica and put major dinks in the plans of mercenaries, led by Finnegan (Williams), who board the ship for greedy motives. Sticks to a reliable action-horror formula with the good sense to not take its characters or slimy creatures too seriously. Sea critters have inventive ways of disposing of extraneous cast members, resulting in gore aplenty. Slacker humor provided by Finnegan's sidekick Pantucci (Kevin J. O'Connor) injects the film with a certain goofiness. Typical B-movie fare that leans more toward guilty pleasure than quality entertainment. **106m/C VHS, DVD.** Treat Williams, Famke Janssen, Anthony Heald, Kevin J. O'Connor, Wes Studi, Derrick O'Connor, Jason Flemyng, Djimon Hounsou; **D:** Stephen Sommers; **W:** Stephen Sommers; **C:** Howard Atherton; **M:** Jerry Goldsmith.

Deep Six ✓✓½ 1958 (R) A WWII drama that examines the conflict between pacifism and loyalty. A staunch Quaker is called to active duty as a lieutenant in the U.S. Navy, where his beliefs put him into disfavor with shipmates. **110m/C VHS.** Alan Ladd, William Bendix, James Whitmore, Keenan Wynn, Efrem Zimbalist Jr., Joey Bishop; **D:** Rudolph Mate.

Deep Space ✓✓½ 1987 A flesh-eating alien lands on earth and, after devouring a cop, is stalked by his partner. An "Alien" rip-off. Some humorous moments keep us from thinking too hard about how much the monster resembles our friend from "Alien." **90m/C VHS.** Charles Napier, Ann Turkel, Ron Glass, Bo Svenson, Julie Newmar; **D:** Fred Olen Ray.

Deep Trouble ✓✓½ 2001 It's strictly amateur hour in this hip-hop urban drama. New York drug kingpin Perry (Stovall) decides that the world of organized crime simply isn't enough, and decides to overtake the business of Star (Scarborough), an entertainment manager who represents up-and-coming actress Diana (Horsford), as well as several stand-up comics. Star and Diana decide that they aren't going to be pushed around by this bully, so they take a stand and the "trouble" begins. Filled with bad acting and amateurish special effects (several characters get shot in the head, which is represented by a simple trickle of blood). The film is very poorly paced, having more scenes of pointless dialogue than action. **102m/C DVD.** Count Stovall, Janel C. Scarborough, Alvah Horsford; **D:** Juney Smith; **W:** Juney Smith.

Deeply ✓✓½ 1999 Fiona McKay (Watson) takes her teenaged daughter Claire (Dunst) to her childhood home on an island off the coast of Nova Scotia. Claire's been traumatized by the sudden death of her boyfriend and is susceptible to the stories told by elderly neighbor, Claire (Redgrave), who has some dark secrets. **102m/C VHS, DVD. CA** Julietta Watson, Lynn Redgrave, Kirsten Dunst, Julia Brendler, Brent Carver; **D:** Sheri Elwood; **W:** Sheri Elwood; **M:** Micki Meuser.

Deepstar Six ✓✓½ 1989 (R) When futuristic scientists try to set up an undersea research and missile lab, a group of subterranean monsters get in the way. **97m/C VHS, DVD.** Taurean Blacque, Nancy Everhard, Greg Evigan, Miguel Ferrer, Matt McCoy, Nia Peeples, Cindy Pickett, Marius Weyers, Thom Bray, Elya Baskin; **D:** Sean S. Cunningham; **W:** Lewis Abernathy, Geof Miller; **C:** Mac Ahlberg; **M:** Harry Manfredini.

Deepwater 🐾🐾 2005 (R) Neo-noir. Young Nat (Black) is just out of rehab and drifting around when he rescues Finch (Coyote) from a road accident and is rewarded by a job in the man's rundown motel. Finch has a lot of shady local interests so the plot confusion deepens, leading to an unexpected twist. Nat's not the most reliable narrator either, and it's this (Maestro)... Adapted from the Matthew F. Jones novel. 93m/C DVD. **C:** Lucas Black, Peter Coyote, Mia Maestro, Lesley Ann Warren, Xander Berkeley; **D:** David S. Marfield; **W:** Mark Brown, Demetria Johnson; **M:** Darren Floyd.

The Deer Hunter 🐾🐾🐾🐾 1978 (R) A powerful and vivid portrait of Middle America with three steel-working friends who leave home to face the Vietnam War. Emotionally shattering, not to be missed. **183m/C VHS, DVD, HD DVD. Robert De Niro, Christopher Walken, Meryl Streep, John Savage, George Dzundza, John Cazale, Chuck Aspegren, Rutanya Alda, Shirley Stoler, Amy Wright, Mady Kaplan, Mary Ann Haenel, Richard Kuss, Pierre Segui, Joe Grifasi, Christopher Colombi Jr., Joe Strnad, Paul D'Amato; D:** Michael Cimino; **W:** Michael Cimino, Deric Washburn, Louis Garfinkle; **C:** Vilmos Zsigmond; **M:** John Williams. Oscars '78: Director (Cimino), Film Editing, Picture, Sound, Support. Actor (Walken); AFI '98: Top. '00; Directors Guild '78: Director (Cimino); Golden Globes '79: Director (Cimino); L.A. Film Critics '78: Director Film, Support. Actor (Walken); Natl. Soc. Film Critics '78: Support. Actress (Streep).

Def by Temptation 🐾🐾½ 1990 (R) A potent horror fantasy about a young black theology student who travels to New York in search of an old friend. There he meets an evil woman who is determined to seduce him and 'force him to give in to temptation. Great soundtrack. **95m/C VHS, DVD. James Bond III, Kadeem Hardison, Bill Nunn, Samuel L. Jackson, Minnie Gentry, Rony Clanton, Cynthia Bond, John Canada Terrell; D:** James Bond III; **W:** James Bond III; **C:** Ernest R. Dickerson. **M:** Paul Lawrence.

Def Jam's How to Be a Player 🐾 1997 (R) Dray (Bellamy) thinks that monogamy is a word used to build furniture. Although he has steady girlfriend Lisa (Voorhies), he also has several other ladies in waiting. He is, in fact, a player. He even teaches others to play. What he needs, however, is a screenplay. His sister Jenny (Desselle), who has been hurt in love, cracks the numerical code to his organizer, and invites all of Dray's harem to one party. The result of this booty intervention is Dray's abandonment of his promiscuous ways. The stand-up comedy roots of much of the cast translate into clunky performances, and the direction is pretty played out, too. **93m/C VHS, DVD. Bill Bellamy, Natalie Desselle, Mari Morrow, Jermaine "Huggy" Hopkins, A.J. (Anthony Johnson), Max Julien, Beverly Johnson, Gilbert Gottfried, Bernie Mac, Elise Neal, Amber Smith, Lark Voorhies; D:** Lionel C. Martin; **W:** Mark Brown, Demetria Johnson; **M:** Darren Floyd.

Def-Con 4 🐾½ 1985 (R) Three marooned space travelers return to a holocaust-stricken Earth to try to start again, but some heavy-duty slimeballs are in charge and they don't want to give it up. Good special effects bolster a weak script. **85m/C VHS, DVD. Maury Chaykin, Kate Lynch, Tim Choate; D:** Paul Donovan.

The Deerslayer 🐾½ 1978 Low-budget snoozer based on the classic novel by James Fenimore Cooper. 'Frontiersman Hawkeye and his Indian companion Chingachgook set out to rescue a beautiful Indian maiden and must fight bands of hostile Indians and Frenchmen along the way. **98m/C VHS. Steve Forrest, Ned Romero, John Anderson, Joan Prather; D:** Richard Friedenberg; **M:** Andrew Belling.

Defenders of the Law 🐾🐾 1931 Early action talkie concerned with gang warfare and law enforcement. **54m/B VHS. John Holland, Mae Busch, Alan Cooke, Joseph Girard, Edmund Breese, Catherine Dale Owen, Robert Gleecker; D:** Joseph Levering.

The Defenders: Payback 🐾🐾½ 1997 (R) E.G. Marshall returns to the lawyer role of Lawrence Preston that he played in the CBS series from 1961-1965. This time around, Preston has his granddaughter, M.J. (Plimpton), joining the family firm along with son Don (Bridges). Their first case together is a doozy—unrepentant Michael Lane (Larroquette) has confessed to killing the recently paroled man who had gone to prison for raping Lane's young daughter. **95m/C VHS. E.G. Marshall, Beau Bridges, Martha Plimpton, John Larroquette, Yaphet Kotto, Roma Maffia, Rachael Leigh Cook, Mimi Kuzyk, Olea Dubois; D:** Andy Wolk; **W:** Andy Wolk, Nicholas Kilbertus; **C:** John Newby; **M:** Mark Isham. **CABLE.**

The Defenders: Taking the First 🐾🐾½ 1998 (R) Don (Bridges) and M.J. (Plimpton) defend a student accused of beating a Latino to death. Their client claims he was incited by white supremist zeal. John Walker (Casnoff), a white supremist's brother, who flies a wrongful death suit against Walker and chooses Don to represent the case. Now the team must try to prove Walker's culpability without disputing his First Amendment rights to free speech. **95m/C VHS. Beau Bridges, Martha Plimpton, Philip Casnoff, Peter Wolk; D:** Andy Wolk; **W:** Andy Wolk, Jeremy London; **C:** John Newby; **M:** Mark Isham. **CABLE.**

Defending Your Life 🐾🐾🐾 1991 (PG) Brooks' cock-eyed way of looking at the world travels to the afterlife in this uneven comedy/romance. In Judgment City, where everyone goes after death, past lives are examined and judged; if you lived a good enough person you get to stay in heaven (where you wear funny robes and eat all you want without getting fat). If not, it's back to earth for another go-round. Brooks plays an L.A. advertising executive who crashes his new BMW and finds himself defending his life. When he meets and falls in love with Streep, his interest in the afterlife multiplies. Occasionally charming, seldom out-right hilarious. **112m/C VHS, DVD. Albert Brooks, Meryl Streep, Rip Torn, Lee Grant, Buck Henry, George D. Wallace, Lillian Lehman, Peter Schuck, Susan Walters; D:** Albert Brooks; **W:** Albert Brooks; **C:** Allen Daviau; **M:** Michael Gore.

Defense of the Realm 🐾🐾🐾½ 1985 (PG) A British politician is accused of selling secrets to the KGB through his mistress and only a pair of dedicated newspapermen believe he is innocent. In the course of finding the answers they discover a national cover-up conspiracy. An acclaimed, taut thriller. **96m/C VHS, DVD, GB Gabriel Byrne, Greta Scacchi, Denholm Elliott, Ian Bannen, Bill Paterson, Fulton Mackay, Robbie Coltrane; D:** David Drury; **C:** Roger Deakins. British Acad. '85. Support. Actor (Elliott).

Defense Play 🐾½ 1988 (PG) Two teenagers are unwittingly stuck in the middle of a Soviet plot to steal the plans that created a technologically advanced helicopter. **95m/C VHS. David Oliver, Susan Ursitti, Monte Markham, William Frankfather, Patch Mackenzie. D:** Monte Markham.

Defenseless 🐾🐾 1991 (R) Hershey tries hard in an unplayable part as a giddy attorney who finds herself trapped in a love-affair/legal case that turns murderous. Good cast and interesting twists contend with a sexist sub-text, which proves a woman can't "have it all." **106m/C VHS, DVD. Barbara Hershey, Sam Shepard, Mary Beth Hurt, J.T. Walsh, Sheree North; D:** Martin Campbell; **W:** James Cresson; **M:** Trevor Jones.

Defiance 🐾🐾 1979 (PG) A former merchant seaman moves into a run-down area of New York City. When a local street gang begins terrorizing the neighborhood, he decides to take a stand. Familiar plotline handled well in this thoughtful film. **101m/C VHS. Jan-Michael Vincent, Art Carney, Theresa Saldana, Danny Aiello; D:** John Flynn; **W:** Thomas Michael Donnelly; **M:** John Beal, Basil Poledouris.

Defiant 🐾🐾 *The Wild Pack; The Sandpit Generals* 1970 Two rival street gangs clash when one admits a young orphan girl. 93m/C VHS. Kent Lane, John Rubinstein, Tisha Sterling; **D:** Hal Bartlett.

Defying Gravity 🐾🐾 1999 Frat boy John Griffiths (Chilson) is hiding a secret from his fellow brothers—he's gay and even has a boyfriend, Pete (Harfield), who's sick of John's lying. Pete is gay-bashed and John agonizes over going to the cops with information if it means his off-campus activities could get out. Good intentions but director/writer Keitel's inexperience (this is his first film) shows in a slow pace and amateurishness. **101m/C VHS, DVD. Daniel Chilson, Niklaus Lange, Don Handfield, Lunia Carter, Seabass Diamond, Lesley Testi; D:** John Keitel; **W:** John Keitel; **C:** Thomas M. Haring; **M:** Tim Westergren.

Degree of Guilt 🐾🐾½ 1995 Good miniseries adaptation of Richard North Patterson's novels "Eyes of a Child" and "Degree of Guilt." Lawyer Chris Paget (Elliot) makes the mistake of falling for associate Teresa Perlita (Zuniga), who's going through a bad divorce from Richie (Ventresca), a loser who wants custody of their daughter and a lot of money from Teresa. Meanwhile, he's taking on the defense of murder suspect Mary Carelli (Lawrence), who's also Chris's ex-lover (Lawrence), and the mother of his son. However this turns out not to be the only murder investigation going when Richie winds up dead and Chris becomes the prime suspect. **180m/C VHS, DVD. David James Elliott, Daphne Zuniga, Sharon Lawrence, Nigel Bennett, Don Francks, Patricia Kalember; D:** Mike Robe; **W:** Cynthia Whitcomb; **C:** Kees Van Oostrum; **M:** Craig Safan. TV.

Definitely, Maybe 🐾🐾🐾 2008 (PG-13) Almost divorced dad Will Hayes (Reynolds), at daughter Maya's (Breslin) request, recounts the great loves that led him to marry her mother in the first place. As a young, idealistic 1992 Clinton campaign worker, Will has a long distance relationship with college girlfriend Emily (Banks), but soon becomes interested in both journalist Summer (Weisz) and freespirit campaign worker April (Fisher, in a standout performance). Both Will's love life and career have their ups and downs as he tries to figure out what he wants in his life, learning some tough and very hilarious lessons on the way, and of course, the flick keeps you guessing as to which woman is actually Mom. Bittersweet, smart, above-average romantic comedy with excellent performances from its leads. **111m/C DVD, GB US Ryan Reynolds, Abigail Breslin, Isla Fisher, Elizabeth Banks, Rachel Weisz, Derek Luke, Kevin Kline, Nestor Serrano, Annie Parisse, Liane Balaban, Kevin Corrigan, Adam Ferrara; D:** Adam Brooks; **W:** Adam Brooks; **C:** Florian Ballhaus; **M:** Clint Mansell.

The Defilers 🐾 1965 (R) Disturbing, low-budget J.D. movie in which two thugs imprison a young girl in a basement and force her to be their love slave. **69m/B VHS. Byron Mabe, Jerome (Jerry Stallon) Eden. D:** David Friedman.

The Defiant Ones 🐾🐾🐾½ 1958 Thought-provoking story about racism revolves around two escaped prisoners (one black, one white) from a chain gang in the rural South. Their societal conditioning to hate each other dissolves as they face constant peril together. Critically acclaimed. **97m/B VHS, DVD. Tony Curtis, Sidney Poitier, Theodore Bikel, Lon Chaney Jr., Charles McGraw, Cara Williams; D:** Stanley Kramer. **W:** Nedrick Young, Harold Jacob Smith; **C:** Sam Leavitt; **M:** Steve Dorff. Oscars '58: B&W Cinematography; Story & Screenplay; British Acad. '58. Actor (Poitier); Golden Globes '59: Film—Drama, N.Y. Film Critics '58: Director (Kramer), Film, Screenplay.

Deja 🐾🐾 1925 and moving between Chicago and Odessa. A Chicago hitman is hired by the mob to kill a traitor who has fled to Odessa. Niczypur, the traitor, has been using the newly opened Chicago-Constantinople-Odessa shipping line for his own smuggling operation. Filled with shootouts, brawls, and chases, in English, Russian, and Polish with English subtitles. **106m/C VHS. Pt. Jerzy Stuhr, Galina Pietrowa, Nikolai Karaczencow, Wladimir Golowin; D:** Juliusz Machulski.

Deja Vu 🐾🐾 1989 Thriller set in Dana (Foyt) has an encounter with a mysterious woman in Israel, she is led on a roundabout way to England's White Cliffs of Dover. There she meets Sean (Dillane) and they quickly fall in love, since they have so much in common, such as being married to other people. This proves to be no problem, for destiny, coincidence and director/screenwriter Jaglom conspire to have the two couples share a house for the weekend. Unfortunately, it's hard to detect the true love, since the two leads have as much chemistry as remedial science class. Vanessa Redgrave and her mother Rachel Kempson appear together for the first time as the sister and mother of the host, played by '60s pop singer Neil Harrison. **115m/C VHS. Victoria Foyt, Stephen (Dillon) Dillane, Vanessa Redgrave, Glynis Barber, Michael Brandon, Vernon Dobtcheff, Noel Harrison, Rachel Kempson, Anna Massey; D:** Henry Jaglom; **W:** Henry Jaglom, Victoria Foyt; **C:** Hanania Baer; **M:** Gaili Schoen.

Deja Vu 🐾🐾½ 1998 (PG-13) After Dana (Foyt)...

Deja Vu 🐾🐾 2006 (PG-13) In their third outing, Scott and Washington tackle action and wormholes and bring pic to as logical a conclusion as can be expected. ATF agent Doug Carlin (Washington) is called to New Orleans when a ferry carrying U.S. sailors is blown up. Carlin discovers victim Claire (Patton) had actually died beforehand and must have some connection to the bomber. Carlin gets pulled in by FBI agent Pryzwara (Kilmer), who tells him about a high-tech project that recreates images from days earlier, but can see Claire prior to the tragedy. Since Claire is a babe, Doug would naturally like to save her, and thanks to this time window, he now has a chance of getting to the bomber first. Scott has always known how to move things along and he sets a brisk pace throughout. **126m/C DVD, Blu-ray Disc, HD DVD. US Denzel Washington, Val Kilmer, Paula Patton, Bruce Greenwood, Adam Goldberg, James (Jim) Caviezel, Elden (Ratliff) Henson, Erika Alexander; D:** Tony Scott; **W:** Terry Rossio, Bill Marsilii; **C:** Paul Cameron; **M:** Harry Gregson-Williams.

The Deli 🐾🐾 1997 Johnny Amico (Starr) runs a New York deli, has a bad gambling habit and a big debt to mobster Tommy Tomacees (Vincent), an outspoken Mama (Malina), and a colorful clientele. Not much happens, the budget is small, but the actors charm. **96m/C VHS, DVD. Joseph (Joe) D'onofrio, Mike Starr, Judith Malina, Matt Keeslar, Frank Vincent, Ice-T, Heather Matarazzo, Ina't, Jerry Stiller; D:** John A. Gallagher; **W:** John A. Gallagher, John Dorrian; **C:** Ron Garcia. **CABLE.**

Deliberate Intent 🐾🐾½ 2001 Well-done fact-based drama follows the case of a triple murder-for-hire and First Amendment issues the case raised. When Lawrence Horn (McDaniel) hires a killer to sue the publisher for abetting the murder that said killer used a book called "Hot Man: A Technical Manual for Independent Contractors" to plan the crime. Lawyer Siegel (Rifkin) brings in First Amendment expert Rod Smolla (Hutton) to sue the publisher for abetting the murder. **120m/C VHS, DVD. Timothy Hutton, Ron Rifkin, James McDaniel, Clark Johnson, Penny Johnson, Cliff DeYoung, Kenneth Welsh; D:** Andy Wolk; **C:** Ron Garcia. **CABLE.**

The Deliberate Stranger 🐾🐾🐾 1986 Harmon is engrossing as charismatic serial killer Ted Bundy, sentenced to death for several Florida murders and suspected in the killings of at least 25 women years later. **95m/C VHS, DVD, GB Mark Harmon, M. Emmet Walsh, Frederic Forrest, George Grizzard, Ben Masters, John Ashton; D:** Marvin J. Chomsky.

Deliberate

celebre on capital punishment as it dragged on for nine years. Bundy was finally executed in 1989. Based on the book "Bundy: The Deliberate Stranger" by Richard W. Larsen. **188m/C VHS.** Mark Harmon, M. Emmet Walsh, Frederic Forrest, John Ashton, George Grizzard, Ben Masters, Glynnis O'Connor, Bonnie Bartlett, Billy Green Bush, Lawrence Pressman; **D:** Marvin J. Chomsky. **TV**

The Delicate Delinquent ♂♂½ **1956** Lewis's first movie without Dean Martin finds him in the role of delinquent who manages to become a policeman with just the right amount of slapstick. **101m/B VHS, DVD.** Jerry Lewis, Darren McGavin, Martha Hyer, Robert Ivers, Horace McMahon; **D:** Don McGuire; **W:** Don McGuire.

Delicatessen ♂♂♂ **1992 (R)** Set in 21st-century Paris, this hilarious debut from directors Jeunet and Caro focuses on the lives of the oddball tenants of an apartment building over a butcher shop. Although there is a famine, the butcher shop is always stocked with fresh meat—made from the building's tenants. Part comedy, part horror, part romance, this film merges a cacophony of sights and sounds with intriguing results. Watch for the scene involving a symphony of creaking bed springs, a squeaky bicycle pump, a cello, and clicking knitting needles. In French with English subtitles. **95m/C VHS, DVD. FR** Marie-Laure Dougnac, Dominique Pinon, Karin Viard, Jean-Claude Dreyfus, Ticky Holgado, Anne Marie Pisani, Edith Ker, Patrick Paroux, Jean-Luc Caron; **D:** Jean-Pierre Jeunet, Marc Caro; **W:** Gilles Adrien, Jean-Pierre Jeunet, Marc Caro; **C:** Darius Khondji; **M:** Carlos D'Alessi. César '92: Art Dir./Set Dec., Writing.

Delightfully Dangerous ♂♂ **1945** Often Deadly Dull. A farfetched musical rooted in yesteryear about mismatched sisters, one a 15-year-old farm girl, the other a New York burlesque dancer, in competition on Broadway. ♫ I'm Only Teasin'; In a Shower of Stars; Mynah Bird; Through Your Eyes to Your Heart; Delightfully Dangerous; Once Upon a Song. **92m/B VHS, DVD.** Jane Powell, Ralph Bellamy, Constance Moore, Arthur Treacher, Louise Beavers; **D:** Arthur Lubin.

Delinquent Daughters ♂½ **1944** Slow-paced drama about a high school girl who commits suicide and the cop and reporter who try to find out why so darn many kids are getting into trouble. **71m/B VHS, DVD.** June Carlson, Fifi d'Orsay, Teala Loring; **D:** Al(bert) Herman.

Delinquent Parents ♂½ **1938** A wayward girl gives up her baby for adoption. She turns her life around and becomes a juvenile court judge. Years later, who should come up before her for misdeeds but her long-lost daughter. The Hound cannot improve on a contemporary critic who renamed this "Delinquent Producers." **62m/B VHS, DVD.** Doris Weston, Maurice Murphy, Helen MacKellar, Terry Walker, Richard Tucker, Morgan Wallace; **D:** Nick Grinde.

Delinquent School Girls woof! *Bad Girls* **1984 (R)** Three escapees from an asylum get more than they bargained for when they visit a Female Correctional Institute to fulfill their sexual fantasies. Buys into just about every conceivable stereotype. **89m/C VHS, DVD.** Michael Pataki, Bob Minos, Stephen Stucker; **D:** Gregory Corarito.

Delirious ♂♂½ **1991 (PG)** A writer for a TV soap opera wakes from a bash on the head to find himself inside the story where murder and mayhem are brewing. Can he write himself back to safety, and find romance along the way? A romantic lead and the film has few laughs. **96m/C VHS, DVD.** John Candy, Mariel Hemingway, Emma Samms, Raymond Burr, David Rasche, Dylan Baker, Charles Rocket, Jerry Orbach, Renee Taylor, Robert Wagner; **D:** Tom Mankiewicz; **W:** Lawrence J. Cohen; **M:** Cliff Eidelman.

Delirium woof! *Psycho Puppet* **1977** Homicidal maniac goes on a killing spree and has just one thing in mind—women. Angry group of citizens inadvertently includes the demonic villain in their vigilante club. Nothing redeeming here. **94m/C VHS.**

Turk Cekovsky, Debi Shanley, Terry Ten Broeck; **D:** Peter Maris.

Deliver Us from Eva ♂♂½ **2003 (R)** Eva (Union) is the overbearing, self-righteous eldest of the four Dandridge sisters. After their parents' untimely death, Eva took on the role of the surrogate mother and since then has become an overpowering influence in their lives. Her sisters' significant others, tired of their lives being dictated by Eva, decide to hire Ray (LL Cool J), a noted ladies man, to woo her out of their lives. The attraction turns real though, and complications arise. Plot is predictable, (it's yet another updating of Shakespeare's "Taming of the Shrew") but you don't mind due to great chemistry between the two solid leads. **105m/C VHS, DVD. US** Gabrielle Union, LL Cool J, Duane Martin, Essence Atkins, Robine Lee, Meagan Good, Mel Jackson, Dartanyan Edmonds, Kym E. Whitley, Royale Watkins, Matt Winston, Ruben Paul, Dorian Gregory; **D:** Gary Hardwick; **W:** Gary Hardwick, James Iver Mattson, B.E. Brauner; **C:** Alexander Grusynski; **M:** Marcus Miller.

Deliverance ♂♂♂ **1972 (R)** Terrifying exploration of the primal nature of man and his alienation from nature, based on the novel by James Dickey, which he adapted for the film (he also makes an appearance as a sheriff). Four urban professionals, hoping to get away from it all for the weekend, canoe down a southern river, encounter crazed backwoodsmen, and end up battling for survival. Excellent performances all around, especially by Voight. Debuts for Beatty and Cox. Watch for O'Neill as a sheriff, and director Boorman's son Charley as Voight's son. "Dueling Banjos" and tune are memorable as is scene where the backwoods boys promise to make the fellows squeal like pigs. **109m/C VHS, DVD, Blu-ray Disc, HD DVD.** Jon Voight, Burt Reynolds, Ronny Cox, Ned Beatty, James Dickey, Bill McKinney, Ed O'Neill, Charley Boorman; **D:** John Boorman; **W:** James Dickey; **C:** Vilmos Zsigmond; **M:** Eric Weissburg.

Delivered ♂♂ *Death by Pizza* **1998 (R)** Pizza deliveryman Will Sherman (Strickland) is the unfortunate witness to a murder by serial killer Reed (Eldard). When Reed realizes Will saw him, he goes after him but the cops have come to the conclusion that it's Will who's the killer—so he has to evade the cops and Reed as well. It's all played for laughs. **90m/C VHS, DVD.** David Strickland, Ron Eldard, Leslie Stefanson, Scott Bairstow, Nicky Katt, Jillian Armenante, Bob Morrisey, Mark Berry; **D:** Guy Ferland; **W:** Andrew Liotta, Lawrence Trilling; **C:** Shane Kelly; **M:** Nicholas Pike.

The Delivery ♂♂ **1999 (R)** Euro-thriller finds buddies Guy (Douglas) and Alfred (van Huet) so desperate for money that they agree to do a job for a crime boss. Seems he needs them to deliver a large shipment of Ecstasy from Barcelona to Amsterdam. Added into the mix is the prerequisite tough babe—in this case, Loulou (Meriel). Drugs, chases, sex, and violence. **100m/C VHS, DVD. NL BE** Fedja Van Huet, Freddy Douglas, Auriele Meriel, Rik Launspach, Esmee De La Bretoniere, Jonathan Harvey, Hidde Maas, Christopher Simon; **D:** Roel Reine; **W:** David Hilton; **C:** Jan van den Nieuwenhuyzen.

Delivery Boys ♂½ **1984 (R)** The "Delivery Boys," three breakdancers aiming to win the $10,000 New York City Break-Off, find unusual perils that may keep them from competing. **94m/C VHS.** Joss Marcano, Tom Sierchio, Jim Soriero, Mario Van Peebles, Samantha Fox; **D:** Ken Handley.

Delos Adventure ♂ **1986 (R)** A geological expedition in South America stumbles upon covert Russian activities and must battle to survive in this overly violent actioner. **98m/C VHS, DVD.** Roger Kern, Jenny Neumann, Kevin Brophy; **D:** Joseph Purcell.

The Delta ♂♂ **1997** White, middleclass Memphis teenager Lincoln Bloom (Gray) is leading a double life. He parties with his girlfriend Monica (Huss) and macho buddies but also sneaks off to cruise the city's gay pick-up spots. Which is where he meets the older John (Chan), an Amerasian immigrant from Vietnam, whose outward manner was a black sol-

dier. The two have a brief romantic idyll but while the openly gay John is desperate for love, Lincoln is still uncertain about his sexual identity and the disparity between their lives. Feature debut for both Sachs and his two lead actors. **85m/C VHS, DVD.** Shayne Gray, Thang Chan, Rachel Zan Huss, Ricky Little; **D:** Ira Sachs; **W:** Ira Sachs; **C:** Benjamin P. Speth; **M:** Michael Rohatyn.

Delta Farce ♂ **2007 (PG-13)** Watching a Larry movie is like dressing squirrels in little ballet outfits. It might seem like a good idea when you're drunk, but you aren't certain you'd like your friends and neighbors to see you doing it, and you'll probably feel bad about yourself when you're done. Three idiotic weekend warriors fall asleep in a cargo plane bound for Iraq. Due to weather problems, the pilot has to dump the cargo (and them) over Mexico, which does not happen to be between the US and Iraq on any map currently in print. They immediately begin to try to 'spread freedom and democracy' by helping a village in trouble, and can't even tell the difference between Mexicans and Iraqis. Ineptly done and poorly funded, at least it does its best to insult anyone who isn't white, male, straight, drunk, and stupid. **89m/C DVD, Blu-ray Disc. US** Larry the Cable Guy, DJ Qualls, Marisol Nichols, Danny Trejo, Bill Engvall, Keith David, Glenn Morshower, Christina Moore, Lisa Lampanelli, Ed O'Ross; **D:** C.B. Harding; **W:** Bear Aderhold, Thomas F.X. Sullivan; **C:** Tom Priestley; **M:** James Levine.

Delta Force ♂ **1986 (R)** Based on the true hijacking of a TWA plane in June 1985. Arab terrorists take over an airliner; the Delta Force, led by Lee Marvin and featuring Norris as its best fighter, rescue the passengers in ways that cater directly to our nationalistic revenge fantasies. Average thriller, exciting and tense at times, with fine work from Marvin, Norris, and Forster. **125m/C VHS, DVD.** Lee Marvin, Chuck Norris, Shelley Winters, Martin Balsam, George Kennedy, Hanna Schygulla, Susan Strasberg, Bo Svenson, Joey Bishop, Lainie Kazan, Robert Forster, Robert Vaughn, Kim Delaney; **D:** Menahem Golan; **W:** James Bruner; **C:** David Gurinkel; **M:** Alan Silvestri.

Delta Force 2: Operation Stranglehold ♂½ **1990 (R)** Delta Force is back with martial artist and military technician Norris at the helm. Action-packed and tense. **110m/C VHS, DVD.** John P. Ryan, Chuck Norris, Billy Drago, Richard Jaeckel, Paul Perri; **D:** Aaron Norris; **W:** Lee Reynolds; **C:** Joao Fernandes; **M:** Frederic Talgorn.

Delta Force 3: The Killing Game ♂½ *Young Commandos* **1991 (R)** A terrorist mastermind plants an atomic bomb in an American city, and the President has only one choice...call in the Delta Force. The leading men in this lackluster thriller are the sons of some of Hollywood's biggest stars. **97m/C VHS, DVD.** Nick Cassavetes, Eric Douglas, Mike Norris, Matthew Penn, John P. Ryan, Sandy Ward; **D:** Sam Firstenberg; **W:** Boaz Davidson.

Delta Force Commando ♂½ **1987 (R)** Two U.S. Fighter pilots fight against terrorism in the deadly Nicaraguan jungle. **90m/C VHS, DVD. IT** Fred Williamson, Bo Svenson; **D:** Frank (Pierluigi Ciriaci) Valenti.

Delta Force Commando 2 ♂ *Priority Red One* **1990 (R)** The celluloid was hardly dry on the first "Delta Force Commando" before the resourceful Italians began grinding out this follow-up, with the lead commando getting the Force entangled in a deadly international conspiracy. **100m/C VHS. IT** Richard Hatch, Fred Williamson; Giannina Facio, Van Johnson; **D:** Frank (Pierluigi Ciriaci) Valenti.

Delta Fox ♂♂ **1977** Delta Fox is carrying $1 million for the mob, but the mob is carrying a grudge and the chase is on. **90m/C VHS.** Priscilla Barnes, Richard Lynch, Stuart Whitman, John Ireland; **D:** Beverly Sebastian, Ferd Sebastian.

Delta Heat ♂ **1992 (R)** A new designer drug hits LA, and detective Mike Bishop (Edwards) follows his partner to the drug's source in Louisiana. When Bishop arrives he discovers his partner has been tortured and murdered in order to keep the drug lord's foes in line. Bishop

must then save himself and find justice in the steamy streets of New Orleans. Routine lone guy vs. bad guys actioner. **91m/C VHS, DVD.** Anthony Edwards, Lance Henriksen, Betsy Russell, Linda Dona, Rod Masterson, John McConnell, Clyde Jones; **D:** Michael Fischa.

Delta of Venus ♂½ **1995 (R)** Paris, 1940—beautiful young American Elena (England), an aspiring author, falls for handsome Lawrence (Mandylor), a writer of dirty books. But she finds out Lawrence isn't faithful and winds up supporting herself as a nude model and writing her own erotic tales. Lots of sex scenes and an equal amount of pretensions. Based on the erotic novel "Delta of Venus" by Anais Nin. Prague substitutes for Paris as the film location. Also availble unrated; the theatrical version came out as NC-17. **100m/C VHS, DVD.** Audie England, Costas Mandylor, Erick Da Silva, Raven Snow; **D:** Zalman King; **W:** Patricia Louisiana Knop, Elisa Rothstein; **C:** Eagle Egilsson; **M:** George S. Clinton.

Deluge ♂♂ **1933** Tidal waves caused by earthquakes have destroyed most of New York (though some may think this is no great loss) in this early sci-fi pic. **72m/B VHS.** Edward Van Sloan, Peggy Shannon, Sidney Blackmer, Fred Kohler Sr, Matt Moore, Samuel S. Hinds, Lane Chandler; **D:** Felix Feist.

The Deluge ♂♂ *Potop* **1973** Romance woven around the Polish-Swedish war in the 17th century. Adapted from the 1886 novel by Nobel prize-winning author Henryk Sienkiewicz, and filmed largely on location in authentic castles of the era. Polish with subtitles. **185m/C VHS, DVD. PL** Daniel Olbrychski, Malgorzata Braunek, Wladyslaw Hancza, Leszek Herdegen, Andrzej Lapicki; **D:** Jerzy Hoffman; **C:** Jerzy Wojcik; **M:** Kazimierz Serocki.

Delusion ♂½ *The House Where Death Lives* **1984 (R)** Gothic thriller in which invalid Cotten and family are harassed by a possibly supernatural killer as told by Cotten's nurse. Filmed in 1980. Ending is a letdown. **93m/C VHS.** Patricia Pearcy, David Hayward, John Dukakis, Joseph Cotten, Simone Griffeth; **D:** Alan Beattie.

Delusion ♂♂ **1991 (R)** A yuppie with an embezzled fortune is held up in the Nevada desert by a psycho hood with a showgirl lover. But who's really in charge here? The snappy, hip, film-noir thriller takes a few unlikely twists and has an open Lady-or-the-Tiger finale that may infuriate. **100m/C VHS.** Jim Metzler, Jennifer Rubin, Kyle Secor, Robert Costanzo, Tracey Walter, Jerry Orbach; **D:** Carl Colpaert; **W:** Carl Colpaert, Kurt Voss; **C:** Geza Sinkovics; **M:** Barry Adamson.

Delusions of Grandeur ♂♂½ *La Folle des Grandeurs* **1976** A French comedy of court intrigue set in 17th-century Spain. In French with English subtitles. Based loosely on Victor Hugo's "Ruy Blas". **85m/C VHS, DVD. FR** Yves Montand, Louis de Funes, Alice Sapritch, Karin Schubert, Gabriele Tinti; **D:** Gerard Oury.

Demented ♂ **1980 (R)** Beautiful and talented woman is brutally gang-raped by four men, but her revenge is sweet and deadly as she entices each to bed and gives them a big dose of their own medicine. All-too-familiar plot offers nothing new. **92m/C VHS.** Sallee Elyse, Bruce Gilchrist; **D:** Arthur Jeffreys, Alex Rebar; **W:** Alex Rebar.

Dementia ♂♂½ **1998** Wild-eyed sexual thriller owes a bit to "Diabolique." Recovering from a breakdown, wealthy Kathrine (Bursel) becomes friendly with her outpatient nurse Luisa (Sanchez). Then Luisa's smarmy ex-husband Sonny (Schulze) shows up and things get twisty. Production values are not top drawer and the cast is not well known, but director Keith keeps things moving nicely. **85m/C DVD.** Marisol Padilla Sanchez, Patricia Bursiel, Matt Schulze, Azura Skye, Matthew Sullivan, Jesus Nebot, Susan Davis; **D:** Woody Keith; **W:** Woody Keith, R.G. Fry; **C:** David Trulli; **M:** Karl Preusser.

Dementia 13 ♂♂½ *The Haunted and the Hunted* **1963** This eerie thriller, set in a creepy castle, is an early Coppola film about the members of an Irish family who are being offed by an axe murderer one by one. **75m/B VHS, DVD.** William Campbell, Luana

Anders, Bart Patton, Patrick Magee, Barbara Dowling, Ethne Dunn, Mary Mitchell, Karl Schanzer; **D:** Francis Ford Coppola; **W:** Francis Ford Coppola; **C:** Charles Hannawalt; **M:** Ronald Stein.

Demetrius and the Gladiators 🐾🐾½ 1954 A sequel to "The Robe," wherein the holy-robe-carrying slave is enlisted as one of the trampy gladiators and mixes with the Caligula's people's perceptions of foreigners has Olivier, as a Russian inventor (?!) who comes along when a group of terrorists empress Messalina. 101m/C VHS, DVD, Victor Mature, Susan Hayward, Michael Rennie, Debra Paget, Anne Bancroft, Jay Robinson, Barry Jones, Richard Egan, William Marshall, Ernest Borgnine; **D:** Delmer Daves; **W:** Philip Dunne; **C:** Milton Krasner.

The Demi-Paradise 🐾🐾½ 1943 Tongue-in-cheek look at people's perceptions of foreigners has Olivier, as a Russian inventor (?!) who comes to England with some trepidation. Though the Brits are plenty quirky, he manages to find romance with Ward in this charming look at British life. 110m/B VHS, GB Laurence Olivier, Penelope Dudley Ward, Margaret Rutherford, Marjorie Fielding, Felix Aylmer, Guy Middleton, Michael Shepley; **D:** Anthony Asquith.

Demolition High 🐾 1995 (R) Adventure for 1943 Tongue-in-cheek look at people's perceptions of foreigners has Olivier, as a Russian inventor (?!) who comes along when a group of terrorists labeled a troublemaker. But real trouble comes along when a group of terrorists fleeing police after a robbery, take over the school and hold the teachers and students as hostages. Fortunately, Lenny is able to lead a secret counterattack. 85m/C VHS, Corey Haim, Alan Thicke, Jeff Kober, Dick Van Patten; **D:** Jim Wynorski; **W:** Steve Jankowski; **C:** Zoran Hochstatter; **M:** Kevin Kiner.

Demolition Man 🐾🐾 1993 (R) No-brain sci-fier rests on the action skills of Stallone and Snipes. Psychoviillain Snipes (sporting a Dennis Rodman 'do) is pursued by equally violent cop Stallone in the late 1990s. Then they're cryogenically frozen, defrosted in 2032 and back to their old tricks. One problem. This is not a fun future: virtual reality sex is the only kind allowed and puritan ethics and political correctness are enforced to the max. Cop and bad guy get to show this highly entertaining but ly society some really violent times. Implausible plot and minimal acting, but lots of action and violence for fans. 115m/C VHS, DVD, Jack Black, Steve Katan, Grand L. Bush, Bill Cobbs, Dan Cortese, Rob Schneider, Jesse Ventura, Sylvester Stallone, Wesley Snipes, Sandra Bullock, Nigel Hawthorne, Benjamin Bratt, Bob Gunton, Glenn Shadix, Denis Leary; **D:** Marco Brambilla; **W:** Daniel Waters, Robert Reneau, Peter M. Lenkov; **C:** Alex Thomson; **M:** Elliot Goldenthal.

The Demolitionist 🐾🐾 1995 (R) Tough undercover cop Alyssa Lloyd (Eggert) is killed by crime-lord Mad Dog Burne (Grieco) and then resurrected by scientist Jack Crowley (Abbott) as a hard-hitting futuristic superheroine who's out to save Metro City from evil. 100m/C VHS, DVD, Nicole Eggert, Richard Grieco, Bruce Abbott, Susan Tyrell, Peter Jason, Sarah Douglas, Andras Jones, Heather Langenkamp, David Anthony Marshall, Jack Nance, Tom Savini; **D:** Robert Kurzman; **W:** Brian DiMuccio, Dino Vincenti; **C:** Marcus Hahn; **M:** Shawn Patterson.

The Demon 🐾½ 1981 (R) A small town may be doomed to extinction, courtesy of a monster's thirst for the blood of its inhabitants. 94m/C VHS, DVD, SA Cameron Mitchell, Jennifer Holmes; **D:** Percival Rubens; **W:** Percival Rubens; **C:** Vincent Cox.

Demon Barber of Fleet Street 🐾🐾½ *Sweeney Todd: The Demon Barber of Fleet Street* 1936 Loosely based on an actual event, this film inspired the 1978 smash play "Sweeney Todd." Slaughter stars as a mad barber who doesn't just cut his client's hair. He happens to have a deal cooked up with the baker to provide him with some nice "juicy" filling for his meat pies. Manages to be creepy and funny at the same time. 68m/B VHS, DVD, GB

Tod Slaughter, Eve Lister, Bruce Seton; **D:** George King.

Demon for Trouble 🐾 1934 Outlaws are murdering land buyers in this routine western. 59m/B VHS, Bob Steele, Don Alvarado, Gloria Shea, Nick Stuart; **D:** Robert F. "Bob" Hill; **W:** Jack Nateford; **C:** William C. Thompson.

Demon Hunter 🐾½ 1988 Terror reigns while a deranged killer stalks his next victim. 90m/C VHS, George Ellis, Erin Fleming, Marianne Gordon; **D:** Massey Cramer; **M:** Bob Corley.

A Demon in My View 🐾🐾½ 1992 (R) In a role similar to his infamous Norman Bates in "Psycho," Perkins stars as a man who kills a terrible secret—he is a former serial killer. When a fellow tenant in his apartment house accidentally destroys his doll, Perkins' tenuous sanity is shaken and he begins killing again. A smart thriller. Perkins last big-screen role, once in reality and then again in a dream (nightmare?). 99m/C VHS, Anthony Perkins, Sophie Ward, Stratford Johns; **D:** Petra Haffter; **W:** Petra Haffter.

The Demon Lover woof! *Devil Master:* *Master of Evil* 1977 (R) Leader of a satanic cult calls forth the devil when he doesn't get his way. Poorly acted and badly produced. Features comic book artists Val "Howard the Duck" Mayerick and Gunnar "Leatherface" Hansen. 87m/C VHS, Gunnar Hansen, Val Mayerick, Gunnar Hansen, Christmas Robbins, Val Mayerick, Sonja Ward, Steve Tom Hutton, David Howard; **D:** Donald G. Jackson, Jerry Younkins; **W:** Donald G. Jackson, Jerry Younkins.

Demon Lust 🐾🐾 2001 "The Sopranos" meet "Dracula" in this ultra low-budget New Jersey independent production. Nick (Teller) and Tony (Vincent) owe $5,000 to a mobster who has sent a thug (Savini) to collect. After some allegedly comic bits, the two guys find themselves hooked up with Amanda (Stevens), a beautiful babe who's really a monster. Most of the lead roles are well acted. 77m/c DVD, Edward Lee Vincent, Zander Teller, Brinke Stevens, Tom Savini; **D:** David A. Goldberg; **W:** Coven Balfour; **C:** Joseph Robert Jobe. **M:** Coven Balfour.

Demon of Paradise woof! 1987 (R) Dynamite fishing off the coast of Hawaii unearths an ancient, man-eating lizard-man. Uneven, unexciting horror attempt. 84m/C VHS, Kathryn Witt, William (Bill) Steis, Leslie Huntly, Laura Banks, Frederick Bailey; **D:** Cirio H. Santiago; **W:** Frederick Bailey; **C:** Ricardo Remias.

Demon Possessed 🐾½ 1993 (R) When Tom is critically injured in a snowmobile race in a remote woods, he and his friends find shelter in a deserted children's camp. It turns out the camp was run by a secret religious cult that practiced occult murder and the demon that haunted the place has never left. When Tom dies this satanic spirit finds the perfect host to return to human form and continue its bloody work. 97m/C VHS, Dawn Laurie, Aaron Kjenass, David Fields, Eve Montgomery; **D:** Christopher Webster; **W:** Julian Weaver. **M:** Gentrost.

Demon Queen 🐾 1980 A vampirish woman seduces, then murders, many men. 70m/C VHS, Mary Fanaro, Dennis Stewart, Cliff Dance; **D:** Donald Farmer.

Demon Rage 🐾½ *Satan's Mistress* *Fury of the Succubus; Dark Eyes* 1982 (R) Neglected housewife drifts under the spell of a phantom lover. 89m/C VHS, DVD, Britt Ekland, Lana Wood, Kabir Bedi, John Carradine, Sherry Scott; **D:** James Polakof.

Demon Seed 🐾🐾🐾 1977 (R) When a scientist (Weaver) and his wife (Christie) separate so he can work on "Proteus," a somewhat biological supercomputer, the terminal within his computer-controlled home allows Proteus to infiltrate, taking over the house and his wife. Proteus' intent? To procreate. Bizarre and taut, based on a Dean Koontz novel. 97m/C VHS, DVD, Julie Christie, Fritz Weaver, Gerrit Graham, Berry Kroeger, Ron Hays, Lisa Lu, Larry J. Blake; **D:** Donald Cammell; **W:** Robert Jaffe, Roger O. Hirson; **C:** Bill Butler; **V:** Robert Vaughn.

Demon Wind 🐾½ 1990 (R) A gateway to Hell opens up on a secluded farm and various heroic types try to close it. Meanwhile, demons attempt to possess

those humans in their midst. Zombies abound in this near-woof. 97m/C VHS, Eric Larson, Francine Lapensée, Rufus Norris; **D:** Charles Philip Moore.

Demonia woof! 1990 Archaeologists digging in Sicily uncover a sealed convent where five nuns were crucified in the 15th century. This discovery unleashes an ancient evil and bizarre murders begin to take place. Unfortunately, that's about as far as the plot goes. Even by Fulci's standards, "Demonia" is slow and ponderous, with many scenes taking place twice, once in reality and then again in a dream (nightmare?). Fulci's trademark gore is scant and the special effects are laughable. Even die-hard Fulci fans will be disappointed. 90m/C DVD, **IT** Brett Halsey, Meg Register, Carla Cassola, A Oliver, Lucio Fulci; **D:** Lucio Fulci; **W:** Lucio Fulci, Piero Regnoli; **C:** Luis Ccarese.

Demonic Toys 🐾🐾 1990 (R) The possessed playthings attack a bunch of unfortunates in a warehouse, and pumped-up lady cop Scoggins deserves an award for keeping a straight face. Skimpily scripted gore from the horror assembly-line at Full Moon Productions. Far more entertaining are the multiple behind-the-scenes featurettes on the tape. 86m/C VHS, DVD, Richard Speight Jr., Tracy Scoggins, Bentley Mitcrum, Michael Russo, Jeff Weston, Daniel Carny, Peter R Schrum; **D:** Peter Manoogian.

Demonlover 🐾🐾 2002 Big business meets the high-stakes game of high tech Internet pornography and results in a confusing, unnecessarily violent thriller. Niel-sen plays Diane, a corporate spy acting as an assistant to Henri-Pierre Volf (Malar-tre), the head of multinational conglomerate VolfGroup. VolfGroup threatens to take over TokyoAnime, producers of revolutionary, animated 3-D smut, which sparks rival companies Mangatronics and Demonlover to get nasty. Nasty pretty much sums up just about all the characters and the rest of the action throughout, led by the particularly immoral Diane. Characters are totally devoid of sympathy while the plot begins to totally unravel halfway through. 120m/C VHS, DVD, FR Connie Nielsen, Charles Berling, Chloe Sevigny, Gina Gershon, Dominique Reymond, Jean-Baptiste Malartre; **D:** Olivier Assayas; **W:** Olivier Assayas; **C:** Denis Lenoir; **M:** Sonic Youth.

Demonoid, Messenger of Death 🐾 *Macabra* 1981 (R) Discovery of an ancient temple of Satan worship drastically changes the lives of a young couple when the husband becomes possessed by the Demonoid, which initially takes on the form of a severed hand. Poor script needs hand, producing a number of unintentionally laughable moments. 85m/C VHS, DVD, Samantha Eggar, Stuart Whitman, Roy Cameron Jenson; **D:** Alfredo Zacharias.

The Demons 🐾 *Les Demons; Los Demonios* 1974 (R) As she slips into death, a tortured woman curses her torturers. Later in turn in a Berlin theatre is so involving that its viewers become the demons they are seeing. The new monsters turn on the other audience members. Virtually plotless, very explicit. Rock soundtrack by Accept, Go West, Motley Crue, and others. Revered in some circles, blasted in others. Followed by "Demons 2" 89m/C VHS, DVD, **IT** Urbano Barberini, Natasha Hovey, Paolo Cozza, Karl Zinny, Fiore Argento, Fabiola Toledo, Nicoletta Elmi, Michele (Michael) Soavi; **D:** Lamberto Bava; **W:** Lamberto Bava, Dario Argento, Franco Ferrini, Dardano Sacchetti; **C:** Gianlo-renzo Battaglia. **M:** Claudio Simonetti.

Demons 🐾½ *Demoni* 1986 (R) A horror film in a Berlin theatre is so involving that its viewers become the demons they are seeing. The new monsters turn on the other audience members. Virtually plotless, very explicit. Rock soundtrack by Accept, Go West, Motley Crue, and others. Revered in some circles, blasted in others. Followed by "Demons 2" 89m/C VHS, DVD, **IT** Urbano Barberini, Natasha Hovey, Paolo Cozza, Karl Zinny, Fiore Argento, Fabiola Toledo, Nicoletta Elmi, Michele (Michael) Soavi; **D:** Lamberto Bava; **W:** Lamberto Bava, Dario Argento, Franco Ferrini, Dardano Sacchetti; **C:** Gianlo-renzo Battaglia. **M:** Claudio Simonetti.

Dempsey 🐾🐾 1983 In this film, based on Jack Dempsey's autobiography, Williams plays the role of the famed world heavyweight champ. His rise through the boxing ranks as well as his personal life are chronicled. A bit slow-moving considering the pounding fists and other action. 110m/C VHS, DVD, Treat Williams, Sam Waterston, Sally Kellerman, Victoria Tennant, Peter Mark Richman, Jesse Vint, Bonnie Bartlett James Naughton; **D:** Gus Trikonis; **M:** Billy Goldenberg. TV

Denial: The Dark Side of Passion 🐾🐾 1991 (R) A strong-willed woman tries to put a destructive love affair behind her—but if she succeeded there'd be no movie. Torrid stuff with a watchable cast. 103m/C VHS, Robin Wright Penn, Jason Patric, Barry Primus, Christina Harnos, Rae Dawn Chong; **D:** Erin Dignam; **W:** Erin Dignam.

Denise Calls Up 🐾🐾½ 1995 (PG-13) Comedy about futility and complications of urban relationships among overworked professionals. A group of six friends date and date entirely via phone, fax, and computer without ever meeting or

quel to "Demons." The son of horror-meister Mario Bava, Lamberto collaborated with Italian auteur Argento (who co-wrote and produced) to create an improbable sequel (storywise) which seems to have been edited by some kind of crazed cutting room employee. Residents of a chi-chi high rise watching a documentary about the events of "Demons"—a sort of high-tech playwithin-a-play plot—when a demon emerges from the TV, spreads his creepy scooties, and causes the tenants to sprout fangs and claws and nasty tempers. Lots of blood drips from ceilings, plumbing fixtures, and various body parts. 88m/C VHS, DVD, **IT** David Edwin Knight, Nancy Brill, Coralina Cataldi-Tassoni, Bobby Rhodes, Asia Argento, Virginia Bryant; **D:** Lamberto Bava, Asia Argento, Lamberto Bava; **C:** Gianlorenzo Battaglia. **M:** Simon Boswell.

Demons in the Garden 🐾🐾🐾 *Demonios En El Jardin* 1982 (R) Centers on the disintegration of a family after the end of the Spanish Civl War, due to sibling rivalries and a variety of indiscretions. Problems mount as two brothers become involved with their stepsister. Story takes on poignancy in its narration by a young boy. Beautiful cinematography. In Spanish with English subtitles. 100m/C VHS, SP Angela Molina, Ana Belen, Encarna Paso, Imanol Arias; **D:** Manuel Gutierrez Aragon; **C:** Jose Luis Alcaine.

Demons of the Mind 🐾🐾 1975 Evil Blood Will Have Blood 1972 (R) A sordid psychological horror film about a baron in 19th century Austria who imprisons his children, fearing that mental illness is a family trait. 85m/C VHS, DVD, GB Michael Hordern, Patrick Magee, Yvonne Mitchell, Robert Hardy, Gillian Hills, Virginia Wetherall, Shane Briant, Paul Jones, Thomas Heathcote, Kenneth J. Warren; **D:** Peter Sykes; **W:** Christopher Wicking; **C:** Arthur Grant.

Demons of Ludlow 🐾 1975 Demons attend a small town's bicentennial celebration intent on raising a little hell of their own. 83m/C VHS, DVD, Paul von Hauser, Stephanie Cushna, James Robinson, Carol Perry; **D:** Steven Kuether.

Demonstone 🐾 *Heartstone* 1989 (R) A TV reporter becomes possessed by a Filipino demon and carries out an ancient curse against the family of a corrupt government official. 90m/C VHS, DVD, R, Lee Ermey, Jan-Michael Vincent, Nancy Everhard; **D:** Andrew Prowse.

Demonstrator 🐾🐾½ 1971 A father and son are at odds when dad heads an Asian military coalition and junior protests that abducted his daughter. 91m/C VHS, George Kennedy, Pamela Gilbert; **D:** Emmett Alston; **W:** Bruce Akiyama.

Demonwarp woof! 1987 A vengeance-minced hunter journeys into an evil, primeval forest to kill the monsters that abducted his daughter. 91m/C VHS, George Kennedy, Pamela Gilbert; **D:** Emmett Alston; **W:** Bruce Akiyama.

Demons 2 🐾½ 1987 (R) Interior sequel to "Demons."

leaving their homes, even for a close friend's funeral who dies, oddly enough, while on the phone). Subplot involves title character, Denise (Ubach) tracking down sperm donor Martin (Gunther) and eventually giving birth, with the help of her cellular coaches. Funny premise is executed well, but doesn't hold up over a (barely) feature length film. **79m/C VHS.** Timothy Daly, Dana Wheeler-Nicholson, Caroleen Feeney, Liev Schreiber, Dan Gunther, Aída Turturro, Alanna Ubach, Sylvia Miles; **D:** Hal Salwen; **W:** Hal Salwen; **C:** Mike Mayers; **M:** Lynne Geller.

Dennis the Menace 🐾🐾½ **1993** (PG) Straight from the Hughes kiddie farm comes Kevin McAllister—oops!—Dennis Mitchell (newcomer Gamble), curious, crafty, and blond five-year-old. He dreams and schemes, but everything he does manages to be a threat to the physical and mental well being of hot-head neighbor Mr. Wilson (Matthau), perfectly cast as the grump). Lloyd is very nasty as protagonist Switchblade Sam; Plowright, Thompson, and Stanton round out the cast as Mrs. Wilson and the Mitchell parents, respectively. Sure to please young kids, but parents may be less enthralled with this adaptation of the popular '50s comic strip and subsequent TV series. **96m/C VHS, DVD.** Walter Matthau, Mason Gamble, Joan Plowright, Christopher Lloyd, Lea Thompson, Robert Stanton, Billie Bird, Paul Winfield, Amy Sakasitz, Kellen Hathaway, Arnold Stang; **D:** Nick Castle; **W:** John Hughes; **C:** Thomas Ackerman; **M:** Jerry Goldsmith.

A Dennis the Menace Christmas 🐾🐾 **2007** In yet another variation of "A Christmas Carol," cutie neighborhood nuisance Dennis Mitchell (Cotton) tries to help grouchy Mr. Wilson (Wagner) learn the true meaning of Christmas. **?m/C DVD.** Robert Wagner, Louise Fletcher, George Newbern, Jack Noseworthy, Maxwell Perry Cotton, Kim Schraner; **D:** Ron Oliver; **W:** Kathleen Laccinole; **C:** C. Kim Miles; **M:** Peter Allen. **VIDEO**

Dennis the Menace: Dinosaur Hunter 🐾🐾½ **1993** (G) Another version of Hank Ketchum's mischievous cartoon character brought to life to have adventures and disturb his neighbor Mr. Wilson. This time Dennis discovers a huge, primitive bone in his backyard and when an archaeologist declares it's a dinosaur bone, news crews, tourists, and scientists are suddenly everywhere. This badly disturbs Mr. Wilson's retirement and Dennis and his friends must save the day (and their neighborhood). **118m/C VHS.** Victor DiMattia, William Windom, Pat Estrin, Jim Jansen, Patsy Garrett; **D:** Doug Rogers.

Dennis the Menace Strikes Again 🐾🐾½ **1998** (G) Direct-to-video sequel finds hyperactive Dennis (Cooper) trying to save curmudgeonly Mr. Wilson (Rickles) from a pair of con men. **75m/C VHS, DVD.** Justin Cooper, Don Rickles, George Kennedy, Betty White, Brian Doyle-Murray, Carrot Top; **D:** Charles Kanganis; **W:** Tim McCanlies; **C:** Christopher Faloona; **M:** Graeme Revell. **VIDEO**

The Dentist 🐾🐾½ **1996** (R) After seeing this movie, you may never want to sit in that dental chair again. When his marriage falls apart, L.A. dental specialist Dr. Alan Feinstone (Bernsen) takes to pill popping and psychotic behavior, including demonic drilling and particularly bloody oral surgery. **93m/C VHS, DVD.** Corbin Bernsen, Ken Foree, Linda Hoffman, Michael Stadvec; **D:** Brian Yuzna; **W:** Charles Finch, Stuart Gordon, Dennis Paoli; **C:** Levie Isaacks; **M:** Alan Howarth.

The Dentist 2: Brace Yourself 🐾 **1998** (R) Allan Feinstone (Bernsen) has escaped from the asylum to which he was sent in the first film. He's settled in a rural community and set up another practice. This is one guy who doesn't claim to be painless. **99m/C VHS,**

DVD. Corbin Bernsen, Jillian McWhirter, Linda Hoffman; **D:** Brian Yuzna; **W:** Brian Yuzna; **C:** Jurgen Baum; **M:** Alan Howarth. **VIDEO**

Dentist in the Chair 🐾½ **1960** Dumb Brit comedy about dental students David (Monkhouse) and Brian (Stevens) who inadvertently get involved with smalltime crook Sam Field (Connor) who gives them a load of expensive dental equipment. But they have to get rid of the goods before they're accused of theft. **87m/B VHS. GB Spill** Monkhouse. Ronnie Stevens, Kenneth Connor, Peggy Cummins, Eric Barker, Stuart Saunders; **D:** Don Chaffey; **W:** Val Guest, Bob Monkhouse; **C:** Reg Wyer; **M:** Kenneth V. Jones.

The Denver & Rio Grande 🐾🐾½ **1951** Action-packed western about two rival railroads competing to be the first to complete a line through the Royal Gorge. Plot is predictable, but the scene featuring two trains crashing into each other is worth it (Haskin used actual trains for this stunt). **89m/C VHS.** Edmond O'Brien, Sterling Hayden, Dean Jagger, Zasu Pitts, J. Carrol Naish; **D:** Byron Haskin.

The Departed 🐾🐾🐾½ **2006** (R) Scorsese goes back to the mob (Irish and in Boston this time) for a complicated and violent tale of identity and betrayal based on the Hong Kong flick "Infernal Affairs." Colin (a strong Damon) is a state police officer who's actually a mole for crazy kingpin Frank Costello (Nicholson, nuttier than ever) while jittery Billy (an equally strong DiCaprio) is the cop who's infiltrated Costello's gang at the behest of his tough bosses Queenan (Sheen) and Dignam (Wahlberg). Both younger men are involved—in different ways—with lone femme, shrink Madolyn (Farmiga). Tension builds, insults and bullets fly, and the truth will out—with some unexpected consequences. Scorsese's at his best (if in familiar territory). **150m/C DVD, Blu-ray Disc, HD DVD.** US Leonardo DiCaprio, Matt Damon, Jack Nicholson, Mark Wahlberg, Martin Sheen, Ray Winstone, Vera Farmiga, Anthony Anderson, Alec Baldwin, James Badge Dale, Mark Rolston, Kevin Corrigan, James Dale, Kristen Dalton; **D:** Martin Scorsese; **W:** William Monahan; **C:** Michael Ballhaus; **M:** Howard Shore. Oscars '06: Adapt. Screenplay, Director (Scorsese), Film, Film Editing; Directors Guild '06: Director (Scorsese); Golden Globes '07: Director (Scorsese); Writers Guild '06: Adapt. Screenplay.

Department Store 🐾 *Bargain Basement* **1935** Confusing crime-drama involving a store manager who mistakes an ex-convict for his employer's heir. Based on a story by H. F. Maltby. **65m/B VHS. GB** Garry Marsh, Eve Gray, Sebastian Shaw, Geraldine Fitzgerald, Jack Melford; **D:** Leslie Hiscott; **C:** William Luff.

Depraved 🐾½ **1998** Opella and Dan spice up their sex lives by acting out their fantasies. But they start to go too far for Dan and he has a fight with his fiance, who storms out. Only the next morning Dan discovers Opella's dead body. Naturally, instead of calling the cops, Dan calls his brother, and they decide to dispose of the body and come up with an alibi. Can you spell trouble? **90m/C VHS, DVD.** Seidy Lopez, Antonio Garcia Guzman, Mario Lopez, Barbara Niven; **D:** Rogelio Lobato. **VIDEO**

The Deputy Drummer 🐾½ **1935** Second-rate early British musical, notable as a later vehicle for silent-era star Lane. He plays a penniless composer who impersonates an aristocrat to attend a party, and catches jewel robbers in the act. **71m/B VHS. GB** Lupino Lane, Jean Denis, Kathleen Kelly, Wallace Lupino, Margaret Yarde, Syd Crossley; **D:** Henry W. George; **W:** Reginald Long.

Deputy Marshal 🐾½ **1950** Hall trails a pair of bankrobbers, fights off landgrabbers, and finds romance as well. **75m/B VHS.** Jon Hall, Frances Langford, Dick Foran; **D:** William Berke; **W:** William Berke.

Der Purimshpiler 🐾🐾½ **1937** *The Purim Player; The Jester; The Jewish Jester* **1937** A drifter embarks on a quest for happiness, which takes him to various small towns. In one, he meets and falls in love with an ingenue, the daughter of a shoemaker's daughter. In Yiddish with English subtitles. **90m/B VHS.** PL Miriam Kressyn, Zygmund Turkow, Hymie Jacobsen; **D:** Joseph Green.

Der Todesking 🐾🐾½ **2005** *The Death King* **1989** From the man who gave us "Nekromantik" comes this story of a chain letter that brings suicide to seven unfortunates, on seven successive days of one week. Each suicide is separated by the image of a naked, progressively decomposing man's body. In German with confusing English subtitles. **80m/C VHS. GE** Herman Kopp, Heinrich Ebber, Michael Krause, Eva M. Kurz, Angelika Hock, Nicholas Petche, Jorg Buttgereit, Manfred O. Jelinski; **D:** Jorg Buttgereit; **W:** Franz Rodenkirchen, Jorg Buttgereit; **C:** Manfred O. Jelinski; **M:** Daktari Lorenz, Herman Kopp.

Derailed 🐾🐾 **2002** (R) Spy Jacques Kristoff (Van Damme) has never told his family what he does for a living, which is a problem when they decide to surprise him on one of his "business trips." It's really bad timing since they're on the same Munich-bound train as thief Galina (Harring) who is carrying vials of mutated smallpox, which is wanted by international criminal Mason Cole (Arana), who hijacks the train. Low-budget but lots of action. **89m/C VHS, DVD.** Jean-Claude Van Damme, Laura Elena Harring, Tomas Arana, Susan Gibney, Jessica Bowring, Lucy Jenner; **D:** Bob Misiorowski; **W:** Adam Gierasch, Jace Anderson; **C:** Ross Clarkson; **M:** Serge Colbert. **VIDEO**

Derailed 🐾½ **2005** (R) Disappointing thriller has Owen as Charles Schine, unhappily married, in the midst of a midlife crisis, and more than willing to be enthralled by the charms of equally unhappy Lucinda (Aniston). However, while in their seedy hotel room, the couple is attacked by psycho-thief Laroche (Cassel), who then threatens to reveal their affair unless they pay him off. Since Owen can't convincingly play a wimp (though he tries), you wait for him to mop the floor with this sleazy Frenchman. First English-language feature for Swedish director Hafstrom; adapted from the James Siegel novel. **110m/C DVD, HD DVD, Blu-ray Disc.** US Clive Owen, Jennifer Aniston, Vincent Cassel, Melissa George, Giancarlo Esposito, David Morrissey, Georgina Chapman, Denis O'Hare, Tom Conti, Addison Timlin, Xzibit, The RZA; **D:** Mikael Hafstrom; **W:** Stuart Beattie.

Deranged 🐾🐾🐾 **1974** (R) Of the numerous movies based on the cannibalistic exploits of Ed Gein ("Psycho," "The Texas Chainsaw Massacre," etc.), this is the most accurate. A dead-on performance by Blossom and a twisted sense of humor help move things along nicely. The two directors, Gillen and Ormsby, previously worked together on the classic "Children Shouldn't Play with Dead Things." An added attraction is the early special effect work of gore wizard Tom Savini. **82m/C VHS, DVD.** CA Roberts Blossom, Cosette Lee, Robert Warner, Marcia Diamond, Brian Sneagle, Leslie (Les) Carlson, Marion Waldman, Micki Moore, Pat Orr, Robert McHeady; **D:** Jeff Gillen, Alan Ormsby; **W:** Jeff Gillen, Alan Ormsby; **M:** Carl Zittrer.

Deranged 🐾½ **1987** (R) A mentally unstable, pregnant woman is attacked in her apartment after her husband leaves town. She spends the rest of the movie engaged in psychotic encounters, real and imagined. Technically not bad, but extremely violent and grim. Not to be confused with 1974 movie of the same name. **85m/C VHS, DVD.** Jane (Veronica Hart) Hamilton, Paul Siederman, Jennifer Delora, James Gillis, Jill Cumer, Gary Goldman; **D:** Chuck Vincent.

Deranged 🐾🐾½ *Anacardium* **2001** Ultra talky thriller dealing with the conversations between renter and landlord. Soon talk of revenge and a husband out for blood creep into play. Sounds ridiculous? Somehow pulled off through decent acting and a tight script. Awarded best picture at the New York Independent Film Festival. **125m/C DVD.** Frank John Hughes, Richard Rucolo, Sean Masterson, Bob Rumnock, Laura Cayouette; **D:** Scott Thomas; **W:** Scott Thomas; **C:** Carl F. Bartels; **M:** Lars Anderson. **VIDEO**

Derby 🐾🐾🐾 **1971** (R) The documentary story of the rise to fame of roller-derby stars on the big rink. **91m/C VHS.** Charlie O'Connell, Lydia Gray, Janet Earp, Ann Colvello, Mike Snell; **D:** Robert Kaylor.

The Derby Stallion 🐾🐾½ **2005** No, it's not a good movie but it's got horses and Efron is as cute as heck, so you think tweener girls will care? Teenager Patrick (Efron) discovers his calling when he befriends alcoholic Houston Jones (Cobbs), who offers to train him to ride in the statewide steeplechase race. But Patrick's father (Moses), a former big leaguer, is pressuring him to stick with baseball. **98m/C DVD.** Zac Efron, Bill Cobbs, William R. Moses, Colton James, Tonja Walker, Michael Nardini, Sarah Blackman, Crystal Hunt, Rob Pinkston; **D:** Craig Clyde; **W:** Kimberly Gough; **C:** John Gunselman; **M:** Billy Preston. **VIDEO**

Dersu Uzala 🐾🐾🐾½ **1975** An acclaimed, photographically breathtaking film about a Russian surveyor in Siberia who befriends a crusty, resourceful Mongolian. They begin to teach each other about their respective worlds. Produced in Russia; one of Kurosawa's stranger films. **140m/C VHS, DVD.** JP RU Yuri Solomin, Maxim Munzuk; **D:** Akira Kurosawa; **W:** Akira Kurosawa, Yuri Nagibin; **C:** Asakazu Nakai, Yuri Gantman, Fyodor Dobronravov; **M:** Isaak Shvarts. Oscars '75: Foreign Film.

Descending Angel 🐾🐾🐾 **1990** (R) The premise is familiar: a swastika-friendly collaborator is forced out of the closet. But the cast and scripting make this cable there's-a-Nazi-in-the-woodwork suspenser better than average, despite its flawed finale. Scott plays a well-respected Romanian refugee—active in the community, in the church, and in Romanian-American activities—whose daughter's fiance (Roberts) suspects him of Nazi collusion. **96m/C VHS, DVD.** George C. Scott, Diane Lane, Eric Roberts, Mark Margolis, Vyto Ruginis, Amy Aquino, Richard Jenkins, Jan Rubes; **D:** George C. Scott, Jeremy Paul Kagan; **W:** George C. Scott. **CABLE**

The Descent 🐾🐾🐾½ **2005** (R) Six adventure-junkie galpals go spelunking in Appalachia and find their vacation ruined by a pack of creepy humanoids who are none too happy to have guests in their cave. So much for the trip serving to distract poor Sarah (MacDonald) from her grief over the deaths of her family. Smart, nerve-jangling terror ensues as the friends battle personal demons and each other while fending off the slimy subterranean creatures. The effects aren't always very special, but horror fans will still dig both the gory splatter and the mental tension. Original ending shown in the film's U.K. version was slightly changed for its U.S. release. **99m/C DVD, Blu-ray Disc. GB** Shauna Macdonald, Natalie Mendoza, Alex Reid, Nora-Jane Noone, Saskia Mulder, Oliver Milburn, MyAnna Buring, Molly Kayall; **D:** Neil Marshall; **W:** Neil Marshall; **C:** Sam McCurdy; **M:** David Julyan.

Descent 🐾½ **2007** (NC-17) Feminist empowerment or just revenge fantasy exploitation? College grad school student Maya (Dawson) is brutally raped by date Jared (Faust) in an attack that leaves her a basket case. She seems to get back some equilibrium by hitting the clubs and getting interested in dominating DJ Adrian (Patrick), which also appears to get Maya focused on planning revenge on Jared. Dawson's worth watching but the film is only so-so. Also available in an R-rated version. **104m/ C DVD.** Rosario Dawson, Chad Faust, Marcus Patrick; **D:** Talia Lugacy; **W:** Talia Lugacy, Brian Priest; **C:** Christopher La Vasseur, Jonathan Furmanski; **M:** Alex Moulton.

Desert Bloom 🐾🐾🐾 **1986** (PG) On the eve of a nearby nuclear bomb test, a beleaguered alcoholic veteran and his family struggle through tensions brought on by a promiscuous visiting aunt and the chaotic, rapidly changing world. Gish shines as the teenage daughter through whose eyes the story unfolds. From a story by Corr and Linda Ramy. **103m/C VHS, DVD.** Jon Voight, JoBeth Williams, Ellen Barkin, Annabeth Gish, Allen (Goorwitz) Garfield, Jay Underwood; **D:** Eugene Corr; **W:** Eugene Corr; **C:** Reynaldo Villalobos; **M:** Brad Fiedel.

Desert Blue 🐾🐾 **1998** (R) Baxter, California is a tiny (pop. 87) desert town whose one claim to fame is a towering recreation of an ice cream cone that has drawn the attention of a pop culture prof Lance (Heard). Lance has come to Baxter with his sncoty teen TV star daughter, Skye (Hudson), and the duo are trapped in town when it's quarantined by a toxic spill. Skye eventually connects to the town's disaffected teens, including Blue (Sexton), Pete (Affleck), and Ely (Ricci). John Heard, Christina Ricci, Casey Affleck, Sara Gilbert, Ethan Suplee, Lucinda Jenney; D: Enrique Chediak; M: Vytas Nagisetty.

Desert Commandos 🐾🐾 1967 When the Allies appear to be winning WWII, the Nazis devise a plan to eliminate all of the opposing forces' leaders at once. 96m/C VHS, DVD. IT GE FR Ken Clark, Horst Frank, Jeanne Valerie, Carlo Hinterman, Gianni Rizzo; D: Umberto Lenzi.

The Desert Fox 🐾🐾🐾 1936 Big-budgeted portrait of German Army Field Marshal Rommel, played by Mason, focuses on the soldier's defeat in Africa during WWII and his subsequent disillusioned return to Hitler's Germany. Mason played Rommel again in 1953's "Desert Rats." 87m/B V-HS, DVD. James Mason, Cedric Hardwicke, Jessica Tandy, Luther Adler; D: Henry Hathaway.

Desert Gold 🐾🐾 1936 A fierce Indian chief battles a horde of greedy white men over his tribe's gold mine. Based on a novel by Zane Grey. 58m/B VHS, DVD. Buster Crabbe, Robert Cummings, Marsha -tunt, Tom Keene, Raymond Hatton, Monte Blue, Leif Erickson; D: Donna Deitch; W: Natalie Cooper; C: Robert Elswit.

Desert Hearts 🐾🐾🐾 1986 (R) An upstanding professional woman travels to Reno, Nevada in 1959 to obtain a quick divorce, and slowly becomes involved in a lesbian relationship with a free-spirited casino waitress. 93m/C VHS, DVD. Helen Shaver, Audra Lindley, Patricia Charbonneau, Andra Akers, Dean Butler, Jeffrey Tambor, Denise Crosby, Gwen Welles; D: Donna Deitch; W: Natalie Cooper; C: Robert Elswit.

Desert Heat 🐾🐾 1999 (R) Loner Eddie Lomax (Van Damme) is left for dead at an abandoned highway stop in the Mojave Desert after a gang steals his motorcycle. An unexpected rescue by an old friend leaves Edd e with one thought—revenge. 95m/C VHS, DVD. Jean-Claude Van Damme, Noriyuki "Pat" Morita, Danny Trejo, Gabrielle Fitzpatrick, Larry Drake, Vincent Schiavelli; D: Danny Mulroon; W: Tom O'Rourke; C: Ross A. Maehl; M: Bill Conti. VIDEO

Desert Kickboxer 🐾🐾 1992 (R) A border guard takes on a cocaine dealer and his henchmen, fighting for go=d and, of course, a beautiful woman. Lots of kickboxing action. 86m/C VHS, John Haymes Newton, Judie Aronson, Sam DeFrancisco, Paul Smith; D: Isaac Florentine.

Desert of the Lost 🐾🐾½ 1927 Wales flees to Mexico after shooting a man in self-defense. He's aided by Montgomery and, in turn, helps save her from a forced marriage. 58m/B VHS. Wally Wales, Peggy Montgomery, William J. Dyer, Edward Cecil, Richard Neill, Kelly Catford, Ray Murro, George Magrill, Charles "Slim" Whitaker; D: Richard Thorpe.

The Desert of the Tartars 🐾 Le Desert des Tartares; Il Deserto dei Tartari 1976 (PG) Story of a young soldier who dreams of war and discovers that the real battle for him is with time. 140m/C VHS, DVD. FR IT IA Vittorio Gassman, Giuliano Gemma, Helmut Griem, Philippe Noiret, Jacques Perrin, Fernando Rey, Jean-Louis Trintignant, Max von Sydow; D: Valerio Zurlini; W: Jean-Louis Bertucelli Andre G. Brunelin; C: Luciano Tovoli; M: Ennio Morricone.

Desert Phantom 🐾½ 1936 Villains threaten to rob a woman of her ranch until a stranger rescues her. 66m/B VHS, DVD. Johnny Mack Brown, Sheila (Manors) Mangan; Price, Nelson McDowell; D: S. Foy Luby.

The Desert Rats 🐾🐾½ 1953 A crusty British captain (Burton) takes charge of an Australian division during WWII. Thinking they are interior to his own British troops, he is stiff and uncaring to the Aussies until a kind-hearted drunk and the courage of the division win him over. Crack direction from Wise and Newton's

performance (as the wag) simply steal the movie. Mason reprises his role as Germany Army Field Marshal Rommel from "The Desert Fox." 88m/B VHS, DVD. Richard Burton, Robert Newton, Charles "Bud" Tingwell, James Mason; D: Robert Wise.

Desert Saints 🐾🐾 2001 (R) Hit-man Banks (Sutherland) picks up hitchhik-er Bennie (Walters) and impulsively decides to use her assistance in his next job. But Bennie turns out to be an FBI agent assigned to hunt Banks down—or maybe she isn't. 86m/C VHS, DVD. Kiefer Sutherland, Melora Walters, Rachel Ticotin, Jamey Sheridan, Leslie Stefanson, William Sage; D: Richard Green; Incornia, Carolyn Jacobs; D: Paul DeNuccio.

Desert Snow 🐾🐾½ 1989 (R) Here's a non-formulaic dope opera oater: cowboys 'n' drug runners battle it out for an out-of-the-way, unpopulated western town. About as clever as the title. 90m/C VHS. Frank Capizzi, Flint Carney, Shelley Hinde, Sam Incornia, Carolyn Jacobs; D: Paul DeNuccio.

The Desert Song 🐾🐾 1953 MacRae secretly leads a band of do-goo-ders against the evil forces of a dastardly sheik. Grayson is in the general's daughter who falls in love with our disguised hero. Third filmed version of the Sigmund Romberg operetta creaks along with the talents of MacRae and Grayson rising about the hackneyed plot. ♪[The Desert Song; Gay Parisienne; Long Live the Night; One Alone; One Flower; The Riff Song; Romance. 96m/C VHS. Gordon MacRae, Kathryn Grayson, Raymond Massey, Steve Cochran, Dick Wesson, Alyn Ann McLerie, Ray Collins, William Conrad; D:-l Bruce Humberstone; W: Roland Kib-bee; C: Robert Burks; M: Max Steiner.

Desert Steel 🐾½ 1994 (PG) Rival racers risk their lives in the big off-road race. 39m/C VHS, David Naughton, Brian Skinner, Amanda Wyss, Russ Tamblyn; D: Glenn Ge-

Desert Thunder 🐾🐾 1999 (R) Lee Miller (Baldwin) is a retired Air Force pilot who rejoins the action when he's called to lead a commando mission to defeat an Iraqi terrorist threat. Low-budget still boasts some good explosions and aerial scenes. 88m/C VHS, DVD. Daniel Baldwin, Richard Portnow, Stacy -taiduk; D: Jim Wynoski; W: Lenny Juliano. VIDEO

Desert Trail 🐾🐾½ 1935 Wayne is a championship rodeo rider, accused of a bank robbery. 57m/B VHS, DVD. John Wayne, Paul Fix, Mary Kornman; D: Robert North Bradbury; W: Lindsley Parsons; C: Archie Stout.

Desert Warrior 🐾 1988 (PG-13) Earth becomes a waste site after a nuclear war. Ferrigno stars as a post-nuke hero in this low-budget action flir. Very bad acting. 89m/C VHS, Lou Ferrigno, Shari Shattuck, Kenneth Peer, Anthony East; D: Jim Goldman; W: Frederick Bailey.

Desert Winds 🐾🐾 1995 Weird little fantastical romance finds Jackie (Graham) who lives near the New Mexican desert, regularly communing with nature on a rocky plateau. Lonely Jackie once heard the voice of Eugene (Nickles), who lives 500 miles away in Arizona, thanks to a rare phenomenon known as a wind tunnel, but it takes seven years before she hears his voice again. 97m/C VHS, DVD. Heather Graham, Michael A. (M.A.) Nickles, Jack Kehler, Adam Ant; D: Michael A. (M.A.) Nickles; W: Michael A. (M.A.) Nickles; C: Denis Maloney; M: James McVay.

The Deserters 🐾🐾½ 1983 Sergeant Hawley, a Vietnam-era hawk, hunts deserters and draft-dodgers in Canada. There, he confronts issues of war and peace head-on. 110m/C VHS, CA Alan Scarfe, Dermot Hennelly, Jon Bryden, Barbara March; D: Jack Darcus; W: Jack Darcus; C: Tony Westman; M: Michael Conway Baker.

The Designated Mourner 🐾½ 1997 (R) Adapted from the play by Wallace Shawn, this pointy-headed inaction movie laments the passing of the class of people who "appreciate the poetry of John Donne" and other forms of high art. It's probably the same class that would like repressive country that resembles a large

table. Nichols plays the eponymous mourner Jack, a journalist who once ran with a literary crowd but betrayed their ideals for survival. Richardson plays his wife Judy, the daughter of final talking head Howard (de Keyser), who is a humanist most don't like people. If you need a lecture on culture written by a man who was in "Mom and Dad Save the World" and playec the geeky social student teacher in "Clueless," then this is your movie. To quote Shawn: "Inconceivable!" 94m/C VHS, DVD. GB Mike Nichols, Miranda Richardson, David de Keyser; D: David Hare; W: Wallace Shawn; C: Oliver Stapleton; M: Richard Hartley.

Designing Woman 🐾🐾🐾 1957 Bacall and Peck star in this mismatched tale of romance. She's a chic high-fashion designer; he's a rumpled sports writer. The fun begins when they try to adjust to married life together. Neither likes the other's friends or lifestyle. Things get even crazier when Bacall has to work with her ex-lover Helmore on a fashion show and Peck's former love Gray shows up as well. And as if that weren't enough, Peck is being hunted by the mob because of a boxing story he's written. It's a fun, quick, witty tale that is all entertainment and no message. Bacall's performance is of note because Bogart was dying of cancer at the time. 119m/C VHS, DVD. Gregory Peck, Lauren Bacall, Dolores Gray, Sam Levene Tom Helmore, Mickey Shaughnessy, Jesse White, Chuck Connors, Edward Platt, Alvy Moore, Jack Cole; D: Vincente Minnelli; W: George Wells; C: John Alton; M: Andre Previn. Oscars '57: Story & Screenplay.

Desire 🐾🐾🐾 1936 Jewel thief Madeleine (Dietrich) manages to involve innocent tourist Tom (Cooper) into carrying her ill-gotten goods across the Spanish border. Then she entices him into joining her crime. By this time Tom is in love—and so is Madeleine but she doesn't think she's good enough for him. Lots of trying until the twosome can figure out what to do. Cooper manages to hold his own with the so-phisticated Dietrich in their second film together (after "Morocco"). 96m/B VHS. Marlene Dietrich, Gary Cooper, John Halliday, William Frawley, Ernest Cossart, Akim Tamiroff, Alan Mowbray; D: Frank Borzage; W: Edwin Justus Mayer, Waldemar Young; M: Frederick "Friederich" Hollander.

Desire 🐾🐾 1993 (R) A free-spirited woman finds herself attracted to a local fisherman. Hardly her intellectual equal but then what she really wants is his body. 108m/C VHS, DVD. Greta Scacchi, Vincent D'Onofrio; D: Andrew Birkin.

Desire 🐾🐾 1995 (R) Security consultant Lauren Allen (Hodge) is working for a perfume manufacturer whose fragrance, Desira, is the fave of a Beverly Hills serial killer who likes to douse his victims in the scent. The prime suspect is scent expert Gordon Lewis (Kemp) and naturally Lauren falls for him. Standard erotic thriller fare. 90m/C VHS. Kate Hodge, Martin Kemp, Deborah Shelton, Robert Miranda; D: Rodney McDonald; W: Rodney McDonald.

Desire and Hell at Sunset Motel 🐾½ 1992 (PG-13) Low-budget thriller takes place at the Sunset Motel in 1950s Anaheim. Fenn is the bombshell wife of a toy salesman who's in town for a sales meeting, while she just wants to visit Disneyland. She's soon fooling around with another guy and her husband hires a psychotic criminal to spy on her as her new lover plots to kill hubby. Very confusing plot isn't worth figuring out. Film's only redeeming quality is the imaginative and creative work used in the visuals. Castle's directorial debut. 90m/C VHS, DVD. Sherilyn Fenn, Whip Hubley, David Hewlett, David Johansen, Paul Bartel, Kenneth Tobey; D: Allen Castle; W: Allen Castle; C: Jamie Thompson.

Desire Under the Elms 🐾🐾 1958 Ives, the patriarch of an 1840s New England farming family, takes a young wife (Loren) who promptly has an affair with her stepson. Based on the play by Eugene O'Neill. 114m/B VHS, DVD. Sophia Loren, An-

thony Perkins, Burl Ives, Frank Overton; D: Delbert Mann; C: Daniel F. Fapp; M: Elmer Bernstein.

Desiree 🐾🐾½ 1954 A romanticized historical epic abo t Napoleon and his 17-year-old mistress, Desiree. Based on the novel by Annemarie Selinko. Slightly better than average historical fiction piece. 110m/C Charlotte Austin, Marlon Brando, Jean Simmons, Merle Oberon, Michael Rennie, Cameron Mitchell, Elizabeth Sellars, Cathleen Nesbitt; D: Henry Koster; W: Daniel Taradash; C: Milton Krasner; M: Alex North.

Desk Set 🐾🐾🐾 His Other Woman 1957 One of the later and less dynamic Tracy/ Hepburn comedies, about an efficiency expert who installs a giant computer in an effort to update a TV network's female-run reference department. Still, the duo spar-kle as they bicker, battle, and give in to love. Based on William Marchant's play. 103m/C VHS, DVD. Spencer Tracy, Katharine Hepburn, Joan Blondell, Gig Young, Dina Merrill, Neva Patterson, Harry Ellerbe, Nicholas Joy; D: Walter Lang; W: Phoebe Ephron, Henry Ephron; C: Leon Shamroy; M: Cyril Mockridge.

Desolation Angels 🐾🐾 1995 Nick Adams (Rodick) returns to New York after a month spent unhappily visiting his mother and discovers his girlfriend Mary (Thomas) has been raped by his best friend Sid (Bassett). At least that's how Nick interprets the situation after an unwilling Mary admits they had sex. Nick goes after Sid, gets beaten up, hires a couple of thugs who botch a retaliation, and just gets increasingly enraged over his inability to settle the situation. The focus is on Nick and Rodrick is more than up to the director McCann's demands. 90m/C VHS, DVD. Michael Rodrick, Peter Bassett, Jennifer Thomas; D: Tim McCann; W: Tim McCann; M: Andy Howe.

Despair 🐾🐾🐾 Eine Reise ins Licht 1978 A chilling and comic study of a victimized chocolate factory owner's descent into madness, set against the backdrop of the Nazi rise to power in the 1930s. Adapted from the Nabokov novel by Tom Stoppard. 120m/C VHS, GE Dirk Bogarde, Andrea Ferreol, Volker Spengler, Klaus Lowitsch; D: Rainer Werner Fassbinder; W: Tom Stoppard; C: Michael Ballhaus; M: Peer Raben.

Desperado 🐾🐾½ El Mariachi 2 1995 (R) Rodriguez's nameless guitar player-turned-gunman returns—this time in the persona of heartthrob Banderas. The director also has a studio budget to play with (a sizable increase over the $7000 for "El Mariachi," so the action's on a bigger, more violent scale (you'll quickly lose count of flying bodies and bullets) as El Mariachi tracks infamous drug lord Bucho (de Almeida). Gringo Buscemi provides assistance, beautiful bookstore owner Carolina (Hayek) offers solace, and Tarantino meets his well-deserved cameo demise. You'll also find Mariachi, Gallardo, in a cameo role as a musician. Filmed in Mexico. 103m/C VHS, DVD. Antonio Banderas, Salma Hayek, Joaquim de Almeida, Steve Buscemi, Richard "Cheech" Marin, Carlos Gomez, Carlos Gallardo; Cameos: Quentin Tarantino, Carlos Gallardo; D: Robert Rodriguez; W: Robert Rodriguez; C: Guillermo Navarro; M: Los Lobos.

The Desperados 🐾🐾 1943 Cheyenne Rogers (Ford) is a gunman trying to go straight. So he heads into the town of Red Valley, Utah, to see o c pal-turned-sheriff Steve Upton (Scott). Unfortunately for Cheyenne this is just after the town's bank has been robbed in a crooked scheme set up by a couple of sk=rpies (Hall, Buchanan) and he is framed for the crime. Now it's up to Cheyenne, Steve, and a couple of wild west gals (Trevor, Keyes) to prove his innocence. Set in 1863; adapted from a story by Max Brand. Columbia's first Technicolor film. 86m/C DVD. Glenn Ford, Randolph Scott, Claire Trevor, Evelyn Keyes, Edgar Buchanan, Porter Hall Guinn "Big Boy" Williams, Raymond Walburn; D: Charles Vidor; W: Robert Carson; C: George Meehan Jr.

Desperados 🐾🐾½ 1969 (PG) After the Civil War, a murderous renegade and two of his sons go on a looting rampage, eventually kidnapping the child of the third son who just wants to live in peace. Mede in Spain. **90m/C VHS.** *SP* Jack Palance, Vince Edwards, Christian Roberts, George Maharis, Neville Brand, Sylvia Syms; **D:** Henry Levin; **W:** Walter Brough; **C:** Sam Leavitt.

The Desperados 🐾½ *Apache Vengeance: Five Savage Men* 1970 When a young woman is raped by outlaws robbing her stagecoach, a bevy of western heroes band together to avenge her. **86m/C VHS, DVD.** Keenan Wynn, Henry Silva, Michele Carey, John Anderson, Joe Turkel; **D:** Ron Joy; **W:** Richard Bakalyan; **M:** Rupert Holmes.

Desperate 🐾🐾½ 1947 An honest truck driver witnesses a mob crime and must escape with his wife in this minor film noir. Eventually, the law is on his tail, too. **73m/B VHS.** Steve Brodie, Audrey Long, Raymond Burr, Jason Robards Sr., Douglas Fowley, William Challee, Ilka Gruning, Nan Leslie; **D:** Anthony Mann.

Desperate Cargo 🐾½ 1941 Two showgirls stranded in a Latin American town manage to get aboard a clipper ship with hoodlums who are trying to steal the vessel's cargo. **69m/B VHS, DVD.** Ralph Byrd, Carol Hughes, Jack Mulhall; **D:** William Beaudine; **W:** Morgan Cox, John T. Coyle; **C:** Jack Greenhalgh.

Desperate Characters 🐾🐾🐾 1971 (R) A slice-of-city-life story about a middle-class couple living in a once-fashionable section of Brooklyn, New York, who watch their neighborhood disintegrate around them. The two find their lives a series of small disappointments, routine work, uncertain friendships, and pervasive violence. Excellent performances, especially by MacLaine as the harried wife, but the film's depressing nature made it a complete boxoffice flop. **87m/C VHS.** Shirley MacLaine, Kenneth Mars, Gerald S. O'Loughlin, Sada Thompson, Michael Higgins, Rose Gregorio, Jack Somack, Chris Gampel, Mary Alan Hokanson, Patrick McVey, Carol Kane; **D:** Frank D. Gilroy; **W:** Frank D. Gilroy.

Desperate Crimes 🐾🐾 *Mafia Docks* 1993 Two rival mobs battle over the prostitution and drug trade. When an innocent woman is murdered her brother looks for revenge with the help of a beautiful prostitute. **92m/C VHS, DVD.** Traci Lords, Denise Crosby, Franco (Columbo) Columbu, Van Quattro, Rena Niehaus, Nicoletta Boris, Elizabeth Kaitan, Randi Ingerman; **D:** Andreas Marfori; **C:** Marco Isoli.

Desperate Hours 🐾🐾🐾 1955 A tough, gritty thriller about three escaped convicts taking over a suburban home and holding the family hostage. Plenty of suspense and fine acting. Based on the novel and play by Joseph Hayes. **112m/B VHS, DVD.** Humphrey Bogart, Fredric March, Martha Scott, Arthur Kennedy, Gig Young, Dewey Martin, Mary Murphy, Robert Middleton, Richard Eyer, Ray Collins, Beverly Garland; **D:** William Wyler; **C:** Lee Garmes. Natl. Bd. of Review '55: Director (Wyler).

Desperate Hours 🐾🐾 1990 (R) An escaped prisoner holes up in a suburban couple's home, waiting for his lawyer/accomplice to take him to Mexico. Tensions heighten between the separated couple and the increasingly nerve-wracked criminals. Terrific, if not downright horrifying, performance by Rourke in an overall tepid remake of the 1955 thriller. **105m/C VHS, DVD.** Mickey Rourke, Anthony Hopkins, Mimi Rogers, Kelly Lynch, Lindsay Crouse, Elias Koteas, David Morse, Shawnee Smith, Danny Gerard, Matt McGrath; **D:** Michael Cimino; **W:** Mark Rosenthal, Larry Konner, Joseph Hayes; **C:** Doug Milsome; **M:** David Mansfield.

Desperate Journey 🐾🐾½ 1942 Flynn and Reagan are two of five Allied fighters shot down over Nazi occupied Poland. They go through various tight squeezes such as stealing Goering's car and eliminating a few Nazis on their way back to England. All the while they are hunted by Massey as Nazi Major Otto Baumester, who of course bumbles and fumbles the whole affair. Strictly propaganda intended to keep up morale on the homefront. Flynn was not pleased about having Reagan as his co-star, seeing as he was usually paired with female leads. **108m/B VHS.** Errol Flynn, Ronald Reagan, Raymond Massey, Nancy

Coleman, Alan Hale, Arthur Kennedy, Helmut Dantine; **D:** Raoul Walsh; **M:** Max Steiner.

Desperate Lives 🐾🐾 1982 High school siblings come into contact with drugs and join their guidance counselor in the war against dope. Average made for TV fare. **100m/C VHS.** Diana Scarwid, Doug McKeon, Helen Hunt, William Windom, Art Hindle, Tom Atkins, Sam Bottoms, Diane Ladd, Dr. Joyce Brothers; **D:** Robert Lewis; **M:** Bruce Broughton. **TV**

Desperate Living 🐾🐾½ 1977 Typical John Waters trash. A mental patient (Stole) is released and becomes paranoid that her family may be out to kill her. After aiding in the murder of her husband (the hefty maid, Hill, suffocates him by sitting on him), Stole and Hill escape to Mortville, a town populated by outcasts such as transsexuals, murderers, and the woefully disfigured. **90m/C VHS, DVD.** Mink Stole, Jean Hill, Edith Massey, Liz Renay, Mary Vivian Pearce, Cookie Mueller, Susan Lowe, Ed Peranio, Pat Moran, George Stover, Turkey Joe, Channing Wilroy; **D:** John Waters; **W:** John Waters; **C:** Thomas Loizeaux.

Desperate Measures 🐾🐾½ 1998 (R) Police officer Frank Connor (Garcia) desperately searches for a bone marrow donor for his dying son. Turns out the perfect match is vicious murderer and prison inmate Pete McCabe (Keaton). McCabe seizes the opportunity to unleash an elaborate and violent prison escape in a San Francisco hospital. Keaton, as a poor man's Hannibal Lecter, offers this movie's only entertainment. The rest of the dying child to propel its already ludicrous story along, it would be a great source for slapstick comedy. Film was held back for several months before its final release and you'll find out why the studio wanted to hide this one. **100m/C VHS, DVD.** Andy Garcia, Michael Keaton, Marcia Gay Harden, Brian Cox, Efrain Figueroa, Joseph Cross, Richard Riehle; **D:** Barbet Schroeder; **W:** Henry Bean, Neal Jimenez, David Klass; **C:** Luciano Tovoli; **M:** Trevor Jones.

The Desperate Mission 🐾🐾 *Distant Drums* 1960 Joaquin Murietta (Montelban) is a Mexican nobleman acting as a Robin Hood for those oppressed by corrupt authorities in gold-rushed 1840s California. Only what the family doesn't realize is that the duo have escaped from an asylum for the criminally insane and want to take over their lives. **92m/C VHS.** Edward (Eddie) Bunker, David Keith, Marg Helgenberger, William Katt, Mel Harris, Mary Crosby, Brian Bonsall, Cyndi Pass; **D:** Andrew Lane; **W:** C. Courtney Joyner.

Desperate Motives 🐾 *Redheads* 1994 (R) Lucy (Karvan) videotapes herself having sex with lawyer Brewster (Hembrow) and then accidentally films his murder. So she's stalked by the killer. **102m/C VHS.** *AU* Claudia Karvan, Catherine McClements, Mark Hembrow; **D:** Danny Vendramini; **W:** Danny Vendramini.

Desperate Moves 🐾🐾 1986 An Oregon-transplanted geek in San Francisco sets out to make himself over in order to win his dream girl. Sometimes effective, often sappy treatment of his coming to terms with the big city. **90m/C VHS.** Isabel Sanford, Steve Tracy, Paul Benedict, Christopher Lee, Eddie Deezen; **D:** Ovidio G. Assonitis.

Desperate Prey 🐾½ 1986 An

having heart palpitations over the hunk). Unfortunately, her current lover is Anne (Chappell) and Dorothea has also decided on a marriage of convenience with ambitious politician William (Hurst). It's all very operatic. **92m/C VHS.** *NZ* Jennifer Ward-Lealand, Kevin Smith, Lisa Chappell, Michael Hurst, Kiri Mills, Clifford Curtis; **D:** Stewart Main, Peter Wells; **C:** Leon Narbey; **M:** Peter Scholes.

Desperate Target 🐾½ 1980 Courageous people fight against all odds to survive. **90m/C VHS.** Chris Mitchum, Victoria Loveland; **D:** George Vieira; **C:** Jack Beckett.

The Desperate Trail 🐾🐾½ 1994 (R) Prostitute, convicted of killing an abusive client, manages to escape from the marshal who's escorting her to her hanging. She teams up with a con man in a plot to rob a bank while the marshal enlists a posse to track her down. Strong performances augmented by blazing guns, hobbled by weak writing. **93m/C VHS, DVD.** Sam Elliott, Linda Fiorentino, Craig Sheffer, Frank Whaley; **D:** P.J. Pesce; **W:** P.J. Pesce, Tom Abrams; **C:** Michael Bonvillain; **M:** Stephen Endelman. **CABLE**

Desperate Women 🐾🐾½ 1978 Western about three unjustly accused female convicts rescued en route to prison by an ex-hired gun. **96m/C VHS.** Susan St. James, Dan Haggerty, Ronee Blakley, Ann Dusenberry, Susan Myers; **D:** Earl Bellamy. **TV**

Desperately Seeking Susan 🐾🐾 1985 (PG-13) Roberta (Arquette) is a bored New Jersey housewife who gets her kicks reading the personals. When she becomes obsessed with a relationship between two lovers who arrange their meetings through the columns, Roberta decides to find out for herself who they are. But after an accident, Roberta loses her memory and thinks she is Susan, the free-spirited woman in the personals. Unfortunately, Susan (Madonna) is in a lot of trouble with all sorts of unsavory folk and our innocent housewife finds herself caught in the middle. Terrific characters, with special appeal generated by Arquette and Madonna. Quinn winningly plays Roberta's bewildered romantic interest. **104m/C VHS, DVD.** Rosanna Arquette, Madonna, Aidan Quinn, Mark Blum, Robert Joy, Laurie Metcalf, Steven Wright, John Turturro, Will Patton, Richard Hell, Annie Golden, Ann Magnuson, Richard Edson; **D:** Susan Seidelman; **W:** Leora Barish; **C:** Edward Lachman; **M:** Thomas Newman. British Acad. '85: Support. Actress (Arquette); Natl. Bd. of Review '85: Support. Actress (Arquette).

Destination Alpha 🐾🐾 *Space: 2100* 1975 In the 21st century, an explosion has destroyed half the moon, causing it to break away from the Earth's orbit. The moon is cast far away, but the 311 people manning Alpha, a research station on the moon, must continue their search for other life forms in outer space. A thankless task. Pilot for the TV series "Space: 1999". **93m/C VHS.** *GB* Martin Landau, Barbara Bain, Barry Morse, Nick (Nicholas) Tate; **D:** Tom Clegg; **W:** Terence Feely; **M:** Derek Wadsworth. **TV**

Destination Moon 🐾🐾½ 1950 Story of man's first lunar voyage contains Chesley Bonstell's astronomical artwork and a famous Woody Woodpecker cartoon. Includes previews of coming attractions from classic science fiction films. **91m/C VHS, DVD.** Warner Anderson, Tom Powers, Dick Wesson, Erin O'Brien-Moore; **D:** Irving Pichel; **W:** Alford "Rip" Van Ronkel, Robert Heinlein, James O'Hanlon; **C:** Lionel Lindon; **M:** Leith Stevens.

Destination Moonbase Alpha 🐾🐾

Destination Saturn 🐾🐾 *Buck Rogers* 1939 Buck Rogers awakens from suspended animation in the 25th century. **90m/B VHS, DVD.** Buster Crabbe, Constance Moore; **D:** Ford Beebe.

Destination Tokyo 🐾🐾 1943 A weathered WWII submarine actioner, dealing with the search-and-destroy mission of a U.S. sub sent into Tokyo harbor. Available in a colorized version. **135m/B VHS, DVD.** Cary Grant, John Garfield, Alan Hale, Dane Clark, John Ridgely, Warner Anderson, William Prince, Robert Hutton, Tom Tully, Peter Whitney, Faye Emerson, John Forsythe; **D:** Delmer Daves.

Destination Vegas 🐾🐾 1995 (R) Attorney Sommerfield is on the lam, driving across the Mojave trying to elude hitmen sent to prevent her testimony in a murder trial. She hooks up with drifter Duhamel, who just happens to be an ex-getaway driver, and it's put the pedal to the metal time. Low-budget familiar story with some saving humor. **78m/C VHS, DVD.** Jennifer Sommerfield, Claude Duhamel, Stephen Polk, Richard Lynch; **D:** Paul Wynne; **W:** Paul Wynne; **C:** William H. Molina; **M:** Peter Tomashek. **VIDEO**

Destiny 🐾🐾🐾 *Der Müde Tod* 1921 Fritz Lang's silent fantasy is a version of the myth of Orpheus. Death takes a young man on the eve of his wedding, but agrees to return him if his fiancee can save three lives. In terms of style, it's really closer to Dreyer's "Vampyr" than to Lang's own "M." **99m/B VHS, DVD.** *GE* Lil Dagover, Rudolf Klein-Rogge, Bernhard Goetzke, Walther Jansson, Eduard von Winterstein, Paul Biensfeldt; **D:** Fritz Lang; **W:** Thea von Harbou; **C:** Fritz Arno Wagner, Erich Nitzschmann, Hermann Saalfrank.

Destiny 🐾🐾🐾 *Al-Massir* 1997 Averroes (el-Cherif) is a 12th century Arab humanist philosopher living in Andalusia, Spain. When one of his disciples is burned at the stake for heresy, the man's son Youssef (Rahouma), following his father's wishes, travels to Andalusia to study with Averroes. Youssef finds that the ruling Caliph (Memida) supports Averroes but a fundamentalist Muslim cult hopes to overthrow the Caliph and destroy Averroes and his students. Arabic with subtitles. **135m/C VHS, DVD.** *EG* Nour (el-Sherif), Fares Rahouma, Mahmoud Hemeida, Khaled el-Nabaoui, Laila Eloui; **D:** Youssef Chahine; **W:** Youssef Chahine, Khaled Youssef.

The Destiny of Marty Fine 🐾 1996 Lame low-budget drama about washed-up boxer Marty Fine (Gelfant), who witnesses the murder of mob boss Capelli (Ironside). He promises old-time gangster Daryl (Fell) he'll keep quiet but Daryl orders a hit anyway. So lowlife Marty tries to get out of L.A. **85m/B VHS.** Mark Ruffalo, Alan Gelfant, Norman Fell, James LeGros, Catherine Keener, Michael Ironside, Glenn Plummer, John Diehl, Sandra Seacat; **D:** Michael Hacker; **W:** Mark Ruffalo, Michael Hacker; **C:** Melinda Sue Gordon.

Destiny Turns on the Radio 🐾 1995 (R) Mystic figure Johnny Destiny (Tarantino) dabbles in the lives of various stock characters in Las Vegas after emerging from a glowing swimming pool. Three years after this grand entrance, he enlists escaped con Julian and partner Thoreau (McDermott and Le Gros, respectively) to help him return to his place of origin. Julian has other plans, which involve getting his ex, Lucille (Travis), back from sleazy casino owner Tuerto (Belushi). Aggressively cheezy, dime novel dialogue and threadbare, convoluted plot wastes talents of interesting cast. Too much time and energy spent trying to be hip. Sadly, Tarantino's only participation was in front of the camera. **101m/C VHS.** Dylan McDermott, Nancy Travis, James LeGros, Quentin Tarantino, Allen (Goorwitz) Garfield, James Belushi, Tracey Walter, Bob(cat) Goldthwait, Richard Edson; **D:** Jack Baran; **W:** Robert Ramsey, Matthew Stone; **C:** James L. Carter; **M:** Steven Soles.

Destroy All Monsters 🐾🐾½ *Kaiju Soshingeki; All Monsters Attack; Operation Monsterland* 1968 (G) When alien babes take control of Godzilla and his monstrous colleagues (, it looks like all is lost for Earth. Adding insult to injury, Ghidra is sent in to take care of the loose ends. Can the planet possibly survive this madness? Classic Toho monster slugfest also features Mothra, Rodan, Son of Godzilla, Anglia, Varan, Baragon, Spigas and others. **88m/C VHS, DVD.** *JP* Akira Kubo, Jun Tazaki, Yoshio Tsuchiya, Kyoko Ai, Yukiko Kobayashi, Kenji Sahara, Andrew Hughes, Yoshifumi Tajima, Nadao Kirino, Susumu Kurobe, Hisaya Ito; **D:** Inoshiro Honda; **W:** Inoshiro Honda, Takeshi Kimura; **C:** Taiichi Kankura; **M:** Akira Ifukube.

Destroy All Planets 🐾🐾½ *Gamera Tai Viras; Gamera Tai Uchukaiju Bairasu; Gamera Vs. Viras; Gamera Vs. Outer Space Monster Viras* 1968 Aliens whose spaceships turn into giant flying squids are attacking Earth. It's up to Gammera, the flying, fire-breathing turtle to save the day. **75m/C VHS, JP** *Peter Williams, Kojiro Hongo, Toru Takatsuka;* **D:** *Noriaki Yuasa.*

Destroyer 🦴 1943 (R) Small-budget film crew goes to an empty prison to shoot, and are stalked by the ghost/zombie remains of a huge serial killer given the electric chair 18 months before. **94m/C VHS,** *Anthony Perkins, Deborah Foreman, Lyle Alzado;* **D:** *Robert Kirk.*

The Destructors 🦴 *The Marseille Contract* 1974 (PG) An American narcotics enforcement officer in Paris seeks the help of a hitman in order to catch a druglord. **89m/C VHS, GB** *Anthony Quinn, Michael Caine, James Mason; Maureen Kerwin, Alexandra Stewart;* **D:** *Robert Parrish;* **W:** *Judd Bernard.*

Destry Rides Again 🦴🦴🦴 1939 An uncontrollably lawless western town is whipped into shape by a peaceful, unarmed sheriff. A vintage Hollywood potpourri with Dietrich's finest post-Sternberg moment, standing on the bar singing "See What the Boys in the Back Room Will Have." The second of three versions of this Max Brand story. First was released in 1932; the third in 1954. **94m/B VHS, DVD,** *James Stewart, Marlene Dietrich, Brian Donlevy, Charles Winninger, Mischa Auer, Irene Hervey, Una Merkel, Billy Gilbert, Jack Carson, Samuel S. Hinds, Allen Jenkins;* **D:** *George Marshall;* **W:** *Gertrude Purcell, Felix Jackson, Henry Myers;* **C:** *Hal Mohr.* **M:** *Frank Skinner. Natl. Film Reg. '96.*

The Detective 🦴🦴🦴 1954 Based on G.K. Chesterton's "Father Brown" detective stories, a slick, funny English mystery in which the famous priest tracks down a notorious, endlessly crafty antique thief. **91m/B VHS,** *GB Alec Guinness; Peter Finch, Joan Greenwood, Cecil Parker, Bernard Lee;* **D:** *Robert Hamer;* **W:** *Maurice Rapf.*

Details of a Duel: A Question of Honor 🦴🦴½ 1989 A butcher and a teacher collide in this comedy and provoked in which they resolve their grievances with a duel before the entire town. In Spanish with English subtitles. **97m/C VHS, SP** *Frank Ramírez, Florine Lemaitre, Vicky Hernandez, Humberto Dorado;* **D:** *Sergio Cabrera;* **W:** *Jerry Goldsmith.*

The Detective 🦴🦴🦴 1968 A New York detective investigating the mutilation murder of a homosexual finds political and police department corruption. Fire, gritty performances prevail in this suspense thriller. Based on the novel by Roderick Thorpe. **114m/C VHS, DVD,** *Frank Sinatra, Lee Remick, Ralph Meeker, Jacqueline Bisset, William Windom, Robert Duvall, Tony Musante, Jack Klugman, Al Freeman Jr., Horace McMahon, Lloyd Bochner, Pat Henry, Patrick McVey, "Sugar Ray" Robinson, Renee Taylor, Tom Atkins, George Plimpton;* **D:** *Gordon Douglas;* **W:** *Abby Mann;* **C:** *Joseph Biroc;* **M:** *Jerry Goldsmith.*

Detective 🦴🦴 1985 Style over substance as Godard has various characters/suspects investigating a murder committed in a Paris hotel two years previously. However, Godard seems more interested in the look than the plot. French with subtitles. **95m/C VHS, FR** *Nathalie Baye, Claude Brasseur, Jean-Pierre Leaud, Johnny Hallyday, Laurent Terzieff, Alain Cuny;* **D:** *Jean-Luc Godard;* **W:** *Philippe Setbon, Alain Sarde;* **C:** *Bruno Nuytten.*

Detective Sadie & Son 🦴🦴 *Sadie & Son* 1984 An elderly detective and her young son crack a case. **96m/C VHS,** *Debbie Reynolds, Sam Wanamaker, Brian McNamara;* **D:** *John Llewelyn Moxey.* **TV**

Detective School Dropouts 🦴 *Dumb Dicks* 1985 (PG) ... detective school, ... are they smart enough to curb a kidnapper? Find out and get a few laughs at the

Detention 🦴½ 2003 (R) Lungren is history teacher and ex-Special Forces soldier Decker, in charge of detention for a group of juvenile delinquents. The school is shut down by a group of drug dealers so they can use it to finish a heroin theft. Decker and the students must fight the bad guys in the usual hail of gunfire and explosions to regain control of the school. Cartoonish action flick isn't helped by the wooden presence of "The Dolphinator." **84m/C DVD** *CA Dolph Lundgren, Alex Karzis, Sidney J. Furie, John Sheppard, Corey Sevier, Dov Tiefenbach, Chris Collins, Mpho Koaho, Larry Day, Danielle Hampton, Kata Dobo;* **D:** *Curtis Petersen;* **M:** *Amin Bhatia.* **VIDEO**

Deterrence 🦴🦴 2000 (R) Stagy one-room thriller set during the presidential campaign of 2008. Veep Walter Emerson (Pollak) became prez when the incumbent died—now he's campaigning for re-election. He's at a Colorado primary when a blizzard forces Emerson and his aides (as well as a TV crew) to take shelter in a small town diner. The diner's cable TV hookup reports an international crisis—Iraq forces have invaded Kuwait and slaughtered American peacekeepers. So Emerson decides the thing to do is nuke Baghdad. Lots of pontificating. **101m/C VHS, DVD,** *Kevin Pollak, Timothy Hutton, Sheryl Lee Ralph, Sean Astin, Clotilde Courau, Badja Djola, Mark Thompson;* **D:** *Rod Lurie;* **C:** *Frank Perl;* **M:** *Lawrence Nash Groupe.*

Detective Story 🦴🦴½ 1951 Intense drama about a New York City police precinct with a wide array of characters noir downer. Well-designed, stylish, and compelling, if a bit contrived and, at times annoyingly shrill. Shot in only six days with six indoor sets. Down-on-his-luck pianist Neal hitches cross-country to rejoin his fiancee. His first wrong turn involves the accidental death of the man who picked him up, then he's en route to Hollywood with a capital "D" when he picks up fatal femme Savage, as vicious a vixen as ever ruined a good man. Told in flashback, it's also been called the most despairing of all "B"-pictures. As noir as they get. **67m/B VHS, DVD,** *Tom Neal, Ann Savage, Claudia Drake, Edmund MacDonald, Tim Ryan, Esther Howard, Don Brodie, Pat Gleason;* **D:** *Edgar G. Ulmer;* **W:** *Martin Goldsmith;* **C:** *Benjamin (Ben H.) Kline;* **M:** *Leo Erdody. Natl. Film Reg. '92.*

Detour 🦴🦴 1992 (R) Remake of the 1945 noir classic even features Neal Jr. in the role that his dad made famous. He's the nightclub musician, hitching his way to rural hometown where one of his old friends (Madsen) is now the sheriff. But Danny still can't escape from his ex-partner (Russo) or the rest of the bad guys. Lots of action in a routine plot. **93m/C VHS, DVD,** *Tom Neal Jr., Lea Lavish, Susanna Foster, Erin McGrane;* **D:** *Wade Williams;* **W:** *Wade Williams;* **M:** *Bill Crain.*

Detour to Danger Woof! 1945 Two young men set out on a fishing expedition and run into crooks and damsels in distress. Unintentionally hilarious "acting" by the no-name cast make this a grade-Z "B" movie. Of interest only because it was filmed in the three-color Kodachrome process used primarily in documentaries. **56m/C VHS, Britt Wood,** *John Day, Nancy Brinckman;* **D:** *Richard Talmadge.* **VIDEO**

Detonator 🦴🦴 *Alistair MacLean's Death Train, Death Train* 1993 (R) A renegade Russian general has stolen a nuclear bomb and is transporting it from Germany to Iraq via a hijacked train commandeered by his hired band of mercenaries. Stewart is the U.N. troubleshooter delegated to stop the plot, aided by a commando team featuring Brosnan and Paul. Based on the novel "Death Train" by Alistair MacLean. **96m/C VHS, DVD,** *Pierce Brosnan, Patrick Stewart, Ted Levine, Alexandra Paul, Christopher Lee;* **D:** *David S. Jackson.*

The Detonator 🦴½ 2006 (R) Yet another ho-hum actioner from Snipes. Homeland Security agent Sonni Griffith is involved in an arms deal that goes bad. After leaving too many dead bodies behind, Sonni is given a chance to redeem himself by escorting witness Nadia (Collocia) to New York. Except the arms dealer just happens to be after Nadia and some traitor in the CIA is providing him with intel. **96m/C DVD,** *Wesley Snipes, Silvia Collocia, Michael Brandon, Matthew Leitch, William Hope;* **D:** *Po Chih Leong;* **W:** *Martin Wheeler;* **C:** *Richard Greatrex;* **M:** *Barry Taylor.* **VIDEO**

Detonator 2: Night Watch 🦴🦴½ *Alistair MacLean's Night Watch; Night Watch* 1995 (R) Brosnan and Paul return as operatives for the secret United Nations Anti-Crime Organization (UNACO). Mike Graham and Sabrina Carver are teamed by their boss Nick Caldwell (Devane) when it's discovered that Rembrandt's "Night Watch" has been replaced by a forgery. This takes our intrepid duo to Hong Kong, a shady computer expert/art collector (Shannon), and a suspicious satellite about to be launched by North Korea. Based on a story by Alistair MacLean. **99m/C VHS, DVD,** *Pierce Brosnan, Alexandra Paul, William Devane, Michael J. Rob Schneider, Yin Shaye, Lim Kay Siu, Irene Ng;* **D:** *David S. Jackson;* **W:** *David S. Jackson.* **CABLE**

Detour 🦴🦴🦴 1946 Considered to be the crème de la crème of "B" movies, a largely unacknowledged but cult-followed noir downer. Well-designed, stylish, and compelling, if a bit contrived and, at times annoyingly shrill...

Detroit 9000 🦴🦴 *Detroit Heat* 1973 (R) A pair of Detroit policemen investigate a robbery that occurred at a black congressman's fundraising banquet. **106m/C VHS, DVD,** *Alex Rocco, Scatman Crothers, Hari Rhodes, Lonette McKee, Herbert Jefferson Jr., Robert Phillips;* **D:** *Arthur Marks;* **W:** *Orville H. Hampton;* **C:** *Harry J. May;* **M:** *Luchi De Jesus.*

Detroit Rock City 🦴🦴 1999 (R) It's 1978, and a group of dim Kiss fans will do anything to get into a sold-out Detroit concert. And non-Kiss fans should do anything to get out of watching this movie. Manages to be tasteless and humorless even when it's not obviously annoying. Co-producer Gene Simmons gets his only perform the title song, so Kiss fans will be left searching their neighborhood for an Old Folks Kabuki Theater for a fix of the elderly in makeup. Director Rifkin recreated the 1978 Kiss Love Gun Show with the band performing in that haven of heavy metal: Hamilton, Ontario? **95m/C VHS, DVD,** *Edward Furlong, Sam Huntington, Giuseppe Andrews, Lin Shaye, James DeBello, Natasha Lyonne, Gene Simmons, Paul Stanley, Ace Frehley, Peter Criss;* **D:** *Adam Rifkin;* **W:** *Carl V. DuPre;* **C:** *John R. Leonetti;* **M:** *J. Peter Robinson.*

Deuce Bigalow: European Gigolo Woof! 2005 (R) Deuce returns to clear the name of his former pimp when he's accused of murder in Amsterdam. Crass, which is not unexpected, with some almost entertaining bits (but not nearly enough). **75m/C DVD, UMD, US** *Rob Schneider, Eddie Griffin, Jeroen Krabbe, Til Schweiger, Hanna Verboom, Dana Min Goodman, Miranda Raison, Douglas Sills, Charles Keating, Carlos Ponce, Oded Fehr, Adam Sandler, Norm MacDonald, Fred Armisen;* **D:** *Mike Bigelow;* **W:** *Rob Schneider, David Garrett, Jason Ward;* **C:** *Marc Felperlaan. '05: Worst Actor (Schneider), Worst Supporting Actor (Schneider), Golden Raspberries '05: Worst Actor (Schneider).*

Deuce Bigalow: Male Gigolo 🦴🦴 1999 (R) Schneider tries to enter the low-brow leading man territory now occupied by Adam Sandler (who exec produced) as Deuce Bigelow, a hapless tropical fish caretaker turned hapless gigolo. When Deuce is asked to nurse a stereotypically ethnic gigolo's fish to health, he proceeds, to practically destroy his "business" so pay for the repairs. With the help of pimp T.J. (Griffin), Deuce finds a clientele and the secret that his women want compassion, not sex. The gags (mostly of the tasteless, toilet humor variety) are very "hit and miss," but they should play well to the intended audience of adolescent boys. **86m/C VHS, DVD, Rob Schneider, William Forsythe, Eddie Griffin, Oded Fehr, Gail O'Grady, Richard Riehle, Jacqueline Obradors;* **D:** *Mike Mitchell;* **W:** *Rob Schneider, Harris Goldberg;* **C:** *Peter Lyons Collister.*

Deuces Wild 🦴🦴 2002 (R) Cliche piles upon cliche in this story of Brooklyn street gangs in the late '50s. The Deuces, led by Leon (Dorff) and his hot-headed younger brother Bobby (Renfro), and their rivals the Vipers, go to war over turf when Vipers leader Marco (Redus) is released from prison. Drug-dealing Marco was responsible for the heroin death of their older brother Sal, and the brothers want to keep their streets clean, which also puts them in conflict with local mobster Fritzy (Dillon) and his thugs. There's even a starcrossed romance since Bobby loves Vipers girl Annie (Baik). Director Kalvert did better with teens and drugs and violence in "The Basketball Diaries." **97m/C VHS, DVD, US** *Stephen Dorff, Brad Renfro, Norman Reedus, Fairuza Balk, Max Perlich, Matt Dillon, Drea De Matteo, Frankie Muniz, Vincent Pastore, Balthazar Getty, James Franco, Louis Lombardi, Deborah Harry, Johnny Knoxville, Paul Sampson;* **D:** *Scott Kalvert;* **W:** *Paul Kimatian, Christopher Gambale;* **C:** *John A. Alonzo;* **M:** *Stewart Copeland.*

Deutschland im Jahre Null 🦴🦴½ 1947 The acclaimed, unsettling vision of post-war Germany, as seen through the eyes of a disturbed boy who eventually kills himself. Lyrical and grim. In German with subtitles. **75m/B VHS, GE** *Franz Gruber;* **D:** *Roberto Rossellini.*

Devastator 🦴 *Kings Ransom; The Destroyers* 1985 (R) A Vietnam vet exacts violent revenge on the murderer of an old army buddy. **79m/C VHS,** *Richard (Rick) Hill, Katt Shea, Crofton Hardester;* **D:** *Cirio H. Santiago.*

Devi 🦴🦴🦴½ *The Goddess* 1960 A mindless, a strange and compelling tale of religious superstition. An Indian farmer becomes convinced that his beautiful daughter-in-law is the reincarnation of the goddess Kali. The girl is then pressured into accepting a worship that eventually drives her mad. In Bengal with English subtitles. **93m/B VHS,** *'N Chhabi Biswas, Sharmila Tagore, Soumitra Chatterjee;* **D:** *Satyajit Ray;* **C:** *Subrata Mitra;* **M:** *Ali Akbar Khan.*

Devices and Desires 🦴🦴🦴 *Devices & Desires* 1991 Typically complicated mystery adapted from the novel by P.D. James. Scotland Yard Commander Adam Dalgliesh (Marsden) is on holiday on the east coast of England where, of course, there's blackmail, murder, suicide, and trouble at a nearby, nuclear power station for him to contend with. Made for TV; on six cassettes. **312m/C VHS, GB** *Roy Marsden, Susannah York, Gemma Jones, James Faulkner, Tony Haygarth, Tom Georgeson, Robert Hines, Harry Burton, Helena McNeill;* **D:** *Thomas Ellice.* **TV**

The Devil and Daniel Johnston 🦴🦴🦴 2005 (PG-13) Having lived in relative cult obscurity in the 1980s, singer/songwriter Daniel Johnston morphed into a quasi-celebrity in the early 1990s after Nirvana's Kurt Cobain wore a T-shirt promoting him. Director Feuerzeig's lively documentary follows Johnston from his teenage years—with material that Johnston captured himself on audio and videotape—to his rise to sort-of fame with some of his music being recorded by well-known acts such as Tom Waits and Pearl Jam. However, his life has been riddled with trouble caused by his manic depression. Tends to look mostly at the bright side of his talents and ignores those who contend that he is perhaps overrated. **110m/C DVD.** *US* *D:* Jeff Feuerzeig; *W:* Jeff Feuerzeig; *C:* Fortunato Procopio; *M:* Daniel Johnston.

The Devil & Daniel Webster 🐾🐾🐾½ *All That Money Can Buy; Here is a Man; A Certain Mr. Scratch* 1941 In 1840s New Hampshire, a young farmer, who sells his soul to the devil, is saved from a trip to Hell when Daniel Webster steps in to defend him. This classic fantasy is visually striking and contains wonderful performances. Adapted from the story by Stephen Vincent Benet who based it on Goethe's Faust. **106m/B VHS, DVD.** James Craig, Edward Arnold, Walter Huston, Simone Simon, Gene Lockhart, Jane Darwell, Anne Shirley, John Qualen, H.B. Warner; *D:* William Dieterle; *M:* Bernard Herrmann. Oscars '41: Orig. Dramatic Score.

Devil & Leroy Basset 🐾 1973 (PG) Keema Gregwolf kills a deputy, breaks from jail with the Basset brothers, hijacks a church bus, kidnaps a family, and gets into other troublesome situations while on a posse-eluding cross-country adventure. **85m/C VHS.** Cody Bearpaw, John Goff, George "Buck" Flower; *D:* Robert E. Pearson; *M:* Les Baxter.

The Devil & Max Devlin 🐾½ 1981 (PG) Good cast wanders aimlessly in Disney family fantasy. The recently deceased Max Devlin strikes a bargain with the devil. He will be restored to life if he can convince three mortals to sell their souls. **95m/C VHS, DVD.** Elliott Gould, Bill Cosby, Susan Anspach, Adam Rich, Julie Budd, Sonny Shroyer, Helene Winston; *D:* Steven Hilliard Stern; *W:* Jimmy Sangster; *C:* Howard Schwartz; *M:* Marvin Hamlisch, Buddy (Norman Dale) Baker.

The Devil & Miss Jones 🐾🐾🐾½ 1941 Engaging romantic comedy finds a big business boss posing as an ordinary salesclerk to weed out union organizers. He doesn't expect to encounter the wicked management or his beautiful co-worker, however. **90m/B VHS.** Jean Arthur, Robert Cummings, Charles Coburn, Edmund Gwenn, Spring Byington, William Demarest, S.Z. Sakall; *D:* Sam Wood; *C:* Harry Stradling Sr.

The Devil at 4 O'Clock 🐾🐾½ 1961 An alcoholic missionary and three convicts work to save a colony of leper children from a South Seas volcano. Quality cast barely compensates for mediocre script. **126m/B VHS, DVD.** Spencer Tracy, Frank Sinatra, Kerwin Mathews, Jean-Pierre Aumont; *D:* Mervyn LeRoy; *C:* Joseph Biroc; *M:* George Duning.

The Devil Bat 🐾🐾 *Killer Bats* 1941 Madman Lugosi trains a swarm of monstrous blood-sucking bats to attack whenever they smell perfume. Followed by the sequel "Devil Bat's Daughter." DVD release is paired with the Lugosi vehicle "Scared to Death" (1946). **67m/B VHS, DVD.** Bela Lugosi, Dave O'Brien, Suzanne Kaaren, Yolande Donlan; *D:* Jean Yarbrough; *W:* John Thomas "Jack" Neville; *C:* Arthur Martinelli.

The Devil Bat's Daughter 🐾½ 1946 A young woman, hoping to avoid becoming insane like her batty father, consults a psychiatrist when she starts to have violent nightmares. Unsuccessful sequel to "The Devil Bat." **66m/B VHS, DVD.** Rosemary La Planche, Michael Hale, John James, Molly Lamont; *D:* Frank Wisbar; *W:* Griffin Jay; *C:* James S. Brown Jr.

Devil Diamond 🐾 1937 Mystery-suspense yarn about two amateur detectives who find themselves facing danger after tracking down a gang of evil jewel thieves. **61m/B VHS, DVD.** Kane Richmond, Frankie Darro, Joan Gale, Robert (Fisk) Fiske; *D:* Leslie Goodwins; *W:* Sherman Lowe; *C:* Jack Greenhalgh.

Devil Dog: The Hound of Hell 🐾 1978 A family has trouble with man's best friend when they adopt a dog that is the son of the "Hound of Hell." **95m/**

C VHS, DVD. Richard Crenna, Yvette Mimieux, Kim Richards, Victor Jory, Ike Eisenmann, Lou Frizzell, Ken Kercheval, R.G. Armstrong, Martine Beswick; *D:* Curtis Harrington; *W:* Elinor Karpf, Stephen Karpf; *C:* Gerald Perry Finnerman; *M:* Artie Kane. **TV**

Devil Dogs of the Air 🐾🐾½ 1935 Cagney and O'Brien team up in another air drama with Cagney once again the cocky pilot who, this time, joins the Marine Air Corps. O'Brien plays his flying idol (and later rival). Cagney finds all his wisecracking and luck are no match for knowledge and experience but he learns. Good stunt flying; shot on location at the San Diego naval air base. **85m/B VHS.** James Cagney, Pat O'Brien, Margaret Lindsay, Frank McHugh, Robert Barrat, Russell Hicks, Ward Bond; *D:* Lloyd Bacon.

Devil Doll 🐾🐾🐾 1936 An escaped convict uses a mad scientist's human-shrinking formula to evil ends—he sends out miniature assassins in the guise of store-bought dolls. Rarely seen horror oldie. **80m/B VHS, DVD.** Lionel Barrymore, Maureen O'Sullivan, Frank Lawton, Rafaela (Rafael, Raphaela) Ottiano, Henry B. Walthall, Arthur Hohl, Grace Ford; *D:* Tod Browning; *W:* Tod Browning, Erich von Stroheim, Guy Endore, Garrett Fort; *C:* Leonard Smith.

Devil Doll 🐾🐾 1964 Ventriloquist's dummy, which contains the soul of a former performer, eyes a beautiful victim in the crowd. Newspaper guy senses trouble. Cut above the usual talking, stalking dummy story. **80m/B VHS, DVD.** *GB* Bryant Holiday, William Sylvester, Yvonne Romain, Sandra Dorne, Karel Stepanek, Francis De Wolff; *D:* Lindsay Shonteff; *W:* Lance Z. Hargreaves, George Barclay; *C:* Gerald Gibbs.

Devil Girl from Mars 🐾½ 1954 Sexy female from Mars and her very large robot arrive at a small Scottish inn to announce that a Martian feminist revolution has occurred. The distaff aliens then undertake a search of healthy Earth males for breeding purposes. Believe it or not, the humans don't want to go and therein lies the rub. A somewhat enjoyable space farce. **76m/B VHS, DVD.** *GB* Hugh McDermott, Hazel Court, Patricia Laffan, Peter Reynolds, Adrienne Corri, Joseph Tomelty, Sophie Stewart, John Laurie, Anthony Richmond; *D:* David MacDonald; *W:* John C. Mather, James Eastwood; *C:* Jack Cox; *M:* Edwin Astley.

Devil Horse 🐾🐾 1932 A boy's devotion to a wild horse marked for destruction to a killer leads him into trouble. A serial in 12 chapters of 13 minutes each. **156m/B VHS.** Frankie Darro, Harry Carey Sr., Noah Beery Sr.; *D:* Otto Brower, Richard Talmadge.

Devil in a Blue Dress 🐾🐾🐾 1995 (R) Down-on-his-luck Easy Rawlins (Washington) is an out of work aircraft worker in 1948 LA. He's hired to find mystery woman Daphne (Sizemore). What he finds are the usual noir staples: government corruption backed by thugs who want him to mind his own business. Easy and Daphne's torrid romance featured in the Walter Mosley novel is missing but the racism and violence are intact. Realism and accuracy in period detail enhance solid performance by Washington, though the deliberate, literary pace is at times lulling. Cheadle takes over whenever he shows up as Mouse, Rawlins' loyal friend and psychotically jealous. After she commits suicide, he must prove to the police that he did not kill her. Original dialogue in German. **102m/B VHS.** *GE* Lilli Palmer, Curt Jurgens, Winnie Markus; *D:* Rolf Hansen.

Devil in the Flesh 🐾🐾🐾 1946 Acclaimed drama about a French soldier's wife having a passionate affair with a high school student while her

husband is away fighting in WWI. From the novel by Raymond Radiguet. Dubbed. Updated and remade in 1987. **112m/B VHS.** *FR* Gerard Philipe, Micheline Presle, Denise Grey; *D:* Claude Autant-Lara; *W:* Jean Aurenche, Pierre Bost; *C:* Michel Kelber; *M:* Rene Cloerec.

Devil in the Flesh 🐾🐾 *Il Diavolo in Corpo* 1987 (R) A angst-ridden, semi-pretentious Italian drama about an obsessive older woman carrying on an affair with a schoolboy, despite her terrorist boyfriend father, who had treated her. Famous for a graphic sex scene, available in the unrated version. Updated remake of the 1946 French film. Italian with subtitles. **110m/C VHS, DVD.** *IT* Riccardo De Torrebruna, Maruschka Detmers, Federico Pitzalis; *D:* Marco Bellocchio; *W:* Ennio de Concini, Enrico Palandri, Marco Bellocchio; *C:* Giuseppe Lanci; *M:* Carlo Crivelli.

Devil in the Flesh 🐾½ *Dearly Devoted* 1998 (R) Troubled Debbie Strand (McGowan) has a crush on teacher Peter Rinaldi (McArthur) and no one is going to stop her getting what (or who) she wants. She tries blackmailing him when he doesn't respond and McArthur learns McGowan has a very deadly past. **92m/C VHS, DVD.** Rose McGowan, Alex McArthur, Sherrie Rose, Phil Morris, Robert Silver; *D:* Steve Cohen. **VIDEO**

Devil in the Flesh 2 🐾½ *Teacher's Pet* 2000 (R) In this sequel to '98 flick, disturbed Debbie (O'Keefe) escapes from the looney bin and causes the accidental death of the college coed who offers her a ride, so she assumes her identity. Passing herself off as wealthy Sydney Hollings, Debbie becomes infatuated with her writing prof Sam (Garcia), who's flattered by the attention. Except that anyone who gets in Debbie's way is permanently disposed of. Sly humor and O'Keefe's remarkably appealing considering she plays a psychopath. **90m/C VHS, DVD.** Jodi Lyn O'Keefe, Katherine Kendall, Jsu Garcia, Jeanette Brox, Bill Gratton, Todd McKee, Christiana Frank, Todd Robert Anderson; *D:* Marcus Spiegel; *W:* Richard Brandes; *C:* M. David Mullen. **VIDEO**

The Devil Is a Woman 🐾🐾🐾 1935 Dietrich vamps as money-hungry beauty Concha Perez, who soon has best friends and fellow military officers Pasqual (Atwill) and Antonio (Romero) dueling for her dubious affections. Turns out the man she desires may not be the man she truly needs. Flashbacks show how Concha seductively destroyed Pasqual some years earlier and how his jealousy lingered on. Based on the novel "The Woman and the Puppet" by Pierre Louys. After protests by the Spanish government over the depiction of the Spanish military, Paramount agreed to supress the film and few prints survived. **79m/B VHS.** Marlene Dietrich, Lionel Atwill, Cesar Romero, Edward Everett Horton, Alison Skipworth; *D:* Josef von Sternberg; *W:* John Dos Passos, S.K. Winston; *C:* Josef von Sternberg, Lucien Ballard.

Devil Monster 🐾 1946 A world-weary traveler searches for a girl's fiance in the South Pacific, and is attacked by a large manta. **65m/B VHS.** Barry Norton, Blanche Mehaffey; *D:* S. Edwin Graham.

Devil of the Desert Against the Son of Hercules 🐾🐾½ 1962 The grandson of Zeus ventures into the wasteland to take on a feisty foe. **93m/C VHS, DVD.** *IT* Kirk Morris, Michele Girardon; *D:* Riccardo Freda.

Devil on Horseback 🐾🐾 1954 A miner's son journeys to London to become a jockey in this comedy/drama. As he tries to bully his way into the racing circuit, he succeeds, but not in the way he anticipated. **88m/B VHS, DVD.** *GB* Googie Withers, John McCallum, Jeremy Spenser, Liam Redmond; *D:* Cyril Frankel; *M:* Malcolm Arnold.

The Devil on Wheels 🐾🐾 1947 Inspired by his dad's reckless driving, a teenager becomes a hot rodder and causes a family tragedy. A rusty melodrama that can't be described as high-performance. **67m/B VHS, DVD.** James B. Cardwell, Noreen Nash, Darryl Hickman, Jan Ford, Damian O'Flynn, Lenita Love; *D:* Crane Wilbur; *W:* Crane Wilbur.

The Devil, Probably 🐾 *Le Diable, Probablement* 1977 Ennui among Parisian youth, lost in their polluted, consumer society. Charles (Monnier) spins deeper into depression, despite the efforts of his friends, and finally makes a bargain with a junkie to shoot him in Pere Lachaise cemetery. French with subtitles. **95m/C VHS.** *FR* Antoine Monnier, Tina Irissari, Henri De Maublanc; *D:* Robert Bresson; *W:* Robert Bresson; *C:* Pasqualino De Santis; *M:* Philippe Sarde.

Devil Riders 🐾½ 1944 Unspectacular horse opera has a crooked lawyer trying to get his grubby hands on some choice land. Enter Crabbe to set things straight. **56m/B VHS.** Buster Crabbe, Al "Fuzzy" St. John, Patti McCarty, Charles "Blackie" King, John Merton, Kermit Maynard, Frank LaRue, Jack Ingram, George Chesebro, Edward Cassidy; *D:* Sam Newfield.

The Devil Rides Out 🐾🐾½ *The Devil's Bride* 1968 Considered by many to be Hammer's finest achievement, though several other of the studio's films rate serious consideration. This one's a solid witchcraft tale written by Richard Matheson. In 1925, the Duc de Richleau (Lee), a "good" warlock, and the evil Mocata battle each other over De Richleau's friend Simon (Mower). Some of the effects are a little dated now, but director Terence Fisher builds suspense through a stately pace. Production values are highlighted by the usual excellent sets and a fleet of vintage cars. Lee's performance is one of his strongest in a conventionally heroic role. **95m/C DVD.** *GB* Christopher Lee, Charles Gray, Nike Arrighi, Leon Greene, Patrick Mower, Gwen Ffrangcon Davies, Sarah Lawson, Paul Eddington; *D:* Terence Fisher; *W:* Richard Matheson; *C:* Arthur Grant; *M:* James Bernard.

The Devil Thumbs a Ride 🐾🐾 1947 A naive traveller picks up a hitchhiker, not knowing he's wanted for murder. Will history repeat itself in this interesting noir? **63m/B VHS.** Ted North, Lawrence Tierney, Nan Leslie; *D:* Felix Feist.

Devil Times Five 🐾½ *People Toys; The Horrible House on the Hill* 1974 (R) To take revenge for being incarcerated in a mental hospital, five children methodically murder the adults who befriend them. **87m/C VHS, DVD.** Gene Evans, Sorrell Booke, Shelley Morrison; *D:* Sean McGregor.

The Devil Wears Prada 🐾🐾½ 2006 (PG-13) This predictable plot (small town girl with big city dreams) gets an extra half-bone for Streep's sleek boss-from-hell. That would be Miranda Priestly, high priestess editor of the Manhattan fashion mag where wide-eyed Andy (Hathaway) is hired as a second assistant. A walking fashion faux pas, Andy slowly loses her ideals (and frumpy appearance) to the beguilement of power and designer trends. Can she be saved? Hathaway struggles to hold her own (she has the least showy role) against both Streep and the scene-stealing Tucci. Based on the chick lit book by Lauren Weisberger. **106m/C DVD, Blu-ray Disc.** *US* Anne Hathaway, Meryl Streep, Adrian Grenier, Simon Baker, Stanley Tucci, Emily Blunt, Tracie Thoms, David Marshall Grant, James Naughton, Daniel Sunjata, Rebecca Mader, Rich Sommer; *D:* Daniel Frankel; *W:* Aline Brosh McKenna; *C:* Florian Ballhaus; *M:* Theodore Shapiro. Golden Globes '07: Actress—Mus./Comedy (Streep).

Devil Wears White 🐾 1986 (R) A student's vacation is disrupted when he becomes involved in a war with an insane arms dealer who wants to take over a Latin American Republic. **92m/C VHS.** Robert Livesy, Jane Higginson, Guy Ecker, Anthony Cordova; *D:* Steven A. Hull.

Devil Woman *woof!* 1976 (R) A Filipino Gorgon-woman seeks reptilian revenge on the farmers who killed her family. Bad news. **79m/C VHS.** *PH* Rosemarie Gil; *D:* Albert Yu, Felix Vilars.

Devilfish 🐾 *Shark: Red on the Ocean* 1984 A small seaside community is ravaged by berserk manta rays in this soggy saga. **92m/C VHS.** *IT* Michael Sopkiw, Valentine Monnier, Gianni "John" Garko, William Berger; *D:* Lamberto Bava; *W:* Gianfranco Clerici, Dardano Sabatini.

The Devils *ళళళ* 1971 (R) In 1631 France, a priest is accused of commerce with the devil and sexual misconduct with nuns. Since he is also a political threat, the accusation is used to denounce and eventually execute him. Based on Aldous Huxley's "The Devils of Loudun," the movie features masturbating nuns and other excesses—shocking scenes typical of film director Russell. Supposedly this was Russell's attempt to wake the public to their desensitization of modern horrors of war. Controversial and flamboyant. 109mC VHS, GB **C:** Oliver Reed, Dudley Sutton, Max Adrian, Gemma Jones, Murray Melvin, Michael Gothard, Georgina Hale, Christopher Logue, Brian Murphy, Kenneth Colley; **D:** Ken Russell; **W:** Ken Russell; **C:** David Watkin; **M:** Peter Maxwell Davies.

The Devil's Advocate *ళళ½* 1997 (R) Forget the actors; this film belongs to cinematographer Bartkowiak and production designer Bruno Rubeo, who offer a lush, rich look that's very enticing. And it's all about anticement—young Florida lawyer Kevin Lomax (Reeves) is seduced by the power and money of a position at an influential New York law firm run by the mysterious John Milton (Pacino). But soon Kevin's beautiful wife Mary Ann (Theron) is having a breakdown, his religious mother (Ivey) is prophesying doom, and Kevin learns the boss is Satan—literally. Reeves is earnest, Pacino relishes his showy role, and the visual effects provide some much needed jolts. Based on the novel by Andrew Neiderman. 144mC VHS, DVD, **C:** Al Pacino, Keanu Reeves, Charlize Theron, Judith Ivey, Craig T. Nelson, Jeffrey Jones, Connie Nielsen, Ruben Santiago-Hudson, Debra Monk, Tamara Tunie, Vyto Ruginis, Laura Harrington, Pamela Gray, Heather Matarazzo, Delroy Lindo, Gloria Lynne Henry, Chris Bauer; **D:** Taylor Hackford; **W:** Tony Gilroy, Jonathan Lemkin; **C:** Andrzej Bartkowiak; **M:** James Newton Howard.

Devil's Angels *ళ* 1967 A motorcycle gang clashes with a small-town sheriff. Cheap 'n sleazy fare. 84mC VHS, **C:** John Cassavetes, Beverly Adams, Mimsy Farmer, Salli Sachse, Nai Bonet, Leo Gordon; **D:** Daniel Haller; **W:** Charles B. Griffith.

The Devil's Arithmetic *ళళ½* 1999 Modern teen Hannah Stern (Dunst) is indifferent to her Jewish faith and reluctant to attend her Aunt Eva's (Fletcher) Passover seder. After getting drunk, she passes out and is mysteriously transported to Poland in 1941, where she and her cousin Rivkah (Murphy) are imprisoned in a concentration camp and Hannah gets a first-hand look at faith and oppression. Pic doesn't play down the Nazi horrors and may not be suitable for the very young. Adapted from Jane Yolen's novel. 101mC VHS, DVD, Kirsten Dunst, Brittany Murphy, Louise Fletcher, Paul Freeman, Mimi Rogers; **D:** Donna Deitch; **W:** Robert J. Avrech; **C:** Jacek Laskus; **M:** Frederic Talgorn. CABLE

The Devil's Backbone *ళళ* 2001 (R) El Espinazo de Diablo. In the final days of the Spanish Civil War, staff and children at a remote orphanage run by loyalists Casares (Luppi) and Carmen (Paredes) prepare for an uncertain fate. Carlos (Tielve) is a new arrival who quickly learns that there are many secrets, including the (possible) ghost of schoolboy Santi. Sinister janitor Jacinto (Noriega) also thinks there's gold hidden somewhere and is determined to find it. Uneasy combination of history and the supernatural. Spanish with subtitles. 106mC VHS, DVD, MX Marisa Paredes, Federico Luppi, Eduardo Noriega, Fernando Tielve, Inigo Garces, Irene Visedo, Berta Ojea; **D:** Guillermo del Toro; **W:** Guillermo del Toro, Antonio Trashorras, David Munoz; **C:** Guillermo Navarro; **M:** Javier Navarrete.

The Devil's Brigade *ళళ* 1968 "Dirty Dozen" style film with Holden as the leader of special command brigade consisting of the usual misfits and oddballs. The team is trained to take on the Nazis in Scandanava but has their assignment cancelled. Instead, they take them on in the Italian Alps, making for some perilous adventures. Non-acting notables include former football great Hornung and former boxing champ Gene Fullmer. 130mC VHS, DVD, William Holden, Cliff Robertson, Vince Edwards, Andrew Prine, Claude Akins, Michael Rennie, Dana Andrews, Gretchen Wyler, Carroll O'Connor, Richard Jaeckel, Jack Watson, Paul Hornung, Jeremy Slate, Don Megowan, Patric Knowles, James Craig, Richard Dawson, Tom Stern, Luke Askew, Harry Carey Jr., Tom Troupe, Norman Alden, David Pritchard, Wilhelm von Homburg; **D:** Andrew V. McLaglen; **W:** William Roberts; **C:** William Clothier; **M:** Alex North.

Devil's Canyon *ళళ* 1953 An ex-lawman, serving time in an Arizona prison, is beset by a jailed killer seeking vengeance for his own incarceration. Filmed in 3-D. 92mB VHS, **C:** Dale Robertson, Virginia Mayo, Stephen McNally, Arthur Hunnicutt, Robert Keith, Jay C. Flippen, Whit Bissell; **D:** Alfred Werker.

Devil's Cargo *ళ½* 1948 One of the final three "Falcon" films, in which Calvert replaced Tom Conway, in which Calvert, Rochelle Hudson, Roscoe Karns, Lyle Talbot, Kennedy; **D:** John F. Link.

The Devil's Daughter *ళ* 1991 (R) Satan, in a desperate bid to take over the planet, orders his minions to flood the earth with horrific evil. Only one woman can prevent the HellMaster from succeeding, and she may be too late! 112mC VHS, **C:** Kelly Curtis, Herbert Lom, Maria Angela Giordano, Michel Hans Adatte, Carla Cassola, Angelika Maria Beck, Tomas Arana; **D:** Michele (Michael) Soavi; **W:** Dario Argento; **M:** Pino Donaggio.

The Devil's Disciple *ళళ* 1959 Entertaining adaptation of a minor George Bernard Shaw play set during the American Revolution. British Gen. Burgoyne (Olivier) and his troops are stuck in a northeastern village in 1777 awaiting orders and dealing with rebels. This includes troublemaking Richard Dudgeon (Douglas), whose father has been hanged by the Brits, and pastor Anthony Anderson (Lancaster), working in secret with the rebels. There's also a romantic triangle between the two men and Anderson's wife Judith (Scott). Film suffers from choppy direction, but the excellent cast more than makes up for it. 88mB VHS, GB Burt Lancaster, Kirk Douglas, Laurence Olivier, Janet Scott, Eva LeGallienne, Harry Andrews, Basil Sydney, George Rose; **D:** Guy Hamilton; **W:** John Dighton, Roland Kibbee; **C:** Jack Hildyard; **M:** Richard Rodney Bennett.

Devil's Eye *ళళ* 1960 The devil dispatches Don Juan to tempt and seduce a young virgin bride-to-be, a reverend's daughter, no less. Based on the Danish radio play "Don Juan Returns." 90mB VHS, SW Stig Jarrel, Bibi Andersson, Jarl Kulle; **D:** Ingmar Bergman; **W:** Ingmar Bergman; **C:** Gunnar Fischer; **M:** Erik Nordgren.

Devil's Gift WOOF! 1984 A young boy's toy is possessed by a demon and havoc ensues. 112mC VHS, Bob Mendelsohn, Vicki Saputo, Steven Robertson; **D:** Kenneth Berton.

Devils on the Doorstep *ళళ* 2000 Chinese film needs some sharp editing before this black comedy about a tiny village's survival during WWII could be anything more than frustrating. Local peasant Ma Dasan is surprised when the Chinese Army dump two prisoners in their remote village—a Japanese POW and his Chinese interpreter. When no one comes for the prisoners after six months, the fearful villagers decide they should be executed and Ma is sent to hire an assassin. When this doesn't work out, the villagers try to return them to nearby Japanese troops. This idea isn't any better and by now the movie's exhausted a viewer's patience. Japanese and Mandarin with subtitles. 162mB VHS, DVD, CH Jiang Wen, Kagawa Teruyuki, Jiang Hongbo, Chen Qiang, Sawada Kenya, Yuan Ding, Jiang Wen; **D:** Jiang Wen; **C:** Gu Changwei; Grand Jury Prize.

Devil's Brother *ళళ* 1933 In Fra Diavolo. Bogus bandits The Virtuous Tramps 1933 In one of their lesser efforts, Laurel and Hardy star as bumbling bandits in this comic operetta based on the 1830 opera by Daniel F. Auber. 88mB VHS, DVD, Stan Laurel, Oliver Hardy, Dennis King, Thelma Todd, James Finlayson, Lucille Browne; **D:** Charles R. Rogers, Hal Roach.

Devil's Island *ళళ* 1996 Djoflaeyjan 1996 An abandoned military base is being used to house poor families outside Reykjavik in the '50s. The trash-filled landscape offers little to those who live there, including four generations of one eccentric no-hope family. The usual family dysfunction is all played for exaggerated caricature. Icelandic with subtitles. 103mC VHS, DVD, IC Gisli Halldorsson, Baltasar Kormakur, Sveinn Geirsson, Sigurveig Jonsdottir; **D:** Fridrik Thor Fridriksson; **W:** Einar Karason; **C:** Ari Kristinsson; **M:** Hilmar Om Hilmarsson.

Devil's Kiss *ళ* 1975 The Wicked Caresses of Satan 1975 Gothic horror including zombies, virgins, sorcery, and the inevitable living dead. 93mC VHS, SP FR Maria Silva, Olivier Matrot, Jose Nero, Dan (Daniel, Danny) Martin; **D:** Georges Gigo; **C:** Julio Perez de Rozas; **M:** Alberto Argudo.

Devil's Knight *ళళ* 2003 (R) Brothers Hector (Serna) and Ruben (Solano) Rivera are expert "low-rider" designers who end up murdered. Their sister Delia (Alvarez) leaves the Army to find their killers. With the help of a Vietnam vet mechanic (Kove), she sets out to take her own brand of revenge, which consists of wearing bikinis and rubbing against pimped-out cars at custom shows. So-so actioner is fueled by the even-more-lovingly-shot Alvarez, and the even-more-lovingly-shot custom street machines. 97mC VHS, DVD, Elizabeth Alvarez, Jose Solano, Alexander Romanov, Martin Kove, Pepe Serna, Jaime Gomez, Gary Marshall; **D:** Quan Phillips; **W:** Quan Phillips; **C:** Robert Hayes. VIDEO

The Devil's Mistress *ళ* 1968 A gang of criminals on a pillaging spree murder a man and rape his Indian wife, only to find out she's a she-demon who won't let bygones be bygones. Lame, 66mC VHS, Joan Stapleton, Robert Gregory, Forrest Westmoreland, Douglas Warren, Oren Williams, Arthur Resley; **D:** Orville Wanzer.

The Devil's Nightmare *ళ½* 1971 (R) A woman leads seven tourists (representing the seven deadly sins) on a tour of a medieval European castle. There they experience demonic tortures. Lots of creepy moments. Euro-horror/sex star Blanc is fantastic in this otherwise mediocre production. 88mC VHS, DVD, BE IT Erika Blanc, Jean Servais, Daniel Emilfork, Lucien Raimbourg, Jacques Monseau, Frederique Hender, Ivana Novak, Shirley Corrigan, Frederique Hender; **D:** Jean Brismee; **W:** Patrice Rhomm, Vertunnio De Angelis, Charles Lecocq; **C:** Andre Goeffers; **M:** Alessandroni.

The Devil's Hand *ళ* Devil's Doll. The Naked Goddess; Live to Love 1961 When Alda finds a doll that represents his ideal woman in a curio shop, the shop's owner (Hamilton, aka Commissioner Gordon) tells him the dream girl who modeled for the doll lives nearby. Trouble is, she's part of a voodoo cult, and guess who's head voodoo-man. Big trouble for Alda, big snooze for you. 71mB VHS, DVD, Linda Christian, Robert Alda, Neil Hamilton, Ariadne Welter; **D:** William Hole Jr.

The Devil's Own *ళళళ* 1996 (R) Irish-American New York cop Tom O'Meara (Ford) and wife Sheila (Colin) take charming Irish emigre Rory Devaney (Pitt) into their home and make him part of the family. But Rory, AKA Frankie McGuire, turns out to be an IRA terrorist who has hustled out of trouble in Belfast and now has a bloody purpose for coming to America. When Tom discovers just what it is, he tries to stop Rory before he destroys any more lives—including his own. More a low-key character study than a slam-bang actioner, with Pitt cooly charismatic as the troubled gunman while Ford does his usual professional work as a good cop caught up in a bad situation. Noteworthy only by virtue of the cast's later TV notoriety—Buchanan and Fouger would later appear on "Petticoat Junction." Nelson played Dr. Rossi on "Peyton Place," and Crane beached a role on "Hawaiian Eye." 107mC VHS, DVD, AV Arthur Dignam, Nick (Nicholas) Tate, Simon Burke, Charles Frawley, Jonathan Hardy, Gerry Dugan, Thomas Keneally; **D:** Fred Schepisi; **W:** Fred Schepisi; **C:** Ian Baker; **M:** Bruce Smeaton; Australian Film Inst. '76: Actor (Tate), Actor (Burke), Cinematog., Director (Schepisi), Film, Screenplay.

The Devil's Partner *ళళ* 1958 Yet another uninspired devil yarn in which an old-timer trades in his senior citizenship by dying and coming back in the form of a new wife and indulges in multiple ritual sacrifices. Noteworthy only by virtue of the cast's later TV notoriety. 75mB VHS, DVD, Ed Nelson, Jean Allison, Edgar Buchanan, Richard Crane, Spencer Carlisle, Byron Foulger, Claire Carleton; **D:** Charles R. Rondeau.

Devil's Party *ళళ* 1938 A tenement boy's reunion party turns into a night of horror when one of the guests is killed. As a result, the childhood friends band together to uncover the murderer's identity. 65mB VHS, DVD, Victor McLaglen, Paul Kelly, William Gargan, Samuel S. Hinds, Scotty Beckett; **D:** Ray McCarey.

The Devil's Playground *ళళళ* 1976 Sexual tension rises in a Catholic seminary, distracting the boys from their theological studies. The attentions of the priests only further their sexual confusion. 107mC VHS, DVD, AU Arthur Dignam, Nick (Nicholas) Tate, Simon Burke, Charles Frawley, Jonathan Hardy; **D:** Fred Schepisi; **W:** Fred Schepisi; **C:** Ian Baker; **M:** Bruce Smeaton.

Devil's Pond *ళళ* 2003 (R) Spoiled rich girl Julianne (Reid) impulsively marries her boyfriend Mitch (Pardue) in order to get away from her controlling family. They honeymoon in an isolated cabin, with no communication to the outside world, and Julianne soon discovers that her new hubby has no intention of ever letting her go. This is one newlywed who wasn't expecting the "till death do us part" to come so soon. You'll have to like the pretty lead actors since it's their adventure. 92mC VHS, DVD, Tara Reid, Kip Pardue, Meredith Baxter, Dan Gunther; **D:** Joel Viertel; **W:** Alex Friedman, Mora Stephens; **C:** Matthew Jensen; **M:** Brad Kane. VIDEO

The Devil's Prey *ళళ* 2001 (R) Partyers attending a rave discover it's a front for satanic cult leader Minister Seth (Bergin) to obtain the young flesh he needs for his blood sacrifices. But Susan (Jones) is willing to fight for her life against the masked cult members. Fast-paced horror. 91mC VHS, DVD, Patrick Bergin, Ashley Jones, Charlie O'Connell, Bryan K Wood, Tim Thomerson; **D:** Bradford May. VIDEO

Devil's Rain *ళళ½* 1975 (PG) The rituals and practices of devil worship, possession, and satanism are gruesomely related. Interesting cast. 86mC VHS, DVD, Ernest Borgnine, Ida Lupino, William Shatner, Eddie Albert, Keenan Wynn, Tom Skerritt, Joan Prather, Claudio Brook, John Travolta, Anton La Vey; **D:** Robert Fuest; **W:** James Ashton, Gabe Essoe, Gerald Hopman; **C:** Alex Phillips Jr.; **M:** Al De Lory.

Devil's Possessed *ళళ* 1974 A Middle Ages despot tortures and maims the peasants in his region until they rise up and enact an unspeakable revenge. 90mC VHS, DVD, Paul Naschy; **D:** Leon Klimovsky.

The Devil's Rejects WOOF! 2005 (R) Tortuous recycling by director Zombie of his senseless "House of 1000 Corpses" tribute-driven horror movie, featuring the psychotic Firefly clan, which was enough of a cult hit for this pointless follow-up that also honors (or insults?) other serial killer and zombie flicks as well. Only Satan would order a third installment. 101m/C DVD, Blu-ray Disc, UMD. US GE William Forsythe, Sid Haig, Sheri Moon, Bill Moseley, Tyler Mane, Leslie Easterbrook, Matthew McGrory, Ken Foree, Michael Berryman, Danny Trejo, Rosario Dawson, Deborah Van Valkenburgh, Geoffrey Lewis, Priscilla Barnes, Kate Norby, Dave Sheridan, Lew Temple, Elizabeth (E.G. Dailey) Daily, Diamond Dallas Page, Tom Towles, P.J. Soles, Chris Ellis, Mary Woronov, Daniel Roebuck, Duane Whitaker, Steve Railsback, Brian Posehn; D: Rob Zombie; W: Rob Zombie; M: Rob Zombie, Tyler Bates.

The Devil's Sleep 1951 When a crusading woman sets out to break up a teen narcotics ring, the threatened thugs attempt to draw her daughter into their sleazy affairs, thus assuring the mother's silence. 81m/B VHS, DVD. Lita Grey Chaplin, Timothy Farrell, John Mitchum, William Thomason, Tracy Lynn; D: W. Merle Connell.

Devil's Son-in-Law WOOF! 1977 (R) A black stand-up comic makes a deal with a devil. 95m/C VHS, DVD. Rudy Ray Moore; D: Cliff Roquemore.

The Devil's Undead 1975 (PG) When a Scottish orphanage is besieged by a rash of cold-blooded murders, the detectives Lee and Cushing are summoned to investigate. Interesting spin on that old possessed by demons theme. 90m/C VHS, DVD. GB Christopher Lee, Peter Cushing; D: Peter Sasdy.

Devil's Wanton Fangelse; Prison 1949 A young girl tries to forget an unhappy relationship by beginning a new romance with an equally frustrated beau. Gloomy, but hopeful. 80m/B VHS, DVD. SW Doris Svedlund, Eva Henning, Hasse (Hans) Ekman; D: Ingmar Bergman; W: Ingmar Bergman.

The Devil's Web 1974 (PG) A demonic nurse infiltrates, manipulates, and corrupts three beautiful sisters. 73m/C VHS. Diana Dors, Andrea Marcovicci, Ed Bishop, Cec Linder, Michael Culver; D: Shaun O'Riordan; W: Brian Clemens. TV

Devil's Wedding Night WOOF! El Retumo di la Drequessa Dracula; The Return of the Duchess Dracula; Full Moon of the Virgins 1973 (R) An archaeologist and his twin brother fight over a ring that lures virgins into Count Dracula's Transylvanian castle. Vampire queen Bay seduces the dimwit twins and strips at every chance she gets. 85m/C VHS, DVD. Mark Damon, Rosalba Neri, Frances Davis; D: Luigi (Paolo Solvay) Batzella.

Devlin 1992 (R) Devlin is a tough cop with an alcohol problem and a bad marriage. His father-in-law, Brennan, is a powerful local political boss. When Brennan's son is murdered, Devlin is the fall guy. Seeking to clear himself, he discovers a conspiracy going back 30 years. 110m/C VHS. Bryan Brown, Lloyd Bridges, Roma Downey, Whip Hubley, Lawrence Dane, Lisa Eichhorn, Carol(e) Shelley, Jan Rubes, Frances Fisher, Gary Klar, Bruce MacVittie, Robert Cicchini, Gabrielle Rose; D: Rick Rosenthal; W: David Taylor; C: Neil Roach; M: John Altman. CABLE

Devon's Ghost: Legend of the Bloody Boy 2005 (R) Slasher flick. As a boy, Devon was nearly murdered by his parents. Now he's back (and not as a ghost) to continue his revenge against any young couple he sees. Which means all those horny teens had better watch out. 86m/C DVD. Matt Moore, John Yong Bosch, Karan Ashely, Reza Bahador, Jonathan Cruz, Kristy Vaughan; D: John Yong Bosch, Koichi Sakamoto; W: Karan Ashely, Ron Day, Tim Grace; C: John Rhode, Sam Lazzara; M: Cody Westheimer. VIDEO

Devonsville Terror 1983 (R) Strange things begin to happen when a new school teacher arrives in Devonsville, a town that has a history of torture, murder and witchcraft. The hysterical townspeople react by beginning a 20th-century witchhunt. 97m/C VHS, DVD. Suzanna Love, Donald Pleasence, Deanna Haas, Mary Walden, Robert Walker Jr., Paul Willson; D: Ulli Lommel; W: Ulli Lommel; C: Ulli Lommel; M: Ray Colcord.

Devotion 1931 A lovesick British miss disguises herself as a governess so she can be near the object of her affection, a London barrister. 80m/B VHS. Ann Harding, Leslie Howard, Robert Williams, O.P. Heggie, Louise Closser Hale, Dudley Digges; D: Robert Milton.

Devotion 1995 (R) Lesbian comic Sheila (Derbyshire) is offered her own sitcom by now-married former lover Lynn (Girling), who admits there's still a spark. Should Sheila rekindle the flame or stay true to free-spirited lover Julie (Twa)? Curtesy at first but takes a welcome dramatic turn as the characters explore their true feelings. 124m/C VHS, DVD. Jan Derbyshire, Cindy Girling, Kate Twa; D: Mindy Kaplan.

Devour 2005 (R) Jake (Ackles) and friends play a deadly Internet game called "The Pathway" that assigns its members bizarre tasks that initially seem harmless, but soon turn violent. Fascinating premise, but too many intertwined plots and themes involving uninteresting characters leave viewers confused and bored. 90m/C DVD. Shannyn Sossamon, Dominique Swain, William Sadler, Martin Cummins, Jensen Ackles, Teach, Robert Stewart; D: David Winkler; W: Adam Gross, Seth Gross; C: Brian Pearson; M: Joseph LoDuca. CABLE

D.I. 1957 A tough drill sergeant is faced with an unbreakable rebellious recruit, threatening his record and his platoon's status. Webb's film features performances by actual soldiers. 106m/B VHS. Jack Webb, Don Dubbins, Jackie Loughery, Lin McCarthy, Virginia Gregg; D: Jack Webb.

The Diabolical Dr. Z Miss Muerte; Dans les Griffes du Maniaque 1965 When dad dies of cardiac arrest after the medical council won't let him make the world a kinder gentler place with his personality-altering technique, his dutiful daughter—convinced the council brought on dad's demise—is out to change some personalities in a big way. 86m/B VHS, DVD. SP FR Mabel Karr, Fernando Montes, Estella Blain, Antonio J. Escribano, Howard Vernon, Jess (Jesus) Franco, Jose Maria Prada, Guy Mairesse; D: Jess (Jesus) Franco; W: Jean-Claude Carriere, Jess (Jesus) Franco; C: Alejandro Ulloa; M: Jess (Jesus) Franco.

Diabolically Yours Diaboliquement Votre 1967 A French thriller about an amnesiac who struggles to discover his lost identity. Tensions mount when his pretty spouse and friends begin to wonder if it's all a game. Dubbed. 94m/C VHS, DVD. FR Alain Delon, Senta Berger; D: Julien Duvivier.

Diabolique Les Diabolique 1955 Sadistic boarding school master Michel (Meurisse) has a wealthy, neurotic wife, Christina (Clouzet, the director's wife), and a cold-blooded mistress, Nicole (Signoret), who conspire to poison and then drown him in the school's swimming pool. But after the plot is carried out, his body is carried out. Remade for TV in 1974 as "Reflections of Murder." 107m/B VHS, DVD. FR Simone Signoret, Vera Clouzot, Paul Meurisse, Charles Vanel, Michel Serrault, Georges Chamarat, Robert Dalban, Therese Dorny, Camille Guerini; D: Henri-Georges Clouzot; W: Henri-Georges Clouzot, Frederic Grendel, Jerome Geronimi, Rene Masson; C: Armand Thirard; M: Georges Van Parys. N.Y. Film Critics 55: Foreign Film.

Diabolique 1996 (R) Remake of the 1955 French noir classic, updated for '90s sensibilities, finds timid teacher Mia (Adjani) married to overbearing school head Guy (Palminteri), who's having an affair with love teacher Nicole (Stone). The two women, who loathe Guy equally, plot to kill him. But when a P.I. (Bates) investigates, it seems possible that Guy isn't dead after all. If you're having trouble accessorizing with leopard skin, watch Stone. Otherwise, watch the far superior original. The usually publicity hungry Stone refused to have anything to do with this picture after its release due to a spat with director Chechik. 105m/C VHS, DVD. Sharon Stone, Isabelle Adjani, Chazz Palminteri, Kathy Bates, Spalding Gray, Shirley Knight, Adam Ham-Byrd, Allen (Goorwitz) Garfield; D: Jeremiah S. Chechik; W: Don Roos; C: Peter James; M: Randy Edelman.

Dial Help Ragno Gelido; Minaccia d'Amore 1988 (R) A lame Italian-made suspenser about a model plagued by ghostly phone calls. 94m/C VHS. IT Charlotte Lewis, Marcello Modugno, Mattia Sbragia, Victor Cavallo, William Berger, Carlo Monni, Carola Stagnaro; D: Ruggero Deodato; C: Renato Tafuri.

Dial "M" for Murder 1954 Unfaithful playboy Tony's (Milland) cash is all thanks to his marriage to heiress Margot (Kelly) and he fears losing her to writer Mark (Cummings). So Tony devises an elaborate plan to murder his wife for her money, but when she accidentally stabs the killer-to-be, with scissors no less, it's Tony who comes under the suspicious eye of Chief Inspector Hubbard (Williams). Filmed in 3-D. Based on the play by Frederick Knotts. Loosely remade in 1998 as "A Perfect Murder" starring Michael Douglas and Gwenyth Paltrow. 123m/C VHS, DVD. Ray Milland, Grace Kelly, Robert Cummings, John Williams, Anthony Dawson; D: Alfred Hitchcock; W: Frederick Knott; C: Robert Burks; M: Dimitri Tiomkin.

Diamond Fleece 1992 Rick (Cross) is a convicted diamond thief who's given a parole just so he can guard the world's largest uncut gemstone. But Inspector Outlaw (Dennehy) figures Rick will never be able to resist stealing the gem himself and the law can finally lock Rick away for good. Oh, and Holly, she thinks a maybe-ex-diamond thief will bring a little romance to her life. 93m/C VHS. Ben Cross, Brian Dennehy, Kate Nelligan; D: Al Waxman; W: Michael Norell.

Diamond Head 1962 A Hawaiian landowner brings destruction and misery to his family via his stubbornness. Based on the Peter Gilman novel. 107m/C VHS, DVD. Charlton Heston, Yvette Mimieux, George Chakiris, France Nuyen, James Darren; D: Guy Green; C: Sam Leavitt; M: John Williams.

Diamond Men 2001 Slice of life Americana that's a showcase for actor Forster. Eddie Miller (Forster), a guy in his fifties, is a longtime diamond salesman who travels to jewelry stores throughout Pennsylvania. After having a heart attack, his company wants Eddie to retire—after he trains brash Bobby Walker (Wahlberg) to take over his route. Bobby's an eager loudmouth who bullies while Eddie knows how to finesse his clientele. Still he wants to learn and to befriend Eddie but the story turns out to more than a reluctant old dog teaching a pup some tricks to get along. 100m/C VHS, DVD. Robert Forster, Donnie Wahlberg, Bess Armstrong, Jasmine Guy, George Coe; D: Daniel M. Cohen; W: Daniel M. Cohen; C: John Huneck; M: Garrett Parks.

The Diamond of Jeru 2001 Helen (Jefferson) and John (Carradine) travel to Borneo in search of adventure (and diamonds) in an effort to put some spice back into their marriage. Too bad Helen is very attracted to their guide, Mike (Zane). John gets jealous and decides he and the missus should head out on their own while Mike pursues them through the jungle in an effort to rescue them from certain doom. Based on the story "Off the Mangrove Coast" by Louis L'Amour. 89m/C VHS, DVD. Billy Zane, Keith Carradine, Paris Jefferson, Jackson Raine, Khoa Do; D: Ian Barry, Dick Lowry; W: Beau L'Amour; C: Stephen Windon; M: Christopher Tyng. VIDEO

Diamond Run 1990 (R) A streetwise American expatriate frantically searches for his girlfriend after unwittingly involving her in an assassination plot. 89m/C VHS. William Bell Sullivan, Ava Lazar, Ayu Azhari, David Thornton, Peter Fox; D: Robert Chappell.

Diamond Run 2000 (R) Convoluted heist movie. J. Sloan (Lynch) leads a special forces unit that's gone over to the dark side. Sloan's planned a big diamond heist but loses the gems to thief Megan Marlow (Ljoka), who in turn is being sought by NYPD detective Jack Gates (Valentine). Gates gets to Megan first, only to have them both be stalked by Sloan's henchman, Walker (Gleek). And it seems Megan has another secret that could prove explosive. 98m/C VHS, DVD. Richard Lynch, Linda Ljoka, Michael J. Valentine, Fred Gleek, Peter Harrington; D: David Giancola; W: Marty Poole, Derrick J. Costa; C: John McAleer. VIDEO

Diamond Trail 1933 East Coast jewel thieves bring their operation to the West, unaware that they're being followed by a New York reporter. 58m/B VHS. Rex Bell, Frances Rich, Bud Osborne, Lloyd Whitlock, Norman Feusier; D: Harry Fraser.

The Diamond Trap 1991 (PG) A Manhatten detective finds himself in the middle of a diamond heist and involved with a con artist. 93m/C VHS. Howard Hesseman, Brooke Shields, Ed Marinaro, Twiggy; D: Don Taylor; W: David Peckinpah. TV

Diamondbacks 1999 Militia group, led by O'Keefe, takes over a remote NASA station in order to reprogram a government weapons satellite for evil. And it's up to engineer Lottimer to stop them. Lots of action in a no-brainer adventure. 90m/C VHS, DVD. Miles O'Keeffe, Chris Mitchum, Timothy Bottoms, Eb Lottimer; D: Bernard Salzman. VIDEO

Diamonds 1972 (PG) A tense film in which the Israeli Diamond Exchange is looted by a motley array of criminal heisters. Shaw plays a dual role as twin brothers. 108m/C VHS, DVD. IS Robert Shaw, Richard Roundtree, Barbara Hershey, Shelley Winters; D: Menahem Golan.

Diamonds 1999 (PG-13) Douglas lends both dignity and humor to his first screen role since recovering from a stroke. Harry Agrensky (Douglas) is a one-time boxing champ (recovering from a stroke) who wants to live as independently as possible. He claims to have a fortune in diamonds, given to him by a mobster, hidden away in Reno and bullies his estranged son, Lance (Aykroyd), and his grandson Michael (Allred) to go on a road trip and retrieve them. There are various adventures and bonding moments and Douglas is re-united with Bacall (as a Nevada madam), with whom he worked in 1950's "Young Man with a Horn." 90m/C VHS, DVD. Kirk Douglas, Dan Aykroyd, Corbin Allred, Lauren Bacall, Kurt Fuller, Jenny McCarthy, John Landis, Mariah O'Brien; D: John Mallory Asher; W: Allan Aaron Katz; C: Paul Elliott; M: Joel Goldsmith.

Diamonds Are Forever 1971 (PG) 007 once again battles his nemesis Blofeld, this time in Las Vegas. Bond tries to destroy the implementation of a plot to destroy Washington through the use of a space-orbiting laser. Fabulous stunts include Bond's wild drive through the streets of Vegas in a '71 Mach 1. Connery returned to play Bond in this film after being offered the then record-setting salary of $1 million. 120m/C VHS, DVD. GB Sean Connery, Jill St. John, Charles Gray, Bruce Cabot, Jimmy Dean, Lana Wood, Bruce Glover, Putter Smith, Norman Burton, Joseph Furst, Bernard Lee, Desmond Llewelyn, Laurence Naismith, Leonard Barr, Lois Maxwell, Margaret Lacey, Joe Robinson, Donna Garrat, Trina Parks; D: Guy Hamilton; W: Tom Mankiewicz; C: Ted Moore; M: John Barry.

Diamond's Edge Just Ask for Diamond 1988 (PG) An adolescent private eye and his juvenescent brother snoop into the affairs of the Fat Man, and find out that the opera ain't over until they find out what's in the Fat Man's mysterious box of bon-bons. A gene-parodying kid mystery, written by Horowitz, based on his novel, "The Falcon's Malteser." 83m/C VHS, DVD. Susannah York, Peter Eyre, Patricia Hodge, Nickolas Grace; D: Stephen Bayly; W: Anthony Horowitz; M: Trevor Jones.

Diamonds of the Night Demanty Noci 1964 A breakthrough masterpiece of the Czech new wave, about two young men escaping from a transport train to Auschwitz and scrambling for survival in the countryside. Surreal, powerfully expressionistic film, one of the most important of its time. In Czech with English subtitles. Accompa-

Diana: Her True Story 🎬🎬½ **1993** Britain's royals are held up to scandalous review in this made for tv adaptation of Andrew Morton's sympathetic bio of the Princess of Wales. Taking Diana from her lonely childhood to her "fairytale" nuptials and subsequent disillusionment with being a royal, including her bulimia and half-hearted suicide attempts, Charles is portrayed as an arrogant, emotional cold fish, only interested in farming and continuing his liaison with Camilla Parker-Bowles. Handsome production with appropriate impersonations by the cast. **180mC VHS, DVD.** Serena Scott Thomas, David Threlfall, Elizabeth Garvie, Jeremy Hammer, Donald Douglas; **D:** Kevin Connor; **W:** Stephen Zito. **TV**

Diane 🎬🎬 **1955** Oversstuffed medieval drama featuring Turner as Diane de Poitier, the mistress of a 16th century French King. Moore plays the king in this Hollywood debut. Gorgeous sets and costumes couldn't boost this film at the boxoffice, which had disappointing figures in spite of the expense bestowed upon it. Based on the novel "Diane de Poitier" by John Erskine. **110mC VHS.** Lana Turner, Pedro Armendariz Sr., Roger Moore, Marisa Pavan, Cedric Hardwicke, Torin Thatcher, Taina Elg, John Lupton, Henry Daniell, Sean McClory, Michael Ansara; **D:** David Miller; **W:** Christophe Isherwood; **M:** Miklos Rozsa.

Diary of a Chambermaid 🎬🎬🎬 **1946** A chambermaid wants to marry a rich man and finds herself the object of desire of a poor servant willing to commit murder for her. Excellent comic drama, but very stylized in direction and set design. Produced during Renoir's years in Hollywood. Adapted from a story by Octave Mirbeau. Remade in 1964 by Luis Buñuel. **86mB VHS.** Paulette Goddard, Burgess Meredith, Hurd Hatfield, Francis Lederer, Judith Anderson, Florence Bates, Almira Sessions, Reginald Owen; **D:** Jean Renoir.

Diary of a Chambermaid 🎬🎬🎬½ **1964** *Le Journal d'une Femme de Chambre; Il Diario di una Cameriera* **1964** Vintage Buñuelian social satire about a young girl taking a servant's job in a provincial French family, and easing into an atmosphere of sexual hypocrisy and decadence. In French with English subtitles. Remake of the 1946 Jean Renoir film. **97mC VHS, DVD.** FP Jeanne Moreau, Michel Piccoli, Georges Geret, Françoise Lugagne, Daniel Ivernel; **D:** Luis Buñuel; **W:** Luis Buñuel, Jean-Claude Carrière; **C:** Roger Fellous.

Diary of a Country Priest 🎬🎬🎬½ *Le Journal d'un Cure de Campagne* **1950** With "Balthazar" and "Mouchette," this is one of Bresson's greatest, subtlest films, treating the story of an alienatec, unrewarded young priest with his characteristic austerity and Catholic humanism. In French and English subtitles. **120mB VHS, DVD.** FR Nicole Maurey, Antonelle Balpetre, Claude Layou, Jean Riveyre, Nicole Ladmiral; **D:** Robert Bresson; **W:** Robert Bresson; **C:** Leonce-Henri Eurel; **M:** Jean Jacques Grunenwald.

Diary of a Hitman 🎬🎬½ **1991** (R) A hitman is hired to knock off the wife and child of a commodities broker who claims his wife is a drug addict and the infant is a crack baby and not his. The hired killer wants out of the business, but needs to pull off one more job for a down payment on his apartment. Beset by doubts, he breaks conduct by conversing with the victim and discovers the broker lied. Based on the play "Insider's Price" by Pressman. **90mC VHS.** Forest Whitaker, James Belushi, Sherilyn Fenn, Sharon Stone, Seymour Cassel, Lewis Smith, Lois Chiles, John Bedford Lloyd; **D:** Roy London; **W:** Kenneth Pressman; **M:** Michel Colombier.

Diary of a Lost Girl 🎬🎬🎬½ *Das Tagebuch einer verlorenen* **1929** The second Louise Brooks/G.W. Pabst collaboration (after "Pandora's Box") in which a frail but mesmerizing German girl plummets into a life of hopeless degradation. Dark and gloomy, the film chronicles the difficulties she faces, from rape to an unwanted pregnancy and prostitution. Based on the popular book by Margarete Boehme. Silent. Made after flapper Brooks left Hollywood to pursue greater opportunities and more challenging roles. Under Pabst's guidance. **116mB VHS, DVD.** GE Louise Brooks, Fritz Rasp, Josef Rovensky, Sybille Schmitz; **D:** G.W. Pabst; **W:** Rucolf Leonhard; **C:** Sepp Allgeier, Fritz Arno Wagner; **M:** Timothy Brock.

Diary of a Mad Black Woman 🎬🎬 **2005** (PG-13) The critics spoke and the intended audience ignored every disparaging comment to make this soap opera a success. After an 18-year marriage, Helen (beautiful Elise) gets tossed out of her Atlanta mansion by nasty hubby Charles (Harris) for his long-time mistress, Brenda (Marcos). Weepy Helen flees to the home of her feisty grandmamma Madea (Perry in outrageous drag) and then learns to get her own back. She even finds a blue-collar prince in handsome, loving Orlando (Moore). Yep, it's a life-affirming, over-the-top fairytale with faith as the cornerstone. Perry plays two other roles as well as adapting the script from his play. **116mC VHS, DVD.** US Kimberly Elise, Steve Harris, Shemar Moore, Tamara Taylor, Cicely Tyson, Lisa Marcos, Tiffany Evans, Tyler Perry; **D:** Darren Grant; **W:** Tyler Perry; **C:** David Claessen; **M:** Tyler Perry, Elvin D. Ross.

Diary of a Mad Housewife 🎬🎬🎬 **1970** (R) Despairing of her miserable family life, a housewife has an affair with a writer only to find him to be even more selfish and egotistical than her no-good husband. Snodgress plays her character perfectly, hearing the insensitive absurdity of her husband and her lover over and over again, enjoying her martyrdom as it drives her crazy. **94mC VHS.** Carrie Snodgress, Richard Benjamin, Frank Langella; **D:** Frank Perry, Golden Globes '71: Actress—Mus./Comedy (Snodgress); Natl. Bd. of Review. '70: Support. Actor (Langella).

Diary of a Mad Old Man 🎬🎬 **1963** *Dagboek Van Een Oude Dwaas* **1988** (PG-13) A wistful drama about an old man who's lost everything except his desire for his daughter-in-law, which sends him into a state of nostalgia. **93mC VHS.** BE FR NL Derek de Lint, Ralph Michael, Beatie Edney; **D:** Lili Rademakers; **W:** Hugo Claus; **M:** Egisto Macchi.

Diary of a Madman 🎬🎬 **1963** Price is once again possessed by an evil force in this gothic thriller. Fairy average Price vehicle, based on Guy de Maupassant's story. **96mC VHS.** Vincent Price, Nancy Kovack, Chris Warfield, Ian Wolfe, Nelson Olmstead, Elaine Devry, Stephen Roberts; **D:** Reginald LeBorg; **W:** Robert E. Kent; **C:** Ellis W. Carter; **M:** Nico Fidenco.

Diary of a Rebel 🎬🎬 *El Che Guevara* **1968** A fictional account of the rise of Cuban rebel leader Che Guevara. **88mC VHS.** IT John Ireland, Francesco Rabal, Howard (Red) Ross, Ancrea Checchi, Giacomo "Jack" Rossi-Stuart, Jose Torres, Susanna Martinkova; **D:** Paolo Heusch; **W:** Adriano Bolzoni; **C:** Luciano Trasatti; **M:** Nico Fidenco.

Diary of a Seducer 🎬🎬 *Le Journal du Séducteur; The Seducer's Diary* **1995** Claire's (Mastroianni) a bored 20-year-old Parisian whose ennui is lifted when she meets philosophy student Gregoire (Pouriaud), who lends her a rare copy of Soren Kierkegaard's "Diary of a Seducer." The volume apparently has seductive powers and manages to affect everyone within Claire's orbit. French with subtitles. **96mC VHS.** FR Danielle Dubroux, Chiara Mastroianni, Melvil Poupaud, Mathieu Amalric, Micheline Presle, Hubert Saint Macary, Jean-Pierre Leaud; **D:** Danielle Dubroux; **C:** Laurent Machuel; **M:** Jean-Marie Senia.

Diary of a Serial Killer 🎬🎬 *Le Journal* **1997** (R) Down-on-his-luck journalist Nelson Keece (Busey) witnesses a murder and then is invited by the killer, Stefan (Vosloo), to conduct an exclusive interview. Stefan keeps killing and Nelson keeps writing, but the cops begin to think that Keece is the killer. Then Stefan decides to target Keece's girlfriend Juliette (Campbell) as his next victim. **92mC VHS, DVD.** Gary Busey, Arnold Vosloo, Michael Madsen, Julia Campbell; **D:** Alan Jacobs; **W:** Jennifer Badham-Stewart; **C:** Keith L. Smith; **M:** Stephen Renzetti.

Diary of a Teenage Hitchhiker 🎬 **1982** Teen girl ignores family restrictions and police warnings where he finds the diary kept by his youngest daughter, Anne. The document recounts their years in hiding from the Nazis. Based on the actual diary of 13-year-old Anne Frank, killed in a death camp during WWII. **95mC VHS, DVD.** Charlene Tilton, Dick Van Patten, Katherine Helmond, Dominique Dunne, Katy Kurtzman, Christopher Knight, James Carroll Jordan, Craig T. Nelson, Noelle North, Karlene Crockett, Don McLean, Patricia Smith, Richard Sanders; **D:** Ted Post. **M:** Joe Renzetti.

Diary of a Young Comic 🎬🎬 **1979** New York comedian searches for the meaning of lunacy. He finds it after improvisation in Los Angeles. **74mC VHS.** Stacy Keach, Dom DeLuise, Richard Lewis, Bill Macy, George Jessel, Gary Muleener, Nina Van Pallandt; **D:** Gary Weis.

The Diary of Anne Frank 🎬🎬🎬½ **1959** In June 1945, a liberated Jewish refugee returns to the hidden third floor of an Amsterdam factory where he finds the diary kept by his youngest daughter, Anne. The document recounts their years in hiding from the Nazis. Based on the actual diary of 13-year-old Anne Frank, killed in a death camp during WWII. **150mB VHS, DVD.** Millie Perkins, Joseph Schildkraut, Shelley Winters, Richard Beymer, Gusti Huber, Ed Wynn, Lou Jacobi, Diane Baker; **D:** George Stevens; **C:** William Mellor. Oscars '59: Art Dir/Set Dec., B&W, Cinematog., Support. Actress (Winters).

The Diary of Ellen Rimbauer 🎬🎬 **2003** (R) Prequel to Stephen King's "Rose Red" shows how to the marriage of innocent Ellen (Brenner) to the unfaithful and twisted John Rimbauer (Brand) eventually found her possessed by the forces surrounding their haunted Seattle mansion. Diary passages highlight a series of deadly encounters on the estate. **88mC VHS, DVD.** Lisa Brenner, Steven Brand, Kate Burton, Tsidii Leloka, Brad Greenquist, Tsai Chin; **D:** Craig R. Baxley; **W:** Ridley Pearson; **C:** Joao Fernandes; **M:** Gary Chang. **TV**

Diary of Forbidden Dreams 🎬🎬 *What?; Che?* **1973** (R) A beautiful young girl finds herself drawn into bizarre incidents at an eccentric millionaire's mansion that cause her to go insane. Set on the Italian Riviera, it's the most offbeat rendition of "Alice in Wonderland" you're apt to find. Unfortunately, the convoluted plot lessens its appeal. Unedited version under the original title "What," released at 113 minutes; is also available. **93mC VHS.** IT Marcello Mastroianni, Hugh Griffith, Sydne Rome, Roman Polanski; **D:** Roman Polanski; **W:** Roman Polanski, Gerard Brach.

Diary of the Dead 🎬🎬 **1980** (PG) A newlywed kills his aggravating mother-in-law, only to have her repeatedly return from the grave. **93mC VHS.** Hector Elizondo, Geraldine Fitzgerald, Salome Jens; **D:** Arvin Brown.

Diary of the Dead 🎬🎬 **2007** (R) George A. Romero's *Diary of the Dead* **2007** (R) Nearly 40 years after Romero's ultra-low-budget "Night of the Living Dead" he's taking another stab at the genre with his fifth zombie flick. This modern incarnation starts with some college kids shooting a horror movie in the woods when their filming is interrupted by radio reports of zombies afoot. Camera rolling, the plucky students head for their professor abandon the shoot to instead get footage of his pals succumbing to zombification. Not too much new here, but the familiarity, nostalgia and gooey gore will make some die-hards happy. Pay attention to the spoofs of the original. **95mC VHS, DVD.** US Joshua Close, Joe Dinicol, Philip Riccio, Michelle Morgan, Shawn Roberts, Amy Lalonde, Scott Wentworth; **D:** George A. Romero; **W:** George A. Romero; **C:** Adam Swica; **M:** Norman Orenstein.

Dick 🎬🎬 **1999** (PG-13) If you think Hollywood is done making fun of Nixon, then you don't know "Dick." Satire puts forth the theory that two dizzy teenage girls (Dunst and Williams) caused the downfall of Richard Nixon (Hedaya). They bump into all the major Watergate players, including Liddy (Shearer), Haldemann (Foley) and Dean (Breuer). The girls are blissfully blind to Tricky Dick's indiscretions, and one of them even develops a hilarious crush on him. When they overhear him abusing the presidential pup, however, they turn on him. Flouting the Constitution is one thing, but being mean to dogs is clearly icky behavior. They decide to become the famed Deep Throat for the bickering reporters Woodward (Ferrell) and Bernstein (McCulloch). Rent this with "All the President's Men" and "Nixon," because this is the movie that Oliver Stone would've made if he had a sense of humor instead of flashbacks. **95mC VHS, DVD.** Kirsten Dunst, Michele Williams, Dan Hedaya, Will Ferrell, Dave Foley, Harry Shearer, Jim McCulloch, Devon Gummersall, Ted McGinley, Ryan Reynolds, Saul Rubinek, Teri Garr, G.D. Spradlin, Ana Gasteyer; **D:** Andrew Fleming; **W:** Andrew Fleming, Sheryl Longin; **C:** Alexander Gruszynski; **M:** John Debney.

Dick Barton Strikes Back 🎬🎬½ **1948** "Mr. French" Cabot has a nuclear weapon and is willing to use it, that is, until Dick Barton arrives to put the Frenchman out of commission. Generally considered the best of the Dick Barton film series. **73mB VHS.** GB Don Stannard, Sebastian Cabot, Jean Lodge; **D:** Godfrey Grayson.

Dick Barton, Special Agent 🎬🎬 **1948** Dick Barton is called in when a mad scientist threatens to attack London with germ-carrying bombs. The first film production for Hammer Studios, later to be known for its horror classics. **70mB VHS.** GB Don Stannard, Geoffrey Ford, Jack Shaw; **D:** Alfred Goulding.

Dick Tracy 🎬🎬 **1937** Serial based on the comic-strip character, in 15 chapters. Tracy tries to find his kidnapped brother as he faces the fiend "Spider." The first chapter is 30 minutes and each additional chapter is 20 minutes. **290mB VHS.** Ralph Byrd, Smiley Burnette, Irving Pichel, Jennifer Jones; **D:** John English, Alan James.

Dick Tracy 🎬🎬🎬 **1990** (PG) Beatty wears the caps of producer director, and star, performing admirably on all fronts. One minor complaint: his Tracy is somewhat flat in comparison to the outstanding performances and makeup of the unique villains, especially Pacino. Stylistically superior, shot in only seven colors, the timeless sets capture the essence rather than the reality of the city, successfully bringing the comic strip to life. Madonna is fine as the seductive Breathless Mahoney, belting out Stephen Sondheim like she was born to do it. People expecting the high technology of "Batman" may be disappointed that moviegoers searching for a memory made real will be thrilled. "Sooner or Later." **105mC VHS, DVD.** Warren Beatty, Madonna, Charlie Korsmo, Glenne Headly, Al Pacino, Dustin Hoffman, James Caan, Mandy Patinkin, Paul Sorvino, Charles Durning, Dick Van Dyke, R.G. Armstrong, Catherine O'Hara, Estelle Parsons, Seymour Cassel, Michael J. Pollard, Ian Wolfe, Kathy Bates, James Tolkan; **D:** Warren Beatty; **W:** Jim Cash, Jack Epps Jr.; **C:** Vittorio Storaro; **M:** Danny Elfman, Stephen Sondheim. Oscars '90: Art Dir/Set Dec., Makeup, Song ("Sooner or Later").

Dick Tracy, Detective 🎬🎬 **1945** The first Dick Tracy feature film, in which Splitface is on the loose, a schoolteacher is murdered, the Mayor is threatened and Tracy the clues needed to connect the crimes. **62mB VHS, DVD.** Morgan Conway, Anne Jeffreys, Mike Mazurki, Jane Greer, Lyle Latell; **D:** William Berke; **W:** Eric Taylor; **C:** Frank Redman; **M:** Roy Webb.

Dick Tracy Meets Gruesome 🎬🎬 **** Dick Tracy's Amazing Adventure; Dick Tracy Meets Karloff **1947** Gruesome and his partner in crime, Melody, stage a bank robbery using the secret formula...

mula of Dr. A. Tomic. Tracy has to solve the case before word gets out and people rush to withdraw their savings, destroying civilization as we know it. **66m/B VHS, DVD.** Boris Karloff, Ralph Byrd, Lyle Latell, Anne Gwynne, Edward Ashley, June Clayworth, Tony Barrett, Skelton Knaggs; **D:** John Rawlins; **W:** Eric Taylor, Robertson White; **C:** Frank Redman; **M:** Paul Sawtell.

Dick Tracy Returns 1938 15-chapter serial. Public Enemy Paw Stark and his gang set out on a wave of crime that brings them face to face with dapper Dick. **100m/B VHS.** Ralph Byrd, Charles Middleton; **D:** William Witney.

Dick Tracy: The Spider Strikes 1937 Dick Tracy, his bumbling sidekick, and his beautiful, brainy assistant go up against the master criminal, The Spider. **60m/B VHS, DVD.** Kay Hughes, Smiley Burnette, Lee Van Atta, Ralph Byrd, Francis X. Bushman; **D:** Alan James, Ray Taylor; **W:** Barry Shipman, Winston Miller; **C:** Edgar Lyons; William Nobles.

Dick Tracy vs. Crime Inc. 1941 Dick Tracy encounters many difficulties when he tries to track down a criminal who can make himself invisible. A serial in 15 chapters. **100m/B VHS.** Ralph Byrd, Ralph Morgan, Michael Owen; **D:** William Witney; **W:** John English.

Dick Tracy vs. Cueball 1946 Dick Tracy has his work cut out for him when the evil gangster Cueball appears on the scene. Based on Chester Gould's comic strip. **62m/B VHS, DVD.** Morgan Conway, Anne Jeffreys, Lyle Latell, Rita (Paula) Corday, Ian Keith, Dick Wessel, Skelton Knaggs; **D:** Gordon Douglas; **W:** Robert E. Kent, Dane Lussier; **C:** George E. Diskant; **M:** C. Bakaleinikoff, Phil Ohman.

Dick Turpin 1925 In this rare film, Mix plays the famed English highwayman who seeks adventure in historical Britain. **60m/B VHS.** Tom Mix, Alan Hale; **D:** John Blystone.

Dickie Roberts: Former Child Star 2003 (PG-13) Spade plays the impish title character, a valet parking attendant who wishes to revive his former child-star sitcom fame. Without much help from his despondent agent (a dead-on Lovitz,) Dickie scores a meeting with Rob Reiner (as himself!) who's casting the lead in his new movie. When Dickie loses the role due to a lack of real character, he hires a family to relive his lost youth and help him get a real life. Pic is at its crackling best when Spade is his usual, smarmy self, but suffers when trying for earnestness. Amusing cameos by the likes of Leif Garrett, Danny Bonaduce, and Corey Feldman, and the final credits include a fun and rousing anthem sung by a gaggle of former child stars. **99m/C VHS, DVD. US** David Spade, Mary McCormack, Craig Bierko, Jon Lovitz, Alyssa Milano, Doris Roberts, Jenna Boyd, Scott Tessa, Edie McClurg; **Cameos:** Rob Reiner, Leif Garrett, Brendan Fraser; **D:** Sam Weisman; **W:** David Spade, Fred Wolf; **C:** Thomas Ackerman; **M:** Christophe Beck, Waddy Wachtel.

Didn't You Hear? 1983 (PG) An alienated college student discovers that dreams have a life of their own when he becomes immersed in his own fantasy world. **94m/C VHS.** Dennis Christopher, Gary Busey, Cheryl Waters, John Kauffman; **D:** Skip Sherwood.

Die Another Day 2002 (PG-13) The 20th film in the James Bond series carries a lot of "in" jokes referring to previous films, including the bikini and knife belt worn by NSA agent Jinx (shades of Ursula Andress in "Dr. No"). Of course, the beautiful Berry is well worth contemplating, which is a good thing since this Bond is fairly tiresome with its convoluted plot and over-the-top action. It starts off well and Brosnan is comfortable in the role (even with the silly double entendres) but with the main villain (Stephens) is another megalomaniac with designs on taking over the world (wrapped around some political cant) and the second half of the film is one chase scene after another. Yawn. **130m/C VHS, DVD. GB** Pierce Brosnan, Halle Berry, Toby Stephens, Judi Dench, John Cleese, Rosamund Pike, Rick Yune, Michael Madsen, Will Yun Lee, Kenneth Tsang, Samantha Bond, Colin Salmon, Emilio Echevarría, Michael Gorevoy, Lawrence Makoare; **D:** Lee Tamahori; **W:** Neal Purvis, Robert Wade; **C:** David Tattersall; **M:** David Arnold. Golden Raspberries '02: Worst Support. Actress (Madonna).

Die! Die! My Darling! 1965 A young widow visits her mad ex-mother-in-law in a remote English village, and is imprisoned by the mourning woman as revenge for her son's death. Bankhead's last role. Based on Anne Blaisdell's novel. **97m/C VHS, DVD. GB** Tallulah Bankhead, Stefanie Powers, Peter Vaughan, Maurice Kaufmann, Donald Sutherland, Gwendolyn Watts, Yootha Joyce, Winifred Dennis; **D:** Silvio Narizzano; **W:** Richard Matheson; **C:** Arthur Ibbetson; **M:** Wilfred Josephs.

Die Grosse Freiheit Nr. 7 *Great Freedom No. 7* 1945 A man tries to stop his niece's love affair with a sailor. Nazi propaganda minister Goebbels banned this film in Germany, since it showed German soldiers getting drunk and also had Hildebrand cast as a prostitute. After the war, however, it enjoyed great popularity throughout Germany. Albers sings the classic "Auf der Reeperbahn." In German with no English translation. **100m/C VHS. GE** Hans Albers, Hilde Hildebrand, Ilse Werner, Hans Söhnker, Helmut Käutner; **D:** Helmut Käutner; **W:** Helmut Käutner; **C:** Werner Krien; **M:** Werner Eisbrenner.

Die Hard 1988 (R) It's Christmas Eve and NYC cop John McClane (Willis) has arrived in L.A. to spend the holiday with his estranged wife Holly (Bedelia) and their kids. Unfortunately, Holly is one of the hostages being held by a band of ruthless high-stakes terrorists in the Century City high-rise headquarters of a Japanese corporation. Soon it's the loner cop against the intruders, who is led by Eurotrash villain Hans Gruber (a marvelous performance by Rickman). A high-voltage action thriller that's just as unbelievable as it sounds, but you'll love it anyway. Based on the novel "Nothing Lasts Forever" by Roderick Thorp. **114m/C VHS, DVD, Blu-ray Disc, UMD.** Bruce Willis, Bonnie Bedelia, Alan Rickman, Alexander Godunov, Paul Gleason, William Atherton, Reginald VelJohnson, Hart Bochner, James Shigeta, Mary Ellen Trainor, De'voreaux White, Robert Davi, Ric(k) Ducommun, Clarence Gilyard Jr., Grand L. Bush, Al Leong, Wilhelm von Homburg; **D:** John McTiernan; **W:** Jeb Stuart, Steven E. de Souza; **C:** Jan De Bont; **M:** Michael Kamen.

Die Hard 2: Die Harder 1990 (R) Fast, well-done sequel brings another impossible situation before the wisecracking, tough-cookie cop. Our hero tangles with a group of terrorists at an airport under siege, while his wife remains in a plane circling above as its fuel dwindles. Obviously a repeat of the plot and action of the first "Die Hard," with references to the former in the script. While the bad guys lack the fiendishness of their predecessors, this installment features energetic and finely acted performances. Fairly gory, especially the icicle-in-the-eyeball scene. Adapted from the novel "58 Minutes" by Walter Wager and characters created by Roderick Thorp. **124m/C VHS, DVD, Blu-ray Disc, UMD.** Bruce Willis, William Atherton, Franco Nero, Bonnie Bedelia, John Amos, Reginald VelJohnson, Dennis Franz, Art Evans, Fred Dalton Thompson, William Sadler, Sheila McCarthy, Robert Patrick, John Leguizamo, Robert Costanzo, Tom Verica, Don Harvey, Tony Ganios, Vondie Curtis-Hall, Colm Meaney; **D:** Renny Harlin; **W:** Doug Richardson, Steven E. de Souza; **C:** Oliver Wood; **M:** Michael Kamen.

Die Hard: With a Vengeance 1996 (R) *Die Hard 3* 1995 (R) Third time is not a charm in the "Die Hard" series. McClane (Willis) is back home in the Big Apple and having another bad day. More Eurotrash terrorists, led by the brilliant and vengeful Simon (Irons), are out to blow things up, snag some gold, and make life miserable for McClane and his reluctant partner, Zeus Carver (Jackson). The claustrophobic settings of the first two outings have been replaced by the exhausting expanse of New York City, to good effect, but frenetic action scenes and good chemistry between Willis and Jackson don't quite compensate for a lackluster script and more cartoony feel. Jackson brings a fresh perspective and vitality. **131m/C VHS, DVD, Blu-ray Disc.** Bruce Willis, Samuel L. Jackson, Jeremy Irons, Graham Greene, Colleen Camp, Larry Bryggman, Tony Peck, Nick Wyman, Sam (Leslie) Phillips; **D:** John McTiernan; **W:** Jonathan Hensleigh; **C:** Peter Menzies Jr.; **M:** Michael Kamen.

Die Laughing woof! 1980 (PG) A cab driver unwittingly becomes involved in murder, intrigue, and the kidnapping of a monkey that has memorized a scientific formula that can destroy the world. Writer/actor/composer Benson might consider renaming it "Die from Embarrassment." **108m/C VHS.** Robby Benson, Charles Durning, Bud Cort, Elsa Lanchester, Peter Coyote; **D:** Jeff Werner; **W:** Robby Benson, Scott Parker; **M:** Robby Benson.

Die Mommie Die! 2003 (R) Angela Arden (co-writer Busch, in drag) is a fading diva trapped in a loveless marriage. Her husband, Sol Hussman (Hall), a movie producer, refuses to give her a divorce. Like all good dysfunctional families, battle lines are drawn between dad, supported by daughter Edith (Lyonne) and Angela, supported by son Lance (Sands). Add in bisexual gigolo Tony Parker (Priestly) and fanatically religious maid Bootsie Carp (Conroy) plus some bawdy humor, and you've got the workings of a campy cult classic. Definitely one for John Waters fans. **90m/C VHS, DVD. US** Charles Busch, Natasha Lyonne, Jason Priestley, Frances Conroy, Philip Baker Hall, Stark Sands, Victor Raider-Wexler, Nora Dunn; **D:** Mark Rucker; **W:** Charles Busch; **C:** Kelly Evans; **M:** Dennis McCarthy.

Die, Monster, Die! *Monster of Terror* 1965 A reclusive scientist experiments with a radioactive meteorite and gains bizarre powers. Karloff is great in this adaptation of H.P. Lovecraft's "The Color Out of Space." **80m/C VHS, DVD. GB** Boris Karloff, Nick Adams, Suzan Farmer, Patrick Magee, Freda Jackson, Terence de Marney, Leslie Dwyer, Paul Farrell; **D:** Daniel Haller; **W:** Jerry Sohl; **C:** Paul Beeson; **M:** Don Banks.

Die Screaming, Marianne *Die, Beautiful Marianne* 1973 A girl is on the run from her father, a crooked judge, who wants to kill her before her 21st birthday, when she will inherit evidence that will put him away for life. **81m/C VHS, DVD. GB** Michael Rennie, Susan George, Karin Dor, Leo Genn; **D:** Pete Walker; **W:** Murray Smith; **C:** Norman G. Langley; **M:** Cyril Ornadel.

Die Sister, Die! 1974 Thriller about a gothic mansion with an eerie secret in the basement features a battle between a senile, reclusive sister and her disturbed, tormenting brother. **88m/C VHS, DVD.** Jack Ging, Edith Atwater, Antoinette Bower, Kent Smith, Robert Emhardt; **D:** Randall Hood.

Die Watching 1993 (R) Sleazy erotic thriller about a video director (Atkins) who not only likes to film some hot Hollywood babes but may also like to kill them as well. His latest discovery just could be the next victim. **92m/C VHS, DVD.** Christopher Atkins, Vali Ashton, Tim Thomerson, Carlos Palomino, Mike Jacobs; **D:** Charles Davis; **W:** Kenneth J. Hall; **C:** Howard Wexler; **M:** Scott Roewe.

Different for Girls 1996 (R) Boyish motorcycle dispatch rider Paul Prentice (Graves) nearly gets run over by a London taxi whose passenger Kim Foyle (Mackintosh) seems strangely familiar. Then Paul discovers Kim used to be his boyhood school chum Karl. After a shaky start, the duo discover a genuine attraction but when they get into an argument that leads to a police call and Paul gets thrown in jail, Kim's first instincts are to retreat to her sister's (Reeves) family and back into her quiet life. Director Spence refrains from camping up the situation and some fine performances, especially from the engaging Graves, make this quirky film well worth a watch. **101m/C VHS, DVD. GB** Rupert Graves, Steven Mackintosh, Miriam Margolyes, Saskia Reeves, Neil Dudgeon, Charlotte Coleman; **D:** Richard Spence; **W:** Tony Marchant; **C:** Sean Van Hales; **M:** Stephen Warbeck. Montreal World Film Fest. '95: Film.

A Different Loyalty 2004 (R) Gleaned from the true story of an American journalist, Sally (Stone), finds love with British government agent Leo (Everett) while in Beirut during the Cold War. They marry, but their happily ever after is interrupted when Leo goes missing. A desperate search takes her to the Soviet Union where his disturbing secret life endangers them both. **96m/C VHS, DVD.** Sharon Stone, Rupert Everett, Julian Wadham, Michael Cochrane, Anne Lambton, Jim Piddock, Richard McMillan, Mimi Kuzyk, Emily Van Camp, Tamara Hope, Damir Andrei, John Bourgeois, Sonja Smits, Edward Hibbert, Joss Ackland, Jack Galloway, Matthew Scurfield, Ron Lea, Mark Rendall; **D:** Marek Kanievska; **C:** Jean Lepine; **M:** Normand Corbeil. VIDEO

Different Story 1978 (PG) Romance develops when a lesbian real estate agent offers a homosexual chauffeur a job with her firm. Resorts to stereotypes when the characters decide to marry. **107m/C VHS, DVD.** Perry King, Meg Foster, Valerie Curtin, Peter Donat, Richard Bull; **D:** Paul Aaron.

DIG! 2004 (R) Seven year documentary chronicle of two indie-rock bands, charting rise of one and downfall of the other. The Dandy Warhols, led by Courtney Taylor, seem to be blessed by the angels as they meteorically rise in the world of alterna-pop. Anton Newcombe and band, Brian Jonestown Massacre, who are great mentors to Taylor's own band, seem to have no one but Newcombe to blame for their lack of success. Belligerent and out-of-control, Newcombe amazingly crafts brilliant album after album, but scares bandmates, record companies and friends away. Truly sad upclose look at the difficulties of remaining uncompromising in the ruthless music business. **110m/C DVD. US D:** Ondi Timoner; **W:** Ondi Timoner; **C:** Ondi Timoner, Vasco Lucas Nunes, David Timoner; **M:** David Brownlow.

Digby, the Biggest Dog in the World 1973 (G) Poor comedy-fantasy about Digby, a sheepdog, who wanders around a scientific laboratory, drinks an experimental fluid, and grows and grows and grows. **88m/C VHS. GB** Jim Dale, Angela Douglas, Spike Milligan, Dinsdale Landen; **D:** Joseph McGrath; **M:** Edwin Astley.

Digger 1994 (PG) Digger (Hann-Byrd) arrives at a Pacific Northwest island to stay with relatives, including his Grandma (Dukakis) who's being romanced by the fun-loving Arthur (Nielsen). He makes friends with another youth who turns out to have a terminal heart ailment. **92m/C VHS. GB** Adam Hann-Byrd, Olympia Dukakis, Leslie Nielsen, Joshua Jackson, Barbara Williams, Timothy Bottoms; **D:** Robert Turner; **W:** Rodney Gibbons; **M:** Todd Boekelheide.

Diggers 2006 (R) Four 30-something buddies face life-changing decisions in this modest slice-of-life drama. In 1976, Long Islanders Hunt (Rudd), Jack (Eldard), Cons (Hamilton), and Lozo (Marino) continue their families' tradition as clam diggers, but their livelihood is threatened by a corporate fishery that's buying up prime water rights. Hunt's dad has just died so maybe he should finally move on but he's worried when lothario Jack starts sniffing around his divorced sister, Gina (Tierney). Meanwhile, Cons supplements his earnings dealing pot (although smoking most of it), and Lozo's large and increasing family strains his marriage and his temper. Charming and poignant despite its well-worn premise of breaking out of small-town working-class life. **90m/C DVD.** US Paul Rudd, Ron Eldard, Josh Hamilton, Ken Marino, Lauren Ambrose, Maura Tierney, Sarah Paulson; **D:** Katherine Dieckmann; **C:** Michael McDonough; **M:** David Mansfield.

Digging to China ♂♂½ 1998 (PG) Directorial debut of Hutton is the sentimental story of a sweet friendship between misfits—precocious 10-year-old Harriet (Wood) and mentally handicapped 30-year-old Ricky (Bacon). Harriet's alcoholic mom (Moriarty) runs a motel in rural New Hampshire film is set in the mid-60s) with Harriet's slutty older sister Gwen (Masterson). Ricky winds up at the motel with his dying mother Leah (Seldes), who was taking Ricky to an institution when her car breaks down. Harriet thinks Ricky is a terrific playmate but after some shocking news, the young girl and her new friend decide to run away—causing a lot of trouble. **98m/C VHS, DVD.** Rachel Wood, Kevin Bacon, Mary Stuart Masterson, Cathy Moriarty, Marian Seldes; *D:* Timothy Hutton; *W:* Karen Janszen; *C:* Jorgen Persson; *M:* Cynthia Millar.

Digging Up Business WOOF! 1991 (PG) Johnson tries to save the family funeral home business from financial ruin with some unique interment services. This film needs a decent burial. **89m/C VHS, DVD.** Lynn-Holly Johnson, Billy Barty, Ruth Buzzi, Murray Langston, Yvonne Craig, Gary Owens; *D:* Mark Byers.

Diggstown ♂♂½ 1992 (R) Lightweight, good-natured sports comedy about a boxing scam. Con man Gabriel Caine (Woods), fresh out of prison, heads for Diggstown and the unregulated boxing matches arranged by town boss, John Gillon (Dern). The bet is that Caine's one boxer can beat any 10 boxers, chosen by Gillon, in a 24-hour period. So Caine decides to hook up with an old friend, former prizefighter "Honey" Roy Palmer (Gossett Jr.), to run the scam of his life. Dern is sufficiently nasty and Woods his usual nervy self but it's Gossett Jr. who manages to hold everything together as the aging boxer. Based on the novel "The Diggstown Ringers" by Leonard Wise. **97m/C VHS, DVD.** James Woods, Louis Gossett Jr., Bruce Dern, Oliver Platt, Heather Graham, Randall "Tex" Cobb, Thomas Wilson Brown, Duane Davis, Willie Green, George D. Wallace, Wilhelm von Homburg; *D:* Michael Ritchie; *W:* Steven McKay; *M:* James Newton Howard.

Digital Man ♂♂½ 1994 (R) High-tech military super-soldier prototype has his programming sabotaged and a team of human and robotic commandoes must prevent him from starting WWIII. **95m/C VHS.** Ken Olandt, Adam Baldwin, Ed Lauter, Matthias Hues, Kristen Dalton, Paul Gleason; *D:* Phillip J. Roth.

Dilemma ♂♂½ 1997 Or Death Row, Rudy Salazar (Trejo) volunteers to be a bone-marrow donor to a sick child. LAPD detective Quin (Howell) realizes that it's a set-up for an escape and he's right. Then the cops have to catch Salazar again, but they can't kill him without sacrificing their lives. **87m/C VHS, DVD.** C. Thomas Howell, Danny Trejo, Sofie Svinas; *D:* Eric Larsen; *W:* Ira Israel, Chuck Conaway; *C:* Mark Melville *M:* Alton MacClain.

Dillinger ♂♂½ 1945 John Dillinger's notorious career, from street punk to public enemy number one, receives a thrilling, fast-paced treatment. Tierney turns in a fine performance in this interesting account of the criminal life. **70m/C VHS, DVD.** Lawrence Tierney, Edmund Lowe, Anne Jeffreys, Elisha Cook Jr.; *D:* Max Nosseck; *M:* Phillip Yordan.

Dillinger ♂♂½ 1973 (R) The most colorful period of criminality in America is brought to life in this story of bank-robber John Dillinger, "Baby Face" Nelson, and the notorious "Lady in Red." **106m/C VHS, DVD.** Warren Oates, Michelle Phillips, Richard Dreyfuss, Cloris Leachman, Ben Johnson, Harry Dean Stanton; *D:* Max Nosseck; *M:* Barry DeVorzon.

Dingo ♂♂½ 1990 In Davis' only film appearance he's, what else, a famous jazz trumpeter. Paris-based Billy Cross (Davis) and his combo are on tour in 1969 and momentarily stuck at a remote Australian airstrip. They give an impromptu concert heard by John "Dingo" Anderson (Friels), who instantly decides that music is the life for him. Over the years Dingo keeps in touch with his idol as he works outback bars and secretly saves to go to Paris and check out the scene—even if it means sacrificing his wife and family. **108m/C VHS, DVD, FR AU.** Colin Friels, Miles Davis, Helen Buday, Bernadette LaPort; *D:* Rolf de Heer; *W:* Marc Rosenberg; *C:* Denis Lenoir; *M:* Miles Davis, Michel Legrand.

The Dining Room ♂♂½ 1986 Six performers play more than 50 roles in this adaptation of A.R. Gurney Jr.'s play set in a dining room, where people live out dramatic and comic moments in their lives. From the "American Playhouse" series. **90m/C VHS.** John Shea, Frances Sternhagen, Pippa Pearthree, Remak Ramsay; *M:* Allan Goldstein.

Dingaka ♂♂½ 1965 A controversial drama from the writer and director of "The Gods Must Be Crazy" about a South African tribesman who avenges his daughter's murder by white man's laws, and is then tried by white man's laws. A crusading white attorney struggles to acquit him. **96m/C VHS.** Stanley Baker, Juliet Prowse, Ken Gampu; *D:* Jamie Uys.

Dillinger and Capone ♂♂½ 1995 (R) Supposedly the FBI has killed the wrong Dillinger and the gangster (Sheen) decides to make a new life. But his old friend Al Capone (Abraham), newly released from prison, is holding Dillinger's wife (Hicks) and son hostage as insurance that first: he'll retrieve $15 million from a mob-owned Chicago bank. **95m/C VHS, DVD.** Martin Sheen, F. Murray Abraham, Catherine Hicks, Stephen Davies, Don Stroud, Clint Howard, Joe Estevez; *D:* Jon Purcy; *W:* Michael B. Druxman; *C:* John Aronson; *M:* David Wurst, Eric Wurst.

Dimples ♂♂½ 1936 (PG) When Shirley's pickpocket grandfather is caught red-handed, she steps in, takes the blame, and somehow ends up in show business. Re-issued version is rare. Also available colorized. ♫Hey, What Did the Bluebird Say?; He Was a Dandy; Picture Me Without You; Oh Mister Man Up in the Moon; Dixie-Anna; Get On Board; Swing Low Sweet Chariot, Frank Morgan, Helen Westley, Berton Churchill, Robert Kent, Delma Byron; *D:* William A. Seiter; *W:* Nat Perrin, Arthur Sheekman; *C:* Bert Glennon; *M:* Louis Silvers.

Diner ♂♂♂ 1982 (R) A group of old high school friends meet at "their" Baltimore diner to find that more has changed than the menu. A bittersweet look at the experiences of a group of Baltimore twentysomethings, circa 1959, who find adulthood hard to face. Particularly notable was Levinson's casting of "unknowns" who have since become household names. Features many humorous moments and fine performances. **110m/C VHS, DVD.** Steve Guttenberg, Daniel Stern, Mickey Rourke, Kevin Bacon, Ellen Barkin, Timothy Daly, Paul Reiser, Michael Tucker, Jessica James, Kathryn Dowling, Colette Blonigan; *D:* Barry Levinson; *W:* Barry Levinson; *C:* Peter Sova *M:* Bruce Brody, Ivan Kral. Natl. Soc. Film Critics '82: Support. Actor (Rourke).

Dinner Rush ♂♂♂ 2000 (R) Louis, owner of a trendy Manhattan restaurant and operator of a bookmaking enterprise, must deal with various problems and people from both of his occupations in one hectic night. His son, Udo has transformed the restaurant from a simple Italian place with his pursuit of nouvelle cuisine fame, two mob guys are trying to muscle him out of the bookie business (having already killed his partner), a snooty gallery owner is hassling his staff, his sous-chef is piling up gambling debts, and a powerful food critic just walked in the door. Although pic is overstuffed, Giraldi's deft direction and excellent performances (especially Aiello's) make for a satisfying treat. Success fully realized at nouvelle cuisine restaurateur Giraldi filmed in one of his own eateries. **99m/C VHS, DVD, US.** Danny Aiello, Edoardo Ballerini, Vivian Wu, Mike McGlone, Kirk Acevedo, Sandra Bernhard, Summer Phoenix, Polly Draper, Mark Margolis, John Corbett, Alex Corrado; *D:* Bob Giraldi; *W:* Brian Kalata, Rick Shaughnessy; *C:* Tim Ives; *M:* Alexander Lasarenko.

Dinotopia ♂♂♂ 2002 TV miniseries based on two books by author/illustrator James Gurney, about a fantasy island paradise where humans and talking dinos co-exist peacefully. Teenaged half-brothers Karl (Leitso) and David (Miller) survive a plane crash and wind up on Dinotopia where they are befriended by young princess Marion (Carr). But the island has problems—rogue carnivorous dinosaurs and sinister human Cyrus Crabb (Thewlis) as well as some magical sunstones that are losing their power. Fanciful storytelling with some fun special effects. **285m/C VHS, DVD.** Tyron Leitso, Wentworth Miller, Katie Carr, David Thewlis, Jim Carter, Alice Krige, Colin Salmon, Hannah Yelland, Stuart Wilson, Anna McGuire; *D:* Marco Brambilla; *M:* Trevor Jones; *TV*

Diplomaniacs ♂♂½ 1933 Wheeler and Woolsey, official barbers on an Indian reservation, are sent to the Geneva peace conference to represent the interests of their tribe. Slim plot nevertheless provides quite a few laughs. Fun musical

---

Vince Edwards, Bruce Abbott; *D:* Rupert Wainwright; *C:* Donald M. Morgan.

Dinner and Driving ♂♂½ 1997 Twentysomething writer Jason (a charming Slotnick) looks like a nebbish but must have something else going for him because he's caught between two babes. One is longtime girlfriend Laura (Devicq), who has pressured the reluctant Jason into a marriage proposal. The other is Grace (Eako), a hottie who was Jason's college sweetie and suddenly makes a reappearance in his life. Jason, who doesn't know if he can commit to one woman for life, seeks advice from his equally clueless friends and realizes that relationships aren't easy. **89m/C VHS, DVD.** Joey Slotnick, Brigitte Bako, Sam Roberts, Molly Shannon, Greg Grunberg; *D:* Lawrence Trilling, Steven Wolfson; *C:* Geary McLeod; *M:* Peter Himmelman.

Dim Sum: A Little Bit of Heart ♂♂♂ 1985 (PG) The second independent film from the director of "Chan is Missing." A Chinese-American mother and daughter living in San Francisco's Chinatown confront the conflict between American life. Gentle, fragile picture made with humor and care. In English and Chinese with subtitles. **88m/C VHS, DVD.** Laureen Chew, Kim Chew, Victor Wong, Ida F.O. Chong, Cora Miao, John Nishio, Joan Chen; *D:* Wayne Wang; *W:* Terrel Seltzer; *M:* Todd Boekelheide.

Dinner at Eight ♂♂♂♂ 1933 Social-climbing Mrs. Jordan (Burke) and her husband Oliver (Lionel Barrymore) throw a dinner party for various members of the New York elite. During the course of the evening, all of the guests reveal too much. Special performances all around, especially John Barrymore as a parody of his drunken career, Dressler as a grande dame sliding down the social ladder, and Harlow as a gold-digging hussy. Superb comedic direction by Cukor. Adapted from the play by Edna Ferber and George Kaufman. **110m/C VHS, DVD.** John Barrymore, Lionel Barrymore, Wallace Beery, Madge Evans, Jean Harlow, Billie Burke, Marie Dressler, Phillips Holmes, Jean Hersholt, Lee Tracy, Edmund Lowe, Karen Morley, May Robson; *D:* George Cukor; *W:* Herman J. Mankiewicz, Frances Marion, Donald Ogden Stewart; *M:* William H. Daniels; *M:* William Axt.

Dinner at Eight ♂♂ 1989 A social-climbing romance novelist throws an elegant dinner party. TV remake of the 1933 film does not compare well. **100m/C VHS.** Lauren Bacall, Charles Durning, Ellen Greene, Harry Hamlin, John Mahoney, Marsha Mason, Tim Kazurinsky; *D:* Ron Lagomarsino. *TV*

Dinner at the Ritz ♂♂½ 1937 Daughter of a murdered Parisian banker vows to find his killer with help from her fiance. **78m/B VHS, DVD, GB** David Niven, Annabella, Paul Lukas, Patricia Medina; *D:* Harold Schuster.

The Dinner Game ♂♂ *Le Dîner de Cons* 1998 (PG-13) Smug publisher Pierre (Lhermitte) dines weekly with equally smug friends, their entertainment being to see who can bring the biggest fool as a dinner guest. This nasty joke gets the turnabout it deserves when Pierre intends to bring bumbling Francois (Villeret) to the party, only to have the man proceed to wreck Pierre's life before they even get there—all while Francois maintains his own sweet dignity. French with subtitles. **82m/C VHS, DVD, FR** Thierry Lhermitte, Jacques Villeret, Alexandra Vandernoot, Catherine Frot, Francis Huster, Daniel Prevost; *D:* Francis Veber; *W:* Francis Veber; *C:* Luciano Tovoli; *M:* Vladimir Cosma. Cesar '99: Actor (Villeret), Support. Actor (Prevost), Writing.

Dinner with Friends ♂♂½ 2001 The main course is a look at the meaning of love, marriage, and friendship with a heaping side of mid-life angst. Happily married couple Gabe (Quaid) and Karen (MacDowell) deal with the fallout of the breakup of their friends' marriage. Beth (Collette) shows up at their door after husband Tom (Kinnear) leaves her for another woman. When Gabe and Karen try to help (read: offer their advice), they're met with a less than enthusiastic response. **95m/C VHS, DVD.** Dennis Quaid, Andie MacDowell, Greg Kinnear, Toni Collette; *D:* Norman Jewison; *W:* Donald Margulies. *CABLE*

Dino ♂♂ 1957 Social worker joins a young woman in helping a 17-year-old delinquent re-enter society. **96m/B VHS.** Sal Mineo, Brian Keith, Susan Kohner; *D:* Thomas Carr.

Dinosaur ♂♂½ 2000 (PG) Young iguanodon Aladar is separated from his parents and raised by lemurs on an isolated island. Aladar must discover his heritage just as a meteor crash threatens to destroy his world. Raises the bar on animated adventures by having the impossibly realistic critters superimposed onto actual jungle footage. P C represents the next step in animation evolution, but the amazing visuals are somewhat undercut by the script, which has a pieced-together feel at times. May be too scary for the wee ones since everything glows look so lifelike. **82m/C VHS, DVD, Blu-ray Disc.** *D:* Ralph Zondag, Eric Leighton; *W:* John Harrison, Robert Nelson Jacobs; *M:* James Newton Howard; *V:* Julianna Margulies, Alfre Woodard, D.B. Sweeney, Ossie Davis, Della Reese, Max Casella, Samuel E. Wright, Joan Plowright, Hayden Panettiere, Peter Siragusa.

Dinosaur Island ♂ 1993 (R) Five military men survive a plane crash and discover an island where scantily clad (leather bikinis being the fashion choice) lascivious ladies live. Will the awesome power of testosterone overcome the fierce dinosaurs which stand between the men and their objects of desire? **85m/C VHS, DVD, Blu-ray Disc.** Ross Hagen, Richard Gabai, Antonia Dorian, Peter Spellos, Tom Shell, Griffin (Griffen) Drew, Steve Barkett, Toni Naples, Michelle (McClellan) Bauer; *D:* Jim Wynorski, Fred Olen Ray; *W:* Bob Sheridan, Christopher Wooden; *C:* Gary Graver; *M:* Chuck Cirino.

Dinosaur Valley Girls ♂½ 1996 Hollywood action hero Tony Markham comes into possession of a magic stone that hurls him backwards through time into a prehistoric world. That just happens to be populated by fierce, beautiful babes in animal-print bikinis. A PG version is also available. **94m/C VHS, DVD.** Karen Black, William D. Russell, Ron Jeffries, Jeff Rector, Griffin (Griffen) Drew, Ed Fury; *D:* Don Glut; *W:* Don Glut.

Dinosaurus! ♂ 1960 Large sadistic dinosaurs appear in the modern world. They eat, burr, and pillage their way through this film. Also includes a romance between a Neanderthal and a modern-age woman. **85m/C VHS, DVD.** Ward Ramsey, Kristina Hanson, Paul Lukather, Fred Engelberg; *D:* Irvin S. Yeaworth Jr.; *W:* Dan E. Weisburd, Jean Yeaworth; *C:* Stanley Cortez; *M:* Ronald Stein.

numbers. **62m/B VHS.** Bert Wheeler, Robert Woolsey, Marjorie White, Hugh Herbert; **D:** William A. Seiter; **W:** Joseph L. Mankiewicz, Henry Myers; **M:** Max Steiner.

Diplomatic Courier 🦴🦴 1952 Cold-war espionage saga has secret agent Power attempting to re-steal sensitive documents from the hands of Soviet agents. Involved and exciting thriller. Michael Ansara, Charles Bronson and Lee Marvin made brief appearances. **97m/B VHS.** Tyrone Power, Patricia Neal, Stephen McNally, Hildegarde Knef, Karl Malden; **D:** Henry Hathaway; **C:** Lucien Ballard.

Diplomatic Siege 🦴🦴 *Enemy* 1999 (R) Vicious killer gets off scot-free due to his diplomatic immunity. That is, until the victim's ex-soldier father follows this low-life to the jungles of Paraguay to exact revenge. A heap o' action. **95m/C VHS.** Bruce Boxleitner, Billy Drago, Meg Foster, Robert Forster; **D:** Peter Maris.

Direct Hit 🦴🦴1/2 1993 (R) A CIA assassin discovers retiring is not an option. John Hatch (Forsythe) decides he wants out, particularly when his next kill, Savannah (Champa), turns out to be an innocent pawn. So Hatch turns protector and decides to beat the agency at its own deadly game. **91m/C VHS, DVD.** William Forsythe, Richard Norton, Jo Champa, John Aprea, Juliet Landau, George Segal; **D:** Joseph Merhi; **W:** Jacobsen Hart. **VIDEO**

Dirkham Detective Agency 🦴1/2 1983 Three children team up to form the Dirkham Detective Agency and are hired by a veterinarian to recover two dognapped poodles. **60m/C VHS.** Sally Kellerman, Stan Shaw, John Quade, Gordon Jump, Randy Morton; **D:** Stuart Margolin; **W:** Chuck Menville, Brenda Wilson.

Dirt Bike Kid 🦴1/2 1986 (PG) A precocious brat is stuck with a used motorbike that has a mind of its own. Shenanigans follow in utterly predictable fashion as he battles bankers and bikers with his bad bike. **91m/C VHS, DVD.** Peter Billingsley, Anne Bloom, Stuart Pankin, Patrick Collins, Sage Parker, Chad Sheets; **D:** Hoite C. Caston; **W:** Lewis Colick, David Brandes.

Dirt Boy 🦴🦴 2001 Ex-heroin addict Matty Matthews (Hedman) has decided to leave New York and take forensic courses in a creepy Cape Cod community where the local celeb is Attwater Bridges (Walsh), the writer of a non-fiction account of a serial killer called "Dirt Boy." But after talking to one near-victim, Matty has own suspicions about what really happened. **90m/C VHS, DVD.** Jacob Lee Hedman, Arthur J. Walsh, Luca Bercovici, Michelle Guthrie; **D:** Gerald L. Frasco; **W:** Gerald L. Frasco; **C:** Jeffrey Greeley; **M:** Robert Robertson.

Dirt Gang 🦴 1971 (R) A motorcycle gang terrorizes the members of a film crew on location in the desert. **88m/C VHS.** Paul Carr, Michael Pataki, Michael Forest; **D:** Jerry Jameson.

Dirty 🦴🦴 2005 (R) Paired on LAPD's anti-gang division with immoral cop Salim Adel (Gooding Jr. in an atypical bad-guy role), former street-thug-turned-good-guy Armando Sancho (Collins Jr.) agonizes over whether to turn Salim over to Internal Affairs for his fatal shooting of an innocent citizen until their commanding officers step in. More than subtle hint of the real-life 1990s Rampart scandal. **97m/C DVD.** *US* Cuba Gooding Jr., Clifton (Gonzalez) Collins Jr., Cole Hauser, Nelust Wyclef Jean, Wood Harris, Robert LaSardo, Lobo Sebastian, Khleo Thomas, Ramirez, Aimee Garcia; **D:** Chris Fisher; **W:** Chris Fisher, Gill Reavill, Eric Saks; **C:** Eliot Rockett, Dani Minnick; **M:** Peter Lopez.

Dirty Dancing 🦴🦴 1987 (PG-13) An innocent 17-year-old (Grey) is vacationing with her parents in the Catskills in 1963. Bored with the program at the hotel, she finds the real fun at the staff dances. Falling for the sexy dance instructor (Swayze), she discovers love, sex, and rock and roll dancing. An old story, with little to save it, but Grey and Swayze are appealing, the dance sequences fun, and the music great. Swayze, classically trained in ballet, also performs one of the sound-track songs. ♪ ("I've Had) the Time of My Life; Be My Baby; Big Girls Don't Cry; Cry to Me; Do You Love Me?; Hey Baby; Hungry Eyes; In the Still of the Nite; Love is Strange. **97m/C VHS, DVD, Blu-ray Disc.** Patrick Swayze, Jennifer Grey, Cynthia Rhodes, Jerry Orbach, Jack Weston, Jane Brucker, Kelly Bishop, Lonny Price, Charles "Honi" Coles, Bruce 'Cousin Brucie' Morrow; **D:** Emile Ardolino; **W:** Eleanor Bergstein; **C:** Jeffrey Jur; **M:** John Morris. Oscars '87: Song ("(I've Had) the Time of My Life"); Golden Globes '88: Song ("(I've Had) the Time of My Life"); Ind. Spirit '88: First Feature.

Dirty Dancing: Havana Nights 🦴🦴 2004 (PG-13) Folks, it's not a sequel, it's not a prequel—it's a "re-imagining." This time around the dirty dancers are in Cuba (although filmed in Puerto Rico) and the year is 1958 on the eve of the Communist Revolution. Young Katey's (Garai) dad transplants the family and, bored, she meets Javier (Luna), the poor yet sexy busboy, and...well...really you know the rest. It's great eye candy and the couple is very appealing but they lack that certain something that Swayze (who makes a cameo) and Grey exuded. **86m/C VHS, DVD.** *US* Diego Luna, Romola Garai, Sela Ward, John Slattery, Jonathan Jackson, January Jones, Mika Boorem, Rene Lavan, Patrick Swayze, Mya; **D:** Guy Ferland; **W:** Boaz Yakin, Peter Sagal, Victoria Arch; **C:** Anthony B. Richmond; **M:** Heitor Pereira.

Dirty Deeds 🦴🦴🦴 2002 (R) In the late 1960s, Barry Ryan (Brown) is a Sydney crime boss who rules the slot machine trade. Having the local police chief (Neill) in his pocket is a help and Barry's Vietnam vet nephew Darcy (Worthington) is just joining the business, but Barry does have some personal trouble with his tough wife Sharon (Collette) and young mistress Margaret (Morassi). Then, a couple of Chicago wiseguys show up: down-to-earth Tony (Goodman) and his hot-headed colleague Sal (Williamson) have been instructed to muscle in on Barry's turf, but Barry is not about to let these interlopers interfere with his business. A bold combination of charm, comedy, and violence. **110m/C VHS, DVD.** *AU* Bryan Brown, Toni Collette, John Goodman, Sam Neill, Sam Worthington, Felix Williamson, Andrew S. Gilbert, Kestie Morassi; **D:** David Caesar; **W:** David Caesar; **C:** Geoffrey Hall; **M:** Paul Healy.

Dirty Dishes 🦴🦴 1978 (R) A French film sardonically examining the fruitless life of the average housewife as she confronts a series of bizarre but pointless experiences during the day. Dubbed and subtitled versions available. The director is the American daughter-in-law of the late Luis Buñuel. **99m/C VHS.** *FR* Carole Laure, Pierre Santini; **D:** Joyce Buñuel.

The Dirty Dozen 🦴🦴🦴 1967 (PG) A tough Army major is assigned to train and command 12 hardened convicts offered absolution if they participate in a suicidal mission into Nazi Germany in 1944. Well-made movie was a standout in its genre. Rough and gruff Marvin is good as the group leader. Three made-for-TV sequels followed in the '80s. **149m/C VHS, DVD, Blu-ray Disc, HD DVD.** Lee Marvin, Ernest Borgnine, Charles Bronson, Jim Brown, George Kennedy, John Cassavetes, Clint Walker, Donald Sutherland, Telly Savalas, Robert Ryan, Ralph Meeker, Richard Jaeckel, Trini Lopez, Robert Webber, Stuart Cooper, Robert Phillips, Al Mancini; **D:** Robert Aldrich; **W:** Nunnally Johnson, Lukas Heller; **C:** Edward Scaife; **M:** Frank DeVol. Oscars '67: Sound FX Editing.

The Dirty Dozen: The Deadly Mission 🦴🦴1/2 1987 A second made-for-TV movie finds Borgnine ordering another suicide mission. Savalas (killed in the original, he's playing a new character) must pick 12 convicted army prisoners for an assault on a Nazi-held French monastery. Their mission is to rescue six scientists who are working on a deadly new nerve gas. Followed by "The Dirty Dozen: The Fatal Mission." **96m/C VHS.** Ernest Borgnine, Telly Savalas, Vince Edwards, Gary (Rand) Graham, James Van Patten, Vincent Van Patten, Bo Svenson; **D:** Lee H. Katzin.

The Dirty Dozen: The Fatal Mission 🦴🦴1/2 1988 This third TV sequel has Borgnine learning of a plan to bring a group of high-ranking Nazis to Instanbul via the Orient Express. Naturally, he assigns Savalas the task of getting his motley gang together to thwart the Nazi schemes. To add intrigue, a female has joined the ranks of the Dirty Dozen and a spy may also have infiltrated the group. **91m/C VHS.** Ernest Borgnine, Telly Savalas, Hunt Block, Jeff Conaway, Erik Estrada, Ray "Boom Boom" Mancini, Heather Thomas, Alex Cord; **D:** Lee H. Katzin.

The Dirty Dozen: The Next Mission 🦴🦴1/2 1985 Disappointing TV sequel to the 1967 hit, with Marvin reprising his role as the leader of the motley pack. In this installment, the rag-tag toughs are sent on yet another suicide mission inside Nazi Germany, this time to thwart an assassination attempt of Hitler. Followed by two more sequels. **97m/C VHS.** Lee Marvin, Ernest Borgnine, Richard Jaeckel, Ken Wahl, Larry Wilcox, Sonny Landham, Rico Ross; **D:** Andrew V. McLaglen. **TV**

Dirty Games 🦴🦴1/2 1989 Nicola Kendra is the head of a team sent to Africa to inspect a nuclear waste site. Once there, the scientists discover terrorists are plotting to blow up the nuclear complex unless Nicola and her new allies can prevent it. **97m/C VHS, DVD.** Jan-Michael Vincent, Valentina Vargas, Ronald France, Michael McGovern; **D:** Gray Hofmeyr.

Dirty Gertie from Harlem U.S.A. 🦴🦴 1946 All-black cast performs a variation of W. Somerset Maugham's "Rain." Gertie goes to Trinidad to hide out from her jilted boyfriend. **60m/B VHS, DVD.** Francine Everett, Katherine Moore, Spencer Williams Jr., Alfred Hawkins; **D:** Spencer Williams Jr.

The Dirty Girls 🦴1/2 1964 Typical Metzger sexcapades featuring two stories about prostitute Garance, who works in Paris, and Monique, who plies her trade in Munich. **82m/B VHS, DVD.** Reine Rohan, Denise Roland, Marlene Sherter, Peter Parten, Lionel Bernier; **D:** Radley Metzger; **W:** Peter Fernandez.

Dirty Harry 🦴🦴🦴1/2 1971 (R) Rock-hard cop Harry Callahan attempts to track down a psychopathic rooftop killer before a kidnapped girl dies. Harry abuses the murderer's civil rights, however, forcing the police to return the criminal to the streets, where he hijacks a school bus and Harry is called on once again. The only answer to stop this vicious killer seems to be death in cold blood, and Harry is just the man to do it. Taut, suspenseful direction by Siegel, who thoroughly understands Eastwood's on-screen character. Features Callahan's famous "Do you feel lucky?" line, the precursor to his "Go ahead, make my day." **103m/C VHS, DVD.** Clint Eastwood, Harry Guardino, John Larch, Andrew (Andy) Robinson, Reni Santoni, John Vernon, Albert "Poppy" Popwell, Josef G. Kelly; **D:** Donald Siegel; **W:** Dean Riesner, Harry Julian Fink, Rita M. Fink; **C:** Bruce Surtees; **M:** Lalo Schifrin.

Dirty Heroes 🦴🦴 *Dalle Ardenne All'Inferno* 1971 (R) A band of escaped WWII POWs battle the Nazis for a precious treasure in the war's final days. **117m/C VHS.** John Ireland, Curt Jurgens, Adolfo Celi, Daniela Bianchi, Michael Constantine; **D:** Alberto De Martino; **M:** Ennio Morricone.

Dirty Laundry woof! 1987 (PG-13) Insipid wreck of a comedy about a klutz who accidentally gets his laundry mixed up with $1 million in drug money. Features Olympians Lewis and Louganis. Never released theatrically. **81m/C VHS.** Leigh McCloskey, Jeanne O'Brien, Frankie Valli, Sonny Bono, Carl Lewis, Greg Louganis, Nicholas Worth; **D:** William Webb. **VIDEO**

Dirty Laundry 🦴🦴1/2 2007 (PG-13) Preachy family comedy about acceptance with an either over-the-top or winning performance by Devine, depending on viewer perception. New York writer Sheldon (Dunbar) returns to his Georgia roots after a call from his mama (Devine). She introduces him to his 10-year-old son (a shocker for Sheldon), who's the product of a one-night stand, and does her best to not see that her boy is gay, even after his boyfriend (Costello) shows up. **100m/C DVD.** Rockmond Dunbar, Loretta Devine, Terri J. Vaughn, Joey Costello, Aaron Grady Shaw, Terri J. Vaughn, Maurice Jamal; **W:** Maurice Jamal; **C:** Rory King, Liz Rubin.

Dirty Little Secret 🦴🦴1/2 1998 (R) Sarah Weatley (Gold) hires some hoods to kidnap the adopted 10-year-old son of a wealthy, hot-tempered sheriff (Wagner). But there's more to this than meets the eye—both Sarah and the sheriff share a nasty secret and, after 10 years of keeping silent, what Sarah really wants is revenge. **92m/C VHS.** Tracey Gold, Jack Wagner, Mary Page Keller; **D:** Robert M. Fresco; **W:** Robert M. Fresco. **CABLE**

Dirty Love woof! 2005 (R) Jenny McCarthy was funny once upon a time. Now, not so much. Rebecca (McCarthy) finds out her idiot boyfriend (Webster) is cheating on her, so she attempts to get back at him by sleeping with a constant stream of nerds, each more nerdy than the last. Her sidekicks Michelle (Electra) and Carrie (Heskin) are trashy, ineffectual and stupid. In fact, everyone's stupid. An embarrassing film with little to recommend. **95m/C DVD.** *US* Jenny McCarthy, Carmen Electra, Eddie Kaye Thomas, Victor Webster, Kam Heskin, Lochlyn Munro, Kathy Griffin, Jessica Collins; **D:** John Mallory Asher; **W:** Jenny McCarthy; **C:** Eric Wycoff. Golden Raspberries '05: Worst Picture, Worst Actress (McCarthy), Worst Director (Asher), Worst Screenplay.

Dirty Mary Crazy Larry 🦴🦴🦴 1974 (PG) A racecar driver, his mechanic, and a sexy girl hightail it from the law after pulling off a heist. Great action, great fun, and an infamous surprise ending. **93m/C VHS, DVD.** Peter Fonda, Susan George, Adam Roarke, Vic Morrow, Roddy McDowall, Craig G. Kelly; **D:** John Hough; **M:** Leigh Chapman.

Dirty Mind of Young Sally woof! 1972 (R) Sally's erotic radio program broadcasts from a mobile studio, which must stay one step ahead of the police. **84m/C VHS, DVD.** George "Buck" Flower, Norman Fields, Sharon Kelly; **D:** Bethel Buckalew.

Dirty Pictures 🦴🦴 2000 (R) Dull telepic on controversial subject that features real-life interviews, which only serve to cut the story's momentum. Dennis Barrie (Woods) is the director of the Cincinnati Contemporary Arts Center who decides to book an exhibition of Robert Mapplethorpe photographs in 1990. He gets indicted on obscenity charges and decides on a court fight based on First Amendment rights though it costs him personally. **104m/C VHS, DVD.** James Woods, Diana Scarwid, Craig T. Nelson, Leon Pownall, David Huband, Judah Katz, R.D. Reid, Matt North; **D:** Frank Pierson; **W:** Ilene Chaiken; **C:** Hiro Narita; **M:** Mark Snow. **CABLE**

Dirty Pretty Things 🦴🦴🦴1/2 2003 (R) Frears revisits the theme of the plight of illegal immigrants living in London with typically moving results. Okwe (Ejiofor), a doctor who once escaped to flee his native Nigeria, is now scraping by as a hotel clerk and cabbie in London, where he befriends his Turkish co-worker Senay (Tautou), a chambermaid who later is forced into sweatshop labor and a compromising relationship with her new boss. Already living in fear of being caught by immigration agents, Okwe discovers an illegal organ-selling ring at the hotel. Engagingly illuminates the mysterious and tense underworld inhabited by illegals and those who seek to exploit them in this sur-

Dirty Rotten Scoundrels 🐾🐾🐾 *1988 (PG)* A remake of the 1964 "Bedtime Story," in which two confidence tricksters on the Riviera endeavor to rip off a suddenly rich American woman, and each other. Caine and Martin are terrific, Martin has some of his best physical comedy ever, and Headly is charming as the prey who's always one step ahead of them. Fine direction from Oz, the man who brought us the voice of Yoda in "The Empire Strikes Back." **112m/C** VHS, DVD, Blu-ray *Steve Martin, Michael Caine, Glenne Headly, Anton Rodgers, Barbara Harris, Dana Ivey; D: Frank Oz; W: Stanley Shapiro, Paul Henning, Dale Launer; C: Michael Ballhaus; M: Miles Goodman.*

A Dirty Shame 🐾🐾 *2004 (NC-17)* Outrageously tasteless fare has Waters back in familiar Baltimore territory with an angry and repressed Sylvia Stickles (Ullman), who runs a convenience store with her unfulfilled hubby Vaughn (Isaak). Their daughter Caprice (Blair) is locked in her room so she can't continue her career as a topless dancer. Sylvia suffers a concussion in a car crash and goes nympho—joining a cult of sex addicts led by local sexual healer Ray-Ray (Knoxville). Suddenly, their quiet blue-collar neighborhood is under siege from fetish freaks! It's all low-rent and tawdry exaggeration with a flimsy plot. It doesn't quite work, but then Waters has never let slick technique interfere with his fun. **89m/C** VHS, DVD, CA Tracey Ullman, Chris Isaak, Selma Blair, Johnny Knoxville, Suzanne Shepherd, Mink Stole, Patty Campbell Hearst, Jackie Hoffman; Cameos: Ricki Lake, David Hasselhoff; D: John Waters; W: John Waters; C: Steve Gainer; M: George S. Clinton.*

Dirty Tricks 🐾🐾½ *1981 (PG)* History professor Gould fights with bad guys for a letter written by George Washington. Thoroughly forgettable comedy lacking in laughs. **91m/C** VHS, CA Elliott Gould, Kate Jackson, Arthur Hill, Rich Little; D: Alvin Rakoff; W: William W. Norton Sr.; M: Hagood Hardy.*

Dirty Work 🐾🐾½ *1992 (R)* A drug-dealing bail bondsman (Ashton) steals counterfeit money from the mob and then sets up his partner (Dobson) as the fall guy. Can Dobson survive long enough to set things straight? **88m/C** VHS, John Ashton, Kevin Dobson, Roxann Biggs-Dawson, Donnelly Rhodes, Jim Byrnes, Mitchell Ryan; D: John McPherson; W: Aaron Julien.*

Dirty Work 🐾 *1997 (PG-13)* You'll notice that star and ex-Saturday Night Live newsguy MacDonald isn't even trying to act, he's just doing his dead-pan wise guy routine with a different name. His delivery and attitude, however, are about the only funny things in this tale of Mitch (MacDonald) and Sam (Lange), two losers who can't keep a job but have a talent for petty revenge. When Sam's father (Warden) has a heart attack, the boys decide to open a business specializing in dirty deeds done dirt cheap to pay for a heart transplant. Although the premise is good, the tricks are mostly of the junior high variety and don't seem quite dirty enough. Several unbilled cameos, including Adam Sandler, John Goodman and the late Chris Farley. **81m/C** VHS, DVD, Fred Wolf, Norm MacDonald, Artie Lange, Chevy Chase, Don Rickles, Jack Warden, Traylor Howard, Christopher McDonald, Chris Farley, Gary Coleman; Cameos: John Goodman, Adam Sandler; D: Bob Saget; W: Fred Wolf; C: Arthur Albert; M: Richard Gibbs.*

Disappearance 🐾🐾 *1981 (R)* A hired assassin discovers an ironic link between his new target and his missing wife. **80m/C** VHS, CA Donald Sutherland, David Hemmings, John Hurt, Christopher Plummer, David Warner, Virginia McKenna; D: Stuart Cooper.*

Disappearance 🐾🐾 *2002 (PG-13)* The vacationing Henley family stumble across the ghost town of Weaver, New Mexico, decide to stop long enough to take some photos, and get stranded.

---

prisingly effective thriller. Ejiofor delivers the goods in a darkly subtle turn while Tautou delightfully broadens her range. **107m/C** VHS, DVD, GB Chiwetel Ejiofor, Audrey Tautou, Sergi Lopez, Sophie Okonedo, Zlatko Buric, Benedict Wong; D: Stephen Frears; W: Steven Knight; C: Chris Menges; M: Nathan Larson.*

town and it probably isn't human. Ending's a let-down. **91m/C** VHS, DVD, Harry Hamlin, Susan Dey, Jeremy Lelliott; D: Walter Klenhard; W: Walter Klenhard; C: David Connell; M: Shirley Walker. C.A.B.L.E.

The Disappearance of Aimee 🐾🐾🐾 *1976* Dramatic re-creation of events surrounding the 1926 disappearance of evangelist Aimee Semple McPherson. She claimed she was abducted, but her mother insisted she ran away to have an affair. Excellent TV movie with an exceptional cast. Originally was to star Ann-Margret. **110m/C** VHS, Faye Dunaway, Bette Davis, James Sloyan, James Woods, John Lehne, Lelia Goldoni, Barry Brown, Severn Darden; D: Anthony Harvey; W: John McGreevey; C: James A. Crabe. TV

The Disappearance of Christina 🐾🐾½ *1993 (PG-13)* Successful entrepreneur Joe Seldon (Stamos) is married to heiress Christina (Yarlett) and they seem to be the perfect couple. But when Christina mysteriously vanishes during a sailing trip, was it really an accident? Detective Nora Davis (Pounder) doesn't think so and naturally, Joe is suspect numero uno. **93m/C** VHS, John Stamos, Kim Delaney, Robert Carradine, Claire Yarlett, CCH Pounder; D: Karen Arthur; W: Camille Thomasson.*

The Disappearance of Garcia Lorca 🐾🐾½ *1996 (R)* Death in Granada; Lorca *1996 (R)* In 1954, Spanish-born journalist Ricardo Fernandez (Morales) returns to Granada to look into the death of his idol, poet/playwright Gabriel Garcia Lorca (Garcia). Ricardo's family fled Spain for Puerto Rico in 1936, at the start of the Spanish Civil War, when anti-fascist Lorca was executed. Ricardo wants to find out just who Lorca's killers were but Franco's Spain is a country eager to bury its past. Based on two books by Ian Gibson. **114m/C** VHS, SP Esai Morales, Andy Garcia, Edward James Olmos, Jeroen Krabbe, Miguel Ferrer, Giancarlo Giannini, Marcela Walerstein, Jose Coronado; D: Marcos Zurinaga; W: Marcos Zurinaga, Neil Cohen, Juan Antonio Ramos; C: Juan Ruiz-Anchia; M: Mark McKenzie.*

The Disappearance of Kevin Johnson 🐾🐾½ *1995 (R)* Mockumentary about a British TV crew, doing a film about successful Brits in Hollywood, stumbling across the disappearance of wanna-be producer and wealthy English-man, Kevin Johnson. So they begin asking questions of the agents, executives, stars, business associates, and women in Johnson's life. So just who is Kevin Johnson? **105m/C** VHS, Michael Brandon, Bridget Bates, Keely Sims, Rick Peters, Keri Beymer, Richard Neil, Michael Laskin, Ian Ogilvy, Stoney Jackson; Cameos: Pierce Brosnan, James Coburn, Dudley Moore; D: Francis Megahy; W: Francis Megahy; C: John Newby; M: John Cooà; Nar: Francis Megahy.*

Disappearing Acts 🐾🐾 *2006 (PG-13)* Quebec Bill (Kristofferson) and his teen-aged son Wild Bill (McDermott) travel into the Canadian backwoods to run bootleg whiskey in 1932 so they can save the family's Vermont farm. Elements of magical realism throw off the simpler family adventure plot. Based on the novel by Howard Frank Mosher. **103m/C** DVD, Kris Kristofferson, Lothaire Bluteau, Luis Guzman, William Sanderson, Charlie McDermott, Gary Farmer, Genevieve Cheate, Boyd Gaines, Luis Achom, Eric Stoltz; D: Bryan Gordon, Steven E. Anderson, Damian Harris, Rupert Wainwright; W: Bryan Gordon.*

Disappearing Acts 🐾🐾 *2000 (R)* Zora Banks (Latham) is a college-educated music teacher with dreams of becoming a singer. She meets high school dropout Franklin (Snipes), who's doing construction work and wants to become a contractor. Neither wants a relationship but opposites still attract and they get involved. But not without trouble. Based on the 1989 novel by Terry McMillan. **115m/C** VHS, DVD, Sanaa Lathan, Wesley Snipes, Regina Hall, Clark Johnson, John Amos, CCH Pounder, Aunjanue Ellis, Lisa Arrindell Anderson, Kamaal Fareed, Michael Imperioli; D: Gina Prince-Bythewood; W: Lisa Jones. C.A.B.L.E.

Disaster at Silo 7 🐾🐾 *1988* When the engine of a Titan missile goes on the fritz, the Air Force tries to prevent a nuclear disaster. Based on an actual Titan II missile incident near Little Rock, Arkansas. **92m/C** VHS, Peter Boyle, Patricia Charbonneau, Perry King, Michael O'Keefe, Joe Spano, Dennis Weaver; D: Larry Elikann; W: Douglas Lloyd McIntosh; C: Roy Wagner. TV

The Disciple 🐾🐾 *1915* Vintage silent western wherein Hart's unsmiling good-bad guy tries to clean up a lawless town and win back his wife, who has shamelessly fallen in with a corrupt saloon-keeper. **80m/B** VHS, William S. Hart, Dorothy Dalton, Robert McKim, Jean Hersholt; D: William S. Hart; M: Thomas Ince.*

Disciple of Death 🐾 *1972 (R)* Reven plays "The Stranger", a ghoul who sacrifices virgins to the Devil. **82m/C** VHS, DVD, GB Mike Raven, Ronald Lacey, Stephen Bradley, Virginia Wetherell; D: Tom Parkinson.*

Disclosure 🐾🐾 *1994 (R)* Likable, responsible executive and family man (Douglas) finds himself sexually harassed by his ex-lover turned dragon-lady boss (Moore). But when he rejects her lusty come-on, she points the finger at him. One-dimensional characters and hollow material turn sexual harassment into a trivial issue. High-tech saga of corporate politics, while flashy, is nothing we haven't seen before. Douglas just can't pass up these "Regular Joe meets beautiful, horny babe, bad things happen" roles, can he? Based on the Michael Crichton novel. **125m/C** VHS, DVD, Michael Douglas, Demi Moore, Donald Sutherland, Caroline Goodall, Dennis Miller, Rosemary Forsyth, Roma Maffia; D: Barry Levinson; W: Paul Attanasio; C: Tony Pierce-Roberts; M: Ennio Morricone. Blockbuster '95; Drama Actress, V. (Moore).*

Disco Pigs 🐾🐾½ *2001* Pig (Murphy) and Runt (Cassidy) were born minutes apart in the same Dublin hospital and have grown up in adjoining houses. They share a telepathic bond as well as their own language and no one can separate them—until their first kiss when they turn 17. But Pig will stop at nothing to keep their bond. Adapted by Walsh from his own play. **94m/C** VHS, DVD, IR Cillian Murphy, Elaine Cassidy, Geraldine O'Rawe, Eleanor Methven, Brian F. O'Byrne; D: Kirsten Sheridan; W: Enca Walsh; C: Igor Jadue-Lillo; M: Gavin Friday, Maurice Seezer.*

Disconnected 🐾½ *1987* "Sorry, Wrong Number" is updated, with more than ample doses of sex and violence, rupted by his meddling ways. **30m/B** VHS, Katherine Griffin, J. Edwin Brown, Charles Harmand, Al(a) D. Blake; D: Lois Weber; W: Lois Weber.*

Discontent 🐾½ *1916* An early silent film by Lois Weber in which a cantankerous old vet goes to live with his wealthy nephew. The harmonious family life is disrupted by his meddling ways. **81m/C** VHS, Mark Walker, Frances Raines; D: Gorman Bechard; W: Gorman Bechard; C: Gorman Bechard.*

The Discovery Program 🐾🐾½ *1989* Four award-winning short films on one video: "Ray's Male Heterosexual Dance Hall," "Greasy Lake," "The Open Window," and "Hearts of Stone." The subjects range from humorous and offbeat to tragic and deadly serious. **106m/C** VHS, Tim Ransom, Eric Achom, Eric Stoltz; D: Bryan Gordon, Steven E. Anderson, Damian Harris, Rupert Wainwright; W: Bryan Gordon.*

The Discreet Charm of the Bourgeoisie 🐾🐾🐾 *1972 (R)* Le Charme Discret de la Bourgeoisie *1972 (R)* Bunuel in top form, satirizing modern society. These six characters are forever sitting down to dinner, yet they never eat. Dreams and reality, actual or contrived, prevent their feast. In French with subtitles. **100m/C** VHS, FR Milena Vukotic, Fernando Rey, Delphine Seyrig, Jean-Pierre Cassel, Bulle Ogier, Michel Piccoli, Stephane Audran, Luis Bunuel; D: Luis Bunuel; W: Luis Bunuel, Jean-Claude Carriere; C: Edmond Richard. Oscars '72: Foreign Film; British Acad. '73: Actress (Seyrig); Screenplay; Natl. Soc. Film Critics '72: Director (Bunuel).*

Discretion Assured 🐾🐾½ *1993 (R)* Successful businessman Trevor McCabe (York) finds himself in a romantic quandary with three women, leading to his involvement in embezzlement and murder. **97m/C** VHS, DVD, Michael York, Jennifer O'Neill, Dee Wallace Stone, Elizabeth Ward Gracen; D: Odorico Mendes.*

The Disenchanted 🐾🐾½ *1990* La Desenchantee *1990* Seventeen-year-old Beth (Godreche) is having a rough time growing up. She's forced to look after her bedridden mother and younger brother and their survival depends on the generosity of her mother's ex-lover, who's now taking a more personal interest in the beautiful teenager. Meanwhile, Beth's arrogant boyfriend decides Beth should prove her love for him by sleeping with the ugliest man she can find. French with subtitles. **78m/C** VHS, DVD, FR Judith Godreche, Ivan Desny, Therese Liotard, Malcolm Conrath, Marcel Bozonnet; D: Benoit Jacquot; W: Benoit Jacquot; C: Caroline Champetier; M: Jorge Arriagada.*

The Dish 🐾🐾🐾 *2000 (PG-13)* Tells the true story of a NASA official (Neill) and his group of local Aussie technicians as they manned the satellite dish responsible for bringing to TV sets around the world man's first footsteps on the moon in 1969. Originally only a backup plan, the Australian dish was called into action when the primary receiver in California became useless after a change in Apollo 11's flight path. Treats the central, spectacular event itself with dignity and appropriate awe, but also squeezes humor and emotion out of all that it meets. But the slacker duo are beset by love (Ward, Elizabeth) and cracks surface in their buddyhood. **96m/C** VHS, DVD, Sam Neill, Patrick Warburton, Tom Long, Kevin Harrington, Billie Brown, John McNeil, Tayler Kane, Eliza Szonert, Carl Snell; D: Rob Sitch; W: Rob Sitch, Santo Cilauro, Tom Gleisner, Jane Kennedy; C: Graeme Wood; M: Edmund Choi.*

Dish Dogs 🐾🐾 *1998 (R)* Morgan (Astin) and Jason (Lillard) are a couple of bachelor best friends who cruise SoCal in their old Chevy looking for the best surfing and work as dishwashers to make ends meet. But the slacker duo are beset by love (Ward, Elizabeth) and cracks surface in their buddyhood. **96m/C** VHS, Matthew Lillard, Sean Astin, Shannon Elizabeth, Maitland Ward, Brian Dennehy, Richard Moll; D: Bob Vince; M: Ashley Scott Meyers, Nathan Ives; C: Mark Vicente; M: Herman Beeffink.*

Dishonorable Discharge 🐾🐾½ Ces Dames Preferent le Mambo; Women Prefer the Mambo *1957* American sailor Burt Brickford (Constantine) gets mixed up with dames, drugs, crooks, and treasure hunters—all in a seedy European coastal town. Loosely based on Ernest Hemingway's "To Have and Have Not." Dubbed. **105m/B** VHS, FR Eddie Constantine, Jacques Castelot, Jean Murat, Pascale Roberts, Joelle Bernard, Robert Berri, Lisa Bourdin, Rene Havard; D: Jacques Lemaire; M: Charles Aznavour.*

Dishonored 🐾🐾½ *1931* Dated spy drama has Dietrich playing secret agent X-27 in WWI and masquerading on the s de as a peasant girl. Although not one of the more famous Dietrich-Sternberg productions, its camp plot and Dietrich's lavish performance make it worth watching. Based on the infamous spy Mata Hari, who was shot by the French in 1917 for espionage. **91m/B** VHS, Marlene Dietrich, Victor McLaglen, Lew Cody, Gustav von Seyffertitz, Warner Oland, Barry Norton, Davison Clark, Wilfrid Lucas; D: Josef von Sternberg; W: Josef von Sternberg, Daniel N. Rubin; C: Lee Garmes.*

Dishonored Lady 🐾🐾½ *1947* After her ex-boyfriend is murdered, a female art director finds that she's the number one suspect. When put on trial for the dastardly deed, she takes the fifth in this mediocre melodrama. **85m/B** VHS, DVD, Hedy Lamarr, Dennis O'Keefe, William Lundigan, John Loder; D: Robert Stevenson.*

Disney's Teacher's Pet 🐾🐾🐾 Teacher's Pet: The Movie *2004 (PG)* Disney strikes again with this zany Pinocchio story about a blue dog who wants to become a real boy like his owner Leonard (Fleming). Wanna-be Spot (Lane) dresses as a boy (named Scott) and follows Leonard to school until he discovers his chance: a

---

examines the controversial figure and the Victorian era his life and career spanned. 208m/C VHS. GB Ian McShane, Mary Peach, Mark Dignam, Leigh Lawson, Rosemary Leach; Anton Rodgers, Margaret Whiting; D: Claude Whatham; W: David Butler.

Disney's The Kid 🦴🦴 2000 (PG) Cynical 40-year-old Willis comes face-to-face with his 8-year-old self (Breslin), who wants to know how he grew up to become such a jerk. It's Disney, so there are important Lessons to be learned, and dramatic changes in behavior to be witnessed, but Breslin, Willis, and Tomlin as his assistant, make the schmaltz bearable with excellent performances. Wells' sophisticated, funny script helps smooth out Turtletaub's heavy-handed direction. 104m/C VHS, DVD. Bruce Willis, Emily Mortimer, Jean Smart, Spencer Breslin, Chi McBride, Lily Tomlin, Dana Ivey, Daniel von Bargen, Nicholas Chinlund; D: Jon Turteltaub; W: Audrey Wells; C: Peter Menzies Jr.; M: Jerry Goldsmith.

Disorder 🦴½ 2006 (R) David Randall was accused of a double murder and sent to a mental hospital where he was diagnosed as a paranoid schizophrenic. Now released, David heads back to his hometown to prove his innocence but soon thinks that the same masked killer is now after his friend Melissa. His shrink and the sheriff think David has gone off his meds and may be dangerous. 103m/C DVD. Darren Kendrick, Lauren Selkaly, Thomas Rudersteller, Alan Samulski, Sean Eager; D: Jack Thomas Smith; W: Jack Thomas Smith; C: Jonathan Belinski; M: Joel Goodman. VIDEO

Disorderlies 🦴🦴 1987 (PG) Members of the popular rap group cavort as incompetent hospital orderlies assigned to care for a cranky millionaire. Fat jokes abound with performances by the Fat Boys. 86m/C VHS, DVD. The Fat Boys, Ralph Bellamy; D: Michael A. Schultz; M: Anne Dudley.

Disorderly Orderly 🦴½ 1964 When Jerry Lewis gets hired as a hospital orderly, nothing stands upright long with him around. Vintage slapstick Lewis running amuck in a nursing home. 90m/C VHS, DVD. Jerry Lewis, Glenda Farrell, Everett Sloane, Kathleen Freeman, Susan Oliver; D: Frank Tashlin.

Disorganized Crime 🦴🦴 1989 (R) On the lam from the law, Bernsen attempts to organize a group of his ex-con buddies to pull off the perfect heist. Before the boys can organize, however, the cops are hot on Bernsen's trail, and have to vacate the meeting place. Good cast attempts to lift this movie beyond script. 101m/C VHS, DVD. Lou Diamond Phillips, Fred Gwynne, Corbin Bernsen, Ruben Blades, Hoyt Axton, Ed O'Neill, Daniel Roebuck, William Russ; D: Jim Kouf; W: Jim Kouf; C: Ron Garcia; M: David Newman, Hoyt Axton.

Disraeli 🦴🦴 1930 Arliss deservedly won the Best Actor Oscar for his title role as the famed British prime minister to Queen Victoria. This particular slice of the cunning statesman's life depicts his efforts to secure the Suez Canal for England against the Russians. Arliss' wife also played his screen spouse. One of Warner's earliest and best biographical pictures. Based on a play by Louis Napoleon Parker. 87m/B VHS. George Arliss, Joan Bennett, Florence Arliss, Anthony Bushell, David Torrence, Doris Lloyd, Ivan Simpson, Gwendolyn Logan; D: Alfred E. Green; C: Lee Garmes. Oscars '30: Actor (Arliss).

Disraeli 🦴🦴 1979 Flamboyant, irreverant, a dandy, and a womanizer, Benjamin Disraeli (McShane) was also England's first Jewish Prime Minister and one of its greatest. This British miniseries

Distant Drums 🦴🦴 1951 A small band of adventurers tries to stop the Seminole War in the Florida Everglades. 101m/C VHS, DVD. Gary Cooper, Mari Aldon, Richard Webb, Ray Teal, Arthur Hunnicutt; D: Raoul Walsh; M: Max Steiner.

Distant Justice 🦴½ 1992 (R) Tokyo police inspector Rio (Sugawara) is vacationing in Boston with his wife and daughter, where he can also visit old friend, Chief Bradfield (Kennedy). But Rio's wife is murdered and his daughter kidnapped by vicious drug dealer Roy Pennola (Carradine) and Bradfield assigns young officer Charlie Givens (Lutes) to see that Rio doesn't get himself killed as well. 91m/C VHS. Bunta Sugawara, George Kennedy, David Carradine, Eric Lutes; D: Toru Murakawa.

Distant Thunder 🦴🦴🦴½ Ashani Sanket 1973 A bitter, unrelenting portrait of a small Bengali neighborhood as the severe famines of 1942, brought about by the "distant thunder" of WWII, take their toll. A mature achievement from Ray, in Bengali with English subtitles. 92m/C VHS. IN Soumitra Chatterjee, Sandhya Roy, Babita, Gobinda Chakravarty, Romesh Mukerji; D: Satyajit Ray; W: Satyajit Ray; C: Soumendu Roy; M: Satyajit Ray. Berlin Intl. Film Fest. '73: Golden Berlin Bear.

Distant Thunder 🦴🦴 1988 (R) A scarred Vietnam vet, who has become a recluse, and his estranged son reunite in the Washington State wilderness, causing him to reflect on his isolation. Strong premise and cast watered down by weak script. 114m/C VHS, DVD. CA John Lithgow, Ralph Macchio, Kerrie Keane, Janet Margolin, Rick Rosenthal; D: Rick Rosenberg; C: Ralf Bode; M: Maurice Jarre.

Distant Voices, Still Lives 🦴🦴🦴 1988 A profoundly executed, disturbing film chronicling a British middle-class family through the maturation of the three children, under the dark shadow of their abusive, malevolent father. An evocative, heartbreaking portrait of British life from WWII on, and of the rhythms of dysfunctional families. A film festival favorite. 87m/C VHS. GB Freda Dowie, Pete Postlethwaite, Angela Walsh, Dean Williams, Lorraine Ashbourne; D: Terence Davies; W: Terence Davies; C: Patrick Duval. L.A. Film Critics '89: Foreign Film.

The Distinguished Gentleman 🦴🦴 1992 (R) A small-time con man (Murphy) manages to scam his way into a political career and winds up in Congress. The other characters serve mostly as foils for Murphy's comedic talent. Viewers will laugh despite the story's predictability. 122m/C VHS, DVD. Eddie Murphy, Lane Smith, Sheryl Lee Ralph, Joe Don Baker, Victoria Rowell, Grant Shaud, Kevin McCarthy, Charles S. Dutton, James Garner, Gary Frank; D: Jonathan Lynn; W: Marty Kaplan; C: Gabriel Beristain; M: Randy Edelman.

District B13 🦴🦴 Banlieue 13 2004 (R) Fast-paced and suspenseful actioner set in 2010 outside Paris. Things are so bad that the authorities have walled off the drug-ridden district and left it to crime boss Taha. Local Leito takes a stand by flushing a shipment of Taha's dope and then runs for his life and into undercover cop Damien, who learns that a massive bomb is now in Taha's possession. French with subtitles. 85m/C DVD, Blu-ray Disc. FR David Belle, Cyril Raffaelli, Larbi (Bibi) Naceri, Dany Verissimo; D: Pierre Morel; W: Luc Besson, Larbi (Bibi) Naceri; C: Manuel Teran.

Disturbance 🦴½ 1989 The two personas of a young schizophrenic get him entangled in a mysterious string of murders. 81m/C VHS. Timothy Greeson, Lisa Geoffreion; D: Cliff Guest.

Disturbed 🦴 1990 (R) Lusty mental hospital director McDowell meets sex-starved and suicidal Gidley in this less-than-stellar erotic creeper. Redeemed only by McDowell's performance and more evidence that the droog's career hasn't been just peachy since "Clockwork Orange." 96m/C VHS. Malcolm McDowell, Geoffrey Lewis, Priscilla Pointer, Pamela Gidley, Clint Howard; D: Charles Winkler; W: Emerson Bixby, Charles Winkler.

Disturbia 🦴🦴½ 2007 (PG-13) Unacknowledged updated teen version of "Rear Window." Troubled Kale (LaBeouf) is placed on house arrest with an electronic ankle monitor after a school incident. His fed-up mom (Moss) cuts off his videogame/cable access, so Kale begins spying on the locals with his handy binoculars. At first he's mostly interested in hottie girl next door, Ashley (Roemer), but then Kale becomes suspicious of neighbor Mr. Turner (Morse) and whether he could actually be the serial killer from local news reports. Kale recruits Ashley and pal Ronnie (Yoo) to be his legs even though they question his accusations. Morse is effectively creepy in what amounts to the Raymond Burr role and LeBeouf makes the most of Kale's foolishness and smart-aleck wit. 105m/C DVD, Blu-ray Disc, HD DVD, US Shia LaBeouf, David Morse, Carrie-Anne Moss, Jose Pablo Cantillo, Sarah Roemer, Aaron Yoo; D: D.J. Caruso; W: Christopher Landon, Carl Ellsworth; C: Rogier Stoffers; M: Geoff Zanelli.

Disturbing Behavior 🦴🦴½ 1998 (R) Gavin (Stahl) welcomes new kid in town Steve (Marsden) by pointing out the social castes at Cradle Bay High School. The Uber-group is the goody-goody Blue Ribbons, an excessively strait-laced and perky group of athletes and cheerleaders. Along with fellow outcasts Rachel (Holmes) and U.V. (Donella), they joke about a possible conspiracy, but when Gavin shows up with a crewcut and an inordinate love of pep rallies and bake sales, his friends know something is up. They discover that parents have allowed the school shrink (Greenwood) to use drugs to tinker with the brains of the Blue Ribbons. They also discover that the Stepford Teens' vanilla lives are topped with sprinkles of homicidal fury. Director Nutter creates just the right creepy and paranoid mood in his feature debut. 84m/C VHS, DVD. James Marsden, Nick Stahl, Katie Holmes, Bruce Greenwood, William Sadler, Chad E. Donella, Ethan (Randall) Embry, Steve Railsback; D: David Nutter; W: Scott Rosenberg; C: John Bartley; M: Mark Snow. MTV Movie Awards '99: Breakthrough Perf. (Holmes).

Diva 🦴🦴🦴½ 1982 (R) While at a concert given by his favorite star, a young French courier secretly tapes a soprano who has refused to record. The film follows the young man through Paris as he flees from two Japanese recording pirates, and a couple of crooked undercover police who are trying to cover-up for the chief who not only has a mistress, but runs a prostitution ring. Brilliant and dazzling photography compliment the eclectic soundtrack. 123m/C VHS, DVD. FR Frederic Andrei, Roland Bertin, Richard Bohringer, Gerard Darmon, Jacques Fabbri, Wilhelminia Wiggins Fernandez, Dominique Pinon; D: Jean-Jacques Beineix; W: Jean-Jacques Beineix; C: Philippe Rousselot; M: Vladimir Cosma. Cesar '82: Cinematog., Sound, Score; Natl. Soc. Film Critics '82: Cinematog.

Distortions 🦴🦴 1987 (PG) Hussey is a widow whose evil aunt (Laurie) is holding her hostage. What the film lacks in suspense throughout most of the movie is made up for in the end. 90m/C VHS. Piper Laurie, Steve Railsback, Olivia Hussey, Edward Albert, Rita Gam, Terence Knox; D: Armand Mastroianni.

The Dive 🦴🦴 1989 (PG-13) Two North Sea oil-rig workers are trapped far below the waves when the lifeline to their diving bell snaps in rough seas. 90m/C VHS. Bjorn Sundquist, Frank Grimes, Eindie Eidsvold, Michael Kitchen; D: Tristan De Vere Cole.

Dive Bomber 🦴🦴🦴 1941 Exciting aviation film that focuses on medical problems related to flying. Flynn stars as an aviator-doctor who conducts experiments to eliminate pilot-blackout. MacMurray, Toomey, and Heydt perform well as three flyboys stationed in Hawaii. Great flying sequences filmed at San Diego's naval base with extra scenes shot at Pensacola. Warner Bros. released this film just months before the Japanese attacked Pearl Harbor. Based on the story "Beyond the Blue Sky" by Frank Wead. 130m/B VHS, DVD. Errol Flynn, Fred MacMurray, Ralph Bellamy, Alexis Smith, Regis Toomey, Robert Armstrong, Allen Jenkins, Craig Stevens, Herbert Anderson, Moroni Olsen, Dennie Moore, Louis Jean Heydt, Cliff Nazarro, Tod Andrews, Ann Doran, Charles Drake, Alan Hale Jr., William Forrest, Creighton Hale, Howard Hickman, Russell Hicks, George Meeker, Richard Travis, Addison Richards; D: Michael Curtiz; W: Frank Wead, Robert Buckner; C: Bert Glennon, Winton C. Hoch; M: Max Steiner.

Divided by Hate 🦴🦴 1996 (PG-13) In 1984, struggling farmer Louis Gibbs (Walsh), wife Carol (Roth), and their children fall under the spell of charismatic preacher Steve Riordan (Skerritt) whose anti-government sentiments lead to the forming of a local militia. Naturally, the FBI gets involved and there's a struggle between the feds and the militia, with the family caught in the middle. If it sounds familiar that's because it's based on the 1995 Branch Davidian incident. 92m/C VHS. Dylan Walsh, Andrea Roth, Tom Skerritt; D: Tom Skerritt; W: Leonard Gross.

Divided We Fall 🦴🦴½ Musime si Pomahat 2000 (PG-13) In 1943, the inhabitants of an unnamed Czechoslovakian town are existing under the Nazi occupation. Josef (Polivka) recognizes his former employer David (Kassal), a Jew who has escaped the camps. Josef and his wife Marie (Siskova) agree to hide David in their home although they are under the scrutiny of Nazi collaborator Horst (Dusek), who keeps making passes at Marie. Although they are childless, Marie claims to be pregnant to get Horst to leave her alone. Which leads Josef to ask a delicate favor of David so they can make good on Marie's lie. Czech with subtitles. 123m/C VHS, DVD. CZ Boleslav Polivka, Anna Siskova, Csongor Kassai, Jaroslav Dusek, Jiri Pecha, Simona Stasova, Marin Huba, Vladimir Marek, Jiri Kodet, Richard Tesarik; D: Jan Hrebejk; W: Petr Jarchovsky; C: Jan Malir; M: Ales Brezina.

Divided We Stand 🦴🦴 2000 (R) Naive college coed Lisa joins the Black Student Coalition and soon accuses fellow member Robey of rape. However, BSC member and law student Jarrod, who knows what really happened, is hesitant to get involved. 81m/C VHS, DVD. Andrea Lisa, Crayton Robey, J.R. Jarrod; D: J.R. Jarrod; W: J.R. Jarrod, John Crawford; M: Charles D. Jackson, Sherwood Seward, Derek Seward.

Divine 🦴🦴 1990 Two Divine flicks from Waters. First, Divine plays a naughty girl who, not surprisingly, since this one is titled "The Diane Linkletter Story," ends up a successful suicide. "The Neon Woman" is a rare live performance, with Divine a woman who owns a strip joint and has a slew of problems you won't read about in Dear Abby. 110m/C VHS. Divine; D: John Waters.

The Divine Enforcer 🦴½ 1991 A monsignor in a crime-ridden L.A. neighborhood reaches his wit's end in trying to stave off perpetrators of injustice. Fortunately, help arrives in the form of a mysterious priest who is equally handy with his fists, nunchakus, and guns. From then on it's no more mister nice guy, and the criminals haven't a prayer. 90m/C VHS. Jan Michael Vincent, Erik Estrada, Jim Brown, Judy Landers, Don Stroud, Robert Z'Dar, Michael Foley, Carrie Chambers, Hiroko; D: Robert Rundle.

Divine Nymph 🦴🦴½ 1971 (R) Charts the erotic adventures of the beautiful and young Manuela, who is dangerously pursued by her two cousins. 100m/C VHS. IT Laura Antonelli, Marcello Mastroianni, Terence Stamp; D: Giuseppe Patroni-Griffi; M: Ennio Morricone.

Divine Secrets of the Ya-Ya Sisterhood 🦴🦴 2002 (PG-13) Southern dramedy with a group of girlfriends (Smith, Flanagan, Knight) who stage an intervention to help about-to-be-married, New York-based playwright Sidda Lee

'Bullock) discover the truth about her ec-centric, alcoholic Southern mama Vivi (Burstyn). Flashbacks ensue as we see the women as children in the 1930s when they formed their secret Ya-Ya society and then later to Vivi as a young woman (played somewhat hysterically by Judd). The most fun bits, however, are those with the slightly cracked Southern belles now in their 70s. Female bonding, estrogen fest gives short shrift to the men in these ladies lives (shocking!). First time director Khouri lets these kooky dames run the plot, run a little too wild. Based on the novels "Divine Secrets of the Ya-Ya Sisterhood" and "Little Altars Everywhere" by Rebecca Wells. 116m/C VHS, DVD, JS Ashley Judd, Sandra Bullock, Ellen Burstyn, Maggie Smith, James Garner, Fionnula Flanagan, Shirley Knight, Cherry Jones, Angus MacFadyen, Gina McKee, Matthew Settle, David Rasche, Frederick Koehler, Leslie Silva, Ron Dorton, David Lee Smith; D: Callie Khouri; W: Callie Khouri, Mark Andrus; C: John Bailey; M: T-Bone Burnett.

The Diving Bell and the Butterfly ✓✓✓ 1/2 [PG-13] 2007 The true story of French "Elle" magazine editor Jean-Dominique Bauby, who suffered a stroke that left him completely paralyzed but for his left eyelid. The film chronicles the process by which Bauby dictated his memoir by blinking that left eye, as each individual letter with every blink. As if Bauby's story isn't tragic enough, he died just two days after his book was published in France. An emotionally wrenching, at times difficult to watch, poetic and richly-cinematic journey ripe with colorful and sensual images from Bauby's past life and his fully-functioning inner world as imagined by director Schnabel. In French with subtitles and named after Bauby's biography. 112m/C DVD. FR Mathieu Amalric, Emmanuelle Seigner, Marie-Josee Croze, Patrick Chesnais, Max von Sydow, Anne Consigny, Isaach de Bankole, Niels Arestrup; D: Julian Schnabel; W: Ronald Harwood; C: Janusz Kaminski. British Acad. '07: Adapt. Screenplay Golden Globes '08: Director; Foreign Film. Ind Spirit '08: Cinematog., Director (Schnabel).

Diving In ✓✓ 1990 [PG-13] Have you heard the one about the acrophobic diver? It seems a paralyzing fear of heights is the only thing between a young diver and Olympic gold. Much splashing about and heartstring-tugging. 92m/C VHS. Matt Adler, Kristy Swanson, Burt Young, Grant, Joe Flynn, Shelley Berman, Martin Gabel, Tom Bosley, Dick Gautier, Eileen Brennan; D: Strathford Hamilton; C: Harania Baer; M: Guy Moon, Paul Buckmaster.

Divorce American Style ✓✓ 1/2 1967 Dated but still amusing look at love, marriage, and the big D. Richard (Van Dyke) and Barbara (Reynolds) have find their longtime marriage in a tailspin as they spend all their time arguing. They split but find single life and the dating game have their own pitfalls. 109m/C VHS, DVD. Dick Van Dyke, Debbie Reynolds, Jason Robards Jr., Jean Simmons, Van Johnson, Lee Grant, Joe Flynn, Shelley Berman, Martin Gabel, Tom Bosley; D: Norman Lear; C: Conrad L. Hall; M: Dave Grusin.

Divorce His, Divorce Hers ✓✓ 1972 The first half of this drama shows the crumbling of a marriage through the husband's eyes. The second half offers the wife's perspective. 144m/C VHS, DVD. Richard Burton, Elizabeth Taylor; D: Waris Hussein. TV

Divorce—Italian Style ✓✓✓ 1/2 Divorzio All'italiana 1962 A middle-aged baron bored with his wife begins directing his amorous attentions to a teenage cousin. Since divorce in Italy is impossible, the only way out of his marriage is murder— he excuses a man from murdering his wife if she is having an affair (since he would merely be defending his honor). A hilarious comedy with a twist ending. Available in English with English subtitles or cubbed in Italian. 104m/B VHS, DVD. /T Marcello Mastroianni, Daniela Rocca, Leopoldo Trieste, Stefania Sandrelli; D: Pietro Germi; W: Pietro Germi, Ennio

de Concini, Alfredo Giannetti; C: Carlo Di Palma, Leonida Barboni; M: Carlo Rustichelli. Oscars '62: Story & Screenplay; British Acad. '63: Actor (Mastroianni); Golden Globes '63: Actor-Mus-Comedy (Mastroianni), Foreign Film.

The Divorce of Lady X ✓✓ 1/2 1938 A spoiled British debutante, in the guise of "Lady X," makes a woman-hating divorce lawyer eat his words through romance and marriage. Based on the play by Gilbert Wakefield. 92m/C VHS, GB Merle Oberon, Laurence Olivier, Ralph Richardson, Binnie Barnes; D: Tim Whelan; C: Harry Stradling Sr.; M: Miklos Rozsa.

The Divorcee ✓✓ 1/2 1930 Early Leonard film (he'd later direct "The Great Ziegfeld" and "Pride and Prejudice") casts Shearer as a woman out to beat her husband at philandering. Married to a journalist, she cavorts with her husband's best friend and a discarded old flame as only a pre-production code gal could. Shearer—who Lillian Hellman described as having "a face unclouded by thought"—grabbed an Oscar. Based on the novel "Ex-Wife" by Ursula Parrott. 83m/B VHS, Norma Shearer, Chester Morris, Conrad Nagel, Robert Montgomery, Mary Doran, Tyler Brooke, George Irving, Helen Johnson; D: Robert Z. Leonard. Oscars '30: Actress (Shearer).

Dixiana ✓✓ 1/2 1930 A Southern millionaire falls for a circus performer shortly before the start of the Civil War. Part color. ♪Dixiana; Here's to the Old Days; A Tear, A Kiss, a Smile; My One Ambition is You; A Lady Loved a Soldier; Mr. & Mrs. Sippi; Guiding Star. 99m/B VHS, DVD. Bebe Daniels, Bert Wheeler, Robert Woolsey, Dorothy Lamour, Bill Robinson; D: Luther Reed; M: Max Steiner.

Dixie: Changing Habits ✓✓ 1/2 1985 A New Orleans madam and a Mother Superior go head to head in this amusing TV movie. In the end all benefit as the nuns discover business sense and pay off a debt, while the former bordello owner cleans up her act. Above-average script. 100m/C VHS. Suzanne Pleshette, Clors Leachman, Kenneth McMillan, John Considine, Geraldine Fitzgerald, Judith Ivey; D: George Englund. TV

Dixie Dynamite ✓ 1976 [PG] The two daughters of a Georgia moonshiner set out to avenge the murder of their father. The music is performed by Duane Eddy and Dorsey Burnette. 88m/C VHS, DVD. Warren Oates, Christopher George, Jane Anne Johnstone, Kathy McAuley, R.G Armstrong, Wes Bishop; D: Lee Frost; W: Lee Frost, Wes Bishop.

Dixie Jamboree ✓ 1944 Low-budget musical has gangster on the lam using an unusual method to escape from St. Louis—the last Mississippi Showboat. ♪Dixie Showboat; No, No, No; If It's a Dream; You Ain't Right with the Lord; Big Stuff. 69m/B VHS, DVD. Guy Kibbee, Frances Langford, Louise Beavers, Charles Butterworth; D: Christy Cabanne.

Dixie Lanes ✓ 1988 A relentlessly nostalgic comedy set in a small town at the end of WWII. A woman, troubled by her nephew's restless antics, puts him to work. Unfortunately she adds to his plight, as her favorite pastime is life at the Market. 92m/C VHS, DVD. Hoyt Axton, Karen Black, Art Hindle, John Vernon, Ruth Buzzi, Tina Louise, Pamela Springsteen, Nina Foch; D: Don Cato.

Django ✓✓ 1/2 1968 [PG] Django is a stranger who arrives in a Mexican-border town (dragging a coffin behind him) to settle a dispute between a small band of Americans and Mexicans. 90m/C VHS, DVD. Franco Nero, Loredana Nussiak, Angel Alvarez, Jose Bodalo, Eduardo Fajardo, Simon Arriaga, Ivan Scratiglia; D: Sergio Corbucci; W: Sergio Corbucci, Bruno Corbucci, Jose Maesso, Piero Vivarelli, Franco (Fred Gardner) Rossetti; C: Enzo Barboni; M: Luis Bacalov.

Django Shoots First ✓✓ 1/2 Djan-go Spara per Primo 1974 Spaghetti western with usual amount of action and plot twists. 96m/C VHS. /T Glen Saxson, Evelyn Stewart, Alberto Lupo; D: Alberto De Martino.

Django Strikes Again ✓✓ Djan-go 2: Il Grande Ritorno 1987 Django (Nero) has abandoned his former life of violence in favor of the peaceful life of a monk. That

is, until his daughter is kidnapped. Then he manages to find that old coffin and go after the dastardly dogs. 96m/C VHS, DVD. Franco Nero, Donald Pleasence, Rodrigo Obregon, Christopher Connelly, William Berger; D: Nello Rossati; M: Gianfranco Plenizio.

DNA ✓ 1/2 1997 [R] Idealistic doctor Ash Mattley (Dacascos) mistakenly revives his radical DNA theories to creepy scientist Wessinger (Prochnow), who uses the knowledge in mutant experiments. One mutant, an insect-like creature who's scary powers, lurks in the rain forest, waiting for prey, while Mattley sets out to destroy it. 94m/C VHS, DVD. Mark Dacascos, Jurgen Prochnow, Robin McKee; D: William Mesa; W: Nick Davis; C: Gerry Lively; M: Christopher Stone.

Do I Love You? ✓✓ 1/2 2002 Biking through the streets of London in search of answers to the mysteries of life and love is 30-something lesbian Marina (writer/director Gornick) who is sent adrift after a difficult split with girlfriend Romy (Cassidy). Overly chatty and rambling, much like her trek. 73m/C DVD, Sarah Patterson, Lisa Gornick, Raquel Cassidy, Hami Alexander; D: Lisa Gornick; W: Lisa Gornick. VIDEO

Do Not Disturb ✓✓ 1/2 1965 Filmed on the studio backlot, though the story is set in England and Paris, this so-so romantic comedy finds Janet Harper (Day) relocating to England with exec. hubby Mike (Taylor). He promptly leaves her to settle in alone while dallying with his secretary, so Janet decides to invent her own admirer. But a real suitor, Paul (Fantoni), shows up and sweeps Janet off to Paris, thus making Mike insanely jealous. 102m/C VHS. Doris Day, Rod Taylor, Sergio Fantoni, Hermione Baddeley, Reginald Gardiner; D: Ralph Levy; W: Richard L. Breen; C: Leon Shamroy; M: Lionel Newman.

Do or Die ✓ 1/2 1991 [R] Former "Playboy" centerfolds Speir and Vasquez team up as a couple of federal agent babes who take on international crime boss Morita. But the crimelord is ready for our scantily clad heroines with a sick game of revenge—and the stakes are their very lives! 97m/C VHS, DVD. Erik Estrada, Dona Speir, Roberta Vasquez, Nonyuki "Pat" Morita, Bruce Penhall, Carolyn Liu, Stephanie Schick; D: Andy Sidaris; W: Andy Sidaris.

Do or Die ✓✓ 1/2 2001 When her young son is diagnosed with leukemia, Dr. Samantha Sheppard (Ashfield) is forced to admit to the cops and then Australian miniseries that has been edited to a fast-moving pace. 90m/C DVD, AU Kate Ashfield, Tom Long, Hugo Speer, William McInnes, Martin Sacks; D: Rowan Woods; W: Christopher Lee. C: Martin McGrath; M: Edmund Butt. TV

Do the Right Thing ✓✓✓ 1/2 1989 [R] An uncompromising, brutal comedy about the racial tensions surrounding a white-owned pizzeria in the Bed-Stuy section of Brooklyn on the hottest day of the summer, and the violence that eventually erupts. Ambivalent and, for the most part, hilarious. Lee's coming-of-age. 120m/C VHS, DVD. Spike Lee, Danny Aiello, Richard Edson, Ruby Dee, Ossie Davis, Giancarlo Esposito, Bill Nunn, John Turturro, John Savage, Rosie Perez, Frankie Faison; D: Spike Lee; W: Spike Lee; C: Ernest R. Dickerson; M: Bill Lee. L.A. Film Critics '89: Director (Lee), Film, Support. Actor (Aiello), Natl. Film Reg. '99; N.Y. Film Critics '89: Cinematog.

D.O.A. ✓✓✓ 1/2 1949 A man is given a lethal, slow-acting poison. As his time runs out, he frantically seeks to learn who is responsible and why he was targeted for death. Dark film noir remade in 1988 as "Color Me Dead." Also available colorized. 83m/B VHS, DVD. Edmund O'Brien, Pamela Britton, Luther Adler, Neville Brand, Beverly Garland, Laurette Luez, Virginia Lee, Jess Kirkpatrick, Cay Forrester, Michael Ross; D: Rudolp; Mate; W: Russell Rouse, Clarence

Greene; C: Ernest Laszlo; M: Dimitri Tiomkin. Natl. Film Reg. '04.

D.O.A. ✓✓ 1/2 1988 [R] Well-done remake of the 1949 thriller with Quaid portraying a college professor who is poisoned and has only 24 hours to identify his killer. His search for the suspect is further complicated by the fact that he is being sought by the police on phony charges of murder. Directed by the same people who brought "Max Headroom" to TV screens. 96m/C VHS, DVD, Dennis Quaid, Meg Ryan, Charlotte Rampling, Daniel Stern, Jane Kaczmarek, Christopher Neame, Jay Patterson; D: Rocky Morton, Annabel Jankel; W: Charles Edward Pogue; M: Chez Janke.

DOA: Dead or Alive ✓✓ 2006 [PG-13] Female-centric martial arts actioner, based on a videogame, follows five woman fighters battling to the death on an island. Okay, not the most original concept in the world, but as a straightforward action-and-chicks, "turn-off-the-brain" time waster, you could do a lot worse. Hey, at least Uwe Boll didn't direct it. Corey Yuen, who knows a thing or two about staging martial arts action, did. And it does look like everyone's having a good time. 87m/C DVD, GB GE US Devon Aoki, Sarah Carter, Natassia Malthe, Jaime Pressly, Eric Roberts, Steve Howey, Matthew Marsden, Collin Chou, Holly Valance, Kane (Takeshi) Kosugi, Kevin Nash, Brian White, Robin Shou, Derek Boyer, Silvio Simac; D: Corey Yuen; W: J.F. Lawton, Adam Gross, Seth Gross; C: Chi Ying Chan, Kwok-Man Keung.

Doc Hollywood ✓✓ 1/2 1991 [PG-13] A hotshot young physician on his way to a lucrative California practice gets stranded in a small Southern town. Will the wacky woodsy inhabitants persuade the city doctor to stay? There aren't many surprises in this fish-out-of-water comedy, but the cast injects it with considerable charm. Adapted from Neil B. Shulman's book "What? Dead Again?" 104m/C VHS, DVD. Michael J. Fox, Julie Warner, Woody Harrelson, Barnard Hughes, Bridget Fonda, George Hamilton, Roberts Bossom, Helen Martin, Macon McCalman, Barry Sobel; D: Michael Caton-Jones; W: Daniel Pyne, Jeffrey Price, Peter S. Seaman; C: Michael Chapman; M: Carter Burwell.

Doc Savage ✓✓ 1975 [PG] Doc and "The Amazing Five" fight a murderous villain who plans to take over the world. Based on the novels of Kenneth Robeson. 100m/C VHS. Ron Ely, Pamela Hensley, Paul Wexler, William Lucking, Michael Anderson Sr.; W: George Pal, Joe Morham; C: Fred W. Koenekamp.

Docks of New York ✓✓✓ 1928 Von Sternberg made his mark in Hollywood with this silent drama about dockside losers finding love amid the squalor. A rarely seen, early masterpiece. 60m/B VHS, George Bancroft, Betty Compson, Olga Baclanova; D: Josef von Sternberg; M: Gaylord Carter; Natl. Film Reg. '99.

The Doctor ✓✓ 1/2 1991 [PG-13] A hotshot doctor develops throat cancer and gets treated at his own hospital, an ordeal that teaches him a respect and compassion for patients that he formerly lacked. Potential melodrama is saved by fine acting and strong direction. Based on the autobiographical book "A Taste of My Own Medicine" by Dr. Edward Rosenbaum. 125m/C VHS, DVD. William Hurt, Elizabeth Perkins, Christine Lehti, Mandy Patinkin, Wendy Crewson, Charlie Korsmo, Adam Arkin, Bill Macy; D: Randa Haines; M: Michael Converrino.

Dr. Akagi ✓✓ Kanzo Sensei 1998 In 1945, the dedicated Dr. Akagi (Emoto) is more worried about a hepatitis epidemic than the seaside village that the Japanese wartime defeat. He becomes obsessed with finding a cure and assembles a ragtag group of compatriots to assist him, including a teenaged prostitute and an escaped Dutch prisoner of war. Based on the novel "Dr. Liver" by Ango Sakaguchi. Japanese with subtitles. **128m/C VHS, DVD, JP** Akira (Tsukamoto) Emoto, Jacques Gamblin, Kumiko Aso, Masanori Sera, Jyuro Kara, Keiko Matsuzaka; **D:** Shohei Imamura, Daisuke Tengan; **C:** Shigeru Komatsubara; **M:** Yosuke Yamashita.

Dr. Alien ♂ 1988 (R) Alien poses as beautiful scientist and turns a college freshman into a sex-addicted satyr. Likewise, the cast turns this flick into a dog. **90m/C VHS, DVD** Billy Jacoby, Olivia Barash, Stuart Fratkin, Troy Donahue, Arlene Golonka, Judy Landers; **D:** David DeCoteau.

The Doctor and the Devils ♂♂½ 1985 (R) Based on an old screenplay by Dylan Thomas, this is a semi-Gothic tale about two criminals who supply a physician with corpses to study, either digging them up or killing them fresh. **93m/C VHS, DVD, GB** Timothy Dalton, Julian Sands, Jonathan Pryce, Twiggy, Stephen Rea, Beryl Reid, Sian Phillips, Patrick Stewart, Phyllis Logan, T.P. McKenna; **D:** Freddie Francis; **W:** Ronald Harwood; **M:** John Morris.

Doctor at Large ♂♂½ 1957 A fledgling doctor seeks to become a surgeon at a hospital for the rich. Humorous antics follow. The third of the "Doctor" series. **98m/C VHS, GB** Dirk Bogarde, Muriel Pavlow, James Robertson Justice, Shirley Eaton, Donald Sinden, Anne Heywood; **D:** Ralph Thomas.

Doctor at Sea ♂♂½ 1956 To escape a troublesome romantic entanglement and the stresses of his career, a London physician signs on as a cargo boat as a ship's doctor and becomes involved with French bombshell Bardot. The second of the "Doctor" series. **93m/C VHS, GB** James Robertson Justice, Dirk Bogarde, Brigitte Bardot; **D:** Ralph Thomas; **W:** Jack Davies.

Dr. Bell and Mr. Doyle: The Dark Beginnings of Sherlock Holmes ♂♂½ 2000 *Murder Rooms: The Dark Origins of Sherlock Holmes* 2000 In 1878, Arthur Conan Doyle (Laing) is a medical student at Edinburgh University. He is mentored by the gruff and brilliant, if unconventional, Dr. Joseph Bell (Richardson), who is a pioneer in the field of forensic science. Arthur is soon assisting Dr. Bell, who is helping the local police investigate the brutal murders of several young women. The case may also take a personal turn for Arthur when it appears his classmate and friend Elspeth (Wells) is a target. Well-done if sometimes gruesome; based in part on the letters and writings of Bell. **116m/C VHS, DVD, GB** Robin Laing, Ian Richardson, Charles Dance, Dolly Wells, Sean McGinley, Alec Newman; **D:** Paul Seed; **W:** David Pirie; **C:** John Kenway; **M:** Jim Parker. **TV**

Dr. Bethune ♂♂♂ *Bethune, The Making of a Hero* 1990 Canadian surgeon Norman Bethune was a larger-than-life hero with equally great flaws. A crusader for socialized medicine and an outspoken opponent of Fascism (as well as an alcoholic womanizer), he worked for the Loyalist forces in the Spanish Civil War and was instrumental in developing mobile medical units for treating battlefield wounded. He's also credited with bringing modern medical care to China, where he attended to Mao's revolutionary forces. Sutherland's strong performance shows the intensity and vision of a complicated man; he previously played the doctor in 1977's "Bethune." Awkward jumps in time and place rob the story of narrative drive. **115m/C VHS, CA FR** Donald Sutherland, Helen Mirren, Helen Shaver, Colm Feore, Anouk Aimee, Ronald Pickup, Harrison Liu; **D:** Phillip Borsos; **W:** Ted Allan; **C:** Raoul Coutard; **M:** Alan Reeves.

Dr. Black, Mr. Hyde ♂ *Dr. Black and Mr. White: The Watts Monster* 1976 (R) Not-so-horrifying tale of a black Jekyll who metamorphoses into a white monster with the help of the special potion. Unintended laughs lessen suspense. **88m/C VHS** Rosalind Cash, Stu Gilliam, Bernie Casey, Marie O'Henry; **D:** William Crain.

Doctor Blood's Coffin ♂♂½ 1962 The aptly named doctor performs hideous experiments on the unsuspecting denizens of a lonely village. Good cast in this effective chiller. **92m/C VHS, DVD, GB** Kieron Moore, Hazel Court, Ian Hunter; **D:** Sidney J. Furie.

Doctor Bull ♂♂½ 1933 Rogers is aw-shucks charming in the title role. George Bull is an opinionated small-town doctor who's subjected to much gossip, especially over his romance with widow Janet (Allen). When the town's water supply is contaminated and many fall ill, Bull diagnoses typhoid. Herbert Banning (Churchill), Janet's brother, tries to blame the good doctor since he's the town's health officer, but Janet defends him. **77m/B DVD, VHS** Will Rogers, Marion Nixon, Berton Churchill, Louise Dresser, Vera Allen, Howard Lally, Andy Devine; **D:** John Ford; **W:** Paul Green; **C:** George Schneiderman; **M:** Samuel Kaylin.

Doctor Butcher M.D. WOOf! *Queen of the Cannibals; Zombie Holocaust; The Island of the Last Zombies* 1980 (R) Mad doctor's deranged dream of creating "perfect people" by taking parts of one person and interchanging them with another backfires as his monstrosities develop strange side effects. The M.D., by the way, stands for "Medical Deviate". Dubbed. **81m/C VHS, DVD, IT** Ian McCulloch, Alexandra Cole, Peter O'Neal, Donald O'Brien, Sherry Buchanan, Walter Patriarca; **D:** Frank Martin, Mariano Laurenti; **W:** Fabrizio de Angelis, Romano Scandariato; **M:** Nico Fidenco; **V:** Walter Sear.

Dr. Caligari ♂♂ 1989 (R) The granddaughter of the original Dr. Caligari promotes "better living through chemistry" in her insane asylum while using her patients as guinea pigs in her bizarre sexual experiments. Nothing outstanding here in terms of story or performance, but "Dick Tracy" has nothing on the visually compelling set designs and make-up. **80m/C VHS, DVD** Madeleine Reynal, Fox Harris, Laura Albert, Jennifer Balgobin, John Durbin, Gene Zerna, David Parry, Barry Phillips; **D:** Stephen Sayadian; **W:** Stephen Sayadian, Jerry Stahl; **C:** Stephen Sayadian.

Doctor Chance ♂♂ *Docteur Chance* 1997 Frustrated Angstel (Hestnes) decides it's time to make a big change in his life. He heads to a nightclub and buys the favors (with counterfeit cash) of dancer Ancetta (Elvire) but events get out of hand. Soon the duo are heading out of the city with a car trunk full of weapons and adventure on their minds. French with subtitles. **97m/C VHS, DVD, FR** Pedro Hestnes, Elvire, Marisa Paredes, Stephane Ferrara, Joe Strummer, Feodor Atkine; **D:** F.J. Ossang; **W:** F.J. Ossang; **C:** Remy Chevrin.

Dr. Christian Meets the Women ♂½ 1940 This entry in the "Dr. Christian" series of films has the small-town physician once again exposing a con man trying to filch the townspeople. **63m/B VHS** Jean Hersholt, Edgar Kennedy, Rod La Rocque, Dorothy Lovett, Veda Ann Borg; **D:** William McGann.

Dr. Cyclops ♂♂½ 1940 The famous early Technicolor fantasia about a mad scientist miniaturizing a group of explorers who happen upon his jungle lab. Landmark F/X and a slow-moving story. Now he seeks to revive his wife. Final role for 77-year-old "Stooge" Moe Howard. **76m/C VHS** Albert Dekker, Janice Logan, Victor Killian, Thomas Coley, Charles Halton, Frank Yaconelli, Paul Fix, Frank Reicher; **D:** Ernest B. Schoedsack; **W:** Tom Kilpatrick; **C:** Winton C. Hoch, Henry Sharp; **M:** Gerard Carbonara, Albert Hay Malotte; **D:** Eddie Saeta.

Dr. Death, Seeker of Souls ♂ 1973 (R) Evil doctor discovers a process for transmigrating his soul into the bodies of people he murdered 1000 years ago. Now he seeks to revive his wife. **93m/C VHS, DVD** John Considine, Barry Coe, Cheryl Miller, Stewart Moss, Leon Askin, Jo Morrow, Florence Marly, Sivi Aberg, Athena Lorde, Moe Howard; **D:** Eddie Saeta.

Doctor Detroit ♂ 1983 (R) Aykroyd is funny in thin film, portraying a meek college professor who gets involved with prostitutes and the mob, later married actress Donna Dixon, whom he worked with on this film. Features music by Devo, James Brown, and Pattie Brooks. **91m/C VHS, DVD, Dan Aykroyd, Howard Hesseman, Donna Dixon, T.K. Carter, Lynn Whitfield, Lydia Lei, Fran Drescher, Kate Murtagh, George Furth, Andrew Duggan, James Brown, Glenne Headly; **D:** Michael Pressman; **W:** Carl Gottlieb, Robert Boris; **M:** Lalo Schifrin.

Doctor Dolittle ♂♂ 1967 An adventure about a 19th century English doctor who dreamed of teaching animals to speak to him. Realistic premise suffers from poor script. Based on Hugh Lofting's acclaimed stories. ♫Doctor Dolittle; My Friend the Doctor; Talk to the Animals; I've Never Seen Anything Like It; Beautiful Things; When I Look in Your Eyes; After Today; Fabulous Places; Where Are the Words?. **151m/C VHS, DVD,** Rex Harrison, Samantha Eggar, Anthony Newley, Richard Attenborough, Geoffrey Holder, Peter Bull; **D:** Richard Fleischer; **W:** Leslie Bricusse; **C:** Robert L. Surtees; **M:** Leslie Bricusse. Oscars '67: Song ("Talk to the Animals"), Visual FX; Golden Globes '68: Support. Actor (Attenborough).

Dr. Dolittle ♂♂½ 1998 (PG-13) Loose non-musical adaption of the 1967 movie has Eddie Murphy playing straight man to a group of furry friends voiced by the likes of Chris Rock. Garry Shandling and Albert Brooks. He is reduced to reacting lamely, and is upstaged throughout by the wisecracking critters created by Jim Henson's Creature Shop. Fellow humans Dr. Weller (Platt) and Calloway (Boyle) are shallow villains created to prop up a shaky plot involving the corporate takeover of Dolittle's vet clinic. May contain a bit too much bathroom humor for some family tastes. No animals were harmed during the making of this movie, but there was probably cruel and unusual treatment of the interns involving pooper-scoopers. **85m/C VHS, DVD,** Eddie Murphy, Oliver Platt, Peter Boyle, Jeffrey Tambor, Ossie Davis, Richard Schiff, Kyla Pratt, Raven, Steven Gilborn; **D:** Betty Thomas; **W:** Nat Mauldin, Larry Levin; **C:** Russell Boyd; **M:** Richard Gibbs; **V:** Julie Kavner, Albert Brooks, Chris Rock, John Leguizamo, Garry Shandling, Norm MacDonald, Reni Santoni, Paul (Pee-wee Herman) Reubens, Gilbert Gottfried.

Dr. Dolittle 2 ♂♂ 2001 (PG) The good doctor (Murphy) returns, along with his furry talking friends, who persuade him to save their forest from human developers. The vet must also find a mate for an endangered Pacific Western bear, but the only candidate is Archie (Zahn), a circus performer who has to be taught how to survive in the wilderness. Gastrointestinal and other bodily functions dominate the humor, and a subplot involving Doolittle's moody teenage daughter (Raven-Symone) nearly undoes the charm, but it's passable entertainment. Add half a bone if you're under 12 years old for this flatulence-obsessed outing. **87m/C VHS, DVD,** US Eddie Murphy, Jeffrey Jones, Kevin Pollak, Raven, Kyla Pratt, Kristen Wilson, Zane R. (Lil' Zane) Copeland Jr., Andy Richter; **D:** Steve Carr; **W:** Larry Levin; **C:** Daryn Okada; **M:** David Newman; **V:** Norm MacDonald, Lisa Kudrow, Steve Zahn, Mike Epps, Michael Rapaport, Jacob Vargas, Isaac Hayes, Andy Dick, Joey Lauren Adams, Richard Sarafian.

Dr. Dolittle 3 ♂♂ 2006 (PG) Maya Dolittle (Pratt) is following in her dad's footsteps by working at his clinic and talking to the animals—who frequently get her into trouble. Mom Lisa (Wilson) thinks Maya needs a timeout and sends her to a summer dude ranch, but Maya finds a way to put her talents to good use. **93m/C DVD,** Kyla Pratt, Kristen Wilson, John Amos, Walker Howard, Luciana Carro, Tommy Snider; **D:** Rich Thorne; **W:** Nina Colman; **C:** Eric Goldstein; **M:** Christopher Lennertz.

Dr. Dolittle 4: Tail to the Chief ♂♂ 2008 (PG) Dog whisperer? In her latest adventure, Maya Dolittle (Pratt) is asked by the president to come to the White House and tame the rambunctious First Dog. **90m/C DVD,** Kyla Pratt, Peter Coyote, Malcolm Stewart, Christine Chatelain, Niall Matter; **D:** Craig Shapiro; **W:** Kathleen Lacciole, Matthew Lieberman; **C:** Ron Stannett; **M:** Don MacDonald. **VIDEO**

Dr. Doolittle 3 ♂½ 2006 (PG) Maya Doolittle (Pratt) can also talk to the animals, which doesn't make being a teenager any easier. When she gets into trouble, mom sends Maya to a Colorado dude ranch, where she tries to make some friends while yakking with the local barnyard critters. Since the ranch is in financial trouble, it's up to Maya and the animals to win big at the local rodeo and

save the day. Harmless and silly cash-in on the Eddie Murphy features. **95m/C DVD,** US Kyla Pratt, Kristen Wilson, John Amos, Walker Howard; **D:** Rich Thorne; **W:** Nina Colman; **C:** Eric Goldstein; **M:** Christopher Lennertz. **VIDEO**

Doctor Faustus ♂½ 1968 A stilted, stagy, but well-meaning adaptation of the Christopher Marlowe classic about Faust, who sold his soul to the devil for youth and the love of Helen of Troy. **93m/C VHS, DVD,** Richard Burton, Andreas Teuber, Elizabeth Taylor, Ian Marter; **D:** Richard Burton, Nevill Coghill.

Dr. Frankenstein's Castle of Freaks ♂ 1974 (PG) Dr. Frankenstein and his dwarf assistant reanimate a few Neanderthals that are terrorizing a nearby Rumanian village. **90m/C VHS, DVD, IT** Rossano Brazzi, Michael Dunn, Edmund Purdom, Christiane Royce, Simone Blondell; **D:** Robert (Dick Randall) Oliver; **W:** William Rose, Mark Smith, Robert Spano; **C:** Mario Mancini.

Dr. Giggles ♂ 1992 (R) Drake plays the psycho-genius Dr. Giggles, an escaped mental patient who sets out to avenge the death of his psycho-genius father (dementia runs in the family). He returns to his family home to procure the necessary medical instruments, most notably a hypodermic needle, and starts killing people—on screen with the tools and in the audience with remarkably stupid one-liners. Opening scenes are especially mired in gore. **96m/C VHS, DVD,** Larry Drake, Holly Marie Combs, Glenn Quinn, Keith Diamond, Cliff DeYoung; **D:** Manny Coto; **M:** Manny Coto; **V:** Rob Draper; **M:** Brian May.

Dr. Goldfoot and the Bikini Machine ♂♂ 1966 A mad scientist employs gorgeous female robots to seduce the wealthy and powerful, thereby allowing him to take over the world. Title song by the Supremes. **90m/C VHS, DVD,** Vincent Price, Frankie Avalon, Dwayne Hickman, Annette Funicello, Susan Hart, Kay Elkhardt, Fred Clark, Deanna Lund, Deborah Walley; **D:** Norman Taurog; **M:** Les Baxter.

Dr. Hackenstein ♂½ 1988 (R) A doctor tries to revive his wife by "borrowing" parts from unexpected (and unsuspecting) guests. **88m/C VHS, DVD,** David Muir, Stacey Travis, Catherine Davis Cox, Dyanne DiRosario, Anne Ramsey, Logan Ramsey; **D:** Richard Clark.

Dr. Heckyl and Mr. Hype ♂♂ 1980 (R) A naughty, comical version of the Jekyll and Hyde story. Exuberantly wicked performances from Reed and Coogan; stellar cast of "B" veterans. **100m/C VHS,** Oliver Reed, Sunny Johnson, Maia Danziger, Mel Welles, Virgil Frye, Kedrick Wolfe, Jackie Coogan, Corinne Calvet, Dick Miller, Lucretia Love; **D:** Charles B. Griffith; **W:** Charles B. Griffith; **M:** Richard Band.

Doctor in Distress ♂♂♂½ 1963 Aging chief surgeon falls in love for the first time. His assistant tries to further the romance as well as his own love life. Comedic fourth in the six-film "Doctor" series. **102m/C VHS, GB** Dirk Bogarde, James Robertson Justice, Leo McKern, Samantha Eggar; **D:** Ralph Thomas.

Doctor in the House ♂♂♂½ 1953 Four medical student/roommates seek only to examine lovely women and make lots of cash. In the process, they are also tempted by the evils of drink, but rally to make their grades. A riotous British comedy with marvelous performances all around. Led to six sequels and a TV series. **92m/C VHS, GB** Dirk Bogarde, Muriel Pavlow, Kenneth More, Donald Sinden, Kay Kendall, James Robertson Justice, Donald Houston, Geoffrey Keen, George Coulouris, Shirley Eaton, Joan Hickson, Richard Wattis; **D:** Ralph Thomas. British Acad. '54: Actor (More).

Dr. Jekyll and Ms. Hyde ♂♂½ 1995 (PG-13) Chemist Richard Jacks (Daily) stumbles across the secret formula of great-grandad Dr. Jekyll and, after trying to improve the potion, he finds himself transformed into wicked woman Helen Hyde (Young). Cheap cross-gender gags abound. **89m/C VHS,** Timothy Daly, Sean Young, Lysette Anthony, Stephen Tobolowsky, Harvey Fierstein, Polly Bergen, Stephen Shellen; **D:** David F. Price; **W:** William Davies, William Osborne, Tim John, Oliver Butcher. '54: Actor (More).

Dr. Jekyll and Mr. Hyde 1920 The first American film version of Robert Louis Stevenson's horror tale about a doctor's experiments that lead to his developing good and evil sides to his personality. Silent. Kino Video's edition also contains the rarely seen 1911 version of the film, as well as scenes from a different 1920 version. ?Barrymore, Martha Mansfield, Brandon Hurst, Charles Lane, J. Malcolm Dunn, Nita Naldi, Louis Wolheim; D: John S. Robertson; W: Clara Beranger; C: Karl Struss, Roy F. Overbaugh.

Dr. Jekyll and Mr. Hyde 1932 The hallucinatory, feverish classic version of the Robert Louis Stevenson story, in which the good doctor becomes addicted to the formula that turns him into a sadistic beast. Upright Dr. Jekyll (March) has a genteel fiance, Muriel (Hobart), while twisted alter-ego Hyde delights in torturing barmaid Ivy (Hopkins)—the bond between violence and sexuality in these scenes is highly charged. Possibly Mamoulian's and March's best work, and a masterpiece of subversive, pseudo-Freudian creepiness. Eighteen minutes from the original version, lost until recently, have been restored, including the infamous whipping scene. 96m/B VHS, DVD. Fredric March, Miriam Hopkins, Halliwell Hobbes, Rose Hobart, Holmes Herbert, Edgar Norton; D: Rouben Mamoulian; W: Samuel Hoffenstein, Percy Heath; C: Karl Struss. Oscars '32: Actor (March); Venice Film Fest. '31: Actor (March).

Dr. Jekyll and Mr. Hyde 1941 Strangely cast adaptation of the Robert Louis Stevenson story about a doctor's experiment on himself to separate good and evil. 113m/B VHS, DVD. Spencer Tracy, Ingrid Bergman, Lana Turner, Donald Crisp, Ian Hunter, Barton MacLane, Sara Allgood, Billy Bevan; D: Victor Fleming; W: John Lee Mahin; C: Joseph Ruttenberg; M: Franz Waxman.

Dr. Jekyll and Mr. Hyde 1973 Dr. Jekyll discovers a potion that turns him into the sinister Mr. Hyde. Based on the classic story by Robert Louis Stevenson. 90m/C VHS, DVD. Kirk Douglas, Michael Redgrave, Susan George, Donald Pleasence; D: David Winters. TV

Dr. Jekyll & Mr. Hyde 1999 (R) Henry Jekyll (Baldwin) is a successful surgeon who is traveling to Hong Kong on his honeymoon. But shortly after his arrival, both he and his bride are killed in an explosion during a gang war. Henry is resurrected by Chinese healer Dr. Chau, although the potion he must take alters him physically and mentally. Henry only seeks revenge but he learns that his arrival was predestined and his fate is to become the legendary fighter known as the White Dragon. Obviously has little or nothing to do with the Robert Louis Stevenson story. 96m/C VHS, DVD. CA AU Adam Baldwin, Steve Bastoni, Chang Tseng, Jason Chong, Richard Chong, Kira Clavell, Karen Cliche; D: Colin Budds; W: Peter M. Lenkov; C: Mark Wareham; M: Gary McDorald. VIDEO

Dr. Jekyll and the Wolfman Dr. Jekyll y el Hombre Lobo; Dr. Jekyll vs. the Werewolf 1971 (R) Naschy's sixth stint as El Hombre Lobo. This time he visits a mysterious doctor in search of a cure but ends up turning into Mr. Hyde, a man who likes to torture women. 85m/C VHS. SP Paul Naschy, Shirley Corrigan, Jack Taylor, Barta Barry, Luis Induni, Mirta Miller; D: Leon Klimovsky; W: Paul Naschy.

Dr. Jekyll and the Sister Hyde 1971 (R) A tongue-in-cheek variation on the good doctor theme, which has the good doctor transforming himself into a sultry, knife-wielding woman who kills prostitutes. 94m/C VHS, DVD. GB Ralph Bates, Martine Beswick, Gerald Sim; D: Roy Ward Baker; W: Brian Clemens; C: Norman Warwick; M: Philip Martell, David Whitaker.

Dr. Orloff and the Invisible Man 1972 In this horror film, Dr. Orloff creates an invisible ape-monster that escapes and goes on a rampage. 91m/C VHS, DVD. FR SP Howard Vernon, Brigitte Carva, Fernand Sancho; D: Pierre Chevalier; M: Pierre Chevalier.

Dr. Orloff's Monster 1964 WOOF! As if "The Awful Dr. Orloff" wasn't awful enough, the doctor is back, this time eliminating his enemies with his trusty killer robot. Awful awful awful. 88m/B VHS, DVD, SP Jose Rubio, Agnes Spaak; D: Jess (Jesus) Franco; C: Alfonso Nieva.

Dr. Otto & the Riddle of the Gloom Beam 1985 (PG) Ernest in your face again. "Fresh from the TV commercials featuring "Ernest" comes Varney playing a villain out to wreck the gloeal economy. He also plays all the other characters, too. Way bizarre; "Know whut I mean?" 92m/C VHS, DVD. Jim Varney; D: John R. Cherry III.

Doctor of Doom WOOF! Wrestling Women vs. the Aztec Ape 1962 An unclassifiable epic wherein female wrestlers battle a mad doctor and his Aztec robot gorilla. Dubbed badly, of course. Much anticipated follow-up to "Wrestling Women vs. the Aztec Mummy." 111m/C VHS, DVD, MX Lorena Velázquez, Armando Silvestre, Roberto Canedo, Chucho Salinas, Scnia Infante; D: Rene Cardona Sr.; W: Alfredo Salazar, Enrique Wallace; M: Antonio Diaz Conde.

Doctor Mordrid: Master of the Unknown 1990 (R) Two immensely powerful sorcerers from the 4th dimension cross over into present time with two very different missions—one wants to destroy the Earth, one wants to save it. 102m/C VHS, Jeffrey Combs, Yvette Nipar, Jay Acovone, Brian Thompson; D: Albert Band, Charles Band; M: Richard Band.

Dr. No 1962 (PG) The world is introduced to British secret agent 007, James Bond, when it is discovered that mad scientist Dr. No (Wiseman) is sabotaging rocket launchings from his hideout in Jamaica. The first 007 film is far less glitzy than any of its successors but boasts the sexiest "Bond girl" of them all in Andress as Honey Ryder who walks out of the surf in a white bikini, and promptly made stars of her and Connery. 111m/C VHS, DVD. GB Sean Connery, Ursula Andress, Joseph Wiseman, Jack Lord, Zena Marshall, Eunice Gayson, Margaret LeMars, John Kitzmiller, Lois Maxwell, Bernard Lee, Anthony Dawson; D: Terence Young; W: Johanna Harwood, Richard Maibaum, Berkley Mather; C: Ted Moore; M: John Barry.

Dr. Seuss' How the Grinch Stole Christmas 2000 (PG) If you've seen the cartoon, then you know it was padded. Just think of the stuff that Ron Howard added!/A new plot line here, an embellishment there, all Carreyed by a big star in green skin and hair/Cross Whos are shown doing frantic Yule shopping, and decoration-envy keeps each neighbor hopping/This anti-shop message is curiously told, considering the junk that this film clearly sold/Cindy Lou Who loses her Christmastime zest, and starts to research the town's Yuletide pest/In a flashback it's shown why the Grinch is so mean, and a love interest is added from when he's a teen/He's elected Cheermeister of the holiday season; but again leaves bitter, arc with good Grinchy reason/Mayor May Who, his rival for Martha May's hand, repeats an insult about too active glands/The stage is now set for his Grinchy attacks, assisted by his trusty reindeer/dog Max/Though he gave back Christmas for all the Whos' sakes, the Grinch got away with huge boxoffice takes./Young tots may think that this Grinch is too scary; but big kids will like the antics of Carrey./Fair holiday flick, even though the plot thins. Narrated by Sir Anthony Hopkins. 102m/C VHS, DVD, HD Jim Carrey, Jeffrey Tambor, Christine Baranski, Taylor Momsen, Molly Shannon, Josh Ryan Evans, Clint Howard, Bill Irwin, Sloane Momsen; D: Ron Howard; W: Jeffrey Price, Peter S. Seaman; C: Don Peterman; M: James Horner; Nar: Anthony Hopkins.

Dr. Kildare's Strange Case 1940 Dr. Kildare administers a daring treatment to a man suffering from a mental disorder of a dangerous nature. One in the film series. 76m/B VHS, DVD. Lew Ayres, Lionel Barrymore, Laraine Day; D: Harold Bucquet.

Dr. Mabuse, The Gambler 1922 Doctor Mabuse der Spieler; Dr. Mabuse, Parts 1 & 2 1922 The massive, two-part crime melodrama, introducing the raving mastermind/extortionist/villain to the world. The film follows Dr. Mabuse (Klein-Rogge) through his life of crime until he finally goes mad. Highly influential and inventive. Lang meant this to be a criticism of morally bankrupt post-WWI Germany. Lang also directed "The Thousand Eyes of Dr. Mabuse" (1932) and "The Crimes of Dr. Mabuse" (1960). 242m/B VHS, DVD. GE Rudolf Klein-Rogge, Aud Egede Nissen, Alfred Abel, Gertrude Welcker, Lil Dagover, Paul Richter, Bernhard Goetzke; D: Fritz Lang; W: Fritz Lang, Thea von Harbou; C: Carl Hoffmann.

Dr. Mabuse vs. Scotland Yard 1964 A sequel to the Fritz Lang classics, this film features the arch-criminal attempting to take over the world with a mind-controlling camera. 90m/B VHS. GE Sabine Bethmann, Peter Van Eyck; D: Paul May.

Doctor Satan's Robot 1940 Indestructible robot is battled by insane Dr. Satan in reedited serial, "Mysterious Dr. Satan." 100m/B VHS. Eduardo Ciannelli, Robert Wilcox, William "Billy" Newell, Ella Neal; D: William Witney, John English.

Dr. Jekyll's Dungeon of Death 1982 (R) Dr. Jekyll and his lobotomized sister, Hilda, scour the streets of San Francisco looking for human blood to recreate his great-grandfather's secret serum. 90m/C VHS. James Mathers, Dawn Carver, Kelly, John Kearney, Jake Pearson; D: James Wood.

Dr. Petiot 1990 Le Docteur Petiot 1990 Based on the true life story of a French WWII doctor who promised to smuggle Jews to freedom but instead killed them for their money and possessions. He was executed in 1946—accused of 60 murders and convicted of 27. The gruesome details are left to the imagination rather than shown. In French with subtitles. 102m/C VHS. FR Michel Serrault, Berangere Bonvoisin, Zbigniew Horoks, Andre de Lacombe, Pierre Romans, Nita Klein, Dominique Marcas, Aurore Prieto, Claude Degliame, Martine Montgermont, Nini Crepon, Andre Julien, Andre Chaumeau, Axel Bogousslavsky, Maxime Collion, Nadege Boscher, Jean Dautremay, Michel Harr; D: Christian de Chalonge; W: Christian de Chalonge, Dominique Garnier; C: Patrick Blossier; M: Michel Portal.

Doctor Phibes Rises Again 1972 (PG) The despicable doctor continues his quest to revive his beloved wife. Fun, superior sequel to "The Abominable Dr. Phibes." 89m/C VHS, DVD. GE Vincent Price, Robert Quarry, Peter Cushing, Beryl Reid, Hugh Griffith, Terry-Thomas, Valli Kemp, Peter Jeffrey, Fiona Lewis, Caroline Munro; D: Robert Fuest; W: Robert Fuest, Robert Blees; C: Alex Thomson; M: John Gale.

Dr. Seuss' Horton Hears a Who! 2008 (G) Big-screen CG-animated adaptation of the Dr. Seuss classic. Toning down his schtick considerably, Jim Carrey voices Horton, an enlightened elephant who discovers an entire planet on a speck of dust. Within this planet is the harmonious city of Who-ville, threatened to be crushed by imagination-hating tyranny. Its mayor (Carell), unaccustomed to dealing with crisis, turns to Horton to save it. A timeless, allegorical story that works for kids and adults alike. Its only fault is in trying to stretch a 10-minute bedtime story into an hour and a half, which leads to obvious interference with the original voice of Dr. Seuss. 88m/C DVD. US D: Steve Martino, Jimmy Hayward; W: Cinco Paul; M: John Powell; V: Jim Carrey, Steven Carell, Carol Burnett, Will Arnett, Seth Rogen, Isla Fisher, Jonah Hill, Dan Fogler, Amy Poehler, Jaime Pressly; Nar: Charles Osgood.

Dr. Seuss' The Cat in the Hat 2003 (PG) Another megastar comedian goes deep under the makeup cover to bring a beloved Dr. Seuss character to life. This time it's Myers, who dons the cat garb to bring some mischief to a bored brother and sister on a rainy afternoon. Conrad (Breslin) is an authority-defying s-o-b, while Sally (Fanning) is an uptight overachieving control freak. They rightfully distrust their overworked real estate agent. First-time helmer Welch reveals his art-director roots in the fully-realized Seussian sets, and in the failure to bring any joy or emotion to the proceedings. The screenwriters must have shared the blame, as well, as they go to extremes to flesh out the book, only to drain the translation of charm. You'd be hard-pressed to 'recognize much that you or your kids love from the book. 82m/C VHS, DVD. US Mike Myers, Dakota Fanning, Spencer Breslin, Kelly Preston, Alec Baldwin, Amy Hill, Sean P. Hayes; D: Bo Welch; W: Alec Berg, David Mandel, Jeff Schaffer; C: Emmanuel Lubezki; M: David Newman; V: Sean P. Hayes.

Dr. Strange 1978 TV pilot based upon the Marvel Comics character who, with the help of a sorcerer, practices witchcraft in order to fight evil. 94m/C VHS. Peter Hooten, Clyde Kusatsu, Jessica Walter, Eddie Benton, John Mills; D: Philip DeGuere. TV

Dr. Strangelove, or: How I Learned to Stop Worrying and Love the Bomb 1964 Sellers plays a tour-de-force triple role in Kubrick's classic black anti-war comedy. When a crazed general (Hayden) initiates a nuclear attack on the Soviets, the U.S. President (Sellers) deals with the consequences, "aided" by a hawkish general (Scott) and a wheelchair-bound advisor with an obvious Nazi past. Famous for Pickens' wild ride on the bomb, Hayden's character's 'purity of essence' philosophy, Scott's gumchewing militarist, and countless other scenes. Based on the novel "Red Alert" by Peter George. 93m/B VHS, DVD. GB Peter Sellers, George C. Scott, Sterling Hayden, Keenan Wynn, Slim Pickens, James Earl Jones, Peter Bull, Tracy Reed, Shane Rimmer, Glenn Beck, Gordon Tanner, Frank Berry, Jack Creley; D: Stanley Kubrick; W: Stanley Kubrick, Terry Southern, Peter George; C: Gilbert Taylor; M: Laurie Johnson. AFI '98: Top 100; British Acad. '64: Film, Natl. Film Reg. '89; N.Y. Film Critics '64; Director (Kubrick).

Dr. Syn, Alias the Scarecrow 1964 (G) A mild-mannered minister is, in reality, a smuggler and pirate avenging King George III's injustices upon the English people. Originally broadcast in three parts on the Disney TV show. 129m/C VHS, DVD. Patrick McGoohan, George Cole, Tony Britton, Michael Hordern, Geoffrey Keen, Kay Cole, Alan Dobie; D: James Neilson. TV

Dr. T & the Women 2000 (R) Gere stars as Dr. Sullivan Travis, a charming and sensitive gynecologist to the affluent women of Dallas, Texas. Yet despite his respect for and adoration of the women in his life, Dr. T, as he is known, cannot truly fathom their complexity. And none are more baffling to him than those closest to him—his wife (Fawcett), who is slowly descending into mental illness, and his daughters (Hudson and Reid). Director Altman has set his sights on ordinary human weaknesses and shortcomings here, staying away from the social commentary and cynicism of some of his earlier films, and often hits his target with a sweet and humorous note. Gere's charm and mannerisms fit the doctor to a "T". while Dern, Hunt, and Long put in good performances as well. Screenwriter Ann Rapp also collaborated with Altman on his previous film, "Cookie's Fortune."

Doctor Takes a Wife 🦴🦴🦴 **1940** A fast, fun screwball comedy wherein two ill-matched career people are forced via a publicity mix-up to "take being married." 89m/B VHS. Ray Milland, Loretta Young, Reginald Gardiner, Gail Patrick, Edmund Gwenn, George Metaxa, Charles Halton; *D:* Alexander Hall; *W:* George Seaton.

Dr. Tarr's Torture Dungeon WOOF! *Dr. Jekyll's Dungeon of Darkness; Mansion of Madness* **1975** (R) A mysterious man is sent to the forest to investigate the bizarre behavior of Dr. Tarr who runs a torture asylum. 90m/C VHS, DVD. MX Claudio Brook, Ellen Sherman, Robert Dumont; *D:* Juan Lopez Moctezuma; *W:* Carlos Illescas.

Dr. Terror's House of Horrors 🦴🦴½ **1965** *The Blood Suckers* 1965 On a train, six traveling companions have their fortunes told by a mysterious doctor. Little do they realize that their final destination has changed. Creepy and suspenseful, especially the severed-hand chase sequence. Amazingly, Christopher Lee and Peter Cushing manage to appear in the movie but not the vampire story. 92m/C VHS. GB Christopher Lee, Peter Cushing, Donald Sutherland, Roy Castle, Neil McCallum, Max Adrian, Ann Bell, Michael Gough, John Martin; *D:* Freddie Francis; *W:* Milton Subotsky; *C:* Alan Hume; *M:* Elisabeth Lutyens.

Doctor Who 🦴🦴½ **1996** The late British sci-fi series, which ended in 1989, has been resurrected in this TV movie. The TARDIS is forced down in 1999 San Francisco and renegade Time Lord The Master's sluglike remains escape from the Doctor (McCoy) and into a temporary host body (Roberts). Meanwhile, the Doctor's been hospitalized and a botched operation by Dr. Grace Holloway (Ashbrook) leaves him clinically dead—until he manages to regenerate once again (as McGann). With Grace's help, the Doctor tries to stop his enemy from destroying the world on New Year's Eve in a plot that will also give the Master the Doctor's body as his new home. Production design and special effects are lavish (particularly in relation to the cheesiness of the series). 89m/C VHS. GB CA Paul McGann, Eric Roberts, Daphne Ashbrook, Yee Jee Tso, Sylvester McCoy; *D:* Geoffrey Sax; *M:* John Debney. TV

Doctor X 🦴🦴🦴½ **1932** An armless mad scientist uses a formula for "synthetic flesh" to grow temporary limbs and commit murder. A classic, rarely seen horror oldie, famous for its very early use of two-color Technicolor. 77m/C VHS, DVD. Lionel Atwill, Fay Wray, Lee Tracy, Preston Foster, Arthur Edmund Carewe, Leila Bennett, Mae Busch; *D:* Michael Curtiz; *W:* Earl Baldwin, Robert Tasker; *C:* Ray Rennahan; Richard Towers.

Doctor Zhivago 🦴🦴🦴 **1965** (PG-13) Sweeping adaptation of the Nobel Prize-winning Boris Pasternak novel. An innocent Russian poet-intellectual is caught in the furor and chaos of the Bolshevik Revolution. Essentially a poignant love story filmed as a historical epic. Panoramic film popularized the song "Lara's Theme." Overlong, with often disappointing performances, but gorgeous scenery. Lean was more successful in "Lawrence of Arabia," where there was less need for ensemble acting. 197m/C VHS, DVD. Omar Sharif, Julie Christie, Geraldine Chaplin, Rod Steiger, Alec Guinness, Klaus Kinski, Ralph Richardson, Rita Tushingham, Siobhan McKenna, Tom Courtenay, Bernard Kay, Gerard Tichy, Noel Willman, Geoffrey Keen, Adrienne Corri, Jack MacGowran, Mark Eden, Erik Chitty, Peter Madden, Jose Maria Caffarell, Jeffrey Rockland, Wolf Frees, Lucy Westmore; *D:* David Lean; *W:* Robert Bolt; *C:* Frederick (Freddie) Young; *M:* Maurice Jarre. Oscars '65: Adapt. Screenplay, Art Dir/Set Dec., Color, Color Cinematog., Costume Des. (C), Orig. Score; AFI '98: Top 100; Golden Globes '66: Actor—Drama (Sharif), Director (Lean), Film—Drama, Screenplay, Score; Natl. Bd. of Review '65.

Doctor Zhivago 🦴🦴½ **2003** Miniseries version of the Pasternak novel focuses more on the story's romantic difficulties and slightly less on the politics of the Russian revolution. Noble doctor/poet Yury Zhivago (Matheson) marries his childhood sweetheart and cousin, Tonya (Lara, Knightley). As if this affair weren't dramatic enough, Lara is the obsession of the powerful Kormarovsky (Neill), who is determined to keep her as his possession and who is much more capable of bending with the changing political winds than the idealistic Yury. And if the ending seems different, you're right, it was changed for this re-telling. 214m/C VHS, DVD. GB Hans Matheson, Keira Knightley, Sam Neill, Kris Marshall, Daniele Liotti, Celia Imrie, Bill Paterson, Alexandra Maria Lara, Maryam D'Abo; *D:* Giacomo Campiotti; *W:* Andrew Davies; *C:* Blasco Giurato; *M:* Ludovico Einaudi. TV

Doctors and Nurses 🦴🦴 **1982** A children's satire of soap operas wherein the adults play the children and vice-versa. 90m/C VHS. Rebecca Rigg, Drew Forsythe, Graeme Blundell; *D:* Maurice Murphy.

Doctors' Wives 🦴🦴½ **1970** (R) An adaptation of the Frank Slaughter potboiler about a large city hospital's doctors, nurses, and their respective spouses, with plenty of affairs, medical traumas, and betrayals. 102m/C VHS. Dyan Cannon, Richard Crenna, Gene Hackman, Carroll O'Connor, Rachel Roberts, Janice Rule, Diana Sands, Ralph Bellamy, John Colicos; *D:* George Schaefer; *W:* Daniel Taradash; *C:* Charles B(ryant) Lang Jr.; *M:* Elmer Bernstein.

Dodes 'ka-den 🦴🦴🦴½ **1970** *Clickety Clack* In this departure from his samurai-genre films, Kurosawa depicts a throng of fringe-dwelling Tokyo slum inhabitants in a semi-surreal manner. Fascinating presentation and content. 140m/C VHS, DVD. JP Yoshitaka Zushi, Junzaburo Ban, Kiyoko Tange; *W:* Shinobu Hashimoto, Hideo Oguni, Akira Kurosawa; *D:* Akira Kurosawa; *C:* Takao Saito, Yasumichi Fukuzawa; *M:* Toru Takemitsu.

Dodge City 🦴🦴🦴 **1939** Flynn stars as Wade Hutton, a roving cattleman who becomes the sheriff of Dodge City. His job: to run a ruthless outlaw and his gang out of town. De Havilland serves as Flynn's love interest (as she did in many previous films. A broad and colorful shoot-em-up! 104m/C VHS, DVD. Errol Flynn, Olivia de Havilland, Bruce Cabot, Ann Sheridan, Alan Hale, Frank McHugh, Victor Jory, Henry Travers, Charles Halton; *D:* Michael Curtiz; *M:* Max Steiner.

Dodgeball: A True Underdog Story 🦴🦴 **2004** (PG-13) Likable, easygoing schmoe (Vaughn) runs a gym for underachievers in direct competition with big box fitness fascist (Stiller) across the street. Stiller finds a way to expose Vaughn's financial failings to put him out of business. Vaughn enlists aid of his misfit patrons to win the pot of a professional dodgeball tournament—but they must beat Stiller's elite team first. Slobs vs. snobs comedy in the "Caddyshack/Meatballs" tradition, with plenty of crotch-crunching and boob humor. Don't miss Tom's crusty coach, who hurls wrenches as training. Nothing too original, but should please the frat crowd. Cameos by William Shatner, Lance Armstrong, David Hasselhoff, and Chuck Norris. 96m/C DVD, UMD. US Ben Stiller, Vince Vaughn, Christine Taylor, Justin Long, Jason Bateman, Gary Cole, Missi Pyle, Stephen (Steve) Root, William Shatner, Rip Torn, Hank Azaria, Chris(topher) Williams, Alan Tudyk, David Hasselhoff; *Cameos:* Chuck Norris, Lance Armstrong; *D:* Rawson Marshall Thurber; *W:* Rawson Marshall Thurber; *C:* Jerzy Zielinski; *M:* Theodore Shapiro.

Dodson's Journey 🦴🦴½ **2001** Worried about the impact their impending divorce will have on 10-year-old Maggie (Morton), dad James (Elliott) decides to take his daughter on a bonding fly-fishing trip. Adapted from Dodson's book "Faithful Travelers." 120m/C VHS, DVD. David James Elliott, Alicia Morton, Ellen Burstyn, Brenda James, Tantoo Cardinal, Nanci Chambers; *D:* Gregg Champion; *W:* John Pielmeier; *C:* Attila Szalay; *M:* Joseph Conlan. TV

Dodsworth 🦴🦴🦴½ **1936** The lives of a self-made American tycoon and his wife are drastically changed when they take a tour of Europe. The success of their marriage seems questionable as they re-evaluate their lives. Huston excels as does the rest of the cast in this film, based upon the Sinclair Lewis novel. 101m/B VHS, DVD. Walter Huston, David Niven, Paul Lukas, John Payne, Mary Astor, Ruth Chatterton, Maria Ouspenskaya, Charles Halton; *D:* William Wyler; *W:* Sidney Howard; *C:* Rudolph Mate; *M:* Alfred Newman. Natl. Film Reg. '90; N.Y. Film Critics '36: Actor (Huston).

The Doe Boy 🦴🦴 **2001** A hemophiliac half-Cherokee youth tries to live up to his father's expectations, free himself from an over-protective mother, and forge an identity for himself. He also has to overcome the stigma of accidently killing a female deer instead of a buck during his first hunting trip (giving him his nickname and the movie its title). Redroad's directorial debut doesn't break much new ground, but deals with the themes in a satisfying way. Fine cast helps things along nicely. 83m/C VHS, DVD. James Duval, Kevin Anderson, Andrew J. Ferchland, Jeri Arredondo, Jim Metzler, Gordon Tootoosis, Robert C. Anthony; *D:* Randy Redroad; *W:* Randy Redroad; *C:* Laszlo Kadar; *M:* Adam Dorn.

Does This Mean We're Married? 🦴🦴 **1990** (PG-13) A stand-up comedian is trying to find success in the comedy clubs of Paris but without her green card she may soon be deported. She finds a sleazy marriage broker who fixes her up with a womanizing songwriter who needs money. As usual, immigration officials suspect that the marriage is a fake and the mismatched couple must live together to prove them wrong. 93m/C VHS. Patsy Kensit, Stephane Freiss; *D:* Carol Wiseman.

Dog Bite Dog 🦴🦴🦴 **2006** Violent, if routine. Hong Kong action pic. A Cambodian hit man (Chen) is up against a cop (Lee) with anger issues. Chinese, Thai, and Cambodian with subtitles. 108m/C DVD. HK JP Edison Chen, Sam Lee, Suet Lam, Weiying Pei, Siu-lai Cheang; *D:* Pou-soi Cheang; *W:* Matt Chow, Kam-yuen Szeto; *C:* Yuen Man Fung; *M:* Ben Cheung.

Dog Day 🦴🦴🦴 **1983** *Canicule* An American traitor, who is on the lam from the government, and his cronies, takes refuge on a small farm. A surprise awaits him when the farmers come up with an unusual plan to bargain for his life. 101m/C VHS, DVD. FR Lee Marvin, Miou-Miou, Victor Lanoux; *D:* Yves Boisset.

Dog Day Afternoon 🦴🦴🦴🦴½ **1975** (R) Based on a true story, this taut, yet fantastic thriller centers on a bi-sexual and his slow-witted buddy who rob a bank to obtain money to fund a sex change operation for the ringleader's lover. Pacino is breathtaking in his role as the frustrated robber, caught in a trap of his own devising. Very controversial for its language and subject matter when released, it nevertheless became a huge success. Director Lumet keeps up the pace, fills the screen with pathos without gross sentiment. 130m/C VHS, DVD, Blu-ray Disc, HD DVD. Dominic Chianese, Al Pacino, David Charles Durning, James Broderick, Chris Sarandon, Carol Kane, Lance Henriksen, Dick Anthony Williams; *D:* Sidney Lumet; *W:* Frank Pierson; *C:* Victor Kemper. Oscars '75: Orig. Screenplay; British Acad. '75: Actor (Pacino); Natl. Bd. of Review '75: Support. Actor (Durning); Writers Guild '75: Orig. Screenplay.

Dog Eat Dog 🦴🦴 **2001** (R) *Eimer Frisst den Anderen; La Morte Vestita di Dollari* 1964 Centering on a heist scheme by Mitchell, this one has nothing to offer except Mansfield's attributes. 86m/B VHS, DVD. Cameron Mitchell, Jayne Mansfield, Isa Miranda; *D:* Ray Nazarro.

Dog Gone Love 🦴🦴½ **2003** (R) While doing research at the local vet office, struggling author Steven meets foxy assistant Rebecca who thinks he's gay. So he figures faking it would be fun until—oh my!—he falls for her. Plot is all bark and no bite. 89m/C VHS, DVD. Lindsay Sloane, Richard Kind, Christopher Coppola, Brian Poth, Tom McGowan, Jordan Ladd, Chris Elwood, Marissa Hall, James Warwick, Alexander Chaplin, Marina Black, John Cantwell, Carmen Mormino, Alexandra Boyd, Jenni Pulos, Paul Korver, Steve Susskind, Mikyla, Brian O'Hare, Laura Pinner, Brian T. Lynch; *D:* Rob Lundsgaard; *W:* Rob Lundsgaard; *C:* Kristian Bernier; *M:* William V. Malpede. VIDEO

A Dog of Flanders 🦴🦴½ **1959** A young Dutch boy and his grandfather find a severely beaten dog and restore it to health. 96m/C VHS, DVD. David Ladd, Donald Crisp, Theodore Bikel, Max Croiset, Monique Ahrens; *D:* James B. Clark.

A Dog of Flanders 🦴🦴 **1999** (PG) Fifth screen version of Marie Louise de la Ramee's 1872 children's story is put to sleep by slow pacing and murky settings. Orphan Nello (Kissner) and his grandfather Jehan (Warden) find an abused dog and nurse it back to health. The boy and his dog team up to support the household as Jehan's health begins to fade. Nello is noticed sketching in the town square by artist Michel (Voight), who then befriends and encourages the boy. As his artistic gifts flower, he attempts to win his childhood sweetheart Aloise (Monet) over the protests of her father. The rather depressing climax of the original story is replaced by a brighter ending in an attempt to make the movie more child-friendly, but the uneven acting and accents won't even fool the kiddies. 100m/C VHS, DVD. Jack Warden, Jon Voight, Jeremy James Kissner, Jesse James, Cheryl Ladd, Bruce McGill, Steven Hartley, Dirk Lavrysen, Andrew Bicknell, Antje De Boeck; *D:* Kevin Brodie; *W:* Robert Singer, Kevin Brodie; *C:* Walther Vanden Ende; *M:* Richard Friedman.

Dog Park 🦴🦴 **1998** (R) Andy (Wilson) and Lorna (Henstridge) have only their doggy companions to keep them warm after their respective lovers take a hike. At least until they find each other while walking their pups. Not that the course of true love (or even dating) will run smoothly. Pleasant enough romantic comedy but Henstridge seems out of her element. 91m/C VHS, DVD. CA Luke Wilson, Natasha Henstridge, Janeane Garofalo, Bruce McCulloch, Kathleen Robertson, Kristen Lehman, Mark McKinney, Gordon Currie, Amie Carey, Harland Williams; *D:* Bruce McCulloch; *W:* Bruce McCulloch; *C:* David Makin; *M:* Craig Northey, Genie '99: Support. Actor (McKinney).

Dog Pound Shuffle 🦴🦴🦴 **1975** (PG) Two drifters form a new song-and-dance act in order to raise the funds necessary to win their dog's freedom from the pound. Charming Canadian production. 98m/C VHS. Ron Moody, David Soul; *D:* Jeffrey Bloom; *W:* Jeffrey Bloom.

The Dog Problem 🦴🦴 **2006** (R) Solo (Ribisi) is at a personal and professional crossroads after squandering the rewards of his success on drugs, women, and therapy. At his last session with Dr. Noumand (Cheadle), the good psychiatrist suggests he get a pet to help overcome his loneliness. Upon doing so, his new pooch is soon chomped by a formidable hound in the care of a spunky stripper (Collins). This leads to a most unusual relationship plagued with canine complications. Holds your interest, develops nicely, with just the right touch of comedic urban disdain. 89m/C DVD. Giovanni Ribisi, Don Cheadle, Lynn Collins, Kevin Corrigan, Mena Suvari, Scott Caan, Joanna Krupa; *D:* Scott Caan; *W:* Scott Caan; *C:* Phil Parmet; *M:* Mark Mothersbaugh.

Dog Soldiers 🦴🦴 **2001** (R) Military werewolf flick finds a British army squad on manuevers in the Scottish highlands. When they find their Special Ops wargame foes half-eaten except for leader Ryan, they're set upon by the creatures. The survivors are rescued by a passing female zoologist and taken to a cabin to hold up for night. Pic becomes an "Assault on Precinct 13"-type siege as the creatures try to get to the soldiers, some of whom have taken on distinctly canine tendencies. Hit-and-miss black humor, paired with too-British banter and low-tech effects make this one a bit hard to swallow for most. 104m/C VHS, DVD. GB LU Sean Pertwee, Kevin McKidd, Liam Cunningham, Thomas Lockyer, Emma Cleasby; *D:* Neil Marshall; *W:* Neil Marshall; *M:* Mark Thomas.

Dog Star Man 🐾🐾🐾 1964 The silent epic by the dean of experimental American film depicts man's spiritual and physical conflicts through Brakhage's characteristically freeform collage techniques. *78m/C VHS, DVD. D: Stan Brakhage. Natl Film Reg. '92.*

The Dog Who Stopped the War 🐾🐾 1984 (R) A Canadian children's film about a dog who puts a hat to an escalating snowball fight between rival gangs. *90m/C VHS, DVD. CA Cedric Jourde, Andre Melancon; W: Roger Cantin, Daniele Patenaud; C: Francois Protat; M: Germain Gauthier.*

Dogfight 🐾🐾🐾 1991 (R) It's 1963 and a baby-faced Marine and his buddies are spending their last night in San Francisco before leaving the U.S. for a tour of duty in Vietnam. They agree to have a "dogfight," a competition to see who can bring the ugliest date to a party. Birdlace (Phoenix) chooses Taylor, a shy, average-looking waitress who dreams of becoming a folk singer and realizes too late that she doesn't deserve the treatment he's about to subject her to. This quiet film didn't see a wide release, but is worth renting due to the splendid performances of Phoenix and Taylor. *94m/C VHS, DVD. River Phoenix, Lili Taylor, Richard Panebianco, Anthony Clark, Mitchell Whitfield, Elizabeth (E.G. Daily) Daily, Holly Near, Brendan Fraser, Margaret "Peg" Phillips; D: Nancy Savoca; M: Jimmie Haskell.*

Dogma 🐾🐾🐾 1999 (R) Smith packs a lot into his brave, controversial comedy on Catholicism and, as a Catholic himself, illustrates that he vents with religion. He vents with a film that's both devilishly funny and agonizingly boring. A great cast does good work, including Affleck and Damon as two cast out angels with a plan to re-enter heaven. Rock plays an angry apostle, Hayek is a muse turned stripper, and Rickman is the voice of God informing an abortion worker (Fiorentino) that she's to stop the angels. Rounding out the motley crew is Carlin as a cardinal. The first half is loaded with on-target jokes, but laughs are hard to find in the second hour, which falls victim to excessive religious yakety-schmakety. Smith's a talented screenwriter, unfortunately this time out, it's his directing that's really a sin. *125m/C VHS, DVD. Ben Affleck, Matt Damon, Linda Fiorentino, Chris Rock, Salma Hayek, Jason Lee, George Carlin, Alan Rickman, Jason Mewes, Janeane Garofalo, Kevin Smith, Alanis Morissette, Bud Cort, Jeff Anderson, Guinevere Turner; D: Kevin Smith; W: Kevin Smith; C: Robert Yeoman; M: Howard Shore.*

The Dogfighters 🐾🐾 1995 (R) Ex-Air Force pilot Rowdy Wells (Davi) is blackmailed into trying to destroy a plutonium plant in an eastern European country. That is, if Rowdy can survive an air battle with nemesis Lothar Krasna (Godunov). Small budget is reflected in the mediocre aerial sequences. *94m/C VHS, Robert Davi, Alexander Godunov, Ben Gazzara, Lara Harrow; D: Barry Zetlin; W: Sean Smith, Anthony Stark; C: Levie Isaacks; M: Jimmie Haskell.*

A Dog's Breakfast 🐾🐾½ 2007 Black comedy at its funniest. Patrick hates his younger sister Marilyn's fiance Ryan so much that he decides to murder him. Title is British slang for making a mess of things, although there is a dog (named Mars), and what he eats is important (and gross). *88m/C DVD. David Hewlett, Paul McGillion, Rachel Luttrell, Christopher Judge, Kate Hewlett; D: David Hewlett; W: David Hewlett; C: Alfred Menard; M: Tim Williams. VIDEO*

Dogs in Space 🐾🐾 1987 A low-budget Australian film about a clique of aimless Melbourne rock kids in '978. Caught somewhere between post-hippie-dom and punk. free love and heroin addiction. Acclaimed. Includes music by "lutchence, Brian Eno, Iggy Pop, and others. *109m/C VHS. AU Michael Hutchence, Saskia Post, Nique Needles, Tony Helou, Deanna Bond; D: Richard Lowenstein; M:*

Dogville 🐾🐾½ 2003 (R) Another "love it or hate it" offering from director von Trier brings us yet another troubled woman, Grace (Kidman), who is on the run from mobsters and picks Dogville (a made-up U.S. locale) to hide out, even offering up free labor to the townsfolk in return for their silence. But things go south for her as she is persecuted and eventually they do an about-face and consider ratting her out for a hefty reward...though she's savvy enough to fight back. Set during the Depression and filmed on a minimalist set similar to the Thorton Wilder classic "Our Town," though the two stories are complete contradictions The Danish von Trier may be perceived as hateful toward the American way of life, whereas many will find his latest effort to be a memorably appalling, thought-provoking tale with Kidman flourishing in the challenging lead role. *178m/C DVD. DK, NL, SW, FR, NO, FI, GE/TN Nicole Kidman, Lauren Bacall, Paul Bettany, Philip Baker Hall, Blair Brown, James Caan, Patricia Clarkson, Jeremy Davies, Ben Gazzara, Siobhan Fallon, Zeljko Ivanek, Udo Kier, Harriet Andersson, Jean-Marc Barr, Thom Hoffman, Bill Raymond, Chloe Sevigny, Stellan Skarsgard; D: Lars von Trier; W: Lars von Trier; C: Anthony Dod Mantle; Nar: John Hurt.*

Dogwatch 🐾🐾 1997 (R) San Francisco police detective Charlie Falon (Elliott) tries to avenge his partner's murder but kills the wrong man. Thus he learns dirty cops are behind the crime. Thriller takes the easy road by solving everything with violence. *100m/C VHS. Sam Elliott, Esai Morales, Paul Sorvino, Dan Lauria, Richard Gilliland, Jessica Steen, Mimi (Meyer) Craven; D: John Langley; W: Martin Zurla; C: Robert Yeoman; M: Lennie Niehaus. CABLE*

The Dogs of War 🐾🐾½ 1981 (R) A graphic depiction of a group of professional mercenaries, driven by nothing but their quest for wealth and power, hired to overthrow the dictator of a new West African nation. Has some weak moments which break up the continuity of the movie. Based on the novel by Frederick Forsyth. *102m/C VHS, DVD. GB Christopher Walken, Tom Berenger, Colin Blakely, Paul Freeman, Hugh Millais, Victoria Tennant, JoBeth Williams; D: John Irvin; W: Gary De Vore; C: Jack Cardiff; M: Geoffrey Burgon.*

Dogs of Hell 🐾½ 1983 (R) The sheriff of an idyllic resort community must stop a pack of killer dogs from terrorizing the residents. *90m/C VHS. Earl Owensby, Bill Gribble, Jerry Rushing; D: Worth Keeter.*

Dogs: The Rise and Fall of an All-Girl Bookie Joint 🐾🐾 1996 On the surface, this is a story about some twentysomething women who are bad at relationships and can't pay the rent. To solve one of their problems they turn their apartment into a bookie joint. However, undemeath there is the story of how girl who has just lost her mother and needs money to pay for her funeral. The thread that weaves it all together is the drive to survive and rise above what life has given you, or sometimes what life limitations, but overall it is a good story with competent acting. *88m/C DVD. Pam Columbus, Pam Gray, Eve Annenberg, Toby Huss, Leo Marks, Amedo D'Adamo; D: Eve Annenberg; W: Eve Annenberg; C: Wolfgang Held.*

Dogtown 🐾🐾 1997 Former beauty queen/cheerleader Dorothy Stiemen feels trapped in her small town of Cuba, Missouri. Her longtime boyfriend Ezra Good is a bitter ex-athlete stuck in a dull job who sometimes gets violent. Then high school classmate Philip returns to town. Although he's a struggling actor, Philip is treated like a celebrity, and Dorothy starts giving him the eye. Tensions arise as they all realize how dissatisfied each of them are. *96m/C VHS, DVD. Mary Stuart Masterson, Trevor St. John, Jon Favreau, Rory Cochrane, Karen Black, Natasha Gregson Wagner, Maureen McCormick, Harold Russell, John Livingston, Shawnee Smith; D: George Hickenlooper; M: George Hickenlooper; C: Kramer Morgenthau; M: Steve Stevens.*

Doing Time on Maple Drive 🐾🐾½ 1992 College boy Matt (McNamara) brings his fiancee Alison (Loughlin) home to meet his seemingly tranquil but secretly dysfunctional family. Mom (Besch) expect their older brother Tim (Carrey) is a perfect but elder brother Tim (Carrey) is a not-so-secret alcoholic, neurotic daughter Karen's (Brock) marriage is in trouble, and Matt himself is hiding a big secret that threatens the harmonious family facade. Made for TV. *90m/C VHS, DVD. William McNamara, James B. Sikking, Bibi Besch, Jim Carrey, Lori Loughlin, Jayne Brook, David Byron; D: Ken Karpman. TV*

Dolemite 🐾½ 1975 (R) An ex-con attempts to settle the score with some of his former inmates. He forms a band of kung-fu savvy ladies. Strange combination of action and comedy. *88m/C VHS, DVD. Rudy Ray Moore, Jerry Jones, D'Urville Martin, Lady Reeds; D: D'Urville Martin; W: Jerry Jones; C: Nicholas Josef von Sternberg; M: Arthur Wright.*

Dolemite 2: Human Tornado 🐾🐾 The Human Tornado 1976 (R) Nobody ever said Moore was for everybody's taste. But, hey, when blaxploitation movies were the rage, Rudy the standup comic was out there rapping through a series of trashy movies that, when viewed today, have survived the test of time. This one's just as vile, violent, and sexist as the day it was released. When Rudy is surprised in bed with a white sheriff's wife, he flees and meets up with a madam and a house of kung-fu-skilled girls who are embroiled in a fight with a local mobster. *96m/C VHS, DVD. Rudy Ray Moore, Lady Reeds, Ernie Hudson, Howard Jackson, Herb Graham, Jerry Jones, Jimmy Lynch; D: Cliff Roquemore; W: Jerry Jones; C: Fred Conde, Bob Wilson; M: Arthur Wright.*

The Doll 🐾🐾 La Poupee; He, She or It 1962 A lonely night watchman happens upon two burglars and, in the chase, the thieves knock over a mannequin. The watchman reports the mannequin stolen, brings it home and begins to have conversations with it. Soon, the doll's needs cause him to steal jewelry and clothes, until his brutish neighbor discovers his secrets. In Swedish with English subtitles. *96m/B VHS. SW Per Oscarsson, Gio Petre, Tor Isedal, Elsa Prawitz; D: Arne Mattson.*

Doin' Time 🐾 1985 (R) At the John Dillinger Memorial Penitentiary, the inmates take over the prison under the supervision of warden "Mongo." Silliness prevails. *80m/C VHS, Jeff Altman, Dey Young, Richard Mulligan, John Vernon, Colleen Camp, Melanie Chartoff, Graham Jarvis, Pat McCormick, Eddie Velez, Jimmie Walker, Judy Landers, Nicholas Worth, Mike Mazurki, Muhammad Ali, Melinda Fee, Francesca "Kitten" Natividad, Ron Palillo; D: George Mendeluk; W: George Mendeluk, Dee Caruso, Ron Zwang, Franelle Silver; M: Charles Fox, Matthau.*

Doing Time for Patsy Cline 🐾🐾 1997 Yearning to make it big in faraway Nashville, Ralph (Day) forsakes his parents' down-under farm with guitar in hand. Hitchhiking with punk Boyd (Roxburgh) and pretty Patsy (Otto)—who claims country crooner Patsy Cline as her namesake—he finds out free rides don't come cheap. Patsy flees, leaving the boys in the pen, though there's not much suspense to their fate as director Kennedy's story repeatedly jumps back and forth in time between locales. *95m/C DVD. Richard Roxburgh, Miranda Otto, Matthew Day, Tony Barry, Kir Paramore, Laurence Coy; D: Chris Kennedy; W: Chris Kennedy; C: Andrew Lesnie; M: Peter Best.*

Doin' Time on Planet Earth 🐾🐾 1988 (PG-13) A young boy feels out of place with his family and is convinced by two strange people (aliens themselves?) that he is really an extraterrestrial. Amusing, aimless fun directed by the son of Walter Matthau. *83m/C VHS. Adam West, Candice Azzara, Hugh O'Brian, Matt Adler, Timothy Patrick Murphy, Roddy McDowall, Maureen Stapleton, Andrea Thompson; D: Charles Matthau.*

Dollar 🐾🐾 1997 Reaming to make it helps move her family to Detroit in the 1940s. Petrie's direction moves the story along and creates a lovely period vision. *140m/C VHS. Jane Fonda, Levon Helm, Geraldine Page, Amanda Plummer, Susan Kingsley; D: Daniel Petrie. TV*

The Doll Squad 🐾 Hustler Squad 1973 (PG) Three voluptuous special agents fight an ex-CIA agent out to rule the world. *95m/C VHS, DVD. Michael Ansara, Francine York, Anthony Eisley, John N. Carter, Rafael Campos, William Bagdad, Lisa Todd, Lillian Garrett, Herb Robbins, Tua Satana; D: Ted V. Mikels; W: Ted V. Mikels, Jack Pichean, Pam Eddy; C: Anthony Salinas; M: Nicholas Carras.*

Doll Face 🐾🐾½ Come Back to Me 1946 Story of a stripper who wants to go legit and make it on Broadway. Film was adapted from the play "The Naked Genius" by tease queen Gypsy Rose Lee. 🐾🐾: Dig You Later; Here Comes Heaven Again; Chico-Chico; Somebody's Walkin' In My Dreams; Red Hot and Beautiful. *80m/B VHS, Vivian Blaine, Dennis O'Keefe, Perry Como, Carmen Miranda, Reed Hadley; D: Lewis Seiler.*

Dollman 🐾🐾 1990 (R) An ultra-tough cop from an Earth-like planet (even swear words are the same) crashes in the South Bronx—and on this world he's only 13 inches tall. The filmmakers squander a great premise and cast with bloody shoot-outs and a sequel-ready non-ending. *86m/C VHS, DVD. Tim Thomerson, Jackie Earle Haley, Kamala Lopez, Humberto Ortiz, Nicholas Guest, Michael Halsey, Eugene Robert Glazer, Judd Omen, Frank Collison, Vincent Klyn; D: Albert Pyun.*

Dollman vs. Demonic Toys 🐾🐾 1993 (R) Let's combine elements from three separate films and make one disgusting sequel. "Dollman," the 13-inch cop from the planet Arturos; his new girlfriend, Dollchick, who was shrunk to a diminutive 10 inches in "Bad Channels"; and tough cop Judith Grey, who's once again battling those loathsome playthings from "Demonic Toys." If you feel the need for a plot—Dollchick is kidnapped by Baby Doll and needs to be rescued. *84m/C VHS. Tim Thomerson, Tracy Scoggins, Melissa Behr, Phil Brock, Phil Fondacaro; D: Charles Band; W: Craig Hamann; M: Richard Band.*

Dollars 🐾🐾🐾 The Heist 1971 (R) A bank employee and his clizzy call-girl assistant plan to steal from the German facility's assets while installing its new security system. Lighthearted fun. *119m/C VHS. Warren Beatty, Goldie Hawn, Gert Frobe, Scott Brady, Robert Webber; D: Richard Brooks; W: Richard Brooks; M: Quincy Jones.*

The Dollmaker 🐾🐾½ 1984 Excellent adaptation of Harriette Arnow's novel. A strong-willed Kentucky mother of five helps move her family to Detroit in the 1940s. Petrie's direction moves the story along and creates a lovely period vision. *140m/C VHS. Jane Fonda, Levon Helm, Geraldine Page, Amanda Plummer, Susan Kingsley; D: Daniel Petrie. TV*

Dolls 🐾🐾🐾 2002 Lyrical Japanese film interviews three character studies into a wistful movie about devotion and lost love. A man literally ties himself to the girl he loves after realizing his weak-mindedness drove her to attempt suicide. A gang lord remembers the promise given to a girlfriend 30 years earlier. Thirty years

Dolls 🐾🐾½ 1987 (R) A group of people is stranded during a storm in an old, creepy mansion. As the night wears on, they are attacked by hundreds of antique dolls. Tongue-in-cheek. *77m/C VHS, DVD. Ian Patrick Williams, Carolyn Purdy-Gordon, Carrie Lorraine, Stephen Lee, Guy Rolfe, Bunty Bailey, Cassie Stuart, Hilary Mason; D: Stuart Gordon; M: Ed Naha; M: Richard Band.*

later he returns to the park where they met, finding her still waiting. The final chapter fumbles the connection a bit, focusing on a famous pop star becoming disfigured in an auto accident. She flees the public eye, only to let one devoted fan into her life. Lush photography and landscapes are pure dazzling eye candy, but may turn off some audiences. **113m/C DVD.** Tatsuya Mihashi, Chieko Matsubara, Miho Kanno, Hidetoshi Nishima, Kyoko Fukada, Sebastian Blenkov; **D:** Takeshi "Beat" Kitano; **C:** Katsumi Yanagijima; **M:** Joe Hisaishi.

A Doll's House ♪♪½ **1959** An all-star cast is featured in this original TV production of Henrik Ibsen's classic play about an independent woman's quest for freedom in 19th-century Norway. **89m/B VHS.** Julie Harris, Christopher Plummer, Jason Robards Jr., Hume Cronyn, Eileen Heckart, Richard Thomas; **D:** George Schaefer. **TV**

A Doll's House ♪♪½ **1973 (G)** Fonda plays Nora, a subjugated 19th-century housewife who breaks free to establish herself as an individual. Based on Henrik Ibsen's classic play; some controversy regarding Fonda's interpretation of her role. **98m/C DVD.** Jane Fonda, Edward Fox, Trevor Howard, David Warner, Delphine Seyrig; **D:** Joseph Losey; **W:** Christopher Hampton; **M:** John Barry.

A Doll's House ♪♪♪ **1973 (G)** A Canadian production of the Henrik Ibsen play about a Norwegian woman's search for independence. **96m/C VHS.** *CA* Claire Bloom, Anthony Hopkins, Ralph Richardson, Denholm Elliott, Anna Massey, Edith Evans; **D:** Patrick Garland.

Dolly Dearest ♪½ **1992 (R)** Strange things happening after an American family takes over a run-down Mexican doll factory. They create a new doll called "Dolly Dearest" with deadly results. In the same tradition as the "Chucky" series. **94m/C VHS, DVD.** Rip Torn, Sam Bottoms, Denise Crosby; **D:** Maria Lease.

The Dolly Sisters ♪♪½ **1946** Competent musical about sisters Jenny (Grable) and Rosie (Haver), who became turn-of-the-century vaudeville stars and also find romance. Good songs, extravagent costuming, fine support work, and the charms of the two leading actresses provide simple enjoyment. ♫ I Can't Begin to Tell You; I'm Always Chasing Rainbows; Powder, Lipstick and Rouge; Give Me the Moonlight; On the Mississippi; We Have Been Around; Carolina in the Morning; Arrah Go On, I'm Gonna Go Back to Oregon; The Darktown Strutter's Ball. **114m/C VHS, DVD.** Betty Grable, June Haver, John Payne, Frank Latimore, S.Z. Sakall, Reginald Gardiner, Gene Sheldon, Sig Rumann; **D:** Irving Cummings; **W:** Marian Spitzer, John Larkin; **C:** Ernest Palmer.

Dolores Claiborne ♪♪♪ **1994 (R)** Stephen King gets the Hollywood treatment again (the check cleared, King approved) with better results than previous outings (remember "Needful Things"?). Successful but neurotic New York journalist Selena (Leigh) confronts her troubled past when coarse, hard-talking mom Dolores (Bates) is accused of murdering her wealthy employer (Parfitt). Plummer is vengeful detective John Mackey who, like everyone else on the fictitious Maine island, believes Dolores murdered her husband 15 years before. Top-notch performances by Bates and Leigh highlight this sometimes manipulative tale. Strathairn is wonderfully despicable as the stereotypically abusive husband and father. **132m/C VHS, DVD.** Kathy Bates, Jennifer Jason Leigh, Christopher Plummer, Judy Parfitt, David Strathairn, John C. Reilly; **D:** Taylor Hackford; **W:** Tony Gilroy; **C:** Gabriel Beristain; **M:** Danny Elfman.

The Dolphin ♪♪½ **1987** A dolphin visits a Brazilian fishing village each full moon, turns himself into a man, and casts a spell of seduction over the women. Villagers are both enchanted and angered by the dolphin-man, since his presence creates desire in local women but scares fish from the waters. In Portuguese with English subtitles. **95m/C VHS.** *BR* Carlos Alberto Riccelli, Cassia Kiss, Ney Latorraca; **D:** Walter Lima Jr.; **W:** Walter Lima Jr.

Domestic Disturbance ♪♪ **2001 (PG-13)** Lame entry in the "evil stepparent" genre features Travolta as Frank, a hard-working boat builder who shares custody of his son Danny (O'Leary) with ex-wife Susan (Polo). Danny starts acting out by getting in trouble and lying after Susan gets involved with suave local businessman Rick (Vaughn). Although Danny is clued into Rick's dark side from the start, it takes the appearance of Ray (Buscemi), a sleazy hood from Rick's shady past, to awaken Frank's suspicion. When Danny hides in Rick's van and witnesses Ray's murder, nobody believes him except his dad. The stage is set for the "good dad" versus "bad dad" showdown, which is handled as clumsily and unbelievably as possible. Most of the performances seem listless, with the exception of Vaughn as the oily villain and O'Leary as the terrorized kid. **89m/C VHS, DVD.** *US* John Travolta, Vince Vaughn, Teri Polo, Matt O'Leary, Ruben Santiago-Hudson, Susan Floyd, Steve Buscemi, Angelica Torn; **D:** Harold Becker; **W:** Lewis Colick; **C:** Michael Seresin; **M:** Mark Mancina.

Dominick & Eugene ♪♪♪ **1988 (PG-13)** Dominick is a little slow, but he makes a fair living as a garbageman—good enough to put his brother through medical school. Both men struggle with the other's faults and weaknesses, as they learn the meaning of family and friendship. Well-acted, especially by Hulce, never melodramatic or weak. **96m/C VHS, DVD.** Ray Liotta, Tom Hulce, Jamie Lee Curtis, Todd Graff, Bill Cobbs, David Strathairn; **D:** Robert M. Young; **W:** Alvin Sargent, Corey Blechman; **C:** Curtis Clark; **M:** Trevor Jones.

Dominion ♪♪½ **1994 (R)** Six buddies take off for a weekend hunting trip that turns deadly when a murderous hunter believes they've trespassed on his territory and begins stalking them. **98m/C VHS.** Michael (Mike) Papajohn, Brad Johnson, Brion James, Tim Thomerson, Woody Brown, Glenn Morshower, Richard Riehle, Geoffrey Blake; **D:** Michael Kehoe; **W:** Woody Brown, Michael Kehoe.

Dominion: Prequel to the Exorcist ♪♪½ **2005 (R)** Paul Schrader's dark and intensely serious horror movie about demon-possession gone wrong. Released less because of the interest in another "Exorcist" spin-off, but more in hopes of cashing in on the curiosity to see such an unusual studio maneuver. This "prequel" disappointed the Morgan Creek execs, who then decided to reshoot the entire movie with a new director and a few new actors. That movie became known as "The Beginning." With nothing to lose, the studio plunked in some CGI and released their original investment under this slightly different title. It's better than the reshoot, and makes for a fascinating experiment when paired up scene-for-scene with "The Beginning." **116m/C DVD.** *US* Stellan Skarsgard, Gabriel Mann, Clara Bellar, Andrew French, Israel Aduramo, Eddie Osei, Antoine Kamerling, Julian Wadham, Ilario Bisi-Pedro; **D:** Paul Schrader; **W:** William Wisher, Caleb Carr; **C:** Vittorio Storaro; **M:** Trevor Rabin, Angelo Badalamenti, Dog Fashion Disco.

Dominique Is Dead ♪♪ **1979 (PG)** A woman is driven to suicide by her greedy husband; now someone is trying to drive him mad. A.K.A. "Dominique" and "Avenging Spirit." **95m/C VHS, DVD.** Cliff Robertson, Jean Simmons, Jenny Agutter, Simon Ward, Ron Moody; **D:** Michael Anderson Sr.

Domino ♪ **1988 (R)** A beautiful woman and a mysterious guy link up for sex, murder and double-crosses. Dubbed. Tries to be arty and avant-garde, but only succeeds in being a piece of soft-core fluff. **95m/C VHS, UMD.** *IT* Brigitte Nielsen, Tomas Arana, Daniela Alzone; **D:** Ivana Massetti.

Domino ♪♪½ **2005 (R)** Scott, who proved that he could hang with the Tarantino crowd in "True Romance," uses every trick in his cinematic arsenal to bring to life the "sort of" true story of model-turned-bounty-hunter Domino Harvey (Knightley). Domino joins the crew of a bail-bondsman, looking for passion and thrills, and finds herself in the center of screenwriter Richard Kelly's perfect storm of bombastic sex, gunplay, criminal conspiracies, and reality TV. The plot tends to drag and the supporting cast overwhelms Knightley a bit, but you've got to love a movie that brings together Christopher Walken, Mickey Rourke, and 90210's Ian Ziering, with every camera shot that Tarantino and Oliver Stone were too chicken to use themselves. **128m/C DVD.** *US* Keira Knightley, Mickey Rourke, Edgar Ramirez, Delroy Lindo, Mo'Nique, Lucy Liu, Jacqueline Bisset, Mena Suvari, Macy Gray, Jacqueline Bisset, Dabney Coleman, Brian A(ustin) Green, Ian Ziering, Stanley Kamel, Peter Jacobson, T.K. Carter, Kel O'Neill, Shondrella Avery, Lew Temple, Tom Waits, Rizwan Abbasi; **D:** Tony Scott; **W:** Richard Kelly, Steve Barancik; **C:** Dan Mindel; **M:** Harry Gregson-Williams.

The Domino Principle ♪½ **1977** *The Domino Killings 1977* **(R)** It's got nothing to do with pizza. Viet vet Hackman is a doltish convict sprung from the joint by a government organization to do some dirty work: working as a political assassin. Heavyhanded direction and lack of suspense make it less than it should be. **97m/C VHS, DVD.** Gene Hackman, Candice Bergen, Richard Widmark, Mickey Rooney, Edward Albert, Eli Wallach; **D:** Stanley Kramer; **C:** Fred W. Koenekamp; **M:** Billy Goldenberg.

Don Daredevil Rides Again ♪ **1951** A greedy political boss tries to take over homesteaders' claims for their mineral rights. One settler adopts the identity of an ancestor (Don Daredevil), and a black mask, and becomes a frontier avenger. A 12-episode serial. **180m/B VHS.** Ken Curtis, Aline Towne, Roy Barcroft; **D:** Fred Brannon.

The Don Is Dead ♪♪½ **1973** *Beautiful But Deadly 1973* **(R)** A violent Mafia saga wherein a love triangle interferes with family business, resulting in gang wars. **96m/C VHS, DVD.** Anthony Quinn, Frederic Forrest, Robert Forster, Al Lettieri, Ina Balin, Angel Tompkins, Charles Cioffi; **D:** Richard Fleischer; **W:** Michael Butler; **M:** Jerry Goldsmith.

Don Juan ♪♪½ **1926** Barrymore stars as the swashbuckling Italian duke with Spanish blood who seduces a castleful of women in the 1500s before falling in love with innocent Astor. Many exciting action sequences, including classic sword fights in which Barrymore eschewed a stunt double. Great attention is also paid to the detail of the costumes and settings in which the Spanish-Moor period. Noted for employing fledgling movie sound effects and as the first film with a synchronized musical score from the Vitaphone Company, which, ironically, were responsible for eclipsing the movie's reputation. Watch for Loy as an Asian vamp and Oland as a pre-Charlie Chan Caesare Borgia. **90m/B VHS.** John Barrymore, Mary Astor, Willard Louis, Estelle Taylor, Helene Costello, Myrna Loy, June Marlowe, Warner Oland, Montagu Love, Hedda Hopper, Gustav von Seyffertitz; **D:** Alan Crosland; **W:** Bess Meredyth; **C:** Byron Haskin; **M:** William Axt.

Don Juan DeMarco ♪♪♪½ **1994 (PG-13)** Burned-out clinical psychiatrist Dr. Jack Meckler (Brando) is romantically inspired by a cape-wearing, suicidal manchild from Queens (Depp), who thinks he's legendary lover Don Juan. Delusional Depp recounts, in a convincing Castilian accent, thousands of conquests as the sympathetic shrink decides it's time to bring some spice to his own ho-hum life and marriage to Dunaway). Depp turns in a sincere, engaging performance that avoids the huge potential for melodrama and compensates for inconsistent pacing. Brando and Dunaway make a charmingly quirky couple. Watch for slain Tejano queen Selena in a musical interlude. **92m/C VHS, DVD.** Marlon Brando, Johnny Depp, Faye Dunaway, Geraldine Pailhas, Rachel Ticotin, Bob (Robert) Dishy, Talisa Soto; **D:** Jeremy Leven; **W:** Jeremy Leven; **C:** Ralf Bode; **M:** Michael Kamen.

Don Juan, My Love ♪♪ **1990** *Don Juan, Mi Querido Fantasma 1990* Sexy comedy finds the ghost of Don Juan given a chance, after 450 years in Purgatory, to perform a good deed and free his soul. In Spanish with English subtitles. **96m/C VHS.** *SP* Juan Luis Gallardo, Rossy de Palma, Maria Barranco, Loles Leon; **D:** Antonio Mercero; **M:** Bernardo Bonezzi.

Don Juan (Or If Don Juan Were a Woman) ♪ *Don Juan 73; Ms. Don Juan; Si Don Juan Etait une Femme* **1973** Offers unintentional amusement when...

Don King: Only in America ♪♪½ **1997 (R)** Rhames reigns in this bio of flamboyant, notorious boxing promoter Don King. King starts off as a Cleveland numbers runner at ease with violence, which eventually sends him to a four-year prison term for manslaughter. Released in 1971, King uses his friendship with R&B singer Lloyd Price (Curtis-Hall) to meet Muhammed Ali (McCrary), leading to his set-up of the 1974 Ali-Foreman fight in Zaire. From there it's just more self-promotion. **112m/C VHS, DVD.** Gabriel Casseus, Ving Rhames, Vondie Curtis-Hall, Jeremy Piven, Darius McCrary, Keith David, Bernie Mac, Loretta Devine, Lou Rawls, Ron Leibman; **D:** John Herzfeld; **W:** Kario Salem; **C:** Bill Butler; **M:** Anthony Marinelli. **CABLE**

Don Q., Son of Zorro ♪♪ **1925** Zorro's son takes up his father's fight against evil and injustice. Silent sequel to the 1920 classic. **111m/B VHS, DVD.** Douglas Fairbanks Sr., Mary Astor, Donald Crisp; **D:** Donald Crisp; **W:** Jack Cunningham; **C:** Henry Sharp.

Don Quixote ♪♪ **1935** *Chaliapin: Adventures of Don Quixote 1935* Miguel de Cervantes' tale of the romantic who would rather be a knight in shining armor than shining armor at night. Chaliapin stars as the knight-errant on his nightly errands, tilting at windmills and charging flocks of sheep. Certain scenes were adapted to fit the pre-WWII atmosphere, as it was filmed during the same time that the Nazis were burning books. **73m/B VHS, DVD.** Feodor Chaliapin Sr., George Robey, Sidney (Sydney) Fox, Miles Mander, Oscar Asche, Emily Fitzroy, Wally Patch; **D:** G.W. Pabst; **W:** Paul Morand, Alexandre Arnoux; **M:** Jacques Ibert.

Don Quixote ♪♪½ *Don Kikhot* **1957** The lauded, visually ravishing adaptation of the Cervantes classic, with a formal integrity inherited from Eisenstein and Dovshenko. In Russian with English subtitles. **110m/B VHS.** *SP RU* Nikolai Cherkassov, Yuri Tolubeyev; **D:** Grigori Kozintsev; **W:** Yevgeni Schwarz; **C:** Appolinari Dudko, Andrei Moskvin; **M:** Kara Karayev.

Don Quixote ♪♪ **2000** Spanish nobleman Alonso Quijano of La Mancha (Lithgow) decides to dedicate himself to chivalry. With his sanity in question, he dubs himself a knight errant—becoming Don Quixote—picks up sidekick Sancho Panza (Hoskins), and finds his lady fair—washerwoman Dulcinea (Williams). Episodic retelling has a number of familiar touches (including windmill-tilting) but doesn't add up to much, although the Spanish scenery is a plus. Based on Miguel de Cervantes' 1605 novel. **150m/C VHS.** John Lithgow, Bob Hoskins, Vanessa L(ynne) Williams, Isabella Rossellini, James Purefoy, Lambert Wilson, Tony Haygarth, Peter Eyre; **D:** Peter Yates; **W:** John Mortimer; **C:** David Connell; **M:** Richard Hartley. **CABLE**

Don Segundo Sombra ♪♪½ **1969** An interesting film seen through the eyes of an old gaucho, who is the mentor of a young boy growing to manhood. Based on the novel by Ricardo Guiraldes. In Spanish with English subtitles. **110m/C VHS.** *SP* Juan Carballido, Juan Carlos Gene, Soledad Silveyra, Alejandra Boero; **D:** Manuel Antin.

Don Winslow of the Coast Guard ♪♪ **1943** Serial in 13 episodes features comic-strip character Winslow as he strives to keep the waters of America safe for democracy. **234m/B VHS.** Don Terry, Elyse Knox; **D:** Ford Beebe, Ray Taylor.

Don Winslow of the Navy ♪♪ **1943** Thirteen episodes centered around the evil Scorpion, who plots to attack the Pacific Coast, but is

Dona Flor and Her Two Husbands *Dois Maridos* 1978 Dona Flor (Braga) is widowed when her philandering husband Vadinho (Wilker) finally expires from drink, gambling, and ladies. She remarries, but her new husband Teodoro (Mendonça) is so boring and proper that she begins fantasizing about number one's return. But is he only in her imagination? Based on the novel by Jorge Amado. Portuguese with subtitles. Remade as "Kiss Me Goodbye." 106m/C VHS, DVD *BR* Sonia Braga, Jose Wilker, Mauro Mendonca; *D:* Bruno Barreto; *W:* Bruno Barreto; *C:* Mauro Salles; *M:* Chico Buarque.

Dona Herlinda & Her Son *Dona Herlinda y Su Hijo* 1986 A Mexican sex comedy about a mother who manipulates her bisexual son's two lovers (one male, one female), until all four together in a seamless unit. In Spanish with English subtitles. Slow, but amusing. 90m/C VHS, DVD, MX Guadalupe Del Toro, Arturo Meza, Marco Antonio Trevino, Leticia Lupersio; *D:* Jaime Humberto Hermosillo; *C:* Miguel Angel Hermosillo; *M:* Michel Legrand.

Donkey Skin *Peau d'Ane* 1970 A charming, all-star version of the medieval French fairy tale about a king searching for a suitable wife in a magical realm after his queen dies. In his quest for the most beautiful spouse, he learns that his daughter is that woman. She prefers Prince Charming, however. In French with English subtitles. 89m/C VHS, DVD *FR* Catherine Deneuve, Jean Marais, Delphine Seyrig, Jacques Perrin; *D:* Jacques Demy; *C:* Ghislain Cloquet; *M:* Michel Legrand.

Donner Pass: The Road to Survival 1984 Tame retelling of the western wagon-train pioneers who were forced to resort to cannibalism during a brutal snowstorm in the Rockies. The tragedy is lightly implied, keeping the film suitable for family viewing. 98m/C VHS Robert Fuller, Diane McBain, Andrew Prine, John Anderson, Michael Callan; *D:* James L. Conway.

Donnie Brasco 1996 (R) Excellent look at the unglamourous working end of the mob and an undercover operation. In the late '70s, FBI agent Joe Pistone (Depp) infiltrates the New York Bonanno crime family, where he's mentored by aging low-level hood Lefty (Pacino). As Joe/Donnie gets deeper into the wiseguy life, Lefty takes a fatherly pride in his protege and the agent also becomes ensnared by his new identity—to the possible detriment of both feds and family. Terrific lead performances. Based on a true story and adapted from the book by Pistone and Richard Woodley. 126m/C VHS, DVD, Blu-ray Disc, Johnny Depp, Al Pacino, Anne Heche, Michael Madsen, Bruno Kirby, James Russo, Zeljko Ivanek, Gerry Becker, Zach Grenier, Robert Miano; *D:* Mike Newell; *W:* Paul Attanasio; *C:* Peter Sova; *M:* Patrick Doyle, Nell. Bd. of Review '97: Support. Actress (Heche).

Donnie Darko 2001 (R) Stylish, exciting debut by writer/director Kelly that, like "Mulholland Drive," leaves much unexplained as dark doings occur in an idyllic suburb, circa 1988. Aptly named Darko family is full of complex characters, including the gifted but schizophrenic Donnie, a teenager able to see the future with the aid of a life-size, doomsday-spewing rabbit named Frank. Donnie's psychiatrist (Ross) discovers he's sleepwalking on Frank's orders, which actually saves his life when a jet engine falls from a plane, landing squarely in the teen's bedroom. Even more mysteriously, no plane has reported a missing engine, which turns out to be just one of the many eerie events that may be real or imagined. McDonnell and Osborne are both fine as Donnie's upper-middle class Republican parents. Like "Harvey" on anti-psychotic meds, this challenging and complex film is worth the effort. 113m/C VHS, DVD, UMD, US-ake Gyllenhaal, Jena Malone, Drew Barrymore, Mary McDonnell, James Duval, Maggie Gyllenhaal, Holmes Osborne, Katharine Ross, Patrick Swayze, Noah Wyle, Arthur Taxier, Stuart Stone, Jr. Richard Kelly; *C:* Steven Poster; *M:* Michael Andrews.

The Donor 1994 (R) Cartel stalks victims and kills them for a human organ black market. 94m/C VHS, Michelle Johnson, Gordon Thomson; *D:* Damian Lee; *W:* Neal Dobrofsky, Tippi Dobrofsky.

Don't Answer the Phone! 1980 (R) Deeply troubled photographer stalks and attacks the patients of a beautiful psychologist talk-show hostess. 94m/C VHS, DVD James Westmoreland, Flo Gerish, Ben Frank; *D:* Robert Hammer; *W:* Robert Hammer, Michael Castle; *C:* James L. Carter, *M:* Byron Allred.

Don't Be a Menace to South Central While Drinking Your Juice in the Hood 1995 (R) Parody of "life in the hood" movies pokes fun at the attitudes and characters that are quickly becoming cliches in the genre. Shawn Wayans plays G-next-door, Ashtray, sent by his mother to discover "what it is to be a man" from his father in South Central L.A. He hooks up with his homey Loc Dog (Marlon Wayans), a gun-crazed beer-swilling gangsta who packs a nuclear warhead. As the title implies, almost every major black film in recent memory is given the Wayans' drive-by treatment, with a majority of the plot lifted from "Boyz N the Hood." Fans of the TV series "In Living Color" will love this twisted look at ghetto life, but others may be offended. 88m/C VHS, DVD, Shawn Wayans, Marlon Wayans, Tracey Cherelle Jones, Chris Spencer, Suli McCullough, Darrell Heath, Helen Martin, Isaiah Barnes, Lahmard Tate; *Cameos:* Keenen Ivory Wayans, Damon Wayans, Marlon Wayans; *D:* Paris Barclay; *W:* Shawn Wayans, Marlon Wayans, Phil Beauman; *C:* Russ Brandt; *M:* John Barnes.

Don't Cry, It's Only Thunder 1982 (PG) A young army medic who works in a mortuary in Saigon becomes involved with a group of Vietnamese orphans and a dedicated army doctor. Based on a true story. 108m/C VHS Dennis Christopher, Susan St. James, Roger Aaron Brown, Li Lu, Thu Thuy, James Whitmore; *D:* Peter Werner; *M:* Maurice Jarre.

Don't Do It *D'½* 1994 (PG-13) Three 20-something couples, attempting to find love, all wind up in the same cafe and try to tell the truth about how they feel and whom they desire. 90m/C VHS, DVD, James Marshall, James LeGros, Sheryl Lee, Esai Morales, Alexis Arquette, Balthazar Getty, Sarah Trigger, Heather Graham; *D:* Eugene Hess; *W:* Eugene Hess; *C:* Jan Fox.

Don't Drink the Water 1969 (G) Based on Woody Allen's hit play, this film places an average Newark, New Jersey, family behind the Iron Curtain, where their vacation photo-taking gets them accused of spying. 100m/C VHS, Jackie Gleason, Estelle Parsons, Joan Delaney, Ted Bessell, Michael Constantine; *D:* Howard Morris.

Donor Unknown 1995 (R) Driven businessman Nicholas Stillman (Onorati) has always put work before his family—and both work before his teenaged daughter Danielle (Herbst) have suffered from his attitude. When Nick is hit by a massive heart attack and gets a transplant, he insists on knowing everything about the donor. What he uncovers is a black market in organ procurement and Nash Creed (Brown), who'll do anything to stop Nick from exposing his lucrative business. Based on the novel "Corazon" by William H. Mooney. 93m/C VHS, Peter Onorati, Alice Krige, Clancy Brown, Beverly Herbst, Sam Robards, Richard Portnow, T.J. Castranova, Leo Garcia, John Dorman; *D:* John Harrison; *C:* Zoltan David; *M:* David Bergeaud.

Donovan's Brain 1953 Dedicated scientist Dr. Cory (Ayres) has succeeded in keeping a dismembered monkey's brain alive and gets his chance to experiment on a human when the victim of a plane crash is brought to his lab. Over the objections of his wife Janice (Davis) and assistant Frank (Evans), Cory keeps the brain alive in a tank. Too bad for him, since the organ belongs to a ruthless, vicious businessman (the titular Donovan) who begins to influence Cory in horrible ways. Based on the novel by Curt Siodmak, and also filmed as "The Lady and the Monster" (1944), "Vengeance" (1963), and "The Brain" (1965). 85m/B VHS, DVD, Lew Ayres, Gene Evans, Nancy Davis, Steve Brodie; *D:* Felix Feist; *W:* Felix Feist, Hugh Brooke; *C:* Joseph Biroc; *M:* Eddie Dunstedter.

Donovan's Reef 1963 Two WWII buddies meet every year on a Pacific atoll to engage in a perpetual bar-brawl, until a stuck-up Bostonian maiden appears to find her dad, a man who has fathered a brood of lovable half-casts. A rollicking, good-natured film from Ford. 109m/C VHS, DVD, John Wayne, Lee Marvin, Jack Warden, Elizabeth Allen, Dorothy .amour, Mike Mazurki, Cesar Romero; *D:* John Ford; *W:* James Edward Grant, Frank Nugent; *C:* William Clothier; *M:* Cyril Mockridge.

Don't Come Knocking 2005 (R) Aging movie star Howard Spence (Shepard) is better known for his life of drugs, booze, and babes. Fed-up with his latest cowboy flick, he literally rides off the set, leaving chaos behind him. Spence heads to Nevada to visit his mother (Saint), whom he hasn't seen in 30 years. She blithely informs him that an ex-flame of his had once come calling with the news of his pregnancy, and Spence tracks down barkeep Doreen (Lange) and their bitter son, Earl (Mann). Seems Spence was more fertile than he knew—when he's later accosted by Sky (Polley), who claims to be his daughter. Spence wants another chance but he's pretty beautiful, though. 110m/C DVD, US Sam Shepard, Jessica Lange, Sarah Polley, Gabriel Mann, Tim Roth, Fairuza Balk, Eva Marie Saint, James Gammon, George Kennedy, Marley Shelton, Rodney A. Grant, Tim Matheson, Julia Sweeney, Kurt Fuller, James Roday; *D:* Wim Wenders; *W:* Sam Shepard, Wim Wenders; *C:* Franz Lustig; *M:* T-Bone Burnett.

Don't Let Me Die on a Sunday *D'½ D'½* 1998 Bizarre, disturbing wallow in Parisian depravity begins in a morgue. That's where attendant Ben (Barr) meets Teresa (Bouchez). The details of that first encounter will not be recounted, but the two begin a downward spiral into joyless sex, angst, alienation, and despair. Not for the fainthearted. French with subtitles. 96m/C VHS, DVD, *FR* Elodie Bouchez, Jean-Marc Barr, Martin Petitguyot, Patrick Catalifo, Gerard Loussine, Jeanne Casilas, Florence Darel; *D:* Didier Le Pecheur; *W:* Didier Le Pecheur; *C:* Denis Rouden; *M:* Philippe Cohen-Solal.

Don't Let Your Meat Loaf *D'½* 1995 Three struggling comedians take their act on the road, including subway stations and street corners, in order to get the money to open their own comedy club. 87m/C VHS, Leander Sales, Dana S. Hubbard, Brad Albright; *D:* Leander Sales.

Don't Look Back 1996 (R) Musician and heroin addict Jesse Parrish (Stoltz) stumbles across a suitcase full of cash after witnessing a drug deal gone bad. He heads back to his family and friends in Texas so he can kick his habit, but is marked for death by the dealers who want their money back. Strong script and performances. 91m/C VHS, DVD, Eric Stoltz, John Corbett, Josh Hamilton, Annabeth Gish, Dwight Yoakam, Amanda Plummer; *D:* Geoff Murphy; *W:* Billy Bob Thornton, Tom Epperson; *C:* CARLE.

Don't Look Back: The Story of Leroy "Satchel" Paige *D'½* 1981 Drama of the legendary baseball pitcher who helped break down racial barriers, based on his autobiography. Made-for-TV fare. Gossett hits a home run in the lead, but the overall effort is a ground-rule couple. 98m/C VHS, Louis Gossett Jr., Beverly Todd, Cleavon Little, Clifton.

Don't Be Afraid of the Dark *D' D'* 1973 A young couple move into their dream house only to find that demonic little critters are residing in their basement and they want more than shelter. Made for TV with creepy scenes and eerie makeup for the monsters. 74m/C VHS, Kim Darby, Jim Hutton, Barbara Anderson, William Demarest, Pedro Armendariz Jr., Felix Silla, Patty Maloney, Tamara DeTreaux; *D:* John Newland; *W:* Giovanni Bergamini; *C:* Andrew Jackson; *M:* Billy Goldenberg. TV

Don't Bother to Knock *D' D'* 1952 As a mentally unstable hotel babysitter, Monroe meets a pilot (Widmark) and has a brief rendezvous with him. When the little girl she is babysitting interrupts, Monroe is furious, and later tries to murder the girl. This is one of Monroe's best dramatic roles. Bancroft's film debut as the Widmark's girlfriend. 76m/B VHS, DVD, Richard Widmark, Marilyn Monroe, Anne Bancroft, Elisha Cook Jr., Jim Backus, Lurene Tuttle, Jeanne Cagney, Donna Corcoran; *D:* Roy Ward Baker; *W:* Daniel Taradash; *C:* Lucien Ballard; *M:* Lionel Newman.

Don't Change My World *D'½* 1983 (G) To preserve the natural beauty of the north woods, a wildlife photographer and a reckless poacher. Eco-correct. 89m/C VHS, Roy Tatum, Ben Jones, Edie Kramer, George Macrenais, Paul Newman, David Eldson; *D:* Robert Rector.

Don't Go to Sleep *D' D'* 1982 After a fatal car crash, a young girl misses her mom and dad so much she returns from the grave to take them where they can be one big happy 'family again. Better than play. So she calls him up to get his person and the two begin a phone relationship that develops from business to romance. 84m/C VHS, *GB* Rosanna Arquette, David Suchet; *D:* Barry Davis; *W:* Tom Kempinski. TV

Don't Hang Up *D' D'½* Separation (Arquette) wants to do a production of an agoraphobic London writer Joe's (Suchet) mission and the two begin a phone...

Don't Go Near the Water *D' D'* 1957 Somewhat amusing comedy about the happenings at a Naval installation on a South Pacific tropical paradise. Clark outshines the others in its role as a frustrated officer. Based on the novel by William Brinkley. 107m/C VHS, Glenn Ford, Gia Scala, Earl Holliman, Anne Francis, Keenan Wynn, Fred Clark, Eva Gabor, Russ Tamblyn; *D:* Charles Walters; *W:* Dorothy Kingsley, George Wells.

Don't Go in the Woods woof! 1981 (R) Routine exercise in 'don't do that" terror genre (includes warnings about going into houses, opening phones, looking into basements, answering windows, etc.). This time four young campers are stalked by a crazed killer armed with prehistoric ax. 88m/C VHS, Richard Einhorn.

Don't Go in the House *D'* 1980 (R) Long-dormant psychosis is brought to life by the death of a young man's mother. 90m/C VHS, DVD Dan Grimaldi, Robert Osth, Ruth Darlick; *D:* Joseph Ellison, Ellen Hammill; *C:* Oliver Wood; *M:* Joseph Einhorn.

Don't Fence Me In *D' D'* 1945 Evans is a magazine publisher who heads west to do a story on a legendary character named Wildcat Kelly, who's supposedly dead. She meets rancher Rogers and sidekick Hayes and, of course, discovers that Rogers is the man she's looking for. 71m/B VHS, Roy Rogers, Dale Evans, George "Gabby" Hayes, Robert "Bob" Livingston, Robert McGowan; *C:* William Bradford.

287 · VideoHound's Golden Movie Retriever

Davis, John Beradino, Jim Davis, Ossie Davis, Hal Williams; **D:** George C. Scott, Richard A. Colla.

Don't Look Down 𝒥½ *Wes Craven Presents: Don't Look Down* 1998 TV reporter Carla (Ward) begins suffering from acrophobia after the falling death of her sister. She joins and extreme therapy group run by radical shrink Dr. Sadowski (Kinney) to overcome her fears. But it doesn't help when her fellow therapy mates beginning dying in fatal falls. 90m/C VHS, DVD. Megan Ward, Billy Burke, Terry Kinney, Angela Moore, William McDonald, Kate Robbins, Tara Spencer-Nairn; **D:** Larry Shaw; **W:** Gregory Goodell; **C:** David Geddes; **M:** J. Peter Robinson. **TV**

Don't Look in the Attic woof! 1981 A couple finds a haunted house with cows in the attic. 90m/C VHS. Beba Loncar, Jean-Pierre Aumont; **D:** Carl Ausino.

Don't Look in the Basement 𝒥½ 1973 (R) Things get out of hand at an isolated asylum and a pretty young nurse is caught in the middle. Straight-jacketed by a low budget. 95m/C VHS, DVD. Rosie Holotik, Anne MacAdams, William (Bill) McGhee, Rhea MacAdams, Gene Ross, Betty Chandler, Camilla Carr, Robert Dracup, Jessie Kirby, Hugh Feagin, Harryette Warren, Jessie Lee Fulton, Michael Harvey; **D:** S.F. Browning; **W:** Tim Pope, Tom Pope; **D:** Robert Farrar.

Don't Look Now 𝒥𝒥𝒥 1973 (R) A psychological creepfest with a chilling climax, based on the novel by Daphne Du Maurier. John (Sutherland) and Laura (Christie) Baxter travel to a dank, off-season Venice in an attempt to put the drowning death of their young daughter behind them. But while working on a church restoration, John begins to have psychic visions which are encouraged by a pair of strange sisters (Matania, Mason). There's a steamy love scene between Sutherland and Christie that became the object of much gossip. 110m/C VHS, DVD. *GB IT* Donald Sutherland, Julie Christie, Hilary Mason, Clelia Matania, Massimo Serato, Leopoldo Trieste, Adelina Poerio; **C:** Anthony B. Richmond; **M:** Pino Donaggio.

Don't Mess with My Sister! 𝒥𝒥½ 1985 A married, New York junkyard worker falls in love with a belly dancer he meets at a party. The affair leads to murder and subsequently, revenge. An interesting, offbeat film from the director of "I Spit on Your Grave." 90m/C VHS, DVD. Joe Perce, Jeannine Lemay, Jack Gurci, Peter Sapienza, Laura Lanfranchi; **D:** Mier Zarchi.

Don't Open the Door! woof! 1974 (PG) A young woman is terrorized by a killer located inside her house. 90m/C VHS, DVD. Susan Bracken, Gene Ross, Jim Harrell; **D:** S.F. Browning.

Don't Open Till Christmas woof! 1984 A weirdo murders various Santa Clauses in assorted gory ways. Best to take this one back to the department store. 86m/C VHS. *GB* Edmund Purdom, Caroline Munro, Alan Lake, Belinda Mayne, Gerry Sundquist, Mark Jones; **D:** Edmund Purdom.

Don't Raise the Bridge, Lower the River 𝒥𝒥½ 2001 (R) Douglas plays the stable family man pushed to the brink once again in this chilly kidnapping thriller. Dr. Nathan Conrad (Douglas) is a psychiatrist whose idyllic life is shattered when his eight-year-old daughter Jessie (Bartusiak) is kidnapped by a gang of thieves. They threaten to kill his little girl unless he can retrieve a six-digit number locked in the brain of Nathan's new patient Elisabeth (Murphy), a raving lunatic who slashed an orderly to death. Meanwhile, the bad guys have rigged surveillance equipment in his apartment and are menacing his wife Aggie (Janssen), as cop Esposito stumbles across the plot, inadvertently threatening

Nathan's efforts. All the plot threads are conveniently tied up in a standard final showdown scene. 112m/C VHS, DVD. *US* Michael Douglas, Sean Bean, Brittany Murphy, Skye McCole Bartusiak, Famke Janssen, Guy Tony, Jennifer Esposito, Shawn Doyle, Victor Argo, Oliver Platt, David Goode, Paul Schulze, Lance Reddick; **D:** Gary Fleder; **W:** Patrick Smith Kelly, Anthony Peckham; **C:** Amir M. Mokri; **M:** Mark Isham.

Don't Talk to Strangers 𝒥𝒥½ 1994 (R) Formula thriller has Brosnan marrying divorcee Reed and becoming instant father to her nine-year-old son. But someone appears to be a whacko—is it the kid's real dad (Quinn) or is Brosnan just too good to be true? 94m/C VHS. Pierce Brosnan, Shanna Reed, Terry O'Quinn; **D:** Robert Lewis; **W:** Neil D. Hicks, Jon George, Nevin Schreiner.

Don't Tell 𝒥𝒥 *La Bestia nel Cuore; The Beast in the Heart* 2005 An inexplicable Oscar nominee, this confusing melodrama concerns a brother and sister and family secrets coming to light. Voiceover actress Sabina (Mezzogiorno) lives in Rome with her actor boyfriend, Franco (Boni). After dubbing a rape scene, Sabina begins having nightmares about a scared child and decides to visit her brother, Daniele (Lo Cascio), who lives in Virginia. She pressures him to tell what he knows. Side stories involving Franco's work on a soap opera and a couple of Sabina's friends finding (and losing) romance dissipate the tension. Attractive cast. Italian with subtitles. 120m/C DVD. *IT* Giovanna Mezzogiorno, Stefania Rocca, Angela Finocchiaro, Alessio Boni, Luigi Lo Cascio, Valerio Binasco, Lewis Lemprèuer Palmer, Jeke-Omer Boyayanlar, Lucy Akhurst, Giuseppe Battiston, Francesca Inaudi; **D:** Cristina Comencini; **W:** Francesca Marciano, Cristina Comencini, Giulia Calenda; **C:** Fabio Cianchetti; **M:** Franco Piersanti.

Don't Tell 𝒥 2005 Lame family drama has three siblings (Eastwood, Root, Wlcek) reuniting in their dreary, small hometown after their hard-drinking farmer dad dies. This is a dysfunctional bunch with family secrets that don't inspire sympathy or involvement. 88m/C DVD. *US* Alison Eastwood, Bonnie Root, James Wlcek; **D:** Isaac H. Eaton; **W:** Julie Anne Koehnen; **C:** Mike King; **M:** Larry Brown.

Don't Tell Her It's Me 𝒥 *The Boyfriend School* 1990 (PG-13) Guttenberg is determined to win the heart of an attractive writer. With the assistance of his sister, he works to become a dream man. Clever premise, promising cast, lame comedy. From the novel by Sarah Bird. 101m/C VHS, DVD. Steve Guttenberg, Jami Gertz, Shelley Long, Kyle MacLachlan, Madchen Amick; **D:** Malcolm Mowbray; **W:** Sarah Bird; **M:** Michael Gore.

Don't Tell Mom the Babysitter's Dead 𝒥½ 1991 (PG-13) Their mother traveling abroad, the title situation leaves a houseful of teenagers with the whole summer to themselves. Eldest daughter Applegate cons her way into the high-powered business world while the metalhead son parties hardy. Many tepid comic situations, not adding up to very much. 105m/C VHS, DVD. Christina Applegate, Keith Coogan, Joanna Cassidy, John Getz, Josh Charles, Concetta Tomei, Eda Reiss Merin; **D:** Stephen Herek; **W:** Neil Landau, Tara Ison; **C:** Tim Suhrstedt; **M:** David Newman.

Don't Torture a Duckling 𝒥𝒥½ *Non Si Sevizia un Paperino* 1972 Newspaperman Andrea Martelli (Milian) investigates the deaths of several young boys in the Sicily village where his father was born. The suspicious villagers take their revenge on a couple of outcast locals but Martelli teams up with seductive Patrizia (Bouchet) to uncover the real killer. Creepy rather a gorefest, although Fulci recycled one of the more violent scenes for his later film, "The Psychic." 102m/C VHS, DVD. *IT* Tomas Milian, Barbara Bouchet, Irene Papas, Florinda Bolkan, Marc Porel; **D:** Lucio Fulci; **W:** Lucio Fulci, Robert Gianviti; **C:** Sergio d'Offizi; **M:** Riz Ortolani.

Doogal 𝒥 *The Magic Roundabout* 2005 (G) Animated kiddie adventure. Doogal the dog frees evil sorcerer Zeebad (Stewart) by mistake, and now the canine and his gang—a sassy cow (Goldberg), geeky

snail (Macy), hippy bunny (Fallon), kind-hearted magician (McKellen), and a little girl (Minogue)—must keep the imp from making the world a big ball of ice. Compared with the inventive and beloved British TV show from the 1960s, the disappointment of this outing overpowers all the big-name celebrity voices involved. 80m/C DVD. **D:** Frank Passingham, Dave Borthwick, Jean Duval; **W:** Paul Bassett Davies, Stephane Sanoussi; **C:** Tad Safran; **M:** Mark Thomas; **V:** Tom Baker, Jim Broadbent, Joanna Lumley, Ian McKellen, Kylie Minogue, Bill Nighy, Ray Winstone, Lee Evans, Robbie Williams.

The Doolins of Oklahoma 𝒥𝒥½ *The Great Manhunt* 1949 Scott is the leader of the last of the southwestern outlaw gangs, pursued by lawmen and changing times with the onset of the modern age. Fast-paced and intelligent. 90m/B VHS. Randolph Scott, George Macready, Louise Allbritton, John Ireland, Virginia Huston, Charles Kemper, Noah Beery Jr.; **D:** Gordon Douglas; **M:** George Duning.

Doom 𝒥𝒥 2005 (R) It's the live-action version of the videogame. If that's your thing, you'll enjoy the flick because everyone involved knows it's a game and they get to play Space Marines (led by the Rock and Urban) and use big guns to blow away flesh-eating mutants. Hey, what could be more fun? Anything else comes to mind. 104m/C DVD, UMD, HD DVD. *US* Karl Urban, Rosamund Pike, DeObia Oparei, Ben Daniels, Raz Adoti, Richard Brake, Dexter Fletcher, Al Weaver, Brian Steele, Dwayne "The Rock" Johnson, Yao Chin; **D:** Andrzej Bartkowiak; **W:** David Callaham, Wesley Strick; **C:** Tony Pierce-Roberts; **M:** Clint Mansell.

Doom Asylum woof! 1988 (R) Several sex kittens wander into a deserted sanatorium and meet up with the grisly beast wielding autopsy instruments. The people involved with this spoof should have been (more) committed. 77m/C VHS, DVD. Patty Mullen, Ruth (Coreen) Collins, Kristen Davis, William Hay, Kenny L. Price, Harrison White, Dawn Alvan, Michael Rogen; **D:** Richard Friedman.

The Doom Generation 𝒥𝒥𝒥 1995 (R) Alienated trio on the road trip to hell (doubling as L.A.). Beautiful 17-year-old druggie Amy Blue (McGowan), her sweetly dim boyfriend Jordan White (Duval), and hot-tempered stud/drifter Xavier Red (Schaech) flee after Red kills a store clerk. They're basically from nowhere, going nowhere, and finding sex and (lots of gruesomely depicted) violence along the way. The subtitle, "A Heterosexual Movie by Gregg Araki," may be technically accurate but the homoerotic subtext is very clear. Terrific performances. Second film in Araki's teen trilogy, following "Totally F*** ked Up," and preceding "Nowhere." An unrated version is also available. 84m/C VHS, DVD. Parker Posey, Lauren Tewes, Christopher Knight, Margaret Cho, Skinny Puppy, Heidi Fleiss, Rose McGowan, James Duval, Johnathon Schaech; **D:** Gregg Araki; **W:** Gregg Araki; **C:** Jim Fealy; **M:** Don Gallo.

Doom Runners 𝒥𝒥 1997 Ah, yes—another dark and dangerous postapocalyptic world. Evil ruler Dr. Kao (Curry) uses "mindwiping" to erase the memories of his victims and maintains order with an army of "Doom Troopers." Teen Jada (Moreno) finds a map that will lead her to New Eden, the only free society left. And she's determined that it, despite Kao's threats. 87m/C VHS. Tim Curry, Lea Moreno, Bradley Michael Pierce, Nathan Jones; **D:** Brendan Maher; **W:** Barney Cohen, Ken Lipman; **C:** Steve Arnold; **M:** Braedy Neal. **CABLE**

Doomed at Sundown 𝒥𝒥½ 1937 Decent Steele vehicle has the tough cowpoke as a sheriff's son known for playing practical jokes. When his father gets knifed, it's no laughing matter and he takes off after the killers. Based on a story by Fred Myton. 55m/B VHS, DVD. Bob Steele, Laraine Day, Warner Richmond, Harold Daniels, David Sharpe; **D:** Sam Newfield; **W:** George Plympton.

Doomed Caravan 𝒥𝒥𝒥 1941 Hoppy and his pals lend a hand when some villains try to monopolize the wagon train business. Location shooting was done in the valleys of central California.

60m/B VHS, DVD. William Boyd, Russell Hayden, Andy Clyde, Minna Gombell, Morris Ankrum, Georgia Hawkins, Trevor Bardette, Pat J. O'Brien; **D:** Lesley Selander.

Doomed Love 𝒥𝒥½ 1983 Love is hell, especially when the object of your affection happens to be deceased. A professor of literature in the throes of unrequited love decides to reunite himself with his lost love. Won awards when released in Berlin. 75m/C VHS. Allen Frame, Rosemary Moore, Jim Neu, Bill Rice; **D:** Andrew Horn; **W:** Andrew Horn; **C:** Carl Teitelaum; **M:** Evan Lurie.

Doomed to Die 𝒥𝒥 1940 Cargo of stolen bonds leads to a tong war and the murder of a shipping millionaire. Part of Mr. Wong series. Worth a look if only for Karloff's performance. 67m/B VHS, DVD. Boris Karloff, Marjorie Reynolds, Grant Withers; **D:** William Nigh.

Doomsday 𝒥𝒥½ 1928 Vidor marries for wealth instead of love and, in classic fashion, finds that money doesn't buy happiness. 73m/B VHS. Florence Vidor, Gary Cooper, Lawrence Grant; **D:** Rowland V. Lee.

Doomsday 𝒥𝒥 2008 (R) In 2035 the Reaper Virus has left Scotland a barren wasteland, quarantined from the rest of the world. But when satellite images reveal that life may still exist, a team of soldiers led by Eden Sinclair (Mitra) return in hopes of curing the survivors, instead discovering an underground civilization of psycho bikers and gutter punks. It's hard to tell if director Marshall has assembled a tribute, spoof, or rip-off of earlier doomsday flicks, because while this one doesn't make a lot of sense, it's still cheesy, over-the-top good fun. 109m/C DVD. *US* Rhona Mitra, Malcolm McDowell, Bob Hoskins, Adrian Lester, Alexander Siddig, David O'Hara, MyAnna Buring, Craig Conway; **D:** Neil Marshall; **W:** Neil Marshall; **C:** Sam McCurdy; **M:** Tyler Bates.

The Doomsday Flight 𝒥𝒥 1966 Uneven thriller in which O'Brien plants an altitude-triggered bomb on a jet in an effort to blackmail the airline. Search for the bomb provides some suspenseful and well-acted moments. 100m/C VHS. Jack Lord, Edmond O'Brien, Van Johnson, John Saxon, Katherine Crawford, Michael Sarrazin, Ed Asner, Greg Morris, Richard Carlson, Don Stewart; **D:** William A. Graham; **W:** Rod Serling. **TV**

Doomsday Gun 𝒥𝒥½ 1994 Fact-based thriller about arms manufacturer Gerald Bull (Langella), who dreams of building the world's biggest gun—a behemoth with a range of 1000 miles. Only problem is Bull's willingness to sell the weapon to the highest bidder, who happens to be Saddam Hussein. This doesn't sit well with Israeli Mossad agent Yossi (Arkin). 110m/C VHS, DVD. Frank Langella, Alan Arkin, Kevin Spacey, Tony Goldwyn, James Fox, Michael Kitchen, Francesca Annis, Marianne (Cuau) Denicourt; **D:** Robert M. Young; **W:** Lionel Chetwynd, Walter Bernstein; **C:** Ian Wilson. **CABLE**

Doomsdayer 𝒥½ 1999 (R) Okay, see how familiar this sounds. Jack Logan (Lara) works for a covert agency. His assignment is to prevent a new explosive from falling into terrorists' hands. The Doomsdayer device is currently held by a ruthless billionaire weapons dealer (Kier) and his equally nasty wife (Nielsen), who have their own island. Logan and his team run into trouble before they save the day. Now you won't have to actually watch the video. 93m/C VHS, DVD. Joe Lara, Udo Kier, Brigitte Nielsen, Sandra Gomez, January Isaac, T.J. Storm, Paige Rowland, Ravil Isyanov; **D:** Michael J. Sarna; **W:** Bob Coutie; **C:** David Rakoczy. **VIDEO**

Doomsdayer 𝒥𝒥 2001 An anti-terrorist organization is trying to track down a weapon called The Doomsdayer, capable of causing the meltdown of nuclear power plants, before it falls into the wrong hands. Mission specialist Jack Logan (Lara) finds the weapon's owner Max Gast (Kier) and discovers the device has been activated and there's seven days until mass destruction. m/C VHS, DVD. Joe Lara, Udo Kier, Brigitte Nielsen, January Isaac; **D:** Michael J. Sarna; **W:** Bob Coutie; **C:** David Rakoczy. **VIDEO**

The Door in the Floor 🐾🐾🐾½ **2004** (R) This compelling feature gets an extra half-bone for Jeff Bridges' standout performance. He's dissolute but celebrated children's author/illustrator Ted Cole (the title refers to one of his books), who is spending the summer of 1958 in a Hamptons beach house with his inconsolable wife Marion (Basinger) and their precocious 16-year-old daughter, Ruth (Fanning). Marion has not recovered from the car crash that killed their couple's two teenaged sons. Ted decides on a trial separation, which means he can continue an affair with wealthy Evelyn (Rogers), and he hires 16-year-old Eddie (Foster) to keep an eye on Marion. Eddie does more than that when he develops an obsession for the lonely woman who begins a sexual relationship with him. Adapted from the first section of John Irving's 1998 novel "A Widow of One Year." **111m/C DVD.** *US* Jeff Bridges, Kim Basinger, Jon Foster, Mimi Rogers, Elle Fanning, Bijou Phillips, Louis Arcella; **D:** Tod Williams; **W:** Tod Williams. **C:** Terry Stacey; **M:** Marcelo Zarvos.

Door to Door 🐾🐾🐾½ **2001** Detective Nero Wolfe (Chaykin) and his investigator Archie Goodwin (Hutton) get involved in the case of an eccentric woman who comes to Wolfe with a tale of FBI harassment that leads to murder. Based on the mystery by Rex Stout. **100m/C VHS, DVD.** Timothy Hutton, Maury Chaykin, Saul Rubinek, Debra Monk, Colin Fox; **W:** Timothy Hutton, Michael Jaffe. **CABLE**

Door to Door 🐾🐾 **1984** Comedy about two door-to-door salesmen who race to stay one step ahead of the law and their own company. Fairly lightweight, but it has its moments. **93m/C VHS.** Ron Leibman, Arliss Howard, Alan Austin; **D:** Patrick Bailey. **CABLE**

Door with the Seven Locks 🐾🐾½ **1962** Bizarre Edgar Wallace story of man who leaves seven keys to a treasure vault in his will. Remake of "Chamber of Horrors." **96m/C VHS, GE.** Eddi Arent, Heinz Drache, Klaus Kinski, Ady Berber. **D:** Alfred Vohrer.

Door to Door Maniac 🐾½ **Five Minutes to Live 1961** Criminals hold a bank president's wife hostage, unaware that the husband was looking to get rid of her in favor of another woman. Cash's screen debut. Aside from the strange cast ensemble, not particularly worth seeing. **80m/B VHS, DVD.** Johnny Cash, Ron Howard, Vic Tayback, Donald Woods, Cay Forrester, Pamela Mason; **D:** Bill Karn.

The Doorbell Rang: A Nero Wolfe Mystery 🐾🐾½ **1991** (R) Stone approaches Jim Morrison with an early incarnation of this docudrama, but it's hard to believe even the Lizard King could play himself with any more convincing abandon than Kilmer, in a great performance. Trouble is, the story—one of drug abuse, and abject self-indulgence—grows tiresome, and the audience, with the exception of die-hard fans, may lose sight of any sympathy they might have had. Ryan is forgettable as Morrison's hippie-chick wife, MacLachlan sports a funny wig and dabbles in sado-masochistic journalist peranour. Based on "Riders on the Storm" by John Densmore. **138m/C VHS, DVD, UMD.** Kelly Hu, Val Kilmer, Meg Ryan, Kevin Dillon, Kyle MacLachlan, Frank Whaley, Michael Madsen, Kathleen Quinlan, Crispin Glover, Josh Evans, John Densmore, William Jordan, Mimi Rogers, Paul Williams, Bill Graham, Billy Vera, William Kunstler, Wes Studi, Costas Mandylor, Billy Idol, Michael Wincott, Dennis Burkley; **D:** Oliver Stone, **W:** Oliver Stone, Ralph Thomas, Randy Johnson, J. Randal Johnson; **C:** Robert Richardson.

The Doors 🐾🐾½ **1991** (R) Stone approaches Jim Morrison with an early incarnation of this docudrama, but it's hard to believe even the Lizard King could play himself with any more convincing abandon than Kilmer, in a great performance. Trouble is, the story—one of drug abuse, and abject self-indulgence—grows tiresome, and the audience, with the exception of die-hard fans, may lose sight of any sympathy they might have had. Ryan is forgettable as Morrison's hippie-chick wife, MacLachlan sports a funny wig and dabbles in sado-masochistic journalist paranour. Based on "Riders on the Storm" by John Densmore.

Dorm That Dripped Blood WOOF! **1982** (R) Five college students volunteer to close the dorm during their Christmas vacation. A series of grisly and barbaric incidents eliminates the youngsters one by one. As the terror mounts, the remaining students slowly realize that they are up against a terrifyingly real psychopathic killer. Merry Christmas. **84m/C VHS, DVD.** Laura Lapinski, Stephen Sachs, Pamela Holland; **D:** Stephen Carpenter, Jeffrey Obrow; **W:** Stephen Carpenter.

Dostoevsky's Crime and Punishment 🐾🐾½ **Crime and Punishment 1999** (PG-13) Muddled TV adaptation of the 1866 Dostoevsky novel is anchored by Dempsey's lead performance as impoverished student Rodya Raskolnikov. He murders the local pawnbroker in a "perfect crime" only to be consumed by guilt. Then he falls under the suspicious eyes of unrelenting inspector Porfiri (Kingsley), who waits for Rodya to make a mistake. **89m/C VHS.** Patrick Dempsey, Ben Kingsley, Julie Delpy, Eddie Marsan, Richard Brenner, Lili Horvath, Carole Nimmons, Penny Downie, Michael Mehlmann, Sara Toth; **D:** Joseph Sargent; **W:** David Stevens; **C:** Elemer Ragalyi. **TV**

Dot the I 🐾🐾 **2003** (R) Carmen (Verbeke) is about to marry boring stiff Barnaby (D'Arcy) when she meets sexy, dashing filmmaker Kit (Garcia Bernal) at her bachelorette party and begins an adulterous affair with him. Surprisingly enough, bad things come of this love triangle, including Barnaby's angry jealousy and Kit's inability to separate his personal life from his work. Add in some additional plot twists that turn the last part of the movie from romantic drama into unpredictable noir, and what you get is a fluffy, hollow movie with little sense of direction. Get away with it. **92m/C DVD.** *US* Gael Garcia Bernal, Natalia Verbeke, James D'Arcy, Thomas O'Brien; **D:** Arthur Jnelius.

Doppelganger: The Evil Within 🐾🐾 **1990** (R) Holly Gooding (Barrymore) seems like such a nice girl—until the police suspect her of the brutal murder of her mother. Her new friend Patrick (Newborn) begins to see another side to the vulnerable Holly—a seductress capable of doing anything to get what she wants. **105m/C VHS, DVD, Drew Barrymore, George Newborn, Dennis Christopher, Sally Kellerman, Leslie Hope; **D:** Avi Nesher; **W:** Avi Nesher; Prime Time.

Dopamine 🐾🐾½ **2003** (R) Rand (Livingston), a partner in a dot-com startup, develops an interactive AI-type computer character. When they decide to test it in a classroom, Rand falls for the teacher, Sarah (Lloyd). Rand tries to sort out his feelings, and intellectual instincts as he ponders whether love is emotional or chemical. Perhaps he's over-thinking a bit. Everything about the film is substandard. Semi-professional writing, acting, and directing. **91m/C DVD.** Prime Time, Thinline, Kid Frost, Cookie, Sean Lever, Tony Dorian; **D:** Patrick McKnight, Jeff Williams; **W:** Patrick McKnight; **C:** Steve Van Dyne; **M:** Prime Time.

Dorian Gray 🐾½ **Das Bildnis des Dorian Gray: Il Dio Chiamato a Dorian; Das Bildnis an Gray; Il Dio Chiamato a Dorian; Das Bildnis des Dorian Gray; The Evils of Dorian Gray 1970** (R) Modern-day version of the famous tale by Oscar Wilde about an ageless young man whose portrait reflects the ravages of time and a life of debauchery. More sex, less acting with Berger in lead. Not nearly as good as the original version. "The Picture of Dorian Gray." **92m/C VHS, Das Bildnis des Dorian Gray; Das Bildnis 1970** Helmut Berger, Herbert Lom, Marie Liljedahl, Margaret Lee, Maria Rohm, Beryl Cunningham, Isa Miranda, Eleanora Rossi-Drago, Renato Romano; **D:** Massimo Dallamano; **W:** Massimo Dallamano, Marcello Coscia; **C:** Otello Spila.

Dope Case Pending 🐾🐾 **2000** Extremely low-budget urban action picture revolves around Devon King (Prime Time), who's got a bright future in athletics ahead of him until the cops are called to a party at his house and he's arrested for drug possession. It's a downward spiral from there on. **75m/C DVD.** *US* John Livingston, Sabrina Lloyd, Bruno Campos, Reuben Grundy, Kathleen Antonia, Nicole Wilder; **D:** Mark Decena; **W:** Mark Decena, Timothy Breithardt; **C:** Robert Humphreys; **M:** Eric Holland.

Double Agent 73 🐾 **1980** (R) The title refers to star Chesty Morgan's amazing bust size. Here, she's a secret agent who has a camera/bomb implanted in her oh, never mind. The result is movie curiosity at best. Director Doris Wishman doesn't care about the plot and neither should you. Saul Meth, Jill Harris, Louis Burdi, Frank Silvano, Saul Meth, Jill Harris, Louis Burdi, Peter Petrillo, Cooper Kent; **D:** Doris Wishman, Andrew Charas, Judy J. Kushner; **C:** Yuri Havir; **D:** Doris Wishman. **VIDEO**

Dope Agents 🐾 **La Nuit Des Espions; Night Encounter 1959** Two double agents are sent on a rendezvous to exchange vital government secrets. Dubbed in English. **81m/B VHS.** Fr Marina Vlady, Michel Etcheverry, Roger Crouzet, Robert Hossein, Robert Le Beal, Clement Harari; **D:** Robert Hossein; **W:** Andre Goselain.

Dot.Kill 🐾½ **2005** (R) Getting a cyber-thrill by broadcasting his victims' deaths via his website, a savage murderer is pursued by gruff, drug-addicted cop Charlie Daines (Assante) who gets put on the case and, as his bad luck would have it, ends up on the psycho's to-do list. Not much of a whodunit. **90m/C VHS, DVD.** Armand Assante, Sonny Marinelli, Raffaello Degruttola, Ciare Holman, Frank Nasso; **D:** John Irvin; **W:** Damian Brom-

Double Bang 🐾🐾 **2001** (R) Honest cop Billy Benson decides to take the law into his own hands when his ex-partner is killed by a smalltime mobster. Standard actioner. **104m/C VHS, DVD.** William Baldwin, Adam Baldwin, Jon Seda, Elizabeth Mitchell, Richard Portnow, John Capodice, Sofia Milos; **D:** Heywood Gould; **C:** Jacques Robin; **M:** Andre Gosselain.

Double Cross 🐾🐾 **1992** (R) Tank Polling (Connery), a British journalist, uses the secrets of an ex-hooker (Donohoe) to get back at a corrupt politician who ruined Polling's life five years earlier. Lots of action and a few graphic murders in this thriller. **96m/C VHS.** Amanda Donohoe, Peter Wyngarde, Jason Connery; **C:** David Rush Morrison. **VIDEO**

Double Cross 🐾🐾 **1994** (R) Man has what seems to be a chance erotic encounter with a beautiful blonde. But this wouldn't be a thriller if it ended there, so there's blackmail and murder to contend with as well. **95m/C VHS.** Patrick Bergin, Jennifer Tilly, Kelly Preston, Matt Craven, Kevin Tighe; **D:** Michael Keusch; **C:** Tobias Schliessler; **M:** Graeme Coleman.

Double Crossbones 🐾🐾½ **1951** Rubbery comedian O'Connor becomes an unlikely scourge of the high seas. Meek Charleston shop assistant Dave is accused of piracy after stumbling onto the governor's (Emery) nefarious schemes. Stowing away on a brigantine, Dave goes through a series of adventures and winds up a notorious pirate captain who's determined to rescue beautiful Lady Sylvia (Carter), the governor's ward, from an arranged marriage. **75m/C DVD.** Donald O'Connor, Helena Carter, John Emery, Will Geer, Charles T. Barton, Hope Emerson; **D:** Charles T. Barton; **W:** Oscar Brodney; **C:** Maury Gertsman; **M:** Frank Skinner.

Double-Crossed 🐾🐾½ **1991** In 1984 Barry Seal agrees to inform on Colombia's Medellin Cartel and its links to the Sandanista government of Nicaragua in exchange for leniency on drug-smuggling charges. Little does he know that the personal consequences will turn deadly when his cover is blown and the government double-crosses him. Hopper's hyped-up performance as drug smuggler turned

Double Agents 🐾 **La Nuit Des Espions; Night Encounter 1959**

Double Deal 🐾🐾 **1939** An honest man and a gangster are rivals in love. The gangster robs a jewelry store and tries to pin the crime on the good guy. This is a low movie with a moral so don't expect him to get away with it. **6?m/C VHS.** Monte Hawley, Jeni Le Gon, Edward Thompson, Florence O'Brien; **D:** Arthur Dreifuss.

Double Deal 🐾½ **1950** Murder, mayhem, and industrial espionage come into play as parties fight over an oil field. **66m/B VHS.** Marie Windsor, Richard Denning, Taylor Holmes; **D:** Abby Berlin.

Double Deal 🐾½ **1984** Unfaithful woman and her lover plot to steal priceless opal from hubby. Liteless and silly. **90m/C VHS.** Louis Jourdan, Angela Punch McGregor; **D:** Brian Kavanagh.

Double Down 🐾½ **Zigs 2001** (R) Five buddies, for whom gambling is a career, owe a lot of moolah to the local L.A. bookies. Naturally, they decide that one last bet will get them out of debt and on their way to their dream of owning a sports bar. Low-budget feature with lots of fang. **93m/C VHS, DVD.** Peter Dobson, Jason Priestley, Orien Richman, Kane Picoy, Richard Portnow, Luca Pa anca, Alicia Coppola, Alex Mars Callahan; **C:** Christopher Pearson.

Double Double Toil and Trouble 🐾🐾½ **1994** The twins come to the financial rescue of their family when Dad's business gets into trouble and their home is threatened. But first they need to get a magic moonstone from their wicked Aunt Agatha (Leachman) and rescue kind Aunt Sophia, all before midnight on Halloween. Made for TV, before kiddies amused. **96m/C VHS, DVD.** Scott Wolf, Mark Decascos, Robert Patrick, Alyssa Milano, Kristina Maarclro Wagner, Julia Nickson-Sinatra, Jane Russell, Groucho Marx, Don Paiva, Lou Nova, Joe Devlin; **D:** Irving Cummings.

Double Dragon 🐾🐾½ **1994** (PG-13) Generally harmless brain candy, based on the videogame, finds orphaned brothers Jimmy (Dacascos) and Billy (Wolf) living in the rubble of post earthquake L.A., circa 2007. They have half of a mystical dragon amulet and obsessed mogul Koga Shuko (Patrick), who possesses the other half, after them. Seems he needs the entire amulet in order to control its vast power. Non-stop action should keep the kiddies amused. **96m/C VHS, DVD.** Scott Wolf, Mark Dacascos, Robert Patrick, Alyssa Milano, Kristina Maarclro Wagner, Julia Nickson-Sinatra, Jane Russell, Groucho Marx, Don McGuire, Howard Freeman, Harry Hayden, Nestor Paiva, Lou Nova, Joe Devlin; **W:** Melville Shavelson.

Double Dynamite 🐾🐾½ **1992** (PG-13) It's Only Money 1951 A bank teller is at a loss when his racetrack winnings are confused with the cash lifted from his bank during a robbery. Forgettable forgotten shambles. Originally filmed in 1948. **80m/B VHS.** Frank Sinatra, Jane Russell, Groucho Marx, Don McGuire, Howard Freeman, Harry Hayden, Nestor Paiva, Lou Nova, Joe Devlin; **W:** Melville Shavelson.

Double Edge 🐾½ **American Dragons 1997** (R) Obsessec NYC cop Tony Luca (Biehn) tries to bring down crime lord Roc-oo (Stark) but things go so badly and instead he's taken off the case. His new assign-

Double Edge 🐾½ **1992** (PG-13) The Palestinian-Israeli conflict is the focus of this drama about an ambitious reporter (Dunaway). On her first foreign assignment, New Yorker Faye Milano finds herself way out of her depth when she covers a colleague's beat in Jerusalem. Unable to remain a detached observer, Faye instead becomes an active participant, alternating between her affair with an Israeli reserves officer and her friendship with a family of Palestinian intifada leaders. Dunaway and Kollek are unfortunately stiff in their performances but the location (Israel and the West Bank) is interesting and the story surprisingly balanced. **85m/C VHS.** *IS* Faye Dunaway, Amos Kollek, Muhamad Bakri, Shmuel Shilo, Makram Khoury, Michael Schneider, Anat Azmon, Ann Belkin; **D:** Amos Kollek; **W:** Amos Kollek.

The Doorway 🐾½ **2000** (R) Four college students are fixing up a house that they discover is built over a doorway to hell—and they've just opened it up. So they ask the local expert on the paranormal (Scheider, whose role is very limited) for help. **91m/C VHS, DVD.** Roy Scheider, Lauren Woodland, Suzanne Bridgham, Teresa De Priest, Christian Harmony, Don Maloney; **D:** Michael B. Druxman; **W:** Yoram Astrakhan. **VIDEO**

Doomwatch 🐾🐾½ **1972** (R) A scientist discovers a chemical company is dumping poison into local waters, deforming the inhabitants of an isolated island when they eat the catch of the day. Unsurprising. **89m/C VHS, DVD.** *GB* Ian Bannen, Judy Geeson, John Paul, Simon Oates, George Sanders; **D:** Peter Sasdy; **W:** Clive Exton; **C:** Ken Talbot.

Double Deal 🐾🐾 **1939** An honest man and a gangster are rivals in love.

ment is investigating yakuza murders in Little Tokyo, which has also drawn the unwanted attention of South Korean detective Kim (Park), who recognizes the killer's MO. But when mobsters also start dying it turns out the bad guy is trying to get rid of the mob and the yakuza and take over. **95m/C VHS.** Michael Biehn, Joong-Hoon Park, Cary-Hiroyuki Tagawa, Don Stark, Byron Mann; **D:** Ralph Hemecker; **W:** Erik Saltzgaber; **C:** Ernest Holzman; **M:** Joel Goldsmith, K. Alexander (Alex) Wilkinson. **VIDEO**

Double Exposure 🦴🦴 **1982 (R)** A young photographer's violent nightmares become the next day's headlines. Unsurprising vision. **95m/C VHS.** Michael Callan, James Stacy, Joanna Pettet, Cleavon Little, Pamela Hensley, Seymour Cassel, David Young, Misty Rowe, Don Potter; **D:** William B. Hillman.

Double Exposure 🦴1/2 **1993 (R)** A possessive husband discovers his wife's infidelity and decides to get revenge, only his plan doesn't work out as he intends. **93m/C VHS.** Ron Perlman, Ian Buchanan, Jennifer Gatti, William R. Moses, James McEachin, Dedee Pfeiffer; **D:** Claudia Hoover; **W:** Christine Colfer, Bridget Hoffman, Claudia Hoover.

Double Exposure: The Story of Margaret Bourke-White 🦴1/2 **1989** Beautifully shot but slow biography of a woman who became a well-known professional photographer for "Life" magazine during the 1930s and 1940s, as well as the first official female photojournalist of WWII. **105m/C VHS.** Farrah Fawcett, Frederic Forrest, Mitchell Ryan, David Huddleston, Jay Patterson, Ken Marshall; **D:** Lawrence Schiller; **C:** Robert Elswit. **CABLE**

Double Face 🦴1/2 **1970** A wealthy industrialist kills his lesbian wife with a car bomb, but she seems to haunt him through pornographic films. **84m/C VHS. IT GE** Christiane Kruger, Gunther Stoll, Sydney Chaplin, Klaus Kinski, Annabella Incontrera; **D:** Riccardo Freda; **W:** Riccardo Freda, Paul Hengge; **C:** Gabor Pogany; **M:** Nora Orlandi.

Double Happiness 🦴🦴🦴 **1994 (PG-13)** Slice of life comedy-drama finds 20-something Chinese-Canadian Jade Li (Oh) struggling to balance her would-be acting career and new world romance with her family's traditional values. Jade wants to please her old world father (Chang) so she endures his arranged dates and puts on a pleasant demeanor for family friends. But Jade must decide who she wants to be when she gets involved with non-Asian college student Mark (Rennie). Fine performances and assured direction from Shum in her feature film debut. **87m/C VHS. DVD. CA** Sandra Oh, Stephen Chang, Alannah Ong, Frances You, Johnny Mah, Callum Keith Rennie; **D:** Mina Shum; **W:** Mina Shum; **C:** Peter Wunstorf. Genie '94: Actress (Oh), Film Editing.

Double Identity 🦴1/2 **1989 (PG-13)** Former college professor turned criminal Mancuso moves to a corn patch called New Hope in hopes of returning to the straight and narrow. He finds a good woman to stand by him, but, alas, crime, like smoking, is easier to start than to quit. Much intrigue and deceit. **95m/C VHS. CA FR** Nick Mancuso, Leah K. Pinsent, Patrick Bauchau, Anne LeTourneau, Jacques Godin; **D:** Yves Boisset.

Double Impact 🦴1/2 **1991 (R)** Van Damme plays twins re-united in Hong Kong to avenge their parents' murder by local bad guys, but this tunkhead kick-em-up doesn't even take advantage of that gimmick; the basic story would have been exactly the same with just one Jean-Claude. Lots of profane dialogue and some gratuitous nudity for the kiddies. **107m/C VHS. DVD.** Jean-Claude Van Damme, Cory (Corinna) Everson, Geoffrey Lewis; **D:** Sheldon Lettich; **W:** Jean-Claude Van Damme, Sheldon Lettich; **C:** Richard H. Kline; **M:** Arthur Kempel.

Double Indemnity 🦴🦴🦴🦴 **1944** The classic seedy story of insurance agent Walter Neff (MacMurray), who's seduced by deadly blonde Phyllis Dietrichson (Stanwyck) into killing her husband (Powers) so they can collect together from his company. But the husband's "accident" invites suspicions from claims adjustor Keyes (Robinson) and Walter and Phyllis begin to turn on each other. Terrific, influential film noir, the best of its kind. Based on the James M. Cain novel. **107m/B VHS. DVD.** Fred MacMurray, Barbara Stanwyck, Edward G. Robinson, Tom Powers, Porter Hall, Jean Heather, Byron Barr, Fortunio Bonanova; **D:** Billy Wilder; **W:** Raymond Chandler, Billy Wilder; **C:** John Seitz; **M:** Miklos Rozsa. AFI '98: Top 100, Natl. Film Reg. '92.

Double Jeopardy 🦴🦴 **1992 (R)** Boxleitner stars as a married man who risks his family and life when his sexy ex-lover returns to town. She easily involves him in deception—and murder. A cakewalk for Ward as the femme fatale. **101m/C VHS.** Bruce Boxleitner, Rachel Ward, Sela Ward, Sally Kirkland; **D:** Lawrence Schiller; **M:** Eduard Artemyew. **CABLE**

Double Jeopardy 🦴1/2 **1999 (R)** This film really doesn't make much sense. But it certainly struck a nerve, as well as box-office gold, as an entertaining thriller, probably because it doesn't give you much time to catch your breathe or think about plot holes. Libby (Judd) does time for murdering hubby Nick (Greenwood) after she's set up by the sleaze. Once she's released, she decides since she can't be tried for the same crime twice (this is actually faulty logic), she might as well get rid of the lowlife for real. Wisecracking parole officer Travis Lehman (Jones) winds up getting deeply involved in ferreting out the truth of the messy situation. **105m/C VHS. DVD.** Ashley Judd, Tommy Lee Jones, Bruce Greenwood, Annabeth Gish, Roma Maffia, Jay Brazeau, Gillian Barber, Davenia McFadden, Spencer (Treat) Clark; **D:** Bruce Beresford; **W:** David Weisberg, Douglas S. Cook; **C:** Peter James; **M:** Normand Corbeil.

A Double Life 🦴🦴🦴 **1947** Colman plays a Shakespearean actor in trouble when the characters he plays begin to seep into his personal life and take over. Things begin to look really bad when he is cast in the role of the cursed Othello. Colman won an Oscar for this difficult role, and the moody musical score garnered another for Rozsa. **107m/B VHS. DVD.** Ronald Colman, Shelley Winters, Signe Hasso, Edmond O'Brien, Ray Collins, Millard Mitchell; **D:** George Cukor; **W:** Ruth Gordon, Garson Kanin; **C:** Milton Krasner; **M:** Miklos Rozsa. Oscars '47: Actor (Colman), Orig. Dramatic Score; Golden Globes '48: Actor—Drama (Colman).

The Double Life of Veronique 🦴🦴🦴 *La Double Vie de Veronique* **1991 (R)** They say everyone has a twin, but this is ridiculous. Two women—Polish Veronika and French Veronique—are born on the same day in different countries, share a singing talent, a cardiac ailment, and, although the two never meet, a strange awareness of each other. Jacob is unforgettable as the two women, and director Krzysztof creates some spellbinding scenes but the viewer has to be willing to forgo plot for atmosphere. **96m/C VHS. DVD. FR PL** Irene Jacob, Philippe Volter, Sandrine Dumas, Aleksander Bardini, Louis Ducreux, Claude Duneton, Halina Gryglaszewska, Kalina Jedrusik; **D:** Krzysztof Kieslowski; **W:** Krzysztof Kieslowski, Krzysztof Piesiewicz; **C:** Slawomir Idziak; **M:** Zbigniew Preisner. Cannes '91: Actress (Jacob); Natl. Soc. Film Critics '91: Foreign Film.

The Double McGuffin 🦴🦴 **1979 (PG)** A plot of international intrigue is uncovered by teenagers—a la the Hardy Boys—when a prime minister and her security guard pay a visit to a small Virginia community. They're not believed, though. Action-packed from the makers of Benji. Dogs do not figure prominently here. **100m/C VHS. DVD.** Ernest Borgnine, George Kennedy, Elke Sommer, Ed "Too Tall" Jones, Lisa Whelchel, Vincent Spano; **D:** Joe Camp; **M:** Euel Box; **V:** Orson Welles.

The Double Negative 🦴1/2 *Deadly Companion* **1980** A photojournalist pursues his wife's killer in a confusing story. Based on Ross MacDonald's "The Three Roads." **96m/C VHS. CA** Michael Sarrazin, Susan Clark, Anthony Perkins, Howard Duff, Kate Reid, Al Waxman, Elizabeth Shepherd, John Candy; **D:** George Bloomfield; **W:** Janis Allen.

The Double O Kid 🦴🦴1/2 **1992 (PG-13)** Lance is a 17-year-old video game master who's interning at the Agency, a covert spy organization. Ordered to rush a package to Los Angeles, Lance discovers that a madman computer virus designer and his henchwoman desperately want what he's carrying. Aided by the prerequisite pretty girl, Lance must avoid all the hazards sent his way. **95m/C VHS.** Corey Haim, Wallace Shawn, Brigitte Nielsen, Nicole Eggert, John Rhys-Davies, Basil Hoffman, Karen Black; *Cameos:* Anne Francis; **D:** Duncan McLachlan; **W:** Andrea Buck, Duncan McLachlan.

Double Obsession 🦴1/2 **1993 (R)** College roommates Heather (Hemingway) and Claire (d'Abo) are inseparable friends—until Claire falls in love. Heather becomes possessive and, though the years pass, her obsession with Claire only grows. When Heather's affections turn deadly, can Claire stop her? **88m/C VHS.** Margaux Hemingway, Maryam D'Abo, Frederic Forrest, Scott Valentine; **D:** Eduardo Montes; **W:** Jeffrey Delman, R.J. Marx, Eduardo Montes.

Double or Nothing 🦴1/2 **1937** Lighthearted musical comedy. An eccentric millionaire believes people are basically honest. In his will, he instructs his lawyer to drop four money-filled wallets on the streets to see if they'll be returned. The honest folk get $5000 and a chance to inherit the rest of the Clark fortune if they double their money (legally) in a month, otherwise it goes to a group of greedy relatives. The four (Crosby, Raye, Devine, Frawley) decide to pool their efforts and Der Bingle takes a shot at opening a nightclub while withstanding a series of dirty tricks. **90m/B DVD.** Bing Crosby, Martha Raye, Andy Devine, William Frawley, Mary Carlisle, Samuel S. Hinds, Fay Holden, William Henry; **D:** Theodore Reed; **W:** Erwin Gelsey, John Moffitt, Charles Lederer, Duke Atteberry; **C:** Karl Struss; **M:** Boris Morros.

Double Parked 🦴🦴1/2 **2000** Meter maid Rita (Thorne) is divorced from an alcoholic abuser and finally has a steady job. Which she needs to support her teenaged son Matt (Read) who suffers from cystic fibrosis and bad judgement since his best friend is a delinquent (Fleiss). Rita's been taken care of business while putting her personal needs on hold but that's about to change. Fine performances. **98m/C VHS. DVD.** Callie (Calliope) Thorne, Rufus Read, Noah Fleiss, William Sage, Anthony De Sando, Eileen Galindo, Michelle Hurd, P.J. Brown; **D:** Stephen Kinsella; **W:** Stephen Kinsella, Paul Solberg; **C:** Jim Denault; **M:** Craig Hazen, David Wolfert.

Double Platinum 🦴🦴1/2 **1999 (PG)** Baby diva Brandy squares off against mega-diva Ross—the mommy who abandoned her for a fabulous career. Eighteen years later Brandy decides to pursue a singing career herself and meets Ross—not knowing about their relationship. But when she finds out, there are a lot of abandonment issues to deal with and this teen is determined to get to know her own mommy dearest at her own game. You go, girl! **91m/C VHS. DVD.** Diana Ross, Brandy Norwood, Harvey Fierstein, Roger Rees, Brian Stokes Mitchell, Christine Ebersole, Tony Payne; **D:** Robert Allan Ackerman; **W:** Nina Shengold, Katie Ford, Renee Longstreet. **TV**

Double Play 🦴🦴1/2 **1996 (PG)** Updated version of "The Prince and the Pauper" finds teenaged computer genius Rudy (Jackson) inheriting his dad's successful computer company. But his evil Uncle Mike (Shatner), who's not the boy's guardian, wants the company for himself and hires some thugs to kidnap the kid and force him to sign over control of the business. But Rudy just happens to have a double—a high school baseball star who's in town for the championship game—and confusion rules when he takes his place. Jackson's brother, Richard Lee Jackson, plays his cousin in the movie. **101m/C VHS.** William Shatner, Richard Lee Jackson, Jay Brazeau; **D:** Stefan Scaini; **W:** Richard Clark; **C:** Maris Jansons; **M:** John Welsman.

Double Revenge 🦴1/2 **1989** Two men feel they have a score to settle after a bank heist gone sour leaves two people dead. **90m/C VHS.** Bobby DiCicco, Joe Dallesandro, Nancy Everhard, Leigh McCloskey, Richard Rust, Theresa Saldana; **D:** Armand Mastroianni.

Double Standard 🦴1/2 **1988** You'll be less concerned with the plot—a community discovers that a prominent judge has maintained two marriages for nearly 20 years—than with the possibility that such dim-witted myopes might actually have existed in the real world. This made-for-TV slice of bigamy is for fans of the oops-I-forgot-I'm-married genre only. **95m/C VHS.** Robert Foxworth, Michele Greene, Pamela Bellwood, James Kee; **D:** Louis Rudolph.

Double Suicide 🦴🦴🦴 *Shinju Ten No Amijima* **1969** From a play by Monzarmon Chikamatsu, a tragic drama about a poor salesman in 18th century Japan who falls in love with a geisha and ruins his family and himself trying to requite the hopeless passion. Stylish with Iwashita turning in a wonderful dual performance. In Japanese with subtitles. **105m/B VHS. DVD. JP** Kichiemon Nakamura, Shima Iwashita, Yusuke Takita, Hosei Komatsu; **D:** Masahiro Shinoda; **W:** Masahiro Shinoda, Toru Takemitsu, Taeko Tomioka; **C:** Toichiro Narushima; **M:** Toru Takemitsu.

Double Take 🦴 **1997 (R)** Writer Connor McEwen (Sheffer) witnesses a murder and identifies the suspect from a police line-up. But when he sees a dead ringer for the alleged murderer, he becomes convinced the police have arrested the wrong guy. **86m/C VHS.** Craig Sheffer, Costas Mandylor, Brigitte Bako, Torri Higginson, Maurice Godin; **D:** Mark L. Lester; **W:** Ed Rugoff, Ralph Rugoff; **M:** Paul Zaza.

Double Take 🦴🦴 **2001 (PG-13)** Businessman Daryl Chase (Jones) is framed as a money-launderer for a drug cartel and assumes the identity of street hustler Freddy (Griffin) in order to clear his name. Fans of "Mad TV" and "Malcolm and Eddie" (Jones and Griffin's TV ventures, respectively) will probably be sorely disappointed with this action-comedy attempt. While the two stars trade zingers and dodge gunfire, you're left to wonder why you didn't rent "Midnight Run," or even "Beverly Hills Cop 3." **88m/C VHS. DVD. US** Orlando Jones, Eddie Griffin, Gary Grubbs, Daniel Roebuck, Sterling Macer, Garcelle Beauvais, Edward Hermann, Benny Nieves, Shawn Elliott, Brent Briscoe, Carlos Carrasco; **D:** George Gallo; **W:** George Gallo; **C:** Theo van de Sande; **M:** Graeme Revell.

Double Tap 🦴🦴 **1998 (R)** Undercover FBI agent becomes personally interested in the vigilante she's pursuing—whose purpose is to bring down a drug cartel. Not much to recommend this one, except Stephen Rea's performance. **99m/C VHS.** Heather Locklear, Stephen Rea, Peter Greene, Mykelti Williamson, Kevin Gage, Robert LaSardo, Richard Edson, A. Martinez; **D:** Greg Yaitanes; **C:** John Peters; **M:** Moby.

Double Team 🦴🦴 **1997 (R)** Counter-terrorist expert Jack Quinn (Van Damme) teams with weapons specialist Yaz (Rodman, in his film debut) to take down international terrorist Stavros (Roarke). After Jack kills Stavros's son, he is sent to a high-security superspy retirement village. When his wife and newborn son are kidnapped, Jack escapes, with Yaz's help, to finish the job and try to save his family. Van Damme teams with his third famous Hong Kong action director, Tsui Hark (the other two are John Woo and Ringo Lam) to create yet another disappointment. He's slightly more charismatic than usual (not saying much), but Rodman easily steals the flick as he gets most of the good lines, and delivers them with relish. **93m/C VHS. DVD.** Jean-Claude Van Damme, Dennis Rodman, Mickey Rourke, Natasha Lindinger, Paul Freeman, Valeria Cavalli, Jay Benedict, Bruno Bilotta; **D:** Tsui Hark; **W:** Paul Mones, Don Jakoby; **C:** Peter Pau; **M:** Gary Chang. Golden Raspberries '97: Worst Support. Actor (Rodman), Worst New Star (Rodman).

Double Threat 🦴🦴 **1992 (R)** An aging sex star makes her return to the screen opposite a younger actor with whom she is having an affair. When the director wants to include nude sex scenes in the film she agrees to use a younger body-double. Then the actress discovers her lover is involved in off-screen action with the double as well. This does not please her and she decides to take a deadly revenge. An unrated version is also available. **94m/C** VHS, Sally Kirkland, Andrew Stevens, Lisa Shane, Richard Lynch, Anthony (Tony) Franciosa, Sherrie Rose, Chick Vennera; **D:** David A. Prior.

Double Whammy 🎬🎬 2001 (R)
DiCillo's attempt at Tarantino crimedy doesn't quite work out. Leary is Ray Pluto, a cop with a bad back with lousy timing and a past that haunts him. When his back gives out during a restaurant shooting, he's put on desk duty and sent to sexy chiropractor Hurley, who eventually heals his love life as well as his vertebrae. Weak subplots include his building super's at-

Double Wedding 🎬🎬🎬 1937
Madcap comedy starring Powell as a wacky painter who doesn't believe in working and Loy as a workaholic dress designer. Loy has chosen a fiance for her younger sister, Irene, to marry, but Irene has plans of her own. When Irene and her beau meet bohemian Powell, the fun really begins. Script suffers slightly from too much slapstick and not enough wit, although the stars (in their seventh outing as a duo) play it well. Based on a play "Great Love" by Ferenc Molnar. **86m/B** VHS, DVD, William Powell, Myrna Loy, Florence Rice, John Beal, Jessie Ralph, Edgar Kennedy, Sidney Toler, Mary Gordon; **D:** Richard Thorpe; .o Swerling.

Double Trouble 🎬🎬 1941
Langdon and Rogers are hired to work in a canning factory and accidentally package a valuable necklace in a can of beans. The rest is a mad chase of cops, criminals, and crying women. A B-side. Based on a story by Marc Brandel. **92m/C** VHS, Elvis Presley, Annette Day, John Williams, Yvonne Romain, Michael Murphy, Chips Rafferty, Helen Winston; **D:** Norman Taurog; **W:** Jo Heims.

Double Trouble 🎬 1967
rock star Presley falls in love with an English heiress. The king belts out "Long Legged Girl" while evading cops, wealthy and politically well-connected businessmen and his righthand men. **87m/C** VHS, David Pau, Peter Paul, James Doohan, Roddy McDowall, Steve Kanaly, A.J. (Anthony) Johnson, David Carradine; **D:** John Paragon.

Double Vision 🎬🎬 1992 (PG-13) Twin brothers—one a cop, one a jewel thief—team up to crack the case of an international jewel smuggling ring headed by a wealthy and politically well-connected murder. The king belts out attempted murder. The king belts out "Long Legged Girl" while evading cops. **C** VHS, David Pau, Peter Paul, James Doohan, Roddy McDowall, Steve Kanaly, A.J. (Anthony) Johnson, David Carradine; **D:** John Paragon.

Double Vision 🎬🎬 2002 (R) FBI agent Kevin Richter (Morse) pairs up with troubled Taiwanese "foreign affairs officer and former detective Huang Huo-tu (Leung Ka-Fai) to hunt for a serial killer who uses random methods that don't seem scientifically possible. But the victims do have cne thing in common—a black fungus found in their brain that appears to cause deadly hallucinations. As Huang digs further he discovers the crimes mimic ritualized murders committed by an ancient mystic cult. English and Chinese with subtitles. **110m/C** VHS, DVD, HK Tony Leung Ka-Fai, David Morse, Fene Liu, Brett Climo, Leon Dai; **D:** Kuo-fu Chen; **W:** Kuo-fu Chen, Chao-Fin Ju; **C:** Arthur Wong Ngo-Tai. **M:** Sin-yun Lee.

Doug's 1st Movie 🎬 1999 (G)
Feature-length version of the children's animated series assumes sequels accordding to the title, but has problem stretching the storyline over an hour. However, kids who like the series will enjoy the adventures of 12-year-old Doug Funnie and his pal Skeeter as they try to hide the lake monster Herman Melville (so named because he tries to eat a copy of "Moby Dick") from the clutches of polluting bad guy Mr. 3luff. He also has to impress Patti before the big Valentine's Day Dance. Not overly preachy, but the animation will not impress children used to the glossy Disney style. **77m/C** VHS, **D:** Maurice Joyce; **W:** Ker Scarborough; **M:** Mark Watters; **V:** Jay Hadley, Eddie Korbich, Thomas McHugh, Fred Newman, Chrs Phillips, Constance Shulman, Frank Welker, Alice Playten, Doris Belack, Doug Preis.

The Dove 🎬🎬 1974 (PG-13) The true story of a 16-year-old's adventures as he sails around the world in a 23-foot sloop. The trip took him five years and along the way he falls in love with a girl who follows him to exotic locales. Photography and scenery are magnificent. **105m/C** VHS, Joseph Bottoms, Deborah Raffin, Dabney Coleman, Peter Gwynne; **D:** Charles Jarrott; **W:** Peter S. Beagle. **C:** Sven Nykvist.

Down Among the Z Men 🎬🎬 1952 Enlisted man helps a girl save an atomic formula from spies. Funny in spots but weighed down by musical numbers from a female entourage. From the pre-Monty Python comedy troupe "The Goons." **71m/B** VHS, DVD, GB Peter Sellers, Spike Milligan, Harry Secombe, Michael Bentine, Carole Carr; **D:** Maclean Rogers.

Down & Dirty 🎬🎬🎬 1955
e Cattivi; Ugly, Dirty and Bad; Dirty, Mean and Nasty 1976 A scathing Italian satire about a modern Ro:nan family steeped in petty crime, incest, murder, adultery, drugs, and arson. In Italian with English subtitles. **115m/C** VHS, IT Nino Manfredi, Francesco Animalli, Maria Bosco; **D:** Ettore Scola; **W:** Ruggero Maccari, Ettore Scola; **C:** Dario Di Palma; **M:** Armando Trovajoli. Cannes '76: Director (Scola).

Down and Out in Beverly Hills 🎬🎬½ 1986 (R) A modern retelling of Jean Renoir's classic "Boudu Saved from Drowning" with some nice star turns. Neurotic and wealthy Beverly Hills married Dave (Dreyfuss) and Barbara (Midler) find

tempted murder by his daughter, and a screenwriting duo who also, coincidentally, want to 3e the next Tarantino. Occasionally inspired, but DiCillo can't make the comedy and romance fit with the sometimes brutal violence. **93m/C** VHS, DVD, Denis Leary, Elizabeth Hurley, Steve Buscemi, Luis Guzman, Victor Argo, Christopher Noth, Donald Adeosun Faison, Maurice Smith; **D:** Tom DiCillo; **W:** Tom DiCillo; **C:** Robert Yeoman; **M:** Jim Farmer.

Doubting Thomas 🎬🎬½ 1935
Rogers' last film, which was in theatres when he was killed in a plane crash. Silly story of a husband and his doubts about his wife and her amateur-acting career. The show goes on in spite of his doubts, her forgotten lines, and wardrobe goofs. Remake of 1922's silent film "The Torch Bearers." **78m/B** VHS, Will Rogers, Billie Burke, Alison Skipworth, Sterling Holloway; **D:** David Butler.

Doughboys 🎬🎬½ 1935 Forward March 1930 Keaton's second talkie is a so-so comedy about a rich man who mistakenly enlists in the Army during WWI. He manages to bumble his way through basic training and win the heart of a pretty girl. There are a few bright moments, particularly a musical number between Keaton and "Ukulele Ike" Edwards. **80m/B** VHS, Buster Keaton, Cliff Edwards, Arnold Brcpny, Sally Eilers, Victor Potel, Arnold Korff, Frank Mayo; **D:** Edward Sedgwick.

Doughnuts & Society 🎬½ 1936 Two elderly ladies who run a coffee-shop suddenly strike it rich and find that life among the bluebloods is not all it's cracked up to be. No sprinkles. **70m/B** VHS, Louise Fazenda, Maude Eburne, Eddie Nugent, Ann Rutherford, Hedda Hopper, Franklin Pangborn; **D:** Lewis D. Collins; **W:** Karen De Wolf, Wallace MacDonell; **C:** Edward Sedgwick.

Down Argentine Way 🎬🎬🎬
1940 A lovely young woman falls in love with a suave Argentinian horse breeder. First-rate Fox musical made a star of Grable and smash hit songs are delivered by South American Way; Down Argentina Sing to Your Senorita. **90m/C** VHS, DVD, Don Ameche, Betty Grable, Carmen Miranda, Charlotte Greenwood, J. Carrol Naish, Henry Stephenson, Leonid Kinskey, Kay Aldridge, Chris-Pin (Eugene) Martin, Charles (Jude, Judels) Judels; **D:** Irving Cummings; **W:** Rian James, Ralph Spence, Karl Tunberg; **C:** Leon Shamroy, Ray Renahan; **M:** Mack Gordon.

Down by Law 🎬🎬🎬 1986 (R) In Jarmusch's follow-up to his successful "Stranger than Paradise," he introduces us to three men: a pimp, an out-of-work disc jockey, and an Italian tourist. When the three 3reak out of prison, they wander through the Louisiana swampland with some regrets about their new-found freedom. Slow-moving at times, beautifully shot throughout. Poignant and hilarious, the film is true to Jarmusch form: some will love the film's offbeat flair, and others will find it bothersome. **107m/B** VHS, DVD, John Lurie, Tom Waits, Rogerto Benigni, Ellen Barkin, Billie Neal, Rockets Redglare, Vernel Bagneris, Nicoleta Braschi; **D:** Jim Jarmusch; **W:** Jim Jarmusch; **C:** Robby Müller; **M:** John Lurie, Tom Waits.

Down Came a Blackbird 🎬🎬½ 1994 (R) Anna Lenka (Redgrave), a Holocaust survivor, runs a clinic for healing both the physical and psychological wounds of torture victims. Journalist Helen McNulty (Dern), herself a survivor, decides to write about the clinic but Anna believes Helen's covering up the pain she's never dealt with. Also at the clinic is Tomas Ramirez (Julia), a former college professor with a terrible secret with whom Helen discovers a special rapport. Conventional script with some fine performances; Julia died shortly after principal photography was completed on the TV film, which is dedicated to his memory. **112m/C** VHS, Vanessa Redgrave, Laura Dern, Raul Julia, Jay O. Sanders, Cliff Gorman, Santa Choudhury, L. Scott Caldwell, Jeffrey DeMunn; **D:** Jonathan Sanger; **W:** Kevin Droney; **C:** Kees Van Oostrum; **M:** Graeme Revell.

Down Dakota Way 🎬🎬 1949
Strange coincidence between a recent murder and a fatal cow epidemic. Rogers helps some locals bring the link to light. **67m/C** VHS, DVD, Roy Rogers, Dale Evans, Pat Brady, Morte Montana, Elisabeth Riston, Byron Barr, James B. Cardwell, Roy Barcroft, Emmett Vogan; **D:** William Witney.

Down in the Delta 🎬🎬🎬 1998 (PG-13) Chicago matriarch Rosa Lynn (Alice) tries to prevent her jobless, single-mom daughter Loretta (Woodard) from succumbing to drugs, alcohol, and the other destructive forces that are a part of her rough neighborhood. She sends her Loretta and her two grandchildren (including an autistic boy) to her brother's home in the Mississippi delta, hoping that they'll reconnect to their roots. Though reluctant at first, Loretta finds herself slowly changing her ways as she works in Uncle Earl's restaurant; she is moved by his love of family, particularly his Alzheimer-ridden wife (Rolle). Poet-novelist Maya Angelou's first outing as a director skillfully demonstrates the importance of connecting to one's heritage. Woodard shines energetically as the strung-out mom and Freeman is near-

their lives turned upside down when they prevent suicidal bum Jerry Baskin (Nolte) from drowning in their pool. Jerry takes over the household—bedding Barbara (Midler), and their daughter Jenny (Nelson), and their surly maid Carmen (Pena)—offering encouragement to a frustrated Dave and his son Max (Richards)—and even solving family dog Matisse's identity crisis. Naturally, Jerry learns there's more to life than being a bum. **103m/C** VHS, DVD, Nick Nolte, Bette Midler, Richard Dreyfuss, Little Richard, Tracey Nelson, Elizabeth Pena, Evan Richards, Valerie Curtin, Barry Primus, Dorothy Tristan, Alexis Arquette; **D:** Paul Mazursky; **W:** Paul Mazursky, Leon Capetanos; **C:** Donald McAlpine; **M:** Andy Summers.

Down in the Valley 🎬🎬 2005 (R) Wannabe cowboy hero Harlan (Edwards) befriends rebellious, aimless teen Tobe (Wood) and her shy younger brother Lonnie (Culkin). They'a the children of tough San Fernando Valley sheriff Wade (Morse), who immediately distrusts this soft-spoken, tale-spinning stranger. And with good reason, since Harlan is delusional at best and dangerous at his worst. No matter the talen't, flick stretches credibility—particularly in its last act. **114m/C** DVD, US Edward Norton, Evan Rachel Wood, David Morse, Rory Culkin, John Diehl, Kat Dennings, Hunter Parrish, Bruce Dern, Muse Watson, Geoffrey Lewis, Aviva, Aaron Fors, Heather Ashleigh; **D:** David Jacobson; **W:** David Jacobson; **C:** Enrique Chediak.

Down Mexico Way 🎬🎬 1941 Two cowboys come to the aid of a Mexican town whose residents have been hoodwinked by a phony movie company. Very exciting chase on horseback, motorcycle, and in automobiles. **78m/B** VHS, DVD, Gene Autry, Smiley Burnette, Fay McKenzie, Duncan Renaldo; **D:** Joseph Santley.

Down Periscope 🎬🎬½ 1996 (PG-13) Tom Dodge (Grammer) dreams of command for Dodge to get this dream assignment, he and his losers must beat the nuclear subs of generic mean authority figure Admiral Graham (Dern), in a war game. Predictable comedy is kept afloat by amusing cast, especially Schneider as the weaselly Executive Officer Pascal. Many jokes revolve around Dodge's tattoo, which is on a body part that is normally private first-class. Denied cooperation from the U.S. Navy, the shipyard scenes were filmed on three barges tied together in the San Francisco Bay area, with empty discarded frigates and destroyers belonging to the U.S. Department of Transportation playing the feet. **92m/C** VHS, DVD, Kelsey Grammer, Lauer Holly, Bruce Dern, Rob Schneider, Rip Torn, Harry Dean Stanton, William H. Macy, Ken H. Campbell, Toby Huss, Duane Martin, Jonathan Penner, Bradford Tatum, Harland Williams; **D:** David S. Ward; **W:** Hugh Wilson, Andrew Kurtzman, Ellor Weald; **C:** Victor Hammer; **M:** Randy Edelman.

Down Texas Way 🎬🎬 1942 One of the "Rough R:ders" series. When one of the boys is accused of murdering his best friend, his two companions search for the real killer. **57m/B** VHS, DVD, Buck Jones, Tim McCoy, Raymond Hatton; **D:** Howard Brether-

Down the Drain 🎬🎬 1989 (R) A broad-as-a-city-b:ock farce about an unscrupulous criminal lawyer and his assortment of crazy clients. A fine first half but someone pulls the plug in the middle of the bath. **90m/C** VHS, Andrew Stevens, Joseph Campanella, Don Metuszak, Teri Copley, Joseph Campanella, Don Stroud, Stella Stevens, Jerry Mathers, Benny "The Jet" Urquidez; **D:** Fot-ert C. Hughes.

Down the Wyoming Trail 🎬 1939 Western hero Ritter battles some rustlers who are terrorizing farmers during the winter, while still managing to find time to warble some tunes. **52m/B** VHS, Tex Ritter, Horace Murphy, Mary Brodel, Bobby Lawson, Charles "Blackie" King, Bob Terry; **D:** Albert) Herman; **W:** Peter Dixon, Roger Merton.

ly perfect as the elegant and tender Uncle Earl. **111m/C** VHS, DVD, Alfre Woodard, Al Freeman Jr., Mary Alice, Wesley Snipes, Esther Rolle, Loretta Devine, Anna-Maria Johnson, Mpho Koaho, Kulani Hassen, Richard Blackburn; **D:** Maya Angelou; **W:** Myron Goble; **C:** William Wages; **M:** Stanley Clarke. **C.A.B.L.E.**

Down, Out and Dangerous 🎬🎬 1995 (R) Expectant couple Brad (Davison) and Monica (Etlinger) Harrington find out that Tim (Thomas), the charming homeless man they've befriended, is really a psycho killer. **96m/C** VHS, Richard Thomas, Bruce Davison, Cynthia Ettinger, Steve Hytner, Christine Cavanaugh, George DiCenzo, Jason Bernard, Melinda Culea, Stuart Pankin; **D:** Noel Nosseck; **W:** Carey Hayes, Chad Hayes; **C:** Paul Maibaum; **M:** Mark Snow.

Down to Earth 🎬🎬🎬 1917 Ever-gallant lover Fairbanks overruns a mental hospital to save his sweetheart. Once inside, he's determined to show the patients that their illness is their illusion, and reality's the cure. A quixotic gem from Fairbanks's pre-swashbuckling social comic days. Director Emerson's wife was the scenarist, and "The Wizard of Oz" and "Gone with the Wind" (to name a few), was the man behind the camera. 68m/B VHS. Douglas Fairbanks Sr., Eileen (Elaine Persey) Percy, Gustav von Seyffertitz, Charles P. McHugh, Charles Gerrard, William H. Keith, Ruth Allen, Frederico Prosperi; **D:** John Emerson.

Down to Earth 🎬🎬 1947 A lackluster musical and boxoffice flop with an impressive cast. Rita Hayworth is the Greek goddess of dance sent to Earth on a mission to straighten out Broadway producer Parks and his play that ridicules the Greek gods. Anita Ellis dubs the singing of Hayworth. A parody of "Here Comes Mr. Jordan," remade in 1980 as "Xanadu." 101m/C VHS, DVD. Rita Hayworth, Larry Parks, Marc Platt, Roland Culver, James Gleason, Edward Everett Horton, Adele Jergens, George Macready, William Frawley, James Burke, Fred F. Sears, Lynn Merrick, Myron Healey; **D:** Alexander Hall; **W:** Edwin Blum; **M:** George Duning.

Down to Earth 🎬🎬 2001 (PG-13) Rock is called to heaven before his time by angel Levy but the only body available sends him back in is that of a 60-ish white businessman. Rock's presence and comic sensibility saves what could've been a lame time-waster but he's the only reason to see it and if you don't like Rock, don't bother. Remake of "Heaven Can Wait," which was a remake of "Here Comes Mr. Jordan." 87m/C VHS, DVD. US Chris Rock, Regina King, Chazz Palminteri, Eugene Levy, Frankie Faison, Mark Addy, Greg Germann, Jennifer Coolidge; **D:** Chris Weitz, Paul Weitz; **W:** Chris Rock, Lance Crouther, Ali LeRoi, Louis CK; **C:** Richard Crudo; **M:** Jamshied Sharifi.

Down to the Bone 🎬🎬 1/2 2004 Sad tale of everyday addiction, portraying the issue with a bleakness that allows for authenticity that few films accomplish. Irene (Farmiga), a mother of two saddled with financial difficulties, begins using cocaine to get through her days working as a cashier in a suburban mega-store. But as time passes, her dependence, lies, and the personal tolls all mount. Eventually she seeks help at a rehab center and meets a nurse, Bob (Dillon), who is also a recovering user. The two become friends as they try to support each other's recovery. 105m/C DVD. US Vera Farmiga, Hugh Dillon, Clint Jordan, Marguerite Courtat, Raymond (Ray) McKee, Clara Bow; **D:** Elmer Clifton; **W:** John L.E. Pell; **C:** Alexander Penrod.

Down to the Sea in Ships 🎬🎬 1/2 The Last Adventurers 1922 Bow made her movie debut in this drama about the whalers of 19th-century Massachusetts. Highlighted by exciting action scenes of an actual whale hunt. Silent with music score and original tinted footage. 83m/B VHS, DVD. Marguerite Courtat, Raymond (Ray) McKee, Clara Bow; **D:** Elmer Clifton; **W:** John L.E. Pell; **C:** Alexander Penrod.

Down to You 🎬🎬 1/2 2000 (PG-13) Light romantic comedy has appealing leads and a predictable plot (and references to about a gazillion similar movies). Aspiring chef Al (Prinze Jr.) and artist Imogen (Stiles) are immediately smitten when they meet at the campus dive. The relationship develops at headlong speed but then they both realize neither of them is ready for a lifelong commitment. So, do they just split or try being friends or slow things down or what? 92m/C VHS, DVD. Freddie Prinze Jr., Julia Stiles, Selma Blair, Shawn Hatosy, Zak Orth, Rosario Dawson, Henry Winkler, Ashton Kutcher, Lucie Arnaz; **D:** Kris Isacsson; **W:** Kris Isacsson; **C:** Robert Yeoman; **M:** Edmund Choi.

Down Twisted 🎬 1989 (R) A young woman gets involved with a thief on the run in this "Romancing the Stone" derivative. The muddled plot deserves such a confusing title. 89m/C VHS.

Carey Lowell, Charles Rocket, Trudi Dochtermann, Thom Mathews, Linda Kerridge, Courteney Cox; **D:** Albert Pyun; **W:** Albert Pyun; **C:** Walt Lloyd; **M:** Eric Allaman.

Down Under 🎬 1986 Two gold-hungry beach boys go to Australia looking for riches, and document their adventures on film. Essentially a crudely shot, tongue-in-cheek travelogue narrated by Patrick Macnee. 90m/C VHS. Don Atkinson, Donn Dunlop; **W:** Robert H. Jamieson; **M:** David Gibney; **Nar:** Patrick Macnee.

Down With Love 🎬🎬 1/2 2003 (PG-13) This uneven but amusing homage/satire to the Rock Hudson/Doris Day sex comedies of the early '60s gets the look and feel right, but loses something in the attitude by superimposing modern sensibilities and perspective over the whole thing. Proto-feminist author Barbara Novak (Zellweger) writes a book proclaiming that women should claim their equality in the workplace by acting like men when it comes to sex. This puts a crimp in the style of Babe magnet/cad Catcher Block (McGregor), a magazine writer who conspires to expose her as an old-fashioned girl at heart. McGregor and Zellweger do a good job channelling Hudson and Day, and the production design and costumes perfectly capture the movie version of 1962 Manhattan that never existed in real life. Pierce is perfect in the old Tony Randall role. 94m/C VHS, DVD. US Renee Zellweger, Ewan McGregor, David Hyde Pierce, Sarah Paulson, Tony Randall, Jack Plotnick, Rachel Dratch, John Aylward, Jeri Ryan, Melissa George, Florence Stanley, Laura Kightlinger; **D:** Peyton Reed; **W:** Dennis Drake, Eve Ahlert; **C:** Jeff Cronenweth; **M:** Marc Shaiman.

Downdraft 🎬🎬 1996 (R) A special forces unit has six hours to penetrate a subterranean bunker, which protects a supercomputer that's about to launch a nuclear attack. Assaulted by a variety of sophisticated weapons, the unit must also outwit the computer's android defender. 101m/C VHS. HK Jackie Chan, Paul Chang, Waise Man Chan, Vincent Spano, Kate Vernon, Paul Koslo; **D:** Jackie Chan; **W:** Jackie Chan; **C:** Chung-Yuen Chan, Chin-Kui Chen.

Downfall 🎬🎬🎬 1/2 Der Untergang 2004 (R) Controversial German film explores the last days of Hitler (Ganz) and his cronies in the bunker before the fall of Berlin in 1945. Overlong but engrossing look at the mundane, very human face of evil. Ganz is amazing in the role of a lifetime, virtually becoming the most hated man in history. All the smaller roles, Hitler's secretary Traudl Junge (Lara) for instance, are wonderfully fleshed out by an incredibly talented cast. 155m/C DVD. GE Bruno Ganz, Agustin Lara, Corinna Harfouch, Ulrich Matthes, Heino Ferch, Christian Berkel, Matthias Habich, Thomas Kretschmann, Ulrich Noethen, Gotz Otto, Juliane Koehler, Donevan Gunia; **D:** Oliver Hirschbiegel; **W:** Bernd Eichinger; **C:** Rainer Klausmann; **M:** Stephan Zacharias.

Downhill Racer 🎬🎬 1/2 1969 (PG) An undisciplined American skier locks skitips with his coach and his new-found love while on his way to becoming an Olympic superstar. Character study on film. Beautiful ski and mountain photography keep it from sliding downhill. 102m/C VHS. Robert Redford, Camilla Sparv, Gene Hackman, Dabney Coleman; **D:** Michael Ritchie.

Downhill Willie 🎬 1996 (PG) Willie (Coogan) isn't the brightest guy around—except on skies. Now he wants to enter the Kamikaze Run, which takes place on an extreme race course, and win the half-million top prize as well as the prettiest snow bunny (Keanan) on the slopes. 90m/C VHS, DVD. Keith Coogan, Staci Keanan, Lochlyn Munro, Estelle Harris, Fred Stoller, Lee Reherman; **D:** David Mitchell; **W:** Stephanie Cedar; **C:** David Pelletier; **M:** Norman Orenstein.

Downtown 🎬🎬 1/2 1989 (R) Urban comedy about a naive white suburban cop who gets demoted to the roughest precinct in Philadelphia, and gains a streetwise black partner. Runs a routine beat. 96m/C VHS, DVD. Anthony Edwards, Forest Whitaker, Joe Pantoliano, Penelope Ann Miller; **D:** Richard Benjamin; **M:** Alan Silvestri.

D.P. 🎬 1985 A black orphan attaches to the only other black in post-WWII Germany. From a story by Kurt Vonnegut Jr. 60m/C VHS. Stan Shaw, Rosemary Leach, Julius Gordon. TV

Drachenfutter 🎬🎬🎬 Dragon's Food; Dragon Chow 1987 Powerful story dealing with a Pakistani immigrant's attempts to enter the Western world. Themes of alienation and hopelessness are emphasized. Dialogues occur in 12 languages, predominantly German and Mandarin Chinese; subtitled in English. 75m/B VHS. GE SI/Bhask-er, Ric Young, Buddy Uzzaman; **D:** Jan Schutte; **W:** Thomas Strittmatter; **M:** Claus Bantzer.

Dracula (Spanish Version) 🎬🎬🎬 1/2 1931 Filmed at the same time as the Bela Lugosi version of "Dracula," using the same sets and the same scripts, only in Spanish. Thought to be more visually appealing and more terrifying than the English-language counterpart. The only thing it's missing is a presence like Lugosi. Based on the novel by Bram Stoker. 104m/B VHS, DVD. Carlos Villarias, Lupita Tovar, Eduardo Arozamena, Pablo Alvarez Rubio, Barry Norton, Carmen Guerrero; **D:** George Melford; **W:** Garrett Fort.

Dracula 🎬🎬🎬 1931 Lugosi, in his most famous role, plays a vampire who terrorizes the countryside in his search for human blood. From Bram Stoker's novel. Although short of a masterpiece due to slow second half, deservedly rated a film classic. What would Halloween be like without this movie? Sequelled by "Dracula's Daughter." The 1999 re-release was re-scored by Philip Glass and performed by the Kronos Quartet. 75m/B VHS, DVD. Bela Lugosi, David Manners, Dwight Frye, Helen Chandler, Edward Van Sloan, Frances Dade, Herbert Bunston; **D:** Tod Browning; **W:** Garrett Fort; **C:** Karl Freund. Natl. Film Reg. '00.

Dracula 🎬🎬 1/2 Bram Stoker's Dracula 1973 Count on squinty-eyed Palance to shine as the Transylvanian vampire who must quench his thirst for human blood. Adaptation of the Bram Stoker novel that really flies. 105m/C VHS, DVD. Jack Palance, Simon Ward, Fiona Lewis, Nigel Davenport, Pamela Brown, Penelope Horner, Murray Brown, Virginia Wetherall, Sarah Douglas, Barbara Lindley; **D:** Dan Curtis; **W:** Richard Matheson; **C:** Oswald Morris; **M:** Wojciech Kilar. TV

Dracula 🎬 2006 Nonsensical adaptation of the Dracula story that uses little of Stoker's tale (and much ridiculous invention). Lord Holmwood (Stevens) discovers he has syphilis, which endangers his marriage to Lucy (Myles). Apparently inviting the fanged one (Warren)—who seems to now be a member of a sinister blood cult—to England will offer a potential cure. 90m/C DVD. Marc Warren, Dan Stevens, Sophia Myles, David Suchet, Tom Burke, Stephanie Leonidas, Rafe Spall; **D:** Bill Eagles; **W:** Stewart Harcourt; **M:** Dominik Scherrer. TV

Dracula 🎬🎬 1/2 1979 (R) Langella recreates his Broadway role as the count who needs human blood for nourishment. Notable for its portrayal of Dracula as a romantic and tragic figure in history. Overlooked since the vampire spoof "Love at First Bite" came out at the same time. 109m/C VHS, DVD. Frank Langella, Laurence Olivier, Kate Nelligan, Donald Pleasence, Janine Duvitsky, Trevor Eve, Tony Haygarth; **D:** John Badham; **W:** W.D. Richter; **C:** Gilbert Taylor; **M:** John Williams.

Dracula 2: Ascension 🎬 1/2 Wes Craven Presents Dracula 2: Ascension 2003 (R) Wheelchair-bound medical scientist Lowell (Sheffer) and his students decide to use the blood from Dracula's burned corpse (from the first film, which is now in the local New Orleans morgue) to find a cure for Lowell's paralysis. But it's always a mistake to resurrect a vampire. Lame sequel to the "Dracula 2000" film that has a cliffhanger ending to be resolved in "Dracula 3: Legacy." 85m/C VHS, DVD. Jason Scott Lee, Jason London, Craig Sheffer, Diane Neal, Stephen Billington, Roy Scheider, Rutger Hauer; **D:** Patrick Lussier; **W:** Patrick Lussier, Joel Soisson; **C:** Doug Milsome; **M:** Kevin Kliesch. VIDEO

Dracula 3: Legacy 🎬🎬 2005 (R) Badass Father Uffizi (Lee) is back, accompanied by sidekick Luke (London), and they travel to Transylvania to hunt Dracula (Hauer) at his castle and get rid of him once and for all. Lots of action and a healthy helping of cheese. If you've seen the first two installments, you know what to expect. 90m/C DVD. Jason Scott Lee, Jason London, Rutger Hauer, Roy Scheider, Diane Neal, Alexandra Wescourt; **D:** Patrick Lussier; **W:** Patrick Lussier, Joel Soisson; **C:** Doug Milsome; **M:** Kevin Kliesch, Cleri Torjussen. VIDEO

Dracula A.D. 1972 🎬🎬 Dracula Today 1972 Lee returned to England for his sixth (and most accounts, worst) go-round as Dracula for Hammer Films, where the creative juices seemed to be drying up. The decision was made to turn Dracula loose in the modern world. The movie actually opens in 1872 with a scene that is one of the highlights of the entire production—an action scene that features Dracula battling his nemesis Van Helsing (Cushing) atop a speeding stagecoach. When the coach is wrecked, Dracula is impaled on a wheel spoke and dies. From that point, the scene immediately jumps ahead one century. A Satanist named Johnny Alucard and a group of naive hippie teenagers revive the long-dead vampire in an abandoned church building in England. The teens and Dracula are opposed by Van Helsing's grandson (Cushing again) and his granddaughter Jessica (Beacham). Hammer's unwillingness to pay Lee to speak more than a few lines, together with a sterile plot that had Dracula essentially paralyzed by the modern world, forced the teenagers to carry the story. It appears that the idea for Dracula A.D. 1972 came from the Count Yorga movies, which had some success in placing an Old World vampire in modern Los Angeles. However, the Yorga movies were only moderately successful and this Hammer copy did not even do that well. Dracula A.D. 1972 was the sequel to The Scars of Dracula (1971) and was followed by The Satanic Rites of Dracula (1973). 95m/C VHS, DVD. GB Christopher Lee, Peter Cushing, Christopher Neame, Stephanie Beacham, Michael Coles, Caroline Munro, Marsha A. Hunt, Philip Miller, Janet Key, William Ellis; **D:** Alan Gibson; **W:** Don Houghton; **C:** Dick Bush; **M:** Michael Vickers.

Dracula and Son 🎬🎬 Dracula Pere et Fils 1976 Badly dubbed French satire finds the elegant Count (Lee) deciding that beautiful Hermaine (Marie-Helene Breillat) would be the perfect vampire mommy. Thus Dracula's son Ferdinand is born. Some 300 years later, Ferdinand (Menez) is proving to be a trial to his father, since he has yet to drink anyone's blood. Driven from their castle, the Count winds up in London and becomes a star in vampire films, while Ferdinand lives in Paris. When the two reunite, it's to feud over the beautiful Nicole (Catherine Breillat), who happens to be a dead ringer for Hermaine. Based on the novel "Paris Vampire" by Claude Klotz. 70m/C VHS. FR Christopher Lee, Bernard Menez, Catherine Breillat, Marie Breillat; **D:** Edouard Molinaro; **W:** Edouard Molinaro.

Dracula Blows His Cool 🎬 1982 (R) Three voluptuous models and their photographer restore an ancient castle and open a disco in it. The vampire lurking about the castle welcomes the party with his fangs. 91m/C VHS, DVD. John Garco, Betty Verges; **D:** Carlo Ombra; **W:** Carlo Ombra.

Dracula: Dead and Loving It WOOF! 1995 (PG-13) King of the spoofs Nielsen takes on the title role as the ever-loving, if clumsy, Count who still enjoys necking—particularly with luscious damsels in distress, Lucy (Anthony) and Mina (Yasbeck). And he's still got his bug-eating minion Renfield (MacNichol) and egomaniacal vampire-hunter Van Helsing (Brooks) around. As usual, Brooks throws everything possible on the screen, hoping some schtick will stick (not very much does). 90m/C VHS, DVD. Leslie Nielsen, Mel Brooks, Peter MacNichol, Lysette Anthony, Amy Yasbeck, Steven Weber, Harvey Korman, Anne

Dracula Has Risen from the Grave 🐶🐶½ 1968 (G) Lee's Dracula is foiled by the local priest before he can drain the blood from innocent villagers. Effectively gory. One of the Hammer series of Dracula films. "followed by "Taste the Blood of Dracula". 92m/C VHS, DVD, GB Christopher Lee, Rupert Davies, Veronica Carlson, Barbara Ewing, Barry Andrews, Michael Ripper, Ewan Hooper, Marion Mathie; D: Freddie Francis; W: John (Anthony Hinds) Elder; C: Arthur Grant; M: James Bernard.

Dracula, Prince of Darkness 🐶🐶 Dracula, Disciple of Dracula; The Bloody Scream of Dracula 1966 Sequel to 1958's "Horror of Dracula" finds the Count (Lee) extending his hospitality at Castle Dracula to four unwary tourists, one of whom is immediately killed for his blood. Then Dracula takes the dead man's wife (Shelley) and turns her into a vampire and the gruesome twosome go after the remaining couple. Standard Hammer horror. 90m/C VHS, DVD, GB Christopher Lee, Barbara Shelley, Andrew Keir, Francis Matthews, Suzan Farmer, Charles "Bud" Tingwell, Thorley Walters, Philip Latham; D: Terence Fisher; W: John Sansom, John (Anthony Hinds) Elder; C: Michael Reed; M: James Bernard.

Dracula Rising 🐶🐶½ 1993 (R) A modern-day art historian (Travis) turns out to have been a witch, burned at the stake, in a past life. She was also the blood-drinking Count's lost love. Now Dracula's brother are captured by the Turkish sultan who rules over their native Romania. During their captivity, the boys' father (the country's regent) is killed and when Vlad returns home years later he seeks to expel the Turks and rule himself. But his dreams of a unified country are undermined by tragedy and his own brutality. 89m/C VHS, DVD, Rudolf Martin, Jane March, Peter Weller, Roger Daltrey, Michael Sutton, Christopher Brand; D: Joe Chappelle; W: Thomas Baum; C: Dermot Downs.

Dracula Sucks 🐶 1979 (R) A softcore edit of a hardcore sex parody about Dracula snacking on the usual bevy of screaming quasi-virgins. 90m/C VHS, Jamie Gillis, Reggie Nalder, Annette Haven, Kay Parker, Serena, Seka, John Leslie; D: Philip Marshak.

Dracula 2000 🐶 Wes Craven Presents: Dracula 2000 2000 (R) Dracula finds his way to New Orleans to terrorize the modern world in this adaptation of the classic vampire tale that borrows freewheelingly from many supernatural legends. Butler plays Dracula well enough, but doesn't add anything memorable to a character that's been done, redone, and overdone so many times, while Plummer struggles to make the most of a bad situation. Horror fans will no doubt enjoy the gore, but the overall cheesiness is hard to take by anyone's standards. Presented by Wes Craven, but directed by Patrick Lussier, Craven's editor on many films, including the "Scream" trilogy. 99m/C VHS, DVD, Jonny Lee Miller, Justine Waddell, Gerard Butler, Colleen (Ann) Fitzpatrick, Jennifer Esposito, Danny Masterson, Omar Epps, Lochlyn Munro, Sean Patrick Thomas, Jeri Ryan, Christopher Plummer; D: Patrick Lussier; W: Joel Soisson; C: Peter Pau; M: Marco Beltrami.

Dracula vs. Frankenstein 🐶 Assignment: Terror 1969 An alien reanimates Earth's most infamous monsters in a bid to take over the planet. Rennie's last role. 91m/C VHS, DVD, IT GE SP Michael Rennie, Paul Naschy, Karin Dor, Patty (Patti) Shepard, Craig Hill; D: Hugo Fregonese, Tulio Demicheli; C: Godfrey Hall.

Bancroft, Dara Haun, Megan Cavanagh, Mark Blankfield, Clive Revill; D: Mel Brooks; W: Rudy DeLuca, Steve Haberman, Mel Brooks; C: Michael D. O'Shea; M: Hummie Mann.

Dracula's Daughter 🐶🐶🐶 1936 Count Dracula's daughter, Countess Marya Zaleska, heads to London supposedly to find the cure to a mysterious illness. Instead she finds she has a taste for human blood, especially female blood. She also finds a man, falls in love, and tries to keep him by casting a spell on him. A good script and cast keep this sequel to Bela Lugosi's "Dracula" entertaining. 71m/ B VHS, DVD, Gloria Holden, Otto Kruger, Marguerite Churchill, Irving Pichel, Edward Van Sloan, Nan Grey, Hedda Hopper; D: Lambert Hillyer; W: Garrett Fort; C: George Robinson.

Dracula's Great Love 🐶 woof! Gran Amore del Conde Dracula; Count Dracula's Virgin Lovers; Vampire Playgirls 1972 (R) Four travellers end up in Dracula's castle for the night, where the horny Count takes a liking to one of the women. Left out in the sun too long. 96m/C VHS, DVD, SP Paul Naschy, Charo Soriano, Haydee Politoff, Rossana Yanni, Ingrid Garbo, Mirta Miller; D: Javier Aguirre; W: Javier Aguirre, Paul Naschy.

Dracula's Last Rites 🐶 woof! Last Rites 1979 (R) Blood-curdling tale of a sheriff and a mortician in a small town who are up to no good. Technically inept; film equipment can be spotted throughout. Don't stick your neck out for this one. 86m/C VHS, Patricia Lee Hammond, Gerald Fielding, Victor Jorge; D: Domonic Paris.

Dracula's Widow 🐶🐶 1988 (R) Countess Dracula, missing her hubby and desperately in need of a substitute, picks innocent Raymond as her victim. His girlfriend and a cynical cop fight to save his soul from the Countess' damnation. Directed by the nephew of Frances Ford Coppola. 85m/C VHS, Sylvia Kristel, Josef Sommer, Lenny Von Dohlen, George Stover; D: Christopher Coppola.

Dragnet 🐶🐶 1954 Sgt. Joe Friday and Officer Frank Smith try to solve a mob slaying but have a rough time. Alexander plays the sidekick in "Dragnet" pre-Morgan days. Just the facts: feature version of the TV show that's suspenseful and well-acted. 88m/C VHS, Jack Webb, Ben Alexander, Richard Boone, Ann (Robin) Robinson; D: Jack Webb.

Dragnet 🐶🐶½ 1987 (PG-13) Semi-parody of the vintage '60s TV cop show. Sgt. Joe Friday's straitlaced nephew (Aykroyd) and his sloppy partner Pep (Hanks) take on a crooked reverend (Plummer) and a pagan organization called P.A.G.A.N. Neither Aykroyd nor Hanks can save this big-budget but lackluster spoof that's full of holes, although they both have their funny moments. 106m/C VHS, DVD, Dan Aykroyd, Tom Hanks, Christopher Plummer, Harry (Henry) Morgan, Elizabeth Ashley, Dabney Coleman, Alexandra Paul, Kathleen Freeman, Jack O'Halloran; D: Tom Mankiewicz; W: Tom Mankiewicz, Alan Zweibel, Dan Aykroyd; C: Matthew F. Leonetti; M: Ira Newborn.

Dragon Fury 🐶 1995 Evil dictator tries to conquer what remains of America in the year 2099—a world peopled by barbarians and victims of a deadly plague. Naturally, there's a martial arts hero around to stop him. 80m/C VHS, Robert Chapin, Richard Lynch, Chona Jason, Deborah Stambler; D: David Heavener.

Dragon Fury 2 🐶½ 1996 Futuristic action finds a heroic female struggling Chicago's dour ER doctor Joe Darrow, righteously widowed when his doctor wife bites the dust tending to the poor in Venezuela, while pregnant, no less. Unable to accept her death, Darrow is convinced she's trying to contact him from Beyond as

Dragonfly 🐶½ 2002 (PG-13) I see dead performances. Cheesy, self-gratifying supernatural snorer has Costner as against a violent gang who want to rule the world (with the help of a computer chip). But a scientist unthaws an ancient warrior to help her out. Of course, things don't go exactly as expected. 90m/C VHS.

Mike Norris, Robert Chapin, Cathleen Ann Garcner, Cole Andersen, Walter O'Neill, Kayla Murphy; D: Bryan Michael Stoller; W: Parker Bostwick.

Dragon Lord 🐶 1982 Young kung-fu hero (Chan) defends his village against greedy outlaws. Comic interludes tend to slow the action. 90m/C VHS, DVD, Jackie Chan.

The Dragon Painter 🐶🐶 1919 Provincial painter Tatsu (Hayakawa) is obsessed with painting dragons, believing that his fantasy princess was captured by such a beast. Celebrated Tokyo artist Kano Indara (Peil) is looking for an apprentice and Tatsu accepts after meeting Kano's daughter Ume Ko (Aoki), whom he believes is his lost princess. They marry and Tatsu is so happy he gives up painting, so Ume Ko decides she must leave him for the sake of his art. 53m/B DVD, Sessue Hayakawa, Edward Peil Sr., Toyo Fujita, Tsuru Aoki; D: William Worthington; W: Richard Schayer; C: Frank D. Williams.

Dragon Seed 🐶🐶½ 1944 The lives of the residents of a small Chinese village are turned upside down when the Japanese invade it. Based on the Pearl S. Buck novel. Lengthy and occasionally tedious, though generally well-made with heart-felt attempts to create Oriental characters, without having Asians in the cast. 145m/B VHS, DVD, Katharine Hepburn, Walter Huston, Agnes Moorehead, Akim Tamiroff, Hurd Hatfield, J. Carrol Naish, Henry Travers, Turhan Bey, Aline MacMahon; D: Jack Conway, Harold S. Bucquet; W: Marguerite Roberts, Jane Murfin; C: Sidney Wagner; M: Herbert Stothart.

Dragon Storm 🐶🐶 2004 (PG-13) In this Sci-Fi Channel original production, medieval men must fight to free the planet from an other-worldly infestation of fearsome, foul, flying, fire-breathing alien dragons. And they didn't even call first! 92m/C VHS, DVD, Tony Amendola, Angel Boris, Maxwell Caulfield, Jeff Rank, Isira Angelova, Max Woon Young Park, Tyrone Pinkham, John Rhys-Davies, Richard Wharton; D: Stephen Furst; W: Patrick Phillips. CABLE

Dragon: The Bruce Lee Story 🐶🐶🐶 1993 (PG-13) Entertaining, inspiring account of the life of Chinese-American martial-arts legend Bruce Lee. Jason Scott Lee (no relation) is great as the talented artist, exuding his joy of life and gentle spirit, before his mysterious brain disorder death at the age of 32. Ironically, this release coincided with son Brandon's accidental death on a movie set. The martial arts sequences in "Dragon" are extraordinary, but there's also romance as Lee meets and marries his wife (Holly), who acquits herself well. Based on the book "Bruce Lee: The Man Only I Knew" by his widow, Linda Lee Caldwell. 121m/C VHS, DVD, Jason Scott Lee, Lauren Holly, Robert Wagner, Michael Learned, Nancy Kwan, Kay Tong Lim, Sterling Macer, Ric Young, Sven-Ole Thorsen; D: Rob Cohen; C: David Eggby; M: Randy Edelman.

Dragonard 🐶½ 1988 (R) Slaves on a West Indies island rebel against their cruel masters. 93m/C VHS, Eartha Kitt, Oliver Reed, Annabel Schofield, Patrick Warburton; D: Warren A. Stevens; W: R.J. Marx.

Dragonfight 🐶½ 1990 (R) Corporations rule the world and vie for supremacy through gladiator combat in this action-adventure saga set in the near future. Fights are to the death and when the current champ refuses a new challenger the corporate honchos decide to provoke him into battle by having the challenger mow down innocent bystanders. Several execs also decide the slaughter has to stop but they may be the next targets. 84m/C VHS, Robert Z'Dar, Michael Pare, Paul Coufos, Charles Napier, James Hong, Alexa Hamilton, Fawna MacLaren; D: Warren A. Stevens; W: Buddy Lewis; C: Curtis Petersen; M: Bob Mithoff.

Dragon Forever 🐶🐶½ ever 1988 A big time lawyer is persuaded to take over a case and to begin work against a chemical plant who wants the beautiful cousin of the fishery's owner. A comic king-fu battle between Chan, Hung, and Biao is the rousing finale. In Cantonese with English subtitles. 88m/C VHS, DVD, CH Jackie Chan, Yuen Biao, Sammo Hung, Pauline Yeung, Yuen Wah; D: Sammo Hung, Corey Yuen; W: Roy Szeto, Gordon Chan.

Dragonslayer 🐶🐶 1981 (PG) A sorcerer's apprentice suddenly finds himself the only person who can save the kingdom from a horrible, fire-breathing dragon. Extreme violence but wonderful special effects, smart writing, and a funny performance by Richardson. 110m/C VHS, DVD, Peter MacNicol, Caitlin Clarke, Ralph Richardson, John Hallam, Albert Salmi, Chloe Salaman; D: Matthew Robbins; W: Matthew Robbins, Hal Barwood; M: Alex North.

Dragonworld 🐶🐶½ 1994 (PG) Five-year-old Johnny McGowan is sent to Scotland to live with his grandfather. A wish for a friend has Johnny mysteriously awakening a baby dragon he names Yowler. Years later, the financially strapped adult Johnny agrees to loan Yowler to an amusement park in order to out the park's owner never intends to give Yowler back. 30th baby dragon and young are unbearably cute. 86m/C VHS.

---

he receives a series of cryptic messages, some from the children in his wife's pediatric oncology ward. Darrow's talking parrot provides some of this sillier scenes in this slow-paced, must-miss melodrama. Bates as the neighbor manages to liven up her scenes, anyway. Director Shadyac ("Patch Adams") certainly didn't want to lead here displaying any of his other doctor's kid-loving antics, and glum and glummer Costner as a dutiful downer as he lead the kids in the ward for info about his dead wife. 103m/C VHS, DVD, US Kevin Costner, Joe Morton, Susanna Thompson, Ron Rifkin, Linda Hunt, Kathy Bates, Jay Thomas, Matt Craven, Robert Bailey Jr., Lisa Banes, Jacob Smith; D: Tom Shadyac; W: David Seltzer, Brandon Camp, Mike Thompson; C: Dean Semler; M: John Debney.

Dragonheart 🐶🐶½ 1996 (PG-13) Okay, get past the fact that Connery's Scottish burr is coming out of the "teeth-filled mouth of an 18 ft. tall, 43 ft. long dragon and you'll be well on your way to enjoying this 10th-century fantasy. Knight Bowen (Quaid) is the one-time mentor of evil-hearted King Einon (Thewlis) and it's up to him, Draco the dragon, feisty Kara (Meyer), and some fearful peasants to band together and free themselves from the king's tyranny. There's some slow spots but Bowen and Draco make for an amusing pairing and the dragon does seem, well, real. Work on Draco took more than a year of Industrial Light & Magic's expertise. 103m/C VHS, DVD, HD DVD, Dennis Quaid, David Thewlis, Pete Postlethwaite, Dina Meyer, Julie Christie, Jason Isaacs, Brian Thompson, Wolf Christian, Terry O'Neill; D: Rob Cohen; V: Sean Connery; M: Randy Edelman.

Dragonheart: A New Beginning 🐶🐶 2000 (PG) Geoff (Masterson) is a monastery stableboy who wants to become a knight. Then he discovers Friar Peter (Woodnutt) has secretly been raising a young dragon called Drake (voiced by Benson). When the evil Lord Osric (Van Gorkum) learns of the beast's existence, he wants to claim its powers for himself. But Geoff, who's aided by two mysterious warriors from the east, is determined to save both Drake and the kingdom. 85m/C VHS, DVD, Chris Masterson, Henry O, Harry Van Gorkum, John Woodnutt, Rona Figueroa, Ken Shorter; D: Doug Lefler; W: Sherri Goodmartz; C: Buzz Feitshans IV; V: Robby Benson. VIDEO

Dragonfly Squadron 🐶🐶 1954 Korean war drama about pilots and their romantic problems. Never gets off the ground. 82m/C VHS, John Hodiak, Barbara Britton, Bruce Bennett, Jess Barker; D: Lesley Selander.

Sam Mackenzie, Courtland Mead, Brittney Powell, John Calvin, Andrew Keir, Lila Kaye, John Woodvine; **D:** Ted Nicolaou, Suzanne Glazener Naha; **M:** Richard Band.

Dragstrip Girl ♂♂ 1957 An 18-year-old girl comes of age while burning rubber at the dragstrip—the world of boys, hot rods, and horsepower. A definite "B" movie that may seem dated. *70m/B VHS.* Paul Blaisdell, Fay Spain, Steven Terrell, John Ashley, Frank Gorshin; **D:** Edward L. Cahn.

Dragstrip Girl ♂♂½ 1994 Remake of the 1857 "B" movie; a part of Showtime's Rebel Highway series. Latino Johnny (Dacascos) works as a valet during the day and goes drag racing at night. He's got big plans that may be derailed by rich white girl Laura (Wagner) who likes taking a walk on the wild side. *82m/C VHS. DVD.* Mark Dacascos, Natasha Gregson Wagner, Raymond Cruz, Traci Lords; **D:** Mary Lambert; **W:** Jerome Gary; **C:** Sandi Sissel. CABLE

The Drake Case ♂♂ 1929 A slight courtroom drama made during the waning days of the silent era. You'll probably recognize Brit Lloyd from her later career. *56m/B VHS.* Robert Frazer, Doris Lloyd, Gladys Brockwell; **D:** Edward Laemmle; **W:** Charles Logue; **C:** Jerome Ash.

The Draughtsman's Contract ♂♂♂ 1982 (R) A beguiling mystery begins when a wealthy woman hires an artist to make drawings of her home. Their contract is quite unusual, as is their relationship. Everything is going along at an even pace until murder is suspected, and things spiral down to darker levels. A simple story turned into a bizarre puzzle. Intense enough for any thriller fan. *103m/C VHS, DVD. GB* Anthony (Corbin) Higgins, Janet Suzman, Anne Louise Lambert, Hugh Fraser; **D:** Peter Greenaway; **W:** Peter Greenaway; **C:** Sacha Vierny; **M:** Michael Nyman.

Draw! ♂♂ 1981 Two has-been outlaws warm up their pistols again in this old-fashioned Western. Star power and some smart moments make it worthwhile. Made for TV. *98m/C VHS.* Kirk Douglas, James Coburn, Alexandra Bastedo, Graham Jarvis; **D:** Steven Hilliard Stern.

Dream a Little Dream ♂♂ 1989 (PG-13) Strange teen transformation drama about an old man and his wife trying mystically to regain their youth. When they collide bikes with the teenagers down the street, their minds are exchanged and the older couple with the now young minds are transported to a permanent dream-like state. Same old switcheroo made bearable by cast. *114m/C VHS, DVD.* Corey Feldman, Corey Haim, Meredith Salenger, Jason Robards Jr., Piper Laurie, Harry Dean Stanton, Victoria Jackson, Alex Rocco, William McNamara; **D:** Marc Rocco; **W:** Marc Rocco.

Dream a Little Dream 2 ♂♂ 1994 (PG-13) *The Dreamcatcher* 1999 With his girlfriend pregnant, Freddy (Compte) hits the road to look for his uncle, who might be able to give him some cash. With no car, he takes to hitchhiking and riding trains, and along the way befriends a klepto. When Freddy finds out his dad is out of prison. Quirky characters and a thoughtful script help this pleasing road flick along. *93m/C VHS, DVD.* Maurice Compte, Paddy Connor, Jeanne Heaton, Joseph Arthur, Larry John Meyers; **D:** Edward A. Radtke; **W:** Edward A. Radtke, M.S. Nieson; **C:** Terry Stacey; **M:** Georgiana Gomez.

Dream Chasers ♂ 1982 (PG) A bankrupt old codger and an 11-year-old boy stricken with cancer run away together during the Great Depression. *97m/C VHS, DVD.* Wesley Bishop, Carolyn Carradine, Harold Gould, Justin Dana; **D:** Arthur Dubs, David

E. Jackson; **W:** Wesley Bishop; **C:** Milas C. Hinshaw; **M:** William Loose.

Dream Date ♂♂½ 1993 (PG-13) Lovely teenager is wooed by hip, playful suitor until trouble ensues when goofball sidekick enters the picture. Family entertainment. *96m/C VHS.* Tempest Bledsoe, Clifton Davis, Kadeem Hardison, Anne-Marie Johnson, Pauly Shore, Richard Moll; **D:** Anson Williams.

Dream Demon ♂ 1988 The appearance of Wilhoite, a visiting American, disrupts the status quo at a spooky British manor where the charming Redgrave debates her impending marriage to wealthy rogue, Greenstreet. Aside from a terrific opening dream sequence, most of the scary bits may have been done before. *89m/C VHS. GB* Jemma Redgrave, Kathleen Wilhoite, Timothy Spall, Jimmy Nail, Mark Greenstreet; **D:** Harley Cokliss.

Dream for an Insomniac ♂♂½ 1996 (R) Irritating characters put the kibobsh on this attempt at twentysomething romantic comedy. Whiny would-be actress Frankie (Skye) works at her Uncle Leo's (Cassel) cafe and hangs out with assorted, equally whiny friends. Frankie seems more interested in finding the "perfect" boyfriend than a career anyway and her interest is sparked by new guy David (a sweet Astin). Lots of overacting. Debut for writer/director DeBartolo. *108m/C VHS, DVD.* Ione Skye, MacKenzie Astin, Jennifer Aniston, Seymour Cassel, Michael Landes, Robert Kelker-Kelly; **D:** Tiffanie DeBartolo; **W:** Tiffanie DeBartolo; **C:** Guillermo Navarro; **M:** Jim Larala.

A Dream for Christmas ♂♂♂ 1973 Earl Hammer Jr. (best known for writing the "The Waltons") wrote this moving story of a black minister whose church in Los Angeles is scheduled to be demolished. *100m/C VHS.* Hari Rhodes, Beah Richards, George Spell, Juanita Moore, Joel Fluellen; Robert DoQui, Clarence Muse; **D:** Ralph Senensky. TV

Dream House ♂♂ 1998 (R) This dream house of the future turns out to be a nightmare for its new owners. The supercomputer that runs everything has been misprogrammed and regards these humans as interlopers who must be killed. Tedious horror. *90m/C VHS. CA* Timothy Busfield, Jennifer Dale, Lisa Jakub; **D:** Graeme Campbell. TV

Dream Lover ♂♂ 1985 (R) Terrifying nightmares after an assault lead McNichol to dream therapy. Treatment causes her tortured unconscious desires to take over her waking behavior, and she becomes a violent schizophrenic. Slow, heavy, and not very thrilling. *105m/C VHS.* Kristy McNichol, Ben Masters, Paul Shenar, Justin Deas, Joseph Culp, Gayle Hunnicutt, John McMartin; **D:** Alan J. Pakula; **W:** Jon Boorstin; **C:** Sven Nykvist.

Dream Lover ♂♂ 1993 (R) Divorced architect Ray (Spader) meets and marries Lena (Amick), beautiful and seemingly perfect, who nonetheless warns him that she's just your average mixed-up gal. Suspense is supposed to come into play as Ray suspects Lena's been lying to him about her past. Visually appealing (considerably helped by the attractive leads) but good looks don't make up for the lack of substance and the minimal number of surprises expected in a thriller. Directorial debut of Kazan. Also available in an unrated version. *103m/C VHS, DVD.* James Spader, Madchen Amick, Frederic Lehne, Bess Armstrong, Larry Miller, Kathleen York, Blair Tefkin, Scott Coffey, William Shockley, Clyde Kusatsu; **D:** Nicholas Kazan; **W:** Nicholas Kazan; **C:** Jean-Yves Escoffier; **M:** Christopher Young.

Dream Lovers *Meng zhong ren* 1986 A supernatural love story which moves back and forth from contemporary Hong Kong to the mysterious Qin dynasty. When an orchestra conductor and the daughter of a noted architect meet at an exhibit featuring the famed terracotta army, an affair from the past is resurrected. In Cantonese with English subtitles. *95m/C VHS, DVD. CH* Chow Yun-Fat, Brigitte Lin, Cher Yeung; **D:** Tony Au; **W:** Yau Da Ah-Pin, Manfred Wong; **C:** Bill Wong.

Dream Machine ♂½ 1991 (PG) A childish teen comedy, based on that old urban legend of the lucky kid given a free Porshe by the vengeful wife of a wealthy philanderer. The gimmick is that the husband's body is in the trunk; the murderer is in pursuit. The tape includes an anti-drug commerical—but nothing against reckless driving, which the picture glorifies. *88m/C VHS.* Corey Haim, Evan Richards, Jeremy Slate, Randall England, Tracy Fraim, Brittney Lewis, Susan Seaforth Hayes; **D:** Lyman Dayton.

Dream Man ♂♂½ 1994 (R) Kris Anderson (Kensit) is a Seattle cop with the clairvoyant ability to see crimes as they're committed. But that doesn't stop her from getting involved with the handsome murder suspect (McCarthy) she's supposed to be investigating. *94m/C VHS.* Patsy Kensit, Andrew McCarthy, Bruce Greenwood; **D:** Rene Bonniere; **M:** Michael Alexander Miller; **M:** Graeme Coleman.

Dream No Evil ♂♂½ 1975 A mentally disturbed woman is forced to commit bizarre murders to protect her warped fantasy world. *93m/C VHS.* Edmond O'Brien, Brooke Mills, Marc Lawrence, Arthur Franz; **D:** John Hayes.

A Dream of Kings ♂♂½ 1969 (R) Quinn is exceptional in this Petrakis story of an immigrant working to get his dying son home to Greece. Last film appearance for Stevens before committing suicide at age 36. *107m/C VHS.* Anthony Quinn, Irene Papas, Inger Stevens, Sam Levene, Val Avery; **D:** Daniel Mann; **M:** Alex North.

A Dream of Passion ♂½ 1978 (R) A woman imprisoned in Greece for murdering her children becomes the object of a publicity stunt for a production of "Medea," and she and the lead actress begin to exchange personalities. Artificial gobbledygook. *105m/C VHS. GR S/* Ellen Burstyn, Melina Mercouri, Andreas Voutsinas; **D:** Jules Dassin; **W:** Jules Dassin; **C:** Yorgos Arvanitis.

Dream Street ♂♂½ 1921 A weak morality tale of London's lower classes. Two brothers, both in love with the same dancing girl, woo her in their own way, while a Chinese gambler plans to take her by force. Silent with music score. Based on Thomas Burke's "Limehouse Nights." *138m/B VHS.* Tyrone Power Sr., Carol Dempster, Ralph Graves, Charles Mack; **D:** D.W. Griffith.

The Dream Team ♂♂ 1989 (PG-13) On their way to a ball game, four patients from a mental hospital find themselves lost in New York City after their doctor is knocked out by murderers. Some fine moments from a cast of dependable comics. Watch for numerous nods to "One Flew Over the Cuckoo's Nest," another Lloyd feature. Keaton fans won't want to miss this one. *113m/C VHS, DVD.* Michael Keaton, Christopher Lloyd, Peter Boyle, Stephen Furst, Lorraine Bracco, Milo O'Shea, Dennis Boutsikaris, Philip Bosco, James Remar, Cynthia Belliveau; **D:** Howard Zieff; **W:** Jon Connolly, David Loucka; **M:** David McHugh.

D.R.E.A.M. Team ♂♂ 1999 (R) Garrison (Sheen) heads a secret United Nations agency that has uncovered terrorist activities in Puerto Rico involving a bomb laced with anthrax. He turns to CIA agent Zack (Kaake) to form a team of agents to stop the madness. Their cover just happens to be as models working on a fashion shoot, which means Zack gets to choose three babes to kick butt. *81m/C VHS, DVD.* Jeff Kaake, Angie Everhart, Traci Lords, Traci Bingham, Martin Sheen, Roger Moore, Ian McShane, James Remar; **D:** Dean Hamilton; **W:** Michael Snyder; **M:** Matthias Weber. TV

Dream to Believe ♂♂½ 1985 Slice of the life of your typical high school coed—mom's dying, stepdad's from hell, sports injury hurts, and, oh yeah, championship gymnastic competitions loom. Designed to make you feel oh-so-good in that MTV kind of way. Reeves is most excellent as the girl's blushing beau. *96m/C VHS, DVD.* Rita Tushingham, Keanu Reeves, Olivia D'Abo, Jessica Steen; **D:** Paul Lynch.

Dream Trap ♂½ 1990 A young man is obsessed with a girl in his dreams. When he meets a girl who really exists, fantasy louses up every opportunity for the

real thing. *90m/C VHS.* Kristy Swanson, Sasha Jenson, Jeanie Moore; **D:** Tom Logan, Hugh Parks; **W:** Tom Logan.

Dream with the Fishes ♂♂½ 1997 (R) Suicidal voyeur Terry (Arquette) is about to jump from a bridge when terminally ill thief Nick (Adams) strikes a strange deal with him. In exchange for funding a few of Nick's fantasies, he will kill Terry in a less messy way. After various strange escapades (including an unplanned robbery and nude bowling), the pair arrive in Nick's hometown, where he attempts to resolve old issues with an ex-girlfriend and his abusive father. As Nick's health fades, Terry reexamines his wish to die. As the story develops, the cliches of both the buddy and road movie genres fall away, letting you actually care about both of these guys. In an homage to the early 70s, the film stock copies their grainy look, gradually dissolving over the course of the movie to a clearer look. Debut for director Finn Taylor. *97m/C VHS, DVD.* David Arquette, Brad Hunt, Kathryn Erbe, Cathy Moriarty, Allyce Beasley, Patrick McGaw, J.E. Freeman; **D:** Finn Taylor; **W:** Finn Taylor; **C:** Barry Stone; **M:** Tito Larriva.

Dreamcatcher ♂½ 2003 (R) Four childhood buddies with telepathic abilities bestowed on them by a mentally retarded boy they protected meet in the Maine woods for an annual hunting trip just in time for a body-snatching alien invasion. Of course, the military is there, too, waiting for the chance to eliminate the aliens by toasting the town, literally. Convoluted story doesn't seem like an adaptation of King's novel, it's more like an adaptation of all of 'em, from "It" to "Stand By Me." With some "The Thing" and "Outbreak" thrown in for good measure. None of it works, unless you like bloody scenes of alien rectal excavation. *134m/C VHS, DVD. US* Morgan Freeman, Thomas Jane, Jason Lee, Damian Lewis, Timothy Olyphant, Tom Sizemore, Donnie Wahlberg, Michael O'Neill, Rosemary Dunsmore, Mike Holekamp, Reece Thompson, Giacomo Baessato, Joel Palmer, Andrew Robb; **D:** Lawrence Kasdan; **W:** Lawrence Kasdan, William Goldman; **C:** John Seale; **M:** James Newton Howard.

Dreamchild ♂♂♂ 1985 (PG) A poignant story of the autumn years of Alice Hargreaves, the model for Lewis Carroll's "Alice in Wonderland." Film follows her on a visit to New York in the 1930s, with fantasy sequences including Wonderland characters created by Jim Henson's Creature Shop invoking the obsessive Reverend Dodgson (a.k.a. Carroll). *94m/C VHS. GB* Coral Browne, Ian Holm, Peter Gallagher, Jane Asher, Nicola Cowper, Amelia Shankley, Caris Corfman, Shane Rimmer, James Wilby; **D:** Gavin Millar; **W:** Dennis Potter; **C:** Billy Williams; **M:** Max Harris, Stanley Myers.

Dreamer ♂♂ 1979 (PG) The excitement of bowling is exploited for all it's worth in this "strike or die" extravaganza. One of a kind. *86m/C VHS.* Tim Matheson, Susan Blakely, Jack Warden, Richard B. Shull; **D:** Noel Nosseck; **M:** Larry Bischof; **M:** Bill Conti.

Dreamer: Inspired by a True Story ♂♂½ 2005 (PG) Family-friendly heart-warmer about a girl and her race horse. Ben Crane (Russell) has a failing Kentucky horse farm, so he's working as a trainer for stable owner Palmer (Morse). When the stable's most promising filly Sonador ("Dreamer") breaks a leg during a race and is supposed to be put down, but Ben's plucky daughter Cale (Fanning) insists the horse is a keeper. So Ben quits his job, takes the filly as severance pay, and decides to not only nurse the horse back to health, but get her racing again. Well-matched cast with some especially good moments between Russell and Fanning. *98m/C DVD. US* Kurt Russell, Dakota Fanning, Kris Kristofferson, Elisabeth Shue, Luis Guzman, Freddy Rodriguez, David Morse, Oded Fehr, Ken Howard, Holmes Osborne; **D:** John Gatins; **W:** John Gatins; **C:** Fred Murphy; **M:** John Debney.

The Dreamers ♂♂ 2003 (NC-17) A carnal odyssey among a trio of cinephiles set against the political background of the 1968 Paris student riots. Matthew (Pitt), an impressionable American student, meets flirtatious Isabelle (Green) and her twin brother Theo (Garrel) at a protest march. He soon joins the siblings at their apartment even though he's uncomfortable at their closeness. Matthew's uncomfortable—and meets sympathetic relations dissolve as he begins a sexual relationship with Isabelle as he begins. Matthew begins to question the insularity of the twins' privileged world. Eventually, Matthew begins to question the insularity of the twins' privileged world. Bertolucci's a meticulous craftsman but here it's in the service of a sometimes overwrought romanticism. Screenwriter Adair adapted from his novel "The Holy Innocents." Some subtitled French. **B VHS, DVD.** *US* Michael Pitt, Robin Renucci, Anna Chancellor, Mike Collier, Lucia Rijker, Florian Cadiou; *D:* Benardo Bertolucci; *W:* Gilbert Adair; *C:* Fabio Cianchetti.

Dreaming of Rita 🐾 1994 Bob
(Oscarsson) named his daughter Rita after long-lost love Sabine's resemblance to Hollywood goddess. *M:* Zbigniew Preisner.

Dreamgirls 🐾🐾🐾 2006 (PG-13) The
stage musical was coyly set in Chicago; Condon starts his movie off in 1962 Detroit, where three young black women—Effie (Hudson), Deena (Knowles), and Lorell (Rose)—are singing in a talent contest. Sharp-war-nabe manager Curtis Taylor Jr. (Foxx) takes them on as backup singers to soul shouter James Early (Murphy) and then sees the girl trio's potential to move into pop stardom, as long as the out-of-place Effie, who's a little too black, is replaced. Follows the up-and-down showbiz cliches with lots of intensity even if the music can't compare to the real Motown sound of the 60s and 70s. (Come on—as if the shades of Diana Ross and the Supremes aren't all over the plot.) Anyway, Hudson can belt out her big number, "And I Am Telling You I'm Not Going" with real heartache, and, man, Murphy just scorches the stage. **130m/C DVD, Blu-ray Disc, HD DVD.** *US* Jamie Foxx, Eddie Murphy, Beyonce Knowles, Anika Noni Rose, Jennifer Hudson, Danny Glover, Sharon Leal, Keith D. Robinson, Loretta Devine; *D:* Bill Condon; *M:* Harry Krieger. Oscars '06: Sound, Support. Actress (Hudson); British Acad. '06: Sound, Support. Actress (Hudson); Golden Globes '07: Film—Mus./Comedy, Support. Actor (Murphy), Support. Actress (Hudson); Screen Actors Guild '06: Support. Actor (Murphy), Support. Actress (Hudson).

Dreaming About You 🐾🐾½
Anoche Sone Contigo 1992 Teenagers Toto (Altomaro) and Quique (Moya) are spending their summer break biking around the neighborhood, dreaming about girls, and spying on Chabelita (Aguirre), Quique's family's pretty maid. But Toto w.l soon be doing more than dreaming when his attractive and experienced cousin Azucena (Perdigon) comes for a visit. Spanish with subtitles. **90m/C VHS, DVD.** *MX* Martin Altomaro, Moises Ivan Mora, Leticia Perdigon, Patricia Aguirre; *D:* Marisa Sistach; *W:* Jose Buil; *C:* Alex Phillips Jr.; *M:* Alberto Delgado.

Dreaming Lips 🐾🐾 1937 An
orchestra conductor's wife falls in love with her husband's violinist friend. Tragedy befalls the couple. Bergner in a standout performance, in a familiar script. **70m/B VHS, GB** Raymond Massey, Elisabeth Bergner, Romney Brent, Joyce Bland, Charles Carson, Felix Aylmer. *D:* Paul Czinner; *C:* Lee Games.

Dreaming of Joseph
Lees 🐾🐾 1999 (R) Eva (Morton) has long had fantasies about her worldly older cousin Joseph Lees (Graves), but he's retreated from society after a terrible accident and lives in Italy. Meanwhile, lonely Eva is stuck in boring rural England in 1958. So she's willing to respond to the romantic gestures of working-class Harry Flyte (Ross) and, shockingly, decides to move in with him. Then Eva re-meets Joseph at a family wedding and, perversely, leads her desire for him only increases, which leads Harry to desperate measures. Strained symbolism pushes the plot but the accomplished performances take up the slack. **92m/C VHS, GB** Rupert Graves, Samantha Morton, Lee Ross, Miriam Margolyes, Frank Finlay, Nicholas Woodeson, Holly Aird; *D:* Eric Styles; *W:* Catherine Linstrum; *C:* Jimmy Dibling; *M:* Zbigniew Preisner.

---

an elderly widower, Bob suddenly decides to try and find Sabine, taking off across the Swedish countryside. The unhappily married Rita (Lagercrantz), leaving husband and children behind, goes after him—and meets sympathetic hitchhiker Erik (Ersgard), who's happy to offer a little romance. Swedish with subtitles. 108m/C VHS, SW/Per Oscarsson, Marika Lagercrantz, Patrik Ersgard, Philip Zanden; *D:* Jon Lindstrom, Rita Holst; *C:* Kjell Lagersno.

Dreamland 🐾🐾 2006 (PG-13) Well-
told (and cast) coming-of-age story. The title refers to the name of the New Mexico trailer park where 18-year-old Audrey (Bruckner) lives with her agoraphobic, hard-drinking, widowed dad Henry (Corbett). Because she's a natural caregiver, Audrey has put her college plans on hold and works at the local mini-mart while also looking out for her best friend Calista (Garner), whose beauty pageant dreams are hindered by her MS. When Mookie (Long) and his family move into the neighborhood, Audrey sets him and Calista up on a date even though she likes the guy herself—and discovers the feeling is mutual. Brian Klugman; *D:* Jason Matzner; *W:* Tom Willett; *C:* Jonathan Sela; *M:* Anthony Marinelli.

The Dreamlife of
Angels 🐾🐾🐾½ *La Vie Revee des Anges*
1998 Deceptively simple debut from director Zouca follows the friendship of two opportunistic working class French women, Marie (Regnier) and Isa (Bouchez). Tensions between the two arise when Marie becomes involved with a brutal nightclub owner Chriss (Colin). Zouca had his female leads live together during filming to create the realistic bickering scenes. French with subtitles. 113m/C VHS, DVD, FR Elodie Bouchez, Natacha Regnier, Gregoire Colin, Jo Prestia, Patrick Mercado; *D:* Erick Zonca; *W:* Erick Zonca, Roger Bohbot; *C:* Agnes Godard; *M:* Yann Tiersen, Cesar '99: Actress (Bouchez), Film.

Dreams 🐾🐾 *Kvin ocrom: Journey into
Autumn* 1955 Unfocused film about the lives and loves of two successful women. Subtitled. 86m/B VHS, SW Harriet Andersson, Gunnar Bjornstrand, Eva Dahlbeck, Ulf Palme; *D:* Ingmar Bergman; *W:* Ingmar Bergman; *C:* Hilding Bladh; *M:* Stuart Goring.

Dreams Come True 🐾 1984 (R)
Silly young comedy-romance about two young lovers who discover the trick of out-of-body travel, and have various forms of spiritual contact while their bodies are sleeping. 95m/C VHS, Michael Sanville, Stephanie Shuford; *D:* Max Kalmanowicz.

Dreams Lost, Dreams
Found 🐾½ 1987 A young widow journeys from the U.S. to Scotland in search of her heritage. The third "Harlequin Romance Movie." 102m/C VHS, Kathleen Quinlan; *D:* Willi Patterson, C.A.B.L.E.

Dreamscape 🐾🐾½ 1984 (PG-13)
When a doctor teaches a young psychic how to enter into other people's dreams in order to end their nightmares, somebody else wants to use this psychic for evil purposes. The special effects are far more convincing than the one man-saves-the-country-with-his-psychic-powers plot. 99m/C VHS, DVD, UHD, Dennis Quaid, Max von Sydow, Christopher Plummer, Eddie Albert, Kate Capshaw, David Patrick Kelly, George Wendt, Jana Taylor; *D:* Joseph Ruben; *W:* Chuck Russell; *C:* Brian Tufano; *M:* Maurice Jarre.

Dresden 🐾🐾½ 2006 (R) Ger-
man nurse Anna Mauth (Woll) discovers an injured British pilot, Robert Newman (Light), hiding in the hospital's cellar. She first helps him believing he's a German deserter, but even after discovering that Anna can't

---

bring herself to betray him since they've fallen in love. But time is not on their side as the Allied bombing of the city of Dresden is about to begin. Made for German TV; English and German with subtitles. 180m/C DVD, GE Heiner Lauterbach, Kai Wiesinger, Felicitas Woll, John Light, Benjamin Sadler, Katharina Meinecke, Marie Baumer; *D:* Roland Suso Richter; *W:* Stefan Kolditz; *C:* Holly Fink; *M:* Harald Kloser, Thomas Wanker; TV.

The Dress 🐾🐾 1996 The title char-
acter turns out to be a very malevolent object indeed, in this Dutch absurdist comedy. The bright blue dress with the striking leaf design first causes havoc for the fabric designer, who's nearly fired, while the garment manufacturers get into a fight over the pattern. The dress goes from wearer to wearer, causing havoc for them all, until it is finally destroyed. Dutch with subtitles. 103m/C VHS, NL Henri Garcin, Ariane Schluier, Alex Van Warmerdam; *D:* Alex Van Warmerdam; *W:* Vincent van Warmerdam.

The Dress Code 🐾 Bruno 1999
(PG-13) Eight-year-old Bruno is the kind of meek kid who gets picked on by school-yard bullies and is a disappointment to his dad. So his grandma comes up with a plan to toughen the kid up. 108m/C VHS, DVD, Alex D. Linz, Gary Sinise, Jennifer Tilly, Kathy Bates, Joey Lauren Adams, Shirley MacLaine, Brett Butler, Gwen Verdon, Stacey Halprin, Kiami Davael; *D:* Shirley MacLaine; *W:* David Ciminel lo; *C:* Jean Kesser; *M:* Chris Boardman.

Dress Gray 🐾🐾🐾 1986 Fine, excit-
ing adaptation of the Lucian K. Truscott IV novel about a coverup at an Eastern military academy. Baldwin is cadet Slaight, an upperclassman who finds more secrets than he can handle when a younger cadet (Cassidy), with whom he had an adversarial relationship, is murdered. He's torn between investigating the death or keeping quiet—for the sake of his career if not his life. 192m/C VHS, Alec Baldwin, Hal Holbrook, Eddie Albert, Lloyd Bridges, Susan Hess, Timothy Van Patten, Patrick Cassidy, Alexis Smith, James B. Sikking, Lane Smith; *D:* Glenn Jordan; *W:* Gore Vidal; *M:* Billy Goldenberg. TV

Dressed for Death 🐾½ Straight
on Till Morning; Till Dawn Do Us Part 1974 (R) A tale of true love gone bad as a woman is chased and murdered in her castle by the psychopath she loves. 121m/C VHS, Andrina Ross, Katya Wyath, Shane Briant, Tom Bell, Annie Ross; *D:* Peter Collinson.

Dressed to Kill 🐾🐾 1946
Sherlock Holmes finds that a series of music boxes holds the key to plates stolen from the Bank of England. The plot's a bit thin, but Rathbone/Bruce, in their final Holmes adventure, are always a delight. 72m/B VHS, DVD, Basil Rathbone, Nigel Bruce, Patricia Morison, Edmund Breon, Tom Dillon; *D:* Roy William Neill; *W:* Frank Gruber, Leonard Lee; *C:* Maury Gertsman; *M:* Hans J. Salter.

Dressed to Kill 🐾🐾½ 1980 (R)
Contemporary thriller merges bombastic DePalma with a tense Hitchcockian flare. Sexually unsatisfied Kate (Dickinson) is told to have an affair by her sympathetic shrink Dr. Elliot (Caine) and ends up in a museum. Then Kate's found brutally murdered by prostitute Liz (Allen). Kate's son Peter (Gordon) teams up with Liz to track down the killer into their trap. Suspenseful and fast paced. Dickinson's murderous scene is wonderfully photographed and edited. DePalma was repeatedly criticized for using a stand-in during the Dickinson shower scene; he titled this next film "Body Double" as a rebuttal. 105m/C VHS, DVD, Angie Dickinson, Michael Caine, Nancy Allen, Keith Gordon, Dennis Franz, David Margulies, Brandon Maggart; *D:* Brian De Palma; *W:* Brian De Palma; *C:* Ralf Bode; *M:* Pino Donaggio.

The Dresser 🐾🐾🐾½ 1983 (PG)
Film adaptation of Harwood's play (he also wrote the screen version) about an aging English actor/manager (Finney), his dresser (Courtenay), and their theatre company touring England during WWII. Marvelous, showbiz tale is lovingly told, superbly acted. 119m/C VHS, DVD, Albert Finney, Tom Courtenay, Edward Fox, Michael Gough, Zena Walker, Eileen Atkins, Cathryn Harrison; *D:*

Peter Yates; *W:* Ronald Harwood; *M:* James Horner. Golden Globes '84: Actor—Drama (Courtenay).

The Dressmaker 🐾🐾½ 1989
comedian Fernando stars as a man's tailor who designs dresses in secret so as not to compete with his dressmaker wife. Lightweight but entertaining; English subtitled. 95m/B VHS, FR Fernandel, Francoise Fabian; *D:* Jean Boyer.

Dressmaker 🐾🐾½ 1956 French

The Dressmaker 🐾🐾½ 1989
Two sisters in WWII Liverpool must deal with their young niece's romantic involvement with an American soldier. Plowright and Whitelaw turn in fine performances as the two siblings with very different outlooks on life. 90m/C VHS, GB Pam(ela) Austin, Joan Plowright, Billie Whitelaw, Pete Postleth waite, Jane Horrocks, Tim Ransom; *D:* Jim O'Brien; *C:* Michael Coulter; *M:* George Fenton.

Drift Fence 🐾🐾 2001 Texas Despera-
does 1936 Good early oater about a Texas ranger who goes in search of a beautiful girl in an L.A. coffee shop as he tries to become a screenwriter. He's living with tenuous when Ryan meets young college student Leo (Roessler) and begins to wonder what would happen if he left Joel to pursue this new relationship. Three talky scenarios are offered. 86m/C DVD, CA R.T. Katherine DeMille, Tom Keene, Benny Baker; *D:* Otho Lovering; *W:* Stuart Anthony, Robert Yost.

Drift 🐾 2001 Angsty relationship
drama concerns Ryan (Lee) who's working in an L.A. coffee shop as he tries to become a screenwriter. He's living with tenuous when Ryan meets young college student Leo (Roessler) and begins to wonder what would happen if he left Joel to pursue this new relationship. Three talky scenarios are offered. 86m/C DVD, CA R.T. Lee, Greyson Deyrre, Jonathon Roessler; *D:* Quentin Lee; *W:* Quentin Lee; *M:* Steven Panto.

The Drifter 🐾🐾 1932 A lumberjack
makes sacrifices for the love between his brother and the lumberjill owner's daughter. 57m/B VHS, William Famum, Noah Beery Sr., Phyllis Barrington; *D:* William A. O'Connor; *M:* Oliver Drake; *C:* William Nobles.

The Drifter 🐾🐾½ 1988 (R) It's psy-
chos, psychos everywhere in this lame produced western has Keene posing as a young woman learns to regret a one-night stand. 90m/C VHS, DVD, Kim Delaney, Timothy Bottoms, Miles O'Keeffe, Al Shannon, Thomas Wagner, Larry Brand; *D:* Larry Brand; *W:* Larry Brand; *C:* David Sperling; *M:* Rick Conrad.

The Driftin' Kid 🐾🐾 1941 Poorly
produced western has Keene posing as a rancher in order to nab a bunch of cattle rustlers. So bad that even the sound of the punches are seconds off from the blows. 57m/B VHS, Tom Keene, Stanley Price, Glenn Strange; *D:* Robert Emmett Tansey; *W:* Robert Emmett Tansey, Frances Kavanaugh.

Driftin' River 🐾🐾½ 1946 A ship-
ment of horses bound for the Army is hijacked and the soldiers sent to investigate the theft are murdered. 57m/B VHS, DVD, Eddie Dean, Rosco Ates, Shirley Patterson, William "Billy" Fawcett, Dennis Moore, Bob Callahan, Lottie Harrison, Forrest Taylor; *D:* Robert Emmett Tansey; *W:* Frances Kavanaugh.

Drifting 🐾🐾½ Nagooa 1982 A contro-
versial Israeli film about a homosexual filmmaker surviving in modern-day Jerusalem. First such movie to be made in Israel. In Hebrew with English titles. 103m/C VHS, /S Jonathan Sagalle, Ami Traub, Ben Levine, Dita Arel; *D:* Amos Guttman.

Drifting Souls 🐾🐾 1932 In order to
save her father's life, a beautiful young woman marries for money instead of love. 65m/C VHS, Lois Wilson, Theodore von Eltz, Shirley Grey, Raymond Hatton, Gene Gowing, Bryant Washburn; *D:* Louis King.

Drifting Weeds 🐾🐾½ 1959 A
remake of Ozu's The Duckweed Story; Ukigusa 1959 A movie about a troupe of traveling actors whose leader visits his illegitimate son and his lover after years of separation. Classic Ozu. In Japanese with English subtitles. 128m/B VHS, DVD, JP Ganjiro Nakamura, Machi-

ko Kyo, Haruko Sugimura, Ayako Wakao; **D:** Yasujiro Ozu.

Drillbit Taylor 🦴🦴 2008 (PG-13) Three freshman dweebs find high-school life a nightmare, especially when two ruthless bullies are out for blood. Pooling together pocket change and savings, they hire Drillbit Taylor (Wilson), a panhandler posing as a freelance body guard with plans to quietly steal from their nice suburban homes. Taylor's scheme is thwarted when he discovers a genuine sympathy for the boys, as well as a budding romance with a teacher (Mann). Wilson is typically sweet and likable, but he's lost in a bland script. **102m/C DVD.** *US* Owen Wilson, Leslie Mann, Troy Gentile, David Dorfman, Alex Frost, Josh Peck, Nate Hartley; **D:** Steven Brill; **W:** Seth Rogen, Kristofor Brown; **C:** Fred Murphy; **M:** Christophe Beck.

Drive 🦴🦴 1996 (R) A technologically enhanced man (Dacascos), running from biotech corporate hitmen, offers a down-on-his-luck stranger (Hardison) $5 million to drive him from San Francisco to L.A. And he won't take no for an answer. **99m/C VHS, DVD.** Mark Dacascos, Kadeem Hardison, Brittany Murphy, John Pyper-Ferguson, Tracey Walter, James Shigeta, Masaya Kato; **D:** Steve Wang.

Drive-In WOOF! 1976 (PG) A low-budget bomb showing a night in the life of teenage yahoos at a Texas drive-in. **96m/C VHS.** Lisa Lemole, Glenn Morshower, Gary Cavagnaro; **D:** Rod Amateau.

Drive-In Massacre WOOF! 1974 (R) Two police detectives investigate a bizarre series of slasher murders at the local drive-in. Honk the horn at this one. **78m/C VHS.** Jake Barnes, Adam Lawrence, Austin Johnson, Douglas Gudbye, Valdesta; **D:** Stu Segall; **W:** George "Buck" Flower, John Goff.

Drive Me Crazy 🦴🦴 1999 (PG-13) Nicole (Hart) and Chase (Grenier) have grown up next door to each other and attend the same high school, but that's all they have in common. Pep rallying Nicole yearns to date BMOC Brad (Carpenter), but he's only interested in a rival cheerleader. Slacker-type Chase just wants to hang out at the coffeehouse with his animal activist girlfriend Dulcie (Larter), but he gets dumped hard. They conspire to win their dream dates to the prom by pretending to be a couple in order to provoke jealousy. As the two grow closer, they inevitably fall in love. Unfortunately, they don't do it in a very entertaining or amusing manner. Slow paced, unfunny and trite is no way to go through life, son. Based on the novel "How I Created My Perfect Prom Date" by Todd Strasser. **91m/C VHS, DVD.** Melissa Joan Hart, Adrian Grenier, Stephen Collins, Faye Grant, Susan May Pratt, Kris Park, Mark Webber, Ali Larter, Mark Metcalf, William Converse-Roberts, Gabriel Carpenter; **D:** John Schultz; **W:** Rob Thomas; **C:** Kees Van Oostrum; **M:** Greg Kendall.

Driven 🦴🦴 2001 (PG-13) Hotshot rookie racer Jimmy Bly (Pardue) is slipping in the rankings thanks to pressure from his promoter brother (Leonard) and his ongoing affair with Sophia (Warren), the girlfriend of top rival Beau (Schweiger). Owner Henry (Reynolds) brings in former hotshot Joe Tanto (Stallone) to straighten the kid out, but Joe has his own demons, including a horrific, nearlydeadly crash, an ex married to his arch-rival (De la Fuente), and a hovering female reporter (Edwards). There's a lot going on, what with all the CGI-created car crashes, the bed-hopping, and the tempers flaring, but it's all over the road, so as not to tax anyone's attention span. It doesn't get anywhere, but at least it gets there fast. **117m/C VHS, DVD.** *US* Sylvester Stallone, Burt Reynolds, Kip Pardue, Til Schweiger, Gina Gershon, Robert Sean Leonard, Stacy Edwards, Estella Warren, Christian de la Fuente, Brent Briscoe; **D:**

Renny Harlin; **W:** Sylvester Stallone; **C:** Mauro Fiore; **M:** BT [Brian Transeau].

Driven to Kill 🦴🦴 1990 No-name cast assemble in low-rent suspenser portraying the ugly side of love: bent on revenge, a man is out to obliterate the thugs who made his life a horrible experience highlighted by misery and boredom. **97m/C VHS.** Jake Jacobs, Chip Campbell, Michele McNeil; **D:** John Gazarian; **W:** Frank Norwood; **C:** Robert Hayes.

The Driver 🦴½ 1978 (PG) A police detective will stop at nothing to catch "The Driver," a man who has the reputation of driving the fastest getaway car around. Chase scenes win out over plot. **131m/C VHS, DVD.** Ryan O'Neal, Bruce Dern, Isabelle Adjani, Ronee Blakley, Matt Clark; **D:** Walter Hill; **W:** Walter Hill.

Driver's Seat WOOF! *Psychotic; Identikit* 1973 (R) Extremely bizarre film with a cult following that was adapted from the novel by Muriel Spark. Liz stars as a deranged woman trying to keep a rendezvous with her strange lover in Rome. In the meantime she wears tacky clothes and delivers stupid lines. **101m/C VHS, DVD.** *IT* Elizabeth Taylor, Ian Bannen, Mona Washbourne, Andy Warhol, Guido Mannari, Maxence Mailfort; **D:** Giuseppe Patroni-Griffi; **W:** Giuseppe Patroni-Griffi, Raffaele La Capria; **M:** Franco Mannino.

Driving Force 🦴 1988 (R) In an effort to capitalize on the popularity of the "Road Warrior" movies, features a lone trucker battling a gang of roadhogs in another post-holocaust desert. Ultimately, runs off the road. **90m/C VHS.** Sam Jones, Catherine Bach, Don Swayze; **D:** A.J. Prowse; **W:** Patrick Edgeworth.

Driving Lessons 🦴🦴½ 2006 (PG-13) Red-headed Grint gets to step out from just being Harry Potter's sidekick in this cozy generational comedy. Ben is a shy teen who's usually dragged into helping steely mom Laura (Linney) with her Christian charity work, even agreeing to her suggestion of a summer job. He ends up with the alcoholic and somewhat delusional Evie (Walters), an over-the-hill actress who convinces Ben to drive her to Edinburgh, a trip that turns out to be quite eventful. It's a case of dueling divas for the carcass of one bewildered boy—predictable, but it's still a laugh. **98m/C DVD, GB** Julie Walters, Rupert Grint, Laura Linney, Nicholas Farrell, Jim Norton, Tamsin Egerton, Michelle Duncan; **D:** Jeremy Brock; **W:** Jeremy Brock; **M:** John Renbourn, Clive Carroll.

Driving Miss Daisy 🦴🦴🦴½ 1989 (PG) Tender and sincere portrayal of a 25-year friendship between an aging Jewish woman and the black chauffeur forced upon her by her son. Humorous and thought-provoking, skillfully acted and directed, it subtly explores the effects of prejudice in the South. The development of Aykroyd as a top-notch character actor is further evidenced here. Part of the fun is watching the changes in fashion and auto design. Adapted from the play by Alfred Uhry. **99m/C VHS, DVD.** Jessica Tandy, Morgan Freeman, Dan Aykroyd, Esther Rolle, Patti Lupone; **D:** Bruce Beresford; **W:** Alfred Uhry; **C:** Peter James; **M:** Hans Zimmer. Oscars '89: Actress (Tandy), Adapt. Screenplay, Makeup, Picture; British Acad. '90: Actress (Tandy); Golden Globes '90: Actress—Mus./Comedy (Freeman), Actor—Mus./Comedy (Freeman), Film—Mus./Comedy; Natl. Bd. of Review '89: Actor (Freeman); Writers Guild '89: Adapt. Screenplay.

The Drop 🦴 2006 (R) Naive college student Carter (Bondies) accepts suspiciously big bucks to drive a sports car from San Francisco to L.A. While waiting in a parking garage for the pickup, Carter gets curious about a briefcase in the trunk and makes the mistake of opening it. Supposed to be spooky; instead, the whole thing is silly and nonsensical. **?m/C DVD.** *US* John Savage, Sean Young, Michael P. Bondies; **D:**

Kevin Lewis; **W:** Kevin Lewis; **C:** Chris Wilson. **VIDEO**

Drop Dead Fred WOOF! 1991 (PG-13) As a little girl, Lizzie Cronin had a manic, imaginary friend named Fred, who protected her from her domineering mother. When her husband dumps her 20 years later, Fred returns to "help" as only he can. Although the cast is fine, incompetent writing and direction make this a truly dismal affair. Plus, gutter humor and mean-spirited pranks throw the whole "heart-warming" premise out the window. Filmed in Minneapolis. **103m/C VHS, DVD.** Phoebe Cates, Rik Mayall, Tim Matheson, Marsha Mason, Carrie Fisher, Daniel Gerroll, Ron Eldard; **D:** Ate De Jong; **W:** Carlos Davis, Anthony Fingleton; **M:** Randy Edelman.

Drop Dead Gorgeous 🦴🦴½ *Dairy Queens* 1999 (PG-13) Oh, the ambitions of stage moms and their daughters in this mockumentary of small-town Minnesota beauty pageants. Satire takes the lowest road whenever possible, because that's where the laughs happen to be. Naive Amber (Dunst) has a trailer-trash babe, Annette (Barkin), for a mom, while rival rich bitch, Becky (Richards), is stuck with the horror that is Gladys (Alley). And someone is taking the contest way too seriously, since other contestants are dropping like flies. Piles it on a little thick sometimes, but overall it works. Watch for Richards' cringe-inducing talent show dance number. **97m/C VHS, DVD.** Denise Richards, Kirsten Dunst, Kirstie Alley, Ellen Barkin, Allison Janney, Sam McMurray, Mindy Sterling, Amy Adams, Tara Redepenning, Sara Stewart, Shannon Nelson, Matt Malloy, Brittany Murphy, Mo Gaffney, Nora Dunn, Amanda Detmer; *Cameos:* Adam West; **D:** Michael Patrick Jann; **W:** Lona Williams; **C:** Michael Spiller; **M:** Mark Mothersbaugh.

Drop Dead Sexy 🦴🦴½ 2005 (R) The ick factor seems high but it's more comic/thriller than disturbing. Frank (Lee) and Eddie (Glover) are a couple of small-time Texas losers: Frank works for a used car dealer, Eddie is a gravedigger, and both moonlight for thug Spider (Vince) to whom they owe money. After seeing the obit of Crystal (Keller), the beautiful blonde wife of the richest man (Berkeley) in town, Frank learns she's been buried with an expensive necklace. He convinces Eddie to dig up the body, only to find the necklace missing. They also can't immediately rebury the corpse. So Eddie takes the body home for safekeeping while Frank tries to come up with another plan. **83m/C DVD.** Jason Lee, Crispin Glover, Pruitt Taylor Vince, Xander Berkeley, Melissa Keller, Brad Dourif, Lin Shaye; **D:** Michael Philip; **W:** Michael Philip; **C:** Thomas Callaway; **M:** Deborah Lurie.

Drop-Out Mother 🦴🦴 1988 A woman gives up her executive position to become a housewife and full-time mom; expected domestic turmoil follows. Standard TV fare and sort of a sequel to "Drop-Out Father," shown in 1982. **100m/C VHS.** Valerie Harper, Wayne Rogers, Carol Kane, Kim Hunter, Danny Gerard; **D:** Charles S. Dubin. **TV**

DROP Squad 🦴🦴 1994 (R) Not quite on target social satire revolving around buppie Buford Jackson Jr. (La Salle), a token minority ad exec who's job is to push questionable products, using gross stereotypes, to the black community. His family's appalled and Buford becomes a prime target of D.R.O.P. (Deprogramming and Restoration of Pride), a vigilante organization that kidnaps erring black brethren and leads them back to their cultural heritage. Frequently intense performances but the script raises some serious issues on which it doesn't deliver. Based on the short story "The Deprogrammer" by David Taylor. **88m/C VHS, DVD.** Eriq La Salle, Vondie Curtis-Hall, Ving Rhames, Kasi Lemmons, Vanessa Williams, Nicole Powell, Afemo Omilami, Spike Lee; **D:** David C(lark) Johnson; **W:** David C(lark) Johnson, David Taylor; **C:** Ken Kelsch; **M:** Michael Bearden.

Drop Zone 🦴🦴½ 1994 (R) Routine action-thriller finds U.S. marshal Pete Nessip (Snipes) and his brother Terry (Warner) assigned to protect drug cartel

snitch Earl Leedy (Jeter). The plane they're on is skyjacked by criminal Moncrief (Busey) who parachutes off with Leedy, Terry's killed, and while Pete's on suspension he decides to go undercover into the world of sky-diving with the aid of ex-con cutie Jessie (Butler). Plot holes are big enough to pilot a plane through but the stunts are good and Snipes is never less than professional. **101m/C VHS, DVD.** Wesley Snipes, Gary Busey, Yancy Butler, Michael Jeter, Corin "Corky" Nemec, Kyle Secor, Luca Bercovici, Malcolm Jamal Warner, Rex Linn, Grace Zabriskie, Sam Hennings, Claire Stansfield, Mickey Jones, Andy Romano; **D:** John Badham; **W:** John Bishop, Peter Barsocchini; **C:** Roy Wagner; **M:** Hans Zimmer.

The Dropkick 🦴🦴🦴 1927 Erstwhile D.W. Griffith leading man Barthelmess stars in this pigskin whodunit: a coach's suicide looks like murder, and the prime suspect is the team's most valuable player. Cast includes ten bona fide university football players and Hedda "nobody's interested in sweetness and light" Hopper, while The Duke makes cameo. Webb later went on to direct a musical with Eddie Cantor and Rudy Vallee ("Glorifying the American Girl"). Silent. Based on the story "Glitter" by Katherine Brush. **62m/B VHS.** Richard Barthelmess, Barbara Kent, Dorothy Revier, Eugene Strong, Alberta Vaughn, Brooks Benedict, Hedda Hopper; *Cameos:* John Wayne; **D:** Millard Webb; **W:** Winifred Dunn.

Drowning by Numbers 🦴🦴🦴½ 1987 (R) Three generations of women, each named Cissie Colpitts, solve their marital problems by drowning their husbands and making deals with a bizarre coroner. Further strange visions from director Greenaway, complemented by stunning cinematography courtesy of Sacha Vierny. A treat for those who appreciate Greenaway's uniquely curious cinematic statements. **121m/C VHS, GB** Bernard Hill, Joan Plowright, Juliet Stevenson, Joely Richardson; **D:** Peter Greenaway; **W:** Peter Greenaway; **C:** Sacha Vierny; **M:** Michael Nyman.

Drowning Mona 🦴🦴 2000 (PG-13) Strident comedy about the low-IQ denizens of small town Verplanck, New York, where everybody still drives a Yugo (the town was a test market). Nasty Mona Dearly (Midler) drives her car into the Hudson River and drowns. It turns out to be murder and Chief Wyatt Rash (DeVito) must investigate. He's not lacking in suspects since Mona was the most hated woman in the community. Everyone in the cast looks like they're enjoying themselves which may be more than the viewer will say. **95m/C VHS, DVD.** Danny DeVito, Bette Midler, Jamie Lee Curtis, Casey Affleck, Neve Campbell, William Fichtner, Peter Dobson, Marcus Thomas, Kathleen Wilhoite, Tracey Walter, Paul Ben-Victor, Paul Schulze, Mark Pellegrino; **D:** Nick Gomez; **W:** Peter Steinfeld; **C:** Bruce Douglas Johnson; **M:** Michael Tavera.

Drowning on Dry Land 🦴🦴 2000 (R) After being fired, Hershey decides to take a cross-country trip—by taxi—to find herself in the desert. Naturally, bonding goes on. **90m/C VHS, DVD.** Barbara Hershey, Naveen Andrews, Carol Lynley, John Doe, Stephen Polk; **D:** Carl Colpaert; **M:** Richard Horowitz. **VIDEO**

The Drowning Pool 🦴🦴 1975 (PG) Newman returns as detective Lew Harper (after 1966's "Harper") to solve a blackmail case. Uneventful script and stodgy direction, but excellent character work from all the cast members keep this watchable. Title is taken from a trap set for Newman, from which he must escape using most of his female companion's clothing. Adapted from Ross MacDonald's novel about detective Lew Archer. **109m/C VHS, DVD.** Paul Newman, Joanne Woodward, Anthony (Tony) Franciosa, Murray Hamilton, Melanie Griffith, Richard Jaeckel; **D:** Stuart Rosenberg; **W:** Tracy Keenan Wynn, Walter Hill; **C:** Gordon Willis; **M:** Charles Fox.

Drug Wars: The Camarena Story 🦴🦴 1990 (PG-13) Enrique "Kiki" Camarena (Bauer) is an undercover DEA agent working in Mexico in 1985. His discovery of a major drug operation leads to a top drug kingpin. When his cover is blown, Kiki is kidnapped, tortured, and murdered and the cover-up highlights corruption in the government itself. Based on the book "Desperados" by Elaine Shannon. **130m/C VHS, DVD.** Steven Bauer, Elizabeth Pena, Miguel Ferrer, Benicio Del Toro, Treat Williams, Craig T. Nelson, Guy Boyd, Tory Plana, Tomas Milian, Raymond J. Barry, Everett McGill, Eddie Velez, Rosalind Chao; **D:** Brian Gibson; **W:** Rose Schacht, Ann Powell, Christopher Cannan; **M:** Charles Bernstein. **TV**

Drugstore Cowboy ✓✓✓½
1989 (R) A gritty, uncompromising depiction of a pack of early 1970s drugstore-robbing junkies as they travel around looking to score. Brushes with the law and tragedy encourage them to examine other life-styles, but the trap seems impossible to leave. A perfectly crafted piece that reflects the "me generation" era, though it tends to glamorize addiction. Dillon's best work to date. Based on a novel by prison inmate James Fogle. **100m/C VHS, DVD.** Matt Dillon, Kelly Lynch, James Remar, James LeGros, Heather Graham, William S. Burroughs, Beah Richards, Grace Zabriskie, Max Perlich; **D:** Gus Van Sant; **W:** Gus Van Sant, Daniel Yost; **C:** Robert Yeoman; **M:** Elliot Goldenthal, Ind. Spirt '90: Actor (Dillon), Cinematog., Screenplay. Support. Actor (Perich); L.A. Film Critics '89: Screenplay; N.Y. Film Critics '89: Director '89, Screenplay.

Druids ✓✓½ *Vercingetorix* **2001 (R)** Gallic chieftain Vercingetorix (Lambert) must rally his people when they are threatened by Roman army commander Julius Caesar (Brandauer) in 60 B.C. The action is well-done even if the story drags occasionally. **115m/C VHS, DVD.** Christopher Lambert, Klaus Maria Brandauer, Max von Sydow, Ines Sastre, Stefan Ivanov, Bernard Pierre Donnadieu; **D:** Jacques Dorfmann; **W:** Jacques Dorfmann, Norman Spinrad; **M:** Pierre Charvet.

Drum wOOf! **1976 (R)** This is a sorry sequel to "Mandingo" deals with the sordid interracial sexual shenanigans at a Southern plantation. Bad taste at its best. **101m/C VHS, DVD.** Ken Norton, Warren Oates, Pam Grier, Yaphet Kotto, Fiona Lewis, Isela Vega, Cheryl "Rainbeaux" Smith; **D:** Steve Carver; **C:** Lucien Ballard.

Drum Beat ✓✓ **1954** An unarmed Indian fighter sets out to negotiate a peace treaty with a renegade Indian leader. Bronson is especially believable as chief. Based on historical incident. **111m/C VHS.** Alan Ladd, Charles Bronson, Marisa Pavan, Robert Keith, Rodolfo Acosta, Warner Anderson, Elisha Cook Jr., Anthony Caruso; **D:** Delmer Daves.

Drum Taps ✓✓ **1933** Maynard saves the day for a young girl who is being pushed off her land by a group of speculators. **55m/B VHS, DVD.** Ken Maynard, Dorothy Dix, Frank "Junior" Coghlan, Kermit Maynard; **D:** (John) Patterson) McGowan.

Drumline ✓✓✓ **2002 (PG-13)** Devon Miles, (Cannon) a hip-hop drummer from Harlem, receives a full music scholarship to the fictitious Atlanta A&T University. Although his hotdogging antics brought him recognition at home, they aren't appreciated by bandleader Dr. Lee, who's philosophy is "one band, one sound." The university president is aching for more show-manship during halftime and supports Devon's hot-shot performing. This, along with Devon's wisecracking attitude grates on section-leader and rival Sean (Roberts). Stone does well dealing with ethnic issues without falling into character cliches or stereotypes, but with so many issues explored, some ideas go undeveloped. Good story is helped along by the fair and power of the marching band scenes. **118m/C VHS, DVD. US** Nick Cannon, Zoe Saldana, Orlando Jones, Leonard Roberts, GQ, Jason Weaver; **D:** Charles Stone III; **W:** Shawn Schepps; **M:** John Powell.

Drums ✓✓½ *The Drum* **1938** A native prince helps to save the British army in India from being annihilated by a tyrant. Rich melodrama with interesting characterizations and locale. **96m/B VHS, GB Sabu, Raymond Massey, Valerie Hobson, Roger Livesey, David Tree; **D:** Zoltan Korda.

Drums Along the Mohawk ✓✓✓ **1939** Grand, action-filled saga about pre-Revolutionary America, detailing the trials of a colonial newlywed couple as their village in the hawk Valley is besieged by Indians. Based on the Walter Edmonds novel, and vintage Ford. **104m/C VHS, DVD.** Henry Fonda, Claudette Colbert, Edna May Oliver, Eddie Collins, John Carradine, Doris Bowdon, Arthur Shields, Ward Bond, Jessie Ralph, Robert Lowery; **D:** John Ford; **C:** Ray Rennahan.

Drums in the Deep South ✓✓ **1951** A rivalry turns ugly as two former West Point roommates wind up on opposite sides when the Civil War breaks out. Historical drama hampered by familiar premise. **87m/C VHS, DVD.** James Craig, Guy Madison, Barbara Payton, Barton MacLane; **D:** William Cameron Menzies; **W:** Philip Yordan.

Drums of Fu Manchu ✓✓✓ **1940** Fu Manchu searches for the scepter of Genghis Khan, an artifact that would give him domination over the East. Brand on this daughter's killer. Cheap copy of "Dr. Fu Manchu," like many others, focuses on smoothly evil as the Devil Doctor. Originally a serial in 15 chapters. **150m/B VHS, DVD.** Henry (Kleinbach) Brandon, Robert Kellard, George Cleveland, Dwight Frye, Gloria Franklin, Tom Chatterton, Philip Ahn; **D:** William Witney, John English; **W:** Barney A. Sarecky, Franklyn Adreon, Norman S. Hall, Morgan Cox; **C:** William Nobles; **M:** Cy Feuer.

Drums of Jeopardy ✓✓ *Mark of Terror* **1931** A father wanders through czarist Russia and the U.S. to seek revenge on his daughter's killer. **65m/B VHS, DVD.** Warren Oland, June Collyer, Lloyd Hughes, George Fawcett, Mischa Auer; **D:** George B. Seitz.

Drums O'Voodoo wOOf! *She Devil* **1934** A voodoo princess fights to eliminate the town bad guy in this all-black feature that is greatly hampered by shoddy production values. **70m/B VHS, Laura Bowman, J. Augustus Smith, Edna Barr; **D:** Arthur Hoerl.

Drunken Angel ✓✓ *Yoidore tenshi* **1948** Alcoholic doctor gets mixed up with local gangster. Kurosawa's first major film aided by strong performances. With English subtitles. **108m/B VHS, DVD.** Takashi Shimura, Choko Iida; **D:** Akira Kurosawa; **W:** Keinosuke Uegusa; **C:** Takeo Ito; **M:** Fumio Hayasaka.

Drunken Monkey ✓✓½ *Chui Ma Lau* **2002 (R)** Wen Biao discovers his brother is conducting criminal acts through their security company and confronts him. Shortly after, Wen Biao goes missing and is assumed dead until he resurfaces again for a final martial arts showdown with his misguided sibling. Unfortunately typical in narrative and combat. With subtitles. **98m/C VHS. HK** Chia-Liang Lu, Wing-sin Lau, Jacky Wu, Shannon Yeo, Chiu-hui Liu; **W:** Pak Ling Li; **C:** Wong Bo Man; **M:** Tommy Wai.

Drunks ✓ **1996 (R)** Ensemble story set in a church basement in Manhattan where a diverse group of people go to their Alcoholics Anonymous meetings. Recovering alcoholic Jim (Lewis) has gone on a bender after his wife's death; Ra-chel's (Wiest) an overworked doctor with drug and alcohol dependencies; alcoholic Becky's (Dunaway) a divorcee with problem kids; Brenda's (Hamilton) an ex-heroin addict who's HIV positive; Joseph's (Rollins) still haunted by his son's death. Was a Lady; Do I Love You, Do I?; Friend-Ship; Well, Did You Evah; Tailostro's Dance; Katie Went to Haiti; Madame; Love Your Crepes Suzettes; Thinking of You, A Cigarette, Sweet Music and You. **112m/C VHS, DVD.** Lucille Ball, Gene Kelly, Red Skelton, Virginia O'Brien, Zero Mostel, Dick Haymes, Rags Ragland, Donald Meek, George Gi-

Dry Cleaning ✓✓ *Nettoyage a Sec* **1997** Marrieds Nicole (Miou-Miou) and Jean-Marie (Berling) Kunstler are sharing a midlife crisis. The hard-working owners of a dry cleaning establishment are bored by their routine and decide to visit a racy nightclub where the featured performers are a brother/sister drag act. And before the Kunstlers know quite how it happened, they are both involved with handsome Loic (Merhar), whose sister has suddenly broken up their performing partnership. So Loic is now both working for and living with the Kunstlers and the erotic waters are getting very murky indeed. French with subtitles. **97m/C VHS, FR Miou-Miou, Charles Berling, Stanislas Merhar, Mathilde Seigner; **D:** Anne Fontaine; **W:** Anne Fontaine, Gilles Taurand; **C:** Caroline Champetier.

A Dry White Season ✓✓✓ **1989 (R)** A white Afrikaner living resignedly with apartheid confronts the system when his black gardener, an old friend, is persecuted and murdered. A well-meaning expose that, like many others, focuses on white people. **105m/C VHS, DVD.** Donald Sutherland, Marlon Brando, Susan Sarandon, Zakes Mokae, Janet Suzman, Jurgen Prochnow, Winston Ntshona, Susan Harker, Thoko Nishinga, Rowan Elmes; **D:** Euzhan Palcy; **W:** Colin Welland.

Drying Up the Streets ✓ **1976** Tepid message tale of a police drug squad out to terminate the pattern that has young women turning to a life of prostitution and drugs. **90m/C VHS. CA** Len Cariou, Don Francks, Sarah Torgov, Calvin Butler; **D:** Robin Spry.

D3: The Mighty Ducks ✓ **1996 (PG)** Estevez proves that he'll quack for a dollar in the latest redux of the Disney franchise. This time the members of the rag-tag team are drafted by an exclusive prep school where, once again, they don't fit in. Go figure! Although billed as the star, Estevez only appears briefly at the beginning and end of the movie, leaving team captain Charlie (Jackson) as the focus of the story. Facing off against the new coach and the snooty elitist varsity team, the players learn lessons about maturity, responsibility and whacking people with sticks. In all probability, Disney will not be surprised if you see "D4: Mighty Old to Still Be Playing Kids" in a theatre near you soon. Cameo from professional Mighty Duck and fellow Disney employee Paul Kariya. **104m/C VHS, DVD.** Emilio Estevez, Jeffrey Nordling, Joshua Jackson, David Selby, Heidi Kling, Joss Ackland, Elden (Ratliff) Henson, Shaun Weiss, Matt Doherty, Michael Cudlitz, Vincent A. Larusso, Colombe Jacobsen, Aaron Lohr, Christopher Orr; **D:** Robert Lieberman; **C:** David Hennings; **M:** J.A.C. Redford.

D2: The Mighty Ducks ✓✓ **1994 (PG)** When an injury forces Gordon (Estevez) out of the minor leagues, he is tapped by promotor Tibbles (Tucker) to coach Team U.S.A. in the Junior Goodwill Games. Upon arriving in LA, the coach's head is turned by the money to be made in endorsements, and he soon gets a lesson in character-building (hey, it's Disney). The duck redux premise is lame, but kids will want ice time to see more of the hockey action that made the first a hit. **107m/C VHS, DVD.** Emilio Estevez, Kathryn Erbe, Shaun Weiss, Kenan Thompson, Ty O'Neal; **Cameos:** Kristi Yamaguchi, Kareem Abdul-Jabbar, Wayne Gretzky; **D:** Sam Weisman; **W:** Steven Brill; **M:** J.A.C. Redford.

ter Cohn; **W:** Gary Lennon; **C:** Peter Hawkins; **M:** Joe Delia.

Dual Alibi ✓✓ **1947** Identical twin trapeze artists murder a colleague for a winning lottery ticket. Lom plays the brothers in a dual role. **81m/B VHS, GB Herbert Lom, Terence de Marney, Phyllis Dixey, Ronald Frankau, Abraham Sofaer, Harold Berens, Sebastian Cabot; **D:** Alfred Travers.

Duane Hopwood ✓✓✓ **2005 (R)** Duane (Schwimmer), a casino pit boss, is a loving husband and father, with a stead-fast unwillingness to deal with his alcoholism. It's a sad but familiar story in which Duane watches as his wife (Garofalo) and daughters drift away, he loses his job as a result of a costly mistake, and his life becomes increasingly defined by his drinking schedule, his drinking friends, and his drinking spots. While Duane's alcoholism is never fully resolved, his life is viewed from an entirely human, even sympathetic point of view. Cast somewhat against type. Schwimmer brings a visceral hear-tache to his portrayal. **83m/C VHS. US** David Schwimmer, Janeane Garofalo, Judah Friedlander, Susan Lynch, Dick Cavett, Steven R. Schirripa, John Krasinski, Lenny Venito; **D:** Matt Mulhern; **W:** Matt Mulhern; **C:** Mauricio Rubenstein; **M:** Michael Rohatyn.

Dubarry ✓✓✓ **1930** Early sound version of the romantic experiences of Madame Dubarry, the alluring French heroine of David Belasco's "DuBarry." Talented attempts at humor, all about a music-hall hooker who meets a bumbling card shark on the make. **105m/C VHS, DVD.** Norma Talmadge, Conrad Nagel, William Farnum, Hobart Bosworth, Alison Skipworth; **D:** Sam Taylor.

Dubeat-E-O ✓✓½ **1984** A filmmaker races against time to finish making a documentary about the Los Angeles underground hardcore punk scene, and the failed attempts at humor, all about a music-hall hooker who meets a bumbling card shark on the make. **84m/C VHS, Ray Sharkey, Joan Jett, Derf Scratch, Len Lesser, Nora Gaye; **D:** Alan Sacks.

The Duchess of Duke Street ✓✓✓ **1978** Cockney Rosa Lewis, (Jones), a clockmaker's daughter born in 1869, goes into service with the ambition to become the best cook in London. She learns from a society house-hold's French chef, where she was a kitchen maid, and eventually won success by an unexpected opportunity to cook for Edward, the Prince of Wales. A marriage-of-convenience and a mysterious legacy allows Rosa to buy the rundown Bentinck Hotel (actually the Cavendish) and cater fashionable dinners. By unceasing hard work, Rosa turns her establishment into an exclusive and discreet haunt for aristocrats, the wealthy, and various celebrities. British series on seven cassettes. **880m/C VHS.** Gemma Jones, Christopher Cazenove, John Welsh, George Pravda, June Brown, Victoria Plucknett, Richard Vernon, Doreen Mantle, Elizabeth Bennett, Donald Burton, John Cater, Holly Dea.org, John Rapley; **D:** Cyril Coke, John Gorrie, Simon Langton, Bill Bain, Raymond Menmuir; **W:** Julian Bond, Julia Jones, Rosemary Anne Sisson, Maggie Wadey, Jeremy Paul, Jack Rosenthal, Bill Craig, John Hawkesworth. **TV**

The Duchess and the Dirtwater Fox ✓✓ **1976 (PG)** Period western strung together with many unfunny incidents involving a con man and a saloon gal. **105m/C VHS, DVD.** George Segal, Goldie Hawn, Conrad Janis, Thayer David; **D:** Melvin Frank; **W:** Barry Sandler; **C:** Joseph Biroc; **M:** Charles Fox.

The Duchess of Idaho ✓✓½ **1950** Williams tries to help her roommate patch up a romance gone bad, but ends up falling in love herself. MGM guest stars liven up an otherwise routine production. ♪Baby Come Out of the Clouds; You Can't Do Wrong Doin' Right; Let's Choo Choo to Idaho Of All Things; Or Was I; Spring; Warm Hands, Cold Heart; Single-foot Serenade; You Won't Forget Me. **98m/ C VHS.** Esther Williams, Van Johnson, John Lund, Paula Raymond, Amanda Blake, Eleanor Powell, Lena Horne; **D:** Robert Z. Leonard.

Duchess

The Duchess of Langeais ✍✍✍ *Ne Touchez pas la Hache. Don't Touch the Axe* 2007 Set in 1820s Paris during the Restoration. The Duchess of Langeais, Antoinette (Balibar), is pursued by general Armand de Montriveau (Guillaume Depardieu—Gerard's son) who falls for her at first sight. She's a smart socialite, schooled in the ways of high living—he's a handsome Napoleonic war hero with stories of bravery. Although married, she's flattered by his attentions and engages him in a skillful game of cat and mouse. Montriveau eventually is angered by her game and attempts to exact his revenge, which finally peaks Antoinette's interest—except now it may be too late. The politics of the period are palpable as the social constraints of the would-be lovers stand sentinel to their unrequited love. Gorgeous settings and painful formalities heighten the cruel irony of the ill-fated lovers, and it's oh-so-enticing to watch. **137m/C DVD.** *FR IT* Jeanne Balibar, Guillaume Depardieu, Bulle Ogier, Michel Piccoli, Barbet Schroeder; **D:** Jacques Rivette; **W:** Jacques Rivette, Pascal Bonitzer, Christian Laurent; **C:** William Lubtchansky; **M:** Pierre Allio.

Duck Season ✍✍✍ *Temporada de patos* 2004 (R) Left alone one afternoon in a Mexico City apartment, two young teenaged boys settle in with video games. A neighbor girl joins them, wanting to use their oven, followed by the pizza guy (who the boys refuse payment for supposedly being seconds late but who won't leave until he gets his money). This sets the stage for some genuinely warm exchanges among the quartet as they chatter about life and act goofy in the way only aimless youths can. Of course the marijuana-spiked brownies the girl cooks up adds to their careless mood. **90m/B DVD.** *MX* Enrique Arreola, Diego Catano, Daniel Miranda, Danny Perea; **D:** Fernando Eimbcke; **W:** Fernando Eimbcke, Paula Markovitch; **C:** Alexis Zabe; **M:** Alejandro Rosso.

Duck Soup ✍✍✍ 1933 The Marx Brothers satiric masterpiece (which failed at the box office). Groucho becomes the dictator of Freedonia, and hires Chico and Harpo as spies. Jam-packed with the classic anarchic and irreverent Marx shtick; watch for the mirror scene. Zeppo plays a love-sick tenor; in this, his last film with the brothers. **70m/B VHS, DVD.** Groucho Marx, Chico Marx, Harpo Marx, Zeppo Marx, Louis Calhern, Margaret Dumont, Edgar Kennedy, Raquel Torres, Leonid Kinskey, Charles Middleton; **D:** Leo McCarey; **W:** Harry Ruby, Nat Perrin, Bert Kalmar, Arthur Sheekman; **C:** Henry Sharp; **M:** Harry Ruby, Bert Kalmar. AFI '98: Top 100, Natl. Film Reg. '90.

DuckTales the Movie: Treasure of the Lost Lamp ✍✍½ 1990 (G) Uncle Scrooge and company embark on a lost-ark quest, ala Harrison Ford, for misplaced treasure. Gibson actually plays three roles: rescue. Gibson actually plays three roles: the rancher's best friend, an aw-shucks cowpoke disguise in order to find out what's going on, and the title character used to bedevil the crooks. **68m/B VHS.** Hoot Gibson, Gloria Shea, Hooper Atchley, Skeeter Bill Robbins, Horace Carpenter, Neal Hart, Lafe (Lafayette) McKee, Gordon DeMain; **D:** George Melford; **W:** Jack Natteford; **C:** Tom Galligan, Harry Neumann.

The Dude Bandit ✍✍ 1933 An unscrupulous money-lender tries to gain control of a ranch but Gibson comes to the rescue. Gibson actually plays three roles: the rancher's best friend, an aw-shucks cowpoke disguise in order to find out what's going on, and the title character used to bedevil the crooks. **58m/B VHS, DVD.** George O'Brien, Irene Hervey, Leroy Mason, Syd Saylor, Henry K. Hall; **D:** Edward F. (Eddie) Cline; **C:** Frank B. Good.

Dude, Where's My Car? ✍✍ 2000 (PG-13) Slow-witted roommates Jesse and Chester wake one morning to a bizarre, seemingly unexplainable situation. To make matters worse, they appear to have trashed their girlfriends' home the night before and, of course, their car is missing. Dude. Too hung over to remember how this all came to be, the two boys set out to piece things together and, in the process, involve themselves with angry transsexuals, ostriches, and extraterrestrials. Follows the grand tradition of stoned and/or goofball duos like Cheech and Chong, Bill and Ted, and Wayne and Garth, but just can't reach their level. **83m/C VHS, DVD, UMD.** Ashton Kutcher, Seann William Scott, Jennifer Garner, Marla Sokoloff, Kristy Swanson, David Herman, Charlie O'Connell, Hal Sparks; **D:** Danny Leiner; **W:** Philip Stark; **C:** Robert M. Stevens; **M:** David Kitay.

Dudes ✍ 1987 (R) Three city kids head for the desert and run afoul of some rednecks. Tired grade-6 revenge story. **90m/C VHS.** Jon Cryer, Catherine Mary Stewart, Daniel Roebuck, Flea, Lee Ving, Calvin Bartlett, Pete Willcox, Glenn Withrow; **D:** Penelope Spheeris; **M:** Charles Bernstein.

Dudley Do-Right ✍✍½ 1999 (PG) Lightning didn't strike twice for Fraser, who successfully starred as Jay Ward's '60s cartoon character "George of the Jungle" and then decided to tackle Ward's brainless-but-noble Canadian Mountie, Dudley. The big goof is still protecting Semi-Happy Valley from the dastardly Snidely Whiplash (Molina), who manages to take over the town and rename it Whiplash City. Snidely is also twirling his mustache in the direction of Dudley's sweetie, fair maiden Nell Fenwick (Parker), which the right-minded Mountie won't allow. Unfortunately, the film only manages a few chuckles. **75m/C VHS, DVD.** Brendan Fraser, Sarah Jessica Parker, Alfred Molina, Robert Prosky, Eric Idle, Alex Rocco, Jack Kehler, Louis Mustillo, Regis Philbin, Kathie Lee Gifford; **D:** Hugh Wilson; **W:** Hugh Wilson; **C:** Donald E. Thorin; **M:** Steve Dorff; **Nar:** Corey Burton.

Due East ✍✍½ 2002 (PG-13) Sixteen-year-old Mary Faith (Bryant) is about to experience, seemingly, every single teenaged girl's secret fear. A docile traveling salesman is repeatedly attacked and threatened by a huge, malevolent tractor-trailer on an open desert highway. Released theatrically in Europe. **90m/C VHS, DVD.** Dennis Weaver, Lucille Benson, Eddie Firestone, Cary Loftin, Jacqueline Scott, Lou Frizzell, Gene Dynarski; **D:** Steven Spielberg; **W:** Richard Matheson; **C:** Jack Marta; **M:** Billy Goldenberg. **TV**

Duel ✍✍ 1971 (PG) Spielberg's first notable film, a truly scary made-for-TV exercise in paranoia. A docile traveling salesman is repeatedly attacked and threatened by a huge, malevolent tractor-trailer on an open desert highway. Released theatrically in Europe. **90m/C VHS, DVD.** Dennis Weaver, Lucille Benson, Eddie Firestone, Cary Loftin, Jacqueline Scott, Lou Frizzell, Gene Dynarski; **D:** Steven Spielberg; **W:** Richard Matheson; **C:** Jack Marta; **M:** Billy Goldenberg. **TV**

Duel at Diablo ✍✍ 1966 An exceptionally violent film that deals with racism in the Old West. Good casting; western fans will enjoy the action. **103m/C VHS, DVD.** James Garner, Sidney Poitier, Bibi Andersson, Dennis Weaver, Bill Travers; **D:** Ralph Nelson.

Duel at Silver Creek ✍✍½ 1952 A group of claim jumpers murder anyone who gets in their way, including the family of the Silver Kid (Murphy), who's deputized by Sheriff Lightning (McNally) to help him get the varmints. **76m/B VHS, DVD.** Audie Murphy, Faith Domergue, Stephen McNally, Susan Cabot, Gerald Mohr, Eugene Iglesias, Kyle James, Lee Marvin; **D:** Donald Siegel; **W:** Gerald Drayson Adams; **C:** Irving Glassberg; **M:** Hans J. Salter.

Duel in the Sun ✍✍ 1946 A lavish, lusty David O. Selznick production of a minor western novel about a vivacious half-breed Indian girl, living on a powerful dynastic ranch, who incites two brothers to conflict. Selznick's last effort at outdoing his epic success with "Gone With the Wind." **130m/C VHS, DVD.** Gregory Peck, Jennifer Jones, Joseph Cotten, Lionel Barrymore, Lillian Gish, Butterfly McQueen, Harry Carey Sr., Walter Huston, Charles Bickford, Herbert Marshall; **D:** King Vidor; **W:** Oliver H.P. Garrett, David O. Selznick; **C:** Ray Rennahan; **M:** Dimitri Tiomkin.

Duel of Champions ✍ *Orazi e Curiazi* 1961 It's ancient Rome, and the prodigal gladiator has come home. Now the family must have a duel to decide who will rule. **90m/C VHS, DVD.** *IT SP* Alan Ladd, Franco Fabrizi, Robert Hundar; **D:** Ferdinando Baldi.

Duel of Fists ✍✍ 1971 When the owner of a boxing institute dies, he instructs his son in his will to go searching for his long-lost brother in Thailand. All he can go on is an old photograph and the knowledge that his brother is a Thai boxer. **111m/C VHS.** *HK* David Chiang, Chen Hsing, Ti Lung, Tang Ti; **D:** Chen Chang; **W:** Kuang Ni.

Duel of Hearts ✍✍ 1992 (PG-13) Beautiful Caroline falls in love with wealthy Lord Vane Brecon, who unfortunately is accused of murder. When Caroline tries to help him clear his name she discovers he's hiding a number of secrets. Based on the romance novel "Duel of Love" by Barbara Cartland. Nothing too inspiring here, although regency romance fans will appreciate the attention to detail. **95m/C VHS.** *GB* Alison Doody, Michael York, Geraldine Chaplin, Benedict Taylor, Billie Whitelaw, Virginia McKenna, Richard Johnson, Jeremy Kemp, Beryl Reid, Suzanna Hamilton, Jolyon Baker, Julie Kate; **D:** John Hough. **CABLE**

Duel to the Death ✍✍ 1982 A legendary battle is held every ten years between the best Japanese and Chinese martial arts experts to determine who's tops. During the Ming Dynasty, as the next duel approaches, the candidates are caught in a war between Shaolin monks and ninjas. Chinese with subtitles. **90m/C VHS, DVD.** *HK* Damian Lau, Borman Chu, Flora Cheung; **D:** Siu-Tung Ching.

The Duellists ✍✍ 1977 (PG) A beautifully photographed picture about the long-running feud between two French officers during the Napoleonic wars. Based on "The Duel" by Joseph Conrad. **101m/C VHS, DVD.** *GB* Keith Carradine, Harvey Keitel, Albert Finney, Edward Fox, Tom Conti, Christina Raines, Diana Quick, William Morgan Sheppard; **D:** Ridley Scott.

Duet for One ✍✍ 1986 (R) A famous concert violinist learns she is suffering from multiple sclerosis and is slowly losing her ability to play. Convinced that her life is meaningless without music, she self-destructively drifts into bitter isolation. From the play by Tom Kempinski. **108m/C VHS.** Julie Andrews, Max von Sydow, Alan Bates, Liam Neeson; **D:** Andrei Konchalovsky.

Duets ✍✍ 2000 (R) Bruce Paltrow misuses the talents of his fine ensemble cast (including daughter Gwyneth) in this off-key comedy-melodrama about karaoke culture. The three subplots each center on a pair of misfits en route to a karaoke contest in Omaha. Ricky (Lewis) is a karaoke hustler who meets his daughter Liv (Paltrow) for the first time after the death of her mother in Las Vegas. Suzi (Bello) is a steely waitress who bullies and beguiles mild cab driver Billy (Speedman) into taking her halfway across the country with the promise of sex. Todd's (Giamatti) a freaked-out businessman fleeing his family and Reggie's (Braugher) a deep-thinking escaped convict with a killer voice. Flashes of feeling and humor offset some of the hokiness of the characters, but not enough to save the movie. **112m/C VHS, DVD.** Gwyneth Paltrow, Maria Bello, Scott Speedman, Andre Braugher, Paul Giamatti, Huey Lewis, Marian Seldes, Kiersten Warren, Angie Phillips, Angie Dickinson; **D:** Bruce Paltrow; **W:** John Byrum; **C:** Paul Sarossy; **M:** David Newman.

The Duke ✍✍½ 1999 (G) Talk about the dog who has everything! Hubert is the faithful bloodhound companion to the Duke of Dingwall (Neville). When the Duke dies, Hubert inherits everything—even the title! Trusted butler Clive (Draper) and his niece Charlotte (Draper) are there to make certain Hubert is safe from the plots of the late Duke's sniveling nephew, Cecil (Muirhead), who wants the estate for himself and even tries to arrange a doggie wedding to get the riches. **88m/C VHS, DVD.** *CA* James Doohan, John Neville, Courtnee Draper, Oliver Muirhead, Sophie Heyman, Judy Geeson; **D:** Philip Spink; **W:** Craig Detweiler, Anne Vince, Robert Vince; **C:** Mike Southon; **M:** Brahm Wenger. **VIDEO**

The Duke Is Tops ✍✍½ 1938 In Horne's earliest existing film appearance, she's off to attempt the "big-time," while her boyfriend joins a traveling medicine show. ♪ I Know You Remember. **80m/C VHS, DVD.** Ralph Cooper, Lena Horne, Lawrence Criner, Monte Hawley, Edward Thompson; **D:** William Nolte; **W:** Phil Dunham; **C:** Robert E. Cline, J. Henry Kruse; **M:** Harvey Brooks, Ben Ellison.

Duke of the Derby ✍✍ *Le Gentleman d'Epsom* 1962 A scheming racehorse handicapper bets over his head and ruins his higher-than-means lifestyle. In French with English subtitles. **83m/C VHS.** *FR* Madeleine Robinson, Frank Villard, Jean (Lefevre) Lefebvre, Jacques Marin, Jean Gabin; **D:** Gilles Grangier; **W:** Gilles Grangier; **C:** Louis Page; **M:** Michel Legrand.

The Duke of West Point ✍✍ 1938 Conceited but ultimately good-hearted Brit Earley (Hayward) immigrates to the States and enrolls at West Point. He immediately alienates everyone with his superior attitude but eventually shows his good side. Fontaine provides a fine performance; plus, she's about the only one who's young enough to make a convincing college student. Hokey and predictable, but pleasant enough if you're wondering why they don't make 'em like that anymore. **109m/B VHS.** Louis Hayward, Joan Fontaine, Richard Carlson, William "Billy" Bakewell, Donald (Don "Red") Barry, Charles D. Brown, Tom Brown, Alan Curtis, Emma Dunn, Edward Earle, Marjorie Gateson, Jonathan Hale, Kenneth Harlan, Mary MacLaren; **D:** Alfred E. Green; **W:** George Bruce; **C:** Robert Planck.

The Dukes of Hazzard ✍✍ 2005 (PG-13) Yee-haw! The '70s TV show jumps (literally!) onto the big screen. Good ole Georgia boys, moonshinin' cousins Bo (Scott) and Luke (Knoxville) Duke try to keep their Hazzard County family farm from corrupt county commissioner Boss Hogg (Reynolds), with the help of Uncle Jessie (Nelson), Daisy (Simpson), and Cooter (Koechner). But then, you knew that, because that was the plot of every episode. This version is a little less lighthearted, but it is funny (thanks to script doctoring by the Broken Lizard troupe), and doesn't take itself as seriously as the show. What it does take seriously are the car chases and stunts, which show off the General Lee, the Dukes' beloved 1969 Dodge Charger, to great effect. If you were a fan then, especially of the General, you'll be pleased. If not, you're probably wondering why they bothered at all. **105m/C DVD, Blu-ray Disc, UMD, HD DVD.** *US* Johnny Knoxville, Seann William Scott, Burt Reynolds, Willie Nelson, M.C. Gainey, Michael Weston, Lynda Carter, David Koechner, Jessica Simpson, Jack Polick, Steve Lemme, Michael Roof, Nikki Griffin, Alice Greczyn, James Roday, Jonathan Davis; **D:** Jay Chandrasekhar; **W:** Jay Chandrasekhar, John O'Brien; **C:** Lawrence Sher; **M:** Nathan Barr.

Duma ✍✍✍ 2005 (PG) Family friendly pic with a kid, a cat, and a beautiful setting. Xan (Michaelos) lives on a South African farm and adopts an orphaned cheetah cub he names Duma. When his father (Scott) dies, and Xan and his mom (Davis) must move to the city, Xan is determined to release Duma into the wild himself. Not a very bright idea, especially when he gets lost in the desert—only to be found by the shifty Ripkuna (Walker). Based on fact; adapted from the book "How It Was With Dooms" by Xan and Carol Hopcraft. And no, you can't have a pet cheetah, no matter how cute they are. **100m/C DVD.** *US* Eamonn Walker, Campbell Scott, Hope Davis, Alexann Michaelos; **D:** Carroll Ballard; **W:** Karen Janszen; **C:** Werner Maritz.

Dumb & Dumber 🐾🐾½ '994
(PG-13) Moronic limo driver Lloyd Christmas (Carrey) and equally dense dog groomer Harry Dunne (Daniels) travel (in the hilarious "sheep dog" van) from Rhode Island to Colorado—at one point going east—to return a briefcase full of cash to a beautiful socialite (Holly). Engaging in all sorts of gross-out humor, this one will definitely not appeal to the stuffy critic or arthouse snob. It will provide plenty of laughs, however embarrassingly rendered, for everyone else. Daniels proves a convincing dimwit sidekick, while Carrey mugs shamelessly. Occasional "Seinfeld" writer Farrelly makes his directorial debut. **AKA:** Dumb and Dumberer. 🏆 MTV Movie Awards '95: Comedic Perf. (Carrey), Kiss (Jim Carrey/Lauren Holly); Blockbuster '96: Comedy Actor, V. (Carrey). **110m/C VHS, DVD, UMD.** *D:* Peter Farrelly; *W:* Bennett Yellin, Bobby Farrelly, Peter Farrelly; *C:* Mark Irwin; *M:* Todd Rundgren, Nellie Hooper. **C:** Jim Carrey, Jeff Daniels, Lauren Holly, Teri Garr, Karen Duffy, Mike Starr, Charles Rocker, Victoria Rowell, Felton Perry, Harland Williams, Rob Moran, Cam Neely, Lin Shaye, Fred Stoller; *D:* Peter "Farrelly; *M:* Brian Eno.

Dumb and Dumberer: When Harry Met Lloyd 🐾 2003 (PG-13)
The title is probably the most inspired part of this flick. Harry (Richardson) and Lloyd (Olsen) meet in high school and are immediately recruited to attend a "special needs" class set up by the corrupt principal (Levy) to steal grant money. The school paper's star reporter (Nichols) investigates the scam, setting up possible romance. Richardson and Olsen do a commendable job impersonating Daniels and Carrey, but the charm of the original has been replaced by a double dose of poo and retard jokes, done with less subtlety and class (!) than the Farrelly outing. Stick with the original. **82m/C VHS, DVD, US** Derek Richardson, Eric Christian Olsen, Eugene Levy, Luis Guzman, Cheri Oteri, Rachel Nichols, Elden (Rattiff) Henson, William Lee Scott, Mimi Rogers, Shi a La3eouri, Lin Shaye, Teal Redmann, Troy Miller; *W:* Troy Miller, Robert Brener; *C:* Anthony B. Richmond; *M:* Eban Schletter.

Dumb Waiter 1987 (R) A mini-play by Harold Pinter about two hitmen awaiting instructions for a job in an empty boardinghouse, and getting comically mixed messages. **65m/C VHS, DVD. US** Conti; *D:* Robert Altman; *W:* Harold Pinter. **TV**

Dumbo 🐾🐾🐾 1941 Animated Disney classic about a baby elephant growing up in the circus who is ridiculed for his large ears, until he discovers he can fly. The little elephant who could fly then becomes a circus star. Expressively and imaginatively animated, highlighted by the hallucinatory dancing pink elephants sequence. Endearing songs by Frank Churchill, Oliver Wallace, and Nec Washington, including "Baby Mine," and "I See an Elephant Fly." **63m/C VHS, DVD.** *D:* Ben Sharpsteen; *W:* Joe Grant, Dick Huemer; *M:* Frank Churchill, Oliver Wallace; *V:* Sterling Holloway, Edward Brophy, Verna Felton, Herman Bing, Cliff Edwards. Oscars '41: Scoring/Musical.

Dummy 🐾🐾 2002 (R) Sappy farce/latent coming-of-ager about a man and his dummy. Shy outsider Steven (Brody), nearly 30 and still living at home with his parents, embarks on his dream career in ventriloquism. His wooden buddy, along with high-school friend Fanny (Jovovich), give Steven the confidence to woo his pretty unemployment counselor Lorena (Farmiga). Ranges from genuinely sweet to annoyingly cloying. Despite a decent turn from Oscar-winner Brody, who did all his own ventriloquism, lovable schmuck routine wears thin rather quickly. Supports are uniformly strong. **90m/C VHS, DVD. US** Adrien Brody, Milla Jovovich, Illeana Douglas, Vera Farmiga, Jessica Walter, Ron Leibman, Jared Harris; *D:* Greg Pritkin; *W:* Greg Pritkin; *C:* Horacio Marquerz; *M:* Paul Wallfisch.

The Dummy Talks 🐾🐾 1943
When a ventriloquist is murdered, a midget goes undercover as a dummy to find the killer. Watch closely and you might see his lips move. **85m/B VHS. GB** Jack Warner, Claude Hulbert, Beryl Orde, Derna Dema-Hazell, Ivy Berson, Manning Whiley; *D:* Oswald Mitchell;

W: Michael Barringer, Jack Clifford, Con West; *C:* James Wilson.

Dune 🐾🐾 1984 (PG-13) Lynch sci-fi opus based on the Frank Herbert novel boasting great set design, muddled script-mess. The mere title is enough to turn off anyone who never played the game as a kid and the target audience will probably nit-pick it to death with "that's not like in the game"-type complaints. **137m/C VHS, DVD, HD DVD, Kyle MacLachlan, Francesca Annis, Jose Ferrer, Sting, Max von Sydow, Jürgen Prochnow, Linda Hunt, Freddie Jones, Dean Stockwell, Virginia Madsen, Brad Dourif, Kenneth McMillan, Silvana Mangano, Jack Nance, Sian Phillips, Paul Smith, Patrick Stewart; *D:* Everett McGill, Sean Young, Patrick Stewart; *D:* David Lynch; *W:* David Lynch; *C:* Freddie Francis; *M:* Brian Eno.

Dune 🐾🐾½ Frank Herbert's Dune 2000
Frank Herbert's 1965 sci-fi classic was previously made into a disappointing 1984 film by David Lynch. This miniseries more successfully combines visuals with character, although the complicated plot is still somewhat overwhelming. Duke Leto (Hurt) of the House of Atreides has been appointed by the Emperor to harvest and export Spice—the most prized commodity on the desert planet of Arrakis (or Dune). But a "rival faction, led by Baron Harkonnen "(McNeice), causes trouble for Atreides and his heir, Paul (Newman), who must look to Dune's native inhabitants for support. **270m/C VHS, Blu-ray** Disc, A.ec Newman, William Hurt, Saskia Reeves, Ian McNeice, P. H. Moriarty, Julie Cox, Matt Keeslar, Giancarlo Giannini, Barbara Kodetová, Robert Russell, Mikiaii Kreka Kijakovic; *D:* John Harrison; *W:* John Harrison; *C:* Vittorio Storaro, Harry B. Miller III; *M:* Graeme Revell. **CABLE**

Dune Warriors 🐾½ 1991 (R) Earth is a parched planet in the year 2040. Renegade bands cruise the desert, making short shrift of civilized people who band together in remote villages. When peaceful farmer Carradine's family falls prey to the pillagers, surely he and the most evil warlord of all must clash. Good action and stunts, if the dummy plot doesn't get you first. **77m/C VHS, David Carradine, Richard (Rick) Hill, Luke Askew, Jillian McWhirter, Blake Boyd; *D:* Cino H. Santiago.

The Dunera Boys 🐾🐾🐾 1985 (R)
Hoskins shines in this story about Viennese Jews who, at the onset of WWII, escape to England where they are suspected as German spies. Subsequently, the British snipped them all to an Australian prison camp, where they recreated in peace their Viennese lifestyle. **150m/C VHS.** *AU* Bob Hoskins, Joe Spano, Warren Mitchell, Joseph Furst, Mary-Anne Fahey, Simon Chilvers, Steven Vidler; *D:* Sam Lewin.

Dungeon of Harrow 🐾 1964 Unbelievably cheap tale of shipwrecked comrades who encounter a maniacal family on an otherwise deserted island. Not your stranded-on-a-desert-island fantasy come true. Filmed in San Antonio, a harrowing bore. **74m/B VHS, DVD, Russ Harvey, Helen Hogan, Bill McNulty, Pat Boyette; *D:* Pat Boyette.

Dungeonmaster 🐾½
1983 (PG-13) A warlord forces a computer wiz to participate in a bizarre "Dungeons and Dragons" styled game in order to save a girl held captive. Consists of seven segments, each by a different director. Save yourself the trouble. **80m/C VHS.** Jeffrey Byron, Richard Moll, Leslie Wing, Danny Dick, Stephen Ford, Peter Manoogian, Ted Nicolaou, Rosemarie Turko; *W:* Allen Actcr; *M:* Richard Band.

Dungeons and Dragons 🐾½
2000 (PG-13) Based (probably very loosely) on the role-playing game of the same name. "D & D" tells the story of the land of Izmer, whose reformer ruler, Empress Savina (Birch), wants to empower the lowly commoners and put them on an equal footing with the ruling Mages. Ar elitist Mage, Prcfion (Irons, in an obvious pay-the-bills role) wants to overthrow her. Luckily, she's aided by young hero Riddey (Whalin)

and his sidek.ck Snalls (Wayans). It's hard to decide what's m:re ridiculous: plot, dialogue, settings, effects, costumes, or the idea that anyone would pay to see this mess. The dialogue may be one of the worst examples of fantasy writing in cinema history. **107m/C VHS, DVD.** Justin Caina Burnett.

Dunston Checks In 🐾🐾½ 1995
(PG) This just in: Hollywood thinks monkeys are funny. But, as far as "stupid people learn important life lessons from a monkey, who wears clothes" movies go, this one's not bad. Robert Grant (Alexander) is the manager of a five-star hotel. His Leona Helmsley-esque boss (Dunaway) is convinced that aristocratic guest Lord Rutledge (Everett) is a travel guide critic who is there to bestow an elusive sixth star on the hotel. Actually he's a jewel thief, and Dunston the orangutan is his accomplice. When Dunston flees from his abusive owner, he's adopted by Grant's two children. Together, Dunston and the kids are left to straighten out the whole mess. **88m/C VHS, DVD.** Jason Alexander, Faye Dunaway, Eric Lloyd, Rupert Everett, Graham Sack, Paul Reubens, Glenn Shadix, Nathan Davis, Jennifer Bassey; *D:* Ken Kwapis; *W:* Bruce Graham, John Hopkins; *C:* Peter Lyons Collister; *M:* Milles Goodman.

The Dunwich Horror 🐾🐾 1970
Young warlock acquires a banned book of evil spells, starts trouble on the astral plane. Stockwell hammy. Loosely based on H. P. Lovecraft story. **90m/C VHS, DVD,** on H. P. Lovecraft story. Sandra Dee, Dean Stockwell, Lloyd Bochner, Ed Begley Sr., Sam Jaffe, Joanna Moore, Talia Shire, Donna Baccala; *D:* Daniel Haller; *W:* Curtis Hanson, Henry Rosenbaum, Beach Dickerson, Michael Fox, Bruce Graham; *C:* Richard C. Glouner; *M:* Les Baxter.

Duplex 🐾🐾 2003 (PG-13) New York yuppies try to bump off a sweet old lady for her rent-controlled apartment in Brooklyn. Alex (Stiller) and Nancy (Barrymore), didn't start out as would-be assassins in the name of real estate. After moving into a picture-perfect duplex downstairs from Mrs. Connell, they discover that although very old and in poor health, she still manages a host of irksome behaviors. With her health not declining nearly fast enough, the senior-crazed couple are driven to desperate measures. Stiller is top-notch and Barrymore a worthy co-star despite a far-fetched plot that revenge comedy special-ist/director DeVito ultimately doesn't sell. **88m/C VHS, DVD,** *D:* Drew Barrymore, Ben Stiller, Eileen Essell, Harvey Fierstein, Justin Theroux, Robert Wisdom, Amber Valletta, James Remar, Maya Rudolph, Swoosie Kurtz, Wallace Shawn; *D:* Danny DeVito; *W:* Larry Doyle; *C:* Anastas Michos; *M:* David Newman.

Duplicates 🐾🐾 1992 (PG-13) Harrison and Greist are a married couple whose young son has disappeared. When the boy is found he has no memory of his former life or parents. The couple discover he's the victim of secret experiments which transfer human memories into computer banks. Will they become the next targets? **92m/C VHS, Gregory Harrison, Kim Greist, Cicely Tyson, Lane Smith, William Lucking, Kevin McCarthy; *D:* Sandor Stern.

Dupont Lajoie 🐾🐾 Rape of Innocence 1974 At a tourist campground Lajoie (Carmet) accidentally kills his son's girlfriend when she resists his sexual advances. To save his life he accuses Arabs cf committing the crime and begins a racist campaign of vengeance. French with subtitles. **103m/C VHS. FR** Jean Carmet; *D:* Yves Boisset.

Durango 🐾🐾½ 1999 Okay, the title sounds western and there is a cattle drive but this whimsical romance is set n the Irish countrys:de in 1939. Mark Doran (Keesiar) and his neighbors get together to drive their cattle to the railway (40 miles distant) when the local buyer tries to cheat

them. He's also in love with a lassie (St. Alban) but is worried about if Mark's plan succeeds, he'll have te confidence to get the girl as well. Based on the novel by John B. Keane. **98m/C VHS, Matt Keeslar, Patrick Bergin, Brenda Fricker, Nancy St. Alban, George Hearn, Paul Ronan, Dermot Martin, Mark Lambert; *D:* Brent Shields; *W:* Walter Bernstein; *C:* Johnson; *M:* Mark McKenzie. **TV**

Dust 🐾🐾½ 1985 A white woman in South Africa murders her father when he shows affection for a young black servant. Controversial and intense. **87m/C VHS, FR** Jane Birkin, Trevor Howard, John Matshikiza, Nadine Uwampa, Lourdes Christina Sayo, Rene Diaz; *D:* Marion Hansel; *W:* Marion Hansel; *M:*

Dust Devil 🐾🐾 1993 (R) Three travelers find themselves in Namibia's vast desert, a policeman, a woman on the run, and her abusive husband. They all have the misfortune of meeting up with a super-natural being known as the "Dust Devil," who kills humans in order to steal their souls and increase his other worldly powers. **87m/C VHS, DVD. GB** Robert John Burke, Chelsea Field, Zakes Mokae, Rufus Swart, John Matsikiza, William Hootkins, Marianne Saege-brecht; *D:* Richard Stanley; *W:* Richard Stanley; *C:* Steven Chivers; *M:* Simon Boswell.

Dust to Glory 🐾🐾🐾 2005 (PG)
Son of "The Endless Summer" creator Bruce Brown, Dana Brown brings his father's sense of kineticism to the races in this high-octane documentary. The Baja 1000 is the world's more dangerous and notorious race, open to dirt bikes, souped-up VW bugs, 4x4s, and just about anything else. Its dusty trails and Mexican highways are captured in all their white-knuckled madness through the use of 50 different cameras, edited seamlessly. However, once a few of the race's more eccentric characters are introduced along the way, things slow down considerably. It takes a few jump starts to get going now and then, but overall it's a whopping 97-minute condensed version of this 16 hour trek. Racing legends Robby Gordon, Mario Andretti, and Jimmy Vasser join in the fun. **97m/C DVD. US** *D:* Dana Brown; *W:* Dana Brown; *C:* Kevin Ward; *M:* Nathan Furst.

Dusty 🐾🐾 1985 Touching story of a wild dingo dog raised by an Australian rancher and trained to herd sheep. Filmed in the Australian bush and based on the children's book by Frank Dalby Davison. **89m/C VHS, AU** Bill Kerr, Noel Trevarthen, Carol Burns, Nicholas Holland, John Stanton; *D:* John Richardson.

Dutch 🐾🐾 1991 (PG-13) Working class boob attempts to pick up his girlfriend's son from boarding school. Their trip together gives them an unexpected chance to connect, if they don't kill each other first. Silly premise from the Hughes factory has little innovation and uses type-casting instead of acting. **107m/C VHS.** Ed O'Neill, Ethan (Randall) Embry, JoBeth Williams, Christopher McDonald, Ari Meyers; *D:* Peter Faiman; *W:* John Hughes; *M:* Alan Silvestri.

Durango Valley Raiders 🐾½
1938 Sheriff is the leader of the outlaws and a young cowboy finds out. **55m/B VHS.** Bob Steele; *D:* Sam Newfield.

liams, Elizabeth (E.G. Dailey) Daily; **D:** Peter Faiman; **W:** John Hughes.

Dutch Girls *Woof!* 1987 Muddled mayhem as a horny high school field hockey team travels through Holland, cavorts about, and discovers the meaning of life. 83m/C VHS, DVD. *GB* Bill Paterson, Colin Firth, Timothy Spall; **D:** Giles Foster.

Dutch Treat ♂ 1986 (R) Two nerds con a sultry, all-girl rock band into thinking they're powerful record company execs. Nobody's buying. 95m/C VHS. Lorin Dreyfuss, David Landsberg; **D:** Boaz Davidson.

Dutchman ♂♂♂ 1967 Film presentation of Amiri Baraka's one act play depicting the claustrophobic reality of the black man's race in America. Black man shares subway conversation with a white woman who questions his race and middle class aspirations. Enraged, one takes the other's life. 55m/C VHS, DVD. *GB* Al Freeman, Jr., Shirley Knight; **D:** Anthony Harvey; **M:** John Barry. Cannes '67: Film.

The Dybbuk ♂♂♂½ *Der Dibuk* 1937 A man's bride is possessed by a restless spirit. Set in the Polish-Jewish community before WWI and based on the play by Sholom Anski. Considered a classic for its portrayal of Jewish religious and cultural mores. In Yiddish with English subtitles. 123m/B VHS, DVD. *PL* Abraham Morewski, Isaac Samberg, Moshe Lipman, Lili Liliana, Dina Halpem, Leon Liebgold; **D:** Michal Waszynski; **W:** S.A. Kacyzna, Marek Arensfeln; **C:** Albert Wywerka; **M:** Krzysztof Komeda.

Dying Game ♂♂ 1994 Sorority girls are being stalked and murdered and the detective investigating the crimes falls for the sorority's president. Now, he has to find the killer before his girlfriend becomes the next victim. 74m/C VHS. Michael Wynn, Mathea Webb, D.J. Boozer; **D:** Kris Hughes.

The Dying Gaul ♂♂♂ 2005 (R) *Susan's Plan* 1998 (R) Slow pacing stunts the humor but doesn't manage to destroy it. Divorced Susan (Kinski) wants her lover, Sam (Zane), to knock off her ex-husband (Paul) so she can collect his life insurance policy. He hires the job out to a couple of losers (Schneider, Biehn), who fail. So the lovers hire a crazy biker (Aykroyd) to finish the job. 90m/C VHS, DVD. Nastassia Kinski, Billy Zane, Dan Aykroyd, Rob Schneider, Lara Flynn Boyle, Adrian Paul, Michael Biehn, Carl Ballantine, Thomas Haden Church, Bill Duke, Sheree North; **D:** John Landis; **C:** Ken Kelsch; **M:** Peter Bernstein.

Dying to Remember ♂½ 1993 (PG-13) A fashion designer (Gilbert) regresses to a past life during hypnotherapy and discovers she was murdered in 1963. She flies to San Francisco to discover more about her past but finds that someone wants to keep things secret—and is willing to kill again. Tedious and predictable. 87m/C VHS. Melissa Gilbert, Ted Shackleford, Scott Plank, Christopher Stone, Jay Robinson; **D:** Arthur Allan Seidelman; **W:** George Schenck, Frank Cardea, Brian Ross.

The Dying Truth ♂♂ 1991 A wrongfully accused prisoner lies dying in his cell. Trouble is, he can't die in peace until he solves the murder they say he committed. Interesting mix of the supernatural and mystery, although perhaps not one of Carradine's more memorable roles. 80m/C VHS. David Carradine, Stephanie Beacham, Stephen Greif, Stephan Chase, Larry Carby, Lesley Dunlop; **D:** John Hough.

Dying Young ♂½ 1991 (R) Muted romance has a wealthy leukemia victim hire a spirited, unschooled beauty as his nurse. They fall in love, but the film is either too timid or too unimaginative to mine emotions denoted by the title. Nobody dies, in fact, a grim ending (faithful to the Marti Leimbach novel on which this was based) got scrapped after testing poorly with audiences. The actors try their best, photography is lovely, and Kenny G's melody music fills the soundtrack, but this is basically overmelodramatic drivel. Scott is the late Dewhurst's son. 111m/C VHS, DVD. Julia Roberts, Campbell Scott, Vincent D'Onofrio, Colleen Dewhurst, Ellen Burstyn, David Selby; **D:** Joel Schumacher; **W:** Richard Friedenberg; **C:** Juan Ruiz-Anchia.

Dynamite ♂ 1949 Romance explodes as two young demolitions experts vie for the same girl. Stand back. 68m/B VHS, DVD. William Gargan, Virginia Welles, Richard Crane, Irving Bacon; **D:** William H. Pine.

Dynamite and Gold ♂ *Where the Hell's the Gold?* 1988 (PG) Nelson and crew embark on a search for lost gold, battling hostile Indians, the Mexican army and assorted bandits along the way. A mediocre TV movie. 91m/C VHS, DVD. Willie Nelson, Delta Burke, Jack Elam, Alfonso Arau, Gregory Sierra, Michael Wren, Gerald McRaney; **D:** Burt Kennedy. **TV**

The Dynamite Brothers ♂ 1974 (R) Two tough guys, one a Hong Kong immigrant with martial arts skills, the other a brother from the streets of the ghetto, team up to rid Los Angeles of a Chinese crimelord. 90m/C VHS, DVD. James Hong, Aldo Ray, Alan Tang, Timothy Brown, Carolyn Ann Speed, Don Oliver; **D:** Al Adamson; **M:** Charles Earland.

Dynamite Canyon ♂ 1941 Average oater has villain Price committing murder in order to keep secret the location of a lode of copper. Standard western fare. 58m/B VHS, DVD. Tom Keene, Evelyn Finley, Sugar Dawn, Stanley Price, Kenne Duncan; **D:** Robert Emmett Tansey; **W:** Robert Emmett Tansey, Frances Kavanaugh.

Dynamite Chicken 1970 (R) Melange of skits, songs, and hippie satire is dated. Includes performances by Joan Baez, Lenny Bruce, B.B. King, and others. 75m/C VHS, DVD. Joan Baez, Richard Pryor, Jimi Hendrix; **D:** Ernest Pintoff.

Dynamite Dan ♂½ 1924 A man knocks out the heavyweight boxing champion after he flirts with his girlfriend and decides to give up his day job to become a championship boxer. He is a success, and in the end he has to face the champion again. Will he win? 62m/B VHS, DVD. Kenneth McDonald, Frank Rice, Boris Karloff, Eddie Harris, Diana Alden, Harry Woods, Jack (H.) Richardson; **D:** Bruce Mitchell.

Dynamite Pass ♂ 1950 Offbeat oater about disgruntled ranchers attempting to stop the construction of a new road. 61m/B VHS. Tim Holt, Richard Martin, Regis Toomey, Lynne Roberts, Denver Pyle; **D:** Lew Landers.

Dynamite Ranch ♂ 1932 Ranchers fight tooth and nail to keep their rights and property in this Maynard oater. 60m/B VHS, DVD. Ruth Hall, Alan Roscoe, Arthur Hoyt, Martha Mattox, Ken Maynard; **D:** Forrest Sheldon; **W:** Barry Barringer; **C:** Ted D. McCord.

Dynasty ♂♂ 1976 Pulitzer Prize-winning author James Michener creates the usual sweeping saga of a family torn by jealousy, deception, and rivalry in love and business as husband, wife, and brother-in-law seek their fortune in the Ohio frontier of the 1820s. 90m/C VHS, DVD. Sarah Miles, Harris Yulin, Stacy Keach, Harrison Ford, Amy Irving, Granville Van Dusen, Charles Weldon, Gerrit Graham; **D:** Lee Philips; **W:** Sidney Carroll; **C:** William Cronjager; **M:** Gil Melle.

Dynasty ♂♂ 1977 A leader of the Ming Dynasty is killed by evil Imperial Court eunuch and his son the monk sets out to avenge him. In 3-D: Run-of-the-mill kung-fu stunts. 94m/C VHS, DVD. Bobby Ming, Lin Tashing, Pai Ying, Tang Wei, Jin Gang; **D:** Zhang Meijun.

Dynasty of Fear ♂½ 1972 (PG) *Night: Honeymoon of Fear* 1972 (PG) Matters get rather sticky at a British boys' school when the headmaster's wife seduces the husband's assistant. Together they conspire to murder her husband and share his fortune. 93m/C VHS, DVD. *GB* Peter Cushing, Joan Collins, Ralph Bates, Judy Geeson, James Cossins, John Bown, Brian Grellis, Gillian Lind; **D:** Jimmy Sangster, Michael Sylvester; **W:** Jimmy Sangster; **C:** Arthur Grant.

E. Nick: A Legend in His Own Mind 1984 Satire of videos and magazines designed for adults. 75m/C VHS. Don Calfa, Cleavon Little, Andra Akers, Pat McCormick; **D:** Robert Hegyes.

Each Dawn I Die ♂♂½ 1939 Cagney stars as a reporter who is a fervent critic of the political system. Framed for murder and imprisoned, he is subsequently befriended by fellow inmate Raft, a gangster. Once hardened by prison life, Cagney shuns his friend and becomes wary of the system. Despite its farfetched second half and mediocre script, the film makes interesting viewing thanks to a stellar performance from Cagney. 92m/B VHS, DVD. James Cagney, George Raft, George Bancroft, Jane Bryan, Maxie "Slapsie" Rosenbloom, Alan Baxter, Thurston Hall, Stanley Ridges, Victor Jory; **D:** William Keighley; **W:** Norman Reilly Raine; **C:** Arthur Edeson; **M:** Max Steiner.

The Eagle ♂♂♂ 1925 In this tale of a young Cossack "Robin Hood," Valentino assumes the persona of the Eagle to avenge his father's murder. The romantic rogue encounters trouble when he falls for the beautiful Banky much to the chagrin of the scorned Czarina Dresser. Fine performances from Valentino and Dresser. Silent, based on a Alexander Pushkin story. Released on video with a new score by Davis. 77m/B VHS, DVD. Rudolph Valentino, Vilma Banky, Louise Dresser, George Nicholls Jr., James A. Marcus; **D:** Clarence Brown; **C:** George Barnes; **M:** Carl Davis.

The Eagle and the Hawk ♂♂♂ 1933 Americans Jerry Young (March), Henry Crocker (Grant), and Mike Richards (Oakie) volunteer for flying duty with the British Army in 1918. Jerry is a heroic pilot but becomes depressed by the horrors of war, while gung ho Henry, who's serving as his observer/gunner, also becomes his rival. On leave, Jerry briefly finds solace with a society babe (Lombard) only to discover on his return that Henry's cockiness has gotten their buddy Mike killed. He denounces the war but Henry manages to ensure Jerry's status as a hero despite his actions. 73m/B VHS. Fredric March, Cary Grant, Jack Oakie, Carole Lombard, Guy Standing, Forrester Harvey, Kenneth Howell, Leyland Hodgson; **D:** Stuart Walker; **W:** Seton I. Miller, Bogart Rogers; **C:** Harry Fischbeck.

The Eagle Has Landed ♂♂♂ 1977 (PG) Duvall, portraying a Nazi colonel in this WWII spy film, commissions Sutherland's Irish, English-hating character to aid him in his mission to kill Prime Minister Winston Churchill. Adapted from the best-selling novel by Jack Higgins. A restored version is available at 134 minutes. 123m/C VHS, DVD. Michael Caine, Donald Sutherland, Robert Duvall, Larry Hagman, Jenny Agutter, Donald Pleasence, Treat Williams, Anthony Quayle; **D:** John Sturges; **W:** Tom Mankiewicz; **C:** Anthony B. Richmond; **M:** Lalo Schifrin.

The Eagle Has Two Heads ♂♂ *L'Aigle a Deux Tetes; The Eagle with Two Heads* 1948 Set during the 19th century, poet/anarchist Marais sets out to assassinate the queen, but when he sees the beautiful monarch, it's love at first sight. Adapted from Cocteau's hugely successful play. In French with English subtitles. 93m/B VHS. *FR* Edwige Feuillere, Jean Marais; **D:** Jean Cocteau; **W:** Jean Cocteau.

Eagle vs. Shark ♂½ 2007 (R) Lily (Horsley) and Jarrod (Clement) are small-town mall employees united by a decided lack of social skills who meet at a costume party dedicated to dressing as their favorite animals. Lily's sweet, Jarrod's completely unlikable, and something resembling clingy love ensues as the two bounce from awkward situation to awkward situation. Tries to be simultaneously edgy and charming but ultimately just makes jokes at the expense of its protagonists. 94m/C DVD. *NZ* Brian Sergent, Craig Hall, Joel Tobeck, Jemaine Clement, Loren Horsley, Rachel House; **D:** Taika Waititi; **W:** Taika Waititi; **C:** Adam Clark; **M:** Phoenix Foundation.

Eagles Attack at Dawn ♂½ *The Big Escape; From Hell to Victory; Hostages in the Gulf* 1970 (PG) After escaping from an Arab prison, an Israeli soldier vows to return with a small commando force to kill the sadistic warden. 96m/C VHS, DVD. *IS* Rick Jason, Peter Brown, Joseph Shiloah, Yehuda Barkan, Yehoram Gaon; **D:** Menahem Golan; **W:** Menahem Golan; **C:** Ya'ackov Kallach; **M:** Dov Seltzer.

Eagle's Shadow ♂ 1984 After a poor orphan boy rescues an aged beggar, the grateful old man tutors the lad in Snake-Fist techniques. 101m/C VHS, DVD. Jackie Chan, Juan Lee, Simon Yuen, Roy Horan; **D:** Yuen Woo Ping.

Eagle's Wing ♂½ 1979 John Briley, screenwriter of the award-winning epic "Gandhi," attempts to weave the threads of allegory smoothly in this white man vs. red man Western from England. The mediocre story finds Native American Waterston dueling white trapper Sheen in a quest to capture an elusive, exotic white stallion. 111m/C VHS. *GB* Martin Sheen, Sam Waterston. Harvey Keitel, Stephane Audran, Caroline Langrishe; **D:** Anthony Harvey; **W:** John Briley; **C:** Billy Williams.

Early Days ♂ 1981 A cantankerous, salty, once-powerful politician awaits death. From the play by David Storey. 67m/C VHS. *GB* Ralph Richardson, Edward Judd, Sheila Ballantyne, Mary Cruickshank; **W:** David Storey. **TV**

Early Frost ♂♂½ 1984 Near suspenseful whodunit centering around a simple divorce investigation that leads to the discovery of a corpse. 95m/C VHS, DVD. Diana McLean, Jon Blake, Janet Kingsbury, David Franklin; **D:** Terry O'Connor.

An Early Frost ♂♂♂½ 1985 Highly praised, surprisingly intelligent drama following the anguish of a successful lawyer who tells his closed-minded family that he is gay and dying of AIDS. Sensitive performance by Quinn in one of the first TV films to focus on the devastating effects of HIV. Rowlands adeptly displays her acting talents as the despairing mother. 97m/C VHS, DVD. Aidan Quinn, Gena Rowlands, Ben Gazzara, John Glover, D.W. Moffett, Sylvia Sidney; **D:** John Erman. **TV**

Early Summer ♂♂♂ *Bakushu* 1951 A classic from renowned Japanese director Ozu, this film chronicles family tensions in post-WWII Japan caused by newly independent women rebelling against the social conventions they are expected to fulfill. Perhaps the best example of this director's work. Winner of Japan's Film of the Year Award. In Japanese with English subtitles. 150m/B VHS, DVD. *JP* Ichiro Sugai, Chishu Ryu, Setsuko Hara, Chikage Awashima, Chieko Higashiyama, Haruko Sugimura, Kuniko Miyake, Kan Nihon-yanagi, Shuji Sano, Toyoko Takahashi, Seiji Miyaguchi; **D:** Yasujiro Ozu.

The Earrings of Madame De... ♂♂♂ *Diamond Earrings; Madame De* 1954 A simple story about a society woman who sells a pair of diamond earrings that her husband gave her, then lies about it. Transformed by Ophuls into his most opulent, overwrought masterpiece, the film displays a triumph of form over content. In French with English subtitles. 105m/C VHS. *FR* Charles Boyer, Danielle Darrieux, Vittorio De Sica, Lea di Lea, Jean Debucourt; **D:** Max Ophuls; **W:** Max Ophuls, Marcel Archard, Annette Wademant; **C:** Christian Matras; **M:** Oscar Straus, Georges Van Parys.

Earth ⅔⅔⅔ *Zemlya; Soil* 1930 Classic Russian silent film with English subtitles. Problems begin in a Ukrainian village when a collective farm landowner resists handing over his land. Outstanding camera work. Kino release runs 70 minutes. **'01m/B VHS, DVD,** *Ru* Semyon Svashenko, Niko... va Yulia Solntseva; *D:* Alexander Dovzhenko; *W:* Alexander Dovzhenko; *C:* Danil Demutsky.

Earth ⅔⅔ 1998 The second of Mehta's projected trilogy (after 1997's "Fire"), "Earth" follows the events surrounding the partitioning of India in 1947, forcing neighbors to take sides in a ferocious religious conflict. The story is seen through the eyes of eight-year-old Lenny, the daughter of a wealthy Parsi family in Lahore who are trying to remain neutral. But Lenny is cared for by her lovely Hindu nanny, Shanta (Das), whose Muslim suitors are deeply affected by the violence. Based on the novel "Cracking India" by Bapsi Sidhwa. Hindi, Urdu, Parsi, and Punjabi with subtitles. **101m/C VHS, DVD, CA** *Aamir Khan, Nandita Das, Rahul Khanna, Maia Sethna; D: Deepa Mehta; W: Deepa Mehta; C: Giles Nuttgers; M: A.R. Rahman.*

Earth & Water ⅔ *Home ke Nero* 1999 Twenty-year-old Nicholas and 18-time they meet. But under pressure from her family, Constantina is forced to break things off—without telling Nicholas she is pregnant. Desperate, Nicholas sinks himself to the bottom of a river but resurfaces to a different world. A love story that crosses the border between dreams and reality. Greek with subtitles. **112m/C VHS, DVD, GR** *Giorgios Karamichos, Photini Papadodi-ma, Lena Kitsopculou, Vassilis Eleftheriadis; D: Glauce Rocha; W: Glauce Rocha; C: Yannis Valaras; M: Yannis Aggelakas; Giorgos Christianakis, Asvitpios Zambalas.*

Earth Entranced ⅔⅔ *Terra em Transe* 1966 A complex political lamentation from Rocha, the premiere director of Brazil's own new wave cinema. Here a writer switches his allegiance from one politician to another, only to find that he (and the masses) lose either way. In Portuguese with English subtitles. **105m/C VHS, BR** *Jose Lewgoy, Paulo Gracindo, Jardel Filho, Glauce Rocha. D: Glauce Rocha; W: Glauce Rocha.*

Earth Girls Are Easy ⅔⅔½ 1989 **(PG)** Valley girl Valerie is having a bad week: first she catches her fiancee with another woman, then she breaks a nail, then furry aliens land in her swimming pool. What more could go wrong? When the aliens are temporarily stranded, she decides to make amends by giving them a head-to-toe makeover. Devoid of their excessive hairiness, the handsome trio of fun-loving extraterrestrials set out to experience the Southern California lifestyle. Sometimes hilarious sci-fi/musical, featuring bouncy shtick and a gleeful dishanciting of modern culture. **100m/C VHS, DVD.** *GP Geena Davis, Jeff Goldblum, Charles Rocket, Julie Brown, Jim Carrey, Damon Wayans, Michael McKean, Angelyne, Larry Linville, Rick Overton, Diane Stilwell, Terrance McNally, Stacey Travis; D: Julien Temple; W: Charlie Coffey, Julie Brown, Terrance McNally; C: Oliver Stapleton; M: Nile Rodgers.*

Earth vs. the Flying Saucers ⅔⅔½ *Invasion of the Flying Saucers* 1956 Extraterrestrials land on Earth and issue an ultimatum to humans concerning their constant use of bombs and missiles. Peace is threatened when military disregards the extraterrestrials' simple warning. Superb special effects by Ray Harryhausen. **83m/B VHS, DVD.** *Hugh Marlowe, Joan Taylor, Donald Curtis, Morris Ankrum; D: Fred F. Sears; W: George Worthing Yates, Bernard Gordon; C: Fred H. Jackman Jr.; M: Mischa Bakaleinikoff.*

Earth vs. the Spider ⅔ *The Spider* 1958 Man-eating giant mutant (teenage ninja?) tarantula makes life miserable for a small town in general and high school partyers in particular. Silly old drive-in fare is agony for many camp treasure for a precious few. **72m/B VHS, DVD.** *Edward Kemmer, June Kenney, Gene Persson, Gene Roth, Hal Torey, Mickey Finn; D: Bert I. Gordon; W: Laszlo Gorog, George Worthing Yates; C: Jack Marta.*

Earthquake ⅔⅔ 1974 **(PG)** Less-than-mediocre drama centers on a major earthquake in Los Angeles and its effect on the lives of an engineer, his spoiled wife, his mistress, his father-in-law, and a suspended policeman. Filmed in much-hyped Sensurround—a technique intended to shake up the theatre a bit but which will have no effect on your TV set. Good special effects, but not enough to compensate for lackluster script. **123m/C VHS, DVD.** *Charlton Heston, Ava Gardner, George Kennedy, Lorne Greene, Genevieve Bujold, Richard Roundtree, Marjoe Gortner, Barry Sullivan, Victoria Principal, Lloyd Nolan, Walter Matthau, Scott Hylands; D: Mark Robson; W: Mario Puzo; C: Philip Lathrop; M: John Williams; Oscars '74: Sound, Visual FX.*

Earthstorm ⅔½ 2006 Cheesy low-budget B-pic from the Sci-F Channel. An asteroid hits the moon, resulting in changes to the ocean's tides that cause massive storms. With the moon now unstable and threatening to treat apart, a crew of scientists, plus a demolitions expert, head into space to see if they can prevent further destruction. **85m/C DVD.** *Stephen Baldwin, Dirk Benedict, John Ralston, Jason Blicker, Anna Silk, Amy Price-Francis, Matt Gordon, Conrad Coates; D: Terry Cunningham; M: Michael Kenyves; C: John Tarver.*

Earthworm Tractors ⅔⅔ 1936 Ambitious tractor salesman Alexander Botts will do anything to make a sale. Brown excels as the fast-talking lead. Comedy is strengthened by its supporting cast. Based on characters first appearing in the "Saturday Evening Post." **63m/B VHS, DVD.** *Joe E. Brown, June Travis, Guy Kibbee, Dick Foran, Carol Hughes, Gene Lockhart, Olin Howlin; D: Ray Enright.*

East and West ⅔⅔⅔ *Ost und West* 1924 Morris Brown, a worldly New York Jew, returns home to Galicia with his daughter Mollie for a traditional family wedding. She teaches the young villagers to dance and box but meets her romantic match in a young yeshiva scholar who forsakes tradition to win her heart. Picon shines as the exuberant flapper. With English and Yiddish intertitles. **85m/B VHS.** *Molly Picon, Jacob Kalish, Sidney Goldin, Dr Ivan Abramson, Sidney Goldin.*

Earthly Possessions ⅔⅔½ 1999 **(R)** Sarandon can't really pass for a drab housewife but she does her best in this adaptation of Anne Tyler's novel. Charlotte Emory (Sarandon) is the very sheltered wife of a smalltown minister (Sanders), who longs for a break from her tedious routine. She gets her chance when she's unexpectedly taken hostage by would-be bankrobber, Jake Simms Jr. (Dorff), who suffers from impulse control problems and continual bad luck. Both their fortunes change when Jake forces Charlotte on the road with him (he wants to see his pregnant girlfriend) and an increasingly close bond forms between the two strangers as they try to stay out of police custody. **120m/C VHS, DVD.** *Susan Sarandon, Stephen Dorff, Jay O. Sanders, Elisabeth Moss, Margo Martindale; D: James Lapine; W: Steven Endelman. CABLE*

Earthling ⅔⅔½ 1980 **(PG)** A terminally ill Holden helps a young Schroder survive in the Australian wilderness after the boy's parents are killed in a tragic accident. Lessons of life and the power of the human heart are passed on in this panoramic, yet mildly sentimental film. **102m/C VHS.** *AU William Holden, Rick Schroder, Jack Thompson, Olivia Hamnett, Alwyn Kurts; D: Peter Collinson; W: Lanny Cotler.*

East Is East ⅔⅔⅔ 1999 **(R)** Culture clash comedy is set in 1971 in the northern working-class community of Salford, England. Pakistani immigrant George Khan (Puri) is the would-be stern patriarch to a brood of six sons and one daughter. While he wants to raise his kids traditionally, they're rebelling. Especially in the marriage department; despite his own long marriage to the English Ella (Bassett), George tries to arrange marriages to fellow Pakistanis for his two eldest sons, with disastrous results. Story is swift, paced, definitely not p.c., and is amusingly broad strokes. Based on Khan-Dir's play. **96m/C VHS, DVD.** *GB Om Puri, Linda Bassett, Archie Panjabi, Chris Bisson, Jimi Mistry, Ian Aspinall, Jordan Routledge, Raji James; D: Damien O'Donnell; W: Ayub Khan-Din; C: Brian Tufano; M: Deborah Mollison. British Acad. '99: Film.*

East of Borneo ⅔½ 1931 Tropical adventure involving a "lost" physician whose wife sets out to find him in the jungle. She locates her love only to discover he has a prestigious new job tending to royalty and didn't want to be found. **76m/B VHS, DVD.** *Charles Bickford, Rose Hobart, Georges Renavent; D: George Melford.*

East of Eden ⅔⅔⅔ 1954 Steinbeck's contemporary retelling of the biblical Cain and Abel story receives superior treatment from Kazan and his excellent cast. Dean, in his first starring role, gives a reading of a young man's search for love and acceptance that defines adolescent pain. Though filmed in the 1950s, this story still rivets today's viewers with its emotional message. **115m/C VHS, DVD.** *James Dean, Julie Harris, Richard (Dick) Davalos, Raymond Massey, Jo Van Fleet, Burl Ives, Albert Dekker; D: Elia Kazan; W: Paul Osborn; M: Leonard Rosenman. Oscars '55: Support. Actress (Van Fleet); Golden Globes '56: Film—Drama.*

East of Elephant Rock ⅔ 1976 In 1948, a young first secretary of the British Embassy returns from leave in England to a tense atmosphere in a colony in southeast Asia. Beautiful scenery can't make up for weak plot. **93m/C VHS, GB** *John Hurt, Jeremy Kemp, Judi Bowker, Christopher Cazenove; D: Don Boyd; W: Don Boyd.*

East of Kilimanjaro ⅔ *The Big Search* 1957 A freelance photographer and a doctor search frantically to find the cause of a fatal disease near the slopes of the majestic Mt. Kilimanjaro. Routine killer virus flick filmed in Africa. **75m/C VHS.** *Marshall Thompson, Gaby Andre, Fausto Tozzi; D: Arnold Belgard.*

East Palace, West Palace ⅔⅔ *Behind the Forbidden City; Donggong, Xigong* 1996 Bold and controversial examination of a shadow world in Chinese society. A-Lan (Han) is a young homosexual, cruising the park outside the Forbidden Palace in Beijing. He's detained in a roundup by a cop, Xiao Shi (Jun), who takes him to the park's police station for interrogation. A-Lan is unashamed of his lifestyle and the cop presses him to tell his life story. It soon becomes clear that the Xiao Shi, though outwardedly homophobic, is actually sexually intrigued by A-Lan's presence as the duo mentally and verbally dance around the charged situation. Chinese with subtitles. **95m/C VHS, DVD, CH** *Si Han, Hu Jun; D: Zhang Yuan; W: Zhang Yuan, Wang Xiaobo; C: Zhang Jian; M: Xiang Min.*

East Side Kids ⅔⅔ 1940 Early Side Kids. A "hoodlum wants to pre-vent his brother from beginning a similar life of crime. **60m/B VHS, DVD.** *Leon Ames, Harris Berger, Dennis Moore, Joyce Bryant; D: Robert F. "Bob" Hill.*

East Side Story ⅔½ 2007 Handsome Diego's (Alvarado) life is in upheaval: he feels obligated to keep working in his grandma's (De Bari) Mexican restaurant rather than pursue his own dreams; his closeted boyfriend (Beron) just broke up with him; he's been outed by his desperate Aunt Blanca (Jimenez); and his job and his chance to marry longtime girlfriend Mary (Biondelli). Meanwhile, gossip columnist Claudius De Wolfe (Cowan) discovers that Denny is actually a long-lost relation of Barrett Sr. **88m/B DVD.** *Joan Blondell, Mischa Auer, Irene Hervey, Bing Crosby, Sir C. Aubrey Smith, Robert Kent, Jerome Cowan; D: David Butler; W: William Conselman; C: George Robinson; M: Johnny Burke.*

East Side of Heaven ⅔⅔ 1939 Denny (Crosby) is hired by drunken Cyrus Barrett Jr. (Kent) to deliver a singing telegram to his crusty father (Smith), who is threatening to take custody of his baby grandson. Mona (Hervey), Junior's wife, is an old friend of Denny's and leaves her son with him to sort out her troubled marriage. **90m/C VHS, DVD.**

East-West ⅔⅔ *Est-Ouest* 1999 **(PG-13)** In 1946, Stalin offered amnesty to any Russians who left the country after the 1917 revolution. But he executed or imprisoned many of the homesick expatriates and others 'ound their gray motherland hard to bear (and impossible to leave). Russian doctor Alexei Golovin (Menshikov) bows to circumstances while his marriage to French wife Marie (Bonnaire) becomes increasingly strained. Marie befriends a champion swimmer, Sasha (Bodrov), with the hopes that they can both escape but things don't go as planned. Old-fashioned storytelling hampers the drama and the story (which leaps ahead months and years) becomes confused. French and Russian with subtitles. **125m/C VHS, DVD, FR** *Sandrine Bonnaire, Oleg Menshikov, Sergei Bodrov Jr., Catherine Deneuve, Tatiana Dogileva; D: Regis Wargnier; W: Regis Wargnier, Sergei Bodrov, Rustam Ibragimbekov, Louis Gardel; C: Laurent Dailland; M: Patrick Doyle.*

East Side, West Side ⅔⅔ 1949 Stanwyck and Mason try hard to make this simple-minded soaper work, with mixed results. A wealthy couple experiences marital woes, aggravated by a ambitious young woman and a soft-hearted men suffering from unrequited love. Based on the popular novel by Marcia Davenport. **110m/B VHS.** *Barbara Stanwyck, James Mason, Ava Gardner, Van Heflin, Gale Sondergaard, William Frawley, Nancy Davis; D: Mervyn LeRoy; C: Charles Rosher; M: Miklos Rozsa.*

Easter Parade ⅔⅔⅔½ 1948 Big musical star Don Hewes (Astaire) splits with his partner Nadine (Miller) claiming that he could mold any girl to replace her in the act. He tries and finally succeeds with clumsy chorus girl Hannah Brown (Garland) after much difficulty. Great Garland in peak form, aided by a classic Irving Berlin score. "Happy Easter; Drum Crazy; It Only Happens When I Dance With You; Everybody's Doin' It; I Want to Go Back to Michigan; Beautiful Faces;

East L.A. Warriors ⅔½ 1989 A mobster, Hilton-Jacobs, manipulates Los Angeles gangs in this non-stop action adventure. **90m/C VHS, DVD.** *Tony Bravo, Lawrence-Hilton Jacobs, Kamar De Los Reyes, William (Bill) Smith; D: Addison Randall.*

Earth vs. the Spider ⅔⅔ 2001 **(R)** Shares the title of the 1958 drive-in feature but not much else. Nerdy comic book fanatic Quentin (Gummersal) works as a security guard at a biotech research lab. After his partner is killed curing a break-in, Quentin injects himself with a drug made from a mutated spider in the hopes of becoming an avenging superhero. Soon Quentin begins to mutate and no one is safe! **90m/C VHS, DVD.** *Devon Gummersall, Dan Aykroyd, Amelia Heinle, Christopher Cousins, John Cho, Theresa Russel, Mario Roccuzzo; D: Scott Ziehl; W: Gary Solomon, Chuck Konzelman, Max Enscoe, Arnie de Young; C: Thomas Callaway; M: Charles Bernstein. CABLE*

Need Beautiful Clothes; A Fella With an Umbrella; I Love a Piano; Snookey Ookums. **103m/C VHS, DVD.** Fred Astaire, Judy Garland, Peter Lawford, Ann Miller, Jules Munshin, Jol Lansing; *D:* Charles Walters; *W:* Sidney Shelden, Frances Goodrich, Albert Hackett; *C:* Harry Stradling Sr.; *M:* Irving Berlin. Oscars '48: Scoring/Musical.

Eastern Condors ✇✇ **1987** At the end of the Vietnam War, a band of Chinese convicts are recruited by the U.S. Army (and promised their freedom) if they can destroy an ammunition dump before the Viet Cong can make use of it. Considered a Hong Kong version of "The Dirty Dozen," with the requisite level of high energy and blood. Dubbed or Chinese with English subtitles. **94m/C VHS, DVD.** HK Sammo Hung, Joyce Godenzi, Yuen Biao, Haing S. Ngor; *D:* Sammo Hung.

Eastern Promises ✇✇✇1/2 **2007** (R) Midwife Anna (Watts) delivers a baby in a London hospital as the baby's mother, Tatiana, a teen prostitute from Russia, dies in Anna's arms. Haunted by the young girl's demise as well as her own demons, Anna's attempts to track down Tatiana's identity lead her to a Russian mafia gang led by Semyon (Mueller-Stahl). Seymon's son Kirill (Cassel) and bodyguard/driver Nikolai (a marvelous Mortenson) dole out a fierce brand of brutality, brought to full-tilt in a bloody bathhouse scene. Director Cronenberg's vision is unflinching, messy, and raw in all the right places in this complicated but resonating morality tale. **96m/C DVD, HD DVD.** GB CA Viggo Mortensen, Naomi Watts, Vincent Cassel, Armin Mueller-Stahl, Sinead Cusack, Jerzy Skolimowski, Donald (Don) Sumpter, Mina E. Mina; *D:* David Cronenberg; *W:* Steven Knight; *C:* Peter Suschitzky; *M:* Howard Shore.

Eastside ✇✇ **1999** After being released from prison, Antonio Lopez pays a visit to his successful lawyer brother and learns that he's a mouthpiece for the mob. So Antonio gets an in with East L.A. kingpin De La Rosa as a strongarm guy. Only when he's asked to intimidate the owner of an inner-city youth center, Antonio's latent conscience begins to bother him. Of course, if he betrays De La Rosa, he's dead. **94m/C VHS, DVD.** Mario Lopez, Erian Figueroa, Mark Espinoza, Elizabeth Bogush, Gulshan Grover, Richard Lynch, Carlos Gallardo; *D:* Lorena David; *W:* Eric P. Sherman; *C:* Lisa Wiegand; *M:* Armando Avila. VIDEO

Easy Come, Easy Go ✇✇ **1967** (PG) Elvis, as a Navy frogman, gets excited when he accidentally discovers what he believes is a vast sunken treasure. Music is his only solace when he finds his treasure to be worthless copper coins. ♪Easy Come, Easy Go; The Love Machine; Yoga Is As Yoga Goes; Sing, You Children; You Gotta Stop; I'll Take Love. **96m/C VHS, DVD.** Elvis Presley, Dodie Marshall, Pat Priest, Elsa Lanchester, Frank McHugh, Pat Harrington, Sonny Tufts; *D:* John Rich.

Easy Kill ✇1/2 **1989** A man takes the law into his own hands to exact revenge on drug lords. **100m/C VHS, DVD.** Jane Badler, Cameron Mitchell, Frank Stallone; *D:* Josh Spencer.

The Easy Life ✇✇✇ **1963** Haunting film about a hedonistic man from a small Italian village who takes a mild-mannered student pleasure-seeking. The ride turns sour and the playboy is ultimately destroyed by his own brutality. **105m/B VHS.** IT Vittorio Gassman, Catherine Spaak, Jean-Louis Trintignant, Luciana Angiolillo; *D:* Dino Risi.

Easy Living ✇✇✇ **1937** Exasperated Wall Street millionaire J.B. Ball (Arnold) throws his spoiled wife's (Nash) fur coat out their apartment window and it just happens to land on poor-but-hardworking secretary Mary Smith (Arthur). Ball insists Mary keep the coat and even buys her a matching hat. Soon, rumors are flying that Mary is the millionaire's tootsie. She meets cute with John (Milland), who turns out to be Ball's son and, after the usual misunderstandings, the twosome realize that they're meant for each other. **91m/B VHS.** Jean Arthur, Edward Arnold, Ray Milland, Franklin Pangborn, Mary Nash, William Demerest; *D:* Mitchell Leisen; *W:* Preston Sturges; *C:* Ted Tetzlaff; *M:* Boris Morros.

Easy Living ✇✇1/2 **1949** Compromised melodrama about an over-the-hill football player who must cope with his failing marriage and looming retirement. Based on an Irwin Shaw story. **77m/B VHS.** Victor Mature, Lucille Ball, Jack Paar, Lizabeth Scott, Sonny Tufts, Lloyd Nolan, Paul Stewart; *D:* Jacques Tourneur.

Easy Money ✇✇ **1983** (R) A basic slob has the chance to inherit $10 million if he can give up his loves: smoking, drinking, and gambling among others. Dangerfield is surprisingly restrained in this harmless, though not altogether unpleasing comedy. **95m/C VHS, DVD.** Rodney Dangerfield, Joe Pesci, Geraldine Fitzgerald, Jennifer Jason Leigh, Tom Ewell, Candice Azzara, Taylor Negron; *D:* James Signorelli; *W:* Rodney Dangerfield, Dennis Blair.

Easy Rider ✇✇✇1/2 **1969** (R) Slim-budget, generation-defining movie. Two young men in late 1960s undertake a motorcycle trek throughout the Southwest in search of the real essence of America. Along the way they encounter hippies, rednecks, prostitutes, drugs, Nicholson, and tragedy. One of the highest-grossing pictures of the decade, undoubtedly an influence on two generations of "youth-oriented dramas," which all tried unsuccessfully to duplicate the original accomplishment. Psychedelic scenes and a great role for Nicholson are added bonuses. Look for the graveyard dancing scene in New Orleans. Features one of the "best '60s rock scores around, including "Mean Streets" and "The Wanderers." **94m/C VHS, DVD.** Peter Fonda, Dennis Hopper, Jack Nicholson, Karen Black, Toni Basil, Robert Walker Jr., Luana Anders, Luke Askew, Warren Finnery, Mac Mashourian, Antonio Mendoza, Sabrina Scharf, Phil Spector; *D:* Dennis Hopper; *W:* Terry Southern, Peter Fonda, Dennis Hopper; *C:* Laszlo Kovacs. AFI '98: Top 100, Natl. Film Reg. '98; N.Y. Film Critics '69: Support. Actor (Nicholson); Natl. Soc. Film Critics '69: Support. Actor (Nicholson).

Easy Street ✇✇✇ **1916** Chaplin portrays a derelict who, using some hilarious methods, reforms the residents of Easy Street. Chaplin's row with the town bully is particularly amusing. Silent with musical soundtrack added. **20m/B VHS, DVD.** Charlie Chaplin; *D:* Charlie Chaplin.

Easy to Love ✇✇1/2 **1953** Williams is in love with her boss, but he pays her no attention until a handsome singer vies for her affections. Set at Florida's Cypress Gardens, this aquatic musical features spectacular water ballet productions choreographed by Busby Berkeley, and the title song penned by Cole Porter. ♪Easy to Love; Coquette; Beautiful Spring; That's What Rainy Day is For; Look Out! I'm Romantic; Didja Ever. **96m/C VHS,** Esther Williams, Van Johnson, Tony Martin, John Bromfield, King Donovan, Carrol Baker; *D:* Charles Walters; *W:* William Roberts.

Easy to Wed ✇✇1/2 **1946** Mild MGM musical remake of 1936's "Libeled Lady." Wealthy J.B. Allenbury (Kellaway) is suing for big bucks after an unflattering write-up of his daughter Connie's (Williams) lifestyle (she's accused of being a playgirl who edits married men). So newspaper editor Warren Haggerty (Wynn) sends suave reporter Bill (Johnson) to pretend to be married and prove the accusations true while Haggerty's fiancee Gladys (Ball) gets caught in the middle of the farce. Williams is winning but Ball steals the picture. **109m/C DVD.** Esther Williams, Van Johnson, Keenan Wynn, Lucille Ball, Cecil Kellaway, Ben Blue, June Lockhart, Grant Mitchell, Paul Harvey, Jonathan Hale, James Flavin; *D:* Edward Buzzell; *W:* Dorothy Kingsley; *C:* Harry Strandling Jr.; *M:* Johnny Green.

Easy Virtue ✇✇1/2 **1927** Hitchcock directs this adaptation of a Noel Coward play as a social melodrama. Larita is an unhappily married socialite with a lover. When her husband discovers her infidelity they divorce and she is marked as a woman whose family disapproves. Her reputation is not enhanced by her marriage to a younger man whose family disapproves. **79m/B VHS, DVD.** GB Isabel Jeans, Ian Hunter, Franklin Dyall, Eric Bransby Williams, Robin Irvine, Violet Farebrother; *D:* Alfred Hitchcock.

Easy Wheels ✇✇1/2 **1989** Like most decent biker movies, "Wheels" is propelled by bad taste and a healthy dose of existentialist nihilism. But there's an usual plot twist in this parody. A biker named She-Wolf and her gang kidnap female babies and let wolves rear the children. Their elaborate plan is to create a race of super women who will subdue the troublesome male population. But can this "noble" plan succeed? **94m/C VHS, DVD.** Paul LeMat, Eileen Davidson, Marjorie Bransfield, Jon Menick, Mark Holton, Karen Russell, Jami Richards, Roberta Vasquez, Barry Livingston, mi, Celia Abrams, David O'Malley; *M:* John Ross.

Eat a Bowl of Tea ✇✇✇ **1989** (PG-13) Endearing light drama-comedy concerning a multi-generational Chinese family. They must learn to deal with the problems of life in America and in particular, marriage, when Chinese women are finally allowed to immigrate with their husbands to the United States following WWII. Adaptation of Louis Chu's story, directed by the man who brought us "Dim Sum." A PBS "American Playhouse" presentation. **102m/C VHS, DVD.** Cora Miao, Russell Wong, Lau Siu Ming, Eric Tsiang Chi Wai, Victor Wong, Jessica Harper, Lee Sau Kee; *D:* Wayne Wang; *W:* Judith Rascoe; *C:* Amir M. Mokri; *M:* Mark Adler.

Eat and Run ✇ **1986** (R) A bloody comedy about a 400-pound alien with a taste for Italian (people, that is). **85m/C VHS.** Ron Silver, R.L. Ryan, Sharon Schlarth; *D:* Christopher Hart.

Eat Drink Man Woman ✇✇✇1/2 **1994** (R) In Taipei, widowed master chef serves weekly feast of elaborate food and familial guilt to his three grown daughters, all of whom still live at home. They spend their time sorting out professional and romantic difficulties, searching for independence, and fulfilling traditional family obligations. Each character has a lot going on, but no one's story gets lost in the mix. Lee uses irony to great effect, introducing us to the culinary artist who has lost his sense of taste and has a daughter who works at a Wendy's. Food preparation scenes (more than 100 recipes are served up) illustrate a careful attention to detail (and are guaranteed to make you hungry). Lee's follow-up to "The Wedding Banquet" is a finely observed, comic tale of generational drift, the richness of tradition, and the power of love to redeem or improve. In Chinese with subtitles or dubbed. **123m/C VHS, DVD.** TW Sihung Lung, Kuei-Mei Yang, Yu-Wen Wang, Chien-Lien Wu, Sylvia Chao, Winston Chao, Ahleh Gua, Lester Chen; *D:* Ang Lee; *W:* Ang Lee, Hui-Ling Wang, James Schamus; *C:* Jong Lin; *M:* Mader. Natl. Bd. of Review '94: Foreign Film.

Eat My Dust ✇✇ **1976** (PG) Teenage son of a California sheriff steals the best stock cars from a race track to take the town's heartthrob for a joy ride. Subsequently he leads the town on a wild car chase. Brainless but fast-paced. **89m/C VHS, DVD.** Ron Howard, Christopher Norris, Warren Kemmerling, Dave Madden, Robert Broyles, Jessica Potter, Don Brodie, Evelyn Russell, Clint Howard, Paul Bartel, Rance Howard, Corbin Bernsen; *D:* Charles B. Griffith; *W:* Charles B. Griffith; *C:* Eric Saarinen; *M:* David Grisman.

Eat the Peach ✇✇1/2 **1986** An idiosyncratic Irish comedy about two young unemployed rebels who attempt to break free from their tiny coast town by becoming motorcycle champs after seeing the Elvis Presley film "Roustabout." Together they create the "wall of death," a large wooden barrel in which they can perform various biker feats. **90m/C VHS.** IR Stephen Brennan, Eamon Morrissey, Catherine Byrne, Niall Toibin, Tony Doyle, Joe Lynch; *D:* Peter Ormrod; *W:* Peter Ormrod, John Kelleher; *M:* Donal Lunny.

Eat the Rich ✇ **1987** (R) A British farce about a group of terrorists who take over the popular London restaurant, Bastard's. Led by a former, disgruntled transvestite employee, they turn diners into menu offerings. Music by Motorhead. **89m/C VHS, DVD.** GB Nosher Powell, Lanah Pellay, Fiona Richmond, Ronald Allen, Sandra Dome, Paul McCartney, Linda McCartney, Bill Wyman, Koo Stark, Miranda Richardson, Angie Bowie, Sandie Shaw; *D:* Peter Richardson; *W:* Peter Richardson; *C:* Witold Stok.

Eat Your Heart Out ✇✇1/2 **1996** (R) Routine romantic comedy about talented but struggling young chef Daniel (Oliver) who gets his shot at success with his own TV cooking show. He doesn't realize his best gal pal (Seagall) loves him, while Daniel becomes intrigued by his sexy agent (San Giacomo). **96m/C VHS, DVD.** Christian Oliver, Laura San Giacomo, Pamela Segall, Linda Hunt; *D:* Felix Adlon; *W:* Felix Adlon; *C:* Judy Irola; *M:* Alex Wurman.

Eaten Alive ✇✇ *Death Trap; Starlight Slaughter; Legend of the Bayou; Horror Hotel Massacre* **1976** (R) A Southerner takes an unsuspecting group of tourists into a crocodile death trap. Director Tobe Hooper's follow-up to "The Texas Chainsaw Massacre." Englund is more recognizable with razor fingernails as Freddy Krueger of the "Nightmare on Elm Street" films. **96m/C VHS, DVD.** Neville Brand, Mel Ferrer, Carolyn Jones, Marilyn Burns, Stuart Whitman, Robert Englund, William Finley, Roberta Collins, Kyle Richards, Janus Blythe; *D:* Tobe Hooper; *W:* Marti Rustam, Alvin L. Fast, Kim Henkel; *C:* Robert Caramico; *M:* Wayne Bell.

Eating ✇✇ **1990** (R) Set in Southern California, women gather to celebrate birthdays for three of their friends who are turning 30, 40 and 50. As the party commences, women from two generations discuss their attitudes towards food and men...and discover hilarious parallels. **110m/C VHS, DVD.** Nelly Alard, Frances Bergen, Mary Crosby, Lisa Richards, Gwen Welles, Daphna Kastner, Elizabeth Kemp, Marlena Giovi, Marina Gregory, Toni Basil; *D:* Henry Jaglom; *W:* Henry Jaglom; *C:* Hanania Baer.

Eating Out 2: Sloppy Seconds ✇1/2 **2006** Goofy low-budget gay comedy. Kyle (Verraros) has been dumped by Marc (Chukerman) so he's on the prowl. He's drawn to hunky-but-dumb art class model Troy (Dapper), who says he's straight. Since Kyle and his gal pals Gwen (Brooke) and Tiffani (Kochan) have their doubts, Kyle claims he's a member of a "going straight" group and decides to take Troy to a meeting and see what happens. **85m/C DVD.** Mink Stole, Jim Verraros, Marco Dapper, Emily Brooke, Rebekah Kochan, Brett Chukerman; *D:* Phillip J. Bartell; *W:* Phillip J. Bartell, Q. Allan Brocka; *C:* Lisa Wiegand; *M:* Cary Berger, Boris Worister.

Eating Raoul ✇✇1/2 **1982** The Blands are a happily married couple who share many interests: good food and wine, entrepreneurial dreams, and an aversion to sex. The problem is, they're flat broke. So, when the tasty swinger from upstairs makes a pass at Mary and Paul accidentally kills him, they discover he's got lots of money; Raoul takes a cut in the deal by disposing of—or rather recycling—the body. This may just be the way to finance that restaurant they've been wanting to open. Wonderful, offbeat, hilariously dark comedy. **83m/C VHS, DVD.** Mary Woronov, Paul Bartel, Robert Beltran, Buck Henry, Ed Begley Jr., Edie McClurg, John Paragon, Richard Blackburn, Hamilton Camp, Billy Curtis, Susan Saiger, Richard Paul, Don Steele, Mark Woods; *D:* Paul Bartel; *W:* Paul Bartel, Richard Blackburn; *C:* Gary Theitges; *M:* Arlon Ober.

Eban and Charley ✇1/2 **2001** Draggy romance about a couple of misfits—one of whom is underage. 29-year-old Eban (Fellows) returns to his parents' home in a coastal Oregon community after leaving his job as a soccer coach. He's hanging around town when he meets the 15-year-old Charley (Andrade), who's been sent to live with his resentful divorced father after Charley's mother dies. Eventually, the relationship becomes physical (there are no depictions of sex) and they're headed for trouble. **88m/C VHS, DVD.** Brent Fellows, Giovanni Andrade, Nolan V. Chard, Ron Upton, Pam Munter; *D:* James Bolton; *W:* James Bolton; *C:* Judy Irola; *M:* Stephin Merritt.

The Ebb-Tide ✇✇1/2 **1997** Capt. Chisholm (Coltrane) is bothered by a scandalous past, so he doesn't ask a lot of questions about transporting a secret cargo to Australia. A storm strands Chisholm

Ebbtide ⬥⬥1/2 **1994 (R)** A mother who claims her son died from chemicals dumped by the Poseidon Pacific Co. Jeff got the case when the previous lawyer died mysteriously but this doesn't stop him checking out the chemical company or its beautiful president. **90m/C VHS.** *D:* Craig Lahiff. *W:* Bob Ellis, Peter Goldsworthy.

and two sailors on an uncharted island that's inhabited by the malevolent Ellstrom (Terry) and has Chisholm in a battle of good versus evil. Based on a novel by Robert Louis Stevenson. **104m/C VHS.** Robbie Coltrane, Nigel Terry, Steven Mackintosh; *D:* Nicholas Renton. *W:* Simon Donald. **CABLE**

Ebenezer ⬥⬥1/2 **1997 (PG)** Lawyer Jeff Ebenezer (Palance) is a crumedgeonly crook in the wild west who doesn't believe in Christmas and even cheats at poker. He's told by the ghostly Jacob Marlowe (Halliday) to change his ways or else—and Ebenezer is visited by several spirits that show him the error of his ways. A western version of Charles Dickens' "A Christmas Carol" that's quite colorful. **94m/C VHS.** Jack Palance, Rick Schroder, Amy Locane, Albert Schultz, Richard Halliday, Richard Comar, Michelle Thrush, Susan Coyne, Joshua Silberg, Morris Chapdelaine; *D:* Ken Jubenvill; *W:* Donald Martin; *C:* Henry Lebo; *M:* Bruce Leitl. **TV**

Ebony Dreams **1980** WWII documentary focuses on the experience of female factory workers during and after the war. Five contemporary women relate their personal endeavors and struggles to retain their jobs once the war ended. Excellent use of newsreel footage and interesting interviews with the women. **85m/C VHS.** Philomena Nowlin; *D:* Bill Brame.

Ebony Tower ⬥⬥1/2 **1986** Based on the John Fowles novel about a crusty old artist who lives in a French chateau with two young female companions. They are visited by a handsome young man, thereby initiating sexual tension and recognizably Fowlesian plot puzzles. Features some partial nudity. **80m/C GB** Laurence Olivier, Roger Rees, Greta Scacchi, Toyah Willcox; *D:* Robert Knights; *M:* Richard Rodney Bennett. **TV**

Echo Murders ⬥1/2 **1945** A Sexton Blake mystery wherein he investigates a mine owner's mysterious death, opening up a veritable can of murdering, power-hungry worms. **75m/B VHS, DVD.** Julien Mitchell, David Farrar, "Ferdy" Mayne, Pamela Stirling, David Farrar; Dennis Price; *D:* John Harlow; *W:* John Harlow. *C:* James Wilson; *M:* Percival Mackey.

Echo of Murder ⬥⬥ *Who Killed Atlanta's Children?***2000** Docudrama focuses on the 29 child murders in Atlanta, which took place in the late 70s and early '80s, from the point of view of investigative journalists Hines and Belushi. Their theory is that convicted killer Wayne Williams is the scapegoat for a police conspiracy and the killings were purpetrated by the Ku Klux Klan. But they seem to spend most of their time yelling at each other so the story's emotional impact is lost. **105m/C VHS, DVD.** James Belushi, Gregory Hines; *D:* Charles Robert Carner; *C:* Michael Goi; *M:* James Verboor. **CABLE**

The Echo of Thunder ⬥⬥1/2 **1998** It's a hard life in the Australian outback for Gladwyn (Davis) and Larry (Sheridan) Ritchie who, with their three children, raise specialty palm trees on their small farm. It's a struggle that's made more uncomfortable for Gladwyn when 15-year-old Lara (Hewett) arrives. Lara is Larry's daughter by his late first wife and Gladwyn doesn't think the city-bred girl will fit in, and she's also worried that Lara's presence will stir up old memories for her husband. Indeed, Lara's only friend seems to be the stray Dingo dog she adopts and names Thunderwith. Based on the novel "Thunderwith" by Libby Hathorn. **98m/C VHS.** Judy Davis, Jamey Sheridan, Bill Hunter, Lauren Hewett, Ernie Dingo, Michael Caton; *D:* Simon Wincer; *W:* H. Haden Yelin; *M:* Laurence Rosenthal. **TV**

Echo Park ⬥⬥1/2 **1986 (R)** An unsung sleeper comedy about three "roommates living in Los Angeles' Echo Park: a body builder, a single-mother waitress, and an itinerant songwriter. Charts their struggles as they aim for careers in show-biz. Offbeat ensemble effort. **93m/C VHS, DVD. AU** Tom Hulce, Susan Dey, Michael Bowen, Richard "Cheech" Marin, Christopher Walker, Shirley Jo Finney, Cassandra Peterson, Yana Nirvana, Timothy Carey. *C:* Karl Kofler; *M:* Michael Ventura.

Echoes ⬥⬥ **1983 (R)** A young painter's life slowly comes apart as he is tormented by nightmares that his stillborn twin brother is attempting to murder him. **90m/C VHS, DVD.** Gale Sondergaard, Mercedes McCambridge, Richard Allen, Ruth Romar, John Spencer, Nathalie Nell; *D:* Arthur Allan Seidelman; *W:* Richard Allen, Richard J. Anthony; *C:* Hanania Baer.

Echoes ⬥⬥1/2 **1988** Shopkeeper's daughter Clare O'Brien (Garahy) and doctor's son David Power (Hines) both want to escape from their 1950s Irish seaside town. They meet again at university in Dublin where their friendship turns to romance but their return home comes complete with family troubles and differing dreams. Based on the novel by Maeve Binchy. **208m/C VHS, DVD. GB** Siobhan Garahy, Alison Doody, Dermot Crowley; *W:* Donald Churchill, Barbara Rennie. **TV**

Echoes in the Darkness ⬥⬥1/2 **1987** Miniseries based on the true-life Joseph Wambaugh bestseller about the "Main Line" murder investigation in Pennsylvania in 1979. Police are baffled when a teacher is murdered and her children vanish. Suspicion falls on a charismatic coworker and the school's principal. **234m/C VHS.** Peter Coyote, Robert Loggia, Stockard Channing, Peter Boyle, Cindy Pickett, Gary Cole, Zeljko Ivanek, Alex Hyde-White, Treat Williams; *D:* Glenn Jordan. **TV**

Echoes of Paradise ⬥1/2 *Shadows of the Peacock* **1986 (R)** After a series of earth-shattering events, a depressed woman journeys to an island where she falls for a Balinese dancer. Soon she must choose between returning home or beginning life anew in paradise. **90m/C VHS. AU** Wendy Hughes, John Lone, Rod Mullinar, Peta Toppano, Steve Jacobs, Gillian Jones; *D:* Phillip Noyce. *C:* Peter James.

The Eclipse ⬥⬥⬥1/2 *L'eclisse* **1966** The last of Antonioni's trilogy (after "L'Avventura" and "La Notte"), wherein another fashionable and alienated Italian woman passes from one lover to another, searching unsuccessfully for truth and love. Highly acclaimed, in Italian with subtitles. **123m/B VHS, DVD. IT** Monica Vitti, Alain Delon, Francesco Rabal, Louis Seigner; *D:* Michelangelo Antonioni; *W:* Tonino Guerra, Elio Bartolini, Ottiero Ottieri, Michelangelo Antonioni; *C:* Gianni Di Venanzo; *M:* Giovanni Fusco.

Eclipse ⬥⬥1/2 **1994** Sexual roundelay set in Toronto shortly before a total solar eclipse, which is apparently affecting all the generally listless characters in such a way that they travel from couple to couple, abandon. First feature for Podeswa. **96m/C VHS, CA GE** Von Flores, John Gilbert, Pascale Montpetit, Manuel Aranguiz, Maria del Mar, Matthew Ferguson, Earl Pastko, Greg Ellwand, Daniel MacIvor, Kirsten Johnson; *D:* Jeremy Podeswa; *C:* Miroslaw Baszak; *M:* Ernie Tollar.

Ecstasy WOOF! Soft core fluff about a film director's wife's erotic adventures. **82m/C VHS.** Tiffany Bolling; *D:* Bud Townsend.

Ecstasy ⬥⬥1/2 *Extase; Ekstase; Symphony of Love* **1933** A romantic, erotic story about a young woman married to an older man, who takes a lover. Features Lamarr, then Hedy Kiesler, before her discovery in Hollywood. Film subsequently gained notoriety for Lamarr's nude scenes. In Czech with English subtitles. **90m/B VHS, DVD. CZ** Hedy Lamarr, Jaromir Rogoz, Aribert Mog; *D:* Gustav Machaty; *W:* Gustav Machaty.

Ed WOOF! **1996 (PG)** A must see for all fans of flatulent animatronic chimpanzees who play third base. Everyone else should stay away. LeBlanc (who should've been tipped off when they couldn't even get a real chimp to appear) plays Coop, a pie-eyed exasperation. Cameo from Tommy Lasorda playing a fat major league manager. **94m/C VHS, DVD.** Matt LeBlanc, Jayne Brook, Bill Cobbs, Jack Warden, Dorenry Payne II, Curt Kaplan, Zack (Zach) Ward, Mike McGhone, James (Jim) Caviezel, Valente Rodriguez; *D:* Bill Couturie; *W:* David Mickey Evans; *C:* Alan Caso; *M:* Stephen Endelman.

Ed Gein ⬥ **2001** Considering the subject matter, this is a mild account of murdering grave-robbing, dismembering psycho/cannibal Ed Gein (Railsback) and the Wisconsin farm community who just can't believe what their neighbor has been up to. **88m/C VHS, DVD.** Steve Railsback, Carrie Snodgress, Pat Skipper, Sally Champlin; *D:* Chuck Parello; *W:* Stephen Johnston; *C:* Vanja Cernjul; *M:* Robert F. McNaughton.

Ed Wood ⬥⬥⬥1/2 **1994 (R)** Leave it to Burton to bring to the screen the story of a director many consider to the worst of all time (he's at least in the top three) and who now occupies a lofty position as a cult icon. In this hilarious and touching tribute to a Hollywood maverick with grace-Z-vision, detailed homage is paid to Wood's single-mindedness and optimism in the face of repeated failure and lack of financing, even down to the black and white photography. Depp is convincing (and engaging) as Ed Wood, Jr., the cross-dressing, angora-sweater-wearing low-budget auteur of such notoriously "bad" cult films as "Glen or Glenda" and "Plan 9 From Outer Space." Depp is supported by terrific portrayals of the motley Wood crew, led by Landau's morphine-addicted, down-on-his-luck Bela Lugosi. Burton focuses on Wood's relationship with Lugosi, whose career is over by the time Wood befriends him. Based on Rudolph Grey's book, "Nightmare of Ecstasy: The Life and Art of Edward D. Wood Jr." **127m/B VHS, DVD.** Johnny Depp, Sarah Jessica Parker, Martin Landau, Bill Murray, Jim Myers, Patricia Arquette, Jeffrey Jones, Lisa Marie, Vincent D'Onofrio, Ned Bellamy, Conrad Brooks, Rance Howard, Juliet Landau, G.D. Spradlin, Mike Starr, George "The Animal" Steele, Gregory Walcott; *D:* Tim Burton; *W:* Scott M. Alexander, Larry Karaszewski; *C:* Stefan Czapsky; *M:* Howard Shore. Oscars '94: Makeup, Support. Actor (Landau); Golden Globes '95: Support. Actor (Landau); L.A. Film Critics '94: Cinematog., Support. Actor (Landau); N.Y. Film Critics '94: Cinematog., Support. Actor (Landau); Nat'l Soc. Film Critics '94: Cinematog., Support. Actor (Landau); Screen Actors Guild '94: Support. Actor (Landau).

Eddie ⬥⬥ **1996 (PG-13)** Basketball nut Edwina (Goldberg) wins a chance to be honorary coach of her beloved Knicks in a free throw contest. When some of her courtside advice works, and the other fans seem to respond to her, the publicity-seeking maverick owner (Langella) gives her the job full-time. Predictable comedy with the usual "new team member leads underdogs to contention" characters won't surprise, or particularly thrill, anyone. Goldberg's lively performance somewhat redeems standard script but reduces everyone around her, including an All-Star roster of NBA players, to window dressing. Basically the hoops version of "Little Big League." **100m/C VHS, DVD.** Whoopi Goldberg, Frank Langella, Dennis Farina, Richard Jenkins, Lisa Ann Walter, John Salley; *D:* Steve Rash; *W:* Jon Connolly, David Loucka, Eric Champnella, Keith Mitchell, Steve Zacharias, Jeff Buhai; *C:* Victor Kemper; *M:* Stanley Clarke.

Ed and His Dead Mother ⬥⬥ **1993 (PG-13)** Ed's just an average guy who happens to really love his mother. So much so that when she dies Ed tries to bring her back from the dead—and succeeds. Only death has made a few changes in Mom's personality. Now she's a bug-eating chainsaw-wielding fiend. Just what's a good son supposed to do? **93m/C VHS, DVD.** Ned Beatty, Steve Buscemi, Jonathan Wacks; *M:* Chuck Hughes.

Eddie and the Cruisers ⬥⬥ **1983 (PG)** In the early 1960s, rockers Eddie and the Cruisers score with one hit album. Then Eddie dies mysteriously in a car accident. Years later, a reporter decides to write a feature on the defunct group, prompting a search for missing tapes of the Cruisers' unreleased second album. Questions posed at the end of the movie are answered in the sequel. Enjoyable soundtrack by John Cafferty and the Beaver Brown Band. **90m/C VHS, DVD.** Tom Berenger, Michael Pare, Ellen Barkin, Joe Pantoliano, Matthew Laurence, Helen Schneider, David Wilson, Michael "Tunes" Antunes, Joe Cates, John Stockwell, Barry Sand, Vince Borge, Howard Johnson, Robin Karfo, Rufus Harley, Bruce Brown, Louis D'Esposito, Michael Toland, Bob Garrett, Joanne Collins; *D:* Martin Davidson; *W:* Martin Davidson, Arlene Davidson; *C:* Fred Murphy; *M:* John Cafferty.

Eddie and the Cruisers 2: Eddie Lives! ⬥1/2 **1989 (PG-13)** A sequel to the minor cult favorite, in which a rock star believed to be dead emerges and is now building a new name in Montreal to lead a new band. The Beaver Brown Band again provides the music. **106m/C VHS, CA** Michael Pare, Marina Orsini, Bernie Coulson, Anthony Sherwood; *Cameos:* Larry King, Bo Diddley, Martha Quinn, Merrill Shindler, Jean-Claude Lord; *W:* Charles Zev Cohen; *C:* Rene Verzier; *M:* Leor Aronovi.

Eddie Macon's Run ⬥⬥ **1983** Based on a true story, Eddie Macon plans an escape to run to Mexico. He is followed by a tough cop who is determined to catch the fugitive. Film debut of Goodman. **95m/C VHS.** Kirk Douglas, John Schneider, Lee Purcell, John Goodman, Leah Ayres; *D:* Jeff Kanew; *M:* Wendy Blackstone.

Eddie Presley ⬥⬥1/2 **1992** Eddie Presley is an Elvis impersonator at the lowest rung of the entertainment industry ladder. He's a true believer whose act is a heartfelt homage. He lives in his van and has a crappy security guard job, and has a gig at a seedy hotel, he has a meltdown on stage and gives a performance the audience will never forget. Well-crafted, bittersweet showbiz drama is packed fine performances. Based on writer/star Whitaker's play. **106m/C VHS.** Duane Whitaker, Stacey Keach, Roscoe Lee Browne, Theodore (Ted) Raimi, Joe Estevez, Tom Everett, Clu Gulager, Julie Lancaster, Francesca "Kitten" Natividad, Ian Ogilvy, Willard Pugh, Daniel Roebuck, Tim Thomerson, Patrick Thomas; *Cameos:* Quentin Tarantino, Bruce Campbell; *D:* Jeff Burr; *W:* Duane Whitaker; *C:* Thomas Callaway; *M:* Jim Manzie.

The Eddy Duchin Story ⬥⬥ **1956** Glossy tearjerker that profiles the tragic life of Eddy Duchin, the famous pianist/bandleader of the 30s and 40s. Features almost 30 songs, including classics by Cole Porter, George and Ira Gershwin, Hammerstein, Chopin, and several others. Victrola Shaw, James Whitmore, Rex Thompson; *D:* George Sidney; *M:* Samuel A. Taylor; *C:* Harry Stradling Sr.; *M:* George Duning.

Eden ⬥⬥ **1993** Eden is a luxury resort designed to cater to personal fantasies and filled with numerous intrigues. Part-owner Eve Sinclair faces a number of professional and personal complications, including the tragic death of her husband, a brother-in-law who's interested in more then business, and an old friend with uncertain motives. Lots of sex in beautiful settings. **107m/C VHS, DVD.** Barbara Alyn Woods, Jack Armstrong, Steve Chase, Darcy Demoss, Jeff

Griggs; **D:** Victor Lobl; **W:** Stephen Black, Henry Stern. **CABLE**

Eden 🦴🦴 **1998 (R)** Frustrated, Multiple Sclerosis-afflicted housewife Helen (Going) deals with the physical and emotional limitations of her life with dreams of astral projection. Husband Bill (Walsh) is a prep school teacher who doesn't want her to work even though she reaches one of his problem students (Flanery) more effectively than he can. First-time director Goldberg won a Sundance competition for his screenplay, but can't quite deliver on its promise. A tight budget and too many unanswered questions keep this one on the intriguing but ultimately disappointing level. **106m/C VHS, DVD.** Joanna Going, Dylan Walsh, Sean Patrick Flanery; **D:** Howard Goldberg; **W:** Howard Goldberg; **C:** Hubert Taczanowski; **M:** Brad Fiedel.

Eden 2 🦴🦴 **1993 (R)** The continuing saga of the luxury resort Eden. Owner Eve is still having erotic dreams of late husband Grant while fending off the very real advances of his brother Josh and becoming attracted to Paul, her late husband's best friend. The guests are equally caught up in erotic dilemmas involving sexual blackmail. **102m/C VHS.** Barbara Alyn Woods, Jack Armstrong, Steve Chase, Darcy Demoss, Jeff Griggs; **D:** Kristine Peterson; **W:** Stephen Black, Henry Stern. **CABLE**

Eden 3 🦴🦴 **1993 (R)** Yet another chapter in this sexy cable saga. Eve Sinclair risks losing her share of the tropical resort unless she remarries, which she doesn't want to do, although fitness trainer Randi would be delighted to pick up the option. Meanwhile, an heiress discovers her new bridegroom has murderous intentions. **?m/C VHS.** Barbara Alyn Woods, Jack Armstrong, Steve Chase, Darcy Demoss, Jeff Griggs, Dean Scofield; **D:** Victor Lobl. **CABLE**

Eden 4 🦴🦴 **1993 (R)** Further adventures in the cable series. Eve, Eden's co-owner, must cope with both Josh's jealous rage and Randi's continuing scheming as she tries to keep her guests happy at the posh resort. One of the guests, a beautiful author, gets too caught up in her sexual fantasies and may find herself in danger. **?m/C VHS.** Barbara Alyn Woods, Jack Armstrong, Steve Chase, Darcy Demoss, Jeff Griggs, Dean Scofield; **D:** Kristine Peterson.

Eden Valley 🦴🦴🦴 **1994** A low-key intensity marks this northeast England drama that's produced, written, and directed by an eight-member film cooperative. Troubled Newcastle teenager Billy (Bell) is put on probation for drug and theft charges and in a last-ditch chance at turning his life around gets to live with his estranged father, Hoggy (Hogg). They haven't seen each other in 10 years and Hoggy lives on a farm in County Durham where he raises and trains horses for harness racing. Naturally, their relationship is strained and there aren't any easy solutions (kinda like in real life). **95m/C VHS.** *GB* Darren Bell, Brian Hogg, Mike Elliott, Jimmy Killeen; **D:** Amber Production Team; **W:** Amber Production Team; **M:** Amber Production Team.

The Edge 🦴🦴½ *Bookworm* **1997 (R)** Wealthy Charles Morse (Hopkins) isn't too pleased that fashion photog Bob Greene (Baldwin) takes such an interest in his lovely fashion model wife (Macpherson) and feels the two are out to kill him. Despite his conspiracy theory, Morse and Greene end up depending on each other for survival when their plane crashes in the Alaskan wilderness. To compound their problems, they must do battle with a stalking killer bear. Mamet screenplay dices things up a bit with cutting dialogue which leads to the mind games Mamet is so famous for. Hopkins and Baldwin give understated, intact performances, with an intensity shared only by Bart the Bear, in this small contemporary parable on the meaning of life. The splendid Alaskan scenery is actually breathtaking aerial and ground footage in Canada. **120m/C VHS, DVD.** Anthony Hopkins, Alec Baldwin, Elle Macpherson, Harold Perrineau Jr., L.Q. Jones; **D:** Lee Tamahori; **W:** David Mamet; **C:** Donald McAlpine; **M:** Jerry Goldsmith.

Edge of Darkness 🦴🦴🦴½ **1943** Compelling war-drama about the underground movement in Norway during Nazi takeover of WWII. Flynn plays a Norwegian fisherman who leads the local underground movement and Sheridan is his loyal fiancee. Although several problems occurred throughout filming, this picture earned high marks for its superb performances and excellent camera work. Based on the novel by William Woods. **120m/B VHS.** Errol Flynn, Ann Sheridan, Walter Huston, Nancy Coleman, Helmut Dantine, Judith Anderson, Ruth Gordon, John Beal; **D:** Lewis Milestone; **W:** Robert Rossen.

Edge of Darkness 🦴🦴 **1986** Miniseries mystery involves a police detective who investigates his daughter's murder and uncovers a web of espionage and intrigue. **307m/C VHS.** *GB* Bob Peck, Joe Don Baker, Jack Woodson, John Woodvine, Joanne Whalley; **D:** Martin Campbell; **M:** Eric Clapton, Michael Kamen. **TV**

Edge of Honor 🦴½ **1991 (R)** Young Eagle Scouts camping in the Pacific Northwest stumble across a woodland weapons cache and wage guerilla war against killer lumberjacks out to silence them. A boneheaded, politically correct action bloodbath; you don't have to like the logging industry to disapprove of the broad slurs against its men shown here. **92m/C VHS, DVD.** Corey Feldman, Meredith Salenger, Scott Reeves, Ken Jenkins, Christopher Neame, Don Swayze; **D:** Michael Spence; **W:** David O'Malley.

Edge of Madness 🦴🦴½ *A Wilderness Station* **2002 (R)** In 1850, naive Annie (Dhavernas) agrees to an arranged marriage with Manitoba homesteader Simon (Fehr). But although Annie befriends Simon's younger brother George (Sevier), her husband turns out to be angry and abusive. So she kills him after he attacks her. At least that's what she tells requisite Mullen (Johansson) when the half-frozen and terrified Annie stumbles into town from her wilderness home. But when Mullen investigates, he finds only more questions. **99m/C VHS, DVD.** *CA* Caroline Dhavernas, Brendan Fehr, Paul Johansson, Corey Sevier, Tantoo Cardinal, Peter Wingfield, Currie Graham, Jonas Chernick; **D:** Anne Wheeler; **W:** Anne Wheeler, Charles Kristian Pitts.

Edge of Sanity 🦴½ **1989 (R)** An overdone Jekyll-Hyde reprise, with cocaine serving as the villainous substance. Dr. Jekyll (Perkins) is working in his lab, testing cocaine for use as an anaesthetic, when a lab monkey knocks a liquid into the coke and the fumes cause the doc to turn into Jack Hyde, a prototype for Jack the Ripper. Perkins knows the schizoid territory and the production values are good but this is not for the easily queazy. Available in a 90' minute, unrated version. **85m/C VHS, DVD.** *GB* Anthony Perkins, Glynis Barber, David Lodge, Sarah Maur-Thorp, Ben Cole, Lisa Davis, Jill Melford; **D:** Gerard Kikoine; **W:** J.P. Felix, Ron Raley; **C:** Tony Spratling; **M:** Frederic Talgorn.

Edge of Seventeen 🦴🦴½ **1999** Perceptive gay coming of age tale set in 1984 Ohio. Naive 16-year-old Eric (Stafford) is eager to explore his burgeoning sexuality with the help of college man, Rod (Gabrych). Unfortunately for Eric, Rod's the love 'em and leave 'em type. Disillusioned, Eric tries to remake himself in Brit-pop, New Wave fashion (think Boy George and Duran Duran), while turning to best friend Maggie (Holmes), without realizing the depths of her feelings for him. Eric's coming out tellingly provides confusion not just for himself but for everyone around him. **100m/C VHS, DVD.** Chris Stafford, Tina Holmes, Andersen Gabrych, Stephanie McVay, Lea DeLaria, John Eby; **D:** David Moreton; **W:** Todd Stephens; **C:** Gina DeGirolamo; **M:** Tom Bailey.

Edge of the Axe **1989** A small town held in the grip of terror by a demented slasher. **91m/C VHS.** Barton Faulks, Christina Marie Lane, Page Moseley, Fred Hollyday; **D:** Joseph (Jose Ramon Larraz) Braunstein.

Edge of the World 🦴🦴🦴 **1937** Moody, stark British drama of a mini-society in its death throes, expertly photographed on a six-square-mile island in the Shetlands. A dwindling fishing community of fewer than 100 souls agonize over whether to migrate to the mainland; meanwhile the romance of a local girl with an off-islander takes a tragic course. Choral effects were provided by the Glasgow Orpheus Choir. **80m/B VHS, DVD.** *GB* Finlay Currie, Niall MacGinnis, Grant Sutherland, John Laurie, Michael Powell; **D:** Michael Powell; **W:** Michael Powell.

Edie & Pen 🦴🦴½ **1995 (PG-13)** Tilly seems to be making a career of playing the ditz who's smarter than she seems as she shows here as Edie, who meets Pen (Channing) in Reno where she seems looking for quickie divorces. They hit a bar to celebrate and hook up with soft-hearted Harry (Glenn), who's been dumped by his wife. Some drunken life discussions follow and then Edie finds out that her fiance is Pen's cold-hearted, newly ex hubby (Wilson). Slight script, charming performances. **97m/C VHS, DVD.** Jennifer Tilly, Stockard Channing, Scott Glenn, Stuart Wilson; *Cameos:* Beverly D'Angelo, Louise Fletcher, Joanna Gleason, Michael McKean, Martin Mull, Michael O'Keefe, Chris Sarandon, Randy Travis, Jean Smart, Victoria Tennant; **D:** Matthew Irmas; **W:** Victoria Tennant; **C:** Alicia Weber; **M:** Shawn Colvin.

Edie in Ciao! Manhattan 🦴🦴 *Ciao! Manhattan* **1972 (R)** Real-life story of Edie Sedgwick, Warhol superstar and international fashion model, whose life in the fast lane led to ruin. **84m/C VHS, DVD.** Edie Sedgwick, Baby Jane Holzer, Roger Vadim, Paul America, Viva, Isabel Jewell, Pat Hartley; **D:** David Weisman, John Palmer; **W:** David Weisman, John Palmer; **C:** John Palmer, Kjell Rostand; **M:** Gino Piserchio.

Edison Force *Edison* **2005 (R)** Pollack (Timberlake) is a junior reporter at a lowly community paper in suburban Edison when he stumbles across information on a police unit whose results at cleaning up crime (at any cost) have left them above the law they purportedly serve. When Pollack asks too many questions, bad things happen. Self-important and heavy-handed. **97m/C DVD.** Morgan Freeman, Kevin Spacey, Justin Timberlake, LL Cool J, Dylan McDermott, Cary Elwes, Piper Perabo, Roselyn Sanchez; **D:** David J. Burke; **W:** David J. Burke; **C:** Francis Kenny. **VIDEO**

Edison, the Man 🦴🦴½ **1940** Story of Tommy Edison's early years of experimentation in the basement. The young genious eventually invents light bulbs, motion pictures, and a sound recording device. Well played by Tracy. **108m/C VHS.** Spencer Tracy, Rita Johnson, Lynne Overman, Charles Coburn, Gene Lockhart, Henry Travers, Felix Bressart; **D:** Clarence Brown.

Edith & Marcel 🦴½ **1983** A fictionalization of the love affair between chanteuse Edith Piaf and boxer Marcel Cerdan (played by his son, Marcel Cerdan Jr.). French with English subtitles. **104m/C VHS.** *FR* Evelyne Bouix, Marcel Cerdan Jr., Charles Aznavour, Jacques Villeret; **D:** Claude Lelouch.

Ed's Next Move 🦴🦴½ **1996 (R)** Genial indie NYC comedy with a Woody Allen feel is littered with whimsical one-liners. Title character Ed (Ross) moves from small-town Wisconsin to New York after a break-up with his girlfriend. Being that he's a rice geneticist, it's not a big leap to conclude that Ed's a bit uptight, so it's imperative that Ed's big city roommate, the suave Ray (Carroll), hip him up to better meet the ladies. Soon, Ed falls for boho Lee (Thorne) leader of a band called "Ed's Redeeming Qualities." Fun fantasy sequence involving Ed, his old girlfriend and two translators is a highlight. Low-budget-er, with a first time writer/director (Walsh), and it shows, but in a good-natured way. Though more could be asked visually, picture does boast good performers and well-drawn characters. **88m/C VHS.** Matt Ross, Callie (Calliope) Thorne, Kevin Carroll, Ramsey Faragallah, Nina Shevalea, James (Jimmy) Cummings; **D:** John Walsh; **W:** John Walsh; **C:** Peter Nelson.

EDtv 🦴🦴½ **1999 (PG-13)** Ed (McConaughey) is a scruffy redneck video clerk who agrees to have his life broadcast 24/7 for a reality show produced by DeGeneres. Of course the show becomes a hit, and an entire nation watches breathlessly as Ed steals his brother's girlfriend Shari (Elfman), restocks shelves, and goes to the bathroom with the door open. His family life immediately turns melodramatic, with Ed learning "shocking secrets" about his mom (Kirkland), dad (Landau), and brother (Harrelson). Compared to the back-to-back release in theatres, but director (and TV child star survivor) Ron Howard's version lacks the biting satire. **122m/C VHS, DVD.** Ellen DeGeneres, Sally Kirkland, Martin Landau, Elizabeth Hurley, Rob Reiner, Dennis Hopper, Adam Goldberg, Viveka Davis, Clint Howard, Larry "Flash" Jenkins, Denny Most, Rick Overton, Rupaul Charles, Geddie Watanabe, Harry Shearer, Jennifer Elise Cox, Matthew McConaughey, Jenna Elfman, Woody Harrelson; **D:** Ron Howard; **W:** Lowell Ganz, Babaloo Mandel; **C:** John Schwartzman; **M:** Randy Edelman.

Educating Rita 🦴🦴🦴 **1983 (PG)** Walters and Caine team beautifully in this adaptation of the successful Willy Russell play which finds Rita, an uneducated hairdresser, determined to improve her knowledge of literature. In so doing, she enlists the aid of tutor Frank; a disillusioned alcoholic, adeptly played by Caine. Together, the two find inspiration in one another's differences and experiences. Ultimately, the teacher receives a lesson in how to again appreciate his work and the classics as he observes his pupil's unique approach to her studies. Some deem this a "Pygmalion" for the '80s. **110m/C VHS, DVD.** *GB* Michael Caine, Julie Walters, Michael Williams, Maureen Lipman; **D:** Lewis Gilbert; **W:** Willy Russell; Film; British Acad. '83: Actor (Caine), Actress (Walters); Golden Globes '84: Actor—Mus./Comedy (Caine), Actress—Mus./Comedy (Walters).

The Education of Little Tree 🦴🦴🦴 **1997 (PG)** Child's eye view of a large scale epic on par with modern classics like "The Secret Garden." In 1935, poor, orphaned, and part Native American Little Tree (Ashton) is sent to live with his grandfather (Cromwell) and Native American grandmother (Cardinal) in the Smokey Mountains of Tennessee. There he learns "The Way" of his Cherokee ancestors and how to make moonshine from his Scottish/Irish grandfather. A nosy, Bible-thumping Aunt tips off authorities and soon Little Tree is shipped off to an evil state institution to cure him of his inappropriate Indian ways. There, the old-fashioned discipline runs fierce and abusive. Adapted from a children's book by Forrest Carter. Cardinal and Cromwell carve out memorable performances alongside first-rate newcomer Joseph Ashton. **112m/C VHS, DVD.** James Cromwell, Tantoo Cardinal, Joseph Ashton, Graham Greene, Lisa Bronwyn Moore; **D:** Richard Friedenberg; **W:** Richard Friedenberg; **C:** Anastas Michos; **M:** Mark Isham.

The Education of Sonny Carson 🦴🦴 **1974 (R)** Chilling look at the tribulations of a black youth living in a Brooklyn ghetto amid drugs, prostitution, crime, and other forms of vice. Based on Sonny Carson's autobiography. Still pertinent some 20 years after its theatrical release. **104m/C VHS, DVD.** Rony Clanton, Don Gordon, Paul Benjamin; **D:** Michael Campus.

The Edukators 🦴🦴 *Die Fetten Jahre sind vorbei* **2004 (R)** In Berlin, three twenty-something political idealists, dogmatic and naïve, commit various property pranks on the bourgeoisie. Roomies Jan (Bruehl) and Peter (Erceg) and Peter's girlfriend Julie (Jentsche) (who likes Jan, too) happily vandalize until ineptly graduating to kidnapping when businessman Hardenberg (Klaussner) comes home early and interrupts them. Clueless, the trio decide to hide out with their captive (who turns out to be a former 60s radical) at a mountain cabin. Much generational talk and romantic tension ensues. German with subtitles. **126m/C DVD.** *GE AT* Daniel Bruhl, Julia Jentsch, Stipe Erceg, Burghart Klaussner; **D:** Hans Weingartner; **W:** Hans Weingartner, Katharina

Edvard Munch 🐾🐾 1974 Biographical portrait of the Norwegian Expressionist painter and his tormented life in the stuffy society of 19th-century Oslo. Concentrates mainly on his early years, including the deaths of his mother and younger sister, his brother's suicide, and his struggle to maintain his sanity. Based on Munch's memoirs. In German and Norwegian with English subtitles. 167m/C VHS, DVD, NC **Geir** Westby, Gro Fraas, Eli Ryg; **D:** Peter Watkins; **W:** Peter Watkins; **C:** Odd Geir Saether.

Edward and Mrs. Simpson 🐾🐾 1980 Dramatic reconstruction of the years leading to the abdication of King Edward VIII, who forfeited the British throne in 1936 so that he could marry American divorcee Wallis Simpson. Originally aired on PBS. 270m/C VHS, DVD, Edward Fox, Cynthia Harris; **D:** Waris Hussein. **TV**

Edward Scissorhands 🐾🐾🐾 1990 (PG-13) Depp's a young man created by loony scientist Price, who dies before he can attach hands to his boy-creature. Then the boy is rescued from his lonely existence outside of suburbia by an ingratiating Avon lady. With scissors in place of hands, he has more trouble fitting into suburbia than would most new kids on the block, and the struggles with being different and lonely in a cardboard-cutout world. Visually captivating fairy tale full of splash and color, however predictable the Hollywood-ereital denouement. 100m/C VHS, DVD, Blu-ray Disc Johnny Depp, Winona Ryder, Dianne Wiest, Vincent Price, Anthony Michael Hall, Alan Arkin, Kathy Baker, Conchata Ferrell, Caroline Aaron, Dick Anthony Williams, Robert Oliveri, John Davidson; **D:** Tim Burton; **W:** Tim Burton, Caroline Thompson; **C:** Stefan Czapsky; **M:** Danny Elfman.

Edward II 🐾🐾½ 1992 (R) Jarman's controversial adaptation of Christopher Marlowe's play "The Troublesome Reign of Edward II" portrays the weak-willed monarch as neglecting his kingdom for love. Unfortunately, it's not for his queen but for his commoner male lover. His neglect of his queen and country lead to a swift and brutal downfall. Jarman's use of contemporary anachronisms, stream of consciousness approach, and heavy symbolism may leave more than one viewer wondering what's going on. 91m/C VHS, DVD, GB Steven Waddington, Kevin Collins, Andrew Tiernan, John Lynch, Dudley Sutton, Tilda Swinton, Jerome Flynn, Jody Graber, Nigel Terry, Annie Lennox; **D:** Derek Jarman; **W:** Derek Jarman.

Edward the King 🐾🐾 1975 British miniseries follows the long life of Prince Edward, who waited some 50 years for his overbearing mother, Queen Victoria, to die so he could ascend the throne. Bertie scandalized with his affairs and carousing but, nevertheless, proved his worth as king-in-waiting. On six cassettes. 708m/C VHS, DVD, GB Timothy West, Annette Crosbie, John Gielgud, Francesca Annis, Robert Hardy; **D:** John Gorrie; **C:** Tony Imi. **TV**

Edwin 🐾🐾½ 1984 Sir Fennimore Truscott (Guinness) is a retired High Court Judge who suspects that his neighbor once had an affair with Truscott's wife. These long-fermenting fears assert themself as Truscott presents his case (to the audience) and even suspects the paternity of his son, Edwin. When Edwin comes for a visit, Truscott's obsessions are forced into the open. 78m/C VHS, DVD, GB Alec Guinness, Paul Rogers, Renée Asherson; **D:** Rodney Bennett; **W:** John Mortimer. **TV**

Eegah! 🐾 1962 Another Arch Hall-directed (under the Nicholas Merriwether pseud.) epic in which an anachronistic Neanderthal falls in love in '60s California. Reputed to be one of the worst films of all time. 93m/C VHS, DVD. Marilyn Manning, Richard Eiel, Arch Hall Jr., William Watters, Carolyn Brandt, William Lloyd, Ray Dennis Steckler; **D:** Arch (archie) Hall Sr.; **W:** John Ottman.

The Eel 🐾🐾🐾 Unagi 1996 Yamashita (Yakusho) has just been paroled after spending eight years in prison for killing his adulterous wife in a jealous rage. While there, he found and cared for an eel, which became his only confidante, and which accompanies him to his new life as a barber in a small town outside Tokyo. The newcomer is soon befriended by the locals but Yamashita's life changes most when he saves the suicidal Keiko (Shimizu) from drowning. She comes to work in his shop and would obviously like a more intimate relationship but some secrets in her past and some strange incidents in the town may jeopardize Yamashita's hopes for a normal life. Based on the novel "Glimmering in the Dark" by Akira Yoshimura. Japanese with subtitles. 117m/C VHS, DVD, Koji Yakusho, Misa Shimizu, Mitsuko Baisho, Fujio Tsuneta, Akira (Tsukamoto) Emoto, Etsuko Ichihara, Tomoroh Taguchi, Ken Kobayashi, Sabu Kawahara; **D:** Shohei Imamura; **W:** Shohei Imamura, Motofumi Tomikawa, Daisuke Tengan; **C:** Shigeru Komatsubara; **M:** Shinichiro Ikebe. Cannes '97. **Film**

The Effect of Gamma Rays on Man-in-the-Moon Marigolds 🐾🐾🐾 1973 (PG) A wonderful drama based on the Pulitzer Prize winning play by Paul Zindel. The story centers around eccentric young Matilda and her depressed family. Matilda is preparing for a science fair experiment to beat her competition. Her exhibit shows how radiation affects the growth of marigolds, but sometimes causes them to grow in mutations. This mirrors Matilda, who flowers even amidst the dullness of her sister. 100m/C VHS, Joanne Woodward, Nell Potts, Roberta Wallach, Judith Lowry, Richard Venture; **D:** Paul Newman; **W:** Alvin Sargent. Cannes '73. Actress (Woodward).

The Efficiency Expert 🐾🐾½ Spotswood 1992 (PG) Lighthearted Australian comedy about a dingy moccasin factory where a rigid efficiency consultant is invited to save the eccentric family-run company from bankruptcy. Predictable ending contains a nevertheless timely message about the importance of the bottom line. 97m/C VHS, DVD, AU Anthony Hopkins, Ben Mendelsohn, Alwyn Kurts, Bruno Lawrence, Angela Punch McGregor, Russell Crowe, Rebecca Rigg, Toni Collette; **D:** Mark Joffe; **W:** Andrew Knight, Max Dann; **M:** Ricky Fataar.

Effi Briest 🐾🐾½ Fontane Effi Briest 1974 A 19th-century tragedy well-played by Schygulla and empowered with Fassbinder's directorial skills. Effi (Schygulla) is a 17-year-old beauty, unhappily married to a much older man. She drifts into a brief affair, which is not discovered for several years. When her husband does discover her past infidelity, the Prussian legal code permits him a chilling revenge. Based on a popular 19th-century novel by Theodor Fontane. In German with English subtitles. 135m/B VHS, DVD, GE Hanna Schygulla, Wolfgang Schenck, Lilo Pempeit, Ulli Lommel, Ursula Stratz; **D:** Rainer Werner Fassbinder; **W:** Rainer Werner Fassbinder; **C:** Jürgen Jürges, Dietrich Lohmann.

Egg 🐾🐾½ 1988 Striking film from Holland chronicles the true-life adventures of a die-aged baker who answers a personal ad from a schoolteacher. After much correspondence, the teacher visits the baker in his village, and the townspeople take great interest in what happens next. In Dutch with English subtitles. 58m/C VHS, NL Johan Leysen, Marijke Vengelers; **D:** Danniel Danniel; **W:** Daniel Danniel.

Egg and I 🐾🐾½ 1947 Based on the best-selling humorist Betty MacDonald. A young urban bride agrees to help her new husband realize his life-long dream of owning a chicken farm. A dilapidated house, temperamental stove, and suicidal chickens test the bride's perseverance, as do the zany antics of her country-bumpkin neighbors, Ma and Pa Kettle, who make their screen debut. Plenty of old-fashioned laughs. 104m/B VHS, DVD. Claudette Colbert, Fred MacMurray, Marjorie Main, Percy Kilbride, Louise Allbritton, Richard Long, Billy House, Donald MacBride; **D:** Chester Erskine; **C:** Milton Krasner.

Eight Below 🐾🐾 2006 (PG) Disney goes to the dogs with appropriately tail-wagging results. Jerry (Walker), a guide at the U.S. National Science Research Base in Antarctica, is deeply devoted to his eight beautiful sled dogs. Ambitious scientist McClaren (Greenwood) gets them involved in a risky mission that results in evacuation for the humans—but not the dogs—due to early winter storms. While the dogs scavenge to survive, Jerry tries to organize a rescue trip to save his best friends. Shot in Canada, Norway, and Greenland. 120m/C DVD, Blu-ray Disc. Paul Walker, Bruce Greenwood, Jason Biggs, Gerard Plunkett, Connor Christopher Levins, August Schellenberg, Wendy Crewson, Moon Bloodgood.

The Egyptian 🐾🐾½ 1954 Based on the sword-and-sandal novel by Mika Waltari, this is a ponderous big-budget epic about a young Egyptian in Akhnaton's epoch who becomes physician to Pharaoh. 140m/C VHS, Angela (Clark) Clarke, Edmund Purdom, Victor Mature, Peter Ustinov, Bella Darvi, Gene Tierney, Henry Daniell, Jean Simmons, Michael Wilding, Judith Evelyn, John Carradine, Carl Benton Reid; **D:** Michael Curtiz; **W:** Philip Dunne, Casey Robinson; **C:** Leon Shamroy.

An Egyptian Story 🐾🐾 1975 Hadduta Misriya 1982 An Egyptian film director (Dine) goes to London for open-heart surgery and as he hovers between life and death, he remembers his past. Scenes from Chahine's other films highlight the director's reminiscences. Part 2 of the autobiographical trilogy, preceded by "Alexandria...Why?" and followed by "Alexandria Again and Forever." Arabic with subtitles. 127m/C VHS, DVD, EG Mohei Dine, Nour (el-Sherif) el-Cherif, Oussama Nadir, Magda El Khatib; **D:** Youssef Chahine; **W:** Youssef Chahine; **C:** Mohsen Nasr; **M:** Gamal Salama.

The Eiger Sanction 🐾🐾 1975 (R) An art teacher returns to the CIA (a fictionalized version of the CIA) as an exterminator hired to assassinate the killers of an American agent. In the process, he finds himself climbing the Eiger. Beautiful Swiss Alps scenery fails to totally compensate for several dreary lapses. Based on the novel by Trevanian. 125m/C VHS, DVD, Clint Eastwood, George Kennedy, Vonetta McGee, Jack Cassidy, Thayer David; **D:** Clint Eastwood; **W:** Hal Dresner, Warren B. Murphy, Rod Whitaker; **C:** Frank Stanley; **M:** John Williams.

8-A 🐾🐾 Ochoa 1992 Reconstructs the 1989 trial and execution of Cuban general Arnaldo Ochoa Sanchez, a hero of the revolution who, along with other government officials, advocated the resignation of Fidel Castro as the solution to the country's economic and political crises. At the trial Ochoa and four other officials were convicted of illegal drug trafficking and shot by a firing squad. Spanish with subtitles. 84m/C VHS, CU **D:** Orlando Jiminez-Leal; **W:** Orlando Jiminez-Leal; **C:** Emilio Guede Jr.

8 1/2 🐾🐾🐾🐾 Otto E Mezzo; Federico Fellini's 8 1/2 1963 The acclaimed Fellini self-portrait of a revered Italian film director struggling with a fated film project wanders through his intermixed life, childhood memories, and hallucinatory fantasies. Subtitled in English. 135m/B VHS, DVD, IT Marcello Mastroianni, Claudia Cardinale, Anouk Aimee, Sandra Milo, Barbara Steele, Rossella Falk, Eddra Gale Mark Herron, Madeleine LeBeau, Caterina Boratto; **D:** Federico Fellini; **W:** Tullio Pinelli, Ennio Flaiano, Brunello Rondi, Federico Fellini; **C:** Gianni Di Venanzo; **M:** Nino Rota. Oscars '63: Costume Des. (B&W), Foreign Film; N.Y. Film Critics '63: Foreign Film.

8 1/2 Women 🐾🐾½ 1999 (R) A typically baffling presentation from Greenaway concerns wealthy Swiss businessman Philip Emmenthal (Standing), who is grief-stricken over the recent death of his wife. His son, Storey (Delamere), comes to Geneva to console his father. After seeing Fellini's "8 1/2," they suddenly decide to assemble their own harem of decidedly offbeat females and pursue sexual fantasies. Remarkably unappealing and dull. 122m/C VHS, DVD, GB John Standing, Vivian Wu, Annie Shizuka Inoh, Matthew Delamere, Toni Collette, Amanda Plummer, Manna Fujiwara, Barbara Sarafian, Polly Walker, Karina Mano, Natacha Amal; **D:** Peter Greenaway; **W:** Peter Greenaway; **C:** Sacha Vierny.

8 Heads in a Duffel Bag 🐾🐾 1996 (R) Mob bag man Tommy (Pesci) in a real stretch) loses his heads, the evidence of a successful hit, to med student Charlie Pritchet (Comeau), who's headed for an uneven directorial debut does little to mask the problem. Newcomer Comeau thinks for a "Bachelor Party" era Tom Hanks thing, but doesn't quite get there. Pesci and Spade save flick from disaster, and get most of the good lines, pitted in a generational "battle of the smart-asses," but neither one strays from their previous personas. Locuso hilariously mekes the most of his role as the naive screen roommate. 95m/C VHS, DVD, Joe Pesci, David Spade, Andy Comeau, Kristy Swanson, George Hamilton, Dyan Cannon, Todd Louiso, Frank Robinson, Anthony Mangano, Joe Basile, Ernestine Mercer, Howard George; **D:** Tom Schulman; **W:** Tom Schulman; **C:** Adam Holender; **M:** Andrew Gross.

Eight Days a Week 🐾🐾½ 1997 (R) Shy, nerdy high-schooler Peter (Schaefer) is obsessed with Erica (Russell), the popular babe who lives across the street. Peter decides a sit-in on her front lawn and constant protestations about his devotion is the way to get her attention. Title comes from the Beatles tune that is the cleverest thing in the movie. 92m/C VHS, Joshua Schaefer, Keri Russell, R.D. Robb, Mark L. Taylor, Catherine Hicks; **D:** Michael Davis; **W:** Michael Davis; **C:** James Lawrence Spencer; **M:** Kevin Bassinson.

800 Bullets 🐾🐾½ 800 Balas 2002 Director Iglesia pays tribute to the films of Sergio Leone in this Spanish dramatic comedy. Fourteen-year-old Carlos (Castro) runs away from his uptight widowed mother, Laura (Maura), in search of his paternal grandfather. He finds his grandfather Julian (Gracia) living in Almeria, a region in the south of Spain that doubled for the American West in countless spaghetti westerns. Julian, a former stuntman, is now an alcoholic employee of a theme park cobbled together from the abandoned sets of old cowboy movies. Julian and his fellow stuntmen welcome Carlos into their band of Lost Boys, that is, until Laura shows up, threatening to close the party down. glesia has great fun orchestrating complex comedic set pieces, but has trouble balancing the dramatic tone in the last act. 125m/C DVD, Sancho Gracia, Carmen Maura, Eusebio Poncela, Terele Pavez, Angel de Andres Lopez, Luis Castro; **D:** Alex de la Iglesia; **C:** Flavio Martinez Labiano; **M:** Roque Banos.

800 Leagues Down the Amazon 🐾½ 1993 (PG-13) A 19th-century journey down the Amazon on a raft with a planter, his daughter, and various complications. Based on a novel by Jules Verne. 100m/C VHS, DVD, Daphne Zuniga, Barry Bostwick, Adam Baldwin, Tom Verica, E.E. Bell; **D:** Luis Llosa; **W:** Lanca Schiff, Jackson Barr; **C:** Pili Flores-Guerra; **M:** Jorge Tafur.

Eight Legged Freaks 🐾🐾½ 2002 (PG-13) Attack of the B-Movie Redos! Boy (Arquette) meets girl (Wuhrer) and battle giant mutant spiders in this updated 1950s sci-fi horror/comedy. Prosperity, Arizona is the unlikely site of a toxic waste mishap near a spider farm, spawning SUV-sized creepy crawlies. Slow-witted but sweet local boy Arquette joins forces with foxy sheriff Wuhrer and a posse of locals to rid the town of the huge spidies. Scary, campy, self-parodying fun. Director Elkayem gives props to the '50s horror cult classic "Them!" which plays in the background of one scene. 99m/C VHS, DVD. US David Arquette, Kari Wuhrer, Scott Terra, Scarlett Johansson, Doug E. Doug, Riley Smith, Leon Rippy; **D:** Ellory Elkayem; **W:** Jesse Alexander, Ellory Elkayem; **C:** John Bartley; **M:** John Ottman.

Eight Men Out 🗡🗡🗡 1988 (PG) Taken from Eliot Asinof's book, a moving, full-blooded drama about the infamous 1919 "Black Sox" scandal, in which members of the Chicago White Sox teamed to throw the World Series for $80,000. A dirge of lost innocence, this is among Sayles' best films. Provides an interesting look at the "conspiracy" that ended "Shoeless" Joe Jackson's major-league career. The actual baseball scenes are first-rate, and Straithairn, Sweeney, and Cusack give exceptional performances. Sayles makes an appearance as Ring Lardner. Enjoyable viewing for even the non-sports fan. 121m/C VHS, DVD. John Cusack, D.B. Sweeney, Perry Lang, Jace Alexander, Bill Irwin, Clifton James, Michael Rooker, Michael Lerner, Christopher Lloyd, Studs Terkel, David Strathairn, Charlie Sheen, Kevin Tighe, John Mahoney, John Sayles, Gordon Clapp, Richard Edson, James Read, Don Harvey, John Anderson, Maggie Renzi, Michael Mantell, Nancy Travis, Michael Laskin, Barbara Garrick, Wendy Makkena; **D:** John Sayles; **W:** John Sayles; **C:** Robert Richardson; **M:** Bill Conti.

8 Mile 🗡🗡🗡 2002 (R) Although claiming to be fiction, director Hanson's thinly veiled bio of star Eminem's escape from the streets of Detroit will please more than the rapper's fans. Rabbit (Eminem) is a joyless autoworker living in the trailer park with his loose mother (Basinger) and little sister Lily (Greenfield). The only time that Rabbit has a chance to shine is at the rap battles organized by pal Future (Phifer), who sees talent in his friend. Also recognizing greatness (and a possible ticket out of the 'hood) is aspiring model Alex (Murphy), who quickly consummates a calculating relationship with Rabbit. The climactic rap battle allows Eminem to showcase the talent that made this "Rocky"-esque vehicle possible, although it wisely ends with Rabbit on the cusp of success and not at the pinnacle. Shot on location in Detroit. 118m/C VHS, DVD, UMD. US Eminem, Kim Basinger, Brittany Murphy, Mekhi Phifer, Evan Jones, Eugene Byrd, Omar Benson Miller, De'Angelo Wilson, Taryn Manning, Michael Shannon, Anthony Mackie, Chloe Greenfield, Paul Bates, Craig Chandler; **D:** Curtis Hanson; **W:** Scott Silver; **C:** Rodrigo Prieto; **M:** Eminem. Oscars '02: Song ("Lose Yourself").

8mm 🗡🗡½ 1998 (R) Surveillance expert Tom Welles (Cage) leads a normal family life until he's hired by widow Mrs. Christian (Carter). She wants him to find out the identity of a young girl apparently slashed to death in a porno film found in her late husband's safe. He descends into the underbelly of the pornography industry, guided by sleazeballs with names like Max California (Phoenix) and Dino Velvet (Stormare), and is both disgusted and fascinated by what he sees and learns. After he ferrets out the villain, he is forced into a showdown in order to save his family. Scripted by "Seven" writer Andrew Kevin Walker, but lacks some of the psychological punch of his previous effort. 123m/C VHS, DVD. Nicolas Cage, Joaquin Rafael (Leaf) Phoenix, James Gandolfini, Peter Stormare, Anthony Heald, Catherine Keener, Chris Bauer, Myra Carter, Amy Morton; **D:** Joel Schumacher; **W:** Andrew Kevin Walker; **C:** Robert Elswit; **M:** Mychael Danna.

8 Million Ways to Die 🗡🗡 1985 (R) An ex-cop hires himself out to rescue a pimp-bound hooker, and gets kneedeep in a mess of million-dollar drug deals, murder, and prostitution. Slow-moving but satisfying. Based on the book by Lawrence Block. 115m/C VHS. Jeff Bridges, Rosanna Arquette, Andy Garcia, Alexandra Paul; **D:** Hal Ashby; **W:** Oliver Stone; **C:** Stephen Burum; **M:** James Newton Howard.

Eight on the Lam 🗡 1967 (PG) Unfunny comedy features widower Henry Dimsdale (Hope) taking off with his kids and family maid Golda (Diller) when he's accused of embezzling bank funds. Jasper Lynch (Winters) is on their trail until Henry can prove who the real culprit is. 103m/C VHS. Bob Hope, Phyllis Diller, Jonathan Winters, Jill St. John, Shirley Eaton; **D:** George Marshall; **W:** Albert Lewin, Arthur Marx, Bob Fisher, Burt Styler; **C:** Alan Stensvold; **M:** George Romanis.

8 Seconds 🗡🗡½ 1994 (PG-13) *The Lane Frost Story* Love, not sports, dominates the true-life story of rodeo star Lane Frost (Perry), a world champion bull rider killed in the ring at the age of 25 in 1990. A decent start, he gains quick success on the rodeo circuit, marries (to Geary), and finds his career getting in the way of their happiness. Bull-riding sequences are genuinely stomach churning, the performances low-key. Title refers to the amount of time a rider must stay aboard his animal. 104m/C VHS, DVD. Luke Perry, Cynthia Geary, Stephen Baldwin, James Rebhorn, Carrie Snodgress, Red Mitchell, Ronnie Clair Edwards; **D:** John G. Avildsen; **W:** Monte Merrick; **C:** Victor Hammer; **M:** Bill Conti.

Eight Witnesses 🗡🗡 1954 Suspense thriller about a man being murdered in front of eight blind witnesses. 67m/B VHS, DVD. *GB* Peggy Ann Garner, Dennis Price; **D:** Lawrence Huntington; **W:** Halsted Welles.

8 Women 🗡🗡🗡 8 femmes 2002 (R) Wacky musical murder mystery starring eight of France's top actresses. Grand dame Gaby (Deneuve) and her daughters, Suzon (Ledoyen) and Catherine (Sagnier), share a remote estate with her husband Marcel (Lamure), her mother Mamy (Darrieux), spinster sister Augustine (Huppert), loyal housemaid Mme. Chanel (Richard), and pouty chambermaid Louise (Beart). Louise discovers Marcel stabbed to death—the phone doesn't work, the car won't start, and there's a blizzard. To make matters more interesting, Marcel's estranged sister Pierrette (Ardant) literally comes in from the cold. Now, the eight women are trapped together. Is one of them a killer? Secrets and accusations spill out in song, like a Technicolor '50s musical melodrama. It may not make sense but with this cast, plot will be the last thing on your mind. Based on the play by Robert Thomas; French with subtitles. 103m/C VHS, DVD. *FR* Catherine Deneuve, Isabelle Huppert, Emmanuelle Beart, Fanny Ardant, Virginie Ledoyen, Danielle Darrieux, Ludivine Sagnier, Firmine Richard, Dominique Lamure; **D:** Francois Ozon; **W:** Francois Ozon, Marina de Van; **C:** Jeanne Lapoirie; **M:** Krishna Levy.

Eighteen 🗡🗡 2004 After leaving his dysfunctional family, Pip (Anthony) is living on the streets where his father (Houde) finds him when Pip turns 18. Dad hands his son a tape that his grandfather (McKellen) recorded about his own experiences at 18, which happened while he was a soldier during WWII. The flashbacks are the best part and, despite the "Pip" name, the story has nothing to do with Charles Dickens or "Great Expectations." 101m/C DVD. *CA* Paul Anthony, Brendan Fletcher, Carly Pope, Serge Houde, Clarence Sponagle, Thea Gill; **D:** Richard Bell; **W:** Richard Bell; **C:** Kevin Van Niekerk; **M:** Bramwell Tovey.

18 Again! 🗡🗡½ 1988 (PG) After a bump on the head, an 81-year-old man and his 18-year-old grandson mentally switch places, giving each a new look at his life. Lightweight romp with Burns in especially good form, but not good enough to make him a superstar. Lee really goes into fighting mode. 87m/C DVD. James Lew, Noriyuki "Pat" Morita, Robin Shou, Lorenzo Lamas, Maurice Patton, Bokeem Woodbine, Don "The Dragon" Wilson, Lisa Arturo, Roark Critchlow; **D:** James Lew; **W:** James Lew; **C:** Jan Michalik; **M:** Eddie Griffin, Aaron Bolden. **VIDEO**

18 Fingers of Death 🗡🗡½ 2005 (PG-13) Kung fu spoof about an actor, Buford Lee (Lew), who has starred in 803 low-budget action movies. When the producers cancel the film that he believes will make him a superstar, Lee really goes into fighting mode. 87m/C DVD. James Lew, Noriyuki "Pat" Morita, Robin Shou, Lorenzo Lamas, Maurice Patton, Bokeem Woodbine, Don "The Dragon" Wilson, Lisa Arturo, Roark Critchlow; **D:** James Lew; **W:** James Lew; **C:** Jan Michalik; **M:** Eddie Griffin, Aaron Bolden. **VIDEO**

1860 🗡🗡 1933 During the Battle of Calatafimi in May of 1860, Sicilian peasants revolted against the King of Naples' army. The story focuses on four people caught up in the fighting: the spouse of a revolutionary, a foppish intellectual, a rebel priest, and the young shepherd who is sent with a message to Genoa asking for assistance. Blasetti made great use of location filming and natural light. In Italian with English subtitles. 72m/C VHS. *IT* Giuseppe Gulino, Aida Bellia, Gianfranco Giachetti, Mario Ferrari; **D:** Alessandro Blasetti; **W:** Alessandro Blasetti; **C:** Anchise Brizzi; **M:** Nino Medin.

The Eighteenth Angel 🗡🗡 1997 (R) The unexpected death of his wife (Crewson) finds Hugh Stanton (McDonald) clinging to his 15-year-old daughter Lucy (Cook), who has fallen into a deep depression. Then a mysterious modeling agent "discovers" Lucy, claiming she has the face of an angel, and offers Lucy a trip to Italy. Unexplainable things happen during their stay and when Hugh investigates it seems that good and evil are in a battle for Lucy's soul. 90m/C VHS. Christopher McDonald, Rachael Leigh Cook, Maximilian Schell, Stanley Tucci, Wendy Crewson, Ted Rusoff; **D:** William Bindley; **W:** David Seltzer; **C:** Thomas Ackerman.

The Eighth Day 🗡🗡½ *Le Huitieme Jour* 1995 Sugary story about workaholic businessman Harry (Auteuil), whose wife Julie (Miou-Miou) has just left him, taking their daughters. Driving home, Harry finds Georges (Duquenne) by the side of the road. Georges, who has Downs syndrome, has left the institution he's been living in and, though Harry tries to take him to the nearest police station, Georges refuses to leave him. Naturally, the emotionally deprived Harry begins to loosen up and, when Georges is finally returned to his group home, all his friends decide to help with Harry's attempts to win back his family. Thick with whimsy but the lead performances are excellent. French with subtitles. 108m/C VHS. *FR BE* Daniel Auteuil, Pascal Duquenne, Miou-Miou, Henri Garcin, Fabienne Loriaux, Isabelle Sadoyan, Helene Roussel, Michele Maes; **D:** Jaco Van Dormael; **W:** Jaco Van Dormael; **C:** Walther Vanden Ende; **M:** Pierre Van Dormael. Cannes '96: Actor (Auteuil), Actor (Duquenne).

The Eighties 🗡🗡½ 1983 A comic, pseudo-documentary romp through the making of a musical. Not just another dime-a-dozen song-and-dance flick, but plays with the genre with humor and intelligence, treating us to an insider's view of a performance arranged at a shopping plaza, from the rigorous auditions to the tedium of the production of songs and routines. Treated in a light-hearted, sensitive, just on the verge of laughable manner, it concludes with 30 minutes of song and dance. In French with English subtitles. 86m/C VHS. *FR* Aurore Clement, Lio, Magali Noel, Pascale Salkin; **D:** Chantal Akerman; **W:** Chantal Akerman, Jean Gruault.

88 Minutes 🗡½ 2008 (R) Predictable thriller sat on the shelves developing mold before Sony studios finally released it, and it's easy to see why. Jack Gramm (Pacino—either indifferent or ranting) is an allegedly hotshot forensic shrink whose testimony put away serial killer Jon Forster (McDonough). Forster is on death row when similar crimes are committed. Gramm gets the fisheye from FBI agent Parks (Forsythe) over the latest murder and then receives a call saying he's got 88 minutes to live. There's no sense of urgency and a viewer can easily discern who's sticking it to Jack, making suspense an afterthought. 108m/C DVD. *US GE* Al Pacino, Alicia Witt, Leelee Sobieski, Amy Brenneman, Neal McDonough, William Forsythe, Deborah Kara Unger, Benjamin) Mckenzie, Stephen Moyer; **D:** Jon Avnet; **W:** Gary Scott Thompson; **C:** Denis Lenoir; **M:** Ed Shearmur.

84 Charing Cross Road 🗡🗡🗡 1986 (PG) A lonely woman in New York and a book-seller in London begin corresponding for business reasons. Over a 20-year period, their relationship grows into a friendship, and then a romance, though they communicate only by mail. Based on a true story and adapted from the book by Helene Hanff. 100m/C VHS, DVD. Anne Bancroft, Anthony Hopkins, Judi Dench, Jean De Baer, Maurice Denham, Eleanor David, Mercedes Ruehl, Daniel Gerroll, Hugh Whitemore; **D:** David Hugh Jones; **W:** Hugh Whitemore; **C:** Brian West; **M:** George Fenton. British Acad. '87: Actress (Bancroft).

84 Charlie MoPic 🗡🗡🗡 1989 (R) A widely acclaimed drama about the horrors of Vietnam seen through the eyes of a cameraman assigned to a special frontline unit. Filled with a cast of unknowns, this is an unsetting film that sheds new light on the subject of the Vietnam war. Powerful and energetic; music by Donovan. 89m/C VHS. Richard Brooks, Christopher Burgard, Nicholas Cascone, Jonathan Emerson, Glenn Morshower, Jason Tomlins, Byron Thames; **D:** Patrick Sheane Duncan; **W:** Patrick Sheane Duncan; **C:** Alan Caso; **M:** Donovan.

Eijanaika 🗡🗡½ *Why Not?* 1981 A gripping story of a poor Japanese man who returns to his country after a visit to America in the 1860s. Memorable performances make this an above-average film. In Japanese with English subtitles. 151m/C VHS. *JP* Ken Ogata, Shigeru Izumiya; **D:** Shohei Imamura.

El 🗡🗡 *This Strange Passion* 1952 Bizarre black-comedy finds virginal middle-aged Francisco (De Cordova) marrying a beautiful young woman (Garces) and becoming jealously paranoid when he believes she's been unfaithful. He's eventually driven to insanity and attempted murder. Spanish with subtitles. 88m/B VHS. *MX* Arturo de Cordova, Delia Garces, Luis Beristain, Aurora Walker; **C:** Gabriel Figueroa; **W:** Luis Bunuel, Luis Alcoriza; **C:** Gabriel Figueroa; **M:** Luis Hernandez Breton.

El Amor Brujo 🗡🗡🗡 *Love, the Magician* 1986 An adaptation of the work of Miguel de Falla, in which flamenco dancers enact the story of a tragic romance. 100m/C VHS. Antonio Gades, Cristina Hoyos, Laura Del Sol; **D:** Carlos Saura.

El Barbaro 🗡 *Conquest* 1984 In the beginning of civilization, when evil powers rule, a barbarian has two ambitions in life: to seek revenge for his friend's death and to rescue the world from a sorcerer's power. 88m/C VHS. *IT SP* Andrea Occhipinti, Gioia Scola, Violeta Cela, Sabrina Siani; **D:** Lucio Fulci; **W:** Gino Capone; **C:** Alejandro Ulloa; **M:** Claudio Simonetti.

El Bola 🗡🗡 *Pellet* 2000 A graphic portrayal of child abuse. 12-year-old Pablo (Ballesta) is nicknamed "Bola" or "Pellet" because he carries a small wooden ball as a good luck charm. Which he needs since his embittered father Mariano (Maron) regularly beats him. New kid in school, Alfredo (Galan), who eventually tells his own father, Jose (Gimenez), about the bruises he's seen on Pablo's body. Jose wants to get involved but it's not as simple as it seems. Spanish with subtitles. 88m/C DVD. *SP* Juan Jose Ballesta, Pablo Galan, Alberto Gimenez, Manuel Maron, Nieve De Medina, Ana Wagener, Gloria Munoz; **D:** Achero Manas; **W:** Achero Manas; **C:** Juan Carlos Gomez; **M:** Eduardo Arbide.

El Bruto 🗡🗡½ *The Brute* 1952 A mid-Mexican-period Bunuel drama, about a brainless thug who is used as a bullying pawn in a struggle between a brutal landlord and discontented tenants. In Spanish with English titles. 83m/B VHS. *MX* Pedro Armendariz Sr., Katy Jurado, Andres Soler, Rosita (Rosa) Arenas; **D:** Luis Bunuel.

El Cantante 🗡🗡 2006 (R) Fiery passion is evident in this ode to a likely little-known artist who may be responsible for bringing salsa to the states. Puerto Rican-born Hector Lavoe—musician, singer, and addict—died of AIDS in 1993 at 46 after firing up the salsa scene in the U.S. The film showcases Lavoe and wife Puchi (Lopez) as they navigate the world of music, drugs, sex, and family. The music throbs but the story bobs, and we can't help but scratch our heads at the pair and their thorny relationship (he shares their bed with myriad others—of both sexes). It's the music that steals the show in this thumping, grinding tribute to a shooting star. 116m/C DVD. *US* Marc Anthony, Jennifer Lopez, John Ortiz, Manny Perez, Vincent Laresca, Federico Castelluccio, Nelson Vasquez; **D:** Leon Ichaso; **W:** Leon Ichaso, David Darmstaedter, Todd Anthony Bello; **C:** Claudio Chea; **M:** Andres Levin.

El Carro 🦴🦴½ *The Car* 2004 Winning Colombian comedy about the Velez family, who dreams of its latest member, a cherry red Chevy. Narrated by the youngest daughter, Paola, recounting the drastic social and moral transformations brought on by this new car—a vehicle both for transportation and for plot development. Divided into quirky little episodes all revolving around the new wheels. Consistently funny. **93m/C DVD.** Cesar Badillo, Luly Bossa, Zaira Valenzuela, Diego Cadavid, Andrea Gomez; **D:** Luis Orjuela; **W:** Jymri Pulido.

El Cid 🦴🦴🦴½ 1961 Charts the life of Rodrigo Diaz de Bivar, known as El Cid, the legendary 11th-century Christian hero who freed Spain from Moorish invaders. Noted for its insanely lavish budget, this epic tale is true to its setting and features elaborate battle scenes. **184m/C VHS, DVD.** Charlton Heston, Sophia Loren, Raf Vallone, Hurd Hatfield, Genevieve Page; **D:** Anthony Mann; **W:** Philip Yordan; **C:** Robert Krasker; **M:** Miklos Rozsa.

El Cochecito 🦴🦴🦴 *The Wheelchair* 1960 Great Spanish actor Isbert stars as the head of a large family whose closest friends are all joined together in a kind of fraternity defined by the fact that they each use a wheelchair. He feels excluded because he does not have or need one, so he goes to great lengths to gain acceptance in this "brotherhood." In Spanish with English subtitles. **105m/C DVD.** *SP IT* **D:** Alex de la Iglesia; **W:** Alex de la Iglesia, Jorge Guerricaechevarria; **C:** Jose L. Moreno; **M:** Miguel Asins Arbo.

El Condor 🦴½ 1970 (R) Two drifters search for gold buried in a Mexican fort. **102m/C VHS.** *SP* Jim Brown, Lee Van Cleef, Patrick O'Neal, Marianna Hill, Iron Eyes Cody, Elisha Cook, Jr.; **D:** John Guillermin; **M:** Maurice Jarre.

El Crimen Perfecto 🦴🦴½ *El Crimen Ferpecto; Perfect Crime* 2004 The "perfect crime"? Seemingly not, but this dark comedy delivers. Rafael, the head salesman in a department store, accidentally kills a rival in a dressing room sci-..fle leaves his arch-nemesis and men's department manager (Varela), dead, and Rafael takes it upon himself to dispose of the body. But unattractive Lourdes (Cervera), a sales assistant in love with Rafael, saw it all and even helps him, only to later blackmail him into marriage. Now Rafael must find a way to loosen Lourdes' clutches. In Spanish with English subtitles. **105m/C DVD.** *SP IT* **D:** Alex de la Iglesia; **W:** Alex de la Iglesia, Jorge Guerricaechevarria; **C:** Jose L. Moreno; **M:** Roque Banos.

El Diablo 🦴🦴½ 1990 (PG-13) A young man finds the West more wild than he expected. He finds "help" in the shape of Gossett as he tries to free a young girl who's being held by the notorious El Diablo. Better than average. **107m/C VHS, DVD.** Anthony Edwards, John Glover, Robert Beltran, M.C. Gainey, Miguel (Michael) Sandoval, Sarah Trigger, Joe Pantoliano; **D:** Peter Markle; **W:** John Carpenter, Bill Phillips; **C:** Ron Garcia; **M:** William Olvis. **CABLE**

El Diablo Rides 🦴½ 1939 A fierce feud between cattlemen and sheepmen develops, with touches of comedy in between. **57m/B VHS.** Bob Steele, Carlson Young, Kit Guard, Claire Rochelle, Ted Adams; **D:** Ira Webb; **W:** Carl Krusada; **C:** Edward Kull.

El Diputado 🦴🦴🦴 *The Deputy* 1978 A famous politician jeopardizes his career when he has an affair with a young man. In Spanish with English subtitles. **111m/C VHS.** *SP* Jose Sacristan, Maria Luisa San Jose, Jose Alonso; **D:** Eloy De La Iglesia.

El Dorado 🦴🦴🦴 1967 A gunfighter rides into the frontier town of El Dorado to aid a reckless cattle baron in his war with farmers over land rights. Once in town, the hired gun meets up with an old friend—the sheriff—who also happens to be the town drunkard. Switching allegiances, the gunslinger helps the lawman sober up and defend the farmers. This Hawks western displays a number of similarities to the director's earlier "Rio Bravo" (1959), staring Wayne, Dean Martin, and Ricky Nelson—with Caan playing a role much like Nelson's, and James Caan does as kick "Colorado" much like Caan does as "Mississippi" in El Dorado." John Wayne, Robert Mitchum, James Caan, Charlene Holt, Ed Asner, Arthur Hunnicutt, Christopher George, R.G. Armstrong, Jim Davis, Paul Fix, Johnny Crawford, Michele Carey; **D:** Howard Hawks.

El Mariachi 🦴🦴🦴 1993 (R) Extremely low-budget but clever mixture of humor and violence in a tale of mistaken identity, set in a small Mexican border town. Unemployed singer/musician Gallardo wanders into a small town and is mistaken for a hit man who carries his weapons in a guitar case. Eventually, the real hit man also shows up. 24-year-old director Rodriguez makes his feature film debut with this $7000 feature, originally intended only for the Spanish-language market. Film festival awards and critical attention brought the work to wider release. Spanish with subtitles or dubbed. **81m/C VHS, DVD.** *MX* Carlos Gallardo, Consuelo Gomez, Peter Marquardt, Jaime de Hoyos, Reinol Martinez, Ramiro Gomez; **D:** Robert Rodriguez; **W:** Robert Rodriguez, Carlos Gallardo; **C:** Robert Rodriguez; **M:** Eric Guthrie. Ind. Spirit '94: First Feature, Sundance '93: Aud. Award.

El Matador 🦴🦴 2003 Wanting to escape the doldrums of his pizza delivery job, young Mexican-American Johnny dreams of emulating his father by becoming a matador. But much about ensues after a not-so-friendly loan shark captures the "family jewels"—bronzed bull testicles—and he must fight to regain the prized family heirloom. **74m/C VHS, DVD.** Robert Wolfskill, Martin Kleba, Gabriel Iglesias, Elilio Rivera; **D:** Joey Medina; **W:** Joey Medina; **C:** Tom Hobbs. **VIDEO**

El Muerto 🦴½ 1975 In 15th-century Buenos Aires, a young man flees his home after killing an enemy. Arriving in Montevideo, he becomes a member of a smuggling ring. In Spanish with English subtitles. **103m/C VHS.** *SP* Thelma Biral, Juan Jose Camero, Francesco Rabal; **D:** Hector Olivera.

El Norte 🦴🦴🦴 1983 (R) Gripping account of a Guatemalan brother and sister, persecuted in their homeland, who make an arduous journey north ("El Norte") to America. Their difficult saga continues as they struggle against overwhelming odds in an attempt to realize their dreams. Passionate, sobering, and powerful. In English and Spanish with English subtitles. Produced in association with the "American Playhouse" series for PBS. Produced by Anna Thomas who also co-wrote the story with Nava. **139m/C VHS.** *SP* David Villalpando, Zaide Silvia Gutierrez, Ernesto Cruz, Eraclio Zepeda, Stella Quan, Alicia del Lugo, Lupe Ontiveros; **D:** Gregory Nava; **W:** Anna Thomas, Gregory Nava. Natl. Film Reg. '95

El Paso Stampede 🦴🦴 1953 Cowboy investigates raids on cattle herds used to feed Americans fighting in the Spanish-American War. **50m/B VHS.** Allan "Rocky" Lane, Eddy (Eddie, Ed) Waller, Phyllis Coates; **D:** Harry Keller.

El Super 🦴🦴½ 1979 A Cuban refugee, still homesick after many years, struggles to make a life for himself in Manhattan as an apartment superintendent. In Spanish with English subtitles: an American production shot on location in New York City. **90m/C VHS.** *SP* Raymundo Hidalgo-Gato, Orlando Jimenez-Leal, Zully Montero, Reynaldo Medina, Juan Granda, Hilda Lee, Elizabeth Pena; **D:** Leon Ichaso; **W:** Leon Ichaso, Manuel Arce.

Ele, My Friend 🦴🦴½ 1993 The British Raj still rules India in the 1920s, when 10-year-old Charles comes across a herd of wild elephants living in the jungle. Charles befriends a baby elephant he names Ele but what can he do when hunters also discover the animals? Filmed on location in south India. **104m/C VHS, DVD.** Amjad Khan, Gazan Khan, R.S. Shivaji, Dharan Mandrayar; **D:** Dharan Mandrayar; **W:** Dharan Mandrayar, Barry Prabhu; **M:** Barry Phillips.

Electra 🦴🦴 1995 Sex-bomb Lorra (Tweed) does her oedipal best with stepson Billy (Tab), who was implanted with the secret of physical regeneration by his late scientist dad. Cybervillian Roach (Erik) wants the info, which can only be obtained through intimate contact, and Lorna's the right woman for the job. Funny how Billy's just so uncooperative. Very over-the-top. **85m/C VHS.** Shannon Tweed, Joe Tab, Sten Blake, Julian Grant; **W:** Damian Lee; **C:** Gerald R. Goozie.

Electra Glide in Blue 🦴🦴🦴 1973 (R) An Arizona motorcycle cop uses his head in a way that's coming apart at the seams. Good action scenes; lots of violence. **113m/C VHS, DVD.** Robert Blake, Billy Green Bush, Mitchell Ryan, Jeannine Riley, Elisha Cook Jr., Royal Dano; **D:** James W. Guercio; **W:** Robert Boris; **C:** Conrad L. Hall.

Electric Dreams 🦴🦴½ 1984 (PG) A young man buys a computer that yearns to do more than sit on a desk. First it takes over his apartment, then it sets its sights on the man's cello-playing neighbor—the same woman his owner is courting. To win her affections, the over-eager computer tries to dazzle her with a variety of musical compositions from his unique keyboard.

Eleanor & Franklin 🦴🦴🦴½ 1976 An exceptional dramatization of the personal lives of President Franklin D. Roosevelt and his wife Eleanor. Based on Joseph Lash's book, this Emmy award-winning film features stunning performances by Alexander and Herrmann in the title roles. **208m/C VHS, DVD.** Jane Alexander, Edward Herrmann, Ed Flanders, Rosemary Murphy, MacKenzie Phillips, Pamela Franklin, Anna Lee, Linda Purl, Linda Kelsey, Lindsay Crouse; **D:** Daniel Petrie; **M:** John Barry. **TV**

Eleanor: First Lady of the World 🦴🦴½ 1982 (G) Stapleton plays the former first lady after her husband's death as she goes on to work at the United Nations and emerges as even more of an influential public figure. **96m/C VHS.** Jean Stapleton, E.G. Marshall, Coral Browne, Joyce Van Patten, Gail Strickland; **D:** John Erman; **M:** John Addison.

Election 🦴🦴🦴 1999 (R) Payne uses a high school student council election to skewer the American political system in general and the election process in particular. Smart comedy has wildly ambitious Tracy (Witherspoon) running for council president unopposed until dedicated but flawed civics teacher Mr. McAllister (Broderick) decides she should be stopped. He recruits likeable but dim jock Paul (Klein) to run against her. Then Paul's lesbian (and anarchic) sister Tammy (Campbell) joins the race. As in Payne's previous effort, "Citizen Ruth," no side of the political spectrum is spared. Everyone's foibles and hypocrisy are shown, to great effect. Witherspoon gives an energized performance, while Broderick is excellent as the respected, conflicted mentor with a touch of Bueller in him. **103m/C VHS, DVD.** Matthew Broderick, Reese Witherspoon, Chris Klein, Jessica Campbell, Mark Harelik, Molly Hagan, Colleen Camp, Frankie Ingrassia, Matt Malloy, Holmes Osborne, Phil Reeves, Delaney Driscoll, Jeanine Jackson; **D:** Alexander Payne; **W:** Alexander Payne, Jim Taylor; **C:** James Glennon; **M:** Rolfe Kent. Ind. Spirit '00: Director (Payne), Film, Screenplay; N.Y. Film Critics '99: Screenplay; Natl. Soc. Film Critics '99: Actress (Witherspoon), Writers Guild '99: Adapt. Screenplay.

Elective Affinities 🦴🦴½ 1996 Adaptation of Goethe's 1809 novel, which the Taviani brothers transport to their native Tuscany. Aristocratic Charlotte (Huppert) and Edouard (Anglade) reunite after 20 years and decide to marry, retiring to a country villa. Their idyll is interrupted by the arrival of Edouard's best friend, Ottone (Bentivoglio), and Charlotte's goddaughter Ottilie (Gillain). Soon, the married duo find themselves in love with their respective houseguests. But though the characters pursue their relationships, tragedy haunts them. French with English subtitles. **98m/C VHS.** *FR IT* Isabelle Huppert, Jean-Hugues Anglade, Fabrizio Bentivoglio, Marie Gillain; **D:** Paolo Taviani, Vittorio Taviani; **W:** Paolo Taviani, Vittorio Taviani; **C:** Giuseppe Lanci; **M:** Carlo Crivelli.

Elektra 🦴 2005 (PG-13) When we last saw her in the movie "Daredevil," Elektra had died, but thanks to the magical healing power of her mentor Stick (Stamp) she's alive and kicking. Regrettably, she came back only to be in yet another wretched film. Elektra is an assassin-for-hire. Her next assignment is to kill 13-year-old Abby (Prout) and Abby's father instead. **97m/C DVD.** *US* Jennifer Garner, Terence Stamp, Goran Visnjic, Cary-Hiroyuki Tagawa, Kirsten Prout, Will Yun Lee; **D:** Rob Bowman; **W:** Zak Penn, Stuart Zicherman, Raven Metzner; **C:** Bill Roe; **M:** Christophe Beck.

The Elegant Criminal 🦴🦴½ 1992 Based on the true story of France's most infamous killer, Pierre Lacenaire. The film begins with Lacenaire in prison, writing his memoirs, receiving his admirers, and awaiting his execution (in 1836). A series of flashbacks detail his life and the supposed social climate which hardened his better instincts and turned him to criminal life. However, Auteuil has such a wonderful time playing the charming bad guy that any blurre to society fails to convince. In French with English subtitles. **120m/C VHS.** *FR* Daniel Auteuil, Jean Poiret, Jacques Weber, Marie-Armelle DeGuy, Maiwenn Le Besco, Patrick Pineau; **D:** Francis Girod; **W:** Georges Conchon, Francis Girod.

The Electric Horseman 🦴🦴½ 1979 (PG) Journalist Fonda sets out to discover the reason behind the kidnapping of a prized horse by an ex-rodeo star. The alcoholic cowboy has taken the horse to return it to its native environment, away from the clutches of corporate greed. As Fonda investigates the story she falls in love with rebel Redford. Excellent. Las Vegas and remote western settings. **120m/ C VHS, DVD.** Robert Redford, Jane Fonda, John Saxon, Willie Nelson, Valerie Perrine, Wilford Brimley, Nicolas Coster, James B. Sikking; **D:** Sydney Pollack; **W:** Robert Garland; **C:** Owen Roizman; **M:** Dave Grusin.

The Electronic Monster 🦴🦴 1957 Insurance claims investigator Cameron looks into the death of a Hollywood starlet and discovers an exclusive therapy center dedicated to hypnotism. At the facility, people vacation for weeks in morgue-like body drawers, while evil Dr. Illing uses electronic device to control the sleeper's dreams and actions. Eerie. Intriguingly, it is one of the first films to explore the possibilities of brainwashing and mind control. **72m/B VHS.** *GB* Rod Cameron, Mary Murphy, Meredith Edwards, Peter Illing; **D:** Montgomery Tully.

Electric Shadows 🦴🦴½ 2004 Delivery man Mao Xiaobing (Xiz) is attacked by a strange young woman in the streets and lands in the hospital. After his release, he visits Ling Ling (Qi) at the police station and discovers they were childhood playmates who were both obsessed with the movies. She asks him to take care of her fish and Mao finds her apartment filled with movie memorabilia and a diary that details her fantasy life. Mandarin with subtitles. **95m/C DVD.** *CH* Xu Xia, Zhongyang Qi, Yihong Jiang; **D:** Xiao Jiang; song Cheng; **C:** Hong Chen, Lun Yang; **M:** Lin Zhao.

The Element of Crime 🦴🦴🦴½ *Forbrydelsens Element* 1984 In a monochromatic, post-holocaust future, a detective tracks down a serial killer of young girls. Made in Denmark, this minor festival favorite features an impressive directorial debut and awaits cult status. Filmed in Sepiatone. **104m/C VHS, DVD.** *DK* Michael Elphick, Esmond Knight, Jerold Wells, Me Me Lai, Astrid Henning-Jensen, Preben Leerdorff-Rye, Gotha Andersen...

dersen; **D:** Lars von Trier. **W:** Lars von Trier, Niels Vorsel; **C:** Tom Elling; **M:** Bo Holten.

Element of Doubt ✓✓½ **1996**
Beth Murray's (McKee) family have always been suspicious of her ambitious husband, Richard (Havers). Although Beth desperately wants children, Richard has persuaded her to wait until after he's closed some mysterious business deal. Suddenly, Richard promises Beth a home in the country and the family she desires. Then, Beth discovers her husband has been in close contact with his ex-wife. So, is Beth merely suffering from hysterics or is Richard actually contemplating murder? **90m/C VHS, DVD.** *GB* Nigel Havers, Gina McKee, Polly Adams, Judy Parfitt, Sarah Berger, Michael Jayston, Dennis (Denis) Lill, Robert Reynolds; **D:** Christopher Morahan; **C:** Brian Tufano; **M:** Stephen Warbeck. **TV**

The Elementary School ✓✓✓
Obecna Skola **1991** Screenwriter Sverak's memories of his childhood are the basis for this child's eye view of the mysteries surrounding the adult world. In 1945, 10-year-old Eda (Jakoubek) is living in a village outside Prague. His school class is so wild that the teacher quits and is replaced by the strict Igor Hnizdo (Triska), who turns out to have a weakness for young women. Czech with subtitles. **100m/C VHS.** *CZ* Jan Triska, Vaclav Jakoubek, Zdenek Sverak, Radoslav Budas, Libuse Safrankova, Rudolf Hrusinsky, Petr Cepek; **D:** Jan Sverak; **W:** Zdenek Sverak; **C:** F.A. Brabec.

Elena and Her Men ✓✓✓ *Paris Does Strange Things; Elena et les Hommes* **1956** The romantic entanglements and intrigues of a poor Polish princess are explored in this enjoyable French film. Beautiful cinematography by Claude Renoir. In French with subtitles. **98m/C VHS, DVD.** *FR* Ingrid Bergman, Jean Marais, Mel Ferrer, Jean Richard, Magali Noel, Pierre Bertin, Juliette Greco; **D:** Jean Renoir; **C:** Claude Renoir.

Eleni ✓✓ **1985 (PG)** The true story of "New York Times" reporter Nicholas Gage and his journey to Athens to discover the truth about his mother's execution by Communists during the Greek rebellion after WWII. Adapted by Steve Tesich from Gage's bestselling book. **117m/C VHS.** John Malkovich, Kate Nelligan, Linda Hunt, Oliver Cotton, Ronald Pickup, Dimitra Arliss, Rosalie Crutchley; **D:** Peter Yates; **W:** Steve Tesich; **C:** Billy Williams; **M:** Bruce Smeaton.

Elephant ✓✓✓ **2003 (R)** Made for HBO film depicting a day in the life at a typical American high school that ends in tragedy. Film lazily follows a number of the boys watching a documentary about Hitler and sharing a brief kiss. Mainly utilizing non-actors and a largely improvised script, Van Sant genuinely imparts the reality of high school life in modern day America without trying to explain it but creates a sense of detachment from the characters and subject matter along the way. **81m/C VHS, DVD.** *US* Alex Frost, Eric Deulen, John Robinson, Elias McConnell, Nathan Tyson, Carrie Finklea, Kristen Hicks, Jordan Taylor, Nicole George, Brittany Mountain, Timothy Bottoms, Matt Malloy; **D:** Gus Van Sant; **W:** Gus Van Sant; Film. **CABLE.**

Elephant Boy ✓✓½ **1937** An Indian boy helps government conservationists locate a herd of elephants in the jungle. Sabu's first film. Available in digitally remastered stereo. **80m/B VHS.** *GB* Sabu, Walter Hudd, W.E. Holloway; **D:** Robert Flaherty, Zoltan Korda. Venice Film Fest. '37: Director (Flaherty).

An Elephant Called Slowly ✓✓½ **1969 (G)** In a sequel of sorts to the 1966 hit "Born Free," McKenna and Travers star as an English couple who trek to Africa to meet game warden George Adamson (here playing himself). Once in Africa, they are introduced to a menagerie of animals, such as lions and hippos. Along the way, they meet Pole Pole (Swahili for "Slowly"), a baby elephant who adopts McKenna and Travers and attempts to travel with them. The first 20 minutes are rather slow, but the last 70 are very watchable with gorgeous cinematography and astounding nature shots. **91m/C VHS, DVD.** *GB* Virginia McKenna, Bill Travers, George Adamson, Joab Collins, Vinay Inambar, Ali Twaha; **D:** James Hill; **W:** Bill Travers, James Hill; **C:** Simon Trevor; **M:** Howard Blake, Bert Kaempfert.

The Elephant Man ✓✓✓
1980 (PG) A biography of John Merrick, a severely deformed man who, with the help of a sympathetic doctor, moved from freak shows into posh London society. Lynch's first mainstream film, shot in black and white, it presents a startlingly vivid picture of the hypocrisies evident in the social mores of the Victorian era. Moving performance from Hurt in title role. **125m/B VHS, DVD.** Michael Elphick, Anthony Hopkins, John Hurt, Anne Bancroft, John Gielgud, Wendy Hiller, Freddie Jones, Kenny Baker; **D:** David Lynch; **W:** Eric Bergren, Christopher DeVore, David Lynch; **C:** Freddie Francis; **M:** John Morris, Samuel Barber. British Acad. '80: Actor (Hurt), Film; Cesar '82: Foreign Film.

Elephant Walk ✓✓½ **1954** Sri Lanka's balmy jungles provide the backdrop for a torrid love triangle in this postprime Dieterle effort. Taylor, ignored by her wealthy drunkard hubby, finds solace in the arms of her spouse's sexy righthand man. As if keeping the affair secret weren't a big enough task, she also braves a cholera epidemic and an unscheduled tour of her humble home. Lethargic lead performances make this more of a sleep walk, but Sofaer and Biberman's supporting roles are worth the price of rental. Taylor replaced Vivian Leigh early in the filming after she fell ill, but footage of Leigh in faraway shots is included. **103m/C VHS, DVD.** Elizabeth Taylor, Dana Andrews, Peter Finch, Abraham Sofaer, Abner Biberman; **D:** William Dieterle; **C:** Loyal Griggs.

11:14 ✓✓ **2003 (R)** Rcounts the half hour of events prior to a tragedy at 11:14 pm from five character perspectives. First time effort by Marcks is laudable—smart writing, well shot, wonderfully cast. Characters could have been given more dimension, but the overall effect is acceptable. **86m/C DVD.** Henry Thomas, Blake Heron, Barbara Hershey, Clark Gregg, Hilary Swank, Shawn Hatosy, Colin Hanks, Ben Foster, Patrick Swayze, Rachael Leigh Cook, Stark Sands, Rick Gomez, Jason Segel; **D:** Greg Marcks; **W:** Greg Marcks; **C:** Shane Hurlbut; **M:** Clint Mansell. **VIDEO**

11 Harrowhouse ✓✓✓ *Anything for Love; Fast Fortune* **1974 (PG)** The Consolidated Selling System at 11 Harrowhouse, London, controls much of the world's diamond trade. Four adventurous thieves plot a daring heist making use of a very clever cockroach. A rather successful stab at spoofing detailed "heist" films. **95m/C VHS.** *GB* Charles Grodin, Candice Bergen, James Mason, Trevor Howard, John Gielgud; **D:** Aram Avakian; **W:** Jeffrey Bloom.

The 11th Hour ✓✓½ **2007 (PG)** Global warming is certainly "the" hot topic, and this film doesn't present anything we haven't heard before, plus throws around enough stats and figures to make your head spin. Leonardo DiCaprio multitasks as narrator, actor, and co-writer; he even helped produce. It's grim, but provides some real solutions. Make no mistake—this is a documentary, not intended to entertain, but to inspire outrage and action. **95m/C DVD.** *US* Leonardo DiCaprio, Leila Conners Petersen, Nadia Conners; **C:** Peter Youngblood Hills, Andrew Roland, Brian Knappenberger; **M:** Jean Pascal Beintus, Eric Avery; **Narr:** Leonardo DiCaprio.

Elf ✓✓✓ **2003 (PG)** As a baby, Buddy (Ferrell) had snuck into Santa's bag and found himself transported to the North Pole. The elves adopted the human and raised him as an elf. When he learns of his human origins (the enormous size difference didn't tip him off?), he goes to New York to search for his real father. Daddy turns out to be a Walter Hobbs (Caan), a highly insensitive children's book publisher who needs a good dose of Christmas cheer. While it's all straight-ahead Christmas movie formula, Ferrell's unabashed innocence and delight in everything helps pull it off. It also helps that he looks so damn funny in a cameo as a doctor. Director Favreau makes a cameo as a doctor. **95m/C VHS, DVD, UMD.** *US* Will Ferrell, James Caan, Bob Newhart, Ed Asner, Mary Steenburgen, Zooey Deschanel, Faizon Love, Daniel Tay, Peter Dinklage, Amy Sedaris, Michael Lerner, Andy Richter, Jon Favreau; **D:** Jon Favreau; **W:** David Berenbaum; **C:** Greg Gardiner; **M:** John Debney.

Eli Eli ✓✓½ **1940** An American Yiddish film about a family forced to live apart because of their farm's failure. Lighthearted and fun. In Yiddish with English titles. **85m/B VHS.** Esther Field, Lazar Fried, Meni Serebroff; **D:** Joseph Seiden; **M:** Sholom Secunda.

The Eliminators ✓✓ **1986 (PG)** A cyborgian creature endeavors to avenge himself on his evil scientist creator with help from a kung fu expert and a Mexican. The group uses time travel and other devices to achieve their mission. **95m/C VHS.** Roy Dotrice, Patrick Reynolds, Denise Crosby, Andrew Prine, Conan Lee; **D:** Peter Manoogian; **W:** Danny Bilson, Paul DeMeo; **M:** Richard Band.

Elisa ✓✓ **1994** Teenaged sexpot Marie (Paradis) has grown up in a reform school, thanks to her mother Elisa's suicide. Along with friends Solange (Courau) and Ahmed (Sall), Marie spends her time on the Paris streets shoplifting and flirting. Obsessed with finding her long-gone father, Marie discovers that Lebovitch (Depardieu), the writer of the popular song "Elisa," is daddy dearest. He's now a drunk, living on a fishing island, and Marie sets out to right the wrongs she believes drove her mother to suicide. Based on the song by Serge Gainsbourg. French with subtitles. **111m/C VHS.** *FR* Vanessa Paradis, Gerard Depardieu, Clotilde Courau, Sekkou Sall, Florence Thomassin; **D:** Jean Becker; **W:** Jean Becker, Fabrice Carazo; **C:** Etienne Becker; **M:** Zbigniew Preisner. Cesar '95: Support. Actress (Courau), Score.

Elisa, Vida Mia ✓✓ *Elisa, My Love; Elisa, My Life* **1977** A long-estranged father and daughter are reunited when he falls ill. She stays to help him write his biography and gradually begins to see things through his perspective. The shifting narrative can confuse but worth seeing are Rey and Chaplin's subtle performances. Spanish with subtitles. **125m/C VHS.** *SP* Fernando Rey, Geraldine Chaplin, Norman Brisky, Isabel Mestres, Joaquin Hinojosa; **D:** Carlos Saura; **W:** Carlos Saura. Cannes '77: Actor (Rey).

Elizabeth ✓✓✓ **1998 (R)** And you thought modern day politics were dirty! Indian director Kapur takes a look at the turbulent life of Queen Elizabeth I of England (a brilliant Blanchett) from her uncertain days as a besieged Protestant Princess to her ascension to the throne and the machinations surrounding her early reign. Elizabeth indeed proves to be her father's daughter as she must keep her head (literally) while dealing with religion, war, assassination, and the vexing question of a political marriage. Rush is notable as spidery spymaster Walsingham and Eccleston's hissably evil as the arrogant Catholic Duke of Norfolk. Wonderful shadowy cinematography by Adefarasin adds to the atmosphere but it does help to know some history in order to keep the plots and plotters straight. **124m/C VHS, DVD, HD DVD.** *GB* Cate Blanchett, Geoffrey Rush, Joseph Fiennes, Christopher Eccleston, Richard Attenborough, Fanny Ardant, Vincent Cassel, Daniel Craig; Kathy Burke, James Frain, Edward Hardwicke, Eric Cantona, John Gielgud, Emily Mortimer; **D:** Shekhar Kapur; **W:** Michael Hirst; **C:** Remi Adefarasin; **M:** David Hirschfelder. Oscars '98: Makeup; British Acad. '98: Actress (Blanchett), Cinematog., Film, Score; Golden Globes '99: Actress—Drama (Blanchett); Natl. Bd. of Review '98: Director (Kapur); Broadcast Film Critics '98: Actress (Blanchett).

Elizabeth of Ladymead ✓✓ **1948** Four generations of a British family live through their experiences in the Crimean War, Boer War, WWI, and WWII. Neagle, playing the wives in all four generations, aptly explores the woman's side of war. Enjoyable performances from husband and wife team Neagle and Wilcox. **97m/C VHS.** Anna Neagle, Hugh Williams, Bernard Lee, Michael Lawrence, Nicholas Phipps, Isabel Jeans; **D:** Herbert Wilcox.

Elizabeth R ✓✓✓ **1972** Jackson is outstanding in the title role of this TV drama focusing on the life of Elizabeth I, from 17 to 70. Constantly besieged by court intrigue and political machinations, the Virgin Queen managed to restore England to glory and power amidst private and public turmoil. Six 90-minute cassettes. **540m/C VHS, DVD.** *GB* Glenda Jackson, Rosalie Crutchley, Robin Ellis, Robert Hardy, Peter Jeffrey, Stephen Murray, Vivian Pickles, Sarah Frampton, Ronald Hines; **D:** Claude Whatham, Herbert Wise, Roderick Graham, Richard Martin, Donald Whatham; **W:** Hugh Whitemore, John Hale, Julian Mitchell, John Prebble, Ian Rodger, Rosemary Anne Sisson.

Elizabeth I ✓✓✓ **2005** Mirren gives an outstanding performance as the imperious British monarch. In 1579, Elizabeth is being pressured to marry, but not her loving Earl of Leicester and confidante, the Earl of Leicester (Irons). Matters are complicated by the rebellion of her cousin, Mary Queen of Scots (Flynn), and war with Spain. On his deathbed, Leicester bequeaths his relationship to his handsome and arrogant stepson, the Earl of Essex (Dancy). Flattered and flustered, Elizabeth gradually realizes that the callow Essex is a threat to her throne. **220m/C DVD.** Helen Mirren, Jeremy Irons, Hugh Dancy, Ian McDiarmid, Patrick Malahide, Barbara Flynn, Toby Jones; **D:** Tom Hooper; **W:** Nigel Williams; **C:** Larry Smith; **M:** Robert (Rob) Lane. **CABLE**

Elizabeth: The Golden Age ✓✓½ **2007 (PG-13)** Kapur's 1998 film dealt with Elizabeth's early reign. She's now been in power 27 years and is still doing an intricate political dance to keep her head and her Protestant throne against the Catholic opposition, who want Mary, Queen of Scots (Morton) ruling in her place. Then there's pesky Philip II of Spain (Molla) and his armada threatening her shores. Blanchett returns in the titular role as does Rush as spymaster Walsingham. Owen's cast as a swashbuckling Sir Walter Raleigh (very Errol Flynn), whom Elizabeth uses as a distraction. Lavish pomp and circumstance, but a disappointingly routine costumer. **114m/C DVD.** *GB* Cate Blanchett, Geoffrey Rush, Clive Owen, Abbie Cornish, Rhys Ifans, Jordi Molla, Samantha Morton, Tom Hollander, David Threlfall, Eddie Redmayne, John Shrapnel, Antony Carrick; **D:** Shekhar Kapur; **W:** Michael Hirst, William Nicholason; **C:** Remi Adefarasin; **M:** Craig Armstrong. Oscars '07: Costume Des.

Elizabeth, the Queen ✓✓ *The Private Lives of Elizabeth and Essex* **1968** Historical drama re-creates the struggle for power by Robert Devereaux, Earl of Essex, whom Queen Elizabeth I both loved and feared, and whose downfall she finally invoked. Part of "George Schaefer's Showcase Theatre." **76m/C VHS.** Judith Anderson, Charlton Heston; **D:** George Schaefer. **TV**

Elizabethtown ✓✓ **2005 (PG-13)** Over-stuffed romantic comedy from Crowe begins with the career meltdown of Drew Baylor (Bloom with a so-so American accent). Before Drew can wallow in suicidal depression, his manic mother Hollie (Sarandon) and sister Heather (Greer) inform Drew that dad died while visiting his hometown of Elizabethtown, Kentucky and Drew must deal with the funeral arrangements. This leads to his meeting cute but psychotically perky flight attendant Claire (Dunst), who decides she must console Drew at all costs. Drew discovers things about himself and his family that you may not care about at all, and takes a road trip—accompanied, as per usual in Crowe's movies, by copious amounts of music. **120m/C DVD.** *US* Orlando Bloom, Kirsten Dunst, Susan Sarandon, Judy Greer, Jessica Biel, Alec Baldwin, Paul Schneider, Loudon Wainwright III, Bruce McGill, Paula Deem, Gailard Sartain, Dan Biggers; **D:** Cameron Crowe; **W:** Cameron Crowe; **C:** John Toll; **M:** Nancy Wilson.

Eliza's Horoscope 🐾🐾½ 1970 A frail Canadian woman uses astrology in her search for love in Montreal, and experiences bizarre and surreal events. An acclaimed Canadian film. Silent with original organ score. 69m/C VHS, Colleen Moore, Harry Langdon, Lloyd Hughes, Jed Prouty, Vera Lewis; **D:** Alfred E. Green.

Ella 1926 The American mania for breaking into the movies is satirized in this look at a girl who wins a trip to Hollywood in a small-town beauty contest. 120m/C VHS, DVD, CA Tommy Lee Jones, Elizabeth Moorman; **D:** Gordon Shepard.

Ella Cinders 🐾🐾½ 1926 The American mania for breaking into the movies is satirized in this look at a girl who wins a trip to Hollywood in a small-town beauty contest. Silent with original organ score. 69m/C VHS, Colleen Moore, Harry Langdon, Lloyd Hughes, Jed Prouty, Vera Lewis; **D:** Alfred E. Green.

Ella Enchanted 🐾🐾🐾 2004 (PG) Enchanting modern Cinderella story is a fresh and funny mix of fantasy, romance, and pop culture. Hathaway appealingly plays the title's Ella of Frell, cursed by her fairy godmother Lucinda (Fox) with the "gift" of obedience, which forces the budding teen to obey every command she is given. She hooks up with the ogres, elves, and giants and begins a crusade for their equal rights. Her quest leads her to the total hottie Prince Charmont (Dancy) who is the intended victim of a coup planned by the throne-seeking Prince Edgar. Updated fairy tale sports top-notch special effects, a cool 70s soundtrack, and fun modern anachronisms. Based on the novel by Gail Carson Levine. 101m/C DVD, Anne Hathaway, Hugh Dancy, Cary Elwes, Vivica A. "Fox, Joanna Lumley, Minnie Driver, Patrick Bergin, Parminder K. Nagra, Jimi Mistry, Heidi Klum; **D:** Tommy O'Haver; **W:** Laurie Craig, Karen McCullah Lutz, Kirsten Smith, Jennifer Heath, Michele J. Wolff; **C:** John de Borman; **M:** Shaun Davey; **V:** Steve Coogan; *Narr:* Eric Idle.

Ellen Foster 🐾🐾½ 1997 (PG-13) Coming-of-age TV drama concerns 10-year-old Ellen (Malone), who lives with her abusive, drunken dad (Levine) and her gentle mom (O'Connor). After mom dies, Ellen is shuffled between uncaring relatives, including a nasty grandma, Leonora (Harris), while trying to draw strength from the few friends and teachers who do care about her. Based on the novel by Kaye Gibbons. 97m/C VHS, Jena Malone, Julie Harris, Ted Levine, Glynnis O'Connor, Debra Monk, Barbara Garrick, Kate Burton, Zeljko Ivanek, Lynne Moody, Bill Nunn, Amanda Peet, Allison Jones, Timothy Olyphant; **D:** John Erman; **W:** Mara Nation, William Hanley; **C:** Brian West; **M:** Chris TV.

Elling 🐾🐾½ 2001 (R) Witty, gentle comedy has two Norwegian misfits, recently released from a mental institution, living together in a government-subsidized Oslo flat in order to learn how to live in the outside world. Elling, who had to be dragged from his mother's home when she died, is extremely agoraphobic, fastidious, and socially inept. His roomie Kjell Bjarne is a hulking man with no sense of personal hygiene and an overdeveloped sexual imagination. Their friendship helps them to slowly and amusingly adapt to, and enter, the world. This allows Kjell to befriend, and become romantic with, their pregnant upstairs neighbor, while Elling writes poetry (and slips it into sauerkraut packages at the market), finally attends a reading, and without being cloying. 89m/C VHS, DVD, NC Per Christian Ellefsen, Sven Nordin, Marit Pia Jacobsson, Jorgen Langhelle, Per Christensen; **D:** Petter Naess; **W:** Axel Hellstenius, Per Christensen; **C:** Philip Swanson; **D:** Christopher Cain.

Elmer 🐾🐾½ 1976 (G) Follows the adventures of a temporarily blinded youth and a lovable hound dog who meet in the wilderness and together set off in search of civilization. 82m/C VHS, Elmer Swanson, Philip Swanson; **D:** Christopher Cain.

Elmer Gantry 🐾🐾🐾 1960 The classic multi-Oscar-winning adaptation of the Sinclair Lewis novel written to expose and denounce the flamboyant, small-town evangelists spreading throughout America at the time in the film. Lancaster is the amoral Southern preacher who exacts wealth and power from his congregation, and takes a nun as a mistress. Jones stars as his ex-girlfriend who resorts to a life of prostitution. 146m/C VHS, DVD, Burt Lancaster, Shirley Jones, Jean Simmons, Dean Jagger, Arthur Kennedy, Patti Page, Edward Andrews, John McIntire, Hugh Marlowe, Rex Ingram, Wendell Holmes; **D:** Richard Brooks; **W:** Richard Brooks; **C:** John Alton; **M:** Andre Previn. Oscars '60: Actor (Lancaster), Adapt. Screenplay, Support. Actress (Jones); Golden Globes '61: Actor—Drama (Lancaster); Natl. Bd. of Review '60: Support. Actress (Jones); N.Y. Film Critics '60: Actor (Lancaster).

Elmore Leonard's Gold Coast 🐾🐾½ 1997 (R) Miami mobster Frank DiCilla (Bradford) is dead and his widow, Karen (Helgenberger) is not happy. Yes, she's inherited $15 mil but Frank's will also stipulates that she has to remain faithful to him forever. Too bad Karen (Caruso) are instantly attracted to one another. And too bad Frank's also left behind loathsome hit man Roland (Kober) to enforce the edict (although if Karen wants him, Roland's willing to be flexible). Based on the novel by Elmore Leonard. 109m/C VHS, David Caruso, Marg Helgenberger, Jeff Kober, Barry Primus, Richard Bradford, Wanda De Jesus; **D:** Peter Weller; **W:** Harley Peyton; **C:** Jacek Laskus; **M:** Peter Harris. CABLE

Eloise at the Plaza 🐾🐾½ 2003 Hyperactive adaptation of the first of Kay Thompson's books about six-year-old enfant terrible Eloise (Vassilieva), who lives with her mother at the Plaza Hotel in New York. Mom is away in Paris, so it's up to Nanny (Andrews) to try to reign in her charge's exuberant behavior and frequently disastrous schemes. This time Eloise is determined to attend the prestigious Debutante's Ball that is being held at the Plaza, despite her age (and the lack of an invitation). 90m/C VHS, DVD, Sofia Vassilieva, Julie Andrews, Jeffrey Tambor, Kenneth Welsh, Debra Monk, Jonas Chernick, Christine Baranski; **D:** Kevin Lima; **W:** Janet Brownell; **C:** James Chressanthis; **M:** Bruce Broughton. TV

The Elusive Corporal 🐾🐾🐾 ½ *Le Caporal Epinglé* 1962 Set in a P.O.W. camp on the day France surrendered to Germany, this is the story of the French and Germans, complete with memories of France that is no more. 108m/B VHS, Jean-Pierre Cassel, Claude Brasseur, O.E. Hasse, Claude Rich; **D:** Jean Renoir.

The Elusive Pimpernel 🐾🐾½ *The Fighting Pimpernel* 1950 Niven sparkles in this otherwise undistinguished adaptation of Baroness Orczy's "The Scarlet Pimpernel." 109m/C VHS, GB David Niven, Margaret Leighton, Jack Hawkins, Cyril Cusack, Robert Coote, Edmund Audran, Danielle Goder, Patrick Macnee; **D:** Michael Powell; **W:** Michael Powell, Emeric Pressburger.

Elsa, Elsa 1985 Satire of moviemaking life finds a scriptwriter-director distracted by the loss of his girlfriend and unable to concentrate on writing a memoir of his career as a child actor. He creates a subplot dealing with his romantic problems, and puts the film in jeopardy. Fine acting and witty dialogue, in French with English subtitles. 85m/C VHS, FR Francois Cluzet, Lio, Tom Novembre, Catherine Frot; **D:** Didier Haudepin; **C:** Gilberto Azevedo; **M:** Eric Lelann.

Elves 🐾 1989 (PG-13) A group of possessed, neo-Nazi elves performs serious human harm at Christmas time in this tongue-in-check thriller. 95m/C VHS, Dan Haggerty, Deanna Lund, Julie Austin, Borah Silver; **D:** Jeffrey Mandel.

Elvira Madigan 🐾🐾🐾 1967 (PG) Chronicles the true 19th-century Swedish romance between teenaged Elvira (Degermark, a beautiful circus tight-rope walker, and young Army officer Sixten Sparre (Berggren) who leaves his wife and children to be with her. Exceptional direction and photography and a notable use of classical music by Mozart and Vivaldi. Swedish with subtitles. 90m/C VHS, DVD, SW Pia Degermark, Thommy Berggren, Lennart Malmer, Nina Widerberg, Cleo Jensen; **D:** Bo Widerberg; **C:** Jorgen Persson; **M:** Ulf Bjorlin, Cannes '67: Actress (Degermark).

Elvira, Mistress of the Dark 🐾🐾½ 1988 (PG-13) A manic comedy based on Peterson's infamous B-movie host character. The mega-bust-ed terror-vixen inherits a house in a conservative Massachusetts town and causes double-entendre chaos when she attempts to sell it. 96m/C VHS, DVD, Cassandra Peterson, Jeff Conaway, Susan Kelleman, Edie McClurg, Daniel Greene, William Morgan Shepherd, Kurt Fuller, Pat Crawford Brown, William Duell, William Cort, John Paragon; **D:** James Signorelli; **W:** Sam Egan, Cassandra Peterson, John Paragon; **C:** Hanania Baer; **M:** James Campbell.

Elvira's Haunted Hills 🐾🐾½ 2002 (PG-13) That bodacious vixen returns as Elvira (Peterson) and her French maid Zou Zou (Smith) are stranded in Carpathia in 1851. They manage to find shelter at the Transylvania castle of the twitchy Vladimir Helsubius (O'Brien) where all sorts of high camp happenings occur. 89m/C VHS, DVD, Cassandra Peterson, Richard O'Brien, Mary Jo Smith, Mary Scheer, Scott Atkinson; **D:** Sam Irvin; **W:** Cassandra Peterson, John Paragon; **C:** Viorel Segovia; **M:** Eric Allaman.

Elvis and Me 🐾🐾½ 1988 TV miniseries based on Priscilla Beaulieu Presley's autobiography of her life with the King. Features many of Presley's biggest hits, sung by country star Ronnie McDowell. Film may aggravate Elvis fans, however, as the King is often depicted negatively from his ex-wife's point of view. 187m/C VHS, Dale Midkiff, Susan Walters, Billy Green Bush, Linda Miller; **D:** Larry Peerce.

Elvis Has Left the Building 🐾½ 2004 (PG-13) Once upon a time Elvis gave Harmony Jones (Basinger) a ride in his pink Caddy, making her feel so indebted to the King that, years later, she travels around the country. When she begins unintentionally offing the Elvis impersonators. While on the lam from the law, Harmony teams up with Miles (Corbett), a down-and-out New York advertising executive who has his own issues with the King. Offbeat yet not amusing. 90m/C VHS, DVD, Kim Basinger, John Corbett, Annie Potts, Sean Astin, Denise Richards, Mike Starr, Phill Lewis, Philip Charles MacKenzie, Billy Ray Cyrus, Richard Kind, David Leisure, Tom Hanks, Joel Zwick, Angie Dickinson, Noriyuki "Pat" Morita; **D:** Joe Zwick; **W:** Adam-Michael Garber, Mitchell Ganem; **C:** Paul Elliott; **M:** David Kitay. VIDEO

Elvis in Hollywood 🐾🐾🐾 1993 A tribute highlighting Presley's first four films, "Love Me Tender," "Loving You," "Jailhouse Rock," and "King Creole," completed prior to his reporting for active duty in the army. Features his 1956 screen test at Paramount Studios; photos from the movie sets; interviews with co-stars, directors, writers, business associates, songwriters, and friends; and home movies as well as out-take footage from "Jailhouse Rock." 65m/C VHS, DVD. **D:** Frank Martin.

Elvis Meets Nixon 🐾½ 1998 (PG-13) Based on the bizarre (but true) visit of Elvis Presley (Peters) to the Nixon (Gunton) White House. 103m/C VHS, Richard Beymer, Edwin Newman, Graham Nash, Wayne Newton, Bob Gunton, Rick Peters, Jackie Burroughs, Curtis Armstrong; **D:** Allan Arkush.

Elvis: The Movie 🐾🐾½ 1979 B-iography of the legendary singer, from his high school days to his Las Vegas comeback. Russell gives a convincing performance and lip syncs effectively to the voice of the King (provided by country singer Ronnie McDowell). Also available in 150-minute version. 117m/C VHS, Kurt Russell, Season Hubley, Shelley Winters, Ed Begley Jr., Dennis Christopher, Pat Hingle, Bing (Neil) Russell, Joe Mantegna; **D:** John Carpenter. TV

The Embalmer 🐾🐾½ *L'imbalsamatore* 2003 Peppino (Mathieux) is a dwarfish middle-aged taxidermist (the Embalmer of the title) who attaches himself to handsome but dumb Valerio (Manzillo). Peppino hires Valerio, gives him a place to live, and uses hookers to put the two men in bed together at the same time. When Valerio meets Deborah, a beautiful drifter, on a business trip, the result is a tug-of-war for Valerio's attention. Mathieux is brilliant as the creepy Peppino, who fills every moment with lurking dread and foreboding, adding distinctive visual flourishes and gritty details. 104m/C DVD, IT Ernesto Mahieux, Valerio Foglia Manzillo, Elisabetta Rocchetti, Pietro Biondi, David Ryall, Bernardino Terracciano, Marcela Granito; **D:** Matteo Garrone; **W:** Matteo Garrone, Ugo Chiti, Massimo Gaudioso; **C:** Marco Onorato; **M:** Banda Osiris.

Embassy 🐾🐾 1985 An American family in Rome unknowingly possesses a secret computer chip, and thus is pursued by ruthless agents. 104m/C VHS, Nick Mancuso, Blanche Baker, Eli Wallach, Sam Wanamaker, Richard Gilliland, Mimi Rogers, George Grizzard, Richard Masur, Kim Darby; **D:** Robert Lewis. TV

Embassy 🐾🐾 Target: *Embassy* 1972 In this mediocre espionage thriller, von Sydow is a Soviet defector under asylum at the U.S. embassy in Beirut. Colonel Connors, a Russian spy, penetrates embassy security and wounds von Sydow. He is caught, escapes, is captured, escapes, is often too wordy and contrived. 90m/C VHS, DVD, GB Richard Roundtree, Chuck Connors, Max von Sydow, Ray Milland, Broderick Crawford, Marie-Josee Nat; **D:** Gordon Hessler.

The Embezzled Heaven 🐾🐾½ 1958 Teta works as a cook for an auspicious Austrian family and aspires to have a better place in heaven. In order to ensure this, she financially supports her nephew's seminary education. When she finally visits him she is rudely awakened to his scam, which sends her on a journey of repentance ending in Rome before the pope. In German with subtitles. 91m/B VHS, Annie Rosar, Hans Holt, Viktor de Kowa, Anne Rosar, Vilma Degischer; **D:** Ernst Marischka; **W:** Helle Eaton, Nicole Coady, Rick Bitzelberger; **C:** Franz Werfel. VIDEO

Embrace of the Vampire 🐾🐾 1995 (R) Innocent young Charlotte (Milano) must make a choice between her college boyfriend Chris (Pruett) and a new nighttime lover (Kemp). Seems Charlotte looks different habits. Seems Charlotte looks different actly alike a love los: hundreds of years ago; and he's not going to take no for an answer. Also available in an unrated version. 92m/C VHS, DVD, Alyssa Milano, Martin Kemp, Harrison Pruett, Charlotte Lewis, Jordan Ladd, Rachel True, Jennifer Tilly; **D:** Anne Goursaud; **W:** Halle Eaton, Nicole Coady, Rick Bitzelberger; **C:** Suki Medencevic; **M:** Joseph Williams. TV

Embryo 🐾🐾 *Created to Kill* 1976 (PG) An average sci-fi drama about a scientist who uses raw genetic material to artificially produce a beautiful woman, with ghastly results. 108m/C VHS, DVD, Rock Hudson, Barbara Carrera, Diane Ladd, Roddy McDowall, Ann Schedeen, John Elerick; **D:** Joyce Brothers; **D:**
Alan Rosen; **C:** Michael Storey; **M:** Larry Brown.

Emanon 🐾½ 1986 (PG-13) A coming-of-age tale about a young kid and his Christ-like vagabond, named Emanon (or "no name" if spelled in reverse), he befriends. 101m/C VHS, Stuart Paul, Cheryl Lynn, Jeremy Miller; **D:** Stuart Paul.

Ellie Parker 🐾🐾🐾 2005 Ellie (Watts) is the typical struggling actress in L.A., frantically driving from audition to audition, transforming her clothes and personality in an instant to please a series of dismissive casting directors. While Ellie wrestles with her integrity and the absurdity of Hollywood, she's friends and manager (Chevy Chase, in an odd cameo role) try to re-inspire her love of acting. Coffey uses 16-millimeter film to emphasize Ellie's disconsolate search for something authentic. A low-budget verite production but Watts' performance is spot-on. 95m/C DVD, US Naomi Watts, Rebecca Rigg, Chevy Chase, Mark Pellegrino, Blair Mastbaum, Scott Coffey; *Cameos:* Keanu Reeves; **D:** Scott Coffey; **W:** Scott Coffey; **C:** Blair Mastbaum, Scott Coffey; **M:** B.C. Smith.

Ellie 🐾½ 1984 (R) A murderous widow's stepdaughter tries to save her father from being added to the woman's extensive list of dearly departed husbands. 90m/C VHS, Shelley Winters, Sheila Kennedy, Pat Paulsen, George Gobel, Edward Albert, Jim Wittman.

Ralph Nelson; **W:** Anita Doohan, Jack W. Thomas; **C:** Fred W. Koenekamp; **M:** Gil Melle.

The Emerald Forest 🦴🦴🦴 **1985 (R)** Bill (Boothe) moves his family to Brazil where he has a job as an engineer working on a dam project. His young son Tommy wanders into the rainforest and is taken in by a primitive tribe of Amazons. Bill searches 10 years for him, finally discovering a happily adjusted teenager named Tomme (Boorman, the director's son), who may not want to return to so-called civilization. An engrossing look at tribal life in the vanishing jungle. Beautifully photographed and based upon a true story. **113m/C VHS, DVD.** Powers Boothe, Meg Foster, Charley Boorman, Dira Paes, Rui Polonah; **D:** John Boorman; **W:** Rospo Pallenberg; **C:** Philippe Rousselot.

Emerald Jungle 🦴½ *Eaten Alive by Cannibals; Eaten Alive; Mangiati Vivi dal Cannibali* **1980** While searching for her missing sister in the jungle, Agren encounters cannibal tribes and a colony of brainwashed cult followers. This Italian feature was cut for its U.S. release. **92m/C VHS, DVD.** *IT* Robert Kerman, Janet Agren, Mel Ferrer, Luciano Martino, Mino Loy, Ivan Rassimov, Paola Senatore, Me Me Lai, Meg Fleming, Franco Fantasia; **D:** Umberto Lenzi; **W:** Umberto Lenzi; **C:** Frederico Zanni.

Emerald of Artama 🦴 *The Girl of the Nile* **1967** Anyone viewing the most precious gem sought after stone in the history of man does not live to tell about it. **93m/C VHS.** *SP* Francisco (Frank) Brana, Pilar Arenas, Rory Calhoun; **D:** Jose Maria Elorrieta; **W:** Jose Maria Elorrieta; **C:** Alfonso Nieva; **M:** Federico Contreras.

The Emigrants 🦴🦴🦴 *Utvandrarna* **1972 (PG)** Farmer von Sydow decides to gather his wife (Ullmann) and family together and leave 19th-century Sweden for the promise of a new life in America. Film is divided into two parts, the voyage over, and the journey to a settlement in Minnesota. Pacing is somewhat slow; notable cinematography (by director Troell). Adapted from the novels by Vilhelm Moberg. Dubbed into English. Followed by the sequel to "The Emigrant Saga." **151m/C VHS.** *SW* Max von Sydow, Liv Ullmann, Allan Edwall, Eddie Axberg, Svenold Bern, Aina Alfredsson, Monica Zetterlund, Pierre Lindstedt; **D:** Jan Troell; **W:** Jan Troell, Bengt Forslund; **C:** Jan Troell; **M:** Erik Nordgren. N.Y. Film Critics '72: Actress (Ullmann).

Emil and the Detectives 🦴🦴½ *Emil Und Die Detektive* **1964** A German ten-year-old is robbed of his grandmother's money by gangsters, and subsequently enlists the help of preadolescent detectives to retrieve it. Good Disney dramatization of the Erich Kastner children's novel. Remake of the 1931 German film starring Rolf Wenkhaus. **99m/C VHS.** Bryan Russell, Walter Slezak, Roger Mobley; **D:** Peter Tewkesbury; **W:** A.J. Carothers.

Emile 🦴🦴½ **2003 (R)** McKellen shines in this story of a man confronting the demons of his past. Emile, a respected British scientist and professor, travels to Canada to receive an honorary degree and visit his niece Nadia (Unger). Although Emile acts like the perfect uncle, in reality he deserted Nadia in an orphanage when her parents died and has never been a part of her life. Reconnecting with his past leads into a series of oddly-shot flashbacks to Emile's youth and his painful relationships with his brothers, and in the end Emile must come to terms with his own painful past as well as his selfish treatment of Nadia. Despite Bessai's efforts to break up the narrative, the story is routine and predictable, with McKellen's performance the most distinctive part of the film. **96m/C VHS, DVD, CA GB** Ian McKellen, Deborah Kara Unger, Tygh Runyan, Ian Tracey, Chris William Martin, Janet Wright; **D:** Carl Bessai; **W:** Carl Bessai; **C:** Carl Bessai; **M:** Vincent Mai.

Emily woof! **1977** Returning from her exclusive Swiss finishing school, licentious young Emily discovers mama is a prostitute and deals with the scalding news by delving into a series of erotic encounters at the hands of her willing "instructors." Stark's first venture into the realm of soft porn. **87m/C VHS.** Koo Stark; **D:** Henry Herbert.

Emily Bronte's Wuthering Heights 🦴🦴½ *Wuthering Heights* **1992 (PG)** Miscast version of the tragic tale of doomed lovers Cathy (Binoche) and Heathcliff (Fiennes). While Fiennes may seem too refined for the role, he manages to be both brooding and brutal. However, the beautiful Binoche can't successfully supress her French accent enough to pass for a heedless Yorkshire lass. Good supporting cast, with O'Connor posing as writer/narrator Bronte. **107m/C VHS, DVD, GB** Ralph Fiennes, Juliette Binoche, Janet McTeer, Sophie Ward, Simon Shepherd, Jeremy Northam, Jason Riddington, Jonathan Firth, Paul Geoffrey, Sinead O'Connor; **D:** Peter Kosminsky; **W:** Anne Devlin; **C:** Mike Southon; **M:** Ryuichi Sakamoto.

Eminent Domain 🦴🦴½ **1991 (PG-13)** A communist party member wakes up to find himself stripped of power in a Kafkaesque purge, not knowing what he is accused of—or why. A potent premise, indifferently handled despite filming on location in Poland. Based on actual events that befell the family of scriptwriter Andrej Krakowski. **102m/C VHS.** Donald Sutherland, Anne Archer, Paul Freeman, Bernard Hepton, Francoise Michaud, Jodhi May; **D:** John Irvin; **W:** Andrzej Krakowski, Richard Greggson; **M:** Zbigniew Preisner.

Emissary 🦴🦴 **1989 (R)** An American politician and his wife are blackmailed in Africa by the Russians into revealing state secrets that could filming out WWIII. **98m/C VHS.** *SA* Robert Vaughn, Ted Leplat, Terry Norton, Andre Jacobs; **D:** Jan Scholtz.

Emma 🦴🦴½ **1972** BBC TV version of the Jane Austen saga with young Emma trying her matchmaking skills on all her friends and neighbors—with disastrous results. Mr. Knightly tries to provide both a voice of reason and romance, if only Emma could realize it. **257m/C VHS, DVD.** *GB* Doran Goodwin, Vivienne Moore, John Carson, Donald Eccles, Debbie Bowen; **D:** John Glenister.

Emma 🦴🦴🦴 **1996 (PG)** Jane Austen's 1816 novel about wealthy, 21-year-old Emma Woodhouse (Paltrow) who neglects to notice the attractive, and exasperated, Mr. Knightley (Northam). McGrath's screenplay makes Emma and Knightley more likable than in the book, but otherwise stays true. After the success of "Sense and Sensibility," Austen's name is making it in the movies in the footsteps of the likes of John Grisham. **120m/C VHS, DVD.** Gwyneth Paltrow, Jeremy Northam, Greta Scacchi, Toni Collette, Alan Cumming, Juliet Stevenson, Polly Walker, Ewan McGregor, James Cosmo, Sophie Thompson, Phyllida Law; **D:** Douglas McGrath; **W:** Douglas McGrath; **C:** Ian Wilson; **M:** Rachel Portman. Oscars '96: Orig. Score.

Emma 🦴🦴🦴 *Jane Austen's Emma* **1997** British TV adaptation of the Jane Austen novel featuring young, matchmaking Emma (Beckinsale) wrecking havoc amongst her friends and neighbors with her would-be romantic alliances. Screenplay is truer to the book, with slightly less screen version. Excellent cast, and beautiful locations and costumes make this one worth seeing. A&E Network offered "Emma" after the overwhelming success of their miniseries "Pride and Prejudice," also adapted from Austen. **107m/C VHS, DVD, GB** Kate Beckinsale, Mark Strong, Samantha Bond, Prunella Scales, Bernard Hepton, Raymond Coulthard, Dominic Rowan, James Hazeldine, Samantha Morton, Lucy Robinson, Olivia Williams; **D:** Diarmuid Lawrence; **W:** Andrew Davis.

Emmanuelle 🦴🦴½ **1974** Filmed in Bangkok, a young, beautiful woman is introduced by her husband to an uninhibited world of sensuality. Above-average softcore skin film, made with sophistication and style. Kristel maintains a vulnerability and awareness, never becoming a mannequin. **92m/C VHS, DVD.** *FR* Sylvia Kristel, Alain Cuny, Marika Green, Daniel Sarky; **D:** Just Jaeckin; **W:** Jean-Louis Richard; **C:** Richard Suzuki; **M:** Pierre Bachelet.

Emmanuelle 4 🦴 **1984 (R)** Emmanuelle flees a bad relationship and undergoes plastic surgery to mask her identity. Ultimately, she becomes a beautiful young model in the form of a different actress, Mia Nygren, of course. **95m/C VHS, DVD.** *FR* Sylvia Kristel, Mia Nygren, Patrick Bauchau; **D:** Francis Giacobetti.

Emmanuelle 5 🦴½ **1987 (R)** This time around sexy Emmanuelle flees aboard a convenient yacht when she's chased by adoring fans at the Cannes Film Festival. But she winds up being forced to join an Arab sheik's harem of slaves. A good example of a series that should have quit while it was ahead. **78m/C VHS, DVD.** *FR* Monique Gabrielle, Charles Foster; **D:** Steve Barnett, Walerian Borowczyk; **M:** Pierre Bachelet.

Emmanuelle 6 🦴 **1988 (R)** The saga of the sexy beauty continues. This time Emmanuelle and a group of models head for the paradise of an Amazon jungle where they promptly become the prized captives of a drug lord. **80m/C VHS, DVD.** *FR* Natalie Uher, Jean-Rene Gossart, Thomas Obermuller, Gustavo Rodriguez; **D:** Jean Rollin, Bruno Zincone; **C:** Serge Godet; **M:** Olivier Day.

Emmanuelle & Joanna 🦴 **1978** A mistreated newlywed bride goes to her sister's whorehouse and stumbles across lots of soft-core antics. **90m/C VHS.** *FR* Sherry Buchanan, Danielle Dublino; **D:** Franco (Enzo Gardner) Rossetti; **C:** Pier Luigi Santi; **M:** Enzo Petti.

Emmanuelle in the Country 🦴 *L'Infermiera di Campagna; Country Nurse* **1978** Emmanuelle becomes a nurse in an attempt to bring comfort and other pleasures to those in need. **90m/C VHS, DVD.** *IT* Laura Gemser, Gabriele Tinti, Aldo Sambrel; **D:** Mario Bianchi; **W:** Luigi Petrini; **C:** Umberto Galeassi; **M:** Ubaldo Continiello.

Emmanuelle on Taboo Island 🦴½ *La Spiaggia del Desiderio; Beach Called Desire* **1976 (R)** Marooned young man discovers a beautiful woman on his island. This delights him. **95m/C VHS, DVD.** *IT* Laura Gemser, Paul(o) Giusti, Arthur Kennedy; **D:** Enzo D'Ambrosio; **W:** Enzo D'Ambrosio; **C:** Riccardo (Pallton) Pallottini; **M:** Marcello Giombini.

Emmanuelle, the Joys of a Woman 🦴 *Emmanuelle l'Antivierge; Emmanuelle's 7th Heaven; Emmanuelle 2* **1976** The amorous exploits of a sensuous, liberated couple take them and their erotic companions to exotic Hong Kong, Bangkok, and Bali. **92m/C VHS, DVD.** *FR* Sylvia Kristel, Umberto Orsini, Catherine Rivet, Frederic Lagache, Laura Gemser, Henri Czarniak, Tom Clark, Caroline Laurence; **D:** Francis Giacobetti; **W:** Francis Giacobetti, Jean-Marc Vasseur; **C:** Robert Fraisse; **M:** Pierre Bachelet, Francis Lai.

Emmanuelle, the Queen 🦴 *Black Emmanuelle; Mavri Emmanouela* **1979** Seeking revenge, Emmanuelle plots the murder of her sadistic husband. The lecherous assassin she hires tries to blackmail her, and she challenges him at his own game of deadly seduction. **90m/C VHS.** *GR* Laura Gemser, Gabriele Tinti, Livia Russo, Vagelis Vartan, Pantelis Agelopou; **D:** Ilias Milonakos; **C:** Vassilis Christomoglou; **M:** Giovanni Ullu.

Emmanuelle's Daughter 🦴 **1979** A Greek-made thriller in which a vapidly sensuous heroine cavorts amid episodes of murder, blackmail, and rape. **91m/C VHS.** *GR* Laura Gemser, Gabriele Tinti, Livia Russa, Vagelis Vartan, Nadia Neri; **D:** Ilias Mylonakos; **W:** Ilias Mylonakos; **C:** Vassilis Christomoglou; **M:** Giovanni Ullu.

Emma's Shadow 🦴🦴 *Skyggen af Emma* **1988** In the 1930s, a young girl fakes her own kidnapping to get away from her inattentive family and comes to befriend an ex-convict sewer worker. In Danish with English subtitles. Winner of the Prix de la Jeunesse at Cannes, it was voted 1988's Best Danish Film. **93m/C VHS.** *DK* Borje Ahlstedt, Line Kruse; **D:** Soeren Kragh-Jacobsen; **W:** Soeren Kragh-Jacobsen; **C:** Dan Laustsen.

The Emperor and the Assassin 🦴🦴 **1999 (R)** Sumptuous historical drama (and a complicated storyline) concerns a united China's first emperor. Set in 320 B.C., China is a collection of seven rival kingdoms with Ying Zheng, the King of Qin (Xuejian) obsessed with uniting the country and then dividing it into provinces for proper ruling (with himself as supreme head). Naturally, this means war. Also involved is his lover, Lady Zhao (Li), who plans a fake assassination attempt to aid Zheng. But the assassin she chooses, Jing Ke (Fengyi), is trying to reform and things don't go exactly according to plan. Remember—power corrupts. Mandarin with subtitles. **161m/C VHS, DVD. CH** Xuejian Li, Gong Li, Fengyi Zhang, Zhiwen Wang, Sun Zhou, Chen Kaige; **D:** Chen Kaige; **W:** Chen Kaige, Wang Peigong; **C:** Fei Zhao; **M:** Jiping Zhao.

Emperor Jones 🦴🦴½ **1933** Loosely based on Eugene O'Neill's play, film portrays the rise and fall of a railroad porter whose exploits take him from a life sentence on a chain gang to emperor of Haiti. Robeson re-creates his stage role in his first screen appearance. **72m/B VHS, DVD.** Paul Robeson, Dudley Digges, Frank Wilson, Fredi Washington, Ruby Elzy; **D:** Dudley Murphy. Natl. Film Reg. '99.

Emperor of the Bronx 🦴 **1989** A look at crime, sleaze, violence, and the actions of bad guys in the inner-city. **90m/C VHS, DVD.** Alex D'Andrea, Adrian Drake, Anthony Gioia, William (Bill) Smith; **D:** Joseph Merhi; **W:** Joseph Merhi, Sean Dash; **C:** Richard Pepin.

Emperor of the North Pole 🦴🦴🦴 *Emperor of the North* **1973 (PG)** Violent and well-done tale of hobos riding the rails during the Depression has Marvin as A#1, a legendary hobo who can get on any train, and his protege Cigaret (Carradine), trying to catch a ride on the train of sadistic conductor Shack (Borgnine), who's been known to kill to keep the hobos away. Tense and gritty, with the usual tight direction of Aldrich, beautiful cinematography, and a gripping screenplay. Borgnine is exceptional among a very strong cast. **118m/C VHS, DVD.** Lee Marvin, Ernest Borgnine, Keith Carradine, Charles Tyner, Malcolm Atterbury, Simon Oakland, Harry Caesar, Hal Baylor, Matt Clark, Elisha Cook Jr., Liam Dunn, Robert Foulk, Ray Guth, Sid Haig, Vic Tayback; **D:** Robert Aldrich; **W:** Christopher Knopf; **C:** Joseph Biroc; **M:** Frank DeVol.

Emperor Waltz 🦴🦴½ **1948** Typical Hollywood musical finds phonograph salesman Crosby travelling to Vienna, hoping to sell his goods to the Austrian royal family of Emperor Franz Joseph. He gets mixed up with the Emperor's snobby niece (Fontaine) and attempts to charm her into an audience with her royal uncle. Naturally the two fall in love and everything ends in a happy fade-out. ♫The Emperor's Waltz; Friendly Mountains; Get Yourself a Phonograph; The Kiss in Your Eyes; I Kiss Your Hand, Madame; The Whistler and His Dog. **106m/C VHS, DVD.** Bing Crosby, Joan Fontaine, Roland Culver, Richard Haydn, Lucile Watson, Sig Ruman, Harold Vermilyea; **D:** Billy Wilder; **W:** Billy Wilder, Charles Brackett; **C:** George Barnes; **M:** Victor Young.

The Emperor's Club 🦴🦴½ *The Palace Thief* **2002 (PG-13)** "A man's character is his fate." This statement is eminently displayed through events both past and present of a prep school teacher (Klein) and his more challenging students (Hirsch). Ethics are questioned, schools of thought examined and hearts changed in this "Dead Poet Society" type drama. Hoffman's development of Ethan Canin's book "The Palace Thief" is unfortunately accomplished through manipulation and fake sincerity. **109m/C VHS, DVD. US** Kevin Kline, Emile Hirsch, Embeth Davidtz, Rob Morrow, Paul Franklin Dano, Edward Herrmann, Harris Yulin, Roger Rees, Jesse Eisenberg, Rishi Mehta, Joel Gretsch, Steven Culp, Patrick Dempsey, Rahul Khanna; **D:** Michael Hoffman; **W:** Neil Tolkin; **C:** Lajos Koltai; **M:** James Newton Howard.

The Emperor's New Clothes 🦴🦴½ **1984** The story of an emperor and the unusual outfit he gets from his tailor. A "Faerie Tale Theatre" presentation. 60m/C VHS, DVD. *Al Carney, Alan Arkin, Dick Shawn, Art Carney;* **Nar:** Timothy Dalton. **C.A.B.L.E.**

The Emperor's New Clothes 𝄞𝄞½ 2001 (PG) Historical comedy about "Napoleon" Bonaparte (Holm). Confined to the island of St. Helena by the British, the former emperor and his advisers plot to regain power in France by recruiting a look-alike named Eugene (Holm again) to trade places while the real Napoleon heads to Paris and restakes his claim to power. The first part of the plan works fine; the second part doesn't. Eugene likes playing the exiled ruler too much to reveal himself as an imposter and Napoleon turns out to enjoy his more simple life, especially with comely widow Pumpkin (Hjejle) proffering her charms. Loosely based on the French novel "The Death of Napoleon" by Simon Leys. 107m/ C VHS, DVD, GB *Ian Holm, Iben Hjejle, Tim McInnerny) Tom Watson, Nigel Terry, Hugh Bonneville, Murray Melvin, Eddie Marsan, Clive Russell;* **D:** *Alan Taylor;* **W:** *Kevin Molony, Herbie Wave;* **C:** *Alessio Gelsini Torresi;* **M:** *Rachel Portman.*

The Emperor's New Groove 𝄞𝄞½ 2000 (G) Animated fantasy about self-centered young emperor Kuzco (Spade) who gets turned into a llama by sorceress Yzma (Kitt) and must team up with peasant Pacha (Goodman) to get his throne back. Refreshingly devoid of "important lessons" and sappy pop tunes, the only mission here is to provide laughs, and that it does. Like the great Warner Bros. cartoons of old, sarcastic and sophisticated humor abounds (Spade really helps out here), and the sidekicks get plenty of face (and hero) time, not to mention some of the best lines, including Warburton as Yzma's distracted and clumsy right-hand villain, Kronk. 79m/C VHS, DVD. **D:** *Mark Dindal;* **W:** *Dave Reynolds;* **M:** *John Debney;* **V:** *David Spade, John Goodman, Eartha Kitt, Patrick Warburton, Wendie Malick, Patti Deutsch, John Fiedler, Kellyann Kelso, Eli Russell Linnetz.* Broadcast "Film Critics '00: Song ("My Funny Friend and Me").

The Emperor's Shadow 𝄞𝄞 *Qin Song* 1996 Saga of two boyhood friends in China around 220 BC. Gao Jianli (You) is a famous musician and the childhood friend of powerful Emperor Ying Sheng (Wen). Jianli basically wants to be left alone to work on his music but the Emperor demands he stick around and compose a stirring imperial anthem. Add into the mix Yueyang (Qing), the Emperor's daughter who has the hots for the musician (and vice versa) although she's betrothed to another, and tragedy is bound to be the result. Mandarin with subtitles. 123m/C VHS, DVD. *CH Ge You, Jiang Wen, Xu Qing;* **D:** *Xiaowen Zhou;* **W:** *Wei Lu;* **C:** *Lu Gengxin;* **M:** *Jiping Zhao.*

Empire 𝄞𝄞½ 2002 (R) Leguizamo is Victor Rosa, a slick South Bronx drug entrepreneur hustling to keep his patch of heroin turf. Through narration, Victor walks us through his seedy world and his decision to leave it. His opportunity arises when he meets Wall Street couple Trish (Richards) and Jack (Sarsgaard). Jack cuts him in on an investment deal that helps launder his money, but Victor soon finds out that even a player can get played. Reyes's gangster flick aspires to the heights of "Scarface" and "The Godfather," but sinks in a quagmire of cliches and obvious plot devices. Excellent cast includes Rosallini as an over-the-top drug queenpin as well as rappers Fat Joe and Treach. 95m/C VHS, DVD. *John Leguizamo, Peter Sarsgaard, Denise Richards, Delilah Cotto, Nestor Serrano, Fat Joe, Treach;* **D:** *Franc Reyes;* **W:** *Franc Reyes;* **C:** *Kramer Morgenthau;* **M:** *Ruben Blades.*

Empire Falls 𝄞𝄞½ 2005 Passive Miles Roby (Harris), manager of the Empire Grill, has been unable to sever ties with either his economically depressed Maine mill town or his demanding family, including his ne'er-do-well father Max (Newman), ex-wife Janice (Hunt), teen daughter Tick (Panabaker), and brother David.

Empire of the Ants 𝄞𝄞 1977 (PG) A group of enormous, nuclear, unfriendly ants stalk a real estate dealer and prospective buyers of undeveloped oceanfront property. Story originated by master science-fiction storyteller H. G. Wells. 90m/C VHS, DVD. *Joan Collins, Robert Lansing, John David Carson, Albert Salmi, Jacqueline Scott, Robert Pine;* **D:** *Bert I. Gordon;* **W:** *Bert I. Gordon;* **C:** *Reginald Morris.*

Empire of the Sun 𝄞𝄞𝄞½ 1987 (PG) Spielberg's mature, extraordinarily vivid return to real storytelling, from the best-selling J.G. Ballard novel. Yearns to be a great film, but occasional flat spots keep it slightly out of contention. Young, wealthy British Jim (Bale) lives in Shanghai, but is thrust into a life of poverty and discomfort when China is invaded by Japan at the onset of WWII and he's separated from his family and interred in a prison camp. A mysterious, breathtaking work, in which Spielberg's heightened juvenile romanticism has a real, heartbreaking context. Two other 1987 releases explored the WWII memories of young boys: "Au Revoir Les Enfants" and "Hope and Glory." 153m/C VHS, DVD. *Christian Bale, John Malkovich, Miranda Richardson, Nigel Havers, Joe Pantoliano, Leslie Phillips, Rupert Frazer, Ben Stiller, Robert Stephens, Burt Kwouk, Masato Ibu, Emily Richard, David Neidorf, Ralph Seymour, Emma Piper, Peter Gale, Zhai Nai She, Guts Ishimatsu, J.G. Ballard;* **D:** *Steven Spielberg;* **W:** *Tom Stoppard, Menno Meyjes;* **C:** *Allen Daviau;* **M:** *John Williams.* Natl. Bd. of Review '87: Director (Spielberg).

Empire Records 𝄞𝄞 1995 (PG-13) Well, the soundtrack's good and that's about all this frantic movie has going for it (besides a photogenic cast). Joe's (La-Paglia) the manager of an independent record store about to be taken over by a faceless conglomerate unless he and his young-and-crisis-prone staff can come up with the cash to buy the place within 24 hours. 91m/C VHS, DVD. *Anthony LaPaglia, Rory Cochrane, Liv Tyler, Renee Zellweger, Johnny Whitworth, Robin Tunney, Ethan (Randall) Embry, Maxwell Caulfield, Debi Mazar;* **D:** *Allan Moyle;* **W:** *Carol Heikkinen;* **C:** *Walt Lloyd;* **M:** *Mitchell Leib.*

Empire State 𝄞 1987 (R) When his friend disappears from a posh London nightclub, a young man searches for him and finds more action and intrigue than he can handle. Even so, this movie's still pretty bland. 102m/C VHS, GB *Ray McAnally, Martin Landau, Ray McAnally;* **D:** *Ron Peck.*

The Empire Strikes Back 𝄞𝄞𝄞½ *Star Wars: Episode 5—The Empire Strikes Back* 1980 (PG) Second film in the epic "Star Wars" trilogy finds young Luke Skywalker and the Rebel Alliance plotting new strategies as they prepare to battle the evil Darth Vader and the forces of the Dark Side. Luke learns the ways of a Jedi knight from master Yoda, while Han and Leia find time for romance and a few adventures of their own. Introduces the charismatic Lando Calrissian and a mind-

---

(Quinn). Also in the picture is the town's manipulative matriarch (Woodward) and plot as super special effects and hearty (Hoff-man). HBO miniseries based on the Pulitzer Prize-winning book by Richard Russo is sometimes slow going but the cast is worth the effort. 240m/C DVD. *Ed Harris, Paul Newman, Joanne Woodward, Helen Hunt, Aidan Quinn, Robin Wright Penn, Philip Seymour Hoffman, Danielle Panabaker, Dennis Farina, William Fichtner, Estelle Parsons, Theresa Russell, Jeffrey DeMunn, Lou Taylor Pucci, Kate Burton, Joshua Lucas;* **D:** *Fred Schepisi;* **W:** *Richard Russo;* **C:** *Ian Baker;* **M:** *Paul Grabowsky.* C.A.B.L.E.

The Empire of Passion 𝄞𝄞𝄞 *In the Realm of Passion* 1976 A peasant woman and her low-life lover kill the woman's husband, but find the future they planned with each other is not to be. The husband's ghost returns to haunt them, and destroy the passionate bond which led to the murder. Oshima's follow-up to "In the Realm of the Senses." In Japanese with English subtitles. 110m/C VHS, DVD. *JP Nagisa Oshima, Kazuko Yoshiyuki, Tatsuya Fuji, Takahiro Tamura, Takuzo Kawatani;* **D:** *Nagisa Oshima.* Cannes '78: Director (Oshima).

Employee of the Month 𝄞𝄞½ 2006 (PG-13) Amy (the ever-clueless Simpson) is the hot new employee at megastore Super Club and rumor has it that she has a serious fetish for the employee of the month. This sparks a battle for the title between slacker Zack (weirdly appealing Cook) and 17-time consecutive winner Vince (Shepard). Dopey comedy is only rescued from complete mediocrity by some sharp jabs at consumerism. 103m/C DVD, Blu-ray Disc. *US Dane Cook, Jessica Simpson, Dax Shepard, Andy Dick, Tim Bagley, Sean Woodham, Efren Ramirez, Harland Williams;* **D:** *Greg Coolidge, Dan Calame, Chris Conroy;* **C:** *Anthony B. Richmond;* **M:** *John Swihart.*

Employees' Entrance 𝄞𝄞𝄞 1933 William stars as a ruthless department store manager in this story about commerce and compromise during the Depression. Young gives an excellent performance as the wife of one of his employees. Outrageous, and racy, this pre-Code film was expertly directed by veteran craftsman Del Ruth. Based on a play by David Boehm. 74m/B VHS. *Warren William, Loretta Young, Wallace Ford, Alice White, Allen Jenkins;* **D:** *Roy Del Ruth;* **W:** *Robert Presnell Sr.;* **C:** *Barney McGill;* **M:** *Bernhard Kaun.*

The Empty Acre Woof! 2007 The idyllic world of Beth and Jacob Nance is shattered when their infant son is missing. Might it have something to do with the creepy acre of land on their property, where nothing grows and cattle die? And of course no one people get abducted into the blackness that starts to rise from it. That's about as exciting and edge of your seat as it gets folks. Seriously suspense challenged. Not even eerie. 90m/C DVD. *Nate Witt, Robert Pralgo, Ari Pavel, Sally Brennerman, Ric Avenll;* **D:** *Patrick Rea;* **W:** *Patrick Rea;* **C:** *Jeremy Osbern;* **M:** *Don James.*

The Empty Beach 𝄞𝄞 1985 A tough private detective investigates the disappearance of a wealthy business tycoon. 87m/C VHS. *AU Bryan Brown, Anna Maria Monticelli;* **D:** *Chris Thomson.*

An Empty Bed 𝄞𝄞𝄞 1990 Award-winning independent production depicting Bill Frayne, an older homosexual, and the challenges of his everyday life. Told mostly in flashbacks as Bill encounters people and places during the course of one day, this is a delicate drama with important statements about homosexuality, aging and honesty. 60m/C VHS, DVD. *John Wylie, Mark Clifford Smith, Conan McCarty, Dorothy Stinnette, Kevin Kelly, Thomas Hill, Harriet Bass;* **D:** *Mark Gasper;* **W:** *Mark Gasper.*

Empty Canvas 𝄞½ 1963 *La Noia L'Ennui Et Sa Diversion; L'Ectisme* 1964 A spiritually bankrupt artist becomes obsessively jealous of his mistress who refuses to marry him, in the hope that someone better will come along. Based on the Alberto Moravia novel. 118m/B VHS, DVD. *IT Horst Buchholz, Catherine Spaak, Bette Davis;* **D:** *Damiano Damiani;* **M:** *Luis Baca ov.*

The Empty Mirror 𝄞𝄞 1999 (PG-13) Boring fictionalized account of Hitler's final hours, hidden away in his bunker, as he realizes his Third Reich dreams have come to nothing. He does a lot of ranting but what is more interesting are the clips from Leni Riefenstahl's "Triumph of the Will" that are screened behind him. 108m/C VHS, DVD. *Norman Rodway, Joel Grey, Camilla Soeberg, Glenn Shadix, Peter Michael Goetz, Doug McKeon;* **D:** *Barry J. Hershey;* **W:** *Barry J. Hershey, R. Buckingham;* **C:** *Frederick Elmes;* **M:** *John (Gianni) Frizzel.*

---

blowing secret from Vadar. Offers the same superb special effects and hearty plot as set by 1977's excellent "Star Wars." Followed by "Return of the Jedi" in 1983. 124m/C VHS, DVD. *Mark Hamill, Carrie Fisher, Harrison Ford, Billy Dee Williams, Alec Guinness, David Prowse, Kenny Baker, Frank Oz, Anthony Daniels, Peter Mayhew, Clive Revill, Julian Glover, John Ratzenberger, Jeremy Bulloch;* **D:** *Irvin Kershner;* **W:** *Leigh Brackett, Lawrence Kasdan;* **C:** *Peter Suschitzky;* **M:** *John Williams;* **V:** *James Earl Jones.* Oscars '80: Sound, Visual FX.

En la Cama 𝄞𝄞 *In Bed* 2005 Think Sunrise," *Daniela* (Lewin) and Bruno (Valenzuela) meet at a party in Santiago and wind up in a seedy motel room. There's some post-coital talk, some more sex, and then Bruno happens to mention he's taken a job in Belgium while a Daniela retaliates that one-nighters mean nothing. The attractive duo reveal secrets because they never expect to meet again but the ending hints of further romantic possibilities. Spanish with subtitles. 85m/C DVD, GB *Blanca Lewin, Gonzalo Valenzuela;* **D:** *Matías Bize;* **W:** *Julio Rojas;* **C:** *Gabriel Díaz, Cristian Castro;* **M:** *Diego Fontecilla.*

Enchanted 𝄞𝄞𝄞 2007 (PG) Princess Giselle (Adams) idly sings in wait for "true love's kiss" to rescue her. Vain Prince Edward (Marsden) hears her love song and falls fast, but meddling Queen Narissa (Sarandon) thinks they'll steal her queendom away so she banishes the princess to New York by tossing her down a wishing well (the film turns from animated to real once they're in the city). Divorce lawyer Robert (Dempsey) and his daughter rescue Giselle from the streets of Manhattan, where she promptly makes herself a new dress from his curtains and calls on her animal friends to clean the apartment. Edward has followed and is combing the streets gallantly searching for Giselle, meanwhile, Robert is falling for the princess. It would be a generally happy and fun little film if it ended about there, but no—the queen has more mayhem to unleash. Some painfully slow and predictable scenes, but Adams, Marsden, and Dempsey keep up the charm. 107m/C DVD. *US Amy Adams, Patrick Dempsey, James Marsden, Timothy Spall, Idina Menzel, Susan Sarandon, Rachel Covey;* **D:** *Kevin Lima;* **W:** *Bill Kelly;* **C:** *Don Burgess;* **Nar:** *Julie Andrews.*

Enchanted April 𝄞𝄞½ 1992 (PG) Lotte (Lawrence) and Rose (Richardson), tired of their overbearing husbands, rent a villa in Portofino, Italy, for a month with two other very different women—Lady Caroline (Walker), a beautiful but bored socialite, and crusty old Mrs. Fisher (Plowright), who has an impeccable literary pedigree. The effects of the charming villa, with plenty of wisteria and sunshine, do wonders for the women. A charming and romantic period piece. Based on the 1922 novel by Elizabeth von Arnim. 93m/C VHS, GB *Miranda Richardson, Joan Plowright, Josie Lawrence, Polly Walker, Alfred Molina, Jim Broadbent, Michael Kitchen, Adriana Facchetti;* **D:** *Mike Newell;* **W:** *Peter Barnes;* **C:** *Rex Maidment;* **M:** *Richard Rodney Bennett.* Golden Globes '93: Actress—Mus./Comedy (Richardson). Support. Actress (Plowright).

The Enchanted Cottage 𝄞𝄞½ 1945 An elderly man teaches a boy about life and the beauty of nature when the boy gets lost in a forest. 78m/C VHS, DVD, AR *Harry Davenport, Edmund Lowe, Brenda Joyce;* **D:** *Lew Landers.*

Enchanted Forest 𝄞½ 1945 Salior stops on an island to find provisions and ends up falling in love with a carnival princess. Thinly based upon Herman Melville's "Typee." 94m/C VHS, DVD. *Jane Powell, Dana Andrews, Arthur Shields;* **D:** *Alan Dwan.*

Enchanted Island 𝄞½ 1958 Saliors stops on an island to find provisions and ends up falling in love with a carnival princess. Thinly based upon Herman Melville's "Typee." 94m/C VHS, DVD, AR *Jane Powell, Dana Andrews, Arthur Shields;* **D:** *Alan Dwan.*

The Enchantress 𝄞½ *I Skiachtra* 1985 A daring boy experiences his first true loves and passions when he journeys through a mystical land in order to find a beautiful fairy. In Greek with subtitles. 93m/ C VHS, GR *Alkis Kourkoulos, Sofia Aliberti, Lily Kokodi, Arragone Amaritou, Vicky Koulianou, Nikos Papaconstantinou, Stratos Panis;* **D:** *Manoussos Manoussakis.*

Encino Man 🐾🐾 *California Man* 1992 (PG) Two, like, totally uncool Valley dudes dig up a 10,000-year-old caveman in the backyard. After giving him a makeover and teaching him the necessities like the four basic food groups (Milk Duds in the dairy group, Sweet Tarts in the fruit group), they use the gnarly caveman as their ticket to popularity and dates to the prom. Juvenile humor appealing to teens; strictly brain candy. 88m/C VHS, DVD. Sean Astin, Brendan Fraser, Pauly Shore, Megan Ward, Robin Tunney, Rick Ducommun, Mariette Hartley, Richard Masur, Michael DeLuise; D: Les Mayfield; W: Shawn Schepps; C: Robert Brinkmann. Golden Raspberries '92: Worst New Star (Shore).

Encore 🐾🐾🐾 1952 The third W. Somerset Maugham omnibus (following "Quartet" and "Trio") which includes: "Winter Cruise," "The Ant and the Grasshopper," and "Gigolo and Gigolette." 85m/B VHS. GB Nigel Patrick, Kay Walsh, Roland Culver, Jom Laurie, Glynis Johns, Ronald Squire, Noel Purcell, Peter Graves; D: Pat Jackson, Anthony Pelissier, Harold French; W: Eric Ambler.

Encounter at Raven's Gate 🐾🐾½ 1988 (R) Punk rockers and extraterrestrials meet amid hard rock and gallons of gore. 85m/C VHS. Eddie Cleary, Steven Vidler. D: Rolf de Heer.

Encounter with the Unknown 🐾🐾½ 1975 Relates three fully documented supernatural events including a death prophecy and a ghost. 90m/C VHS, DVD. Rosie Holotik, Gene Ross; D: Harry Z. Thomason; Nar: Rod Serling.

The End 🐾🐾🐾 1978 (R) Reynolds plays a young man who discovers he is terminally ill. He decides not to prolong his suffering and attempts various tried-and-true methods for committing suicide, receiving riotous but incompetent help from the crazed DeLuise. 100m/C VHS, DVD. Burt Reynolds, Sally Field, Dom DeLuise, Carl Reiner, Joanne Woodward, Robby Benson, Kristy McNichol, Norman Fell, Pat O'Brien, Myrna Loy, David Steinberg; D: Burt Reynolds; W: Jerry Belson; C: Bobby Byrne; M: Paul Williams.

End of August 🐾🐾½ 1982 (PG) A spinster of New Orleans Creole aristocracy, circa 1900, breaks out of her sheltered life and experiences new sexual and romantic awareness. Adapted from "The Awakening" by Kate Chopin. 104m/C VHS. Sally Sharp, David Marshall Grant, Paul Roebling; D: Bob Graham; W: Anna Thomas, Gregory Nava; C: Robert Elswit.

End of Days 🐾🐾½ 1999 (R) Alcoholic ex-cop Jericho Cane (Schwarzenegger) becomes a reluctant savior, who must battle a literal Satan (Byrne) who has the opportunity to rule both Heaven and Hell if he can make young Christine (Tunney) his bride before the millennial midnight. There's lots of action, Arnold looks great (post heart surgery), and Byrne is a very sexy devil but there's also an excessive amount of gore and silly mumbo-jumbo to suffer through. 123m/C VHS, DVD, HD DVD, UMD. Arnold Schwarzenegger, Gabriel Byrne, Robin Tunney, Kevin Pollak, CCH Pounder, Rod Steiger, Derrick O'Connor, Miriam Margolyes, Udo Kier; D: Peter Hyams; W: Andrew Marlowe; C: Peter Hyams; M: John Debney.

End of Desire 🐾🐾 1962 Schell discovers that her husband, Marquand, has married her for her money and is having an affair with the maid in this melodrama based on De Maupassant's story, "Une Vie." A period piece that is a little on the slow side. In French with English subtitles. 86m/C VHS. FR Maria Schell, Christian Marquand, Pascale Petit, Ivan Desny; D: Alexandre Astruc.

The End of Innocence 🐾🐾 1990 (R) In her attempts to please everyone in her life, a woman experiences a nervous breakdown. Released two years after Schaeffer's murder. 102m/C VHS, DVD. Dyan Cannon, John Heard, George Coe, Lola Mason, Rebecca Schaeffer, Stephen Meadows, Billie Bird, Viveka Davis; D: Dyan Cannon; W: Dyan Cannon; M: Michael Convertino.

The End of St. Petersburg 🐾🐾🐾½ 1927 (R) A Russian peasant becomes a scab during a workers' strike in 1914. He is then forced to enlist in the army prior to the 1917 October Revolution. Fascinating, although propagandistic film commissioned by the then-new Soviet government. Silent. 75m/B VHS, DVD. Ivan Chuvelov; D: Vsevolod Pudovkin.

End of Summer 🐾🐾½ 1997 (R) Bisset's performance is the highlight of this romantic drama. She's spinster Christine Van Buren who is spending the summer at a Saratoga Springs resort, circa 1890. She's stunned to encounter Theo (Weller), the man she loved and lost 20 years before. Christine and Theo are both willing to take a second chance but soon others are complicating the situation. 95m/C VHS. Jacqueline Bisset, Amy Locane, Elizabeth Shepherd, Michael Hogan; D: Linda Yellen; W: Linda Yellen, Jonathan Platnick; C: David Bridges; M: Patrick Seymour. CABLE

End of the Affair 🐾🐾 1955 In WWII London, Sarah (Kerr), the wife of a British civil servant (Cushing), falls in love with her neighbor Maurice (Johnson). The two make plans for their future together, but suddenly and mysteriously, Sarah brings the affair to an end. 106m/B DVD. GB Deborah Kerr, Van Johnson, John Mills, Peter Cushing; D: Edward Dmytryk; W: Lenore Coffee; C: Wilkie Cooper; M: Benjamin Frankel.

The End of the Affair 🐾🐾🐾 1999 (R) During the Blitz of WWII, married Londoner Sarah Miles (Moore) suddenly breaks off her affair with writer Maurice Bendrix (Fiennes). An unexpected meeting with her husband, Henry (Rea), leads Bendrix to believe Sarah is having a new affair and he hires a detective (Hart) to follow her. Instead, Bendrix discovers her reasons for breaking off with him and her spiritual reawakening. Compellingly adult drama about love, faith, and moral dilemmas that is based on the 1955 novel by Graham Greene. 101m/C VHS, DVD. GB Ralph Fiennes, Julianne Moore, Stephen Rea, Ian Hart, Sam Bould, Jason Isaacs; D: Neil Jordan; W: Neil Jordan; C: Roger Pratt; M: Michael Nyman. British Acad. '99: Adapt. Screenplay.

End of the Century: The Story of the Ramones 🐾🐾🐾 2003 Documents the underground music scene in New York (and abroad) during the late 1970s and chronicles the music, addictions, lineup changes, and pressures of life on the road, as well as just about every petty squabble the Ramones ever had. 110m/C DVD. D: Michael Granaglia, Jim Fields; C: Jim Fields.

End of the Line 🐾🐾½ 1988 (PG) Two old-time railroad workers steal a locomotive for a cross-country jaunt to protest the closing of the local railroad company. Produced by Steenburgen. 103m/C VHS, DVD. Wilford Brimley, Levon Helm, Mary Steenburgen, Kevin Bacon, Holly Hunter, Barbara Barrie, Bob Balaban, Howard Morris, Bruce McGill, Clint Howard, Trey Wilson, Rita Jenrette; D: Jay Russell; W: John Wohlbruck; M: Andy Summers.

End of the Road 🐾🐾½ 1970 (X) Keach is a troubled college professor whose bizarre treatment by his psychologist (Jones) produces tragic results. He eventually enters into an affair with the wife of a co-worker. Fascinating, if uneven script adapted from John Barth's story. Rated X upon release for adult story and nudity. 95m/C VHS. Stacy Keach, James Earl Jones, James Coco, Harris Yulin, Dorothy Tristan; D: Aram Avakian; W: Terry Southern; C: Gordon Willis.

End of the Spear 🐾🐾 2006 (PG-13) Based on the true events of a 1956 missionary trip during which five Americans were speared to death by the very Ecuadorian tribesmen they were seeking to convert. Unfortunately, studio production values coat the jungle and its visitors with a big bottle of syrup. To its credit, it at least tries to develop the tribesmen into something more than savages. Anyone looking for something more than an overt martyr's tale will be disappointed. 112m/C DVD. US Chad Allen, Chase Ellison, Louie Leonardo, Sara Kathryn Bakker, Cara Stoner, Jack Guzman, Christina Souza; D: Jim Hanon; W: Bart Gavigan, Jim Hanon, Bill Ewing; C: Robert A. Driskell Jr.; M: Ronald Owen.

End of the World WOOF! 1976 (PG) A coffee machine explodes, sending a man through a window and into a neon sign, where he is electrocuted. A priest witnesses this and retreats to a convent where he meets his alien double and heads for more trouble with outer space invaders. Interesting premise. 88m/C VHS, DVD. Christopher Lee, Sue Lyon, Lew Ayres, MacDonald Carey, Dean Jagger, Kirk Scott; D: John Hayes; M: Andrew Belling.

The End of Violence 🐾🐾 1997 (R) Slick, manipulative action-movie producer Mike Max (Pullman) evolves from his Hollywood roots to tranquility as a gardener after his own life is touched by the violence so pervasive in his pictures. There's a sinister government agent (Benzali) and a reclusive surveillance expert (Byrne) and Max gets kidnapped, only the kidnappers mysteriously wind up dead, and then he disappears. And, no, the plot doesn't really make much sense and all the characters are paranoid anyway. But it does give you something to try to figure out. Director Wenders drastically re-edited his movie after its lukewarm work-in-progress appearance at the 1997 Cannes Film Festival. 122m/C VHS, DVD. FR Bill Pullman, Gabriel Byrne, Andie MacDowell, Daniel Benzali, Traci Lind, Rosalind Chao, Loren Dean, Nicole Ari Parker, Enrique Castillo, K. Todd Freeman, John Diehl, Pruitt Taylor Vince, Peter Horton, Udo Kier, Marshall Bell, Frederic Forrest, Henry Silva, Samuel Fuller; D: Wim Wenders; W: Nicholas Klein; C: Pascal Rabaud; M: Ry Cooder.

Endangered 🐾🐾½ 1994 Environmentalists battle bad guys for survival in the wilderness. 91m/C VHS. Rick Aiello, Martin Kove, Sandra Hess, Tim Quill, Richard Hench, Dale Dye, Craig Alan, Kent MacLachlan, Renee Estevez; D: Nick Kellis; M: Nick Kellis.

Endangered Species 🐾🐾½ 1982 (R) Offbeat thriller with sci-fi leanings about a retired New York cop on vacation in America's West who is drawn into a female sheriff's investigation of a mysterious series of cattle killings. Could it be UFOs? Based on a true story. 97m/C VHS. Robert Urich, JoBeth Williams, Paul Dooley, Hoyt Axton, Peter Coyote, Harry Carey Jr., Dan Hedaya, John Considine; D: Alan Rudolph; W: Alan Rudolph, John Binder.

Endangered Species 🐾 2002 (R) A spree of bizarre health spa murders and missing victims stumps police detective Sullivan (Roberts) until the culprit is an up-to-no-good alien who just wants human skin to make an out-of-this-world fashion statement. Luckily there's a rival alien who arrives to aide the confused copper. 90m/C VHS, DVD. Eric Roberts, Arnold Vosloo, John Rhys-Davies, Tony LoBianco, Al Sapienza, James W. Quinn, Sarah Kaite Coughlan, Miranda Coughlan, Sophie Bielders, Alisa Hensley, Monika Verbutaite, Evgeniza Zakarevieute; D: Kevin S. Tenney; W: Kevin S. Tenney; C: Chris Manley; M: Harry Manfredini. VIDEO

Endgame 🐾🐾 1985 Grotesquely deformed survivors of WWIII fight their way to get stoked about this long-awaited sequel that once again follows two surfer dudes in their quest for the perfect wave. This time out pro surfers O'Connell and Weaver circle the globe seeking adventure and the world's best waves. Traces the evolution of surfing from the lazy, goldon days of the '60s to the worldwide phenomenon it is today, complete with its own pro tour circuit. Breathtaking scenery and spectacular surfing sequences highlight this look at a unique subculture. Thirty years later and it's still a great ride, though London gangster George Norris (McGann), who uses him in blackmail schemes. Norris is also involved in drug distribution with crooked cop Dunstan (Benfield). When Tom accidentally kills Norris during a fight, he goes to married

Endgame 🐾🐾 2001 Tom (Newman) is a troubled rent boy beholden to sadistic

neighbors Max (Johnson) and Nikki (Barry) for help in escaping Dunstan's wrath. Only Nikki has a personal fascination for Tom that comes out when she agrees to hide him. Moody and sometimes brutal. 113m/C VHS, DVD. GB Daniel Newman, Mark McGann, John Benfield, Toni Barry, Corey Johnson; D: Gary Wicks; W: Gary Wicks; C: David Bennett; M: Adrian Thomas.

Endless Descent WOOF! *La Grieta* 1990 (R) At least it seems endless. A group of scientist-types set out in search of a sunken sub, but somehow take a wrong turn into the rift, the deepest chasm at the bottom of the sea. There, they discover unimaginable horrors—that is, if you've never seen "Alien," or just about any other icky-monster flick. A Spanish film, shot in English, by director Simon, whose other works of art include "Pieces" and "Slugs." 79m/C VHS. SP Jack Scalia, R. Lee Ermey, Ray Wise, Deborah Adair, Ely Pouget; D: (Juan) Piquer Simon; W: David Coleman.

The Endless Game 🐾🐾 1989 (PG-13) Cold War suspenser has British secret-agent-man Finney attempting to solve the murder of his erstwhile fellow agent/lover, much to the dismay of the government. Written by director Forbes, this cable would-be thriller is a decidedly mediocre waste of a talented cast. Also of note, it was actor-director Sir Anthony Quayle's final appearance. 123m/C VHS. GB Albert Finney, George Segal, Derek de Lint, Monica Guerritore, Ian Holm, John Standing, Anthony Quayle, Kristin Scott Thomas; D: Bryan Forbes; W: Bryan Forbes; M: Ennio Morricone. CABLE

Endless Love 🐾🐾 1981 (R) Although only 17, David and Jade are in love. Her parents think they are too serious and demand that the two spend time apart. David attempts to win her parents' affection and approval, goes mad in the process, and commits a foolish act (he burns the house down) that threatens their love forever. Based on the novel by Scott Spencer. Of interest only to those with time on their hands or smitten by a love so bad that this movie will seem grand in comparison. Features Cruise's first film appearance. 115m/C VHS. Brooke Shields, Martin Hewitt, Don Murray, Shirley Knight, Beatrice Straight, Richard Kiley, Tom Cruise, James Spader, Robert Moore, Jami Gertz; D: Franco Zeffirelli; W: Judith Rascoe; C: David Watkin.

Endless Night 1971 An adaptation of an Agatha Christie tale. Focuses on a young chauffeur who wants to build a dream house, and his chance meeting with an American heiress. 95m/C VHS, DVD. GB Hayley Mills, Hywel Bennett, Britt Ekland, George Sanders, Per Oscarsson, Peter Bowles; D: Sidney Gilliat; W: Sidney Gilliat; C: Harry Waxman; M: Bernard Hermann.

The Endless Summer 🐾🐾🐾 1966 Classic surfing documentary about the freedom and sense of adventure that surfing symbolizes. Director Brown follows two young surfers around the world in search of the perfect wave. (They finally find it at a then-unknown break off Cape Saint Francis in South America.) Besides the excellent surfing photography, Big Kahuna Brown provides the amusing tongue-in-cheek narrative. Considered by many to be the best surf movie ever. 90m/C VHS, DVD, UMD. Mike Hynson, Robert August; D: Bruce Brown; W: Bruce Brown; Nar: Bruce Brown. Natl. Film Reg. '02.

The Endless Summer 2 🐾🐾🐾 *Bruce Brown's The Endless Summer 2; Bruce Brown's The Endless Summer Revisited* 1994 (PG) You don't have to personally hang ten the travelogue wears thin and the sub-culture's now fairly well exploited. 107m/C VHS, DVD, Robert "Wingnut" Weaver, Pat O'Connell, Robert August; W: Bruce Brown. Narr: Bruce Brown.

Endplay 1975 An Australian-made crime/horror drama in which two brothers cover for each other in a series of murders involving blonde hitchhikers. Based on a novel by Russell Braddon. 110m/C VHS, AU George Mallaby, John Waters, Ken Goodlet, Delvene Delaney, Charles "Bud" Tingwell, Robert Hewett, Kevin Miles; D: Tim Burstall.

Enduring Love 2004 (R) Brit psychodrama, based on Ian McEwan's 1997 novel, is triggered by a bizarre accident. A runaway hot air balloon disturbs the country picnic of science prof Joe Rose (Craig) and his girlfriend Claire (Morton). Several men, including Joe, try to rescue the boy trapped inside the balloon's basket and one would-be rescuer is killed. Joe doesn't know how to react and his conflict is echoed by loner/misfit Jed (Ifans), also on the scene. In fact, Jed is convinced that he and Joe now share a profound connection. His increasingly chilling persistence leads to the break-down of Joe and Claire's relationship and Joe's own fury. Film heads down a predictable path and the characters become clichés but Craig and Ifans manage to overcome three limitations. 99m/C DVD, Daniel Craig, Rhys Ifans, Samantha Morton, Joe Dunton, Susan Lynch, Helen McCrory, Andrew Lincoln, Corin Redgrave; D: Roger Michell; W: Joe Penhall; C: Haris Zambarloukos; M: Jeremy Sams.

Enemies, a Love Story 1989 (R) A wonderfully resonant, subtle tragedy based on the novel by Isaac Bashevis Singer. A post-Holocaust Jew, living in Coney Island, can't choose between three women—his current wife (who hid him during the war), his tempestuous lover, and his reappearing pre-war wife he presumed dead. A hilarious, confident tale told with grace and patience. 119m/C VHS, DVD, Ron Silver, Lena Olin, Anjelica Huston, Margaret Sophie Stein, Paul Mazursky, Alan King, Judith Malina, Rita Karin, Phil Leeds, Elya Baskin, Marie-Adele Lismieux; D: Paul Mazursky; W: Paul Mazursky; C: Fred Murphy; M: Maurice Jarre. N.Y. Film Critics '89: Director (Mazursky), Support. Actress (Olin); Natl. Soc. Film Critics '89: Support. Actress (Huston).

Enemies of Laughter 2000 Aspiring playwright and TV sitcom writer Paul is dejected as his first big stage venture totally tanks—and he can't seem to find true love either despite a steady string of prospects. But as fate would have it this buddy makes a successful documentary about Paul's romantic woes that attracts the attention of a gorgeous producer who rattles him with her desire to revive his failed play. 91m/C VHS, DVD, David Payner, Judge Reinhold, Rosalind Chao, Beatrice Arthur, Peter Falk, Vanessa Angel, Kathy Griffin, Mariu Henner, Kristina Fulton, Daphne Zuniga, Shera Danese, Leila Kenzle, Glen Merzer; D: Joey Travolta; W: Glen Merzer; C: Kristian Bernier; M: Jeremy Coffing. VIDEO

The Enemy 2001 (R) Mike Ashton (Perry) lives in Canada with his retired cherist father (Buchholz) who has been keeping secrets from his son. But they don't stay hidden when the bad guys come looking for dad and his work on bio-weapons making. A kidnapping attempt and a murder bring in the authorities, including Penry (d'Abo) who has a past with Mike and isn't adverse to fanning some flames. Story gets too convoluted for its own good but the pace is fast. 96m/C VHS, DVD, Luke Perry, Olivia D'Abo, Roger Moore, Horst Buchholz, Tom Conti, Hendrick Haese; D: Tom Kinnimont, Charlie Watson; W: John Penney; C: Mike Garfath; M: Gast Waltzing.

Enemy at the Gates 2000 (R) World War II saga set during the siege of Stalingrad in 1942 as Russian sniper Zaitsev (Law) tracks his equal in German sniper Konig (Harris). Law is also involved in a romantic triangle with a female Russian soldier (Weisz) and smarmy commissar Danilov (Fiennes). Only the sniper story is based on actual events and real people, from William Craig's historical account. Otherwise, the story as put on screen leaves out a lot, namely any real exploration of either the German or the Russian social and political stances of the time. We're left with good-looking men shooting it out in front of dramatic scenery, and a World War II lacking historical commentary. 131m/C VHS, DVD, GE GB IR US Jude Law, Ed Harris, Joseph Fiennes, Rachel Weisz, Bob Hoskins, Gabriel Marshall-Thomson, Eva Mattes, Ron Perlman, Matthias Hazicht; D: Jean-Jacques Annaud; W: Jean-Jacques Annaud, Alain Godard; C: Robert Fraisse; M: James Horner.

Enemy Below 1957 Suspenseful WWII sea epic, r which an American destroyer and a German U-Boat chase one another and square off in the South Atlantic. 98m/C VHS, DVD, Robert Mitchum, Curt Jurgens, David Hedison, Theodore Bikel, Doug McClure, Russell Collins; D: Dick Powell.

Enemy Gold 1993 (R) A crime czar and a beautiful killer without a conscience go after federal agents who have stumbled across a cache of Confederate gold. Basically, a babes-with-guns blowout. 92m/C VHS, DVD, Bruce Penhall, Rodrigo Obregon, Mark Barriere, Suzi Simpson, Tai Collins, Julie Strain; D: Drew Sidaris; W: Wess Rahn, Christian Sidaris.

Enemy Mine 1985 (PG-13) A space fantasy in which two pilots from warring planets, one an Earthling, the other an asexual reptilian Drac, crash land on a barren planet and are forced to work together to survive. 108m/C VHS, DVD, Dennis Quaid, Louis Gossett Jr., Brion James, Richard Marcus, Lance Kerwin, Carolyn McCormick; D: Wolfgang Petersen; W: Edward Khmara; C: Tony Imi; M: Maurice Jarre.

Enemy of the Law 1945 Texas rangers battle evil in an old frontier town. 59m/B VHS, DVD, Tex Ritter, Dave O'Brien; D: Harry Fraser.

Enemy of the State 1998 (R) Paranoia-thriller shows what the nerds would do if they really "wanted revenge. After a friend slips him a videocassette without his knowledge, lawyer Robert Dean (Smith) is targeted by a surveillance-and-gizmo-happy government agency headed by the sinister Reynolds (Voight). They hound Dean relentlessly, cutting him off from everything he holds dear by ruining his career and marriage, forcing him underground. Just when he has no place left to turn, he is aided by Brill (Hackman), a remorseful ex-agent who helped create the cyber-surveillance monster. From this point, our two heroes bicker, buddy-film fashion, and then blow up until the inevitable shootout crescendo. Smith's good guy who sustains interest in tale of technology run amok. 132m/C VHS, DVD, Blu-ray Disc, Will Smith, Gene Hackman, Jon Voight, Jason Lee, Regina King, Gabriel Byrne, Barry Pepper, Scott Caan, Loren Dean, Jake Busey, Lisa Bonet, Stuart Wilson, Tom Sizemore, James LeGros, Ian Hart, Dan E. Butler, Jamie Kennedy, Rebeca Silva, Jason Robards Jr., Bobby Boriello, Anna Gunn, Seth Green, Philip Baker Hall, Lillo Brancato, John Capodice, Jack Black, Bodhi (Pine) Elfman; D: Tony Scott; W: David Marconi; C: Dan Mindel; M: Trevor Rabin, Harry Gregson-Williams.

Enemy Territory 1987 (R) A handful of citizens trapped in a New York City housing project after dark are stalked by a violent, murderous street gang. 39m/C VHS, Ray Parker Jr., Jan-Michael Vincent, Gary Frank, Frances Foster; D: Peter Manoogian.

Enemy Unseen 1991 (R) A dickering squad of mercenaries slog through the African jungle to find a girl abducted by crocodile-worshipping natives. Dull Jungle-Jim-style adventure, notable for the hilariously phony crocs that occasionally clamp onto the characters. 90m/C VHS, Vernon Wells, Stack Pierce, Ken Gampu, Michael McCabe, Angela O'Neill; D: Elmo De Witt.

The Enemy Within 1994 Cable TV remake of the 1964 political thriller "Seven Days in May." Set in the late 1990s, President William Foster's (Waterston) approval rating is at an all-time low and his heavy defense cuts have certain government officials plotting a coup. Hero of the tale is Joint Chief of Staffs officer, Col. Mac Casey (Whitaker), whose military career is warring with his sense of ethics. The updating is fairly clunky; for true suspense stick with the original. 86m/C VHS, DVD, Forest Whitaker, Sam Waterston, Josef Sommer, Jason Robards Jr., Dana Delany, George Dzundza; D: Jonathan Darby; W: Darryl Ponicsan, Ronald Bass; C: Kees Van Oostrum. CABLE

The Enforcer Murder, Inc 1951 A district attorney goes after an organized gang of killers in this film noir treatment of the real-life "Murder, Inc." case. 87m/B VHS, DVD, Humphrey Bogart, Zero Mostel, Ted de Corsia, Everett Sloane, Roy Roberts, Michael "Lawrence, Tolan, King Donovan, Bob Steele, Adelaide Klein, Don Beddoe, Tito Vuolo; D: Bretaigne Windust, Raoul Walsh; W: Martin Rackin; C: Robert Burks.

The Enforcer 1976 (R) Dirty Harry takes on a female partner and a vicious terrorist group that is threatening the city of San Francisco. See how many "punks" feel lucky enough to test the hand of the tough cop. 96m/C VHS, DVD, Clint Eastwood, Tyne Daly, Harry Guardino, Bradford Dillman, John Mitchum, Albert "Poppy" Popwell, Will MacMillan, John Crawford, Jocelyn Jones, DeVeren Bookwalter, Dick Durock, Joe Spano; D: James Fargo; W: Stirling Silliphant, Stuart Hagmann; C: Charles W. Short; M: Jerry Fielding.

Enforcer from Death Row 1978 An ex-con is recruited by a secret international peacekeeping organization to track down and eliminate a band of murderous spies. 87m/C VHS, Cameron Mitchell, Leo Fong, Darnell Garcia, Booker T. Anderson, John Hammond, Marvin Roberts; D: Efren C. Pinon; W: Leo Fong.

The English Patient 1996 (R) Filled with flashbacks and moral ambiguities, this adult romance is a complicated WWII saga that finds fragile French-Canadian nurse Hana (Binoche) caring for a badly burn patient, in an abandoned monastery in Tuscany. Hana's joined by thief-turned-spy Caravaggio (Dafoe), who has a private score to settle with Almasy, and two British bomb disposal experts, Kip (Andrews), a Sikh who falls in love with Hana, and Sgt. Hardy (Whately). Almasy spends his days recalling his illicit love affair with Katharine Clifton (Scott Thomas), as they map the North African desert. Exquisitely ph'otographed in a golden glow by Seale with wonderful performances by the entire cast. Based on novel by Michael Ondaatje. 162m/C VHS, DVD, Ralph Fiennes, Kristin Scott Thomas, Juliette Binoche, Willem Dafoe, Naveen Andrews, Colin Firth, Julian Wadham, Jurgen Prochnow, Kevin Whately, Clive Merrison, Nino Castelnuovo; D: Anthony Minghella; W: Anthony Minghella; C: John Seale; M: Gabriel Yared, Oscars '96: Art Dir/Set Dec, Cinematog., Costume Des, Director (Minghella), Film Editing, Picture, Sound, Support. Actress (Binoche); Orig. Dramatic Score; British Acad. '96: Adapt. Screenplay, Cinematog., Film, Support. Actress (Binoche), Score; Directors Guild '96: Director (Minghella); Golden Globes '97: Film-Drama, Score; L.A. Film Critics '96: Cinematog., Score; N.Y. Film Critics '96: Cinematog.; Natl. Bd. of Review '96: Support. Actress (Binoche), Score; Writers Guild '96: Adapt. Screenplay; Broadcast Film Critics '96: Director (Minghella). Screenplay

An Englishman Abroad 1983 During a cultural exchange, British actress Coral Browne (playing herself in a pointed recreation) visits Moscow in 1961 and chances to meet notorious English spy/defector Guy Burgess (Bates). Behind their gossip and small talk is a tragicomic portrait of the exiled traitor/spy. Made for British TV; nuances may be lost on yank viewers. Winner of several British awards. 63m/C VHS, GB Alan Bates, Coral Browne, Charles Gray; D: John Schlesinger; W: Alan Bennett; M: George Fenton. TV

The Englishman Who Went up a Hill But Came down a Mountain 1995 (PG) Charming if slight tale of town pride based on writer/director Monger's family stories. In 1917 two English cartographers—pompous George (McNeice) and naive Reginald (Grant)—travel to Wales to measure the height of Ffynon Garw (a running gag has the surveyors struggling with the Welsh language). To the proud locals it is the first mountain in Wales, and without that designation they might as well redraw the maps and be part of England—God forbid. But in order to be designated a mountain Ffynon Garw must be 1000 feet high, and she measures only 984. Grant stammers boyishly as the English-man who is not only captivated by the village, but by spirited local lass Betty (Fitzgerald, with whom he starred in "Sirens"). Meaney slyly shines as innkeeper Morgan the Goat, leading the townful of color characters. Wales is shown to great advantage by cinematographer Layton. 96m/C VHS, DVD, GB Hugh Grant, Tara Fitzgerald, Colm Meaney, Ian McNeice, Ian Hart, Kenneth Griffith; D: Christopher Monger; W: Christopher Monger; C: Vernon Layton; M: Stephen Endelman.

Enid Is Sleeping Over Her Dead Body 1990 (R) Well-done comedy noir in the now-popular there's-a-corpse-in-the-closet subgenre. A woman in a mythical New Mexican town tries to hide the body of her sister Enid, who she's accidentally killed. Enid, it turns out, wasn't thrilled to discover her sister sleeping with her police-officer husband. Phillips and Perkins restore the film to its original state after it was ruthlessly gutted by the studio. 105m/C VHS, DVD, Elizabeth Perkins, Judge Reinhold, Rhea Perlman; D: Maurice Phillips; C: Alfonso Beato.

Enigma 1982 Trapped behind the Iron Curtain, a double agent tries to find the key to five pending murders by locating a Russian coded microprocessor holding information that would unravel the assassination scheme. 101m/C VHS, DVD, FR GB Martin Sheen, Brigitte Fossey, Sam Nell, Derek Jacobi, Frank Finlay, Michael (Michel) Lonsdale, Warren Clarke; D: Jeannot Szwarc; W: John Briley.

Enigma 2001 (R) Tom Jericho (Scott) is a British codebreaker working at Bletchley Park during WWII. He has a breakdown after a romantic breakup with colleague Claire (Burrows), who's mysteriously disappeared. Could she have been working for the Germans? Tom is determined to find out, aided by Claire's roommate Hester (Winslet). Meanwhile, intelligence operative Wigram (Northam) is keeping an eye on them both, thinking they know more than they appear to. Excessive subplots make for some confusion but the story's still compelling. Based on a novel by Robert Harris. 117m/C VHS, DVD, GB Dougray Scott, Kate Winslet, Saffron Burrows, Jeremy Northam, Nikolaj Waldau, Tom Hollander, Corin Redgrave, Robert Pugh, Matthew MacFadyen, Donald (Don) Sumpter; D: Michael Apted; W: Tom Stoppard; C: Seamus McGarvey; M: John Barry.

Enigma Secret 1979 Three Polish mathematicians use their noggins to break the Nazi secret code machine during WWII. Based on a true story. In Polish with English subtitles. 158m/C VHS, DVD, PL Tadeusz Borowski, Piotr Fronczewski, Piotr Garlicki; D: Roman Wionczek; W: Rom Wionczek; C: Jacek Zygadlo; M: Henryk Kuzniak.

Enjo Conflagration; The Flame of Torment 1958 True story of a tormented young monk, studying at the Golden Pavilion in Kyoto, who becomes disillusioned by the pervasive corruption of the temple. In desperation, he sets fire to the national shrine in an attempt to preserve the monument from further contamination. Very disturbing yet beautiful to watch. Adapted from Mishima's novel "Temple of the Golden Pavilion." Japanese with subtitles. 98m/B VHS, JP Raizo Ichikawa, Ganjiro Nakamura, Tatsuya Nakadai; D: Kon Ichikawa; W: Natto Wada, Keiji Hasebe, Toshio Mayuzumi; C: Kazuo Miyagawa.

Enola Gay: The Men, the Mission, the Atomic Bomb 🦴🦴 1980 Based on the best-selling book by Gordon Thomas and Max Gordon Witts, this drama tells the story of the airmen aboard the B-29 that dropped the first atomic bomb. Details the events during WWII leading up to the decision to bomb Hiroshima and the concerns of the crew assigned the task. 150m/C VHS. Patrick Duffy, Billy Crystal, Kim Darby, Gary Frank, Gregory Harrison, Ed Nelson, Robert Walden, Stephen Macht, Robert Pine, James Shigeta, Henry Wilcoxon; **D:** David Lowell Rich; **M:** Maurice Jarre. TV

Enormous Changes 🦴🦴🦴 *Enormous Changes at the Last Minute* 1983 Three stories about New York City women and their personal relationships. Based on the stories of Grace Paley. 115m/C VHS. Ellen Barkin, David Strathairn, Ron McLarty, Maria Tucci, Lynn Milgrim, Kevin Bacon; **D:** Mirra Bank; **W:** John Sayles.

Enough 🦴🦴 2002 (PG-13) Revenge fantasy that's been compared to both "Sleeping with the Enemy" (Julia Roberts) and "Double Jeopardy" (Ashley Judd). Working-class waitress Slim (Lopez) marries wealthy contractor Mitch (Campbell) and for a while everything appears perfect. But Mitch turns out to be an abusive, cheating, control freak who forces Slim to take their daughter and run. When Mitch finds and threatens her, Slim decides to literally toughen up and give Mitch a taste of his own medicine. Okay, it's nice to see Lopez kick butt but this movie has a very nasty taste and some lame advice for battered women (who probably won't discover that their biological fathers are filthy rich and can help them out financially). 115m/C VHS, DVD. *US* Jennifer Lopez, Billy Campbell, Juliette Lewis, Dan Futterman, Noah Wyle, Tessa Allen, Fred Ward, Bill Cobbs, Christopher Maher, Janet Carroll; **D:** Michael Apted; **W:** Nicholas Kazan; **C:** Rogier Stoffers; **M:** David Arnold.

Enrapture 🦴½ 1990 (R) A chauffeur is the prime suspect when a promiscuous passenger is murdered in his limousine. The driver did it? 87m/C VHS. Ona Simms, Harvey Siegel, Richard Parnes; **D:** Chuck Vincent.

Ensign Pulver 🦴🦴 1964 A continuation of the further adventures of the crew of the U.S.S. Reluctant from "Mister Roberts," which was adapted from the Broadway play. 104m/C VHS. Walter Matthau, Robert Walker Jr., Larry Hagman, Jack Nicholson, Millie Perkins, James Coco, James Farentino, Burl Ives, Gerald S. O'Loughlin, Al Freeman Jr.; **D:** Joshua Logan.

Enron: The Smartest Guys in the Room 🦴🦴🦴½ 2005 Based on the book by Fortune magazine reporters Bethany McLean and Peter Elkind. Director Alex Gibney deftly compiles vast amounts of in-house video and audio footage along with after-the-fact interviews and Congressional hearings chronicling the devastating downfall in 2001 of corporate behemoth Enron. An engaging, thorough, and coherent profile of the hustle created by chief executives Kenneth Lay, Jeffrey Skilling, and Andy Fastow and the resulting economic destruction, from the loss of 20,000 jobs and $2 million in employee pensions to the $30 billion cost of California's energy crisis. Matter-of-fact narration by Peter Coyote contrasts well with sly use of several pop music songs. 110m/C DVD. *US* **D:** Alex Gibney; **W:** Alex Gibney; **C:** Maryse Albert; **M:** Matt Hauser. Ind. Spirit '06: Feature Doc.; Writers Guild '05: Feature Doc.

Entangled 🦴🦴 1993 (R) David Mirkin (Nelson) is a struggling writer living in Paris with his beautiful girlfriend Annabelle (Treil). As she becomes ever more successful as a fashion model, David becomes ever more jealous and mistrustful. So he hires a detective (Brosnan) to spy on her. And then there's the small matter of a murder. Adapted from the novel "Les Veufs" by Boileau Narcejac. 98m/C VHS. Judd Nelson, Pierce Brosnan, Laurence Treil, Roy Dupuis;

Enter Laughing 🦴🦴 1967 Based on Reiner's semi-autobiographical novel and play, depicts the botched efforts of a Bronx-born schlump to become an actor. Worthwhile, but doesn't live up to the original. 112m/C VHS. Reni Santoni, Jose Ferrer, Elaine May, Shelley Winters, Jack Gilford, Don Rickles, Michael J. Pollard, Janet Margolin, Rob Reiner; **D:** Carl Reiner; **W:** Carl Reiner; **C:** Joseph Biroc; **M:** Quincy Jones.

Enter the Dragon 🦴🦴🦴 *The Deadly Three* 1973 (R) The American film that broke Bruce Lee worldwide combines Oriental conventions with 007 thrills. Spectacular fighting sequences including Karate, Judo, Tae Kwon Do, and Tai Chi Chuan are featured as Lee is recruited by the British to search for opium smugglers in Hong Kong. 98m/C VHS, DVD, UMD, HD DVD. Bruce Lee, John Saxon, Jim Kelly, Anna Capri, Shih Kien, Bob Wall, Angela (Mao Ying) Mao, Betty Chung, Jackie Chan, Tony Liu, Chuck Norris; **D:** Robert Clouse; **W:** Michael Allin; **C:** Gil Hubbs; **M:** Lalo Schifrin. Natl. Film Reg. '04.

Enter the Ninja 🦴 1981 (R) First and most serious of the Cannon canon of relatively well-done ninja epics (faint praise) that created original boxoffice stir for genre (mostly among adolescents needing outlet). Ninja Nero visits old friend in Philippines who's being terrorized by ruthless evil guy George. Nero dispatches numerous thugs before indulging in ninja slugfest with Kosugi. Just because you should, take it seriously doesn't mean you should. 99m/C VHS. Franco Nero, Susan George, Sho Kosugi, Christopher George, Alex Courtney; **D:** Menahem Golan; **W:** Judd Bernard.

The Entertainer 🦴🦴🦴½ 1960 Splendid drama of egotistical, third-rate vaudevillian Archie Rice (Olivier), who tries vainly to gain the fame his dying father Billy (Livesey) once possessed. His blatant disregard for his alcoholic wife Phoebe (De Banzie), his superficial sons (Bates and Finney), and his loyal daughter (Plowright) brings his world crashing down around him, as Archie discovers how self-destructive his life has been. Adapted from the play by John Osborne. Remade for TV in 1975 with Jack Lemmon. 104m/B VHS, DVD. *GB* Laurence Olivier, Brenda de Banzie, Roger Livesey, Joan Plowright, Daniel Massey, Alan Bates, Shirley Anne Field, Albert Finney, Thora Hird; **D:** Tony Richardson; **W:** Nigel Kneale, John Osborne; **C:** Oswald Morris; **M:** John Addison.

Entertaining Angels: The Dorothy Day Story 🦴🦴½ 1996 (PG-13) Dorothy Day (Kelly) was a social activist who founded the left-wing publication The Catholic Worker and was dedicated to sheltering and feeding the poor, founding soup kitchens across America. A radical journalist and New York bohemian, Day converts to Catholicism in the '20s and is soon working with the city's poor and homeless. Episodic story works mainly on indignation and its heroine's compassion. 110m/C VHS. Moira Kelly, Martin Sheen, Melinda Dillon, Lenny Von Dohlen, Heather Graham, Geoffrey Blake, Boyd Kestner, Allyce Beasley, Brian Keith; **D:** Michael Ray Rhodes; **W:** John Wells; **C:** Mike Fash; **M:** Bill Conti, Ashley Irwin.

Entertaining Mr. Sloane 🦴🦴½ 1970 Playwright Joe Orton's masterpiece of black comedy concerning a handsome criminal who becomes the guest and love interest of a widow and her brother. 90m/C VHS. *GB* Beryl Reid, Harry Andrews, Peter McEnery, Alan Webb; **D:** Douglas Hickox; **W:** Clive Exton, Joe Orton; **C:** Wolfgang Suschitzky.

The Entity 🦴🦴 1983 (R) Supposedly based on a true story about an unseen entity that repeatedly rapes a woman. Hershey's the victim whom nobody believes. She eventually ends up at a university for talks with parapsychologist Silver. Pseudo-science is frozen dead in its tracks. Exploitative violence, gore, and nudity aplenty, balanced to a degree by Hershey's strong performance. 115m/C VHS, DVD. Barbara Hershey, Ron Silver, Alex Rocco; **D:** Sidney J. Furie; **W:** Frank De Felitta; **C:** Stephen Burum; **M:** Charles Bernstein.

Entrapment 🦴🦴½ 1999 (PG-13) Too tricky for its own good crime caper features insurance investigator Virginia Baker (Zeta-Jones) convincing her boss, Hector Cruz (Patton), that master thief Mac MacDougall (Connery) is behind the theft of a Rembrandt. Only when Gin catches up to Mac, she convinces him that she's also a thief and she has a very rich heist in mind, that needs his expertise. However, nobody involved in anything that goes on in this movie is exactly what they seem. Nice scenery (and not just that offered by the beautiful Zeta-Jones). 112m/C VHS, DVD, Blu-ray Disc. Sean Connery, Catherine Zeta-Jones, Ving Rhames, Will Patton, Maury Chaykin; **D:** Jon Amiel; **W:** Ronald Bass, William Broyles Jr.; **C:** Phil Meheux; **M:** Christopher Young.

Entre-Nous 🦴🦴🦴½ *Between Us; Coup de Foudre; At First Sight* 1983 (PG) Two attractive, young French mothers find in each other the fulfillment their husbands cannot provide. One of the women was confined in a concentration camp during WWII; the other is a disaffected artist. In French with English subtitles. 112m/C VHS, DVD. *FR* Jean-Pierre Bacri, Patrick Bauchau, Jacqueline Doyen, Isabelle Huppert, Miou-Miou, Guy Marchand; **D:** Diane Kurys; **W:** Alan Henry, Diane Kurys; **C:** Bernard Lutic; **M:** Luis Bacalov.

Entropy 🦴🦴 1999 Dorff gives a gifted lead performance in this excessively stylistic romantic drama. It spans a year in the life of arrogant moviemaker Jake Walsh (Dorff), who describes how he meets French model Stella (Godreche) and experiences love at first sight. Although they live together, their careers frequently keep them apart and Jake's emotional immaturity eventually separates them. The cliched film-within-a-film narrative only manages to slow the main story down. 104m/C VHS. Stephen Dorff, Judith Godreche, Kelly Macdonald, Lauren Holly, Jon Tenney, Frank Vincent, Paul Guilfoyle, Hector Elizondo; **D:** Phil Joanou; **W:** Phil Joanou; **M:** George Fenton.

Envy 🦴🦴 2004 (PG-13) Tim (Stiller) and Nick (Black) are buddies, neighbors, and coworkers at a sandpaper plant. Nick is a dreamer who's constantly coming up with wacky inventions that Tim reminds him are impossible or impractical. One of these ideas is Vapoorize, a spray that makes dog doo disappear. When Tim passes on a chance to get in on the deal and the spray becomes a monster success, his wife's (Weisz) scorn triggers a jealousy that sends him on a trail of petty revenge on Nick. Uneven comedy is elevated by the gleefully manic performance of Walken, as Tim's criminal inspiration, the J-Man. Black's clueless immersion in the overly opulent lifestyle is a kick, as well. 99m/C DVD. *US* Ben Stiller, Jack Black, Rachel Weisz, Amy Poehler, Christopher Walken, Hector Elias, Edward "Blue" Deckert, Ariel Gade, Sam Lerner, Lily Jackson, Connor Matheus; **D:** Barry Levinson; **W:** Steve Adams; **C:** Tim Maurice-Jones; **M:** Mark Mothersbaugh.

Epic Movie woof! 2007 (PG-13) Another cobbled together, extremely unfunny spoof of popular movies. Four orphans (Mays, Penn, Chambers, Campbell) wind up in a chocolate factory where Glover is an even more sinister candy maker than Johnny Depp's Willy Wonka. Then they escape to a parody of "Narnia" (although Coolidge makes a fairly cool ice queen) and it just goes downhill from there. Someone somewhere must still finds this stuff funny. 85m/C DVD. *US* Kal Penn, Adam Campbell, Jennifer Coolidge, Faune A. Chambers, Jayma Mays, Crispin Glover, Fred Willard, Hector Jimenez, Darrell Hammond, Carmen Electra, David Carradine; **D:** Jason Friedberg, Aaron Seltzer; **W:** Jason Friedberg, Aaron Seltzer; **C:** Shawn Maurer; **M:** Ed Shearmur.

Epoch 🦴🦴 2000 (PG-13) Alien monolith suddenly appears and hovers over Bhutan, seemingly causing worldwide power disruptions and earthquakes. National security adviser Lysander (O'Neal) assigns special ops Kasia Czaban (Niznik) and weapons specialist Mason Rand (Keith) to figure out just what the object is—and wants—and, if necessary, to destroy it. 97m/C VHS, DVD. David Keith, Stephanie Niznik, Ryan O'Neal, James Hong, Brian Thompson, Craig Wasson, Donna Magnani, Shannon Lee; **D:** Matt Cold; **C:** Ken Stipe. CABLE

Epoch: Evolution 🦴🦴 2003 (R) It's been 10 years since the alien monolith, Torus, wreaked havoc with the planet. In this passable sequel to 2000's Epoch, Rand (Keith) must now summon it as a drastic measure to prevent a catastrophic third world war. 90m/C VHS, DVD. David Keith, Angel Boris, Billy Dee Williams, Brian Thompson; **D:** Ian Watson; **M:** Jason Christopherson. CABLE

Equal Impact 🦴½ 1996 Identical twin brothers Josh and Dave (Jay and Joe Gates) find themselves caught up in a deadly counterfeiting ring, headed by the sinister Donald Moss (Estevez). To escape, they enlist old friend Ray Tobin (Z'dar) and their own martial arts skills. 105m/C VHS. Jay Gates, Joe Gates, Joe Estevez, Robert Z'Dar; **D:** Jon Steven Ward; **W:** Jon Steven Ward; **C:** Lon Magolin; **M:** Darin Isaacs.

Equalizer 2000 🦴🦴 1986 (R) A warrior in a post-holocaust future plots to overthrow a dictatorship by using a high-powered gun. 85m/C VHS. Richard Norton, Corinne Wahl, William (Bill) Steis; **D:** Cirio H. Santiago.

Equilibrium woof! 2002 (R) It's the near future, in which society self-administers Prozium daily to thwart all emotions. The emotion cops, Grammaton Cleric, arrest sense offenders using the time-tested method of massive gun-kata battles. Agent John Preston's (Bale) position is compromised when he's attracted to Mary (Watson), a woman working with a resistance group. Poor attempt at sci-fi drama raises the question "Would the future suck less if we stopped making lousy movies about it in the present?" 106m/C VHS, DVD. *US* Christian Bale, Emily Watson, Taye Diggs, Angus MacFadyen, Sean Bean, William Fichtner, Matthew Harbour; **D:** Kurt Wimmer; **W:** Kurt Wimmer; **C:** Dion Beebe; **M:** Klaus Badelt.

Equinox 🦴🦴🦴 *The Beast* 1971 (PG) Young archaeologists uncover horror in a state forest. The ranger, questing for a book of spells that the scientists have found, threatens them with wonderful special effects, including winged beasts, huge apes, and Satan. Though originally an amateur film, it is deemed a minor classic in its genre. 80m/C VHS, DVD. Edward Connell, Barbara Hewitt, Frank Bonner, Robin Christopher, Jack Woods, Fritz Leiber Jr., Patrick Burke, Jim Phillips; **D:** Dennis Muren, Jack Woods; **W:** Jack Woods; **C:** Mike Hoover; **M:** John Caper Jr.

Equinox 🦴🦴 1993 (R) Modine gets to try his hand (and does well) at a dual role, with his portrayal of identical twins, separated at birth and raised in completely different environs. Garage worker Henry lives in a tenement while slick brother Freddie is a gangster's chauffeur married to the materialistic Sharon (Singer). Fate brings the brothers together when a janitor discovers a letter that reveals their parentage and the fate that a fortune has been left to them. Set in the near future, in the surreal and decaying city of Empire, this is typical Rudolph with its moody stylized appearance and convoluted plot. 110m/C VHS. Matthew Modine, Lara Flynn Boyle, Lori Singer, Marisa Tomei, Fred Ward, M. Emmet Walsh, Tyra Ferrell, Tate Donovan, Kevin J. O'Connor, Gailard Sartain; **D:** Alan Rudolph; **W:** Alan Rudolph; **C:** Elliot Davis.

Equinox Flower 🦴🦴½ 1958 Ozu's first color film tells the sensitive story of two teenage girls who make a pact to protect each other from the traditional prearranged marriages their parents have set up. Lovely film that focuses on the generation gap between young and old in the Japanese family. In Japanese with English subtitles. 118m/C VHS. *JP* Shin Saburi, Kinuyo Tanaka, Ineko Arima, Miyuki Kuwano, Chishu Ryu; **D:** Yasujiro Ozu.

Equus 🦴🦴½ 1977 (R) A psychiatrist undertakes the most challenging case of his career when he tries to figure out why a stable-boy blinded horses. Based upon the successful play by Peter Shaffer, but not well transferred to film. 138m/C VHS, DVD. Richard Burton, Peter Firth, Jenny Agutter, Joan Plowright, Colin Blakely, Harry Andrews; **D:** Sidney Lumet; **W:** Peter Shaffer; **C:** Oswald Morris; **M:** Richard Rodney Bennett. British Acad. '77: Support. Actress (Agutter); Golden Globes '78: Actor—Drama (Burton), Support. Actor (Firth).

Era Notte a Roma 🎬🎬 *by Night; Blackout in Rome 1960* An American, Russian, and British soldier each escape from a concentration camp and find refuge in the home days of WWII and find refuge in the waning days of WWII and find refuge in the home of a young woman. 145m/C VHS, IT Giovanna Ralli, Renato Salvatori, Leo Genn, Serge Bondarchuk, Peter Baldwin; D: Roberto Rossellini; W: Roberto Rossellini; C: Carlo Carlini; M: Renzo Rossellini.

Eragon 🎬🎬 *2006 (PG)* The dragon, voiced with maternal concern by Weisz, is a lot more charismatic than its rider—the teenaged farm boy of the title (Speleers in his film debut). A sword-and-sorcery flick, based on the first novel in a trilogy by Christopher Paolini (who was a teen himself when he wrote it), has a bad king (Malkovich) oppressing the little people in a mythic land—until Eragon and his dragon Saphira, aided by mentor Brom (Irons), can rally the rebels (there's always rebels). The kids will probably enjoy the adventure—even though the film is left open-ended for a sequel—but it doesn't hold much cross-over appeal for adults. 104m/C DVD, Blu-ray Disc; US Jeremy Irons, Sienna Guillory, Robert Carlyle, John Malkovich, Ed Speleers, Djimon Hounsou, Garrett Hedlund, Joss Stone, Alun Armstrong, Gary Lewis, Christopher Egan Richard Rifkin, Caroline Chikezie, Andrea Fazekas Steve Speirs; D: Stefan Fangmeier; W: Peter Buchman; C: Hugh Johnson; M: Patrick Doyle; V: Rachel Weisz.

Eraser 🎬🎬½ *1996 (R)* Arnold returns to familiar big-budget action territory and looks right at home. He plays elite U.S. Marshal John Kruger, who protects federal witnesses by "erasing" their previous identities. When a beautiful witness unexpectedly lead to some shady corporate dealings that eventually lead to some shady corporate dealings covers a high-level conspiracy, he two go on the run to stay alive long enough to expose the truth. Fans of the big bang Schwarzenegger of yore will not be disappointed. Rumors of production celays and budget overruns, not to mention difficulties between director Russell and producer Kopelson, brought up the spectre of "Waterworld," but the final result is more reminiscent of the success of "True Lies." 115m/C VHS, DVD. Arnold Schwarzenegger, Vanessa Llymei Williams, James Caan, James Coburn, Robert Pastorelli, Andy Romano, James Cromwell, Danny Nucci, Nicholas Chinlund Mark Rolston, Garry Becker, Joe (Johnny) Viterelli, Michael Papajohn; D: Chuck Russell; W: Tony Puryear, Walon Green; C: Adam Greenberg; M: Alan Silvestri.

Eraserhead 🎬🎬🎬 *1978* The infamous cult classic about a num2-brained everyman wandering through what amounts to a sick, ironic parody of the modern urban landscape. Innocently impregnating his girlfriend and fathering a pestilent embryonic mutant. Surreal and bizarre, the film has an inner, completely unpredictable logic all its own. Lynch's first feature-length film stars Nance, who later achieved fame in Lynch's "Twin Peaks" as Pete the Logger. 90m/B VHS, DVD. Jack Nance, Charlotte Stewart, Allen Joseph, Jeanne Bates, Judith Anna Roberts, Laurel Near, V. Phipps-Wilson, Jack Fisk, Jean Lange, Darwin Joston, Hal Landon Jr., Jennifer Lynch, Gill Dennis; D: David Lynch; W: David Lynch; C: Frederick Elmes, Herbert Cardwell; M: David Lynch, Fats Waller, Peter Ivers. Natl. Film. Reg. '04.

Erendira 🎬🎬½ *1983* Based on Gabriel Garcia-Marquez's story about a teenage girl prostituting herself to support her witch-like grandmother after accidentally torching the elder's house. The film follows the two as they travel across the desert trying out new and inventive ways to survive. Unusual ending tops off a creative, if not eclectic, movie. In Spanish with English subtitles. 103m/C VHS, FP MX GE Irene Papas, Claudia Ohana, Michael (Michel) Lonsdale, Rufus, Jorge Fegar; D: Guy Guerra; W: Gabriel Garcia Marquez; C: Denys Clerval; M: Maurice Lecoeur.

Eric 🎬🎬🎬 *1975* Tear-jerker about a young athlete who fights for his life after he's diagnosed with leukemia. Based on the true-life account written by Eric's mother. Doris Lund. 100m/C VHS. Patricia Neal, John Savage, Claude Akins, Sian Barbara Allen, Mark Hamill, Nehemiah Persoff, Tom Clancy; D: James Goldstone; M: Dave Grusin. TV

Erik 🎬🎬 *One Man Out 1989* An ex-government agent working in Central America torn between his loyalties divided when he is approached by a female activist and his old CIA friends. They want him to help expose his current boss as a drug smuggler. 90m/C VHS, Stephen McHattie, Deborah Van Valkenburgh; D: Michael Kennedy; W: Michael Kennedy.

Erik, the Viking 🎬 *1965* The Norse Warrior discovers not only the New World but outrageous subordinates among his crew, calling for drastic measures. 95m/ C VHS. IT SP Giuliano Gemma, Gordon Mitchell, Elissa Pichelli; D: Mario Caiano; W: Mario Caiano; C: Enzo Barboni; M: Carlo Franci.

Erik the Viking 🎬½ *1989 (PG-13)* A mediocre Monty Pythonesque farce about a Viking who grows dissatisfied with his barbaric way of life and decides to set out to find the mythical Asgaard, where Norse gods dwell. Great cast of character actors is wasted. 104m/C VHS, DVD, GE Tim Robbins, Terry Jones, Mickey Rooney, John Cleese, Imogen Stubbs, Anthony Sher, Gordon Cady, Neil Innes, Jim Broadbent, Andrew MacLachlan, Charles McKeown; D: Terry Jones; W: Terry Jones; M: Neil Innes.

Erin Brockovich 🎬🎬🎬 *2000 (R)* Erin Brockovich (Roberts) is a divorced mom desperate for a job. She bullies her way into a file clerk position at the small law office of Ed Masry (Finney) where her salty language, take-no-prisoners attitude, and scanty attire unnerve her co-workers. But that's just the appeal that Erin needs when she uncovers and investigates some shady corporate dealings that eventually lead to a multimillion dollar settlement against a public utility over contaminated water. Standout role for Roberts who's ably backed-up by the rumpled Finney. Based on a true story and yes, the real Erin is a looker who dresses every bit as provocatively as her screen counterpart. 131m/C VHS, DVD, HD DVD, Julia Roberts, Albert Finney, Aaron Eckhart, Marg Helgenberger, Cherry Jones, Yeanne Cox, Conchata Ferrell, Tracey Walter, Peter Coyote; D: Steven Soderbergh; W: Susannah Grant; C: Edward Lachman; M: Thomas Newman. Oscars '00: Actress (Roberts); Golden Globes '01: Actress—Drama (Roberts); L.A. Film Critics '00: Actress (Roberts); Director (Soderbergh); Natl. Bd. of Review '00: Actress (Roberts); N.Y. Film Critics '00: Director (Soderbergh); Natl. Soc. Film Critics '00: Actress (Roberts), Support. Actor (Finney); Broadcast Film Critics '00: Actress (Roberts), Director (Soderbergh).

Ermo 🎬🎬 *1994* Hard-working noodle-maker Ermo (Ailia) supports her slothful husband, Chief (Zhijun), and their son in their northern China village. Her smitten truck-driver neighbor Blindman (Peiqi) has an equally unpleasant wife, Fat Woman (Haiyan), with whom Ermo has an ongoing rivalry. They own a color TV (the only one in the village) and Ermo becomes determined to get a bigger and better set by selling her noodles in a nearby town and compulsively saving her money. Of course, her entrepreneurship has some unexpected consequences. Mardarin Chinese with subtitles. 93m/C VHS. CH Ailia, Peiqi Liu, Ge Zhijun, Zhang Haiyan; D: Xiaowen Zhou; W: Lang Yun; C: Lu Gengxin; M: Xiaowen Zhou.

Ernest Goes to Africa 🎬½ *1997 (PG)* Ernest P. Worrel (Varney) finds himself in a heap 0 trouble when he's accused of buying some stolen diamonds and he and would-be girlfriend Renee are kidnapped and taken to Africa where a prince wants his kajchery returned. Lots of sight gags and low humor. 90m/C VHS, DVD. Jim Varney, Linda Kash, Jamie Bartlett; D: John R. Cherry III; W: John R. Cherry III; C: James Robb.

Ernest Goes to Camp 🎬½ *1987 (PG)* Screwball, slapstick summer camp farce starring the character Ernest P Worrell as an inept camp counselor. When progress threatens the camp, Ernest leads the boys on a turtle-bombing, ship-shooting attack on the construction company. Followed by "Ernest Saves Christmas" and "Ernest Goes to Jail." 92m/C VHS, DVD, Richard Speight Jr., Jim Varney, Victoria Racimo, John Vernon, Iron Eyes Cody, Lyle Alzado, Gailard Sartain, Daniel Butler, Hakeem Abdul-Samad; D: John R. Cherry III; W: John R. Cherry III.

Ernest Goes to Jail 🎬🎬 *1990 (PG)* The infamous loon Ernest P. Worrel winds up in the jury box and the courtroom suddenly becomes hard-time in the slammer for poor Ernest when he is mistaken for a big-wig organized crime boss. Sequel to "Ernest Goes to Camp" and "Ernest Saves Christmas." 81m/C VHS, DVD, Jim Varney, Gailard Sartain, Randall "Tex" Cobb, Bill Byrge, Barry Scott, Charles Napier; D: John R. Cherry III; W: Charlie Cohen; M: Bruce Arntson.

Ernest Goes to School 🎬🎬½ *1994 (PG)* Ernest must finish high school if He's "aided" to keep his job as school janitor. He's "aided" by two crazy science teachers who give him an experimental IQ booster. 89m/C VHS, Jim Varney, Linda Kash, Bill Byrge; D: Coke Sams.

The Ernest Green Story 🎬🎬½ *1993* Drama based on the integration of Central High in Little Rock, Arkansas, by nine black students in 1957. Green was the only senior in the graduate. 92m/C VHS, Sonny Shroyer, Morris Chestnut, CCH Pounder, Gary Grubbs, Tina Lifford, Avery Brooks, Ruby Dee, Ossie Davis; D: Eric Laneuvile. C-A-B-L-E.

Ernest in the Army 🎬½ *1997 (PG)* Ernest is talked into joining the Army reserves and promptly causes all sorts of trouble when he's assigned to drive various military vehicles. 85m/C VHS, DVD. Jim Varney, Hayley Tyson, David Muller, Ivan Lucas; D: John R. Cherry III; W: Jeffrey Pillars; C: James Robb; M: Mark Adler.

Ernest Rides Again 🎬🎬½ *1993 (PG)* Ernest P. "Knowwhutimean?" Worrell (Varney) is back, aiding a college professor friend who has a cockamamie theory that the British crown jewels were hidden in a Revolutionary War cannon. Naturally he's right and Ernest must battle British spies and a greedy antiquities collector to get the gems back. Goofy slapstick sticks to the formula of the other films. 93m/C VHS. Jim Varney, Ron James, Duke Ernsperger, Jeffrey Pillars, Linda Kash, Tom Butler; D: John R. Cherry III; W: John R. Cherry III, Daniel Butler; M: Bruce Arntson, Kirby Shelstad.

Ernest Saves Christmas 🎬½ *1988 (PG)* Ernest P. Worrell is back. When Santa decides that it's time to retire, Ernest must help him recruit a has-been Ernest's show host who is a bit reluctant. For Ernest fans only, and only the most dedicated of them. Second in the series featuring the nimble-faced Varney, the first of which was "Ernest Goes to Camp," followed by "Ernest Goes to Jail." 91m/C VHS, DVD, Jim Varney, Douglas Seale, Oliver Clark, Noelle Parker, Billie Bird; D: John R. Cherry III.

Ernest Scared Stupid 🎬½ *1991 (PG)* Pea-brained Ernest P. Worrell returns yet again in this silly comedy. When he accidentally releases a demon from a sacred tomb a 200-year-old curse threatens to destroy his hometown, unless Ernest can come to the rescue. Would you want your town depending on Ernest's heroics? Who would have thought that the annoying Ernest P. Worrell could appear in one movie, let alone four? 93m/C VHS. Jim Varney, Eartha Kitt, Austin Nagler, Jonas Moscartolo, Shay Astar; D: John R. Cherry III; W: Charlie Cohen, Coke Sams; M: Bruce Arntson.

Ernesto 🎬½ *1979* A lushly erotic Italian film depicting the troubled relationship between a young, devil-may-care gay youth and his older, coolly seducing lover. In Italian with subtitles. 98m/C VHS. IT Martin Ham, Michele Placido; D: Salvatore Sampeti.

The Errand Boy 🎬½ *1961* Jerry Lewis's patented babbling schnook hits Hollywood in search of a job. Holly-wood may never be the same again in this prototypical comedy; a must for Lewis

Ernie Kovacs: Between the Laughter 🎬🎬 *1984* The television comic's life and career, ending with his tragic death in a car accident in 1962. Shows the brand of humor that made Kovacs famous as well as the devastation that he suffered after the tragic kidnapping of his children by his first wife during divorce proceedings. Kovac's second wife, Edie Adams, makes a brief appearance. 95m/C VHS. Jeff Goldblum, Cloris Leachman, Melody Anderson, Madolyn Smith, John Glover, Cammy Bars; D: Lamont Johnson; M: Ralph Burns. TV

Eros 🎬🎬½ *2004 (R)* Three short films by renowned d rectors intended to convey their own interpretation of eroticism. Whether or not they're actually intended to be erotic is for you to be determined. Wong Kar-Wai's "The Hand" nails it. It's nc nudity, no explicit sex, nothing to tell you what to feel. But it's poetic and stays with you. Steven Soderbergh's "Equilibrium" stars Robert Downey, Jr. as a patient explaining his sexually-obscure dream to over. The doc doesn't listen much. Neither do we. Finally, director Michelangelo Antonioni closes the program with a real stinker. His Zabriskien roots place the characters in a land of causal nudity and dopey music. Trilogies need to get better with each installment, but this one rolls downhill the entire way. 104m/C DVD, US FR IT LU Gong Li, Chang Chen, Tin Fung, Zhou Jianun, Robert Downey Jr., Alan Arkin, Ele Keats, Christopher Buchholz, Regina Nemni, Luisa Ranieri; D: Wong Kar-Wai, Steven Soderbergh, Michelangelo Antonioni; W: Wong Kar-Wai, Steven Soderbergh, Michelangelo Antonioni; C: Tonino Guerra, Christopher Doyle, Marco Pontecorvo; M: Peer Raben, Enrica Antonioni, Vinicio Milani, Chico O'Farril, Roger Fellous; W: Raymond Ruer.

Erotic Escape 🎬 *Les Bananes Mecaniques; Mechanical Bananas 1972* Soft-core fun about party girls taking over a small French town. Originally in French, but dubbed in English. Check your brain at the door. 86m/C VHS. FR Marie-Claire Davy, Pauline Larrieu, Anne Libert; D: Jean-Francois Davy; C: Jean-Francois Davy; M: Raymond Ruer.

Erotic Images *woof! 1985 (R)* A beautiful psychology teacher publishes her doctoral thesis on sex and becomes a best-selling author, which threatens her marriage. 93m/C VHS. Britt Ekland, Edd 3ymes, John McCann; D: Declan Langan.

Erotic House of Wax 🎬½ *1997 1965* Sex, murder, false identities, car crashes, and striptease in the Riviera. Young woman inherits her uncle's bizarre wax museum with its death and discovers that the museum's inhabitants have the habit of coming to life and acting out their sexual fantasies. 78m/B VHS. Fabienne Dali, Sophie Hardy, Jean Valmont, Francois Dzyek; D: Max Pecas.

Erotique 🎬🎬 *1994* Sex quartet from female filmmakers. "Let's Talk About Sex" finds struggling Latina actress Rosie (Lopez-Dawson) supporting herself by working at a phone sex agency where a caller (Cranston) wants to know about her sexual fantasies. "Taboo Parlor" finds lesbian lovers Claire (Barnes) and Julia (Soeberg) picking up boy toy Victor (Carr) and planning some s/m games. "Wonton Soup" has Australian-born Chinese Adrian (Louriibos) reuniting with his lover Ann (Man) in Hong Ko.g and deciding to hold her interest by practicing some ancient Chinese sexual techniques. And in "Final Call," a school teacher (Ohana) tries a sexual adventure with a stranger. 120m/C VHS, DVD. Kamala Lopez, Bryan Cranston, Priscilla Barnes, Camilla Soeberg, Michael Carr, Tim Lounibos, Hayley Man, Claudia Ohana; D: Lizzie Borden, Monika Treut, Clara Law, Ana Maria Magalhaes; W: Lizzie Borden, Monika Treut, Susie Bright, Eddie Ling-Ching Fong; C: Larry Banns, Elfi Mikesch, Arthur Wong Ngok Tai.

fans only. **92m/B VHS, DVD**. Jerry Lewis, Brian Donlevy, Dick Wesson, Howard McNear, Felicia Atkins, Fritz Feld, Sig Rumann, Renee Taylor, Doodles Weaver, Mike Mazurki, Lorne Greene, Michael Landon, Dan Blocker, Pernell Roberts, Snub Pollard, Kathleen Freeman; **D:** Jerry Lewis; **W:** Jerry Lewis.

The Errors of Youth 🐶🐶🐶 *Wild Oats* 1978 Dimitri (Zhdanko), a construction worker in Siberia, is disillusioned over a failed love affair and moves to Leningrad where he falls in with black marketeers and a marriage of convenience. Because of political problems, director Frumin left the film unfinished when he emigrated to the U.S. and it wasn't until 1989 that he returned to Leningrad to complete the project. Russian with subtitles. **87m/C VHS.** *RU* Stanislav Zhdanko, Marina Neyolova, Natalia Varley, Mikhail Vaskov; **D:** Boris Frumin.

Erskinville Kings 🐶🐶½ 1999 The plot borders on the cliched but White's debut feature has strong performances to carry it along. It's summer in a grimy Sydney suburb filled with run-down stores, bars, and neglected houses. Barky (screenwriter Chooney acting under the pseudonym Martin Denniss) is returning home after two years for his drunken, abusive father's funeral. He's hoping to have some kind of reconciliation with his brother Wace (Jackman) but Wace's bitterness may prevent that. **85m/C VHS.** *AU* Anik (Martin Denniss) Chooney, Hugh Jackman, Leah Vandenberg, Aaron Blabey, Andrew Wholley, Joel Edgerton; **D:** Alan White; **W:** Anik (Martin Denniss) Chooney; **C:** John Swaffield; **M:** Don Miller-Robinson.

Escanaba in da Moonlight 🐶🐶 2001 (PG-13) If you're not a "Yooper" or familiar with those denizens of Michigan's Upper Peninsula, Daniel's film (based on his play) will probably be lost on you. This is the kind of local humor that rarely travels well. The story is basically a tall tale—middleaged Reuben Soady (Daniels) has reached his advanced years without ever having bagged a deer on his annual hunting trip with his dad (Presnell) and brother (Albright). He is a community laughingstock but that is about to change. **90m/C VHS, DVD.** *US* Jeff Daniels, Harve Presnell, Joey Albright, Wayne David Parker, Randall Goodwin, Kimberly Norris Guerrero; **D:** Jeff Daniels; **W:** Jeff Daniels; **C:** Richard Brawer.

Escapade 🐶🐶 1955 Sons thinking their parents are en route to divorce court create a scheme to achieve peace worldwide. The pacifist father's reaction juxtaposes idealistic youth with the cynicism of adulthood. Adapted from a play by Roger MacDougall. **87m/B VHS.** *GB* John Mills, Yvonne Mitchell, Alastair Sim, Jeremy Spenser, Andrew Ray, Marie Lohr, Peter Asher; **D:** Philip Leacock; **W:** Donald Ogden Stewart.

Escapade in Florence 🐶🐶 1962 As two students in Florence paint their way to immortality, an elaborate art-forging ring preys upon their talents. **81m/C VHS.** Tommy Kirk, Ivan Desny; **D:** Steve Previn.

Escape 🐶½ 1990 (R) A woman attempts to track down her brother's killer and finds an entire town mysteriously controlled by a sadistic and powerful man. Features General Hospital's bad-boy Shriner. **100m/C VHS.** Elizabeth Jeager, Kim Richards, Kin Shriner; **D:** Richard Styles.

Escape 🐶🐶 1990 (PG) A fun-loving, care-free Irish officer is sent to oversee the toughest POW prison in Scotland. There, he becomes consumed with keeping the facility secure despite the intricate escape plans laid out by a group of rioters. **90m/C VHS.** Brian Keith, Helmut Griem; **D:** Lamont Johnson.

The Escape 🐶½ 1995 Prisoner Clayton (Dempsey) manages to escape incarceration and is then on the lam from sadistic prison guard, Hickman (Feore). Moody flashbacks show his crime, while in the present Clayton finds some sexual solace with the accommodating Sarah (Bako) as he tries to outwit his pursuers. **91m/C VHS.** Patrick Dempsey, Brigitte Bako, Colm Feore, Vincent Gale, Nathaniel DeVeaux, William Morgan Sheppard; **D:** Stuart Gillard; **W:** Scott Busby; **C:** Tobias Schliessler; **M:** Loek Dikker. **VIDEO**

The Escape Artist 🐶🐶🐶 1982 (PG) Award-winning cinematographer Deschanel's first directorial effort is this quirky film about a teenage escape artist who sets out to uncover the identity of his father's killers. **96m/C VHS, DVD.** Griffin O'Neal, Raul Julia, Teri Garr, Joan Hackett, Desi Arnaz Sr., Gabriel Dell, Huntz Hall, Jackie Coogan, Elizabeth (E.G. Dailey) Daily; **D:** Caleb Deschanel; **W:** Melissa Mathison; **C:** Stephen Burum; **M:** Georges Delerue.

Escape Clause 🐶🐶 1996 (R) Insurance exec Richard Ramsay (McCarthy) gets a call from a hitman informing him that his wife Sarah (McNeil) has hired him to kill Richard. The hitman says if Richard will pay him, the contract's off. Instead Richard tries to figure out what's going on, with some help from police detective Ferrand (Sorvino), who discovers Richard has been treated for paranoid delusions. Fast-paced mystery with a few too many twists. **131m/C VHS.** Andrew McCarthy, Paul Sorvino, Kate McNeil, Peter Donaldson, Kenneth Welsh, Connie Britton, Stan(ford) Egi, John Evans; **D:** Brian Trenchard-Smith; **W:** Danilo Bach; **M:** Ken Thorne, Richard (Rick) Marvin. **VIDEO**

Escape from Alcatraz 🐶🐶🐶 1979 (PG) A fascinating account of the one and only successful escape from the maximum security prison at Alcatraz in 1962. The three men were never heard from again. **112m/C VHS, DVD.** Clint Eastwood, Patrick McGoohan, Roberts Blossom, Fred Ward, Jack Thibeau, Paul Benjamin, Larry Hankin, Carl Lumbly, Danny Glover; **D:** Donald Siegel; **W:** Richard Tuggle; **C:** Bruce Surtees; **M:** Jerry Fielding.

Escape from Atlantis 🐶🐶½ 1997 (PG-13) Workaholic attorney and single dad, Matt Spencer (Speakman), charters a sailboat and plans a cruise to the Bahamas so he and his three teenagers can have some quality time. The sailboat heads into the Bermuda Triangle and capsizes in a hurricane; when the Spencers come to, they're in the land of Atlantis, where fantasy is reality. **93m/C VHS.** Jeff Speakman, Brian Bloom, Tim Thomerson, Mercedes McNab, Michael Lee Goggin, Justin Burnette, Breck Wilson; **D:** Strathford Hamilton; **W:** Arne Olsen.

Escape from Cell Block 3 🐶 *Women Unchained* 1974 Five escaped female convicts take it on the lam for Mexico and freedom. **82m/C VHS.** Carolyn Judd, Teri Guzman, Bonita Kalem; **D:** Ken Osborne; **W:** Ken Osborne; **C:** Clancy B. Grass III; **M:** Hank Webster.

Escape from Death Row 🐶 *Dio, Sei Proprio un Padreterno!* 1973 (R) Convicted criminal mastermind, sentenced to die, devises a brilliant and daring plan of escape on the eve of his execution. **85m/C VHS, DVD.** *IT* Lee Van Cleef, Jean Rochefort, Tony LoBianco, Edwige Fenech, Fausto Tozzi, Mario Erpichini, Jess Hahn; **D:** Michele Lupo; **W:** Nicola Badalucco, Sergio Donati, Luciano Vincenzoni; **C:** Joe D'Amato, Aldo Tonti; **M:** Riz Ortolani.

Escape from DS-3 🐶🐶 1981 Bobstwick and "Police Academy" alumnus Smith team up in a familiar story: framed for a serious crime, a man attempts to escape from a maximum security satellite prison. About as good as you'd expect. **88m/C VHS.** Jackson Bostwick, Bubba Smith; **D:** Bob Emenegger; **W:** Peter Dawson.

Escape from El Diablo 🐶🐶 1983 (PG) Two juvenile delinquents harass guards at a Mexican prison. Being from California, they use frisbees and skateboards to help their escape. **92m/C VHS.** *SP GB* Jimmy (James Vincent) McNichol, Timothy Van Patten, John Ethan Wayne; **D:** Gordon Hessler.

Escape from Fort Bravo 🐶🐶½ 1953 A Civil War era western set in an Arizona stockade. Holden is the hard-bitten Union cavalry officer who ruthlessly guards his Confederate prisoners, who are led by Forsythe. Parker is a southern spy whose job is to break the rebels out of jail by seducing Holden from his duty, which she does. When Holden discovers what's happened, he recaptures his prisoners only to be beset by hostile Mescalero Indians while trying to get everyone back to the fort. It's an old story but well-executed with lots of action. **98m/C VHS.** William Holden, Eleanor Parker, John Forsythe, William Demarest, William Campbell, Polly Bergen, Richard Anderson, Carl Benton Reid, John Lupton, Howard McNear, Alex Montoya, Forrest Lewis, Fred Graham, William "Billy" Newell; **D:** John Sturges; **W:** Frank Fenton; **C:** Robert L. Surtees.

Escape from Galaxy Three 🐶 1981 (G) A pair of space travelers fight off a bevy of alien aliens. **90m/C VHS.** *IT* James Milton, Cheryl Buchanan; **D:** Sandro Mancori; **M:** Don Powell.

Escape from Hell woof! *Hellfire on Ice, Part 2: Escape from Hell; Femmine Infernali* 1979 Two scantily clad women escape from a jungle prison and are pursued by their sadistic warden. **93m/C VHS, DVD.** *IT SP* Anthony Steffen, Ajita Wilson; **D:** Edward (Edoardo Mulargia) Muller.

Escape from L.A. 🐶🐶½ 1996 (R) Well, *Carpenter's Escape from L.A.* Snake Plissken is back (Russell once again) and so's Carpenter, who did the original "Escape from New York" saga, and technology's advanced a lot in 15 years, so sit back and enjoy the action. In 2013, L.A.'s been turned into a gang-infested island, thanks to a 9.6 earthquake, where Snake is forced to find a doomsday weapon in just 10 hours. Seems he's been injected with a virus that will kill him unless he can complete his job and escape to get the antidote. Naturally, there's lots of bad guys who'll try to stop him. Russell not only reprises his old role but found Snake's original leathers, which still fit, and wore the outfit in some scenes of the sequel. **101m/C VHS, DVD.** Kurt Russell, Georges Corraface, Stacy Keach, Pam Grier, Steve Buscemi, Pam Grier, Valeria Golino, Cliff Robertson, Michelle Forbes, Bruce Campbell, A.J. (Allison Joy) Langer; **D:** John Carpenter; **W:** Kurt Russell, John Carpenter, Debra Hill; **C:** Gary B. Kibbe; **M:** John Carpenter, Shirley Walker.

Escape from Mars 🐶🐶 1999 (PG) Astronauts make the first manned trip to Mars in the 21st century and must battle any number of internal and external problems to survive. **90m/C VHS.** *CA* Christine Elise, Peter Outerbridge, Allison Hossack, Michael Shanks; **D:** Neill Fearnley; **W:** Jim Henshaw; **C:** Peter Woeste; **M:** Peter Allen. **TV**

Escape from New York 🐶🐶🐶 1981 (R) The ultimate urban nightmare: a ruined, future Manhattan is an anarchic prison for America's worst felons. When convicts hold the President hostage, a disgraced war hero unwillingly attempts an impossible rescue mission. Cynical but largely unexceptional sci-fi action, putting a good cast through tight-lipped peril. **99m/C VHS, DVD, UMD.** Kurt Russell, Lee Van Cleef, Ernest Borgnine, Donald Pleasence, Isaac Hayes, Adrienne Barbeau, Harry Dean Stanton, Season Hubley, Tom Atkins, Charles Cyphers, George "Buck" Flower; **D:** John Carpenter; **W:** John Carpenter, Nick Castle; **C:** Dean Cundey; **M:** John Carpenter; **V:** Jamie Lee Curtis.

Escape from Planet Earth 🐶 *The Doomsday Machine* 1967 A spaceship is damaged deep in space and only a few of the crew can make it back to Earth. But who will decide who lives or dies? (Unfortunately, the Earth has been totally destroyed so who cares anyway.) Lousy special effects. **91m/B VHS.** Grant Williams, Bobby Van, Ruta Lee, Henry Wilcoxon, Mala Powers, Casey Kasem, Mike Farrell, Harry Hope; **D:** Lee Sholem.

Escape from Safehaven woof! 1988 (R) Brutal slimeballs rule a mad, sadistic world in the post-apocalyptic-future, and a family tries to escape them. In very poor taste. **87m/C VHS.** Rick Gianasi, Mollie O'Mara, John Wittenbauer, Roy MacArthur, William Beckwith; **D:** Brian Thomas Jones, James McCalmont.

Escape from Sobibor 🐶🐶🐶 1987 (PG-13) Nail-biting, true account of the largest successful escape from a Nazi prison camp, adapted from Richard Rashke's book. Made for TV. **120m/C VHS, DVD.** Alan Arkin, Joanna Pacula, Rutger Hauer, Hartmut Becker, Jack Shepherd; **D:** Jack Gold; **M:** Georges Delerue. **TV**

Escape from the Bronx 🐶 1985 (R) Invading death squads seek to level the Bronx. Local street gangs cry foul and ally to defeat the uncultured barbarians. Sequel to "1990: The Bronx Warriors." **82m/C VHS.** Mark Gregory, Henry Silva, Valeria (Valerie Dobson) D'Obici, Giancarlo Prete, Andrea Coppola; **D:** Enzo G. Castellari.

Escape from the KGB woof! 1987 A CIA agent escapes from a Soviet prison, taking plans for a new space installation with him. **99m/C VHS.** Thomas Hunter, Ivan Desny, Marie Versini, Walter Barns; **D:** Harald Philipp.

Escape from the Planet of the Apes 🐶🐶🐶 1971 (G) Reprising their roles as intelligent, English-speaking apes, McDowall and Hunter flee their world before it's destroyed, and travel back in time to present-day America. In L.A. they become the subjects of a relentless search by the fearful population, much like humans Charlton Heston and James Franciscus were targeted for experimentation and destruction in simian society in the earlier "Planet of the Apes" and "Beneath the Planet of the Apes." Sequelled by "Conquest of..." and a TV series. **98m/C VHS, DVD.** Roddy McDowall, Kim Hunter, Sal Mineo, Ricardo Montalban, William Windom, Bradford Dillman, Natalie Trundy, Eric (Hans Gudegast) Braeden, Jason Evers, Harry Lauter, John Randolph, M. Emmet Walsh; **D:** Don Taylor; **W:** Paul Dehn; **C:** Joseph Biroc; **M:** Jerry Goldsmith.

Escape from Wildcat Canyon 🐶½ 1999 Grandfather Weaver and his young grandson must fight for survival after their small plane crashes in the mountains. **96m/C VHS, DVD.** Dennis Weaver, Michael Calcz, Peter Keleghan, Frank Schorpion, Vlasta Vrana; **D:** Marc Voizard. **CABLE**

Escape: Human Cargo 🐶🐶🐶 *Human Cargo* 1998 Suspenseful and fact-based drama set in 1977. Texan John McDonald (Williams) thinks he's scored big when he gets a contract to build housing in Dhahran, Saudi Arabia. Despite government warnings, McDonald decides to travel there himself to oversee the deal. But his partners prove deceitful and when McDonald tries to enforce the contract, he's eventually released, but with his passport confiscated, the only way for McDonald to get out of the Middle East is to try smuggling himself home as cargo. Based on the book "Flight from Dhahran" by John McDonald and Clyde Burleson. **110m/C VHS, DVD.** Treat Williams, Stephen Lang, Sasson Gabai; **D:** Simon Wincer; **W:** William Mickelberry, Dan Vining; **C:** David Burr; **M:** Eric Colvin. **CABLE**

Escape Me Never 🐶🐶½ 1947 Flynn plays a struggling composer in this sappy period piece about poverty-stricken artists in Italy at the turn of the century. Flynn falls for his brother's wealthy fiancee (Parker), although he is married to the faithful Lupino. Atypical role for Flynn and definitely not one of his best. Based on the novel "The Fool of the Family," by Margaret Kennedy and the play "Escape Me Never" by Kennedy. **101m/B VHS.** Errol Flynn, Ida Lupino, Eleanor Parker, Gig Young, Reginald Denny, Isobel Elsom; **D:** Peter Godfrey; **W:** Thomas Williamson.

Escape to Athena 🐶🐶½ 1979 (PG) A motley group is stuck in a German P.O.W. camp on a Greek island during WWII. **102m/C VHS.** *GB* Roger Moore, Telly Savalas, David Niven, Claudia Cardinale, Richard Roundtree, Stefanie Powers, Sonny Bono, Elliott Gould, William Holden; **D:** George P. Cosmatos; **W:** Edward Anhalt; **M:** Lalo Schifrin.

Escape to Burma 🐶🐶 1955 A man on the run for a murder he did not commit finds refuge and romance in an isolated jungle home. **86m/C VHS, DVD.** Barbara Stanwyck, Robert Ryan, Reginald Denny; **D:** Allan Dwan.

Escape to Paradise 𝟙½ 1982 Beautiful stuntman helps a famous dissident escape from Poland, only to lose him to another heroic venture. 105m/C Cara Perryman; Louis Jourdan. **D:** Herbert Stein.

Escape to the Sun 𝟙½ 1939 ... as a South American motorcycle-taxi driver acting as a guide for tourist Taylor. When Breen sets Taylor up with Shelton, trouble ensues. "Tra-La-La," "Rhythm of the Rio." AV, AV, AV, 60m/B VHS, Bobby Breen, Kent Taylor, Maria Shelton, Joyce Compton, Rosina Galli, Frank Yaconelli. **D:** Erle C. Kenton.

Escapes 𝟙𝟙 1986 In the tradition of "The Twilight Zone," Vincent Price introduces five short thrillers featuring time travel, aliens, and telepathy. Produced with computer assistance for sharper, more contrasted images. 72m/C VHS. Vincent Price, Jerry Grisham, Lee Canfield, John Mitchum, Gil Reaza; **D:** David Steensland. **VIDEO**

Escapist WOOF! 1983 A professional escape artist becomes involved in a perverted corporate plot and must escape to save his life and livelihood. 87m/C VHS. Bill Shirk, Peter Lupus. **D:** Eddie Beverly Jr.

The Escort 𝟙𝟙 1997 (R) Debra Grey (Hall) runs a highly successful (and respectable) escort service and has just hired the charming Suzanne Lane (O'Brien). But behind Suzanne's charm lies the dreaded face of a psycho and she takes a very personal interest in Debra and her family. The unrated version is 90 minutes. 85m/C VHS. Shauna O'Brien, Landon Hall; **D:** Gary Graver; **W:** Sean O'Bannon; **C:** Gary Graver. **VIDEO**

Esmeralda Comes by Night 𝟙𝟙½ De Noche Vienes, Esmeralda 1998 (R) Flaky Mexican comedy about a very nurturing nurse named Esmeralda (Rojo) who just loves men so much that she's married to five of them—at the same time. When she decides to take a sixth ...

Escape to Witch Mountain 𝟙𝟙𝟙 1975 (G) Two young orphans with supernatural powers find themselves on the run from a greedy millionaire who wants to exploit their amazing gift. Adapted from a novel by Alexander Key. 97m/C VHS, DVD. Kim Richards, Ike Eisenmann, Eddie Albert, Ray Milland, Donald Pleasence; **D:** John Hough.

Escape under Pressure 𝟙𝟙½ 2000 (R) C-neaple version of "Die Hard" holds interest thanks to its action. Engineer John Spencer (Lowe) and wife Chloe (Miller) are aboard a Greek ferry that get hijacked by lowlifes who are after ... 100m/C VHS, DVD. Rob Lowe, Larisa Miller, Craig Wasson, Harry Van Gorkum, Stanley Kamel; **D:** Jean Pellerin. **M:** James Christopher; **C:** Richard Clabaugh. **CABLE.**

Escape 2000 WOOF! Turkey Shoot 1981 (R) In a future society where individuality is considered a crime, those who refuse to conform are punished by being hunted down in a jungle. Gross, twisted takeoff of Richard Connell's "The Most Dangerous Game." 80m/C VHS, AU Steve Railsback, Olivia Hussey, Michael Craig; **D:** Brian Trenchard-Smith; **M:** Brian May.

Escape Velocity 𝟙𝟙 1999 (R) Scientists Cal (Bergin), Billie (Crewson) and their daughter Ronnie (Beaudoin) are on a deep space project when they discover ... a priceless ancient statue of Artemis. They manage to protect the statue but have to save themselves from the Killers. 90m/C VHS, DVD. Rob Lowe, ... 100m/C VHS, DVD. Patrick Bergin, Wendy Crewson, Peter Outerbridge, Michelle Beaudoin; **D:** Lloyd A. Simandl. **M:** Peter Allen. **VIDEO**

Espionage in Tangiers ½ Marc Matz, Agent S.077 1965 Bond rip-off with Davila as super-spy Mike Murphy, who's assigned to find a ray gun stolen from a lab. From there it's all gadgets, cars, villains, and babes (who get slapped around when they don't cooperate). Attractive settings in Nice and Tangiers; dubbed. Available as a Drive-In Double Feature with "Assassination in Rome." 92m/C DVD, IT SP Luis Davila, Perla Cristal, Jose Greci, Ana Castor, Alfonso Rojas; **D:** Gregg Tallas; **C:** Alvaro Mancori.

Essex Boys 𝟙𝟙 1999 (R) British gangster movie inspired by the true-crime 1995 murders of three criminals. Ambitious young Billy (Creed-Miles) is hired to chauffeur violent Jason Locke (Bean), who's just out of prison. Jason partnered with John Dyke (Wilkinson) in the drug trade but times have changed and double-crosses are the new name of the game. Billy gets sucked in and betrayed, but becomes the deadlier than the male (Kingston) does ... 102m/C VHS, DVD, GB Charlie Creed-Miles, Sean Bean, Tom Wilkinson, Alex Kingston, Larry Lamb, Terence Rigby, Billy Murray, Amelie Lowdell; **D:** Terry Winsor; **W:** Terry Winsor, Jeff Pope; **C:** John Daly; **M:** Colin Towns.

Estate of Insanity 𝟙 1970 An English lord and his second wife become involved in a web of death when a maniac stalks their ancient estate. 90m/C VHS. John Turner, Heather Sears, Ann Lynn; **D:** Robert Hartford-Davis.

Esther 𝟙𝟙½ 1998 Biblical story of a young Jewish girl named Esther who is sought as the bride of Ahasuerus, the King of Persia. She persuades him to stop the slaughter of her people. 91m/C VHS. Louise Lombard, Thomas Kretschmann, F. Murray Abraham, Jurgen Prochnow, Ornella Muti; **D:** Raffaele Mertes. **CABLE**

Esther and the King 𝟙½ 1960 Biblical costumer with Egan as Persian king and Collins as the Judean maiden he wants in place of the murdered queen. Long, rambling, and torturous. 109m/C VHS, DVD, IT. Joan Collins, Richard Egan, Denis O'Dea, Sergio Fantoni, Rik Battaglia; **D:** Raoul Walsh, Mario Bava. **M:** Angelo Francesco Lavagnino.

Esther Kahn 𝟙𝟙 2000 (PG) Esther (Phoenix) is growing up in the poor East End of London at the end of the 19th century—the daughter of a Jewish tailor. When Esther attends a Yiddish stage play, she decides that she must become an actress and approaches a local theatre for work. She is later taken under the wing of older actor Nathan (Holm), who advises her to take a lover for emotional experience. Esther gets involved with drama critic, Philip Haygard (Desplechin), is betrayed, but achieves a more-desired stage triumph. Adapted from a short story by Arthur Symons. 145m/C VHS, DVD, FR GB Summer Phoenix, Ian Holm, Emmanuelle Devos, Fabrice Desplechin, Frances Barber, Laszlo Szabo; **D:** Arnaud Desplechin; **W:** Arnaud Desplechin, Emmanuel Bourdieu; **C:** Eric Gautier; **M:** Howard Shore.

Eternal Sunshine of the Spotless Mind 𝟙𝟙𝟙½ 2004 (R) Unhappy couple uses latest technology to try and vacuum their minds clean of each other and all associated memories in this black comedy. Carrey plays it mostly straight here as Joel, a lovesick sap who undergoes the memory-erasing procedure when he finds out his stolid girlfriend Clementine (Winslet) had similar sci-fi style treatment to wipe him out of her trendy blue-streaked head. Carrey begins to have second thoughts, however, playing hide and seek with his memories of Clementine from the thoroughly unprofessional mind-erasing technicians (Ruffalo and Wood) who trash his apartment in the process. Clever story penned by Kaufman in his second venture with director Gondry. Leads earn their stellar salaries here, along with excellent supports, including Wood, Ruffalo, Wilkinson, and Dunst. 108m/C DVD, HD DVD, US Jim Carrey, Kate Winslet, Elijah Wood Mark Ruffalo, Thomas Jay Ryan, Jane Adams David Cross, Kirsten Dunst, Tom Wilkinson, Ellen Pompeo, Paulie (Litowsky) Litt; **D:** Michel Gondry; **W:** Michel Gondry, Charlie Kaufman; **C:** Ellen Kuras; **M:** Jon Brion. Oscars '04: Orig. Screenplay; British Acad. '04: Film Editing, ...

E.S.P. 1983 A young man is given the amazing power of extra-sensory perception. 96m/C VHS. Jim Stafford, George Deaton; **D:** Julian Cole.

The Eternal 𝟙𝟙 The Eternal Kiss of the Mummy 1999 (R) Nora (Elliot) plays a young wife and mother who's tormented by binding headaches and dizziness. Along with her husband and young son, she decides to return to her childhood home in Ireland to visit her ailing grandmother. But her symptoms worsen as she gets to her ancestral home, and Elliott discovers that her creepy uncle (Walken) has retrieved the body of a witch she's not quite dead. 95m/C VHS, DVD. Alison Elliott, Jared Harris, Christopher Walken, Lois Smith, Karl Geary; **D:** Michael Almereyda; **W:** Michael Almereyda; **C:** Jim Denault; **M:** Simon Fisher Turner.

Eternal 𝟙 2004 (R) Remarkably dull erotic vampire thriller (which only hints at kink). Detective Raymond Pope (Pla) is searching for his missing wife, which leads him to the Montreal estate of wealthy Elizabeth Kane (Neron) and her maid, Irina (Sanchez). Seems Elizabeth is actually 16th-century Countess Elizabeth Bathory, who kills and then bathes in the blood of young women to maintain her own beauty and immortality. Eventually, the obsessed Pope follows Elizabeth to a masked ball in Venice in order to stop the bloodletting. 107m/C DVD, CA Conrad Pla, Caroline Neron, Victoria Sanchez, Liane Balaban, Sarah Manninen, Ilona Elkin, Nick Baillie; **D:** Wilhelm Liebenberg, Frederico Sanchez; **C:** Jamie Thompson.

Eternal Evil 𝟙 1987 (R) A bored TV director is taught how to have out-of-body experiences by his devil-worshipping girlfriend. He eventually realizes that when he leaves his body, it runs around killing people. 85m/C VHS, DVD. Karen Black, Winston Rekert, Lois Maxwell; **D:** George Mihalka; **W:** Robert Geoffrion; **C:** Paul Van der Linden.

Eternal Return 𝟙𝟙½ L'Eternel Retour, Love Eternal 1943 A lush modern retelling of the Tristan/Isolde legend. Patrice (Marais) brings the beautiful Nathalie (Sologne) to his family's castle, as his uncle's intended bride. But thanks to a love potion, it's Nathalie and Patrice who fall in love—with tragic results. In French with English subtitles. 111m/B VHS, FR Jean Marais, Alexandre Rignault, Roland Toutain, Yvonne de Bray, Jean Murat, Jean Delannoy; **W:** Jean Cocteau; **C:** Roger Hubert; **M:** Georges Auric.

Eternally Yours 𝟙𝟙 1939 A witty magician's career threatens to break up his marriage. 95m/B VHS, DVD. David Niven, Loretta Young, Hugh Herbert, Broderick Crawford, Sir C. Aubrey Smith, Billie Burke, Eve Arden, Zasu Pitts; **D:** Tay Garnett.

The Eternal Waltz 𝟙𝟙 Ewiger Walzer 1954 Overly sentimental chronicle of the life of composer Johann Strauss. Only director Verhoeven's touch holds the viewer's interest, though the production values are excellent. 97m/C VHS. Bernhard Wicki, Hilde Krahl, Annemarie Duerringer, Friedl Loor, Eduard Strauss Jr., Gert Frobe, Arnulf Schroeder; **D:** Paul Verhoeven.

Eternity 𝟙 1990 (R) While trying to uncover corrupt corporate America, a TV reporter falls in love with a model who works for a media king and puts his credibility on the line. He believes that this woman shared romance in a past life. 122m/C VHS, DVD. Jon Voight, Armand Assante, Wilford Brimley, Eileen Davidson, Kaye Ballard, Lainie Kazan, Joey Villa, Steven Keats, Eugene Roche, Frankie Valli, John P. Ryan; **D:** Steven Paul.

Eternity and a Day 𝟙𝟙 Mia Eoniotita Ke Mia Mera 1997 Seriously ill writer Alexander (Ganz) is putting his affairs in order and revisiting his past, particularly moments with his beloved late wife, Anna (Renauld). But the present isn't finished with Alexander yet. He rescues a young boy (Skevis), an illegal immigrant from Albania, who says he was taken from his grandmother. Alexander decides to take the boy home and the two set out on the journey that will surely be Alexander's last. Greek with subtitles. 134m/C VHS, DVD, GR Bruno Ganz, Isabelle Renauld, Achilleas Skevis, Fabrizio Bentivoglio; **D:** Theo Angelopoulos; **W:** Theo Angelopoulos; **C:** Yorgos Arvanitis, Andreas Sinanos; **M:** Eleni Karaindrou. Cannes '98: Film.

Ethan 𝟙½ 1971 A missionary in the Philippines falls in love with a woman and exiles himself for his fall from grace. 91m/C VHS. Robert Sampson, Rosa Rosal, Eddie Infante; **D:** Michael Du Pont.

Ethan Frome 𝟙𝟙 1992 (PG) Neeson stars as the lonely, poverty-stricken 19th-century New England farmer who has long and faithfully cared for his invalid wife. When his wife's distant young cousin comes to take over as housekeeper they both succumb to their forbidden passion while she tends to overwhelm the film's sluggish pacing, where the bleak setting of Massachusetts in winter tends to overwhelm the events. Based on the novel by Edith Wharton. 107m/C VHS, DVD, Liam Neeson, Patricia Arquette, Joan Allen, Tate Donovan, Katharine Houghton, Stephen Mendillo; **D:** John Madden; **W:** Richard Nelson; **C:** Bobby Bukowski.

Eubie! 𝟙𝟙 1982 The popular Broadway musical revue based on the life and songs of Eubie Blake is presented in a video transfer. Some of Eubie's best-known songs, performed here by members of the original cast, include "I'm Just Wild About Harry," "Memories of You," "The Charleston Rag." 100m/C VHS. Gregory Hines, Maurice Hines, Leslie Dockery, Alaina Reed, Lynnie Godfrey, Mel Johnson Jr., Jeffrey V. Thompson; **D:** Julianne Boyd.

Eulogy 𝟙½ 2004 (R) Unworkable ensemble black comedy that wastes its good cast. The dysfunctional Collins family is forced back together to bury their toxic family patriarch (Tom). Accommodating granddaughter Kate (Deschanel) is expected to deliver the eulogy but neither her brooding father (Azaria) nor his crude brother (Romano), or their neurotic sisters (Winger, Preston) have anything good to say. No wonder all the bickering is driving Grandma Charlotte (Laurie) to multiple suicide attempts. And yes, the contrivances extend to a not-unexpected surprise at the reading of the will. 91m/C DVD. Hank Azaria, Jesse Bradford, Zooey Deschanel, Glenne Headly, Famke Janssen, Piper Laurie, Kelly Preston, Ray Romano, Rip Torn, Debra Winger, Curtis Garcia, Keith Garcia, Rene Auberjonois; Orig. Screenplay; Writers Guild '04; Orig. Screenplay.

berjonois; **D:** Michael Clancy; **W:** Michael Clancy; **C:** Michael Chapman; **M:** Richard (Rick) Marvin.

Eureka! ♂♂½ **1981 (R)** A bizarre, wildly symbolic slab of Roegian artifice that deals with the dream-spliced life of a rich, bored gold tycoon who becomes tortured over his dubious marriage and the own useless wealth. Eventually he is bothered by the Mafia and led to the courtroom by business competitors. From the book by Paul Mayersberg. 130m/C VHS, DVD. **GB** Gene Hackman, Theresa Russell, Joe Pesci, Rutger Hauer, Mickey Rourke, Ed Lauter, Jane Lapotaire; **D:** Nicolas Roeg.

Eureka Stockade ♂♂ Massacre Hill **1949** Four early Australian gold prospectors join forces to fight their governor and the police for the rights to dig on the continent. 103m/B VHS. **AU** Chips Rafferty, Peter Finch, Jane Barrett, Peter Illing; **D:** Harry Watt.

Europa, Europa ♂♂♂½ Hitlerjunge Salomon **1991 (R)** The incredible, harrowing and borderline-absurdist true story of Solomon Perel, a young Jew who escaped the Holocaust by passing for German at an elite, Nazi-run academy. Such a sharp evocation of the era that the modern German establishment wouldn't submit it for the Academy Awards. In German and Russian with English subtitles. 115m/C VHS, DVD. **GE** Marco Hofschneider, Klaus Abramowsky, Michele Gleizer, Rene Hofschneider, Nathalie Schmidt, Delphine Forest, Julie Delpy; **D:** Agnieszka Holland; **W:** Agnieszka Holland; **C:** Jacek Petrycki, Jacek Zaleski; **M:** Zbigniew Preisner. Golden Globes '92: Foreign Film; Natl. Bd. of Review '91: Foreign Film; N.Y. Film Critics '91: Foreign Film.

Europa '51 ♂♂½ The Greatest Love **1952** The despairing portrait of post-war malaise, as an American woman, whose son committed suicide, lives in Rome searching for some semblance of meaning, and ends up in an asylum. One of Bergman & Rossellini's least-loved films. In Italian with subtitles. 110m/B VHS. Ingrid Bergman, Alexander Knox, Ettore Giannini, Giulietta Masina, **D:** Roberto Rossellini.

The Europeans ♂♂♂ **1979** Fine adaptation of Henry James's satiric novel. British brother and sister visit their staid American cousins in 19th-century New England in an effort to improve their prospects through fortuitous marriages. 90m/C VHS, DVD. Lee Remick, Lisa Eichhorn, Robin Ellis, Wesley Addy, Tim Woodward; **D:** James Ivory; **W:** Ruth Prawer Jhabvala.

Eurotrip ♂½ **2004 (R)** Straight-arrow Scotty, freshly dumped by his girlfriend, realizes his German pen-pal is not a man coming on to him over the internet but an insanely hot girl. What's a boy to do? Why, jet off to Europe with three friends to meet her, of course! Scott and Cooper (Pitts) get cheap tickets to England and plan to meet up with twins Jamie (Wester) and Jenny (Trachtenberg). At that point, the plot goes out the window as the movie descends into an endless string of insulting, laugh-free jokes about mimes, soccer hooligans, hookers, gay train passengers, and the Vatican. Recommended if you think bottom-of-the-barrel gags based on European stereotypes make a movie. Everyone else should avoid this Trip. 89m/C DVD. **US** Scott Mechlowicz, Jacob Pitts, Michelle Trachtenberg, Travis Wester, Jessica Boehrs, Fred Armisen, Lucy Lawless, Vinnie Jones, Kristen Kreuk, J.P. Manoux, Rade Serbedzija, Steve Hytner, Patrick Malahide, Joanna Lumley; **D:** Jeff Schafler; **W:** Jeff Schaffer, Alec Berg, David Mandel; **C:** David Eggby; **M:** James L. Venable.

Eva ♂♂½ Eva the Devil's Woman **1962** Writer Tyvian (Baker) becomes obsessed with prostitute Eva (Moreau), spends all his money on her, leaves his fiancee Francesca (Lisi) for her, but all she does is taunt and abandon him. He marries Francesca but leaves his bride (who kills herself) for Eva, who discards him again, leaving Tyvian broke and betrayed. Based on the novel "Eve" by James Hadley Chase. 103m/B VHS, DVD. **FR IT** Jeanne Moreau, Stanley Baker, Virna Lisi, James Villiers, Giorgio Albertazzi, Riccardo Garrone; **D:** Joseph Losey; **W:** Hugo Butler, Evan Jones; **C:** Gianni Di Venanzo; **M:** Michel Legrand.

Evan Almighty ♂♂ **2007 (PG)** Holy spinoff! Former TV anchor-turned-politician Evan (Carell) is about to give up his values and ruin the environment when God (Freeman), reprising his "Bruce Almighty" role) orders him to build an ark. Wife Joan (Graham) and his sons are doubtful, but eventually get on the boat. Smarmy blend of animal-based potty humor and tepid life-lessons about taking care of the environment and being nice fails to take advantage of Carell's talents. 95m/C DVD, Blu-ray Disc. **US** Steve Carell, Morgan Freeman, Lauren Graham, John Goodman, John Michael Higgins, Wanda Sykes, Jimmy Bennett, Johnny (John W.) Simmons, Jonah Hill, Ed Helms, Rachael Harris, Molly Shannon, Graham Phillips; **D:** Tom Shadyac; **W:** Steve Oedekerk, Josh Stolberg, Bob Florsheim; **C:** Ian Baker; **M:** John Debney.

Evangeline ♂♂♂½ **1929** Based on the Henry Wadsworth Longfellow poem about the struggles of Evangeline and the tragedy of lost love. Evangeline lives in an Acadian (with ties to France) village in Nova Scotia and is engaged to Gabriel. But when France and England declare war, the village sides with France and the men are forcibly deported to Louisiana. But Evangeline is determined to be reunited with her love. 90m/B VHS, DVD. Dolores Del Rio, Roland (Walter Goss) Drew, Alec B. Francis, George F. Marion Sr., Donald Reed; **D:** Edwin Carewe; **W:** Finis Fox; **C:** Robert B. Kurrle; **M:** Hugo Riesenfeld, Philip Carli.

Eve of Destruction WOOF! **1990 (R)** Hell knows no fury like a cutting-edge android-girl on the warpath. Modeled after her creator, Dr. Eve Simmons, Eve VII has android-babe good looks and a raging nuclear capability. After her trial run, and debutante Eve turns into a PMS nightmare machine, blasting all the good Doctor's previous beaux. That's where military agent Hines comes in, though you wonder why. Dutch actress Soutendijk plays dual Eves in her first American film. 101m/C VHS, DVD. Gregory Hines, Renee Soutendijk, Kurt Fuller, Ross Malinger, Eugene Robert Glazer, John M. Jackson, Loren Haynes, Michael Greene; **D:** Duncan Gibbins; **W:** Duncan Gibbins, Yale Udoff; **C:** Alan Hume.

Evel Knievel ♂♂ **1972 (PG)** The life of motorcycle stuntman Evel Knievel is depicted in this movie, as portrayed by George Hamilton. Stunts will be appreciated by Evel Knievel fans. 90m/C VHS, DVD. George Hamilton, Bert Freed, Rod Cameron, Sue Lyon; **D:** Marvin J. Chomsky; **W:** John Milius; **C:** David M. Walsh; **M:** Patrick Williams.

Evelyn ♂♂♂ **2002 (PG)** Lovable but ale-soaked Desmond Doyle (Brosnan) is abandoned by his wife in 1953. At that time it was believed that a man couldn't care for his children alone, so the children are placed in a church orphanage. A barmaid (Margulies) takes pity on him and convinces him to sober up and seek legal counsel to regain custody. Beresford's straightforward classic style thankfully only alludes to the punishment the children faced rather than exploiting it, choosing instead to focus on the true story of the case against the Family Act of 1941. Faithful retelling brings pertinent items to light, with notable character development. It's refreshing to see Brosnan as an average bloke vs. his 007 persona, and Vavasseu, as the nine-year old Evelyn is one to watch. 94m/C VHS, DVD. **IR GB** Pierce Brosnan, Aidan Quinn, Julianna Margulies, Sophie Vavasseur, Stephen Rea, Alan Bates, John Lynch, Andrea Irvine, Karen Ardiff, Niall Beagan, Hugh MacDonagh; **D:** Bruce Beresford; **W:** Paul Pender; **C:** Andre Fleuren; **M:** Stephen Endelman.

Evelyn Prentice ♂♂½ **1934** Powell and Loy again team up as a married couple (after their "The Thin Man" success) but this time things aren't so rosy. He is an attorney with a wandering eye who has an affair with Russell (in her film debut). Loy finds out and turns for sympathy to Stephens but then she decides to stay with her husband after all. Only she's written some steamy letters to Stephens and he tries blackmailing her—and winds up dead. Dramatic courtroom scene straightens things out. Adapted from the novel by W.E. Woodward. Film was remade as "Stronger Than Desire" in 1939. 78m/B VHS, DVD. Myrna Loy, William Powell, Harvey Stephens, Isabel Jewell, Una Merkel, Rosalind Russell, Henry Wadsworth, Edward Brophy, Cora Sue Collins, Jessie Ralph, Sam Flint, Pat O'Malley, **D:** William K. Howard; **W:** Lenore Coffee.

Even Angels Fall ♂♂ **1990** One of heartthrob singer Humperdinck's scattered dramatic projects, a mystery thriller about a romance novelist moving into a New York brownstone whose previous inhabitant committed suicide—or was it murder? 7m/C VHS. Morgan Fairchild, Engelbert Humperdinck; **D:** Adrian Biddle; **M:** Michael Kamen. **TV**

Even Cowgirls Get the Blues ♂½ **1994 (R)** '70s counterculture loses its ill-defined charm in a meandering adaptation of cult author Tom Robbins' 1976 novel. An interesting failure, but likely to alienate both Van Sant and Robbins fans. Sissy Hackshaw (Thurman) possesses enormous thumbs which she hopes will make her the greatest hitchhiker in the world. But first they take her to a NYC modeling career for The Countess (Hurt in a high camp performance), who sends her to the Rubber Rose ranch, recently liberated by female cowhands, who are happy to welcome her. Theatrical release was delayed numerous times as Van Sant recut but it doesn't matter—the only successful feature is the soundtrack. 106m/C VHS, DVD. Uma Thurman, John Hurt, Rain Phoenix, Lorraine Bracco, Noriyuki "Pat" Morita, Angie Dickinson, Keanu Reeves; *Cameos:* Sean Young, Crispin Glover, Roseanne, Ed Begley Jr.; **D:** Gus Van Sant; **W:** Gus Van Sant; **C:** Eric Alan Edwards, John Campbell; **M:** k.d. lang, Ben Mink.

Even Money ♂♂ **2006 (R)** Dull ensemble drama despite some over-the-top performances. Basinger, DeVito, and Whitaker are gambling addicts who lie, cheat, and steal for another chance at that big score, despite having family and book-ie problems. 108m/C DVD. Danny DeVito, Kim Basinger, Forest Whitaker, Tim Roth, Kelsey Grammer, Jay Mohr, Ray Liotta, Nick Cannon, Carla Gugino, Grant Sullivan; **D:** Mark Rydell; **W:** Robert Tannen; **C:** Robbie Greenberg; **M:** Dave Grusin.

Evening ♂½ **2007 (PG-13)** Ann (Redgrave, chewing scenery) is on her deathbed, and she flashes back to a time when her younger self (Danes) experienced love and loss and possibly caused the death of a friend's brother. Meanwhile, her grown daughters (Collette and Richardson) struggle with their own issues while tending to their dying mother. Adapted by Minot from her novel, the film fails to escape its leaden dialogue, miscast actors, and unlikable, stereotypical characters. 117m/C DVD, Blu-ray Disc. **US** Vanessa Redgrave, Natasha Richardson, Toni Collette, Meryl Streep, Claire Danes, Patrick Wilson, Hugh Dancy, Eton Moss-Bachrach, Mamie Gummer, Eileen Atkins, Glenn Close, Barry Bostwick; **D:** Lajos Koltai; **W:** Susan Minot, Michael Cunningham; **C:** Gyula Pados; **M:** Jan A.P. Kaczmarek.

The Evening Star ♂♂½ **1996 (PG-13)** Sequel to 1983's "Terms of Endearment" starts in 1988 and finds the overbearing Aurora (MacLaine) now wreaking havoc on the lives of her three grown grandchildren (and vice versa). And Aurora's lovelife is as active as ever—old beau Hector Scott (Moffat) is hanging around, young psychiatrist Jerry Bruckner (Paxton) becomes her lover, and former astronaut flame Garrett Breedlove (Nicholson) also makes a brief appearance to cock an eyebrow at the shenanigans. Last screen role for Johnson as neighbor Arthur Cotten. Based on the novel by Larry McMurtry. Bring a hankie for the tears. 128m/C VHS, DVD. Shirley MacLaine, Juliette Lewis, George Newbern, MacKenzie Astin, Bill Paxton, Miranda Richardson, Marion Ross, Ben Johnson, Donald Moffat, Scott Wolf, China Kantner, Jack Nicholson; **D:** Robert Harling; **W:** Robert Harling; **C:** Don Burgess; **M:** William Ross.

The Event ♂♂ **2003 (R)** Unbalanced effort begins with AIDS-stricken Matt dying at his so-called farewell party, arousing the suspicions of Assistant D.A. Nick (Posey). As Matt's suffering is recounted in flashbacks, Nick has a hard time pursuing the case after recently witnessing her father's painful death. 112m/C VHS, DVD. **CA** Parker Posey, Don McKellar, Sarah Polley, Jane Leeves, Brent Carver, Olympia Dukakis, Joanna Adler, Rejean Coumoyer, Christina Zorich, Dick Latessa, Cynthia (Cyndy, Cindy) Preston, Gianna Marciante, Jaclyn Markowitz, Glen Michael Grant, Ruth Moore, Chaz Thorne; **D:** Thom Fitzgerald; **W:** Thom Fitzgerald, Steven Hillyer, Tim Marback; **C:** Thomas M. Harting; **M:** Christophe Beck. **VIDEO**

Event Horizon ♂♂½ **1997 (R)** Cross between "Alien" and "The Shining" has Fishburne heading an ensemble cast out to rescue a prototype spaceship that's been missing for seven years. Their own ship is sabotaged by their own demons and certain extraterrestrial ones, too, that cause much mayhem on their once peaceful mission. 97m/C VHS, DVD. Laurence Fishburne, Sam Neill, Kathleen Quinlan, Joely Richardson, Richard J. Jones, Jack Noseworthy, Sean Pertwee, Jason Isaacs; **D:** Paul W.S. Anderson; **W:** Philip Eisner; **C:** Adrian Biddle; **M:** Michael Kamen.

Ever After: A Cinderella Story ♂♂½ **1998 (PG-13)** The adorable Barrymore takes on Cinderella, renamed Danielle and very capable, in this not-quite-a-fairytale version set in 16th-century France. Huston's the peeved stepmom, Rodmilla, who reduces Danielle to the role of servant in her own home after her beloved father (Krabbe) dies. Danielle still falls for handsome Prince Henry (Scott), only she's not above trying to change the arrogant snob's opinions and tweak him about his privileged upbringing. Artist/genius Leonardo da Vinci (Godfrey) serves as the prince's confidante and there's still a lovely masked ball and a shoe to be lost (and found). 122m/C VHS, DVD. Drew Barrymore, Anjelica Huston, Dougray Scott, Patrick Godfrey, Megan Dodds, Melanie Lynskey, Timothy West, Judy Parfitt, Jeroen Krabbe; *Cameos:* Jeanne Moreau; **D:** Andy Tennant; **W:** Andy Tennant, Susannah Grant, Rick Parks; **C:** Andrew Dunn; **M:** George Fenton.

Evergreen ♂♂½ **1934** The daughter of a retired British music hall star is mistaken for her mother and it is thought that she has discovered the secret of eternal youth. ♪Daddy Wouldn't Buy Me a Bow-Wow; When You've Got a Little Springtime in Your Heart; If I Give in to You; Tinkle, Tinkle, Tinkle; Dear, Dear; Dancing on the Ceiling; Just by Your Example; Over My Shoulder. 91m/B VHS. **GB** Jessie Matthews, Sonnie Hale, Betty Balfour, Barry Mackay, Ivor McLaren, Hartley Power, Patrick Ludlow, Marjorie Gaffney; **D:** Victor Saville; **W:** Emlyn Williams; **C:** Glen MacWilliams; **M:** Richard Rodgers, Harry Woods, Lorenz Hart, Harry Woods.

Evergreen ♂♂ **2004 (PG-13)** Troubled mother Kate (Seymour) and daughter Henri (Land) move to a new community in hope of a fresh start. Henri resents her family's dire position and sets out to create a better niche with her newfound boyfriend's affluent but screwed up family. Dreary independent coming-of-age film is helped by good performances, especially from Land, but offers few surprises. 85m/C DVD. **US** Cara Seymour, Mary Kay Place, Noah Fleiss, Gary Farmer, Bruce Davison, Addie Land; **D:** Enid Zentelis; **W:** Enid Zentelis; **C:** Matthew Clark; **M:** John Sirrat, Patrick Sansone.

An Everlasting Piece ♂♂½ **2000 (R)** Director Levinson moves from working-class Baltimore to working-class Belfast in the 1980s in this goofball comedy. Best pals and fellow barbers Colm (McEvoy) and George (O'Byrne) don't let their different religions come between them. In fact, they decide it will be an advantage when they take on a new toupee business (called The Piece People)—Colm can sell to the Catholics and George will handle the Protestants. But it turns out they have a rival firm, Toupee or Not Toupee, and then Colm winds up with a substantial order from the IRA. He's willing to separate politics for business but is anyone else? 103m/C VHS, DVD. **US** Barry McEvoy, Brian F. O'Byrne, Anna Friel, Billy Connolly, Pauline McLynn, Laurence Kinlan, Ruth McCabe; **D:** Barry Levinson; **W:** Barry McEvoy; **C:** Seamus Deasy; **M:** Hans Zimmer.

The Everlasting Secret Family 🐾🐾 1988 Politics and family life make strange bedfellows. A top political figure joins a secret homosexual organization in his search for power. 93m/C VHS, DVD . *AU* Arthur Dignam, Mark Lee, Dennis Miller, Heather Mitchell; *D:* Michael Thornhill.

Eversmile New Jersey 🐾🐾 1989 (PG) A dentist travels through Patagonia, offering dental care and advice to anyone in need, and a young woman, taken with the dental knight, dumps her boyfriend and slows away with him. When he discovers his latest potential victim of his porn business. But it's more Connie (Cheryl Ladd) to the rescue. 92m/C VHS. Cheryl Ladd, Jordan Ladd, Ted McGinley, Vincent Gale, Robert Wisden, Tom Butler; *D:* Bill W.L. Norton; *W:* Robert Bensink. **CABLE.**

Every Other Weekend 🐾🐾🐾
Un Week-end sur Deux 1991 Camille Valmont (Baye) is an actress who has sacrificed everything for her now-fading career. She's divorced and given him custody of their two young children—often ignoring her every

Every Girl Should Be Married 🐾🐾½ 1948 A shopgirl sets her sights on an eligible bachelor doctor. 84m/B VHS. Cary Grant, Betsy Drake, Diana Lynn, Franchot Tone; *D:* Don Hartman.

Every Girl Should Have One 🐾½ 1978 A rambunctious comedy about a chase following a million-dollar diamond theft. 90m/C VHS. Zsa Zsa Gabor, Robert Alda, Alice Faye, Sandra Vacey, John Lazar; *D:* Robert Hyatt; *W:* Robert Hyatt; *C:* Michael Jones; *M:* Johnny Pate.

Every Man for Himself & God Against All 🐾🐾🐾🐾
Kaspar Hauser; Jeder fur Sich und Gott gegen Alle; The Enigma of Kaspar Hauser 1975 Kaspar Hauser is a young man who mysteriously appears in the town square of Nuremberg, early in the 19th century. He cannot speak or stand upright and is found to have been kept in a dungeon for the first 18 years of his life. He becomes an attraction in society with his alternate vision of the world and attempts to reconcile with reality. A lovely, though demanding film which is based on a true story. In German with English subtitles. 110m/C VHS, DVD. *GE* Bruno S., Brigitte Mira, Walter Ladengast, Hans Musaus, Willy Semmelrogge, Michael Kroecher, Henry van Lyck; *D:* Werner Herzog; *W:* Werner Herzog; *C:* Jorge Schmidt-Reitwein; *M:* Orlando Di Lasso.

Every Mother's Worst Fear 🐾🐾 1996 (PG-13) When her boyfriend dumps her, 16-year-old Martha Hoagland (Jordan Ladd) checks out the Internet chat rooms. She begins an online romance with Drew (Gale) but doesn't realize that hacker Mitch Carson (McGinley) is manipulating the entire situation. Soon Martha decides to slip away and meet Drew, and winds up Mitch's prisoner and the latest potential victim

Everybody Says I'm Fine! 🐾🐾½ 2006 A horrible accident during his childhood that left Xen (Ergineer) an orphan also gave him the power as an adult to hear people's thoughts as he cuts hair for a living. While he uses his gift for the greater good by helping customers with problems in their lives, he's otherwise lonely and unhappy. He becomes intrigued by the beautiful Nikita (Puri) but is baffled when her thoughts are silent; his interest in her may be a dire mistake. 103m/C DVD. *IN* Fardeen Engineer, Koel Purie, Rahul Bose, Pooja Bhatt, Anahita Oberoi; *D:* Rahul Bose; *W:* Rahul Bose.
VIDEO

Everybody Sing 🐾🐾 1938 A down-on-their-luck theatrical 'family,' including Garland (who is kicked out of boarding school for singing Mendelssohn with a swing beat) decides to put on a show in hopes of making a comeback. Dumb plot and boring songs make this one for die-hard Garland fans only. ♪Swing, Mr. Mendelssohn, Swing; The One I Love; Down on Melody Farms; The Show Must Go On; I Wanna Swing; Never Was There Such a Perfect Day; Quainty Dainty Me; Why? Because; Snooks. 80m/B VHS. Allan Jones, Fanny Brice, Judy Garland, Reginald Owen, Billie Burke, Reginald Gardiner, Lynne Carver, Monty Woolley; *D:* Edwin L. Marin; *M:* George Bassman.

Everybody Wins 🐾 1990 (R) A mystery-romance about a befuddled private eye trying to solve a murder and getting caught up with the bizarre prostitute who hired him. Arthur Miller based this screenplay on his stage drama "Some Kind of Love Story." Confused arc, given its pedigree, disappointing mystery. 110m/C VHS, DVD. Nick Nolte, Debra Winger, Will Patton, Jack Warden, Kathleen Wilhoite, Frank Converse, Frank Military, Judith Ivey; *D:* Karel Reisz; *W:* Arthur Miller; *C:* Ian Baker.

Everybody's All American 🐾🐾 1988 (R) Shallow, sentimental melodrama about a college football star and his cheerleader wife

Every Breath 🐾🐾 1993 (R) A kinky couple's games can be deadly and now they have someone new to play with. Jimmy couldn't resist the wife's seductive allure and if he wants to survive, he'll have to beat them at their own game. 88m/C VHS. Judd Nelson, Joanna Pacula, Patrick Bauchau; *D:* Steve Bing; *W:* Judd Nelson, Andrew Fleming, Steve Bing; *M:* Nils Lofgren.

Every Day's a Holiday 🐾🐾½ 1938 In the 1890s, West stars as confidence woman Peaches O'Day who sells the Brooklyn Bridge and is run out of New York City. But she comes back, in disguise as a French singer, to expose some crooked cops. The Hays office again came down heavily on Mae's suggestive behavior, which left her with little to rely on. West's last film for Paramount. 79m/B VHS, Mae West, Edmund Lowe, Charles Butterworth, Charles Winninger, Walter Catlett, Lloyd Nolan, Herman Bing; *D:* Edward Sutherland; *W:* Mae West.

Every Time We Say Goodbye 🐾🐾½ 1986 (PG-13) In 1942, Jerusalem, an American flyboy falls in love with a young Sephardic Jewish girl, whose family resists the match. 97m/C VHS, DVD. Tom Hanks, Christina Marsillach, Benedict Taylor, Anat Atzmon, Gila Almagor; *D:* Moshe Mizrahi; *W:* Moshe Mizrahi, Leah Appet; *M:* Philippe Sarde.

Every Which Way But Loose 🐾🐾 1978 (R) Fairly pointless Eastwood foray featuring Clint as a beer-guzzling, country-music loving truck driver earning a living as a barroom brawler. He and his orangutan travel to Colorado in pursuit of the woman he loves. Behind him are a motorcycle gang and an L.A. cop. All have been victims of his fists. Sequel is "Any Which Way You Can." 115m/C VHS. DVD. Clint Eastwood, Sondra Locke, Geoffrey Lewis, Beverly D'Angelo, Ruth Gordon; *D:* James Fargo; *W:* Jeremy Joe Kronsberg; *C:* Rexford Metz; *M:* Steve Dorff.

Every Woman Knows a Secret 🐾🐾 1999 Twenty-something Rob (Bettany) is blamed for the death of divorced, fortyish Jess's (Redmond) son as a drunk driving crash. Oddly drawn together by grief and guilt, the two begin an affair that reveals more secrets. 95m/C VHS, GB English subtitles. Paul Bettany, Siobhan Redmond; *D:* Paul Seed; *C:* Ian Punter; *M:* Nigel Hess. TV

Everybody's Fine 🐾🐾½ *Stanno Tutti Bene* 1990 Mastroianni stars in this bittersweet story of a father on a mission to reunite his five grown children. His journey takes him all over Italy as he tries to bring them together in this touching film about enduring family love. In Italian with English subtitles. 115m/C VHS. *IT* Marcello Mastroianni, Salvatore Cascio, Valeria Cavalli, Norma Martelli, Marino Cenna, Roberto Nobile, Michele Morgan, Fabio Iellini; *D:* Giuseppe Tornatore; *W:* Giuseppe Tornatore, Tonino Guerra; *M:* Ennio Morricone.

Everyman's Law 🐾½ 1936 A cowboy who poses as a hired gunman is almost lynched by ranchers who think he is a murderer. 60m/B VHS. Johnny Mack Brown, Beth Marion, Frank Campeau, Lloyd Ingraham, John (Jack) Beck, Charles "Slim" Whitaker; *D:* Albert Ray; *W:* Earle Snell; *C:* Jack Greenhalgh.

Everyone Says I Love You 🐾🐾 1996 (R) Woody sings! Granted, he doesn't sing very well, but who else could twist a story of love among the neurotic rich with lavish production numbers from the golden age of movie musicals? The excellent cast (who weren't told that they were in a musical until after they signed) prove that as singers, they're pretty good actors. The plot centers around the wandering love lives of Steffi (Hawn), her husband Bob (Alda), her ex-husband Joe (Allen) and their assorted children, especially the preppy Skylar (Barrymore) and her fiance Holden (Norton). Some of the musical productions are shaky (Allen's duet with Julia Roberts in a straight shot out of Tin Ear Alley), but the feeling behind them is genuine. Besides, where else are you going to hear Groucho's "Hooray for Captain Spaulding" sung in French or a chorus of pregnant women sing "Makin' Whoopee"? 105m/C VHS, DVD. Woody Allen, Goldie Hawn, Gaby Hoffman, Edward Norton, Natalie Portman, Julia Roberts, Tim Roth, Natasha Lyonne, Lukas Haas, David Ogden Stiers; *D:* Woody Allen; *W:* Woody Allen; *C:* Carlo Di Palma; *M:* Dick Hyman.

Everyone's Hero 🐾🐾 2006 (G) Reeve completed pre-production on this lackluster animated feature before his death, which is why he's sharing directorial credit (pic is also dedicated to both Christopher and Dana Reeve). During the 1932 World Series between the Yankees and the Chicago Cubs, Babe Ruth's lucky bat Darlin' (Goldberg), is stolen. Pint-sized baseball fan Yankee Irving (Austin) hops the rails, accompanied by wisecrack-ing baseball Screwie (Reiner), to find the

other weekend visitation rights. In financial straits, Camille takes a job out of town and decides to take the kids with her, without telling Adrian. Self-centered and easily distracted, Camille tries to get close but manages to destroy what little rapport she has with her children. Camille isn't likable but Baye is such a gifted actress that you'll still feel pity. Director Garcia's debut. French with subtitles. 100m/C VHS, FR Nathalie Baye, Miki (Predrag) Manojlovic, Joachim Serreau, Felicie Pasotti; *D:* Nicole Garcia; *W:* Nicole Garcia, Jacques Fieschi; *C:* William Lubtchansky; *M:* Oswald D'Andrea.

Everybody's Dancin' 🐾½ 1950 A ballroom proprietor's business is married by random killings in her establishment as the bands play on. 127m/C VHS, DVD. Spade Cooley, Dick Lane, Hal Derwin, Roddy McDowall; *D:* Will Jason. tragedies. Decently acted and based on Frank Deford's novel. 127m/C VHS, DVD. Jessica Lange, Dennis Quaid, Timothy Hutton, Jean (De Pauw), John Goodman, Carl Lumbly, Ray Baker, Savannah Smith; *D:* Taylor Hackford; *M:* James Newton Howard.

Everybody's Famous! 🐾🐾½
Iedereen Beroemd! 2000 (R) Factory worker Jean (De Pauw) is convinced that his teenaged daughter Marva (Van der Groot) has the talent to become a famous singer, though she suffers from stage fright and seems hopeless. Devoted dad goes to the extreme of kidnapping Debbie (Reuten), a Belgian pop star burned out by her successful career. Jean's demand is that Debbie's lowlife manager (Loew) make Marva a star. Meanwhile, Debbie falls for her young co-kidnapper Willy (De Smedt). It's all played for laughs as it skewers the idea of media madness and fame at any price but there's a warped sweetness at the core as well. Dutch, Flemish, and French with subtitles. 95m/C VHS, DVD. *BE* Josse De Pauw, Eva Van de Gucht, Werner De Smedt, Thekla Reuten, Victor Low, Gert Portael; *D:* Dominique Deruddere; *W:* Dominique Deruddere; *C:* Willy Stassen; *M:* Raymond van het Groenewoud.

Everything is Illuminated 🐾🐾🐾 2005 (PG-13) Based on a novel by Jonathon Safran Foer, the film follows the journey of Jonathon (Wood), a fastidious New Yorker attempting to locate the Ukrainian woman who saved his grandfather from the Nazis. After traveling to the Ukraine, Jonathon employs Alex (Hutz), who narrates the film, and his grandfather (Leskin) as tour guides. The two specialize in taking "rich Jewish people" on trips to their ancestral homes and relatives. The beauty of the film is in finding its way from the humorous early scenes to the solemn conclusion. 104m/C DVD. *US* Elijah Wood, Eugene Hutz, Boris Leskin, Laryssa Lauret; *D:* Liev Schreiber; *W:* Liev Schreiber; *C:* Matthew Libatique; *M:* Paul Cantelon.

Everything Put Together 🐾🐾½ 2000 Suburban housewife Angie (Mitchell) is pregnant as are her best friends Judith (Burns) and Barbie (Mullally). But Angie seems overly anxious and her worst fears are realized when her seemingly healthy son dies in the hospital from SIDS. Although husband Russ (Louis) tries to be as understanding and caring as possible, Angie sinks into severe depression, especially when her friends, in their discomfort, begin to withdraw from her. 88m/C VHS, DVD. Radha Mitchell, Megan Mullally, Justin Louis, Catherine Lloyd Burns, Alan Ruck, Matt Malloy, Michele Hicks; *D:* Marc Forster; *W:* Catherine Lloyd Burns, Adam Forgash; *C:* Roberto Schaefer; *M:* Thomas Koppel.

Everything Relative 🐾🐾½ 1996 Seven college buddies reunite and spend a weekend in the country together in this lesbian twist on "The Big Chill." A brisk held by partners Katie and Sarah for their new baby brings the mostly single forty-something women together, and bring out the unfulfilled desires and regrets of the six lesbians and one straight woman. Standouts include Weber as the stunt woman mourning the loss of a lover to a car accident 15 years prior, as well as the relationship between Josie (McLaughlin) and Maria (Negron), the woman who left her to get married and have children, and now relates how her lesbian desires are now divorced and losing her children. 110m/C VHS, DVD. Stella Pence, Harriet Sansom Harris, Ellen McLaughlin, Gabriella Messina, Andrea Weber, Monica Bell, Carol Schlanger, Olivia Negron; *D:* Sharon Pollack.

Everything for Sale 🐾🐾🐾 *Wszystko na Sprzedaz* 1968 An unacknowledged tribute to actor Zbigniew Cybulski, an actor who starred in several films for Wajda and who died in the same manner as the actor in this behind-the-scenes look at moviemaking. The lives of a director and actors are disrupted when their leading man, who lead a complicated officscreen life, is killed during filming. Polish with subtitles. 94m/C DVD. *PL* Andrzej Lapicki, Daniel Olbrychski, Beata Tyszkiewicz, Elzbieta Czyzewska; *D:* Andrzej Wajda; *W:* Andrzej Wajda; *C:* Witold Sobocinski; *M:* Andrzej Korzynski.

Everything Happens at Night 🐾🐾½ 1939 Rival reporters Milland and Cummings are torn between the land and the big game. Anachronistic adventure might distract the younger kiddies (the far and booger jokes will probably help). 88m/C DVD. *US* Christopher Reeve, Daniel St. Pierre, Colin Brady; *W:* Christopher Kurtz, Jeff Hand; *C:* Andy Wang, Jan Carlee; *M:* John Debney; *V:* Jake T. Austin, Rob Reiner, Whoopi Goldberg, William H. Macy, Stanley Jordan, Raven, Robert Wagner, Forest Whitaker, Brian Dennehy, Robin Williams, Joe Torre, Dana Reeve.

bat, stolen by unhygienic Cubs pitcher Lefty (Macy), and get it to the Bambino in time to win the big game.

ages to keep the characters and their stories engaging, but loses something with neatly pat solutions to the intricate problems facing these women. **110m/C VHS, DVD.** *Stacey Neikin, Ellen McLaughlin, Olivia Negron, Monica Bell, Andrea Weber, Gabriella Messina, Carol Schneider;* **D:** *Sharon Pollack;* **W:** *Sharon Pollack;* **C:** *Rachel Othmer;* **M:** *Frank London.*

Everything That Rises 🦴🦴½ **1998** Quaid directs (his debut) and stars in this movie about tough rancher Jim Clay who struggles to hold onto the land that's been in his family for generations. An uncommunicative man, Jim is forced to re-examine his life when his young son Nathan (Merriman) is rendered a paraplegic after an auto accident caused by his dad. Winningham is devoted, stoic wife Kyle and Presnell is aging cowpoke/family friend Garth. **90m/C VHS.** *Dennis Quaid, Mare Winningham, Harve Presnell, Ryan Merriman, Meat Loaf Aday, Bruce McGill;* **D:** *Dennis Quaid;* **W:** *Mark Spragg;* **C:** *Jack Conroy;* **M:** *David Robbins.* **CABLE**

Everything You Always Wanted to Know about Sex (But Were Afraid to Ask) 🦴🦴🦴 **1972 (R)** Satiric comical sketches about sex includes a timid sperm cell, an oversexed court jester, a sheep folly, and a giant disembodied breast. Quite entertaining in its own jolly way. Based on the book by Dr. David Reuben. **88m/C VHS, DVD.** *Woody Allen, John Carradine, Lou Jacobi, Louise Lasser, Anthony Quayle, Geoffrey Holder, Lynn Redgrave, Tony Randall, Burt Reynolds, Gene Wilder, Robert Walden, Jay Robinson;* **D:** *Woody Allen;* **W:** *Woody Allen;* **C:** *David M. Walsh;* **M:** *Mundell Lowe.*

Everything's Gone Green 🦴🦴½ **2006 (R)** Happy-go-lucky slacker Ryan (Costanzo) loses his job and girlfriend in one worst-day-of-his-life swoop. New employment at a lottery magazine draws him into a money laundering scheme that produces loot, ladies, and lots of opportunity for moral growth. Cleverly and hilariously weaves recurrent "green" references into each outlandish circumstance (dare you to tally them). Not a waste to watch but does lack that secret box-office hit ingredient. **95m/C DVD. CA** *Paulo Costanzo, Steph Song, J.R. Bourne, Aidan Devine, Susan Hogan, Tom Butler, Gordon Michael Woolvett, Katharine Isabelle;* **D:** *Paul Fox;* **W:** *Douglas Coupland;* **C:** *David Frazee.*

Eve's Bayou 🦴🦴🦴½ **1997 (R)** Eve (newcomer Smollett) comes from the upper-middle class Batiste family that seems all too perfect on the outside, but secrets and lies slowly surface when she mistakenly catches her doctor father Louis (Jackson) doing more than a routine check-up with a female patient. With her innocence shattered by the discovery, Eve's torment soon affects her emotionally strained mother Roz (Whitfield) and adolescent tease older sister Cisely (Good). Impressive, multi-layered directorial debut from Lemmons didn't draw much attention during theatrical run, but has gained a following since. **109m/C VHS, DVD.** *Samuel L. Jackson, Lynn Whitfield, Debbi (Deborah) Morgan, Diahann Carroll, Jurnee Smollett, Meagan Good, Vondie Curtis-Hall, Lisa Nicole Carson, Jake Smollett, Ethel Ayler;* **D:** *Kasi Lemmons;* **W:** *Kasi Lemmons;* **C:** *Amy Vincent;* **M:** *Terence Blanchard;* **Nar:** *Tamara Tunie.* Ind. Spirit '98: First Feature, Support. Actress (Morgan).

The Evictors woof! **1979 (PG)** Young couple moves into an abandoned, haunted farmhouse in a small Louisiana town. Unfortunately, they don't know anything about its horrible bloody history. And the real estate agent acts kinda funny. AIP Amityville scare-a-thon. **92m/C VHS.** *Vic Morrow, Michael Parks, Jessica Harper, Sue Ane Langdon, Dennis Fimple;* **D:** *Charles B. Pierce;* **W:** *Charles B. Pierce.*

Evidence of Blood 🦴🦴½ **1997 (PG-13)** Crime writer investigates a 40-year-old murder in a small town that would rather keep its secrets to itself. Based on the book by Thomas H. Cook. **109m/C VHS.** *David Strathairn, Mary McDonnell;* **D:** *Andrew Mondshein;* **W:** *Dalene Young;* **C:** *Philip Linzey;* **M:** *Mason Daring.*

The Evil 🦴🦴 **1978 (R)** A psychologist must destroy an evil force that is killing off the members of his research team residing at an old mansion. **80m/C VHS.** *Richard Crenna, Joanna Pettet, Andrew Prine, Victor Buono, Cassie Yates, George O'Hanlon Jr., Lynne Moody, Mary Louise Weller, Milton Selzer;* **D:** *Gus Trikonis;* **W:** *Donald G. Thompson;* **C:** *Mario DiLeo.*

Evil 🦴🦴🦴 *Ondskan* **2003** Wanting her son to escape his stepdad's beatings, Erik's (Wilson) mom scrapes up the funds to send him to a supposedly classy boarding school. Unfortunately it's ruled by upperclassmen who like to keep the pecking order alive by tormenting younger students. But Erik's violent past—including his expulsion from his last school as a gang leader—makes him a poor target for their abuse, and despite his desire to please his mom he must fight to protect himself and the other victims. Based on Swede Jan Guillou's 1981 autobiographical novel "Ondskan." **113m/C DVD. SW** *Marie Richardson, Andreas Wilson, Henrik Lundstrom, Gustaf Skarsgard, Linda Zilliacus, Johan Rabeus, Kjell Bergqvist, Magnus Roosman;* **D:** *Mikael Hafstrom;* **W:** *Mikael Hafstrom, Hans Gunnarsson;* **C:** *Peter Mokrosinski;* **M:** *Francis Shaw.*

Evil Altar 🦴 **1989 (R)** A man controls a small town, but only so long as he offers sacrifices to the devil! **90m/C VHS.** *William (Bill) Smith, Robert Z'Dar, Pepper Martin, Theresa Cooney, Ryan Rao;* **D:** *James R. Winburn.*

The Evil Below 🦴 **1987** A couple hits the high seas in search of the lost treasure ship "El Diablo," resting on the ocean floor. In the process they trigger an evil curse and must attempt to thwart it. **90m/C VHS. SA** *June Chadwick, Wayne Crawford;* **D:** *Jean-Claude Dubois.*

Evil Clutch 🦴½ **1989 (R)** A young couple vacationing in the Alps encounter several creepy locals when they find themselves in the midst of a haunted forest. The cinematography is extremely amateurish in this Italian gorefest and the English dubbing is atrocious. However, the special makeup effects are outstanding and the musical score adds a touch of class to this otherwise inept horror film. **88m/C VHS, DVD. IT** *Coralina Cataldi-Tassoni, Diego Ribba, Elena Cantarone, Luciano Crovato, Stefano Molinari;* **D:** *Andreas Marfori;* **W:** *Andreas Marfori;* **C:** *Marco Isoli.*

Evil Dead 🦴🦴½ **1983 (NC-17)** Five college students, vacationing in the Tennessee mountains, take refuge in an abandoned cabin. They find a tape and a Book of the Dead, which unwittingly lets them resurrect demons, which transform the students into evil monsters until only Ash (Campbell) remains to fight the evil. Exuberantly gory low-budgeter followed by two sequels. **85m/C VHS, DVD, UMD.** *Bruce Campbell, Ellen Sandweiss, Betsy Baker, Hal Delrich, Sarah York, Theodore (Ted) Raimi, Sam Raimi, Scott Spiegel;* **D:** *Sam Raimi;* **W:** *Sam Raimi;* **C:** *Tim Philo;* **M:** *Joseph LoDuca.*

Evil Dead 2: Dead by Dawn 🦴🦴½ **1987 (R)** A gory, tongue-in-cheek sequel/remake of the original festival of gag and gore, in which an ancient book of magic invokes a crowd of flesh-snacking, joke-tossing ghouls. Followed by yet a third bloodfest. **84m/C VHS, DVD, Blu-ray Disc, UMD.** *Bruce Campbell, Sarah Berry, Dan Hicks, Kassie Wesley, Theodore (Ted) Raimi, Denise Bixler, Richard Domeier, Scott Spiegel, Josh Becker, Lou Hancock;* **Cameos:** *Sam Raimi;* **D:** *Sam Raimi;* **W:** *Sam Raimi, Scott Spiegel;* **C:** *Peter Deming;* **M:** *Joseph LoDuca.*

Evil Dead Trap 🦴🦴½ **1988** Nami (Miyuki Ono), a Japanese late-night TV show host, is sent a tape that appears to show a brutal murder. Her cheap boss refuses to do anything, but she and her female crew decide to follow up on the tape and find the location where it was made. What follows is an abandoned factory owes much to Argento with even more visceral sex and violence. Director Ikeda's camera is almost never still. The script combines supernatural elements with a realistic setting and believable characters. **90m/C VHS, DVD. JP** *Miyuki Ono, Fumi Katsuragi, Hitomi Kobayashi, Eriko Nakagawa;* **D:** *Toshiharu Ikeda;* **W:** *Takashi Ishii.*

Evil Ed 🦴½ **1996 (R)** Formerly mild-mannered film editor Ed (Ruebeck) becomes obsessed with the horror series he's working on, goes off the deep end, and begins a series of killings that mimic the ones from the films. Lots of splatter. **90m/C VHS, DVD. SW** *Johan Ruebeck, Olof Rhodin, Pete Lorberg;* **D:** *Anders Jacobsson;* **W:** *Anders Jacobsson;* **C:** *Anders Jacobsson;* **M:** *Goran Lundstrom.*

Evil Eyes 🦴🦴 **2004 (R)** Hard-up screenwriter Jeff Stenn (Baldwin) is happy to accept a producer's (Kier) offer to pen a horror flick about a guy who went psycho and offed his family with an axe. But Jeff starts suffering from violent hallucinations and is soon living out his character's nightmare. Familiar plot moves briskly but if you really need see a crazy guy with an axe, watch "The Shining." **80m/C DVD.** *Adam Baldwin, Udo Kier, Mark Sheppard, Jennifer Gates, Kristin Lorenz;* **D:** *Mark Atkins;* **W:** *Naomi L. Selfman;* **C:** *Mark Atkins.* **VIDEO**

Evil Has a Face 🦴🦴 **1996 (R)** Chicago police sketch artist Gwen McGarrell (Young) travels to rural Minnesota to help investigator Tom Sawyer (Moses) locate a child molester. But the face she draws turns out to be that of her abusive stepfather (Ross), who's been presumed dead. **92m/C VHS.** *Sean Young, William R. Moses, Joe Guzaldo, Chelcie Ross, Brighton Hertford, Richard (Dick) Cusack;* **D:** *Robert M. Fresco;* **W:** *Robert M. Fresco;* **C:** *Stephen Lighthill;* **M:** *Joseph Vitarelli.* **CABLE**

Evil Judgment 🦴½ **1985** A young girl investigates a series of murders and finds the culprit is a psychopathic judge. **93m/C VHS.** *Pamela Collyer, Jack Langedijk, Nanette Workman;* **D:** *Claude Castravelli.*

Evil Laugh woof! **1986 (R)** Medical students and their girlfriends party at an abandoned orphanage, until a serial killer decides to join them. **90m/C VHS, DVD.** *Tony Griffin, Kim McKamy, Jody Gibson, Dominick Brascia;* **D:** *Dominick Brascia.*

Evil Lives 🦴🦴½ *Soulmates* **1992** Now here's a horror premise you don't run into every day. Horror novelist Richard Wayborn (Rodgers) leaves a trail of dead women during his lecture tours. Seems he's really 700-years-old and his long-dead wife can temporarily resurrect herself using the nubile forms of other women. Now, Wayborn has chosen a new babe but so far she's managing to elude his deadly charms. **90m/C VHS, DVD.** *Tristan Rogers, Arabella Holzbog, Tyrone Power Jr., Soledad Curtis, Griffin O'Neal, Melissa Moore, Wendy Barry, Paul Bartel, Dawn Wells;* **D:** *Thunder Levin.* **VIDEO**

The Evil Mind 🦴🦴½ *The Clairvoyant* **1934** A fraudulent mind reader predicts many disasters that start coming true. **80m/B VHS, DVD. GB** *Claude Rains, Fay Wray, Jane Baxter, Felix Aylmer;* **D:** *Maurice Elvey;* **W:** *Charles Bennett.*

Evil Obsession 🦴 **1996** Disturbed Homer (Feldman) obsessed with super-model Margo (Stevens) and later becomes a suspect in the murders of 12 other models. **93m/C VHS.** *Corey Feldman, Kimberly Stevens, Mark Derwin, Brion James, Stacie Randall;* **D:** *Richard W. Munchkin.* **VIDEO**

The Evil of Frankenstein 🦴🦴 **1964** The third of the Hammer Frankenstein films, with the mad doctor once again finding his creature preserved in ice and thawing him out. Preceded by "The Revenge of Frankenstein" and followed by "Frankenstein Created Woman." **84m/C VHS, DVD. GB** *Peter Cushing, Duncan Lamont, Peter Woodthorpe, Sandor Eles, Kiwi Kingston, Katy Wild;* **D:** *Freddie Francis;* **W:** *John (Anthony Hinds);* **C:** *John Wilcox;* **M:** *Don Banks.*

Evil Roy Slade 🦴🦴½ **1971** Goofy family comedy (a failed TV pilot) that's a parody of every western cliche imaginable. Roy (Astin) is the meanest gunslinger in the west (he was raised by vultures) who's trying to turn over a new leaf after he falls for a pretty schoolteacher. He's aided by a shrink, who wants Roy to give up his weapons fetish, but singing glamour boy lawman Bing Bell (Shawn) has a score to settle with Roy. **97m/C VHS.** *John Astin, Dick Shawn, Mickey Rooney, Pam(ela) Austin, Henry Gibson, Edie Adams, Milton Berle, Dom DeLuise, Noriyuki "Pat" Morita, Penny Marshall, John Ritter;* **Cameos:** *Jerry Paris;* **D:** *Jerry Paris;* **W:** *Garry Marshall, Jerry Belson;* **C:** *Sam Leavitt;* **Nar:** *Pat Buttram.* **TV**

Evil Spawn 🦴 *Deadly Sting; Alive by Night; Alien Within* **1987** A fading movie queen takes an experimental drug to restore her youthful beauty, but it only turns her into a giant silverfish. Releases under several alternate titles, and with varying running times. **70m/C VHS, DVD.** *Bobbie Bresee, John Carradine, Drew Godderis, John Terrance, Dawn Wildsmith, Jerry Fox, Pamela Gilbert, Forrest J. Ackerman;* **D:** *Kenneth J. Hall;* **W:** *Kenneth J. Hall;* **C:** *Christopher Condon.*

Evil Spirits 🦴½ **1991 (R)** Boarding-house tenants are murdered while the crazy landlady cashes their social security checks. This seedy horror cheapie doesn't take itself seriously, and like-minded genre buffs may enjoy the cult-film cast. **95m/C VHS, DVD.** *Karen Black, Arte Johnson, Virginia Mayo, Michael Berryman, Martine Beswick, Bert Remsen, Yvette Vickers, Robert Quarry, Mikel Angel, Debra Lamb;* **D:** *Gary Graver;* **W:** *Mikel Angel.*

The Evil That Men Do 🦴🦴 **1984 (R)** A hitman comes out of retirement to break up a Central American government's political torture ring and, in the process, brings a friend's killer to justice. Based on the novel by R. Lance Hill. **90m/C VHS, DVD.** *Charles Bronson, Theresa Saldana, Joseph Maher, Jose Ferrer, Rene Enriquez, John Glover, Raymond St. Jacques, Antoinette Bower, Enrique Lucero, Jorge Luke;* **D:** *J. Lee Thompson;* **W:** *John Crowther;* **C:** *Xavier Cruz;* **M:** *Ken Thorne.*

Evil Toons 🦴½ **1990 (R)** A quartet of lovely coeds on a cleaning job venture into a deserted mansion. There they accidentally release a vulgar, lustful, animated demon who proceeds to cause their clothes to fall off. Can the girls escape the haunted mansion with their sanity, virtue and wardrobes intact? **86m/C VHS, DVD.** *Suzanne Ager, Stacy Nix, Madison Stone, Don Dowe, Arte Johnson, Dick Miller, Monique Gabrielle, David Carradine;* **D:** *Fred Olen Ray.*

Evil Town 🦴 **1987 (R)** In this poorly made film, a wandering guy discovers a town overrun with zombies created by a mad doctor. **88m/C VHS.** *Dean Jagger, James Keach, Robert Walker, Jr., Doria Cook, Michele Marsh;* **D:** *Edward Collins.*

Evil under the Sun 🦴🦴 **1982 (PG)** An opulent beach resort is the setting as Hercule Poirot attempts to unravel a murder mystery. Based on the Agatha Christie novel. **112m/C VHS, DVD. GB** *Peter Ustinov, Jane Birkin, Maggie Smith, Colin Blakely, Roddy McDowall, Diana Rigg, Sylvia Miles, James Mason, Nicholas Clay;* **D:** *Guy Hamilton;* **W:** *Anthony Shaffer;* **C:** *Christopher Challis;* **M:** *Cole Porter.*

The Evil Within woof! *Baby Blood* **1989 (R)** Parasitic beast, with an unquenchable thirst for blood, slithers from the center of the earth into the convenient womb of a young woman. She takes to murder in order to keep everyone within reach while preparing to give birth. As disgusting as it sounds. **88m/C VHS, DVD.** *Emmanuelle Escourrou, Jean-Francois Guillote;* **D:** *Alain Robak;* **W:** *Alain Robak, Serge Cukier.*

Evils of the Night 🦴 **1985** Teenage campers are abducted by sex-crazed alien vampires. Bloody naked mayhem follows. **85m/C VHS, DVD.** *John Carradine, Julie Newmar, Tina Louise, Neville Brand, Aldo Ray, Karrie Emerson, Bridget Holloman;* **Cameos:** *Pat Buttram;* **W:** *Marti Rustam, Phillip D. Connors.*

Evilspeak woof! **1982 (R)** Bumbling misfit enrolled at a military school is mistreated by the other cadets. With the help of his computer, he retaliates with satanic power. Bits, bytes, and gore. **89m/C VHS, DVD.** *Clint Howard, Don Stark, Lou Gravance, Lauren Lester, R.G. Armstrong, Joe Cortese, Claude Earl Jones, Haywood Nelson;* **D:** *Eric Weston.*

Evita 🐾🐾½ 1996 (PG) Rock opera about the life and death of Eva Peron finally comes to the big screen with all its extravaganza intact. Madonna's in the title role (in fine voice, lavishly costumed but unflatteringly lit) about an ambitious poor girl willing to do anything to make her mark—in this version by sleeping her way up the ladder of power to Argentine strongman Juan Peron (Pryce as wax dummy). Evita becomes a would-be champion of the people, even as the government ruthlessly suppresses their freedoms. The surprisingly strong-voiced Banderas (perhaps his emphatic enunciation is to make his English as clear as possible) is everyman narrator Che (changed from the stage version's revolutionary Che Guevara), "but some of the other songs are drowned by loud orchestration. Director Parker has a cameo as a frustrated film director trying to work with Evita. **FA** Cine-Oh, What A Circus; On This Night of a Thousand Stars; Eva and Magaldi; Eva Beware of the City; Buenos Aires; Another Suitcase in Another Hall; Goodnight and Thank You. **133m/C** VHS, DVD, Madonna, Antonio Banderas, Jonathan Pryce, Jimmy Nail, Victoria Sus, Julian Littman, Olga Meedis, Laura Pallas, Julia Worsley; **Cameos:** Alan Parker; **D:** Alan Parker; **W:** Oliver Stone, Alan Parker; **C:** Darius Khondji; **M:** Andrew Lloyd Webber, Tim Rice. Oscars '96: Song ("You Must Love Me"); Golden Globes '97: Actress—Mus./Comedy (Madonna), Film—Mus./Comedy, Song ("You Must Love Me").

Evolution 🐾½ 2001 (PG-13) A meteor containing microscopic organisms crashes in the New Mexico desert and they begin evolving at an enormous rate. A misfit team consisting of community college prof Duchovny, government scientist Moore, wannabe fireman Scott, and kooky geologist Jones try to prevent the spores (which evolve into a number of crazy critters) from taking over the planet. It's supposed to be sci-fi comedy, but the effectively scary monsters eliminate whatever comedic elements the writers and Reitman forgot to kill. **101m/C** VHS, DVD, David Duchovny, Julianne Moore, Orlando Jones, Seann William Scott, Ted Levine, Ethan Suplee, Michael Ray Bower, Katharine Towne, Dan Aykroyd, Richard Moll, Gregory Itzin, Ty Burrell; **D:** Ivan Reitman; **W:** David Diamond, David Weissman, Don Jakoby; **C:** Michael Chapman; **M:** John Powell.

The Ewok Adventure 🐾🐾½ 1984 (G) Those adorable, friendly and funny characters from "Return of the Jedi," detailing their battle against an evil queen to retain their forest home. Preceded by "The Ewok Adventure." **98m/C** VHS, DVD, Wilford Brimley, Warwick Davis, Aubree Miller, Fionnula Flanagan. **Nar:** Burl Ives. **TV**

Evolver 🐾½ 1994 (R) Teenager Kyle Baxter (Randall) wins a robot patterned after a video arcade game but the robot has a secret military weapon's program built into its brain, causing it to evolve into a killing machine. **90m/C** VHS, DVD, Ethan Embry, John de Lancie, Cassidy Rae, Cindy Pickett, Paul Dooley; **D:** Mark Rosman; **V:** William H. Macy.

The Ewoks: Battle for Endor 🐾🐾½ 1985 TV movie based on the furry creatures from "Return of the Jedi." Another adventure from George Lucas. In this installment the Ewoks save a miraculous child from harm with the help of a young human. This fun-filled adventure has Lucas's thumbprint all over it and great special effects. Followed by "Ewoks: The Battle for Endor." **96m/C** VHS, DVD, Warwick Davis, Eric Walker, Aubree Miller, Fionnula Flanagan. **Nar:** Burl Ives. **TV**

The Ex 🐾🐾½ 1996 (R) Architect David Kenyon (Mancuso) has a new life, with a sweet second wife (Amis) and a five-year-old son. Then the ex, Deirdre (Butler), comes sauntering back and it seems she and David had a very kinky relationship. Now Deirdre decides it's time to get revenge. Familiar plotline is given a high gloss and some chills. **87m/C** VHS, Yancy Butler, Nick Mancuso, Suzy Amis; **D:** Mark L. Lester; **W:** John Lutz, Larry Cohen; **M:** Paul Zaza.

The Ex 🐾 Fast Track 2007 (PG-13) Tom (Braff) loses his job after his wife (Peet) quits hers to raise their first child. To save the family, he moves them from New York to Ohio to accept an advertising job with his father-in-law. Then he discovers that his new boss is a wheelchair-bound paraplegic who had a one-time relationship with his wife in high school, and has been obsessing over her ever since. Plays like a mean sitcom, but without the laughs that would normally accompany black comedies. Although it might make you squirm like one. **90m/C** VHS, DVD, Zach Braff, Amanda Peet, Jason Bateman, Charles Grodin, Mia Farrow, Donal Logue, Lucian Maisel, Amy Poehler, Fred Armisen, Bob Stephenson, Josh Charles, Paul Rudd, Amy Adams, Romany Malco; **D:** Jesse Peretz; **W:** Michael Handelman, Paul Guion; **C:** Tom Richmond; **M:** Ed Shearmur.

Ex-Cop 🐾🐾 1993 Pete Danberg is a cop with a drinking problem. He's fired from the force but not before he puts away the "Las Vegas Slasher." Unfortunately for Pete the Slasher makes parole and is out for revenge—using Pete's kidnapped daughter as bait. **97m/C** VHS, Rick Savage, Sandy Hackett, Joan Chamberlain, Douglas Tany, Angi Davidson, Richard Connell, Jim Williams; **D:** Paul Wendkos; **M:** Georges Delerue.

Ex-Lady 🐾🐾 1933 Davis stars as a liberated woman who loves advertising writer Raymond, but doesn't want to marry him. However, she believes living together is the most suitable arrangement. The two open up and an agency and complications ensue. Remake of "Illicit," which was filmed only two years earlier with Barbara Stanwyck in the lead role. **65m/B VHS,** Bette Davis, Gene Raymond, Frank McHugh, Claire Dodd, Monroe Owsley, Ferdinand Gottschalk; **D:** Robert Florey.

Ex-Mrs. Bradford 🐾🐾🐾 1936 Amateur sleuth Dr. Bradford teams up with his ex-wife to solve a series of murders at the race track. Sophisticated comedy-mystery; witty dialogue. **80m/B VHS,** William Powell, Jean Arthur, James Gleason, Eric Blore, Robert Armstrong; **D:** Stephen Roberts.

Excalibur 🐾🐾🐾½ 1981 (R) A sweeping, visionary retelling of the life of King Arthur, from his conception, to the sword in the stone, to the search for the holy Grail and the final battle with Mordred. An imperfect, sensationalized version, but still the best yet filmed. **140m/C VHS, DVD, HD DVD,** Robert Addie, Keith Buckley, Helen Mirren, Cherie Lunghi, Paul Geoffrey, Gabriel Byrne, Liam Neeson, Patrick Stewart, Nicol Williamson, Nigel Terry, Nicholas Clay; **D:** John Boorman; **W:** Rospo Pallenberg, John Boorman; **C:** Alex Thomson; **M:** Trevor Jones.

Excellent Cadavers 🐾🐾½ 1999 (R) Giovanni Falcone (Palminteri) was an incorruptible Italian prosecutor who took on the Mafia in Sicily in the 1980s. By the end of the decade, and with the help of informer Tommaso Buscetta (Abraham), Falcone had 300 convictions and sealed his own grim fate. Title refers to the corpses of public officials who challenged the mobsters. Based on the book by Alexander Stille. **86m/C VHS, DVD,** Chazz Palminteri, F. Murray Abraham, Anna Galiena, Bruno Ganz; **D:** Ricky Tognazzi; **W:** Peter Pruce; **M:** Joseph Vitarelli. **CABLE**

Excess Baggage 🐾🐾 1996 (PG-13) Attention-seeking rich girl Emily (Silverstone) fakes her own kidnapping to get her dad at dear old dad, involving car thief Vincent Roche (del Toro) in the crime. Things get out of control when her creepy "Uncle" Ray (Walken), who's an ex-CIA assassin, is hired by Emily's father to get her back. Silverstone's character is alternately whiny and pouting, you'll wonder why dad would want her back and why Vincent hangs on at all. First picture in Silverstone's pricey production deal with Columbia went through the rumor mill (for supposed clashes between Silverstone and director Brambilla) and was originally scheduled for release in the fall of '96. **101m/C** VHS, DVD, Alicia Silverstone, Benicio Del Toro, Christopher Walken, Harry Connick Jr., Jack Thompson, Nicholas Turturro, Michael Bowen, Leland Crser, Robert Wisden, Sally Kirkland; **D:** Marco Brambilla; **W:** Mikhalla Max Adems, Dick Clement, Ian La Frenais; **C:** Jean-Yves Escoffier; **M:** John Lurie.

Excessive Force 🐾🐾½ 1993 (R) Routine actioner lives up to its title by offering lots of violence, but little else. Gang leader Young seeks revenge on the cops who ruined a $3 million drug deal. Loner cop Griffith is the only one to survive the grudge killings and goes after hieves. Limited theatrical release sent this one straight to video. **89m/C VHS, DVD,** Thomas Ian Griffith, Lance Henriksen, James Earl Jones, Charlotte Lewis, Tony Todd, Burt Young, W. Earl Brown; **D:** Jon Hess; **M:** Thomas Ian Griffith; **C:** Donald M. Morgan; **M:** Charles Bernstein.

Excessive Force 2: Force on Force 🐾🐾 1995 (R) Special agent Harry Cordell (Randall) volunteers to hunt down an assassination squad that is turning L.A. into murder central. Seems her former lover Francis Lydell (Gauthier) is head killer and Harry's got a score to settle. Lots of action and nifty weapons. **88m/C VHS,** Stacie Randall, Dan Gauthier, Jay Patterner; **D:** Jonathan Winfrey; **W:** Mark Sevi; **C:** Russ Brandt; **M:** Kevin Kiner.

The Execution 🐾🐾 1985 Five female friends who discover that the Nazi doctor who brutalized them in a concentration camp during WWII is now living a normal life in California. Together they plot his undoing. **92m/C VHS, DVD,** Loretta Swit, Valerie Harper, Sancy Dennis, Jessica Walter, Rip Torn, Barbara Barrie, Robert Hooks, Michael Lerner; **D:** Paul Wendkos; **M:** Georges Delerue.

Execution of Justice 🐾🐾 1999 (R) Emily Mann's play focused on the trial of city supervisor Dan White for the deaths of San Francisco Mayor George Moscone (Young) and openly gay elected official Harvey Milk (Coyote). You may remember the infamous "Twinkie Defense." This sporadically compelling cable docudrama delves into the mind of White (Daly) himself. **103m/C VHS,** Timothy Daly, Peter Coyote, Stephen Young, Amy Van Nostrand, Tyne Daly, Khali Kain, Frank Pellegrino, Shannon Hile; **D:** Leon Ichaso; **W:** Michael Butler; **C:** Claudio Chea. **CABLE**

The Execution of Private Slovik 🐾🐾🐾 1974 This quiet powerhouse of a TV movie recounts in straightforward terms the case of Eddie Slovik, a WWII misfit who became the only American soldier executed for desertion since the Civil War. The Levinson/Link screenplay (based on the book by William Bradford Huie) ends up defying Slovik, which some might find hard to take. But there's no arguing the impact of the drama, or of Sheen's unaffected lead performance. Based on a true story. **104m/C VHS, DVD,** Martin Sheen, Mariclare Costello, Ned Beatty, Gary Busey, Matt Clark, Ben Hammer, Warren Kemmerling; **D:** Lamont Johnson; **W:** Richard Levinson, William Link; **C:** Bill Butler. **TV**

The Executioner 🐾 Like Father, Like Son, Massacre Mafia Style 1978 (R) A very cheap, very "Godfather"-like story of a mafia family gone awry. **84m/C VHS,** Duke Mitchell, Vic Caesar, Dominic Miceli, John Strong, Jim Williams, Lorenzo Dodo; **D:** Duke Mitchell.

The Executioner 🐾🐾½ 1985 The lawyers and family of Raymond Graham struggle to keep him from being executed for murder. Based on a true story. **107m/C VHS,** Morgan Freeman, Jeff Fahey, Kate Reid, Laurie Metcalf, Josef Sommer; **D:** Daniel Petrie. **TV**

The Executioner 🐾🐾 1970 (PG) A thriller wherein a British spy must prove that his former colleague is a double agent. Elements of backstabbing betrayal and espionage abound. **107m/C VHS,** George Peppard, Joan Collins, Keith Michell, Oscar Homolka, Charles Gray, Nigel Patrick; **D:** Sam Wanamaker.

The Executioner, Part 2: Frozen Scream 🐾 1984 (R) Brutal feud rocks the Mafia, and a crime kingpin's passionate son seeks revenge on his father's slayers. Not a sequel to any other films bearing similar titles. Strange thing is, no "Executioner, Part I" was ever made. Pretty laughable. **150m/C VHS,** Chris Mitchum, Aldo Ray, Antoine John Mottel, Renee Harmon; **D:** James Bryant.

The Executioners 🐾🐾½ 1993 When a nuclear explosion contaminates most of the city's drinking water, the remainder falls under the harsh control of the Black Knight. Now, it's up to the Heroic Trio to defeat their nemesis. Chinese with subtitles. **100m/C VHS, DVD, HK** Anita Mui, Michelle Yeoh, Maggie Cheung, Ching Siu Tung; **W:** Susan Chan; **C:** Hang-Seng Poon; **M:** Cacima Wong.

The Executioner's Song 🐾🐾🐾½ 1982 European version of the TV movie based on Norman Mailer's Pulitzer Prize-winner, recounting the life and death of convicted murderer Gary Gilmore. Features adult-minded footage not seen in the U.S. version. **157m/C VHS,** Tommy Lee Jones, Rosanna Arquette, Eli Wallach, Christine Lahti, Jerry Wright, Jordan Clark, Steven Keats; **D:** Lawrence Schiller.

Executive Action 🐾🐾 1973 (PG) Political thriller providing a plausible look at the events leading to the assassination of JFK. In this speculation, a millionaire pays a professional spy to organize a secret conspiracy to kill President Kennedy. Ryan's final film. Adapted by Dalton Trumbo from Mark Lane's "Rush to Judgement." **91m/C VHS,** Burt Lancaster, Robert Ryan Will Geer, Gilbert Green, John Anderson; **D:** David Miller; **C:** Robert Steadman; **M:** Randy Edelman.

Executive Decision 🐾🐾 1996 (R) Those wacky terrorists are at it again. You would think that after getting their butts kicked in almost every action picture since 1980 that they would learn. But here they are, hijacking a 747, cutting off communications, and affixing a nerve gas bomb to the plane. This time a group of high tech commandos, led by Russell and (briefly) Seagal, must sneak onto the plane and generally mess up the bad guys' plans. Brave stewardess Berry helps tango with the central casting mad dog terrorists. The title refers to the difficult decision on whether or not to blow the plane up in order to avert disaster. Or maybe "Die Hard: Ad Nauseum" wasn't available. **132m/C VHS, DVD,** Kurt Russell, Halle Berry, Oliver Platt, John Leguizamo, Steven Seagal, Joe Morton, David Suchet, B.D. Wong, Len Cariou, Whip Hubley, J.T. Walsh; **D:** Stuart Baird; **W:** Jim Thomas, John Thomas; **C:** Alex Thomson; **M:** Jerry Goldsmith.

Executive Power 🐾🐾 1998 (R) The President has a secret and his people will do anything to prevent a scandal. Secret Service agent Nick (Schiefer) realizes this when a staffer who knows turns up dead. Above average thriller. **115m/C VHS,** Craig Sheffer, Andrea Roth, Joanna Cassidy, John Heard, William Atherton, Denise Crosby, John Capodice; **D:** David Corley; **M:** David Corley. **VIDEO**

Executive Suite 🐾🐾🐾 1954 One of the first dog-eat-dog dramas about high finance and big business. The plot centers on the question of a replacement for the freshly buried owner of a gigantic furniture company. **104m/B VHS,** William Holden, June Allyson, Barbara Stanwyck, Fredric March, Walter Pidgeon, Louis Calhern, Shelley Winters, Paul Douglas, Nina Foch, Dean Jagger; **D:** Robert Wise; **W:** Ernest Lehman; **C:** George J. Folsey.

Executive Target 🐾 1997 (R) Stunt-car driver Nick James (Madsen) is grabbed by a gang of mercenaries who want him as their getaway man when they attempt to kidnap the president (Schneider) and overthrow the U.S. government. He agrees because the gang have also taken his wife as a hostage. Lots of action sequences show where the money went. **96m/C VHS, DVD.** Michael Madsen, Keith David, Angie Everhart, Roy Scheider, Dayton Callie, Kathy Christopherson; *D:* Joseph Merhi; *W:* Dayton Callie; *C:* Ken Blakey. **VIDEO**

Exiled *2006 (R)* High-octane Hong Kong actioner. In 1998, Macau's gangsters are settling old scores and divvying up their loot before the Portuguese island is turned over to communist China. Wo (Nick Cheung) has just returned from exile but Boss Fay (Yam), whom he tried to kill, still wants revenge and sends Blaze (Wong Chau-Sang) and Fat (Lam) to do the deed. But when gangsters Tai (Ng) and Cat (Roy Cheung) show up, it's to prevent Wo's death. Turns out, all five men once belonged to the same gang and they agree to first hijack a gold shipment before finishing other business. Cantonese with subtitles or dubbed. **109m/C DVD.** *HK* Nick Cheung, Roy Cheung, Frances Ng, Suet Lam, Anthony Wong Chau-Sang, Ka-tung Lam, Simon Yam, Josie Ho, Richie Jen; *D:* Johnny To; *W:* Kam-yeun Szeto, Tin-Shing Yip; *C:* Sui-keung Cheung; *M:* Guy Zerafa.

Exiled in America *1990* A Central American freedom fighter (Albert) flees his country for the United States, settling in a small town with his wife. She gets a waitressing job at a local diner, telling the owner her husband died in an accident, and the owner's son winds up falling in love with her. Things get complicated when the death squad, led by a corrupt CIA agent, follows Albert to his hiding place, and the local sheriff threatens to blow his cover. **84m/C VHS.** Maxwell Caulfield, Viveca Lindfors, Kamala Lopez, Stella Stevens, Wings Hauser; *D:* Paul Leder.

Exiled to Shanghai *1937* A couple of newsreel men invent a television device that revolutionizes the business. **65m/B VHS.** Wallace Ford, June Travis, Dean Jagger, William "Billy" Bakewell, Arthur Lake, Jonathan Hale, William Harrigan, Sarah Padden; *D:* Nick Grinde.

eXistenZ *1999 (R)* Typically scary and weird Cronenberg production finds security guard Law saving the life of computer-game designer Leigh. They both get sucked into one of her alternate-reality creations and are pursued by assassins. In this future world, game players are literally hooked up to their computer with an umbilical-like cord plugged directly into their spines—no doubt the fantasy of teenage boys everywhere. Surreal visuals and excellent performances won't help the viewer keep track of what's going on, but for Cronenberg linear plotting is rarely the point. **97m/C VHS, DVD.** *CA* Jennifer Jason Leigh, Jude Law, Ian Holm, Willem Dafoe, Sarah Polley, Christopher Eccleston, Don McKellar, Callum Keith Rennie; *D:* David Cronenberg; *W:* David Cronenberg; *C:* Peter Suschitzky; *M:* Howard Shore. Genie '99: Film Editing.

Exit *1995 (R)* Gang of criminals, lead by pscho Charles (Bradley), take a strip club's dancers as hostages when their robbery attempt goes bad. Exotic dancer Diane (Whirry) manages to escape and hook up with ex-ATF agent Alex (Bucci) to stop the creeps. Lame action, silly dialogue, very attractive Whirry. **90m/C VHS.** Shannon Whirry, David Bradley, Larry Manetti, Joe Bucci; *D:* Ric Roman Waugh; *W:* Joe Augustyn, Brent Friedman, David Robinson; *C:* David B. Nowell; *M:* Kevin Kiner.

Exit in Red *1997 (R)* Beverly Hills psychiatrist Ed Altman (Rourke) is hiding out after the suicide of one of his patients lead to professional misconduct charges. But he just can't leave the womanizing job and gets involved with unhappily married Ally (Schofield). When her husband turns up dead, Ed's charged with murder. It's a frame but just how's he going to prove it. **96m/C VHS.** Mickey Rourke, Annabel Schofield, Anthony Michael Hall, Carre Otis; *D:* Yurek Bogayevicz; *W:* David Womack; *C:* Ericson Core; *M:* Michael Lorenc.

Exit to Eden *1994 (R)* Anne Rampling's (AKA Anne Rice) novel focused on fulfilling S&M sexual fantasies, but director Marshall goes for laughs with a buddy cops-out-of-water sitcom subplot, as undercover cops Aykroyd and O'Donnell track a suspected jewel thief to the fantasy resort of Eden, run by dominatrix Delany. (What was the pitch for this one? Think "Another Stakeout" meets "Tie Me Up, Tie Me Down"? It'll be great. Really.) Neither plot works, resulting in a kinky movie with no kink, and a comedy with few laughs. O'Donnell holds up her end, providing what few yuks there are. Everyone else, especially Aykroyd and Delany, seem to be sleepwalking. Lucky for them. **113m/C VHS, DVD.** Dana Delany, Paul Mercurio, Dan Aykroyd, Rosie O'Donnell, Hector Elizondo, Stuart Wilson, Iman, Sandi Kom, Laura Elena Harring; *D:* Garry Marshall; *W:* Deborah Amelon, Bob Brunner; *M:* Patrick Doyle. Golden Raspberries '94: Worst Support. Actress (O'Donnell).

Exit Wounds *2001 (R)* Unpredictable, unorthodox Detroit police detective Orin Boyd (Seagal, of course) gets sent to the baddest part of town after successfully, but unconventionally, breaking up a plot to kill the Vice President. There, along with his rambunctious new partner (Washington), he uncovers corrupt cops and a drug-running scheme involving the notorious crime lord Walker (DMX). Lots of martial arts sequences and loads of gunfire from, presumably, really bad shots. Romance also blossoms between Mr. Loose Canon and a precinct commander played by Hennessy. Typical Seagal flick, sure to be enjoyed by fans. Others should be wary. **98m/C VHS, DVD.** *US* Steven Seagal, DMX, Isaiah Washington IV, Anthony Anderson, Michael Jai White, Bill Duke, Jill(ian) Hennessey, Tom Arnold, Bruce McGill, David Vadim, Eva Mendes; *D:* Andrzej Bartkowiak; *W:* Ed Horowitz, Richard D'Ovidio; *C:* Glen MacPherson; *M:* Jeff Rona, Damon Blackman.

Exodus *1960* Chronicles the post-WWII partition of Palestine into a homeland for Jews; the anguish of refugees from Nazi concentration camps held on ships in the Mediterranean; the struggle of the tiny nation with forces dividing it from within and destroying it from the outside; and the heroic men and women who saw a job to be done and did it. Based on the novel by Leon Uris; filmed in Cyprus and Israel. Preminger battled the Israeli government, the studio, and the novel's author to complete this epic. Cost more than $4 million, a phenomenal amount at the time. **208m/C VHS, DVD.** Paul Newman, Eva Marie Saint, Lee J. Cobb, Sal Mineo, Ralph Richardson, Hugh Griffith, Gregory Ratoff, Felix Aylmer, Peter Lawford, Jill Haworth, John Derek, David Opatoshu, Marius Goring, Alexandra Stewart, Michael Wager, Martin Benson, Paul Stevens, George Maharis; *D:* Otto Preminger; *W:* Dalton Trumbo; *M:* Ernest Gold. Oscars '60: Orig. Dramatic Score; Golden Globes '61: Support. Actor (Mineo).

Exorcism *Exorcismo 1974* A satanic cult in a small English village commits a series of gruesome crimes that have the authorities baffled. **90m/C VHS, DVD.** *SP* Paul Naschy, Maria Perschy, Maria Kosti, Grace Mills, Jorge Torras, Marta Avile; *D:* Juan Bosch; *W:* Juan Bosch, Paul Naschy; *C:* Francisco Sanchez.

The Exorcism of Emily Rose *2005 (PG-13)* Nineteen year old student Emily Rose (Carpenter) died during an exorcism performed by Father Richard Moore (Wilkinson), who is being tried for negligent homicide. Attorney Erin Bruner (Linney) hopes her defense of the priest will propel her career to the next level. This courtroom drama is interwoven with horror as the freakish circumstances of Emily's death are recounted from the stand. Somewhat predictable, but well worth the viewing for fans of the genre. **114m/C DVD, UMD.** *US* Laura Linney, Tom Wilkinson, Campbell Scott, Jennifer Carpenter, Colm Feore, Joshua Close, Kenneth Welsh, Duncan Fraser, J.R. Bourne, Mary Beth Hurt, Henry Czerny, Shohreh Aghdashloo; *D:* Scott Derickson; *W:* Scott Derrickson, Paul Harris Boardman; *C:* Tom Stern; *M:* Christopher Young.

Exorcism's Daughter *House of Insane Women 1974 (R)* While running an insane asylum, a man discovers that a woman has lost her mind because as a child, she witnessed her mother's death during an exorcism. Pretty grim but interesting for genre fans. A natural double feature with "House of Psychotic Women." **93m/C VHS.** *SP* Amelia Gade, Francesco Rabal, Espartaco (Spartaco) Santoni; *D:* Rafael Morena Alba.

The Exorcist *1973 (R)* Truly terrifying story of a young girl who is possessed by a malevolent spirit. Brilliantly directed by Friedkin, with underlying themes of the workings and nature of fate. Impeccable casting and unforgettable, thought-provoking performances. A rare film that remains startling and engrossing with every viewing, it spawned countless imitations and changed the way horror films were made. Based on the bestseller by Blatty, who also wrote the screenplay. Not for the squeamish. When first released, the film created mass hysteria in theatres, with people fainting and paramedics on the scene. **120m/C VHS, DVD.** Ellen Burstyn, Linda Blair, Jason Miller, Max von Sydow, Jack MacGowran, Lee J. Cobb, Kitty Winn, Barton Heyman, Peter Masterson; *D:* William Friedkin; *W:* William Peter Blatty; *C:* Owen Roizman, Billy Williams; *M:* Jack Nitzsche; *V:* Mercedes McCambridge. Oscars '73: Adapt. Screenplay, Sound; Golden Globes '74: Director (Friedkin), Film—Drama, Screenplay, Support. Actress (Blair).

The Exorcist 2: The Heretic *1977 (R)* Unnecessary sequel to the 1973 hit "The Exorcist" which featured extensive recruiting by Boorman. After four years, Blair is still under psychiatric care, suffering from the effects of being possessed by the devil. Meanwhile, a priest investigates the first exorcist's work as he tries to help the head-spinning lass. Decent special effects. **118m/C VHS, DVD.** Richard Burton, Linda Blair, Louise Fletcher, Kitty Winn, James Earl Jones, Ned Beatty, Max von Sydow, Paul Henreid; *D:* John Boorman; *W:* William Goodhart; *C:* William A. Fraker; *M:* Ennio Morricone.

Exorcist 3: Legion *1990 (R)* Apparently subscribing to the two wrongs make a right school of sequels, this time novelist Blatty is the director. The result is slightly better than the first sequel, but still a far cry from the original. Fifteen years later, Detective Kinderman (Scott) is faced with a series of really gross murders bearing the mark of a serial killer who was flambeed in the electric chair on the same night as the exorcism of the pea-soup expectorating devil of the original. With the aid of priests Flanders and Dourif, the detective stalks the transmigratory terror—without the help of Linda Blair, who was at the time spoofing "The Exorcist" in "Repossessed". **105m/C VHS, DVD.** George C. Scott, Ed Flanders, Jason Miller, Nicol Williamson, Scott Wilson, Brad Dourif, Nancy Fish, George Dicenzo, Viveca Lindfors, Patrick Ewing, Fabio; *D:* William Peter Blatty; *W:* William Peter Blatty; *C:* Gerry Fisher; *M:* Barry DeVorzon.

Exorcist: The Beginning *2004 (R)* Once upon a time, Paul Schrader was set to make a prequel to the 1973 horror classic "The Exorcist." He shot his film, which was rejected by the producer as insufficiently scary. So Renny Harlin was hired to basically re-shoot (and recast) the entire movie. This backstory has got to be more interesting than what finally showed up on screen. In 1949, Merrin (holdover Skarsgard) has temporarily rejected the priesthood and is working as an archeologist. He agrees to travel to Kenya and bring back an artifact unearthed at a mysteriously preserved Byzantine church. Scary, possibly supernatural, things begin to happen—a child even becomes possessed! Would that any of the cheap theatrics could, more than momentarily, hold a viewer's interest. Schrader's version is also expected to be released on DVD. **114m/C DVD.** Stellan Skarsgard, James D'Arcy, Izabella Scorupco, Remy Sweeney, Julian Wadham, Andrew French, Ben Cross, David Bradley; *D:* Renny Harlin; *W:* William Wisher, Caleb Carr, Alexi Hawley; *C:* Vittorio Storaro; *M:* Trevor Rabin.

Exotica *1994 (R)* Daunting look at eroticism, secrecy, and despair. Christina (Kirshner) is at the center of some complicated relationships. She dresses as a schoolgirl while working at the Exotica strip club in Toronto, where her former lover Eric (Koteas) is the creepily suggestive DJ. Christina's also the obsession of seemingly mild-mannered tax man Francis (Greenwood), who has turned her table dancing into a strange private ritual. Lest this seem to make sense be assured that director Egoyan has much, much, much more going on—not all of it clear and most of it disturbing. **104m/C VHS, DVD.** *CA* Mia Kirshner, Elias Koteas, Bruce Greenwood, Don McKellar, Calvin Green, Arsinee Khanjian, Sarah Polley, Calvin Green, David Hemblen; *D:* Atom Egoyan; *W:* Atom Egoyan; *C:* Paul Sarossy; *M:* Mychael Danna. Genie '94: Art Dir./Set Dec., Cinematog., Costume Des., Director (Egoyan), Film, Orig. Screenplay, Support. Actor (McKellar), Score; Toronto-City '94: Canadian Feature Film.

Expect No Mercy *1995 (R)* Government agent must rescue a fellow agent being held in a virtual reality center that trains assassins to commit murder. **91m/C VHS, DVD.** Wolf Larson, Laurie Holden, Real Andrews, Billy Blanks, Jalal Merhi; *D:* Zale Dalen; *W:* J. Stephen Maunder; *C:* Curtis Petersen; *M:* Varouje.

Expectations *Swedish Heroes; Svenska Hjaltar 1997* Several interconnected tales follow a divorcing couple, a man trying to reconcile with his father, two young lovers, and an older man and woman poised on the edge of an affair. Swedish with subtitles. **95m/C VHS, DVD.** *SW* Niclas Olund, Kent-Arne Dahlgren, Stefan Sundstrom, Emma Warg, Anki Liden, Cajsa-Lisa Ejemyr, Janne Carlsson, Hans Klinga; *D:* Daniel Bergman; *W:* Reider Jonsson; *C:* Esa Vuorinen; *M:* Nicklas Frisk.

The Expendables *1989 (R)* A rugged captain turns a platoon of criminals and misfits into a tough fighting unit for a particularly dangerous mission from which they might not return. See the "Dirty Dozen" instead. **89m/C VHS.** Anthony Finetti, Peter Nelson, Loren Haynes, Kevin Duffis; *D:* Cirio H. Santiago; *W:* Philip Alderton.

Experience Preferred... But Not Essential *1983 (PG)* An English schoolgirl gets her first job at a resort where she learns about life. **77m/C VHS.** *GB* Elizabeth Edmonds, Sue Wallace, Geraldine Griffith, Karen Meagher, Ron Bain; *D:* Peter Duffell; *W:* June Roberts; *C:* Phil Meheux. **TV**

The Experiment *2001 (R)* A prestigious medical institute recruits 20 men to spend two weeks in a controlled prison environment for a psychology experiment. Eight are chosen as guards and the remaining 12 are prisoners. The guards, led by sadist Berus (von Donnanyi), soon begin abusing their power and their prisoners while the prisoners, led by Tarek (Bleibtreu), challenge their authority and the scientists simply lose control of their experiment. Based on the novel "Black Box" by Giordano. German with subtitles. **119m/C VHS, DVD.** *GE* Moritz Bleibtreu, Christian Berkel, Justus von Dohmanyi, Oliver Stokowski, Wotan Wilke Möhring, Nicki von Tempelhoff, Timo Dexters, Antoine Munot Jr., Edgar Selge, Andrea Sawatzki, Philip Hochmair; *D:* Oliver Hirschbiegel; *W:* Don Bohlinger, Mario Giordano, Christoph Darnstadt; *C:* Rainer Klausmann; *M:* Alexander von Bubenheim.

Experiment in Terror *1962* A psychopath kidnaps a girl in order to blackmail her sister, a bank teller, into embezzling $100,000. **123m/B VHS, DVD.** Lee Remick, Glenn Ford, Stefanie Powers, Ross Martin; *D:* Blake Edwards; *M:* Henry Mancini.

Experiment Perilous *1945* A psychologist and a recently widowed woman band together to find her husband's murderer. An atmospheric vintage mystery. **91m/B VHS.** Hedy Lamarr, Paul Lukas, George Brent, Albert Dekker; *D:* Jacques Tourneur.

The Expert *1995 (R)* Special operations expert John Lomax (Speakman) helps catch the creep who murdered his sister. But the killer gets a slap-on-the-wrist sentence, ticking Lomax off mightily. Now, the pro prepare for a deadly last

Exper. Weapon ✗✗ 1989 92m/C VHS, UMD. Jeff Speakman, James Brolin, Michael Shaner, Alex Datcher, Wolfgang Bodison, Elizabeth (Ward) Gracen, Red West, Jim Varney. *D:* Rick Avery. *W:* Max Allan Collins. *C:* Levie Isaacks; *M:* Ashley Irwin.

The Experts ✗✗ 1989 (PG-13) When the KGB needs real Americans for their spies to study, they kidnap two out-of-work "New Yorkers" who mistakenly believe that they have been hired to open a nightclub in Nebraska. Shot on location in Canada. Sometimes funny and directed by former Second City TV MacKenzie Brother, Dave Thomas. 94m/C VHS. John Travolta, Arye Gross, Charles Martin Smith, Kelly Preston, James Keach, Deborah Foreman, Brian Doyle-Murray; *D:* Dave Thomas; *W:* Nick Thiel; Eric Alter; *M:* Marvin Hamlisch.

Explorers ✗✗½ 1985 (PG) Intelligent family fare involving three young boys who use a contraption from their makeshift laboratory to travel to outer space. From the director of "Gremlins," displaying Dante's characteristic surreal wit and sense of irony. 107m/C VHS, DVD. Ethan Hawke, River Phoenix, Jason Presson, Amanda Peterson, Mary Kay Place, Dick Miller, Robert Picardo, Dana Ivey, Meshach Taylor, Brooke Bundy; *D:* Joe Dante; *W:* Eric Luke; *M:* Jerry Goldsmith.

Explosion ✗½ 1969 (R) Distraught and disturbed young man evades the draft after losing a brother in Vietnam. Arriving in Canada, he meets another draft-dodger with whom he embarks on a murderous rampage. 96m/C VHS. Don Stroud, Gordon Thomson, Michèle Chicoine, Richard Conte; *D:* Jules Bricken.

Expose WOOF! 1997 Congressman's daughter Tiffany gets mistaken for a call girl and propositioned by one of dad's colleagues. When the geezer pays her off to keep quiet, Tiff decides extortion is a viable career option. 78m/C VHS. *D:* Tracy Tucker, Kevin E. West, Daneen Boone, Libby George; *D:* B.A. Fredrick.

Exposed ✗✗ 1983 (R) High fashion model Kinski falls in with a terrorist gang through a connection with violinist Nureyev. Weak plotting undermines the end of award. Martha Stewart-like Susan Andrews (Strong) Brit wit Jade Blake (Carliart, stripping the barrier between performance and audience. 100m/C VHS. Nastassja Kinski, Rudolf Nureyev, Harvey Keitel, Ian McShane, Bibi Andersson; *D:* James Toback; *W:* James Tcback; *C:* Henri Decae; *M:* Georges Delerue.

Exposed ✗ 2003 (R) Bob Smith (Donovan) hosts a TV tabloid show that is digging for dirt on three popular female TV personalities who are all up for a big award. 95m/C VHS.

Exposure ✗ 1991 (R) A rugged American photographer (Coyote) on assignment in Rio turns vigilante to locate the vicious killer of a young prostitute. Coyote and his girlfriend (Pays) get caught up in the deadly underworld of international arms trading and drug running as they search for the murderer. 99m/C VHS. Peter Coyote, Amanda Pays, Tcheky Karyo; *M:* Todd Boekelheide.

Express to Terror ✗½ 1979 Passengers aboard an atomic-powered train en route to Los Angeles attempt to kill a sleazy theatrical agent. Pilot for the "Supertrain" series. 120m/C VHS. Steve Lawrence, George Hamilton, Vic Morrow, Broderick Crawford, Robert Alda, Don Stroud, Fred Williamson, Stella Stevens, Don Meredith; *D:* Dan Curtis. TV

Expresso Bongo ✗✗½ 1959 Soho singer/bongo player (Richards) is "discovered" by seedy talent agent Johnny Jackson (Harvey) who manages to turn young man into a teen idol with a 50-50 contract. But women come between the duo and Johnny finds himself without a star. 111m/B VHS, DVD, GB Laurence Harvey, Sylvia Syms, Yolande Donlan, Cliff Richard; *D:* Val Guest; *W:* Wolf Mankowitz; *C:* John Wilcox.

Exquisite Corpses ✗✗½ 1988 An Oklahoma hayseed charges to New York with a new, slick image. He meets the wife of a wealthy man, and together they organize a murderous operation. 95m/C VHS. Zoe Tamerlis, Gary Knox, Daniel Chapman, Ruth (Coreen) Collins; *D:* Temistocles Lopez.

The Exterminating Angel ✗✗✗½ *El Angel exterminador* 1962 A fierce, funny surreal nightmare, wherein dinner guests find they cannot, for any definable reason, leave the dining room; full of dream imagery and characteristically scatological satire. One of Buñuel's best, in Spanish with English subtitles. 95m/B VHS. MX SP Claudio Brook, Cesar del Campo, Lucy Gallardo, Enrique Garcia Alvarez, Tito Junco, Ofelia Montesco, Bertha Moss, Pancho Cordova, Silvia Pinal, Enrique Rambal, Jacqueline Andere, Jose Baviera, Augusto Benedico, Luis Beristain; *D:* Luis Buñuel; *W:* Luis Alcoriza, Luis Buñuel; *M:* Raul Lavista.

Exterminator ✗ 1980 (R) Vietnam veteran hunts down the gang that assaulted his friend and becomes the target of the police, the CIA and the underworld in this bloody banal tale of murder and intrigue. Followed by creatively titled "Exterminator II." 101m/C VHS, DVD, UMD, Christopher George, Samantha Eggar, Robert Ginty, Steve James, Tony DiBenedetto, Dick Boccelli, Patrick Farrelly, Michelle Harrell, Stan Getz, Roger Grimsby; *C:* James Glickenhaus; *W:* James Glickenhaus; *D:* Mark Buntzman; *M:* Joe Renzetti.

Exterminator 2 ✗ 1984 (R) The Exterminator battles the denizens of New York's underworld after his girlfriend is crippled, then murdered by the ruthless Mr. X. Violence galore. 88m/C VHS. Robert Ginty, Mario Van Peebles, Deborah Geffner, Frankie Faison; *D:* Mark Buntzman; *W:* Mark Buntzman.

Exterminators in the Year 3000 WOOF! 1983 (R) The Exterminator and his mercenary girlfriend battle with nuclear mutants over the last remaining tanks of purified water on Earth. Low-budget Road Warrior rip-off. 91m/C VHS, IT SP Robert Jannucci, Alicia Moro, Alan Collins, Fred Harris; *D:* Jules Harrison.

The External ✗✗ *Michael Almereyda's The Mummy, Trance* 1999 (R) Alcoholic Nora (Elliott) keeps experiencing strange trances that have nothing to do with her drinking. So, Nora, her husband (Harris) and their young son travel to Ireland to visit Nora's freaky uncle (Walken) in hopes of some kind of explanation. Yep, it all has something to do with a 2,000-year-old druid he's keeping in the basement of the family castle. No, it doesn't make much sense. 95m/C VHS, DVD. Alison Elliott, Jared Harris, Christopher Walken, Karl Geary; *D:* Michael Almereyda.

Extra Girl ✗✗ 1923 A silent melodrama/farce about a farm girl, brilliantly played by Normand, who travels to Hollywood to be a star. Once in the glamour capital, she gets used and abused for her trouble. 87m/B VHS, DVD. Mabel Normand, Ralph Graves, Vernon Dent; *D:* F. Richard Jones; *W:* Mack Sennett.

Extramarital ✗✗ 1998 (R) Magazine editor Fahey assigns reporter Lords to investigate a woman whose affair with a mystery man turns deadly. 90m/C VHS, DVD. Jeff Fahey, Traci Lords, Brian Bloom, Maria Isabel Diaz; *D:* Yael Russool.

Extramuros ✗✗ 1985 A nun (Maura), living in a convent during the Spanish Inquisition, tries to repress her lesbian desires while the convent vies for fame and money through faked visions. Spanish with subtitles. 120m/C VHS. SP Carmen Maura; *D:* Miguel Picazo.

Extreme Measures ✗✗½ 1996 (R) Dr. Grant, Action Guy! Cast against type, Grant takes on action-suspense in this urbane medical thriller, and it works. Plot is pretty standard for the genre—doctor Luthan (Grant) suspects foul play when homeless people are turning up in his ward. Seeking to expose what he believes is a medical conspiracy, his "darn meddling" gets him in all kinds of trouble. Enter Dr. Lawrence Myrick (Hackman), a genius neurologist who reeks of suspicion. Luthan must get by him to uncover the dangerous human experimentation that's been going on. Producer and real-life love Hurley may have had something to do with the fact that Grant pulls off a mostly convincing turn, where his normally comic persona is used to humanize an otherwise cardboard form. Adapted from a book by Michael Palmer. 118m/C VHS, DVD. J.K. Simmons, Hugh Grant, Gene Hackman, Sarah Jessica Parker, David Cronenberg, Bill Nunn, Debra Monk, John Toles-Bey, Paul Guilfoyle, Andre De Shields, Shaun Austin-Olsen, Peter Appel; *D:* Michael Apted; *W:* Tony Gilroy; *C:* John Bailey; *M:* Danny Elfman.

Extreme Limits ✗✗ 2001 (R) CIA agent Williams heads to Alaska to find a plane that has crashed in the mountains. As well as helping the survivors, he must find a mystery bomb that's also being sought by terrorists. Typical action fare. Wynorski directed under the pseudonym Jay Andrews. 105m/C VHS, DVD. Treat Williams, Hannes Jaenicke, John Beck, Susan Blakely, Gary Hudson, Julie St. Claire; *D:* Jim Wynorski; *C:* Andrea V. Rossotto. VIDEO

Extreme Justice ✗✗½ 1993 (R) A violent exposé of the Special Investigations Section of the Los Angeles Police Department, an elite, undercover squad which specialized in catching violent repeat offenders. But their tactics left something to be desired. They were accused of stalking their prey until they committed a crime and then dealing with the criminal by shooting them in the act. Lots of gunplay. Originally a theatrical film that was pulled for release in the wake of the Rodney King verdict. 96m/C VHS, DVD. Scott Glenn, Yaphet Kotto, Lou Diamond Phillips, Scott Glenn, William Forsythe, Chelsea Field; *D:* Mark L. Lester; *W:* Robert Boris; *C:* Mark Irwin; *M:* David Michael Frank.

Extreme Dating ✗ 2004 (R) Four young ad execs head to a ski resort to continue their concept of extreme dating, which has so far been a disaster. The latest scheme is: equally stupid: Troy (Keegan) and his crush Amy (DiScala) will get kidnapped, Troy will save the day, and Amy will be forever grateful and in love. Only the ex-cons hired by their pals Daniel (Sawa) and Lindsay (Detmer) decide to change the plan. No hilarity ensues, just embarrassment. 96m/C DVD. Devon Sawa, Amanda Detmer, Andrew Keegan, Jamie-Lynn Sigler, Ian Virgo, Meat Loaf Aday, Lee Thompson Young; *W:* William Mastrosimone; *D:* J.A.C. Redford.

Extreme Honor ✗ 2001 (R) This is an action movie with little action until the finale and a too-familiar storyline. Brascoe (Anderson) is forced out of the Navy SEALs when he's framed by his partner (Gruner). Now he needs a lot of cash in order to pay for his son's cancer treatments. So Brascoe teams up with two crooks (Madsen, Bush) to rip off a billionaire (Ironside). 95m/C VHS, DVD. Dan Anderson, Michael Madsen, Olivier Gruner, Grand L. Bush, Martin Kove, Antonio Fargas, Edward Albert, Charles Napier, Ollie Corso; *D:* Steven Rush; *W:* Steven Rush; *C:* Ken Blakey; *M:* David Powell, Geoff Levin. VIDEO

The Extraordinary Adventures of Mr. West in the Land of the Bolsheviks ✗✗✗ 1924 The first achievement from the Kuleshov workshop, a wacky satire on American insularity depicting a naive and prejudiced American can visiting Russia and being taken advantage of. Silent. 55m/B VHS. Vsevolod Pudovkin, Boris Barnet; *D:* Lev Kuleshov.

The Extreme Adventures of Super Dave ✗✗½ 1998 (PG) Cable TV character Super Dave Osborne (Einstein) comes to the big screen as Super Dave comes out of retirement for one last megastunt. He and protégé Van Wormer plot a death-defying leap to raise money for neighbor Carides who has an ill son (Lindner). 91m/C VHS, DVD, Bob Einstein, Gia Carides, Carl Michael Lindner, Steve Van Wormer, Dan Hedaya; *D:* Peter Macdonald; *W:* Lorne Cariden, Don Lake; *C:* Bernd Heinl; *M:* Scott Gilman. VIDEO

Extreme Ops ✗½ 2002 (PG-13) Shameless attempt to cash in on the popularity of extreme sports does a faceplant. Once best friends, they now fight for justice and the woman they both love. 104m/C VHS, DVD. Rufus Sewell, Heino Ferch, Liliana Komorowska, Klaus Lowitsch, Jean-Pierre Castaldi, Joe Absolom, Jana Pallaske, David Scheller; *C:* Hannes Hubach; *M:* Normand Corbeil, Stanislas Syrewicz. VIDEO

Extreme Vengeance ✗✗ 1990 Police officer David plots mafia crime boss Mario Blanco away for ten years, then exposes police corruption and goes into hiding. When Blanco gets out, he seeks revenge on David's family, forcing David out of hiding to protect what is his. Available in Spanish subtitles. 97m/C VHS, David Cox, Lisa Gay Hamilton, Michael De Costa, Tanya George; *D:* Raja Zahr; *C:* Edward Zare.

Extreme Prejudice ✗✗ 1987 (R) A redneck Texas Ranger fights a powerful drug kingpin along the U.S.-Mexican border. Once best friends, they now fight for justice and the woman they both love. 104m/C VHS, DVD. Nick Nolte, Powers Boothe, Michael Ironside, Rip Torn, Clancy Brown, Matt Mulhern, William Forsythe, Tommy (Tiny) Lister, Larry B. Scott, Maria Conchita Alonso; *D:* Walter Hill; *W:* Deric Washburn; *M:* Jerry Goldsmith.

Extremedays ✗½ 2001 (PG) Four buddies take an aimless road California trip after graduating from college, indulging in their love of extreme sports such as surfing, skateboarding, dirt bike racing, and snowboarding. But when one of the guys learns of his grandfather's death, they decide to make the trip into a pilgrimage to pay their respects. For the most part it's silly fluff. 93m/C VHS, DVD. Dante Basco, Ryan Browning, A.J. Buckley, Derek Hamilton, Cassidy Rae; *D:* Eric Hannah. VIDEO

Extremely Dangerous ✗✗½ 1999 Convoluted thriller that originated as a four-part British miniseries. Neil Byrne (Bean) was a British intelligence agent working deep undercover after infiltrating a group of gangsters. But his life is blown apart when Neil is convicted of the brutal murders of his wife and daughter. Naturally, he's innocent and when he makes his escape from prison transport, he heads back to find the true killers and get his revenge while being pursued by mobsters, police, and the agency he worked for. Some of the violence is very nasty. 200m/C VHS, DVD, Sean Bean, Juliet Aubrey, Ralph Brown, Anthony Booth, Ron Donachie, Sean Gallagher; *D:* Sallie Aprahamian; *W:* Peter Middleton; *M:* Rupert Gregson-Williams. TV

Extremities ✗✗ 1986 (R) An adaptation of the topical William Mastrosimone play about an intended rape victim who turns on her attacker, captures him, and plots to kill him. Violent and exploitive. 83m/C VHS, DVD, CA Genevieve Bujold, Farrah Fawcett, Diana Scarwid, James Russo, Alfre Woodard; *D:* Robert M. Young; *W:* William Mastrosimone; *C:* Curtis Clark; *M:* J.A.C. Redford.

Eye ✗✗ *Dead Innocent* 1996 (R) When attorney Suzanne St. Laurent's (Bujold) daughter is kidnapped, only mom can cut with the video-obsessed culprit before her child is killed. 30m/C VHS, DVD, CA Genevieve Bujold, Graham Greene, Jonathan Scarre, Emily Hampshire, Nancy Beatty, Susan Glover; *D:* Sara

Botsford; **W:** Mort Pattigo, Dolores Payne; **C:** Rodney Gibbons; **M:** David Findlay.

The Eye 🦴🦴 *2008 (R)* Stylish Asian ghost story follows the blind-since-childhood Mun (Lee), who receives a corneal transplant that restores her sight. Some adjustment is expected, but Mun sees shadowy figures lurking about that no one else sees, accident scenes miles from where they occurred, and, yes, dead people. Mun goes to a shrink, Dr. Wah (Chou), who doesn't think his patient is crazy. Instead, the doctor investigates the cornea donor—and is not reassured to discover the young woman committed suicide. Cantonese, Mandarin, and Thai with subtitles. **98m/C VHS, DVD.** *HK* Sin-Je (Angelica) Lee, Lawrence Chou, Chutcha Rujinanon, Candy Lo; **C:** Oxide Pang, Danny Pang; **W:** Oxide Pang, Danny Pang, Jojo Hui; **C:** Decha Seementa.

The Eye 🦴½ *2008 (PG-13)* Sydney Wells (Alba) is a concert violinist who has been blind since a childhood firecracker accident. As an adult, she undergoes a corneal transplant and promptly begins seeing ghouls, fire, premonitions of death, and eventually the image of the cornea donor (Romero), who it seems is trying to communicate something important through her eyes. Naturally her doctor and everyone else around her assume she is merely struggling with her transition to the sighted world; boy, are they wrong. Another ho-hum Hollywood re-make of a popular Asian formula horror film, but Alba fans will appreciate the tight, lingering shots of her lovely face and her obligatory shower scene. **97m/C DVD.** *US* Jessica Alba, Alessandro Nivola, Parker Posey, Rade Serbedzija, Rachel Ticotin, Chloe Grace Moretz, Fernanda Romero, Obba Babatunde, Danny Mora; **D:** David Moreau, Xavier Palud; **W:** Sebastian Gutierrez; **C:** Jeffrey Jur; **M:** Marco Beltrami.

The Eye Creatures 🦴 *1965* Alien creatures in the form of eyeballs are fought off by a teenager and his girlfriend. A low-budget, gory, science fiction feature. **80m/B VHS, DVD.** John Ashley, Cynthia Hull, Warren Hammack, Chet Davis, Bill Peck; **D:** Larry Buchanan.

An Eye for an Eye 🦴 *1981 (R)* A story of pursuit and revenge with Norris as an undercover cop pitted against San Francisco's underworld and high society. **106m/C VHS, DVD.** Chuck Norris, Christopher Lee, Richard Roundtree, Matt Clark, Mako, Maggie Cooper; **D:** Steve Carver; **W:** James Bruner; **C:** Roger Shearman; **M:** William Goldstein.

An Eye for an Eye 🦴 *1995 (R)* A made-for-TV script that ended up on the feature film pile (and we do mean pile). Manipulative story has Karen McCann (Field) listening on the phone as her daughter is raped and killed by a scuzzball drifter (Sutherland). He's caught, but released on a technicality, driving Mom to join a vigilante group and plot revenge. Not a great career move for the director or surprisingly distinguished cast, who are given nothing but cardboard characters and push-button emotional cliches to work with. Shamelessly plays on middle class fears of crime and doubts about the judicial system. Based on the novel by Erika Holzer. **102m/C VHS, DVD.** Sally Field, Ed Harris, Kiefer Sutherland, Beverly D'Angelo, Joe Mantegna, Keith David; **D:** John Schlesinger; **W:** Amanda Silver, Rick Jaffa; **C:** Amir M. Mokri; **M:** James Newton Howard.

Eye of God 🦴🦴🦴 *1997 (R)* Darkly dramatic story of lonely small-town waitress Ainsley (Plimpton), who marries newly released, born-again ex-con Jack (Anderson) with whom she has been corresponding. Movie kicks off when veteran sheriff (Holbrook) questions a shaken up youth, Tommy (Stahl), who is mysteriously covered in blood but rendered mute by his experience. First-time director Nelson's spare narrative seeks to explore deep issues like faith and violence in the Bible Belt locale. Performances are universally powerful, especially Plimpton's lovable dim-bulb and Anderson's maniacal Jack, giving credence to the clever but sometimes overly flashy cinematic style. **88m/C VHS, DVD.** Martha Plimpton, Kevin Anderson, Hal Holbrook, Nick Stahl, Richard Jenkins, Margo Martindale, Maggie Moore, Mary Kay Place; **D:** Tim Blake Nelson; **W:** Tim Blake Nelson; **C:** Russell Fine; **M:** David Van Tieghem.

Eye of the Beholder 🦴 *1999 (R)* Disengaged surveillance expert, known only as "The Eye" (McGregor), works for British intelligence out of their embassy in Washington. His latest assignment is to keep track of blackmailing Joanna (Judd) who turns out to be a psychotic serial killer of many identities. This must provide some strange turn-on, since instead of calling the cops, he proceeds to track her cross-country, protecting her from capture. Judd's an attractive femme fatale but the picture makes little sense and soon falls into the jaw-dropping, I-don't-believe-what-I'm-seeing category. Based on the novel by Marc Behm. **101m/C VHS, DVD.** Ewan McGregor, Ashley Judd, Patrick Bergin, k.d. lang, Jason Priestley, Genevieve Bujold; **D:** Stephan Elliott; **C:** Guy Dufaux; **M:** Marius De Vries.

Eye of the Demon 🦴 *1987* A couple moves to a small town in Massachusetts and discovers that the area had once been a haven for witchcraft. To their horror, they soon find that old habits die hard, and the spellcasting continues in a nearby graveyard. **92m/C VHS, DVD.** Tim Matheson, Pamela Sue Martin, Woody Harrelson, Barbara Billingsley, Susan Ruttan; **D:** Carl Schenkel. **CABLE**

Eye of the Dolphin 🦴🦴½ *2006 (PG)* Come on, who doesn't love a dolphin? After her mother's death, troubled teen Alyssa (Schroeder) is sent to live with her previously unknown father Hawk (Dunbar), who runs a dolphin research facility in the Bahamas. Alyssa discovers she has a natural ability to communicate with the dolphins and when the facility is threatened with closure, she and a wild dolphin pal come to the rescue. Good family fare. **100m/C DVD.** Carly Schroeder, Adrian Dunbar, Katharine Ross, Christine Adams, Jane Lynch, George Harris; **D:** Michael D. Sellers; **W:** Michael D. Sellers, Wendell Morris; **C:** Guy Livneh; **M:** Alan Derian. **VIDEO**

Eye of the Eagle 🦴½ *1987 (R)* A special task force is given a dangerous assignment during the Vietnam war. **84m/C VHS, DVD.** Brett (Baxter) Clark, Ed Crick, Robert Patrick, William (Bill) Steis, Cec Verrell; **D:** Cirio H. Santiago.

Eye of the Eagle 2 🦴 *1989 (R)* When his platoon is betrayed and killed in Vietnam, a surviving soldier joins with a beautiful girl and seeks revenge. **79m/C VHS, DVD.** Todd Field, Andy Wood, Ken Jacobson, Ronald Lawrence; **D:** Carl Franklin.

Eye of the Eagle 3 🦴½ *1991 (R)* Filipino-made Vietnam-War shoot-em-up, rack-em-up, shoot-em-up again, with U.S. forces pinned down against seemingly overwhelming odds. Violent. **90m/C VHS, DVD.** Steve Kanaly, Ken Wright, Peter Nelson, Carl Franklin; **D:** Cirio H. Santiago; **W:** Carl Franklin.

Eye of the Killer 🦴🦴½ *1999 (R)* Mickey Hayden is a drunken detective who is forced to re-open the serial killer case that led to his present wretched state. But this time Mickey finds himself having psychic visions when he touches the victims' belongings that put him into the mind of the killer. Now he's tracking a serial killer that may tie into a ten-year-old case. **100m/C VHS, DVD.** Kiefer Sutherland, Henry Czerny, Polly Walker, Gary Hudson; **D:** Paul Marcus; **W:** Jeff Miller; **C:** Brian Pearson; **M:** Michael Hoenig.

Eye of the Needle 🦴🦴½ *1981 (R)* Based on Ken Follett's novel about a German spy posing as a shipwrecked sailor on a deserted English island during WWII. Lonely, sad, yet capable of terrible violence, he is stranded on an isolated island while en route to report to his Nazi commander. He becomes involved with an English woman living on the island, and begins to contemplate his role in the war. **112m/C VHS, DVD.** Donald Sutherland, Kate Nelligan, Ian Bannen, Christopher Cazenove, Philip Brown, Stephen MacKenna, Faith Brook, Colin Rix, Alex McCrindle, John Bennett, Sam Kydd, Rik Mayall, Bill Fraser; **D:** Richard Marquand; **W:** Stanley Mann; **C:** Alan Hume; **M:** Miklos Rozsa.

Eye of the Storm 🦴🦴½ *1991 (R)* At the highway gas station/motel/diner where they live, two young brothers witness their parent's murder. Their younger brother is blinded in the same incident. Ten years later both brothers are still there and the tragedy may have turned one of them psychotic. When the abusive Gladstone and his young and sexy wife are stranded at the gas station it brings out the worst in everyone, with a violent climax during an equally violent thunderstorm. **98m/C VHS, DVD.** Craig Sheffer, Bradley Gregg, Lara Flynn Boyle, Dennis Hopper, Leon Rippy, Wilhelm von Homburg; **D:** Yuri Zeltser.

Eye of the Storm 🦴½ *The Farmhouse 1998 (R)* What's the elegant Danner during in this horror mishmash? (Maybe it worked better as a stage play.) College student Jenny (Kendall) is forced to shelter with because of a tornado. Seems mom Irma (Danner) went whacko and killed daughter Sally and the event was covered up by her husband and adult son. Now, Irma's delusions mistake Jenny for Sally and the local sheriff is also snooping into Sally's disappearance. Adapted by co-scripter Watson from his play "The Farmhouse". **100m/C VHS, DVD.** Katherine Kendall, Blythe Danner, Leo Burmester, Guy Ale, Kurt Deutsch, Keith Reddin; **D:** Marcus Spiegel; **W:** Marcus Spiegel, Randy Watson; **C:** Horacio Marquinez; **M:** Anton Sanko.

Eye of the Stranger 🦴½ *1993 (R)* Suspenser about a nameless stranger who sets out to solve the mystery of a small western town and its corrupt mayor. **96m/C VHS, DVD.** David Heavener, Sally Kirkland, Martin Landau, Don Swayze, Stella Stevens, John Pleshette, Joe Estevez, Thomas F. Duffy; **D:** David Heavener; **W:** David Heavener; **M:** Robert Garrett.

Eye of the Tiger 🦴🦴 *1986 (R)* A righteous ex-con battles a crazed, crack-dealing motorcycle gang that terrorized and murdered his wife, and is moving on to infest his town. **90m/C VHS, DVD.** Gary Busey, Yaphet Kotto, Seymour Cassel, Bert Remsen, William (Bill) Smith, Judith Barsi; **D:** Richard Sarafian; **W:** Michael Thomas Montgomery; **C:** Peter Lyons Collister; **M:** Don Preston.

Eye of the Wolf 🦴🦴½ *1995 (PG-13)* Zoologist (Fahey) brings a wild wolf into civilization and then must fight to save the animal from execution. Kazan (a wolf-dog mix) is the true star—and rightly so. **96m/C VHS.** Jeff Fahey, Sophie Duez.

Eye on the Sparrow 🦴🦴½ *1991 (PG)* A couple (Winningham and Carradine) desperately want to raise a child of their own, but the system classifies them as unfit parents since they are both blind. Together they successfully fight the system in this inspiring movie that was based on a true story. **94m/C VHS.** Mare Winningham, Keith Carradine, Conchata Ferrell, Sandy McPeak, Karen Lee, Bianca Rose; **D:** John Korty. **TV**

Eye See You 🦴½ *D-Tox 2001 (R)* Substandard cop vs. serial killer yarn has FBI man Jake Malloy (Stallone) tracking a serial killer who likes to remove his victims' eyes with a drill. When his girlfriend becomes the maniac's latest victim, Sly goes on the sauce and ends up, in a Wyoming detox center for cops. Shortly after he arrives, the patients start dying in apparent suicides and Malloy suspects his old nemesis might be on the premises. The plot wavers between illogical and laughable, while everybody involved overacts in an apparent attempt to figure out what the heck's going on. **95m/C VHS, DVD.** Sylvester Stallone, Tom Berenger, Charles S. Dutton, Sean Patrick Flanery, Christopher Fulford, Dina Meyer, Robert Patrick, Jeffrey Wright, Kris Kristofferson, Stephen Lang, Rance Howard; **D:** Jim Gillespie; **W:** Ron L. Brinkerhoff; **C:** Dean Semler; **M:** John Powell.

Eye Witness 🦴🦴½ *Your Witness 1949* An American attorney goes abroad to free a friend from the British legal system. A book of poems becomes the necessary device in deducing the whereabouts of the witness testifying to his friend's alibi. **104m/B VHS.** *GB* Robert Montgomery, Felix Aylmer, Leslie Banks, Michael Ripper, Patricia Wayne; **D:** Robert Montgomery; **M:** Malcolm Arnold.

Eye Witness 🦴🦴 *1970 (PG)* The murder of an African dignitary is witnessed by a young boy who has trouble convincing his parents and the police about the incident. Suspenseful but less than original. Shot on location in Malta. **95m/C VHS, DVD.** *GB* Mark Lester, Lionel Jeffries, Susan George, Tony Bonner; **D:** John Hough; **W:** Bryan Forbes; **C:** David Holmes.

Eyeball woof! *Gatto Rossi in Un Labirinto Do Vetro 1978 (R)* An intrepid policeman is stumped by a madman who is removing eyeballs from his victims. At least they won't have to watch this movie. **87m/C VHS.** *IT* John Richardson, Martine Brochard; **D:** Umberto Lenzi.

Eyes Behind the Stars 🦴🦴½ *Occhi Dalle Stelle 1972* A news photographer accidentally gets a few pictures of invading aliens, but nobody takes him seriously, particularly the government. **95m/C VHS, DVD.** *IT* Martin Balsam, Robert Hoffman, Nathalie Delon, Sherry Buchanan; **D:** Mario Gariazzo.

Eyes of a Stranger woof! *1981 (R)* Terrifying maniac stalks his female prey by watching their every move. Tewes is cast as a journalist, the stronger of the two sisters in this exploitative slasher. **85m/C VHS.** Lauren Tewes, John Disanti, Jennifer Jason Leigh; **D:** Ken Wiederhorn; **W:** Eric L. Bloom; **M:** Richard Einhorn.

Eyes of a Witness 🦴🦴½ *1994* American businessman Roy Baxter (Travanti) travels to Kenya to rescue his daughter (Grey) from danger in the African bush. But Roy is falsely charged with murdering a government official and must take on the police to prove his innocence. **90m/C VHS.** Daniel J. Travanti, Jennifer Grey, Carl Lumbly; **D:** Peter R. Hunt; **W:** Charles Robert Carner, Walter Clayton III; **C:** James Davis; **M:** Charles Gross.

Eyes of an Angel 🦴🦴 *1991 (PG-13)* A widower (Travolta), who's heavily involved in gambling, is forced to go on the run with his young daughter (Raab) when a deal goes sour. She must abandon the family dog, who manages to follow them from Chicago to California anyway. Talk about loyalty! **91m/C VHS, DVD.** John Travolta, Ellie Raab, Jeffrey DeMunn; **D:** Robert Harmon.

Eyes of Fire 🦴🦴 *1984 (R)* In early rural America, a group of pioneers set up camp in the wilderness and are besieged during the night by Indian witchcraft. **86m/C VHS.** Dennis Lipscomb, Rebecca Stanley, Fran Ryan, Rob Paulsen, Guy Boyd, Karlene Crockett; **D:** Avery Crounse; **W:** Avery Crounse; **M:** Brad Fiedel.

Eyes of Julia Deep 🦴🦴 *1918* Rare silent film featuring the ill-fated Minter as Julia, a woman who prevents Terry (Forrest) from killing himself. Piano scored. **54m/B VHS.** Mary Miles Minter, Alan Forrest, Alice Wilson, George Periolat; **D:** Lloyd Ingraham.

Eyes of Laura Mars 🦴🦴½ *1978 (R)* A photographer exhibits strange powers—she can foresee a murder before it happens through her snapshots. In time she realizes that the person responsible for a series of killings is tracking her. Title song performed by Barbra Streisand. **104m/C VHS, DVD.** Faye Dunaway, Tommy Lee Jones, Brad Dourif, Rene Auberjonois, Raul Julia, Darlanne Fluegel, Michael Tucker; **D:** Irvin Kershner; **W:** John Carpenter, David Zelag Goodman; **C:** Victor Kemper.

Eyes of Texas 🦴🦴½ *1948* Bryant, a lawyer who uses a pack of killer dogs to get the land she wants, is pursued by a U.S Marshal played decently by Rogers. **54m/B VHS, DVD.** Roy Rogers, Lynne Roberts, Andy Devine, Nana Bryant, Roy Barcroft; **D:** William Witney.

The Eyes of the Amaryllis 🦴½ *1982 (R)* A young girl becomes involved in a mysterious game when she arrives in Nantucket to care for her insane, invalid grandmother. Based on the story by Natalie Babbitt and filmed on location on Nantucket Island. **94m/C VHS.** Martha Byrne, Ruth Ford, Guy Boyd, Jonathan Bolt, Katharine King Keller.

Eyes of the Beholder ♂♂ 1992 (R) Janice is a psychopathic serial killer who suffered brain damage from a botched surgical attempt to reverse his insanity. Now he's escaped from the state mental institution, heading straight for the secluded home of the doctor who made him crazier than ever. During a raging storm, Janice stalks the doctor, his wife, and their two hapless dinner guests in a sadistic game of cat-and-mouse. 89mC VHS. Lanny Von Dohlen, Joanna Pacula, Matt McCoy, George Lazenby, Kyle Travis, Charles Napier. D: Lawrence L. Simeone; W: Lawrence L. Simeone; M: Greg Turner.

Eyes of the Panther 1990 One of Shelley Duvall's "Nightmare Classics" series, this adaptation of an Ambrose Bierce story concerns a pioneer girl haunted for years by the animal urges of a wild cat. 60mC VHS. Daphne Zuniga, C. Thomas Howell.

The Eyes of Youth ♂♂ 1919 A young woman searches her soul for answers: to marry or not to marry is the question. A little foresight, in the form of a glimpse into the hypothetical future, helps her make the right choice. Very early Valentino fare in which the sheik plays a cad. 78mB VHS. Clara Kimball Young, Edmund Lowe, Rudolph Valentino; D: Albert Parker; W: Albert Parker. C: Arthur Edeson.

Eyes Right! ♂♂ 1926 Based on a story by Ernest Grayman, this portrayal of life in a military prep school has its main character experience struggle, recognition, love, jealousy, and triumph. Silent. 46mB VHS. Francis X. Bushman, Larry Kent, Frederick Vroom, Florence Fair, Dora Dean, Robert Hale; D: Louis Chaudet; C: Allen Derey.

The Eyes, the Mouth ♂♂ 1983 (R) A young man has an affair with his dead twin brother's fiancee. Happiness eludes them as they are haunted by the deceased's memory and the family's grief. In Italian with English subtitles. 100mC VHS. Fll /T Lou Castel, Angela Molina; D: Marco Bellocchio; W: Marco Bellocchio.

Eyes Wide Shut ♂♂ 1999 (R) Kubrick's psychosexual drama (two years in the making), and last film, turned out to be visual interesting (if just because you know everything was done on soundstages) but less than compelling. Society doc William Harford (Cruise) and wife Alice (Kidman) seem to have it all, until a stoned Alice confesses to having lustful thoughts for others besides he hubby. Bill can't admit to the same (he's kind of a chilly guy), but this revelation sends him reeling out into the Manhattan night looking for adventure. He ends his evening observing, but not joining in, an aristocratic, anonymous orgy before heading home, presumably a wiser man. Kicmar's role basically fades out after her bravura confessional and Cruise seems more like an interested bystander than a man whose known world has crumbled. Based on Arthur Schnitzler's 1926 novel "Traumnovelle. 159mC VHS, DVD, Blu-ray Disc, HD DVD. Treva Etienne, Tom Cruise, Nicole Kidman, Sydney Pollack, Marie Richardson, Vnessa Shaw, Todd Field, Rade Serbedzija, Leeee Sobieski, Alan Cumming, Tromas Gibson, Sky Dumont, Fay Masterson; D: Stanley Kubrick; W: Stanley Kubrick; C: Larry Smith; M: Jocelyn Pook.

Eyewitness ♂♂½ The Janitor 1981 (R) When a murder occurs in the office building of a star-struck janitor, he fabricates a tale in order to initiate a relationship with the TV reporter covering the story. Unfortunately the killers think he's telling the truth, which plunges the janitor and reporter into a dangerous and complicated position, pursued by both police and foreign agents. Somewhat contrived, but always interesting. Woods turns in a wonderful psychotic best friend. 102mC VHS, DVD. William Hurt, Sigourney Weaver, Christopher Plummer, James Woods, Kenneth McMillan, Pamela Reed, Irene Worth, Steven Hill, Morgan Freeman; D: Peter Yates; W: Steve Tesch.

Eyewitness to Murder ♂♂½ 1993 Stevens plays a cop who is assigned to protect beautiful artist Walter. They both have their tragic flaws: he is a grieving widower, she has been blinded by an unknown attacker. Their flaws may draw them together. Somewhat more engaging than a TV police action drama. 75mC VHS. Andrew Stevens, Adrian Zmed, Sherilyn Wolter, Carl Strano, Robin Drue; D: Jag Mundhra.

F. Scott Fitzgerald in Hollywood ♂♂ 1976 Dramatization begins in the late 1930s when Fitzgerald was lured to Hollywood to work in the burgeoning film industry. It covers the period when, with his wife in a mental institution, he lived with Sheila Graham and struggled against alcoholism. Interesting story made dull and depressing by Miller's uninspired performance but it's almost saved by Weld's portrayal of Zelda. 98mC VHS, Jason Miller, Tuesday Weld, Julia Foster, Dolores Sutton, Michael Lerner, James Woods, John Randolph; D: Anthony Page. TV

F/X ♂♂♂ 1986 (R) Follie Tyler (Brown) is a New York-based special effects expert who is contracted by government agent Lipton (DeYoung) to fake an assassination in order to protect mob informer DeFranco (Orbach). After completing the assignment, Rollie learns that he's become involved in a real crime and is forced to reach into his bag of F/X tricks to survive, aided by tough cop Leo McCarthy (Dennehy), who's trying to figure out just what's going on. Twists and turns abound in this fast-paced story that was the sleeper hit of the year. Followed by a sequel. 109mC VHS, DVD. Bryan Brown, Cliff DeYoung, Diane Venora, Brian Dennehy, Jerry Orbach, Mason Adams, Joe Grifasi, Martha Gehman, Angela Bassett; D: Robert Mandel; W: Robert T. Megginson, Gregory Freeman; C: Miroslav Ondricek; M: Bill Conti.

F/X 2: The Deadly Art of Illusion ♂♂ 1991 (PG-13) Weak follow-up finds the special-effects specialist set to pull off just one more illusion for the police. Once again, corrupt cops use him as a chump for their scheme, an over-complicated business involving a stolen Vatican treasure. 107mC VHS, DVD. Bryan Brown, Brian Dennehy, Rachel Ticcrin, Philip Bosco, Joanna Gleason; D: Richard Franklin; W: Bill Condor; C: Victor Kemper; M: Michael Boddicker; Lalo Schifrin.

Fabiola ♂♂ 1948 This first of the big Italian spectacle movies, this one opened the door for a flood of low-budget imitators. Fabiola, the daughter of a Roman senator, becomes a Christian when her father's Christian servants are accused of murdering him. In the meantime, Rome to convert to Christian status. You can bet plenty of Christians will lose their heads, be thrown to the lions and generally burn at the stake before he does. 96mC VHS. /T Michel Simon, Henri Vidal, Michele Morgan, Gino Cervi; D: Alessandro Blasetti.

The Fable of the Beautiful Pigeon Fancier ♂♂♂½ Bella Palomera 1988 A powerful man who has always gotten what he wanted spies a beautiful young married woman and sets out to make her his own. Based on the Time of Cholera." In Spanish with English subtitles. 73mC VHS. SP Ney Latorraca, Claudia Ohana, Tonia Carrero, Dina Stat, Chico Diaz; D: Ruy Guerra; W: Ruy Guerra, Gabriel Garcia Marquez; C: Edgar Moura.

Fabled ♂½ 2002 (R) Is it all in his head? And do you care? Paranoid Joseph Fable (Askew) believes his ex-girlfriend Liz (Winnick) is in cahoots with his shrink and that his co-workers have stolen his dog. His friend Alex (Nash) thinks Joe should stop mixing booze and his meds. 84mC DVD. US Desmond Askew, Katheryn Winnick, Michael Panes, J. Richey Nash; D: Ari Kirschenbaum; W: Ari Kirschenbaum; C: Yaron Orbach; M: Jack Lingo.

Fabulous Adventures of Baron Munchausen ♂♂ Munchausen; The Fabulous Baron Munchausen; The Original Fabulous Adventures of Baron Munchausen; Baron Prasil 1961 The legendary Baron Munchausen, known for his tall tales, relates the story of his trek to the strange and beautiful land of Trukesan in a mixture of live action and animation. Wonderful special effects but a boring story. 84mC VHS, GE Milos Kopecky, Hana Brejchova, Rudolf Jelinek, Jan Werich; D: Karel Zeman; W: Karel Zeman; C: Jiri Tarantik; M: Zdenek Liska.

The Fabulous Baker Boys ♂♂♂ 1989 (R) Two brothers have been performing a tired act as nightclub pianists for 15 years. When they hire a sultry vocalist to revitalize the routine, she inadvertently triggers long-suppressed hostility between the "boys." The story may be a bit uneven, but fine performances by the three leading actors the price of the rental. 116mC VHS, DVD. Michelle Pfeiffer, Jeff Bridges, Beau Bridges, Elle Raab, Jennifer Tilly; D: Steven Kloves; W: Steven Kloves; C: Michael Ballhaus; M: Dave Grusin.

Golden Globes '90: Actress—Drama (Pfeiffer); L.A. Film Critics '89: Actress (Pfeiffer), Cinematog.; Natl. Bd. of Review '89: Actress (Pfeiffer); N.Y. Film Critics '89: Actress (Pfeiffer), Cinematog.; Support Actor (Bridges).

The Fabulous Dorseys ♂♂ 1947 The musical lives of big band leaders Tommy and Jimmy Dorsey are portrayed in this less than fabulous biography that's strong on song but weak on plot. Guest stars include Art Tatum, Charlie Barnet, Ziggy Elman, Bob Eberly and Helen O'Connell. Highlights are the tunes. 87mC VHS. Walter Abel, Donald Meek, Margot Grahame, Marie Wilson; D: Harve Foster.

Facade ♂♂ 1998 (R) American real-estate mogul, Colin Wentworth, and French-man Frederic Colbert team up for a shady business deal to build a luxury hotel in Malibu. They use murder, so no one will stand in their way. Frederic even encourages Colin to kill his murdered partner's wife, Caroline. But strange things keep happening and what Colin believes to be true, turns out to be very far from reality. 93mC VHS. Eric Roberts, Angus MacFadyen, Camilla Overbye Roos, Joe (Johnny) Vitereli; D: Carl Colpaert; W: Carl Colpaert, Lance Smith VIDEO

Face ♂♂ 1997 (R) A violent Brit-take on "Reservoir Dogs" has a group of East End armed robbers realizing someone in their gang has betrayed them after a heist goes wrong. Chief among the crooks are Ray (Carlyle) and his partner Dave (Winstone), plus three rookies and the unexpected involvement of a crooked cop. Lots of energy but not much that's new. 107mC VHS, DVD, GB Robert Carlyle, Steven Waddington, Ray Winstone, Philip Davis, Damon Albarn, Peter Vaughan, Lena Headey, Andrew Tiernan; D: Antonia Bird; W: Ronan Bennett; C: Fred Tammes; M: Andy Roberts.

Face Down ♂♂ 1997 (R) You've got your standard wisecracking New York ex-cop-turned-PI Bob Signorelli (Mantegna), who has a one-nighter with your blonde bombshell type client Merre (Maroney), who has ties to a mystery man (Ant). There's a murder, there's Bob's ex-partner Lt. Cooper (Riegert), who's no friend investigating the murder, and there's Bob trying to find the killer first. And you've certainly seen it all before. 107mC VHS. J.K. Simmons, Joe Mantegna, Peter Riegert, Kelli Maroney, Adam Ant; D: Thom Eberhardt; W: Thom

The Face at the Window ♂♂ 1939 Melodramatic crime story of a pair of ne'er-do-well brothers who terrorize Paris to conceal their bank robberies. 65mB VHS, DVD. Tod Slaughter, Marjorie Taylor, John Warwick, Robert Adair, Harry Terry; D: George King.

A Face in the Crowd ♂♂♂½ 1957 Journalist (Neal) discovers a country-home philosopher (Griffith) and puts him on her TV show. His aw-shucks personality soon wins him a large following and increasing influence—even political clout. Off the air he reveals his true nature to be insulting, vengeful, and power-hungry—all of which Nea decides to expose. Marks Griffith's spectacular film debut as a thoroughly despicable character and debut of Remick as a pretty cheerleader in whom he takes an interest. Schulburg wrote the screenplay from his short story "The Arkansas Traveler." He and director Kazan collaborated equally well in "On the Waterfront." 126mB VHS, DVD, Andy Griffith, Patricia Neal, Lee Remick, Walter Matthau, Anthony Franciosa; D: Elia Kazan; W: Budd Schulberg; C: Harry Stradling Sr.

A Face in the Fog ♂♂ 1936 Two newspaper reporters set out to solve a number of murders that have plagued the cast of a play. A so interested in solving this case leads him to alienation, rape, infidelity, and murder. In Japanese with English subtitles. 124mB VHS. JP Minoru Chiaki, Robert Dunham, Kyoko Kishica, Beverly (Bihari) Maeda, Eiji Okada, Koreya Senda, Tatsuya Nakadai, Machiko Kyo; D: Hiroshi Teshigahara, W: Kobe Abe; C: Hiroshi Segawa; M: Toru Takemitsu.

Face of Another ♂♂ Tanin nc kao; I Have a Stranger's Face; Stranger's Face 1966 A severely burned man gets a second chance when a plastic surgeon makes a mask to hide the disfigurement. Unfortunately this face leads him to alienation, rape, infidelity, and murder. In Japanese with English subtitles. 124mB VHS. JP Minoru Chiaki, Robert Dunham, Kyoko Kishica, Beverly (Bihari) Maeda, Eiji Okada, Koreya Senda, Tatsuya Nakadai, Machiko Kyo; D: Hiroshi Teshigahara, W: Kobe Abe; C: Hiroshi Segawa; M: Toru Takemitsu.

Face of the Screaming Werewolf ♂½ La Casa Del Terror; House of Terror 1959 Originally a Mexican horror/comedy that was bought for U.S. distribution by Jerry Warren, who earned his spot in the horror hall of fame with "The Incredible Petrified World" and "Teenage Zombies." A scientist brings a mummy back to life, but when he removes the bandages (gasp), the subject turns out to be a werewolf. Suffers from comic evisceration; not much to scream about. 60mB VHS. MX Lon Chaney Jr., Landa Varle, Raymond Gaylord; D: Gilberto Martinez Solares, Jerry Warren.

Face/Off ♂♂♂½ 1997 (R) Woo returns to his blood-soaked, violence-as-poetry-in-motion roots with the story of a fed who assumes the identity of the presumed-dead terrorist whom killed his son. When the master criminal wakes up, he takes on the fed's identity. Travolta is back for another wild ride, eating up the scenery when he takes on the bad-guy role. Cage, fresh from action hits in "The Rock" and "Con Air" gets to study the nature of good and evil (another Woo specialty) while he learns the nuances of the "leap across the room with two pistols blazing" move. Woo's Hong Kong efforts have always explored the blurry line between the good guys and the bad guys, and with Cage and Travolta, he has the perfect actors to display his findings. Woo cultists will welcome the return to the old style, while those only familiar with his stateside work will understand what all the fuss was about. 140mC VHS, DVD, Blu-ray Disc, HD DVD. John Travolta, Nicolas Cage, Joan Allen, Alessandro Nivola, Gina Gershon, Nick Cassavetes, Dominique Swain, Harve Presnell, Margaret Cho, CCH Pounder, Com Feore, John Carroll Lynch, Matt Ross; D: Jona Woo; W: Mike Webb, Michael Colleary; C: Oliver Wood; M: John Powell. NTV

Eberhardt; C: John Holosko; M: Gunther Schuler. C.A.R.L.E.

Face

Movie Awards '98: On-Screen Duo (John Travolta/ Nicolas Cage). Action Seq.

Face the Evil 🎬🎬½ **1997 (R)** TV star Sharon (Tweed) gets taken hostage in an art gallery where she's filming by a gang of thieves. But that's not the real problem—seems their leader, Dangler (Henriksen), wants to retrieve a shipment of nerve gas that's been hidden in some art work. **92m/C VHS, DVD.** Shannon Tweed, Lance Henriksen, Bruce Payne, Jayne Heitmeyer; **D:** Paul Lynch; **W:** Richard Beattie; **C:** Barry Gravelle; **M:** Paul Zaza. **VIDEO**

Face the Music 🎬🎬 **1992 (PG-13)** Ringwald and Dempsey were once stormily married and pursuing successful, collaborative careers as singer/songwriters for the movies. But they've abandoned the work, along with the marriage, until a movie producer makes them a new song. Only Dempsey's new girlfriend has some voracious objections. **93m/C VHS.** Patrick Dempsey, Molly Ringwald, Lysette Anthony; **D:** Carol Wiseman; **W:** Randee Russell; **C:** Yves Dahan; **M:** Didier Vasseur.

Face to Face 🎬🎬½ **1952** Dramatic adaptation of two short stories, "The Secret Sharer," by Joseph Conrad, and Stephen Crane's "The Bride Comes to Yellow Sky." The Conrad story features Mason as a sea captain who discovers a fugitive stowaway aboard his ships. The Crane story features Preston as a sheriff threatened by an old-time gunfighter. **92m/ B VHS.** Bretaigne Windust, James Mason, Michael Pate, Robert Preston, Marjorie Steele, Gene Lockhart, Minor Watson; **D:** John Brahm.

A Face to Kill For 🎬🎬 **1999**

Faceless 🎬🎬 *Les Predateurs de la Nuit* **1988** Franco gorefest has model Barbara disappear after going to a plastic surgery clinic run by the crazed Dr. Flamand. Her father sends a P.I. to find her, and he finds much more, as beautiful women are being killed for their skin and other needed accessories for the doctor's sister, who was disfigured in an acid-throwing incident. Bigger budget and better production values than Franco usually uses provides quality scares and squirms for fans of his work. Others may not be as enamored. **98m/C DVD. SP FR** Helmut Berger, Brigitte La-

haie, Chris Mitchum, Telly Savalas, Stephane Audran, Anton Diffring, Caroline Munro, Howard Vernon; **D:** Jess (Jesus) Franco; **W:** Fred (Rene Chateau) Castle, Pierre Ripert, Jean Mazarain, Michele Lebrun; **C:** Roger Fellous; **M:** Romano Musumarra.

Faces 🎬🎬½ **1968 (R)** Cassavetes' first independent film to find mainstream success portrays the breakup of the 14-year marriage of middle-aged Richard (Marley) and Maria (Carlin) Forst. Both seek at least momentary comfort with others—Richard with prostitute Jeannie (Rowlands) and Maria with aging hippie Chet (Cassel). The director's usual improvisational and documentary style can either be viewed as compelling or tedious but the performances are first-rate. **129m/B VHS, DVD.** John Marley, Lynn Carlin, Gena Rowlands, Seymour Cassel, Val Avery, Dorothy Gulliver, Joanne Moore Jordan, Fred Draper, Darlene Conley; **D:** John Cassavetes; **W:** John Cassavetes; **C:** Al Ruban; **M:** Jack Ackerman. Natl. Soc. Film Critics '68: Screenplay, Support. Actor (Cassel).

Faces of Women 🎬🎬 **1985** Two stories about women in contemporary Africa. In the first, an unhappy young woman is married to a very jealous man. When her brother-in-law visits, she decides to give her husband something to worry about. The second story finds a businesswoman running into problems when she tries to open a restaurant—problems that her daughter helps to solve. French and indigenous languages with English subtitles. **103m/C VHS.** Eugenie Cisse Roland, Sidiki Bakaba, Albertine N'Guessan; **D:** Desire Ecare.

Facing the Enemy 🎬🎬 **2000 (R)** Harlan Moss (Caulfield) believes in revenge and he blames Detective Griff McCleary (Ashby) for the death of his wife (Preston). So his idea is to seduce McCleary's estranged wife (Paul)—and then kill her. The surprise ending isn't very much of a surprise if you're in the mood for a cop thriller, this one will pass the time. **98m/C VHS, DVD.** Linden Ashby, Maxwell Caulfield, Alexandra Paul, Cynthia (Cyndy, Cindy) Preston, Max Gail, Bruce Weitz, Melanie Wilson; **D:** Rob Malenfant; **W:** Martin Kitrosser; **C:** Steve Adcock; **M:** Richard Bowers. **VIDEO**

Facing Windows 🎬🎬½ *La Finestra di Fronte* **2003 (R)** Unhappy Giovanna (Mezzogiorno) is a working wife and mother with an oblivious husband, Filippo (Nigro), and a dull job in a chicken factory. Her only sliver of excitement is her handsome neighbor, Lorenzo (Bova), whom she ogles from her kitchen window (as he watches back). Things change when Filippo brings home a confused elderly gentleman who thinks his name is Davide (Girotti). Giovanna reluctantly allows the stranger to stay the night after spotting a concentration camp number tattooed on his arm. In a round about way, this leads to Giovanna getting involved with Lorenzo, learning about Davide's lost love, and even satisfying her secret dream of becoming a pastry chef. Poignant if undemanding slice of life drama. Girotti's last role; Italian with subtitles. **106m/C DVD. IT GB PT TU** Giovanna Mezzogiorno, Massimo Girotti, Raoul Bova, Filippo Nigro, Serra Yilmaz, Massimo Poggio, Ivan Bacchi; **D:** Ferzan Ozpetek; **W:** Ferzan Ozpetek, Gianni Romoli; **C:** Gianfilippo Corticelli; **M:** Andrea Guerra.

Factory Girl 🎬🎬½ **2006 (R)** The brief life of Warhol wild child Edie Sedgwick (Miller) is retold in a conventional biopic. Blonde, beautiful, and from a wealthy-but-troubled family, Sedgwick trades in art school for the sixties New York scene and her chance as Warhol's (Pearce) latest muse. But Edie falls into a drug-fueled trap and bad romantic choices, including a seductive musician (Christensen). While Miller certainly looks the part, there's nothing substantial or particularly interesting about her performance or the flick. **90m/C DVD. US** Sienna Miller, Guy Pearce, Hayden Christensen, Jimmy Fallon, Mena Suvari, Shawn Hatosy, Illeana Douglas, James Naughton, Beth Grant, Jack Houston; **D:** George Hickenlooper; **W:** Captain Mauzner; **C:** Michael Grady; **M:** Ed Shearmur.

Factotum 🎬🎬🎬 **2006 (R)** Adaptation of Charles Bukowski's 1975 book of the same name is a bleak, darkly funny examination of ideals and ambivalence. Bukoswki's booze-soaked alter-ego Hank Chinaski (Dillon) lives by the slacker code with his series of changeable jobs and changeable women while he tends to his mediocre writing. Girlfriends Jan (Taylor) and Laura (Tomei) are excellent as Hank's enablers, but it's Dillon who brings style and swagger to a "man of many jobs" (a definition of the movie's title) who eschews soul-sucking opportunity and success in favor of being true to his distasteful, deep self. **94m/C DVD. US GE NO** Matt Dillon, Lili Taylor; **M:** Jack Ackerman. US **GE NO** Matt Dillon, Lili Taylor, Marisa Tomei, Fisher Stevens, Didier Flamand, Adrienne Shelly, Karen Young, Tom Lyons; **D:** Bent Hamer; **W:** Bent Hamer, Jim Stark; **C:** John Christian Rosenlund; **M:** Kristin Asbjornsen.

The Facts of Life 🎬🎬 **1960 (PG-13)** Risque bedroom comedy finds Larry Gilbert (Hope) and Kitty Weaver (Ball) running off from boredom in suburbia and their respective spouses (Hussey and DeFore) to have a little interlude together. **103m/B VHS.** Bob Hope, Lucille Ball, Ruth Hussey, Don DeFore, Louis Nye, Philip Ober; **D:** Melvin Frank; **W:** Melvin Frank, Norman Panama; **C:** Charles Bryant) Lang Jr.; **M:** Leigh Harline. Oscars '60: Costume Des. (B&W).

The Faculty 🎬🎬½ **1998 (R)** Nerd (Wood), beauty queen (Brewster), jock (Hatosy), new girl (Harris), rebel (Hartnett), and lovelorn girl (DuVall) come up against the greatest challenge of their lives. No, not the SATs. Parasitic aliens have nested in their high school and re-placed the rumpled, frumpy staff with pleasure-seeking sexpots out for excitement. It's "The Breakfast Club" against "Them" in a battle royale! More style, less substance dictates the union between indie director Rodriguez and screenwriter Williamson. As expected, the dialogue is hip, the fashions are crisp, and kids are spunky, but pic never explains the aliens' visit. The multi-generational cast is enjoyable enough and the scares (however recycled they may be) are effective if you like icky scenes of alien projectiles sprouting from a human orrifice or two. **102m/C VHS, DVD.** Jon Abrahams, Elijah Wood, Robert Patrick, Bebe Neuwirth, Salma Hayek, Jon Stewart, Piper Laurie, Famke Janssen, Christopher McDonald, Jordana Brewster, Clea DuVall, Laura Harris, Josh Hartnett, Usher Raymond; **D:** Robert Rodriguez; **W:** Kevin Williamson; **C:** Enrique Chediak; **M:** Marco Beltrami.

Fade to Black woof! **1980 (R)** Young man obsessed with movies loses his grip on reality and adopts the personalities of cinematic characters (Hopalong Cassidy and Dracula among them) to seek revenge on people who have wronged him. Thoroughly unpleasant, highlighted by clips from old flicks. **100m/C VHS, DVD.** Dennis Christopher, Tim Thomerson, Linda Kerridge, Mickey Rourke, Melinda Fee, Gwynne Gilford, Norman Burton, Morgan Paull, James Luisi, John Steadman, Marcie Barkin, Eve Brent; **D:** Vernon Zimmerman; **W:** Vernon Zimmerman; **C:** Alex Phillips Jr.; **M:** Craig Safan.

Fade to Black 🎬🎬 **1993 (R)** Business-field stars as a college professor with voyeuristic tendencies and a handy camcorder. After viewing his latest tape, he realizes he's filmed his neighbor's murder and that he can recognize the killer. Before he can warn the girlfriend, she disappears and our nosy prof is framed for death. **84m/C VHS.** Timothy Busfield, Heather Locklear, Michael Beck, Louis Giambalvo, Cloris Leachman, David Byron; **D:** John McPherson; **W:** Douglas Barr.

Fade to Black 🎬🎬🎬 **2004 (R)** Jay-Z's brilliant goodbye letter to the public eye. What's touted as the final concert of his career is magnificently captured in an exploding Madison Square Gardens in November of 2003, along with studio time during the making of "The Black Album." Jay-Z waxes ill-osophic about the methods to his badness, gets a haircut, and scowls as his posse bumrush his Coleco-Vision, dropping furious rhymes everywhere he turns. The entire affair is a little too long, but the energy carries well. **109m/**

C DVD. US Michael John Warren; **C:** Scott Lochmus, Theron Smith, Paul Bozymowski, Luke McCoubrey.

Fahrenheit 451 🎬🎬🎬 **1966** Chilling adaptation of the Ray Bradbury novel about a totalitarian futuristic society that has banned all reading material and the firemen whose job it is to keep the fires at 451 degrees: the temperature at which paper burns. Werner is Montag, a fireman who begins to question the rightness of his actions when he meets the book-loving teacher Clarisse (Christie)—who also plays the dual role of Werner's TV-absorbed wife, Linda. Truffaut's first color and English-language film. **112m/C VHS, DVD. FR GB** Oskar Werner, Julie Christie, Cyril Cusack, Anton Diffring, Alex Scott, Anna Palk, Ann Bell, Mark Lester, Tom Watson; **D:** Francois Truffaut; **W:** Francois Truffaut, Helen Scott, Jean-Louis Richard, David Rudkin; **C:** Nicolas Roeg; **M:** Bernard Herrmann.

Fahrenheit 9/11 🎬🎬🎬 **2004 (R)** A nail-biting Michael Moore's indictment of the Bush administration's handling of the Iraq War begins with the 2000 election and follows Bush up to and through the 9/11 attacks, pointing out lost opportunities to stop Bin Laden's plot. Continues through the War on Terrorism and the Iraq War. Party affiliation will determine viewer opinion, but Moore's poisoned pen letter of a documentary is effective and bracing. This is pure propaganda, but of the strongest kind. Moore uses every weapon in his arsenal to attack Bush and his cronies, with outtakes and bloopers by Ashcroft, Rumsfeld, and Bush especially juicy. Sobering, horrific footage of ongoing carnage in Iraq—the stuff they don't show on the nightly news—balances out some of the more outlandish buffoonery and lampooning. Viciously funny and gut-wrenchingly heartbreaking. **110m/C DVD. US D:** Michael Moore; **W:** Michael Moore; **C:** Mike Desjarlais; **M:** Bob Golden, Jeff Gibbs. Golden Raspberries '04: Worst Actor (Bush), Worst Support. Actor (Rumsfeld), Worst Support. Actress (Spears).

Fail-Safe 🎬🎬🎬½ **1964** A nail-biting nuclear age nightmare, in which American planes have been erroneously sent to bomb the USSR, with no way to recall them. An all-star cast impels this bitterly serious thriller, the straight-faced flipside of "Dr. Strangelove." **111m/B VHS, DVD.** Henry Fonda, Dan O'Herlihy, Walter Matthau, Larry Hagman, Fritz Weaver, Dom DeLuise; **D:** Sidney Lumet; **W:** Walter Bernstein; **C:** Gerald Hirschfeld.

Fail Safe 🎬🎬🎬 **2000** Claustrophobic remake of the 1964 Cold War thriller shown originally as a live CBS TV broadcast. Thanks to a computer glitch, a nuclear strike is launched against the USSR and the president and the military must find a way to recall the bombers or deal with the consequences. **86m/B DVD.** George Clooney, Richard Dreyfuss, Noah Wyle, Brian Dennehy, Sam Elliott, Don Cheadle, Harvey Keitel, Hank Azaria, James Cromwell, John Diehl, Norman Lloyd; **D:** Stephen Frears; **W:** Walter Bernstein; **C:** John Alonzo. **TV**

Failure to Launch 🎬🎬 **2006 (PG-13)** Finally, a movie that lives up to its title. Tripp (McConaughey) is a 35-year-old slacker still living with his parents (Bradshaw and Bates). They want him out, so they hire a woman, Paula (Parker), who specializes at getting grown men to move out of their parents' homes. Along the way characters are bitten by a chipmunk, a lizard, a dolphin, even a mockingbird. Both Parker and McConaughey play their usual smiling, glowing selves. Since this is a romantic comedy, they eventually fall in love. Guess Paula's not used to these freeloaders being buff and charming. **97m/C DVD, Blu-ray Disc, HD DVD. US** Matthew McConaughey, Sarah Jessica Parker, Zooey Deschanel, Justin Bartha, Bradley Cooper, Terry Bradshaw, Kathy Bates, Katheryn Winnick, Tyrell Jackson Williams, Patton Oswalt, Stephen Tobolowsky, Peter Jacobson, Kate McGregor-Stewart; **D:** Tom Dey; **W:** Tom J. Astle, Matt Ember; **M:** Rolfe Kent.

Fair Game woof! **1982 (R)** Three young women decide to ditch their private school for a weekend of fun but find out the resort town they've chosen is run by sociopaths who get their kicks by stalking our chicks. **90m/C** VHS, AU Kiri Trengove, Kerry Mack, Marie O'Loughlina, Karen West; **D:** Christopher Fitchatt.

Fair Game WOOF! **1985** In the Australian outback, three loathesome excuses for human beings come across a beautiful woman alone on a remote farm. Naturally, they try to do despicable things but she fights back. **83m/C** VHS, DVD, AU Cassandra Delaney, Peter Ford, David Sandford, Gary Who; **D:** Mario Andreacchio; **W:** Rob George; **C:** Andrew Lesnie; **M:** Ashley Irwin.

Fair Game 𝄢𝄢 **1989** (R) A psychotic but imaginative ex-police detective Max (Baldwin) defies orders so he can protect family attorney Kate (Crawford, in her big-screen debut) from high-tech assassins. Nice work if you can get it. Generic action plot provides Crawford and first-time director Sipes with relatively safe proving ground. Cindy wears the "Die Hard" dirty white tank top look fetchingly enough (and showers when the action slackens), while Baldwin is no slouch in the babe department (male division) either. Based on Paula Gosling's 1978 novel "Fair Game," which was previously filmed as 1986's "Cobra." **91m/C** VHS, DVD, William Baldwin, Cindy Crawford, Steven Berkoff, Miguel (Michael) Sandoval, Christopher McDonald, Johann Carlo, Salma Hayek, John Bedford Lloyd, Jenette Goldstein; **D:** Andrew Sipes; **Prod.** Irwin Corey, Brenda Fogarty; **By:** Richardson, Nat Bonet, Martha Reeves; **D:** Harry Hurwitz) Tampa.

Fairy Tales 𝄢 **1976** (R) A ribald musical fantasy follows the equally risque "Cinderella," in order to save the kingdom, the prince must produce an heir. The problem is that only the girl in the painting of "Princess Beauty" can "interest" the prince and she must be found. Good-natured smut. **83m/C** VHS, DVD, Don Sparks, Prof. Irwin Corey, Brenda Fogarty, Sy Richardson, Nat Bonet, Martha Reeves; **D:** Harry Hurwitz) Tampa.

FairyTale: A True Story 𝄢𝄢½ Illumination **1997** (PG) Discovery of hope and fantasy in bleak reality when two girls in 1917 war-torn England claim to have photographed fairies in their garden. Skeptical debunker Harry Houdini (Keitel) and spiritual believer Sir Arthur Conan Doyle (O'Toole) show up to investigate the photos of cousins Elsie (Hoath) and Frances (Earl). The issues of science and spiritualism are profusely debated between the two men, getting a little in the way of the girls and their story. Tries to appeal to both adult's and children, which may leave both feeling a bit unsatisfied. Perky pixies flitting about throughout picture, courtesy of special f/x wizard Tim Webber, are bound to delight even hardened audience skeptics. Don't blink for Mel Gibson's cameo as Frances' father. This same true story known as the Cottingley Fairies, is also part of the plotline in the surreal British film "Photographing Fairies. **99m/C** VHS, DVD, Harvey Keitel, Peter O'Toole, Florence Hoath, Elizabeth Earl, Paul McGann, Phoebe Nicholls, Bill Nighy, Bob Peck, Tim (McInnany) McInnerny; **Cameos:** Mel Gibson; **D:** Charles Sturridge; **W:** Ernie Contreras; **C:** Michael Coulter; **M:** Zbigniew Preisner.

Faith 𝄢 **1990** (R) When young dancer Faith's parents are killed in an accident she winds up in a frightening foster home. Running away, she meets a gentleman/mobster who keeps her attain her dance dreams. Laughably implausible. **104m/C** VHS, Sylvia Seidel, Ami Dolenz, Richard Maldone; **D:** Ted Mather; **W:** Ted Mather; **M:** Guido de Angelis, Maurizio de Angelis.

Faith 𝄢𝄢 **1994** Nick Simon (Hannah) is a widowed tabloid journalist who falls in love with Holly (Harker), daughter of politician Peter Moreton (Gambon). Nick gets

an unexpected scoop when -tolly tells him about her father's affair and now must choose between using the information or protecting his girlfriend's dad even as Peter struggles to save his career. The film takes place on RKO's back lot for a behind-the-scenes view of Hollywood. **DVD, GB** John Hannah, Michael Gambon, Susan Peter Fearon. TV

Faithful 𝄢𝄢½ **1995** (R) Black comedy about depressed, rich housewife Margaret (Cher) who is rudely interrupted by Tony the hitman (Palminteri) while trying to commit suicide on her 20th wedding anniversary. Unfaithful hubby Jack (O'Neal), who has put the contract out on Margaret, is conveniently away on business. As Margaret sits tied to a chair and Tony waits for a call to confirm the hit, the two connect and decide to turn the tables. Director Mazursky succeeds in bringing Palminteri's three-character play to the screen, even if it does suffer at times from too much stage talk and not enough action. First film for Cher since 1990's "Mermaids" and the first for O'Neal since 1989's "Chances Are." Big rift between Mazursky and the film's producers over final cut led him to threaten to pull his name from the credits. Mazursky cameos as the hitman's therapist. **91m/C** VHS, DVD, Cher, Ryan O'Neal, Chazz Palminteri; **Cameos:** Paul Mazursky, Paul Mazursky; **W:** Chazz Palminteri; **C:** Fred Murphy.

Faithless 𝄢𝄢𝄢½ Trolsa **2000** (R) Ullman again directs a Bergman screenplay about raw emotions and the pain of broken relationships. Evidently semi-autobiographical (it's set on Bergman's island home of Faro), an aging filmmaker (Josephson) in a spare office contemplates his newest screenplay when he's visited by an actress. This visitation is wholly in his mind, however, as Marianne (Endre) aids "Bergman" in writing about a painful affair in his past. Married to Markus (Hanzon), Marianne falls into an affair with close family friend David, who turns out to be the filmmaker in his younger days. The affair wreaks havoc on all three, while Marianne and David's daughter becomes a pawn. While the older filmmaker is thoughtful and even wistful, Bergman shows his younger, more reckless self literally "Bergman" in writing about a painful affair in his past. Married to Markus (Hanzon), Marianne falls into an affair with close family friend David, who turns out to be the filmmaker in his younger days. The affair wreaks havoc on all three, while Marianne and David's daughter becomes self literally in Swedish with subtitles. **142m/C** VHS, DVD, SW Lena Endre, Erland Josephson, Thomas Hanzon, Krister Henriksson, Philip Zanden, Marie Richardson, Michelle Gylemo, Juni Dahr, Therese Brunnander; **D:** Liv Ullmann; **W:** Ingmar Bergman; **C:** Jorgen Persson.

Fake Out 𝄢 Nevada Heat **1982** Nightclub singer is caught between the mob and the police who want her to testify against her gangland lover. Typical vanity outing for Zadora. **89m/C** VHS, DVD, Pia Zadora, Telly Savalas, Desi Arnaz Jr.; **D:** Matt Cimber.

Fakers 𝄢𝄢 **2004** A London con man (Rhys) orchestrates an art heist to pay back a $50,000 debt. With the help of an artist buddy (Chambers), who came to possess a lost sketch by an Italian master, they hope to produce five copies and sell them to various London galleries in one single morning, and then blow town before anyone is the wiser. Chirpy crime caper with a lackluster plot. **85m/C** DVD, GB Matthew Rhys, Kate Ashfield, Art Malik, Tony Haygarth, Tom Chambers; **D:** Richard James; **W:** Paul Gerstenberger; **C:** Balazs Bolygo; **M:** Kevin Sargent.

The Falcon and the Snowman 𝄢𝄢𝄢 **1985** (R) True story of Daulton Lee and Christopher Boyce, two childhood friends who, almost accidentally, sell American intelligence secrets to the KGB in 1977. Hutton and Penn are excellent, creating a relationship we care about, creating characterizations. **110m/C** VHS, DVD, Sean Penn, Timothy Hutton, Lori Singer, Pat Hingle, Dorian Harewood, Richard Dysart, David Suchet, Jennifer Runyon, Priscilla Pointer, Nicholas Pryor, Joyce Van Patten, Mady Kaplan, Michael Ironside; **D:** John Schlesinger; **W:** Steven Zaillian; **C:** Allen Daviau; **M:** Lyle Mays, Pat Metheny.

Fall 𝄢𝄢 **1997** Brainy supermodel falls for literary critic in this portrait of life in the Big Apple. Within minutes of a chance encounter in a cab, married 'fare Sarah Easton (DeCadenet) is willing the hours away, listening to romantic hack Michael's poetry and writhing seductively while feasting on carry-out like it's "9 1/2 Weeks." Schaeffer places himself opposite yet another gorgeous model and egotisticaly pens his character as a supersensitive writer (who does this guy think he is. Woody Allen?) faced with overwhelming acclaim after his first novel, who decides to chuck it all and drive a cab. Although nicely acted and not bad to look at, the main characters and both their dilemmas are just a little hard to relate to. **92m/C** VHS, DVD, Eric Schaefer, Amanda DeCadenet, Francie Swift, Lisa Vidal, Rudolf Martin; **D:** Eric Schaefer; **W:** Eric Schaefer; **C:** Joe DeSalvo; **M:** Amanda Kravat.

The Fall 𝄢𝄢 **1998** (R) Or should that be "The Patsy"? American novelist Sheffer, who's living in Budapest, gets chosen as the savior of femme de Fourgerolles, who is being stalked by Prochnow. Or so she says—and she wants Sheffer to kill her tormentor. **90m/C** VHS, DVD, Craig Sheffer, Jurgen Prochnow, Helene de Fourgerolles; **D:** Andrew Piddington. VIDEO

Fall from Grace 𝄢𝄢½ **1994** American and British intelligence officers take deadly risks in 1943 Europe in an effort to convince Hitler to end the war. **180m/C** VHS, GB James Fox, Michael York, Patsy Kensit, Gary Cole; **D:** Waris Hussein.

Fall from Innocence 𝄢½ **1983** A girl is driven to a life of prostitution and drugs by the sexual abuse inflicted upon her by her father. **81m/C** VHS, Isabelle Mejias, Thom Haverstock, Amanda Smith, Rob McEwan.

Fall Guy 𝄢𝄢 **1947** Cocaine-addled Tom Cochrane (Penn) can't explain to the cops why he's covered in blood. He's accused of murder but escapes from jail and tries to convince Hitler to end the war. gets his girl, Lois (Loring). In help him figure out what's happened. Dead bodies and a set-up are involved. Adapted from the Cornell Woolrich story "Cocaine." **64m/B** VHS, Reginald LeBorg, Mack Stengler, Teala Loring, Robert Armstrong, Clifford Penn, Elisha Cook Jr., Douglas Fowley, Charles Arnt, Virginia Dale; **W:** Jerry Warner.

The Falcon in Hollywood 𝄢𝄢½ **1944** The falcon gets caught up with the murder of an actor who was part of a Tinseltown love triangle. **DVD, GB** John Hannah, Michael Gambon, Susan-Part of the popular "Falcon" series from the 1940s. **67m/B** VHS, Tom Conway, Barbara Hale, Veda Ann Borg, Sheldon Leonard, Frank Jenks, Rita (Paula) Corday, John Abbott; **D:** Gordon Douglas.

The Falcon in Mexico 𝄢𝄢½ **1944** When paintings from a supposedly dead artist turn up for sale in New York City, the Falcon and the artist's daughter wind up journeying to Mexico to solve the mystery. Part of "The Falcon" series. **70m/B** VHS, Tom Conway, Mona Maris, Nestor Paiva; **D:** William Berke.

The Falcon's Brother 𝄢𝄢 **1942** Enemy agents intent on killing a South American diplomat are foiled by the Falcon's brothers at a steep personal cost. The plot enabled Sanders' real-life brother Conway to take over the title role in "The Falcon" mystery series, a role which he played nine more times. **64m/B** VHS, Tom Conway, George Sanders, Keye Luke, Jane Randolph; **D:** Stanley Logan.

The Falcon Takes Over 𝄢𝄢 **1942** Escaped con Moose Malloy (Bond) is trying to track down his missing ex-girlfriend Velma in New York. The Falcon (Sanders) becomes interested in the case Riordan (Barl), uncovering a gambling operation. **65m/B** VHS, George Sanders, Lynn Bari, Ward Bond, James Gleason, Allen Jenkins, Helen Gilbert, Edward (Ed) Gargan, Anne Revere; **D:** Irving Reis; **M:** Lynn Root, Frank Felton; **C:** George Robinson.

The Fall of the House of Usher 𝄢 **1949** Lord Roderick Usher is haunted by his sister's ghost in this poor adaptation of the Poe classic. **70m/B** VHS, DVD, GB Kay Tendeler, Gwen Watford, Irving Steen, Lucy Pavey; **D:** Ivan Barnett.

The Fall of the House of Usher 𝄢𝄢 *House of Usher* **1960** The moody Roger Corman/Vincent Price interpretation, the first of their eight Poe adaptations, depicting the collapse of the family doomed to destruction. Stray to the Roger Corman/Vincent Price version to see how it should have been done. **101m/C** VHS, DVD, Martin Landau, Robert Hays, Charlene Tilton, Ray Wa ston; **D:** James L. Conway.

The Fall of the Roman Empire 𝄢𝄢𝄢 **1964** An all-star, big budget extravaganza set in ancient Rome praised for its action sequences. The licentious son of Marcus Aurelius arranges for his father's murder and takes over as emperor while Barbarians gather at the gate. Great sets, fine acting, and thundering battle scenes. **187m/C** VHS, DVD, Sophia Loren, Alec Guinness, James Mason, Stephen Boyd, Christopher Plummer, John Ireland Anthony Quayle, Eric Porter, Mel Ferrer, Omar Sharif; **D:** Anthony Mann; **W:** Philip Yordan; **C:** Robert Krasker; **M:** Golden Globes '65. Score.

Fall Time 𝄢𝄢 **1994** (R) Crime drama set in small-town Minnesota, circa 1957. Three high schoolers set in motion a prank that turns bad when they pull up in front of the local bank. David (Arquette), Joe (Blechman), and Tim (London) intend to stage a mock robbery—but a real robbery is going down and the teens wind up the terrified hostages of creepy criminals Florence (Rourke) and Leon (Baldwin). Promising premise derailed by narrative inadequacies. **88m/C** VHS, DVD, Mickey Rourke, Stephen Baldwin, Jason London, David Arquette, Sheryl Lee; **D:** Paul Warner; **W:** Steve Alden, Paul Skemp; **C:** Mark J. Gordon; **M:** Hummie Mann.

Fallen 𝄢𝄢 **1997** (R) Take a police-story suspense thriller, add the occult and a big dose of the supernatural, stir in a big, heaping helping of philosophy, a dash of a wrong-man subplot, shake vigorously, and out pours the bitter "Fallen." Heart of the excution of serial killer Edgar Reese (Koteas), crack cop Hobbes (Washington) is soon chasing down copycat killings springing up everywhere. The real culprit is not Reese, but a fallen angel who inhabits body after body, creating new killer's with each new host. Washington manages to hold his own as the pic gets messy and overly complicated. Goodman's character provides needed earthbound common sense when the banter gets a bit too lofty, debating things like the meaning of life, existence of God, and other issues that don't belong here. Hobbit's second feature tries to take on way too much in it's already lengthy span. With a mish-mash of conflicting film styles and dicey dialogue, film manages to land on the careers of an

Fall Guy 𝄢𝄢 Kamata Koshin-Kyoku **1982** Ginshiro Kuraoka (Kazama) is a megalomaniac actor whose once-hot career is on the skids. He's planned a spectacular fight scene for his latest picture in order to one-up his acting rival, but it's so dangerous that no stuntman will play it for him. Until desperate and loyal bit player Yasu (Hirata) comes along. Ginshiro has already foisted his pregnant mistress Konetsu (Matsuzaka) off on his lackey and 'to provide for his new bride (whom he has always loved) Yasu is ready to tackle the dangerous stunt. **108m/C DVD, JP** Keiko Matsuzaka, Sonny Chiba, Morio Kazama, Mitsuru Hirata, Chika Takami, Keizo Kanie; **D:** Kinji Fukasaku; **W:** Kouhei Tsuka; **C:** Kiyoshi Kitasaka; **M:** Masato Kai.

The Fall of the House of Usher 𝄢½ **1980 (PG)** Another version of Edgar Allan Poe's classic tale of a family doomed to destruction. **101m/C** VHS, DVD, Martin Landau, Robert Hays, Charlene Tilton, Ray Wa ston; **D:** James L. Conway.

otherwise talented cast and crew. 124m/C VHS, DVD. Denzel Washington, Donald Sutherland, John Goodman, Elias Koteas, Embeth Davidtz, James Gandolfini, Robert Joy, Gabriel Casseus; D: Gregory Hoblit; W: Nicholas Kazan; C: Newton Thomas (Tom) Sigel; M: Tan Dun.

The Fallen ♂♂♂ 2005 Set in the beautiful Italian countryside during the latter stage of World War II, follows the daily struggles of German, Italian, and American soldiers in October 1944 as Italian rebels battle with Italian and German troops forcing common villagers to choose between fascism and communism. The Allies head north to attack Germany's "Gothic Line." Intimate look at the common soldier's life filmed on a modest budget (under $1 million) unusual to modern war films. 105m/C DVD. US Fabio Sartor, Sergio Leone, John McVay, Thomas Pohn, Ruben Pla, Dirk Schmidt; D: Ari Taub; W: Caio Ribeiro, Nick Day; C: Claudia Amber, Ian Dudley; M: Sergei Dreznin.

Fallen Angel ♂♂½ 1981 Relationship between a child pornographer and a particular young girl he finds easily exploitable because of her unbalanced home situation. Fine cast, solid direction. 100m/C VHS. Dana Hill, Richard Masur, Melinda Dillon, Ronny Cox; D: Robert Lewis; M: Richard Bellis. TV

Fallen Angel ♂½ Revenge 1999 (R) Mystery woman seduces and murders her victims and a police detective tries to undercover the link between the crimes. 90m/C VHS, DVD. Alexandra Paul, Vlasta Vrana, Anthony Michael Hall, Michelle Johnson; D: Marc S. Grenier; W: Neil Goldberg; C: Georges Archambault; M: Milan Kymlicka. VIDEO

Fallen Angels 1 ♂♂ Duoluo Tianshi 1995 The visuals dazzle but the disjointed narrative proves a challenge in what Kar-Wai originally intended to be a third story for his film "Chungking Express." Contract killer Wong Chi-Ming (Lai) has been getting his assignments from a nameless female agent (Reis) who's fallen for him. Wong wants to retire, which upsets her. Then there's mute ex-con He Zhiwo (Kaneshiro) who gets involved with a strange young woman named Cherry (Young) who still loves her ex-boyfriend, and everybody crosses paths but there's really no connection and nothing makes much sense anyway. 97m/C VHS, DVD. HK Leon Lai, Michelle Reis, Takeshi Kaneshiro, Charlie Young, Karen Mok; D: Wong Kar-Wai; W: Wong Kar-Wai; C: Christopher Doyle; M: Frankie Chan.

Fallen Angels 1 ♂♂½ 1993 Trilogy of hard-boiled, film noirish tales set in Los Angeles. "The Frightening Frammis" concerns a grifter (Gallagher) who meets his match in a mystery woman (Rossellini) in this adaptation of a Jim Thompson story. "Murder, Obliquely" finds a plain Jane (Dern) falling for a heel (Rickman) who may have murdered his previous girl in a Cornell Woolrich tale. "Since I Don't Have You" has Buzz Meeks (Busey) hired to find a dame sought by both Howard Hughes (Mathesen) and gangster Mickey Cohen (Woods). From a story by James Elroy. 90m/C VHS. Peter Gallagher, Isabella Rossellini, Nancy Travis, John C. Reilly, Bill Erwin, Laura Dern, Alan Rickman, Diane Lane, Robin Bartlett, Gary Busey, Tim Matheson, James Woods, Aimee Graham, Dick Miller, Ken Lerner; D: Tom Cruise, Alfonso Cuaron, Jonathan Kaplan; W: Jon Robin Baitz, Amanda Silver, Steven Katz; M: Elmer Bernstein. CABLE

Fallen Angels 2 ♂♂♂ 1993 Three more film noir stories set in L.A. "Dead End for Delia" finds a police detective (Oldman) arriving at a murder scene to find his estranged wife (Anwar) the victim. Based on a short story by William Campbell Gault. "I'll Be Waiting" has Kirby as a hapless hotel detective who falls for a beautiful guest (Helgenberger) and winds up a mob pawn. Adaptation of a Raymond Chandler tale. "The Quiet Room" has Bedelia and Mantegna as a pair of corrupt cops who find their shakedown schemes going very wrong. From a story by Jonathan Craig. 90m/C VHS. Gary Oldman, Gabrielle Anwar, Meg Tilly, Patrick Massett, Vondie Curtis-Hall, Paul Guilfoyle, Dan Hedaya, John Putch, Wayne Knight, Bruno Kirby, Marg Helgenberger, Jon Polito, Peter Scolari, Dick Miller, Joe Mantegna, Bonnie Bedelia, Vinessa Shaw, J.E. Freeman, Peter Gallagher, Patrick Breen, Genia Michaela, Wayne Grace; Cameos: Tom Hanks; D: Phil Joanou, Tom Hanks, Steven Soderbergh; W: Scott Frank, C. Gaby Mitchell. CABLE

Fallen Champ: The Untold Story of Mike Tyson ♂♂♂ 1993 Director Kopple's provocative documentary on the boxing champ, from his roots in a Brooklyn ghetto to his conviction for rape in 1991. Tyson is shown as pathetic, vulnerable, and violent—psychologically unprepared for both acclaim and responsibility, as well as easily manipulated by promoters and opportunists. A mixture of ring footage and interviews with sportswriters, promoters, trainers, and others as well as media coverage of Tyson. 93m/C VHS. D: Barbara Kopple. TV

The Fallen Idol ♂♂♂ The Lost Illusion 1949 A young boy wrongly believes that a servant he admires is guilty of murdering his wife. Unwittingly, the child influences the police investigation of the crime so that the servant becomes the prime suspect. Richardson as the accused and Henrey as the boy are notable. Screenplay adapted by Greene from his short story, "The Basement Room." 92m/B VHS, DVD. GB Ralph Richardson, Bobby Henrey, Michele Morgan, Sonia Dresdel, Jack Hawkins, Bernard Lee, Denis O'Dea, Dora Bryan, Walter Fitzgerald, Karel Stepanek, Geoffrey Keen, James Hayter, Dandy Nichols, George Woodbridge, John Ruddock, Joan Young, Gerard Heinz; D: Carol Reed; W: Graham Greene, Lesley Storm, William Templeton; C: Georges Perinal. British Acad. '48: Film; Natl. Bd. of Review '49: Actor (Richardson); N.Y. Film Critics '49: Director (Reed).

The Fallen Sparrow ♂♂♂ 1943 Garfield is superb as a half-mad veteran of the Spanish Civil War. Captured and brutalized, he never reveals the whereabouts of a valuable possession. His return to the U.S. continues his torture as Nazi agent Slezak uses the woman Garfield loves to set a trap and finish the job. Solid performances and good plot are highlights. 94m/B VHS. John Garfield, Maureen O'Hara, Walter Slezak, Patricia Morison, Martha O'Driscoll, Bruce Edwards, John Miljan, John Banner, Hugh Beaumont; D: Richard Wallace.

Falling ♂♂ Fallen 2006 Intimate character study of five women who reunite at the funeral of their former teacher. Together they crash a wedding, kick up their heels at a nightclub, and share secrets that liberate them. As things are packed to a close, one is left feeling empty and unfulfilled, much like the lives of our five friends. German with subtitles. 88m/C DVD. AT Birgit Minichmayr, Ursula Strauss, Kathrin Resetarits, Nina Proll, Gabriela Hegedus; D: Barbara Albert; W: Barbara Albert; C: Bernhard Keller.

Falling Down ♂♂ 1993 (R) Douglas is "D-FENS" (taken from his license plate), a normally law-abiding white-collar geek who snaps while stuck in a traffic jam on a hot day in LA. Like Charles Bronson in "Death Wish," he decides to take matters into his own hands. Unlike Bronson, he is not avenging an attack by a specific criminal, but raging against whomever gets in his way. Duvall is a detective on his last day before retirement, Hershey has the thankless role of Douglas' ex. Essentially a revenge fantasy that was vilified by some for catering to the baser emotions. 112m/C VHS, DVD, Michael Douglas, Robert Duvall, Barbara Hershey, Rachel Ticotin, Tuesday Weld, Frederic Forrest, Lois Smith, D.W. Moffett, Dedee Pfeiffer, Vondie Curtis-Hall, Michael Paul Chan, Raymond J. Barry, Jack Kehoe, John Diehl; D: Joel Schumacher; W: Ebbe Roe Smith; C: Andrzej Bartkowiak; M: James Newton Howard.

Falling Fire ♂♂½ The Cusp 1997 (R) Good visual effects highlight this cable sci-fier that combines terrorists and asteroids. Daryl Boden (Pare) has the task of getting his spacecraft to steer an asteroid into earth orbit for the purpose of mining its resources. But an eco-terrorist group, led by Lopez (Vidosa), want to force the asteroid to crash into the planet, thus "cleansing" it of man. Oh, there's a terrorist aboard Boden's craft to help things along, while his ex-wife Marilyn (von Palleske) fights the eco-villains back on earth. 84m/C VHS, DVD. CA Michael Pare, Heidi von Palleske, Christian Vidosa, Zehra Leverman; D: Daniel D'or; W: Daniel D'or; C: Jonathan Freeman; M: Donald Quan. CABLE

Falling for a Dancer ♂♂♂½ 1998 When young Elizabeth Sullivan (Dermot-Walsh) gets pregnant after a brief affair, there's not much she can do since she lives in Ireland during the 1930s. She's forced by her family into marriage with a drunken widower and resigns herself to loneliness until love is found again. 200m/C VHS, DVD. GB Elisabeth Dermot-Walsh, Dermot Crowley, Liam Cunningham, Rory Murray, Brian McGrath, Maureen O'Brien, Colin Farrell; D: Richard Standeven; W: Deirdre Purcell; C: Kevin Rowley; M: Stephen McKeon. TV

Falling from Grace ♂♂½ 1992 (PG-13) Bud Parks (Mellencamp) is a successful country singer who, accompanied by his wife and daughter, returns to his small Indiana hometown to celebrate his grandfather's 80th birthday. He's tired of both his career and his marriage and finds himself taking up once again with an old girlfriend (Lenz), who is not only married to Bud's brother but is also having an affair with his father. Bud believes he's better off staying in his old hometown but the problems caused by his return may change his mind. Surprisingly sedate, although literate, family drama with good ensemble performances. Actor-director debut for Mellencamp. 100m/C VHS, DVD. John Cougar Mellencamp, Mariel Hemingway, Kay Lenz, Claude Akins, Dub Taylor, Brent Huff, Deirdre O'Connell, Larry Crane; D: John Cougar Mellencamp; W: Larry McMurtry.

Falling in Love ♂♂½ 1984 (PG-13) Two married New Yorkers unexpectedly fall in love after a coincidental meeting at the Rizzoli Book Store. Weak but gracefully performed reworking of "Brief Encounter," where no one seems to ever complete a sentence. An unfortunate re-teaming for Streep and De Niro after their wonderful work in "The Deer Hunter." 106m/C VHS, DVD. Robert De Niro, Meryl Streep, Harvey Keitel, Dianne Wiest, George Martin, Jane Kaczmarek, David Clennon; D: Ulu Grosbard; W: Michael Cristofer; C: Peter Suschitzky; M: Dave Grusin.

Falling in Love Again ♂♂½ In Love 1980 (PG) Romantic comedy about middle-aged dreamer Gould and realistic wife York. They travel from Los Angeles to their hometown of New York for his high school reunion, where Gould is suddenly attacked by nostalgia vibes for his youth, seen in countless flashbacks, and prominently featuring Pfeiffer, notable in her film debut. Like watching a home movie about people you don't care about. 103m/C VHS, DVD. Elliott Gould, Susannah York, Michelle Pfeiffer; D: Steven Paul; W: Ted Allan; C: Michael Mileham; M: Michel Legrand.

Fallout ♂♂½ 2001 It is horribly ironic that filmmaker Palumbo chose to film the introduction to his independent feature on top of one of the World Trade Center towers. His film concerns the interplay among four high-rise office workers who flee a disaster of uncertain origin and find themselves trapped in a basement fallout shelter. His story really has nothing to do with the 9/11/01 atrocities. It's a well-made character study that attempts to work with some serious ideas within the limitations of a modest budget. It's mostly successful, too, and certainly doesn't need any extra baggage. Parallels to reality are difficult to ignore, however. 88m/C DVD. Claire Beckman, Mark Deakins, Keith Randolph Smith, David Wasson; D: Robert Palumbo; W: Robert Palumbo, Mark Gallini; C: Wolfgang Held; M: Frank Ferrucci.

False Arrest ♂♂½ 1992 A woman is falsely accused of killing her husband's business partner and winds up in prison where she continues to fight to prove her innocence. Mills does well in this less-than-glamorous role. Based on a true story. 102m/C VHS, DVD. Donna Mills, Steven Bauer, James Handy, Lane Smith, Lewis Van Bergen, Dennis Christopher, Robert Wagner; D: Bill W.L. Norton. TV

False Colors ♂ 1943 Hopalong Cassidy unmasks a crook posing as a ranch heir. This was the 49th Hopalong Cassidy feature. 54m/B VHS, DVD. William Boyd, Robert Mitchum, Andy Clyde, Jimmy Rogers; D: George Archainbaud.

False Faces ♂♂½ 1932 A ruthless, money-hungry quack is hounded by the law and the victims of his unscrupulous plastic surgery. 80m/B VHS. Lowell Sherman, Peggy Shannon, Lila Lee, Joyce Compton, Berton Churchill, David Landau, Eddie Anderson, Ken Maynard, Veda Ann Borg; D: Lowell Sherman.

False Faces ♂½ 1918 Secret agent known as The Lone Wolf is working in France for the Allies when he learns a German master spy is headed for the U.S. to cause trouble. So he heads for New York to stop him. Lots of thrills. 65m/B VHS. Henry B. Walthall, Lon Chaney Sr., Mary Anderson, Milton Ross; D: Irvin Willat.

False Identity ♂½ 1990 (PG-13) A radio psychologist buys a Purple Heart medal at a garage sale and then tries to find out about the original recipient. But her questions are making a number of folks uneasy, including a potentially dangerous stranger. 97m/C VHS. Genevieve Bujold, Stacy Keach, Veronica Cartwright, Tobin Bell, Mimi Maynard; D: James Keach; W: Sandra K. Bailey.

False Prophets ♂½ 2006 (R) Waitress Maggie (Heuring) is pregnant and wants an abortion until a fundamentalist group talks her into adoption because they believe there's something miraculous about the baby. Except Maggie gets suspicious and runs away and winds up at a rural gas station with a spiritually-minded attendant named Manny (Lyons), who helps her give birth in a field. There's supposed to be some meaning to all this. ?m/C DVD. Lori Heuring, Patrick Bergin, Clayne Crawford, Tucker Smallwood, Antonio David Lyons; C: David Gossard; M: Brian Arbuckle. VIDEO

False Witness ♂♂½ 1989 A New Orleans district attorney and her lover, a private investigator, find themselves working the same rape-murder case. When their methods disagree both find themselves in danger. Adapted from a novel by Dorothy Uhnak. 96m/C VHS. Phylicia Rashad, Philip Michael Thomas, Terri Austin, George Grizzard; D: Arthur Allan Seidelman; M: Charles Fox.

Fame ♂♂♂ 1980 (R) Follows eight talented teenagers from their freshman year through graduation from New York's High School of Performing Arts. Insightful and absorbing, director Parker allows the kids to mature on screen, revealing the pressures of constantly trying to prove themselves. A faultless parallel is drawn between these "special" kids and the pressures felt by high schoolers everywhere. Great dance and music sequences. Basis for a TV series. ♪Fame; Red Light; I Sing the Body Electric; Dogs in the Yard; Hot Lunch Jam; Out Here On My Own; Is It OK If I Call You Mine?. 133m/C VHS, DVD. Irene Cara, Barry Miller, Paul McCrane, Anne Meara, Joanna Merlin, Richard Belzer, Maureen Teefy, Albert Hague; D: Alan Parker; M: Michael Gore. Oscars '80: Song ("Fame"), Orig. Score; Golden Globes '81: Song ("Fame").

Fame Is the Spur ♂♂½ 1947 A lengthy but interesting look at the way power corrupts, plus an insight into the Conservative versus Labor dynamics of British government. Redgrave is a poor, idealistic worker who decides to help his

The Family 🐶🐶½ *Violent City* 1970 As Con man Donald "Doc" Holiday (Coulier) must become the perfect family man (complete with kids and dog) before he can inherit his uncle's estate. He finds a couple of cute, mouthy orphans who have run away so they won't be separated in foster care and hires a nanny who doesn't realize it's also a 'holiday-set film, everything will turn out 'or the best. 94m/C DVD. *D:* Ken Loach. **TV**

fellow workers by running for Parliament. There he falls prey to the trappings of office with surprising consequences. Look hard for Tomlinson, who went on to star in "Mary Poppins" and "Bedknobs and Broomsticks" for Disney. 116m/B VHS, GB Michael Redgrave, Rosamund John, Bernard Miles, Hugh Burden, Guy Verney, Carla Lehmann, Sir Seymour Hicks, David Tomlinson; *D:* Roy Boulting.

The Family 🐶🐶½ *Violent City* 1970 As a New Orleans hit-men who resists joining the mob. Bronson initiates an all-out war on the syndicate. A poorly dubbed Italian action film. 94m/C VHS, DVD. *IT* Charles Bronson, Jill Ireland, Telly Savalas, George Savalas, Michel Constantin, Umberto Orsini; *D:* Aldo Tonti; *M:* Sergio Solima; *C:* Aldo Tonti; *M:* Ennio Morricone.

Family 🐶🐶🐶 1994 Petty thief Charlo Spencer (McGinley) abuses wife Paula (Ryan) and their kids, with young son John Paul in danger of following in his dad's footsteps and teenage daughter Nicola just discovering her emerging sexuality. Narrative is divided into four chapters, each devoted to a different family member. Ordinary life with no melodrama but many priceless moments. Will seem familiar to followers of Roddy Doyle's Barrytown trilogy. 119m/C VHS, GB Sean McGinley, Ger Ryan, Neil Conroy, Barry Ward; *D:* Michael Winterbottom; *W:* Roddy Doyle.

A Family Affair 🐶🐶½ 2001 Rachel (Lesnick), a Jewish lesbian New Yorker, has been brutally dumped by her manipulative girlfriend Reggie (Greene). She flees to San Diego for the succor of her PFLAG mom (Golonka), who's more than happy to help her daughter find Ms. Right. And that seems to be blonde and perky WASP Christine (Shaffer). Insecurity leads to romance leads to love—and the sudden re-appearance of Reggie. 107m/C VHS, DVD. Helen Lesnick, Arlene Golonka, Erica Shaffer, Michele Greene, Suzanne Westenhoefer, Barbara Stuart; *D:* Danny De La sla, Kelly Neil, Robert Westlind.

Family Business 🐶🐶 1989 (R) A bright Ivy Leaguer, impressed by the exploits and vitality of his criminal grandfather, recruits him and his ex-con dad to pull off a high-tech robbery, which goes awry. Caper film, with its interest in family relationships and being true to one's nature. Casting Connery, Hoffman, and Broderick as the three leaves a big believability problem in the family department. 107m/C VHS, DVD. Sean Connery, Dustin Hoffman, Matthew Broderick, Rosanna Desoto, Janet Carroll, Victoria Jackson, Bill McCutcheon, Deborah Rush, Marilyn Cooper, Salem Ludwig, Rex Everhart, James Tolkan, Tony DiBenedetto, Wendell Pierce, John Capodice, Luis Guzman; *D:* Sidney Lumet; *W:* Vincent Patrick; *C:* Andrzej Bartkowiak; *M:* Cy Coleman.

Family Enforcer 🐶 *Death Collector* 1976 (R) A small-time hoodlum is bent on becoming the best enforcer in an underworld society. 82m/C VHS, DVD. Joe Cortese, Lou Criscoula, Joe Pesci, Anne Johns, Keith Davis; *D:* Ralph De Vito; *W:* Ralph De Vito; *C:* Bob Bailin.

The Family Game 🐶🐶🐶 *Kazoku geimu; Kazoku Game* 1983 An obsessive satire about a poor, belligerent college student hired by a wealthy contemporary Japanese family to tutor their spoiled teenage son. Provides an all-out cultural assault on the Japanese bourgeoisie. From an original story by Yohei Honma. In Japanese with English subtitles. 107m/C VHS, DVD. *JP* Junichi Tsujita, Yusaku Matsuda, Juzo Itami, Saori Yuki, Ichirota Miwagawa; *D:* Yoshimitsu Morita; *W:* Yoshimitsu Morita; *C:* Yonezo Maeda.

The Family Holiday 🐶🐶 2007 Con man Donald "Doc" Holiday (Coulier) must become the perfect family man (complete with kids and dog) before he can inherit his uncle's estate. He finds a couple of cute, mouthy orphans who have run away so they won't be separated in foster care and hires a nanny who doesn't realize it's also a 'holiday-set film, everything will turn out 'or the best. 94m/C DVD. Dave Coulier, Christina Pickles, Craig Clyde, Alexa Fischer, Terisa Greenan; *C:* Paul Mayne; *M:* Justin Melland. **CABLE**

Family Jewels 🐶🐶 1965 A spoiled child-heiress has to choose among her six uncles to decide which should be her new father. If you like Jerry Lewis, you can't miss this! In addition to playing all six uncles, Lewis plays the chauffeur, as well as serving as producer, director, and coauthor of the script. 100m/C VHS, DVD. Jerry Lewis, Donna Butterworth, Sebastian Cabot, Robert Strauss; *D:* Jerry Lewis. **TV**

Family Life 🐶🐶 1971 *Wednesday's Child* 1971 A portrait of 19-year-old Janice Baldwin, who's forced to get an abortion by her parents and battles them constantly to establish her own identity. She is eventually sent to a mental institution for depression, where she is subjected to increasingly vigorous psychological interventions, including electro-shock. Documentary-style effort originally made for British TV. 108m/C VHS, GB Sandy Ratcliff, Bill Dean, Grace Cave; *D:* Ken Loach. **TV**

Family Life 🐶🐶½ *Zycie Rodzinne* 1971 Melancholy mood piece finds an engineer reluctantly returning to his family's delapidated country mansion after six years in Warsaw. He must confront his own life as well as his alcoholic father and slightly mad sister. Polish with subtitles. 93m/C VHS. *PL* Daniel Olbrychski, Jan Nowicki, Jan Kreczmar, Maja Komorowska, Halina Mikolajska; *D:* Krzysztof Zanussi; *W:* Krzysztof Zanussi; *M:* Wojciech Kilar.

The Family Man 🐶🐶 1979 A brief encounter between a married Manhattanite (Asner) and a much younger single woman (Baxter Birney) is sensitively handled in this film which explores their passionate affair. 98m/C VHS. Ed Asner, Meredith Baxter, Paul Clemens, Mary Joan Negro, Anne Jackson, Martin Short, Michael Ironside; *D:* Glenn Jordan; *M:* Billy Goldenberg. **TV**

Family Man 🐶🐶🐶 2000 (PG-13) With the help of a guardian angel/taxi driver (Cheadle), money-loving investment banker Jack Campbell (Cage) gets to see how life could have been if he'd married college sweetie Leoni, had kids, and was living in New Jersey and working as a tire salesman. Lost in this new world of responsibility and funnel cakes, Jack can't help but pine for his old life. But, in the end, will he choose ambition and "freedom" over love? Darker and not as tidy as "It's a Wonderful Life," it's obvious inspiration. "Family Man" seeks to teach Jack a lesson we see coming miles off. 125m/C VHS, DVD. Nicolas Cage, Tea Leoni, Don Cheadle, Amber Valletta, Jeremy Piven, Saul Rubinek, Josef Sommer, Harve Presnell, Mary Beth Hurt, Kate Walsh; *D:* Brett Ratner; *W:* David Diamond, David Weissman; *C:* Dante Spinotti; *M:* Danny Elfman.

A Family Matter 🐶🐶 *Vendetta: Secrets of a Mafia Bride* 1991 (R) A Mafia chieftain adopts a child whose father was killed by hit men. She grows into a beautiful woman bent on revenge. Melodramatic Italian-American co-production, made for TV. 100m/C VHS. Eric Roberts, Carol Alt, Eli Wallach, Burt Young; *D:* Stuart Margolin; *W:* Stuart Margolin; *M:* Bruce Ruddell.

Family of Cops 🐶🐶½ 1995 (PG-13) Trouble comes calling on Inspector Paul Fein's (Bronson) close-knit Milwaukee family when his party girl daughter Jackie (Featherstone) comes home to visit. She's soon accused of murdering a wealthy businessman she ponied up in a drunken stupor and her cop family gets deeply involved in the investigation. Made for TV. 90m/C VHS, DVD. Charles Bronson, Daniel Baldwin, Angela Featherstone, Sebastian Spence, Lesley-Anne Down, Barbara Williams, Simon MacCorkindale; *D:* Ted Kotcheff; *W:* Joel Blasberg. **TV**

Family of Cops 2: Breach of Faith 🐶🐶 2007 *Breach of Faith; A Family of Cops 2* 1997 (PG-13) The investigation of a priest's murder makes inspector Paul Fein (Bronson) and his cop family the target of Russian mobsters. TV movie once again filmed in Toronto, which substitutes for Milwaukee. 90m/C VHS, DVD. Charles Bronson, Joe Penny, Angela Featherstone, Barbara Williams, Kim Weeks, Sebastian Spence, Diane Ladd; *D:* Sheldon Larry; *W:* Noah Jubelirer, Nikki Je Boer; *D:* Sheldon Larry. **TV**

Family of Cops 3 🐶🐶 1998 Police inspector Paul Fein (Bronson) decides to run for chief while detective son Ben (Penny) investigates the murder of a banker. There's also a corruption problem and a love affair for a little romance. 96m/C VHS, DVD. Charles Bronson, Joe Penny, Milwaukee. 90m/C VHS, Real Andrews; *D:* Charles Bronson, Joe Penny, Diane Ladd, Sebastian Spence, Kim Weeks, David Henson, Joe Penny, Diane Ladd; *D:* Sheldon Larry; *W:* David Oreux; *M:* Manning Robinson. **TV**

Family Pictures 🐶🐶🐶 1993 A photographer remembers growing up in the '50s with her autistic brother, the mother who lavished her attention on him almost to the exclusion of her five other children, and the father who blamed his wife for their son's deficiencies. Interesting portrait of an American family, which eventually cracks under pressure and splits up. Adapted from the novel by Sue Miller (no relation to screenwriter Jennifer). 240m/C VHS, Anjelica Huston, Sam Neill, Kyra Sedgwick, Dermot Mulroney, Gemma Barry, Tara Strong, Toni Higginson, Jamie Harrold; *D:* Philip Saville; *W:* Jennifer Miller.

The Family Plan 🐶🐶½ 2005 (PG) Charlie Mackenzie (Spelling), wants to keep her executive job, but new boss Ed Walcott (Germann) insists on family values and mistakenly believes Charlie is married. When she is forced to invite Ed and his wife (Vernon) to dinner, Charlie borrows a house and child (Breslin) from a friend and hires actor Buck (Bridges) to play her husband. Their ruse works for the evening, but Charlie is horrified to learn that the Walcotts are planning to rent the house next door. Should she keep lying or will the truth set Charlie free (or just make her unemployed)? 85m/C DVD. Tori Spelling, Greg Germann, Jordan Bridges, Kate Vernon, Abigail Breslin, Jon Polito, Kali Rocha, Christopher Cass; *D:* David S. Cass Sr.; *W:* Richard Gitelson; *C:* James W. Wrenn; *M:* David Kitay. **CABLE**

Family Plot 🐶🐶🐶 1976 (PG) Alfred Hitchcock's last film "focuses on the search for a missing heir which is undertaken by a phony psychic and her private-eye boyfriend, with all becoming involved in a diamond theft. Campy, lightweight mystery that states with time and doesn't fit well into Hitchcock's genre. 120m/C VHS, DVD. Karen Black, Bruce Dern, Barbara Harris, William Devane, Ed Lauter, Katherine Helmond, Cathleen Nesbitt, Warren Kemmerling, Edith Atwater, William Prince, Nicholas Colasanto, Alfred Hitchcock; *D:* Alfred Hitchcock; *W:* Ernest Lehman; *C:* Leonard J. South; *M:* John Williams.

Family Prayers 🐶🐶½ 1991 (PG) Coming-of-age drama, set in 1969 Los Angeles, about a 13-year-old Andrew and his family troubles. His father Martin (Mantegna) is a compulsive gambler which causes wife Rita (Archer) untold anxiety and constant friction between the two. Tension is heightened by Nan (LuPone) and Rita's opinionated older sister who has trailed the family out of their money problems more than once. Meanwhile, Andrew tries to look out for h s younger sister and prepare for his bar-mitzvah. A little too much of a nostalgic golden glow surrounds what is essentially a family tragedy. 109m/C VHS. Tzvi Ratner-Stauber, Joe Mantegna, Anne Archer, Patti LuPone, Paul Reiser, Allen (Goorwitz) Garfield, Conchata Farrell, David Margulies; *D:* Scott Rosenfelt; *W:* Steven Ginsburg.

A Family Thing 🐶🐶🐶 1996 (PG-13) Racial issues are addressed in this character-driven story of two brothers. Southerner Earl Pilcher (Duvall) learns his recently deceased woman who raised him, Earl discovers she also has a half brother, Ray (Jones), who is black and living in Chicago. He drives to Chicago, and seeks out Ray, who to Earl's surprise knows about him already, and is not exactly thrilled about the family ties either. As the two brothers, expertly played by Duvall and Jones, slowly find common ground, Hall steals the show as the irascible Aunt T. 109m/C VHS, DVD. Robert Duvall, James Earl Jones, Irma P. Hall, Michael Beach, Grace Zabriskie, Regina Taylor, Mary Jackson, Paula Marshall, Jim Harrell; *D:* Richard Pearce; *W:* Billy Bob Thornton, Tom Epperson; *C:* Fred Murphy.

Family Reunion 🐶🐶 1979 The Andrews family is on vacation and visiting the ghost town of Sutterville. Grandpa Henry didn't want to stop and for good reason—it seems the town was once in the grip of a satanic cult. Forty years before, when Tom Andrews was a child, he was rescued by Henry, who adopted him. Now Tom's real father has willed the family back to Sutterville to complete the ritual. 88m/C VHS, DVD. Mel Novak, John Andes, A.J. Woods, Kaylin Cool, Pam Phillips, Mark McTague; *D:* Michael Hawes; *W:* Jack Anderson.

Family Secrets 🐶🐶½ 1984 Drama about a daughter, mother, and grandmother overprotecting and manipulating each other during a weekend reunion where they recently dumped him). 97m/C VHS, David Eisner, Rebecca Jenkins, Henry Beckman. **TV**

The Family Stone 🐶🐶🐶 2005 (PG-13) Parker plays against her "Sex in the City" role. She's still a New Yorker here, but an uptight one—who's dragged home for the holidays. Mix of characters are rare. No one likes Meredith and they're not shy about it! Another attempt at screwball holiday comedy with a decent cast that delivers on low expectations. 102m/C DVD. US Claire Danes, Diane Keaton, Rachel McAdams, Dermot Mulroney, Craig T. Nelson, Sarah Jessica Parker, Luke Wilson, Tyrone Giordano, Brian White, Elizabeth Reaser, Paul Schneider; *D:* Thomas Bezucha; *C:* Jonathan Brown; *M:* Michael Giacchino.

Family Sins 🐶🐶 1987 A domineering father dotes on his sports-oriented son while willfully neglecting the other. Eventually this leads to calamity. 93m/C VHS. James Farentino, Jill Eikenberry, Andrew Bendarski, Mimi Kuzyk, Brent Spiner, Michael Durrell, Tom Bower; *D:* Jerrold Freedman. **TV**

Family Tree 🐶🐶½ 2000 (G) Slow-paced and preachy. A small town, suffering from high unemployment, is happy when a plastics company agrees to build a new factory. Only problem is that it means cutting down the town landmark—an ancient oak tree with generations of initials carved into its bark. However, young Mitch (Lawrence) decides to start a save-the-tree movement. 90m/C VHS, Robert Forster, Cliff Robertson, Naomi Judd, Andy Lawrence, Matthew Lawrence; *D:* Duane Clark; *W:* Paul Canterna; *C:* John Peters; *M:* Michael Curp, Randy Miller.

Family Upside Down 🐶🐶 1978 An aging couple fight their separation after the husband has a heart attack and is put into a nursing home. The fine cast received several Emmy nominations, with Astaire the winner. 100m/C VHS. Helen Hayes, Fred Astaire, Efrem Zimbalist Jr., Patty Duke; *D:* David Lowell Rich; *M:* Henry Mancini. **TV**

Family Viewing 🐾🐾🐾 1987 Surrealistic depiction of a family—obsessed with television and video—whose existence is a textbook model of home sweet dysfunctional home. An early, experimental film from Canada's Egoyan, it won considerable praise for its social commentary. **92m/C VHS, DVD.** *CA* David Hemblen, Adian Tierney, Gabrielle Rose, Arsinee Khanjian; *D:* Atom Egoyan; *W:* Atom Egoyan; *C:* Robert MacDonald; Peter Mettler; *M:* Mychael Danna. Toronto-City '87. Canadian Feature Film.

Famous Five Get into Trouble 🐾🐾 1987 Four precocious youngsters and a dog get involved with a criminal plot and cutely wile their way out of it. Scandinavian; dubbed in English. **90m/C VHS.** Astrid Villaume, Ove Sprogøe, Lily Broberg; *D:* Trine Hedman.

The Fan 🐾🐾 1981 (R) A Broadway star is threatened and later on circle cut down when a lovestruck fan feels he has been rejected by his idol. The stellar cast makes this bloody and familiar tale seem better than it is. **95m/C VHS, DVD.** Lauren Bacall, Maureen Stapleton, James Garner, Hector Elizondo, Michael Biehn, Griffin Dunne; *D:* Edward Bianchi; *W:* Priscilla Chapman; *C:* Dick Bush; *M:* Pino Donaggio.

The Fan 🐾🐾½ 1996 (R) Obsessed baseball fan Gil Renard (De Niro, who owns the copyright on playing deranged) stalks favorite player Bobby Rayburn (Snipes) who just signed a big contract with the hometown team. When Rayburn goes into a slump, Renard figures he can help his idol—by any means necessary. As an added bonus, Gil's a knife salesman. De Niro does the psycho thing with his usual aplomb, while Snipes successfully returns to the diamond. Scott keeps the familiar storyline from becoming tedious. Based on the book by Peter Abrahams. **117m/C VHS, DVD.** Jack Black, Chris Mulkey, Brandon Hammond, Charles Hallahan, Dan E. Butler, Michael Jace, Frank Medrano, M.C. Gainey, Eric Bruskotter, Kim Robillard, Robert De Niro, Wesley Snipes, Ellen Barkin, John Leguizamo, Benicio Del Toro, Patti D'Arbanville; *D:* Tony Scott; *W:* Phoef Sutton; *C:* Darius Wolski; *M:* Hans Zimmer.

Fanatic woof! *The Last Horror Film* 1982 (R) Beautiful queen of horror films is followed to the Cannes Film Festival by her number one fan who, unbeknownst to her, is slowly murdering members of her entourage in a deluded and vain attempt to capture her attentions. Fine performances all around. 🎵 *Fancy Pants*; *Home Cookin'.* **92m/C VHS, DVD.** Bob Hope, Lucille Ball, Bruce Cabot, Jack Kirkwood, Lea Penman, Eric Blore, John Alexander, Norma Varden; *D:* George Marshall; *C:* Charles B(ryant) Lang Jr.

Fanci's Persuasion 🐾🐾½ 1995 San Francisco-set gay farce features lesbian Fanci (Patton) 24 hours away from marrying lover Loretta (Boa) and in panic mode. Her parents refuse to come to the ceremony and inexplicable complications to deal with. Deliberately over-the-top performances and contrived dialogue and situations can't really take the strain despite the pic's good looks. **78m/C VHS.** Jessica Patton, Boa, Justin Bond, Robert Coffman, Charles Herman-Wurmfeld; *D:* Charles Herman-Wurmfeld; *W:* Charles Herman-Wurmfeld; *C:* David Rush Morrison.

Fancy Pants 🐾🐾½ 1950 Remake of "Ruggles of Red Gap" features Hope, a British actor posing as a butler. Also featuring Ball, an amusing contrast. Fine performances all around. 🎵 *Fancy Pants*; *Home Cookin'.* **92m/C VHS, DVD.** Bob Hope, Lucille Ball, Bruce Cabot, Jack Kirkwood, Lea Penman, Eric Blore, John Alexander, Norma Varden; *D:* George Marshall; *C:* Charles B(ryant) Lang Jr.

Fandango 🐾🐾½ 1985 (PG) Five college friends take a wild weekend drive across the Texas Badlands for one last fling before graduation and the prospect of military service. Expanded by Reynolds with assistance from Steven Spielberg, from his student film. Provides a look at college and life during the Vietnam crisis. **91m/C VHS, DVD.** Judd Nelson, Kevin Costner, Sam Roberts, Chuck Bush, Brian Cesak, Elizabeth (E.G.) Daily) Daily, Suzy Amis, Glenne Head-

ly, Pepe Serna, Marvin J. McIntyre; *D:* Kevin Reynolds; *W:* Kevin Reynolds; *M:* Alan Silvestri.

Fanfan la Tulipe 🐾🐾 *Fanfan the Tulip; Fearless Little Soldier* 1951 Fanfan (Philipe) escapes an unwanted marriage by joining the army of Louis XV (Herrand) after being promised an illustrious career and a royal marriage. And after many heroics, it all comes true. Amusing satire of swashbucklers and historical romance movies. French with subtitles. **98m/B VHS, DVD.** *FR* Gerard Philipe, Gina Lollobrigida, Marcel Herrand, Sylvia Pelayo, Genevieve Page, Noel Roquevert; *D:* Christian-Jaque; *W:* Rene Wheeler, Jean Fallet, Christian-Jaque; *C:* Christian Matras; *M:* Georges Van Parys, Maurice Thiriet. Cannes '52: Director (Christian-Jaque).

Fangs 🐾½ 1975 (R) Unfriendly reptile-stomping villagers take the life of Mr. Snakey's favorite serpent. He sends his slithering pets on a vengeful and poisonous spree. **90m/C VHS.** Les Tremayne, Janet Wood, Bebe Kelly, Marvin Kaplan, Alice Nunn; *D:* Vittorio Schiraldi.

Fangs of Fate 🐾½ 1925 A gang of bad guys battles the town's new marshal. **67m/B VHS.** Billy(y) (William Patten) Patton, Dorothy Donald; *D:* Horace Carpenter; *W:* Horace Carpenter; *C:* Paul H. Allen.

Fangs of the Living Dead 🐾½ *Malenka, the Vampire; La Nipote del Vampiro; The Niece of the Vampire; The Vampire's Niece* 1968 When a young woman inherits a castle, her uncle, who happens to be a vampire, tries to persuade her to remain among the undead. **80m/C VHS, DVD.** *SP IT* Anita Ekberg, Rossana Yanni, Diana Lorys, Fernando Bilbao, Paul Muller, Julian Ugarte, Andriana Ambesi; *D:* Armando de Ossorio; *W:* Armando de Ossorio.

Fangs of the Wild 🐾🐾 *Follow the Hunter* 1954 When a young boy witnesses a murder at his father's hunting lodge, no one but the killer believes him. When the killer decides to get rid of the boy, Buck the Wonder Dog gets involved. **72m/B VHS.** Charles Chaplin Jr., Onslow Stevens, Margia Dean, Freddy Ridgeway, Phil Tead, Robert Stevenson; *D:* William Claxton.

Fanny 🐾🐾🐾 1932 Second part of Marcel Pagnol's trilogy depicting the lives of the people of Provence, France. The poignant tale of Fanny, a young woman who marries an older man when Marius, her young lover, leaves her pregnant when he goes to sea. Remade several times but the original holds its own very well. "Marius" was first in the trilogy; "Cesar" was third. **128m/B VHS, DVD.** *FR* Raimu, Orane Demazis, Pierre Fresnay, Alida Rouffe; *D:* Marc Allegret; *W:* Marcel Pagnol; *M:* Vincent Scotto.

Fanny 🐾🐾🐾 1961 Young girl falls in love with an adventurous sailor, and finds herself pregnant after he returns to the sea. With the help of the sailor's parents, she finds, marries, and eventually grows to love a much older man, who in turn cares for her and adores her son as if he were his own. When the sailor returns, all involved must confront their pasts and define their futures. Beautifully made, with fine performances and a plot which defies age or nationality. Part of the "A Night at the Movies" series, this tape simulates a 1961 movie evening, with a Tweety Pie cartoon, a newsreel and coming attractions for "Splendor in the Grass" and "The Roman Spring of Mrs. Stone." **148m/C VHS.** *FR* Leslie Caron, Maurice Chevalier, Charles Boyer, Horst Buchholz, Lionel Jeffries; *D:* Joshua Logan; *W:* Julius J. Epstein; *C:* Jack Cardiff.

Fanny and Alexander 🐾🐾🐾🐾 *Fanny Och Alexander* 1983 (R) The culmination of Bergman's career, this autobiographical film is set in a rural Swedish town in 1907. It tells the story of one year in the lives of the Ekdahl family, as seen by the young children, Fanny and Alexander. Magic and religion, love and death, reconciliation and estrangement are skillfully captured in this carefully detailed, lovingly photographed film. In Swedish with English subtitles or dubbed. **197m/C VHS, DVD.** *SW* Pernilla Allwin, Bertil Guve, Gunn Wallgren, Allan Edwall, Ewa Froling, Erland Josephson, Harriet Andersson, Jarl Kulle, Jan Malmsjo; *D:* Ingmar Bergman; *W:* Ingmar Bergman; *C:* Sven Nykvist; *M:* Daniel Bell.

Oscars '83: Art Dir./Set Dec., Cinematog., Costume Des., Foreign Film; Cesar '84: Foreign Film; Golden Globes '84: Foreign Film; L.A. Film Critics '83: Cinematog., Foreign Film; N.Y. Film Critics '83: Director (Bergman), Foreign Film.

Fanny Hill 🐾🐾 1983 (R) A softcore adaptation of the racy Victorian classic. **80m/C VHS, DVD.** *GB* Alfred Marks, Lisa Raines, Shelley Winters, Wilfrid Hyde-White, Oliver Reed; *D:* Gerry O'Hara; *W:* Stephen Chesley; *C:* Tony Spratling; *M:* Paul Hoffert.

Fanny Hill: Memoirs of a Woman of Pleasure woof! 1964 Sexual exploits of an innocent in bawdy 18th-century London, as directed by notorious "Super Vixen" Meyer (though by Meyer standards, proceedings are fairly innocuous, if inept). Based on the novel. **105m/B VHS.** *GE* Miriam Hopkins, Walter Giller, Alexander D'Arcy, Leticia Roman, Billy Frick, Heidi Hansen, Chris Howland, Ulli Lommel; *D:* Russ Meyer; *W:* Robert J. Hill; *C:* Heinz Hoelscher; *M:* Erwin Halletz.

Fantasia 🐾🐾🐾 1940 Disney's most personal animation feature first bombed at the boxoffice and irked purists who couldn't take the plotless, experimental mix of classical music and cartoons. It became a cult movie, embraced by more liberal generations of moviegoers. Reissue of the original version, painstakingly restored, ceased because of a planned remake. 🎵 *Toccata & Fugue in D; The Nutcracker Suite; The Sorcerer's Apprentice; The Rite of Spring; Pastoral Symphony; Dance of the Hours; Night on Bald Mountain; Ave Maria; The Cossack Dance.* **116m/C VHS, DVD.** *D:* Ben Sharpsteen, James Nelson Algar, Samuel Armstrong, Ford Beebe, Jim Handley, T. Hee, Wilfred Jackson, Hamilton Luske, Bill Roberts, Paul Satterfield; *W:* Lee Blair, Phil Dike, Otto Englander, Carl Fallberg, Campbell Grant, Albert Heath, Graham Heid, Arthur Heinemann, Bianca Majolie, William Martin, John McLeish, Sylvia Moberly-Holland, Perce Pearce, Bill Peet, Edward Penner, Joseph Sabo, Webb Smith, Leo Thiele, Norman Wright; *M:* Leopold Stokowski; *V:* Walt Disney; *Nar:* Deems Taylor. AFI '98: Top 100, Natl. Film. Reg. '90.

Fantasia/2000 🐾🐾½ 2000 (G) Lightweight continuation of Disney's 1940 film hangs on to Mickey Mouse's popular "The Sorcerer's Apprentice" and adds seven new animated sequences of varying charm with celebrity introductions. Probably the most fun sequence is that of Saint-Saens' "Carnival of the Animals." Music is conducted by James Levine and performed by the Chicago Symphony Orchestra. Originally released in the IMAX format. 🎵 *Symphony No. 5 (Ludwig Van Beethoven); Pines of Rome (Ottorino Respighi); Rhapsody in Blue (George Gershwin); Piano Concerto No. 2, Allegro, Opus 102 (Dmitri Shostakovich); Carnival of the Animals (Camille Saint-Saens); The Sorcerer's Apprentice (Paul Dukas); Pomp and Circumstance (Edward Elgar); Firebird Suite (Igor Stravinsky).* **75m/C VHS, DVD.** *D:* Hendel Butoy, Eric Goldberg, James Nelson Algar, Gaetan Brizzi, Paul Brizzi, Pixote Hunt, Francis Glebas.

Fantasies woof! *And Once Upon a Love* 1973 (R) Teenage lovers Derek and Hooten return to their Greek island home and decide to improve their village by turning it into a tourist haven. First collaboration of the Dereks is a loser, lacking plot, direction, and decent acting. Bo shows no talent but the obvious one and is actually credited as Kathleen Collins. **81m/C VHS, DVD.** Bo Derek, Peter Hooten, Anna Alexiades; *D:* John Derek.

The Fantasist 🐾 1989 (R) Sex crime thriller features a deranged killer who makes obscene, yet seductive phone calls to young ladies before murdering them. **98m/C VHS.** Timothy Bottoms, Christopher Cazenove; *D:* Robin Hardy.

Fantastic Balloon Voyage 🐾 *Viaje Fantastico en Globo* 1976 (G) Three men embark on a journey across the equator in a balloon, experiencing myriad adventures along the way. Much hot air. **100m/C VHS.** *MX* Hugo Stiglitz, Jeff Cooper, Carlos East, Carmen; *D:* Rene Cardona Jr.

Fantastic Four 🐾 2005 (PG-13) Or, more like the "So-So-Four." The Stan Lee/Jack Kirby "Marvel Comic foursome, who made their print debut in 1961, finally get on the big screen, though beyond introducing them and showing off the newly-acquired superpowers from exposure to outer-space radiation, they don't have much to do. Lee cameos as mailman Willy Lumpkin. **105m/C DVD, Blu-ray Disc, UMD.** *US* Ioan Gruffudd, Jessica Alba, Michael Chiklis, Chris Evans, Julian McMahon, Kerry Washington, Stan Lee, Laurie Holden; *D:* Tim Story; *W:* Mark Frost, Michael France, Simon Kinberg; *C:* Oliver Wood; *M:* John Ottman.

Fantastic Four: Rise of the Silver Surfer 🐾½ 2007 (PG) They weren't fantastic the first time and this sequel is almost as dull. Mr. Fantastic (Gruffudd) keeps getting distracted while trying to marry invisible sweetie Sue (Alba). But he's got good reason, with intergalactic traveler Silver Surfer deciding to visit our little planet. Seems dead planets follow in the visitor's wake and the mild foursome doesn't want that happening to Earth. At least the 3-D animation for the Surfer deserves a look-see. **92m/C DVD, Blu-ray Disc.** *US* Ioan Gruffudd, Jessica Alba, Chris Evans, Michael Chiklis, Julian McMahon, Doug Jones, Andre Braugher, Kerry Washington, Gonzalo Menendez; *D:* Tim Story; *W:* Don Payne, Mark Frost; *C:* Larry Blanford; *M:* John Ottman; *V:* Laurence Fishburne.

The Fantastic Night 🐾🐾🐾 *La Nuit Fantastique* 1942 Considering that this film was made in France during the Nazi occupation, it is a remarkably clear work. It's a fantasy about Denis (Gravey), who is visited by a beautiful woman (Presle) as he sleeps and then follows her through a series of adventures. According to the box copy, the star was working with the Resistance while he was making the film. French with subtitles. **90m/B VHS, DVD.** *FR* Fernand Gravey, Micheline Presle, Marcel Levesque, Christiane Nere; *D:* Marcel L'Herbier; *W:* Louis Chavance, Marcel L'Herbier; *C:* Pierre Montazel; *M:* Maurice Thiriet.

Fantastic Planet 🐾🐾🐾 *La Planete Sauvage; Planet of Incredible Creatures; The Savage Planet* 1973 (PG) A critically acclaimed French, animated, sci-fi epic based on the drawings of Roland Topor. A race of small humanoids are enslaved and exploited by a race of giants until one of the small creatures manages to unite his people and fight for equality. **72m/C VHS, DVD.** *FR* Roland Topor, Rene Laloux; *W:* Roland Topor, Steve Hayes, Rene Laloux; *C:* Boris Baromykin, Lubomir Rejthar; *M:* Alain Goraguer; *V:* Barry Bostwick.

Fantastic Seven 🐾🐾 1979 The Fantastic Seven is a daredevil team sent to rescue a Hollywood sex symbol who has been kidnapped and held for ransom while shooting on location off the coast of Miami. **96m/C VHS.** Christopher Connelly, Christopher Lloyd, Soon-Teck Oh, Morgan Brittany, Bill Macy, Peter Haskel, Patrick Macnee, Elke Sommer; *D:* John Peyser; *C:* Frank Holgate; *M:* Bill Conti. TV

Fantastic Voyage 🐾🐾 *Microscopia; Strange Journey* 1966 An important scientist, rescued from behind the Iron Curtain, is so severely wounded by enemy agents that traditional surgery is impossible. After being shrunk to microscopic size, a medical team journeys inside his body where they find themselves threatened by the patient's natural defenses. Great action, award-winning special effects. **100m/C VHS, DVD.** Stephen Boyd, Edmond O'Brien, Raquel Welch, Arthur Kennedy, Donald Pleasence, Arthur O'Connell, William Redfield, James Brolin, Barry Coe, Brendan Fitzgerald, Shelby Grant, Ken Scott; *D:* Richard Fleischer; *W:* Harry Kleiner; *C:* Ernest Laszlo; *M:* Leonard Roseman. Oscars '66: Art Dir./Set Dec., Color, Visual FX.

The Fantastic World of D.C. Collins 🐾🐾 1984 Gary Coleman plays a daydreaming teenager who thinks he is being pursued by mysterious strangers seeking a videotape that was unknowingly slipped to him. **100m/C VHS.** Gary Coleman, Bernie Casey, Shelley Smith, Fred (John F.) Dryer, Marilyn McCoo, Philip Abbott, George Gobel, Michael Ansara; *D:* Leslie Martinson. TV

The Fantasticks 🐾🐾½ 1995 (PG) The stage's longest-running musical gets the big-screen treatment with a story about two fathers (Grey and Hughes) who decide to matchmake for their children, Matt (McIntyre) and Luisa (Kelly). They hire the Fantasticks) of a traveling carnival (called the Fantasticks) to kidnap Luisa, so that Matt can play the hero and rescue her. The plan seems to work but the course of true love never runs that smoothly. Adapted by Jones and Schmidt from their play. **AKA:** The Fantasticks. 105m/C **VHS.** Bryan Brown, Helen Morse. **D:** Gordon Pinsent. **TV**

Far Cry from Home 🐾 1981 A battered wife attempts to escape from her domineering husband before it's too late. 87m/C **VHS.** CA Mary Ann McDonald, Richard Monette. **M:** Henry Mancini.

Far East 🐾½ 1985 Two ex-lovers meet in Southeast Asia and join forces to find the woman's missing husband, a reporter. 105m/C **VHS.** Bryan Brown, Helen Daniels. **D:** John Duigan.

Far and Away 🐾🐾½ 1992 (PG-13) Meandering old-fashioned epic about immigrants, romance, and settling the American West. In the 1890s, Joseph Donelly (Cruise) is forced to flee his Irish homeland after threatening the life of his landlord, and emigrates to America in the company of the landlord's daughter, feisty Shannon Christie (Kidman). Particularly brutal scenes of Cruise earning his living as a bare-knuckled boxer contrast with the expansiveness of the land rush ending. Slow, spotty, and a little too slick for its own good, though real-life couple Cruise and Kidman are an attractive pair. Filmed in 70-mm Panavision on location in Ireland and Montana. 140m/C **VHS. DVD.** Tom Cruise, Nicole Kidman, Thomas Gibson, Robert Prosky, Barbara Babcock, Colm Meaney, Eileen Pollock, Michelle Johnson, Cyril Cusack, Clint Howard, Rance Howard; **D:** Ron Howard; **W:** Bob Dolman; **C:** Mikael Salomon; **M:** John Williams.

Far Away and Long Ago 🐾🐾 1974 Based on the autobiographical novel by Guillermo Hudson which details the memories which haunted his childhood—the Argentinian pampas, its gauchos, witchcraft, and women. In Spanish with English subtitles. 91m/C **VHS.** AR Juan Jose Camero, Leonor Manso; **D:** Manuel Antin.

Far Country 🐾🐾🐾 1955 Cattlemen must battle the elements and frontier lawlessness in this classic. Stewart leads his herd to the Yukon in hopes of large profits, but ends up having to kidnap it back from the crooked sheriff and avenging the deaths of his friends. Entertaining and the usual Western arena. 97m/C **VHS. DVD.** James Stewart, Ruth Roman, Walter Brennan, Harry (Henry) Morgan, Corinne Calvet, Jay C. Flippen, John McIntire; **D:** Anthony Mann; **C:** William H. Daniels; **M:** Henry Mancini.

Far from the Madding Crowd 🐾🐾🐾 1967 (PG) A lavish, long adaptation of Thomas Hardy's 19th-century classic about the beautiful Bathsheba (Christie) and the three very different men who love her. Her first love is handsome and wayward soldier Sgt. Troy (Stamp), her second love is the noble lord William Boldwood (Finch), and her third the ever-loving and long-patient farmer Gabriel Oaks (Bates). Christie is well cast as the much-desired beauty. Gorgeous cinematography by Nicolas Roeg. Remade for British TV in 1997. 165m/C **VHS. DVD.** GB Julie Christie, Terence Stamp, Peter Finch, Alan Bates, Prunella Ransome; **C:** Nicolas Roeg; **M:** Richard Rodney Bennett. Natl. Bd. of Review '67. Actor (Finch).

Far from the Madding Crowd 🐾🐾🐾 1997 TV version of the Thomas Hardy novel (filmed for the big screen in 1967) that follows the adventures of young Bathsheba (Baeza), who's the object of desire for three very different men in 19th-century rural England. Independent-minded Bathsheba Everdene inherits a farm and insists on managing it herself. She's aided by steadfast head man Gabriel Oak (Parker), who loves her but doesn't feel he can offer her anything, wealthy older neighbor William Boldwood (Terry), whose love for Bathsheba comes as an obsession; and rakish Sgt. Frank Troy (Firth), who captivates and stiff-upper-lipped but Irving is so appropriately noble was based on the romantic bestseller by M.M. Kaye. 108m/C **VHS. DVD.** GB Paloma Baeza, Nigel Terry, Nathaniel Parker, Jonathan Firth; **D:** Nicholas Renton.

Far from Home 🐾🐾 1989 (R) Drew Barrymore is the seductive teen being scoped by a psychotic killer while on vacation with her father. Lots of over-the-top performances by the familiar cast. 86m/C **VHS. DVD.** Matt Frewer, Drew Barrymore, Richard Masur, Karen Austin, Susan Tyrrell, Anthony Rapp, Jennifer Tilly, Andras Jones, Dick Miller; **D:** Meiert Avis; **C:** Paul Elliott; **M:** Jonathan Elias.

Far from Home: The Adventures of Yellow Dog 🐾🐾 1994 (PG) Stalwart lad Angus (Bradford) and his faithful pooch Yellow (Dakota) battle the elements, wild animals and fatigue as they try to get back home after being shipwrecked on a remote island in British Columbia. Good thing Dad (Davidson) gave them all those cool survival tips before they left, or else they never would've known that you can eat bugs. (Okay, the dog probably knew that already.) Mom (Rogers) does her bit by making sure the search mission stays focused. You usually can't go wrong with a kid and his dog lost in the wilderness, but this one is really short—on time and on loving good. Nice scenery, though. 81m/C **VHS. DVD.** Jesse Bradford, Bruce Davison, Mimi Rogers, Tom Bower; **D:** Phillip Borsos; **W:** Phillip Borsos.

Far North 🐾🐾½ 1988 (PG-13) Quirky comedy about a woman who returns to her rural family homestead after her father is seriously injured by a horse, and tries to deal with her eccentric family's travails. Fine cast never reaches its potential. Shepard's directing debut. 96m/C **VHS. DVD.** Jessica Lange, Charles Durning, Tess Harper, Donald Moffat, Ann Wedgeworth, Patricia Arquette, Nina Draxton; **D:** Sam Shepard; **W:** Sam Shepard; **C:** Robbie Greenberg.

A Far Off Place 🐾🐾 1993 (PG-13) Adolescent boy, adolescent girl, adolescent bushperson, and mature dog set out across the African desert to escape elephant poachers who want to kill them. The boy and girl find romance in the sand, bushperson finds water by listening, and dog gets very nice walk. Strong performances by the youthful leads lend charm to this Disney/Amblin flick, particularly Bok as the bushperson. Unusually violent film for studios involved (animals and people bite sand), though care is taken to edit actual blood shed on screen. Filmed in Zimbabwe and Namibia and based on the books "A Story Like the Wind" and "A Far Off Place" by Laurens van der Post. 107m/C **VHS. DVD.** Reese Witherspoon, Ethan (Randall) Embry, Sarel Bok, Jack Thompson, Maximilian Schell, Robert Burke, Miles Anderson; **D:** Mikael Salomon; **W:** Robert Caswell, Jonathan Hensleigh, Sally Robinson; **C:** Juan Ruiz-Anchia; **M:** James Horner.

Far from Heaven 🐾🐾🐾½ 2002 (PG-13) Perfect '50s homemaker, mother, and wife Cathy (Moore) faces her husband Frank's (Quaid) emerging homosexual desires, which culminate in her witnessing him in an intimate kiss with another man at the office. When Cathy seeks comfort from her black gardener (Haysbert), scandal and hatred spread and wrenching truths are found. Melodramatic (in the Douglas Sirk tradition) tale of social/racial taboos and a woman's sacrifice is intriguing. Moore's performance is Oscar caliber (she got a nomination), Quaid's fearless, and Lachman's retro-chic visuals also exhibit stunning craftsmanship, while Bernstein's lush score sets the proper Hollywood studio bigwig, and fragile hostess, Ellie (Connally), who's written a screenplay based on her own traumas. 99m/C **VHS.** Edward Atterton, Jennifer Connelly, Dan Futterman, Marcia Gay Harden, George Newbern, Jim True-Frost, Andrew Lauren, Tracee Ellis Ross; **D:** John Huddles; **W:** John Huddles; **C:** Tami Reiker.

Far from Home 🐾🐾 1999 (R) Julianne Moore, Dennis Quaid, Dennis Haysbert, Patricia Clarkson, James Rebhorn, Celia Weston, Viola Davis; **D:** Todd Haynes; **W:** Todd Haynes; **C:** Edward Lachman; **M:** Elmer Bernstein. Ind. Spirit '02: Actor, Cinematog., Director (Haynes), Film, Support. Actor (Quaid); L.A. Film Critics '02: Actress (Moore), Cinematog., Score, Natl. Bd. of Review '02: Actress (Moore), N.Y. Film Critics '02: Actress (Moore), Cinematog., Director (Haynes), Film, Support. Actress (Clarkson); Nat. Soc. Film Critics '02: Cinematog., Support. Actress (Clarkson).

The Far Horizons 🐾🐾 1955 Meriwether Lewis (MacMurray) and William Clark (Heston) lead an expedition to survey the territory after the Louisiana Purchase. Along the way they gain the assistance of Sacajawea, played by blue-eyed Donna Reed. Vintage Hollywood at its best: takes a historical premise and turns it into comical love-triangle that comes full circle—in the White House, no less. Check your knowledge of history at the door, but enjoy the beautiful scenery and some unintentional giggles. 107m/C **VHS.** Fred MacMurray, Charlton Heston, Donna Reed, Barbara Hale, William Demarest, Eduardo Noriega, Herbert (Hayes) Heyes, Lester Matthews, Alan Reed, Larry Pennell; **D:** Rudolph Maté; **W:** Winston Miller, Edmund H. North; **C:** Daniel F. Fapp; **M:** Hans J. Salter.

Far Harbor 🐾🐾 1996 An attractive group of yuppie failures gather in a Long Island mansion to whine and snipe at each other over dinner. Among them is Frick (Atterton), a persona non grata English filmmaker, who becomes obsessed with a moored yacht that belongs to a old yuppies gather in a Long [...]. **C:** Jack Maria; **M:** R. Dale Butts.

Far Side of the Moon 🐾🐾 La Face Cachée de la Lune 2003 Lepage directed, wrote (an adaptation of his play), and stars as Quebec brothers Philippe and André. Philippe is a failed doctoral student obsessed with space, while gay younger brother André is a vacuous TV weatherman. They are brought into each other's orbit by the death of their mother, although noticing the changes (not necessarily for the better). Angelic companion Raphaele (Kinski) watches events passively, including an old man's (Runemark) reflections on life and the philosophical musings of Emil Fiesti (Datoe, Time itself, get it??), even as Cassiel impulsively chooses humanity over his heavenly world. Falk makes a return appearance to little effect. Overlong and under-developed. 146m/C **VHS. DVD.** GE Otto Sander, Peter Falk, Heinz Buchholz, Nastassja Kinski, Heinz Ruhmann, Bruno Ganz, Solveig Dommartin, Ruediger Vogler, Willm Datoe, Lou Castel; **D:** Wim Wenders; **W:** Ulrich Zieger, Richard Reitinger, Wim Wenders; **C:** Jurgen Jurges; **M:** David Darling, Laurent Petitgand. Cannes '93: Grand Jury Prize.

Faraway, So Close! 🐾🐾 In Weiter, So Nah! 1993 (PG-13) Wenders er-ratic follow-up to his magnificent "Wings of Desire." Cassiel (Sander), the angel left behind when Damiel (Ganz) chose to become human, once again surveys Berlin, noticing the changes ('not necessarily for the better). Angelic companion Raphaele (Kinski) watches events passively, including an old man's (Runemark) reflections on life and the philosophical musings of Emil Fiesti (Datoe, Time itself, get it??), even as Cassiel impulsively chooses humanity over his heavenly world. Falk makes a return appearance to little effect. Overlong and under-developed.

Far Frontier 🐾🐾 1948 Roy Rogers saves the day by thwarting a band of outlaws who are being smuggled across the border in soybean oil cans. Includes musical numbers and horse tricks. 60m/B **VHS.** Roy Rogers, Andy Devine, Francis Ford, Gail Davis, Roy Barcroft, Clayton Moore, Robert Strange, Holly (Mike Ragan) Bane, Lane Bradford, Edmund Cobb; **D:** William Witney; **W:** Sloan Nibley; **C:** Jack Marta; **M:** R. Dale Butts.

The Far Side of Jericho 🐾🐾½ 2006 (R) In the 1880s, the widows of three executed outlaw brothers are forced to flee their homes and are pursued by a posse determined to find their husbands' buried ill-gotten gains. Routine oater. 99m/C **DVD.** Patrick Bergin, James Gammon, Lawrence Pressman, C. Thomas Howell, Suzanne Andrews, Judith Burnett, Lissa Negrin, Josh Dien, Jason Connery; **D:** Tim Hunter; **W:** Rob Sullivan, James Crumley; **C:** Patrick Cady; **M:** Mark Adler. **VIDEO**

Fantasy Island 🐾 1977 Three people fly "De plane, boss!") to an island paradise and get to live out their fantasies for a price. Pilot for the TV series. 100m/C **VHS.** Ricardo Montalban, Bill Bixby, Sandra Dee, Peter Lawford, Carol Lynley, Hugh O'Brian, Eleanor Parker, Dick Sargent, Victoria Principal; **D:** Richard Lang. **TV**

Fantasy Man 🐾½ 1984 A restless middle-aged man tries to relieve his midlife crisis with the help of three women. 86m/C **VHS.** AU Harold Hopkins, Jeanie Drynan, Kerry Mack, Kate Fitzpatrick; **D:** John Meagher; **W:** John Meagher.

Fantasy Mission Force 🐾 1984 In this indescribably silly action comedy, Japanese troops capture an international group of generals (some in Civil War-era uniforms). An invasion of Canada is underway. Jackie is part of a group trying to rescue them. Jackie is part of a group trying to rescue them. 90m/C **VHS. DVD.** HK Jackie Chan, Brigitte Lin, Adam Cheng, Jimmy Wang Yu; **D:** Yen Ping Chu.

Far Out Man Woof! Soul Man 2 1989 (R) An unalterable middle-aged hippie is sent by his worried family and his psychiatrist on a cross-country journey to rediscover himself. The script makes no sense and has very few laughs. 81m/C **VHS. DVD.** Thomas Chong, Rae Dawn Chong, C. Thomas Howell, Shelby Chong, Martin Mull, Paris Chong, Paul Bartel, Judd Nelson, Michael Winslow, Richard "Cheech" Marin; **D:** Thomas Chong; **W:** Thomas Chong.

The Far Pavilions 🐾🐾½ Blade of Steel 1984 A British officer falls in love with an Indian princess during the second Afghan War. Cross is appropriately noble as his ethnic love. This lavish production was based on the romantic bestseller by M.M. Kaye. 108m/C **VHS. DVD.** GB Ben Cross, A. Alonzo; **W:** David Zelag Goodman; **C:** John A. Alonzo; **D:** [...]

Farewell My Concubine 🐾🐾 Bawang Bie Ji 1993 (R) Exotic film covers 50 years of sexual, social, and political Chinese history wrapped around the story of two male Peking Opera stars. Deposited as boys at the Opera's training school by their hermetically sealed world, but their friendship is tested during the chaos of Communism and the cultural revolution. Sumptuous and well-acted, but the sheer length and emotional detachment prove to be drawbacks. Adapted from a novel by Lee, who based the work on a 2000-year-old Chinese opera about an imperial concubine. Filmed on location in Beijing. In Mandarin Chinese with subtitles. 157m/C **VHS. DVD.** HK Leslie Cheung, Fengyi Zhang, Gong Li, Lu Qi, Dalemei) Ying, Ge You, Fei Yang, Ma Mingwei; **D:** Chen Kaige; **W:** Lilian Lee, Lu Wei; **C:** Gu Changwei; **M:** Jiping Zhao. British Acad. '93: Foreign Film; Cannes '93: Film; Golden Globes '94: Foreign Film; L.A. Film Critics '93: Foreign Film; Natl. Bd. of Review '93: Foreign Film, Support. Actor.

Farewell, My Lovely 🐾🐾🐾 1975 (R) A remake of the 1944 Raymond Chandler mystery, "Murder, My Sweet," featuring private eye Phillip Marlowe hunting for an ex-convict's lost sweetheart in 1941 Los Angeles. Perhaps the most accurate of Chandler adaptations, but far from the best; this film often leaves a nicely detailed production. Mitchum is a bit too world-weary as the seen-it-all detective. 95m/C **VHS. DVD.** GB Robert Mitchum, Charlotte Rampling, Sylvia Miles, John Ireland, Anthony Zerbe, Jack O'Halloran, Harry Dean Stanton, Sylvester Stallone, Joe Spinell, Jim Thompson; **D:** Dick Richards; **W:** Jerry Goodman; **C:** John A. Alonzo; **M:** David Shire.

A Farewell to Arms ♂♂♂ 1932 The original film version of Ernest Hemingway's novel about the tragic love affair between an American ambulance driver and an English nurse during the WWI campaign of WWI. The novelist disavowed the film. Fine performances and cinematography. 85m/B VHS, DVD. Helen Hayes, Gary Cooper, Adolphe Menjou, Mary (Phillips) Philips, Jack La Rue, Blanche Frederici; D: Frank Borzage; W: Oliver H.P. Garrett, Benjamin Glazer; C: Charles B(ryant) Lang Jr. Oscars '33: Cinematog., Sound.

Farewell to the King ♂♂½ 1989 (PG-13) During WWII, a ship-wrecked American deserter becomes the chief of a tribe of Borneo headhunters until his jungle kingdom is caught between the forces of the U.S. and Japanese. With the help of a British officer he helps them defend themselves when the Japanese invade. An old-fashioned war epic with a beautiful location and solid if uninspired-performances by the leads. Based on Pierre Schoendoerffer's novel "L'Adieu Au Roi." 114m/C VHS. Nick Nolte, Nigel Havers, Marius Weyers, Frank McRae, Marilyn Tokuda, Elan Oberon, William Wise, James Fox, Aki Aleong; D: John Milius; W: John Milius; C: Dean Semler; M: Basil Poledouris.

Fargo ♂♂♂ 1996 (R) Another malicious, extra-dark comedy from the Coen brothers. Car salesman Jerry Lundegaard (Macy) hires a couple of losers to kidnap his wife so he can swindle the ransom money out of his father-in-law. Naturally, the scheme begins to unravel and the very pregnant police chief Marge Gunderson (McDormand) treks through the frozen tundra of Minnesota to put the pieces of the puzzle together. McDormand's performance as the chatty competent chief is first rate. Needing the flat-accented Midwesterners of their youth, the Coens have also returned to their filmmaking roots after the disappointing big-budget "Hudsucker Proxy." Because Minneapolis was having its warmest, driest winter in 100 years, the Coens were forced to shoot most of the exteriors in wintery North Dakota. 97m/C VHS, DVD. William H. Macy, Frances McDormand, Steve Buscemi, Peter Stormare, Harve Presnell, Steve Reevis, Steve Park, Jose Feliciano; D: Joel Coen; W: Ethan Coen, Joel Coen; C: Roger Deakins; M: Carter Burwell. Oscars '96: Actress (McDormand), Orig. Screenplay; AFI '98: Top 100; '96: Director (Coen); Cannes '96: Director (Coen); Ind. Spirit '97: Actor (Macy), Actress (McDormand), Cinematog., Director (Coen), Film, Screenplay; Natl. Bd. of Review '96: Actress (McDormand), Director (Coen), Natl. Film Reg. '06; N.Y. Film Critics '96: Film; Screen Actors Guild '96: Actress (McDormand); Writers Guild '96: Orig. Screenplay; Broadcast Film Critics '96: Actress (McDormand), Film. Australian Film Inst. '96: Foreign Film; British Acad.

Fargo Express ♂½ 1932 When the kid brother of Maynard's true love is falsely accused of robbing a stagecoach, Maynard works to clear his name. Routine stuff. 60m/B VHS, DVD. Ken Maynard, Helen Mack, Paul Fix; D: Alan James.

Farinelli *Il Castrato* 1994 (R) A movie to make men cringe. Floridly depicts the complex professional and personal ties of 18th-century opera composer Riccardo Broschi (Dionisi) and his younger brother Carlo (Dionisi), a celebrated castrato singer under the stage name "Farinelli." In part, because of an early church prohibition against women singing in public, boys were castrated before puberty to preserve their pure soprano voices while vocal power and agility grew as they became men. Castrati were the rock stars of their day and Farinelli lived a flamboyant life before retiring to the Spanish court of Philip V. The castrato voice heard in the movie is an electronic mixture of counter-tenor Derek Lee Ragin and soprano Ewa Mallas Godlewska. French and Italian with subtitles. 110m/C VHS, DVD. *FR IT BE* Stefano Dionisi, Enrico Lo Verso, Jeroen Krabbe, Elsa Zylberstein, Caroline Cellier, Omero Antonutti, Jacques Boudet; D: Gerard Corbiau; W: Gerard Corbiau, Andree Corbiau, Marcel Beaulieu; C: Walther Van den Ende; M: Christopher Rousset. Cesar '95: Art

Dir/Set Dec., Sound; Golden Globes '95: Foreign Film.

Farmer & Chase ♂♂ 1996 (R) It's always nice to see an old pro like Gazzara but it's a shame it couldn't have been in something less predictable. Farmer's (Gazzara) a hold-up man who's been working with partner Ollie (Jones) for 20 years. But when Ollie's killed, Farmer, who wants to pull one last job before retiring, makes the mistake of teaming up with his pacifist son Chase (Field). And then Chase involves his new gal pal Hillary (Boyle) in con the scheme. Dumb move, dumb movie. 97m/C VHS. Ben Gazzara, Todd Field, Lara Flynn Boyle, Steven Anthony Jones, Ron Kaell, David Booth; D: Michael Seltzman; W: Michael Seltzman; M: Tony Saunders.

The Farmer Takes a Wife ♂♂½ 1935 Henry Fonda's first film, recreating his stage role, as a mid-19th century farmer at odds with the Erie canal builders and struggling to court the woman he loves. Remade as a musical in 1953. 91m/B VHS. Janet Gaynor, Henry Fonda, Charles Bickford, Slim Summerville, Jane Withers; D: Victor Fleming.

The Farmer Takes a Wife ♂♂ 1953 Poor musical remake of the 1935 drama, about the trials of a struggling 1850s farmer and the Erie canal boat cook he loves. Contains no memorable music and Robertson can't compete with Henry Fonda's original role as the 'farmer. ♫We're in Business; On the Erie Canal; We're Doing it for the Natives in Jamaica; When I Close My Door; Today I Love Everybody; Somethin' Real Special; With The Sun Warm Upon Me; Can You Spell Schenectady?. 81m/C VHS. Betty Grable, Dale Robertson, Thelma Ritter, John Carroll, Eddie Foy Jr., Charlotte Austin, Merry Anders, Gwen Verdon, Kathleen Crowley, May Wynn; D: Henry Levin; W: Sally Benson, Walter Bullock, Joseph Fields; C: Arthur E. Arling; M: Cyril Mockridge, Harold Arlen.

The Farmer's Daughter ♂♂ 1947 Young portrays Katrin Holmstrom, a Swedish farm girl who becomes a maid to Congressman Cotten and winds up running for office herself (not neglecting to find romance as well). The outspoken and multi-talented character charmed audiences and was the basis of a TV series in the 1960s. 97m/B VHS. Loretta Young, Joseph Cotten, Ethel Barrymore, Charles Bickford, Harry Davenport, Lex Barker, James Arness, Rose Hobart; D: H.C. Potter; C: Milton Krasner. Oscars '47: Actress (Young).

The Farmer's Other Daughter ♂♂ *Farm Girl* 1965 A rural comedy about Farmer Brown whose lovely daughter is eyed by all the farmhands. Meanwhile, his lovely housekeeper would be the perfect candidate. Based on Eden Philpott's play. 97m/B VHS, DVD. *GB* Jameson Thomas, Lillian Hall-Davis, Gordon Harker; D: Alfred Hitchcock; W: Alfred Hitchcock; C: Jack Cox.

Fascination WOOF! 2004 (R) Bisset's beauty at 60 is the only fascinating thing in this mess of a thriller. Dad (Naughton) dies in a mysterious swimming accident, son (Garcia) thinks foul play, Mom remarries quickly, son sleeps with new stepsister (Evans). The plot twists and surprise revelations stretch things beyond the point of believability, the dialogue is terrible, and the performances lack any spark. It all adds up to a shallow, painful movie that will either induce groans or laughs. 102m/C DVD. Jacqueline Bisset, Adam Garcia, Alice Evans, James Naughton, Stuart Wilson; D: Klaus Menzel; W: Klaus Menzel; C: Reinhart Pesche, Reinhart Pesche; M: John Du Prez, John Du Prez.

Fashions of 1934 ♂♂ *Fashions 1934* A typical, lightweight '30s musical with impressive choreography by Busby Berkeley. Powell plays a disreputable clothing designer who goes to Paris to

steal the latest fashion designs and winds up costuming a musical and falls in love. ♫Spin a Little Web of Dreams; Broken Melody. 78m/B VHS. Bette Davis, William Powell, Frank McHugh, Hugh Herbert, Reginald Owen, Busby Berkeley; D: William Dieterle.

Fass Black ♂♂ 1977 (R) Yet another man against the mob flick straight out of Bartlett's familiar plotlines. Amidst gratuitous music and violence, a disco owner locks horns with the syndicate after they try to take over his place. There's a good reason disco is dead. 105m/C VHS. John Poole, Jeannie Bell, Cal Wilson, Harold Nicholas, Nicholas Lewis; D: D'Urville Martin.

The Fast and the Furious ♂♂ 1954 On the lam after being falsely charged with murder, Ireland picks up a fast car and a loose woman (or is it a loose car and a fast woman?) and makes a run for the border by entering the Pebble Beach race. 73m/B VHS, DVD. John Ireland, Dorothy Malone, Bruce Carlisle, Iris Adrian; D: Edwards Sampson, John Ireland; W: Jerome Odlum, Jean Howell; C: Floyd Crosby; M: Alexander Gerens.

The Fast and the Furious ♂♂½ 2001 (PG-13) Rookie L.A. cop Brian (Walker) goes undercover to infiltrate a street gang that adapts sports cars for illicit street racing and other, even less legal, uses. But first he has to earn the respect and trust of their leader, Dominic (Diesel), and the love of Dom's sister Mia (Brewster). Dominic is the head of a tight-knit "family" of quirky thieves hopped up on car exhaust and adrenaline, very much in the B-movie tradition of "Gone in 60 Seconds" (the original), "Eat My Dust," and "Grand Theft Auto." And hey, let's face it, kids. That's all this is, a summer B-movie where reality, plot, and dialogue have no place. Diesel does impress (again) in the patriarch-philosopher-thief role. 101m/C VHS, DVD, UMD. HD DVD. US Vin Diesel, Paul Walker, Jordana Brewster, Michelle Rodriguez, Rick Yune, Ted Levine, Ja Rule, Thom Barry, Chad Lindberg, Johnny Strong, Matt Schulze, Vyto Ruginis; D: Rob Cohen; W: Gary Scott Thompson, Erik Bergquist, David Ayer; C: Ericson Core; M: BT (Brian Transeau).

The Fast and the Furious: Tokyo Drift ♂♂½ 2006 (PG-13) The franchise heads to Japan (just like the Bad News Bears!) with new anti-hero Sean (Black), a bad-attitude teenager sent to live with his estranged military dad. Sean soon finds himself involved in the illegal neon world of drift racing and rebel gangster types out to teach this gaijin some hard lessons. Pic delivers on its fast-cars-fast-races premise. 105m/C DVD, HD DVD. US Lucas Black, Bow Wow, Sung Kang, Jason J. Tobin, Zachery Ty Bryan, Leonardo Nam, Brian Tee, Nathalie Kelley, Brian Goodman, Sonny Chiba, Nikki Griffin, Lynda Boyd, Keiko Kitagawa, Vincent Laresca, Vin Diesel; D: Justin Lin; W: Chris Morgan; C: Stephen Windon; M: Brian Tyler.

Fast Break ♂½ 1979 (PG) New York deli clerk who is a compulsive basketball fan talks his way into a college coaching job. He takes a team of street players with him, with predictable results on and off the court. Kaplan's screen debut. 107m/C VHS. Gabe Kaplan, Harold Sylvester, Randee Heller; D: Jack Smight; M: David Shire.

Fast Bullets ♂½ 1936 Texas Rangers fight a gang of smugglers and rescue a kidnap victim in this typical western. 52m/B VHS. Tom Tyler, Rex Lease, Alan Bridge, William (Bill) Gould, Margaret Nearing, Robert Walker, Charles "Slim" Whitaker, George Chesebro, Jimmy Aubrey; D: Harry S. Webb; W: Carl Krusada; C: Pliny Goodfriend.

Fast, Cheap & Out of Control ♂♂♂½ 1997 (PG) Director Morris' use of odd camera angles, unusual editing, and dark humor increases with each outing but always seems to enhance interest in the subject matter rather than detract from it. While his previous films have focused on just one subject, this one features four: a wild-animal trainer, a topiary gardener, a scientist who creates robotic insects, and a man who studies mole rats. Through inter-cutting and the overlapping of the subjects (at times audio

from one is played over the visuals of another), Morris gives the impression that they are all linked together. Old movie footage is used to add an unreal quality, and the score by Caleb Sampson of the Alloy Orchestra hypnotically completes the surrealism. This is the story of four obsessed men, but none as obsessed as director Morris himself, with his need to show that truth is stranger than fiction. 82m/C VHS, DVD. D: Errol Morris; C: Robert Richardson; M: Caleb Sampson. Natl. Bd. of Review '97: Feature Doc.; N.Y. Film Critics '97: Feature Doc.; Natl. Soc. Film Critics '97: Feature Doc.

Fast Company ♂♂ 1978 The life story of champion race car driver Lonnie Johnson including women, money, and the drag racing sponsors. 90m/C VHS, DVD. William (Bill) Smith, John Saxon, Claudia Jennings, Nicholas (Nick) Campbell, Don Francks; D: David Cronenberg; W: David Cronenberg.

Fast Food ♂ 1989 A super-cheap, strangulated attempt at low comedy, wherein an entrepreneurial hamburger peddler invents a secret aphrodisiac sauce. Look for former porn-star Traci Lords. 90m/C VHS, DVD. Clark Brandon, Tracy Griffith, Randal Patrick, Traci Lords, Kevin McCarthy, Michael J. Pollard, Jim Varney; D: Michael A. Simpson; W: Clark Brandon.

Fast Food Nation ♂♂ 2006 (R) Director Richard Linklater's attempt to show the public that fast food is both figuratively and literally crappy suffers from some slow pacing and wandering plotlines, but its point is effectively supersized. After Don (Kinnear), an executive at fictional restaurant chain Mickey's, discovers that some cows may have dropped a chalupa in the meat patties, he starts an investigation that crosses ethnic and class barriers. The story then weaves the lives of illegal immigrants (Moreno, Valderrama), cattle ranchers (Kristofferson, Willis) and suburbanites (Arquette, Hawke, Johnson) together to show why most burger shack value meals should be called the "number two." Linklater wrote the screenplay with Eric Schlosser, whose eponymous non-fiction book provided inspiration. Salad, anyone? 114m/C DVD. GB US Patricia Arquette, Paul Franklin Dano, Luis Guzman, Ethan Hawke, Bobby Canavale, Greg Kinnear, Ashley Johnson, Kris Kristofferson, Avril Lavigne, Esai Morales, Catalina Sandino Moreno, Wilmer Valderrama, Bruce Willis; D: Richard Linklater; W: Richard Linklater, Eric Schlosser; C: Lee Daniel; M: Dean Martinez.

Fast Forward ♂½ 1984 (PG) A group of eight teenagers from Ohio learn how to deal with success and failure when they enter a national dance contest in New York City. A break-dancing variation on the old show business chestnut. ♫Fast Forward; How Do You Do; As Long As We Believe; Pretty Girl; Mystery; Curves; Showdown; Do You Want It Right Now?; Hardrock. 110m/C VHS. John Scott Clough, Don Franklin, Tracy Silver, Cindy McGee; D: Sidney Poitier; W: Richard Wesley; M: Tom Bahler.

Fast Getaway ♂♂½ 1991 (PG) Chases scenes proliferate when a teen criminal mastermind plots bank heists for his outlaw father. Relatively painless adolescent action-comedy, cleverly acted, quickly forgotten. 91m/C VHS. Corey Haim, Cynthia Rothrock, Leo Rossi, Ken Lerner, Marcia Strassman; D: Spiro Razatos.

Fast Getaway 2 ♂♂½ 1994 (PG-13) Ex-bank robber Nelson (Haim) has given up a life of crime to open a business with gal pal Patrice (Buxton) while waiting for his partner/dad Sam (Rossi) to get out of jail. Then Nelson gets set up by Lily (Rothrock) and finds himself trying to convince an FBI agent of his innocence. Innocuous. 90m/C VHS. Corey Haim, Sarah Buxton, Leo Rossi, Cynthia Rothrock, Peter Paul Liapis; D: Oley Sassone; W: Mark Sevi; M: David Robbins.

Fast Girl ♂½ 2007 (PG) After her dad is killed in a racing accident, Alex (Monroe) wants to prove she can win in the male-dominated sport. But her Uncle Bill (Brown), who runs the local speedway, refuses to allow her to compete, and a romance with driver Darryl (Guarini) messes with Alex's concentration. 85m/C

Fast Gun 🐶 *1973 (P)* Weapons-loving ex-CIA spook decides to take over a town—with your basic one lone hero to stop him. **90m/C VHS.** Richard Gates, Robert Dryer, Brenda Bakke, Cirio H. Santiago; **D:** Cirio H. Santiago; **W:** Joe Mari Avellana; **C:** Frederick Bailey; **C:** Ricardo Remias; **M:** Lorenio.

Fast Kill 🐶 *1973 (R)* A terrorist plot begins to fall apart when the conspirators fight among themselves. **94m/C VHS.** Tom Adams, Susie Hampton, Norman Shelley, Peter Halliday; **D:** Lindsay Shonteff.

Fast Money 🐶🐶 *1996 (R)* Car thief Jack Martin (and everyone else) with a brief-case containing $2.7 million. **93m/C VHS.** Yancy B-ller, Matt McCoy, John Ashton, Trevor Goddard, Andy Romano, Carole Cook, Patrika Darbo; **D:** Alexander Wright; **M:** Alexander Wright; **C:** Thomas Jewett; **M:** Tony Riparetti.

Fast Money 🐶🐶½ *1983* Three pals can't resist the temptation of big bucks from flying drugs in from Mexico, but they find danger along the way. **92m/C VHS.** Sammy Allred, Sonny Carl Davis; **D:** Doug Holloway.

The Fast Runner 🐶🐶🐶 *at the Fast Runner 2001 (R)* The first Inuktitut language feature film is a remarkably compelling drama based on an ancient Inuit legend. Atanarjuat (Natar Ungalaaq) movie-producer husband (Robert Dryer)... **172m/C VHS, DVD.** CA Pakkak Innuksuk, Natar Ungalaaq, Peter Henry Arnatsiaq, Sylvia Ivalu, Lucy Tulugarjuk; **D:** Zacharias Kunuk; **W:** Paul Apak Angilirq; **C:** Norman Cohn; **'01:** Director (Kunuk), Cannes '01: First Feature, Genie play, Score.

Fast Sofa 🐶🐶 *2001 (R)* Lowlife, smalltime L.A. drug dealer Rick (Busey) has a one-nighter with porn actress Ginger (Tilly) and decides to follow her to Palm Springs. Too bad her jealous (and violent) movie-producer husband (Roberts) is also about to show up. Based on the book by Bruce Craven. **91m/C VHS, DVD.** Jake Busey, Jennifer Tilly, Eric Roberts, Adam Goldberg, Crispin Glover, Natasha Lyonne, Bijou Phillips; **D:** Salome Breziner; **W:** Salome Breziner, Peter Chase, Bruce Craven; **C:** Dean Lent; **M:** William V. Malpede.

Fast Talking 🐶🐶🐶 *1986* The story of a quick-talking, incorrigible, 15-year-old Australian boy's humorous though tragic criminal schemes. The young protagonist slides his way through a life marked by a degenerate home life, a brother who holds no promise. **93m/C VHS, AU Steve Bisley, Tracy Mann, Peter Hehir, Dennis Moore, Rod Zuanic, Toni Allaylis, Chris Truswell; **D:** Ken Cameron; **W:** Ken Cameron.

Fast Times at Ridgemont High 🐶🐶🐶 *1982 (R)* Teens at a Southern California high school revel in sex, drugs, and rock 'n' roll. A full complement of student types meet at the Mall—that great suburban microcosm percolating with angst-ridden teen trials—to contemplate losing their virginity, plot skipping homeroom, and move inexorably closer to the end of their adolescence. The talented young cast became household names; Sean Penn is most excellent as the California surfer dude who antagonizes teacher Walston, aka "Aloha Mr. Hand." Based on the best-selling book by Cameron Crowe, it's one of the best of the genre. **91m/C VHS, DVD, HD DVD.** Sean Penn, Jennifer Jason Leigh, Judge Reinhold, Robert Romanus, Brian Backer, Phoebe Cates, Ray Walston, Scott Thomson, Vincent Schiavelli, Amanda Wyss, Forest Whitaker, Kelli Maroney, Eric Stoltz, Pamela Springsteen, James Russo, Martin Brest, Anthony Edwards, Nicolas Cage; **W:** Cameron Crowe; **C:** Matthew F. Leonetti. Natl. Film Reg. '05.

Fast Walking 🐶🐶 *1982 (R)* A prison guard sure hunting teens, a tycoon's daughter, his cousin has contracted to the same man his cousin has contracted to. **115m/C VHS.** James Woods, Kay Lenz, M. Emmet Walsh, Robert Hooks, Tim McIntire, Timothy Carey, Susan Tyrrell; **D:** James B. Harris.

Faster, Pussycat! Kill! Kill! 🐶🐶🐶 *The Leather Girls; Pussycat 1965* It doesn't get any better than this! Three sexy go-go dancers get their after-work kicks by hot-rodding in the California desert. They soon find themselves enwrapped in murder, kidnapping, lust and robbery after a particular race gets out of hand. Easily the most watchable, fun and funny production to spring from the mind of Russ Meyer. Those who haven't seen this cannot truly be called "cool." **83m/B VHS, DVD.** Tura Satana, Haji, Lori Williams, Susan Bernard, Stuart Lancaster, Paul Trinka, Dennis Busch; **D:** Russ Meyer, Mickey Foxx; **D:** Russ Meyer; **W:** Jack Moran, Russ Meyer; **C:** Walter Schenk; **M:** Paul Sawtell, Bert Shefter, The Bostweeds.

Fastest Guitar Alive 🐶½ *1968* Debut of the legendary Orbison is strictly for inveterate fans only. Rebel operative/crooner during the Civil War, whose rhythm is good but timing is bad, steals a Union gold supply, but the war ends before he makes it back to the land of Dixie. Seems that makes him a common thief. **88m/C VHS.** Roy Orbison, Sammy Jackson, Margaret Pierce, Joan Freeman; **D:** Michael D. Moore; **M:** Fred Karger.

Fastest Gun Alive 🐶🐶🐶 *1956* Suspenseful western with ex-gunfighter Ford challenged to a showdown by Crawford. **89m/C VHS.** Glenn Ford, Jeanne Crain, Broderick Crawford, Russ Tamblyn, Allyn Joslyn, Leif Erickson, John Dehner, Noah Beery Jr., J.M. Kerrigan, Rhys Williams; **D:** Russell Rouse; **W:** Russell Rouse, Frank D. Gilroy; **C:** George J. Folsey; **M:** Andre Previn.

Fat Albert 🐶🐶½ *2004 (PG)* Clunky live-action version of Bill Cosby's standup routines and the animated series "Fat Albert and the Cosby Kids." Depressed South Philly teen Doris (Pratt) is watching TV Land reruns of the show when a magic portal opens up allowing Fat Albert (an agreeable Thompson) and his gang to pop into her living room. F.A. feels obliged to offer advice to help Doris gain some self-esteem and even develops a crush on Doris' popular foster sister, Lauri (Ramirez). Meanwhile, the '70s-era tooners react to the real world of the 21st century in expected fish-out-of-water ways. Hey, hey, hey is more why, why, why? **93m/C VHS, DVD.** US Kenan Thompson, Kyle Pratt, Marques Houston, Dania Ramirez, Omari (Omarion), Shedrack Anderson III, Jermaine Williams, Keith D. Robinson, Alphonso McAuley, Aaron A. Frazier, J. Mack Slaughter; **Cameos:** Bill Cosby; **D:** Joel Zwick; **W:** Bill Cosby, Charles Kipps; **C:** Paul Elliot; **M:** Richard Gibbs.

Fat City 🐶🐶🐶½ *1972 (PG)* One of Huston's later triumphs, a seedy, street-level drama based on the Leonard Gardner novel about an aging alcoholic boxer trying to make a comeback and his young worshipful protege. Highly acclaimed. Tyrrell earned an Oscar nomination as the boxer's world-weary lover. **93m/C VHS, DVD.** Stacy Keach, Jeff Bridges, Susan Tyrrell, Candy Clark, Nicholas Colasanto; **D:** John Huston. **C:** Conrad L. Hall; **M:** Marvin Hamlisch.

Fat Guy Goes Nutzoid woof! *1986* A crude farce about an obese mental patient who escapes from the mental hospital and joins two teenagers on a wild trip to New York City. **85m/C VHS.** Tibor Feldman, Peter Linari, John MazKay, Joan Allen; **D:** John Golden; **M:** Leo Kottke.

Fat Man and Little Boy 🐶🐶½ *1989 (PG-13)* A lavish, semi-fictional account of the creation of the first atomic bomb, and the tensions between J. Robert Oppenheimer and his military employer, Gen. Leslie Groves. Overlong but interesting. Cusack whose character never existed, is especially worthwhile as an idealistic scientist. **127m/C VHS, DVD.** Paul Newman, Dwight Schultz, Bonnie Bedelia, John Cusack, Laura Dern, John C. McGinley, Natasha Richardson, Ron Frazier; **D:** Roland Joffe; **W:** Bruce Robinson, Tony Garnett, Roland Joffe; **M:** Ennio Morricone.

Fatal Beauty 🐶½ *1987 (R)* A female undercover cop in Los Angeles tracks down a crazy dealer selling cocaine (from which the title is taken). Elliott is the mob bodyguard who helps her out. Violent and sensational, the film tries to capitalize on the success of "Beverly Hills Cop" and falls miserably. Goldberg is wasted in this effort and the picture tiptoes around the interracial romance aspects that are implied. **104m/C VHS, DVD.** Whoopi Goldberg, Sam Elliott, Ruben Blades, Harris Yulin, Brad Dourif; **D:** Tom Holland; **W:** Hilary Henkin, Dean Riesner; **C:** David M. Walsh; **M:** Harold Faltermeyer.

Fatal Bond 🐶🐶 *1991 (R)* Blair plays a small-town hairdresser caught in an obsessive love affair with a drifter. When she suspects her boyfriend is committing a string of rape-murders, will she turn him in or protect him? Or is she next? **89m/C VHS.** Linda Blair, Jerome Ehlers, Stephen Leeder, Donal Gibson, Caz Lederman, Tao Gerbert, Penny Pedersen, Joe Bugner; **D:** Vincent Monton; **W:** Phillip Avalon.

Fatal Charm 🐶🐶 *1992 (R)* There's a serial killer at work in a small town. So far six women have been raped and murdered. But cute-teen Valerie can't believe it when the townspeople accuse that sweet guy Adam, especially since he's the one boy Valerie is so very attracted to. **90m/C VHS.** Amanda Peterson, Mary Frann, James Remar, Andrew Robinson, Peggy Lipton; **D:** Alan Smithee; **W:** Nicholas Niciphor.

Fatal Chase 🐶🐶 *Nowhere to Hide 1977* Van Cleef is a U.S. Marshal assigned to protect ex-hitman Musante from his vengeful former employers. And you thought you didn't get along with your boss. Typical made-for-TV fodder written by Anhalt, who usually manages to be a trifle more entertaining. **78m/C VHS.** Lee Van Cleef, Tony Musante, Charles Robinson, Lelia Goldoni, Noel Fournier, Russell Johnson, Edward Anhalt; **D:** Jack Starrett; **W:** Edward Anhalt.

Fatal Error 🐶🐶½ *1999* Digicron, the world's largest media company, is about to connect all the televisions and computers worldwide. But Dr. Nick Baldwin (Sabato Jr.) and Army medical researcher Samantha Carter (Turner) discover that people are dying from an untraceable virus. So is the virus linked to Digicron. Well, what do you think? Adapted from the novel "Reaper" by Ben Mezrich. **91m/C VHS, DVD.** Antonio Sabato Jr., Janine Turner, Robert Wagner, Malcolm Stewart; **C:** David Geddes; **M:** Ron Ramin. **CABLE**

Fatal Exposure 🐶🐶 *1990* The inevitably sanguinary Jack the Ripper lives on in the form of his great grandson, who evades himself of modern technology to capture those magic moments on videotape. Just goes to show home movies can be bland. **96m/C VHS.** Blake Bahner, Ena Henderson, Julie Austin, Dan Schmale, Renee Cline, Gary Wise, Joy Ovington; **D:** Peter B. Good; **W:** Christopher Painter; **C:** Peter B. Good; **M:** Dean Richard Marino.

Fatal Exposure 🐶🐶 *1991 (PG-13)* A divorcee on vacation with her young sons accidentally picks up the wrong snapshots at the developers'. It turns out she has her hands on some incriminating photos, and the subject will resort to anything, even murder, to keep her quiet. **89m/C VHS.** Mare Winningham, Nick Mancuso, Christopher McDonald, Geoffrey Blake, Christopher Pettiet; **D:** Alan Metzger. **TV**

Fatal Fix 🐶½ *1984* Young female athletes are mysteriously disappearing at the Falcon Academy of Athletics and a crazed killer is responsible. **88m/C VHS.** Sally Kirkland, Lynn Banashek, Sean Masterson, Teal Roberts; **D:** Michael Elliot; **W:** Michael Elliot; **C:** Alfred Taylor; **M:** Shuki Levy.

Fatal Attraction 🐶🐶 *Head On 1980 (R)* Couple meet after an auto accident. They begin an affair which turns dark and bizarre. Fine cast doesn't get far with this peculiar premise, although every one tries hard. **90m/C VHS.** CA Sally Kellerman, Stephen Lack, John Huston, Lawrence Dane; **D:** Michael Grant.

Fatal Attraction 🐶🐶🐶 *1987 (R)* When a very married New York lawyer is seduced by a beautiful blonde associate, the one-night stand leads to terror as she continues to pursue the relationship. She begins to threaten his family and home with possessive, violent acts. An expertly made, manipulative thriller, one of the most hotly discussed films of the 1980s. A successful change of role for Close as the sexy, scorned, and deadly other woman. Also available in a special "director's edition," featuring Lyne's original, controversial ending. **120m/C VHS, DVD.** Michael Douglas, Glenn Close, Anne Archer, Stuart Pankin, Ellen Hamilton-Latzen, Ellen Foley, Fred Gwynne, Meg Mundy, J.J. Johnston; **D:** Adrian Lyne; **W:** James Dearden; **C:** Howard Atherton; **M:** Maurice Jarre.

The Fat Spy woof! *1966* Campy beach movie parody has a gaggle of treasure hunting teens, a tycoon's daughter, her boyfriend, his twin brother, and the twin's girlfriend descending on an island off the Florida coast looking for the Fountain of Youth. Flick tries hard, with plenty of (awful) "rock" music by The Wild Ones, Jayne Mansfield, and Phyllis Diller among the participants wildly mugging for laughs. None of it works, as parody or straight comedy. Unless you're a fan of ultra-bad quickie exploitation, don't bother. **75m/C VHS, DVD.** Phyllis Diller, Jack E. Leonard, Brian Donlevy, Jayne Mansfield, Joseph Brun, Joel Hirschborn, Al Kasha; **D:** Joseph Brun; **M:** Al Kasha.

Fatal Combat 🐶½ *No Exit 1996 (R)* Reclusive billionaire Houston Armstrong (Fitzpatrick) privately broadcasts a program called "No Exit" that features a convict forced to run out of combatants so strong tends to run out of combatants so hard with all these people running around screaming and dying. **83m/C VHS, Jooly Fichardson, Scott Cohen, Stacy Keach, Justina Machado, Ann Cusack, David Ramsey; **D:** Richard Pearce; **W:** Ron McGee; **C:** Ivan Strasburg; **M:** Mark Adler. **TV**

Fatal Contact: Bird Flu in America 🐶 *2006* Oh no! Another really terrible disaster flick! Avian flu has mutated and is now transmittable from human to human, which causes widespread panic. Poor scientist Iris Varnack (Richardson) is trying to come up with a vaccine or something but gosh darn, it's just too hard with all these people running around screaming and dying! **83m/C VHS, DVD.** Joely Richardson, Scott Cohen, Stacy Keach, Justina Machado, Ann Cusack, David Ramsey; **D:** Richard Pearce; **W:** Ron McGee; **C:** Ivan Strasburg; **M:** Mark Adler. **TV**

Fatal Confinement 🐶🐶½ *1564* Wrenching drama finds Crawford, having lived 15 years in seclusion with her young daughter, forced to sell her land to a giant corporation bent on expansion. Interesting also for the similarities to Crawford's real life "Mommie Dearest" lifestyle. **70m/C VHS.** GB Joan Crawford, Paul Burke, Charles Bickford; **D:** Robert Guest.

Fatal Games 🐶½ *1984 Young female athletes are mysteriously disappearing at the Falcon Academy of Athletics and a crazed killer is responsible. Music by the Pretenders. **90m/C VHS.** FR Helmut Berger, Corinne Clery; **D:** Massimo Pirri.

hend Dion in Hong Kong and bring him back to face charges in the Philippines. But Dion escapes and the duo are forced to deal with local officer Philip in order to get Dion back. Dubbed into English. **96m/C VHS.** HK Robin Shou, Yukari Oshima, Waise Lee; **D:** Ki Yee Chik.

The Fatal Hour ♂♂½ **1940** Karloff is enlisted to aid police in solving the murder of a detective. As Karloff is rounding up suspects, three more murders take place. Feeble. **66m/B VHS, DVD.** Boris Karloff, Marjorie Reynolds, Grant Withers, Charles Trowbridge, John Hamilton, Frank Puglia, Jason Robards Sr.; **D:** William Nigh; **W:** Scott Darling, George Wagner; **C:** Harry Neumann.

The Fatal Image ♂♂½ **1990** A mother and daughter on vacation in Paris inadvertently videotape the photographer to investigate. **90m/C VHS.** Lane Coyle; **D:** Dennis Devine; **W:** Dennis Devine, Mike Bowler, Steve Jarvis.

Fatal Images ♂ **1989** A camera mysteriously causes all the models who pose for it to die, prompting the photographer to investigate. **90m/C VHS.** Lane Coyle; **D:** Dennis Devine; **W:** Dennis Devine, Mike Bowler, Steve Jarvis.

Fatal Instinct ♂½ **1992 (R)** A tough-guy cop trying to solve a murder instead finds himself a victim of sexual obsession in this erotic thriller. Also available in an unrated version. Not to be confused with (but doesn't everything sound familiar) "Basic Instinct." **93m/C VHS.** Michael Madsen, Laura Johnson, Antony (Tony) Hamilton; **D:** John Dirlam.

Fatal Instinct ♂♂ **1993 (PG-13)** Spoof on erotic thrillers such as "Fatal Attraction" and "Basic Instinct." Suave Assante plays a guy with dual careers—he's both cop and attorney, defending the criminals he's arrested. Young plays a lovelorn psycho who's lost her panties. Plot is worth mentioning only in passing, since the point is to mercilessly skewer the entire film noir tradition. The gags occasionally hit dead-chuckle level, though for every good joke there's at least three that misfire. Clemons of "E Street Band" fame wanders around with sax for background music purposes, typical of the acute self-consciousness of the film. **90m/C VHS, DVD.** Armand Assante, Sean Young, Sherilyn Fenn, Kate Nelligan, Christopher McDonald, James Remar, Tony Randall; **Cameos:** Clarence Clemons, Doc Severinsen; **D:** Carl Reiner; **W:** David O'Malley; **M:** Richard Gibbs.

A Fatal Inversion ♂♂½ **1992** When 19-year-old Hodge inherits a remote English estate from his great-uncle, he invites best friend Northam to spend a carefree summer, after both have told their parents they're vacationing in Greece. The boys are soon joined by Todd, Ford, and Warnecke in an informal commune but several disasters cause them to break off all contact for 12 years—until the remains of two bodies are discovered on the grounds and a police investigation is started. Made for British TV, based on the psychological thriller by Ruth Rendell (writing as Barbara Vine). **150m/C VHS. GB** Douglas Hodge, Jeremy Northam, Saira Todd, Julia Ford, Gordon Warnecke, Nicholas Woodeson, Peter Attard, Rachel Joyce, Nicholas Le Prevost, Ben Chaplin; **D:** Tim Fywell; **W:** Sandy Welch; **C:** Barry McCann; **M:** David Ferguson. **TV**

Fatal Justice ♂ **1993** Mars is a topnotch assassin who's been in the business too long and knows too much so the agency he works for decides to kill him off. They send young and beautiful professional Diana to do the job but will she be able to when she discovers Mars is actually her father? **90m/C VHS, DVD.** Suzanne Ager, Richard Folmer, Tom Bertino, Joe Estevez; **D:** Gerald Cain; **W:** Bret McCormick; **C:** Gerald Cain; **M:** Jeff Walton.

Fatal Mission ♂ **1989 (R)** A Vietnam soldier captures a female Chinese guerilla and uses her as his hostage and guide through the jungle. **84m/C VHS, DVD.** Peter Fonda, Mako, Tia Carrere, Ted Markland, Jim Mitchum; **D:** George Rowe; **C:** Phil Parmet.

Fatal Passion ♂♂ **1994** Two sisters escape from the city after an accidental murder but run straight into the middle of a sacrificial backwoods cult. **90m/C VHS, DVD.** Lisa Hayland, Joe Pilato; **D:** Hugh Parks; **C:** Greg Patterson.

Fatal Past ♂♂ **1994 (R)** Bodyguard gets up close and personal with his client—who happens to be a mobster's mistress. As if this weren't trouble enough their pasts provide doom and gloom as well. **85m/C VHS.** Costas Mandylor, Kasia (Katarzyna) Figura; **D:** Clive Fleury; **W:** Richard Ryan.

Fatal Pulse Woof! **1988** Sorority girls are being killed off in grisly ways. Basic slasher/gore. **90m/C VHS.** Michelle McCormick, Ken Roberts, Joe Estevez, Alex Courtney; **D:** Anthony J. Christopher; **W:** James Hundhausen; **C:** David Lewis; **M:** Martin Mayo.

Fatal Skies ♂ **1990** An evil schemer plots to dump toxic waste in a small town's water supply until a group of teens comes to the rescue. **88m/C VHS.** Tim Burke, J. Michael Esposito, Maureen Burns, Timothy Leary; **D:** Thomas Dugan; **C:** Glenn Kershaw; **M:** Daniel May.

Fatal Vision ♂♂½ **1984** TV-murder-of-the-week version of Joe McGinniss's controversial book about the murder trial of Dr. Jeffrey MacDonald, the former Green Beret physician accused of murdering his whole family and blaming the killings on crazed hippies. McGinniss first believed MacDonald may have been innocent but his subsequent investigation, and his book, proved otherwise. Starring debut for Cole, who would go on to play a much better TV dad. MacDonald still protests his innocence. **192m/C VHS.** Gary Cole, Karl Malden, Eva Marie Saint, Wendy Schaal, Barry Corbin, Gary Grubbs, Scott Paulin, Albert Salmi; **D:** David Greene; **W:** John Gay; **C:** Stevan Larner; **M:** Gil Melle. **TV**

Fatally Yours ♂♂ **1995** Real-estate agent Danny (Rossovich) decides to restore a long-vacant house where a mob massacre occurred in 1928. While in the house, he's "contacted" by the ghostly Sara (MacDonnell), whose husband and gangster father were among the dead. Sara tells him about a hidden treasure of jewels, which leads some present-day gangsters to take an interest in Danny's new property. **90m/C VHS.** Rick Rossovich, George Lazenby, Roddy McDowall, Sage Stallone, Sarah MacDonnell; **D:** Tim Everitt; **C:** Tim Everitt.

Fate ♂♂½ **1990 (PG-13)** Sweet comedy. A young man plans his love-affair carefully, but his biggest problem is meeting the girl of his dreams. Cheerful acting from Lynn and Paul. Stylish and charming. **115m/C VHS.** Cheryl Lynn, Stuart Paul, Kaye Ballard, Susannah York; **D:** Stuart Paul.

Fateless ♂♂♂½ *Sorstalanság* **2005** Gyuri is a 14-year-old Hungarian Jewish boy subjected to the horrors of three different concentration camps, surviving only to find isolation in the world around him. An emphasis on the dehumanization of the Jews as they were corralled into these camps gives a unique look and tone from that of other Holocaust pictures. Muddy and miserable perspective is nonetheless visually beautiful. Adapted from a novel by Nobel Prize-winning author Imre Kertesz. **114m/C DVD. HU GE GB** Marcell Nagy, Daniel Craig, Aron Dimeny, Andras M. Kecskes, Jozsef Gyabronka, Endre Harkanyi, Janos Ban, Judit Schell; **D:** Lajos Koltai; **W:** Imre Kertesz; **C:** Gyula Pados; **M:** Ennio Morricone.

Father ♂♂ *Apa* **1967** After WWII, a Hungarian youth makes up stories about his dead father's heroism that enhance his own position. Eventually he becomes obsessed with the facts surrounding his father's death at the hands of the enemy and, learning the truth, lays the past to rest. In Hungarian with English subtitles. **85m/B VHS, DVD. HU** Andras Balint, Miklos Gabor; **D:** Istvan Szabo; **W:** Istvan Szabo.

Father ♂♂ **1990 (PG-13)** A woman receives an anonymous telephone call telling her to watch a TV news program and learn the truth about her beloved father. What she sees is her father's face superimposed over that of a young Nazi soldier and an aging, unstable woman accusing her father of war crimes. The daughter fiercely believes her father to be a victim of mistaken identity but questions keep nagging at her. Very similar in plot to "Music Box" and just as pedestrian in spite of some good performances. **106m/C VHS. AU**

Max von Sydow, Carol Drinkwater, Julia Blake, Steve Jacobs; **D:** John Power. Australian Film Inst. '90: Actor (von Sydow), Actress (Blake).

Father and Scout ♂♂ **1994 (PG)** Would-be Eagle Scout Michael (Bonsall) has a problem when he takes his citybred, whiny, basically incompetent, dad Spenser (Saget) on a camping trip. Made for TV. **92m/C VHS, DVD.** Bob Saget, Brian Bonsall, Heidi Swedberg, Stuart Pankin, Troy Evans; **D:** Richard Michaels; **M:** David Kitay. **TV**

Father and Son ♂♂♂ **2003** Intense look at a father-son relationship. The father (Sheltin), a widower, and son (Neimyshev) have lived a largely hermetic life, creating a relationship that more closely resembles partners than of father and son (and not in the business sense either). As each face new choices, however, they are forced to realize that they may have to let go of their dependence on each other. Second chapter of Alexander Sokurov's trilogy on family relationships, the first being "Mother and Son". **83m/C DVD. GE** Andrei Shetinin, Alexei Neimyshev, Alexander Rasbash; **D:** Alexander Sokurov; **W:** Sergei Potepalov; **C:** Alexander Burov; **M:** Andrei Sigle.

The Father Clements Story ♂♂½ **1987** The true story of a black priest in Chicago who battled the Roman Catholic hierarchy in order to adopt a troubled teenager. **100m/C VHS.** Louis Gossett Jr., Malcolm Jamal Warner, Carroll O'Connor, Leon Robinson, Rosetta LeNoire, Ron McClarty; **D:** Edwin Sherin. **TV**

Father Figure ♂♂½ **1980** When a divorced man attends his ex-wife's funeral, he discovers that he must take care of his estranged sons. Well-done drama based on young adult writer Richard Peck's novel. **94m/C VHS.** Hal Linden, Timothy Hutton, Cassie Yates, Martha Scott, Jeremy Licht; **D:** Jerry London; **M:** Billy Goldenberg. **TV**

Father Goose ♂♂½ **1964** During WWII, a liquor-loving plane-spotter stationed on a remote Pacific isle finds himself stuck with a group of French refugee schoolgirls and their teacher. Some predictable gags, romance, and heroism fill out the running time pleasantly. Scriptwriters Stone and Tarloff, who were competitors, not collaborators on the project, shared an Oscar. **116m/C VHS, DVD.** Cary Grant, Leslie Caron, Trevor Howard; **D:** Ralph Nelson; **W:** Peter Stone, Frank Tarloff; **C:** Charles B(ryant) Lang Jr.; **M:** Cy Coleman. Oscars '64: Story & Screenplay.

Father Hood ♂ **1993 (PG-13)** Family drama has Swayze playing a small-time criminal whose daughter tracks him down after leaving the foster-care shelter where she and her brother are being abused. The family takes to the road, running from both the police and a journalist (Berry) who wants to expose the corrupt foster-care system. The children are obnoxious, Swayze is miscast, and the entire film is a misfire. **94m/C VHS, DVD.** Patrick Swayze, Halle Berry, Sabrina Lloyd, Brian Bonsall, Diane Ladd, Michael Ironside, Bob Gunton; **D:** Darrell Roodt; **W:** Scott Spencer.

Father of Lies ♂♂½ **2007** Bishop Calvin Jacobs (Powell) has a drinking problem and a church that's deep in debt and he's willing to go to some unscrupulous means to save his ministry. He learns that not trusting in the Lord is his biggest mistake. **102m/C DVD.** Clifton Powell, Vivica A. Fox, DMX, Clyde Jones, Veronica Berry, Lucius Basten; **D:** Phenomenon; **W:** Anthony Faia, Evan Scott.

Father of the Bride ♂♂♂½ **1950** A classic, quietly hilarious comedy about the tribulations of a father preparing for his only daughter's wedding. Tracy is suitably overwhelmed as loving father Stanley Banks and Taylor radiant as the bride, Kay. A warm vision of American family life, accompanied by the 1940 MGM short "Wedding Bills." Followed by "Father's Little Dividend" (1951) and later a TV series. Remade in 1991. **106m/C VHS, DVD.** Spencer Tracy, Elizabeth Taylor, Joan Bennett, Billie Burke, Leo G. Carroll, Russ Tamblyn, Don Taylor, Moroni Olsen; **D:** Vincente Minnelli; **W:** Frances Goodrich, Albert Hackett; **C:** John Alton.

Father of the Bride ♂♂ **1991 (PG)** Remake of the 1950 comedy classic portrays one of the most overextravagant weddings in recent film history, but falls short of the original. Predictable plot and characters don't hide any surprises, but nothing detracts from the purpose of the film: to be a nice, charming movie. Martin is fine as the reluctant dad but Keaton is little more than window dressing as the bride's mom; Short is annoying as a pretentious wedding coordinator. Williams pulls off a nice film debut—and was almost immediately cast in a TV ad as a young-bride-to-be calling her dad long distance to tell him she's engaged. Adapted from a novel by Edward Streeter. **105m/C VHS, DVD.** Steve Martin, Diane Keaton, Kimberly Williams, Kieran Culkin, George Newbern, Martin Short, B.D. Wong, George Michael Goetz, Kate McGregor-Stewart, Martha Gehman, Eugene Levy; **D:** Charles Shyer; **W:** Charles Shyer, Nancy Meyers; **C:** John Lindley; **M:** Alan Silvestri.

Father of the Bride Part 2 ♂♂½ **1995 (PG)** Sweetly sentimental update of the 1951 film "Father's Little Dividend" finds George Banks (Martin) once again thrown for a loop—first by his beloved daughter Annie's (Williams) pregnancy and then by wife Nina's (the radiant Keaton) announcement that they are about to become parents themselves. George doesn't deal very well with either situation but, aided by fey party planner Franck (Short), he manages to get through the predictable chaos. Martin's physical expressiveness and sly charm are a big plus. **106m/C VHS, DVD.** Steve Martin, Diane Keaton, Kimberly Williams, Martin Short, George Newbern, Kieran Culkin, Peter Michael Goetz, Kate McGregor-Stewart, Eugene Levy, B.D. Wong, Jane Adams; **D:** Charles Shyer; **W:** Nancy Meyers, Charles Shyer; **C:** William A. Fraker; **M:** Alan Silvestri.

Father Was a Fullback ♂♂½ **1949** College football coach (MacMurray) has a losing team, problems with the administration and alumni, and two daughters with growing pains at home. Wife O'Hara supplies the sympathetic shoulder. **99m/B VHS.** Fred MacMurray, Maureen O'Hara, Betty Lynn, Rudy Vallee, Thelma Ritter, Natalie Wood, Jim Backus; **D:** John M. Stahl; **W:** Mary Loos, Casey Robinson, Richard Sale; **C:** Lloyd Ahern; **M:** Cyril Mockridge.

Fatherland ♂♂½ **1994** It's 1964 and 20 years earlier Hitler has won WWII in this what-if TV movie. The Nazi leader is about to sign a historic alliance with the U.S. President in Berlin when a series of murders of high-ranking Third Reich officers begins. SS detective Xavier March (Hauer) investigates, along with visiting American journalist Charlie Maguire (Richardson), leading the two to the Gestapo coverup of the Holocaust. If the secret gets out it could ruin the summit, so guess who's in big danger? Intriguing premise but the thriller fails to sustain tension. Based on the novel by Robert Harris. Filmed in Prague, Czech Republic. **106m/C VHS.** Rutger Hauer, Miranda Richardson, Peter Vaughan, Jean Marsh, Michael Kitchen, John Woodvine, John Shrapnel, Clare Higgins; **D:** Christopher Menaul; **W:** Stanley Weiser, Ron Hutchinson; **C:** Peter Sova; **M:** Gary Chang.

Fathers and Sons ♂♂½ **1992** Max is a brooding, former bad-boy movie director living on the Jersey Shore. His wife's death causes him to rethink his life and deal with his drinking problem. He also tries to get to know his equally brooding teenage son, Ed. Turns out addiction may run in the family as Ed experiments with drugs. Ill-fitting subplot deals a serial killer stalking the community. Goldblum brings an uneasy gentleness to the father's role in an otherwise slow, talky, and obviously symbolic flick. **100m/C VHS.** Jeff Goldblum, Rory Cochrane, Mitchell Marchand, Famke Janssen, Natasha Gregson Wagner, Ellen Greene, Samuel L. Jackson, Joie Lee, Rosanna Arquette, Michael Disend; **D:** Paul Mones; **W:** Paul Mones; **C:** Ron Fortunato; **M:** Mason Daring.

Father's Day ♂♂½ **1996 (PG-13)** The comedy team of Williams and Crystal makes its feature film debut in this affable take on fatherhood. Freelance writer Putley (Williams) unites with attorney Law-

Faust: Love of the Damned ♦♦ 2000 (R) Very gory, visually impressive horror flick finds artist John Jaspers (Frost) selling his soul to Lucifer minion "M" (Divoff) in exchange for revenge on his wife's killers. Eventually, he gets sent to hell but returns as avenger Faust (in a red rubber suit). There's also a good guy detective (Combs) and a troubled shrink named Jade (Brook) involved in the action. Based on the comic book by Tim Vigil and David Quinn. An unrated version is also available. **96m/C VHS, DVD.** *Mark Frost, Andrew Divoff, Jeffrey Combs, Isabel Brook;* **D:** *Brian Yuzna;* **W:** *David Quinn;* **C:** *Jacques Haitkin;* **M:** *Xavier Capellas.*

Faust ♦♦♦½ *Faust-Eine deutsche Volkssage* 1526 The classic German silent based upon the legend of Faust, who sells his soul to the devil in exchange for youth. Based on Goethe's poem, and directed by Murnau as a classic example of Germanic expressionism. Remade as "All That Money Can Buy" in 1941. 117m/B VHS, DVD. GE *Emil Jannings, Werner Fuetterer, Gosta Ekman, Camilla Horn;* **D:** *F.W. Murnau;* **W:** *Hans Kyser;* **C:** *Carl Hoffmann;* **M:** *Timothy Brock, Werner R. Heymann.* **VIDEO**

Father's Little Dividend ♦♦♦ 1951 Tracy expects a little peace and quiet now that he's successfully married off Taylor. If this charming sequel to "Father of the Bride." However, he's quickly disillusioned by the news he'll soon be a grandfather—a prospect that causes nothing but dismay. Reunited the stars, director, writers, and producer from the successful first film. **82m/B VHS, DVD.** *Spencer Tracy, Joan Bennett, Elizabeth Taylor, Don Taylor, Billie Burke, Russ Tamblyn, Moroni Olsen;* **D:** *Vincente Minnelli;* **W:** *Frances Goodrich, Albert Hackett;* **C:** *John Alton;* **M:** *Albert Sendrey.*

A Father's Revenge ♦♦½ 1988 (R) Dennehy is the only reason to bother with this average hostage drama. He's the father of a stewardess who's one of a group being held by terrorists. They're scheduled to die in 72 hours unless Dennehy can find a way to rescue them. **93m/C VHS, DVD.** *Brian Dennehy, Joanna Cassidy, Ron Silver;* **D:** *John Herzfeld.* **TV**

Fathom ♦♦½ 1967 Welch and her bikini fill out the title role as Fathom Harvill, a parachutist who is hired to find a nuclear triggering device that has been lost in the Mediterranean. She eventually hooks up with spy guy Peter Merriweather (Franciosa) and gets involved in a case involving priceless jewelry stolen from China. Spy spoof is on so '60s. Based on the novel by Larry Forrester. **104m/C VHS, DVD.** *Raquel Welch, Anthony (Tony) Franciosa, Ronald Fraser, Clive Revill, Richard Briers, Tom Adams;* **D:** *Leslie Martinson;* **W:** *Lorenzo Semple Jr.;* **C:** *Douglas Slocombe;* **M:** *John Dankworth.*

Fatso ♦♦½ 1980 (PG) After the shocking death of his obese cousin, an obsessive overeater struggles to overcome his neurosis with the aid of his sister and a self-help group called "Chubby Checkers." Bancroft's first work as both writer and director. **93m/C VHS, DVD.** *Dom DeLuise, Anne Bancroft, Ron Carey, Candice Azzara;* **D:** *Anne Bancroft.*

Fatty Finn ♦♦½ 1984 A children's gagfest about young kids and bullies during the Depression, on Syd Nicholls comic strip. **91m/C VHS, AU** *Ben Oxenbould, Bart Newton;* **D:** *Maurice Murphy.*

Fatwa ♦♦ 2006 Junior senator Maggie Davidson (Holly) lets her ambitions get the better of her when she takes a hard-line stance on Islamic terrorism. She attracts the notice of a D.C. sleeper cell that may decide to make a point. **91m/C DVD.** *National Mall to make a point.* **91m/C DVD. US** *Lauren Holly, Rachel Miner, John Doman, Lacey Chabert, Angus MacFadyen, Mykelti Williamson, Ryan Sands;* **D:** *John Carter;* **W:** *Scott Schafer;* **C:** *Brian Gurley.* **VIDEO**

Fay Grim ♦♦ 2006 (R) Hartley's sequel to 1998's "Henry Fool" follows the misbegotten adventures of Henry's estranged wife Fay (Posey). Henry's been on the lam for years, but CIA op Fulbright (Goldblum) suddenly turns up and informs Fay that A) Henry's dead; B) Henry was in the CIA; C) his notebook memoirs are actually coded secrets; and D) Fay needs to retrieve them from Paris. So Fay agrees to capture the wretched excess of the book. Thompson's screen alter-ego Duke (Depp) packs his Caddy with illicit drugs and his equally wasted lawyer (Del Toro), and heads for his next writing assignment—to cover a drug enforcement conference in Vegas. Depp does a great job of impersonating the completely wasted Thompson, while Del Toro passes out and pukes a lot in the sidekick role. It's most definitely a one-of-a-kind trip, but not one that most people will be willing to take. **118m/C VHS, DVD, HD DVD.** *Johnny Depp, Benicio Del Toro, Christina Ricci, Gary Busey, Craig Bierko, Ellen Barkin, Cameron Diaz, Flea, Mark Harmon, Katherine Helmond, Michael Jeter, Penn Jillette, Lyle Lovett, Tobey Ma-*

FBI Girl ♦♦ 1952 An FBI clerk is used as bait to trap a murderer and break up a gang. Burr, pre-Perry Mason, plays a bad guy. **74m/B VHS, DVD.** *Cesar Romero, George Brent, Audrey Totter, Raymond Burr, Tom Drake;* **D:** *William Berke.*

The Favor, the Watch, & the Very Big Fish ♦♦ 1992 (R) Set in a fairytale version of Paris, Hoskins is a photographer of religious subjects searching for a man to pose as Jesus. He discovers his subject in the hirsute Goldblum, a mad bar pianist who actually thinks he's the savior. Richardson plays the object of Hoskins's shy affections, an actress who does dubbing work by providing the moan—attempt at screwball-comedy with some brief humorous moments. **89m/C VHS, GB** *FR Jack Arnold, Bob Hoskins, Jeff Goldblum, Natasha Richardson, Michel Blanc, Jacques Villeret, Angela Pleasence, Jean-Pierre Cassel, Bruce Altman;* **D:** *Ben Lewin;* **W:** *Ben Lewin;* **C:** *Bernard Zitzermann;* **M:** *Vladimir Cosma.*

The Favorite Son ♦♦♦ *Le Fils Préféré* 1994 Troubled family history is examined between three adult French brothers and their Italian immigrant father. A dutiful son, hotel manager Jean-Paul (Lanvin) regularly visits elderly father Raphael (Herlitzka). But Jean-Paul has problems. Desperate for cash to pay his loan shark, he approaches estranged younger brother Philippe (Barr), a wealthy lawyer, who is loath to help, while older school teacher brother Francis (Giraudeau) has little spare cash. Jean-Paul decides to take out a life insurance policy on dad—who promptly disappears—leaving the brothers to reluctantly come to terms in order to find him. French with subtitles. **100m/C VHS.** *FR Gerard Lanvin, Jean-Marc Barr, Bernard Giraudeau, Roberto Herlitzka, Marguerite Buy;* **D:** *Nicole Garcia;* **W:** *Nicole Garcia;* **C:** *Eric Gautier;* **M:** *Philippe Sarde.* César '95, Actor (Lanvin).

The Favor ♦♦½ 1992 (R) Lighthearted romance rife with comic confusion, vivid fantasies, secrets, and the all-important favor. Kathy (Kozak) seeks to relieve the boredom of her marriage through best friend Emily's (McGovern) torrid love affairs. Tom. Or so she thinks, until Em spills all the juicy details. In a change of pace, the males take a back seat to the women. Good comic performances from Kozak and McGovern and witty dialogue are his subplot. Theatrical release was delayed three years due to financial crisis at Orion Pictures. **97m/C VHS, DVD.** *Harley Jane Kozak, Elizabeth McGovern, Bill Pullman, Brad Pitt, Ken Wahl, Larry Miller, Holland Taylor;* **D:** *Donald Petrie;* **M:** *Thomas Newman.*

Fear ♦♦ 1990 (R) A young psychic chologist (Sheedy) delves into the minds of serial killers and writes novels about her experiences. But what happens when the next killer is also a psychic and decides to play mind-games with her? Above-average suspense sustains this cable thriller. **96m/C VHS, DVD.** *Ally Sheedy, Lauren Hutton, Michael O'Keefe, Stan Shaw, Dina Merrill, John Agar, Marki DuBois;* **D:** *Rockne S. O'Bannon;* **M:** *Henry Mancini.* **CABLE**

Fear ♦♦½ 1996 (R) Wahlberg (the former Marky Mark) is a parents' worse nightmare: the violent, obsessed boyfriend of a 16-year-old girl (Witherspoon) as "Fatal Attraction" goes to the prom. Some cleverness, but ultimately follows a familiar, clichéd path littered with one-dimensional characters and predictable plot twists. Gory, unconvincing climax kills any credibility that was left. The one standout is Petersen as the girl's protective father. **96m/C VHS, DVD.** *Reese Witherspoon, Mark Wahlberg, William L. Petersen, Amy Brenneman, Alyssa Milano, Tracy Fraim, Christopher Gray, Todd Caldecott;* **D:** *James Foley;* **W:** *Christopher Crowe;* **C:** *Thomas Kloss;* **M:** *Carter Burwell.* MTV Movie Awards '97: Song ("Machinehead").

Fear ♦♦ 1946 An impoverished medical student murders the professor he believes is tormenting him and his life suddenly gets better. He falls in love and gets a scholarship but the police are closing in on his crime. Except...did any of it really happen? Or is he suffering from hallucinations. Low-budget psycho-drama with some good paranoid moments. **68m/B VHS.** *Peter Cookson, Warren William, Anne Gwynne, James B. Cardwell, Nestor Paiva;* **D:** *Alfred Zeisler.*

Fear ♦ *Honor Betrayed* 1988 (R) A vacationing family is plagued by a murderous Vietnam vet and other psychotic consciences. **96m/C VHS, DVD, Edward (Eddie) Bunker, Frank Stallone, Cliff DeYoung, Kay Lenz, Robert Factor;** **D:** *Robert A. Ferretti.*

The FBI Story ♦♦♦ 1959 Mr. Stewart goes to Washington in this anatomy of the Federal Bureau of Investigation. If you're a fan of the gangster genre (LeRoy earlier directed "Little Caesar"), and not especially persnickety about fidelity to the facts, this actioner offers a pseudo-factual (read fictional) glimpse—based on actual cases from the 1920s through the 1950s—into the life of a fictitious agent-family man. **149m/C VHS, DVD.** *James Stewart, Vera Miles, Nick Adams, Murray Hamilton, Larry Pennell, Diane Jergens, Jean Willes, Joyce Taylor, Ann Doran, Parley Baer, Victor Millan;* **D:** *Mervyn LeRoy;* **W:** *Richard L. Breen, John Twist;* **C:** *Joseph Biroc;* **M:** *Max Steiner.*

Fear, Anxiety and Depression ♦♦½ 1989 (R) A neurotic aspiring playwright in New York has various problems with his love life. Subtle Woody Allen comedy attempt, with a few bright spots. The dregs of New York, with all the violence and degradation, are brought to the screen here. **84m/C VHS.** *Todd Solondz, Stanley Tucci;* **D:** *Todd Solondz.*

The Fear Chamber WOOf! *Torture Zone; Chamber of Fear; La Camara del Terror; Torture Chamber* 1968 Hardly a Karloff vehicle. Boris isn't the footage for this and three other Mexican "horror" films in LA, an unfortunate swan song to his career, though he was fortunate to be quickly written out of this story. The near plot concerns a mutant rock that thrives on human fear. Doctor Karloff and his assistants make sure the rock is rolling in sacrificial victims (women, of course). A prodigious devaluation of the "B" grade horror flick. It's so bad it's just bad. **88m/C VHS, DVD.** MX *Boris Karloff, Yerye Beirut, Julissa, Carlos East, Sandra Chavez, Eva Muller, Pamela Rosas, Santanon, Isela Vega;* **D:** *Juan Ibanez, Jack Hill;* **C:** *Juan Enrique Vergara;* **C:** *Austin McKinney;* **M:** *Raul Dominguez.*

Fear City ♦♦½ 1985 (R) Two partners who own a talent agency are after the psychopath who is killing off their prized strippers with the aid of a local cop. Sleazy look at Manhattan low life. **93m/C VHS, DVD.** *Billy Dee Williams, Tom Berenger, Jack Scalia, Melanie Griffith, Rae Dawn Chong, Joe Santos, Maria Conchita Alonso, Rossano Brazzi, Rae Ferrara;* **W:** *Nicholas St. John;* **C:** *James Lemmo;* **M:** *Dick Halligan.*

The Fear: Halloween Night ♦ *Fear 2; Fear: Resurrection* 1999 (R) Mike Hawthorne, the son of a psycho killer, has been plagued by blackouts. According to the streets. **90m/C VHS.** *T Michael Constantine, Fred Williamson, Gianni Manera.*

Fear in the City ♦ 1981 The Sicilian Mafia and a black crime gang battle for control of the streets. **90m/C VHS.** *Gianni Manera.* **VIDEO**

Fear in the Night ♦♦ 1947 Suspenseful tale of a murder committed by a man under hypnosis. Fearing his tive friend into investigating his detective friend into investigating his "crime," which leads them to a mansion, a mirrored room, and a plot that takes some clever and unexpected twists. Remade in 1956 as "Nightmare." **72m/B VHS, DVD.** *Paul Kelly, DeForest Kelley, Ann Doran, Kay Scott, Robert Emmett Keane;* **D:** *Maxwell Shane;* **W:** *Maxwell Shane;* **C:** *Jack Greenhalgh;* **M:** *Rudolph (Rudy) Schrager.*

The Fear Inside ♦♦½ 1992 (R) Lahti plays a woman suffering from agoraphobia who, because of her fear, has not left her home in more than a year. To help out, Lahti invites a seemingly charming college student to live with her. When the young woman's equally charming "brother" comes to visit, Lahti discovers the two aren't so charming after all. A standard woman-in-terror film with a better-than-average cast. **100m/C VHS, Christine Lahti, Jennifer Rubin, Dylan McDermott, David Ackroyd, Thomas Ian Nicholas, Paul (Link) Link, Jenette Goldstein;* **D:** *Leon Ichaso;* **W:** *David Birke;* **C:** *Bojan Bazelli.* **CABLE**

Fear No Evil ♦♦ 1980 (R) A teenager who is the human embodiment of the demon Lucifer commits acts of demonic murder and destruction. His powers are challenged by an 8-year-old girl, who is the embodiment of the archangel Gabriel.

The Fear ♦♦½ 1994 (R) Student psychologist (Bowz) takes a group to a remote cabin to explore their fears as part of his research project. Then, they begin to die horribly and gradually figure out that the cabin's wooden mascot, Morty (Weiss), is coming to life and doing them in. **98m/C VHS, DVD.** *Eddie Bowz, Darin Heames, Anna Karin, Leland Hayward, Monique Mannen, Heather Medway, Antonio Todd, Erick Weiss, Vince Edwards, Ann Turkel, Wes Craven;* **D:** *Vincent Robert;* **W:** *Ron Ford;* **C:** *Bernd Heinl;* **M:** *Robert O. Ragland.*

Fear 335

First feature from La Loggia is better than it sounds. **90m/C VHS, DVD.** Stefan Angrim, Kathleen Rowe McAllen, Elizabeth Hoffman; **D:** Frank Lalogia.

Fear of a Black Hat ⟊⟊ 1994 (R) Think "Spinal Tap" as gangsta rap and you've the plot of this good-natured imitator. The dim-witted Ice Cold (Cundieff), Tone-Def (Lawrence), and Tasty-Taste (Scott), the trio known as NWH (Niggaz With Hats), are touring in support of their album and trying to convince filmmaker Nina Blackburn (Lemmons) of their street cred. Like Tap's metalheads, the more they explain themselves, the less sense they make. **87m/C VHS, DVD.** Larry B. Scott, Mark Christopher Lawrence, Kasi Lemmons, Rusty Cundieff, Lamont Johnson, Howie Gold, Faizon Love, Deezer D, Barry (Shabaka) Henley, Penny Johnson, Eric Laneuville; **D:** Rusty Cundieff; **W:** Rusty Cundieff; **C:** John L. (Ndiaga) Demps Jr.

Fear of Fear ⟊⟊ *Angst vor der Angst* 1975 Middleclass housewife Margot (Carstensen) begins experiencing intense fear after having her second child but her husband and family dismiss her concerns. So she turns to drugs and alcohol for relief, which only makes her situation worse. German with subtitles. **88m/C VHS, DVD. GE** Margit Carstensen, Brigitte Mira, Irm Hermann, Ulrich Faulhaber, Armin Meier, Adrian Hoven; **D:** Rainer Werner Fassbinder; **W:** Rainer Werner Fassbinder; **M:** Peer Raben.

Fear of the Dark ⟊⟊ 2002 (PG-13) Brian doesn't sleep at night because he knows something in the dark is after him. His brother Dale thinks he's just trying to get attention, until the two are home alone when a storm knocks out the power. Creepy and atmospheric, but anyone over the age of 15 will be disappointed by the lack of gore or any over-the-top scares. **86m/C VHS, DVD. CA** Jesse James, Kevin Zegers, Linda Purl, Charles Powell, Rachel (Racheal) Skarsten; **D:** K.C. Bascombe; **W:** K.C. Bascombe, John Sullivan; **C:** Marc Charlebois; **M:** Sari Dijani. **VIDEO**

Fear Runs Silent ⟊⟊ 1999 (R) High school class heads to the woods for an overnight campout. They get stranded. Can you guess what happens? Yes, someone or something tries to kill them! Busy production tries to make up for lack of storyline freshness. **90m/C VHS, DVD.** Stacy Keach, Billy Dee Williams, Dan Lauria, Bobby Jacoby, Suzanne Davis, Ethan Erickson, Elizabeth Low; **D:** Serge Rodnunsky; **W:** Serge Rodnunsky; **C:** Pierre Chemaly. **VIDEO**

Fear Strikes Out ⟊⟊⟊ 1957 Perkins plays Jimmy Piersall, star outfielder for the Boston Red Sox, and Malden, his demanding father, in the true story of the baseball star's battle for sanity. One of Perkins' best screen performances. **100m/B VHS, DVD.** Anthony Perkins, Karl Malden, Norma Moore, Adam Williams, Perry Wilson; **D:** Robert Mulligan; **W:** Raphael David Blau; **M:** Elmer Bernstein.

Fear X ⟊⟊⟊ 2003 (PG-13) Grim, intense thriller stars Turturro as Harry, a security guard at a Wisconsin shopping mall obsessed with finding the truth about his wife's murder. His pursuit takes him across the Midwest into Montana and directly into the path of respected cop Peter (Remar) and his wife, Kate (Unger). Minimal in dialogue and feel, the movie depends on Turturro to hold it together and he does so impressively, portraying Harry as a man so disturbed by grief that the chase becomes more important than finding the truth. Swedish director Refn's American debut. **91m/C VHS, DVD.** John Turturro, Deborah Kara Unger, William Allen Young, James Remar, Stephen McIntyre, Eugene M. Davis, Mark Houghton, Jacqueline Ramel; **D:** Nicolas Winding Refn; **W:** Nicolas Winding Refn, Hubert Selby Jr.; **C:** Larry Smith; **M:** Brian Eno, J. Peter Schwalm.

Feardotcom ⟊ *fear dot com* 2002 (R) Cyber-thriller features a killer virus loose in Manhattan. All the victims shared one thing—48 hours before they logged onto the same web site, which features a live feed of sicko Alistair (Rea) torturing and murdering women. Detective Mike (Dorff) and Health Department investigator Terry Huston (McElhone) investigate the visuals are actually interesting;

too bad everything else about the movie is awful. **101m/C VHS, DVD. US GB GE LU** Stephen Dorff, Natascha (Natasha) McElhone, Stephen Rea, Jeffrey Combs, Udo Kier, Nigel Terry, Michael Sarrazin, Amelia Curtis; **D:** William Malone; **W:** Josephine Coyle; **C:** Christian Sebaldt; **M:** Nicholas Pike.

Fearless ⟊ 1977 An Italian detective has found a Viennese banker's daughter, but continues to pursue the unanswered questions of the case, embroiling himself in a web of intrigue and plotting. **89m/C VHS, DVD. IT** Joan Collins, Maurizio Merli, Frank Antel; **D:** Stelvio Massi; **W:** Stelvio Massi; **C:** Riccardo (Palton) Pallottini; **M:** Stelvio Cipriani.

Fearless ⟊⟊⟊ 1993 (R) Two plane crash survivors reach out to each other as they try and cope with everyday life. Bridges is riveting as the transformed Max, and Perez compelling as the sorrowful Carla. Hulce provides dead-on amusement as a casualty lawyer who knows he's slime but can't help himself. Opening sequences of smoke in the corn fields are haunting as are flashbacks of the crash itself. Weir provides an engrossing look at facing death, both psychological and spiritual, but the ending is something of a letdown in its happiness. Based on the novel by Yglesias. **122m/C VHS, DVD.** Jeff Bridges, Isabella Rossellini, Rosie Perez, Tom Hulce, John Turturro, Benicio Del Toro, Deirdre O'Connell, John de Lancie; **D:** Peter Weir; **W:** Rafael Yglesias; **C:** Allen Daviau; **M:** Maurice Jarre. LA Film Critics '93: Support. Actress (Perez).

Fearless Tiger ⟊½ 1994 (R) Martial arts action flick includes the usual combination of fierce swordplay, hand-to-hand showdowns, and the intrigue of exotic locations. **88m/C VHS. CA** Bolo Yeung, Monica Schnarre, Jamie Farr, Jalal Merhi; **D:** Ron Hulme; **W:** Ron Hulme; **M:** Varouje.

The Fearless Vampire Killers ⟊⟊⟊ *Pardon Me, Your Teeth Are in My Neck; Dance of the Vampires* 1967 Underrated, off-beat, and deliberately campy spoof of vampire films in which Tate is kidnapped by some fangy villains. Vampire trackers MacGowran and Polanski pursue the villains to the haunted castle and attempt the rescue. Only vampire movie with a Jewish bloodsucker ("Boy, have you got the wrong vampire," he proclaims to a maiden thrusting a crucifix at him). Inside the castle, Polanski is chased by the count's gay vampire son. Highlight is the vampire ball with a wonderful mirror scene. Many other amusing moments. **98m/C VHS, DVD. GB** Jack MacGowran, Roman Polanski, Alfie Bass, Jessie Robins, Sharon Tate, Ferdinand "Ferdy" Mayne, Iain Quarrier, Terry Downes, Fiona Lewis, Ronald Lacey; **D:** Roman Polanski; **W:** Gerard Brach, Roman Polanski; **C:** Douglas Slocombe; **M:** Krzysztof Komeda.

Fearmaker ⟊½ *House of Fear; Violent Rage* 1989 (PG) After the mysterious death of her father, the heiress to his fortune is tangled in a web of treachery created by other potential inheritors. **90m/C VHS. MX** Katy Jurado, Paul Picerni, Sonia Amelio, Carlos East; **D:** Antonio Carras.

Feast ⟊½ 2006 (R) The third (and last) of Bravo's "Project Greenlight" series finds strangers hanging out in a dive desert bar when Hero (Dane) barges in with a shotgun and a thing's decapitated head. Hero quickly bites it but his wife, Heroine (Rawat), takes over and warns everyone that they are about to be attacked by carnivorous creatures and must work together to survive. Familiar horror story although fast-paced and mildly amusing. Also available unrated. **85m/C DVD, HD DVD.** US Navi Rawat, Balthazar Getty, Henry Rollins, Krista Allen, Clu Gulager, Judah Friedlander, Duane Whitaker, Eric Dane, Jenny Wade; **D:** John Gulager; **W:** Marcus Dunstan, Patrick Melton; **C:** Thomas Callaway; **M:** Stephen (Steve) Edwards.

Feast for the Devil ⟊½ *Feast of Satan* 1971 A woman searches for her missing sister in a mysterious coastal village, only to fall under the occult spell of a mad doctor. **90m/C VHS, DVD. SP** Krista Nell, Teresa Gimpera; **D:** Jose Maria Elorrieta; **W:** Jose Maria Elorrieta; **C:** Emmanuele Di Cola.

Feast of July ⟊⟊ 1995 (R) Victorian-era drama, adapted from an H. E. Bates novel, has young Bella (Davidtz) pregnant and abandoned by super-cad Arch (Wise) whom she sets out to find. After a miscarriage, she is taken in by the Wainwright family where she becomes the object of the affections of the three grown sons. Predictably, she falls for and weds the troubled loafer, Con (Chaplin). Naturally (this being Victorian England) tragedy results. Well-crafted, a given considering the producers, but ultimately a familiar telling of an average story. Feature film debut for director Menaul, after an award-winning career in British TV. **116m/C VHS, DVD.** Embeth Davidtz, Ben Chaplin, Tom Bell, Gemma Jones, James Purefoy, Kenneth Anderson, Greg Wise; **D:** Christopher Menaul; **W:** Christopher Neame; **C:** Peter Sova; **M:** Zbigniew Preisner.

Feast of Love ⟊⟊ 2007 (R) University professor Harry (Freeman) dispenses wisdom at his friend Bradley's (Kinnear) coffee shop. And Bradley sure needs it: his wife Kathryn (Blair) has left him for another woman, and his new girlfriend Diana (Mitchell) is still sleeping with her married lover. Meanwhile, Harry also contemplates the love affair between Bradley's teenage employees Chloe (Davalos) and Oscar (Hemingway). As the narrator of these stories of love and loss, Harry doesn't seem to have any problems at all. Hmm. A strange movie that tries to be profound but is largely weightless. **102m/C DVD. US** Morgan Freeman, Greg Kinnear, Jane Alexander, Radha Mitchell, Billy Burke, Selma Blair, Alexa Davalos, Toby Hemingway, Fred Ward, Stana Katic; **D:** Robert Benton; **W:** Allison Burnett; **C:** Kramer Morgenthau; **M:** Stephen Trask.

Federal Agent ⟊⟊ 1936 Lots of clichés fill this crime film about a federal agent chasing foreign spys who are looking for a new explosive. **53m/B VHS.** William Boyd, Charles A. Browne, Irene Ware, George Cooper, Lentia Lace, Dan Alvarado; **D:** Sam Newfield.

Federal Agents vs. Underworld, Inc. ⟊⟊ *Golden Hands of Kurigal* 1949 Super G-Man Dave Worth goes up against Nila, a greedy villainess bent on finding the golden hands of Kurigal so she may rule the world. A 12-episode serial edited onto two cassettes. **167m/B VHS.** Kirk Alyn, Rosemary La Planche, Roy Barcroft, Carol Forman, James Dale, Bruce Edwards; **D:** Fred Brannon.

Federal Hill ⟊⟊⟊ 1994 (R) Familiar plot and characters are still well-handled by cast and first time writer/director Corrente. Federal Hill is a working-class, Little Italy section of Providence, Rhode Island. Five buddies, mostly losers, hang out together at a weekly card game. Nicky's (De Sando) a small-time dealer who meets his uptown Brown University sweetie, Wendy (Langdon), when he sells her cocaine. His friends try to warn him, especially short-fused burglar Ralphie (Turturro). And, of course, things go very wrong for practically everyone. The video is available colorized or in the director's version in B&W. **100m/B VHS, DVD.** Anthony De Sando, Nicholas Turturro, Libby Langdon, Michael Raynor, Jason Andrews, Frank Vincent, Robert Turano, Michael Corrente; **D:** Michael Corrente; **W:** Michael Corrente; **C:** Richard Crudo; **M:** Bob Held, David Bravo.

Federal Operator 99 ⟊⟊½ 1945 A fortune in stolen jewels, a chemical plant, and a priceless violin all figure in this 12 chapter serial. And it's up to Jerry Blake, Federal Operator 99, to save the day. Part of "The Cliffhanger Serials" series. **169m/B VHS.** Marten Lamont, Helen Talbot, George Lewis; **D:** Yakima Canutt, Spencer Gordon Bennett, Wallace Grissell; **W:** Albert DeMond, Jesse Duffy, Basil Dickey, Joseph Poland; **C:** Bud Thackery.

Federal Protection ⟊⟊ 2002 (R) Chicago mobster Frank Carbone (Assante) decides to go into the witness protection program after barely surviving a hit. But his suburban neighborhood heats up when next-door neighbor Leigh (Featherstone) finds out her husband is cheating on her with her own sister (Meyer) and she turns to Frank for comfort. Meanwhile,

Frank is finding life a little too quiet and decides to stir things up by contacting his former partners. Slickly made genre piece if you don't mind watching a familiar story. **94m/C VHS, DVD.** Armand Assante, Angela Featherstone, Dina Meyer, David Lipper, Maxim Roy, Tony Calabretta; **D:** Anthony Hickox; **W:** Craig Smith.

Feds ⟊½ 1988 (PG-13) Two women enter the FBI Academy and take on the system's inherent sexism with feebly comic results. **82m/C VHS.** Rebecca De Mornay, Mary Gross, Ken Marshall, Fred Dalton Thompson, Larry Cedar, James Luisi, Raymond Singer; **D:** Dan Goldberg; **W:** Dan Goldberg, Len Blum; **M:** Randy Edelman.

Feed *woof!* 2005 Yuck. A police officer investigates a fetish website where a dominant feeder controls submissive gainers. Only he goes too far and they are force-fed to death. Will definitely put you off your dinner. **105m/C DVD. AU** Jack Thompson, Alex O'Loughlin, Patrick Thompson, Rose Ashton, Gabby Millgate; **D:** Brett Leonard; **W:** Kieran Galvin; **C:** Steve Arnold; **M:** Gregg Leonard. **VIDEO**

Feeders *woof!* 1996 Ya gotta love a low-budget film with the tagline "Earth was just an appetizer!" Okay, so maybe "love" isn't exactly what you'll be thinking. Anyway, Derek and Bennett are heading to the east coast for a vacation when they have a deadly UFO encounter with some flesh-eating aliens, who think earthlings are the perfect snack food. **80m/C VHS, DVD.** Jon McBride, Grant Polonia, Sebastian Barran, Melissa Torpy, Maria Russo, Todd Carpent, Gary LeBlanc; **D:** Jon McBride, John Polonia, Mark Alan Polonia; **W:** Jon McBride, Mark Alan Polonia; **C:** Arthur Daniels.

Feel My Pulse ⟊⟊ 1928 Silent comedy about a rich fanatic who leaves everything in his will to his young niece on the stipulation that she lead a germ-free life; when she reaches 21, she moves into the sanitarium that's inherited, not knowing it has become a base for prohibition-era rum runners. **86m/B VHS.** Bebe Daniels, Richard Arlen, William Powell; **D:** Gregory La Cava.

Feel the Motion ⟊ 1986 A female auto-mechanic wants to make it big in the music biz. She sees her chance when she slips her demo tape onto a hit TV-music show. **98m/C VHS. GE** Sissy Kelling, Frank Meyer-Brockman, Ingold Locke, Falco, Meat Loaf Aday; **D:** Wolfgang Buld; **W:** Wolfgang Buld; **C:** Roland Willaert.

Feel the Noise ⟊½ 2007 (PG-13) Familiar scenario plays out to the sultry beat of reggaeton. When Harlem rapper Rob (Grandberry) tangles with a local gangster, his mom ships him off to Puerto Rico to live with his estranged dad (Esposito) and his family. Stepbrother Javi (Rasuk) introduces Rob to the local scene and music as well as sexy sweet dancer C.C. (Henao). She pushes Rob's musical ambitions, which eventually leads everyone back to New York. The soundtrack will probably do better than the movie. **86m/C DVD. US** Omari (Omarion) Grandberry, Victor Rasuk, James McCaffrey, Giancarlo Esposito, Zulay Henao, Kellita Smith, Melonie Diaz; **D:** Alejandro Chomski; **W:** Albert Leon; **C:** Zoran Popiv; **M:** Andres Levin.

Feelin' Screwy ⟊ 1990 A couple of misfit dweebs attempt to rid their town of the local drug dealer in order to impress a couple of babes in this limp coming-of-ager. **90m/C VHS.** Quincy Reynolds, Larry Gambal, Darin McBride, Hassan Jamal, Marsha Canter, Brooks Morales, Anna Fuentes; **D:** Riffat A. Khan; **W:** Riffat A. Khan.

Feelin' Up *woof!* 1976 (R) A young man sells all his possessions to come to New York in search of erotic adventures. **84m/C VHS.** Malcolm Groome, Kathleen Seward, Rhonda Hansome, Tony Collado, Charles Douglass; **D:** David Secter.

Feeling Minnesota ⟊ 1996 (R) A truly stupid movie about truly stupid, mostly nasty people. Petty criminal Jjaks (Reeves) shows up at sleazy older brother Sam's (D'Onofrio) wedding and promptly falls for beautiful-but-unhappy bride Freddie (Diaz), who's being forced into the marriage by local crime boss Red (Lindo).

Manipulative Freddie easily convinces Jakks to run away to Vegas with her but Sam isn't willing to let his bride go so easily. The only character who comes off with any dignity is the diner waitress played by Love. A very lame first effort from Baigelman. Title's from a Soundgarden song about "looking California and feeling Minnesota." **86m/C VHS, DVD**. *Keanu Reeves, Cameron Diaz, Vincent D'Onofrio, Delroy Lindo; Dan Ayroyd, Courtney Love, Tuesday Weld, Leon Haim; W: Steven Baigelman; C: Wat Lloyd*.

Feet First 🐾🐾½ *1930* A shoe salesman puts on "upper crust" airs as he begins a shipboard romance with a girl who thinks he's wealthy. Lloyd's second sound film shows him grappling with technique in some scenes that recall highlights of his silent hits. **85m/B VHS, DVD**. *Harold Lloyd, Barbara Kent, Robert McWade; D: Clyde Bruckman*.

Felicia's Journey 🐾🐾🐾 *1999* (PG-13) Joseph Ambrose Hilditch (Hoskins) is a mild-mannered, fastidious, middle-aged Brit whose mother problems have turned him into a serial killer. He's a catering manager who watches tapes of his flamboyant late mother Gaa's (Khanji-an) cooking show, where young Hilditch was an embarassed foil. Into his structured world stumbles pregnant Irish teen, Felicia (Cassidy) who's trying to find the father of her baby. Hilditch begins to take a warped interest in Felicia, who may be naive but who isn't dumb. Cold and elegant adaptation of William Trevor's novel. **111m/C VHS, DVD, CA, GB** *Bob Hoskins, Elaine Cassidy, Arsinee Khanjian, Peter McDonald, Gerard McSorley, Brid Brennan, Claire Benedict; D: Atom Egoyan; W: Atom Egoyan; C: Paul Sarossy; M: Mychael Danna, Genie '99: Actr. (Hoskins). Adapt. Screenplay, Cinematog., Score*.

Felicidades 🐾🐾 *Merry Christmas 2000* A not exactly joyous story set on Christmas Eve but probably much more realistic about the expectations that the holiday brings to people. A random group of men and women randomly cross paths during the evening—a doctor eager to seduce a beautiful woman, a father doing some last-minute shopping, a man in a wheelchair, a writer—all looking for some connection that they're not finding. Bittersweet rather than bitter but also frustrating because you learn so little about the characters. Spanish with subtitles. **100m/C VHS, DVD**. *Lucho Bender; W: Pablo Cedron, Silke Klein, Luis Machin, Pablo Cedron, Carlos Belloso, Marcello Mazzarello; D: Lucho Bender; C: Daniel Sorelo; M: Andres Goldstein, Daniel Tarras*.

Felix the Cat: The Movie 🐾½ *1991* Classic cartoon creation Felix returns in a title feature. The feline and his bag of tricks enter a dimension filled with Heman/Mutant Ninja Turtles leftovers; newage princess, comic reptiles, robots and a Darth Vader clone who's defeated with ridiculous ease. Strictly for undemanding kids. **83m/C VHS**. *D: Tibor Hernadi; V: Chris Phillips, Alice Playten, Maureen O'Connell*.

Fellini: I'm a Born Liar 🐾🐾 *Fellini: Je suis un grand menteur/ Federico Fellini: Sono un gran bugiardo; Fellini: Je suis un grand menteur/ Federico Fellini: Sono un gran bugiardo* **2003** Documentary includes an interview with the filmmaker Frederico Fellini, as well as with those who worked on him, most notably Donald Sutherland and Roberto Eanighi. Director Pettigrew uses Fellini's interview as the foundation of the film, but focuses on Fellini the enigma rather than his work or his life. Clips from Fellini's films are used frequently but not labeled; nor are the numerous interviews with the people who have been part of the filmmaker's career. You get a sense of his style, but very little information about his life or his films. For dedicated Fellini fans only—everyone else should just start with his movies. **89m/C VHS, DVD, GE** *Federico Fellini, Donald Sutherland, Terence Stamp, Giuseppe Rotuno, Roberto Benigni, Olivier Gal; C: Peco Wiser; W: Damian Pettigrew; D: Damian Pettigrew*.

Fellini Satyricon 🐾🐾 *Satyricon* **1969** (R) Fellini's famous, garish, indulgent pastiche vision of ancient Rome, based on the novel "Satyricon" by Petronius, follows the adventures of two young men through the decadences of Nero's reign. Actually an exposition on the excesses of the 1960s, with the actors having little to do other than look good and react to any number of sexual situations. Crammed with excesses of every variety. In Italian with English subtitles. **129m/C VHS, DVD, IT** *Martin Potter, Hiram Keller, Salvo Randone, Max Born, Alain Cuny; D: Federico Fellini; W: Federico Fellini, Bernardino Zapponi; C: Giuseppe Rotunno; M: Nino Rota*.

Fellini's Roma 🐾🐾🐾 *Roma* **1972** (R) Fellini reviews his youth in this stream-of-consciousness homage to Rome and Italy. Best left for fervent Fellini fans. **C VHS, DVD, FR** *Peter Gonzales, Britta Barnes, Pia de Doses, Fiona Florence, Vterne Meitland, Renato Giovanoli; Cameos: Gore Vidal, Anna Magnani, Marcello Mastroianni; D: Federico Fellini*.

Fellow Traveler 🐾🐾🐾 *1989* Two old friends, an actor and a screenwriter, both successful, get blacklisted for repudiated Communist leanings in 1950s Hollywood. Good performances and a literate script. **97m/C VHS**. *Ron Silver, Hart Bochner, Imogen Stubbs, Katherine Borowitz, Jonathan Hyde; D: Philip Saville; M: Colin Towns. CABLE.*

Felony 🐾½ *1995* (R) Police seek revenge when 12 cops are murdered. Turns out the culprit is a rogue CIA agent, whose spree was captured on video by a tabloid-show cameraman. **90m/C VHS, DVD**. *Lance Henriksen, Leo Rossi, Joe Don Baker, Charles Napier, Ashley Laurence, Cory (Corinne) Everson; D: David A. Prior; W: David A. Prior; M: Jan A.P. Kaczmarek*.

Female 🐾🐾½ *1933* Feminist look at life in the '30s stars Chatterton as the domineering president of an auto factory who gives them the strictly business line the next day. However, she finally meets her match when Brent walks through the door. (The two stars were a real-life married couple at the time.) Funny, role-reversal story directed by Curtiz of "Casablanca" fame. Based on a story by Donald Henderson Clark. **60m/B VHS**. *Ruth Chatterton, George Brent, Philip Reed, Ruth Donnelly, Johnny Mack Brown, Lois Wilson, Gavin Gordon, Ferdinand Gottschalk; D: Michael Curtiz, William Dieterle; W: Gene Markey, Kathryn Scola*.

The Female Bunch WOOF! *1969* (R) The man-free world of an all-woman settlement is shattered by the arrival of a handsome stranger. Some of this garbage was filmed on location at the notorious Charles Manson ranch, and that's the least of its flaws. **86m/C VHS**. *Jennifer Bishop, Russ Tamblyn, Lon Chaney Jr., Nesa Renet, Geoffrey Land, Regina Carrol; D: Al Acarson, John Cardos*.

The Female Jungle 🐾 *The Hangover* **1956** Below-average whocares whodunnit directed by Roger Corman stock-company actor Ve Sota. Police sergeant Tierney is caught between a rock and a hard place. The prime suspect in a murder case, Tierney discovers a series of clues that implicate his friend Carradine. Interesting only for the screen debut of nympho-typecast Miss Jayne—of whom Bette Davis said "Dramatic art in her option is knowing how to fill a sweater". **56m/B VHS**. *Lawrence Tierney, John Carradine, Jayne Mansfield, Burt Kaiser, Kathleen Crowley, Jayne Kodi, Duane Grey, Jack Hill, Bruno VeSota; C: Elwood "Woody" Bredell; M: Nicholas Carras*.

Female Perversions 🐾🐾 *1996* (R) Psycho-sexual story of Los Angeles attorney Eve Stephens (Swinton), who, because of bizarre dreams and fantasies, leads a dual life. Successful Eve is being considered for appointment as a judge, but her enormous insecurity and neuroses consider their plausibility as Laure goes from thief to grieving widow to ambassador's wife and back, while toying with paparazzo Banderas. **112m/C VHS, DVD, FR** *Tilda Swinton, Amy Madigan, Karen Sillas, Laila Robins, Clancy Brown, Frances Fisher, Paulina Porizkova, Lisa Jane Persky, Dale Shuger; D: Susan Streitfeld; W: Susan Streitfeld, Julie Hebert; C: Teresa Medina; M: Debbie Wiseman*.

Femalien 🐾 *1996* (R) Advanced alien beings, composed of pure light energy, travel to earth to assume corporal form so they can once again experience sexual pleasure. **90m/C VHS, DVD**. *Venessa Taylor, Kiri Kelly, Paige Turco, Dirk Benedict, Conrad Janis, Bo Hopkins, George Segal, Eliott Gould, Lois Nettleton, Virginia Capers, Billy Zane; Kline, Warren Beringer; D: Conrad Janis; W: Markie Grimm; C: Francis Mohajerin, Monty Rowan; M: Tony Humecke*.

The Feminine Touch 🐾🐾½ *1995* Journalist Jennifer Barron (Turco) discovers a deadly conspiracy to take over U.S. politics by killing off presidential candidates. And the hitman who's doing the job thinks Jennifer's in possession of an informative computer disk so he goes after her. **95m/C VHS**. *Paige Turco, Dirk Benedict, Conrad Janis, Bo Hopkins, George Segal, Elliott Gould, Lois Nettleton, Virginia Capers; Kline, Warren Beringer*.

Femme Fatale 🐾🐾½ *Fatal Woman* **1990** (R) When a man's new bride disappears he teams up with an artist pal to track her down. Their search reveals her secret double life and leads them to L.A.'s avant-garde art scene—and deeper into deception and mystery. Billy Zane (Elijah) and Lisa Zane are brother and sister. **96m/C VHS**. *Colin Firth, Lisa Zane, Billy Zane, Scott Wilson, Lisa Blount; D: Andre Guttfreund; W: John Biancato; Michael Ferris*.

Femme Fatale 🐾🐾½ *2002* (R) De-Palma's latest exercise in leering style over substance works because he does stunning, sparkling visuals so well and because he uses Rebecca Romijn-Stamos to show them off. She's Laure, a sleek jewel thief who, when we first see her, is seducing the diamond-encrusted bra off a supermodel at Cannes. Convoluted heist-doublecross-mistaken-identity plot keeps the surprises coming, often enough that you don't have much time to consider their plausibility as Laure goes from thief to grieving widow to ambassador's wife and back, while toying with paparazzo Banderas. **112m/C VHS, DVD, FR** *Rebecca Romijn, Antonio Banderas, Peter Coyote, Gregg Henry, Eriq Ebouaney, Edouard Montoute, Rie Rasmussen, Thierry Fremont; D: Brian De Palma; W: Brian De Palma; C: Thierry Arbogast; M: Ryuichi Sakamoto*.

zation on the part of both sisters about their dysfunctional behavior. Filled with detailed symbolism, powerful imagery, and dream sequences. Rife with Freudian psychology, movie is based on Louise J. Kaplan's feminist study on female behavior and sexuality, "Female Perversions." Ex-tremely glossy visuals and rich production design brings life to this rather heavy story. **110m/C VHS, DVD**.

Female Trouble 🐾🐾½ *1974* (R) Divine leads a troublesome existence in this $25,000 picture. She turns to a life of crime and decadence, seeking to live out her philosophy. "Crime is beauty." Look closely at the Divine rape scene where she plays both rapist and victim. Climax of her deviant ways comes with her unusual night club act for which the law shows no mercy. Trashy, campy; for die-hard Waters fans. **95m/C VHS, DVD, Divine, David Lochary, Mary Vivian Pearce, Mink Stole, Edith Massey, Cookie Mueller, Susan Walsh, Michael Potter, Ed Peranio, Paul Swift, George Figgs, Susan Lowe, Channing Wilroy, Jack Taylor, Alice Anne; D: John Waters; W: John Waters; C: John Waters*.

Female Vampire 🐾 *Erotikill, The Bare Breasted Contessa* **1973** Franco's dreamy, sanguine, produced-on-a-dime tale of a vampiress who cruises the Riviera, seducing and nibbling on a variety of men and women. Not for most tastes. **95m/C VHS, DVD, FR SP GE** *Lina Romay, Monica Swinn, Jack Taylor, Alice Arno; D: Jess (Jesus) Franco; C: Jess (Jesus) Franco; M: Daniel White*.

Femme Fontaine: Killer Babe for the C.I.A. WOOF! *1995* (R) Beautiful assassin Drew "Killer Babe" Fontaine (Hope) gets help from CIA-agent-turned-monk Master Sun (Hong) in order to avenge her father's death. Fishnet-clad women with big guns are always a Troma treat. **93m/C VHS**. *Margot Hope, James Hong, Arthur Roberts, Catherine Dao, David "Shark" Fralick, Kevin Fry, Harry Mok; D: Margot Hope; W: Margot Hope; C: Gary Graver; M: Gardner Cole, Jim Cox*.

Femmes de Paris 🐾🐾 *Women of Paris* **1953** A funny and risque French musical comedy about the comings and goings of the cast of a naughty nightclub shows. In French with English subtitles. **79m/C VHS, FR** *Robert Michel Simon, Brigitte Auber, German Kerjean, Georges Galley, Micheline Dax; D: Jean Boyer; W: Alex Joffe; C: Charles Suin; M: Paul Misraki*.

The Fence 🐾🐾½ *1994* Interesting presentation of standard bad boy grows up, attempts to go straight. Terry Griff (Wirth) has been bounced from juvenile detention to prison since he was 15. On the streets for the first time in 14 years, Terry wants to lead a clean life with potential girlfriend Jackie (Gimp). But when Terry gets on the wrong side of his dishonest parole officer, the harsh world of the streets pulls him back. Bleak urban drama with sincere performances. **90m/C VHS, DVD**. *Billy Wirth, Erica Gimpel, Marc Alaimo, Paul Benjamin, Lorenzo Clemons; D: Peter Tistor; W: Peter Fedorenko; C: John Newby; M: Jeff Beal*.

The Fencing Master 🐾🐾🐾½ *1992* The fencing master is the aristocratic Don Jaime de Astarloa (Antonutti) who secretly takes on female pupil, Adela de Otero (Serna), whom he begins to fall in love. But when another pupil is murdered by de Astarloa's signature thrust to the throat, Don Jaime finds himself caught up in a bewildering world of political intrigue. Adapted from the novel by Antonio Perez Reverte. Spanish with subtitles. **88m/C VHS, SP** *Assumpta Serna, Omero Antonutti, Joaquim de Almeida; D: Pedro Olea; W: Pedro Olea; C: Alfredo Mayo*.

Fer-De-Lance 🐾½ *Operation Serpent* **1974** A stricken submarine is trapped at the bottom of the sea, with a nest of deadly snakes crawling through the ship. **120m/C VHS, DVD, David Janssen, Hope Lange, Ivan Dixon, Jason Evers; D: Russ Mayberry. TV*.

Fergie & Andrew: Behind Palace Doors 🐾🐾½ *1993* More soap-opera from the British royals in this tale of feisty redhead, Sarah Ferguson, and the neglectful Prince Andrew. He's cheating partners get in the way. **92m/C VHS** *FR Fernandel, Suzy Delair, Francoise Fabian, Georges Chamarat; D: Michael Switzer. TV*.

Fernandel the Dressmaker 🐾🐾½ *1957* Fernandel dreams of designing exquisite dresses, but when the opportunity arises, he finds his cheating partners get in the way. In French with English subtitles. **95m/B VHS, FR Fernandel, Suzy Delair, Francoise Fabian, Georges Chamarat; D: Michael Switzer. TV*.

Ferngully: The Last Rain Forest 🐾🐾½ *1992* (G) Animated eco-musical follows the adventures of independent-minded flying sprite Crysta, who lives in a rain forest beset by pollution. She discovers the outside world and becomes smitten with the human Zak, who is helping to cut down the forest. Crysta decides to reduce him to her size and show him the error of his ways. She's aided by fellow sprite, Pips, and a crazy bat (Batty Koda with a voice provided by the lively Williams). So-so script with politically throwing enlivens the tale. **80m/C VHS, DVD, D: Bill Kroyer; W: Jim Cox; M: Alan Silvestri; V: Samantha Mathis, Christian Slater, Robin Williams, Tim Curry, Jonathan Ward, Grace Zabriskie, Rich-ard "Cheech" Marin, Thomas Chong, Tone Loc, Jim Cox*.

Ferocious Female Freedom Fighters 1988 A typical foreign-made action flick with female wrestlers is spoofed by the L.A. Connection comedy troupe which did the totally ridiculous dubbed dialog. 90m/C VHS, DVD. Eva Arnaz, Barry Prima, Leyli Sagita, Wieke Widowati, Ruth Pelupessi, Aminah Cendrakasih; D: Yopi Burnama; W: Deddy Armand, Charles Kaufman, Joey Gaynor; C: Asmawi; M: Gatot Sudarto.

Ferris Bueller's Day Off 1986 (PG-13) It's almost graduation and if Ferris can get away with just one more sick day—it had better be a good one. He sweet talks his best friend into borrowing his dad's antique Ferrari and sneaks his girlfriend out of school to spend a day in Chicago. Their escapades lead to fun, adventure, and almost getting caught. Broderick is charismatic as the notorious Bueller with Grey amusing as his tattle-tale sister doing everything she can to see him get caught. Early Sheen appearance as a juvenile delinquent who pesters Grey. Led to TV series. One of Hughes' more solid efforts. 103m/C VHS, DVD. Matthew Broderick, Mia Sara, Alan Ruck, Jeffrey Jones, Jennifer Grey, Cindy Pickett, Edie McClurg, Charlie Sheen, Del Close, Virginia Capers, Max Perlich, Louie Anderson, Richard Edson, Lyman Ward, Kristy Swanson, Larry "Flash" Jenkins, Ben Stein; D: John Hughes; W: John Hughes; C: Tak Fujimoto; M: Ira Newborn.

Ferry to Hong Kong 1959 World-weary, heavy drinking traveler comes aboard the "Fat Annie," a ship skippered by the pompous Captain Hart. The two men clash, until an act of heroism brings them together. Embarrassingly hammy performance by Welles as the ferry skipper. 103m/C VHS. Curt Jurgens, Orson Welles, Sylvia Syms; D: Lewis Gilbert.

Festival at Cannes 2002 (PG-13) That would be the Cannes Film Festival where everyone is hustling in one way or another. American actress Alice (Scacchi) is looking for financing for her first directorial effort and offers the lead to aging actress Millie Marquand (Aimee). But Millie has been offered major moolah to play a mother role in a big studio pic by desperate producer Rick Yorkin (Silver). Then there's Millie's flagrantly unfaithful director/husband Viktor (Schell), wheeler-dealer Kaz (Norman), and Blue (Gabrielle), a starlet promoting an indie pic that's an unexpected hit, as well as numerous other associates, assistants, and hangers-on. 99m/C VHS, DVD. US Greta Scacchi, Anouk Aimee, Ron Silver, Zack Norman, Jenny Gabrielle, Maximilian Schell, Kim Kolavich, Rachel Bailit, Alex Craig Mann, Peter Bogdanovich, Camilla Campanale; D: Henry Jaglom; W: Henry Jaglom; C: Hanania Baer; M: Gaili Schoen.

Festival Express 2003 (R) In 1970, rock promoters Ken Walker and Thor Eaton orchestrated a lollapalooza featuring Janis Joplin, the Grateful Dead, the Band, the Flying Burrito Bros, Delaney & Bonnie, Ian & Sylvia, Buddy Guy and Sha Na Na. For five days the musicians travelled by private train across Canada, playing concerts, socializing, trading riffs, and partying. A film crew recorded the event, but in the chaos following the tour the footage was lost for decades, only to later be restored by the producer's son. The electrifying sequences of Janis Joplin capture her at the height of a self-consuming talent months prior to her death. A must-see for fans of the bands, the era, and its music. 90m/C DVD. CA D: Bob Smeaton; C: Bob Fiore, Peter Biziou.

The Feud 1990 (R) Wacky comedy about the ultimate "family feud." The Bullards of Millville and the Bealers of Hornbeck engage in a battle of the witless, and no one in either town is safe. A silly, irreverent comedy of the slapstick variety. Based on a novel by Thomas Berger. 87m/C VHS. Rene Auberjonois, Ron McLarty, Joe Grifasi, David Strathairn, Gale Mayron; D: Bill D'Elia; W: Bill D'Elia.

Feud Maker 1938 Steele rides to the rescue in this range war between guys and the cowmen. Hackett, schemer who falsely befriends ...ting to buy up cheap land when the participants have killed each other off. Based on a story by Harry F. Olmsted. 55m/B VHS, DVD. Bob Steele, Marion Weldon, Karl Hackett, Frank Ball, Budd Buster, Lew Meehan, Roger Williams; D: Sam Newfield; W: George Plympton.

Feud of the Trail 1937 A cowboy saves a range family's gold and falls in love with the villain's daughter in the process. Tyler plays both the hero and the villain here. 56m/B VHS. Tom Tyler, Harlin Wood, Guinn "Big Boy" Williams; D: Robert F. "Bob" Hill.

Feud of the West 1935 Old West disagreements settled with guns in this outing for cowboy star Gibson, here portraying a rodeo performer. 60m/B VHS. Hoot Gibson, Buzz Barton, Joan Barclay, Nelson McDowell, Reed Howes, Lew Meehan; D: Harry Fraser.

Fever 1981 Controversial Polish film based on Andrzej Strug's novel "The Story of One Bomb." Focusing on a period in Polish history marked by anarchy, violence, resistance, and revolution, it was banned before it won eventual acclaim at the Gdansk Film Festival. In Polish with English subtitles. 115m/C VHS. PL Adam Ferency, Barbara Grabowska, Boguslaw Linda, Olgierd Lukaszewicz; D: Agnieszka Holland; W: Krzysztof Teoplitz; C: Jacek Petrycki; M: Jan Pawluskiewicz.

Fever 1988 (R) A once-honest cop trades his good life in for a shot at dealing drugs. Meanwhile, his wife's lover wants to murder him. 83m/C VHS. Bill Hunter, Gary Sweet, Mary Regan, Jim Holt; D: Craig Lahiff.

Fever 1991 (R) An ex-con and a high-powered lawyer join forces to rescue the woman both of them love from a vicious killer. Available in Spanish. 99m/C VHS, DVD. Armand Assante, Sam Neill, Marcia Gay Harden, Joe Spano, John Dennis Johnston, Mark Boone Jr., Jon(athan) Gries, Gordon Clapp, Gregg Henry, John Capodice, Rainbow Harvest, John David (J.D.) Cullum; D: Larry Elikann; W: Larry Brothers; C: Bojan Bazelli; M: Michel Colombier. CABLE

Fever 1999 (R) Twentysomething Nick Parker (Thomas) is a struggling artist living in a Brooklyn tenement and fighting a losing battle to keep both his physical health and his sanity. Neither are helped when his landlord's murder leads to a police investigation; a suspicious new tenant moves into the apartment above Nick's; and Nick realizes that he's been sleepwalking. Since the film is told from his fractured point-of-view, the viewer can never be sure just what's real. 90m/C VHS, DVD. Henry Thomas, David O'Hara, Bill Duke, Teri Hatcher, Sandor Tecsy, Ima St. Paule, Marisol Padilla Sanchez; D: Alex Winter; W: Alex Winter; C: Joe DeSalvo; M: Joe Della.

The Fever 2004 Works because of Redgrave's outstanding performance, although the idea teeters (if not topples) into pretension. A nameless privileged woman decides to shake up her life by traveling to a nameless country that's in the midst of a civil war. Falling ill, she has hallucinations, seeing images of violence and revolutionaries (including Jolie) who condemn her indifference and discuss oppression. Based on the play by Wallace Shawn. 83m/C DVD. Vanessa Redgrave, Angelina Jolie, Geraldine James, Joely Richardson, Rade Serbedzija, Michael Moore; D: Carlo Gabriel Nero; W: Wallace Shawn; C: Mark Moriarty; M: Claudio Capponi. CABLE

Fever Mounts at El Pao 1959 Los Ambiciosos 1959 A minor effort from director Bunuel about the regime of a dictator in an imaginary South American country. In Spanish with English subtitles. 97m/B VHS. MX Gerard Philipe, Jean Servais; D: Luis Bunuel.

Fever Pitch WOOF! 1985 (R) Sordid story of a sports writer (O'Neal) who becomes addicted to gambling. Very poor script. 95m/C VHS. Ryan O'Neal, Catherine Hicks, Giancarlo Giannini, Bridgette Andersen, Chad Everett, John Saxon, William (Bill) Smith, Patrick Cassidy, Chad McQueen; D: Richard Brooks; W: Richard Brooks; M: Thomas Dolby.

Fever Pitch 1996 (R) Mildly amusing sports/romance based on Nick Hornby's 1992 sports memoir and set in late '80s London. English teacher/school coach Paul Ashworth (Firth) is an obsessed fan of the Arsenal football (soccer) club. Although completely opposite in temperament, Paul begins a romance with fellow teacher, Sarah (Gemmell), who's only mildly interested in sports. When Sarah gets pregnant, they drift apart as Sarah begins more and more to resent Paul's perpetual adolescent behavior. Finally, it all comes down to Arsenal's championship match and how they both react. 103m/C VHS, DVD. GB Colin Firth, Ruth Gemmell, Neil Pearson, Mark Strong, Holly Aird, Ken Stott, Stephen, Rea, Lorraine Ashbourne; D: David Evans; W: Nick Hornby; C: Chris Seager; M: Neil MacColl, Boo Hewerdine.

Fever Pitch 2005 (PG-13) Math teacher Ben meets unlucky-in-love career woman Lindsey. Looking for a change from the usual (successful) guys she dates, she agrees to go out with him, and a relationship ensues. Then the other spike drops. He's an obsessive Red Sox fan and must choose between his love for Lindsey and the Sox. Standard romantic comedy is raised a level by coinciding with the Red Sox historic 2004 comeback against the Yankees and subsequent World Series victory. Adapted from Nick Hornby's novel about an obsessive soccer fan. A solid outing, but the brothers Farrelly show signs of losing a little zip off their fastball. 98m/C DVD. US Jimmy Fallon, Drew Barrymore, KaDee Strickland, Jone Skye, Willie Garson, James B. Sikking, Jobeth Williams, Jack Kehler, Lenny Clarke, Siobhan Fallon, Marissa Jaret Winokur, Evan Helmuth, Scott Severance, Zen Gesner; D: Peter Farrelly, Bobby Farrelly; W: Lowell Ganz, Babaloo Mandel; C: Matthew F. Leonetti; M: Craig Armstrong.

A Few Days in September Quelques Jours en Septembre 2006 Confusing spy thriller. CIA agent Elliott (Nolte) disappears ten days before 9/11 after contacting French agent Irene (Binoche). Elliott makes Irene responsible for his two children, half-siblings Orlando (Forestier) and David (Riley). But setting up a meeting proves difficult as they follow his trail from Paris to Venice, pursued by an over-the-top assassin (Turturro), in an effort to discover what Elliott's learned that's so dangerous. English, French, and Arabic with subtitles. 112m/C DVD. FR IT Juliette Binoche, Nick Nolte, John Turturro, Sara Forestier, Tom Riley, Mathieu Demy, Said Amadia; D: Santiago Amigorena; W: Santiago Amigorena; C: Christophe Beaucarne; M: Laurent Martin.

A Few Good Men 1992 (R) Strong performances by Cruise and Nicholson carry this story of a peacetime military coverup. Cruise is a smart-aleck Navy lawyer sleepwalking through his comfortable career in DC. He's ready to write off two soldiers pinned for the murder of their cohort until he interviews their commanding officer, Nicholson. Cruise smells a rat, but Nicholson practically dares him to prove it. Moore is another military lawyer assigned to the case, though her function seems to be holding Kaffee's hand (there's no actual romance between the two). Incredible fireworks between Cruise and Nicholson in the courtroom. Based on the play by Sorkin, who also wrote the screenplay. 138m/C VHS, DVD, Blu-ray Disc. Tom Cruise, Jack Nicholson, Demi Moore, Kevin Bacon, Kevin Pollak, Kiefer Sutherland, James Marshall, J.T. Walsh, Christopher Guest, J.A. Preston, Matt Craven, Wolfgang Bodison, Xander Berkeley, Cuba Gooding Jr., Noah Wyle; D: Rob Reiner; W: Aaron Sorkin; C: Robert Richardson; M: Marc Shaiman. MTV Movie Awards '93: Film; Natl. Bd. of Review '92: Support. Actor (Nicholson).

ffolkes 1980 (PG) Assault Force; North Sea Hijack 1980 (PG) Rufus Excalibur Ffolkes is an eccentric underwater expert who is called upon to stop a madman (Perkins, indulging himself) from blowing up an oil rig in the North Sea. Entertaining farce with Moore spoofing the opposite of his usual suave James Bond character. 99m/C VHS, DVD. Roger Moore, James Mason, Anthony Perkins, David Hedison, Michael Parks; D: Andrew V. McLaglen.

The Fiance 1996 (R) Faith (Anthony) suspects husband Richard (Cassidy) of being unfaithful and confides her suspicions to the friendly Walter (Moses). Only the unbalanced guy then becomes unhealthily involved in Faith's life. 94m/C VHS, DVD. William R. Moses, Lysette Anthony, Patrick Cassidy, Alina Thompson, Wanda Acuna, Gordon Thomson; D: Martin Kitrosser; W: Greg Walker, Frank Rehwaldt; C: M. David Mullen; M: Richard Bowers. VIDEO

Fiances / The Engagement; I Fidanzati 1963 Young man from Milan takes a welding job in Sicily that will separate him from his fiancee for 18 months. He thinks the separation will be good for them but loneliness and the strange environment makes him long for her. Non-professional leads provide strength. Italian with subtitles. 84m/B VHS, DVD. IT Carlo Carbrini, Anna Canzi; D: Ermanno Olmi; W: Ermanno Olmi; C: Lamberto Caimi; M: Gianni Ferrio.

Fiction Makers 1967 Roger Moore stars as Simon Templar, also known as "The Saint," a sophisticated detective who is hired to help Amos Klein. Klein turns out to be an alias for a beautiful novelist who is being threatened by the underworld crime ring. Based on the Leslie Charteris character. 102m/C VHS. GB Roger Moore, Sylvia Syms, Justine Lord, Kenneth J. Warren, Philip Locke, Tom Clegg; D: Roy Ward Baker; W: Harry Junkin, John Kruse; C: Michael Reed; M: Edwin Astley.

Fictitious Marriage 1988 Eldad Ilan, a high school teacher experiencing a mid-life crisis, travels to Israel to get away from his family in order to consider his life's direction. In Hebrew with English subtitles. 90m/C VHS, DVD. Shlomo Bar-Aba, Irit Sheleg, Ofra Veingarten; D: Haim Bouzaglo.

Fiddler on the Roof 1971 (G) Based on the long-running Broadway musical. The poignant story of Tevye, a poor Jewish milkman at the turn of the century in a small Ukrainian village, and his five dowry-less daughters, his lame horse, his wife, and his companionable relationship with God. Topol, an Israeli who played the role in London, is charming, if not quite as wonderful as Zero Mostel, the Broadway star. Finely detailed set decoration and choreography, strong performances from the entire cast create a sense of intimacy in spite of near epic proportions of the production. Play was based on the Yiddish stories of Tevye the Dairyman, written by Sholem Aleichem. ♫Tradition; Matchmaker, Matchmaker; If I Were a Rich Man; Sabbath Prayer; To Life; Miracle of Miracles; Tevye's Dream; Sunrise, Sunset; Wedding Celebration. 184m/C VHS, DVD. Chaim Topol, Norma Crane, Leonard Frey, Molly Picon, Paul Mann, Rosalind Harris, Michele Marsh, Neva Small, Paul Michael Glaser, Ray Lovelock; D: Norman Jewison; W: Joseph Stein; C: Oswald Morris; M: John Williams. Oscars '71: Cinematog., Sound, Orig. Song Score and/or Adapt.; Golden Globes '72: Actor—Mus./Comedy (Topol), Film—Mus./Comedy.

The Fiddlin' Buckaroo 1933 Maynard plays a government agent who disguises himself as a musical ventriloquist to capture Kohler and his band of outlaws. Everybody sings a lot. 63m/B VHS, DVD. Ken Maynard, Gloria Shea, Fred Kohler Sr., Frank Rice, Jack Mower, Charles "Slim" Whitaker, Robert F. (Bob) Kortman, Hank Bell, Jack Rockwell; D: Ken Maynard; W: Nate Gatzert.

Fidel 2002 Excellent bio of Fidel Castro's rise to power in Cuba loses a little steam in its later moments but keeps interest with a strong performance by Martin in the title role. The politics are also kept simple; Castro is an idealistic lawyer who fights for the underdog as a rebel leader after his country's military takeover by Batista (Plana). But once he himself takes power, Castro blurs the lines into a dictatorship of his own. Based on the books "Guerilla Prince" by Georgie Anne Geyer and "Fidel Castro" by Robert E. Quirk. 140m/C VHS, DVD. Victor Hugo Martin, Gael Garcia Bernal, Patricia Velasquez, Maurice Compte, Tony Plana, Guillermo Diaz, Margarita d'Francisco, Enrique Arce; D: David Attwood; W:

Fido 🦴🦴 2006 (R) Amusing—if mild—zom-com. In the near-future (although it looks like the 1950s), a radioactive cloud has turned the dead into zombies. But a shady corporation has domesticated some zombies (thanks to electronic collars), and turned them into household help. When Timmy's (Ray) family finally acquires one, the lonely kid names his loyal zombie Fido. Despite Fido's unwavering desire to eat the neighbors (hey, that old lady was mean!), 91m/C DVD, CA Billy Connolly, Carrie-Anne Moss, Dylan Baker, Henry Czerny, Tim Blake Nelson, K'Sun Ray, Sonja Bennett; D: Andrew Currie. W: Andrew Currie, Robert Chomiak, Dennis Heaton; C: Jan Kiesser; M: Don MacDonald.

The Field 🦴🦴🦴½ 1990 (PG-13). After an absence from the big screen, intense and nearly over the top Harris won acclaim as an iron-willed peasant fighting to retain a patch of Irish land he's tended all his life, now offered for sale to a wealthy American. His uncompromising stand divides the community in this glowing adaptation of John B. Keane's classic play, an allegory of Ireland's internal conflicts. 113m/C VHS, DVD, GB Richard Harris, Tom Berenger, John Hurt, Sean Bean, Brenda Fricker, Frances Tomelty, John Cowley, Sean McGinley, Jenny Conroy; D: Jim Sheridan; W: Jim Sheridan; C: Jack Conroy; M: Elmer Bernstein.

Field of Dreams 🦴🦴🦴½ 1989 (PG) Uplifting mythic fantasy based on W.P. Kinsella's novel "Shoeless Joe." Iowa corn farmer Ray Kinsella (Costner) heecs a mysterious voice that instructs "If you build it, he will come" and cuts a baseball diamond in his corn field. Soon the ball field is inhabited by the spirit of Joe Jackson (Liotta) and others who were disgraced in the notorious 1919 "Black Sox" baseball scandal. Jones is reluctantly pulled into the mystery. It's all about chasing a dream, maintaining innocence, finding redemption, reconciling the child with the adult, and celebrating the mythic lure of baseball. Costner and Madigan are strong, believable characters. 106m/C VHS, HD DVD, DVD, Kevin Costner, Amy Madigan, James Earl Jones, Burt Lancaster, Ray Liotta, Timothy Busfield, Frank Whaley, Gaby Hoffman, Dwier Brown; D: Phil Alden Robinson; W: Phil Alden Robinson; C: John Lindley; M: James Horner.

Field of Fire 🦴🦴 1992 (R) One of America's top military experts has been taken hostage and it's up to a top general to rescue him. But the rescue doesn't come off as planned and all must fight their way through the Cambodian jungle to safety. 96m/C VHS, David Carradine; D: Cirio H. Santiago; W: Thomas McKelvey Cleaver.

Field of Honor 🦴🦴½ 1986 (R) A look at the harrowing experience of jungle combat through the eyes of a Dutch infantryman in Korea. 93m/C VHS, Everett McGill, Ron Bradsbeker; Hey Young Lee; D: Hans Scheepmaker.

Field of Honor 🦴🦴½ d'Honneur 1987 (PG) A quiet French anti-war drama set during the Franco-Prussian war in 1859 in which a peasant boy volunteers to fight in place of a rich man's son. He is befriended behind enemy lines by a young boy and both try to avoid capture. In French with English subtitles. 87m/C VHS, FR Cris Campion, Eric Wapler, Pascale Rocard, Frederic Mayer; D: Jean-Pierre Denis, Cesar '88: Score

The Fiend 🦴 1971 (R) A religious cultist, already unbalanced, grabs a knife and starts hacking away Jack-the-Ripper style. 87m/C VHS, DVD, GB Ann Todd, Patrick Magee, Tony Beckley, Madeline Hinde, Suzanna Leigh, Percy Herbert; D: Robert Hartford-Davis.

Fiend WOOF! 1983 Glowing supernatural thing flits around graveyard before animating dead guy who needs to kill in order to go on living. Murderous dead guy becomes a small-town music teacher feeding parasitically on his students to satisfy his supernatural hunger. His neighbor suspects some discord. Low-budget time waster. 93m/C VHS, DVD, Don Leifert, Richard Nelson, Elaine White, George Stover; D: Donald M. Dohler.

The Fiend Who Walked the West 🦴🦴½ 1958 Brutal western has incarcerated bankrobber Dan letting slip the location of his loot to fellow inmate Griffin, who unfortunately turns out to be psychotic and due for release. When Dan's family is endangered lawmen release him for a showdown with Griffin. Tense remake of "Kiss of Death" provides effective atmosphere and graphic violence in an Old West setting. 101m/B VHS, Hugh O'Brian, Robert Evans, Dolores Michaels, Linda Cristal, Stephen Mcnally, Ron Ely, Edward Andrews, Ken Scott, Emile Meyer, Gregory Morton; D: Gordon Douglas; W: Philip Yordan; C: Joe MacDonald; M: Leo Baxter.

Fiend without a Face 🦴🦴 1958 An isolated air base in Canada is the site for a scientist using atomic power in an experiment to make a person's thoughts materialize. Only his thoughts are evil and reveal themselves as flying brains with spinal cords that suck human brains right out of the skull. Tons of fun for '50s SF fans and anyone who appreciates the sheer silliness of it all. 77m/B VHS, DVD, Marshall Thompson, Kim Parker, Terence Kilburn, Michael Balfour, Gil Winfield, Shane Cordell, Kynaston Reeves; D: Arthur Crabtree; W: Herbert J. Leder; C: Lionel Banes; M: Buxton Orr.

The Fiendish Plot of Dr. Fu Manchu WOOF! 1980 (PG) A sad farewell from Sellers, who in his last film portrays Dr. Fu in his desperate quest for the necessary ingredients for his secret life-preserving formula. Sellers portrays both Dr. Fu and the Scotland Yard detective on his trail, but it's not enough to save this picture, flawed by poor script and lack of direction. 100m/C VHS, GB Peter Sellers, David Tomlinson, Sid Caesar, Helen Mirren, Simon Williams, Steve Franken, Stratford Johns, John Le Mesurier, John Sharp, Clement Harari; D: Piers Haggard; W: Rudy Dochtermann, Jim Mooney; C: Jean Tournier; M: Marc Wilkinson.

Fierce Creatures 🦴🦴 1996 (PG-13) This not-really-a-sequel features the same cast as "A Fish Called Wanda" and was jokingly known as "Death Fish II" until a more appropriate title was thought of. A failing London zoo gets a new lease on life, and officious new manager Rollo Lee (Cleese) is again in fine form thought of destroying the zoo's cuddly current occupants. Kline is again in fine form as Willa Weston, Vince's more sympathetic partner. Despite inspired moments, flick's not as tightly told or as wickedly funny as "Fish," (an admittedly tough act to follow). A family-friendlier attitude has effectively declawed this "Creature." Many scenes were reshot after unfavorable advance screenings, necessitating a new director and recall of the actors from far and wide. 93m/C VHS, DVD, John Cleese, Jamie Lee Curtis, Kevin Kline, Michael Palin, Ronnie Corbett, Robert Lindsay, Carey Lowell, Billie Brown, Derek Griffiths, Cynthia Cleese; D: Robert M. Young, Fred Schepisi; W: John Cleese, Iain Johnstone; C: Adrian Biddle, Ian Baker; M: Jerry Goldsmith.

Fierce People 🦴 2005 (R) In 1980, fifteen-year-old Finn (Yelchin) is supposed to summer in South America with his wayward anthropologist father. Instead, they wreck addict/masseuse mom (Lane), who's trying her luck at sobriety, plucks him from their New York City existence to spend the season at the New Jersey country estate of super-loaded and super-eccentric Osborne (Sutherland), where the idle rich pursue their own brand of summer fun. Finn falls for the billionaire's granddaughter (Stewart), and a twisted coming-of-age story unfolds amid the darkness. Be warned: a brutal rape sequence is totally jarring, and the already bizarre twists, and outrageous characters top as the icy villain with a distinct southern accent, which makes him more of a bad gag than a bad guy. Jumbled story

Fifth Day of Peace 🦴🦴 1972

Fifth Avenue Girl 🦴🦴½ 1939 An unhappy millionaire brings home a poor young woman to pose as his mistress to make his family realize how they've neglected him. As this below-par social comedy drones toward its romantic conclusion, the rich folks see the error of their ways and love conquers all. 83m/B VHS, Ginger Rogers, Walter Connolly, Tim Holt, James Ellison, Franklin Pangborn; D: Gregory La Cava.

Fifth Avenue Girl — see above.

Fiesta 🦴🦴 1995 Young, idealistic Spanish aristocrat Rafael (Colin) has been studying in the Spanish Republic during the years since it's 1936 and he has been summoned home to fight against the Communists. Messagual assigns Rafael to the firing squad to toughen him up but Rafael eventually rediscovers his convictions and double-crosses his mentor. Based on an autobiographical novel by Jose Luis de Vilallonga. French with subtitles. 108m/C VHS, FR Jean-Louis Trintignant, Gregoire Colin, Dayle Haddon, Marc Lavoine, Jean-Philippe Ecofey, Laurent Terzieff; D: Pierre Boutron; W: Pierre Boutron, Jean-Yves Escoffier; C: Javier Aguirresarobe; M: Wim Mertens.

15 Minutes 🦴🦴 2001 (R) New York cop and publicity hound De Niro teams up with arson investigator Burns to hunt down a couple of violent criminals who are videotaping their crimes for celebrity. Grammer tries exploring our culture's fascination with violence, nihilism, and fame, or just using information as currency. 120m/C VHS, DVD, US Robert De Niro, Edward Burns, Kelsey Grammer, Avery Brooks, Melina Kanakaredes, Vera Farmiga, Karel Roden, Oleg Taktarov, John DiResta, James Handy, Darius McCrary, Charlize Theron, Kim Cattrall, David Alan Grier; D: John Herzfeld; W: John Herzfeld; M: Anthony Marinelli, J. Peter Robinson.

15 Amore 🦴🦴 1998 Dorothy's husband is off fighting in WWII while she struggles with the family farm and three young kids in rural Australia. But soon she gets the help of two Italian POWs, Alfredo and Joseph, who settle right in. Then, Dorothy takes in German Jewish refugees Frau Gutman and her daughter Rachel. While Dorothy and Alfredo have an unacknowledged love for each other, Joseph and Rachel engage in a secret romance. Secret until Rachel's disappearing mother finds out. A last-minute bombshell accusation needlessly skewers everything that's gone before. Title refers to a tennis score, one of the local pastimes. 92m/C VHS, AU Lisa Hensley, Steve Bastoni, Domenic Galati, Tara Jaskzewicz, Gertraud Ingeborg; D: Maurice Murphy; W: Maurice Murphy; C: John Brock; M: Carlo Giacco.

The Fifth Element 🦴🦴½ 1997 (PG-13) Besson's view of the future is colorful, loud and fashionable. Dressed in costumes by Jean Paul Gaultier, Willis (in a blonde dye job) is New York City cab driver turned unwilling hero Korban Dallas, who must save earth from destruction at the hands of evil arms dealer Zorg (Oldman). Bruce is up to the old heroics that made him a household name, and takes time to romance orange-haired nymph Jovovich, who holds the key to all the madness going on. Oldman is over-the-top as the icy villain with a distinct southern accent, which makes him more of a bad gag than a bad guy. Jumbled story fortunately takes a backseat to weird aliens and stunning visuals which makes this an eye-catching (albeit confusing) sci-fi trip. 126m/C VHS, DVD, Blu-ray Disc, UMD, Bruce Willis, Gary Oldman, Ian Holm, Milla Jovovich, Luke Perry, Lee Evans, Chris Tucker, Brion James, Tommy (Tiny) Lister, Ian Neeson; D: Luc Besson; W: Luc Besson, Robert Mark Kamen; C: Thierry Arbogast; M: Eric Serra. British Acad. '98: Art Dir/Set Dec., Cinematog., Director (Besson).

The Fifth Floor WOOF! 1980 (R) College disco dancer overdoses on drugs and winds up in an insane asylum, complete with menacing attendant Hopkins and apathetic doctor Ferrer. Pathetic, exploitative trash. 90m/C VHS, Bo Hopkins, Dianne Hull, Patti D'Arbanville, Mel Ferrer, Bob Hoskins; D: Howard (Hikmet) Avedis; W: Howard (Hikmet) Avedis.

The Fifth Horseman Is Fear 🦴🦴 1964. In Nazi-occupied Prague, Dr. Braun is forbidden from practicing medicine because he is a Jew. Instead, he catalogs confiscated property in a warehouse. But when a wounded resistance fighter is secretly brought to Braun for treatment, he journeys throughout the chaotic city trying to find morphine for his patient, whom he is hiding in his apartment building. But he fears his scared neighbors may become informers. Czech with subtitles. 100m/B VHS, CZ Jiri Adamira, Miroslav Machacek, Josef Vinklar, Jiri Vrtala, Zbynek Brynch; W: Zbynek Brynch; C: Jan Kalis.

The Fifth Monkey 🦴½ 1990 (PG-13) A man embarks on a journey to sell four monkeys in order to fill a dowry for his bride, but along the way he encounters all sorts of obstacles and adventures. Filmed on location in Brazil. 93m/C VHS, Ben Kingsley; D: Eric Rochant; W: Eric Rochant.

The Fifth Musketeer 🦴🦴 Behind the Iron Mask 1979 (PG) A campy adaptation of Dumas's "The Man in the Iron Mask," wherein a monarch's evil twin impersonates him while imprisoning the true king. A good cast; and rich production shot in Austria makes for a fairly entertaining swashbuckler. 90m/C DVD, GB Beau Bridges, Sylvia Kristel, Ursula Andress, Cornel Wilde, Ian McShane, Alan Hale Jr., Helmut Dantine, Olivia de Havilland, Jose Ferrer, Rex Harrison; D: Ken Annakin; W: David Ambrose; C: Jack Cardiff.

The Fifth Seal 🦴🦴 1976 A group of friends are arrested when one makes a casual remark that offends a commandant. This leads to a series of tasks that test their commitment to their moral ideals. Set at the close of WWII in Hungary. In Hungarian with English subtitles. 116m/C VHS, HU Laos Oze, Laszlo Markus, Ferenc Bencze, Sandor Horvath; D: Zoltan Fabri; M: Gyorgy Vukan.

Yelchin, Chris Evans, Kristen Stewart, Elizabeth Perkins, Christopher Shyer, Blu Mankuma; D: Griffin Dunne; W: Dirk Wittenborn; C: William Rexer; M: Nick Laird-Clowes.

50 First Dates 🦴🦴½ 2004 (PG-13) Barrymore is the sweet girl with no short-term memory and Sandler is the love-struck island veterinarian who tries to woo her, over and over again. Sweetly charming at times, as Sandler tones down his more outrageous behavior for a decent romantic comedy. Clark does a fine job as Barrymore's slightly over-protective but loving father. Astin goes 180 degrees from anything resembling a hobbit as the pumped-up brother. 96m/C DVD, Blu-ray Disc, UMD, US Adam Sandler, Drew Barrymore, Rob Schneider, Sean Astin, Blake Clark, Dan Aykroyd, Amy Hill, Allen Covert, Maya Rudolph, Missi Pyle, Lusia Strus, Pomaika'i Brown; D: Peter Segal; W: George Wing; C: Jack N. Green; M: Teddy Castellucci.

$50,000 Reward 🦴🦴 1925 Maynard's first western finds him being victimized by an unscrupulous banker who wants Maynard's land deeds for property on which a new dam is being built. 49m/B VHS, Ken Maynard, Esther Ralston, Edward Peil Sr., Bert Lindley, Lillian (Lillianne, Lylian) Leighton, Frank Whitson; D: Clifford S. Elliott; W: Frank Howard Clark; C: Bert Longenecker.

52 Pick-Up 🦴🦴½ 1986 (R) After a fling at a wealthy industrialist is blackmailed by a trio of repulsive criminals and determines to save himself. First he becomes deeply caught in their web of murder. Based on an Elmore Leonard novel with lots of gruesome violence and good performances. **111m/C VHS.** Roy Scheider, Ann-Margret, Vanity, John Glover, Doug McClure, Clarence Williams III, Kelly Preston, Robert Trebor, Lonny (Lonnie) Chapman; **W:** John Frankenheimer; **D:** John Steppling, Elmore Leonard; **M:** Gary Chang.

54 *1998 (R)* The days of '70s disco, drugs, and hedonism rear their heads in this look back at New York's infamous Studio 54. Myers takes the drama route as druggie club co-owner Steve Rubell, while Phillippe starts off as innocent New Jersey boy Shane O'Shea, who gets a job as a bartender and is soon taking the low road to debauchery. Others hitting the dance floor include pouty soap star Julie (Campbell), coat-check girl/would-be disco diva Anita (Hayek), and her busboy hubby Greg (Meyer). But Shane is a dunce and his story a bore, while the effective Myers takes a decided backseat storywise. Film went through a lot of last-minute re-editing but it didn't seem to help. **92m/C VHS, DVD.** Mike Myers, Ryan Phillippe, Breckin Meyer, Salma Hayek, Neve Campbell, Sela Ward, Sherry Stringfield, Ellen A. Dow, Heather Matarazzo, Skipp (Robert L.) Sudduth, Cindy Crawford; **Cameos:** Lauren Hutton, Michael York; **D:** Mark Christopher; **W:** Mark Christopher; **C:** Alexander Gruszynski.

55 Days at Peking *1963* A costume epic depicting the Chinese Boxer Rebellion and the fate of military Britishers caught in the midst of the chaos. Standard fare superbly handled by director Ray and an all-star cast. **150m/C VHS, DVD.** Charlton Heston, Ava Gardner, David Niven, John Ireland, Flora Robson, Paul Lukas, Jacques Sernas; **D:** Nicholas Ray; **W:** Philip Yordan; **C:** Jack Hildyard.

The Fig Tree *1987* After her mother passes away, Miranda becomes tormented by the fear of death. Now her aunt must help her cope with this difficult part of life. Adapted from the short story by Katherine Anne Porter. Aired on PBS as part of the "Wonderworks" family movie series. **58m/C VHS.** Olivia Cole, William Converse-Roberts, Doris Roberts, Teresa Wright, Karron Graves; **D:** Calvin Skaggs.

Fight Club *1999 (R)* Young, male, repressed rage comes in the form of Norton's disillusioned yuppie, emotionally numbed by chronic insomnia, who meets a kindred spirit in malcontent Pitt. Tyler's his name and anarchy's his game as the duo eventually establish fight clubs where the participants beat each other up and stage massive acts of terrorism to undermine the allure of consumerism. Bonham Carter plays a kinky, death-obsessed woman both men fancy. Fincher heads for the dark side again and puts a middle finger on the pulse of several hot topics without missing a beat or skirting the issues. Film's dark humor and stylistic vision of young male malaise is made even more biting by newcomer Uhl's faithful adaptation of Chuck Palahniuk's debut novel. Performances by all three leads are equal to the powerful subject matter. **139m/C VHS, DVD, UMD.** Brad Pitt, Edward Norton, Helena Bonham-Carter, Meat Loaf Aday, Jared Leto, Eion Bailey; **D:** David Fincher; **W:** Jim Uhls; **C:** Jeff Cronenweth; **M:** Howard Shore.

Fight for Gold *1986* In the frozen wastes of the North, a man becomes embroiled in a violent quest for gold. **107m/ C VHS. GE** Doug McClure, Harald Leipnitz, Heinz Reinl, Roberto Bianco, Angelica Ott, Kristina Nel; **D:** Harald Reinl.

A Fight for Jenny *1990 (PG)* Miami Viceroy Thomas and Warren play an interracial couple who fight for custody of the wife's child from a previous marriage. Standard made-for-TV meaningful drama (bite-sized issues served with a modicum of melodrama). **95m/C VHS.** Philip Michael Thomas, Lesley Ann Warren, Jean Smart, Lynne Moody, William Atherton; **D:** Gilbert Moses.

Fight for the Title *1957* Benny Leonard's reign as the lightweight boxing champ has just begun when WWII is declared. Against his manager's wishes, Benny decides to enlist. **30m/C VHS, DVD.** Michael Landon, George Brenlin; **D:** Eric Kenton.

Fight for Us *L'Insoumis 1989 (R)* A social activist, recently released from prison, takes on the death squads terrorizing the countryside in post-Marcos Philippines. In Spanish with English subtitles. **92m/C VHS.** Philip Salvador, Dina Bonnevie, Gina Alajar, Benbol Roco; **D:** Lino Brocka; **W:** Jose F. Lacaba; **C:** Rody Lacap; **M:** Hugo Crotti.

Fight for Your Life *Getting Even; Held Hostage; Staying Alive 1977 (R)* Three escaped convicts—a white bigot, an Asian, and a Chicano—crash a black minister's family hostage. After suffering all manner of vicious torture, the family exacts an equally brutal revenge. Shades of "The Desperate Hours" and "Extremities," but with much more graphic violence and a racial twist. **89m/C VHS, DVD. CA** William Sanderson, Robert Judd, Lela Small, Reggie Rock Bythewood; **D:** Robert A. Endelson; **W:** Straw Weisman; **C:** Lloyd Freidus; **M:** Jeff Slevin.

The Fighter *The First Time 1952* A Mexican patriot, involved in a struggle to overthrow a dictator, falls for a co-revolutionist. Flashbacks show the destruction of his family and village, and his pugilistic expertise, which he uses to fight for a huge purse to help the cause. Adapted from Jack London's "The Mexican." **78m/B VHS, DVD.** Richard Conte, Vanessa Brown, Lee J. Cobb, Frank Silvera, Roberta Haynes, Hugh Sanders, Claire Carleton, Martin Garralaga; **D:** Herbert Kline; **W:** Herbert Kline, Aben Kandel; **C:** Floyd Crosby, James Wong Howe; **M:** Vincente Gomez.

The Fighter *1995 (R)* French soldier Charlemont (Gruner) gets involved with desperate farmers opposing a greedy landlord (Ermey) and during a mission to destroy a Nazi supply station. He meets with a woman of the Italian underground, and succeeds in destroying his target with her help. **80m/C VHS.** Sterling Hayden, J. Carrol Naish, Joy Page; **D:** Lesley Selander.

Fighter Attack *1953* Story of a WWII pilot, based in Corsica, who is shot down during a mission to destroy a Nazi supply station. He meets with a woman of the Italian underground, and succeeds in destroying his target with her help. **80m/C VHS.** Sterling Hayden, J. Carrol Naish, Joy Page; **D:** Lesley Selander.

The Fighting American *1924* A frat boy proposes to a girl on a brotherly dare, and, unflattered by the fraternal proposal, the girl flees to the Far East to return to the bosom of her family. But it turns out the boy really does love the girl, by golly, and he's got enough of that fighting American spirit to prove it. Predates Oland's Charlie Chan career by seven years. **65m/B VHS.** Pat O'Malley, Mary Astor, Raymond Hatton, Warner Oland; **D:** Tom Forman.

Fightin' Ranch *Fighting Thru 1930* A famous lawman saves his reputation, previously tainted. **60m/B VHS.** Jeanette Loff, Wallace MacDonald, Carmellita Geraghty, Ken Maynard; **D:** William Nigh; **W:** John Nattefrod; **C:** Ted D. McCord.

Fighting Back *Death Vengeance 1982 (R)* Reactionary tale of an angry resident in a crime-ridden Philadelphia neighborhood who organizes a patrol of armed civilian vigilantes. The police attempt to head off a racial confrontation in this effective drama graced with some fine performances. **96m/C VHS.** Tom Skerritt, Patti LuPone, Michael Sarrazin, Yaphet Kotto; **D:** Lewis Teague; **W:** David Zelag Goodman; **C:** Franco Di Giacomo.

Fighting Black Kings *1976 (PG)* Martial arts and karate masters appear in this tale of action. **90m/C VHS.** William Oliver, Charles Martin, Willie Williams, Mas Oyama; **D:** Shuji Goto; **C:** Kimlaki Kimura; **M:** Keisuke Hidaka.

Fighting Caballero *1935* Lease and his pals effectively handle a gang of mine-harassing outlaws. **60m/B VHS.** Dorothy Gulliver, Earl Douglas, George Chesebro, Robert Walker, Wally Wales, Rex Lease; **D:** Elmer Clifton; **W:** Elmer Clifton; **C:** Bert Longenecker.

Fighting Caravans *Blazing Arrows 1931* In this early big-budget western, based on a story by Zane Grey, a wagon train sets out west from Missouri. Cooper emerges as the hero after warding off an Indian attack that takes the lives of the original leaders. **80m/B VHS, DVD.** Gary Cooper, Ernest Torrence, Tully Marshall, Fred Kohler Sr., Lili Damita; **D:** Otto Brower, David Burton.

Fighting Champ *1933* Cow-punching gives way to boxing as Steele steps into the ring and takes on all comers. Poor combination of riding and boxing makes for a disappointing Western. **57m/B VHS.** Bob Steele, Arletta Duncan, George "Gabby" Hayes, Charles "Blackie" King, Lafe (Lafayette) McKee, Kit Guard, George Chesebro; **D:** John P. McCarthy; **W:** Wellyn Totman.

Fighting Cowboy *1933* Bill settles a tungsten mine dispute with a greedy miner and some outlaws. **50m/B VHS.** Buffalo Bill Jr., Allen Holbrook; **D:** Victor Adamson; **C:** Brydon Baker.

Fighting Devil Dogs *1943* Two Marine lieutenants are assigned the task of obtaining a deadly secret weapon controlled by crooks. A serial in 12 chapters. **195m/B VHS.** Lee Powell, Bruce Bennett; **D:** John English, William Witney.

Fighting Elegy *Kenka Eregi 1966* A high school boy longs for an unattainable girl and channels all those teenaged hormones into brawling with street gangs. Then he has an encounter with an ultra-right wing militarist that changes his life and sets him on the path to fascism. Japanese with subtitles. **86m/B VHS. JP** Hideki Takahashi, Yusuke Kawazu, Jinko Asano, Mitsuo Kataoka; **D:** Seijun Suzuki.

Fighting Father Dunne *1948* Mega-hokey Hollywood steamroller about a tough priest caring for St. Louis newsboys in the early 1900s. Based on a true story. **92m/B VHS.** Pat O'Brien, Darryl Hickman, Charles Kemper, Una O'Connor, Arthur Shields, Harry Shannon, Joseph (Joe) Sawyer, Anna Q. Nilsson, Donn Gift, Myrna Dell; **D:** Ted Tetzlaff.

The Fighting Fists of Shanghai Joe *1965* Fearsome fighting man about the Far East engages a vile American land baron in a battle of honor. **94m/C VHS, DVD.** Klaus Kinski, Gordon Mitchell, Carla Romanelli, Claudio Undari, Chen Lee; **D:** Mario Caiano.

The Fighting Kentuckian *1949* Homeward bound from the Battle of New Orleans in 1814, a Kentucky rifleman lingers in a French settlement in Alabama. His romance with the daughter of a French general is blocked by the father until the American saves the community from an assault by land grabbers. Hardy as a frontiersman is well worth the view. An action-packed, well-photographed film. **100m/B VHS.** John Wayne, Oliver Hardy, Vera Hruba Ralston, Marie Windsor, Philip Dorn, Ernie Adams, Stanley Blystone, Frank Rice; **D:** George Waggner.

The Fighting Legion *1930* Maynard shows his foresight here, making this one of the first westerns to fully exploit sound by adding music and singing. Standard plot has Maynard going after the villain who murdered his brother. **69m/B VHS.** Ken Maynard, Dorothy Dwan, Ernie Adams, Stanley Blystone, Frank Rice; **D:** Harry Joe Brown.

Fighting Mad *1939* A singing Mountie tangles with border-crossing robbers and saves the reputation of a woman they exploit. One of the "Renfrew of the Mounties" series. **57m/B VHS.** James Newill, Milburn Stone, Sally Blane; **D:** Sam Newfield.

Fighting Mad *1976 (R)* A peaceful land owner is driven to violence when he discovers that the business men who want his property are planning to murder two of his family members in order to get it. The local sheriff's apathy forces the man to take the law into his own hands. Unlike other Fonda films of the time which consist of chaotic violence and car crashes, this story is a well performed character study. **90m/C VHS, DVD.** Peter Fonda, Lynn Lowry, John Doucette, Phil Carey, Scott Glenn, Kathleen Miller; **D:** Jonathan Demme; **W:** Jonathan Demme.

Fighting Mad *Fierce 1977 (R)* Soldiers leave their buddy for dead in wartime Vietnam. He is alive, but captured by Japanese soldiers who believe they are still fighting in WWII. **96m/C VHS, DVD.** James Iglehart, Jayne Kennedy, Leon Isaac Kennedy; **D:** Cirio H. Santiago.

Fighting Marines *1936* U.S. Marines are trying to establish an air base on Halfway Island in the Pacific, but are thwarted by the "Tiger-Shark," a modern-day pirate. First appeared as a serial. **69m/ B VHS, DVD.** Jason Robards Sr., Grant Withers, Ann Rutherford, Pat O'Malley; **D:** Joseph Kane, B. Reeves Eason; **W:** Barney A. Sarecky.

The Fighting Marshal *1932* After serving time for a crime he didn't commit, McCoy assumes the identity of a dead sheriff and tries to find the felons who done him wrong. **58m/B VHS.** Tim McCoy, Dorothy Gulliver, Mary Carr, Matthew Betz, Pat O'Malley; **D:** David Ross Lederman.

Fighting Parson *1935* In order to infiltrate a lawless town Gibson, a gunsling cowboy, dresses as a revivalist preacher. **65m/B VHS.** Hoot Gibson, Marceline Day, Robert Frazer, Stanley Blystone, Skeeter Bill Robbins, Charles 'Blackie' King; **D:** Harry Fraser.

Fighting Pilot *1935* Talmadge is a real fighter in this classic talkie. His assignment is to rescue the plans for a secret aircraft from ill fate. **62m/B VHS, DVD.** Richard Talmadge, Victor Mace, Gertrude Messinger, Eddie Davis, Robert Frazer; **D:** Noel Mason Smith.

The Fighting Prince of Donegal *1966* An Irish prince battles the invading British in 16th Century Ireland. Escaping their clutches, he leads his clan in rescuing his mother and his beloved in this Disney swashbuckler. Based on the novel "Red Hugh, Prince of Donegal" by Robert T. Reilly. **110m/C VHS, DVD.** Peter McEnery, Susan Hampshire, Tom Adams, Gordon Jackson, Andrew Keir; **D:** Michael O'Herlihy; **M:** George Bruns.

The Fighting Rats of Tobruk *The Rats of Tobruk 1944* Australian film about the Egyptian campaign against Rommel in World War II attempts to take a slightly documentary approach to the subject. It's notable mostly for providing an early role for Peter Finch. **71m/B VHS, DVD. AU** Grant Taylor, Peter Finch, Chips Rafferty, Pauline Garrick; **D:** Charles Chauvel; **C:** George Heath.

The Fighting Redhead *1950* Final entry in the "Red Ryder" series has Hart as a cattle rustling murderer and Bannon as the hero, Red Ryder. Based on the comic strip, "Red Ryder." **55m/C VHS, DVD.** Jim Bannon, Don Reynolds, Emmett Lynn, Marin Sais, Peggy Stewart, John Hart, Lane Bradford; **D:** Lewis D. Collins; **W:** Paul Franklin, Jerry Thomas.

Fighting Renegade *1939* The search for an Indian burial ground in Mexico prompts two murders and McCoy, disguised as a notorious bandit part of the time, is wrongly accused. Justice triumphs in the end. **60m/B VHS, DVD.** Joyce Bryant, Ben (Benny) Corbett, Ted Adams, Tim McCoy; **D:** Sam Newfield; **W:** William Lively; **C:** Arthur Reed.

The Fighting Rookie *1934* LaRue, better known for playing hoods, is a rookie cop set up and disgraced by the mob. But he fights back to regain his honor and bring the gang to justice. **65m/B VHS.** Ada Ince, DeWitt Jennings, Matthew Betz, Wally Wales, Arthur Belasco, Jack La Rue; **D:** Spencer Gordon Bennet; **C:** George Morgan; **C:** James S. Brown Jr.

Fighting Seabees ✍✍½ 1944 As a hot-tempered construction foreman who battles Navy regulations as well as the Japanese, Wayne emerges as a larger-than-life hero in this action-packed saga of the Pacific theater of WWII. Extremely popular patriotic drama depicts the founding of the Seabees, the naval construction corps, amidst the action and the would-be romance with a woman reporter. Also available colorized. 100m/B VHS, DVD, John Wayne, Susan Hayward, Dennis O'Keefe, Wally Wales, Paul Fix, William Frawley, Grant Withers, Tom London, J.M. Kerrigan, Leonid Kinskey, Duncan Renaldo, Addison Richards, Ben Welden, Crane Whitley, Charles Trowbridge; **D:** Edward Ludwig; **W:** Borden Chase, Aeneas MacKenzie; **C:** William Bradford. **M:** Walter Scharf, Roy Webb.

The Fighting Sheriff ✍ 1931 Routine oater mixes action and romance when a sheriff is thrown together with a society debutante. 65m/B VHS, Buck Jones, Loretta Sayers, Robert Ellis, Harlan E. Knight, Paul Fix, Lillian Worth; **D:** Louis King; **W:** Stuart Anthony.

The Fighting 69th ✍✍½ 1940 Combat but entertaining WW drama with lots of action. Cagney is a Brooklyn street tough who joins the all-Irish 69th New York regiment but could care less about its famed military history. He promptly defies his superiors and barely scrapes through his training. Sent to France, the swaggering Cagney turns coward when confronted by the horrors of war but even-tually redeems himself. O'Brien is the famed regimental chaplain Father Duffy, while Brent is commander "Wild Bill" Donovan, who would later found the OSS in WWII. Lots of heart-tugging emotion backed with a fine supporting cast. 90m/B VHS, DVD, James Cagney, Pat O'Brien, George Brent, Jeffrey Lynn, Alan Hale, Frank McHugh, Dennis Morgan, William Lundigan, Dick Foran, Guinn "Big Boy" Williams, Henry O'Neill, John Litel, George Reeves, Frank "Junior" Coghlan, Sammy Cohen, Joseph Crehan, Eddie Dew, William Hopper, Frank Mayo, Herbert Anderson, Harvey Stephens, Charles Trowbridge, Roland Varno; **D:** William Keighley; **W:** Fred Niblo, Norman Reilly Raine, Dean Franklin; **C:** Gaetano Antonio "Tony" Gaudio; **M:** Adolph Deutsch.

The Fighting Stallion ✍✍½ 1926 Canutt stars as a drifter hired by a rancher who's determined to capture a beautiful wild stallion (played by Boy the Wonder Horse). Silent with original organ score. 78m/B VHS, Yakima Canutt, Nava Gerber, Bud Osborne; **D:** Ben F. Wilson; **W:** George W. Pyper; **C:** Joseph Walker.

The Fighting Sullivans ✍✍½ The Sullivans 1942 The true story of five brothers killed on the Battleship Juneau at Guadalcanal during WWII. The tale tells of the family felt by the siblings after Pearl Harbor, their enlistment to fight for their country, and their tragic fate in the heat of battle. Truly a stirring tribute to all lives lost in combat. 110m/B VHS, DVD, Anne Baxter, Thomas Mitchell, Selena Royle, Eddie Ryan, Trudy Marshall, James B. Cardwell, Roy Roberts, Ward Bond, Mary McCarty, Bobby Driscoll, Addison Richards, Selmer Jackson, Mae Marsh, Harry Strang, Barbara Brown, George Offerman Jr., John Campbell, John Alvin, Patrick Curtis, Nancy June Robinson; **D:** Lloyd Bacon, **W:** Edward Doherty, Mary C. McCall, Jules Schermer; **C:** Lucien N. Andriot; **M:** Cyril Mockridge, Alfred Newman.

The Fighting Temptations ✍✍ 2003 (PG-13) New York adman Darrin marries a witch and hilarity ensues. Oh wait, that's something else. Okay, Darrin (Gooding, Jr.) is an adman in New York...for about 15 minutes. Before long he's unemployed and heading to his small Georgia hometown in order to collect an inheritance. Only there's a catch—he must return a gospel choir to its former greatness in order to collect. Water-thin plot is merely filler connecting the great gospel and R&B music that is the real star of this show. Beyonce Knowles is the love interest and mainstay of the choir, but she's only one of the prominent musical talents who help to raise this flick above the mundane. Shirley Caesar, Melba Moore, The O'Jays, Faith Evans, Eddie LeVert, and Montel Jordan are among the luminaries. 123m/C VHS, DVD, US Cuba Gooding Jr., Beyonce Knowles, Mike Epps, LaTanya Richardson, Jackson, Steve Harvey, Melba Moore; **D:** Jonathan Lynn; **W:** Elizabeth Hunter, Saladin Patterson; **C:** Affonso Beato; **M:** Jimmy Jam, Terry Lewis, James "Big Jim" Wright.

Fighting Shadows ✍½ 1935 McCoy plays a tough lawman who rids his town of an unscrupulous bandit gang by some excellent trick riding for which Western star McCoy was known. 58m/B VHS, Tim McCoy, Robert "Tex" Allen, Geneva Mitchel, Ward Bond, Si Jenks; **D:** David Selman.

Fighting Texans ✍ 1933 An entire town invests in an oil well, on the advice of young salesman Bell, that the bankers are sure is a dud. Imagine their surprise when it turns out to be a gusher. 60m/B VHS, Rex Bell, Luana Walters, Betty Mack, Gordon DeMain, Lyons.

Fighting Thru ✍ California in 1878 tough loner takes on a vicious motorcycle gang that's terrorizing a small town, and realizes that they're also responsible for his family's death. 60m/B VHS, Ken Maynard, Jeanette Loff; **D:** William Nigh.

The Fighting Trooper ✍½ 1934 Based on the James Oliver Curwood story. "Footprints," this frontier tale presents a Mountie who goes undercover as a trapper in the Northwest. He is out to catch a murderer. 57m/B VHS, Kermit Maynard, Barbara Worth, Leroy Mason, Charles Delaney, Robert Frazer, George Regas, Walter Miller, Joseph Girard; **D:** Ray Taylor; **W:** Forrest Sheldon; **C:** Edgar Lyons.

Fighting Valley ✍✍ 1943 Texas Rangers O'Brien, and Wilkerson ride off to break up an outlaw gang that is trying to monopolize the ore smelting business. O'Brien later went on to directing for TV and also wrote for Red Skelton. 60m/B VHS, Dave O'Brien, James Newill, Guy Wilkerson, Patti McCarty, John Merton, Curley Dresden; **D:** Oliver Drake; **W:** Oliver Drake.

Fighting Vigilantes ✍✍ 1947 A villainous food distributor is terrorizing his rivals until LaRue whips him. Holt and her father put together a committee called "The Vigilantes" to help out Holt. A daughter of a movie good guy Jack Holt. 61m/B VHS, Lash LaRue, Al "Fuzzy" St. John, Jennifer Holt, George Chesebro, Lee Morgan, Russell Arms, Steve Clark; **D:** Ray Taylor.

The Fighting Westerner ✍½ Rocky Mountain Mystery 1935 Scott stars as a mining engineer who becomes entangled in mysterious murders. Mrs. Leslie Carter stars in a rare screen role. 54m/B VHS, DVD, Randolph Scott, Charles "Chic" Sale, Ann Sheridan, Charles T. Barton.

Film Geek ✍✍½ 2006 Pitiful Scotty (Makkasian) loses his video store job because of the pain and suffering he's caused coworkers and customers (and viewers) alike with his endless chit-chat about the cinema and his lame zero-visitor movie website. The forlorn film fanatic gets really bummed out until his life takes an undue fairytale-ending twist thanks in part to a cool movie-loving chick he's preoccupied with. 78m/C DVD, GB John (Johnny Rotten) Lydon, Paul Cook, Steve Jones, Malcolm McLaren, Sid Vicious, Glen Matlock, Nancy Spungen; **D:** Julien Temple; **M:** John (Johnny Rotten) Lydon.

Fighting with Kit Carson ✍✍ 1933 Famous guide and Indian fighter lead bands of settlers westward. Action-packed. Twelve chapters. 230m/B VHS, DVD, Johnny Mack Brown, Noah Beery Sr., Noah Beery Jr., Betsy King Ross; **D:** Armand Schaefer, Colbert Clark.

The Filth and the Fury ✍✍½ 1999 (R) British punk anarchists The Sex Pistols get their documentary due. Combines new and old footage and interviews of the (surviving) band members (Sid Vicious died of a heroin overdose). Director Temple previously covered the group in 1980's "The Great Rock 'n' Roll Swindle," which was told from the viewpoint of their former manager Malcolm McLaren. 105m/C VHS, DVD, GB John (Johnny Rotten) Lydon, Paul Cook, Steve Jones, Malcolm McLaren, Sid Vicious, Glen Matlock, Nancy Spungen; **D:** Julien Temple; **M:** John (Johnny Rotten) Lydon.

Final ✍✍½ 2001 (R) Bill (Leary) wakes up confused in a Connecticut psychiatric hospital after an apparent suicide attempt. He's assigned to Ann (Davis), a young staff therapist who tries to help Bill sort out his memories from his delusions, which include the fear that he's to be executed by lethal injection and must escape. The story takes on some strange twists, including patients' rights and conspiracy theories. 111m/C VHS, DVD, Denis Leary, Hope Davis, J.C. MacKenzie, Jim Gaffigan; **D:** Campbell Scott; **W:** Bruce McIntosh; **C:** Dan Gillham; **M:** Guy Davis.

The Final Alliance ✍ 1989 (R) A tough loner takes on a vicious motorcycle gang that's terrorizing a small town, and realizes that they're also responsible for his family's death. 90m/C VHS, David Hasselhoff, John Saxon, Bo Hopkins, Jeanie Moore; **D:** Mario DiLeo.

Final Analysis ✍✍ 1992 (R) A Glossy thriller starring Gere as a San Francisco psychiatrist who falls for the glamorous sister of one of his patients. Basinger plays the femme fatale and Thurman is Gere's sexually neurotic patient. Although heavily influenced by "Vertigo," this film never comes close to attaining the depth of Hitchock's cinematic masterpiece. Roberts gives the most gripping performance in this slick suspense movie as Basinger's sleazy gangster husband. 125m/C VHS, DVD, Richard Gere, Kim Basinger, Uma Thurman, Eric Roberts, Paul Guilfoyle, Keith David, Robert Harper, Jolyon Baker, Harris Yulin, Agustin Rodriguez; **D:** Phil Joanou; **W:** Wesley Strick, Robert Berger; **C:** Jordan Cronenweth; **M:** George Fenton.

Final Appeal ✍✍½ 1993 (PG-3) Christine Biorci (Williams) is an abused wife, living in terror of her drug-addicted doctor husband, Ed. When Christine walks in on Ed and his mistress, she's forced to kill him in self-defense. But Ed's mistress swears it was murder and Christine's on trial. Now her only chance is her hard-drinking lawyer brother Perry (Dennehy)—who doesn't believe her story. Fact-based made for TV fare. 94m/C VHS, JoBeth Williams, Brian Dennehy, Lindsay Crouse, Tom Nason, Eddie Jones, Ashley Crow, Betsy Brantley, Michael Beach; **M:** Charles Bernstein. TV

Final Approach ✍✍ 1991 (R) Test pilot Jason Halsey (Sikking) crashes in the desert and awakens in the office of psychiatrist Dio Gottlieb (Elizondo). Halsey can't remember anything about his past, or his own name for that matter, but through word association games and psychological tests, he begins to remember as Gottlieb tries to pry information from his brain. Showy computer effects are excellent, but they only serve to fill holes in a story that has an unsatisfying ending. Notable as first film made with digital sound. Also available in a letterboxed version. 100m/C VHS, James B. Sikking, Hector Elizondo, Madolyn Smith, Kevin McCarthy, Cameo Kneuer, Wayne Duvall; **D:** Eric Steven Stahl.

Final Approach ✍✍ 2004 Hijackers take control of a plane full of elementary students and, to make things worse, the pilot collapses. Luckily 10-year-old Ricky (Garrett)—who has mastered computer flight simulation games—is put in charge of landing the plane. He and his friends must keep the terrorists at bay. Family-oriented though perhaps a little scary for the younger set. 92m/C DVD, Jordan Garret, Larry Miller, Eric Roberts, Mark Dacascos, Angela Watson, Dean Rasche, Tim Thomerson, Steve Hynter; **D:** James Becket; **W:** James Becket; **C:** Denis Maloney; **M:** Peter Tomashek. VIDEO

Final Assignment ✍ The Moscow Chronicle 1980 A Canadian TV reporter agrees to smuggle a dissident Soviet scientist's ill granddaughter out of Russia for treatment along with a videotape documenting tragic experiments on children with steroids. She manages to evade the KGB while carrying on with a Russian press officer, and enlists the support of a Jewish fur trader. Location shooting in Canada instead of Russia is just one pitfall of this production. 101m/C VHS, CA Genevieve Bujold, Michael York, Burgess Meredith, Colleen Dewhurst; **D:** Paul Almond.

Final Combination ✍½ 1993 Boxer Welton (Stretch) lures two girls to his hotel room where he rapes and beat them to death. Trying to catch the psycho is hard-bitten, hard-drinking L.A. cop Matt Dickson (Madison), who figures out he's after a serial killer using the names of famous boxers as aliases. Also involved is mous journalist Catherine Briggs (Boltner), who offers into to Dickson but has her own age-ola. Ordinary thriller with silli-er-than-usual dialogue. 92m/C VHS, Michael Madsen, Lisa Eonel, Gary Stretch, Tim Russ, Damian Chapa, Carmen Argenziano, Susan Byun; **D:** Nigel Dick; **W:** Larry Golin; **M:** Rolfe Kent.

Final Comedown ✍ 1972 (R) A black revolutionary attempts to get white radicals behind his war against racism as is polished for world domination but fears another savior is born. Several monks and many babies meet gruesome deaths before he gets his consequence. The last theatrical release; the next entry was made for TV. 108m/C VHS, DVD, Sam Neill, Lisa Harrow, Barnaby Holm, Rossano Brazzi, Don Gordon, Mason Adams, Marc Boyle, Tommy Duggan, Richard Oldfield, Kirk Doug-las, Martin Sheen, Katharine Ross, James Farentino, Charles Durning; **D:** Don Taylor; **M:** Thomas G. Brown.

The Final Conflict ✍✍✍ Omen 3: The Final Conflict 1981 (R) Unwelcomed third installment in the "Omen" series; concerned back to 1941, just hours before the bombing of Pearl Harbor. The command-ers face the ultimate decision—leave history intact or stop the incident and thus avoid WWII. Excellent photography and a surprise ending. 92m/C VHS, DVD, Kirk Douglas, Martin Sheen, Katharine Ross, James Farentino, Charles Durning; **D:** Don Taylor; **M:** Lalo Schifrin.

The Final Countdown ✍✍✍ 1980 (PG) A U.S. nuclear-powered aircraft carrier, caught in a time warp, is transported back to 1941, just hours before the bombing of Pearl Harbor. The command-ers face the ultimate decision—leave history intact or stop the incident and thus avoid WWII. Excellent photography and a surprise ending. 92m/C VHS, DVD, Carla De Lane, T.J. Kennedy, Joe Rainer, Brett Rice, Jordan Williams; **D:** Larry Hunter, David Amorose.

Final Cut ✍½ 1988 While filming in a secluded swampland, a crew stumbles on a local sheriff's crooked scheme and by one by the crew members disappear. 92m/C VHS, DVD, Kirk Doug-las, Martin Sheen, Katharine Ross, James Farentino, Charles Durning; **D:** Don Taylor.

Final Cut ✍✍ 1995 Follows "House of Cards" and "To Play the King" in portraying the political adventures of Francis Urquardt (Richardson). Prime Minister. At 65, Urquardt has two goals: he wants to beat Margaret Thatcher's 11-year reign and he wants to establish a secret retirement fund (the plot involves Cyprus and could—finally—leads to Urquardt's downfall). Author Michael Dobbs objected to the adaptation and insisted his name be removed from the script. On two cassettes. 200m/C VHS, DVD, GB Ian Richardson, Diane Fletcher, Paul Freeman, Isla Blair, Nick Brimble, Erika Hoffman, Nickolas Grace, Julian Fellowes; **D:** Mike Vardy; **W:** Andrew Davies; **C:** Ian Punter; **M:** Jim Parker.

The Final Cut ✍✍ 1998 (R) John Pierce (Elliott) is a retired bomb squad specialist who's unwillingly called back to active duty to stop a bomber who's target ing Seattle. Along with ambitious officer Kathleen Hardy (Ramsay), Pierce tries to discover the bomber's next move—only to have suspicion fall upon himself. 95m/C VHS, Sam Elliott, Charles Martin Smith, Amna Elizabeth Ramsay, Matt Craven, Ray Baker, John Hannah, Amanda Plummer; **D:** Roger Christian; **W:** Paul Inglis; **C:** Mike Southon; **M:** Ross Vannelli.

Final Cut ✍ 1998 (R) A self-indulgent, apparently largely improvised mess. Jude (Law) has died and his friends pay their respects at his funeral, his wife Sadie (Frost) insists they view the home video he'd been working on for the past two years. It turns out Jude must have recorded his pals at their worst behavior, all of which is now revealed to the uncomfortable ensemble. **93m/C VHS, DVD. GB** Jude Law, Sadie Frost, Ray Winstone, Ray Burdis, Dominic Anciano, Perry Benson, John Beckett; **D:** Ray Burdis, Dominic Anciano; **W:** Ray Burdis, Dominic Anciano; **C:** John Ward; **M:** John Beckett.

The Final Cut ♪♪½ **2004 (PG-13)**
After "One Hour Photo" Williams plays another guy involved in images, this time in a subdued sci-fi thriller. In the near-future, newborns are implanted with a chip that records their entire life—good, bad, and in-between. Alan Hakman (Williams) is a cutter who splices the appropriate footage of the deceased together as a funeral memorial. Then Hakman is asked to create a memorial of the recently-deceased chipmaker, a guy with some shady dealings that put Hakman in danger. Caviezel plays an anti-chip activist who wants an expose and Sorvino is Williams' ex-girlfriend who didn't care for his video obsession. The premise has certainly been done before and in much more enthralling movies. **104m/C DVD. CA GE** Robin Williams, Mira Sorvino, James (Jim) Caviezel, Mimi Kuzyk, Brendan Fletcher, Vincent Gale, Thom Bishops, Casey Dubois, Liam Ranger; **D:** Omar Naim; **W:** Omar Naim; **C:** Tak Fujimoto; **M:** Brian Tyler.

The Final Days ♪♪♪½ **1989 (PG)**
TV drama follows the presidency of Richard Nixon (Smith) from Watergate through his resignation. Based on the Pulitzer Prize-winning book by Bob Woodward and Carl Bernstein. **150m/C VHS.** Lane Smith, Richard Kiley, David Ogden Stiers, Ed Flanders, Theodore Bikel; **D:** Richard Pearce.

Final Destination ♪♪ **2000 (R)**
Teenager Alex (Sawa) predicts that a plane filled with classmates will explode. It does but he and some others manage to make it off the plane beforehand. Things get interesting (and a little philosophical) when the survivors start dying. Seems Death feels cheated and is getting even. Typical body count slasher genre gets a twist from the machinations of fate...or whatever. Filmmakers paid tribute to some of their favorite horror stars and directors with the characters' surnames. **97m/C VHS, DVD.** Devon Sawa, Ali Larter, Kristen Cloke, Daniel Roebuck, Roger Guenveur Smith, Chad E. Donella, Seann William Scott, Tony Todd, Kerr Smith, Amanda Detmer; **D:** James Wong; **W:** Glen Morgan, James Wong, Jeffrey Reddick; **C:** Robert McLachlan; **M:** Shirley Walker.

Final Destination 2 ♪♪ **2003 (R)**
Sequel has the same premise as the original. Kimberly (Cook) has a horrifying vision of a traffic accident as she heads onto the highway. She blocks the ramp with her SUV, thus saving the lives of the drivers behind her. However, Death doesn't like to be cheated and the drivers start to die in bizarre accidents. Less philosophical than the first one, it ups the ante on the gore factor. Death also has a tendency to lay elaborate, convoluted plans to bring the intended victims to their gruesome deaths (kinda like Bond villains). The accidents can be so improbable that it borders on being tiresome, but if you accept the premise on a certain level you can enjoy it as a guilty pleasure. Larter returns as the sole survivor from the first movie and Tony Todd has a cameo as a morgue attendant. **100m/C VHS, DVD. US** Ali Larter, A.J. Cook, Michael Landes, Terrence "T.C." Carson, Lynda Boyd, Jonathan Cherry, Keegan Connor Tracy, Sarah Carter, Tony Todd, Justina Machado, David Paetkau, James N. Kirk; **D:** David R. Ellis; **W:** J. Mackye Gruber, Eric Bress; **C:** Gary Capo; **M:** Shirley Walker.

Final Destination 3 ♪♪ **2006 (R)**
Death stalks a whole new batch of interchangeable teenagers who survive a huge rollercoaster crash thanks to the premonition of Wendy (Winstead). You weren't really expecting anything different, were you? Demises come in really gross, over-the-top, more-gore-the-better ways as the Grim Reaper makes like a deranged Wile E. Coyote. **92m/C DVD. US** Mary Elizabeth Winstead, Ryan Merriman, Kris Lemche, Texas Battle, Jesse Moss, Crystal Lowe, Chelan Simmons, Alexz Johnson, Gina Holden, Sam Easton, Amanda Crew; **D:** James Wong; **W:** James Wong, Glen Morgan; **C:** Robert McLachlan; **M:** Shirley Walker.

Final Embrace ♪♪½ **1992 (R)**
When Laurel's famous sister is murdered she decides to do a little investigating on her own. She's aided by a young cop who just happened to be obsessed with the murdered woman. **88m/C VHS.** Robert Rusler, Nancy Valen, Dick Van Patten, Linda Dona; **D:** Oley Sassone; **W:** R.J. Robertson, Jim Wynorski; **M:** Daniel Licht.

Final Encounter ♪ *For the Cause* **2000 (R)** Confusing sci-fier based on the Warhammer videogame. A 100-year-old war between two technologically advanced colonies may finally be decided by witches (Whalen) is told by Gen. Murran (Cain) to lead a unit into enemy territory and stop the devastation. They're aided by witches who can turn computer programs into physical monsters but they also have to deal with a traitor. **96m/C DVD.** Dean Cain, Justin Whalin, Thomas Ian Griffith, Jodi Bianca Wise; **D:** David Douglas, Tim Douglas; **W:** David Douglas, Christopher Salazar; **C:** Adolfo Bartoli; **M:** Kevin Memley. **VIDEO**

Final Equinox ♪♪½ **1995** Mysterious alien artifact, which has the power to spontaneously create new life, is stolen and both the government and the mob try to be the first to find—and control—it. Cop Kove opposes them both. **90m/C VHS.** Martin Kove, Joe Lara, David Warner, Gary Kasper; **D:** Serge Rodnunsky; **W:** Serge Rodnunsky.

Final Exam woof! **1981 (R)** Psychotic killer stalks college students during exam week. This one's too boring to be scary. You root for the psycho to rid everyone just to have the movie over. **90m/C VHS.** Cecile Bagdadi, Joel Rice; **D:** Jimmy Huston.

Final Exam ♪♪½ **1998** Ghetto drama about racism. High school basketball star Javon Robinson (McCray) is counting on getting a scholarship to college to get away from the drugs and violence that surrounds him. But when he fails English, he takes his teacher hostage at gunpoint and blames his failure on racism. **93m/C VHS.** Alvin O. McCray, John Mollica, Mario Velasquez, Gregor Manns, Augustina Montesino; **D:** John Mollica; **C:** Mike Dolgetta. **VIDEO**

The Final Executioner ♪ *The Last Warrior* **1983** A valiant man finds a way to stop the slaughter of innocent people in a post-nuclear world. **95m/C VHS.** William Mang, Marina Costa, Harrison Muller, Woody Strode; **D:** Romolo Guerrieri.

Final Fantasy: The Spirits Within ♪♪½ **2001 (PG-13)** Photorealistic computer-generated animation may be the highlight of this fantasy adventure, which is based on the videogame series. In the year 2065, life on Earth is threatened by aliens who steal energy from all living things on the planet. A team of scientists, led by Aki Ross (Ming-Na) and Dr. Sid (Sutherland) are at odds with the military, in the form of General Hein (Woods) over how to deal with the creatures. Plot, dialogue, and characterization, the movie's obvious weaknesses, definitely take a back seat to the visuals. The human characters, while not completely lifelike, are the closest anyone's come so far. Where the techology shines is in the landscapes and non-human creatures, which are all striking. **104m/C VHS, DVD, Blu-ray Disc, UMD. US D:** Hironobu Sakaguchi; **W:** Al Reinert, Jeff Vintar; **M:** Elliot Goldenthal; **V:** Ming Na, Alec Baldwin, Steve Buscemi, Peri Gilpin, Ving Rhames, Donald Sutherland, James Woods, Keith David, Jean Simmons, Matt McKenzie.

The Final Goal ♪½ **1994 (R)** Evil businessman (and ex-soccer star) Paulo Ramirez (Estrada) meddles with his country's current soccer star, who's playing in the Global Cup of Soccer. He wants the player to throw the game and thinks death threats will accomplish his goal. **85m/C VHS, DVD.** Erik Estrada, Steven Nijjar, Dean Butler; **D:** Jon Cassar.

The Final Hit ♪♪ **2002 (R)** Washed-up Hollywood producer Sonny Wexler (Reynolds) prefers to reminisce about his past success than raise the money to option a hot script and get back in the game. Maybe he should stick with his memories, since Sonny hooks up with a shady businessman who expects a guaranteed return on his investment—or else. **90m/C VHS, DVD.** Burt Reynolds, Lauren Holly, Benjamin Bratt, Sean Astin; **D:** Burt Reynolds.

Final Impact ♪♪½ **1991 (R)** Nick Taylor seeks vengeance on reigning kickboxing champ Jake Gerard through his prodigy, Danny Davis. Will sweet revenge for the wicked beating, suffered at the hands of Gerard years earlier, be his? **99m/C VHS, DVD.** Lorenzo Lamas, Kathleen Kinmont, Mimi Lesseos, Kathrin Lautner, Jeff Langton, Mike Worth; **D:** Joseph Merhi; Stephen Smoke; **M:** John Gonzalez.

Final Judgment ♪♪ **1992 (R)** Daniel Tyrone (Douif) is a former gang member, now a troubled priest, who's the prime suspect in the Los Angeles murder of a beautiful stripper. Determined to find the killer Father Tyrone heads into L.A.'s underground sex industry to search for clues, which brings him face to face with evil and his own desires. **90m/C VHS.** Brad Dourif, Isaac Hayes, Maria Ford, Karen Black, Orson Bean, David Ledingham; **D:** Louis Morneau; **M:** Kirk Honeycutt, Louis Morneau.

Final Justice ♪ **1984 (R)** A small-town Texan sheriff wages a war against crime and corruption that carries him to Italy and the haunts of Mafia hitmen. **90m/C VHS, DVD.** Joe Don Baker, Rossano Brazzi, Patrizia Pellegrino, Venantino Venantini; **D:** Greydon Clark; **W:** Greydon Clark; **C:** Nicholas Josef von Sternberg; **M:** David Bell.

Final Justice ♪ **1994 (R)** Icky revenge drama has bad guys Red (Huff) and Bobby (Marotta) hiding out in a woodsy cabin that's owned by lawyer Alan Massard (Brolin) and his wife Amy (Fitzgerald). Unfortunately for them, the Massards have chosen to invite some friends and hang out at the cabin for the weekend, where the bad guys do nasty things before Alan manages to kill Bobby and trap Red. Then there's a stupid debate on just what to do with Red and more violence. **92m/C VHS.** James Brolin, Annie Fitzgerald, Brent Huff, Rick Marotta, Beau Billingslea; **D:** Brent Huff; **W:** Brent Huff.

Final Justice ♪♪½ **1998** Teacher Gwen (O'Toole) is outraged when a sleazy attorney (McKean) gets her murdered gay brother's killer acquitted. So she kidnaps him from L.A. and metes out rough justice of her own but then winds up on trial herself. **120m/C VHS, DVD.** Annette O'Toole, Michael McKean, CCH Pounder, Brian Wimmer; **D:** Tommy Lee Wallace; **W:** Babs Greyhosky; **M:** Brian Tyler. **CABLE**

Final Mission ♪ **1984** Vengeful one-man army follows the professional hit of a man who slaughtered his family from L.A. to Laos. His pursuit leads to a jungle showdown. Gee, sounds like "Rambo, First Blood," though obviously less grand and glorious. **97m/C VHS.** Richard Young, John Dresden, Kaz Garas, Christine Tudor; **D:** Cirio H. Santiago.

Final Mission ♪♪ **1993 (R)** Virtual reality becomes a weapon in a military conspiracy when pilots start dying. Air Force jets are supposed to be unstoppable thanks to the new technology and a general is only too willing to blame the deaths on pilot error but one fly boy is out to find the truth. **91m/C VHS.** Billy Wirth, Corbin Bernsen, Elizabeth (Ward) Gracen, Steve Railsback.

Final Move ♪ **2006 (R)** After using his psychic powers to help the LAPD solve a chess-related serial-killer case, former detective Dan Marlowe (Schulze) becomes obsessed by thoughts that he might have put an innocent man to death. A rash of similar slayings seems to confirm his worst fears, causing him to rejoin the force to crack the case. Produces a serious case of deja vu for the onslaught of rehashed plot twists. **90m/C DVD.** Matt Schulze, Lochlyn Munro, Amanda Detmer, Daniel Baldwin, David Carradine; **D:** Joey Travolta; **W:** Richard Preston Jr., David Shoshan. **VIDEO**

Final Notice ♪ **1989** A detective tracking a serial killer has as his only evidence a trail of shredded photos of nude women. Not released theatrically. **91m/C VHS.** Gil Gerard, Steve Landesberg, Jackie Burroughs, Melody Anderson, Louise Fletcher, David Ogden Stiers, Kevin Hicks; **D:** Steven Hilliard Stern; **W:** John Gay; **M:** Tom Scott.

The Final Option ♪ *Who Dares Wins* **1982 (R)** An agent of England's Special Air Services team goes undercover as one of a band of anti-nuclear terrorists that take over the U.S. Embassy in London. Violent, but unconvincing. **125m/C VHS. GB** Lewis Collins, Judy Davis, Richard Widmark, Robert Webber, Edward Woodward, Ingrid Pitt, Kenneth Griffith, Tony Doyle, John Duttine; **D:** Ian Sharp; **W:** Reginald Rose; **C:** Phil Meheux.

Final Payback woof! **1999** A cast of faded TV stars long since past their prime time (Richard Grieco of "21 Jump Street," Corbin Bernsen of "L.A. Law," Martin Kove of "Cagney and Lacey," Priscilla Barnes of "Three's Company") collect their paychecks for this ineptly directed thriller that leaves no direct-to-video cliche unturned. Grieco stars as an ex-cop who finds himself "pushed over the fence" after he is framed for the murder of the police chief's wife. Gee, you think the police chief himself (B-movie vet John Saxon) may be involved in the conspiracy? No nudity and only one car explosion. Why bother? **102m/C VHS, DVD, UMD.** Richard Grieco, Corbin Bernsen, Martin Kove, Priscilla Barnes, John Saxon; **D:** Art Camacho.

The Final Programme ♪♪½
The Last Days of Man on Earth **1973** In this futuristic story, a man must rescue his sister—and the world—from their brother, who holds a microfilmed plan for global domination. Meanwhile, he must shield himself from the advances of a bisexual computer programmer who wants to make him father to a new, all-purpose human being. Based on the Michael Moorcock "Jerry Cornelius" stories, the film has gained a cult following. **85m/C VHS, DVD. GB** Hugh Griffith, Harry Andrews, Jon Finch, Jenny Runacre, Sterling Hayden, Patrick Magee, Sarah Douglas; **D:** Robert Fuest; **W:** Robert Fuest; **C:** Norman Warwick; **M:** Gerry Mulligan, Paul Beaver; Bernard Krause.

Final Round ♪♪½ **1993 (R)** A kickboxer and his girlfriend are kidnapped by a millionaire who stages hunts the humans games for the pleasure of his gambling syndicate. Stiff but with a few good action sequences. **90m/C VHS.** Lorenzo Lamas, Anthony de Longis, Kathleen Kinmont, Clark Johnson, Isabelle Jamieson; **D:** George Erschbamer; **W:** Arne Olsen; **M:** Graeme Coleman.

Final Sanction ♪♪½ **1989** After a nuclear holocaust exhausts their military resources, the U.S. and the Soviets each send one-man armies to battle each other for final control of the world. **90m/C VHS.** Robert Z'Dar, Ted Prior; **D:** David A. Prior; **W:** David A. Prior.

The Final Season ♪♪ **2007 (PG)**
A tiny city in Iowa revels in the success of the local high school baseball team, with its multiple state championships. But administrators are plotting to merge the school with a neighboring high school, putting both coaches and players in jeopardy. Brand new head coach Kent Stock (Astin) wants the team to end their legendary final game. Yet another based-on-a-true-story sports drama that makes up for its flaws with a whole lotta heart. **114m/C DVD. US** Sean Astin, Powers Boothe, Rachael Leigh Cook, James Gammon, Larry Miller, Marshall Bell, Tom Arnold, Michael Angarano, Angela Paton; **D:** David Mickey Evans; **W:** Art D'Alessandro, James Grayford; **C:** Stephen Blake; **M:** Stanley Clarke.

Final Shot: The Hank Gathers Story ♪♪½ **1992** Inspirational story of Gathers, who rose from the ghetto to become one of America's top college basketball stars at Loyola Marymount, until tragedy strikes during a game. **92m/C VHS, DVD.** Victor Love, Duane Davis, Nell Carter, George Kennedy; **D:** Charles Braverman; **W:** Fred Johnson; **C:** Stephen Blake; **M:** Stanley Clarke.

The Final Terror ♪♪ *Campsite Massacre; Bump in the Night; The Forest Primeval* **1983 (R)** Group of young campers is stalked by a mad killer in a desolate, back-

Final Voyage 🐾🐾 1999 (R) Hijackers, lec by Ice-T, take over the cruise ship Britannica and their robbery of the vault leads to a threat to sink the boat as well. Bodyguard Walsh manages to escape and wages a one-man war against the bad guys throughout the ship. It's better than "Speed 2." Wynorski directed under the pseudonym Jay Andrews. **95m/C VHS, DVD.** Ice-T, Dylan Walsh, Erika Eleniak, Claudia Christian (Rick) Ducommun; **D:** Jim Wynorski; **W:** Jim Wynorski, J. Everitt Morley; **C:** Ken Blakey; **M:** David Wurst, Eric Wurst. **VIDEO**

Final Warning 🐾🐾½ 2006 (R) *Chernobyl: The Final Warning* 1990 A dramatization of actual events surrounding the 1986 meltdown of the nuclear power plant at Chernobyl. **94m/C VHS.** Jon Voight, Jason Robards Jr., Sammi Davis; **D:** Anthony Page. **TV**

Find Me Guilty 🐾🐾🐾 2006 (R) Amusingly cutting mockery of courtroom ritual from master Lumet that's based on a true story. From 1986-88, 20 members of the New Jersey-based Lucchese crime family were prosecuted by the feds; all had attorneys except for low-level goombah Giacomo "Jackie Dee" DiNorscio (Diesel), who represented himself. Jackie wisecracks throughout the trial, garnering unexpected sympathy while causing agita in both the presiding judge (Silver) and mob boss Nick Calabrese (Rocco). Performances are excellent; note Sciorra's cameo as Jackie's bitter ex-wife. **125m/C DVD.** US Vin Diesel, Peter Dinklage, Linus Roache, Ron Silver, Alex Rocco, Annabella Sciorra, Richard Portnow, Robert Stanton, Raul Esparza, Domenick Lombardozzi, Paul Borghese, Jerry Adler, Marcia Jean Kurtz; **D:** Sidney Lumet; **W:** Sidney Lumet, T.J. Mancini, Robert J. McCrea; **C:** Ron Fortunato; **M:** Richard Glasser.

Find the Lady 🐾🐾 2001 (R) *Call the Cops!* Kopek and Broom 1976 (R) Candy assumes a supporting role as a bumbling cop who is part of an incompetent police team trying to rescue a kidnapped socialite. **100m/C VHS.** CA John Candy, Peter Cook, Mickey Rooney, Lawrence Dare, Alexandra Bastedo, Robert McHeady, Dick Emory, Michael Kirby, Delroy Lindo; **D:** John Trent; **W:** David Main, Claude Harz; **C:** Harry Waxman.

Finder's Fee 🐾🐾 2001 (R) A basic psycho-thriller set primarily in a New York apartment. Tepper (Palladino) finds a wallet in the street and contacts the owner, Avery Phillips (Jones). Later, Tepper also discovers a lottery ticket worth $6 mil inside the wallet and spills the news to his poker buddy, Fishman (Lillard), who can't keep the news from the other guys—Quigley (Reynolds) and Bolan (Milrok). Then, Avery shows up and sits in on the game, supposedly unaware of his potential good fortune. Now, does Tepper keep the ticket? And will his buddies also keep quiet? **99m/C VHS, DVD.** Erik Palladino, James Earl Jones, Matthew Lillard, Ryan Reynolds, Dash Mihok, Carly Pope, Robert Forster, Frances Bay; **D:** Jeff Probst; **C:** Francis Kenny; **M:** B.C. Smith.

Finders Keepers 🐾🐾 1984 (R) A wild assortment of characters on board a train en route from California to Nebraska search for $5 million hidden in the baggage car. **96m/C VHS.** Michael O'Keefe, Beverly D'Angelo, Ed Lauter, Louis Gossett Jr., Pamela Stephenson, Jim Carrey, David Wayne, Brian Dennehy, John Schuck; **D:** Richard Lester; **W:** Ronny Graham.

Finding Buck McHenry 🐾🐾½ 2000 When 11-year-old Jason (Schiffman) gets cut from Little League, he decides to form his own team. He persuades school custodian Buck McHenry (Davis) to coach but the man's knowledge about the game leads Jason to suspect that Buck is a Negro

---

woods area. Better-than-average stalked-teens entry is notable for the presence of some soon-to-be stars. **90m/C VHS, DVD.** John Freidrich, Rachel Ward, Adrien Zmed, Daryl Hannah, Joe Pantoliano, Ernest Harden Jr., Mark Metcalf, Lewis Smith, Cindy Harrel, Akosua Busia; **D:** Andrew Davis.

Final Verdict 🐾🐾½ 1991 (R) A trial lawyer defends a man he knows is guilty, throwing his life and his family into turmoil. **93m/C VHS.** Treat Williams, Glenn Ford, Amy Wright, Olivia Burnette; **D:** Jack Fisk; **C:** Paul Elliott. **CABLE**

Finding Forrester 🐾🐾 2000 (PG-13) Underprivileged kid (Brown) from the Bronx, who has smarts and basketball skills, wins a scholarship to an Upper East Side prep school where he's befriended by wealthy classmate Paquin and eccentric writer Connery. Predictable, cloying script almost undermines excellent performances by Connery and newcomer Brown. The only good thing about the screenplay is their dialogue together. **133m/C VHS, DVD.** Anna Paquin, Sean Connery, Rob Brown, F. Murray Abraham, Busta Rhymes, April Grace, Michael Nouri, Zane F. (Lil' Zane) Copeland Jr.; **D:** Gus Van Sant; **W:** Mike Rich; **C:** Harris Savides; **M:** Hal Willner.

Finding Graceland 🐾🐾½ 1998 (PG-13) Down-on-his-luck Byron (Schaech) is driving his 1959 Cadillac convertible through New Mexico when he stops for a hitchhiker and Elvis impersonator (Keitel), who's on his way to Memphis. Except this Elvis believes he's the real thing and he's heading for his Graceland home. Odd things seem to happen to Byron as long as Elvis is around. Not the least being his finding Marilyn Monroe impersonator, Ashley (Fonda). **97m/C VHS, DVD.** Johnathon Schaech, Harvey Keitel, Bridget Fonda, Gretchen Mol; **D:** David Winkler; **W:** Jason Horwich; **C:** Elliot Davis; **M:** Stephen Endelman.

Finding Home 🐾🐾 2004 (PG-13) Workaholic exec Amanda (Brenner) inherits her grandmother Esther's (Fletcher) B&B, located on a remote island off the Maine coast. When Amanda travels there to decide if she should sell the property, she begins having flashbacks of some terrible childhood event that she has repressed. But maybe things are better left forgotten. Conventional family melodrama in a picturesque setting. **124m/C DVD.** Lisa Brenner, Genevieve Bujold, Louise Fletcher, Johnny Messner, Justin Henry, Jason Miller, Misha Collins; **D:** Lawrence Foldes; **W:** Lawrence Foldes, Graton S. Harper; **C:** Jeffrey Seckendorf; **M:** Jo-

Finding Nemo 🐾🐾🐾 2003 (G) Despite the dead mom beginning, this is Pixar (of "Toy Story" fame). Little clown fish Nemo (Gould) was born with an undersized fin and is the sole survivor of a barracuda attack. This makes nervous dad Marlin (Brooks) overprotective. When curious Nemo is scooped up by a scuba diver for life in a fish tank, it's dad to the rescue! He's aided by chipper blue tang Dory (DeGeneres), who unfortunately suffers from short-term memory loss, a sea turtle (director Stanton), and other denizens of both sea and air (including a helpful pelican), while Nemo is making new friends (and escape plans) with his tank mates. Since water is considered the hardest thing to animate, the underseas sequences are particularly breathtaking. There's the usual humor to keep adults interested as well as the irrepressible sweetness amidst the comedy. **101m/C VHS, DVD.** US **D:** Andrew Stanton; **W:** Andrew Stanton, Bob Peterson, David Reynolds; **C:** Sharon Calahan, Jeremy Lasky; **M:** Thomas Newman; **V:** Albert Brooks, Ellen DeGeneres, William Dafoe, Alexander Gould, Barry Humphries, Andrew Stanton, Brad Garrett, Allison Janney, Austin Pendleton, Stephen (Steve) Root, Vicki Lewis, Joe Ranft, Geoffrey Rush, Eric Bana, Bruce Spence, Elizabeth Perkins, Erik Per Sullivan, John Ratzenberger, Bill Hunter, LuLu Ebeling, Erica Beck, Bob Peterson. Oscars '03: Animated Film

Finding Neverland 🐾🐾🐾 2004 (PG) Genteel drama takes the usual biographical license and makes sometimes-obvious conclusions between the life and work of author J.M. Barrie (an equally genteel Depp). A celebrated writer in Edwardian London, Barrie is looking for inspiration when he meets recent widow Sylvia Llewelyn Davies (Winslet) and her four young sons: Peter (Highmore), Jack (Prospero), George (Roud), and Michael (Spill). The

---

gro League legend who's long dropped out of sight and he decides to uncover the truth. **88m/C VHS, DVD.** Ossie Ruby Dee, Ernie Banks, Michael Schiffman, Duane McLaughlin, Karl Pruner, Megan Bower, Catherine Blythe; **D:** Charles Burnett; **W:** Alfred Slote; **C:** John L. (Nslaga Demps Jr.; **M:** Stephen James Taylor. **CABLE**

childless Barrie, detached from his own marriage, becomes increasingly involved with their lives, leading them in games and telling stories that revitalize his own creative juices, which result in the successful play by Allan Knee. **106m/C DVD, Blu-ray, Disc.** US Johnny Depp, Kate Winslet, Julie Christie, Radha Mitchell, Dustin Hoffman, Kelly Macdonald, Ian Hart, Eileen Essell, Freddie Highmore, Joe Prospero, Nick Roud, Luke Spill; **D:** Marc Forster; **W:** David Magee; **C:** Roberto Schaefer; **M:** Jan A.P. Kaczmarek. Oscars '04: Orig. Score.

Finding North 🐾🐾 1997 Predictable dramedy about the friendship between a straight woman and gay man. Talkative, bored bank clerk Rhonda (Makkena) meets suicidal yuppie, Travis (Hickey), who's just lost his lover to AIDS, and decides to help him regain his emotional balance. Even if this means following him from New York to the small Texas town where Travis' late lover grew up. **95m/C VHS, DVD.** Wendy Makkena, John Benjamin Hickey, Angela Pietropinto, Freddie Roman, Molly McClure; **D:** Tanya Wexler; **C:** Michael Barrett; **V:** Jonathan Walker.

Fine Gold 🐾🐾 1988 (R) Tale of embezzlement leaves a man without home and family, so he decides to turn the tables on those who betrayed him. **91m/C VHS.** Andrew Stevens, Ray Walston, Ted Wass, Stewart Granger, Lloyd Bochner, Jane Badler; **D:** Jose Antonio De La Loma.

A Fine Madness 🐾🐾🐾 1966 A near-classic comedy about a lusty, rebellious poet thrashing against the pressures of the modern world, and fending off a bevy of lobotomy-happy psychiatrists. Shot on location in New York City, based on Elliot Baker's novel. **104m/C VHS, DVD.** Sean Connery, Joanne Woodward, Jean Seberg, Patrick O'Neal, Colleen Dewhurst, Clive Revill, John Fiedler, Werner Peters, Kay Medford, Jackie Coogan, Zohra Lampert, Sorrell Booke, Sue Ane Langdon, Bibi Osterwald, Gerald S. O'Loughlin, Richard S. Castellano; **D:** Irvin Kershner; **W:** Elliot Baker; **C:** Ted D. McCord; **M:** John Addison.

A Fine Mess 🐾½ 1986 (PG) Two buffoons cash in when one overhears a plan to dope a racehorse, but they are soon fleeing the plotters' slapstick pursuit. The plot is further complicated by the romantic interest of a gangster's wife. The TV popularity of the two stars did not translate to the big screen; perhaps it's Edwards's fault. **100m/C VHS, DVD.** Ted Danson, Howie Mandel, Richard Mulligan, Stuart Margolin, Maria Conchita Alonso, Paul Sorvino; **D:** Blake Edwards; **W:** Blake Edwards; **C:** Harry Stradling Jr.; **M:** Henry Mancini.

A Fine Romance 🐾🐾 1992 (PG-13) An improbable romance set in Paris features Andrews and Mastroianni as abandoned spouses falling in love. Andrews is the prim English Pamela who has been abandoned by her doctor husband. Mastroianni is the irrepressible Cesareo, whose wife has just happened to run off with the aforementioned doctor. They meet to plan how to get their spouses back and wind up with opposites attracting. Not much story and the charm is spread thin. Based on the play "Tchin Tchin" by Francois Billetdoux. **83m/C VHS, DVD.** Julie Andrews, Marcello Mastroianni, Ian Fitzgibbon, Catrin Castaldi, Jean-Jacques Dulon, Maria Machado, Jean-Michel Cannone, Catherine Jarrett, Gene Saks; **W:** Ronald Harwood; **M:** Pino Donaggio.

The Finest Hour 🐾🐾 1991 (R) Two Navy buddies have a falling out when they both fall for the same woman. But they must put aside their differences when their next mission sends them to Iraq to deal with the deadly threat of biological warfare. **105m/C VHS.** Rob Lowe, Gale Hansen, Tracy Griffith, Eb Lottimer; **D:** Shimon Dotan; **W:** Shimon Dotan.

The Finger Man 🐾🐾½ 1955 An ex-con cooperates with the feds rather than return to jail. The deal is that he gets the dirt on an underworld crime boss. Solid performances. **82m/B VHS.** Frank Lovejoy, Forrest Tucker, Peggy Castle, Timothy Carey, Glenn Gordon, John Cliff, William P. Leicester, John Close, Hugh Sanders, Joi Lansing, Charles Maxwell; **D:** Harold Schuster; **W:** Warren Douglas; **C:** William Sickner; **M:** Paul Dunlap.

Finger on the Trigger 🐾🐾 1965 El Dedo En El Gatillo 1965 Veterans from both sides of the Civil War are after a hidden supply of gold, but find that they must band together to fend off an Indian attack. Routine. **89m/C VHS.** Rory Calhoun, James Philbrook, Todd Martin, Silvia Solar, Brad Talbot; **D:** Sidney W. Pink.

Fingerprints Don't Lie 🐾 1951 A fingerprint expert pins the murder of the town mayor on an innocent guy, then subpects a frame-up. **56m/B VHS.** Richard Travis, Sheila Ryan, Tom Neal; **D:** Sam Newfield.

Fingers 🐾🐾🐾 1978 (R) Keitel is Johnny Fingers, a mobster's son, reluctantly working as a mob debt-collector, all the while dreaming of his ambitions to be a concert pianist. The divisions between his dreams and reality cause him to crack. Toback's first film generates psychological tension and excellent performances. **89m/C VHS, DVD.** Harvey Keitel, Tisa Farrow, Jim Brown, Danny Aiello, Tanya Roberts, Marian Seldes, Michael V., Gazzo, James Toback; **D:** James Toback; **W:** James Toback; **C:** Michael Chapman; **M:** George Barrie.

Finian's Rainbow 🐾🐾🐾 1968 (G) A leprechaun comes to America to steal back a pot of gold taken by an Irishman and his daughter in this fanciful musical comedy based on a 1947 Broadway hit. Both the sprite and the girl find romance, the share-cropping locals are saved by the cash; a bigot learns the error of his ways; and Finian (Astaire) dances off to new adventures. The fine production and talented cast are not used to their best advantage by the director who proved much better suited for "The Godfather." Entertaining, nonetheless. ♫How Are Things in Glocca Morra?; Look To the Rainbow; That Old Devil Moon; If This Isn't Love; Something Sort of Grand-ish; The Be-Gat; This Time of Year; The Great Come and Get It Day; When I'm Not Near the Girl I Love. **141m/C VHS, DVD.** Fred Astaire, Petula Clark, Tommy Steele, Keenan Wynn, Al Freeman Jr., Don Francks, Susan Hancock, Dolph Sweet; **D:** Francis Ford Coppola.

Finish Line 🐾🐾½ 1989 A high school track star turns to steroids to enhance his performance after being pushed by an overzealous father. The father-and-son drama pulls the pair. **100m/C VHS.** James Brolin, Josh Brolin, Mariska Hargitay, Kristen Bauer; **D:** John Finnegan, Billy Vera, Stephen Lang; **D:** John Nicolella. **CABLE**

Finishing School 🐾🐾 1933 Girls' school roommates Rogers and Dee experience heartaches and loves lost while enduring disinterested parents and snobbish peers. Boxoffice bomb when released on peers. Boxoffice bomb when released despite a strong cast. **73m/B VHS.** Ginger Rogers, Frances Dee, George Nichols Jr., Beulah Bondi, Bruce Cabot, Billie Burke, John Halliday, Sara Haden, Jack Norton, Joan Barclay, Jane Darwell, John David Horsley; **D:** George Nichols Jr.; **W:** Max Steiner.

The Finishing Touch 🐾🐾 1992 (R) Someone is stalking L.A.'s most gorgeous women and Detective Sam Store (Nader) is assigned to the case. Store discovers his prime suspect is a video artist with a taste for pornography. When Stone's investigation is cut short, his exwife, Detective Hannah Stone (Hack)'s brought in to take over the case. Unfortunately, she finds herself falling for the suspect in this erotic thriller. **82m/C VHS.** Michael Nader, Shelley Heck, Arnold Vosloo, Art Evans, Clark Johnson, Theodore (Ted) Raimi; **D:** Fred Gallo.

Finnegan Begin Again 🐾🐾 1984 A middle-aged schoolteacher and a grouchy, 65-year-old newspaper editor find romance despite their other college-tions. Winning performances and charm to this cable TV movie. **112m/C VHS.** Mary Tyler

---

Moore, Robert Preston, Sam Waterston, Sylvia Sidney, David Huddleston; *D:* Joan Micklin Silver. **CABLE**

Finnegan's Wake *Passages from "Finnegans Wake"; Passages from James Joyce's Finnegans Wake* **1965** Portions of the filmed adaptation of James Joyce's novel are shown in this program along with an interview with producer/director Mary Ellen Bute. **92m/B VHS.** Peter Haskell, Martin J. Kelley, Jane Reilly, Page Johnson; *D:* Mary Ellen Bute; *W:* Mary Ellen Bute; *C:* Ted Nemeth; *M:* Elliot Kaplan.

Fiona **1998** Fiona was abandoned as a baby, raised in an abusive foster home, and is now a crack-smoking hooker on the streets of New York. After casually killing three cops, she hides out in a crackhouse where she hooks up with Anita—who naturally turns out to be Fiona's long-lost mama. Film is a blend of fiction and documentary footage of real prostitutes and drug houses. **85m/C VHS, DVD.** Anna Thomson, Mike Hodge, Anna Grace, Felicia Maguire; *D:* Amos Kollek; *W:* Amos Kollek; *C:* Ed Talavera; *M:* Alison Gordy.

Fiorile *Wild Flower* **1993 (PG-13)** Covers several generations of a Tuscan clan living under a family curse which dates back to Napoleon's invasion of Italy. At that time Jean, a handsome French lieutenant, falls in love with Tuscan peasant girl Elisabetta, nicknamed Fiorile. When Jean is executed for a theft committed by her brother, the pregnant Fiorile vows revenge. Throughout successive generations, haunted by the past, the family's personal bad luck persists. Several of the actors play their character's ancestors, lending continuity. Attractive cast does well with the Taviani brothers' visual style and romantic narrative. In Italian with English subtitles. **118m/C VHS.** *IT* Michael Vartan, Galatea Ranzi, Claudio Bigagli, Lino Capolicchio, Constanze Engelbrecht, Athina Cenci, Giovanni Guidelli, Chiara Caselli; *D:* Paolo Taviani, Vittorio Taviani; *W:* Paolo Taviani, Vittorio Taviani, Sandro Petraglia; *C:* Giuseppe Lanci; *M:* Nicola Piovani.

Fire **1977** A fire started by an escaped convict rages through Oregon timberland in this suspenseful Irwin Allen disaster drama. **98m/C VHS.** Ernest Borgnine, Vera Miles, Patty Duke, Alex Cord, Donna Mills; *D:* Earl Bellamy. **TV**

Fire **1996** Follows the relationship of two sisters-in-law in New Delhi—both stuck in frustrating, loveless marriages—while examining the harsh patriarchal culture of India. Radha (Azmi) is married to Ashok (Kharbanda), a video store clerk who has taken a vow of celibacy under the teachings of a scruffy swami. Sita (Das) is married to Ashok's brother Jatin (Jaafer), who is openly having an affair with a Chinese Canadian woman. As her frustration grows, the younger Sita acts on her attraction to her sister-in-law and the two begin a lesbian affair, which is taboo in the strict Hindu culture. Dialogue is in "Hinglish," or English with occasional Hindi phrases thrown in. The attitudes portrayed must exist, because the film was banned in India. **104m/C VHS, DVD.** *CA* Shabana Azmi, Nandita Das, Kulbashan Kharbanda, Jaaved Jaaferi, Ranjit (Chaudry) Chowdhry, Kushal Rekhi; *D:* Deepa Mehta; *W:* Deepa Mehta; *C:* Giles Nuttgens; *M:* A.R. Rahman.

Fire Alarm **1932** A change of scene for Western star Brown as he portrays a fireman who, in-between his work, romances a career girl. **67m/B VHS, DVD.** Johnny Mack Brown, Noel Francis; *D:* Karl Brown; *W:* Karl Brown, I.E. Chadwick.

Fire and Ice **1983 (PG)** An animated adventure film that culminates in a tense battle between good and evil, surrounded by the mystical elements of the ancient past. Designed by Frank Frazetta. **81m/C VHS, DVD.** Randy Norton, Cynthia Leake; *D:* Ralph Bakshi; *W:* Ralph Bakshi, Willy Bogner, Gerry Conway; *V:* Susan Tyrrell, William Ostrander.

Fire and Ice **1987 (PG)** A tale of love on the slopes. Two skiers realize that their feelings for each other are perhaps even stronger than their feelings about skiing. You won't care though, except for some fine ski footage. **83m/C VHS.** Suzy

Chaffee, John Eaves; *D:* Willy Bogner; *W:* George Schlatter; *M:* Harold Faltermeyer; *Nar:* John Denver.

Fire and Rain **1989** Based on the real-life crash of a Delta Airlines plane in Dallas and the rescue efforts made following the disaster. Familiar cast-members turn in decent performance. **89m/C VHS.** Angie Dickinson, Charles Haid, Tom Bosley, David Hasselhoff, Robert Guillaume, Susan Ruttan, John Beck, Patti LaBelle, Dean Jones, Lawrence Pressman, Penny Fuller; *D:* Jerry Jameson; *W:* Gary Sherman. **TV**

Fire and Sword **1982** A Cornish knight must choose between loyalty for king and country and the love of an Irish woman in this medieval drama. A not very inspired retelling of the Tristan and Isolde legend. **84m/C VHS.** *GB* Peter Firth, Leigh Lawson, Antonia Preser, Christopher Waltz; *D:* Veith von Furstenberg.

Fire Birds *Wings of the Apache* **1990 (PG-13)** Army attack helicopters and the people who fly them are used in the war on drugs in South America. Failed to match the exciting flight sequences, the romantic interest, or the boxoffice of "Top Gun." **85m/C VHS, DVD.** Nicolas Cage, Tommy Lee Jones, Sean Young, Bryan Kestner, Dale Dye, Mary Ellen Trainor, J.A. Preston, Peter Onorati; *D:* David Green; *W:* Dale Dye, Nick Thiel, Paul F. Edwards; *M:* David Newman.

Fire Down Below **1957** Hayworth is the been-around-the-block beauty who persuades Mitchum and Lemmon, two small-time smugglers, to take her to a safe haven, no questions asked. Both men fall for her obvious charms, causing them to have a falling out until a life or death situation puts their friendship to the test. An unoriginal melodrama indifferently acted by everyone but Lemmon. Good location work in Trinidad and Tobago. **116m/C VHS, DVD.** *GB* Robert Mitchum, Jack Lemmon, Rita Hayworth, Herbert Lom, Anthony Newley; *D:* Robert Parrish; *W:* Irwin Shaw; *C:* Desmond Dickinson; *M:* Arthur Benjamin, Douglas Gamley.

Fire Down Below **1997 (R)** Seagal comes armed with his trademark ponytail, martial arts expertise, big leather jackets, and environment-friendly message to the Appalachians in this hoedown showdown. As undercover (yeah, he blends right in) EPA agent Jack Taggart, Seagal must stop evil industrialist Hanner (Kristofferson) from dumping toxic waste. Of course, the company town sends the usual band of thugs (thoughtfully attacking one at a time) to make him go away. He finds allies in the local outcasts (Helgenberger and Stanton) for the final confrontation. Not Seagal's worst, but that's not saying much. Even the usually impressive fight scenes become tedious after a while. At least he didn't try to direct this one. Originally conceived as a Bruce Willis project at Columbia. **105m/C VHS, DVD.** Steven Seagal, Marg Helgenberger, Kris Kristofferson, Harry Dean Stanton, Stephen Lang, Levon Helm, Brad Hunt, Richard Masur, Ed Bruce, Randy Travis, Mark Collie, Alex Harvey; *D:* Felix Alcala; *W:* Jeb Stuart; *C:* Tom Houghton; *M:* Nick Glennie-Smith.

Fire, Ice and Dynamite **1991 (PG)** Moore is onscreen only briefly as an eccentric tycoon who fakes suicide to watch several teams of challengers scramble in a madcap winter-sports contest for his millions. A German-made avalanche of crazy stunts, bad jokes, and product plugs for countless European companies, commencing with a literal parade of guests, from astronaut Buzz Aldrin to soul man Isaac Hayes. Numbing; must be seen to be believed. **106m/C VHS.** Roger Moore, Shari Belafonte, Simon Shepherd, Uwe Ochsenknecht, Marjoe Gortner; *D:* Willy Bogner.

Fire in the Night **1985** In a small Southern town, a beautiful and surefooted woman battles the limitless resources of the town's predominant dynastic family. **89m/C VHS.** Patrick St. Esprit, Muni Zano, Graciela Casillas, John Martin; *D:* John Steven Soet; *C:* Gene Jackson.

Fire in the Sky **1993 (PG-13)** Mysterious disappearance of Sweeney sparks a criminal investigation, until he returns, claiming he was abducted by aliens. Though everybody doubts his story, viewers won't, since the alleged aliens have already made an appearance, shifting the focus to Sweeney as he tries to convince skeptics that his trauma is genuine. Perhaps this mirrors what director Lieberman went through while trying to convince backers the film should be made. He could have benefitted by understanding the difference between what he was telling viewers and what he was showing them. Captivating special effects are one of the few bright spots. Based on a story that might be true. **98m/C VHS, DVD.** D.B. Sweeney, Robert Patrick, Craig Sheffer, Peter Berg, James Garner, Henry Thomas; *D:* Robert Lieberman; *W:* Tracy Torme; *M:* Mark Isham.

The Fire in the Stone **1985** A young boy discovers an opal mine and dreams of using the treasure to reunite his family. However, when the jewels are stolen from him, he enlists his friends to help get them back. Based on the novel by Colin Thiele. **97m/C VHS.** *AU* Paul Smith, Linda Hartley, Theo Perisindis; *D:* Gary Conway; *W:* Roger Dunn; *C:* Ross Berryman; *M:* Isabel Meier, Matthias Bonnefoy.

Fire Maidens from Outer Space **1956** Fire maidens prove to be true to the space opera code that dictates that all alien women be in desperate need of male company. Astronauts on an expedition to Jupiter's 13th moon discover the lost civilization of Atlantis, which, as luck would have it, is inhabited by women only. Possibly an idea before its time, it might've been better had it been made in the '60s, when space-exploitation came into its own. **80m/B VHS, DVD.** *GB* Anthony Dexter, Susan Shaw, Paul Carpenter, Harry Fowler, Jacqueline Curtiss, Sydney Tafler, Maya Koumani, Jan Holden, Kim Parker, Rodney Diak, Owen Berry; *D:* Cy Roth; *C:* Cy Roth; *M:* Ian Struthers.

Fire Monsters Against the Son of Hercules *Maciste Contro i Mostri* **1962** The son of the muscular one in this average sword and sandal adventure. **82m/C VHS, DVD.** *IT* Reg Lewis, Margaret Lee; *D:* Guido Malatesta; *W:* Guido Malatesta, Arpad De Riso; *C:* Giuseppe La Torre; *M:* Guido Robuschi, Gian Stellari.

The Fire Next Time **1993** In the year 2017, the United States is being ravaged by an ecological holocaust caused by a deadly combination of pollution and global warming. Nelson, Bedelia, and their children are forced from their Louisiana home by a natural disaster and decide to head for better times in Canada. Their travels aren't easy. **195m/C VHS, DVD.** Craig T. Nelson, Bonnie Bedelia, Jurgen Prochnow, Richard Farnsworth, Justin Whalin, Charles Haid, Sal Lopez, Shawn Toovey, Ashley Jones; *Cameos:* Odetta; *D:* Tom McLoughlin; *W:* James Henerson. **TV**

Fire on the Amazon **1993 (R)** Really dumb "save-the-environment" movie with Bullock the rainforest activist and Sheffer the photojournalist. The duo hook up to investigate the assassination of an environmentalist. The big woo-hoo is Bullock's brief nude sex scene with Sheffer. **81m/C VHS, DVD.** Sandra Bullock, Craig Sheffer, Judith Chapman, Juan Fernandez; *D:* Luis Llosa; *W:* Catherine Cyran, Jane Gray; *C:* Pili Flores-Guerra; *M:* Roy J. Ravio.

Fire Over England **1937** Young naval officer volunteers to spy at the Spanish court to learn the plans for the invasion of his native England and to identify the traitors among the English nobility. He arouses the romantic interest of his queen, Elizabeth I, one of her ladies, and a Spanish noblewoman who helps with his missions, and later leads the fleet to victory over the huge Spanish Armada. The first on-screen pairing of Olivier and Leigh is just one of the many virtues of this entertaining drama. **81m/B VHS, DVD.** *GB* Flora Robson, Raymond Massey, Laurence Olivier, Vivien Leigh, Leslie Banks, James Mason; *D:* William K. Howard; *W:* Clemence Dane, Sergei Nolbandor; *C:* James Wong Howe; *M:* Richard Addinsell.

Fire Serpent WOOF! **2007 (R)** Another laughably bad cheapie from the Sci-Fi Channel. Solar flares cast off living flames that occasionally make it to Earth, not only starting fires but possessing people. A firefighter (Brendon) is drawn into a government conspiracy involving flame hunter Dutch Fallon (Mantooth), an arson investigator (Holt), and a Fed (Beltran). **89m/C DVD.** Nicholas Brendon, Randolph Mantooth, Sandrine Holt, Robert Beltran; *D:* John Terlesky; *W:* Judith Reeves-Stevens, Garfield Reeves-Stevens; *C:* Patrick Mcgowan; *M:* Chuck Cirino. **CABLE**

Fire with Fire **1986 (PG-13)** A boy at a juvenile detention center and a Catholic school girl fall in love. However, they find themselves on the run from the law when he escapes to be with her. Sheffer and Madsen are appealing in this otherwise unspectacular film. **103m/C VHS.** Craig Sheffer, Virginia Madsen, Jon Polito, Kate Reid, Jean Smart, D.B. Sweeney; *D:* Duncan Gibbins; *W:* Bill Phillips, Paul Boorstin, Sharon Boorstin; *M:* Howard Shore.

The Fire Within *Le Feu Follet; Fuoco Fatuo* **1964** Ronet plays an alcoholic writer recently released from a sanitorium after a breakdown. Believing his life will only continue its downward spiral, he pays a final visit to friends and calmly plots his suicide. Malle clearly and pitilessly describes a man beyond despair. Based on a novel by Pierre Drieu La Rochelle, which itself fictionalized the suicide of writer Jacques Rigaut. In French with English subtitles. **104m/B VHS.** *FR* Bernard Noel, Jeanne Moreau, Alexandra Stewart, Henri Serre, Maurice Ronet, Lena Skerla, Yvonne Clech, Hubert Deschamps, Jean-Paul Moulinot; *D:* Louis Malle; *W:* Louis Malle; *C:* Ghislan Cloquet.

Fireback **1978** A Vietnam vet's wife is kidnapped by the mob, causing him to take up arms and spill blood yet again. **90m/C VHS, DVD.** Bruce Baron, Richard Harrison; *D:* Teddy Page; *M:* Patrick Wales.

Fireball 500 **1966** Your basic low-budget teen flick from AIP finds Frankie and Fabian as rival stock car drivers in South Carolina. Newcomer Frankie makes a play for Annette, who's already Fabian's girl. But then Frankie switches cars to romance wealthy raceway owner Parrish. Bootleggers try to trick Frankie into illegal doings during a cross-country race, but he wises up and helps the Feds close the moonshiners down. He also croons a few tunes and spill the action is a little more adventurous than in the "Beach Party" series. **92m/C DVD.** Frankie Avalon, Annette Funicello, Fabian, Julie Parrish, Chill Wills, Harvey Lembeck; *D:* William Asher; *W:* William Asher, Leo Townsend; *C:* Floyd Crosby; *M:* Les Baxter.

Fireball Forward **1972 (PG)** A battalion fighting in France during WWII is having a bad time until Gazzara takes over and turns them into a crack fighting team. Uses some battle footage from the movie "Patton." **100m/C VHS.** Ben Gazzara, Eddie Albert, Ricardo Montalban, Dana Elcar, L.Q. Jones, Anne Francis; *D:* Marvin J. Chomsky. **TV**

Fireballs **1990** Sexploitaton pic set at a firehouse, where a batch of female recruits turn up the heat for three stud hose-bearers. The title should give you some idea of the intellectual level. **89m/C VHS.** Mike Shapiro, Goren Kalezik; *D:* Mike Shapiro.

Firebird 2015 A.D. **1981 (PG)** Dreary action adventure set in a 21st century society where automobile use is banned because of an extreme oil shortage. Private cars are hunted down for destruction by the Department of Vehicular Control. One over-zealous enforcer decides to make it a package deal and throws in the owners as well. Everyone connected with effort should have been cited for running stop sign. **97m/C VHS.** Darren McGavin, George Touliatos, Doug McClure; *D:* David Robertson.

Firecracker **1971** Female martial arts expert retaliates against the crooks who murdered her sister. **83m/C VHS.** Jillian Kesner, Darby Hinton; *C:* James Wong Howe; *M:* Cirio H. Santiago.

Firecreek 🐾🐾½ **1968** Fonda and his thugs terrorize a small town protected by part-time sheriff Stewart. Beautiful photography and competent cast, but meandering and long. 104m/C VHS, DVD. Henry Fonda, James Stewart, Inger Stevens, Gary Lockwood, Dean Jagger, Ed Begley Sr. Jay C. Flippen, Jack Elam, Barbara Luna; **D:** Vincent McEvety; **C:** William Clothier.

Firefall 🐾🐾½ *Freefall* **1994** Wildlife photog Katy Mazur (Gidley) has a brief affair with sportsman Grant Orion (Roberts) while on assignment in Africa. When they meet again, Orion tells Katy he's actually an Interpol agent who's assigned to protect her—although she has no idea why. But that's not Jonas's only problem—bad guy Wolf (Baldwin) learns about the crime and he's determined to get the cash for himself. 94m/C VHS, DVD, Pamela Gidley, Eric Roberts, Jeff Fahey; **D:** John Irvin.

Firefight 🐾 **1987** After a nuclear holocaust, convicted criminals endeavor to rule the wasteland. 100m/C VHS, James Pfeiffer, Janice Carraher, Jack Tucker; **D:** Scott Pfeiffer.

Firefight 🐾🐾½ **2003 (R)** Armored car driver Jonas (Bacic) is desperate to save his family's restaurant from bankruptcy so, aided by chopper pilot George (Mancuso), he robs his own vehicle and uses a forest fire as cover. 94m/C VHS. **M:** Ken Williams.

The Firefly 🐾🐾 **1937** Although slow-paced and long, this adaptation of the 1912 Rudolf Friml operetta was one of MacDonald's most popular films. Co-star Jones gets to sing the best song in the film, "Donkey Serenade," while MacDonald sings most of the others. ♪Love is Like a Firefly; English March; A Woman's Kiss; He Who Loves and Runs Away; When a Maid Comes Knocking at Your Heart; When the Wine Is Full of Fire; The Donkey Serenade; Giannina Mia; Sympathy. 140m/B VHS. Jeanette MacDonald, Allan Jones, Warren William, Billy Gilbert, Henry Daniell, Douglass Dumbrille, George Zucco; **D:** Robert Z. Leonard.

Firefox 🐾🐾½ **1982 (PG)** A retired pilot sneaks into the Soviet Union for the Pentagon to steal a top-secret, ultra-sophisticated warplane and fly it out of the country. Best for the low-altitude flight and aerial battle sequences, but too slow on the ground. Best for the low-altitude flight and aerial battle sequences, but too slow to show getting started. 136m/C VHS, DVD. Clint Eastwood, Freddie Jones, David Huffman, Warren Clarke, Ronald Lacey, Kenneth Colley, Nigel Hawthorne, Kai Wulff; **D:** Clint Eastwood; **C:** Bruce Surtees; **M:** Maurice Jarre.

Firehawk 🐾🐾 **1992 (R)** Several American soldiers survive the crash of their helicopter into the jungles of Vietnam. They think their only enemy is the Vietcong but when they discover the cop has been sabotaged the hunt is on for the traitor among them. 92m/C VHS. Martin Kove, Matt Salinger, Vic Trevino; **D:** Cirio H. Santiago; **W:** Jeff Yonis.

Firehead 🐾🐾½ **1990 (R)** A pyrokinetic Soviet detector begins using his powers to destroy American munitions in the name of peace. When a clandestine pro-war organization hears of this, they attempt to capture the man and use him for their own evil purposes. 88m/C VHS. Christopher Plummer, Chris Lemmon, Martin Landau, Gretchen Becker, Brett Porter; **D:** Peter Yuval.

Firehouse 🐾 **1972** Tempers ignite in a lily-white firehouse when a black rookie replaces an expired veteran. March—of "Paper Lion" renown—directed this made-for-TV emergency clone, which ran ever-so-briefly as an adventure series on TV in 1974 (with a largely different cast). 73m/C VHS, DVD. Richard Roundtree, Vince Edwards, Andrew Duggan, Richard Jaeckel, Sheila Frazier, Val Avery, Paul LeMat, Michael Lerner; **D:** Alex March; **M:** Tom Scott. TV

Firehouse 🐾 **1987 (R)** In the style of "Police Academy," three beautiful and sex-starved fire-fighting recruits klutz up an urban firehouse. A softcore frolic. 91m/C VHS. Barrett Hopkins. Shannon Vi-

---

olet Brown, John Anderson, Julia Roberts; **D:** J. Christian Ingvordsen; **W:** J. Christian Ingvordsen, Steven Kaman, Rick Marx; **C:** Steven Kaman; **M:** Michael Montes.

Firehouse Dog 🐾🐾 **2007 (PG)** Movie dog Rexx, aka Dewey, is lost during an airplane stunt and ends up in the reluctant care of sullen 12-year-old Shane Fahey (Hutcherson). Shane and his dad, Connor (Greenwood), are going through a rough time as Connor has taken charge of an embattled inner-city fire station called Dogpatch. But the kid soon realizes that Dewey is no ordinary mutt and his furry pal becomes both a rescue dog and the perfect PR tool. There's lots of bonding and hey, it's a dog movie! What could be better? Okay there are a few things better than this particular dog movie, like a trip to the vet. 111m/C DVD. US Josh Hutcherson, Bruce Greenwood, Dash Mihok, Steven Culp, Bill Nunn, Bree Turner, Mayte Garcia; **D:** Todd Holland; **W:** Mike Werb, Michael Colleary, Claire-Dee Lim; **C:** Victor Hammer; **M:** Jeff Cardoni.

The Fireman 🐾🐾½ **1916** Chaplin portrays a fireman who becomes a hero. Silent with musical soundtrack added. 20m/B VHS, DVD. Eric Campbell, Edna Purviance, Charlie Chaplin; **D:** Charlie Chaplin.

The Firemen's Ball 🐾🐾 *Horí, ma panenko* **1968** A critically acclaimed comedy about a small-town ball held for a retiring fire chief. Plans go amusingly awry as beauty contestants refuse to show themselves, raffle prizes and other items—including the gift for the guest of honor—are stolen, and the firemen are unable to prevent an old man's house from burning down. Forman's second film is sometimes interpreted as political allegory. Czech with subtitles. 73m/C VHS, DVD, CZ Vaclav Stockel, Josef Svet; **D:** Milos Forman; **W:** Ivan Passer, Jaroslav Papousek, Vaclav Sasek, Milos Forman; **C:** Miroslav Ondricek; **M:** Karel Mares.

Firepower 🐾 **1979 (R)** Loren blames her chemist husband's death on a rich industrialist and hires hitman Coburn to take care of the matter. Less than compelling. 104m/C VHS. Dominic Chianese, Sophia Loren, James Coburn, O.J. Simpson, Christopher Chad McQueen, Gary Daniels, Jim Hellwig, Jo F. Bean; **D:** Michael Winner; **M:** Gato Barbieri.

Firepower 🐾½ **1993 (R)** Two cops chase "The Swordsman" into a federally sanctioned area of legalized gambling, prostitution and crime (Las Vegas?), risking life and limb in the treacherous "Caged Ring of Death." 95m/C VHS, DVD. Chad McQueen, Gary Daniels, Jim Hellwig, Jo Chad McQueen, George Murdock; **D:** Richard Pepin; **W:** Michael January; **C:** Ken Blakey.

Fires on the Plain 🐾🐾 *Nobi* **1959** A grueling Japanese antiwar film about an unhinged private in the Philippines during WWII who roams the war-torn countryside encountering all manner of horror and devastation. In Japanese with English subtitles. 105m/B VHS, DVD. JP Eiji Funakoshi, Osamu Takizawa, Mickey Curtis, Asao Sano, Kyu Sazanka, Yoshihiro Hamaguchi, Hikaru Hoshi, Yasushi Sugita, Masaya Tsukida, Mantaro Ushio; **D:** Kon Ichikawa; **W:** Natto Wada; **C:** Setsuo Kobayashi; **M:** Yasushi Akutagawa.

Fires Within 🐾🐾 **1991 (R)** A curiously flat romance with political overtones. After eight years as a political prisoner in Cuba, Nestor (Smits) is released and goes to Miami to be reunited with his wife and daughter. Once there he finds his wife has fallen in love with another man. Now Nes-

---

tor must choose between his politics and the chance to win back his family. Secondary plotlines fizzle out and a talented cast is largely wasted. Scacchi is beautiful but hardly believable as the Cuban wife. 90m/C VHS, DVD. Jimmy Smits, Greta Scacchi, Vincent D'Onofrio; **D:** Gillian Armstrong; **W:** Cynthia Cidre; **C:** David Gribble; **M:** Maurice Jarre.

Firestarter 🐾🐾 **1984 (R)** A C.I.A.-like organization is after a little girl who has the ability to set anything on fire in this filmed adaptation of Stephen King's bestseller. Good special effects help a silly plot. 115m/C VHS, DVD, David Keith, Drew Barrymore, Freddie Jones, Martin Sheen, George C. Scott, Heather Locklear, Louise Fletcher, Moses Gunn, Art Carney; **W:** Stanley Mann; **C:** Giuseppe Ruzzolini; **M:** Tangerine Dream.

Firestarter 2: Rekindled 🐾🐾 **2002** Original sequel to the 1984 film, based on the Stephen King novel. A now-adult Charlie (Moreau) is researching the project that sparked her fire-starting powers, without realizing that her former mentor (McDowell) wants to eliminate all survivors of the Lot 6 project. Meanwhile, insurance agent Vincent Storza (Nucci) is looking for Charlie and a mysterious scientist (Hopper) is also involved. 168m/C VHS, DVD. Marguerite Moreau, Malcolm McDowell, Danny Nucci, Dennis Hopper, Skye McCole Bartusiak, John Dennis Johnston, Darrell Williams, Deborah Van Valkenburgh; **D:** Robert Iscove; **W:** Philip Eisner; **C:** David Boyd. C.A.B.L.E.

Firestorm 🐾½ **1997 (R)** Ex-NFL tough guy Long plays Jesse Graves, a parachuting firefighter with a really square head in his first starring role. Jesse, along with "smoke jumping" mentor Wynt (Glenn), must drop into a raging Wyoming forest fire in order to save a group of trapped firemen. Except they aren't really firemen, they're convicts in disguise who have escaped through a hole in the plot. Ringleader Shaye (Forsythe) had his lawyer set the fire so that he could use the cover of the volunteer murderer/fire fighter release program to escape and find the $37 million he has hidden. Happens all the time. The smoky chain gang also stumble across beautiful bird-watcher Jennifer (Amis) and take her hostage. Jesse must foil the bad guys, save the girl and douse the fire; all the while lugging around his humongous chin and speaking in monotone. Fire effects were enhanced by computer generated graphics. 89m/C VHS, DVD. Howie Long, Scott Glenn, William Forsythe, Suzy Amis, Christiane Hirt, Garwin Sanford, Sebastian Spence, Michael Greyeyes, Benjamin Ratner, Barry Pepper, Vladimir Kulich; Tom McBeath; **D:** Dean Semler; **W:** Chris Soth; **C:** Stephen Windon; **M:** J. Peter Robinson.

Firestorm: 72 Hours in Oakland 🐾½ **1993** Residents of an Oakland community face the threat of a big brush fire. 94m/C VHS, LeVar Burton, Jill Clayburgh, Michael Gross; **D:** Michael Tuchner.

Firetrap 🐾🐾½ **2001 (R)** Combo heist/disaster flick is routine material. Thief Jack (Cain) is hired to steal a computer chip from a L.A. high-rise corporate headquarters but is double-crossed by a crooked company insider (Tyson) who sets fire to the building, trapping Jack and the other occupants. 99m/C VHS, DVD. Dean Cain, Richard Tyson, Lori Petty, Mel Harris, Jeana Storm, Vanessa Angel, John O'Hurley, Elena Sahagun, Steven Williams; **D:** Harris Done; **W:** Richard Gosset Jr., Preston Jr., Diane Fine; **C:** Mark W. Gray; **M:** Sean Murray. VIDEO

Firewalker 🐾 **1986 (PG)** An "Indiana Jones" clone about of three mercenaries endeavoring to capture a fortune in hidden gold. Paper-mache sets and a villain with an eye patch that consistently charges eyes are just some of the gaffes that make this one of the worst edited movies in history. 106m/C VHS, DVD. Chuck Norris, Louis Gosset Jr., Melody Anderson; **D:** J. Lee Thompson; **M:** Gary Chang.

Firewall 🐾🐾 **2006 (PG-13)** The 60-something Ford does the heroic family man thing again. Here he plays Jack Stanfield, a security specialist at a Seattle bank, whose family is held hostage by psycho thief Bill Cox (Bettany) and his

---

gang. Cox needs Jack to circumvent his own security system so that $100 million can be transferred to an offshore account. Jack, of course, decides to thwart their nefarious plan and save his family. Ford is his usual stalwart self, but the movie is a drag, bringing nothing new to the well-worn genre. 105m/C DVD, Blu-ray Disc, HD DVD. US Harrison Ford, Paul Bettany, Virginia Madsen, Lynn Rajskub, Robert Patrick, Robert Forster, Alan Arkin, Carly Schroeder, Jimmy Bennett, Vince Vieluf, Kett Turton, Vincent Gale, Nikolaj Coster-Waldau; **D:** Richard Loncraine; **W:** Joe Forte; **C:** Marco Pontecorvo; **M:** Alexandre Desplat.

Fireworks 🐾🐾 *Hana-Bi* **1997** Idiosyncratic mixture of drama, comedy, violence, and sentiment. Nishi (Kitano) is a tough detective whose wife, Miyuki (Kishimoto), is dying from leukemia. He's visiting her in the hospital when his partner Horibe (Osugi) is gunned down and paralyzed. Deciding to get justice on his own terms, Nishi quits the force and decides to settle his debts with the yakuza (by robbing a bank) (which also funds a last trip with his wife). Takeshi (who uses his acting alias of Beat Kitano) is the strong, silent, violent type and a very visual director. Those are Kitano's own paintings in the scenes where Horibe takes up art as his new hobby. Japanese with subtitles. 103m/C VHS, DVD. JP Takeshi "Beat" Kitano, Kayoko Kishimoto, Ren Osugi, Susumu Terajima, Tetsu Watanabe; **D:** Hideo Yamamoto; **W:** Takeshi "Beat" Kitano; **C:** Hideo Yamamoto; **M:** Joe Hisaishi.

The Firing Line 🐾🐾 **1991** The Central American government hires a mercenary rebel-buster to squash insurgents. Everything's great until he finds out he agrees with the rebel cause, and he trains them to fight the government. Below average renegade-with-a-hidden-heart warpic. 93m/C VHS, DVD. Reb Brown, Shannon Tweed, Michael Monty, Kathleen Marie, Melvin Davidson, Carl Terry, Andy Jacobson; **D:** John Gale; **W:** John Gale, Sonny Sanders; **C:** Carl Sommers; **M:** Martia Manue.

The Firm 🐾🐾🐾½ **1993 (R)** Top-flight cast promises a good time—the script, based on the top-selling 1991 novel by John Grisham nearly guarantees it. Ambitious, idealistic Ivy League law school grad Cruise accepts a great offer from a small but wealthy Memphis law firm. As with anything that seems too good to be true, he discovers involved makes up for predictability. Sorvino has an uncredited cameo as a mob boss. Book fans beware: the script is fairly faithful until the end. The movie rights were snapped up before the book was published. Placed third in the 1993 race for top boxoffice gross. 154m/C VHS, DVD. Tom Cruise, Jeanne Tripplehorn, Gene Hackman, Hal Holbrook, Terry Kinney, Wilford Brimley, Ed Harris, Holly Hunter, David Strathairn, Gary Busey, Steven Hill, Tobin Bell, Barbara Garrick, Jerry Hardin, Karina Lombard, John Beal, Paul Sorvino, Joe (Johnny) Viterelli; **D:** Sydney Pollack; **W:** Rocter Towne, David Rayfiel; **C:** John Seale; **M:** Dave Grusin.

First a Girl 🐾🐾½ **1935** Delivery girl Elizabeth (Matthews) is dropping off costumes at the local theatre, which is where she meets a female impersonator with throat trouble. He gets Elizabeth to take his place on stage and she becomes famous overnight. So she keeps up the charade until a princess (Lee) and her boyfriend (Jones) become suspicious and decide to uncover the truth. If the plot sounds familiar it's because the film was remade as "Victor/Victoria" (1982). 93m/B VHS. GB Jessie Matthews, Sonnie Hale, Anna Lee, Griffith Jones, Alfred Drayton, Martita Hunt; **D:** Victor Saville; **W:** Marjorie Gaffney; **C:** Glen MacWilliams.

First Affair **1983** A young girl undergoes the pressures of freshman life at college, including her first love affair, which is with the husband of a female professor. 95m/C VHS, Loretta Swit, Melissa Sue Anderson, Joel Higgins; **D:** Gus Trikonis. TV

First & Ten: The Team Scores Again 🐾 **1985** A sequel to the cable comedy "First and Ten" about a football team's relationship with their female owner. 101m/C VHS. Delta Burke, Geoffrey Scott, Ruta Lee, Reid Shelton, Clayton Landry, Fran Tarkenton. CABLE

First Blood 1982 (R) Stallone is a former Green Beret survivor of Vietnam whose nightmares of wartime horrors are triggered by a wrongful arrest in a small town. He escapes into the mountains of the Northwest and leads his pursuers to all manner of bloody ends. Finally, the Army is summoned to crush him. Extremely violent and frequently confused, fueled on the revenge fantasy and not much concerned with the rules of plot realism. Screen debut of Caruso. Based on David Morrell's novel. A boxoffice hit that launched the "Rambo" series. Followed by "Rambo: First Blood, Part 2." 96m/C VHS, DVD, Blu-ray Disc, UMD. Sylvester Stallone, Richard Crenna, Brian Dennehy, Jack Starrett, David Caruso; D: Ted Kotcheff; W: Sylvester Stallone; C: Andrew Laszlo; M: Jerry Goldsmith.

First Born 1984 (PG-13) In search of romance, divorced mother Garr finds an intriguing man, Weller. Trouble erupts when her son learns Weller is a cocaine dealer. Talented cast makes most of story. 100m/C VHS. Teri Garr, Peter Weller, Christopher Collet, Corey Haim, Sarah Jessica Parker, Robert Downey Jr.; D: Michael Apted; C: Ralf Bode.

First Daughter 1999 Alex McGregor (Hemingway) is a Secret Service agent who saves President Johnathan Hayes's (Harrison) life and is rewarded for her efforts by being assigned to protect his bratty teen daughter, Jess (Keena), on a Colorado rafting trip. (Actually filmed in Australia.) The teen gets kidnapped by a paramilitary group and agent Alex, aided by river guide Grant Carlson (Savant), is determined to get her back. 94m/C VHS. Mariel Hemingway, Doug Savant, Monica Keena, Gregory Harrison; D: Armand Mastroianni; W: Carey Hayes, Chad Hayes; C: Mark Wareham; M: Louis Febre. CABLE

First Daughter 2004 (PG) Ever hear of a flick called "Chasing Liberty" about a president's daughter who wants to escape from her duties and just have a little fun? Well, let's just play follow the government leader. Samantha Mackenzie (Holmes) chafes under the restrictions of being presidential dad's (Keaton) properly offspring. So she heads to college in California where she tries to ditch her security detail to party with diva roommate Mia (Amerie), getting into some mild hijinks that cause mom Melanie (Colin) to lay down the law (it's an election year), even as Sam gets flirty with faculty adviser James (Blucas). Everyone seems to be sleepwalking (even director Whitaker) as if it's too much effort to pump some hot air into this snoozefest. 104m/C VHS, DVD. US Katie Holmes, Marc Blucas, Margaret Colin, Michael Keaton, Marc Blucas, Lela Rochon Fuqua; D: Forest Whitaker; W: Jessica Bendinger, Kate Kondell; C: Toyomichi Kurita; M: Michael Kamen, Blake Neely, Damon Elliot; Nar: Forest Whitaker.

The First Deadly Sin 1980 (R) Police lieutenant Sinatra tracks down a homicidal killer in spite of wife Dunaway's illness and his impending retirement. Read Lawrence Sanders' bestselling novel; it's a lot more exciting than this. 112m/C VHS, DVD. Frank Sinatra, Faye Dunaway, David Dukes, Brenda Vaccaro, James Whitmore; D: Brian G. Hutton; M: Mann Rubin; C: Jack Priestley; M: Gordon Jenkins.

First Degree 1995 (R) N.Y.C. homicide detective Rick Mallory (Lowe) goes up against the mob while investigating the murder of a rich man and falling for the widow. 98m/C VHS, DVD. CA Rob Lowe, Leslie Hope, Tom McCamus, Nadia Capone, Brett Halsey; D: Jeff Woolnough; W: Ron Base; C: Glen MacPherson. CABLE

First Degree *Charades; Felons* 1998 (R) Quinn (Wilder) and wife Lara (Kates) invite some friends and co-workers to their house for a barbecue. But there's more than hamburgers about to be grilled. Seems widow Jude (Black) is convinced that her husband Paul's killer is attending the festivities. And she soon has everyone turning on each other. 80m/C VHS, DVD. Erika Eleniak; C. Thomas Howell, Jack Scalia, James Wilder, James Russo, Karen Black, Kimberley Kates, James Andronica; D: Stephen Eckelberry; W: S.P. Somtow; C: Susan Emerson. VIDEO

First Descent 2005 (PG-13) Documentary attempts to chronicle the history as well as the current state of free-ride snowboarding. Nick Perata, Shawn Farmer, Terji Haakonsen, Shaun White and Hannah Teter ride virgin powder throughout Alaska's spectacular Chugach Mountains. The narration darts around a bit but the obvious enthusiasm more than makes up. 110m/C DVD, UMD. US D: Kevin Harrison, Kemp Curley; C: Scott Duncan; M: Mark Mothersbaugh.

First Do No Harm 1997 (PG-13) Well-intentioned but routine TV movie depicts the crisis of the farming Reimuller family when the youngest child, four-year-old Robbie (Adkins), is diagnosed with epilepsy. Their health insurance won't cover Robbie's drug treatment and the bank is about to foreclose on the farm so dad Dave (Ward) takes up truck driving while mom Lori (Streep) tries to hold things together. Dismayed at Robbie's doctors, Lori also pursues an unorthodox treatment for Robbie that involves diet therapy rather than drugs. Director Abraham's own son has his epilepsy controlled by this alternative method. 94m/C VHS, DVD. Meryl Streep, Fred Ward, Seth Adkins, Allison Janney, Michael Yarmush; D: Jim Abrahams; W: Ann Beckett; C: Pierre Letarte. TV

First Encounter 1997 Warming—when exploring space and encountering a mysteriously abandoned, apparently deserted ship—Leave It Alone! This crew decides to go sightseeing and it doesn't work out well. 88m/C VHS. Redge Mahaffey, Roddy Piper, Trevor Goddard; D: Redge Mahaffey; W: Redge Mahaffey. VIDEO

First Family 1980 (R) Flat satire of life in the White House. The humor is weak and silly at best, despite the excellent comedy cast. Henry's first directorial effort. 100m/C VHS. Bob Newhart, Madeline Kahn, Gilda Radner, Richard Benjamin; D: Buck Henry; W: Buck Henry; M: Ralph Burns.

First Kid 1996 (PG) Formulaic "Home Alone Guarding Tess" does have its moments, but if you're over 14, probably not enough of them. Latest in a bevy of films to be inaugurated into the white hot "White House" genre-of-the-moment. Innocuous family comedy casts Sinbad as agent who is given the menial job of guarding Prez's bratty son Luke (Pierce). Simms sees that Luke is a misunderstood misfit like himself, and helps the lad have more fun than a Presidential son is allowed. Flick's clean, inoffensive humor makes it hard to dislike. Watch for cameo from Sonny Bono. 101m/C VHS, DVD. Sinbad, Brock Pierce, James Naughton, Blake Boyd, Timothy Busfield, Art LaFleur, Robert Guillaume, Lisa Eichhorn, Zachery Ty Bryan, Bill Cobbs; D: David Mickey Evans; W: Tim Kelleher; C: Anthony B. Richmond; M: Richard Gibbs.

First Knight 1995 (PG-13) King Arthur/Camelot legend comes to life again, but isn't worth the time it takes to watch. Wandering swordsman Lancelot (Gere) saves beautiful Guinevere (Ormond), soon to be Arthur's (Connery) queen, from evil renegade knight Malagant. They yearn, they gaze, they kiss—you gag. Written like a Harlequin romance, the dialogue (especially when uttered by Gere) is unintentionally funny, and the plot will cause much eye-rolling. Connery's regal (he knows his costume epics) and Ormond's lovely, but Gere is badly miscast. He offers a contemporary take on the flawed hero complete with American accent, an amazing feat in the 13th century. Big-scale battles, betrayals, passion, even Disneyland-like Camelot sets—the pieces for a tremendous epic are all here, it just doesn't work. 134m/C VHS, DVD. Sean Connery, Richard Gere, Julia Ormond, Ben Cross, John Gielgud, Liam Cunningham, Christopher Villiers, Valentine Pelka; D: Jerry Zucker; W: William Nicholson; C: Adam Greenberg; M: Jerry Goldsmith.

First, Last and Deposit 2000 Christine and her daughter 13-year-old Tessa end up living in their car when Christine is unable to cover the rent on her cashier's salary after her boyfriend moves them to Santa Barbara, loses his job, and splits. Tessa tries to get along with her new classmates by lying about her home life as the bonds between mother and daughter begin to strain under the pressure of their situation. First-time director Hyoguchi's use of digital video helps convey the desperation and immediacy of the family's plight, as well as giving a sense of gritty realism. Mostly inexperienced cast does a fine job. 92m/C VHS, DVD, Sara Wilcox, Jessica Alcorn, Don Margolin, Alanna Learned, Robin Alcorn, Katie Hatcher, Jason Hallows; D: Peter Hyoguchi; W: Peter Hyoguchi; Duffy Hecht.

First Legion 1951 Boyer and Addy are seminarians struggling with their faith when they are confronted with a supposed miracle. Low-key examination of religion and conflict within a religious community. 77m/B VHS. Charles Boyer, Barbara Rush, William Demarest, Leo G. Carroll; D: Douglas Sirk.

First Love 1939 Best known for Durbin's first screen kiss, this light-weight romance finds orphaned Connie Harding moving to New York to live with her wealthy Uncle James Clinton (Pallette) and his family. Connie meets handsome rich boy Ted Drake (Stack's screen debut) but her snobby debutante cousin Barbara (Parrish) already has Ted in her sights. Barbara tries to prevent Connie from going to the Drakes fancy dance but, in Cinderella fashion, the Clinton family servants help her become the belle of the ball. Durbin also does some singing. ♪One Fine Day; Amapola; Sympathy; A Change of Heart; Deserted; Spring In My Heart; Home Sweet Home. 85m/B VHS, DVD. Deanna Durbin, Robert Stack, Eugene Pallette, Helen Parrish, Leatrice Joy, June Storey, Frank Jenks, Kathleen Howard, Charles Coleman, Mary Treen; D: Henry Koster; W: Bruce Manning, Lionel Houser; C: Joseph Valentine; M: Frank Skinner.

First Love 1970 (R) A 16-year-old falls in love with a slightly older woman only to have his feelings rejected and to discover that she's his father's mistress. Actor Schell's directorial debut. 90m/C VHS. GE SI John Moulder-Brown, Dominique Sanda, Maximilian Schell, Valentina Cortese; D: Maximilian Schell; C: Sven Nykvist.

First Love 1977 (R) A story of an idealistic college student who takes love (and especially making love) more seriously than the rest of his peers, including his girlfriend. Based on Harold Brodkey's story "Sentimental Education." Darling's directorial debut. 92m/C VHS. William Katt, Susan Dey, John Heard, Beverly D'Angelo, Robert Loggia; D: Joan Darling; M: John Barry.

First Love and Other Pains / One of Them 1999 Two gay shorts explore first love. In "First Love" (50 minutes), Hong Kong college student Mark begins an English lit course with a stern British professor, Hugh Graham. Depressed by creative burnout, Hugh is flattered by Mark's attentions and they have a one-nighter—at least in Hugh's mind because Mark is looking for a longer-lasting romance. Cantonese and English with subtitles. In "One of Them" (47 minutes), two gay teens in the 60s strike up a friendship that makes their small, boring town almost bearable. 97m/C VHS, DVD. Edward Strode, Alex Wong, Ciaran Pennington, Cameron J. Watt; D: Simon Chung, Stewart Main; W: Simon Chung, Peter Wells; C: Ping Hung Wong, Stewart Main.

First Love, Last Rites 1998 (R) Peretz moved his atmospheric debut feature (adapted from a short story by Ian McEwan) from the English coast to the bayous of Louisiana. There local gal Sissel (Gregson Wagner) is shacking up with fish-out-of-water Brooklyn boy Joey (Ribisi). They have a lot of sex. Sissel finally introduces Joey to her crazy father Henry (Burke) and the two men get involved in an eel-catching business. Then Sissel and Joey start spatting and soon they're not having sex anymore and their romance drifts away. The film does look really good. 93m/C VHS. Natasha Gregson Wagner, Giovanni Ribisi, Robert John Burke, Eli Marienthal; D: Jesse Peretz; W: Jesse Peretz, David Ryan; C: Tom Richmond; M: Craig (Shudder to Think) Wedren.

First Man into Space *Satellite of Blood* 1959 An astronaut returns to Earth covered with strange space dust and with an organism feeding inside him (shades of "Alien"). The alien needs human blood to survive and starts killing in order to get it. 78m/B VHS, DVD. Marshall Thompson, Maria Landi, Bill Edwards; D: Robert Day; W: John C. Cooper, Lance Z. Hargreaves; C: Geoffrey Faithfull; M: Buxton Orr.

First Men in the Moon 1964 A fun, special effects-laden adaptation of the H. G. Wells novel about an Edwardian civilian spacecraft visiting the moon and the creature found there. Visual effects by Ray Harryhausen. Finch makes a brief appearance. 103m/C VHS, DVD. GB Martha Hyer, Edward Judd, Lionel Jeffries, Erik Chitty, Peter Finch; D: Nathan "Jerry" Juran; W: Nigel Kneale, Jan Read; C: Wilkie Cooper; M: Laurie Johnson.

First Monday in October 1981 (R) Clayburgh, as the first woman appointed to the Supreme Court, finds a friendly rival in colleague Matthau, a crusty but benign liberal judge. Though based on a Broadway hit, it ended up seeming to foreshadow the real-life appointment of Sandra Day O'Connor, which occurred at about the time the film was released. The title refers to the date the court begins its sessions. 99m/C VHS, DVD. Walter Matthau, Jill Clayburgh, Barnard Hughes, James Stephens, Jan Sterling, James Stephens, Joshua Bryant, Noble Willingham; D: Ronald Neame; C: Fred W. Koenekamp; M: Ian Fraser.

First Name: Carmen *Prenom: Carmen* 1983 Carmen, although posing as an aspiring filmmaker, really is a bank robber and terrorist. She is also such a femme fatale that during a bank robbery one of the guards decides to run away with her. Godard casts himself as Carmen's uncle. Amusing late Godard. French with subtitles. 95m/C VHS, DVD. FR Maruschka Detmers, Jacques Bonnaffe, Jean-Luc Godard, Myriem Roussel, Christophe Odent; D: Jean-Luc Godard; W: Anne-Marie Mieville; C: Raoul Coutard.

The First 9 1/2 Weeks woof! 1998 (R) Prequel to "9 1/2 Weeks" finds investor Matt Wade trying to close the biggest deal of his career with eccentric New Orleans businessman Francois Dubois. But Dubois' wife starts raising Wade's temperature even more than steamy New Orleans. 99m/C VHS, DVD. Paul Mercurio, Clara Bellar, Malcolm McDowell, Frederic Forrest, Dennis Burkley, James Black, Anna Jacyszyn, William Keane, Richard Durden; D: Alexander Wright; W: Alexander Wright; C: John Tarver; M: Norman Orenstein.

The First Nudie Musical 1975 (R) A producer tries to save his studio by staging a 1930s style musical, but with a naked cast and risque lyrics. Has attained semi-cult/trash status. ♪The First Nudie Musical; The Lights and the Smiles; Orgasm; Lesbian Butch Dyke; Dancing Dildos; Perversion; Honey, What Ya Doin' Tonight; Let 'Em Eat Cake; I Don't Have to Hide Anymore. 100m/C VHS, DVD. Cindy Williams, Stephen Nathan, Diana Canova, Bruce Kimmel, Alan Abelew, Alexandra Morgan, Frank Doubleday, Kathleen Hietala, Leslie Ackerman, Ron Howard; D: Mark Haggard, Bruce Kimmel; W: Bruce Kimmel; C: Douglas Knapp; M: Bruce Kimmel.

The First Olympics: Athens 1896 1984 Recounts the organization and drama surrounding the first modern-day Olympic games when the inexperienced American team shocked the games with their success. 260m/C VHS, DVD. Louis Jourdan, Angela Lansbury, David Ogden Stiers, Virginia McKenna, Jason Connery, Alex Hyde-White, Honor Blackman, Bill Travers; D: Alvin Rakoff; M: Bruce Broughton. TV

The First Power 1989 A detective and psychic join forces to track down a serial killer who, after being executed, uses his satanic powers to kill again. 90m/C VHS, DVD. Lou Diamond Phillips,

First Snow 🎬🎬 2007 (R) A traveling salesman Jimmy (Pearce) impulsively gets his fortune told by Vacaro (Simmons), who suffers a seizure and abruptly ends their session. After his other predictions come true Jimmy returns and insists that the psychic tell him the rest—which is of Jimmy's death by the first snowfall. Jimmy starts to unravel as his impending doom is in him but maybe prophecy. Pearce (angular and spooked) past mistakes catch up to him but maybe his underachieves. 102m/C DVD, VHS, DVD. **C:** Theo van de Sande. **M:** Stewart Copeland.

First Spaceship on Venus 🎬 *Der Schweigende Stern; Milczaca Gwiazda* 1960 Eight scientists from various countries set out for Venus and find the remains of a civilization far in advance of Earth's that perished because of nuclear weapons. A sometimes compelling anti-nuclear sci-fi effort made with German and Polish backing. Originally released. 78m/C VHS, DVD, GE **C:** Yoko Tani, Oldrich Lukes, Ignacy Machowski, Julius Ongewe, Michal Postnikow, Kurt Rackelmann. **D:** Kurt Maetzig. **C:** Joachim Hasler.

First Strike 🎬 1985 The United States and the USSR engage in nuclear submarine warfare when the Soviets hijack a U.S. sub and aim its weapons at Arab oil fields. 90m/C VHS. **C:** Stuart Whitman, Persis Khambatta. **D:** Allan Kuskowski. **W:** Allan Kuskowski. **C:** Glenn Roland.

First Sunday 🎬 2008 (PG-13) Durell (Ice Cube) and LeeJohn (Morgan) are buddies who both find themselves in need of some large money in a big hurry. In order to escape 'tight spots. Naturally, they hatch a plan to rob the local Baltimore neighborhood church since, hey, who else has that kind of cash? Just one problem: someone has already unloaded the safe, and a handful of church officials are on hand to witness the whole caper. Undaunted, the two pals take the whole lot hostage, setting up a few lame attempts at humor as the characters find themselves stuck together. The overly sweet choirmaster (Williams) proves to be a high point in a mostly predictable and ridiculous movie. See this one if you have the entire N.W.A catalogue on your iPod. 98m/C DVD. **C:** Ice Cube, Katt Micah Williams, Tracy Morgan, Loretta Devine, Michael Beach, Chi McBride, Keith David, Regina Hall, Malinda Williams. **D:** David E. Talbert. **C:** Alen Caso. **M:** Stanley Clarke.

The First Time 🎬½ *You Don't Need Pajamas at Rosie's; The Beginners; The Beginners; They Don't Wear Pajamas at Rosie's; Doin' It* 1982 (R) It's pre-Porky's zaniness as a vacationing youth understandably wants to spend his 'first time' with Bisset. Other than her presence, this film has little to offer. 90m/C VHS. **C:** Jacqueline Bisset, Wes Stern, Rick Kelman, Wink Roberts. **D:** James Neilson.

First Time Felon 🎬🎬½ 1997 (R) Based on the true story of a young Chicago drug dealer Greg Yance (Epps), who's convicted as a first-time offender and sent to a prison boot camp to straighten up. But the real challenge is when he's released and returns to his old neighborhood, with its old temptations, and tries to find an honest job. 106m/C VHS, DVD, Omar Epps, William Forsythe, Rachel Ticotin, Delroy Lindo. **D:** Charles S. Dutton. **W:** Daniel Therriault. CABLE.

The First to Go 🎬🎬 1997 (PG-13) Impulsive Adam is the first of his crowd to get engaged. His friends don't approve of his decision and decide to take him on vacation to get him to change his mind. Only his fiancee decides to come along and she has pans of his own. 91m/C VHS, DVD, Zach Galligan, Laurel Holloman, Mark Harmon, Conn "Corky" Nemec, Steve Parlavecchio, Jennifer Jostyn, Lisanne Fall. **D:** John Jacobs.

First Turn On 🎬 1983 (R) Not to be confused with "The Thomas Edison Story," this sex-comedy follows the adventures of several young campers who decide to die happy when an avalanche leaves them trapped in a cave. A longer unrated version is available. 88m/C VHS, DVD. Georgia Harrell, Michael Sarville, Googy Gress, Jenny Johnson, Heidie Bassett, Vincent D'Onofrio, Sheila Kennedy. **D:** Michael Herz, Lloyd Kaufman. **W:** Michael Herz, Lloyd Kaufman, Stuart Strutin, Georgia Harrell. **C:** Lloyd Kaufman.

The First $20 Million is Always the Hardest 🎬 2002 (PG-13) Dismal "comedy" about the late dot-com economy is itself late by at least a year. Not that timeliness would've helped this muddled, desperate-for-laughs mess. Marketing whiz Andy (Garcia) leaves his corporate gig to "do something important." He joins a hot tech firm run by digital guru Francis (Colantoni) who immediately resents him and assigns him to the hopeless project of trying to create a $99 PC. He assembles a quirky team of misfits that Dawson, as Andy's love interest; escapes with any dignity. Based on the P.J Bronson novel. 105m/C VHS, DVD. Adam Garcia, Rosario Dawson, Jake Busey, Enrico Colantoni, Ethan Suplee, Gregory Jbara, Dan E. Butler, Linda Hart, Anjul Nigam. **D:** Mick Jackson. **W:** Jon Favreau, Gary Tieche. **C:** Ron Garcia. **M:** Marco Beltrami.

The First Wives Club 🎬🎬½ 1996 (PG) As the first Mrs. Trump, who makes a most appropriate cameo, so wisely puts it, "Don't get mad, get everything." But to the three rich, middle-aged friends who are dumped by their husbands so the guys can play a younger "trophy" wives, there's just nothing like revenge. Comedy begins in 1969 with the young and idealistic Annie (Keaton), Brenda (Midler), Elise (Hawn) and Cynthia present with the wronged Cynthia (Chandling) ledge-diving from her swanky Manhattan apartment because her husband left her. The remaining mistreated trio goes into action, using their exes' own money, businesses, power, and various mistresses against them. This film's appeal and success had Hollywood tongues wagging, predicting the dawn of new roles for older actresses. Based on the dark Olivia Goldsmith. 104m/C VHS, DVD. Goldie Hawn, Diane Keaton, Bette Midler, Sarah Jessica Parker, Heather Locklear, Marcia Gay Harden, Elizabeth Berkley, Victor Garber, Dan Hedaya, Stephen Collins, Maggie Smith, Stockard Channing, Bronson Pinchot, Jennifer (Jennie) Dundas, Lowe, Eileen Heckart, Philip Bosco, Rob Reiner, James Naughton, Dina Spybey, J. Hugh Winston. **W:** Robert Harling. **C:** Donald E. Thorin. **M:** Marc Shaiman.

First Yank into Tokyo 🎬🎬 *Mask of Fury* 1945 An American army pilot who grew up in Japan undergoes plastic surgery in order to infiltrate Japanese lines and get information from an American scientist. Some last minute editing to capitalize on current events made this the first American film to deal with the atomic bomb. 83m/B VHS. Tom Neal, Richard Loo, Barbara Hale, Marc Cramer. **D:** Gordon Douglas.

A Fish Called Wanda 🎬🎬🎬 1988 (R) Absurd, high-speed farce about four criminals trying to retrieve $20 million they've stolen from a safety deposit box—and each other. Meanwhile, barrister Archie Leech (Cleese) falls in love with female thief, Wanda (Curtis). Some sick, but tastelessly funny, humor involves Palin's problem with stuttering and some very dead doggies. Written by Monty Python alum Cleese and director Crichton, who understand that silence is sometimes funnier than speech, and that timing is everything. Wickedly funny. 98m/C VHS, John Cleese, Kevin Kline, Jamie Lee Curtis, Michael Palin, Tom Georgeson, Maria Aitken, Patricia Hayes, Geoffrey Palmer, Andrew MacLachlan. **D:** Charles Crichton. **W:** Charles Crichton, John Cleese. **C:** Alan Hume. **M:** John Du Prez. Oscars '88: Support. Actor (Kline); British Acad. '88: Actor (Cleese), Support. Actor (Palin).

Fish in a Barrel 🎬 2001 (R) Familiar heist gone wrong flick is supposed to be played for laughs but doesn't have any. Four petty thieves are surprised to find themselves with four million in uncut diamonds and then wind up with two more partners to split the loot—a hitwoman and a dirty cop. 85m/C VHS, DVD. Jeremy Renner, Andy Jover, Kent Dallian, Stephen Ingle, Rene Rigal, David Keeley. **D:** Kent Dallian. **C:** Lisa Wiegand. **M:** Matt Sorum, Lanny Cordola.

The Fish that Saved Pittsburgh 🎬🎬 1979 (PG) A floundering basketball team hires an astrologer to try and change their luck. She makes sure all the team members' signs are compatible with their star's Pisces sign (the team also hooks up with her caring, study costar Ben (Green). Her lesbian best friend Vicki also has a thing for her. 104m/C VHS. Produced a disco soundtrack with several Motown groups who also performed in the movie. 104m/C VHS, Julius Erving, Margaret Avery, Meadowlark Lemon, Nicholas Pryor, Debbie Allen. **D:** Gilbert Moses. **M:** Thom Bell.

Fish Without a Bicycle 🎬 *Girls Will Be Girls* 2003 (R) Too many dating cliches floating around in a lead actress/writer Mattison's story of a woman who dumps her dutiful and handsome beau Danny (Rowe) to pursue her dreams of acting—and other men, including the self-absorbed director Michael (Callen). She still does. But while this picture runs it weaves a spell that pulls you in, especially in its quiet moments. Your reaction to the silly ending depends entirely on how well you're bamboozled by a script that equates madness with enlightenment and the homeless with holy tools. Filmed on the streets of New York, with many street people playing themselves. 138m/C VHS, DVD. Robin Williams, Jeff Bridges, Amanda Plummer, Mercedes Ruehl, Michael Jeter, Harry Shearer, John de Lance, Kathy Najimy, David Hyde Pierce. **D:** Terry Gilliam. **W:** Richard LaGravenese. **C:** Roger Pratt. **M:** George Fenton. Golden Globes '92: Actor—Mus./Comedy (Williams), Support. Actor (Ruehl); L.A. Film Critics '91: Actress (Ruehl).

The Fisher King 🎬🎬🎬 1991 (R) A derelict-infested Manhattan and-out radio ceejay meets a crazed vagabond (Williams) obsessed with medieval history and in search of the Holy Grail. At first the whimsical mix of Arthurian myth and modern urban hell seems amazingly wrongheaded. In retrospect it still does. But while this picture runs it silly ending depends entirely on how well... **VIDEO**

The Fishing Trip 🎬🎬 1998 Jessie (Hood) and her younger sister Kristi (Erwin) are determined to track down the stepfather who molested them as children. They discover he's on a fishing trip at a remote British Columbia cabin and head when his aunt and bratty cousin come to live with them. 72m/B VHS, DVD. Bobby Breen, Leo Carrillo, Henry Armetta, Lee Patrick, Rosina Galli, Leon Belasco. **D:** Bernard Vorhaus.

Fisherman's Wharf 🎬🎬 1939 Breen stars as an orphan adopted by a San Francisco fisherman who runs away when his aunt and bratty cousin come to live with them. 72m/B VHS, DVD. Bobby Breen, Leo Carrillo, Henry Armetta, Lee Patrick, Rosina Galli, Leon Belasco. **D:** Bernard Vorhaus.

Fish Hawk 🎬½ 1979 (G) When an alcoholic Indian, Fish Hawk, meets a young boy in the forest, they strike up a friendship and he attempts to clean up his act. Attempts to be heartwarming. 95m/C VHS, DVD. CA Will Sampson, Charlie Fields. **D:** Donald Shbib.

Fist 🎬 *Black Fist; The Black Streetfighter; Homeboy* 1976 (?) Street fighter battles his way through the urban jungle seeking personal freedom and revenge. 84m/C VHS, DVD. Richard Lawson, Annazette Chase, Dabney Coleman, Philip Michael Thomas. **D:** Timothy Galfas, Richard Kaye. **W:** Tim Kelly. **M:** Ed Townsend.

F.I.S.T. 🎬🎬½ 1978 (R) A young truck driver turns union organizer for idealistic reasons, but finds himself teaming with gangsters to boost his cause. His rise to the top of the union comes at the cost of his integrity, as Stallone does a character resembling Jimmy Hoffa. 145m/C VHS, DVD. Sylvester Stallone, Rod Steiger, Peter Boyle, David Huffman, Melinda Dillon, Tony LoBianco, Kevin Conway, Peter Donat, Cassie Yates, Brian Dennehy. **D:** Norman Jewison. **W:** Sylvester Stallone, Joe Eszterhas. **C:** Laszlo Kovacs. **M:** Bill Conti.

Fist Fighter 🎬 1988 (R) The ups and downs of a professional bare-knuckle fighter as he avenges a friend's murder. 99m/C VHS. Jorge (George) Rivero, Edward Albert, Brenda Bakke, Mike Connors, Simon Andreu, Matthias Hues. **D:** Frank Zuniga. **W:** Max Bloom.

Fist of Fear, Touch of Death 🎬 *Girls Will Be Girls* 2003 (R) ... **C:** Cook, Maurice Smith, Robert Marius, Eric Hahn. **D:** Joe Man Avellana.

Fist of Glory 🎬½ 1995 (R) In the waning days of the Vietnam War, a commando searches for the comrade who saved his life. Too many dating cliches floating around drug-addicted POW who's forced to fight in order to survive. 93m/C VHS, DVD, Dale "Apollo" Cook, Maurice Smith, Robert Marius, Eric Hahn. **D:** Joe Man Avellana.

Fist of Honor 🎬 1992 (R) A young boxer seeks to avenge his fiance's death, a beautiful girl squares off against a bad cop, and two mobster leaders try to take control of the same city. When a member of one family breaks a truce and begins killing rival family members, the violence escalates and old scores will be settled. 90m/C VHS, DVD. Sam Jones, Joey House, Harry Guardino, Nicholas Worth, Frank Sivero, Abe Vigoda, Bubba Smith. **D:** Richard Pepin. **W:** Charles Kanganis.

Fist of Legend 🎬🎬 1994 (R) Chen Zuen (Li) is a martial arts practitioner studying abroad during WWII, who returns to his homeland to avenge his teacher's death at the hands of the invading Japanese. Homage to Bruce Lee's 1972 "Fists of Fury" AKA "Chinese Connection." Cantonese with subtitles or dubbed. 92m/C VHS, DVD. HK jet Li, Yasuka Kurata. **D:** Woo-ping Yuen, Gordon Chen. **M:** Joseph Koo.

Fist of Steel 🎬½ 1993 In this futuristic martial arts film, modern day gladiators fight to the death in tournaments run by a vicious syndicate. When top gladiator Amp makes an escape bid he's hunted by henchman Mainframe, who plans to meet Amp in a fixed fight in order to become the new champion. 97m/C VHS, DVD. Cook, Greg Douglass, Cynthia Khan, Don Nakaya Nielsen, Jim Gaines, Ned Hourani, Nick Nicholson, Kris Aguilar. **D:** Irvin Johnson. **W:** Anthony Jesu.

Fist of the North Star 🎬🎬 1995 (R) Legendary warrior Kenshiro (Daniels) returns from the grave to avenge the death of his father. He must battle evil Lord Shin (Mandylor) and his henchmen in a post-apocalyptic future. Based on the Japanese comic book series, which is also available in anime form. 90m/C VHS, DVD. Gary Daniels, Costas Mandylor, Christopher Penn, Julie Brown, Malcolm McDowell, Melvin Van Peebles, Isako Washio. **D:** Tony Randel. **W:** Tony Randel. **C:** Jacques Haitkin. **M:** Christopher Stone.

Fistful of Death 🎬 *Ballad of Django; Stinky; Giu la Testa...Hombre* 1971 A truly weird and completely illogic Italian spaghetti western that somehow includes the characters of Butch Cassidy and the Sundance Kid (and Kinski—the John Carradine)...

Henry, Jim Kenney, Diana Tayback, T.J Grist. **D:** Ammon Buchbinder. **C:** Derek Rogers. Gene '98: Song ("River Blue").

dine of European cinema—apparently out to make a buck). **84m/C VHS.** *IT* Klaus Kinski, Jack Betts, Gordon Mitchell, Giancarlo Prete; *D:* Demofilo Fidani; *W:* Demofilo Fidani; *C:* Joe D'Amato; *M:* Coriolano Gori.

A Fistful of Dollars ✶✶✶ **1964** (R) The epitome of the "spaghetti western" pits Eastwood as "the man with no name" against two families who are feuding over land. A remake of Kurosawa's "Yojimbo," and followed by Leone's "For a Few Dollars More." and "The Good, The Bad, and The Ugly." **101m/C VHS, DVD.** *IT* Clint Eastwood, Gian Marie Volonte, Marianne Koch; *D:* Sergio Leone; *W:* Sergio Leone, Victor Andres Catena, Duccio Tessari, G. Schock; *M:* Massimo Dallamano, Federico G. Larraya; *M:* Ennio Morricone.

A Fistful of Dynamite ✶✶✶ *Duck, You Sucker; Giu la Testa* **1972** (PG) A spaghetti western, with Leone's trademark humor and a striking score by Morricone. An Irish demolitions expert and a Mexican peasant team up to rob a bank during a revolution in Mexico. **138m/C VHS, DVD.** *IT* James Coburn, Rod Steiger, Romolo Valli; *D:* Sergio Leone; *M:* Ennio Morricone.

Fistful of Lead ✶✶✶ **1970** Hilton is Sartana, this film's version of Clint Eastwood's "Man with No Name" in a blatant rip-off of "Fistful of Dollars." Of the many copycats that came in the wake of Leone's classic, this is one of the better efforts, which considering the field is damning with faint praise. **92m/C VHS, DVD.** *IT* George Hilton, Charles Southwood, Pierro Lulli, Erika Blanc; *D:* Giuliano Carnimeo; *W:* Tito Carpi; *C:* Stelvio Massi; *M:* Francesco De Masi.

Fists of Blood ✶✶½ **1987** A martial arts expert seeks revenge on the drug baron who murdered his friend and kidnapped his girl. **90m/C VHS.** *AU* Eddie Stazak; *D:* Brian Trenchard-Smith.

Fists of Fury ✶✶✶ *Tang Shan da Xiong* **1973** (R) *The Big Boss*; Bruce Lee stars in this violent but charming Kung Fu action adventure in which he must break a solemn vow to avoid fighting in order to avenge the murder of his teacher by drug smugglers. **102m/C VHS, DVD.** Bruce Lee, Maria Yi; *D:* Lo Wei; *W:* Lo Wei, Bruce Lee; *C:* Chen Ching Chur, *M:* Fu-ling Wang.

Fists of Iron ✶✶ **1994** (R) Tough guy, skilled in martial arts, seeks revenge on the fighter and promoter who caused the death of his best friend. **94m/C VHS.** Mike Worth, Matthias Hues, Sam Jones, Marshall Teague, Jenilee Harrison; *D:* Richard W. Munchkin; *W:* Sean Dash; *C:* Garett Griffin; *M:* Louis Febre.

Fit for a King ✶✶ **1937** A reporter becomes a princess' knight in shining armor when he foils an assassination plot in this screwball romance. **73m/B VHS, DVD.** Joe E. Brown, Leo Carrillo, Helen Mack, Paul Kelly, Harry Davenport; *D:* Edward Sedgwick; *C:* Paul Vogel.

Fit to Kill ✶✶½ **1993** (R) Once again special agents Donna Hamilton and Nicole Justine (former Playboy centerfolds Speir and Vasquez) reteam for an adventure that matches them with an old enemy, double agents, diamonds, and revenge. Filmed on location in Hawaii. **94m/C VHS, DVD.** Dona Speir, Roberta Vasquez, R.J. (Geoffrey) Moore, Bruce Penhall, Julie Strain, Rodrigo Obregon, Cynthia Brimhall, Tony Peck; *D:* Andy Sidaris; *W:* Andy Sidaris.

Fitzcarraldo ✶✶✶✶ **1982** (PG) Although he has failed to build a railroad across South America, Fitzcarraldo is determined to build an opera house in the middle of the Amazon jungles and have Enrico Caruso sing there. Based on a true story of a charismatic Irishman's impossible quest at the turn of the century. Of note: No special effects were used in this movie—everything you see actually occurred during filming, including hauling a large boat over a mountain. **157m/C VHS, DVD.** *GE* Klaus Kinski, Claudia Cardinale, Jose Lewgoy, Miguel Angel Fuentes, Paul Hittscher; *D:* Werner Herzog; *M:* Popul Vuh. Cannes '82: Director (Herzog).

Five Came Back ✶✶ **1939** When a plane with 12 passengers crashes in the South American jungle, only five can ride in the patched-up wreck. Since the remainder will be left to face head hunters, intense arguments ensue. Same director remade this as "Back from Eternity" in 1956. **93m/B VHS.** Lucille Ball, Chester Morris, John Carradine, Wendy Barrie, Kent Taylor, Joseph Calleia, Sir C. Aubrey Smith, Patric Knowles; *D:* John Farrow.

Five Card Stud ✶✶½ **1968** (PG) Five members of a lynching party are being killed one by one, and a professional gambler, who tried to prevent the lynching, attempts to ensnare the killer with the aid of a preacher with a gun. The poor script was based on a novel by Ray Gaulden. **103m/C VHS, DVD.** Robert Mitchum, Dean Martin, Inger Stevens, Roddy McDowall, Yaphet Kotto, John Anderson, Katherine Justice; *D:* Henry Hathaway; *W:* Marguerite Roberts; *C:* Daniel F. Fapp; *M:* Maurice Jarre.

Five Cartridges ✶✶ *Funf Patronenhulsen* **1960** Five soldiers during the Spanish Civil War hide their dying commander's final message in five empty bullet casings to keep the message from falling into enemy hands. Now, they have to survive the fighting in order to deliver the message. German with subtitles. **85m/B VHS.** *GE* Erwin Geschonneck, Manfred Krug, Armin Mueller-Stahl, Ulrich Thein, Edwin Marran, Ernst-Georg Schwill; *D:* Frank Beyer; *W:* Walter Gorrish; *C:* Gunter Marczinkowski.

Five Corners ✶✶✶ **1988** (R) A quixotic, dramatic comedy about the inhabitants of the 5 Corners section of the Bronx in 1964, centering around a girl being wooed by a psychotic rapist, her crippled boyfriend, and the hero-turned-racial-pacifist who cannot rescue her out of principle. **92m/C VHS, DVD.** Jodie Foster, John Turturro, Todd Graff, Tim Robbins, Elizabeth Berridge, Rose Gregorio, Gregory Rozakis, Rodney Harvey, John Seitz; *D:* Tony Bill; *W:* John Patrick Shanley; *C:* Fred Murphy; *M:* James Newton Howard. Ind. Spirit '89: Actress (Foster).

5 Dark Souls ✶✶½ **1996** Three high schoolers, anxious to be part of the "in" crowd, are sent by five members of the most popular clique on a sinister woodland adventure as stars in a snuff film. **90m/C VHS.** Tina Ona Paukstelis, Mick Wynhoff, Matthew Winkler, Christopher D. Harder, Karen Dilloo, Sy Stevens, William Krekling; *D:* Jason Paul Collum.

Five Days ✶✶½ **2007** Leanne (Tremarco) and her two children disappear from their car while at a rest stop—all of which is captured by CCTV cameras. The children are later found but the police investigation becomes a major news story and the action unfolds on days 1, 3, 28, 33, and 79. As the story proceeds, it becomes clear that nothing (and no one) is quite as it seems, even when the missing persons case turns into a murder inquiry. **300m/C DVD.** *GB* David Oyelowo, Hugh Bonneville, Janet McTeer, Penelope Wilton, Patrick Malahide, Edward Woodward, Sarah Smart, Christine Tremarco, Philip Davis, Rory Kinnear, Niki Amuka-Bird; *D:* Simon Curtis, Otto Bathurst; *W:* Gwyneth Hughes; *C:* Florian Hoffmeister; *M:* Magnus Fiennes. TV

Five Days One Summer ✶✶ **1982** (PG) Set in 1932, the story of a haunting and obsessive love affair between a married Scottish doctor and a young woman who happens to be his niece. While on vacation in the Swiss Alps, the doctor must vie for her love with their handsome young mountain climbing guide. Based on a story by Kay Boyle. **108m/C VHS.** Sean Connery, Betsy Brantley, Lambert Wilson; *D:* Fred Zinnemann; *W:* Michael Austin; *M:* Elmer Bernstein.

Five Dolls for an August Moon ✶✶ **1970** A group of investment speculators try to talk scientist Gerry Farrell (Berger) into selling them the rights to a new formula, while at a wild weekend retreat on an isolated island. As the competitors try to cheat one another with secret bids, Farrell seems disinterested, and tempers rise with the stakes. The wives and girlfriends along for the fun and games feel the tension as their men stray, or try to get them to use sex to close a deal. But once the murders begin, the possibility of anyone trusting anyone is left far behind. Allegedly a professional assignment given Bava with just two days' notice, the film is a fair murder mystery in which even this director's visual tricks can't sustain interest. The cast of connivers is interchangeable and hard to keep straight, and in some cases more easily identifiable by their now-hideous 1970 fashions than their faces. **78m/C DVD.** *IT* William Berger, Ira von Furstenberg, Edwige Fenech, Howard (Red) Ross, Helena Ronee, Teodoro Corra, Ely Galleani, Edith Meloni, Mauro Bosco, Maurice Poli; *D:* Mario Bava; *W:* Mario di Nardo; *C:* Antonio Rinaldi; *M:* Pierro Umiliani.

Five Easy Pieces ✶✶✶✶ **1970** (R) Nicholson's superb acting brings to life this character study of a talented musician who has given up a promising career and now works on the oil rigs. After a few years he returns home to attempt one last communication with his dying father and perhaps, reconcile himself with his fear of failure and desire for greatness. Black, Anspach, and Bush create especially memorable characters. Nicholson orders toast via a chicken salad sandwich is a classic. **98m/C VHS, DVD.** Jack Nicholson, Karen Black, Susan Anspach, Lois Smith, Billy Green Bush, Fannie Flagg, Ralph Waite, Sally Struthers, Helena Kallianiotes, Richard Stahl, Lorna Thayer; *D:* Bob Rafelson; *W:* Adrien (Carole Eastman) Joyce, Bob Rafelson; *C:* Laszlo Kovacs. Golden Globes '71: Support. Actress (Black); Natl. Bd. of Review '70: Support. Actress (Black); Natl. Film Reg. '00; N.Y. Film Critics '70: Director (Rafelson), Film, Support. Actress (Black); Natl. Soc. Film Critics '70: Support. Actress (Smith).

Five Fingers ✶✶✶½ *Operation Cicero* **1952** Under the alias "Cicero," Albanian valet Mason joins the espionage ring, selling highly confidential British war papers to the Germans during WWII. True story with odd real-life ending—unconvinced of document authenticity, the Nazis never acted on the information, even when they had the time and date of the European invasion! Fast-paced and absorbing. Adapted from the book "Operation Cicero" by L.C. Moyzisch. **108m/B VHS.** James Mason, Danielle Darrieux, Michael Rennie, Walter Hampden, Oscar Karlweis, Herbert Berghof, John Wengraf, Michael Pate, Ivan Tresault, Hannelore Axman, David Wolfe, Nestor Paiva, Richard Loo, Keith McConnell; *D:* Joseph L. Mankiewicz; *W:* Michael Wilson; *M:* Bernard Herrmann; *Nar:* John Sutton. Golden Globes '53: Screenplay.

Five for Hell ✶✶ **1967** The army picks five of its meanest men for a suicide mission during WWII. They must go behind German lines and find the plans for the German offensive. Parolini used the pseudonym Frank Kramer. **88m/C VHS. DVD.** *IT* Klaus Kinski, Gianni "John" Garko, Aldo Canti, Margaret Lee; *D:* Gianfranco Parolini.

Five Giants from Texas ✶✶ *Cinque Della Vendetta* **1966** El cheapo spaghetti western features Madison, TV's former Wild Bill Hickock, as a rancher fighting off displaced Mexican peasants and outlaws. **103m/C VHS.** *IT* Guy Madison, Monica Randall; *D:* Aldo Florio.

Five Golden Dragons ✶✶ **1967** A typical action film about an American running afoul of ruthless gold trafficking in Hong Kong. Even this stellar cast can't help the script. **92m/C VHS.** *GB* Robert Cummings, Christopher Lee, Brian Donlevy, Klaus Kinski, George Raft, Dan Duryea, Margaret Lee; *D:* Jeremy Summers.

Five Graves to Cairo ✶✶✶ **1943** Tense WWII thriller finds British soldier John Bramble (Tone) stranded in a small desert town after the defeat of the British garrison by General Rommel's (Von Stroheim) Afrika Korps. Arab hotel owner Farid (Tamiroff) agrees to let Bramble assume the identity of a dead hotel waiter, whose only interest is in getting her brother out of a German POW camp. The real waiter turns out to have been a secret Nazi spy, fortunately known to Rommel only by name, so Bramble attempts to learn where the German supply depots have been hidden (the "five graves" of the title)—that is, unless Moush decides to betray him to win her brother's release. Based on the play "Hotel Imperial" by Lajos Biro. **97m/B VHS.** Franchot Tone, Anne Baxter, Erich von Stroheim, Akim Tamiroff, Peter Van Eyck, Fortunio Bonanova, Miles Mander, Konstantin Shayne, Leslie Denison, Ian Keith, Frederick Giermann, Fred Numey; *D:* Billy Wilder; *W:* Billy Wilder, Charles Brackett; *C:* John Seitz; *M:* Miklos Rozsa.

The Five Heartbeats ✶✶✶ **1991** (R) Well told story of five black singers in the 1960s, their successes and failures as a group and as individuals. Although every horror story of the music business is included, the story remains fresh and the acting excellent. Music is fine, but secondary to the people. Well written characters with few cliches. Skillfully directed by Townsend (of "Hollywood Shuffle") who did research by talking to the Dells. Less than memorable showing at the boxoffice but fun and entertaining. **122m/C VHS, DVD.** Robert Kevin Townsend, Tressa Thomas, Michael Wright, Harry J. Lennix, Diahann Carroll, Leon, Hawthorne James, Chuck Patterson, Roy Fegan, Tico Wells, John Canada Terrell, Harold Nicholas, Paul Benjamin, Norma Donaldson, Eugene Robert Glazer, Lamont Johnson; *D:* Robert Kevin Townsend; *W:* Keenen Ivory Wayans, Robert Kevin Townsend; *C:* Bill Dill; *M:* Stanley Clarke.

Five Minutes to Love ✶ *The Rotten Apple; It Only Take Five Minutes* **1963** McClanahan (one of TV's "Golden Girls") plays a young, sleazy hussy named "Poochie, the girl from the shack." This exploitation schlocker appears to be McClanahan's first film. **85m/B VHS, DVD.** Rue McClanahan, Paul Leder, King Moody; *D:* John Hayes.

The Five of Me ✶✶½ **1981** A man with five personalities finds that livin' ain't easy and seeks professional help. Based on the autobiography of Henry Hawksworth. **100m/C VHS.** David Birney, Dee Wallace Stone, Mitchell Ryan, John McLiam, James Whitmore Jr., Ben Piazza; *D:* Paul Wendkos. TV

The Five Pennies ✶✶½ **1959** Sentimental biography starring Kaye as famed jazzman Red Nichols features performances by legendary musicians Bob Crosby, Bobby Troup, Ray Anthony and Louis Armstrong. This movie marked Weld's film debut. ♫ Good Night Sleep Tight; The Five Pennies; Battle Hymn of the Republic; When the Saints Go Marching In; The Music Goes 'Round and Around; Jingle Bells; Carnival of Venice; Paradise. **117m/C VHS, DVD.** Danny Kaye, Louis Armstrong, Barbara Bel Geddes, Tuesday Weld, Harry Guardino; *D:* Melville Shavelson; *W:* Melville Shavelson, Jack Rose; *C:* Daniel F. Fapp.

The Five Senses ✶✶½ **1999** Follows the trials of five urbanites, each of whom is linked to a missing child, as well as being linked to one of the five senses. Massage therapist Ruth (Rose) is losing her sense of touch; cake baker Rona (Parker) has an impaired sense of taste; housecleaner Robert (MacIvor) believes his acute sense of smell will lead to love; optholmologist Richard (Volter) is losing his hearing; and teenager Rachel (Litz) is drawn into spying games (sight) with a voyeur. Suprisingly accessible given the complex construct, each story is not only well-acted but frequently warm and witty. **105m/C VHS, DVD.** *CA* Mary-Louise Parker, Philippe Volter, Gabrielle Rose, Daniel MacIvor, Molly Parker, Pascale Bussieres, Marco Leonardi, Brendan Fletcher, Nadia Litz; *D:* Jeremy Podeswa; *W:* Jeremy Podeswa; *C:* Gregory Middleton; *M:* Alex Pauk, Alexina Louie. Genie '99: Director (Podeswa); Toronto-City '99: Canadian Feature Film.

The 5000 Fingers of Dr. T ✶✶✶ **1953** (G) In Dr. Seuss' only non-animated movie, a boy tries to evade piano lessons and runs right into the castle of the evil Dr. Terwilliger, where hundreds of boys are held captive for piano lessons. Worse yet, they're forced to wear silly beanies with "happy fingers" waving on top. Luckily, the trusted family plumber is on hand to save the day through means of an atomic bomb. Wonderful satire, horrible music, mesmerizing Seussian sets. The skating brothers (who are joined at their beards) are a treat. **88m/C VHS, DVD.** Peter Lind Hayes, Mary Healy, Tommy Rettig, Hans Conried, Noel Cravat; *D:* Roy Rowland; *W:* Theodore "Dr. Seuss" Geisel, Allan Scott; *C:* Franz Planer; *M:* Frederick "Friedrich" Hollander; Hans J. Salter.

5x2 *♂½ Cinq fois deux; Five Times Two*
2004 (R) The unhappy marriage of Marion (Bruni-Tedeschi) and Gilles (Freiss) is chronicled backwards in five scenes (with two characters, hence the title), beginning with their divorce and ending with their first meeting and includes a dinner party, childbirth, and their wedding night. The couple is basically a disaster from the beginning of their relationship and you won't be terribly sympathetic (or surprised) about what happens. French with subtitles. **90m/C DVD. FR** Valeria Bruni-Tedeschi, Stephane Freiss, Geraldine Pailhas Françoise Fabian, Michael (Michel) Lonsdale, Antoine Chappey; **D:** François Ozon; **W:** Francois Ozon, Emmanuele Bernheim; **C:** Yorick Le Saux; **M:** Philippe Rombi.

The $5.20 an Hour Dream *♂ 1980* Lavin is a divorced mother and factory worker burdened with debt and determined to get and keep a job on the higher-paying, traditionally all-male assembly line. "Lesser feminist drama on the heels of "Norma Rae." **96m/C VHS.** Linda Lavin, Richard Jaeckel, Nicholas Pryor, Pamela McNalier, May! Nutter, Taurean Blacque, Robert Davi, Dennis Fimple, Dana Hill, Ernie Hudson; **D:** Russ Mayberry. **TV**

Five Weeks in a Balloon *♂♂ 1962* (PG) This adaptation of the Jules Verne novel follows the often-comic exploits of a 19th-century British expedition that encounters many adventures on a balloon trek across Africa. Pleasant fluff with a good cast. **101m/C VHS, DVD.** Fabian, Peter Lorre, Red Buttons, Cedric Hardwicke, Barbara Eden; **D:** Irwin Allen; **W:** Charles Bennett, Irwin Allen; **C:** Winton C. Hoch.

The Fix *♂ The Agitators 1984* A group of cocaine smugglers get their just desserts as the federal government catches them in a sting operation. **95m/C VHS.** Vince Edwards, Richard Jaeckel, Julie Hill, Charles Dierkop, Byron Cherry, Robert Tessier; **D:** Will Zens.

Fixed Bayonets! *♂♂♂½ 1951* Fuller's second Korean War epic is just as gritty as his first ("Steel Helmet"), and it stood in direct contrast to the sappy and nostalgic WWII pictures of the time. A unit covering the retreat of a division from an icy mountainous terrain sees its commanding officers killed off until Corporal Menno (Basehear) remains to lead the men. Menno, hesitant to kill, learns whether he can do what needs to be done for the survival of his men. One of Fuller's best films, and that's saying a lot: Strong **DVD.** Richard Basehart, Gene Evans, Michael O'Shea, Richard Hylton, Craig Hill, Skip Homeier, Richard Monahan, James Dean, John Doucette; **D:** Samuel Fuller; **W:** Samuel Fuller; **C:** Lucien Ballard; **M:** Roy Webb.

The Fixer *♂ 1968* (PG-13) Based on the true story of a Jewish handyman (Bates) in 1911 Tsarist Russia who's accused of murdering a gentile boy. Wrongly imprisoned he's tortured to confess to the crime, which he refuses to do. Bogarde is the lawyer who tries to help him. Strong direction and acting in an unrelieving drama. Adapted from Bernard Malamud's Pulitzer Prize-winning novel. **132m/C VHS.** Alan Bates, Dirk Bogarde, Georgia Brown, Hugh Griffith, Elizabeth Hartman, Ian Holm, David Opatoshu, David Warner, Carol White, Murray Melvin, Peter Jeffrey, William Hutt; **D:** John Frankenheimer; **W:** Dalton Trumbo; **M:** Maurice Jarre.

The Fixer *♂♂½ 1997* Jack Killoran (Voight) is a corrupt Chicago lawyer who can get anything done for a price. But after he's temporarily paralyzed in an accident, Jack has a crisis of conscience and decides he'd like to go legit. However, his bosses decide he knows too much to let him go. **105m/C VHS.** Jon Voight, Brenda Bakke, J.J. Johnston, Miguel (Michael) Sandoval, Karl Pruner, Brent Jennings, Jack Wallace; **D:** Charles Robert Carner; **W:** Charles Robert Carner; **C:** Michael Goi; **M:** Lennie Niehaus. **CABLE**

Flags of Our Fathers *♂♂½ 2006* (R) Director Eastwood tells the dark and ultimately sad story behind Joe Rosenthal's iconic 1945 photograph, the flagraising by six soldiers at Iwo Jima. It's most ambitious outing to date. The government decides to whisk the three survivors home and use them on a nationwide war bonds drive, although only marine...

Rene Gagnon (Bradford) takes to the hoopla. Navy corpsman "Doc" Bradley (Phillippe) is haunted by the deaths and those left behind while alcoholic Pima Indian Ira Hayes (Beach) would rather fight than fra... Joseph Schildkraut, William Frawley, Ann Dvorak, Joseph Kane.

Flambards *♂♂½ 1978* In the early 1900s, teenaged orphan Christine is sent to live with her tyrannical Uncle Russell William, who's obsessed with the new-fangled airplane. Quarrels intensify as both young men fall in love with Christine and WWI begins, leading to sacrifice and tragedy. Based on the trilogy by K.M. Peyton. **678m/C VHS, DVD. GB** Christina McKenna, Stephen Grives, Alan Parnaby, Edward Judd, Sebastian Abineri, Peter Settelen, Carol Leader, Frank Mills; **D:** Lawrence Gordon-Clark, Peter Duffell. **TV**

The Flame & the Arrow *♂♂♂ 1950* Dardo the Arrow, a Robin Hood-like outlaw in medieval Italy, leads his band of mountain fighters against a mercenary warlord who has seduced his wife and kidnapped his son. Spectacular acrobatics, with Lancaster performing his own stunts, add interest to the usual swashbuckling. **88m/C VHS.** Burt Lancaster, Virginia Mayo, Aline Allenby; **D:** Jacques Tourneur; **M:** Max Steiner.

The Flame Is Love *♂½ 1979* Adaptation of one of Barbara Cartland's romantic novels. A turn-of-the-century American heiress falls tragically in love with a Parisian journalist despite her engagement to an Englishman. **96m/C VHS.** Linda Purl, Timothy Dalton, Shane Briant; **D:** Michael O'Herlihy. **TV**

Flame of Araby *♂♂ 1951* When Princess Tanya's (O'Hara) father is murdered, she's threatened with an unwanted marriage and loss of the throne. But if she can win a horse race, Tanya has a chance for freedom. Now, if she can only convince handsome Bedouin chief Tamerlane (Chandler), who has the fastest black stallion in the desert, to come to her aid. **78m/C VHS.** Maureen O'Hara, Jeff Chandler, Lon Chaney Jr., Buddy Baer, Maxwell Reed, Susan Cabot, Royal Dano, Richard Egan; **D:** Charles Lamont; **W:** Gerald Drayson Adams; **C:** Russell Metty.

The Flame of New Orleans *♂♂♂ 1941* Dietrich is naturally the flame in question as Claire, Countess of New Orleans. She becomes engaged to Girard (Young) but then is attracted to sailor Robert (Cabot) and strings both men along while she tries to decide what to do. Claire's temporary solution is a harebrained plan involving her posing as a lookalike cousin, just come to town. French director Clair's first U.S. film was critically panned upon its release. **79m/B VHS.** Marlene Dietrich, Bruce Cabot, Roland Young, Mischa Auer, Andy Devine, Frank Jenks, Franklin Pangborn, Laura Hope Crews; **D:** Rene Clair; **W:** Norman Krasna; **C:** Rudolph Mate; **M:** Frank Skinner.

Flame of the Barbary Coast *♂♂½ 1945* A rancher from Montana vies with a gambling czar for a beautiful dance hall queen and control of the Barbary Coast section of San Francisco. The great earthquake of 1906 provides the plot with a climax. Also available colorized. **91m/B DVD.** John Wayne, Ann Dvorak, Joseph Schildkraut, William Frawley, Ann Dvorak, Joseph Kane.

The Flaming Teen-Age *♂ 1956* Schlocky pseudo-documentary demonstrating the evils of drugs and alcohol. Exploitative, and the teenagers look really old. Cheaply made, and it shows. **67m/B VHS, DVD.** Noel Reyburn, Ethel Barrett, Jerry Frank; **D:** Irvin S. Yeaworth Jr., Charles Edwards.

Flaming Star *♂♂♂ 1960* In the 1870s Texas, a family with a white father and an Indian mother is caught in the midst of an Indian uprising. The mixed-blood youth, excellently played by Presley, must choose a side with tragic results for all. A stirring, well-written drama of frontier prejudice and one of Presley's best films. **101m/C VHS, DVD.** Elvis Presley, Dolores Del Rio, Barbara Eden, Steve Forrest, John McIntire, Richard Jaeckel, L.Q. Jones, Douglas Dick, Rodolfo Acosta, Ford Rainey, Karl Swenson; **D:** Don Siegel; **W:** Nunnally Johnson, Clair Huffaker; **C:** Charles Clarke; **M:** Cyril Mockridge.

Flaming Signal *♂½ 1933* Featuring Flash the Wonder Labrador, this action-packed film deals with a pilot who crash-lands near a Pacific island, just as the natives, provoked by an exploitative German trader, are rising up against the whites. Both Flash and his master manage to rescue the missionary's pretty daughter. **64m/B VHS.** Noah Beery Sr., Marceline Day, Carmelita Geraghty, Mischa Auer, Henry B. Walthall, John David Horsley; **D:** Charles E. Roberts, George Jeske; **W:** Charles E. Roberts; **C:** Irvin Akers; **M:** Lee Zahler.

Flaming Lead *♂½ 1939* A hard-drinkin' ranch owner hires a nightclub cowboy to help him get an Army horse contract. **57m/B VHS, DVD.** Ken Maynard, Eleanor Stewart, Walter Long, Tom London; **D:** Sam Newfield.

Flaming Frontiers *♂♂ 1938* A frontier scout matches wits against gold mine thieves, in 15 episodes. **300m/B VHS, DVD.** Johnny Mack Brown, Eleanor Hanson, Ralph Bowman; **D:** Ray Taylor.

Flaming Bullets *♂♂ 1945* Last of the Texas Rangers series has solid action scenes, but little else. Ritter leads the Texas Rangers in breaking up a gang with a devious scheme: breaking men out of jail, then killing them for the cash reward. **55m/B VHS.** Tex Ritter, Dave O'Brien, Guy Wilkerson, Charles "Blackie" King, Patricia Knox, I. Stanford Jolley; **D:** Harry Fraser; **W:** Harry Fraser; **C:** Ian Wilson; **M:** Alan Blaakley.

Flame Over India *♂♂ North-west Frontier 1960* When Moslems lay siege to a British fortress in India, Governess Wyatt (Bacall) and Captain Scott (More) save the Maharaja's son and escape by commandeering a train. Along the way they find treason, adventure, and love. **130m/C VHS.** GB Kenneth More, Lauren Bacall, Herbert Lom, Wilfrid Hyde-White, I.S. Johar, Ursula Jeans, Ian Hunter, Eugene Deckers, Jack (Ursula) Gwillim, Govind Raja Ross, Frank Olegario; **D:** J. Lee Thompson; **C:** Geoffrey Unsworth.

Flame to the Phoenix *♂♂½ 1985* A WWII drama with the Polish cavalry forces' decimation to German Panzer tanks. **80m/C VHS.** GB Paul Geoffrey, Annie(l) Firbank, Frederick Treves; **D:** William Brayne.

The Flame Trees of Thika *♂♂♂ 1981* In 1913, a British family travels to East Africa to start a coffee plantation. Seen through the eyes of the young daughter, her childhood consists of the exotic and sometimes unhappy English neighbors, and the wild animals that roam the plains. Based on the memoirs of writer Elspeth Huxley. Four cassettes; shown on PBS "Masterpiece Theatre." **366m/C VHS, DVD.** GB Hayley Mills, Holly Aird, David Robb, Ben Cross; **D:** Roy Ward Baker; **C:** ...

Flame of the Islands *♂♂ 1955* De Carlo plays a smoldering, passionate chanteuse who struggles with love and gangsters for possession of a Bahamian casino in this tropical heat wave. **92m/C VHS.** Yvonne De Carlo, Howard Duff, Zachary Scott, James Arness, Kurt Kaszner, Barbara O'Neil; **D:** Edward Ludwig.

Flanders *♂ 2006* Dumont's work (with nonprofessionals) is an acquired, frequently polarizing taste, and in this case, numbingly boring. Andre (Boldin) is a brute of a farmer who boffs local trollop Barbe (Leroux). He gets drafted and goes off to fight some nameless war in the desert. One of his fellow soldiers is Blondel (Cretel), who also knew Barbe in the biblical sense. She's back home having an abortion and going temporarily nuts while the soldiers pay the price for brutal acts against the local militia. French with subtitles. **91m/C DVD. FR** Samuel Boidin, Adelaide Leroux, Henri Cretel; **D:** Bruno Dumont; **C:** Yves Cape.

Flannel Pajamas *♂♂ 2006* (R) Raw but talky look at the nearly-three year relationship between two New Yorkers from their first date to their final breakup. Jewish Stuart (Kirk) and Catholic Nicole (Nicholson) date, marry, and try to settle into domestic life while family dilemmas (Nicole's mother is an anti-Semite, among other problems) and personal and professional disappointments take their toll. Equal opportunity nudity by both leads. **124m/C DVD.** Julianne Nicholson, Justin Kirk, Rebecca Schull, Chelsea Altman; **D:** Jeff Lipsky; **C:** Matira Radwan; **M:** Paul Hsu.

The Flash *♂♂ 1990* When police scientist Barry Allen is accidentally doused by chemicals and then struck by lightning, the combination makes him into a new superhero. His super quickness help his...

Flaming Road *♂♂♂ 1949* A scandalously entertaining melodrama in which Crawford portrays a carnival dancer who intrigues Scott and Brian in a small Southern town where the carnival stops. Crawford shines in a role that demands her to be both tough and sensitive in a corrupt world full of political backstabbing and sleazy characters. Remade as a TV movie and television soap-opera series in 1980. **94m/B VHS.** Joan Crawford, Zachary Scott, David Brian, Sydney Greenstreet, Gertrude Michael, Gladys George, Virginia Huston, Fred Clark, Alice White; **D:** Michael Curtiz; **W:** Edmund H. North, Ronald MacDougall; **M:** Max Steiner.

Flamingo Rising *♂♂½ 2001* Impetuous Herbert T. Lee (Benben) decides to build the world's largest drive-in movie theatre in his '60s Florida community. Unfortunately, the spot he picks is right across the street from the funeral parlor run by Turner Knight (Hurt), who doesn't see it as an appropriate venue. Caught in the middle are Lee's two adopted children and his wife, Edna (McGovern), who tries to make both men see reason. Based on the novel by Larry Baker. **96m/C VHS.** Brian Benben, William Hurt, Elizabeth McGovern, Angela Bettis, Erin Broderick, Joe Tony, Chris Larkin, Oliver via Oguma; **D:** Martha Coolidge; **W:** Richard Russo; **C:** Johnny E. Jensen; **M:** David Newman. **TV**

The Flamingo Kid *♂♂♂ 1984* (PG-13) Brooklyn teen Jeffrey Willis (Dillon) gets a summer job at a fancy beach club on Long Island. His plumber father, Arthur (Elizondo), remembers how to dream but is so aware of how rough the world is on dreamers. Suddenly making lots of money at a menial job, the kid's attracted to the high style of local sports car dealer Phil Brody (Crenna), and finds his father's solid life a bore. By the end of the summer, he's learned the true value of both men, and the kind of man he wants to be. Excellent performances all around, nice ensemble acting among the young men who play Dillon's buddies. Great sound track. Film debut of Jones, who seems a little old for her part as a California college sophomore. **100m/C VHS, DVD.** Matt Dillon, Hector Elizondo, Molly McCarthy, Martha German, Richard Crenna, Jessica Walter, Carole (Raphaelle) Davis, Janet Jones, Fisher Stevens, Bronson Pinchot; **D:** Garry Marshall; **W:** Garry Marshall, Neil Marshall; **C:** James A. Contner; **M:** Curt Sobel.

The Flaming Urge *♂ 1953* A small town is plagued by mysterious fires. Could a pyromaniac be on the loose? **67m/B VHS, DVD.** Harold Lloyd Jr., Cathy Downs; **D:** Harold Ericson; **W:** Harold Ericson; **C:** Clark Ramsey; **M:** Raoul Kraushaar.

Flash *(continued)* quest in fighting crime in Central City where he's aided by fellow scientist Tina McGee (the only other person to know his secret). In this adventure, the Flash seeks out the violent and mesmerizing leader of a biker gang who caused the death of Barry's brother. Based on the DC comic book character, this is the pilot episode for the short-lived TV series. The look is dark and stylized and not played for camp. **94m/C VHS.** John Wesley Shipp, Amanda Pays, Michael Nader; *M:* Danny Elfman. **TV**

Flash 1998 Fourteen-year-old Connor's (Black) best friend is a horse named Flash. When his family hits hard times, Connor's dad (Kerwin) joins the merchant marines, his grandmother (Burstyn) goes to work in a factory, and Connor is forced to sell Flash. The teen takes a job in the new owner's stables and when he sees how badly the animal is treated, Connor steals Flash and sets off to meet his father's ship in New York. **90m/C VHS, DVD.** Lucas Black, Ellen Burstyn, Brian Kerwin, Shawn Toovey, Tom Nowicki, Dan Biggers; *D:* Simon Wincer. **TV**

Flash & Firecat 1975 (PG) A beautiful blonde and a crazy thief steal and race their way across the country in a dune buggy with the police hot on their trail. **90m/C VHS.** Roger Davis, Tricia Sembera, Dub Taylor, Richard Kiel; *D:* Ferd Sebastian.

Flash Gordon 1980 (PG) Camp version of the adventures of Flash Gordon in outer space. This time, Flash and Dale Arden are forced by Dr. Zarkov to accompany him on a mission to far-off Mongo, where Ming the Merciless is threatening the destruction of Earth. Music by Queen. **111m/C VHS, DVD.** Sam Jones, Melody Anderson, Chaim Topol, Max von Sydow, Ornella Muti, Timothy Dalton, Brian Blessed; *D:* Mike Hodges; *W:* Lorenzo Semple Jr.; *C:* Gilbert Taylor; *M:* Howard Blake.

Flash Gordon Conquers the Universe *Purple Death from Outer Space* 1940 Ravaging plague strikes the earth and Flash Gordon undertakes to stop it. A serial in 12 chapters. **240m/B VHS, DVD.** Buster Crabbe, Carol Hughes, Charles Middleton, Frank Shannon, Anne Gwynne, John Hamilton, Herbert Rawlinson, Tom Chatterton; *D:* Ford Beebe, Ray Taylor; *W:* George Plympton, Basil Dickey, Barry Shipman; *C:* Jerome Ash, William Sickner.

Flash Gordon: Mars Attacks the World *The Deadly Rays from Mars; Flash Gordon's Trip to Mars* 1939 The earth is plagued by the evil Ming, but Flash Gordon steps in. From the serial. **97m/B VHS, DVD.** Buster Crabbe, Jean Rogers, Charles Middleton; *D:* Robert F. "Bob" Hill, Ford Beebe.

Flash Gordon: Rocketship *Spaceship to the Unknown; Perils from Planet Mongo; Space Soldiers; Atomic Rocketship* 1940 Re-edited from the original Flash Gordon serial in which Flash and company must prevent the planet Mongo from colliding with Earth. Good character acting and good clean fun. **82m/B VHS, DVD.** Buster Crabbe, Jean Rogers, Frank Shannon, Charles Middleton, Priscilla Lawson, Jack Lipson; *D:* Frederick Stephani.

A Flash of Green 1985 A crooked politician is helping a construction firm exploit valuable waterfront property. He enlists the influence of a hesitant local journalist, who then falls for the woman leading the homeowner's conservation drive against the development plan. Made for American Playhouse and produced by costar Jordon. D. MacDonald. **122m/C VHS.** Ed Harris, Blair Brown, Richard Jordan, George Coe; *D:* Victor Nunez; *W:* Victor Nunez; *M:* Charles Engstrom.

Flashback 1989 (R) FBI agent Sutherland's assignment sounds easy: escort aging 1960s radical Hopper to prison. But Hopper is cunning and decides not to go without a fight. He uses his brain to outwit the young Sutherland and to turn against himself. Good moments between the two leads and with Kane, as a woman who never left the '60s behind. **108m/C VHS.** Dennis Hopper, Kiefer Sutherland, Carol Kane, Cliff DeYoung, Paul Dooley, Michael McKean, Richard Masur; *D:* Franco Amurri; *M:* Barry Goldberg.

Flashdance 1983 (R) 18-year-old Alex (Beals) wants to dance. She works all day as a welder, has a hot affair going with her boss Nick (Nouri), dances at a local bar at night, and hopes someday to get enough courage to audition for a spot at the School of Ballet. Glossy music video redeemed somewhat by exciting choreography with Marine Jahan doing the dancing for Beals. Oscar-winning title song sung by Irene Cara. Inspired the torn-sweatshirt trend in fashion of the period. ♫Flashdance...What a Feeling; I Love Rock 'n Roll; Manhunt; Gloria; Lady, Lady, Lady; Seduce Me Tonight. **95m/C VHS, DVD.** Jennifer Beals, Michael Nouri, Belinda Bauer, Lilia Skala, Cynthia Rhodes, Sunny Johnson, Lee Ving, Kyle T. Heffner, Ron Karabatsos, Robert Wuhl, Elizabeth Sagal; *D:* Adrian Lyne; *W:* Joe Eszterhas; *C:* Don Peterman; *M:* Giorgio Moroder. Oscars '83: Song ("Flashdance...What a Feeling"); Golden Globes '84: Song ("Flashdance...What a Feeling"), Score.

Flashfire 1994 (R) The torching of an apartment building and the murder of a cop seem unrelated until troubled detective Jack Flinder (Zane) becomes involved. Soon, he and murder witness Lisa (Minter) are on the run from the arsonists and crooked police. **88m/C VHS, DVD.** Billy Zane, Kristin Minter, Louis Gossett Jr.; *D:* Elliot Silverstein; *W:* John Warren, Dan York; *C:* Albert J. Dunk; *M:* Sylvester Levay.

Flashpoint 1984 (R) A pair of Texas border patrolmen discover an abandoned jeep that contains a fortune in cash, apparently from the 1960s. As they try to figure out how it got there, they become prey to those who want to keep the secret. With this cast, flick ought to be better. **95m/C VHS, DVD.** Treat Williams, Kris Kristofferson, Tess Harper, Rip Torn, Miguel Ferrer, Roberts Blossom; *D:* William (Bill) Tannen; *W:* Michael Butler.

Flashpoint Africa 1984 When a news team follows a terrorist group's activities it winds up in a power struggle with terrifying consequences. **99m/C VHS.** Trevor Howard, Gayle Hunnicutt, James Faulkner, Ken Gampu; *D:* Francis Megahy.

Flatbed Annie and Sweetiepie: Lady Truckers *Flatbed Annie* 1979 A couple of good ol' gals hit the road and encounter a variety of bad guys out to steal their truck. **100m/C VHS.** Annie Potts, Kim Darby, Harry Dean Stanton, Arthur Godfrey, Rory Calhoun, Billy Carter, Avery Schreiber; *D:* Robert Greenwald. **TV**

Flat Top 1952 The training of Navy fighter pilots aboard "flat top" aircraft carriers during WWII provides the drama here. A strict commander is appreciated only after the war when his role in their survival. The film makes good use of actual combat footage; fast-paced and effective. **85m/C VHS, DVD.** Sterling Hayden, Richard Carlson, Keith Larsen, John Bromfield; *D:* Lesley Selander.

Flatfoot *The Knock-Out Cop* 1978 (PG) Tough police officer will let nothing stop him from finding and arresting drug smugglers. Good for laughs as well as lots of action. **113m/C VHS.** *IT GE* Bodo, Werner Pochath, Bud Spencer, Enzo Cannavale, Dagmar Lassander, Joe Stewardson; *D:* Steno.

Flatliners 1990 (R) A group of medical students begin after-hours experimentation with death and out-of-body experiences. Some standard horror film images but Roberts and Sutherland create an energy that makes it worth watching. **111m/C VHS, DVD, Blu-ray Disc.** Kiefer Sutherland, Julia Roberts, William Baldwin, Oliver Platt, Kevin Bacon, Kimberly Scott, Joshua Rudoy, Aeryk Egan; *D:* Joel Schumacher; *W:* Peter Filardi; *C:* Jan De Bont; *M:* James Newton Howard.

Flawless 1999 (R) Former New York City cop and resident tough guy Walt Koontz (De Niro) lives across the hall from nosily outrageous drag queen Rusty (Hoffman). The odd couple have a mutual animosity that's put to the test when Walt suffers a stroke and it's recommended that he take singing lessons to help him recover his ability to speak. So he makes an offer to Rusty who needs the cash. Soon they're not only tolerating each other but bonding as well. There are distracting subplots about hidden drug money and a drag queen beauty contest that take the focus off of what could have worked as a two-character study about an unlikely friendship. **111m/C VHS, DVD.** Robert De Niro, Philip Seymour Hoffman, Barry Miller, Chris Bauer, Skipp (Robert L.) Sudduth, Wanda De Jesus, Daphne Rubin-Vega, Rory Cochrane; *D:* Joel Schumacher; *W:* Joel Schumacher; *C:* Declan Quinn; *M:* Bruce Roberts.

Flawless 2007 (PG-13) A soon-to-retire janitor (Caine) of the London Diamond Corporation convinces the company's only female executive (Moore) to help him make off with the merchandise—a scheme she easily agrees to after years of sexist, lying bosses stepping on her head to climb higher on the ladder. Set in 1960's London, told in flashback by an elderly, heavily made-up Moore. Slow pace and cheesy ending keep the drama and suspense in mediocrity. **108m/C VHS, DVD.** *LU GB US* Demi Moore, Michael Caine, Joss Ackland, Lambert Wilson; *D:* Michael Radford; *W:* Edward A. Anderson; *C:* Richard Greatrex; *M:* Stephen Warbeck.

Fled 1996 (R) Charles Piper (Fishburne) and Luke Dodge (Baldwin) are combative prison escapees who need to find a stash of cash and a computer disk that could save them from both the Cuban mob and the cops. Bombshell Cora (Hayek) decides to help the duo and tries to get steamy with Piper. Lots of chases, lots of violence, not much sense. The climatic battle (the film was shot around Atlanta) takes place in a sightseeing gondola at Georgia's Stone Mountain. **98m/C VHS, DVD.** Laurence Fishburne, Stephen Baldwin, Salma Hayek, Will Patton, Robert John Burke; *D:* Kevin Hooks; *W:* Preston A. Whitmore II; *C:* Matthew F. Leonetti; *M:* Graeme Revell.

Fleeing by Night *Ye Ben* 2000 Old-fashioned romantic melodrama set in 1930s China. A small town businessman owns a theater and invites a Beijing opera company to perform there. His naive daughter Wei Ing-er (Liu) is smitten by moody performer Lin Chung (Yin) as is (unexpectedly) her American-schooled fiance Hsu Shao-dung (Huang). But the twosome have a rival for Lin Chung's affections—the wealthy and jealous Huang Zilei (Tai), whose sexual interest is blatant. The dialogue is frequently florid (as probably befits the setting) and it's operatic soap all the way. Mandarin with subtitles. **123m/C DVD.** *TW* Rene Liu, Lei Huang, Chao-te Yin, Li-jen Tai, Ah-Leh Gua; *D:* Li-Kong Hsu, Chi Yin; *W:* Hui-Ling Wang, Ming-xia Wang; *C:* Cheng-hui Tsai; *M:* Chris Babida.

Flesh *Andy Warhol's Flesh* 1968 An Andy Warhol-produced seedy urban farce about a bisexual street hustler who meets a variety of drug-addicted, deformed, and sexually deviant people. Dalesandro fans will enjoy his extensive exposure (literally). **90m/C VHS, DVD.** Joe Dalesandro, Geraldine Smith, Patti D'Arbanville, Candy Darling, Jackie Curtis, Geri Miller, Barry Brown; *D:* Paul Morrissey; *W:* Paul Morrissey; *C:* Paul Morrissey.

Flesh and Blood 1922 An unjustly convicted lawyer is released from prison to find out his wife has died. He vows revenge on those who falsely imprisoned him and assumes the disguise of a crippled beggar to begin his plot. Silent with musical score. **75m/B VHS, DVD.** Lon Chaney Sr.; *D:* Irving Cummings.

Flesh and Blood *The Rose and the Sword* 1985 (R) A rowdy group of 16th Century hellions makes off with a princess who is already spoken for and pillage and plunder their way to revenge. Hauer leads the motley group through sword fights, raids, and the like. Dutch director Verhoeven's first English language film. Not for children; with rape scenes, nudity, and graphic sex. **126m/C VHS, DVD.** Rutger Hauer, Jennifer Jason Leigh, Tom Burlinson, Susan Tyrrell, Jack Thompson, Ronald Lacey, Brion James, Bruno Kirby; *D:* Paul Verhoeven; *W:* Paul Verhoeven, Gerard Soeteman; *C:* Jan De Bont; *M:* Basil Poledouris.

Flesh and Blood Show *Asylum of the Insane* 1973 (R) Rehearsal turns into an execution ritual for a group of actors at a mysterious seaside theatre. Truth in titling: features blood, gore, and some sex. Shot in part in 3-D. **93m/C VHS, DVD.** *GB* Robin Askwith, Candace Glendenning, Tristan Rogers, Ray Brooks, Jenny Hanley, Luan Peters, Patrick Barr, Judy Matheson, Penny Meredith; *D:* Pete Walker; *W:* Alfred Shaughnessy; *C:* Peter Jessop.

Flesh and Bone 1993 (R) Quaid is exact as a vending machine distributor with a desolate rural Texas circuit, haunted by the memory of a decades-old murder committed by his father (Caan) during a botched farm-house robbery. Alcoholic Ryan (Quaid's real-life wife) emerges from a bad marriage and helps Quaid rebuild his life, never suspecting that they may have met before. Challenging but successful role for Ryan, better known for her girlish, romantic-comedy appeal. Paltrow's unforgettable as a heartless casket robber and Caan's partner/girlfriend. Director Kloves extracts moments of earthy beauty from the bleak, humble West Texas setting. **127m/C VHS, DVD.** Dennis Quaid, Meg Ryan, James Caan, Gwyneth Paltrow, Scott Wilson; *D:* Steve Kloves; *W:* Steven Kloves; *M:* Thomas Newman.

The Flesh and the Devil 1927 Classic Garbo at her seductive best as a woman who causes a feud between two friends. Gilbert is an Austrian officer, falls for the married Garbo and winds up killing her husband in a duel. Banished to the African Corps he asks his best friend (Hanson) to look after his lady love. But Hanson takes his job too seriously and falls for the lady himself. Great silent movie with surprise ending to match. The first Gilbert and Garbo pairing. **112m/B VHS, DVD.** John Gilbert, Greta Garbo, Lars Hanson, Barbara Kent, George Fawcett, Eugenie Besserer; *D:* Clarence Brown; *C:* William H. Daniels. Natl. Film Reg. '06.

The Flesh and the Fiends *Mania; Fiendish Ghouls; Psycho Killers* 1960 Fine adaptation of the Burke and Hare grave robbing legend. Cushing is the doctor who needs corpses and Pleasence and Rose provide them by any means. Highly atmospheric representation of dismal, 19th century Edinburgh. Very graphic for its time. **87m/B VHS, DVD.** *GB* Peter Cushing, June Laverick, Donald Pleasence, George Rose, Dermot Walsh, Renee Houston, Billie Whitelaw, John Cairney, Michael Balfour; *D:* John Gilling; *W:* John Gilling, Leon Griffiths; *C:* Monty Berman; *M:* Stanley Black.

Flesh and the Spur 1957 A cowboy tracks the killer of his brother. Future Mannix Mike Connors (nicknamed 'Touch' at the time) joins the search. Undefying western with oddball touches, notably a theme song by Chipmunks creator Ross Bagdasarian. **78m/C VHS.** John Agar, Maria English, Mike Connors, Raymond Hatton, Maria Monay, Joyce Meadows, Kenne Duncan; *D:* Edward L. Cahn.

The Flesh Eaters 1964 A claustrophobic low-budget thriller about a film queen and her secretary who crash-land on an island inhabited by your basic mad scientist. His latest experiment is with tiny flesh-eating sea creatures. Shock ending. **87m/C VHS, DVD.** Martin Kosleck, Rita Morley, Byron Sanders, Barbara Wilkin, Ray Tudor; *D:* Jack Curtis; *W:* Arnold Drake; *C:* Carson Davidson.

Flesh Eating Mothers 1989 Housewives are transformed into cannibals after a mystery virus hits their town. Their kids must stop the moms from eating any more people. **90m/C VHS, DVD.** Robert Lee Oliver, Donatella Hecht, Valorie Hubbard, Neal Rosen, Terry Hayes; *D:* James Aviles Martin.

Flesh Feast WOOF! 1969 Classically horrendous anti-Nazi bosh, in which a mad female plastic surgeon (Lake) rejuvenates Hitler and then tortures him to death with maggots to avenge her mother's suffering. Lake's last film, and the sorriest sign-off any actress ever had. **72m/C VHS, DVD.** Veronica Lake, Phil Philbin, Heather Hughes, Martha Mischon, Yanka (Doris Keating)

Flesh Gordon 🎬 1972 Soft-core spoof of the "Flash Gordon" series. Flesh takes it upon himself to save Earth from the evil Wang's sex ray. Wang, of course, is eager to claim it. During his cown-home trip he becomes involved in a murder and must use his disguise skills tc solve it before he becomes the next victim. Based on the novels of Gregory MacDonald. Look for cameo by real-life porn starlet Candy Samples. The restored (90-minute) version also includes the theatrical trailer. A 72-minute R-rated version is also available. **90min/C VHS, DVD.** Jason Williams, Suzanne Fields, Joseph Hudgins, John Hoyt, Howard Ziehm; **D:** Michael Benveniste, Howard Ziehm, Michael Benveniste; **W:** Michael Benveniste; **C:** Howard Ziehm; **M:** Ralph Ferraro; **V:** Craig T. Nelson.

Flesh Gordon 2: Flesh Gordon Meets the Cosmic Cheerleaders 🎬 1990 Emperor Wang (Hunt) threatens the Universe with his powerful impotence ray. Flesh (Murdocco), along with Dale (Kelly) and Dr. Flexi Je'koff (Travis), do battle with a belt of farting asteroids and other weirdos. Director Ziehm delivers this one on a shoestring of under $1 million, even improving technically on the original. The sex scenes are, however, more watered down in an apparent attempt to gain a wider audience. Scatological jokes are the basis for much of the humor. **98m/C VHS, DVD.** *CA* Vince Murdocco, Tony Travis, William Dennis Hunt, Robyn Kelly, Morgan Fox, Melissa Mounds; **D:** Howard Ziehm; **W:** Howard Ziehm; **C:** Danny Nowak.

Fleshburn 🎬 1984 (R) An Indian Vietnam War veteran escapes from a mental institution to get revenge on the four psychiatrists who committed him. **91m/C VHS, DVD.** Steve Kanaly, Karen Carlson, Sonny Landham, Macon McCalman; **D:** George Gage; **W:** George Gage, Beth Gage, Brian Garfield; **M:** Arthur Kempel.

Fleshpot on 42nd Street 🎬 1971 Stark, realistic look at the streetwalking profession. Dusty leaves her blue collar boyfriend to move in with a transvestite and then she meets a dashing young Staten Island native (like the director). Their romance blooms until he is run over by a car, sending Dusty into a tailspin which lands her back on 42nd Street. Along the way, various rustic hookers and venerable old floozies liven up director Mulligan's version of New York. Less emphasis on the sleaze than the grittiness. **78m/C VHS.** Diana Lewis, Lynn Flanagan, Boc Walters, Andy Milligan.

Fleshtone 🎬 1994 (R) Artist Matthew Greco's (Kemp) work is not for the faint-hearted since he paints grisly suicides and murders. No wonder he's lonely—so lonely that he answers a phone-sex ad and is hooked up with Edna, who doesn't exist. Just what has Matthew gotten himself into? Provocative but ending is a letdown. An unrated version is also available. **89m/C VHS.** Martin Kemp, Lise Cutter, Tim Thomerson; **D:** Harry Hurwitz; **W:** Harry Hurwitz.

Fletch 🎬 1985 (PG) Somewhat charming comedy. When newspaper journalist Fletch goes undercover to get the scoop on the local drug scene, a wealthy young businessman enlists his help in dying. Something's rotten in Denmark when the man's doctor knows nothing of the illness and Fletch comes nothing of the drug scene than he realizes. Throughout the entire film, Chevy Chase assumes a multitude of flippant comic characters to discover the truth. Based on Gregory McDonald's novel. **98m/C VHS, DVD.** Chevy Chase, Dana Wheeler-Nicholson, M. Emmet Walsh, Kenneth Mars, Geena Davis, Richard Libertini, George Wendt, Kareem Abdul-Jabbar, Alison La Placa, George Wyner, Tony Longo, James Avery, William Sanderson, Beau Starr, Raph Seymour, Larry "Flash" Jenkins; **D:** Michael Ritchie; **W:** Andrew Bergman; **C:** Fred Schuler; **M:** Harold Faltermeyer.

Fletch Lives 🎬 1989 (PG) In this sequel to "Fletch," Chase is back again as the super-reporter. When Fletch learns of his inheritance of a Southern estate he is eager to claim it. During his down-home trip he becomes involved in a murder and must use his disguise skills tc solve it before he becomes the next victim. Based on the novels of Gregory MacDonald. **95m/C VHS, DVD.** Chevy Chase, Hal Holbrook, Julianne Phillips, Richard Libertini, R. Lee Ermey, Cleavon Little, Randall "Tex" Cobb, Richard Belzer, Geoffrey Lewis, Patricia Kalember, Phil Hartman, George Wyner; **D:** Michael Ritchie; **M:** Harold Faltermeyer.

Flicka 🎬🎬½ 2006 (PG) A girl and her horse. Katy McLaughlin (Lohman) is happy to return to her family's struggling Wyoming ranch after having blown her year at boarding school. She would much rather help her older brother, Howard (McGraw), breed quarter horses, although her traditionalist father, Rob (Kwanten). Mom Nell (Bello) plays peacemaker. The situation worsens when black stallion of the title. But when dad sells Flicka to the rodeo, Katy is determined to get the horse back. C-W singing star McGraw is a natural while the twenty-something Lohman can still pass for teen. A big-hearted, hard-headed teen. **94m/C DVD.** *US* Alison Lohman, Tim McGraw, Maria Bello, Ryan Kwanten, Dallas Roberts, Nick Searcy, Jeffrey Nordling, Danny Pino; **D:** Michael Mayer; **W:** Mark Rosenthal, Larry Konner; **C:** J.(James)Michael Muro; **M:** Aaron Zigman.

Flickering Lights 🎬½ *Blinkende Lygter* 2001 Trokild (Pilmark) is deeply in debt to gangster Eskimo (Andersson). He and pals Peter (Thomsen), Arne (Mikkelsen), and Stefan (Kaas) are surprised to discover the briefcase they've been forced to steal contains a lot of money. They decide to keep the cash and are heading for Spain when their getaway truck breaks down in the woods. The foursome finds refuge in an abandoned inn and Torkild, who's tired of the criminal life, decides to back up so they can all start new lives. Of course, Eskimo may have other ideas when he finds them. An uncertain mixture of dark humor and sentimentality. Danish with subtitles. **109m/C VHS, DVD, DK** Soren Pilmark, Ulrich Thomsen, Mads Mikkelsen, Nikolaj Lie Kaas, Peter Andersson, Sofie Grabol, Iben Hjejle, Frits Helmuth; **D:** Anders Thomas Jensen; **W:** Anders Thomas Jensen; **C:** Eric Kress; **M:** Bent Fabricius-Bjerre, Jeppe Kaas.

Flickers 🎬🎬½ 1980 Uncouth, ambitious Cockney Arnie Cole (Hoskins) wants to go from bioscope exhibitor to owner of his own silent-film production company. But he needs money—and up per middle-class Maud (de la Tour) needs a husband since she's pregnant and can make a business arrangement that turns a single mum won't do. The oddball duo make a business arrangement that turns he's a fireplug) and a delight as sparring partners. 6 episodes. **307m/C VHS, DVD, GB** Bob Hoskins, Frances de la Tour, Peggy Wood, Dickie Arnold, Valerie Holliman, Fraser Cairns, Granville Saxon, Jim Hooper, Joanna Foster; **D:** Cyril Coke; **W:** Roy Clarke. **TV**

Flicks *Hollyweird* 1985 (R) A compilation of skits parodying the tradition of Saturday afternoon matinees, including coming attractions and a cartoon. Never released theatrically. **79m/C VHS.** Martin Mull, Pamela Sue Martin, Betty Kennedy, Richard Belzer; **D:** Peter Winograd.

The Flight 🎬🎬½ 1989 A non-narrative view of glider planes as they soar over the countryside and rivers of the Laurentians and Canadian Rockies. Useful in language arts classes. **96m/C VHS.** Eli Danker, Sandy McPeak, Lindsay Wagner; **D:** Paul Wendkos.

Flight from Glory 🎬🎬½ 1937 A group of pilots fly supplies over the Andes from their isolated base camp to even more isolated mines. Morris is their leader who watches as, one by one, the men are killed on their dangerous flights. To make a bad situation worse, Heflin arrives as a new recruit—along with his pretty wife. **66m/B VHS, DVD.** Chester Morris, Onslow Stevens, Whitney Bourne, Van Heflin; **D:** Lew Landers.

Flight from Singapore 🎬½ 1962 Transporting desperately needed blood to Malaysia, a flight crew is forced to crash land in the jungle. Nicely done if escape in order to prove his loyalty. Cold war drama hangs together on strength of Bikel's performance. **74m/B VHS, GB** Patrick Allen, Patrick Holt, William Abney, Harry Fowler; **D:** Dudley Birch; **W:** Dudley Birch.

Flight from Vienna 🎬🎬 1956 A high-ranking Hungarian security officer, disenchanted with communism, stages a daring escape from his country. In Vienna, he asks the British for political asylum, but is sent back to Hungary to help a scientist escape to the West. **54m/B VHS.** Theodore Bikel, John Bentley, Donald Gray, Adrienne Scott, Carine Hartman; **D:** Denis Kavanagh; **W:** Denis Kavanagh; **C:** Hal Morey.

Flight of Black Angel 🎬🎬½ 1991 (R) Wacked-out F-16 pilot fancies himself an angel of death, and, after annihilating a number of trainees, sets out to make Las Vegas a nuked-out ghost town. Squadron commander Strauss, however, is not pleased with his pilot's initiative. Made-for-cable script runs out of gas and heads into a nosedive. **102m/C VHS, DVD.** Peter Strauss, William O'Leary, James O'Sullivan, Mike Genovese, Marijke Mercken; **D:** Jonathan Mostow; **W:** John Brancato. **CABLE**

Flight of Dragons 🎬🎬½ 1982 Animated tale takes place between the Age of Magic and the Age of Science, in a century when dragons ruled the skies. **98m/C VHS.** *D:* Arthur Rankin Jr., Jules Bass; **V:** John Ritter, Victor Buono, James Earl Jones, Donald E. Messick, Larry Storch.

A Flight of Rainbirds 🎬🎬 1981 In a dual role, Krabbe plays a biologist who dreams he must lose his virginity within a week or die and his alter ego who joins him in the search for the perfect woman. In Dutch with English subtitles. **94m/C VHS.** *NL* Jeroen Krabbe, Willeke Van Ammelroy, Marijke Merckens; **D:** Ate De Jong; **W:** Ate De Jong; **C:** Paul van den Bos; **M:** Laurens van Rooyen.

Flight of the Eagle 🎬🎬½ 1982 Based on the actual ill-fated expedition of Salomon Andree who, with two friends, attempted to fly from Sweden to the North Pole in a hydrogen balloon in 1897. The last half of the film crags somewhat as the three struggle to survive in the frozen north after their balloon crashes. Beautifully photographed adventure. In Swedish with English subtitles. **115m/C VHS, SW Max** von Sydow, Goran Stangertz, Clement Harari, Sverre Anker; **D:** Jan Troell.

Flight of the Grey Wolf 🎬½ 1976 A tame, innocent wolf is mistaken for a killer and must run for his life with the help of his boy-owner. **82m/C VHS, DVD.** Bill Williams, Barbara Hale, Jeff East; **D:** Frank Zuniga; **W:** Calvin Clements Jr.

Flight of the Innocent 🎬🎬½ 1993 (R) The innocent 10-year-old Vito comes from a family who make their living as kidnappers. He is the only witness (and the only survivor) when his family is massacred by a rival gang. Vito flees the carnage and sets off to find this cousin who lives in Rome. But his journey truly ends when he is taken in by a wealthy industrialist family whose own son has been kidnapped. Directorial debut of Cartei who tends to rely on striking visuals rather than his characters. In Italian with English subtitles. **105m/C VHS, DVD.** *IT* Manuel Coleo, Francesca Neri, Jacques Perrin, Frederico Pacifici, Sal Borgese; **D:** Carlo Cartei; **W:** Carlo Cartei, Gualtiero Rosella.

Flight of the Intruder 🎬 1990 (PG-13) Vietnam naval pilots aboard an aircraft carrier don't take any rogue war is being handled, so they go rogue and decide to go on a mission to bomb an enemy air base in Hanoi. Loads of male bonding. **115m/C VHS, DVD.** Danny Glover, William Defoe, Brad Johnson, Rosanna Arquette, Tom

Flight of the Living Dead: Outbreak on a Plane 🎬🎬 Plane Dead 2007 Campy, fast-paced gore. A scientist brings a corpse infected with a genetically engineered virus aboard a flight from L.A. to Paris. The zombie escapes from the cargo hold and infects the passengers, who really have nowhere to escape. When he returns home eight years later, a NASA investigation ensues. Paul Reubens, better known as Pee-wee Herman, provides the voice of the robot. **90m/C VHS, DVD.** Joey Cramer, Veronica Cartwright, Cliff DeYoung, Sarah Jessica Parker, Matt Adler, Howard Hesseman; **D:** Randal Kleiser; **W:** Michael Burton, Matt MacManus; **M:** Alan Silvestri; **V:** Paul (Pee-wee Herman) Reubens.

The Flight of the Phoenix 🎬🎬 1965 A group of men stranded in the Arabian desert after a plane crash attempt to rebuild their plane in order to escape before succumbing to the elements. Big budget, all-star survival drama based on the Elleston Trevor novel. Frank Towns (Quaid) is the tough, cynical pilot of a rusty C-119 cargo plane who has just picked up a disparate group of oil rig workers, including lone woman Kelly (Otto), from the Mongolian desert. They crash during a sandstorm and their survival comes to depend on arrogant occidtal Elliott (Ribisi). Claiming to be an aircraft designer, Elliott announces he can make a new plane from the crash pieces, if the reluctant Towrs will cede him authority. Tensions grow, supplies dwindle, and desert nomads wait like vultures to prey on the weakening survivors. Remake has CGI advantages but less-compelling characters. **112m/C VHS, DVD, Blu-ray Disc. US** Dennis Quaid, Miranda Otto, Giovanni Ribisi, Tyrese Gibson, Hugh Laurie, Tony Curran, Kirk "Sticky Fingaz" Jones, Jacob Vargas, Scott Michael Campbell, Kevork Malikyan; **D:** John Moore; **W:** Scott Frank, Edward Burns; **C:** Brendan Galvin; **M:** Marco Beltrami.

Flight of the Phoenix 🎬🎬½ 2004 (PG-13) Old-fashioned remake of Robert Aldrich's 1965 film makes use of both Lukas Heller's original screenplay

Flight of the Red Balloon 🎬🎬 *Le Voyage du Ballon Rouge* 2008 Hou's homage to Albert Lamorisse's 1956 film "The Red Balloon" does have a red balloon, a little boy, and Paris, but Simon (Iteanu) doesn't wander the streets accompanied by the balloon so much as he wanders with his new nanny Song (Fang), a Taiwanese film student who serves as Hou's calm observer. Simon's single mom is frazzled bleach-blonde Suzanne (Binoche), who doesn't seem to be coping with her son, her career, or her emotions very well. Not much actually happens so the film can be something of a slog but it looks beautiful. French with subtitles. **113m/C DVD. FR, TW** Juliette Binoche, Hippolyte Girardot, Simon Iteanu, Song Fang, Louise Margolin, Anna Sigalevitch; **D:** Hou Hsiao-Hsien; **W:** Hou Hsiao-Hsien, Francois Margolin; **C:** Mark Lee Ping-Bin; **M:** Constance Lee.

Flight to Fury 🎬½ 1966 A cheap independent adventure film, featuring the novice Hellman-Nicholson team, about a few assorted mercenaries searching for a horde of diamonds when their plane crashes in the wilderness of the Philippines. Based on a story by director/producer Hellman. **73m/B VHS.** Jack Nicholson, Dewey Martin, Fay Spain, Vic Diaz, Jacqueline

Mann, Dianne Wilhite, Chris Martel; **D:** Brad F. Ginter.

Sizemore, Ving Rhames, David Schwimmer; **D:** John Millus; **W:** Robert Dillon; **C:** Fred W. Koenekamp; **M:** Basil Poljedouris.

Flight of the Navigator 🎬🎬½ 1986 (PG) A boy boards an alien space-craft and embarks on a series of time-travel adventures with a crew of wisecracking extraterrestrial creatures. When he returns home eight years later, a NASA investigation ensues. Paul Reubens, better known as Pee-wee Herman, provides the voice of the robot. **90m/C VHS, DVD.** Joey Cramer, Veronica Cartwright, Cliff DeYoung, Sarah Jessica Parker, Matt Adler, Howard Hesseman; **D:** Randal Kleiser; **W:** Michael Burton, Matt MacManus; **M:** Alan Silvestri; **V:** Paul (Pee-wee Herman) Reubens.

Flight to Mars 🐾🐾 1952 An expedition crash lands on the red planet and discovers an advanced underground society that wants to invade earth using the U.S. spacecraft. Includes previews of coming attractions from classic science fiction films. First movie of this genre to be shot in color. 72m/C VHS, DVD. Cameron Mitchell, Marguerite Chapman, Arthur Franz, Virginia Huston; D: Lesley Selander; W: Arthur Strawn; C: Harry Neumann; M: Marlin Skiles.

Flight to Nowhere WOOF! 1946 An FBI agent tracks down a stolen map of atomic bomb source material with the help of a charter pilot and a dizzy blonde. Muddled plot and no discernable acting. 74m/B VHS. Alan Curtis, Evelyn Ankers, Jack Holt; D: William Rowland.

Flightplan 🐾🐾1/2 2005 (PG-13) Kyle Pratt (Foster) and her daughter Julia (Lawston) are on the flight from Berlin to New York to bury Kyle's husband who, she's told, died after falling (or jumping?) from their apartment roof. She happens to be a propulsion engineer who knows planes inside and out. Kyle wakes from a nap to find Julia simply gone. Worse, the crew and even the passengers don't recall Julia being there, as flight and boarding lists seem to confirm that she wasn't. Tense, psychological and.... implausible, but Foster makes it work. Not for the claustrophobic—most of the film's 90 minutes is spent inside the plane. 93m/C DVD, Blu-ray Disc. US Jodie Foster, Peter Sarsgaard, Erika Christensen, Sean Bean, Kate Beahan, Greta Scacchi, Judith Scott, Michael Irby, Brent Sexton, Marlene Lawston, Haley Ramm, Stephanie Faracy; D: Robert Schwentke; W: Billy Ray, Peter A. Dowling; M: James Horner.

Flim-Flam Man 🐾🐾 One Born Every Minute 1967 A con man teams up with an army deserter to teach him the fine art of flim-flamming as they travel through small southern towns. Love may lead the young man back to the straight and narrow, but not his reprobate mentor. Scott is wonderful; and the slapstick episodes move at a good pace. 104m/C VHS. George C. Scott, Michael Sarrazin, Slim Pickens, Sue Lyon, Jack Albertson, Harry (Henry) Morgan; D: Irvin Kershner; C: Charles B(ryant) Lang Jr.; M: Jerry Goldsmith.

Flinch 🐾🐾 1994 (R) Two models, who work as live mannequins, witness a murder and wonder if they'll be the next victims. 90m/C VHS. Judd Nelson, Nick Mancuso, Gina Gershon; D: George Erschbamer.

The Flintstones 🐾🐾1/2 1994 (PG) Preceded by massive hype, popular '60s cartoon comes to life thanks to a huge budget and creative sets and props. Seems that Fred's (Goodman) being set up by evil corporate types Cliff Vandercave (MacLachlan) and Miss Rosetta Stone (Berry) to take the fall for their embezzling scheme. Soon he gives up dining at RocDonald's for Cavern on the Green and cans best buddy Barney (Moranis). Forget the lame plot (32 writers took a shot at it) and sit back and enjoy the spectacle. Goodman's an amazingly true-to-type Fred, O'Donnell has Betty's giggle down pat, and Perkins looks a lot like Wilma. Wilma's original voice, VanderPyl, has a cameo as Mrs. Feldspar; listen for Korman's voice as the Dictabird. Add half a bone if you're under 12. 92m/C VHS, DVD. John Goodman, Rick Moranis, Elizabeth Perkins, Rosie O'Donnell, Elizabeth Taylor, Kyle MacLachlan, Halle Berry, Jonathan Winters, Richard Moll, Irwin Keyes, Dann Florek; Cameos: Laraine Newman, Jean Vander Pyl, Jay Leno; D: Brian Levant; W: Tom S. Parker, Jim Jennewein, Steven E. de Souza; C: Dean Cundey; M: David Newman; V: Harvey Korman. Golden Raspberries '94: Worst Support. Actress (O'Donnell), Worst Screenplay.

The Flintstones in Viva Rock Vegas 🐾🐾 2000 (PG) In a prequel to the 1994 film, a young Fred (Addy) and his best pal Barney (Baldwin) take their girlfriends Wilma (Johnson) and Betty (Krakowski) on a would-be romantic weekend to Rock Vegas. There's a whole lot going on, as runaway society girl Wilma is being wooed by playboy Chip Rockefeller (Gibson), Chip's trying to bankrupt and frame Fred, and the Great Gazoo (Cumming) is on hand to observe earthly mating habits.

Everything is appropriately cartoonish, including the story and the acting. Unfortunately, the only ones who'll be entertained are the ones who are too young to remember the original series (or the original movie for that matter). 90m/C VHS, DVD. Mark Addy, Kristen Johnston, Stephen Baldwin, Jane Krakowski, Thomas Gibson, Joan Collins, Alan Cumming, Harvey Korman, Alex Meneses; D: Brian Levant; W: Harry Elfont, Deborah Kaplan, Jim Cash, Jack Epps Jr.; C: Jamie Anderson; M: David Newman.

Flipper 🐾🐾🐾 1963 A fisherman's son befriends an injured dolphin, is persuaded to return him to the wild, and earns the animal's gratitude. Prime kids' fare, as its sequels and TV series attest. 87m/C VHS, DVD. Chuck Connors, Luke Halpin, Kathleen Maguire, Connie Scott; D: James B. Clark.

Flipper 🐾🐾🐾 1996 (PG) They still call him Flipper! Flipper, who in some scenes is played by a robot dolphin, reappears in a feature film for the first time since 1966. Sullen 14-year-old city boy Sandy Ricks (Wood) must spend the summer with crusty bachelor uncle Porter (Hogan), who would rather fish than look after his troublesome nephew. The duo witness the heartless killing of Flipper's family and are adopted by him. In addition to causing their seafood bill to skyrocket, the dolphin helps them uncover an illegal toxic waste dumper, who happens to be the same guy who made Flipper's mama sleep with the fishes. Updated along with the story is the soundtrack, which features a version of the famous theme song by Matthew Sweet. 97m/C VHS, DVD. Elijah Wood, Paul Hogan, Chelsea Field, Isaac Hayes, Jonathan Banks; D: Alan Shapiro; W: Alan Shapiro; C: Bill Butler; M: Joel McNeely.

Flipper's New Adventure 🐾🐾 Flipper and the Pirates 1964 Believing they are to be separated, Flipper and Sandy travel to a remote island. Little do they know, a British family is being held for ransom on the island they have chosen. It's up to the duo to save the day. An enjoyable, nicely done family adventure. 103m/C VHS, DVD. Luke Halpin, Pamela Franklin, Tom Helmore, Francesca Annis, Brian Kelly, Joe Higgins, Ricou Browning; D: Leon Benson.

Flipper's Odyssey 🐾🐾 1966 Flipper has disappeared and his adopted family goes looking for him, but when one of the boys gets trapped in a cave, Flipper is his only hope. 77m/C VHS. Luke Halpin, Brian Kelly, Tommy Norden; D: Paul Landres.

Flipping 🐾🐾 1996 (R) Quartet of none-too-bright wiseguy wanna-bes serve as debt collectors for gangster Leo Richards (David). Turns out gay undercover cop Billy (Proval) has infiltrated the gang—only to fall for ambitious hoodlum Michael (Amos)—and violent double-crosses abound. Debut for writer/director Mitchell. 102m/C VHS. David Amos, David Proval, Gene Mitchell, Keith David, Shant Benjamin, Barry Primus, Mike Starr, Tony Burton, Paul Klar; D: Gene Mitchell; W: Gene Mitchell; C: Phil Parmet.

Flirt 🐾🐾1/2 1995 (R) Three variations on the same theme: love, jealousy, and the problems of committing are what comprise this interesting portrait of modern romance in three countries. One character in each of the three stories is faced with an ultimatum to commit and is given a 90-minute deadline. Each are already involved in various other romantic entanglements. The best scenes show the confused flirts receiving very amusing advice from strangers. First episode is the best, as the pace subsequently slows. 84m/C VHS. GE JP William Sage, Parker Posey, Martin Donovan, Dwight Ewell, Dominik Bender, Geno Lechner, Miho Nikaido, Toshizo Fujisawa; D: Hal Hartley; W: Hal Hartley; C: Michael Spiller; M: Hal Hartley.

Flirtation Walk 🐾🐾1/2 1934 West Point musical that has cadet Powell falling in love with the general's daughter (Keeler), who is already engaged to lieutenant Eldredge. Some fairly good numbers, including "Mr. and Mrs. Is The Name" and "Flirtation Walk." In an attempt to change

her image, Keeler hardly dances at all, which is too bad for the viewer. Based on a story by Lou Edelman and Delmer Daves. 98m/B VHS. Dick Powell, Ruby Keeler, Pat O'Brien, Ross Alexander; D: Frank Borzage; W: Delmer Daves.

Flirting 🐾🐾🐾 1989 (R) Set in an Australian boarding school in 1965, a charming story following the misadventures of the adolescent Danny Embling, who has the misfortune to be both bright and sensitive, putting him seriously at odds with his masculine peers. He finds love with an outcast at the neighboring girls boarding school, the daughter of a diplomat from Uganda. Kidman has a supporting role as a snobbish older boarding school girl, not quite as bad as she seems. Tender and amusing. The second of director Duigan's coming-of-age trilogy, preceded by "The Year My Voice Broke" (the third film isn't yet completed). 100m/C VHS, DVD. AU Noah Taylor, Thandie Newton, Nicole Kidman, Bartholomore Rose, Felix Nobis, Josh Picker, Kiri Paramore, Marc Gray, Joshua Marshall, David Wieland, Craig Black, Leslie Hill; D: John Duigan; W: John Duigan. Australian Film Inst. '90: Film.

Flirting with Disaster 🐾🐾🐾 1995 (R) Mel Coplin (Stiller) is your average neurotic New York entomologist searching for his birth parents so he can finally name his four-month-old child and make love to his wife. Tagging along on his bumpy ride are his wife Nancy (Arquette), a beautiful quirky adoption agency shrink (Leoni), and a pair of bisexual FBI agents. The excellent cast also features Moore as Mel's bra-baring adoptive mother, Segal as his weirdly paranoid adoptive father, and Alda and Tomlin as hilarious send-ups of ex-hippie mentality. As events spin madly out of control, every type of relationship is satirized, and every character is left in their underwear. This is director Russell's first big-budget movie, and is as close to a vintage screwball comedy as you'll see in the '90s. 92m/C VHS, DVD. Ben Stiller, Patricia Arquette, Tea Leoni, Alan Alda, Mary Tyler Moore, George Segal, Lily Tomlin, Josh Brolin, Richard Jenkins, Celia Weston, Glenn Fitzgerald, Beth Ostrosky, Cynthia Lamontagne, David Patrick Kelly, John Ford Noonan, Charles Oberty; D: David O. Russell; W: David O. Russell; C: Eric Alan Edwards; M: Stephen Endelman.

Flirting with Fate 🐾🐾🐾 1916 Early Fairbanks-cum-acrobat vehicle. Having hired a hitman to rub himself out, a young man decides he doesn't want to die, after all. Seems there's a girl involved.... 51m/B VHS. Douglas Fairbanks Sr., Jewel Carmen, Howard Gaye, William E. Lawrence, George Beranger, Dorothy Hadel, Lillian Langdon; D: Christy Cabanne.

Floating 🐾🐾 1997 Van (Reedus) is a moody 20-year-old ex-high school swimming champ who's basically treading water. He looks after his drunken paraplegic father (Lyman) in their run-down cottage and drifts into home burglaries with two equally loser friends. It's Van's idea to stash their ill-gotten gains in the basement of his former family home—of course the empty dwelling immediately gets a new owner—and Van winds up befriending the family's son, Doug (Lowe), who's not only a swimming champ but has Dad problems as well. This male bonding leads to some (predictable) attitude changes but the sincerity of the cast goes a long way in overcoming the cliches. 91m/C VHS, DVD. Norman Reedus, Chad Lowe, Will Lyman, Jonathan Quint, Josh Marchette, Sybil Temchen; D: William Roth; W: William Roth; C: Wolfgang Held; M: David Mansfield.

Floating Life 🐾🐾 1995 The Chans have decided to emigrate from Hong Kong before the mainland China takeover and join daughter Bing (Yip) and her family in Sydney. High-strung Bing's determined to assimilate as much as possible into Australian society and bullies her newly arrived family, who are naturally disoriented. The arrival of laggard son Gar Ming (Wong) and easy-going daughter Yen (Shun-Wah), who's been living in Germany, only provide further complications for a family completely adrift in their new world. Cantonese, German, and English dia-

logue. 95m/C VHS. AU Annie Yip, Annette Shun-Wah, Anthony Wong, Edwin Pang, Cecilia Fong Sing Lee, Toby Wong, Toby Chan, Bruce Poon; D: Clara Law; W: Clara Law, Eddie Ling-Ching Fong; C: Dion Beebe; M: Davood A. Tabrizi.

The Flock 🐾🐾 2007 (R) Burned-out federal agent Erroll Babbage (Gere) is training his replacement, Alliscn Laurie (Danes), while investigating a missing girl he thinks is the victim of a paroled sex offender. First English-language pic for Hong Kong director Lau, best-known for "Infernal Affairs," but the reshoots were done by Niels Mueller. Having another director take over is not considered a good sign. Sleazy and confusing, but features some good work by Gere and Danes. 91m/C DVD. US Richard Gere, Claire Dares, KaDee Strickland, Matt Schulze, Russell Sams, Avril Lavigne, Ray Wise, French Stewart, Kristina Sisco; D: Andrew Lau; W: Hans Bauer, Craig Mitchell; C: Enrique Chediak; M: Guy Farley.

Flood! 🐾🐾 1976 Irwin Allen's first made-for-TV disaster film. A dam bursts and devastates a small town, good casting pilot must save the day. Good cast is swept along in a current of disaster-genre cliches. 98m/C VHS. Robert Culp, Martin Milner, Barbara Hershey, Richard Basehart, Carol Lynley, Roddy McDowall, Cameron Mitchell, Teresa Wright, Francine York; D: Earl Bellamy. TV

Flood: A River's Rampage 🐾🐾1/2 1997 (PG-13) Community struggles to rebuild after a devastating flood. 92m/C VHS, DVD. Richard Thomas, Kate Vernon, Jan Rubes; D: Bruce Pittman. TV

Flooding 🐾🐾1/2 1997 Clever homage to Alfred Hitchcock on a budget. Joyce Calloway (Gibson) has become agoraphobic after the unsolved murder of her husband and has spent the past six months in her house. She is working with a new doctor (who comes to the house, of course) to get over her fear of the outside world, and she better hurry, because her parents are selling the house in an effort to get her to go outside. After a fling, a man comes to her back door, falls inside, and dies after uttering a name she doesn't recognize. The tension mounts as it becomes clear that her subconscious mind is holding out on her and that someone wants her dead or at least out o' the way. The why of the story is the weak link in the film; it is the journey to the answer that is absorbing. This is not a perfect film, but it is worth watching for fans of suspense. 86m/C DVD. Brenna Gibson, Lauren Bailey, Kary Cawley; D: Todd Portugal; W: Todd Portugal.

The Floorwalker 🐾🐾🐾 1917 Chaplin becomes involved with a dishonest floorwalker in a department store. Silent. 20m/B VHS, DVD. Charlie Chaplin; D: Charlie Chaplin.

Flor Silvestre 🐾 Wild Flower 1958 The son of a rich rancher romances a young woman against the background of the Mexican Revolution. 90m/B VHS. MX Dolores Del Rio, Pedro Armendariz Sr.; D: Emilio Fernandez.

The Florentine 🐾🐾 1998 (R) A decaying steel town is home to a bar called The Florentine, its owner Whitey (Madsen), and the usual drinking denizens. But with profits sinking, Whitey may lose his livelihood. And then there's his sister Molly's (Madsen) problems. Her wedding to Frankie (Perry) is in jeopardy because of a con man (Belushi) and her ex-fiance, Teddy (Sizemore), who's back in town. 104m/C VHS, DVD. Michael Madsen, Virginia Madsen, Luke Perry, Tom Sizemore, James Belushi, Mary Stuart Masterson, Christopher Penn; D: Nick Stagliano. VIDEO

The Florida Connection 🐾 1974 An action thriller set in the Florida Swamps with a collection of villains and a vague plot about smuggling. 90m/C VHS. Dan Pastorini, June Wilkinson, Bill (Billy) Thurman; D: Robert Emery; W: Robert Emery.

Florida Straits 🐾🐾 1987 (PG-13) A recently released Cuban prisoner hires a few losers and their boat to return to the island, supposedly to find the girl he loves. The real quest is for gold buried during the Bay-of-Pigs invasion in this none-too-original cable movie that at least offers a good

Floundering 🦴🦴½ 1994 (R) Misguided satire uses the 1992 L.A. riots as a backdrop to tell the saga of unemployed James Boyz (LeGros), whose life is a walking disaster. He owes the IRS, his unemployment compensation has run out, his brother (Hawke) has fled from a drug rehab clinic, and he finds his girlfriend (Zane) in bed with another man. John drags himself among the city's downtrodden as he fantasizes about life. Drag pretty much sums up the film despite good performances by LeGros and Hawke. 97m/C VHS, DVD. James LeGros, Ethan Hawke, Steve Buscemi, John Cusack, Lisa Zane, Sy Richardson, Jeremy Piven, Billy Bob Thornton; **D:** Peter McCarthy; **W:** Peter McCarthy; **C:** Denis Maloney; **M:** Pray for Rain.

Flowers of Reverie 🦴🦴 1984 A former soldier is imprisoned for his work in the resistance during the Hungarian Revolution (1848-9), leading to tragedy. In Hungarian with English subtitles. 106m/C VHS HU Gyorgy Cserhalmi, Grazyna Szapolowska, Jiri Adamira, Boguslew Linda; **D:** Laszlo Lugossy; **W:** Laszlo Lugossy; **C:** Elemer Ragalyi; **M:** Gyorgy Selmecz.

Flowers in the Attic 🦴½ 1987 (PG-13) Based on the V.C. Andrews bestseller, a would-be thriller about four young siblings locked for years in their family's old mansion by their grandmother with their mother's selfish acquiescence. A chicken-hearted, clumsy flop that skimps on the novel's trashier themes. 93m/C VHS, DVD. Victoria Tennant, Kristy Swanson, Louise Fletcher, Jeb Stuart Adams; **D:** Jeffrey Bloom; **W:** Jeffrey Bloom; **C:** Gil Hubbs; **M:** Christopher Young.

Fluke 🦴🦴 1995 (PG) "Ghost" meets "Oh, Heavenly Dog" as Tom (Modine) dies in a suspicious car accident and is reincarnated as a dog who remembers his past life. He returns to his former family (Travis and Pomerance) to protect them from his former business partner (Stoltz), battling such puppy perils as cosmetic testing labs and dogcatchers along the way. While there's plenty of squishy sentimentality to go around, some of the scenes involving animal abuse may be a little much for the target audience of preteen kids. Jackson and Stoltz trade "Pulp Fiction" for pup fiction, but this dog won't hunt. Based on the novel by James Herbert. 96m/C VHS, DVD. Matthew Modine, Nancy Travis, Eric Stoltz, Max Pomerance, Ron Perlman; Jon Polito, Bill Cobbs, Frederico Pacifici, Collin Wilcox-Paxton; **D:** Carlo Carlei; **C:** Raffaele Mertes; **M:** Carlo Siliotto; **V:** Samuel L. Jackson.

Flourish 🦴🦴 2006 (PG-13) Desperate for cash, Gaby (Morrison) agrees to babysit precocious 16-year-old Lucy (Meester), who soon disappears from the house. Now Gaby spends an increasingly wild night, running into lots of very strange people, trying to find Lucy before her parents get home. 96m/C DVD. Jenny (Jennifer) Morrison, Leighton Meester, Jesse Spencer, Connie Ray, Daniel Roebuck, Olivia Burnette; **D:** Kevin Palys; **W:** Kevin Palys; **C:** Maximilian Gutierrez; **M:** Luigi Pittorino, Melinda Doring.

The Flower of My Secret 🦴🦴🦴 1995 (R) *La Flor de My Secreto* Emotional yet restrained story about middle-aged Leo (Paredes), whose long-time marriage is fast ending and it's not working. Leo writes hugely popular romance novels under a pseudonym but her current work is so bleak it's unpublishable. So, Leo gets a job at a newspaper where editor Angel (Echanove) immediately falls for her, and indeed, lives up to his name as her guardian. Willfully myopic about her own life, Leo undergoes further trials until she slowly realizes the mess she's in and becomes willing to change. Surprisingly subdued given Almodovar's usual flamboyance but it's a welcome change of pace. Spanish with subtitles. 107m/C VHS, DVD. SP FR Marisa Paredes, Juan Echanove, Imanol Arias, Carmen Elias, Rossy de Palma, Chus Lampreave, Joaquin Cortes, Manuela Vargas; **D:** Pedro Almodovar; **W:** Pedro Almodovar; **C:** Alfonso Beato; **M:** Alberto Iglesias.

Flower Drum Song 🦴🦴 1961 The Rodgers and Hammerstein musical played better on Broadway than in this overblown adaptation of life in San Francisco's Chinatown. Umeki plays the young girl who arrives from Hong Kong for an arranged marriage. Her intended (Soo) is a fast-living nightclub owner already enjoying the love of singer Kwan. Meanwhile Umeki falls for the handsome Shigeta. Naturally, everything comes together in a happy ending. ♪ Enjoy Being A Girl; Don't Marry Me; Grant Avenue; You Are Beautiful; A Hundred Million Miracles; Fan Tan Fanny; Chop Suey; The Other Generation; I Am Going to Like It Here. 133m/C VHS, DVD. Nancy Kwan, Jack Soo, James Shigeta, Miyoshi Umeki, Juanita Hall; **D:** Henry Koster; **C:** Russell Metty; **M:** Richard Rodgers.

Flowers of St. Francis 🦴🦴🦴 *Francesco, giullare di Dio; Francis, God's Jester* 1950 Rossellini's presentation of St. Francis and his friars' attainment of spiritual harmony. In Italian with English subtitles. This is the British release version, 10-15 minutes longer than the U.S. version. 75m/B VHS, DVD. IT Aldo Fabrizi, Brother Nazario Gerardi, Arabelle Lemaitre; **D:** Roberto Rossellini; **W:** Father Antonio Lisandrini, Father Felix Morion, Federico Fellini, Roberto Rossellini; **C:** Otello Martelli; **M:** Enrico Buondonno, Renzo Rossellini.

Flowers of Shanghai 🦴🦴 *Hai Shang Hua* 1998 Slow costume drama/soap opera set in the brothels of late 19th-century Shanghai. In this self-contained world, the elegant "flower girls" depend on their ability to hold onto wealthy clients who will marry her. Based on the novel "Biographies of Flowers of Shanghai" by Han Ziyun. Mandarin with subtitles. 125m/C VHS, DVD. JP TW Tony Leung Chiu-Wai, Michiko Hada, Hsiao-hui Wei, Jack Kao, Michelle Reis, Annie Shizuka Inoh, Fang Hsuan, Simon Chang; **D:** Hou Hsiao-Hsien; **W:** Tien-wen Chu; **C:** Mark Lee Ping-Bin; **M:** Yoshihiro Yanno.

The Fluffer 🦴🦴 2001 Naive aspiring filmmaker Sean (Cunio) has his romantic illusions destroyed and is rather rudely forced to grow up. Gay Sean gets a job with a Hollywood porn production company and falls for one of the company's stars—the immature and self-destructive gay-for-pay Mikey (Gurney) whose nominal de-porn is Johnny Rebel. Mikey's on a downward slide despite Sean's admiration and the love of his stripper girlfriend Julie (Day) and if the two aren't careful, Mikey will take them with him. Title refers to one of the personal services Sean is expected to offer Mikey. 94m/C VHS, DVD. Michael Cunio, Scott Gurney, Roxanne Day, Richard Riehle, Taylor Negron, Tim Bagley, Adina Porter, Deborah Harry; **D:** Richard Glatzer, Wash West; **W:** Wash West; **C:** Mark Putnam.

Flubber 🦴🦴 1997 (PG) Bland remake of Disney's "The Absent-Minded Professor" with Williams as the betuddled, yet brilliant Prof. Brainard. Putting his wedding on the back Bunsen burner, much to the dismay of his fiancee Sara Jean (Harden), Brainard invents a bouncy, flying green slime named "flubber." As the substance becomes the cure-all for romantic turmoil and fledgling school basketball teams, it also attracts the attention of a corrupt businessman and his moronic henchmen. Due to the dull subplots, kids doesn't have much screen time. Williams, and adults will be disappointed that the main attraction (the cute green goo) oddly enough, seems comfortable playing second banana to a substance that could describe his comedic skills. 93m/C VHS, DVD. Robin Williams, Marcia Gay Harden, Christopher McDonald, Raymond J. Barry, Clancy Brown, Ted Levine, Wil Wheaton, Edie McClurg; **D:** Les Mayfield; **W:** John Hughes; **C:** Dean Cundey; **M:** Danny Elfman.

The Fly 🦴🦴🦴 1958 The historic, chilling original '50s sci-fi tale about a hapless scientist experimenting with teleportation that accidentally gets anatomically confused with a housefly. Campy required viewing. Followed by two sequels and a 1986 remake which itself has spawned one sequel. 94m/C VHS, DVD. David Hedison, Patricia Owens, Vincent Price, Herbert Marshal, Kathleen Freeman, Betty Lou Gerson, Charles Herbert; **D:** Kurt Neumann; **W:** James Clavell; **C:** Karl Struss; **M:** Paul Sawell.

The Fly 🦴🦴🦴 1986 (R) A sensitive, humanistic remake of the 1958 horror film about a scientist whose flesh is genetically intermixed with a housefly via his experiment. A thoughtful, shocking horror film, with fine performances from Goldblum and Davis and a brutally emotional conclusion. Followed by "The Fly II" in 1989. 96m/C VHS, DVD. Jeff Goldblum, Geena Davis, John Getz, Joy Boushel, Cosetta Lee; **D:** David Cronenberg; **W:** David Cronenberg, Charles Edward Pogue; **C:** Mark Irwin; **M:** Howard Shore. Oscars '86: Makeup.

The Fly 2 🦴½ 1989 (R) Inferior sequel to Cronenberg's opus, in which the offspring of Seth Brundle achieves full maturity in three years, falls in love, and discovers the evil truth behind his father's teleportation device. 105m/C VHS, DVD. Eric Stoltz, Daphne Zuniga, Lee Richardson, John Getz, Harley Cross; **D:** Chris Walas; **W:** Ken Wheat, Frank Darabont, Mick Garris, Jim Wheat; **C:** Robin Vidgeon; **M:** Christopher Young.

Fly Away Home 🦴🦴🦴 1996 (PG) Does for geese what "Babe" did for pigs. Young Amy (Paquin) is forced to live with her estranged father, Thomas (Daniels), a thoughtful, scruffy sculptor/inventor, in rural Ontario. Still ceaking with her own mother's death, Amy suddenly becomes a mother herself to a tiny gaggle of goslings when she happens upon a nest of uprooted eggs. Extraordinary technical achievements make up for some unnecessary melodrama in the second half as the geese head South, led by Amy, in a glider built by her father. Touching but unsentimental, mostly well scripted and acted, and extraordinarily shot. Based on the true story of inventor Bill Lishman, who led domesticated geese on a winter migration from Toronto, Canada to North Carolina, leading the formation in his motor-powered glider. 107m/C VHS, DVD. Jeff Daniels, Anna Paquin, Dana Delany, Terry Kinney, Jeremy Ratchford; **D:** Carroll Ballard; **W:** Robert Rodat, Vince McKewin; **C:** Caleb Deschanel; **M:** Mark Isham.

Fly Boy 🦴🦴½ 1999 (PG) Gramps (Karen) a still-adventurous WWII vet whose remote-controlled model airplanes are the terror of the neighborhood and the delight of his 10-year-old grandson, Ray (Hughes). In fact, Ray would like to help Gramps fulfill his big dream—to fly a real plane one last time. 86m/C VHS. Miko Hughes, James Karen, Kathleen Lloyd, Gregory Itzin; **D:** Richard Stanley.

Flush 🦴🦴 1981 Unorthodox comedy involving funny noises. 90m/C VHS, William Callaway, William Bronder, Jeannie Linero; **D:** Andrew J. Kuehn.

Flushed Away 🦴🦴🦴 2006 (PG) The Aardman studio ventures from its usual clay figure stop-motion look into computer animation but the inventiveness remains. Roddy (Jackman) is a posh London pet mouse who is unceremoniously flushed down the loo by baddie sewer rat Sid (Richie). Roddy discovers a raucous underground community that is threatened by evil gangster The Toad (McKellen) and his French cousin Le Frog (Reno). Fortunately, the pampered Roddy is taken in by tough working-class rat Rita (Winslet) as they try to save the day. The harmonizing singing slugs are an added highlight. 84m/C DVD. US GB **D:** Dick Clement, Ian La Frenais, Chris Lloyd, Joe Keenan; **W:** Hugh Jackman, Kate Winslet, Ian McKellen, Jean Reno, Bill Nighy, Andy Serkis, Kathy Burke, David Suchet, Shane Richie, Miriam Margolyes, Rachel Rawlinson.

Fly by Night 🦴🦴 1993 (PG-13) Vis-matched New York rappers Rich and I join forces to make it big as hard-core gangstas. When they're propelled to the top of the charts, forces both personal and professional work to tear them apart. 93m/C DVD. Jeffrey D. Sams, Ron Brice, Daryl (Chili) Mitchell, Todd Graff, Leo Burmester, Soulfood Jael, Larry (Lawrence) Gilliard Jr., Omar Carter, Maura Tierney, Yul Vazquez, M.C. Lyte, Christopher-Michael Gerrard, Ebony Jo-Ann; **D:** Steve Gomer; **W:** Todd Graff; **C:** Larry Banks; **M:** Kris Parker, Sidney Mills, Dwayne Sumal. Sundance '93: Filmmakers Trophy.

Fly with the Hawk 🦴🦴 1985 A troubled teenager gets lost in the wilderness for a year, and learns some important things from nature to take back to civilization. 90m/C VHS. Shelley Lynne Sceigel; **D:** Robert Tanos.

Flyboys 🦴🦴 2006 (PG-13) Old-fashioned war flick based on the exploits of the Lafayette Escadrille—young American men who volunteered for the French military during WWI, before the U.S. entered the war. Formulaic script has the new recruits, who had a life expectancy as biplane pilots of six weeks, training under the paternal eye of Capt. Thenault (Reno). Besides the heroics, there's a corny romance between laconic Texan Rawlings (Franco) and local beauty Lucienne (Decker). Extensive CGI is combined with actual footage for the dynamic air sequences. 139m/C DVD, Blu-ray Disc. James Franco, Martin Henderson, Jean Reno, Philip Winchester, David Ellison, Jennifer Decker, Tyler Labine, Abdul Salis, Christian Arnold; **D:** Tony Bill; **W:** Blake T. Evans, David S. Ward, Phil Sears; **C:** Henry Braham; **M:** Trevor Rabin.

Flying Blind 🦴½ Foreign agents are thwarted in their attempt to steal a vital air defense secret. Unconvincing espionage plot cobbled into a story about a Los Angeles-Las Vegas puddle jumper. 69m/B VHS, DVD. Richard Arlen, Jean Parker, Marie Wilson, Nils Asther, Roger Pryor, Eddie Quillan, Grady Sutton, Dick Purcell; **D:** Frank McDonald; **W:** Richard Murphy, Maxwell Shane; **C:** Fred H. Jackman Jr.; **M:** Dimitri Tiomkin.

The Flying Deuces 🦴🦴🦴 *Flying Aces* 1939 Ollie's broken heart lands Laurel and Hardy in the Foreign Legion. The comic pair escape a firing squad only to suffer more indignities. A musical interlude with a Laurel soft shoe while Hardy sings "Shine On, Harvest Moon" is ore of the film's highlights. 65m/B VHS, DVD. Stan Laurel, Oliver Hardy, Jean Parker, Reginald Gardiner, James Finlayson; **D:** Edward Sutherland; **W:** Ralph Spence, Charles R. Rogers, Harry Langdon, Alfred Schiller; **C:** Elmer Dyer, Art Lloyd; **M:** Leo Shuken, John Leopold.

Flying Down to Rio 🦴🦴½ 1933 The first Astaire-Rogers musical, although they are relegated to supporting status behind Del Rio and Raymond. Still, it was enough to make them stars and a team that epicirnizes the height of American musical entities. The slim story revolves around singer Del Rio's two suitors and receives a splendid, art deco production. Showgirls dancing on plane wings in flight provide another memorable moment. ♪ Music Makes Me; The Carioca; Orchids in the Moonlight; Flying Down to Rio. 89m/B VHS, DVD. Fred Astaire, Ginger Rogers, Dolores Del Rio, Eric Blore, Gene Raymond, Franklin Pangborn; **D:** Thornton Freeland; **M:** Vincent Youmans, Max Steiner.

The Flying Fool 🦴🦴 1929 Ace pilot Bill returns from the war to find his younger brother has fallen for a singer. When Bill meets the lady, he also notices her charms and the two brothers have a duel in the skies to see who'll get the girl. 75m/B VHS. William Boyd, Marie Prevost, Russell Gleason; **D:** Tay Garnett; **W:** James Gleason.

Flying from the Hawk 🦴🦴½ 1966 A 12-year-old boy sees something he shouldn't and soon finds that his friends and relatives are mysteriously vanishing...

The Flying Irishman 1939 Film version of aviator "Wrong Way" Corrigan's life story and his 1938 flight from New York to California—that landed him near Dublin, Ireland instead. Only screen appearance of Corrigan, whose trip was suspected to be a publicity stunt since he was eager to emulate the exploits of friend Charles Lindbergh. 71m/B VHS. Paul Kelly, Robert Armstrong, Gene Reynolds, Eddie Quillan, Donald MacBride, J.M. Kerrigan, Douglas Corrigan; D: Leigh Jason; W: Dalton Trumbo, Ernest Pagano; C: J. Roy Hunt.

Flying Leathernecks 1951 Tough squadron leader Wayne fights with his fellow officer Ryan in Guadalcanal when their leadership styles clash. But when the real fighting begins all is forgotten as Wayne leads his men into victorious battle, winning the admiration and devotion of his fliers. Memorable WWII film deals with war in human terms. 102m/C VHS, DVD. John Wayne, Robert Ryan, Janis Carter, Don Taylor, James Bell, James Dobson, Jay C. Flippen, Gordon Gebert, William Harrigan, Brett King, Adam Williams, Carleton Young, Dick Wessel, Gail Davis, Harlan Warde, Michael (Steve Flagg) St. Angel, Maurice Jara, John Mallory, Britt Nelson, Lynn Stalmaster; D: Nicholas Ray; W: Kenneth Gamet, James Edward Grant; C: William E. Snyder; M: Roy Webb.

The Flying Saucer 1950 U.S. and Russian scientists clash over their search for a huge flying saucer that is hidden under a glacier. The first movie to deal with flying saucers. The cassette includes animated opening and closing sequences plus previews of coming attractions. 71m/B VHS, DVD. Mikel Conrad, Pat Garrison, Hanz Von Teuffen; D: Mikel Conrad; W: Howard Irving Young, Mikel Conrad; C: Philip Tannura; M: Darrell Calker.

The Flying Scotsman 1929 A fired railroad worker tries to wreck an express train on the engineer's last journey. The daughter of the intended victim saves the day. Silent, with sound added. 60m/B VHS, DVD. Ray Milland, Pauline Johnson, Moore Marriott; D: Castleton Knight.

The Flying Scotsman 2006 (PG-13) Based on the story of Graeme Obree, a Scottish amateur cyclist who broke several world speed records using a bike of his own design made from, among other things, parts from a washing machine. "Scotsman" highlights his nightmarish problems of self doubt and depression. Despite the litany of cliches, it's well enough done, and there are good moments, though some will find it a definite downer. 96m/C DVD. GB Johnny Miller, Sean Brown, Julie Austin, Billy Boyd, Laura Fraser, Brian Cox, Ron Donachie, Morven Christie, Steven Berkoff, Philip Wright, Adrian Smith, Joseph Carney, Niall Macgregor, Christopher Anderson, Moray Hunter, Niall Greig Fulton, Daniel Andre Pageon, Gudrun Mangel, Muzaffer Cakar; D: Douglas Mackinnon; W: John Brown, Declan Hughes, Simon Rose; C: Gavin Finney; M: Martin Phipps.

Flying Tigers 1942 Salutes the All-American Volunteer Group which flew for China under General Claire Chennault against the Japanese before the U.S. entered WWII. A squadron leader and a brash new recruit both vie for the affections of a pretty nurse in-between their flying missions. Romance and a few comic touches take a back seat to graphic scenes of aerial battles and dramatization of heroic sacrifice in this rousing war film. 101m/B VHS, DVD. John Wayne, Paul Kelly, John Carroll, Anna Lee, Mae Clarke, Gordon Jones; D: David Miller.

Flying Wild 1941 A gang of saboteurs is out to steal top-secret airplane blueprints. Who else but the Bowery Boys could conceivably stop them? 62m/B VHS, DVD. Leo Gorcey, Bobby Jordan, Donald Haines, Joan Barclay, David Gorcey, Bobby Stone, Sammy (Earnest) Morrison; D: William West; W: Al Martin; C: Fred H. Jackman Jr.; M: Johnny Lange, Lew Porter.

Flynn My Forgotten Man 1996 Details the adventurous early years of Tasmania-born Errol Flynn (Pearce) before he became the swashbuckling hero of Hollywood films. His sexual exploits get him kicked out of school and he makes his way as gigolo, thief, liar, and alleged spy. 96m/C VHS, DVD. AU Guy Pearce, Claudia Karvan, Steven Berkoff; D: Frank Howson; W: Frank Howson; C: John Wheeler; M: Anthony Marinelli.

Flypaper 1997 (R) Parking-lot bigshot Marvin (Loggia) and his business associate Jack (Brolly) help out junkie Natalie (Frost), who is being pressured by low-rent hood Bobby Ray (Sheffer). There's actually three separate but connected stories revolving around a big score and the various lowlifes who want to get their hands on it one California afternoon. 111m/C VHS, DVD. Robert Loggia, Sadie Frost, Craig Sheffer, Shane Brolly, Lucy Liu, James Wilder, Illeana Douglas, Talisa Soto, John C. McGinley; D: Klaus Hoch; W: Klaus Hoch; C: Jurgen Baum; M: Peter Manning Robinson.

FM Citizen's Band 1978 (PG-13) The disc jockeys at an L.A. radio station rebel in the name of rock'n'roll. Despite the promising cast and setting (Mull makes his movie debut as a memorable space case), this is just disjointed and surprisingly unhip; one producer took his name off it due to creative difficulties. The decent soundtrack includes concert footage of Jimmy Buffet and Linda Ronstadt. JFM: Do It Again; FM Reprise; Livingston Saturday Night; The Key To My Kingdom; Green Grass and High Tides; Life In The Fast Lane; Bad Man; Poor, Poor, Pitiful Me. 104m/C VHS, DVD. Eileen Brennan, Alex Karras, Cleavon Little, Martin Mull, Cassie Yates, Linda Ronstadt, Jimmy Buffett; D: John A. Alonzo; W: Ezra Sacks; C: David Myers.

Focus 2001 (PG-13) Based on a 1945 novel by playwright Arthur Miller, and bigotry features Macy as Larry Newman, a nebbish personnel worker who lives with his invalid mother. After 20 years on the job, he is demoted after he gets glasses because they make him look "too Jewish" to his bosses. After quitting his job in protest, he is interviewed for a new job by Gertrude (Dern), a woman that he had turned away from his firm because she may or may not have been a Jew. A whirlwind romance ensues, and the two are soon married as their neighborhood's becoming a battleground of ethnic tension. Strong-arm tactics are used on local newsstand owner Finkelstein (Paymer), and he warns the Newmans about collective hate. Macy gives a great performance, but the material is a bit blunt and preachy. 106m/C VHS, DVD. William H. Macy, Laura Dern, David Paymer, Meat Loaf Aday, Michael Copeman, Kenneth Welsh, Kay Hawtrey, Joseph Ziegler, Arlene Meadows; D: Neil Slavin; W: Kendrew Lascelles; C: Juan Ruiz-Anchia; M: Mark Adler.

The Fog 1978 (R) John Carpenter's blustery follow-up to his success with "Halloween." An evil fog containing murderous, vengeful ghosts envelops a sleepy seaside town and subjects the residents to terror and mayhem. 91m/C VHS, DVD. Hal Holbrook, Adrienne Barbeau, Jamie Lee Curtis, Janet Leigh, John Houseman, Tom Atkins; D: John Carpenter; W: John Carpenter, Debra Hill; C: Dean Cundey; M: John Carpenter.

The Fog 2005 (PG-13) Remake of the 1980s film of the same name, this foggy feature is updated by utterly ludicrous special effects. It does, however, stay true to the original film's roots, where a misty fog overtakes the sleepy (and fictional) town of Antonio Bay, bringing in the ghosts of some seafarers murdered 100 years ago. Of course, the ghosts are ticked off and they exact revenge on the poor townsfolk. The original was at least scarier, and even better-acted, which isn't saying a whole lot. 100m/C VHS, DVD, UMD. US Tom Welling, Maggie Grace, Selma Blair, DeRay Davis, Kenneth Welsh, Sara Botsford, Rade Serbedzija, Adrian Hough; D: Rupert Wainwright; W: Cooper Layne; C: Nathan Hope; M: Graeme Revell.

Fog Island 1945 Murder and terror lurk after a greedy inventor, who was framed for fraud by his business partner, is released from prison. He plots revenge by inviting his foes to his island home. 72m/B VHS, DVD. George Zucco, Lionel Atwill, Terry Morse, Jerome Cowan, Veda Ann Borg; D: Terry Morse; W: Pierre Gendron; C: Ira Morgan.

The Fog of War: Eleven Lessons from the Life of Robert S. McNamara 2003 (PG-13) Oscar winner for Best Documentary not only gave prolific documentarian Morris his first Academy Award, but also presents a startlingly honest and three-dimensional portrayal of one of the major architects of twentieth-century American history, Robert McNamara. A former president of the Ford Automotive Company and the Secretary of Defense for both Kennedy and Johnson, McNamara speaks frankly about his role in the Bay of Pigs and the Vietnam War, alternating between offering fascinating insights and arguing with his off-screen interviewer. He'll make you love him one moment and cringe the next. A must-see for history buffs. 106m/C DVD. US D: Errol Morris; C: Peter Donahue, Robert Chappell; M: Philip Glass. Oscars '03: Feature Doc.; Ind. Spirit '04: Feature Doc; L.A. Film Critics '03: Feature Doc.; Natl. Bd. of Review '03: Feature Doc.

Folks! 1992 (PG-13) Selleck is a Chicago stockbroker whose wife and kids have left him, the FBI is after him, and, worst of all, his parents don't want to be a burden, so Selleck decides that the best way to solve his financial woes is to help his parents commit suicide so he can collect on their insurance policies. Tasteless comedy that makes fun of aging and Alzheimer's Disease. Selleck is too sweet and cuddly for his role, but Ameche is good as the senile father, and Ebersole is great as Selleck's unpleasant sister. 109m/C VHS, DVD. Tom Selleck, Don Ameche, Anne Jackson, Christine Ebersole, Wendy Crewson, Robert Pastorelli, Michael Murphy, Kevin Timothy Chevalia, Margaret Murphy; D: Ted Kotcheff; M: Michel Colombier.

Follies Girl 1943 There's folly in expecting that this wartime tuner would hold up today. An army private romances a dress designer and a musical show somehow results. JKeep the Flag A-Flying; No Man In The House; Someone to Love; I Told A Lie; Shall We Gather at the Rhythm?; Fascination; I Knew Your Father's Son; Thoity Poiple Boids. 74m/B VHS. Wendy Barrie, Doris Nolan, Gordon Oliver, Anne Barrett, Arthur Pierson; D: William Rowland.

Follies in Concert 1985 A filmed record of the famed Stephen Sondheim musical play, performed at Lincoln Center in New York with an all-star cast. Songs include "I'm Still Here," "Losing My Mind," "Broadway Baby," and "The Ladies Who Lunch." 90m/C VHS, DVD. Carol Burnett, Lee Remick, Betty Comden, Andre Gregory, Adolph Green, Mandy Patinkin, Phyllis Newman, Elaine Stritch, Jim Walton, Licia Albanese.

Follow Me 1969 (G) Round-the-world odyssey of three moon doggies searching for adventure—and the perfect wave. Spectacular surfing scenes are complemented by songs performed by Dino, Desi, and Billy. 90m/C VHS. Claude Codgen, Mary Lou McGinnis, Bob Purvey; D: Gene McCabe.

Follow Me, Boys! 1966 A Disney film about a simple man who decides to put down roots and enjoy the quiet life, after one year too many on the road with a ramshackle jazz band. That life is soon interrupted when he volunteers to lead a high-spirited boy scout troop. 120m/C VHS, DVD. Fred MacMurray, Vera Miles, Lillian Gish, Charlie Ruggles, Elliott Reid, Kurt Russell, Luana Patten, Ken Murray; D: Norman Tokar; W: Louis Pelletier; M: George Bruns.

Follow Me Quietly 1949 Serial strangler who only kills in the rain is stalked by Lundigan. Very good little thriller which packs a punch in less than an hour. 59m/B VHS. William Lundigan, Dorothy Patrick, Jeff Corey, Nestor Paiva, Charles D. Brown, Paul Guilfoyle; D: Richard Fleischer.

Follow That Camel Carry On Follow That Camel 1967 Foreign Legion sergeant who invents acts of heroism finally gets a chance to really help out a friend in need. Part of the "Carry On" series. 95m/C VHS. GB Phil Silvers, Kenneth Williams, Anita Harris, Jim Dale; D: Gerald Thomas.

Follow That Car 1980 (PG) Three southern kids become FBI agents and begin a thigh-slappin', rip-snortin' down-home escapade. 96m/C VHS. Dirk Benedict, Tanya Tucker, Teri Nunn; D: Daniel Haller.

Follow That Dream 1961 (G) Elvis plays a musical hillbilly whose family is trying to homestead on government land along the sunny Florida coast. Based on Richard C. Powell's novel "Pioneer Go Home." The songs—the only reason to see this movie—include "Angel," "What a Wonderful Life," and the title track. 111m/C VHS, DVD. Elvis Presley, Arthur O'Connell, Anne Helm, Simon Oakland, Jack Kruschen, Joanna Moore, Howard McNear; D: Gordon Douglas; W: Charles Lederer; C: Leo Tover; M: Hans J. Salter.

Follow That Rainbow 1966 Believing that her long-lost father is a popular touring singer, a young lass pursues him from Switzerland to South Africa. 90m/C VHS. Joe Stewardson, Memory Jane, Joan Blickhill; D: Louis Burke.

Follow the Boys 1944 Vaudeville performer Tony West (Raft) heads out to California to try his luck and gets a double break when he's noticed by leading lady Gloria Vance (Zorina). Not only does he become a star but he marries Gloria as well. When WWII breaks out Tony's turned down for military service, so he organizes camp shows for the soldiers. They're a big success but misunderstandings have put his marriage in jeopardy. Plot's merely an excuse to have haute Hollywood (including Marlene Dietrich, Orson Welles, Jeanette MacDonald, and W.C. Fields) sing, dance, and tell jokes. JBeyond the Blue Horizon; I'll See You In My Dreams; The Bigger the Army and the Navy; Some of These Days; I'll Get By; I'll Walk Alone; Mad About Him Blues; The House I Live In. 111m/B VHS. George Raft, Vera Zorina, Grace McDonald, Charles Butterworth, Martha O'Driscoll, Charley Grapewin, Elizabeth Patterson; D: Edward Sutherland; W: Lou Breslow, Gertrude Purcell.

Follow the Fleet 1936 A song-and-dance man joins the Navy and meets two sisters in need of help in this Rogers/Astaire bon-bon featuring a classic Berlin score. Look for Betty Grable, Lucille Ball, and Tony Martin in minor roles. Hilliard went on to be best known as the wife of Ozzie Nelson in TV's "The Adventures of Ozzie and Harriet." JLet's Face the Music and Dance; We Saw the Sea; I'm Putting All My Eggs In One Basket; Get Thee Behind Me, Satan; But Where Are You?; I'd Rather Lead a Band; Let Yourself Go. 110m/B VHS, DVD. Fred Astaire, Ginger Rogers, Randolph Scott, Harriet Hilliard Nelson, Betty Grable, Lucille Ball; D: Mark Sandrich; M: Irving Berlin, Max Steiner.

Follow the Leader East of the Bowery 1944 On leave from the Army, Hall and Gorcey discover that one of the gang has been jailed on a trumped-up charge and set about finding the real culprit. JNow and Then; I All Want to Do Play the Drums. 65m/B VHS. Leo Gorcey, Huntz Hall, Gabriel Dell, Jack La Rue, Joan Marsh, William Benedict, Mary Gordon, Sammy (Earnest) Morrison; D: William Beaudine; M: Gene Austin.

Follow the River 1995 (PG) It's 1775 and Mary Ingles (Lee) is living with her husband and family on a frontier farm in the Blue Ridge Mountains. The community is raided by the Shawnee, lead by Wildcat (Schweig), who take Mary and several other settlers miles away to their home camp. Once there, Mary befriends another captive, the older Gretten Wildcat, and plots to escape and find her way home. Based on the 1981 novel by James Alexander Thom; filmed in North Carolina. 93m/C VHS, DVD. Sheryl Lee, Eric Schweig, Ellen Burstyn, Tim Guinee, Renee O'Connor; D: Martin Davidson.

Follow the Stars Home 2001 Dianne (Williams) falls for charming fisherman Mark McCune (Close), they get married, and she's soon pregnant. But when Dianne learns that their baby daughter will be born with severe disabilities, Mark can't cope and leaves her. Flash forward six years, with Dianne making a life for herself and Julia—aided by her mother (Brown); and Mark's steadfast pediatrician brother, David (Scott), who obviously loves her. Then an accident brings Mark back into their lives, but will Dianne make a different choice this time? Based on the novel by Luanne Rice. A Hallmark Hall of Fame production that's a predictable tear-jerker. **97m/C** VHS, DVD, Kimberly Williams, Debby, **84m/C** VHS, Jonathan Penner, Sandra Bullock, Gerald Orange, George Plimpton; **D:** Daniel Adams.

Follow the Sun 🐾🐾½ 1951 Ford excels as Ben Hogan, who was seriously injured in a car accident and fought his way back to become a golf legend. Details his painful recovery and the support he received from his wife Valerie (Baxter). Real life pros (acting) in their own right) Sam Snead, Jimmy Demaret, and Cary Middlecoff have cameos. **93m/B** VHS. Glenn Ford, Anne Baxter, Dennis O'Keefe, June Havoc, Larry Keating, Roland Winters, Nana Bryant, Myrtle Anderson. **Cameos:** Sam Snead; **D:** Sidney Lanfield; **W:** Frederick Hazlitt Brennan; **C:** Leo Tover; **M:** Cyril Mockridge.

Following 🐾🐾 1999 (R) Nolan's feature debut is an odd little neo-noir about a young man named Bill (Theobald) who likes to follow strangers. He picks the wrong guy in burglar Cobb (Haw) who has his own voyeuristic tastes. Cobb turns the tables on Bill and decides to become his mentor in crime. And sticking with the noir tradition, there's a mysterious blonde femme (Russell) whose relationship to the men is gradually revealed. As in his 2001 film "Memento," Nolan plays twister with the chronology, which means more than one viewing may be necessary to figure things out. **71m/B** VHS, DVD. Jeremy Theobald, Alex Haw, Lucy Russell, John Nolan; **D:** Christopher Nolan; **W:** Christopher Nolan; **M:** David Julyan.

A Fond Kiss 🐾🐾 2004 (R) A modern-day Scottish "Romeo & Juliet," with star-crossed mediocrity between a Pakistani DJ and a Catholic music teacher. The culture-clash throws both families into panic (you know the story). Another notch in a series of socially-adept films from director Ken Loach and writer Paul Laverty. This tire around they bring a little less humor and a little more drama, albeit stilted, which, along with weak performances and nearly unintelligible accents may turn off a majority of Western audiences. **104m/C** VHS, DVD. Eva Birthistle, Atta Yaqub, Ahmad Riaz, Shabana Akhtar, Shamshad Akhtar, Ghizala Avan, Pasha Bocarie, Gerard Kelly; **D:** Ken Loach; **C:** Barry Ackroyd; **M:** George Fenton.

Food of Love 🐾🐾 2002 Melodramatic gay romance set in the world of classical music. 18-year-old piano student Paul Porterfield (Bishop) is hired as a page turner for a concert giver by his idol, middle-aged pianist Richard Kennington (Rhys). While traveling in Barcelona with his clinging mother Pamela (Stevenson), Paul re-meets Richard and they have a fling, which means more to Paul than to Richard whose longtime lover is his manager Joseph (Corduner). At school in New York, Paul happens to meet Joseph (lots of coincidences here) and Pamela finally realizes her son is gay. Based on the novel "The Page Turner" by David Leavitt. Spanish director Pons's English-language debut feels abrupt and Paul is an unsympathetic character. **112m/C** VHS, DVD, SP, GF. Kevin Bishop, Paul Rhys, Juliet Stevenson, Allan Corduner, Geraldine McEwan; **D:** Ventura Pons; **W:** Ventura Pons; **C:** Mario Montero; **M:** Carles Cases.

Food of the Gods WOOF! 1976 (PG) On a secluded island giant rats, chickens, and other creatures crave human flesh, blood, bones, etc. This cheap, updated version of the H. G. Wells novel suffers from lousy performances and lack of imagination. **88m/C** VHS, Marjoe Gortner, Pamela Franklin, Ralph Meeker, Ida Lupino, Jon Cypher; **D:** Bert I. Gordon.

Food of the Gods: Part 2 WOOF! *Gnaw: Food of the Gods 2* 1988 (R) The killer beasts and animals of the first film (and of H.G. Wells' classic novel) strike again: gigantic rats maim young

girls. Easily as bad as the original. **93m/C** VHS. Paul Coufos, Lisa Schrage; **D:** Damian Lee; **W:** E. Kim Brewster.

A Fool and His Money 🐾½ 1988 (R) Adnan Morris Codman (Penner) decides to market a shady new religion based on greed but, naturally, finds the true road. Bullock is skeptical girlfriend Debby. **84m/C** VHS. Jonathan Penner, Sandra Bullock, Gerald Orange, George Plimpton; **D:** Daniel Adams.

Fool for Love 🐾🐾½ 1985 (R) Explores the mysterious relationship between a modern-day drifter and his long-time lover, who may or may not be his half-sister, as they confront each other in a seedy New Mexico motel. Adapted by Shepard from his play. **108m/C** VHS, DVD. Sam Shepard, Kim Basinger, Randy Quaid, Harry Dean Stanton; **D:** Robert Altman; **W:** Sam Shepard; **M:** George Burt.

The Fool Killer 🐾🐾½ *Violent Journey* 1965 In the post-Civil War south, a 12-year-old boy learns that a terrifying legend may be all too real. Offbeat film with striking visuals and other choice psycho role for Perkins. **100m/B** VHS. Anthony Perkins, Edward Albert, Dana Elcar, Henry Hull, Salome Jens, Arnold Moss; **D:** Servando Gonzalez.

A Fool There Was 🐾🐾 1914 The rocket that blasted Theda Bara to stardom and launched the vamp film genre. One of the few extant Bara films, it tells the now familiar story of a good man whom crumbles from the heights of moral rectitude thanks to the inescapable influence of an unredeemable vamp. Bette Davis described Bara as "divinely, hysterically, insanely malevolent." Much heavy emoting; subtitled (notoriously) "Kiss Me, My Fool!" Based on Rudyard Kipling's "The Vampire." **70m/B** VHS, DVD, Mabel Frenyear, Victor Benoit, Theda Bara, Edward Jose, Runa Hodges, Clifford Bruce; **D:** Frank Powell; **W:** Roy L. McCardell; **C:** George Schneiderman.

Foolin' Around 🐾🐾 1980 (PG) An innocent Oklahoma farm boy arrives at college and falls in love with a beautiful heiress. He will stop at nothing to win her over, including crashing her lavish wedding ceremony. **101m/C** VHS. Michael Talbot, William H. Macy, Gary Busey, Annette O'Toole, Eddie Albert, Tony Randall, Cloris Leachman; **D:** Richard T. Heffron; **W:** Michael Kane; **C:** Philip Lathrop; **M:** Charles Bernstein.

Foolish WOOF! 1999 (R) Foolish? You bet it is. Eddie Griffin stars as the title character, a struggling comic who runs the old Eddie Murphy routines to a hip-hop beat. He butts heads with his brother Fifty Dollah, played by rapper/sports agent/bad actor Master P, who also wrote and executive produced this clunker. The troom mike falls into the picture so often that you expect Master P to grab it and bust a rhyme at any given moment. Strictly for sucka MCs. **96m/C** VHS, DVD, Eddie Griffin, Master P, Frank Sivero, Amy Petersen, Jonathan Banks, Andrew (Dice Clay) Silverstein, Marla Gibbs, Daphne Lynn Duplaix, Sver-Ole Thorsen, Bill Nunn, Bill Duke; **D:** Dave Meyers; **W:** Master P; **C:** Steve Gainer; **M:** Wendy Melvin, Lisa Coleman.

Foolish Wives 🐾🐾🐾 1922 A remake of Von Stroheim's classic depicting the confused milieu of post-war Europe as reflected through the actions of a young woman estranged from her husband—start a warm romance when they meet in San Francisco. The husband reacts violently. Good cast seems lost. original film. **107m/B** VHS, DVD. Erich von Stroheim, Mae Busch Maur[le] (Ford) George, Cesare Gravina, Harrison Ford; **D:** Erich von Stroheim; **C:** William H. Daniels; **M:** Sigmund Romberg.

Fools 🐾 1970 (PG) Two lonely people—he an aging horror film actor and she a young woman estranged from her husband—start a warm romance when they meet in San Francisco. The husband reacts violently. Good cast seems lost. **93m/C** VHS, Jason Robards Jr., Katharine Ross, Scott Hylands; **D:** Tom Gries.

Fool's Gold 🐾🐾½ 2008 (PG-13) 112m/ C DVD, US Matthew McConaughey, Kate Hudson, Donald Sutherland, Alexis Dziena, Ewen Bremner, Ray Winstone, Kevin Hart, Malcolm Jamal Warner.

Fool's Gold: The Story of the Brink's-Mat Robbery 🐾🐾½ 1992 True story focuses on a robbery that nets the thieves a windfall—and the problems that follow. In November of 1983, mickey McAvoy (Bean) has set up a heist to rob the high-security warehouse of Brink's-Mat at Heathrow airport. The thieves are after gold bullion but what they find in the vaults are 6,800 gold bars, worth roughly eight times more than their intended haul. The police are quickly on to various members of the gang, but just what happened to all that loot? (Most of the bars have never been recovered; the police believe some were smelted down, but many may be buried. McAvoy was sentenced in 1984 to 25 years in prison.) **93m/C** VHS, DVD. GF. Sean Bean, Larry Lamb, David Cardy, Jeremy Child, Rob Spendlove; **D:** Terry Winsor; **W:** Terry Winsor, Jeff Pope; **C:** Dick Pope; **M:** William Wooll. TV.

Fools of Fortune 🐾🐾½ 1990 (PG-13) Adaptation of William Trevor's novel depicting Willie Clinton's childhood and adult experiences of family dramatics giant; it's a rather disjointed and straying shamrock opera. **104m/C** VHS, GF Mary Elizabeth Mastrantonio, Iain Glen, Julie Christie, Michael Kitchen, Sean McClory, Frankie McCafferty, Niamh Cusack; **D:** Pat O'Connor; **W:** Michael Hirst; **M:** Hans Zimmer.

Fools Rush In 🐾🐾 1997 (PG-13) Uptight eastern yuppie Alex Whitman (Perry) meets cute in Vegas with beautiful Latina casino worker Isabel Fuentes (Hayek) and the duo spend the night together. Three months later, Isabel shows up at Alex's New York door to announce her pregnancy and say she's keeping the baby. Movie clichés collide with movie stereotypes when they decide to marry but find the relationship suffers over their vast ethnic and cultural differences. At least he plays his character's real-life dad plays his character's father. Perry's real-life dad. **110m/C** VHS, DVD. Matthew Perry, Salma Hayek, Jon Tenney, Jill Clayburgh, Stanley DeSantis, Anne Betancourt, Carlos Gomez, Tomas Milian, John Bennett Perry, Siobhan Fallon, Marjorie Ann Mutchie, Irving Bacon, Danny Mummert; **D:** Frank Strayer; **W:** Karen De Greenberg; **M:** Alan Silvestri.

Footlight Glamour 🐾🐾 1943 Dagwood is actually hired to run a new tool manufacturing plant but Blondie causes trouble when she casts the boss' daughter in a local play. **68m/B** VHS. Penny Singleton, Arthur Lake, Larry Simms, Jonathan Hale, Thurston Hall, Ann Savage, Marjorie Ann Mutchie, Irving Bacon, Danny Mummert; **D:** Frank Strayer; **W:** Karen De Wolf; **C:** Philip Tannura.

Footlight Parade 🐾🐾🐾 1933 Broadway producer Cagney is out of work. Sound films have scared off his backers until his idea for staging live musical numbers before the cinema features lures them back. Lots of authentic backstage action produces three spectacular Busby Berkeley-choreographed numbers that climax the film, including the giant water ballet featuring more than 100 performers. ♫Ah, the Moon is Here; Sittin' on a Backyard Fence; Honeymoon Hotel; By A Waterfall; Shanghai Lil. **104m/B** VHS. James Cagney, Joan Blondell, Dick Powell, Ruby Keeler, Guy Kibbee, Ruth Donnelly; **D:** Lloyd Bacon; **M:** George Barnes. Natl. Film Reg. '92.

Footlight Serenade 🐾🐾½ 1942 A boxer falls for a beautiful dancer with whom he's costarring in a Broadway play. Unfortunately, she's secretly married to another of the actors and her husband is becoming jealous of the boxer's intentions. Light, fun musical. One of a series of Grable movies made to boost morale during WWII. ♫Are You Kidding?; I'm Still Crazy About You; I Hear the Birdies Sing; Living High; I'll Be Marching to a Love Song; Land On Your Feet; I'm Stepping

Out With a Memory Tonight. **80m/B** VHS. Betty Grable, Victor Mature, John Payne, Jane Wyman, Phil Silvers, James Gleason, Mantan Moreland; **D:** Gregory Ratoff; **C:** Lee Garmes.

Footloose 🐾🐾½ 1984 (PG) When a city boy moves to a small Midwestern town, he discovers some disappointing news: rock music and dancing have been forbidden by the local government. Determined to bring some '60s-style life into the town, he sets about changing the rules and eventually enlists the help of the daughter of the man responsible for the law. Rousing music, talented young cast, and plenty of trouble make this an entertaining musical-drama. ♫Footloose; Let's Hear it for the Boy; The Girl Gets Around; Dancing in the Sheets; Somebody's Eyes; Almost Paradise; I'm Free; Never; Holding Out for a Hero. **107m/C** VHS, DVD. Kevin Bacon, Lori Singer, Christopher Penn, John Lithgow, Dianne Wiest, John Laughlin, Sarah Jessica Parker; **D:** Herbert Ross; **M:** Miles Goodman.

Footsteps 🐾🐾 1998 (R) *Exposé* 1941 Fairly amusing comedy-mystery with investment counselor Flynn doubling as detective. Based on the play "Blondie White" by Ladislaus Fodor, Bernard Merivale, and Jeffrey Dell; **96m/B** VHS. Errol Flynn, Brenda Marshall, Ralph Bellamy, Alan Hale, Lee Patrick, Allan Jenkins, Lucile Watson, William Frawley, Roscoe Karns, Grant Mitchell, Maris Wrixon, Noel Madison, Jack La Rue, Turhan Bey; **D:** Lloyd Bacon, Hugh MacMullen; **W:** Lester Cole, John Wexley.

Footsteps in the Dark 🐾🐾½ 1941 (R) Reporter Jason Davis (Chapa) gets a tip that makes him an eyewitness to a judge's murder. Separated from wife Nancy (Alonso), Jason gets involved with photographer Amber (Lombard), who is also connected to D.A. Steve Carlen (Schanley). When Jason turns up evidence that links Amber and Carlen to the murdered judge and he begins to receive threatening messages, Jason can trust only himself to catch the killer. **93m/C** VHS, DVD. Damian Chapa, Karina Lombard, Tom Schanley, Maria Conchita Alonso, Steven Bauer, Sandra Bernhard, Tippi Hedren; **D:** Daphna Edwards; **W:** Daphna Edwards; **C:** David J. Miller; **M:** Alex Wurman. VIDEO

For a Few Dollars More 🐾🐾½ 1965 (PG) The Man With No Name returns as a bounty hunter who teams up with a gunslinger/rival to track down the sadistic leader of a gang of bandits. Violent. Sequel to "A Fistful of Dollars" (1964) and followed by "The Good, The Bad, and The Ugly." **127m/C** VHS, VHS, DVD, Blu-ray Disc. /T Clint Eastwood, Lee Van Cleef, Klaus Kinski, Gian Maria Volonte; **D:** Sergio Leone; **W:** Sergio Leone, Luciano Vincenzoni; **C:** Massimo Dallamano; **M:** Ennio Morricone.

For a Lost Soldier 🐾🐾 *Voor een Verloren Soldaat* 1993 Middle-aged Dutch choreographer Jeroen (Krabbe), working on a piece about the Allied liberation, recalls his relationship with a Canadian soldier more than 40 years before. During WWII, the 13-year-old Jeroen (Smit) is sent from Amsterdam to live in the country with a foster family. With the first twinges of puberty and sexuality he longs for a special friend, whom he finds in Walt (Kelley), a young gay American soldier who is part of the Allied liberation forces. Very provocative subject, delicately handled without any implication of child abuse. In English and Dutch with subtitles. **92m/C** VHS, DVD. Ni Marten Smit, Andrew Kelley, Jeroen Krabbe, Freark Smink, Elsje de Wijn, Derk-Jan Kroon; **D:** Roeland Kerbosch; **W:** Roeland Kerbosch; **C:** Nils Post; **M:** Joop Stokkermans.

For Better and for Worse 🐾🐾½ 1992 (R) A nice young couple is planning to have your average nice wedding when one of their friends gets hold of an invitation and decides to jokingly invite the Pope to attend. But the joke is on them when the Pope accepts. Talk about upstaging the bride! **94m/C** VHS. W: Tony Gilroy; **C:** Yves Dahan; **M:** John Goodstein.

For Better or Worse 🦴🦴 1995 (PG-13) Pathetic loser Michael Makeshift (Alexander, also making his directorial debut) falls in love with his new sister-in-law Valerie (Davidovich) even as he gets entangled in his brother Reggie's (Woods) business scams. 95m/C VHS. Jason Alexander, Lolita (David) Davidovich, James Woods, Joe Mantegna, Jay Mohr, Beatrice Arthur, Robert Costanzo, John Amos, Eda Reiss Merin; Cameos: Rob Reiner, Rip Torn; D: Jason Alexander; W: Jeff Nathanson; C: Wayne Keenan; M: Miles Goodman. CABLE

For Ever Mozart 🦴🦴 1996 Godard's film puzzle makes references to literature, music, and cinema itself without making any particular sense. Veteran film director Vicky Vitalis (Messica) agrees to help his daughter Camille (Assas) stage a comedic play by Alfred de Musset in Sarajevo, in order to cheer up its war-tired residents. This doesn't go well, but the director has already abandoned the project to return to his latest film idea, which also turns out to be a disaster. French with subtitles. 85m/C VHS. FR SI Vicky Messica, Madeleine Assas, Frederic Pierrot, Ghalia Lacroix; D: Jean-Luc Godard; W: Jean-Luc Godard; C: Christophe Pollock.

For Heaven's Sake 🦴🦴🦴 1926 Lloyd's first film for Paramount has him making an accidental donation to a skid row mission, then marrying the preacher's daughter and converting all the neighborhood tough guys. 60m/B VHS, DVD. Harold Lloyd, Jobyna Ralston, Noah Young, James Mason, Paul Weigel; D: Sam Taylor.

For Heaven's Sake 🦴🦴½ Heaven Only Knows 1979 A bumbling basketball team is lent some heavenly assistance in the form of a meddling angel. But can he hit the jumper? 90m/C VHS. Ray Bolger, Kent McCord; D: Jerry Thorpe; W: William Blinn. TV

For Hire 🦴🦴½ 1998 Suffering from cancer and a pregnant wife, Chicago cabbie Mitch Lawrence (Lowe) is desperate for money. So, he agrees to kill an associate of famous writer Louis Webber (Mantegna) for $50,000. When the job is done, Mitch learns just why he was chosen to do the deed. 96m/C VHS, DVD. Rob Lowe, Joe Mantegna, Dominic Philie, Bronwen Black; D: Jean Pellerin; M: Alan Reeves.

For Keeps 🦴½ 1988 (PG-13) Two high school sweethearts on the verge of graduating get married and suffer all the trials of teenage parenthood. Tends toward the unrealistic and trite. 98m/C VHS, DVD. Molly Ringwald, Randall Batinkoff, Kenneth Mars; D: John G. Avildsen; W: Tim Kazurinsky, Denise DeClue; M: Bill Conti. TV

For Ladies Only 🦴🦴 1981 A struggling actor takes a job as a male stripper to pay the rent. Among the leering ladies is Davis, daughter of former President Reagan. 100m/C VHS. Gregory Harrison, Patricia (Patti) Davis, Dinah Manoff, Louise Lasser, Lee Grant, Marc Singer, Viveca Lindfors, Steven Keats; D: Mel Damski. TV

For Love of Ivy 🦴🦴 1968 (PG) Poitier is a trucking executive who has a gambling operation on the side. Ivy is the Black maid of a rich white family who is about to leave her job to look for romance. The two are brought together but the road to true love doesn't run smooth. Based on a story by Poitier. 102m/C VHS, DVD. Sidney Poitier, Abbey Lincoln, Beau Bridges, Carroll O'Connor, Nan Martin; D: Daniel Mann; M: Quincy Jones.

For Love of the Game 🦴🦴 1999 (PG-13) The baseball glove has long been gold for Costner. In his third baseball outing, he moderately scores as veteran Detroit Tigers pitcher Billy Chapel, facing a crossroad in his professional and personal life. In 1-2-3 manner, he learns that the team he's played on for 20 years has been sold, the new owners want to trade him, and his longtime girlfriend, Jane (Preston), is dumping him prior to an important game with the Yankees. Magically, he's this close to pitching a perfect game, as the last five years of his life flash before him. Sudsy, predictable romance overshadows the game action, but harder-edged Raimi, with his own love for the game, injects some striking visual flair. Costner pitched a fit against the studio for editing out his infamous penis shot to ensure a kid-friendly rating. Based on the novel by Michael Shaara. 137m/C VHS, DVD, HD DVD. Michael (Mike) Papajohn, Kevin Costner, Kelly Preston, John C. Reilly, Jena Malone, Brian Cox, J.K. Simmons, Bill E. Rogers, Vin Scully, Carmine D. Giovinazzo, Hugh Ross, Steve Lyons; D: Sam Raimi; W: Dana Stevens; C: John Bailey; M: Basil Poledouris.

For Love or Country: The Arturo Sandoval Story 🦴🦴½ 2000 (PG-13) Biopic of Cuban trumpeter Arturo Sandoval (Garcia) who stays in Cuba for the sake of wife Marianela (Maestro) and their children, all the while chafing under his artistic restrictions. Finally, his wife agrees to defect and during a tour in Athens, Sandoval asks for political asylum. Both Garcia and Maestro have a believable chemistry but also look for Dutton's portrayal of Dizzy Gillespie, who hired Sandoval for his U.N. Orchestra, allowing the musician to travel abroad. 120m/C VHS, DVD. Andy Garcia, Mia Maestro, Charles S. Dutton, David Paymer, Gloria Estefan, Tomas Milian, Freddy Rodriguez, Jose Zuniga, Steven Bauer, Fionnula Flanagan, Michael O'Hagan; D: Joseph Sargent; W: Timothy J. Sexton; C: Donald M. Morgan; M: Arturo Sandoval. CABLE

For Love or Money 🦴🦴 1963 A super-rich hotel owner wants her lawyer to find her three beautiful daughters. However, she doesn't trust him enough not to meddle in the search. Lavish production and a good cast can't overcome the mediocrity of the script and direction. 108m/C VHS. Kirk Douglas, Mitzi Gaynor, Thelma Ritter, William Bendix, Julie Newmar, Gig Young, Leslie Parrish, William Windom, Dick Sargent; D: Michael Gordon.

For Love or Money 🦴½ 1984 Game-show contestants find money and romance. 91m/C VHS. Jamie Farr, Suzanne Pleshette, Gil Gerard, Ray Walston, Lawrence Pressman, Mary Kay Place; D: Terry Hughes; M: Billy Goldenberg. TV

For Love or Money 🦴🦴 1988 (PG-13) A real estate man with Career on the mind has to choose between the woman in his life and the condo development that stands firmly between them and happily-ever-afterdom. 89m/C VHS. Timothy Daly, Haviland (Hayle) Morris, Kevin McCarthy, David Doyle, Shelley Fabares; D: Todd Hallowell; W: Bart Davis; C: Igor Sunara; M: Jim Lang.

For Love or Money 🦴🦴½ 1993 (PG) Struggling hotel concierge with a heart of gold finds himself doing little "favors" for a slimy entrepreneur who holds the key to his dreams—the cash to open an elegant hotel of his own. Romantic comedy is reminiscent of the classic screwball comedies of the '30s and '40s, but lacks the trademark tight writing and impeccable timing. Fox is appealing and likable as the wheeling and dealing concierge, a role undermined by a mediocre script offering too few laughs. 89m/C VHS, DVD. Michael J. Fox, Gabrielle Anwar, Isaac Mizrahi, Anthony (Corlan) Higgins, Michael Tucker, Bobby Short, Dan Hedaya, Bob Balaban, Udo Kier, Patrick Breen, Paula Laurence; D: Barry Sonnenfeld; W: Mark Rosenthal, Larry Konner; M: Bruce Broughton.

For Me and My Gal 🦴🦴½ 1942 In his film debut, Kelly plays an opportunistic song-and-dance man who lures a young vaudevillian (Garland) away from her current partners. WWI interrupts both their career and romance, but you can count on them being reunited. Loaded with vintage tunes. ♫ For Me and My Gal; They Go Wild, Simply Wild Over Me; The Doll Shop; Oh, Johnny, Oh; Oh, You Beautiful Doll; When You Wore A Tulip; Don't Leave Me Daddy; Do I Love You; By The Beautiful Sea. 104m/B VHS, DVD. Gene Kelly, Judy Garland, George Murphy, Martha Eggerth, Ben Blue, Richard Quine, Keenan Wynn, Stephen McNally, D: Busby Berkeley; M: George Bassman.

For One More Day 🦴½ Oprah Winfrey Presents: Mitch Albom's For One More Day 2007 As the sap rises, Chick Benetto (Imperioli) is a washed-up baseball player turned alcoholic who's made such a mess of his life that he's suicidal. Suddenly, Chick's dead mom Posey (Burstyn) shows up and leads Chick on a trip down memory lane to show him that he can still turn his life around. A weepie family drama adapted from Albom's novel. 92m/C DVD. Michael Imperioli, Ellen Burstyn, Samantha Mathis, Alice Drummond, Vadim Imperioli, Scott Cohen, Emily Wickersham; D: Lloyd Kramer; W: Mitch Albom; C: Tami Reiker; M: Lennie Niehaus. TV

For Pete's Sake 🦴🦴½ 1974 (PG) Topsy-turvy comedy about a woman whose efforts to get together enough money to put her husband through school involve her with loan sharks, a madame, and even cattle rustling in NYC. Not one of Streisand's best. 90m/C VHS, DVD. Barbra Streisand, Michael Sarrazin, Estelle Parsons, William Redfield, Molly Picon; D: Peter Yates; W: Stanley Shapiro, Maurice Richlin; C: Laszlo Kovacs; M: Artie Butler.

For Real 🦴🦴½ 2002 (PG-13) Mac (Reid) is a wealthy, workaholic middle-aged black record promotor, living in the suburbs of Richmond, Virigina, and looked after by his housekeeper Hardy (Lepart). When Hardy's inner-city, 18-year-old niece CeCe (Curry) gets into serious trouble, Hardy and Mac ask for leniency from the judge and Mac is expected to keep CeCe on the straight and narrow. But there's a generation clash since CeCe thinks Mac is a sellout and Mac thinks CeCe is a punk with a fatalistic attitude. But CeCe's opportunities may be threatened by her own insecurities and her narrow notions of what being "real" mean, while Mac has to learn to loosen up. 95m/C VHS, DVD. Tim Reid, Tamara Curry, Kwelli Leary, Eugene Long, Susan Fales-Hill; D: Tim Reid; W: Tim Reid, Shirley Pierce. VIDEO

For Richer, for Poorer 🦴½ Father, Son and the Mistress 1992 (PG) A very rich, successful businessman notices his son is happy just to sit back and let dad earn all the dough while he waits for his share. In order to teach his son a lesson, Dad decides to give all his money away. But the plan backfires when both realize that earning a second fortune may not be as easy as they assumed. Below average cable fare. 90m/C VHS, DVD. Jack Lemmon, Talia Shire, Joanna Gleason, Jonathan Silverman, Madeline Kahn, George Wyner; D: Jay Sandrich; W: Stan Daniels. CABLE

For Richer or Poorer 🦴🦴 1997 (PG-13) Definitely poorer. Don't pity the Amish because they can't defend themselves against movies like this—envy them because they don't have to see it. Shallow New York real-estate hustler Brad (Allen) is supposed to be divorcing socialite wife Caroline (Alley). Their inept accountant (Knight), however, has cooked the books, causing them to head for the Pennsylvania hills. They hide out with a community of Amish people, rediscovering their love along with a bunch of manure jokes. Proves once again the inherent unfunniness of butter churns and barn raisings. 122m/C VHS, DVD. Tim Allen, Kirstie Alley, Wayne Knight, Larry Miller, Jay O. Sanders, Michael Lerner, Miguel A. Nunez Jr., Megan Cavanagh, John Pyper-Ferguson, June Claman, Katie Moore; D: Bryan Spicer; W: Jana Howington, Steve Lukanic; C: Buzz Feitshans IV; M: Randy Edelman.

For Roseanna 🦴🦴½ Roseanna's Grave 1996 (PG-13) Romantic comedy (despite the subject matter) about Marcello (Reno), the owner of a trattoria in an Italian village and his ailing wife Cecilia (Ruehl), whose dream is to be buried next to their daughter in one of the three remaining plots in their ancient local cemetery. Marcello goes to great lengths to ensure the health of the town's more at-risk citizens to save his wife's spot. Pleasant enough comedy boasts a fine job by an excellent cast, and the Italian scenery is beautiful. Overlooked at the time of its theatrical release, but worth a look for the sentimentally inclined. 99m/C VHS, DVD. Jean Reno, Mercedes Ruehl, Polly Walker, Mark Frankel, Trevor Peacock, Fay Ripley, Giuseppe Cederna, Luigi Diberti, Renato Scarpa, George Rossi, Roberto Della Casa, Romano Ghini; D: Paul Weiland; W: Saul Turteltaub; C: Henry Braham; M: Trevor Jones.

For Sale 🦴🦴 A Vendre 1998 After France (Kiberlain) leaves her groom-to-be at the altar, he hires private detective Luigi (Castellito) to track her down and bring her back. Luigi discovers France has left a string of lovers in her wake and that she has been charging them for her favors. The more he learns, the more obsessed he becomes with a woman he has yet to meet in the flesh. French with subtitles. 116m/C VHS, DVD. FR Sandrine Kiberlain, Sergio Castellito, Jean-Francois Stevenin, Chiara Mastroianni, Aurore Clement, Samuel Le Bihan; D: Laetitia Masson; W: Laetitia Masson; C: Antoine Hebale; M: Siegfried.

For the Boys 🦴🦴 1991 (R) Midler stars as Dixie Leonard, a gutsy singer-comedian who hooks up with Eddie Sparks (Caan) to become one of America's favorite USO singing, dancing, and comedy teams. The movie spans 50 years and three wars—including Korea and Vietnam—and raises such issues as the blacklist and the role of politics in showbiz. Glitzy Hollywood entertainment falters despite Midler's strong performance. ♫ Billy-A-Dick; Come Rain or Come Shine; In My Life; Stuff Like That There. 120m/C VHS, DVD. Bette Midler, James Caan, George Segal, Patrick O'Neal, Christopher Rydell, Arye Gross, Norman Fell, Rosemary Murphy, Dori Brenner, Bud Yorkin, Jack Sheldon, Melissa Manchester, Brandon Call, Arliss Howard; D: Mark Rydell; W: Marshall Brickman, Neal Jimenez, Lindy Laub; C: Stephen Goldblatt; M: Dave Grusin. Golden Globes '92: Actress—Mus./Comedy (Midler).

For the First Time 🦴🦴 1959 In his last film, Lanza plays an opera singer who tours European cities to raise money for his deaf girlfriend's medical treatment. ♫ Oh Mon Amour; Bavarian Drinking Song; Ave Maria; Vesti La Giubba; La Donna e Mobile; Niun Mi Tema; Grand March; O Solo Mio; Ich Liebe Dich. 97m/C VHS. Mario Lanza, Zsa Zsa Gabor, Johanna von Koczian, Kurt Kasznar, Hans Sohnker, Peter Capell, Renzo Cesana, Sandro Giglio; D: Rudolph Mate; W: Andrew Solt.

For the Love of Angela 🦴🦴 1982 Pretty and young shop clerk involves herself with both the shopkeeper and his son. 90m/C Sarah Rush, David Winn, Margaret Fairchild, Barbara Malloy, Peter Paul Liapis, Louis Jourdan; D: Rudy Veyar; W: Paul C. Elliot.

For the Love of Benji 🦴🦴½ 1977 (G) In this second "Benji" film, the adorable little dog accompanies his human family on a Greek vacation. He is kidnapped to be used as a messenger for a secret code, but escapes, to have a series of comic adventures in this entertaining family fare. 85m/C VHS, DVD. Benji, Patsy Garrett, Cynthia Smith, Allen Fintzat, Ed Nelson; D: Joe Camp; W: Joe Camp; C: Don Reddy; M: Euel Box.

For the Love of It 🦴½ 1980 TV stars galore try to hold together this farce about car chases in California, stolen secret documents, and (of course) true love. Outstandingly mediocre. 100m/C VHS. Deborah Raffin, Jeff Conaway, Tom Bosley, Norman Fell, Don Rickles, Henry Gibson, Norijuki "Pat" Morita, William (Bill) Christopher, Lawrence-Hilton Jacobs, Adrian Zmed, Barbi Benton, Adam West; D: Hal Kanter. TV

For the Love of Mary 🦴🦴½ 1948 Durbin retired after this fluff romantic comedy (with some musical numbers) in which she played White House switchboard operator Mary Peppertree. Mary has three potential suitors and juggling her romances causes job-related problems. Includes a second ending and song, which runs an additional eight minutes. ♫ Moonlight Bay; Let Me Call You Sweetheart; I'll Take You Home Again, Kathleen; On the Wings of a Song; Largo al Factotum. 91m/B VHS. Deanna Durbin, Edmond O'Brien, Don Taylor, Jeffrey Lynn, Harry Davenport, Ray Collins, Hugo Haas; D: Fred de Cordova; W: Oscar Brodney; C: William H. Daniels.

For the Moment 🐾🐾½ 1994 Aussie aviator Lachlan (Crowe) has joined the British Commonwealth Air Training Plan in 1942, a crash course for fighter pilots that drew men from several countries to bases across Canada. Stationed with best buddy Johnny (Outerbridge) in Manitoba, Lachlan falls for the married Lill (Hirt), sister of Johnny's honey Kate (McMillan), whose husband is away fighting. The emotional stakes are high for all concerned since they know the fliers will soon be sent off to combat. Old-fashioned (and sometimes slow-moving) romance with excellent performances and some gorgeous scenery. 120m/C VHS, DVD. *CA* Russell Crowe, Christianne Hirt, Peter Outerbridge, Sara McMillan, Wanda Cannon, Scott Kraft; *D:* Aaron Kim Johnston; *W:* Aaron Kim Johnston; *C:* Ian Elkin; *M:* Victor Davies.

For Which He Stands 🐾🐾 1998 The life and assassination of civil rights activist Medgar Evers are dramatically presented in this production of "American Playhouse" for PBS. Provides insight into the events surrounding his life. Adapted from the biography written by Evers' widow. 84m/C VHS. Howard E. Rollins Jr., Rocky Aoki, Paul Winfield, Irene Cara, Margaret Avery, Roscoe Lee Browne, Laurence Fishburne, Janet MacLach len, Dick Anthony Williams; *D:* Michael A. Schultz.

For Whom the Bell Tolls 🐾🐾🐾½ 1943 Hemingway novel gorgeously translated to the big screen, features a star-crossed romantic tale of derring-do. American schoolteacher Robert Jordan (Cooper) decides to join the Spanish Civil War and fight the fascists. He's ordered to rendezvous with peasant guerillas, to aid in blowing up a bridge, and in the rebel camp Jordan meets the beautiful Maria (Bergman). Lots of heroics (and some romance under the stars). Both leads were personally selected by the author. Originally released at 170 minutes. 130m/C VHS, DVD. Gary Cooper, Ingrid Bergman, Akim Tamiroff, Katina Paxinou, Arturo de Cordova, Vladimir Sokoloff, Mikhail Rasumny, Joseph Calleia, Alexander Granach; Yakima Canutt, George Coulouris, Yvonne De Carlo, Martin Garralaga, Soledad Jimínez, Duncan Renaldo, Tito Renaldo, Pedro de Cordoba, Frank Puglia, John (Jack) Mylong, Eric Feldary, Lio Yarson, Leo Bulgakov, Antonio Molina; *D:* Sam Wood; *W:* Dudley Nichols; *C:* Ray Rennahan; *M:* Victor Young. Oscars '43: Support. Actress (Paxinou).

For Your Consideration 🐾🐾½ 2006 (PG-13) Writing team Guest and Levy drop their patented "mockumentary" format, but not their sly satire in this send-up of Hollywood's awards season. Marilyn Hack ('O'Hara) is a fading actress stuck in a bad low-budget movie until an internet rumor deems her performance Oscar-worthy. As the buzz grows, she and her costars (Shearer, Posey) begin campaigning for nominations (Shearer, Posey) begin campaigning for nominations. Levy and Guest (as the studio head (Gervais)) becomes interested. Levy and Guest get the most out of their ensemble cast (including themselves), especially O'Hara. Fred Willard and Jane Lynch are a highlight as clueless entertainment show hosts. 86m/C DVD. *US* Catherine O'Hara, Harry Shearer, Parker Posey, John Michael Higgins, Christopher Moynihan, Jennifer Coolidge, Fred Willard, Jane Lynch, Ricky Gervais, Bob Balaban, Michael McKean, Ed Begley Jr., Jim Piddock, Rachael Harris, Eugene Levy, Carrie Aizley, Christopher Guest; *D:* Christopher Guest; *W:* Eugene Levy, Christopher Guest; *C:* Robert Schaefer; *M:* C.J. Vanston.

For Your Eyes Only 🐾🐾🐾 1981 (PG) In this James Bond adventure, 007 must keep the Soviets from getting hold of a valuable instrument aboard a sunken British spy ship. Sheds the gadgetry of its more recent predecessors in the series in favor of some spectacular stunt work and the usual beautiful girl and exotic locale. Glen's first outing as director, though he handled second units on the hit title tune. Sheena Easton sang the hit title tune. 136m/C VHS, DVD. *GB* Roger Moore, Carole Bouquet, Chaim Topol, Lynn-Holly Johnson, Julian Glover, Cassandra Harris, Jill Bennett, Michael Gothard, John Wyman, Jack Hedley, Lois Maxwell, Desmond Llewelyn, Geoffrey Keen, Walter Gotell, Charles Dance; *D:* Alan Hume; *M:* Bill Conti, Michael G. Wilson.

For Your Love Only 🐾🐾 1979 A beautiful young student falls in love with her teacher and is blackmailed, leading her to murder her tormentor. Soap opera made for German TV. Dubbed in English. 90m/C VHS. *GE* Nastassja Kinski, Christian Quadflieg, Judy Winter, Klaus Schwarzkopf; *D:* Wolfgang Petersen. **TV**

Forbidden 🐾🐾 1985 In Nazi Germany, a German countess has an affair with a Jewish intellectual, and she winds up hiding him from the S.S. Based on the novel "The Last Jews of Berlin" by Leonard Gross. Slow made-for-cable movie. 116m/C VHS. Jacqueline Bisset, Jürgen Prochnow, Irene Worth, Peter Vaughan, Amanda Cannings, Avis Bunnage; *D:* Anthony Page; *W:* Leonard Gross. **CABLE**

Forbidden Choices 🐾🐾 *The Beans of Egypt, Maine* 1994 (R) Problems and attractions of the white trash Bean family as observed by enthralled neighbor girl Earlene (Plimpton). Hot-tempered Reuben Bean (Hauer) has just landed a long prison term, leaving his brood of nine in the care of lover Roberta (Lynch), who's also too eager to give in to hand some Beal's charms, leading to more heartbreak. Based on Carolyn Chute's novel "The Beans of Egypt, Maine." Directorial debut of Warren. 109m/C VHS. Martha Plimpton, Kelly Lynch, Rutger Hauer, Patrick McGaw, Richard Sanders; *D:* Jennifer Warren; *W:* Bill Phillips; *C:* Stevan Larner; *M:* Peter Manning Rob.

The Forbidden Christ 🐾🐾 *Il Cristo Proibito* 1950 Bruno (Valone) returns from the war to his Tuscan village after years as a POW, only to learn his younger brother, a Resistance fighter, was killed by the Nazis after being betrayed by someone in the town. Bruno wants revenge but when no one will help him find the truth, his rage leads him to kill the wrong man. The only film made by writer Malaparte, which was inspired by actual events, was a boxoffice disaster and caused him to abandon future film plans. Italian with subtitles. 98m/B VHS. *IT* Raf Vallone, Gino Cervi, Alain Cuny, Elena Varzi; *D:* Curzio Malaparte; *W:* Curzio Malaparte; *C:* Gabor Pogany; *M:* Curzio Malaparte.

The Forbidden City 🐾🐾 1918 San San is a young Chinese maiden who has the misfortune of falling in love with a Western diplomat. After he is sent away on business San San keeps secret the fact she has born her a child but her actions are unforgiven by her father, a deposed mandarin. 72m/B VHS. Norma Talmadge, Thomas Meighan; *D:* Sidney Franklin.

The Forbidden Dance WOOF! 1990 (PG-13) The first of several quickies released in 1990 applying hackneyed plots to the short-lived Lambada dance craze. The nonsensible plot has a Brazilian princess coming to the U.S. in order to stop further destruction of the rain forest. Instead, she winds up falling for a guy, teaching him to Lambada, and going on TV for a dance contest. Features an appearance by Kid Creole and the Coconuts. 90m/C VHS, DVD. Laura Elena Harring, Jeff James, Sid Haig, Richard Lynch; *D:* Greydon Clark.

Forbidden Fruit 🐾 *Le Fruit Défendu* 1952 Widowed country doctor (Fernandel), who lives with his domineering mother (Sylvie), marries an equally demanding woman (Nollier) and then finds himself involved with a compliant young prostitute (Arnoul). Comic Fernandel does very well with his change of pace role as a very well with his change of pace role as a man whose illusions of middle-class respectability are destroyed. Based on "Letter à Mon Juge" by Georges Simenon. French with subtitles. 103m/B VHS. *FR* Fernandel, Françoise Arnoul, Claude Nollier, Sylvie, Jacques Castelot; *D:* Henri Verneuil; *W:* Jacques Companeez, Jean Manse, Henri Verneuil; *C:* Henri Alekar; *M:* Paul Durand.

Forbidden Games 🐾🐾🐾 *Jeux Interdits* 1952 Famous anti-war drama about two French children play-acting the dramas of war amid the carnage of WWII. Young refugee Fossey sees her parents and dog killed. She meets a slightly older boy whose family takes the girl in. The children decide to bury the animals they have seen killed in the same way that people are buried—even stealing crosses from the cemetery to use over the animal graves. Eventually they are discovered and Fossey is again separated from her newfound home. Acclaimed; available in both dubbed and English-subtitled versions. 90m/B VHS, DVD. *FR* Brigitte Fossey, Georges Poujouly, Amedee, Louis Herbert, Suzanne Courtal, Jacques Marin, Laurence Badie, Andre Wasley, Louis Saintève; *D:* Rene Clement; *W:* Rene Clement, Jean Aurenche, Pierre Bost, Francois Boyer; *C:* Robert Juillard; *M:* Narciso Yepes. Oscars '52: Foreign Film; British Acad. '53: Film; N.Y. Film Critics '52: Foreign Film; Venice Film Fest. '52: Film.

Forbidden Homework 🐾🐾 *La Taree Prohibida* 1992 A young man (Pastor) neects to complete an assignment for his film class and persuades middle-aged Maria (Rojo), a friend of the family, to let him rehearse a scene. What she doesn't know is that he's recording their rehearsal—which happens to be a simulated sexual encounter that turns all too real. Spanish with subtitles. 80m/C VHS, DVD, MX Maria Rojo, Julian Pastor, Esteban Soberanes; *D:* Jaime Humberto Hermosillo; *W:* Jaime Humberto Hermosillo; *C:* Alex Phillips Jr.; *M:* Omar Guzman.

The Forbidden Kingdom 🐾🐾½ 2008 (PG-13) Introduce the kiddies to kung fu action-lite in this mild adventure (that could easily be a PG). Boston teen Jason (Angarano) is magically transported back to ancient China thanks to a golden staff that must be returned to its imprisoned owner, the Monkey King (Li). He's helped by drunken fighter Lu Yan (Chan), orphaned babe Golden Sparrow (Yifei), and a guy known as the Silent Monk (Li again). They're opposed by the Jade Warlord (Chou), white-haired witch Ni Chang (Bing Bing Li), and various evil minions. Plays it safe but it's the first pairing between martial art stars Chan and Li, so that's a treat. 105m/C VHS. *US* Michael Angarano, Jackie Chan, Jet Li, Collin Chou, Bingbing Li, Lu Yifei, Morgan Benoit; *D:* Rob Minkoff; *W:* John Fusco; *C:* Peter Pau; *M:* David Buckley.

Forbidden Love 🐾 1982 A man in his early 20s falls in love with a woman twice his age, much to the chagrin of her daughters. 96m/C VHS, Andrew Stevens, Yvette Mimieux, Dana Elcar, Lisa Lucas, Jerry Houser, Randi Brooks, Lynn Carlin, Hildy Brooks, John Considine; *D:* Steven Hilliard Stern; *M:* Hagood Hardy. **TV**

Forbidden Passion: The Oscar Wilde Movie 🐾🐾 *Oscar* 1985 A British-made look at Wilde's later years, emphasizing his homosexuality and the Victorian repression that accompanied it. 120m/C VHS. *GB* Michael Gambon, Robin Lermitte; *D:* Henry Herbert; *W:* John Hawkesworth; *C:* Garth Tucker; *M:* Carl Davis.

Forbidden Zone 🐾🐾 1980 (R) A sixth dimension kingdom is ruled by a midget, King Fausto, and inhabited by dancing frogs, bikini-clad tootsies, robot boxers, and degraded beings of all kinds. Original music by Ongo Boingo, and directed by founding member Elfman. 75m/B VHS, DVD. Herve Villechaize, Susan Tyrrell, Viva, Marie-Pascale Elfman, Joe Spinell, Richard Elfman, Danny Elfman; *D:* Richard Elfman; *W:* Matthew Bright, Richard Elfman; *C:* Gregory Sandor; *M:* Danny Elfman.

Forbidden Zone: Alien Abduction 🐾 1996 (R) Three babes sharing a sauna also share sexual confidences and discover they've each had an encounter with the same unusual men. Then one of the girls figures out they've had an alien encounter of the very close kind. 90m/C VHS, DVD, Darcy Demoss, Pia Reyes, Dumitri Bogmaz, Carmen Lacatus, Alina Chivulesсu, Flo'ın Chiriac, Meredyth Holmes; *D:* Lucian S. Diaconde; *W:* Vernon Lumley; *C:* Adelfo Bartoli; *M:* Reg Powell.

The Force 🐾 1994 (R) Rookie LAPD cop Cal Warner (Gedrick) crosses paths with maverick homicide detective Des Flynn (Hudson), who's on the trail of a brutal killer. But when Flynn dies mysteriously, it's Cal who's haunted by bizarre dreams—and finding the truth could be dangerous. 88m/C VHS, DVD. Jason Gedrick, Kim Delaney, Gary Hudson, Cyril O'Reilly, Suki Kaiser; *D:* Mark Rosman.

Forbidden Planet 🐾🐾🐾½ 1956 In A.D. 2200, a space cruiser visits the planet Altair-4 to uncover the fate of a previous mission of space colonists. They are greeted by Robby the Robot and discover the only survivors of the Earth colony which have been preyed upon by a deadly space monster. A classic science-fiction version of the Shakespearean classic "The Tempest." 98m/C VHS, DVD, NL. DVD. Walter Pidgeon, Anne Francis, Leslie Nielsen, Warren Stevens, Jack Kelly, Richard Anderson, Earl Holliman, George D. Wallace, Robert Dix, Jack Holland; *D:* Fred M. Wilcox; *W:* Cyril Hume; *C:* George J. Folsey; *M:* Bebe Barron, Louis Barron; *V:* Marvin Miller. *Narr:* Les Tremayne.

The Forbidden Quest 🐾🐾 1993 In 1941, a journalist (Ward) tracks down the only survivor of Holland's 1905 expedition to Antarctica. Maureen's search for the truth soon takes her into forbidden territory, in opposition to the ship's carpenter husband, the detective assigned to the case. 87m/C VHS, DVD. Shannon Tweed, Corbin Timbrook; *D:* Robert Angelo; *W:* Daryl Haney, Hell Styverson; *C:* Michael Goi; *M:* Herman Beeftink.

Forbidden Sins 🐾🐾 1999 (R) Defense attorney Maureen Doherty (Tweed) is hired to defend an arrogant multi-millionaire accused of murdering a stripper during kinky sex games. Maureen's justice is meted out by the girls. 88m/C VHS, DVD, Lauren Hutton, Cliff DeYoung, Renée Estevez; *D:* Zalca Baron.

Forbidden Sun 🐾 1989 (R) An Olympic gymnastics coach and her dozen beautiful students go to Crete to train. When one of them is brutally raped, vengeance is meted out by the girls. 88m/C VHS, DVD. Lauren Hutton, Cliff DeYoung, Renée Estevez; *D:* Zalca Baron.

Forbidden Trails 🐾½ 1941 Rough Riders adventure has Silver the horse saving his owner from the vengeance of two outlaws. Two more heroes go under cover to bring the bad guys to justice. 60m/B VHS, DVD. Buck Jones, Tim McCoy, Raymond Hatton; *D:* Robert North Bradbury.

Forbidden World WOOF! 1982 (R) Lives of a genetic research team become threatened by the very life form they helped to create; a man-eating organism capable of changing its genetic structure as it grows and matures. Corman-produced quickie follow-up to "Alien." 82m/C VHS. Jesse Vint, Dawn Dunlap, June Chadwick, Linden Chiles, Scott Paulin, Michael Bowen; *D:* Allan Holzman; *W:* Jim Wynorski, Tim Curnen, R.J. Robertson; *C:* Tim Suntisext; *M:* Susan Justin.

equally deadly. **94m/C VHS.** Jason Gedrick, Gary Hudson, Cyndi Pass, Kim Delaney; **D:** Mark Rosman; **W:** Randall Frakes, Mitch Marcus; **C:** Jacques Haitkin; **M:** Louis Febre.

Force Five 🦴🦴 **1975** A group of ex-cons form an anti-crime undercover force turning their skills toward justice. Nothing new in this TV pilot. **78m/C VHS.** Gerald Gordon, Nicholas Pryor, James Hampton, David Spielberg, Leif Erickson, Bradford Dillman, Victor Argo; **D:** Walter Grauman. **TV**

Force: Five 🦴 **1981 (R)** Mercenary gathers a group of like-minded action groupies together to rescue the daughter of a powerful man from a religious cult. All action and no brains. **95m/C VHS.** Joe Lewis, Pam Huntington, Master Bong Soo Han; **D:** Robert Clouse; **W:** Robert Clouse; **M:** William Goldstein.

Force of Evil 🦴🦴🦴 **1949** A cynical attorney who works for a mob boss and for Wall Street tries to save his brother from the gangster's takeover of the numbers operation. The honorable, though criminal, brother refuses the help of the amoral lawyer, and he is finally forced to confront his conscience. Garfield's sizzling performance and the atmospheric photography have made this a film noir classic. **82m/B VHS, DVD.** John Garfield, Thomas Gomez, Marie Windsor, Sheldon Leonard, Roy Roberts; **D:** Abraham Polonsky; **W:** Abraham Polonsky; **C:** George Barnes. Natl. Film Reg. '94.

Force of Evil 🦴 **1977** A paroled murderer returns to his hometown to brutalize the family that refused to fabricate an alibi for him. **100m/C VHS.** Lloyd Bridges, Eve Plumb, William Watson. Pat(ricia) Crowley; **D:** Richard Lang. **TV**

Force of Impulse 🦴 **1960** J.D. schlocker featuring an impressive cast involved with everything from hot rods to robbery to parental problems. **84m/B VHS.** J. Carrol Naish, Robert Alda, Tony Anthony, Christina Crawford, Jody McCrea, Lionel Hampton; **D:** Saul Swimmer; **W:** Richard Bernstein, Francis Swann; **C:** Clifford Poland; **M:** Joseph Liebman.

Force of One 🦴🦴 **1979 (PG)** A team of undercover narcotics agents is being eliminated mysteriously, and karate expert Norris saves the day in this sequel to "Good Guys Wear Black." **91m/C VHS, DVD, UMD.** Chuck Norris, Bill Wallace, Jennifer O'Neill, Clu Gulager; **D:** Paul Aaron.

Force on Thunder Mountain 🦴 **1977** A father and son go camping and encounter ancient Indian lore and flying saucers. **93m/C VHS, DVD.** Christopher Cain, Todd Dutson.

Force of the Ninja 🦴🦴 **1988 (R)** When Kazuko Tokugawa (Ball), the daughter of a member of Japan's imperial family, is kidnapped and two of her friends are killed, Kenji (Ivan) is forced to take action. A U.S. agent studying the art of the ninja, he learns that the kidnapping is part of an international arms deal lead by a mercenary named Ryan (Williams). Now Kenji must return home and save the situation using his new warrior skills. **100m/C VHS.** Douglas Ivan, Patricia Ball, Brook Lynne, Lee Thomas; **D:** Emmett Alston; **M:** Dan Slider.

Force 10 from Navarone 🦴🦴 **1978 (PG)** So-so sequel to Alistair MacLean's "The Guns of Navarone," follows a group of saboteurs whose aim is to blow up a bridge vital to the Nazi's in Yugoslavia. Keep an eye out for Ford, Nero, and Bach. Lots of double-crosses and action sequences, but doesn't quite hang together. **118m/C VHS, DVD.** Robert Shaw, Harrison Ford, Barbara Bach, Edward Fox, Carl Weathers, Richard Kiel, Franco Nero; **D:** Guy Hamilton; **W:** Robin Chapman; **C:** Christopher Challis; **M:** Ronald Goodwin.

Forced Entry 🦴 *The Last Victim* **1975 (R)** Psychopathic killer-rapist hesitates over one of his victims, and she murders him instead. **92m/C VHS, DVD.** Tanya Roberts, Ron Max, Nancy Allen; **D:** Jim Sotos.

Forced March 🦴🦴½ **1990** On location in Hungary, an actor portrays a poet who fought in WWII and became a victim of the Holocaust. However, the line between illusion and reality becomes... Flat drama. **104m/C VHS.** Chris Sarandon, Renee Soutendijk, Josef Sommer, John Seitz; **D:** Rick King.

Forced to Kill 🦴🦴½ **1993 (R)** A repo man is on his way to deliver a Jaguar when he's captured by a bizarre family and forced to fight in an illegal bare-fist tournament run by the local lunatic sheriff. Professional stuntman Eubanks has his work cut out for him in this actioner. **91m/C VHS, DVD.** Corey Michael Eubanks, Michael Ironside, Rance Howard, Don Swayze, Clint Howard, Brian Avery, Kari Whitman, Mickey Jones, Carl Ciarfalio, Cynthia J. Blessington, Alan Gelfant; **D:** Russell Solberg; **W:** Corey Michael Eubanks; **M:** Martin D. Bolin.

Forced Vengeance 🦴🦴 **1982 (R)** Vietnam vet pits himself against the underworld in Hong Kong. With Norris in the lead, you can take it for granted there will be plenty of martial arts action. **103m/C VHS, DVD.** Chuck Norris, Mary Louise Weller; **D:** James Fargo; **M:** William Goldstein.

Forces of Nature 🦴🦴 **1999 (PG-13)** Lightweight romantic screwball comedy has straight-laced nice guy Ben (Affleck) trying to get to Savannah in time for his wedding with Tierney. When his plane skids off the runway, he's paired up with free spirit Sarah (Bullock) on an obstacle-filled trip down south. Some fine moments and unusually well done characterization are undone by inconsistency and a lack of chemistry. Enjoyment of the conclusion depends on your opinion of romantic comedy conventions. **104m/C VHS, DVD.** Jack Kehler, Sandra Bullock, Ben Affleck, Maura Tierney, Steve Zahn, Blythe Danner, Ronny Cox, Michael Fairman, Janet Carroll, Richard Schiff, Meredith Scott Lynn, George D. Wallace, John Doe, Steve Hytner, David Strickland; **D:** Bronwen Hughes; **W:** Marc Lawrence; **C:** Elliot Davis; **M:** John Powell.

Ford: The Man & the Machine 🦴🦴½ **1987** Episodic biography of ruthless auto magnate Henry Ford I from the building of his empire to his personal tragedies. The cast lacks spark and Robertson (Ford) is positively gloomy. The only one appearing to have any fun is Thomas (Ford's mistress). Based on the biography by Robert Lacey. **200m/C VHS, DVD.** Cliff Robertson, Hope Lange, Heather Thomas, Michael Ironside, Chris Wiggins, R.H. Thomson; **D:** Allan Eastman; **C:** Thomas Burstyn.

A Foreign Affair 🦴🦴🦴 **1948** Amusing comedy finds straitlaced congresswoman Phoebe Frost (Arthur) heading a committee that travels to Berlin to check on the morale (and morals) of American troops stationed there. Phoebe is suspicious of sultry singer Erika Von Schuetow (Dietrich), whose under the protection of a mysterious American officer. After Phoebe falls for Captain John Pringle (Lund), guess who turns out to be the heel in question? Of course, he's got a perfectly reasonable explanation. **115m/B VHS.** Marlene Dietrich, Jean Arthur, John Lund, Millard Mitchell, Stanley Prager, Peter Von Zerneck, Freddie (Fred) Steele; **D:** Billy Wilder; **W:** Billy Wilder, Charles Brackett, Richard L. Breen; **C:** Charles B(ryant) Lang Jr.; **M:** Frederick "Friedrich" Hollander.

Foreign Affairs 🦴🦴 **1993** Vinnie Miller (Woodward) is a prim New England college teacher off to London on a research sabbatical. On the flight Vinnie's seatmate is boisterous good-ole-boy Chuck Mumpson (Dennehy), with whom she appears to have nothing in common. Naturally the two middle-aged romantics find a funny, though bittersweet, love together. A rather distracting subplot find's Vinnie's young colleague Fred (Stolz) involved in an affair with an older, eccentric British actress (Beacham). Based on the novel by Alison Lurie. **100m/C VHS.** Joanne Woodward, Brian Dennehy, Eric Stoltz, Stephanie Beacham, Ian Richardson, Robert Hardy; **D:** Jim O'Brien; **W:** Chris Bryant; **C:** Michael Coulter. **CABLE**

Foreign Body 🦴🦴½ **1986 (PG-13)** An Indian (played by "Passage to India" star, Banerjee) visiting London pretends to be a doctor and finds women flocking to him. Excellent overlooked British comedy. Based on the novel by Roderick Mann. **108m/C VHS.** GB Victor Banerjee, Warren Mitchell, Trevor Howard, Geraldine McEwan, Amanda Donohoe, Denis Quilley, Eve Ferret, Anna Massey; **D:** Ronald Neame; **W:** Celine La Freniere; **M:** Ken Howard.

Foreign Correspondent 🦴🦴🦴🦴 **1940** A classic Hitchcock tale of espionage and derring-do. A reporter is sent to Europe during WWII to cover a pacifist conference in London, where he becomes romantically involved with the daughter of the group's founder and befriends an elderly diplomat. When the diplomat is kidnapped, the reporter uncovers a Nazi spy-ring headed by his future father-in-law. **120m/B VHS, DVD.** Joel McCrea, Laraine Day, Herbert Marshall, George Sanders, Robert Benchley, Albert Bassermann, Edmund Gwenn, Eduardo Ciannelli, Harry Davenport, Martin Kosleck, Charles Halton; **D:** Alfred Hitchcock; **W:** George Benchley, Charles Bennett, Joan Harrison, James Hilton; **M:** Alfred Newman.

A Foreign Field 🦴🦴½ **1993** Comedy/drama focuses on several WW2 veterans returning on the Normandy beaches in honor of the 50th anniversary of the invasion. Blustery British Cyril (McKern) and equally demanding Yank Waldo (Randolph) also must deal with their 50-year rivalry over their wartime love, the cheerfully vulgar Angelique (Moreau). Veteran performers get the chance to show their stuff but film descends into pathos. **90m/C VHS, DVD.** GB Leo McKern, John Randolph, Jeanne Moreau, Lauren Bacall, Alec Guinness, Edward Hermann, Geraldine Chaplin; **D:** Charles Sturridge; **W:** Roy Clarke; **M:** Geoffrey Burgon.

Foreign Land 🦴🦴 *Terra Estrangeira* **1995** Twenty-one-year-old Paco is an impoverished student living in Sao Paulo who naively agrees to take a suitcase to Lisbon for shady businessman Igor (Melo) and give it to his compatriot, Miguel (Borges). But Paco discovers Miguel has been murdered—leading him to the dead man's girl-friend, unhappy Brazilian exile, Alex (Torres). The two bond while seeking to avoid the newly arrived Igor and Miguel's other treacherous associates. Portuguese with subtitles. **100m/B VHS, DVD,** BR PT Alexandre Borges, Tcheky Karyo, Fernanda Torres, Laura Cardoso, Joao Lagarto, Luis Mello, Fernando Pinto; **D:** Walter Salles; **W:** Walter Salles, Marcos Bernstein, Daniela Thomas; **C:** Walter Carvalho; **M:** Jose Miguel Wisnik.

Foreign Student 🦴🦴½ **1994 (R)** In 1956 Philippe (Hofschneider) is a French exchange student at a traditionbound Virginia college. At a professor's home he meets part-time housekeeper April (Givens), who wants to practice her schoolbook French (among other things). They begin a romance but, since April is black, there's trouble. Hofschneider is charming though Givens appears too glamorous and self-aware. Dutton and Battle are notable in their small roles as blues musicians. Howlin' Wolf and Sonny Boy Williamson. Directorial debut for Sereny. Based on the novel "The Foreign Student" by Philippe Labro. **96m/C VHS.** Marco Hofschneider, Robin Givens, Jack Coleman, Edward Hermann, Rick Johnson, Charlotte Ross, Charles S. Dutton, Hinton Battle; **D:** Eva Sereny; **W:** Menno Meyjes; **C:** Franco Di Giacomo; **M:** Jean-Claude Petit.

The Foreigner 🦴 **1978** Secret agent who comes to New York City to meet his contact becomes entrapped in a series of mysterious events revolving around the underground club scene. **90m/ B VHS, DVD.** Eric Mitchell, Patti Astor, Deborah Harry; **D:** Amos Poe; **W:** Amos Poe.

The Foreigner 🦴🦴 **2003 (R)** Ludicrous would-be actioner stars immovable hulk Seagal as a former spy turned mercenary. His latest job is to carry the black box recorder from a downed plane from France to Germany but the sinister Van Arken (Van Gorkum) has other ideas. **96m/ C VHS, DVD.** Steven Seagal, Harry Van Gorkum, Sherman Augustus, Anna-Louise Plowman; **D:** Michael Oblowitz; **W:** Darren O. Campbell; **C:** Michael Slovis; **M:** David Wurst, Eric Wurst. **VIDEO**

The Foreman Went to France 🦴🦴½ *Somewhere in France* **1942** Industrial engineer travels to France during WWII to help prevent secret machinery from falling into the hands of the Nazis and their allies. **88m/B VHS.** GB Clifford Evans, Constance Cummings, Robert Morley, Gordon Jackson, Ernest Milton, Charles Victor, Mervyn Johns, Bill Blewitt, Paul Bonifas, Ronald Adam; **D:** Charles Frend; **W:** Leslie Arliss, John Dighton, Angus MacPhail; **C:** Wilkie Cooper; **M:** William Walton.

Foreplay woof! *The President's Women* **1975** Inane trilogy of comedy segments involving characters with White House connections. Stories are introduced by former President Mostel discussing his downfall in a TV interview. Lame rather than risque, wasting talents of all involved. Each segment was scripted and directed by a different team. **100m/C VHS, DVD.** Pat Paulsen, Jerry Orbach, Estelle Parsons, Zero Mostel; **D:** Bruce Malmuth, John G. Avildsen; **C:** Ralf Bode.

Forest of Little Bear 🦴🦴 **1987** A man returns to his impoverished family in 1928 and decides to seek the reward put on the head of a one-eared man-eating bear. He kills the bear but faces a dilemma when he sees the bear left a helpless cub behind. In Japanese with English subtitles. **124m/C VHS.** JP Takahiro Tamura, Junko Sakurado, Hiroshi Miyata; **D:** Toshio Goto; **W:** Ryunosuke Ono; **C:** Takaya Yamazaki; **M:** Masaru Sato.

Forest Warrior 🦴🦴 **1995 (PG)** Children fight to save the local forests of Tanglewood Mountain from greedy developer Kiser with the help of ghostly mountain man John McKenna (Norris), who was murdered in the same woods a century before. Mild adventure with good ecology theme. **98m/C VHS,** Chuck Norris, Terry Kiser, Max Gail, Roscoe Lee Browne, William Sanderson; **D:** Aaron Norris; **W:** Ron Swanson; **C:** Joao Fernandes.

Forever 🦴🦴½ **1978** A teenage girl experiences true love for the first time and struggles with its meaning. Adaptation of Judy Blume's novel. **100m/C VHS.** Stephanie Zimbalist, Dean Butler, John Friedrich, Beth Raines, Diana Scarwid; **D:** John Korty. **TV**

Forever: A Ghost of a Love Story 🦴🦴½ **1992 (R)** Coogan is a hot-shot music video director who moves into a haunted house and soon meets the resident ghost, who just happens to be a beautiful woman. He falls for the ghostly presence but his all-too-real female agent is also making her moves. **93m/C VHS.** Keith Coogan, Sean Young, Diane Ladd, Sally Kirkland, Terence Knox, Nicholas Guest, Renee Taylor, Steve Railsback; **D:** Thomas Palmer Jr.; **W:** Thomas Palmer Jr.

Forever Amber 🦴🦴½ **1947** Seventeenth century rags to riches story features Darnell as the poverty stricken girl who uses sex to gain wealth and status. She makes it to the bed of King Charles II, only to lose the one man she ever really loved (Wilde). The censorship of the 1940s hindered the film's erotic potential. Adapted from the best-selling novel by Kathleen Winsor. **140m/C VHS.** Linda Darnell, Cornel Wilde, Richard Greene, George Sanders, Richard Haydn, Jessica Tandy, Anne Revere, John Russell, Leo G. Carroll, Robert Coote, Margaret Wycherly, Alma Kruger, Edmund Breon, Alan Napier, Jane Ball, Richard Bailey, Skelton Knaggs, Norma Varden, Edith Evanson, Ellen Corby; **D:** Otto Preminger; **W:** Philip Dunne, Ring Lardner Jr.; **C:** Leon Shamroy; **M:** David Raksin.

Forever and a Day 🦴🦴🦴 **1943** Tremendous salute to British history centers around a London manor originally built by an English admiral during the Napoleonic era and the exploits of succeeding generations. The house even manages to survive during wartime. Once-in-a-lifetime casting and directing. **104m/B VHS, DVD.** Brian Aherne, Robert Cummings, Ida Lupino, Charles Laughton, Herbert Marshall, Ray Milland, Anna Neagle, Merle Oberon, Claude Rains, Victor McLaglen, Buster Keaton, Jessie Matthews, Roland Young, Sir C. Aubrey Smith, Edward Everett Horton, Elsa Lanchester, Edmund Gwenn; **D:** Rene Clair, Edmund Goulding, Cedric Hardwicke, Frank Lloyd, Victor Saville, Robert Stevenson; **W:** Christopher Isherwood, Gene Lockhart, Donald Ogden Stewart, Charles Bennett, Michael Hogan, Peter Godfrey; **C:** Robert De Grasse, Lee Garmes, Russell Metty, Nicholas Musuraca; **M:** Anthony Collins.

Forever Darling 🐾🐾 1956 Mixed effort from the reliable comedy duo sees Desi playing a dedicated chemist who neglects his wife while pursuing the next great pesticide. Lucy calls on her guardian angel (Mason) to help her rekindle her marriage. He advises her to go with Desi when he tests his new bug killer, and a series of hilarious, woodsy calamities occur. Lucy and Desi are always fun to watch, but '60s TV sitcom fans will enjoy the fact that Mrs. Howell (Schaefer) and Jane Hathaway (Kulp) appear in the same picture. **91m/C VHS, DVD.** Lucille Ball, Desi Arnaz Sr., James Mason, Louis Calhern, John Emery, John Hoyt, Natalie Schafer, Nancy Kulp; **D:** Alexander Hall.

Forever Emmanuelle 🐾 Laure 1975 (R) Sensual young woman finds love and the ultimate erotic experience in the wilds of the South Pacific in this sequel to the porn-with-production-values "Emmanuelle." **89m/C VHS.** IT FR Annie Belle, Emmanuelle Arsan, Al Cliver; **D:** Emmanuelle Arsan, Ovidio G. Assonitis; **W:** Roger Evans; **M:** Franco Micalizzi; **C:** Horacio Fernandez; **M:** Marianne Pendino.

Forever Evil 🐾 1987 The vacation cabin are almost killed off by the cult followers of a mythic god. Predictable, designed to be a tear jerker, though it serves mostly as a star vehicle for Gibson who bumbles with '90s technology, finds his true love, and escapes from government heavies, adorable as ever. Through all the schmaltz, the relations grip Gibson develops with the young Wood turns out to be the most authentic and endearing love in the film. **102m/C VHS, DVD.** Mel Gibson, Jamie Lee Curtis, Elijah Wood, Isabel Glasser, George Wendt, Joe Morton, Nicolas Surcy, David Marshall Grant, Art LaFleur, John David (J.D.) Cullum; **D:** Steve Miner; **W:** J.J. (Jeffrey) Abrams; **C:** Russell Boyc; **M:** Jerry Goldsmith.

Forever Female 🐾🐾🐾 1953 Bright comedy about show business, egos, and love. Holden is a young playwright whose first play is accepted by stage producer Douglas on the condition that the lead role, featuring a 19-year-old heroine, be rewritten for his ex-wife Rogers. She's an aging leading lady smitten by Holden's charms—as is the ingenue Crowley, who would be perfect for the role as written. Complications and manipulations abound as the play makes its way to production. Adaptation of the Sir James Barrie play "Rosalind." **93m/B VHS.** Ginger Rogers, William Holden, Paul Douglas, Patricia Crowley, James Gleason, Jesse White, George Reeves, Marjorie Rambeau, King Donovan, Vic Perrin, Marion Ross; **D:** Irving Rapper; **W:** Julius J. Epstein, Philip G. Epstein. TV

Forever Love 🐾🐾 1998 Lizzie Brooks (McEntire) is a wife and mother who has just awakened from a 20-year coma. Her daughter Emma (Stephens) is a grownup, her husband Peter (Matheson) is a stranger, and she discovers her best friend Gail (Armstrong) has taken her place in both her home and Peter's heart. Now Lizzie seeks to find her own place in a totally new world. Based on a true story. **120m/C VHS.** Reba McEntire, Tim Matheson, Bess Armstrong, Heather Stephens, Richard Biggs, Scott Foley; **D:** Michael Switzer; **W:** Holt Boetman. TV

Forever, Lulu 🐾 1987 Crazy Streets (R) A cown-on-her-luck novelist winds up involved with the mob and a gangster's girlfriend. Completely laughless comedy with amateurish direction. **86m/C VHS, DVD.** Hanna Schygulla, Deborah Harry, Alec Baldwin, Annie Golden, Paul Gleason, Dr. Ruth Westheimer; **D:** Amos Kollek.

Forever Mary 🐾🐾🐾 Mery, per sempre 1989 A teacher tries to better the lives of the boys sentenced to a reformatory in Palermo, Sicily, when a teenage transvestite prostitute (the title character) is admitted to the school. In Italian with English subtitles. **100m/C VHS.** IT Michele Placido, Alessandro DiSanzo, Francesco Benigno; **D:** Marco Risi; **W:** Sandro Petraglia.

Forever Mine 🐾🐾 1999 (R) In 1973, cabana boy Alan (Fiennes) meets Ella (Mol), the seductive young wife of political Mark (Liotta) at the Miami Beach resort where he works. It's lust at first sight but ends badly when Mark discovers the affair. But in 1987, Alan re-enters both their lives with a new identity, a new occupation, and a desire for revenge. Noir wannabe whose story doesn't always hold together (but is at least titillating for the sex scenes) **117m/C VHS, DVD.** Joseph Fiennes, Ray Liotta, Gretchen Mol, Vincent Laresca.

Forever Together 🐾🐾½ Can't Be Heaven 2000 (PG) The perils of young, first love are sweetly explored as fatherless seventh-grader Danny (Burke) thinks he's falling in love with best friend, Julie (Tracenberg). His widowed mom (Ticotin) is having her own romantic troubles, so Danny turns for advice to a friendly jazz musician (Macchio). **88m/C VHS, DVD.** Michelle Trachtenberg, Rachel Ticotin, Ralph Macchio, Shyan Burke, Matt McCoy, Diane Ladd, Garry Marshall; **D:** Richard Friedman. VIDEO

Forever Young 🐾🐾½ 1992 (PG) When test pilot Gibson's girlfriend is hit by a car and goes into a coma, he volunteers to be cryogenically frozen for one year. Oops!—he's left frozen for 50 years, until he's accidentally thawed out by a couple of kids. Predictable, designed to be a tear jerker, though it serves mostly as a star vehicle for Gibson who bumbles with '90s technology, finds his true love, and escapes from government heavies, adorable as ever. Through all the schmaltz, the relationship Gibson develops with the young Wood turns out to be the most authentic and endearing love in the film. **102m/C VHS, DVD.** Mel Gibson, Jamie Lee Curtis, Elijah Wood, Isabel Glasser, George Wendt, Joe Morton, Nicolas Surcy, David Marshall Grant, Art LaFleur, John David (J.D.) Cullum; **D:** Steve Miner; **W:** J.J. (Jeffrey) Abrams; **C:** Russell Boyc; **M:** Jerry Goldsmith.

Forger of London 🐾🐾 1961 Edgar Wallace tale in which Scotland Yard investigates a counterfeit ring connected to a prime suspect, an amnesiac playboy. **91m/C VHS.** GE Eddi Arent, Karin Dor, Viktor de Kowa, Helmut Lange, Robert Graf; **D:** Harald Reinl.

Forget About It 🐾🐾 2006 (PG-13) In a trailer park outside Phoenix, retired war vets Sam (Reynolds), Carl (Loggia), and Eddie (Durning) genially vie for the attention of sexy neighbor Christine (Welch) while enjoying their golden years. Then wiseguy Angelo Nitti (Paloma) is located as part of the Witness Protection Program without admitting that he's stolen four million bucks from his cohorts. When the trio find the cash and begin to live it up, they also find themselves pursued by the mob and the feds. **85m/C DVD.** Burt Reynolds, Raquel Welch, Robert Loggia, Charles Durning, Richard Grieco, Tim Thomerson, Phyllis Diller, Joanna Pacula, Michael Paloma; **D:** B.J. Davis; **W:** Julia Davis; **C:** Mark Trengove.

Forget Mozart 🐾🐾 Zaruditne na Mozara 1985 On the day of Mozart's death, the head of the secret police gathers a group together for questioning. They include the composer's wife, his lyricist, the head of a Masonic lodge, and Salieri, Mozart's rival. Each has a different story to tell to the investigator about the composer's life and death. The film makes use of a number of sets and costumes from "Amadeus" and was also filmed on location in "Prague." In German with English subtitles. **93m/C VHS.** GE Armin Mueller-Stahl, Catarina Raacke; **D:** Salvo Luther.

Forget Paris 🐾🐾½ 1995 (PG-13) Pro basketball referee Mickey (Crystal) and airline executive Ellen (Winger) meet in Paris, fall in love and get married. But once the honeymoon is over, the marital bliss unravels due to conflicting work schedules and the lack of romantic scenery. This look at yuppie love and court-ship finds Crystal in pre-"City Slickers 2" form, launching three-point one-liners and "When Harry Met Sally" sentiment. Bland direction and an obligation to be cute intensify the "been-there-seen-that" feeling. Winger's presence may hint of miscasting, but she has one of the films funniest scenes involving a stray pet and a pigeon. **101m/C VHS, DVD.** Billy Crystal, Debra Winger, Joe Mantegna, Cynthia Stevenson, Richard Masur, Julie Kavner, William Hickey, Cathy Moriarty, John Spencer; **D:** Billy Crystal; **W:** Lowell Ganz, Babaloo Mandel, Billy Crystal; **C:** Don Burgess; **M:** Marc Shaiman.

The Forgotten 🐾🐾 2004 (PG-13) Convoluted conspiracy-minded sci-fi thriller. Telly (Moore) is still acutely grieving over her young son's death in a plane crash 14 months before. Despite the help of hubby Jim (Edwards) and shrink Jack Munce (Sinise). Telly can't let go of the pain until the mementos of her son's life disappears. Now Jim claims they never had a child. Ash (West), the father of a daughter killed on the same flight, can't remember his child and thinks Telly is nuts. But Telly knows she's not—someone is erasing the evidence of her kids' existence and she's going to find out who and why (even if it means getting chased by those nasty men in black). **89m/C VHS, DVD.** Julianne Moore, Dominic West, Gary Sinise, Alfre Woodard, Robert Wisdom, Jessica Hecht, Anthony Edwards, Linus Roache; **D:** Joseph Ruben; **W:** Gerald Di Pego; **C:** Anastas Michos; **M:** James Horner, Paul Kelly.

Forgotten City 🐾🐾 The Vivero Letter 1998 (R) James Wheeler is out to uncover a city from the Mayan civilization, but he faces a rival expedition, an unhappy native tribe, and mysterious disappearances and deaths that point to someone—or something—wanting the city and its treasures to remain undisturbed. Based on the novel "The Vivero Letter" by Desmond Bagley. Filmed on location in Costa Rica. **96m/C VHS, DVD.** Robert Patrick, Fred Ward, Chiara Caselli; **D:** H. Gordon Boos; **W:** Denne Bart Petticlerc, Arthur Sellers; **C:** Fabrizio Lucci. VIDEO

The Forgotten One 🐾½ 1989 (R) An uninspired author and a female reporter become mixed up in a century-old murder and the restless ghost it spawned. **89m/C VHS.** Kristy McNichol, Terry O'Quinn, Blair Parker, Elisabeth Brooks; **D:** Phillip Badger; **C:** James Mathers.

Forever Young 🐾🐾 1985 A young boy immerses himself in Catholicism. Adventure, but he is unaware that the priest's friend is involved with his mother. **85m/C VHS.** GE James Aubrey, Nicholas Gecks, Alec McGowen; **D:** David Drury; **M:** Ray Connolly. TV

The Forgotten 🐾🐾 1989 After 17 years as POWs, six Green Berets are freed, only to face a treacherous government conspiracy aimed at eliminating them. **96m/C VHS.** Keith Carradine, Steve Railsback, Stacy Keach, Pepe Serna, Don Opper, Richard Lawson; **D:** James Keach; **W:** Mark Burt; **C:** Kevin Rowley; **M:** Hal Lindes.

Forgive and Forget 🐾🐾 1999 Macho London construction worker David (Shepherd) can't admit to himself or anyone else that he's gay, including his best mate since childhood, Theo (Simon). But when Theo decides to move in with his girlfriend Hannan (Fraser), David schemes to break them up. He also declares his love by appearing with Theo on a TV talk show, with unforgettable consequences. **96m/C VHS.** DVD. GB Steve John Shepherd, John Simm, Laura Fraser, Maurice Roeves, Ger Ryan, Meera Syal; **D:** Aisling Walsh; **W:** Mark Burt; **C:** Charlie Ordonez.

Forgetting Sarah Marshall 🐾🐾 2008 (R) Apatow produced comedy that stars (and was written by) second-banana Segel. Slacker couch potato Pater is an underachieving L.A. composer of TV music who's devastated when he's dumped by ambitious woebegone Peter eventually decides to vacation at a Hawaiian resort but—tada!—finds Sarah and her new beau, self-absorbed Brit rocker Aldous Snow (Brand), are also guests. Despite frequent humiliations, Peter sticks it out, supported by brunette beauty Rachael (Kunis) and various odd hotel encounters. Segel is more likely to say "get over it already" than be amused. **112m/C DVD.** US Jason Segel, Kristen Bell, Mila Kunis, Bill Hader, Russell Brand, Jonah Hill, Paul Rudd, William Baldwin, Jason Bateman, Maria Thayer, Steve Landesberg, Jack McBrayer, Liz Cackowski, Gedde Waterabe; **D:** Nicholas Stoller; **W:** Jason Segel; **C:** Russ T. Alsobrook; **M:** Lyle Workman.

Forgotten Silver 🐾🐾🐾 1996 Jackson's mockumentary finds the director and co-director Botes "discovering" the lost films of Colin McKenzie, a pioneering New Zealand filmmaker of the early 1920s. These include McKenzie's epic film "Salome" which the duo decide to restore. The entire escapade is a fiction, including the silent film footage that's shown. The tape also includes the short film "Signing Off" and special request he has trouble fulfilling. English subtitles. **131m/C VHS, RU** Leonid Filatov, Tatiana Dogileva, Irina Kupchenko; **D:** Edgar Ryazanov.

A Forgotten Tune for the Flute 🐾🐾🐾 1988 A delightful, Glasnost-era romantic comedy. A bureaucrat caught up in a dull, stuffy existence has a heart attack and winds up falling in love with his nurse. He then must decide to love which beckons him. In Russian with English subtitles. **131m/C VHS, RU** Leonid Filatov, Tatiana Dogileva, Irina Kupchenko; **D:** Edgar Ryazanov.

Forlorn River 🐾½ 1937 Nevada and Weary, two law-abiding men, seek to return their hometown to peace by eliminating a gang of outlaws. Based on a novel by Zane Grey. **62m/B VHS.** Buster Crabbe, June Martel, John D. Patterson, Harvey Stephens, Chester Conklin, Lew Kelly, Syd Saylor; **D:** Charles T. Barton.

Forgotten Warrior 🐾½ 1986 (R) Vengeance is the name of the game as a Vietnam vet tracks down the fellow officer who tried to kill him and shot his commander. **76m/C VHS.** Quincy Frazer, Sam T. Labpuzz, Ron Marchini, Joe Meyer; **D:** Nick Cacas, Charlie Ordonez.

The Formula 🐾½ 1980 (R) Convoluted story about a secret formula for synthetic fuel that meanders its way from the end of WWII to the present. A U.S. soldier and a reclusive oil billionaire. Scott and Brando have one good confrontation scene but the rest of the movie is just hot air. From the novel by Steve Shagan. **117m/C VHS.** Marlon Brando, George C. Scott, Marthe Keller, G.D. Spradlin, Beatrice Straight, John Gielgud, Richard Lynch; **D:** John G. Avildsen.

Formula 51 🐾🐾 The 51st State 2001 (R) Good cast is wasted in this ridiculous yet revolting around drugs and crime lords. Elmo (Jackson) is a pharmacology grad student who loses his ability to work in the field due to a marijuana bust. He ends up toiling for drug kingpin Lizard (Meat Loaf) telling for crack, heroin or ecstasy. After he arranges an unpleasant surprise and invents a drug that is allegedly more powerful thar crack, heroin or ecstasy. Lizard, he flees to Liverpool in an attempt to sell his formula to English criminal Durant (Tomlinson). Aside from the asinine plot, the film is allegedly more plicably forced to parade around in a kilt for most of the film. Just say no. **92m/C VHS, DVD. GB CA** Samuel L. Jackson, Robert Carlyle, Emily Mortimer, Meat Loaf Aday, Sean Pertwee, Ricky Tomlinson, Rhys Ifans; **D:** Ronny Yu, David Wu; **W:** Stel Paviou; **C:** Harg-Seng Poon.

Forgotten Prisoners 🐾🐾 1990 Forgotten Prisoners: The Amnesty Files 1990 (R) Celluloid proof that conviction and true grit do not always entertain. Greenwald—whose credits range from "Xanadu" to "The Burning Bed"—directed this righteous but stationary drama about an Amnesty International official (Silver) who's assigned to look into the incarceration and egregious mistreatment of Turkish citizens. **92m/C VHS.** Ron Silver, Roger Daltrey, Hector Elizondo; **D:** Robert Greenwald; **M:** Brad Fiedel. CABLE

Formula for a Murder ✍ 1985 A very rich but paralyzed woman marries a scheming con artist who plots to kill her and inherit everything. 88m/C VHS. IT Christina Nagy, David Warbeck, Rossano Brazzi; D: Alberto De Martino; C: Gianlorenzo Battaglia; M: Francesco De Masi.

Formula 17 ✍✍ Shi qi sui de tian kong 2004 Classic romantic comedy—that is if you live in director DJ Chen's world set in an apparent hetero-free Taipei. This is a boy meets boy tale about young, attractive, sexually innocent country boy Tien's (Tang) move to the big city in search of love. Soon after arriving he runs into an old friend from home, Yu (Chin), who is a gay club bartender. Naturally he's swept into a hilarious circle of new friends including flamer CC (Jl) and fitness trainer Alan (Yang). Tien meets a hot one-night-stand artist named Bai (Duncan) who deflowers Tien but can't deliver the relationship Tien expects. High energy sino-pop soundtrack and attractive cast carries this light-hearted film. 93m/C DVD. Tony Yang, Duncan, King Chin, Dada Jl, Jimmy Yang, Jason Chang; D: D.J. Chen; W: Rady Fu; C: Chen Huei-Sheng; M: George Chen, Hung Tze-Li.

Forrest Gump ✍✍✍½ 1994 (PG-13) Grandly ambitious and slightly flawed, amounting to a wonderful bit of movie magic. As the intelligence-impaired Gump with a heart of gold and more than enough character and dignity, Hanks supplies another career highlight. Field contributes a nice turn as his dedicated mama (they were last together in "Punchline"), while Sinise is particularly effective as a handicapped Vietnam veteran with a bad attitude. Incredible special effects put Gump in the middle of historic events over a four decade period, but the real story is the life-affirming, non-judgmental power of Gump to transform the lives of those around him. From the novel by Winston Groom. 142m/C VHS, DVD. Tom Hanks, Robin Wright Penn, Sally Field, Gary Sinise, Mykelti Williamson, Haley Joel Osment, Michael Conner Humphreys, Hanna Hall, Sonny Shroyer, Siobhan Fallon, Peter Dobson, Michael Jace, Geoffrey Blake, Mary Ellen Trainor, David Brisbin; D: Robert Zemeckis; W: Eric Roth; C: Don Burgess; M: Alan Silvestri. Oscars '94: Actor (Hanks), Adapt. Screenplay, Director (Zemeckis), Film Editing, Picture, Visual FX; AFI '98: Top 100; Directors Guild '94: Director (Zemeckis); Golden Globes '95: Actor—Drama (Hanks), Director (Zemeckis), Film—Drama; Natl. Bd. of Review '94: Actor (Hanks), Film, Support. Actor (Sinise); Screen Actors Guild '94: Actor (Hanks); Writers Guild '94: Adapt. Screenplay; Blockbuster '95: Movie, T., Drama Actor, T. (Hanks); Blockbuster '96: Drama Actor, V. (Hanks).

Forsaking All Others ✍✍½ 1935 Screwball comedy featuring several MGM superstars. Friends since childhood, Gable has been in love with Crawford for 20 years, but she never realizes it and plans to marry Montgomery. Crawford is very funny in this delightful story of a wacky romantic triangle. 84m/B VHS. Joan Crawford, Clark Gable, Robert Montgomery, Charles Butterworth, Billie Burke, Rosalind Russell, Frances Drake; D: Woodbridge S. Van Dyke; W: Joseph L. Mankiewicz; C: George J. Folsey.

Fort Apache ✍✍✍½ 1948 The first of director Ford's celebrated cavalry trilogy, in which fanatical Lt. Col. Owen Thursday (a decidedly unsympathetic Fonda) leads his reluctant men to an eventual slaughter when he battles Apache chief Cochise (Inclan), recalling George Custer at Little Big Horn. Wayne is his seasoned second-in-command Kirby Yorke, who's unable to prevent what occurs. In residence: Ford hallmarks of spectacular landscapes and stirring action, as well as many vignettes of life at a remote outpost. Don't forget to catch "She Wore a Yellow Ribbon" and "Rio Grande," the next films in the series. 125m/B VHS, DVD. Henry Fonda, John Wayne, Shirley Temple, John Agar, Pedro Armendariz Sr., Victor McLaglen, Ward Bond, Anna Lee, Guy Kibbee, Miguel Inclan, Mae Marsh; D: John Ford; W: Frank Nugent; C: Archie Stout; M: Richard Hageman.

Fort Apache, the Bronx ✍✍✍ 1981 (R) A police drama set in the beleaguered South Bronx of NYC, based on the real-life experiences of two former New York cops who served there. Newman is a decent cop who goes against every kind of criminal and crazy and against his superiors in trying to bring law and justice to a downtrodden community. 123m/C VHS, DVD. Paul Newman, Ed Asner, Ken Wahl, Danny Aiello, Rachel Ticotin, Pam Grier, Kathleen Beller; D: Daniel Petrie; W: Heywood Gould; C: John Alcott; M: Jonathan Tunick.

Fort Saganne ✍ 1984 Charles Saganne (Depardieu), a soldier from a peasant background, is posted to the French Sahara, where he becomes a natural leader. He gains fame and fortune, marries, and then WWI begins. Good, if cliched, adventure saga. Based on the novel by Louis Gardel. French with subtitles. 180m/C VHS. FR Gerard Depardieu, Catherine Deneuve, Philippe Noiret, Sophie Marceau, Michel Duchaussoy; D: Alain Corneau; W: Alain Corneau, Louis Gardel; M: Philippe Sarde.

Fortress ✍ 1985 (R) A teacher and her class are kidnapped from their one-room schoolhouse in the Australian outback. They must use their ingenuity and wits to save their lives in this violent suspense drama. 90m/C VHS, DVD. AU Rachel Ward, Sean Garlick, Rebecca Rigg; D: Arch Nicholson; M: Danny Beckerman. CABLE

Fortress ✍ 1993 (R) How come the future is never a place you'd want to be? Thanks to overpopulation a woman is only allowed one pregnancy. When John and Karen Brennick are caught trying to have a second child they are shipped to the Fortress, an underground prison in the middle of the desert. Discipline is enforced with numerous sadistic toys, including the intestinator, so-called because it's implanted in the stomach of each prisoner and infractions result in excruciating laser-activated pain. Lambert does well with his action hero but it's character actor Smith as the warden, a techno-human with some sick fantasies, who has the real fun in this horrific depiction of the future. 91m/C VHS, DVD. Christopher Lambert, Kurtwood Smith, Loryn Locklin, Lincoln Kilpatrick; D: Stuart Gordon; W: Steve Feinberg, Troy Neighbors, Terry Curtis Fox; C: David Eggby.

Fortress 2: Re-Entry ✍✍ 1999 (R) John Brennick (Lambert) and his wife and son have escaped from a maximum security prison known as The Fortress. But Brennick is re-captured and his new prison is in orbit, 26,000 miles from Earth. Brennick wants to escape here but there's mucho surveillance to overcome (including a camera placed inside his body) and the problem of returning to Earth. 92m/C VHS, DVD. Christopher Lambert, Pam Grier, Patrick Malahide, Nick Bimble; D: Geoff Murphy; W: Steve Feinberg, Troy Neighbors. VIDEO

Fortress of Amerikka ✍✍½ 1989 In the not-too-distant future, mercenaries get their hands on a secret weapon that could allow them to take over the USA. 97m/C VHS, DVD. Gene Le Brock, Kellee Bradley; D: Eric Louzil; W: Eric Louzil; C: Ron Chapman; M: Dave Ouimet.

Fortune and Men's Eyes ✍✍ 1971 (R) Exploitative and depressing film about life in a Canadian prison. A naive young man is sent to prison for marijuana possession and has to make a difficult choice—be regularly sodomized by a man who will protect him or be raped by everyone else. Based on the play by John Herbert. 102m/C VHS. Wendell Burton, Michael Greer, Zooey Hall, Danny Freedman; D: Harvey Hart; W: John Herbert.

The Fortune Cookie ✍✍✍ Meet Whiplash Willie 1966 After receiving a minor injury during a football game, a TV cameraman is convinced by his seedy lawyer brother-in-law to exaggerate his injury and start an expensive lawsuit. A classic, bitter comedy by Wilder. First of several Lemmon-Matthau comedies. 125m/B VHS, DVD. Jack Lemmon, Walter Matthau, Ron Rich, Cliff Osmond, Judi West, Lurene Tuttle; D: Billy Wilder; W: Billy Wilder, I.A.L. Diamond; C: Joseph LaShelle; M: Andre Previn. Oscars '66: Support. Actor (Matthau).

Fortune Dane ✍½ 1986 (PG) Police detective Fortune Dane goes undercover to clear his name after he is framed for murder. 83m/C VHS. Carl Weathers, Adolph Caesar; D: Nicholas Sgarro; W: Charles Correll.

Fortunes ✍✍ 2005 (R) Three thirty-something buddies are having early mid-life crises in this surprisingly appealing comedy-drama. After a bar night, two of the guys impulsively stop at a fortune teller. Married Phil (Hale) is told his young son is in danger and he becomes neurotically overprotective, while Lewis (Urbaniak) becomes a weird recluse after suddenly quitting his stressful job. This leaves cocky James (McGlone) to help out his boys while dealing with a career setback when he fails to get an expected promotion. 91m/C DVD. James Urbaniak, Mike McGlone, Tony Hale, Diana Henry; D: Parker Cross; W: Matt Salzberg; M: Tobin Sprout.

Fortune's Fool ✍ 1921 A beef king and profiteer marries a younger woman and soon discovers the problems that ambition can cause. Silent. 50m/B VHS. GE Emil Jannings, Daguey Servaes, Reinhold Schunzel; D: Reinhold Schunzel.

Fortunes of War ✍✍ 1987 British professor Guy Pringle arrives with his bride, Harriet, to take up a teaching post in the Balkans in 1939. The idealistic Guy soon becomes enmeshed in anti-fascist politics and involved with the local members of the British embassy. When threatened by war they travel to Athens and then Cairo, where Guy's increasing involvement in the political situation, and his neglect of Harriet, causes a crisis in their marriage. Slow-moving drama with some self-centered characters is redeemed by the acting skills of those involved. Based on the autobiographial novels of Olivia Manning. Originally shown on "Masterpiece Theater" on PBS. 160m/C VHS, DVD. GB Kenneth Branagh, Emma Thompson, Rupert Graves, Ronald Pickup, Robert Stephens, Charles Kay, James Villiers, Harry Burton, Ciaran Madden, Diana Hardcastle, Greg Hicks, Alan Bennett, Jeremy Brudell, Jeremy Sinden; D: James Cellan Jones; W: Alan Plater.

Fortunes of War ✍✍ 1994 (R) Peter Kernan (Salinger) is a burned-out relief worker in Thailand. Desperate for money, he agrees to smuggle a rare medicine across the Cambodian border to a rural war lord. Travelling with refugee Khoy Thoun (Ngor) and French Red Cross worker, Johanna (Jenkins), Peter begins to realize his need to do the right thing, even if the cost is high. Filmed on location in Manila. 107m/C VHS, DVD. Matt Salinger, Michael Ironside, Haing S. Ngor, Sam Jenkins, Martin Sheen, Michael Nouri; D: Thierry Notz; W: Mark Lee.

Forty Carats ✍✍½ 1973 (PG) Ullmann plays the just-turned 40 divorcee who has a brief fling with the half-her-age Albert while on vacation in Greece. She figures she'll never see him again but, back in New York, he turns up on the arm of her beautiful daughter (Raffin). Except he's still interested in mom. The rest of the movie is spent trying to convince Ullmann that love can conquer all. Ullmann's very attractive but not well-suited for the part; Raffin's screen debut. Based on the Broadway hit. 110m/C VHS. Liv Ullmann, Edward Albert, Gene Kelly, Binnie Barnes, Deborah Raffin, Nancy Walker; D: Milton Katselas; W: Jay Presson Allen; C: Charles B(ryant) Lang Jr.

40 Days and 40 Nights ✍✍½ 2002 (R) Abstinence comedy has womanizer Matt (Hartnett) suffering from a brutal romantic break-up, so for Lent he vows to go cold turkey in the sack. His always-supportive friends and co-workers rush to place odds on when Matt's self-control will eventually crumble, even posting his progress on the Internet. With babes aplenty seemingly everywhere, Matt's vow is really tested when, of course, he meets the girl of his dreams (Sossamon). Director Lehmann deftly directs the crew of likeable characters, keeping things light and moving along. Memorable funny scenes includes a dinner with Matt's dad describing sex with a hip replacement, and any with Bagel Guy (Maronna). 94m/C VHS, DVD. US Josh Hartnett, Shannyn Sossamon, Maggie Gyllenhaal, Vinessa Shaw, Paulo Costanzo, Glenn Fitzgerald, Emmanuelle Vaugier, Michael Maronna, Mary Gross, Stanley Anderson, Adam Trese, Barry Newman, Griffin Dunne, Monet Mazur, Dylan Neal, Chris Gauthier; D: Michael Lehmann; W: Rob Perez; C: Elliot Davis; M: Rolfe Kent.

Forty Days of Musa Dagh ✍✍ 1985 Based on the true story of Armenia's fight for freedom against Turkey in the 1914 uprising and the dreadful cost. From the novel by Franz Werfel. 120m/C VHS. Kabir Bedi, Maurice Sherbanee, Ronnie Carol, Victoria Woodbeck, Michael Constantine, David Opatoshu; D: Sarky Mouradian; W: Alex Hakobian; C: Gregory Sandor; M: Jaime Mendoza-Nava.

48 Angels ✍✍½ 2006 (PG-13) Nine-year-old Seamus (newcomer Flynn) is terminally ill. Inspired by the story of Saint Columcille, he sets off in a rowboat to find God and ask for a miracle. When Seamus meets wounded Darry (Brolly) and teenaged runaway James (Travers), the unlikely trio decides to stay together and help each other. Touching but not maudlin story; beautiful Irish scenery. 90m/C DVD. IR Shane Brolly, John Travers, Darragh Kelly, Ciaran Flynn; D: Marion Comer; W: Marion Comer; M: Patrick Duffner.

44 Minutes: The North Hollywood Shootout ✍✍½ 2003 (R) In 1997, two heavily-armed, media-junkie bank robbers (Bryniarski, Taktarov) hold the ill-prepared LAPD at bay for 44 minutes when their heist goes wrong. Told from the point-of-view of various officers, detectives, and SWAT team members called to the scene. 120m/C VHS, DVD. Michael Madsen, Ron Livingston, Mario Van Peebles, Andrew Bryniarski, Oleg Taktarov, Ray Baker, Douglas Spain, Alex Meneses, Dale Dye, J.E. Freeman; D: Yves Simoneau; W: Tim Metcalfe; C: David Franco; M: George S. Clinton. CABLE

Forty Guns ✍✍½ 1957 Typically over-the-top Fuller production filled with melodrama, violence, and lots of sexual innuendo. Griff (Sullivan), Wes (Barry), and Chico (Dix) are lawmen out to arrest Brockie (Ericson), the nasty younger brother of tough, whip-cracking Jessica Drummond (Stanwyck). Jessica basically owns and runs everything and everyone around her with the help of her hired guns. Griff falls for this western wildcat, making his job more difficult. A climactic shootout helps the movie live up to its title. 79m/B DVD. Barbara Stanwyck, Barry Sullivan, Gene Barry, Robert Dix, John Ericson, Dean Jagger, Eve Brent; D: Samuel Fuller; W: Samuel Fuller; C: Joseph Biroc; M: Harry Sukman.

The Forty-Niners ✍ 1932 A forgettable oater about the hysteria surrounding the finding of gold in California. 59m/B VHS. Tom Tyler, Betty Mack, Alan Bridge, Fern Emmett, Gordon Wood, Frank Ball; D: John P. McCarthy.

The Forty-Ninth Parallel ✍✍✍ The Invaders 1941 Six Nazi servicemen, seeking to reach neutral American land, are trapped aboard their U-boat sunk by Royal Canadian Air Force bombers, forcing them into Canada on foot, where they run into an array of stalwart patriots. Dated wartime propaganda made prior to the U.S. entering the war, riddled with entertaining star turns. **90m/B VHS, DVD, GB** Laurence Olivier, Leslie Howard, Eric Portman, Raymond Massey, Glynis Johns, Finlay Currie, Anton Walbrook; **D:** Michael Powell; **W:** Emeric Pressburger, Rodney Ackland. Oscars '42: Story.

40 Pounds of Trouble ⅋⅋½
1962 Lake Tahoe casino/hotel manager Steve McCluskey (Curtis) likes to avoid complications in his life. But first he's charmed by his boss niece Chris (Pleshette), the hotel's new headliner, and then he becomes a surrogate father to five-year-old Penny (Wilcox), abandoned by her dad-ridden dad. So what does Steve decide to do? Why take them to Disneyland, of course! Director Jewison's feature film debut. **106m/C VHS,** Tony Curtis, Suzanne Pleshette, Claire Wilcox, Phil Silvers, Larry Storch, Howard Morris, Stubby Kaye, Edward Andrews, Mary Murphy, Kevin McCarthy, Sharon Farrell; **D:** Norman Jewison; **W:** Marion Hargrove; **M:** Mort Lindsey.

42nd Street ⅋⅋⅋ 1933 A Broadway musical producer faces numerous problems in his efforts to reach a successful opening night. Choreography by Busby Berkeley. A colorized version of the film is also available. ♫You're Getting to Be a Habit with Me; Shuffle off to Buffalo; Young and Healthy; 42nd Street; It Must Be June. **89m/B VHS, DVD.** Warner Baxter, Ruby Keeler, Bebe Daniels, George Brent, Dick Powell, Guy Kibbee, Ginger Rogers, Una Merkel, Busby Berkeley, Ned Sparks, George E. Stone; **D:** Lloyd Bacon; **W:** Rian James, James Seymour; **C:** Sol Polito; **M:** Harry Warren, Al Dubin. Natl. Film Reg. '98.

.45 ⅋⅋ 2006 (R) New York bad girl Kat (Jovovich) hates being controlled by her violent, gun-selling boyfriend Big Al (MacFayden). She stars making her own deals and is willing to go to any lengths to break free, with the help of the hopelessly-devoted Riley (Dorff) and her lesbian friend Vic (Strange). Good tough role for Jovovich in a woman's revenge flick. **97m/C DVD.** Milla Jovovich, Stephen Dorff, Angus MacFadyen, Aisha Tyler, Sarah Strange, Vincent Laresca; **D:** Gary Lennon; **W:** Gary Lennon; **C:** Teodoro Maniaci; **M:** John Robert Wood.

VIDEO

Forty Shades of Blue ⅋⅋½
2005 Character study set in Memphis in which music industry legend Alan James (Tom), his much younger Russian live-in, Laura (Korzun), and adult son from a previous marriage, Michael (B.rows) are brought together when Alan is given a prestigious music industry award. The film unwinds painfully slowly as each character's flawed motivations and dark compromises are examined. Use of local music is a high point in this Sundance award winner. **107m/C DVD, US** Rip Torn, Dina Korzun, Darren E. Burrows, Paprika Steen, Red West, Jennifer O'Hara; **D:** Ira Sachs; **W:** Ira Sachs; **M:** Michael Rohayn, Dickon Hinchliffe.

Forty Thousand
Horsemen ⅋⅋½ 1941 The story of the ANZACS of Australia, created to fight Germany in the Middle East during WWII. This Australian war drama is full of cavalry charges, brave young lads, and "Waltzing Matilda." **86m/B VHS.** Au Chips Rafferty, Grant Taylor, Betty Bryant, Pat Twohill; **D:** Charles Chauvel; **W:** Elsa Chauvel; **C:** George Heath; **M:** Lindley Evans.

The 40 Year Old Virgin ⅋⅋⅋
2005 (R) Forty year old Andy (Carrell) is a virgin, obsessed with pre-teen pursuits like video games, action heroes and collectibles. His work buddies find out his terrible secret and take on the task of initiating Andy into the world of adulthood and sex. Yes, it's raunchy and sophomoric, but the underlying sweetness and the well-done slapstick humor are worth it. Along with "Wedding Crashers," helped bring back the successful R-rated comedy. **116m/C DVD. HD DVD.** *US* Steven Carell, Catherine Keener, Paul Rudd, Romany Malco, Elizabeth Banks, Leslie Mann, Jane Lynch, Seth Rogen, Kat Dennings, David Koechner, Loudon Wainwright III; **D:** Judd Apatow; **W:** Steven Carell, Judd Apatow; **C:** Jack N. Green; **M:** Lyle Workman. L.A. Film Critics '05: Actress (Keener).

Foul Play ⅋⅋⅋ 1978 (PG) Hawn is a librarian who picks up a hitchhiker which leads to nothing but trouble. She becomes involved with San Francisco detective Chase in an effort to expose a plot to kill the Pope during his visit to the city. Also involved is Moore as an English orchestra conductor with some kinky sexual leanings. Chase is charming (no mugging here) and Hawn both bubbly and brave. A big winner at the boxoffice; features Barry Manilow's hit tune "Ready to Take a Chance Again." **116m/C VHS, DVD.** Goldie Hawn, Chevy Chase, Dudley Moore, Burgess Meredith, Billy Barty, Rachel Roberts, Eugene Roche, Brian Dennehy, Chuck McCann, Bruce Solomon, Marc Lawrence, Don Calfa, Marilyn Sokol, Frances Bay; **D:** Colin Higgins; **W:** Colin Higgins; **C:** David M. Walsh; **M:** Charles Fox.

Found Alive ⅋ 1934 After a painful divorce, a woman kidnaps her son and steals away into the Mexican jungle, but only with the help of her faithful butler. **65m/B VHS.** Barbara Bedford, Maurice Murphy, Robert Frazer; **D:** Charles Hutchison.

The Fountain ⅋⅋ 2006 (PG-13) Given the pic's long and troubled production history, maybe Aronofsky getting anything onscreen is a miracle. Of course this fantastical odyssey may be considered as a new "2001" and best seen by an audience in the same trippy condition. Anyway, Jackman and Weisz tackle three time periods and three characters but not in a linear fashion. In the 16th-century, Spanish conquistador Tomas is dispatched by Queen Isabel to find the Tree of Life worshipped by the Mayans. In the

---

47 Ronin, Part 1 ⅋⅋⅋ *The Loyal 47 Ronin; 47 Samurai* 1942 Turn of the 18th-century epic chronicling the samurai legend. The warriors of Lord Asano plan to avenge their leader, tricked into committing a forced seppuku, or hara-kiri. The photography is generously laden with views of 18th century gardens as well as panoramic vistas. This is the largest and most popular film of the Kabuki version of the story by Seika Mayama. In Japanese with English subtitles. **111m/C VHS, DVD.** *JP* Yoshisaburo Arashi, Utaemon Ichikawa, Chojuro Kawarazaki, Kunitaro Kawarazaki, Mantoyo Mimasu, Mieko Takamine; **D:** Kenji Mizoguchi; **W:** Yoshikata Yoda; **C:** Kohei Sugiyama; **M:** Shiro Fukai.

47 Ronin, Part 2 ⅋⅋⅋ 1942 Second half of the film in which the famous Japanese folklore tale of Lord Asano and his warriors is told. The film follows Asano's samurai as they commit themselves to avenging their leader in 1703. In Japanese with English subtitles. **108m/C VHS, DVD.** *JP* Yoshisaburo Arashi, Utaemon Ichikawa, Chojuro Kawarazaki, Kunitaro Kawarazaki; **D:** Kenji Mizoguchi; **W:** Kenchiro Hara, Yoshikata Yoda; **C:** Kohei Sugiyama; **M:** Shiro Fukai.

48 Hrs. ⅋⅋⅋ 1982 (R) An experienced San Francisco cop (Nolte) springs a convict (Murphy) from jail for 48 hours to find a vicious murdering escaped con. Murphy's film debut is great and Nolte is perfect as his gruff foil. **97m/C VHS, DVD.** Nick Nolte, Eddie Murphy, James Remar, Annette O'Toole, David Patrick Kelly, Sonny Landham, Brion James, Denise Crosby; **D:** Walter Hill; **W:** Walter Hill, Larry Gross, Steven E. de Souza, Roger Spottiswoode; **M:** James Horner.

48 Hours to Live ⅋ *Men in the Midnite* 1960 A reporter travels to a nuclear scientist's secluded island only to find the scientist held hostage by nuclear weapon-seeking terrorists. **86m/B VHS.** *SW* Anthony Steel, Ingemar Johansson, Marlies Behrens; **D:** Peter Bourne; **W:** Peter Bourne; **C:** Bengt Lindstrom; **M:** Harry Arnold.

---

47 Ronin, Part 1 *The Loyal 47 Ronin; 47 Samurai* 1942 Turn of the 18th-century epic chronicling the samurai legend. [continued]

Four Adventures of Reinette and Mirabelle ⅋⅋⅋ 1989 Small but touching Rohmer tale of the friendship between two women—one a naive country girl (Miquel, as Reinette), the other a sophisticated Parisian (Forde, as Mirabelle)—who share an apartment and a number of experiences, but who have a very different manner of inhabiting those experiences. A thoroughly French human comedy, one of Rohmer's better studies. In French with English subtitles. **95m/C VHS, DVD.** *FR* Joelle Miquel, Jessica Forde, Philippe Laudenbach, Marie Rivière, Beatrice Romand, Emily Baer; **C:** Joaquin Baca-Asay; **M:** Jason Frederick.

Four Bags Full ⅋⅋ 1956 A bitter comedy about two smugglers during WWII who try to get a slaughtered pig to the black market under the Nazis' noses. In French with English subtitles. **82m/C VHS, FR** Jean Gabin, Louis de Funes, Andre Bourvil, Jeanette Batti; **D:** Claude Autant-Lara.

Four Brothers ⅋⅋½ 2005 (R) Urban remake of "The Sons of Katie Elder." Mama Mercer (Flanagan) is gunned down in a Detroit market hold-up, which brings her four adopted sons, two white and two black, to reunite and avenge her not-so-accidental death, leading to an elaborate conspiracy implicating the upper echelons of Motor City politics. For all its action scenes, violence and verbal ugliness, the final result is disappointing. **109m/C DVD, Blu-ray Disc, UMD, HD DVD.** *US* Mark Wahlberg, Andre Benjamin, Tyrese Gibson, Garrett Hedlund, Josh Charles, Chiwetel Ejiofor, Fionnula Flanagan, Terrence Howard, Sofia Vergara, Taraji P. Henson, Barry (Shabaka) Henley, Kenneth Welsh; **D:** John Singleton; **W:** David Elliot, Paul Lovett; **C:** Peter Menzies Jr.

Four Daughters ⅋⅋⅋ 1938 Classic, three-hankie outing in which four talented daughters of music professor Reins fall in love and marry. Garfield shines, in a role tailor-made for him, as the world-weary suitor driven to extremes in the name of love. Great performances from all. Based on the novel "Sister Act" by Fannie Hurst. **90m/B VHS.** Claude Rains, John Garfield, May Robson, Priscilla Lane, Lola Lane, Rosemary Lane, Gale Page, Dick Foran, Jeffrey Lynn, Frank McHugh; **D:** Michael Curtiz; **M:** Max Steiner.

Four Days ⅋⅋½ 1999 (R) Four-year-old Simon (Zegers) is devoted to his small-time crook dad Milt (Forsythe) who's just double-crossed his partner, Fury (Meany), in a bank robbery after arranging for Simon to get the money and meet him in a pre-selected location. But

---

47 Ronin, Part 1 *The Loyal 47 Samurai* 1942 Turn of the 18th century, who is trying to cure his dying wife, Izzi, who is writing a novel called "The Fountain." And in the 26th century, Tom is floating in a space bubble towards a nebula and Izzi shows up in his dreams. Or something. Feel free to interpret as you wish or just call it hooey and forget it. **95m/C DVD, Blu-ray Disc, HD DVD, UMD.** *US* Hugh Jackman, Rachel Weisz, Ellen Burstyn, Clifford Curtis, Mark Margolis; **D:** Darren Aronofsky; **W:** Darren Aronofsky; **C:** Matthew Libatique; **M:** Clint Mansell.

The Fountainhead ⅋⅋⅋ 1949 Cooper is an idealistic, uncompromising architect who refuses to change his design. When he finds out his plans 'for a public housing project have been radically altered he blows up the building and winds up in court defending his actions. Neal is the sub-plot love interest. Based on the novel by Ayn Rand. **113m/C VHS, DVD.** Gary Cooper, Patricia Neal, Raymond Massey, Ray Collins, Henry Hull, Robert Douglas, Kent Smith, Moroni Olsen, Ann Doran; **D:** King Vidor; **C:** Robert Burks; **M:** Max Steiner.

Four and a Half
Women ⅋⅋½ *Chocolate for Breakfast* 2005 Cute comedy about four roommates dealing with the day-to-day shuffle of being young, female, and running wild around the Big Apple. Things get complicated when one of the girls becomes pregnant after a one-night-stand and decides to keep the baby. **125m/C VHS, DVD.** *US* Gillies, Marin Hinkle, Callie (Calliope) Thorne, Isabelle Maron; **D:** Emily Baer; **W:** Yasmine Haury; **C:** Eric Rohmer.

---

present, Tommy is a medical researcher who is trying to cure his dying wife, Izzi, and Fury is on his trail—at least Simon has gotten a lift from over-sexed Crystal (Davidovitch), so things may not be so bad. Based on the novel by John Buell. **88m/C VHS, CA** Kevin Zegers, Lolita (David) Davidovich, Colm Meaney, William Forsythe, Anne-Marie Cadieux, Patrick Goyette; **D:** Curtis Wehrfritz; **W:** Pickney Benedict; **C:** Miroslaw Baszak; **M:** Tom Third.

Four Days in July ⅋⅋ 1985 Two couples from Belfast, one Catholic and one Protestant, find they have something in common when they meet with a Marxist revolutionary group protesting the Depression. Comedy and action combine with elements of strong language, strong sex, and strong violence. **97m/C VHS, DVD.** *GB* Des McAleer, Brid Brennan, Charles Lawson, Paula Hamilton, Shane Connaughton, Eileen Pollock, Stephen Rea; **D:** Mike Leigh. TV

Four Days in September ⅋⅋ 1997 (R) Based on the true story of Charles Burke Elbrick (Arkin), the American ambassador to Brazil who, in 1969, was kidnapped by four idealistic students, part of a group of political prisoners who's expecting the goods. So they come up with another scheme that involves collecting on another's life insurance policies (to pay off the gangster)—which means one of them will have to die. Sketchy thriller. **99m/C VHS, DVD.** Olivia Williams, Balthazar Getty, Stacy Edwards, Danie London, Tim Curry, Forest Whitaker, George Lazenby, John Taylor; **D:** Paul Rachman; **W:** Thomas Durham, William Quist; **C:** Claudio Rocha; **M:** Brian Tyler, Scott Hackwith.

Four Dogs Playing
Poker ⅋½ 2000 (R) Four friends plan an art heist and then lose the prize, which gets them into trouble with the gangster who's expecting the goods. So they come up with another scheme that involves collecting on another's life insurance policies (to pay off the gangster)—which means one of them will have to die. Sketchy thriller. **98m/C VHS, DVD.** Olivia Williams, Balthazar Getty, Stacy Edwards, Danie London, Tim Curry, Forest Whitaker, George Lazenby, John Taylor; **D:** Paul Rachman; **W:** Thomas Durham, William Quist; **C:** Claudio Rocha; **M:** Brian Tyler, Scott Hackwith.

Four Deuces ⅋⅋ 1975 Gang war is underway between the Chico Hamilton mob and Vic Morano and the Four Deuces during the Depression, part of a Marxist revolutionary group protesting their government's military dictatorship. Their leader, Fernando Gabeira (Cardoso), wants the release of political prisoners and gives the government four days to meet his terms. Adapted from the book "What's Up, Comrade?" by Gabeira. **105m/C VHS, DVD, BR** Alan Arkin, Pedro Cardoso, Marco Ricca, Fernenca Torres; **D:** Bruno Barreto; **W:** Leopoldo Serrari; **C:** Felix Monti; **M:** Stewart Copeland.

---

unbeknownst to Simon, Milt has been killed and Fury is on his trail—at least Simon has gotten a lift from over-sexed Crystal (Davidovitch) [continued]

Four Faces West ⅋⅋½ 1948 McCrea is an honest rancher who nevertheless robs the local bank in order to save his father's ranch from foreclosure. His humanity in helping a diphtheria-ridden family leads to his capture, but the sheriff promises a light sentence, since 'ne is not a typical bad guy. Fine performances strengthen this low-key western. **90m/B VHS, DVD.** Joel McCrea, Frances Dee, Charles Bickford; **D:** Alfred E. Green.

The Four Feathers ⅋⅋⅋ 1939 A grand adventure from a story by A.E.W. Mason. After resigning from the British Army a young man is branded a coward and given four white feathers as symbols of his disgrace. Determined to prove them wrong he joins the Sudan campaign of 1898 and rescues each of the men from

Four Eyes and Six
Guns ⅋⅋½ 1993 In 1882 a New York optometrist, who's a fan of the popular dime-store western novels, moves to Tombstone, Arizona, in search of adventure. He's just in time, too, because Wyatt Earp is trying to rid the town of those pesky Dcom Brothers but is having a problem with his eyesight (causing his gunshots to go astray). Now if the green-horn can just get Earp to wear his new glasses. Silly but harmless fluff. **92m/C VHS.** Judge Reinhold, Patricia Clarkson, Dan Hedaya, M. Emmet Walsh, Austin Pendleton, Fred Ward; **D:** Piers Haggard; **W:** Leon Prochnik. **CABLE**

certain death. They then take back their feathers as does his girl upon learning of his true courage. Excellent performances by Smith and Richardson. **99m/C VHS, DVD.** *GB* Alexander Knox, John Clements, Ralph Richardson, Sir C. Aubrey Smith, June Duprez, Donald Gray, Jack Allen, Allan Jeayes, Frederick Culley, Hal Walters, Henry Oscar, John Laurie, Clive Baxter, Robert Rendel, Derek Elphinstone, Norman Pierce, Amid Taffazani, Archibald Batty, Hay Petrie; *D:* Zoltan Korda; *W:* R.C. Sherriff, Lajos Biro, Arthur Wimperis; *C:* Osmond H. Borradaile, Georges Perinal, Jack Cardiff; *M:* Miklos Rozsa.

The Four Feathers 1978 Determined to return the symbols of cowardice, four feathers, to his friends and fiancee, a man courageously saves his friends' lives during the British Sudan campaign and regains the love of his lady, in this fifth remake of the story. **95m/C VHS, DVD.** Beau Bridges, Jane Seymour, Simon Ward, Harry Andrews, Richard Johnson, Robert Powell; *D:* Don Sharp. **TV**

The Four Feathers 2002 (PG-13) Featherweight remake has Ledger as Harry, a British officer in the late 1800's in love and engaged to marry hottie Ethne (Hudson), sporting an unfortunate English accent). Best friend and fellow officer Jack (Bentley) also fancies English muffin Ethne, unbeknownst to Harry. When Harry resigns from service with battle in the Sudan looming, he's labeled a coward and given four white feathers as a sign of his cowardice. Ditched and dissed, a suitably shamed Harry, determined to prove his courage, disguises himself as an African native (Riiight) and implausible, but action scenes are well done. Based on A.E.W. Mason's 1902 novel. **130m/C VHS, DVD.** *US* Heath Ledger, Wes Bentley, Kate Hudson, Djimon Hounsou, Michael Sheen, Kris Marshall, Rupert Penry-Jones, Tim Pigott-Smith, Alex Jennings; *D:* Shekhar Kapur; *W:* Michael Schiffer, Hossein Amini; *C:* Robert Richardson; *M:* James Horner.

Four for Texas 1963 Perhaps Aldrich's later success with "The Dirty Dozen" can be attributed, in part, to his exercise in how not to make a comic western; poorly made, over long, and far too dependant on the feminine charisma of Ekberg and Andress. Slow-moving Sinatra-Martin vehicle tells the tale of con men in the Old West who battle bandits and bad bankers for a stash of loot. **124m/C VHS, DVD.** Frank Sinatra, Dean Martin, Anita Ekberg, Ursula Andress, Charles Bronson, Victor Buono, Jack Elam, Arthur Godfrey, Moe Howard, Larry Fine, Joe DeRita; *D:* Robert Aldrich; *W:* Robert Aldrich, Teddi Sherman; *C:* Ernest Laszlo; *M:* Nelson Riddle.

Four Friends 1981 (R) *Georgia's Friends* 1981 The magical good and bad dream of the 1960s is remembered in this story of four friends. A young woman and the three men in love with her first come together in high school and then separate, learning from college, war and drug abuse, and each other in this ambitious movie from Steve Tesich, the writer of "Breaking Away." Good performances by all. **114m/C VHS, DVD.** James Leo Herlihy, Craig Wasson, Jodi Thelen, Michael Huddleston, Jim Metzler, Reed Birney; *D:* Arthur Penn; *W:* Steve Tesich; *C:* Ghislan Cloquet.

The Four Horsemen of the Apocalypse 1921 Silent classic and star maker for Valentino concerning an Argentine family torn apart by the outbreak of WWI. Valentino is a painter who moves from his native Argentina to France and is persuaded to enlist by a recruiter who invokes the image of the Biblical riders. His excellence as a soldier, however, proves to be his undoing. The 1962 remake can't hold a candle to original, adapted from a novel by Vicente Blasco-Ibanez. **110m/B VHS.** Rudolph Valentino, Alice Terry, Pomeroy Cannon, Josef Swickard, Alan Hale, Mabel van Buren, Nigel de Brulier, Bowditch Turner, Wallace Beery, Bridgetta Clark, Virginia Warwick, Stuart Holmes, John St. Polis, Mark Fenton, Derek Ghent; *D:* Rex Ingram; *W:* June Mathis; *C:* John Seitz; *M:* Louis F. Gottschalk. Natl. Film Reg. '95.

The Four Horsemen of the Apocalypse 1962 The members of a German family find themselves fighting on opposite sides during WWII. This remake of the vintage Valentino silent failed at the boxoffice, with complaints about its length, disjointed script, and uninspired performances. The title refers to the horrors of conquest, pestilence, war, and death. Adapted from the book by Vincente Blasco-Ibanez. **153m/C VHS, DVD.** Glenn Ford, Charles Boyer, Lee J. Cobb, Paul Henreid, Yvette Mimieux; *D:* Vincente Minnelli; *W:* John Gay; *C:* Milton Krasner; *M:* Andre Previn.

The 400 Blows 1978 *Les Quatre Cents Coups* 1959 The classic, groundbreaking semi-autobiography that initiated Truffaut's career and catapulted him to international acclaim, about the trials and rebellions of 12-year-old French schoolboy, Antoine Doinel (Leaud). One of the greatest and most influential of films, and the first of Truffaut's career-long Doinel series. French with subtitles. **97m/B VHS, DVD.** *FR* Francois Truffaut, Jean-Pierre Leaud, Claire Maurier, Albert Remy, Guy Decomble, Georges Flament, Patrick Auffay, Jeanne Moreau, Jean-Claude Brialy, Jacques Demy, Robert Beauvais; *D:* Francois Truffaut; *W:* Francois Truffaut, Marcel Moussey; *C:* Henri Decae; *M:* Jean Constantin. Cannes '59: Director (Truffaut); N.Y. Film Critics '59: Foreign Film.

Four in a Jeep 1951 In Vienna in 1945, soldiers from different countries are serving as an international military police force. They clash as a result of political demands and their love for the same woman. Shot on location in Austria. **83m/B VHS.** Ralph Meeker, Viveca Lindfors, Joseph Yadin, Michael Medwin; *D:* Leopold Lindberg.

Four Jacks and a Jill 1941 Four musicians are left in the lurch when their band singer leaves them for her gangster boyfriend and they must frantically search for a replacement. Not completely uninteresting, but rather bland and old now. Earlier versions of the story were released as "Street Girl" and "That Girl from Paris." ♪I'm in♪ "Good Shape For the Shape I'm In; You Go Your Way and I'll Go Crazy; I Haven't A Thing to Wear; Wherever You Are; Boogie Woogie Conga. **68m/B VHS.** Anne Shirley, Ray Bolger, Desi Arnaz Sr., Jack Durant, June Havoc, Eddie Foy Jr., Fritz Feld; *D:* Jack B. Hively.

Four Last Songs 2006 Lounge pianist Larry (Tucci) is trying for musical acclaim by holding a tribute concert to a late classical composer, who was a native of his Mediterranean resort town. However, life keeps getting in his way. There's his long-lost daughter, neurotic lovers and friends, and eccentric neighbors ruining his big chance. Lots of overacting. **110m/C DVD.** *GB SP* Stanley Tucci, Rhys Ifans, Hugh Bonneville, Jena Malone, Jessica Stevenson, Marisa Paredes, Emmanuelle Seigner, Karl Johnson, Virgile Bramly; *D:* Francesca Joseph; *W:* Francesca Joseph; *C:* Javier Salmones; *M:* Dan (Daniel) Jones.

Four Men and a Prayer 1938 The four Leigh brothers (Greene, Sanders, Niven, Henry) seek the truth behind their colonel father's (Smith) dismissal from military service in India and his alleged suicide, which they believe was murder. Stiff upper lips prevail as the siblings travel from India to Argentina to Egypt and back home to England to restore the family honor. **85m/B DVD.** Richard Greene, George Sanders, David Niven, William Henry, Sir C. Aubrey Smith, Loretta Young, Alan Hale Jr., John Carradine, Reginald Denny, J. Edward Bromberg, Berton Churchill, Barry Fitzgerald; *D:* John Ford; *W:* Sonya Levien, Richard Sherman, Walter Ferris; *C:* Ernest Palmer.

Four Minute Mile 1988 Four athletes become determined to break the record of running the mile in under four minutes. **186m/C VHS.** *GB* Richard Huw, Nique Needle, John Philbin, Lewis Fitzgerald, Michael York; *D:* Jim Goddard; *W:* David Williamson; *C:* Ian Warburton.

4 Months, 3 Weeks, 2 Days 2007 *4 Luni, 3 Saptamani si 2 Zile* 2007 Stunning, intense thriller about two college roommates who seek an illegal abortion for one of them in the hellish totalitarian state of 1987 Romanian. To do so they must enter the Romanian underworld and find someone to do the procedure while dealing with low-lifes who threaten them with violence, blackmail, and humiliation every step of the way. A tightly crafted noir that uses the challenging issue of abortion as a backdrop rather than a centerpiece, instead focusing on the struggles of the two women in the face of a dangerous world they aren't meant to see. **113m/C DVD.** *RO* Laura Vasiliu, Anamaria Marinca, Alex Potocean, Vlad Ivanov; *D:* Cristian Mungiu; *W:* Cristian Mungiu; *C:* Oleg Mutu.

The Four Musketeers 1975 (PG) *The Revenge of Milady* 1975 (PG) A fun-loving continuation of "The Three Musketeers," reportedly filmed simultaneously. Lavish swashbuckler jaunts between France, England, and Italy, in following the adventures of D'Artagnan and his cohorts. Pictures give an amusing depiction of Lester-interpreted 17th-century Europe, with fine performances especially by Dunaway as an evil countess seeking revenge on our heroes and Welch as the scatterbrained object of York's affections. Followed, in 1989, by "The Return of the Musketeers." **108m/C VHS, DVD.** Michael York, Oliver Reed, Richard Chamberlain, Frank Finlay, Raquel Welch, Christopher Lee, Faye Dunaway, Jean-Pierre Cassel, Geraldine Chaplin, Simon Ward, Charlton Heston, Roy Kinnear, Nicole Calfan; *D:* Richard Lester; *W:* George MacDonald Fraser; *C:* David Watkin; *M:* Lalo Schifrin.

The 4 Musketeers 1974 *D'Artagnan et les Trois Mousquetaires; D'Artagnan and the Three Musketeers* 2005 (R) Yet another (remarkably dull and silly) version of the Dumas swashbuckler, only this time the evil Milady de Winter (Beart) has made a pact with the devil for some supernatural powers. The musketeers still use their swords a lot and battle the corrupt Cardinal Richelieu (Karyo) as well. Made for French TV; dubbed into English. **190m/C DVD.** *FR* Emmanuelle Beart, Tcheky Karyo, Vincent Elbaz, Gregori Derangere, Heino Ferch, Stefania Rocca, Tristan Ulloa, Gregory Gadebois, Diana Amft; *D:* Pierre Aknine; *W:* Pierre Aknine; *C:* Allen Smith; *M:* Matt Dunkley. **TV**

Four Robbers 1987 The ruthless Ma initiates his series of crimes throughout the Far East, somehow staying ahead of the cops. When the final showdown occurs, it's an all out kung fu massacre. **90m/C VHS.** *HK* Lau Chun, Shek Hon, Kong Seng, Lee Wing Shan; *D:* Gam Loi Sung; *W:* Gam Loi Sung.

Four Rode Out 1969 A Mexican outlaw is pursued by his girlfriend, onetime partner, and the law. Brutal, inferior western. **99m/C VHS, DVD.** Pernell Roberts, Sue Lyon, Leslie Nielsen, Julian Mateos; *D:* John Peyser.

Four Rooms 1995 (R) Four stories by four hot indie filmers told in the same L.A. hotel on New Year's Eve are tied together by bellboy Roth, stumbling around in a Jerry/Carrey-like stupor. Leading off is Anders's roomful of witches trying to resurrect spirit of '50s stripper De Cadenet. After this disappointing start is Rockwell's bland look at infidelity, with wife Beals tied and gagged by her husband (Proval) over an alleged fling with Roth. Bandaras heads the best seg as a mobster who leaves his demonic children in Roth's hands. Tarantino is the anchor man with his take on Hitchcock, dealing with a macabre bet involving the removal of body parts. Altogether disjointed and uninspired. **98m/C VHS, DVD.** Tim Roth, Antonio Banderas, Jennifer Beals, Paul Calderon, Sammio Davis, Valeria Golino, Madonna, Ione Skye, Marisa Tomei, Tamlyn Tomita, Bruce Willis, David Proval, Lili Taylor, Alicia Witt, Amanda DeCadenet, Danny Verduzco, Lana McKissack, Quentin Tarantino; *Cameos:* Salma Hayek; *D:* Quentin Tarantino, Alexandre Rockwell, Robert Rodriguez, Allison Anders; *W:* Quentin Tarantino, Alexandre Rockwell, Robert Rodriguez, Allison Anders; *C:* Phil Parmet, Guillermo Navarro, Andrzej Sekula, Rodrigo Garcia; *M:* Combustible Edison, Esquivel, Goldo on Raspberries '95: Worst Support. Actress (Madonna).

The Four Seasons 1981 (PG) Three upper-middle-class New York couples share their vacations together, as well as their friendship, their frustrations and their jealousies. Alda's first outing as a film director is pleasant and easy on the eyes. **108m/C VHS, DVD.** Alan Alda, Carol Burnett, Sandy Dennis, Len Cariou, Jack Weston, Rita Moreno, Bess Armstrong; *D:* Alan Alda; *W:* Alan Alda.

Four Sheets to the Wind 2007 (R) Seminole-Cree Cufe Smallhill discovers that his ill father has committed suicide. When his older sister Miri comes home for the funeral, she persuades Cufe that he needs a break from their small hometown and should come and stay with her in Tulsa. Miri is a party-hard gal and Cufe finds more sympathy from her neighbor Francie and a chance to decide what's next in his life. **81m/C DVD.** Cody Lightning, Jeri Arredondo, Christian Kane, Tamara Podemski, Laura Bailey; *D:* Sterlin Harjo; *W:* Sterlin Harjo; *C:* Frederick Schroeder; *M:* Jeff Johnson.

Four Sided Triangle 1953 Two mad scientists find their friendship threatened when they discover that they are both in love with the same woman. So they do what anyone would do in this situation—they invent a machine and duplicate her. **81m/B VHS, DVD.** *GB* James Hayter, Barbara Payton, Stephen Murray, John Van Eyssen, Percy Marmont; *D:* Terence Fisher; *W:* Terence Fisher, Paul Tabori; *C:* Reg Wyer; *M:* Malcolm Arnold.

Four Sons 1928 Mother Bernie lives with her four sons in Burgendorf, Bavaria. Joseph has a job offer in America and his mother gives him money to help him immigrate. The other three boys enlist in WWI and when America enters the war, Joseph enlists on the other side. After the war is over, and after much hardship and sorrow, Mother Bernie goes through Ellis Island herself. **100m/B DVD.** Margaret Mann, James Hall, George Meeker, June Collyer, Charles Morton, Ralph Bushman, Earle Foxe, Albert Gran; *D:* John Ford; *W:* Philip Klein; *C:* George Schneiderman.

Four Times That Night 1969 (R) *Quante Volte...Quella Notte* 1969 Though he's known for his work in horror, Mario Bava also made one sex comedy and it's not a bad little movie, though its appeal is mostly nostalgia. Technically, it's a "Rashomon" story with the events of one night told from different points of view. What happens when Gianni (Halsey) takes the lovely Tina (Giordano) to his bachelor pad? Is it date rape or does she seduce him? The film is still grand stuff for '60s fans. The shagadelic apartment must be seen to be believed. **83m/C DVD.** *IT* Brett Halsey, Daniela Giordano, Pascale Petit, Brigitte Skay; *D:* Mario Bava; *M:* Lallo Gori.

Four Ways Out 1957 Four average guys are fed up by their lot in life and stage a boxoffice robbery of their local soccer stadium. They don't get to enjoy their ill-gotten gains. In Italian with subtitles or dubbed. **77m/B VHS.** *IT* Gina Lollobrigida, Renato Baldini, Paul Muller; *D:* Pietro Germi.

Four Weddings and a Funeral 1994 (R) Refreshing, intelligent adult comedy brimming with stiff upper-lip wit and sophistication. Thirtyish Brit bachelor Charles (Grant) spends his time attending the weddings of his friends, but manages to avoid taking the plunge himself. Then he falls for American Carrie (MacDowell), who's about to wed another. Great beginning offers loads of laughs as the first two weddings unfold, then becomes decidedly bittersweet. While Grant makes this a star turn as the romantic bumbler, MacDowell charms without seeming particularly needed. Supporting characters are superb, especially Coleman as the "flirty" Scarlett and Atkinson as a new minister. Surprising boxoffice hit found a broad audience. **118m/C VHS, DVD.** *GB* Hugh Grant, Andie MacDowell, Simon Callow, Kristin Scott Thomas, James Fleet, John Hannah, Charlotte Coleman, David Bower, Corin Redgrave, Rowan Atkinson, Rosalie Crutchley, Kenneth Griffith, Jeremy Kemp, Sophie Thompson; *D:* Mike Newell; *W:* Richard Curtis; *C:* Michael Coulter; *M:* Richard Rodney Bennett. Australian Film Inst. '94:

Foreign Film; British Acad. '94: Actor (Grant). Director (Newell). Film. Support. Actress (Scott Thomas). Golden Globes '95: Actor-Mus./Comedy (Grant). Writers Guild '94: Orig. Screenplay.

The 4D Man ♫♫½ 1959 A physicist makes two fateful discoveries while working on a special project that gets out of control, leaving him able to pass through matter and see around corners. He also finds that his touch brings instant death. Cheap but effective sci-fier. Young Duke has a small part. 85m/C VHS, DVD. W: Jackson Davies. M: Ralph Carmichael.

The Foursome ♫♫½ 2006 (PG-13) Four buddies reunite at their twentieth college reunion, discussing work, money, wives, and sex. Still competitive, the guys goes about the business of tracking down warnings of manager Gerald Olin (Jackson) that it's just plain evil. The room persona. and awkward revelations. Harmless enough but leans toward boring and dumb. 90m/C DVD. Kevin Dillon, Shi Banac, Chris Gauthier, Paul Jarrett, John Shaw; D: William Dear. W: L.A. Film Critics '84: Foreign Film.

1408 ♫♫ ½ 2007 (PG-13) Professional skeptic Mike Enslin (Cusack) specializes in debunking haunted houses and other paranormal spots in his bestselling books. His next target is room 1408 at Manhattan's Dolphin Hotel, despite the warnings of manager Gerald Olin (Jackson) that it's just plain evil. The room preys on an occupant's deepest, darkest fears and since Mike is grieving the death of his young daughter Katie (Anthony), should he be surprised when she shows up? Creepiness builds effectively. Adapted from a Stephen King short story. 94m/C DVD. US John Cusack, Samuel L. Jackson, Mary McCormack, Jasmine Jessica Anthony; D: Mikael Hafstrom. W: Matt Greenberg, Scott U. Alexander, Larry Karaszewski. C: Benoit Delhomme. M: Gabriel Yared.

1492: Conquest of Paradise ♫♫½ 1992 (PG-13) Large-scale Hollywood production striving for political correctness is a drawn-out account of Columbus's (Depardieu) discovery and subsequent exploitation of the "New World." Skillful directing by Ridley Scott and impressive scenery add interest, yet don't make up for a script which chronicles events but tends towards trite dialogue and characterization. Available in both pan-and-scan and letterbox formats. 142m/C VHS, DVD. Gerard Depardieu, Sigourney Weaver, Armand Assante, Frank Langella, Loren Dean, Angela Molina, Fernando Rey, Michael Wincott, Steven Waddington, Tcheky Karyo, Kario Salem; D: Ridley Scott. W: Roselyne Bosch. M: Vangelis.

The Fourth Angel ♫♫ 2001 (R) London-based journalist Jack Elgin (Irons) is on holiday with his family when their plane is hijacked by terrorists. Jack's wife and two daughters are among the dead. He's naturally outraged after learning the hijackers have been released and decides to hunt the criminals himself, which draws the attention of CIA agents Bernard (Whitaker) and Davidson (Priestley). A not unfamiliar revenge thriller. Based on the novel "Angel" by Robin Hunter. 95m/C VHS, DVD. Jeremy Irons, Forest Whitaker, Jason Priestley, Charlotte Rampling, Lois Maxwell, Timothy West, Ian McNeice; D: John Irvin. W: Allan Scott. C: Mike Molloy. M: Paul Zaza.

The 4th Floor ♫♫ 1999 (R) Lewis, who's engaged to older and successful TV weatherman Hurt, inherits a rent-controlled apartment and is then terrorized by her neighbor, who may be working for someone else. Twist ending leaves viewer with more questions than answers. 90m/C VHS, DVD. Juliette Lewis, William Hurt, Austin Pendleton, Shelley Duvall, Artie Lange, Tobin Bell; D: Josh Klausner. W: Josh Klausner. C: Michael Slovis. M: Brian Tyler.

The 4th Man ♫♫♫½ 1979 Steeped in saturated colors and jet black comedy, with an atmospheric score, Verhoeven's nouveau noir mystery enjoyed considerable art-house success but was not released in the US until 1984. The story is decidedly non-linear, the look stylish and symbolic. Krabbe is an alcoholic bisexual Catholic writer who inadvertently becomes the hypotenuse of a love triangle involving Herman, a young man he encounters at a railway station, and his lover Christine, who owns the Sphinx beauty parlor and whose three husbands died, shall we say, mysteriously. In Dutch with English subtitles. 102m/C VHS, DVD, NL Jeroen Krabbe, Renee Soutendijk, Thom Hoffman, Dolf DeVries, Geert De Jong; D: Paul Verhoeven. W: Gerard Soeteman; C: Jen De Bont. M: Loek Dikker. L.A. Film Critics '84: Foreign Film.

The 4th Tenor ♫♫½ 2002 (PG-13) Well, Rodney proves he's not much of a misfit detective is hired by a beautiful woman to find her missing husband. The investigation reveals some unsavory facts about the gentleman. Characterizations and plot twists keep this mystery interesting. 91m/C VHS, Mark Harmon, Mimi Rogers, Cliff DeYoung, Paul Gleason, M. Emmet Walsh; D: Ivan Passer. W: Andrew Guerdat. C.A.B.L.E.

The Fourth Sex ♫½ 1961 Le Quatrieme Sexe 1961 Wealthy American, Sand, spends her time in Paris painting her girlfriends in the nude and throwing wild parties. When she meets newcomer Caroline, she immediately sets out to add her to her harem. 82m/B VHS, FR Nicole Berger, Brigitte Juslin, Richard Winckler; D: Michel Wichard.

Fourth Story ♫♫♫ 1990 (PG-13) A woman to find her beautiful husband. For one of his operatic singing waitress (Gurvitch) but she doesn't return his interest. So he decides he has to learn to sing himself in order to impress her and flies to Italy for professional coaching, only to be taken in by a couple of con men. 97m/C VHS, DVD. Rodney Dangerfield, Robert Davi, Annabelle Gurvitch, Anita De Simone, Charles Fleischer, Harry Basil, Vincent Schiavelli; D: Harry Basil. M: Christopher Lennertz. VIDEO

The Fourth War ♫♫ 1990 (R) Schneider and Prochnow are American and Russian colonels, respectively, assigned to guard the West German-Czechoslovakian border against each other. With the frustrated warriors begin to taunt each other and their interest. So he decides he has to learn threatening to touch off a major superpower conflict. 109m/C VHS, Roy Scheider, Jurgen Prochnow, Tim Reid, Lara Harris, Harry Dean Stanton, Dale Dye; D: John Frankenheimer. M: Bill Conti.

The Fourth Protocol ♫♫♫ 1987 (R) Well-made thriller based on the Frederick Forsyth bestseller about a British secret agent trying to stop a young KGB agent from destroying NATO and putting the world in nuclear jeopardy. Brosnan, as the totally dedicated Russkie, gives his best performance to date while Caine, as usual, is totally believable as he warns his friend the fox to stay clear of their hunting grounds, for the master is come his master's best hunting dog and Pierce Brosnan, Ned Beatty, Joanna Cassidy, Julian Glover, Ray McAnally, Michael Gough, Ian Richardson, Betsy Brantley, Matt Frewer, Peter Cartwright, David Conville; D: John MacKenzie. W: Frederick Forsyth, Richard Burridge, George Axelrod. C: Phil Meheux. M: Lalo Schifrin, Francis Shaw.

Fourth Wise Man ♫♫ 1985 A Biblical Easter story about a rich physician searching for Christ in Persia. 72m/C VHS, DVD. Martin Sheen, Lance Kerwin, Alan Arkin, Harold Gould, Eileen Brennan, Ralph Bellamy, Adam Arkin, Richard Libertini; D: Michael Ray Rhodes. W: Tom Fontana; C: Jon Krahouse; M: Bruce Langhorne.

Fourth Wish ♫♫ 1975 When a single father learns that his son is dying, he vows to make his son's last months as fulfilling as possible. Bring lots of hankies. 107m/C VHS. John Meillon, Robert Bettles, Robyn Nevin; D: Don Chaffey; C: Geoff Burton. Australian Film Inst. '75: Actor (Meillon).

Fowl Play Woof! 1975 Supercock; Super-chicken; A Fistful of Feathers 1975 (PG) An unlikely threesome encounter various hard-ships and mishaps on their way to the first cock-fighting Olympics. Let's hope it's the last cock-fighting Olympics. 90m/C VHS. Nancy Kwan, Ross Hagen.

Foxfire ♫♫♫ 1987 (PG) In the role that won her Tony and Emmy awards, Tandy stars as Annie Nations, a woman who has lived her entire life in the Blue Ridge Mountains. Widowed, all she has left are the memories of her beloved husband, with whom she regularly communes. Her son tries to convince her to move, and it becomes a clash of the wills as Annie tries to decide to stay in her past or change her future. 118m/C VHS, DVD. Jessica Tandy, Hume Cronyn, John Denver, Gary Grubbs, Harriet Hall; D: Jud Taylor; C: Thomas Burstyn. TV.

Foxfire ♫♫ 1996 (R) Not much more than "The Craft" without the hocus-pocus. Lusty Legs Sadovsky (Jolie) is a liberated drifter who empowers a quartet of abused teens to take action against their molester. Based on the book by Joyce Carol Oates originally written in the 1950s, modern adaptation suffers from time warp, most notably when the girls expose their teacher's behavior to their principal and he promptly suspends them without further ado. After some bonding and tattooing in an abandoned house, flick descends into the more masculine and mundane territory of car chases, kidnapping and gunplay. Filmmakers rather timidly back off of leather-clad Legs' obvious lesbianism and her relationship with the adoring Maddy (Burress). Decent acting by most would've benefitted from a more cohesive screenplay. 102m/C VHS, DVD Angelina Jolie, John Diehl, Jenny Lewis, Cathy Moriarty, Richard Beymer, Hedy Burress, Jenny Shimizu, Sarah Rosen-

Foxes ♫♫ 1980 (R) Four young California girls grow up with little supervision from parents still trying to grow up themselves. They rely on each other in a world where they have to make adult choices, yet are not considered grown-up. They look for no more than a good time and no tragic mistakes. 106m/C VHS, DVD. Jodie Foster, Cherie Currie, Marilyn Kagan, Scott Baio, Sally Kellerman, Randy Quaid, Laura Dern; D: Adrian Lyne. W: Gerald Ayres.

The Fox and the Hound ♫♫♫ 1981 (G) Sweet story of the friendship shared by a fox and hound Young and naive, the animals become friends and swear their allegiance to one another when they are separated for a season. Upon return, the hound has become his master's best hunting dog and warns his friend the fox to stay clear of their hunting grounds, for the master is determined the fox retreats but soon finds himself boldly standing his ground against a bear that attacks the hound, and the hound inevitably protects the fox from the mean-spirited hunter. Very good animation, but not in the same class as other Disney favorites like "Beauty and the Beast." 83m/C VHS, DVD. D: Art Stevens, Ted Berman, Richard Rich. W: Art Stevens, Peter Young, Steve Hulett, Earl Kress, Vance Gerry, Larry Clemmons, Dave Michener, Burny Mattinson. M: Buddy (Norman Dale) Baker; V: Mickey Rooney, Kurt Russell, Pearl Bailey, Jack Albertson, Sandy Duncan, Jeanette Nolan, Pat Buttram, John Fiedler, John McIntire, Richard Bakalyan, Paul Winchell, Keith Coogan, Corey Feldman.

The Fox and His Friends ♫♫♫½ 1975 Faustrecht der Freiheit; Fist Right of Freedom 1975 Fassbinder's breakthrough tragi-drama, about a lowly gay carnival barker who wins the lottery, thus attracting a devious, exploiting lover, who takes him for everything he has. In German with English subtitles. 123m/C VHS, DVD. GE Rainer Werner Fassbinder, Peter Chatel, Karl-Heinz Boehm, Adrian Hoven, Harry Baer, Ulla Jacobsson, Kurt Raab; D: Rainer Werner Fassbinder. C: Michael Ballhaus.

The Fox and the Hound 2 ♫♫ 2006 (G) Fox Tod and hound dog Copper are still buddies but their friendship is tested when Copper's head is turned by a group of hound dog howlers. 69m/C DVD. D: Jim Kammerud. M: Rich Burns, Roger, S.H. Schulman; M: Jeff Foxworthy, Patrick Swayze, Reba McEntire, Jeff Foxworthy, Patrick Swayze, Roz Paulsen. VIDEO

Ross Hagen, Gus Trikonis; C: Fred C. Soriano Jr.; M: Tito Soto.

Fox and His Friends ♫♫♫½

Foxtrap ♫ 1985 An L.A. courier is hired to find a runaway girl and, upon finding her in Europe, discovers he's been led into a trap. A low budget Italian co-production. 89m/C VHS. //Fred Williamson, Christopher Connelly, Arlene Golonka; D: Fred Williamson.

Foxtrot ♫♫ 1976 The Other Side of Paradise 1976 (R) A wealthy count isolates himself his wife, and their two servants, on an island but cannot escape his past or the horrors of WWII. Even the good cast can't save the pretentious script and inadequate production. 91m/C VHS, SI MX Peter O'Toole, Charlotte Rampling, Max von Sydow, Jorge Luke; D: Arturo Ripstein.

Foxy Brown ♫ 1974 (R) A bitter woman poses as a prostitute to avenge the mob-backed deaths of her drug dealer brother and undercover cop boyfriend. Extremely violent. Black exploitation flick. 92m/C VHS, DVD. Pam Grier, Terry Carter, Antonio Fargas, Kathryn Loder, Peter Brown, Sid Haig, Juanita Brown; D: Jack Hill. W: Jack Hill. C: Brick Marquard; M: Willie Hutch.

Foxstyle ♫½ 1973 A wealthy nightclub owner struggles with his country's roots and his city sophistication. 84m/C VHS. Juanita Moore, Richard Lawson, John Taylor, Jovita Bush; D: Clyde Houston.

Foxfire Light ♫ 1982 (PG) A young woman vacationing in the Ozarks is drawn into a romance with a cowboy. But her mother's social ambitions and her own indecision may tear them apart. 102m/C VHS. Tippi Hedren, Lara Parker, Leslie Nielsen, Barry Van Dyke; D: Allen Baron; C: Thomas Ackerman.

F.P. 1 1933 An artificial island (Floating Platform 1) in the Atlantic is threatened by treason. This slow-moving thriller was the English-language version of the German "F.P. 1 Antwortet Nicht" ("F.P. 1 Doesn't Answer"). Both were directed at the same time by Hartl, using different casts. 74m/B VHS, GE Leslie Fenton, Conrad Veidt, Jill Esmond; D: Karl Hartl.

F.P. 1 Doesn't Answer ♫♫ F.P. 1 Antwortet Nicht 1933 A mid-Atlantic refueling station (Floating Platform 1) is threatened by treason and a pilot sets out to put things right. Features pre-Hollywood vintage Lorre; Albers was Germany's number one boxoffice draw at the time. In German. 74m/B VHS, GE Hans Albers, Sybille Schmitz, Paul Hartmann, Peter Lorre, Hermann Speelmann; D: Karl Hartl.

Fracture ♫♫½ 2007 (R) Old Turk vs. young Turk as Hopkins and Gosling play mind games. Arrogant Ted Crawford (Hopkins) shoots his adulterous trophy wife Jennifer (Davitz). Prosecutor Willy Beachum (Gosling) is leaving for a cushy private job when he gets the case, which proceeds to fall apart. Since Ted's taunting him, Willy can't let things go, no matter what it costs. Hopkins plays his part with sadistic relish (yes, Hannibal Lecter will come to mind), while Gosling handles an emotional roller-coaster from cockiness to vulnerability to determination. 112m/C DVD. US Anthony Hopkins, Ryan Gosling, David Strathairn, Rosamund Pike, Embeth Davidtz, Billy Burke, Clifford Curtis, Fiona Shaw, Bob Gunton, Xander Berkeley, Josh Stamberg, Zoe Kazari; D: Gregory Hoblit; W: Daniel Pyne, Glen Gers; C: Kramer Morgenthau; M: Michael Danna, Jeff Danna.

Frailty ♫♫ 2002 (R) Impressive directorial debut by Paxton has him as Dad, a seemingly normal West Texas widower. One day, however, he tells his boys that their family has been chosen by God to destroy demons who are disguised as normal people. This sounds okay by impressionable nine year old Adam (Sumpter), but older Fenton (O'Leary) seems skeptical. Told mostly in flashback from the point of view of now-grown, haunted Fenton (McConaughey), the story keeps the gore mostly offscreen, while focusing on fanaticism, the trust between parents and their kids, and toll of insanity. Screenwriting debut for Hanley. Paxton acquits himself well on both sides of the camera, but

Foxfire Light ♫ 1982
berg, Peter Facinelli; D: Annette Haywood-Carter; W: Elizabeth White; C: Newton Thomas (Tom) Sigel; M: Michel Colombier

---

it's O'Leary who shines. McConaughey turns in his best performance to date. **100m/C VHS, DVD.** *US* Bill Paxton; Matthew McConaughey, Powers Boothe, Luke Askew, Matt O'Leary, Jeremy Sumpter, Derk Cheetwood, Missy (Melissa) Crider, Alan Davidson, Cynthia Ettinger, Vincent Chase, Levi Kreis; *D:* Bill Paxton; *W:* Brent Hanley; *C:* Bill Buller; *M:* Brian Tyler. **CABLE**

Frame by Frame 1995 (R) Cop partners Ekberg (Helgenberger) and Stash (Biehn), who share a passion on and off the job, become implicated in the mob-style murder of Stash's wife. **97m/C VHS.** Michael Biehn, Marg Helgenberger, Ron White, Dan Lett, Von Flores; *D:* Douglas Barr; *C:* Rodney Charters; *M:* Mark Snow. **CABLE**

Frame Up 1991 (R) A small town sheriff is trying to investigate a murder tied to a fraternity's initiation. However, he runs into opposition from the most powerful man in town. **90m/C VHS.** Wings Hauser, Bobby DiCicco, Frances Fisher, Dick Sargent, Robert Picardo; *D:* Paul Leder.

Framed 1975 (R) A nightclub owner is framed for murder, which understandably irks him. He's determined to get paroled and then seek revenge on the crooked cops responsible for his incarceration. This action melodrama features the writer, director and star of "Walking Tall." **106m/C VHS.** Joe Don Baker, Gabriel Dell, Brock Peters, Conny Van Dyke, John Marley; *D:* Phil Karlson; *W:* Mort Briskin.

Framed 1990 An art forger gets tripped up by a beautiful con artist. However, when they meet again he is willingly drawn into her latest swindle. **87m/C VHS.** Jeff Goldblum, Kristin Scott Thomas, Todd Graff; *D:* Dean Parisot.

Framed 1993 British miniseries about a mediocre cop and a master criminal. Sgt. Larry Jackson (Morrissey) is on vacation in Spain when he spots the supposedly dead master thief/murderer Eddie Myers (Dalton). Once back in London, Larry's assigned the dubious task of guarding Eddie and finding out the names of his associates. Only the sophisticated Eddie starts to dangle temptation in front of the younger man until Larry begins to waver in his duty. Intricate plotting, with Dalton particular fine as the suave, immoral crook. LaPlante also wrote the very successful "Prime Suspect" police dramas for TV. **115m/C VHS, DVD.** *GB* Timothy Dalton, David Morrissey, Timothy West, Annabelle Apsion, Penelope Cruz, Rowena King, Francis Johnson, Glyn Grimstead, Wayne Foskett, Trevor Cooper; *D:* Geoffrey Sax; *W:* Lynda La Plante. *M:* Nick Bicat. **TV**

Fran 1985 A young woman is torn between her desperate need for a male companion and the care of her children. Well made, albeit depressing, Australian production. **92m/C VHS.** *AU* Noni Hazlehurst, Annie Byron, Alan Fletcher; *D:* Glenda Hambly. Australian Film Inst. '85; Actress (Hazlehurst).

Frances 1982 The tragic story of Frances Farmer, the beautiful and talented screen actress of the '30s and early '40s, who was driven to a mental breakdown by bad luck, drug and alcohol abuse, a neurotic, domineering mother, despicable mental health care, and her own stubbornness. After being in and out of mental hospitals, she is finally reduced to a shadow by a lobotomy. Not nearly as bleak as it sounds, this film works because Lange understands this character from the inside out, and never lets her become melodramatic or weak. **134m/C VHS, DVD.** Jessica Lange, Sam Shepard, Jeffrey DeMunn, Gerald S. O'Loughlin, Chris Pennock, John Randolph, Lane Smith; *D:* Graeme Clifford; *W:* Christopher DeVore, Nicholas Kazan, Eric Bergren; *C:* Laszlo Kovacs; *M:* John Barry.

Francesco 1993 (PG-13) Set in 13th-century Italy and depicting the life of St. Francis of Assisi. Follows the pleasure-loving son of a wealthy merchant through his religious awakening, and the founding of the Franciscan order of monks. Rourke, in a definite change-of-pace role, is actually believable, while Bonham Carter offers fine support as a devoted disciple. **119m/C VHS, DVD.** Mickey Rourke, Helena Bonham-Carter, Paolo Bonacelli, Andrea Ferreol, Hanns Zischler, Diego Ribon; *C:* Liliana Cavani; *C:* Giuseppe Lanci, Ennio Guarnieri; *M:* Vangelis.

The Franchise Affair 1952 A teenage girl in need of an alibi accuses two reclusive women of kidnapping and abusing her. It's up to a lawyer to sort out the truth. Based on the novel by Josephine Tey. **149m/C VHS.** *GB* Michael Denison, Dulcie Gray, Anthony Nicholls, Marjorie Fielding, Athene Seyler, Ann Stephens, Patrick Troughton; *D:* Lawrence Huntington.

The Franchise Affair 1988 A scandal is about to overtake the sleepy village of Milford in 1947. An elderly lady and her daughter, the owners of a forbidding country house, are accused of kidnapping and beating a teenaged girl until she agreed to work as their servant. A British TV production based on the novel by Josephine Tey and previously filmed for the big screen in 1952. **155m/C VHS.** *GB* Patrick Malahide, Rosalie Crutchley, Joanna McCallum, Alex Jennings; *D:* Leonard Lewis; *W:* James Andrew Hall; *M:* Paul Hart. **TV**

Francis Covers the Big Town 1953 The fourth in the series finds Peter Stirling (O'Connor) trying to become an ace reporter with a New York newspaper. Thanks to Francis he gets some big scoops but then runs afoul of the mob and is accused of murder. And it's up to his smarter pal to come to the rescue. **86m/B VHS, DVD.** Donald O'Connor, Yvette Dugay, Gene Lockhart, Nancy Guild, Larry Gates, Gale Gordon; *D:* Arthur Lubin; *W:* Oscar Brodney; *C:* Carl Guthrie; *M:* Joseph Gershenson; *V:* Chill Wills.

Francis Gary Powers: The True Story of the U-2 Spy 1976 Dramatization of the true experiences of Gary Powers, a CIA spy pilot whose plane was shot down over the Soviet Union in 1960. His capture, trial, and conviction are all portrayed in detail, taken from Power's own reminiscences. **120m/C VHS.** Lee Majors, Noah Beery Jr., Nehemiah Persoff, Lew Ayres, Brooke Bundy; *D:* Delbert Mann. **TV**

Francis Goes to the Races 1951 The second in the talking-mule series finds O'Connor and Francis taking up residence on Kellaway's failing horse ranch. When mobsters seize control of the property to pay off a debt, Francis decides to check with the horses at the Santa Anita race track and find a sure winner to bet on. **88m/B VHS, DVD.** Donald O'Connor, Piper Laurie, Cecil Kellaway, Jesse White, Barry Kelley, Hayden Rorke, Vaughn Taylor, Larry Keating; *D:* Arthur Lubin; *W:* Oscar Brodney; *M:* Frank Skinner; *V:* Chill Wills.

Francis Goes to West Point 1952 Peter (O'Connor) and Francis get into West Point where the unfortunate freshman winds up last in his class. But thanks to Francis, Peter makes it past school hazing, grades, and other campus hijacks. Look for Leonard Nimoy in the bit role of a football player. Third in the series. **81m/B VHS, DVD.** Donald O'Connor, Lori Nelson, William Reynolds, Gregg (Hunter) Palmer, Alice Kelley, Les Tremayne, David Janssen, Paul Burke; *D:* Arthur Lubin; *W:* Oscar Brodney; *C:* Carl Guthrie; *M:* Joseph Gershenson; *V:* Chill Wills.

Francis in the Haunted House 1956 The sixth and last entry in the series finds star Donald O'Connor, director Arthur Lubin, and even Chill Wills (the voice of Francis) all abandoning the sinking series. So, its left to Rooney (as hapless David Prescott) to get himself into trouble (trapped in a haunted house with thieves) and for Francis to get him out. Ho-hum. **80m/B VHS.** Mickey Rooney, Virginia Welles, James Flavin, Paul Cavanagh, David Janssen, Richard Deacon; *D:* Charles Lamont; *W:* Herbert Margolis, William Raynor; *C:* George Robinson; *M:* Joseph Gershenson; *V:* Paul Frees.

Francis in the Navy 1955 The precocious talking mule, Francis, is drafted, and his buddy, played by O'Connor, comes to the rescue. The loquacious beast proves he has the superior grey matter however, and ends up doing all the thinking. Look for Clint Eastwood in his second minor role. **80m/B VHS, DVD.** Donald O'Connor, Martha Hyer, Jim Backus, Paul Burke, David Janssen, Clint Eastwood, Martin Milner; *D:* Arthur Lubin.

Francis Joins the WACs 1954 The fifth entry in the series finds O'Connor working as a bank clerk when he is mistakenly drafted back into the military—and sent to a WAC base. Francis tries to keep him out of trouble with the ladies. Wills, the voice of Francis, also turns up as a general. **94m/B VHS.** Donald O'Connor, Julie Adams, Chill Wills, Mamie Van Doren, Lynn Bari, Zasu Pitts, Joan Shawlee, Mara Corday, Allison Hayes; *D:* Arthur Lubin; *V:* Chill Wills.

Francis the Talking Mule *Francis* 1949 The first of the silly but funny series about, what else, a talking mule. Peter Stirling (O'Connor) is the dim-bulb G.I. who hooks up with Francis while fighting in Burma. Francis helps Peter become a war hero but of course everyone thinks he's crazy when Peter insists the mule can talk. The joke is that Francis is smarter than any of the humans. O'Connor starred in six of the films, with Mickey Rooney taking over the final adventure. Director Lubin went on to create the TV series "Mr. Ed," about a talking horse. Watch for Tony Curtis in a small role. **91m/B VHS, DVD.** Donald O'Connor, Patricia Medina, Zasu Pitts, Ray Collins, John McIntire, Eduard Franz, Howland Chamberlain, Frank Faylen, Tony Curtis; *D:* Arthur Lubin; *M:* Frank Skinner; *V:* Chill Wills.

Frank and Jesse 1994 (R) Another revisionist western finds outlaw Jesse James (Lowe) brooding about his violent existence while brother Frank (Paxton) keeps the gang together and they all try to avoid capture by a vengeful Alan Pinkerton (Atherton) and his detective agency. **106m/C VHS, DVD.** Rob Lowe, Bill Paxton, Randy Travis, William Atherton, Alexis Arquette; *D:* Robert Boris; *W:* Robert Boris; *C:* Walt Lloyd; *M:* Mark McKenzie.

Frank McKlusky, C.I. 2002 (PG-13) Frank McKlusky (Sheridan) is a klutzy but dedicated insurance claims investigator with an over-protective mama (Parton) who worries that her sonny boy will end up in a coma like his daredevil dad (Quaid). But Frank learns it can't always be safety first when he and his gay partner Jimmy (Farley) investigate a couple of silly lawyers (Pollak, Morgan). **83m/C VHS.** Dave Sheridan, Dolly Parton, Randy Quaid, Kevin Farley, Eugene Collier, Sean Patterson; *D:* Mark Dippe; *W:* Simon Barret, Scott Clevenger; *C:* Eliot Rockett; *M:* Ryan Beveridge. **VIDEO**

Frankenfish 2004 (R) Hungry, jumbo-sized mutant fish feast on any human they can get their fins on in the Louisiana Bayou whether they're on land or water. **84m/C VHS, DVD.** Tory Kittles, K.D. Aubert, China Chow, Tomas Arana, Richard Edson, Muse Watson, Raoul Trujillo, Matthew Rauch, Donna Biscoe, Mark Boone Jr., Reggie Lee, Noelle Evans, Eugene Collier, Sean Patterson; *D:* Mark Dippe; *W:* Simon Barret, Scott Clevenger; *C:* Eliot Rockett; *M:* Ryan Beveridge. **VIDEO**

Frankenhooker 1990 (R) Jeffrey Franken is a nice guy; he didn't mean to mow his fiancee down on the front lawn. But sometimes bad things just happen to good people. Luckily Jeff thought to save her head and decides to pair it up with the body of some sexy streetwalkers. Voila! You have Frankenhooker: the girlfriend with (someone else's) heart of gold. The posters say it best, "A Terrifying Tale of Sluts and Bolts." **90m/C VHS, DVD.** James Lorinz, Patty Mullen, Charlotte J. Helmkamp, Louise Lasser, Shirley Stoler, Joseph Gonzalez, Beverly Bonner, John Zacherle; *D:* Frank Henenlotter; *W:* Frank Henenlotter, Robert Martin; *C:* Robert M. "Bob" Baldwin Jr.; *M:* Joe Renzetti.

Frankenstein 1931 The definitive expressionistic Gothic horror classic that set the mold. Adapted from the Mary Shelley novel about Dr. Henry Frankenstein (Clive), the scientist who creates a terrifying, yet strangely sympathetic monster aided by his hunchbacked assistant, Fritz (Frye). Great performance by Karloff as the creation, which made him a monster to Jack Pierce's makeup). Several powerful scenes, excised from the original version, have been restored, including that of young Maria (Marilyn Harris), who is spotted by the monster innocently picking flowers by a pond. The first in the Universal series. **71m/B VHS, DVD.** Boris Karloff, Colin Clive, Mae Clarke, John Boles, Dwight Frye, Edward Van Sloan, Frederick Kerr, Lionel Belmore, Arletta Duncan; *D:* James Whale; *W:* Garrett Fort, John Lloyd Balderston, Robert Florey, Francis Edwards Faragoh; *C:* Arthur Edeson; *M:* David Broekman. AFI '98; Top 100, Natl. Film Reg. '91.

Frankenstein 1973 A brilliant scientist plays God, unleashing a living monster from the remains of the dead. A TV movie version of the legendary horror story. Good atmosphere provided by producer Dan "Dark Shadows" Curtis. **130m/C VHS, DVD.** Robert Foxworth, Bo Svenson, Willie Aames, Susan Strasberg; *D:* Glenn Jordan.

Frankenstein 1982 A remake of the horror classic, closely following the original story, wherein the creature speaks (and waxes philosophical), the doctor sees him as his dark subconscious, and the two die in an arctic confrontation. **81m/C VHS.** Robert Powell, Carrie Fisher, David Warner, John Gielgud; *D:* James Ormerod.

Frankenstein 1993 Yet another remake of Mary Shelley's 1818 novel. Bergin stars as Dr. Victor Frankenstein, fanatically believing in the power of science to solve all mankind's ills. This leads him to prove his theories on the "secret of life" with his creation of the monster (Quaid), which Frankenstein finds he cannot ultimately control. Slow-moving story but while the monster isn't really terrifying, he's vengeful and intelligent enough to be a good enemy. **117m/C VHS.** Patrick Bergin, Randy Quaid, John Mills, Lambert Wilson, Fiona Gillies, Jacinta Mulcahy, Timothy Stark; *D:* David Wickes; *W:* David Wickes. **CABLE**

Frankenstein and Me 1996 (PG) Monster-mad 12-year-old Earl Williams (Boulanger) lives in a small Mojave desert town and dreams about bringing Frankenstein's creature back to life. On Halloween, Earl and his friends visit a traveling carnival that claims to have the "authentic" monster, which happens to fall off the truck when the show leaves. Earl finds the dummy and makes numerous attempts to bring the creature back to life. Lots of fantasy sequences and the picture's fun without being too scary. **91m/C VHS.** *CA* Jamieson Boulanger, Ricky Mabse, Louise Fletcher, Burt Reynolds, Myriam Cyr; *D:* Robert Tinnell; *W:* David Sherman, Richard Goudreau; *C:* Roxanne Di Santo; *M:* Normand Corbeil.

Frankenstein and the Monster from Hell 1974 (R) A young doctor is discovered conducting experiments with human bodies and thrown into a mental asylum run by none other than Dr. Frankenstein himself. They continue their gruesome work together, creating a monster who develops a taste for human flesh. This really lame film was the last of the Hammer Frankenstein series. **93m/C VHS, DVD.** *GB* Peter Cushing, Shane Briant, Madeleine Smith, David Prowse, John Stratton, Bernard Lee, Patrick Troughton, Sydney Bromley; *D:* Terence Fisher; *W:* John (Anthony Hinds) Elder; *C:* Brian Probyn; *M:* James Bernard.

Frankenstein Created Woman 1966 In Hammer's fourth take on the Frankenstein story, traditional lab scenes are replaced with less expensive "soul" translocations, though the filmmakers retain an ongoing fascination with decapitations. Oddly, the story has a warmth that's often lacking in the genre, and it's aimed at a younger audience, reflecting the changes that were going on when it was made. **86m/C DVD.** Peter Cushing, Susan Denberg, Thorley Walters, Robert Morris, Duncan Lamont, Peter Blythe, Alan MacNaughton, Peter Madden, Barry Warren, Derek Fowlds; *D:* Terence Fisher; *W:* John (Anthony Hinds) Elder; *C:* Arthur Grant.

Frankenstein '80 WOOf! *Mosaic* 1979 Guy named Frankenstein pieces together a monster who goes on a killing spree. Bottom of the barrel Italian production with funky music and lots of gore. **88m/C VHS.** *IT GE* John Richardson, Gordon Mitchell, Leila Parker, Dada Gallotti, Marisa Travers, Xiro

Frankenstein General Hospital WOOF! 1988 A completely laughless horror spoof wherein the 12th grandson of the infamous scientist duplicates his experiments in the basement of a modern hospital. A must see for Frankenstein fans; considered by some the worst Frankenstein movie ever made. 90m/C VHS, Mark Blankfield, Kathy Shower, Leslie Jordan, Irwin Keyes, Jonathan Farwell, Hamilton Mitchell, Lou (Cutel) Cutell, Bobby 'Boris' Pickett; **D:** Deborah Roberts; **W:** Robert Deel, Michael F. Kelly; **C:** Tom Fraser.

Frankenstein Island 1981 (PG) Four balloonists get pulled down in a storm and up on a mysterious island. They are greeted by one Sheila Frankenstein and encounter monsters, amazons, and other obstacles. Completely inept. Carradine "appears" in a visionary sequence wearing his pajamas. 97m/C VHS, DVD, Cameron Mitchell, Andrew Duggan, John Carradine, Dr Jerry Warren.

Frankenstein Meets the Space Monster WOOF! 1965 Mars Invades Puerto Rico; Frankenstein Meets the Spacemen; Duel of the Space Monsters 1965 A classic grade-Z epic about a space robot gone berserk among Puerto Rican disco dancers. 80m/B VHS, DVD, James Karen, Nancy Marshall, Marvn Hanold, David Kerman, Robert Reilly, Lou (Cutel) Cutell; **D:** Robert Gaffney; **W:** George Garret; **C:** Saul Midwall.

Frankenstein Meets the Wolfman 1942 The two famous Universal monsters meet and battle it out in this typical grade-B entry, the fifth from the series. The Werewolf wants Dr. Frankenstein to cure him, but only his monster (played by Lugosi) remains. 73m/C VHS, DVD, Lon Chaney Jr., Bela Lugosi, Patric Knowles, Lionel Atwill, Maria Ouspenskaya, Ilona Massey, Dwight Frye; **D:** Roy William Neill; **W:** Curt Siodmak; **C:** George Robinson.

Frankenstein Must Be Destroyed 1969 Evil Dr. Frankenstein (Cushing) gets interested in brain transplants but discovers the expert, Dr. Pravda, he hoped to work with has gone mad and is in an asylum. He forces a young medical couple to help him free Pravda but the man is accidentally killed. Nevertheless, Frankenstein transplants Pravda's brain into the body of an asylum inmate that Frankenstein has murdered. These things never work out as intended. Followed by "The Horror of Frankenstein." 97m/C VHS, DVD, GB Peter Cushing, Veronica Carlson, Freddie Jones, Maxine Audley, Simon Ward, Thorley Walters, George Pravda, Colette O'Neil; **D:** Terence Fisher; **W:** Bert Batt; **C:** Arthur Grant.

Frankenstein Reborn 1998 (PG) Thirteen-year-old Anna Frankenstein is impressed with her eccentric scientist uncle, Victor, but things get a little spooky when she meets his latest creation Yes, Uncle Vic is still working on creating a man from stitched together parts of dead bodies and this time his creature has a human soul. DeCoteau used the pseudonym Julian Breen. 70m/C VHS, DVD, Jason Simmons, Ben Gould, Haven Burton, Ethan Wilde; **D:** David DeCoteau. **VIDEO**

Frankenstein Sings... The Movie 1995 (PG) Musical horror spoof fincs young couple seeking shelter in a creepy mansion that happens to belong to Dr. Frankenstein. Also visiting (it just happens to be Halloween) are Mr. and Mrs. Dracula, the Wolfman and his mother, and the mummified remains of Elvis and his agent. Some amusing one-liners and mediocre music; adapted from a stage musical. 83m/C VHS, Candace Cameron, Ian Bohen, Jimmie Walker, Anthony Crivello; **D:** Joel Cohen, Alec Sokolow.

Frankenstein Unbound 1990 Roger Corman's Frankenstein Unbound 1990 (R) Corman returns after nearly 20 years with a better than ever B movie. Hurt plays Dr. Joseph Buchanan, a nuclear physicist time traveler who accidentally goes back to 1816 and runs into Lord Byron (Patric), Percy (Hutchence) and Mary (Fonda)

Papas, Ranato Romano; **D:** Mario Mancini; **W:** Mario Mancini, Ferdinando De Leone; **C:** Emilio Variano.

Shelley and their neighbor Baron Frankenstein (Julia) and his monster (Brimble). But Frankenstein is not done experimenting just yet. Great acting, fun special effects, intelligent and subtle message, with a novel combining his obsession with the cosmos and his mother's erotic history; Raymo adapts from the 1993 novel. 85m/B VHS, DVD, John Hurt, Raul Julia, Bridget Fonda, Jason Patric, Michael Hutchence, Catherine Rabett, Nick Brimble, Catherine Corman, Mickey Knox; **D:** Roger Corman; **W:** F.X. Feeney, Roger Corman; **C:** Armando Nannuzzi; **M:** Carl Davis; **V:** Terri Treas.

Frankenstein's Daughter WOOF! 1958 Demented descendant of Dr. Frankenstein sans a den of gruesome monsters loose, including the corpse of a teenaged girl he revitalizes, as he continues his mad experiments in his forefathers. 85m/B VHS, DVD, John Ashley, Sandra Knight, Donald Murphy, Felix Locher, Sally Todd, Harry Wilson; **D:** Richard Cunha; **C:** Meredith Nicholson; **M:** Nicholas Carras.

Frankenstein's Great Aunt Tillie WOOF! 1983 An excruciatingly bad send up of the Frankenstein sega with the good doctor about to be evicted from his estate because of back taxes. Gabor appears for a few seconds in a 'flashback. 99m/C VHS, DVD, Donald Pleasence, Yvonne Furneaux, Aldo Ray, June Wilkinson, Zsa Zsa Gabor; **D:** Myron G. Gold; **W:** Myron G. Gold.

Frankenweenie 1984 (PG) "Frankenweenie" is the tale of a lovable spunky dog named Sparky and his owner, Victor Frankenstein. When Sparky is hit by a car, Victor brings him back to life through the use of electric shock. This affectionate parody of "Frankenstein" launched renowned director Burton's career. 27m/B VHS, DVD, Shelley Duvall, Daniel Stern, Barret Oliver, Paul Bartel, Joseph Maher, Jason Hervey; **D:** Tim Burton; **C:** Thomas Ackerman; **M:** Michael Convertino, David Newman.

Frankie and Johnny 1936 Based on the song of the same name, famed torch singer Morgan portrays a singer in a bordello who shoots her unfaithful lover. Release was delayed two years by the Hays Office's intervention in how a house of prostitution could be portrayed on screen. Too bad they reached an agreement. Not even Morgan's rendition of the title song redeems this. 68m/B VHS, Helen Morgan, Chester Morris; **D:** Chester Erskine.

Frankie and Johnny 1965 Elvis is a riverboat gambler/singer whose lousy luck until Kovack changes the odds. This upsets his girlfriend Douglas who shoots him (but not fatally). Elvis wears period costumes, but this is otherwise similar to his contemporary films. 97m/C VHS, Elvis Presley, Donna Douglas, Harry (Henry) Morgan, Audrey Christie, Anthony Eisley, Sue Ane Langdon, Robert Strauss, Nancy Kovack; **D:** Fred de Cordova; **W:** Alex Gottlieb; **C:** "Jack" Marquette; **M:** Fred Karger.

Frankie and Johnny 1991 (R) Ex-con gets a job as a short-order cook and falls for a world-weary waitress. She doesn't believe in romance, but finally gives into his pleas for a chance and finds out he may not be such a bad guy after all. Nothing can make Pfeiffer dowdy enough for this 'role, but she and Pacino are charming together. In a change of pace role, Neligan has fun as a fellow waitress who loves men. Based on the play "Frankie and Johnny in the Clair de Lune" by McNally who also wrote the screenplay. 117m/C VHS, DVD, Al Pacino, Michele Pfeiffer, Hector Elizondo, Nathan Lane, Kate Neligan, Jane Morris, Greg Lewis, Al Fann, K. Callan Phil Leeds, Tracy Reiner, Dey Young; **D:** Garry Marshall; **W:** Terrance McNally; **C:** Dante Spinotti; **M:** Marvin Hamlisch, British Acad. '91: Support. Actress (Neligan); Natl. Bd. of Review '91: Support. Actress

---

Shelley and their family/of customs officer Jack Kelly (Byrne), who instills in the boy lifelong love of the stars. The adult Frankie (Walker) becomes a celebrity who writes a novel combining his obsession.

Frantic 1988 (R) While in Paris, an American surgeon's wife is kidnapped when she inadvertently picks up the wrong suitcase. Her kidnappers want their hidden treasure, which forces the husband into the criminal underground and into unexpected heroism when he seeks to rescue her. Contrived ending weakens on the whole, but Polanski is still master of the dark film thriller. 120m/C VHS, Harrison Ford, Betty Buckley, John Mahoney, Emmanuelle Seigner, Jimmie Ray Weeks, Yorgo Voyagis, David Huddleston, Gerard Klein; **D:** Roman Polanski; **W:** Roman Polanski, Gerard Brach; **C:** Witold Sobocinski; **M:** Ennio Morricone.

Franz 1972 A French mercenary and an insecure woman struggle with a doomed love affair. In French with English subtitles. 90m/C VHS, FR Danielle Evenou, Barbara Louis Navarre, Jacques Brel; **D:** Jacques Brel; **W:** Paul Andreota, Jacques Brel; **C:** Alain Levent; **M:** Jacques Brel.

Frasier the Sensuous Lion Frasier the Lovable Lion 1973 (PG) A zoology professor is able to converse with Frasier, a lion known for his sexual stamina and whose potency is coveted by a billionaire (shadow of monkey glands rejuvenation therapy.) A fairly typical, if slightly risque, talking critter film. 97m/C VHS, Michael Callan, Katherine Justice, Frank Da Kova, Malachi Throne, Victor Jory, Peter Lorre Jr., Marc Lawrence; **D:** Pat Shields.

Frauds 1993 (R) Collins is an immoral insurance investigator who takes his victims for everything he can. Then he meets a couple who are out to beat him at his own game. 94m/C VHS, Phil Collins, Hugo Weaving, Josephine Byrnes; **D:** Stephan Elliott; **W:** Stephan Elliott; **C:** Geoff Burton; **M:** Guy Gross.

The Fraternity 1985 (R) Despite the title, these aren't frat boys but a group of elite boarding school students who call themselves "The Circle" and run Runice Academy until headmaster Williams discovers their involvement in a cheating scandal and one of them is expelled. When the alleged informant winds up dead, another (Dunne) in the group decides he has to come clean about the group's other activities. 100m/C VHS, DVD, Treat Williams, Robin Dunne, Gordon Currie; **D:** Sidney J. Furie. **VIDEO**

Fraternity Vacation 1985 (R) Two college fraternity men show a nerd the greatest time of their lives on vacation in Palm Springs. 95m/C VHS, DVD, Stephen Geoffreys, Sheree J. Wilson, Cameron Dye, Leigh McCloskey, Tim Robbins, Matt McCoy, Amanda Bearse, John Vernon, Nita Talbot, Barbara Crampton, Kathleen Kinmont, Max Wright, Julie Payne, Franklin Ajaye, Charles Rocket, Britt Ekland; **D:** James Frawley; **W:** Lindsay Harrison; **C:** Paul Ryan; **M:** Brad Fiedel.

---

taken in by the family of customs officer Jack Kelly (Byrne), who instills in the boy lifelong love of the stars. The adult Frankie (Walker) becomes a celebrity who writes a novel combining his obsession.

Frantic Elevator to the Gallows; Ascenseur pour l'Echefaud 1958 From Louis Malle comes one of the first French New Wave film noir dramas. A man kills his boss with the connivance of the employer's wife, his lover, and makes it look like suicide. Meanwhile, teenagers have used his car and gun in the murder of a tourist couple and he is indicted for that crime. Their perfectly planned murder begins to unravel into a panic-stricken nightmare. A suspenseful and captivating drama. Direction by Malle's first feature film. Musical score by jazz legend Miles Davis. 92m/B VHS, DVD, FR Maurice Ronet, Jeanne Moreau, Georges Poujouly; **D:** Louis Malle; **C:** Henri Decae; **M:** Miles Davis.

Frantic 1988 (R) Elevator to the Gallows; an American surgeon's wife is kidnapped when she inadvertently picks up the wrong suitcase. Her kidnappers want their hidden treasure, which forces the husband into the criminal underground and into unexpected heroism when he seeks to rescue her. Contrived ending weakens on the whole, but Polanski is still master of the dark film thriller. 120m/C VHS, Harrison Ford, Betty Buckley, John Mahoney, Deahbla Molloy, Niall Tobin, Karl Davies; **D:** Michael Lindsay-Hogg; **W:** Chef Raymo, Renan O'Leary; **C:** Paul Laufer; **M:** Elmer Bernstein.

Freaked 1993 (PG-13) Bizarre little black comedy throws everything at the screen, hoping some of the gross-out humor will prove amusing (and some does). Greedy TV star Ricky Coogin (Winter) agrees to be the spokesman for E.E.S. Corporation which markets a toxic green slime fertilizer to the third world. He's sent to South America to promote the product and is captured by the mad scientist proprietor (Quaid) of a mysterious sideshow, who douses him with the fertilizer. Before you know it he's an oozing half-man, half-beast, perfect to join other freaks as the latest attraction. Lots of yucky makeup. Reeves has an uncredited cameo as the Dog Boy. 80m/C VHS, DVD, Alex Winter, Randy Quaid, Megan Ward, Michael Stoyanov, Brooke Shields, William Sadler, Derek McGrath, Alex Zuckerman, Karyn Malchus, Mr. T, Morgan Fairchild; **Cameos:** Keanu Reeves, Tom Stern, Tim Burns; **D:** Alex Winter, Tom Stern; **W:** Alex Winter, Tom Stern, Tim Burns; **C:** Jamie Thompson, Jane Omens; **M:** Kevin Kiner; **V:** Bob(cat) Goldthwait.

The Freakmaker Mutations; The Mutation 1973 (R) Mad professor attempts to breed plants with humans in his lab and has the usual bizarre results. Experiments that fail go to Dunn, a dwarf who runs a freak show. Shamelessly includes real freaks as if plot was not strange enough. 90m/C VHS, DVD, GB Donald Pleasence, Tom Baker, Brad Harris, Julie Ege, Michael Dunn, Jill Haworth, Olga Anthony, Lisa Collings, Scott Antony; **D:** Jack Cardiff; **W:** Edward Andrew (Santos A.ocoer) Mann, Robert D. Weinbach; **C:** Paul Beeson; **M:** Basil Kirchin.

Freaks 1932 Nature's Mistakes; Forbidden Love; The Monster Show 1932 The infamous, controversial, cult-horror classic about a band of circus freaks that exact revenge upon a beautiful aerialist and her strongman lover after enduring humiliation and exploitation. Based on Ted Robbins story "Spurs." "Frankenstein" but was so successful that it was repeatedly banned. Browning's film may be a shocker but it is never intended the only compassionate, loyal, and loving people around. 66m/B VHS, DVD, Wallace Ford, Olga Baclanova, Leila Hyams, Roscoe Ates, Harry Earles, Henry Victor, Daisy Earles, Madame Rose (Dion) Dione, Daisy Hilton, Violet Hilton; **D:** Tod Browning; **C:** Al Boasberg; **M:** Gunnar Leon Gordon, Edgar Allen Woolf; **D:** William Cooke, Paul Tabot.

Freakshow 1995 (R) Two teens wander into the sideshow at a local carnival and meet the Freakmaster (Hansen), whose grisly exhibits have equally grisly stories to tell. Campy horror with routine special effects. 102m/C VHS, DVD, Gunnar Hansen, Veronica Carlson, Brian D. Kelly, Shannon Michelle Parsons; **D:** William Cooke, Paul Talbot.

Freaky Friday 1976 (G) A housewife and her teenage daughter inadvertently switch bodies and each then tries to carry on the other's normal routine. Mary Rodgers' popular book is brought to the screen with great charm in this above average Disney film. 95m/C VHS, DVD, Barbara Harris, Jodie Foster, Patsy Kelly, John Astin, Dick Van Patten, Ruth Buzzi, Kaye Ballard, Charlene Tilton, James van Patten; **D:** Gary Nelson; **M:** Mary Rodgers.

Freaky Friday 2003 (PG) Worthy remake of the 1976 Disney original breathes some life into the body-switch genre. Curtis plays Tess, a widowed psychiatrist and mom to rebellious 15-year-old Anna (Lohan). Anna's upset that her mom is about to remarry. Following a fight over said wedding at a Chinese restaurant, mom and daughter are hexed by a cursed fortune cookie and wake up the next day in each other's body. After the initial shock wears off, the two leads seem right at home in the other's role, resulting in more laughs than you'd expect from a Disney remake. Curtis is especially fun to watch, whether she's tapping into her inner teen and kicking out the jams in Anna's garage band. Light comedy by deftly blends with morality in fun family comedy. 93m/C VHS, DVD, US Jamie Lee Curtis, Lindsay Lohan, Mark Harmon, Heroic Gould,

---

VideoHound's Golden Movie Retriever 365

Freaky

Chad Michael Murray, Ryan Malgarini, Stephen Tobolowsky, Christina Vidal, Rosalind Chao, Willie Garson, Dina Sprybey; D: Mark S. Waters; W: Leslie Dixon, Heather Hach; C: Oliver Wood; M: Rolfe Kent.

Fred Claus 2007 (PG) Vaughn attempts to bring his familiar shtick to preteens and fails miserably in this story about Santa's repo man brother, who's looking to make a quick buck in order to start a restaurant. Santa (Giamatti) offers Fred (Vaughn) money if he comes back to the North Pole to help with the Christmas rush, and something that fails to resemble hilarity ensues. The laughs are few, and the considerable talents of Vaughn, Giamatti, and fellow cast members Spacey, Weisz, and Bates are frittered, as the pic seems to rely exclusively on Vaughn's trademark big mouth and cliched family-movie sap. 115m/C DVD. US Vince Vaughn, Paul Giamatti, Miranda Richardson, Rachel Weisz, John Michael Higgins, Kathy Bates, Trevor Peacock, Chris Bridges, Elizabeth Banks, Jeremy Swift, Elizabeth Berrington, Kevin Spacey; D: David Dobkin; W: Dan Fogelman; C: Remi Adefarasin; M: Christophe Beck.

Freddie the Frog 1992 (G) Prince Frederick's life is shattered when his father is killed by his evil Aunt Messina, who wants to rule the kingdom. She even changes Frederick into a frog—but he manages to escape her with the help of friendly sea monster Nessie. But Freddie discovers that he has also been given super-frog powers, just in time to save Britain's landmarks, which are disappearing thanks to Aunt Messina's spells. 72m/C VHS. GB D: Jon Acevski; W: Jon Acevski, David Ashton; V: Ben Kingsley, Nigel Hawthorne, Jenny Agutter, John Sessions, Brian Blessed, Billie Whitelaw, Jonathan Pryce, Phyllis Logan, Michael Hordern; Nar: James Earl Jones.

Freddy Got Fingered woof! 2001 (R) Green, making his feature directorial debut, is a dedicated slacker who refuses to get a job and move out of his father's (Tom) house. Green the director loves Green the "actor," almost as much as he loves human and animal bodily fluids—all of them. What he does to horses and elephants will poison forever your fond memories of trips to the zoo. Forever. Taken in small doses, Green's act can induce "I can't believe I'm laughing at this"-type chuckles, but an hour and a half could cause permanent brain damage. Look what its apparently done to him! To say "Freddy" wallows in the gutter is to besmirch the gutter's good name. 88m/C VHS, DVD. US Tom Green, Rip Torn, Harland Williams, Eddie Kaye Thomas, Julie Hagerty, Anthony Michael Hall, Marisa Coughlan; D: Tom Green; W: Tom Green, Derek Harvie; C: Mark Irwin; M: Mike Simpson. Golden Raspberries '01: Worst Picture, Worst Actor (Green), Worst Director (Green), Worst Screenplay.

Freddy vs. Jason 2003 (R) Highly anticipated cinematic showdown between Freddy Krueger and Jason Vorhees begins with the clever premise that Freddy is dying of neglect. The children of Elm Street have forgotten about him, so Freddy is ceasing to exist. Freddy gets it into his head to inject a little horror into the real world and summons Jason from whatever hell he's been languishing in and sets him loose. The only problem is that Jason is taking center stage, which displeases Freddy. Ronny Yu's frenetic direction sets a suitable pace, but after the setup, it all settles into standard "slasher film" mode until the climactic battle. Forgettable cast of victims adequately plays off of Robert Englund's scene-devouring Freddy. 97m/C VHS, DVD, UMD. US Robert Englund, Ken Kirzinger, Monica Keena, Jason Ritter, Kelly Rowland, Katharine Isabelle, Brendan Fletcher, Tom Butler, Lochlyn Munro, James Callahan; D: Ronny Yu; W: Damian Shannon, Mark Swift; C: Fred Murphy; M: Graeme Revell.

Freddy's Dead: The Final Nightmare A Nightmare on Elm Street 6: Freddy's Dead 1991 (R) Freddy's daughter journeys to Springwood, Ohio, to put a stop to her father's evil ways. Will she be able to destroy this maniac, or is a new reign of terror just beginning? The sixth film in the "Nightmare" series; followed by "Wes Craven's New Nightmare." 96m/C VHS, DVD. Robert Englund, Lisa Zane, Shon Greenblatt, Lezlie (Dean) Deane, Ricky Dean Logan, Breckin Meyer, Yaphet Kotto, Elinor Donahue, Roseanne, Johnny Depp, Alice Cooper, Tom Arnold; D: Rachel Talalay; W: Michael De Luca; C: Declan Quinn.

Frederick Forsyth's Icon 2005 (PG-13) Based on bestseller Frederick Forsyth's book icon. Jason Monk (Swayze), an ex-CIA agent, comes out of retirement to save an entire country from the brink of ruin. Russian presidential candidate Igor Komarov (Bergin) promises his people a new Russia, but his plan is based on a secret "Black Manifesto" that lays a foundation for dictatorship and military rule, among other evils. Monk's also charged with seeking out Anatoli Grishin (Cross), an evil KGB officer whom Monk has a personal vendetta against. Forsyth fans may be disappointed by the many deviations from the book; breathtaking Russian scenery and some thrilling suspense may make up for it. 180m/C DVD. Patrick Swayze, Patrick Bergin, Michael York, Ben Cross, Annika Peterson, Jeff Fahey, Joss Ackland; D: Charles Martin Smith; W: Adam Armus, Nora Kay Foster; C: David Carnell; M: Daniel Licht. CABLE.

Free Amerika Broadcasting 1989 A drama about an alternate reality in which Richard Nixon was assassinated, leaving Spiro Agnew president. As a result, the country turns to violent revolution. 80m/C VHS. Brian Kincaid; D: Dean Wilson.

Free and Easy Easy Go 1930 Keaton plays the incompetent manager of a beauty contest winner (Page) and her overbearing mother, accompanied by Keaton, go to Hollywood to make the girl a star. They gate-crash the MGM studio where all cause havoc and it turns out Keaton is the one who lands in front of the cameras (Page has to settle for romancing Montgomery). Provides a behind-the-scenes look at the MGM studio, with a number of MGM stars making cameo appearances. 92m/B VHS, DVD. Buster Keaton, Anita Page, Robert Montgomery, Trixie Friganza, Fred Niblo; Cameos: Cecil B. DeMille, Jackie Coogan, Lionel Barrymore, William Haines; D: Edward Sedgwick.

Free Enterprise 1998 (R) Funny and inventive semi-autobiographical tale of a couple of aspiring filmmakers facing 30 without a clue about becoming adults. Schlock screenwriter Robert (Weigel) and best bud, film editor Mark (McCormack), filter their existence through sci fi and '70s TV shows. The two are completely geeked by a chance meeting with their "Star Trek" idol William Shatner (who slyly pokes fun at his own persona), who offers them encouragement. The duo actually make some attempts at that grown-up thing by the clever finale. 114m/C VHS, DVD. Eric McCormack, Rafer Weigel, William Shatner, Audie England, Deborah Van Valkenburgh, Jonathan Slavin, Maury LaMar; D: Robert Meyer Burnett; W: Robert Meyer Burnett, Mark Altman; C: Charles L. Barbee; M: Scott Spock.

Free Grass Scream Free! 1969 A gang of thoughtless hippie drug smugglers and abusers escape from the police, drink acid-spiked wine, shoot each other, and have love-ins. 82m/C VHS. Russ Tamblyn, Richard Beymer, Casey Kasem, Lana Wood, Warren Finnerty, Elizabeth Thompson, Lindsay Crosby, Jody McCrea; D: Bill Brame, John Lawrence; W: Robert Meyer Burnett; C: Charles L. Barbee; M: Scott Spock.

Free Money 1999 (R) Kinda dumb buddy comedy finds Bud (Sheen) and Larry (Church) stuck in North Dakota and forced to marry the twin daughters of local prison warden The Swede (Brando, overacting as usual). The two losers decide the best way to get away from their father-in-law's watchful eye is to rob a train loaded with cash. 94m/C VHS, DVD. Charlie Sheen, Marlon Brando, Donald Sutherland, Thomas Haden Church, Mira Sorvino, David Arquette; D: Yves Simoneau; W: Tony Peck, Joseph Brutsman; C: David Franco.

Free of Eden 1998 Successful New York businessman Poitier reluctantly agrees to mentor a troubled inner-city teenaged girl (played by Poitier's daughter). 97m/C VHS, DVD. Sidney Poitier, Sydney Tamiia Poitier, Phylicia Rashad, Robert Hooks; D: Leon Ichaso; W: Delle Chatman, Yule Caise; C: Claudio Chea; M: Terence Blanchard. CABLE.

Free Ride 1986 (R) A kooky kid steals a sportscar to impress a girl, and gets involved with local hoods. They chase each other around. 92m/C VHS. Gary Hershberger, Reed Rudy, Dawn Schneider, Peter DeLuise, Brian MacGregor; W: Robert Bell, Ron Zwang.

A Free Soul 1931 Tippling litigator Barrymore helps low-life mobster Gable beat a murder rap, only to discover the hood has stolen his daughter's heart. Bargaining with his ditzy daughter, he vows to eschew the bottle if she'll stay away from good-for-nothing Gable. Directed by Brown, and based on the memoirs of Adela Rogers St. John. The final courtroom scene—a cloak-and-gavel classic—cinched Barrymore's Oscar. Remade with Liz Taylor as "The Girl Who Had Everything" (although, ironically, the earlier version is the racier of the two). 94m/B VHS. Norma Shearer, Leslie Howard, Lionel Barrymore, Clark Gable, James Gleason, Lucy Beaumont; C: William H. Daniels. Oscars '31: Actor (Barrymore).

Free to Love 1925 Screen idol Bow plays a young woman, fresh out of prison, who is taken in by a kindly, affluent patron. But, as the silent drama axiom would have it, there's no escaping the past, and she's forced to defend her former life when her guardian is murdered. 61m/B VHS. Clara Bow, Donald Keith, Raymond (Ray) McKee; D: Frank O'Connor.

Free, White, and 21 1962 A black motel owner is accused of raping a white civil rights worker. Produced in a "pseudo-documentary" form which sometimes drags. 104m/B VHS. Frederick O'Neal, Annalena Lund, George Edgely, John Hicks, Hugh Crenshaw, George Russell; D: Larry Buchanan.

Free Willy 1993 (PG) Sentimental story about a 12-year-old runaway (Richter) who befriends a whale. Should appeal to children for its heartwarming story and delightful sea acrobatics. An electronically operated stand-in whale was used for far-off shots; a domesticated performing whale named Keiko for the close-ups. Director Wincer was known to grumble about the temperamental Keiko during shooting. Suggested viewing for students of animal behavior. Proof that family films can make money, "Free Willy" placed tenth for total boxoffice receipts in 1993. 112m/C VHS, DVD. Jason James Richter, Lori Petty, Jayne Atkinson, August Schellenberg, Michael Madsen; D: Simon Wincer; W: Keith A. Walker, Corey Blechman; C: Robbie Greenberg; M: Basil Poledouris. MTV Movie Awards '94: Song ("Will You Be There").

Free Willy 2: The Adventure Home 1995 (PG) While camping in the Pacific Northwest, Jesse is reunited with his orca/pal Willy, who has found a new home along with his whale siblings. But an offshore oil spill separates Willy from his family and threatens their lives, so his human friends must once again come to the rescue. All the principal characters are back, except for Willy (real name Keiko), who is recuperating from a skin virus in Mexico. Animatronics and Gump-like digital effects were used to replicate the real Willy. 98m/C VHS, DVD. Jason James Richter, Michael Madsen, Jayne Atkinson, August Schellenberg, Jon Tenney, Elizabeth Pena; D: Dwight Little; W: Corey Blechman, John Mattson; C: Laszlo Kovacs; M: Basil Poledouris.

Free Willy 3: The Rescue 1997 (PG) Isn't this poor whale ever going to be left in peace? This time around an illegal whaling operation threatens Willie and his orca pod. But 17-year-old Jesse (Richter), who has a summer job as a whale tracker on a research vessel, is determined to rescue his friend, aided by 10-year-old Max (Berry), who's horrified to discover his commercial fisherman father (Kilpatrick) is one of the whalers. 86m/C VHS, DVD. Jason James Richter, Vincent Berry, August Schellenberg, Annie Corley, Patrick Kilpatrick; D: Sam Pillsbury; W: John Mattson; C: Tobias Schliessler; M: Cliff Eidelman.

Free Zone 2005 Three women with ethnic ties to the Middle East converge in Jordan and become traveling companions for dissimilar reasons. An American with Israeli roots, Rebecca (Portman) kicks things off in a 10-minute crying jag in a cab by the Wailing Wall, though her sorrow appears connected not to religion but to her break-up with her fiance after he makes an appalling admission to her. The cab driver is Hanna (a spirited Laslo), an Israeli woman who has endured the regional turmoil but needs to collect cash that an associate of her husband owes to her. Woman number three, Leila (Abbass), is a Palestinian who works at Hanna's husband's office, who informs Hanna that the associate has vanished, causing the women to embark on a road trip to the Free Zone to look for him—and the cash. While an interesting trip, the political lessons stall out along the way. 94m/C DVD. BE FR IS SP Natalie Portman, Uri Klauzner, Carmen Maura, Hiam Abbass, Hanna Laslo, Makram Khoury, Aki Avni; D: Amos Gitai; W: Amos Gitai, Marie-Jose Sanselme; C: Laurent Brunel.

Freebie & the Bean 1974 (R) Two San Francisco cops nearly ruin the city in their pursuit of a numbers-running mobster. Top-flight car chases and low-level, bigoted humor combine. Watch for Valerie Harper's appearance as Arkin's wife. Followed by a flash-in-the-pan TV series. 113m/C VHS. Alan Arkin, James Caan, Loretta Swit, Valerie Harper, Jack Kruschen, Mike Kellin; D: Richard Rush.

Freedom 1982 A young man finds the price of freedom to be very high when he tries to escape from Australian society in a silver Porsche. 102m/C VHS. AU Jon Blake, Candy (Candy) Raymond, Jad Capelja, Reg Lye, John Clayton, Charles "Bud" Tingwall, Chris Haywood; D: Scott Hicks; W: John Emery; C: Ron Johanson; M: Don Walker.

Freedom Is Paradise 1989 With his mother dead and his father missing, 13-year-old Sasha is growing up in a bleak reform school. Every time he runs away he is caught and severely beaten upon his return. When Sasha learns of his father's whereabouts in the gulag-style prison, on where is father is being held. Bodrov's directorial debut. In Russian with English subtitles. 75m/C VHS. RU Volodya Kozyrev, Svetlana Gaitan, Vitautas Tomkus; D: Sergei Bodrov; W: Sergei Bodrov; C: Yuri Skhirtladze. Montreal World Film Fest. '89: Film.

Freedom Road 1979 Drama about a Reconstruction Era ex-slave, portrayed by heavyweight champion Ali, who is elected to the U.S. Senate and subsequently killed while trying to obtain total freedom for his race. Based on a novel by Howard Fast. 186m/C VHS. Ron O'Neal, Edward Herrmann, John McLiam, Ernest Dixon, Alfre Woodard, Kris Kristofferson, Muhammad Ali; D: Jan Kadar. TV

Freedom Song 2000 In Mississippi in 1961, Will Walker (Glover) is a black man both angry and afraid. Civil rights, freedom rights and increasing racial violence make for tense times for the Walker family as teenaged Owen (Shannon) is drawn to organizer Daniel Wall (Curtis-Hall). Complex, conflicted people and situations make for a fine drama. 150m/C VHS, DVD. Danny Glover, Vondie Curtis-Hall, Vicellous Shannon, Loretta Devine, Glynn Turman, Stan Shaw, Michael Jai White, Rae'ven (Alyia Larrymore) Kelly, John Beasley, Jason Weaver, Marcello Thedford, Phil Alden Robinson; D: Phil Alden Robinson, Stanley Weiser; M: James Horner. CABLE. TV

Freedom Strike 🐾½ 1998 (R) Navy pilots Stone and MacDonald are sent on a covert mission to sabotage an Iraqi nuclear reactor before terrorists can use it. 93m/C VHS, DVD. Michael Dudikoff, Tone Loc, Felicity Waterman; **D:** Jerry P. Jacobs.

Freedom Writers 🐾🐾½ 2007 (PG-13) Oh so earnest (yet affecting) dedicated teacher true story set in 1994. White-bread newbie Erin Gruwell (Swank) is unprepared for teaching freshman English to an ethnically diverse, underprivileged class at a Long Beach high school. In order to get their attention, Erin, inspired by "The Diary of Anne Frank," gives her students journals to write about their own lives in their own raw vernacular. A collection of entries is eventually published as "The Freedom Writers Diary," which continues to cause classroom/parental clashes for its eye-opening depictions of teen experience. Swank, complete with gleaming smile and pearls, is filled with can-do spirit while Dempsey is wasted as her neglected hubby. 123m/C DVD, Blu-ray Disc, HD DVD, US Hilary Swank, Patrick Dempsey, Scott Glenn, Imelda Staunton, John Benjamin Hickey, Pat Carroll, April Lee Hernandez, Deaf'ce Wyatt, Mario, Vanetta Smith; **D:** Richard LaGravenese; **C:** Richard LaGravenese; **M:** Mark Isham.

Freedomland 🐾🐾½ 2006 (R) White girl (Moore) from "the right side of the tracks" walks into a medical center in the projects with the story of a carjacking/kidnapping of her son. Black detective Lorenzo (Jackson) must find out the truth and prevent a riot as they, one of whom (Eldard) is her brother, lock down the neighborhood. Tension is effectively built as Lorenzo works the case while trying to balance his allegiances to his instincts, his neighborhood, and his job. Jackson's presence is vital to keeping the movie from spinning out of control into preachy "good-for-you" territory. Still gets a bit heavy, and more than a little depressing. 113m/C DVD. US Samuel L. Jackson, Julianne Moore, Edie Falco, Ron Eldard, William Forsythe, Aunjanue Ellis, Anthony Mackie, LaTanya Richardson Jackson, Clarke Peters; **D:** Joe Roth; **W:** Richard Price; **C:** Anastas Michos; **M:** James Newton Howard.

Freejack 🐾🐾½ 1992 (R) Futuristic thriller set in the year 2009, where pollution, the hole in the ozone layer, and the financial gap between the social classes have grown to such horrific proportions that the rich must pillage the past to find young bodies to replace their own. Estevez is a young race car driver whose sudden death makes him an ideal candidate for this bizarre type of surgery. Once "transported to the future, he becomes a "Freejack" who must run for his life. Good cast including Jagger and Hopkins brings this one up slightly. Adapted from the novel "Immortality Inc." by Robert Sheckley. 110m/C VHS, DVD. Emilio Estevez, Mick Jagger, Rene Russo, Anthony Hopkins, Jonathan Banks, David Johansen, Amanda Plummer, Grand L. Bush, Frankie Faison, Esai Morales, John Shea; **D:** Geoff Murphy; **W:** Dan Gilroy, Ronald Shusett, Steven Pressfield; **C:** Amir M. Mokri; **M:** Trevor Jones.

Freelance 🐾½ 1988 (R) A nurse attempts to find the obsessive killer who shot her husband. The murderer phones a radio psychiatrist from his car, using Biblical quotes, while cruising for new victims. Okay thriller, based on the L.A. freeway shootings. 91m/C VHS, DVD. Darlanne Fluegel, James Russo, Billy Drago, Richard Belzer, Michael Callan, Steve Franken, Kenneth Tobey, Clint Howard; **D:** Francis Delia; **W:** Larry Ketron, Darrell Fetty. Francis Delia; **M:** Joe Delia.

Freeway 🐾½ 1995 (R) Grubby modern retelling of "Little Red Riding Hood" finds surly 16-year-old Vanessa (Witherspoon) escaping from her parole officer to avoid foster care when the cops arrest her mom and stepdad. She takes the family car and heads off to grandma's but car trouble on the freeway leads to a ride from the big bad wolf—Bob Wolverton (Sutherland)—a serial killer preying on young women. Lots of lurid unpleasantness exact and the teamwork with Witherspoon, Kiefer Sutherland, Brooke Shields, Wolfgang Bodison, Dan Hedaya, Amanda Plummer, Bokeem Woodbine, Brittany Murphy, Michael T. Weiss, Guillermo Diaz, Susan Barnes, Alanna Ubach, Conchata Ferrell, Tara Subkoff, Sydney Lassick; **D:** Matthew Bright; **W:** Matthew Bright; **C:** Danny Elfman.

Freeway 2: Confessions of a Trickbaby 🐾 1999 (R) The 1995 film was a violent modern update of "Little Red Riding Hood" and the sequel is a twisted fairytale "Hansel and Gretel." Crystal (Lyonne) escapes from juvenile prison with cell buddy Cyclona (Celedonio) and heads to Tijuana where she hopes psychic Sister Gomez (Gallo) can cure her of her compulsion to murder. The body count rises a lot on their journey. As grubby and unappealing as its predecessor. 90m/C VHS, DVD. Natasha Lyonne, Maria Celedonio, Vincent Gallo, David Alan Grier, Michael T. Weiss, John Landis, Max Perlich; **D:** Matthew Bright; **C:** Joel Ransom; **M:** Kennard Ramsey. VIDEO

The Freeway Maniac 🐾 1988 (R) A low budget thriller about an escaped convict who ends up on a movie set where he continues his former career: murder. Music by former "Doors" guitarist Robby Krieger. 94m/C VHS. Loren Winters, James Courtney, Shepard Sanders, Donald Hotton; **D:** Paul Winters; **C:** Robby Krieger.

Freeze-Die-Come to Life 🐾🐾🐾 Zamri Oumi Voskresni 1990 First feature film from Kanevski, who spent eight years in a labor camp before overcome the crushing poverty and bleakness of life in a remote mining community with friendship and humor. Beautifully filmed images, fine acting, touching but never overly sentimental story. The title comes from a children's game of tag. In Russian with English subtitles. 105m/B VHS, RU Pavel Nazarov, Dinara Drukarova; **D:** Vitaly Kanevski; **W:** Vitaly Kanevski; **C:** Vladimir Brylyakov; **M:** Sergei Banevich.

Freeze Frame 🐾🐾½ 1992 Dicher-ty is a high school TV reporter who's determined to capture a biotech conspiracy on video in this funny, fast-paced action flick. Nothing objectionable here. 78m/C VHS. Shannen Doherty, Charles Hald, Robyn Douglass, Seth Michaels; **D:** William Bindley.

Freeze Frame 🐾🐾½ 2004 (R) Sean Vail (Evans) was accused of multiple murders but released on a 'technicality. Ten years later, Sean's paranoia is in full bloom and he obsessively videotapes every moment of his life so he will have an alibi if it's ever needed, which happens when a new victim is discovered. But Sean can't account for his whereabouts because the tapes of those specific hours are mysteriously missing. Brt Evans is best known for his comedy so this psycho-thriller is a real departure. Strong visually, if the flick falls apart at the end. 90m/C DVD, IR GB Lee Evans, Sean McGinley, Rachael Stirling, Ian McNeice, Colin Salmon, Rachel O'Riordan; **D:** John Simpson; **W:** John Simpson; **C:** Mark Garret; **M:** Debbie Wiseman.

French Can-Can 🐾🐾🐾 Only the French Can! 1955 Dramatically sparse but visually stunning depiction of the can-can's revival in Parisian nightclubs. Gabin plays the theatre impressario who discovers the laundress Arnoul and decides to turn her into the dancing star of his new revue at the Moulin Rouge. In French with English subtitles. 93m/C VHS, DVD. FR Jean Gabin, Francoise Arnoul, Maria Felix, Jean-Roger Caussimon, Edith Piaf, Patachou; **D:** Jean Renoir.

The French Connection 🐾🐾🐾½ 1971 (R) Popeye Doyle (Hackman) and his partner Buddy Russo (Scheider) are a couple of hard-nosed NYC narcotics detectives who stumble onto what turns out to be one of the biggest narcotics rings of all time, involving French mastermind Alain Charnier (Rey). Cat-and-mouse thriller will keep you on the edge of your seat; contains one of the most exciting chase scenes ever filmed. Hackman's portrayal of Doyle is special. Based on a true story from the book by Robin Moore. Followed in 1975 by "French Connection 2." 102m/C VHS, DVD. Gene Hackman, Roy Scheider, Fernando Rey, Tony LoBianco, Eddie Egan, Sonny Grosso, Marcel Bozzuffi; **D:** William Friedkin; **W:** Ernest Tidyman; **C:** Owen Roizman; **M:** Don Ellis. Oscars '71: Actor (Hackman), Adapt. Screenplay, Director (Friedkin), Film Editing, Picture; AFI '98: Top 100; British Acad. '72: Actor (Hackman); Directors Guild '71: Director (Friedkin); Golden Globes '72: Actor—Drama (Hackman); Director (Friedkin), Film—Drama; Natl. Bd. of Review '71: Actor (Hackman), Natl. Film Reg. '05; N.Y. Film Critics '71: Actor (Hackman); Writers Guild '71: Adapt. Screenplay.

French Connection 2 🐾🐾🐾 1975 (R) New York policeman "Popeye" Doyle goes to Marseilles to crack a heroin ring headed by his arch nemesis, Frog One, whom he failed to stop in the United States. Dour, super-gritty sequel to the 1971 blockbuster, and featuring one of Hackman's most uncompromising performances. 118m/C VHS, DVD. Gene Hackman, Fernando Rey, Bernard Fresson; **D:** John Frankenheimer; **W:** Robert Dillon; **C:** Claude Renoir; **M:** Don Ellis.

The French Detective 🐾🐾🐾 Adieu Poulet 1975 Two detectives, one an old-time tough guy and the other a young cynic, are after a ruthless politician and his pet hood. Grim but entertaining. 90m/C VHS. FR Lino Ventura, Patrick Dewaere, Victor Lanoux; **D:** Pierre Granier-Deferre.

French Exit 🐾🐾 1997 (R) Another "meet cute" Hollywood romantic comedy. Neophyte screenwriters David Lake (Silverman) and Zina Hart (Amick) have a fender bender in an L.A. intersection. Flirtatious sparks fly amid their bickering but later they discover they're vying for the same big break script job. So will professional rivalry destroy the romantic fire? What do you think. 88m/C VHS. Kurt Fuller, Beth Broderick, Jonathan Silverman, Madchen Amick, Molly Hagan; **D:** Daphna Kastner; **W:** Daphna Kastner, Mari Lerner; **C:** Geza Sinkovics; **M:** Alex Wurman.

French Fried Vacation 🐾🐾 Les Bronzes 1979 Zany antics erupt when a group of unattached people on an adults vacation in Africa. French with English subtitles. 90m/C VHS, DVD. FR Josiana Balasko, Michel Blanc, Mariann (Marie-Anne) Chezel, Thierry Lhermitte, Gerard Jugnot, Dominique Lavanant; **D:** Patrice Leconte.

French Intrigue 🐾🐾 Cannabis 1970 (R) International agents track drug lords from the U.S. to France in a so-so spy thriller. 99m/C VHS, Serge Gainsbourg, Paul Nicholas, Gabriele Ferzetti, Jane Birkin, Cur. Jurgens; **D:** Pierre Koralnik; **W:** Franz-Andre Burguet; **C:** Willy Kurant; **M:** Serge Gainsbourg.

French Kiss 🐾🐾½ 1995 (PG-13) Ultra cute Kate (Ryan) has a fear of flying but she's more afraid of losing her fiance (Hutton) to a newly met French babe. She jets off to Paris and on the way meets a dashing, but disheveled, French rogue (Kline). What happens next is predictable, but amusing just the same. Plot drags a bit in the middle, but the scenery and banter between Ryan and Kline are a pleasant enough diversion. Kline is at his charming best, while Ryan is typically perky. Watch for Spielvogel's stereotypically rude French hotel concierge. He's a hoot. 111m/ C VHS, DVD. Meg Ryan, Kevin Kline, Timothy Hutton, Jean Reno, Francois Cluzet, Renee Humphrey, Michael Riley, Susan Anbeh, Laurent Spiel-vogel; **D:** Lawrence Kasdan; **W:** Adam Brooks; **C:** Owen Roizman; **M:** James Newton Howard.

The French Lesson 🐾🐾½ The Frog Prince 1986 (PG) A romantic British farce from a screenplay by cartoonist Simmonds, dealing with an English girl who goes to school in Paris and finds love. 90m/C VHS, GB Alexandre Sterling, Jane Snowdon; **D:** Brian Gilbert; **W:** Posy S. Simmonds.

The French Lieutenant's Woman 🐾🐾🐾½ 1981 (R) Romantic stories, that cut in the form of two parallel stories, that cut in the form of two parallel love and tragedy in the form of two parallel stories, that cut between the present who keeps her mysterious past from the scientist who loves her, and the lead actor and actress in the film of the same story filmed. An illicit affair on the set. Extraordinary performances and beautifully shot. Based on the John Fowles novel. 124m/C VHS, DVD. Meryl Streep, Jeremy Irons, Leo McKern, Lynsey Baxter, Harold Pinter; **C:** Freddie Francis; **M:** Carl Davis. British Acad. '81: Actress (Streep); Golden Globes '82: Actress—Drama (Streep); L.A. Film Critics '81: Actress (Streep).

The French Line 🐾🐾 1954 A millionaires beauty travels incognito while trying to sort out which men are after her money, and which ones aren't. The 3-D presentation of Russell's physique in skimpy costumes earned this the condemnation of the Catholic Legion of Decency, which pumped the boxoffice even higher. Lacks the charm of "Gentlemen Prefer Blonds," which it imitates. 102m/C VHS. Jane Russell, Gilbert Roland, Arthur Hunnicutt, Scott Elliott, Joi Lansing; **D:** Lloyd Bacon.

French Postcards 🐾🐾 1979 (PG) Three American students study all aspects of French culture when they spend their junior year of college at the Institute of French Studies in Paris. By the same writers who penned "American Graffiti" a few years earlier. 95m/C VHS. Miles Chapin, Blanche Baker, Valerie Quennessen, Debra Winger, Mandy Patinkin, Marie-France Pisier; **D:** Willard Huyck; **W:** Gloria Katz, Willard Huyck.

French Quarter 🐾🐾½ 1978 (R) A dual story about a young girl in the modern-day French Quarter of New Orleans who is also the reincarnation of a turn-of-the-century prostitute. Everyone gets to play two roles but this film is more curiosity than anything else. 101m/C VHS. Bruce Davison, Virginia Mayo, Lindsay Bloom, Alisha Fontaine, Lance LeGault, Anne Michelle; **D:** Dennis Kane.

French Quarter Undercover 🐾 1985 (R) Two undercover cops in New Orleans thwart a terrorist plot aimed at the World's Fair. 84m/C VHS. Michael Parks, Bill Holiday; **D:** Joe Catalanotto.

French Silk 🐾🐾 1994 (PG-13) Homicide detective (Horsley) falls for a lingerie designer (Lucci) who's a murder suspect. Filmed on location in New Orleans. Made for TV production with additional footage. "R" rating is for nudity (not Lucci's). Based on the novel by Sandra Brown. 90m/C VHS. Susan Lucci, Lee Horsley, Shari Belafonte, R. Lee Ermey, Sarah Marshall, Bobby Hosea, Jim Metzler, Joe Warfield, Paul Rosenberg; **D:** Noel Nosseck. TV

The French Touch 🐾🐾½ Coup de Torchon 1954 Romantic comedy about a shepherd who decides to pass himself off as a chronic philanderer, a very appealing stranger Marijo (Balasko), a hit among the Parisiennes. Fair to middling comedy. 84m/B VHS. FR Fernandel, Renee Devillers, Georges Chamarat; **D:** Jean Boyer.

French Twist 🐾🐾½ Gazon Maudit 1995 (R) Romantic comedy about housewife Loli (Abril), tiredly coping with her realtor/husband Laurent (Chabat) covers her hubby is a chronic philanderer. Loli gets revenge by inviting Marijo to move in with them. Laurent realizes he loves this hot but she's having too much fun and there is finally an interesting showdown between Laurent and Marijo over matter-of-fact lesbian, and when she discovers their two sons. Then Loli meets appealing stranger Marijo (Balasko), a very life-term for lesbian. French with subtitles. 100m/C VHS, DVD. FR Victoria Abril, Alain Chabat, Josiane Balasko, Ticky Holgado; **D:** Josiane Balasko; **W:** Josiane Balasko, Telsche Boorman.

C: Gerard de Battista; **M:** Manuel Malou. Cesar '96: Writing.

The French Way 🐾🐾½ **1940** One of the legendary Baker's few films, in which she portrays a Parisian nightclub owner playing matchmaker for a young couple. In French with English subtitles. 72m/B VHS. *FR* Josephine Baker, Micheline Presle, Georges Marchal; *D:* Jacques de Baroncelli.

The French Woman 🐾 **1979 (R)** Soft-core story of blackmail, murder, and sex involving French cabinet ministers mixing passion and politics. From the director of "Emmanuelle." 97m/C VHS, DVD. Francoise Fabian, Klaus Kinski; *D:* Just Jaeckin; *M:* Serge Gainsbourg.

Frenchman's Creek 🐾🐾½ **1944** Adventure set in the 17th century features English noblewoman Lady Dona (Fontaine) fleeing her spineless husband Harry St. Columb (Forbes) and his lecherous friend, Lord Rockingham (Rathbone). She finds a Frenchman's ship anchored in a creek off her country estate and becomes dazzled by its dashing pirate captain (de Cordova). Unfortunately, the pirate is also a spy (since the Frenchies and the Brits are fighting as usual) and Rockingham discovers their secrets. When the Frenchman is captured, Lady Dona risks all to rescue him. Based on the novel by Daphne du Maurier and remade for British TV in 1998. 112m/C VHS. Joan Fontaine, Arturo de Cordova, Basil Rathbone, Ralph Forbes, Nigel Bruce, Cecil Kellaway, Moyna MacGill; *D:* Mitchell Leisen; *W:* Talbot Jennings; *C:* George Barnes; *M:* Victor Young. TV

Frenchman's Creek 🐾🐾½ **1998** Lady Dona St. Columb (Fitzgerald) is bored both with London society and her husband, Sir Harry (Fleet), so she and her children head for her family's estate on the Cornish coast. There, Dona discovers dashing French privateer, Jean Aubrey (Delon), is using a nearby cove to anchor his ship while he spies on the English. Dona and the pirate get very, very close when he discovers that his wife is having an affair, turns to his art for solace...and seals his wife's corpse in a statue. Creepy. 75m/B VHS, DVD. *GB* Derrick DeMarney, Frederick Valk, Joan Greenwood, Joan Seton, Valentine Dyall, Martin Miller; *D:* Vernon Sewell; *W:* Vernon Sewell.

Frenzy 🐾🐾½ **1972** *Latin Quarter* **1946** A sculptor, pushed over the brink of sanity when he discovers that his wife is having an affair, turns to his art for solace...and seals his wife's corpse in a statue. Creepy. 75m/B VHS, DVD. *GB* Derrick DeMarney, Frederick Valk, Joan Greenwood, Joan Seton, Valentine Dyall, Martin Miller; *D:* Vernon Sewell; *W:* Vernon Sewell.

Frenzy 🐾🐾🐾 **1972 (R)** The only film in which Hitchcock was allowed to totally vent the violence and perverse sexuality of his distinctive vision, in a story about a strangler stalking London women in the late '60s. Finch plays the convicted killer-only he's innocent and must escape prison to find the real killer. McGowen is wonderful as the put-upon police inspector. A bit dated, but still ferociously hostile and cunningly executed. 116m/C VHS, DVD. *GB* Jon Finch, Barry Foster, Barbara Leigh-Hunt, Anna Massey, Alec McCowen, Vivien Merchant, Billie Whitelaw, Jean Marsh, Bernard Cribbins, Michael Bates, Rita Webb, Jimmy Gardner, Clive Swift, Madge Ryan, George Tovey, Noel Johnson; *D:* Alfred Hitchcock; *W:* Anthony Shaffer; *C:* Gilbert Taylor; *M:* Ronald Goodwin.

Frequency 🐾🐾½ **2000 (PG-13)** In 1999, New York cop John (Caviezel) finds he can communicate with his dead father (Quaid) through dad's old ham radio. Since his father was a fireman who died in a warehouse fire almost exactly 30 years ago, John decides to tell him how not to get killed. This leads to changes in the present (messing with the past always does), including the murder of John's mother by a serial killer. Father and son must solve and prevent the killings in the past and the present using their knowledge of the 1969 World Series. It's all very convoluted and ridiculous (especially the ending), but the underlying sentiment, and the fine work of Caviezel and Quaid make it easy to suspend disbelief and go along for the ride. 117m/C VHS, DVD. Dennis Quaid, James (Jim) Caviezel, Elizabeth Mitchell, Andre Braugher, Shawn Doyle, Noah Emmerich, Jordan Bridges, Melissa Errico, Daniel Henson; *D:* Gregory Hoblit; *W:* Toby Emmerich; *C:* Alar Kivilo; *M:* Michael Kamen.

Fresh 🐾🐾½ **1994 (R)** Intelligent 12-year-old boy runs heroin in the morning and sells crack after school in a tough Brooklyn neighborhood. Enterprising young man draws life lessons from chess-hustler father Jackson and heroin-dealing mentor Esposito, so he looks for a way out of the dead-end business. First time director Yakin plays it straight, foregoing the usual Hollywood-style rap and automatic weapons approach to convey the message that circumstances can kill innocence just as effectively as a bullet. Startling but subdued atmosphere allows the plot and characters to become more complicated than first suspected. Excellent performance by newcomer Nelson as the kid. 114m/C VHS, DVD. Samuel L. Jackson, Giancarlo Esposito, Sean Nelson, N'Bushe Wright, Ron Brice, Jean LaMarre, Luis Lantigua, Yul Vazquez, Cheryl Freeman; *D:* Boaz Yakin; *W:* Boaz Yakin; *C:* Adam Holender. Ind. Spirit '95: Debut Perf. (Nelson); Sundance '94: Special Jury Prize, Filmmakers Trophy.

Fresh Cut Grass 🐾🐾½ **2004** Debut for writer/director Coppola is an overly earnest story about college grad and wannabe writer Zac (Wilke). After his father's death, Zac's biding his time cutting lawns while deciding what to do next. He finds romance with the exotically named Eastern Star (Hansz), who helps him on the path to adulthood. 101m/C DVD. Katy Hansz, James McCaffrey, Bobby Cannavale, Dylan Bruno, David Wilke, Alicia Coppola; *D:* Matthew Coppola; *W:* Matthew Coppola; *C:* Tom Agnello.

Fresh Kill 🐾 **1987** A young guy from Chicago goes to Hollywood, and gets mixed up in drugs and murder. 90m/C VHS. Flint Keller, Patricia Parks; *D:* Joseph Merhi. VIDEO

The Freshman 🐾🐾🐾 **1925** Country boy Lloyd goes to college and, after many comic tribulations, saves the day with the winning touchdown at the big game and wins the girl of his dreams. This was one of the comedian's most popular films. 75m/B VHS, DVD. Harold Lloyd, Jobyna Ralston, Brooks Benedict, James Anderson, Hazel Keener; *D:* Fred Newmeyer, Sam Taylor; *W:* Sam Taylor. Natl. Film Reg. '90.

The Freshman 🐾🐾½ **1990 (PG)** Brando, in an incredible parody of his Don Corleone character, makes this work. Broderick is a college student in need of fast cash, and innocent enough to believe that any work is honest. A good supporting cast and a twisty plot keep things interesting. Sometimes heavy handed with its sight gags, but Broderick and Brando push the movie to hilarious conclusion. Don't miss Bert Parks's musical extravaganza. 102m/C VHS, DVD. Marlon Brando, Matthew Broderick, Penelope Ann Miller, Maximilian Schell, Bruno Kirby, Frank Whaley, Jon Polito, Paul Benedict, Richard Gant, B.D. Wong, Bert Parks; *D:* Andrew Bergman; *W:* Andrew Bergman; *C:* William A. Fraker; *M:* David Newman.

Freud Leaving Home 🐾🐾 **1991** Freud (Roor) is the nickname of 25-year-old Angelique, who lives with her Jewish family in Stockholm. Problems erupt when her sister and brother return home for their mother's 60th birthday and all learn of her fatal illness. The siblings are forced to confront themselves and their relationships with each other and their mother. 100m/C VHS with subtitles. *SW* Gunilla Roor, Ghita Norby, Philip Zanden, Jessica Zanden; *D:* Suzanne Bier.

Frida 🐾🐾½ **1984** The life of controversial Mexican painter Frido Kahlo is told via deathbed flashbacks using the artist's paintings to set the scenes. In Spanish with English subtitles. 108m/C VHS, DVD. *SP* Ofelia Medina, Juan Jose Gurrola, Max Kerlow; *D:* Paul Leduc.

Frida 🐾🐾🐾 **2002 (R)** Biography of nonconformist Mexican artist Frida Kahlo (Hayek) from her teen years to her death at the age of 44. The story relies heavily on her stormy marriage and continued relationship with famed muralist Diego Rivera (Molina). Director Julie Taymor also surrealistically brings to life several of Kahlo's paintings, although her glamorization of the famously uni-browed and mustachioed painter drew fire from ardent fans. Based on the book by Hayden Herrera. 120m/C VHS, DVD. *US* Salma Hayek, Alfred Molina, Ashley Judd, Geoffrey Rush, Antonio Banderas, Roger Rees, Edward Norton, Valeria Golino, Mia Maestro, Saffron Burrows, Patricia Reyes Spindola, Margarita Sanz, Diego Luna; *D:* Julie Taymor; *W:* Gregory Nava, Anna Thomas, Clancy Sigeland, Diane Lake; *C:* Rodrigo Prieto; *M:* Elliot Goldenthal. Oscars '02: Makeup, Score; British Acad. '02: Makeup; Golden Globes '03: Score.

Friday 🐾🐾½ **1995 (R)** It's "Boyz N' the Hood" meets "Good Times." Ice Cube wrote and stars as Craig in this humorous look into life in the 'hood. Craig's just lost his job and spends his time sitting on the porch with his pot smoking sidekick Smokey (Tucker), with the two getting mixed up in a variety of crazy antics involving their kooky neighbors. The laughs come at the expense of overworn cliches and stereotypical characters, but there's originality in the movie's energy and boldness (i.e. the local dope dealer is also the neighborhood ice cream man). To some, this "Friday" could be something to look forward to. 91m/C VHS, DVD, UMD. Ice Cube, Chris Tucker, Bernie Mac, John Witherspoon, Regina King, Nia Long, Tommy (Tiny) Lister, Anna Maria Horsford, LaWanda Page; *D:* F. Gary Gray; *M:* Frank Fitzpatrick.

Friday After Next 🐾½ **2002 (R)** Third installment of the series shows Christmas in the 'hood, as heroes Craig (Ice Cube) and Day-Day (Epps) are forced to take jobs as mall security guards after a ghetto Santa (Smiley) steals their presents and rent money. The usual brand of lowbrow humor is shoveled out in heaping piles and most of the regulars return, including John Witherspoon as Craig's chronically flatulent father. 85m/C VHS, DVD. *US* Ice Cube, Mike Epps, John Witherspoon, Don "DC" Curry, Anna Maria Horsford, Clifton Powell, Terry Crews, BeBe Drake, Sommore, Starletta Du-Pois, K.D. Aubert, Katt Micah Williams, Rickey Smiley, Joel McKinnon Miller, Reggie Gaskins; *D:* Marcus Raboy; *W:* Ice Cube; *C:* Glen MacPherson; *M:* John Murphy.

Friday Foster 🐾½ **1975 (R)** A beautiful, young photographer investigates an assassination attempt and uncovers a conspiracy against black politicians. Based on the Chicago Tribune comic strip. 90m/C VHS, DVD. Pam Grier, Yaphet Kotto, Thalmus Rasulala, Carl Weathers, Godfrey Cambridge; *D:* Arthur Marks; *W:* Orville H. Hampton; *C:* Harry J. May; *M:* Luchi De Jesus.

Friday Night 🐾🐾🐾 *Vendredi Soir* **2002** Laure (Lemercier) is packing up her Paris apartment one wintery evening prior to moving in with her lover. She's a little uncertain about the upcoming changes as she heads out to dinner with friends. There's a public transport strike and a massive traffic jam, so Laure takes to watching the stranded commuters, one of whom is burly and calm Jean (Lindon). It's bitterly cold and Laure decides to offer Jean a ride. Laure also decides to cancel her plans and make new ones (the one-night stand kind) with Jean. Based on the novel by Emmanuele Bernheim. French with subtitles. 90m/C DVD. *FR* Valerie Lemercier, Vincent Lindon; *D:* Claire Denis; *W:* Claire Denis, Emmanuele Bernheim; *C:* Agnes Godard; *M:* Dickon Hinchliffe.

Friday Night Lights 🐾🐾🐾 **2004 (PG-13)** Excellent tale about West Texas and its love for high school football. Based on the 1990 nonfiction account written by H.G. Bissinger of the 1988 season of the Odessa-Permian Panthers team, the film showcases the be-all, end-all small town fervor for the game and the all-consuming impact that has on its teenaged players. Among those are arrogant star running back James "Boobie" Miles (Luke), shy and insecure quarterback Mike Winchell (Black), and troubled tailback Don Billingsley (Hedlund), who's abused by his alcoholic dad (country singer McGraw, making a notable debut). Thornton gives a fine performance as Coach Gaines, a reserved man who knows his job is on the line if the team doesn't bring the state championship. 117m/C VHS, DVD, UMD, HD DVD. *US* Billy Bob Thornton, Derek Luke, Jay Hernandez, Lucas Black, Garrett Hedlund, Connie Britton, Lee Jackson, Lee Thompson Young, Tim McGraw, Grover Coulson; *D:* Peter Berg; *W:* Peter Berg, David Aaron Cohen; *C:* Tobias Schliessler; *M:* Brian Reitzell, David Torn.

Friday the 13th 🐾🐾 **1980 (R)** Notable as among the first in a very long series of slasher flicks, with effects by Tom Savini. A New Jersey camp reopens after it's been closed for 20 years after a history of "accidental" deaths. And the horror begins again. Six would-be counselors arrive to get the place ready. Each is progressively murdered; knifed, speared, and axed. Followed by numerous, equally gory sequels. 95m/C VHS, DVD. Betsy Palmer, Adrienne King, Harry Crosby, Laurie Bartram, Mark Nelson, Kevin Bacon, Jeannine Taylor, Robbi Morgan, Peter Brouwer, Walt Gorney; *D:* Sean S. Cunningham; *W:* Victor Miller; *C:* Barry Abrams; *M:* Harry Manfredini.

Friday the 13th, Part 2 woof! **1981 (R)** New group of teen camp counselors are gruesomely executed by the still undead Jason. Equally as graphic as the first installment; followed by several more gorefests. 87m/C VHS, DVD. Amy Steel, John Furey, Adrienne King, Betsy Palmer, Kirsten Baker, Stu Charno, Warrington Gillette, Walt Gorney, Marta Kober, Bill Randolph, Jack Marks; *D:* Steve Miner; *W:* Ron Kurz; *C:* Peter Stein; *M:* Harry Manfredini.

Friday the 13th, Part 3 woof! **1982 (R)** Yet another group of naive counselors at Camp Crystal Lake fall victim to the maniacal Jason. The 3-D effects actually helped lessen the gory effects, but this is still awful. Followed by more disgusting sequels. 96m/C VHS, DVD. Dana Kimmell, Paul Kratka, Richard Brooker, Catherine Parks, Jeffrey Rogers, Tracie Savage, Larry Zerner; *D:* Steve Miner; *W:* Martin Kitrosser, Carol Watson; *C:* Gerald Feil.

Friday the 13th, Part 4: The Final Chapter woof! **1984 (R)** Jason escapes from the morgue to once again slaughter and annihilate teenagers at a lakeside cottage. Preceded by three earlier "Friday the 13th" films, equally as graphic. The title's also a lie since there's several more sequels to look forward to. 90m/C VHS, DVD. Erich Anderson, Judie Aronson, Kimberly Beck, Peter Barton, Tom Everett, Corey Feldman, Crispin Glover, Richard Brooker; *D:* Joseph Zito; *W:* Barney Cohen; *C:* Joao Fernandes.

Friday the 13th, Part 5: A New Beginning woof! **1985 (R)** Jason rises from the dead to slice up the residents of a secluded halfway house. The sequels, and the sameness, never stop. See Part 6... 92m/C VHS, DVD. John Shepherd, Melanie Kinnaman, Shavar Ross, Richard Young, Juliette Cummins, Corey Feldman, Carol Lacatell, Vernon Washington; *D:* Danny Steinmann; *W:* Danny Steinmann, David M. Cohen, Martin Kitrosser; *C:* Stephen Posey.

Friday the 13th, Part 6: Jason Lives woof! **1986 (R)** One of the few youths not butchered by Jason digs him up and discovers he's not (and never will be) dead. Carnage ensues...and the sequels continue. 87m/C VHS, DVD. Thom Mathews, Jennifer Cooke, David Kagen,

Friday the 13th, Part 7: The New Blood WOOF! 1988 (R) A young camper with telekinetic powers accidentally unchains Jason from his underwater lair with the now-familiar results. There's still another bloody sequel to go. 90m/C VHS, DVD. Lar Park-Lincoln, Kevin Blair Spitras, Susan Blu, Terry Kiser, Kane Hodder, Elizabeth Kaitan, John Otrin, Heidi Kozak; D: John Carl Buechler; W: Daryl Haney; C: Paul Elliot.

Friday the 13th, Part 8: Jason Takes Manhattan ⚬ 1989 (R) Yet another sequel, with the hockey-masted walking slaughterhouse transported to New York. Most of the previous action in the movie takes place on a cruise ship. This one is less gruesome than others in the series. Followed by "Jason Goes to Hell: The Final Friday." 96m/C VHS, DVD. Kelly Hu, Jensen (Jennifer) Daggett, Scott Reeves, Peter Mark Richman, Barbara Bingham, Kane Hodder, Martin Cummins, Sharlene Martin, Vincent Craig Dupree; D: Rob Hedden; W: Rob Hedden; C: Bryan England.

Fridays of Eternity ⚬⚬⚬ 1981 A romantic comedy about loyalty, fidelity, love, and lovers all with a tinge of the supernatural. In Spanish with English subtitles. 89m/C VHS. AFI Thelma Biral, Hector Alterio; D: Hector Olivera.

Fried Green Tomatoes ⚬⚬⚬ 1991 (PG-13) Two stories about four women, love, friendship, Southern charm, and eccentricity all unfold together by wonderful performances. Unhappy, middle-aged Evelyn (Bates), meets the talkative 83-year-old Ninny Threadgoode (Tandy) and Ruth (Parker), who ran the local cafe. Back-and-forth narrative as it tracks multiple storylines is occasionally confusing, though strong character development holds interest. Surprising box office hit adapted by Fannie Flagg from her novel "Fried Green Tomatoes at the Whistle Stop Cafe." 130m/C VHS, DVD. Kathy Bates, Jessica Tandy, Mary Stuart Masterson, Mary-Louise Parker, Cicely Tyson, Chris O'Donnell, Stan Shaw, Gailard Sartain, Timothy Scott, Gary Basaraba, Lois Smith, Grace Zabriskie; D: Jon Avnet; W: Fannie Flagg, Carol Sobieski; C: Geoffrey Simpson; M: Thomas Newman.

Frieda ⚬⚬½ 1947. An RAF officer brings his German wife home after the war and she is naturally distrusted by his family and neighbors. An interesting look at post-war bigotry. 98m/B VHS, GB David Farrar, Glynis Johns, Mai Zetterling, Flora Robson, Albert Lieven; D: Basil Dearden.

Friend of the Family ⚬½ 1995 While backpacking across the U.S., Elke (O'Brien) is invited to stay in Malibu with the Stillman family—husband Jeff, with Linda, and their 20-something children, Josh and Montana. Naturally the sexy Elke becomes very involved with the family. 96m/C VHS, DVD. Shauna O'Brien, C.T. Miller, Griffin (Griffen) Drew, Lisa Boyle; D: Edward Holzman; W: Edward Holzman, April Mostowitz; C: Kim Heun; M: Richard Bronskill.

Friend of the Family 2 ⚬ 1996 (R) Disturbed young woman decides to get revenge on the man who used and abandoned her by becoming his family's nanny. Also available in an unrated version. Ray used the pseudonym Nicholas Medina. 90m/C VHS, DVD. Shauna O'Brien, Paul Michael Robinson, Jenna Bodnar, Jeff Rector; D: Fred Olen Ray; W: Henry Krinkle; C: Gary Graver.

Friendly Fire ⚬⚬⚬ 1979 Based on a true story of an American family in 1970 whose soldier son is killed by "friendly fire" in Vietnam, and their efforts to uncover the circumstances of the tragedy. Touching and powerful, with an excellent dramatic performance by Burnett. 146m/C VHS. Carol Burnett, Ned Beatty, Sam Waterston, Timothy Hutton; D: David Greene. TV

Kerry Noonan, Renee Jones, Tom Fridley, C.J. Graham, Darcy Demoss; D: Tom McLoughlin; W: Tom McLoughlin; C: Jon Kranhouse; M: Harry Manfredini.

Friendly Persuasion ⚬⚬⚬ Except for Me and Thee 1956 Earnest, solidly acted tale about a peaceful Quaker family struggling to remain true to its ideals in spite of the Civil War which touches their lives in southern Indiana. Cooper and McGuire are excellent as the parents with Perkins fine as the son worried he's using his religion to hide his cowardice. Based on a novel by Jessamyn West. 140m/C VHS, DVD. Gary Cooper, Dorothy McGuire, Anthony Perkins, Marjorie Main, Charles Halton; D: William Wyler; W: Michael Wilson; C: Ellsworth Fredericks; M: Dimitri Tiomkin. Cannes '57. Film.

Friends ⚬ 1971 (R) Ho-hum drama about an orphaned French girl and an unloved English boy who meet, become friends, and decide to run away together. They even have a baby before they're discovered. Provides no insight into the teenagers dilemmas. Followed by "Paul and Michelle." 101m/C VHS, GB Sean Bury, Anicee Alvina, Pascale Roberts, Sady Rebbot, Ronald Lewis; D: Lewis Gilbert; M: Elton John.

Friends ⚬⚬ 1995 Story of three South African women sharing an apartment in Johannesburg and Kente, a black teacher. When Fox plants a bomb that takes two innocent lives, their loyalties are tested. Debut for director Proctor. 109m/C VHS. Kerry Fox, Michele Burgers, Dambisa Kente; D: Elaine Proctor.

Friends & Crocodiles ⚬⚬ 2005 Flashy real estate mogul Paul Reynolds (Lewis) is living a hedonistic lifestyle in 1980s London. He hires practical Lizzie Thomas (May) as his secretary but she's disturbed by his reckless, sometimes criminal, behavior and soon quits. Over a 20-year period, Paul's fortunes unravel while life is kinder to Lizzie, and the two maintain a sometimes strained friendship. 105m/C DVD, GB Damian Lewis, Jodhi May, Robert Lindsay, Patrick Malahide, Eddie Marsan, Allan Corduner, Chris Larkin; D: Stephen Poliakoff; W: Stephen Poliakoff; C: Barry Ackroyd; M: Adrian Johnston. TV

Friends and Family ⚬⚬½ 2001 Very broad comedy tries to shoehorn in a few too many subplots but it's slickly-done and harmless. Danny (Gartin) and Stephen (Lauren) are enforcers for New York mobster Victor Patrizzi (Lo Bianco), who has no problem with the fact that they are gay. Nor do Stephen's parents, who decide to make a surprise visit to the city to celebrate Mr. Torcelli's (Pellegrino) birthday. But what Stephen's parents don't know is what the two actually do for a living—the guys have been passing themselves off as caterers. With Patrizzi's assistance, they arrange a celebration that unexpectedly turns into an inept hostage situation. 87m/C VHS, DVD. Greg Lauren, Christopher Gartin, Tony LoBianco, Rebecca Creskoff, Brian Lane Green, Meshach Taylor, Edward Hibbert, Beth Fowler, Frank Pellegrino, Tovah Feldshuh, Anna Maria Alberghetti, Frank Vinucci, Patrick Collins; D: Kristen Coury; M: Joseph Triebwasser; C: Jon Leuba; M: Kurt Hoffman.

Friends & Lovers ⚬½ 1999 Nonsensical and mediocre would-be romantic comedy about wealthy widower, Richard (Rasche), who invites his estranged son, Ian (Newbern), and his son's L.A. friends to spend Christmas with him at his Park City chalet. Everyone has some kind of sexual agenda except for Richard, who just wants to come to terms with Ian. 104m/C VHS, DVD. David Rasche, George Newbern, Stephen Baldwin, Danny Nucci, Robert Downey Jr., Leon, Alison Eastwood, Suzanne Cryer, Neill Barry, Claudia Schiffer; D: George Haas; W: George Haas; C: Carlos Montaner; M: Emilio Kauderer.

Friends Forever ⚬⚬½ 1986 Conformity, sexuality, and friendship are explored in this coming-of-age drama. Kristian is a shy, conformist 16-year-old, starting off at a new school. He finds himself drawn to two different young men who equally dominate his class. Herrik's androgynous sexual charm is equaled by the leader of a band of troublemakers. Kristian gains in self-confidence by their friendship but is tested when he learns Patrick is gay. 95m/C VHS, DK Stefan Christian Henszelman, Claus Bender Mortensen, Thomas Elholm, Christine Skou; D: Stefan Christian Henszelman; M: Kim Sagild.

Friends, Lovers & Lunatics ⚬½ Me Crazy 1989 A weekend turns into a romantic nightmare/laugh-fest when a man between three wealthy, married, middle-aged women...

Fright ⚬ Spell of the Hypnotist 1956 A woman—convinced that she died in 1889 as part of a suicide pact with Prince Rudolph of Austria—seeks help from a psychiatrist who promptly falls in love with her (didn't Freud say it was supposed to be the other way around?). 66m/B VHS, DVD. Nancy Malone, Eric Fleming, Frank Marth, Humphrey Davis, Ned Glass, Norman Burton; D: W. Lee Wilder.

A Friendship in Vienna ⚬⚬½ 1988 The friendship of two young teenage girls, one Jewish, and the other the daughter of a Nazi collaborator, is tested as WWII looms over Europe and the Nazis begin their persecution of Austrian Jews. Adapted from the book "Devil in Vienna" by Doris Orgel. 100m/C VHS. Jenny Lewis, Ed Asner, Jane Alexander, Stephen Macht, Rosemary Forsyth, Ferdinand "Ferdy" Mayne, Richard Arthur Allan Seidelmar; W: Richard Alfieri; Mari Jaan Simmons. CABLE

Friends with Money ⚬⚬½ 2006 (R) L.A.-set story about the friendship between three wealthy, married, middle-aged women and their slightly younger, unmarried, and decidedly not-rich pal. That's Olivia (Aniston), who has quit her teaching job in a fit of ennui to become a maid. Her friend Franny (Cusack) is a generous stay-at-home mom with a great marriage to Matt (Germann), while Jane (McDermott) is a continuously furious fashion designer whose merctsexual Brit hubby Aaron (McBurney) is suspected of being gay. Screenwriting partners Christine (Keener) and David (Isaacs) discover they can't even like each other after a marriage fractures. The women talk and support one another (and of the actresses are great fleshing out some thin characters) but not much happens. 88m/C DVD, US Jennifer Aniston, Joan Cusack, Catherine Keener, Frances McDormand, Jason Isaacs, Scott Caan, Simon McBurney, Greg Germann, Ty Burrell, Bob Stephenson; D: Nicole Holofcener; M: Craig Richey, Rickie Lee Jones. Ind. Spirit '07: Support. Actress (McDormand).

Fright ⚬ Night Legs 1971 A baby-sitter is menaced by a mental hospital escapee. He turns out to be the father of the boy she is watching. Tense but violent thriller. 87m/C VHS, DVD, GB Susan George, Honor Blackman, Ian Bannen, John Gregson, George Cole, Dennis Waterman, Tara Collinson, Maurice Kaufmann, Michael Brennan, Roger Lloyd-Pack; D: Peter Collinson; W: Tudor Gates; C: Ian Wilson; M: Harry Robinson.

Fright House ⚬ 1989 (R) Two stories of terror. "Fright House" features witches preparing an old mansion for a visit from the Devil. "Abandon" explains the prolonged youth of a teacher to her young student. 110m/C VHS. Al Lewis, Duane Jones; D: Len Anthony.

Fright Night ⚬⚬½ 1985 (R) It's Dracula-versus-the-teens time when Charley suspects that his new neighbor descends from Count Vlad's line. He calls in the host of "Fright Night," the local, late-night, horror-flick series, to help de-ghoul the neighborhood. But they have a problem when the vampire discovers that anybody believes them anyway. Sarandon is properly seductive as the bloodsucker. 106m/C VHS, DVD. William Ragsdale, Chris Sarandon, Amanda Bearse, Roddy McDowall, Stephen Geoffreys, Jonathan Stark, Dorothy Fielding, Art Evans; D: Tom Holland; W: Tom Holland; M: Brad Fiedel.

Frightmare ⚬ 1981 (R) Great horror star dies, but he refuses to give up his need for adoration and revenge. 84m/C VHS. Ferdinand "Ferdy" Mayne, Luca Bercovici, Nita Talbot, Peter Kastner; D: Norman Thaddeus Vane.

Frightmare ⚬⚬½ Frightmare 2 1974 (R) A seemingly quiet British couple don't indulge in one strange habit—they're cannibals. Released on video as "Frightmare 2" to avoid confusion with the 1981 film. 86m/C VHS, DVD, GB Deborah Fairfax, Kim Butcher, Rupert Davies, Sheila Keith; D: Pete Walker; W: David McGillivray; C: Peter Jessop; M: Stanley Myers.

Fright Night 2 ⚬⚬½ 1988 (R) The sequel to the 1985 release "Fright Night," in which the harassed guy from the original film learns slowly that the vampire's roost around him at his college. Not quite as good as the original but the special effects are worth a look. 108m/C VHS, DVD. Roddy McDowall, William Ragsdale, Traci Lind, Julie Carmen, Jonathan Gries, Russ Clark, Brian Thompson; D: Tommy Lee Wallace; W: Tommy Lee Wallace, Tim Metcalfe, Miguel Tejada-Flores; C: Mark Irwin; M: Brad Fiedel.

The Frighteners ⚬⚬½ 1996 (R) Con man Frank Bannister (Fox) has a unique scam—he works with a group of ghosts who haunt a home until Frank comes along to drive them out, for the right price. But the small town of Fairwater is plagued by a serial killer's evil spirit and Frank and his spiritual cronies face the challenge of getting rid of the ghost before the police decide to get rid of Frank. Interesting horror-comedy takes a lot of twists and turns to get where its going, but the fans of the genre. New Zealand helmer Jackson makes his American directorial debut. 106m/C VHS, DVD, HD DVD. Michael J. Fox, Trini Alvarado, Peter Dobson, Dee Wallace Stone, John Astin, Jeffrey Combs, Troy Evans, Chi McBride, Jake Busey, R. Lee Ermey, Jim Fyfe; D: Peter Jackson; W: Peter Jackson, Fran Walsh; C: Alun Bollinger; M: Danny Elfman.

The Frightened Woman ⚬⚬ 1971 Wealthy Sayer (Leroy) likes to get his sexual kicks by playing master and slave in his villa outside Rome. When his usual hired call girl isn't available, he decides to lure a lovely journalist (Lassander) into his domination games. 90m/C VHS, DVD. /T: Phillippe LeRoy, Dagmar Lassander; D: Piero Schivazappa; W: Piero Schivazappa; M: Stelvio Cipriani.

The Frightened City ⚬⚬ 1961 Waldo Zhernikov (Lom) decides to unite all six of London's crime syndicates into one conglomerate that would control the city. But when he gets power-mad, rival gangster Harry Foulcher (Connery) breaks away and forms his own organization. Naturally, there's a war between the factions. Paddy Damion (Connery in an early role), one of Waldo's gunsels, is sent to get rid of Foulcher. 91m/B VHS, DVD, GB Herbert Lom, John Gregson, Sean Connery, Alfred Marks, Yvonne Romain, Kenneth Griffith, Olive McFarland, Frederick Piper, John Stone, David Davies, Tom Bowman, Robert Cawdron, Norrie Paramor; D: John Lemont; W: Leigh Vance; C: Desmond Dickinson; M: Norrie Paramor.

The Fringe Dwellers ⚬⚬½ 1986 (PG) An Aborigine family leave their shantytown and move to the white, middle-class suburbs of Australia, encountering prejudice and other difficulties. Well acted and interesting but the ending's a letdown. 98m/C VHS. Kristina Nehm, Justine Saunders, Bob Maza, Kylie Belling, Denis Walker, Ernie Dingo; D: Bruce Beresford; W: Bruce Beresford, Rhoisin Beresford; M: George Dreyfus.

The Frisco Kid ⚬⚬ No Knife 1979 (R) An innocent orthodox rabbi (Wilder) from Poland is sent to the wilds of San Francisco during the 1850s gold rush to lead a new congregation. He lands in Philadelphia, joins a wagon train and is eventually robbed and abandoned. He eventually meets up with a not-too-bright robber (Ford) who finds himself unexpectedly befriending the man and undergoing numerous tribulations in order to get them both safely to their destination. This isn't a ...

laugh riot and some scenes fall distinctly flat but Wilder is sweetness personified and lends the movie its charm. **119m/C VHS, DVD.** Gene Wilder, Harrison Ford, Ramon Bieri, Val Bisoglio, George DiCenzo, Penny Peyser, William (Bill) Smith; **D:** Robert Aldrich; **W:** Michael Elias; **C:** Robert B. Hauser.

Frisk ✍✍ 1995 Disturbing depictions of sex/murder fantasies come courtesy of letters written by Dennis (Gunther), a part of the L.A. S&M scene, to his former boyfriend, Julian (Laplante). Just exactly how far Dennis has gone with these sick likeminded sexual partners is the question. Has he become the killer he claims to be? Adapted from Dennis Cooper's 1991 novel. **87m/C VHS, DVD.** Michael Gunther, Jaie Laplante, Craig Chester, Parker Posey, James Lyons, Alexis Arquette, Raoul O'Connell, Michael Stock; **D:** Todd Verow; **W:** Todd Verow, Jim Dwyer, George LaVoo; **C:** Greg Watkins.

Fritz the Cat ✍✍ 1972 Ralph Bakshi's animated tale for adults about a cat's adventures as he gets into group sex, college radicalism, and other hazards of life in the '60s. Loosely based on the underground comics character by Robert Crumb. Originally X-rated. **77m/C VHS, DVD.** **D:** Ralph Bakshi; **W:** Ralph Bakshi; **C:** Ted C. Bemiller, Gene Borghi; **M:** Ed Bogas, Ray Shanklin; **V:** Skip Hinnant, Rosetta LeNoire, John McCurry.

Frog and Wombat ✍✍1/2 1998 Alli, whose codename is "Frog," tries to convince her best friend Jane, code named "Wombat," that their new school principal (Cox) is up to no good, especially when she discovers the man's niece is missing. So the intrepid duo prepare to investigate. **90m/C VHS.** Katie Stuart, Ronny Cox, Lindsay Wagner, Ross Malinger, Emily Lipoma; **D:** Laurie Agard; **W:** Laurie Agard; **C:** Ray Preziosi; **M:** Greg Edmonson.

Frogs ✍✍1/2 1972 (PG) An environmental photographer working on a small island in Florida interrupts the birthday celebration of a patriarch. He and the folks at the party soon realize that various amphibians animals in the surrounding area are going berserk and attacking humans. One of the first environmentally motivated animal-vengeance films, and one of the best to come out of the '70s. **91m/C VHS, DVD.** Ray Milland, Sam Elliott, Joan Van Ark, Adam Roarke, Judy Pace, Lynn Borden, Mae Mercer, David Gilliam, George Skaff, Holly Irving; **D:** George McCowan; **W:** Robert Blees, Robert Hutchison; **C:** Mario Tosi; **M:** Les Baxter.

Frogs for Snakes ✍✍ 1998 (R) Self-conscious black comedy about New York loan shark Al Santana (Coltrane) who also spends his time as a wanna-be East Village theatrical impressario. And how everybody who works for Al as a collector is even more desperate to be an actor, including his struggling ex-wife Eva (Hershey). And how all the characters suddenly break into monologues from their favorite movies. And how none of this makes much sense and the actors have really done better work elsewhere. **98m/C VHS.** Barbara Hershey, Robbie Coltrane, Harry Hamlin, Ian Hart, John Leguizamo, Lisa Marie, Debi Mazar, David Deblinger, Ron Perlman, Clarence Williams III, Justin Theroux, Nicholas Chinlund, Mike Starr, Taylor Mead; **D:** Amos Poe; **W:** Amos Poe; **C:** Enrique Chediak.

Frolics on Ice ✍✍ *Everything's on Ice* 1939 Pleasant musical-comedy about a family man saving to buy the barber shop at which he works. Irene Dare is featured in several ice skating production numbers. **65m/B VHS.** Roscoe Karns, Lynne Roberts, Irene Dare, Edgar Kennedy, Eric Linden, George Meeker, Bobby Watson, Mary Currier; **D:** Erle C. Kenton; **W:** Sherman Lowe, Adrian Landis; **C:** Russell Metty.

From a Far Country: Pope John Paul II ✍✍ 1981 TV biography of Polish Pope John Paul II begins in 1926 as Karol Wojtila celebrates Christmas with his father and continues through the important highlights of his life. **120m/C VHS, DVD. PL, GB** Sam Neill, Christopher Cazenove, Warren Clarke, Kathleen Byron, Maurice Denham, Lisa Harrow; **D:** Krzysztof Zanussi; **W:** Krzysztof Zanussi; **C:** Slawomir Idziak; **M:** Wojciech Kilar; **Nar:** Michael Jayston. **TV**

Campbell. **121m/C VHS, DVD, Blu-ray Disc.** *US* Johnny Depp, Heather Graham, Ian Holm, Robbie Coltrane, Ian Richardson, Jason Flemyng, Katrin Cartlidge, Terence Harvey, Susan Lynch, Lesley Sharp, Annabelle Apsion; **D:** Albert Hughes, Allen Hughes; **W:** Terry Hayes, Rafael Yglesias; **C:** Peter Deming; **M:** Trevor Jones.

From Hell to Borneo ✍1/2 1964 A mercenary must defend his secluded island from pirates and gangsters. **90m/ C VHS.** George Montgomery, Torin Thatcher, Julie Gregg, Lisa Moreno; **D:** George Montgomery.

From Hell to Victory ✍✍ 1979 (PG) Group of friends of different nationalities vow to meet each year in Paris on the same date but WWII interrupts their lives and friendships. Director Lenzi alias Hank Milestone. Good battle scenes but nothing special. **100m/C VHS, DVD.** *SP FR* George Peppard, George Hamilton, Horst Buchholz, Jean-Pierre Cassel, Capucine, Sam Wanamaker, Anny (Annie Legras) Duperey, Ray Lovelock; **D:** Umberto Lenzi.

From Here to Eternity ✍✍✍✍ 1953 Complex, hard-hitting look at the on and off-duty life of soldiers at the Army base in Honolulu in the days before the Pearl Harbor attack. There's sensitive Pvt. Prewitt (Clift), his always in trouble best friend Maggio (Sinatra), and their goodguy top sergeant (Lancaster) who just happens to be having a torrid affair with the commander's wife (Kerr). Prewitt, meanwhile, is introduced to a club "hostess" (Reed) who is a lot more vulnerable than she's willing to admit. A movie filled with great performances. Still has the best waves-on-the-beach love scene in filmdom. Based on the novel by James Jones, which was toned down by the censors. **118m/B VHS, DVD.** Burt Lancaster, Montgomery Clift, Frank Sinatra, Deborah Kerr, Donna Reed, Ernest Borgnine, Philip Ober, Jack Warden, Mickey Shaughnessy, George Reeves, Claude Akins, Harry Bellaver, John Dennis, Tim Ryan, John Bryant, John Cason, Douglas) Henderson, Robert Karnes, Robert J. Wilke, Carleton Young, Merle Travis, Arthur Keegan, Barbara Morrison, Tyler McVey; **D:** Fred Zinnemann; **W:** Daniel Taradash; **C:** Burnett Guffey; **M:** George Duning, Oscars '53: B&W Cinematog., Director (Zinnemann), Film Editing, Picture, Screenplay, Sound, Support. Actor (Sinatra), Support. Actress (Reed); AFI '98: Top 100; Directors Guild '53: Director (Zinnemann); Golden Globes '54: Support. Actor (Sinatra), Natl. Film Reg. '02; N.Y. Film Critics '53: Actor (Lancaster), Director (Zinnemann), Film.

From Here to Eternity ✍✍1/2 1979 (PG-13) From here to eternity...and back on the silver screen. Remake of the 1953 classic is based on James Jones's novel about old life on a Hawaiian military base just before WWII. Decent actioner, but no Oscar-winner this time around. **110m/C VHS.** Natalie Wood, Kim Basinger, William Devane, Steve Railsback, Peter Boyle, Will Sampson, Andy Griffith, Roy Thinnes, Barbara Hershey; **D:** Buzz Kulik; **W:** Harold Gast. **TV**

From Here to Maternity ✍✍1/2 1985 A soap opera-based spoof about modern maternity. Three women want to be pregnant but their significant others aren't interested in paternity. **40m/C VHS.** Carrie Fisher, Arleen (Arlene) Sorkin, Lauren Hutton, Griffin Dunne, Paul Reiser; **D:** Tom Schiller. **TV**

From Hollywood to Deadwood ✍✍ 1989 (R) A beautiful starlet is kidnapped and the private eye searching for her discovers blackmail and danger. **90m/C VHS.** Scott Paulin, Jim Haynie, Barbara Schock; **D:** Rex Pickett; **W:** Rex Pickett; **C:** Peter Deming.

From Justin to Kelly woof! 2003 (PG) Justin Guarini and Kelly Clarkson hurry to cash in on another "American Idol" success with another remake of "Where the Boys Are." Justin and Kelly chase romance between ludicrous dance numbers. In the pantheon of bad pop star flicks, this ranks well south of Elvis's worst fare, and even manages to sneak under the Unholy Trinity of Vanilla Ice-Mariah-Britny. **90m/C VHS, DVD.** Justin Guarini, Kelly Clarkson, Katherine Bailess, Anika Noni Rose, Greg Siff, Brian Dietzen; **D:** Robert Iscove; **W:** Kim Fuller; **C:** Francis Kenny; **M:** Michael Wandmacher.

From Beyond ✍✍ 1986 (R) A gruesome, tongue-in-cheek adaptation of the ghoulish H.P. Lovecraft story. Scientists discover another dimension through experiments with the pineal gland. From the makers of "Re-Animator," and just as funny. **90m/C VHS.** Jeffrey Combs, Barbara Crampton, Ted (Theodore) Sorel, Ken Foree, Carolyn Purdy-Gordon, Bunny Summers, Bruce McGuire; **D:** Stuart Gordon; **W:** Dennis Paoli, Brian Yuzna; **C:** Mac Ahlberg; **M:** Richard Band.

From Beyond the Grave ✍✍ *Creatures* 1973 (PG) This horror compendium revolves around a mysterious antique shop whose customers experience various supernatural phenomena, especially when they try to cheat the shop's equally mysterious owner. **98m/C VHS, DVD.** *GB* Peter Cushing, David Warner, Ian Bannen, Donald Pleasence, Margaret Leighton, Lesley-Anne Down, Diana Dors, Ian Ogilvy; **D:** Kevin Connor.

From Dusk Till Dawn ✍✍1/2 1995 (R) Escaped cons Seth and Richie Gecko (Clooney and Tarantino) pick up an ex-preacher (Keitel) and his two kids (Lewis and Liu) as hostages en route to their Mexican rendezvous spot, a raunchy biker joint run (unbeknownst to them) by vampires. Feels like two movies in one, as Rodriguez's and Tarantino's styles don't necessarily mesh as much as they coexist. The first half features Tarantino's gift for snappy dialogue and somewhat sympathetic scumbags while the barroom finale shows off Rodriguez's mastery of the go-for-broke action set piece. Clooney proves the jump from TV to movies can be made successfully. Penned by Tarantino in 1990 during his video store days, he used the fee to get "Reservoir Dogs" off the ground. **108m/C VHS, DVD, UMD.** George Clooney, Quentin Tarantino, Harvey Keitel, Juliette Lewis, Ernest Liu, Fred Williamson, Richard "Cheech" Marin, Salma Hayek, Michael Parks, Tom Savini, Kelly Preston, John Saxon, Danny Trejo, Tia Texada; **D:** Robert Rodriguez; **W:** Quentin Tarantino; **C:** Guillermo Navarro; **M:** Graeme Revell. MTV Movie Awards '96: Breakthrough Perf. (Clooney).

From Dusk Till Dawn 2: Texas Blood Money 1998 (R) *Texas Blood Money* 1998 (R) Buck (Patrick) and his partner-in-crime Luther (Whitaker) decide to get a few bad men together and knock over a bank in Mexico. However, the group unwittingly come into contact with the vampire denizens of the Titty Twister bar and soon join the ranks of the undead. Except for Buck, who's somehow managed to avoid having the bite put on him—for now. Direct-to-video sequel is set two weeks after the first film's carnage. **88m/C VHS, DVD.** Robert Patrick, Bo Hopkins, Muse Watson, Duane Whitaker, Raymond Cruz, Tiffani-(Amber) Thiessen, Brett Harrelson, Danny Trejo, Bruce Campbell; **D:** Scott Spiegel; **W:** Duane Whitaker, Scott Spiegel; **C:** Philip Lee; **M:** Joseph Williams. **VIDEO**

From Dusk Till Dawn 3: The Hangman's Daughter ✍✍ 1999 (R) This is actually a prequel to the "From Dusk Till Dawn" mayhem. In 1914, a group of refugees wind up in an isolated Mexican saloon, "La Tetilla del Diablo," that's the home of Santanico Pandemonium, the Queen of the Vampires (Braga). Oh, and the hangman's daughter is lovely Esmeralda (Celi), who doesn't know that Santanico is her mom. **94m/C VHS, DVD.** Michael Parks, Sonia Braga, Marco Leonard, Rebecca Gayheart, Temuera Morrison, Lenny Y. Loftin, Danny Trejo, Ara Celi; **D:** P.J. Pesce. **VIDEO**

From Hell ✍✍✍ 2001 (R) The Hughes brothers take on the legend of Jack the Ripper in this grisly period thriller. Inspector Abberline (Depp) is the fictional opium-addled detective charged with finding the notorious killer of London's ladies of the night in 1888. With the help of his police sidekick Godley (Coltrane) and the cockney hooker-with-a-heart-of-gold Mary (Graham), Abberline pries into the medical community, the royal family and other less respectable areas in his search for the Ripper. Beautiful visuals and taut suspense raise this effort a notch above other adaptions of the material. Based on a graphic novel (a.k.a. fancy-schmancy comic book) by Alan Moore and Eddie

From Noon Till Three ✍✍1/2 1976 (PG) A change of pace role for Bronson as a two-bit gunfighter in a spoof of western legends. Bronson has a brief romance with Ireland who, believing him dead, fictionalizes their relationship in a series of books and builds the mediocre Dorsey into a western hero. When he turns up alive no one, including Ireland, believes that he is the real Dorsey and he's gradually driven crazy. Good script, weak direction but Bronson is likeable. **99m/C VHS.** Charles Bronson, Jill Ireland, Douglas Fowley, Stan Haze, Damon Douglas; **D:** Frank D. Gilroy; **W:** Frank D. Gilroy; **C:** Lucien Ballard; **M:** Elmer Bernstein.

From Other Worlds ✍1/2 2004 Dull sci-fi comedy. Depressed Brooklyn housewife Joanne believes she has been abducted by aliens and decides to meet with a group of fellow abductees, who include Abraham. They bond and begin to look for clues, meeting an alien who gives them advice on saving Earth from destruction. **88m/C DVD.** Cara Buono, Isaach de Bankole, David Lansbury, Joel de la Fuente, Robert Peters, Melissa Leo; **D:** Barry Strugatz; **W:** Barry Strugatz; **C:** Morris Flam; **M:** Pierre Foldes.

From Russia with Love ✍✍✍1/2 1963 (PG) Bond is back and on the loose in exotic Istanbul looking for a super-secret coding machine. He's involved with a beautiful Russian spy and has the SPECTRE organization after him, including villainess Rosa Klebb (she of the killer shoe). Lots of exciting escapes but not an overreliance on the gadgetry of the later films. The second Bond feature, thought by many to be the best. **125m/C VHS, DVD. GB** Sean Connery, Daniela Bianchi, Pedro Amendariz Sr., Lotte Lenya, Robert Shaw, Eunice Gayson, Walter Gotell, Lois Maxwell, Bernard Lee, Desmond Llewelyn, Nadja Regin, Alizia Gur, Martine Beswick, Leila; **D:** Terence Young; **W:** Johanna Harwood, Richard Maibaum; **C:** Ted Moore; **M:** John Barry.

From the Dead of Night ✍✍✍ 1989 A spooky chiller about a near-death experience. Fashion designer Wagner narrowly escapes death but gets close enough to the other side that six of the dead feel cheated that she didn't join them. They decide to rectify the mistake and Wagner is pursued by the shadowy figures. Based on the novel "Walkers" by Gary Bradner. **192m/C VHS, DVD.** Lindsay Wagner, Bruce Boxleitner, Diahann Carroll, Robert Prosky, Robin Thomas, Merritt Butrick, Joanne Linville; **D:** Paul Wendkos. **TV**

From the Earth to the Moon ✍✍✍ 1958 A mad scientist invents a new energy source and builds a rocket which takes him, his daughter, and two other men for some adventures on the moon. Based on the novel by Jules Verne. **100m/C VHS.** George Sanders, Joseph Cotten, Debra Paget, Don Dubbins; **D:** Byron Haskin; **W:** Robert Blees.

From the Earth to the Moon ✍✍✍ 1998 Executive producer Tom Hanks shows off his fascination with the space program in this 12-part series covering the Apollo space program through the 1960s and '70s. Covers behind-the-scenes at NASA, the heroics of the astronauts and their missions, and the families that are left behind to wait and worry. On six cassettes. **720m/C VHS, DVD.** David Andrews, Bryan Cranston, Timothy Daly, Al Franken, Tony Goldwyn, Chris Isaak, Cary Elwes, Brett Cullen, Robert John Burke, Peter Scolari, Nick Searcy, Lane Smith, Dan Lauria, Mark Rolston, Mason Adams, Ronny Cox, Dakin Matthews, Kevin Pollak, Ben Marley, Joe Spano, Daniel Hugh-Kelly, Stephen (Steve) Root, Dann Florek, John Slattery, Ted Levine, Ann Cusack, Jo Anderson, James Rebhorn, Mark Harmon, Rita Wilson, Tom Amandes, John Aylward, Dylan Baker, Adam Baldwin, Reed Birney, Betsy Brantley, Bart Braverman, David Brisbin, Jimmy Buffett, Dan E. Butler, David Clennon, Gary Cole, Matt Craven, Wendy Crewson, Blythe Danner, Dave Foley, Jack Gilpin, John Michael Higgins, Peter Horton, Clint Howard, Zeljko Ivanek, Tcheky Karyo, John Carroll Lynch, Ann Magnuson, Joshua Malina, Andrew Masset, DeLane Matthews, Paul McCrane, Doug McKeon, Jay Mohr, Kieran Mulroney, Holmes Osborne, Connor O'Farrell, Elizabeth Perkins, Ethan Phillips, Andrew Rubin, Alan Ruck, Diana Scarwid, Grant Shaud, Cynthia Stevenson, Tom Verica, Gareth

...Williams, JoBeth Williams, Max Wright, Steve Zahn; **D:** Tom Hanks, David Franke, Lili Fini Zanuck, Graham Yost, Frank Marshall, Jon Turteltaub, Gary Flecer, David Carson, Sally Field, Jonathan Mostow; **W:** Tom Hanks, Graham Yost, Stephen Katz, Remi Aubuchon, Al Reinert, Andy Wolk, Jeffrey Alladin Fiskin, Karen Janszen, Jonathan Marc Feldman; **C:** Gale Tattersall; **M:** Michael Kamen, Mark Mancina. **CABLE**

From the Edge of the City 1998 Sasha (Papadopoulos) is a teenaged émigré from Russia, who's working the Athens streets as a hustler. His older (and ruthless) mentor Giorgos (Papoulidis) is a pimp and offers Sasha the chance to move up by temporarily turning over the management of one of his girls—fellow emigre, Natasha (Tzimou). But Sasha, who isn't nearly as hardened as some of his friends, struggles not to become emotionally involved with the girl, to disastrous effect. Greek with subtitles. **94m/C VHS, DVD, GR** Stathis Papadopoulos, Theadora Tzimou, Costas Cotsiandis; **D:** Constantine Giannaris; **W:** Constantine Giannaris; **C:** George Argiriollpoulos; **M:** Akis Daoutis.

From the Hip 1986 (PG) A young lawyer (Nelson) gets the chance of a lifetime when his office assigns a murder case to him. The only problem is that he suspects his client is very guilty indeed and must discover the truth without breaking his case a bit out of hand, as he flares his nostrils at every opportunity. The movie is encumbered by a weak script and plot as well as a mic-story switch from comedy to drama. **111m/C VHS, DVD,** Judd Nelson, Elizabeth Perkins, John Hurt, Ray Walston; **D:** Bob Clark; **W:** Bob (Benjamin) Clark, David Kelly; **C:** Dante Spinotti; **M:** Paul Zaza.

From the Journals of Jean Seberg 1995 An imaginary look at the life of the ill-fated actress, who began her career as a 17-year-old miscast in Otto Preminger's "Saint Joan," achieved fame in Godard's "Breathless," and became a suicide at age 40 in 1979. Seberg (Hurt) dispassionately narrates her life story as she views film clips, from small-town Iowa teenager to would-be star, through abusive relationships, drugs and drinking, political activism, and FBI harassment. **97m/C VHS, DVD,** Mary Beth Hurt; **D:** Mark Rappaport; **W:** Mark Rappaport; **C:** Mark Daniels.

From the Life of the Marionettes 1980 (R) A repressed man in a crumbling marriage rapes and kills a young prostitute. Another look at the powers behind individual motivations from Bergman, who uses black and white and color to relate details of the incident. **104m/C VHS, DVD, SW** Robert Atzorn, Christine Buchegger, Martin Benrath, Rita Russek, Lola Muethel, Walter Schmidinger, Heinz Bennent; **D:** Ingmar Bergman; **W:** Ingmar Bergman; **C:** Sven Nykvist.

From the Manger to the Cross 1915 This version of the Passion play was the first film to be done on location in Palestine. Re-enacts the Nativity, the flight into Egypt, and the crucifixion. Color-tinted. **71m/B VHS, DVD,** R. Henderson-Bland, Alice Hollister, Gene Gauthier; **D:** Sidney Olcott; **W:** Gene Gauthier, Sidney Olcott. Natl Film Reg. '98.

From the Mixed-Up Files of Mrs. Basil E. Frankweiler 1995 (PG) Runaway siblings (Barnwell and Lee) secretly hide out in a New York art museum. They get caught up in trying to determine the authenticity of a sculpture (could it be the work of Michelangelo?) and turn to the statue's last owner, elusive art patron Mrs. Basil E. Frankweiler (Bacall). Based on the Newbery Award-winning novel by E.L. Konigsburg. Made for TV. **92m/C VHS, DVD,** Lauren Bacall, Jean Marie Barnwell, Jesse Lee; **D:** Marcus Cole. **TV**

From the Terrace 1960 Newman is a wealthy Pennsylvania boy who goes to New York and marries into even more money and social position when he weds Woodward. He gets a job with her family's investment company and neglects his wife for business. She turns to another man and when he goes home which leads to some emotional soul searching. The explicitness of O'Hara's very long novel was diluted by the censors and Newman's performance is a stilted disappointment. Loy, as Newman's alcoholic mother, earned the best reviews. **144m/C VHS, DVD,** Paul Newman, Joanne Woodward, Myrna Loy, Ina Balin, Felix Aylmer, George Grizzard, Patrick O'Neal, Barbara Eden, Mae Marsh; **D:** Mark Robson; **W:** Ernest Lehman; **C:** Leo Tover; **M:** Elmer Bernstein.

The Front 1976 (PG) Woody is the bookmaker who becomes a "front" for blacklisted writers during the communist witch hunts of the 1950s in this satire comedy. The scriptwriter and several of the performers suffered blacklisting themselves during the Cold War. Based more or less on a true story. **95m/C VHS, DVD,** Woody Allen, Zero Mostel, Herschel Bernardi, Michael Murphy, Danny Aiello, Andrea Marcovicci; **D:** Martin Ritt; **W:** Walter Bernstein; **C:** Michael Chapman; **M:** Dave Grusin.

The Front Line 2006 Joe (Ebouaney), a political refugee from the Congo, is working as a bank security guard in Dublin. Psycho Eddie (Frain) and his gang kidnap Joe's family, using them as leverage to make Joe their heist. Only Joe isn't the innocent man for their heist. When things go wrong, he seems an underground network of fellow African immigrants to track the gang down, including crime boss Erasmus (Kae-Kazim), another Congolese native. **90m/C DVD, GB IrE** Eriq Ebouaney, James Frain, Gerard McSorley, Ian McElhinney, Hakeem Kae-Kazim; **D:** David Gleeson; **W:** David Gleeson; **C:** Volker Tittel; **M:** Patrick Cassidy.

The Front Page 1974 (PG) A remake of the Hecht-MacArthur play about the managing editor of a 1920s Chicago newspaper who finds out his ace reporter wants to quit the business and get married. But first an escaped convicted killer offers the reporter an exclusive interview. **105m/C VHS, DVD,** Jack Lemmon, Walter Matthau, Carol Burnett, Austin Pendleton, Vincent Gardenia, Charles Durning, Susan Sarandon; **D:** Billy Wilder; **W:** I.A.L. Diamond, Billy Wilder; **C:** Jordan Cronenweth; **M:** Billy May.

The Front Page 1931 The original screen version of the Hecht-MacArthur play about the shenanigans of a battling newspaper reporter and his editor in Chicago. O'Brien's film debut here is one of several hilarious performances in this breathless pursuit of an exclusive with an escaped death row inmate. **101m/B VHS, DVD,** Adolphe Menjou, Pat O'Brien, Edward Everett Horton, Mae Clarke, Walter Catlet; **D:** Lewis Milestone; **C:** Hal Mohr.

Frontier Days 1934 Cody goes undercover to capture the leader of a gang of stagecoach robbers. He also manages to capture a killer along the way. **60m/B VHS,** Bill Cody, Ada Ince, Wheeler Oakman; **D:** Sam Newfield.

Frontier Fugitives 1945 When a trapper is murdered—allegedly by Indians—the Texas Rangers ride in to investigate. **58m/B VHS,** Tex Ritter, Dave O'Brien, Guy Wilkerson, Lorraine Miller, I. Stanford Jolley, Jack Ingram; **D:** Harry Fraser.

Frontier Horizon 1939 Wayne and the Three Mesquiteers help out ranchers whose land is being bought up by crooked speculators. **55m/B VHS,** John Wayne, Jennifer Jones, Ray Corrigan, Raymond Hatton; **D:** George Sherman.

Frontier Justice 1935 Gibson is the foolish son of a cattle owner who has been forced into an insane asylum because of a battle over water rights. Naturally, he must take on responsibility and rescue his father. **58m/B VHS, DVD,** Hoot Gibson, Richard Cramer; **D:** Robert McGowan.

Frontier Law 1943 Hayden and the boys ride into town to clean out the bed guys and clear a friend wrongly accused of murder. **55m/B VHS, DVD,** Russell Hayden, Jennifer Holt, Dennis Moore, Fuzzy Knight, Jack Ingram, Hal Taliaferro; **D:** Elmer Clifton; **W:** Elmer Clifton.

Frozen 1998 Flashback look at the suicide of struggling Beijing performance artist Qi Lei (Hongshen), who freezes himself to death in an "ice burial" as part of his art. Focuses on the aftermath of Tiananmen Square and its disaffected younger generation. Mandarin with subtitles. Working without authorization, the director hid behind a pseudonym that translates as "No Name." The film was smuggled out of China and completed in Amsterdam. **80m/B VHS, DVD, GB GE** Jia Hongshen, Bai Yu, Li Geng, Wei Ye; **D:** Wang Xiaoshuai; **W:** Pang Ming; **C:** Yang Shu; **M:** Roeland Dol.

Frozen Alive 1964 A scientist experiments with suspended animation but, wouldn't you know, someone murders his wife while he's on ice. Apparently being frozen stiff does not an alibi make, and he becomes the prime suspect. Much unanimated suspense. **80m/B VHS, DVD, GB GE** Mark Stevens, Marianne Koch, Delphi Lawrence, Joachim Hansen, Walter Rilla, Wolfgang Lukschy; **D:** Bernard Knowles.

Frostbiter: Wrath of the Wendigo 1994 (R) Disappointing Troma entry takes itself a bit too seriously. It wants to be an "Evil Dead on ice." We even see a movie poster for same flick; the plot involves hunters trapped in the frozen woods of Northern Michigan by the evil spirit "Wendigo." It's short on original horror and the laff-factor is not up to usual Troma standards (although the killer chill was a nice touch). The only saving grace is the quirky soundtrack, including said chill's theme song by Rancall and Alan Lynch, "March of the Undead" by the 3-D Invisibles, and "I'm a Hellbilly" by Elvis Hitler. Based on the comic book character of the same name. **90m/C VHS,** Ron Asheton, Lori Baker, Patrick Butler, Devlin Burton; **D:** Tom Chaney; **W:** Tom Chaney; **C:** Tom Chaney.

The Frontiersmen 1938 Things plod along at the little red schoolhouse until Hoppy and the guys have to take off after some rustlers. Features the schoolboys. Unusual for its lack of gunplay until near the end. **71m/B VHS,** William Boyd, George "Gabby" Hayes, Russell Hayden, Evelyn Venable, Clara Kimball Young, Charles Hughes, Dickie Jones, Roy Barcroft, Emory Parnell; **D:** Lesley Selander.

Frontier Pony Express 1939 Roy and Trigger do their best to help the Pony Express riders who are being attacked by marauding gangs in California during the time of the Civil War. **54m/B VHS,** Roy Rogers; **D:** Joseph Kane.

Frontier Scout 1938 Action-packed western has Wild Bill Hickok, portrayed by former opera singer Houston, trying to gain control of California for the U.S. Based on the short story "Gil Carson" by George Bruce. **58m/B VHS,** George Houston, Mantan Moreland; **D:** Sam Newfield.

Frontier Uprising 1961 **68m/B VHS,** Jim Davis, Nancy Hadley, Ken Mayer, Nestor Paiva, Don O'Kelly; **D:** Edward L. Cahn; **W:** Owen Harris.

Frontier Vengeance 1940 Barry is falsely accused of murder and works to clear his name while at the same time romancing a stagecoach criver who's trying to win a race with a rival stagecoach line. **54m/B VHS,** Donald (Don "Red") Barry, Betty Moran, George "Gabby" Hayes, Russell Hayden; **D:** Nate Watt; **W:** Barry Shipman, Bennett Cohen; **C:** Reggie Lanning; **M:** Cindy Walker.

Frontier Outlaws 1944 A gang of villains is selling stolen cattle, and Crabbe poses as an interested buyer to catch them in the act. Laughs are provided by Lynn as a judge, and as "Fuzzy" St. John as Crabbe's sidekick. **58m/B VHS,** Buster Crabbe, Al "Fuzzy" St. John, Frances Gladwin, Marin Sais, Charles "Blackie" King, Jack Ingram, Kermit Maynard, Edward Cassidy, Emmett Lynn, Budd Buster; **D:** Sam Newfield.

Frozen Assets 1992 (PG-13) Pathetic attempt at comedy from Long and Bernsen. He's an ambitious executive who finds the "bank" of his corporation's latest acquisition deals in sperm and not cash. Still, he expects this acquisition to be a success and comes up with a number of tacky ways, much to the horror of the facility's administrator, to make that profit margin grow. **93m/C VHS,** Corbin Bernsen, Shelley Long, Larry Miller, Dody Goodman, Gerrit Graham, Paul Sand, Teri Copley, Matt Clark, John Bloom; **D:** George Miller; **W:** Don Klein, Tom Kartozian.

Frozen in Fear *The Flying Dutchman* 2000. Variation on the 1933 film "The Mystery of the Wax Museum" and "The Vincent Price 1953 remake "House of Wax." Admiring art dealer Oxenberg tracks reclusive painter Roberts down to his remote cabin in Montana. Turns out the artist uses real female bodies for his work—killing young women, arranging them in provocative poses, and then encasing them in ice. Will Oxenberg become part of his next tableau? **91m/C VHS, DVD,** Eric Roberts, Catherine Oxenberg, Rod Steiger, Scott Plank, Barry Sigismondi, Joan Benedict, Douglas Sebern; **D:** Robin P. Murray. **VIDEO**

The Fugitive 1948 Fonda is a priest devoted to God and the peasants under his care when he finds himself on the run after religion is outlawed in this nameless South-of-the-border dictatorship. Despite the danger of capture, he continues to minister to his flock. His eventual martyrdom unites the villagers in prayer. Considered Fonda's best performance; Ford's favorite film. Shot on location in Mexico. Excellent supporting performances. Based on the Graham Greene novel "The Power and the Glory" although considerably cleaned up for the big screen—Greene's priest had lost virtually all of his faith and moral code, here the priest is a genuine Ford hero. A gem. **99m/B VHS,** Henry Fonda, Dolores Del Rio, Pedro Armendariz Sr., J. Carrol Naish, Leo Carrillo, Ward Bond, Robert Armstrong, John Qualen; **D:** John Ford; **W:** Dudley Nichols.

The Fugitive 1993 (PG-13) Exciting big-screen version of the '60s TV series with the same basic storyline: Dr. Richard Kimble's (Ford) wife (Ward) is murdered and he's convicted, so he's as determined as the mysterious one-armed man. Dogged marshal Sam Gerard (Jones) is determined to retrieve his man. Lots of mystery and action, particularly a spectacular train/bus crash sequence, keeps the tension high. Due to illness, Richard Jordan had begun, then replaced by Krabbe after production had begun. Alec Baldwin was originally slated to star as Kimble, but backed out and Ford was cast. Sound familiar? Ford also replaced Eadlwin as Jack Ryan in "Patriot Games." **127m/C VHS, DVD, Blu-ray Disc, HD DVD,** Harrison Ford, Tommy Lee Jones, Jeroen Krabbe, Julianne Moore, Sela Ward, Joe Pantoliano, Andreas Katsulas, Daniel Roebuck; **D:** Andrew Davis; **W:** David N. Twohy, Jeb Stuart; **C:** Michael Chapman; **M:** James Newton Howard. Oscars '93: Support. Actor (Jones); L.A. Film Critics '93: Support. Actor (Jones); Golden Globes '94: Support. Actor (Jones); MTV Movie Awards '94: On-Screen Duo (Harrison Ford/Tommy Lee Jones), Action Seq., Blockbuster '95: Action Actor (Ford).

Fugitive Among Us 1992 Dedicated cop is determined to return an escaped rapist to a life behind bars and he's aided by a victim who would really rather forget the whole thing. Made for TV. **97m/C VHS, DVD,** Peter Strauss, Eric Roberts, Elizabeth Pena, Lauren Holly. **TV**

Fugitive Champion 1999 Gangsters bust motor-cross champion Jake McKnight (Mayer) out of a chain gang so that he can search for his kidnapped daughter, a participant in an interstate sex site. The silly plot is a framework upon which to hang some inventive lively chase scenes. Standard action for a video premiere with a generic title. **94m/C DVD,** Chip (Christopher) Mayer, Charlene Blaine, Thomas Alan Ford, Carlos Cervantes...

Fugitive

W: Steven Baio, Jack Burkhead Jr.; C: Jason C. Poteet; M: Ennio di Berardo. VIDEO

The Fugitive Kind 🦴🦴½ 1960 A young drifter walks into a sleepy Mississippi town and attracts the attention of three of its women with tragic results. Based upon the Tennessee Williams' play "Orpheus Descending." good performances but the writing never hangs well enough together for coherence. 122m/B VHS, DVD. Marlon Brando, Anna Magnani, Joanne Woodward, Victor Jory, R.G. Armstrong, Maureen Stapleton; D: Sidney Lumet; C: Boris Kaufman.

Fugitive Mind 🦴½ 1999 (PG-13) Robert Dean (Dudikoff) is suffering from severe memory loss. As he begins to piece together his past, Dean discovers his mind has been programmed to carry out bizarre crimes. So now what does he do? 94m/C VHS, DVD. Michael Dudikoff, Heather Langenkamp, Michele Greene, David Hedison, Ian Ogilvy; D: Fred Olen Ray; W: Sean McGinley, Tripp Reed; C: Theo Angell; M: David Wurst, Eric Wurst. VIDEO

Fugitive Rage 🦴🦴 1996 (R) Tara McCormick (Schumacher) winds up behind bars when she shoots the mobster who was acquitted for murdering her sister. She teams up with her cellmate Josie (O'Brien) to fight back against the mob who's put a bounty on her head and a covert government agency also out to use her. Prerequisite prison shower sequences, tough babes, and lots of action. 90m/C VHS. Wendy Schumacher, Shauna O'Brien, Jay Richardson; D: Fred Olen Ray.

Fugitive Road 🦴🦴 1934 The great von Stroheim stars as a crusty but soft-hearted border guard who arbitrarily detains people at the crossing. 69m/B VHS. Erich von Stroheim, Wera Engels, Leslie Fenton, Harry Holman; D: Frank Strayer.

The Fugitive: Taking of Luke McVane 🦴🦴 1915 An early silent western in which Hart upholds the cowboy code of honor. 28m/B VHS. William S. Hart, Enid Markey, Clifford(?) Smith; D: William S. Hart, Clifford Smith.

Fugitive Valley 🦴½ 1941 Muddled plot has villains-turned-heroes on the trail of some outlaws and stolen money. Terhune shows off some of his vaudeville skills, and King sings some songs. 61m/B VHS, DVD. Ray Corrigan, John "Dusty" King, Max Terhune, Julie Duncan, Glenn Strange, Robert F. (Bob) Kortman, Tom London, Reed Howes; D: S. Roy Luby.

Fulfillment 🦴🦴½ 1996 *The Fulfillment of Mary Gray* 1989 (PG-13) Ladd stars as Mary Gray, a turn-of-the-century woman comfortably married to good but unexciting farmer, Jonathan (Levine). He's unable to give his wife the child they both desperately want and when his younger brother, Aaron (Smith), visits, the hope is Aaron can be persuaded to help out. The naturally volatile situation is heightened by the fact Mary is very drawn to the handsome Aaron anyway, and the feeling is mutual. Based on the novel "The Fulfillment" by LaVyrle Spencer. 96m/C VHS. Cheryl Ladd, Ted Levine, Lewis Smith; D: Piers Haggard. TV

Full Body Massage 🦴🦴 1995 (R) Wealthy art gallery owner Nina (Rogers) spends much of her time alone at her California dream home—except for a weekly appointment with young masseur Douglas (Burgard). But one week, the older Fitch (Brown) comes instead and begins discussing life and personal spirituality while he massages away the self-indulgent cares of the world-weary Nina. Good work by the leads in a chatty cable movie. 93m/C VHS. Mimi Rogers, Bryan Brown, Christopher Burgard, Elizabeth Barondes; D: Nicolas Roeg; W: Dan Gurskis; C: Anthony B. Richmond; M: Harry Gregson-Williams. CABLE

Full Circle 🦴🦴 *The Haunting of Julia* 1977 (R) Peter Straub wrote this eerie tale about a grief-stricken young woman whose child has recently died. To overcome her loss, she moves into a new house—which is haunted by the ghost of a long-dead child. 122m/B VHS, DVD. Mia Farrow, Keir Dullea, Tom Conti, Jill Bennett, Robin Gammell; D: Richard Loncraine; M: Colin Towns.

Full Contact 🦴🦴 *Xia dao Gao Fei* 1992 Nightclub bouncer Jeff helps his friend Sam escape from a loan shark. But Sam has doublecrossed him and now thinks that Jeff is dead in an arranged explosion. But Jeff's survived and plans to seek a suitable revenge. Cantonese with subtitles. 99m/C VHS, DVD. HK Chow Yun-Fat, Anthony Wong, Simon Yam, Bonnie Fu, Franklin Chin, Ann Bridgewater, Chan Chi Leung; D: Ringo Lam; W: Yin Nam; M: Teddy Robin Kwan.

Full Count 🦴🦴 1993 (R) Farmhand Luke Powers heads for the decadence of Los Angeles to find his older brother. When there thugs make the mistake of trying to rob him, Luke shows off his martial arts skills. When Luke finds out his brother has been murdered by gamblers involved in an illegal back alley kickboxing circuit, he vows to get revenge. 97m/C VHS, DVD. Jerry Trimble, Howard Jackson, Alvin Prouder, Gerry Blanck, Denise Buick; D: Rick Jacobson; W: Beverly Gray.

Full Count 🦴🦴 *Lenexa, 1 Mile* 2006 (R) Sports figure in, but this is more a story about friendship despite the curves in the plot. Five high school buddies are spending their last summer in their Kansas hometown before separating to go to college. They play a money game of basketball against the local cops and celebrate their win by getting drunk and driving. When disgruntled cop Russ pulls the boys over, he gets even by taking the money back and threatening them with arrest. They retaliate and things go downhill until there's another showdown between the boys (who have joined a softball league) and Russ' team. (And no, there's no showing of the "big game".) 90m/C DVD. Austin Nichols, Paul Wesley, Jason Ritter, Chris Klein, Josh Stewart, Timothy Ryan Hensel, Michael Rooker, William Baldwin, Michael Beach; D: Jason Wiles; W: Jason Wiles, Shawn Bitterman; C: David Boyd; M: Gary Clark Jr.

Full Disclosure 🦴🦴½ 2000 (R) Veteran journalist McWhirter (Ward) gets an incredible opportunity when a group of radicals he sent to prison ask him to protect a Palestinian operative (Ticotin) involved in the murder of a pro-Israeli media mogul. But neither an FBI agent (Plummer) nor an assassin (Miller) want McWhirter in the way and he'll have to decide just how badly he wants this story. 137m/C VHS, DVD. Fred Ward, Christopher Plummer, Penelope Ann Miller, Rachel Ticotin, Virginia Madsen, Kim Coates, Nicholas (Nick) Campbell, Dan Lauria, Roberta Maxwell; D: John Bradshaw; W: Tony Johnston; C: Barry Stone; M: Claude Desjardins, Eric N. Robertson. VIDEO

Full Eclipse 🦴🦴 1993 (R) Max Dire (Van Peebles) is seduced by the fetching Casey (Kensit) into joining a fierce elite group of underground cops whose mission is to wipe out crime. However, Max soon learns that the secret of their power is a serum which turns them into werewolves. Max is now faced with a decision: join forces with them, or expose them. Either way, blood will flow. Interesting special effects. Unrated version also available. 97m/C VHS, DVD. Mario Van Peebles, Patsy Kensit, Bruce Payne, Anthony John (Tony) Denison; D: Anthony Hickox; W: Richard Christian Matheson; C: Sandi Sissel.

Full Exposure: The Sex Tape Scandals 🦴½ 1989 (R) Sleazy drama about a murdered call girl who was blackmailing her clients with sex videos. A cop and his inexperienced female partner are assigned to catch the killer. 95m/C VHS, DVD. Jennifer O'Neill, Lisa Hartman Black, Vanessa (Lynne) Williams, Anthony John (Tony) Denison, Peter Jurasik; D: Noel Nosseck; W: Stephen Zito; M: Dana Kaproff. TV

Full Fathom Five 🦴½ 1990 (PG) Central American militants, angered by America's invasion of Panama, hijack a submarine and threaten a nuclear assault on Houston. Boring and dumb. 81m/C VHS. Michael Moriarty, Maria Rangel, Michael Cavanaugh, John Lafayette, Todd Field, Daniel Faraldo; D: Carl Franklin; W: Bart Davis.

Full Frontal 🦴½ 2002 (R) Despite its suggestive title, Soderbergh's film is arty, meandering, and uninvolving. Shot mostly on digital video in 18 days, the director's unofficial sequel to "sex, lies and videotape" tracks the loosely related lives and loves of various Los Angeles movie business types working on a film called "Rendezvous" over a 24-hour period. Katt, hilarious as a self-involved stage actor playing Hitler; Keener, as the somewhat demented Lee; and masseuse McCormack are the real standouts. However, improv-feel performances are good all around, with canny insider humor. The film's ambiguous presentation, including voice-overs, plays within movies, and movies-within-movies-within movies (whew!), undermine its intention to reveal the whole Hollywood circus that is really best kept under wraps. 101m/C VHS, DVD. US David Duchovny, Nicky Katt, Catherine Keener, Mary McCormack, David Hyde Pierce, Julia Roberts, Blair Underwood, Enrico Colantoni, Dina Spybey; D: Steven Soderbergh; C: Steven Soderbergh.

Full Hearts & Empty Pockets 🦴½ 1963 Follows the happy-go-lucky adventures of a young, handsome, impoverished gentleman on the loose in Rome. Dubbed in English. 88m/B VHS. IT GE Linda Christian, Gino Cervi, Senta Berger; D: Camillo Mastrocinque.

Full Metal Jacket 🦴🦴🦴½ 1987 (R) A three-act Vietnam War epic, about a single Everyman impetuously passing through basic training then working in the field as a Marine Corps photojournalist and fighting at the onset of the Tet offensive. First half of the film is the most realistic bootcamp sequence ever done. Unfocused but powerful. Based on the novel by Hasford, who also co-scripted. 116m/C VHS, DVD, Blu-ray Disc, HD DVD. Matthew Modine, R. Lee Ermey, Vincent D'Onofrio, Adam Baldwin, Dorian Harewood, Arliss Howard, Kevyn Major Howard, Ed O'Ross, John Terry, Jon Stafford, Marcus D'Amico, Kieron Jecchinis, Bruce Boa, Kirk Taylor, Tim Colceri, Ian Tyler, Gary Landon Mills, Sal Lopez, Ngoc Le, Peter Edmund, Tan Hung Francione, Leanne Hong, Costas Dino Chimona; D: Stanley Kubrick; W: Stanley Kubrick, Michael Herr, Gustav Hasford; C: Doug Milsome; M: Abigail Mead.

Full Metal Ninja 🦴 1989 When his family is kidnapped, a trained martial artist trails their abductors and swears revenge. 90m/C VHS. Patrick Allen, Pierre Kirby, Sean Odel, Jean Paul, Renato Sala; D: Godfrey Ho.

The Full Monty 🦴🦴🦴 1996 (R) A group of laid off Yorkshire mill workers come up with a unique way to earn some money in this amusing Britcom. When exuberant Gaz (Carlyle) notices the local women lining up to see the Chippendale dancers, he persuades his mates to launch a striptease act themselves. But these guys are hardly cover boy material—they're variously overweight, middle-aged, depressed, and shy. Nevertheless, they turn out to be an unexpected success despite numerous mishaps and misunderstandings. Title refers to the fact that they strip down to their birthday suits. The film audience merely gets the moon view. 90m/C VHS, DVD. GB Robert Carlyle, Tom Wilkinson, Mark Addy, Steve Huison, William Snape, Paul Barber, Hugo Speer, Lesley Sharp, Emily Woof, Deirdre Costello; D: Peter Cattaneo; W: Simon Beaufoy; C: John de Borman; M: Anne Dudley. Oscars '97: Orig. Mus./Comedy Score; British Acad. '97: Actor (Carlyle), Film, Support. Actor (Wilkinson); Screen Actors Guild '97: Cast.

Full Moon in Blue Water 🦴🦴 1988 (R) His wife's been dead a year, he owes back taxes on his bar, his father has Alzheimer's, and his only form of entertainment is watching old home movies of his wife. Floyd has problems. Enter Louise, a lonely spinster who feels that it's her personal duty to change his life. If she doesn't do it, the bizarre things that happen after her arrival will. 96m/C VHS, DVD. Gene Hackman, Teri Garr, Burgess Meredith, Elias Koteas, Kevin Cooney, David Doty; D: Peter Masterson; W: Bill Bozzone; C: Fred Murphy; M: Phil Marshall.

Full Moon in Paris 🦴🦴🦴½ *Les Nuits de la Pleine* 1984 (R) A young woman in Paris moves out on her architect lover in order to experience freedom. Through a couple of random relationships, she soon finds that what she hoped for is not what she really wanted. The fourth of Rohmer's Comedies and Proverbs series. French with subtitles. 101m/C VHS, DVD. FR Pascale Ogier, Tcheky Karyo, Fabrice Luchini; D: Eric Rohmer; W: Eric Rohmer; C: Renato Berta. Venice Film Fest. '84: Actress (Ogier).

Full of It 🦴🦴 2007 (PG-13) Mildly amusing teen comedy. Sam (Pinkston) is the small, geeky kid who tries to fit it at his new high school by telling a few white lies. Only by the next morning they've magically come true. But it's a definite case of "be careful what you wish for," including Sam almost losing out on the right girl (Mara) because of his typical teen boy cheerleader (Walsh) fantasy. 91m/C VHS, DVD. US Kate Mara, Craig Kilborn, John Carroll Lynch, Cynthia Stevenson, Amanda Walsh, Derek McGrath, Teri Polo, Joshua Close, Ryan Pinkston; Cameos: Carmen Electra; D: Christian Charles; W: Jon Lucas, Scott Moore; C: Kramer Morgenthau; M: John Swihart.

Full of Life 🦴🦴½ 1956 Holliday stars in this domestic comedy about a non-religious young woman who had married, in a civil ceremony, into a strict, Italian-Catholic family. Although Emily is now eight months pregnant the family still wants her and husband Nick (Conte) to have a church wedding. Holliday is a winning personality and charming. Fante adapts from his own novel. 91m/B VHS. Judy Holliday, Richard Conte, Salvatore Baccaloni, Esther Minciotti; D: Richard Quine; W: John Fante.

Full Speed 🦴🦴 *A Toute Vitesse* 1996 Quentin (Cervo) has published a semi-autobiographical novel about disenfranchised youth that's based on his friends from a Lyon housing project, including drug-dealing DJ, Jimmy (Rideau). Although he has a girlfriend, Julie (Bouchez), Quentin flirts with Algerian-born Samir (Bardadi) in order to learn about Samir's murdered boyfriend, so he can use the story in his writing. Julie, meanwhile, becomes involved with the charismatic Jimmy when Quentin decides to go to Paris. There are several melodramatic twists in Morel's feature debut about love-for-today youth and racial tensions. French with subtitles. 84m/C VHS. FR Pascal Cervo, Stephane Rideau, Elodie Bouchez, Meziane Bardadi; D: Gael Morel; W: Gael Morel, Catherine Corsini; C: Jeanne Lapoirie.

Full Tilt Boogie 🦴🦴½ 1997 (R) Director Sarah Kelly's documentary films the making of hipster crime-vampire flick "From Dusk Till Dawn" by Quentin Tarantino and Robert Rodriguez. Watching this clash of show biz egos is actually more fun than watching the movie they made. Probes the inner workings of big shots Tarantino, Clooney, Keitel, and the interns that hate to go to Taco Bell for them. Keitel, in his best "I can't believe you talked me into making this movie" tone, has a brief monologue about...well, he probably had a point when he started talking. Also shows the problems that went on during the production, including the destruction of a set by fire and the process of saving it. Included on the "From Dusk Till Dawn" special edition DVD. 110m/C VHS, DVD. Sarah Kelly; C: Chris Gallo; M: Cary Berger, Dominic Kelly.

The Fuller Brush Girl 🦴🦴½ 1950 Lots of slapstick with Ball as a door-to-door saleswoman unexpectedly involved in a murder. She and dim-bulb boyfriend Albert are chased by cops, murderers, and smugglers (who has a cameo) 1948 film "The Fuller Brush Man." 84m/B VHS. Lucille Ball, Eddie Albert, Carl Benton Reid, Gale Robbins, Jeff Donnell, John Litel, Fred

Fun 🎥🎥 1994 Another in the thrill kill genre. 14-year-old Bonnie (Witt) and 15-year-old Hillary (Humphrey) are best friends (and possibly lovers) who have stabbed to death an old woman—seemingly for kicks and to cement their loyalty to each other. (Can you say Leopold and Loeb?) Convicted and in a reformatory, they're documenting their actions, separately (in black & white sequences), to counselor Jane (Hope) and tabloid journalist John (Moses). Bleak dysfunction adapted by Bosley from his play. **95m/C VHS, DVD.** Alicia Witt, Renee Humphrey, Leslie Hope, William R. Moses, Ania Suli; **D:** Rafal Zielinski; **W:** James Bosley; **C:** Jens Sturup; **M:** Marc Tschanz.

Fun & Fancy Free 🎥🎥🎥 1947 **(G)** Part-animated, part-live-action Disney feature is split into two segments: "Bongo" with Dinah Shore narrating the story of a happy-go-lucky circus bear looking for love; and "Mickey and the Beanstalk"—a "new" version of an old fairy tale, Disney's last performance as the voice of Mickey and the only film to star Mickey, Donald Duck, Jimmy Cricket and Goofy. **73m/C VHS, DVD.** **D:** Jack Kinney, Hamilton Luske, William M. Morgan; **C:** Charles P. Boyle; **W:** Paul J. Smith, Oliver Wallace, Eliot Daniel; **V:** Walt Disney, Cliff Edwards, Billy Gilbert, Clarence Nash, Anita Gordon; **Nar:** Edgar Bergen, Dinah Shore.

Fun Down There Woof! 1988 This small-town boy-comes-to-the-big-city tale is so bad. It's—bad. A naive—and unsympathetic—gay man from upstate New York moves to Greenwich Village in a climactic dive down there (and they don't mean Australia). **110m/C VHS, DVD.** Michael Waite, Nickolas Nagourney, Gretchen Somerville, Martin Goldin, Kevin Och; **D:** Roger Stigliano; **W:** Michael Waite, Roger Stigliano.

Fun in Acapulco 🎥🎥 1963 **(PG)** Former trapeze artist Elvis romances two beauties and acts as a part-time lifeguard and night club entertainer. He must conquer his fear of heights for a climactic dive from the Acapulco cliffs. Features ten musical numbers. 🎵Fun in Acapulco; Vino, Dinero y Amor; Mexico; The Bullfighter Was A Lady; El Toro; Marguerita; (There's) No Room To Rhumba (In A Sports Car); I Think I'm Going To Like It Here; You Can't Say No In Acapulco. **97m/C VHS, DVD.** Elvis Presley, Ursula Andress, Elsa Cardenas, Paul Lukas, Alejandro Rey, Larry Domasin, Howard McNear; **D:** Richard Thorpe; **M:** Ernest Gold.

Fun with Dick and Jane 🎥🎥 1977 **(PG)** An upper-middle class couple turn to armed robbery to support themselves when the husband is fired from his job. Though it has good performances, the film never develops its intended title. **104m/C VHS, DVD.** George Segal, Jane Fonda, Ed McMahon; **D:** Ted Kotcheff; **W:** Jerry Belson, David Giler, Mordecai Richler; **C:** Fred W. Koenekamp; **M:** Ernest Gold.

Fun with Dick and Jane 🎥🎥 2005 **(PG-13)** Recycled version of the 1977 film with Jane Fonda and George Segal. Dick (Carrey) has a great life with gorgeous wife Jane (Leoni), a super house and an important executive position. Then Dick's company goes bust in a big way, and his efforts to find a comparable job (or any job) go bust as well. So what do they do? Why, of course, they turn to a life of crime. None-too-subtle political message (an Enron-esque company blowup) is rendered ineffective by too much gas and not enough go. If Jim Carrey's trademark slapstick doesn't drive you nuts, you'll get a few laughs out of it. **90m/C DVD, UMD, HD DVD. US** Jim Carrey, Tea Leoni, Alec Baldwin, Richard Jenkins, Angie Harmon, John Michael Higgins, Richard Burgi, Gloria Garayua; **D:** Dean Parisot; **W:** Judd

---

Graham, Lee Patrick; **Cameos:** Red Skelton; **D:** Lloyd Bacon; **W:** Frank Tashlin.

The Fuller Brush Man 🎥🎥½ 1948 A newly hired Fuller Brush man becomes involved in murder and romance as he tries to win the heart of his girlfriend. A slapstick delight for Skelton fans. **93m/B VHS.** Red Skelton, Janet Blair, Don McGuire, Adele Jergens; **D:** Frank Tashlin.

Apatow, Nicholas Stoller; **C:** Jerzy Zielinski; **M:** Theodore Shapiro, Randall Poster.

The Funeral 🎥🎥🎥½ 1984 A sharp satire of the clash of modern Japanese culture and corruption at the old. The hypocrisies, rivalries and confusion run amok as an average family are displayed at the funeral of this patriarch who also happened to own a house of ill repute. Itami's break-through film. Japanese with subtitles. **112m/C VHS, DVD.** JP Tsutomu Yamazaki, Nobuko Miyamoto, Kin Sugai, Ichiro Zaitsu, Nekohachi Edoya, Hideji Otaki; **D:** Juzo Itami; **C:** Yonezo Maeda; **M:** Joji Yuasa.

The Funeral 🎥🎥🎥 1996 **(R)** Ferrara fuels fantastic performances from his famous threesome in this fatalistic tale of a family of gangsters in 1930s New York. Flashbacks from the opening funeral scene show a complex and troubled family of Italian brothers (Walken, Penn, and Gallo), from their formative years through their quest for justice after youngest brother Johnny is murdered. Not just another mob movie; characters are multi-dimensional, sprints into his role. More subtle than "Bad Lieutenant" and less pretentious than "The Addiction." **99m/C VHS, DVD.** Christopher Walken, Benicio Del Toro, Vincent Gallo, Christopher Penn, Isabella Rossellini, Annabella Sciorra, John Ventimiglia, Paul Hipp, Gretchen Mol; **D:** Abel Ferrara; **W:** Nicholas St. John; **C:** Ken Kelsch; **M:** Joe Delia.

Funeral for an Assassin 🎥½ 1977 **(PG)** A professional assassin seeks revenge for his imprisonment by the government of South Africa, a former client. Planning to kill all of the country's leading politicians, he masquerades as a black apartheid establishment. **92m/C VHS, DVD.** Vic Morrow, Peter Van Dissel; **D:** Ivan Hall.

Funeral Home 🎥½ 1982 2 Cries in the Night 1982 Terrified teen spends her summer vacation at her grandmother's tourist home, a former funeral parlor. Rip-off of "Psycho." **90m/C VHS, DVD.** CA Lesleh Donaldson, Kay Hawtrey; **D:** William Fruet.

Funeral in Berlin 🎥🎥 1966 **(R)** Second of the Caine/Harry Palmer espionage films (following up "Ipcress File"), in which the deadpan antihero British secret serviceman arranges the questionable defection of a Russian colonel (Homolka). Good look at the spy biz and postwar Berlin. Based on the novel by Len Deighton. "Billion Dollar Brain" continues the series. **102m/C VHS, DVD.** Michael Caine, Eva Renzi, Oscar Homolka, Paul (Christian) Hubschmid, Guy Doleman, Hugh Burden; **D:** Guy Hamilton; **W:** Evan Jones; **C:** Otto Heller; **M:** Konrad Elfers.

The Funhouse 🎥½ 1981 **(R)** Four teenagers spend the night at a carnival funhouse, witness a murder, and become next on the list of victims. From the director of cult favorite "The Texas Chainsaw Massacre," but nothing that hasn't been seen before. **96m/C VHS, DVD.** Elizabeth Berridge, Shawn Carson, Cooper Huckabee, Largo Woodruff, Sylvia Miles, Miles Chapin, Kevin Conway, William Finley, Wayne Doba; **D:** Tobe Hooper; **W:** Larry Block; **C:** Andrew Laszlo; **M:** John Beal.

Funland 🎥 1989 **(PG-13)** In the world's weirdest amusement park a clown goes nuts over the place and decides to seek revenge for the place and decides to seek revenge. From the new corporate owners' plans quest to contribute to the population count. Lahti after having problems on the cartoonist Wilder who strays from wife fertile college co-ed Masterson in his conception and into the welcoming arms of by right. Roth and Watts turn in harrowing performances as the tortured husband and wife, with Watts also credited as producer. Deliberately shocking and manipulative, which may validate its premise, but still a nasty little flick. **107m/C VHS, DVD.** David Lander, William Windom, Bruce Mahler, Michael McManus; **D:** Michael A. Simpson.

Funny About Love 🎥½ 1990 **(PG-13)** Fairly absurd tale with cashes of inappropriate black humor about a fellow (Pitt) and Corbett, who descend upon a family, first as annoying guests, then as vicious sadists out for blood. Haneke had always said this movie would work better in America as social commentary, and he's probably right. Roth and Watts turn in harrowing performances. **86m/C VHS, DVD.** Gene Wilder, Christine Lahti, Mary Stuart Masterson, Robert Prosky, Stephen Tobolowsky, Anne Jackson, Susan Ruttan, David Margulies; **D:** Leonard Nimoy; **W:** Norman Steinberg, David Frankel.

Funny Games 🎥🎥🎥 1997 Georg (Muhe), his wife, Anna (Lothar), and young son, Georgie (Clapczynski) are vacationing at their lakeside cottage when their peace is invaded by psycho Paul (Frisch) and his sniveling partner Peter (Giering). The family is tied up and forced to play humiliating games with a couple of amoral killers. Most of the physical violence occurs off-screen but the psychological torture is relentless. German with subtitles. **103m/C VHS, DVD.** AT Susanne Lothar, Ulrich Muhe, Frank Giering, Arno Frisch, Stefan Clapczynski; **D:** Michael Haneke; **W:** Michael Haneke; **C:** Jurgen Jurges.

Funny Games 🎥🎥🎥 2007 **(R)** Haneke's shot-by-shot remake of his 1997 German art house thriller about two preppy 20-somethings, Paul and Peter (Pitt and Corbet), who descend upon a family, first as annoying guests, then as vicious sadists out for blood. Haneke had always said this movie would work better in America as social commentary, and he's probably right. Roth and Watts turn in harrowing performances as the tortured husband and wife, with Watts also credited as producer. Deliberately shocking and manipulative, which may validate its premise, but still a nasty little flick. **112m/C DVD.** IT GE FR GB US Naomi Watts, Tim Roth, Michael Pitt, Brady Corbet, Devon Gearhart; **D:** Michael Haneke; **W:** Michael Haneke; **C:** Darius Khondji.

Funny Valentine 🎥 2005 **(R)** Josh (Hall) is having trouble with New York's singles scene but has his buddies Tim (Lord Jamar) and Sean (Martin) offer dating advice, including placing a personal ad and vetting the responses. Embittered single mom Doreen (Marron) is not one of their choices but Josh decides to follow his heart. A romantic comedy that's weak on both the romance and the comedy. There is a lot of unwarranted semi-nudity that is more appropriate to softcore porn. **90m/C DVD.** Anthony Michael Hall, Mario Marron, Ivan Martin, Larry Storch, Lord Jamar; **D:** Jeff Oppenheim; **C:** Stephen Treadway.

Funnyman 🎥🎥 1994 **(R)** Cartoon splatter courtesy of a demon dressed in classic British jester regalia. Rock 'n' roll mogul Young obtains Lee's creepy ancestral home in a card game but when he visits with his family everyone but Young is killed by the Funnyman, who uses his victims own weaknesses to dispatch them. A second set of likely candidates arrives when Young's brother Devitt shows up with a motley collection of hangers-on, including psychic Black, who's the only one to realize something's seriously off. **89m/C VHS, DVD. GB** Tim James, Benny Young, Matthew Devitt, Pauline Black, Ingrid Lacey; **Cameos:** Christopher Lee; **D:** Simon Sprackling; **W:** Simon Sprackling.

Funny Bones 🎥🎥🎥 1994 **(R)** Struggling comedian Tommy Fawkes (Platt) bombs in Vegas big-time while his Mr. Showbiz father George (Lewis) easily overshadows him at every turn. So Tommy decides to head back to his childhood home in Blackpool, England and figure out his life. What he discovers are the Parkers, a family of British vaudevillians and, briefly, Mrs. Parker (Caron), resulting in half-brother Jack (Evans) who has all the natural talent Tommy can only dream about. Serious, funny, and hostile with no-table performances from Platt and Evans. **128m/C VHS, DVD.** Oliver Platt, Lee Evans, Leslie Caron, Jerry Lewis, Oliver Reed, Ian McNeice, Ruta Lee, Richard Griffith, George Carl, Freddie Davies; **D:** Peter Chelsom; **W:** Peter Flannery; **C:** Eduardo Serra; **M:** John Altman.

Funny Dirty Little War 🎥🎥🎥½ No Habra mas Penas ni Olvido; Funny Little Dirty War 1983 An Argentinian farce about the petty rivalries in a small village erupting into a violent, mini-civil war. Based on the novel by Osvaldo Soriano. In Spanish with English subtitles. **80m/C VHS, DVD.** AR Federico Luppi, Julio de Grazia, Miguel Angel Sola; **D:** Hector Olivera; **W:** Hector Olivera, Roberto Cossa; **C:** Leonardo Solis; **M:** Oscar Cardozo Ocampo.

Funny Face 🎥🎥🎥 1957 Musical satire on beatniks and the fashion scene also features the May-December romance between Astaire and the ever-lovely Hepburn. He is a high-fashion photographer (based on Richard Avedon); she is a Greenwich Village bookseller fond of sha-peless, drab clothing. He decides to take her to Paris and show her what modeling's all about. The elegant musical score features classic Gershwin. 🎵Let's Kiss and Make Up; He Loves and She Loves; Funny Face; How Long Has This Been Going On?; Clap Yo' Hands; S'Wonderful; Bonjour Paris; On How To Be Lovely; Marche Funebre. **103m/C VHS, DVD.** Audrey Hepburn, Kay Thompson, Suzy Parker; **D:** Stanley Donen; **M:** Ira Gershwin.

The Funny Farm 🎥½ 1982 Comics about a group of ambitious young comics striving to make it in the crazy world of comedy at Los Angeles' famous comedy club, The Funny Farm. **90m/C VHS.** CA Tracy Bregman, Miles Chaplin, Eileen Brennan, Peter Aykroyd; **D:** Ron Clark.

Funny Farm 🎥🎥 1988 **(PG)** Chevy Chase as a New York sportswriter finds that life is in the country is not quite what he envisioned. The comedy is uneven throughout, with the best scenes coming at the end. **101m/C VHS, DVD.** Chevy Chase, Madolyn Smith, Joseph Maher, Jack Gilpin, Brad Sullivan, Macintyre Dixon; **D:** George Roy Hill; **W:** Jeffrey Boam; **C:** Miroslav Ondricek; **M:** Elmer Bernstein.

Funny Girl 🎥🎥🎥 1968 **(G).** Follows the early career of comedian Fanny Brice, her rise to stardom with the Ziegfeld Follies, and her stormy romance with gambler Nick Arnstein in a fun and funny look at 1900s Broadway's film debut followed her auspicious performance of the role on Broadway. Score was augmented by several tunes sung by Brice during her performances. Excellent performances from everyone, captured beautifully by Wyler in his musical film debut. Followed by "Funny Lady." 🎵I'm The Greatest Star; Sadie, Sadie; His Love Makes Me Beautiful; You Are Woman, I Am Man; Don't Rain On My Parade; I'd Rather Be Blue Over You; People; Second Hand Rose. **151m/C VHS, DVD.** Barbra Streisand, Omar Sharif, Walter Pidgeon, Kay Medford, Anne Francis; **D:** William Wyler; **W:** Isobel Lennart; **C:** Harry Stradling Sr.; **M:** Jule Styne, Walter Scharf; Oscars '68: Actress (Streisand); Golden Globes '69. Actress-Mus./Comedy (Streisand).

Funny Lady 🎥🎥½ 1975 **(PG).** A continuation of "Funny Girl," recounting Fanny Brice's tumultuous marriage to showman Billy Rose in the 1930s and her lingering affection for first husband Nick Arnstein. One of the rare sequels which are just as good, or at least almost, as the original. 🎵How Lucky Can You Get?; Great Day; More Than You Know; Blind Date; So Long, Honey Lamb; Isn't This Better; Let's Hear It For Me; I Like Him/I Like Her; It's Only a Paper Moon. **137m/C VHS, DVD.** Barbra Streisand, James Caan, Roddy McDowall, Ben Vereen, Carole Wells, Larry Gates, Heidi O'Rourke; **D:** Herbert Ross; **W:** Jay Presson Allen, Arnold Schulman; **C:** James Wong Howe.

Funny Money 🎥 1982 Pointed, satirical look at the British habit of financing life with the almighty credit card. Sometimes uneven comedy. **89m/C VHS, GB** Gregg Henry, Elizabeth (E.G. Bailey) Daily, Gareth Hunt, Derren Nesbitt, Annie Ross; **D:** James Kenneth Clarke.

A Funny Thing Happened on the Way to the Forum 🎥🎥🎥 1966 A bawdy Broadway farce set in ancient Rome where a conniving slave plots his way to freedom by aiding in the romantic escapades of his master's inept son. Terrific performances by Mostel and Gilford. Keaton's second-to-last film role. The Oscar-winning score includes such high-lights as "Comedy Tonight," "Lovely," and "Everybody Ought to Have a Maid." **100m/C VHS, DVD.** Zero Mostel, Phil Silvers, Jack Gilford, Buster Keaton, Michael Hordern, Michael Crawford, Annette Andre; **D:** Richard Lester; **W:** Melvin Frank, Michael Pertwee; **C:** Nicolas Roeg; **M:** Ken Thorne. Oscars '66 Adapt. Score.

Fur: An Imaginary Portrait of Diane Arbus 2006 (R) Imaginary indeed as tall, pale Kidman looks nothing like the small, dark Arbus, not to mention that Downey's character Lionel Sweeney suffers from an extreme form of hirsuteness that covers him in hair so he's reduced to acting with eyes and voice. So here's this married 1950s New York housewife who helps out husband Allan (Burrell) with his commercial photography career suddenly transforming herself into a snapper of those marginalized by society. Apparently Diane is tired of being the good girl and wants to take a walk on the wild side and fulfill her own artistic desires. It's a well-intentioned but somehow unsatisfactory effort. 120m/C DVD. *US* Nicole Kidman, Robert Downey Jr., Ty Burrell, Harris Yulin, Jane Alexander; *W:* Steven Shainberg; *C:* Bill Pope; *M:* Carter Burwell.

The Further Adventures of Tennessee Buck 1988 (R) Mercenary adventurer travels through tropical jungles acting as a guide to a dizzy couple. Along the way, they encounter cannibals, headhunters, and other bizarre jungle things in this lame take on "Indiana Jones." Shot on location in Sri Lanka. 90m/C VHS, DVD. David Keith, Kathy Shower, Brant Van Hoffman; *D:* David Keith; *M:* John Debney.

Further Adventures of the Wilderness Family, Part 2 *Wilderness Family, Part 2* 1977 (G) Depicts the Robinson family who left civilization for the freedom of the Colorado wild. Predictable retreat, but more good family adventure drama from the makers of "Adventures of the Wilderness Family." 104m/C VHS. Heather Rattray, Ham Larsen, George "Buck" Flower, Robert F. Logan, Susan Damante-Shaw; *D:* Frank Zuniga.

Fury 1936 Tracy gives an excellent performance as an innocent young man framed for kidnapping and then nearly murdered by a lynch mob. His plans for revenge are thwarted by his girlfriend, who fears that he will turn into the murderer he has been accused of being. Powerful anti-violence message is well-made, with strong ensemble acting. Lang's favorite of his American-made films. 96m/B VHS, DVD. Spencer Tracy, Sylvia Sidney, Walter Abel, Bruce Cabot, Edward Ellis, Walter Brennan, Frank Albertson; *D:* Fritz Lang; *C:* Joseph Ruttenberg. Natl. Film Reg. '95.

The Fury 1978 (R) The head of a government institute for psychic research finds that his own son is snatched by supposed terrorists who wish to use his lethal powers. The father tries to use another young woman with psychic power to locate him, with bloody results. A real chiller. 117m/C VHS, DVD. Kirk Douglas, John Cassavetes, Carrie Snodgress, Andrew Stevens, Amy Irving, Charles Durning, Carol Rossen, Rutanya Alda, William Finley, Jane Lambert, Joyce Easton, Daryl Hannah, Dennis Franz, James Belushi; *D:* Brian De Palma; *W:* John Farris; *C:* Richard H. Kline; *M:* John Williams.

The Fury of Hercules *La Furia Di Ercole; Fury of Samson* 1961 It's up to the mighty son of Zeus to free an enslaved group of people from an oppressive, evil ruler. Surely all who stand in his way will be destroyed. Another Italian muscleman film. 95m/C VHS. *IT* Brad Harris, Luisella Boni, Mara Berni, Carlo Tamberlani, Serge Gainsbourg, Elke Arendt, Alan Steel; *D:* Gianfranco Parolini.

The Fury of the Wolfman *La Furia del Hombre Lobo* 1970 A murdering werewolf is captured by a female scientist who tries to cure his lycanthropy with drugs and brain implants. Pretty slow going, but hang in there for the wolfman versus werewoman climax. 80m/C VHS, DVD. *SP* Paul Naschy, Perla Cristal, Michael Rivers, Mark Stevens, Veronica Lujan; *D:* Jose Maria Zabalza; *W:* Paul Naschy.

Fury on Wheels *Jump* 1971 (PG) Tale of men who race cars and wreak havoc and vice versa. 89m/C VHS. Tom Ligon, Collin Wilcox-Paxton, Sudie Bond, Conrad Bain, Sally Kirkland, Jack Nance, Judd Hirsch; *D:* Joseph Manduke; *W:* Richard Wheelwright; *C:* Gregory Sandor.

Fury to Freedom: The Life Story of Raul Ries 1985 A young man raised in the volatile world of abusive and alcoholic parents grows into an abusive and violent adult. One night, however, he meets something he can't beat up, and it changes his life. 78m/C VHS, DVD. Gil Gerard, John Quade, Tom Silardi; *D:* Eric Jacobson; *W:* Eric Jacobson; *C:* Don Burgess.

The Fury Within 1998 (PG-13) Mike (Mandylor) and Jo (Sheedy) Hanlon are an estranged couple who, along with their two young children, are terrorized by the supernatural. Turns out the poltergeist is a manifestation of Jo's anger about her upcoming divorce. Gives new meaning to the saying about scorned women. 91m/C VHS, DVD. Ally Sheedy, Costas Mandylor, Vincent Berry; *D:* Noel Nosseck. CABLE

Fuse 2003 Two years after the civil war, the Bosnian town of Tesanj expects a visit from President Bill Clinton. The entire community is determined to present a wholesome image (turning the brothel into a cultural center) but a black marketeer, a crazy ex-police chief, and a continuing Serbian rivalry could derail the process. Bosnian and Serbian with subtitles. 105m/C DVD. *BS* Bogdan Diklic, Enis Beslagic, Sasa Petrovic, Izudin Bajrovic; *D:* Pjer Zalica; *W:* Pjer Zalica; *C:* Mirsad Herovic; *M:* Sasa Losic.

Future Cop 1976 A hard-nosed, old-fashioned cop is forced to team with the ultimate partner—a robot. Silly made-for-TV movie, but likable leads. 78m/C VHS. Ernest Borgnine, Michael J. Shannon, John Amos, John Larch, Herbert Nelson, Ronnie Clair Edwards; *D:* Jud Taylor; *W:* Danny Bilson, Paul DeMeo.

Future Fear 1997 (R) Genetic scientist Dr. John Denniel (Wincott) has to find a solution to a flesh-eating virus that threatens mankind. Along with wife Anna (Ford), John tries combining human DNA with that of other species. But it turns out the virus was engineered by maniacal General Wallace (Keach) as a form of human cleansing—and he's not happy when he hears about a potential cure. 82m/C VHS, DVD. Shawn Thompson, Jeff Wincott, Maria Ford, Stacy Keach; *C:* Lewis Baumander; *W:* Lewis Baumander; *C:* Graeme Mears; *M:* Donald Quan. VIDEO

Future Force 1989 (R) In the crime-filled future cops can't maintain order. They rely on a group of civilian mercenaries to clean up the streets. 90m/C VHS, DVD. David Carradine, Robert Tessier, Anna Rapagna, William Zipp; *D:* David A. Prior; *W:* David A. Prior; *C:* Andy Parke; *M:* Mark Mancina.

Future Hunters 1988 In the holocaust-blitzed future, a young couple searches for a religious artifact that may decide the future of the planet. 96m/C VHS. Robert Patrick, Linda Carol, Ed Crick, Bob Schott; *D:* Cirio H. Santiago.

Future Kill 1985 (R) Anti-nuclear activists battle fraternity brothers in this grim futuristic world. Shaky political alliances form between revenge-seeking factions on both sides. 83m/C VHS, DVD. Edwin Neal, Marilyn Burns, Doug Davis; *D:* Ronald W. Moore; *W:* Ronald W. Moore.

Future Shock 1993 (PG-13) Dr. Russell Langdon is a psychiatrist who has been experimenting with virtual reality technology. Unbeknownst to three of his patients he decides to use them as guinea pigs in his work. But confronting their deepest fears only leads to new terrors. Also available in an unrated version. 93m/C VHS, DVD. Bill Paxton, Vivian Schilling, Brion James, Martin Kove; *D:* Eric Parkinson, Matt Reeves, Oley Sassone; *W:* Vivian Schilling.

Future Zone 1990 (R) In an attempt to save his father from being murdered, a young man travels backwards in time. 88m/C VHS. David Carradine, Charles Napier, Ted Prior; *D:* David A. Prior.

Futurekick 1991 (R) In the not so distant future, a kickboxer with an attitude and cyborg capabilities must use every ounce of strength in a battle against evil. 80m/C VHS, DVD. Don "The Dragon" Wilson, Meg Foster, Christopher Penn, Eb Lottimer, Linda Dona, Maria Ford; *D:* Damian Klaus; *W:* Damian Klaus, Catherine Cyran; *C:* Ken Arlidge; *M:* Stan Ridgway.

Futuresport 1998 (R) In 2025, Tre Ramsey (Cain) is the arrogant star of a popular violent sport that's a combo of skateboarding and basketball. Only the key game turns out to have more on the line than endorsements when terrorists take over the arena. Tre's mentor, and Futuresport creator Orbike Fixx (Snipes), suggests it's just a gigantic turf war and that matters can be settled by an arena match to the death. Caught in the middle is newscaster Alejandra (Williams), the woman Tre once loved and left behind. 89m/C VHS, DVD. Dean Cain, Vanessa (Lynne) Williams, Wesley Snipes, Bill Smitrovich, Francoise Yip; *D:* Ernest R. Dickerson; *W:* Robert Hewitt Wolfe. TV

Futureworld 1976 (PG) In the sequel to "Westworld," two reporters junket to the new "Futureworld" theme park, where they first support a scheme to clone and control world leaders. Includes footage shot at NASA locations. 107m/C VHS, DVD. Peter Fonda, Blythe Danner, Arthur Hill, Yul Brynner, Stuart Margolin; *D:* Richard T. Heffron; *W:* George Schenck.

Futz 1969 Story from off-Broadway is of a man who loves his pig and the world that can't understand the attraction. Better in original stage production. 90m/C VHS. John Pakos, Victor Lipari, Sally Kirkland; *D:* Tom O'Horgan.

Fuzz 1972 (R) Reynolds in the Boston cop on the track of a bomber killing policemen, punks setting winos on fire, and some amorous fellow officers. Combines fast action and some sharp-edged humor. 92m/C VHS, DVD. Burt Reynolds, Tom Skerritt, Yul Brynner, Raquel Welch, Jack Weston, Charles Martin Smith, Albert "Poppy" Popwell; *D:* Richard A. Colla; *M:* Dave Grusin.

Fyre 1978 (R) Young beautiful girl moves from the Midwest to Los Angeles and becomes a prostitute. 90m/C VHS. Allen (Goorwitz) Garfield, Lynn Theel, Tom Baker, Cal Haynes, Donna Wilkes, Bruce Kirby; *D:* Richard Grand.

G 2002 (R) Black urban adaptation of "The Great Gatsby." Successful hip-hop mogul Summer G (Jones) uses his bling to buy a mansion in the Hamptons and throw lots of parties. G is still upset that lover Sky (Maxwell) ran off long ago to marry old-money rich Chip Hightower (Underwood). Chip's cheating on his wife so G figures it's time to get Sky back. Journalist Tre (Royo) documents the happenings. Contrived mish-mash was filmed in 2001. 96m/C DVD. *US* Richard T. Jones, Chenoa Maxwell, Blair Underwood, Andrew Lauren, Laz Alonso, Andre Royo; *D:* Christopher Scott Cherot; *W:* Andrew Lauren, Charles E. Drew Jr.; *C:* Horacio Marquinez; *M:* Bill Conti.

"G" Men 1935 Powerful story based loosely on actual events that occurred during FBI operations in the early 1930s, with Cagney on the right side of the law, though still given to unreasonable fits of anger. Raised and educated by a well-known crime kingpin, a young man becomes an attorney. When his friend the FBI agent is killed in the line of duty, he joins the FBI to seek vengeance on the mob. But his mob history haunts him, forcing him to constantly prove to his superiors that he is not under its influence. Tense and thrilling classic. 86m/B VHS, DVD. James Cagney, Barton MacLane, Ann Dvorak, Margaret Lindsay, Robert Armstrong, Lloyd Nolan, William Harrigan, Regis Toomey; *D:* William Keighley; *W:* Seton I. Miller; *C:* Sol Polito.

G-Men Never Forget *Code 645* 1948 Moore, former stunt-man and future Lone Ranger, stars in this 12-part serial about FBI agents battling the bad guys. Lots of action. On two cassettes. 167m/B VHS. Clayton Moore, Roy Barcroft, Ramsay Ames, Drew Allen, Tommy Steele, Eddie Acuff; *D:* Fred Brannon, Yakima Canutt.

G-Men vs. the Black Dragon 1943 Reedited serial of "Black Dragon of Manzanar" stars Cameron as Fed who battles Asian Axis agents during WWII. Action-packed. 244m/B VHS. Rod Cameron, Roland Got, Constance Worth, Nino Pipitone, Noel Cravat; *D:* William Witney.

G2: Mortal Conquest 1999 (R) In the year 2003, Steven Colin (Bernhardt) unknowingly possesses the secret of an ancient martial arts power he learned in a former incarnation. Now the foes from the ancient battle have returned and Colin must remember his past if he's to save his present. 93m/C VHS, DVD. Daniel Bernhard, James Hong; *D:* Nick Rotundo; *W:* Nick Rotundo; *M:* Gary Koftinoff. VIDEO

G. Whilliker! 1993 Brothers have decided a guy named Gus Whilliker is the perfect match for their older sister/guardian. Too bad she's already dating someone. 93m/C VHS. Dan Brook, Robin Brooks, Matthew Tompkins, Jay Michael Ferguson, William Ryan Tilk, Chris Lloyd, Jody Miller; *D:* David McClendon; *W:* Brenda Brown-Canary, Michael Haldeman; *M:* Drew F. Barlow.

Gabbeh 1996 Gabbeh is not only the name of the film's heroine (Djobat), it is also the name of the finely embroidered woolen rugs that the nomadic Ghashgai tribe is known for. Gabbeh has a simple desire—she wishes to marry a mysterious horseman but her father keeps placing obstacles in her path. She tells her story to an old married couple, who are washing their own gabbeh in a stream. The film is visually lush but a challenge for Western sensibilities with its slow pace and allegorical content. Farsi with subtitles. 75m/C VHS, DVD. *IA* Shaghayek Djodat, Hossein Moharami, Rogheih Moharami, Abbas Sayahi; *D:* Mohsen Makhmalbaf; *W:* Mohsen Makhmalbaf; *C:* Mahmoud Kalari; *M:* Hossein Alizadeh.

Gabriel Over the White House 1933 Part political satire, part fantasy, and completely fascinating. Huston, completely in thrall to his crooked cohorts, who manages to get elected President. While recuperating from an auto accident Hammond thinks he sees a vision of the Archangel Gabriel, who essentially tells him to change his crooked ways. From bought man Hammond changes to righteous do-gooder, much to the dismay of his criminal companions, who'll stop at nothing to get rid of the man they think has simply gone insane. Huston gives a powerful performance in this decidedly oddball film. 86m/B VHS. Walter Huston, Karen Morley, Arthur Byron, Franchot Tone, Dickie Moore, C. Henry Gordon, David Landau, Samuel S. Hinds, Jean Parker; *D:* Gregory La Cava; *W:* Carey Wilson.

Gabriela 1984 (R) A sultry romance develops between a Brazilian tavern keeper and the new cook he's just hired. Derived from Jorge Amado's novel. In Portuguese with English subtitles. 102m/C VHS. *BR* Sonia Braga, Marcello Mastroianni, Nelson Xavier, Antonio Cantafora; *D:* Bruno Barreto; *W:* Bruno Barreto; *C:* Carlo Di Palma; *M:* Antonio Carlos.

Gabriela 2001 (R) Student Gabriela (Lopez) takes a job at a mental health clinic where she meets social worker Mike (Gomez). She's pretty, he's handsome, there's a strong mutual attraction but Gabriela is engaged to Pat (Galligan) even though she doesn't really love him and only agreed to please her strict mother (Fernandez). So will this twosome manage to overcome their romantic obstacles and be together? Expect the expected. 93m/C VHS, DVD. Seidy Lopez, Jaime Gomez, Zach Galligan, Troy Winbush, Evelina Fernandez, Lupe Ontiveros, Stacy Haiduk; *D:* Vincent Jay Miller; *W:* Vincent Jay Miller; *C:* Adrian Rudomin; *M:* Craig Stuart Garfinkle.

Gabrielle 2005 French superstars give this highly stylized French period piece some bite despite one set and a whole lot of arguing, crying, and talking. Wealthy publisher Jean (Gregory) is living the high life, complete with a statue-filled mansion, an army of servants and a beautiful but dissatisfied wife, Gabr-

Gaby: A True Story ✓✓✓ 1987 (R) The story of a woman with congenital cerebral palsy who triumphs over her condition with the help of family and loved ones, and ends up a college graduate and acclaimed author. Based on a true story. 115m/C VHS. Rachel Levin, Liv Ullmann, Norma Aleandro, Robert Loggia, Lawrence Monoson, Robert Beltran, Tony Goldwyn; **D:** Luis Mandoki; **W:** Martin Salinas, Michael James Love; **C:** Lajos Koltai; **M:** Maurice Jarre.

Gal Young 'Un ✓✓✓ 1979 Set during the Prohibition era, a rich, middle-aged woman living on her property in the Florida backwoods finds herself courted by a much younger man. She discovers she is being used to help him set up a moonshining business. Unsentimental story of a strong woman. Based on a Marjorie Kinnan Rawlings story. 105m/C VHS. Dana Preu, David Peck, J. Smith, Timothy McCormack, Gena Densmore, Jenny Stringfellow; **D:** Victor Nunez; **C:** Victor Nunez; **Sundance** '81: Grand Jury Prize.

Galactic Gigolo Woof! 1987 (R) An alien broccoli (yes, the vegetable) descends to earth on vacation, and discovers he's irresistible to Connecticut women. Must be something in the water. Amateurish effort intended as science-fiction satire, but there's more sleaze than humor. 80m/C DVD. Carmine Capobianco, Debi Thibeault, Ruth (Coreen) Collins, Angela Nicholas, Frank Stewart; **D:** Gorman Bechard.

Galaxies Are Colliding ✓✓½ 1995 (R) The physically impressive Nielsen stars as space- and time-traveling freedom fighter Lancera, who beams down to Earth to battle your basic evil, intergalactic villain Kya (Moll) who has the power source that could save her civilization. 91m/C VHS. Brigitte Nielsen, James D. Hinton, Ronald J. Knight, Lionel Mark Smith, Tad Horino, Herb Kaplowitz, Nancy McCauley; **D:** William Sachs; **W:** William Sachs; **C:** Dean Cundey.

Galaxina ✓✓½ 1980 (R) In the 31st century, a beautiful robot woman capable of human feelings is created. Stumbling parody of superspace fantasies features murdered Playmate Stratten in one of few film appearances. 95m/C VHS, DVD. Dorothy Stratten, Avery Schreiber, Stephen Macht, James D. Hinton, Ronald A. Ryman; **W:** William Sachs; **C:** Philip Lee; **M:** Stephen Barber.

Galaxis ✓✓ 1995 (R) The physically impressive Nielsen stars as space- and time-traveling freedom fighter Lancera, who beams down to Earth to battle your basic evil, intergalactic villain Kya (Moll) who has the power source that could save her civilization. 91m/C VHS, DVD, HD DVD. Brigitte Nielsen, James D. Hinton, Ronald A. Ryman; **D:** William Sachs.

Galaxy Invader ✓ 1985 (PG) Chaos erupts when an alien explorer crash lands his spacecraft in a backwoods area of the United States. 79m/C VHS, DVD. Richard Ruxton, Faye Tilles, Don Leifert, D: Donald M. Dohler; **M:** Donald M. Dohler.

Galaxy of Terror ✓✓½ 1981 (R) An Infinity of Terror; Planet of Horrors; Mindwarp. Astronauts sent to rescue a stranded spaceship get killed by vicious aliens. Big First: Moran (Joanie on "Happy Days") explodes. Interior Corman-produced "Alien" imitation still manages to shock and displays generous gore. Followed by "Forbidden World." 80m/C VHS. Erin Moran, Edward Albert, Ray Walston, Grace Zabriskie, Zalman King, Taaffe O'Connell, Robert Englund, Bernard Behrens, Jack Blessing, Sid Haig. (E.D.)

Galaxy Quest ✓✓½ 1999 (PG) An ingratiating goof on "Star Trek" and other cheesy TV shows that draw rabid fans and typecast actors. At a sci-fi convention, the actors from the long-running TV space series "Galaxy Quest" are mistaken for real space traveling heroes by naive aliens who need them to aid in an intergalactic war and whisk the troupe off to a galaxy far, far away (or thereabouts). Naturally, the "crew" is ill-prepared for their latest mission. Playful acting includes Allen's babe Gwen DeMarco (Weaver), and cynical Brit, Alexander Dane (Rickman). 104m/C VHS, DVD. Tim Allen, Sigourney Weaver, Alan Rickman, Tony Shalhoub, Sam Rockwell, Daryl (Chill) Mitchell, Robin Sachs, Enrico Colantoni, Missi Pyle; **D:** Dean Parisot; **W:** David Howard, Robert Gordon; **C:** Jerzy Zielinski; **M:** David Newman.

Gale Force ✓✓½ 2001 (R) The reality TV show "Treasure Hunt" involves eight contestants, one of whom is L.A. detective Sam Garrett (Williams), competing to find 10 million buried on the remote island on which they are marooned. But Sam is suspicious of executive producer Stuar. McMahon (DeYoung), who'll do anything for ratings, and show host Jack MacRae (Nozick), who has a pot to get the money for himself. Oh, and then Mother Nature decides to make things even more interesting. Lots of action, including a good storm sequence. Wynorski directs under his own name. 96m/C VHS, DVD. Treat Williams, Michael Dudikoff, Tim Thomerson, Curtis Armstrong, Clif DeYoung, Bruce Nozick; **D:** Jim Wynorski. VIDEO

Galgameth ✓✓½ 1996 (PG) The Adventures of Galgameth. Old-fashioned tale of a boy-hero and a friendly monster. 14-year-old Prince Davin (Oatway) accidentally injures his father during a joust and blames himself when the king suddenly dies. But knight El El (Macht), who declares himself regent and terrorizes the kingdom. Davin's only hope to restore peace is a magical statue called Galgameth that the prince is able to bring to life. Romanian location provides proper storybook castles and medieval villages. 99m/C VHS. Devin Oatway, Stephen Macht, Sean McNamara, Johna Stewart, Tom Dugan; **D:** Sean McNamara; **W:** James Angel; **C:** Christian Sebaldt; **M:** Richard (Rick) Marvin.

Gallagher's Travels ✓ 1987 A screwball male/female reporting team chase an animal smuggling ring through the wilds of Australia. 94m/C VHS. AU Ivar Kants, Joanne Samuel, Stuart Campbell, Jennifer Hagan; **D:** Michael Caulfield.

The Gallant Fool ✓✓½ 1933 A man is wrongly accused of murder and tries to clear his name while eluding the law. 57m/B VHS. Bob Steele, Arletta Duncan, George "Gabby" Hayes, John Elliott; **D:** Robert North Bradbury.

The Gallant Hours ✓✓½ 1960 Biography of Admiral "Bull" Halsey (Cagney) covers five weeks, October 18 through December 1, 1942, in the WWII battle of Guadalcanal in the South Pacific. Director Montgomery forgoes battle scenes to focus on the human elements in a war and what makes a great leader. Fine performance by Cagney. 115m/B VHS. James Cagney, Dennis Weaver, Ward (Edward) Costello, Richard Jaeckel, Les Tremayne, Robert Burton, Raymond Bailey, Karl Swenson, Harry Landers, James T. Goto, Leon Lontoc, Carleton Young, James Yagi, Carl Benton Reid, Selmer Jackson, Nelson Leigh, John McKee, Tyler McVey, William Schallert, John Zaremba, Richard Carlyle, Herbert Lytton, Sydney Smith, Art Gilmore; **D:** Robert Montgomery; **W:** Frank D. Gilroy, Beirne Lay Jr.; **C:** Joe MacDonald; **M:** Roger Wagner.

Gallipoli ✓✓✓ 1981 (PG) History as the destiny of two friends as they become part of the legendary WWI confrontation between Australia and the German-allied Turks. A superbly filmed, gripping commentary on the wastes of war. Haunting score; excellent performances by Lee and a then-unknown Gibson. Remake of a lesser 1931 effort "Battle of Gallipoli." 111m/C VHS, DVD, AU Mel Gibson, Mark Lee, Bill Kerr, David Argue, Tim McKenzie, Robert Grubb, Graham Dow, Stan Green, Heath Harris, Harold Hopkins, Charles Yunupingu, Ronny Graham, Gerda Nicolson; **D:** Peter Weir; **M:** Peter Weir, David Williamson; **C:** Russell Boyd; **M:** Brian May, Australian Film Inst. '81: Actor (Gibson), Film.

Galloping Dynamite ✓✓ 1937 Early western based on a James Oliver Curwood story. A ranger avenges the death of his brother killed for gold. 58m/B VHS, DVD. Kermit Maynard; **D:** Harry Fraser.

The Galloping Ghost ✓✓½ 1931 A 12-chapter serial starring football great "Red" Grange about big games, gambling, and underworld gangs. Grange is ousted from football when he's accused of throwing a game and he sets out to prove his innocence. 226m/B VHS, DVD. Harold "Red" Grange, Dorothy Gulliver, Walter Miller, Tom Dugan; **D:** B. Reeves Eason.

Galloping Romeo ✓✓ 1933 59m/B VHS, DVD. Bob Steele, Doris Hill, George Hayes, Frank Ball, Ernie Adams; **D:** Robert North Bradbury; **W:** Harry Fraser.

Gallowglass ✓✓✓ 1995 A "gallowglass" is an ancient Gaelic term for a servant, willing to sacrifice his life for his master. In this moody TV mystery that is dim Joe (Sheen), whose life was saved by manipulative, handsome Sandor (Rhys), who now demands his help in kidnapping Nina (Whitley), an unhappy ex-model who was the victim of a kidnapping years before in Italy and now lives with her husband in wealthy seclusion in the country. There, Nina is under the protection of bodyguard/chauffeur Paul (McArdle), and their mutual attraction leads to unexpected complications. Based on the thriller by Ruth Rendell (writing as Barbara Vine). 150m/C VHS. Paul Rhys, Michael Sheen, Arkie Whiteley, John McArdle, Claire Hackett, Gary Waddhorn; **D:** Tim Fywell; **C:** Rex Maidment. TV

Galyon ✓ 1977 (PG) Soldier of fortune is recruited by an oil tycoon to find his daughter and son-in-law who have been kidnapped by terrorists in South America. 92m/C VHS. Stan Brock, Lloyd Nolan, Ina Bain, Ron Hayes; **D:** Ivan Tors.

Gambit ✓✓ 1966 Caine's first Hollywood film casts him as a burglar who develops a "Topkapi"-style scheme to steal a valuable statue with MacLaine as the lure and Lom as the equally devious owner. Once Caine's careful plan is put into operation, however, everything begins to unravel. 109m/C VHS. Shirley MacLaine, Michael Caine, Herbert Lom, Roger C. Carmel; **D:** Ronald Neame; **W:** Alvin Sargent, Jack Davies; **M:** Maurice Jarre.

The Gamble ✓✓ 1988 (R) A young man (Modine) seeks to rescue his father from gambling debts by wagering himself against a lustful countess (Dunaway). When he loses the bet, however, he flees into operation, however, everything begins to unravel. Once Caine's careful plan is put into operation. 108m/C VHS, DVD. Matthew Modine, Jennifer Beals, Faye Dunaway; **D:** Carlo Vanzina.

Gamble on Love ✓ 1986 Woman returns to her father's Las Vegas casino and falls for the man who manages the gaming room. 90m/C VHS. Beverly Garland; **D:** Jim Balsen.

The Gambler ✓✓✓ 1974 (R) College professor Axel Freed has a gambling problem so vast that it nearly gets him killed by his bookies. He goes to Las Vegas to recoup his losses and wins big, only to blow the money on stupid sports bets that get him deeper into trouble. Excellent character study of a compulsive loser on a downward spiral. 111m/C VHS. James Caan, James Woods, Jacqueline Brookes, Burt Young, James Woods; **D:** Karel Reisz; **W:** James Toback; **C:** Victor Kemper; **M:** Jerry Fielding.

Gambling Ship ✓✓ 1933 Tired of life as a gambling boss, Ace Corbin (Grant) decides to retire and assumes a new identity as a businessman on a cross-country train trip. He meets Eleanor (Hume), who's pretending to be a socialite but is really the mistress of Joe (Vinton), who owns a failing gambling ship. Ace winds up buying the venture to settle a score with rival Pete (LaRue) but Pete doesn't take kindly to his new competition. 72m/B VHS. Cary Grant, Benita Hume, Glenda Farrell, Roscoe Karns, Arthur Vinton, Jack LaRue; **D:** Louis Gasnier, Max Marcin; **W:** Max Marcin; Charles (Bryant) Lang Jr.; **M:** Werner R. Heymann.

The Gambling Terror ✓✓ 1937 A cowboy goes after a mobster selling protection to hapless ranchers. 53m/B VHS. Johnny Mack Brown, Charles "Blackie" King; **D:** Sam Newfield.

The Game ✓ 1989 Three friends arrange a puzzle-murder-mystery for a selected group of guilty people, with $1 million as the prize—and death for the loser. 91m/C VHS. Tom Elair, Debbie Martin; **D:** Curtis Brown.

The Gambling Samurai ✓✓ Kunisada Chuji 1960 A samurai returns to his village to find it besieged by a ruthless government. Instead of attacking, he bides his time and works to undermine the government—finally achieving his revenge. In Japanese with English subtitles. 101m/C VHS. JP Toshiro Mifune, Michiyo Arata; **D:** Senkichi Taniguchi.

Gambler's Choice ✓✓ 1944 A police lieutenant and his boyhood friend find themselves on opposite sides of the law in this crime drama. Even though both men are romantically involved with the same woman, their friendship remains intact. 66m/B VHS, DVD. Chester Morris, Nancy Kelly, Russell Hayden, Sheldon Leonard, Lee Patrick, Lloyd Corrigan, Tom Dugan, Lyle Talbot, Charles Arnt; **D:** Frank McDonald; **W:** Maxwell Shane, Irving Reis, James Edward Grant, Howard Emmett Rogers; **C:** Fred H. Jackman Jr.

The Gambling Samurai ✓✓ 1993 You'll see lots of familiar western TV stars as Rogers returns yet again as debonair gambler Brady Hawkes. This time he's on the biggest card game around—only this time he must stop him playing a cross country trip to San Francisco and gangsters who would like to take over his clubs. Dull direction and a mediocre script. 96m/C VHS, DVD. Kenny Rogers, Reba McEntire, Rick Rossovich, Chuck Connors, Patrick Macnee, Linda Evans, James Drury, Mickey Rooney, Jere Burns, Clint Walker, Claude Akins, Gene Barry, Doug McClure, Hugh O'Brian, Brian Keith, Park Overall, Jack Kelly, David Carradine, Johnny Crawford, Marianne Rogers; **D:** Dick Lowry. TV

The Gambler Returns: The Luck of the Draw ✓✓½ 1993 You'll see lots of familiar western TV stars as Rogers returns yet again as debonair gambler Brady Hawkes. This time he's on the biggest card game around—only this time he must stop him playing a cross country trip to San Francisco and gangsters who would like to take over his clubs. Dull direction and a mediocre script. 180m/C VHS, DVD. Kenny Rogers, Reba McEntire, Rick Rossovich, Chuck Connors, Patrick Macnee, Linda Evans, James Drury, Mickey Rooney, Jere Burns, Clint Walker, Claude Akins, Gene Barry, Doug McClure, Hugh O'Brian, Brian Keith, Park Overall, Jack Kelly, David Carradine, Johnny Crawford, Marianne Rogers; **D:** Dick Lowry. TV

The Gambler & the Lady ✓✓ 1952 A successful London-based gambler and casino owner endeavors to climb the social ladder by having an affair with a member of the British aristocracy. He not only has to contend with this jilted nightclub singer girlfriend but also with the gangsters who would like to take over his clubs. Dull direction and a mediocre script. 72m/B VHS, DVD. GB Dane Clark, Naomi Chance, Kathleen Byron, Meredith Edwards, Eric Pohlmann, George Pastell; **D:** Patrick Jenkins, Sam Newfield; **W:** Sam Newfield; **C:** Walter J. (Jimmy W.) Harvey; **M:** Ivor Slaney.

The Gambler ✓✓ 1997 In St. Petersburg in 1866, Russian writer Dostoyevsky (Gambon) is a middle-aged compulsive gambler who is currently indebted to his publisher Stellovsky (Jansen) and must now write a new novel in 27 days to pay him off. He hires poverty-stricken Anna (May) to be his secretary and the dictated novel Lurns out to be the story of a gambling couple who are trying to get out of hock at a German resort. The real and fictional intertwine as Anna becomes more and more protective of Dostoyevsky and determined to help him succeed. 97m/C VHS, DVD, GB NL HU Michael Gambon, Jodhi May, Polly Walker, Dominic West, Luise Rainer, John Wood, Johan Leysen, Thom Jansen, Angeline Ball; **D:** Karoly Makk; **W:** Charles Cohen, Nick Dear; **C:** Katalin Oegern; **C:** Jules Van Den Steenhoven; **M:** Brian Lock.

The Game 🎬🎬🎬 1997 (R) Investment banker Nicholas Van Orton (Douglas) is an uptight corporate control freak. He receives a dangerous birthday present from his blacksheep younger brother Conrad (Penn). It's a subscription to Consumer Recreation Services, a real life-and-death version of a role-playing game that is designed to tap the hidden emotional and physical resources of the client. His life is overrun with an escalating series of traps and terrors, with the game reaching into every facet of his life. Excellent portrayal by Douglas as a man stuck in a Hitchcockian nightmare. 128m/C VHS, DVD, HD DVD. Michael Douglas, Sean Penn, Deborah Kara Unger, Armin Mueller-Stahl, James Rebhorn, Peter Donat, Carroll Baker, Anna (Katerina) Katarina; **D:** David Fincher; **W:** John Brancato, Michael Ferris; **C:** Harris Savides; **M:** Howard Shore.

Game for Vultures 🎬1½ 1986 (R) Racial unrest in Rhodesia is the backdrop for this tale of a black revolutionary who fights racists sanctions. The noble topic suffers from stereotypes and oversimplification. 113m/C VHS. Richard Harris, Richard Roundtree, Joan Collins, Ray Milland; **D:** James Fargo.

The Game Is Over 🎬🎬1½ 1966 (R) *La Curee* 1966 (R) A wealthy neglected wife falls in love with her grown stepson, causing her to divorce her husband and shatter her life. A good performance by Fonda, then Vadim's wife. Modern version of Zola's "La Curee." 96m/C VHS, DVD. *FR* Jane Fonda, Peter McEnery, Michel Piccoli, Tina Aumont; **D:** Roger Vadim; **W:** Roger Vadim; **C:** Claude Renoir; **M:** Jean Bouchety.

Game of Death 🎬 *Goodbye Bruce Lee: His Last Game of Death; Bruce Lee's Game of Death* 1979 (R) Bruce Lee's final kung fu thriller about a young martial arts movie star who gets involved with the syndicate. Lee died halfway through the filming of this movie and it was finished with outtakes and a double. 100m/C VHS, DVD. Bruce Lee, Dean Jagger, Kareem Abdul-Jabbar, Colleen Camp, Chuck Norris; **D:** Robert Clouse; **M:** John Barry.

The Game of Love 🎬🎬 1990 (PG) Olin presides over Henry's bar, the lost and found of lonely hearts and lust, where people go to quench that deep thirst for love. 94m/C VHS. Ed Marinaro, Belinda Bauer, Ken Olin, Robert Rusler, Tracy Nelson, Max Gail, Janet Margolin, Brynn Thayer; **D:** Bobby Roth.

Game of Seduction 🎬 1986 A murdering, womanizing playboy pursues a married woman and gets caught up in a treacherous cat-and-mouse game. Dubbed. 81m/C VHS. Sylvia Kristel, Jon Finch, Nathalie Delon; **D:** Roger Vadim.

Game of Survival 🎬 1989 A young rebel warrior from another planet is sent to earth to battle six of the galaxy's most brutal warriors. 85m/C VHS. Nikki Hill, Cindy Coatman, Roosevelt Miller Jr.; **D:** Armand Gazarian.

The Game of Their Lives 🎬 2005 (PG) Bland account of the United States' long-shot 1950 soccer team—a hodgepodge of players haphazardly rounded up—that jolted a heavily superior English team in the first round of the World Cup in Brazil. Weak script that, while it scores on facts, gives the cast of mostly cookie-cut pretty boys very little to get fired up about. 101m/C VHS, DVD. Gerard Butler, Wes Bentley, Jay Rodan, Gavin Rossdale, Costas Mandylor, Louis Mandylor, Zachery Ty Bryan, Patrick Stewart, Jimmy Jean-Louis, Terry Kinney, John Rhys-Davies, Marilyn Dodds Frank, Richard Jenik, Bill Smitrovich; **D:** David Anspaugh; **W:** Angelo Pizzo; **C:** Johnny E. Jensen; **M:** William Ross.

The Game Plan 🎬1½ 2007 (PG) The Rock is the only one who scores in this Disney retread. Swaggering star quarterback Joe Kingman (Johnson) suddenly finds his bachelor lifestyle cramped by the sudden arrival of Peyton (Pettis), the eight-year-old daughter he never knew he had. In a premise that somehow could serve up, Peyton is from a previous marriage, although the idea that somehow Joe had no idea that his ex-wife had a child is not the most ridiculous aspect of the movie. This sets up an endless series of gags

based on Joe not knowing how to interact with a little girl or, really, anyone outside of his agent (Sedgwick). Johnson's charm is undeniable, and Pettis is button-cute, but the rest is lukewarm family fare. 110m/C DVD, Blu-ray Disc. Dwayne "The Rock" Johnson, Kyra Sedgwick, Roselyn Sanchez, Morris Chestnut, Madison Pettis, Brian White, Paige Turco, Gordon Clapp, Hayes Macarthur, Jamal Duff, Jackie Flynn; **D:** Andy Fickman; **W:** Nichole Millard, Kathryn Price; **C:** Greg Gardiner; **M:** Nathan Wang.

Game 6 🎬🎬1½ 2005 (R) It's October 25, 1986, and Nicky (Keaton) has quite the dilemma—should he attend his play's opening night or watch his beloved Bosox battle the New York Mets in the soon-to-be-legendary game six of the World Series? With his crumbling marriage (having a mistress doesn't help), distant daughter, stalled career, and a cutthroat theater critic set to make or break his new work, he feels just as wrapped in failure as his once-cursed baseball team. Keaton cleanly fields his distressed-man act but the story flubs the grounder. 87m/C DVD. *US* Michael Keaton, Robert Downey Jr., Griffin Dunne, Catherine O'Hara, Bebe Neuwirth, Shalom Harlow, Roger Rees, Ari Graynor, Nadia Dajani, Harris Yulin, Tom Aldredge, Lillias White, Amir Ali Said; **D:** Michael Hoffman; **W:** Don DeLillo; **C:** David M. Dunlap; **M:** Yo La Tengo.

Gamebox 1.0 🎬🎬 2004 (PG-13) Video game tester Charlie gets hooked on a new virtual-reality system that's plugged directly into a user's brain. The object is to rescue the Princess, who looks suspiciously like Charlie's dead girlfriend. The game infests Charlie's brain so the only way for him to survive is to win. The CGI's not bad considering the low budget, but the story's formulaic. 83m/C DVD. Danielle Fishel, Patrick Kilpatrick, Patrick Cavanaugh, Nate Richert; **D:** David Hillenbrand, Scott Hillenbrand; **W:** Patrick Casey, Worm Miller; **C:** Philip D. Schwartz. VIDEO

Gamera, the Invincible 🎬1½ *Gamera; Gammera; Daikaiju Gamera* 1966 This Japanese monster flick features the ultimate nuclear super-turtle who flies around destroying cities and causing panic. First in the series of notoriously bad films, this one is cool in black and white and has some impressive special effects. Dubbed in English. 86m/B VHS, DVD. *JP* Eiji Funakoshi, Harumi Kiritachi, Junichiro Yamashiko, Yoshiro Uchida, Brian Donlevy, Albert Dekker, Diane Findlay, John Baragrey, Dick O'Neill; **D:** Noriaki Yuasa; **W:** Fumi Takahashi; **C:** Nobuo Munekawa.

Gamera vs. Barugon 🎬1½ *Gamera Tai Barugon; Gambara vs. Barugon; The War of the Monsters* 1966 The monstrous turtle returns to Earth from his outer space prison, now equipped with his famous leg-jets. He soon wishes he had stayed airborne, however, when he is forced to do battle with 130-foot lizard Barugon and his rainbow-melting ray. Tokyo and Osaka get melted in the process. 101m/C VHS, DVD. *JP* Kojiro Hongo, Kyoko Enami; **D:** Shigeo Tanaka.

Gamera vs. Gaos 🎬🎬1½ 1967 *Gamera vs. Gyaos; Gyaos; Boyichi and the Supermonster; Gamera vs. the Giant Monster; Gamera Tai Gaos* 1967 Now fully the good guy, Gamera slugs it out with a bat-like critter named Gaos. Suspense rules the day when Gaos tries to put out the super turtle's jets with his built-in fire extinguisher but luckily for Earth, Gamera has a few tricks of his own up his shell. 87m/C VHS, DVD. *JP* Kojiro Hongo, Naoyuki Abe, Naoyaki Ueda; **D:** Noriaki Yuasa.

Gamera vs. Guiron 🎬 *Attack of the Monsters; Gamera Tai Guiron* 1969 Gamera risks it all to take on an evil, spear-headed monster on a distant planet. Highlight is the sexy, leotard clad aliens who want to eat the little Earth kids' brains. 88m/C VHS, DVD. *JP* Nobuhiro Kashima, Christopher Murphy, Miyuki Akiyama, Yuko Hamada, Eiji Funakoshi; **D:** Noriaki Yuasa.

Gamera vs. Zigra 🎬 *Gamera Tai Shinkai Kaiju Jigara; Gamera vs. the Deep Sea Monster Zigra* 1971 Gamera the flying turtle chose an ecological theme for this, his final movie. It seems that the alien Zigrans have come to Earth to wrest the planet from the hands of the pollutive humans who have nearly destroyed it. The aliens

kill the staunch turtle, but the love and prayers of children revive him that he may defend Earth once more. 91m/C VHS. *JP* Reiko Kasahara, Mikiko Tsubouchi, Koji Fujiyama, Arlene Zoellner, Gloria Zoellner; **D:** Noriaki Yuasa.

Games 🎬🎬1½ 1967 Bored married Manhattanites Paul (Caan) and Jennifer (Ross), who are looking for some kinky entertainment, get involved with amateur medium Lisa (Signoret). Suddenly what's "real," isn't and there's more than one double-cross to cope with. Lots of atmosphere but not enough suspense. 100m/C VHS. Simone Signoret, James Caan, Katharine Ross, Don Stroud, Kent Smith, Estelle Winwood, Marjorie Bennett, Ian Wolfe; **Cameos:** Florence Marly, Luana Anders; **D:** Curtis Harrington; **W:** Gene R. Kearney; **C:** William A. Fraker; **M:** Samuel Matlovsky.

Games Girls Play 🎬1½ *The Bunny Caper; Sex Play* 1975 The daughter of an American diplomat organizes a contest at a British boarding school to see which of her classmates can seduce important dignitaries. 90m/C VHS. Christina Hart, Jane Anthony, Jill Damas, Drina Pavlovic; **D:** Jack Arnold.

Games of Love and Chance 🎬🎬 *Lesquive* 2003 Centered around North African immigrant Krimo (Elkharraz), a closed-up teenager living in a Paris suburb whose emotional walls force girlfriend Magali (Ganito) to dump him. He quickly finds a new love interest in the extroverted Lydia (Forestier) and pushes his way into a school play to be near her. The camera provides a close view of the many effusive confrontations between the teenaged cast, all of whom are played by acting neophyte residents of the working class suburb where the film is set. Many of the themes explored are universal to the teen movie genre. This film, Kechiche's second effort, has been an award-winning hit in France. 119m/C DVD. *FR* Osman Elkharraz, Sara Forestier, Sabrina Ouazani, Nanou Benhamou, Aurelie Ganito, Rachid Hami; **D:** Abdellatif Kechiche; **W:** Abdellatif Kechiche; **C:** Lubomir Bakchev.

The Gamma People woof! 1956 A journalist discovers a Balkan doctor shooting children with gamma rays, creating an army of brainless zombies. Cult-renowned grade-Z tripe. 83m/B VHS. *GB* Walter Rilla, Paul Douglas, Eva Bartok; **D:** John Gilling; **C:** Ted Moore.

Gandhi 🎬🎬🎬 1982 (PG) The biography of Mahatma Gandhi, from the prejudice he encounters as a young attorney in South Africa, to his role as spiritual leader to the people of India and his use of passive resistance against the country's British rulers, and his eventual assassination. Kingsley is a marvel in his Academy Award-winning role and the picture is a generally riveting epic worthy of its eight Oscars. 188m/C VHS, DVD. *GB* Ben Kingsley, Candice Bergen, Edward Fox, John Gielgud, John Mills, Saeed Jaffrey, Trevor Howard, Ian Charleson, Roshan Seth, Athol Fugard, Martin Sheen, Daniel Day-Lewis, Rohini Hattangady, Ian Bannen, Geraldine James, Nigel Hawthorne, Om Puri, John Ratzenberger; **D:** Richard Attenborough; **W:** John Briley; **C:** Billy Williams; **M:** George Fenton. Oscars '82: Actor (Kingsley), Art Dir./Set Dec., Cinematog., Costume Des., Director (Attenborough), Film Editing, Orig. Screenplay, Picture, Sound; British Acad. '82: Actor (Kingsley), Director (Attenborough), Film, Support. Actress (Hattangady); Directors Guild '82: Director (Attenborough); Golden Globes '83: Actor—Drama (Kingsley), Director (Attenborough), Foreign Film, Screenplay; L.A. Film Critics '82: Actor (Kingsley); Natl. Bd. of Review '82: Actor (Kingsley); N.Y. Film Critics '82: Actor (Kingsley).

Gang Boys 🎬1½ 1997 When a young man is brutally beaten by an L.A. street gang, mom Blair does not take things lying down. She contacts her estranged, ex-cop husband Hauser and he organizes a group of local victims to fight back. This time it's the gang members who should watch out. 87m/C VHS, DVD. *JP* Nobuhiro Kashima, Linda Blair, Cole Hauser, Daryl Roach, Carmen Zapata, Ernest Harden Jr., Talbert Morton, Dave Buzzotta; **D:** Wings Hauser; **W:** Maria Dylan, Wings Hauser; **C:** Francis Grumman; **M:** Geoff Levin, Chris May. VIDEO

Gang Bullets 🎬 1938 Mobster tries to continue his dirty systems in a new town, but finds the legal force incorruptible. 62m/B VHS. Anne Nagel, Robert Kent, Charles Trowbridge, Morgan Wallace, J. Farrell MacDonald, Arthur Loft, John Merton; **D:** Lambert Hillyer.

Gang Busters 🎬🎬 1942 Men battle crime in the city in this serial in 13 episodes based on the popular radio series of the same name. 253m/B VHS, DVD. Kent Taylor, Irene Hervey, Robert Armstrong, Ralph Morgan, Richard Davies, Ralf Harolde; **D:** Ray Taylor, Noel Mason Smith; **W:** Morgan Cox, Phillips Lord, Victor McLeod, George Plympton; **C:** John Boyle, William Sickner.

Gang Busters 🎬1½ 1955 Prisoners plan a breakout. Slow and unexciting adaptation of the successful radio series. Filmed in Oregon. 78m/B VHS, DVD. Myron Healey, Sam Edwards, Frank Gerstle; **D:** Bill Karn.

Gang in Blue 🎬🎬1½ 1996 (R) Black officer Michael Rhoades (Van Peebles) is secretly investigating a white supremacist group of cops, called the Phantoms, within the LAPD. Marine Corp vet and police rookie Keith DeBruler (Brolin) becomes Rhoades's new partner and his racial comments make him a likely initiate for the Phantoms. So can he be trusted to be Rhoades's inside man and help Michael expose the corruption within the ranks? 99m/C VHS, DVD. Mario Van Peebles, Josh Brolin, Melvin Van Peebles, J.T. Walsh, Cynda Williams, Stephen Lang, Sean McCann; **D:** Mario Van Peebles, Melvin Van Peebles; **W:** David Fuller, Flick Natkin; **C:** Rhett Monta; **M:** Larry Brown. CABLE

Gang Justice 🎬 1994 Low-budget melodrama finds sensitive Asian student Paul (Kim) battling racists at school and his crippled alcoholic father at home. Some martial arts fight scenes but this is amateur time. 92m/C VHS, DVD. Joon Kim, Jonathan Gorman, Erik Estrada, Angel Dashek; **D:** Richard W. Park.

Gang of Roses 🎬🎬 2003 (R) In the old west, Rachel, Chasity, Kim, Ming Li, and Maria formed the Rose Gang. Successful bank robbers, they retired after five years but regroup when Rachel's sister is killed. 88m/C VHS, DVD. Monica Calhoun, Stacey Dash, LisaRaye, Marie Matiko, Kimberly (Lil' Kim) Jones, Bobby Brown, Louis Mandylor; **C:** Ben Kuffrin; **M:** Michael Cohen. VIDEO

Gang Related 🎬1½ 1996 (R) Rodriguez (Shakur) and Divinci (Belushi) are a couple of scuzzball homicide cops who set up drug deals with impounded dope, then kill the customers. They keep the dope and the money, and call the murders "gang-related." Their plan unravels when they whack an undercover DEA agent posing as a dealer. They try to play a game of "pin the crime on the wino" with a derelict (Quaid) who the duo thinks is easy prey. As their scheming spins out of control, Rodriguez tries to hold things together, while Divinci rips them apart. Shakur rises above the average material as the most likable of the entirely distasteful cast of characters. 109m/C VHS, DVD. James Belushi, Tupac Shakur, Dennis Quaid, Leila Rochon, James Earl Jones, David Paymer, Wendy Crewson, Gary Cole, Terrence "T.C." Carson, Brad Greenquist, James Handy, Victor Love, Robert LaSardo, Gregory Scott Cummins; **D:** Jim Kouf; **W:** Jim Kouf; **C:** Brian Reynolds; **M:** Mickey Hart.

Gang War 🎬 1940 Low-budget gangster film with an all-black cast about two gangs fighting for control of the city's jukebox business. 60m/B VHS, DVD. Ralph Cooper, Gladys Snyder, Reggie Fenderson, Lawrence Criner, Monte Hawley, Jesse C. Brooks, Maceo B. Sheffield; **D:** Leo Popkin.

Gang Wars 🎬 *Devil's Express* 1975 (R) There's a riot going on as Puerto Rican, Black, and Chinese gangs fight it out for control of the city. 82m/C VHS. Warhawk Tanzania, Larry Fleishman, Sam DeFazio, Wilfred Roldan, Elsie Roman, Sarah Nyrick; **D:** Barry Rosen.

The Gang's All Here 🎬 1940 Darro joins a trucking firm whose rigs are being run off the road and hijacked by a competitor. Features "Charlie Chan" regulars Luke and Moreland. 63m/B VHS, DVD. Frankie Darro, Marcia Mae Jones, Jackie Moran, Mantan Moreland, Keye Luke; **D:** Jean Yarbrough.

The Gang's All Here 🐾🐾 *Girls He Left Behind* 1943 Produced smack in the middle of World War II, the film has... On leave from his army post, playboy Benny Goodman and his crew. Eddie Allee (Miranda), sweeping her off her feet for an evening of romance that leaves her swooning, only to leave for duty the next morning. He returns, but with a secret. *103m/C VHS.* Carmen Miranda, Phil Baker, Benny Goodman, Eugene Pallette, Charlotte Greenwood, Edward Everett Horton, Alice Faye, Dave Willock q, Tony De Marco, son. *D: Busby Berkeley. W: Nancy Winner, George Root Jr.*

Gangs, Inc. *Crimes, Inc., Paper Bullets* 1941 A woman is sent to prison for a hit-and-run accident, actually the fault of a wealthy playboy. When she learns his identity she vows revenge and turns to crime to achieve her evil ends. Okay thriller suffers from plot problems. Ladd has a minor role filmed before he became a star. *72m/B VHS, DVD.* Joan Woodbury, Jack LaRue, Linda Ware, John Archer, Vince Barnett, Alan Ladd, Gavin Gordon, Selmer Jackson, George Pembroke. *D: Phil Rosen. W: Martin Mooney. C: Arthur Marinelli.*

Gangs of New York 🐾🐾🐾 2002 (R) Scorsese's flawed but rich and powerful epic recounts the mid-19th Century struggles in New York's Five Points section between the Irish immigrant gangs the Dead Rabbits and the second-generation nativist gangs led by the brutal but mesmerizing Bill the Butcher (Day-Lewis). Young Amsterdam Vallon (DeCaprio) witnesses the death of his father 'Priest' (Neeson), the leader of the Rabbits, in a bloody street melee and is sent away. When he returns, unrecognized, he insinuates himself into Bill's inner circle, waiting for his chance at vengeance and catching the eye of pickpocket Jenny (Diaz). This plot is set against the backdrop of New York corruption of 'Boss' Tweed's New York empire and the draft riots that were tearing the city apart at the time. Scorsese's vision is realized through meticulous attention to period detail, a standout performance by Day-Lewis, and the willingness to show hero and villain alike as well-rounded characters. Uneven pacing and underuse (crooaally out of necessity of excellent supporting cast are the only complaints. Loosely based on the 1928 book by Herbert Asbury. *166m/C VHS, DVD. US* Leonardo DiCaprio, Daniel Day-Lewis, Cameron Diaz, Liam Neeson, Jim Broadbent, John C. Reilly, Henry Thomas, Brendan Gleeson, Gary Lewis, Stephen Graham, Eddie Marsan, Alec McCowen, David Hemmings, Larry (Lawrence) Gilliard Jr., Cara Seymour, Roger Ashton-Griffiths, Cian McCormack. *Cameos:* Martin Scorsese; *D:* Martin Scorsese; *W:* Jay Cocks, Steven Zaillian, Kenneth Lonergan; *C:* Michael Ballhaus; *M:* Howard Shore. *British Acad. '02: Actor (Day-Lewis); Golden Globes '03: Director (Scorsese), Song ("The Hands That Built America"); L.A. Film Critics '02: Actor (Day-Lewis); N.Y. Film Critics '02: Actor (Day-Lewis); Screen Actors Guild '02: Actor (Day-Lewis).*

Gangster No. 1 🐾🐾½ 2000 (R) An aging London crime boss—who's only known as 'Gangster 55' (McDowall)—learns that his mentor Freddie Mays (Thewlis) is just out of prison after a 30-year stretch for murder. Flashback to 1968, when a young, ruthless Gangster (a ferocious Bettany) earns his place by taking on (Burrows) and learns of a plot to rub out Freddie. He pans on setting up his boss and becoming head man but never comes jealous of Freddie's rivals. Then Gangster becomes jealous of Freddie's girlfriend, Karen (Burrows). *103m/C VHS, DVD.* Malcolm McDowell, Paul Bettany, David Thewlis, Saffron Burrows, Kenneth Cranham, Jamie Foreman, Eddie Marsan, Andrew Lincoln; *D:* Paul McGuigan; *W:* Johnny Ferguson; *C:* Peter Sova; *M:* John Dankworth.

The Gangster 🐾🐾½ 1947 Sullivan plays a small-time slum-bred hood who climbs to the top of the underworld, only to lose his gang because he allows his fears to get the better of him. There's nothing to ear except crime with an interesting psychological perspective, though a bit sluggish at times. Noir. *84m/B VHS.* Barry Sullivan, Joan Lorring, Akim Tamiroff, Harry Morgan, John Ireland, Fifi d'Orsay, Shelley Winters. *D: Gordon Wiles.*

Ganked 🐾 2005 (PG-13) Ricky (Mitchell) is an undiscovered songwriter living in his parents' basement hoping to hit the big-time any day now. When he wins a contest and is offered a position in a record company he thinks he's made it. Instead, he's stuck working in their mailroom, while the company's sexy singer Kennedy Ross (Bombay) steals his song got his revenge. *108m/C DVD.* Kel Mitchell, Katt Micah Williams, Antwon Tanner, Bombay; *D:* Kel Mitchell; *W:* Kel Mitchell; *C:* Kenn Michael; *M:* John Dankworth.

Ganja and Hess 🐾🐾½ *Black Vampire; Double Possession; 'Back Out; Blood Couple; Black Evil* 1973 (R) Jones plays a professor of African studies who is turned into a vampire by another vampire. He then marries the villain's ex-wife, played by Clark, a veteran of Russ Meyer films. Not much of a story but the acting is actually quite good and there are some creepy moments thanks mainly to an interesting score. *110m/C VHS, DVD.* Duane Jones, Marlene Clark, Bill Gunn, Sam Waymon, Leonard Jackson, Candece Tarpley, Mabel King; *D:* Bill Gunn; *W:* Bill Gunn; *C:* James E. Hinton; *M:* Sam Waymon.

Ganjasaurus Rex 🐾 1987 (R) Monster spoof about a giant green dinosaur emerging from the pot-laden hills of California. Maybe it's all in your head. *100m/C VHS.* Paul Bassis, Dave Fresh, Rosie Jones. *D: Ursi Reynolds.*

Gangster Wars 🐾🐾 1981 A specially edited-for-video version of the TV miniseries "The Gangster Chronicles." Based on fact, it deals with the growth of organized crime in America from the early days of this century, through up to become three ghetto kids who grow up to become powerful mobsters. *121m/C VHS.* Michael Nouri, Joe Penny, Brian Benben, Kathleen Lloyd, Madeleine Stowe, Robert Davi; *D:* Richard Sarafian. TV

Gangster World 🐾🐾 1998 (R) In the 21st century, Gangster World is an adult theme park that caters to fulfilling a human's most decadent fantasies—aided by cyborgs in a 1930s setting. But with a name like this, it's easy to believe that a battle for control turns the park into the most dangerous place in the universe. Lots of action and decent enough special effects. *91m/C VHS, DVD.* Xavier DeCille, David Leisure, Gabriel Dell Jr., Stacey Williams, Bridget Flannery; *D:* David Bishop. VIDEO

Gangsters 🐾 1979 City is ruled by the mob and nothing can stop their bloody grip except "The Special Squad." *90m/C VHS.* 🐾 Michael V. Gazzo, Tony Page, Vicki Sue Robinson, Nai Bonet; *D:* Mac Ahlberg.

Gangster's Den 🐾 1945 A gang of renegades scare a woman out of buying a gold-laden piece of land and Billy the Kid comes to her rescue. *56m/B VHS, DVD.* Buster Crabbe, Kermit Maynard, Al "Fuzzy" St. John, Charles "Blackie" King; *D:* Sam Newfield.

Gangster's Law woof! 1986 A look at a seedy gangster's downfall. Filmed on location in Italy. Dubbed. *89m/C VHS.* Klaus Kinski, Maurice Poli, Susy Andersen, Max Delys; *D:* Siro Marcellini.

Gangsters of the Frontier 🐾 1944 The people of Red Rock are forced to work in the town mines by two prison escapees until Ritter and his friends ride to the rescue. Part of the "Texas Ranger" series. *56m/B VHS.* Tex Ritter, Dave O'Brien; *D:* Elmer Clifton. *W:* Elmer Clifton.

Gangway 🐾½ 1937 Pat Wayne (Matthews), a London newspaper reporter, is mistaken for a jewel thief and kidnapped by gangsters aboard a New York-bound ocean liner. In the meantime, the real thief is aboard posing as a Hollywood actress (Blakeney), and it's up to Scotland Yard inspector Bob Deering (Mackay) to solve the crime. Matthews was considered by many to be the English equivalent of America's Eleanor Powell. Based on an original story by Dwight Taylor. *90m/B VHS.* GB Jessie Matthews, Barry Mackay, Olive Blakeney, Liane Ordeyne, Patrick Ludlow, Nat Pendleton, Noel Madison, Alastair Sim, Doris Rogers; *W:* Sonnie Hale, Lesser Samuels.

The Garbage-Picking, Field Goal-Kicking Philadelphia Phenomenon 🐾🐾½ 1998 Sports recruiters discover the natural kicking talents of sanitation engineer Barney Gorman (Danza) and turn his life upside down by giving him the chance to be the new place-kicker for the Philadelphia Eagles. *104m/C VHS, DVD.* Tony Danza, Jessica Fisher, Catherine Hicks, Steven Hill, Howard Cal; *D:* Tim Kelleher. TV

Garbo Talks 🐾🐾 1984 (PG-13) A dying eccentric's last request is to meet the reclusive screen legend Greta Garbo. Bancroft amusingly plays the dying woman whose son goes to extreme lengths in order to fulfill his mother's last wish. *104m/C VHS, DVD.* Anne Bancroft, Ron Silver, Carrie Fisher, Catherine Hicks, Steven Hill, Howard Da Silva, Dorothy Loudon, Harvey Fierstein, Hermione Gingold; *D:* Sidney Lumet; *C:* Andrzej Bartkowiak.

The Garden 🐾🐾 1990 Eternally provocative director Jarman does another take on sex and religion. He examines the role of the Church in the persecution of homosexuality by recreating the story of Christ in some sequences with two male lovers, who are arrested, humiliated, and tortured. *90m/C VHS.* GB Tilda Swinton, Johnny Mills, Philip MacDonald, Roger Cook, Kevin Collins, Pete Lee-Wilson, Spencer Lee, Jody Graber; *D:* Derek Jarman; *W:* Derek Jarman; *M:* Simon Fisher Turner.

The Garden of Allah 🐾🐾 1936 Dietrich finds hyper-romantic encounters in the Algerian desert with Boyer, both. This early Technicolor production flawed, is an absolute must for Dietrich fans. Yuma, Arizona substituted for the exotic locale. *85m/C VHS, DVD.* Marlene Dietrich, Charles Boyer, Basil Rathbone, Sir C. Aubrey Smith, Tilly Losch, Joseph Schildkraut, Henry (Kleinbach) Brandon, John Carradine; *D:* Richard Boleslawski; *W:* W.P Lipscomb, Lynn Riggs; *C:* William Howard Greene; *M:* Max Steiner.

Gappa the Triffian Monster 🐾🐾 *Daikyoju Gappa; Monster from a Prehistoric Planet* 1967 (PG) Researchers visiting a tropical island find an egg and take it back to Tokyo with them, dismaying the egg's giant monster parents. Dubbed. *90m/C VHS, DVD.* JP Tamio Kawaji, Yoko Yamamoto, Tatsuya Fuji, Koji Wada, Yuji Okada; *D:* Hiryasu Hoguchi; *M:* Ryuzo Nakanishi; *C:* Muneo Ueda. VIDEO

Garage Days 🐾🐾½ 2003 (R) Sydney, Australia garage band tries to hit it big in this goofy comedy directed by Proyas. Freddy (Gurry) just wants to make it big as the singer of a rock and roll band, but he has to cope with the quirks and problems of his bandmates: girlfriend/bassist Tanya (Miranda), guitarist with an identity crisis Joe (Stiller), and dedicated drug user/drummer Lucy (Sadrinna) who spends more time creating pharmaceutical cocktails than practicing the drums. Further complicating the mix is the attraction between Freddy and Joe's girlfriend Kate (Stange) and the band's misguided attempt to blackmail a big-time manager (Csokas) to come see them play. Proyas fills the movie with inventive visuals and keeps the comedy level high, but with plot, some may find too little substance to go with the style. *105m/C VHS, DVD. AU* Maya Stange, Russell Dykstra, Andy Anderson, Marton Csokas, Kick (Christopher) Gurry, Pia Miranda, Brett Stiller, Chris Sadrinna, Tiriel Mora; *D:* Alex Proyas; *W:* Alex Proyas, Dave Warner; *C:* Simon Duggan; *M:* Antony Partos, Dave McCormack.

The Garbage Pail Kids Movie woof! 1987 (PG) The disgusting youngsters, stars of bubblegum cards, make their first and last film appearance in this live action dud. The garbage is where it should be thrown. *100m/C VHS.* Anthony Newley, Mackenzie Astin, Katie Barberi; *D:* Rod Amateau.

The Garden of Redemption 🐾🐾 Italian priest Don Paolo (LaPaglia) has his faith tested when his Tuscan village is occupied in 1944 by German troops and he has to decide whether to overcome his fears and join with the partisan resistance movement. Village beauty Adriana (Davidtz) is eager to help him with the decision only complicates matters more. *99m/C VHS.* Anthony LaPaglia, Embeth Davidtz, Dan Hedaya, Peter Firth, David Neal, Jorge Sanz, James Acheson; *D:* Thomas Michael Donnelly; *W:* John Altman.

Garden State 🐾🐾🐾 2004 (R) Zach Braff stars in his directorial debut (which he also wrote) as Andrew Largeman, a struggling actor whose biggest role so far has been a retarded quarterback in a cable movie. Things aren't going well. He works at a Vietnamese restaurant, is in a perpetually medicated state, and his father just called home to tell him his mother died. Large flies home to New Jersey for the funeral, leaving his...

The Garden of the Finzi-Continis 🐾🐾🐾 *Il Giardino Dei Finzi-Contini* 1971 (R) Acclaimed from the novel by De Sica about an aristocratic Jewish family living in Italy under increasing Fascist oppression on the eve of WWII. The garden wall symbolizes the distance between the Finzi-Continis and the Nazi reality about to engulf them. Flawless acting and well-defined direction. Based on the novel by Giorgio Bassani, who collaborated on the script but later repudiate the film. Music by De Sica's son, Manuel. In Italian with English subtitles or dubbed. *94m/C VHS, DVD.* IT Dominique Sanda, Helmut Berger, Lino Capolicchio, Fabio Testi, Romolo Valli; *D:* Vittorio De Sica; *W:* Cesare Zavattini; *C:* Ennio Guarnieri; *M:* Bill Conti, Manuel De Sica. Oscars '71: Foreign Film; Berlin Intl. Film Fest. '71: Golden Berlin Bear.

The Garden of Delights 🐾🐾 1970 A wicked black comedy about a millionaire, paralyzed and suffering from amnesia after a car accident. His horrendously greedy family tries to get him to remember and reveal his Swiss bank account number. Acclaimed; in Spanish with English subtitles. *95m/C VHS.* SP Jose Luis Lopez Vasquez, Lina Canellas, Luchy Soto, Francisco Pierra, Charo Soriano; *D:* Carlos Saura.

The Garden of Eden 🐾🐾🐾 1928 Milestone—whose "Two Arabian Nights" had won an Academy Award the previous year, and who went on to direct "All Quiet on the Western Front" and "Of Mice and Men"—directed this sophisticated, so-called "Orchid Lady," is a young girl who dreams of diva-dom but falls deep into the underbelly of the seedy side of Budapest. With the aid of a fallen baroness, however, she finds her way to Monte Carlo and has her turn in the limelight. A handsome production designed by William Cameron Menzies, art director for "Gone With the Wind." *115m/B VHS, DVD.* Corinne Griffith, Louise Dresser, Charles Ray, Lowell Sherman; *D:* Lewis Milestone; *W:* Hans Kraly; *C:* John Arnold.

Garden of Evil 🐾🐾½ 1954 On their way to the gold fields, Hooker (Cooper), Fiske (Widmark), and Daly (Mitchell) are stranded in a Mexican village. Leah (Hayward) offers three strangers big bucks if they'll rescue her husband (Marlowe), who was injured in a gold mining accident. The mine is located in a remote mountain region and the group find themselves besieged by Apaches. Equal excitement went on behind the camera as a temperamental Hayward walked off the set whenever she didn't like Hathaway's brusque directing. *100m/C DVD.* Gary Cooper, Susan Hayward, Richard Widmark, Cameron Mitchell, Hugh Marlowe, Victor Manuel Mendoza, Rita Moreno; *D:* Henry Hathaway; *W:* Frank Fenton; *C:* Milton Krasner; *M:* Bernard Herrmann.

medication behind. Reunited with his high school friends, who form a motley crew ranging from a gravedigger to a millionaire who invented silent Velcro. Large begins to experience life again. His awakening is further helped by the arrival of Sam (Portman), a cute, quirky free spirit. While there are some minor flaws, the stellar cast and some genuinely amusing moments are well worth a look. 109m/C **DVD**. *US* Zach Braff, Ian Holm, Ron Leibman, Method Man, Natalie Portman, Ann Dowd, Denis O'Hare, Peter Sarsgaard, Michael Weston, Jean Smart, Jim Parsons, Jackie Hoffman, Amy Ferguson, Ato Essandoh; **D:** Zach Braff; **C:** Lawrence Sher; **M:** Chad Fisher. Ind. Spirit '05: First Feature.

Gardens of Stone 🐾🐾 1987 (R)
A zealous young cadet during the Vietnam War is assigned to the Old Guard patrol at Arlington Cemetery, and clashes with the patrol's older officers and various pacifist civilians. Falls short of the mark, although Jones turns in an excellent performance. 112m/C **VHS, DVD.** James Caan, James Earl Jones, D.B. Sweeney, Anjelica Huston, Dean Stockwell, Lonette McKee, Mary Stuart Masterson, Bill Graham, Sam Bottoms, Casey Siemaszko, Laurence Fishburne, Dick Anthony Williams, Elias Koteas, Peter Masterson, Carlin Glynn, Eric Holland; **D:** Francis Ford Coppola; **W:** Ronald Bass; **C:** Jordan Cronenweth; **M:** Carmine Coppola.

Garfield: A Tail of Two Kitties 🐾🐾½ 2006 (PG) Jon (Meyer), his fat (CGI-rendered) kitty (voiced again by Murray), and dumb dog Odie follow vet Liz (Hewitt) to London where Garfield eventually switches places with a spoiled look-alike named Prince (Curry) who just inherited a country estate. Except Lord Dargis (Connolly), next in line to inherit, wants to do the feline in. It's like a furry version of "The Prince and the Pauper." 80m/C **DVD.** *US* Jennifer Love Hewitt, Breckin Meyer, Billy Connolly, Lucy Davis, Ian Abercrombie, Roger Rees, Lucy Davis; **D:** Tim Hill; **W:** Joel Cohen, Alec Sokolow; **C:** Peter Lyons Collister; **M:** Christophe Beck; **V:** Bill Murray, Tim Curry, Bob Hoskins, Jane Leeves, Jane Horrocks, Sharon Osbourne, Richard E. Grant, Vinnie Jones, Rhys Ifans, Roscoe Lee Browne.

Garfield: The Movie 🐾½ 2004 (PG) The best thing that this escapee from the comic pages has going for it is that fat, nap-taking, lasagna-loving orange cat Garfield (a CGI-creation) is perfectly voiced by the sardonic Murray. The lazy feline dominates nice guy owner Jon (Meyer) and is appalled when life in paradise is threatened by the arrival of excitable mongrel Odie, who arrives via Garfield's sexy vet, Dr. Liz (Hewitt). Naturally, Garfield does his best to get rid of his doggy nuisance until Odie winds up in the clutches of nasty TV show host Happy Chapman (Tobolowsky), who's a decidedly unhappy guy. So it's Garfield to the rescue! Despite the daily comic strip, Garfield's long past his cultural prime, so it's a mystery how he made it to the big screen, especially in this unfunny, slapstick exercise in tedium. 80m/C **DVD.** *US* Breckin Meyer, Jennifer Love Hewitt, Stephen Tobolowsky, Mark Christopher-Lawrence, Evan Arnolds Christopher; **D:** Peter Hewitt; **W:** Joel Cohen, Alec Sokolow; **C:** Dean Cundey; **M:** Christophe Beck; **V:** Bill Murray, Debra Messing, Brad Garrett, Alan Cumming, David Eigenberg, Nick Cannon, Jimmy Kimmel.

Gargantua 🐾½ 1998 Marine biologist Jack Ellway (Baldwin) and his son are studying the effects of seismic activity on marine life on a Polynesian island, that's also been the scene of a number of mysterious drownings. Then Jack discovers a nearby underwater trench houses a family of giant reptiles. When a two-foot long baby lizard comes ashore, it's clear mom and dad must be close behind. Kinda the small screen version of "Godzilla," and you know how successful that was. 91m/C **VHS.** Adam Baldwin, Julie Carmen, Bobby Hosea, Emile Hirsch; **D:** Bradford May; **W:** Ronald Parker; **C:** John Stokes. **TV**

Gargoyles, The Movie: The Heroes Awaken 🐾🐾½ 1994 (G) Mythical crimefighting creatures, trapped in stone by day thanks to a sorcerer's spell but released to live at night, are displaced in time from their medieval Scottish home, winding up in modern-day New York City.

But they discover they still have old enemies to fight. First aired as a five-episode part of the animated TV series. 80m/C **VHS, DVD.** *D:* Saburo Hashimoto; *W:* Eric Luke, Michael Reaves; **M:** Carl Johnson; *V:* Ed Asner, Keith David, Jonathan Frakes, Marina Sirtis, Bill Fagerbakke, Salli Richardson, Frank Welker, Thom Adcox, Jeff Glenn Bennett.

Garringo 🐾🐾 1969 Lawmen attempt to bring to justice a man who is intent on killing the soldiers responsible for his father's death. 95m/C **VHS.** *IT SP* Anthony Steffen, Peter Lee Lawrence, Jose Bodalo; **D:** Rafael Romero Marchent.

Gas woof! 1981 (R) This dog has tycoon Hayden buying up all the gas stations in town to create a crisis that will make him richer. Everyone in the cast wastes their time, especially Sutherland as a hip DJ reporting on the gas shortage. 94m/C **VHS.** *CA* Donald Sutherland, Susan Anspach, Sterling Hayden, Peter Aykroyd, Howie Mandel, Helen Shaver; **D:** Les Rose; **W:** Dick Wolf.

Gas Food Lodging 🐾🐾🐾 1992 (R) Saga casts Adams as Nora, a weary waitress in Laramie, New Mexico, trying her best to raise two teenaged daughters on her own. The daughters, Skye and Balk, are disillusioned about love and family. Balk's special friend is Darius, an eccentric window dresser, played by Leitch, Skye's brother. Nothing works out quite as intended but multi-dimensional characters, poignant situations, and enormous emotional appeal highlight the directorial debut of Anders. Based on the Richard Peck novel "Don't Look and It Won't Hurt." 100m/C **VHS, DVD.** Brooke Adams, Ione Skye, Fairuza Balk, James Brolin, Robert Knepper, Donovan Leitch, David Lansbury, Jacob Vargas, Chris Mulkey, Tiffany Anders; **D:** Allison Anders; **W:** Allison Anders; **C:** Dean Lent; **M:** J. Mascis, Barry Adamson. Ind. Spirit '93: Actress (Balk).

Gas Pump Girls 🐾½ 1979 (R) _Gas-s-s-s... or, It May Become Necessary to Destroy the World in Order to Save It_ 1970 (PG) A gas main leak in an Alaskan defense plant kills everyone beyond 30-something and the post-apocalyptic pre-boomer survivors are left to muddle their way through the brume. Trouble is, AIP edited the heck out of the movie, much to Corman's chagrin, and the result is a truncated comedy. Corman was so displeased, in fact, he left to create New World studios. 79m/C **VHS, DVD.** Robert Corff, Elaine Giftos, Pat Patterson, George Armitage, Alex Wilson, Ben Vereen, Cindy Williams, Bud Cort, Talia Shire; **D:** Roger Corman; **W:** George Armitage; **C:** Ron Dexter; **M:** Barry Melton.

Gaslight 🐾🐾🐾½ _Angel Street_ 1940 A forgotten British classic that fell victim to the American production of the same title and theme that was filmed only four years later. Set in late Victorian London, Wynyard is the rich innocent married to the calculating Walbrook, who slowly tries driving his bride insane in order to discover some hidden family jewels. She comes under the protection of a Scotland Yard detective (Pettingell) who suspects Walbrook has already murdered once. An outstandingly eerie psychological thriller. Based on the play "Angel Street" by Patrick Hamilton. 88m/C **VHS, DVD.** *GB* Anton Walbrook, Diana Wynyard, Frank Pettingell, Cathleen Cordell, Robert Newton, Jimmy Hanley, Minnie Rayner, Mary Hinton, Marie Wright, Jack Barty, Moyna MacGill, Darmora Ballet; **D:** Thorold Dickinson; **W:** A.R. Rawlinson, Bridget Boland; **C:** Bernard Knowles; **M:** Richard Addinsell.

Gaslight 🐾🐾🐾½ _The Murder in Thornton Square_ 1944 Lavish remake of the 1940 film, based on the Patrick Hamilton play "Angel Street." A man tries to drive his beautiful wife insane while searching for priceless jewels. Her only clue to his evil acts is the frequent vanishing of their gaslights. A suspenseful Victorian era mystery. Lansbury's film debut, as the tarty maid. 114m/B **VHS, DVD.** Charles Boyer, Ingrid Bergman, Joseph Cotten, Angela Lansbury, Terry Moore, May Whitty, Barbara Everest, Emil Ra-

meau, Edmund Breon, Halliwell Hobbes, Tom Stevenson; **D:** George Cukor; **W:** John Van Druten, Walter Reisch, John Lloyd Balderston; **C:** Joseph Ruttenberg; **M:** Bronislau Kaper. Oscars '44: Actress (Bergman); Golden Globes '45: Actress—Drama (Bergman).

The Gate 🐾🐾 1987 (PG-13) Kids generally like to explore and Dorff and Tripp are no exception. When a large hole is exposed in their backyard, it would be a childhood sin not to see what's in it, right? What they don't know is that this hole is actually a gateway to and from Hell. The terror they unleash includes more than just run-of-the-mill demons. Good special effects. Followed by "Gate 2." 85m/C **VHS, DVD.** Christa Denton, Stephen Dorff, Louis Tripp, Kelly Rowan, Jennifer Irwin; **D:** Tibor Takacs; **W:** Michael Nankin; **C:** Thomas Vamos.

Gate 2 🐾½ 1992 (R) Tripp returns in his role as Terry, a young student of demonology in this lame sequel to "The Gate." Terry and a couple of his teen buddies call up a group of demons that have been confined behind a gate for billions of years. The demons are used to grant modest wishes, but the wishes end up having very evil effects. Incredibly weak plot saved only by the special monster effects, which include live action and puppetry. 90m/C **VHS, DVD.** Louis Tripp, Simon Reynolds, Pamela Segall, James Villemaire, Neil Munro, James Kidnie, Andrea Ladanyi; **D:** Tibor Takacs; **W:** Michael Nankin; **C:** Bryan England; **M:** George Blondheim.

Gate of Flesh 🐾🐾 _Nikutai No Mon_ 1964 In postwar Japan, four prostitutes survive the American Occupation by sticking to their own code of conduct, including a restriction on anyone giving away their services for free. However, conduct becomes a flexible point when the women harbor a wounded black marketeer whom each comes to desire. Based on a novel by Taijiro Tamura. Japanese with subtitles. 90m/C **VHS.** *JP* Joe Shishido, Yumiko Nogawa, Kayo Matsuo, Satoko Kasai, Misako Tominaga, Tomiko Ishii; **D:** Seijun Suzuki.

Gate of Hell 🐾🐾🐾½ _Jigokumen_ 1954 Set in 12th-century Japan. A warlord desires a beautiful married woman and seeks to kill her husband to have her. However, he accidentally kills her instead. Filled with shame and remorse, the warlord abandons his life to seek solace as a monk. Heavily awarded and critically acclaimed; the first Japanese film to use color or photography. In Japanese with English subtitles. 89m/C **VHS.** *JP* Kazuo Hasegawa, Machiko Kyo, Isao Yamagata, Koreya Senda; **C:** Kohei Sugiyama; **M:** Yashushi Akutagawa. Oscars '54: Costume Des., (C), Foreign Film; Cannes '54: Film.

Gates of Hell woof! _City of the Living Dead; The Fear; Twilight of the Dead; Fear in the City of the Living Dead_ 1980 The Seven Gates of Hell have been opened and in three days the dead will rise and walk the earth. A reporter (George) and a psychic (MacColl) fight to close the portals before Salem, Massachusetts is overrun by the risen dead. A gorefest that tried to disguise itself under many other titles. 93m/C **VHS, DVD.** *IT* Christopher George, Janet Agren, Katherine (Katriona) MacColl, Robert Sampson, Carlo De Mejo, Antonella Interlenghi, Luciano Rossi, Venantino Venantini; **D:** Lucio Fulci, Michele (Michael) Soavi; **C:** Sergio Salvati; **M:** Fabio Frizzi.

Gates of Hell 2: Dead Awakening 🐾 1996 Occultists performing an initiation rite reopen the portal to hell and a creature from its depths reawakens to cause the usual unholy terror. 87m/C **VHS, DVD.** Tom Campitelli, Tamara Hext, Randy Strickland; **D:** G.D. Marcum.

The Gathering 🐾🐾 1977 A dying man seeks out the wife and family he has alienated for a final Christmas gathering. James Poe authored this well-acted holiday tearjerker that won the 1977-78 Emmy for outstanding TV drama special. 94m/C **VHS.** Ed Asner, Maureen Stapleton, Lawrence Pressman, Stephanie Zimbalist, Bruce Davison, Gregory Harrison, Veronica Hamel, Gail Strickland; **D:** Randal Kleiser; **M:** John Barry. **TV**

The Gathering 🐾🐾 2002 (R) Backpacker Cassie (Ricci) is headed for the English village of Ashby Wake when she's hit by a car. The driver, Marion Kirkman (Fox), takes Cassie to her house to recover since she's lost her memory. Marion's husband Simon (Dillane) is researching a recently uncovered first-century church with some unusual iconography that's drawing a number of strangers to the site. Cassie begins to have premonitions about the Kirkmans and the church and her possible ties to the mystery. 92m/C **DVD.** *US GB* Christina Ricci, Ioan Gruffudd, Kerry Fox, Stephen (Dillon) Dillane, Simon Russell Beale, Robert Hardy, Peter McNamara; **D:** Brian Gilbert; **W:** Anthony Horowitz; **C:** Martin Fuhrer; **M:** Anne Dudley.

A Gathering of Eagles 🐾🐾½ 1963 Hudson portrays a hard-nosed Air Force colonel during peacetime whose British wife must adjust to being a military spouse. 115m/C **VHS.** Rock Hudson, Rod Taylor, Mary Peach, Barry Sullivan, Kevin McCarthy, Henry Silva, Leif Erickson; **D:** Delbert Mann; **M:** Jerry Goldsmith.

The Gathering: Part 2 🐾🐾
1979 Sequel in which a widow has a Christmas reunion with her family, but conflict arises when she introduces a new man in her life. Not as effective as the original, also made for TV. 98m/C **VHS.** Maureen Stapleton, Efrem Zimbalist Jr., Jameson Parker, Bruce Davison, Lawrence Pressman, Gail Strickland, Veronica Hamel; **D:** Charles S. Dubin. **TV**

The Gathering Storm 🐾🐾 1974 Based on the first book of memoirs from Sir Winston Churchill, this drama examines the pre-WWII years. 72m/C Richard Burton, Virginia McKenna, Ian Bannen; **D:** Herbert Wise.

The Gathering Storm 🐾🐾🐾
2002 Finney stars as a typically pugnacious Winston Churchill, who in the mid-1930s is in the political wilderness as he tries to warn an indifferent England about German re-armament and Hitler's rise to power. But he also has problems at home, since he beloved wife Clemmie (Redgrave) has gone off on an extended trip abroad to ease some marital strain and Winston is feeling lonely, jealous, and vulnerable. 96m/C **VHS, DVD.** Albert Finney, Vanessa Redgrave, Jim Broadbent, Linus Roache, Lena Headey, Tom Wilkinson, Derek Jacobi, Ronnie Barker, Celia Imrie, Hugh Bonneville; **D:** Richard Loncraine; **W:** Hugh Whitemore; **C:** Peter Hannan; **M:** Trevor Jones. **C A B L E**

The Gatling Gun 🐾½ _King Gun_ 1972 (PG) Poor tale of the Cavalry, Apache Indians, and renegades all after the title weapon. 93m/C **VHS, DVD.** Guy Stockwell, Woody Strode, Patrick Wayne, Robert Fuller, Barbara Luna, John Carradine, Pat Buttram, Phil Harris; **D:** Robert Gordon.

Gator Bait 🐾½ 1973 (R) The Louisiana swamp is home to the beautiful Desiree, and woe be unto any man who threatens her family. Aims to please fans of the raunchy and violent. Followed by an equally vile sequel. 91m/C **VHS.** Claudia Jennings, Clyde Ventura, Bill (Billy) Thurman, Janit Baldwin; **D:** Ferd Sebastian, Beverly Sebastian; **W:** Ferd Sebastian, Beverly Sebastian.

Gator Bait 2: Cajun Justice 🐾 1988 (R) A city girl comes to the Louisiana swamp and turns violent in an effort to exact revenge on the men who have been tormenting her. 94m/C **VHS.** Jan MacKenzie, Tray Loren, Paul Muzzcat, Brad Kepnick, Jerry Armstrong, Ben Sebastian; **D:** Ferd Sebastian, Beverly Sebastian; **W:** Ferd Sebastian, Beverly Sebastian.

Gator King 🐶½ 1970 (R) Villainous Santos (Fargas) imports Chinese crocodiles to serve them up as dinner at his restaurant and for other nefarious purposes. Spunky journalist Maureen (Foley) and her ex-beau Ranger Ronny (Richardson) decide to investigate. It's a standardissue micro-budget action flick with nothing really to recommend it, even to fans of the genre. **86m/C DVD.** Antonio Fargas, Jay Richardson, Sharron K. Foley, Michael Berryman, L. Denk; **C:** Richard Lacy; **M:** Joe Pegram.

Gattaca 🐶🐶🐶 1997 (PG-13) It's a future world where genetic tinkering allows parents to tweak their children's DNA before birth and a caste system of "perfect" humans exists. Vincent (Hawke) dreams of employment, which could uncover his true identity. Thinking man's sci-fi (read: no spaceships or explosions) along the lines of George Lucas' "THX-1138." **112m/C VHS, DVD, Blu-Ray Disc.** Ethan Hawke, Uma Thurman, Jude Law, Gore Vidal, Alan Arkin, Loren Dean, Jayne Brook, Elias Koteas, Tony Shalhoub, Ernest Borgnine; **D:** Andrew Niccol; **W:** Andrew Niccol; **C:** Slawomir Idziak; **M:** Michael Nyman.

The Gaucho 🐶🐶 1927 Fairbanks stars as the title character, an immortal swashbuckler who lusts after a virginal religious (Grear) before undergoing a change of heart (but not before dancing a red-hot tango with the less-than-virginal Velez). **95m/B VHS, DVD.** Douglas Fairbanks Sr., Lupe Velez, Geraine Greear, Gustav von Seyffertitz; **D:** F. Richard Jones; **W:** Lotta Woods; **C:** Gaetano Antonio "Tony" Gaudio.

Gaucho Serenade 🐶🐶½ 1940 Former rodeo stars Gene (Autry) and Frog (Burnette) set out to help the son of their ex-partner, who's the kidnapping target of gangsters. Lots of singing, not much action. ♪Gaucho Serenade; A Song in the Night; The Singing Hills; Give Out with a Song; Wooing of Kitty MacFuty. **66m/B VHS.** Gene Autry, Smiley Burnette, Duncan Renaldo, June Storey, Mary Lee; **D:** Frank McDonald; **W:** Bradford Ropes; **C:** Reggie Lanning.

Gaudi Afternoon 🐶🐶 2001 Cassandra (Davis) is a translator, working in Barcelona, who gets caught up in the volatile relationship between transsexual Frankie (Harden) and her estranged female lover Ben (Taylor), who is now involved with hippo April (Lewis). It seems that Frankie and Ben also share a daughter and a custody fight is brewing that Cassandra doesn't want to get caught up in. On the other hand, all the melodrama is making her life quite interesting. Based on a novel by Barbara Wilson. **88m/C VHS, DVD. SP** Judy Davis, Marcia Gay Harden, Lili Taylor, Juliette Lewis, Maria Barranco, Christopher Bowen, Courtney Jines; **D:** Susan Seidelman; **W:** James Myhre; **C:** Josep Civit; **M:** Bernardo Bonezzi.

The Gauntlet 🐶🐶 1977 (R) Clint is a broken-down cop ordered to Las Vegas to bring back a key witness for an important trial—but the witness turns out to be a beautiful prostitute being hunted by killers. Violence-packed action with some decent set-pieces. **111m/C VHS, DVD.** Clint Eastwood, Sondra Locke, Pat Hingle, Bill McKinney; **D:** Clint Eastwood; **W:** Michael Butler; **C:** Rexford Metz; **M:** Jerry Fielding.

The Gay Deceivers 🐶🐶 1969 (R) Unmistakably grounded in the '60s, the performances of this comedy are still fresh, but the script is a little stale. Danny (Coughlin) and Elliot (Casey) are two straight guys who avoid the draft by posing as a loving couple. When an army Colonel appears to be investigating the duo they move into a gay apartment complex to carry on their scam. Naturally, hilarity ensues. The jokes are stereotype-based and show no true skill from the writer or director. Unfortunately, the film is credited with ruining the careers of its leads. **97m/C DVD.** Kevin Coughlin, Lawrence Casey, Brooke Bundy; **D:** Bruce Kessler; **W:** Gil Lasky, Jerome Wish; **C:** Richard C. Glouner; **M:** Stu Phillips.

The Gay Desperado 🐶🐶½ 1936 Mexican bandit Pablo (Carrillo), who styles himself after American screen gangsters, kidnaps singing caballero Chivo (Martini) and heiress Jane (Lupino). The reason everybody is so gay is that they're always singing in this goofy musical comedy. **85m/B VHS, DVD.** Leo Carrillo, Nino Martini, Stanley Fields, Mischa Auer; **D:** Rouben Mamoulian; **W:** Wallace Smith; **C:** Lucien N. Andriot; **M:** Alfred Newman.

The Gay Divorcee 🐶🐶🐶 The Gay Divorce 1934 Astaire pursues Rogers in an English seaside resort, where she mistakes him for the hired correspondent in her divorce case. Based on the musical play "The Gay Divorce" by Dwight Taylor and Cole Porter. The title was slightly changed for the movie because of protests from the Hays Office. ♪Don't Let It Bother You; A Needle in a Haystack; Let's K-nock K-nees; Night and Day; The Continental. **107m/B VHS, DVD.** Fred Astaire, Ginger Rogers, Edward Everett Horton, Eric Blore, Alice Brady, Erik Rhodes, Betty Grable; **D:** Mark Sandrich; **M:** Max Steiner. Oscars '34: Song ("The Continental").

Gay Purr-ee 🐶🐶 1962 Delightful tale of feline romance in the City of Lights. For all ages. **85m/C VHS, DVD.** ♪ D: Abe Levitow; **V:** Judy Garland, Robert Goulet, Red Buttons, Hermione Gingold, Mel Blanc.

The Gay Lady 🐶🐶½ Trottie True 1949 Light romantic comedy set in the 1890s about an actress who climbs to stardom in London theatre and winds up marrying into the aristocracy. Look for Christopher Lee and Roger Moore in early bit parts. **95m/C VHS.** Jean Kent, James Donald, Hugh Sinclair, Lana Morris, Bill Owen, Michael Medwin, Andrew Crawford; **D:** Brian Desmond Hurst.

The Gay Ranchero 🐶🐶 1942 Rogers, without Dale Evans, in an average tale of old west meets new crooks. Rogers is the sheriff who foils gangsters trying to take over an airport. The action doesn't stop him from singing a duet with leading lady Frazee on "Waitil I Get My Sunshine in the Moonlight." **55m/B VHS, DVD.** Roy Rogers, Andy Devine, Tito Guizar, Jane Frazee, Estelita Rodriguez; **D:** William Witney.

The Gazebo 🐶🐶🐶 1959 Wacky comedy about a TV writer who is being blackmailed by someone who has nude photos of his Broadway star wife. He decides murder is the only solution to this problem. Reynolds sings "Something Called Love." Based on a play by Myra and Alec Coppel from a story by Alec McLeod (of "Love Boat" fame). **102m/B VHS.** Glenn Ford, Debbie Reynolds, Carl Reiner, John McGiver, Doro Merande, Bert Freed, Martin Landau; **D:** George Marshall; **W:** George Wells.

Geek Maggot Bingo 🐶 The Freak from Suckweasel Mountain 1983 It's too bad director Zedd waited until he did "Bingo" to post a sign warning: "Leave Now. It isn't cult classic, this horror spoof is too long on in-jokes and short on substance to even number in the cult hall of fame. It does, however, boast Death as a Spaghetti vampire queen and Hell as a punk cowboy crooner (before alternative country hit the airwaves). **TV** horror-meister Zacherle narrates. **70m/C VHS, DVD.** Robert Andrews Richard Hell, Donna Death, Brenda Bergman, Tyler Smith, Bruno Zeus, John Zacherle; **C:** Nick Zedd; **D:** Nick Zedd; **GE** Alexander Golling; **D:** Herbert Selpin.

A Geisha 🐶🐶 1953 Miyoharu (Kogure) is a passive elderly geisha who agrees to train the naive young Eiko (Wakao) in her new role. But Eiko discovers her romantic notion of the geisha life are far from it's modern reality. Poignant look at the changing status of the geisha in Japan after WWII.

Geheimakte WB1 🐶 Secret Paper WB1 1942 Historical drama centering on the invention of the U-boat by Sergeant Wilhelm Bauer during Denmark's WWII blockade of the ports of Schleswig-Holstein. In German with no subtitles. **91m/B VHS. GE** Alexander Golling; **D:** Herbert Selpin.

Geheimnisse einer Seele see Secrets of a Soul

Genealogies of a Crime 🐶🐶 Genealogies d'un Crime 1997 Complex puzzle with the ever-beautiful Deneuve in two roles. In one role, she's Solange, a criminal lawyer who agrees to defend a young man, Rene (Poupaud), who's accused of murdering his psychologist aunt Jeanne (Deneuve again, in flashback), a criminal with homicidal tendencies, became his shrink, and even expected to be killed by him. Solange believes Jeanne's ministrations programmed Rene to kill. As Solange investigates Rene's background, she becomes too involved with the unstable young man—leading her down the path to madness as well. French with subtitles. **114m/C VHS, DVD.** FF Catherine Deneuve, Melvil Poupaud, Michel Piccoli, Andrzej Seweryn, Bernadette LaFont, Hubert Saint Macary; **D:** Paul Ruiz; **W:** Raul Ruiz, Pascal Bonitzer; **C:** Stefan Ivanov; **M:** Jorge Arriagada.

The General 🐶🐶🐶🐶 1926 Keaton's masterpiece and arguably the most formally perfect and funniest of silent comedies. Concerns a plucky Confederate soldier who single-handedly retrieves a pivotal train from Northern territory. Full of eloquent man-vs-machinery images and outrageous sight gags. Remade as "The Great Locomotive Chase" in 1956

and the country's social upheavals, in Japanese with English subtitles. **86m/B VHS.** JP Michiyo Kogure, Ayako Wakao, Seizaburo Kawazu, Chieko Naniwa, Eitaro Shindo; **D:** Kenji Mizoguchi; **W:** Yoshikata Yoda; **M:** Ichiro Saito.

The Geisha Boy 🐶🐶 1958 Jerry is a floundering magician who joins the USO and tours the Far East. His slapstick confrontations with the troupe leader and an officer who dreams of attending his own funeral provide hearty laughs, plus Lewis finds romance with a Japanese widow after her son claims him as a father. Pleshette's film debut with an appearance by the Los Angeles Dodgers. **98m/C VHS.** Jerry Lewis, Marie McDonald, Sessue Hayakawa, Barton MacLane, Suzanne Pleshette, Nobu McCarthy; **D:** Frank Tashlin.

Geisha Girl 🐶½ 1952 Forgotten sci-fi film about a mad scientist and his Japanese cohorts who develop small explosive pills that are more powerful than nuclear bombs. Their plans of world conquest are thwarted when the pills inadvertently fall into the hands of two American G.I.s. **67m/B VHS.** Martha Hyer, William Andrews, Archer MacDonald, Kekao Yokoo, Teddy Nakamura; **D:** George Breakston; **C:** Ray Stahl.

Gemini Affair 🐶 1974 Two women go to Hollywood to become rich and famous but end up being very disappointed. **88m/C VHS.** Marta Kristen, Kathy Kersh, Anne Seymour; **D:** Matt Cimber.

Gen-X Cops 🐶🐶 Tejing Xinrenlei 1999 (R) Hong Kong police break a ring of smugglers, who are selling a massive shipment of explosives. But the cops then lose the goods to major criminal, Akatora (Nakamura). So a rebellious trio of young cops go undercover and discover the bad guy has very sinister plans. Cantonese with subtitles. **113m/C VHS, DVD, HK** Nicholas Tse, Stephen Fung, Sam Lee, Grace Kip, Toru Nakamura, Jackie Chan; **D:** Benny Chan; **W:** Benny Chan; **C:** Arthur Wong Ngok Tai.

The Gendarme of Saint-Tropez 🐶🐶½ 1964 Officer Ludovic Cruchot's plans for career advancement are on shaky ground after he is transferred to St. Tropez where his daughter has a little too much fun at the beach. Also available dubbed. **80m/C VHS.** FR Louis de Funes, Michel Galabru, Genevieve Grad, Jean (Lefevre) Lefebvre, Christian Marin; **D:** Jean Girault; **C:** Marc Fossard; **M:** Raymond Lefevre.

The Gene Krupa Story 🐶🐶½ 1959 The story of the famous jazz drummer and his career plunge after a drug conviction. Krupa recorded the soundtrack, mimed by Mineo, who was too young for a convincing portrayal. Gavin part as Mineo's dad. **101m/B VHS, DVD.** Sal Mineo, James Darren, Susan Kohner, Susan Oliver, Anita O'Day, Red Nichols; **D:** Don Weis.

The General 🐶🐶🐶 1998 (R) Biopic of maverick Dublin crime lord Martin Cahill (Gleeson), nicknamed "The General" for his planning abilities. Film is one, long flashback as it begins in 1994 with Cahill's assassination. Cahill supports his family through various burglaries, making a mockery of the local cops, the local mobster is noted by the IRA and when he refuses to cut them in on his profits, things turn very dicey for the cocky, ruthless Cahill. **123m/B VHS, DVD, IR** Brendan Gleeson, Adrian Dunbar, Sean McGinley, Jon Voight, Maria Doyle Kennedy, Angeline Ball, Ciaran Fitzgerald, Eamon Owens; **D:** John Boorman; **C:** Seamus Deasy; **M:** Richie Buckley. Cannes '98: Director (Boorman).

The General Line 🐶🐶🐶 Old and the New 1929 Eisenstein's classic only feature "Our Gang" comedy goofed by transplanting them to a Civil War milieu popular at the time. Confederate kids Spanky and Alfa play soldier, ultimately outsmarting Union troops. The rascals are still funny sometimes, but Buckwheat's role as an eager slave is disturbing today. **73m/B VHS.** George "Spanky" McFarland, Phillip Holmes, Ralph Morgan, Irving Pichel, Rosina Lawrence, Billie "Buckwheat" Thomas, Carl "Alfalfa" Switzer, Louise Beavers; **D:** Fred Newmeyer.

General Spanky 🐶🐶 1936 The General Spanky 1936 A clever, atmospheric suspense film about an American mercenary in Shanghai falling in love with a beautiful spy as she battles a fierce Chinese warlord who wants to take over the city. Playwright-to-be Odets' first screenplay; he, O'Hara and '30s gossip hound Skolsky have cameos as reporters. **93m/B VHS.** Gary Cooper, Madeleine Carroll, Akim Tamiroff, Dudley Digges, Porter Hall, William Frawley, Philip Ahn; Cameos: John O'Hara, Clifford Odets, Sidney Skolsky; **D:** Lewis Milestone; **W:** Clifford Odets; **C:** Victor Milner.

Generale Della Rovere 🐶🐶🐶½ Il Generale Della-Rovere 1960 A WWII black marketeer is forced by the Nazis to go undercover in a local prison. To find out who makes the leaders are, he poses as a general. But when prisoners begin to look to him for guidance, he finds the line between his assumed role and real identity diminished, leading to a bravura lead performance by veteran director De Sica. In Italian with English subtitles. **139m/B VHS.** IT Vittorio De Sica, Otto Messmer, Sandra Milo; **D:** Roberto Rossellini; **W:** Roberto Rossellini, Sergio Amidei, Diego Fabbri, Indro Montanelli; **C:** Carlo Carlini; **M:** Renzo Rossellini.

The General's Daughter 🐶🐶 1999 (R) Disturbing and convoluted military thriller based on the 1992 bestseller by Nelson DeMille. Paul Brenner (Travolta) is an Army criminal investigator whose latest case is the rape and murder of Capt. Elisabeth Campbell (Stefanson), whose father (Cromwell) is a legendary general. Elisabeth specialized in psychological warfare but she had more than a few mental problems of her own. Naturally, for the good of the service, everyone but Brenner would like a quick and tidy solution to the sleazy goings-on. Goes a little too over the top (including some performances) and you may come to wonder what it's all done about. **116m/C VHS, DVD.** John Travolta, Madeleine Stowe, James Cromwell, Timothy Hutton, James Woods, Leslie Stefanson, Clarence Williams III, Daniel von Bargen, Boyd Kestner, Mark Boone Jr.; **D:** John Eeessey; **W:** Peter Weireter, Mark Boone Jr.

with Fess Parker. **78m/B VHS, DVD.** Buster Keaton, Marion Mack, Glen Cavender, Jim Farley, Joe Keaton, Frederick Vroom, Charles Smith, Frank Barnes, Mike Donlin; **D:** Clyde Bruckman, Buster Keaton; **W:** Clyde Bruckman, Al Boasberg, Charles Henry Smith, Buster Keaton; **C:** Bert Haines, Devereaux Jennings. Natl. Film Reg. '89.

General's

Benjamin Hickey, Rick Dial, Brad Beyer; **D:** Simon West; **W:** William Goldman, Christopher Bertolini; **C:** Peter Menzies Jr.; **M:** Carter Burwell.

A Generation 🎬🎬🎬 *Pokolenie* 1954 During WWII, a young man escapes from the Warsaw Ghetto and finds his way to the Polish Resistance. He falls in love with the leader of the local group and finds the courage to fight for his freedom. Strong directorial debut from Wajda. Part 1 of his "War Trilogy," followed by "Kanal" and "Ashes and Diamonds." Scripted by Czeszko from his novel "Pokolenie." **PL** Tadeusz Lomnicki, Urszula Modrzynska, Zbigniew Cybulski, Roman Polanski; **D:** Andrzej Wajda; **W:** Bohdan Czeszko; **C:** Jerzy Lipman; **M:** Andrzej Markowski.

Generation 🎬🎬 *A Time For Caring* 1969 A very pregnant bride informs everyone she'll give birth at home without doctors, and creates a panic. Based on the Broadway play by William Goodhart. 109m/C **VHS.** David Janssen, Kim Darby, Carl Reiner, Peter Duel, Andrew Prine, James Coco, Sam Waterston; **D:** George Schaefer; **W:** William Goodhart; **C:** Lionel Lindon; **M:** Dave Grusin.

Genevieve 🎬🎬🎬 1953 A 1904 Darracq roadster is the title star of this picture which spoofs "classic car" owners and their annual rally from London to Brighton. Two married couples challenge each other to a friendly race which becomes increasingly intense as they near the finish line. 86m/C **VHS, DVD. GB** John Gregson, Dinah Sheridan, Kenneth More, Kay Kendall, Geoffrey Keen, Reginald Beckwith, Arthur Wontner, Joyce Grenfell, Leslie Mitchell, Michael Medwin, Michael Balfour, Edie Martin, Harold Siddons; **D:** Henry Cornelius; **W:** William Rose; **C:** Christopher Challis; **M:** Larry Adler. British Acad. '53: Film; Golden Globes '55: Foreign Film.

Genghis Cohn 🎬🎬½ 1993 Black comedy follows the misadventures of a former Nazi concentration camp commander (Lindsay) who has settled in a small Bavarian town and taken on the position of police chief. But his quiet life is rocked by a series of murders, an affair with a kinky Baroness (Rigg), and by the ghost of Jewish comedian Genghis Cohn (Sher), a victim of the camps whose haunting presence exacts a particularly appropriate revenge. Adapted from Romain Gary's novel "The Dance of Genghis Cohn." Made for British TV. 100m/C **VHS. GB** Robert Lindsay, Diana Rigg, Antony Sher; **D:** Elijah Moshinsky; **W:** Stanley Price.

Genie of Darkness 🎬 1962 The ashes of Nostradamus himself are retrieved in a bid to destroy his vampiric descendent. Edited from a Mexican serial; if you were able to sit through this one, look for "Curse of Nostradamus" and "The Monster Demolisher." 77m/B **VHS. MX** German Robles; **D:** Frederick Curiel.

Gentle Giant 🎬🎬 1967 An orphaned bear is taken in by a boy and his family and grows to be a 750 pound giant who must be returned to the wild. "Gentle Ben" TV series was derived from this feature. 93m/C **VHS.** Dennis Weaver, Vera Miles, Ralph Meeker, Clint Howard, Huntz Hall; **D:** James Neilson.

Gentle Savage 🎬🎬½ *Camper John* 1973 (R) When an Indian is wrongly accused of raping and beating a white woman, the white community seeks revenge. The vengeful mob, led by the victim's step-father, is unaware that it's really their ringleader who is responsible for the crime. When the accused's brother is slain, the Indian community retaliates. Violent but well-crafted. 85m/C **VHS.** William (Bill) Smith, Gene Evans, Barbara Luna, Joe Flynn; **D:** Sean McGregor.

A Gentle Woman 🎬🎬½ *A Gentle Creature; Une Femme Douce* 1969 Adaptation of Dostoevsky's short story about a young married woman who kills herself. Sanda marries pawnbroker Frangin, is miserable in her marriage, toys with killing her husband, and commits suicide instead, leaving the bewildered Frangin to try to figure out why. Several theories are offered but nothing is ever made clear. Debut of Sanda; Bressons' first film in color. French with subtitles. 89m/C **VHS. FR** Dominique San-

da, Guy Frangin, Jane Lobre; **D:** Robert Bresson; **W:** Robert Bresson; **C:** Ghislain Cloquet; **M:** Jean Wiener.

A Gentleman After Dark 🎬🎬 1942 Poor script but a good lead performance by Donlevy. Harry Melton escapes from prison in order to protect his daughter (who was raised by others) from his blackmailing wife, Flo (Hopkins). This monster mom is threatening to spoil the girl's upcoming marriage by revealing her sordid antecedents. A remake of 1936's "Forgotten Faces." 78m/B **VHS.** Brian Donlevy, Miriam Hopkins, Preston Foster, Harold Huber, Philip Reed, Gloria Holden, Douglass Dumbrille, Sharon Douglas; **D:** Edwin L. Martin; **W:** George Bruce, Patterson McNutt; **C:** Milton Krasner; **M:** Dimitri Tiomkin.

Gentleman Bandit 🎬🎬 1981 So-so drama about a Mexican landowner returns home and finds his people's land stolen from them by greedy tax collectors. Based on a true story. 96m/C **VHS.** Ralph Waite, Julie Bovasso, Jerry Zaks, Joe Grifasi, Estelle Parsons, Tom Aldredge; **D:** Jonathan Kaplan. **TV**

The Gentleman from California 🎬 *The Californian* 1937 The dashing son of a Mexican landowner returns home and finds his people's land stolen from them by greedy tax collectors. 56m/B **VHS, DVD.** Ricardo Cortez, Marjorie Weaver, Katherine DeMille; **D:** Gus Meins.

Gentleman from Dixie 🎬🎬 1941 After LaRue is released from prison, he looks to change his life by joining his brother on a farm and seeking revenge on the man who put him in the pokey. 61m/B **VHS.** Jack La Rue, Marian Marsh, Clarence Muse, Mary Ruth, Robert Kellard, John Holland, Herbert Rawlinson; **D:** Albert Herman.

Gentleman from Texas 🎬 1946 Ropin', ridin', and romance figure in this less than dramatic oater. 55m/B **VHS.** Johnny Mack Brown, Raymond Hatton, Claudia Drake, Reno Blair, Christine McIntyre; **D:** Lambert Hillyer.

Gentleman Jim 🎬🎬½ 1942 A colorful version of the life of old-time heavyweight boxing great Jim Corbett, transformed from a typical Warner Bros. bio-pic by director Walsh into a fun-loving, anything-for-laughs donnybrook. Climaxes with Corbett's fight for the championship against the great John L. Sullivan. One of Flynn's most riotous performances. 104m/ **B VHS, DVD.** Errol Flynn, Alan Hale, Alexis Smith, Jack Carson, Ward Bond, Arthur Shields, William Frawley; **D:** Raoul Walsh.

The Gentleman Killer 🎬 1969 A man-with-no-name clears a ravaged border town of murdering bandits. 95m/C **VHS.** **IT SP** Anthony Steffen, Silvia Solar; **D:** Giorgio Stegani; **W:** Jaime Jesus Balcazar; **C:** Francis Marin; **M:** Bruno Nicolai.

Gentleman's Agreement 🎬🎬🎬 1947 Magazine writer Phil Green (Peck) looks for a new angle when he agrees to write a series of articles on anti-Semitism for publisher John Minify (Dekker). Phil pretends to be Jewish, and his new identity pervades his life in unexpected ways, almost destroys his relationships. Garfield has a small but powerful role as Phil's Jewish friend Dave, who has long had to deal with both overt and covert prejudice. This movie was Hollywood's first major attack on anti-Semitism. Controversial in its day, yet still timely. 118m/B **VHS, DVD.** Gregory Peck, Dorothy McGuire, John Garfield, Celeste Holm, Anne Revere, June Havoc, Albert Dekker, Jane Wyatt, Dean Stockwell, Nicholas Joy; **D:** Elia Kazan; **W:** Moss Hart; **C:** Arthur C. Miller; **M:** Alfred Newman. Oscars '47: Director (Kazan), Picture, Support. Actress (Holm); Golden Globes '48: Director (Kazan), Film—Drama, Support. Actress (Holm); N.Y. Film Critics '47: Director (Kazan), Film.

A Gentleman's Game 🎬🎬½ 2001 (R) Twelve-year-old Timmy (Gamble) is a gifted young golfer who is pushed by his father to improve his game. He becomes a caddy at the local country club and manages to get tips from reluctant club pro Foster Pearce (Sinise) but learns about more than just golf. Based on the novel by Coyne, who co-scripted. 91m/C **VHS, DVD.** Mason Gamble, Gary Sinise, Philip Baker Hall, Dylan Baker, Henry Simmons, Ellen Muth, Brian Doyle-Murray; **D:** J. Mills Goodloe; **W:**

J. Mills Goodloe, Tom Coyne; **C:** Conrad W. Hall; **M:** Jeff Beal.

Gentlemen Prefer Blondes 🎬🎬🎬 1953 Amusing satire involving two show-business girls from Little Rock trying to make it big in Paris. Seeking rich husbands or diamonds, their capers land them in police court. Monroe plays Lorelei Lee, Russell is her sidekick. Despite an occasionally slow plot, the music, comedy, and performances are great fun. Film version of a Broadway adaption of a story by Anita Loos. Followed by (but without Monroe) "Gentlemen Marry Brunettes." ♫A (Two) Little Girl(s) From Little Rock; Bye, Bye Baby; Ain't There Anyone Here For Love?; When Love Goes Wrong; Diamonds Are A Girl's Best Friend. 91m/C **VHS, DVD.** Marilyn Monroe, Jane Russell, Charles Coburn, Elliott Reid, Tommy Noonan, George Winslow; **D:** Howard Hawks; **W:** Charles Lederer; **C:** Harry Wild; **M:** Leo Robin, Jule Styne, Lionel Newman.

Gentlemen's Relish 🎬🎬½ 2001 Artist Kingdom Swann (Connolly) is dismayed to learn Edwardian London finds his paintings of his naughty but vibrant Violet (Lancashire) buys him a camera so he can experiment. With the help of unscrupulous assistant Marsh (Henshall), Swann becomes a successful society photographer, progressing into "artistic" nudes. However, Marsh is selling the increasingly naughty pics to a specialist clientele without the naïve Swann's knowledge. 89m/C **DVD. GB** Billy Connolly, Sarah Lancashire, Douglas Henshall, Katie Blake; **D:** Douglas Mackinnon; **W:** David Nobbs; **C:** Gavin Finney; **M:** Julian Nott. **TV**

Genuine Risk 🎬½ 1989 (R) Gorgeous young woman turns off her crime boss boyfriend bigtime when she seduces his bodyguard. Genuine tripe. 89m/C **VHS.** Terence Stamp, Michelle Johnson, Peter Berg, Michael (M.K.) Harris; **D:** Kurt Voss; **W:** Kurt Voss.

George! 🎬½ 1970 (G) A carefree bachelor takes his girlfriend and his 250-pound St. Bernard on a trip to the Swiss Alps where he proves that a dog is not always man's best friend. 87m/C **VHS, DVD.** Marshall Thompson, Jack Mullaney, Inge Schoner; **D:** Wallace C. Bennett; **W:** Wallace C. Bennett.

George A. Romero's Land of the Dead 🎬🎬🎬 *Land of the Dead* 2005 (R) Romero brings the walkers back for a fourth time, but with a tasty new twist—they aren't as dumb as they used to be. And worse yet, they've stumbled upon some ammo. But the upper-crust think they're now safe in their walled-in super tower until a renegade supplies runner, who's living among the poverty-plagued street people and angry because the elite won't invite him in, threatens their comfy confines. Compelling statement about societal classes embedded within usual gore. 93m/C **DVD, UMD, HD DVD. FR CA US** Simon Baker, John Leguizamo, Asia Argento, Robert Joy, Dennis Hopper, Eugene Clark, Boyd Banks, Joanne Boland, Krista Bridges, Jennifer Baxter, Pedro Miguel Arce, Boyd Banks, Phil Fondacaro, Simon Pegg; **D:** George A. Romero; **W:** George A. Romero; **C:** Miroslaw Baszak; **M:** Reinhold Heil, Johnny Klimek.

George Balanchine's The Nutcracker 🎬🎬½ 1993 (G) Pas de deux redeux. Tchaikovsky's classic ballet about the magic of Christmas and a little girl (Cohen) who dreams on Christmas Eve that she is in an enchanted kingdom. Culkin lamely grins through his wooden performance as the Nutcracker Prince, but the talent of the dancers is such that conventional camera techniques sometimes fail to keep up with their exacting moves. Adapted from the 1816 story by E.T.A. Hoffmann. 93m/C **VHS, DVD.** Macaulay Culkin, Jessica Lynn Cohen, Bart Robinson Cook, Wendy Whelan, Gen Horiuchi, Kyra Nichols, Damian Woetzel, Nilas Martins, Nancy McFadden; **W:** Susan Cooper; **C:** Ralf Bode; **Nar:** Kevin Kline.

(Mann) falls in love with George and takes him back to San Francisco, leaving behind obnoxious fiancee Lyle (Church). But when poachers capture George's "brother" Ape (voiced by Cleese), he returns to save the day (aided by various jungle companions), Fraser is an appealing lead, and the script is sweetly funny while retaining creator Ward's smart, subversive edge. The stunts are more impressive than you'd usually expect from a cartoon adaptation. 91m/C **VHS, DVD.** Brendan Fraser, Leslie Mann, Thomas Haden Church, Holland Taylor, Richard Roundtree, Greg Cruttwell, Abraham Benrubi, John Bennett Perry, Kelly Miller; **D:** Sam Weisman; **W:** Dana Olson, Audrey Wells; **C:** Thomas Ackerman; **M:** Marc Shaiman; **V:** John Cleese; **Nar:** Keith Scott.

George Wallace 🎬🎬½ 1997 Follows 20 years (1955-1975) in the life of politician George Wallace (Sinise) from his career as a state circuit judge, his four terms as Alabama's hard-line segregationist governor, to the first years after he was paralyzed by a would-be assassin while campaigning for the presidency. Some elements are disturbingly dramatized, including Archie (Williams), the fictional black manservant who serves as Wallace's conscience. Based on the book "Wallace" by co-scripter Frady. 178m/C **VHS.** Gary Sinise, Mare Winningham, Clarence Williams III, Joe Don Baker, Angelina Jolie, Mark Valley, Cliff DeYoung, Skipp (Robert L.) Sudduth, Mark Rolston, Michael Jensen, Terry Kinney; **D:** John Frankenheimer; **W:** Marshall Frady, Paul Monash; **C:** Alan Caso; **M:** Gary Chang. **CABLE**

George Washington 🎬🎬½ 1984 Bostwick stars as the father of our country in this made TV adaptation of James Thomas Flexner's biography. The destitute young Washington develops a close friendship with the wealthy Will Fairfax (Dukes), who provides him with the support to pursue his dreams, even though Washington has secretly fallen in love with Sally (Smith). Will's flirtatious wife. George himself has married the widowed Martha (Duke) and begins his military career, leading the American colonies against the Brits in the Revolutionary War. 398m/C **VHS.** Barry Bostwick, David Dukes, Jaclyn Smith, Patty Duke, Hal Holbrook, Lloyd Bridges, Jose Ferrer, Trevor Howard, Richard Kiley, James Mason, Clive Revill, Robert Stack; **W:** Richard Fielder. **TV**

George Washington Slept Here 🎬🎬🎬 1942 Hilarious side-splitter about a couple who moves from their Manhattan apartment to an old, broken-down country home in Connecticut. It's one catastrophe after another as the couple tries to renovate their home and deal with a greedy neighbor. Based on the play by George S. Kaufman and Moss Hart. 93m/B **VHS.** Jack Benny, Ann Sheridan, Charles Coburn, Percy Kilbride, Hattie McDaniel, William Tracy; **D:** William Keighley.

George White's Scandals 🎬🎬 1945 A lightweight musical comedy look at the show biz world and why the show must go on. Based on White's Broadway extravaganzas. Jazz numbers by Gene Krupa and his orchestra are preceded by "George White's Scandals" of 1934 and 1935. ♫Bolero in the Jungle; E.H.S.; Leave Us Leap; I Want to be a Drummer in the Band; How Did You Get Out of My Dreams?; I Wake Up in the Morning; Who Killed Vaudeville?; Scandals; Liza. 95m/B **VHS.** Joan Davis, Jack Haley, Jane Greer, Phillip Terry, Margaret Hamilton, Martha Holliday; **D:** Felix Feist.

George's Island 🎬🎬🎬 1991 (PG) When young George is placed with the worst foster parents in the world, his eccentric grandfather helps him escape. They wind up on Oak's Island, where, leg-

A Gentleman After Dark

George of the Jungle 🎬🎬 1997 (PG) The '60s cartoon hero goes big screen and live-action with Fraser starring as the clumsy (but very hunky) jungle hero. While on safari, socialite Ursula

Georgia 🎬🎬 1987 Tough lawyer Nina Bailey (Davis) explores her past when she begins a search for information on her biological mother, Georgia, a photographer who drowned herself years before. Only Nina has no idea about the to's parenting skills leave something to be desired and soon she sets off to Georgia's unleash. Frequent flashbacks to Georgia's mysterious life and death (Davis well plays both roles). 90m/C VHS. AU Judy Davis, Julia Blake, John Bach; D: Ben Lewin.

Georgia 🎬🎬🎬 1995 (R) Character study about sibling rivalry, self-destruction, and the Seattle music scene. Struggling rock singer Sadie (Leigh), who relies on booze, drugs, and men to help her make it through the night, returns to Seattle to crash with big-sister Georgia (Winningham). Settled, with loving husband and kids, the much more talented Georgia is also a popular folk icon and has the type of personal/career success angry and ambitious Sadie can only dream about. Fine performances—particularly from the charmenlike Leigh; both leads do their own singing. Screenwriter Turner 's Leigh's mother. 117m/C VHS, DVD. Mina (Badly) Badie, Jennifer Jason Leigh, Mare Winningham, Ted Levine, Max Perlich, John Doe, John C. Reilly, Jimmy Witherspoon; D: Ulu Grosbard; W: Barbara Turner; C: Jan Kiesser; Ind. Spirit '96: Actress (Winningham); Montreal World Film Fest. '95; Film '95: N.Y. Film Critics '95: Actress (Leigh).

Georgia, Georgia 🎬½ 1972 (R) Sands is a black entertainer on tour in Sweden who falls for a white photographer. Her traveling companion, who hates whites, takes drastic action to separate the lovers. Poor acting, script, and direction. Based on a book by Maya Angelou. 91m/C VHS. Diana Sands, Dirk Benedict, Minnie Gentry; D: Stig Bjorkman; W: Maya Angelou.

Georgia Rule 🎬½ 2007 (R) Generally misbegotten female family saga from director Marshall takes a decided turn into the unpleasant. Rebellious troubled teen Rachel (Lohan) finally screws up so badly that her alcoholic mom Lily (Huffman) sends her off for a summer of tough love at her own estranged mother Georgia's (Fonda) small-town home in Idaho Mormon territory. Rachel proceeds to be both outrageous and obnoxious, casually revealing that she's been molested by stepdad Arnold (Elwes), although she's such a liar no one knows what to believe. Then Lily shows up, also seeking a safe haven and adding to the family tension. Yes, this is the film where Lohan's own outrageous and obnoxious behavior drew public reprimands from the producer and others. 113m/C DVD. US Jane Fonda, Lindsay Lohan, Felicity Huffman, Dermot Mulroney, Cary Elwes, Garrett Hedlund, Laurie Metcalf, Hector Elizondo; D: Gary Marshall; W: Mark Andrus; C: Karl Walter Lindenlaub; M: John Debney.

Georgy Girl 🎬🎬 1966 Fedgrave finely plays the overweight ugly-duckling Georgy who shares a flat with the beautiful and promiscuous Meredith (Rempling). Georgy is, however, desired by the wealthy and aging Mason and soon by Meredith's lover (Bates) who recognizes her good heart. When Meredith becomes pregnant, Georgy persuades her to let her raise the baby, leaving Georgy with the dilemma of marrying the irresponsible Bates (the baby's father) or the settled Mason. Tha film and title song (sung by the Seekers) were both huge hits. Based on the novel by Margaret Foster who also co-wrote the screenplay. 100m/B VHS, DVD. GB Lynn Redgrave, James Mason, Charlotte Rampling, Alan Bates, Bill Owen, Claire Kelly, Peggy Thorpe-Bates, Dandy Nichols; D: Silvio Narizzano; W: Margaret Foster, Peter Nichols; C: Ken Higgins; Golden Globes '67: Actress—Mus./Comedy (Redgrave); N.Y. Film Critics '66: Actress (Redgrave).

Geronimo 🎬🎬 1962 In typical Hollywood casting Connors stars as the Indian leader on the warpath against the cavalry over broken treaties. Lots of action and the Indians are actually the good guys. 101m/C VHS. Chuck Connors, Ross Martin, Pat Conway, Kamala Devi, Adam West, Lawrence (Larry) Dobkin, Denver Pyle, Enid Jaynes, Armando Silvestre, John Anderson; D: Arnold Laven.

Geronimo 🎬🎬 1993 Not to be confused with the big screen version, this made-for-cable drama uses three actors to portray the legendary Apache warrior at various stages of his life. The intrepid teenager who leads attacks on Mexican troops, the adult fighting the duplicitous bluecoats, and the aged man witnessing the destruction of his way of life. The true story is told from the point of view of Native American culture and history. Somewhat overly earnest. 120m/C VHS. Joseph Runningfox, Jimmy Herman, Michael Greyeyes, Tailinh Forest Flower, Kimberly Norris, August Schellenberg, Geno Silva; D: Roger Young; W: J.T. Allen; M: Patrick Williams; CABLE.

Gepetto 🎬🎬 2000 Kince goopy Pinocchio update that focuses on toymaker dad, Geppetto (Carey). His longing for a kid of his own is granted by the Blue Fairy (Louis-Dreyfus), who makes puppet Pinocchio (Adkins) come alive. But Geppetto's parenting skills leave something to be desired and soon he sets off to Pinocchio with travelling showman, Stromboli (Spiner), and gets into all kinds of trouble. Some catchy tunes. 90m/C VHS, DVD. Drew Carey, Seth Adkins, Julia Louis-Dreyfus, Brent Spiner, Rene Auberjonois, Usher Raymond, Ana Gasteyer, Wayne Brady; D: Tom (Thomas R.) Moore; C: Stephen M. Katz; M: Stephen Schwartz; TV.

Germany in Autumn 🎬🎬 Deutschland im Herbst 1978 Twelve West German filmmakers offer political statements and artistic commentary on the political situation in their country after the kidnapping and murder of industrialist Hans Martin Schleyer. In German with English subtitles. 124m/C VHS. GE D: Volker Schlöndorff, Rainer Werner Fassbinder, Alf Brustellin, Alexander Kluge, Maximiliane Mainka, Edgar Reitz, Katja Rupe, Hans Peter Cloos, Bernhard Sinkel, Beate Mainka-Jellinghaus, Peter Schubert, Heinrich Boll; W: Heinrich Boll.

Germany, Pale Mother 🎬🎬 Deutschland, Bleiche Mutter 1980 In 1939, young, pregnant German hausfrau Lene (Mattes) sends her husband, Hans (Jacobi), to the front lines. Lene and her daughter struggle for survival through the war years until she has a bittersweet reunion with the embittered Hans. Director Sanders-Brahms based her story on her own mother's wartime experiences but the film suffers from the relentless parade of atrocities. German with subtitles. 123m/C VHS. GE Eva Mattes, Ernst Jacobi; D: Helma Sanders-Brahms; C: Jürgen Jurges; M: Jürgen Knieper.

Germinal 🎬🎬🎬 1993 (R) Recounts the struggle of working-class coal miners in France, led by Depardieu and wife Miou-Miou, to stave off poverty. While greedy investors debate how far they should lower miners' wages, the Maheu family, spurred on by newly arrived Marxst and off-camera French pop star Renaud, lead a strike. Minor themes revolving around management's adulterous adventures provide some momentary relief to relieve short attention spans. Seems so self-consciously an epic drama, however, that the overall effect is ponderous. Adaptation of the 19th century novel by Zola. In French with English subtitles. 158m/C VHS. FR Gerard Depardieu, Miou-Miou, Jean-Roques Renaud, Jacques Dacqmine, Jean-Pierre Bisson, Jean Carmet, Laurent Terzieff, Anny (Annie Legras) Duperey, Renaud; D: Claude Berri; C: Yves Angelo; M: Jean-Louis Roques, Cesar '94: Cinematog., Costume Des.

Germicide 🎬 1974 Scientist tries to warn the world of the threat posed by a horrifying bacterial weapon. Terrorists and his mistress hatch plots against him. 90m/C Rod Taylor, Bibi Andersson, Mathieu Carriere, Christian Barbier; D: Sergio Gobbi; C: Jean Badal.

Gerry 🎬🎬 2002 (R) Even for Van Sant, this is a bizarro film with a number of obscure (and-not-so-obscure) influences. Two young men, both named Gerry (Damon and Affleck), are driving along a desert highway when they decide to get out of the car and hike along a wilderness trail. They get lost and start wandering around. They have no food or water and, after a couple of days, start to hallucinate, even tually the Affleck Gerry can't go on (but the film does). Something to make you go hmmmmmmm. Or maybe, what were they thinking?! 103m/C DVD. US Matt Damon, Casey Affleck; D: Gus Van Sant; W: Matt Damon, Casey Affleck, Gus Van Sant; C: Harris Savides; M: Arvo Part.

Geronimo: An American Legend 🎬🎬 1993 (PG-13) Well-intentioned bio-actioner about the legendary Apache leader who fought the U.S. Army over forcing Native Americans onto reservations. The division of young Army officer Gatewood (Patric) is to round up the renegades led by Geronimo (Studi), whom Some 'respectively steal any scene they're in although the leads manage to hold their own. An unknown Damon plays the narrator, Lt. Britton Davis. Too noble for its own good and somewhat plodding. Great location filming around Moab, Utah. 115m/C VHS, DVD. Wes Studi, Jason Patric, Robert Duvall, Gene Hackman, Matt Damon, Rodney A. Grant, Kevin Tighe, Carlos Palomino, Stephen McHattie; D: Walter Hill; W: John Milius, Larry Gross; C: Lloyd Ahern II; M: Ry Cooder.

Geronimo's Revenge 🎬½ 1960 When Geronimo starts a battle with the settlers, a rancher he has befriended finds himself caught in the middle. The fourth soggy Disney TV oater from the "Tales of Texas John Slaughter" series. 77m/C VHS. Tom Tryon, Darryl Hickman; D: Harry Keller.

Gertrud 🎬🎬½ 1964 The simple story of an independent Danish woman rejecting her husband and lovers in favor of isolation. Cold, dry, minimalistic but manages to make up Dreyer's final film. In Danish with subtitles. 116m/B VHS, DVD. DK Nina Pens Rode, Bendt Rothe, Ebbe Rode, Baard Owe; D: Carl Theodor Dreyer; W: Carl Theodor Dreyer, Anne Abrahamsen, Henning Bendtsen; M: Jorgen Jersild.

Gervaise 🎬🎬🎬 1956 The best of several films of Emile Zola's "L'Assommoir." A 19th-century middle-class family is destroyed by the father's plunge into alcoholism despite a mother's attempts to save them. Well acted but overwhelmingly depressing. In French with English subtitles. 116m/B VHS. FR Maria Schell, Francois Perier, Suzy Delair, Armand Mestral; D: Rene Clement; M: Georges Auric. British Acad.'56: Actor (Perier), Film; N.Y. Film Critics '57: Foreign Film; Venice Film Fest. '56: Actress (Schell).

Get a Clue! 🎬🎬 1998 (PG) Teenaged Turtle discovers her body of a millionaire recluse and then learns that whoever can find the murderer will be awarded $20 million. Adapted from the book "The Westing Game." 95m/C VHS. Cliff DeYoung, Ray Walston, Lewis Arquette, Billy Morrisette, Ernest Liu, Sirene West, Sandy Faison; D: Terence H. Winkless; M: Dylan Kelsey Hadley; C: Kurt Brabbee; M: Parmer Fuller. VIDEO

Get a Clue 🎬½ 2002 (G) Pampered rich girl and school gossip columnist (Lohan) becomes an amateur detective when one of her teachers goes missing. Lohan fans will love this good-natured Disney Channel teen mystery, others probably not so much. 107m/C DVD. Lindsay Lohan, Bug Hall, Ian Gomez, Brenda Song, Amanda Plummer, Charles Shaughnessy, Dan Lett, Kimberly Roberts; D: Maggie Greenwald; W: Alana Sanko; C: Rhett Morita; M: David Mansfield. CABLE

Get Carter 🎬🎬🎬 1971 (R) Tough and stylish crime drama that has gained infamy since its release. Small-timer London hood Jack Carter (Caine) arrives in Newcastle determined to find out who killed his brother. After meeting local crime boss Cyril Kinnear (Osborne), Carter is told to go back home and leave things alone. But he doesn't turn out exactly as expected. Caine shows just how ruthless he can make a character. Film debut for director Hodges. Based on the novel "Jack's Return Home" by Ted Lewis. Remade in 2000. 112m/C VHS, DVD. GB Michael Caine, Ian Hendry, John Osborne, Geraldine Moffatt, Glynn Edwards, Dorothy White, Petra Markham, Bryan Mosley, Britt Ekland, Tony Beckley, George Sewell, Alan Armstrong, Bernard Hepton, Terence Rigby; D: Mike Hodges; W: Mike Hodges; D: Mike Hodges; W: Roy Budd.

Get Carter 🎬🎬 2000 (R) Stallone is Las Vegas tough guy Jack Carter, who goes home to Seattle for his brother's funeral and decides that his death wasn't natural. Hoping to redeem himself in the eyes of sister-in-law Gloria (Richardson) and niece Doreen (Cook), Carter searches the seedy uncelebrly for the killers. Or he may be searching for some decent lighting, since most of the scenes are dark even for a seedy underbelly. His injury-inducing tour of this underworld leads him to a sleazy pornographer (Roarke) and whiny billionaire (C.unning), setting the stage for a climactic showdown involving Doreen. Remake falls because Stallone's at all time on New Year's Eve 1983, and can't bring a thriving doing empire to it knees. The outcome: a TV series. Graves previously appeared on TV as the original 1971 Brit thriller, Michael Caine (two pearance as a wily bar owner. 104m/C VHS, DVD. Sylvester Stallone, Michael Caine, Rachael Leigh Cook, Alan Cumming, Miranda Richardson, Mickey Rourke, John Cassini, Gretchen Mol; D: Stephen Kay; M: Tyler Bates.

Get Christie Love! 🎬🎬 1974 Vintage blaxploitation from the genre's halcyon days, when going undercover meant a carte blanche for skimpy outfits. Based on Dorothy Uhnak's detective novel, the eponymous policewoman goes undercover to bring a drug-running operation to its knees. The outcome: a TV series. Graves previously appeared on TV as the original title role) makes an appearance as a wily bar owner. 104m/C VHS, DVD. Teresa Graves, Harry Guardino, Louise Sorrel, Paul Stevens, Andy Romano, Debbie Dozier; D: William A. Graham; TV.

Get Crazy 🎬🎬½ 1983 Flip Out The owner of the Saturn Theatre is attempting to stage the biggest rock-and-roll concert of all time on New Year's Eve 1983, and everything is going wrong in this hilarious, off-beat film. 90m/C VHS, DVD. Malcolm McDowell, Allen (Goorwitz) Garfield, Daniel Stern, Gail Edwards, Ed Begley Jr., Lou Reed, Bill Henderson, Fabian, Bobby Sherman, Miles Chapin, Howard Kaylan, Franklin Ajaye, Mary Woronov, Paul Bartel, Jackie Joseph, Dick Miller, Lee Ving, Clint Howard; D: Allan Arkush; W: Henry Rosenbaum, Danny Opatoshu, David Taylor; C: Thomas Del Ruth; M: Michael Boddicker.

Get On the Bus 🎬🎬½ 1996 (R) Lee looks at the personal side of the Million Man March through a fictional group of men who board a bus in south central L.A. and head for Washington, D.C. Practically ignoring the event itself, Lee and writer Bythewood focus on the men, who participated, their reasons, and their interaction with each other. Standouts in the melting pot of characters include Dutton as the attentive bus driver, a brash young actor (Braugher), a likable old man (Davis), an absentee father (Byrd) and his potentially delinquent son (Bonds), and a cop (Smith). Despite low budget (2.4 mil) and tight shooting schedule (21 days), Lee manages to drive the story home with the dialogue and characterization that (for the most part) avoids stereotypes. 122m/C VHS, DVD. Andre Braugher, Ossie Davis, Charles S. Dutton, DeAundre Bonds, Gabriel Casseus, Albert Hall, Hill Harper, Harry J. Lennix, Bernie Mac, Wendell Pierce, Roger Guenveur Smith, Isaiah Washington IV, Steve White, Thomas Jefferson Byrd, Richard Belzer, Randy Quaid; D: Spike Lee; W: Reggie Rock Bythewood; C: Elliot Davis; M: Terence Blanchard.

Get Out Your Handkerchiefs *Preparez Vous Mouchoirs* 1978 (R) Unconventional comedy about a husband desperately attempting to make his sexually frustrated wife happy. Determined to go to any lengths, he asks a Mozart-loving teacher to become her lover. She is now, however, bored by both men. Only when she meets a 13-year-old genius at the summer camp where the three adults are counselors does she come out of her funk and find her sexual happiness. Laure is a beautiful character, but Depardieu and Dewaere are wonderful as the bewildered would-be lovers. Academy Award winner for Best Foreign Film. In French with English subtitles. 109m/C VHS, DVD. *FR* Gerard Depardieu, Patrick Dewaere, Carole Laure; *D:* Bertrand Blier; *W:* Bertrand Blier; *C:* Jean Penzer; *M:* Georges Delerue. Oscars '78: Foreign Film; Cesar '79: Score; Natl. Soc. Film Critics '78: Film.

Get Over It! 2001 (PG-13) Professes to be thematically related to "A Midsummer Night's Dream," but don't let this get your hopes up. Thankfully, there's little chance of that happening, as the practice of basing teen comedies on Shakespeare plays reached the saturation point not too long ago and audiences realized that a film claiming to have been inspired by the Bard rarely met such high expectations. So it goes with this below-average kiddie comedy, which follows the sad breakup of Berke Landers (Foster), the nice but slightly dull boy, and Alison (Sagemiller), his popular former girlfriend, who soon takes up with Striker (West), the hot new boy in school. Berke's obsession with his old flame seems unrelenting until Kelly (Dunst) enters the scene. 90m/C VHS, DVD. *US* Kirsten Dunst, Ben Foster, Colin Hanks, Melissa Sagemiller, Sisqo, Shane West, Martin Short, Swoosie Kurtz, Ed Begley Jr., Zoe Saldana, Mila Kunis, Carmen Electra; *Cameos:* Coolio, Colleen (Ann) Fitzpatrick; *D:* Tommy O'Haver; *W:* R. Lee Fleming Jr.; *C:* Maryse Alberti; *M:* Steve Bartek.

Get Rich or Die Tryin' 2005 (R) Gangsta melodrama loosely based on the experiences of star/rapper 50 Cent. Thug Marcus wants easy money by selling drugs; instead he gets into some nasty turf wars and winds up in prison. He reconnects with homeboy Bama (Howard) who offers to be his manager if Marcus wants to pursue that rap career. He also gets a good woman, Charlene (Bryant), who loves and believes in him. None of this is particularly interesting, maybe because familiarity breeds, if not contempt, then indifference. 134m/C DVD. *US* Curtis "50 Cent" Jackson, Terrence Howard, Joy Bryant, Bill Duke, Adewale Akinnuoye-Agbaje, Omar Benson Miller, Viola Davis, Tory Kittles, Marc John Jefferies, Brian O'Hara, Sullivan Walker, Russell Hornsby, Ashley Walters, Serena Reeder; *D:* Jim Sheridan; *W:* Terence Winter; *C:* Declan Quinn; *M:* Quincy Jones, Gavin Friday, Maurice Seezer.

Get Real 1999 (R) Gay coming of age tale about Brit suburban teen, Steven (Silverstone), deciding to come out of the closet. Steven's only confidante is fellow outsider Linda (Brittain). Then he has an unexpected encounter with popular jock John (Gorton), who's confused about his sexuality and terrified that anyone will suspect he's gay, even to the point of helping his jock buddies gay-bash Steven. Eventually, Steven decides secrecy is not worth the pain. Good performances in a somewhat self-conscious drama. Adapted from Wilde's play "What's Wrong with Angry?" 111m/C VHS, DVD. *GB* Ben Silverstone, Brad Gorton, Charlotte Brittain, Stacy A. Hart, Kate McEnery, Jacquetta May, David Lumsden, Louise J. Taylor, Tim Harris; *D:* Simon Shore; *W:* Patrick Wilde; *C:* Alan Almond; *M:* John Lunn.

Get Rita *Gun Moll; Poopsie; Oopsie Poopsie; La Puppa del Gangster* 1975 Italian prostitute sets up her gangster boyfriend for a murder she committed and she winds up as mob boss. 90m/C VHS. Sophia Loren, Marcello Mastroianni; *D:* Tom Rowe.

Get Shorty 1995 (R) Low-level Miami loan shark and film buff Chili Palmer (Travolta) heads to Hollywood via Las Vegas, looking for a deadbeat dry-cleaner (Paymer), and a grade-Z movie producer (Hackman) who owes Vegas $150,000. Aided by B-movie screen-queen Russo, Palmer is pitted against a variety of shady Hollywood-types, including an egomaniacal star (DeVito) while trying to get into showbiz himself. Snappy scripting and performances finally do screen justice to an Elmore Leonard novel. DeVito, with the smaller title role, was originally cast as Chili Palmer, a role Travolta twice turned down until the ubiquitous Quentin Tarantino advised him to take it. 105m/C VHS, DVD. John Travolta, Gene Hackman, Danny DeVito, Rene Russo, Dennis Farina, Delroy Lindo, David Paymer, James Gandolfini, Bobby Slayton; *Cameos:* Bette Midler, Harvey Keitel, Penny Marshall; *D:* Barry Sonnenfeld; *W:* Scott Frank; *C:* Don Peterman; *M:* John Lurie. Golden Globes '96: Actor--Mus./Comedy (Travolta).

Get Smart 2008 (PG-13) So this adaptation of the '60s TV show does have some smart casting. Carell stars as the over-eager wannabe spy Maxwell Smart, who finally gets his chance to work in the field, although he's partnered with lethally lovely Agent 99 (Hathaway) rather than his hero, CONTROL superstar Agent 23 (Johnson). Will Smart's clumsy obliviousness (and some spy gadgetry) be enough to defeat crime syndicate KAOS and its evil leader Siegfried (Stamp)? Maybe the Chief (Arkin) should have a backup plan just in case. Not yet reviewed. ?m/C Steve Carell, Anne Hathaway, Dwayne "The Rock" Johnson, Alan Arkin, Terence Stamp, Terry Crews, David Koechner, Ken Davitian, Bill Murray, Masi Oka, Bernie Kopell; *D:* Peter Segal; *W:* Tom J. Astle, Matt Ember; *C:* Dean Semler; *M:* Trevor Rabin.

Get Smart, Again! 1989 Would you believe Maxwell Smart is back and as CONTROL's most incompetent agent? How about Agent 99 as his sidekick? Hymie the robot and a true no-good-niks at KAOS? Well, it's all true. This second reunion movie (following "The Nude Bomb") from the '60s TV show highlights all the wacky gadgetry, including the shoe phone, but fails to find the show's original outlandishness. 93m/C VHS, DVD. Don Adams, Barbara Feldon, Dick Gautier, Bernie Kopell, Kenneth Mars, Harold Gould, Roger Price, Fritz Feld, Robert Karvelas, King Moody; *D:* Gary Nelson. TV

Get That Girl 1932 Minor western action pic marred by former silent-screen player Talmadge's heavy German accent which soon lead to him giving up acting for a directing career. 54m/B VHS. Richard Talmadge, Shirley Grey, Carl Stockdale; *D:* George Crone.

Get That Man 1935 When a cabby is mistaken for the murdered heir to a vast fortune, his life suddenly becomes complex. 57m/B VHS. Wallace Ford, Leon Ames, Lillian Miles, E. Alyn (Fred) Warren; *D:* Spencer Gordon Bennet.

Get Well Soon 2001 (R) Disjointed romantic comedy finds midnight TV talk show host Bobby Bishop (Gallo) suffering a nervous breakdown that results in a number of scandals. Bobby takes off to see ex-girlfriend Lily (Cox) in New York but she's not happy to see him when he arrives and neither is her new boyfriend (Donovan). 95m/C VHS, DVD. Vincent Gallo, Courteney Cox, Jeffrey Tambor, Tate Donovan, Elina Lowensohn, Anne Meara; *D:* Justin McCarthy; *W:* Justin McCarthy; *M:* Vincent Gallo, Ric Markmann.

The Getaway 1972 (PG) McQueen plays a thief released on a parole arranged by his wife (McGraw) only to find out a corrupt politician wants him to rob a bank. After the successful holdup, McQueen finds out his cohorts and trying to double-cross him. McQueen and McGraw are forced into a feverish chase across Texas to the Mexican border, pursued by the politician's henchmen and the state police. Completely amoral depiction of crime and violence with McQueen tacitum as always and McGraw again showing a complete lack of acting skills. Based on a novel by Jim Thompson. McQueen and McGraw had a romance during filming and later married. Remade in 1993. 123m/C VHS, DVD, Blu-ray Disc, HD DVD. Steve McQueen, Ali MacGraw, Ben Johnson, Sally Struthers, Al Letieri, Slim Pickens, Jack Dodson, Dub Taylor, Bo Hopkins; *D:* Sam Peckinpah; *W:* Walter Hill; *C:* Lucien Ballard; *M:* Quincy Jones.

The Getaway 1993 (R) It was a bad movie in 1972 and the remake hasn't improved the situation. Doc and Carol are husband and wife crooks (played by marrieds Basinger and Baldwin). Doc gets double-crossed and winds up in a Mexican jail; Carol gets a well-connected crook (Woods) to spring her hubby--by sleeping with him and promising Doc will pull off another heist. The robbery's botched, there are double-crosses galore, and the couple go on the run. The stars are pretty but everything's predictable. An unrated version is also available. 110m/C VHS, DVD, HD DVD. Alec Baldwin, Kim Basinger, James Woods, Michael Madsen, Jennifer Tilly, David Morse; *D:* Roger Donaldson; *W:* Walter Hill, Amy Holden Jones; *C:* Peter Menzies Jr.; *M:* Mark Isham.

Getting Away With Murder woof! 1996 (R) An utterly distasteful bomb that proves the Holocaust just isn't as funny as it used to be. College professor Aykroyd takes matters into his own hands when he learns that his kindly neighbor (Lemmon) is a Nazi war criminal. After finding out he may have been a wee bit hasty, he marries the coot's daughter as penance. Writer-director Miller tries to squeeze gags out of such topics as Nazi death camps and Holocaust denial. Definitely career lows for everyone involved. (What were they thinking?) One of the last films released (with no advance warning and no advance screenings) by Savoy pictures. 92m/C VHS, DVD. Dan Aykroyd, Lily Tomlin, Jack Lemmon, Bonnie Hunt, Brian Kerwin; *D:* Harvey Miller; *W:* Harvey Miller; *C:* Frank Tidy; *M:* John Debney.

Getting Even 1986 (R) A maniac threatens to poison the entire population of Texas with a deadly gas unless he gets $50 million. An adventurous businessman sets out to stop him. 90m/C VHS. Edward Albert, Joe Don Baker, Audrey Landers; *D:* Dwight Little; *C:* Peter Lyons Collister.

Getting Even 1992 (R) Dundee and Evans served together in Vietnam. Fifteen years later they're reunited by the FBI to track a former Marine, who once betrayed Evans to the enemy. Seems he's now a drug trafiker and arms dealer who also gets his sadistic pleasures by killing women. The two ex-Marines find they have one last battle to fight. 93m/C VHS. Richard Roundtree, Michael J. Aronin; *D:* Leandro Lucchetti.

Getting Even with Dad 1994 (PG) Crook Danson can't find the money he stole in his last heist. Why? Because his precocious son has hidden it with the intention of blackmailing dear old dad into going straight and acting like a real father. Title is unintentionally funny in light of Mac's domineering dad Kit, who makes everybody in Hollywood want to go hide when he appears. Fairly bland family film squanders charm of Danson and Culkin, running formulaic plot into ground. Headly is likewise wasted as district attorney who prosecutes and then falls for Pops. 108m/C VHS, DVD. Macaulay Culkin, Ted Danson, Glenne Headly, Hector Elizondo, Saul Rubinek, Gailard Sartain, Kathleen Wilhoite, Sam McMurray, Dann Florek; *D:* Howard Deutch; *W:* Tom S. Parker, Jim Jennewein; *C:* Tim Suhrstedt; *M:* Miles Goodman.

Getting Gertie's Garter 1945 Light romantic farce that hinges on the fact the befuddled lead doesn't dare mention a lady's undergarment in public. (Yes, Virginia, there was a time when O'Keefe) has just obtained a swell promotion and is happily married to Patty (Ryan). But in his reckless youth, he gave former flame Gertie (McDonald) a bejeweled garter as a token of his affections. Now, Gertie is about to get married to Ken's friend Ted (Sullivan) and that darn garter is wantd by the District Attorney as evidence in a robbery. Ken needs to quietly retrieve the garter before Patty, Ted, the D.A., and Ken's stuffy board of directors gets wind of the scandalous trinket. Lots of slapstick farce moments such as hiding in closets and shimmying down drainpipes. 72m/B VHS, DVD. Dennis O'Keefe, Marie McDonald, Barry Sullivan, Binnie Barnes, Sheila Ryan, J. Carrol Naish, Jerome Cowan; *D:* Allan Dwan; *W:* Alan Dwan, Karen DeWolf; *C:* Charles Lawton Jr.

Getting Gotti 1994 (R) Story of the seven-year investigation and six-month trial by U.S. Attorney's Office prosecutor Diane Giacalone (Bracco) against reputed mobster "Teflon Don" John Gotti. (She lost.) 93m/C VHS, DVD. Lorraine Bracco, Anthony John (Tony) Denison, Kathleen Lasky, August Schellenberg; Kenneth Welsh, Ellen Burstyn, Lawrence Bayne; *D:* Roger Young; *W:* James Henerson; *M:* Patrick Williams. TV

Getting In *Student Body* 1994 (R) Pressured by the family tradition of attending Johns Hopkins Medical School, Gabriel Higgs (Mailer) decides to bribe the rivals ahead of him on the waiting list. But one of them (McCarthy) decides the easiest thing to do is murder the other candidates and frame Gabe. 94m/C VHS. Steven Mailer, Kristy Swanson, Andrew McCarthy, Dave Chappelle; *D:* Doug Liman; *W:* P.J. Posner, Joel Posner, Jonathan Lewin.

Getting It 2006 Teen sex comedy hero Silver is unlucky in love until by some twist of fate a rumor spreads about town that he has a two-foot (fill in the blank). Suddenly the ladies are lined up around the block to boyfriend young Silver. But alas, true love rules as he decides to woo back his dream girl. 97m/C DVD. Patrick Censoplano, Cheryl Dent, Sajen Corona, Sandra Staggs, Salvatore Crivello; *D:* Nick Gaitatjis; *W:* Nick Gaitatjis; *M:* Holly Amber Church. VIDEO

Getting It On 1983 (R) High school student uses his new-found video equipment for voyeuristic activity. 100m/C VHS, DVD. Martin Yost, Heather Kennedy, Jeff Edmond, Kathy Rockmeier, Mark Alan Ferri; *D:* William Olsen.

Getting It Right 1989 (R) A sweet-natured British comedy about an inexperienced, shy adult male who is quite suddenly pursued by a middle-aged socialite, a pregnant, unstable rich girl, and a modest single mother. Novel and screenplay by Elizabeth Jane Howard. 101m/C VHS. *GB* Jesse Birdsall, Helena Bonham-Carter, Lynn Redgrave, Peter Cook, John Gielgud, Jane Horrocks, Richard Huw, Shirley Anne Field, Pat Haywood, Judy Parfitt, Bryan Pringle; *D:* Randal Kleiser; *W:* Elizabeth Jane Howard; *M:* Colin Towns, Steve Tyrell.

The Getting of Wisdom 1977 A 13-year-old girl from the Australian outback tries to establish her identity and her individuality, within the restricting confines of a Victorian girl's boarding school. Based on the novel by Henny Handel Richardson. 100m/C VHS. *AU* Susannah Fowle, Hilary Ryan, Alix Longman, Sheila Helpmann, Patricia Kennedy, Barry Humphries, John Waters; *D:* Bruce Beresford.

Getting Out 1994 Arlie (DeMornay) is an ex-con on her way home to Georgia and what she hopes will be a reunion with the son she bore in jail. She thinks he's in a foster home but instead her mother (Burstyn) had the child adopted and if she interferes, Arlie's parole will be revoked. Arlie's trying desperately to rehabilitate herself but the system and old contacts are close to dragging her back down. TV movie adapted from Marsha Norman's 1977 play. 92m/C VHS, DVD. Rebecca De Mornay, Ellen Burstyn, Robert Knepper, Richard Jenkins, Carol Mitchell-Leon, Tandy Cronyn, Norman Skaggs; *D:* John Korty; *W:* Eugene Corr, Ruth Shapiro; *M:* Mason Daring.

Getting Over 1981 A black promoter is hired as a figurehead by a bigoted record company president and proceeds to try to run the company his own way. He develops an all-girl group called

|

"The Love Machine" and gets involved in a singer's kidnapping and a record company run by gangsters. Filled with clichés in shape and enters the work of 'female body building.' Crammed with workout scenes and disco music. 95m/C VHS, Alexandra Paul, Sandahl Bergman, David Naughton; "Buzz" Cooper. D: Bernie Rollins.

The Ghastly Ones woof! 1968 Three couples must stay in a haunted mansion to inherit an estate, but they're soon being violently killed off. No budget and no talent. Remade as "Legacy of Blood." 81m/C VHS, DVD. Don Williams, Maggie

Getting Physical ✓✓½ 1984 After being mugged, a secretary decides to get in shape and enters the world of 'female body building.' Crammed with workout scenes and stereotypes. 108m/C VHS, Gwen Bresc, Mary Hopkins, John Joff, Andrew

Getting Played ✓✓½ 2005

Getting Straight ✓✓ 1970 (R) A returning Vietnam soldier (Gould) goes back to his alma mater to secure a teaching degree and gets involved in the lives of his fellow students and the turbulence of the end of the '60s, including campus riots. A now-dated "youth" picture somewhat watchable for Gould's performance. 124m/C VHS, Elliott Gould, Candice Bergen, Jeff Corey, Cecil Kellaway, Jeannie Berlin, Harrison Ford, John Rubinstein, Robert F. Lyons, Max Julien; D: Richard Rush. VIDEO

Getting Up and Going Home ✓✓½ 1992 Jack (Sherritt) is a married man with a midlife crisis. So what does he do? Get involved with not one, but two, other women. Is he asking for trouble or what? Adapted from the book by Robert Anderson. 93m/C VHS Tom Sherritt, Blythe Danner, Roma Downey, Julianne Phillips, Bruce Kirby, Gary Frank, Dorian Harewood, Paul Sand; D: Steven Schachter; W: Peter Nelson.

Getting Wasted ✓✓½ 1980 (PG) Set in 1969 at a military academy for troublesome young men, chaos ensues when the cadets meet hippies. 96m/C VHS, DVD. Brian Kerwin, Stephen Furst, Cooper Huckabee, David Caruso, Stefan Angrim; D: Paul Fritzler; C: Daniel Pearl.

Gettysburg ✓✓✓ 1993 (PG) Civil War buff Ted Turner (who has a cameo as a Confederate soldier) originally intended Michael Shaara's Pulitzer Prize-winning novel "The Killer Angels" to be adapted as a three-part miniseries for his "TNT" network, but the lure of the big screen prevailed, marking the first time the battle has been committed to film and the first time a film crew has been allowed to film battle scenes on the Gettysburg National Military Park battlefield. The greatest battle of the war and the bloodiest in U.S. history is realistically staged by more than 5,000 Civil War re-enactors. The all-male cast concentrates on preserving the human cost of the war, with Daniels particularly noteworthy as the scholarly Colonel Chamberlain, determined to hold Little Round Top for the Union. Last film role for Jordan, to whom the movie is co-dedicated. The full scale recreation of Pickett's Charge is believed to be the largest period scale motion-picture sequence filmed in North America since D.W. Griffith's "Birth of a Nation." 254m/C VHS, DVD. Jeff Daniels, Martin Sheen, Tom Berenger, Sam Elliott, Richard Jordan, Stephen Lang, Kevin Conway, C. Thomas Howell, Maxwell Caulfield, Andrew Prine, James Lancaster, Royce D. Applegate, Brian Mallon, Cooper Huckabee, Bo Brinkman, Kieran Mulroney, Patrick Gorman, William Morgan Sheppard, James Kane, Warren Burton, Macintyre Dixon, George Lazenby, Alex Harvey, Joseph Fuqua, Ivan Kane, Patrick Stuart, Tim Ruddy, Richard Anderson, Billy Campbell, David Carpenter, Donal Logue, Dwier Brown, Mark Moses, Ken Burns, Ted Turner; D: Ronald F. Maxwell; W: Ronald F. Maxwell; C: Kees Van Oostrum; M: Randy Edelman.

Ghetto Blaster ✓ 1989 (R) A Vietnam vet takes on out-of-control street gangs to make his neighborhood safe. 86m/C VHS, R.G. Armstrong, Richard Hatch, Rich-ard Jaeckel, Harry Caesar, Rose Marie, Kamar De Los Reyes; D: Alan L. Stewart.

Ghetto Dawg ✓ 2002 (R) Standard urban actioner finds Tariq (J-King) wanting to escape his job working for mobster Gresh (Winslow) after falling for Robin (Coe). But Gresh wants Tariq to help him in his illegal pit bull fights and threatens to hurt Tariq's loved ones if he won't cooperate. 88m/C VHS, DVD. Drena De Niro, ...King, Portia Coe, Gianna Palminteri, Law-Rence Winslow, P.J. Marshal, Brian Averill; W: Allen Cognata; C: Shawn Kim; M: Wendell Hanes.
VIDEO

Ghetto Dawg 2: Out of the Pits ✓½ 2005 (R) Aimless teen Donte (Outlaw) has revenge on his mind when his brother is murdered. He joins the brother's violent crew but discovers he's not the killer type. Hooker girlfriend Brynn (Faith) comes up with a scheme to rip off crime boss Big Daddy (Torres) but there's one last thing Donte needs to do before blow-ing town with his squeeze and it involves dog-fighting competitions. A basic rehash of the first flick. 88m/C VHS, DVD. Daniel Out-law, Jianstra Faith, Lou Torres, Paris Campbell, J-King, Tany Sweating; D: Wendell Franklin; W: Horace Jackson, Robert H. Raff, Mike Rhodes; C: Mike Rhodes; M: Tom McIntosh.
VIDEO

Ghetto Revenge The Bus is Coming 1971 An embittered Vietnam vet gets caught between white supremacists and black 'radical activists in this coming home story. He returns and tries to build a life but succumbs to the desire for vengeance and things are never the same. 109m/C VHS, Mike Sims, Stephanie Faulkner, Burl Bullock, Tony Sweating; D: Wendell Franklin; W: Horace Jackson, Robert H. Raff, Mike Rhodes; C: Mike Rhodes; M: Tom McIntosh.

Ghidrah the Three Headed Monster ✓✓½ Ghidora; Ghidrah Sandai Kaiju Chikyu Saidai No Kessen; Ghidrah, the Three-Headed Monster; Ghidrah; The Greatest Battle on Earth; The Biggest Fight on Earth; Monster of Monsters 1965 When a three-headed monster from outer-space threatens the world, hu-mans, having nowhere else to turn, appeal to the friendly Mothra, Rodan, and Godzilla. Rock'em, sock 'em giant thrashing about as Tokyo once again gets trampled. Dependable afternoon monster 'ere complete with usual dubious dubbing. 85m/C VHS, JP Akiko Wakabayashi, Yosuke Natsuki, Yu-riko Hoshi, Hiroshi Koizumi, Takashi Shimura, Emi Ito, Yumi Ito, Keni Sahara, Hisaya Itc; D: Inoshiro Honda; W: Shinichi Sekizawa; C: Hajime Koizumi; M: Akira Ifukube.

The Ghost ✓½ Lo Spettro; Lo Spettro de Dr. Hitchcock; The Spectre 1963 A woman is driven mad by her supposedly dead husband and their evil housekeeper. Sequel to "The Horrible Dr. Hitchcock." 96m/C VHS, DVD. IT Barbara Steele, Peter Baldwin, Leonard Elliot, Harriet White, Harriet Medin, Umberto Raho; D: Riccardo Freda; W: Ricardo Freda, Oreste Biancoli; C: Raffaele Masciocchi; M: Franco Man-nino, Roman Vlad.

The Ghost ✓✓✓ 1990 (PG-13) Zucker, known for overboard comedies like "Air-plane!" and "Ruthless People," changed tack and directed this undemanding ro-mantic thriller, which was the surprising top grosser of 1990. Murdered investment consultant Sam Wheast (Swayze) at-tempts (from somewhere near the hereaf-ter) to protect his lover, Molly (Moore), from imminent danger when he learns he was the victim of a hit gone afoul. Gold-berg is medium Oda Mae Brown, who suddenly discovers that the powers she's been faking are real. A winning blend of action, special effects (from Industrial Light and Magic) and romance 127m/C VHS, DVD. Stephen (Steve) Root, Patrick Swayze, Demi Moore, Whoopi Goldberg, Tony Goldwyn, Rick Aviles, Vincent Schiavelli, Gail Boggs, Anne-Bruce Joel Rubin; D: Jerry Zucker; W: Bruce Joel Rubin; C: Adam Greenberg; M: Mau-rice Jarre. Oscars '90; Orig. Screenplay, Support. Actress (Goldberg); British Acad. '90; Support. Ac-tress (Goldberg); Golden Globes '91; Support. Ac-tress (Goldberg).

The Ghost and Mrs. Muir ✓✓✓ 1947 A charming, beauti-fully orchestrated fantasy about a feisty widow who, with her young daughter, buys a seaside house and refuses to be intimi-dated by the crabby ghost of its former sea captain owner. When the widow falls into debt, the captain dictates his sea ad-ventures, which she adapts into a suc-cessful novel. The ghost also falls into love with the beautiful lady. Tierney is exquisite and Harrison is sharp-tongued and comical. Based on R. A. Dick's novel. 104m/B VHS, DVD. Gene Tierney, Rex Harrison, George Sand-ers, Edna Best, Anna Lee, Vanessa Brown, Robert Coote, Natalie Wood, Isobel Elsom; D: Joseph L. Mankiewicz; W: Philip Dunne; C: Charles B'ryant; M: Bernard Herrmann.

The Ghost and Mr. Chicken ✓✓½ 1966 Fraidy cat Lu-ther Heggs (Knotts) works for a small town newspaper and longs to be a hot-shot re-porter. One night he thinks he sees a woman's corpse at the vacant Simmons mansion but of course there's no body when the cops come. The house is con-sidered haunted and there is a 20-year-old murder scandal, so Luther is very reluc-tantly persuaded to spend the night and solve the sinister goings-on. 90m/C VHS, Don Knotts, Joan Staley, Dick Sargent, Liam Redmond, Skip Homeier, Reta Shaw, Lurene Tut-tle, Philip Ober; D: Alan Rafkin; W: James Fritzell; C: William Margulies; M: Vic Mizzy.

The Ghost and the Darkness ✓✓½ 1996 (R) Based on the true story of two man-eating lions who killed 130 people and nearly derailed the building of the East African railroad in 1896. Engineer John Patterson (Kilmer) is sent to build a bridge over the Tsavo river, but as African liaison Samuel (Kani) in-forms him, Tsavo prophetically means place of slaughter. The workers become convinced the lions, nicknamed "The Ghost" and "The Darkness" are actually demons and, try as he might, Patterson has little luck killing the beasts. Then, leg-endary big game hunter Remington (Douglas) is called in—but the lions still seem to have the advantage. Lots of crunching bones, slurping blood, and quick cut editing is used to depict the lions' attacks. 110m/C VHS, DVD. Val Kilmer, Michael Douglas, Tom Wilkinson, Emily Mortimer, Henry Cele; D: Stephen Hopkins; M: Jerry Goldsmith, Oscars '96; Sound FX Editing.

The Ghost and the Guest ✓ 1943 Newlyweds spend their honeymoon in a house in the country only to find that gangsters are using the place as a hideout. Chases involving se-cret passages ensue. 59m/B VHS, DVD. James Dunn, Florence Rice, Mabel Todd, Robert Bice, Anthony Warde, Anthony Caruso, Edward Foster; D: William Nigh; M: Morey Amsterdam; C: James N. Toney, Robert E. Cline.

The Ghost Breakers ✓✓✓ 1940 As a follow-up to the Hope/Goddard 1939 comedy thriller "The Cat and the Ca-nary," this spooky comedy even bet-ter. Lots of laughs and real chills as Hope and Goddard investigate a haunted man-sion that she's inherited in Cuba. Effective horror scenes are expertly handled by di-rector Marshall. Remade in 1953 as "Scared Stiff" with Dean Martin and Jerry Lewis. Based on the play by Paul Dickey and Charles Goddard. 83m/B VHS, DVD. Bob Hope, Paulette Goddard, Richard Carlson, Paul Lukas, Willie Best, Pedro de Cordoba, Noble John-son, Anthony Quinn; D: George Marshall; W: Wal-ter DeLeon; C: Charles B'ryant; Lang Jr.

The Ghost Brigade ✓✓½ The Killing Box; Grey Knight 1993 (R) Civil War ghost story finds a Union general (Sheen) trying to discover who's slaughtering both Confederate and Union soldiers in the battlefield. So he sends Captain Harling (Pasdar) to investigate, with the help of rebel prisoner Strayn (Bernsen) and a slave (Williams). What they find is an evil brigade of soldiers—who already happen to be dead—and are eager for new re-

cruits. 80m/C VHS, DVD. Corbin Bernsen, Martin Sheen, Adrian Pasdar, Ray Wise, Cynda Williams, Roger Wilson, Billy Bob Thornton, Alexis Arquette, David Arquette, Roger Wilson, Dean Cameron, A.J. (Allison Joy) Langer, Matt LeBlanc; D: George Hickenlooper; W: Matt Greenberg; C: Kent Wake-ford.

The Ghost Camera ✓✓½ 1933 Slight story of a man falsely accused of murder. A photograph taken at the murder scene can prove his innocence if only the missing camera can be discovered. 68m/B VHS, GB Henry Kendall, Ida Lupino, John Mills; D: Bernard Vorhaus.

Ghost Chase ✓½ 1988 (PG-13) A young filmmaker desperate for funds in-herits his dead relative's clock, from which issues the ghost of the deceased's butler. The departed's secret fortune. Neither scary nor funny. 89m/C VHS, DVD. Jason Lve-ly, Jill Whitlow, Tim McDaniel, Paul Gleason, Chuck "Porky" Mitchell; D: Roland Emmerich; W: Roland Emmerich, Oliver Eberle; C: Karl Walter Lindenlaub.

Ghost Chasers ✓✓½ 1951 The Bowery Boys become mixed up in super-natural hijinks when a séance leads to the appearance of a ghost that only Sach can see. 70m/B VHS. Leo Gorcey, Huntz Hall, William Benedict, David Gorcey, Buddy Gorman, Bernard Gorcey, Jan Kayne, Philip Van Zandt, Lloyd Corri-gan; D: William Beaudine.

Ghost City ✓ 1932 Our hero must deal with a masked gang that is 'haunt-ing' a town. 60m/B VHS. Bill Cody, Helen Fos-ter, Ann Rutherford, John Shelton, Reginald Owen; D: Harry Fraser.

Ghost Crazy ✓✓ Crazy Knights 1944 Three wild comedians and a gorilla create mayhem in a haunted house. 63m/B VHS. Shemp Howard, Billy Gilbert, Maxie 'Slapsie' Ro-senbloom, Tim Ryan; D: William Beaudine W: Tim Ryan; C: Marcel Le Picard.

Ghost Dad ✓ 1990 (PG) A widowed workaholic dad is prematurely killed and returns from the dead to help his children prepare for the future. Cosby walks through doors, walls, and other solid ob-jects for the sake of comedy—only none of it is funny. 84m/C VHS, DVD. Bill Cosby, Denise Nicholas, Ian Bannen, Christine Ebersole, Dana Ashbrook, Arnold Stang; D: Sidney Poitier; W: S.S. Wilson, Brent Maddock; M: Henry Mancini.

Ghost Dance ✓ 1983 Sacred Indi-an burial ground is violated, with grim re-sults. 93m/C VHS, DVD. Sherman Hemsley, Hen-ry Bal, Julie Amato; D: Peter Buta.

Ghost Dog: The Way of the Samurai ✓✓½ 1999 (R) Jarmusch takes a Far Eastern approach to the Mob-hit man genre with "Dog," whose title character, a contract killer played excel-lantly by Whitaker, pledges himself to small-time hood Louie in the tradition of the Samurai after Louie saves his life. When one of his hits goes wrong, Ghost Dog is targeted for elimination, which leads to many dead bodies. Like most Jar-musch offerings, this one's quirky, disjoint-ed, and not for everyone, but Whitaker's performance and the offbeat humor make up for a lot. 116m/C VHS, DVD. Forest Whit-aker, Cliff Gorman, Henry Silva, John Tormey, Isaach de Bankole, Tricia Vessey, Victor Argo, Gene Ruffini, Richard Portnow, Camille Winbush; D: Jim Jarmusch; W: Jim Jarmusch; M: Robby Muller.

Ghost Fever woof! 1987 (PG) Two bumbling cops try to evict the inhabitants of a haunted house and get nowhere. A bad rip-off of "Ghostbusters." Alan Smi-thee is a pseudonym used when a director does not want his or her name on a film—no wonder. 86m/C VHS. Sherman Hemsley, Luis Avalos; D: Alan Smithee; W: Oscar Brodney.

The Ghost Goes West ✓✓✓ 1936 A brash American family buys a Scottish castle and transports the pieces to the United States along with the Scott-ish family ghost (Donat). Also along is the ghost's modern-day descendant (also payed by Donat) who comes to love the caretaker and in love with the new owner's daughter. It turns out to be up to the ghost to settle the two lovers together and find his own eternal rest. A rather lovable fantasy, Rene Clair's first English film. Available in digitally remastered stereo with original movie trailer. **90m/B VHS.** *GB* Robert Donat, Jean Parker, Eugene Pallette, Elsa Lanchester, Ralph Bunker, Patricia Hilliard, Everley Gregg, Morton Selten, Chili Bouchier, Mark Daly, Herbert Lomas, Elliot Mason, Jack Lambert, Hay Petrie; *D:* Rene Clair; *W:* Robert Sherwood, Geoffrey Kerr; *C:* Harold Rosson.

Ghost in the Machine ♂♂½
1993 (R) Serial killer dies while undergoing an X-ray scan and somehow, because of a lightning storm and a power outage, his soul manages to infiltrate the hospital's computer and go on to terrorize more victims via their home computers and appliances. (You expect this to make sense?) Outlandish, predictable flick hovers between high-tech horror and satiric comedy and wastes some pretty decent talent. Horror buffs may get a kick out of it but be forewarned: You may never view your microwave, dishwasher, or electrical outlets in quite the same way again. **104m/C VHS, DVD.** Karen Allen, Chris Mulkey, Ted Marcoux, Jessica Walter, Ric(k) Ducommun, Wil Horneff, Nancy Fish, Brandon Adams; *D:* Rachel Talalay; *W:* William Davies, William Osborne; *M:* Graeme Revell.

Ghost in the Noonday Sun woof! 1974 Crew of a treasure-seeking pirate ship sets sail for high sea silliness in this slapstick adventure film. Not a theatrical release for one obvious reason—it's terrible. **90m/C VHS.** *GB* Peter Sellers, Spike Milligan, Anthony (Tony) Franciosa, Clive Revill, Rosemary Leach, Peter Boyle; *D:* Peter Medak.

Ghost in the Shell ♂♂♂ Koukaku Kidoutai 1995 Major Motoko Kusanagi of the Security Police Section 9 is on the trail of a super hacker known as the Puppet Master. His techniques are so advanced that almost nothing is known about him. The time is 2029 and many people are cybernetically enhanced which allows the Puppet Master to make almost anyone his pawn. The more the Major works on the case, the more conflicted she becomes, for all that remains of her original body is a small slice of brain. In a world where the only humanity some people have are their ghosts (or souls), where they may or may not be within the shells (or bodies) they are born with, what happens when a ghost exists where it should not? Along with the philosophical questions about the nature of humanity that are heavily interlaced within the plot, this anime features a slick science fiction story and top-quality animation. Based on the story by Masamune Shirow. A special edition is available which includes the 30-minutes documentary "The Making of Ghost in the Shell." **82m/C VHS, DVD, UMD.** *JP D:* Mamoru Oshii; *W:* Kazunori Ito.

Ghost Keeper ♂ 1980 Three girls are trapped in a mansion with an old hag and various supernatural apparitions. **87m/C VHS.** Riva Spier, Murray Ord, Georgie Collins; *D:* Vernon Sewell.

Ghost of a Chance ♂♂ Eonios Filtis 2001 Vera is a dealer at a casino where med student Takis tries to make some cash. After becoming lovers, they rig a roulette game, take the money, and leave it with Vera's mother while they hide out at a friend's house. But their romantic dreams soon succumb to reality and when Vera returns home for her father's funeral, she's confronted by the casino boss who threatens her unless he gets his money back. Greek with subtitles. **100m/C VHS, DVD.** *GR* Maria Solomou, Emilios Chilakis, Mae Savastopoulou, Spyros Stavrinidis; *D:* Vangelis Seitanidis; *C:* Alekos Yannaros; *M:* Fotini Baxevani, Dimitris Tsakas.

The Ghost of Frankenstein ♂♂½ 1942 Fourth Frankenstein film in the Universal Studios series with Chaney filling in for Karloff as the monster. Not as good as its predecessors, but the cast is enjoyable, especially Lugosi as the monster's deformed sidekick, Ygor. Based on a story by Eric Taylor. **68m/B VHS, DVD.** Cedric Hardwicke, Lon Chaney Jr., Lionel Atwill, Ralph Bellamy, Bela Lugosi, Evelyn Ankers, Dwight Frye; *D:* Erle C. Ken-

ton; *W:* Scott Darling; *C:* Milton Krasner; *M:* Charles Previn.

The Ghost of Rashmon Hall ♂ *Night Comes Too Soon* 1947 Doctor tries to rid his home of the ghosts of a sailor, his wife and her lover. **52m/B VHS, DVD.** *GB* Valentine Dyall, Anne Howard, Alex Flavorsham, Howard Douglas, Beatrice Marsden, Arthur Brander, Antony Baird, Monti DeLyle, Nina Erber, John Desmond; *D:* Denis Kavanagh; *W:* Pat Dixon; *C:* Ray Densham.

The Ghost of Spoon River ♂♂♂ *The Mystery of Spoon River* 2000 (R) Chicago lawyer Emma Masters (Sinclair) heads home to defend her brother-in-law Jesse (McNamara) who's been accused of killing the local game warden. A killing that seems racially motivated and seems to tie into the town's dark past and a 1941 lynching. And despite the title, this standard thriller has really nothing to do with Edgar Lee Masters' "Spoon River Anthology." **90m/C VHS, DVD.** Lauren Sinclair, Brian McNamara, Richard Portnow, Michael Monks; *D:* Scott A. Meehan. **VIDEO**

Ghost of the Needle ♂ 2003 (R) Jacob (Avenet-Bradley) is a serial killer who likes to drug, photograph, and vacuum seal his female victims—watching as they suffocate. Except his latest victim, Aimee (Christian), is apparently getting her revenge from beyond the grave. **86m/C DVD.** Brian Avenet-Bradley, Frank Warlick, Greg Thompson, Leigh Hill; *D:* Brian Avenet-Bradley; *W:* Brian Avenet-Bradley; *C:* Laurence Avenet-Bradley; *M:* Mark Lee Fletcher.

The Ghost of Yotsuya ♂♂½ 1958 Based on the Japanese legend of a man who must betray his wife to gain the power he seeks. When he does, however, what follows is a horrifying revenge. In Japanese with English subtitles. **76m/C VHS.** *JP* Shigeru Amachi, Noriko Kitazawa; *D:* Nobuo Nakagawa; *W:* Yoshihiro Ishikawa; *C:* Tadashi Nishimoto; *M:* Michiaki Watanabe.

Ghost on the Loose ♂♂ 1943 The Bowery Boys take on Nazi spies. **65m/C VHS, DVD.** Leo Gorcey, Huntz Hall, Bela Lugosi; *D:* William Beaudine.

Ghost Patrol ♂♂½ 1936 A cowboy duo kidnaps the inventor of a ray gun in order to hijack mail planes, but they're stopped by G-man McCoy and friends. An odd hybrid of science fiction and western, to say the least. **57m/B VHS, DVD.** Tim McCoy, Walter Miller, Wheeler Oakman; *D:* Sam Newfield.

Ghost Rider ♂ 1935 A lawman is aided in his outlaw-nabbing efforts by the ghost of a gunfighter. **56m/B VHS.** Rex Lease, Bobby Nelson, Franklyn Farnum, Lloyd Ingraham, Eddie (Ed, Eddy, Edwin) Parker, Lafe (Lafayette) McKee; *D:* Jack Levine.

Ghost Rider ♂♂ 1943 Former footballer Brown rides the range once again, this time with an element of the supernatural nipping at his heels. **58m/B VHS.** Johnny Mack Brown, Raymond Hatton, Tim Seidel, Beverly Boyd, Milburn (Mit) Morante; *D:* Wallace Fox.

Ghost Rider ♂♂½ 2007 (PG-13) Critic-proof nonsense based on the Marvel comic character with the flaming skull head and motorcycle. Stunt rider Johnny Blaze (Cage) makes a deal with the devil (Fonda) who, naturally, doesn't follow through as intended. So Johnny is left as hell's bounty hunter, up against devil spawn Blackheart (Bentley). Beautiful Mendes is wasted in the girl role while Cage and Bentley overact; Fonda and Elliott stay cool, and viewers wait for some superhero fire to ignite. **108m/C DVD, Blu-ray Disc, UMD.** *US* Nicolas Cage, Eva Mendes, Wes Bentley, Sam Elliott, Donal Logue, Peter Fonda, Brett Cullen, Matt Long, Raquel Alessi; *D:* Mark Steven Johnson; *W:* Mark Steven Johnson; *C:* Russell Boyd; *M:* Christopher Young.

The Ghost Ship ♂♂½ 1943 A young sailor signs on as third mate on a ship, only to find out that the captain is a sadistic martinet who doesn't mind endangering his crew to prove his authority. Better than it should have been B-picture was supposedly commissioned because the studio had an expensive leftover ship set and wanted an excuse to use it. **69m/B VHS, DVD.** Richard Dix, Russell Wade, Edith Barrett, Lawrence Tierney, Steve Forrest, Ben Bard, Edmund Glover; *D:* Mark Robson; *W:* Don-

ald Henderson Clarke; *C:* Nicholas Musuraca; *M:* Roy Webb.

Ghost Ship ♂½ 1953 Young couple is tortured by ghostly apparitions when they move into an old yacht with a dubious past. Grade-B haunting featuring the murdered wife of the ship's former owner as the poltergeist. **69m/B VHS, DVD.** *GB* Dermot Walsh, Hazel Court, Hugh Burden, John Robinson; *D:* Vernon Sewell.

Ghost Ship ♂ 2002 (R) Promising premise sinks into formulaic horror-on-the-high-seas after a gruesome and startling beginning. A boat salvage crew led by Murphy (Byrne) is working in a remote area of the Bering Sea when they're led to the remains of a passenger liner that's been missing for more than 40 years. First mate Epps (Margulies) is the first crewmember to figure out that things are not as they should be, but the rest are caught in a web of greed that may have been the undoing of the ship's original passengers. **88m/C VHS, DVD.** *US* Julianna Margulies, Ron Eldard, Desmond Harrington, Isaiah Washington IV, Gabriel Byrne, Alex Dimitriades, Karl Urban, Emily Browning, Francesca Rettondini; *D:* Steve Beck; *W:* John Pogue, Mark Hanlon; *C:* Gale Tattersall; *M:* John (Gianni) Frizzell.

Ghost Son ♂♂½ 2006 Mark (Hannah) and his American wife Stacey (Harring) live on a ranch in South Africa. When he dies in a car crash, the suicidal Stacey begins to see (and feel) his ghost. After delivering a son, Stacey is certain that her baby is possessed by Mark's spirit and is out to kill her. **97m/C DVD.** Laura Elena Harring, John Hannah, Pete Postlethwaite, Coralina Cataldi-Tassoni, Mosa Kaiser, Mary Twala; *D:* Lamberto Bava; *W:* Lamberto Bava, Silvia Ranfagni; *C:* Tani Canivari; *M:* Paolo Vivaldi.

Ghost Story ♂♂ 1981 (R) Four elderly men, members of an informal social club called the Chowder Society, share a terrible secret buried deep in their pasts—a secret that comes back to haunt them to death. Has moments where it's chilling, but unfortunately they're here. Based on the best-selling novel by Peter Straub. **110m/C VHS, DVD.** Fred Astaire, Melvyn Douglas, Douglas Fairbanks Jr., John Houseman, Craig Wasson, Alice Krige, Patricia Neal; *D:* John Irvin; *W:* Lawrence D. Cohen; *C:* Jack Cardiff; *M:* Philippe Sarde.

Ghost Town ♂ 1937 Good guy Carey saves a mine from claim jumpers, but before he is mistakenly incarcerated as his friend's murderer, and then proved innocent. **65m/B VHS.** Harry Carey Sr.; *D:* Harry Fraser.

Ghost Town ♂♂½ 1988 (R) Fine sleeper about a modern sheriff who follows a gal through a supernatural sandstorm and discovers a literal ghost town of bad guys. **85m/C VHS.** Franc Luz, Catherine Hickland, Jimmie F. Skaggs, Penelope Windust, Bruce Glover, Blake Conway, Laura Schaefer; *D:* Richard Governor; *W:* Duke Sandefur; *M:* Harvey R. Cohen.

Ghost Town Gold ♂ 1936 The Three Mesquiteers series continues as the trio outwits bank robbers who have hidden their loot in a ghost town. **53m/B VHS, DVD.** Robert "Bob" Livingston, Ray Corrigan, Max Terhune; *D:* Joseph Kane.

Ghost Town Law ♂½ 1942 The Rough Riders step in to save the day when a group of outlaws defend their hideout by murdering anyone who approaches. **62m/B VHS, DVD.** Buck Jones, Tim McCoy, Raymond Hatton; *D:* Howard Bretherton.

Ghost Town Renegades ♂ 1947 A pair of government agents prevent a crook from gaining control of a mining town. **57m/B VHS.** Lash LaRue, Al "Fuzzy" St. John, Jennifer Holt; *D:* Ray Taylor.

Ghost Town Riders ♂½ 1938 An outlaw gang is holed up in an abandoned town, threatening to steal Shannon's gold mine, until Baker comes to the rescue. **55m/B VHS.** Bob Baker, Fay McKenzie, George Cleveland, Glenn Strange, Forrest Taylor, Hank Worden, Murdock MacQuarrie; *D:* George Waggner.

The Ghost Train ♂½ 1941 Badly dated mystery/thriller. Grating musical hall comedian Tommy Gander (Askey) causes a group of passengers to miss their con-

necting train and they are all forced to wait overnight in an eerie Cornish station. The stationmaster (Lornas) tells them that the station is haunted by a ghost train (the result of a deadly rail disaster) and that very night is the anniversary of the original tragedy. But what happens next turns out to be far less supernatural (note the film was made during wartime). **82m/B DVD.** *GB* Arthur Askey, Richard Murdock, Kathleen Harrison, Peter Murray-Hill, Herbert Lomas, Morland Graham, Carole Lynne, Betty Jardine, Stuart Latham; *D:* Walter Forde; *W:* Val Guest, J.O.C. Orton, Marriott Edgar; *C:* Jack Cox.

Ghost Valley ♂♂½ 1932 When Keene and Kennedy inherit land rich in unmined ore, the administrator (Harris) attempts to scare them off. To foil his plan, Keene conceals his identity and takes a job as the administrator's assistant. Based on a story by Adele Buffington. **54m/B VHS.** Tom Keene, Merna Kennedy, Mitchell Harris, Billy Franey, Harry Bowen, Kate Campbell, Ted Adams, Buck Moulton, Harry Semels, Al Taylor, Charles "Slim" Whitaker; *D:* Fred Allen.

The Ghost Walks ♂♂ 1934 A playwright has his new masterpiece acted out in front of an unsuspecting producer, who thinks that a real murder has taken place. But when the cast really does start disappearing, who's to blame? **69m/B VHS, DVD.** John Miljan, June Collyer, Richard Carle, Spencer Charters, Johnny Arthur, Henry Kolker; *D:* Frank Strayer.

Ghost World ♂♂♂ 2001 (R) Zwigoff makes his feature debut with this dark comedy that contains echoes of his documentary "Crumb." Enid (Birch) and Rebecca (Johansson) are not your typical acid-tongued teenage outsiders. Instead of struggling to fit in, they wear their contempt for the empty mall culture that surrounds them like a badge of honor. On a whim, the girls answer a personal ad from Seymour, a middle-aged schmoe who collects old records. Seymour, whose personal quirks are-similar to those of former Zwigoff documentary subject R. Crumb, is also baffled by modern culture and Enid is eventually drawn to him. She decides to help him in his attempt to find a woman, developing a special yet strange bond with him. Swinging from bleak to hilarious, the plot refuses to follow your standard romantic formula. That would be, like, so mainstream. Based on the underground comics of Daniel Clowes. **111m/C VHS, DVD.** *US* Thora Birch, Scarlett Johansson, Steve Buscemi, Brad Renfro, Illeana Douglas, Bob Balaban, Teri Garr, Stacey Travis, Dave Sheridan, Brian George; *D:* Terry Zwigoff; *W:* Daniel Clowes, Terry Zwigoff; *C:* Alfonso Beato; *M:* David Kitay. Ind. Spirit '02: Support. Actor (Buscemi); N.Y. Film Critics '01: Support. Actor (Buscemi); Natl. Soc. Film Critics '01: Support. Actor (Buscemi).

Ghost Writer ♂ 1989 (PG) A writer discovers the ghost of a movie star haunting her beach house, and together they solve the dead vamp's murder. **94m/C VHS.** Audrey Landers, Judy Landers, Jeff Conaway, David Doyle, Anthony (Tony) Franciosa, Joey Travolta, John Matuszak, David Paul, Peter Paul; *D:* Kenneth J. Hall.

Ghostbusters ♂♂♂ 1984 (PG) After losing their scholastic funding, a group of "para-normal" investigators decide to go into business for themselves, aiding New York citizens in the removal of ghosts, goblins and other annoying spirits. Comedy-thriller about Manhattan being overrun by ghosts contains great special effects, zany characters, and some of the best laughs of the decade. Oscar nominated title song written and sung by Ray Parker Jr. Followed by a sequel. **103m/C VHS, DVD, UMD.** Bill Murray, Dan Aykroyd, Harold Ramis, Rick Moranis, Sigourney Weaver, Annie Potts, Ernie Hudson, William Atherton, David Margulies, Steven Tash, Reginald VelJohnson, Timothy Carhart; *D:* Ivan Reitman; *W:* Dan Aykroyd, Harold Ramis; *C:* Laszlo Kovacs; *M:* Elmer Bernstein.

Ghostbusters 2 ♂♂½ 1989 (PG) After being sued by the city for the damages they did in the original "Ghostbusters," the boys in khaki are doing kiddie shows at birthday parties. When a river of slime that is actually the physical version of evil is discovered running beneath the city, the Ghostbusters are back in action. They must do battle with a wicked spirit in a painting or the entire world will fall prey to its ravaging whims. Murray is the high-light of this serviceable sequel, although MacNicol gives him a good run as the painting's henchman. 102m/C VHS, DVD, Bill Murray, Dan Aykroyd, Sigourney Weaver, Harold Ramis, Rick Moranis, Ernie Hudson, Peter Machi-chol, David Margulies, Wilhelm von Homburg, Har-ris Yulin; "Cheech" Marin, Brian Doyle-Murray, Janet Mar-golin, Mary Ellen Trainor; D: Ivan Reitman; W: Dan Aykroyd, Harold Ramis; C: Michael Chapman; M: Randy Edelman.

Ghosthouse *1988* It looks like an average suburban house, but it's haunted by the ghost of a little girl—and when she comes, evil is sure to follow. 91m/C VHS. Lara Wendel, Gregg Scott; D: Humphry Humbert.

Ghostriders *1987* One hundred years after their hanging, a band of ghost-descendents take revenge on the townfolk's descendents. 85m/C VHS. Bill Shaw, Jim Pe-ters, Ricky Long, Carl Powell, Mike Ammons, Ar-land Bishop; D: Alan L. Stewart.

Ghosts Can Do It *1990 (R)* Those jumping to conclusions, but is it possible this obscurity was titled to be reminiscent of the more publicized Bo Derek vehicle "Ghosts Can't Do It" comedy about a man who returns to his sexy wife despite her efforts at killing him. 88m/C VHS, AU Garry McDonald, Pamela Stephenson; D: Ted Robinson; W: Steve J. Spears; C: David Burr, M: Philip Scott.

Ghosts Can't Do It *1990 (R)* Dear Departed *1989* The Hound doesn't like jumping to conclusions, but is it possible this obscurity was titled to be reminiscent of the more publicized Bo Derek vehicle "Ghosts Can't Do It." comedy about a man who returns to his sexy wife despite her efforts at killing him. 91m/C VHS. Bo Derek, Anthony Quinn, Don Murray, Leo Damian; D: John Derek. Golden Raspberries '90: Worst Picture, Worst Ac-tress (Derek), Worst Director (Derek).

Ghosts Never Sleep *2005*

Ghosts of Berkeley Square *1947* The ghosts of two retired soldiers of the early 18th cen-tury are doomed to haunt their former home, and only a visit from a reigning monarch can free them. 85m/B VHS. Robert Morley, Felix Aylmer; D: Ver-non Sewell.

The Ghosts of Hanley House *1968* No-budget spooker with no-brain plot. Several unlucky guests spend an evening in a creepy man-sion...sound familiar? Shot in Texas. 80m/c VHS, DVD. Barbara Chase, Wilkie Je Martel, Elsie Baker, Cliff Scott; D: Louise Sherrill; M: Louise Sherrill; M: Craig Stuart Garfinkle. VIDEO

Ghosts of Mississippi *1996 (PG-13)* Director Reiner attempts to tell the story of civil rights leader Medgar Evers, murdered in 1963, and the three trials of Byron De la Beckwith (Woods), who was finally con-victed (after two hung juries) in 1994. Un-fortunately, he filters the story through the eyes of white assistant D.A. Bobby De Laughter (Baldwin) while ignoring Evers' accomplishments almost completely. Woods chews up the scenery as the wily old racist, bringing perhaps a bit too much glee into a portrait of true evil. Gold-berg sleepwalks through her role as Evers' widow, Myrlie; Evers' sons, Darrell and Van, play themselves; daughter Ree-na plays a juror while her character is played by Yolanda King, the daughter of slain civil rights leader Martin Luther King, Jr. Filmed on location in Jackson, Missis-sippi. 123m/C VHS, DVD. Alec Baldwin, Whoopi Goldberg, James Woods, Craig T. Nelson, Wayne Rogers, William H. Macy, Michael O'Keefe, Yolan-da King, Susanna Thompson, Lucas Black, James Pickens Jr., Virginia Madsen, Bill Cobbs, Alexa Vega, Jerry Levine, Bill Smitrovich, Terry O'Quinn.

Ghosts That Still Walk *1977* Spooky phenomena occur. The demons possessing a young lad's soul may be re-sponsible. 92m/C VHS, Ann Nelson, Matt Bos-ping Around. Tonight Is So Right For Love; What's She Really Like?; Pocketful of Rainbows; Got the Best I Can; Blue Suede Shoes. 104m/C VHS, DVD, Elvis Pres-ley, Juliet Prowse, Robert Ivers, Leticia Roman, Ludwig Stossel, James Douglas, Jeremy Slate; D: Norman Taurog; C: Loyal Griggs.

GhostWatcher *2002 (R)* A hor-rid ordeal makes Laura too scared to leave the house but then some evil spirits get worse when the ghost hunter she hires turns out to be a fraud. 94m/C VHS, DVD. Andy Wood, John Cross; C: Mac Ahlberg.

Ghostwarrior *Swordkill 1986 (R)* A 16th-century samurai warrior's ice-packed body is revived and runs amuck in the streets of modern-day Los Angeles. 86m/C VHS. Hiroshi Fujioka, Janet (Jckinson) Julian, Charles Howe, Rita Crafts; D: James T. Flocker.

Ghostwriter *1984* Based on Philip Roth's best-selling novel, the story of a writer coming to terms with his past. Roth co-wrote the screenplay. First seen on PBS. 90m/C VHS, Sam Wanamaker, Clare Bloom, Rose Arrick, Macintyre Dixon, Paulette Smit; D: Tristam Powell; W: Philip J. Roth. VIDEO

The Ghoul *1975 (R)* An eccen-tric English Egyptologist desires a sacred jewel to be buried with him and vows to come back from the grave if the gem is stolen. When that happens, he makes good on his ghostly promise. A minor hor-ror piece with Karloff only appearing at the beginning and end of the film. This leaves the middle very dull. 73m/B VHS, DVD, GB Boris Karloff, Cedric Hardwicke, Ernest Thesiger, Dorothy Hyson, Ralph Richardson, Anthony Bu-shell, Kathleen Harrison, Harold Huth, D. A. Clarke-Smith, Jack Raine; D: T. Hayes Hunter; W: Roland Pertwee, John Hastings Turner, Rupert Downing; C: Gunther Krampf.

The Ghoul *1934* An eccen-tric English Egyptologist desires a sacred jewel to be buried with him and vows to come back from the grave if the gem is stolen. When that happens, he makes good on his ghostly promise. A minor hor-ror piece with Karloff only appearing at the beginning and end of the film. This leaves the middle very dull. 73m/B VHS, DVD, GB Boris Karloff, Cedric Hardwicke, Ernest Thesiger, Dorothy Hyson, Ralph Richardson, Anthony Bu-shell, Kathleen Harrison, Harold Huth, D. A. Clarke-Smith, Jack Raine; D: T. Hayes Hunter; W: Roland Pertwee, John Hastings Turner, Rupert Downing; C: Gunther Krampf.

Ghoul School *1990 (R)* A young man gets more than he bargained for when he conjures up a batch of evil crea-tures in dark hallways. 90m/C VHS, DVD, Joe Franklin, Nancy Sirianni, William Friedman; D: Tim-othy O'Rawe; W: Timothy O'Rawe; C: Michael Raso; M: Rodney Shields.

Ghoulies *1984 (PG-13)* A young man who dabbled in the occult. Ridicu-lous but successful. Followed by three se-quels. 81m/C VHS, DVD, Lisa Pelikan, Jack Nance, Scott Thomson, Tamara DeTraux, Mars-Lisa Bercovici; C: Mac Ahlberg; D: Luca Bercovici; W: Luca Bercovici; M: Richard Band.

Ghoulies 2 *1987 (R)* Inept sequel to "Ghoulies" (1985), wherein the little de-mons haunt a failing carnival horror house, whose revenues begin to soar. Followed by a second sequel. 89m/C VHS, DVD. Damon Martin, Royal Dano, Phil Fondacaro; D: Albert Band.

Ghoulies 3: Ghoulies Go to College *1991 (R)* Third in the series has the best special effects and the worst storyline. Not satisfied with ripping off "Gremlins," this one imposes Three Stooges personae upon a trio of demons at large on a beer- and babe-soaked cam-pus. 94m/C VHS with Kevin McCarthy, Griffin O'Neal, Evan MacKenzie; D: John Carl Buechler.

Ghoulies 4 *1993 (R)* Dopey se-ries continues with the satanic creatures roaming the streets of Los Angeles, searching for a way to return to the r neth-e-world home. They get their chance when they meet a Satan-worshipping dominatrix out on a killing spree. 84m/C

Rex Linn, Richard Riehle, Bonnie Bartlett, Diane Ladd, Andy Romano, Rance Howard, Margo, Mar-Seale; M: Marc Shaiman.

G.I. Blues *1960 (PG)* Three G.I.'s form a musical combo while sta-tioned in Germany. Prowse is the ni-first film after his military service. *Shop-

VHS, Bobby DiGicco, Barbara Alyn Woods, Peter Paul Llapsis; D: Jim Wynorski; W: Mark Sevi.

Gia *1998 (R)* Based on the life of self-destructive supermodel/drug addict Gia Carangi (Jolie), who died from AIDS at the age of 26. Gia grew up in an abusive Philadelphia family and hid her insecuri-ties under a tough and wanton persona. Taken under the wing of New York model-ing exec Wilhelmina Cooper (Dunaway), Gia's exactness gets her noticed but the hedonistic lifestyle of the late 70s quickly leads to her downfall. Jolie goes all out for the title role. 120m/C VHS, DVD, Angelina Jolie, Mercedes Ruehl, Kylie Travis, Faye Dunaway, Edna Fe:ber novel, this epic saga covers Elizabeth Mitchell, Louis Giambalvo, John Consi-dine, Scot Cohen; D: Michael Cristofer; W: Mi-chael Cristofer, Jay McInerney; C: Rodrigo Garcia; M: Terence Blanchard. CABLE.

Giant *1956* Based on the Edna Fe:ber novel, this epic saga covers two generations of a wealthy Texas cattle baron (Hudson) who marries a strong-willed Virginia woman (Taylor) and takes her to live on his vast ranch. It explores the problems they have adjusting to life together, as well as the politics and preju-dice of the time. Dean plays the resentful ranch hand (who secretly loves Taylor) who wincs up striking oil and beginning to

G.I. Jane *1951* A TV producer faints when he gets his draft notice and dreams his company is stranded at a lone-ly army post with a lot of WACs. 62m/B Jordan O'Neil, Moore endures grueling training exercises and sexist remarks from male colleagues as she struggles to make a movie look great, even if it means writing doesn't quite measure up. 124m/C VHS, DVD, Blu-ray Disc. Demi Moore, Viggo Mor-tensen, Anne Bancroft, Jason Beghe, Scott Wil-son, Anne Chestnut, Lucinda Jenney, James (Jim) Caviezel; D: Ridley Scott; W: David N. Twohy, Danielle Alexandra; C: Hugh Johnson; M: Trevor Jones, Golden Raspberries '97: Worst Ac-tress (Moore).

G.I. Jane *1951*

G.I. War Brides *1946* Linda Powell (Lee) stows away aboard a ship heading for the States to find her soldier beau. She assumes the identity of English war bride Joyce Giles, who has decided she wants to stay in England. When Linda arrives, she discovers her G.I. no longer loves her and reporter Steve (Ellison) dis-covers Linda's deception but falls too in pretty English rose anyway. 69m/B VHS, Anna Lee, James Ellison, Harry Davenport, Wil-liam Henry, Robert Armstrong, Joseph (Joe) Saw-yer, Stephanie Bachelor,; Doris Lloyd, Mary McLeod, Carol Savage; D: George Blair; W: Jack K. Butler; C: Alfred S. Keller; M: Ernest Gold, Jo-seph Dubin.

Giant Steps *1992* Williams plays Slate Hopson, a moody jazz legend idolized by a talented young trumpet play-er. When the two meet Hopson clues the boy into some of life's lessons and redis-covers his own joy at making music. 94m/C VHS, Billy Dee Williams, Michael Mahonen; D: Richard Rose; W: Paul Quarrington, Greg Dum-mett; C: Paul Sarossy; M: Eric Leeds, Eric Leeds.

Giants of Rome *1963*

Giants of Thessaly *1960* Jason and Orpheus search for the Golden Fleece, encountering and defeat-ing monsters, wizards, and a scheming witch. 86m/C VHS, DVD, IT Roland Carey, Ziva Rodann, Massimo Girotti, Alberto (Albert Farley) Farnese; D: Riccardo Freda.

G.I. Executioner *Wit's End; Drag on Lady 1971 (R)* An adventure set in Singa-pore featuring a Vietnam veteran turned executioner. 86m/C VHS, DVD. Tom Keene, Victoria Racimo, Angelique Pettyjohn, Janet Wood, Walter Hill; D: Joel M. Reed.

The Giant Claw *1957* Giant winged (and stringed) bird attacks from outer space and scientists Morrow, Cor-day and Ankrum attempt to pluck it. Good, bad movie. Corday was Playboy's Miss October, 1958. 76m/B VHS, Jeff Morrow, Mara Corday, Morris Ankrum, Louis D. Merrill, Edgar Barrier, Robert Shayne, Morgan Jones, Clark Ho-well; D: Fred F. Sears.

Giant from the Unknown *Woof! 1958* Giant conquis-tador is revived after being struck by light-ning and goes on a murderous rampage. Unbelievably bad. 80m/B VHS, Edward Kemmer, Buddy Baer, Bob Steele, Sally Fraser, Morris Ankrum; D: Richard Cunha; W: Ralph Brooke, Frank Hart Taussig; C: Richard Cunha; M: Albert Glasser.

The Giant Gila Monster *1959* A giant lizard feels the nerve to disrupt teens to play Philipsdies, a marathoner (who uses a horse) trying to save Greece from invading Persian hordes. Lots of muscle on display but not much talent. 90m/C VHS, /T Steve Reeves, Mylene Demongeot, Daniela Rocca, Ivo Garrani, Alberto Lupo, Sergio Fantoni; D: Jacques Tourneur; C: Mario Bava.

The Giant of Metropolis *1961* Muscle-bound hero goes shirtless to take on the evil, sa-distic ruler of Atlantis (still above water) in 10,000 B.C. Ordinary Italian adventure, but includes interesting sets and bizarre torture scenes. 92m/C VHS, DVD, IT Gordon Mitchell, Roldano Lupi, Bella Cortez, Liana Orfei; D: Umberto Scarcel.

The Giant of Marathon *1960 (PG)* A meteorite carrying spider eggs crashes to Earth and soon the alien ara-chnids are growing to humongous propor-tions. Notoriously bad special effects, but the veteran "B" cast has a good time. 76m/C VHS, Steve Brodie, Barbara Hale, Leslie Parrish, Robert Easton, Alan Hale Jr., Dianne Lee Hart, Bill Williams, Christiane Schmidtmer, Kevin Brodie; D: Bill Rebane; W: Bill Rebane, Richard L. Huff, Robert Easton; C: Jack Willoughby.

The Giant Spider Invasion *1975 (PG)*

The Giants of Rome *1963*

fortune to rival that of his former boss. Dean's last movie—he died in a car crash shortly before filming was completed. 201m/C VHS, DVD. Elizabeth Taylor, Rock Hud-son, James Dean, Carroll Baker, Chill Wills, Den-nis Hopper, Rod Taylor, Earl Holliman, Jane With-ers, Sal Mineo, Mercedes McCambridge; D: George Stevens; W: Ivan Moffat, Fred Guiol; C: William Mellor; Oscars '56: Director (Stevens); AFI '98: Top 100; Directors Guild '56: Director (Ste-vens), Natl. Film Reg. '05.

ton Heston, Shirley Jones, Mike Connors, Harvey Korman, Barbara Bain, Taylor Nichols, Crystal Bernard, Mykelti Williamson, Christopher McDonald; **D:** Claudia Hoover; **W:** Brad Mirman; **C:** Joao Fernandes; **M:** Anthony Marinelli.

Gideon's Daughter ♂♂ 2005 Public relations whiz Gideon Warner (Nighy) is a professional star and a personal disaster. As he struggles to maintain some kind of relationship with estranged daughter Natasha (Blunt), Gideon finds unexpected romance with Stella (Richardson), who's grieving over the death of her young son. **144m/C DVD. GB** Bill Nighy, Miranda Richardson, Emily Blunt, Robert Lindsay; **D:** Stephen Poliakoff; **W:** Stephen Poliakoff; **C:** Barry Ackroyd; **M:** Adrian Johnston. **TV**

Gideon's Trumpet ♂♂1/2 1980 True story of Clarence Earl Gideon, a Florida convict whose case was decided by the Supreme Court and set the precedent that everyone is entitled to defense by a lawyer, whether or not they can pay for it. Based on the book by Anthony Lewis. **104m/C VHS.** Henry Fonda, Jose Ferrer, John Houseman, Dean Jagger, Sam Jaffe, Fay Wray; **D:** Robert E. Collins. **TV**

Gidget ♂♂1/2 1959 A plucky, boy-crazy teenage girl (whose nickname means girl midget) discovers romance and wisdom on the beaches of Malibu when she becomes involved with a group of college-aged surfers. First in a series of Gidget/surfer films. Based on a novel by Frederick Kohner about his daughter. **95m/C VHS.** Sandra Dee, James Darren, Cliff Robertson, Mary Laroche, Arthur O'Connell, Joby Baker; **D:** Paul Wendkos; **W:** Gabrielle Upton; **C:** Burnett Guffey.

Gidget Goes Hawaiian ♂♂ 1961 Gidget is off to Hawaii with her parents and is enjoying the beach (and the boys) when she is surprised by a visit from boyfriend "Moondoggie." Sequel to "Gidget" and followed by "Gidget Goes to Rome." **104m/C VHS, DVD.** Cindy Carol, James Darren, Jeff Donnell, Cesare Danova, Peter Brooks, Jessie Royce Landis; **D:** Paul Wendkos; **M:** John Williams.

Gidget Goes to Rome ♂1/2 1963 Darren returns in his third outing as boyfriend "Moondoggie" to yet another actress playing "Gidget" as the two vacation in Rome and find themselves tempted by other romances. Second sequel to "Gidget." **104m/C VHS, DVD.** Cindy Carol, James Darren, Jeff Donnell, Cesare Danova, Peter Brooks, Jessie Royce Landis; **D:** Paul Wendkos; **M:** John Williams.

The Gift ♂♂ 2000 (R) Widowed mom Blanchett uses her psychic gifts to help find the murderer of rich girl Holmes in their Georgia town. Among those involved are battered wife Swank, abuser Reeves, Holmes's fiance Kinnear and mentally slow tow-truck driver Ribisi. By-the-numbers thriller loses steam after a promising start, but is saved by the performances of a fine cast. The characters are stock Southern Gothic types, but they're given dimension by the portrayals. Raimi shows (early on) that he still knows how to startle an audience and create a creepy atmosphere. **112m/C VHS, DVD.** Cate Blanchett, Katie Holmes, Hilary Swank, Keanu Reeves, Greg Kinnear, Giovanni Ribisi, Rosemary Harris, J.K. Simmons, Chelcie Ross, John Beasley; **D:** Sam Raimi; **W:** Billy Bob Thornton, Tom Epperson; **C:** Jamie Anderson; **M:** Christopher Young.

The Gift Horse ♂♂ 1952 A WWII British naval officer dispatches his duties with an iron hand in an attempt to overcome the legacy of a court-martial eight years earlier. Angry rumblings from his crew threaten to upset the ship's stability. Against this foreboding backdrop, the Nazis give battle. Not historically accurate, but exciting. Based on a story by Ivan Goff and Ben Roberts. **99m/B VHS. GB** Trevor Howard, Richard Attenborough, Sonny Tufts, Bernard Lee; **D:** Compton Bennett; **W:** William Fairchild; **C:** Harry Waxman; **M:** Clifton Parker.

The Gift of Love ♂1/2 1990 Sacharine TV adaption of O. Henry's Christmas romance "The Gift of the Magi." **96m/C VHS, DVD.** James Woods, Marie Osmond, Timothy Bottoms, June Lockhart, David Wayne; **D:** Don Chaffey. **TV**

The Gig ♂♂1/2 1985 In this small, independently made film, a band of middle-aged amateur jazz musicians give up their stable occupations for a once-in-a-lifetime shot at a two-week gig in the Catskills. Film succeeds on the strength of it's well fleshed-out characters. **95m/C VHS.** Wayne Rogers, Cleavon Little, Warren Vache, Joe Silver, Daniel Nalbach, Andrew Duncan, Jay Thomas, Jerry Matz; **D:** Frank D. Gilroy; **W:** Frank D. Gilroy.

Gigi ♂♂♂♂ 1958 Based on Colette's story of a young Parisian girl (Caron) trained to become a courtesan to the wealthy Gaston (Jourdan). But he finds out he prefers her to be his wife rather than his mistress. Chevalier as always admiring eye on the ladies. Gingold is Gigi's grandmother and former Chevalier flame, and Gabor amuses as Gaston's current, and vapid, mistress. One of the first MGM movies to be shot on location, this extravaganza features some of the best tributes to the French lifestyle ever filmed. Score includes memorable classics. ♫Gigi; Ah Yes, I Remember It Well; Thank Heaven For Little Girls; The Night They Invented Champagne; She's Not Thinking of Me; It's a Bore; Gossip; I'm Glad I'm Not Young Anymore; The Parisians. **119m/C VHS, DVD.** Leslie Caron, Louis Jourdan, Maurice Chevalier, Hermione Gingold, Eva Gabor, Isabel Jeans, Jacques Bergerac; **D:** Vincente Minnelli; **W:** Alan Jay Lerner; **C:** Joseph Ruttenberg; **M:** Frederick Loewe. Oscars '58: Adapt. Screenplay, Art Dir./Set Dec., Color Cinematog., Costume Des., Director (Minnelli), Film Editing, Picture, Song ("Gigi"), Scoring/Musical; Directors Guild '58: Director (Minnelli); Golden Globes '59: Director (Minnelli), Film—Mus./Comedy, Support. Actress (Gingold); Natl. Film Reg. '91.

Gigli ♂ 2003 (R) The one where Ben met Jen. The title is pronounced "Geely" and is the last name of smalltime mobster hitman Larry (Affleck). His latest job is to kidnap and babysit a prosecutor's mentally impaired brother (Bartha in his film debut) as leverage in mob boss Starkman's (an overacting Pacino) trial, but he begins to feel sorry for his hostage. So his worried boss Louis (Venito) decides to send Ricki (Lopez), another contract killer, to keep an eye on them. Oh, and Ricki's a lesbian, which doesn't preclude Larry hitting on her. Not quite as bad as the film that made Hayworth into a Hollywood sex goddess. **124m/C VHS, DVD.** Ben Affleck, Jennifer Lopez, Justin Bartha, Christopher Walken, Al Pacino, Lainie Kazan, Missy (Melissa) Crider, Lenny Venito; **D:** Martin Brest; **W:** Martin Brest; **C:** Robert Elswit; **M:** John Powell. Golden Raspberries '03: Worst Picture, Worst Actor (Affleck), Worst Actress (Lopez), Worst Director (Brest), Worst Screenplay.

Gilda ♂♂♂1/2 1946 An evil South American gambling casino owner hires young American Ford as his trusted aide, unaware that Ford and his sultry wife Hayworth have engaged in a steamy affair. Hayworth does a striptease to "Put the Blame on Mame" in this prominently sexual film. This is the film that made Hayworth into a Hollywood sex goddess. **110m/B VHS, DVD.** Rita Hayworth, Glenn Ford, George Macready, Joseph Calleia, Steven Geray; **D:** Charles Vidor; **W:** Jo Eisinger, Marion Parsonnet; **C:** Rudolph Mate.

The Gilded Cage ♂♂ 1954 Two brothers are falsely accused of art theft and must find the real crooks in order to clear their names. **77m/B VHS. GB** Alex Nicol, Veronica Hurst, Clifford Evans, Ursula Howells, Elwyn Brook-Jones, John Stuart; **D:** John Gilling.

Gildersleeve on Broadway ♂♂1/2 1943 Longtime bachelor Throckmorton Gildersleeve (Peary) has finally proposed to girlfriend Matilda (Doran) when he decides to make a trip to New York. He has two purposes: to track down niece Margie's (Landry) wandering beau Jimmy (Road) and to help out town druggist Mr. Peavey (LeGrand), which leads him into the clutches of lonely widow (and pharmaceutical company owner) Laura (Burke). Soon there are three women, including blonde babe Francine (Carleton), after our man. Third of four films based on the radio serial "The Great Gildersleeve." **65m/B VHS.** Harold (Hal) Peary, Billie Burke, Claire Carleton, Ann Doran, Hobart Cavanaugh, Margaret Landry, Richard LeGrand, Freddie Mercer, Michael Road; **D:** Gordon Douglas; **W:** Robert E. Kent; **C:** Jack MacKenzie.

Gimme an F WOOf! ♂ T & A Academy 2 1985 (R) The handsome cheerleading instructor at Camp Beaver View ruffles a few pom-poms when he discovers that the camp's owner is about to enter into a shady deal with some foreigners. The film certainly deserves an "F" for foolishness if nothing else. **100m/C VHS.** Stephen Shellen, Mark Keyloun, John Karlen, Jennifer Cooke; **D:** Paul Justman.

Gimme Shelter ♂♂1/2 1970 The '60s ended as violence occurred at a December 1969 free Rolling Stones concert attended by 300,000 people in Altamont, California. This "Woodstock West" became a bitter remembrance in rock history, as Hell's Angels (hired for security) do some ultimate damage to the spectators. A provocative look at an out-of-control situation. **91m/C VHS, DVD.** Mick Jagger, Keith Richards, Charlie Watts, Bill Wyman, Mick Taylor, Mick Bailin, Grace Slick, Paul Kantner, Jerry Garcia, David Crosby, Stephen Stills, Graham Nash, Tina Turner, Ike Turner, Melvin Belli, Bill Graham; **D:** David Maysles, Albert Maysles, Charlotte Zwerin; **C:** Haskell Wexler; **M:** Rolling Stones.

Gin Game ♂♂♂ 1984 Taped London performance of the Broadway play about an aging couple who find romance in an old age home. Two-character performance won awards; touching and insightful. **82m/C VHS, DVD.** Jessica Tandy, Hume Cronyn; **D:** Mike Nichols.

Ginger ♂ 1972 Fabulous super-sleuth Ginger faces the sordid world of prostitution, blackmail and drugs. Prequel to "The Abductors" and followed eventually by "Girls Are for Loving." **90m/C VHS, DVD.** Cheri Caffaro, William Grannel, Calvin Culver, Cindy Barnett, Lise Mauer, Michele Norris, Linda Susoeff; **D:** Don Schain; **W:** Don Schain; **C:** R. Kent Evans; **M:** Robert G. Orpin.

Ginger Ale Afternoon ♂ 1989 A smutty comedy revolving around a triangle formed by a married couple and their sexy next-door neighbor. The film tries for fizz but only comes up flat. **88m/C VHS.** Dana Anderson, John M. Jackson, Yeardley Smith; **D:** Rafal Zielinski; **W:** Gina Wendkos; **M:** Willie Dixon.

Ginger and Cinnamon ♂ Dillo con Parole Mie 2003 Fun in the summer sun in this equally light romance set on a picturesque Greek island. Thirty-year-old Stefania (Montorsi) has broken up with longtime beau Andrea (Morelli) and ends up vacationing with 14-year-old neice, Meggy (Merlino), on Ios. Meggy's decided her vacation is the perfect opportunity to lose her virginity and she's found the perfect guy—who turns out to be Andrea. Italian with subtitles. **105m/C DVD. IT** Stefania Montorsi, Giampaolo Morelli, Martina Merlino, Alberto Cucca; **D:** Daniele Luchetti; **W:** Stefania Montorsi, Daniele Luchetti, Ivan Cotroneo; **C:** Paolo Camera.

Ginger & Fred ♂♂♂ 1986 (PG-13) An acclaimed story of Fellini-esque poignancy about an aging dance team. Years before they had gained success by reverently impersonating the famous dancing duo of Astaire and Rogers. Now, after 30 years, they reunite under the gaudy lights of a high-tech TV special. Wonderful performances by the aging Mastroianni and the still sweet Masina. Italian with English subtitles. **126m/C VHS, DVD. IT** Marcello Mastroianni, Giulietta Masina, Franco Fabrizi, Friedrich Von Ledenberg, Martin Blau, Toto Mignone; **D:** Federico Fellini; **W:** Federico Fellini, Tonino Guerra, Tullio Pinelli; **C:** Tonino Delli Colli; **M:** Nicola Piovani.

Ginger in the Morning ♂♂ 1973 A salesman is enamored of a young hitchhiker whom he picks up on the road. This is the same year Spacek played the innocent-gone-twisted in "Badlands." **90m/C VHS, DVD.** Sissy Spacek, Slim Pickens, Monte Markham, Susan Oliver, Mark Miller; **D:** Gordon Wiles.

Ginger Snaps ♂♂ 2001 (R) Modern teen horror goes for quite a ride. Teenaged sisters Ginger (Isabelle) and Brigitte (Perkins) are proud misfits in their quiet Canadian community. Then they're attacked by a werewolf in the woods and Ginger starts behaving very strangely (even for her). Brigitte turns to local pot dealer Sam (Lemche) for help while Ginger just gets more and more aggressive. **107m/C VHS, DVD. CA** John Bourgeois, Peter Keleghan, Emily Perkins, Katharine Isabelle, Kris Lemche, Mimi Rogers, Jesse Moss, Danielle Hampton; **D:** John Fawcett; **W:** Karen Walton; **C:** Thom Best; **M:** Michael Shields.

Ginger Snaps Back: The Beginning ♂♂ Ginger Snaps 3 2004 (R) The trilogy snaps back from the depths of hell in this prequel that finds sisters Ginger and Brigitte time-warped to 19th century Canada and seeking shelter from the woods at an all-male trading fort that—unbeknownst to them—has been trying to fend off those pesky werewolves. **94m/C VHS, DVD. CA** Katharine Isabelle, Emily Perkins, Nathaniel Arcand, J.R. Bourne, Hugh Dillon, Adrien Dorval, Brendan Fletcher, David La Haye, Tom McCamus, Matthew (Matt) Walker; **D:** Grant Harvey; **W:** Stephen Massicotte, Christina Ray; **C:** Michael Marshall. **VIDEO**

Ginger Snaps: Unleashed ♂ Ginger Snaps 2: The Sequel 2004 (R) In this why-did-they-bother sequel, it's Brigitte's turn to be afflicted with a case of the lycanthropy, but she keeps it at bay with wolfsbane. The whole thing goes haywire when she's taken to a rehab clinic after being mauled by another werewolf and can't take her meds. **93m/C VHS, DVD. CA** Emily Perkins, Katharine Isabelle, Janet Kidder, Tatiana Maslany, Eric Johnson, Pascale Hutton, Jack Mackinnon; **D:** Brett Sullivan; **W:** Megan Martin; **C:** Gavin Smith; **M:** Kurt Swinghammer. **VIDEO**

The Gingerbread Man ♂♂1/2 1997 (R) Lawyer Rick Macgruder (Branagh) falls for a scheming femme (Davidtz) who hires him to have her deranged, stalker father (Duvall) committed. Set in steamy Savannah, as Rick's unusual mousy partner, surprises with an unusually good performance. Grisham's first original screenplay. Studio Polygram disliked Altman's original cut, replaced his editor, and recut the movie to its own specifications, angering Altman who threatened to remove his name from the film. Though not an Altman masterpiece, sly thriller doesn't fail to entice. **114m/C VHS, DVD.** Kenneth Branagh, Embeth Davidtz, Robert Duvall, Tom Berenger, Daryl Hannah, Robert Downey Jr., Famke Janssen, Mae Whitman, Jesse James; **D:** Robert Altman; **W:** John Grisham, Al Hayes; **C:** Gu Changwei; **M:** Mark Isham.

The Girl ♂♂♂ 1968 The first of Meszaros' trilogy, dealing with a young girl who leaves an orphanage to be reunited with her mother, a traditional country peasant. In Hungarian with English subtitles. Meszaros' first film. Followed by "Riddance" (1973) and "Adoption" (1975). **86m/B VHS. HU** Adam Szirtes, Kati Kovacs, Teri Horvath; **D:** Marta Meszaros, Marta Meszaros; **W:** Marta Meszaros; **C:** Tamas Somlo; **M:** Levente Szorenyi.

The Girl ♂♂1/2 1986 (R) Nero is a wealthy attorney who agrees to pay Powney 300 crowns to have his way with her. Although somewhat ambivalent because of her scandalous age, he takes her anyway. Soon he informs his wife he needs to go on a long business trip, which fits in with her own adulterous plans. A snooping reporter (Brennan) out for some dirt upsets the apple cart, eventually leading to

Girl 🎬½ 1998 (R) 18-year-old Andrea Marr (Swain) is bored by her usual life and her virginity. She decides to try on the local club scene and spots musician Todd Sparrow (Flanery), becoming his groupie, and also taking up with cool chick singer Cybil (Reid) and her friends who are in a band. This try at self-discovery ultimately proves less-than-satisfying for Andrea. Lots of cliched issues are dealt with in the most cursory fashion. Based on the novel by Blake Nelson. 99m/C VHS, DVD. Dominique Swain, Sean Patrick Flanery, Tara Reid, Summer Phoenix, Selma Blair, Channon Roe, Portia de Rossi, Christopher K. Masterson, Rosemary Forsyth, James Karen; D: Jonathan Kahn; W: David E. Tolchinsky; C: Tami Reiker. M: Michael Tavera.

The Girl 🎬🎬 1998 (R) Suburban 18-year-old Andrea Marr (Swain) is bored by murder. 104m/C VHS. Franco Nero, Christopher Lee, Bernice Stegers, Clara Powney, Frank Brennan; D: Arne Mattson.

Girl from Chicago 🎬🎬 1932 In this crime melodrama a secret service agent falls in love while on assignment in Mississippi. When he's back in New York he finds a good friend of his girl's in serious trouble with the numbers racket. 69m/B C VHS, DVD. Starr Calloway, Grace Smith, Eugene Brooks, Frank Wilson; D: Oscar Michaeux.

Girl from Calgary 🎬½ 1932 A female rodeo champ ropes her boyfriends much like she ropes her cows, but not without a knock-down, drag-out fight between the two which forces our cowgirl to make the choice she seems to know is fated. Stock rodeo footage is intercut with the heroine riding an obviously mechanical bucking bronc. 66m/B VHS, DVD. Fifi d'Orsay, Paul Kelly; D: Phillip H. (Phil, P.H.) Whitman.

A Girl, 3 Guys and a Gun 🎬🎬 2001 (R) Stylish lesbian love story has a Paris artist meeting sultry nightclub singer and initiating a one-night stand which becomes a torrid affair. This upsets the club owner, who considers the singer his property. First-time director (and co-writer) Zeig has confidence and an eye for subtle nuance, but occasionally wanders into pretentiousness (an occupational hazard for a first-time director). Clare Keim, Agathe ce la Boulaye, Sandra N'Kake, Cyril Lecomte; D: Sande Zeig; W: Monique Wittig.

A Girl, a Guy and a Gob 🎬🎬 1932 The Navy Steps Out 1941 A shy rich boy falls in love with a girl who has her sights on another. Silly but enjoyable comedy. 91m/B VHS. Lucille Ball, Edmond O'Brien, George Murphy, Franklin Pangborn, Henry Travers, Lloyd Corrigan; D: Richard Wallace.

The Girl Can't Help It 🎬🎬 1956 Satiric rock and roll musical comedy about a retired mobster who hires a hungry talent agent to promote his girlfriend, a wanna-be no-talent singer. Mansfield's first starring role. Classic performances by some of the early greats including Eddie Cochran, Gene Vincent, the Platters, Little Richard, and Fats Domino. 99m/B VHS, DVD. Jayne Mansfield, Tom Ewell, Edmond O'Brien, Julie London, Ray Anthony, Henry Jones, John Emery, Juanita Moore, Barry J. Gordon Fats Domino, Abbey Lincoln, Eddie Fontaine, Little Richard, Eddie Cochran, Gene Vincent; D: Frank Tashlin; W: Frank Tashlin, Herbert Baker; C: Leon Shamroy; M: Lionel Newman.

Girl Crazy 🎬🎬 When the Girls Meet the Boys 1943 A wealthy young playboy is sent to an all-boy school in Arizona to get his mind off girls. Once there, he still manages to fall for a local girl who can't stand the sight of him. The eighth film pairing for Rooney and Garland. 7Sam and Delilah; Embraceable You; I Got Rhythm; Fascinating Rhythm; Treat Me Rough; Bronco Busters; Bidin' My Time; But Not For Me; Do. 99m/B VHS. Mickey Rooney, Judy Garland, Nancy Walker, June Allyson; D: Norman Taurog; C: William H. Daniels; M: Ira Gershwin.

Girl Happy 🎬🎬 1965 The King's fans will find him in Fort Lauderdale, Florida this time as the leader of a rock 'n' roll group. His mission: to chaperone the daughter of a Chicago mobster who naturally falls for him. Why not? 7Girl Happy; Cross My Heart and Hope to Die; Do Not Disturb; Spring Fever; Wolf Call; Do the Clam; Fort Lauderdale Chamber of Commerce; Puppet On a String; I've Got to Find About My Baby. 96m/C VHS, DVD. Elvis Presley, Shelley Fabares, Gary Crosby, Nita Talbot, Mary Ann Mobley, Jackie Coogan; D: Boris Sagal; W: Harvey Bullock.

Girl Hunters 🎬🎬½ 1963 That intrepid private eye, Mike Hammer (played by his creator, Spillane), is caught up with communist spies, wicked women, and a missing secretary. Hammer is his usual self.

Girl from Hunan 🎬🎬🎬 1986 Turn-of-the-century China, a 12-year-old girl is married to a two-year-old boy in a typical arranged marriage. She grows into womanhood treating her toddler husband with sibling affection, but conducts a secret love affair with a farm laborer. Intolerant village laws against adultery place her life in jeopardy. In Mandarin with English subtitles. 99m/C VHS. Na Renhua, Deng Xiaoguang, Yu Zhang; D: Xie Fei.

The Girl from Missouri 🎬🎬🎬 One Hundred Percent Pure 1934 Cute comedy in which Harlow tries to snag a millionaire without sacrificing her virtues. Lots of laughs and hilarious action, especially the scene where Harlow arrives at the yacht in Florida. Kelly is great as Harlow's wise-cracking girlfriend. Witty dialogue by Emerson and Loos, who also wrote "Gentlemen Prefer Blondes." 75m/B VHS. Jean Harlow, Lionel Barrymore, Franchot Tone, Lewis Stone, Patsy Kelly, Alan Mowbray, Clara Blandick, Russell Hopton, John David Horsley; D: Jack Conway; W: Anita Loos, John Emerson.

The Girl from Paris 🎬🎬🎬 Une Hirondelle a Fait le Printemps 2002 A Parisian internet worker leaves the city and buys a mountaintop farm from a cranky farmer, Sandrine (Seigner) gives up her high-stress city life and buys a goat farm from Adrien (Serrault), who's ready to be done with farming but resentfully agrees to stick around for 18 months to help out. Sandrine initially does big business through internet advertising, crawling visitors who buy the farm's products and sleep in the barn, but soon must confront the harsh, relentless realities of managing a farm by herself. As she does, her adversarial relationship with Adrien evolves into a friendship. Moves a bit slowly, but farm-raised Carion directs it with sincerity and precision, and creates an honest story of country life and the relationships it builds. 103m/ C DVD. FR Michel Serrault, Mathilde Seigner, Jean-Paul Roussillon, Frederic Pierrot, Marc Berman, Francoise Bette; D: Christian Carion; W: Christian Carion, Eric Assous; C: Antoine Heberle; M: Philippe Rombi.

The Girl from Petrovka 🎬½ 1974 (PG) A high-spirited Russian ballerina falls in love with an American newspaper correspondent. Their romance is complicated by the suspicious KGB. Bittersweet with a bleak ending. 103m/C VHS. Goldie Hawn, Hal Holbrook, Anthony Hopkins; D: Robert Ellis Miller; W: Chris Bryant, Allan Scott; M: Henry Mancini.

The Girl from Tobacco Row 🎬 1966 A Southern slut involved with a cache of stolen cash fools with both a convict and the sheriff. 90m/C VHS. Tex Ritter, Rachel Romen, Earl Richards, Tim Ormond, Rita Faye, Ralph Emery; D: Ron Ormond.

The Girl Getters 🎬🎬 The System 1966 Tinker (Reed) and his rowdy London pals take a vacation at a seaside resort, where they proceed to pick fights, chase girls, and cause general (minor) mayhem. Tinker's busy chasing Nicola (Merrow) but surprises himself when he actually stars to fall for her. 79m/B VHS. GB Oliver Reed, Jane Merrow, David Hemmings, John Alderton, Harry Andrews; D: Michael Winner; W: Peter Draper; C: Nicolas Roeg.

Girl in Gold Boots 🎬 1969 Aspiring starlet meets up with a draft evader and a biker on her way to Hollywood where she gets a job as a go-go dancer in a sleazy club. But things don't go smoothly when a murder and a drug theft are revealed. 7Do You Want to Laugh or Cry?; For You; Hello, Michelle; One Good Time; One Good Place; Lonesome Man; You Gotta Come Down; Everything I Touch Turns to Gold; Cowboy Santa; Wheels of Love. 91m/C VHS, DVD. Jody Daniels, Leslie McRae, Tom Pace, Mark Herron; D: Ted V. Mikels; W: Art Names, Leighton J. Peatman, John T. Wilson; C: Robert Maxwell; M: Nicholas Carras.

Girl in His Pocket 🎬🎬 Amour de Poche; Nude in His Pocket 1957 Mad scientist creates a potion that turns things into three-inch statues. He uses it mostly to have trysts with his lab assistant so his fiancee won't find out. Based on "The Diminishing Draft" by Waldemar Kaempfert.

The Girl in a Swing 🎬🎬 1989 (R) An Englishman impulsively marries a beautiful German girl and both are subsequently haunted by phantoms from her past—are they caused by her psychic powers? Cliche-ridden silliness. Based on the Richard Adams novel. 119m/C VHS, DVD. Meg Tilly, Rupert Frazer, Elspet Gray, Lynsey Baxter, Nicholas Le Prevost, Jon Kroll; D: Gordon Hessler.

Girl in Black 🎬🎬 To Koritsi Me Ta Mavra 1956 The shy daughter of a once wealthy household gets the chance to experience her genteel poverty when she falls in love with the young man boarding with her family. He is attracted to her but a shocking tragedy changes everything. In Greek with English subtitles. 100m/B VHS, DVD. GR Elli Lambetti, Eleni Zafirou, Georges Foundas, Dimitri Horne, Stefanos Stratigos; D: Michael Cacoyannis; W: Michael Cacoyannis; C: Walter Lassally; M: Manos Hadjidakis.

Girl in Black Stockings 🎬🎬 1957 Beautiful women are mysteriously murdered at a remote, Utah hotel. Interesting little known thriller similar to Hitchcock's "Psycho," but pre-dating it by three years. 75m/B VHS. Lex Barker, Anne Bancroft, Mamie Van Doren, Ron Randell, Marie Windsor, John Dehner, John Holland, Diana Van Der Vlis; D: Howard W. Koch; M: Les Baxter.

The Girl in Blue 🎬🎬 1974 (R) A lawyer, ill at ease with his current romance, suddenly decides to search for a beautiful woman he saw once, and instantly fell in love with years before. 103m/ C VHS, DVD, CA Maud Adams, David Selby, Gay Rowan, William Osler, Diane Dewey, Michael Kirby; D: George Kaczender.

A Girl in Every Port 🎬 1928 Sailors Spike (McLaglen) and Salami (Armstrong) travel the world in search of adventure and games. Spike thinks he's found true love with French gold-digger Marie (flapper Brooks) but Salami convinces him otherwise. 62m/B VHS. Victor McLaglen, Robert Armstrong, Louise Brooks, Natalie Joyce; D: Howard Hawks; W: Seton I. Miller; C: L.W. O'Connell, Rudolph Bergquist.

A Girl in Every Port 🎬½ 1952 Navy buddies acquire an ailing racehorse and try to conceal it aboard ship along with a healthy horse they plan to switch it with in an upcoming race. Groucho flies without his brothers in this film. 86m/B VHS. Groucho Marx, William Bendix, Marie Wilson, Don DeFore, Gene Lockhart; D: Chester Erskine.

A Girl in a Million 🎬🎬 1946 Williams dumps his verbose wife and seeks peace and quiet in a men-only War Department office. All is well until the arrival of a colonel and his daughter, mute from trauma. Finding her silence appealing, he marries her, but another trauma restores her speech. Sexist comedy may have played better in its day. 90m/B VHS. GB Hugh Williams, Joan Greenwood, Naunton Wayne, Wylie Watson, Garry Marsh; D: Francis Searle.

Girl, Interrupted 🎬🎬½ 1999 (R) Ryder stars as neurotic 18-year-old Susanna who, after making a half-hearted suicide attempt, is diagnosed with borderline personality disorder. So, in 1967, she's sent to Claymoore, a psychiatric hospital outside Boston, where she'll spend the next two years. There, Susanna meets some young woman who are truly disturbed, including compelling sociopath, Lisa (Jolie). Yes, the story's predictable but it's also touching—just don't expect the fireworks of "One Flew Over a Cuckoo's Nest." Based on the 1993 memoir by Susanna Kaysen. 127m/C VHS, DVD. Winona Ryder, Angelina Jolie, Vanessa Redgrave, Whoopi Goldberg, Clea DuVal, Brittany Murphy, Elisabeth (Elisabeth, Elizabeth, Liz) Moss, Jared Leto, Jeffrey Tambor, Mary Kay Place; D: James

judge-and-jury character but the action is fast-paced. 103m/B VHS, DVD. Mickey Spillane, Lloyd Nolan, Shirley Eaton, Hy Gardner, Scott Peters, Charles Farrell; D: Roy Rowland; W: Roy Rowland, Robert Fellows; C: Ken Talbot; M: Phillip Green.

The Girl in the Cadillac 🎬🎬½ 1994 (R) Modern-day B-movie wanna-be loosely adapted from the James M. Cain novella "The Enchanted Isle." 17-year-old freespirited Amanda (Eleniak) wants to get out of stifling small town Texas. She buys a bus ticket to find her long-gone daddy and winds up with not-too-smart cowpoke Rick (McNamara) instead. An El Dorado convertible, and Rick's partners, can't overcome the cliches. 89m/C VHS. Erika Eleniak, William McNamara, Michael Lerner, Bud Cort, Valente Pernie, Ed Lauter, William Shockley; D: Lucas Platt; W: John Warren; C: Nancy Schreiber; M: Anton Sanko.

The Girl in the Cafe 🎬🎬 2005 When a tender but offbeat romance develops between Lawrence (Nighy), a mellow-and-lonely middle-aged British public official, and Gina (MacDonald), a younger New Agar, he decides to take her along on his trip to the G8 Summit in Iceland but is taken aback when she abruptly shocks the crowd with a rant about starvation of African children. 95m/C DVD. Bill Nighy, Kelly Macdonald, Ken Stott, Penny Downe, Meneka Das; D: David Yates; W: Richard Curtis. C.A.B.L.E.

The Girl in the Picture 🎬🎬½ 1986 (PG-13) Sinclair stars in this light comedy as an unlucky photo clerk who discovers only too late that his ex-girlfriend may be the woman of his dreams. Typical understated but entertaining effort. 89m/C VHS. GB John Gordon-Sinclair, Irina Brook, David McKay, Catherine Guthrie, Paul Young, Gregor Fisher; D: Cary Parker.

The Girl in the Red Velvet Swing 🎬🎬 1955 Rather genteel reworking of a 1906 New York society scandal. Evelyn Nesbit (Collins) is a hotsy showgirl who's being courted by famous married architect Stanford White (Milland). However, Evelyn marries wealthy-but-unstable society boy Harry Thaw (Granger), who is pathologically jealous of Evelyn's relationship with White and shoots him dead in public. Then he uses an insanity plea (and family money) to avoid the death penalty in the ensuing trial. Collins is catnip but her character is depicted as boringly naive. 109m/C DVD. Joan Collins, Ray Milland, Farley Granger, Luther Adler, Glenda Farrell, Cornelia Otis Skinner, Frances Fuller, Philip Reed, Gale Robbins, John Hoyt, Harvey Stephens, Emile Meyer, Richard Travis, Jack Raine, Ainslie Pryor, Kay Hammond, Kay Hammond, Edith Evanson; D: Richard Fleischer; W: Walter Reisch, Charles Brackett; C: Milton Krasner; M: Leigh Harline, Edward B. Powell.

Girl in the Cadillac 82m/C VHS, FR Jean Marais, Genevieve Page, Agnes Laurent, D: Pierre Kast; C: Ghislain Cloquet.

The Girl in Lover's Lane 🎬🎬 1960 A drifter falls in love with a small town girl but becomes a murder suspect when she turns up dead. Interesting mainly for Elam's uncharacteristic portrayal of a village idiot. 78m/B VHS, DVD. Brett Halsey, Joyce Meadows, Lowell Brown, Jack Elam; D: Charles R. Rondeau.

The Girl in Room 2A woof! 1976 (R) A young woman is trapped in a mansion with the elderly owner and her demented son. Routine horrorfest. 90m/C VHS. Raf Vallone, Daniela Giordano; D: William

Mangold; **W:** James Mangold, Anna Hamilton Phelan, Lisa Loomer; **C:** Jack N. Green; **M:** Mychael Danna. Oscars '99: Support. Actress (Jolie); Golden Globes '00: Support. Actress (Jolie); Screen Actors Guild '99: Support. Actress (Jolie); Broadcast Film Critics '99: Support. Actress (Jolie).

The Girl Most Likely 🦴🦴½
1957 Light musical comedy about a romance-minded girl who dreams of marrying a wealthy, handsome man. She runs into a problem when she finds three prospects. Remake of 1941's "Tom, Dick and Harry" with Ginger Rogers. Choreography by great Gower Champion. ♫The Girl Most Likely; All the Colors of the Rainbow; I Don't Know What I Want; Balboa; We Gotta Keep Up With the Joneses; Crazy Horse. **98m/C VHS.** Jane Powell, Cliff Robertson, Tommy Noonan, Kaye Ballard, Una Merkel; **D:** Mitchell Leisen; **C:** Leon Shamroy; **M:** Cyril Mockridge.

The Girl Next Door 🦴🦴½ 1953
Widowed comic strip writer Bill Carter (Dailey) is a single dad to 10-year-old son Joe (Gray). Then pretty nightclub star Jeannie (Haver) moves in next-door and their romance causes friction. Haver's last film before she decided to enter a convent for several months. **92m/C DVD.** Dan Dailey, June Haver, Billy Gray, Dennis Day, Cara Williams, Natalie Schafer; **D:** Richard Sale; **W:** Isobel Lennart; **C:** Leon Shamroy; **M:** Cyril Mockridge.

The Girl Next Door 🦴🦴 1998 (R)
Married doctor Czerny agrees to keep an eye on his neighbor's 18-year-old hotbabe daughter (Shannon) while her parents are out of town. Only he takes the good neighbor relationship too far. When the teen winds up dead, the local Sheriff (Busey) is out to discover just what happened. **100m/C VHS, DVD.** CA Henry Czerny, Gary Busey, Polly Shannon, Robin Gammell, Alberta Watson, Simon MacCorkindale; **D:** Eric Till.

The Girl Next Door 🦴🦴 2004 (R)
Porn goddess Danielle (Cuthbert) moves to suburbia to taunt and tease nerdy teen next door, Matt (Hirsch). The two meet cute and a "Risky Business" redo ensues: Matt hooks up with Danielle, to the delight of his two geeky friends (Marquette and Dano), who inform Matt of the illicit past Danielle is trying to leave behind. That past includes former producer Olyphant, who shows up to woo Danielle back to "the life" while schooling the studious Matt in the ways of the world. He must then juggle a trip to a Vegas porn convention and work on a speech on morality to win a scholarship to Georgetown. Though Cuthbert and Hirsch are attractive and have decent chemistry, it's Olyphant that scores with an above average comedic performance in this otherwise uninspired genre fare. **108m/C DVD.** US Elisha Cuthbert, Emile Hirsch, Timothy Olyphant, James Remar, Christopher Marquette, Paul Franklin Dano, Timothy Bottoms, Donna Bullock, Amanda Swisten, Jacob Young, Brian Kolodziej; **D:** Luke Greenfield; **W:** David T. Wagner, Brent Goldberg, Stuart Blumberg; **C:** Jamie Anderson; **M:** Paul Haslinger.

Girl of the Golden West 🦴🦴 1938 A musical version of the David Belasco chestnut about a Canadian frontier girl loving a rogue. One of Eddy and MacDonald's lesser efforts but features Ebsen's song and dance talents. ♫Camptown Races; Shadows on the Moon; Soldiers of Fortune; Soldiers on the Moon Reprise; The Wind in the Trees; Liebestraum; Ave Maria; Senorita. **120m/B VHS.** Jeanette MacDonald, Nelson Eddy, Walter Pidgeon, Leo Carrillo, Buddy Ebsen, Leonard Penn, Priscilla Lawson, Bob Murphy, Olin Howlin, Cliff Edwards, Billy Bevan; **D:** Robert Z. Leonard.

A Girl of the Limberlost 1990 A young Indiana farmgirl fights to bring her estranged parents back together, in spite of a meddling aunt and the unexplained phenomena that haunt her. Fine acting and beautiful scenery. Originally broadcast as part of PBS's "Wonderworks" family movie series, it's best appreciated by young teens. Adapted from Gene Stratton Porter's much-filmed novel. **120m/C VHS, DVD.** Annette O'Toole, Joanna Cassidy, Heather Fairfield; **D:** Burt Brinckerhoff; **W:** Pamela Douglas; **C:** Gordon C. Lonsdale; **M:** Misha Segal. TV

The Girl of Your Dreams 🦴🦴½
(R) La niña de tus ojos 1999 Macarena Granada (Cruz) headlines a troop of Spanish actors who travel from their war-torn country to Berlin in 1938 to turn an Andalusian musical into a movie. Things get grimly messy when she seeks to rescue a prisoner from a nearby concentration camp. In Spanish, with subtitles. **121m/C VHS, DVD.** Penelope Cruz, Antonio Resines, Jorge Sanz, Rosa Maria Sarda, Santiago Segura, Loles Leon, Jesus Bonilla, Neus Asensi, Miroslav Taborsky, Karel Dobry, Johannes Silberschneider, Goetz Otto, Hanna Schygulla, Maria Barranco, Juan Luis Gallardo, Heinz Rilling, Jan Preucil, Borivoj Navratil, Martin Fafyn, Otto Sevcik; **D:** Fernando Trueba; **W:** Rafael Azcona, Miguel Angel Egea, Carlos Lopez, David Trueba; **C:** Javier Aguirresarobe; **M:** Antoine Duhamel. VIDEO

Girl on a Chain Gang woof!
1965 A girl on the run gets caught by police and does her time on a chain gang—predictable. **96m/B VHS.** William Watson, Julie Ange, R.K. Charles; **D:** Jerry Gross; **W:** Jerry Gross.

The Girl on a Motorcycle 🦴🦴
Naked under Leather; La Motocyclette 1968 (R) Singer Faithfull is a bored housewife who dons black leather and hops on her motorcycle to meet up with her lover (Delon), all the while remembering their other erotic encounters. **92m/C VHS, DVD.** GB Alain Delon, Marianne Faithfull, Roger Mutton; **D:** Jack Cardiff; **W:** Gillian Freeman, Ronald Duncan; **C:** Jack Cardiff; **M:** Les Reed.

A Girl on Her Own 🦴🦴 1976 A young actress embarking on her first big role in Paris must also deal with family and political considerations in this drama set during the political upheaval of 1935. **112m/C VHS.** FR Sophie Chemineau, Bruno La Brasca; **D:** Philippe Nahon.

The Girl on the Bridge 🦴🦴🦴
Le Fille sure le Pont 1998 (R) An unconventional romance that finds middle-aged professional knife-thrower Gabor (Auteuil) calmly engaging in conversation with suicidal Adele (Paradis), the titular character. After a young lifetime of perpetual bad luck, what could be better for Adele than to risk everything every night by becoming Gabor's new partner. The duo seem to have a telepathic communication that makes their characters maintain a hands-off relationship. French with subtitles. **92m/B VHS.** FR Daniel Auteuil, Vanessa Paradis, Demetre Georgalas, Isabelle Petit-Jacques; **D:** Patrice Leconte; **W:** Serge Frydman; **C:** Jean-Marie Dreujou. Cesar '00: Actor (Auteuil).

Girl Play 🦴🦴 2004 When two lesbians meet while doing a play they begin to fall for one another despite the fact Robin (Greenspan) has a long-term partner and Lacie (Harmon) loathes commitment. Drawn from the real-life story of the lead actresses who adapted the script from their play "Real Girls." **74m/C VHS, DVD.** Mink Stole, Dom DeLuise, Robin Greenspan, Lacie Harmon, Katherine Randolph; **D:** Lee Friedlander; **W:** Lee Friedlander, Robin Greenspan, Lacie Harmon. VIDEO

Girl Rush 🦴 1944 Two bad vaudeville comics are stuck in California during the gold rush and are promised sacks of gold if they can persuade some women to come to a rowdy mining town. ♫Annabela's Bustle; Rainbow Valley; Walking Arm in Arm With Jim. **65m/B VHS.** Wally Brown, Alan Carney, Frances Langford, Barbara Jo Allen, Robert Mitchum, Paul Hurst, Patti Brill, Sarah Padden, Cy Kendall; **D:** Gordon Douglas.

The Girl Said No 🦴½ With Words and Music 1937 A sleazy bookie poses as a theatrical producer in order to get even with a dance hall floozy who once stiffed him. **72m/B VHS.** Robert Armstrong, Irene Hervey, William Haines; **D:** Andrew L. Stone; **W:** Andrew L. Stone.

Girl Shy 🦴🦴🦴 1924 Harold is a shy tailor's apprentice who is trying to get a collection of his romantic fantasies published. Finale features Lloyd chasing wildly after girl of his dreams. **65m/B VHS, DVD.** Harold Lloyd, Jobyna Ralston, Richard Daniels; **D:** Fred Newmeyer; **W:** Sam Taylor.

Girl 6 🦴🦴½ 1996 (R) Aspiring actress (Randle) takes job as a phone sex operator in order to make ends meet. After finally finding stardom in the world of titillating telecommunications, she starts to take her work home. Bound to be compared, unfairly and probably unfavorably, to Lee's debut "She's Gotta Have It." Terrific performance by Randle is hampered by the lack of a strong story and too many unresolved subplots. Features the obligatory Lee cameo, while Tarantino shows up as a young hotshot director. Prince provides old and new tunes (as well as his previous moniker, apparently) to the proceedings. **107m/C VHS, DVD.** Theresa Randle, Isaiah Washington IV, Ron Silver, Jim Turturro, Naomi Campbell, Halle Berry, Madonna, Quentin Tarantino, Debi Mazar, Peter Berg, Richard Belzer, Spike Lee, Jenifer Lewis, Michael Imperioli, Kristen Wilson, Dina Pearlman, Maggie Rush, Desi Moreno, Susan Batson; **D:** Spike Lee; **W:** Suzan-Lori Parks; **C:** Malik Hassan Sayeed; **M:** Prince.

The Girl, the Body and the Pill 🦴 1967 Sexploitation pic from director Lewis has a high school instructor getting fired for her sex education lectures—so she continues them in the privacy of her own home. Meanwhile, her students take up playing musical beds and learn about "the pill." **80m/C VHS.** Pamela Rhae, Bill Rogers, Nancy Lee Noble, George Brown, Roy Collodi, Todd Harris, James Nelson, Ray Sager, Valedia Hill; **D:** Herschell Gordon Lewis; **W:** Allison Louise Downe; **C:** Roy Collodi; **M:** Larry Wellington.

A Girl Thing 🦴🦴 2001 In four individual stories, shrink Dr. Noonan (Channing) listens to her female patients' dreams and woes. Macpherson is a successful lawyer who finds herself attracted to Capshaw in a complicated affair. Headly and her sisters DeMornay and Janney bicker over their mother's final request—they must spend a week together in her house in order to collect their inheritance. Whitfield suspects her husband Bakula is having an affair and hires Hamilton to check things out. Manheim stars as a deeply disturbed patient who forces the doctor to re-evaluate her own life and profession. **237m/C VHS, DVD.** Stockard Channing, Elle Macpherson, Kate Capshaw, Glenne Headly, Rebecca De Mornay, Allison Janney, Lynn Whitfield, Linda Hamilton, Camryn Manheim, Scott Bakula, Bruce Greenwood, Brent Spiner, Mia Farrow; **D:** Lee Rose. CABLE

A Girl to Kill For 🦴½ 1990 (R) A temptress lures a randy college guy into a plot of murder and betrayal. **85m/C VHS.** Sasha Jenson, Karen Austin, Alex Cord, Rod McCary, Karen Medak; **D:** Richard Oliver.

Girl Under the Sheet 🦴 1961 A con-man/archaeologist moves into an ancient castle and begins romancing a beautiful resident ghost. **89m/C VHS.** IT Chelo Alonso, Walter Chiari; **D:** Marino Girolami; **W:** Marino Girolami; **C:** Augusto Tiezzi; **M:** Carlo Savina.

The Girl Who Had Everything 🦴🦴 1953 Good melodrama with top cast, intelligent script and smooth direction. Taylor plays the spoiled daughter of a criminal lawyer (Calhern) who falls for her father's client (Lamas), a suave, underground syndicate boss. Remake of the 1931 film "A Free Soul," which starred Norma Shearer, Clark Gable, and Lionel Barrymore. Based on the novel of the same name by Adela Rogers St. John. **69m/B VHS.** Elizabeth Taylor, Fernando Lamas, William Powell, Gig Young, James Whitmore, Robert Burton; **D:** Richard Thorpe; **M:** Andre Previn.

The Girl Who Knew Too Much 🦴🦴½ La Ragazza Che Sapeva Troppo; The Evil Eye 1963 Ten years ago in Italy a string of "alphabet murders" began on "A" and ended on "C." Now a pretty young American named Nora Davis (Roman) is visiting a family friend in Italy. When the friend dies and Nora goes for help—in the middle of the night, in the rain, wearing only a raincoat, alone, through an empty plaza—she witnesses a murder that happened ten years ago or does she? She shouldn't worry, though, because handsome young Dr. Marcello Bassi (Saxon speaking fluent Italian) wants to help her. Typically fun and frightening Bava fare with the script, cinematography and direction working much more smoothly than usual. **86m/B DVD.** IT Leticia Roman, John Saxon, Valentina Cortese, Robert Buchanan; **D:** Mario Bava; **W:** Mario Bava, Ennio de Concini, Mino Guerrini; **C:** Mario Bava.

The Girl Who Spelled Freedom 🦴🦴🦴 1986 A young Cambodian girl, speaking little English, strives to adjust to life in Chattanooga, Tennessee. She faces her challenges by becoming a champion at the national spelling bee. Based on a true story. **90m/C VHS.** Wayne Rogers, Mary Kay Place, Jade Chinn, Kieu Chinh, Kathleen Sisk; **D:** Simon Wincer. TV

Girl with a Pearl Earring 🦴🦴🦴½ 2003 (PG-13) Based on the novel by Tracy Chevalier about the fictional relationship between the famous Dutch painter Vermeer and the servant girl who posed for his most famous work. Griet (Johansson, bearing an uncanny similarity to the actual painting) is sent to work for Vermeer after her father can no longer support the family. Vermeer (Firth) is intrigued by her intuitive sensibilities to art and soon has her helping in the studio and then posing for him. Johansson gives an exceptionally flawless performance in an intelligent and visually stunning film. **95m/C VHS, DVD.** GB LU Colin Firth, Scarlett Johansson, Tom Wilkinson, Judy Parfitt, Essie Davis, Cillian Murphy, Alakina Mann, Joanna Scanlan; **D:** Peter Webber; **W:** Olivia Hetreed; **C:** Eduardo Serra; **M:** Alexandre Desplat. L.A. Film Critics '03: Cinematog.

The Girl with a Suitcase 🦴🦴
La Ragazza con la Valgia 1960 Young nightclub singer Aida (Cardinale) falls for rich cad Marcello (Pani) and leaves her job to follow him to his family home in Parma. He was just stringing her along and instructs his 16-year-old brother Lorenzo (Perrin) to get rid of Aida. But instead Lorenzo decides to become her protector and the unlikely duo fall in love. Italian with subtitles; the original release was 135 minutes. **111m/B VHS, DVD.** IT Claudia Cardinale, Jacques Perrin, Corrado Pani, Luciana Angiolillo, Romolo Valli, Gian Marie Volonte; **D:** Valerio Zurlini; **W:** Valerio Zurlini; **C:** Tino Santoni; **M:** Mario Nascimbene.

Girl with Green Eyes 🦴🦴
1964 Kate Brady (Tushingham) is a young Catholic farm girl who comes to Dublin for work and falls in love with much older divorced writer Eugene Gaillard (Finch). She moves in with him despite her moral misgivings but both discover their differences are too great to sustain their relationship. O'Brien adapted the screenplay from her novel "The Lonely Girl." **91m/B VHS, DVD.** GB Peter Finch, Rita Tushingham, Lynn Redgrave, Marie Kean, Julian Glover, T.P. McKenna, Yolande Finch, Arthur O'Sullivan; **D:** Desmond Davis; **W:** Edna O'Brien; **C:** Manny Wynn; **M:** John Addison.

The Girl with the Hat Box 🦴🦴 1927 Early Russian production about a poor working girl who's paid with a lottery ticket rather than rubles (an ironic pre-communist theme?). When she strikes it rich in the lottery, her boss gives chase and silent antics ensue. Silent with orchestral score. **67m/B VHS, DVD.** RU Anna Sten, Vladimar Fogel, Serafina Birman, Ivan Kovalsky; **D:** Boris Barnet.

The Girl with the Hungry Eyes 🦴🦴 1994 (R) In 1937, top fashion model and hotel owner Louise (Fulton) kills herself over a cheating fiancee. Except Louise doesn't die, instead she becomes a vampire and, in the present-day, decides to return to her now-derelict haunts. Louise is determined to restore her hotel to its former glory and get her revenge on men in general. Filmed in Miami's South Beach. Adapted from a short story by Fritz Leiber. **84m/C VHS, DVD.** Christina (Kristina) Fulton, Isaac Turner, Leon Herbert, Bret Carr, Susan Rhodes; **D:** Jon Jacobs; **W:** Jon Jacobs; **M:** Paul Inder.

Girlfight ♂♂♂ 1999 (R) Scrappy feminist coming-of-age drama is the feature debut from director Karyn Kusama. Diana (Rodriguez) is a high-school senior with a bad temper and a penchant for trouble. Her single dad, Sandro (Calderon), encourages her boxing trainer but refuses to work with a daughter to participate. Diana decides to train anyway, and her determination finds her becoming the gym's first female champ. She falls in love with fellow promising amateur Adrian (Douglas), setting the stage for an unlikely mixed gender bout between the two. The movie strains reality when it has Diana fight Adrian, but the feeling throughout is heartfelt without being overly sentimental. And at least she doesn't howl "Yo Adrian" afterwards. **90m/C VHS, DVD.** Jamie Tirelli, Michelle Rodriguez, Santiago Douglas, Ray Santiago, Elisa Bocanegra, Paul Calderon, John Sayles; **D:** Karyn Kusama; **W:** Karyn Kusama; **C:** Patrick Cady; **M:** Theodore Shapiro. Ind. Spirit '01: Debut Perf. (Rodriguez); Sundance '00: Director (Kusama), Grand Jury Prize.

Girlfriend from Hell ♂ 1989 (R) The Devil inhabits the body of a teenage wallflower and turns her into an uncontrollable vamp. **95m/C VHS.** Liane (Alexandra) Curtis, Dana Ashbrook, Lezlie (Dean) Deane, James Daughton, Anthony Barrile, James Karen; **D:** Daniel M. Peterson; **W:** Daniel M. Peterson.

Girlfriends ♂♂♂ 1978 (PG) Bittersweet story of a young Jewish photographer learning to make it on her own. Directorial debut of Weill reflects her background in documentaries as the true-to-life episodes unfold. **87m/C VHS.** Melanie Mayron, Anita Skinner; Viveca Lindfors, Bob Balaban, Amy Wright, Christopher Guest, Kathryn Walker, Kristopher Tabori, Mike Kellin, Kenneth McMillan; **D:** Claudia Weill; **W:** Vicki Polon; **C:** Fred Murphy. Sundance '78: Grand Jury Prize.

Girls Are for Loving ♂ 1973 Undercover agent Ginger faces real adventure when she battles it out with her counterpart, a seductive enemy agent. Her third adventure following "Ginger" (1970) and "The Abductors" (1971). **90m/C VHS, DVD.** Cher Cattaro, Timothy Brown, William Grannell, Scott Ellsworth, Robert C. Jefferson, Jocelyn Peters, Yukii Shimoda, Fred Vincent; **D:** Don Schain; **W:** Don Schain; **M:** Robert G. Orin.

Girls Can't Swim ♂♂ 1973 Ne Savent Pas Nager 1999 Fifteen-year-old Gwen (Le Besco) and her best friend Lise (Alyx) always spend their summers together on the Brittany coast where Gwen lives and Lise's family rents a cottage. But when there's a family tragedy, Lise must stay home until the gloomy atmosphere has her traveling to Gwen's on her own. Gwen's parents (who have their own problems) let Lise stay but things between the friends have changed. Gwen has been flaunting her sexuality with the local boys and comes to resent Lise, who feels abandoned. Gwen's thoughtless sexual impulses finally cause the divisions between the girls to spin out of control. French with subtitles. **98m/C VHS.** FR Isild Le Besco, Karen Alyx, Pascal Elso, Pascale Bussières, Julien Cottereau, Marie Rivière; **D:** Anne-Sophie Birot, Christophe Honcre; **C:** Nathalie Durand; **M:** Ernest Chausson.

A Girl's Folly ♂♂1/2 1917 A country girl falls in love with the leading man of a film shooting on location. She wants to become a rich actress, but fails miserably. The actor offers her all the luxuries she wants if she'll become his mistress. When she finally agrees, her mother shows up. What will our country maid do now? **66m/B VHS.** Robert Warwick, Doris Kenyon, June Elvidge, Johnny Hines; **D:** Maurice Tourneur.

Girls! Girls! Girls! ♂♂1/2 1962 (PG) Poor tuna boat fisherman Elvis moonlights as a nightclub singer to get his father's boat out of hock. He falls for a rich girl pretending to be poor, and after some romantic trials, there's the usual happy ending. ♫The Nearness of You; Never Let Me Go; Girls, Girls, Girls; Return to Sender; We're Coming in Loaded; A Boy Like Me, A Girl Like You; Song of the Shrimp; Earth Boy; The Walls Have Ears. **106m/C VHS, DVD.** Elvis Presley, Stella Stevens, Laurel Goodwin, Jeremy Slate, Benson Fong, Robert Strauss.

Girls in Chains ♂♂1/2 1943 Girls in a reformatory, a teacher, a corrupt school official, and the detective willing to nail 'em. There's also a murder at the beginning of the film. **72m/B VHS.** Arline Judge, Roger Clark, Robin Raymond, Barbara Pepper, Dorothy Burgess, Clancy Cooper, Sid Melton, Betty Blythe, Peggy Stewart, Francis Ford; **D:** Edgar G. Ulmer; **W:** Albert Beich; **C:** Ira Morgan; **M:** Leo Erdody.

Girls in Prison ♂♂1/2 1956 Anne Carson is sent to prison for a bank robbery she didn't commit, and although the one chaplain believes her story, the other prisoners think she knows where the money is hidden. They plan a prison break, forcing Carson to go with them and get the money, but they soon run across the real robber, also searching for the loot. A below-average "B" prison movie, lacking the psychotic killer inhabiting the place that's a good idea. **87m/B VHS.** Richard Denning, Joan Taylor, Adele Jergens, Helen Gilbert, Lance Fuller, Jane Darwell, Raymond Hatton; **D:** Edward L. Cahn.

Girls in Prison ♂♂ 1994 (R) Not exactly a remake of the same-titled 1956 film (although it's still set in the '50s) but it's a familiar "babes behind bars" saga. Aspiring country singer Aggie (Crider) is wrongfully convicted of murdering a record company exec and winds up in the big house. Then she learns an inmate has been contracted to kill her. Can she find the hit girl before it's too late (and find out who's framing her)? **82m/C VHS.** Missy (Melissa) Crider, Ione Skye, Anne Heche, William Boyett, Tom Towles, Miguel (Michael) Sandoval, Jon Polito, Richmond Arquette; **D:** John McNaughton; **W:** Christa Lang, Samuel Fuller; **C:** Jean De Segonzac; **M:** Hummie Mann. CABLE

Girls Just Want to Have Fun ♂♂ 1985 (PG) An army brat and their friends pull out all the stops and defy their parents for a chance to dance on a national TV program. **90m/C VHS, DVD.** Sarah Jessica Parker, Helen Hunt, Ed Lauter, Holly Gagnier, Morgan Woodward, Lee Montgomery, Shannen Doherty, Biff Yeager; **D:** Alan Metter; **W:** Janice Hirsch, Amy Spies; **C:** Thomas Ackerman; **M:** Thomas Newman.

Girls' Night ♂♂1/2 1997 The acting's fine but the story's weak in this old-fashioned weepie. Britt wives Dawn (Blethyn) and Jackie (Walters) are best friends, and in-laws, who even work at the same factory. But women are also suffering from the marriage blues and find solace at the local bingo parlor. When Dawn wins very big, she splits the money with Jackie and then discovers that she has cancer. The duo decide this is the time for their dream Las Vegas vacation, where they even meet a Prince Charming—in the form of cowpoke Cody (Kristofferson). **106m/C VHS.** GB Brenda Blethyn, Julie Walters, Kris Kristofferson, George Costigan, James Gaddas, Philip Jackson; **D:** Nick Hurran; **W:** Kay Mellor; **C:** David Odd; **M:** Ed Shearmur.

Girls Next Door ♂ 1979 (R) A bevy of boisterous beauties cavort and cause havoc in buffoon-cluttered suburbia. **85m/C VHS.** Kirsten Baker, Perry Lang, Leslie Cederquist, Richard Singer; **D:** James Hong.

Girls Night Out ♂ 1983 (R) Ex-cop must stop a killer who is murdering participants in a sorority house scavenger hunt and leaving cryptic clues on the local radio station. **96m/C VHS, DVD.** Hal Holbrook, Rutanya Alda, Julia Montgomery, James Carroll; **D:** Robert Deubel.

The Girls of Huntington House ♂♂ 1973 A teacher in a school for unwed mothers finds herself becoming increasingly absorbed in her students' lives. **73m/C VHS.** Shirley Jones, Mercedes McCambridge, Sissy Spacek, William Windom, Pamela Sue Martin, Darrell Larson; **D:** Alf Kjellin. TV

Girls of the White Orchid ♂ Death Ride to Osaka 1985 A naive American girl thinks she's getting a job singing in a Japanese nightclub, but it turns out to be a front for a prostitution ring run by the Japanese Yakuza. Based on real stories.

Giuliani Time ♂♂♂♂ 2005 A mostly-warts documentary on Rudy Giuliani, from his early career at the Department of Justice to his controversial two terms as the mayor of New York City and his response to the disaster of 9/11, ending with his speech at the 2004 Republican National Convention. Filmmaker Keating is not as far. **119m/C DVD.** US **D:** Kevin Keating; **W:** William Farnum; **D:** Joseph Kane. Shirley Burnette, William Farnum; **C:** Kevin Keating; **M:** David Carbonara.

Git Along Little Dogies ♂♂1/2 1937 It's cattle ranchers versus oil men with Autry caught in the middle of the petrol/cow war. But Gene still finds a little time to romance the town banker's pretty daughter. **60m/B VHS.** Gene Autry, Judith Allen, Smiley Burnette, William Farnum; **D:** Joseph Kane.

Git! ♂♂1/2 1965 A young runaway and his faithful dog are taken in by a wealthy dog-breeder and trained by him into a crack hunting team. **90m/C VHS.** Jack Chaplin, Richard Webb, Heather North; **D:** Ellis Kadison.

Girly ♂ Mumsy, Nanny, Sonny, and Girly 1970 (R) An English gothic about an excessively weird family that lives in a crumbling mansion and indulges in murder, mental aberration, and sexual compulsion. **101m/C VHS.** GB Michael Bryant, Ursula Howells, Pat Heywood, Howard Trevor, Vanessa Howard, Michael Ripper; **D:** Freddie Francis.

Girls Town ♂ 1995 (R) Tough look at the lives of three working-class high school seniors who are shattered by the suicide of Nikki (Ellis), the fourth member of their group, who killed herself from guilt over an undisclosed rape. Single mom Patti (Taylor), ambitious Emma (Grace), and strong-willed Angela (Harris) argue, commiserate, battle their foes (Patti's abusive boyfriend, Nikki's rapist), and learn about each other as they struggle to figure out themselves and their ambiguous futures. Lots of time is spent in the girls' bathroom at school (how realistic can you get?) **90m/C VHS.** Lili Taylor, Anna Grace, Bruklin Harris, Aunjanue Ellis, Guillermo Diaz, John Ventimiglia; **D:** Jim McKay; **W:** Denise Casano, Jim McKay, Lili Taylor, Anna Grace, Bruklin Harris, Aunjanue Ellis; **C:** Russell Fine. Sundance '96: Filmmakers Trophy.

Girls on the Road ♂♂1/2 1973 (PG) Two girls are just out for fun cruising the California coast, but that handsome hitchhiker turns out to be a deadly mischief. **91m/C VHS.** CA Kathleen (Kathy) Cody, Michael Ontkean, Dianne Hull, Ralph Waite, Rigg Kennedy; **D:** Thomas J. Schmidt.

Girls Riot ♂♂ 1988 Young, female juvenile delinquents have had enough! They decide to give their warden-like headmistress a taste of her own violence. **106m/C VHS, DVD.** Mollie O'Mara, Sharon Christopher, Vera Gallagher; **D:** John P. Finegan; **W:** John P. Anka.

Girls School Screamers ♂ 1986 (R) Six young women and a nun are assigned to spend the weekend checking the contents for sale in a scary mansion bequeathed to their school. Unfortunately, the psychotic killer inhabiting the place doesn't think that's a good idea. **85m/C VHS, DVD.** Jocelyne Boisseau, Cornelia Calwer, Argelis Dominose, Ute Freight; **D:** Manfred Purzer.

Give Me a Sailor ♂♂1/2 1938 Hope and Whiting play brothers, and 'fellow Naval officers, who meet sisters Grable and Raye on shore leave. Naturally, there's comic romantic complications until a double wedding ends the farce. Not much of a musical score from Ralph Rainger and Leo Robin but the movie's fun. Based on a play by Anne Nichols. ♫What Goes Here in My Heart?; A Little Kiss at Twilight; Give Me a Sailor; The US and You; It Don't Make Sense. **80m/B VHS.** Bob Hope, Martha Raye, Betty Grable, Jack Whiting, Clarence (C. William) Kolb, Nana Bryant, Emerson Treacy; **D:** Elliott Nugent; **W:** Frank Butler, Doris Anderson.

Give 'Em Hell, Harry! ♂♂♂ 1975 James Whitmore's one-man show as Harry S. Truman filmed in performance on stage; Whitmore was nominated for a Best Actor Oscar. **103m/C VHS.** James Whitmore; **D:** Steve Binder.

Give My Regards to Broad Street ♂♂ 1984 (PG) McCartney film made for McCartney fans. Film features many fine versions of the ex-Beatle's songs that accompany his otherwise lackluster portraya of a rock star in search of his stolen master recordings. ♫Eleanor Rigby; Ballroom Dancing; Good Day, Sunshine; Silly Love Songs; No Values; No More Lonely Nights; Yesterday; Not Such a Bad Boy; The .ong and Winding Road. **109m/C VHS, DVD.** GB Paul McCartney, Bryan Brown, Ringo Starr, Barbara Bach, Tracey Ullman, Ralph Richardson, Linda McCartney; **C:** Peter Webb.

Giving It Up ♂♂1/2 Casanova Falling 1999 (R) Bland and predictable romantic comedy. Successful New York ad exec Ralph (Feuerstein) is a sexaholic. This pleases his boss Jonathan (Coleman) but makes him a pariah in his female co-workers. He meets his match in sophisticated Elizabeth (Redford) and decides to change his horn dog ways for true love. Only Ralph slips when he gets a chance with supermodel Amber (Larter). It ain't pretty when Liz finds out. **90m/C VHS, DVD.** Mark Feuerstein, Catney Coleman, Ali Larter, Amy Redford, Callie (Calliope) Thorne, James Tolkac; **D:** Christopher Kublan; **W:** Christopher Kublan; **C:** Leland Krane.

The Gladiator ♂♂1/2 1938 Los Angeles citizen turns vigilante against drunk drivers after his brother is one of their victims. **70m/B VHS.** Joe E. Brown, Man Mountain Dean, June Travis, Dickie Moore, Lucien Littlefield, Robert Kent, Ethel Wales; **D:** Edward Sedgwick.

The Gladiator ♂♂1/2 1992 (R) When suburban Golden Gloves boxing champion Tommy Riley (Marshall) is forced to move to the inner city because of his father's gambling debts, he becomes involved with an evil boxing promoter who thrives on an illegal boxing matches. Eventually Riley is forced to fight his black friend Lincoln (Gooding), even though Lincoln has been warned that another blow to the head could be fatal. **94m/C VHS, DVD.** Ken Wahl, Nancy Allen, Robert Culp, Stan Shaw, Rosemary Forsyth; **D:** Abel Ferraa. TV

though the producers concentrate on the seamy side. **96m/C VHS, DVD.** Thomas Jefferson Byrd, Carolyn Seymour, Mako, Ann Jillian, Jennifer Jason Leigh; **D:** Jonathan Kaplan; **C:** John Lindley; **M:** Brad Fiedel. TV

of the various men associated with the production, each starlet thinks she's a shoe-in for the part. Entertaining but undistinguished musical with appealing dance routines of Fosse and the Champions. Ira Gershwin, collaborating for the first and only time with Burton Lane, wrote the lyrics to two of the songs. ♫Give the Girl a Break; In Our United State; It Happens Every Time; Nothing is Impossible; Applause, Applause; Challenge Dance; Debbie Reynolds; Harry James; **84m/C VHS.** Marge Champion, Gower Champion, Debbie Reynolds, Helen Wood, Bob Fosse, Kurt Kaszner, Richard Anderson, William Ching, Larry Keating, Donna (Dona Marel) Martell; **D:** Stanley Donen; **M:** André Previn.

head could mean his life. Although this film tries to serve some moral purpose, it falls flat on the mat. **98m/C VHS, DVD.** Cuba Gooding Jr., James Marshall, Robert Loggia, Ossie Davis, Brian Dennehy, Cara Buono, John Heard, Jon Seda, Lance Slaughter; **D:** Rowdy Herrington; **W:** Lyle Kessler, Robert Mark Kamen; **C:** Tak Fujimoto; **M:** Brad Fiedel.

Gladiator ♂♂♂ 2000 (R) Emperor Marcus Aurelius (Harris) decides to name victorious general Maximus (Crowe) his heir over the ruler's own son, the decadent Commodus (Phoenix). But Commodus manages to take over the Empire anyway. Maximus is betrayed, his family killed, and he is sold as a slave, eventually learning the ways of a gladiator. Then he returns to Rome to get his revenge. Last role for Reed (playing owner/trainer Proximo), who died during production. Unlike the cheesy Italian muscle epics of the early '60s this is swords, sandals, and killer beasts for a new generation, with a compelling hero in Crowe. **154m/C VHS, DVD.** Russell Crowe, Joaquin Rafael (Leaf) Phoenix, Connie Nielsen, Djimon Hounsou, Ralph (Ralf) Moeller, Derek Jacobi, Oliver Reed, Richard Harris, David Schofield, John Shrapnel, Tomas Arana, Spencer (Treat) Clark, Tommy Flanagan, David Hemmings, Sven-Ole Thorsen; **D:** Ridley Scott; **W:** David Franzoni, John Logan, William Nicholson; **C:** John Mathieson; **M:** Hans Zimmer. Oscars '00: Actor (Crowe), Costume Des., Film, Sound, Visual FX; British Acad. '00: Cinematog., Film; Golden Globes '01: Film—Drama, Score; Natl. Bd. of Review '00: Support. Actor (Phoenix); Broadcast Film Critics '00: Actor (Crowe), Cinematog., Film, Support. Actor (Phoenix).

Gladiator Cop: The Swordsman 2 ♂1/2 1995 (R) A legendary sword, believed to have magic powers, is stolen and an ex-detective winds up fighting modern-day gladiators and a man who believes himself to be a reincarnation of Alexander the Great. **92m/C VHS, DVD.** James Hong, Frank Anderson, Christopher Lee Clements, Heather Gillan, Lorenzo Lamas; **D:** Nick Rotundo; **W:** Nick Rotundo; **C:** Edgar Egger; **M:** Guy Zerafa.

The Gladiators ♂♂ *The Peace Game*; *Gladiatorerna* 1970 Televised gladiatorial bouts are designed to subdue man's violent tendencies in a futuristic society until a computer makes a fatal error. **90m/C VHS.** Arthur Pentelow, Frederick Danner; **D:** Peter Watkins.

Gladiator of Rome ♂ *Il Gladiatore Di Roma* 1963 A gladiator flexes his pecs to save a young girl from death at the hands of evil rulers. **105m/C VHS, DVD.** *IT* Gordon Scott, Wandisa Guida, Roberto Risso, Ombretta Colli, Alberto (Albert Farley) Farnese; **D:** Mario Costa.

Gladiators 7 ♂1/2 1962 Sparta must be freed from the tyrannical rule of the Romans. In lieu of samurai or cowboys, who better than the Gladiators 7 to do the deed? Plenty of sword-to-sword action and scantily clad Italian babes. **92m/C VHS, DVD.** *SP IT* Richard Harrison, Loredana Nusciak, Livio Lorenzon, Gerard Tichy, Edoardo Toniolo, Joseph Marco, Barta Barry; **D:** Pedro Lazaga.

Glam ♂♂ 1997 (R) Eccentric writer Sonny Daye (McNamara) arrives in L.A. and is promptly exploited. His cousin Franky (Frank) takes Sonny's journal to a pair of schlocky producers who are impressed by the writing. So vain and ruthless Sid Dalgren (Danza) decides to control Sonny even while- his tootsie, Vanessa (Wagner), begins to fall for the oddball's sweetness. Very talky. Director Evan's mom, Ali McGraw, has a cameo. **93m/C VHS, DVD.** William McNamara, Frank Whaley, Natasha Gregson Wagner, Tony Danza, Valerie Kaprisky, Caroline Lagerfelt, Lou (Cutel) Cutell, Robert DoQui, Jon Cryer, Donal Logue; *Cameos:* Ali MacGraw; **D:** Josh Evans; **W:** Josh Evans; **M:** Josh Evans.

Glass ♂1/2 1990 A normally complacent man is driven to the brink of savagery when a killer begins stalking his employees. **92m/C VHS.** Alan Lovell, Lisa Peers, Adam Stone, Natalie McCurry; **D:** Chris Kennedy; **W:** Chris Kennedy; **C:** Peter De Vries; **M:** Mario Gregorie.

The Glass Bottom Boat ♂♂1/2 1966 A bubbly but transparent Doris Day comedy, in which she falls in love with her boss at an aerospace lab. Their scheme to spend time together gets her mistaken for a spy. Made about the time they stopped making them like this anymore, it's innocuous slapstick romance with a remarkable 1960s cast, including a Robert Vaughn cameo as the Man From U.N.C.L.E. Doris sings "Que Sera, Sera" and a few other numbers. **110m/C VHS, DVD.** Doris Day, Rod Taylor, Arthur Godfrey, Paul Lynde, Eric Fleming, Alice Pearce, Ellen Corby, John McGiver, Dom DeLuise, Dick Martin, Edward Andrews; *Cameos:* Robert Vaughn; **D:** Frank Tashlin; **W:** Everett Freeman; **C:** Leon Shamroy.

The Glass Cage ♂♂ 1996 (R) Ex-CIA agent Paul Yeager (Tyson) takes a bartending job in New Orleans' French Quarter in order to get back his exotic dancer girlfriend Jacqueline (Lewis) but the bar's jealous owner and dirty cop Montrachet (Roberts) have other plans in mind for the duo. **96m/C VHS.** Richard Tyson, Charlotte Lewis, Eric Roberts, Stephen Nichols, Joseph Campanella; **D:** Michael Schroeder; **W:** David Keith Miller; **C:** John Aronson.

The Glass House ♂♂♂ *Truman Capote's The Glass House* 1972 Alda stars as a middle-aged college professor, convicted on a manslaughter charge, who is sent to a maximum security prison and must learn to deal with life inside. Filmed at Utah State Prison, real-life prisoners as supporting cast add to the drama. Still has the power to chill, with Morrow particularly effective as one of the inmate leaders. Adapted from a Truman Capote story. **92m/C VHS, DVD.** Alan Alda, Vic Morrow, Clu Gulager, Billy Dee Williams, Dean Jagger, Kristopher Tabori; **D:** Tom Gries; **M:** Billy Goldenberg. **TV**

The Glass House ♂1/2 2001 (PG-13) With a brittle plot you can see right through, this flick is aptly named. After their parents are killed in a car accident, 16-year-old Ruby (Sobieski) and her little brother Rhett (Morgan) are sent to live with their former neighbors Erin and Terry Glass (Lane and Skarsgaard). The Glasses live in a swanky glass mansion with all the charm of a Windex bottle. Although the kids with clothes and gadgets, Ruby begins to suspect what we already know: evil stepparents! Ruby then tries to tell all the adults in her life that the Glasses have ugly streaks, but no one believes her or even suggests a rinsing agent. Obvious plot devices and cliched techniques (including the ever-popular "tinkling danger piano music") shatter what could have been a great thriller given the cast and concept. **111m/C VHS, DVD.** *US* Leelee Sobieski, Stellan Skarsgaard, Diane Lane, Trevor Morgan, Bruce Dern, Kathy Baker, Christopher Noth, Rita Wilson, Michael O'Keefe, Vyto Ruginis; **D:** Daniel Sackheim; **W:** Wesley Strick; **C:** Alar Kivilo; **M:** Christopher Young.

Glass House: The Good Mother ♂♂ 2006 (R) Orphaned Abby (Hinson) and her younger brother Ethan (Coleman) are adopted by a seemingly perfect couple, Eve (Harmon) and Raymond (Gretsch) Goode. Soon uptight Eve is doting exclusively on Ethan, who suddenly gets sick, and Abby is suspicious. She learns the Goodes have previously fostered several young boys who have all disappeared. She also figures out that Raymond has been covering for his wife. But Abby is determined her brother will not become their next victim. **93m/C VHS, DVD.** Angie Harmon, Joel Gretsch, Jason London, Jordan Hinson, Bobby Coleman; **D:** Steve Antin; **W:** Brett Merryman; **C:** Bobby Bukowski; **M:** Steve Gutheinz. **VIDEO**

The Glass Jungle ♂♂ 1988 Will a cab driver save Los Angeles? When armed terrorists save Los Angeles? It all out in sunny California city an innocent cabby seems to hold the solution to survival. **94m/C VHS.** Lee Canalito, Joe Filbeck, Diana Frank, Mark High, Frank Scala; **D:** Joseph Merhi.

The Glass Key ♂♂ 1942 Previously filmed in 1935, this version of Dashiell Hammett's novel is a vintage mystery concerning nominally corrupt politician Madvig (Donlevy) being framed for murder, and his assistant Ed Beaumont (Ladd) sleuthing out the real culprit. One of Ladd's first starring vehicles; Lake is the mystery woman who loves him, and Bendix a particularly vicious thug. **85m/B VHS.** Alan Ladd, Veronica Lake, Brian Donlevy, William Bendix, Bonita Granville, Richard Denning, Joseph Calleia, Moroni Olsen, Dane Clark; **D:** Stuart Heisler; **W:** Jonathan Latimer; **C:** Theodor Sparkuhl; **M:** Victor Young.

The Glass Menagerie ♂♂♂ 1987 (PG) An aging Southern belle deals with her crippled daughter Laura, whose one great love is her collection of glass animals. The third film adaptation of Tennessee Williams classic, which preserves the performances of the Broadway revival cast, is a solid-but-not-stellar adaptation of the play. All-star acting ensemble. **134m/C VHS, DVD.** Joanne Woodward, Karen Allen, John Malkovich, James Naughton; **D:** Paul Newman; **W:** Tennessee Williams; **C:** Michael Ballhaus; **M:** Henry Mancini.

The Glass Shield ♂♂♂ 1995 (PG-13) Timely look at racism and corruption in the Los Angeles sheriff's department as seen through the eyes of African American rookie J.J. Johnson (Boatman). His dream of being a police officer turns to disillusionment when he slowly realizes his own department is framing a black man (Ice Cube) for a murder he did not commit. First half grabs your attention, but the momentum is lost in murky plot twists and a rushed ending. Made on a shoestring, but has an interesting cast, including the reliably slimy Ironside as one of the bad cops and an almost unrecognizable Petty, who becomes Johnson's only ally on the force. **109m/C VHS, DVD.** Michael Boatman, Lori Petty, Michael Ironside, Ice Cube, Richard Anderson, Elliott Gould; **D:** Charles Burnett; **W:** Charles Burnett; **C:** Elliot Davis; **M:** Stephen James Taylor.

The Glass Slipper ♂♂ 1955 In this version of the "Cinderella" saga, Caron plays an unglamourous girl gradually transformed into the expected beauty. Winwood is the fairy godmother who inspires the girl to find happiness, rather then simply providing it for her magically. The film is highlighted by the stunning dance numbers, choreographed by Roland Petit and featuring the Paris ballet. **93m/C VHS.** Leslie Caron, Michael Wilding, Keenan Wynn, Estelle Winwood, Elsa Lanchester, Barry Jones, Amanda Blake, Lurene Tuttle; **D:** Charles Walters; *Nar:* Walter Pidgeon.

Glass Tomb ♂♂ 1955 At a circus, a man performs the world's longest fast inside a glass cage, and becomes the raison d'etre for murder. **59m/B VHS, DVD.** John Ireland, Honor Blackman, Eric Pohlmann, Tonia Bern, Sidney James; **D:** Montgomery Tully.

The Glass Trap ♂1/2 2004 (PG-13) It's never pretty when an experiment goes afoul, resulting in freakishly large, angry, and human-hungry ants. Naturally, this can't be good for the demons when they get stuck in a really big skyscraper with them. **90m/C VHS, DVD.** C. Thomas Howell, Stella Stevens, Siri Baruc, Brent Huff, Chick Vennera; **D:** Fred Olen Ray; **W:** Lisa Morton, Brett Thompson. **VIDEO**

Gleaming the Cube ♂1/2 1989 (PG-13) A skateboarding teen investigates his brother's murder. Film impresses with its stunt footage only. For those with adolescent interests. **102m/C VHS, DVD.** Christian Slater, Steven Bauer, Min Luong, Art Chudabala, Le Tuan; **D:** Graeme Clifford; **W:** Michael Tolkin; **M:** Jay Ferguson.

The Gleiwitz Case ♂♂ *Der Fall Gleiwitz; The Affair Gleiwitz* 1961 A reconstruction of an actual event. On August 31, 1939, six Germans living in Poland are selected for a secret mission: to take over a radio transmitter near Gleiwitz on the German-Polish border. Under the command of an SS officer, the attack will appear to come from Polish insurgents and thus justify the Nazi invasion of Poland. German

---

with subtitles. **70m/B DVD.** *GE* Hilmar Thate, Hannjo Hasse, Herwart Grosse, Georg Leopold; **D:** Gerhard Klein; **W:** Wolfgang Kohlaas, Gunther Ruckert; **C:** Jan Curik; **M:** Kurt Schaaen.

Glen and Randa ♂♂1/2 1971 (R) Two young people experience the world after it has been destroyed by nuclear war. Early McBride, before the hired-gun success of "The Big Easy." **94m/C VHS.** Steven Curry, Shelley Plimpton; **D:** Jim McBride; **W:** Rudy Wurlitzer, Jim McBride.

Glen or Glenda? WOOF! *He or She; I Changed My Sex; I Led Two Lives; The Transvestite; Glen or Glenda: The Confessions of Ed Wood* 1953 An appalling, quasi-docudrama about transvestism, interspersed with meaningless stock footage, inept dream sequences and Lugosi sitting in a chair spouting incoherent prattle at the camera. Directorial debut of Wood, who, using a pseudonym, played the lead; one of the phenomenally bad films of this century. An integral part of the famous anti-auteur's canon. **67m/B VHS, DVD.** Edward D. Wood Jr., Bela Lugosi, Lyle Talbot, Timothy Farrell, Dolores Fuller, Charles Crafts, Shirley Speril, Conrad DeZita, Evelyn Wood, Shirley Speril, Captain Brooks, Henry Bederski, William C. Thompson, Mr. Walter, Harry Thomas, George Weiss; **D:** Edward D. Wood Jr.; **W:** Edward D. Wood Jr.; **C:** William C. Thompson.

Glengarry Glen Ross ♂♂♂ 1992 (R) Seven-character study chronicling 48 hours in the lives of some sleazy real estate men in danger of getting the ax from their hard-driving bosses. A standout cast includes Pacino as the glad-handing sales leader, Lemmon as the hustler fallen on dim prospects, and Baldwin, briefly venomous, as the company hatchet-man. Brutal and hard-edged with very strong language. Mamet scripted from his Tony-award winning Broadway play. **100m/C VHS, DVD.** Al Pacino, Jack Lemmon, Ed Harris, Alec Baldwin, Alan Arkin, Kevin Spacey, Jonathan Pryce, Bruce Altman, Jude Ciccolella; **D:** James Foley; **W:** David Mamet; **C:** Juan Ruiz-Anchia; **M:** James Newton Howard. Natl. Bd. of Review '92: Actor (Lemmon); Venice Film Fest. '93: Actor (Lemmon).

The Glenn Miller Story ♂♂♂ 1954 (G) The music of the Big Band Era lives again in this warm biography of the legendary Glenn Miller, following his life from the late '20s to his untimely death in a WWII plane crash. Stewart's likably convincing and even belies the trombone playing well. ♪Moonlight Serenade; In the Mood; Tuxedo Junction; Little Brown Jug; Adios; String of Pearls; Pennsylvania 6-5000; Stairway to the Stars; American Patrol. **113m/C VHS, DVD.** James Stewart, June Allyson, Harry (Henry) Morgan, Gene Krupa, Louis Armstrong, Ben Pollack; **D:** Anthony Mann; **W:** Oscar Brodney, Valentine Davies; **C:** William H. Daniels; **M:** Henry Mancini. Oscars '54: Sound.

The Glimmer Man ♂♂1/2 1996 (R) When a vicious LA serial killer starts dispatching whole families, NY detective Jack Cole (Seagal) is teamed with local homicide detective Jim Campbell (Wayans). Since, however, this is a Seagal movie, things have to be a little different. Cole, for example, is an ex-CIA operative who has been convinced by a Buddhist monk to stop killing people and start wearing goofy Nehru jackets and prayer beads. Campbell is a couch potato who cries over old movies (or perhaps he was watching the dailies from this one). After Cole's ex-wife is killed, he's implicated; and then somehow the Russian Mafia and the CIA are brought into the mix. Cole uses his unique brand of non-violence to slash, chop and impale his way to justice. Predictable when it's not being unbelievable, this could have been called "Hard to Watch." **92m/C VHS, DVD.** Steven Seagal, Keenen Ivory Wayans, Michelle Johnson, Brian Cox, Bob Gunton, Stephen Tobolowsky, Johnny Strong, Ryan Cutrona, Peter Jason, Nikki Cox, Richard Gant, Alexa Vega; **D:** John Gray; **W:** Kevin Brodbin; **C:** Rick Bota; **M:** Trevor Rabin.

A Glimpse of Hell ♂♂1/2 2001 (PG-13) Excellent depiction of the 1989 explosion aboard the USS Iowa, and the subsequent investigations by the Navy, Congress. Lt. Dan Meyer (Leonard) is put in charge of a gun turret but soon finds

Glitch! ♂1⁄2 **1988 (R)** A throng of beautiful Hollywood hopefuls draw two youngsters unconnected with the film into posing as the film's director and producer in the hopes of conducting personal interviews on the casting couch. **88m/C VHS, DVD.** Julia Nickson-Soul, Will Egan, Steve Donmyer, Dan Speaker, Dallas Cole, Ji-Tu Cumbuka, Dick Gautier, Ted Lange, Teri Weigel, Fernando Carzon, John Kreng, Lindsey Carr; **D:** Nico Mastorakis; **W:** Nico Mastorakis; **C:** Peter C. Jensen; **M:** Tom Marolda. **VIDEO**

The Glitter Dome ♂1⁄2 **1984** Two policemen discover the sleazier side of Hollywood when they investigate the murder of a pornographer. Based upon the novel by Joseph Wambaugh. **90m/C VHS.** Stuart Margolin, John Marley, James Garner, John Lithgow, Margot Kidder, Colleen Dewhurst. **TV**

Glitter WOOF! **2001 (PG-13)** Following in the footsteps of "Cool as Ice" and "Spice World," this may be the third in the pop star "why was this allowed to happen?" trilogy. Mariah Carey, showing her acting range of two emotions ("Yay" and "Huh?"), stars as Billie Frank, a backup singer who climbs to stardom with the help from her svengali boyfriend Dice (Bees-ley). Together they struggle through the hard times and the wooden dialogue. Will "A Star is Born" tear them apart? You'll be wishing that wild dogs will tear her apart before the end of this mess. So bad it's nearly unintentionally funny. The key word is nearly. **104m/C VHS, DVD.** Mariah Carey, Max Beesly, Tia Texada, Da Brat, Valarie Pettiford, Ann Magnuson, Terrence Howard, Dorian Harewood; **C:** Geoffrey Simpson; **M:** Terence Blanchard. **Golden Raspberries '01: Worst Actress (Carey)**

A Global Affair ♂1⁄2 **1963** Hope is a department head in the United Nations who finds an abandoned baby in the building. The inept bachelor is wooed by a number of international beauties seeking to adopt the child for their various countries but he becomes increasingly attached to the little tyke. **84m/B VHS.** Bob Hope, Lilo (Lisselotte) Pulver, Michele Mercier, Yvonne De Carlo, Miiko Taka, Robert Sterling, Nehemiah Persoff, John Dehner, Mickey Shaughnessy; **D:** Jack Arnold; **W:** Charles Lederer, Arthur Marx, Bob Fisher; **C:** Joseph Ruttenberg.

Glitz ♂1⁄2 **1988** A Miami cop and an Atlantic City lounge singer team up to investigate a call-girl's death and wind up too close to a drug ring. Based on the novel by Elmore Leonard. **96m/C VHS.** Jimmy Smits, John Diehl, Markie Post, Ken Foree, Madison Mason, Robin Strasser; **D:** Sandor Stern. **TV**

Gloomy Sunday ♂♂♂ **2002** Story of a complex love triangle and Nazi oppression in 1930's Budapest, told in extended flashback. Jewish restaurant owner Laszlo (Krol), his waitress/lover Ilona (Narozsan) and pianist Andras (Dionisi) are all involved with one another when German salesman Hans (Ben Becker) fals for Ilona and eventually befriends the trio, inspired by Ilona. Andras composes a hit song (the titular "Gloomy Sunday") that causes a rash of suicides. Three years later, Hans returns to Budapest as an SS colonel and is immediately torn between his dedication to the ideals of the Third

Reich and his three friends. The characters are complex and well-written, and the tension is thick as they all struggle with the ethical implications of their actions as war encroaches on Budapest. Somewhat marred by stilted, melodramatic moments, but the excellent story and fine acting more than makes up for it. **114m/C VHS, DVD, GE.** Joachim Krol, Stefano Dionisi, Ben Becker, Erika Marozsan, Sebastian Koch, Laszlo I. Kish, Rolf Becker; **D:** Rolf Schuebel; **W:** Rolf Schuebel, Ruth Toma; **C:** Edward Klosinski; **M:** Detlef Petersen, Rezso Seress.

Gloria ♂♂1⁄2 **1980 (PG)** She used to be a Mafia moll, now she's ourturning the entist who is running in the son of a slain neighbor. He's got a book that they want, and they're willing to kill to get it. Trademark Cassavetes effort in which he has actors plumb their souls to discomfiting levels. **123m/C VHS, DVD.** Gena Rowlands, John Adams, Buck Henry, Julie Carmen; **D:** John Cassavetes; **M:** Bill Conti, Venice Film Fest '80: Film; Golden Raspberries '80: Worst Support. Actor (Adams).

Gloria ♂♂ **1993 (R)** Remake of the 1980 Cassavetes film, with Stone as title character, a gang moll who reluctantly becomes the guardian of a boy whose parents were killed by her low-life boyfriend Kevin (Northam). Entertainment value is derived from listening to Stone mangle her Noo Yawk accent. Stick with the original. **108m/C VHS, DVD.** Sharon Stone, Jeremy Northam, Cathy Moriarty, George C. Scott, Mike Starr, Don Billett, Tony DiBenedetto, Bonnie Bedelia, Jean-Luke Figueroa, Barry McEvoy, Jerry Dean, Teddy Atlas; **D:** Sidney Lumet; **M:** Steve Antin; **C:** David Watkin; **M:** Howard Shore.

Glorifying the American Girl ♂♂ **1930** Eaton's a chorus girl performing in the Ziegfeld Follies, which lends itself to numerous production numbers. The only film Ziegfeld ever produced. ♂1⁄2 What I Wouldn't Do For That Man; Blue Skies; I'm Just a Vagabond Lover; Baby Face; At Sundown; Beautiful Changes; Sam the Old Accordian Man; There Must Be Someone Waiting For Me. **96m/B VHS, DVD.** Mary Eaton, Dan Healey, Eddie Cantor, Rudy Vallee; **D:** Millard Webb.

Glory ♂♂ **1956** O'Brien is a racehorse owner who tussles with her grandmother over how to keep the family farm open on a shoestring budget. Brennan enters the picture as the financial guru who lends them back on track, with enough left over to enter their prize filly in the Kentucky Derby. Lucas plays O'Brien's love interest. No surprises here. **100m/C VHS.** Margaret O'Brien, Walter Brennan, Charlotte Greenwood; **D:** David Butler.

Glory ♂♂♂ **1989 (R)** A rich, historical spectacle chronicling the 54th Massachusetts, the first black volunteer infantry unit in the Civil War. The film manages to artfully focus on both the 54th and their white commander, Robert Gould Shaw. Based on Shaw's letters, the film uses thousands of accurately costumed "living historians" (re-enactors) as extras in this panoramic production. A haunting, bittersweet musical score pervades what finally becomes an anti-war statement. Stunning performances throughout, with exception-al work from Freeman and Washington. **122m/C VHS, DVD.** Matthew Broderick, Morgan Freeman, Denzel Washington, Cary Elwes, Jihmi Kennedy, Andre Braugher, John Finn, Donovan Leitch, John David (J.D.) Cullum, Bob Gunton, Jane Alexander, Raymond St. Jacques, Cliff DeYoung, Alan North, Jay O. Sanders, Richard Riehle, Ethan Phillips, RonReaco Lee, Peter Michael Goetz; **D:** Edward Zwick; **W:** Kevin Jarre, Marshall Herskovitz; **C:** Freddie Francis; **M:** James Horner. Oscars '89: Cinematog., Sound, Support. Actor (Washington); Golden Globes '90: Support. Actor (Washington).

Glory & Honor ♂♂1⁄2 **1998** Covers explorer Robert Peary's (Czerny) treks to the North Pole and his finally successful in 1909). Peary was accompanied by his black valet Matthew Henson (Lindo), who proved to be resourceful and a source of calm to the driven explorer, and was eventually credited as a co-discoverer. Filmed on location near the Arctic Circle. **94m/C VHS.** Henry Czerny, Delroy Lindo; **D:** Kevin Hooks. **CABLE**

Glory Daze ♂♂ **1996 (R)** Gen-X comedy about graduation week for five Santa Cruz college friends/housemates. There's Jack (Affleck), Mickey (DeRamus), Rob (Rockwell), Josh (Hong), and Dennis (Stewart) who basically party and kvetch about their uncertain futures, with various girlfriends, professors, and parents around to nag the boys. Not much you haven't seen before, although a number of the cast have gone on to bigger and better things. **100m/C VHS, DVD.** Ben Affleck, Sam Rockwell, French Stewart, Vinnie DeRamus, Vien Hong, Alyssa Milano, Megan Ward, John Rhys-Davies, Elizabeth Ruscio, Spalding Gray, Mary Woronov, **Cameos:** Matthew McConaughey, Brendan Fraser, Matt Damon, Meredith Salenger; **D:** Rich Wilkes; **W:** Rich Wilkes; **C:** Christopher Taylor.

Glory Enough for All: The Discovery of Insulin ♂♂1⁄2 **1992** The drama behind the discovery of insulin in the 1920s focuses on the research of four men, sometimes not-so-friendly rivals, searching for a treatment for diabetes mellitus. Dr. Frederick Banting and science student Charles Best are granted permission by James Macleod, a Professor of Physiology at the University of Toronto, to conduct experiments on the pancreas. Macleod then assigns biochemist James Collip to assist them on developing a viable serum, an extract named insulin. Banting and Macleod were awarded the Nobel prize in 1923 for their discovery (though Banting felt Macleod was undeserving). Adapted from "The Discovery of Insulin" by Michael Bliss. **195m/C VHS.** CA R.H. Thomson, Robert Wisden, John Woodvine, Michael Zelniker, Martha Henry, Heather Hess; **D:** Eric Till; **W:** Grahame Woods. **TV**

Glory! ♂♂1⁄2 **1990 (R)** Slashing satire about TV evangelism. Thomas as the meek son of founder of Church of the Champions of Christ brings in lewd female rock singer to save the money-machine ministry from financial ruin. Rock music, sex, and MTV-like camera work make it work with seeing. Whitmore is a treat. **152m/C VHS.** Ellen Greene, Richard Thomas, Barry Morse, James Whitmore, Winston Rekert; **D:** Lindsay Anderson; **W:** Stan Daniels.

Glory Road ♂♂1⁄2 **2006 (PG)** Yet another inspirational, fact-based sports drama. In 1966, the Miners, an under-funded basketball team at small Texas Western, became legends by defeating the sport's Goliaths—the all-white University of Kentucky Wildcats—in a championship. Their coach, Don Haskins, made history when he recruited seven black players and had five of them in his starting lineup. Naturally, there are problems leading up to their triumph, which are dealt with efficiently by first-time director Gartner. End credits showcase Haskins and several of the actual players reflecting on the game. **106m/C DVD, Blu-ray, Disc.** US Josh(ua) Lucas, Derek Luke, Austin Nichols, Jon Voight, Evan Jones, Alphonso McAuley, San Jones III, Emily Deschanel, Al Shearer, Schin A.S. Kerr, Mencad Brooks, Damaine Radcliff; **D:** James Gartner; **W:** Chris Cleveland, Bettina Gilois; **C:** John Toon, Jeffrey L. Kimball; **M:** Trevor Rabin.

The Glory Boys ♂1⁄2 **1984** A secret agent is hired to protect an Israeli scientist who is marked for assassination by the PLO and IRA. **78m/C VHS.** Rod Steiger, Anthony Perkins, Gary Brown, Aaron Harris; **D:** Michael Ferguson.

The Glory Stompers WOOF! **1967** Hopper prepares for his Easy Rider role as the leader of a motorcycle gang who battles with a rival leader over a woman. Very bad, atrocious dialogue, and a "love-in" scene that will be best appreciated by insomniacs. **85m/C VHS.** Dennis Hopper, Jody McCrea, Chris Noel, Jock Mahoney, Lindsay Crosby, Robert Tessier, Casey Kasem; **D:** Anthony M. Lanza.

The Glory Trail ♂1⁄2 Glorious Sacrifice **1936** A group of railroad workers and soldiers are constantly harassed by Indian attacks. **63m/B VHS.** Tom Keene, Joan Barclay, James Bush, Frank Melton, Walter Long; **D:** Lynn Shores.

Go ♂♂♂ **1999 (R)** Episodic tale of grocery clerk Ronna (Polley) as she takes over a shift to Vegas-bound co-worker Simon (Askew) and also agrees to sub as a go-between for a drug deal between two actors (Mohr and Wolf) and Simon's dealer Todd (Olyphant). Three-part narrative for a few of the cast members, most notably Polley and Diggs. Based on a children's novel, by Upton Sinclair. **103m/C VHS, DVD.** Water Brennan, Richard Deacon, Ed Wynn, Karen Dotrice, Matthew Garber; **D:** Robert Stevenson; **C:** Edward Colman; **M:** Buddy (Norman Dale) Baker.

Go Down Death ♂1⁄2 **1941** In this early all-black film, a minister is caught in a moral dilemma literally between Heaven and Hell. Scenes of the afterlife are taken from early silent films. **63m/B VHS, DVD.** Myra D. Hemmings, Samuel H. James, Eddy L. Houston, Spencer Williams Jr., Amos Droughan; **D:** Spencer Williams Jr.

Go Fish ♂♂♂1⁄2 **1994 (R)** Low-budget girl-meets-girl romantic comedy finds Kia (McMillan) playing matchmaker for her roommate, energetic Max (Turner) by setting her up with shy Ely (Brodie). The opposites do, eventually, attract, with their friends eager for every detail. Good-natured and candid, with a welcome lack of melodrama. **87m/B VHS, DVD.** Guinevere Turner, V.S. Brodie, T. Wendy McMillan, Anastasia Sharp, Migdalia Melendez; **D:** Rose Troche; **W:** Guinevere Turner, Rose Troche; **C:** Ann T. Rossetti; **M:** Brendan Dolan, Jennifer Sharpe.

Go for Broke! ♂♂1⁄2 **1951** Inexperienced officer Johnson heads a special WWII attack force which is made up of Japanese Americans. Sent to fight in Eu-

Glory Years ♂ **1987** Three old friends find themselves in charge of the scholarship fund at their 20th high school reunion. Unfortunately, they decide to increase the fund by gambling in Las Vegas and lose it all on a fixed fight! **150m/C VHS, DVD.** George Dzundza, Archie Hahn, Tim Thomerson, Tawny Kitaen, Donna Pescow, Donna Denton; **D:** Arthur Allan Seidelman.

The Glove ♂♂ The Glove: Lethal Terminator; Blood Mad **1978 (R)** Ex-cop turned bounty hunter has his toughest assignment ever: It's his job to bring in a six-and-a-half foot, 250-pound ex-con who's been wreaking havoc with an unusual glove—it's made of leather and steel. **93m/C VHS, DVD.** John Saxon, Roosevelt "Rosie" Grier, Joanna Cassidy, Joan Blondell, Jack Carter, Aldo Ray; **D:** Ross Hagen.

The Gnome-Mobile ♂♂ **1967** A lumber baron and his two grandchildren with a lost gnome colony. Brennan has a dual role as both a human and a gnome grandfather. Wynn's last film. Based on a children's novel, by Upton Sinclair. **103m/C VHS, DVD.** Water Brennan, Richard Deacon, Ed Wynn, Karen Dotrice, Matthew Garber; **D:** Robert Stevenson; **C:** Edward Colman; **M:** Buddy (Norman Dale) Baker.

The Go-Between ♂♂♂1⁄2 **1971 (PG)** Wonderful tale of hidden love. Young boy Guard acts as a messenger between the aristocratic Christie and her former lover Bates. But tragedy befalls them all when the lovers are discovered. The story is told as the elderly messenger (now lover Bates, but tragedy befalls them all as the go-between and builds to a messenger for the lady he loved long ago. Based on a story by L.P. Hartley. **116m/C VHS.** GB Julie Christie, Alan Bates, Dominic Guard, Margaret Leighton, Michael Redgrave, Michael Gough, Edward Fox, Edward Losey; **W:** Harold Pinter; **C:** Gerry Fisher; **M:** Michel Legrand. British Acad. '71: Screenplay, Support. Actor (Fox), Support. Actress (Leighton); Cannes '71: Film.

rope, they prove their bravery and loyalty to all. Good, offbeat story. **92m/B VHS, DVD.** *US* Van Johnson, Gianna Maria Canale, Warner Anderson, Lane Nakano, George Miki; *C:* Paul Piroshi; *W:* Robert Pirosh; *M:* Alberto Colombo.

Go for It 1983 (PG) Oddball supercops go after a mad scientist—who has created a deadly "K" bomb—and they encounter killer whales, karate busboys and malevolent Shirley Temple clones along the way. **109m/C VHS.** *IT* Bud Spencer, Terence Hill, David Huddleston; *D:* E.B. (Enzo Barboni) Clucher.

Go for the Gold 1984 A young marathon runner risks his girlfriend's love when he decides to pursue fame and fortune. **98m/C VHS.** James Ryan, Cameron Mitchell, Sandra Horne; *D:* Jackie Cooper; *M:* David McHugh.

Go for Zucker *Alles Auf Zucker!* 2005 Two estranged Jewish brothers, one living in eastern Germany, the other in the west, must clean up their act in order to receive the inheritance their recently-deceased mother left behind. As stated in the will, they must reconcile their differences and, more importantly, adhere to strict Jewish Orthodox conventions. Contrived storyline and loads of Jewish stereotypes drag this one into sitcom territory. A hit in Germany, but something is lost in translation for sure. **90m/C DVD.** Henry Hubchen, Hannelore Elsner, Udo Samel, Sebastian Blomberg, Rolf Hoppe, Golda Tencer, Steffen Groth, Anja Franke, Elena Uhlig; *D:* Dani Levy; *W:* Dani Levy, Holgar Franke; *C:* Carl F. Koschnick; *M:* Niki Reiser.

Go Further ½ 2003 Documentary follows Woody Harrelson and his "Merry Hempsters" as they travel up and down the Pacific coast by bike, preaching the virtues of a Green lifestyle. Pushing its message to the converted, film is cloying and about as subtle as a jackhammer. Harrelson does, however, come across as surprisingly intelligent and well-informed. Who could have guessed? **80m/C DVD.** *CA* Woody Harrelson; *D:* Ron Mann; *C:* Robert Fresco; *M:* Guido Luciani.

Go-Get-'Em-Haines 1935 Newsman Boyd follows a fleeing bankrupt utilities tycoon over an ocean liner for an interview only to end up trying to solve the tycoon's murder. **61m/C VHS, DVD.** William Boyd, Sheila Terry, Eleanor Hunt, Leroy Mason, Lloyd Ingraham, Jimmy Aubrey, Clarence Geldart, Louis Natheaux, Lee Shumway; *D:* Sam Newfield.

The Go-Getter 1954 Wild slapstick fun in the world of business. **78m/C VHS.** Hank McCune, Beverly Garland, Thurston Hall, Ray Collins, Andrew Tombes; *D:* Leslie Goodwins, Leigh Jason; *W:* Earl Baldwin, Charles Maxwell; *C:* Charles Straumer.

Go, Johnny Go! 1959 Rock promoter Alan Freed molds a young orphan into rock sensation "Johnny Melody." Musical performances include Ritchie Valens (his only film appearance), Eddie Cochran, Jackie Wilson, Chuck Berry, Jimmy Clanton, Eddie Cochran, Jackie Wilson, Ritchie Valens; *D:* Paul Landres.

Go Kill and Come Back 1968 (PG) A bounty hunter tracks down a notoriously dangerous train robber. **95m/C VHS, DVD.** Gilbert Roland, George Helton, Edd Byrnes; *D:* Enzo G. Castellari.

The Go-Masters 1982 *Taikyoku* Historic co-production between Japan and China, centering on the ancient strategy board game "Go." A young competitor becomes obsessed with winning at any price. Episodic tale of the relationships between a Japanese and Chinese family spans 30 years and Japan. In Japanese and Chinese with English subtitles. **134m/C VHS.** *JP CH* Huang Zong-Ying, Du Peng, Yu Shao-Kang, Lui Xin, Yoshiko Mita, Keiko Matsuzaka, Mayumi Ogawa, Rentaro Mikuni, Daolin Sun, Shen Guan-Chu, Misako Honno; *D:* Junya Sato, Duan Jishun. Montreal World Fest. '83: Film.

Go Now ½ 1996 Regular guy Nick (Carlyle), a soccer-playing construction worker meets and falls in love with hotel management trainee Karen (Au-brey). All is going well until Nick starts experiencing physical problems—dropping things, double vision, numbness. As his condition worsens, it's confirmed that he's been stricken with Multiple Sclerosis. Nick goes through the usual stages of dealing with the disease, but Winterbottom's film doesn't go through the usual disease-of-the-week motions. Straightforward look at the effects of a debilitating disease doesn't create martyrs or heroes, opting instead for realistic characters and honest emotions or situations. First-rate performance by Carlyle. **87m/C VHS.** *GB* Robert Carlyle, Juliet Aubrey, James Nesbitt, Sophie Okonedo, Berwick Kaler, Tom Watson; *D:* Michael Winterbottom; *W:* Jimmy McGovern, Paul Powell; *C:* Daf Hobson; *M:* Alastair Gavin.

Go Tell It on the Mountain 1984 Young black boy tries to gain the approval of his stern stepfather in this fine adaptation of James Baldwin's semiautobiographical novel. Set in the 1930s; originally a PBS "American Playhouse" presentation. **100m/C VHS, DVD.** Paul Winfield, Olivia Cole, Ruby Dee, Alfre Woodard, James Bond III, Rosalind Cash, Linda Hopkins; *D:* Stan Lathan.

Go Tell the Spartans 1978 (R) In Vietnam, 1964, a hard-boiled major is ordered to establish a garrison at Muc Wa with a platoon of burned out Americans and Vietnamese mercenaries. Blundering but politically interesting war epic pre-dating the flood of 1980s American-Vietnam apologetics. Based on Daniel Ford's novel. **114m/C VHS, DVD.** Burt Lancaster, Craig Wasson, David Clennon, Marc Singer, Jonathan Goldsmith, Joe Unger, Dennis Howard, Evan C. Kim, John Megna, Hilly Hicks, Dolph Sweet, Clyde Kusatsu, James Hong; *D:* Ted Post; *W:* Wendell Mayes; *C:* Harry Stradling Jr.; *M:* Dick Halligan.

Go West ½ *Marx Brothers Go West* 1940 The brothers Marx help in the making and un-making of the Old West. Weak, late Marx Bros., but always good for a few yucks. **80m/B VHS, DVD.** Groucho Marx, Chico Marx, Harpo Marx, John Carroll, Diana Lewis, Walter Woolf King, George Lessey, Robert Barrat, June MacCloy; *D:* Edward Buzzell; *W:* Irving Brecher; *C:* Leonard Smith; *M:* George Bassman, Roger Edens.

Go West 2005 Ambitious but not always successful stew of ethnic hatred, war, romance, and identity. Kenan (Drmac) is Muslim; his lover Milan (Filpovic) is a Bosnian Serb and when the ethnic conflicts break out in Sarajevo in 1992, the two decide to flee to the Netherlands. Only their train is stopped by Bosnian soldiers, so Milan disguises Kenan as a woman and says she's his wife. Forced to find refuge with Milan's father Ljubo (Serbedzija) in his Bosnian hometown, the two attempt to continue their deception. Then Milan gets drafted and barkeep Ranka (Burina) discovers Kenan's secret. Bosnian with subtitles. **97m/C DVD.** *BS* Rade Serbedzija, Mirjana Karanovic, Tarik Filpovic, Mavio Drmac, Haris Burina; *Cameos:* Jeanne Moreau; *D:* Ahmed Imamovic; *W:* Ahmed Imamovic, Enver Puska; *C:* Mustafa Mustafic; *M:* Enes Zlatar.

Go West, Young Man ½ 1936 West is a movie star whose latest film is premiering in a small town, where she's naturally a sensation. Scott is the muscular farm boy who catches her eye and she decides to hang around in order to catch the rest of him as well. The censors again cut West's most overt sexual and satiric barbs. **80m/B VHS, DVD.** Mae West, Randolph Scott, Warren William, Alice Brady, Elizabeth Patterson, Lyle Talbot, Isabel Jewell; *D:* Henry Hathaway; *W:* Mae West; *C:* Karl Struss.

Goal! The Dream Begins ½ 2006 (PG) Illegal Mexican immigrant Santiago Munez (Becker) dreams of making it big playing soccer. L.A. talent scout Foy (Dillane), who's got U.K. contacts, offers a tryout with Newcastle United. First, the poor Santiago has to get across the pond (grandma helps) but his adjustment is difficult until his partying superstar teammate Gavin (Nivola) gives him a boost. Hits all the inspirational sports cliches (it's a Disney release) but it's good-hearted and good-looking (and that's not just the players). First of a planned trilogy. **118m/C DVD.** *US* Kuno Becker, Alessandro Nivola, Marcel Iures, Stephen (Dillon) Dillane, Anna Friel, Kieran O'Brien, Sean Pertwee, Gary Lewis, Cassandra Bell, Tony Plana, Miriam Colon, Jorge Cervera, Lee Ross, Ashley Walters, Frances Barber, Kevin Knapman; *Cameos:* Kieron Dyer, David Beckham; *D:* Danny Cannon; *W:* Dick Clement, Ian La Frenais, Adrian Butchart; *C:* Michael Barrett; *M:* Graeme Revell, Graeme Revell.

The Goalie's Anxiety at the Penalty Kick ½ *Die Angst Tormannes beim Elfmeter* 1971 A chilling landmark film that established Wenders as one of the chief film voices to emerge from post-war Germany. The story deals with a soccer player who wanders around Vienna after being suspended, commits a random murder, and slowly passes over the brink of sanity and morality. A suspenseful, existential adaptation of the Peter Handke novel. In German with English subtitles. **101m/C VHS.** *GE* Arthur Brauss, Erika Pluhar, Kai (Kay) Fischer; *D:* Wim Wenders; *W:* Peter Handke, Wim Wenders; *C:* Robby Muller; *M:* Jurgen Knieper.

Goblin woof! 1993 Newlywed couple regret the purchase of their new home when the devilish creature once brought to life by the previous homeowner, is raised from the witch-craft performing farmer, is raised from the depths of hell to rip to pieces anyone in its view. Any movie whose promo says "You won't believe your eyes...until he rips them from their sockets" is sure to be a crowd pleaser. Enjoy. **75m/C VHS.** Bobby Westrick, Jenny Admire; *D:* Todd Sheets.

God Bless the Child 1988 A young single mother loses her home and her seven-year-old daughter are forced to live on the streets. Harrowing TV drama providing no easy answers to the plight of the homeless. **93m/C VHS, DVD.** Mare Winningham, Dorian Harewood, Grace Johnston, Charlaine Woodard, Obba Babatunde, L. Scott Caldwell; *D:* Larry Elikann; *W:* Dennis Nemec; *M:* David Shire. TV

God Grew Tired of Us 2006 (PG) Continuation of 2003's "The Lost Boys of Sudan," which revisits three young Sudanese men—John Bul Dau, Panther Bior, and Daniel Abul Pach—and their adjusting to life in the U.S. as refugees. **89m/C DVD.** *US* John Bul Dau, Panther Bior, Daniel Abul Pach; *D:* Christopher Quinn; *C:* Paul Daley; *M:* Mark Nelson, Mark McAdam, Jamie Staff.

God is My Co-Pilot 1945 Based on the book by Col. Robert Lee Scott (played by Morgan), an ace fighter pilot with Maj. Gen. Chennault's (Massey) famed Fighting Tigers squadron. After multiple engagements against the Japanese in the air over China, Scott is battling illness and nerves in 1942 when he's grounded just before a major air assault. Fairly standard hero story, told in flashbacks, although there's an emphasis on Scott's faith sustaining him, as you might guess from the title. **88m/B VHS.** Dennis Morgan, Raymond Massey, Dane Clark, Alan Hale, Andrea King, John Ridgely, Stanley Ridges, Craig Stevens, Richard Loo, Warren Douglas; *D:* Robert Florey; *W:* Abem Finkel, Peter Milne; *C:* Sid Hickox; *M:* Franz Waxman.

God, Man and Devil ½ 1949 A wager between God and Satan begins this allegory of money versus the spirit. A poor Torah scribe, Hershele Dubrovner, has a life that glorifies God until Satan, disguised as a business partner, turns him greedy and dishonest. Dubrovner's success destroys both his religion and his community leaving only betrayal and abandonment. In Yiddish with English subtitles. **100m/B VHS.** Mikhal Mikhalesko, Gustav Berger; *D:* Joseph Seiden.

God Said 'Ha!' 1999 (PG-13) Julia Sweeney recounts a very trying year in her life in this adaptation of her one-woman Broadway show. She tells of her brother's fight with lymphoma, which caused him (as well as her parents) to move in with her, as well as her own battle with cervical cancer. Sweeney's wry observations and loving remembrances prevent melodrama from seeping in. As with most monologues-turned-movies, this one works much better in the small-screen setting. **87m/C VHS.** Julia Sweeney; *D:* Julia Sweeney; *W:* Julia Sweeney; *C:* John Hora; *M:* Anthony Marinelli.

God Told Me To 1976 (R) A religious New York cop is embroiled in occult mysteries while investigating a series of grisly murders. He investigates a religious cult that turns out to be composed of half-human, half-alien beings. A cult-fave Larry Cohen epic. **89m/C VHS, DVD.** Tony LoBianco, Deborah Raffin, Sylvia Sidney, Sandy Dennis, Richard Lynch, Sam Levene, Andy Kaufman, Robert Drivas, Mike Kellin; *D:* Larry Cohen; *W:* Larry Cohen; *C:* Paul Glickman; *M:* Frank Cordell. *Demon*

The Goddess 1958 Sordid story of a girl who rises to fame as a celluloid star by making her body available to anyone who can help her career. When the spotlight dims, she keeps going with drugs and alcohol to a bitter end. **105m/B VHS.** Kim Stanley, Lloyd Bridges, Patty Duke; *D:* John Cromwell; *W:* Paddy Chayefsky.

The Godfather 1972 (R) Coppola's award-winning adaptation of Mario Puzo's novel about a fictional Mafia family in the late 1940s. Revenge, envy, and parent-child conflict mix with the rituals of Italian mob life in America. Minutely detailed, with excellent performances by Pacino, Brando, and Caan as the violence-prone Sonny. Film debut of Coppola's daughter Sophia, the infant in the baptism scene, who returns in "Godfather III." The horrific horse scene is an instant classic. Indisputably an instant piece of American culture. Followed by two sequels. **171m/C VHS, DVD.** Marlon Brando, Al Pacino, Robert Duvall, James Caan, Diane Keaton, John Cazale, Talia Shire, Richard Conte, Richard S. Castellano, Abe Vigoda, Alex Rocco, Sterling Hayden, John Marley, Al Lettieri, Sofia Coppola, Al Martino, Morgana King; *D:* Francis Ford Coppola; *W:* Mario Puzo, Francis Ford Coppola; *C:* Gordon Willis; *M:* Nino Rota. Oscars '72: Actor (Brando), Adapt. Screenplay, Picture; AFI '98: Top 100; Directors Guild '72: Director (Coppola); Golden Globes '73: Actor—Drama, Screenplay, Score; Natl. Bd. of Review '72: Support. Actor (Pacino), Natl. Film Reg. '90; N.Y. Film Critics '72: Support. Actor (Duvall); Natl. Soc. Film Critics '72: Actor (Pacino); Writers Guild '72: Adapt. Screenplay.

The Godfather 1902-1959: The Complete Epic 1981 Coppola's epic work concerning the lives of a New York crime family. Comprises the first two "Godfather" films, reedited into a chronological framework of the Corleone family history, with much previously discarded footage restored. **386m/C VHS.** Marlon Brando, Al Pacino, Robert Duvall, James Caan, Richard S. Castellano, Diane Keaton, Robert De Niro, John Cazale, Lee Strasberg, Talia Shire, Michael V. Gazzo, Troy Donahue, Joe Spinell, Abe Vigoda, Alex Rocco, Sterling Hayden, John Marley, Richard Conte, G.D. Spradlin, Bruno Kirby, Harry Dean Stanton, Roger Corman, Al Lettieri; *D:* Francis Ford Coppola; *W:* Mario Puzo, Francis Ford Coppola.

The Godfather, Part 2 1974 (R) A continuation and retracing of the first film, interpolating the young Vito Corleone and its founding by the young Vito (De Niro, in a terrific performance) 60 years before in NYC's Little Italy. Often considered the second half of one film, the two films stand as one of American film's greatest efforts, and as a 1970s high-water mark. Combined into one work for TV presentation. Followed by a sequel. **200m/C VHS, DVD.** Al Pacino, Robert De Niro, Diane Keaton, Robert Duvall, James Caan, Danny Aiello, John Cazale, Lee Strasberg, Talia Shire, Michael V. Gazzo, Troy Donahue, Joe Spinell, Abe Vigoda, Marianna Hill, Fay Spain, G.D. Spradlin, Bruno Kirby, Harry Dean Stanton, Roger Corman, Kathleen Beller, John Aprea, Morgana King, Dominic Chianese, Frank Sivero, Gianni Russo, Peter Donat; *D:* Francis Ford Coppola; *W:* Francis Ford Coppola, Mario Puzo; *C:* Gordon Willis; *M:* Nino Rota, Carmine Coppola. Oscars '74: Adapt. Screenplay, Art Dir/Set Dec, Director (Coppola), Picture, Support. Actor (De Niro), Orig. Dramatic Score; AFI '98: Top 100; Directors Guild '74: Director (Coppola), Natl. Film Reg. '93; Natl. Soc. Film Critics '74: Director (Coppola); Writers Guild '74: Adapt. Screenplay.

The Godfather, Part 3 🎬🎬🎬
1990 (R) Don Corleone, now aging and guilt-ridden, determines to buy his salvation in the Catholic Church, which he finds to be a more corrupt brotherhood than his own. Meanwhile, back on the homefront, his young daughter discovers her sexuality as she falls in love with her first cousin. Weakest entry of the trilogy is still a stunning and inevitable conclusion to the story; Pacino adds exquisite finishing touches to his time-worn character. Beautifully photographed in Italy by Gordon Willis. Video release contains the final director's cut featuring nine minutes of footage not included in the theatrical release. **170m/C VHS, DVD.** Al Pacino, Diane Keaton, Andy Garcia, Joe Mantegna, George Hamilton, Talia Shire, Sofia Coppola, Eli Wallach, Don Novello, Bridget Fonda, John Savage, Al Martino, Raf Vallone, Franc D'Ambroso, Dona Donnelly, Richard Bright, Helmut Berger, George Hamilton; **D:** Francis Ford Coppola; **W:** Mario Puzo, Francis Ford Coppola; **C:** Gordon Willis; **M:** Carmine Coppola. Golden Raspberries '90: Worst Support. Actress (Coppola), Worst New Star (Coppola).

Godmoney 🎬🎬½ **1997** (R) Nathan (Rodney) is a New York street kid who tries to clean up his life of drugs and crime by moving to the Los Angeles suburbs where he is recruited by Matthew (Field), a dealer who tries to get him back into his old ways. Director Doane's debut made an impression on the festival circuit, and it deserves its reputation. Despite a background in music videos, he is able to tell a coherent story about interesting characters without letting style overpower substance. **99m/C VHS, DVD.** Rick Rodney, Bobby Field, Christi Allen; **D:** Darren Doane. **W:** Darren Doane, Sean Atkins, Sean Nelson; **M:** Nicholas Rivera.

Gods and Generals 🎬🎬 **2003** (PG-13) Maxwell's ambitious second film in his "Civil War trilogy" is exquisite in its attention to period detail, and grand in its depiction of the battles it covers, but suffers when it gets to the stories of the men it portrays. A prequel to 1993's "Gettysburg," this one covers the years 1861-63, beginning with Gen. Lee (Duvall) declining command of the Union Army, through the battles of First Manassas, Fredericksburg, and Chancellorsville, and finishing with Stonewall Jackson's death and the events leading up to Gettysburg. The main problem is that the dialogue (housed in many self-important and overlong speeches) is stilted, lifeless, and humorless, which handcuffs a very talented cast. Historic personages are raised to icon status, showing none of the real-life flaws that would've made them more interesting. Based on the novel by Jeffrey M. Shaara. **220m/C VHS, DVD, Blu-ray Disc, HD DVD. US** Jeff Daniels, Stephen Lang, Robert Duvall, Kevin Conway, C. Thomas Howell, Patrick Gorman, Brian Mallon, Matt Letscher, William Sanderson, Mira Sorvino, Frankie Faison, Jeremy London, Kali Rocha, Bruce Boxleitner, Billy Campbell, Bo Brinkman, Mia Dillon, Stephen Spacek, Royce D. Applegate, William Morgan Sheppard; **Cameos:** Ted Turner; **D:** Ronald F. Maxwell; **C:** Kees Van Oostrum; **M:** John (Glenn) Frizzell, Randy Edelman.

Gods and Monsters 🎬🎬🎬½ **1998** Although British director James Whale (McKellen) had a varied (if short) Hollywood career in the '30s and '40s, his name rested on his Universal horror films: "The Invisible Man," "Frankenstein," and "The Bride of Frankenstein." Now long-retired and suffering from ill-health, the openly gay Whale lives quietly in L.A. with his protective housekeeper, Hanna (Redgrave). Whale does enjoy the company of his new gardener—Clayton Boone (Fraser)—but a stroke has left the director with a confusing sense of reality—returning him to his soldiering days in WWI and "Frankenstein." Brilliant performance from McKellen, with solid support from Fraser and Redgrave. Based on the novel "Father of Frankenstein" by Christopher Bram. **105m/C VHS, DVD.** an McKellen, Brendan Fraser, Lynn Redgrave, Lolita (David) Davidovich, David Dukes, Kevin J. O'Connor, Brandon

Kleyla, Jack Plotnick, Rosalind Ayres, Arthur Dignam, Jack Betts, Martin Ferrero, David Millbern; **D:** Bill Condon; **W:** Bill Condon; **C:** Stephen M. Katz; **M:** Carter Burwell. Oscars '98: Adapt. Screenplay; Golden Globes '99: Actor (McKellen), Ind. Spirit '99: Actor (McKellen), Film, Support, Actress (Redgrave); L.A. Film Critics '98: Actor (McKellen), Natl. Bd. of Review '98: Actor (McKellen), Natl. Bd. of Review '98: Actor (McKellen); Broadcast Film Critics '98: Actor (McKellen), Chiyang; **D:** Harry Kerwin.

God's Bloody Acre woof! **1975** (R) Three backwoods mountain-dwelling brothers kill construction workers in order to defend their land, and then begin preying on vacationers. **90m/C VHS, Scott Lawrence, Jennifer Gregory, Sam Moree, Shiang Hwa Chyang; **D:** Harry Kerwin.

God's Comedy 🎬🎬 A Comedia de Deus **1995** Joao de Deus (Montero) is a lecherous ice-cream maker who indulges himself with the ice cream counter girls that Joao needs to be taught a lesson. Portuguese with subtitles. **163m/C VHS,** Manuela de Freitas, Raquel Ascenso, Sarana Serrano; **D:** Joao Cesar Montero; **W:** Joao Cesar Montero; **C:** Joao Barroso.

God's Country 🎬🎬 **1946** A loner kills a man in self-defense and escapes the pursuing law by disappearing into California Redwood country with his dog. **62m/C VHS,** Robert Lowery, Helen Gilbert, William Farnum, Buster Keaton; **D:** Robert Emmet Tansey.

God's Country and the Man 🎬🎬 **1937** Typical western adventurer about a cowboy out to nab a gunman who's been threatening the life of a dance hall girl. Plenty of two-fisted action when law-abiding Keene shows up. **56m/B VHS, DVD.** Tom Keene, Betty Compson, Charlotte Henry, Charles "Blackie" King, Billy Bletcher, Eddie (Ed. Eddy, Edwin) Parker; **D:** Robert North Bradbury.

God's Gun 🎬 A Bullet from God **1975** (R) Preacher who was once a gunfighter seeks revenge on the men who tried to kill him. Parolini used the pseudonym Frank Kramer. **93m/C VHS, DVD.** Richard Boone...see Van Cleef, Jack Palance, Sybil Danning; **D:** Gianfranco Parolini.

God's Little Acre 🎬🎬🎬 **1958** Delves into the unexpectedly passionate lives of Georgia farmers. One Tyan, convinced there's buried treasure on his land, nearly brings himself and his family to ruin trying to find it. Based on the novel by Erskine Caldwell. **110m/B VHS, DVD.** Robert Ryan, Tina Louise, Michael Landon, Buddy Hackett, Vic Morrow, Jack Lord, Aldo Ray, Fay Spain; **D:** Anthony Mann; **W:** Philip Yordan; **C:** Hans J. Haller; **M:** Elmer Bernstein.

God's Lonely Man 🎬🎬 **1996** Ernest Reckman (Wyle) is one of life's losers. He gets fired from his videostore job and suffers bouts of violence and suicidal impulses. Then he poses as a police officer in order to "rescue" teenaged prostitute Christiane (McComb) so they can begin a new life together but this also doesn't go as planned. **98m/C VHS, DVD.** Michael Wyle, Heather McComb, Justine Bateman, Paul Dooley, Roxana Zal, Wallace (Wally) Langham, Kieran Mulroney; **D:** Frank Von Zerneck; **W:** Frank Von Zerneck; **C:** Dennis Smith; **M:** James Fearnley.

The Gods Must Be Crazy 🎬🎬🎬 **1984** (PG) An innocent and charming film. A peaceful Bushman travels into the civilized world to return a Coke bottle "to the gods." Along the way he meets a transplanted schoolteacher, an oafishly clumsy microbiologist and a gang of fanatical terrorists. A very popular film disarmingly crammed with slapstick and broad humor of every sort. Followed by a weak sequel. **109m/C VHS, DVD, SA** Nixau, Marius Weyers, Sandra Prinsloo, Louw Verwey, Jamie Uys, Michael Thys, Nic de Jager; **D:** Jamie Uys; **W:** Jamie Uys; **C:** Robert M. Lewis, Buster Reynolds; **M:** John Boshoff, Johnny Bishop.

The Gods Must Be Crazy 2 🎬🎬½ **1989** (PG) A slapdash sequel to the original 1981 African chortler, featuring more ridiculous shenanigans of the bush. This time the bushman's children find themselves in civilization and Nixau

must use his unique ingenuity to secure their safe return. **90m/C VHS, DVD.** Nixau, Lena Faruga, Hans Strydom, Eiros Nadies, Eric Bowen; **D:** Jamie Uys; **M:** Charles Fox.

Gods of the Plague 🎬🎬🎬 Götter der Pest **1969** Fassbinder goes noir—or grey with lots of sharp lighting—in this gangster-auteur tale of robbery gone awry. The requisite trappings of the crime genre (guys and dolls and cops and robbers) provide a vague backdrop (and a vague plot) for a moody story full of teutonic angst and alienation, and that certain Fassbinder feeling (which, need we say, isn't to everyone's taste). An early effort by the director, who remade the story later the same year as "The American Soldier." German with subtitles. **92m/C VHS, DVD, GE** Hanna Schygulla, Harry Baer; **D:** Rainer Werner Fassbinder.

God's Sandbox 🎬½ Tahara **2002** This one takes a strange turn from family drama and romance into politics and religion and never finds its proper path again. At a Sinai Desert resort, Liz is mistrustful of Rachel's friendship with co-worker Mustapha because he is a Bedouin, but he is eager to regale her with a local legend. Seems in the 1960s another wild child Israeli, Leila, fell in love with a local sheik's son, but her acceptance into the tribe revolves around her agreeing to the ritual of female circumcision. And yes, the two stories tie together. Arabic and Hebrew with subtitles. **66m/C DVD. /S** Razia Israeli author Liz tries to reconnect with rebellious daughter Rachel, who is working at a Sinai Desert resort. Orl Perel, Sami Samir, Meital Doran, Juliano Mer, Ori Perel; **C:** Claudio Steinberg; **M:** Arik Rudich.

The Godsend 🎬 **1979** (R) "Omen" rip-off about a little girl who is thrust upon a couple. After adopting her, they lose their natural family to her evil ways. **93m/C VHS, CA** Cyd Hayman, Malcolm Stoddard, Angela Pleasence, Patrick Barr; **D:** Gabriele Beaumont.

Godsend 🎬🎬 **2004** (PG-13) Playing like a dozen similar demon-child redos, pic tries for originality by combining modern technology with typical genre supernatural creepiness. Cute 8-year-old Adam Duncan is killed in a freak auto accident. Grieving parents Paul (Kinnear) and Jessie (Romijn-Stamos) have no sooner buried their adored son when they are approached by Dr. Wells (De Niro) who offers to harvest their dead son's cells for cloning and subsequent rebirth via Jessie. Naturally, the couple agree. When the Adam clone reaches his eighth birthday, however, things start to go eerily awry. **102m/C VHS, DVD. US** Greg Kinnear, Rebecca Romijn, Cameron Bright, Robert De Niro, Merwin Mondesir, Deborah Odell, Jack Simons, Elle Downs, Zoie Palmer; **D:** Nick Hamm; **W:** Mark Bomback; **C:** Kramer Morgenthau; **M:** Brian Tyler.

The Godson 🎬 **1998** (PG-13) When Giuseppe "the Guppy" Calzone becomes the head of his crime family, he realizes his son and heir will need some tutoring to become the next big boss. So he sends the kid to Mafia U. to pick up some tricks of the trade. But the head of a rival family sees this as the perfect opportunity to get rid of the Calzone clan. Really, really dumb, despite the comic cast. **100m/C VHS, DVD.** Rodney Dangerfield, Dom Deluise, Kevin McDonald, Fabiana Udenio, Lou Ferrigno, Barbara Crampton; **D:** Bob Hoge; **W:** Bob Hoge; **C:** Tom Lappin; **M:** Boris Elkis. **VIDEO**

Godspell 🎬🎬½ **1973** (G) Musical retelling of the story of Jesus, set in New York City. Adapted from an enjoyable Broadway play but the film version comes off as silly. Good dancing and interesting score. Songs include "Day by Day By My Side; Alas For You; On the Willows; O, Bless the Lord My Soul; Prepare Ye the Way of the Lord; Turn Back O Man; Beautiful City; Save the People. **103m/C VHS, DVD.** Victor Garber, David Haskell, Jerry Sroka, Lynne Thigpen, Gilmer McCormick; **D:** David Greene; **M:** Stephen Schwartz.

Godzilla 🎬🎬½ **1998** (PG-13) Overthe-top remake of the 1954 cult classic has nuclear testing in France creating a giant mutant lizard to destroy all boats, piers, people and buildings that happen to get in its way. Gone are the days of a man in a rubber suit menacing Tokyo, replaced by state-of-the-art special effects. Third rate storyline has wimpy biologist Niko Tatopolos (Broderick) hired to track down and connect with the creature that Godzilla has chosen as the Big Apple as the birthing place for its huge brood. When the eggs hatch, look out. Burr's various supporting characters (including Reno as a French secret agent out to destroy Godzilla) cross paths with the creature, and its sequel. Ending leaves door wide open for an inevitable sequel of its own. **139m/C VHS, DVD, UMD.** Matthew Broderick, Jean Reno, Maria Pitillo, Hank Azaria, Kevin Dunn, Michael Lerner, Harry Shearer, Arabella Field, Vicki Lewis, Doug Savant, Malcolm Danane; **D:** Roland Emmerich, Dean Devlin; **C:** Ueli Steiger; **M:** David Arnold. Golden Raspberries '98: Worst Remake/Sequel, Worst Support. Actress (Pitillo).

Godzilla, King of the Monsters 🎬🎬½ Gojira **1956** An underwater prehistoric reptile emerges from the depths to terrorize Tokyo after he has been awakened by atomic testing. Burr is called in (as the only living American witness to Godzilla's destructive 1955 outburst) to help mediate the conflict. Film released to coincide with the 30th anniversary of the original. **91m/C VHS, DVD. JP** Raymond Burr, Takashi Shimura, Akira Takarada, Akihiko Hirata, Momoko Kochi, Sachio Sakai, Fuyuki Murakami, Ren Yamamoto; **D:** Inoshiro Honda, Terry Morse; **W:** Guy Roe; **M:** Akira Ifukube.

Godzilla 1985 🎬½ **1985** (PG) Godzilla is awakened from underwater slumber by trolling nuclear submarines belonging to the superpowers near Japan. The giant monster's newly acquired appetite for nuclear energy inadvertently precipitates an international incident. Burr is back in the U.S. **80m/B VHS, DVD. JP** Raymond Burr, Keiju Kobayashi, Ken Tanaka, Raymond Burr, Yasuka Sawaguchi, Shin Takuma; **D:** Kohji Hashimoto, Robert J. Kizer; **W:** Shuichi Nagahara, Lisa Tomei; **C:** Kazutami Hara; **M:** Reijiro Koroku.

Godzilla on Monster Island 🎬 **1998** Godzilla vs. Gigan **1972** Even giant monster's cannot hope to take on both Ghidra and Gigan alone and hope to succeed. Therefore he summons his pal Angilus for help. Together, they offer Earth its only hope of survival. Though the terror may repel you, the film is a must for Godzilla fans; it's his first speaking part. **89m/C VHS, DVD. JP** Hiroshi Ichikawa, Tomoko Umeda, Yuriko Hishimi, Minoru Takashima, Zan Fujita; **D:** Jun Fukuda.

Godzilla 2000 🎬🎬½ **1999** (PG) Any other bigger-than-life movie-house hero staring in a series of films that span almost 50 years would have to answer some serious questions about plot repetition—but not Godzilla. The familiarity is what you pay to see. If Godzilla didn't clumsily destroy Tokyo office buildings and knock commuter trains off their elevated tracks, you'd be asking for a refund, pronto. So, with the latest Japanese flick to make it to our shores—featuring the REAL Godzilla, not that sophisticated

Godzilla Raids Again 🎬🎬 Gigantis, the Fire Monster; Godzilla's Counter Attack **1955** Warner Bros. had a problem securing rights to Godzilla's name, so they opted to destroy Osaka instead of Tokyo, but the spiny Angorous is terror when the battle royale begins. The first Godzilla sequel. **78m/B VHS, DVD. JP** Hugo Grimaldi, Makoyama, Minoru Chiaki; **D:** Mictoyoshi Oda; **W:** Shigeaki Hidaka; **C:** Seichi Enco; **M:** Masaru Sato.

American excuse for a Godzilla from a couple of years back—all is well. Funny dubbing, rubber suits, miniature sets—perfect comfort food on a rainy afternoon. As far as the plot goes...in short, spacecraft attacks Tokyo—the radioactive dinosaur comes to the rescue. **97m/C VHS, DVD.** JP Takehiro Murata, Shiro Sano, Hiroshi Abe, Naomi Nishida, Mayu Suzuki; **D:** Takao Okawara; **W:** Hiroshi Kashiwabara, Wataru Mimura; **C:** Katsuhiro Kato; **M:** Takayuki Hattori.

Godzilla vs. Biollante 🐱🐱 *Gojira tai Biorante* **1989 (PG)** Five years after Japan was destroyed, scientists are studying Godzilla's cells. Desperate spies, who apparently can't find their own Godzilla cells on all the ruined buildings, release Godzilla from his volcanic prison. When one scientist's attempt to create a super-plant goes awry and creates the behemoth Biollante, the monsters go at it in a giant territorial rumble. Japan (or a really small model thereof) is once again underfoot. Sequel to "Godzilla 1985." **104m/C VHS.** JP Koji Takahashi, Yoshiko Tanaka, Megumi Odaka, Kunihiko Mitamura, Masahiro Takashima, Kenpachiro Satsuma; **D:** Kazuki Omori; **W:** Kazuki Omori; **C:** Yudai Kato.

Godzilla vs. King Ghidora 🐱½ **1991** Tokyo begins to panic when aliens from the 23rd century make an appearance. But these aliens supposedly come in peace—warning that Godzilla will soon reawaken and destroy Japan unless he can be destroyed first. But it turns out these beings aren't so benign and soon Godzilla is confronted by his arch-enemy—flying, three-headed King Ghidora. **89m/C VHS, DVD.** JP Richard Berger, Kiwako Harada, Kent Gilbert, Shoji Kobayashi; **D:** Kazuki Omori; **W:** Kazuki Omori; **C:** Yoshinori Sekiguchi; **M:** Akira Ifukube.

Godzilla vs. Mechagodzilla II 🐱½ **1993** Mechagodzilla II, a mammoth robot fueled by a nuclear reactor and sheathed in a synthetic diamond shield, is supposed to protect Japan from Godzilla. The mechanical monster has its work cut out for it now that Godzilla and Rodan have both arrived to claim the recently hatched baby Godzilla from a team of scientists. **108m/C VHS, DVD.** JP Masahiro Takashima, Leo Mangetti; **D:** Takao Okawara.

Godzilla vs. Megalon 🐱🐱 **1976 (G)** Godzilla's creators show their gratitude to misguided but faithful American audiences by transforming the giant monster into a good guy. This time, the world is threatened by Megalon, the giant cockroach, and Gigan, a flying metal creature, simultaneously. Fortunately, the slippery hero's robot pal Jet Jaguar is on hand to slug it out side by side with Tokyo's ultimate defender. **80m/C VHS, DVD.** JP Katsuhiko Sasaki, Hiroyuki Kawase, Yutaka Hayashi, Robert Dunham, Kotaro Tomita; **D:** Jun Fukuda; **W:** Jun Fukuda, Shinichi Sekizawa; **C:** Yuzuru Aizawa; **M:** Richiro Manabe.

Godzilla vs. Monster Zero 🐱🐱 *Monster Zero; Battle of the Astros; Invasion of the Astro-Monsters; Invasion of Planet X; Kaiju Daisenso; The Great Monster War; War of the Monsters* **1968 (G)** Novel Godzilla adventure with the big guy and Rodan in outer space. Suspicious denizens of Planet X require the help of Godzilla and Rodan to rid themselves of the menacing Ghidra, whom they refer to as Monster Zero. Will they, in return, help Earth as promised, or is this just one big, fat double cross? **93m/C VHS, DVD.** JP Akira Takarada, Nick Adams, Kumi Mizuno, Jun Tazaki, Akira Kubo, Keiko Sawai, Yoshio Tsuchiya, Noriko Sengoku, Fuyuki Murakami; **D:** Inoshiro Honda; **W:** Shinichi Sekizawa; **C:** Hajime Koizumi; **M:** Akira Ifukube.

Godzilla vs. Mothra 🐱🐱 *Godzilla vs. the Thing; Godzilla vs. the Giant Moth; Godzilla Fights the Giant Moth; Mothra vs. Godzilla; Mosura tai Gojira* **1964** Mighty Mothra is called in to save the populace from Godzilla, who is on a rampage; and he's aided by two junior Mothras who hatch in the nick of time. The hesitant moth avoids the fire-breathing behemoth until succumbing to the pleadings of the Peanut Sisters to save humanity. Hilarious special effects inspire more laughter from derision than anything

---

else. **88m/C VHS, DVD.** JP Akira Takarada, Yuriko Hoshi, Hiroshi Koizumi, Emi Ito, Yumi Ito, Yoshifumi Tajima, Kenji Sahara, Yu Fujiki; **D:** Inoshiro Honda; **W:** Shinichi Sekizawa; **C:** Hajime Koizumi; **M:** Akira Ifukube.

Godzilla vs. the Cosmic Monster 🐱🐱 *Godzilla Versus the Bionic Monster; Godzilla vs. Mechagodzilla; Gojira Tai Meka-Gojira* **1974 (G)** Godzilla's worst nightmares become a reality as he is forced to take on the one foe he cannot defeat—a metal clone of himself! To make matters worse, Earth is in dire peril at the hands of cosmic apes. We all need friends, and Godzilla is never more happy to see his buddy King Seeser, who gladly lends a claw. **80m/C VHS, DVD.** JP Masaki Daimon, Kazuya Aoyama, Reiko Tajima, Barbara Lynn, Akihiko Hirata; **D:** Jun Fukuda.

Godzilla vs. the Sea Monster WOOF! *Nankai No Kai Ketto; Ebirah, Terror of the Deep; Big Duel in the North* **1966** Godzilla makes friends with former rival Mothra (a giant moth) and together they bash on Ebirah, an enormous lobster backed by an evil cache of (human) totalitarians. The unrepentant crusteacean turns the tables on our heroes, however, by growing a new tentacle everytime one is ripped off. Meanwhile, a frenzied batch of helpless humans are trapped on an island about to explode, if they aren't drowned first in a shower of reptilian backwash. **80m/C VHS, DVD.** JP Kumi Mizuno, Choraro Togin, Hideo Sunazuka, Akira Takarada; **D:** Jun Fukuda; **W:** Shinichi Sekizawa, Kazuo Yamada; **C:** Masaru Sato.

Godzilla vs. the Smog Monster 🐱 *Gojira Tai Hedora; Godzilla vs. Hedora* **1972 (G)** Godzilla battles a creature borne of pollution, a 400-pound sludge blob named Hedora. Early 1970s period piece conveys interesting attitude towards pollution; it's treated as a sinister force that people are powerless to stop. Japanese teenagers marshal their dancing talents to combat the threat amid the hypnotic swirl of disco lighting. Great opening song: "Save the Earth." Dubbed in English. **87m/C VHS, DVD.** JP Akira Yamauchi, Hiroyuki Kawase, Toshio Shibaki; **D:** Yoshimitu Banno.

Godzilla's Revenge 🐱 *Oru Kaiju Daishingeki* **1969** A young boy who is having problems dreams of going to Monster Island to learn from Minya, Godzilla's son. Using the lessons in real life, the boy captures some bandits and outwits a bully. Uses footage from "Godzilla vs. the Sea Monster" and "Son of Godzilla" for battle scenes. One of the silliest Godzilla movies around. **70m/C VHS, DVD.** JP Kenji Sahara, Tomonori Yazaki, Machiko Naka, Sachio Sakai, Chotaro Togin, Yoshitumi Tajima, Eisei Amamoto, Ikio Sawamura; **D:** Inoshiro Honda; **M:** Kunio Miyauchi.

The Goebbels Experiment 🐱🐱 **2005** Documentary on Joseph Goebbels, Hitler's minister of propaganda, taken from diaries covering 1924 to 1945. Archival footage illustrates the readings. Kenneth Branagh narrates the English version; Udo Samel the German one. **107m/C DVD.** **D:** Lutz Hachmeister; **W:** Lutz Hachmeister, Michael Kloft; **C:** Hajo Schomerus; **M:** Hubert Bittman.

Goin' Coconuts 🐱 **1978 (PG)** Donny and Marie are miscast as Donny and Marie in this smarmy story of crooks and jewels. Seems someone covets the chanteuse's necklace, and only gratuitous crooning can spare the twosome from certain swindling. Big bore on the big island. **90m/C VHS.** Donny Osmond, Marie Osmond, Herb Edelman, Kenneth Mars, Ted Cassidy, Marc Lawrence, Harold Sakata; **D:** Howard Morris.

Goin' South 🐱🐱 **1978 (PG)** An outlaw is saved from being hanged by a young woman who agrees to marry him in exchange for his help working a secret gold mine. They try to get the loot before his old gang gets wind of it. A tongue-in-cheek western that served as Nicholson's second directorial effort. Movie debuts of Steenburgen and Belushi. **109m/C VHS, DVD.** Jack Nicholson, Mary Steenburgen, John Belushi, Christopher Lloyd, Veronica Cartwright, Richard Bradford, Danny DeVito, Luana Anders,

---

Ed Begley Jr., Anne Ramsey; **D:** Jack Nicholson; **W:** Charles Shyer; **C:** Nestor Almendros; **M:** Perry Botkin.

Goin' to Town 🐱½ **1935** Complicated yarn with West as a woman who inherits an oil field and becomes the wealthiest woman in the state. She falls for British engineer Cavanagh and decides to become a "lady," in order to get his attention. There's a subplot about Buenos Aires and a crooked horse race, an in-name-only marriage to a high society type, and a murder before Mae finally gets her man. **71m/B VHS, DVD.** Mae West, Paul Cavanagh, Gilbert Emery, Ivan Lebedeff, Marjorie Gateson, Tito Coral, Monroe Owsley; **D:** Alexander Hall; **W:** Mae West; **C:** Karl Struss.

Goin' to Town 🐱 **1944** Radio team Lum and Abner in one of their last films, as two conmen who scheme to make money from a phony oil well. **77m/B VHS.** Chester Lauck, Norris Goff, Barbara Hale, Grady Sutton, Florence Lake; **D:** Leslie Goodwins; **W:** Charles E. Roberts, Charles Marion; **C:** Robert Pittack; **M:** Lud Gluskin.

Going All the Way 🐱🐱½ **1997 (R)** Korean War vets Sonny Burns (Davies) and Gunner Casselman (Affleck) find themselves becoming best buds after returning to their Indianapolis hometown in 1954. Gunner's the self-confident stud, who vaguely wants to be an artist, while aspiring photographer Sonny's an anxious geek. The boys have mom troubles (Sonny's is a bible-thumper while Gunner's is a seductive flirt) and chase girls with varying success but the true bonding is strictly male. Davies is appropriately twitchy while Affleck gets to effectively use his natural charisma. Wakefield adapted from his 1970 novel. **110m/C VHS, DVD.** Jeremy Davies, Ben Affleck, Jill Clayburgh, Lesley Ann Warren, Rose McGowan, Rachel Weisz, Amy Locane; **D:** Mark Pellington; **W:** Dan Wakefield; **C:** Bobby Bukowski.

Going Ape! 🐱🐱 **1981 (PG)** Danza inherits a bunch of orangutans. If the apes are treated well, a legacy of $5 million will follow. This is all you need to know. **87m/C VHS.** Tony Danza, Jessica Walter, Danny DeVito, Art Metrano, Rick Hurst; **D:** Jeremy Joe Kronsberg; **M:** Elmer Bernstein.

Going Back 🐱½ **1983** Four friends reunite after college to relive a memorable summer they spent together after graduating from high school. **85m/C VHS.** Bruce Campbell, Christopher Howe, Perry Mallette, Susan W. Yamasaki; **D:** Ron Teachworth.

Going Bananas 🐱🐱 **1988 (PG)** Wacky adventure about a chimp who is being chased by a sinister circus owner. The monkey runs through Africa dragging along a boy, his caretaker, and a guide. **95m/C VHS.** Dom DeLuise, Jimmie Walker, David Mendenhall, Herbert Lom; **D:** Boaz Davidson.

Going Berserk 🐱½ **1983 (R)** The members of SCTV's television comedy troupe are featured in this comedy which lampoons everything from religious cults to kung fu movies. Has moments of inspired lunacy, interspersed with more pedestrian fare. Includes wicked send-up of "Father Knows Best," with former cast member Donahue. **85m/C VHS.** CA John Candy, Joe Flaherty, Eugene Levy, Paul Dooley, Pat Hingle, Richard Libertini, Ernie Hudson, Alley Mills, Dixie Carter, Murphy Dunne, Elinor Donahue; **D:** David Steinberg.

Going for the Gold: The Bill Johnson Story 🐱🐱 **1985** Biographical tale of the American downhill skier who went from hard-luck punk to Olympic champion in the 1984 games at Sarajevo, Yugoslavia. **100m/C VHS.** Anthony Edwards, Dennis Weaver, Sarah Jessica Parker, Deborah Van Valkenburgh, Wayne Northrop; **D:** Don Taylor.

Going Greek 🐱½ **2001 (R)** College freshman/football star Jake (Bruno) is in school on a scholarship and must keep up his grades. That's not going to be easy when his geeky cousin Gil (James) wants to join a fraternity and won't be accepted unless Jake agrees to pledge as well. Jake finds himself loosening up with all the raucous antics of his frat brothers, but his grades begin to suffer as does his rela-

---

tionship with girlfriend Paige (Harris), who despises all fraternities. Gross-out gags and gratuitous nudity abound as you might expect. **90m/C VHS, DVD.** Dylan Bruno, Laura Harris, Simon Rex, Dublin James, Corey Pearson, Oliver Hudson, Steve Monroe; **D:** Justin Zackham; **W:** Justin Zackham; **C:** Kirk Douglas; **M:** Nathan Barr. **VIDEO**

Going Hollywood 🐱🐱 **1933** Amusing musical/romantic fluff about a French teacher (Davies) who falls in love with a radio crooner (Crosby in his first MGM film). He's got the movie bug and heads for Hollywood, where he becomes an overnight sensation with a sultry costar (D'Orsay). Davies follows and proceeds to get Crosby out of D'Orsay's clutches and winds up replacing her rival in the film, promptly becoming a star herself. The underrated Davies was a fine light comedienne and supplied glamour to the production as well. Kelly, in her film debut, supplied the slapstick. The last Hearst-Cosmopolitan production made with MGM. ♫Temptation; We'll Make Hay While the Sun Shines; Going Hollywood; Our Big Love Scene; After Sundown; Cinderella's Fella; Beautiful Girl; Just an Echo in the Valley. **78m/B VHS.** Marion Davies, Bing Crosby, Fifi d'Orsay, Stuart Erwin, Patsy Kelly, Ned Sparks; **D:** Raoul Walsh; **W:** Donald Ogden Stewart; **C:** George J. Folsey.

Going Home 🐱½ **1986** During WWI, Canadian soldiers held in British camps awaiting transport back home stage a riot over the endless delays and intolerable conditions. A fact-based story of the events leading up to this tragedy. **91m/C VHS, DVD.** George Burns, Art Carney, Lee Strasberg; **D:** Martin Brest; **W:** Martin Brest.

Going in Style 🐱🐱½ **1979 (PG)** Three elderly gentlemen, tired of doing nothing, decide to liven up their lives by pulling a daylight bank stick-up. They don't care about the consequences because anything is better than sitting on a park bench all day long. The real fun begins when they get away with the robbery. Great cast makes this a winner. **96m/C VHS, DVD.** George Burns, Art Carney, Lee Strasberg; **D:** Martin Brest; **W:** Martin Brest.

Going My Way 🐱🐱🐱½ **1944** A musical-comedy about a progressive young priest assigned to a downtrodden parish who works to get the parish out of debt, but clashes with his elderly curate, who's set in his ways. Followed by "The Bells of St. Mary's." Fitzgerald's Oscar-winning Supporting Actor performance was also nominated in the Best Actor category. ♫The Day After Forever; Swinging on a Star; Too-ra-loo-ra-loo-ra; Going My Way; Silent Night; Habanera; Ave Maria. **126m/B VHS, DVD.** Bing Crosby, Barry Fitzgerald, Rise Stevens, Frank McHugh, Gene Lockhart, Porter Hall; **D:** Leo McCarey; **W:** Frank Butler, Frank Cavett, Leo McCarey; **C:** Lionel Lindon. Oscars '44: Actor (Crosby), Director (McCarey), Picture, Screenplay, Song ("Swinging on a Star"), Story, Support. Actor (Fitzgerald); Golden Globes '45: Director (McCarey), Film—Drama, Support. Actor (Fitzgerald); Natl. Film Reg. '04; N.Y. Film Critics '44: Actor (Fitzgerald), Director (McCarey). Film.

Going Overboard 🐱 *Babes Ahoy* **1989 (R)** Cruise ship waiter dreams of becoming a comedian and his big break when the ship's comic disappears. **99m/C VHS, DVD.** Adam Sandler, Burt Young, Billy Zane, Peter Berg; **D:** Valerie Breiman.

Going Places 🐱🐱 *Les Valseuses; Making It* **1974 (R)** A cynical, brutal satire about two young thugs traversing the French countryside raping, looting and cavorting as they please. Moreau has a brief role as an ex-con trying to go straight. An amoral, controversial comedy that established both its director and two stars. In French with English subtitles or dubbed. **122m/C VHS, DVD.** FR Gerard Depardieu, Patrick Dewaere, Miou-Miou, Isabelle Huppert, Jeanne Moreau, Brigitte Fossey; **D:** Bertrand Blier; **W:** Bertrand Blier; **C:** Bruno Nuytten; **M:** Stephane Grappelli.

Going Postal 🐱🐱 *Postal Worker* **1998 (R)** Psychologist Dr. Nicolas Brink (Portnow) is hired to create an early warning system to prevent the ticking timebombs of the postal world from going off. But he may be

Going Shopping ✗✗ 2005 (PG-13) Jaglom indulges his penchant for talky, femme-centered comedies by focusing on Holly (Foyt), the deeply in debt (a man done her wrong) owner of a trendy boutique. She searches for an infusion of cash while hoping a big Mother's Day sale will draw in customers and help salvage her enterprise. Interspersed with Holly's travails is a chorus of women who offer their thoughts on what shopping means to them. 106m/C DVD. *W:* Henry Jaglom, Victor Harnet; *C:* Hanaria Baer; *M:* Harriet Schock.

Going Under 1991 (PG) Subsurface military satire about the U.S.S. Sub Standard the worst nuclear vessel in the Navy. It's so poorly constructed that the brass would rather sink than inspect it—if only they could. Interesting cast sinks with script headed for dry dock. 81m/C VHS. Bill Pullman, Wendy Schaal, Ned Beatty, Robert Vaughn, Bud Cort, Michael Winslow; *D:* Mark W. Travis; *W:* Randolph Davis, Darryl Zanuck; *C:* Victor Harner; *M:* David Michael Frank.

Going Undercover ✗ 1988 (PG-13) A bumbling private investigator is hired to protect a rich, beautiful, and spoiled young woman on her European vacation. Poor excuse for a comedy. 90m/C VHS, DVD. Lea Thompson, Jean Simmons, Chris Lemmon; *D:* James Kenwin Clarke.

Going Upriver: The Long War of John Kerry ✗✗✗½ 2004 Director Butler has former senator and 2004 presidential candidate John Kerry for some 40 years and has been photographing him since 1969. This matter-of-fact documentary looks at Kerry's military service (with some archival footage shot in Vietnam) and his later role in helping establish the group Vietnam Veterans Against the War. Based on the nonfiction book "Tour of Duty" by Douglas Brinkley. 89m/C DVD. *US D:* George Butler; *W:* Joseph Dorman; *C:* Sandi Sissel; *M:* Philip Glass.

The Gold & Glory ✗ Coolangatta Gold 1988 [FG-13] Two brothers, one a musician, the other an athlete, vie for the affections of the same girl by competing in a footrace for a golden purse. 102m/C VHS. *AU:* Colin Friels, Josephine Smulders, Grant Kenny; *D:* Igor Auzins; *W:* Peter Schreck; *C:* Keith Wagstaff; *M:* Bill Conti.

Gold Diggers of 1933 ✗✗✗½ 1933 In the famous period musical, show-girls help a songwriter save his Busby Berkeley-choreographed show. Followed by two sequels. ♫We're in the Money; Shadow Waltz; I've Got to Sing a Torch Song; Pettin' in the Park; Remember My Forgotten Man. 96m/B VHS, DVD. Joan Blondell, Ruby Keeler, Aline MacMahon, Dick Powell, Guy Kibbee, Warren William, Ned Sparks, Ginger Rogers; *D:* Mervyn LeRoy.

Gold Diggers of 1935 ✗✗✗ 1935 The second Gold Diggers film, having something to do with a New England resort, romance, and a charity show put on at the hotel. Plenty of Berkeleian large-scale drama, especially the bizarre, mock-tragic "Lullaby on Broadway" number, which derails the last days of a Broadway baby. ♫I'm Going Shopping With You; The Words Are in My Heart; Lullaby of Broadway. 95m/B VHS, DVD. Dick Powell, Adolphe Menjou, Gloria Stuart, Alice Brady, Frank McHugh, Glenda Farrell, Grant Mitchell, Hugh Herbert, Wini Shaw; *D:* Busby Berkeley; *C:* George Barnes. Oscar '35: Song ("Lullaby of Broadway").

Gold Diggers: The Secret of Bear Mountain ✗✗½ 1995 (PG) Thirteen-year-old Beth (Ricci) moves to the small town of Wheaton, Washington, and forms an unlikely friendship with rebellious tomboy Jody (Chlumsky). Together, the girls set out on a treasure hunt that takes them into a dangerous trek through sea-coast mountain terrain. The grownups are dumb (and the story's fairly boring) but the two heroines have real appeal. 94m/C VHS, Christina Ricci, Anna Chlumsky, Polly Draper, Brian Kerwin, Diana Scarwid, David Keith; *W:* Barry Glasser; *C:* Ross Berryman; *M:* Joel Michael.

The Gold of Naples ✗✗ L'Oro Di Napoli 1954 A four-part omnibus film about life in Naples, filled with romance, funny and sad tragedies, by turns poignant, and pensive. Originally six tales; two were trimmed for U.S. release. In Italian with subtitles. 107m/B VHS. *IT:* Vittorio De Sica, Silvana Mangano; *D:* Vittorio De Sica.

Gold of the Amazon Women ✗ Amazon Women 1979 When two explorers set out to find gold, they stumble onto a society of man-hungry women who follow them into the urban jungle of Manhattan. There is also a European "R"-rated version. 94m/C VHS, DVD. Bo Svenson, Anita Ekberg, Bond Gideon, Donald Pleasence; *D:* Mark L. Lester; *W:* Stanley Ralph Ross; *C:* David Quaid; *M:* Gil Melle. TV

Gold Raiders ✗ 1951 Larry, Moe, and Shemp team up with an insurance agent to take on the bad guys in the wild west. The Stooges are long past their prime. 56m/B VHS. George O'Brien, Moe Howard, Shemp Howard, Larry Fine, Sheila Ryan, Clem Bevans, Lyle Talbot; *D:* Edward L. Bernds.

Gold Raiders ✗✗½ 1963 Team of secret agents are sent to the Jungles of Laos to find a plane carrying $200 million worth of gold, and nothing will get in their way. 106m/C VHS. *GB* Robert Ginty, Sarah Langenfelc, Steven, Dusty Rhodes; *D:* P. (Philip) Chalong.

The Gold Rush ✗✗✗ 1925 Chaplin's most critically acclaimed film. The best definition of his simple approach to film form; adept manuevering of visual pathos. The "Little Tramp" searches for gold and romance in the Klondike in the mid-1800s. Includes the dance of the rolls, and Chaplin's lovely music, pantomime sequence of eating the shoe, and Chaplin's lovely music. 85m/B VHS, DVD. Charlie Chaplin, Mack Swain, Tom Murray, Georgia Hale; *D:* Charlie Chaplin; *W:* Charlie Chaplin; *C:* Roland H. Totheroh, Jack Wilson; *M:* Charlie Chaplin. AFI '98: Top '00, Natl. Film Reg. '92.

The Golden Bowl ✗✗✗ 1972 Wealthy widower Adam Verver (Morris) and his naive daughter, Maggie (Townsend), are utterly devoted to each other. A situation that doesn't change with Maggie's marriage to an impoverished Italian prince (Massey). Then Maggie decides her lonely father should also remarry and who could be better than Maggie's old chum, the beautiful Charlotte (Hunnicutt). But what the Ververs don't realize is how well the Prince and Charlotte already know each other. However, a gilced crystal cup—the Golden Bowl—will bring unwelcome knowledge. Based on the novel by Henry James. 270m/C VHS. *GB* Barry Morse, Jill Townsend, Daniel Massey, Gayle Hunnicutt, Cyril Cusack, Kathleen Byron; *D:* James Cellan Jones; *W:* Jack Pulman. TV

The Golden Bowl ✗✗½ 2000 (R) Beautiful but bloodless Merchant/Ivory adaptation of Henry James' complex 1904 novel set in turn-of-the-century London. Wealthy American aesthete Adam Verver (Nolte) dotes on his only daughter, Maggie (Beckinsale), and even buys her a husband—an impoverished Italian aristocrat, Prince Amerigo (a miscast Northam), whom she loves. But, unknown to both of them, the prince and Maggie's best friend, the equally poor Charlotte (Thurman), had a long ago affair that gets rekindled, even through Charlotte has become the wife of Adam. A studied menage a quatre where just what anyone knows (or suspects) is never made clear. 130m/C VHS, DVD, *GB US FR* Nick Nolte, Uma Thurman, Kate Beckinsale, Jeremy Northam, Anjelica Huston, James Fox, Madeline Potter, Peter Eyre; *D:* Ismail Merchant; *W:* Ruth Prawer Jhabvala; *C:* Tony Pierce-Roberts; *M:* Richard Robbins.

Golden Boy ✗✗✗ 1939 Holden plays a young and gifted violinist who earns money for his musical education by working as a part-time prizefighter. Fight promoter Menjou has Stanwyck cozy up to the impressionable young man to convince him to make the fight game his prime concern. She's successful but it leads to tragedy. Holden's screen debut, with Cobb as his immigrant father and Stanwyck successfully slinky as the corrupting love interest. Classic pugilistic drama with well-staged fight scenes. Based on Clifford Odets play with toned down finale. 99m/B VHS. William Holden, Adolphe Menjou, Barbara Stanwyck, Lee J. Cobb, Joseph Calleia, Sam Levene, Don Beddoe, Charles Halton, Beatrice Blinn; *D:* Rouben Mamoulian; *W:* Daniel Taradash, Victor Heeman, Sarah Y. Mason.

The Golden Child ✗✗ 1986 (PG-13) When a Tibetan child with magic powers is kidnapped and transported to Los Angeles, Chandler, a professional "finder of lost children" must come to the rescue. The search takes him through Chinatown in a hunt that cliches every Oriental swashbuckler ever made. Good fun. 94m/C VHS, DVD. Eddie Murphy, Charlotte Lewis, Charles Dance, Victor Wong, Randall "Tex" Cobb, James Hong; *D:* Michael Ritchie; *W:* Dennis Feldman; *C:* Donald E. Thorin; *M:* Michel Colombier.

The Golden Coach ✗✗✗ Le Carrosse D'Or 1952 Based on a play by Prosper Merimee, the tale of an 18th-century actress in a South America that takes on all comers, including the local viceroy who creates a scandal by presenting her with his official coach. Rare cinematography by Claude Renoir. 101m/C VHS, DVD. *FR* Anna Magnani, Odoardo Spadaro, Nada Fiorelli, Dante Rino, Duncan Lamont; *D:* Jean Renoir; *W:* Ginette Doynel, Jack Kirkland, Giulio Macchi, Jean Renoir; *C:* Claude Renoir, Ronald Hill; *M:* Antonio Vivaldi.

The Golden Compass ✗✗ 2007 (PG-13), 12-year-old Lyra (Richards) lives in a world similar to Victorian England and ruled by the church-like Magisterium, who seem dead set on controlling the minds of everyone in the world and eliminating free will. When best friend Roger (Walker) disappears, Lyra, along-side a strange assortment of allies including a 'talking, armored bear (McKellan) and a pilot with a Texas accent (Elliot), travels north to rescue him, despite the Magisterium and their ice-queen agent Ms. Coulter's(Kidman) best efforts to stop her. The all-star cast is exceptional, but the story may confound without the book as a roadmap. The film stirred a minor controversy because of the anti-religion themes of the book upon which it was based (the first installment of Philip Pullman's popular British fantasy trilogy), even though writer/director Weitz mostly cut those parts from the movie. 113m/C DVD. *US* Nicole Kidman, Daniel Craig, Eva Green, Christopher Lee, Dakota Blue Richards, Sam Elliott, Ben Walker, Tom Courtenay, Derek Jacobi, Kathy Bates; *D:* Chris Weitz; *W:* Chris Weitz; *C:* Henry Braham; *M:* Alexandre Desplat; *V:* Kristin Scott-Thomas, Freddie Highmore, Ian McKellan, Ian McShane. Oscars '07: Visual FX.

Golden Demon ✗✗½ Konjiki Yasha 1953 An acclaimed Japanese epic, from the novel by Koyo Ozaki, about the destructive powers of wealth on the lives of two star-crossed lovers in medieval Japan. In Japanese with English subtitles. 95m/C VHS. *JP* Jun Negami, Fujiko Yamamoto; *D:* Koji Shima.

Golden Earrings ✗✗½ 1947 Enjoyable, yet incredulous story about British agent Milland joining up with gypsy Dietrich for espionage work in Nazi Germany. Absurd film was so bad it became a camp classic overnight. Although Dietrich and Milland couldn't stand each other and battled constantly during production, the movie did quite well at the boxoffice. Based on a novel by Yolanda Foldes. 95m/B VHS, DVD. Ray Milland, Marlene Dietrich, Bruce Lester, Dennis Hoey, Quentin Reynolds, Reinhold Schunzel, Ivan Triesault; *D:* Mitchell Leisen; *W:* Abraham Polonsky, Frank Butler, Helen Deutsch; *C:* Daniel F. Fapp.

Golden Gate ✗✗ 1993 (R) Young Fed Dillon is thrown into the hysteria of the communist witch hunt in 1952 San Francisco. He snares Song, a Chinese labor activist, on some very dubious charges. Ten years later he finds himself getting involved with Song's daughter Marilyn (Chen), who knows nothing about her lover's involvement with her family. Then she finds out. Ever-changing moods, sometimes times film noir, sometimes a love story, sometimes a nostalgic look back are confusing. Promising storyline meanders and fades as Director Madden tries to tie too much in a short time. Beware of broad stereotypes in every character. 95m/C VHS. Matt Dillon, Joan Chen, Bruno Kirby, Tzi Ma, Stanford; Eg, Peter Murnik, Jack Shearer, Amir Harris, David Janssen, John Vernon, Bright gess Meredith; *D:* John Madden; *W:* David Henry Hwang; *C:* Bobby Bukowski; *M:* Elliot Goldenthal.

Golden Lady ✗½ 1979 Beautiful woman leads her female gang in a deadly game of international intrigue. 90m/C VHS. Christina World, Suzanne Danielle, June Chadwick; *D:* Joseph (Jose Ramon) Larraz.

Golden Rendezvous ✗✗ Nuclear Terror 1977 A tale of treachery aboard a "gambler's paradise" luxury liner which is hijacked and held for ransom. Based on Alistair MacLean's novel. 103m/C VHS, Richard Harris, David Janssen, John Carradine, Burgess Meredith, Ann Turkel, John Vernon, Dorothy Malone, Keith Baxter, Gordon Jackson; *D:* Ashley Lazarus.

The Golden Salamander ✗✗ 1951 Howard shines in otherwise lackluster adventure about archaeologist searching for ancient ruins in Tunisia who must deal with gun runners and their evil leader, while torridly romancing a beautiful Tunisian girl. Filmed on location in Tunis. Based on the novel by Victor Canning. 96m/B VHS. *GB* Trevor Howard, Anouk Aimee, Herbert Lom, Miles Malleson, Walter Rilla, Jacques Sernas, Wilfrid Hyde-White, Peter Copley, Eugene Deckers, Henry Edwards, Marcel Poncin, Percy Walsh, Sybilla Binder, Kathleen Boutall, Valentine Dyall; *D:* Frank Zuniga; *M:* Oswald Morris.

The Golden Seal ✗✗½ 1983 (PG) Tale of a small boy's innocence put in direct conflict, because of his love of a rare wild golden seal and her pup, with the greed of adults. Filmed in the Aleutian Islands, it's a scenic film with themes of failed dreams, pride and ordinary greed of adults. 94m/C VHS, DVD. Steve Railsback, Michael Beck, Penelope Milford, Torquil Campbell; *D:* Frank Zuniga; *M:* John Barry.

The Golden Spiders: A Nero Wolfe Mystery ✗✗✗ 2000 It's actually the pilot of a mystery but writer Rex Stout's eccentric sleuth Wolfe (Chaykin) and his idiosyncratic cast of helpers as well as the setting (Manhattan in the late '40s) make for some amusing moments. Gourmand and orchid grower Wolfe never leaves his brownstone, preferring right-hand man Archie Goodwin (Hutton) take care of the legwork. The golden spiders of the title are a pair of flashy earrings worn by a damsel in distress that leads to several hit-and-run deaths, blackmail, and fraud. 100m/C VHS, DVD. Maury Chaykin, Timothy Hutton, Bill Smitrovich, Saul Rubinek, Mimi Kuzyk, Beau Starr, Robert Clark, Larissa Lauchinski, Gary Reineke, Nicky Guadagni, Robert Bockstael, Trent McMullen, Bill Duke; *W:* Paul Monash; *C:* Mike Fash; *M:* Michael Small. C.A.B.L.E

The Golden Stallion ✗✗ 1949 Trigger falls in love with a stunning mare. He sees her villainous owners abusing her and kills them. Roy takes the blame for his equine pal, but true love triumphs to save the day. 67m/B VHS, Roy Rogers, Dale Evans, Estelita Rodriguez, Pat Brady, Douglas Evans, Frank Fenton; *D:* William Witney.

The Golden Voyage of Sinbad ✗✗½ 1973 (G) In the mysterious ancient land of Lemuria, Sinbad and his crew encounter magical and mystical creatures, including a one-eyed centaur and a griffin. Ray Harryhausen can once again claim credit for the unusual and wonderful mythical creatures.

---

springing to life. **105m/C VHS, DVD.** John Phillip Law, Caroline Munro, Tom Baker, Douglas Wilmer, Martin Shaw, John David Garfield, Gregoire Aslan; **D:** Gordon Hessler; **W:** Brian Clemens; **C:** Ted Moore; **M:** Miklos Rozsa.

Goldeneye 🐾🐾🐾 1995 (PG-13) Bond is back, in the long-awaited (eight years) debut of Brosnan as legendary Brit agent 007. Since we're through the Cold War, Bond has to make do with the villainy of the Russian Mafia, who are planning to sabotage global financial markets utilizing the "Goldeneye" satellite weapon. There's a spectacularly impossible stunt to start things out in familiar territory and lots more noisy (if prolonged) action pieces. Brosnan (who looks great in a tux) is slyly self-aware that his character is more myth than man and Janssen does a suitably over-the-top job as bad Bond girl Xenia Onatopp. Tina Turner sings the dreary title track. **130m/C VHS, DVD.** Pierce Brosnan, Famke Janssen, Sean Bean, Izabela Scorupco, Joe Don Baker, Robbie Coltrane, Judi Dench, Tcheky Karyo, Gottfried John, Alan Cumming, Desmond Llewellyn, Michael Kitchen, Serena Gordon, Samantha Bond, Minnie Driver; **D:** Martin Campbell; **W:** Jeffrey Caine, Michael France; **C:** Phil Meheux; **M:** Eric Serra. Blockbuster '96: Action Actor, T. (Brosnan).

Goldeneye: The Secret Life of Ian Fleming 🐾🐾🐾½ *Spymaster* 1989 James Bond's creator lead quite an interesting life himself. The debonair author joins His Majesty's Secret Service and gets involved in numerous romantic exploits. Not to be confused with the British TV movie "Spymaker," which also covered Fleming's early career. **103m/C VHS.** *GB* Charles Dance, Phyllis Logan, Julian Fellowes, Patrick Ryecart, Ed Devereaux; **D:** Don Boyd; **W:** Reg Gadney; **C:** Mike Southon; **M:** Michael Berkeley. **TV**

Goldengirl 🐾🐾 1979 (PG) Ian Nazi doctor tries to make a superwoman of his daughter who has been specially fed, exercised, and emotionally conditioned since childhood to run in the Olympics. Anton's starring debut. **107m/C VHS.** Susan Anton, James Coburn, Curt Jurgens, Robert Culp, Leslie Caron, Harry Guardino, Jessica Walter; **D:** Joseph Sargent; **M:** Bill Conti.

Goldenrod 🐾½ 1977 A successful rodeo champion is forced to reevaluate his life when he sustains a crippling accident in the ring. **100m/C VHS.** CA Tony LoBianco, Gloria Carlin, Donald Pleasence, Donnelly Rhodes; **D:** Harvey Hart. **TV**

Goldfinger 🐾🐾🐾 1964 (PG) Ian Fleming's James Bond, Agent 007, attempts to prevent international gold smuggler Goldfinger and his pilot Pussy Galore from robbing Fort Knox. Features villainous assistant Oddjob and his deadly bowler hat. The third in the series is perhaps the most popular. Shirley Bassey sings the theme song. **117m/C VHS, DVD.** *GB* Sean Connery, Gert Frobe, Shirley Eaton, Tania Mallet, Harold Sakata, Cec Linder, Bernard Lee, Lois Maxwell, Desmond Llewellyn, Nadja Regin; **D:** Guy Hamilton; **W:** Paul Dehn, Richard Maibaum; **C:** Ted Moore; **M:** John Barry. Oscars '64: Sound FX Editing.

Goldilocks & the Three Bears 🐾🐾½ 1983 Entry from "Faerie Tale Theatre" tells the story of Goldilocks, who wanders through the woods and finds the home of three bears—only in this version Goldilocks is a nasty child, and it's the bears who'll get your sympathy. **60m/C VHS, DVD.** Tatum O'Neal, Alex Karras, Brandis Kemp, Donovan Scott, Hoyt Axton, John Lithgow, Carole King; **D:** Gilbert Cates.

Goldrush: A Real Life Alaskan Adventure 🐾🐾½ 1998 Well-bred Frances (Milano) decides to leave New York society life behind and join an expedition to Alaska (as a would-be gold miner) during the 1899 gold rush. **89m/C VHS.** Alyssa Milano, Bruce Campbell, Stan Cahill, Tom Scholte, William Morgan Sheppard; **D:** John Power; **W:** Jacqueline Feather, David Seidler.

Goldstein 🐾🐾½ 1964 After strolling out of Lake Michigan, a mysterious old man roams around Chicago and causes a profound reaction in the people he meets. One man, a sculptor, becomes so affected that he scours the city for him while trying

to make up with his pregnant ex-girlfriend, who decides to have an abortion that becomes an oddly comical experience. Unique debut film of notable director Kaufman was filmed in various locations throughout Chicago in the 1960s. **79m/B DVD.** Lou Gilbert, Tomas Erhart, Severn Darden, Ellen Madison, Benito Carruthers; **D:** Philip Kaufman, Benjamin Manaster; **W:** Philip Kaufman, Benjamin Manaster; **C:** Jean-Phillippe Carson; **M:** Meyer Kupferman.

The Goldwyn Follies 🐾🐾 1938 Lavish disjointed musical comedy about Hollywood. A movie producer chooses a naive girl to give him advice on his movies. George Gershwin died during the filming. ♫Romeo and Juliet; Water Nymph; Here, Pussy, Pussy; Serenade To a Fish; Love Walked In; Love is Here to Stay; Spring Again; I Was Doing Alright; La Serenata. **115m/C VHS, DVD.** Adolphe Menjou, Vera Zorina, Al Ritz, Harry Ritz, Jimmy Ritz, Helen Jepson, Phil Baker, Bobby Clark, Ella Logan, Andrea Leeds, Edgar Bergen; **C:** George Marshall; **C:** Gregg Toland; **M:** George Gershwin, Ira Gershwin.

The Golem 🐾🐾🐾½ *Der Golem, wie er in die Welt kam* 1920 A huge clay figure is given life by a rabbi in hopes of saving the Jews in the ghetto of medieval Prague. Rarely seen Wegener expressionist mythopus that heavily influenced the "Frankenstein" films of the sound era. **80m/B VHS, DVD. GE** Paul Wegener, Albert Steinruck, Ernst Deutsch, Lyda Salmonova, Otto Gebuehr, Max Kronert, Loni Nest, Greta Schroder, Hans Sturm; **D:** Carl Boese, Paul Wegener; **W:** Henrik Galeen, Paul Wegener; **C:** Karl Freund; **M:** Hans Landsberger.

Goliath Against the Giants 🐾½ *Goliath Contro I Giganti; Goliath at Contra Los Gigantes; Goliath and the Giants* 1963 Goliath takes on Bokan, who has stolen his throne. Goliath must fight Amazons, storms, and sea monsters to save the lovely Elea. Goliath conquers all. **95m/C VHS. IT** *SP* Brad Harris, Gloria Milland, Fernando Rey, Barbara Carroll; **D:** Guido Malatesta.

Goliath and the Barbarians 🐾🐾 *Il Terror Dei Barabari* 1960 Goliath and his men go after the barbarians who are terrorizing and ravaging the Northern Italian countryside during the fall of the Roman Empire. A basic Steve Reeves muscleman epic. **86m/C VHS. IT** Steve Reeves, Bruce Cabot; **D:** Carlo Campogaliani; **M:** Les Baxter.

Goliath and the Sins of Babylon 🐾🐾 *Maciste, L'Eroe Piu Grande Del Mondo* 1964 Well-sculpted Forest plays yet another mesomorph to the rescue in this poorly dubbed spaghetti legend. Goliath must spare 24 virgins whom the evil Crisa would submit as human sacrifice. There—who played the mighty Maciste in a number of films—was randomly assigned the identity of Goliath, Hercules, or Samson for U.S. viewing; go figure. **80m/C VHS. IT** Mark Forest, Eleanora Bianchi, Jose Greci, Giuliano Gemma, Paul Muller; **D:** Michele Lupo.

Goliath Awaits 🐾🐾 1981 Harmon plays an oceanographer who discovers a ship that was sunk by German U-boats during WWI. Nothing much new there, except that the survivors still reside on board the vessel, some 40 years after the oceanliner was torpedoed. And get this: they're living a quasi-Utopian existence. Kind of hard to swallow. Made for TV, it originally aired in two parts. **110m/C VHS, DVD.** H.B. Halicki, Marion Busia, George Cole, James McIntyre, Jerry Daugirda; **D:** H.B. Halicki; **W:** H.B. Halicki; **C:** Jack Vacek; **M:** Philip Kachaturian.

Gone Are the Days 🐾🐾½ 1974 *The Man From C.O.T.T.O.N.; Purlie Victorious* 1963 Shaky adaptation of the play, "Purlie Victorious." A black preacher wants to cause

the ruin of a white plantation owner. Alda's screen debut. **97m/B VHS, DVD.** Ossie Davis, Ruby Dee, Sorrell Booke, Godfrey Cambridge, Alan Alda, Beah Richards; **D:** Nicholas Webster; **W:** Ossie Davis; **C:** Boris Kaufman.

Gone Are the Days 🐾🐾 1984 Government agent (Korman) is assigned to protect a family who witnessed an underworld shooting, but the family would like to get away from both the mob and the police. Disney comedy is well-acted but done in by cliches. **90m/C VHS, DVD.** Harvey Korman, Susan Anspach, Robert Hogan; **D:** Gabrielle Beaumont. **CABLE**

Gone Baby Gone 🐾🐾🐾 2007 (R) In working-class Dorchester (Boston), four-year-old Amanda McCready has been abducted. Cops Jack Doyle (Freeman) and Remy Bressant (Harris) are on the scene, but it's not enough for Amanda's Aunt Beatrice (Madigan). She hires private detectives Patrick Kenzie (the younger Affleck) and Angie Gennaro (Monaghan), locals with better access to neighborhood folks who might not talk to police. Mom Helene (Ryan) is tough to sympathize with—a drinker and druggie who lives in near squalor and who seems apathetic at best about her daughter's disappearance. Stellar performances, nuance, plot twists, and a distinctly unHollywood gritty Boston backdrop create a crime thriller that offers an uncomfortable edge of moral dilemma. The brothers Affleck and the rest of the crew put out a commendable effort, with Ben a pleasant surprise behind the camera and Casey an equally pleasant surprise in front of it. **115m/C DVD, Blu-ray Disc.** *US* Casey Affleck, Michelle Monaghan, Morgan Freeman, Ed Harris, John Ashton, Amy Ryan, Amy Madigan, Titus Welliver, Michael K. Williams, Edi Gathegi, Jill Quigg; **C:** John Toll; **M:** Harry Gregson-Williams.

Gone Dark 🐾½ *The Limit* 2003 (R) Out to score a big drug bust, undercover agent Monica (Forlani) is in too deep as she has affairs with the kingpin and his right-hand man. Denny, all while becoming addicted to heroin. When Denny ends up dead, Monica fears that an elderly neighbor, May (Bacall), might know too much and in her frenzied state she holds her captive but May's not about to succumb. Forlani and Bacall do their best to redeem director Webb's freshman effort as it labors through jerky scene cuts. **83m/ C VHS, DVD.** Claire Forlani, Lauren Bacall, Henry Czerny, Pete Postlethwaite; **D:** Lewin Webb; **W:** Matt Holland; **C:** Curtis Petersen; **M:** Norman Orenstein. **VIDEO**

Gone Fishin' woof! 1997 (PG) Long delayed comedy (thanks to some on-set disasters and true believers' doubts about quality) finds best friends and bassmasters of disaster Gus (Glover) and Joe (Pesci) thinking they're going on a peaceful fishing trip. Instead they meet two women (Arquette and Whitfield) who are on the trail of a dangerous British con artist (Brimble). Pesci and Glover have reeled in one stinky old shoe of a movie here. Granted, it's not entirely their fault, but they should've known better. There are no surprises (or laughs) as every joke and set piece is tipped way ahead of time, just so you won't miss it. Less fun than a fish hook in the eye. **94m/C VHS, DVD.** Danny Glover, Joe Pesci, Rosanna Arquette, Lynn Whitfield, Willie Nelson, Nick Brimble, Gary Grubbs, Carol Kane, Edythe Davis; **D:** Christopher Cain; **W:** J.J. (Jeffrey) Abrams, Jill Mazursky Cody; **C:** Dean Semler; **M:** Randy Edelman.

Gone in 60 Seconds 🐾🐾 1974 (PG-13) Car thief working for an insurance adjustment firm gets double-crossed by his boss and chased by the police. Forty minutes are consumed by a chase scene which destroyed more than 90 vehicles. **105m/C VHS, DVD.** H.B. Halicki, Marion Busia, George Cole, James McIntyre, Jerry Daugirda; **D:** H.B. Halicki; **W:** H.B. Halicki; **C:** Jack Vacek; **M:** Philip Kachaturian.

Gone in 60 Seconds 🐾🐾 2000 (PG-13) Cage is an ex-car thief who must steal 50 cars in one night in order to save his ne'er-do-well brother (Ribisi) while gung-ho cop Castleback (Lindo) stays on

his tail. "Rounding-up-the-old-crew" montage ensues, followed by much highway mayhem and the odd humorous one-liner. As with most Bruckheimer-produced epics, flash and stunts run roughshod over plot and character, but the target audience won't care because the cars just look so damn cool. Jolie is woefully underutilized in the girlfriend/partner-in-crime role. Remake of the 1974 film notable for its 40-minute chase scene. **117m/C VHS, DVD, Blu-ray Disc, UMD.** Nicolas Cage, Angelina Jolie, Giovanni Ribisi, Robert Duvall, Scott Caan, Vinnie Jones, Will Patton, Delroy Lindo, Chi McBride, Christopher Eccleston, Timothy Olyphant, William Lee Scott, Frances Fisher, Grace Zabriskie, James Duval, TJ Cross, Arye Gross, Bodhi (Pine) Elfman; **Master P; D:** Dominic Sena; **W:** Scott Rosenberg; **C:** Paul Cameron; **M:** Trevor Rabin.

Gone to Ground 🐾 1976 Mad killer terrorizes a group of vacationers who are trapped in an isolated beach house. **74m/C VHS. AU** Charles "Bud" Tingwell, Elaine Lee, Eric Oldfield, Marion Johns, Robyn Gibbes, Judy Lynne, Dennis Grosvenor, Alan Penney, Marcus Hale; **D:** Kevin James Dobson; **W:** Bruce A. Wishart; **C:** Russell Boyd. **TV**

Gone with the West 🐾½ 1972 Little Moon and Jud McGraw seek revenge upon the man who stole their cattle. **92m/C VHS, DVD.** James Caan, Stefanie Powers, Sammy Davis Jr., Aldo Ray, Michael Conrad, Michael Walker Jr.; **D:** Bernard Giraudeau.

Gone with the Wind 🐾🐾🐾 1939 Epic Civil War drama focuses on the life of petulant southern belle Scarlett O'Hara. Starting with her idyllic lifestyle on a sprawling plantation, the film traces her survival through the tragic history of the South during the Civil War and Reconstruction, and her tangled love affairs with Ashley Wilkes and Rhett Butler. Classic Hollywood doesn't get any better than this; one great scene after another, equally effective in intimate drama and sweeping spectacle. The train depot scene, one of the more technically adroit shots in movie history, involved hundreds of extras and dummies, and much of the MGM lot was razed to simulate the burning of Atlanta. Based on Margaret Mitchell's novel, screenwriter Howard was assisted by producer Selznick and novelist F. Scott Fitzgerald. For its 50th anniversary, a 231-minute restored version was released that included the trailer for "The Making of a Legend: GWTW." **231m/C VHS, DVD.** Clark Gable, Vivien Leigh, Olivia de Havilland, Leslie Howard, Thomas Mitchell, Hattie McDaniel, Butterfly McQueen, Evelyn Keyes, Harry Davenport, Ann Darwell, Ona Munson, Barbara O'Neil, William "Billy" Bakewell, Rand Brooks, Ward Bond, Laura Hope Crews, Yakima Canutt, George Reeves, Marjorie Reynolds, Ann Rutherford, Victor Jory, Paul Hurst, Isabel Jewell, Cliff Edwards, Eddie Anderson, Oscar Polk, Eric Linden, Violet Kemble-Cooper, Fred Crane, Howard Hickman, Leona Roberts, Fred Crane, Howard Hickman, Leona Roberts, Many Anderson, Frank Faylen; **D:** Victor Fleming; **W:** Sidney Howard; **C:** Ray Rennahan; **M:** Max Steiner. Oscars '39: Actress (Leigh), Color Cinematog., Director (Fleming), Film Editing, Picture, Screenplay, Support. Actress (McDaniel); AFI '98: Top 100, Natl. Film Reg. '89; N.Y. Film Critics '39: Actress (Leigh).

Gonza the Spearman 🐾🐾½ 1986 A gifted samurai lancer is accused of having an affair with the wife of the lord of his province. The lancer must leave to save the woman's honor, because to stay would mean death to them both. In Japanese with English subtitles. **126m/C VHS. JP** Hiromi Goh, Shima Iwashita; **D:** Masahiro Shinoda.

Good Advice 🐾🐾½ 2001 In a sparsely populated North Carolina community, loner Raymond Toker (Thomas) discovers an abandoned newborn in the

Stockbroker Ryan Turner (Sheen) loses all his money on a bad stock tip and decides to ghostwrite his ex-girlfriend's (Richards) lame newspaper advice column. Suddenly the column is hot and the newspaper's publisher (Harmon) is showing interest in more than Ryan's byline. **93m/C VHS, DVD.** Charlie Sheen, Denise Richards, Angie Harmon, Jon Lovitz, Rosanna Arquette, Estelle Harris, Barry Newman; **D:** Steve Rash; **W:** Robert Horn, Daniel Margosis; **C:** Daryn Okada; **M:** Teddy Castellucci.

A Good Baby 🐾🐾½ 1999

woods. He rescues the infant and attempts to find the baby's parents but no one will claim her. Toker gets more and more attached to the baby when slick traveling salesman Truman Lester (Strthaim) suddenly appears in town and the child's origins are finally revealed. Hesty ending mars an otherwise notably affecting debut for director Dieckmann. **98m/C VHS, DVD.** Henry Thomas, David Strathairn, Danny Nelson; **D:** Katherine Dieckmann; **W:** Katherine Dieckmann; **C:** Jim Denault; **M:** David Mansfield.

Good Boy! 🐾🐾 **2003 (PG)** "E.T." meets "Benji" in this amiable talking dog pic with very young kiddie appeal. Twelve-year-old Owen (Aiken)'s a lonely little boy who begs his parents for a pup of his own when a doggie-piloted spacecraft conveniently crashes into his neighborhood carrying the adorable Hubble, who comes from (where else?) the Dog Star. Owen adopts Hubble but quickly realizes this is no ordinary pooch. Soon Owen is speaking dog while Hubble tries to train Earthling dogs to begin taking charge or face the threat of an en-masse canine "recall" to the home planet. While visual mechanics of the animal's speech are crude, vital performances of both humans and hounds alike elevate this recycled plot. **89m/C VHS, DVD.** Liam Aiken, Molly Shannon, Kevin Nealon, Brittany Moldowan, Hunter Elliot; **D:** John Hoffman; **W:** John Hoffman; **V:** Matthew Broderick, Delta Burke, Donald Adeosun Faison, Vanessa Redgrave, Richard "Cheech" Marin, Brittany Murphy, Carl Reiner.

Good Burger 🐾🐾½ **1997 (PG)** Teen actors Kel and Kenan from Nickelodeon fame make their feature film debut in this innocent, silly romp as employees trying to prevent the takeover of their fast food restaurant by the mega burger-conglomerate across the street. Similar to comedy teams of the past, Kel is the dim-witted Ed and Kenan is the schemer Dexter, always looking for a quick way out of hard labor. The pre-adolescent humor of the film is as goofy as it is charming and the energetic duo of K&K serves up an entertaining meal for the kiddies. Shaquille O'Neal makes a cameo as does funk meister George Clinton. And yes, that fry machine! **95m/C VHS, DVD.** Sylvia Krisel, Umberto Orsini, Jean-Pierre Bouvier, Charlotta Alexandra; **D:** Francois Leterrier; **C:** Jean Badal; **M:** Serge Gainsbourg.

Good Bye, Lenin! 🐾🐾🐾 **2003 (R)** Communism has come to an end as the Berlin Wall falls in 1989 which may be too much of a shock for Alex's (Brühl) mom Christiane (Sass)—a staunch Socialist—who has a heart attack right before the event and slips into an eight-month coma. In an effort to protect her from the changes capitalism has brought, he comically yet believably revives the vestiges of the fallen 'regime and even goes so far as to stage a newscast as part of the ruse. Although the practicality of the scenario is stretched, Brühl impressively delivers in this offbeat farce. In German, with English subtitles. Winner of the 2003 European Film Awards for best picture. **121m/C DVD.** Chulpan Khamatova, Alexander Beyer, Daniel Brühl, Katrin Sass, Maria Simon, Florian Lukas; **D:** Wolfgang Becker; **W:** Bernd Lichtenberg; **C:** Martin Kukula; **M:** Yann Tiersen.

Good-bye, Emmanuelle 🐾½ **1977 (R)** Follows the further adventures of Emmanuelle in her quest for sexual freedom and the excitement of forbidden pleasures. The second sequel to "Emmanuelle." **92m/C VHS, DVD.**

Good Day to Die 🐾🐾½ **1995 (R)** Western made-for-TV saga, set during the 1880s land rush of the Oklahoma Territory, and adapted from the novel by Clancy Carlile. Half-black, half-Cherokee gunslinger Gypsy Smith (Poitier) reluctantly agrees to lead a wagon of freed slaves west to found their own community. Naturally, there's trouble with the Klan and Gypsy isn't the only one involved—young Cherokee brave White Wolf (Wirth), who has been raised among whites, has a forbidden romance with his foster sister, Rachel (Going), leading to lots of heartbreak. Fawcett has a brief role as the young Rachel's high-strung mother. Filmed in Alberta, Canada. **120m/C VHS, DVD.** Sidney Poitier, Michael Moriarty, Joanna Going, Billy Wirth, Regina Taylor, Hart Bochner, Sidney Franklin; **C:** Karl Freund. Oscars '37: Actress (Rainer), Cinematog.

The Good Earth 🐾🐾🐾½ **1937** Pearl S. Buck's classic re-creation of the story of a simple Chinese farm couple beset by greed and poverty. Outstanding special effects. MGM's last film produced by master Irving Thalberg and dedicated to his memory. Rainer won the second of her back-to-back Best Actress Oscars for her portrayal of the self-sacrificing O-Lan. **138m/B VHS, DVD.** Paul Muni, Luise Rainer, Charley Grapewin, Keye Luke, Walter Connolly; **D:** Sidney Franklin; **C:** Karl Freund. Oscars '37: Actress (Rainer), Cinematog.

Good Evening, Mr. Wallenberg 🐾🐾½ **1993** Raoul Wallenberg was an upper-class Swede who imported luxury goods from Hungary. He was also responsible for saving thousands of Hungarian Jews from extermination by the Nazis. Using phony documents he first has small groups of Jews smuggled to safety but when he learns that the 65,000 Jews of the Budapest ghetto are to be killed he uses a bluff to prevent the deaths. Later taken prisoner by the Soviet Army, Wallenberg's fate has never been determined. Characters are dwarfed by the immensity of the events arc Wallenberg remains an enigma. In Swedish, German, and Hungarian with English subtitles. **115m/C VHS, DVD.** Sw Stellan Skarsgard, Erland Josephson, Katharina Thalbach; **D:** Kjell Grede; **W:** Kjell Grede.

The Good Fairy 🐾🐾🐾 **1935** Charming romantic comedy based on the play by Ferenc Molnar and given the stardust touch of screenwriter Sturges. Luisa (a charming Sullavan) has just left a Budapest orphanage for a job where she attracts the amorous advances of millionaire Konrad (a scene-stealing Morgan). She pretends to be married and picks the first name out of the phone book as her "husband," that of struggling lawyer Max Sporum (Marshall), who goes along with the deception because he's instantly smitten with Luisa. She decides she can play "good fairy" to Max by using Konrad's bankroll but it's not real estate to fix his "I'll Be Yours" with Deanna Durbin in the lead. **98m/B VHS, DVD.** Margaret Sullavan, Herbert Marshall, Frank Morgan, Reginald Owen, Alan Hale, Beulah Bondi, Cesar Romero; **D:** William Wyler; **W:** Preston Sturges; **C:** Norbert Brodine.

The Good Father 🐾🐾🐾 **1987 (R)** An acclaimed British TV movie about a bitter divorced man trying to come to terms with his son, his ex-wife, and his divorce battle of a friend. **90m/C VHS, DVD. GB** Anthony Hopkins, Jim Broadbent, Harriet Walter, Frances Viner, Joanne Whalley, Simon Callow, Michael Byrne; **D:** Mike Newell; **W:** Christopher Hampton; **C:** Michael Coulter; **M:** Richard Hartley.

A Good Day to Die — (continued above)

Good Fences 🐾½ **2003 (R)** In the mid-1970s, upwardly mobile black lawyer Tom Spader (Glover) moves with his wife Mabel (Goldberg) and their kids into a posh Greenwich, Connecticut, suburb and much to Mabel's disgust. Self-indulgent and simplistic satire. Based on the novel by Ericka Ellis. **119m/C VHS, DVD.** Danny Glover, Whoopi Goldberg, Mo'Nique, D: Ernest R. Dickerson; **W:** Trey Ellis; **C:** Jonathan Freeman; **M:** George Duke. **CABLE.**

The Good Fight 🐾🐾½ **1992** Grace Cragin (Lahti) is a lawyer at a small firm who's asked by her son's best friend to represent him in a tough case against a powerful corporation. The young man is dying of mouth cancer and he wants to sue the tobacco company that makes the chewing tobacco he blames for his illness. Grace is wary of the high-powered litigation necessary but with the increasingly personal aid of her prominent lawyer ex-husband (O'Quinn), she is ready to battle the odds. Another fine performance by Lahti in this cable drama. **91m/C VHS, Christine Lahti, Terry O'Quinn, Kenneth Welsh, Lawrence Dane, Adam Trese, Tony Rosato, Andrea Roth, Jonathan Crombie; **D:** John David Coles; **M:** Mark Snow.

The Good German 🐾🐾🐾½ **2006 (R)** A throwback to 1940s noir, director Soderbergh makes it the real deal by only using technology of the era, with mixed results. The black-and-white drama begins during WWII as war correspondent Jake (Clooney) has an affair with the married Lena (an intense Blanchett). After the war ends he returns on assignment with hopes of finding her but is disheartened to see that she's taken up hooking with Tully (Maguire), a boyish pimp who fronts as a motor-pool soldier and becomes Jake's driver. The desolate Lena is desperate to leave Germany and her misery behind but can't because the U.S. and Russian governments are searching for her possibly dead husband—a Nazi scientist—who's disappeared. Visually nifty tribute to classic Hollywood might have pulled it off if the story were better. Based on Joseph Kanon's 2001 novel of the same name. **107m/B DVD.** US George Clooney, Cate Blanchett, Tobey Maguire, Beau Bridges, Tony Curran, Leland Orser, Jack Thompson, Robin Weigert, Christian Oliver, Ravil Isyanov, Don Pugsley; **D:** Steven Soderbergh; **W:** Paul Attanasio; **C:** Steven Soderbergh; **M:** Thomas Newman.

The Good Girl 🐾🐾🐾 **2002 (R)** Justine (Aniston) spends her days in the retail hell of Retail Rodeo, a West Texas discount mart, and her nights with her pot-head Housepainter hubby (Reilly), while longing for something better. In director Arteta's excellent and biting indie dramedy. She finds just that in college dropout and new employee, the self-named Holden (as in Caulfield) played by Gyllenhaal. Justine and Holden's brooding, malcontent Cheryl, who makes creative use of the store's PA system for the benefit of the unaware, zombie-like customers. Nelson is the narrow-minded boss who provides a good portion of the comedy. Successful re-teaming of Arteta and actor/writer White. **93m/C VHS, DVD.** US Jennifer Aniston, Jake Gyllenhaal, John C. Reilly, Tim Blake Nelson, Zooey Deschanel, Mike White, Deborah Rush, John Carroll Lynch, John Doe, Roxanne Hart; **D:** Miguel Arteta; **W:** Mike White; **C:** Enrique Chediak. Ind. Spirit '03: Screenplay.

The Good Guys and the Bad Guys 🐾🐾½ **1969 (PG)** When Kennedy is abandoned by his gang of outlaws for being too old to keep up, he finds himself being hunted by lifelong marshal

Good Girls Don't 🐾½ **1995** Jeannie (Estevez) and Bettina (Parton) are framed for murder and take it on the lam in a red convertible with a half million in cash. It's a comedy. Mary Woronov, Christopher Knight; **D:** Rick Sloane; **W:** Rick Sloane.

A Good Man in Africa 🐾½ **1994 (R)** Bumbling low-level British diplomat gets caught up in the high-level political turmoil of a newly independent African state. Confusing plot has borderline incompetent blackmailed by corrupt politician into bribing respected doctor for local land rights. Wow corrupt officials, ineffectual bureaucrats—go figure! Does to the British diplomats' corps what "A Fish Called Wanda" did to England's legal community. Perfor- mances by Connery, Gossett and Lithgow almost make up for shortcomings in key areas such as writing and direction. Adapted from the novel by William Boyd. **95m/C VHS.** Colin Friels, Sean Connery, Louis Gossett Jr., John Lithgow, Joanne Whalley, Diana Rigg; **D:** Bruce Beresford; **W:** William Boyd; **C:** Andrzej Bartkowiak.

Good Luck 🐾🐾½ **1996 (R)** Inspirational buddy movie that manages to avoid the worst of sentimental excess. Tony Olezniak (D'Onofrio) is a football player left blind because of a game injury. He's dating Mt. Rushmore (Garcia) kill time smoking weed and playing pranks. They and their buddies crash a party where Jay meers Wendy (Robinson) and there's a brawl with some jocks that results in a stabbing. When the boy later dies, suspicions point to Mt. Rushmore as the culprit and Jay tries to stay loyal through a bad situation. **112m/C DVD.** Jorge Garcia, Cameron Richardson, Jason Segel, Kelsey Grammer, Nathan Stevens, James Ransone, Elise Robertson; **D:** Tenney Fairchild; **W:** Tenney Fairchild; **C:** Scott Henriksen; **M:** Robin Trower.

Good Luck Chuck WOOF! **2007 (R)** Charlie Logan (Cook) is a successful dentist whose office is conveniently adjacent to that of his long-time buddy, boob-obsessed plastic surgeon Stu (Fogler). Charlie's requisite fatal flaw is that he carries a curse placed on him during his preteen years by a rebuffed goth girl. As a result every woman he dates dumps him and immediately meets the man of her dreams. So legendary is the curse that heaps of women pursue him to ensure Mr. Right's arrival. When he meets klutzy but sweet beauty Cam (Alba), he faces a double dilemma: what to do with the Mr. Right-seeking bimbos, and how to hang on to Cam in light of the curse. Charlie and Cam are cute, but the gags are crude and the sex scenes are gross. **96m/C DVD, Blu-ray Disc.** US Dane Cook, Jessica Alba, Dan Fogler, Ellia English, Chelan Simmons, Lonny Ross; **D:** Mark Helfrich; **W:** Josh Stolberg; **C:** Anthony B. Richmond; **M:** Aaron Zigman.

Good Man in Africa — (see above)

Good Morning 🐾🐾🐾 **Ohayo 1959** One of Ozu's first color efforts, "Good Morning," is a light social comedy revolving around two young Japanese boys who try to talk their parents into buying them one of those new-fangled television sets. Not likely, since the Dad feels that the boob tube will cull the senses of the Japa-

Good Guys Wear Black 🐾🐾 **1978 (PG)** A mild-mannered professor keeps his former life as leader of a Vietnam commando unit under wraps until he discovers that he's "number one on the CIA hit list. Sequel is "A Force of One." **96m/C VHS, DVD.** Chuck Norris, Anne Archer, James Franciscus; **D:** Ted Post; **W:** Mark Medoff.

The Good Humor Man 🐾🐾 **2005 (R)** Coming of age story set in 1976. Underachieving high school buddies Jay (Stevens) and Mt. Rushmore (Garcia) kill time on a downward spiral and winds up in jail, which is where paraplegic Bernard Lemley (Hines), once Tony's tutor, finds him. Bernard wants to enter a rigorous whitewater raft race held on Oregon's Rogue River and he needs Tony's strength to help him do it. The emotional payoff comes as the two bicker and bond. Lots of charm. **95m/C VHS, DVD.** Vincent D'Onofrio, Gregory Hines, Max Gail, James Earl Jones, Sarah Trigger, Joe Theismann; **D:** Richard LaBrie; **W:** Bob Comfort; **C:** Maximo Munzi; **M:** Tim Truman.

nemesis Mitchum. **91m/C VHS, DVD.** Robert Mitchum, George Kennedy, David Carradine, Tina Louise, Douglas Fowley, Lois Nettleton, Martin Balsam, John Carradine; **C:** Burt Kennedy; **W:** Ronald M. Cohen; **C:** Harry Stradling Jr.

nese youth...talk about your ESP. The kids feel that there's too much small talk going on. Ozu keeps the camera at kids' eye-level, emphasizing the sympathetic perspective of the children and giving a unique look to the film. Bold colors populate the screen and Ozu keeps the story whimsical while commenting on Japanese society (very much like Juzo Itami would years later). The characters are well-fleshed out and likable. **94m/C DVD**. *JP* Masahiko Shimazu, Koji Shigaraji, Chishu Ryu, Kuniko Miyake; *D:* Yasujiro Ozu; *W:* Yasujiro Ozu, Kogo Noda; *C:* Yuuharu Atsuta; *M:* Toshiro Mayuzumi.

Good Morning, Babylon 🐾🐾🐾

Good Morning Babilonia 1987 (PG-13) The Taviani brothers' first American film. Two young Italian brothers skilled in cathedral restoration come to America and find success building the sets to D.W. Griffith's "Intolerance." Eventually, their fortune is shattered by the onslaught of WWI. **113m/ C VHS**. Vincent Spano, Joaquim de Almeida, Greta Scacchi, Charles Dance, Desiree Becker, Omero Antonutti; *D:* Paolo Taviani, Vittorio Taviani; *W:* Paolo Taviani, Vittorio Taviani; *M:* Nicola Piovani.

Good Morning, Vietnam 🐾🐾🐾

1987 (R) Based on the story of Saigon DJ Adrian Cronauer, although Williams' portrayal is a bit more extroverted than the personality of Cronauer. Williams spins great comic moments that may have been scripted but likely were not as a man with no history and for whom everything is manic radio material. The character ad-libs, swoops, and swerves, finally accepting adult responsibility. Engaging all the way with an outstanding period soundtrack. **121m/C VHS, DVD**. Robin Williams, Forest Whitaker, Bruno Kirby, Richard Edson, Robert Wuhl, J.T. Walsh, Noble Willingham, Floyd Vivino, Tung Thanh Tran, Chintara Sukapatana, Richard Portnow, Juney Smith, Cu Ba Nguyen, Dan Stanton, Don Stanton; *D:* Barry Levinson; *W:* Mitch Markowitz; *C:* Peter Sova; *M:* Alex North. Golden Globes '88: Actor—Mus./Comedy (Williams).

The Good Mother 🐾🐾½ 1988

(R) A divorced mother works at creating a fulfilling life for herself and her daughter, with an honest education of how far this education is being taken, fights her for custody of their eight-year-old daughter after allegations of sexual misconduct against the mother's new lover. Well acted, weakly edited and scripted. **104m/C VHS, DVD**. Diane Keaton, Liam Neeson, Jason Robards Jr., Ralph Bellamy, James Naughton, Teresa Wright, Asia Vieira, Joe Morton, Katey Sagal, Tracy Griffith, Charles Kimbrough, Matt Damon; *D:* Leonard Nimoy; *W:* Michael Bortman; *C:* David Watkin; *M:* Elmer Bernstein.

Good Neighbor Sam 🐾🐾½

1964 A married advertising executive (Lemmon) agrees to pose as a friend's husband in order for her to collect a multi-million-dollar inheritance. Complications ensue when his biggest client mistakes the friend for his actual wife and decides they're the perfect couple to promote his wholesome product—milk. **130m/C VHS**. Jack Lemmon, Romy Schneider, Dorothy Provine, Mike Connors, Edward G. Robinson, Joyce Jameson, David Swift; *D:* David Swift; *W:* James Fritzell, Everett Greenbaum, David Swift; *C:* Burnett Guffey; *M:* Frank DeVol.

Good News 🐾🐾🐾½ 1947 A vintage

Comden-Green musical about the love problems of a college football star, who will flunk out if he doesn't pass his French exams. Revamping of the 1927 Broadway smash features the unlikely sight of Lawford in a song-and-dance role. ♪*Varsity Drag; He's a Lady's Man; Good News; Tait Song; Students Are We; Just Imagine; If You're Not Kissing Me; Football; I Feel Pessimistic; Pass That Peace Pipe*. **93m/C VHS, DVD**. June Allyson, Peter Lawford, Joan McCracken, Mel Torme; *D:* Charles Walters; *W:* Betty Comden; *C:* Charles E. Schoenbaum; *M:* Hugh Martin, Ralph Blane, Roger Edens.

The Good Night 🐾🐾½ 2007 (R)

Has-been pop star Gary (Freeman) composes commercial jingles and lives in Manhattan with his nagging girlfriend Dora (Paltrow). But Gary transcends his humdrum existence in his own mind with Anna (Cruz), literally the girl of his dreams—and she's more than happy to cater to his every whim. After a frustrated Dora skips town, Gary hires dream expert Mel (DeVito) to find Anna. Mel delivers model Melodia, who hardly lives up to her dreamy counterpart. Director Jake Paltrow's (yes, Gwyneth's brother) feature debut has some clever moments and does pull some charm, but never quite manages to keep afloat. **93m/C DVD**. *US* Martin Freeman, Penelope Cruz, Gwyneth Paltrow, Simon Pegg, Danny DeVito; *D:* Jake Paltrow; *W:* Jake Paltrow; *C:* Giles Nuttgens; *M:* Alec Puro.

Good Night, and Good Luck 🐾🐾🐾½ 2005 (PG)

Nearly flawless portrayals and script combine with smoky black and white shooting to transport you back to the McCarthy era, where television newsman Edward R. Murrow (Strathairn) faces off with Senator Joseph McCarthy and the House Un-American Activities Committee. Murrow is pressured to back down, but he and CBS staff are intent on exposing McCarthy's fear-based witch-hunt for communist activity. McCarthy plays his own role by way of archival footage; performances by Jeff Daniels and Robert Downey Jr. don't disappoint. A labor of love for George Clooney, he co-wrote and directed, and plays Fred Friendly, Murrow's producer at CBS. Though spare, the dialogue and acting create a scene and mood that, whether you remember the era or not, makes it completely real and utterly believable. **93m/B DVD, Blu-ray Disc, UMD, HD DVD**. *US GB FR JP* David Strathairn, Patricia Clarkson, George Clooney, Jeff Daniels, Robert Downey Jr., Frank Langella, Ray Wise, Robert John Burke, Reed Edward Diamond, Tate Donovan, Grant Heslov, Thomas (Tom) McCarthy, Matt Ross, Alex Borstein, Peter Jacobson, Robert Knepper, Dianne Reeves, Rose Abdoo, John David (J.D.) Cullum, Glenn Morshower; *D:* George Clooney; *W:* George Clooney, Grant Heslov; *C:* Robert Elswit. Ind. Spirit '06: Cinematog.; L.A. Film Critics '05: Cinematog.; Natl. Bd. of Review '05: Film.

The Good Old Boys 🐾🐾½

1995 Debuting as both director and co-writer, Jones also stars as aging cowpoke Hewey Calloway. The n'er-do-well Hewey makes a surprise visit to the hardscrabble 1906 Texas farm of brother Walter (Kinney), whose wife Eve (McDormand) is none too happy to see the wanderer. But Walter needs help, the local banker (Brimley) is about to foreclose, and Hewey is also taken with spirited schoolmarm Spring Renfro (Spacek), who also starred with Jones in "Coal-Miner's Daughter"). And even Hewey realizes that the 20th century is going to change his way of life forever. Easy-going drama with a fine cast. **118m/C VHS**. Tommy Lee Jones, Sissy Spacek, Terry Kinney, Frances McDormand, Wilford Brimley, Sam Shepard, Walter Olkewicz, Matt Damon, Bruce McGill, Park Overall, Richard Jones; *D:* Tommy Lee Jones; *W:* J.T. Allen, Tommy Lee Jones; *C:* Alan Caso; *M:* John McEuen.

Good Sam 🐾🐾 1948 An incurable

"Good Samaritan" finds himself in one jam after another as he tries too hard to help people. Lots of missed opportunities for laughs with McCrarey's mediocre direction. **116m/B VHS**. Gary Cooper, Ann Sheridan, Ray Collins, Edmund Lowe, Joan Lorring, Ruth Roman; *D:* Leo McCarey.

The Good Shepherd 🐾🐾 2006

(R) The birth of the CIA was apparently accomplished by a bunch of gray-faced, unassuming men from the same social milieu, who wore dull suits and neglected their private lives for the good of their country. Edward Wilson (Damon) knocks up and then marries senator's daughter Clover (Jolie), but that is about the most human behavior he'll show in decades as he moves from WWII through the Cold War with paranoia as his distinguishing characteristic. De Niro's second directorial effort is a long slog through the spy biz where everyone lies and betrays. If you

want to see a spymaster at work, watch Alec Guinness in any of his incarnations as George Smiley; at least he's more human than robotic. **160m/C DVD, HD DVD**. *US* Matt Damon, Angelina Jolie, Alec Baldwin, Tammy Blanchard, Billy Crudup, Michael Gambon, William Hurt, Timothy Hutton, Keir Dullea, John Turturro, Joe Pesci, Gabriel Macht, Eddie Redmayne, Lee Pace, John Sessions, Robert De Niro, Martina Gedeck, Mark Ivanir; *D:* Robert De Niro; *W:* Eric Roth; *C:* Robert Richardson; *M:* Marcelo Zarvos, Bruce Fowler.

The Good Son 🐾🐾 1993 (R) In a

grand departure from cute, Culkin tackles evil as a 13-year-old obsessed with death and other unseemly hobbies. During a stay with his uncle, Mark (Wood) watches as his cousin (Culkin) gets creepier and creepier, and tries to alert the family. But will they listen? Nooo—they chose to ignore the little warning signs like the doll hanging by a noose in Culkin's room. And then there's the untimely death of a sibling. Hmmm. Culkin isn't as bad as expected, but doesn't quite get all the way down to bone-chilling terror either. Original star Jesse Bradford was dropped when Papa Culkin threatened to pull Mac of "Home Alone 2" if he wasn't cast in the lead. **87m/ C VHS, DVD**. Macaulay Culkin, Elijah Wood, Wendy Crewson, David Morse, Daniel Hugh-Kelly, Quinn Culkin; *D:* Joseph Ruben; *W:* Ian McEwan; *C:* John Lindley; *M:* Elmer Bernstein.

The Good, the Bad, and Huckleberry Hound 1988 Journey-

ing out West to begin a ranch, Huckleberry Hound winds up becoming a sheriff in the small town of Two-Bit. Huckleberry stands up against a group of bully brothers who have been terrorizing the town. **94m/C VHS**. *D:* Ray Patterson; *V:* Daws Butler.

The Good, the Bad and the Ugly 🐾🐾🐾½ 1967 Leone's grandilo-

quent, shambling tribute to the American Western. Set during the Civil War, it follows the seemingly endless adventures of three dirtbags in search of a cache of Confederate gold buried in a nameless grave. Violent, exaggerated, beautifully crafted, it is the final and finest installment of the "Dollars" trilogy: a spaghetti Western chef d'oeuvre. **161m/C VHS, DVD**. *IT* Clint Eastwood, Eli Wallach, Lee Van Cleef, Chelo Alonso, Luigi Pistilli, Rada Rassimov, Livio Lorenzon, Mario Brega; *D:* Sergio Leone; *W:* Sergio Leone, Sergio Donati, Furio Scarpelli, Luciano Vincenzoni, Agenore Incrocci; *C:* Tonino Delli Colli; *M:* Ennio Morricone.

The Good Thief 🐾🐾🐾 2003 (R)

Jordan's stylish reworking of Jean-Pierre Melville's "Bob le Flambeur" serves as a showcase for Nolte's magnificent performance. Nolte is Bob, an American inveterate gambler, heroin addict, and master thief whom everyone likes, including the French cop (Karyo) who wants to save him from himself. When Bob loses the last of his money at the track, he's talked into masterminding an art heist at a casino with the usual band of multinational partners. Along the way, he rescues a young waitress from a pimp, taking her under his wing. Jordan provides plenty of atmosphere and noir-heist dialogue, although some head-scratching at the end. **109m/C VHS, DVD**. *FR GB IR* Nick Nolte, Tcheky Karyo, Said Taghmaoui, Gerard Darmon, Nutsa Kukhianidze, Emir Kusturica, Marc Lavoine, Mark Polish, Michael Polish, Ouassni Embarek, Sarah Bridges; *Cameos:* Ralph Fiennes; *D:* Neil Jordan; *W:* Neil Jordan; *C:* Chris Menges; *M:* Elliot Goldenthal.

Good Times 🐾🐾½ 1967 Pop sil-

liness as Sonny and Cher (playing themselves) are offered a movie deal by an eccentric tycoon (Sanders). Sonny thinks the script is terrible and dreams up various parts that he and Cher could play. Friedkin's directorial debut. **91m/C VHS, DVD**. Cher, Sonny Bono, George Sanders, Norman Alden, Edy Williams, China Lee, Larry Duran, Kelly Thordsen; *D:* William Fredkin; *W:* Tony Barrett; *C:* Robert Wyckoff; *M:* Sonny Bono.

The Good Wife 🐾🐾½ *The Umbrel-*

la Woman 1986 (R) A bored and sexually frustrated wife scandalizes her small Australian town by taking up with the new hotel barman. There's no denying Ward's sexuality, but overall the movie is too predictable. **97m/C VHS, DVD**. *AU* Rachel Ward,

Bryan Brown, Sam Neill, Steven Vidler, Bruce Barry, Jennifer Claire; *D:* Ken Cameron; *W:* Peter Kenna; *C:* James Bartle; *M:* Cameron Allan.

Good Will Hunting 🐾🐾 1997

(R) Good, if predictable, first effort from screenwriting actors Damon and Affleck. Troubled, young Will Hunting (Damon) is a janitor at MIT who also happens to be an unsung mathematical genius. This gift is discovered by big-shot Professor Lambeau (Skarsgard), who must vouch for Will with the parole board by giving him weekly math sessions and taking him to a therapist to work on his anger. Naturally, only the equally troubled shrink Sean Maguire (Williams) is willing to help Hunting get beyond his blue-collar roots. But Will resists the help—not sure that he wants to leave his neighborhood and best friends behind. The Damon/Williams scenes are affecting but the southie Boston accents offer an unexpected challenge. **126m/C VHS, DVD**. Matt Damon, Robin Williams, Ben Affleck, Stellan Skarsgard, Minnie Driver, Casey Affleck, Cole Hauser; *D:* Gus Van Sant; *W:* Matt Damon, Ben Affleck; *C:* Jean-Yves Escoffier; *M:* Danny Elfman. Oscars '97: Orig. Screenplay, Support. Actor (Williams); Golden Globes '98: Screenplay; Screen Actors Guild '97: Support. Actor (Williams); Broadcast Film Critics '97: Breakthrough Perf. (Damon), Orig. Screenplay.

A Good Woman 🐾🐾½ (PG)

Lackluster reworking of Oscar Wilde's 1892 drawing room comedy "Lady Windermere's Fan" that is now set on Italy's Amalfi coast in 1930. Penniless adventuress Mrs. Erlynne (Hunt) sets her apparently greedy eyes on wealthy American newlywed Robert Windermere (Umbers), who's honeymooning with wife Meg (Johansson). Meanwhile, devilish Lord Darlington (Campbell Moore) has designs on the naive bride. But appearances generally deceive. Hunt and Johansson are miscast and can't comfortably manage Wilde's arch bon mots, though the British actors do much better. Pic at least looks very good. **99m/C DVD**. *US GB IT SP* Helen Hunt, Scarlett Johansson, Mark Umbers, Stephan Campbell Moore, Tom Wilkinson, Milena Vukotic, Roger Hammond, John Standing, Diana Hardcastle; *D:* Mike Barker; *W:* Howard Himelstein; *C:* Ben Seresin; *M:* Richard G. Mitchell.

A Good Year 🐾🐾 2006 (PG-13)

Certainly everyone involved had a wonderful time swilling wine and eating foie gras in Provence, but Crowe should be forbidden from taking any role that calls for him to play a Hugh Grant-ish floppy-haired Brit. Max is a London bonds trader who lives off on the fast track. When he unexpectedly inherits his Uncle Max's (Finney) vineyard, he travels down to the property with the intention of selling it quickly. That is until all that wine, not to mention French babe Fanny (Cotillard), start Max thinking he's missing out on life's true pleasures. The setting is really, really pretty. **118m/C DVD**. *US* Russell Crowe, Albert Finney, Marion Cotillard, Abbie Cornish, Tom Hollander, Freddie Highmore, Kenneth Cranham, Archie Panjabi, Didier Bourdon, Isabelle Candelier; *D:* Ridley Scott; *W:* Marc Klein; *C:* Philippe Le Sourd; *M:* Marc Streitenfeld.

Goodbye Again 🐾🐾 *Aimez-*

Vous Brahms 1961 A romantic drama based on the novel by Francoise Sagan. Bergman is a middle-aged interior decorator whose lover, Montand, has a roaming eye. She finds herself drawn to the younger (Perkins) of a client and begins an affair—flattered by the young man's attentions. Montand is outraged and vows to change his ways and marry Bergman if she will give up the young man. A bit soapy, but a must for Bergman fans. **120m/B VHS**. Jessie Royce Landis, Ingrid Bergman, Anthony Perkins, Yves Montand, Diahann Carroll; *D:* Anatole Litvak; *W:* Samuel A. Taylor. Cannes '61: Actor (Perkins).

The Goodbye Bird 🐾🐾½ 1993

(G) Frank is accused by his high school principal of stealing her prized talking parrot. With the aid of a kindly veterinarian Frank tries to discover who the thief really is. **91m/C VHS**. Cindy Pickett, Concetta Tomei, Wayne Rogers, Christopher Pettiet; *D:* William Clark.

Goodbye Charlie 🐾🐾 1964 Very much a product of its time with the swingin' '60s playboy aura. Hollywood writer Charlie Sorel is murdered by film producer Leopold Sartori (Matthau) when he catches Charlie with his wife. But the playboy is reincarnated as a woman (Reynolds)—much to the confusion of the male Charlie's best friend, George (Curtis). And other half lives, loves, and gets revenge. Based on the play by George Axelrod. 117m/C VHS, DVD. Debbie Reynolds, Tony Curtis, Pat Boone, Walter Matthau, Joanna Barnes, Ellen Burstyn, Laura Devon, Martin Gabel, Roger C. Carmel; D: Vincente Minnelli; W: Harry Kurnitz; C: Milton Krasner; M: Andre Previn.

Goodbye Columbus 🐾🐾🐾 1969 (PG) Philip Roth's novel about a young Jewish librarian who has an affair with the spoiled daughter of a nouveau riche family is brought to late-'60s life, and vindicated by superb performances all around. Benjamin and McGraw's first starring roles. 105m/C VHS, DVD. Richard Benjamin, Ali MacGraw, Jack Klugman, Nan Martin, Jaclyn Smith; D: Larry Peerce; W: Arnold Schulman; C: Gerald Hirschfeld. Writers Guild '68. Adapt. Screenplay.

Goodbye Cruel World 🐾½ 1982 (R) Black comedy about a suicidal TV anchorman who decides to spend his last day filming the relatives who drove him to the brink. 90m/C VHS. Dick Shawn, Cynthia Sikes, Chuck "Porky" Mitchell; D: David Irving.

Goodbye, Dragon Inn 🐾🐾🐾 2003 Long on atmosphere and short on plot, this slow-moving drama's centered around a decaying movie palace in Taiwan that appears to have become a gay cruising spot. A Japanese tourist wanders in to get in out of the rain (or maybe for other reasons), the crippled ticket girl decides to finally act on her crush on the film projectionist, and two elderly patrons weep as they watch the feature, King Hu's 1966 epic, "Dragon Inn." Melancholy but forgettable. ♪Fill The World With Love; And The Sky Smiled. 81m/C VHS, DVD. Chinese with subtitles. Shiang-chyi Chen, Shih Chun; D: Ming-liang Tsai. W: Ming-liang Tsai. C: Liao Pen-yung.

The Goodbye Girl 🐾🐾🐾 1977 (PG) Neil Simon's story of a former actress, her precocious nine-year-old daughter and the aspiring actor who moves in with them. The daughter serves as catalyst for the other two to fall in love. While Mason's character is fairly unsympathetic, Dreyfuss is great and Simon's dialogue witty. 111m/C VHS, DVD. Richard Dreyfuss, Marsha Mason, Quinn Cummings, Barbara Rhoades, Marilyn Sokol; D: Herbert Ross; W: Neil Simon; M: Dave Grusin. Oscars '77: Actor (Dreyfuss); British Acad. '78: Actor (Dreyfuss); Golden Globes '78: Actor—Mus./Comedy (Dreyfuss), Actress—Mus./Comedy (Mason), Film—Mus./Comedy, Screenplay; L.A. Film Critics '77: Actor (Dreyfuss).

Goodbye, Love 🐾½ 1934 Dull comedy about a group of ex-husbands who refuse to pay alimony and end up in jail. 65m/B VHS. Charlie Ruggles, Verree Teasdale, Sidney Blackmer, Mayo Methot, Phyllis Barry, Ray Walker, John Kelly, Hale Grace, Luis Alberni; D: Herbert Ross.

Goodbye, Mr. Chips 🐾🐾 1969 Ross debuted as director with this big-budget (but inferior musical re-make) of the classic James Hilton novel about a gentle teacher at an English all-boys private school and the woman who helps him demonstrate his compassion and overcome his shyness. O'Toole, although excellent, is categorically a non-singer, while Clark, a popular singer at the time Older; Walk Through the World; What Shall I Do with Today?; What a Lot of Flowers; Schooldays. 151m/C VHS, DVD. Peter O'Toole, Petula Clark, Michael Bryant, Jack Hedley, Elspeth March, Herbert Ross, Sian Phillips; M: Leslie Bricusse, John Williams; Golden Globes '70: Actor—Mus./Comedy (O'Toole); Natl. Bd. of Review '69: Actor (O'Toole); Natl. Soc. Film Critics '69: Support. Actress (Phillips).

Goodbye, Mr. Chips 🐾🐾 1939 An MGM classic, the sentimental rendering of the James Hilton novel about shy Latin professor Charles Chipping (Donat), who teaches in an English public school, marrying the vivacious Katherine (Garson) only to tragically lose her. He spends the rest of his life devoting himself to his students and becoming a school legend. Multi award-winning soaper featuring Garson's first screen appearance, which was Oscar nominated. Remade in 1969 as a fairly awful musical starring Peter O'Toole. 115m/B VHS, DVD. Robert Donat, Greer Garson, Paul Henreid, John Mills, Terence Rattigan; D: Sam Wood; W: R.C. Sherriff, Sidney Franklin, Claudine West, Eric Maschwitz; C: Frederick A. (Freddie) Young. Oscars '39: Actor (Donat).

Goodbye, Miss 4th of July 🐾🐾½ 1988 Inspired by the true story of the teenage daughter of Greek immigrants living in pre-WWI West Virginia, the prejudice they encounter, and the relationship that begins between the family and an aging African-American ex-boxer, and the girl's efforts in the influenza epidemic. Based on the 1985 book by her brother. 89m/C VHS. Richard Speight Jr., Roxana Zal, Louis Gossett Jr., Chris Sarandon, Chantal Contouri, Chynna Phillips, Mildred Anderson, Conchata Ferrell, Ed Lauter; D: George Miller.

Goodbye, My Lady 🐾🐾 1956 Based on the novel by James Street, this is a tear-jerking film about a young Mississippi farmboy who finds and cares for a special dog that is found eventually must give up. 95m/B VHS. Brandon de Wilde, Walter Brennan, Sidney Poitier, Phil Harris, Louise Beavers; D: William A. Wellman.

Goodbye, New York 🐾 1985 (R) A New York yuppie on a vacation finds herself penniless and stranded in Israel. She makes the best of the situation by joining a kibbutz and falling for a part-time soldier. Well, of course. 90m/C VHS, IS: Julie Hagerty, Amos Kollek, Shmuel Shilo; D: Amos Kollek; M: Michael Adene.

Goodbye, Norma Jean 🐾 1975 (R) Detailed and sleazy re-creation of Marilyn Monroe's early years in Hollywood. Followed by "Goodnight, Sweet Marilyn." 95m/C VHS, DVD. Misty Rowe, Terrance Locke; D: Larry Buchanan; M: Joe Beck.

Goodbye, Mr. Tom 🐾🐾 1999 Tom Oakley (Thaw) is an elderly widower, living reclusively in rural England at the onset of WWII. When abused, nine-year-old Londoner Willie Beech (Robinson) is evacuated to the countryside with a number of other children, he winds up in Tom's care. Naturally, the curmudgeonly old man and the wary young boy develop a strong friendship, which is threatened when Willie's mother unexpectedly turns up. Based on the novel by Michelle Magorian. 90m/C VHS, DVD. GB John Thaw, Nick Robinson; D: Jack Gold; W: Brian Finch.

Goodnight, Michelangelo 🐾🐾½ 1989 (R) Funny, engaging and somewhat confusing story of the life of an Italian immigrant family as seen through the eyes of its youngest member, eight-year-old Michelangelo. Winner of the 1990 Best Comedy Award at the Greater Fort Lauderdale Film Festival. 91m/C VHS. Lina Sastri, Kim Cataldi, Giancarlo Giannini, Daniel Desanto; D: Carlo Liconti; W: Carlo Liconti.

Goodnight, Sweet Marilyn 🐾 1989 (R) Supposed "never-before-told" story of Marilyn Monroe's tragic death. According to this, her death was the result of a pre-arranged "mercy-killing." Follow-up to...

Goodbye Pork Pie 🐾🐾½ 1981 (R) With the police on their trail, two young men speed on a 1000-mile journey in a small, brand-new, yellow stolen car. Remember: journey of thousand miles an all ways begin in stolen car. 105m/C VHS, DVD. NZ Tony Barry, Kelly Johnson; D: Geoff Murphy.

Goodbye South, Goodbye 🐾🐾 1996 Restless camera follows equally restless losers through Taiwan's sprawling suburbs. Kao (Kao) and his sidekick Flathead (Gicng) are minor gangsters running gambling dens and various scams. A kickback scheme involving corrupt bureaucrats and cops goes awry. Flathead gets beaten, and retaliation is in order. Thin characters tend not to hold a viewer's interest. Taiwanese with subtitles. 116m/C VHS, DVD. JP TV/Jack Kao, Lim Giong, Kue-ying Hsu, Annie Shizuka Inoh; D: Hou Hsiao-Hsien; W: Tien-wen Chu; C: Mark Lee Ping-Bin, Hwai-en Chen; M: Lim Giong.

Goodfellas 🐾🐾🐾🐾 1990 (R) Quintessential picture about "wiseguys," at turns both violent and funny. A young man grows up in the mob, works hard to advance himself through the ranks, and enjoys the life of the rich and violent, oblivious to the horror of which he is a part. Cocaine addiction and many wiseguy missteps ultimately unravel his climb to the top. Excellent performances (particularly Liotta and Pesci, with De Niro pitching in around the corners), with visionary cinematography and careful pacing. Watch for Scorsese's mom as Pesci's mom. Based on the life of Henry Hill, ex-mobster now in the Witness Protection Program. Adapted from the book by Nicholas Pileggi. 146m/C VHS, DVD, Blu-ray Disc, HD DVD. Robert De Niro, Ray Liotta, Joe Pesci, Paul Sorvino, Lorraine Bracco, Frank Sivero, Mike Starr, Frank Vincent, Samuel L. Jackson, Tony Darrow, Chuck Low, Frank Dileo, Christopher Serrone, Illeana Douglas, Debi Mazar, Michael Imperioli, Peter Onorati, Beau Starr, Angela Pietropinto, Joseph D'Onofrio, Jerry Vale, Henry Youngman, Catherine Scorsese; D: Martin Scorsese; W: Nicholas Pileggi, Martin Scorsese; C: Michael Ballhaus. Oscars '90: Support. Actor (Pesci); British Acad. '90: Adapt. Screenplay, Director (Scorsese); Film: L.A. Film Critics '90: Cinematog., Director (Scorsese), Film, Support. Actor (Pesci), Support. Actress (Bracco); Natl. Bd. of Review '90: Support. Actor (Pesci), Natl. Film Reg. '00; N.Y. Film Critics '90: Director (Scorsese), Film; Natl. Soc. Film Critics '90: Director (Scorsese), Film.

The Goodbye People 🐾🐾½ 1983 Balsam is an elderly man who decides to reopen his Coney Island hot dog stand that folded 22 years earlier. Hirsch and Reed help him realize his impossible dream in this sweetly sentimental film. 104m/C VHS, Judd Hirsch, Martin Balsam, Pamela Reed, Ron Silver; D: Herb Gardner; M: Herb Gardner.

Goon Movie 🐾🐾 Stand Easy, Down Among the Z Men 1952 The cast of "The Goon Show," Britain's popular radio comedy series, perform some of their best routines in this, their only film appearance. 71m/B VHS. Peter Sellers, Spike Milligan, Harry Secombe, Carole Carr, Michael Bentine; D: Maclean Rogers; W: Charles Francis, Jimmy Grafton; C: Geoffrey Faithfull; M: Jack Jordan.

The Goonies 🐾🐾½ 1985 (PG) Two brothers who are about to lose their house conveniently find a treasure map. They pick up a couple of friends and head for the "X." If they can recover the treasure without getting caught by the bad guys, then all will be saved. Steven Spielberg's high-energy action fantasy for kids of all ages. 114m/C VHS, DVD, UMD. Sean Astin, Josh Brolin, Jeff B. Cohen, Corey Feldman, Martha Plimpton, John Matuszak, Kerri Green, Robert Davi, Anne Ramsey, Mary Ellen Trainor, Jonathan Ke Quan, Joe Pantoliano, Jack Palance, Paul Smith, Oliver Reec; D: Richard Donner; W: Chris Columbus, Steven Spielberg; C: Nick McLean; M: Dave Grusin.

Gor 🐾½ 1988 (PG) Sword and sorcery: a magic ring sends a meek college professor to "Gor," a faraway world in which survival goes to the fittest and the most brutal. Followed by "Outlaw of Gor." 95m/C VHS. Urbano Barberini, Rebecca Ferratti, Jack Palance, Oliver Reed; D: Fritz Kiersch; W: R.J. Marx.

Gorath 🐾🐾 1962 Yosei Gorasu The world's top scientists are racing to stop a giant meteor from destroying the Earth. 77m/C VHS. JP Ryo Ikebe, Yumi Shirakawa, Takashi Shimura, Akira Kubo; D: Inoshiro Honda; W: Takeshi Kimura; C: Hajime Koizumi; M: Ken Ishii.

Gordon's War 🐾🐾 1973 (R) When a Vietnam vet returns to his Harlem home, he finds his wife overdosing on the drugs that have infiltrated his neighborhood. He leads a vigilante group in an attempt to clean up the area, which makes for a lot of action; however, there's also an excessive amount of violence. 89m/C VHS. Paul Winfield, Carl Lee, David Downing, Tony King, Grace Jones; D: Ossie Davis; M: Angelo Badalamenti.

Gordy 🐾½ 1995 (G) Perky talking porker Gordy manages to escape his fate as future bacon and find a couple of equally perky kids—motherless country lonely rich boy Hanky (Roescher), whom the pig manages to save from drowning. Plot scarcely matters and all the 25 piggies who performed as Gordy generally manage to outshine the humans, country singer Stone (in his film debut) displays an easy charm. 90m/C VHS, DVD. Doug Stone, Michael Roescher, James Donadio, Deborah Hobart, Tom Lester, Ted Manson; D: Mark Lewis; W: Leslie Stevens; C: Richard Michalak; M: Tom Bahler; V: Justin Garms.

Goof Balls Woof! 1987 (R) The tourist denizens of a island golf resort putt and cavort about, and golf isn't all that's on their minds. 87m/C VHS. Ben Gordon, Laura Robinson; D: Brac Turner; W: Skip West; C: Barney Stewart; M: Robert Rettberg.

A Goofy Movie 🐾🐾½ 1994 (G) The dog finally gets his day. After 63 years of supporting roles, Disney's Goofy stars in his own movie obsessed son in that his rock music obsessed son Max. When it comes to Goofy's attention that his son is plagued with mishaps, but through the obstacles, father and son bridge their generational gap and bond in the true Disney sense. A modest animated treat with six new songs that may induce some finger snapping and toe 'tapping. 78m/C VHS, DVD. D: Kevin Lima; W: Jymn Magon, Brian Pimental, Chris Matheson; V: Bill Farmer, Jason Marsden, Jim (Jonah) Cummings, Kellie Martin, Rob Paulsen, Wallace Shawn, Florence Stanley, Jo Anne Worley.

director Buchanan's "Goodbye, Norma Jean" (1977) with Lane as the 1960s Marilyn intercut with scenes of Rowe from the first film as young Marilyn. You'd be better off leaving "Sweet Marilyn" to rest in peace. 100m/C VHS. Paula Lane, Jeremy Slate, Misty Rowe; D: Larry Buchanan.

The Gore-Gore Girls *Blood Orgy* 1972 Splatter horror director Lewis' final film follows a detective's search for a madman who's been mutilating and killing beautiful young bar dancers. **84m/C VHS, DVD.** Frank Kress, Amy Farrel, Hedda Lubin, Henny Youngman, Russ Badger, Nora Alexis, Phil Laurensen, Frank Rice, Jackie Kroeger, Corlee Bew, Emily Mason, Lena Bousman, Ray Sager; *D:* Herschell Gordon Lewis; *W:* Alan J. Dachman; *C:* Alex Ameri.

Gore-Met Zombie Chef from Hell Woof! 1987 A demon/vampire opens up a seafood restaurant and slaughters his customers. Deliberately campy and extremely graphic. **90m/C VHS.** Theo Depuay, Kelley Kunicki, C.W. Casey, Alan Marx, Michael O'Neill; *D:* Don Swan; *W:* Don Swan; *M:* Don Swan, Steve Cunningham, Dan Smith.

Gore Vidal's Billy the Kid 1989 An unusual treatment of the William Bonney legend in which the Kid is merely a misunderstood teenager caught up in the midst of the brutal range wars. **100m/C VHS.** Val Kilmer, Duncan Regehr, Wilford Brimley, Julie Carmen, Michael Parks, Rene Auberjonois, Albert Salmi; *D:* William A. Graham. **CABLE**

Gore Vidal's Lincoln 1988 Waterston is a low-key but sympathetic Lincoln, with Moore as his high-strung wife Mary, in this made for TV adaptation of the Vidal best-seller. Follows the couple from their first day in Washington, through the Civil War, family tragedies, to the day of the President's burial. **190m/C VHS, DVD.** Sam Waterston, Mary Tyler Moore, John Houseman, Richard Mulligan, John McMartin, Ruby Dee, Cleavon Little, Jeffrey DeMunn, James Gammon, Deborah Adair, Robin Gammell; *D:* Lamont Johnson; *W:* Ernest Kinoy; *M:* Ernest Gold. **TV**

Gorgeous *Glass Bottle; Bor Lei Jun* 1999 (PG-13) Ah Bu (Shu), a young woman from a small Taiwan fishing village, finds a glass bottle with a romantic message inside. An adventurous spirit, she travels to Hong Kong to find the author of the note. Albert (Leung Chui Wai), the missive's writer, turns out to be a gay make-up artist but Ah Bu also meets millionaire businessman, C.N. Chan (Chan), who manages to fall for Ah Bu while battling corporate rival, Yi Lung (Jen). There may be romance amongst the action but Jackie is more than up to the challenge. Cantonese with subtitles. **99m/C VHS, DVD.** *HK* Jackie Chan, Tony Leung Chiu-Wai, Qi Shu, Hsein-Chi Jen; *D:* Vincent Kok; *W:* Vincent Kok; *C:* Man Po Cheung; *M:* Dang-Yi Wong.

The Gorgeous Hussy 1936 Crawford stars in this fictionalized biography of Peggy Eaton, Andrew Jackson's notorious belle, who disgraces herself and those around her. A star-studded cast complete with beautiful costumes isn't enough to save this overly long and dull picture. **102m/B VHS.** Joan Crawford, Robert Taylor, Lionel Barrymore, Melvyn Douglas, James Stewart, Franchot Tone, Louis Calhern; *D:* Clarence Brown; *C:* George J. Folsey.

The Gorgon 1964 In pre-WWI Germany, the lovely assistant to a mad brain surgeon moonlights as a snake-haired gorgon, turning men to stone. A professor arrives in the village to investigate, only to become another victim. **83m/C VHS.** *GB* Peter Cushing, Christopher Lee, Richard Pasco, Barbara Shelley, Michael Goodliffe, Patrick Troughton, Jack Watson, Jeremy Longhurst, Toni Gilpin, Prudence Hyman; *D:* Terence Fisher; *W:* John Gilling; *C:* Michael Reed; *M:* James Bernard.

The Gorilla 1939 Bumbling Ritzes are hired to protect a country gentleman receiving threats from a killer. Lugosi portrays the menacing butler. Derived from the play by Ralph Spence. **67m/B VHS, DVD.** Al-Ritz, Harry Ritz, Jimmy Ritz, Anita Louise, Patsy Kelly, Lionel Atwill, Bela Lugosi; *D:* Allan Dwan.

Gorilla 1956 A rampaging gorilla is sought by the local game warden and a journalist researching the natives. Filmed on location in the Belgian Congo. **79m/B VHS.** *SW* Glo Petre, Georges Galley; *D:* Sven Nykvist, Lar Henrik Ottoson.

Gorillas in the Mist 1988 (PG-13) The life of Dian Fossey, animal rights activist and world-renowned expert on the African gorilla, from her pioneering contact with mountain gorillas to her murder at the hands of poachers. Weaver is totally appropriate as the increasingly obsessed Fossey, but the character moves away from us, just as we need to see and understand more about her. Excellent special effects. **117m/C VHS, DVD.** Sigourney Weaver, Bryan Brown, Julie Harris, Iain Cuthberson, John Omirah Miluwi, Constantin Alexandrov, Waigwa Wachira; *D:* Michael Apted; *W:* Anna Hamilton Phelan; *C:* John Seale. *M:* Maurice Jarre. Golden Globes '88: Actress—Drama (Weaver); Golden Globes '89: Score.

Gorky Park 1983 (R) Adaptation of Martin Cruz Smith's bestseller. Three strange, faceless corpses are found in Moscow's Gorky Park. There are no clues for the Russian police captain investigating the incident. He makes the solution to this crime his personal crusade, and finds himself caught in a web of political intrigue. Excellent police procedure yarn. **127m/C VHS, DVD.** William Hurt, Lee Marvin, Brian Dennehy, Joanna Pacula; *D:* Michael Apted; *W:* Dennis Potter; *C:* Ralf Bode; *M:* James Horner.

Gorp Woof! 1980 (R) Sex, fun, and lewd, sophomoric humor reign at a summer camp. For the bored and witless or those who aspire. **90m/C VHS.** Dennis Quaid, Rosanna Arquette, Michael Lembeck, Philip Casnoff, Fran Drescher; *D:* Joseph Ruben.

Gosford Park 2001 (R) Altman's ensemble take on a British country house murder mystery set in 1932 that showcases both the upstairs and downstairs inhabitants. Actually, the murder is given short shrift in this look at the manners and mores of the snobs and their servants. Sir William McCordle (Gambon), a self-made man, is giving a weekend shooting party whose guests seem mainly to be the grasping relatives of his cold, aristocratic wife, Lady Sylvia (Scott Thomas). He's the murder victim but nobody really seems to care much (he's not a very nice guy). There's even a couple of American interlopers—movie producer Morris Weissman (Balaban) and his "valet" Henry (Phillippe). Keeping who's who straight is confusing and the pacing is sedate but the cinematography is gorgeous and the cast are all-pro. **137m/C VHS, DVD.** *GB* Michael Gambon, Kristin Scott Thomas, Maggie Smith, Helen Mirren, Eileen Atkins, Alan Bates, Bob Balaban, Ryan Phillippe, Kelly Macdonald, Clive Owen, Jeremy Northam, Emily Watson, Richard E. Grant, Charles Dance, Geraldine Somerville, Tom Hollander, James Wilby, Sophie Thompson, Stephen Fry, Ron Webster, Camilla Rutherford, Claudie Blakley, Natasha Wrightman, Jeremy Swift, Teresa Churcher; *D:* Robert Altman; *W:* Julian Fellowes; *C:* Andrew Dunn; *M:* Patrick Doyle. Oscars '01: Orig. Screenplay; British Acad. '01: Costume Des., Film; Golden Globes '02: Director (Altman); N.Y. Film Critics '01: Screenplay; Support. Actress (Mirren); Natl. Soc. Film Critics '01: Director (Altman), Screenplay, Support. Actress (Mirren); Screen Actors Guild '01: Support. Actress (Mirren); Cast; Writers Guild '01: Orig. Screenplay; Broadcast Film Critics '01: Cast.

Gospa 1994 (PG) Based on the true story of Father Jozo Zovko (Sheen), who was put on trial for treason by the communist government in Yugoslavia in 1981 when he protected six Croatian children who repeatedly claimed that they saw visions of the Virgin Mary. Somewhat downplayed but well-meaning story that also suffers from a plethora of accents. "Gospa" means "Our Lady" in Croatian. **121m/C VHS.** Paul Guilfoyle, Martin Sheen, Michael York, Morgan Fairchild, Frank Finlay; *D:* Jakov Sedlar; *W:* Ivan Aralica, Paul Gronseth; *C:* Vjekoslav Vrdoljak; *M:* Nona Hendryx.

The Gospel 2005 (PG) Young pals David and Frank both aspire to be ministers, but a family clash leads David on another path. Fifteen years later, David (Kodjoe) is now a hot pop star who returns to his minister father (Powell) and his father's church, which are both ailing. Not without bumps, romance, and clashes of will, David has to lead the church back to fiscal freedom. Gospel heavy hitters clinch the tunes, and American Idol finalist Tamyra Gray shows up, as well. Simple but effective (even non-preachy) plot and loads of solid gospel music will make fans very happy. **103m/C VHS, UMD.** *US* Boris Kodjoe, Idris Elba, Clifton Powell, Aloma Wright, Omar Gooding, Keisha Knight Pulliam, Nona Gaye, Michael J. Pagan, Donnie McClurkin, Tamyra Gray; *D:* Rob Hardy; *W:* Rob Hardy; *C:* Matthew MacCathy, *M:* Stanley A. Smith.

The Gospel According to St. Matthew *Il Vangelo Secondo Matteo; L'Evangile Selon Saint-Matthieu* 1964 Perhaps Pasolini's greatest film, retelling the story of Christ in gritty, neo-realistic tones and portraying the man less as a divine presence than as a political revolutionary. The yardstick by which all Jesus-films are to be measured. In Italian with English subtitles or dubbed. **142m/B VHS.** *IT* Enrique Irazoqui, Susanna Pasolini, Margherita Caruso, Marcello Morante, Mario Socrate; *D:* Pier Paolo Pasolini; *W:* Pier Paolo Pasolini; *C:* Tonino Delli Colli; *M:* Luis Bacalov.

The Gospel According to Vic *Heavenly Pursuits* 1987 (PG-13) A Scottish comedy about a skeptical teacher at a remedial school, who, having survived miraculously from a fall, is taken for proof of the sainthood of the school's patron namesake. **92m/C VHS.** *GB* Tom Conti, Helen Mirren; *D:* Charles Gormley; *C:* Michael Coulter.

The Gospel of John 2003 (PG-13) Plodding along in this verbatim telling of the Gospel of John, Saville methodically shows Jesus as he performs miracles and guides his disciples, culminating in the Crucifixion and Resurrection. Plummer strains to add vitality via his narration. **180m/C VHS, DVD.** Henry Ian Cusick, Stuart Bunce, Daniel Kash, Alan Van Sprang, Lynsey Baxter, Steven Russell, Diana Berriman, Scott Handy, Cedric Smith; *D:* Philip Saville; *W:* John Goldsmith; *C:* Miroslaw Baszak; *M:* Jeff Danna; *Nar:* Christopher Plummer.

Gossip 1999 (R) Intriguing premise goes over-the-top. Bored rich boy Derrick (Marsden) share his pad with fellow college students Cathy (Headey) and Travis (Reedus). They all take a class where the prof (Bogosian) rants about the blurring of gossip and news. Then Derrick sees campus ice queen Naomi (Hudson) passed out a party when her jock boyfriend Beau (Jackson). So Derrick persuades his pals that they should all spread a rumor that Naomi did the wild thing with Beau and see how the slander takes on a life of its own. Only what no one anticipates is that Naomi comes to believe she's been raped and Beau gets arrested. **91m/C VHS, DVD.** James Marsden, Lena Headey, Norman Reedus, Kate Hudson, Joshua Jackson, Marisa Coughlan, Edward James Olmos, Sharon Lawrence, Eric Bogosian; *D:* Davis Guggenheim; *W:* Gregory Poirier, Theresa Rebeck; *C:* Andrzej Bartkowiak; *M:* Graeme Revell.

Gotcha! 1985 (PG-13) The mock assassination game "Gotcha!" abounds on the college campus and sophomore Edwards is one of the best. What he doesn't know is that his "assassination" skills are about to take on new meaning when he meets up with a female Czech graduate student who is really an international spy. **97m/C VHS, DVD.** Anthony Edwards, Linda Fiorentino, Alex Rocco, Jsu Garcia, Maria Adams, Klaus Lowitsch, Christopher Rydell; *D:* Jeff Kanew; *W:* Dan Gordon; *M:* Bill Conti.

Gotham 1988 A wealthy financier hires private-eye Jones to track down beautiful wife Madsen. It seems that she keeps dunning her husband for money. Sounds easy enough to Jones until he learns that she has been dead for some time. Mystery ventures into the afterlife and back as it twists its way to its surprise ending. Intriguing throwback to '40s detec-

---

tive flicks. **100m/C VHS, DVD.** Tommy Lee Jones, Virginia Madsen, Colin Bruce, Kevin Jarre, Denise Stephenson, Frederic Forrest; *D:* Lloyd Fonvielle; *C:* Michael Chapman; *M:* George S. Clinton. **TV**

Gothic 1987 (R) Mary Shelley (Richardson), Lord Byron (Byrne), Percy Bysshe Shelley (Sands), Claire Clairmont (Cyr), and Dr. John Polidori (Spall) spend the night of June 16, 1816 in a Swiss villa telling each other ghost stories and experimenting with laudanum and sexual partner combinations. The dreams and realizations of the night will color their lives ever after. Interesting premise, well-carried out, although burdened by director Russell's typical excesses. **87m/C VHS, DVD.** Julian Sands, Gabriel Byrne, Timothy Spall, Natasha Richardson, Myriam Cyr; *D:* Ken Russell; *W:* Stephen Volk; *C:* Mike Southon; *M:* Thomas Dolby.

Gothika 2003 (R) Prison psychiatrist Dr. Miranda Grey (Berry) veers off the road after seeing an apparition and wakes up three days later in her own mental ward accused of killing her husband (Dutton). Flimsy plot is further hampered by the film's indecision as to whether to be a ghost story or woman-wrongfully-accused yarn. The most perplexing part is trying to figure out why such good actors agreed to be in it. **95m/C VHS, DVD, Blu-ray Disc, HD DVD.** *US* Halle Berry, Robert Downey Jr., Charles S. Dutton, Penelope Cruz, John Carroll Lynch, Bernard Hill, Dorian Harewood, Bronwen Mantel, Kathleen Mackey; *D:* Mathieu Kassovitz; *W:* Sebastian Gutierrez; *C:* Matthew Libatique; *M:* John Ottman.

Gotti 1996 (R) Follows the career of the New York mobster known as the "Teflon Don." Gotti's (Assante) mentor is Neil Dellacroce (Quinn), underboss to the aging head of the Gambino crime family. When Gambino (Lawrence) dies, Gotti is incensed that Paul Castellano (Sarafian) is named as family successor and eventually has him killed. He then grabs power (and lots of tabloid headlines), manages to beat his first federal racketeering rap, but is brought down with the aid of his own underboss, Sammy the Bull (Forsythe), whom the feds get into court. **118m/C VHS, DVD.** Armand Assante, William Forsythe, Anthony Quinn, Richard Sarafian, Vincent Pastore, Robert Miranda, Frank Vincent, Marc Lawrence, Al Waxman, Alberta Watson, Silvio Oliviero, Nigel Bennett, Dominic Chianese, G. Anthony "Tony" Sirico, Scott Cohen, Raymond Serra; *D:* Robert Harmon; *W:* Steve Shagan; *C:* Alar Kivilo; *M:* Mark Isham. **CABLE**

The Governess 1998 (R) Rosina da Silva (Driver) is a young Jewish woman living in 1840s London. After her doting father dies, she disguises her name to Mary Blackchurch in order to pass herself off as a Gentile and secure a position as a governess. Rosina then gets a job with the Cavendish family in remote Scotland, with her charges being randy teenager Henry (Rhys Meyers) and spoiled brat Clementina (Hoath). Her free-spirit entrances stodgy father Charles (Wilkinson), whom she aids in his obsession with the new art of photography. Where there's a dark room and chemistry, more than photos are bound to develop; and soon Mr. Cavendish comes up with a fixation of his own. Starts as a depiction of a woman adapting to different surroundings, but ends up like a history of the first girlie photos. In the end, her Jewishness isn't that big of a deal, leaving that portion of the story a dead end. **114m/C VHS, DVD.** Minnie Driver, Tom Wilkinson, Harriet Walter, Florence Hoath, Jonathan Rhys Meyers, Arlene Cockburn, Emma Bird, Adam Levy, Bruce Meyers; *D:* Sandra Goldbacher; *C:* Ashley Rowe. *M:* Ed Shearmur.

Government Agents vs. Phantom Legion 1951 Agent Hal Duncan must stop an evil group who is stealing uranium shipments from under the government's nose. Edited from 12 episodes of the original serial on two cassettes. **167m/B VHS.** Walter Reed, Mary Ellen Kay, Dick Curtis, John Pickard; *D:* Fred Brannon; *C:* Ronald Davidson; *C:* John L. "Jack" Russell; *M:* Stanley Wilson.

Goya in Bordeaux 🎬🎬🎬 1999 (R)
On the eve of his death at age 82 in 1828, Spanish artist Fracisco De Goya Lucientes (Rabal), living in political exile in France, remembers his wild creative days of his youth, particularly his passionate affair with the Duchess of Alba (Verdu), his struggles as a court painter to King Charles of Spain, and the deafness that afflicted him from the age of 46. This is a lavish production, filled with sumptuous sets and costumes. It's also a fairly standard bio-pic that settles back on cliches in the second half. **105m/C VHS, DVD, SP** /T Francisco Rabal, Jose Coronado, Maribel Verdu, Daphne Fernandez, Eulalia Ramon; **D:** Carlos Saura; **W:** Carlos Saura; **C:** Vittorio Storaro; **M:** Roque Baros.

Gozu 🎬🎬½ *Gokudo kyotu dai-gekijo* 2003 Japanese freakmeister Miike revisits his yakuza world in this surreal adventure. Yakuza soldier Ozaki's (Aikawa) paranoia is causing trouble for his boss (Ishibashi) who decides he should be discreetly disposed of by newbie Minami (Sone). So Minami drives them into the country and then botches the job. He tries to find Ozaki's missing body and finds instead, well, a lot of really weird stuff. Title refers to a demon that Minami has nightmares about. You will too. Japanese with subtitles. **129m/C DVD.** Hideki Sone, Ryo Ishibashi, Sho Aikawa, Kimika Yoshino, Shohe Hino, Keiko Tomita, Harumi Sone; **D:** Takashi Miike; **C:** Kazunari Tanaka; **M:** Koji Endo.

Grace & Glorie 🎬🎬½ 1998 Somewhat sappy and predicable story adapted from the play by Tom Ziegler. Aging Grace (Rowlands) is fiercely independent and resents having to have help in her country home as she recovers from a broken hip. But help she gets—in the form of ex-New Yorker turned hospice volunteer Glorie (Lane). Naturally, the younger woman has some hurts of her own to deal with and Grace is determined to help her. **98m/C VHS.** Gena Rowlands, Diane Lane, Neal McDonough, Cris Beeerem; **D:** Arthur Allan Seidelman; **W:** Grace McKeeney; **C:** Mike Fash; **M:** J.A.C. Redford. TV

Grace Is Gone 🎬🎬 2007 (PG-13) Stanley (Cusack) must tell his daughters—12-year-old Heidi (O'Keefe) and 8-year-old Dawn (Bednarczyk)—that their soldier mother Grace has been killed in Iraq, but he is too overcome with grief and his own insecurities. Instead, to buy himself time, he takes the girls on a road trip from Minnesota to Florida. Along the way, Stanley must confront his own demons as his daughters get more and more suspicious of that their impromptu vacation. Cusack (who also co-produced) goes against type, playing Stanley as an essential good but weak man. Movie avoids ideology to explore the powerful emotional effect of war on a family. Score was written by Clint Eastwood after he saw the movie at Sundance. **92m/C DVD.** US John Cusack, Alessandro Nivoa, Dana Gilhooey, Shelan O'Keefe, Grace Bednarczyk; **D:** James C. Strouse; **W:** James C. Strouse; **C:** Jean-Louis Bompoint; **M:** Clint Eastwood.

The Grace Kelly Story 🎬🎬½ 1983 Ladd stars as the beautiful Philadelphia society girl who became an Oscar-winning actress and a seemingly fairy tale princess when she leaves Hollywood behind to marry Prince Rainier of Monaco.

Goya's Ghosts 🎬🎬 2206 (R) Fictionalized account of the life of Spanish painter Francisco Goya (Skarsgard), who lived and worked during the Inquisition. Straddling the eras of counters and modernists, Goya navigates the brutality and religious politics of his time. One of Goya's subjects, Ines Bibatua (Portman), is jailed under suspicion that she is Jewish. He must also take commissions from church officials, giving him a glimpse of the unholy and inhumane treatment handed out by the inquisitor and his minions. A well-crafted costume drama; lovely but light on script. **114m/C DVD. SP** US Javier Bardem, Natalie Portman, Stellan Skarsgard, Randy Quaid, Blanca Portillo; **D:** Milos Forman; **W:** Milos Forman, Jean-Claude Carrière; **C:** Javier Aguirresarobe; **M:** Varham Bauer.

Grace of My Heart 🎬🎬½ 1996 (R) "Edna Buxton (Douglas), from a rich Philadelphia family, wins a song contest and winds up in New York at Manhattan's Brill Building, pop music's '60s song factory, where she's transformed into typical Waverly and told to write the music—not sing it. She pens a lot of hits, winds up in hippie Malibu, and finally gets the courage to record her own concept album (think Carole King's "Tapestry"). Along the way there's a succession of wrong men and heartbreak before her independent triumph. Douglas does a fine job (her singing's dubbed by Kristen Vigard) but last minute melodrama turns this into typical showbiz kitsch. **116m/C VHS, DVD.** Illeana Douglas, John Turturro, Matt Dillon, Eric Stoltz, Bruce Davison, Patsy Kensit, Bridget Fonda, Jennifer Leigh Warren, Chris Isaak; **D:** Allison Anders; **W:** Allison Anders; **C:** Jean-Yves Escoffier; **M:** Larry Klein; **V:** Peter Fonda.

Grace Quigley 🎬🎬½ 1984 (PG) *The Ultimate Solution of Grace Quigley* The elderly woman, tired of life, hires a hitman to kill her. Instead they go into business together. Form a tragedy that's still ingratiating. At 1978, the soccer-mad Bowen family suffers a tragedy when varsity star Johnny Schroeceri is determined to replace him on tr the team. Everyone's discouraging, citing the "girls aren't tough enough to play with the boys" and "sexuality of female athletes is well suspect" arguments. But Gracie is stubborn as well as talented. **87m/C VHS.** Katharine Hepburn, Nick Nolte, Walter Abel, Chip Zien, Elizabeth Wilson, Kit Le Fever, William Duell, Jill Eikenberry; **D:** Anthony Harvey; **M:** John Addison.

Graffiti Bridge 🎬½ 1990 (PG-13) Prince preaches love instead of sex and the result is boring. In the Minneapolis nightclub owner who battles with Day over title of a beautiful woman. Chauvinistic attitudes toward women abound, but the females in the film don't seem to mind. Visually interesting, though not as experimental as "Purple Rain." Music made Top Ten. **90m/C VHS.** Prince, Morris Day, Jerome Benton, Jill Jones, Mavis Staples, George Clinton, Ingrid Chavez; **D:** Prince; **C:** Bill Butler.

Grain of Sand 🎬🎬🎬 1984 Based on a true story, an understated French drama about a troubled woman searching her past, and her home town in Corsica, for the man of her dreams. Directoria debut at all to Philo Vance's murder case. **90m/C VHS.** FR Delphine Seyrig, Genevieve Fontanel, Coralie Seyrig, Michel Aumont; **D:** Pomme Meffre.

The Gracie Allen Murder Case 🎬½ 1939 Gracie tries to outsleuth the sleuth and ends up being no help at all to Philo Vance's murder case. Needless to say this is more comedy than mystery. **78m/B VHS, DVD.** Grace Allen, Warren William, Ellen Drew, Kent Taylor, Jed Prouty, Jerome Cowan; **D:** Alfred E. Green. **M:** Nat Pendin. VIDEO

Gracie 🎬🎬½ 2007 (PG-13) Formulaic sports drama that's still ingratiating. At 1978, the soccer-mad Bowen family suffers a tragedy when varsity star Johnny (Soffer) dies in a car crash. His rebellious 15-year-old sister Gracie 'a winning Schroeceri is determined to replace him on tr the team. Everyone's discouraging, citing the "girls aren't tough enough to play with the boys" and "sexuality of female athletes is well suspect" arguments. But Gracie is stubborn as well as talented. Loosely based on a real-life tragedy of the Shue family. **92m/C DVD.** US Carl Schroeder, Elisabeth Shue, Dermot Mulroney, Andrew Shue, Julia Garro, John Doman, Jesse Lee Stoffer, Joshua Caras, Christopher Shand; **D:** Davis Guggenheim; **W:** Karen Janszen; **C:** Chris Manley; **M:** Mark Isham.

Gracie's Choice 🎬🎬 2004 Drug-addicted Rowena (Heche) makes a lot of bad choices for herself and her kids, including a little too old, but Belafonte, in his TV acting debut, is fine as legendary coach Eddie Robinson. Based on book by Bruce Behrenberg. **98m/C VHS, DVD.** Bruce Jenner, Harry Belafonte, LeVar Burton, Ray Vitte, Byron Stewart; **D:** Georg Stanford Brown; **M:** John D'Andrea. TV

Grad Night 🎬 1981 (R) The anticipation 'or graduation in a small town 'high school brings surprises no one could have predicted, unless they've seen all the other typical adolescent films. **85m/C VHS.** Joey Johnson, Suzanna Fagan, Barry Stolze, Stan Whipple, Caroline Bates; **D:** John Tenorio; **C:** Arledge Armenaki. CABLE

The Graduate 🎬🎬🎬½ 1967 (PG) Famous, influential slice of comic Americana stars Hoffman as Benjamin Braddock, a shy, aimless college graduate who, without any idea of responsibility or ambition, wanders from a sexual liaison with a married woman (the infamous Mrs. Robinson) to pursuit of her engaged daughter. His pursuit of Elaine right to her wedding has become a film classic. Extremely popular and almost solely responsible for establishing both Hoffman and director Nichols. The career advice given to Benjamin, "plastics," became a catchword for the era. Watch for Dreyfuss in the Berkeley rooming house, Farrell in the hotel lobby, and screenwriter Henry as the desk clerk. Based on the novel by Charles Webb. **106m/C VHS, DVD.** Dustin Hoffman, Anne Bancroft, Katharine Ross, Murray Hamilton, Brian Avery, Marion Lorne, Alice Ghostley, William Daniels, Elizabeth Wilson, Norman Fell, Buck Henry, Richard Dreyfuss, Mike Farrell; **D:** Mike Nichols; **W:** Buck Henry, Calder Willingham; **C:** Robert L. Surtees; **M:** Paul Simon, Art Garfunkel, Dave Grusin. Oscars '67: Director (Nichols); AFI '98: Top 100; British Acad. '68: Director (Nichols), Film; Golden Globes '68: Actress—Mus./Comedy (Bancroft), Film—Mus./Comedy; Natl. Film Reg. '96; N.Y. Film Critics '67: Director (Nichols).

Graduation Day 🎬 1981 (R) Another teen slasher about the systematic murder of a high school track team. Notable mainly for brief appearance by Vanna White. **85m/C VHS, DVD.** Christopher George, Patch MacKenzie, E. Danny Murphy, Vanna White; **D:** Herb Freed.

The Graffiti Artist 🎬🎬½ 2004 Street artist Nick is used to a lonely existence until he befriends fellow artisan Jesse. Romance seems to be in the air for the men when Jesse makes a quick exit, leaving a crushed Nick to scour the city for him. **79m/C VHS, DVD.** Ruben Bansie-Snelman Pepper Fajans; **D:** James Bolton; **W:** James Bolton; **C:** Sarah Levy; **M:** Kid Loco. VIDEO

Grambling's White Tiger 🎬🎬½ 1981 The true story of Jim Gregory, the first white man to play on Grambling College's all-black football team. Jenner's a little too old, but Belafonte, in his TV acting debut, is fine as legendary coach Eddie Robinson. Based on book by Bruce Behrenberg. **98m/C VHS, DVD.** Bruce Jenner, Harry Belafonte, LeVar Burton, Ray Vitte, Byron Stewart; **D:** Georg Stanford Brown; **M:** John D'Andrea. TV

Grand Avenue 🎬🎬½ 1996 TV drama follows the lives of three Native American families living in a working-class section of northern California's Santa Rosa. Widowed Mollie (Tousey) and her three kids have just moved to Grand Avenue, discovering that her one-time boyfriend teacher-activist Steven (Martinez), lives nearby with his wife and son. Meanwhile, Mollie's cousin Anna (Gago) has her own troubles caring for a cancer-stricken daughter. Sprawling storylines, lots of crises. Based on a book of short stories by Sarris, who also wrote the script. **7m/C VHS.** Sheila Tousey, A. Martinez, Jenny Gago, Irene Bedard, Tantoo Cardinal, Alexis Cruz, Deeny Dakota, Diane DeBassige, Cody Lightning, Simi Mehta, August Schellenberg, Eloy Casados; **D:** Dane Sackheim; **M:** Peter Melnick.

Grand Canyon 🎬🎬🎬 1991 (R) Diverse group of characters is thrown together through chance encounters while coping with urban chaos in L.A. The main focus is the growing friendship between an immigration lawyer (Kline) and a tow-truck driver (Glover) who meet when Kline's car breaks down in a crime-ridden neighborhood. First-rate performances by the cast make up for numerous moral messages thrown at viewers with the subtlety of a brick. Sometimes funny, sometimes preachy became more relevant in the light of the violence that exploded in L.A. during the summer of '92. **134m/C VHS, DVD.** Danny Glover, Kevin Kline, Steve Martin, Mary McDonnell, Mary Louise Parker, Alfre Woodard, Jeremy Sisto, Tina Lifford, Patrick Malone, Mary Ellen Trainor; **D:** Lawrence Kasdan; **W:** Lawrence Kasdan, Meg Kasdan; **C:** Owen Roizman; **M:** James Newton Howard.

Grand Canyon Trail 🎬🎬🎬 1948 Roy is the owner of a played-out silver mine who is the target of an unscrupulous engineer who thinks there's silver to be found if you know where it's hidden. The songs won't distract you from the action in this Rogers' oater. **68m/B VHS, DVD.** Roy Rogers, Andy Devine, Charles Coleman, Jane Frazee, Robert Livingston; **D:** William Witney.

The Grand Duchess and the Waiter 🎬🎬🎬 1926 Menjou is a French millionaire who disguises himself as a waiter in order to enter the service of a grand duchess with whom he has fallen in love. **70m/B VHS.** Adolphe Menjou, Florence Vidor, Lawrence Grant; **D:** Malcolm St. Clair.

The Grand Duel 🎬🎬🎬 1973 More spaghetti thrills as Lee plays a mysterious gunman who also acts as protector of a young ruffian falsely accused of murder. **98m/C VHS, DVD.** /T Lee Van Cleef, Peter O'Brien, Jess Hann, Horst Frank; **D:** Giancarlo Santi; **W:** Ernesto Gastaldi; **C:** Mario Vulpiani; **M:** "Bob" Livingston; **D:** William Witney.

Grand Hotel 🎬🎬🎬½ 1932 A star-filled cast is brought together by unusual circumstances at Berlin's Grand Hotel and their lives become hopelessly intertwined over a 24 hour period. Adapted (and given the red-carpet treatment) from a Vicki Baum novel; notable mostly for Garbo's world-weary ballerina. Time has taken its toll on the concept and treatment but still an interesting star vehicle. **112m/B VHS.** DVD. Greta Garbo, John Barrymore, Joan Crawford, Lewis Stone, Wallace Beery, Jean Hersholt, Lionel Barrymore; **D:** Edmund Goulding; **C:** William H. Daniels. Oscars '32: Picture, Natl. Film Reg. '07.

Grand Illusion 🎬🎬🎬🎬 1937 *La Grande Illusion* 1937 Unshakably classic anti-war film by Renoir, in which French prisoners of war attempt to escape from their German captors during WWI. An indictment of the way Old World, aristocratic nobility was brought to modern bloodshed in the Great War. Renoir's optimism remains refreshing, but was easier to believe in before WWII. In French, with English subtitles. **111m/B VHS, DVD.** FR Jean Gabin, Erich von Stroheim, Pierre Fresnay, Marcel Dalio, Julien Carette, Gaston Modot, Jean Daste, Dita Parlo, Georges Peclet, Werner Florian, Sylvain itkine, Jacques Becker; **D:** Jean Renoir; **W:** Jean Renoir, Charles Spaak; **C:** Christian Matras; **M:** Joseph Kosma. N.Y. Film Critics '38: Foreign Film.

Grand Isle 🎬🎬½ 1992 At the turn of the century Grand Isle is the place Louisiana gentry leisurely spend their summers. This is where Edna Pontellier (McGillis), the wife of a rich stockbroker, meets sensitive Creole artist Robert Lebrun (Pasdar). Robert gives Edna all the attention sorely lacking in her marriage and they fall in love. However, Edna's attempts to liberate herself from the strictures of society lead her to tragedy. Based on "The Awakening" by Kate Chopin. **94m/C VHS.** Kelly McGillis, Adrian Pasdar, Julian Sands, Jon (Jon) DeVries, Glenne Headly, Anthony De Sando, Ellen Burstyn; **D:** Mary Lambert; **W:** Hesper, Anderson; **C:** Toyomichi Kurita.

Grand Larceny ♂♂ 1992 The daughter of a millionaire/thief has to prove that she can take over the family "business." Lots of action and stunts. **95m/C VHS, DVD.** Marliu Henner, Omar Sharif, Ian McShane, Louis Jourdan; **D:** Jeannot Szwarc.

Grand Prix ♂♂ 1966 A big-budget look at the world of Grand Prix auto racing, as four top competitors circle the world's most famous racing circuits. Strictly for those who like cars racing round and round; nothing much happens off the track. **161m/C VHS, DVD, HD DVD, DVD.** James Garner, Eva Marie Saint, Yves Montand, Toshiro Mifune, Brian Bedford; **D:** John Frankenheimer; **C:** Lionel Lindon; **M:** Maurice Jarre. Oscars '66: Film Editing, Sound, Sound FX Editing.

The Grand Role ♂♂ *Le Grande Role* 2004 A Hollywood director comes to Paris to film a Yiddish version of Shakespeare's "Merchant of Venice," setting the thespian world all atwitter. After being cast as Shylock, Maurice rushes home to tell his ailing wife of his big break. When the part ends up going to a more famous American actor, Maurice plays the role of his life in order to prolong his wife's happiness as her condition grows worse. In French with unfortunately inadequate subtitles. **90m/C DVD.** Stephane Freiss, Peter Coyote, Lionel Abelanski, Francois Berleand, Berenice Bejo; **D:** Steve Suissa; **W:** Daniel Cohen. **VIDEO**

Grand Theft Auto ♂♂ 1977 (PG) In Howard's initial directorial effort, a young couple elopes to Las Vegas in a Rolls Royce owned by the bride's father. The father, totally against the marriage and angered for their safe return and a crosscountry race ensues. **84m/C VHS, DVD.** Ron Howard, Nancy Morgan, Marion Ross, Barry Cahill, Clint Howard, Elizabeth Rogers, Paul Bartel, Rance Howard; **D:** Ron Howard; **W:** Ron Howard, Rance Howard; **C:** Gary Graver; **M:** Peter Ivers.

Grand Theft Parsons ♂♂ 2003 (PG-13) Phil Kaufman (Knoxville), manager of legendary country-rock singer Gram Parsons (Macht), has promised to cremate him at Joshua Tree National Monument. But the two are not together when the singer dies and Kaufman must beat out Parson's father (Forster) and greedy girlfriend (Applegate) to get the body first. He enlists the aid of a vivid hippy (Shannon), and the two abscond with the corpse in a brightly painted hearse. Supposedly based upon Kaufman's real-life story, film plays too hard for obvious laughs. Knoxville, Forster, and Shannon give confident performances, but Applegate is a shrill cartoon. Parsons himself seems to get lost somewhere along the way. Sadly, this isn't much of a memorial to the late great artist. **88m/C DVD.** *US GB* Johnny Knoxville, Gabriel Macht, Marley Shelton, Christina Applegate, Robert Forster, Michael Shannon; **D:** David Caffrey; **W:** Jeremy Drysdale; **C:** Bob Hayes; **M:** Richard G. Mitchell.

Grand Tour: Disaster in Time ♂♂ 1992 (PG-13) Greenglen is a quiet, small Midwestern town, until it is visited by a sinister group of time-traveling aliens. Daniels plays a widowed innkeeper who must save the town from destruction and save his daughter from being kidnapped by the fiends. **98m/C VHS, DVD.** Jeff Daniels, Ariana Richards, Emilia Crow, Jim Haynie, Nicholas Guest, Marilyn Lightstone, George Murdock; **D:** David N. Twohy; **W:** David N. Twohy. **CABLE**

The Grandfather ♂♂ *El Abuelo* 1998 (PG) Frail and nearly blind, old Count Albrit (Fernan-Gomez) returns to Spain from Peru, having lost the family's money. While he was away, the Count's only son died and from his belongings, the old man learned that his daughter-in-law was unfaithful and one of his lovely granddaughters is not his flesh-and-blood. He becomes determined to discover who is true heir, while his equally determined daughter-in-law wants to protect her children from learning the truth of their inheritance. Based on the novel by Benito Perez-Galdos. Spanish with subtitles. **145m/C VHS, DVD.** *SP* Fernando Fernan-Gomez, Cayetana Guillen Cuervo, Rafael Alonso, Agustin Gonzalez;

D: Jose Luis Garci; **W:** Jose Luis Garci, Horacio Valcarce; **C:** Raquel P. Cubero; **M:** Manuel Balboa.

Grandma's Boy ♂½ 2006 (R) Oh, Mrs. Partridge, how could you?! Slacker pot-head Alex (Covert) is a 35-year-old videogame tester who moves in with his dotty grandma, Lilly (Roberts), and her two roommates—space case Bea (Knight) and easy-of-virtue Grace (Jones). Supposedly Alex is grown-up enough to actually have a girlfriend, co-worker Samantha (Cardellini), but this doesn't seem credible. Of course, neither does the flick but what do you expect since it comes from Adam Sandler's production company. Rob Schneider and David Spade cameo. **96m/C DVD.** *US* Allen Covert, Doris Roberts, Shirley Jones, Shirley Knight, Linda Cardellini, Joel David Moore, Kevin Nealon, Rob Schneider, David Spade, Peter Dante, Nick Swardson, Jonah Hill, Jonathan Loughran; **D:** Nicholaus Goossen; **W:** Allen Covert, Nick Swardson, Barry Wernick; **C:** Mark Irwin; **M:** Waddy Wachtel.

Grandma's House ♂ *Grandmother's House* 1988 (R) A brother and sister discover that the house in which they live with their grandmother is chock-full of secrets and strange happenings, including madness, incest, and murder. **90m/C VHS, DVD.** Eric Foster, Kim Valentine, Brinke Stevens, Ida Lee, Len Lesser; **D:** Peter Rader; **W:** Peter C. Jensen; **C:** Peter C. Jensen.

Grandview U.S.A. ♂♂½ 1984 (R) A low-key look at low-rent middle America, centering on a foxy local speedway owner and the derby-obsessed boys she attracts. Pre-"Dirty Dancing" choreography from Patrick Swayze and wife Lisa Niemi. **97m/C VHS.** Jamie Lee Curtis, Patrick Swayze, C. Thomas Howell, M. Emmet Walsh, Troy Donahue, William Windom, Jennifer Jason Leigh, Ramon Bieri, John Cusack, Joan Cusack, Jason Court; **D:** Randal Kleiser; **M:** Thomas Newman.

The Granny ♂½ 1994 (R) Evil Granny Gargoli (Stevens) is so mean that just before she dies she swallows an ancient potion, enabling her to haunt her survivors. When Kelly (Whirry), the only one to really care for Granny, is cheated out of her inheritance, the rest of the family is in for some nasty shocks from the zombiefied oldster. Can't decide whether to be camp or horrific. **85m/C VHS.** Shannon Whirry, Stella Stevens; **D:** Luca Bercovici; **W:** Luca Bercovici.

The Grapes of Wrath ♂♂♂♂ 1940 John Steinbeck's classic American novel about the Great Depression. We follow the impoverished Joad family as they migrate from the dust bowl of Oklahoma to find work in the orchards of California and as they struggle to maintain at least a little of their dignity and pride. A sentimental but dignified, uncharacteristic Hollywood epic. **129m/B VHS, DVD.** Henry Fonda, Jane Darwell, John Carradine, Charley Grapewin, Zeffie Tilbury, Doris Bowdon, Russell Simpson, John Qualen, Eddie Quillan, O.Z. Whitehead, Grant Mitchell; **D:** John Ford; **W:** Nunnally Johnson; **C:** Gregg Toland. Oscars '40: Director (Ford), Support. Actress (Darwell); AFI '98: Top 100; Natl. Film Reg. '89; N.Y. Film Critics '40: Director (Ford), Film.

The Grass Harp ♂♂½ 1995 (PG) Rather dull retelling (with an excellent cast of the Truman Capote novella covering the eccentricities of small town Southern life in the '30s and '40s. Teenaged Collin Fenwick (Furlong) is sent to live with his maiden aunts, artistic, impractical Dolly (Laurie) and shrewd, hard businesswoman Verena (Spacek). Charlie Cool's (Matthau) the retired judge who's sweet on Dolly, Morris Ritz (Lemmon) is a shady Chicago entrepreneur with plans for Verena's money, and there are various opinionated townspeople with stories to tell as well. Screen nostalgia directed by Matthau's son Charles. **107m/C VHS, DVD.** Sissy Spacek, Piper Laurie, Edward Furlong, Walter Matthau, Nell Carter, Jack Lemmon, Mary Steenburgen, Roddy McDowall, Joe Don Baker, Charles Durning, Sean Patrick Flanery, Mia Kirshner; **D:** Charles Matthau; **W:** Stirling Silliphant; **C:** John A. Alonzo; **M:** Patrick Williams.

The Grass Is Always Greener Over the Septic Tank ♂♂ 1978 Based on Erma Bombeck's best-seller. A city family's flight to the supposed peace

---

of the suburbs turns out to be a comic compilation of complications. **98m/C VHS.** Carol Burnett, Charles Grodin, Linda Gray, Alex Rocco, Robert Sampson, Vicki Belmonte, Craig Richard Nelson, Anne Walterhouse, Eric Stoltz; **D:** Robert Day. **TV**

The Grass Is Greener ♂♂½ 1961 An American millionaire invades part of an impoverished Earl's mansion and falls in love with the lady of the house. The Earl, who wants to keep his wife, enlists the aid of an old girlfriend in a feeble attempt to make her jealous. The two couples pair off properly in the end. **105m/C VHS, DVD.** Cary Grant, Deborah Kerr, Jean Simmons, Robert Mitchum; **D:** Stanley Donen; **W:** Hugh Williams; **C:** Christopher Challis; **M:** Noel Coward.

The Grave ♂♂½ 1995 (R) Rednecks King (Scheffer) and Tyn (Charles) escape from a North Carolina prison farm after learning about a possible fortune buried in a grave. Unfortunately, they can't keep their mouths shut and soon every other lowlife around them is hunting as well. **90m/C VHS.** Craig Shefer, Josh Charles, Gabrielle Anwar, Donal Logue, John Diehl, Anthony Michael Hall, Eric Roberts; **D:** Jonas Pate; **W:** Jonas Pate, Josh Pate; **C:** Frank Prinzi.

Grave Indiscretions ♂♂ *The Grotesque; Gentlemen Don't Eat Poets* 1996 (R) Eccentric aristocrat, and amateur paleontologist, Sir Hugo Coal (Bates) is much more interested in the dinosaur skeleton he's attempting to assemble than in his crumbling estate or unsatisfied wife Harriet (Russell). Although he does take a dislike to the married servants his wife hires—sly butler Fledge (Sting) and his dipso cook/wife Doris (Styler). And then there's daughter Cleo (Headey) who's about to marry useless poet Sidney (Mackintosh) until he suddenly disappears. Which raises all sorts of questions, including just what the pigs have been eating recently. Based on McGrath's 1989 novel, "The Grotesque." **97m/C VHS.** *GB* Sting, Alan Bates, Theresa Russell, Trudie Styler, Lena Headey, Steven Mackintosh, Anna Massey, Jim Carter, James Fleet, Maria Aitken; **D:** John-Paul Davidson; **W:** Patrick McGrath; **C:** Andrew Dunn; **M:** Anne Dudley.

Grave of the Fireflies ♂♂♂ *Hotaru no Haka* 1988 In post-war Japan, in the city of Kobe's train station, a young boy lies dying. A janitor finds a metal canister lying next to the boy and when he opens it ashes fall out. As fireflies gather around, ghostly figures of the story flashes back to the orphaned, homeless Seita and his sister. The two youngsters struggle in the Japanese countryside but find they cannot escape the hardships of war and have no chance for survival. Stunning animated testimony to the human spirit. Based on the novel by Akiyuki Nosaka. In Japanese with English subtitles. **88m/C VHS, DVD.** *JP* **D:** Isao Takahata; **W:** Isao Takahata.

Grave of the Vampire ♂ *Seed of Terror* 1972 (R) A vampire rapes and impregnates a modern-day girl. Twenty years later, their son, who grows up to be a bitter bloodsucker, sets out to find his father and kill him. **95m/C VHS, DVD.** William (Bill) Smith, Michael Pataki, Lyn Peters, Diane Holden, Jay Adler, Kitty Vallacher, Jay Scott, Lieux Dressler; **D:** John Hayes.

Grave Secrets ♂½ 1989 (R) A professor of psychic phenomena teams up with a medium to find out who—or what—is controlling the life of a young woman. **90m/C VHS.** Paul LeMat, Renee Soutendijk, David Warner, Olivia Barash, Lee Ving; **D:** Donald P. Borchers.

Grave Secrets: The Legacy of Hilltop Drive ♂ 1992 The Williams family finds out their dream house is built on the site of an old graveyard. The spirits are not only restless, they're deadly. Based on a true story. **94m/C VHS, DVD.** Jonelle Allen, Patty Duke, David Soul, Blake Clark; **D:** John D. Patterson.

Gravesend ♂♂½ 1997 (R) Big cajones, puny budget: mini-Scorsese Stabile delivers the goods. Tracks a night in the life of four delinquent Brooklyn buddies

---

who find themselves with a dead body on their hands. To avoid police involvement, the boys recruit local drug dealer JoJo (Aquilino) to aid in the body's disposal. JoJo demands $500 and a finger from the victim in return. Rest of pic deals with the fellows' quest for cash and incorporates a deluge of dark humor which, outside of the pat, in your face dialogue and action, is the picture's real draw. Nineteen at the time of shooting, film school dropout's $5,000 auspicious first picture grabbed the attention of such heavyweights as Spielberg (Stabile now has a two picture deal with his Dreamworks SKG) and Oliver Stone. **85m/C VHS, DVD.** Tony Tucci, Michael Parducci, Tom Malloy, Thomas Brandise, Macky Aquilino; **D:** Salvatore Stabile; **W:** Salvatore Stabile; **C:** Joseph Dell'Olio; **M:** Bill Laswell.

The Graveyard ♂♂ *Persecution; Terror of Sheba; Sheba* 1974 A mommy spends many years torturing her little boy, David. In one blood-filled day, the fellow seeks his revenge. **90m/C VHS.** Lana Turner, Trevor Howard, Ralph Bates, Olga Georges-Picot, Suzan Farmer; **D:** Don Chaffey.

Graveyard of Honor ♂♂½ *Shin Jingi No Hakaba* 2002 Mike's remake of the 1975 classic follows Rikuo Ishimatsu, a lowly dishwasher, to the height of gang power, after he unknowingly saves the life of a gang leader. Well-executed script delves more deeply into the relationship Rikuo has with his heroin-addicted girlfriend and brings a comedic flair to gangster leader Ishimatsu's character. Japanese with subtitles. **131m/C DVD.** *JP* Goro Kishitani, Shingo Yamashiro, Narumi Arimori, Ryosuke Miki; **D:** Takashi Miike; **W:** Shigenori Takechi; **C:** Hideo Yamamoto; **M:** Koji Endo.

Graveyard of Horror ♂ 1971 His wife and baby dead, a man seeking revenge discovers a horrible secret: his brother, a doctor, is stealing the heads from corpses. Dubbed. **105m/C VHS, DVD.** *SP* Bill Curran, Francisco (Frank) Brana, Beatriz Lacy; **D:** Miguel Madrid.

Graveyard Shift ♂½ 1987 (R) A New York cabby on the night shift is actually a powerful vampire who uses his fares to build an army of vampires. Not to be confused with the 1990 Stephen King scripted film. Followed by "Understudy: Graveyard Shift II." **89m/C VHS, DVD.** *IT* Silvio Oliviero, Helen Papas, Cliff Stoker; **D:** Gerard Ciccoritti.

Graveyard Shift ♂ *Stephen King's Graveyard Shift* 1990 (R) Just because Stephen King wrote the original story doesn't mean its celluloid incarnation is guaranteed to stand your hair on end; unless that's your response to abject boredom. Dull, all-semi-star suspenser. **111m/C VHS, DVD.** Chariton Heston, David Carradine, Stacy Keach, Ned Beatty, Ronny Cox, Christopher Reeve, Michael O'Keefe, Rosemary Forsyth; **D:** David Greene.

Gray Lady Down ♂♂ 1977 (PG) A nuclear submarine sinks off the coast of Cape Cod and with their oxygen running out, a risky escape in an experimental diving craft seems to be their only hope. Dull, all-semi-star suspenser. **111m/C VHS, DVD.** Chariton Heston, David Carradine, Stacy Keach, Ned Beatty, Ronny Cox, Christopher Reeve, Michael O'Keefe, Rosemary Forsyth; **D:** David Greene.

Gray Matters ♂♂ 2006 (PG-13) Artificial screwball comedy finds loft-sharing siblings Gray (Graham) and Sam (Cavanagh) deciding they're too co-dependent and each needs to find a romantic partner—except they don't realize they'll want the same woman. Sam and beautiful Charlie (Moynahan) meet and are soon planning to elope to Vegas, with Gray as a witness. The gals share a drunken night out and an impulsive kiss (which Charlie doesn't remember) and suddenly the thirty-something Gray realizes she really, really likes girls. Fanciful if awkward debut from writer/director Kramer. **96m/C DVD.** *US* Heather Graham, Tom Cavanagh, Bridget Moynahan, Alan Cumming, Molly Shannon, Sissy Spa-

---

Grayeagle 1977 When a frontier trapper's daughter is kidnapped by Cheyenne Indians, he launches a search for her recovery. More style than pace in this Western, but worth a look for fans of this genre. 104m/C VHS. Ben Johnson, Iron Eyes Cody, Lana Wood, Alex Cord, Jack Elam, Paul Fix, Cindy Butler, Charles B. Pierce; **C:** Charles B. Pierce; **D:** Charles B. Pierce. cek. Rachel Shelley, *Cameos* Glora Gaynor; **D:** Sue Kramer; **W:** Sue Kramer; **C:** John Bartley; **M:** Andrew Hollander.

Gray's Anatomy 1996 Yet another monologue from Gray, this time about his medical crisis involving a rare eye disease. 80m/C VHS, DVD. Spalding Gray; **D:** Steven Soderbergh.

The Great Adventure 1975 Two farm boys capture and attempt to train a wild otter. Unfortunately, the otter longs to once again join his kind despite the boys' efforts. Arne Sucksdorff won an Oscar for his arresting view of animal life. 73m/B VHS. SW Anders Norberg, Kjell Sucksdorff; **W:** Arne Sucksdorff.

The Great Adventure *Det Stora Aventyret* 1953 Two farm boys capture and attempt to train a wild otter...

Grbavica: The Land of My Dreams 2006 In postwar Sarajevo, single mother Esma is forced to work as a waitress in a gangster-run club in order to supplement the government aid she needs to raise defiant adolescent daughter Sara. They argue over many things, including the truth about Sara's father, whom she believes died fighting for Bosnia. Title refers to the rundown district, formerly the site of a prison camp, where they live. Bosnian with subtitles. 90m/C DVD. AT3S GE Mirjana Karanovic, Bogdan Diklic, Luna Mijovic, Leon Lucev, Kenan Catic; **D:** Jasmila Zbanic; **W:** Jasmila Zbanic; **C:** Christine A. Maier; **M:** Enes Zlatar.

Grease 1978 (PG) Film version of the hit Broadway musical about summer love. Set in the 1950s, this spirited musical follows a group of high-schoolers throughout their senior year. The story offers a responsible moral, act like a tart and you'll get your guy; but hey, it's all in fun anyway. Followed by a weak sequel. ♫ Grease; Summer Nights; Hopelessly Devoted to You; You're the One That I Want; Sandy; Beauty School Dropout; Look at Me, I'm Sandra Dee; Greased Lightnin'; It's Raining on Prom Night. 110m/ C VHS, DVD. John Travolta, Olivia Newton-John, Jeff Conaway, Stockard Channing, Didi Conn, Eve Arden, Frankie Avalon, Sid Caesar, Dinah Manoff, Joan Blondell, Alice Ghostley, Dody Goodman, Kelly Ward, Michael Tucci, Barry Pearl, Edd Byrnes, Susan Buckner, Lorenzo Lamas, Fannie Flagg, Eddie Deezen, Michael Biehe; **D:** Randal Kleiser; **W:** Allan Carr; **C:** Bill Butler; **M:** John Farrar, Barry Gibb.

Grease 2 1982 (PG) Continuing saga of the T-Birds, the Pink Ladies, and young love at Rydell High. Newton-John and Travolta have graduated, leaving Pfeiffer to lead on love-struck book-neb Caulfield. Some okay tunes, though lame story lacks good-humor flair of the original. 115m/C VHS, DVD. Maxwell Caulfield, Michelle Pfeiffer, Adrian Zmed, Lorna Luft, Didi Conn, Eve Arden, Sid Caesar, Tab Hunter, Christopher McDonald; **D:** Patricia Birch; **M:** Artie Butler.

Greased Lightning 1977 (PG) The story of the first black auto racing champion, Wendell Scott, who had to overcome racial prejudice to achieve his success. Slightly better-then-average Pryor comedy vehicle. 95m/C VHS, DVD. Richard Pryor, Pam Grier, Beau Bridges, Cleavon Little, Vincent Gardenia; **D:** Michael A. Schultz; **W:** Leon Capetanos, Melvin Van Peebles; **M:** Fred Karlin.

Greaser's Palace 1972 *Zoot Suit Jesus* 1972 Seaweedhead Greaser, owner of the town's saloon, faces his arch-nemesis in this wide-ranging satiric Christ allegory from the director of "Putney Swope." 91m/C VHS, DVD. Albert Henderson, Allan Arbus, Michael Sullivan, Luana Anders, James Antonio, Ronald Nealy, Larry Moyer, John Paul Hudson, Herve Villechaize; **D:** Robert Downey; **W:** Robert Downey; **C:** Peter Powell; **M:** Jack Nitzsche.

Great Balls of Fire 1989 (PG-13) A florid, comic-book film of the glory days of Jerry Lee Lewis, from his first band to stardom. Most of the drama is derived from his marriage to his 13-year-old cousin. Somewhat overacted but full of energy. The soundtrack features many of the "killer's" greatest hits re-recorded by Jerry Lee Lewis for the film. 108m/C VHS, DVD. Dennis Quaid, Winona Ryder, Alec Baldwin, Trey Wilson, John Doe, Lisa Blount, Steve Allen, Stephen Tobolowsky, Lisa Jane Persky, Michael St. Gerard, Peter Cook; **D:** Jim McBride; **W:** Jack Baran, Jim McBride.

Great Bank Hoax *Great Georgia Bank Hoax; Shenanigans* 1978 *The* (PG) Three bank managers decide to rob their own bank to cover up the fact that all the assets have been embezzled. 89m/C VHS. Richard Basehart, Ned Beatty, Burgess Meredith, Michael Murphy, Paul Sand, Arthur Godfrey; **D:** Joseph Jacoby; **C:** Walter Lassally.

Great Adventure 1975 (PG) In the severe environment of the gold rush days on the rugged Yukon territory, a touching tale unfolds of a young orphan boy and his eternal bond of friendship with a great northern dog. Based on a Jack London story. Baldanello used the pseudonym Paul Elliotts and Fred Romer is actually Fernando Romero. 90m/C VHS, DVD. IT SP Jack Palance, Joan Collins, Fred Romer, Elisabetta Virgili, Remo de Angelis, Manuel de Blas; **D:** Gianfranco Baldanello.

The Great Alligator *Il Fiume del Grande Caimano; Alligators* 1981 As if you couldn't guess, this one's about a huge alligator who does what other 'uge alligators do...terrorizes the people at a resort. 89m/C VHS, DVD. Barbara Bach, Mel Ferrer, Richard Johnson, Claudio Cassinelli, Romano Puppo; **D:** Sergio Martino; **W:** Sergio Martino, Ernesto Gastaldi, Luigi Montefiore, Maria Chiaretta; **C:** Giancarlo Ferrando.

The Great American Broadcast 1941 Two WWI vets want more than anything to strike it rich. After many failed endeavors, the two try that new-fangled thing called radio. The station takes off, as does the plot. The girlfriend of one vet falls for his partner and numerous other misunderstandings and complications ensue. Charming and crazy musical with an energetic cast. ♫I've Got a Bone To Pick With You; It's All In a Lifetime; I Take to You; Long Ago Last Night; Where You Are; The Great American Broadcast; Albany Bound; Give My Regards to Broadway; If I Didn't Care. 92m/B VHS. Alice Faye, John Payne, Jack Oakie, Cesar Romero, James Newill, Mary Beth Hughes; **D:** Archie Mayo; **C:** Leon Shamroy.

The Great American Sex Scandal *Jury Duty* 1994 (PG-13) Sanford Lagelfust (Pinchot) is an meek accountant on trial for embezzlement, but when the prosecution's main witness turns out to be his sexy girlfriend Hope (Scoggins) the case turns into a courtroom sex scandal. Silly Canadian TV production. 94m/C VHS, DVD. C4 Bronson Pinchot, Tracy Scoggins, Heather Locklear, Stephen Baldwin, Lynn Redgrave, Alan Thicke, Meredith Amick, Barbara Bosson, Ilene Graff, Mark Blankfield, Danny Pintauro, Reginald Veloohnson, Jacklyn Zeman; **D:** Michael A. Schultz.

Great American Traffic Jam *Gridlock* 1980 (PG) Farce about the humorous variety of characters interacting on the interstate during a massive California traffic jam. 97m/C VHS. Ed McMahon, Vic Tayback, Howard Hasseman, Abe Vigoda, Noah Beery Jr., Desi Arnaz Jr., John Beck, Shelley Fabares, James Gregory; **D:** James Frawley. TV

The Great Armored Car Swindle 1964 An anonymous English businessman becomes involved in international intrigue when he becomes a pawn in a plan to transfer money to a Middle Eastern government under communist rule. But thanks to his wife things don't go off as planned. 58m/B VHS. Peter Reynolds, Dermot Walsh, Joanna Dunham, Lisa Gaston, Eiran Cozby; **D:** Lance Comfort.

Great Day in the Morning 1956 A rebel sympathizer and a Northern spy are both after Colorado gold to help finance the Civil War. But our Southern gentlemen soon find themselves equally interested in the local ladies. 92m/C VHS, Robert Stack, Ruth Roman, Raymond Burr, Virginia Mayo, Alex Nicol, Regis Toomey; **D:** Jacques Tourneur.

The Great Debaters 2007 (PG-13) Inspirational story focusing on the debate team from all black Wiley College in East Texas who took on—and beat—all comers, including vaunted white rivals, during the 1930s. Debate coach (and labor/civil rights organizer) Melvin B. Tolson (director Washington) winnows down his prospects to four: earnest Hamilton Burgess (Williams), debonair Henry Lowe (Parker), aspiring lawyer and rare female debater Samantha Booke (Smollett), and Jr. (Denzel Whitaker), who's trying to please his theology professor father (Forest Whitaker; no relation). Naturally in the Jim Crow south they run into lots of problems before the big confrontation with the oh-so-superior Harvard team. The pros graciously step back to allow their younger colleagues room to shine. 127m/C DVD. US Denzel Washington, Forest Whitaker, Nathaniel Parker, Jurnee Smollett, Denzel Whitaker, Jermaine Williams, Gina Ravera, John Heard, Kimberly Elise; **D:** Denzel Washington; **W:** Robert Eisele; **C:** Philippe Rousselot; **M:** James Newton Howard, Peter Golub.

Great Bikini Off-Road Adventure 1994 (R) Duke Abbey is about to lose his jeep tour company because business is so slow that he can't pay the rent. Then Duke's niece Lori decides to get her bikini-clad friends to hire on as drivers, showing lots of sights on their desert tours. 95m/C VHS. Avalon Anders, Lauren Hays, Floyd Irons, Laura Huspeth, Dan Frank; **D:** Gary Orona.

The Great Caruso 1951 The story of opera legend Enrico Caruso's rise to fame, from his childhood in Naples, Italy, to his collapse on the stage of the Metropolitan Opera House. Lanza is superb as the singer, and there are 27 musical numbers to satisfy the opera lover. ♫The Loveliest Night of the Year; Over the Waves; Vesti la Giubba; M'Appari; Celeste Aida; Numi, Pieta; La Fatal Pietra; Sextet from Lucia di Lammermoor; La Donne a Mobile. 113m/C VHS, DVD. Mario Lanza, Ann Blyth, Dorothy Kirsten; **D:** Richard Thorpe; **C:** Joseph Ruttenberg; **M:** Johnny Green. *Oscars '51: Sound.*

The Great Challenge *Les Fils du Vent; Sons of the Wind* 2004 Extreme athletes travel to Bangkok to set up a gym and explore the city. But they encounter a Thai gang who are allied with Japanese yakuza to take control of the city. For fans of the martial arts genre; Maurice (Moscovitch) masterminds. French with subtitles. 93m/C VHS, DVD. FR Williams Belle, Chau Belle, Malik Diouf, Yann Hnautra; **D:** Julien Seri; **W:** Julien Seri; **C:** Michel Taburiau; **M:** Christian Henson.

The Great Commandment 1941 Young man throws himself into a revolution against the overbearing Roman Empire in A.D. 30. The man, who has become influenced by the teachings of Christ, decides to give up his revolution and go along with his brother's widow. (He always loved her anyway). 78m/B VHS, DVD. John Beal, Marjorie Cooley, Warren McCollum; **D:** Irving Pichel.

Great Dan Patch 1949 The story of the great horse Dan Patch, the horse that went on to become the highest-earning harness racer in history. 92m/B VHS, DVD. Dennis O'Keefe, Gail Russell, Ruth Warrick, Charlotte Greenwood, Henry Hull, Arthur Hunnicutt, Clarence Kolb; **D:** Joseph M. Newman; **W:** John Taintor Foote; **C:** Gilbert Warrenton.

Great Day 1946 A soap opera set around the wartime visit of first lady Eleanor Roosevelt to a small British town. It focuses mainly on the wife and daughter of a bitter, alcoholic WWI vet. 62m/B VHS. Eric Portman, Flora Robson, Sheila Sim, Isabel Jeans, Walter Fitzgerald, Philip Friend, Marjorie Rhodes, Maire O'Neill, Beatrice Varley; **D:** Lance Comfort.

The Great Escape 2: The Untold Story 1988 Bland actioner can't decide whether it's a remake of the original or a sequel; it pretends to be a sequel yet spends a lot of time retelling—poorly—the first great escape. Once it gets around to the sequel part, it dispenses with protocol: Pleasence, an escapee in the original, is a Nazi bad guy in this go-round. Poor casting, especially Reeves, unconvincing as a German-speaking British officer who rallies the surviving escapees in revenge against their WWII captors. TV movie was originally shown in two parts, but mercifully shortened for video. 93m/C VHS. Christopher Reeve, Judd Hirsch, Ian McShane, Donald Pleasence, Anthony John (Tony) Denison, Michael Nader, Charles Haid; **D:** Jud Taylor, Paul Wendkos. TV

The Great Dictator 1940 Chaplin's first all-dialogue film, a searing satire on Nazism in which he has dual roles as a Jewish barber with amnesia who is mistaken for a Hitlerian dictator, Adenoid Hynkel. A classic scene involves Hynkel playing with a gigantic balloon of the world. Hitler banned the film's release to the German public due to its highly offensive portrait of him. The film also marked Chaplin's last wearing of the Little Tramp's (and Hitler's, equally little) mustache. 126m/B V-HS, DVD. Charlie Chaplin, Paullette Goddard, Jack Oakie, Billy Gilbert, Reginald Gardiner, Henry Daniell, Maurice (Moscovitch) Moscovich, Emma Dunn, Bernard Gorcey, Paul Weigel, Chester Conklin, Grace Hayle, Carter De Haven; **D:** Charlie Chaplin; **W:** Charlie Chaplin; **C:** Roland H. Totheroh, Karl Struss; **M:** Meredith Willson. *Natl. Film Reg. '97.; N.Y. Film Critics '40: Actor (Chaplin).*

The Great Elephant Escape 1995 Vacationing American teen Gordon-Levitt teams up with Kenyan M'Cormac, who works at an animal orphanage, to save a baby elephant from an unscrupulous businessman and his poacher friends. Made for TV. 90m/C VHS. Joseph Gordon-Levitt, Frederick M'Cormac, Stephenie Zimbalist, Leo Burmester, Julian Sands; **D:** George Miller; **W:** John Sweet, Christopher Canaan. TV

The Great Escape 1963 During WWII, troublesome allied POWs are thrown by the Nazis into an escape-proof camp, where they join forces in a single mass break for freedom. One of the great war movies, with a superb ensemble cast and lots of excitement. The story was true, based on the novel by Paul Brickhill. McQueen performed most of the stunts himself, against the wishes of director Sturges. Followed by a made for TV movie 25 years later. 170m/C VHS, DVD. Tom Adams, Steve McQueen, James Garner, Richard Attenborough, Charles Bronson, James Coburn, Donald Pleasence, David McCallum, James Donald, Gordon Jackson, Hannes Messemer, John Leyton, Nigel Stock, Jud Taylor, Hans Reiser, Robert Freitag, Karl Otto Alberty, Angus Lennie, Robert Graf, Harry Riebauer; **D:** John Sturges; **M:** Elmer Bernstein.

Great Expectations 1934 (PG-13) Inspirational adaptation of the Dickens novel, easily dwarfed by the brilliant 1946 version. Holmes is Pip, the orphan who rises in the world thanks to a mysterious benefactor (Hull), with Wyatt as Pip's disdainful love, Estella. 102m/B VHS, Phillips Holmes, Henry Hull, Jane Wyatt, Florence Reed, Francis L. Sullivan, Alan Hale, Anne Howard; **D:** Stuart Walker; **W:** Gladys Unger; **C:** George Robinson.

Hunt's slightly mad and pathetic Miss Havisham. Remake of the 1934 film. **118m/B VHS, DVD.** *GB* John Mills, Valerie Hobson, Anthony Wager, Alec Guinness, Finlay Currie, Jean Simmons, Bernard Miles, Francis L. Sullivan, Martita Hunt, Freda Jackson, Torin Thatcher, Hay Petrie, Eileen Erskine, George "Gabby" Hayes, Everley Gregg, O.B. Clarence; *D:* David Lean; *W:* David Lean, Ronald Neame; *C:* Guy Green; *M:* Walter Goeher. Oscars '47: Art Dir/Set Dec.; B&W, B&W Cinematog.

Great Expectations 1981
Miniseries adaptation of the Dickens epic about Pip and his mysterious benefactor in Victorian London. **300m/C VHS, DVD.** *GB* Gerry Sundquist, Stratford Johns, Joan Hickson; *D:* Julian Amyes; *W:* James Andrew Hall. **TV**

Great Expectations 1989
Dickens classic retold on three cassettes. A mysterious benefactor turns a poor orphan boy into a gentleman of means. **325m/C VHS.** *GB* Jean Simmons, Anthony Hopkins, John Rhys-Davies; *D:* Kevin Connor. **TV**

Great Expectations 1997 (R)
Expecting "Great Expectations?" The title and basic storyline are about all the filmmakers took for their contemporary updating of Dickens' story. The artistic, orphaned Finn (Hawke) is living a meager existence with his trashy sister and his "uncle" Joe in a Florida fishing town. His destiny is intertwined with an escaped convict (De Niro) he aids, the rich and loony Ms. Dinsmoor (Bancroft) and Dinsmoor's beautiful niece Estella (Paltrow). After being spurned by Estella as a teen, Finn quits painting and drawing entirely. Years later a mysterious art dealer offers him a one-man show in New York if he will move there and start creating again. Estella inevitably reappears in his life, providing more than a little inspiration. More style than substance. Although the visuals are stunning, the director should have learned that beauty on the surface isn't all it's cracked up to be from, say...hmm..."Great Expectations" by Charles Dickens maybe? **112m/C VHS, DVD.** Ethan Hawke, Robert De Niro, Gwyneth Paltrow, Hank Azaria, Anne Bancroft, Chris Cooper, Josh Mostel, Kim Dickens, Nell Campbell, Stephen Spinella; *D:* Alfonso Cuaron; *W:* Mitch Glazer; *C:* Emmanuel Lubezki; *M:* Patrick Doyle.

Great Expectations 1999
British TV version of the Dickens story about the expectations of Pip (Gruffudd). As a boy, he helps escaped convict Magwitch (Hill), a kindness that will change the course of Pip's life, though he doesn't realize it. Also a continuing part of his life is haughty beauty, Estella (Waddell), who has been raised by the eccentric Miss Havisham (Rampling) to wreak havoc on the male gender. A respectable retelling and rather dull. **180m/C VHS, DVD.** Ioan Gruffudd, Justine Waddell, Charlotte Rampling, Bernard Hill, Clive Russell, Lalla Morse, Nicholas Woodeson, Lesley Sharp, Emma Cunniffe, Daniel Evans; *D:* Julian Jarrold; *W:* Tony Marchant. **TV**

Great Expectations: The Untold Story 1987 Magwitch is an escaped convict, hiding out in the Victorian English countryside, who is aided by the young orphan, Pip. Captured and sent to the penal colonies in Australia, Magwitch serves his time and then discovers a fortune in gold, which he decides to use to make Pip into a gentleman. But Magwitch's enemies would like to get Pip's inheritance for themselves. Based on the Dickens classic, this three-tape miniseries is also available in a 102-minute feature length version. **287m/C VHS.** John Stanton, Sigrid Thornton, Robert Coleby, Todd Boyce, Anne Louise Lambert, Ron Haddrick, Noel Ferrier; *D:* Tim Burstall. **TV**

Great Flamarion 1945 A woman-hating trick-shot artist is nevertheless duped into murdering the husband of his femme fatale assistant after he comes to believe she loves him. He's wrong. **78m/B VHS.** Dan Duryea, Erich von Stroheim, Mary Beth Hughes; *D:* Anthony Mann.

The Great Gabbo 1929 A ventriloquist can express himself only through his dummy, losing his own identity and going mad at the end. Von Stroheim's first talkie. May quite possibly be the first mentally-twisted-ventriloquist story ever put on film. Von Stroheim hated the movie, believing it to be analogous to his own life. When he tried to buy the rights to the film, presumably to destroy the prints, he found that the property had been already purchased by real-life ventriloquist, Edgar Bergen. Based on a story by Ben Hecht. ♫The New Story; I'm Laughing Ickey; I'm in Love With You; The Ga-Ga Bird; The Web of Love; Every Now and Then. **82m/B VHS, DVD.** Erich von Stroheim, Betty Compson, Don Douglas, Marjorie "Babe" Kane; *D:* James Cruze; *W:* Ben Hecht, F. Hugh Herbert; *C:* Ira Morgan; *M:* Howard Jackson, Charley Chase.

The Great Gatsby 1949
Follows the silent 1926 version of F. Scott Fitzgerald's Jazz Era novel. Mysterious Jay Gatsby (Ladd) is a wealthy gangster and bootlegger who tries to buy his way into fast-living New York society. He befriends well-bred but penniless Nick Carraway (Carey), who serves as Gatsby's one true friend and eyewitness to the unfolding events. Gatsby rekindles his love for decorative Daisy (Field), who married into money and society and merely toys with leaving it all behind for Gatsby. Finally, the shallowness and selfishness all about prove to be Gatsby's undoing. **92m/B VHS.** Alan Ladd, Betty Field, MacDonald Carey, Ruth Hussey, Barry Sullivan, Howard da Silva, Shelley Winters, Henry Hull, Ed Begley Sr., Elisha Cook Jr.; *D:* Elliott Nugent; *W:* Cyril Hume, Richard Maibaum; *C:* John Seitz; *M:* Robert Emmett Dolan.

The Great Gatsby 1974 (PG) Adaptation of F. Scott Fitzgerald's novel of the idle rich in the 1920s. A mysterious millionaire crashes Long Island society, and finds his heart captured by an impetuous and emotionally impoverished girl. Skilful acting and directing captures the look and feel of this era, but the movie doesn't have the power of the book. **144m/C VHS, DVD.** Robert Redford, Mia Farrow, Bruce Dern, Karen Black, Patsy Kensit, Sam Waterston, Howard da Silva, Edward Herrmann; *D:* Jack Clayton; *W:* Francis Ford Coppola; *M:* Nelson Riddle. Oscars '74: Costume Des., Orig. Song Score and/or Adapt.; Golden Globes '75: Support. Actress (Black).

The Great Gatsby 2001 Wealthy Jay Gatsby (Stephens) was a poor boy with a questionable past who fell in love with rich girl Daisy (Sorvino), who married another (Donovan). Now Jay, who wants to make it in Jazz Age Newport society, renews his involvement with superficial Daisy, which leads to tragedy. All the drama is observed by Daisy's cousin Nick (Rudd). Adapted from the 1925 F. Scott Fitzgerald novel. **100m/C VHS, DVD.** Toby Stephens, Mira Sorvino, Martin Donovan, Paul Rudd, Francie Swift, Matt Malloy; *D:* Robert Markowitz; *W:* John McLaughlin; *C:* Guy Dufaux; *M:* Carl Davis. **CABLE**

The Great Gildersleeve 1943 Throckmorton P. Gildersleeve adds another problem to his list; the sister of a local judge wants to marry him. His niece and nephew won't allow it and his attempts to juggle everyone's desires make for fine fun. Peary was also the voice for the popular radio series of the same name. **62m/B VHS.** Harold (Hal) Peary, Jane Darwell, Nancy Gates, Charles Arnt, Thurston Hall; *D:* Gordon Douglas.

Great Gold Swindle 1984 A dramatization of the 1982 swindling of the Perth Mint in Australia of over $650,000 worth of gold. **101m/C VHS.** John Hargreaves, Robert C. Hughes, Tony Rickards, Barbara Llewellyn; *D:* John Power; *W:* David White; *C:* David Sanderson; *M:* John Stuart.

The Great Gundown 1975 A violent tale set in the Old West. The peace of frontier New Mexico erupts when a half-breed Indian leads a brutal assault on an outlaw stronghold. **98m/C VHS.** Robert Padilla, Richard Rust, Milila St. Duval; *D:* Paul Hunt.

Great Guns 1941 Stan and Ollie enlist in the army to protect a spoiled millionaire's son but wind up being targets at target practice instead. Not one of their better efforts. **74m/B VHS, DVD.** Stan Laurel, Oliver Hardy, Sheila Ryan, Dick Nelson; *D:* Montague (Monty) Banks.

Great Guy *Pluck of the Irish* 1936 One of Cagney's lesser roles as an ex-boxer turned food inspector who wipes out graft in his town. **50m/B VHS, DVD.** James Cagney, Mae Clarke, Edward Brophy; *D:* John Blystone.

The Great Impostor 1961 The true story of Ferdinand Waldo Demara Jr. who, during the 1950s, hoodwinked people by impersonating a surgeon, a college professor, a monk, a prison warden, and a schoolteacher, with the FBI always one step behind him. **112m/C VHS.** Tony Curtis, Edmond O'Brien, Arthur O'Connell, Gary Merrill, Raymond Massey, Karl Malden, Mike Kellin, Frank Gorshin; *D:* Robert Mulligan; *C:* Robert Burks; *M:* Henry Mancini.

Great Jesse James Raid 1949 Jesse James comes out of retirement to carry out a mine theft. Routine. **73m/C VHS, DVD.** Willard Parker, Barbara Payton, Tom Neal, Wallace Ford; *D:* Reginald LeBorg.

Great K & A Train Robbery 1926 A railroad detective is hired to find and stop the bandits who have been preying on the K & A Railroad. Silent. **55m/B VHS.** Tom Mix, Dorothy Dwan, William Walling, Harry Grippe, Carl Miller; *D:* Lewis Seiler.

The Great Land of Small 1986 (G) Two children enter a fantasy world and try to save it from Evil. For kids. **94m/C VHS.** Karen Elkin, Michael Blouin, Michael Anderson Jr., Ken Roberts; *D:* Vojtech Jasny.

The Great Lie 1941 A great soaper with Davis and Astor as rivals for the affections of Brent, an irresponsible flyer. Astor is the concert pianist who marries Brent and then finds out she's pregnant after he's presumed dead in a crash. The wealthy Davis offers to raise the baby so Astor can continue her career. But when Brent does return, who will it be to? Sparkling, catty fun. Astor's very short, mannish haircut became a popular trend. **107m/B VHS.** Bette Davis, Mary Astor, George Brent, Lucile Watson, Hattie McDaniel, Grant Mitchell, Jerome Cowan; *D:* Edmund Goulding; *C:* Gaetano Antonio "Tony" Gaudio; *M:* Max Steiner. Oscars '41: Support. Actress (Astor).

The Great Locomotive Chase 1956 During the Civil War, Parker and his fellow Union soldiers head into Confederate territory to disrupt railroad supply lines. They take over a locomotive, but are pursued by Confederate Hunter, the conductor of another train; and soon a pursuit is underway. Based on the true story of Andrews' Raiders. **85m/C VHS, DVD.** Fess Parker, Jeffrey Hunter, Kenneth Tobey; *D:* Francis D. Lyon; *W:* Lawrence Edward Watkin; *C:* Charles P. Boyle; *M:* Paul J. Smith.

The Great Los Angeles Earthquake 1990 *Great Los Angeles Earthquake* Made-for-TV disaster movie is the same old story; multiple soap-opera plotlines are spun around terrifying special effects, as L.A. is devastated by three major earth tremors and attendant disasters. Condensed from a two-part miniseries. **106m/C VHS, DVD.** Ed Begley Jr., Joanna Kerns; *D:* Larry Elikann.

The Great Lover 1949 Aboard an ocean liner, a bumbler chaperoning school kids gets involved with a gambler, a duchess and a murder. Vintage Bob Hope. **80m/B VHS, DVD.** Bob Hope, Rhonda Fleming, Roland Young, Roland Culver, George Reeves, Jim Backus, Jack Benny; *D:* Alexander Hall; *W:* Edmund Beloin, Melville Shavelson, Jack Rose; *C:* Charles B(ryant) Lang Jr.

The Great Madcap 1949 A wealthy man believes in lavishly indulging himself which drives his excessively conservative family crazy. Bunuel satirizes behavioral extremes, Christianity, advertising, sex, and a number of other popular absurdities. In Spanish with English subtitles. **90m/B VHS.** *MX* Fernando Soler, Rosario Granados, Ruben Rojo; *D:* Luis Bunuel.

The Great Man Votes 1938 Alcoholic college professor Barrymore falls into a deep depression after his wife's death. His children then plan to create a situation wherein his vote will decide the fate of the new town mayor, thus instilling in him a newly found sense of importance for himself and his children. Satiric and funny. **72m/B VHS.** John Barrymore, Peter Holden, Virginia Weidler, Katherine Alexander, Donald MacBride, Elisabeth Risdon, Granville Bates, Luis Alberni, J.M. Kerrigan, William Demarest, Roy Gordon; *D:* Garson Kanin; *C:* Russell Metty.

The Great Man's Lady 1942 Stanwyck stars in a "stand by your man" story in which she supported and was responsible for the good deeds of a now past town hero. Told in flashback sequence, Stanwyck's character, 109-year-old Hanna Sampler, reveals to a young biographer the trials and tribulations of her life with Ethan Hoyt, founder of Hoyt City, who is being honored with the dedication of a statue in the opening of the film. The picture reveals their secrets and the truth about the woman behind the man. Based on the story "The Human Side" by Vina Delmar. **91m/B VHS.** Barbara Stanwyck, Joel McCrea, Brian Donlevy; *D:* William A. Wellman; *W:* Seena Owen, W.L. Rivers, Adela Rogers St. John; *C:* William Mellor; *M:* Victor Young.

The Great McGinty 1940 *Down Went McGinty* Sturges' directorial debut, about the rise and fall of a small-time, bribe-happy politician is an acerbic, ultra-cynical indictment of modern politics that stands, like much of his other work, as bracingly courageous as anything that's ever snuck past the Hollywood censors. Political party boss Tamiroff chews the scenery with gusto while Donlevy, in his first starring role, is more than his equal as the not-so-dumb political hack. **82m/B VHS.** Brian Donlevy, Muriel Angelus, Akim Tamiroff, Louis Jean Heydt, Arthur Hoyt, William Demarest; *D:* Preston Sturges; *W:* Preston Sturges; *C:* William Mellor. Oscars '40: Orig. Screenplay.

Great McGonagall 1975 Tale of an unemployed Scot trying to become Britain's poet laureate. Sellers adds a semi-bright spot with his portrayal of Queen Victorial **95m/C VHS.** *GB* Peter Sellers, Spike Milligan, Julia Foster; *D:* Joseph McGrath.

The Great Mike 1944 Unlikely but moving story of a young boy who convinces track management that his work horse has a chance against the touted thoroughbred. Sentimental, with little innovation, but generally well-acted. **72m/C VHS, DVD.** Stuart Erwin, Robert "Buzzy" Henry, Pierre Watkin, Gwen Kenyon, Carl "Alfalfa" Switzer, Edythe Elliott, Marion Martin; *D:* Wallace Fox.

Great Missouri Raid 1951 Follows the famous adventures of the James/Younger gang and their eventual demise. **81m/C VHS.** Wendell Corey, MacDonald Carey, Ellen Drew, Ward Bond; *D:* Gordon Douglas; *C:* Ray Rennahan.

The Great Moment 1944 Story of the Boston dentist who discovered ether's use as an anesthetic in 1845. Confusing at times, changing from comedy to drama and containing flashbacks that add little to the story. Surprisingly bland result from ordinarily solid cast and director. **87m/B VHS.** Joel McCrea, Betty Field, Harry Carey Sr., William Demarest, Franklin Pangborn, Porter Hall; *D:* Preston Sturges; *C:* Victor Milner.

The Great Mouse Detective 1986 (G) *The Adventures of the Great Mouse Detective* 1986 (G) Animated version of the book "Basil of Baker Street" by Eve Titus. Fun adventure concerning the Sherlock-of-the-mouse-world, Basil, who must prevent his arch nemesis, Professor Ratigan, from overthrowing Queen Moustoria. Not as good as some of the other Disney animated features, but kids will enjoy it nonetheless. **74m/C VHS, DVD.** *D:* John Musker, Ron Clements, Dave Michener; *M:* Henry Mancini; *V:* Vincent Price, Barrie Ingham, Val Bettin, Susanne Pollatschek, Candy Candido, Eve Brenner, Alan Young, Melissa Manchester.

The Great Muppet Caper 1981 (G) A group of hapless reporters (Kermit, Fozzie Bear, and Gonzo) travel to London to follow up on a major jewel robbery. **95m/C VHS, DVD.** Charles Grodin, Diana Rigg, John Cleese, Robert Morley, Peter Ustinov, Peter Falk, Jack Warden; *D:*

The Great New Wonderful 🦴½ 2006 (R) Five stories about neurotic New Yorkers that are linked by occurring in September 2002, a year after the terrorist attacks (which are never directly mentioned). So you're just left to guess how the characters were actually affected, making for some dull story-telling. 86m/C DVD. Thomas (Tom) McCarthy, Judy Greer, Naseeruddin Shah, Tony Shalhoub, Jim Gaffigan, Olympia Dukakis, Dick Latessa, Sharat Saxena, Edie Falco, Stephen Colbert, Jeremy Shamos, Will Arnett, Rosemarie DeWitt, Seth Gilliam, Jim Parsons, Bill Donner, Ed Serralian, Ari Graynor, Martha Millan, Priscilla Shanks, Sam Catlin; **D:** Danny Leiner; **W:** Sam Catlin; **C:** Harlan Bosmajian; **M:** John Swihart.

The Great Northfield Minnesota Raid 🦴🦴½ 1972 (PG) The Younger/James gang dec ides to rob the biggest bank west of the Mississippi, but everything goes wrong. Uneven, offbeat western, but Duvall's portrayal of the psychotic Jesse James and Robertson's cunning Cole Younger are notable. 91m/C VHS. Cliff Robertson, Robert Duvall, Elisha Cook Jr., Luke Askew, R.G. Armstrong, Donald Moffat, Matt Clark; **D:** Philip Kaufman; **W:** Philip Kaufman; **C:** Bruce Surtees; **M:** Dave Grusin.

The Great Outdoors 🦴🦴 1988 (PG) Good cast is mostly wasted in another John Hughes's tale of vacation gone bad. A family's peaceful summer by the lake is disturbed by their uninvited, troublesome relatives. Aykroyd and Candy are two funny guys done in by a lame script that awkwardly examines friendship and coming of age and throws in a giant bear when things get unbearably slow. May be fun for small fry. 91m/C VHS, DVD. Dan Aykroyd, John Candy, Stephanie Faracy, Annette Benning, Chris Young, Lucy Deakins, John Bloom; **D:** Howard Deutch; **W:** John Hughes; **C:** Ric Waite; **M:** Thomas Newman.

The Great Plane Robbery 🦴½ 1940 Gang leader Joe Colson (Madison) has insured his life for big bucks, which has his insurance company worried. So they hire PI Mike Henderson (Holt) to make sure Colson stays alive until his policy runs out. Not an easy task when the plane they're flying in is hijacked by racketeer Frankie Toller (Fields) who wants Colson to reveal where he's hiding his dough. 61m/B VHS. Jack Holt, Stanley Fields, Noel Madison, Milburn Stone, Paul Fix, Vickie Lester; **D:** Lewis D. Collins; **W:** Albert DeMond; **C:** James S. Brown Jr.; **M:** Lee Zahler.

The Great Race 🦴🦴 1965 A dastardly villain, a noble hero, and a spirited suffragette are among the competitors in an uproarious New York-to-Paris auto race circa 1908 complete with pie fights, saloon brawls, and a confrontation with a feisty polar bear. Overly long and only sporadically funny. 160m/C VHS, DVD. Jack Lemmon, Tony Curtis, Natalie Wood, Peter Falk, Keenan Wynn, George Macready; **D:** Blake Edwards; **M:** Henry Mancini. Oscars '65: Sound FX Editing.

The Great Raid 🦴🦴 2005 (R) Workmanlike retelling of the 1944 rescue of more than 500 American POWs from a Japanese prison camp located in a remote area of the Philippines. You've got the outside planners, Army Rangers Mucci (Bratt) and Prince (Franco) and their Filipino allies, led by Pajota (Montano); the insiders, led by malaria sufferer Gibson (Fiennes); and nurse Margaret (Nielsen), who's also a resistance leader. Film has a loooong build-up before the raid comes off, which dissipates the tension. Completed in 2002, flick sat on the Miramax shelves until its brief 2005 big screen release. 132m/C DVD, Blu-ray Disc. US Benjamin Bratt, James Franco, Connie Nielsen, Joseph Fiennes, Marton Csokas, Robert Mammone, Natalie Mendoza, Motoki Kobayashi, Cesar Montano, Maximilian Martini, James Carpinello, Craig McLachlan, Dale Dye, Paolo Montalban, Gotaro Tsunashima; **D:** John Dahl; **W:** Carlo Bernard, Doug Miro; **C:** Peter Menzies Jr.; **M:** Trevor Rabin.

Great Ride 🦴 1978 State police are after two dirt bikers who are riding through areas where bike riding is illegal. 90m/C VHS. Perry Lang, Michael MacRae, Michael Sullivan; **D:** Don Hulette.

The Great Riviera Bank Robbery 🦴½ 1979 A genius axecutes a bank robbery on the French Riviera netting $15 million. Based on a true story, the film chronicles the unfolding of the heist. 98m/C VHS. Ian McShane, Warren Clarke, Stephen Greif, Christopher Malcolm; **D:** Francis Megahy.

The Great Rupert 🦴🦴🦴 *A Christmas Wish* 1950 Durante and family are befriended by a helpful squirrel (a puppet) in obtaining a huge fortune. Good fun; Durante shines. 86m/B VHS, DVD. Jimmy Durante, Terry Moore, Tom Drake, Frank Orth, Sara Haden, Queenie Smith; **D:** Irving Pichel; **W:** Laszlo Vadnay; **C:** Lionel Lindon.

The Great St. Louis Bank Robbery 🦴🦴½ 1959 Three career criminals (Denton, Clarke, Dukas) and chael are brought together for a bank heist. They don't trust each other, which proves fatal when the heist goes bad. Based on a true story and filmed in semi-documentary style. Nineteen-year-old McQueen's follow-up to "The Blob." 86m/B VHS, DVD. Graham Denton, David Clarke, James Dukas, Steve McQueen, Molly McCarthy; **D:** Charles Guggenheim; **W:** Richard T. Heffron; **C:** Victor Duncan; **M:** Bernardo Segall.

The Great St. Trinian's Train Robbery 🦴🦴 1966 Train robbers hide their considerable loot in an empty country mansion only to discover, upon returning years later, it has been converted into a girls' boarding school. When they try to recover the money, the thieves run up against a band of pestiferous adolescent girls, with hilarious results. Sequel to the cartoon by Ronald Searle. Based on "The Pure Hell of St. Trinian's." 90m/C VHS. GB Dora Bryan, Frankie Howerd, Reg Varney, Desmond Walter-Ellis; **D:** Sidney Gilliat, Frank Launder; **M:** Malcolm Arnold.

The Great Santini 🦴🦴🦴 *Ace; The Great Santini* 1980 (PG) Lt. Col. Bull Meechum, the "Great Santini", a Marine pilot stationed stateside, fights a war involving his frustrated career goals, repressed emotions, and family. His family becomes his company of marines, as he abuses them in the name of discipline, because he doesn't allow himself any other way to show his affection. With a standout performance by Duvall, the film successfully blends warm humor and tenderness with the harsh cruelties inherent with dysfunctional families and racism. Based on Pat Conroy's autobiographical novel, the movie was virtually undistributed when first released, but re-released due to critical acclaim. 118m/C VHS, DVD. Robert Duvall, Blythe Danner, Michael O'Keefe, Julie Ann Haddock, Lisa Jane Persky, David Keith; **D:** Lewis John Carlino; **C:** Ralph Woolsey; **M:** Elmer Bernstein. Montreal World Film Fest. '80: Actor (Duvall).

Great Scout & Cathouse Thursday 🦴½ 1976 (PG) Marvin and Reed vow to take revenge on their third partner, Culp, who made off with all their profits from a gold mine. The title refers to Marvin's May-December romance with prostitute Lenz. Already forgotten, unfunny, all-star comedy with cutesy title. 96m/C VHS. Lee Marvin, Oliver Reed, Robert Culp, Elizabeth Ashley, Kay Lenz; **D:** Don Taylor.

Great Smokey Roadblock 🦴🦴 *Last of the Cowboys* 1976 (PG) While in the hospital, a 60-year-old truck driver's rig is repossessed by the finance company. Deciding that it's time to make one last perfect cross country run, he escapes from the hospital, steals his truck, picks up six prostitutes, heads off into the night with

The Great Skycopter Rescue 🦴 1982 Ruthless businessmen hire a motorcycle gang to terrorize and scare away the inhabitants of an oil-rich town. A local teenage flying enthusiast organizes his friends into an attack force to fight back. 96m/C VHS. William Marshall, Aldo Ray, Russell Johnson, ?ery Mict?os, Terry Taylor; **D:** Lawrence Foldes.

the police on his tail, and becomes a folk hero. 84m/C VHS, DVD. Henry Fonda, Eileen Brennan, Susan Sarandon, John Byner; **D:** John Leone.

The Great Texas Dynamite Chase 🦴½ *Dynamite Women* 1976 (R) Two sexy young women drive across Texas with a carload of dynamite. They leave a trail of empty banks with the cops constantly on their trail. 90m/C VHS, DVD. Claudia Jennings, Jocelyn Jones, Johnny Crawford, Chris Pennock, Tara Strohmeier, Miles Watkins, Bart Braverman; **D:** Michael Pressman; **C:** Jamie Anderson; **M:** Craig Safan.

The Great Train Robbery 🦴🦴🦴 *The First Great Train Robbery* 1979 (PG) A dapper thief arranges to heist the Folkstone bullion express in 1855, the first moving train robbery. Well-designed, fast-moving costume piece based on Crichton's best-selling novel. 111m/C VHS, DVD. GB Sean Connery, Donald Sutherland, Lesley-Anne Down, Alan Webb; **D:** Michael Crichton; **W:** Michael Crichton; **C:** Geoffrey Unsworth; **M:** Jerry Goldsmith.

Great Treasure Hunt 🦴 1972 Four 'Western rogues help a blind man steal a wealthy crook's gold. 90m/C VHS. Mark Damon, Stevio Rossi, Luis Marin; **D:** Tonino Ricci.

The Great Wall 🦴🦴 *The Great Wall* 1986 (PG) A Chinese-American can family travels to mainland China to discover the country of their ancestry and to visit relatives. They experience racial culture shock. Wang's first independent feature. In English and Chinese with subtitles. 103m/C VHS, DVD. Peter Wang, Sharon Iwai, Kelvin Han Yee, Lin Qinqin, Hy Xiaoguang; **D:** Peter Wang; **W:** Peter Wang, Shirley Sun; **M:** David Liang, Ge Ganu.

The Great Waldo Pepper 🦴🦴🦴 1975 (PG) Low key and [for Hill] less commercial film about a WWI pilot-turned-barnstormer who gets hired as a stuntman for the movies. Features spectacular vintage aircraft flying sequences. 107m/C VHS, DVD. Robert Redford, Susan Sarandon, Margot Kidder, Bo Svenson, Scott Newman, Geoffrey Lewis, Edward Herrmann; **D:** George Roy Hill **W:** William Goldman; **C:** Robert L. Surtees; **M:** Henry Mancini.

The Great Wallendas 🦴🦴 1978 The true story of the tragedies and triumphs of the Wallendas, a seven-person acrobatic family, who were noted for their daring act on the high wire without nets below them. 96m/C VHS. Lloyd Bridges, Britt Ekland, Cathy Rigby; **D:** Larry Elikann. TV

The Great Waltz 🦴🦴🦴 1938 The first of two musical biographies on the life of Johann Strauss sees the musician quit his banking job to pursue his dream of becoming a successful composer. A fine, overlooked production rich with enjoyable music and romantic comedy. ♪Tales of Vienna Woods; There'll Come A Time; One Day When We Were Young; Voices of Spring; Du und Du; The Bat; I'm In Love With Vienna; Revolutionary March. 102m/B VHS, DVD. Luise Rainer, Fernand Gravey, Miliza Korjus, Hugh Herbert, Lionel Atwill, Curt Bois, Leonid Kinskey, Al Shean, Minna Gombell, George Houston, Bert Roach, Herman Bing, Alma Kruger, Sig Rumann; **D:** Julien Duvivier; **C:** Joseph Ruttenberg. Oscars '38: Cinematog.

The Great War 🦴🦴 *La Grande Guerre* 1959 Two Italian soldiers find themselves in the midst of WWI, much against their will. They try a number of schemes to get out of fighting and working, but their circumstance dictates otherwise. Slightly muddled, but generally good acting. 113m/B VHS. FR IT Vittorio Gassman, Alberto Sordi, Silvana Mangano, Folco Lulli; **D:** Mario Monicelli; **M:** Nino Rota.

The Great Water 🦴🦴 *Golemata voda; Velika voda* 2004 Aging Macedonian politician Lem Nikodinoski (Jovanovski) is rushed to the hospital after suffering a heart attack and has the time to reflect on his childhood, which was spent in a Stalinist camp intended to indoctrinate the young into proper communists. There, an orphaned 12-year-old Lem (Kekenovski) is taken under the wing of charismatic teen Isak (Stankovska, an actress cast as a boy), which ultimately leads to a wrenching betrayal. Based on the novel by Zivko Cirgo; in English and Macedonian with subtitles. 90m/C DVD. Nikolina Kujaca, Meto Jovanovski, Saso Kekenovski, Maja Stankovska, Mitko Apostolovski, Verica Nedeska, Risto Gogovski; **D:** Ivo Trajkov; **W:** Ivo Trajkov, Vladimir Blazevski; **C:** Suki Medencevic; **M:** Kiril Dzajkovski.

The Great White Hope 🦴🦴½ 1970 (PG-13) A semi-fictionalized biography of boxer Jack Johnson, played by Jones, who became the first black heavyweight world champion in 1910. Alexander makes her film debut as the boxer's white lover, as both battle the racism of the times. Two Oscar-nominated performances in what is essentially an "opened-out" version of the Broadway play. 103m/C VHS. James Earl Jones, Jane Alexander, Lou Gilbert, Joel Fluellen, Chester Morris, Robert Webber, Hal Holbrook, R.G. Armstrong, Moses Gunn, Scatman Crothers; **D:** Martin Ritt; **C:** Burnett Guffey.

The Great White Hype 🦴🦴½ 1996 (R) Screenwriter Shelton, who penned "Bull Durham" and "White Men Can't Jump," returns to the sports arena with this satire of the sleazy world of boxing. Jackson's the Don King-esque promoter and manager of heavyweight champ Wayans. Noticing it at pay-per-view revenues are slipping, he searches for a white boxer to generate interest and dollars and finds champ-in-the-making Berg, who beat the boxer-turned-musician Berg. Jackson's performance as the flamboyant Rev. Fred Sultan fuels the entire movie. Concentrating on the shady wheeling and dealing, the boxing action is kept to a minimum. 95m/C VHS, DVD. Samuel L. Jackson, Damon Wayans, Peter Berg, Jeff Goldblum, Jon Lovitz, Corbin Bernsen, Salli Richardson, Rocky Carroll, Jamie Foxx, Michael Jace; **D:** Reginald (Reggie) Hudlin; **W:** Ron Shelton, Tony Hendra; **C:** Ron Garcia; **M:** Marcus Miller.

Great World of Sound 🦴🦴 2007 (R) Martin (Healy) sees an ad to become a record producer and joins the shady company of the title. He's partnered with exuberant (and once homeless) Clarence (Holliday) to hit those southern highways and byways and audition and "sign" musical talent. It's a scam, but both men need the job too badly to let their consciences guide them. 106m/C DVD. Pat Healy, Kene Holliday, Rebecca Mader, Jonathan Bakly, Robert Longstreet, Adam Stone, Tricia Paoluccio; **D:** Craig Zobel; **W:** Craig Zobel, George Smith; **M:** David Wingo.

The Greatest 🦴🦴½ 1977 (PG) Autobiography of Cass us Clay, the fighter who could float like a butterfly and sting like a bee. Ali plays himself, and George Benson's hit "The Greatest Love of All" is introduced. 100m/C VHS, DVD. Muhammad Ali, John Marley, Roger E. Mosley, Dina Merrill, Paul Winfield; **D:** Tom Gries; **W:** Ring Lardner Jr.; **C:** Harry Stradling Jr.; **M:** Michael Masser.

The Great Ziegfeld 🦴🦴🦴½ 1936 (PG) Big bio-pic of the famous showman; acclaimed in its time as the best musical biography ever done, still considered the textbook for how to make a musical. Look for cameo roles by many famous stars, as well as a walk-on role by future First Lady Pat Nixon. The movie would have stood up as a first-rate biography of Ziegfeld, even without the drop-dead wonderful songs. ♪Won't You Come Play With Me?; It's Delightful to be Married; If You Knew Susie; Shine On Harvest Moon; A Pretty Girl is Like a Melody; You Gotta Pull Strings; She's a Follies Girl; You; You Never Looked So Beautiful. 179m/B VHS, DVD. William Powell, Luise Rainer, Myrna Loy, Frank Morgan, Reginald Owen, Nat Pendleton, Ray Bolger, Virginia Bruce, Harriet Hocter, Ernest Cossart, Robert Greig, Gilda Gray, Leon Errol, Dennis Morgan, Mickey Daniels, William Demarest. Cameos: Fanny Brice; **D:** Robert Z. Leonard; **W:** William Anthony McGuire. Oscars '36: Actress (Rainer), Picture, N.Y. Film Critics '36: Actress (Rainer).

The Greatest Game Ever Played ✶✶½ 2005 (PG) Classic kid-from-the-wrong-side-of-the-tracks story tells how 20-year-old amateur golfer Francis Ouimet beat his boyhood idol and defending champ Harry Vardon (Dillane) to win the 1913 U.S. Open. Ouimet's working-class background precludes him from playing at the country club course where he caddies, but he learns to play on his own. Class barriers abound, and there's lots and lots of golfing. The draw of the underdog, the fact that it's a true story, and some fine performances, ultimately carries the day. 115m/C DVD. *US* Shia LaBeouf, Stephen (Dillon) Dillane, Elias Koteas, Marnie McPhail, Stephen Marcus, Peter Firth, Michael Weaver, Josh Flitter, Peyton List, James Paxton, Matthew Knight, Len Cariou, Luke Askew; **D:** Bill Paxton; **W:** Mark Frost; **C:** Shane Hurlbut; **M:** Brian Tyler.

The Greatest Question ✶✶½ 1919 Gish is a girl menaced by a married couple whom she saw commit a murder years before. A rush job by Griffith to fulfill his studio obligations but Gish's performance is fine. 80m/C VHS. Lillian Gish, Robert "Bobbie" Harron, Ralph Graves, Eugenie Besserer, George Fawcett, George Nicholls Jr., Josephine Crowell, Carl Stockdale; **D:** D.W. Griffith.

The Greatest Show on Earth ✶✶✶ 1952 DeMille is in all his epic glory here in one of a traveling circus wrought with glamour, romance, mysterious clowns, a tough ringmaster, and a train wreck. 149m/C VHS, DVD. Betty Hutton, Cornel Wilde, James Stewart, Charlton Heston, Dorothy Lamour, Lawrence Tierney, Gloria Grahame; **D:** Cecil B. DeMille. Oscars '52: Picture, Story; Golden Globes '53: Director (DeMille), Film—Drama.

The Greatest Story Ever Told ✶✶ 1965 Christ's journey from Galilee to Golgotha is portrayed here in true international-all-star-epic treatment by director Stevens. A lackluster version of Christ's life, remarkable only for Heston's out-of-control John the Baptist. 196m/C VHS, DVD. Max von Sydow, Charlton Heston, Sidney Poitier, Claude Rains, Jose Ferrer, Telly Savalas, Angela Lansbury, Dorothy McGuire, John Wayne, Donald Pleasence, Carroll Baker, Van Heflin, Robert Loggia, Shelley Winters, Ed Wynn, Roddy McDowall, Pat Boone; **D:** George Stevens; **W:** George Stevens, James Lee Barrett; **C:** William Mellor, Loyal Griggs; **M:** Alfred Newman.

Greed ✶✶✶ 1924 A wife's obsession with money drives her husband to murder. Although the original version's length (eight hours) was trimmed to 140 minutes, it remains one of the greatest and most highly acclaimed silent films ever made. Effective use of Death Valley locations. Adapted from the Frank Norris novel, "McTeague." 140m/B VHS. Dale Fuller, Gibson Gowland, Zasu Pitts, Jean Hersholt, Chester Conklin; **D:** Erich von Stroheim. Natl. Film Reg. '91.

The Greed of William Hart ✶ *Horror Maniacs* 1948 Reworking of the Burke and Hare legend has grave robbers providing Edinburgh medical students with the requisite cadavers. 78m/B VHS, DVD. *GB* Tod Slaughter, Henry Oscar, Jenny Lynn, Winifred Melville; **D:** Oswald Mitchell.

Greedy ✶½ 1994 (PG-13) Money-grubbing family suck up to elderly millionaire uncle (Douglas) when they fear he'll leave his money to the sexy, young former pizza delivery girl (d'Abo) he's hired as his nurse. Fox is the long-lost nephew who comes to the rescue. Wicked comedy from veterans Ganz and Mandel should zing, but instead falls flat thanks to a descent into the maudlin. Fox bares his backside and Douglas has fun as the mean old miser, but check out Hartman, a riot as a snarky relative. 109m/C VHS, DVD. Michael J. Fox, Olivia d'Abo, Phil Hartman, Nancy Travis, Ed Begley Jr., Bob Balaban, Colleen Camp, Jere Burns, Khandi Alexander, Jonathan Lynn; **D:** Jonathan Lynn; **W:** Lowell Ganz, Babaloo Mandel; **C:** Gabriel Beristain; **M:** Randy Newman.

Greedy Terror ✶ *The Great Ride* 1978 A cross-country motorcycle trip becomes a real nightmare when two young men realize they're being stalked by a maniac with a thirst for blood. 90m/C VHS. Michael MacRae, Perry Lang; **D:** Don Hulette; **W:** Walter Dallenbach; **M:** Don Hulette.

Greek Street ✶✶ *Latin Love* 1930 The owner of small cafe in London discovers a poor girl singing in the street for food. He takes her in and spotlights her songs in his cafe. 51m/B VHS. *GB* Sari Maritza, Arthur Ahmbling, Martin Lewis; **D:** Sinclair Hill.

The Greek Tycoon ✶½ 1978 (R) Old familiar story about widow of an American president who marries a billionaire shipping magnate and finds that money cannot buy happiness. A transparent depiction of the Onassis/Kennedy marriage, done to a turn. 106m/C VHS. Anthony Quinn, Jacqueline Bisset, James Franciscus, Raf Vallone, Edward Albert; **D:** J. Lee Thompson.

Green Archer ✶✶ 1940 Fifteen episodes of the famed serial, featuring a spooked castle complete with secret passages and tunnels, trapdoors, and the mysterious masked figure, the Green Archer. 283m/B VHS, DVD. Victor Jory, Iris Meredith, James Craven, Robert (Fisk) Fisk; **D:** James W. Horne.

The Green Berets WOOF! 1968 (G) Cliched wartime heroics co-directed by the Duke stars as a Special Forces colonel, leading his troops against the Viet Cong. Painfully insipid pro-war propaganda, notable as the only American film to come out in support of U.S. involvement in Vietnam. Truly embarrassing but did spawn the hit single "Ballad of the Green Beret" by Barry Sadler. 135m/C VHS, DVD. John Wayne, David Janssen, Jim Hutton, Aldo Ray, George Takei, Raymond St. Jacques, Bruce Cabot, Jack Soo, Patrick Wayne, Luke Askew, Irene Tsu, Edward Faulkner, Jason Evers, Mike Henry, Chuck Roberson, Eddy Donno; **D:** John Wayne; **W:** James Lee Barrett; **C:** Winton C. Hoch; **M:** Miklos Rozsa.

The Green Butchers ✶½ *De Gronne Slagtere* 2003 (R) Beware the sausage you're eating-particularly if it came from a certain Danish butcher shop. Friends and coworkers Svend (Mikkelsen) and Bjarne (Kaas) decide to open their own shop but business isn't going so well until Svend discovers the body of an electrician who accidentally froze to death in their store's meat locker. For some reason, Svend decides to add some human flesh to his sausage recipe and soon can't sell enough of the resulting delicacy. In order to keep up with demand, Svend turns to murder. It's a comedy. Danish with subtitles. 100m/C DVD. Mads Mikkelsen, Line Kruse, Nicolas Bro, Nikolaj Lie Kaas; **D:** Anders Thomas Jensen; **W:** Anders Thomas Jensen; **C:** Sebastian Blenkov; **M:** Jeppe Kaas.

Green Card ✶✶½ 1990 (PG-13) Some marry for love, some for money, others for an apartment in the Big Apple. Refined, single MacDowell covets a rent-controlled apartment in Manhattan, but the lease stipulates that the apartment be let to a married couple. Enter brusque and burly Depardieu, who covets the elusive MacDowell, as a stuffy horticulturist, and Depardieu, as a French composer works well, and the two adroitly play a couple whose relationship covers the romantic continuum. Director Weir wrote the screenplay with Depardieu in mind. Depardieu's English-language debut. 108m/C VHS, DVD. Gerard Depardieu, Andie MacDowell, Bebe Neuwirth, Gregg Edelman, Robert Prosky, Jessie Keosian, Ann Wedgeworth, Ethan Phillips, Mary Louise Wilson, Lois Smith, Simon Jones; **D:** Peter Weir; **W:** Peter Weir; **M:** Hans Zimmer. Golden Globes '91: Actor—Mus./Comedy (Depardieu), Film—Mus./Comedy.

Green Dolphin Street ✶✶½ 1947 Flimsy romantic epic set in 19th century New Zealand. A young girl marries the beau she and her sister are battling over in this Oscar-winning special effects show which features one big earthquake. Based on the Elizabeth Goudge novel, this was one of MGM's biggest hits in 1947. 161m/B VHS. Lana Turner, Van Heflin, Donna Reed, Edmund Gwenn; **D:** Victor Saville; **C:** George J. Folsey.

Green Dragon ✶✶½ 2001 (PG-13) Tai (Duong) is a former Army translator now appointed camp manager at a Vietnamese refugee camp in 1975. He brings a nephew, Minh, and a niece, Anh, as well as a boatload of guilt over leaving their mother behind. He forms a bond with his boss, Jim (Swayze) who seems gruff but has his own issues. The camp cook (Whitaker) helps Minh open up by teaching him to paint and working with him on a mural depicting an idealized American melting pot, with the titular Green Dragon at its center. Various subplots and periods of heavy-handed sentimentality threaten to overwhelm fine character study, but overall this is an engaging look at a period of American history previously ignored. 113m/C VHS, DVD. Don Duong, Patrick Swayze, Forest Whitaker, Hiep Thi Le, Kieu Chinh, Billinger C. Tran, Trung Hieu Nguyen, Long Nguyen, Jennifer Tran; **D:** Timothy Linh Bui; **W:** Tony Bui, Timothy Linh Bui; **C:** Kramer Morgenthau; **M:** Mychael Danna, Jeff Danna.

Green Eyes ✶½ 1934 A costume party in a country mansion sets the scene for a routine murder mystery when the guests find their host stabbed to death in a closet. Based on the novel "The Murder of Stephen Kester" by H. Ashbrooke. 68m/B VHS, DVD. Shirley Grey, Charles Starrett, Claude Gillingwater, John Wray, Dorothy Revier; **D:** Richard Thorpe; **M:** Melville Shyer.

Green Eyes ✶✶✶½ 1976 Winfield, an ex-GI, returns to postwar Vietnam to search for his illegitimate son who he believes will have green eyes. A highly acclaimed drama featuring moving performances from Winfield and Jonathan Lippe. 100m/C VHS, DVD. Paul Winfield, Rita Tushingham, Jonathon Lippe, Victoria Racimo, Royce Wallace, Claudia Bryar; **D:** John Erman. TV

Green Fields ✶✶½ *Gruner Felder* 1937 A quiet romance based on Peretz Hirschbein's legendary tale of a young scholar of the Talmud who leaves the shelter of the synagogue in order to learn about people in the real world. The search takes him to the countryside where he finds himself in the middle of a battle between two families who both want him as a tutor and a suitor for their daughters. In Yiddish with English subtitles. 95m/B VHS, DVD. Michael Goldstein, Herschel Bernardi, Helen Beverly; **D:** Jacob Ben-Ami.

Green Fire ✶✶½ 1955 The screen sizzles when emerald miner Granger meets plantation-owner Kelly in the exotic jungles of South America. Usual plot complications muddle the story, but who cares when the stars are this attractive? 100m/C VHS, Stewart Granger, Grace Kelly, Paul Douglas, John Ericson, Murvyn Vye, Jose Torvay, Robert Tafur, Nacho Galindo; **D:** Andrew Marton; **M:** Miklos Rozsa.

Green for Danger ✶✶✶ 1947 A detective stages a chilling mock operation to find a mad killer stalking the corridors of a British hospital during WWII. Sim's first great claim to fame (pre-"A Christmas Carol"). 91m/B VHS, DVD. *GB* Trevor Howard, Alastair Sim, Leo Genn; **D:** Sidney Gilliat.

The Green Glove ✶✶½ 1952 A jewel thief steals a beautiful relic from a tiny church. WWII makes it impossible for him to fence it and the church finds a relentless ally to track the thief. Excellent action sequences lift this standard plot slightly above the ordinary. 88m/B VHS, DVD. Glenn Ford, Geraldine Brooks, Cedric Hardwicke, Gaby Andre, Roger Treville, Juliette Greco, Jean Brochard; **D:** Rudolph Mate; **W:** Charles Bennett.

Green Grow the Rushes ✶✶ *Brandy Ashore* 1951 The English government tries to put a stop to brandy smuggling on the coast, but the townspeople drink up the evidence. A young Burton highlights this watered-down comedy. Based on a novel by co-scripter Harold Clewes. 77m/B VHS, DVD. *GB* Roger Livesey, Honor Blackman, Richard Burton, Frederick Leister; **D:** Derek Twist.

Green Horizon ✶½ *Afurika Monogatari; A Tale of Africa* 1980 A bucolic old codger faces a dilemma when he must choose between his granddaughter's future and his disaster-prone natural environment. 80m/C VHS. James Stewart, Philip Sayer, Elenora Vallone; **D:** Simon Trevor; **C:** Simon Hani; **W:** Shintaro Tsuji; **C:** Tsuguzo Matsumae.

The Green Hornet ✶✶ 1939 The feature version of the original serial, in which the Green Hornet and Kato have a series of crime-fighting adventures. 100m/B VHS, DVD. Gordon Jones, Keye Luke, Anne Nagel, Wade Boteler, Walter McGrail, Douglas Evans, Cy Kendall; **D:** Ford Beebe, Ray Taylor; **W:** George Plympton, Basil Dickey; **C:** Jerome Ash, William Sickner.

The Green House ✶✶ *The Greenhouse; Le Jardin des Plantes* 1996 Fernand Bonard (Rich) is the aged caretaker of the Paris zoo's botanical gardens during the waning days of WWII. His son Armand (Labarthe) is a collaborator who arrives at his father's home with eight-year-old daughter, Philippine (Stevenin), to celebrate her birthday. When Armand is suddenly killed by the Gestapo, Fernand begins an elaborate deception for his granddaughter, portraying her father as a hero of the French Resistance but his illusions take an unexpected turn. French with subtitles. 93m/C VHS. *FR* Claude Rich, Salome Stevenin, Samuel Labarthe, Catherine Jacob, Rose Thiery; **D:** Philippe de Broca; **W:** Philippe de Broca, Alexandre Jardin; **C:** Janos Kende; **M:** Charles Court.

Green Ice ✶½ 1981 An American electronics expert gets involved with a brutal South American government dealing with emeralds and plans a heist with his girlfriend and other cohorts. A little bit of romance, a little bit of action, a lot of nothing much. 109m/C VHS, DVD. *GB* Ryan O'Neal, Anne Archer, Omar Sharif, John Larroquette; **D:** Ernest Day; **W:** Edward Anhalt, Robert De Laurentis.

Green Inferno ✶ *Tarzan and the Jungle Mystery* 1972 A wealthy eccentric who lives deep in the South American jungle incites the natives to rebel. Mercenary agents are then hired to kill him. 90m/C VHS. *SP* Richard Yesteran, Didi Sherman, Caesar Burner; **D:** Miguel Iglesias.

The Green Man ✶✶ 1991 Maurice Allington (Finney), the alcoholic and randy owner of the Green Man Inn in rural England, jokes about the spirits that supposedly haunt the inn. It's not too funny, however, when he discovers the spirits are real and he has to figure out who the spirit of a 17th-century murderer is inhabiting before he kills again. A classy ghost story based on the novel by Kingsley Amis. 150m/C VHS. *GB* Albert Finney, Sarah Berger, Linda Marlowe, Michael Hordern, Nickolas Grace, Michael Culver; **D:** Elijah Moshinsky; **W:** Malcolm Bradbury.

Green Mansions ✶✶ 1959 Screen adaptation of W. H. Hudson's novel suffers due to miscasting of Hepburn as Rima the Bird Girl, who is not permitted to leave her sanctuary. Perkins is good as the male lead who fled to the jungle in search of wealth and instead finds a powerful love. Hepburn was married to director Ferrer at the time. 104m/C VHS. Audrey Hepburn, Anthony Perkins, Lee J. Cobb, Sessue Hayakawa, Henry Silva, Nehemiah Persoff, Michael Pate; **D:** Mel Ferrer; **W:** Dorothy Kingsley; **C:** Joseph Ruttenberg.

The Green Mile ✶✶½ 1999 (R) Lightning didn't exactly strike twice when Darabont directed this follow-up to "The Shawshank Redemption," another period prison drama by Stephen King. Paul Edgecomb (Hanks) is the decent head guard at Louisiana's Cold Mountain Penitentiary in 1935. He works E block, which is death row (title refers to the color of the floor). Among his prisoners is hulking black man John Coffey (Duncan), whose intimidating size belies a sweet nature. And something else—it seems Coffey has the power to heal. Overlong and watching the executions takes a strong stomach; characters are more symbols than human beings. 187m/C VHS, DVD, Blu-ray Disc. Tom Hanks, Michael Clarke Duncan, David Morse, Bonnie Hunt, Michael Jeter, Sam Rockwell, James Cromwell, Patricia Clarkson, Graham Greene, Barry Pepper, Doug Hutchison, Jeffrey DeMunn, Harry Dean Stanton, Dabbs Greer, Eve Brent, William Sadler, Gary Sinise; **D:** Frank Darabont; **W:** Frank Darabont; **C:** David Tattersall; **M:** Thomas Newman. Broadcast "Tim Critics '99. Adapt. Screen-play, Support. Actor (Duncan).

Green Pastures 🐾🐾🐾 1936 An adaptation of Marc Connelly's 1930 Pulitzer Prize-winning play, which attempts to retell Biblical stories in black English vernacular of the '30s. Southern theatre owners boycotted the controversial film which had an all-Black cast. **33m/C VHS, DVD.** Rex Ingram, Oscar Polk, Eddie Anderson, George Reed, Abraham Gleaves, Myrtle Anderson, Frank Wilson; **D:** William Keighley, Marc Connelly; **C:** Hal Mohr.

Green Plaid Shirt 🐾🐾 1996. In 1978, Phillip and Guy are exploring first love while their friends, Devon, Jerry, and Todd are exploring life. Ten years later, Phillip is the only one to survive the AIDS impact on the gay community as he tries to make sense of what happened and what comes next. **90m/C VHS, DVD.** Gregory Phelan, Kevin Blair Spirtas, Russell Scott Lewis, Richard Israel, Jonathan Klein; **D:** Richard Natale; **W:** Richard Natale; **C:** Amil Bhattacharya; **M:** Norman Noll.

The Green Promise 🐾🐾 1949 A well-meaning but domineering farmer and his four motherless children face disaster as a result of the father's obstinacy. But when he is laid up, the eldest daughter takes over, tries modern methods and equipment, and makes the farm a success. **90m/B VHS.** Walter Brennan, Marguerite Chapman, Robert Paige, Natalie Wood; **D:** William D. Russell; **W:** Monty Collins Jr.; **C:** John L. "Jack" Russell; **M:** Rudolph (Rudy) Schrager.

The Green Room 🐾🐾 *La Chambre verte* 1978 Truffaut's haunting tale of a man who, valuing death over life, erects a shrine to all the dead he has known. Offered a chance at love, he cannot overcome his obsessions to take the risk. Based on the Henry James story "Altar of the Dead." In French with subtitles. **95m/C VHS.** *FR* Antoine Vitez, Jane Lobre Marcel Berbert, Francois Truffaut, Nathalie Baye, Jean Daste; **D:** Francois Truffaut; **W:** Jean Gruault; **C:** Nestor Almendros; **M:** Maurice Jaubert.

The Green Slime WOOF! 1968 *Gamma Sango Uchu Daisakusen; Battle Beyond the Stars; Death and the Green Slime* 1968 G) Danger and romance highlight the journey of a space ship assigned to intercept an on-screen asteroid. Little do the astronauts realize, but they have brought aboard the ship the malevolent alien creatures known as green slime (and we ain't talking jello here). Cheap, U.S./Japanese co-production will leave you feeling lousy in the morning. The title song is legendary among genre aficionados. **90m/C VHS. JP** Robert Horton, Richard Jaeckel, Luciana Paluzzi, Bud Widom, Ted Gunther, Robert Dunham; **D:** Kinji Fukasaku; **W:** Ivan Reiner, Charles Sinclair, Bill Finger; **C:** Yoshikazu Yamasawa; **M:** Charles Fox, Toshiaki Tsushima.

Green Snake 🐾🐾 1993 Combo of mysticism and action based on a Chinese fable. Green Snake (Cheung), and Son Ching (Wong) are actual reptiles who have been practicing taking human form. When self-righteous Buddhist monk Fa-Hai discovers them, he thinks it's a sin to tamper with the natural order. The snakes don't appreciate his lack of compassion and plot destruction. Cantonese with subtitles. **102m/C VHS, DVD. HK** Maggie Cheung, Joey Wong; **D:** Tsui Hark.

Green Street Hooligans 🐾🐾½ 2005 (R) Matt Buckner (Wood) is expelled from Harvard weeks before graduating when he's forced to take the fall for his wealthy roommate after cocaine is found in their room. He accepts $10,000 in hush money, and takes off for London to visit his sister Shannon (Forlani) and brother-in-law Steve (Warren). Steve's younger brother Pete (Hunnam) takes Matt to a West Ham football match, where he's introduced to the violent world of the Green Street Elite, the gang of rabid fans committed to supporting the West Ham football club through the gritty nature of soccer hooliganism will

leave you both fascinated and repelled. **106m/C DVD. GB US** Elijah Wood, Charlie Hunnam, Claire Forlani, Marc Warren, Leo Gregory, Henry Goodman, Geoff Bell, Ross McCall, Rafe Spall, Kieran Bew, Francis Pope, Christopher Hehir, Terence Jay; **D:** Lexi Alexander; **W:** Lexi Alexander, Dougie Brimson, Josh Shelov; **C:** Alexander Buono; **M:** Christopher Franke.

The Green Wall 🐾🐾🐾 1970 A city-dwelling young man attempts to homestead with his family in the Amazon. A lovely and tragic film with stunning photography of the Peruvian forests. First Peruvian feature to be shown in the U.S. In Spanish with English subtitles. **110m/C VHS. SP** Julio Aleman, Sandra Riva; **D:** Armando Robles Godoy; **W:** Armando Robles Godoy.

Greenfingers 🐾🐾½ 2000 (R) One of those strange-but-true stories that barely stays ahead of being twee, thanks to its cast. Surly prisoner Colin Briggs (Owen) has just been transferred to Edgefield, an "open" prison that aims at building job skills. When Colin accidentally turns out to be a prime gardener (with greenfingers in British parlance), warden Hodge (Clarke) assigns him to garden detail along with his twinkly, dying, elderly cellmate Fergus (Kelly). Then the prison garden comes to the attention of TV star gardener Georgina Woodhouse (Mirren) and she sponsors their efforts in a very prestigious flower show. Remember the Brits take their gardening very seriously indeed. **90m/C VHS, DVD. GB US** Clive Owen, Helen Mirren, David Kelly, Warren Clarke, Danny Dyer, Peterson Joseph, Natasha Little, Adam Fogerty; **D:** Joel Hershman; **W:** Joel Hershman; **C:** John Daly; **M:** Guy Dagul.

Greenmail 🐾 2001 (R) A Seattle serial bomber is targeting corporations that harm the environment. Naturally, the bomb squad must stop him. Even things getting blowed up good can't save this one. **92m/C VHS, DVD.** Stephen Baldwin, Tom Skerritt, Kelly Rowan; **D:** Jonathan Heap; **W:** Raul Inglis, James Makichuk; **C:** Michael G. Wojciechowski. **VIDEO**

Greenwich Village 🐾🐾 1944 Would-be classical composer Kenneth Harvey (Ameche) finds his work being adapted for a musical revue by speakeasy owner Danny O'Mara (Bendix). But Harvey isn't too upset when he discovers singer Bonnie Watson (Blaine in her screen debut) is working on the show. Miranda is the club's fortune-telling comic foil. **82m/C DVD.** Don Ameche, William Bendix, Vivian Blaine, Carmen Miranda, Felix Bressart; **D:** Walter Lang; **W:** Earl Baldwin, Ernest Pagano, Michael Fessier, Walter Bullock; **C:** Leon Shamroy, Harry Jackson; **M:** Emil Newman, Chuck Henderson.

Greetings 🐾🐾🐾 1968 (R) De Niro stars in this wild and crazy comedy about a man who tries to help his friend flunk his draft physical. One of DePalma's first films, and a pleasantly anarchic view of the late '60s, wrought with a light, intelligent tone. Followed by the sequel "Hi, Mom!" **88m/C VHS, DVD.** Robert De Niro, Jonathan Warden, Gerrit Graham, Allen (Goorwitz) Garfield, Megan McCormick, Bettina Kugel, Jack Cowford, Richard Hamilton; **D:** Brian De Palma; **W:** Brian De Palma, Charles Hirsch; **C:** Robert Fiore.

Gregory's Girl 🐾🐾🐾½ 1980 Sweet, disarming comedy established Forsyth. An awkward young Scottish schoolboy falls in love with the female goalie of his soccer team. He turns to his 10-year-old sister for advice, but she's more interested in ice cream than love. His best friend is no help, either, since he has yet to fall in love. Perfect mirror of teenagers and their instantaneous, raw, and all-consuming loves. Very sweet scene with Gregory and his girl lying on their backs in an open space illustrates the simultaneous simplicity and complexity of young love. **91m/C VHS, DVD. GB** Gordon John Sinclair, Dee Hepburn, Jake D'Arcy, Chic Murray, Alex Norton, John Bett, Clare Grogan; **D:** Bill Forsyth; **W:** Bill Forsyth; **C:** Michael Coulter; British Acad. '81: Screenplay.

Gremlins 🐾🐾🐾 1984 (PG) Comedy horror with deft satiric edge. Produced by Spielberg. Fumbling gadget salesman Rand Peltzer is looking for something really special to get his son Billy. He finds it in a small store in Chinatown. The wise shopkeeper is reluctant to sell him the

adorable "mogwai" but relents after fully warning him "Don't expose him to bright light, don't ever get him wet, and don't, ever, ever feed him after midnight." Naturally, this all happens and the result is a gang of nasty gremlins who decide to tear up the town on Christmas Eve. Followed by "Gremlins 2: The New Batch" which is less black comedy, more parody, and perhaps more inventive. **106m/C VHS, DVD.** Zach Galligan, Phoebe Cates, Hoyt Axton, Polly Holliday, Frances Lee McCain, Keye Luke, Dick Miller, Corey Feldman, Judge Reinhold, Glynn Turman, Scott Brady, Jackie Joseph; **D:** Joe Dante; **W:** Chris Columbus; **C:** John Hora; **M:** Jerry Goldsmith; **V:** Howie Mandel.

Gremlins 2: The New Batch 🐾🐾½ 1990 (PG-13) The sequel to "Gremlins" is superior to the original, which was quite good. Set in a futuristic skyscraper in the Big Apple, director Dante presents a less violent but far more campy vision, paying myriad surreal tributes to scores of movies, including "The Wizard of Oz" and musical extravaganzas by the dozen. Also incorporates a Donald Trump parody, takes on TV news, and body slams modern urban living. Great fun. **107m/C VHS, DVD.** Zach Galligan, Phoebe Cates, John Glover, Christopher Lee, Robert Prosky, Robert Picardo, Haviland (Haylie) Morris Dick Miller, Jackie Joseph, Keye Luke, Belinda Balaski Gizson, Leonard Maltin, Hulk Hogan, Charles S. Haas; **Cameos:** Jerry Goldsmith; **D:** Joe Dante; **W:** Charles S. Haas; **C:** John Hora; **M:** Jerry Goldsmith; **V:** Howie Mandel, Tony Randall.

Grendel, Grendel, Grendel 🐾🐾 1982 An utterly urbane dragon wants to be friends, but for some reason people are just terrified of Grendel. It's true, he bites a head off once in a while, but nobody's perfect! An ingenious, animated retelling of Beowulf. **60m/C VHS.** Pl Janusz Grabowski, Agnieszka Kruszewska, Eva Sorowik, Tomasz Grochoczk, Andrze Precig; **D:** Krzysztof Gruber.

Greta 🐾🐾🐾 1986 During WWII, a young Polish boy escapes from a detention camp. Now on the run, several bizarre twists of fate place him in the care of Greta, a young girl whose father is an officer in the S.S. In Polish with English subtitles. **60m/C VHS.** Pl, Janusz Grabowski, Agnieszka Kruszewska, Eva Sorowik, Tomasz Grochoczk, Andrze Precig; **C:** Krzysztof Gruber.

The Grey Fox 🐾🐾🐾½ 1983 (PG) Based on the true story of Canada's most colorful and celebrated outlaw. Gentle-manly old stagecoach robber Bill Miner (Farnsworth) tries to pick up his life after 30 years in prison. Unable to resist another heist, he tries train robbery, and winds up hiding out in British Columbia where he meets photographer Kate Flynn (Burroughs), come to document the changing West. Farnsworth is perfect as the man who suddenly finds himself in the 20th century trying to work at the only craft he knows. Borso's first feature film after his work as a documentary filmmaker. **92m/C VHS. CA** Richard Farnsworth, Jackie Burroughs, Wayne Robson, Timothy Webber, Ken Pogue; **D:** Phillip Borsos; **W:** John Hunter; **C:** Frank Tidy; **M:** Michael Conway Baker. Genie '83: Director (Borsos), Film, Support. Actress (Burroughs).

Grey Owl 🐾🐾½ 1999 (PG-13) Interesting old-fashioned biopic suffers from miscasting (and it's not Brosnan, although he takes a little getting used to). Based on the true story of Archie Grey Owl (Brosnan), an Ojibway trapper in 1930s Canada who changes his occupation and becomes an ardent early environmentalist and celebrity lecturer and writer. Only hitch is that his death does the truth come out—Archie was in fact Englishman Archibald Belaney. Film bogs down in its romantic aspects with Galipeau, as Grey Owl's young Mohawk girlfriend, sadly out of her depths. **117m/C VHS, DVD. CA** Pierce Brosnan, Annie Galipeau, Vlasta Vrana, Nathaniel Arcand, David Fox, Charles Powell, Renee Asherson, Stephenie Cole, Graham Greene; **D:** Richard Attenborough; **W:** William Nicholson; **C:** Roger Pratt; **M:** George Fenton. Genie '99: Costume Des.

Greyfriars Bobby 🐾🐾½ 1961 A true story of a Skye terrier named Bobby who, after his master dies, refuses to leave the grave. Even after being coaxed by the local children into town, he still returns to the cemetery each evening. Word of his loyalty spreads, and Bobby becomes the pet of 19th century Edinburgh. Nicely told, with fine location photography and good acting. Great for children and animal lovers. **91m/C VHS, DVD.** Donald Crisp, Laurence Naismith, Kay Walsh; **D:** Don Chaffey.

Greystoke: The Legend of Tarzan, Lord of the Apes 🐾🐾 1984 (PG) The seventh Earl of Greystoke becomes a shipwrecked orphan in darkest Africa. Ruling the ape-clan in the tree-swinging persona of Tarzan, he still reddiscovered by an anthropologist and returned to his ancestral home in Scotland, where he is immediately recognized by his grandfather. The contrast between the behavior of man and ape is interesting, and Tarzan's introduction to society is fun, but there's no melodrama or cliff-hanging action, as we've come to expect of the Tarzan genre. Due to her heavy southern accent, Andie MacDowell (as Jane) had her voice dubbed by Glenn Close. **130m/C VHS, DVD.** Christopher Lambert, Ralph Richardson, Ian Holm, James Fox, Andie MacDowell, Ian Charleson, Cheryl Campbell, Nigel Davenport; **D:** Hugh Hudson; **W:** Michael Austin, N.Y. Film Critics '84.

Gridiron Gang 🐾🐾 2006 (PG-13) Based on the true story of correctional officer Sean Porter (The Rock), who recruits a bunch of gangbangers stuck in a juvie camp for this football team. Naturally, the teens find hope through the help of the game and their tough coach. Heavily motivational sports cliche, the documentary footage shown at the end of the real team pair are thrown into the switches of social services programs and government offices where they snuffle endlessly but nothing happens. Think "Waiting for Godot" meets "Waiting for the Man." Meanwhile, their dealer is murdered and they're the prime suspects, pursued by the cops and the actual killers, who believe that they've stolen said dealer's stash. Shakur shows flashes of the brilliance that might have been as its long-crazy siblings him perfectly as its bug-crazy short-sighted partner. Fellow actor Curtis-Hall's directorial debut. **91m/C VHS, DVD.** Tim Roth, Tupac Shakur, Thandie Newton, Charles Fleischer, Howard Hesseman James Pickens Jr., John Sayles, Tom Towles, Eric Payne; **Cameos:** Vondie Curtis-Hall; **D:** Vondie Curtis-Hall; **W:** Vondie Curtis-Hall; **C:** Bill Pope; **M:** Stewart Copeland.

Gridlock'd 🐾🐾 1996 (R) Junkies Spoon (Shakur) and Stretch (Roth) decide to kick the habit after their singer Cookie (Newton) overdoses and slips into a coma. The hapless pair are thrown into the switches of social services programs and government offices where they snuffle endlessly but nothing happens. Think "Waiting for Godot" meets "Waiting for the Man." Meanwhile, their dealer is murdered and they're the prime suspects, pursued by the cops and the actual killers, who believe that they've stolen said dealer's stash. Shakur shows flashes of the brilliance that might have been as its long-crazy siblings him perfectly as its bug-crazy short-sighted partner. Fellow actor Curtis-Hall's directorial debut. **91m/C VHS, DVD.** Tim Roth, Tupac Shakur, Thandie Newton, Charles Fleischer, Howard Hesseman James Pickens Jr., John Sayles, Tom Towles, Eric Payne; **Cameos:** Vondie Curtis-Hall; **D:** Vondie Curtis-Hall; **W:** Vondie Curtis-Hall; **C:** Bill Pope; **M:** Stewart Copeland.

Grief 🐾🐾 1994 Mark (Chester) is a writer on the syndicated daytime TV show "The Love Judge." Still numb from his lover's death from AIDS the previous year, Mark begins to take an interest in fellow writer Bill (Arquette), while writer Paula (Gutteridge) desires to become the show's new producer and secretary Leslie (Doug-

The Grey Zone 🐾🐾 2001 (R) Nelson adapted his own play, which centers on the Sonderkommandos, Jewish prisoners who worked in the crematoriums (in this case at Auschwitz), disposed of remains, and were given special privileges by the Nazis. In October of 1944, the prisoners plan an uprising and blow up two of the gas chambers. The film isn't transcend its theatrical origins and is both surreal and excruciating (since Nelson doesn't spare depicting the atrocities) to watch. **108m/C VHS, DVD. US** David Arquette, Daniel Benzali, Steve Buscemi, David Chandler, Allan Corduner, Harvey Keitel, Natasha Lyonne, Mira Sorvino; **D:** Tim Blake Nelson; **C:** Russell Fine; **M:** Jeff Danna.

Grief

las) wants to take her place as the new writer. Present producer Jo (Beat) tries to keep her office family in line while sorting out her personal life. Writer-director Glatzer knows his territory since he spent five years writing for "Divorce Court." **86m/C VHS, DVD.** Craig Chester, Alexis Arquette, Lucy Gutteridge, Illeana Douglas, Jackie Beat, Carlton Wilborn, Paul Bartel, Mary Woronov; **D:** Richard Glatzer; **W:** Richard Glatzer; **C:** David Dechant.

Grievous Bodily Harm 🦴🦴 **1989 (R)** Morris Martin's wife Claudine is missing. When he finds a videotape of Claudine in very compromising positions, he becomes murderously determined to find out where she has gone. **136m/C VHS.** John Waters, Colin Friels, Bruno Lawrence; **D:** Mark Joffe.

Griffin and Phoenix: A Love Story 🦴🦴½ **1976** A sentimental film about the mortality of two vital people. Falk deserts his family when he learns he has terminal cancer. Clayburgh, also terminally ill, meets him for a short but meaningful affair. Good performances help overcome the tear-jerker aspects of the story. **110m/C VHS.** Peter Falk, Jill Clayburgh, Dorothy Tristan, John Lehne; **D:** Daryl Duke. **TV**

The Grifters 🦴🦴🦴½ **1990 (R)** Evocative rendering of a terrifying subculture. Huston, Cusack, and Bening are con artists, struggling to stay on top in a world where violence, money, and lust are the prizes. Bening and Huston fight for Cusak's soul, while he's determined to decide for himself. Seamless performances and dazzling atmosphere, along with superb pacing, make for a provocative film. Based on a novel by Jim Thompson. **114m/C VHS, DVD.** Anjelica Huston, John Cusack, Annette Bening, Pat Hingle, J.T. Walsh, Charles Napier, Henry Jones, Gailard Sartain, Jeremy Piven; **D:** Stephen Frears; **W:** Donald E. Westlake; **C:** Oliver Stapleton; **M:** Elmer Bernstein. Ind. Spirit '91: Actress (Huston), Film; L.A. Film Critics '90: Actress (Huston); Natl. Soc. Film Critics '90: Actress (Bening). Support. Actress (Bening).

Grilled 🦴½ *Men Don't Quit* **2006 (R)** Struggling meat salesmen Maurice (Romano) and Dave (James) have their bacon on the line if they don't make a big sale. There's also a mobster, his girl, and a couple of hitmen that also involve the guys. The duo did much better on the small screen, having misplaced their comedy chops while making this yawner. **77m/C VHS, DVD. US** Ray Romano, Kevin James, Juliette Lewis, Sofia Vergara, Michael Rapaport, Barry Newman, Burt Reynolds, Kim Coates, Eric Allen Kramer, Jack Kehler, Jon Polito, Lisa Jane Persky, Mary Lynn Rajskub, Caroline Aaron, Richard Libertini, Lisa Edelstein; **D:** Jason Ensler; **W:** William Tepper; **C:** Lawrence Sher; **M:** Adam Cohen. **VIDEO**

Grim 🦴 **1995 (R)** Lives up to its title as an extremely icky and evil subterranean creature is awakened from a long sleep by miners. Apparently not long enough, since he proceeds to rip apart anyone he comes in contact with. **86m/C VHS, DVD.** Emmanuel Xuereb, Tres Handley, Peter Tregloan; **D:** Paul Matthews; **W:** Paul Matthews; **C:** Alan M. Trow; **M:** Dennis Michael Tenney.

Grim Prairie Tales 🦴🦴 **1989 (R)** A city slicker and a crazed mountain man meet by a campfire in the high plains one night and pass the time sharing four tales of Western horror. Dourif and Jones are funny, their stories scary, making for an interesting twist on both the horror and the Western genres. **90m/C VHS.** Brad Dourif, James Earl Jones, Marc McClure, William Atherton, Scott Paulin, Lisa Eichhorn; **D:** Wayne Coe; **W:** Wayne Coe; **C:** Janusz Kaminski.

The Grim Reaper 🦴🦴🦴 **1962** *La Commare Secca* 22-year-old Bertolucci directed his first feature with this grim and brutal treatment of the investigation of murder of a prostitute, told via flashbacks and from the disparate perspectives of three people who knew the woman. A commercial bust, the critics were no kinder than the public at the time; not until two years later, with "Before the Revolution," did Bertolucci earn his directorial spurs. The script was written by Pasolini, with whom the erstwhile poet had collaborated on "Accattone" the previous year (as assistant). In Italian with English subti-

tles. **100m/B VHS, DVD. IT** Francesco Rulu, Giancarlo de Rosa; **D:** Bernardo Bertolucci; **W:** Pier Paolo Pasolini.

Grim Reaper 🦴½ **1981 (R)** Mia Farrow's sister is one of a group of American students vacationing on a Greek island. Farrow learns of the twisted cannibalistic murderer who methodically tries to avenge the tragic deaths of his family. **81m/C VHS, DVD. IT** Tisa Farrow, George Eastman; **D:** Joe D'Amato.

Grind 🦴🦴 **1996** Dysfunctional blue-collar family saga set in New Jersey, Eddie Dolan (Crudup), just out of the joint, moves in with brother Terry (Schulze) and sister-in-law Janey (Shelly). He gets a dull factory job and fixes up old cars to go drag-racing on the weekend—as well as helping out Terry, who has a sideline working with a car theft ring. Since gorgeous Eddie works nights, he and sulky stay-at-home-with-the-baby Janey get to be real close daytime buddies. Naturally their affair causes trouble for all. A paint-by-numbers plot with some decent acting. **96m/C VHS.** Billy Crudup, Adrienne Shelly, Paul Schulze, Frank Vincent, Saul Stein, Amanda Peet, Steven Beach, Tim Devlin; **D:** Chris Kentis; **W:** Chris Kentis, Laura Lau; **C:** Stephen Kazmierski; **M:** Brian Kelly.

Grind 🦴🦴 **2003 (PG-13)** Lightweight tale of teens and their quest for fame and the booty that comes with it rides the rails of the newly-hip extreme sports genre. The straight-outta-Central Casting group of grinders consists of good-looking Eric (Vogel); ladies man Sweet Lou (Kem); goofy, sex-crazed Matt (Vieluf); and the nerdy Dustin (Brody). They follow their skateboarding hero Jimmy Wilson (London) on tour and hope to grab the pro's attention with their skateboarding antics in order to win a coveted sponsorship and ensuing fame and fortune. Pic finds moderate success when sticking to the 'board action (even if it's obviously stand-in work) while gross-out and slacker humor too often misses the mark. **100m/C VHS, DVD. US** Vince Vieluf, Mike Vogel, Adam Brody, Joey Kern, Jenny (Jennifer) Morrison, Jason London, Randy Quaid, Christopher McDonald, Summer Altice; **D:** Casey La Scala; **W:** Ralph Sall; **C:** Richard Crudo; **M:** Ralph Sall.

Grisbi 🦴🦴 *Touchez Pas au Grisbi; Honour Among Thieves; Touchez Pas Au Grisbi* **1953** King of the French underworld, Gabin finds there's no honor among thieves when a gold heist goes wrong and the loot comes up missing. Moreau is the quintessential moll. French with subtitles. **94m/B VHS, DVD. FR** Jean Gabin, Jeanne Moreau, Lino Ventura, Daniel Cauchy, Gaby Basset; **D:** Jacques Becker; **W:** Jacques Becker, Maurice Griffe; **M:** Jean Wiener. Venice Film Fest. '54: Actor (Gabin).

The Grissom Gang 🦴🦴 **1971 (R)** Remake of the 1948 British film "No Orchids for Miss Blandish." Darby is a wealthy heiress kidnapped by a family of grotesques, led by a sadistic mother. The ransom gets lost in a series of bizarre events, and the heiress appears to be falling for one of her moronic captors. Director Robert Aldrich skillfully blends extreme violence with dark humor. Superb camera work, editing, and 1920s period sets. **127m/C VHS, DVD.** Kim Darby, Scott Wilson, Tony Musante, Robert Lansing, Wesley Addy; **D:** Robert Aldrich; **W:** Leon Griffiths; **C:** Joseph Biroc; **M:** Gerald Fried.

Grizzly 🦴🦴 *Killer Grizzly* **1976 (PG)** Giant, killer grizzly terrorizes a state park in this blatant "Jaws" rip-off. From the same folks who produced "Abby," a blatant "Exorcist" rip-off. Filmed in Georgia. **92m/C VHS, DVD.** Christopher George, Richard Jaeckel, Andrew Prine, Victoria (Vicki) Johnson, Charles Kissinger; **D:** William Girdler; **W:** Harvey Flaxman, David Sheldon; **M:** Robert O. Ragland.

Grizzly Adams: The Legend Continues 🦴½ **1990** A small town is saved from three desperados by Grizzly and his huge grizzly bear pet, Martha. **90m/C VHS.** Gene Edwards, Link Wyler, Red West, Tony Caruso, Acquanetta, L.Q. Jones; **D:** Ken Kennedy.

Grizzly Falls 🦴🦴½ **1999 (PG)** Old-fashioned family fare, set in 1913, finds 13-year-old Harry (Clark) setting out on a wilderness adventure in the Canadian Rockies with his dad, Tyrone (Brown). Tyrone is out to capture a grizzly and bring it back (alive) for study. But when Tyrone finds a female grizzly and captures the bear's two cubs, Mom Grizzly gets back at him by making off with Harry. The boy and the bear bond but this interspecies relationship can't last and eventually boy and cubs end up with the right species of parent. **94m/C VHS, DVD. CA GB** Daniel Clark, Bryan Brown, Tom Jackson, Oliver Tobias, Richard Harris; **D:** Stewart Raffill; **W:** Richard Beattie; **C:** Thom Best; **M:** Paul Zaza, David Reilly.

Grizzly Man 🦴🦴🦴½ **2005 (R)** Timothy Treadwell spent 13 summers, beginning in 1990, in the Alaskan wilderness living among grizzly bears until 2003, when he and his girlfriend were killed in a bear attack. Director Herzog is an ideal choice to tell the story of one self-absorbed man's obsession (tinged with madness) as the animals' self-appointed guardian and protector. Herzog includes amateur naturalist Treadwell's video footage as well as interviews and his own narration. **103m/C VHS, DVD. US D:** Werner Herzog; **C:** Peter Zeitlinger; **M:** Richard Thompson. Directors Guild '05: Feature Doc. (Herzog); L.A. Film Critics '05: Feature Doc.; N.Y. Film Critics '05: Feature Doc.; Natl. Soc. Film Critics '05: Feature Doc.

Grizzly Mountain 🦴🦴½ **1997 (G)** Dylan (Dylan Haggerty) and his sister Nicole (Lund) are camping in Oregon with their parents when they decide to explore a cave. After some mysterious rumbling and shaking, the siblings emerge in the 1870s. They meet mountain man Jeremiah (Haggerty), who promises to help them return home, but he's got problems of his own—bad guy Burt (Stephens) wants to dynamite the mountain so the railroad can come through. Pic wanders back and forth between the two time periods and the kids learn a lesson in ecology (and are reunited with their parents). Easy-going; some beautiful scenery. **96m/C VHS, DVD.** Dan Haggerty, Dylan Haggerty, Nicole Lund, Perry Stephens, Kim Morgan Greene, Martin Kove, Robert Budaska, E.E. Bell, Marguerite Hickey, Don Borza; **D:** Jeremy Hatt; **W:** Peter White, Jeremy Hatt; **C:** Andy Parke; **M:** Jon McCallum.

The Groomsmen 🦴🦴 **2006 (R)** Writer, director, actor Ed Burns mines familiar territory with yet another story of Irish-American males struggling with growing up. This time Burns casts himself as a reluctant father-to-be who gets together with his longtime pals to discuss, continuously, their individual plights and struggles, none of which are very interesting or extraordinary, before resigning himself to a life of monogamy and responsibility. Nearly everything is a retread of past Burns' flicks except for the excellent ensemble cast, which includes Jay Mohr as still juvenile cousin Mike and John Leguizamo as T.C., the prodigal friend who returns with a long-held secret. Burns' first version of this story, "The Brothers McMullen" (1995), is still his best. **99m/C DVD. US** Edward Burns, Donal Logue, Jay Mohr, John Leguizamo, Matthew Lillard, Shari Albert, Spencer Fox, John A. Russo, Heather Burns, Jessica Capshaw, Brittany Murphy, Arthur J. Nascarella, Marion McCorry, Joe Pistone, John F. O'Donohue, Jamie Tirelli, Kevin Kash, Catharine Bolz, Amy Leonard; **D:** Edward Burns; **W:** Edward Burns; **C:** William Rexer; **M:** Robert Gray, P.T. Walkley.

could have been told about a homecoming dance or spring break. The changes and discoveries the characters make have not changed. Even though the film was made on a restricted budget—actually shot in Super 16mm.—it looks very good. **86m/C VHS, DVD.** Steve Van Wormer, Lola Glaudini, Hamish Linklater, Denny Kirkwood, Rachel True, MacKenzie Firgens, Nick Offerman, Ari Gold; **D:** Greg Harrison; **W:** Greg Harrison; **C:** Matthew Irving.

The Groove Tube 🦴🦴½ **1972 (R)** A TV series called "The Groove Tube" is the context for these skits that spoof everything on TV from commercials to newscasts. Chevy Chase's movie debut. **75m/C VHS, DVD.** Ken Shapiro, Chevy Chase, Richard Belzer, Marcy Mendham, Bill Kemmill, Ken Shapiro, Alex Stephens, Berkeley Harris, Buzzy Linhart, Richmond Baier; **D:** Ken Shapiro; **W:** Lane Sarasohn, Ken Shapiro; **C:** Bob Bailin.

Gross Anatomy 🦴🦴½ **1989 (PG-13)** Lightweight comedy/drama centers on the trials and tribulations of medical students. Modine is the very bright, but somewhat lazy, future doctor determined not to buy into the bitter competition among his fellow students. His lack of desire inflames Lahti, a professor dying of a fatal disease who nevertheless believes in modern medicine. She pushes and inspires him to focus on his potential, and his desire to help people. Worth watching, in spite of cheap laughs. Interesting cast of up-and-comers. **107m/C VHS, DVD.** Matthew Modine, Daphne Zuniga, Christine Lahti, John Scott Clough, Alice Carter, Robert Desiderio, Zakes Mokae, Todd Field; **D:** Thom Eberhardt; **W:** Ron Nyswaner; **M:** David Newman.

Gross Misconduct 🦴🦴 **1993 (R)** Charismatic university professor Justin Thorne (Smits) makes the nearly fatal mistake of getting involved with his student, Jennifer (Watts). Seems she's one of those obsessive types and when Thorne wants to break off the affair for the sake of his marriage, Jennifer goes over the edge. Thorne's charged with rape and unless Jennifer changes her story his life is over. Based on a true story that happened in the '50s but this version is set in the '90s. **97m/C VHS. AU** Jimmy Smits, Naomi Watts, Sarah Chadwick, Adrian Wright, Alan Fletcher; **D:** George Miller; **W:** Lance Peters, Gerard Maguire; **C:** David Connell.

Grosse Fatigue 🦴🦴 **1994 (R)** *Dead Tired* Diminutive comic everyman Blanc successfully takes up the challenge of a dual role of mistaken identity (as well as directing and writing chores). He first plays himself, bewildered by accusations of lechery and other escapades, who learns he has a psychopath double who's stolen his celebrity. So it's up to Michel and pal Carole (the gorgeous Bouquet) to track down the mischief-maker before Blanc's reputation is in complete tatters: French with subtitles. **85m/C VHS, DVD. FR** Michel Blanc, Carole Bouquet, Philippe Noiret, Josiane Balasko; **Cameos:** Charlotte Gainsbourg, Mathilda May, Thierry Lhermitte, Roman Polanski; **D:** Michel Blanc; **W:** Michel Blanc; **C:** Eduardo Serra; **M:** Rene Marc Bini.

Grosse Pointe Blank 🦴🦴🦴 **1997 (R)** Stressed-out Martin Q. Blank (Cusack) debates with his nervous shrink (Arkin) about whether to attend his 10-year high school reunion. He doesn't want to deal with the Debi (Driver), the girl he ditched on prom night, the incessant small talk, or the prospect of telling his classmates that he's a professional hit man. Then there's the matter of rival pro Grocer (Aykroyd), who wants to start an assassins union. Dark comedy with excellent writing, a charmingly off-center lead by Cusack, who attended his own reunion as research, and a surprising amount of action. Pasadena fills in for most of Grosse Pointe, but the Detroit shots are real. **107m/C VHS, DVD.** John Cusack, Minnie Driver, Dan Aykroyd, Alan Arkin, Joan Cusack, Jeremy Piven, Mitchell Ryan, Hank Azaria, Michael Cudlitz, Benny "The Jet" Urquidez, Barbara Harris, Ann Cusack, K. Todd Freeman; **D:** George Armitage; **W:** Tom Jankiewicz, D.V. DeVincentis, Steve Pink; **M:** Tom Jankiewicz; **C:** Jamie Anderson; **M:** Joe Strummer.

Grotesque 🐺 woof! *1987 (R)* After slaughtering a young woman's family as they vacationed in a remote mountain cabin, a gang of bloodthirsty punks are attacked by the family secret, the deformed son. The title says it all. *79m/C VHS.* Linda Blair, Nels Van Patten, Brad Wilson, Sharon Hughes, Robert Z'Dar, Billy Frank, Michele Bensoussan, Mikel Angel. *D:* Joe Tornatore; *W:* Mikel Angel.

Ground Control 🎬🎬 *1998 (PG-13)* Jack Harris (Sutherland) is a former air traffic controller, who retired after a fatal plane crash. Years later, a old friend asks Jack to help out during a busy night at the Phoenix airport and Jack finds himself being forced to aid in a plane with no radar, contact or control. *98m/C VHS, DVD.* Kiefer Sutherland, Robert Sean Leonard, Kelly McGillis, Henry Winkler, Michael Gross, Margaret Cho, Charles Fleischer, Farrah Forke, Bruce McGill, Kristy Swanson. *D:* Richard Howard.

The Ground Truth 🎬🎬½ *2006 (R)* Compelling but unabashedly biased, go-for-the-jugular documentary about the effect of the Iraq War on the soldiers who've fought it. Filmmaker Foulkrod interviews scores of vets whose the violence of the war (especially against Iraqi civilians) and the struggle to reintegrate into American society in the face of an uncaring government bureaucracy. The movie raises important points about the effect of war on those who wage it, but doesn't reach out to those who think otherwise. *72m/C DVD. US D:* Patricia Foulkrod; *C:* Reuben Aaronson. *M:* Dave Hodge.

Ground Zero 🎬½ *1988 (R)* Ground Zero is the term used to describe the site of a nuclear explosion. San Francisco is threatened with just such a new name in this story of nuclear blackmail. Someone plants an atomic bomb on the Golden Gate Bridge. It must be defused and the culprit caught. *50m/C VHS.* Ron Castee, Melvin Bell, Yvonne D'Angiers. *D:* James T. Flocker.

Ground Zero 🎬🎬 *1988 (R)* Political thriller, set in the Australian outback in the '50s, in which a man searches for the reasons for his father's murder in the films of the British nuclear tests. *109m/C VHS. AU D:* Michael Patterson.

Groundhog Day 🎬🎬🎬 *1993 (PG)* Phil (Murray), an obnoxious weatherman, is in Punxatawney, PA to cover the annual emergence of the famous rodent from its hole. After he's caught in a blizzard that he didn't predict, he finds himself trapped in a time warp, doomed to relive the same day over and over again until he gets it right. Lighthearted romantic comedy, takes a funny premise and manages to carry it through to the end. Murray has fun with the role, although he did get bitten by the groundhog during the scene when they're driving. Elliott is perfectly cast as a smartmouthed cameraman. *103m/C VHS, DVD.* Bill Murray, Andie MacDowell, Chris Elliott, Stephen Tobolowsky, Brian Doyle-Murray, Marita Geraghty, Angela Paton; *D:* Harold Ramis; *C:* John Bailey. *W:* George Fenton. British Acad. '93: Orig. Screenplay, Natl. Film Reg. '06.

The Groundstar Conspiracy 🎬🎬🎬 *1972 (PG)* Spy thriller brings to life L.P. Davias' novel, "The Alien." After an explosion kills all but one space project scientist, Peppard is sent to investigate suspicions of a cover-up. Meanwhile, the surviving scientist (Sarrazin) suffers from disfigurement and amnesia. He pursues his identity while Peppard accuses him of being a spy. Splendid direction by Lamont Johnson. Sarrazin's best role. *96m/C VHS, DVD. CA* George Peppard, Michael Sarrazin, Christine Belford, Cliff Potts, James Olson, Tim O'Connor, James McEachin, Alan Oppenheimer; *D:* Lamont Johnson; *W:* Paul Hoffert.

The Group 🎬🎬½ *1966* Based upon the novel by Mary McCarthy, the well-acted story deals with a group of graduates from a Vassar-like college as they try to adapt to life during the Great Depression. Has some provocative subject matter, including lesbianism, adultery, and mental breakdowns. Soapy, but a good cast with film debuts of Bergen, Hackett, Pettet, Widdoes, and Holbrook. *150m/C VHS.* Candice Bergen, Joanna Pettet, Shirley Knight, Joan Hackett, Elizabeth Hartman, Jessica Walter, Larry Hagman, James Broderick, Kathleen Widdoes, Hal Holbrook, Mary-Robin Redd, Richard Mulligan, Carrie Nye; *D:* Sidney Lumet; *C:* Boris Kaufman.

The Grudge 🎬🎬 *2004 (PG-13)* "Ju-On" and there are still minced groans (of disbelief) than shrieks. Studying social work as an exchange student in Tokyo, Karen (Gellar) discovers elderly Emma (Zabriskie) home alone, her family (Matpother, DuVall) missing. She sees a ghostly boy (Ozeki, who was in two of the Japanese films) and his demonic mother (Fuji, who's been in all five). Karen's scruffy boyfriend (Behr) is lured in, as is her boss (Raimi) and a local detective (Ishibashi). Pullman also appears briefly as an American professor who was an early victim of the house of horrors. Gellar's an old hand at battling things that go bump in the night but this experience isn't worth the expertise. *96m/C DVD, UMD. US D:* Sarah Michelle Gellar, Jason Behr, William Mapother, Clea DuVall, KaDee Strickland, Grace Zabriskie, Bill Pullman, Rosa Blasi, Theodore (Ted) Raimi, Ryo Ishibashi, Yuya Ozeki, Takako Fuji, Yoko Maki; *D:* Takashi Shimizu; *W:* Takashi Shimizu; *C:* Hideo Yamamoto.

The Grudge 2 🎬½ *2006 (PG-13)* Same shriek, different day. Hospitalized in Japan after her last ordeal, Karen (Gellar in a cameo) kills herself in front of her horrified sister Aubrey (Tamblyn). Naturally, Aubrey now wants to discover what lead her sis to suicide, which involves those weird mother-child demons and a haunted house best left alone. It's creepy, but lacks new ideas since writer-director Shimizu sticks to his formula, which has served him through four "Ju-Or" flicks and two American remakes. *96m/C DVD. US* Amber Tamblyn, Arielle Kebbel, Sarah Michelle Gellar, Jennifer Beals, Christopher Cousins, Edison Chen, Takako Fuji, Kim Miyori, Oga Tanaka, Teresa Palmer, Misako Uno; *D:* Takashi Shimizu; *W:* Stephen Susco; *C:* Katsumi Yanagijima; *M:* Christopher Young.

Gruesome Twosome 🐺 *1967* Another gutsy/cannibalism/mutilation funfest by Lewis, about someone who's marketing the hair of some very recently deceased college coeds. *75m/C VHS, DVD.* Elizabeth Davis, Gretchen Wells, Chris Martell, Rodney Bedell, Ronnie Cass, Karl Stoeber, Dianne Wilhite, Andrea Barr, Dianne Raymond, Sherry Robinson, Barrie Walton, Michael Lewis, Ray Sager; *D:* Herschel Gordon Lewis; *W:* Allison Louise Downe; *C:* Roy Collodi; *M:* Larry Wellington.

Grumpier Old Men 🎬🎬 *1995 (PG-13)* Max (Matthau) and John (Lemmon) are back at each other's throats, but with John happily married to Ariel (Ann-

---

Margaret), he's not much of an adversary. Enter Maria (Loren), who wants to turn the boys' favorite bait shop into an Italian restaurant. In a twist that should surprise no one, Max soon falls for the beautiful Maria, and she with him. Jokes are similar but more adolescent than in the first, and subplots involving John and Max's kids' wedding and Grandpa's (Meredith) romantic interests are forced. Suffers the standard sequel fate of not measuring up to the original. *101m/C VHS, DVD.* Jack Lemmon, Walter Matthau, Ann-Margret, Sophia Loren, Kevin Pollak, Burgess Meredith, Daryl Hannah, Ann Guilbert; *D:* Howard Deutch; *W:* Mark Steven Johnson.

Grumpy Old Men 🎬🎬 *1993 (PG-13)* Lemmon and Matthau team for their seventh movie, in parts that seem written just for them. Boyhood friends and retired neighbors, they have been feuding for so long that neither of them can remember why. Doesn't matter much, when it provides a reason for them to spout off at each other every morning and play nasty practical jokes every night. This, and ice-fishing, is life as they know it, until feisty younger woman Ann-Margret moves into the neighborhood and lights some long-dormant fires. 83-year-old Meredith is a special treat playing Lemmon's 90-something father. Filmed in Wabasha, Minnesota, and grumpy, in the most pleasant way. *104m/C VHS, DVD.* Jack Lemmon, Walter Matthau, Ann-Margret, Burgess Meredith, Daryl Hannah, Kevin Pollak, Ossie Davis, Buck Henry, Christopher McDonald; *D:* Donald Petrie; *W:* Mark Steven Johnson. *C:* Johnny E. Jensen; *M:* Alan Silvestri.

Grunt! The Wrestling Movie 🐺 woof! *1985 (R)* A spoof of documentaries about the behind-the-scenes world of wrestling. For fans only. *91m/C VHS.* Wally Greene, Steven Cepello, Dick Murdoch, John Tolos; *D:* Allan Holzman.

Gryphon *1988* Ricky's new teacher can do all sorts of magical things. Hidden among her tricks are lessons about creativity, beauty, and imagination. Adapted from the short story by Charles Baxter. Aired on PBS as part of the "Wonderworks" family movie series. *58m/C VHS.* Amanda Plummer, Sully Diaz, Alexis Cruz; *D:* Mark Cullingham.

Guadalcanal Diary 🎬🎬½ *1943* A vintage wartime flag-waver, with a typical crew of Marines battling the "Yellow Menace" over an important base on the famous Pacific atoll. Based on Richard Tregaskis' first-hand account. *93m/B VHS, DVD.* Preston Foster, Lloyd Nolan, William Bendix, Richard Conte, Anthony Quinn, Richard Jaeckel, Roy Roberts, Minor Watson, Miles Mander, Ralph Byrd, Lionel Stander, Reed Hadley, John Archer, Eddie Acuff, Lester Jackson, Paul Fung; *D:* Lewis Seiler; *W:* Lamar Trotti, Jerome Cady; *C:* Charles Clarke; *M:* David Buttolph.

Guantanamera 🎬🎬🎬 *1995* A famous singer arrives to her hometown of Guantanamo for the first time in 50 years, is reunited with her first sweetheart, and promptly dies. Her niece Georgina (Ibarra) comes to take her remains back to Havana, along with her husband Adolfo (Cruz), an oafish Communist Party worker who has devised a bizarre relay system to transport corpses in order to save gasoline. Also in the caravan is Mariano (Perugorria), a former student of Georgina's who had a crush on her. Mariano attempts to seduce Georgina, while Adolfo attempts to get a clue. Celebrates the lives of everyday Cubans and skewers bumbling government bureaucrats. The final collaboration between directors Gutierrez Alea, who died in 1996, and Tabio. Spanish with subtitles. *104m/C VHS, DVD. CU* Carlos Cruz, Mirta Ibarra, Jorge Perugorria, Raul Eguren, Pedro Fernandez; *D:* Tomas Gutierrez Alea, Juan Carlos Tabio; *W:* Tomas Gutierrez Alea, Juan Carlos Tabio; *C:* Hans Burman; *M:* Jose Nieto.

The Guardian 🎬½ *1984 (R)* Residents of a chic New York apartment building hire a security expert/ex-military man to aid them in combatting their crime problem. But one of the liberal tenants thinks their guard's methods may come at too

---

high a cost. *102m/C VHS.* Martin Sheen, Louis Gossett Jr., Arthur Hill; *D:* David Greene; *M:* Jonathan Goldsmith. *CABLE.*

The Guardian 🎬 *2000 (R)* A young couple unwittingly hires a human sacrificial child. Based on the book "The Nanny" by Dan Greenburg. *92m/C VHS, DVD.* Jenny Seagrove, Dwier Brown, Carey Lowell, Brad Hall, Miguel Ferrer, Natalija Nogulich, Pamela Brull, Gary Swanson; *D:* William Friedkin; *W:* William A. Alonzo; *M:* Jack Hues.

The Guardian 🎬½ *2001 (R)* So soldier Van Peebles witnesses the escape of a demon while stationed in the middle east (although they doesn't know what he's really seen) and 12 years later must battle said demon to save the world. There are other plot threads but they don't make much sense either. *89m/C VHS, DVD.* James Remar, Ice-T, Mario Van Peebles; *D:* John Terlesky, Gary J. Tunnicliffe; *W:* Jeff Yagher.

The Guardian 🎬🎬½ *2006 (PG-13)* Costner has settled comfortably into mentor mode in this familiar action story. Legendary Coast Guard rescue swimmer Ben Randall's wife has left him, his crew died during their last mission, and he's become an unwilling and unorthodox instructor to the Guard's latest recruits. Naturally, his biggest challenge is a cocky, younger version of himself—Jake Fischer (Kutcher). But Ben is just the guy to whip Jake into shape as they bond over past mistakes and insecurities. Kutcher's a surprisingly good match for Costner as the troubled newbie. *139m/C DVD. US* Kevin Costner, Ashton Kutcher, Melissa Sagemiller, Clancy Brown, Bonnie Bramlett, Sela Ward, Neal McDonough, John Heard, Brian Geraghty, Dule Hill, Shelby Fenner, Alex Daniels; *D:* Andrew Davis; *W:* Ron L. Brinkerhoff. *C:* Stephen St. John; *M:* Trevor Rabin.

Guardian Angel 🎬🎬 *1994 (R)* Detective Christy McKay (Rothrock) quits the force after her partner/lover is killed by icy seductress Nina (Denier), who manages to escape from jail. When McKay is hired to protect playboy Lawton Hobbs (McVicar), she firds that the threat comes from a psycho ex-girlfriend. Guess who? *90m/C VHS, DVD.* Cynthia Rothrock, Lydie Denier, Daniel McVicar, Kenneth McLeod, Marshall Teague, John O'Leary, Dale Jacoby; *D:* Richard W. Munchkin.

Guardian of the Abyss 🎬 *1982* Beyond Justice A young couple who buy an antique mirror get more than they bargained for when they discover that it is the threshold to Hell and the devil wants to come through. *60m/C VHS, DVD.* Ray Lonnen, Rosalyn Landor, Paul Darrow, Barbara Ewing; *D:* Don Sharp.

Guarding Eddy 🎬½ *2004 (PG)* Autistic 18-year-old Eddy Patterson (Presley) runs away from home to fulfill his dream of playing basketball with the Los Angeles Clippers. He winds up in a homeless shelter and meets injured NBA hopeful Mike Jeffreys (Ellsworth), who's doing community service. Naturally, the two bond in this sappy inspirational flick. *96m/C DVD.* Brian Presley, Kiko Ellsworth, Lee Garlington, Anna Maria Hostord; *D:* Scott McKinsey; *W:* Paul Davidson; *C:* Christopher Norr; *M:* Scott Kay. *VIDEO*

Guarding Tess 🎬🎬 *1994 (PG-13)* Long-suffering Secret Service agent Cage is nearing the end of his three-year assignment to crotchety widowed First Lady MacLaine when the Prez extends his tour of duty. Feels like a TV movie, not surprising since writers Torckvei and Wilson have several sitcoms to their credit, including "WKRP" in Cincinnati." Nice chemistry between Cage and MacLaine results in a few funny moments, but there are too many formulaic plot twists. End result: a pleasant, if somewhat slow buddy comedy. **98m/C VHS, DVD.** Shirley MacLaine, Nicolas Cage, Austin Pendleton, Edward Albert, Richard Griffiths, Dale Dye; **D:** Hugh Wilson; **W:** Hugh Wilson, Peter Torokvei; **C:** Brian Reynolds; **M:** Michael Convertino.

The Guardsman ♪♪♪ 1931 Broadway's illustrious couple Lunt and Fontanne shine in this adaptation of the clever marital comedy by French playwright Molnar in which they also starred. This sophisticated comedy was their only starring film, although they were offered large sums of money to appear in other movies—they just couldn't tear themselves away from the stage. Remade as "The Chocolate Soldier" and "Lily in Love." **89m/B VHS.** Alfred Lunt, Lynn Fontanne, Roland Young, Zasu Pitts, Maude Eburne, Herman Bing, Ann Dvorak; **D:** Sidney Franklin.

Guerilla Brigade ♪♪½ *Riders* 1939 A rarely seen Ukrainian epic about Russian/Ukrainian solidarity during the Civil War. In Russian with English subtitles. **90m/B VHS.** *RU* Stephan Shkurat, Lev Sverdlin, Pyotr Masokha, Vladimir Osvetsimsky; **D:** Igor Savchenko; **W:** Vsevolod Pavlovsky; **C:** Vladimir Okulich; **M:** Sergei Pototsky.

Guess What We Learned in School Today? woof! 1970 (R) Parents in a conservative suburban community protest sex education in the schools. Intended as a satire, but it only reinforces stereotypes. **85m/C VHS.** Richard Carballo, Devin Goldenberg; **D:** John G. Avildsen.

Guess Who ♪♪ 2005 (PG-13) Guess who thought it was a good idea to remake the classic 1967 Spencer Tracy/ Sidney Poitier drama as a tepid comedy starring two sitcom actors? Columbia Pictures, apparently, but they're definitely in the minority. On the eve of his anniversary, successful black businessman Percy Jones (Mac) is introduced to his daughter's new boyfriend, goofy white dude Simon (Kutcher). Unnerved by the interracial relationship, Percy struggles to cope, while Simon tries his best to fit in and win Percy over. Mac works overtime to rise above the material, but the repetitive "white guy" jokes and inappropriate slapstick diminish the film's message of racial tolerance, making it come across instead as a low-rent "Meet the Parents" rip-off. **105m/C DVD, UMD.** *US* Bernie Mac, Ashton Kutcher, Zoe Saldana, Judith Scott, Hal Williams, RonReaco Lee, Kellee Stewart, Robert Curtis Brown, Nicole Sullivan, Jessica Cauffiel, Kimberly Scott, Denise Dowse, Niecy Nash, Sherri Shepherd, Paula Krumholtz; Mike Epps; **D:** Kevin Rodney Sullivan; **W:** Peter Tolan, Jay Scherick, David Ronn; **C:** Karl Walter Lindenlaub; **M:** John Murphy.

Guess Who's Coming to Dinner ♪♪♪ 1967 Controversial in its time. A young white woman brings her black fiance home to meet her parents. The situation truly tests their open-mindedness and understanding. Hepburn and Tracy (in his last film appearance) are wonderful and serve as the anchors in what would otherwise have been a rather sugary film. Houghton, who portrays the independent daughter, is the real-life niece of Hepburn. Spencer Tracy, Sidney Poitier, Katharine Hepburn, Cecil Kellaway, Beah Richards, Roy Glenn, Isabel Sanford; **D:** Stanley Kramer; **W:** William Rose; **C:** Sam Leavitt; **M:** Frank DeVol. Oscars '67: Actress (Hepburn), Story & Screenplay; AFI '98: Top 100; British Acad. '68: Actor (Tracy), Actress (Hepburn).

Guest in the House ♪♪½ 1944 A seemingly friendly young female patient is invited to stay in the family home of her doctor. She skillfully attempts to dissect the family's harmony in the process. **121m/B VHS, DVD.** Anne Baxter, Ralph Bellamy, Ruth Warrick, Marie McDonald, Margaret Hamilton, Aline McMahon, Scott McKay, Jerome Cowan, Percy Kilbride, Connie Laird; **D:** John Brahm; **W:** Ketti Frings; **C:** Lee Garmes; **M:** Werner Janssen.

Guest Wife ♪♪½ 1945 Determined to impress his sentimental boss, a quick-thinking bachelor talks his best friend's wife into posing as his own wife, but the hoax gets a bit out of hand and nearly ruins the real couple's marriage. **90m/B VHS.** Claudette Colbert, Don Ameche, Dick Foran, Charles Dingle, Wilma Francis; **D:** Sam Wood; **C:** Joseph Valentine.

A Guide for the Married Man ♪♪♪ 1967 One suburban husband instructs another in adultery, with a cast of dozens enacting various slapstick cameos. Based on Frank Tarloff's novel of the same name. Followed by "A Guide for the Married Woman." **91m/C VHS, DVD.** Walter Matthau, Robert Morse, Inger Stevens, Sue Ane Langdon, Claire Kelly, Elaine Devry; *Cameos:* Lucille Ball, Sid Caesar, Jack Benny, Wally Cox, Jayne Mansfield, Louis Nye, Carl Reiner, Phil Silvers, Terry-Thomas, Sam Jaffe, Jeffrey Hunter, Polly Bergen; **D:** Gene Kelly; **W:** Frank Tarloff; **M:** John Williams.

A Guide for the Married Woman ♪½ 1978 A bored housewife tries to take the romantic advice of a girlfriend to add a little spice to her life. A poor TV follow-up to "A Guide for the Married Man." **96m/C VHS, DVD.** Cybill Shepherd, Barbara Feldon, Eve Arden, Chuck Woolery, Peter Marshall, Charles Frank; **D:** Hy Averback. TV

A Guide to Recognizing Your Saints ♪♪♪ 2006 (R) More than anything Dito Montiel (LeBeouf) wants to get out of his 1986 Queens' Astoria neighborhood and away from his irascible father Monty (Palminteri). But for now, Dito hangs out with his pals, especially tough thug Antonio (Tatum) and Irish newcomer Mike (Compston), as well as girlfriend Laurie (Diaz). But the streets are changing—and not for the better. Years later, Dito (now played by Downey Jr.) returns home because his dad is dying. However, not everyone he knew is there to say hello. Based on debut writer/director Montiel's coming-of-age memoir. **98m/C DVD.** *US* Shia LaBeouf, Robert Downey Jr., Chazz Palminteri, Dianne Wiest, Channing Tatum, Melonie Diaz, Martin Compston, Eric Roberts, Rosario Dawson; **D:** Dito Montiel; **W:** Dito Montiel; **C:** Eric Gautier; **M:** Jonathan Elias.

The Guilty ♪♪ 1999 (R) Lawyer Callum Crane (Pullman) has a drunken sexual tryst with his new secretary, Sophie (Anwar), and suddenly his life is spiraling out-of-control. Sophie tries to blackmail him when Crane is appointed a federal judge and he decides to hire Nathan (Sawa), a young man who's just been released from prison, to bump her off. But Nathan's not exactly who he seems and, of course, nothing goes exactly as planned. It's a complex thriller with a good ensemble cast. **112m/C VHS, DVD.** Bill Pullman, Gabrielle Anwar, Devon Sawa, Angela Featherstone, Joanne Whalley, Jaimz Woolvett, Ken Tremblett, Camilla Overbye Roos; **D:** Anthony Waller; **W:** William Davies; **C:** Tobias Schliessler; **M:** Debbie Wiseman.

Guilty as Charged ♪½ 1992 (R) A butcher rigs his own private electric chair and captures and executes paroled killers in his personal quest for justice. But when a politician frames an innocent man for murder how far will this vigilante go? **95m/C VHS, DVD.** Rod Steiger, Lauren Hutton, Heather Graham, Isaac Hayes; **D:** Sam Irvin; **M:** Steve Bartek.

Guilty as Sin ♪♪ 1993 (R) Johnson is a ruthless Casanova accused of murdering his very wealthy wife and decides lawyer DeMornay is just the woman to defend him. Question is, who'll defend DeMornay from him? Johnson has fun as the menacing smoothie but DeMornay's supposedly hotshot criminal attorney is just plain dumb. It sounds like "Jagged Edge" but there's no sexual involvement between client and lawyer and no thrill in this thriller. **120m/C VHS, DVD.** Don Johnson, Rebecca De Mornay, Jack Warden, Stephen Lang, Dana Ivey, Ron White, Sean McCann, Luis Guzman; **D:** Sidney Lumet; **W:** Larry Cohen; **C:** Andrzej Bartkowiak.

Guilty by Association ♪♪ 2003 Very graphic look at street life and its consequences set in Washington, DC. A young man tries to support his girlfriend and their daughter without turning to drug dealing and other criminal activities but the local gang members show him the supposed lure of easy money and what it can buy. Although Freeman's name and face on prominently featured on the box art, his part as a good cop is small. **80m/C VHS, DVD.** Daemon Moore, Jeff Edward, Morgan Freeman; **D:** Po Johns; **W:** Howard Gibson; **C:** Sean Morrison; **M:** Nicholas Rivera. VIDEO

Guilty by Suspicion ♪♪½ 1991 (PG-13) Examination of the 1950s McCarthy investigations by the House Un-American Activities Committee comes off like a bland history lesson. De Niro plays a director who attended a Communist party meeting in the '30s but who otherwise doesn't have any red connections. He takes the moral high ground and refuses to incriminate his buddies (Wendt) to get off the hook and finds himself blacklisted. Characterized by average performances (excepting Wettig who goes overboard) and a lightweight script. "The Front" (1976) does a better job on this topic. Directorial debut for producer Winkler. **105m/C VHS, DVD.** Robert De Niro, Annette Bening, George Wendt, Patricia Wettig, Sam Wanamaker, Chris Cooper, Ben Piazza, Martin Scorsese, Barry Primus, Gailard Sartain, Stuart Margolin, Barry Tubb, Roxann Biggs-Dawson, Robin Gammell, Brad Sullivan, Luke Edwards, Adam Baldwin, Stephen (Steve) Root, Tom Sizemore, Illeana Douglas, Jon Tenney; **D:** Irwin Winkler; **W:** Irwin Winkler; **C:** Michael Ballhaus; **M:** James Newton Howard.

Guilty Conscience ♪♪♪ 1985 Anthony Hopkins plays a successful attorney who plots his wife's murder, but is it fantasy or reality? Excellent cast and intricate plot combine for a satisfying mystery. **90m/C VHS.** Anthony Hopkins, Blythe Danner, Swoosie Kurtz; **D:** David Greene; **W:** Richard Levinson, William Link; **C:** Stevan Larner; **M:** Billy Goldenberg. TV

Guilty of Innocence ♪♪ 1987 (PG) A young African-American man finds he's guilty until proven innocent when he runs into the law in Texas. A bold lawyer joins his fight for justice. Based on a true story. **95m/C VHS.** Dorian Harewood, Dabney Coleman, Hoyt Axton, Paul Winfield, Dennis Lipscomb, Debbi (Deborah) Morgan, Marshall Colt, Victor Love; **D:** Richard T. Heffron. TV

Guilty of Treason ♪♪½ 1950 A documentary on the life and times of Joszaf Cardinal Mindszenty of Hungary, who was imprisoned by the communists as an enemy of the state for speaking out against the totalitarian regime. At the trial, it was revealed that the Cardinal's confession was obtained only by the use of drugs, hypnosis, and torture. A realistic look at the dark side of Communism. **86m/B VHS, DVD.** Charles Bickford, Paul Kelly, Bonita Granville, Richard Derr, Berry Kroeger, Elisabeth Risdon, Roland Winters, John Banner; **D:** Felix Feist.

The Guinea Pig ♪♪½ *The Outsider* 1948 Jack Read (Attenborough), the son of a tobacconist, is sent to a posh public school as an experiment but finds problems between his simple upbringing and the reactions of teachers and other students. **97m/B VHS.** *GB* Richard Attenborough, Joan Hickson, Bernard Miles, Sheila Sim, Robert Flemyng, Timothy Bateson; **D:** Roy Boulting; **W:** Bernard Miles, Roy Boulting.

Guinevere ♪♪ 1999 (R) Harper (Polley) is an uncertain, inexperienced 20-year-old in San Francisco who ditches family responsibilities at her sister's wedding reception in order to talk to forty-something photographer Connie Fitzpatrick (Rea). Worldly wise and a natural charmer, Connie soon has Harper as his latest "Guinevere," the innocent young women he beds and nurtures until they outgrow the need for his guidance. Harper certainly doesn't seem to have much personality on her own but Connie also needs something of a lifeline as his drinking increases while his job prospects decline. Polished production with compelling performances by both Polley and Rea. **104m/C VHS, DVD.** Stephen Rea, Sarah Polley, Jean Smart, Gina Gershon, Paul Dooley, Francis Guinan, Jasmine Guy, Sandra Oh, Emily Procter, Gedde Watanabe; **D:** Audrey Wells; **W:** Audrey Wells; **C:** Charles Minsky; **M:** Christophe Beck. Sundance '99: Screenplay.

Guitarman ♪ 1995 Modern version of "The Pied Piper of Hamlin" finds a mysterious musician saving a farming community's crops from a plague of locusts. But when the mayor reneges on paying the piper (so to speak), he takes the town's children instead. **92m/C VHS.** Nicholas (Nick) Campbell, Donnelly Rhodes, Andrea Martin, Shawn Ashmore, Jack Semple; **D:** Will Dixon.

Gulag ♪♪½ 1985 An American sportscaster is wrongly sentenced to ten years of hard labor in a Soviet prison, and plans his escape from the cruel guards. Good suspense. **130m/C VHS, DVD.** *GB* David Keith, Malcolm McDowell, Wally Suter, Warren Clarke, John McEnery; **D:** Roger Young; **M:** Elmer Bernstein. TV

Gulliver's Travels ♪♪ 1939 The Fleischer Studio's animated version of Jonathan Swift's classic about the adventures of Gulliver, an English sailor who is washed ashore in the land of Lilliput, where everyone is about two inches tall. **74m/C VHS, DVD. D:** Dave Fleischer; **W:** Dan Gordon, Tedd Pierce, Edmond Seward, Izzy Sparber; **C:** Charles Schettler; **V:** Lanny Ross, Jessica Dragonette.

Gulliver's Travels ♪♪½ 1977 (G) In this partially animated adventure the entire land of Lilliput has been constructed in miniature. Cartoon and real life mix in a 3-dimensional story of Dr. Lemuel Gulliver and his discovery of the small people in the East Indies. From the classic by Jonathan Swift. **80m/C VHS, DVD.** *GB* Richard Harris, Catherine Schell; **D:** Peter Hunt.

Gulliver's Travels ♪♪½ 1995 (PG) Faithful TV version of Jonathan Swift's 1726 satiric novel. Lemuel Gulliver (Danson) is constructed to Bedlam, an English insane asylum, after having been lost at sea for eight years. While in the asylum he relates his very odd adventures—in the tiny land of Lilliput, among the giants of Brobdingnag, with the silly and impractical intellectuals of Laputa, and finally amidst the brutish human Yahoos, who are ruled by rational talking horses, the Houyhnhnms. Meanwhile, Gulliver's wife Mary (Steenburgen) and son Tom (Sturridge) struggle to prove his sanity and win his release. On two cassettes. **187m/C VHS, DVD.** Ted Danson, Mary Steenburgen, Edward Fox, Thomas Sturidge, Edward Woodward, Nicholas Lyndhurst, Peter O'Toole, Phoebe Nicholls, Ned Beatty, Kate Maberly, Alfre Woodard, Geraldine Chaplin, John Standing, Warwick Davis, Robert Hardy, Shashi Kapoor, Karyn Parsons, Edward Petheridge; **D:** Charles Sturridge; **W:** Simon Moore; **C:** Howard Atherton; **M:** Trevor Jones. TV

Gumball Rally ♪♪ 1976 (PG) An unusual assortment of people converge upon New York for a cross country car race to Long Beach, California where breaking the rules is part of the game. **107m/C VHS, DVD.** Michael Sarrazin, Gary Busey, Raul Julia, Nicholas Pryor, Tim McIntire, Susan Flannery; **D:** Charles "Chuck" Ball; **W:** Leon Capetanos.

Gumby: The Movie ♪♪½ 1995 (G) Gumby and his musical group, the Clayboys, seek to save their neighbors' farms from foreclosure by putting on a benefit concert. And yes, pal Pokey is along to help out. But 90 minutes of our gentle clay hero stretches the patience of even the most enthusiastic fan. **90m/C VHS. D:** Art Clokey; **W:** Art Clokey.

Gummo woof! 1997 (R) "Kids" scripter and first time helmer Korine shamelessly parades out the freaks and calls it entertainment. More like a series of grisly images than a cohesive narrative when nihilism pervades a group of disaffected Xenia, Ohio teens who explore every brand of atrocity for kicks. Disturbing, not only in the graphic violence of the bored juvies but also in the frightening lack of a point to this uneven and self-indulgent shock-fest. Touted as modern movie's golden-boy, 23 year-old Korine doesn't let any dark rumor slip in to detract from the purely revolting scenarios. The images that do summon up some truth about growing up in a dead-end town are far overshadowed by the collection of images as a whole. Renowned French cinematographer Escoffier lends style to this lost cause. **88m/C VHS, DVD.** Chloe Sevigny, Jacob Reynolds, Jacob Sewell, Nick Sutton, Carisa Bara, Darby Dougherty, Max Perlich, Linca Manz; **D:** Harmony Korine; **W:** Harmony Korine; **C:** Jean-Yves Escoffier.

The Gumshoe Kid 𝒵𝒵 *The Detective Kid* 1990 (R) A college-bound kid enters the family detective business to prevent his mother from being evicted. He gets in over his head though, trying to track the fiancee of a wealthy mobster. Naturally, as in all good noir worlds, he must save a femme fatale blonde (Thompson) from a killer. **101m/C VHS, DVD.** Jim Metzler, Billy Bob Thornton, Andrea Thompson, John Ritter, Kay Lenz, Victoria Lenz, Paula Marshall; **D:** Stefani Ames; **W:** Stefani Ames, Tom Epperson; **C:** Carlos Gaviria; **M:** Larry Manfredini.

Gun Cargo 𝒵 1949 Muddled story about a conniving shipowner who fires his crew for demanding shore leave. He replaces them with assorted low-lifes, resulting in the usual hijinks. A terrible performance by an otherwise great cast. **49m/C VHS.** Rex Lease, Smith Ballew, William Farnum, Gibson Gowrand; **D:** Jack Irwin; **W:** Jack Irwin; **C:** Edward A. Full.

Gun Code 𝒵1/2 1940 The white-hatted cowboy hero puts a stop to small-town racketeering. **52m/B VHS.** Tim McCoy, Ina Guest; **D:** Sam Newfield.

Gun Crazy 𝒵𝒵𝒵1/2 *Deadly is the Female* 1949 Annie Laurie Starr—Annie Oakley in a Wild West show—meets gun-lovin' Bart Tare, who says a gun makes him feel good inside, "like I'm somebody." Sparks fly, and the two get married and live happily ever after—until the money runs out and fatal femme Laurie's craving for excitement and "violence starts to flare up. The two become lovebirds-on-the-lam. Now a cult fave, it's based on a MacKinlay Kantor story. Ex-stuntman Russell Harlan's photography is daring; the realism of the impressive robbery scenes is owed in part to the technical consultation of former train robber Al Jennings. And watch for a young Tamblyn as the 14-year-old Bart. **87m/B VHS, DVD.** Peggy Cummins, John Dall, Berry Kroeger, Morris Carnovsky, Anabel Shaw, Nedrick Young, Trevor Bardette, Russ Tamblyn, Harry Lewis, Mickey Little, Paul Frison, Dave Bair, Stanley Prager, Virginia Farmer, Anne O'Neal, Frances Irwin, Don Beddoe, Robert Osterloh, Shimen Ruskin, Harry Hayden; **D:** Joseph H. Lewis; **W:** Dalton Trumbo; **C:** Russell Harlan; **M:** Victor Young. Natl. Film Reg. '98.

Gun Fury 𝒵𝒵1/2 1953 A panoramic western about a Civil War veteran pursuing the bandits who kidnapped his beautiful bride-to-be. First screened as a 3-D movie. **83m/C VHS, DVD.** Rock Hudson, Donna Reed, Phil Carey, Lee Marvin; **D:** Raoul Walsh.

A Gun, a Car, a Blonde 𝒵𝒵 1997 Paraplegic Richard Spraggins (Metzler) escapes from his pain-filled life by imagining himself to be living in a '50s film noir world, where he takes on the persona of tough private eye Rick Stone. Naturally, as in all good noir worlds, he must save a femme fatale blonde (Thompson) from a killer. **101m/C VHS, DVD, GB** Jim Metzler, Billy Bob Thornton, Andrea Thompson, John Ritter, Kay Lenz, Victoria Lenz, Paula Marshall; **D:** Stefani Ames; **W:** Stefani Ames, Tom Epperson; **C:** Carlos Gaviria; **M:** Larry Manfredini.

A Gun in the House 𝒵 1981 While being attacked in her own home, a woman shoots one of her assailants. The police find no conclusive evidence of attack and arrest the woman for murder. Exploitive drama on gun control. **100m/C VHS.** Sally Struthers, David Ackroyd, Joel Bailey, Jeffrey Tambor; **D:** Ivan Nagy. **TV**

Gun Law 𝒵1/2 1933 The hero tackles the Sonora Kid, an outlaw terrorizing Arizona folk. One of the few sound westerns with Hoxie, a silent-era star who hung up his spurs when his voice proved non-photogenic. **59m/B VHS.** Jack Hoxie, Paul Fix, Mary Carr, Edmund Cobb, Robert Burns; **D:** Lewis D. Collins.

Gun Lords of Stirrup Basin 𝒵𝒵 1937 A cattleman and the daughter of a homesteader are in love in the Old West, but a seedy lawyer wants to douse their flame. Bullets and fists fly as a result. **55m/B VHS.** Bob Steele, Louise Stanley, Karl Hackett, Ernie Adams, Frank LaRue, Frank Ball, Steve Clark; **D:** Sam Newfield.

Gun Packer 𝒵𝒵 1938 When an outlaw gang robs stagecoaches of their gold and causes the body to salt barren mine shafts so the unsuspecting can be swindled out of their money on worthless gold mine certificates, hard-riding Randall is called in to save the day. **51m/B VHS.** Jack "Blackie" King, Glenn Strange; **D:** Wallace Fox; **W:** Robert Emmett.

The Gun Ranger 𝒵𝒵1/2 1934 Our hero plays a Texas Ranger who becomes fed up with soft judges and shady prosecutors and decides to take the law into his own hands. Mexican bandits believe the rancher's property houses a revolutionary fortune, and set about recovering it. The brother defends his father's ranch along with a sidekick, who sweeps the sister off her feet. **56m/B VHS, DVD.** Bob Steele, Eleanor Stewart, John Merton, Ernie Adams, Charles French; **D:** Albert Herman.

Gun Girls 𝒵 1956 Campy exploitation flick about a gun-toting gang of girls who rob anything or anyone. The guy who fences their goods ends up getting one of them pregnant. **67m/C VHS.** Timothy Farrell, Jean Ferguson, Jacquelyn Park, Eve Brent; **D:** Robert Dertano.

Gun Glory 𝒵𝒵1/2 1957 Granger plays Tom Early, a gunslinger who returns home after three years to find the town has no respect when he stops a murderer from invading their town with his cattle herd. Based on the novel "Man of the West" by Phillip Yordan. **88m/C VHS.** Stewart Granger, Rhonda Fleming, Chill Wills, Steve Rowland, James Gregory, Jacques Aubuchon, Arch Johnson, William "Bill" Fawcett, Lane Bradford, Michael Dugan, Bud Osborne, Max McAvoy, Charles Herbert, Carl Pitti; **D:** Roy Rowland; **W:** William Ludwig; **M:** Jeff Alexander.

Gun Grit 𝒵 1936 An FBI agent is sent west to break up a protection racket. **51m/B VHS.** Jack Perrin, Ethel Beck, David Sharpe, Roger Williams, Budd Buster; **D:** William Berke.

The Gun in Betty Lou's Handbag 𝒵𝒵 1992 (PG-13) Shy, small-town librarian with a dull marriage is looking for excitement when she stumbles across a gun used in a murder. She decides excitement will follow her (false) confession to the crime, leaving her husband and thunderstruck, the police confused, and the gossip line humming. She also intrigues the real bad guy, who comes looking for her. Lame silliness is redeemed somewhat by Miller, but there's some surprisingly nasty violence given the comedy label. **89m/C VHS, DVD.** Penelope Ann Miller, Eric Thal, Alfre Woodard, Cathy Moriarty, William Forsythe, Julianne Moore, Xander Berkeley, Michael O'Neill, Christopher John Fields; **D:** Richard Allan Moyle; **W:** Grace Cary Bickley; **M:** Richard Gibbs.

A Gunfight 𝒵𝒵 1971 (PG) When Cash is stranded n a small Western town, he meets up with fellow old-time gunfighter Douglas. The two strike up a friendship, but discover the town folk expect a gun battle. Needing money, the two arrange a gunfight for paic admission—winner take all. Cash makes his screen debut. **90m/C** Kirk Douglas, Johnny Cash, Jane Alexander, Karen Black, Dana Elcar, Keith Carradine, Raf Vallone; **D:** Lamont Johnson; **W:** Harold Jack Bloom.

The Gunfight at Dodge City 𝒵𝒵 1959 Bat Masterson (McCrea) is pressured to become the sheriff of Dodge City and immediately has problems with the crooked local politicians and the more trouble when his old gang shows up in town. Typical oater that McCrea originally intended to be his final picture before his retirement from the screen. **80m/C DVD.** Joel McCrea, Julie Adams, John McIntire, Nancy Gates, Richard Anderson, Don Haggerty, James Westerfield; **D:** Joseph M. Newman; **W:** Martin Goldsmith, Daniel Ullman; **C:** Carl Guthrie; **M:** Hans J. Salter.

Gunfight at Red Sands 𝒵𝒵 *Gringo; Duello Nel Texas* 1963 Landmark western in the history of Italian cinema. Long before Leone's Eastwood trilogy, this film

Gun Riders 𝒵1/2 *Five Bloody Graves; Five Bloody Days to Tombstone; Lonely Man* 1969 Gunman must seek out and stop a murderer of innocent people. **88m/C VHS, DVD.** Scott Brady, Jim Davis, John Carradine; **D:** Al Adamson.

Gun Shy 𝒵𝒵 2000 (R) Psychiatry and organized crime collide again, but this time it's the cops in therapy. Well, one of them is scared. Charlie (Neeson) is a burnedout DEA agent forced back undercover as a go-between for an Italian gangster (Platt) who knows he's cliche and a Colombian drug cartel leader (Zuniga) who believes investing in bean futures is some sort of ethnic no-no. Charlie's work problems lead him to a men's therapy group and a nurse (Bullock) dubbed the "Enema Queen." Yep, it's mostly that kind of humor. The crime figures are thin, and Blakely needs to work on his comic and scene timing, but Neeson fares pretty well. The group sessions are highlights, but the payoff isn't as big as one would hope. **102m/C VHS, DVD.** Liam Neeson, Oliver Platt, Sandra Bullock, Jose Zuniga, Richard Schiff, Andrew Lauer, Mitch Pileggi, Paul Ben-Victor, Mary McCormack, Frank Vincent, Michael Mantell, Louis Giambavo, Gregg Daniel, Michael Delorenzo; **D:** Eric Blakeney; **W:** Eric Blakeney; **C:** Tom Richmond; **M:** Rolfe Kent.

Gun Smoke 𝒵𝒵 1931 A gang of big city thugs high-tails it west when they're glad to get busted for murder and robbery. They land in a small western town in Idaho, where their fancy suits and brim hats get them quickly mistaken for a different type of gang—one with big bucks who will invest in the city. It doesn't take the city boys long to figure out that they can take the town over, and soon reinforcements are arriving by train to help them. But one smart cowboy has them pegged for trouble from the get-go. **71m/B VHS.** Richard Arlen, Mary Brian, William Boyd, Eugene Palette, Charles Winninger, Louise Fazenda, Brooks Benedict; **D:** Edward Sloman; **W:** Grover Jones.

Gunblast 𝒵 1974 A convict is released from San Quentin and wastes no time in getting involved with mob-powered drug smuggling. **70m/C VHS.** Lloyd Allan, Christine Cardan, James Cunningham; **D:** Nick Millard; **W:** Nick Millard.

Guncrazy 𝒵𝒵 1992 (R) Girl from the wrong side of the tracks, abused her entire life, finds her freedom in a gun. She winds up killing the man who raped her, takes up with an equally lost ex-con and the two armed misfits go on the run from the law. Barrymore's convincing and the movie is another well-made variation on the lovers-on-the-run theme. Film was inspired by, but is not a remake of, the 1949 movie "Gun Crazy." **97m/C VHS, DVD.** Drew Barrymore, Ione Skye, Joe Dallesandro, Michael Ironside; **D:** Tamra Davis; **W:** Matthew Bright; **C:** Lisa Rinzler.

Gunfire 𝒵1/2 1950 A Frank James look-alike cavorts, robs and loots the countryside until the real James decides to set things straight. **59m/B VHS, DVD.** Don (Red) Barry, Robert Lowery, Pamela Blake, Wally Vernon, Jan Sterling; **D:** William Berke.

Gung Ho! 𝒵𝒵 1943 Carlson's Raiders are a specially trained group of Marine jungle fighters determined to retake the Pacific island of Makin during WWII. **88m/B VHS, DVD.** Robert Mitchum, Randolph Scott, Noah Beery Jr., Alan Curtis, Grace McDonald; **D:** Ray Enright; **C:** Milton Krasner.

Gung Ho 𝒵𝒵 *China 9, Liberty 37* 1985 (PG-13) A Japanese film takes over a small-town U.S. auto factory and causes major cultural collisions. Keaton plays the go-between as the double-crossing gunman. Keaton's part is pretty puny in this leisurely norse opera. **90m/C VHS, DVD.** ƒƒ Fabio Testi, Warren Oates, Jenny Agutter, Sam Peckinpah; **D:** **M:** Pino Donaggio.

Gunfighter's Moon 𝒵1/2 1996 (PG-13) Legendary gunslinger Frank Morgan (Henriksen) is called on by former lover, Linda (Lenz) to help her sheriff husband prevent a ailbreak. Frank's tired of his constant challengers but can't seem to make another life for himself. **95m/C VHS, DVD.** Lance Henriksen, Kay Lenz, David McIlwraith, Ivan Sergei, Nikki Delbach; **D:** Larry Ferguson; **W:** Larry Ferguson; **C:** James L. Carter; **M:** Lee Holdridge.

Gunfighter 𝒵𝒵 1998 (PG) Gunfighter Sheen is out to avenge the murder of some townsfolk. Then an outlaw kidnaps his girlfriend and things get even more personal. **85m/B VHS.** Angela (Clark) Clarke, Gregory Peck, Helen Westcott, Millard Mitchell, Jean Parker, Karl Malden, Skip Homeier, Mae Marsh; **D:** Clay Boris. **TV**

The Gunfighters 𝒵1/2 1987 Lackluster pilot of a proposed Canadian series pits three individualistic relatives against a powerful empire-builder. **100m/C VHS, DVD.** George Kennedy, Michael Kane, Lori Haller; **D:** CA Art Hindle, Reiner Schone, Anthony Addabbo.

Gunfight at the O.K. Corral 𝒵𝒵𝒵1/2 1957 The story of Wyatt Earp and Doc Holliday joining forces in Dodge City to rid the town of the criminal Clanton gang. Filmed in typical Hollywood style, but redeemed by its great stars. **122m/C VHS, DVD.** Burt Lancaster, Kirk Douglas, Rhonda Fleming, Jo Van Fleet, John Ireland, Kenneth Tobey, Lee Van Cleef, Frank Faylen, DeForest Kelley, Earl Holliman, Dennis Hopper, Martin Milner, Jack Elam, Olive Carey, Joan Camden; **D:** John Sturges; **W:** Leon Uris; **C:** Charles Bryan; **M:** Dimitri Tiomkin.

The Gunfighter 𝒵𝒵1/2 1950 A mature, serious, Hollywood-western character study about an aging gunfighter searching for peace and quiet but unable to avoid his reputation. One of King's best films. **85m/B VHS.** Gregory Peck, Helen Westcott, Millard Mitchell, Jean Parker, Karl Malden, Skip Homeier, Mae Marsh, Jean Parker; **D:** Henry King; **C:** Arthur C. Miller.

introduced the theme of an avenging stranger to the genre. Harrison stars as the dark, brooding hero whose family has been attacked by a gang of bandits. **97m/C VHS, DVD.** **SP** ff Richard Harrison, Giacomo "Jack" Rossi-Stuart, Sara Lezana, Dar (Daniel) Danny) Martin; **D:** Ricardo Blasco; **W:** Albert Band, Ricardo Blasco; **C:** Massimo Dallamano; **M:** Ennio Morricone.

The Gunfighter 𝒵𝒵1/2 1950 A mature, serious, Hollywood-western character study about an aging gunfighter searching for peace and quiet but unable to avoid his reputation. One of King's best films, it invites, it invites. Long naps his reputation and the duel-challenges it invites. One of King's best films. Long maps his reputation and the duel-challenges. Martin Sheen, Clu Gulager; **D:** Christopher Coppola.

VideoHound's Golden Movie Retriever

411

Gunga Din 1939 The prototypical "buddy" film. Three veteran British sergeants in India try to suppress a native uprising, but it's their water boy, the intrepid Gunga Din, who saves the day. Friendship, loyalty, and some of the best action scenes ever filmed. Based loosely on Rudyard Kipling's famous poem, the story is credited to Ben Hecht, Charles MacArthur, and William Faulkner (who is uncredited). Also available colorized. 117m/B VHS, DVD. Cary Grant, Victor McLaglen, Douglas Fairbanks Jr., Sam Jaffe, Eduardo Ciannelli, Montagu Love, Joan Fontaine, Abner Biberman, Robert Coote, Lumsden Hare, Cecil Kellaway, Roland Varno, George Regas, Reginald (Reggie, Reggy) Sheffield, Clive Morgan; D: George Stevens; W: Fred Guiol, Joel Sayre, Ben Hecht, William Faulkner; C: Joseph August; M: Alfred Newman. Natl. Film Reg. '99.

The Gunman 2003 (R) Already tormented by the murder of his wife, crime detective Ben Simms (Flanery) is plunged further into turmoil when given the duty of catching a vigilante who enjoys offing the bad guys...and he discovers that her killer is up next. 91m/C VHS, DVD. Sean Patrick Flanery, Joey Lauren Adams, Mimi Rogers, Brian McNamara, Tom Wright, Jeff Speakman, Emma Nicolas, Steve Krieger, Alaina Kalanj, Daniel Millican; D: Daniel Millican; W: Daniel Millican. VIDEO

Gunman from Bodie 1941 Second of the Rough Rider series. Jones, McCoy, and Hatton rescue a baby orphaned by rustlers and then go after the bad guys. 62m/B VHS, DVD. Tim McCoy, Buck Jones, Raymond Hatton; D: Spencer Gordon Bennet.

Gunman's Walk 1958 Rancher Lee Hackett (Heflin) gained his power through his gunslinging skill but wants his two sons to be respectable citizens. However, hot-tempered eldest son Ed (Hunter) wants to best the old man's reputation while younger son Davy (Darren) has his own problems when he falls for Sioux half-breed Clee (Grant), whose brother was murdered by Ed. As Ed gets more ruthless, his father must decide how far he's willing to go to protect him. 95m/C VHS. Van Heflin, Tab Hunter, James Darren, Kathryn Grant, Mickey Shaughnessy, Robert F. Simon, Edward Platt, Bert Convy; D: Phil Karlson; W: Frank Nugent; C: Charles Lawton Jr.

Gunmen 1993 (R) A reluctant buddy team face down some bad guys. DEA agent Cole (Van Peebles) teams up with smuggler Dani (Lambert) and his violence-loving henchman (Leary). Adds comedy to the mix as well as shameless action rip-offs from spaghetti westerns. 90m/C VHS, DVD. Christopher Lambert, Mario Van Peebles, Denis Leary, Patrick Stewart, Kadeem Hardison, Sally Kirkland; Cameos: Big Daddy Kane, Ed Lover, Eric B. Rakim, Dr. Dre; D: Deran Sarafian; W: Stephen Sommers; M: John Debney.

Gunner Palace 2004 (PG-13) Frenetic documentary follows the 2/3 Field Artillery Division (known as "The Gunners") of the U.S. Army's First Armored Division as they serve their tour of duty in Iraq. The Gunners have set up camp in a once-opulent Iraqi palace, formerly occupied by one of Saddam Hussein's sons. Tucker and Epperlein ignore the politics behind the war, but rather emphasize the chaotic existence of the soldiers on the frontlines. We watch them daily routines, see them laugh and interact, and listen to them express their feelings about putting their lives on the line. The ugly, grainy camerawork might turn some off, but after all, it presents a compelling snapshot of life during wartime. 85m/C DVD. US D: Michael Tucker, Petra Epperlein; C: Michael Tucker.

Gunners & Guns 1934 Vintage western starring King. 51m/B VHS. Black King, Edmund Cobb, Edna Asetin, Eddie Davis; D: Robert Hoyt.

Gunplay 1951 Two cowboys befriend a boy whose father has been killed and search for the murderer. 61m/B VHS. Tim Holt, Joan Dixon, Richard Martin, Robert Bice, Harper Carter, Mauritz Hugo; D: Lesley Selander; W: Ed Earl Repp; C: J. Roy Hunt; M: Paul Sawtell.

Gunpowder 1987 Two Interpol agents endeavor to stop a crime lord from causing the collapse of the world economy. 85m/C VHS. David Gilliam, Martin Potter, Gordon Jackson, Anthony Schaeffer; D: Norman J. Warren; W: Roy MacLean; C: Alistair Cameron; M: Jeffrey Wood.

The Gunrunner 1984 (R) Costner plays a Canadian mobster, involved in liquor smuggling, who aids a Chinese rebellion in this 1920s drama. Interesting rebellion concept. Received more attention after Costner gained notoriety in later films. 92m/C VHS. CA Kevin Costner, Sara Botsford, Paul Soles; D: Nardo Castillo.

Guns 1990 (R) An international gunrunner puts the moves on buxom women between hair-raising adventures. 95m/C VHS, DVD. Erik Estrada, Dona Speir; D: Andy Sidaris; W: Andy Sidaris.

The Guns and the Fury 1983 Two American oil riggers in the Middle East, circa 1908, are forced to fight off an attack by a vicious Arab sheik and his tribe. 90m/C VHS. Peter Graves, Cameron Mitchell, Michael Ansara, Albert Salmi; D: Tony Zarindast.

Guns at Batasi 1964 Attenborough plays a tough British Sergeant Major stationed in Africa during the anti-colonial 1960s. Ultimately the regiment is threatened by rebel Africans. Fine performances make this rather predictable film watchable. 103m/B VHS, DVD. GB Richard Attenborough, Jack Hawkins, Mia Farrow, Flora Robson, John Leyton; D: John Guillermin; M: John Addison.

Guns Don't Argue 1957 Entertaining schlocker about the rise and fall of famous criminal Dillinger. Non-stop action also features Bonnie and Clyde, Pretty Boy Floyd and Baby Face Nelson. 92m/C VHS, DVD. Myron Healey, Jim Davis, Lyle Talbot, Paul Dubov, Sam Edwards, Richard Crane; D: Bill Karn; W: Phillips Lord; C: William Clothier; M: Paul Dunlap.

Guns for Dollars They Call Me Hallelujah 1973 Mex-Western has four men, including a secret agent and a cossack, tangled up in a fortune in smuggled jewels. Southwood, Agata Flory, Roberto Camardiel, Paolo Gozlino, Rick Boyd; D: Giuliano Carnimeo.

Guns in the Dark 1937 A cowboy vows never to use a gun again when he believes that he accidentally shot his best friend. 60m/C VHS, DVD. Johnny Mack Brown, Claire Rochelle; D: Sam Newfield.

Guns of Diablo 1964 Wagon train master Bronson has to fight a gang that controls the supply depot, all the while showing his young helper (beardless boy Russell) the fascinating tricks of the trade. 91m/C VHS, DVD. Charles Bronson, Kurt Russell, Susan Oliver; D: Boris Sagal.

Guns of Justice Colorado Ranger 1950 Undercover Colorado rangers stop a swindler from forcing homesteaders off their land. 60m/B VHS. James Ellison, Russell Hayden, Tom Tyler, Raymond Hatton; D: Thomas Carr.

The Guns of Navarone 1961 During WWII, British Intelligence on the Middle East sends six men to the Aegean island of Navarone to destroy guns manned by the Germans. Consistently interesting war epic based on the Alistair MacLean novel, with a vivid cast. 159m/C VHS, DVD, Blu-ray Disc. Gregory Peck, David Niven, Anthony Quinn, Richard Harris, Stanley Baker, Anthony Quayle, James Darren, Irene Papas, Gia Scala, James Robertson Justice, Bryan Forbes, Allan Cuthbertson, Michael Trubshawe, Percy Herbert, Walter Gotell, Tutte Lemkow; D: J. Lee Thompson; W: Carl Foreman; C: Oswald Morris; M: Dimitri Tiomkin. Golden Globes '62: Film—Drama, Score.

Guns of the Law 1944 The Texas Rangers try to stop a shifty lawyer who attempts to swindle a family out of a potential fortune in property. 56m/B VHS, DVD. Dave O'Brien, James Newill, Guy Wilkerson, Jack Ingram, Robert F. (Bob) Kortman, Bob (Robert) Barron; D: Elmer Clifton; W: Elmer Clifton.

Guns of the Magnificent Seven 1969 (G) The third remake of "The Seven Samurai." Action-packed western in which the seven free political prisoners and train them to kill. The war party heads out to rescue a Mexican revolutionary being held in an impregnable fortress. 106m/C VHS, DVD. George Kennedy, Monte Markham, James Whitmore, Reni Santoni, Bernie Casey, Joe Don Baker, Scott Thomas, Michael Ansara, Fernando Rey; D: Paul Wendkos; M: Elmer Bernstein.

Gunshy 1998 (R) Familiar crime genre has some fine performances and an intelligent script. Journalist Jake Bridges (Petersen) heads to Atlantic City after catching his wife cheating on him. His drunken ranting gets him trouble, but Jake is rescued by likeable smalltime mob guy Frankie (Wincott) and his hot girlfriend, Melissa (Lane). Jake hangs around watching Frankie work and making passes at Melissa but it just might be that Jake has his own hidden agenda, as well. 101m/C VHS, DVD. William L. Petersen, Michael Wincott, Diane Lane, Kevin Gage, Michael Byrne, Meat Loaf Aday, Eric Schaeffer, Musetta Vander, John Fleck, Bada (Medu) Djola, R. Lee Ermey, Natalie Canerday; D: Jeff Celentano; W: Larry Gross; C: John Aronson; M: Hal Lindes.

The Gunslinger 1956 A woman marshall struggles to keep law and order in a town overrun by outlaws. Unique western with a surprise ending. 83m/C VHS, DVD. John Ireland, Beverly Garland, Allison Hayes, Jonathan Haze, Dick Miller, Bruno VeSota, William Schallert; D: Roger Corman; W: Charles B. Griffith, Mark Hanna; C: Frederick E. West; M: Ronald Stein.

Gunslinger's Revenge Mio West 1998 (PG-13) After 20 years Doc Lowen's (Pieraccioni) gun-toting, outlaw father Johnny (Keitel) resurfaces much to Doc's dismay as he's devoted his life to a peace-loving existence with his wife and young son. While they try to resolve their issues Johnny must also contend with the return of his former nemesis Jack Sikora (Bowie) who's bent on revenge. Pace is slow on the draw (even for a Western) and a dubbed-over Keitel shoots a blank though Bowie followers will want to lasso this one. In Italian with English subtitles. 87m/C DVD. Harvey Keitel, David Bowie, Sandrine Holt, Vincenzo Pardini, Leonardo Pieraccioni; D: Giovanni Veronesi; W: Giovanni Veronesi, Vincenzo Pardini. VIDEO

Gunsmoke 1953 Reb Kittredge (Murphy) is a gun-for-hire who's offered a job by greedy rancher Matt Telford (Randolph). Instead, Kittredge decides to go with Telford's enemy, Dan Saxon (Kelly), so Telford hires another gunslinger (Drake) to get rid of them both. Cabot provides the usual romantic lure as Saxon's daughter. Based on the novel "Roughshod" by Norman A. Fox. 78m/C VHS. Audie Murphy, Susan Cabot, Paul Kelly, Charles Drake, Mary Castle, Jack Kelly, Jesse White, William Reynolds; D: Nathan "Jerry" Juran; W: D.D. Beauchamp; C: Charles P. Boyle.

Gunsmoke: Return to Dodge 1987 The first of the TV movies that reunited most of the cast of the classic TV western. Matt Dillon returns to Dodge and Miss Kitty after 12 years only to be trailed by a ruthless adversary. 100m/C VHS, DVD. James Arness, Amanda Blake, Buck Taylor, Fran Ryan, Earl Holliman, Steve Forrest; D: Vincent McEveety. TV

Gunsmoke Trail 1938 Cowpoke Randall saves an heiress from losing her estate to a phony uncle in low-budget Western. Also features the prolific "Fuzzy" St. John in his cowboy's sidekick stage (interestingly), St. John, a nephew of Fatty Arbuckle, later co-starred in the "Lone Rider" series with Randall's brother, Robert Livingston). 59m/C VHS, DVD. Louise Stanley, Henry Roquemore, Ted Adams, John Merton, Addison "Jack" Randall, Al "Fuzzy" St. John; D: Sam Newfield; W: Fred Myton; C: Jack Greenhalgh.

The Guru 2002 (R) Naïve dance instructor Ramu Gupta (Mistry) leaves India to pursuit stardom in New York. After being fired from his job as a waiter, he auditions for a movie company, but it turns out to be for a porn film. Unable to perform despite coaching from Sharrona (Graham), a porn starlet, Ramu is fired from his job as well. As luck (and script) would have it, he's re-hired by his former boss to replace the drunken swami that was scheduled to appear at a party for socialite Lexi (Tomei). Regurgitating his porn co-star's advice, Ramu becomes a hit as a sex guru. Soon Ramu is the toast of the town as the mystical sex therapist (think Deepak Chopra as Dr Ruth). The movie has some genuinely funny moments, but suffers for trying to be both a light-hearted romantic comedy and a social satire. 91m/C VHS, DVD. GB FR US Jimi Mistry, Heather Graham, Marisa Tomei, Michael McKean, Christine Baranski, Rob Morrow, Malachy McCourt, Dash Mihok; D: Daisy von Scherler Mayer; W: Tracey Jackson; C: John de Borman; M: David Carbonara.

Gus 1976 (G) A Disney film about the California Atoms, a football team that has the worst record in the league until they begin winning games with the help of their field goal kicking mule of a mascot, Gus. The competition then plots a donkey-napping. Enjoyable comedy for the whole family. 96m/C VHS, DVD. Ed Asner, Tim Conway, Dick Van Patten, Ronnie Schell, Bob Crane, Tom Bosley; D: Vincent McEveety; W: Arthur Alsberg; M: Robert F. Brunner.

The Guy from Harlem 1977 He's read, he's from Harlem, and he's not going to take it any more. 86m/C VHS. Loye Hawkins, Cathy Davis, Patricia Fulton, Wanda Starr; D: Rene Martinez Jr.

A Guy Named Joe 1944 A sentimental, patriotic Hollywood fantasy about the angel of a young pilot through battle and also helping him to romance his girl, who's still too devoted to his memory. Remade in 1989 as "Always." 121m/B VHS. Spencer Tracy, Irene Dunne, Van Johnson, Ward Bond, James Gleason, Lionel Barrymore, Esther Williams; D: Victor Fleming; W: Dalton Trumbo; C: Karl Freund.

A Guy Thing 2003 (PG-13) Paul (Lee), wakes up after his bachelor party to find free spirit Becky (Stiles) besides him in bed. Of course his fiancee walks in just as Paul is able to shoo Becky out, thus avoiding a rather embarrassing situation. Or not. Becky turns-out to be his fiancee's cousin and keeps popping up into Paul's life, as does her insanely possessive, cop ex-boyfriend. Lee and Stiles are likable enough, unfortunately the material is too bland to make anything out of their chemistry. 101m/C VHS, DVD. US Jason Lee, Julia Stiles, Selma Blair, Shawn Hatosy, James Brolin, Diana Scarwid, Larry Miller, Julie Hagerty, Jackie Burroughs, David Koechner, Thomas Lennon; D: Chris Koch; W: Matt Tarses, Bill Wrubel, Greg Glienna, Pete Schwaba; C: Robbie Greenberg; M: Mark Mothersbaugh.

The Guyana Tragedy: The Story of Jim Jones 1980 Dramatization traces the story of the Reverend Jim Jones and the People's Temple from its beginnings in 1953 to the November 1978 mass suicide of more than 900 people. Boothe is appropriately hypnotic as the Reverend. 240m/C VHS. Powers Boothe, Ned Beatty, Randy Quaid, Brad Dourif, Brenda Vaccaro, LeVar Burton, Colleen Dewhurst, James Earl Jones; D: William A. Graham; C: Gil Hubbs; M: Elmer Bernstein. TV

The Guys ♂♂♂½ 2002 (PG) Cinematic adaptation of Anne Nelson's timely play about September 11. A fateful introduction brings a journalist (Weaver) to collaborate with an emotionally wrought, inarticulate New York City Fire Department captain (LaFaglia) on poignant, heartfelt eulogies for his fallen brothers. Both leads do a fine job bringing their characters from stage to screen. Some archival footage feels awkwardly placed but on the whole film presents a dignified and humanistic perspective on an event whose worth impact is still unfolding. Shot on location in New York, with very little budget in just two weeks, after discovering some lighting equipment had failed. Simpson and Weaver's daughter makes a cameo appearance along with Nelson's two sons. **98m/C VHS, DVD** US Sigourney Weaver, Anthony LaPaglia, Jim Simpson; **C:** Maryse Alberti; **M:** Ron Carter.

The Guyver ♂♂½ 1991 A young college student is transformed into a superhuman fighting machine thanks to his discovery of an alien device, "The Guyver." A CIA agent (Hamill) must keep the secret device from falling into the hands of human mutants, the Zoanoids. Based on a Japanese comic book. **92m/C VHS, DVD.** Mark Hamill, Vivian Wu, David Gale, Jeffrey Combs, Michae Berryman; **D:** Steve Wang.

Guyver 2: Dark Hero ♂♂½ 1994 (R) The Guyver discovers an alien ship filled with weapons capable of destroying the planet. Naturally, he must battle the evil mutant Zoanoids in order to save the world. Adapted from a Japanese comic book. **127m/C VHS, DVD.** David Hayter, Kathy Christopherson, Christopher Michael; **D:** Steve Wang; **W:** Nathan Long.

The Gymnast ♂♂½ 2006 A devastating injury ended the Olympic gymnastic hopes of Jane Hawkins. Years later, the unhappily married, middle-aged Jane gets a chance at performing in Las Vegas in a cirque-style aerial act with the beautiful younger Serena. As they practice for the show, Jane is surprised to feel so close to her new partner. Great shots of the aerial fabric act and a romantic story. **98m/C DVD.** Allison Mackie, Dreya Webber, Addie Yungmee, David De Simone, Mam Smith; **D:** Ned

---

Guys and Dolls ♂♂♂½ 1955 New York gambler Sky Masterson takes a bet that he can romance a Salvation Army lady. Based on the stories of Damon Runyon with Blaine, Kaye, Pully, and Silver recreating their roles from the Broadway hit. Brando's not-always-convincing musical debut. ♪More I Cannot Wish You; My Time of Day; Guys and Dolls; Fugue for Tinhorns; Follow the Fold; Sue Me; Take Back Your Mink; If I Were a Bell; Luck Be a Lady. **150m/C VHS, DVD,** Marlon Brando, Jean Simmons, Frank Sinatra, Vivian Blaine, Stubby Kaye, Sheldon Leonard, Veda Ann Borg, Regis Toomey; **D:** Joseph L. Mankiewicz; **W:** Joseph L. Mankiewicz; **C:** Harry Stradling Sr.; **M:** Frank Loesser. Golden Globes '56: Actress—Mus./Comedy (Simmons), Film—Mus./Comedy.

Guys and Balls ♂♂ 2004 (R) Small-town, baker's son Ecki (Bruckner) is the goalie on the local soccer team. After losing an important game, Ecki is discovered in a drunken embrace with another man and his teammates throw him off the squad. Vowing to get even, Ecki decides to put together an all-gay team and challenge his hometown's homophobes to a grudge match. So he heads to the city to recruit players and, naturally, finds mostly stereotypical oddballs. Lots of good-natured crass humor and rowdiness. German with subtitles. **106m/C DVD, GE** Christian Berkel, Maximilian Bruckner, Rolf Zacher, Lisa Maria Potthoff, David Rott, Mariele Millowitsch; **D:** Sherry Horman; **W:** Benedikt Gollhardt; **C:** Hanno Lentz; **M:** Martin Todsharow.

The Guyver ♂♂½

Gypsy ♂♂♂ 1962 The life story of America's most famous striptease queen, Gypsy Rose Lee (Wood). Russell gives a memorable performance as the infamous Mama Rose, Gypsy's stage mother. Based on both Gypsy Rose Lee's memoirs and the hit 1959 Broadway play by Arthur Laurents. ♪Small World; All I Need Is the Girl; You'll Never Get Away From Me; Let Me Entertain You; Some People; Everything's Coming Up Roses; You Gotta Have a Gimmick; Baby June and the Newsboys; Mr. Goldstone, I Love You. **144m/C VHS, DVD,** Rosalind Russell, Natalie Wood, Karl Malden, Ann Jillian, Parley Baer, Paul Wallace, Betty Bruce; **D:** Mervyn LeRoy; **W:** Arthur Laurents, Leonard Spigelgass; **C:** Harry Stradling Sr.; **M:** Jule Styne, Stephen Sondheim. Golden Globes '63: Actress—Mus./Comedy (Russell).

Gypsy ♂♂½ 1993 If you like Bette brassy and larger than life, as only she can be, then this is the production for you. This TV re-creation of the 1959 Broadway musical stars Midler as notorious stage mother Mama Rose, who tries to realize all her frustrated ambitions by pushing her two young daughters, June and Louise, into vaudeville show biz. Her wish eventually comes true, in an unexpected fashion, when an adult Louise (Gibb) transforms herself into stripper Gypsy Rose Lee. ♪Everything's Coming Up Roses; You've Gotta Have a Gimmick; All I Need Is the Girl; Rose's Turn; Some People; Mr. Goldstone, I Love You; You'll Never Get Away From Me; Together, Wherever We Go. **150m/C VHS, DVD,** Bette Midler, Peter Riegert, Cynthia Gibb, Ed Asner, Christine Ebersole, Michael Jeter, Andrea Martin, Jennifer Beck, Linda Hart, Rachel Sweet; **D:** Emile Ardolino; **W:** Arthur Laurents; **M:** Jule Styne, Stephen Sondheim. **TV**

Gypsy ♂♂♂ 1975 A modern day gypsy-blooded Robin Hood cavorts behind heists and romantic trysts. Dubbed. **90m/C VHS.** Alain Delon, Annie Girardot, Paul Meurisse; **D:** Jose Giovanni.

Gypsy Angels ♂ 1994 (R) A daredevil stunt pilot has a terrifying accident and develops amnesia. With the help of a stripper (who is in love with him), he tries to rebuild his life, this time with her in it. White's no actress and unless you like stunt flying (and there's a lot of it), fly by this one. (You'll note the director won't admit to this, since Smithee is a pseudonym.) **92m/C VHS.** Vanna White, Richard Roundtree, Gene Bicknell; **D:** Alan Smithee.

Gypsy Blood ♂♂ 1918 One of the first screen versions of "Carmen," closer to Prosper Merrimee's story than to the opera, depicting the fated love between a dancing girl and a matador. Lubitsch's first notable film. Silent. **104m/B VHS, DVD.** Pola Negri; **D:** Ernst Lubitsch.

Gypsy Colt ♂♂½ 1954 (G) Gypsy is the horse beloved by the young Corcoran. But a drought forces her family to sell the animal to a racing stable 500 miles from their home. Gypsy is having none of this, escapes the stables, and returns home to be with Corcoran. Both horse and child actress are naturally appealing. **72m/** **C VHS.** Donna Corcoran, Ward Bond, Frances Dee, Lee Van Cleef, Larry Keating; **D:** Andrew Marton.

Gypsy 83 ♂♂ 2001 Rue is goth girl Gypsy Vale, a Stevie Nicks wanna-be named after her idol's famous song, who unhappily resides in decidedly un-hip Sandusky, Ohio with her hippie dad and abandoned by her still-aspiring rock star mother. Desperate to flee the quiet Midwestern life where she and her only friend Clive (Turton) serve merely as social outcasts, the two black-clad souls head to a New York nightclub to participate in the "Night of 1000 Stevies" Nicks tribute bash. The two encounter some predictable problems along the way, including being hassled about the way they look by various smallminded locals but also meet some reassuring kindred spirits, including wash-up lounge singer Black and Amish boy Scoville. Typical rebel without a cause premise made slightly better by a decent Rue

---

Farr; **W:** Ned Farr; **C:** Marco Fargnoli; **M:** Craig Richey.

Gypsy ♂♂♂ 1962

---

and Turton. **94m/C VHS, DVD, US** Sara Rue, Karen Black, John Doe, Paulo Costanzo, Kett Turton, Arson Scoville; **C:** Gina DeGirolamo; **W:** Todd Stephens; **C:** Gina DeGirolamo; **M:** Marty Beller.

The Gypsy Moths ♂♂ 1969 It's not actually about a bug infestation. Instead, it's a Frankenheimer melodrama about three barnstorming skydivers arriving in a small Kansas town to give an exhibition. They're staying with the aunt (Kerr) and uncle (Windom) of young Malcolm (Wilson) and Aunt Elizabeth is immediately drawn to fatalistic, taciturn leader Mike Rettig (Lancaster). After their one-night stand, Rettig is scheduled to perform an extremely risky jump, but tragedy strikes. Because Malcolm and Joe (Hackman) need money to bury Mike, Malcolm decides to perform the same stunt to draw a big crowd. **106m/C VHS, DVD,** Burt Lancaster, Deborah Kerr, Gene Hackman, Scott Wilson, William Windom, Bonnie Bedelia, Sheree North, Ford Rainey; **D:** John Frankenheimer; **W:** William Hanley; **C:** Philip Lathrop; **M:** Elmer Bernstein.

The Gypsy Warriors ♂½ 1978 Two Army captains during WWII infiltrate Nazi-occupied France in order to prevent the distribution of a deadly toxin and are aided by a band of Gypsies. Ex. **77m/C VHS.** Tom Selleck, James Whitmore Jr., Joseph Ruskin, Lina Raymond; **D:** Lou Antonio. **TV**

H ♂♂ 1990 Two junkies try to kick their heroin addiction and face the difficult withdrawal period. Includes glimpses into their past that shed light on the reasons they turned to drugs. Contains explicit footage. **93m/C VHS, CA** Martin Neufeld, Pascale Montpetit; **D:** Darrell Wasyk. Gene s '91: Actress (Montpetit), Toronto-City '90: Canadian Feature Film.

H-Bomb woof! 1971 Mitchum stars as a CIA agent who is sent to Bangkok to retrieve two stolen nuclear warheads from a terrorist. It just so happens that his exgirlfriend's father is the terrorist he must contend with in this stupid movie. **98m/C VHS.** Olivia Hussey, Chris Mitchum, Kung Savilai; **D:** P. (Philip) Chalong.

H-Man woof! Bijo to Ekitainingen 1959 A Japanese sci-fi woofer about a radioactive mass of slime festering under Tokyo. Extremely lame special effects get quite a few unintentional laughs. Dubbed. **79m/C VHS.** JP Koreya Senda, Kenji Sahara, Yumi Shirakawa, Akihiko Hirata; **D:** Inoshiro Honda.

Habit ♂♂ 1997 A very low-budget film. Wastrel Sam (Fessenden) is at loose ends when he meets intriguing Anna (Shaidar). This first encounter is a bust (Sam's very drunk) but a later meeting leads to an intense sexual encounter—and Sam waking up alone in Battery Park with a prominently cut lip and some hazy memories. All their encounters are similarly intense (and in public places) but Anna refuses to reveal anything about herself. Sam is soon a confused physical wreck but when Anna's around, he just doesn't care. **112m/C VHS, DVD,** Larry Fessenden, Meredith Snaider, Aaron Beall, Heather Woodbury, Patricia Coleman; **C:** Frank DeMarco; **M:** Geoffrey Kidde.

Habitat ♂♂½ 1997 (R) Nature goes wild when high school student Andreas (Getty) moves with his scientist parents, Hank (Kanyo) and Clarissa (Krige), to the small Southwestern burg of Pleasanton. Hank's experiment with accelerated evolution takes some unexpected blips, with Hank turning into particles of matter, their house transformed into a vegetation-covered fortress, and Clarissa becoming a very earthy earth mother. Some eerie special effects. **103m/C VHS, DVD.** Alice Krige, Balthazar Getty, Tcheky Karyo, Kenneth Welsh, Lara Harris; **D:** Rene Daalder; **W:** Rene Daalder; **C:** Jean Lepine; **M:** Ralph Grierson. **CABLE**

The Habitation of Dragons ♂♂½ 1991 Family feuds and melodrama in 1930s West Texas. Wandering lawyer George Tolliver (Davis) argues with successful businessman brother Leonard (Forrest) while matriarch Leonora (Stapleton) presides and family skeletons rattle. Confusing hodgepodge. **94m/C VHS.** Jean Stapleton, Frederic Forrest, Brad Davis, Pat Hingle, Hallie Foote, Maureen O'Sullivan; **D:** Mi-

---

chael Lindsay-Hogg; **W:** Horton Foote; **M:** David Shire. **TV**

Hack! ♂♂ 2007 (R) Horror fans Vincent King (Kanan) and his wife Mary (Landau) want to create the ultimate slasher flick—with the unwitting participation of a group of college students. Emily (McKellar) and her pals are on a biology field trip at a remote island where they find the number of clever horror movie references. **100m/C DVD,** Sean Kanan, Jay Kenneth Johnson, Juliet Landau, Danica McKellar, Lochlyn Munro, Adrienne Frantz, Burt Young, William Forsythe, Kane Hodder; **D:** Matt Flynn; **W:** Matt Flynn; **C:** Roger D'Ingriani; **M:** Scott Glasgow. **VIDEO**

Hack O'Lantern ♂ Halloween Night 1987 Granddad worships Satan, and gets his grandson involved; the result is much bloodshed, violence, and evil. **90m/C VHS.** Hy Pyke, Gregory Scott Cummins, Katrina Garner, Carla Baron; **D:** Jag Mundhra; **M:** Greg Haggard.

Hackers ♂♂ 1995 (PG-13) Group of teenaged computer cyber-geeks surf the 'net and become the prime suspects in an industrial conspiracy when hacker Dade (Miller) breaks into the computer at Ellingson Oil Company. It's "really an inside job but just try getting anyone (read "adult") to believe him. So the techno whiz kids band together, with cops and security all wanting to shut them down. Jolie (hacker Acid Burn) is the daughter of actor Jon Voight. **105m/C VHS, DVD.** Felicity Huffman, Jonny Lee Miller, Angelina Jolie, Fisher Stevens, Lorraine Bracco, Jesse Bradford, Wendell Pierce, Alberta Watson, Laurence Mason, Renoly Santiago, Matthew Lillard, Penn Jillette; **D:** Iain Softley; **W:** Rafael Moreu; **C:** Andrzej Sekula; **M:** Simon Boswell.

The Hades Factor ♂½ 1984 Loosely based on the novel by Robert Ludlum and Gayle Lynds. **184m/C DVD, US** Stephen Dorff, Mira Sorvino, Blair Underwood, Colm Meaney, Danny Huston, Sophia Myles, Josh Hopkins, Jeffrey DeMunn, Kenneth Welsh, Anjelica Huston; **D:** Mick Jackson; **W:** Elwood Reid; **C:** Ivan Strasburg; **M:** Peter Robinson. **TV**

Hadley's Rebellion ♂½ 1984 (PG) A Georgia farm boy adjusts to relocation at an elitist California boarding school by flaunting his wrestling abilities. **96m/C VHS.** Griffin O'Nea, Charles Durning, William Devane, Adam Baldwin, Dennis Hage, Lisa Lucas; **D:** Fred Walton; **W:** Fred Walton.

Haiku Tunnel ♂♂ 2000 (R) Josh (Kornbluth) takes a temp job with high-powered attorney Bob Shelby (Keith) and then accepts an offer for a permanent position. This soon begins to freak commitment-phobic Josh out, resulting in his inability to complete the simple task of mailing out 17 important letters. As his anxiety grows, Josh has even more trouble dealing with his chipper co-workers and his impatient boss. **88m/C VHS, DVD.** Josh Kornbluth, Warren Keith, Helen Shumaker, June Lomena, Amy Resnick; **D:** Josh Kornbluth, Jacob Kornbluth; **W:** Josh Kornbluth, Jacob Kornbluth; **C:** Don Matthew Smith.

Hail ♂ Hail to the Chief, Washington, B.C. 1973 (PG) A biting satire of what-mighthave-been if certain key cabinet members had their way. **95m/C VHS, DVD,** Anthony Michael Hall, Robert Downey Jr., Frank Gorshin, Samuel L. Jackson, Joan Nelson, Nicholas Pryor, Dick O'Neill, Phil Foster, Joseph Sirola, Dan Resin, Willard Waterman, Gary Sandy; **D:** Fred Levinson.

Hail, Hero! ♂♂½ 1969 (PG) A dated Vietnam War era drama about a confused hippie rebelling against his parents and the draft. First film for both Douglas and

Strauss. Adapted from the novel by John Weston. Includes music by Gordon Lightfoot. **97m/C VHS.** Michael Douglas, Arthur Kennedy, Teresa Wright, John Larch, Charles Drake, Deborah Winters, Peter Strauss; **D:** David Miller; **C:** Robert B. Hauser.

Hail Mary ⚁⚁½ *Je Vous Salue Marie* 1985 (R) A modern-day virgin named Mary inexplicably becomes pregnant in this controversial film that discards notions of divinity in favor of the celebration of a live-ly, intellectual humanism. Godard rejects orthodox narrative structure and bourgeois prejudices. Very controversial, but not up to his breathless beginning work. In French with English subtitles. **107m/C VHS.** **FR SI GB** Myriem Roussel, Thierry Rode, Philippe Lacoste, Manon Anderson, Juliette Binoche, Johan Leysen; **D:** Jean-Luc Godard; **W:** Jean-Luc Godard.

Hail the Conquering Hero ⚁⚁⚁½ 1944

A slight young man is rejected by the Army. Upon returning home, he is surprised to find out they think he's a hero. Biting satire with Demarest's performance stealing the show. **101m/B VHS.** Eddie Bracken, Ella Raines, William Demarest, Franklin Pangborn, Raymond Walburn, Freddie (Fred) Steele; **D:** Preston Sturges.

Hair ⚁⚁⚁½ 1979 (PG) Film version of the explosive 1960s Broadway musical about the carefree life of the flower children and the shadow of the Vietnam War that hangs over them. Great music, as well as wonderful choreography by Twyla Tharp help portray the surprisingly sensitive evocation of the period so long after the fact. Forman has an uncanny knack for understanding the textures of Americana life. Watch for a thinner Nell Carter. **122m/C VHS, DVD.** Treat Williams, John Savage, Beverly D'Angelo, Annie Golden, Nicholas Ray, Nell Carter; **D:** Milos Forman; **W:** Michael Weller, James Rado; **C:** Miroslav Ondricek; **M:** Galt MacDermot.

The Hairdresser's Husband ⚁⚁⚁ *Le Mari de la coiffeuse*

1992 (R) Antoine (Rochefort) has had an odd obsession since boyhood—hairdressers—and in middle age he finds love with Mathilde (Galiena), a hairdresser he meets and proposes to as she cuts his hair. She accepts, and the two live their quiet lives in their barber shop as she cuts hair and he watches, occasionally breaking out in Arabian dances. A dark and odd yet refreshing film with fine performances by Rochefort and Galiena in this story about fetishism, obsession, and hair. In French with English subtitles. **84m/C VHS.** **FR** Jean Rochefort, Anna Galiena, Roland Bertin, Maurice Chevit, Philippe Clevenot, Jacques Mathou, Claude Aufaure; **D:** Patrice Leconte; **W:** Claude Klotz, Patrice Leconte; **C:** Eduardo Serra; **M:** Michael Nyman.

Hairspray ⚁⚁⚁ 1988 (PG) Waters' first truly mainstream film, if that's even possible, and his funniest. Details in the struggle among teenagers in 1962 Baltimore for the top spot in a local TV dance show. Deals with racism and stereotypes, as well as typical "teen" problems (hairdo's and don'ts). Filled with refreshingly tasteful, subtle social satire (although not without typical Waters touches that will please die-hard fans), Lake is lovable and appealing as Divine's daughter; Divine, in his last film, is likable as an iron-toting

mom. Look for Waters in a cameo and Divine as a man. Great '60s music, which Waters refers to as "the only known remedy to today's Hit Parade of Hell." **94m/C VHS, DVD.** Ricki Lake, Divine, Jerry Stiller, Colleen (Ann) Fitzpatrick, Sonny Bono, Deborah Harry, Ruth Brown, Leslie Ann Powers, Michael St. Gerard, Shawn Thompson, Clayton Prince, Pia Zadora, Ric Ocasek, Mink Stole, Mary Vivian Pearce, Alan J. Wendl, Susan Lowe, George Stover, Toussaint McCall; **Cameos:** John Waters; **D:** John Waters; **W:** John Waters; **C:** David Insley; **M:** Kenny Vance.

Hairspray ⚁⚁⚁ 2007 (PG) Remake of the 1988 John Waters surprise hit that later became a Broadway musical. In spite of the rehash, this new iteration finds its freshness by upping the bounce and fun. The story remains intact, with less-than-popular teenager Tracy Turnblad (newcomer Blonsky, a treat) shaking up her 1960s-era town with her efforts to integrate the local television dance show. Supported by her mother Edna (Travolta in plus-size drag), she turns dance into social activism and has a blast doing it. **115m/C DVD, Blu-ray Disc.** **US** John Travolta, Christopher Walken, Michelle Pfeiffer, Queen Latifah, Nicole Blonsky, Amanda Bynes, James Marsden, Zac Efron, Brittany Snow, Allison Janney, Elijah Kelley, Jerry Stiller, Paul Dooley, Taylor Parks; **D:** Adam Shankman; **W:** Leslie Dixon, Thomas Meehan, Mark O'Donnell; **C:** Bojan Bazelli; **M:** Marc Shaiman.

The Hairy Ape ⚁⚁ 1944 Screen

adaptation of the Eugene O'Neill play. A beast-like coal stoker becomes obsessed with a cool and distant passenger aboard an ocean liner. **90m/B VHS.** William Bendix, Susan Hayward, John Loder, Dorothy Comingore, Roman Bohnen, Alan Napier; **D:** Alfred Santell.

Half a Lifetime ⚁⚁ 1986 The stakes are too high for four friends playing a game of poker. **85m/C VHS.** C4 Keith Carradine, Gary Busey, Nick Mancuso, Saul Rubinek; **D:** Daniel Petrie; **W:** Stephen Metcalfe.

Half a Loaf of Kung Fu ⚁ *Dian Zhi Gong Fu Gan Chian Chan* 1978 The worthy bodyguards of Sem Chuan are called upon to deliver a valuable jade statue. Thwarted again and again by ruthless robbers, they falter. Only Chan carries on, meeting the enemy alone. Fast action, good story. **98m/C VHS, DVD.** **HK** Jackie Chan, James Tien; **D:** Chi-Hwa Chen; **W:** Ming Chi Tang; **C:** Chin-Kui Chen; **M:** Frankie Chen.

Half a Sixpence ⚁⚁ 1967 Former musician Sidney, who earlier directed "Showboat" and "Kiss Me Kate," shows a bit less verve in this production. Based on H.G. Wells' 1905 novel, "Kipps," it sports much of the original cast from its Broadway incarnation. Edwardian orphan Steele, a cloth-dealer-in-training, comes into a large sum of money and proceeds to lose it with great dispatch. Somewhere along the way he loses his girlfriend, too, but she takes him back because musicals end happily. ♫Half a Sixpence; Flash, Bang, Wallop!; All In The Cause Of Economy; I'm Not Talking To You; Money To Burn; The Race Is On; I Don't Believe A Word Of It; A Proper Gentleman; She's Too Far Above Me. **148m/B VHS, DVD.** Tommy Steele, Julia Foster, Penelope Horner, Cyril Ritchard, Grover Dale; **D:** George Sidney; **W:** Beverley Cross; **C:** Geoffrey Unsworth.

Half a Soldier ⚁⚁ *Half a Sinner* 1940 A spoiled girl gets a big surprise when she steals a car and discovers the body of a gangster in the trunk. **59m/B VHS.** Constance Collier, Tom Dugan, Heather Angel, John "Dusty" King; **D:** Al Christie; **W:** Fred Jackson Jr.; **C:** Charles Van Enger.

Half-Baked ⚁ 1997 (R) Four seedy roommates whose problems stem from their love of marijuana float through life with loser jobs that give them just enough money to buy their next bag. When Kenny (H. Williams) is arrested for killing a diabetic police horse during a munchies run, the three remaining friends must put their resinated brains together and come up with a way to bail him out. Thurgood (Chapelle), a custodian for a pharmaceutical company, decides to steal some high-grade grass from the lab; and along with Brian (Breuer, doing a very convincing stoned) and Scarface (Diaz), he begins dealing.

This puts them afoul of the law as well as local drug lord Samson Simpson (C. Williams). Just say no. Trust me, dude, this stuff is bogus and it won't get you off. **83m/C VHS, DVD, HD DVD.** Tracy Morgan, Harland Williams, Dave Chappelle, Jim Breuer, Guillermo Diaz, Rachel True, Clarence Williams III, Thomas Chong, Jon Stewart, Stephen Baldwin, Willie Nelson, Janeane Garofalo, Steven Wright, Laura Silverman, Snoop Dogg; **D:** Tamra Davis; **W:** Neal Brennan, Dave Chappelle; **C:** Steven Bernstein; **M:** Alf Clausen.

The Half-Breed ⚁⚁ 1951 Routine oater with settlers and Apaches fighting, and the obligatory half-breed stuck in the middle. **81m/B VHS.** Robert Young, Jack Buetel, Janis Carter, Barton MacLane, Reed Hadley, Porter Hall, Connie Gilchrist; **D:** Stuart Gilmore.

Half-Caste ⚁ 2004 (R) See Bobby go to South Africa with his buddies to capture on film the fabled "Half-Caste"—half man, half leopard—that finds humans to be tasty treats. See Bobby's friends go bye-bye in not-at-all-surprising hideousness leaving him to persuade the coppers that he isn't the evil-doer. Look elsewhere for scary horror movie. **86m/C VHS, DVD.** Sebastian Apodaca, Kim Te Roller, Robert Pike Daniel, Rob Zazzali, Kathy Wagner, Greg Good, Kelly Cohen; **D:** Sebastian Apodaca; **W:** Sebastian Apodaca; **C:** Cooper Donaldson; **M:** Charlie Brissette, Manu Hanu, Hanu-Manu. **VIDEO**

Half Human ⚁½ 1958 Dull Japanese monster movie about an ape-human who terrorizes Northern Japan. When released in the U.S., Carradine and Morris were added. Without subtitles, just Carradine's narration. Director Honda made better movies before and after, with Godzilla and Rodan. **78m/B VHS, JP** John Carradine, Akira Takarada, Morris Ankrum; **D:** Inoshiro Honda.

Half Light ⚁⚁ 2005 (R) Rachel's (Moore) life as a well-known writer is sent spiraling when her five-year-old son accidentally drowns and she finds herself unable to write. Attempting to revive her career and escape her sorrow, she treks to a remote Scottish village where she seeks comfort from a local lighthouse operator. On cue, the tranquil setting is disrupted by not only visions of her dead child but by a shocking murder in town. Moore somewhat makes up for what's lacking in this not-quite-so-spooky tale. **102m/C DVD.** Demi Moore, Henry Ian Cusick, Nicholas Gleaves, Beans El-Balawi, Kate Isitt; **D:** Craig Rosenberg; **W:** Craig Rosenberg. **VIDEO**

Half Moon Street ⚁⚁ *Escort Girl* 1986 (R) A brilliant woman scientist supplements her paltry fellowship salary by becoming a hired escort and prostitute, which leads her into various incidents of international intrigue. Adapted from a story by Paul Theroux, "Dr. Slaughter." **90m/C VHS, DVD.** Sigourney Weaver, Michael Caine, Keith Buckley, Ian MacInnes; **D:** Bob Swaim.

The Half Naked Truth ⚁⚁½ 1932 Carnival barker Jimmy Bates (Tracy) has big plans, which are realized when he transforms sideshow hoochie dancer Teresita (Velez) into Princess Exotica and makes her a Broadway star. But when she begins dating the show's producer (Morgan), Jimmy gets jealous and tries to sabotage the dame's career (all in the name of love of course). **77m/B VHS.** Lee Tracy, Shirley Chambers, Lupe Velez, Eugene Pallette, Frank Morgan, Franklin Pangborn; **D:** Gregory La Cava; **W:** Gregory La Cava; **C:** Bert Glennon; **M:** Max Steiner.

Half Nelson ⚁⚁⚁ 2006 (R) Get high, Mr. Chips. Crackhead Brooklyn schoolteacher Dan Dunne (Gosling) manages to do the inspiring inner-city educator thing until 12-year-old Drey (Epps in a stellar debut performance), no stranger to addicts, discovers him passed out in a bathroom stall after a basketball game, pipe in hand. This leads to a tentative, complicated relationship between the two, with Dan's ironic efforts to save Drey from a drug dealer's plans to bring her into his fold somehow offering the pair the possibility of salvation. Gosling is raw and sympathetic portraying Dan's contradictions, and the film smartly avoids the usual feel-good trappings. **106m/C DVD.** **US** Ryan Gos-

ling, Anthony Mackie, Tina Holmes, Deborah Rush, Shareeka Epps, Monique Gabriela Cumen, Jay O. Sanders, Karen Chilton; **D:** Ryan Fleck; **W:** Ryan Fleck, Anna Boden; **C:** Andrij Parekh. Ind. Spirit '07: Actor (Gosling), Actress (Epps).

Half of Heaven ⚁⚁⚁ *La Mitad del Cielo* 1986 A critically popular film about a young Spanish woman who begins to share certain telepathic powers with her wizened grandmother. In Spanish with English subtitles. **95m/C VHS. SP** Angela Molina, Margarita Lozano; **D:** Manuel Gutierrez Aragon.

Half Past Dead ⚁ 2002 (PG-13) Steven Seagal hauls his bloated carcass through the motions in this action dud that's far past half dead. He plays Sascha, an undercover government agent working in a new-fangled Alcatraz prison. During the planned execution of thief/murderer Lester (Weitz), a corrupt government official (Chestnut) and his kickboxing henchwoman (Peeples) take a Supreme Court justice (Thorson) hostage in an effort to find out where Lester hid his loot. Seagal allies with Nick (Ja Rule), his former FBI sting target, in order to save the day. Peeples delivers the film's only standout fight scene, although the backstage duel between Seagal and the buffet table must have been quite a sight. TV producer/novelist Stephen J. Cannell appears as a prison bureau chief. **97m/C VHS, DVD.** Steven Seagal, Morris Chestnut, Ja Rule, Nia Peeples, Michael "Bear" Taliferro, Claudia Christian, Linda Thorson, Bruce Weitz, Kurupt, Mo'Nique, Matt Battaglia, Richard Bremner, Stephen J. Cannell, Don Michael Paul, Tony Plana; **D:** Don Michael Paul; **W:** Don Michael Paul; **C:** Michael Slovis; **M:** Tyler Bates.

Half-Shot at Sunrise ⚁⚁ 1930 Madcap vaudeville comedians play AWOL soldiers loose in the 1918 Paris. Continuous one-liners, sight gags, and slapstick nonsense. First film appearance of comedy team Wheeler and Woolsey. **78m/B VHS, DVD.** Bert Wheeler, Robert Woolsey, Dorothy Lee, Robert Rutherford, Edna May Oliver; **D:** Paul Sloane; **M:** Max Steiner.

Half Slave, Half Free ⚁⚁½ *Solomon Northrup's Odyssey* 1985 The true story of a free black man in the 1840s who is kidnapped and forced into slavery for 12 years. Part of the "American Playhouse" series on PBS. Followed by "Charlotte Forten's Mission: Experiment in Freedom." **113m/C VHS, DVD.** Avery Brooks, Mason Adams, Petronia Paley, John Saxon, Joe Seneca, Michael (Lawrence) Tolan, Lee Bryant, Rhetta Greene, Janet League; **D:** Gordon Parks. **TV**

The Halfback of Notre Dame ⚁⚁½ 1996 (G) Star football

player (and coach's son) Craig Modeau (Hogan) is a lumbering misfit, ripe for high school teasing, anywhere but on the gridiron. But French exchange student Esmeralda (Vaugier) thinks he's sweet—much to the dismay of current boyfriend, obnoxious quarterback Archie (Cutler). Then Craig decides to quit the team right before the big game when dad says no fraternizing and it's up to his French flame to get the jock to change his mind. Made for TV reworking of Victor Hugo's "The Hunchback of Notre Dame." **97m/C VHS.** Gabriel Hogan, Emmanuelle Vaugier, Scott Hylands, Sandra Nelson, Allen (Cutler) Cutler; **D:** Rene Bonnière; **W:** Richard Clark, Mark Trafficante; **C:** Maris Jansons; **M:** George Blondheim. **TV**

Halfmoon ⚁⚁ *Paul Bowles: Halbmond* 1995 Trilogy of stories by Paul Bowles. "Merkala Beach" looks at the friendship of two young Moroccan men who are both seduced by the same mysterious woman. "Call at Corazon" finds the honeymoon journey of a mismatched British couple turning into a voyage as they sail up the Amazon on a crowded cargo boat. "Allal" is a Moroccan boy who's an outcast in his village because of his illegitimacy. He befriends an old snake dealer and steals one of his cobras in order to charm the reptile. Then Allal winds up in a magical transformation with the creature. English and Arabic with subtitles. **90m/C VHS, DVD. GE GE** Samir Guesmi, Khalid Ksouri, Sondos Belhassan, Veronica Quillogan, Sam Cox, Said Zakir, Mohammed Belfquih; **D:** Irene von Alberti, Frieder Schlaich; **W:** Irene von Alberti, Frieder Schlaich; **C:** Volker Tittel; **M:** Roman Bunka; **Nar:** Paul Bowles.

Hallelujah! 🐾🐾½ *1929* Haynes plays an innocent young man who finds religion and becomes a charismatic preacher after a family tragedy. He retains all his human weaknesses, however, including falling for the lovely but deceitful McKinney. Great music included tradition al spirituals and songs by Berlin, such as "At the End of the Road" and "Swanee Shuffle." Shot on location in Tennessee. The first all-black feature film and the first talkie for director Vidor was given the go ahead by MGM production chief Irving Thalberg, though he knew the film would be both controversial and get minimal release in the deep South, such as its predecessor. It relies on old-fashioned buckets of blood. No chills, just trauma. Co-scripted by Carpenter, director of the original. **90m/C VHS, DVD.** Daniel L. Haynes, Nina Mae McKinney, William Fontaine, Harry Gray, Fannie Belle DeKnight, Everett McGarrity. *D:* King Vidor. *M:* Irving Berlin. *W:* Ben Hecht. *S,N:* Behrman. *M:* Richard Rodgers, Lorenz Hart.

Hallelujah, I'm a Bum 🐾🐾½ *1933* *Happy Go Lucky; Lazy Bones 1933 A happy-go- lucky hobo reforms and begins a new life for the sake of a woman. Bizarre Depres- sion-era musical with a Rodgers and Hart score and continuously rhyming dialogue. The British version, due to the slang meaning of "bum," was retitled, substitut- ing "tramp." "Aryou Are Too Beautiful; I'll Do It Again; I've Got To Get Back To New York; That We Do You Want With Money?; Dear June; Bumper Found a G and 83m/B York." *D:* Al Jolson, Madge Evans, Frank Mor- gan, Chester Conklin, Edgar Connor; *C:* Lewis Milestone; *W:* Ben Hecht, S.N, Behrman; *M:* Rich- ard Rodgers, Lorenz Hart.

Hallelujah, I'm a Bum 🐾🐾½ *Halleluja, I'm a Tramp; The Heart of New York;*

The Hallelujah Trail 🐾🐾 *1965* Denver mining town in the late 1800s is about to batten down the hatches for a long winter, and there's not a drop of whis- key to be had. The U.S. Cavary sends a shipment to the miners, but temperance leader Cora Templeton Massingale (Rem- ick) and her bevy of ladies against liquor stand between the shipment and the would-be whistle whetters. Limp Western satire directed by Preston Sturges' broth- er, who fared much better when he kept a straight face (he also directed "The Great Escape"). Based on Bill Gulick's novel, "The Hallelujah Train." **166m/C VHS, DVD. C DVD.** Burt Lancaster, Lee Remick, Jim Hutton, Pamela Tiffin, Donald Pleasence, Brian Keith, Martin Lan- dau; *D:* John Sturges; *W:* John Gay; *C:* Robert L. Surtees; *M:* Elmer Bernstein; *Nar:* John Dehner.

Halloween 🐾🐾🐾½ *1978 (R)* John Carpenter's horror classic has been ac- claimed "the most successful independent motion picture of all time." *A* deranged youth returns to his hometown with mur- derous intent after 15 years in an asylum. Very, very scary—you feel this movie more than see it. **90m/C VHS, DVD, Blu-ray Disc, UMD.** Jamie Lee Curtis, Donald Pleasence, Nancy Loomis, P.J. Soles, Charles Cyphers, Kyle Richards, Brian Andrews, John Michael Graham, Nancy Stephens, Arthur Malet, Mickey Yablans, Brent Le Page, Adam Hollander, Robert Phalen, Sandy Johnson, David Kyle, Nick Castle; *D:* John Carpenter; *W:* John Carpenter, Debra Hill; *C:* Dean Cundey; *M:* John Carpenter. Natl. Film Reg. '06.

Halloween 🐾🐾 *2007 (R)* Director Rob Zombie trades suspense and chills for action and shock in this remake of the classic 1970s horror movie and loses what made the original so scary in the first place. The tale is essentially the same, but this time crazed serial killer Michae Myers (Mane) gets an extended backstory, com- plete with a goodhearted stripper mom (Moon-Zombie) and evil step-dad (For- sythe). Once we get to the actual story, in which Myers stalks and murders his long- lost sister's (Taylor-Compton) friends, it's been shortened so much that there's bare- ly any time to build any tension, instead just going for your standard action-crazed stabfest. Diehard fans will deem it far bet-

ter than most of the films in the series, but it doesn't hold a candle to the original. (Williams). They are accompanied by fel- low lust-ridden Michael fodder Charlie **110m/C DVD.** US Malcolm McDowell, Tyler Mane, Scout Taylor-Compton, Brad Dourif, Danny Trejo, William Forsythe, Danielle Harris, Hanna Hall, Sheri Moon-Zombie, Dee Wallace Stone; *D:* Rob Zombie; *W:* Rob Zombie; *C:* Phil Parmet; *M:* Tyler Bates.

Halloween 2: The Nightmare Isn't Over! 🐾½ *1981 (R)* Trying to pick up where "Halloween" left off, the se- quel begins with the escape of vicious killi- er Michael, who continues to murder and terrorize the community of Haddonfield, Il- linois. Lacking the innovative intentions of its predecessor, it relies on old-fashioned buckets of blood. No chills, just trauma. Co-scripted by Carpenter, director of the original. **92m/C VHS, DVD.** Jamie Lee Curtis, Donald Pleasence, Jeffrey Kramer, Charles Cy- phers, Lance Guest; *D:* Rick Rosenthal; *W:* John Carpenter, Debra Hill; *C:* Dean Cundey; *M:* John Carpenter.

Halloween 3: Season of the Witch 🐾🐾 *1982 (R)* Modern druid plans to kill 50 million children with his die returns home to kill his niece. **89m/C VHS, DVD.** Donald Pleasence, Ellie Cornell, Dan- ielle Harris, Michael Pataki, George P. Wilbur, Beau Starr, Kathleen Kinmont, Sasha Jenson, Gene Ross; *D:* Dwight Little; *W:* Alan B. McElroy; *C:* Peter Lyons Collister; *M:* Alan Howarth, John Carpenter.

Halloween 4: The Return of Michael Myers 🐾 *1988 (R)* The third sequel, wherein the lunatic that won't pick up with the escape of vicious killi- franchise, and that the entire genre has been parodied into the ground. You should ignore this movie instead. Internet group of stupid kids to stay in Michael Myers' house as a publicity stunt for a live webcast. Naturally, Mike doesn't like the interlopers and proceeds to permanently cut their internet connections. Nothing new is added to the series, and drug-use for the young uns to get an interesting new piercing, and sexual hi-inks are still the best way and as sexual hi-inks are still the best way **86m/C VHS, DVD.** US Busta Rhymes, Sean Pat- rick Thomas, Jamie Lee Curtis, Bianca Kajlich, Tyra Banks, Thomas Ian Nicholas, Ryan Merri- man, Luke Kirby, Brad Loree, Daisy McCrackin, Katee Sackhoff; *Cameos:* Rick Rosenthal; *D:* Rick Rosenthal; *W:* Larry Brand, Sean Hood; *C:* David Geddes; *M:* Danny Lux.

Halloween 5: The Revenge of Michael Myers 🐾½ *1989 (R)* Fifth in the series, this Halloween is an im- provement over 2, 3, and 4, thanks to a few well directed scare scenes. Unfortu- nately, the plot remains the same: a psy- cho behemoth chases down and kills more teens. An open ending promises yet another installment. **96m/C VHS, DVD.** Donald Pleasence, Ellie Cornell, Danielle Harris, Don Shanks, Betty Carvalho, Beau Starr, Wendy Ka- plan, Jeffrey Landman; *D:* Dominique Othenin-Gi- rard; *W:* Dominique Othenin-Gi- rard, Michael Jacobs; *C:* Rob Draper; *M:* Alan Howarth.

Halloween 6: The Curse of Michael Myers 🐾 *Halloween: The Ori- gin of Michael Myers 1995 (R)* First the return. Then his revenge. And now, his curse. aimed square at the viewer. Lame series entry connects Michael Myers to an an- cient Celtic ritual that drives him to murder whole families in his old stompin' grounds of Haddonfield. Before he finishes his reign of terror, Myers has to contend with Dr. Loomis (Pleasence), the man who making monster (the entire franchise had grossed over \$200 million and a combined budget of \$20 million and ing out the group's criminal behavior. In should probably join Freddy and Jason at the old slashers' retirement home. Film marks the final screen appearance of Pleasence, who died shortly after its com- pletion. **88m/C VHS, DVD.** Donald Pleasence, Mitchell Ryan, Marianne Hagan, Leo Geter, George P. Wilbur, Kim Darby, Bradford English, Devin Gardner, Paul Rudd; *D:* Joe Chappelle; *W:* Daniel Farrands; *C:* Billy Dickson; *M:* Alan Ho- warth.

Halloween: H20 🐾🐾 *H20 (Twenty Years Later); Halloween 7 1998 (R)* Jamie Lee Curtis treads familiar water in this return to the wellspring of the slasher genre. She reprises her role as Laurie Strode, sister of relentless psycho-killer Michael Myers. After faking her own death and changing her name, she becomes the headmistress of a private school in Cali- fornia. Now an overprotective single mom, she battles with the spirit of her brother, as well as the spirit of vodka. Her rebellious

Halloween Night 🐾🐾 *1990 (R)* An- cient evil rises up to destroy the perfect small town. **90m/C VHS, DVD.** Hy Pyke, Katrina Gar- ner; *D:* Emilio P. Miraglio.

Halloween: Resurrection 🐾½ *2002 (R)* The producers would like you to ignore the fact that psycho Michael Myers has been killed about 957 times in this son John (Harnett) blows off a field trip for

a romantic weekend with girlfriend Molly (Williams). They are accompanied by fel- low lust-ridden Michael fodder Charlie (Harn-Byrd) and Sarah (O'Keefe) on the Curtis, Adam Arkin, Josh Harnett, Michelle Wil- liams, Adam Ham-Byrd, Jodi Lyn O'Keefe, Janet Leigh, LL Cool J, Joseph Gordon-Levitt, Nancy Stephens, Branden Williams, Chris Duranc; *D:* Daryn Okada; *M:* John Ottman, John Carpenter.

The Halls of Montezuma 🐾🐾½ *1950* Large, bombastic WWII combat epic. Depicts the Marines fighting the Japanese in the Pa- cific. **113m/C VHS, DVD.** Richard Widmark, Jack Palance, Reginald Gardiner, Robert Wagner, Karl Malden, Richard Boone, Richard Hylton, Skip Homeier, Jack Webb, Neville Brand, Martin Milner, Bert Freed; *D:* Lewis Milestone; *W:* Michael Blank- fort, *C:* Winton C. Hoch, Harry Jackson; *M:* Sol Kaplan.

Halloween with the Addams Family 🐾 *1979 A* really, pathetic production spawned during the "reunion" craze of the late '70s, sparked only by the lively performance of Coogan's Uncle Fes- ter and the always lovable Lurch. **87m/C VHS.** John Astin, Carolyn Jones, Jackie Coogan, Ted Cassidy; *D:* George Tibbles, David Steinmetz; *C:* Jacques Marquette. *M:* Vic Mizzy, TV

Hallucination 🐾 *Hallucination;* *Generation 1967* Early flower-power exploiter about expatriate acid heads who murder an antique dealer under the influence of LSD and then attempt to hide at a moras- tery. Depicts LSD as the catalyst in bring- sepia while everyone's cool, breaking into color during the head trips. **90m/C VHS** George Montgomery, Danny Stone; *D:* Edward An- drew (Santos Alcocer) Mann, *W:* Edward Andrew (Santos Alcocer) Mann.

Hallucinations of a Deranged Mind 🐾 *Delirios de Um Anormal 1978 A* compilation of all the magic moments ever censored by the Brazilian military dictator- ship. Includes scenes banned from over 10 different Mojica Marins films, including his "Coffin Joe" character. In Portuguese with English subtitles. **86m/C VHS, BR Jose Mojica Marins.** *D:* Jose Mojica Marins; *W:* Jose Mojica Marins.

Hambone & Hillie 🐾🐾 *1984 (PG)* An elderly woman makes a 3000-mile trek across the United States to search for the dog she lost in an airport. **97m/C VHS.** Lillian Gish, Timothy Bottoms, Candy Clark, O.J. Simp- son, Robert Walker Jr., Jack Carter, Alan Hale Jr., Anne Lockhart; *D:* Roy Watts; *W:* Sandra K. Ba- ley.

Hamlet 🐾🐾🐾½ *1990 (PG)* Zeffirelli— in his fourth attempt at Shakespeare— brings to the screen his stage perfor- mance as the classic Shakespeare char- acter. Something is lost in the process, although there are some redeeming mo- ments including those with Faithfull as Ophelia. **114m/C VHS, GB** Nicol Williamson An- thony Hopkins, Marianne Faithfull, Gordon Jack- son, Judy Parfitt, Mark Dingham, Anjelica Huston; *D:* Tony Richardson.

Hamlet 🐾🐾🐾½ *1990 (PG)* Williamson brings to the screen his stage perfor- mance as the classic Shakespeare char- acter; something is lost in the process, although there are some redeeming mo- ments including those with Faithfull as creates a surprisingly energetic and ac- cessible interpretation of the Bard's moody play. Gibson brings charm, humor and a carefully calculated sense of vio- lence, not to mention a good deal of solid flesh, to the eponymous role, and handles the language skillfully (although if you seek a poetic Dane, stick with Olivier). Ex- ceptional work from Scofield and Bates. Close seems a tad hysterical (not to men- tion too young to play Gibson's mother), but brings insight and nuance to her role. Purists beware: this isn't a completely faithful adaptation. Beautifully costumed; shot on location in Northern Scotland. Those who prefer a traditional, "if you like your Shakespeare this isn't the version for you," but move the action ahead 600 years to the 19th century adds an interest- ing external political dimension to the pal- ace intrigue and gives this sixth screen adaptation the stature of Olivier's 1948

Hamburger Hill 🐾🐾 *1987 (R)* Popular war epic depicting the famous battle between Americans and Viet Cong over a useless hill in 1980s Vietnam backlash, and heyday of 1980s Vietnam backlash, and possibly the most realistic and bloodiest of the lot. **104m/C VHS, DVD.** Michael Dolan, Dan- iel O'Shea, Dylan McDermott, Tommy Swerdlow, Courtney B. Vance, Anthony Barille Michael Eoat- man, Don Cheadle, Tim Quill, Don James, Michael A. (M.A.) Nickles, Harry O'Reilly, Steven Weber, Tegan West, Ken Chinh, Doug Goodman, J.C. Falmore; *D:* John Irvin; *W:* James (Jim) Carabat- sos; *C:* Peter Macdonald; *M:* Philip Glass.

Hamburger... The Motion Picture 🐾 *1986 (R)* The life and times of students at Busterburger U., the only college devoted to hamburger franchise management. **90m/C VHS.** Leigh McCloskey, Dick Butkus, Randi Brooks, Sandy Heckett; *D:* Mike Marvin; *M:* Elmer Bernstein.

The Hamburg Cell 🐾🐾½ *2004* Based on the events leading up to 9/11 from the hijackers' perspective, Ziad Jar- rah (who will take over United Flight 93) is studying in Hamburg and begins going to a better Muslim A desire to belong recruit- ed by Al Qaeda. Alongside jihadists Mo- hammad Atta and Ramzi bin al Shibh, Jar- rah's plans begin to take shape; the story ends with the hijackers boarding their vari- ous flights. **101m/C DVD, GB** Karam Saleh, Ka- mel, Agni Tsangaridon, Kammy Darweish, Omar Berdouni, Adnar Maral; *D:* Antonia Bird; *W:* Ronan Bennett, Alice Bernard; *C:* Paul Conboy, T.V.

Hamlet 🐾🐾🐾½ *1948* Splendid acap- tation of Shakespeare's dramatic play, a better Muslim A desire to belong recruit- where soon leads to Jarrah being recruit- cut, including all of Rosencrantz and Guil- densterm. Beautifully photographed in Denmark. An Olivier triumph. Remade several times. **153m/B VHS, DVD, GB** au- rence Olivier, Basil Sydney, Felix Aylmer, Jean Simmons, Stanley Holloway, Peter Cushing, Chris- topher Lee, Eileen Herlie, John Laurie, Esmond Knight, Anthony Quayle; *D:* Laurence Olivier. *W:* Alan Dent; *C:* Desmond Dickinson; *M:* William Walton; *V:* John Gielgud. Oscars '48: Actor (Olivi- er), Art Dir./Set Dec., B&W, Costume Des. (B&W), Picture British Acad. '48: Film; Golden Globes '49: Actor—Drama (Olivier); N.Y. Film Critics '48: Actor

Hamlet 🐾🐾🐾 *1969 (G)* Williamson brings to the screen his stage perfor- mance as the classic Shakespeare char- acter; something is lost in the process, although there are some redeeming mo- ments including those with Faithfull as Ophelia. **114m/C VHS, GB** Nicol Williamson An- thony Hopkins, Marianne Faithfull, Gordon Jack- son, Judy Parfitt, Mark Dingham, Anjelica Huston; *D:* Tony Richardson.

Hamlet 🐾🐾🐾 *1996 (PG-13)* Bran- agh tackles Shakespeare once again with the uncut, four-hour long story of the mel- anchoy Dane (played by you-know-who), text, and move the action ahead 600 years to the 19th century adds an interest- ing external political dimension to the pal- ace intrigue and gives this sixth screen adaptation the stature of Olivier's 1948 masterpiece. Jacobi and Christie stand out among a very large and brilliant cast. Lemmon and Crystal, however, should stick to American comedy. A two and a half hour version was also prepared for those with shorter attention spans, but the uncut version is well worth the time invested. **242m/C VHS, GB** Kenneth Branagh, Kate Winslet, Julie Christie, Derek Jacobi, Richard Briers, Brian Blessed, Michael Maloney, Timothy Spall, Reece Dinsdale, Jack Lemmon, Nicholas Farrell, Charlton Heston, Rosemary Harris, Gerard Depardieu, Robin Williams, Billy Crystal, Simon Russell Beale, Michael Bryant, John Gielgud, Richard Attenborough, Rufus Sewell, Judi Dench, Ian McElhinney, John Mills; **D:** Kenneth Branagh; **W:** Kenneth Branagh; **C:** Alex Thomson; **M:** Patrick Doyle.

Hamlet 🦴🦴🦴 **2000 (R)** It's mopey Hawke's turn as the title character but in this update he's hardly a Danish prince. Instead he's an experimental filmmaker in New York whose murderous uncle Claudius (MacLachlan) runs the family conglomerate, Denmark, Inc. Thanks to Almereyda's respect for Shakespeare's language, as well as his excellent adaptation to present-day corporate America, this interpretation loses none of the play's power, and adds some insights that prove its timelessness. **111m/C VHS, DVD.** Ethan Hawke, Kyle MacLachlan, Sam Shepard, Diane Venora, Bill Murray, Julia Stiles, Liev Schreiber, Karl Geary, Paula Malcomson, Steve Zahn, Dechen Thurman, Jeffrey Wright, Paul Bartel, Rome Neal, Casey Affleck; **D:** Michael Almereyda; **W:** Michael Almereyda; **C:** John de Borman; **M:** Carter Burwell.

The Hammer 🦴🦴½ **2007 (R)** After getting dumped by his girlfriend on his 40th birthday, carpenter/boxing instructor Jerry Ferro (Carolla), aka "The Hammer" quits his lousy day job for a return to the ring with Olympic hopes. He soon sparks up a romance with one of his students (Juergensen) and catches the eye of big-time boxing coach Eddie Bell (Quinn), who takes him under his wing. Not so much a spoof of triumphant sports movies, but a realistic underdog comedy that works as a goofy "Rocky" tribute. Nearly autobiographical, written by Carolla, an actual former Golden Glover (and carpenter), who plays his usual self-deprecating, snarky self with surprising success. **93m/C DVD. US** Adam Carolla, Heather Juergensen, Jonathan Hernandez, Oswaldo Castillo, Tom Quinn, Raimu; **D:** Charles Herman-Wurmfeld; **W:** Kevin Hench; **C:** Marco Fagnoli; **M:** John Swihart, Matt Mariano.

Hammers over the Anvil 🦴🦴½ **1991** Young Alan Marshall (Outhred) has a case of hero worship for local horse trainer East Driscoll (Crowe). But East has also caught the eye of the upper-class (and married) English beauty, Grace McAlister (Rampling), with whom he is having an affair, and which Alan witnesses. But East wants Grace more than just part-time and is determined to force her to run away with him—with disastrous consequences. **98m/C VHS, DVD. AU** Charlotte Rampling, Russell Crowe, Alexander Outhred, John Rafter Lee, Kirsty McGregor, Jake Frost; **D:** Ann Turner; **W:** Ann Turner, Peter Hepworth; **C:** James Bartle.

Hammersmith Is Out 🦴🦴 **1972 (R)** A violent lunatic cons an orderly into letting him escape. Chases, romance and craziness follow. **108m/C VHS.** Richard Burton, Elizabeth Taylor, Peter Ustinov, Beau Bridges, John Schuck; **D:** Peter Ustinov.

Hammett 🦴🦴 **1982 (PG)** After many directors and script rewrites, Wenders was assigned to this arch neo-noir what-if scenario. Depicts Dashiell Hammett solving a complex crime himself, an experience he uses in his novels. Interesting, but ultimately botched studio exercise, like many from executive producer Francis Coppola, who is said to have reshot much of the film. **98m/C VHS, DVD.** Frederic Forrest, Peter Boyle, Sylvia Sidney, Elisha Cook Jr., Marilu Henner; **D:** Wim Wenders; **C:** Joseph Biroc; **M:** John Barry.

Hamsin 🦴🦴🦴 **1983** A Jewish landowner and an Arab worker encounter difficulties in their relationship when the government announces plans to confiscate Arab land. In Hebrew with English subtitles. **90m/C VHS.** Shlomo Tarshish, Yasin Shawap, Hemda Levy, Ruth Geler; **D:** Daniel Wachsmann.

Hamsun 🦴🦴 **1996** Highly regarded Norwegian Nobel Prize-winning writer Knut Hamsun (von Sydow) stunned his countrymen when he sided with the Nazis in WWII and urged them to stop resisting the invaders of their homeland. An ardent nationalist, the elderly Hamsun apparently heard only what he wanted to about Hitler's policies and regarded Britain as the greater threat to Europe. After the war Hamsun and his equally outspoken pro-German wife, Marie (Norby), are deemed traitors and are put on trial. Based on a book by Thorkild Hansen. Swedish, Danish, and Norwegian with subtitles. **154m/C VHS, DVD. NO DK SW** Max von Sydow, Ghita Norby, Sverre Anker Ousdal, Ernst Jacobi, Anette Hoff, Erik Hivju; **D:** Jan Troell; **W:** Per Olof Enquist; **C:** Jan Troell; **M:** Arvo Part.

Hancock 🦴🦴 **2008** Hancock (Smith) is a superhero with a big image problem. Edgy and sarcastic (and a drunk), he gets the job done but leaves a LOT of damage behind and the citizens of L.A. are tired of cleaning up the mess. With his bad rep, it's a good thing Hancock just saved the life of PR exec Ray Embrey (Bateman) because he really needs a spin doctor. Of course, what's not going to help is Hancock hitting on Embrey's hot babe wife (Theron). Not yet reviewed. **?m/C** Will Smith, Jason Bateman, Charlize Theron; **D:** Peter Berg; **W:** Vince Gilligan, Vy Vincent Ngo; **C:** Tobias Schliessler; **M:** John Powell.

The Hand 🦴🦴 **1960** During WWII, three British POWs are tortured by the Japanese. Refusing to give information, two of them have their right hands cut off. The third opts to talk, thereby keeping his hand. After the war, a series of murders occur in London where the victims have their hands amputated. Could there be a connection? **61m/B VHS, DVD. GB** Derek Bond, Ronald Lee Hunt, Reed de Rouen, Ray Cooney, Brian Coleman; **D:** Henry Cass.

The Hand 🦴🦴🦴 **1981 (R)** A gifted cartoonist's hand is severed in a car accident. Soon, the hand is on the loose with a mind of its own, seeking out victims with an obsessive vengeance. Stone's sophomore directorial outing is a unique, surreal psycho-horror pastiche consistently underrated by most critics. **105m/C VHS, DVD.** Michael Caine, Andrea Marcovicci, Annie McEnroe, Bruce McGill, Viveca Lindfors; **Cameos:** Oliver Stone; **D:** Oliver Stone; **W:** Oliver Stone; **C:** King Baggot; **M:** James Horner.

Hand Gun 🦴🦴½ **1993 (R)** Jack McCallister (Cassel) is wounded in a shoot-out with police but still manages to get away with half-a-million from a robbery. When word gets out, everybody begins looking for Jack, including his two sons—gun happy George (Williams) and small time con artist Michael (Schulze). **90m/C VHS, DVD.** Seymour Cassel, Treat Williams, Paul Schulze, Michael Rapaport; **D:** Whitney Ransick; **W:** Whitney Ransick; **C:** Michael Spiller; **M:** Douglas J. Cuomo.

The Hand that Rocks the Cradle 🦴🦴½ **1992 (R)** DeMornay is Peyton Flanders, the nanny from hell, in an otherwise predictable thriller. Sciorra's role is a thankless one as pregnant and unbelievably naive Claire Bartel, who unwittingly starts a horrific chain of events when she levels charges of molestation against her obstetrician. Transparent plot preys on the worst fears of viewers, and doesn't offer anything innovative or new. See this one for DeMornay's Jekyll and Hyde performance. **110m/C VHS, DVD.** Annabella Sciorra, Rebecca De Mornay, Matt McCoy, Ernie Hudson, Julianne Moore, Madeline Zima, John de Lancie, Mitchell Laurance; **D:** Curtis Hanson; **W:** Amanda Silver; **C:** Robert Elswit; **M:** Graeme Revell. MTV Movie Awards '92: Villain (De Mornay).

A Handful of Dust 🦴🦴 **1988 (PG)** A dry, stately adaptation of the bitter Evelyn Waugh novel about a stuffy young aristocrat's wife's careless infidelity and how it sends her innocent husband to a tragic downfall. A well-meaning version that captures Waugh's cynical satire almost in spite of itself. Set in post-WWI England. **114m/C VHS, DVD. GB** James Wilby, Kristin Scott Thomas, Rupert Graves, Alec Guinness, Anjelica Huston, Judi Dench, Cathryn Harrison, Pip Torrens, John Junkin; **D:** Charles Sturridge; **W:** Charles Sturridge, Tim Sullivan, Derek Granger; **C:** Peter Hannan; **M:** George Fenton. British Acad. '88: Support. Actress (Dench).

The Handmaid's Tale 🦴🦴½ **1990 (R)** A cool, shallow but nonetheless chilling nightmare based on Margaret Atwood's bestselling novel, about a woman caught in the machinations of a near-future society so sterile it enslaves the few fertile women and forces them into being child-bearing "handmaids." **109m/C VHS, DVD.** Natasha Richardson, Robert Duvall, Faye Dunaway, Aidan Quinn, Elizabeth McGovern, Victoria Tennant, Blanche Baker, Traci Lind; **W:** Harold Pinter; **C:** Igor Luther; **M:** Ryuichi Sakamoto.

Hands Across the Border 🦴🦴 **1943** A musical western in which Roy helps a woman find the men who killed her father. **72m/B VHS, DVD.** Roy Rogers, Ruth Terry, Guinn "Big Boy" Williams, Onslow Stevens, Mary Treen, Joseph Crehan; **D:** Joseph Kane.

Hands Across the Table 🦴🦴🦴 **1935** Regi Allen (Lombard) is a fortune-hunting manicurist in a swanky hotel barber shop. Has-been millionaire playboy Theodore Drew III (MacMurray) falls for her but he's about to marry money (Allwyn) and Regi's got a wheelchair-bound rich man (Bellamy) just waiting for her to say "I do." Snappy dialogue and light-hearted performances. Based on the story "Bracelets" by Vina Delmar. **80m/B VHS, DVD.** Carole Lombard, Fred MacMurray, Ralph Bellamy, Astrid Allwyn, Ruth Donnelly, Marie Prevost, William Demarest, Edward (Ed) Gargan; **D:** Mitchell Leisen; **W:** Norman Krasna, Vincent Lawrence, Herbert Fields; **C:** Ted Tetzlaff.

Hands of a Murderer 🦴🦴½ **1990** Sherlock Holmes and the Prince of Crime faithful Dr. Watson (Hillerman) are in pursuit of the great detective's most evil nemesis—the nefarious Moriarty (Andrews). This time, the fiend has escaped the gallows and stolen government secrets from the safe of Holmes' brother Mycroft. TV movie. **100m/C VHS, DVD.** Edward Woodward, John Hillerman, Anthony Andrews, Kim Thomson, Peter Jeffrey, Warren Clarke; **D:** Stuart Orme; **W:** Charles Edward Pogue.

Hands of a Stranger 🦴🦴½ **1962** Another undistinguished entry in the long line of remakes of "The Hands of Orlac." A pianist who loses his hands in an accident is given the hands of a murderer, and his new hands want to do more than tickle the ivories. Kellerman has a very small role as does former "Sheena" McCalla. **95m/B VHS, DVD.** Paul Lukather, Joan Harvey, James Stapleton, Sally Kellerman, Irish McCalla; **D:** Newton Arnold; **C:** Henry Cronjager Jr.

Hands of a Stranger 🦴🦴½ **1987** Policeman's wife is raped during an adulterous tryst. As the painful truth dawns on the cop, he himself dallies with a compassionate lady D.A. while hunting the attacker. About as sordid as a network TV-movie gets without toppling into sleaze; strong acting and a sober script pull it through. But the plot, from Robert Daly's novel, doesn't justify miniseries treatment; the two-cassette package is excessively long. **179m/C VHS.** Armand Assante, Beverly D'Angelo, Blair Brown, Michael Lerner, Philip Casnoff, Arliss Howard; **D:** Larry Elikann; **W:** Arthur Kopit. TV.

The Hands of Orlac 🦴🦴 *Orlacs Hände* **1925** Classic silent film about a pianist whose hands are mutilated in an accident. His hands are replaced by those of a murderer, and his urge to kill becomes overwhelming. Contains restored footage. **92m/B VHS. AT** Conrad Veidt, Fritz Kortner, Carmen Cartellieri, Paul Askonas, Alexandra Sorina, Fritz Strassny; **D:** Robert Wiene; **W:** Ludwig Nerz; **C:** Gunther Krampf, Hans Androschin.

The Hands of Orlac 🦴🦴 *Hands of the Stranger; Hands of a Strangler* **1960** Third remake of Maurice Renard's classic tale. When a concert pianist's hands are mutilated in an accident, he receives a graft of a murderer's hands. Obsession sweeps the musician, as he believes his new hands are incapable of music, only violence. Bland adaptation of the original story. **95m/B VHS, DVD. GB FR** Mel Ferrer, Christopher Lee, Felix Aylmer, Basil Sydney, Donald Wolfit, Donald Pleasence, Dany Carrel, Lucile Saint-Simon, Peter Reynolds, Campbell Singer, David Peel; **D:** Edmond T. Greville; **W:** Edmond T. Greville, John Baines, Donald Taylor; **C:** Desmond Dickinson; **M:** Claude Bolling.

Hands of Steel WOOF! **1986 (R)** A ruthless cyborg carries out a mission to find and kill an important scientist. Terrible acting, and lousy writing: an all-around woofer! **94m/C VHS, DVD,** Daniel Greene, John Saxon, Janet Agren, Claudio Cassinelli, George Eastman; **D:** Sergio Martino.

Hands of the Ripper 🦴🦴½ **1971 (R)** Jack the Ripper's daughter returns to London where she works as a medium by day and stalks the streets at night. Classy Hammer horror variation on the perennial theme. **85m/C VHS. GB** Eric Porter, Angharad Rees, Jane Merrow, Keith Bell, Derek Godfrey, Dora Bryan, Marjorie Rhodes, Norman Bird; **D:** Peter Sasdy; **W:** L.W. Davidson; **C:** Ken Talbot; **M:** Christopher Gunning.

Hands Up 🦴🦴½ **1926** Jaunty Confederate spy (played by much-overlooked American comedian Griffith) attempts, amidst much comic nonsense, to thwart Yankee gold mining during the Civil War. Silent. **50m/B VHS.** Raymond Griffith, Mack Swain, Marion (Marian) Nixon, Montagu Love; **D:** Clarence Badger. Natl. Film Reg. '05.

Hands Up 🦴🦴🦴 *Rece do Gory* **1981** Famed Polish film finished in 1967 but not released until 1981 for political reasons (prologue shot in '81 included). Doctors at a medical school reunion reflect upon the effect of Stalinist rule on their education and lives. In Polish with English subtitles. **78m/C VHS. PL** Tadeusz Lomnicki, Bogumil Kobiela, Alan Bates, Joanna Szczerbic, Jerzy Skolimowski; **W:** Jerzy Skolimowski, Andrzej Kostenko; **M:** Jozef Skrzek.

Hang 'Em High 🦴🦴🦴½ **1967 (PG-13)** A cowboy is saved from a lynching and vows to hunt down the gang that nearly killed him in this American-made spaghetti western. Eastwood's first major vehicle made outside of Europe. **114m/C VHS, DVD. IT** Clint Eastwood, Inger Stevens, Ed Begley Sr., Pat Hingle, James MacArthur; **D:** Ted Post; **W:** Leonard Freeman, Mel Goldberg; **C:** Richard H. Kline, Leonard J. South; **M:** Dominic Frontiere.

Hangar 18 🦴🦴🦴 *Invasion Force* **1980 (PG)** Silly sci-fi drama about two astronauts who collide with a UFO during a shuttle flight. Later they learn that the government is hiding it in a hangar and they try to prove its existence. Shown on TV as "Invasion Force" with an entirely new ending. **97m/C VHS, DVD.** Darren McGavin, Robert Vaughn, Gary Collins, James Hampton, Philip Abbott, Pamela Bellwood, Tom Hallick, Cliff Osmond, Joseph Campanella; **D:** James L. Conway; **W:** David O'Malley.

The Hanged Man 🦴🦴 **1974** Tale of a gunslinger in the Old West who mystically escapes death by hanging. Reborn, he re-evaluates the meaning of justice. **78m/C VHS, DVD.** Steve Forrest, Cameron Mitchell, Sharon Acker, Dean Jagger, Will Geer, Barbara Luna, Rafael Campos; **D:** Michael Caffey. TV.

Hangfire 🦴🦴 **1991 (R)** When a New Mexican prison is evacuated thanks to a nasty chemical explosion, several prisoners decide it's time for a furlough, and they elect the local sheriff's wife as a traveling companion. Another mediocre actioner from director Maris, it gets an extra bone for stunts kids shouldn't try at home. **91m/C VHS.** Brad Davis, Yaphet Kotto, Lee DeBroux, Jan-Michael Vincent, George Kennedy, Kim Delaney, James Tolkan, Lou Ferrigno, Lyle Alzado, Collin Bernsen. *D:* Peter Maris. *W:* Brian D. Jeffries. *C:* Mark Morris.

Hangin' with the Homeboys 1991 (R) One night in the lives of four young men. Although the Bronx doesn't offer much for any of them, they have little interest in escaping 'ts confines, and they are more than willing to complain. Characters are insightful, ly written and well portrayed, with strongest work from Serrano as a Puerto Rican who is trying to pass himself off as Italian. Lack of plot may frustrate some viewers. **89m/C VHS, DVD.** Mario Joyner, Doug E. Doug, John Leguizamo, Nestor Serrano, Kimberly Russell, Mary B. Ward, Christine Claravell, Reggie Montgomery. *D:* Joseph B. Vasquez; *W:* Joseph B. Vasquez; *C:* Anghel Decca. Sundance '91: Screenplay.

The Hanging Garden 1997 (R) Bizarre family drama mixes the matter-of-fact and the surreal. Gay 25-year-old Sweet William (Leavins) returns to his rural Nova Scotia home and family after a 10-year absence for the marriage of his sister, Rosemary (Fox). The reunion brings up lots of painful memories and flashes back to the 15-year old Sweet William (Veinotte), when 1e was spectacularly abused by his psycho father Whiskey Mac (MacNeill). After more crises, the teen hangs himself from a backyard tree. Oh yes, everyone in the present can still see the teen's ghost hanging there, including the adult William. You figure it out. **91m/C VHS, DVD, CA** Chris Leavins, Peter MacNeill, Kerry Fox, Seana McKenna, Troy Veinotte, Sarah Polley, Christine Dunsworth, Joel S. Keller, Joan Orenstein; *D:* Thom Fitzgerald; *W:* Thom Fitzgerald; *C:* Daniel Jobin. Genie '97: Screenplay; Support. Actor (MacNeill). Support. Actress (McKenna); Toronto-City '97: Canadian Feature Film.

Hanging on a Star 1978 (PG) A small 'rock band encounters many comic adventures as it climbs its way up the charts. Raffin stars as the band's persistent and competent road agent. **92m/C VHS.** Deborah Raffin, Lane Caudell, Wolfman Jack, Jason Parker, Danil Torppe. *D:* Mike MacFarland.

The Hanging Tree 1959 Cooper plays a frontier doctor who rescues a thief (Piazza) from a lynch mob (Schell). Malden is the bad guy who tries to attack Schell and Cooper shoots him. The townspeople take Cooper out to "The Hanging Tree" but this time it's Schell and Piazza who come to his rescue. Slow-paced western with good performances. Scott's screen debut. **108m/B VHS.** Gary Cooper, Maria Schell, Ben Piazza, Karl Malden, George C. Scott, Karl Swenson, Virginia Gregg, King Donovan; *D:* Delmer Daves. *M:* Max Steiner.

Hanging Up 1999 (PG-13) Strident, schmaltzy comedy about family. Married working mom and middle sister Eve (Ryan) seems to be the one that has to deal with family dilemmas, in this case her cantankerous dying father Lou (Matthau). Older sis Georgia (Keaton) is a workaholic Manhattan magazine exec while ditzy younger sis Maddy (Kudrow) is an actress working on a soap. They check in by phone but duck out on their share of the responsibilities although sibling rivalry rears its head. Based on the nove by Delia Ephron. **94m/C VHS, DVD,** Meg Ryan, Diane Keaton, Lisa Kudrow, Walter Matthau, Adam Arkin, Cloris Leachman, Jesse James, Duke Moosekian, Ann Bortolotti; *D:* Diane Keaton; *W:* Delia Ephron, Nora Ephron. *C:* Howard Atherton. *M:* David Hirschfelder.

The Hanging Woman *Return of the Zombies; Beyond the Living Dead; La Orgia de los Muertos; Dracula, the Terror of the Living Dead; Orgy of the Dead; House of Terror.* 1972 (R) A man is summoned to the reading of a relative's will, and discovers the corpse of a young woman hanging in a cemetery. As he investigates the mystery, he uncovers a local doctor's plans to zom-

bify the entire world. Not bad at all and quite creepy once the zombies are out in force. Euro-horror star Naschy plays the necrophiliac grave digger, Igor. **91m/C DVD. SP/IT** Stelvio Rosi, Vickie Nesbitt, Catherine Gilbert, Gerald Tichy, Paul Naschy; Dianik Zurakowska, Maria Pia Conte, Carlos Quiney. *D:* Jose Luis Merino; *M:* Jose Luis Merino.

Hangman 2000 (R) A serial killer plays a lethal game of hangman, sending a videotape of each murder to detective Nick Roos (Phillips). Roos joins psychiatrist Grace Mitchell (Arnick) to catch the killer but she may be the killer's next intended victim. **95m/C VHS, DVD.** Lou Diamond Phillips, Madchen Amick, Dan Laura, Mark Wilson, Vincent Corazza. *D:* Ken Girotti; *W:* Vladimir Nemirovsky. *C:* Gerald Packer. *M:* Steven Stern.

VIDEO

Hangman's Curse 2003 (PG-13) It's the jocks vs. the Goths in a high school with a deadly disease. No one's sure whether the deaths are caused by the ghost of a bullied student, drugs, or witchcraft, so an undercover family of occult investigators is brought in to solve the mystery. Convoluted plot with a predictable erring doesn't work as horror, because it's not all that scary, and the mystery elements don't hold up. Christians looking for a "family values thriller" might like it, though. **106m/C VHS, DVD.** David Keith, Mel Harris, Edwin Hodge, William R. Moses, Leighton Meester, Douglas Smith, Bobby Brewer, Daniel Farber, Andrea Morris, Frank Peretti, George Humphreys; *W:* Kathy Mackel, Stan Foster.

Hangman's House 1928 Dying "hanging" judge James O'Brien (Bosworth) tries to ensure his daughter Connaught's (Collyer) happiness by marrying her to wealthy James D'Arcy (Foxe), even though she despises him. Meanwhile, exiled patriot Hogan (McLaglen) returns to Ireland to kill the man responsible for his sister's suicide (guess who). **72m/B DVD.** Victor McLaglen, June Collyer, Earle Foxe, Hobart Bosworth, Larry Kent; *D:* John Ford; *W:* Malcolm Stuart Boylan; *C:* George Schneidamsn.

Hangmen woofl 1987 (R) Ex-CIA agents battle it out on the East side of New York. If you're into very violent, very bad, acted films, then this one's for you. **88m/C VHS, DVD.** Jake LaMotta, Rick Washburne, Dog Thomas, Sandra Bullock. *D:* J. Christian Ingvordsen, Steven Kaman. *C:* Steven Kaman. *M:* Michael Montes.

Hangmen Also Die 1942 Lang's anti-Nazi propaganda film was inspirated by the actual May, 1942 assassination of Reinhard Heydrich. Franz Svoboda (Donlevy) is the member of the Czech resistance who assassinates Heydrich. The Nazis seek revenge and begin rounding up and executing Czech citizens, aided by the traitorous Emil (Lockhart). Franz wants to give himself up to prevent further slaughter but is persuaded to turn the tables on Emil and make him appear to be the assassin. Bertolt Erecht had a hand in the original screenplay but did not receive screen credit and last said most of his work was cut out. **134m/B VHS, DVD.** Brian Donlevy, Gene Lockhart, Walter Brennan, Anna Lee, Dennis O'Keefe, Alexander Granach, Jonathan Hale, Margaret Wycherly, Hans von Twardowski; *D:* Fritz Lang; *W:* John Wexley; *C:* James Wong Howe; *M:* Hans Esser.

Hangover Square 1945 Foggy, gaslit London, 1903. High-strung composer George (Cregar) 'nas periodic blackouts and thinks he's a murderer although the police clear him. Then he gets involved with lush music hall singer Netta (Darnell), who strings him along. When George discovers her betrayal, his black-

outs get worse and he really does become a killer. And what happens to the two-film Netta is still genuinely shocking. Cregar's last film—he died of a heart attack before its release. **77m/B DVD,** Laird Cregar, Linda Darnell, George Sanders, Glenn Langan, Alan Napier; *D:* John Brahm; *W:* Barre Lyndon; *C:* Joseph LaShelle. *M:* Bernard Herrmann.

Hank Aaron: Chasing the Dream 1995 Docudrama combines archival footage, interviews, and reenactments to tell the story of the life and career of Henry Aaron. Follows Aaron's development as a Hall of Fame outfielder for the Milwaukee and Atlanta Braves and as a leader in the civil rights movement. Emphasis on personal and societal issues, as well as on-the-field accomplishments, raises this one above most sports biography documentaries. **120m/C VHS.** *D:* Mike Tollin; *W:* Mike Tollin; *C:* Chuck Cohen, Derek Britt; *M:* Ed Smart; *Narr:* Dorian Harewood.

Hanky Panky 1982 (PG) Insipid comic thriller in which Wilder and Radner become involved in a search for top secret plans. **107m/C VHS, DVD,** Gene Wilder, Gilda Radner, Richard Widmark, Kathleen Quinlan; *D:* Sidney Poitier.

Hanna K. 1983 (R) Story of divided passions set in the tumultuous state of Israel. American lawyer Clayburgh tries to settle her personal and political affairs with various Middle Eastern men. Medic-cre and disappointing. Release generated controversy over pro-Palestine stance. **111m/C VHS. FR** Jill Clayburgh, Gabriel Byrne, Jean Yanne, Muhamad Bakri, David Clennon, Oded Kotler. *D:* Constantin Costa-Gavras.

Hannah and Her Sisters 1986 (PG) Allen's grand epic about a New York showbiz family, its three adult sisters and their various romantic entanglements. Excellent performances by the entire cast, especially Caine and Hershey. Classic Allen themes of life, love, death, and desire are explored in an urbane, witty and sensitive manner. Witty, ironic, and heartwarming **103m/C VHS, DVD.** Mia Farrow, Barbara Hershey, Dianne Wiest, Michael Caine, Woody Allen, Maureen O'Sullivan, Lloyd Nolan, Sam Waterston, Carrie Fisher, Max von Sydow, Julie Kavner, Daniel Stern, Tony Roberts, John Turturro; *D:* Woody Allen; *C:* Carlo Di Palma. Oscars '86: Orig. Screenplay, Support. Actor (Caine), Support. Actress (Wiest); British Acad. '86: Director (Allen), Orig. Screenplay; Golden Globes '87: Screenplay; Support. Actress (Wiest); L.A. Film Critics '86: Film, Screenplay, Support. Actress (Wiest); Natl. Soc. Film Critics Review '86: Director (Allen), Support. Actress (Wiest); N.Y. Film Critics '86: Director (Allen), Film, Support. Actress (Wiest); Natl. Bd. of Review '86: Support. Actress (Wiest); Writers Guild '86: Orig. Screenplay.

Hanna's War 1988 (PG-13) A moving film about Hanna Senesh, a young Hungarian Jew living in Palestine, who volunteered for a suicide mission behind Nazi lines during WWII. After her capture by the Germans, she was killed, and Detmers is very believable as a martyr. **148m/C VHS.** Ellen Burstyn, Maruschka Detmers, Anthony Andrews, Donald Pleasence, David Warner, Denholm Elliott, Vincenzo Ricotta, Ingrid Pitt; *D:* Menahem Golan; *W:* Menahem Golan; *M:* Dov Seltzer.

Hannibal 2001 (R) The long-awaited sequel to the much loved "Science of the Lambs." Dettmers is now considered by many to have been a martyr. equally praised "Manhunter" is more gruesome than scary, but it still managed to bring loads of people to the theatre, most likely to enjoy a heapin' helping of Hopkins's Hannibal. This time the infamous Dr. Lecter and FBI agent Clarice Starling (now played by Moore) are brought together by one of Hannibal's vengeful victims, the severely disfigured Verger (played by Oldman, under layers of prosthetics), and his trained wild pigs. Based on the novel by Thomas Harris. **131m/C VHS, DVD, US** Anthony Hopkins, Julianne Moore, Gary Oldman, Ray Liotta, Frankie Faison, Giancarlo Giannini, Francesca Neri, Zeljko Ivanek, Hazelle Goodman, David Andrews, Francis Guinan, Enrico Lo Verso; *D:* Ridley Scott; *W:* David Mamel, Steven Zaillian; *C:* John Matheson; *M:* Hans Zimmer.

Hannibal Rising 2007 (R) How Hannibal became a cannibal. Harris adapts his own novel but the fiendish spark is gone. A teenaged Hannibal (Ulliel) and his family fall prey to vicious roving thugs in 1944. His plump little sister suffers an especially nasty fate). He's then taken in by his widowed Japanese aunt, Lady Murasaki (Li), who introduces him to the ways of the samurai and a handy stash of swords. Hannibal then tracks his quarry and dispatches them in gory ways while practicing his superstitious sneer. A distinct comedown for a franchise character. **117m/C VHS, DVD, US GB FR** Gaspard Ulliel, Gong Li, Rhys Ifans, Kevin McKidd, Dominic West, Aaron Thomas, Helena-La Tachovska; *D:* Peter Webber; *W:* Thomas Harris; *C:* Benjamin Davis; *M:* Ilan Eshkeri, Shigeru Umebay Ashi.

Hansel and Gretel 1982 From Shelly Duvall's "Faerie Tale Theatre" comes the story of two young children who get more than they bargained for when they eat a gingerbread house, though he can foresee the outcome of their reign. In German with English subtitles. **110m/C VHS. GE HU** Klaus Maria Brandauer, Erland Josephson, Walter Schmidinger; *D:* Peter Dobai, Istvan Szabo; *C:* Lajos Koltai; *M:* Gyorgy Vukan.

Hanussen 1988 (R) The third of Szabo and Brandauer's price-of-power trilogy, (after "Mephisto" and "Colonel Redl"), in which a talented German magician and clairvoyant (based on a true life figure) collaborates with the Nazis during his rise 'o power in the 1930s, a

The Happening 2008 (R) Actually the problem is no one can figure out what IS happening. Wahlberg is a high school science teacher who's worried about an environmental disaster. And he's right. Soon he and his family are on the run, trying to find a safe haven from a crisis that threatens humanity. Did the govern-

Hanover Street 1979 (PG) An American bomber pilot and a married British nurse fall in love in war-torn Europe. Eventually the pilot must work with the husband of the woman he loves on a secret mission. A sappy, romantic tearjerker. **109m/C VHS, DVD,** Harrison Ford, Lesley-Anne Down, Christopher Plummer, Alec McCowen. *D:* Peter Hyams; *W:* Peter Hyams; *C:* David Watkin.

Hannie Caulder 1972 (R) A woman hires a bounty hunter to avenge her husband's murder and her own rape at the hands of three bandits. Excellent casting but uneven direction. Boyd is uncredited as the preacher. **87m/C VHS, DVD.** Raquel Welch, Robert Culp, Ernest Borgnine, Strother Martin, Jack Elam, Christopher Lee, Diana Dors, Stephen Boyd; *D:* Burt Kennedy; *W:* Burt Kennedy.

Hanoi Hilton 1987 (R) A brutal drama about the sufferings of American POWs in Vietnamese prison camps. Non-classic tale. **105m/C VHS, DVD,** Robin Askwith, Eleanor Parker, Richard Basehart, Cyril Shaps, John Gregson; *D:* Robert Schenkel.

Hans Brinker 1969 Young drama about Hans and his sister participate in an ice skating race, hoping to win a pair of silver skates. A musical version of the classic tale. **103m/C VHS, DVD.** Richard Basehart, ... *D:* Robert Scheerer.

Hans Christian Andersen 1952 Sentimental musical story of Hans Christian Andersen, a young cobbler who remastered editions available with stereo sound and original trailer. ♪♪The King's New Clothes; I'm Hans Christian Andersen; Wonderful Copenhagen; Thumbelina; The Inch Worm; No Two People. **112m/C VHS, DVD.** Danny Kaye, Farley Granger, Zizi Jeanmaire, Joey Walsh; *D:* Charles Vidor. *W:* Moss Hart. *C:* Harry Stradling Sr.; *M:* Frank Loesser. CABLE ment accidentally release a biological weapon that got out of control and is decimating the population or is Mother Nature taking revenge? Let's hope that M. Night has his scary movie mojo back after 2006's disappointing "The Lady in the Water." Not yet reviewed. **?m/C** Mark Wahlberg, Zooey Deschanel, John Leguizamo, Spencer Breslin, Betty Buckley, Joel de la Fuente, Frank Collison, Ashlyn Sanchez; **D:** M. Night Shyamalan; **W:** M. Night Shyamalan; **C:** Tak Fujimoto; **M:** James Newton Howard.

Happenstance 🐾🐾½ *The Beating of the Butterfly's Wings; Le Battement d'Ailes du Papillon* **2000** (R) Is it fate? destiny? chance? that brings people together? Clerk Irene (Tautou) chats with a woman on the subway who tells her that she will meet her true love that day. He turns out to be Faudel (Younes) but of course the made-for-each-other duo's actually getting together is a maze of complications. Amusing romantic comedy. French with subtitles. **97m/C VHS, DVD.** *FR* Audrey Tautou, Faudel, Eric Savin, Eric Feldman, Nathalie Besancon, Lysaine Meis, Lily Boulogne, Francoise Bertin, Frederique Bouraly, Irene Ismailoff; **D:** Laurent Firode; **W:** Laurent Firode; **C:** Jean-Rene Duveau; **M:** Peter Chase.

The Happiest Days of Your Life 🐾🐾🐾 **1950** During the London Blitz, a girls' academy is evacuated to the country and mistakenly billeted with a boys' school. The headmaster and headmistress clash and the bewildered students all try to get along. Good cast, lots of laughs. Adapted from a play by John Dighton. **81m/B VHS.** *GB* Alastair Sim, Margaret Rutherford, Joyce Grenfell, Edward Rigby, Guy Middleton, John Bentley, Bernadette O'Farrell, Richard Wattis, Muriel Aked, Patricia Owens, John Turnbull, Arthur Howard; **D:** Frank Launder; **W:** Frank Launder, John Dighton; **M:** Mischa Spoliansky.

The Happiest Millionaire 🐾🐾 **1967** A Disney film about a newly immigrated lad who finds a job as butler in the home of an eccentric millionaire. Based on the book "My Philadelphia Father," by Kyle Chrichton. ♫What's Wrong With That?; Watch Your Footwork; Valentine Candy; Strengthen the Dwelling; I'll Always Be Irish; Bye-Yum Pum Pum; I Believe in This Country; Detroit; There Are Those. **118m/C VHS, DVD.** Fred MacMurray, Tommy Steele, Greer Garson, Geraldine Page, Lesley Ann Warren, John Davidson; **D:** Norman Tokar; **W:** A.J. Carothers; **C:** Edward Colman; **M:** Richard M. Sherman, Robert B. Sherman.

Happily Ever After 🐾🐾 **1982** Las Vegas star-maker recruits and manipulates two preteen performers. Show business life in Vegas is given a truthful treatment in this drama. **95m/C VHS.** Suzanne Somers, John Rubinstein, Eric (Hans Gudegast) Braeden; **D:** Robert Scheerer. **TV**

Happily Ever After 🐾½ *Alem Da Paixao* **1986** A Brazilian housewife meets a bisexual transvestite and has a passionate affair, bringing her into the depths of the criminal underworld. In Portuguese with English subtitles. Contains nudity. **106m/C VHS.** *BR* Regina Duarte, Paul Castelli; **D:** Bruno Barreto; **C:** Alfonso Beato.

Happily Ever After 🐾½ **1993** (G) Sequel to "Snow White" begins where the original ends, but isn't connected to the Walt Disney classic. Snow White and her Prince prepare for their wedding when the Wicked Queen is found dead by her brother, who vows revenge. So it's up to Snow and the Dwarfelles (Disney said no to using the Dwarfs), female cousins of the original Dwarfs, to rescue him. Interesting choices from the casting department. Diller is Mother Nature and Asner provides the voice of a rapping owl. Poorly animated drivel designed to ride in on Disney's coattails. While the kids might enjoy it, save your money for the original, finally slated for a video release. **74m/C VHS, DVD.** **D:** John Howley; **V:** Dom DeLuise, Phyllis Diller, Zsa Zsa Gabor, Ed Asner, Sally Kellerman, Irene Cara, Carol Channing, Tracey Ullman.

Happily Ever After 🐾🐾 *Ils se Marient et Eurent Beaucoup D'Enfants; ...And They Lived Happily Ever After* **2004** The wandering eye of the married man. Vincent (writer/director Attal) is happily married to Gabrielle (Gainsbourg) but, when egged on by his horndog bachelor pal Fred (Cohen), has sex with a hot masseuse (David). When Gabrielle finds out, she's hurt but gives a Gallic shrug and decides it's nothing she can't handle, especially since infantile Vincent knows he's being stupid. And Gabrielle knows she can find someone else, too. Depp has a cameo as a tempting stranger. French with subtitles. **100m/C DVD.** Yvan Attal, Charlotte Gainsbourg, Alain Chabat, Emmanuelle Seigner, Alain Cohen, Johnny Depp, Anouk Aimee, Claude Berri; **D:** Yvan Attal; **W:** Yvan Attal; **C:** Remy Chevrin.

Happily N'Ever After 🐾🐾 **2007** (PG) Animated spoof of fairytales where the bad guys take over. A wizard (Carlin) goes on vacation and his two idiot assistants (Shawn, Dick) lose control of Fairy Tale Land to wicked stepmother Frieda (Weaver). Now, everyone from Cinderella to Rapunzel has their stories rewritten, and not for the better. Good voice work makes up for lackluster animation. **87m/C DVD, Blu-ray Disc.** *US* GE Lisa Kaplan; **D:** Paul J. Bolger; **W:** Rob Moreland; **V:** David Dulac; **M:** Paul Buckley; **V:** Sarah Michelle Gellar, Freddie Prinze Jr., Sigourney Weaver, Andy Dick, Wallace Shawn, Patrick Warburton, George Carlin, Michael McShane, Kath Soucie.

Happiness 🐾🐾 **1932** Another zany comedy from the land of the hammer and sickle. Banned in Russia for 40 years, it was deemed to be risque and a bit too biting with the social satire. Silent with orchestral score. **69m/B VHS, DVD.** *RU* Nikolai Cherkassov, Mikhail Gipsi, Yelena Yegorova; **D:** Alexander Medvedkin, Alexander Medvedkin; **W:** Alexander Medvedkin; **C:** Gleb Troyanski.

Happiness 🐾🐾 **1998** Very disturbing film made for the "love it or hate it" category. There are three middleclass New Jersey sisters—perky housewife Trish (Stevenson), underachieving Joy (Adams) and glamourous writer Helen (Boyle). Trish is married to shrink Bill (Baker) and they have an 11-year-old son, Billy (Read), who's getting curious about sex. His dad is the wrong person to ask since he's a pedophile who abuses his son's friends. Then there's Allen (Hoffman), one of Bill's patients. He makes obscene phone calls to Helen, who turns out to be turned on by the dirty talk. Suburban hell, indeed. Some riveting performances, especially Baker and Hoffman. **139m/C VHS, DVD.** Dylan Baker, Cynthia Stevenson, Lara Flynn Boyle, Jane Adams, Philip Seymour Hoffman, Ben Gazzara, Louise Lasser, Rufus Read, Jared Harris, Jon Lovitz, Camryn Manheim, Elizabeth Ashley, Marla Maples; **D:** Todd Solondz; **W:** Todd Solondz; **C:** Maryse Alberti; **M:** Robbie Kondor.

Happy Accidents 🐾🐾½ **2000** (R) Quirky sci-fi/romance offers a breath of fresh air by going against the grain of both genres. Ruby (Tomei) is a neurotic loser in romance who always tries to "fix" the men she dates. She meets Sam (D'Onofrio), who appears to be the well-adjusted guy she doesn't have to change. They fall for each other, and then Sam drops the other shoe. He claims to be a time-traveler from the year 2470, and he's come back to save her life by breaking the "causal chain of events" that will result in a fatal accident. Ruby then has to decide whether to believe him or write him off as another lunatic. D'Onofrio amusingly goes from seemingly normal to spouting surreal "history" without blinking. Light on the special effects (especially for sci-fi), but they're effective when they are used. Pic went through a time warp of its own, as it was shot in 1999, debuted at Sundance in 2000 and released in theatres in 2001. **110m/C VHS, DVD.** *US* Marisa Tomei, Vincent D'Onofrio, Tovah Feldshuh, Nadia Dajani, Holland Taylor, Richard Portnow, Sean Gullette, Cara Buono, Liana Pai, Tamara Jenkins, Jose Zuniga; **Cameos:** Anthony Michael Hall; **D:** Brad Anderson; **W:** Brad Anderson; **C:** Terry Stacey; **M:** Evan Lurie.

Happy Birthday, Gemini 🐾½ **1980** (R) A coming-of-age comedy about a young man on his 21st birthday worrying about his sexual identity. Based on the play "Gemini" by Albert Innaurato. The closeness of the characters on stage did not translate to the screen. **107m/C VHS.** Robert Viharo, Madeline Kahn, Rita Moreno, Alan Rosenberg, Sarah Holcomb, David Marshall Grant, David McIlwraith; **D:** Richard Benner; **W:** Richard Benner.

Happy Birthday to Me 🐾½ **1981** (R) Several elite seniors at an exclusive private school are mysteriously killed by a deranged killer who has a fetish for cutlery. **108m/C VHS, DVD.** CA Melissa Sue Anderson, Glenn Ford, Tracy Bregman, Jack Blum, Matt Craven, Lawrence Dane, Lenore Zann, Sharon Acker, Frances Hyland, Earl Pennington, David Eisner, Richard Rebere, Lesleh Donaldson; **D:** J. Lee Thompson; **W:** Timothy Bond, Peter Jobin, John C.W. Saxton, John Beaird; **C:** Miklos Lente; **M:** Bo Harwood, Lance Rubin.

Happy Campers 🐾🐾 **2001** (R) Director of Camp Bleeding Dove (Stormare) is sidelined by an injury, so his teen counselors take charge and seek to spice up their boring daily routines. Routine summer camp flick with a better-than-average cast. **94m/C VHS, DVD.** Brad Renfro, Dominique Swain, Emily Bergl, Jaime (James) King, Jordan Bridges, Peter Stormare, Justin Long, Keram Malicki-Sanchez; **D:** Daniel Waters; **W:** Daniel Waters; **C:** Elliot Davis; **M:** Rolfe Kent. **VIDEO**

The Happy Ending 🐾🐾½ **1969** (PG) Woman struggles with a modern definition of herself and her family, causing pain and confusion for her family. Simmons is solid as the wife and mother seeking herself. Michel LeGrand's theme song "What Are You Doing With The Rest of Your Life?" was a big hit. **112m/C VHS.** Jean Simmons, John Forsythe, Lloyd Bridges, Shirley Jones, Teresa Wright, Dick Shawn, Nanette Fabray, Bobby Darin, Tina Louise; **D:** Richard Brooks; **W:** Richard Brooks; **C:** Conrad L. Hall.

Happy Endings 🐾🐾½ **2005** (R) Director Roos somewhat successfully juggles several storylines about life, love, gay love, blackmail, deceit, and making babies that focus on two women whose paths eventually cross. There's Mamie (Kudrow) whose teenage fling with her unrelated stepbrother Charley (Coogan) resulted in a forsaken child and a cheerless, regret-filled life; meanwhile, vagabond Jude (a dynamic Gyllenhaal) manages to weasel her way into her gay friend Otis' home and his widowed father's heart. **128m/C DVD.** *US* Tom Arnold, Jesse Bradford, Steve Coogan, Laura Dern, Maggie Gyllenhaal, Lisa Kudrow, Jason Ritter, David Sutcliffe, Hallee Hirsh, Eric Jungmann, Johnny Galecki; **D:** Don Roos; **W:** Don Roos; **C:** Clark Mathis.

The Happy Face Murders 🐾🐾½ **1999** (R) A puzzling murder and witnesses who keep changing their stories are the problem in this mystery, inspired by true events, that doesn't quite live up to its potential. Dowdy grandmother Lorraine Petrovich (Ann-Margaret) accuses abusive younger boyfriend Rusty (Campbell) of murder. Cynical detective Jen Powell (Heigenberger) and her naive assistant, Dylan (Thomas), must try and find the truth as everyone else keeps lying. Only dramatizes the gore. **99m/C VHS.** Ann-Margret, Marg Heigenberger, Henry Thomas, Nicholas (Nick) Campbell, Rick Peters, David McIlwraith, Bruce Gray, Emily Hampshire; **D:** Brian Trenchard-Smith; **W:** John Pielmeier; **C:** Albert J. Dunk; **M:** Elmer Bernstein. **CABLE**

Happy Feet 🐾🐾🐾 **2006** (PG) Beautifully computer animated tale of Mumbles (Wood), a penguin who can't sing after being dropped as an egg by his father (Jackman). Instead, he hoofs like Savion Glover, whose moves were motion-captured for Mumbles' dance sequences. Exiled from his group and his love Gloria (Murphy), Mumbles has adventures with predators, other penguins and a certain two-legged animal that is apparently ruining the planet. Some situations may scare smaller children and the ecological message is a little ominous, so assure them that it will all work out fine and you'll remember to cut up those plastic six-pack

---

thingies before you throw them out. **87m/C DVD, Blu-ray Disc, HD DVD.** *US* D: George Miller; **W:** George Miller, John Collee, Judy Morris, Warren Coleman; **M:** John Powell; **V:** Elijah Wood, Robin Williams, Brittany Murphy, Hugh Jackman, Nicole Kidman, Hugo Weaving, Anthony LaPaglia, Magda Szubanski, Elizabeth (E.G. Dailey) Daily, Steve Irwin, Miriam Margolyes. Oscars '06: Animated Film; British Acad. '06: Animated Film; Golden Globes '07: Song ("The Song of the Heart").

Happy Gilmore 🐾🐾 **1996** (PG-13) Skating-impaired hockey player Gilmore (Sandler) translates his slap shot into a 400-yard tee shot and joins the pro golf tour. His unique style brings a new, less refined breed of fan to the game and upsets the reigning tour hotshot (McDonald). Sandler improves on "Billy Madison," which isn't saying much. There's still plenty of ammo for his many detractors, but the laughs are more frequent and consistent. Replacing bathroom humor with abusive behavior, the mis-named Happy swears at or beats up about 90% of the supporting cast, including Bob Barker in a charity pro-am. **92m/C VHS, DVD, UMD, HD DVD.** Adam Sandler, Christopher McDonald, Carl Weathers, Julie Bowen, Frances Bay, Ben Stiller, Richard Kiel, Joe Flaherty, Kevin Nealon, Allen Covert, Robert Smigel, Bob Barker, Dennis Dugan; **D:** Dennis Dugan; **W:** Adam Sandler, Tim Herlihy; **C:** Arthur Albert; **M:** Mark Mothersbaugh. MTV Movie Awards '96: Fight (Adam Sandler/Bob Barker).

Happy Go Lovely 🐾🐾 **1951** Chorus girl Janet (Vera-Ellen) is part of an American troupe that's in Scotland hoping to open a show. Producer Frost (Romero) needs financial backing and, after seeing Janet exit a limo, thinks she's found a rich beau and offers her the show's lead in hopes of getting her boyfriend's money. When the limo's owner, stodgy millionaire B.G. Bruno (Niven), does show up, Janet mistakes him for a reporter and falls in love with the guy. Tired plot, but good performances in this lightweight musical. ♫One-Two-Three; Would You, Could You; London Town. **95m/C VHS, DVD.** *GB* Sandra Dorne, Vera-Ellen, David Niven, Cesar Romero, Bobby Howes; **D:** H. Bruce Humberstone; **W:** Val Guest; **C:** Erwin Hillier; **M:** Mischa Spoliansky.

Happy Hell Night 🐾🐾 **1992** (R) A fraternity prank helps a crazed priest escape from a mental institution and again take up his hobby fom 25 years ago—killing local fraternity members. Oh, the irony is delicious! Unfortunately, the direction and script are not, and they bury some genuinely scary moments. Look for a pre-stardom Rockwell and pre-"CSI" Fox, along with McGavin making a mortgage payment or two. **84m/C DVD.** Nick Gregory, Darren McGavin, Sam Rockwell, Jorja Fox, Ted Clark, Frank John Hughes, Ifran Mensur, Gala Videnovic, Laura Carney, Charles Cragin; **C:** Brian Owens; **W:** Brian Owens; **C:** Sol Negrin.

The Happy Hooker 🐾🐾 **1975** (R) Xaviera Hollander's cheeky (and best-selling) memoir of her transition from office girl to "working girl" has been brought to the screen with a sprightly (though sanitary) air of naughtiness, with Redgrave enjoyable in title role. Followed by "The Happy Hooker Goes to Washington" and "The Happy Hooker Goes Hollywood." **96m/C VHS.** Lynn Redgrave, Jean-Pierre Aumont, Nicholas Pryor; **D:** Nicholas Sgarro.

The Happy Hooker Goes to Hollywood 🐾 **1980** (R) Third film inspired by the title of Xaviera Hollander's memoirs, in which the fun-loving Xaviera comes to Hollywood with the intention of making a movie based on her book, but soon meets up with a series of scheming, would-be producers. **86m/C VHS.** Martine Beswick, Chris Lemmon, Adam West, Phil Silvers; **D:** Alan Roberts.

The Happy Hooker Goes to Washington 🐾½ **1977** (R) Further adventures of the world's most famous madam. Heatherton (not Redgrave) is Xaviera Hollander this time, testifying before the U.S. Senate in defense of sex. Fairly stupid attempt to milk boxoffice of original. Second in the holy trilogy of Happy Hooker pictures, which also include "The Happy Hooker" and "The Happy Hooker Goes Hollywood." **89m/C VHS.** Joey Heatherton,

---

George Hamilton, Ray Walston, Jack Carter; **D:** William A. Levey.

Happy Hour 🦴🦴½ 1987 (R) A young brewing scientist discovers a secret formula for beer, and everyone tries to take it from him. Little turns in a good performance as a superspy. 88m/C VHS. Richard Gilliland, Jamie Farr, Tawny Kitaen, Ty Henderson, Rich Little; **D:** John DeBello. **W:** John DeBello.

Happy, Texas 🦴🦴🦴 1999 (PG-13) Producer/director Mark Illsley's quirky little debut hearkens back to such classic Hollywood comedies as "Some Like It Hot." Escaped prisoners Harry Sawyer (Northam) and Wayne Wayne Wayne Jr. (Zahn), steal a camper and assume the identity of its owners in order to evade the law. The trouble is that the owners are a pair of gay men who organize kiddie beauty pageants. When they arrive in the town of Happy, Texas, the populace thinks that they're there to stage the Little Miss Fresh Squeezed contest and greet them with open arms. Wayne is forced to summon up fashion and choreography skills not commonplace for your average hardened criminal, while Harry hobnobs with the local gentry while plotting to knock over the town bank. Romantic complications involving a schoolmarm (Douglas), lady banker (Walker) and a sexually confused

Happy Since I Met You 🦴🦴🦴 1989 Comedy-drama about a scatterbrained drama teacher and a struggling young actor who become romantically involved. 55m/C VHS. **GB** Julie Walters, Duncan Preston; **Cameos:** Tracey Ullman, Jim Bowen; **D:** Baz Taylor. **W:** Victoria Wood.

Happy New Year! 🦴🦴½ 1987 (PG) Two sophisticated thieves plan and execute an elaborate jewel heist that goes completely awry. Remake of the 1974 French film of the same name. 86m/C VHS. Peter Falk, Wendy Hughes, Tom Courtenay, Charles Durning, Joan Copeland; **D:** John G. Avildsen; **W:** Warren Lane; **M:** Bill Conti.

A Happy New Year 🦴🦴🦴 1979 Two men and a woman, all engineers in a chemical plant, try to fight off a hangover as they deal with the comings and goings of friends throughout the day and night in Hungarian with English subtitles. 84m/C VHS. HU Istvan Bujtor, Erika Bodnar, Cecilia Esztergalyos, Andras Balint; **D:** Reszo Szorenyi.

Happy Landing 🦴🦴½ 1938 Predictable, yet entertaining Henie vehicle about a plane that makes a forced landing in Norway near Henie's home. Romance follows with bandleader Romero and manager Ameche. 🎵Hot and Happy; Yonny and his Oompah; You Are The Music to the Words in my Heart; A Gypsy Told Me; You Appeal to Me. 84m/C VHS. Sonja Henie, Don Ameche, Jean Hersholt, Ethel Merman, Cesar Romero, Billy Gilbert, Wally Vernon, El Brendel; **D:** Roy Del Ruth; **W:** Milton Sperling, Boris Ingster.

Happy New Year 🦴🦴½ The Happy New Year Caper; La Bonne Année 1973 Charming romantic comedy in which two thieves plan a robbery but get sidetracked by the distracting woman who works next door to the jewelry store that's their target. Available in both subtitled and dubbed versions. Remade in 1987. 114m/C VHS. FR/IT Francoise Fabian, Lino Ventura, Andre Falcon, Charles Gerard; **D:** Claude Lelouch; **W:** Claude Lelouch Pierre Uytterhoeven.

Happy Times 🦴🦴½ Xingfu Shiguang 2000 (PG) Underneath this light comedy is an intimate tale of an aging loser and his unexpected relationship with a young, blind teenager. When Zhao (Benshan) tries to woo plus-sized divorcée (Li-hua) by pretending that he is a hotel owner, she demands that he give her blind stepdaughter Wu Ying (Jie) a job, unaware that Zhao's only experience in hotel management was renting out a dilapidated bus to couples by the hour. With the help of friends, Zhao sets up an elaborate ruse: outfitting an abandoned factory as the "hotel" where Wu, a masseuse, employs her craft on Zhao's friends posing as clients who pay her in phony money. Zhao finds redemption for a sort in the sullen but honest Wu, who in turn blossoms in her new job. Acclaimed Chinese director Yimou elicits excellent performances in his scaled-down allegory. In Mandarin with subtitles. 106m/C VHS, DVD, CH Benshan Zhao, Jie Dong, Xueqian Li, Lifan Dong, Qibin Leng, Biao Fu, Ben Nu; **D:** Yimou Zhang; **M:** San Bao.

Happy Together 🦴 1989 (PG-13) An eager freshman accidentally gets a beautiful, impulsive girl as his roommate. Together they meet the challenges of secondary education. 102m/C VHS, DVD. Helen Slater, Patrick Dempsey, Dan Schneider, Marius Weyers, Barbara Babcock, Brad Pitt; **D:** Mel Damski; **M:** Robert Folk.

Happy Together 🦴🦴 Cheun Gwong Tsa Sit 1996 Lovers ...Lai Yiu-Fai (Leung) and Ho Po-Wing (Cheung) travel to Argentina from Hong Kong looking for adventure but soon go their separate ways. Lai is working as a doorman at a tango bar when a badly beaten Ho unexpectedly re-enters his life. Lai looks after the self-destructive Ho but his restlessness causes him to desert Lai once again, even as Lai begins to suffer from depression and serious homesickness, as well as still worrying about Ho. Edgy visuals and playful performances belie a serious nature. Chinese and Spanish with subtitles. 92m/C VHS, DVD. HK Leslie Cheung, Tony Leung Chiu-Wai, Chang Chen; **D:** Wong Kar-Wai; **W:** Wong Kar-Wai; **C:** Christopher Doyle; **M:** Danny Chung.

Harakiri 🦴🦴🦴½ Seppuku 1962 An old samurai (Nakadai) wishes to commit ritual suicide on the grounds of a feudal lord, where he learns that his son-in-law, also a samurai, was forced to commit seppuku with a bamboo blade while seeking work. He tells the younger warrior's story to the assembled warlords, who abandoned the samurai when they were no longer needed. Beautifully told and shot film is a scathing indictment of the treatment of men of honor after the battles that defined them have been fought. A classic of the genre, focusing on the aftermath rather than the glory. 135m/B VHS, DVD. JP Tatsuya Nakadai, Rentaro Mikuni, Masao Mishima, Shima Iwashita, Yoshio Inaba, Akira Ishihama, Shimsuya Nakadai, Tetsuro Tamba, Shichisaburo Amatsu, Yoshio Aoki, Jo Azumi, Akiji Kobayashi, Ichiro Nakaya, Kei Sato, Ryo Takeuchi; **D:** Masaki Kobayashi; **W:** Shinobu Hashimoto, Yasuhiko Takiguchi; **C:** Yoshio Miyajima; **M:** Toru Takemitsu.

Hard As Nails 🦴🦴½ 2001 (R) Overachieving video premiere is a genre piece that leaves no cliche unturned, but it also has moments of real style. Gangster Alex (Scott) and stripper Kat (Yates) are caught between Russian and Japanese gangs in Los Angeles. A cop (Craig) and a hooker (Farentino) are involved, too. Doublecrosses abound. Some of the stunt work is wonderfully acrobatic. Director Katkin makes the most of a pocket-change budget. 88m/C DVD. Allen Scott, Kim Yates, Andrew Craig, Matt Westmore, Lorissa McComas, Stella Farentino; **D:** Brian Katkin; **W:** Brian Katkin. **C:** Marco Cappetta. **M:** Chris Farrell

Hard Choices 🦴🦴🦴 1984 A 15-year-old Tennessee boy is unjustly charged as an accessory to murder, until a female social worker decides to help him. From then on, nothing is predictable. Excellent work by Klenck, McCleery, and Seitz. Don't miss Sayles as an unusual drug dealer. Intelligent, surprising, and powerful. Based on a true story, this is a low profile film that deserves to be discovered. 90m/C VHS. Margaret Klenck, Gary McCleery, John Seitz, John Sayles, Liane (Alexandra) Curtis, J.T. Walsh, Spalding Gray; **D:** Rick King; **W:** Rick King.

Hard Core Logo 🦴🦴 1996 (R) Mockumentary about a group of Canadian veteran punk rock musicians who, at thirtysomething, have reunited for one last benefit concert. The semi-legendary Van-... sheriff (Macy) arise, setting the stage for a happy, but unnecessarily tidy, ending. 104m/C VHS, DVD. Steve Zahn, Jeremy Northam, Ally Walker, Illeana Douglas, William H. Macy, M.C. Gainey, Ron Perlman, Michael Hitchcock, Paul Dooley; **D:** Mark Illsley; **C:** Bruce Douglas Johnson; **M:** Stone, Mark Illsley. Ind. Spirit '00: Support Actor (Zahn), Peter Harris.

Hard-Boiled 🦴🦴🦴½ Lashou Shentan 1992 Police Inspector Yuen (Woo regular Yun-Fat) is investigating, with his usual excessive force, the Triads organized crime syndicate and a group of gun smugglers who killed his partner. He joins forces with Tony, an undercover cop who's working as a gangster hitman. There's lots of gunplay and betrayals among all the participants. Usual Woo way with violence and action sequences although the plot is more contrived. In Mandarin and Chinese with English subtitles. 126m/C VHS, DVD. HK Chow Yun-Fat, Tony Leung Chiu-Wai, Philip Chan, Anthony Wong, Teresa Mo, Bowie Lam, Hoi-Shan Kwan, Philip Kwok, John Woo; **D:** John Woo; **W:** Barry Wong; **M:** Michael Gibbs.

Hard-Boiled Mahoney 🦴🦴½ 1947 Slip, Sach, and the rest of the Bowery Boys try to solve a mystery involving mysterious women and missing men. The last film in the series for Bobby Jordan, whose career was ended when he was injured in an accident involving a falling elevator. 64m/B VHS. Leo Gorcey, Huntz Hall, Bobby Jordan, William Benedict, David Gorcey, Gabriel Dell, Teala Loring, Dan Seymour, Bernard Gorcey, Patti Brill, Betty Compson; **D:** William Beaudine.

Hard Bounty 🦴🦴½ 1994 (R) After five years of chasing desperadoes, bounty hunter Martin B. Kanning hangs up his guns to open a saloon—complete with whores. When one of his ladies is murdered, the other gals decide to chase after the killer. Naturally, Kanning can't let them go alone. 90m/C VHS, DVD. Matt McCoy, Kelly Le Brock, Rochelle Swanson, Felicity Waterman, Kimberly Kelley; **D:** Jim Wynorski. **W:** Karen Kelly; **C:** Zoran Hochstatter; **M:** Tel...

Hard Candy 🦴🦴 2006 (R) Page ... scary-good as 14-year-old Hayley, a seeming Lolita out to tempt 32-year-old photographer Jeff (Wilson). They first flirt in an online chat room and then face-to-face in a coffee shop. Jeff invites pixie-ish Hayley back to his home for drinks, only whatever you think may happen, doesn't. Hayley drugs Jeff, ties him to a chair, and accuses him of being a child pornographer, pedophile, and possible murderer before threatening him with castration 'for his "crimes." Is she right or just a very dangerous hysteric? First feature for commercial/video director Slade. 103m/C DVD. US Ellen Page, Patrick Wilson, Sandra Oh, Odessa Rae, Gilbert John; **D:** David Slade; **W:** Brian Nelson; **C:** Jo Willems; **M:** Molly Nyman, Harry Escott.

Hard Cash 🦴🦴 Run for the Money 2001 (R) Thief Tom Taylor (Slater) wants to go legit after being released from prison but instead hooks up with a new crew for a job. When they discover the money is marked, Taylor finds himself embroiled with corrupt FBI agent Mark Cornell (Kilmer). Despite the billing, Kilmer has limited screen time and this caper film is a predictable yawner. 96m/C VHS, DVD. Christian Slater, Balthazar Getty, Vincent Laresca, Peter Woodward, William Forsythe, Sara Downing; **D:** Pedrag (Peter) Antonijevic; **W:** Willie King. **M:** Rick King.

Hard Drivin' 🦴 1960 Rowdy action featuring Southern stock car drivers with well shot race scenes from the Southern 500. 92m/C VHS. Roy Calhoun, John Gentry, Alan Hale Jr. **D:** Paul Helmick.

Hard Evidence 🦴🦴½ 1994 (R)

A Hard Day's Night 🦴🦴🦴½ 1964 The Beatles' first film is a joyous romp through an average "day in the life" of the Fab Four, shot in a pseudo-documentary style with great flair by Lester and noted as the first music video. 🎵A Hard Day's Night; Tell Me Why; I Should Have Known Better; She Loves You; I'm Happy Just to Dance with You; If I Fell; And I Love Her; This Boy; Can't Buy Me Love. 90m/B VHS, DVD. GB John Lennon, Paul McCartney, George Harrison, Ringo Starr, Wilfrid Brambell, Norman Rossington, John Junkin, Victor Spinetti, Anna Quayle, Deryck Guyler, Richard Vernon, Lionel Blair, Eddie Malin, Robin Ray, Alison Seebohm, David Saxon, Patti Boyd; **D:** Richard Lester; **W:** Alun Owen; **C:** Gilbert Taylor; **M:** George Martin, John Lennon, Paul McCartney.

Hard Country 🦴🦴½ 1981 (PG) Caught between her best friend's success as a country singer and the old values of a woman's place, a small town girl questions her love and her life style. A warm and intelligent rural drama. Basinger's debut. 104m/C VHS. Jan-Michael Vincent, Kim Basinger, Michael Parks, Gailard Sartain, Tanya Tucker, Ted Neeley, Gary Hannah, Richard Moll; **D:** David Greene; **W:** Michael Kane; **M:** Michael Martin Murphey.

Hard Drive 🦴½ 1994 A high tech, interactive network offers shared fantasies to Will and Delilah. Then they become obsessed with making their dreams a reality. 92m/C VHS, DVD. Matt McCoy, Christina (Kristina) Fulton, Edward Albert, Leo Damian, Stella Stevens; **D:** James Merendino; **W:** James Merendino; **C:** Sead Muhanovic; **M:** Nels Cline.

Hard Eight 🦴🦴🦴½ 1996 (R) Performances are the highlight of this low-key story set in Reno, Nevada. Sydney (Hall) is a professional gambler who decides to take under his wing the destitute John (Reilly) and teach him the trade. (Paltrow) but there has to be some snake in this gambler's would-be paradise and it shows up in the malevolent form of the scary Jimmy (Jackson), who the dim John befriends despite Sydney's warnings. Debut for writer/director Anderson. 101m/C VHS, DVD. Philip Baker Hall, John C. Reilly, Gwyneth Paltrow, Samuel L. Jackson, F. William Parker, Philip Seymour Hoffman, Nathanael Cooper, Wynn White, Robert Ridgely, Michael J. Rowe, Kathleen Campbell, Melora Walters; **D:** Paul Thomas Anderson; **C:** Robert Elswit; **M:** Michael Penn, Jon Brion.

Hard Frame 🦴½ Hunters Are for Killing 1970 An ex-con returns home hoping all will turn to sweetness and light when he attempts to make nice-nice with his stepdad, who wouldn't stick by him during his trial. Reynolds' debut into TV moviedom; could be the hirsute actor was thinking of...

this one when he said his movies were the kind they show in prisons and airplanes because nobody can leave. 100m/C VHS. Burt Reynolds, Melvyn Douglas, Suzanne Pleshette, Larry Storch, Martin Balsam, Peter Brown, Jill Banner, Don (Don "Red") Barry, Angus Duncan, Ivor Francis, A. Martinez; **D:** Bernard Girard; **W:** Charles Kuenstle; **C:** Gerald Perry Finnerman; **M:** Jerry Fielding.

Hard Hombre 1931 Gibson rides and shoots across the screen in one of his best western adventures. 60m/B VHS, DVD. Hoot Gibson, Lena Basquette, Skeeter Bill Robbins, Jack Byron, Glenn Strange; **D:** Otto Brower.

Hard Hunted 1992 (R) Three macho undercover agents try to avoid death at the hands of high-tech guerillas trying to steal nuclear weapons. No-brain actioner, heavy on the display of feminine charms. 97m/C VHS, DVD. Dona Speir, Roberta Vasquez, Cynthia Brimhall, Bruce Penhall, R.J. (Geoffrey) Moore, Tony Peck, Rodrigo Obregon, Al Leong, Michael J. Shane; **D:** Andy Sidaris; **W:** Andy Sidaris.

Hard Justice 1995 (R) Bureau of Alcohol, Tobacco & Firearms agent Nick Adams (Bradley) goes undercover in prison to find his partner's killer and discovers that Warden Pike (Napier) is running an illegal gun operation. Now, who's he gonna trust? Lots of action thrills in a routine story. 95m/C VHS. David Bradley, Charles Napier, Yuji Okumoto, Vernon Wells; **D:** Greg Yaitanes; **W:** Nicholas Amendolare, Chris Bold; **C:** Moshe Levin; **M:** Don Peake.

Hard Knocks 1979 An excon goes from one tragic situation to another, and is eventually stalked by shotgun-wielding rednecks in this grim, powerful drama. Excellent performance by Mann holds this picture together. 85m/C AU Tracy Mann, John Arnold, Bill Hunter, Max Cullen, Tony Barry; **D:** Don McLennan; **W:** Don McLennan. Australian Film Inst. '80: Actress (Mann).

Hard Knocks 1/2 1980 A young man on the run is tormented by an aging actress and her husband. His attempt to leave a past of violence and pain creates even more havoc. 90m/C VHS. Michael Christian, John Crawford, Donna Wilkes, Keenan Wynn.

Hard Labour 1973 Middle-aged housekeeper is humiliated at home by her children and tyrannical daughter-in-law. 70m/C VHS, DVD. GB Alison Steadman, Ben Kingsley, Clifford Kershaw; **D:** Mike Leigh. **TV**

Hard Lessons 1/2 1986 *The George McKenna Story* 1986 Washington stars as the newly appointed principal of George Washington High in Los Angeles. The school is located in South Central, a gang and drug-infested war zone where the students are armed for their own protection. The situation appears hopeless but McKenna refuses to give up. Based on a true story. 95m/C VHS, DVD. Denzel Washington, Lynn Whitfield, Akosua Busia, Richard Masur; **D:** Eric Laneuville; **W:** Charles Eric Johnson; **C:** Isidore Mankofsky; **M:** Herbie Hancock. **TV**

Hard Luck 2001 Trevor "Lucky" O'Donnell's life certainly doesn't live up to his nickname. He's doing time in a mental ward when his childhood sweetheart Sheryl visits to let him know that his buddy, her brother Eric, is dying of cancer. So Lucky escapes and heads to his home town of Gold Beach, Oregon, determined that the threesome will take one last trip together to their favorite childhood haunt. Too bad they're being pursued by Sheryl's cop husband Matt and her and Eric's dad, who just happens to be the Chief of Police. 85m/C VHS, DVD. Kirk Harris, Renee Humphrey, Matthew Faber, Ron Gilbert, Gareth Williams, Karen Black, Joanne Baron, Darrell Bryan, Tony Longo, Luca Bercovici, Jon Jacobs; **D:** Jack Rubio; **W:** Kirk Harris.

Hard Part Begins 1973 A naive country singer gets sucked into the pratfalls of show business. 87m/C VHS. CA Donnelly Rhodes, Nancy Belle Fuller, Paul Bradley; **D:** Paul Lynch; **W:** John Hunter; **C:** Robert Saad; **M:** Ian Guenther.

Hard Pill 2005 Tim (Slavin) is young, lonely, and gay—uncomfortable with the club scene and the personals. So when he learns about a new pill that claims to turn homosexuals straight, he decides to be a test case and finds himself dealing with the consequences. Debut feature for Baumgartner. 94m/C DVD. US Jonathan Slavin, Jennifer Elise Cox, Scotch Ellis Loring, Susan Slome, Mike Begovich, Jason Bushman, John Baumgartner; **D:** John Baumgartner; **W:** John Baumgartner; **M:** Mike Petrone.

Hard Promises 1992 (PG) Absence doesn't necessarily make the heart fonder, as Joey finds out when he's accidentally invited to his wife's wedding. He's been away from home for so long he doesn't even realize he's been divorced and hightails it home to win his sweetheart back. Average performances and script round out this innocuous domestic comedy-drama. 95m/C VHS, DVD. Sissy Spacek, William L. Petersen, Brian Kerwin, Mare Winningham, Peter MacNichol, Ann Wedgeworth, Amy Wright, Lois Smith, Rip Torn; **D:** Martin Davidson; **W:** George S. Clinton. **CABLE**

Hard Rain 1997 (R) Armored car guards Tom (Slater) and his uncle Charlie (Asner) are transporting $3 million to high ground during a flood in a small Indiana town. When their truck gets stuck in the mud, a band of jet-skiin' motor boatin' thieves arrive and try to steal the money. Tom hides the dough and alerts the local sheriff (Quaid) who, being your normal American elected official, decides he wants to steal it, too. Tom forms an uneasy alliance with head bad guy Jim (Freeman) to thwart the lawman and his toadies. While all this is happening, Tom manages to find love interest Karen (Driver), who's there to protect her church restoration work and wear wet blouses. And now the weather report: floods are the least cinematic disasters. Everything just gets soggy and waterlogged (especially the action sequences). Director Salomon created the huge flooded town set inside a tank in Palmdale, California. 96m/C VHS, DVD. Morgan Freeman, Christian Slater, Randy Quaid, Minnie Driver, Ed Asner, Richard Dysart, Betty White, Mark Rolston, Peter Murnik, Dann Florek, Wayne Duvall, Michael Goorjian; **D:** Mikael Salomon; **W:** Graham Yost; **C:** Peter Menzies Jr.; **M:** Christopher Young.

The Hard Ride 1/2 1971 (R) Above average biker movie about a Vietnam vet who brings the body of a black buddy back home, then tries to persuade the dead man's white girlfriend and the leader of his motorcycle gang to attend the funeral. 93m/C VHS. Robert Fuller, Sherry Bain, Tony Russell, Marshall Reed, Biff (Elliott) Elliott, William Bonner, R.L. Armstrong; **D:** Burt Topper; **W:** Burt Topper.

Hard Ticket to Hawaii 1987 (R) A shot-on-video spy thriller about an agent trying to rescue a comrade in Hawaii from a smuggling syndicate. Supporting cast includes many Playboy Playmates. 96m/C VHS, DVD. Ron Moss, Dona Speir, Hope Marie Carlton, Cynthia Brimhall, Harold Diamond, Rodrigo Obregon, Rustam Branaman, Kwan Hi Lim; **D:** Andy Sidaris; **W:** Andy Sidaris; **C:** Howard Wexler; **M:** Gary Stockdale.

Hard Times 1975 (PG) A Depression-era drifter becomes a bare knuckle street fighter, and a gambler decides to promote him for big stakes. One of grade-B meister Hill's first genre films. A quiet, evocative drama. 92m/C VHS, DVD. Charles Bronson, James Coburn, Jill Ireland, Strother Martin; **D:** Walter Hill; **W:** Walter Hill, Bryan Gindoff, Bruce Henstell; **C:** Philip Lathrop; **M:** Barry DeVorzon.

Hard to Die 1990 *Tower of Terror.* Director Wynorski's comic homage to Carol Frank's "Sorority House Massacre." Five beauties (former Playboy Playmates Harris, Taylor, Dare, Moore, and Carney) find employment moving boxes in a deserted lingerie factory. The film takes off from there as they uncover a mysterious spirit called the Sorority House Killer in an ancient "Soul Box." Desperate to extinguish the evil threat, they focus their efforts in an armed struggle involving high-powered weaponry against the building maintenance man, whom they fear is possessed by the spirit. Accompanied by a lovely, touching group shower scene. 77m/C VHS. Robin Harris, Melissa Moore, Debra (Deborah Dutch) Dare, Lindsay Taylor, Bridget Carney, Forrest J Ackerman, Orville Ketchum; **D:** Jim Wynorski.

Hard Rock Zombies 1985 (R) Four heavy metal band members die horribly on the road and are brought back from the dead as zombies. This horror/heavy metal spoof is somewhat amusing in a goofy way. 90m/C VHS, DVD. E.J. Curcio, Sam Mann; **D:** Krishna Shah; **W:** David Ball.

Hard Target 1/2 1993 (R) Van Damme continues his action-hero ways as Chance Boudreaux, a Cajun (which explains the accent) merchant seaman, who comes to the rescue of Natasha (Butler), albeit with lots of violence. Brimley provides the humor as Chance's bayou uncle. It's another variation of "The Most Dangerous Game" story but it moves. American directorial debut of over-the-top Hong Kong action director Woo who had to trim down his usual stylistic effects and repeatedly cut some of the more violent scenes to earn an "R" rating. 97m/C VHS, DVD. Jean-Claude Van Damme, Lance Henriksen, Yancy Butler, Arnold Vosloo, Wilford Brimley, Kasi Lemmons, Eliott Keener, Theodore (Ted) Raimi, Chuck Pfarrer; **D:** John Woo; **W:** Chuck Pfarrer; **C:** Russell Carpenter; **M:** Graeme Revell.

Hard to Hold 1/2 1984 (PG) Rockin' Rick's lukewarm film debut where he falls in love with a children's counselor after an automobile accident. Springfield sings "Love Somebody" with music by Peter Gabriel. 93m/C VHS, DVD. Rick Springfield, Janet Eilber, Patti Hansen, Albert Salmi, Monique Gabrielle; **D:** Larry Peerce.

Hard to Kill 1989 (R) Policeman Seagal is shot and left for dead in his bedroom, but survives against the odds, though his wife does not. After seven years, he is well enough to consider evening the score with his assailants. He hides while training in martial arts for the final battle. Strong outing from Seagal, with good supporting cast. 96m/C VHS, DVD. Steven Seagal, Kelly Le Brock, William Sadler, Frederick Coffin, Bonnie Burroughs, Zachary Rosencrantz, Dean Norris; **D:** Bruce Malmuth; **W:** Steven McKay; **C:** Matthew F. Leonetti; **M:** Charles Fox.

Hard Traveling 1985 (PG) An unemployed Depression-era farmworker is accused of murder. He must fight a hostile court system to maintain his dignity and salvage the love and respect of his wife. Based on a novel by Alvah Bessie. 99m/C VHS. J.E. Freeman, Ellen Geer, Barry Corbin, James Gammon, Jim Haynie; **D:** Dan Bessie; **W:** Dan Bessie; **C:** David Myers.

The Hard Truth 1/2 1994 (R) By-the-book actioner finds cop Jonah (Rooker) suspended for having an itchy trigger finger. His gal Lisa (Anthony) knows her sleazy boss has lots of mob money handy and proposes they grab it. But then Lisa gets a look at Chandler (Roberts), the electronic whiz blackmailed to assist in the heist, and the triangle leads to trouble. 100m/C VHS. Michael Rooker, Eric Roberts, Lysette Anthony, Ray Baker, Don Yesso; **D:** Kristine Peterson; **W:** Jonathan Tydor; **C:** Ross Berryman.

Hard Vice 1/2 1994 (R) Vice cops Joe Owens (Jones) and Andrea Thompson (Tweed) have their work cut out for them on their Las Vegas beat. When the bodies start piling up, the prime suspects turn out to be a group of high-priced hookers. 86m/C VHS, DVD. Shannon Tweed, Sam Jones, James Gammon, Rebecca Ferratti; **D:** Joey Travolta; **W:** Joey Travolta, Lem Dobbs; **C:** F. Smith Martin; **M:** Jeff Lass.

Hard Way 1980 A world-weary assassin is pressured by his boss to perform one last assignment. A surprise awaits him if he accepts. 88m/C VHS. Patrick McGoohan, Lee Van Cleef, Donal McCann, Edna O'Brien; **D:** Mihael Dryhurst.

The Hard Way 1991 (R) Hollywood superstar Fox is assigned to hardened NYC cop Woods to learn the ropes as he trains for a role. Nothing special in the way of script or direction, but Woods and Fox bring such intensity and good humor to their roles that the package works. Fox pokes fun at the LA lifestyle as the annoying, self-absorbed actor, and Marshall has an entertaining appearance as his agent. Woods is on familiar over-the-edge turf as the brittle but dedicated detective. Silly finale almost destroys the film, but other small vignettes are terrific. 91m/C VHS, DVD. James Woods, Michael J. Fox, Annabella Sciorra, Stephen Lang, Penny Marshall, LL Cool J, John Capodice, Christina Ricci, Karen (Lynn) Daniel Pyne, Lem Dobbs; **D:** John Badham; **W:** Daniel Pyne, Lem Dobbs; **C:** Robert Primes; **M:** Arthur B. Rubinstein.

The Hard Word 1/2 2002 (R) Pearce is Dale, the eldest of three criminal brothers who are enticed into one last job upon their release from prison. Since they've been pulling jobs all along, thanks to a "work-release" program cooked up by their slimy lawyer, Frank Malone (Taylor), and some crooked cops, it doesn't seem like a bad idea. Problems arise when Dale finds out that Frank is setting them up, and having an affair with his femme-fatale wife Carole (Griffiths). Aussie caper flick sizzles on the strength of lived-in performances by Pearce and Griffiths, as well as a grungy feel that makes the whole thing resonate with suspicion. 102m/C VHS, DVD. AU GB Guy Pearce, Rachel Griffiths, Robert Taylor, Joel Edgerton, Damien Richardson, Rhonda Findleton, Kate Atkinson, Vince Colosimo, Paul Sonkkila, Kim Gyngell, Dorian Nkono; **D:** Scott Roberts; **W:** Scott Roberts; **C:** Brian J. Breheny; **M:** David Thrussell.

Hardball 2001 (PG-13) Loosely based on Daniel Coyle's book "Hardball: A Season in the Projects," the plot plays like a watered down "Bad News Bears" with a dark edge. Conor O'Neill (Reeves) is a gambler who owes money all over Chicago. He asks broker pal Jimmy (McGlone) for financial help, but it comes at a cost. Jimmy has him take over a baseball team from the Cabrini-Green projects as part of his company's community outreach program. Conor and the foul-mouthed little tykes inevitably get off on the wrong foot, setting up the eventual "rag-tag bunch of misfits turn into champions" scenario. Grimmer overtones show up, however, with the realities of the projects and a tragedy that deeply affects Conor and the team. The kids' teacher Elizabeth (Lane) is the guiding influence/unfulfilled love interest. The kids, especially Griffith and Warren, steal pic from the grown-ups with their performances. 106m/C VHS, DVD. US Keanu Reeves, Diane Lane, John Hawkes, Bryan C. Hearne, Julian Griffith, A. Delon Ellis Jr., DeWayne Warren, Michael B. Jordan, D.B. Sweeney, Mike McGlone, Graham Beckel, Mark Margolis; **D:** Brian Robbins; **W:** John Gatins; **C:** Tom Richmond; **M:** Mark Isham.

Hardbodies 1984 (R) Three middle-aged men hit the beaches of Southern California in search of luscious young girls. They find them. Mid-life crisis done stupidly. Followed by a sequel. 88m/C VHS, DVD. Grant Cramer, Teal Roberts, Gary Wood, Michael Rapport, Sorrels Pickard, Courtney Gains, Kristi Somers, Cindy Silver, Crystal Shaw, Kathleen Kinmont, Joyce Jameson; **D:** Mark Griffiths; **W:** Eric Alter.

Hardbodies 2 woof! 1986 (R) A sequel to the original comedy hit, dealing with film crew in Greece that is distracted by hordes of nude natives. Sophomoric humor dependent on nudity and profanity for laughs. 89m/C VHS. Brad Zutaut, Brenda Bakke, Fabiana Udenio, James Karen; **D:** Mark Griffiths; **W:** Eric Alter; **M:** Eddie Arkin.

Hardcase and Fist 1989 (R) A framed cop leaves prison with his mind on revenge. The godfather who used him is just his first target. 92m/C VHS, DVD. Maurice Lavette, Ted Prior, Tony Zarindast, Christine Lunde, Carter Wong; **D:** Tony Zarindast; **W:** Tony Zarindast; **M:** Robert Hayes. **VIDEO**

Hardcore 🐾🐾½ *The Hardcore Life* **1979** (R) A Midwestern businessman who is raising a strict Christian family learns of his daughter's disappearance while she is on a church trip. After hiring a streetwise investigator, he learns that his daughter has become an actress in pornographic films out in California. Strong performance by Scott and glimpse into the hardcore pornography industry prove to be convincing points of this film, though it exploits what it condemns. 106m/C VHS, DVD, George C. Scott, Season Hubley, Peter Boyle, Dick Sargent; *D:* Paul Schrader; *W:* Paul Schrader; *C:* Michael Chapman; *M:* Jack Nitzsche.

Hardcore 🐾🐾½ **2004** Two teenage prostitutes partner up for a string of power plays that eventually lead to murder. In Greek with subtitles 96m/C DVD. Dimitris Liolios, Andreas Marianos, Konstadinos Markoulakis, Ioannis Papazisis; *D:* Denis Iliade; *W:* Dennie Iliade. VIDEO

The Harder They Come 🐾🐾½ **1972** (R) A poor Jamaican youth becomes a success with a hit reggae record after he has turned to a life of crime out of desperation. Songs, which are blended nicely into the framework of the film, include "You Can Get It If You Really Want It" and "Sitting in Limbo." 93m/C VHS, DVD, JM Jimmy Cliff, Janet Barkley, Carl Bradshaw, Bobby Charlton, Ras Daniel Hartman, Basil Keane, Winston Stona; *D:* Perry Henzell; *W:* Perry Henzell; Trevor D. Rhone; *C:* Peter Jessop, David McDonald; *M:* Desmond Dekker, Jimmy Cliff.

The Harder They Fall 🐾🐾🐾 **1956** A cold-eyed appraisal of the scum-infested boxing world. An unemployed reporter (Bogart) in his last role) promotes a fighter for the syndicate, while doing an expose on the fight racket. Bogart became increasingly debilitated during filming and died soon afterward. Based on Budd Schulberg's novel. 109m/B VHS, DVD, Humphrey Bogart, Rod Steiger, Jan Sterling, Mike Lane, Max Baer Sr., Alber "Poppy" Popwell; *D:* Mark Robson; *W:* Philip Yordan; *C:* Barnett Guffey.

Hardhat & Legs 🐾🐾 **1980** Comic complications arise when a New York construction worker falls in love with the woman who's teaching the modern sexuality course in which he's enrolled. 96m/C VHS, Sharon Gless, Kevin Dobson, Raymond Serra, Eva Josephson, Bobby Short, Jacqueline Brookes, Deanna Lund; *D:* Jerry Lewis; *W:* Jerry Lewis.

Hardly Working 🐾 **1981** (PG) A circus clown finds it difficult to adjust to real life as he fumbles about from one job to another. Lewis's last attempt at resuscitating his directorial career. His fans will love it, but others need not bother. 96m/C VHS, Jerry Lewis, Susan Oliver, Roger C. Carmel, Gary Lewis; *D:* Jerry Lewis; *W:* Jerry Lewis.

Hardware 🐾 **1990** (R) Fag-tag ripoff in which McDermot is a post-apocalyptic garbage picker who gives girlfriend Travis some robot remains he collected (ours is not to ask why), oblivious to the fact that the tidy android was a government-spawned population controller, programmed to destroy warm bodies. Seems old habits die hard, and that spells danger. Will Robinson. Much violence excised to avoid x-rating. 94m/C VHS, DVD, Dylan McDermott, Stacey Travis, John Lynch, Iggy Pop; *D:* Richard Stanley; *M:* Simon Boswell.

Harem 🐾 **1985** A beautiful stockbroker gets kidnapped by a wealthy OPEC oil minister and becomes part of his harem. Kingsley stars as the lonely sheik who longs for the love of a modern woman. 107m/C VHS, Ben Kingsley, Nastassja Kinski; *D:* Arthur Joffe.

Harem 🐾🐾 **1986** In the early 1900s, a dastardly Turkish sultan kidnaps an American beauty to add to his harem—mightily displeasing his jealous first wife. Lots of overwrought romance and drama until she is finally rescued. 200m/C VHS, Omar Sharif, Nancy Travis, Ava Gardner, Julian Sands, Art Malik, Sarah Miles, Yaphet Kotto, Chere Lunghi; *D:* William (Billy) Hale. TV

Harem Suare **1999** (R) Exotic but not particularly erotic saga of young beauty Safiye (Gillain) who is sold as a concubine to the Sultan of the Ottoman Empire. She becomes his favorite and official wife but this does not prevent her from turning to palace eunuch Nadir (Descas) for affection. Nor does it protect Safiye or the rest of the Sultan's women when the empire falls, the Sultan flees to Europe, and the women are abandoned to fend for themselves. Turkish, French, and Italian with subtitles. 107m/C VHS, DVD, /T Marie Gillain, Alex Descas, Valeria Golino, Lucia Bose; *D:* Ferzan Ozpetek; *W:* Ferzan Ozpetek, Gianni Romoli; *C:* Pasquale Mari; *M:* Aldo De Scalzi.

Harlan County, U.S.A. 🐾🐾🐾 **1976** (PG) The emotions of 180 coal mining families are seen up close in this classic documentary about their struggle to win a United Mine Workers contract in Kentucky. Award-winning documentary. 103m/C VHS, DVD, *D:* Barbara Kopple; *C:* Phil Parmet. Oscars '75: Feature Doc., Natl. Film Reg. '90.

Harlan County War 🐾🐾½ **2000** Ruby Kincaid (Hunter) is the wife of striking Kentucky coal miner Silas (Levine). After a court order severely restricts the union members' protests, Ruby leads the wives into action, even allowing her arrest to be used as propaganda by union rep Warren Jakopovich (Skarsgard) to her husband's dismay. Good lead performances, although the dramatic power of the story is subdued. Inspired by Barbara Kopple's 1976 documentary, "Harlan County, U.S.A." 104m/C VHS, DVD, Holly Hunter, Stellan Skarsgard, Ted Levine, Wayne Robson; *D:* Tony Bill; *W:* Peter Silverman; *C:* Flavio Martinez Labiano; *M:* Van Dyke Parks. CABLE

Harlem Nights 🐾🐾 **1989** (R) Two Harlem nightclub owners in the 1930s battle comically against efforts by the Mob and crooked cops to take over their territory. High-grossing, although screwhat disappointing effort from Murphy, who directed, wrote, produced, and starred in this film. 118m/C VHS, DVD, Eddie Murphy, Richard Pryor, Redd Foxx, Danny Aiello, Jasmine Guy, Michael Lerner, Arsenio Hall, Della Reese, Eugene Robert Glazer; *D:* Eddie Murphy; *M:* Herbie Hancock. Golden Raspberries '89: Worst Screenplay.

Harlem on the Prairie 🐾 *Bad Man of Harlem* **1938** This first-ever western with an all-black cast has Jeffries helping a young lady find hidden gold and helping a local all-black cast and crew. 54m/B VHS, Herbert Jeffries, Mantan Moreland, F.E. (Flournoy) Miller, Connie Harris, Macoe B. Sheffield, William Spencer Jr.; *D:* Sam Newfield.

Harlem Rides the Range 🐾½ **1939** Jeffries must outsnarl villainous Brooks, who means to swindle a radium mine away from its rightful owner. Early oater of interest only because of its atypical all-black cast and crew. 59m/B VHS, DVD, Herbert Jeffries, Spencer Williams Jr., Clarence Brooks, Tom Southern, Wade Dumas, Leonard Christmas; *D:* Richard C. Kahn; *W:* F.E. (Flournoy) Miller, Spencer Williams Jr.

Harley 🐾🐾 **1990** (PG) Diamond is Harley, an L.A. thug-on-a-hog, who's on his way to an extended stay at one of the state's luxury institutions when he's sent to a Texas rehabilitation community. There, he bonds with an ex-biker, and may just find his way back down the straight and narrow. And the local long-horn rednecks applaud his efforts...not. 80m/C VHS, Lou Diamond Phillips, Elf Cummins, DeWitt Jan, Valentine Kim; *D:* Free Holmes; *W:* Frank Kuntz, Sandy Kuntz.

Harley Davidson and the Marlboro Man 🐾 **1991** (R) An awful rehash of "Butch Cassidy and the Sundance Kid" with blatant vulgarity and pointless sci-fi touches. The title duo are near-future outlaws who rob a bank to save their favorite bar, then find they've stolen mob money. Some action, but it's mostly talk: lewd, meant-to-be-whimsical soul-probing chats between H.D. and M.M. that would bore even the biker crowd—and did. 98m/C VHS, DVD, Mickey Rourke, Don Johnson, Chelsea Field, Tom Sizemore, Daniel Baldwin, *D:* Simon Wincer; *W:* Don Michael Paul; *C:* David Eggby; *M:* Basil Poledouris.

Harlow 🐾🐾½ **1965** The more lavish of the two Harlow biographies made in 1965, both with the same title. A sensationalized "scandal sheet" version of Jean Harlow's rise to fame that bears little resemblance to the facts of her life. 125m/C VHS, Carroll Baker, Martin Balsam, Red Buttons, Mike Connors, Angela Lansbury, Peter Lawford, Raf Vallone, Leslie Nielsen; *D:* Gordon Douglas; *W:* John Michael Hayes; *C:* Joseph Ruttenberg.

Harmon of Michigan 🐾🐾 **1941** College football hero Harmon starred in this loosely adapted story of his life in this real-life tale of success and decides to put together his own as a cappella group—a musical sextet known as "The Comedian Harmonists," who find great success in Germany. Unfortunately, as the '20s give way to the '30s and the rise of Nazism, the group begins to run into trouble since three of its members are Jewish. Eventually, the political pressures force the group to disband and send its Jewish members into exile. German with subtitles. 114m/C VHS, GE Ulrich Noethen, Ben Becker, Heino Ferch, Heinrich Schafmeister, Max Tidof, Kai Wiesinger, Meret Becker, Katja Riemann, Dana Vavrova; *D:* Joseph Vilsmaier; *W:* Klaus Richter; *C:* Joseph Vilsmaier; *M:* Harald Kloser.

The Harmonists 🐾🐾 **1999** (R) Actor/singer Harry Frommermann (Noethen) is frustrated by his lack of success and decides to put together his own as a cappella group—a musical sextet known as "The Comedian Harmonists," who find great success in Germany. Unfortunately, as the '20s give way to the '30s and the rise of Nazism, the group begins to run into trouble since three of its members are Jewish. Eventually, the political pressures force the group to disband and send its Jewish members into exile. German with subtitles. 114m/C VHS, GE Ulrich Noethen, Ben Becker, Heino Ferch, Heinrich Schafmeister, Max Tidof, Kai Wiesinger, Meret Becker, Katja Riemann, Dana Vavrova; *D:* Joseph Vilsmaier; *W:* Klaus Richter; *C:* Joseph Vilsmaier; *M:* Harald Kloser.

Harmony Lane 🐾🐾 **1935** Highly romanticized rendition of the life of American composer, Stephen Collins Foster (1826-1864). Montgomery as Foster, manages to lend a hint of credibility to the syrupy, melodramatic script. Very little attention is given to orchestrated fact and almost every scene is orchestrated to show-case the composer's songs. The music steals the show. ♫Beautiful Dreamer; Old Folks at Home; Swanee River; Oh! Susanna; De Camptown Races. 84m/B VHS, Douglass Montgomery, Evelyn Venable, Adrienne Ames, Joseph Cawthorn, William Frawley, Florence Roberts, Smiley Burnette, Hattie McDaniel; *D:* Joseph Santley.

Harnessing Peacocks 🐾🐾½ **1992** Hebe (Scott Thomas) has a one-night stand with a mystery man during carnival time in Venice, gets pregnant, and winds up living a very independent life with her son in a British seaside community. She supports herself as both a chef and as an expensive mistress, with a very select group of admirers, but always drawn of reuniting with her son's father. Based on the novel by Mary Wesley. 108m/C VHS, GB Serena Scott Thomas, Peter Davison, Renee Asherson. TV

Harold & Kumar Escape from Guantanamo Bay 🐾🐾½ **2008** (R) Scatological, un-PC stoner comedy finds amiable dopers Harold (Cho) and Kumar (Penn) in federal trouble when Kumar can't resist lighting up his homemade bong in the airplane lavatory on their Amsterdam-bound flight. The bong is mistaken for a bomb and overzealous, idiotic Homeland Security dude Fox (Corddry) is sure the boys are terrorists (can you say ethnic profiling?). So they wind up at Git-mo, where predictable humiliations follow, before escaping and going on a road trip to Texas (an amiable fake Dubya makes an appearance), where they hope Harold's well-connected pal Colton (Winter) can keep them from wearing orange jump-suits for the rest of their days. If you liked their first buddy adventure (NPH?), this is way more of the same. 102m/C DVD, US John Cho, Kal Penn, Rob Corddry, Jack Conley, Roger Bart, Paula Garces, Neil Patrick Harris, Missi Pyle, Danneel Harris, Eric Winter, James Adomian, Beverly D'Angelo, David Krumholtz, Eddie Kaye Thomas, Ed Helms, Clyde Kusatsu, Christopher Meloni; *D:* Jon Hurwitz, Hayden Schlossberg; *W:* Jon Hurwitz, Hayden Schlossberg; *C:* Daryn Okada; *M:* George S. Clinton.

Harper 🐾🐾🐾 *The Moving Target* **1966** A hip, fast-moving genre piece about cynical LA private eye Lew Harper (Newman) who is hired by Mrs. Sampson (Bacall) to investigate the disappearance of her wealthy husband. Along the way he gets involved with an aging actress (Winter), a junkie singer (Harris), a religious nut (Martin), and a smuggling operation. From the Ross McDonald novel "The Moving Target." Later sequelled in "The Drowning Pool." 121m/C VHS, DVD, Paul Newman, Shelley Winters, Lauren Bacall, Julie Harris, Robert Wagner, Janet Leigh, Arthur Hill, Pamela Tiffin; *D:* Jack Smight; *W:* William Goldman; *C:* Conrad L. Hall; *M:* Johnny Mandel.

Harper Valley P.T.A. 🐾½ **1978** (PG) Eden raises hell in Harper Valley after the PTA questions her parental capabilities. Brain candy was adapted from a hit song; TV series followed. 93m/C VHS, DVD, Barbara Eden, Nanette Fabray, Louis Nye, Pat Paulsen, Ronny Cox, Ron Masak, Audrey Christie, John Fiedler, Bob Hastings; *D:* Richard Bennett; *W:* Barry Schneider.

Harrad Experiment 🐾🐾½ **1973** (R) Adaptation of Robert Rimmer's love-powered bestseller in which an experiment-minded college establishes a campus policy of sexual freedom. Famous for the Hedren/Johnson relationship, shortly before a down-son married Hedren's real-life daughter Melanie Griffith. Followed by "The Harrad Summer." 98m/C VHS, James Whitmore, Tippi Hedren, Don Johnson, Bruno Kirby, Laurie Walters, Victoria Thompson, Elliot Street, Sharon Taggart, Robert Middleton, Billy (Billie) Dee; *D:* Ted Post; *W:* Ted Cassedy, Michael Werner; *C:* Richard H. Kline; *M:* Artie Butler.

Harold and Kumar Go to White Castle 🐾🐾½ **2004** (R) Up-tight junior banker Harold (Cho) and his laid-back med student pal Kumar (Penn) take the edge of encroaching adulthood by getting high A lot. One such session produces cravings for White Castle hamburgers and sets the pair on a convoluted quest, despite Harold's need to finish an important work project. The journey is complicated by broken down vehicles, side trips for weed, creepy tow-truck drivers, skateboard punks, over-enthusiastic cops, and a hilariously Ecstasy-fueled Neil Patrick Harris. The pair's odd-couple chemistry helps smooth over the more ridiculous plot twists, and the target audience, properly medicated, should enjoy themselves for the final credits have rolled. 96m/C DVD, UMD, John Cho, Kal Penn, Paula Garces, David Krumholtz, Eddie Kaye Thomas, Fred Willard, Ethan (Randall) Embry, Neil Patrick Harris, Christopher Meloni, Ryan Reynolds, Anthony Anderson, Kate Kelton, Brooke D'Orsay; *D:* Danny Leiner; *W:* Jon Hurwitz, Hayden Schlossberg; *C:* Bruce Douglas Johnson; *M:* David Kitay.

Harold and Maude 🐾🐾🐾 **1971** (PG) Cult classic pairs Cort as a death-obsessed disillusioned 20-year-old obsessed with suicide (his staged attempts are a thesis of UCLA student Higgins, who showed it to his landlady, wife of film producer Lewis. Features music by the pre-Islamic Cat Stevens. 92m/C VHS, DVD, Ruth Gordon, Bud Cort, Cyril Cusack, Vivian Pickles, Charles Tyner, Ellen Geer, Eric Christmas, Gleorge) Wood, Gordon Devol; *D:* Hal Ashby; *W:* Colin Higgins; *C:* John A. Alonzo; *M:* Cat Stevens. Natl. Film Reg. '97.

Harold Robbins' Body Parts 🐾🐾 *Body Parts; Vital Parts* **1999** (R) An unsurprising formula revenge flick. Ty Kinnick (Grieco) is double-crossed by his best friend (Stewart) and wife (Massey) during a drug deal. Five years later, he's back and finds that the intrigues are still being played out. 87m/C DVD, Richard Grieco, Will Foster Stewart, Athena Massey; *D:* Craig Corman; *W:* Craig Corman.

Harrad Summer ♂♂♂ *1974 (R)* Sequel to "The Harrad Experiment." College coeds take their sex-education to the bedroom where they can apply their knowledge by more intensive means. **103m/C VHS.** Angela (Clark), Richard Doran, Victoria Thompson, Laurie Walters, Robert Reiser, Bill Dana, Marty Allen; **D:** Steven Hilliard Stern.

Harriet Craig ♂♂♂ *1950* Tailormade Crawford role finds her as seemingly perfect wife Harriet Craig. In reality, she's a domineering shrew, who's also a bully and a clean freak. Harriet squelches husband Walter's (Corey) promotion because it means he'll be travelling abroad, ruins his relationship with best friend Billy (Joslyn), and manages to sabotage her young cousin Clare's (Stevens) romance before anyone stands up to her. Third film adaptation of George Kelly's 1925 play "Craig's Wife." **94m/B VHS.** Joan Crawford, Wendell Corey, Allyn Joslyn, William Bishop, K.T. Stevens, Lucile Watson, Raymond Greenleaf, Ellen Corby; **D:** Vincent Sherman; **W:** James Gunn; **C:** Joseph Walker; **M:** George Duning.

Harriet the Spy ♂♂½ *1996 (PG)* Sixth-grade, 11-year-old tomboy Harriet M. Welsch (Trachtenberg) spies on everyone around her and, encouraged by her nanny Ole Golly (O'Donnell), writes down everything going on in her secret notebook, because she's determined to become a great writer. Unfortunately, Harriet's imagination sometimes gets the best of her and when her notebook is found, her friends and family are not too happy about its contents. Based on the award-winning novel by Louise Fitzhugh. Lovers of the book may not be enthusiastic about some of the changes but generally it's enjoyable fare. **102m/C VHS, DVD.** Michelle Trachtenberg, Rosie O'Donnell, Vanessa Lee Chester, Gregory Edward Smith, Robert Joy, Eartha Kitt, J. Smith-Cameron; **D:** Bronwen Hughes; **W:** Douglas Petrie, Theresa Rebeck; **C:** Francis Kenny; **M:** Jamshied Sharifi.

Harrison's Flowers ♂♂ *2002 (R)* Sometimes goopy, sometimes harrowing story of a naive woman searching for her missing husband. Newsweek photojournalist Harrison Lloyd (Strathairn) promises wife Sarah (MacDowell) that his '91 assignment to Yugoslavia (at the beginning of the Balkan conflict) will be his last. Maybe in more ways than one, since he's reported missing, which Sarah doesn't believe. So she's takes off for Croatia and promptly gets a hard lesson in the confusion of war. Fellow correspondents Kyle (Brody), Stevenson (Gleeson), and Yeager (Koteas) agree to help Sarah even though they think she's nuts. Watch the guys, particularly Brody, since all MacDowell has to do is alternate between noble, frightened, and stubborn. **122m/C VHS, DVD. FR** Andie MacDowell, David Strathairn, Elias Koteas, Adrien Brody, Brendan Gleeson, Alun Armstrong, Caroline Goodall, Diane Baker, Gerard Butler, Marie Trintignant; **D:** Elie Chouraqui; **W:** Elie Chouraqui, Didier Le Pecheur, Isabel Ellsen; **C:** Nicola Pecorini; **M:** Cliff Eidelman.

Harry and Max ♂ *2004* Harry (Johnson) is a teenage pretty boy in a pop band, younger than brother Max (Williams). They're a slightly younger pretty boy model. They're jealous of one another, and steal one another's sex partners, one being a quite older adult yoga teacher (Gilroy). While there is never any real sex or nudity on screen, one has to wonder what kind of audience this movie meant to please. Truly awful, in spite of cast's dire attempts to inject some believability into the absurd story. **74m/C DVD. US** Bryce Johnson, Cole Williams, Rain Phoenix, Tom Gilroy, Michelle Phillips, Katherine Ellis, Justin Zachary, Roni Deitz; **D:** Christopher Munch; **W:** Christopher Munch; **C:** Rob Sweeney; **M:** Michael Tubbs.

Harry & Son ♂♂ *1984 (PG)* A widowed construction worker faces the problems of raising his son. Newman is miscast as the old man and we've all seen Benson play the young role too many times. **117m/C VHS.** Paul Newman, Robby Benson, Ellen Barkin, Wilford Brimley, Judith Ivey, Ossie Davis, Morgan Freeman, Joanne Woodward; **D:** Paul Newman; **M:** Henry Mancini.

Harry and the Hendersons ♂♂½ *1987 (PG)* Ordinary American family vacationing in the Northwest has a collision with Bigfoot. Thinking that the big guy is dead, they throw him on top of the car and head home. Lo and behold, he revives and starts wrecking the furniture and in the process, endears himself to the at-first frightened family. Nice little tale efficiently told, with Lithgow fine as the frustrated dad trying to hold his Bigfoot-invaded home together. Basis for the TV series. **111m/C VHS, DVD.** John Lithgow, Melinda Dillon, Don Ameche, David Suchet, Margaret Langrick, Joshua Rudoy, Kevin Peter Hall, Lainie Kazan, M. Emmet Walsh, John Bloom; **D:** William Dear; **W:** William Dear, William E. Martin, Ezra D. Rappaport; **C:** Allen Daviau; **M:** Bruce Broughton. Oscars '87: Makeup.

Harry and Tonto ♂♂♂ *1974* A gentle comedy about an energetic septuagenarian who takes a cross-country trip with his cat, Tonto. Never in a hurry, still capable of feeling surprise and joy, he makes new friends and visits old lovers. Carney deserved his Oscar. Mazursky has seldom been better. **115m/C VHS, DVD.** Art Carney, Ellen Burstyn, Larry Hagman, Geraldine Fitzgerald, Chief Dan George, Arthur Hunnicutt, Josh Mostel, Cliff DeYoung, Philip Bruns, Rene Enriquez, Herbert Berghof, Michael (Mick) McCleery, Melanie Mayron, Michael C. Butler; **Cameos:** Paul Mazursky; **D:** Paul Mazursky; **W:** Paul Mazursky; **C:** Michael C. Butler; **M:** Bill Conti. Oscars '74: Actor (Carney); Golden Globes '75: Actor—Mus./Comedy (Carney).

Harry & Walter Go to New York ♂♂ *1976 (PG)* At the turn of the century, two vaudeville performers are hired by a crooked British entrepreneur for a wild crime scheme. The cast and crew try their hardest, but it's not enough to save this boring comedy. The vaudeville team of Caan and Gould perhaps served as a model for Beatty and Hoffman in "Ishtar." **111m/C VHS, DVD.** James Caan, Elliott Gould, Michael Caine, Diane Keaton, Burt Young, Jack Gilford, Charles Durning, Lesley Ann Warren, Carol Kane; **D:** Mark Rydell; **W:** John Byrum; **M:** David Shire.

Harry Black and the Tiger ♂♂ *1958* Jungle adventure involving a one-legged hunter and a man-eating tiger. The hunter initially teams up with the old war buddy who cost him his leg. The motivation grows with each failure to catch the beast and to make matters worse, the friend's wife and son are lost somewhere in the perilous jungle. Filmed in India. **107m/C VHS. GB** Stewart Granger, Barbara Rush, Anthony Steel; **D:** Hugo Fregonese.

Harry Potter and the Chamber of Secrets ♂♂♂½ *2002 (PG)* Action-packed sequel tops its predecessor with less exposition and more adventure as Harry (Radcliffe) and his friends at Hogwarts try to discover who may lie somewhere in the halls of the school, unbeknownst to professors Rickman, Smith, and even headmaster Harris. Everything about this outing is bigger and better, including a delightfully expanded, labyrinthine Hogwarts. Sometimes over-the-top thrills may be a lot for younger viewers. Book two in Rowling's series. **161m/C VHS, DVD, Blu-ray Disc, HD DVD. US** Daniel Radcliffe, Rupert Grint, Emma Watson, Kenneth Branagh, Robbie Coltrane, Richard Harris, Maggie Smith, Alan Rickman, Jason Isaacs, Tom Felton, Alan Rickman, Warwick Davis, Richard Griffiths, Fiona Shaw, Julie Walters, Shirley Henderson, Mark Williams, Julian Glover, Miriam Margolyes, Christian Coulson, Gemma Jones, David Bradley, Bonnie Wright; **D:** Chris Columbus; **W:** Steven Kloves; **C:** Roger Pratt; **M:** John Williams; **V:** Toby Jones.

Harry Potter and the Goblet of Fire ♂♂♂½ *2005 (PG-13)* If you aren't already swept up in the book-turned-film craze created by Rowling, this film might just do it. Harry (Radcliffe) and his trusty pals Ron (Grint) and Hermione (Watson), now teens in their fourth year at Hogwarts, battle the forces of evil that swirl around Harry's mysterious past. Lord Voldemort makes a showing, and new character Mad Eye Moody (Gleeson) joins forces with the good guys to help Harry compete in the frightening and dangerous Tri-Wizard Tournament. Special effects are even better than the previous three films—old fans won't be disappointed; new fans will want to play catch-up. **157m/C DVD, Blu-ray Disc, UMD, HD DVD. US** Daniel Radcliffe, Rupert Grint, Emma Watson, Robbie Coltrane, Ralph Fiennes, Michael Gambon, Brendan Gleeson, Jason Isaacs, Gary Oldman, Miranda Richardson, Alan Rickman, Maggie Smith, Timothy Spall, Frances de la Tour, Pedja Bjelac, David Bradley, Warwick Davis, Tom Felton, Robert Hardy, Shirley Henderson, Roger Lloyd-Pack, Mark Williams, Stanislav Ianevski, Robert Pattinson, Clarence Poesy, David Tennant, James Phelps, Oliver Phelps, Bonnie Wright, Katie Leung, Matthew Lewis, Afshan Azad, Shefali Chowhury; **D:** Mike Newell; **W:** Steven Kloves; **C:** Roger Pratt; **M:** Patrick Doyle.

Harry Potter and the Order of the Phoenix ♂♂ *2007 (PG-13)* Warner Brothers turned to Yates, their least recognizable director yet, for this fifth chapter of the Potter series and, regrettably, he doesn't bring much to the table. Angsty Potter (Radcliffe) returns to Hogwarts to discover that most of the wizarding world doesn't believe him about the Dark Lord's return, so he begins training for wizard-on-wizard combat under the nose of Ministry stooge Dolores Umbridge (Staunton). It's all quite dark and moody, but the story is nearly incomprehensible, and Yates bungles most of the sequences that made the book so much fun to read **139m/C DVD, Blu-ray Disc, HD DVD. US** Daniel Radcliffe, Emma Watson, Rupert Grint, Michael Gambon, Alan Rickman, Gary Oldman, Imelda Staunton, Jason Isaacs, Ralph Fiennes, Helena Bonham-Carter, David Thewlis, Robbie Coltrane, Fiona Shaw, Maggie Smith, Tom Felton, Emma Thompson, Tom Wilkinson, Brendan Gleeson, Julie Walters, Evanna Lynch, Mark Williams, Bonnie Wright, Warwick Davis, Robert Hardy, David Bradley; **D:** David Yates; **W:** Michael Goldberg; **C:** Slawomir Idziak; **M:** Nicholas Hooper.

Harry Potter and the Prisoner of Azkaban ♂♂♂½ *2004 (PG)* Harry's back at Hogwarts, but he's still dealing with evil entities trying to kill him. Sirius Black (oldman), a roguwe wizard and convicted murderer has escaped from Azkaban Prison. Harry also has to deal with the onset of puberty and the trials of being a teenager. Michael Gambon takes over the role of Dumbledore from the late Richard Harris. Cauron is more faithful to the spirit of the books, driven more by emotion and feeling, and less by the marketing department. Cuaron was author J.K. Rowling's choice to direct the franchise from the start. **141m/C DVD, Blu-ray Disc, HD DVD.** Daniel Radcliffe, Emma Watson, Rupert Grint, Michael Gambon, Gary Oldman, Robbie Coltrane, Alan Rickman, Maggie Smith, Julie Walters, David Thewlis, Tom Felton, Emma Thompson, Julie Christie, Timothy Spall; **D:** Alfonso Cuaron; **W:** Steven Kloves; **C:** Michael Seresin; **M:** John Williams.

Harry Potter and the Sorcerer's Stone ♂♂♂ *2001 (PG)* Much-anticipated screen adaptation of J.K. Rowling's first book about a Dickensian orphan who discovers his wizardly legacy, didn't disappoint its legions of built-in fans. Director Columbus remains painstakingly faithful to the book, although film plays, understandably, like a highlights version and sometimes lacks any personality of its own. This may have been intentional (directors Steven Spielberg and Terry Gilliam were perhaps passed over because their personal stamp would override the material), and it doesn't detract from the outstanding production and captivating storytelling. Stellar all-Brit cast are what you'd expect given a $125-million budget and use of no less than nine effects houses. Even those not familiar with the book will enjoy the film's many charms. Good mix of entertainment for kids and adults, although a bit long for the very young. **152m/C VHS, DVD, Blu-ray Disc, UMD, HD DVD. US** Daniel Radcliffe, Rupert Grint, Emma Watson, Robbie Coltrane, Richard Harris, Maggie Smith, Zoe Wanamaker, Alan Rickman, Ian Hart, John Hurt, Tom Felton, Harry Melling, Richard Griffiths, Fiona Shaw, John Cleese, Warwick Davis, Julie Walters, Sean Biggerstaff, David Bradley, Matthew Lewis; **D:** Chris Columbus; **W:** Steven Kloves; **C:** John Seale; **M:** John Williams.

Harry Tracy ♂♂½ *Harry Tracy—Desperado 1983 (PG)* Whimsical tale of the legendary outlaw whose escapades made him both a wanted criminal and an exalted folk hero. **111m/C VHS, DVD. CA** Bruce Dern, Gordon Lightfoot, Helen Shaver, Michael C. Gwynne; **D:** William A. Graham; **C:** Allen Daviau.

Harry's War ♂♂ *1984 (PG)* A middle-class, middle-aged American declares military war on the IRS in this overdone comedy. **98m/C VHS.** Edward Herrmann, Geraldine Page, Karen Grassle, David Ogden Stiers; **D:** Keith Merrill.

Harsh Times ♂♂ *2005 (R)* Bale's truly scary as Jim Davis, a haunted Gulf War vet who drinks and drugs too much, which only exacerbates his natural volatility. Jim also manages to drag best bud, weak-willed Mike (Rodriguez), into his twilight life, which takes a crazy turn when, after being turned down by the LAPD, Jim is offered a job with Homeland Security. But it's in Colombia, which means choosing between work and love with his Mexican honey (Trull). Since writer/director Ayer also wrote "Training Day," you know this isn't going to end well. **119m/C DVD, HD DVD. US** Christian Bale, Freddy Rodriguez, Eva Longoria, Terry Crews, Tammy Trull, J.K. Simmons, Noel Guglielmi; **D:** David Ayer; **W:** David Ayer; **C:** Steve Mason; **M:** Graeme Revell.

Hart's War ♂♂½ *2002 (R)* Willis is leathery Col. McNamara, ranking U.S. POW officer in a German stalag who clashes with newly imprisoned Lt. Thomas Hart (Farrell), Yale law student and son of a U.S. Senator. Hart is recruited to lead a court martial proceeding against African-American prisoner Scott (Howard), accused of killing racist fellow prisoner Bedford (Hauser). McNamara seems to have ulterior motives for this court martial, however, and seems to be undermining Hart at every turn. Howard shines as the accused who doesn't even begin to expect a fair trial, and lures is brilliant as the urbane, Yankee culture loving German Col. Visser, who also happens to be a Yale alum. Beautiful cinematography helps offset occasional heavy-handed direction and, at times, overwrought plot. **128m/C VHS, DVD, Blu-ray Disc. US** Bruce Willis, Colin Farrell, Terrence Howard, Cole Hauser, Marcel lures, Linus Roache, Rory Cochrane, Michael Weston, Vicelious Shannon, Scott Michael Campbell, Adrian Grenier, Jonathan Brandis, Joe Spano, Sam Worthington; **D:** Gregory Hoblit; **W:** Billy Ray, Terry George; **C:** Alar Kivilo; **M:** Rachel Portman.

Harum Scarum ♂♂ *Harem Holiday 1965* Elvis tune-fest time! When a movie star (Presley) travels through the Middle East, he becomes involved in an attempted assassination of the king and falls in love with his daughter. He also sings at the drop of a veil: "Shake That Tambourine," "Harem Holiday," and seven others. **95m/C VHS, DVD.** Elvis Presley, Mary Ann Mobley, Fran Jeffries, Michael Ansara, Billy Barty, Theo Marcuse, Jay Novello; **D:** Gene Nelson; **W:** Gerald Drayson Adams; **C:** Fred H. Jackman Jr.; **M:** Fred Karger.

Harvard Man ♂♂½ *2001 (R)* Dropping a metric ton of acid while getting chased by the Mafia and the FBI: it's all just a day in the life of Harvard student Alan Jensen (Grenier). Meanwhile, the busy scholar/basketball player is also juggling two girlfriends: a mobster's daughter/cheerleader (Gellar), and older philosophy professor (Adams), as well as the throw-out for a basketball game. Stoltz and Gayheart play the mobster's bookies and use a twist. Inspired by his own '60s acid trip, director Toback's modern coming-of-age comedy is long on mayhem-inspired action and dialogue but short on characters to care about and isn't as fun as it sounds. The all-too-real depiction of a bad trip al-

Harvest ✝✝✝ one, however, is worth a look. **'00m/C VHS, DVD, US** Adrian Grenier, Sarah Michelle Gellar, Joey Lauren Adams, Eric Stoltz, Rebecca Gayheart, Gianni Russo, Ray Allen, Michael Aparo, Al Franken. **D:** James Toback. **W:** Ryan Shore.

The Harvest ✝✝✝1/2 1992 (R) Sultry temptress Leilani senses Miguel's internal thermometer into convulsions with her preference for ice during lovemaking. However, their tryst turns sour (for him) when she takes Miguel to the beach where mystery thugs beat him unconscious and swipe his kidney. Bizarre story sure to ignite a small cult following. **97m/C VHS, DVD, US** Miguel Ferrer, Leilani Sarelle Ferrer, Harvey Fierstein, Anthony John (Troy) Denison, Tim Thomerson, Matt Clark, Henry Silva. **D:** David Marconi. **W:** David Marconi.

Harvest Melody ✝✝ 1943 Singing star Glida Parker travels to farm country for a mere publicity stunt but decides to stay. Corny in more ways than one. ♪You Could Have Knocked Me Over With A Feather; Put It in Reverse; Let's Drive Out To The Drive-In; Tenderly. **70m/B VHS, DVD,** Wil Horneff, Jeffrey DeMunn, John Slattery, Lisa Emery, Mary McCormack, James Van Der Beek, Evan Handler, Frederick Weller. **D:** Stuart Burkin. **W:** Stuart Burkin, James Biederman, David A. Kohn. **C:** Oliver Bokelberg.

Harvest of Fire ✝✝1/2 1995 (PG) A close-knit Amish farming community in Iowa has been the target of a series of barn burnings, which come under the investigation of FBI agent Sally Russell (Davidovich). But the community doesn't want an outsider around and Sally needs some help, which she finds with Annie widow help, which she finds with Amish widow Annie Beiler (Duke). And gradually the disparate duo find some common ground. A Hallmark Hall of Fame presentation. **90m/C VHS** Patty Duke, Lolita (David) Davidovich, J.A. Preston, Jean (Louisa) Kelly, Tom Aldredge, James Read, Craig Wasson. **D:** Arthur Allan Seidelman. **W:** Richard Alfieri. **C:** Neil Roach. **M:** Lee Holdridge. **TV**

Harvey ✝✝✝1/2 1950 Straightforward version of the Mary Chase play about a friendly drunk with an imaginary six-foot rabbit friend named Harvey, and a sister who tries to have him committed. A fondly remembered, charming comedy. Hull is a standout, well deserving her Oscar. **104m/B VHS, DVD,** James Stewart, Josephine Hull, Victoria Horne, Peggy Dow, Cecil Kellaway, Charles Drake, Jesse White, Wallace Ford, Nana Bryant. **D:** Henry Koster. **W:** Oscar Brodney. **C:** William H. Daniels. **M:** Frank Skinner. Oscars '50: Support. Actress (Hull); Golden Globes '51: Support. Actress (Hull).

The Harvey Girls ✝✝✝ 1946 Lightweight musical about a restaurant chain that sends its waitresses to work in the Old West. ♪In the Valley Where the Evening Sun Goes Down; Wait and See; On the Atchison, Topeka and Santa Fe; It's a Great Big World; The Wild Wild West. **102m/C VHS, DVD,** Judy Garland, Ray Bolger, John Hodiak, Preston Foster, Angela Lansbury, Virginia O'Brien, Marjorie Main, Chill Wills, Kenny L. Baker, Selena Royle, Cyd Charisse. **D:** George Sidney. **C:** George J. Folsey. **M:** Harry Warren, Johnny Mercer. Oscars '46: Song ("On the Atchison, Topeka and Santa Fe").

Hat Box Mystery ✝✝ 1947 A detective's secretary is tricked into shooting a woman and private eye Neal is determined to save her from prison. Although not outstanding, it's worth seeing as perhaps the shortest detective film (a mere 44 min.) to ever make it out following. **44m/B VHS, DVD,** Tom Neal, Pamela Blake, Allen Jenkins. **D:** Lambert Hillyer.

Hatari! ✝✝ 1962 An adventure-loving team of professional big game hunters ventures to East Africa to round up animals for zoos around the world. Led by Wayne, they get into a couple of scuffs along the way, including one with lady photographer Martinelli who is doing a story on the expedition. Extraordinary footage of Africa and the animals brought to life by a fantastic musical score **158m/C VHS, DVD,** John Wayne, Elsa Martinelli, Red Buttons, Hardy Kruger, Gerard Blain, Bruce Cabot. **D:** Howard Hawks. **W:** Leigh Brackett. **C:** Russell Harlan. **M:** Henry Mancini.

Hatchet for the Honeymoon ✝ Blood Brides; Una Hacha para la Luna de Miel; Il Rosso Segno della Follia; An Axe for the Honeymoon; The Red Sign of Madness 1970 A rather disturbed young man goes around hacking young brides to death as he tries to find out who murdered his wife. Typical sick Bava horror flick; confusing plot, but strong on vivid imagery. **90m/C VHS, DVD, SP II** Stephen Forsyth, Dagmar Lassander, Laura Betti, Gerard Tichy, Femi Benussi, Alan Collins, Jesus Puente. **D:** Mario Bava. **W:** Mario Bava, Santiago Moncada, Mario Musy. **C:** Santa Maria Romitelli.

Hate ✝✝✝ La Haine; Hatred 1995 Twenty-hours in the lives of young, disenfranchised Said (Taghmaoui), Vinz (Cassel), and Hubert (Kounde), who are living in a housing project outside Paris. A riot breaks out, thanks to police brutality of an Arab resident, and Vinz finds a gun the cops lost. A Paris sojourn leads to a police interrogation of Hubert and Said, a fight with some skinheads, a return to their home turf, and an unexpected conclusion. Intelligent look at the idiocy engendered by societal oppression and a buildup of hatred. French with subtitles. **95m/B VHS, DVD, FR** Vincent Cassel, Hubert Kounde, Said Taghmaoui, François Levantal. **D:** Mathieu Kassovitz. **C:** Pierre Aim, Georges Diane. Cannes '95: Director (Kassovitz), Cesar '96:

Hate Crime ✝✝ 2005 Overwrought melodrama. Robbie (Peterson) and Trey (Smith) are a contented gay couple whose neighbor, Chris (Donella), is the homophobic son of a fundamentalist pastor (Davison). Naturally the neighbors soon clash. When Trey is beaten to death at a local park, Robbie is sure who's guilty, but the cops aren't. **103m/C DVD, US** Bruce Davison, Chad E. Donella, Cindy Pickett, Brian J. Smith, Seth Peterson, Susan Blakey, Giancarlo Esposito, Farah White. **D:** Tommy Stovall. **W:** Tommy Stovall. **M:** Ebony Tay.

Hatfields & the McCoys ✝✝ 1975 A re-telling of the most famous feud in American history—the legendary mountain war between the Hatfields and the McCoys. **90m/C VHS,** Jack Palance, Steve Forrest, Richard Hatch, Karen Lamm. **D:** Clyde Ware. **TV**

Hats Off ✝ 1937 Clarke and Payne star as opposing press agents in this tedious musical. The only bright spot is the finale which features white-roped girls on a cloud-covered carousel. ♪Where Have You Been All My Life?; Little O c Rhythm; Another; Zilch's Hats; Hats Off. **65m/B VHS,** Mae Clarke, John Payne, Helen Lynd, Luis Alberni, Richard "Skeets" Gallagher, Franklin Pangborn. **D:** Boris L. Petroff.

The Hasty Heart ✝✝ 1986 A rowdy, terminally ill Scotsman brings problems and friendships in this makeshift wartime hospital built in the jungles of Burma. Remake of 1949 flick with Richard Todd and Ronald Reagan in leading roles. **100m/C VHS,** Gregory Harrison, Cheryl Ladd, Perry King. **D:** Martin Speer.

The Haunted ✝ 1979 The ancient curse of an Indian woman haunts a present day family by possessing the body of a beautiful girl. Through the girl, a horrible vengeance is carried out. **81m/C VHS,** Aldo Ray, Virginia Mayo, Anne Michelle, Jim Negele. **D:** Michael de Gaetano.

Haunted ✝✝1/2 1995 (R) At their Sussex home, David Ash watches helplessly as his younger sister Juliet drowns. Flash-forward to 1925 and the grownup David (Quinn) returns to teach a university course debunking the supernatural. Still he's drawn to a supposedly haunted mansion, inhabited by artist Robert Mariell (Andrews), his sister Christina (Beckinsale), brother Simon (Lowe), and their elderly nanny (Massey). David starts experiencing visions of his dead sister, while mysterious fires and other unexplained manifestations occur—all of which seem tied to the unholy Mariell trio. Based on a novel by James Herbert. **108m/C VHS, DVD, GB** Aidan Quinn, Kate Beckinsale, Anthony Andrews, Alex Lowe, Anna Massey, Geraldine Somerville, Victoria Shalet. **Cameos:** John Gielgud. **D:** Lewis Gilbert. **W:** Lewis Gilbert, Bob Kellett, Tim Prager. **C:** Tony Pierce-Roberts. **M:** Debbie Wiseman.

The Haunted Castle ✝✝✝ 1986 The first production of the play "Turpitude" resulted in a number of mysterious accidents and the opening night death of the star. Kay Taggart. Fifteen years later, producer Sol Broski wants to take another shot mounting a new production at the original theatre. Problems arise almost immediately and people claim the ghost of Kay Taggart is haunting the play. Parapsychologist Charles Mooreland is called in to discover whether it's a spirit or a corporeal form wreaking havoc. **91m/C VHS,** Peter Tomarken, Suzan Spann, Yvette McClendon. **D:** Dennis DeVine. **W:** Steve Jarvis.

The Haunted Castle ✝✝✝1/2 Schloss Vogelod 1921 One of Murnau's first films, and a vintage, if crusty, example of German expressionism. A nobleman entertains guests at his country estate when strange things start to occur. Silent with English titles. **56m/B VHS, DVD, GB** Arnold Korff, Lulu Keyser-Korff. **D:** F.W. Murnau.

Haunted Gold ✝✝ 1932 A young Wayne, in his first Western for Warners, battles gold-hungry desperadoes and a mysterious cloaked phantom. Remake of "The Phantom City." **57m/B VHS, DVD,** John Wayne, Sheila Terry, Harry Woods. **D:** Mack V Wright. **W:** Adele Buffington.

Haunted Harbor ✝✝1/2 Pirate's Harbor 1944 A high-seas financier has been murdered by a crooked crony and Captain Jim Marsden's alibi is all wet. He's got to find the gold, the girl, and avoid the goons. Part of "The Cliffhanger Serials" series. **243m/B VHS,** Kane Richmond, Kay Aldridge, Roy Bancroft.

Haunted Highway ✝ Death Ride 2005 Photographer Greg (Gamble) has an affair with his model, Yumi (Yoshikawa) which takes his wife, Amanda (Putney), finds out about. Greg accidentally kills Amanda during an argument and puts her body in his car trunk for disposal in a remote location. Then Amanda starts to haunt him. Dumb rather than scary. **83m/C DVD, US** Rand Gamble, Junichi Suzuki. **W:** Junichi Suzuki. **C:** Takuo Ishizaka. **VIDEO**

Haunted Honeymoon ✝✝ 1986 (PG) Arthritic comedy about a haunted house and a couple trapped there. Sad times for the Mel Brooks alumni participating in this lame horror spoof. **82m/C VHS, DVD,** Gene Wilder, Gilda Radner, Dom DeLuise, Jonathan Pryce, Paul Smith, Peter Vaughan, Bryan Pringle, Roger Ashton-Griffiths, Jim Carter, Eve Ferret. **D:** Gene Wilder. **W:** Gene Wilder, Terence Marsh. **M:** John Morris.

The Haunted Mansion ✝1/2 2003 (PG) Inspired by the popular Disney ride of the same name, Jim Evers (Murphy) is a workaholic real estate agent who takes his family along to see a mansion whose owner wants to sell. They soon find out that the mansion is inhabited with ghosts, lots of them. Coincidentally enough, it turns out that Evers's wife Sara

Haunted: The Ferryman ✝1/2 1963 A subtle, bloodless horror film adapted a week-end spent in a monstrously haunted mansion by a parapsychologist (Johnson), the mansion's skeptic heir (Tamblyn), and two

(Thomason) bears a striking resemblance to the owner's long dead lover, who had committed suicide. So why wouldn't they let Red's ranch, warring The production design of the mansion is quite impressive, it still doesn't make up for the lack of an original story or dialogue. Murphy's comedic talent s largely wasted. Skip the movie, go for the ride. **99m/C VHS, DVD, Blu-ray Disc, US** Eddie Murphy, Marsha Thomason, Terence Stamp, Wallace Shawn, Jennifer Tilly, Nathaniel Parker, Marc John Jeffries, Aree Davis, Dina Spybey. **D:** Rob Minkoff. **W:** David Berenbaum. **C:** Remi Adefarasin. **M:** Mark Mancina.

The Haunted Palace ✝✝✝1/2 1963 Price plays both a 17th-century warlock burned at the stake and a descendant who returns to the family dungeon and gets possessed by the mutant-breeding forebearer. The movie has its own identity crisis, with title and ambience from Poe but story from H.P. Lovecraft's "The Case of Charles Dexter Ward." Respectable but rootless chills. **87m/C VHS, DVD,** Vincent Price, Debra Paget, Lon Chaney Jr., Frank Maxwell, Leo Gordon, Elisha Cook Jr., John Dierkes, Barboura Morris, Bruno VeSota. **D:** Roger Corman. **W:** Charles Beaumont, Floyd Crosby. **M:** Ronald Stein.

Haunted Ranch ✝✝1/2 1943 Reno Red has been murdered and a shipment of gold bullion is missing. A gang on the lookout for the gold tries to convince people that Red's ranch is haunted by his ghost. **56m/B VHS, DVD,** John "Dusty" King, Dave O'Brien, Max Terhune, Rex Lease, Julie Duncan. **D:** Robert Emmett Tansey.

The Haunted Sea ✝✝ 1997 (R) The crew of the Patra discovered an abandoned ship that's filled with Aztec treasure. But when the Patra's crew members begin disappearing, those remaining must discover what's guarding the treasure. **74m/C VHS,** James Brolin, Joanna Pacula, Krista Allen, Don Stroud. **D:** Dan Golden; **C:** John Aronson; **D:** David Wurst, Eric Wurst.

The Haunted Strangler ✝✝1/2 The Grip of the Strangler 1958 Boris Karloff is a writer investigating a 20-year-old murder who begins copying some of the killer's acts. **78m/B VHS, DVD, GB** Boris Karloff, Anthony Dawson, Elizabeth Allan, Timothy Turner, Diane Aubrey, Dorothy Gordon, Jean Kent, Vera Day. **D:** Robert Day. **W:** John C. Cooper, Jan Carino. **C:** Lionel Banes. **M:** Buxton Orr.

Haunted Summer ✝✝ 1988 (R) Soft-focus, sex-and-drugs period piece of the bacchanalian summer of 1816 spent by free spirits Lord Byron, Percy Shelley, Mary Shelley, and John Polidori and others, that led Mary Shelley to write "Frankenstein." Based on the novel of the same name by Anne Edwards. **106m/C VHS,** Alice Krige, Eric Stoltz, Philip Anglim, Laura Dern, Alex Winter. **D:** Ivan Passer. **W:** Lewis John Carino.

Haunted Symphony ✝✝ 1998 (R) Blood Song; Last Resurrection; Hellfire 1994 (R) In the 18th century, a deranged composer novelist who is mysteriously confronted for the devil an killed by a mob. Years later, his niece Gabrielle (Burns) discovers the unfinished symphony hidden in an old piano and hires choir master Marius (Cross) to complete the score. But when he tries, demonic things begin to occur. **85m/C VHS,** Jennifer Burns, Ben Cross, Doug Wert, Beverly Garland. **D:** David Tausik. **W:** Gray; David Hartwell.

HauntedWeen ✝1/2 1991 All trick, no treat, as a guy nailed by a frat house prank 20 years ago comes-back-for-revenge. **88m/C VHS,** Brien Blakely, Blake Pickett with various events and macabre set-pieces from his own novel, including a dead ferryman rising from the grave. **50m/C VHS, GB** Jeremy Brett, Natasha Parry, Lesley Dunlop. **D:** John Irvin.

The Haunting ✝✝✝1/2 1963 A

mediums (Harris and Bloom). A chilling adaptation of Shirley Jackson's "The Haunting of Hill House," in which the psychology of the heroine is forever in question. There's a silly 1999 remake that's all special effects and no scares. **113m/B VHS, DVD.** *GB* Julie Harris, Claire Bloom, Russ Tamblyn, Richard Johnson, Fay Compton, Rosalie Crutchley, Lois Maxwell, Valentine Dyall, Diane Clare; **D:** Robert Wise; **W:** Nelson Gidding; **C:** Davis Boulton; **M:** Humphrey Searle.

The Haunting ♂♂½ *The Haunting of Hill House* **1999 (PG-13)** Tiny Lili Taylor gets to play avenging angel with an assortment of ghosties and ghoulies in this silly would-be frightener based on the novel by Shirley Jackson and originally filmed in 1963. Dr. Marrow (Neeson) enlists three subjects to stay at Hill House for a study in insomnia that's (unknown to them) actually a study in fear response. There's brash Theo (Zeta-Jones), dopey Luke (Wilson), and fragile Nell (Taylor), who turns out to have unexpected ties to the haunted mansion. Big-budget doesn't make for big frights, just big, mocking laughter from the audience—certainly not what director De Bont must have intended. Dern appears briefly as the scruffy caretaker, with Seldes his Mrs. Danvers-like wife. **114m/C VHS, DVD.** Lili Taylor, Liam Neeson, Catherine Zeta-Jones, Owen Wilson, Bruce Dern, Marian Seldes, Virginia Madsen, Todd Field, Alix Koromzay; **D:** Jan De Bont; **W:** David Self; **C:** Caleb Deschanel; **M:** Jerry Goldsmith.

Haunting of Harrington House ♂ **1982** Tame teenage haunted house film. **50m/C VHS.** Dominique Dunne, Roscoe Lee Browne, Edie Adams, Phil Leeds; **D:** Murray Golden. **TV**

The Haunting of Hell House ♂ *Henry James' The Ghostly Rental; The Ghostly Rental* **1999 (R)** Remember when Hammer Studios made all those horror movies based on Edgar Allan Poe stories and they were a lot of campy fun (if not truly creepy)? Well, that's what this Victorian Gothic wants to (or should) be and isn't. Tormented James (Bowen) took his girlfriend to an abortionist and she died. James seeks advice from the mysterious Professor Ambrose (York), whose family past is also filled with tragedy. **90m/C VHS, DVD.** Andrew Bowen, Michael York, Claudia Christian, Aideen O'Donnell; **D:** Mitch Marcus; **W:** Mitch Marcus, L.L. Shapira; **C:** Russ Brandt; **M:** Ivan Koutikov.

The Haunting of Morella ♂ **1991 (R)** Poe-inspired cheapjack exploitation about a an executed witch living again in the nubile body of her teen daughter. Ritual murders result, in between lesbian baths and nude swims. Producer Roger Corman did the same story with more class and less skin in his earlier anthology "Tales of Terror." **82m/C VHS, DVD.** David McCallum, Nicole Eggert, Maria Ford, Lana Clarkson; **D:** Jim Wynorski; **W:** Jim Wynorski, R.J. Robertson.

Haunting of Sarah Hardy ♂½ **1989** Ward, as a recently wed heiress, returns to the scene of her unhappy childhood home. In a standard plot, Ward is torn between an apparent haunting and the question of her own sanity. TV film is redeemed by the creditable acting. Wendy McCallum, Nicole Eggert, Maria Ford, Lana Clarkson; **D:** Jim Wynorski; **W:** Jim Wynorski, R.J. Robertson. **94m/C VHS.** Sela Ward, Michael Woods, Roscoe Born, Polly Bergen, Morgan Fairchild; **D:** Jerry London; **C:** Bojan Bazelli. **TV**

The Haunting of Seacliff Inn ♂♂½ **1994 (PG-13)** Susan and Mark Enright struggle to start a bed-and-breakfast in their newly acquired Mendocino Victorian manse. But psychic Susie senses something—seems the former owner was accused of murdering his wife a hundred years ago, an owner was accused of murdering his wife in the house. Not-too-frightening ghost story but good cast work. **94m/C VHS.**

Ally Sheedy, William R. Moses, Louise Fletcher, Lucinda Weist, Maxine Stuart, Tom McCleister, James Horan; **D:** Walter Klenhard; **W:** Walter Klenhard, Tom Walla. **CABLE**

The Haunting Passion ♂♂½ **1983** Newlywed Seymour moves into a haunted house only to be seduced by the ghost of the former occupant's dead lover. Effective and erotic presentation. **100m/C VHS, DVD.** Jane Seymour, Gerald McHaney, Millie Perkins, Ruth Nelson, Paul Rossilli, Ivan Bonar; **D:** John Korty. **TV**

Haunts ♂½ *The Veil* **1977 (PG)** Tormented woman has difficulty distinguishing between fantasy and reality after a series of brutal slayings lead police to the stunning conclusion that dead people have been committing the crimes. **97m/C VHS.** Cameron Mitchell, Aldo Ray, May Britt, William Gray Espy, Susan Nohr; **D:** Herb Freed; **M:** Pino Donaggio.

Haunts of the Very Rich ♂♂½ **1972** A loose remake of "Outward Bound" in which a group of spoiled people on a vacation find themselves spiritually dead. Made for TV. **72m/C VHS.** Lloyd Bridges, Anne Francis, Donna Mills, Tony Bill, Robert Reed, Moses Gunn, Cloris Leachman, Ed Asner; **D:** Paul Wendkos. **TV**

Hav Plenty ♂♂♂ **1997 (R)** Moving in the circles of young black professionals, Lee Plenty (Cherot) is an unemployed would-be writer who doesn't seem to care too much about getting a job. The materialistic and ambitious Havilland (Maxwell),a friend of his from college, invites him to a New Year's Eve party when she finds that her fiance Michael (Harper) is playing around on her. The sedate holiday weekend turns into a frenzy of surprises, as Lee is chased by Hav's hairdo-happy friend Caroline (Jones) and newlywed sister Leigh (Lee). Screwball romantic comedy comes off as a hybrid of Spike Lee and Woody Allen, with writer/director/editor Cherot's own personal touches thrown in. Performances are excellent, especially Cherot himself, who only starred when the actor hired to play his part bowed out as filming started. **87m/C VHS, DVD.** Christopher Scott Cherot, Chenoa Maxwell, Hill Harper, Tammi Katherine Jones, Robine Lee, Betty Vaughn, Reginald James, Kenneth "Babyface" Edmonds; **D:** Christopher Scott Cherot; **W:** Christopher Scott Cherot; **C:** Kerwin Devonish; **M:** Wendy Melvoin, Lisa Coleman.

Havana ♂♂ **1990 (R)** During the waning days of the Batista regime, a gambler travels to Havana in search of big winnings. Instead, he meets the beautiful wife of a communist revolutionary. Unable to resist their mutual physical attraction, the lovers become drawn into a destiny which is far greater than themselves. Reminiscent of "Casablanca." **145m/C VHS, DVD.** Robert Redford, Lena Olin, Alan Arkin, Raul Julia, Tomas Milian, Tony Plana, Betsy Brantley, Lise Cutter, Richard Farnsworth, Mark Rydell, Daniel Davis; **D:** Sydney Pollack; **W:** Judith Rascoe, David Rayfiel; **C:** Owen Roizman; **M:** Dave Grusin.

Havana Widows ♂♂ **1933** Gold-digging chorus girls Mae (Blondell) and Sadie (Farrell) squeeze some money out of Herman Brody (Jenkins) and take off for Havana on a mission to bilk money from the millionaires there. They pose as wealthy widows and have their sights set on Deacon Jones (Kibbee), when their whole plot goes to pot as Brody suddenly shows up. Plus, Mae finds herself attracted to Deacon's son Bob-only he's broke. **62m/B VHS.** Joan Blondell, Glenda Farrell, Guy Kibbee, Allen Jenkins, Lyle Talbot, Frank McHugh; **D:** Ray Enright; **W:** Earl Baldwin.

Have No Fear: The Life of Pope John Paul II ♂♂ **2005** Cut-and-dried made-for-TV bio is told in flashback after the Pontiff (Kretschmann) begins to review his life after a pilgrimage to Jerusalem in 2000. He reflects on growing up as Karol Wojtyla in Nazi-occupied Poland and his journey from entering the clergy, up the priestly ladder to his election to Pope John Paul II. **87m/C DVD.** Thomas Kretschmann, Bruno Ganz, John Albasiny, Charles Kay, Joaquim DeAlmeida, Sabrino Javor; **D:** Jeff Bleckner; **W:** Michael Hirst, Judd Parkin; **C:** Roberto Benvenuti; **M:** Carlo Siliotto. **TV**

Have Rocket Will Travel ♂♂ **1959** Three janitors (guess who) help a scientist who is about to lose her job if she can't send a rocket to Venus. They accidently initiate the launch while still on board and introduce their brand of slapstick to a whole new planet. First of the late '50s-early '60s feature films to capitalize on the renewed popularity of the Three Stooges. **76m/B VHS.** Moe Howard, Larry Fine, Joe DeRita, Anna-Lisa, Jerome Cowan, Bob Colbert; **D:** David Lowell Rich; **W:** Raphael Hayes.

Haven ♂♂½ **2004 (R)** Overly-complicated story begins with corrupt businessman Carl Ridley (Paxton) taking his daughter Pippa (Bruckner) and getting out of Miami with a suitcase full of cash just ahead of the feds. Ridley goes to the Caymans, hoping to arrange something with his double-dealing attorney Allan (Dillane). Meanwhile, dock worker Shy (Bloom) makes the mistake of romancing wealthy Andrea (Saldana), greatly upsetting her violent brother Hammer (Mackie). A local crime boss (Adoti) is clued into Ridley's money, and things just get more confusing. **98m/C DVD.** *US GB GE SP* Orlando Bloom, Agnes Bruckner, Bill Paxton, Zoe Saldana, Anthony Mackie, Bobby Cannavale, Stephen (Dillon) Dillane, Victor Rasuk, Raz Adoti, Robert Wisdom; **D:** Frank E. Flowers; **W:** Frank E. Flowers; **C:** Michael Bernard; **M:** Heitor Pereira.

Having It All ♂♂ **1982** A wry comedy about a love triangle. Dyan Cannon stars as a successful business woman with a husband on each coast, who finds dividing her time is more than she bargained for. **100m/C VHS.** Dyan Cannon, Barry Newman, Hart Bochner, Melanie Chartoff, Sylvia Sidney; **D:** Edward Zwick; **M:** Miles Goodman. **TV**

Having Our Say: The Delany Sisters' First 100 Years ♂♂½ **1999** Based on the book and the Broadway play that looks at life through the aging eyes of the black Delany sisters: 103-year-old Sadie (Carroll) and 101-year-old Bessie (Dee). They share their experiences with New York Times reporter Amy Hill Hearth (Madigan), who has come to interview them in 1991. Their father was born a slave but all 12 of the Delany children graduated from college, with Bessie becoming a teacher and Sadie a dentist in Harlem. (The real Bessie died in 1995 and Sadie in 1999.) **90m/C VHS.** Diahann Carroll, Ruby Dee, Mykelti Williamson, Lonette McKee, Lisa Arrindell Anderson, Audra McDonald, Richard Roundtree, Della Reese; **D:** Lynne Littman; **W:** Emily Mann; **C:** Frank Byers. **TV**

Having Wonderful Crime ♂♂½ **1945** Madcap comedy-thriller about a newly married couple who combine sleuthing with a honeymoon. With their criminal lawyer friend along, the trio winds up searching for a magician who has vanished. Fast-paced action and quick dialogue. **70m/B VHS.** Pat O'Brien, George Murphy, Carole Landis, Lenore Aubert, George Zucco, Gloria Holden, Richard Martin, Blanche Ring, Charles D. Brown; **D:** Edward Sutherland; **W:** Howard J. Green; **C:** Frank Redman; **M:** Leigh Harline.

Having Wonderful Time ♂♂½ **1938** A young girl tries to find culture and romance on her summer vacation at a resort in the Catskills. Film debut of comic Red Skelton, who wasn't always as old as the hills. Based on a Broadway hit by Arthur Kober. **71m/B VHS.** Ginger Rogers, Lucille Ball, Eve Arden, Red Skelton, Douglas Fairbanks Jr.; **D:** Alfred Santell.

Havoc 2: Normal Adolescent Behavior ♂ *Normal Adolescent Behavior* **2007 (R)** It's kinda scary to think that this is a realistic portrait of modern teen life. Six teens, who have known each other since kindergarten, have decided to have sexual relationships only with each other (Tamblyn) falls for her new neighbor Sean (Holmes) and wants to change the rules, leaving clique leader Billie (Garner) very unhappy. **89m/C DVD.** Amber Tamblyn, Ashton Holmes, Kelli Garner, Ricky Ullman, Stephen Colletti, Hilarie Burton, Daryl Sabara, Kelly Lynch, Julia Garro, Edward Tournier; **D:** Beth Schacter; **W:**

Beth Schacter; **C:** Harlan Bosmajian; **M:** Craig DeLeon.

Hawaii ♂♂♂ **1966** James Michener's novel about a New England farm boy who decides in 1820 that the Lord has commanded him to the island of Hawaii for the purpose of "Christianizing" the natives. Filmed on location. Also available in a 181 minute version with restored footage. Available in director's cut version with an additional 20 minutes. **161m/C VHS, DVD.** Max von Sydow, Julie Andrews, Richard Harris, Carroll O'Connor, Bette Midler, Gene Hackman, Jocelyn Lagarde; **D:** George Roy Hill; **W:** Daniel Taradash, Dalton Trumbo; **M:** Elmer Bernstein. Golden Globes '67: Support. Actress (Lagarde), Score.

Hawaii Calls ♂♂ **1938** Two young stowaways on a cruise ship are allowed to stay on after one of them (Breen) struts his stuff as a singer. The two then turn sleuth to catch a gang of spies. More ham than a can of Spam, but still enjoyable. ♫That's The Hawaiian In Me; Hawaii Calls; Down Where The Trade Winds Blow; Macushla; Aloha Oe. **72m/B VHS.** Bobby Breen, Ned Sparks, Irvin S. Cobb, Warren Hull, Gloria Holden, Pua Lani, Raymond Paige, Philip Ahn, Ward Bond; **D:** Edward F. (Eddie) Cline.

Hawaiian Buckaroo ♂ **1938** A couple of cowboys fight to save their pineapple plantation from a sneaky foreman. **62m/B VHS.** Smith Ballew, Evalyn Knapp, Benny Burt, Harry Woods, Pat J. O'Brien; **D:** Ray Taylor.

The Hawk ♂♂½ **1993 (R)** Okay thriller about suburban housewife Annie (Mirren) who suspects that her husband Stephen (Costigan) is a serial killer known as The Hawk. Since Annie has a history of depression and her husband is a known louse, her suspicions are dismissed as delusional. Some surprise twists help the weak story along. Contains some graphic views of corpses. Based on the novel by Ransley. **84m/C VHS, DVD.** *GB* Helen Mirren, George Costigan, Owen Teale, Rosemary Leach; **D:** David Hayman; **W:** Peter Ransley; **M:** Nick Bicat.

Hawk and Castle *The Hawk of Castile* **1967** Bandits murder, pillage, and terrorize the nobility in Medieval Europe until the Hawk comes onto the scene. **95m/C VHS.** *SP* Alvaro de Luna, Julio Perez Tabernero, Nuria Torray, German Cobos, Felix Defauce, Mari Real; **D:** Jose Maria Elorrieta; **W:** Jose Maria Elorrieta; **C:** Alfonso Nieva; **M:** Fernando Garcia Morcillo.

The Hawk Is Dying ♂♂½ **2006** And so's the flick. Gloomy George Gattling (Giamatti) is stuck in a boring life, helping his sister (Schwimmer) with her autistic son, Fred (Pitt). When tragedy strikes, George becomes obsessed with catching and taming a wild red-tail hawk, seeking to control something in his life, no matter the cost or consequences. Williams shows up occasionally as a stoner co-ed willing to boff George. Based on the novel by Harry Crews. **106m/C DVD.** Paul Giamatti, Michelle Williams, Michael Pitt, Robert Wisdom, Rusty Schwimmer, Ann Wedgeworth; **D:** Julian Goldberger; **C:** Bobby Bukowski; **M:** Julian Goldberger.

The Hawk of Powder River ♂ **1948** Cheapie western has Dean getting involved with a beautiful outlaw gang leader with a murderous streak. A large part of this film was lifted from earlier Dean oaters, as are all the tunes. **54m/B VHS.** Eddie Dean, Roscoe Ates, Jennifer Holt, June Carlson, Terry Frost, Lane Bradford; **D:** Ray Taylor.

Hawk of the Wilderness ♂♂ **1938** A man, shipwrecked as an infant and reared on a remote island by native Indians, battles modern day pirates after an explorer finds a cache of treasure. Serial in 12 episodes. **213m/B VHS.** Bruce Bennett, Mala, William Royle; **D:** William Witney.

Hawk the Slayer ♂♂½ **1981** A comic book fantasy. A good warrior struggles against his villainous brother to possess a magical great powers of destruction. Violent battle scenes; Palance makes a great villain. **93m/C VHS, DVD.** Jack Palance,John Terry, Harry Andrews, Roy Kinnear, Ferdinand "Ferdy"

Hawken's Breed ✂️ 1987 (R) Drifter meets American Indian beauty and hears her tale of woe; the two fall for each other and set out together to avenge the murder of her husband and son. Nothing much to crow about. 93m/C VHS. Peter Fonda, Serene Hedin, Jack Elam; *D:* Charles B. Pierce.

Hawkeye ✂️½ 1988 (R) After his best friend is murdered by gangsters in a seedy drug deal, Hawkeye, a rough and tumble Texas cop, heads out to the streets of Las Vegas with a vengeance. 90m/C VHS. Troy Donahue, Chuck Jeffreys, George Chung, Stan Wertlieb; *D:* Leo Fong.

Hawks ✂️½ 1989 (R) Somewhere on the road to black-comedy this film gets waylaid by triviality. Two terminally ill men break out of the hospital, determined to make their way to Amsterdam for some last-minute fun. Mediocre at best. 105m/C VHS. *GB* Anthony Edwards, Timothy Dalton, Janet McTeer, Jill Bennett, Sheila Hancock, Connie Booth, Camille Coduri; *D:* Robert Ellis Miller; *W:* Roy Clarke; *C:* Doug Milsome.

The Hawks & the Sparrows ✂️✂️✂️ *Uccellacci e Uccellini* 1967 Shortly after "Mr. Ed" came Pasolini's garrulous crow, which follows a father and son's travels through Italy spouting pithy bits of politics. A comic Pasolinian allegory-fest full of then-topical political allusions. The story comes off a bit wooden. Worth watching to see Toto, the Italian comic, in his element. 91m/B VHS, DVD. *IT* Toto, Ninetto Davoli, Femi Benussi; *D:* Pier Paolo Pasolini; *W:* Pier Paolo Pasolini; *M:* Ennio Morricone.

Hawks's Vengeance ✂️½ 1996 (R) While investigating his police detective stepbrother's murder British Royal Marine Lt. Eric "Hawk" Kelly (Daniels) discovers a bizarre connection between a skinhead gang called the Death Skulls, a martial arts master crime boss (Magda), a real life incident. Silent with orchestral score. 96m/C VHS, DVD. James Hampton, Christopher Connelly, Sam Pickens, Denver Pyle; *D:* Joe Camp; *W:* William Bickley.

Hawmps! *WOOF!* 1976 (G) Idiotic comedy about a Civil War lieutenant who trains his men to use camels. When the soldiers and animals begin to grow fond of each other, Congress orders the camels to be set free. Hard to believe this was based on a real life incident. 98m/C VHS. James Hampton, Christopher Connelly, Slim Pickens, Denver Pyle; *D:* Joe Camp; *W:* William Bickley.

Hawthorne of the USA ✂️✂️½ 1919 Reid stars as Anthony Hamilton Hawthorne, American extraordinaire. After gambling a fortune away in Monte Carlo, Hawthorne heads to mainland Europe for rest and revelry. Instead, he finds the love of a princess and a Communist coup in the making. Silent with orchestral score. 55m/B VHS. Wallace Reid, Harrison Ford, Lila Lee, Tully Marshall; *D:* James Cruze.

Haxan: Witchcraft through the Ages ✂️✂️✂️ *Haxan; Witchcraft through the Ages* 1922 The demonic Swedish master-piece in which witches and victims suffer against various historical backgrounds. Nightmarish and profane especially the appearance of the Devil as played under much make-up by Christiansen himself. Silent. 74m/B VHS, DVD. *SW* Maren Pedersen, Clara Pontoppidan, Oscar Stribolt, Benjamin Christiansen, Tora Teje, Elith Pio, Karen Winther, Emmy Schonfeld, John Andersen, Astrid Holm, Gerda Madsen; *D:* Benjamin Christiansen; *C:* Johan Ankerstjerne; *Nar:* William S. Burroughs.

Hazel's People ✂️½ *Happy as the Grass Was Green* 1973 (G) Bitter and hostile college student attends his friend's funeral in Mennonite country. He discovers not only a way of life he never knew existed, but a personal faith in a living Christ. From the Merle Good novel, "Happy as the Grass Was Green." 105m/C VHS. Geraldine Page, Pat Hingle, Graham Beckel, Rachel Thomas; *D:* Charles Davis; *C:* Stan Martin; *M:* Gordon Zahler.

Mayne, William Morgan Sheppard; *D:* Terry Marcel.

The Hazing ✂️½ *Dead Scared* 2004 A demon is set loose at a campus mansion where college frat students spend a grisly initiation evening possessed by the wicked dude. 87m/C VHS, DVD. Brad Dourif, Tiffany Shepis, Parry Shen, David Tom, Robert Donovan, Philip Andrew, Jeremy Maxwell, Nectar Rose, Charmaine DeGrate, Brooke Burke, Jeff Lee; *Cameos:* Robert Donovan; *D:* Rolfe Kanefsky; *W:* Rolfe Kanefsky; *M:* Chris Farrell.

He Died With a Felafel in His Hand ✂️✂️ 2001 Ya gotta love the title—if nothing else about this adaptation of John Birmingham's semicomic 1994 novel. Three distinct Australian cities play their part: subtropical Brisbane inspires indolence and wacky sunstruck behavior; cool Melbourne fosters navel-gazing and an overly-earnest dedication to causes; and seaside Sydney is dedicated to hedonism. Wanabe Brisbane writer Danny (Taylor) is looking for some kind of purpose in life and turns to friend Sam (Hamilton) for advice. The duo wind up in Melbourne after Sam's breakup with gal pal Anya (Bohringer) and finally make their way to Sydney where their chaotic lives don't become any more stable. Oh, and the title refers to one of the duo's many strange roommates. 107m/C DVD. *AU* IT Noah Taylor, Emily Hamilton, Romane Bohringer, Sophie Lee, Francis McMahon, Brett Stewart; *D:* Richard Lowenstein; *W:* Richard Lowenstein; *C:* Andrew de Groot.

He Got Game ✂️✂️½ 1998 (R) Lee hops all over the place with this basketball drama that reveals more of his love for the game than cohesive filmmaking. Actually two movies in one: High school basketball great Jesus Shuttlesworth (newcomer and Milwaukee Bucks player Allen) must decide between college or a lucrative NBA contract. Then up pops his incarcerated pops, Jake, (a haggard Washington) to pressure him to chose his warden's alma mater, which turns the film into a shallow look at a strained father-son relationship. Washington is dynamic as the embittered father and Allen is evenly effective. Yet, the reunion is never fully developed and sometimes abandoned, while Lee scores visually by beautifully photographing the glorious hoop moves. Extraneous, stereotypical characters and raunchy sex sequences drag the film further from its dramatic resonance. 134m/C VHS, DVD. Denzel Washington, Ray Allen, Milla Jovovich, Rosario Dawson, Hill Harper, Zelda Harris, Jim Brown, Ned Beatty, Lonette McKee, John Turturro, Michele Shay, Bill Nunn, Thomas Jefferson Byrd; *D:* Spike Lee; *W:* Spike Lee; *C:* Malik Hassan Sayeed.

He Is My Brother ✂️½ 1975 (G) Two boys survive a shipwreck landing on an island that houses a leper colony. 90m/C VHS. Keenan Wynn, Bobby Sherman, Robbie (Reiss) Rist; *D:* Edward Dmytryk.

He Kills Night After Night After Night ✂️½ *Night After Night After Night* 1969 British police are baffled as they seek the man who has been killing women in the style of Jack the Ripper. And he keeps doing it. 88m/C VHS. *GB* Donald (Don) Sumpter, Terry Scully, Jack May, Linda Marlowe, Justine Lord, Gilbert Wynne; *D:* Lindsay Shonteff; *W:* Dail Ambler.

He Knows You're Alone ✂️ 1980 (R) Lame horror flick that focuses on a psychotic killer terrorizing a bride-to-be and her bridal party in his search for a suitable bride of his own. 94m/C VHS, DVD. Don Scardino, Caitlin O'Heaney, Tom Rolling, Paul Gleason, Elizabeth Kemp, Tom Hanks, Patsy Pease, Lewis Arlt, James Rebhorn, Joseph Leon, James Carroll; *D:* Armand Mastroianni; *W:* Scott Parker; *C:* Gerald Feil; *M:* Alexander Peskanov, Mark Peskarov.

He Lives: The Search for the Evil One ✂️ 1967 A man who was imprisoned by Nazis as a child attempts to keep Hitler, now living in Buenos Aires, from starting a 4th Reich. 90m/C VHS. Henry (Kleinbach) Brandon, Lisa Pera, Pitt Herbert, Lee Patterson; *D:* Joseph Kane; *C:* Gay Galbraith; *M:* John Caper Jr.

He Loves Me ... He Loves Me Not ✂️ *A la Folie...Pas de Tout* 2002 Art student Angelique (Tautou) is obsessively enthralled with her married lover, cardiolo-

---

gist Loïc (Le Bihan), and refuses to believe that he won't leave his pregnant wife Rachel (Care). When Loïc stands in Angelique up before they are about to take a holiday, she begins to unravel and attempts suicide. Then the film takes us back to the beginning and shows Loïc's very different point-of-view: Angelique is delusional and stalking Loïc who barely knows the girl. And her madness just excels from there. French with subtitles. 92m/C VHS, DVD. *FR* Audrey Tautou, Samuel Le Bihon, Isabelle Care, Sophie Guillemin, Clément Sibony; *D:* Laetitia Colombani; *W:* Laetitia Colombani; *C:* Pierre Aïm; *M:* Jerome Coullet.

He Said, She Said ✂️✂️ 1991 Romance is the topic, but this isn't a typical dating film, instead a couple's relationship unfolds from differing points of view: first, the guy's (by Silver), and then the girl's (by Kwapis) and then Baltimore journalists and professional rivals, tell how their romance wound up on the rocks, and why (or so they say). The end result is overlong and lacks the zing of other war between the sexes movies, but moderately highlight the fact that men and women often view the same incidents very differently. Bacon overacts, Perkins over-reacts, and Stone shines as Bacon's ex-girl. 115m/C VHS, DVD, Elizabeth Perkins, Kevin Bacon, Sharon Stone, Nathan Lane, Anthony LaPaglia, Stanley Anderson, Charlaine Woodard, Danton Stone, Phil Leeds, Rita Karin; *D:* Marisa Silver, Ken Kwapis; *W:* Brian Hohlfield; *C:* Stephen Burum; *M:* Miles Goodman.

He Sees You When You're Sleeping ✂️½ 2002 (PG) Recently deceased stockbroker Sterling's superficial life doesn't pass muster with the powers-that-be at the pearly gates. But his guardian angel sets him up with one last selfless earthly task to make amends— save a single mom and her seven-year-old daughter from the evil clutches of local mob. A Christmas-themed Mary Higgins Clark adaptation. 100m/C VHS, DVD. Cameron Bancroft, Erika Eleniak, Greg Evigan, Udo Kier, Sean Campbell, Pam Hyatt, David Palffy, Roger Haskett, Rheta Hutton, Jason Low, Craig March, Claire Riley; *D:* David Winning; *W:* Carl Binder; *C:* David Pelletier; *M:* Michael Richard Plowman. TV

He Walked by Night ✂️✂️✂️½ 1948 Los Angeles homicide investigators track down cop killer Ray Morgan (Basehart) in this excellent drama. The final confrontation takes place in the L.A. County Flood Control System, consisting of some 700 miles of underground tunnels. Based on a true story from the files of the Los Angeles police, this first rate production reportedly inspired Webb to create "Dragnet." 80m/B VHS, DVD. Richard Basehart, Scott Brady, Roy Roberts, Jack Webb, Whit Bissell; *D:* Alfred Werker, Anthony Mann; *W:* John C. Higgins; *C:* John Alton; *M:* Leonid Raab.

He Was a Quiet Man ✂️½ 2007 Milquetoast Bob Maconel (Slater) is a paranoid and angry office drone who likes to keep a loaded gun in his desk. He accidentally becomes a hero when a co-worker, or does go postal and Bob kills him. This earns him a promotion. But he's dismayed to find out that his secret crush, Vanessa (Cuthbert), was paralyzed by a bullet and wants Bob to help her die. He can't, so they start a romance instead, or do they? Ending leaves a lot to puzzle out. 95m/C DVD. Christian Slater, Elisha Cuthbert, William H. Macy, Sascha Knopf, John Gulager, Jamison Jones; *D:* Frank A. Cappello; *W:* Frank A. Cappello; *C:* Brandon Trost; *M:* Jeff Beal.

He Who Gets Slapped ✂️✂️✂️ 1924 Chaney portrays a brilliant scientist whose personal and professional humiliation causes him to join a travelling French circus as a masochistic clown (hence the title). There he falls in love with a beautiful circus performer and plans a spectacular revenge. Brilliant use of lighting and Expressionist devices by director Sjostrom (who used the Americanized version of his name—Seastrom—in the credits). Adapted from the Russian play "He, The One Who Gets Slapped" by Leonid Andreyev. 85m/B

VHS. Lon Chaney Sr., Norma Shearer, John Gilbert, Tully Marshall, Ford Sterling, Marc McDermott; *D:* Victor Sjostrom; *W:* Carey Wilson, Victor Sjostrom.

He Who Walks Alone ✂️✂️½ 1978 Documents the life of Thomas E. Gilmore, who became the South's first elected black sheriff in the 1960s. 74m/C VHS. Louis Gossett Jr., Clu Gulager, Mary Alice, James McEachin, Barton Heyman, Barry Brown, Lonny (Lonnie) Chapman; *D:* Jerrold Freedman. TV

The Head ✂️✂️ 1959 A scientist comes up with a serum that can keep the severed head of a dog alive. Before too long, he tries the stuff out on a woman, backed body to that of a beautiful stripper. Weird German epic sports poor special effects and unintentional laughs, but is interesting nonetheless. 92m/B VHS, DVD. GE Horst Frank, Michel Simon, Paul Dahlke, Karin Kernke, Helmut Schmidt; *D:* Victor Trivas; *W:* Victor Trivas.

Head ✂️✂️ 1968 (G) Infamously plotless musical comedy starring the TV fab four of the '60s, the Monkees, in their only film appearance. A number of guest stars appear and a collection of old movie clips are also included. "Circle Sky; Can You Dig It; Long Title: Do I Have to Do This All Over Again; Daddy's Song; As We Go Along; The Porpoise Song." 86m/C VHS, DVD. Peter Tork, Mickey Dolenz, Davy Jones, Michael Nesmith, Frank Zappa, Annette Funicello, Teri Garr, Timothy Carey, Logan Ramsey, Victor Mature, Jack Nicholson, Bob Rafelson, Dennis Hopper; *D:* Bob Rafelson; *W:* Jack Nicholson, Bob Rafelson; *C:* Michael Hugo; *M:* Ken Thorne.

Head Above Water ✂️✂️ 1996 (PG-13) Remake of same-titled 1993 Norwegian black comedy is now set on an island off the Maine coast where married Nathalie (Diaz) and George (Keitel) are vacationing at her family's cottage. George goes off on an overnight fishing trip, but Nathalie isn't alone for long—former boyfriend Kent (Zane) shows up, the duo get drunk catching up on old times, and Nathalie wakes up the next morning with Kent's corpse. This unstable Nathalie hides the body, which is quickly found by George, who discards the corpse in a more permanent manner involving cement. Then Natalie suddenly decides George must have murdered Kent and is now after her. Plot doesn't hang together well and Keitel is frequently too low-key but Diaz is watchable, and Zane is also good. 92m/C VHS, DVD. Cameron Diaz, Harvey Keitel, Craig Sheffer, Billy Zane; *D:* Jim Wilson; *W:* Theresa Marie; *C:* Richard Bowen; *M:* Christopher Young.

Head in the Clouds ✂️✂️ 2004 (R) Beautiful Theron turns heads as hedonistic socialite Gilda, who briefly storms into the life of shy Irishman Guy (Townsend) in 1933. His torch remains ablaze as she later summons him to Paris, where Gilda is dabbling as a photographer and with a Spanish refugee named Mia (Cruz). Their triangular idyll is troubled by the political idealism displayed by both Mia and Guy, who are committed to the anti-fascist cause in the Spanish Civil War. Gilda feels betrayed when they leave her behind. When Guy finally sees her again in 1944, he's a British spy smuggled into France and Gilda is romancing Nazi officer Bietrich (Kretschmann). But is she really the un-feeling collaborator she seems? A plush potboiler with a pretty cast. 124m/C DVD. GB CA Charlize Theron, Penelope Cruz, Stuart Townsend, Thomas Kretschmann, Steven Berkoff, Karine Vanasse, Gabriel Hogan, David LaFaye, Peter Cockett, John Jorgenson, John Robinson, Lisa Bronwyn Moore; *D:* John Duigan; *W:* John Duigan; *C:* Paul Sarossy; *M:* Terry Frewer.

Head of State ✂️✂️ 2003 (PG-13) Just because Rock played a director in "Jay and Silent Bob Strike Back" doesn't mean he can do it in real life, at least not yet. Rock plays Mays Gilliam, a D.C. alderman drafted to run for President after the unnamed party's candidates die in a plane crash. The party leadership doesn't want him to win, just provide diversity cred for the next election. With his brother Mitch (Mac) as running mate, Mays fights his handlers to create his own identity. Un-

---

fortunately, in the hands of writer and director Rock, candidate Rock isn't given much consistent identity to work with. Maybe with a proven director, and more than token effort at plot and characterization, this one might've been better. **95m/C VHS, DVD.** *US* Chris Rock, Bernie Mac, Dylan Baker, Nick Searcy, Lynn Whitfield, Robin Givens, Tamala Jones, Stephanie March, James Rebhorn, Keith David, Tracy Morgan, Robert Stanton, Jude Ciccolella, Nate Dogg; *D:* Chris Rock; *W:* Chris Rock, Ali LeRoi; *C:* Donald E. Thorin; *M:* Marcus Miller, David "DJ Quik" Blake.

Head of the Family 🦴🦴½ **1971 (PG)** After a woman sacrifices her political ideals and career goals for her role as a family matriarch, she eventually falls apart. **105m/C VHS.** *IT FR* Nino Manfredi, Leslie Caron, Ugo Tognazzi, Claudine Auger; *D:* Nanni Loy; *W:* Nanni Loy.

Head of the Family 🦴🦴½ **1996 (R)** Lance (Bailey) moves to Nob Hollow and discovers the Stackpool family's dreadful secrets—they're telepathic quadruplets under the control of brother Myron (Perra), who just happens to be a giant head that gets around in a wheelchair. Lance decides to use the whacko family to get rid of babe girlfriend Loretta's (Lovell) inconvenient husband. **82m/C VHS, DVD.** Blake Bailey, Jacqueline Lovell, Bob Schott, J.W. Perra; *D:* Robert Talbot; *W:* Benjamin Carr; *C:* Adolfo Bartoli; *M:* Richard Band.

Head Office 🦴🦴 **1986 (PG-13)** A light comedy revolving around the competition between corporate management and the lower echelon for the available positions of chairman. **90m/C VHS, DVD.** Danny DeVito, Eddie Albert, Judge Reinhold, Rick Moranis, Jane Seymour; *D:* Ken Finkleman; *M:* James Newton Howard.

Head On 🦴🦴 **1998** Nineteen-year-old Ari (Dimitriades) is forced to confront his Greek heritage and its idea of manhood with the homosexuality he keeps secret from his traditional family. Much of his day is spent killing time with his friends until he can meet Sean (Garner), the young man Ari is attracted to, at a bar that night. Bored and restless, Ari is out to have a good time with as little pain to himself as possible. Adapted from the book "Loaded" by Christos Tsiolkas. **104m/C VHS, DVD.** *AU* Alex Dimitriades, Paul Capsis, Julian Garner, Damien Fotiou, Elena Mandalis, Andrea Mandalis, Tony Nikolakopoulos, Eugenia Fragos, Maria Mercedes; *D:* Ana Kokkinos; *W:* Ana Kokkinos, Mira Robertson, Andrew Bovell; *C:* Jaems Grant; *M:* Ollie Olsen.

Head On 🦴🦴🦴 *Gegen die Wand* **2004** Cahit (Unel) is a Turkish immigrant in Hamburg whose drunken, self-destructive behavior lands him in a psych ward. He meets fellow immigrant Sibel (Kekilli), a wrist-slasher who needs to escape her conservative Muslim family either by death or a marriage of convenience. Cahit figures he has nothing to lose and agrees when Sibel says she will keep him in alcohol. But their arrangement eventually spirals into mad love and violent consequences. Turkish and German with subtitles. **118m/C DVD.** Birol Unel, Sibel Kekilli, Catrin Striebeck, Guven Kirac, Meltem Cumbul, Cem Akin, Aysel Iscan, Demir Gokgol, Stefan Gebelhoff, Hermann Lause, Adam Bousdoukos, Ralph Misske, Mehmet Kurtulus; *D:* Fatih Akin; *W:* Fatih Akin; *C:* Rainer Klausmann.

Head Over Heels 🦴🦴🦴 **1967** A model married to an older man has an affair with a younger one and cannot decide between them. In French with subtitles. **89m/C VHS.** *FR* Brigitte Bardot, Laurent Terzieff, Michael Sarne; *D:* Serge Bourguignon.

Head Over Heels 🦴🦴½ **2001 (PG-13)** New York art restorer Amanda (Potter) has sworn off men after a bad breakup, but finds herself back in the game when she meets her dashing and mysterious neighbor, Jim (Prinze). Having conveniently taken up residence in an apartment that offers a perfect view of the one occupied by Jim, her attraction grows as she and her supermodel roommates follow the young man's every move. Works well during its romantic comedy stretches, but loses points for its reliance on an ill-conceived plot point revolving around a possible murder, and for lowering itself to much crude, scatological humor. **86m/C VHS, DVD.** *US* Monica Potter, Freddie Prinze Jr., Shalom Harlow, Ivana Milicevic, China Chow, Stanley Brazeau, Sarah O'Hare, Tomiko Fraser, Stanley DeSantis; *D:* Mark S. Waters; *W:* Ron Burch, David Kidd; *C:* Mark Plummer; *M:* Randy Edelman, Steve Porcaro.

Head Winds 🦴🦴 **1925** Silent romance in which Mr. Right spares helpless girl against her will from marrying Mr. Wrong. **52m/B VHS.** House Peters Sr., Patsy Ruth Miller; *D:* Herbert Blache; *W:* Edward T. Lowe; *C:* John Stumar.

Headhunter 🦴🦴½ **1989** Voodoo-esque killers are leaving headless bodies all around Miami. Plenty of prosthetic make-up. **92m/C VHS.** Kay Lenz, Wayne Crawford, John Fatooh, Sam Kanaly, June Chadwick, Sam Williams; *D:* Francis Schaeffer.

Headhunter 🦴🦴 **2005** Ben Caruso (Parrillo) wants a new job and a chance to see Sarah (Clainos), a professional headhunter. Sarah gets Ben a higher-paying desk job but it's on the graveyard shift, and weird things immediately start happening. When Ben does some investigating, he learns Sarah was a murder victim who was decapitated and has been using her "clients" to find her missing head. And if they can't, they may have to look for their own. Offers some surprises for the indie horror genre. **90m/C DVD.** Ben Parrillo, Kristi Clainos, Mark Aiken; *D:* Paul Tarantino; *W:* Paul Tarantino; *C:* Seth Kotok; *M:* Vincent Gillioz. **VIDEO**

Headin' for the Rio Grande 🦴 **1936** A cowboy and his sheriff brother drive off cattle-rustlers in this Western saga. Ritter's film debut. Songs include "Campfire Love Song," "Jailhouse Lament," and "Night Herding Song." **60m/B VHS, DVD.** Tex Ritter, Eleanor Stewart, Syd Saylor, Warner Richmond, Charles "Blackie" King; *D:* Robert North Bradbury.

Headin' Home 🦴🦴½ **1920** A very early version of the Babe Ruth story—starring none other than the Babe himself. A fair print, this film is orchestra scored. **56m/B VHS, DVD.** Babe Ruth, Margaret Seddon, Ruth Taylor, William Sheer; *D:* Lawrence Windom; *W:* Arthur Baer.

Heading for Heaven 🦴🦴 **1947** A mistaken medical report leaves a frazzled realtor believing he has only three months to live, and when he disappears the family suspects the worst. A minor comedy based on a play by Charles Webb. **65m/B VHS, DVD.** Stuart Erwin, Glenda Farrell, Russ Vincent, Irene Ryan, Milburn Stone, George O'Hanlon; *D:* Lewis D. Collins.

Heading South 🦴🦴🦴 *Vers le Sud* **2005** French pic set in the late '70s tells the story of three women "of a certain age," as the euphemism goes, who travel to an accommodating beachside resort in Haiti to satisfy their still-burning sexual needs. Each woman has her own backstory and reason for seeking out the pleasures of a more-than-willing local teenager, and each take a turn explaining this frankly and directly to the camera. The wretched conditions and dangers of life for the locals are shown in frightening, sharp contrast to the self-indulgence of the foreigners. Veteran French director Laurent Cantet elicits excellent performances from cast, most notably Charlotte Rampling as queen bee Ellen. Based on short stories by Haitian writer Dany Laferrière. **105m/C DVD.** *CA FR* Charlotte Rampling, Karen Young, Louise Portal, Menothy Cesar, Lys Ambroise, Jackenson Pierre Olmo Diaz, Wilfried Paul; *D:* Laurent Cantet; *W:* Laurent Cantet, Robin Campillo; *C:* Pierre Milon.

Headless Body in Topless Bar 🦴🦴½ **1996** Based on a famous New York Post headline and the crime that inspired it, this black comedy contains more than its lurid title lets on. Except for street footage at the opening and closing, the entire movie is set in a seedy strip club. After shooting the bartender in a robbery attempt, a crazed ex-con holds the patrons and employees hostage. He forces them to play a mind game called "Nazi truth," revealing the distasteful truth about the captives. Director Bruce and screenwriter Koper first worked together filming re-creations for "America's Most Wanted." The cast worked for "hostage scale," meaning if those playing captives stole the gun from the robber (a plot point), they got his pay for the day. If not, then he got their wages. **105m/C VHS, DVD.** Raymond J. Barry, Jennifer MacDonald, David Selby, Taylor Nichols, Paul Williams, Biff Yeager, Rustam Branaman, April Grace; *D:* James Bruce; *W:* Peter Koper; *C:* Kevin Morrisey; *M:* Charles P. Barrett.

Headless Eyes 🦴½ **1983** Gory entry into the psycho-artist category. An artist is miffed when mistaken by a woman as a burglar he loses an eye. Not one to forgive and forget, he becomes quite the eyeball fetishist, culling donations from unsuspecting women. An eye for an eye ad infinitum. **78m/C VHS.** Bo Brundin, Gordon Raman, Mary Jane Early; *D:* Kent Bateman; *W:* Kent Bateman.

Headline Woman 🦴🦴 **1935** An ongoing feud between a police commissioner and a newspaper's city editor causes a reporter to make a deal with a policeman in exchange for news. A good cast makes this otherwise tired story tolerable. **75m/B VHS, DVD.** Heather Angel, Roger Pryor, Jack La Rue, Ford Sterling, Conway Tearle; *D:* William Nigh.

Heads 🦴🦴½ **1993 (R)** Unassuming copyreader Guy Franklin (Cryer) gets promoted to reporter and his first assignment is a doozy. He's to cover a series of decapitation murders in a small town. Can he do the job without become the next victim—or being accused of the crimes? Filmed in Manitoba, Canada. **102m/C VHS.** *CA* Jon Cryer, Jennifer Tilly, Ed Asner, Roddy McDowall; *D:* Paul Shapiro; *W:* Adam Brooks; *M:* Jonathan Goldsmith. **CABLE**

Headspace 🦴½ **2002 (R)** Something triggers Alex's (Denham) brain into hyperdrive and gives him immense mental abilities, including super-fast speed reading and chess-playing invincibility. But the drawbacks are wicked, as his repressed childhood memory of dad blowing away mom returns, along with hellish visions of ghastly monsters. To make things worse, the people around him are winding up dead, causing him the all-too-obvious concern that he's in some way responsible. **90m/C DVD.** *US* Sean Young, Larry Fessenden, William Atherton, Dee Wallace Stone, Christopher Denham, Erick Kastel, Olivia Hussey, Mark Margolis, Udo Kier; *D:* Andrew van den Houten; *W:* Steve Klausner, William M. Miller; *C:* William M. Miller; *M:* Ryan Shore.

Healer 🦴½ *Little Pal* **1936** A doctor forgets his pledge to help the lame and becomes a fashionable physician. A young crippled lad helps him eventually remember. **80m/B VHS, DVD.** Mickey Rooney, Ralph Bellamy, Karen Morley, Judith Allen, Robert McWade; *D:* Reginald Barker.

The Healer 🦴🦴 *Julie Walking Home* **2002** When her cancer-stricken son is unable to take traditional treatment, Julie frantically seeks out a mystic healer in Poland to cure him. In the midst of a divorce from her cheating husband she unexpectedly finds romance there as well. **113m/C VHS, DVD.** Miranda Otto, William Fichtner, Lothaire Bluteau, Jerzy Nowak, Ryan Smith, Bianca Crudo, Boguslawa Schubert; *D:* Agnieszka Holland; *W:* Agnieszka Holland, Arlene Sarner; *C:* Jacek Petrycki; *M:* Antoni Lazarkiewicz. **TV**

Hear My Song 🦴🦴½ **1991 (R)** Mickey O'Neill (Dunbar) is an unscrupulous club promoter, who books singers with names like Franc Cinatra, while trying to revive his failing nightclub in this charming, hilarious comedy. He hires the mysterious Mr. X, who claims he is really the legendary exiled singer Josef Locke, only to find out he is an imposter. To redeem himself with his fiancee and her mother, he goes to Ireland to find the real Locke (Beatty) and bring him to Liverpool to sing. Dunbar is appealing in his role, and Beatty is magnificent as the legendary Locke—so much so that he was nominated for a Golden Globe for Best Supporting Actor. **104m/C VHS.** *GB* Ned Beatty, Adrian Dunbar, Shirley Anne Field, Tara Fitzgerald, William Hootkins, David McCallum, Gladys Sheehan; *D:* Peter Chelsom; *W:* Peter Chelsom; *C:* Sue Gibson; *M:* John Altman.

Hear No Evil 🦴½ **1993 (R)** Below average thriller with a deaf victim (Matlin) involved in a game of cat-and-mouse with a corrupt cop (Sheen) who's looking for a valuable coin. Weak script plays up the woman in jeopardy theme but lacks the crucial element of suspense. A waste of an otherwise talented cast. **98m/C VHS, DVD.** Marlee Matlin, D.B. Sweeney, Martin Sheen, John C. McGinley, Christina Carlisi, Greg Elam, Charley Lang; *D:* Robert Greenwald; *W:* Randall Badat, Kathleen Rowell; *M:* Graeme Revell.

Hearing Voices 🦴½ **1990** Joyless Erica is a commercial model who suffers from a form of scoliosis. If she capitalized on her infirmity by advertising medical aids, she could make a lot of money but she firmly refuses her lover's pleas to do this. When her doctor suggests reconstructive surgery, she storms out of his office but not before attracting the attention of Lee, his gay lover. Erica and Lee begin a complex emotional relationship, upsetting to everyone around them. Uninvolving characters, inert direction, and amateurish acting work against Greytak's feature film debut. **87m/C VHS.** Erika Nagy, Stephen Gatta, Tim Ahearn, Michael Davenport; *D:* Sharon Greytak; *W:* Sharon Greytak.

The Hearse WOOF! **1980 (PG)** Incredibly boring horror film in which a young school teacher moves into a mansion left to her by her late aunt and finds her life threatened by a sinister black hearse. **100m/C VHS, DVD.** Trish Van Devere, Joseph Cotten, Donald Hotton, David Gautreaux; *D:* George Bowers; *W:* William Bleich; *C:* Mori Kawa.

The Hearst and Davies Affair 🦴🦴 **1985** Married, middle-aged newspaper tycoon William Randolph Hearst falls for teenage Ziegfeld girl Marion Davies and tries to turn her into a Hollywood star. Davies was generally thought to be talented as a comedienne but Hearst insisted on choosing ill-suited dramatic roles for the blonde and her career was problematic. Their lavish lifestyle was enhanced when Hearst built San Simeon for Davies and their scandalous affair lasted 35 years. **97m/C VHS.** Robert Mitchum, Virginia Madsen, Fritz Weaver; *D:* David Lowell Rich. **TV**

Heart 🦴🦴 **1987 (R)** A down-and-out small-time boxer is given a chance to make a comeback, and makes the Rocky-like most of it. **93m/C VHS, DVD.** Brad Davis, Jesse Doran, Sam Gray, Steve Buscemi, Frances Fisher; *D:* James (Momel) Lemmo.

Heart 🦴½ **1999 (R)** Gruesome wannabe thriller (told in flashback) finds Gary Ellis (Eccleston) suffering a jealousy-induced heart attack after discovering wife Tess's (Hardie) philandering with Alex (Ifans). Gary gets a heart transplant—the donor being a young man killed in a motorcycle accident—and contacts the man's mother, Maria Ann (Reeves) after he gets out of the hospital. Too bad she's crazy. **85m/C VHS, DVD.** *GB* Christopher Eccleston, Saskia Reeves, Kate Hardie, Rhys Ifans, Bill Paterson, Anna Chancellor, Matthew Rhys; *D:* Charles McDougall; *W:* Jimmy McGovern; *C:* Julian Court; *M:* Stephen Warbeck.

Heart and Souls 🦴🦴½ **1993 (PG-13)** Reincarnation comedy casts Downey Jr. as a mortal whose body is inhabited by four lost souls who died on the night he was born. Now an adult, he must finish what they could not, no matter how outrageous it may be. Talented cast wears plot that's old hat. Downey Jr. must be looking to do a trilogy of tired reincarnated soul roles—this is his second, "Chances Are"

Heart Beat 🦴🦴½ **1980 (R)** The fictionalized story of Jack Kerouac (author of "On the Road"), his friend and inspiration Neal Cassady, and the woman they shared, Carolyn Cassady. Based on Carolyn Cassady's memoirs. Strong performances, with Nolte as Cassady and Spacek as his wife, overcome the sometimes shaky narrative. 105m/C VHS, Nick Nolte, John Heard, Sissy Spacek, Ann Dusenberry, Ray Sharkey, Tony Bill, Steve Allen, John Larroquette; **D:** John Byrum; **W:** John Byrum; **M:** Jack Nitzsche.

Heart Condition 🐾🐾½ 1990 (R)
A deceased black lawyer's heart is donated to a bigoted Los Angeles cop who was stalking the screen when the film debuts. Soon afterwards the lawyer's ghost returns to 'taunt the police officer, hoping the officer will help to avenge his murder. Both Hoskins and Washington display fine performances given the unlikely script. 95m/C VHS, DVD, Bob Hoskins, Denzel Washington, Chloe Webb, Ray Baker, Janet DuBois, Alan Rachins, Roger E. Mosley, Jeffrey Meek; **D:** James D. Parriott; **C:** Arthur Albert.

The Heart Is a Lonely Hunter 🐾🐾½ 1968 (G) Set in the South, Carson McCuller's tale of angst and ignorance, loneliness and beauty comes to the screen with the film debuts of Keach and Locke. Arkin gives an instinctive, gentle performance as the deaf mute. 124m/C VHS, DVD, Alan Arkin, Chuck Tyson, Sondra Locke, Stacy Keach, Cicely Tyson, Laurinda Barrett; **D:** Robert Ellis Miller; **C:** James Wong Howe; **M:** Dave Grusin. N.Y. Film Critics '68.

The Heart Is Deceitful Above All Things 🐾 2004 (R) The worst kind of trailer trash—an alcoholic druggie who doesn't say no to any scum's sexual advances—yet social services returns her 7-year-old boy Jeremiah to her, taking him from stable foster parents. After corrupting him very religiously parents for three years, but just as the damage is undone, skanky Sarah returns and takes him on the road for more misery. Based on a supposed autobiographical novel by J.T. LeRoy that was later outed as written by writer Laura Albert. 98m/C DVD. US Asia Argento, Jimmy Barrett, Cole Sprouse, Dylan Sprouse, Peter Fonda, Ben Foster, Ornella Muti, Kip Pardue, Michael Pitt, Asia Argento; **W:** Asia Argento; **D:** Asia Argento; **C:** Eric Alan Edwards; **M:** Alessandro Magania; **C:** Sonic Youth.

Heart Like a Wheel 🐾🐾½ 1983 (PG) The story of Shirley Muldowney, who rose from the daughter of a country-western singer to the leading lady in drag racing. The film follows her battles on the race or a family. Bedelia's performance is outstanding. Fine showings from Bridges and Axton in supporting roles. 113m/C VHS, DVD. Bonnie Bedelia, Beau Bridges, Bill McKinney, Leo Rossi, Hoyt Axton, Dick Miller, Anthony Edwards; **D:** Jonathan Kaplan; **W:** Ken Friedman.

Heart of a Champion: The Ray Mancini Story 🐾🐾 1985
Made-for-TV movie based on the life of "Boom Boom" Mancini, former lightweight boxing champion. Inspired by the career his father never had due to WWII. 94m/C VHS, Robert (Bobby) Blake, Doug McKeon, Mariclare Costello; **D:** Richard Michaels.

Heart of a Nation 🐾🐾🐾 Pere et Fils; Immortal France 1943 Saga of the Montmare family and their life during three wars, beginning with the Franco-Prussian War and ending with the Nazi occupation in France. Although ordered to be destroyed by the Nazis, this film was saved, along with many others, by the French "Cinema Resistance." In French with English subtitles. 111m/B VHS, DVD, FR Louis Jouvet, Raimu, Suzy Prim, Michèle Morgan, Renée Devillers, Harry Krimer; **D:** Julian Duvivier. Nar: Charles Boyer.

Heart of America Woof! 2003 (R)
You might know Boll from his embarrassingly bad video game movies, but this school-shooting melodrama is easily the director's worst film yet. Your mind will boggle at now shamelessly Boll milks the Columbine tragedy in his desperate attempt to reinvent himself as a serious filmmaker. So on the last day of high school, the film leaves no Afterschool Special cliché unturned as it follows various students and teachers hours before two brooding loners decide to take out their angst Charlton Heston-style. In-material, but Boll is no Michael Moore. Instead, he prefers to shoot inappropriate softcore T&A in a scene where a bully molests a mentally-handicapped girl known as "Slow White." Yeah, classy stuff all around. 87m/C DVD, CA GE Jürgen Prochnow, Michael Paré, Patrick Muldoon, Kett Turton, Elissabeth (Elisabeth, Elizabeth, Liz) Moss, Maria Conchita Alonso, Clint Howard, Brendan Fletcher, Lochlyn Munro, Maeve Quinlan, Michaela Mann, Will Sanderson; **D:** Uwe Boll. **W:** Uwe Boll, Robert Dean Klein; **C:** Mathias Neumann; **M:** Reinhard 3asser.

Heart of Darkness 🐾🐾 1993 Joseph Conrad's 1902 menacing novella set in the Belgian Congo is told through flashbacks by Marlow (Roth), whose employers, a Belgian trading company, hire him to find Kurtz (Malkovich), head of a remote trading station, who is rumored to be hoarding a huge cache of ivory. Marlow's journey up the river is beset by obstacles and Kurtz is rumored to be either insane or a prophet in his jungle kingdom. Filmed in Belize. Francis Ford Coppola's updated adaptation became "Apocalypse Now." 120m/C VHS. Tim Roth, John Malkovich, James Fox, Isaach de Bankole, Patrick Ryecart, Geoffrey Hutchings, Peter Vaughan, Phoebe Nicholls, Alan Corduner, Alan Scarfe, Iman, Timothy Bateson; **D:** Nicolas Roeg; **W:** Benedict Fitzgerald; **M:** Stanley Myers. TV

The Heart of Dixie 🐾🐾 1989 (PG) Three college co-eds at a southern university in the 1950s see that lives and values change with the influence of the civil rights movement. College newspaper reporter Sheedy takes up the cause of a black man victimized by racial violence. Lightweight social-conscience 'are. 96m/C VHS, DVD, Virginia Madsen, Ally Sheedy, Phoebe Cates, Treat Williams, Kyle Secor, Francesca Roberts, Barbara Babcock, Don Michael Paul, Kurtwood Smith, Richard Bradford; **D:** Martin Davidson; **W:** Tom McConway; **C:** Robert Elswit; **M:** Kenny Vance.

Heart of Dragon 🐾🐾 1985 Police officer Chan takes care of his mentally challenged brother Hung, who gets mistaken for a robbery suspect. So Chan has to track down the real crooks. Features a 20-minute fight finale. Chinese with subtitles or dubbed. 85m/C VHS, DVD, HK Jackie Chan, Sammo Hung, Emily Chu; **D:** Sammo Hung; **W:** Barry Wong; **C:** Arthur Wong Ngok Tai; **M:** Man Yee Lam.

Heart of Glass 🐾🐾🐾 Herz aus Glas 1974 A pre-industrial Bavarian village becomes deeply troubled when their glassblower dies without imparting the secret of making his unique Ruby glass. The townspeople go to extremes, from madness to murder to magic, to discover the ingredients. From German director Herzog (who hypnotized his cast daily), this somewhat apocalyptic tale is based on legend. The colors are incredible in their intensity. In German with English subtitles. 93m/C VHS, DVD, GE Josef Bierbichler, Stefan Guttler, Clemens Scheitz, Volker Prechtel, Sonia Skiba; **D:** Werner Herzog; **W:** Werner Herzog, Herbert Achternbusch; **C:** Jörg Schmidt-Reitwein; **M:** Popul Vuh.

Heart of Humanity 1918 An intense drama of love, patriotism, and sacrifice just before the war in a small Canadian village. A traveler who is really a Prussian army lieutenant finds his way to the house of a young man who is about to wed. He ends up falling in love with his fiancée and war is declared just before the wedding. A silent film with music score. 133m/B VHS, Dorothy Phillips, Erich von Stroheim; **D:** Allen Holubar.

Heart of Light 🐾🐾 Lysets Hjerte 1997 Marginalized Inuit family living in Danish-occupied Greenland, suffer from being cut off from their native culture. Teenager Nisi has a breakdown, goes on a killing spree, and then turns the gun on himself. His drunken father, Rasmus, decides to leave the community on an old dogsled and encounters a hermit who leads him on a mystical journey into the past. Filmed on location in Greenland. In-

Heart of Midnight 🐾🐾½ 1989 (R) An emotionally unstable young woman inherits a seedy massage parlor. She works hard to turn it, and herself, into something better. Nice performance by Leigh. 93m/C VHS, Jennifer Jason Leigh, Brenda Vaccaro, Frank Stallone, Peter Coyote, Gale Mayron, Sam Schacht, Denise Dumont; **D:** Matthew Chapman; **W:** Matthew Chapman; **M:** Yanni.

Heart of Stone 🐾🐾 2001 (R) Sexy L.A. mom (Everhart) is suffering from a stale marriage and empty nest syndrome when her daughter goes off to college. So she's easy prey for the seductive Steve (Wilder), who becomes violently obsessed with Mary. And then there's a little problem of a killer targeting college coeds—could Mary's daughter become the next victim? And is Mary's unhinged over the killer? 90m/C VHS, DVD, Angie Everhart, James Wilder, Peter J. Lucas, Gregor Torzs; **D:** Dale Trevillion, Mary Pistone. VIDEO

Heart of Texas Ryan 🐾½ 1917 Flamboyant cowboy star fights his win nappers and wins in this silent film. 50m/B VHS, Tom Mix, George Fawcett, Bessie Eyton, Frank Campeau, Charles Gerrard; **D:** E.A. Martin; **W:** Gilson Willets.

The Heart of the Game 🐾🐾½ 2005 (PG-13) Filmed over seven years, director Serrill follows Bill Resler's unorthodox approach to coaching the Roughriders, the girls' varsity basketball team at Seattle's middle-class Roosevelt High School. He turns the losing team into winners over the seasons, especially after recruiting gifted and volatile Darnellia Russell, an African-American from the inner-city, to join the predominantly white team. 97m/C DVD. US D: Ward Serrill; **W:** Ward Serrill.

Heart of the Golden West 🐾🐾 1942 Roy protects ranchers of Cherokee City from unjust shipping charges. 65m/B VHS, Roy Rogers, Smiley Burnette, George "Gabby" Hayes, Bob Nolan; **D:** Joseph Kane.

Heart of the Rio Grande 🐾½ 1942 Spoiled young rich girl tries to trick her father into coming to her "rescue" at a western dude ranch. 70m/B VHS, DVD, Gene Autry, Smiley Burnette, Fay McKenzie, Edith Fellows, Joseph Strauch Jr.; **D:** William M. Morgan.

Heart of the Rockies 🐾½ 1937 The Three Mesquiteers stop a mountain family's rustling and illegal game trappers. 54m/B VHS, DVD, Robert "Bob" Livingston, Ray Corrigan, Max Terhune, Lynne Roberts, Yakima Canutt, (John) Pickerson) McGowan; **D:** Joseph Kane.

Heart of the Rockies 🐾½ 1951 Roy, along with his trusty horse and dog, takes care of a highway construction project. 67m/B VHS, DVD, Roy Rogers, Penny Edwards, Gordon Jones, Ralph Morgan, Fred Graham, Mira McKinney; **D:** William Witney.

Heart of the Stag 🐾🐾 1984 (R) On an isolated sheep ranch in the New Zealand outback, a father and daughter suffer the repercussions of an incestuous relationship when she becomes enamored with a hired hand. 94m/C VHS, DVD, NZ Bruno Lawrence, Mary Regan, Terence Cooper; **D:** Michael Firth.

Heartaches 🐾🐾 1947 A reporter tries to track down a murderer who has killed twice. 71m/B VHS, Ann Staunton, Chill Wills, Sheila Ryan, Edward Norris, James Seay, Frank Orth, Lash LaRue; **D:** Basil Wrangell; **W:** Frank Ryan, Terence Cooper; **D:** Mi-

The Heart of Me 🐾🐾½ 2002 (R) Rather staid adaptation of Rosamond Lehmann's 1953 novel "The Echoing Grove," which focuses on the romantic trials of bohemian Dinah (Bonham Carter) and her adulterous affair with her chilly older sister Madeleine's (Williams) husband, Rickie (Bettany). Soapy melodrama covers approximately the mid-thirties to the post-war period. 96m/C VHS, DVD, GB Helena Bonham Carter, Olivia Williams, Paul Bettany, Eleanor Bron; **D:** Thaddeus O'Sullivan; **W:** Lucinda Coxon; **C:** Gyula Pados; **M:** Nicholas Hooper.

Heartaches 🐾🐾 1982 A young pregnant woman (Potts) meets up with a Parisian school for pickpockets, but DVD. DK Rasmus Lyberth, Anda Kristensen, Viivi Nielsen, Niels Platou; **D:** Jacob Gronlykke; **W:** Jacob Gronlykke; **D:** Dan Laustsen; **M:** Joachim Holbek.

Heartaches 🐾🐾 1982 A young pregnant woman (Potts) meets up with a crazy girlfriend (Kidder) in this touching film about love and friendship. Although on a study in contrasts, the two end up sharing an apartment together in Toronto. Fine performances from Potts and Kidder give life to this romantic comedy. 90m/C VHS, CA Margot Kidder, Annie Potts, Robert Carradine, Winston Rekert; **D:** Donald Shebib, Genie '82. Actress (Kidder).

Heartbeat 🐾🐾 1946 If you thought pointless Hollywood remakes of French films were a new phenomenon (see "Pure Luck," for example), then note this lighthearted remake of a 1940 Gallic farce. Rogers becomes the best student in when she tries out her skills on a dashing diplomat they fall in love instead. 100m/C VHS, Ginger Rogers, Jean-Pierre Aumont, Adolphe Menjou, Basil Rathbone, Melville Cooper, Mona Maris, Henry Stephenson, Eduardo Ciannelli; **D:** Sam Wood; **C:** Joseph Valentine.

Heartbeeps 🐾½ 1981 (PG) Mildly amusing romantic comedy about a couple of robot household servants (Kaufman and Peters) who fall in love, escape from domestic service, and begin a family of their own (they assemble a child robot from spare parts). 88m/C VHS, Andy Kaufman, Bernadette Peters, Randy Quaid, Kenneth McMillan, Melanie Mayron, Christopher Guest, Richard B. Shull, Dick Miller, Kathleen Freeman, Mary Wronovo, Paul Bartel; **D:** Allan Arkush; **C:** Charles Rosher Jr.; **M:** John Williams.

Heartbreak Hotel 🐾🐾½ 1988 (PG-13) Johnny Wolfe kidnaps Elvis Presley from his show in Cleveland and drives him to his mother, a die-hard Elvis fan. Completely unbelievable, utterly ridiculous, and still a lot of fun. 101m/C VHS, DVD, David Keith, Tuesday Weld, Charlie Schlatter, Angela Goethals, Jacque Lynn Colton, Chris Mulkey, Karen Landry, Tudor Sherrard, Paul Harkins; **D:** Chris Columbus; **W:** Chris Columbus; **M:** Georges Delerue.

The Heartbreak Kid 🐾🐾½ 1972 (PG) Director May's comic examination of love and hypocrisy. Grodin embroils himself in a triangle with his new bride and a woman he can't have, an absolutely gorgeous and totally unloving woman he shouldn't want. Walks the fence between tragedy and comedy, with an exceptional performance from Berlin. Based on Bruce Jay Friedman's story. 106m/C VHS, DVD, Charles Grodin, Cybill Shepherd, Eddie Albert, Jeannie Berlin, Audra Lindley, Art Metrano; **D:** Elaine May; **W:** Neil Simon; **C:** Owen Roizman; **M:** Garry Sherman, Cy Coleman, Sheldon Harnick. N.Y. Film Critics '72: Support. Actress (Berlin); Natl. Soc. Film Critics '72: Support. Actor (Albert), Support. Actress (Berlin).

The Heartbreak Kid 🐾½ 2007 (R) In the hands of the increasingly uninspired Farrelly brothers, this lame remake of the 70s film about an unlikable putz who marries too quickly and finds the real girl of his dreams on his honeymoon turns into yet another showcase of gross-out jokes and Stiller-style neuroses. He plays unsympathetic Eddie, who's desperately trying to get out of his marriage to sexpot Lila (Akerman) so he can woo nice girl Miranda (Monaghan). Portrays none of the original's wit or bite, and Stiller blows what little chance the movie has with a by-the-numbers, unappealing performance. 115m/C DVD, HD DVD, US Ben Stiller, Michelle Monaghan, Malin Akerman, Jerry Stiller, Rob Corddry, Danny McBride, Scott Wilson, Carlos Mencia; **D:** Bobby Farrelly, Peter Farrelly; **W:** Bobby Farrelly, Peter Farrelly, Scot Armstrong, Leslie Dixon, Kevin Barnett; **C:** Matthew F. Leonetti; **M:** Bill Ryan, Brendan Ryan.

George Bricker, Monte (Mcnty) Collins Jr.; **C:** Jack Greenhalgh; **M:** Emil Cadkin.

Heartbreak Ridge 🎬🎬🎬 1986 (R) An aging Marine recon sergeant is put in command of a young platoon to whip them into shape to prepare for combat in the invasion of Grenada. Eastwood whips this old story into shape too, with a fine performance of a man who's given everything to the Marines. The invasion of Grenada, though, is not epic material. (Also available in English with Spanish subtitles.) 130m/C VHS, DVD. Clint Eastwood, Marsha Mason, Everett McGill, Arlen Dean Snyder, Bo Svenson, Moses Gunn, Eileen Heckart, Boyd Gaines, Mario Van Peebles, Vincent Irizarry, Ramon Franco, Tom Villard, Pete Koch, Richard Venture, J.C. Quinn, Peter Jason, Thom Sharp; D: Clint Eastwood; M: Lennie Niehaus.

Heartbreaker 🎬🎬½ 1983 (R) Eastern Los Angeles explodes with vicious turf wars when Beto and Hector battle for the affection of Kim, the neighborhood's newest heartbreaker. 90m/C VHS, DVD. Fernando Allende, Dawn Dunlap, Michael D. Roberts, Robert Dryer, Apollonia; D: Frank Zuniga.

Heartbreakers 🎬🎬🎬 1984 (R) Two male best friends find themselves in the throes of drastic changes in their careers and romantic encounters. On target acting makes this old story new, with a fine performance by Wayne, in her last film before her death. 98m/C VHS. Peter Coyote, Nick Mancuso, Carole Laure, Max Gail, James Laurenson, Carol Wayne, Jamie Rose, Kathryn Harrold; D: Bobby Roth; W: Bobby Roth; C: Michael Ballhaus; M: Tangerine Dream.

Heartbreakers 🎬🎬½ 2001 (PG-13) Max and Page, played by Weaver and Hewitt, are a mother-daughter con-artist team who delight in seducing men right out of their bank accounts and billfolds. Tobacco billionaire William B. Tensy is Max's latest target, but proves to be a tougher case than she realized. Meanwhile, daughter Page has her sights set on Jack, the handsome Palm Beach bar owner, but can't decide if it's just another con, or true love. Hackman excels as the obnoxious Tensy. Director Mirkin's first feature since "Romy and Michelle's High School Reunion." 123m/C VHS, DVD. US Sigourney Weaver, Jennifer Love Hewitt, Gene Hackman, Ray Liotta, Jason Lee, Anne Bancroft, Jeffrey Jones, Nora Dunn, Julio Oscar Mechoso, Ricky Jay, Stacey Travis; D: David Mirkin; W: Paul Guay, Robert Dunn, Stephen Mazur; C: Dean Semler; M: John Debney.

Heartburn 🎬🎬🎬 1986 (R) Based on Nora Ephron's own semi-autobiographical novel about her marital travails with writer Carl Bernstein, this is a tepid, bitter modern romance between writers already shell-shocked from previous marriages. 109m/C VHS, DVD. Meryl Streep, Jack Nicholson, Steven Hill, Richard Masur, Stockard Channing, Jeff Daniels, Milos Forman, Catherine O'Hara, Maureen Stapleton, Karen Akers, Joanna Gleason, Mercedes Ruehl, Caroline Aaron, Yakov Smirnoff, Anna Maria Horsford, Wilfrid Hyde-White; D: Mike Nichols; W: Nora Ephron; C: Nestor Almendros; M: Carly Simon.

Heartland 🎬🎬🎬 1981 (PG) Set in 1910, this film chronicles the story of one woman's life on the Wyoming frontier, when she contracts to become a housekeeper for a rancher. Elinore (Ferrell) and her young daughter arrive at the home of Clyde Stewart (Torn) and face any number of hazards, which test her courage and spirit. Stunningly realistic and without cliche. Based on the diaries of Elinore Randall Stewart. 95m/C VHS, DVD. Conchata Ferrell, Rip Torn, Barry Primus, Lilia Skala, Megan Folson; D: Richard Pearce; W: Beth Ferris; C: Fred Murphy. Sundance '81: Grand Jury Prize.

Hearts & Armour 🎬🎬 1983 A holy war between Christians and Moors erupts when a Moorish princess is kidnapped. Based on Ludovico Ariosto's "Orlando Furioso." 101m/C VHS. IT Tanya Roberts, Leigh McCloskey, Ron Moss, Rick Edwards, Giovanni Visentin; D: Giacomo Battiato.

Heart's Desire 🎬½ 1937 Opera great Tauber stars in this musical of an unknown Viennese singer who falls in love with an English girl. 79m/B VHS. GB Richard Tauber, Lenora Corbett, Kathleen Kelly, Paul Graetz; D: Paul Stein.

Heart's Haven 🎬🎬½ 1922 An insensitive wife (Adams), who doesn't appreciate how wonderful her husband is, winds up running away with another man. 61m/B VHS. Claire Adams, Robert McKim, Carl Gantvoort, Jean Hersholt; D: Benjamin B. Hampton.

Hearts in Atlantis 🎬🎬½ 2001 (PG-13) Coming-of-age tale tinged with creeps benefits from the odd combination of a story by Stephen King and direction from Scott Hicks, who also directed "Shine" and "Snow Falling on Cedars." Bobby (Yelchin) is an 11-year-old boy living in lower middle class Connecticut circa 1960 with his widowed mother Liz (Davis). When enigmatic Ted (Hopkins) rents a room in their attic, he offers the boy a job reading him the daily newspaper. He also has Bobby keep an eye out for the "low men" (CIA agents? Mafia?) he believes are pursuing him. Ted offers the male role model and adult attention Bobby craves and the two quickly become close. Ted, it seems, has some kind of psychic ability, which he also sees in Bobby. Although lushly filmed, the plot seems a bit stagnant and listless for a story about young people. 101m/C VHS, DVD. US Anthony Hopkins, Anton Yelchin, Hope Davis, Mika Boorem, David Morse, Alan Tudyk, Tom Bower, Celia Weston, Adam LeFevre, Timothy Reifsnyder, Deirdre O'Connell, Will Rothhaar; D: Scott Hicks; W: William Goldman; C: Piotr Sobocinski; M: Mychael Danna.

Hearts of Darkness: A Filmmaker's Apocalypse 🎬🎬🎬 1991 (R) This riveting, critically acclaimed documentary about the making of Francis Ford Coppola's masterpiece "Apocalypse Now" is based largely on original footage shot and directed by his wife Eleanor. Also included are recent interviews with cast and crew members including Coppola, Martin Sheen, Robert Duvall, Frederic Forrest and Dennis Hopper. 96m/C VHS. Sam Bottoms, Eleanor Coppola, Francis Ford Coppola, Robert Duvall, Laurence Fishburne, Frederic Forrest, Albert Hall, Dennis Hopper, George Lucas, John Milius, Martin Sheen; D: Fax Bahr, George Hickenlooper; W: Fax Bahr, George Hickenlooper; M: Todd Boekelheide. Natl. Bd. of Review '91: Feature Doc.

Hearts of Fire 🎬 1987 A trio of successful rock 'n' roll stars work out their confused romantic entanglements. Barely released at all, and not even in the U.S. Sad outing for the cast, especially legendary Dylan. 90m/C VHS. Bob Dylan, Fiona, Rupert Everett, Julian Glover; D: Richard Marquand; W: Joe Eszterhas; M: John Barry.

Hearts of Humanity 🎬🎬 1932 Mawkish melodrama concerning a Jewish antique dealer and his relationship with the son of an Irish cop. An early "Chico and the Man" variant. 56m/B VHS. Jean Hersholt, Jackie Searl, J. Farrell MacDonald, Claudia Dell, Charles Delaney, Lucille LaVerne, George Humbert; D: Christy Cabanne.

Hearts of the West 🎬🎬🎬½ 1975 (PG) Hollywood Cowboy A fantasy-filled farm boy travels to Hollywood in the 1930s and seeks a writing career. Instead, he finds himself an ill-suited western movie star in this small offbeat comedy-drama that's sure to charm. 103m/C VHS. Jeff Bridges, Andy Griffith, Donald Pleasence, Alan Arkin, Blythe Danner; D: Howard Zieff; M: Rob Thompson. N.Y. Film Critics '75: Support. Actor (Arkin).

Hearts of the World 🎬🎬🎬 1918 A vintage Griffith epic about a young boy who goes off to WWI and the tribulations endured by both him and his family on the homefront. Overly sentimental but powerfully made melodrama, from Griffith's waning years. Silent with music score. 152m/B VHS. Lillian Gish, Robert "Bobbie" Harron, Dorothy Gish, Erich von Stroheim, Ben Alexander, Josephine Crowell, Noel Coward, Mary Gish; D: D.W. Griffith.

Heartstopper 🎬 1992 Benjamin Latham, an innocent physician in Pittsburgh, was accused of being a vampire in colonial times and hung. 200 years later, he emerges from the grave, unscathed. While trying to figure out what has hap-

pened, he falls in love with a photojournalist, who helps him find his own descendent, Matthew Latham. Unfortunately, his deep freeze has left him with the compulsion to kill, but only evil members of society. 96m/B VHS. Moon Zappa, Tom Savini, Kevin Kindlin; D: John A. Russo; W: John A. Russo; C: John Rice.

Heartstrings 🎬🎬 The Perfect Man 1993 Melissa wants everything in her life to be perfect, including having the perfect man, which she thinks is New York gallery owner Peter. But will Melissa's heart compromise her ambitions? 94m/C VHS. CA Garwin Sanford, Brian Jensen, Michelle Little, Phyllis Diller; D: Wendy Hill-Tout; W: Wendy Hill-Tout; C: Peter Wunstorf; M: George Blondheim.

Heartwood 🎬🎬 1998 (PG-13) Frank (Mills) is an outcast living in the woods of a falling lumber town. He falls for Sylvia (Swank), the daughter of the engineer hired by mill owner Logan Reese (Robards) to save the mill and the town as well. But when Frank discovers gold, he's the one who comes up with a plan. 92m/C VHS, DVD. Eddie Mills, Hilary Swank, Jason Robards Jr., Randall Batinkoff, Stanley DeSantis; D: Lanny Cotler.

Heat 🎬🎬🎬 Andy Warhol's Heat 1972 Another Andy Warhol-produced journey into drug-addled urban seediness. Features a former child actor/junkie and a has-been movie star barely surviving in a run-down motel. This is one of Warhol's better film productions; even non-fans may enjoy it. 102m/C VHS, DVD. Joe Dallesandro, Sylvia Miles, Pat Ast, Andrea Feldman, Ray Vestal; D: Paul Morrissey; W: Paul Morrissey; C: Paul Morrissey; M: John Cale.

Heat 🎬½ 1987 (R) A Las Vegas bodyguard avenges the beating of an old flame by a mobster's son, and incites mob retaliation. Based on the William Goldman novel. 103m/C VHS, DVD. Burt Reynolds, Karen Young, Peter Machichol, Howard Hesseman; D: R.M. Richards; W: William Goldman; M: Michael Gibbs.

Heat 🎬🎬🎬 1995 (R) Pacino and De Niro in the same scene. Together. Finally. Obsessive master thief McCauley (De Niro) leads a crack crew on various military-style heists across L.A. while equally obsessive detective Hanna (Pacino) tracks him. Each man recognizes and respects the other's ability and dedication, even as they express the willingness to kill each other, if necessary. Excellent script with all the fireworks you'd expect, as well as a surprising look into emotional and personal sacrifice. Beautiful cinematography shows industrial landscape to great effect. Writer-director Mann held onto the screenplay for 12 years. 171m/C VHS, DVD, UMD. Robert De Niro, Al Pacino, Val Kilmer, Jon Voight, Diane Venora, Ashley Judd, Wes Studi, Tom Sizemore, Mykelti Williamson, Amy Brenneman, Ted Levine, Dennis Haysbert, William Fichtner, Natalie Portman, Hank Azaria, Henry Rollins, Kevin Gage, Tone Loc, Bud Cort, Jeremy Piven, Tom Noonan, Xander Berkeley; D: Michael Mann; W: Michael Mann; C: Dante Spinotti; M: Elliot Goldenthal.

Heat and Dust 🎬🎬🎬 1982 (R) A young bride joins her husband at his post in India and is inexorably drawn to the country and its prince of state. Years later her great niece journeys to modern day India in search of the truth about her scandalous and mysterious relative. More than 50 years span these two romances, this is the tale of women rebelling against an unseen caste system which keeps them second-class citizens. Ruth Jhabvala wrote the novel and screenplay. 130m/C VHS, DVD. GB Julie Christie, Greta Scacchi, Shashi Kapoor, Christopher Cazenove, Nickolas Grace, Julian Glover, Susan Fleetwood, Charles Godfrey, Jennifer Kendal, Madhur Jaffrey, Barry Foster, Amanda Walker, Sudha Chopra, Sajid Khan, Zakir Hussain, Ratna Pathak, Charles McCaughan, Parveen Paul; D: James Ivory; W: Ruth Prawer Jhabvala, Saeed Jaffrey, Harish Khare; C: Walter Lassally; M: Richard Robbins. British Acad. '83: Adapt. Screenplay.

Heat and Sunlight 🎬🎬½ 1987 A photographer becomes obsessively jealous of his lover as their relationship comes to an end. Director Nilsson again used a unique improvisational, video-to-film technique, as he did with his previous film,

"Signal 7." 98m/B VHS, DVD. Rob Nilsson, Consuelo Faust, Bill Bailey, Don Bajema, Ernie Fossellus; D: Rob Nilsson; W: Rob Nilsson; C: Tomas Tucker. Sundance '88: Grand Jury Prize.

Heat of Desire 🎬🎬 Plein Sud 1984 (R) A philosophy professor abandons everything (including his wife) for a woman he barely knows and is conned by her "relatives." With English subtitles. 90m/C VHS. FR Clio Goldsmith, Patrick Dewaere, Jeanne Moreau, Guy Marchand; D: Luc Beraud.

The Heat of the Day 🎬🎬½ 1991 A British officer is accused of treason. As he attempts to find those who framed him, he meets a lovely woman all too willing to help. But whose side is she really on? Set in WWII. Tense and well-acted; made for TV. 120m/C VHS. Michael York, Patricia Hodge, Peggy Ashcroft, Anna Carteret, Michael Gambon; W: Harold Pinter. TV

Heat of the Flame 🎬 1976 A vicious woodsman captures and rapes a beautiful girl. Psychological games, eroticism and exploitive nudity ensue. 88m/C VHS. SP Tony Ferrandis, Ellie MacLure, Raymond Young, Anthony (Jose, J. Antonio, J.A.) Mayans; D: Rafael Romero Marchent.

Heat of the Sun 🎬🎬🎬 1999 Former Scotland Yard detective Albert Tyburn (Eve) has been sent to work in Nairobi, Kenya in the hedonistic expatriate community of the 1930s, known as "Happy Valley." But despite his disdain for the community's racial and social lines, Tyburn is soon involved in the murder of a young boy against the backdrop of Nairobi's premier social event, Race Week. 360m/C VHS, DVD. GB Trevor Eve, Michael Byrne, Susannah Harker, Tim Woodward, Daniel Betts, James Callis, Freddie Annobil-Dodoo, Kate McKenzie, Hugh Bonneville, Cathryn Harrison, Julian Rhind-Tutt, Diana Quick, Deborah Findlay, Joss Ackland, Richard McCabe, Sonya Walger; D: Adrian Shergold, Diarmuid Lawrence, Paul Seed; W: Russell Lewis; Tim Prager. TV

Heat Street 🎬 1987 Two thugs exact revenge on street gangs for the murders of loved ones. Made for video. 90m/C VHS. Quincy Adams, Deborah Gibson, Wendy MacDonald, Del Zamora; D: Joseph Merhi. VIDEO

Heat Wave 🎬🎬½ The House Across the Lake 1954 A writer gets involved with a "femme fatale" who kills her wealthy husband for the love of a young pianist. 60m/B VHS, DVD. GB Alex Nicol, Hillary Brooke, Sidney James, Susan Stephen, Paul Carpenter; D: Ken Hughes; W: Ken Hughes; C: Walter J. (Jimmy W.) Harvey; M: Ivor Slaney.

Heat Wave 🎬🎬🎬 1990 (R) The Watts ghetto uprising of 1965 is a proving ground for a young black journalist. Excellent cast and fine script portrays the anger and frustration of blacks in Los Angeles and the U.S. in the 1960s and the fear of change felt by blacks and whites when civil rights reform began. Strong drama with minimal emotionalism. 92m/C VHS, DVD. Blair Underwood, Cicely Tyson, James Earl Jones, Sally Kirkland, Margaret Avery, David Strathairn, Robert Hooks, Adam Arkin, Paris Vaughan, Charlie Korsmo; D: Kevin Hooks; W: Kevin Hooks, Michael Lazarou; C: Mark Irwin; M: Thomas Newman. CABLE

Heated Vengeance 🎬 1987 (R) A Vietnam vet returns to the jungle to find the woman he left behind, and runs into some old enemies. 91m/C VHS. Richard Hatch, Michael J. Pollard, Dennis Patrick, Mills Watson, Cameron Dye; D: Edward Murphy.

Heater 🎬🎬 1999 Two homeless men come into possession of an electric space heater that, despite the December cold, is useless to them since they don't have any place to plug in. So they decide to travel from their inner city haunt to a suburban shopping mall—by foot—in hopes they can return the heater for a cash refund. 87m/C VHS, DVD. CA Gary Farmer, Stephen Ouimette. *D:* Terrance Odette; *W:* Terrance Odette; *C:* Arthur E. Cooper; *M:* Neil Clark.

Heathers 1989 (R) Clique of stuck-up girls named Heather rule the high school social scene until the newest member (not a Heather) decides that enough is enough. She and her outlaw boyfriend (Slater) embark accidentally on her part, intentionally on his) on a murder spree disguised as a rash of teen suicides. Dense, take-no-prisoners black comedy that buckets of potent teen slang, satire and unforgiving hostility. Humor this dark is rare; sharply observed and acted, though the end is out of place. Slater does his best Nicholson impression. 102m/C VHS, DVD. Winona Ryder, Christian Slater, Kim Walker, Shannen Doherty, Lisanne Falk, Penelope Milford, Glenn Shadix, Lance Fenton, Patrick Labyorteaux, Jeremy Applegate, Renee Estevez; *D:* Michael Lehmann; *W:* Daniel Waters; *C:* Francis Kenny; *M:* David Newman. Ind. Spirit '90: First Feature.

The Heat's On *Tropicana* 1943 Gaxton is a Broadway producer with a failing musical and an unhappy star in West. He cranks up the publicity machine and gets the show declared immoral by the Legion of Purity which results in its closing (not what he expected). Gaxton then runs a scam to become the producer of West's new show, which just happens to be financed by some Legion members. Very uneven plot and performances with thrown-in musical numbers. West wrote her own dialogue but unlike her early films she had little control over the production and it showed. West didn't make another movie for 27 years (the appalling "Myra Breckenridge"). "Just a Stranger in Town. Hello, Mi Amigo; The White Keys; and the Black Keys; There Goes That Guitar; Antonio; The Caissons Go Rolling Along; There Goes My Heart. 79m/B VHS. Mae West; William Gaxton, Victor Moore, Almira Sessions, ...ester Allen, Mary Roche, Alan Dinehart, Lloyd Bridges; *D:* Gregory Ratoff; *W:* Fitzroy Davis, George S. George, Fred Schiller.

Heatseeker 1995 (R) Corporations use mechanical fighters to participate in brutal kickboxing contests in 2019 New America. Human Chance (Cooke) must battle cyborg opponent Xao if he wants to save his kidnapped trainer. Lots of action and even some intentional humor. 91m/C VHS. Keith Cooke, Gary Daniels, Norbert Weisser, Thom Mathews, Tina Cote; *D:* Albert Pyun.

Heatwave 1983 (R) Local residents oppose a multi-million dollar residential complex in Australia. Davis portrays a liberal activist, who wages war with the developers, and, in return, becomes involved with a possible murder case. 92m/C VHS. Judy Davis, Richard Mor, Chris Haywood, Bill Hunter, John Gregg, Anna Maria Monticelli; *D:* Phillip Noyce.

Heaven 1987 (PG-13) An exploration of "heaven" including the idea, the place, and people's views about it. Questions such as "How do you get there?" and "What goes on up there?" are discussed. Offbeat interviews mixed with a collage of celestial images. 80m/C VHS, DVD. *D:* Diane Keaton; *M:* Howard Shore.

Heaven 1999 (R) Robert Marling (Donovan) is an architect with a broken marriage and a compulsion to gamble (and lose) at a sleazy strip joint owned by the odious and brutal Stanner (Schiff). One of the performers is a psychic transvestite named Heaven (Edwards), who predicts that Robert will win big in the lottery. This info gets back to evil shrink Melrose (Maahide), who has both Robert and Heaven as patients, and who just happens to be having an affair with Robert's bitter wife, Jennifer (Going). And the coincidental silliness doesn't stop there. Based on a novel by Chad Taylor. 103m/C VHS, DVD. NZ Danny Edwards, Joanna Going, Patrick Malahide, Martin Donovan, Karl Urban, Richard Schiff; *D:* Scott Reynolds; *C:* Simon Raby; *M:* Victoria Kelly.

Heaven 2001 (R) Themes of despair and redemption fuel this story of Philippa (Blanchett), a woman who has accidentally killed four innocent people while trying to assassinate drug lord Vendice. As she's questioned by the authorities (who are in cahoots with Vendice), young police translator Filippo (Ribisi) falls in love with her. The two escape thanks to police incompetence and go after Vendice. Directed by Tom Tykwer from a script written by late film legend Krzysztof Kieslowski ("The Decalogue" series and "Three Colors" trilogy) 96m/C VHS, DVD. US GE Cate Blanchett, Giovanni Ribisi, Stefania Rocca, Remo Girone, Mattia Sbragia, Alberto Di Stasio, Stefano Santospago, Alessandro Sperduti; *D:* Tom Tykwer; *W:* Krzysztof Kieslowski, Krzysztof Piesiewicz; *C:* Frank Griebe.

Heaven & Earth 1993 (R) Conclusion of Stone's Vietnam trilogy (after "Platoon" and "Born on the Fourth of July") focuses on Vietnamese woman (film debut of Le) and her life under the French and American occupations. Jones is the American soldier who marries her and eventually brings her to the U.S. Not one for subtleties, Stone chases melodramatic excess with finesse from a sawing away at guilt and remorse from a "woman's point of view." Cranky Tommy Lee shows up too late to save flick and is saddled with a perplexing I.D. to boot. Flawed, ambitious, and interesting if a student of Ly Haslip. Based on the two autobiographies of Le Ly Haslip, "When Heaven and Earth Changed Places" and "Child of War, Woman of Peace." Filmed on location in Thailand. 142m/C VHS, DVD. Hiep Thi Le, Tommy Lee Jones, Joan Chen, Haing S. Ngor, Debbie Reynolds, Conchata Ferrell, Dustin Nguyen, Liem Whatley, Dale Dye; *D:* Oliver Stone; *W:* Oliver Stone; *C:* Robert Richardson; *M:* Kitaro. Golden Globes '94: Score.

Heaven and Earth 1990 104m/C VHS. JP Masahiko Tsugawa, Takaaki Enoki, Atsuko Asano, Tsunehiko Watase, Naoki Zaizen, Binpachi Ito; *D:* Haruki Kadokawa; *W:* Haruki Kadokawa; *M:* Daisuke Hinata; *Nar:* Stuar Whitman.

Heaven Before I Die 1996 (PG) Sheltered Jacob (Velasquez) travels from the Middle East to Toronto and is taken under the questionable wing of a small-time thief (Giannini) and a beautiful waitress (Pacula). But when Jacob finds a measure of success as a Charlie Chaplin impersonator, his innocence gets a dose of culture shock. 98m/C VHS, DVD. C4 Andy Velasquez, Giancarlo Giannini, Joanna Pacula, Omar Sharif, Burt Young, Joseph Bologna; *D:* Izidore K. Musallam.

Heaven Can Wait 1943 Social satire in which a rogue tries to convince the Devil to admit him into Hell by relating the story of his philandering life and discovers that he was a more valuable human being than he thought. A witty Lubitsch treat based on the play "Birthdays." 112m/C VHS, DVD. Don Ameche, Gene Tierney, Laird Cregar, Charles Coburn, Marjorie Main, Eugene Palette, Allyn Joslyn, Spring Byington, Signe Hasso, Louis Calhern, Dickie Moore, Florence Bates, Scotty Beckett, Charles Halton; *D:* Ernst Lubitsch.

Heaven Can Wait 1978 (PG) A remake of 1941's "Here Comes Mr. Jordan." L.A. Rams quarterback Joe Pendleton (Beatty) is summoned to heaven before his time. When archangel Mr. Jordan (Mason) realizes the mistake, Joe is returned to Earth but it's in the body of a wealthy industrialist who's about to be murdered by his unfaithful wife Julia (Cannon) and his nervous secretary, Tony (Grodin). But Joe is about to let a little thing like murder prevent him from playing in the Super Bowl—new tccy or not. Next to be confused with the 1943 film of the same name. 101m/C VHS, DVD. Warren Beatty, Julie Christie, James Mason, Jack Warden, Buck Henry; *D:* Warren Beatty, Buck Henry; *W:* Elaine May, Warren Beatty; *C:* William A. Fraker; *M:* Dave Grusin. Oscars '78: Art Dir/Set Dec.; Golden Globes '79: Actor--Mus./Comedy (Beatty), Film--Mus./Comedy; Support. Actress (Cannon); Writers Guild '78: Adapt. Screenplay.

Heaven Help Us 1985 (R) *Catholic Boys* 1985 (R) Three mischievous boys find themselves continually in trouble with the priests running their Brooklyn Catholic high school during the mid-1960s. Realistic and humorous look at adolescent life. 104m/C VHS. Andrew McCarthy, Mary Stuart Masterson, Kevin Dillon, Malcolm Danare, Jennifer Dundas Lowe, Kate Reid, Wallace Shawn, Jay Patterson, John Heard, Donald Sutherland, Yeardley Smith, Sherry Steiner, Calvert Deforest, Philip Bosco, Patrick Dempsey, Christopher Durang; *D:* Michael Dinner; *M:* Patrick O'Hearn.

Heaven Is a Playground 1991 (R) On Chicago's South Side an inner city basketball coach and an idealistic young lawyer are determined to change the fate of a group of high school boys. The men use the incentive of athletic scholarships to keep their team in school and away from drugs and gangs. 104m/C VHS, DVD. D.B. Sweeney, Michael Warren, Richard Jordan, Victor Love; *D:* Randall Fried; *W:* Randall Fried; *C:* Tom Richmond; *M:* Patrick O'Hearn.

Heaven Knows, Mr. Allison 1957 Terrific two-character WWII drama finds tough (but tender-hearted) Marine sergeant Allison (Mitchum) stranded with Irish nun, Sister Angela (Kerr), on a Pacific island overrun by Japanese troops. The duo hide out during the day and forage for food by night, gradually revealing their pasts to each other. He falls hard while she resists his advances and they struggle to stay alive until U.S. forces invade the island. Lots of action and good performances. Based on the novel by Charles Shaw. 106m/C VHS, DVD. Robert Mitchum, Deborah Kerr; *D:* John Huston; *W:* John Huston, John Lee Mahin; *C:* Oswald Morris; *M:* Georges Auric.

Heaven on Earth 1989 The story of two orphaned British children who, along with thousands of orphans shipped from England to Canada between 1867 and 1914, try to make new lives in the Canadian wilderness. 101m/C VHS. C4 R.H. Thomson, Sian Leisa Davies, Torquil Campbell, Fiona Reid; *D:* Allan Kroeker; *W:* Margaret Atwood.

Heaven or Vegas 1998 (R) Rachel (Bileeth) is a part-time Vegas prostitute who falls for gigolo Navy (Grieco), who offers her a new life with him in Montana. But first Rachel wants to visit the home she ran away from years before. Too bad Rachel's sister Lilli starts making eyes at her man and when Navy appears interested, Rachel runs away again. Can Navy find her and convince Rachel he loves only her? It's a modern-day fairytale so what do you think? 97m/C VHS. Yasmine Bleeth, Richard Grieco; *D:* Gregory C. Haynes; *W:* Gregory C. Haynes. VIDEO

Heaven Tonight 1993 (R) Ex-rock star dad copes with midlife crisis by trying to hit the big comeback, this time with his son. 97m/C VHS. AU John Waters, Rebecca Gilling, Guy Pearce, Kim Gyngell; *D:* Pino Amenta; *C:* David Connell.

Heavenly Bodies WOOF! 1984 (R) A young woman who dreams of owning a health club will stop at nothing to accomplish 'ner goals. When a rival tries to put her out of business, a "dance-down" takes place in this lame low-budget aerobics musical. 99m/C VHS. C4 Cynthia Dale, Richard Rebiere, Laura Henry, Stuart Stone, Walter George Alton, Cec Linder; *D:* Lawrence Dane; *W:* Lawrence Dane, Ron Base; *C:* Thomas Burstyn.

Heavenly Creatures 1994 (R) Haunting and surreal drama chronicles the true-life case of two young schoolgirls, Pauline and Juliet, who were charged with clubbing to death Pauline's mother in Christchurch, New Zealand, in 1954. Opens two years before the murder, and follows the friendship as the two teens become obsessed with each other, retreating into a rich fantasy life. They create an elaborate, medieval kingdom where they escape to their dream lovers and romantic alter egos. Elaborate morphing and animation effects vividly express the shared inner fantasy world, while innovative camera work creates the sensations of hysteria and excitement that the girls experience as their infatuation becomes uncontrollable. Leads Lynsky and Winslet are convincing in the awkward, quiet Pauline and the pretty, intelligent, upper class Juliet. Bizarre crime story is stylish and eerily compelling; and made more so by real life events; after the film was released, mystery writer Anne Perry was revealed as Juliet Hulme. 99m/C VHS, DVD. NZ Melanie Lynskey, Kate Winslet, Sarah Pierse, Diana Kent, Clive Merrison, Simon O'Connor, Peter Jackson; *D:* Peter Jackson; *W:* Peter Jackson, Fran Walsh; *C:* Alun Bollinger; *M:* Peter Dasent.

The Heavenly Kid 1985 Leather-jacketed "cool" guy who died in a '60s hot rod crash finally receives an offer to exit limbo and enter heaven. The deal requires that he educate his dull earthly son on more hip and worldly ways. A big problem is that the soundtrack and wardrobe are 1955, whereas the cocky cool greaser supposedly died 17 years ago in 1968. Mildly entertaining. 92m/C VHS, DVD. Lewis Smith, Jane Kaczmarek, Jason Gedrick, Richard Mulligan; *D:* Cary Medoway; *M:* Kennard Ramsey.

Heaven's a Drag *To Die For* 1994 Low-budget British comedy. a tearjerker and a supernatural comedy. HIV-positive London drag performer Mark (Williams) lives with Simon (Arklie), a TV repairman who keeps his sexuality a secret from his co-workers and his emotional distance from his stricken lover. When Mark dies, Simon is quick to get on with his life—too quick for Mark, who's ghostly presence puts a damper on Simon's dating possibilities and brings up some old resentments. 95m/C VHS, DVD. GB Thomas Arkle, Ian Patrick Williams, Dilly Keane, Tony Slattery, Jean Boht, John Altman; *D:* Peter MacKenzie Litten; *W:* Johnny Byrne; *C:* John Ward. *Nar:* Ian McKellen.

Heaven's Above 1963 A sharp, biting satire on cleric life in England. Sellers stars as the quiet, down-to-earth reverend who is appointed to a new post in space. 113m/B VHS, DVD. GB Peter Sellers, Cecil Parker, Isabel Jeans, Eric Sykes, Ian Carmichael; *D:* John Boulting, Roy Boulting; *W:* Richard Rodney Bennett.

Heaven's Burning 1997 (R) Fast-paced road movie with some unexpected twists. Midori (Kudon) is a young Japanese woman who is honeymooning in Sydney with new hubby Yukio (Isomura). But Midori takes her own kidnapping to wait for her lover to arrive (who doesn't show). Yukio and the cops quickly discover her plotting but, in the meantime, Midori's been caught up in the midst of a bank robbery. When the robbery goes wrong, she becomes the quasi-hostage of driver Colin (Crowe), who takes off across Australia, pursued by the cops, his ex-partners, and the humiliated husband who wants revenge. Midori and Colin bond and things get increasingly stranger. 96m/C VHS, DVD. AU Youki Kudon, Russell Crowe, Kenji Isomura, Ray Barrett, Robert Mammone, Petru Gheorghiu, Matthew Dyktynski, Anthony Phelan, Colin Hay, Susan Prior, Norman Kaye; *D:* Craig Lahiff; *W:* Louis Nowra; *C:* Brian J. Breheny; *M:* Michael Atkinson.

Heaven's Fall 2006 (PG-13) Nine young blacks are pulled off an Alabama freight train in 1931, accused of raping two white women. Quickly convicted, they were all sentenced to the electric chair. Their case is appealed to the U.S. Supreme Court and, in 1933, New York attorney Sam Leibowitz (Hutton) travels to the deeply segregated South to work on their defense. Straightforward retelling of the case of the Scottsboro Boys and a landmark judicial decision. 105m/C DVD. Timothy Hutton, David Strathairn, Bill Sage, Leelee Sobieski, Anthony Mackie, Azura Skye, Bill Smitrovich, James Tolkan, Maury Chaykin; *D:* Terry Green; *W:* Terry Green; *C:* Paul Sanchez; *M:* David Reynolds.

Heaven's Fire 1999 Dean (Roberts) finds himself trying to prevent former co-worker Quentin (Prochnow) from stealing U.S. currency engraving plates from the treasury building. Dean foils the attempt but the crooks (and a

Heaven's

group of tourists) are trapped in the building by a couple of explosions. So Dean then tries to protect the innocent while keeping Quentin at bay. **91m/C VHS, DVD.** Eric Roberts, Jurgen Prochnow, Carl Timmins; **D:** David Warry-Smith; **W:** Rob Kerchner, Charles Philip Moore; **C:** Gordon Verheul; **M:** Deddy Tzur. **CABLE**

Heaven's Gate ♫♫ **1981 (R)** The uncut version of Cimino's notorious folly. A fascinating, plotless, and exaggerated account of the Johnson County cattle war of the 1880s. Ravishingly photographed, the film's production almost single-handedly put United Artists out of business. **220m/C VHS, DVD.** Kris Kristofferson, Christopher Walken, Isabelle Huppert, John Hurt, Richard Masur, Mickey Rourke, Brad Dourif, Joseph Cotten, Jeff Bridges, Sam Waterston, Terry O'Quinn, Geoffrey Lewis; **D:** Michael Cimino; **W:** Michael Cimino; **C:** Vilmos Zsigmond. Golden Raspberries '81: Worst Director (Cimino).

Heaven's Prisoners ♫♫ **1995 (R)** Dave Robicheaux (Baldwin) is an ex–New Orleans homicide detective who is recovering alcoholic, living a quiet life on a bayou with patient wife Annie (Lynch). They witness a plane crash and Dave rescues the only survivor, a young Salvadoran girl, whom they adopt. But the crash wasn't an accident and Dave's snooping around involves him with drug runners and local crime bosses, including old high school buddy, Bubba Rocque (Roberts), and his sirenish wife, Claudette (Hatcher). Convoluted plot with some moody touches but Baldwin scores as the flawed hero. Based on the mystery series by James Lee Burke. **135m/C VHS, DVD.** Paul Guilfoyle, Alec Baldwin, Kelly Lynch, Mary Stuart Masterson, Eric Roberts, Teri Hatcher, Vondie Curtis-Hall, Badja (Medu) Djola, Joe (Johnny) Viterelli, Hawthorne James; **D:** Phil Joanou; **W:** Scott Frank, Harley Peyton; **C:** Harris Savides; **M:** George Fenton.

Heavy ♫♫ **1994 (R)** Sensitive character study supported by an excellent ensemble, led by Vince as Victor, an obese, painfully withdrawn, 30-ish cook. He lives with his domineering mother (a subdued Winters) and helps her run their roadside diner, along with veteran waitress Delores (Harry). Then beautiful teenager Callie (Tyler) is hired and Victor develops a suitably massive crush. Tyler is all pout and promise as Callie, making it clear why a guy like Victor could fall hard for her. Harry brings a rich cynical and sexual edge to Delores. Director Mangold's feature debut is both eloquent and economical, though at times paced to a near stand-still. **104m/C VHS, DVD.** Pruitt Taylor Vince, Shelley Winters, Liv Tyler, Deborah Harry, Evan Dando, Joe Grifasi; **D:** James Mangold; **W:** James Mangold; **C:** Michael Barrow; **M:** Thurston Moore. Sundance '95: Special Jury Prize.

Heavy Metal ♫♫♫ **1981 (R)** Yes, the animated cult flick is now legally available on video, its copyright disputes finally resolved. A collection of science-fiction and fantasy stories, inspired by the similarly titled magazine and offered in a variety of graphic styles, that all encompass the theme of good versus evil. And don't always banter on the good. Features a soundtrack compiled from the work of many top metal artists of the time as well as Bernstein's score with the London Philharmonic Orchestra. A three-minute transitional segment, called "Neverwhere Land," that was cut from the original version has been restored as an epilogue. **90m/C VHS, DVD, UMD.** CA **D:** Gerald Potterton; **W:** Dan Goldberg, Len Blum; **C:** Brian Tufano; **M:** Elmer Bernstein; **V:** John Candy, Joe Flaherty, Don Francks, Eugene Levy, Rodger Bumpass, Jackie Burroughs, Harold Ramis, Richard Romanus, Doug Kenney.

Heavy Metal 2000 ♫♫½ **2000 (R)** The original 1981 film was cutting edge but this video game-ish sequel is average at best. Warrior babe Julie is tracking a group of space pirates, led by villain Lord Tyler, who destroyed her home and forced her sister into slavery. Julie assumes a new name, F.A.K.K. (Federation Assigned Ketogenic Killzone), and the usual avenger mission. **88m/C VHS, DVD. D:** Michael Coldewey, Michel Lemire; **W:** Robert Payne Cabeen; **C:** Bruno Philip; **M:** Frederic Talgom; **V:** Julie Strain, Michael Ironside, Billy Idol, Sonja Ball.

Heavy Petting ♫♫½ **1989** A hilarious compilation of "love scene" footage from feature films of the silent era to the '60s, newsreels, news reports, educational films, old TV shows, and home movies. **75m/C VHS, DVD.** David Byrne, Josh Mostel, Sandra Bernhard, Allen Ginsberg, Ann Magnuson, Spalding Gray, Laurie Anderson, John Oates, Abbie Hoffman, Jacki Ochs; **D:** Obie Benz; **C:** Sandi Sissel.

Heavy Traffic ♫♫♫ **1973** Ralph Bakshi's animated fantasy portrait of the hard-edged underside of city life. A young cartoonist draws the people, places, and paranoia of his environment. **77m/C VHS, DVD.** Joseph Kaufmann, Beverly Hope Atkinson, Michael Brandon,* Frank De Kova, Terri Haven, Mary Dean Lauria, Lillian Adams, Jamie Farr, Robert Easton; **D:** Ralph Bakshi; **W:** Ralph Bakshi; **C:** Ted C. Bemiller, Gregg Heschong; **M:** Ed Bogas.

Heavyweights ♫ **1994 (PG)** A product of Disney's sometimes assembly line approach to family entertainment (think "Mighty Ducks"). Nothing new saga of overweight youngsters sent to a fat camp run by tyrannical fitness guru Tony Perkis (Stiller). His methods cause the kids to band together and overthrow him and his "evil" tactics. Oh, by the way, there's a baseball competition with the more athletic camp kids on the other side of the lake. Guess who wins. Stiller as the fame obsessed fitness fanatic, sporting a David Copperfield-make-over, is the only highlight in this exercise of excess fluff. Directorial debut of Brill. **98m/C VHS, DVD.** Jeffrey Tambor, Ben Stiller, Jerry Stiller, Anne Meara, Shaun Weiss, Kenan Thompson; **D:** Steven Brill; **W:** Judd Apatow, Steven Brill; **C:** Victor Hammer; **M:** J.A.C. Redford.

Heck's Way Home ♫♫½ **1995** Heck is the Neufeld family dog and best friend of 11-year-old Luke (Krowchuk). The family is moving from Winnipeg to Australia and have a three-day layover in Vancouver. Heck is supposed to come along but instead, unbeknownst to the family, he gets captured by the local dogcatcher (Arkin) and the family are forced to leave without him. Naturally, Heck escapes and starts off on a 2000-mile journey to find his family before they fly away forever. **92m/C VHS, DVD.** Chad Krowchuk, Alan Arkin, Michael Riley, Shannon Lawson; **D:** Michael Scott; **C:** Maris Jansons. **CABLE**

Hedd Wyn ♫♫ **1992** True story of talented young poet Ellis Evans (Garmon), writing under the pseudonym Hedd Wyn, who dreams of winning a coveted literary prize. His hopes are put on hold when he's forced to fight in WWI, although he submits his antiwar poem "The Hero" to the competition. Welsh with subtitles. **123m/C VHS. GB** Huw Garmon, Catrin Fychan, Ceri Cunnington, Lilo Silyn; **D:** Paul Turner; **W:** Alan Llwyd; **C:** Ray Orton; **M:** John E.R. Hardy.

Hedda ♫♫½ **1975** A dramatization of the Henrik Ibsen play, "Hedda Gabler," about a middle-class pregnant woman. The story finds her frustrated with her life and manipulating those around her with tragic results. **102m/C VHS. GB** Glenda Jackson, Peter Eyre, Timothy West, Jennie Linden, Patrick Stewart; **D:** Trevor Nunn.

Hedwig and the Angry Inch ♫♫♫ **2000 (R)** Creator-star Mitchell adapted and directed his Off Broadway stage rock musical along with composer-lyricist Trask (who's also in the film) and opened up his gender-bending '70s kitsch fantasy. Hedwig was once Hansel, an East Berlin boy, whose sex-change operation was botched and who was abandoned in a Kansas trailer park by her G.I. husband. Betrayed in love by teenaged boy toy Tommy (Pitt), who also steals Hedwig's songs, Hedwig and her band embark on a low-rent tour while Hedwig slips her life story to the disinterested and stalks a much-more successful Tommy. **95m/C VHS, DVD. US** John Cameron Mitchell, Michael Pitt, Andrea Martin, Miriam Shor, Alberta Watson, Maurice Dean Wint, Rob Campbell, Stephen Trask, Theodore Liscinski, Michael Aranov; **D:** John Cameron Mitchell; **W:** John Cameron Mitchell; **C:** Frank DeMarco; **M:** Stephen Trask.

Heidi ♫♫½ **1937** Johanna Spyri's classic tale puts Shirley Temple in the hands of a mean governess and the loving arms of her Swiss grandfather. Also available colorized. Remade in 1967. **88m/B VHS, DVD.** Shirley Temple, Jean Hersholt, Helen Westley, Arthur Treacher, Sidney Blackmer, Marcia Mae Jones, Mary Nash; **D:** Allan Dwan; **W:** Walter Ferris; **C:** Arthur C. Miller; **M:** Julien Josephson.

Heidi ♫♫½ **1952** The Swiss do their own version of the children's classic by Johanna Spyri. A precocious little girl enjoys life in the Swiss Alps with her grandfather, until her stern aunt takes her away to live in the village in the valley. **98m/B VHS. SI** Elsbeth Sigmund, Heinrich Gretler, Thomas Klameth, Elsie Attenoff; **D:** Luigi Comencini.

Heidi ♫♫♫ **1965** The classic story from Johanna Spyri's novel is filmed beautifully in the Swiss Alps in Eastmancolor. Heidi is kidnapped by her mean aunt and forced to work as a slave for a rich family. Her kindly old grandfather comes to her rescue. Family entertainment for all, dubbed in English. **95m/C VHS. AT GE** Eva Maria Singhammer, Gustav Knuth, Lotte Ledl; **D:** Werner Jacobs.

Heidi ♫♫♫ **1967** The second American adaptation of the classic Johanna Spyri novel tells the story of an orphaned girl who goes to the Swiss Alps to live with her grandfather. **100m/C VHS, DVD.** Maximilian Schell, Jennifer Edwards, Michael Redgrave, Jean Simmons; **D:** Delbert Mann; **W:** Earl Hammer; **M:** John Williams. **TV**

Heidi ♫♫♫ **1993 (G)** Yet another version of the children's classic, from German writer Johanna Spyri's 1881 novel. Thornton is charming as the orphan shuttled from relative to relative until she happily ends up with her crotchety grandfather (Robards) in his mountain cabin. Then her cousin comes along and whisks her off to the city to be a companion to the invalid Klara (Randall). Seymour is the snobbish, scowling governess. This "Heidi" is spunky enough to keep the sugar level tolerable. Filmed on location in Austria. **167m/C VHS, DVD.** Noley Thornton, Jason Robards Jr., Jane Seymour, Lexi (Faith) Randall, Sian Phillips, Patricia Neal, Benjamin Brazier, Michael Simkins, Andrew Bicknell, Jane Hazlegrove; **C:** Michael Rhodes; **W:** Jeanne Rosenberg; **M:** Lee Holdridge. **TV**

The Heidi Chronicles ♫♫ **1995** Some 25 years of boomer angst and friendship are covered in this cable adaptation of Wasserstein's 1988 Pulitzer Prize-winning play. Heidi Holland (Curtis) goes from prep school to Vassar to an art history career while searching for self-fulfillment, feminist ideals, and some romance along the way. The romance is on-and-off, thanks to caddish journalist Scoop (Friedman), but Heidi can always depend on soul mate, gay pediatrician Peter (Hulce), and Susan (Cattrall), her follow-the-fads confidante. Heidi's sometimes too morose for her own good but you won't mind spending a couple of hours in her company. **94m/C VHS.** Jamie Lee Curtis, Tom Hulce, Kim Cattrall, Peter Friedman, Eve Gordon, Shari Belafonte, Sharon Lawrence, Julie White, Debra Eisenstadt, Roma Maffia; **D:** Paul Bogart; **W:** Wendy Wasserstein; **C:** Isidore Mankofsky; **M:** David Shire.

Height of the Sky ♫♫½ **1999** In rural Arkansas, 1935, the poor Jones family farms a small plot of land, which barely rent from the rich Caldwells. When Gabriel Jones (Moninger) succumbs to tuberculosis, family patriarch Wendel Jones (Stewart) decides to hide Gabriel in an old cabin thereby leaving the strong-willed Leora (Weedon) in charge of the family. Jennifer must convince Mr. Caldwell (Palazzo) that all is well on their farm while she covers for her father's absence. Written and directed by Lyn Clinton, cousin of President Bill Clinton. **116m/C DVD.** Grant Moninger, Evan Palazzo, Jackie Stewart, Jennifer Weedon; **D:** Lyn Clinton; **W:** Lyn Clinton; **C:** John R. Zilles; **M:** Boris Zelkin.

Heights ♫♫½ **2004 (R)** Mildly entertaining debut from Terrio follows the lives of several New Yorkers over 24 hours. Diana (Close) is an award-winning diva who gives acting classes at Juilliard. Struggling Alec (Bradford) auditions for Diana and she decides to use him to console herself about her husband's latest romance by inviting Alec to her big birthday bash. Meanwhile, her photographer daughter Isabel (Banks) is worried about her upcoming wedding to handsome lawyer Jonathan (Marsden), who is dodging journalist Peter (Light) for suspicious reasons. Based on co-writer Fox's play. **93m/C DVD. US** Glenn Close, Elizabeth Banks, James Marsden, Jesse Bradford, Thomas Lennon, Matthew Davis, Isabella Rosellini, John Light, George Segal, Eric Bogosian, Michael Murphy; **D:** Chris Terrio; **W:** Amy Fox; **C:** Jim Denault; **M:** Martin Erskine, Ben Butler.

Heimat 1 ♫♫½ **1952** *Heimat-Eine deutsche Chronik* 1984 Sixteen-hour series follows the lives, loves, and tragedies of the German Simon family from the end of WWI to 1982. Based on Reitz's own family and his childhood. Shot over two years, the series has 28 lead performances and more than 140 speaking roles. German with subtitles. **924m/C VHS. GE** Marita Breuer; **D:** Edgar Reitz; **W:** Edgar Reitz, Peter F. Steinbach; **C:** Gernot Roll; **M:** Nikos Mamangakis.

Heimat 2 ♫♫½ **1992** The continuation of the saga is composed of 25 half-hour segments and follows Hermann Simon's life in Munich from 1960 to 1970. A modernist musician and composer, Hermann falls in with a group of students, artists, and rebels. German with subtitles. **750m/C VHS. GE** Daniel E. Smith, Henry Arnold, Salome Kammer, Hannelore Hoger, Anke Sevenich, Noemi Steuer; **D:** Edgar Reitz; **W:** Edgar Reitz; **C:** Gernot Roll, Gerard Vandenburg, Christian Reitz; **M:** Nikos Mamangakis.

The Heiress ♫♫♫ **1949** Based on the Henry James novel "Washington Square." Catherine (de Havilland) is the plain, awkward daughter of wealthy widowed doctor Austin Sloper (Richardson), who is a belittling tyrant to his only child. Catherine has no suitors until handsome, fortune-seeking Morris Townsend (Clift) approaches her. Naturally, Dr. Sloper dismisses his interest and warns that his daughter will only end up with a broken heart. No happy endings here but the performances are superb. Remade as "Washington Square" in 1997. **115m/B VHS, DVD.** Olivia de Havilland, Montgomery Clift, Ralph Richardson, Miriam Hopkins, Vanessa Brown, Mona Freeman, Ray Collins, Selena Royle; **D:** William Wyler; **W:** Ruth Goetz, Augustus Goetz; **C:** Leo Tover; **M:** Aaron Copland. Oscars '49: Actress (de Havilland), Art Dir/Set Dec., B&W, Costume Des. (B&W), Orig. Dramatic Score; Golden Globes '50: Actress—Drama (de Havilland); Natl. Bd. of Review '49: Actor (Richardson), Natl. Film Reg. '96; N.Y. Film Critics '49: Actress (de Havilland).

The Heirloom ♫♫½ **2005** A wealthy family commits mass suicide and 20 years later the mystery remains. James (Chang) inherits the abandoned Taipei mansion and decides to move in with girlfriend Yo (Kwan). Nasty things begin to happen. James' character fades into the background while Yo fights off the creepies. Chinese with subtitles. **97m/C DVD. TW** Jason Chang, Terri Kwan, Yu-Chen Chang, Tender Huang; **D:** Leste Chen; **W:** Dorian Li; **C:** Pung-Leung Kwan; **M:** Jeffrey Cheng.

The Heist ♫♫ **1989** An ex-con, upon regaining his freedom, sets out to rip off the crook who framed him. Entertaining enough story with a first-rate cast. **97m/C VHS, DVD.** Pierce Brosnan, Tom Skerritt, Wendy Hughes, Noble Willingham, Tom Atkins, Robert Prosky; **D:** Stuart Orme; **C:** Jiri (George) Tirl; **M:** Arthur B. Rubinstein. **CABLE**

The Heist ♫♫½ **1996** Con artist plots the hijacking of a transport company's fleet and starts out by taking off the firm's employees hostage. But one of the workers is an ex-cop who failed once to stop a robbery and is not about to fail again. **99m/C VHS, DVD. GE** Hannes Jaenicke, Cali Timmins, Andrew McCarthy, Cynthia Geary, Wolf Larson; **D:** Michael Kennedy; **W:** Michael Januay; **C:** Bruce Worrall. **TV**

Heist ✗✗✗ 2001 (R) Hackman is Joe, a master-thief who's planning to retire after his latest job, but fence Bergman (DeVito) has other ideas, holding Joe's payoff until he agrees to a big-time gold heist. And just to make things interesting, Bergman sends in his nephew Silk (Rockwell) along. This complicates things even more, especially with Joe's wife, Fran (Pidgeon). In classic Mamet fashion, doublecrosses, plot twists, misdirection, great dialogue and perfect casting combine to create an excellent caper film. Lin-do and Jay add plenty of spark as Joe's loyal crew members. 107m/C VHS, DVD. US Gene Hackman, Danny DeVito, Delroy Lindo, Sam Rockwell, Rebecca Pidgeon, Ricky Jay, Patti Lu-Pone, Jim Frangione; D: David Mamet; W: David Mamet; C: Robert Elswit; M: Theodore Shapiro.

Held for Murder ✗ 1994 Perplexing, contemplative film on faith and over—and maybe a miracle. Told in flashback, publisher Alexander Klimt (Verley) travels to a Swiss lakeside town where it's rumored that the beautiful Rachel Donnadieu (Masitah) has been "visited" by God, who wishes to experience the pleasures of love, in the form of her own husband, simple fisherman Simon (Depardieu). Story is derived from the Greek myth concerning Zeus, who seduced Alcmene in the shape of her husband Amphitryon. French with subtitles. 84m/C VHS, FR S/ Gerard Depardieu, Laurence Masitah, Bernard Verley; D: Jean-Luc Godard; W: Jean-Luc Godard; C: Caroline Champetier.

Held Up ✗½ *Inconvenienced* 2000 (PG-13) Engaged couple Foxx and Long are having a hard time staying together when after they have a fight and Foxx becomes a hostage during a botched convenience store robbery in a sleepy southwestern town. Broad comedy works in all but they're all been done before by funnier writers. Foxx has some appeal, but not enough to overcome the material. Video included. 88m/C VHS, DVD. Jamie Foxx, Nia Long, Jake Busey, John Cullum, Barry Corbin, Eduardo Yanez, Mike Weiss, Sarah Paulson, Julie Hagerty; D: Steve Rash; W: Jeff Eastin; C: David Makin; M: Robert Folk.

Helen of Troy ✗½ 1956 Mythological fantasy finds Helen (Podesta), the beautiful daughter of Zeus, falling in love with Trojan prince Paris (Sernas)—an event that leads to the siege of Troy. Ignores script for lavish effects. Video includes behind-the-scenes footage. 135m/C VHS, DVD. Rossana Podesta, Jacques Sernas, Cedric Hardwicke, Stanley Baker, Niall MacGinnis, Nora Swinburne, Robert Douglas, Torin Thatcher, Harry Andrews, Janette Scott, Ronald Lewis, Brigitte Bardot; D: Robert Wise; W: John Twist, N. Richard Nash; C: Harry Stradling Sr.; M: Max Steiner.

Helen of Troy ✗✗½ 2003 Since Helen was the face that launched a thousand ships for the Trojan War, she needs to be a looker and, in the person of Guillory, she is. Which is good, since the cable miniseries is fairly ordinary. Helen is married to weak-willed Menelaus (Callis), the King of Sparta but falls crazy in love with Paris (Marsden), a Prince of Troy. The lovers hightail it to Troy, where King Priam (Rhys-Davies) offers protection. Menelaus's brother Agamemnon (a snakey Sewell) leads the Spartans on a 10-year battle to get Helen back. Remember the Trojan Horse is a big deal. 177m/C VHS, DVD.
CABLE

Helas pour Moi ✗✗ *Oh Woe is Me* 1994 Perplexing, contemplative film on faith and woe—and maybe a miracle. Told in flashback, publisher Alexander Klimt (Verley) travels to a Swiss lakeside town where it's rumored that the beautiful Rachel Donnadieu (Masitah) has been "visited" by God, who wishes to experience the pleasures of love, in the form of her own husband, simple fisherman Simon (Depardieu). Story is derived from the Greek myth concerning Zeus, who seduced Alcmene in the shape of her husband Amphitryon. French with subtitles. 84m/C VHS, FR S/ Gerard Depardieu, Laurence Masitah, Bernard Verley; D: Jean-Luc Godard; W: Jean-Luc Godard; C: Caroline Champetier.

Hell Comes to Frogtown ✗ 1988 (R) In a post-nuclear land run by giant frogs, a renegade who is one of the few normal non-sterile men left on earth must rescue some fertile women and impregnate them. Sci-fi spoof is extremely low-budget, but fun. Stars "Rowdy" Roddy Piper of wrestling fame. 88m/C VHS, DVD. Roddy Piper, Sandahl Bergman, Rory Calhoun, Cec Verrell; D: Robert J. Kizer, Donald G. Jackson; W: Randall Frakas; M: David G. Jackson.

Hell Commandos ✗ 1969 Soldiers in WWII struggle to prevent the Nazis from releasing a deadly bacteria that will kill millions. Dubbed. 90m/C DVD. IT Guy Madison, Stelvio Rosi; D: Jose Luis Merino.

Hell Fire Austin ✗½ 1932 Maynard finds himself mixed up with outlaws in the Old West. 60m/B VHS, Ken Maynard, Nat Pendleton, Jack Perrin; D: Forrest Sheldon.

Hell Harbor ✗✗ 1930 Caribbean love, murder and greed combine to make this early talkie. Exterior shots were filmed on the west coast of Florida in the 1930s. 65m/B VHS, Lupe Velez, Gibson Gowland, Jean Hersholt, John Holland; D: Henry King.

Hell High ✗ 1986 (R) Four high schoolers plan a night of torture and humiliation for an annoying teacher, only to find she has some deadly secrets of her own. Dumber than it sounds. 84m/C VHS, DVD. Christopher Stryker, Christopher Cousins, Millie Prezioso, Jason Brill; D: Douglas Grossman.

Hell Hounds of Alaska ✗ 1973 (G) The Yukon. Yugoslav-style. European co-production goes back to the Gold Rush days for an adventure about a frontiersman tracking down a stolen shipment of the precious ore while trying to save the life of an injured boy. 90m/C VHS, Doug McClure, Harald Leipnitz, Angelica Ott; D: Harald Reinl.

Hell Hunters ✗ 1987 Nazi-hunters foil the plot of an old German doctor to poison the population of L.A. Meanwhile, a daughter avenges the death of her mother by blowing up the doctor's jungle compound. 96m/C VHS, Stewart Granger, Maud Adams, George Lazenby, Candice Daly, Romulo Arantes, William Berger; D: Ernst R. von Theumer; W: James Dalesandro, Louis LaRussa II; C: Mario DiLeo, Barry Samson; M: Larry Fallon.

Hell in the Pacific ✗✗✗ 1969 (PG) A marvelously photographed (by Conrad Hall) psycho/macho allegory about an American and a Japanese soldier stranded together on a tiny island during the mini-war they fight by themselves. Overly obvious anti-war statement done with style. 101m/C VHS, DVD. Lee Marvin, Toshiro Mifune; D: John Boorman; W: Eric Bercovici, Alexander Jacobs; C: Conrad L. Hall; M: Lalo Schifrin.

Hell Is for Heroes ✗✗✗ 1962 McQueen stars as the bitter leader of a small infantry squad outmanned by the Germans in this tight WWII drama. A strong cast and riveting climax make this a must for action fans. 90m/B VHS, DVD. Steve McQueen, Bobby Darin, Fess Parker, Harry Guardino, James Coburn, Mike Kellin, Nick Adams, Bob Newhart, L.Q. Jones, Don Haggerty, Joseph Hoover, Michele Montau, Bill Mullikin; D: Donald Siegel; W: Robert Pirosh, Richard Carr; C: Harold Lipstein; M: Leonard Rosenman.

Hell Night WOOF! 1981 (R) Several young people must spend the night in a mysterious mansion as part of their initiation into Alpha Sigma Rho fraternity in this extremely dull low-budget horror flick. 100m/C VHS, DVD, Linda Blair, Vincent Van Patten, Kevin Brophy, Peter Barton, Jenny Neumann; D: Tom De Simone; W: Randy Feldman; M: Dan Wyman.

Hell of the Living Dead WOOF! *Apocalipsis Canibal; Night of the Zombies; Zombie Creeping Flesh* 1983 Staff of a scientific research center are killed and then resurrected as cannibals who prey on the living. The living will suffer again if trapped into watching. Matta is pseudonym for director Vincent Dawn. Cheap, dubbed, and possessing minimal coherence. 103m/C VHS, DVD. IT SP Margi Evelyn Newton, Frank Garfield, Selan Karay; D: Bruno Mattei; W: J.M. Cunilles, Claudio Fragasso; C: John Cabrera.

Hell on Frisco Bay ✗✗½ 1955 An ex-waterfront cop, falsely imprisoned for manslaughter, sets out to clear his name. His quest finds him taking on the Mob, in this '30s-style gangster film. Good performances all around, especially Robinson, who steals every scene he's in. 93m/C VHS. Alan Ladd, Edward G. Robinson, Joanne Dru, Fay Wray, William Demarest, Jayne Mansfield; D: Frank Tuttle; M: Max Steiner.

Hell on the Battleground ✗½ 1988 (R) Group of inexperienced recruits are led into combat by two battle-hardened veterans. That's their only hope for survival as a counterattack by U.S. tanks. 91m/C VHS. David A. Prior, William (Bill) Smith, Ted Prior, Fritz Matthews; D: David A. Prior.

Hell on Wheels ✗ 1967 Two successful brothers in the racing industry are torn apart by the same girl. Brotherly love diminishes into a hatred so deep that murder becomes the sole purpose of both. 96m/C VHS. Marty Robbins, Jennifer Ashley, John Ashley, Gigi Perreau, Robert Doman, Connie Smith, Frank Gerstle; D: Will Zens.

Hell Raiders ✗½ 1968 A force invades a supposedly defenseless Pacific island, and finds itself fiercely attacked. 90m/C VHS. John Agar, Richard Webb, Joan Huntington; D: Larry Buchanan.

Hell River ✗✗ 1975 (PG) In 1941 Yugoslavia, Yugoslav partisans and Nazis battle it out at a place called Hell River. 100m/C VHS. Rod Taylor, Adam West; D: Stole Jankovic.

Hell-Ship Morgan ✗✗ 1936 Bancroft is a womanizing tuna boat captain who falls for and marries Sothern. When they set up married life on the boat she starts eying first mate Jory. And Bancroft finds out. 65m/B VHS. George Bancroft, Ann Sothern, Victor Jory, George Regas, Howard Hickman, Ralph Byrd; D: David Ross Lederman

Hell Ship Mutiny ✗✗½ 1957 Marcomes to the aid of a lovely island principality during WWII, five American GIs wander through the desert. They find numerous pitfalls and unexpected help. Overall, dismal and disappointing. 66m/B VHS. Wally Campo, Brandon Carroll; D: Burt Topper.

Hell Squad ✗ 1985 (R) Unable to release his son from the Middle Eastern terrorists who kidnapped him, a U.S. ambassador turns to the services of nine Las Vegas showgirls. These gals moonlight as vicious commandos in this low-budget action film with skin. 88m/C VHS. Bainbridge Scott, Glen Hartford, Tina Lederman; D: Kenneth Hartford; W: Kenneth Hartford; M: Charles P. Barnett.

Hell Squad ✗ 1958 Lost in North Africa during WWII, five American GIs wander through the desert. They find numerous pitfalls and unexpected help. Overall, dismal and disappointing. 64m/B VHS. Wally Campo, Brandon Carroll; D: Burt Topper.

Hellbenders ✗½ *I Crudeli; Los Despiadados* 1967 (PG) A confederate veteran and must fight through Union train adversity. Dubbed. *Il Crudeli; Los Despiadados*. Joseph Cotten, Norma Bengell, Julian Mateos; D: Sergio Corbucci; M: Ennio Morricone.

Hellbent ✗½ 1988 A crazed musician and a revenge-obsessed housewife embark on an unusual adventure that challenges their very sanity. 90m/C VHS. IT SP Margit Evelyn Newton, Frank Garfield; D: Richard Casey; W: Richard Casey.

Hellblock 13 ✗½ 1997 Anthology of three low-budget horror tales is told with grainy, raw-edged energy and a distinct regional flavor. Tara (Rochon) writes stories while she's on Death Row and shows them to her stolid guard (Hansen). "Leatherface" from "Texas Chainsaw Massacre") Rochon brings a welcome note of humor to what might have been your basic madwoman stereotype. The individual films get better and funnier as they go along. 31m/C VHS, DVD. Debbie Rochon, Gunnar Hansen, J.J. North, Jennifer Peluso, David G. Holland; D: Paul Talbot; W: Paul Talbot; Jeff Miller, Michael R. Smith.

Hellbound ✗✗ 1994 (R) Prosatanos (Nearne), a powerful 12th-century wizard, is imprisoned and the source of his power (a scepter) is supposedly destroyed. Fast-forward several hundred years when Prosatanos manages to free himself and seek out the pieces of his scepter. Which happens to lead him to Chicago and a couple of unsuspecting cops (Norris, Levels). 95m/C VHS, DVD. Chuck Norris, Christopher Nearne, Calvin Levels, Sheree J. Wilson; D: Aaron Norris.

Hellbound: Hellraiser 2 ✗✗ *Hellraiser 2* 1988 (R) In this, the first sequel to Clive Barker's inter-dimensional nightmare, the traumatized daughter from the first film is pulled into the Cenobites' universe. Gore and weird imagery abound. An uncut, unrated version is also available. 96m/C VHS, DVD. GB Ashley Laurence, Clare Higgins, Kenneth Cranham, Imogen Boorman, William Hope, Oliver Smith, Sean Chapman, Doug Bradley; D: Tony Randel; W: Peter Atkins; C: Robin Vidgeon; M: Christopher Young.

Hellboy ✗✗✗½ 2004 (PG-13) Faithful adaptation of the cult Dark Horse comic is a success, thanks mostly to del Toro's smart direction and Perlman's amusing, yet complex portrayal of the titular demon/hero. During WWII, the Nazis and Rasputin team up to try to bring about the Apocalypse. Perlman gives Hellboy depth (even under all the prosthetics), but he has lots of help from a strong supporting cast. 125m/C DVD, Blu-ray Disc, UMD. US Ron Perlman, John Hurt, Selma Blair, Rupert Evans, Karel Roden, Jeffrey Tambor, Biddy Hodson, Doug Jones, Ladislav Beran, Kevin Trainor, Corey Johnson, Stephen H. Fisher; D: Guillermo del Toro; W: Guillermo del Toro, Peter Briggs; C: Guillermo Navarro; M: Marco Beltrami; V: David Hyde Pierce.

Hellboy 2: The Golden Army ✗✗✗ 2008 (PG-13) The big red guy from the Dark Horse comic returns (after this 2004 big screen adventure) as the truce between humankind and the world of the fantastic (which is dying, is broken). This means makes the situation even worse. Not yet reviewed. ?m/C Ron Perlman, Selma Blair, Doug Jones, Luke Goss, Roy Dotrice, John Hurt, Jeffrey Tambor, Brian Steele, Anna Walton; D: Guillermo del Toro; W: Guillermo del Toro; C: Guillermo Navarro; M: Danny Elfman; V: Thomas Kretschmann, Seth MacFarlane.

Hellcats woof! 1968 (R) A mob of sleazy, leather-clad female bikers terrorize small Midwestern towns in this violent girl-gang thriller. Even biker movie fans might find this one unworthy. 90m/C VHS. Ross Hagen, Dee Duffy, Sharyn Kinzie, Del (Sonny) West, Bob Slatzer. **D:** Bob Slatzer.

Hellcats of the Navy ½ 1957 Soggy true saga of the WWII mission to sever the vital link between mainland Asia and Japan. The only film that Ronald and Nancy Davis starred in together and the beginning of their grand romance. 82m/B VHS, DVD. Ronald Reagan, Nancy Davis, Arthur Franz, Robert Arthur; **D:** Nathan "Jerry" Juran; **W:** Bernard Gordon, David Lang.

Helldorado Heldorado 1946 A lively western starring the singing cowboy, Roy Rogers. 54m/B VHS, DVD. Roy Rogers, George "Gabby" Hayes, Dale Evans, Paul Harvey; **D:** William Witney.

Heller in Pink Tights 1960 Offbeast western, based on a novel by Louis L'Amour, that follows the adventures of a seedy vaudeville troupe in the 1880s. Manager Tom Healy (Quinn) stays barely ahead of his creditors, with Angela (Loren) as his leading asset (and Loren's assets the film's highlight). She dallys with gunslinger Clint Mabry (Forest), who pursues her out of town and there's an Indian attack and more gunslinging until the troupe manages to find a safe haven. The story was hardly sophisticated director Cukor's specialty, which may account for the unbelievable characters and confused plot. 100m/C VHS, DVD. Sophia Loren, Anthony Quinn, Margaret O'Brien, Steve Forrest, Edmund Lowe, Ramon Novarro, Eileen Heckart; **D:** George Cukor; **W:** Walter Bernstein; **C:** Harold Lipstein; **M:** Daniele Amfitheatrof.

Hellfighters 1968 (G) Texas oil well fire fighters experience trouble between themselves and the women they love. 121m/C VHS, DVD. John Wayne, Katharine Ross, Jim Hutton, Vera Miles, Bruce Cabot, Jay C. Flippen; **D:** Andrew V. McLaglen; **W:** Clair Huffaker; **C:** William Clothier; **M:** Leonard Rosenman.

Hellfire 1948 A gambler promises to build a church and follow the precepts of the Bible after a minister sacrifices his life for him. 90m/B VHS. William (Wild Bill) Elliot, Marie Windsor, Forrest Tucker, Jim Davis; **D:** R.G. Springsteen.

The Hellfire Club 1961 In 18th century Britain, a young man reaches adulthood and attempts to claim the estate of his father. No ordinary dad, his led the infamous Hellfire Club, an organization specializing in debauchery and depravity. His cousin challenges his claim and kidnaps his fiancee. Historical hokum, complete with swordplay. 88m/C VHS, GB Keith Michell, Kai (Kay) Fischer, Adrienne Corri, Peter Arne, David Lodge, Bill Owen, Peter Cushing, Francis Matthews, Desmond Walter-Ellis; **D:** Robert S. Baker, Monty Berman; **W:** Jimmy Sangster.

Hellgate woof! 1989 (R) A woman hitchhiking turns out to be one of the living dead. Her benefactor lives to regret picking her up. 96m/C VHS, DVD. Abigail Wolcott, Ron Palillo, Carel Trichardt, Petrea Curran, Evan J. Klisser, Joanne Ward; **D:** William A. Levey; **W:** Michael O'Rourke; **C:** Peter Palmer.

Hellhole 1985 (R) A young woman who witnesses her mother's murder is sent to a sanitarium where the doctors are perfecting chemical lobotomies. Extremely weak script and poor acting make this a suspenseless thriller. 93m/C VHS. Judy Landers, Ray Sharkey, Mary Woronov, Marjoe Gortner, Edy Williams, Mary Woronov, Dyanne Thorne, Lynn Borden; **D:** Pierre De Moro; **W:** Vincent Mongol; **C:** Stephen Posey; **M:** Jeff Sturges.

Hellmaster 1992 Your basic sicko mad scientist experiments on some unsuspecting college students by injecting them with an addictive drug. The drug also causes some horrifying mutations and makes its victims superhuman (but also super-ugly). Lots of gore. Creative special effects and make-up will appeal to fans of horror. 92m/C VHS, DVD, John Saxon, David Emge, Amy Raasch; **D:** Douglas Schulze; **W:** Douglas Schulze.

Hello Again 1987 (PG) The wife of a successful plastic surgeon chokes to death on a piece of chicken. A year later she returns to life, with comical consequences, but soon discovers that life won't be the same. 96m/C VHS, DVD. Shelley Long, Corbin Bernsen, Judith Ivey, Gabriel Byrne, Sela Ward, Austin Pendleton, Carrie Nye, Robert Lewis, Madeleine Potter; **D:** Frank Perry; **M:** William Goldstein.

Hello, Dolly! 1969 (G) Widow Dolly Levi, while matchmaking for her friends, finds a match for herself. Based on the hugely successful Broadway musical adapted from Thornton Wilder's play "Matchmaker." Lightweight story needs better actors with stronger characterizations. Original Broadway score helps. ♫Hello Dolly; Just Leave Everything to Me; Love is Only Love; Dancing; Walter's Gavotte; It Only Takes a Moment; Ribbons Down My Back; Elegance; It Takes a Woman. 146m/C VHS, DVD. Barbra Streisand, Walter Matthau, Michael Crawford, Louis Armstrong, E.J. Peaker, Marianne McAndrew, Tommy Tune; **D:** Gene Kelly; **W:** Ernest Lehman; **C:** Harry Stradling Sr.; **M:** Jerry Herman. Oscars '69: Art Dir./Set Dec., Sound, Scoring/Musical.

Hello Down There ½ 1969 (G) Harmless—if dated—family comedy. Inventor Fred Miller (Randall) persuades his reluctant family to participate in a month-long experiment that has them living in a prototype underwater home. Wife Vivian (Leigh) is afraid of the water and his teenaged children are distressed because their pop band has a chance at a record deal. Meanwhile, the living room pool attracts sharks and an overly-friendly seal. Shot in Florida. 97m/C DVD. Tony Randall, Janet Leigh, Jim Backus, Ken Berry, Charlotte Rae, Richard Dreyfuss, Roddy MacDowall; **D:** Jack Arnold; **W:** Frank Telford, John McGreevey; **C:** Clifford Poland; **M:** Jeff Barry.

Hello, Frisco, Hello ½ 1943 San Francisco's wild Barbary Coast is the setting for this romantic musical. Smoothie Payne opens up a saloon that features Faye, who's in love with him, as the star singing attraction. Unfortunately, Payne is involved with a society snob and Faye heads off to European success. When she returns, it's to a sadder and wiser man. ♫Hello, Frisco, Hello; You'll Never Know; San Francisco; Ragtime Cowboy Joe; Sweet Cider Time; Has Anybody Here Seen Kelly; King Chanticleer; When You Wore a Tulip; Strike Up the Band, Here Comes a Sailor. 98m/C VHS. Alice Faye, John Payne, Jack Oakie, Lynn Bari, Laird Cregar, June Havoc, Ward Bond, Aubrey Mather, John Archer; **D:** H. Bruce Humberstone; **W:** Robert Ellis, Helen Logan. Oscars '43: Song ("You'll Never Know").

Hello Mary Lou: Prom Night 2 ½ The Haunting of Hamilton High: Prom Night 2 1987 (R) A sequel to the successful slasher flick, wherein a dead-for-30-years prom queen relegates the current queen to purgatory and comes back to life in order to avenge herself. Wild special effects. 97m/C VHS. C4 Michael Ironside, Wendy Lyon, Justin Louis, Lisa Schrage, Richard Monette; **D:** Bruce Pittman; **W:** Ron Oliver; **C:** John Herzog.

Hello Trouble ½ 1932 A Texas Ranger accidentally kills his friend, who was a former Ranger turned bandit, causing him to hang up his guns. 63m/C VHS. Buck Jones, Lena Basquette, Wallace MacDonald, "Spec" (Walter) O'Donnell, Ward Bond, Frank Rice, Ruth Warren; **D:** Lambert Hillyer.

Hellraiser ½ 1987 (R) A graphic, horror fantasy about a woman who is manipulated by the monstrous spirit of her husband's dead brother. In order for the man who was also her lover to be brought back to life, she must lure and kill human prey for his sustenance. Grisly and inventive scenes keep the action fast-paced; not for the faint-hearted. 94m/C DVD, UMD. GB Andrew (Andy) Robinson, Clare Higgins, Ashley Laurence, Sean Chapman, Oliver Smith, Robert Hines, Doug Bradley, Nicholas Vince, Dave Atkins; **D:** Clive Barker; **W:** Clive Barker; **M:** Christopher Young.

Hellraiser 3: Hell on Earth 1992 (R) Pinhead is back in this film based on characters created by horrormeister Clive Barker. A strange black box holds the key to sending Pinhead back to Hell and is sought by the heroine, a TV newswoman (Farrell). But Pinhead's human henchman, a nasty nightclub owner, isn't going to make things easy. Imaginative special effects and Bradley's commanding presence as Pinhead aid this shocker, which becomes unfortunately mired in excessive gore. An unrated version at 97 minutes is also available. 91m/C VHS, DVD. Doug Bradley, Terry Farrell, Kevin Bernhardt, Paula Marshall, Ken Carpenter, Peter Boynton, Ashley Laurence; **D:** Anthony Hickox; **W:** Peter Atkins; **C:** Gerry Lively.

Hellraiser 4: Bloodline 1995 (R) You can't keep a bad Pinhead in Hell, as this unfortunate sequel demonstrates. Bradley reprises his role as the big bad S&M pincushion in the latest and supposedly last installment of Clive Barker's blood drenched series. Tracing the origin of the infernal Rubik's Cube that releases Pinhead, the plot jumps between 18th century France, present day New York, and a 22nd century space station. Along the way, the Pointy One gets to flay, skewer, and impale to his evil heart's content. Special f/x guru Kevin Yeagher was so embarrassed by this outing that he took his director's credit off of the picture. Bad acting, bad plot, bad complexion. 81m/C VHS, DVD. Bruce Ramsay, Valentina Vargas, Doug Bradley, Kim Myers, Christina Harnos, Charlotte Chatton, Paul Perri, Mickey Cottrell; **D:** Alan Smithee, Kevin Yagher; **W:** Peter Atkins; **M:** Daniel Licht.

Hellraiser 5: Inferno 2000 (R) Los Angeles detective Joseph (Sheffer), wakes up one day literally in hell. In order to escape he must find the puzzle box, which is in Pinhead's possession. This one is not only boring, it's confusing, and Pinhead has little more than a cameo appearance. 99m/C VHS, DVD. Craig Sheffer, Doug Bradley, Nicholas Turturro, James Remar, Lindsay Taylor; **D:** Scott Derrickson; **W:** Scott Derrickson, Paul Harris Boardman. VIDEO

Hellraiser: Deader Hellraiser 7: Deader 2005 (R) Wanting to break the big story about a freaky Bucharest cult that supposedly rouses the deceased, a female reporter unearths the terrifying truth behind who they want to bring back to life. 88m/C VHS, DVD. Doug Bradley, Kari Wuhrer, Paul Rhys, Marc Warren, Georgina Rylance; **D:** Rick Bota; **W:** Neal Marshall Stevens, Tim(othy) Day; **M:** Henning Lohner. VIDEO

Hellraiser: Hellseeker 2002 (R) The fifth sequel in the 15-year-old series looks great, thanks to debuting director Bota, who's a veteran cinematographer. But the story doesn't have enough ple murder suspect. 89m/C VHS, DVD. Ashley Laurence, Dean Winters, Doug Bradley; **D:** Rick Bota; **W:** Carl DuPre, Tim(othy) Day; **C:** John Drake; **M:** Stephen (Steve) Edwards. VIDEO

Hellraiser: Hellworld 2005 (R) Pinhead (Bradley) and the Cenobites torment some computer hackers through the use of the hellworld.com site (possibly by manning the tech support phones). Ridiculously resilient franchise plods along, helped by the presence of Henriksen, on hiatus from whatever Alien sequel they're probably working on. 2005m/C DVD. Doug Bradley, Lance Henriksen, Henry Cavill, Kathryn Winnick; **D:** Rick Bota; **W:** Joel Soisson, Carl DuPre; **C:** Gabriel Kosuth; **M:** Lars Anderson. VIDEO

Hellriders woof! 1984 (R) A motorcycle gang rides into a small town and subjects its residents to a reign of terror. 90m/C VHS. Adam West, Tina Louise, Ross Alexander, Renee Harmon; **D:** James Bryan; **W:** Renee Harmon, James Bryan.

Hell's Angels 1930 Classic WWI aviation movie is sappy and a bit lumbering, but still an extravagant spectacle with awesome air scenes. Studio owner Hughes fired directors Howard Hawks and Luther Reed, spent an unprecedented $3.8 million, and was ultimately credited as director (although Whale also spent some time in the director's chair). Three years in the making, the venture cost three pilots their lives and lost a bundle. Harlow replaced Swedish Greta Nissen when sound was added and was catapulted into blond bombshelldom as a two-timing dame. And the tinted and two-color scenes—restored in 1989—came well before Ted Turner ever wielded a crayola. 135m/B VHS, DVD. Jean Harlow, Ben Lyon, James Hall, John Darrow, Lucien Prival, Frank Clarke, Roy "Baldy" Wilson, Douglas Gilmore, Jane Winton, Evelyn Hall; **D:** Howard Hughes; **W:** Harry Behn, Howard Estabrook, Joseph Moncure March; **C:** Elmer Dyer, Harry Perry, E. Burton Steene, Dewey Wrigley, Gaetano Antonio "Tony" Gaudio; **M:** Hugo Riesenfeld.

Hell's Angels Forever 1983 (R) A revealing ride into the world of honor, violence, and undying passion for motorcycles on the road. Documentary was filmed with cooperation of the Angels. Features appearances by Willie Nelson, Jerry Garcia, Bo Diddley, Kevin Keating and Johnny Paycheck. 93m/C VHS. Willie Nelson, Jerry Garcia, Johnny Paycheck, Bo Diddley; **D:** Richard Chase, Leon Gast, Kevin Keating.

Hell's Angels on Wheels 1967 Low-budget, two-wheeled Nicholson vehicle that casts him as a gas station attendant who joins up with the Angels for a cross country trip. Laszlo Kovacs is responsible for the photography. One of the better 1960s biker films. 95m/C VHS, DVD. Jack Nicholson, Adam Roarke, Sabrina Scharf, Jana Taylor, John Garwood, Sonny Barger, Bruno VeSota; **D:** Richard Rush; **W:** Robert W(right) Campbell; **C:** Laszlo Kovacs; **M:** Stu Phillips.

Hell's Angels '69 ½ 1969 (PG) Figuring on robbing Caesar's Palace for the thrill, two wealthy brothers plot a deadly game by infiltrating the ranks of the Hell's Angels. Upon figuring out that they've been duped, the Angels seek revenge. Average biker epic filmed in Nevada features Hell's Angels Oakland chapter. 97m/C VHS, DVD. Tom Stern, Jeremy Slate, Conny Van Dyke, G.D. Spradlin, Sonny Barger, Steve Sandor; **D:** Lee Madden; **W:** Tom Stern, Jeremy Slate, Don Tait; **C:** Paul Lohmann.

Hell's Belles ½ Girl in the Leather Suit 1969 Biker has his ride stolen by a rival, who leaves a chick as payment. The two team up to get revenge, chasing the gang across the Arizona desert and picking them off one by one. 96m/C VHS, DVD. Jeremy Slate, Adam Roarke, Jocelyn Lane, Angelique Pettyjohn, Michael Walker, William Lucking; **D:** Maury Dexter; **W:** James Gordon White, Robert McMullen; **M:** Les Baxter.

Hell's Brigade: The Final Assault woof! 1980 (PG) Low-budget, poorly acted film in which a small band of American commandos is ordered on the most dangerous and important mission of WWII. 99m/C VHS. Jack Palance, John Douglas, Carlos Estrada; **D:** Henry Mankiewik.

Hell's Gate Bad Karma 2001 (R) Dangerous and crazy Agnes Thatcher (Kensit) believes her shrink, Dr. Trey Cambell (Muldoon), is the reincarnation of Jack the Ripper and that she was his mistress. She escapes from the looney bin and decides to eliminate Trey's family so that they can be reunited. Standard psycho-horror fare with some nudity for titillation (no pun intended). 92m/C VHS, DVD. Patsy Kensit, Patrick Muldoon, Amy Locane, Damian Chapa; **D:** John Hough; **C:** Jacques Haitkin; **M:** Harry Manfredini. VIDEO

Hell's Headquarters 1932 A startling tale of murder and greed involving a hunt for a fortune in African ivory. 59m/B VHS, DVD. Jack Mulhall, Barbara Weeks, Frank Mayo; **D:** Andrew L. Stone.

Hell's Hinges 🎬🎬 1916 The next to last Hart western, typifying his good/bad cowboy character. This time he's a gunslinger who falls for the new preacher's sister, while the minister himself is led astray by a saloon gal. Perhaps Hart's best film. **65m/B VHS, DVD**, William S. Hart, Clara Williams, Jack Standing, Robert McKim; **D:** William S. Hart, Fed. Film Reg. '94.

Hell's House 🎬🎬 1932 After his mother dies, young lad Durkin goes to the city to live with relatives, gets mixed up with mol. Davis and her bootlegger boyfriend O'Brien, and is sent to a brutal reform school. Interesting primarily for early appearances by Davis and O'Brien (before he was typecast as the indefatigable good-guy). **80m/B VHS, DVD**, Junior Durkin, Pat O'Brien, Bette Davis, Frank "Junior" Coghlan, Charley Grapewin, Emma Dunn; **D:** Howard Higgin.

Hell's Kitchen NYC 🎬🎬½ 1997 **(R)** Ex-con Johnny Miles (Phifer) returns home to New York's notorious Hell's Kitchen after serving five years for a crime he did not commit. More or less a redemption drama, the film benefits from a good cast, especially Jolie as a revenge-driven street urchin and Arquette as her drugged-out mom. Despite the trappings of his "convict-into-street angel" role, Phifer exudes a quiet strength that never seems out of place, even when the action gets hysterical. Director Cinciripini scores points in creating scenes of drug addiction that invoke a kind of horrific absurdity, guiding seemingly over-the-top moments with a sure hand and a rock-solid purpose. It's in the more preachy aspects of his script where he loses control, the rising saccharine quotient potentially diluting the potency of his worthwhile message. **101m/C DVD**, Rosanna Arquette, William Forsythe, Michael Spiller, Angelina Jolie, Mekhi Phifer, Johnny Whitworth, Michael Nicolosi, Ryan Slater, Sharif Rashed; **D:** Tony Cincirpini; **W:** Tony Cincirpini; **C:** Derek Weselah; **M:** Tony Cincirpini, Nat Robinson.

Helltown 🎬🎬 *Born to the West* 1938 A western programmer based on Zane Grey's novel in which Wayne tracks down a cattle rustler. **60m/B VHS, DVD**, John Wayne, Marsha Hunt, Johnny Mack Brown, Monte Blue, Syd Saylor, John D. Patterson; **D:** Charles T. Barton; **W:** Stuart Anthony, Robert Yost; **C:** Devereaux Jennings.

The Hellstrom Chronicle 🎬🎬🎬 1971 **(G)** A powerful quasi-documentary about insects, their formidable capacity for survival, and the conjectured battle men will have with them in the future. **90m/C VHS**, Lawrence Pressman; **D:** Walon Green; **W:** David Seltzer, Lawrence Feature Doc.

Help! 🎬🎬🎬 *Eight Arms to Hold You* 1965 **(G)** Ringo's ruby ring is the object of a search by Arab cult members. Clang (McKern) and Ahme (Bron) who chase the Fab Four all over the globe in order to acquire the bauble. A crazy scientist (Spinelli) and his assistant (Kinnear) also want the ring and join in the pursuit. ♪Help!; You're Gonna Lose That Girl; You've Got to Hide Your Love Away; The Night Before; Another Girl; Ticket to Ride; I Need You. **90m/C VHS, DVD, GB** John Lennon, Paul McCartney, Ringo Starr, George Harrison, Leo McKern, Eleanor Bron, Victor Spinetti, Roy Kinnear, John Bluthal, Patrick Cargill, Alfie Bass, Warren Mitchel, Peter Copley, Bruce Lacey; **D:** Richard Lester; **M:** George Martin, Ken Thorne, John Lennon, Paul McCartney, Ringo Starr, George Harrison.

Help Wanted Female 🎬 1968 Jo, a prostitute with kung fu skills who likes to rob traveling salesmen, is in a quandary over her lesbian roommate's acid dropping friends, including Mr. Gregory, who has a penchant for murder. After recounting a previous trip in which he murdered an acquaintance, he succeeds in alienating his current companions, who must fight for their life to escape him. **77m/C VHS, DVD**, Anthony (Tony) Vorno, Inga Olsen; **D:** Harold Perkins.

Help Wanted: Male 🎬🎬½ 1982 When a magazine publisher discovers that her fiancé cannot have children, she looks for someone else who can do the job right. **97m/C VHS**, Suzanne Pleshette, Gil Gerard, Bert Convy, Dana Elcar, Harold Gould, Caren Kaye; **D:** William Wiard, TV.

Helter Skelter 🎬🎬½ 1976 The harrowing story of the murder of actress Sharon Tate and four others at the hands of Charles Manson and his psychotic "family." Based on the book by prosecutor Vincent Bugliosi, adapted by J.P. Miller. Features an outstanding performance by Railsback as Manson. **194m/C VHS, DVD**, Steve Railsback, Nancy Wolfe, George DiCenzo, Marilyn Burns, Christina Hart, Alan Oppenheimer, Cathy Paine; **D:** Tom Gries; **W:** James P(indney) Miller; **M:** Billy Goldenberg, TV.

Helter Skelter Murders woof! 1971 **(R)** An independently made version of the Charles Manson story, with sequences filmed at Spawn Ranch. Includes Manson's own recording of his songs "Mechanical Man" and "Garbage Dump" on the soundtrack. **83m/B VHS, DVD**, Brian Klinkner, Debbie Duff, Phyllis Estes; **D:** Frank Howard. **W:** J.J. Wilkie, Duke Howze; **C:** Frank Howard.

The Henderson Monster 🎬🎬½ 1980 Experiments of a genetic scientist are questioned by a community and its mayor. A potentially controversial drama turns into typical romantic fluff. **105m/C VHS, DVD**, Jason Miller, Christine Lahti, Stephen Collins, David Spielberg, Nehemiah Persoff, Larry Gates; **D:** Waris Hussein, TV.

Hendrix 🎬🎬½ 2000 **(R)** Biopic of legendary rock guitarist Jimi Hendrix (Harris) from his first teenaged band to his drug overdose death in 1970. There are some fine re-creations of such notable Hendrix performances at the 1967 Monterey Pop Festival and Woodstock. **103m/C VHS, DVD**, Wood Harris, Vivica A. Fox, Billy Zane, Christian Potenza, Dorian Harewood, Kris Holden-Ried, Christopher Ralph, Michie Mee; **D:** Leon Ichaso; **W:** Art Washington, Hal Roberts, Butch Stein; **C:** Claudio Chea **M:** Daniel Licht. C.ABLE.

Hennessy 🎬🎬½ 1975 **(PG)** An IRA man plots revenge on the Royal family and Parliament after his family is violently killed. Tense political drama, but slightly far-fetched. **103m/C VHS, DVD, GB** Rod Steiger, Lee Remick, Richard Johnson, Trevor Howard, Peter Egan, Eric Porter; **D:** Don Sharp; **W:** John Gay.

Henri Langlois: The Phantom of the Cinematheque 🎬🎬🎬 *Le Fantome D'henri Langlois* 2004 Documentary follows the career of the eccentric, longtime curator and film preservationist, co-founder of the Paris Cinematheque Francaise, founded by Langlois and Georges Franju in 1936. A fanatical collector, Langlois began by preserving silent films and hiding banned works from the Nazis during the occupation of Paris. Later, Langlois offered screenings of his collection, which heavily influenced such budding directors as Godard and Truffaut. Langlois also had a fractious relationship with the French government, who provided a subsidy and fired him for Richard; French with English subtitles. **128m/B DVD**, **D:** Jacques Richard; **C:** Jerome Blumberg; **M:** Nicolas Baby, Liam Farell.

Henry IV 🎬🎬½ 1985 The adaptation of the Luigi Pirandello farce about a modern-day recluse who shields himself from the horrors of the real world by pretending to be mad and acting out the fantasy of being the medieval German emperor Henry IV. In Italian with English subtitles. **94m/C VHS, DVD.** /T Marcello Mastroianni, Claudia Cardinale, Leopoldo Trieste, Paolo Bonacelli, Luciano Bartoli, Latou Chardons; **D:** Marco Bellocchio; **W:** Marco Bellocchio, Tonino Guerra, Astor Piazzolla.

Henry V 🎬🎬🎬 1944 Classic, epic adaptation of the Shakespeare play, and Olivier's first and most successful directorial effort, dealing with the medieval British monarch that defeated the French at Agincourt. Distinguished by Olivier's brilliant formal experiment of beginning the drama as a 16th Century performance of the play in the Globe Theatre, and having the stage eventually transform into realistic historical settings of storybook color. Filmed at the height of WWII suffering in Britain (and meant as a parallel to the British fighting the Nazis), the film was not released in the U.S. until 1946. **136m/C VHS, DVD, GB** Laurence Olivier, Robert Newton, Leslie Banks, Esmond Knight, Renee Asherson, Leo Genn, George Robey, Ernest Thesiger, Felix Aymer, Ralph Truman, Harcourt Williams, Max Adrian, Valentine Dyall, Russell Thorndike, Roy Emerton, Robert Helpmann, Freda Jackson, Griffith Jones, John Laurie, Niall MacGinnis, Michael Shepley; **D:** Laurence Olivier; **W:** Alan Dent, Dallas Bower, Laurence Olivier; **C:** Robert Krasker; **M:** William Walton, Natl. Bd. of Review '46; N.Y. Film Critics '46. Actor (Olivier).

Henry V 🎬🎬🎬 1989 Stirring, expansive retelling of Shakespeare's drama about the warrior-king of England, Branagh (who also adapted the screenplay). Wonderful supporting cast includes some of Britain's finest actors. **138m/C VHS, DVD, GB** Kenneth Branagh, Derek Jacobi, Brian Blessed, Alec McGowen, Ian Holm, Richard Briers, Robert Stephens, Robbie Coltrane, Christian Bale, Judi Dench, Paul Scofield, Michael Maloney, Emma Thompson, Patrick Doyle, Richard Clifford, Charles Kay, Geraldine McEwan, Christopher Ravenscroft, John Sessions, Simon Shepherd, Jay Villiers, Danny (Daniel) Webb; **D:** Kenneth Branagh; **W:** Kenneth Branagh; **C:** Kenneth Mac millan; **M:** Patrick Doyle, Oscars '89: Costume Des.; British Acad. '89; Director (Branagh); Natl. Bd. of Review '89; Director (Branagh).

Henry & June 🎬🎬🎬½ 1990 **(NC-17)** Based on the diaries of writer Anais Nin which chronicled her triangular relationship with author Henry Miller and his wife June, a relationship that provided the erotic backdrop to Miller's "Tropic of Capricorn." Set in Paris in the early '30s, the setting moves between the impecunious expatriate's cheap room on the Left bank—filled with artists, circus performers, prostitutes, and gypsies—to the conservative, well-appointed home of Nin and her husband. Captures the heady atmosphere of Miller's gay Paris; no one plays an American better than Ward (who replaced Alec Baldwin). Notable for having prompted the creation of an NC-17 rating. **136m/C VHS, DVD**, Fred Ward, Uma Thurman, Maria De Medeiros, Richard E. Grant, Kevin Spacey; **D:** Philip Kaufman; **W:** Phillip Kaufman; **C:** Philippe Rousselot; **M:** Mark Adler.

Henry & Verlin 🎬🎬 1994 Verlin (Macintosh) is a nine-year-old who doesn't talk. He lives in rural Ontario (during the Depression) with his overprotective mother Minnie (Beatty) and indifferent father Ferris (Joy), as well as Ferris' childlike brother Henry (Farmer) who befriends Verlin. The misfit duo develop a strong bond that includes disabled retired prostitute Mabel (Kidder)—much to the resentment of some of the less-enlightened townsfolk. There's some melodramatic excess. **87m/C VHS, DVD, CA** Gary Farmer, Keegan Macintosh, Nancy Beatty, Robert Joy, Margot Kidder, Eric Peterson; **D:** Gary Ledbetter, **M:** Georges Delerue.

Henry Fool 🎬🎬🎬 1998 **(R)** Simon Grim (Urbaniak) is a socially inept garbage man treated with contempt by his depressed mother (Porter) and caustic sister (Posey). Henry Fool (Ryan), an alcoholic homeless man, claims to be a great writer and sees a bit of poet in Simon as well. After he moves Henry into the family's basement, Simon takes his first steps as a poet and Henry takes his ties with both of the women. Simon turns out to be a natural artist, and writes a poem that profoundly moves and/or shocks the public and creates a controversy on the Internet. As Simon is courted by publishers, he champions Henry's unread work as well. Their respective fortunes rise and fall as Henry's work is unveiled. Director Hartley pulls very different elements such as the artistry of Samuel Beckett and the myth of Faust together to create a bizarre urban fable. **138m/C VHS, DVD**, Thomas Jay Ryan, James Urbaniak, Parker Posey, Maria Porter, Kevin Corrigan, James Saito; **D:** Hal Hartley; **W:** Hal Hartley; **C:** Michael Spiller.

Henry Hill 🎬🎬 2000 Misfit Henry (Harold) was a childhood musical prodigy who left his rural Maine home for New York City. But his extreme stage fright means his dreams of becoming a concert violinist are remote and a failed suicide attempt finds Henry returning to his loony family who run a gas station/diner. To Henry's rescue is Cynthie (Kelly), a troubled loner in a red car who takes an interest in Henry and decides to hang around until she can persuade him to go back to New York with her and try again. The film is straight-forward and uncommon—showing the high cost of war—showing the high doubts, and subterfuge that underlie conflicts. Marvelous film-directorial debut for Branagh. **85m/C VHS, DVD**, Jamie Harold, Moira Kelly, Susan Blommaert, John Griesemer, Eden Riegel; **D:** David G. Kantar; **W:** David G. Kantar; **C:** Luke Eder; **M:** Dave Eggar.

Henry: Portrait of a Serial Killer 🎬🎬🎬🎬 1990 **(R)** Based on the horrific life and times of serial killer Henry Lee Lucas, this film has received wide praise for its straight-forward and uncommon, promising look into the minds of madmen. The film follows ex-cons Henry (Rooker) and his roommate Otis (Towles) as they set out on mindless murder spree (one of which they videotape). Extremely disturbing and graphic film. Unwary viewers should be warned of the grisly scenes and use their own discretion when viewing this otherwise genuinely moving film. **90m/C VHS, DVD**, Michael Rooker, Tom Towles, Tracy Arnold, David Katz; **D:** John McNaughton; **W:** John McNaughton, Richard Fire; **C:** Charlie Lieberman; **M:** Robert F. McNaughton.

Henry: Portrait of a Serial Killer 2: Mask of Sanity 🎬🎬½ *Henry 2: Portrait of a Serial Killer* 1996 **(R)** Michael Rooker gave a chilling performance as serial killer Henry in part 1 but Giuntoli is merely dull. A sullen drifter, Henry manages to get a job and fellow worker Kai (Komenich) invites him to crash at his place. Turns out Kai is a part-time arsonist for hire and Henry helps him out—also, in introducing Kai to the pleasures of casual murder. The gore is actually limited to a few bloody scenes (usually more is heard than shown) but the whole project is boring. **84m/C VHS, DVD**, Neil Giuntoli, Rich Komenich, Kate Walsh, Carri Levinson, Penelope Milford; **D:** Chuck Parello; **W:** Chuck Parello; **C:** Michael Kohnhurst; **M:** Robert F. McNaughton.

Her Alibi 🎬🎬 1988 **(PG)** When successful murder-mystery novelist Phil Blackwood runs out of ideas for good books, he seeks inspiration in the criminal courtroom. There he discovers a beautiful Romanian immigrant named Nina who is accused of murder. He goes to see her in jail and offers to provide her with an alibi. Narrated by Blackwood in the tone of one of his thriller novels. Uneven comedy, with appealing cast and arbitrary plot. **95m/C VHS**, Tom Selleck, Paulina Porizkova, William Daniels, James Farentino, Hurd Hatfield, Patrick Wayne, Tess Harper, Joan Copeland; **D:** Bruce Beresford; **W:** Charlie Peters; **C:** Freddie Francis; **M:** Georges Delerue.

Her and She and Him 🎬🎬½ *The Right Man* 1940 Mixed-up romance with Fellows and Wells as sisters. Lincoln their cousin, and Ladd her fiance. The sisters fall for Evans and use Ladd in their schemes, causing him to believe Evans is actually after Linden. Eventually, everyone...

Her First Romance 🎬🎬 1969 Young Swedish beauty Greta arrives in Paris with only her guitar Penniless, she takes up with another woman but soon feels she's only a sexual prisoner. So Greta seduces a young painter who is having an obsessive affair with a gay artist. Dubbed into English. **90m/C VHS**, Astrid Frank, Yves Vincent; **D:** Max Pecas; **C:** Robert Lefebvre.

pairs up properly. **77m/B VHS.** Edith Fellows, Julie Bishop, Alan Ladd, Judith Linden, Wilbur Evans, Roger Daniel; **D:** Edward Dmytryk; **W:** Adele Comandini.

Her Husband's Affairs ⅃ 1947
Tone is an advertising wonder and Ball is his loving wife who always gets credit for his work. Tone does the advertising for an inventor who is searching for the perfect embalming fluid in this rather lifeless comedy. **83m/B VHS.** Lucille Ball, Franchot Tone, Edward Everett Horton, Gene Lockhart, Larry Parks; **D:** S. Sylvan Simon; **M:** George Duning.

Her Life as a Man ⅃½ 1983 A female reporter is refused a job as a sportswriter because of her gender. She makes herself up as a man, gets the job, and creates havoc when she has to deal with lustful women on the job. **93m/C VHS.** Robyn Douglass, Joan Collins, Robert Culp, Marc Singer, Laraine Newman; **D:** Robert Ellis Miller. **TV**

Her Majesty ⅃⅃ 2001 Young New Zealander Elizabeth Wakefield (Andrews) can't believe it when, in 1953, she learns that her hero, Queen Elizabeth II, will be visiting her hometown during a commonwealth tour. Elizabeth is friends with Hira Mata (Haughton), an aged Maori whose shack is considered an eyesore by town busybody Virginia Hobson (Holloway). When Virginia wants to clean up the community by displacing the old woman, things take a turn for the worst thanks to Elizabeth's spiteful brother (Elliott). **105m/C DVD.** *NZ* Vicky Haughton, Sally Andrews, Craig Elliott, Liddy Holloway, Annabel Leach; **D:** Mark J. Gordon; **W:** Mark J. Gordon; **C:** Stephen M. Katz; **M:** William Ross.

Her Name Is Cat ⅃⅃½ 1999 (R) Yet another Hong Kong hitwoman (Almen Wong) agrees to yet another "last job" before retiring...fans know the drill. Explosions and slo-mo shoot outs are plentiful, though the fight choreography isn't going to make anyone forget John Woo or Ringo Lam. **94m/C DVD.** *HK* Michael Wong, Almen Wong, Kent Masters King; **D:** Clarence (Fok) Ford; **W:** Wong Jing. **VIDEO**

Her Silent Sacrifice ⅃½ 1918 A silent melodrama about a French girl torn between material wealth and true love. **42m/B VHS.** R. Payton Gibb, Edmund Pardo, Blanche Craig, Benjamin Struckman, Alice Brady, Henry Clive; **D:** Edward Jose; **W:** Eve Unsell.

Herbie: Fully Loaded ⅃⅃ 2005 (G) On her way out of town, college graduate Maggie Peyton (Lohan) spends 75 bucks to free a '63 VW Beetle from the junkyard scrap pile and has boy pal Kevin (Long) restore it. Lo and behold, it's Herbie and he helps Maggie prove her driving skills to her NASCAR champ daddy (Keaton)—who's spent his energies on his not-as-talented son—as they race against pompous archenemy Trip Murphy (Dillon). The sassy Lohan, in her third Disney venture, picks up the speed for an uninspired-and-somewhat-CGI Herbie. Fifth feature in a series that, 15 years before, seemed out of gas. **101m/C DVD. UMD. US** Lindsay Lohan, Matt Dillon, Justin Long, Breckin Meyer, Michael Keaton, Jill Ritchie, Cheryl Hines, Thomas Lennon, Jimmi Simpson, Jeremy Roberts; **D:** Angela Robinson; **W:** Robert Ben Garant, Alfred Gough, Miles Millar, Thomas Lennon; **C:** Greg Gardiner; **M:** Mark Mothersbaugh.

Herbie Goes Bananas ⅃½ 1980 (G) While Herbie the VW is racing in Rio de Janeiro, he is bothered by the syndicate, a pickpocket, and a raging bull. The fourth and final entry in the Disney "Love Bug" movies, but Herbie later made his way to a TV series. **93m/C VHS. DVD.** Cloris Leachman, Charles Martin Smith, Harvey Korman, John Vernon, Alex Rocco, Richard Jaeckel, Fritz Feld; **D:** Vincent McEveety.

Herbie Goes to Monte Carlo ⅃ 1977 (G) While participating in a Paris-to-Monte-Carlo race, Herbie the VW takes a detour and falls in love with a Lancia. Third in the Disney "Love Bug" series. **104m/C VHS. DVD.** Dean Jones, Don Knotts, Julie Sommars, Roy Kinnear, Don McEveety; **W:** Arthur Alsberg.

Herbie Rides Again ⅃ ⅃ ½ 1974 (G) In this "Love Bug" sequel, Herbie comes to the aid of an elderly woman who is trying to stop a ruthless tycoon from

---

raising a skyscraper on her property. Humorous Disney fare. Two other sequels followed. **88m/C VHS. DVD.** Helen Hayes, Ken Berry, Stefanie Powers, John McIntire, Keenan Wynn; **D:** Robert Stevenson; **M:** George Bruns.

Hercules ⅃ ⅃ ½ *La Tatiche de Ercole* 1958 The one that started it all. Reeves is perfect as the mythical hero Hercules who encounters many dangerous situations while trying to win over his true love. Dubbed in English. **107m/C VHS. DVD.** *IT* Steve Reeves, Sylva Koscina, Fabrizio Mioni, Gianna Maria Canale, Arturo Dominici; **D:** Pietro Francisci; **C:** Mario Bava.

Hercules ⅃ 1983 (PG) Lackluster remake of 1957 original finds legendary muscle guy Hercules in the person of Ferrigno's Hulkster fighting against the evil King Minos for his own survival and the love of Cassiopeia, a rival king's daughter. **100m/C VHS.** *IT* Lou Ferrigno, Sybil Danning, William Berger, Brad Harris, Ingrid Anderson, Mindi Miller; **D:** Lewis (Luigi Cozzi) Coates; **W:** Lewis (Luigi Cozzi) Coates; **M:** Pino Donaggio. Golden Raspberries '83: Worst Support. Actress (Danning), Worst New Star (Ferrigno).

Hercules ⅃ ⅃ ½ 1997 (G) After a couple of animated downers, Disney's latest adventure goes for a happy heroic tone by taking on Greek myths. Baby Herc is the son of Zeus, who rules on Mt. Olympus. Hades, Lord of the Underworld, plans a takeover and learns that only Hercules' strength will stand in his way. Hades manages to kidnap the tyke and turn him mortal but when the teenaged Herc learns his true origins, he also discovers that if he proves himself to be a hero he can regain his immortality and return to Mt. Olympus. He's aided by his flying horse Pegasus, satyr-like trainer Phil, and smart gal Meg, while Hades has his less-than-bright minions Pain and Panic. Lots of fun and lots of merchandising (even the movie makes fun of the inevitable tie-ins). ♫The Gospel Truth; Go the Distance; One Last Hope; I Won't Say; Zero to Hero. **92m/C VHS. DVD.** Ron Clements; Bob Shaw, Donald McEnery, Irene Mecchi; **M:** Alan Menken, David Zippel; **V:** Tate Donovan, James Woods, Danny DeVito, Matt Frewer, Bob(cat) Goldthwait, Susan Egan, Rip Torn, Samantha Eggar, Paul Shaffer, Barbara Barrie, Hal Holbrook, Amanda Plummer, Carol(e) Shelley; **Nar:** Charlton Heston.

Hercules 2 ⅃ *The Adventures of Hercules* 1985 (PG) The muscle-bound demi-god returns to do battle with more evil foes amidst the same stunningly cheap special effects. **90m/C VHS. DVD.** *IT* Lou Ferrigno, Claudio Cassinelli, Milly Carlucci, Sonia Viviani, William Berger, Carlotta Green; **D:** Lewis (Luigi Cozzi) Coates; **M:** Pino Donaggio.

Hercules against the Moon Men ⅃ *Maciste la Regina di Samar* 1964 It's no holds barred for the mighty son of Zeus when evil moon men start killing of humans in a desperate bid to revive their dead queen. **88m/C VHS. DVD.** *IT* FR Alan Steel, Jany Clair, Anna Maria Polani, Nando Tamberlani, Delia D'Alberti, Jean-Pierre Honore; **D:** Giacomo Gentilomo; **W:** Arpad De Riso, Nino Scolaro; **C:** Oberdan Troiani; **M:** Carlo Franci.

Hercules and the Captive Women ⅃ *Hercules and the Haunted Women; Hercules and the Conquest of Atlantis; Ercole Alla Conquista di Atlantide* 1963 Hercules' son is kidnapped by the Queen of Atlantis, and the bare-chested warrior goes on an all-out rampage to save the boy. Directed by sometimes-lauded Cottafavi. **93m/C VHS.** *IT* Reg Park, Fay Spain, Ettore Manni; **D:** Vittorio Cottafavi.

Hercules and the Princess of Troy ⅃ ⅃ ½ 1965 Hercules is up to his pecs in trouble as he battles a hungry sea monster in order to save a beautiful maiden. Originally a pilot for a prospective TV series, and shot in English, not Italian, with Hercules played by erstwhile Tarzan Scott. Highlights are special effects and color cinematography. **50m/C VHS. DVD.** *IT* Gordon Scott, Diana Hyland, Paul Stevens, Everett Sloane; **D:** Albert Band; **W:** Larry Forrester; **C:** Enzo Barboni; **M:** Fred Steiner. **TV**

Hercules in New York ⅃½
Hercules: The Movie; Hercules Goes Bananas 1970 (G) Motion picture debut of Schwarzenegger (his voice is dubbed) as a Herculean mass of muscle sent by dad Zeus to Manhattan, where he behaves likes a geek out of water and eventually becomes a professional wrestling superstar. 250 pounds of stupid, lighthearted fun. **93m/C VHS. DVD.** Arnold Schwarzenegger, Arnold Stang, Deborah Loomis, James Karen, Ernest Graves, Taina Elg; **D:** Arthur Allan Seidelman; **W:** Aubrey Wisberg; **C:** Leo Lebowitz; **M:** John Balamos.

Hercules in the Haunted World ⅃ ⅃ ½ *Ercole al Centro Della Terra* 1964 Long before the days of 24-hour pharmacies, Hercules—played yet again by Reeves-clone Park—must journey to the depths of Hell in order to find a plant that will cure a poisoned princess. Better than most muscle operas, thanks to Bava. **91m/C VHS. DVD.** *IT* Reg Park, Leonora Ruffo, Christopher Lee, George Ardisson; **D:** Mario Bava.

Hercules, Prisoner of Evil ⅃ 1964 Spaghetti myth-opera in which Hercules battles a witch who is turning men into werewolves. Made for Italian TV by director Dawson (the nom-de-cinema of Antonio Margheriti). **90m/C VHS.** *IT* Reg Park; **D:** Anthony M. Dawson. **TV**

Hercules the Legendary Journeys, Vol. 1: And the Amazon Women ⅃ ⅃ ½ 1994 Half-man, half-god Hercules (Sorbo) and his friend Ioleus (Hurst) are summoned to a village to kill the beasts stealing livestock. Turns out those responsible are the village's women, who are mad at their husbands and have formed a band of Amazons, lead by Hippolyta (Downey), who happens to be working for Hercules' immortal enemy, the goddess Hera. Now it's up to Herc to convince Hippolyta that men and women can work together and outsmart Hera at the same time. **91m/C VHS. DVD.** Kevin Sorbo, Michael Hurst, Roma Downey, Anthony Quinn, Lucy Lawless; **D:** Bill W.L. Norton; **M:** Joseph LoDuca. **TV**

Hercules the Legendary Journeys, Vol. 2: The Lost Kingdom ⅃ ⅃ ½ 1994 Hera has hidden the kingdom of Troy and only a magic compass can point Hercules (Sorbo) in the right direction. He rescues a sacrificial virgin (O'Connor) and the duo manage to find the compass and get into Troy where she learns her father was once its king. Turns out dad sent his daughter away so he wouldn't have to sacrifice her to Hera and lost his kingdom instead. Now she wants her kingdom back and Hera still wants her sacrifice—especially if it's Hercules. **91m/C VHS. DVD.** Kevin Sorbo, Michael Hurst, Anthony Quinn, Renee O'Connor, Robert Trebor; **D:** Harley Cokliss; **M:** Joseph LoDuca. **TV**

Hercules the Legendary Journeys, Vol. 3: The Circle of Fire ⅃ ⅃ ½ 1994 Here's stolen fire from mankind, which is slowly freezing to death, keeping one eternal torch for herself. A villager named Deianeira (Kitaen) enlists Hercules (Sorbo) to search for Prometheus (Ferguson), the god of fire, but Hera's stolen his flame as well. When Herc finds the torch it's encircled in a ring of fire, which Hera knows can destroy Hercules' immortality. **92m/C VHS.** Kevin Sorbo, Michael Hurst, Anthony Quinn, Tawny Kitaen, Mark Ferguson; **D:** Doug Lefler; **M:** Joseph LoDuca. **TV**

Hercules the Legendary Journeys, Vol. 4: In the Underworld ⅃ ⅃ ½ 1994 Having married Deianeira (Kitaen), Herc's a pretty happy guy until a mysterious maiden, Iole, comes to him for help. Seems a deadly crack has opened up in the earth and is swallowing villagers. But Iole has actually been sent by Hera to destroy Hercules and when Deianeira discovers her treachery she goes to warn her husband. Only Hera manages to trick her into walking off a cliff and falling to her death. Hercules must go into the underworld to save the world from Hera but when he learns Deianeira's fate, he accepts an impossible challenge from Hades (Ferguson) to bring

---

his wife back to life. **91m/C VHS.** Kevin Sorbo, Michael Hurst, Anthony Quinn, Tawny Kitaen, Mark Ferguson; **D:** Bill W.L. Norton; **M:** Joseph LoDuca. **TV**

Hercules Unchained ⅃ ⅃ *Ercole e la Regina de Lidia* 1959 Sequel to "Hercules" finds superhero Reeves must use all his strength to save the city of Thebes and the woman he loves from the giant Antaeus. **101m/C VHS. DVD.** *IT* Steve Reeves, Sylva Koscina, Silvia Lopel, Primo Carnera; **D:** Pietro Francisci.

Hercules vs. the Sons of the Sun ⅃ ½ *Hercules Against the Sons of the Sun; Ercole Contro I Figli del Sole* 1964 Herc (Forest) battles the evil King of the Incas by building unstoppable fighting machines. Typical of the genre. **91m/C VHS. DVD.** *IT SP* Mark Forest, Giuliano Gemma, Riccardo Valle, Andrea Scotti, Anna Maria Pace, Angela Rhu, Giulio Donnini; **D:** Osvaldo Civirani; **W:** Osvaldo Civirani; **C:** Osvaldo Civirani, Julio Ortas; **M:** Coriolano Gori.

Here and Elsewhere ⅃ ⅃ ½ *Ici et Ailleurs* 1976 Godard, Gorin, and Mieville contrast the story of a French family with a look at the Palestine revolution as seen through the media of television, books, and pictures. The film was originally titled "Until Victory," and was commissioned by the Palestinians to examine life in the Palestinian camps. After the defeat of the Palestinian army in the Six Day War, Godard and his cohorts transformed the film with their French family ("Here") and their impressions of Palestine ("Elsewhere"). French with subtitles. **60m/C VHS.** *FR* Anne-Marie Mieville; **D:** Jean-Pierre Gorin, Jean-Luc Godard; **W:** Jean-Pierre Gorin, Jean-Luc Godard.

Here Come the Co-Eds ⅃ ⅃ ½ 1945 Bud & Lou are the caretakers of an all-girl college which is about to go bankrupt unless the boys can find a way to pay off the mortgage. And come to the rescue they do, including Bud getting into the wrestling ring with the "Masked Marvel" (Chaney Jr. as the villain). There's also a classic silent scene with Lou served a bowl of oyster stew containing a live oyster, which promptly grabs his tie, bites his fingers, and squirts in his face. **90m/B VHS. DVD.** Bud Abbott, Lou Costello, Lon Chaney Jr., Peggy Ryan, Martha O'Driscoll, June Vincent, Donald Cook, Charles Dingle; **D:** Jean Yarbrough; **W:** Arthur T. Horman, John Grant.

Here Come the Girls ⅃ ½ 1953 An unfunny musical-comedy about a chorus boy (Hope) fired for incompetence and then rehired to set a trap when the new singer (Martin) is stalked by a killer. Weak script, weak songs. ♫Girls Are Here To Stay; Never So Beautiful; You Got Class; Desire; When You Lose Someone; Ali Baba Be My Baby; Heavenly Days; See the Circus; Peace. **100m/C VHS.** Bob Hope, Tony Martin, Arlene Dahl, Rosemary Clooney, Millard Mitchell, William Demarest, Fred Clark, Robert Strauss; **D:** Claude Binyon; **W:** Hal Kanter.

Here Come the Littles: The Movie ⅃ ½ 1985 A 12-year-old boy finds many new adventures when he meets The Littles—tiny folks who reside within the walls of people's houses. Adapted from the books and TV series. **76m/C VHS. D:** Bernard Deyries.

Here Come the Marines ⅃ ⅃ *Tell It To the Marines* 1952 The Bowery Boys accidentally join the marines and wind up breaking up a gambling ring. **66m/B VHS.** Leo Gorcey, Huntz Hall, Tim Ryan; **D:** William Beaudine.

Here Come the Nelsons ⅃ ⅃ ½ 1952 In between the radio show, "The Adventures of Ozzie and Harriet," and the TV series came this feature film. Ad man Ozzie is trying to develop a campaign for a women's wear company while the town's centennial celebration is causing problems on the homefront. Seems Harriet's houseguest for the festivities is Rock Hudson! **76m/B VHS.** Ozzie Nelson, Harriet Hilliard Nelson, David Nelson, Ricky Nelson, Rock Hudson, Barbara Lawrence, Sheldon Leonard, Jim Backus; **D:** Fred de Cordova; **W:** Don Nelson, Ozzie Nelson.

Here Come the Waves 🐾🐾🐾 1945 Easy-going wartime musical finds Der Bingle as a singing idol drafted into the Navy, assigned to direct WAVE shows. The crooner meets identical twins (both played by Hutton) and falls hard. Only problem: is he can't tell the gals apart—and one twin can't stand him. Amusing romantic complications mix well with some spoofing of a star's life. *Ac-cent-tchu-ate the Positive; I Promise You; Let's Take the Long Way Home; That Old Black Magic; There's a Fellow Waiting in Poughkeepsie; Here Come the Waves; My Mama Thinks I'm a Star; Join the Navy; Sorry. **96m/C VHS** **C:** Bing Crosby, Betty Hutton, Sonny Tufts, Ann Doran, Noel Nelly, Mae Clarke, Gwen Crawford, Catherine Craig; **D:** Mark Sandrich; **W:** Zion Myers.

Here Comes Cookie 🐾🐾 1935 Amusing farce finds Gracie (Allen) the daughter of wealthy Harrison Allen (Barbier), who's afraid of the fortune hunters eyeing other daughter Phyllis (Furness). So he temporarily turns over the family fortune to Gracie, who promptly turns their Park Avenue mansion into a home for down-on-their-luck vaudevillians. Lots of specialty acts and Burns is around as straight man. **65m/B VHS, DVD, Gracie Allen, George Barbier, Betty Furness; D:** Norman Z. McLeod; **W:** Don Hartman, Sam Mintz. **C:** Gilbert Warrenton.

Here Comes Kelly 🐾½ 1943 Controlling his temper and hanging on to his job is more than our hero can handle. **65m/C VHS, Eddie Quillan, Joan Woodbury, Maxie Rosenbloom. D:** William Beaudine.

Here Comes Mr. Jordan 🐾🐾🐾 1941 Montgomery is the young prizefighter killed in a plane crash because of a mix-up in heaven. He returns to life in the body of a soon-to-be murdered millionaire. Rains is the indulgent and advising guardian angel. A lovely fantasy/romance remade in 1978 as "Heaven Can Wait." **94m/B VHS, DVD, Robert Montgomery, Claude Rains, James Gleason, Evelyn Keyes, Edward Everett Horton, Rita Johnson, John Emery; D:** Alexander Hall; **W:** Sidney Buchman, Seton I. Miller; **M:** Frederick Hollander. **Oscars '41:** Screenplay, Story.

Here Comes Santa Claus 🐾½ 1984 A young boy and girl travel to the North Pole to deliver a very special wish to Santa Claus. **78m/C VHS, DVD; D:** Christian Gion.

Here Comes the Groom 🐾🐾 1951 Late, state Capra-corn, involving a rogue journalist who tries to keep his girlfriend from marrying a millionaire by becoming a charity worker. Includes a number of cameos. *In the Cool, Cool, Cool of the Evening; Bonne Nuit, Good Night; Mis-ter Cristofo; Your Own Little House. **114m/B VHS, DVD, Bing Crosby, Jane Wyman, Franchot Tone, Alexis Smith, James Barton, Connie Gilchrist, Robert Keith, Anna Maria Alberghetti, Charles Halton; Cameos:** Dorothy Lamour, Phil Harris, Louis Armstrong; **D:** Frank Capra. **Oscars '51:** Song ("In the Cool, Cool, Cool of the Evening").

Here is My Heart 🐾🐾 1934 It's a classic plot: someone pretends to be someone they're not, all for love, in this musical comedy a famous (and wealthy) singer pretends to be a waiter, all to position himself nearer to the woman of his dreams. Only she's a European princess. Will she even notice him? **77m/B VHS, Bing Crosby, Kitty Carlise Hart, Roland Young, Alison Skipworth, Reginald Owen, William Frawley; D:** Frank Tuttle; **W:** Alfred Savoir; **M:** Leo Robin, Ralph Rainger.

Here on Earth 🐾🐾 2000 (PG-13) Predictable teary teen romantic drama with a very pretty cast doing what they can with one-note roles. Smalltown beauty Samantha (Sobieski) waits tables at the family diner and hangs out with long-time boyfriend Jasper (Hartnett), who's a bit snotty. Kelley (Klein). Their rivalry causes a disaster for Sam and her family that the boys must rectify, even as Kelley and Sam turn to each other. Oh yeah, and then Sam's recurring knee problems turn out to be cancer and everyone has to pull together. **96m/C VHS, DVD, Chris Klein, Leelee Sobieski, Josh Hartnett, Michael Rooker, Annie Corley, Bruce Greenwood, Annette O'Toole, Stuart Wilson, Tac Fitzgerald; D:** Mark Piznarski; **W:** Michael Seitzman; **C:** Michael D. O'Shea; **M:** Andrea Morricone.

Here We Go Again! 🐾🐾 1942 Fibber McGee and Molly are planning a cross-country trip for their 20th anniversary celebration, but complications abound. Based on the popular NBC radio series. **76m/B VHS, DVD, Marian Jordan, Jim Jordan, Harold (Hal) Peary, Gale Gordon, Edgar Bergen, Ray Noble. D:** Allan Dwan.

Heritage of the Desert 🐾½ 1933 One of the earlier westerns based on the rugged Scott. **62m/B VHS, DVD, Randolph Scott, Sally Blane, Guinn "Big Boy" Williams; D:** Henry Hathaway.

The Hero 🐾½ 1992 (PG-13) Interesting twist on Cinderella fable and modern media satire has TV reporter Davis looking for the man who saved her life, expecting a genuine hero, and accepting without question the one who fits her vision. Critically considered disappointing, in fact, and Davis is fetching as the vulnerable media person. Strong language and cark edges may keep away some of the kids, but otherwise this is a fine fable. **116m/C VHS, DVD, Geena Davis, Dustin Hoffman, Andy Garcia, Joan Cusack, Kevin J. O'Connor, Chevy Chase, Maury Chaykin, Stephen Tobolowsky, Christian Clemenson, Tom Arnold, Warren Bering-er, Susie Cusack, James Madio, Richard Riehle, Don Yesso, Darrell Larson; D:** Stephen Frears. **W:** David Peoples; **C:** Oliver Stapleton; **M:** George Fenton.

Hero 🐾🐾🐾 Ying Xiong 2003 (PG-13) Visually stunning movie combines martial arts, tragedy, historical drama, and philosophy into one complex, satisfying epic. Set in 3rd century B.C. China, the story revolves around swordsman Nameless (Li), who hunts down three assassins for the ruthless King (Chen), who used brutal methods to bring the various states of China under his leadership. Told mostly in flashback, Nameless unveils his encounters with the warriors (Leung, Cheung, and Yen) to the King, but all is not as it seems, and in the end Nameless faces a choice of what his place in the King's newly unified China should be. Features revolutionary fight sequences (each segment has its own color theme) and beautiful martial arts sequences, but is hindered by inconsistent performances. The most expensive Chinese production ever made at $30 million, it has been criticized for appearing to endorse the government's stance on a unified China. **98m/C DVD, Blu-ray Disc, UMD, HK DVD, Jet Li, Maggie Cheung, Donnie Yen, Zhang Ziyi, Tony Leung Chiu-Wai, Daoming Chen; D:** Yimou Zhang; **W:** Yimou Zhang, Feng Li, Bin Wang; **C:** Christopher Doyle; **M:** Tan Dun.

Hero and the Terror 🐾½ 1988 (R) Perennial karate guy Norris plays a sensitive policeman who conquers his fear of a not-so-sensitive maniac who's trying to kill him. Plenty of action and a cheesy subplot to boot. **96m/C VHS, DVD, Chuck Norris, Brynn Thayer, Steve James, Jack O'Halloran, Ron O'Neal, Billy Drago; D:** William (Bill) Tannen; **W:** Michael Blodgett; **C:** Eric Van Haren Noman; **M:** David Michael Frank.

A Hero Ain't Nothin' but a Sandwich 🐾½ 1978 (PG) A young urban black teenager gets involved in drugs and is eventually saved from ruin. Slow-moving, over-directed and talky. However, Scott turns in a fine performance. Based on Alice Childress' novel. **107m/C VHS, DVD, Cicely Tyson, Paul Winfield, Larry B. Scott, Helen Martin, Glynn Turman, David Groh; D:** Ralph Nelson.

Heroes in Blue 🐾🐾 1939 Two brothers join the police force, but one goes astray and hooks up with gangsters. Plenty of action distracts from the clichéd story. **60m/B VHS, Dick Purcell, Charles Quigley, Bernadene Hayes, Edward (Ed Kean, Keene) Keane. D:** William Watson.

Heroes Die Young 🐾🐾 1960 A cheap independent feature depicting an American command mission with orders to sabotage German oil fields during WWII. **75m/B VHS, Erika Peters, Scott Borland, Robert Getz, James Strother; D:** Gerald Shepard; **W:** Gerald Shepard; **C:** Glen R. Smith; **M:** Al Pellegrini.

Heroes for Sale 🐾🐾🐾 1933 Fascinating melodrama about a WWI veteran who returns home and manages to survive one disaster after another. Barthelmess is great in his performance as an American Everyman who must deal with everything from morphine addiction to finding work during the Depression. Fest-paced, patriotic film is helped by ambitious script and the expert direction of Wellman. **72m/B VHS, Richard Barthelmess, Loretta Young, Aline MacMahon, Robert Barrat, Grant Mitchell, Douglass Dumbrille, Charley Grapewin, Ward Bond; D:** William A. Wellman; **W:** Robert Lord, Wilson Mizner.

Heroes in Hell 🐾½ Eroi All'inferno 1973 Escaped WWII POW joins the Allied underground in an espionage conspiracy against the Third Reich by kidnapping a

---

Hero at Large 🐾🐾½ 1980 (PG) An unemployed actor foils a robbery while dressed in a promotional "Captain Avenger" suit, and instant celebrity follows. Lightweight, yet enjoyable. **98m/C VHS, DVD, John Ritter, Anne Archer, Bert Convy, Kevin McCarthy, Kevin Bacon; D:** Martin Davidson; **W:** A.J. Carothers.

Hero Bunker 🐾🐾 1971 Hero trunk about a platoon of heroic Greek soldiers who attempt, at the expense of their personal longevity, to defend an important bunker from enemy invasion. **93m/C VHS, Giannis Vogllis, Mania Xenia; D:** George Andrews.

Hero of Rome 🐾½ 1963 Rome has many who could be called "hero," but one stands, biceps and pecs above the rest. **90m/C VHS, DVD, Rancoph Antonini, Gordon Scott, Gabriella Pallotta, Antonino Visonti; D:** Giorgio Feroni; **W:** Alberta Montani. **C:** Augusto Tiezzi; **M:** Angelo Francesco Lavagni-no.

Hero of the Year 🐾½ 1985 The characters from Falk's "Top Dog" return in this story of a Polish TV personality who loses his job and is forced to face unemployment and job-seeking. **115m/C VHS, Pl. Jerzy Stuhr, Mieczyslaw Franaszek, Piotr Machalica, Marian Opania; D:** Feliks Falk; **W:** Feliks Falk; **C:** Witold Adamek; **M:** Jan Pawluskiewicz.

Hero Wanted 🐾🐾 2008 (R) Garbage collector Liam Case (Gooding) becomes a local hero when he rescues a young girl from a burning car, but that one moment doesn't bring the changes to his life Liam anticipates. He happens to be at the bank, flirting with a pretty teller, when a heist is attempted. Liam and the teller are among the shooting victims and Liam's on the case gets suspicious about Liam's revenge. But the detective (Licitra) true to the life as the hero gets to be at the bank, and a few plot twists. Lots of flashbacks and a few plot twists. **95m/C DVD, Cuba Gooding Jr., Ray Liotta, Christa Campbell, Jean Smart, Norman Reedus, Tommy Flanagan, Kim Coates, Ben Cross; D:** Chad Law; **W:** Evan Law, Evan Law; **C:** Larry Blanford; **M:** Kenneth Burgomaster. VIDEO

Herod the Great 🐾 1960 Biblical epic of the downfall of Herod, the ruler of ancient Judea. Scantily clad women abound. Dubbed. **93m/C VHS, IT Edmund Purcom, Sandra Milo, Alberto Lupo; D:** Arnaldo Genoi-ro.

Heroes 🐾🐾 1977 (PG) An institutionalized Vietnam vet (Winkler) escapes, hoping to establish a worm farm which will support all his crazy buddies. On the way to the home of a friend he hopes will help him, he encounters Field. Funny situations don't always mix with serious underlying themes of mental illness and post-war adjustment. **97m/C VHS, Henry Winkler, Sally Field, Harrison Ford; D:** Jeremy Paul Kagan; **W:** James (Jim) Carabatsos; **M:** Jack Nitzsche.

Heroes of the Hills 🐾½ 1938 The Three Mesquiteers back up a plan that allows trusted prisoners to work for neighboring ranchers. Part of "The Three Mesquiteers" series. **54m/B VHS, Robert "Bob" Livingston, Ray Corrigan, Max Terhune, Priscilla Lawson, Leroy Mason, James Eagles, Roy Barcroft, Carleton Young; D:** George Sherman; **W:** Betty Burbridge; **C:** Reggie Lanning; **M:** Cy Feuer.

Heroes Shed No Tears 🐾 The Sunset Warrior 1986 Chinese mercenaries are hired by the Thai government to capture a drug lord from the Golden Triangle. Cantonese with subtitles. **93m/C VHS, DVD, HK Eddy Ko, Ching-Ying Lam, Chen Yue Sang, Kuo Sheng; D:** John Woo.

Heroes Stand Alone 🐾 1989 (R) When a U.S. spy plane is downed in Central America, a special force is sent to rescue the crew. Another "Rambo" rip-off. **84m/C VHS, Bradford Dillman, Chad Everett, Wayne Grace, Rick Dean; D:** Mark Griffiths; **W:** Thomas McKelvey, Cleaver.

Heroes Three 🐾🐾 1984 When his crewmate is murdered while on leave in the Far East, a Navy officer enlists the aid of a Chinese detective to track down the killer. **90m/C VHS, Rowena Cortes, Mike Kelly, Laurens C. Postma, Lawrence Tan; D:** S.H. Lau.

The Heroic Trio 🐾🐾½ Dong Fang San Xia 1993 Three superheroines battle the evil Underground to prevent him from stealing any more human babies. Lots of martial arts and supernatural action. Chinese with subtitles or dubbed. **87m/C VHS, DVD, HK Damian Lau, Michele Yeoh, Maggie Cheung, Anita (Yim-Fong) Mui, Anthony Wong; D:** Ching Siu Tung; **W:** Sandy Shaw; **C:** Hang-Seng Poon, Tom Lau; **M:** William Hu.

The Heroes of Desert Storm 🐾🐾 1991 The human spirit of the people who fought in the high-tech Persian Gulf War is captured in this film that also features real war footage from ABC News. **93m/C VHS, Daniel Baldwin, Angela Bassett, Marshall Bell, Michael Alan Brooks, William Bumiller, Michael Champion, Maria Isabel Diaz; D:** Don Ohlmeyer; **W:** Lionel Chetwynd.

The Heroes of Telemark 🐾🐾½ 1965 In 1942, Norway is under Nazi occupation and Nazi scientists are dangerously close to producing an essential element for making an atomic bomb in a secret factory. Uncer-ground leader Knut Straud (Harris) enlists the help of Norwegian scientist Rolf Pedersen (Douglas) and a group of saboteurs to destroy the factory. But their raid only provides a short delay and our heroes must now prevent shipment of the components from ever reaching Germany. Filmed on location in Norway, with former members of the underground serving as technical advisors for director Mann. **130m/C VHS, DVD, GB Richard Harris, Kirk Douglas, Michael Redgrave, Ulla Jacobsson, David Weston, Sebastian Breaks, Alan Howard, Roy Dotrice, Patrick Jordan, Anton Diffring, Eric Porter, Ralph Michael; D:** Anthony Mann; **W:** Ben Barzman; **C:** Robert Krasker; **M:** Malcolm Arnold.

Heroes of the Alamo 🐾½ 1937 Remember the Alamo...but forget this movie. Dull, threadbare dramatization of the battle that was scorned even back in '37. **75m/B VHS, DVD, Rex Lease, Lane Chandler, Roger Williams, Earle Hodgins, Julian Rivero; D:** Harry Fraser.

Heroes of the Heart 🐾🐾½ 1994 Residents of a West Virginia trailer park are devastated when their homes are destroyed in a flood. But then Basquette claims she was visited by God, who's directed her to bring the poor community together so that each can be granted their most secret wish. Nicely eccentric characters, serious theme with some whimsical touches, and a country-music soundtrack. **102m/C VHS, DVD, Lena Basquette, Larry Groce, Dusty Rhodes, Webb Wilder, John McIntira, Jennifer Gurney, Johnny Paycheck; D:** Daniel Boyd; **W:** Daniel Boyd.

German general. **90m/C VHS. IT Klaus Kinski, Ettore Manni; D:** Joe D'Amato, Joe D'Amato; **C:** Joe D'Amato.

He's Just Not That Into You

2008 Based on the relationship book by Greg Behrendt and Liz Tuccillo. It's a series of interconnecting stories about (mis)reading human behavior, including Barrymore as a single confused by dating. Connelly in a stale marriage to a cheating Cooper, Goodwin interested in Connelly (who doesn't know she exists), and other romantic travails. Not yet reviewed. **?m/C** Drew Barrymore, Jennifer Aniston, Kevin Connolly, Jennifer Connelly, Bradley Cooper, Ginnifer Goodwin, Justin Long, Scarlett Johansson, Ben Affleck, Wilson Cruz, Kris Kristofferson; **D:** Ken Kwapis; **W:** Abby Kohn, Marc Silverstein; **C:** John Bailey; **M:** Cliff Eidelman.

He's My Girl ✓✓½ **1987** (PG-13)

When a rock singer wins a trip for two to Hollywood, he convinces his agent to dress up as a woman so they can use the free tickets. **104m/C VHS.** David Hallyday, T.K. Carter, Misha McK, Jennifer Tilly; **D:** Gabrielle Beaumont; **W:** Terence H. Winkless, Taylor Ames, Charles F. Bohl; **C:** Peter Lyons Collister.

Hester Street ✓✓✓½ **1975** Set at

the turn of the century, the film tells the story of a young Jewish immigrant who ventures to New York City to be with her husband. As she re-acquaints herself with her husband, she finds that he has abandoned his Old World ideals. The film speaks not only to preserving the heritage of the Jews, but to cherishing all heritages and cultures. Highly regarded upon release, unfortunately forgotten today. **92m/B VHS, DVD.** Carol Kane, Doris Roberts, Steven Keats, Mel Howard, Dorrie Kavanaugh, Stephen Strimpell; **D:** Joan Micklin Silver; **W:** Joan Micklin Silver; **C:** Kenneth Van Sickle; **M:** William Bolcom.

Hexed ✓½ **1993** (R) Walter Mitty lives

in the person of bellboy Matthew Welsh, who enjoys masquerading as a debonair bon vivant. He finagles his way into the life of Hexina, a beautiful psychotic model who has checked into the hotel where Matthew works in order to murder her blackmailer. She tries to kill Matthew, apparently getting in a little practice, but he'll still follow her anywhere. Inane, charmless comedy that intends to satirize "Fatal Attraction" and similar films. **93m/C VHS, DVD.** Arye Gross, Claudia Christian, Adrienne Shelly, R. Lee Ermey, Norman Fell, Michael E. Knight; **D:** Alan Spencer; **W:** Alan Spencer.

Hey Arnold! The Movie ✓✓

2002 (PG) Kidpic based on the Nickelodeon series has the cranial oddity cast getting civic-minded about saving their endangered 'hood from an evil corporate developer. Eerily upbeat Arnold battles strangely Ronald Reagan-sounding Scheck who wants to raze their inner-city neighborhood. Together with his more realistic, flat-topped friend Gerald, Arnold employs a variety of ways to save his diverse urban home, from organizing a block party (good) to breaking and entering (hmm...this is for kids?). Castellaneta is the voice of Grandpa, who has explosive plans of his own to save the street. Big names (well, their voices) cameo. Some of the charm of the series remains but lacks feature-length punch. Animation suffers from the big screen treatment, as well. **76m/C VHS, DVD, US D:** Tuck Tucker; **W:** Craig Bartlett, Steve Viksten; **M:** Jim Lang; **V:** Spencer Klein, Francesca Marie Smith, Jamil Walker Smith, Dan Castellaneta, Tress MacNeille, Paul Sorvino, Christopher Walberg, Christopher Lloyd, Vincent Schiavelli, Maurice LaMarche.

Hey, Babu Riba ✓✓½ **1988** (R)

A popular Yugoslavian fit of nostalgia about four men convening at the funeral of a young girl they all loved years before, and their happy, Americana-bathed memories therein. In Serbo-Croatian with English subtitles. **109m/C VHS, DVD.** YU Gala Videnovic, Nebojsa Bakocevic, Dragan Bielogic, Marko Todorovic, Goran Radakovic, Relja Basic, Milos Zutic; **D:** Jovan Acin; **W:** Jovan Acin.

Hey Good Lookin' ✓✓½ **1982**

Ralph Bakshi's irreverent look at growing up in the 1950s bears the trademark qualities that distinguish his other adult animated features, "Fritz the Cat" and "Heavy Traffic." **87m/C VHS. D:** Ralph Bakshi; **W:** Ralph Bakshi.

Hey, Happy! ✓✓ **2001** Camp com-

edy set in a post-apocalyptic Winnipeg, where survivors of some type of environmental plague seem blase about a coming flood of biblical proportions. So enterprising DJ Sabu (Yuen) decides to hold an end-of-the-world rave party on the appropriately named Garbage Hill. That is after he fulfills his sexual quest of sleeping with 2,000 men. And his choice for the magic number is schizo Happy (Afanas), who hears alien voices on his radio urging him to give in. But the path to sexual conquest does not run smooth as Sabu has a stalker/rival in pierced punk Spanky (Godson). Sometimes slick, sometimes outrageous, sometimes surreal and just plain weird. **75m/C VHS, DVD, CA** Jeremie Yuen, Craig Aftanas, Clayton Godson; **D:** Noam Gonick; **W:** Noam Gonick; **C:** Paul Suderman.

Hey There, It's Yogi Bear ✓✓

1964 When Yogi Bear comes out of winter hibernation to search for food, he travels to the Chizzling Brothers Circus. The first feature-length cartoon to come from the H-B Studios. **98m/C VHS, DVD.** Joseph Barbera, William Hanna; **W:** Joseph Barbera, William Hanna; **M:** Marty Paich; **V:** Daws Butler, James Darren, Mel Blanc, J. Pat O'Malley, Julie Bennett.

Hi-De-Ho ✓✓ **1935** The great Cab

Calloway and his red hot jazz are featured in this film, which has the band caught in crossing that law-abiding line. **72m/B VHS, DVD.** Adolphe Menjou, Martha Scott, Dennis O'Keefe, Pola Negri; **D:** Andrew L. Stone.

Hi Diddle Diddle ✓✓½ **1943** Topsy-turvy

comedy features young lovers who long for conventional happiness. Instead they are cursed with con-artist parents who delight in crossing that law-abiding line. **72m/B VHS, DVD.** Adolphe Menjou, Martha Scott, Dennis O'Keefe, Pola Negri; **D:** Andrew L. Stone.

Hi, Good Lookin'! ✓✓½ **1944** A

radio station employee pretends to be a bigshot executive to help a pretty girl become a singer. Ozzie Nelson and His Orchestra are featured. **62m/B VHS.** Harriet Hilliard Nelson, Eddie Quillan, Kirby Grant, Roscoe Karns, Fuzzy Knight, Milburn Stone, Betty Kean; **D:** Edward Lilley; **W:** Bradford Ropes, Paul Girard Smith, Claudie Blakley; **C:** Jerome Ash.

Hi-Jacked ✓ **1950** When a parolee

trucker's cargo is stolen, he inevitably becomes a suspect and must set out to find the true culprits. **66m/B VHS.** Jim Davis, Paul Cavanagh, Marsha Jones, Sid Melton, David Bruce, Ralph Sanford, Iris Adrian, George Eldredge; **D:** Sam Newfield; **W:** Orville H. Hampton, Fred Myton, Raymond L. Schrock; **C:** Philip Tannura; **M:** Paul Dunlap.

Hi-Life ✓✓½ **1998** (R) Talky, Christ-

mastime, Manhattan-set ensemble comedy features compulsive gambler and out of work actor Jimmy (Stoltz) owing bookie Fatty (Durning) $900. To get the money, he tells girlfriend Susan (Kelly) it's to finance an abortion from his slutty sis Maggie (Hannah). Then Maggie's ex-boyfriend Ray (Scott) gets involved and Fatty's associate Miner (Reigart) and numerous other players who all wind up at the Hi-Life Bar and discover Jimmy's scams. **82m/C VHS, DVD.** Eric Stoltz, Moira Kelly, Daryl Hannah, Campbell Scott, Peter Riegert, Katrin Cartlidge, Charles Durning, Saundra Santiago, Anne DeSalvo, Bruce MacVittie, Tegan West; **D:** Roger Hedden; **W:** Roger Hedden; **M:** David Lawrence.

The Hi-Lo Country ✓✓½ **1998**

(R) For years, Sam Peckinpah wanted to make this movie. It took Martin Scorsese to resurrect the project and to secure Walon Green to adapt the 1961 Max Evans novel for the screen. Pete Calder (Crudup) returns to New Mexico from WWII. While waiting for buddy Big Boy Matson (Harrelson) to return from the Marines, Pete falls for Mona (Arquette), a saucy woman whose husband works for the area's biggest rancher, Jim Love (Elliott). When Big Boy does return, it becomes obvious that Pete and Mona are hot for each other, so Big Boy bows out. Big Boy is the last real cowboy (a favorite Peckinpah theme),

who loves the land, fears no one, and knows his times are coming to an end. Director Frears may not completely understand the American mythic West, but thanks to Oliver Stapleton's cinematography, the film has a look close to what a Peckinpah or a Ford might have given it. **114m/C VHS, DVD.** Woody Harrelson, Patricia Arquette, Billy Crudup, Penelope Cruz, Sam Elliott, Cole Hauser, Darren E. Burrows, Jacob Vargas, James Gammon, Lane Smith, Katy Jurado, John Diehl, Enrique Castillo, Rosaleen Linehan; **D:** Stephen Frears; **W:** Walon Green; **C:** Oliver Stapleton; **M:** Carter Burwell.

Hi, Mom! ✓✓✓ **1970** (R) DePalma's

follow-up to "Greetings" finds amateur pornographer/movie maker De Niro being advised by a professional in the field (Garfield) of sleazy filmmaking. De Niro films the residents of his apartment building and eventually marries one of his starlets. One of De Niro's earlier and better efforts with De Niro playing a crazy as only he can. **87m/C VHS, DVD.** Robert De Niro, Charles Dunham, Allen (Goorwitz) Garfield, Lara Parker, Jennifer Salt, Gerrit Graham; **D:** Brian De Palma; **W:** Brian De Palma.

Hi-Riders ✓ **1977** (R) A revenge-

based tale about large, mag-wheeled trucks and their drivers. **90m/C VHS.** Mel Ferrer, Stephen McNally, Neville Brand, Ralph Meeker; **D:** Greydon Clark.

Hidalgo ✓✓½ **2004** (PG-13) Inspired

by real-life U.S. Calvary horseman Frank T. Hopkins (Mortensen)—meaning it takes liberties with the truth (which Hopkins himself has been accused of). Old-fashioned adventure story hows the devotion he had for his mixed-breed horse, Hidalgo, as they travel 3,000 miles in 1890 to the "Ocean of Fire" endurance race, going against thoroughbreds and the wild elements of Arabia per the invitation of Sheikh Riyadh (Sharif). Mortensen looks stunning riding his steed, the elegant Sharif stirs up wonderful memories of Lawrence of Arabia, and the visual effects of sandstorms, colossal locusts, and the competition are captivating; however, this kind of story has been told before, with more dramatic twists and turns. **135m/C VHS, DVD.** Viggo Mortensen, Omar Sharif, Louise Lombard, Said Taghmaoui, Peter Mensah, J.K. Simmons, Adoni Maropis, Floyd "Red Crow" Westerman, Zuleikha Robinson, Adam Alexi-Malle, Silas Carson, Harsh Nayyar, Elizabeth Berridge, Victor Talmadge, Frank Collison, Jerry Hardin, C. Thomas Howell, Malcolm McDowell; **D:** Joe Johnston; **W:** John Fusco; **C:** Shelly Johnson; **M:** James Newton Howard.

Hidden ✓✓✓½ *Caché* **2005** (R)

Georges Laurent (Auteuil) and his wife Anne (Binoche) are upper middle class professionals living a comfortable life with their young son in Paris when suddenly a disturbing surveillance video tape of their own home is left at their front door, followed by another and another. This invasion plunges Georges into a world of repressed memories and disquieting dreams as he tries to make sense of these events as well as his past. On the surface a whodunit mystery not unlike any other from the post modern-age France, and the story unfolds as a metaphor for personal and societal responsibility in the post-9/11 modern-age France, followed by an increasingly uncomfortable revelation from previously held under thumb. **121m/C DVD.** Daniel Auteuil, Juliette Binoche, Annie Girardot, Maurice Benichou, Bernard Le Coq, Lester Makedonsky, Walid Afkir; **D:** Michael Haneke; **W:** Michael Haneke; **C:** Christian Berger. L.A. Film Critics '05; Foreign Film.

The Hidden ✓✓ **1987** (R) A sea-

soned cop (Nouri) and a benign alien posing as an FBI agent (MacLachlan) team up to track down and destroy a hyper-violent alien who survives by invading the bodies of humans, causing them to go on murderous rampages. Much acclaimed, high velocity action film with state-of-the-art special effects (at least for the time). Followed by a minor 1994 sequel with a different cast. **98m/C VHS, DVD.** Kyle MacLachlan, Michael Nouri, Clu Gulager, Ed O'Ross, Claudia Christian, Clarence Felder, Richard Brooks, William Boyett, Chris Mulkey; **D:** Jack

Sholder; **W:** Bob Hunt, Jim Kouf; **C:** Jacques Haitkin; **M:** Michael Convertino.

The Hidden 2 ✓✓½ **1994** (R) The

hyper-violent alien of the 1987 movie returns. With its love of fast cars, high-caliber weapons, and heavy metal music, this body-possessing creature appears to be unstoppable. **91m/C VHS, DVD.** Raphael Sbarge, Kate Hodge, Michael Nouri; **D:** Seth Pinsker; **W:** Seth Pinsker; **M:** David McHugh.

Hidden Agenda ✓✓½ **1990** (R) A

human rights activist and an American lawyer uncover brutality and corruption among the machinations on the British police system. Generally worthwhile. **108m/C VHS, DVD.** Frances McDormand, Brian Cox, Brad Dourif, Mai Zetterling, John Benfield, Des McAleer, Jim Norton, Maurice Roeves; **D:** Ken Loach; **W:** Jim Allen; **C:** Clive Tickner; **M:** Stewart Copeland. Cannes '90: Special Jury Prize.

Hidden Agenda ✓✓ **1999** (R) Ar-

riving in Berlin, American tourist Dillon learns his brother has been murdered. He decides to do some investigating on his own and winds up caught between CIA spies and the German secret police. **97m/C VHS, DVD.** Kevin Dillon, Christopher Plummer, Andrea Roth, Michael Wincott, J.T. Walsh; **D:** Iain Paterson; **W:** Iain Paterson; **C:** Thom Best; **M:** Harry Manfredini. **VIDEO**

Hidden Agenda ✓✓ **2001** (R)

Former NSA agent Jason Price (Lundgren) is still doing covert government work by making people vanish. His latest client is a mobster (Houde) but Price finds that a legendary hit man (Roy) has taken an unhealthy interest in his operation. **94m/C VHS, DVD.** Dolph Lundgren, Maxim Roy, Brigitte Paquette, Serge Houde, Patrick Kerton, Christian Paul; **D:** Marc S. Grenier; **W:** Les Weldon; **C:** Sylvain Brault. **VIDEO**

Hidden Assassin ✓ *The Shooter*

1994 (R) French hit woman Simone (Detmers) supposedly shoots the Cuban ambassador to the U.N. and escapes back to her home base in Prague, followed by Czech-born U.S. Marshal Mickey Dane (Lundgren). Mickey starts to doubt that Simone is the killer (she claims she's long retired and is being set up) and the duo try to find the truth amid lots of double-crosses. Doesn't make much sense in any case. **89m/C VHS, DVD.** Dolph Lundgren, Maruschka Detmers, Assumpta Serna, Gavan O'Herlihy, John Ashton, Simon Andreu; **D:** Ted Kotcheff; **W:** Meg Thayer, Billy Ray, Yves Andre Martin; **C:** Fernando Arguelles; **M:** Stefano Mainetti.

The Hidden Blade ✓✓½ **2004** (R) *Kaku-*

shi Ken: Oni No Tsume Set in 1861, Katagiri (Nagase) is a lower-caste samurai who has a forbidden love for serving girl Kie (Matsu), who he rescues from domestic abuse. He's also troubled by being ordered to kill an old comrade, Hazama (Ozawa), who plotted against the Shogunate and has escaped from confinement. Based on the short stories of Shuhei Fujisawa. The Japanese title, "Hidden Blade: The Devil's Claw", refers to a unique sword maneuver. Japanese with subtitles. **132m/C DVD. JP** Masatoshi Nagase, Min Tanaka, Nenji Kobayashi, Ken Ogata, Takako Matsu, Hidetaka Yoshioka, Yukishi Ozawa, Tomoko Obata, Reiko Takashima; **W:** Yoji Yamada; **D:** Yoji Yamada; **C:** Mutsuo Naganuma; **M:** Isao Tomita.

Hidden City ✓✓ **1987** A film archi-

vist and a statistician become drawn into a conspiracy when a piece of revealing film is spliced onto the end of an innocuous government tape. **112m/C VHS.** Charles Dance, Cassie Stuart, Alex Norton, Tusse Silberg, Bill Paterson; **D:** Stephen Poliakoff.

Hidden Enemy ✓½ **1940** During

WWII, a scientist develops a new metal alloy that is stronger than steel yet lighter than aluminum. His nephew must protect his scientist/uncle from spies who would steal the formula to use against the Allies. **63m/B VHS.** Warren Hull, Kay Linaker, Wilhelm von Brinken, George Cleveland; **D:** Howard Bretherton.

Hidden Fears ♦♦½ 1993 Maureen Dietz (Foster) carries the gruesome memories of her husband's murder with her. Years later she goes to the police with new evidence to reopen her husband's case. Only the killers find out and return to finish off the eyewitnesses, and she's next! Based on the novel "Exercise in Terror" by Kaminsky, who also wrote the screenplay. 90m/C VHS, Meg Foster, Frederic Forrest, Wally Taylor, Beverleigh Banfield, Marc Macaulay, Patrick Cherry, Scott Hayes; D: Jean Bodon; W: Stuart Kaminsky.

The Hidden Fortress ♦♦♦½ 1958 *Kakushi Toride No San Akunin; Three Bad Men in the Hidden Fortress* 1958 Kurosawa's tale of a warrior who protects a princess from warring feudal lords. An inspiration for George Lucas' "Star Wars" series and deserving of its excellent reputation. In Japanese with English subtitles. 139m/B VHS, DVD, JP Toshiro Mifune, Misa(to) Uehara, Kamatari Fujiwara, Susumu Fujita, Eiko Miyoshi, Takashi Shimura, Kichijiro Ueda, Koji Mitsui, Minoru Chiaki, Toshiko Higuchi, Shiten Oheashi; D: Akira Kurosawa; W: Akira Kurosawa, Shinobu Hashimoto, Ryuzo Kikushima, Hideo Oguni; C: Kazuo Yamazaki; M: Masaru Sato. Berlin Intl. Film Fest. '59: Director (Kurosawa).

The Hidden Room ♦♦♦ *Obsession* 1949 A doctor finds out about his wife's affair and decides to get revenge on her lover. He kidnaps him, imprisons him in a cellar, and decides to kill him—slowly. Tense melodrama. 98m/B VHS, DVD, GB Robert Newton, Sally Gray, Naunton Wayne, Phil...

Hidden Gold ♦½ 1933 Routine western for Mix, which has him going undercover to win the confidence of three outlaws and discover where they have hidden their loot. 57m/B VHS, Tom Mix, Judith Barrie, Raymond Hatton; D: Arthur Rosson.

Hidden Guns ♦½ 1956 Above-average tale of father-and-son lawmen out to reform a town and put the bad guys away. When dad is killed, the son goes up against the villain alone. A Greek chorus adds an interesting twist to the action. Erich von Stroheim Jr. is listed as assistant director. 66m/B VHS, Bruce Bennett, Richard Arlen, John Carradine, Faron Young, Angie Dickinson, Guinn "Big Boy" Williams; D: Albert C. Gannaway.

Hidden in America ♦♦½ 1996 (PG-13) Bill Januson (Bridges) has lost his auto-plant job because of downsizing and his wife to cancer. His savings exhausted and his prospects bleak, Januson struggles to put food on the table for his two kids, who increasingly begin to suffer the effects of poverty. Produced in conjunction with the End Hunger Network, whose co-founder, Jeff Bridges, has a cameo. 96m/C VHS, DVD, Beau Bridges, Bruce Davison, Jena Malone, Shelton Dane, Alice Krige, Josef Sommer, Frances McDormand; Cameos: Jeff Bridges; D: Martin Bell; W: Peter Silverman, Michael deGuzman; C: James R. Bagdonas; M: Mason Daring. CABLE

Hidden Obsession ♦♦ 1992 (R) Newscaster Ellen is taking a much needed vacation at an isolated cabin when she learns that a serial killer has escaped from a nearby prison. Luckily, she has a hunky police officer neighbor for protection. But though the escaped killer is captured, the killings go on—with Ellen as the next target. 92m/C VHS, Heather Thomas, Jan-Michael Vincent, Nicholas Celozzi; D: John Stewart; W: David Reskin.

Hidden Places ♦♦½ 2006 Widowed mom Eliza (Penny) is struggling through the Depression on her father-in-law's farm when he suddenly dies. Eliza has to get in the orange crop or risk foreclosure on the debt-ridden property. Her Aunt Batty (Jones) says to have faith and when charming veteran Gabe (Gedrick) shows up, he may be the answer to their prayers. Gabe agrees to help out with the harvest and falling in love with the young widow may be his bonus. Based on the novel by Lynn Austin. 7m/C DVD, Sydney Penny, Jason Gedrick, Shirley Jones, Barry Corbin, Tom Bosley, John Diehl; D: Yelena Lanskaya; W: Robert Tate Miller; C: James Wrenn; M: Roger Bellen. CABLE

Hidden Valley ♦ 1932 Early Steele western in which everyone is fighting over a map that leads to hidden treasure in the valley. 60m/B VHS, Bob Steele, Gertrude Messinger, Francis McDonald; D: Rene Borniere; W: Barry Wexler.

Hide and Go Shriek ♦½ 1988 (R)...

Hide and Seek ♦ 1977 When a high school hacker converts his computer into a nuclear weapon, he finds that it has developed a mind of its own. 60m/C VHS, Daryl Hannah, Ingrid Veninger, David Patrick; D: Skip Schoolnik.

Hide and Seek ♦♦ 1980 A study of children living in the land that would soon become Israel. Although they play as normal children, life is particularly difficult. This adversity will lay the foundation for their Israeli citizenry. In Hebrew with English subtitles. 90m/C VHS, Gila Almagor, Doron Tavor, Chaim Hadaya; D: Dan Wolman.

Hide and Seek ♦♦ *Cord* 2000 (R) Pregnant Ann (Hannah) is kidnapped by a crazy childless couple (Tilly and Gallo) and it's no kids' game when husband Jack (Greenwood) tries to find her. 100m/C Gallo, Bruce Greenwood, Johanna Black; D: Sidney J. Furie; W: Joel Hladecek, Ya's Takata; M: Robert Garll. VIDEO

Hide and Seek ♦♦ 2005 (R) Nine-year-old Emily (Fanning) witnesses her mother's bloody suicide. Her father (De Niro), a psychologist, decides to take the traumatized girl from bustling Manhattan to a peaceful, rural community to help her cope. Once settled in, it's pretty clear that Emily isn't coping very well. Her issues manifest in the form of an imaginary friend named Charlie, who does some rather scary things when he's angry. Stellar cast and high production values can't hide the fact that it's still a run-of-the-mill horror movie. Fanning sports the best child gold since Christina Ricci's Wednesday Addams. 100m/C DVD, US Robert De Niro, Dakota Fanning, Famke Janssen, Elisabeth Shue, Amy Irving, Dylan Baker, Melissa Leo, Robert John Burke, David Chandler, Molly Grant Kallins; D: John Polson; W: Ari Schlossberg; C: Darius Wolski.

Hide in Plain Sight ♦♦½ 1980 (PG) A distraught blue-collar worker searches for his children who disappeared when his ex-wife and her mobster husband are given new identities by federal agents. Caan's fine directorial debut is based on a true story. 96m/C VHS, James Caan, Jill Eikenberry, Robert Viharo, Kenneth McMillan, Josef Sommer, Danny Aiello; D: James Caan.

Hide-Out ♦♦½ 1934 A man running from the law winds up at a small farm, falls in love, and becomes reformed by the good family that takes him in. Good supporting cast includes a very young Rooney. 83m/B VHS, Robert Montgomery, Maureen O'Sullivan, Edward Arnold, Elizabeth Patterson, Mickey Rooney, Edward Brophy; D: Woodbridge S. Van Dyke.

Hideaway ♦♦ 1994 (R) Hodgepodge movie finds Hatch Harrison (Goldblum) brought back from the other side after suffering injuries from a near-fatal car accident. He returns with the ability to psychically connect with Vassago (Sisto), a sadistic serial killer of young girls. Coincidentally, Harrison has a teenage daughter, Regina (Silverstone), and Vassago has her lined up as his next victim. The visual effects of spirits floating down a cosmic vortex are entertaining, but plot originality must have been hidden away to make room for the nifty special effects. Based on a novel by Dean F. Koontz. 103m/C VHS, DVD, Jeff Goldblum, Christine Lahti, Alicia Silverstone, Jeremy Sisto, Rae Dawn Chong; D: Brett Leonard; W: Andrew Kevin Walker, Neal Jimenez; C: Gale Tattersall; M: Trevor Jones.

Hideous ♦½ 1997 (R) Eccentric collector's greatest prize is a seemingly petrified toxic waste mutant that's not so petrified afterall. If this mutants to come to life and even spawn little mutants to go on a killing spree. 82m/C VHS, DVD, Jacqueline Lovell, Michael Citriniti, Rhonda Griffin, Mel Johnson Jr., Tracy Scoggins; D: Charles Band; W: Benjamin Carr; M: Richard Band.

Hideous Kinky ♦♦½ 1999 (R) Julia (Winslet) is a free-spirited single mom who decides to leave London and take her two daughters, Bea and Lucy, to live in Morocco in 1972. She gets by on sales of homemade dolls and the occasional check from the girls' father. Julia looks for a conversion to the Sufi life and looks good doing it, as does the whole movie. The Moroccan locales are brilliantly displayed. Character development and consistent narrative are sometimes lacking. 97m/C VHS, DVD, GB FR Kate Winslet, Said Taghmaoui, Bella Riza, Carrie Mullan, Pierre Clementi, Abigail Cruttenden, Sira Stampe; D: Gillies Mackinnon; W: Billy Mackinnon; C: John de Borman; M: John Keane.

Hideous Sun Demon ♦½ 1959 *Blood on His Lips; Terror from the Sun; The Sun Demon* 1959 A physicist exposed to radiation must stay out of sunlight or he will turn into a scaly, lizard-like creature. Includes previews of coming attractions from classic sci-fi films. 75m/B VHS, DVD, Robert Clarke, Patricia Manning, Nan Peterson, Patrick Whyte, Peter Similuk, Fred La Porta, Robert Garry, Del Courtney; D: Thomas Boutross, Robert Clarke; W: Doane R. Hoag, E.S. Seeley Jr.; C: Vilis Lapenieks, John Morrill, Stan Follis; M: John Seeley.

Hider in the House ♦♦½ 1990 (R) In a peaceful neighborhood of a family is about to spend an evening of terror when they discover a psychopath is hiding in the attic of their home. 109m/C VHS, Michael McKean, Gary Busey, Mimi Rogers, Kurt Christopher Kinder, Candy Hutson, Elizabeth Ruscio, Bruce Glover; D: Michael Patrick.

Hiding Out ♦♦ 1987 (PG-13) A young stockbroker testifies against the Mafia and must find a place to hide in order to avoid being killed. He winds up at his cousin's high school in Delaware, but can he really go through with passing himself off as a teenager and avoid the troubles once again? 99m/C VHS, DVD, Jon Cryer, Keith Coogan, Gretchen Cryer, Annabeth Gish, Tim Quill; D: Bob Giraldi; W: Jeff Rothberg, Joe Menosky; C: Daniel Pearl; M: Anne Dudley.

The Hiding Place ♦♦ 1975 True story of two Dutch Christian sisters sent to a concentration camp for hiding Jews during WWII. Film is uneven but good cast pulls it through. Based on the Corrie Ten Boom book and produced by Billy Graham's Evangelistic Association. 145m/C VHS, Julie Harris, Eileen Heckart, Arthur O'Connell, Jeanette Clift; D: James F. Collier.

High & Low ♦♦♦½ 1962 *Tengoku To Jigoku* 1962 (R) Fine Japanese film noir about a wealthy businessman who is being blackmailed by kidnappers who claim to have his son. When he discovers that they have mistakenly taken his chauffeur's son he must decide whether to face financial ruin or risk the life of a young boy. Based on an Ed McBain novel. In Japanese with English subtitles. 143m/B VHS, DVD, JP Toshiro Mifune, Tatsuya Nakadai; D: Akira Kurosawa; W: Evan Hunter, Ryuzo Kikushima, Hideo Oguni, Akira Kurosawa; C: Asakazu Nakai, Takao Saito; M: Masaru Sato.

The Hideaways ♦♦½ 1973 *From the Mixed-Up Files of Mrs. Basil E. Frankweiler* 1973 A 12-year-old girl and her younger brother run away and hide in the Metropolitan Museum of Art. The girl becomes enamored of a piece of sculpture and sets out to discover its creator. Based on the children's novel by E.L. Konigsburg. 105m/C VHS, DVD, Ingrid Bergman, Sally Prager, Johnny Doran, Madeline Kahn; D: Fielder Cook.

The High and the Mighty ♦♦♦ 1954 One of Wayne's most sought-after films finally makes it to DVD, as it took 10 years for Wayne's daughter-in-law to restore a negative found in a pool of water in a warehouse. Wayne is Dan Roman, who steps up to the situation on a trans-Pacific airline flight in deep trouble. In a device that'll be familiar to viewers of "Lost" many flashbacks give backstory on passengers and crew. Unfortunately, this serves mostly to slow down the action and suspense of their current situation. Excellent performance by an all-star cast cover for some of the more cated elements of the film, which was, after all, a precursor to the popular disaster flicks of the 70s. 148m/C DVD, John Wayne, Claire Trevor, Laraine Day, Robert Stack, Jan Sterling, Phil Harris, Robert Newton, David Brian, Paul Kelly, Sidney Blackmer, Julie Bishop, John Howard, Wally Brown, William Campbell, Ann Doran, John Qualen, Paul Fix, Joy Lim, George Chandler, Douglas Fowley, Regis Toomey, Carl "Alfalfa" Switzer, William Hopper, William Schallert, Julie Mitchum; D: William A. Wellman; W: Ernest K. Gann; C: Archie Stout; M: Dimitri Tiomkin. Oscars '54: Orig. Dramatic Score; Golden Globes '55: Support. Actress (Sterling).

High Anxiety ♦♦ 1977 (PG) Brooks tries hard to please in this low-brow parody of Hitchcock films employing dozens of references to films like "Psycho," "Spellbound," "The Birds," and "Vertigo." Tells the tale of a high-learning psychiatrist caught up in a murder mystery. The title song performed a la Sinatra by Brooks is one of the film's high moments. Brooks also has a lot of fun with Hitchcookian camera movements. Uneven but amusing tribute. 92m/C VHS, DVD, Mel Brooks, Madeline Kahn, Cloris Leachman, Harvey Korman, Ron Carey, Howard Morris, Dick Van Patten; D: Mel Brooks; W: Mel Brooks, Ron Clark, Barry Levinson, Rudy DeLuca.

High Art ♦♦ 1998 (R) A trio of women play romantic games in New York's art community. Ambitious magazine editor-in-training Syd (Mitchell) has a boyfriend, James (Mann), but "feels something's missing." Noticing a leak in her apartment ceiling, Syd heads upstairs to confront her neighbor and meets Lucy Berliner (Sheedy), a once-celebrated, now-retired photographer with a heroin problem and an equally hooked girlfriend, Greta (Clarkson). Syd and Lucy begin a friendship that leads to an affair, while Syd also wants to revitalize Lucy's career. Ex-Brat Packer Sheedy's the real revelation with her standout performance. 102m/C VHS, DVD, Radha Mitchell, Ally Sheedy, Patricia Clarkson, Tammy Grimes, Gabriel Mann, Lisa Cholodenko; D: Lisa Cholodenko; W: Lisa Cholodenko; C: Tami Reiker; M: Craig (Shudder to Think) Wedren. Ind. Spirit '99: Actress (Sheedy); L.A. Film Critics '98: Actress (Sheedy); Natl. Soc. Film Critics '98: Actress (Sheedy); Sundance '98: Screenplay.

High Ballin' ♦♦ 1978 (PG) Truckers Fonda and Reed team up with lady trucker Shaver to crush the independent drivers. 100m/C VHS, DVD, Peter Fonda, Jerry Reed, Helen Shaver, David Ferry; D: Peter Carter; W: Paul F. Edwards.

High Command ♦♦ 1937 To save his daughter from an ugly scandal, the British general of an isolated Colonial African outpost traps a blackmailer's killer. 84m/B VHS, DVD, GB Lionel Atwill, Lucie Mannheim, James Mason; D: Thorold Dickinson.

High Country ♦♦ 1981 *The First Hello* 1981 (PG) Two misfits, one handicapped, the other an ex-con, on the run from society, learn mutual trust as they travel through the Canadian Rockies. 101m/C VHS, CA Timothy Bottoms, Linda Purl, George Sims, Jim Lawrence, Bill Berry; D: Harvey Hart.

High Crime ♦♦ 1973 A "French Connection"-style suspense story about the narcotics trade. Features high-speed chases and a police commissioner obsessed with capturing the criminals. 91m/C VHS, James Whitmore, Franco Nero, Fernando Rey; D: Enzo G. Castellari.

High Crimes ♂♂½ 2002 (PG-13) Military courtroom thriller is only average but does have Freeman, who's always worth watching. He's reteamed with "Kiss the Girls" co-star Judd, who plays spunky California attorney Claire Kubik. Claire gets a big surprise when her contractor hubby Tom (Caviezel) is suddenly arrested by the FBI and sent to a military prison. Turns out Tom, then known as Ron Chapman, was in an elite Marine special unit and is accused of a 1988 civilian massacre in El Salvador. She looks to recovering alcoholic and ex-JAG lawyer Charlie Grimes (Freeman) for assistance but sinister plots are afoot. Based on the 1998 novel by Joseph Finder. 115m/C VHS, DVD. US Ashley, Judd, James (Jim) Caviezel, Morgan Freeman, Amanda Peet, Tom Bower, Adam Scott, Bruce Davison, Michael Gaston, Juan Carlos Hernandez, Jude Ciccolella, Michael Shannon; D: Carl Franklin; W: Yuri Zeltser, Cary Bickley; C: Theo van de Sande; M: Graeme Revell.

The High Crusade ♂½ 1992 (PG-13) A group of 13th-century English crusaders are heading for the Holy Land when they're interrupted on their journey by an alien spacecraft. They overpower the space guys and take over the vessel, hoping it will take them to Jerusalem, but since the spacecraft's on autopilot, the knights wind up heading for the aliens' home planet instead. 100m/C VHS, DVD. GB GE John Rhys-Davies, Michael Des Barres, Rick Overton; D: Holger Neuhauser.

High Desert Kill ♂♂ 1990 (PG) A science-fiction tale that will keep you guessing. Aliens landing in the New Mexican desert want something totally unexpected, and a trio of friends will be the first to find out what it is. Writer Cook was also responsible for "The China Syndrome." 93m/C VHS. Chuck Connors, Marc Singer, Anthony Geary, Micah Grant; D: Harry Falk; W: T.S. Cook. CABLE

High Fidelity ♂♂♂ 2000 (R) Frears, Cusack, and the writing team from "Grosse Pointe Blank" successfully bring Nick Hornby's 1995 novel to the screen, transplanting it from London to Chicago in the process. Cusack is Rob, a stuck-in-adolescence record store owner who just broke up with Laura (Hjejle), his long-time, live-in love. This gets him to thinking about his Top Five All-Time Breakups. Cue flashbacks. It also sends him on some hilarious conversations with his employees: know-it-all Barry (Black) who wields his musical tastes like a weapon, and Dick (Louiso), who's bashful to the point of invisibility. Cusack does his usual fine job, but Black and Louiso take over whenever they're on screen. 113m/C VHS, DVD. John Cusack, Todd Louiso, Jack Black, Iben Hjejle, Tim Robbins, Joan Cusack, Lisa Bonet, Catherine Zeta-Jones, Lili Taylor, Natasha Gregson Wagner, Sara Gilbert, Chris Rehmann, Ben Carr, Joelle Carter, Bruce Springsteen; D: Stephen Frears; W: John Cusack, D.V. DeVincentis, Steve Pink, Scott Rosenberg; C: Seamus McGarvey; M: Howard Shore.

High Frequency ♂♂ 1988 Two young men monitoring a satellite relay station witness the murder of a woman. Believing they know who the killer's next victim will be, they set out to warn her. Lack of development mars what could have been a tidy little thriller. 105m/C VHS. IT Oliver Benny, Vincent Spano, Isabelle Pasco, Anne Canovas; D: Faliero Rosati.

High Gear ♂ 1933 Heartstring-tugger about a race car driver, his girlfriend and the orphan son of a driver killed in a crash. Try to guess the outcome. 65m/B VHS. James Murray, Joan Marsh, Jackie Searl, Theodore von Eltz, Lee Moran, Gordon DeMain; D: Leigh Jason.

High Heels ♂ Docteur Popaul; Scandrel in White 1972 A black comedy about a doctor who believes beauty is only skin deep and marries a plain woman. However, when he meets her beautiful sister, he begins to wonder. In French with English subtitles. 100m/C VHS. FR Laura Antonelli, Jean-Paul Belmondo, Mia Farrow, Daniel Ivernel; D: Claude Chabrol.

High Heels ♂♂ Tacones Lejanos 1991 (R) An outrageous combination murder-melodrama-comedy from Almodovar. Rebecca is a TV anchorwoman in Madrid whose flamboyant singer/actress mother has returned to the city for a concert. Rebecca happens to be married to one of her mother's not-so-ex-flames. When her husband winds up dead, Rebecca confesses to his murder during her newscast—but is she telling the truth or just covering up for her mom? Mix in a drag queen/judge, a dancing chorus of women prison inmates, and a peculiar police detective, and see if the plot convolutions make sense. In Spanish with English subtitles. 113m/C VHS. SP Victoria Abril, Marisa Paredes, Miguel Bose, Feodor Atkine, Bibi Andersen, Rocio Munoz; C: Alfredo Mayo; M: Ryuichi Sakamoto. Cesar '93: Foreign Film.

High Heels and Low Lifes ♂♂ 2001 (R) Brit nurse Shannon (Driver) and American actress Frances (McCormack) overhear a plot to rob a London safe deposit box center and immediately go to the cops. When the cops seem uninterested, the girls decide to blackmail the crooks into giving them a cut. Nice premise and an enjoyable performance by Driver are wasted by Smith's flat direction, which misses almost all comic opportunities in the script. 85m/C VHS, DVD. US GB Minnie Driver, Mary McCormack, Kevin McNally, Mark Williams, Danny Dyer, Michael Gambon, Kevin Eldon, Len Collin, Darren Boyd, Julian Wadham; D: Mel Smith; W: Kim Fuller; C: Steven Chivers; M: Charlie Mole.

High Hopes ♂♂♂ 1988 A moving yet nasty satiric comedy about a pair of ex-hippies maintaining their countercultural lifestyle in Margaret Thatcher's England, as they watch the signs of conservative "progress" overtake them and their geriatric, embittered Mum. Hilarious and mature. 110m/C VHS. GB Philip Davis, Ruth Sheen, Edna Dore, Philip Jackson, Heather Tobias, Leslie Manville, David Bamber; D: Mike Leigh; W: Mike Leigh; C: Roger Pratt; M: Rachel Portman, Andrew Dixon.

High Ice ♂½ 1980 Forest ranger and a lieutenant colonel are involved in a clash of wills over a rescue mission high in the snow-capped Washington state peaks. 97m/C VHS. David Janssen, Tony Musante; D: Eugene S. Jones.

High Lonesome ♂♂½ 1950 Barrymore is a drifter in Big Bend country, suspected in a series of mysterious murders. While he is being held captive, the real killers—thought dead—return to exact revenge on those they hold responsible for the range war in which they were wounded. This was LeMay's only stint as a director. 80m/C VHS, DVD. John Drew (Blythe) Barrymore Jr., Chill Wills, John Archer, Lois Butler, Kristine Miller, Basil Ruysdael, Jack Elam; D: Alan LeMay; W: Alan LeMay; C: William Howard Greene; M: Rudolph (Rudy) Schrager.

High Noon ♂♂♂ 1952 Landmark Western about Hadleyville town marshal Will Kane (Cooper) who faces four professional killers alone, after being abandoned to his fate by the gutless townspeople who profess to admire him. Cooper is the ultimate hero figure, his sheer presence overwhelming. Note the continuing use of the ballad written by Dimitri Tiomkin, "Do Not Forsake Me, Oh My Darlin'" (sung by Tex Ritter) to heighten the tension and action. ♫High Noon (Do Not Forsake Me, Oh My Darlin'). 85m/B VHS, DVD. Gary Cooper, Grace Kelly, Lloyd Bridges, Lon Chaney Jr., Thomas Mitchell, Otto Kruger, Katy Jurado, Lee Van Cleef, Harry (Henry) Morgan, Robert J. Wilke, Sheb Wooley; D: Fred Zinnemann; W: Carl Foreman; C: Floyd Crosby; M: Dimitri Tiomkin. Oscars '52: Actor (Cooper), Film Editing, Song ("High Noon (Do Not Forsake Me, Oh My Darlin')"), Orig. Dramatic Score; AFI '98: Top 100; Golden Globes '53: Actor—Drama (Cooper), Support. Actress (Jurado), Score, Natl. Film Reg. '89; N.Y. Film Critics '52: Director (Zinnemann), Film.

High Noon ♂♂ 2000 (PG-13) Generally faithful but needless TV remake of the 1952 western classic. Stoic marshal Will Kane (Skerritt), having just married the Quaker Amy (Thompson), is about to give up his badge when he learns that outlaw Frank Miller (Madsen) will be coming in on the noon train with revenge on his mind. Everyone thinks Will should just skedaddle out of town and save them all some grief but, hey, he's a hero and has to do what's right! 93m/C VHS, DVD. Tom Skerritt, Susanna Thompson, Reed Edward Diamond, Maria Conchita Alonso, Michael Madsen, Dennis Weaver, August Schellenberg; D: Rod Hardin; W: Carl Foreman, T.S. Cook; C: Robert McLachlan; M: Allyn Ferguson. CABLE

High Noon: Part 2 ♂ 1980 Majors attempts to fill Gary Cooper's shoes, as Marshal Kane returns a year after the events of the original "High Noon" to remove the corrupt marshal who replaced him. Subtitled "The Return of Will Kane." 96m/C VHS. Lee Majors, David Carradine, Pernell Roberts, Katherine (Kathy) Cannon; D: Jerry Jameson. TV

High Plains Drifter ♂♂½ 1973 (R) A surreal, violent western focusing on a drifter who defends a town from gunmen intent on meting out death. One of Eastwood's most stylistic directorial efforts, indebted to his "Man with No Name" days with Sergio Leone. Laser format is letterboxed and includes chapter stops and the original theatrical trailer. 105m/C VHS, DVD. Clint Eastwood, Verna Bloom, Mitchell Ryan, Marianna Hill, Jack Ging, Stefan Gierasch; D: Clint Eastwood; W: Ernest Tidyman, Dean Riesner; C: Bruce Surtees; M: Dee Barton.

High Risk ♂½ 1981 (R) Improbable action-adventure of four unemployed Americans who battle foreign armies, unscrupulous gunrunners, and jungle bandits in a harrowing attempt to steal $5 million from an expatriate American drug dealer living in the peaceful splendor of his Columbian villa. Interesting in its own run-on way. 94m/C VHS, DVD. James Brolin, Anthony Quinn, Lindsay Wagner, James Coburn, Ernest Borgnine, Cleavon Little, Chick Vennera; D: Stewart Raffill; W: Stewart Raffill; C: Alex Phillips Jr.; M: Mark Snow.

High Road to China ♂♂ 1983 (PG) A hard-drinking former WWI air ace is recruited by a young heiress who must find her father before his ex-partner takes over his business. Post-"Raiders of the Lost Ark" thrills and romance, but without that tale's panache. 105m/C VHS. Bess Armstrong, Tom Selleck, Jack Weston, Robert Morley, Wilford Brimley, Brian Blessed; D: Brian G. Hutton; M: John Barry.

High Rolling in a Hot Corvette ♂ High Rolling 1977 (PG) Two carnival workers leave their jobs and hit the road in search of adventure and excitement, eventually turning to crime. 82m/C VHS. AU Joseph Bottoms, Greg Taylor, Judy Davis, Wendy Hughes; D: Igor Auzins.

High School Caesar ♂ 1960 A seedy teenage exploitation flick about a rich teenager, with no parental supervision, who starts his own gang to run his high school. 75m/B VHS, DVD. Steve Stevens, Lowell Brown, Gary Vinson, Judy Nugent, Daria Massey, John Ashley; D: O'Dale Ireland; W: Ethelmae Wilson Page, Robert Slaven; C: Harry Birch; M: Nicholas Carras.

High School Confidential ♂ Young Hellions 1958 Teen punk Tamblyn transfers to Santo Bello high school from Chicago and causes havoc among the locals. He soon involves himself in the school drug scene and looks to be the top dog in dealing, but what no one knows is that he's really a narc! A must for midnight movie fans thanks to high camp values, "hep cat" dialogue and the gorgeous Van Doren as Tamblyn's sex-crazed "aunt." 85m/B VHS, DVD. Russ Tamblyn, Jan Sterling, John Drew (Blythe) Barrymore Jr., Mamie Van Doren, Diane Jergens, Jerry Lee Lewis, Ray Anthony, Jackie Coogan, Charles Chaplin Jr., Burt Douglas, Michael Landon, Jody Fair, Phillipa Fallon, Robin Raymond, James Todd, Lyle Talbot, William Wellman Jr.; D: Jack Arnold; W: Robert Blees, Lewis Meltzer; C: Harold Marzorati.

High School High ♂♂½ 1996 (PG-13) Idealistic teacher Richard Clark (Lovitz) leaves the private school world for notorious inner city Marion Barry High. This school is so bad it has its own cemetery (it's a parody, folks), but Clark is determined to get through to the kids. "Clockers" star Phifer shows up as a helpful student. Penned by David Zucker of "Airplane!" fame, so don't expect a "Mr. Holland's Opus". 86m/C VHS, DVD. Jon Lovitz, Tia Carrere, Mekhi Phifer, Louise Fletcher, Malinda Williams; D: Hart Bochner; W: Pat Proft, David Zucker, Robert Locash; C: Vernon Layton; M: Ira Newborn.

High School Musical ♂♂½ 2006 (PG) Bouncy musical with catchy tunes, made for the Disney Channel, finds high school basketball star Troy (Efron) falling for studious Gabriella (Hudgens) on vacation (they do karaoke together). When they realize they go to the same school, Troy is pressured to stay with the status quo—especially when he wants to try out for the school musical with Gabriella against the very ambitious Evans siblings. 98m/C DVD. Zac Efron, Ashley Tisdale, Lucas Grabeel, Bart Johnson, Monique Coleman, Vanessa Anne Hudgens, Alyson Reed, Corbin Bleu; D: Kenny Ortega; W: Peter Barsocchini; C: Gordon C. Lonsdale; M: David Lawrence. CABLE

High School Musical 2 ♂♂½ 2007 (G) Just as lively (if not as fresh) as its predecessor. Gabriella is hoping to enjoy the summer with Troy but he needs to save some cash for college. The Wildcats get jobs at the Lava Springs Country Club, which happens to be owned by the parents of scheming Sharpay and Ryan. Sharpay dangles basketball perks and other incentives for Troy to sing with her in the club talent contest, which leaves Gabriella feeling neglected, but none of it is anything that a few song-and-dance numbers can't solve. 111m/C DVD, Blu-ray Disc. Zac Efron, Vanessa Anne Hudgens, Ashley Tisdale, Corbin Bleu, Lucas Grabeel, Monique Coleman; D: Kenny Ortega; W: Peter Barsocchini; C: Daniel Aranyo; M: David Lawrence. CABLE

High School USA ♂½ 1984 A high-school class clown confronts the king of the prep-jock-bullies. Antics ensue in this flick that features many stars from '50s and '60s sitcoms. 96m/C VHS, DVD. Michael J. Fox, Nancy McKeon, Bob Denver, Angela Cartwright, Elinor Donahue, Dwayne Hickman, Lauri Hendler, Dana Plato, Tony Dow, David Nelson; D: Rod Amateau; M: Miles Goodman. TV

High Season ♂♂½ 1988 (R) A satire about a beautiful English photographer (Bisset) stranded on an idyllic Greek island with neither money nor inspiration, and the motley assembly of characters who surround her during the tourist season. 95m/C VHS. GB Jacqueline Bisset, James Fox, Irene Papas, Sebastian Shaw, Kenneth Branagh, Robert Stephens, Leslie Manville; D: Clare Peploe; W: Mark Peploe, Clare Peploe; C: Chris Menges; M: Jason Osborn.

High Sierra ♂♂½ 1941 Bogart is Roy "Mad Dog" Earle, an aging gangster whose last job backfires, so he's hiding out from the police in the High Sierras. Bogart's first starring role. Based on the novel by W.R. Burnett. Remade in 1955 as "I Died A Thousand Times." Also available colorized. 96m/B VHS, DVD. Humphrey Bogart, Ida Lupino, Arthur Kennedy, Joan Leslie, Cornel Wilde, Henry Travers, Henry Hull; D: Raoul Walsh; W: John Huston, W.R. Burnett; C: Gaetano Antonio "Tony" Gaudio.

High Society ♂♂ 1956 A wealthy man attempts to win back his ex-wife who's about to be remarried in this enjoyable remake of "The Philadelphia Story." ♫High Society Calypso; Little One; Who Wants to Be a Millionaire?; True Love; You're Sensational; I Love You, Samantha; Now You Has Jazz; Well, Did You Evah?; Mind if I Make Love to You? 107m/C VHS, DVD. Frank Sinatra, Bing Crosby, Grace Kelly, Louis Armstrong, Celeste Holm, Sidney Blackmer, Louis Calhern; D: Charles Walters; C: Paul Vogel; M: Cole Porter.

High Spirits ♂♂ 1988 (PG-13) An American inherits an Irish castle and a sexy 200-year-old ghost. A painful, clumsy comedy by the fine British director that was apparently butchered by the studio before its release. 99m/C VHS, DVD. Daryl Hannah, Peter O'Toole, Steve Guttenberg, Beverly D'Angelo, Liam Neeson, Martin Ferrero, Peter Gallagher, Jennifer Tilly; D: Neil Jordan; W: Neil Jordan; C: Alex Thomson; M: George Fenton.

High Stakes 🐾🐾 *Melanie Rose* 1989 (R) Kirkland stars as a prostitute who's battling the Mob and falling in love. Limited release in theatres but another fine performance from Kirkland. 102m/C VHS. Sally Kirkland, Robert LuPone, Richard Lynch, Sarah Michelle Gellar, Berly Miller, Maia Danziger, Jesse Conti, Hatch, Berly Miller, Maia Danziger, Jesse Conti, Samantha Lousa, Larry Block, June Stein, Michael Steinhardt, Maggie Warner, William Kennedy; **D:** Amos Kollek; **W:** Amos Kollek; **C:** Mac Hirschfeld; **M:** Bob Dylan, Mira Spektor.

High Stakes 🐾🐾½ *The Disappearance of Nora* 1993 Nora Fremont (Hamel) wakes up in the Nevada desert bloodied and bruised from a beating and suffering from amnesia. She makes it to Vegas where she meets Denton (Farina), who does casino security, and he agrees to help her find her way back. But when her husband (Collins) comes to claim her, Nora's nightmare is really just beginning. You'll hope he dies sooner since the movie is so lame. Beware, Carrey has very little screen time in spite of the advertising. 96m/C VHS, DVD. Veronica Hamel, Dennis Farina, Stephen Collins, Stan Ivar, Bryan Cranston; **C:** Joyce Chopra; **W:** Tom Cole, Alan Ormsby; **C:** James Glennon; **M:** Mark Snow. TV

High Strung 🐾½ 1991 (PG) Writer Thane Furrows (Oedekerk) thinks his life can't get any worse since he's plagued by a nagging mom, pressuring boss, and an insurance salesman. Then mysterious voices and images (played by Carrey) tell him he'll die that night. Naturally, Thane tries to think of a way out of his predicament. You'll hope he dies sooner since the movie is so lame. Beware, Carrey has very little screen time in spite of the advertising. 96m/C VHS. Steve Oedekerk, Steve Oedekerk, Thomas F. Wilson, Fred Willard, Jim Carrey; **D:** Roger Nygard; **W:** Steve Oedekerk, Robert Kuhn; **C:** Alan Oltman; **M:** Thomas Lieberman.

High Tension woof! *Haute tension* 2003 (R) French splatter exploitation film finds college friends Marie (De France) and Alex (Maiwenn) spending the weekend at the isolated farmhouse of Alex's parents. Your standard gross killer (Nahon), who enjoys decapitation, kills Alex's family and kidnaps Alex so he can torture her at his leisure. Marie sets out to rescue her. There's a lot more gore and even more bad dubbing. Americans do these things much better. 91m/C DVD. FR/Cecile de France, Maiwenn Le Besco, Philippe Nahon, Franck Khalfoun, Andrei Finti, Oana Pellea, Marco Claudiu Pascu; **D:** Alexandre Aja; **W:** Alexandre Aja, Gregory Levasseur; **C:** Maxime Eudes.

High Tide 🐾🐾🐾 1987 (PG-13) A strong and strange drama once again coupling the star and director of "My Brilliant Career." A small-time rock 'n' roll singer who is stranded in a small, beach town fortuitously meets up with her previously abandoned teenage daughter. Acclaimed. 120m/C VHS. AU Judy Davis, Jan Adele, Claudia Karvan, Colin Friels, John Clayton, Mark Hembrow, Frankie J. Holden, Monica Trapaga; **D:** Gillian Armstrong; **W:** Laura Jones; **C:** Russell Boyd; **M:** Peter Best, Ricky Fataar, Mark Moffatt, Australian Film Inst. '87. Actress (Davis); Nat. Soc. Film Critics '88. Actress (Davis).

High Velocity 🐾½ 1976 (PG) Lame adventure about two mercenaries involved in the challenge of a lifetime—rescuing a kidnapped executive from Asian terrorists. Filmed in Manila. 105m/C VHS. Ben Gazzara, Paul Winfield, Britt Ekland, Keenan Wynn; **D:** Remi Kramer; **M:** Jerry Goldsmith.

High Voltage 🐾🐾 1998 (R) Tough guy Johnny Clay (Sabato Jr.) winds up in unexpected trouble when he and his cohorts rob a bank that's laundering money for the Asian mob. Mob boss Cheung decides they need to be taught a lesson. 92m/C VHS, DVD. Antonio Sabato Jr., Lochlyn Munro, William Zabka, George Kee Cheung, Amy Smart, James Lew, Antonio (Tony) Sabato, Shannon Lee; **D:** Isaac Florentine; **W:** Mike Mains; **C:** Philip D. Schwartz; **M:** Stephen (Steve Edwards. VIDEO

High Voltage 🐾🐾 1929 A fast-moving comedy adventure set in the High Sierras. 62m/B VHS, DVD. Carole Lombard, William Boyd, Gwen Moore, Billy Bevan; **D:** Howard Higgin.

Higher and Higher 🐾🐾 1944 Bankrupt aristocrat conspires with servants to regain his fortune, and tries to marry his daughter into money. Sinatra's first big-screen role. 🎵You Belong In a Love Song; A Most Important Affair; The Music Stopped; Today I'm A Debutante; A Lovely Way To Spend An Evening; I Couldn't Sleep a Wink Last Night; You're On Your Own; I Saw You First; Disgustingly Rich. 90m/B VHS. Frank Sinatra, Leon Errol, Michele Morgan, Jack Haley, Mary McGuire; **D:** Tim Whelan.

Higher Education 🐾🐾 1988 (R) Andy leaves his small town for a big city college and falls head over heels for a student and a teacher. He didn't know college could be so much fun. 83m/C VHS. Kevin Hicks, Isabelle Mejias, Lori Hallier, Maury Chaykin, Richard Monette; **D:** John Sheppard.

Higher Learning 🐾🐾 1994 (R) Racism, idealism, and the struggle for identity converge in this stylistically shot but rarely enlightening commentary on campus life and strife, focusing on three very different freshmen at fictional Columbus University—a bright track star (Epps) who questions the exploitation of black student athletes; a sheltered, sexually confused beauty from the 'burbs (Swanson); and a group of skinheads (Rapaport). Single-goony, paranoid loner who falls in with a group of skinheads (Rapaport). Single-ton's honorable intention—to make a movie that makes a difference—is marred by cardboard supporting characters, a penchant for in-your-face irony, and a predictable, simplistic conclusion. 122m/C VHS, DVD. Omar Epps, Kristy Swanson, Michael Rapaport, Laurence Fishburne, Jennifer Connelly, Ice Cube, Tyra Banks, Jason Wiles, Cole Hauser, Regina King, Colleen (Ann) Fitzpatrick; **D:** Jon Singleton; **W:** John Singleton; **C:** Peter Lyons Collister.

The Highest Honor 🐾🐾½ 1984 (R) True story set during WWII of a friendship between an Australian army officer, captured while attempting to infiltrate Singapore, and a Japanese security officer. Too long, but gripping. 99m/C VHS. AU John Howard, Atsuo Nakamura, Stuart Wilson, Michael Aitkens, Steve Bisley; **D:** Peter Maxwell.

Highlander 🐾🐾🐾 1986 (R) A strange tale about an immortal 16th-century Scottish warrior who has had to battle his evil immortal enemy through the centuries. The feud comes to blows in modern-day Manhattan. Connery makes a memorable appearance as the good warrior's mentor. Spectacular battle and death scenes. A cult favorite which spawned a weak sequel and a TV series. Based on a story by Gregory Widen. 110m/C VHS, DVD. Christopher Lambert, Sean Connery, Clancy Brown, Roxanne Hart, Beatie Edney, Alan North, Sheila Gish, Jon Polito; **D:** Russell Mulcahy; **W:** Gregory Widen, Peter Bellwood, Larry Ferguson; **C:** Gerry Fisher; **M:** Michael Kamen.

Highlander 2: The Quickening 🐾½ 1991 (R) The saga of Connor MacLeod and Juan Villa-Lobos continues in this sequel set in the year 2024. An energy shield designed to block out the sun's harmful ultraviolet rays has left planet Earth in perpetual darkness, but there is evidence that the ozone layer has repaired itself. An environmental terrorist and her group begin a sabotage effort and are joined by MacLeod and Villa-Lobos in their quest to save Earth. Stunning visual effects don't make up for the lack of substance. The Renegade version is a director's cut, which has been reedited and contains some 19 additional minutes of footage. 90m/C VHS, DVD. Christopher Lambert, Sean Connery, Virginia Madsen, Michael Ironside, John C. McGinley; **D:** Russell Mulcahy; **W:** Peter Bellwood; **C:** Phil Meheux; **M:** Stewart Copeland.

Highball 🐾🐾 1997 (R) Newlyweds try to expand their social life by throwing a series of theme parties. Charmingly owkey indie. 90m/C VHS, DVD. Justine Bateman, Peter Bogdanovich, Rae Dawn Chong, Christopher Eigeman, Annabella Sciorra, Ally Sheedy, Eric Stoltz, Catherine Kellner, Dean Cameron, Andrea Bowen; **D:** Noah Baumbach; **W:** Noah Baumbach; **C:** Steven Bernstein. VIDEO

Highlander: The Gathering 🐾🐾½ 1992 (PG-13) Re-edited episodes from the syndicated TV series finds good immortals Connor MacLeod (Lambert) and distant relative Duncan (Paul) banding against an evil immortal misguided human (Vanity). Lots of sword-play and a little bit of romance (courtesy of Vandernoot). 96m/C VHS, DVD. Christopher Lambert, Adrian Paul, Richard Moll, Vanity, Alexandra Vandernoot, Stan Kirsch; **W:** Lorain Despres, Dan Gordon. TV

Highpoint 🐾 1980 (PG) When an unemployed man becomes the chauffeur of a wealthy family, he finds himself in the middle of a mysterious murder and part of an international CIA plot. Hard to figure what's happening in this one, and it's all best forgotten. 91m/C VHS. Christopher Plummer, Beverly D'Angelo, Kate Reid, Saul Rubinek; **D:** Peter Carter.

Highway 🐾🐾 2001 (R) Vegas pool cleaner Jack Hayes (Leto) decides to make make a quick getaway when he gets caught in bed with a mobster's wife. So he and best pal Pilot Kelson (Gyllenhaal) score some drugs and head out on the road, along with hitchhiking hooker Cassie (Blair). And they even have a destination—to attend a vigil for the recently deceased Kurt Cobain in Seattle. 97m/C VHS, DVD. Jared Leto, Jake Gyllenhaal, Selma Blair, Jake Gyllenhaal, Kimberley Kates, Jeremy Piven, John C. McGinley, James Cox; **W:** Scott Rosenberg; **C:** Mauro Fiore. VIDEO

Highway Hitcher 🐾🐾 *The Pass* 1998 (R) Comic strip salesman Charles Duprey (Forsythe) is in the midst of a mid-life crisis, including having his wife Shirley (Allen) leave him. Charles' friend Willie (McKean) convinces him to hit the road to Reno for a little R&R. On a backroad Charles crosses paths with Hunter (LeGros), who's having car trouble, and reluctantly offers him a ride. He should have trusted his instincts, since this is the beginning of trouble. 83m/C VHS, DVD, William Forsythe, James LeGros, Elizabeth Pena, Jamie Kennedy, Nancy Allen, Michael McKean, Jason Simmons, John Doe; **D:** Kurt Voss; **M:** Kurt Voss; **C:** Denis Maloney; **M:** Vinnie Gioia.

Highlander: Endgame 🐾🐾½ *rutiero* 2000 (R) Fourth series installment ignores the two middle films but harkens back to the 1985 original, Lambert returns as immortal Connor MacLeod, teaming up with his equally immortal clansman, Duncan (TV "Highlander" Paul), to battle baddie Jacob Kell (Payne). Kell has a long-standing grudge against Connor and doesn't follow the rules of the "game." Numerous flashbacks could be confusing for newcomers but fans will find enjoyment and there is much action and swordplay. Story is so fast-paced that some subplots and release contains 12 more minutes of footage and a new ending. 101m/C VHS, DVD. Christopher Lambert, Adrian Paul, Bruce Payne, Lisa Barbuscia, Peter Wingfield, Jim Byrnes, Donnie Yen, Beatie Edney, Sheila Gish; **D:** Douglas Aarniokoski; **W:** Joel Soisson; **C:** Doug Milsome; **M:** Stephen Graziano.

Highlander: The Final Dimension 🐾🐾½ *Highlander 3: The Magician; Highlander 3: The Sorcerer* 1994 (R) Immortal Connor MacLeod (Lambert) battles master illusionist Kane (Van Peebles), who seeks to rule the world. Aiding MacLeod is Alex Smith (Unger), a research scientist who discovers Kane was once buried beneath a mystical mountain along with three other immortal warriors some 300 years before. MacLeod returns to his old Scottish stomping grounds to prepare for battle. Lots of action and special effects, really dumb storyline and overacting—even for a fantasy film. Original theatrical release was PG-13 and 94 minutes; footage added. 99m/C VHS, DVD. Christopher Lambert, Mario Van Peebles, Deborah Kara Unger, Mako; **D:** Andrew Morahan; **W:** Paul Ohl; **C:** Steven Chivers; **M:** J. Peter Robinson.

Highway 13 🐾½ 1948 When a trucker witnesses an "accidental" death at the loading warehouse, he falls under suspicion. He then sets out to clear his name, corpse of an unknown young man in the same small town. So begins a wild road trip. Lacklus-ter direction undercuts much of the first-rate acting and amusing story quirks. 110m/C VHS, DVD. Valerie Juhagiar, Don McKellar, Earl Pastko, Peter Breck, Art Bergmann; **W:** Bruce McDonald; **M:** Don McKellar.

Highway 61 🐾🐾 1991 (R) Shy barber Pokey Jones lives in the small Canadian town of Pickerel Falls and becomes a celebrity when the mysterious, frozen corpse of an unknown young man in his backyard. Jackie Bangs, a rock roadie who's stolen her band's stash of drugs, finds herself stranded in the same small town. So begins a wild road trip. Lackluster direction undercuts much of the first-rate acting. 110m/C VHS, DVD. Valerie Buhagiar, Don McKellar, Earl Pastko, Peter Breck, Art Bergmann; **W:** Bruce McDonald; **M:** Don McKellar.

Highway to Hell 🐾🐾 1992 (R) Bergen plays the devil in a horror-comedy about going to hell—even if you're not dead yet. Lowe and Swanson are newlyweds on their way to Las Vegas when they're stopped by a "hellcop," who kidnaps the bride and takes her to the nether-world to be the devil's new plaything. Her human hubby doesn't take kindly to this and goes to hell to rescue his bride. Campy flick is played for laughs and has some good special effects. 93m/C VHS. Patrick Bergin, Adam Storke, Chad Lowe, Kristy Swanson, Richard Farnsworth, C.J. Graham, Lita Ford, Kevin Peter Hall, Pamela Gidley, Brian Helgeland; **Cameos:** Gilbert Gottfried; **D:** Are De Jong.

Highwaymen 🐾🐾 2003 (R) Rennie (Caviezel) uses a fast car and a police scanner to get a bead on the serial killer who murdered his wife by running her down with a '72 El Dorado. Along for the ride is Molly (Mitra), the one woman to survive the attacks. Intriguing premise is run off the road by the short run-time, which doesn't leave much time to make the plot very cohesive. 80m/C DVD. US James (Jim) Caviezel, Rhona Mitra, Frankie Faison, Gordon Currie, Colm Feore; **D:** Robert Harmon; **W:** Hans Bauer, Craig Mitchell; **C:** Rene Ohashi; **M:** Mark Isham.

Highway Patrolman 🐾🐾 *El Patrullero* 1991 Young Pedro Rojas (Sosa) has just graduated from the National Highway Patrol Academy and is sent to a desolate stretch of Mexican desert. Pedro's more depressed as his ideals are destroyed and his rage increases. Spanish with subtitles. 104m/C VHS. MX Roberto Sosa, Zaide Silvia Gutierrez, Bruno Bichir, Vanessa Bauche; **D:** Alex Cox; **W:** Lorenzo O'Brien; **C:** Miguel Garzon; **M:** Zander Schloss.

Highway Catastrophe: 9/11, Fear and the Selling of America 🐾🐾½ 2004 Another in a series of Anti-Bush documentaries to come out in 2004. The one suggests a much larger and darker conspiracy behind the Bush administration's agenda post-9/11. Hermann Goering is quoted at 11. Hermann Goering is quoted at start, offering a frightening parallel that may or may not be too out there, depending on your party affiliation. Many partisan and non-partisan authorities are interviewed, notably Noam Chomsky and Nor-

The Highway Man 🐾🐾 1999 (R) Middleaged Frank Drake (McHattie) is running telephone scams and winds up getting framed by his nasty boss (Gossett) for fraud and then accused of murder. Into this mess strolls Ziggy (Harris), who thinks Frank is her daddy, along with her boyfriend/thief Walter (Priestly), who's just made a big score. It plays more like two separate stories that never really come together. 97m/C VHS, DVD. Jason Priestley, Louis Gossett Jr., Stephen McHattie, Laura Harris, Callum Keith Rennie, Gordon Michael Woolvett, Bernie Coulson; **D:** Kenni Waxman; **W:** Richard Beattie.

man Mailer. **66m/C** *DVD.* **D:** Jeremy Earp, Sut Jhally; **C:** David Rabinovitz; **M:** Thom Monahan.

Hijacking Hollywood 🦴🦴 **1997** Modest Hollywood satire finds naive Kevin Conroy (Thomas) using family ties to land a menial job with distant relative Michael Lawrence (Metcalf), a tyrannical producer. Kevin's supervisor is the petty Russell (Thompson), who enjoys sending the kid on useless errands. Kevin's one important task is to pick up film rushes at the airport and he tells hustling roommate Tad (Mandt) that if someone took the dailies, a production could be held hostage. Naturally, Tad is all for the idea. **91m/C** *VHS, DVD.* Henry Thomas, Scott Thompson, Mark Metcalf, Paul Hewitt, Art LaFleur, Neil Mandt; **D:** Neil Mandt; **W:** Jim Rossow, Neil Mandt; **C:** Anton Floquet.

Hilary and Jackie 🦴🦴🦴 **1998 (R)** Based on the true story of cover girl cellist Jacqueline Du Pre (Watson) and her relationship with her sister Hilary (Griffiths). As Jackie takes the world of classical music by storm, Hilary gives up her musical ambitions and marries conductor Kiffer (Morrissey). The story switches perspectives between the two women after Jackie arrives at Hilary's doorstep and asks if she may sleep with her husband. Hilary reluctantly agrees, and there go all those stereotypes you had about girls who play classical music. The second half details Jackie's decline and eventual death from multiple sclerosis and the sisters' mutual bonds developed during her illness, including some actual Du Pre performances, make this a pleaser for those who liked "Shine." **124m/C** *VHS, DVD.* *GB* Emily Watson, Rachel Griffiths, James Frain, David Morrissey, Charles Dance, Celia Imrie, Rupert Penry-Jones, Nyree Dawn Porter, Bill Paterson, Vernon Dobtcheff, Auriol Evans, Keeley Flanders; **D:** Anand Tucker; **W:** Frank Cottrell-Boyce; **C:** David C(lark) Johnson; **M:** Barrington Pheloung.

The Hill 🦴🦴½ **1965** British soldiers in a WWII North African military prison are subjected to the brutal discipline of the sadistic Staff Sgt. Williams (Hendry). One of the harshest punishments is the "Hill," a man-made sand wall that the men must climb in full gear. When one of the men dies, it provokes a confrontation between the prisoners, led by Connery, and Williams and his C.O. (Andrews). Harrowing, disturbing look at British Army life and discipline excels on the strength of taut script and great work by the fine cast. **121m/B** *VHS, DVD.* *GB* Sean Connery, Harry Andrews, Ian Hendry, Ian Bannen, Ossie Davis, Alfred Lynch, Jack Watson, Roy Kinnear, Michael Redgrave, Norman Bird, Neil McCarthy, Howard Goorney, Tony Caunter; **D:** Sidney Lumet; **W:** Ray Rigby, R.S. (Ray) Allen; **C:** Oswald Morris.

Hill Number One **1951** A dramatization of the story of Easter, featuring Dean in one of his first major roles as John the Baptist. **57m/B** *VHS, DVD.* James Dean, Michael Ansara, Leif Erickson, Ruth Hussey, Roddy McDowall; **D:** Arthur Pierson. *TV*

Hill 24 Doesn't Answer 🦴🦴🦴 **1955** Four Zionist soldiers defend a strategic entrance to Jerusalem. While at their posts, they reflect on their lives and devotion to the cause. Made in Israel, in English. The first Israeli feature film. **101m/B** *VHS.* *IS* Edward Mulhare, Haya Harareet, Michael Wager; **D:** Thorold Dickinson.

Hillbillies in a Haunted House WOOF! *Hillbillys in a Haunted House* **1967** Two country and western singers en route to the Nashville jamboree encounter a group of foreign spies "haunting" a house. Features Rathbone's last film performance. Sequel to "Las Vegas Hillbillies" (1966). Giant step down for everyone involved. **88m/C** *VHS, DVD.* Ferlin Husky, Joi Lansing, Don Bowman, John Carradine, Lon Chaney Jr., Basil Rathbone, Merle Haggard, Sonny James, Linda Ho, Molly Bee, George Barrows; **D:** Jean Yarbrough; **W:** Duke Yelton; **C:** Vaughn Wilkins; **M:** Hal Borne.

Hillbilly Blitzkrieg 🦴 *Enemy Round-Up* **1942** Two soldiers are sent to the boonies to guard a top-secret missile site from enemy agents. Come-to-life comic strip characters Snuffy Smith, Barney Google and Spark Plug join in the antics. **63m/B** *VHS, DVD.* Bud Duncan, Cliff Nazarro, Edgar Kennedy, Doris Linden, Lucien Littlefield, Alan Baldwin; **D:** Roy Mack.

The Hills Have Eyes 🦴🦴 **2006 (R)** Unnecessary remake of Wes Craven's 1977 lunatic-fest. Not much has been altered in way of the storyline—family stranded in the desert with a pack of inbred killers on their tail, but this time around there's an actual budget. Most of it's blown on fake blood. Slick and humorless, desperate to cash in on (hopefully) short-lived sadism genre resurrected by Rob Zombie. Thanks, Rob. **107m/C** *DVD, UMD.* *US* Aaron Stanford, Emilie de Ravin, Vinessa Shaw, Kathleen Quinlan, Ted Levine, Desmond Askew, Dan Byrd, Tom Bower, Billy Drago, Robert Joy, Michael Bailey Smith, Laura Ortiz; **D:** Alexandre Aja; **W:** Gregory Levasseur; **C:** Maxime Alexandre; **M:** Tomandandy.

The Hills Have Eyes WOOF! **1977 (R)** Desperate family battles for survival and vengeance against a brutal band of inbred hillbilly cannibals. Craven gorefest followed by Hills II. **83m/C** *VHS, DVD.* Susan Lanier, Robert Houston, Martin Speer, Dee Wallace Stone, Russ Grieve, John Steadman, James Whitworth, Michael Berryman, Virginia Vincent, Janus Blythe; **D:** Wes Craven; **W:** Wes Craven; **C:** Eric Saarinen; **M:** Don Peake.

The Hills Have Eyes 2 🦴🦴 **2007 (R)** The unnecessary sequel to the unnecessary 2006 remake (not to be confused with 1984's unnecessary sequel to the gory 1977 original). The inbred mutant cannibal Carter clan were unfortunately not quite wiped out and are hiding in some New Mexico caves just waiting to pick off the members of a National Guard patrol and feed on their intestines. The Craven father and son screenwriting team isn't showing us anything we haven't seen before—or want to see again. **88m/C** *DVD, Blu-ray Disc.* *US* Flex Alexander, Jacob Vargas, Michael Bailey Smith, Lee Thompson Young, Michael McMillian, Jessica Stroup, Daniella Alonso, Eric Edelstein; **D:** Martin Weisz; **W:** Wes Craven, Jonathan Craven; **C:** Sam McCurdy; **M:** Trevor Morris.

The Hills Have Eyes, Part 2 🦴 **1984** Craven reprises Hills with Eyes number one to ill effect. Ignorant teens disregard warnings of a "Hills Have Eyes" refugee, and go stomping into the grim reaper's proving grounds. Predictably bad things happen. **86m/C** *VHS, DVD.* Michael Berryman, Kevin Blair Spirtas, John Bloom, Janus Blythe, John Laughlin, Tamara Stafford, Peter Frechette; **D:** Wes Craven; **W:** Wes Craven; **C:** David Lewis.

The Hills of Home 🦴🦴 *of Lassie* **1948 (G)** Warm sentimental tale about a Scottish doctor and his beloved pet collie. One of the better films in the "Lassie" series. **97m/C** *VHS, DVD.* Edmund Gwenn, Donald Crisp, Tom Drake, Janet Leigh; **D:** Fred M. Wilcox; **W:** William Ludwig.

Hills of Oklahoma 🦴🦴 **1950** Allen stars as the leader of a cattlemen's association who decides not to deal with dishonest meatpacker Keane, so he drives his herd across the desert to a slaughterhouse run by an honest businesswoman. Based on an original story by Cooper. **67m/B** *VHS.* Rex Allen, Elisabeth Fraser, Elisabeth Risdon, Fuzzy Knight, Roscoe Ates, Robert Emmett Keane, Trevor Bardette; **D:** R.G. Springsteen; **W:** Olive Cooper, Victor Arthur.

Hills of Utah 🦴🦴½ **1951** Autry finds himself in the middle of a feud between the local mine operator and a group of cattlemen, while searching for his father's murderer. **70m/B** *VHS.* Gene Autry, Pat Buttram, Denver Pyle; **D:** John English.

The Hillside Strangler 🦴½ **1989** Crime-of-the-week drama about the investigation to apprehend the serial killer responsible for 10 deaths in 1977-78. **91m/C** *VHS.* Richard Crenna, Dennis Farina, Billy Zane, Tony Plana, James Tolkan, Tasia Valenza; **D:** Steven Gethers. *TV*

The Hillside Strangler 🦴½ **2004 (R)** Okay dramatization of the serial murder cases that occurred over a 14-month period in California in 1977-78 and were originally thought to have been the work of one man. Instead, the crimes were committed by cousins Kenneth Bianchi (Howell) and Angelo Buono (Turturro) after their try at running an escort service went bad and Bianchi strangled one of the hookers. Flick ignores the police investigation in favor of showing the murders. Both lead actors are gung-ho about their roles but this is hardly Oscar-worthy material. **97m/C** *DVD.* Nicholas Turturro, C. Thomas Howell, Allison Lange, Lin Shaye, Aimee Brooks, Julia Lee; **D:** Chuck Parello; **C:** John Pirozzi.

Himalaya 🦴🦴 *Himalaya - L'Enfance d'un Chef; Himalaya - The Youth of a Chief; Caravan* **1999** The age-old struggle of generations deciding between tradition and progress plays itself out once more against the spectacular scenery of the Tibetan mountains. Although the story is nothing new, the film gives a detailed look into a traditional lifestyle that is fast dying out, using non-professional actors, location shooting, and not an ounce of special effects. A bit of the film's grandeur is lost on the small screen, but it is still breathtaking. **104m/C** *VHS, DVD.* *FR SI GB* Thinlen Lhondup, Karma Wangiel, Lhakpa Tsamchoe; **D:** Eric Valli; **W:** Eric Valli, Olivier Dazat; **C:** Eric Guichard, Jean-Paul Meurisse; **M:** Bruno Coulais.

Himatsuri 🦴🦴🦴 *Fire Festival* **1985** An acclaimed film detailing the conflicts between man and nature, as a lumberjack in a Japanese forest believes he's the protector of the mountains through his divine relationship with the ancient gods. Outraged by the destruction, pollution, and commercial exploitation of the land he turns to violence. In Japanese with English subtitles. **120m/C** *VHS.* *JP* Kinya Kitaoji, Kiwako Taichi, Ryota Nakamoto, Norihei Miki; **D:** Mitsuo Yanagimachi; **W:** Kenji Nakagami; **C:** Masaki Tamura; **M:** Toru Takemitsu.

The Hindenburg 🦴🦴 **1975 (PG)** A dramatization of what might have happened on the fateful night the Hindenburg exploded. Scott plays an investigator who is aware that something is up, and has numerous suspects to interrogate. The laser edition features widescreen format, digital Stereo Surround, the original trailer, and chapter stops. **126m/C** *VHS, DVD.* George C. Scott, Anne Bancroft, William Atherton, Roy Thinnes, Gig Young, Burgess Meredith, Charles Durning, Richard Dysart; **D:** Robert Wise; **W:** Nelson Gidding, Richard Levinson, William Link; **C:** Robert L. Surtees; **M:** David Shire. Oscars '75: Sound FX Editing, Visual FX.

Hindsight 🦴 **1997** Ah, Hollywood. Joanne (Shower), the bored wife of studio exec Vincent (Law), is having an affair with younger, not-too-bright, aspiring actor Jason (Steadman). Joanne's finally agreed to run off when Jason happens to meet party girl Cassandra (Pass). Thanks to her studio connections, Jason soon has an important agent (Forster) and a studio deal that leaves Joanne in the back lot. But Cassandra is a wild woman with an agenda that doesn't bode well for our self-ish himbo. **93m/C** *VHS.* Ken Steadman, Cyndi Pass, Kathy Shower, John Phillip Law, Robert Forster; **D:** John Bowen; **W:** Steve Tymon; **C:** Keith Holland. *VIDEO*

Hip Hip Hurrah! 🦴🦴🦴 **1987** At the end of the 19th-century, a group of famous painters travel each summer to the northernmost cape of Skagen in Denmark to capture the beauty around them. The most talented of their group is Soren Kroyer (Skarsgard) who has a beautiful wife, Marie (Vieth), and a mistress Lille Marie, who was mad, he was born to her in an insane asylum, and the very light dims around him. Danish with subtitles. **110m/C** *VHS.* *DK* Stellan Skarsgard, Lene Brondum, Pia Vieth, Helge Jordal; **D:** Kjell Grede; **W:** Kjell Grede.

Hip Hop 4 Life 🦴🦴 **2002 (PG-13)** Devon is an eloquent wordsmith at the crossroads of life: pursue college or battle rap his way to the top? Despite his girlfriend and father pushing for college, Devon's dreams of becoming an mc drive him to the stage. Half-baked storyline begins to drag quickly, but to its credit, the film avoids the clichéd misogyny and profanity that so many urban dramas cling to. Rough enough to keep younger audiences watching, but nice enough to satisfy the older crowd. Features a slew of Cleveland, Ohio's lesser-known, but decent, rap acts contributing stage time. **98m/C** *VHS, DVD.* Michael Bell, Q-Nice, Danielle Green; **D:** David Velo Stewart; **W:** David Velo Stewart. *VIDEO*

Hips, Hips, Hooray 🦴🦴½ **1934** Two supposed "hot shot" salesmen are hired by a cosmetic company to sell flavored lipstick. This lavish musical comedy is one of Wheeler and Woolsey's best vehicles. ♪"Tired of It All; Keep Romance Alive; Keep On Doin' What You're Doin'. **68m/B** *VHS.* Robert Woolsey, Bert Wheeler, Ruth Etting, Thelma Todd, Dorothy Lee; **D:** Mark Sandrich.

Hired Hand 🦴🦴 **1971** Two drifters settle on a farm belonging to one of their wives, only to leave again seeking to avenge the murder of a friend. TV prints include Larry Hagman in a cameo role. **93m/C** *VHS, DVD.* Peter Fonda, Warren Oates, Verna Bloom, Severn Darden, Robert Pratt; *Cameos:* Larry Hagman; **D:** Peter Fonda; **W:** Alan Sharp; **C:** Vilmos Zsigmond; **M:** Bruce Langhorne.

Hired to Kill 🦴🦴½ *The Italian Connection* **1973 (R)** A pair of Mafia hoods plot against each other over a $6 million drug shipment. **90m/C** *VHS.* Henry Silva, Woody Strode, Adolfo Celi, Mario Adorf; **D:** Fernando Di Leo; **W:** Fernando Di Leo; **C:** Franco Villa; **M:** Armando Trovajoli.

Hired to Kill 🦴🦴 **1991 (R)** The granite-hewn Thompson plays a male-chauvinist commando grudgingly leading a squad of beautiful mercenary-ettes on an international rescue mission. Not as bad as it sounds (mainly because the ladies aren't complete bimbos), but between senseless plotting, gratuitous catfights, and a love scene indistinguishable from rape, there's plenty to dislike. **91m/C** *VHS, DVD.* Brian Thompson, George Kennedy, Jose Ferrer, Oliver Reed, Penelope Reed, Michelle Moffett, Barbara Lee (Niven) Alexander, Jordanna Capra; **D:** Nico Mastorakis, Peter Rader; **W:** Nico Mastorakis.

Hiroshima 🦴🦴🦴 **1995 (PG)** Haunting depiction re-creates the circumstances surrounding the dropping of the first atomic bomb in 1945. Juxtaposes scenes between the U.S., Japan, and their leaders—President Truman (Welsh) and Emperor Hirohito (Umewaka)—with the development of the Manhattan Project, the bombing itself, and its consequences. Filmed primarily in B&W, with newsreel and contemporary witness interviews in color. Japanese sequences are subtitled in English. Filmed on location in Montreal and Tokyo. **180m/C** *VHS, DVD.* *JP CA* Kenneth Welsh, Naohiko Umewaka, Wesley Addy, Richard Masur, Hisashi Igawa, Ken Jenkins, Jeffrey DeMunn, Leon Pownall, Saul Rubinek, Timothy West, Koji Takahashi, Kurara Kato; **D:** Roger Spottiswoode, Koreyoshi Kurahara; **M:** John Hopkins, Toshiro Ishido; **C:** Pierre Mignot, Shohei Ando. *CABLE*

Hiroshima Maiden **1988** An American family gains new perspective when they meet a young survivor of the atomic bomb. Based on true stories of Japanese women who stayed with Americans while undergoing surgery to minimize their scars. Originally aired on PBS as part of the "Wonderworks" family movie series. **58m/C** *VHS.* Susan Blakely, Richard Masur, Tamlyn Tomita; **D:** Joan Darling.

Hiroshima, Mon Amour 🦴🦴🦴 **1959** Presented in a complex network of flashbacks this profoundly moving drama explores the shadow of history over the personal lives of a lonely French actress (Riva), who's working in Hiroshima, and the Japanese architect (Okada) with whom she's having an affair. She has suffered during the war in occupied France, while he has survived the city's bombing—and their pasts deeply affect their present. Resnais' first feature film and highly influential; adapted by Marguerite Duras from her book. Japanese with subtitles. **88m/B** *DVD.* *JP FR* Emmanuelle Riva, Eiji Okada, Bernard Fresson, Stella Dassas, Pierre Barbaud; **D:** Alain Resnais; **W:** Marguerite Duras; **C:** Sacha Viemy, Michio Takahashi; **M:** Georges Delerue, Giovanni Fusco. N.Y. Film Critics '60: Foreign Film.

Hiroshima: Out of the Ashes &&½ 1990 (PG) The terrible aftermath of the bombing of Hiroshima, August, 1945, as seen through the eyes of American and Japanese soldier's, the Japanese people, and a priest. Carefully detailed and realistic, creates an emotional response. Don't miss the scene in which Nelson and his buddy find themselves surrounded by Japanese—find themy—only to realize that their "captors" have been just as blinded by the blast. Created as an homage for the 45th anniversary of the bombing. **98m/C VHS.** Max von Sydow, Judd Nelson, Mako, Tamlyn Tomita, Stanford Egi, Sab Simono, Noriyuki "Pat" Morita, Kim Miyori. **D:** Peter Werner.

His Bodyguard && 1998 (PG-13) A deaf young man (Natale) is witness to a break-in at the pharmaceutical lab that his family owns, where thieves steal a secret experimental drug. Jenny Farrell (Kapture), the head of lab security, is assigned to protect him from the perpetrators and the two end up running from the bad guys and getting quite friendly. **88m/C VHS.** Mitzi Kapture, Robert Guillaume, Anthony Natale, Vanessa Vaughan, Michael Copeman, Robin Gammell; **D:** Artie Mandelberg; **W:** Emma Sams. **CABLE.**

His Brother's Ghost && 1945 When Fuzzy is rubbed out by bandits, Billy Carson (no longer called Billy the Kid thanks to mothers' protestations) convinces his twin brother to impersonate him in order to make the bandits believe they are the victims of hocus pocus from the otherworld. Crabbe—who dressed up before it was chic—made this during his post sci-fi western period, when he slugged it through some 50 low-rent oaters (usually under the direction of Newfield) at PRC studios, here called "Blackie" Carson. **54m/C VHS.** Buster Crabbe, Al "Fuzzy" St. John, Charles "Blackie" King, Bud Osborne, Karl Hackett, Arch Hall Sr.; **D:** Sam Newfield.

His Butler's Sister && 1944 Bachelor composer Charles Gerard (Tone) hires a sybarite's life in his Manhattan penthouse, which is run by his butler Martin Murphy (O'Brien). When Murphy's stepsister Ann Carter (Durbin) arrives unexpectedly, she's delighted to hear who Murphy works for because she's a singer and wants an audition—an absolute taboo in Gerard's household. So she fools him into thinking she's the new maid until she can get her big break. Nothing new but Durbin gets to work her pretty pipes. Nessun Dorma. In the Spirit of the Moment; When You're Away; Is It True What They Say About Dixie?; In the Spirit of the Moment. **87m/B VHS, DVD.** Deanna Durbin, Franchot Tone, Pat O'Brien, Evelyn Ankers, Akim Tamiroff, Alan Mowbray, Frank Jenks, Walter Catlett, Hans Conried, Florence Bates, Roscoe Karns, Franklin Pangborn; **D:** Frank Borzage. **V:** Samuel Hoffenstein, Betty Reinhardt; **C:** Elwood "Woody" Bredell; **M:** Hans J. Salter.

His Double Life &&½ 1933 Bachelor composer Charles Gerard (Tone) lives a sybarite's life in his Manhattan penthouse, which is run by his butler Martin Murphy (O'Brien)... **67m/B VHS, DVD.** Roland Young, Lillian Gish, Montagu Love; **D:** Arthur Hopkins.

His Fighting Blood &&½ 1935 Tom Elliott joins the Mounties but his first assignment is to bring in the Marsden gang and his brother Phil is a member. Based on a James Oliver Curwood story. **63m/B V+S, DVD.** Kermit Maynard, Polly Ann Young, Paul Fix, Ted Adams, Ben Hendricks Jr., Charles "Blackie" King, Joseph Girard, Frank La Rue; **D:** John English; **W:** Joseph O'Donnell; **C:** Jack Greenhalgh.

His First Command &&& 1929 An early talkie wherein a playboy falls in love with the daughter of a cavalry officer, and enlists in order to win her affections. **60m/B V+S.** William Boyd, Dorothy Sebastian, Gavin Gordon; **D:** Gregory La Cava.

His First Flame && 1926 A classic Langdon silent romantic comedy. **62m/B VHS, DVD.** Harry Langdon, Vernon Dent, Natalie Kingston; **D:** Frank Capra.

His Girl Friday &&&& 1940 Classic, unrelentingly hilarious war-between-the-sexes comedy. Cynical newspaper editor Walter Burns (Grant) wants to get a big scoop on political corruption, which involves convincing star reporter (and ex-wife) Hildy Johnson (Russell, in top form) to come back to work and put off her marriage to dull Bruce Baldwin (Bellamy). Hildy can't resist covering a good story, even when it mean helping a condemned man (Qualen) escape the law. One of Hawk's most furious and inventive screen comedies, in which women are given uniquely equal (for Hollywood) footing, with staccato dialogue and wonderful performances. Based on the Hecht-MacArthur play "The Front Page," which was filmed in 1931, remade in 1974, and again in 1988 (as "Switching Channels"). **92m/B VHS, DVD.** Cary Grant, Rosalind Russell, Ralph Bellamy, Gene Lockhart, John Qualen, Porter Hall, Roscoe Karns, Abner Biberman, Cliff Edwards, Billy Gilbert, Helen Mack, Ernest Truex, Clarence (C. William) Kolb, Frank Jenks; **D:** Howard Hawks; **W:** Charles Lederer; **C:** Joseph Walker. **M:** Morris Stoloff. Nat'l. Film Reg. '93.

His Greatest Gamble &&½ 1934 Tearjerker. Philip Eden (Dix) escapes from prison after 15 years when he learns his estranged daughter, Alice (Wilson), has become a neurotic wimp out of her vengeful mother, Florence (O'Brien-Moore). And there's no way to treat daddy's little girl. **72m/B VHS.** Richard Dix, Dorothy Wilson, Bruce Cabot, Erin O'Brien-Moore, Shirley Grey, Leonard Carey; **D:** John S. Robertson; **W:** Sidney Buchman, Harry Hervey; **C:** Ted Tetzlaff.

His Kind of Woman &&& 1951 Sleazy, campy crime drama that turns out to be compelling fun. Unlucky gambler Dan Milner (Mitchum) accepts a big payday for an unknown job that takes him to a Mexican resort. He gets an eyeful of charteuse Lenore (Russell) and the hot two-some hook-up, even though her married boyfriend, Mark (Price), is also hanging around. Then Dan learns his job is to be the "fall guy" for racketeer Nick Ferraro (Burr), who wants to get back into the States, and he doesn't go for the idea. **120m/B VHS, DVD.** Robert Mitchum, Jane Russell, Vincent Price, Tim Holt, Charles McGraw, Raymond Burr, Jim Backus, Marjorie Reynolds; **D:** John Farrow; **W:** Frank Fenton, Jack Leonard; **C:** Harry Wild; **M:** Leigh Harline.

His Majesty O'Keefe &&½ 1953 Lancaster stars as a South Seas swashbuckler dealing in the lucrative copra-coconut-oil trade of the mid-1800s. The natives see him as a god and allow him to marry a beautiful maiden. When his reign is threatened by unscrupulous traders, Lancaster springs into action to safeguard his kingdom. Based on a real-life American adventurer; this was the first movie ever filmed in the Fiji Islands. **92m/C VHS.** Burt Lancaster, Joan Rice, Benson Fong, Philip Ahn, Grant Taylor; **D:** Byron Haskin.

His Majesty, the American && 1919 William Brooks (Fairbanks) is a young man whose heritage is unknown to him. It turns out he's an heir to a small European kingdom. When Brooks arrives in Alaine he discovers the present king is trying to overthrow the war minister and the usual dash our hero saves the day and also wins the hand of a beautiful princess. First picture released by United Artists studios, formed by Fairbanks, Mary Pickford, Charles Chaplin, and D.W. Griffith. **100m/B VHS.** Douglas Fairbanks Sr., Marjorie Daw, Lillian Langdon, Frank Campeau; **D:** Joseph Henabery.

His Name Was King woof! 1985 A man goes after the gang who murdered his brother and raped his young wife in the old West. **90m/C VHS.** Richard Harrison, Klaus Kinski, Anne Puskin; **D:** Don Reynolds.

His Picture in the Papers && 1916 An early silent comedy wherein the robust, red-meat-eating son of a health food tycoon must get his father's permission to marry by getting his picture favorably in the paper for advertising's sake. **68m/B VHS.** Douglas Fairbanks Sr., Clarence Handysides, Rene Boucicault, Jean Temple.

His Private Secretary &&½ 1933 Wayne plays the jet-setting son of a wealthy businessman who wants his boy to settle down. And he does—after he meets the minister's beautiful daughter. **60m/B VHS, DVD.** John Wayne, Evalyn Knapp, Alec B. Francis, Reginald Barlow, Natalie Kingston, Arthur Hoyt, Al "Fuzzy" St. John; **D:** Philip H. (Phil. P.H.) Whitman.

His Secret Life &&& Fate ignorante *It: Blind Fairies: Ignorant Fairies* 2001 (R) Antonia (Buy) is devastated when her husband Massimo (Renzi) is killed in a car accident. But her grief turns to shock when she accidentally discovers she was having a long-time affair. She goes to confront her husband's mistress and learns it's a mister—Michele (Accorsi), who resents Antonia's interference in this life. But Antonia is desperate to learn about her husband's secret life and other love and they are finally drawn together by their mutual bereavement and curiosity. Italian with subtitles. **105m/C VHS, DVD, FR /T Margherita Buy, Stefano Accorsi, Serra Yilmaz, Andrea Renzi, Erika Blanc, Gabriel Garko, Rosario De Cicco, Lucrezia Valia, Koray Candemir; D:** Ferzan Ozpetek; **W:** Ferzan Ozpetek, Gianni Romoli; **C:** Pasquale Mari; **M:** Andrea Guerra.

His Wife's Lover &&& *Zayn Vaybs Lubovnik* 1931 An actor disguised as an old man wins the heart of a lovely young woman. He decides to test her fidelity by reverting to his handsome young self and attempting to seduce her. An enchanting comedy in Yiddish with English subtitles. **77m/B VHS.** Ludwig Satz, Michael Rosenberg, Isadore Cashier, Lucy Levine; **D:** Sidney Goldin.

The History Boys &&½ 2006 (R) Bennett adapted his own play, which also features the same cast and director an old man wins the heart of a lovely young woman. He decides to test her fidelity by reverting to his handsome young self... and may seem more stagebound than cinematic. In 1983, at a Sheffield grammar school, eight senior boys are being specially tutored in history for a chance to pass the entrance exams to Oxford and Cambridge. To this end, the headmaster Posner (Barnett), who has a crush on fellow grown-ups show off. But Bennett can write some very good monologues. **109m/C VHS, DVD.** Richard Griffiths, Frances de la Tour, James Corden, Samuel Barnett, Dominic Cooper, Jamie Parker, Sacha Dhawan, Russell Tovey, Georgia Taylor, Andrew Knot, Clive Merrison, Penelope Wilton, Adrian Scarborough; **D:** Nicholas Hytner; **W:** Alan Bennett; **C:** Andrew Dunn; **M:** George Fenton.

History Is Made at Night &&& 1937 A wife seeks a divorce from a jealous husband while on an Atlantic cruise. She ends up finding true love and heartbreak in this story of a love triangle at sea. **90m/B VHS.** Charles Boyer, Jean Arthur, Leo Carrillo, Colin Clive; **D:** Frank Borzage; **M:** Gregg Toland.

The History of Mr. Polly &&½ 2007 Victorian everyman Alfred Polly (Evans) finds himself desperately unhappy since he's stuck with a nagging wife (Duff) and a failing business. So he decides to take drastic action to transform himself from a downtrodden loser into a hero. Based on a novel by H.G. Wells. **93m/C VHS, DVD, GB** Lee Evans, Anne-Marie Duff, Julie Graham, Richard Coyle, Roger Lloyd-Pack, Trevor Cooper; **D:** Gilles Mackinnon; **W:** Adrian Hodges; **C:** Nigel Willoughby; **M:** James Edward Barker; Tim Despic. **TV**

History of the World: Part 1 &&½ 1981 (R) More misses than hits in this Brooks parody of historic epics. A bluntly satiric vision of human evolution, from the Dawn of Man to the French Revolution told in an episodic fashion. Good

---

Charles Butler, Homer Hunt, Loretta Blake, Helena Rupport; **D:** John Emerson; **W:** John Emerson, Anita Loos.

for a few laughs. **90m/C VHS, DVD.** Mel Brooks, Dom DeLuise, Madeline Kahn, Harvey Korman, Cloris Leachman, Gregory Hines, Pamela Stephenson, Paul Mazursky, Beatrice Arthur, Fritz Feld, John Hurt, Jack Carter, John Hillerman, John Gavin, Barry Levinson, Ron Carey, Howard Morris, Sid Caesar, Jackie Mason, Charlie Callas, Henry Youngman, Hugh Hefner; **D:** Mel Brooks; **W:** Mel Brooks; **C:** John Morris, Woody Omens; **M:** Shecky Greene; **Nar:** Orson Welles.

A History of Violence &&& 2005 (R) Unassuming small-town diner owner and family man Tom Stall (Viggo Mortensen) foils a robbery, killing the hold-up men, and becomes a hero. This new status brings the unwanted attention of a trio of men who comes to the town from Tom's past. And a very violent past it turns out to be. Cronenberg, working from a script by Josh Olson, delivers another deceptively cool and engrossing, but intelligent fable with the notion of identity and reality, while he takes a jab at the audience's knowledge of and expectations. It's all very cool and engrossing, but intelligent and their conventions. It's all very cool and engrossing, but intelligent and playing with the ride. **96m/C DVD, US** Viggo Mortensen, Maria Bello, William Hunt, Stephen McHattie, Peter MacNeill, Ed Harris, Ashton Holmes, Heidi Hayes; **D:** David Cronenberg; **W:** Josh Olson; **C:** Peter Suschitzky; **M:** Howard Shore, L.A. Film Critics '05; Support. Actor (Harris). N.Y. Film Critics '05: Support. Actor (Hurt), Support. Actress (Bello); Natl. Soc. Film Critics '05: Director (Cronenberg), Support. Actor (Harris).

Hit! && 1973 (R) When the 15-year-old daughter of a government agent dies of a drug overdose, he deals his revenge on the top French heroin traffickers. **135m/C VHS.** Billy Dee Williams, Richard Pryor, Gwen Welles, Paul Hampton, Warren Kemmerling, Sid Melton; **D:** Sidney J. Furie; **W:** Alan R. Trustman, David M. Wolf; **M:** Lalo Schifrin.

The Hit &&½ 1985 (R) A feisty young hooker gets mixed-up with two strong-armed hired killers as they escort an unusual stool-pigeon from his exile in Spain to their angry mob bosses. Minor cult-noir from the director of "My Beautiful Laundrette" and "Dangerous Liaisons." **105m/C VHS, DVD, GB** Terence Stamp, John Hurt, Laura Del Sol, Tim Roth, Fernando Rey, Bill Hunter; **D:** Stephen Frears; **W:** Peter Prince; **C:** John A. Alonzo; **M:** Eric Clapton.

The Hit &&½ 2001 (R) A not-very-thrilling thriller that finds Baltimore reporter Keith Hen (Underwood) wants to unite all rival rap labels under one black-owned company that will also be a community power. But he crosses the mob, bent on shutting down Hen's efforts. **97m/C DVD.** Blair Underwood, DeRay Davis, Ernest Harden Jr., James Russo, Michelle Flowers, Nicki Norris; **D:** Ryan Combs; **W:** Ryan Combs; **C:** Daniel Moder; **M:** Brad Fiedel.

Hit & Run && 2006 *Revenge Squad* 1982 David Marks, a Manhattan cab driver, is haunted by recurring flashbacks of a freak hit-and-run accident in which his wife was struck down on a city street. **96m/C VHS, DVD.** US Michael Pardoci, Peter Jacobson, Kerr Smith, Judy Prescott, J.K. Simmons, Teresa De Priest, Hoyt Richards, John Fiore, Steve Singer; **D:**

Hit and Runway && 2001 (R) Alex (Pardoci) works at his family's restaurant, although he really wants to be a screenwriter. He comes up with the idea for a movie for a big action star named Jagger Stevens (Richards), although Alex turns to playwright Elliot (Jacobson), whom he meets at the restaurant, for professional help. In return, Alex promises to help Elliot win the body of cute waiter Joey (Smith). It's all cute and predictable. **90m/C VHS, DVD. US** Michael Parducci, Peter Jacobson, Kerr Smith, Judy Prescott, J.K. Simmons, Teresa De Priest, Hoyt Richards, John Fiore, Steve Singer; **D:**

Christopher Livingston; **W:** Christopher Livingston, Jaffe Cohen; **C:** David Tumbley; **M:** Frank Piazza.

Hit Lady 🦴🦴 1974 An elegant cultured woman becomes a hit lady for the syndicate in this predictable, yet slick gangster movie. **74m/C VHS, DVD.** Yvette Mimieux, Dack Rambo, Clu Gulager, Keenan Wynn; **D:** Tracy Keenan Wynn; **W:** Yvette Mimieux; **M:** George Aliceson Tipton. **TV**

The Hit List 🦴🦴 1988 (R) A regular guy fights back brutally when his wife and child are mistakenly kidnapped by the Mafia. Fast-paced action makes up for thin plot. **87m/C VHS.** Jan-Michael Vincent, Leo Rossi, Lance Henriksen, Charles Napier, Rip Torn; **D:** William Lustig; **W:** Peter Brosnan.

The Hit List 🦴🦴1/2 1993 (R) Charles Pike (Fahey) is a professional hitman working for attorney Peter Mayhew (Coburn) to wipe out drug lords. Then Mayhew gives Pike a new assignment. He introduces him to sexy widow Jordan Henning (Butler), who wants Pike to kill the man who murdered her husband. Pike finds himself mixing business with pleasure in a deadly combination that sees him dodging crooked cops and trained assassins. **97m/C VHS.** Jeff Fahey, Yancy Butler, James Coburn; **D:** William Webb; **W:** Reed Steiner.

The Hit Man 🦴🦴 *Il Sicario* 1960 A crime drama that profiles the crisis of a man unfit to commit murder but who does for a price. **100m/B VHS.** Andrea Checchi, Sergio Fantoni, Pietro Germi, Sylva Koscina, Belinda Lee, Alberto Lupo; **D:** Damiano Damiani; **C:** Cesare Zavattini; **C:** Pier Ludovico Pavoni; **M:** Roberto Nicolosi.

Hit Me 🦴🦴1/2 1996 (R) Bleak neo-noir based on Jim Thompson's novel "A Swell-Looking Babe." Sonny (Koteas) is a thirtysomething bellhop at the downscale Stillwell hotel who goes home to a scuzzy apartment and the responsibilities of caring for his retarded brother Leroy (Legett). His first slip is falling for troubled guest Monique (Marsac)—the femme fatale of the flick. And then Sonny makes an even bigger mistake by agreeing to help his "friend" Del (Ramsay) rob the hotel's safe deposit boxes of cash intended for a big poker game. **125m/C VHS, DVD.** Elias Koteas, Laure Marsac, Bruce Ramsay, Jay Leggett, Kevin J. O'Connor, Philip Baker Hall, J.C. Quinn, Haing S. Ngor, William H. Macy; **D:** Steven Shainberg; **W:** Denis Johnson; **C:** Mark J. Gordon.

Hit Men 🦴🦴 *Black Kingpin* 1973 Double crosses and gun battles highlight this tale of inner-city crime. **90m/C VHS.** IT Henry Silva, Mario Adorf, Woody Strode, Adolfo Celi, Luciana Paluzzi, Franco Fabrizi, Femi Benussi, Peter Berling, Cyril Cusack, Sylva Koscina; **D:** Fernando Di Leo; **W:** Fernando Di Leo, Augusto Finochi; **C:** Franco Villa; **M:** Armando Trovajoli.

Hit the Deck 🦴🦴1/2 1955 Second-rate studio musical about sailors on leave and looking for romance. Based on the 1927 Broadway musical. ♪Sometimes I'm Happy; Hallelujah; Why, Oh Why; Keeping Myself For You; More Than You Know; I Know That You Know; Lucky Bird. **112m/C VHS.** Jane Powell, Tony Martin, Debbie Reynolds, Walter Pidgeon, Vic Damone, Gene Raymond, Ann Miller, Russ Tamblyn, J. Carrol Naish, Kay Armen, Richard Anderson; **D:** Roy Rowland; **C:** George J. Folsey.

Hit the Dutchman 🦴🦴 1992 (R) Routine gangster flick about Dutch Schultz trying to rise to the top of the New York crime community—with or without the help of underworld pals Legs Diamond and Lucky Luciano. An unrated version is also available. **116m/C VHS.** Bruce Nozick, Sally Kirkland, Will Kempe, Jenny (Jennifer) McShane; **D:** Menahem Golan.

Hit the Ice 🦴🦴 1943 Newspaper photographers Bud and Lou are mistaken as gangsters in Chicago and the usual complications ensue. Includes an appearance by Johnny Long & His Orchestra. ♪I'm Like A Fish Out Of Water; Happiness Bound; I'd Like to Set You to Music; Slap Polka. **89m/C VHS.** Bud Abbott, Lou Costello, Patric Knowles, Elyse Knox, Ginny Simms; **D:** Charles Lamont.

Hit the Saddle 🦴🦴 1937 The Three Mesquiteers track down a gang involved in capturing wild horses in protected areas although one of three is more interested in the charms of a dance hall girl (played by starlet Rita Hayworth) who would soon become Rita Hayworth). **54m/B VHS.** Robert "Bob" Livingston, Ray Corrigan, Max Terhune, (John) (Paterson) McGowan, Yakima Canutt, Rita Hayworth; **D:** Mack V. Wright.

Hit Woman: The Double Edge 🦴🦴1/2 1993 (R) Lucci plays a dual role as an FBI agent and the look-alike killer-for-hire that she's tracking. Originally made for TV; the video version contains additional footage that earned the "R" rating. **92m/C VHS.** Susan Lucci, Robert Urich, Michael Woods, Robert Prosky; **D:** Stephen Stafford; **W:** Alan Oltman, Joe Reb Moffly; **C:** Gideon Porath; **M:** Gerald Gouriet. **TV**

Hitch 🦴🦴1/2 2005 (PG-13) The charming Smith tackles romantic comedy to winnable effect as the title character. Alex "Hitch" Hitchens is a professional dating doctor, the hero of schlubs everywhere. This time his client is shy, hefty accountant Albert (James), who's in love with Allegra (Valletta), a wealthy beauty far out of his league. While Hitch works on Albert, he's also falling for cynical gossip columnist Sara (Mendes) but his every smooth move turns disastrous in her hot babe presence. Everyone pulls their weight and looks like they're having fun. So should the audience. **119m/C DVD, Blu-ray Disc, UMD.** US Will Smith, Eva Mendes, Amber Valletta, Kevin James, Adam Arkin, Kevin James, Julie Ann Emery; **D:** Andy Tennant; **W:** Kevin Bisch; **C:** Andrew Dunn; **M:** George Fenton.

The Hitch-Hiker 🦴🦴🦴 1953 Two young men off on the vacation of their dreams pick up a psychopathic hitchhiker with a right eye that never closes, even when he sleeps. Taut suspense makes this flick worth seeing. **71m/B VHS, DVD.** Edmond O'Brien, Frank Lovejoy, William Talman, Jose Torvay; **D:** Ida Lupino; **W:** Ida Lupino, Daniel Mainwaring, Lucille Fletcher, Robert L. Joseph; **C:** Nicholas Musuraca; **M:** Leith Stevens. Natl. Film Reg. '98.

Hitched 🦴🦴 2001 Housewife Eve (Lee) doesn't suspect that her salesman hubby Ed (Hall) is cheating on her. But then he winds up in the hospital after a drunk-driving accident that also involved his lady friend of the moment. So Eve decides to get even by shackling him in their soundproof basement and filing a missing person's report. Detective Cary Grant (Carter) is immediately smitten and makes his move on Eve but gets confused when Ted reappears and Eve goes missing. **89m/C VHS, DVD.** Sheryl Lee, Anthony Michael Hall, Alex Carter; **D:** Wesley Strick; **W:** Wesley Strick; **C:** Jonathan Freeman; **M:** Randy Miller. **CABLE**

The Hitcher 🦴🦴1/2 1986 (R) A young man picks up a hitchhiker on a deserted stretch of California highway only to be terrorized by the man's repeated appearances: is he real or a figment of his imagination? Ferociously funny, sadomasochistic comedy with graphic violence. **98m/C VHS, DVD.** Rutger Hauer, C. Thomas Howell, Jennifer Jason Leigh, Jeffrey DeMunn, John M. Jackson, Billy Green Bush; **D:** Robert Harmon; **W:** Eric Red; **C:** John Seale; **M:** Mark Isham.

The Hitcher 🦴🦴1/2 2007 (R) Bean can't out-spook Rutger Hauer's title character from the 1986 original as this remake gets gutted (and not in a scary way) into generic action-horror. Jim (Knighton) and girlfriend Grace (Bush) are traveling that lonely desert highway, only to have repeated run-ins with psychopath John Ryder. Many of the original's set action pieces are recreated but, except for the addition of the nubile Bush, the '86 version is a lot more terrifying (if not as loud). **83m/C DVD, HD DVD, UMD.** US Sean Bean, Sophia Bush, Zachary Knighton, Neal McDonough; **W:** Jake Wade Wall, Eric Bernt; **C:** Dave Meyers, James Hawkinson; **M:** Steve Jablonsky.

The Hitcher 2: I've Been Waiting 🦴🦴 2003 (R) Jim Halsey (Howell) reprises his role from the 1986 film) goes back to West Texas to confront his fear of the past accompanied by his girlfriend Maggie (Wuhrer). They travel the same stretch of desolate road and—surprise!—encounter a psycho hitchhiker, Jake (Busey, who certainly looks the part). **93m/C VHS, DVD.** C. Thomas Howell, Kari Wuhrer, Jake Busey; **D:** Louis Morneau; **W:** Molly Meeker, Charles Meeker, Leslie Scharf; **C:** George Mooradian; **M:** Joe Kraemer. **VIDEO**

Hitchhikers woof! 1972 (R) Trash film about a bunch of scantily clad female hitchhikers who rob the motorists who stop to pick them up. Keep right on going when you spot this roadkill. **90m/C VHS.** Misty Rowe, Norman Klar, Linda Avery; **D:** Ferd Sebastian.

The Hitchhiker's Guide to the Galaxy 🦴🦴🦴 1981 The six-episode BBC TV adaptation of Douglas Adams's hilarious science-fiction books. Features the intergalactic Ford Prefect, sent to Earth to update its planetary listing in the Hitchhiker's Guide; hapless hero Arthur Dent, a typical Englishman caught up in space mayhem; and an odd assortment of aliens, including Marvin the Paranoid Android. The show's sheer cheesiness is part of the charm. **194m/C VHS, DVD.** GB Simon Jones, David Dixon, Sandra Dickinson, Mark Wing-Davey; **D:** Alan Bell; **W:** Douglas Adams. **TV**

The Hitchhiker's Guide to the Galaxy 🦴🦴 2005 (PG) Douglas Adams' absurdist sci-fi classic finally makes it to the big screen. When the Earth is demolished, Arthur Dent (Freeman) hitches a ride of the planet with Ford Prefect (Def), a writer for the HGTG, a Fodors-esque guidebook to the universe. Arthur and Ford fall in with Zaphod Beeblebrox (Rockwell), the sublimely blase President of the Galaxy, and his girlfriend, Trillian (Deschanel), in their quest to find the Ultimate Question to life, the universe, and everything. The script's slavish devotion to Adams' text weighs down certain scenes, dampening their sound more like audiobook recitations, but Jennings does a praiseworthy job of bringing the author's eccentric vision to life. The cast is uniformly strong, particularly Rockwell, who gleefully chews the scenery as two-headed egotist Zaphod. **110m/C DVD, UMD.** GB US Martin Freeman, Mos Def, Sam Rockwell, Zooey Deschanel, John Malkovich, Bill Nighy, Warwick Davis, Simon Jones, Anna Chancellor, Albie Woodington, Jason Schwartzman, Dominique Jackson, Jack Stanley; **D:** Garth Jennings; **W:** Douglas Adams, Karey Kilpatrick; **C:** Igor Jadue-Lillo; **M:** Joby Talbot; **V:** Alan Rickman, Thomas Lennon, Helen Mirren, Stephen Fry, Richard Griffiths, Ian McNeice.

Hitler: Dead or Alive 🦴🦴 1943 Three ex-cons devise a scheme to gain a million-dollar reward for capturing Adolf Hitler in this low-budget production. **64m/B VHS, DVD.** Ward Bond, Dorothy Tree, Bruce Edwards, Warren Hymer, Paul Fix, Russell Hicks, Bobby Watson; **D:** Nick Grinde.

Hitler: The Last Ten Days 🦴🦴 1973 (PG) Based on an eyewitness account, the story of Hitler's last days in an underground bunker gives insight to his madness. **106m/C VHS.** Alec Guinness, Simon Ward, Adolfo Celi, Phyllida Law; **D:** Ennio de Concini.

Hitler: The Rise of Evil 🦴🦴 2003 General overview of the insecure but ambitious Hitler (Carlyle) during his rise to power. He goes from World War I soldier to member of the nationalist German Worker's Party and leader of the Nazi Party. Filmed on location in Vienna and Prague. **186m/C DVD.** Robert Carlyle, Stockard Channing, Liev Schreiber, Peter O'Toole, Jena Malone, Julianna Margulies, Matthew Modine, Peter Stormare, Chris Larkin; **D:** Christian Duguay; **W:** John Pielmeier, G. Ross Parker; **C:** Pierre Gill; **M:** Normand Corbeil. **TV**

Hitler's Children 🦴🦴 1943 Two young people, a German boy and an American girl, are caught in the horror of Nazi Germany. He's attracted to Hitler's rant, she's repelled. Exploitative yet engrossing. **83m/B VHS.** Tim Holt, Bonita Granville, Otto Kruger, H.B. Warner, Irving Reis, Hans Conried, Lloyd Corrigan; **D:** Edward Dmytryk.

Hitler's Daughter 🦴 1990 (R) Made for TV movie following the trials and tribulations of the illegitimate daughter of Adolf Hitler. She's all grown up now...and wants to rule the United States. She secures a position of power during an election and now Nazi-hunters must figure out her identity before she takes over the world! **88m/C VHS.** Kay Lenz, Veronica Cartwright, Melody Anderson, Patrick Cassidy, Carolyn Dunn, Lindsay Merrithew, George R. Robertson; **D:** James A. Contner. **TV**

The Hitman 🦴🦴 1991 (R) Norris plays a cop undercover as a syndicate hit man in Seattle, where he cleans up crime by triggering a three-way mob bloodbath between beastly Italian mafiosi, snooty French-Canadian hoods, and fanatical Iranian scum. But he teaches a black kid martial arts, so you know he's politically correct. Action addicts will give this a passing grade; all others need not apply. **95m/C VHS, DVD.** Chuck Norris, Michael Parks, Al Waxman, Alberta Watson, Salim Grant, Ken Pogue, Marcel Sabourin, Bruno Gerussi, Frank Ferrucci; **D:** Aaron Norris; **C:** Joao Fernandes.

Hitman woof! 2007 (R) Just like the videogame on which the film is based, orphaned kids are recruited by a top-secret organization that trains them as assassins. Grown, the killers are all bald with their heads tattooed with large bar codes, and they roam around the rest of the world with large guns, knocking off whomever needs knocking off. One of these guys, known only as "47" (Olyphant), is on task to murder Russian President Belicoff (Thomsen), which he does with brutal (and predictable) violence. But when Belicoff later shows up alive on television, 47 realizes he's been had, and now he's running from police, Interpol, and worse yet, a handful of his old cronies. Somehow gorgeous Nika (Kurylenko) gets tossed into the mix and is on the lam with 47. She lends some eye-candy and a touch of humanity, but that's about it. The violence is over the top, the plot is less than thin, and the acting perfunctory at best. **100m/C DVD.** US Timothy Olyphant, Olga Kurylenko, Dougray Scott, Robert Knepper, Ulrich Thomsen, Henry Ian Cusack, Michael Offei; **D:** Skip Woods, Xavier Gens; **C:** Laurent Bares; **M:** Geoff Zanelli.

Hitman's Journal 🦴🦴 *18 Shades of Dust* 1999 (R) Vincent Dianni (Aiello) is a mob enforcer for Don Cucci and his son Tommy (Forsythe). But when info leaked to the feds gets the Don life in prison, Vincent comes under suspicion as the squealer. All Vincent wants to do is quietly retire but first he has to square things with his bosses. **95m/C VHS, DVD.** Danny Aiello, William Forsythe, Polly Draper, Vincent Pastore, Aida Turturro; **D:** Danny Aiello III. **VIDEO**

Hitman's Run 🦴🦴 1999 (R) Former Mafia hitman Roberts has double-crossed his bosses and is now in the FBI's Witness Protection Program. However, his safety is hardly guaranteed. **93m/C VHS, DVD.** Eric Roberts, Damian Chapa, Esteban Louis Powell; **M:** Mark L. Lester; **W:** Eric Barker; **C:** Zoltan David; **M:** Roger Bellon. **VIDEO**

The Hitter 🦴🦴 1979 (R) A former prizefighter, his girlfriend, and a washed-up promoter are all on the run in this adventure tale. **94m/C VHS.** Ron O'Neal, Adolph Caesar, Sheila Frazier; **D:** Christopher Leitch.

Hittin' the Trail 🦴🦴 1937 The Good Cowboy is mistaken for a murdering varmint, and must prove his innocence. **57m/C VHS, DVD.** Tex Ritter, Charles "Blackie" King, Ray Whitley, The Range Ramblers; **D:** Robert North Bradbury.

Hitz 🦴🦴1/2 *Judgment* 1989 (R) In a Los Angeles barrio, Musico, a Loco gang member, kills two rival gang members. Arrested and convicted when a young boy named Pepe is coerced into testifying against him, Musico is killed in the courtroom. But the violence doesn't stop. The judge, who wants to reform the juvenile court system, tries to protect Pepe, and both are targeted for death by the Loco gang. **90m/C VHS.** Elliott Gould, Emilia Crow, Karen Black, Cuba Gooding Jr.; **D:** William Sachs;

The Hoax ✂️✂️ 2006 (R) In 1971, egocentric writer Clifford Irving's dreams collapse when his book deal falls through. To bolster his bruised ego, Irving tells his publisher (Davis) that he's new tome will be a sensation—and then has to come up with an idea. With the help of loyal researcher Dick Suskind (Molina), Irving schemes to sell a bogus autobiography of reclusive Howard Hughes and greed wins out over corporate suspicions before his case: do well but this long-forgotten hoax has to work hard to attract the interest of a casual viewer. 115m/C DVD. *US* Richard Gere, Alfred Molina, Hope Davis, Marcia Gay Harden, Stanley Tucci, Julie Delpy; *D:* Lasse Hallstrom; *W:* William Wheeler; *C:* Oliver Stapleton; *M:* Carter Burwell.

The Hobbit ✂️✂️✂️ 1978 An animated interpretation of J.R.R. Tolkien's novel of the same name. The story follows Bilbo Baggins and his journeys in Middle Earth and encounters with the creatures who inhabit it. He joins comrades to battle against evil beings and creatures. 76m/C VHS, DVD. *D:* Arthur Rankin Jr, Jules Bass; *M:* Maury Laws; *V:* Cyril Ritchard, Brother Theodore, Paul Frees, Donald E. Messick, Hans Conried, Thurl Ravenscroft, Orson Bean, John Huston, Otto Preminger, Richard Boone. TV

Hobo's Christmas ✂️✂️✂️ 1987 A man who left his family to become a hobo comes home for Christmas 25 years later. Hughes turns in a delightful performance as the hobo. 94m/C VHS, Barnard Hughes, Gerald McRaney, Wendy Crewson; *D:* Will MacKenzie. TV

Hobgoblins ✂️ 1987 Little creatures escape from a studio vault and wreak havoc. 92m/C VHS, DVD. Jeffrey Culver, Tom Bartlett; *D:* Rick Sloane.

Hobson's Choice ✂️✂️ 1953 A prosperous businessman in the 1890s tries to keep his daughter from marrying, but the strong-willed daughter has other ideas. 107m/B VHS. *GB* Charles Laughton, John Mills, Brenda de Banzie; *D:* David Lean; *C:* Jack Hildyard; *M:* Malcolm Arnold. British Acad. '54.

Hobson's Choice ✂️✂️1/2 1983 Remake of the old family comedy about a crusty, penny-pinching businessman whose headstrong daughter proves to him she'll not become an old maid. Instead she marries one of his employees. Not bad, but not as good as the original. 95m/C VHS. Jack Warden, Sharon Gless, Richard Thomas, Lillian Gish; *D:* Gilbert Cates. TV

Hockey Night ✂️✂️1/2 1984 A moving story for pre- and early teens in which a girl goalie makes the boys' hockey team. 77m/C VHS, DVD. *CA* Megan Follows, Rick Moranis, Gail Youngs, Martin Harburg, Henry Ramer; *D:* Paul Shapiro.

Hocus Pocus ✂️✂️ 1993 (PG) The divine Miss M is back, but this time she's not so sweet. Midler, Najimy, and Parker are 17th century witches accidentally conjured up in the 20th century, appropriately enough on Halloween in Salem, Massachusetts. Seems they were hung 300 years back and they take their revenge in some surprisingly gruesome ways, given the Disney label. They rant, they rave, they sing (only once), they fly. See this one for the three stars who make up for it's lack of substance with their comedic talents. 95m/C VHS, DVD. Bette Midler, Kathy Najimy, Sarah Jessica Parker, Thora Birch, Doug Jones, Omri Katz, Vinessa Shaw, Stephanie Faracy, Charles Rocket; *Cameos:* Penny Marshall, Garry Marshall; *D:* Kenny Ortega; *W:* Neil Cuthbert, Mick Garris; *M:* John Debney.

Hoffa ✂️✂️✂️ 1992 (R) The story of union organizer James R. Hoffa, who oversaw the rise of the Teamsters, a labor union composed mostly of truck drivers, from its fledgling infancy during the Great Depression to the 1970s. Powerful performances by Nicholson in the title role and DeVito, who plays a union aide, a fictitious composite of several men who actually served Hoffa. This almost affectionate biographical treatment stands out in contrast from a career bristling with tension and violence. Proceeds through a series of flashbacks from the day Hoffa disappeared, July 30, 1975. 140m/C VHS, DVD. Jack Nicholson, Danny DeVito, Armand Assante, J.T. Walsh, Frank Whaley, Kevin Anderson, John P. Ryan, Robert Prosky, Natalija Nogulich, Nicholas Pryor, John C. Reilly, Karen Young, Cliff Gorman, Paul Guilfoyle, Jennifer Nicholson, Richard Schiff; *D:* Danny DeVito; *W:* David Mamet; *C:* Stephen Burum; *M:* David Newman.

Hoffman ✂️1/2 1970 Lonely, middle-aged business Benjamin Hoffman (Sellers) has a yen for his secretary Janet (Cusack). When he discovers her boyfriend Tom (Mitchell) is involved in some illegal activities, Hoffman blackmails her into spending the weekend with him. Very minor Sellers and not very funny. Gebler adapted from his own novel. 113m/C VHS, DVD. *GB* Peter Sellers, Sinead Cusack, Jeremy Bulloch; *D:* Alvin Rakoff; *W:* Ernest Gebler; *C:* Gerry Turpin; *M:* Ron Grainer.

Hog Wild ✂️1/2 1980 (PG) A clique of high school nerds exact revenge on bullies from the local mean motorcycle gang. 94m/C VHS. Patti D'Arbanville, Tony Rosato, Michael Biehn; *D:* Les Rose.

The Holcroft Covenant ✂️✂️ 1985 (R) Based upon the complex Robert Ludlum novel. Details the efforts of a man trying to release a secret fund that his Nazi father humanistically set up to relieve the future sufferings of Holocaust survivors. Confusing, and slow, but interesting, nonetheless. 112m/C VHS, DVD. *GB* Michael Caine, Victoria Tennant, Anthony Andrews, Lilli Palmer, Mario Adorf, Michael (Micha) Lonsdale; *D:* John Frankenheimer; *W:* Edward Anhalt, John Hopkins, George Axelrod.

Hold 'Em Jail ✂️✂️1/2 1932 Some good laughs with Wheeler and Woolsey starring as a competitive football team at Kennedy's Bidemore Prison. 65m/B VHS. Bert Wheeler, Robert Woolsey, Edgar Kennedy, Betty Grable, Edna May Oliver; *D:* Norman Taurog.

Hold Me, Thrill Me, Kiss Me ✂️✂️1/2 1993 (R) "Offbeat" barely begins to describe this comedy about a hapless loser who finds true love. Eli (Parrish) has escaped marriage to a rich girl named Twinkie (Young), unfortunately it took a little shooting to do it and now Eli's hiding out in a tacky pink trailer park where Sabra (Naschak), an insatiable stripper with a fondness for sex toys, immediately goes after Eli's bod. But he falls for her naive (and virginal) sister, Darnie (Shelly). Hershman manages to keep all three-wheeling goings on under control. Film debut of former mocel Parrish; directorial debut feature of Hershman. 92m/C VHS. Max Parrish, Adrienne Shelly, Andrea Naschak, Sean Young, Diane Ladd, Bela Lehoczky, Ania Suli; *Cameos:* Timothy Leary; *D:* Joel Hershman; *W:* Joel Hershman; *C:* Kent Wakeford; *M:* Gerald Gouriet.

Hold That Ghost ✂️✂️✂️ 1941 Oh, Charlie and Costello inherit an abandoned roadhouse where the illicit loot of its former owner, a "rubbed out" mobster, is supposedly hidden. Abbott, O'Connell, Ricky Jay, Molly Parker; *D:* Bud Abbott, Lou Costello, Joan Davis, Richard Carlson, Mischa Auer, The Andrews Sisters, Shemp Howard, Evelyn Ankers, Nestor Paiva; *D:* Arthur Lubin; *W:* Robert Lees, Frederic Rinaldo, John Grant; *C:* Elwood "Woody" Bredell; *M:* Hans J. Salter.

Hold the Dream ✂️✂️1/2 1986 Barbara Taylor Bradford's sequel to "A Woman of Substance." Kerr plays the adult Emma Harte while Seagrove, who played young Emma in the original miniseries, now plays her granddaughter Paula, who has been chosen to take over the family's retailing empire. But will her ambitions clash with her romantic possibilities? 200m/C VHS, DVD. Jenny Seagrove, Deborah Kerr, Claire Bloom, James Brolin, Stephen Collins, Nicholas Farrell, Nigel Havens, John Mills, Liam Neeson, Valentine Pelka; *D:* Don Sharp; *C:* John Coquillon; *M:* Barrie Guard. TV

Hold Your Man ✂️✂️✂️ 1933 Great star vehicle that turns from comedy to drama with Harlow falling for hustler Gable. See how Harlow makes the kids dig holes in the desert to "build character." She's really looking for an Old West outlaw's treasure, and her ancestors' past may be connected to Stanley's family. Faithfully adapted by Sachar, from his own award-winning children's book, the movie keeps all the elements that make the book so popular with the early adolescent crowd: it doesn't talk down to the audience, it has an involving, complex plot, the characters are not caricatures, and it handles real issues with honesty. You won't find that in many movies aimed at any age nowadays. 111m/C VHS, DVD. *US* Sigourney Weaver, Jon Voight, Patricia Arquette, Shia LaBeouf, Tim Blake Nelson, Dule Hill, Henry Winkler, Nathan Davis, Khleo Thomas, Jake M. Smith, Byron Cotton, Brenden Jefferson, Miguel Castro, Max Kasch, Noah Poletiek, Rick Fox, Scott Plank, Roma Maffia, Eartha Kitt, Siobhan Fallon; *D:* Andrew Davis; *W:* Louis Sachar; *C:* Stephen St. John; *M:* Joel McNeely.

Hold the Dream — continued... [fragment]

A Hole in One ✂️✂️ 2004 It's not about golf. Anna (Williams) is a sweet but troubled small-town girl in the 1950s whose boyfriend is the pathological jealous and violent Billy (Aday). Emotionally fragile, Anna becomes convinced that the way out of her troubles is to undergo that ice pick cure-all—a lobotomy—at the hands of crackpot Dr. Ashton (Raymond). Billy hopes in different employee Tom (Guinee) to pose as a rival doc and dissuade Anna but the twosome end up falling in love. 97m/C DVD. Michelle Williams, Meat Loaf Aday, Tim Guinee Bill Raymond, Wendell Pierce, Eleanor Parker, Eddie Hodges, Keenan Wynn, Joi Lansing; *D:* Frank Capra. Oscars '59: Song ("High Hopes"). *D:* Richard Ledes; *W:* Richard Ledes; *C:* Stephen Kazmierski; *M:* Stephen Trask.

A Hole in the Head ✂️✂️1/2 1959 A comedy-drama about a shiftless but charming lout who tries to raise money to save his hotel from foreclosure and learn to be responsible for his young son. Notable for the introduction of the song "High Hopes." 120m/C VHS, DVD. Frank Sinatra, Edward G. Robinson, Thelma Ritter, Carolyn Jones, Eleanor Parker, Eddie Hodges, Keenan Wynn, Joi Lansing; *D:* Frank Capra. Oscars '59: Song ("High Hopes").

The Hole ✂️1/2 2001 Teen psychodrama offers cheap thrills. A terrified Liz (Birch) is discovered to be the only survivor of four students who have been missing for 18 days. Liz talks to psychologist Mike (Harrington), which she reveals an unrequited crush on her. Seeking to escape a school trip, Liz persuades Martin (Fox) and Frankie (Knightley) spend the time in a disused WWII underground steel bunker he's discovered. Only jealous Martin locks them in. Or does he? Liz's story is full of holes and the police investigation offers another theory of what happened. Based on the novel "After the Hole" by Guy Burt. 102m/C VHS. *GB* Thora Birch, Keira Knightley, Desmond Harrington, Embeth Davidtz, Daniel Brocklebank, Keira Knightley, Steven Waddington, Laurence Fox; *D:* Nick Hamm; *W:* Ben Court, Caroline Ip; *C:* Denis Crossan; *M:* Clint Mansell.

Hole in the Sky ✂️✂️1/2 *The Rangers, the Crook and a Hole in the Sky* 1995 (PG) Teenaged Mac (O'Connell) is working for the Montana forestry service in the summer of 1919 under the tutelage of taciturn legend Bill Bell (a mustache-less Elliott). Mac learns some lessons about growing up, first love, card-playing—and never to rile the camp cook. Based on an autobiographical story by Norman MacLean. Made for TV; filmed on location in British Columbia. 94m/C VHS, DVD. Sam Elliott, Jerry O'Connell, Ricky Jay, Molly Parker; *D:* John Kent Harrison; *W:* Robert W. Lenski. TV

The Holes *Les Gaspards* 1972 (PG) A Parisian book shop owner's daughter vanishes along with other local citizens and American tourists, and he decides to investigate when the police won't. In French with subtitles. 92m/C VHS, DVD. *FR* Philippe Noiret, Charles Denner, Michel Serrault, Gerard Depardieu; *D:* Pierre Tchernia; *W:* Pierre Tchernia, Rene Goscinny; *C:* Jean Tournier; *M:* Gerard Calvi.

Holes ✂️✂️1/2 2003 (PG) Poor Stanley Yelnats VI. As a result of a family curse, he's just been convicted of a crime he didn't commit and sent to a juvenile facility. While there, he's met with a nasty overseer, Mr. Sir (Voight), and a proverbial camp counselor (Nelson), and scariest of all the Warden (Weaver) an intimidating figure who makes the kids dig holes in the desert to "build character." She's really looking for an Old West outlaw's treasure, and her ancestors' past may be connected to Stanley's family. Faithfully adapted by Sachar.

Hole in the Head — continued...

The Holiday ✂️✂️1/2 2006 (PG-13) *Free to Live; Unconventional Linda* 1938 The classically genteel screwball comedy about a rich girl who steals her sister's fiance. A yardstick is years to come for sophisticated, urbane Hollywood romanticism. Based on the play by Philip Barry who later wrote "The Philadelphia Story." 95m/B VHS, DVD. Cary Grant, Katharine Hepburn, Doris Nolan, Edward Everett Horton, Ruth Donnelly, Lew Ayres, Binnie Barnes, Henry Kolker; *D:* George Cukor; *W:* Donald Ogden Stewart, Sidney Buchman.

Holiday ✂️✂️1/2 1938 Chick romance lite. LA careerist Amanda (Diaz) has just discovered her boyfriend (Burns) cheating; London journalist Iris (Winslet) loves Jasper (Sewell), who's just announced his engagement. Naturally, Christmas joy is the furthest thing from their minds, until, thanks to an Internet site, the two women decide to swaps digs for the holidays. Iris gets Beverly Hills luxury and Amanda gets cozy, snowy English countryside cottage. At least they each have holidays to all 135m/C DVD, Blu-ray Disc. *US* Cameron Diaz, Kate Winslet, Jude Law, Jack Black, Eli Wallach, Edward Burns, Rufus Sewell, Shannyn Sossamon, Bill Macy, Shelley Berman, Kathryn Hahn, John Krasinski; *D:* Nancy Meyers; *W:* Nancy Meyers; *C:* Dean Cundey; *M:* Hans Zimmer.

Holiday Affair ✂️✂️1/2 1949 Hollywood yuletide charmer about a pretty widow being courted by two very different men. 86m/B VHS, Robert Mitchum, Janet Leigh, Wendell Corey, Esther Dale, Harry Morgan, Larry J. Blake; *D:* Don Hartman.

Holiday Heart ✂️✂️ 2000 (R) Macho big man Rhames may not be the first actor to spring to mind to play a drag queen but he does a fine job in this melodramatic adaptation of the play by West. Holiday Heart (Rhames) comes to the rescue of ex-addict Warda (Woodard) who has a 12-year-old daughter, Niki (Reynolds), and lousy taste in men. Wanda just can't make that final break with her dealer boyfriend Silas (Williamson), even though it leads to her sliding back into crack addiction and means that Heart has to draw on his maternal skills to give Niki a stable home. 97m/C VHS, DVD. Ving Rhames, Alfre Woodard, Mykelti Williamson, Jesika Reynolds; *D:* Robert Kevin Townsend; *W:* Cheryl L. West; *C:* Jan Kiesser; *M:* James Taylor.

Holiday Hotel 🦴🦴 1977 (R) A group of wild French vacationers let loose at their favorite little resort hotel along the Brittany coast. Available in French with English subtitles or dubbed into English. 109m/C VHS, FR Sophie Barjac, Daniel Ceccaldi; D: Michael (Michel) Lang.

Holiday in Havana 🦴🦴 1949 Desi Arnaz is back in Cuba winning hearts and dance contests. Watch only for Desi's presence. ♫Holiday in Havana; The Arnaz Jam; Straw Hat Song; Rhumba Rumbero; Copacobana; Made For Each Other; I'll Take Romance. 73m/B VHS. Desi Arnaz Sr., Lolita Valdez, Mary Hatcher, Ann Doran; D: Jean Yarbrough.

Holiday in Mexico 🦴🦴½ 1946 Pidgeon plays the U.S. ambassador to Mexico whose teenage daughter (Powell) tries to run his life along with his household. He falls for a singer while she develops a crush on an older, respected pianist (Iturbi playing himself). Lots of lively production numbers featuring Xavier Cugat and his orchestra. ♫I Think Of You; Walter Winchell Rhumba; Yo Te Amo Mucho—And That's That; And Dreams Remain; Holiday in Mexico; Ave Maria; Les Filles de Cadiz; Italian Street Song; Polonaise in A Flat Major. 127m/C VHS. Walter Pidgeon, Jane Powell, Ilona Massey, Jose Iturbi, Roddy McDowall, Xavier Cugat, Hugo Haas; D: George Sidney; W: Isobel Lennart; C: Harry Stradling Sr.; M: Georgie Stoll.

Holiday Inn 🦴🦴🦴 1942 Fred Astaire and Bing Crosby are rival song-and-dance men who decide to work together to turn a Connecticut farm into an inn, open only on holidays. Remade in 1954 as "White Christmas." ♫White Christmas; Be Careful, It's My Heart; Plenty to Be Thankful For; Abraham; Abraham; Let's Say It With Firecrackers; I Gotta Say I Love You Cause I Can't Tell A Lie; Let's Start the New Year Right; Happy Holidays; Song of Freedom. 101m/B VHS. Bing Crosby, Fred Astaire, Marjorie Reynolds, Walter Abel, Virginia Dale; D: Mark Sandrich. Oscars '42: Song ("White Christmas").

Holiday Rhythm 🦴½ 1950 A TV promoter is knocked out and dreams of a world-wide trip full of entertainment, comedy, and insanity. 61m/B VHS. Mary Beth Hughes, Tex Ritter, David Street, Donald MacBride; D: Jack Scholl; W: Lee Wainer; C: Benjamin (Ben H.) Kline; M: Bert Shefter.

The Hollow 🦴½ 2004 (R) Updated remake of the classic Legend of Sleepy Hollow. Ian (Zegers), who is the great-great-grandson of Ichabod Crane, moves to town. Once he hears of his lineage, chaos ensues for the teens of Sleepy Hollow on Halloween eve, and it's up to Ian to settle the score with the Headless Horseman. Love interest Karen (Cuoco), nemesis Brody (Carter) and Claus Van Ripper (Keach) are among the cast. Strangely enough this film first aired on the ABC Family channel in 2004, though the violence would preclude many families from watching it. 82m/C DVD. Kevin Zegers, Kaley Cuoco, Nick Carter, Ben Scott, Stacy Keach, Judge Reinhold, Nicholas Turturro, Eileen Brennan; D: Kyle Newman; W: Hans Rodionoff; C: Scott Kevan; M: Todd Haberman. CABLE

Hollow City 🦴🦴🦴 2004 A group of children, fleeing the Angolan civil war, are taken to the capitol of Luanda by a nun. Young N'Dala (Roldan) leaves the group to explore the city and he meets a variety of characters who seek to influence his life. Portuguese with subtitles. 90m/C DVD, PT Joao Roldan, Custodio Francisco, Carlao Machado; D: Maria Joao Ganga; W: Maria Joao Ganga; C: Jacques Besse; M: Manu Dibango, Ne Goncalves.

Hollow Gate 🦴🦴 1988 Trick or Treat?? Four kids find out when they run into a guy with hungry dogs. 90m/C VHS. Katrina Alexy, Richard Dry, Patricia Jacques, Addison Randall; D: Ray Di Zazzo; W: Ray Di Zazzo; C: Vojislav Mikulic; M: John Gonzales.

Hollow Man 🦴🦴 2000 (R) Scientist Caine (Bacon) heads a team that discovers the ability to make humans invisible. He decides to test it on himself and the process works, in fact it's irreversible, and his newfound unexpected side effects when he gives into his worst impulses and terrorizes his colleagues, including ex-girlfriend Linda (Shue) and her new beau (Brolin). Stunning visual effects can't hide script's lack of imagination and creepy sexual kink. Degenerates into body-count slasher flick as the intriguing moral questions are dropped in favor of cheap scares. 114m/C VHS, DVD, Blu-ray Disc, UMD. Kevin Bacon, Elisabeth Shue, Josh Brolin, William Devane, Kim Dickens, Greg Grunberg, Mary Jo Randle, Joey Slotnick; D: Paul Verhoeven; W: Andrew Marlowe; C: Jost Vacano; M: Jerry Goldsmith.

Hollow Man 2 🦴½ 2006 (R) Volunteer soldier/assassin Michael Griffin (Slater) goes mad when he becomes invisible thanks to a research project. He needs certain drugs to stay alive so Michael goes after scientist Maggie Dalton (Regan), who is being protected by cop Frank Turner (Facinelli). Slater has little actual screen time since his character's invisible and does mostly voice work. 91m/C DVD. Christian Slater, Peter Facinelli, Laura Regan, David McIlwraith, Sarah Deakins, William Macdonald; D: Claudio Fah; W: Joel Soisson; C: Peter Wunstorf; M: Marcus Trump. VIDEO

Hollow Point 🦴🦴 1995 (R) After FBI agent Diane Norwood (Carrere) and DEA agent Max Perish (Griffith) get in each other's way, they reluctantly team up to bring down crime kingpin Oleg Krezinsky (Hemblen). Only Krezinsky and his partner Livingston (Lithgow) learns she's a fed and hires assassin Lawton (Sutherland) to teach her a lesson. 103m/C VHS, DVD. Thomas Ian Griffith, Tia Carrere, John Lithgow, Donald Sutherland, David Hemblen; D: Sidney J. Furie; C: David Franco; M: Brahm Wenger.

Hollow Reed 🦴🦴🦴 Believe Me 1995 Heart-wrenching, though not maudlin, drama revolves around nine-year-old Oliver Wyatt (Bould). His parents, Martyn (Donovan) and Hannah (Richardson), have bitterly divorced after Martyn finally acknowledges his homosexuality and moves in with his lover, Tom (Hart). Hannah's new live-in boyfriend Frank (Flemyng) turns out to be abusive towards Oliver, who's reluctant to say anything to destroy his mother's new happiness. But when Martyn discovers what's happening, he instigates a custody battle for his son that has everyone at each other's throats, with the terrified Oliver caught in the crossfire. Compelling performances. 105m/C VHS. GB Martin Donovan, Joely Richardson, Ian Hart, Jason Flemyng, Sam Bould, Edward Hardwicke, Annette Badland, Douglas Hodge; D: Angela Pope; W: Paula Milne; C: Remi Adefarasin; M: Anne Dudley.

Hollywood after Dark 🦴 1965 Behind-the-scenes glimpse of McClanahan plays a young starlet trying to make it big in Hollywood. Pure exploitation schlock. Not released theatrically until 1968. 74m/C VHS. Anthony (Tony) Vorno, Rue McClanahan, Paul Bruce, Ernest Macias, John Barrick; D: John Patrick Hayes; W: John Patrick Hayes; C: Vilis Lapenieks; M: Bill Marx.

Hollywood Boulevard 🦴🦴🦴½ 1976 (R) Behind-the-scenes glimpse of shoestring-budget movie making offers comical sex, violence, sight gags, one-liners, comedy bits, and mock-documentary footage. Commander Cody and His Lost Planet Airmen are featured. 93m/C VHS, DVD. Candice Rialson, Mary Woronov, Rita George, Jonathan Kaplan, Jeffrey Kramer, Dick Miller, Paul Bartel, Charles B. Griffith, Richard Doran; D: Joe Dante, Allan Arkush; W: Patrick Hobby; C: Jamie Anderson; M: Andrew Stein.

Hollywood Boulevard 2 🦴 1989 (R) A "B" movie studio finds its top actresses being killed off and terror reigns supreme as the mystery grows more intense. Could that psycho-bimbo from outer space make making offers to do with it? 82m/C VHS. Ginger Lynn Allen, Kelly Monteith, Eddie Deezen, Ken Wright, Steve Vinovich, Mindi Miller; D: Steve Barnett.

Hollywood Canteen 🦴🦴🦴 1944 Star-studded extravaganza with just about every Warner Bros. lot actor in this tribute to love and nationalism. Lovesick G.I. Hutton falls for Leslie, wins a date with her in a phony raffle set up at the Hollywood Canteen, and the sparks fly right away. But he thinks she tricked him as he boards his train and she's not there to see him off. Lame story is redeemed by the talented cast and wonderful musical numbers which make this picture fly with charm and style. Before production began there were arguments over "unpatriotic" actors—labeled as such due to their lack of participation in this, and other similar movies produced at the time. ♫Don't Fence Me In; Sweet Dreams, Sweetheart; You Can Always Tell A Yank; We're Having a Baby; What Are You Doin' the Rest of Your Life; The General Jumped At Dawn; Gettin' Corns For My Country; Voodoo Moon; Tumblin' Tumbleweeds. 124m/B VHS. Robert Hutton, Dane Clark, Janis Paige, Jonathan Hale, Barbara Brown, James Flavin, Eddie Marr, Ray Teal, Bette Davis, Joan Leslie, Jack Benny, Jimmy Dorsey, Joan Crawford, John Garfield, Barbara Stanwyck, Ida Lupino, Eddie Cantor, Jack Carson, Eleanor Parker, Alexis Smith, S.Z. Sakall, Peter Lorre, Sydney Greenstreet, Helmut Dantine; D: Delmer Daves; W: Delmer Daves.

Hollywood Chainsaw Hookers 🦴🦴 1988 (R) A campy, sexy, very bloody parody about attractive prostitutes who dismember their unsuspecting customers. 90m/C VHS, DVD. Linnea Quigley, Gunnar Hansen, Jay Richardson, Michelle (McClellan) Bauer, Dawn Wildsmith, Dennis Mooney, Jerry Fox; D: Fred Olen Ray; W: Fred Olen Ray, T.L. Lankford; C: Scott Ressler; M: Michael Perlstein.

Hollywood Chaos 🦴½ 1989 Director Ballantine's stars quit his production before it even starts, so he gets the next best thing—star look-alikes. However, his problems are just beginning. One of his new "stars" is kidnapped, and his reclusive stage manager is hunted as the object of desire for a female motorcycle gang. 90m/C VHS. Carl Ballantine, Tricia Leigh Fisher, Kathleen Freeman; D: Sean McNamara.

Hollywood Confidential 🦴🦴 1997 (R) TV movie stars Olmos as former LAPD cop Stan Navarro, who now runs a struggling detective agency specializing in the seamier sides of Hollywood. His latest cases involve getting dirt on a studio actress, seeing if a bartender at the newest hotspot is skimming the receipts, and "persuading" the mistress of a well-known director to take a hike. 90m/C VHS, DVD. Edward James Olmos, Anthony Yerkovich, Rick Aiello, Richard T. Jones, Charlize Theron, Angela Alvarado, Christina Harmos, Thomas Jane, Amanda Pays; D: Reynaldo Villalobos; W: Anthony Yerkovich; C: Reynaldo Villalobos; M: Marc Bonilla. TV

Hollywood Cop 🦴½ 1987 (R) A tough cop in Hollywood goes up against the mob for the sake of a kidnapped boy. 101m/C VHS, Jim Mitchum, David Goss, Cameron Mitchell, Troy Donahue, Aldo Ray; D: Amir Shervan.

The Hollywood Detective 🦴🦴 1989 (PG) An average TV movie that spoofs "Kojak." A TV detective tries it out for real, and gets into troubles for which he can't pause "for a message from our sponsor." 88m/C VHS. Telly Savalas, Helene Udy, George Coe, Joe Dallesandro, Tom Reese; D: Kevin Connor. TV

Hollywood Dreams 🦴🦴½ 1994 (R) Starlet on the Hollywood casting couch saga of a midwestern gal that comes to California with dreams of making it big. 90m/C VHS, DVD. Kelly Cook, Danny Smith, Debra Beatty; D: Ralph Portillo.

Hollywood Ending 🦴🦴 2002 (PG-13) Allen continues two recent disturbing trends: making mediocre comedies, and making creepy casting choices when picking his female leads. This time he's Val Waxman, a a down-on-his-luck, nuerotic director about ten years past his prime with a hot ex-wife, Ellie (Leoni) who's engaged to a smarmy studio head (Williams). He's also managed to snag a hot dim-bulb wannabe-actress girlfriend (Messing). When Ellie uses her connections to get Val a job directing an "Ode to New York" pic, his hypochodriac tendencies go into haywire and go blind. Woody's made some great comedies in the past, and if this was 10-15 years ago, the joke might've been great, too. But his overwhelmingly annoying screen persona, and the missed execution of some pretty good setups, this one goes to the forgettable file. Leoni, Williams, and Rydell do well with what they're given. 114m/C VHS, DVD. US Woody Allen, Tea Leoni, Treat Williams, Debra Messing, George Hamilton, Tiffani-Amber Thiessen, Mark Rydell, Isaac Mizrahi, Marian Seldes, Peter Gerety, Greg Mottola, Mark Webber, Lu Yu, Barney Cheng, Jodie Markell; D: Woody Allen; W: Woody Allen; C: Wedigo von Schultzendorff.

Hollywood Harry 🦴 Harry's Machine 1986 (PG-13) A private-eye mystery/parody, about an inept detective who searches for a missing porn actress. 99m/C VHS. Robert Forster, Kathrine (Kate) Forster, Joe Spinell, Shannon Wilcox; D: Robert Forster; W: Curt Allen.

Hollywood Heartbreak 🦴 1989 It's heartbreak in tinseltown for a young writer who's trying to pitch his movie script but winds up defending himself from slimy agents and persistent starlets. Another entry for Bartlett's familiar plotlines. 90m/C VHS, Mark Moses, Carol Mayo Jenkins, Ron Karabatsos, Richard Romanus, James LeGros; D: Lance Dickson.

Hollywood High 🦴 1977 (R) Four attractive teen couples converge on the mansion of an eccentric silent-film star for an unusual vacation experience in this teenage skin flick. Followed by a sequel. 81m/C VHS. Marcy Albrecht, Sherry Hardin, Rae Sperling, Susanne Kevin Mead; D: Patrick Wright.

Hollywood High, Part 2 🦴 1981 (R) Ignored by their boyfriends for the lure of sun and surf, three comely high school students try their best to regain their interest. 86m/C VHS. April May, Donna Lynn, Camille Warner, Lee Thornburg; D: Caruth C. Byrd.

Hollywood Homicide 🦴🦴 2003 (PG-13) In 2003, director Shelton released the hard-edged corrupt cop film "Dark Blue." And then this buddy cop comedy. The first works, this doesn't (much), although the premise had possibilities. Veteran L.A. homicide detective Joe Gavilan (Ford) has three ex-wives, a couple of kids he never sees, money troubles thanks to his off-duty job peddling real estate, and an Internal Affairs investigator (Greenwood) dogging him. His dewy partner, K.C. Calden (Hartnett) isn't sure he even wants to be a detective—he'd rather be an actor. Meanwhile, he moonlights as a yoga instructor. Their on-and-off duty jobs collide as they investigate multiple homicides at a rap club. Ford's relaxed and grumpy; Hartnett's naive and cute but they don't have much rapport and the story's generally weak. 111m/C VHS, DVD. US Harrison Ford, Josh Hartnett, Lena Olin, Master P, Bruce Greenwood, Keith David, Isaiah Washington IV, Lolita (David) Davidovich, Martin Landau, Dwight Yoakam, Kurupt, Lou Diamond Phillips, Gladys Knight, Meredith Scott Lynn, James MacDonald, Clyde Kusatsu, Frank Sinatra Jr., Smokey Robinson, Robert Wagner; Cameos: Eric Idle; C: Ron Shelton, Robert Souza; C: Barry Peterson; M: Alex Wurman.

Hollywood Hot Tubs 🦴 1984 (R) Teen sex romp has adolescent picking up some extra cash and a lot of fun repairing the hot tubs of the rich and famous. 103m/C VHS, Donna McDaniel, Michael Andrew, Katt Shea, Paul Gunning, Edy Williams, Jewel Shepard; D: Chuck Vincent.

Hollywood Hot Tubs 2: Educating Crystal 🦴🦴 1989 (R) A softcore comedy about a well-tanned ingenue learning about business in Hollywood during numerous hot tub trysts. 103m/C VHS. Jewel Shepard, Patrick Day, Remy O'Neill, David Tiefen, Bart Braverman; D: Ken Raich.

Hollywood in Trouble 🦴 1987 A bumbling middle-aged fool decides to break into the wacky movie-making business. 90m/C VHS. Vic Vallard, Jean Levine, Jerry Tiffe, Pamela Dixon, Jerry Cleary; D: Joseph Merhi; W: Joseph Merhi; C: Bob Vose.

The Hollywood Knights 🦴🦴 1980 (R) Cheap imitation of "American Graffiti" is not without its funny moments. Beverly Hills teens, lead by Newbomb Turk (Wuhl), are displeased that their hangout—Tubby's Drive-in—is being shut down by those no-fun adults. So they decide to retaliate. Set on Halloween Night,

1965. 91m/C VHS, DVD. Robert Wuhl, Michelle Pfeiffer, Tony Danza, Fran Drescher, Leigh French, Gary (Rard) Graham, James Jeter, Stuart Pankin, Gailard Sartain, Mike Binder, T.K. Carter, Moosie Drier, Debra Feuer, Garry Goodrow, Joyce Hyser, Roberta Wallach, Doris Hargrave, Walter Janovitz, Art LaFleur, Glenn Withrow, Sandy Helberg; **D:** Floyd Mutrux; **W:** Floyd Mutrux; **C:** William A. Fraker.

Hollywood Man 🦴🦴 **1976 (R)** A Hollywood actor wants to make his own film but when his financial support comes from the mob there's trouble ahead. 90m/C VHS. William (Bill) Smith, Don Stroud, Jennifer Billingsley, Mary Woronov; **D:** Jack Starrett.

Hollywood Mystery 🦴🦴½ **2003 (R)** *Hollywood Hoodlum* 1934 A publicity agent stops at nothing to promote his would-be starlet girlfriend. 53m/B VHS, DVD. June Clyde, Frank Albertson, Joe Crespo; **D:** B. Reeves Eason.

Hollywood North 🦴🦴½ **2003 (R)** Amusing satire on Canadian 'filmmaking' when the government doesn't give incentives for 'films made in Canada. Novice film producer Bobby Meyers (Modina) is trying to raise money to film a classic Canadian novel. But he needs a name actor and winds up with gun-toting paranoid Michael (Bates). Things just get worse—he's stuck with oversexed actress Gillian (Tilly), and numerous script changes turn Bobby's vision into something unrecognizable. All the while his trials are being documented by director Sandy (Unger). 89m/C VHS, DVD. **CA** Matthew Modine, Alan Bates, Deborah Kara Unger, Jennifer Tilly, Alan Thicke, John Neville, Kim Coates, Clare Coulter, Joe Golden, Saul Rubinek, Lindy Booth; **D:** Peter O'Brien; **W:** Barry Healey, John Hunter, Tony Johnston; **C:** Barry Stone; **M:** Terence Gowan, Blair Packham.

Hollywood or Bust 🦴🦴½ **1956** The zany duo take their act on the road as they head for Tinsel Town in order to meet Lewis' dream girl Ekberg. This was the last film for the Martin & Lewis team and it's not the swan song their fans 'would have hoped for. 95m/C VHS. Dean Martin, Jerry Lewis, Anita Ekberg, Patricia Crowley, Maxie 'Slapsie' Rosenbloom, Willard Waterman; **D:** Frank Tashlin.

Hollywood Party 🦴🦴½ **1934** Durante plays a film star who decides to throw a Hollywood bash. Any pot is incidental as it is mainly an excuse to have numerous stars of the day appear in brief comic bits or musical numbers. Mickey Mouse and the Big Bad Wolf of Disney age also appear in color animated footage combined with live action. Numerous MGM directors worked on parts of the film but Dwan was given the task of trying to pull the various scenes together (he is uncredited onscreen). ♪♫Hollywood Party; Hello; Reincarnation; I've Had My Moments; Feeling High; Hot Chocolate Soldiers. 72m/B VHS. Jimmy Durante, Stan Laurel, Oliver Hardy, Lupe Velez, Ted Healy, Moe Howard, Curly Howard, Larry Fine, Robert Young, Charles Butterworth, Polly Moran, George Givot, Tom Kennedy, Arthur Treacher; **D:** Allan Dwan, Richard Boleslawski; **W:** Howard Dietz, Arthur Kober; **C:** James Wong Howe; **V:** Walt Disney, Billy Bletcher.

Hollywood Safari 🦴🦴 **1996 (PG)** Jane (Boone) and Troy (Leisure) Johnson train animals for the movies. But Kensho-the mountain lion escapes into the woods after a transport accident and is eventually captured by the police who think it's the wild cat that recently attacked a local teen. The Johnsons try to prevent the sheriff's deputy (Savage) from having Kensho killed before they can prove their claims, but their best defense would be to find the renegade cougar. It's a pleasant enough 'time-waster,' with Muldy, the Johnson's dog, providing some fine heroics. 85m/C VHS, DVD. John Savage, Ted Jan Roberts, David Leisure, Debbie Boone, Ken Tigar, Don 'The Dragon' Wilson; **D:** Henri Charr; **W:** Robert Newcastle; **C:** Guido Verweyen. VIDEO

Hollywood Shuffle 🦴🦴½ **1987 (R)** Townsend's autobiographical comedy about a struggling black actor in Hollywood trying to find work and getting nothing but stereotypical roles. Written, directed, financed by Townsend, who created this often clever and appealing film on a $100,000 budget. 81m/C VHS, DVD. Robert Townsend, Anne-Marie Johnson, Starletta DuPois, Helen Martin, Keenen Ivory Wayans, Damon Wayans, Craigus R. Johnson, Eugene Robert Glazer; **D:** Robert Townsend; **W:** Keenen Ivory Wayans, Robert Townsend; **C:** Peter Deming; **M:** Patrice Rushen, Udi Harpaz.

The Hollywood Sign 🦴🦴 **2001 (R)** Tom Greener (Berenger) and Kage Mulligan (Reynolds) have seen their acting careers fade away as has that of veteran actor Floyd Benson (Steiger). The three get together to drink and talk at the foot of the Hollywood sign where they happen to stumble across the body of a dead gangster. Doing some investigating, Germans who thrived under the Nazi regime from a Vegas casino. They include Tom's girlfriend Paula (Kim) in their plan to get the money, finance Paula's script, and jump start their careers. 93m/C VHS, DVD. **US GE NL** Rod Steiger, Burt Reynolds, Tom Berenger, Jacqueline Kim; **Cameos:** Gary Marshall; **D:** Sonke Wortmann; **M:** Leon de Winter; **C:** Wedigo von Schultzendorff.

Hollywood Stadium Mystery 🦴🦴 **1938** A boxer turns up dead before a big match and a D.A. investigates. Performances hold this one up, especially by Hamilton who later played Commissioner Gordon on TV's 'Batman.' 66m/B VHS, DVD. Neil Hamilton, Evelyn Venable, Jimmy Wallington, Barbara Pepper, Lucien Littlefield, Lynne Roberts, Charles Williams, James Spottswood, Reed Hadley, Smiley Burnette; **D:** David Howard.

The Hollywood Strangler Meets the Skid Row Slasher WOOF! *The Model Killer* **1979 (R)** Voiced-over narration, canned music, and an unfathomable plot are but a few of this would-be fright fest's finer points. Uninhibited by any narrative connection, two terrors strike fear in the heart of Tinseltown. While a psycho photographer cruises L.A. taking pictures of models he subsequently strangles, a woman working in a bare-burns magazine store takes a stab (with a knife) at lowering the city's derelict population. There's a word for this sort of dribble, and it isn't versimilitude. Steckler used an alias (not surprisingly) for this one—Wolfgang Schmidt. 72m/C VHS. Pierre Agostino, Carolyn Brandt, Forrest Duke, Chuck Alford; **D:** Ray Dennis Steckler, Ray Dennis Steckler.

Hollywood Vice Squad 🦴 **1986 (R)** Explores the lives of Hollywood police officers and the crimes they investigate. Contains three different storylines involving prostitution, child pornography, and organized crime. The film can't decide to be a comedy send-up of crime stories or a drama and is also crippled by a poor script. Written by the real-life chief of the L.A. vice squad. 90m/C VHS, DVD. Trish Van Devere, Ronny Cox, Frank Gorshin, Leon Isaac Kennedy, Carrie Fisher, Ben Frank, Robin Wright Penn; **D:** Penelope Spheeris; **W:** James J. Docherty; **M:** Michael Convertino.

Hollywood Zap WOOF! **1986 (R)** Two losers, one a Southern orphan, the other a video game nut, hit Hollywood and engage in antics that are meant to be funny, but are actually tasteless. 85m/C VHS. Ben Frank, Ivan E. Roth, De Waldron, Annie Gaybis, Chuck 'Porky' Mitchell; **D:** David M. Cohen; **W:** David M. Cohen.

Hollywoodland 🦴🦴½ **2006 (R)** Low-rent detective Louis Simo (Brody) is hired by the mother (Smith) of actor George Reeves (Affleck) to investigate his suspicious death. In 1959, middle-aged Reeves allegedly shot himself in his bedroom—probably because of his failing career and his frustration at being typecast as TV's Superman. But Louis isn't so sure, George had dumped his longtime lover, aging beauty Toni Mannix (Lane), for young starlet Leonore (Tunney). Maybe Toni's protective tough hubby Eddie (Hoskins), an MGM exec, arranged something anyway. Louis' poking around doesn't sit well with those in power and if he's not careful he may end up like Reeves. The self-aware Lane is the cast standout, though Affleck is comfortably capable while Brody is overly twitchy. 126m/C DVD, HD DVD, **US** Adrien Brody, Diane Lane, Ben Affleck, Bob Hoskins, Lois Smith, Robin Tunney, Jeffrey DeMunn, Brad Willis...

Hollywood's New Blood 🦴 **1988** Young actor's making a movie are haunted by a film crew from hell. 90m/C VHS. Bobby Johnston, Francine Lapensee; **D:** James Shyman.

Holocaust 🦴🦴🦴½ **1978** The war years of 1935 to 1945 are relived in this account of the Nazi atrocities, focusing on the Jewish Weiss family, destroyed by the monstrous crimes, and the Dorf family, who thrived under the Nazis. Highly acclaimed riveting miniseries with an exceptional cast. Won eight Emmy's. 475m/C VHS. Michael Moriarty, Fritz Weaver, Meryl Streep, James Woods, Joseph Bottoms, Tovah Feldshuh, David Warner, Ian Holm, Michael Beck, Marius Goring; **D:** Marvin J. Chomsky. TV

Holocaust Survivors... Remembrance of Love 🦴🦴 *Remembrance of Love* **1983** A concentration camp survivor and his daughter attend the 1981 World Gathering of Holocaust Survivors in Tel-Aviv and both find romance. 100m/C VHS. Kirk Douglas, Pam Dawber, Chana Eden, Yoram Gal, Robert Clary; **D:** Jack Smight; **M:** William Goldstein. TV

Hologram Man 🦴🦴 **1995 (R)** Futuristic thriller finds psycho/terrorist Slash Gallagher (Lurie) captured by rookie cop Kurt Decoda (Lara). His prison term is to be served in Holographic Stasis, which means his mind is stored on a computer. Slash's gang menges to break his mind out of the computer but since his body is destroyed, Slash roams as a powerful electro-magnetic hologram. And it's up to cop Decoda to get Slash back. 96m/C VHS, DVD. Joe Lara, Evan Lurie, William Sanderson, Tommy (Tiny) Lister, Michael Nouri, John Amos; **D:** Richard Pepin; **W:** Evan Lurie; **M:** John Gonzalez.

Holy Girl 🦴🦴🦴 *La Niña Santa; The Holy Child* **2004 (R)** Martel's second feature film, in Spanish with English subtitles, explores themes of sexual power, shame and longing through the comings and goings and chance encounters of doctors and hotel staff during an otolaryngologists' conference. At the center is the hotel manager's teenage and very Catholic daughter who is discovering the vulnerability and power of her own sexuality. The story unfolds in a not-so-orderly fashion but patience finds an intricate and startling conclusion. 106m/C DVD. **AR NL SP IT** Mercedes Moran, Carlo Belloso, Alejandro Urdapilleta, Maria Alche, Julieta Zylberberg; **D:** Lucrecia Martel; **W:** Lucrecia Martel; **C:** Felix Monti; **M:** Andres Gerszenzon.

The Holy Innocents 🦴🦴🦴 *Los Santos Inocentes* **1984 (PG)** A peasant family is torn asunder by their feudal obligations to their patrons. Set in the 1960s in Franco's Spain. In Spanish with English subtitles. 108m/C VHS. **SP** Alfredo Landa, Francesco Rabal; **D:** Mario Camus. Cannes '84: Actor (Rabal).

Holy Man 🦴🦴 **1998 (PG)** This satire of home shopping networks is supposed to shell American consumerism, but ends up shooting itself in the foot instead. Murphy is G, a New Age-babble spouting wise man who is used by home shopping execs Goldblum and Preston to boost flagging sales. G lectures about the joy of spiritual over material happiness, but sales scar anyway. Misuses Murphy's wisecracking ability in what could have been a good premise, and reduces his character to a sight gag. 113m/C VHS, DVD. Eddie Murphy, Jeff Goldblum, Kelly Preston, Robert Loggia, Jon Cryer, Eric McCormack, Marc Macaulay, Sam Kitchin, Robert Small, Morgan Fairchild; **D:** Stephen Herek; **W:** Tom Schulman; **C:** Adrian Biddle; **M:** Alan Silvestri.

Holy Matrimony 🦴🦴½ **1994 (PG-13)** Mild-mannered and pleasant comedy in spite of its potentially salacious plot. Thieves Peter (Donovan) and Havana (Arquette) take off to Canada to hide out in the Hutterite religious community where Peter grew up and where he's welcomed as the prodigal son. Peter hides their stolen loot but neglects to pass the word on before he's killed in an accident. Wanting to stay and search for the money, Havana uses the colony's reliance on biblical law to marry Peter's brother, Zeke (Gordon-Levitt). Only problem is Zeke is 12 and doesn't even like girls. Strictly brother-sister affection develops between the two. 93m/C VHS, DVD. Patricia Arquette, Joseph Gordon-Levitt, Armin Mueller-Stahl, Tate Donovan, John Schuck, Lois Smith, Courtney B. Vance, Jeffrey Nordling, Richard Riehle; **D:** Leonard Nimoy; **C:** Bobby Bukowski; **M:** Bruce Broughton.

The Holy Terror 🦴🦴 **1937** A Naval Air officer's daughter, Jane (Withers), unwittingly uncovers a group of spies while she entertains the troops with her musical shows. 68m/B VHS. Jane Withers, Tony Martin, Leah Ray, El Brendal, Joe E. Lewis, Joan Davis; **D:** James Tinling; **W:** Lou Breslow, John Patrick.

Holt of the Secret Service 🦴🦴 **1942** Secret service agent runs afoul of saboteurs and fifth-columnists in this 15-episode serial. 290m/B VHS, DVD. Jack Holt, Evelyn Brent, C. Montague Shaw, Tristram Coffin, John Ward, George Chesebro; **D:** James W. Home.

Holy Smoke 🦴🦴 **1999 (R)** Free-spirited Ruth (Winslet) travels to India and finds would-be spiritual enlightenment with an Indian guru. Her behavior terrifies her parents and her mother (Hamilton) manages to lure Ruth back home to Australia. They've hired American cult specialist, macho PJ Waters (Keitel), to rescue and deprogram her. Isolated in the Australian bush, the balance of power between Ruth and PJ begins to shift as sexual obsession takes hold. Complex characters but the strident storyline gets annoying and some scenes seem staged for needless shock value. Based on the novel by the Campion sisters. 114m/C VHS, DVD. **AU** Harvey Keitel, Kate Winslet, Julie Hamilton, Tim Robertson, Sophie Lee, Pam Grier, Paul Goddard, Daniel Wyllie; **D:** Jane Campion; **W:** Jane Campion, Anna Campion; **C:** Dion Beebe; **M:** Angelo Badalamenti.

Holy Terror 🦴🦴 **1965** The story of Florence Nightingale, who shocked Victorian society by organizing a nursing staff to aid British soldiers in the Crimean War, is told in this presentation from 'George Schaefer's Showcase Theatre.' 76m/C VHS. Julie Harris, Denholm Elliott, Torin Thatcher, Kate Reid; **D:** George Schaefer. TV

Homage 🦴🦴 **1995 (R)** Archie's (Whaley) an emotionally disturbed mathematical nerd who needs a break from academia and persuades widowed ex-teacher Katherine Samuel (Danner) to hire him as caretaker for her New Mexico ranch. The duo achieve a strange serenity that shatters when Katherine's TV star daughter, self-absorbed Lucy (Lee), arrives seeking shelter because of her drug and drinking problems. A nasty triangle ensues as Lucy makes the mistake of sexually enticing, then rejecting, the needy Archie. In fact, the mistake's fatal. Based on Medoff's play 'The Homage That Follows.' 100m/C VHS, DVD. Frank Whaley, Blythe Danner, Sheryl Lee, Bruce Davison, Danny Nucci; **D:** Ross Kagan Marks; **W:** Mark Medoff; **C:** Tom Richmond; **M:** W.G. Snuffy Walden.

Hombre 🦴🦴🦴 **1967** A white man in the 1880s, raised by a band of Arizona Apaches, is forced into a showdown. Based on a story by Elmore Leonard. 111m/C VHS, DVD. Paul Newman, Fredric March, Richard Boone, Diane Cilento, Cameron Mitchell, Barbara Rush, Martin Balsam; **D:** Martin Ritt, Harriet Frank Jr., Irving Ravetch; **C:** James Wong Howe.

Hombres Armados 🦴🦴🦴 *Men with Guns* **1997** Fiercely independent filmmaker John Sayles' men with guns are not characters; they're an inevitable force helping a stage-coach full of settlers across treacherous country; he not only faces the... Alan Silvestri.

lows a well-to-do physician (Luppi) who trains doctors to work in the countryside among the local Mayan Indians. What he doesn't realize is that a civil war is engulfing his country, the Indians are practically enslaved, and his students have been murdered by the government that trained them. He picks up a ragged bunch of stragglers whose lives have been shattered by ever-present soldiers from either side of the war. Together they trudge through the jungle, searching for a place devoid of war or politics. Sayles based his idea on the 36-year-long civil war in Guatemala, which began in 1960. Spanish with subtitles. **126m/C VHS, DVD.** Federico Luppi, Damian Delgado, Dan Rivera Gonzalez, Tania Cruz, Damian Alcazar, Iguandili Lopez, Nandi Luna Ramirez, Rafael De Quevedo, Mandy Patinkin, Kathryn Grody, Roberto Sosa; **D:** John Sayles; **W:** John Sayles; **C:** Slawomir Idziak; **M:** Mason Daring.

Hombres Complicados 🦴🦴 **1997** Petty crook Roger (De Pauw) can't pay his debts to a group of gangsters. So he convinces gullible brother Bruno (Roofthooft) that they should use the small inheritance left to them by their mother to take a bonding road trip. Roger wants to buy some time until he can come up with a get-rich-quick scheme but, as usual in his sad-sack life, Roger's scheming leads to some bizarre happenings. Flemish and French with subtitles. **83m/C VHS.** *BE* Josse De Pauw, Dirk Roofthooft, Lies Pauwels; **D:** Dominique Deruddere; **W:** Dominique Deruddere, Marc Didden; **C:** Willy Stassen.

Home 🦴½ **2005** Roommates Susan and Rose throw a party in their Brooklyn brownstone one hot summer night. Bobby shows up in hopes of re-connecting with his ex Harper, who's more interested in making a play for Rose's crush, Tommy. So Bobby gets to know Susan until HER ex shows up. Frankly, this is a pretty dull gathering although the situations and conversations will sound familiar. **91m/C DVD.** Nicol Zanzarella, E. Jason Liebrecht, Erin Stacey Visslailli, Minerva Scelza, T. Stephen Neave, Bradley Spinelli; **D:** Matt Seitz; **W:** Matt Seitz; **C:** Jonathan Wolff.

Home Alone 🦴🦴🦴 **1990 (PG)** Eight-year-old Kevin is accidentally left behind when his entire (and large) family makes a frantic rush for the airport. That's the plausible part. Alone and besieged by burglars, Kevin turns into a pint-sized Rambo defending his suburban castle with the wile and resources of a boy genius with perfect timing and unlimited wherewithal. That's the implausible part. Pesci and Stern, the targets of Macauley's wrath, enact painful slapstick with considerable vigor, while Candy has a small but funny part as the leader of a polka band traveling cross-country with mom O'Hara. The highest-grossing picture of 1990, surpassing "Ghost" and "Jaws." **105m/C VHS, DVD.** Macaulay Culkin, Catherine O'Hara, Joe Pesci, Daniel Stern, John Heard, Roberts Blossom, John Candy, Billie Bird, Angela Goethals, Devin Ratray, Kieran Culkin; **D:** Chris Columbus; **W:** John Hughes; **C:** Julio Macat; **M:** John Williams.

Home Alone 2: Lost in New York 🦴🦴½ **1992 (PG)** In an almost exact duplication of the original blockbuster, the harebrained McCallister family leaves Kevin behind in the shuffle to start his Florida vacation. Boarding the wrong plane, Kevin lands in NYC, where wonder of wonders, he meets crooks Pesci and Stern, prison escapees who somehow survived the torture meted out in the first film. And they want revenge. Loaded with cartoon violence and shameless gag replicas from HA1, mega-hit still produces genuine laughs and manages to incorporate as ever, with supporting cast all delivering fine performances. Filmed in New York City. **120m/C VHS, DVD.** Macaulay Culkin, Joe Pesci, Daniel Stern, Catherine O'Hara, John Heard, Tim Curry, Brenda Fricker, Devin Ratray, Hillary Wolf, Eddie Bracken, Gerry Bamman, Donald Trump; **D:** Chris Columbus; **W:** John Hughes; **C:** Julio Macat; **M:** John Williams.

Home Alone 3 🦴 **1997 (PG)** Regardless of the new faces, the story and cartoon violence seems all too familiar. Linz (taking over for the teenaged Culkin) is stricken with the chicken pox but able to booby trap his suburban house with to foil the plans of international criminals trying to recover a microchip stashed in a toy car. Film fails to carry the charm of its predecessors and sends the wrong messages; it's okay for parents to leave underaged kids home by themselves and electrocuting people is fun. Writer Hughes should be left home alone to rethink his skills as a screenwriter. **102m/C VHS, DVD.** Alex D. Linz, Kevin Kilner, Olek Krupa, Rya Kihlstedt, Lenny Von Dohlen, David Thornton, Haviland (Haylie) Morris, Marian Seldes, Scarlett Johansson, Christopher Curry, Baxter Harris, Seth Smith; **D:** Raja Gosnell; **W:** John Hughes; **C:** Julio Macat; **M:** Nick Glennie-Smith.

The Home and the World 🦴🦴🦴½ *Ghare Baire* **1984** Another masterpiece from India's Ray, this film deals with a sheltered Indian woman who falls in love with her husband's friend and becomes politically committed in the turmoil of 1907-08. Based on Rabindranath Tagore's novel. In Bengali with English subtitles. **130m/C VHS.** *IN* Victor Banerjee, Soumitra Chatterjee; **D:** Satyajit Ray.

Home at Last 🦴🦴 **1988** An orphan in turn of the century New York finds himself shipped to Nebraska on an orphan train. There he works on the farm of his adopted family, whose own son has died. The boy finds that he must adjust to a new lifestyle as well as strive to be accepted as someone other than a replacement for the couple's son. From the "Wonderworks" series. **58m/C VHS, DVD.** Adrien Brody, Frank Converse, Caroline Lagerfelt, Sascha Radetsky.

A Home at the End of the World 🦴🦴½ **2004 (R)** Cunningham adapted his 1990 novel, but the beauty of his prose gets lost in the transition. Sweet-but-awkward Bobby Morrow (Farrell) meets shy outsider Jonathan Glover (Roberts) in 1967 Cleveland. When Bobby is orphaned, he moves in with the Glovers (Spacek, Frewer) and stays with them even after Jonathan takes off for gay life in the New York. Bobby later follows and then bunks with Jonathan and his older, platonic roommate Clare (Wright Penn). Jonathan so seduces him and gets pregnant. When the threesome move out of the city and try to raise the baby together, Clare soon realizes that the emotional intimacy between the two men leaves no room for her. Farrell is tender, but the storytelling is disjointed and the ending somewhat abrupt. Farrell's controversial frontal nude scene, allegedly cut for being distracting, was not restored for the DVD release. **95m/C VHS, DVD.** *US* Colin Farrell, Robin Wright Penn, Dallas Roberts, Sissy Spacek, Matt Frewer, Erik Smith, Harris Allan, Andrew Chalmers, Ryan Donowho; **D:** Michael Mayer; **W:** Michael Cunningham; **C:** Enrique Chediak; **M:** Duncan Sheik.

Home Before Midnight 🦴½ **1984** A young songwriter falls in love with a 14-year-old, is discovered, and is subsequently charged with statutory rape. **115m/C VHS, DVD.** James Aubrey, Alison Elliott; **D:** Pete Walker.

Home for Christmas 🦴🦴 **1990** An elderly homeless man, with the love of a young girl, teaches a wealthy family the spirit of Christmas. **96m/C VHS.** Mickey Rooney, Joel Kaiser; **D:** Peter McCubbin.

Home for Christmas 🦴🦴½ *Lite Miss Millions* **1993 (PG)** A 12-year-old has run away from her wicked stepmom who hires a bounty hunter to bring her back—for a half a million bucks. Only when he finds the girl stepmom doesn't want to pay up and she tells anyone who will listen that the 12-year-old who isn't a fool and knows stepmom is a lying witch, can help. **90m/C VHS, DVD.** Howard Hesseman, Anita Morris, Jennifer Love Hewitt, James Avery, Steve Landesberg, Terri Treas, Deanna (Dee) Booher; **D:** Jim Wynorski; **W:** Jim Wynorski, R.J. Robertson; **C:** Zoran Hochstatter; **M:** Joel Goldsmith.

Home for the Holidays 🦴🦴 *Deadly Desires* **1972** Four daughters are called home on Christmas by their father who is convinced they their second wife is trying to poison him. **74m/C VHS.** Eleanor Parker, Walter Brennan, Sally Field, Jessica Walter, Julie Harris; **D:** John Llewellyn Moxey. **TV**

Home for the Holidays 🦴🦴½ **1995 (PG-13)** Frantic dysfunctional family saga finds eldest daughter Claudia Larson (Hunter) on her way to Baltimore to spend Thanksgiving with her family. Frazzled Claudia must deal with badly bewigged mom Adele (Bancroft), genial dad Henry (Durning), and her siblings—frenzied gay brother Tommy (Downey Jr.) and self-righteous sister Joanne (Stevenson), as well as screwy Aunt Glady (Chaplin) and Tommy's handsome friend Leo Fish (McDermott). Yes, there are moments of deja vu about your very own family holidays but the film seems badly paced and ultimately irritating. Adapted from a short story by Chris Radant. **103m/C VHS, DVD.** Holly Hunter, Anne Bancroft, Charles Durning, Robert Downey Jr., Dylan McDermott, Cynthia Stevenson, Geraldine Chaplin, Steve Guttenberg, Claire Danes, David Strathairn, Austin Pendleton; **D:** Jodie Foster; **W:** W.D. Richter; **C:** Lajos Koltai; **M:** Mark Isham.

Home Free All 🦴🦴½ **1984** A Vietnam vet turned revolutionary, turned writer, tries to reacquaint himself with childhood friends only to find one has joined the mob and another is settled in suburbia and none of them are dealing well with adulthood. **92m/C VHS.** Allan Nicholls, Roland Caccavo, Maura Ellyn, Shelley Wyant, Lucille Rivim; **D:** Stuart Bird.

Home Fries 🦴🦴 **1998 (PG-13)** Things go from bad to worse for pregnant fast-food cashier, Sally (Drew Barrymore), as she learns that the father of her child is not only married, but dead! The catch is that the philanderer's stepsons are responsible and believe that Sally may have overheard their dastardly deed on her drive-through headset. Brother Dorian (Luke Wilson) takes a job at the Burger-Matic to find out just what Sally knows, but predictably falls in love with her instead. Tries to be a quirky dark comedy in a sweet love story, but the result is a bad mix of bleak humor and saccarine-sweet puppy love. Barrymore's cute and convincing performance manages to keep the whole thing from spoiling. Unfortunately, first-time director Parisot leaves the audience thinking, "this isn't what I ordered." **94m/C VHS, DVD.** Drew Barrymore, Luke Wilson, Catherine O'Hara, Jake Busey, Shelley Duvall, Kim Robillard, Daryl (Chill) Mitchell, Lanny Flaherty, Chris Ellis, Edward "Blue" Deckert; **D:** Dean Parisot; **W:** Vince Gilligan; **C:** Jerzy Zielinski; **M:** Rachel Portman.

Home from the Hill 🦴🦴🦴 **1960** A solemn, brooding drama about a southern landowner and his troubled sons, one of whom is illegitimate. This one triumphs because of casting. **150m/C VHS, DVD.** Robert Mitchum, George Peppard, George Hamilton, Eleanor Parker, Everett Sloane, Luana Parker, Constance Ford; **D:** Vincente Minnelli; **W:** Harriet Frank Jr., Irving Ravetch; **C:** Milton Krasner. Natl. Bd. of Review '60: Actor (Mitchum).

The Home Front 🦴🦴½ *The Scoundrel's Wife* **2002 (R)** During World War II, Camille (O'Neal), a Louisiana widow with two kids, Blue (McCullough) and Florida (Chabert), takes a job as an assistant to an exiled German doctor. They are both outcasts, she because of an incident years before involving her husband, and he because he is German. When German U-boats begin attacking ships in the harbor, they both fall under suspicion. Complicating matters is Florida's romance with a Nazi-hunting Coast Guard ensign. A little disjointed, and the conclusion isn't exactly believable, but the movie looks good, and has a great sense of the time and place based it on stories he heard growing up in the same town in which the tale is set. **102m/C VHS, DVD.** Tatum O'Neal, Julian Sands, Tim Curry, Lacey Chabert, Eion Bailey, Rudolf Martin, Patrick McCullough; **D:** Glen Pitre; **W:** Glen Pitre, Michelle Benoit; **C:** Uta Briesewitz; **M:** Ernest Troost.

Home in Oklahoma 🦴🦴 **1947** A boy will be swindled out of his inheritance and a killer will escape justice until Roy comes to the rescue. Standard series fare. **72m/B VHS, DVD.** Roy Rogers, Dale Evans, George "Gabby" Hayes, Carol Hughes; **D:** William Witney.

Home Is Where the Hart Is 🦴🦴 **1988 (PG-13)** A rich 103-year-old is kidnapped by a nurse wanting to marry him and become heir to his estate. It's up to his sons, all in their 70s, to rescue him. **94m/C VHS.** Martin Mull, Leslie Nielsen, Valri Bromfield, Stephen E. Miller, Eric Christmas, Ted Stidder; **D:** Rex Bromfield; **W:** Rex Bromfield.

Home Movies 🦴½ **1979 (PG)** Brian DePalma and his film students at Sarah Lawrence College devised this loose, sloppy comedy which hearkens back to DePalma's early films. Tells the story of a nebbish who seeks therapy to gain control of his absurdly chaotic life. **89m/C VHS, DVD.** Kirk Douglas, Nancy Allen, Keith Gordon, Gerrit Graham, Vincent Gardenia, Mary Davenport; **D:** Brian De Palma; **W:** Brian De Palma; **C:** James L. Carter; **M:** Pino Donaggio.

Home of Angels 🦴🦴½ **1994** Billy sneaks his granddad out of his nursing home in Philadelphia and together the twosome begin a perilous journey back to Billy's home in Long Island, New York so they can have a family Christmas. They're aided by a homeless man when they run into trouble with a street gang. **90m/C VHS.** Lance Robinson, Abe Vigoda, Sherman Hemsley, Joe Frazier; **D:** Nick Stagliano.

A Home of Our Own 🦴🦴 **1975** An American priest sets up a home in Mexico for orphan boys and changes their lives for the better. A true story of Father William Wasson. **100m/C VHS.** Pancho Cordova, Pedro Armendariz Jr., Carmen Zapata, Enrique Novi, Richard Angarola, Jason Miller; **D:** Robert Day; **W:** Blanche Hanalis; **C:** Jacques 'Jack' Marquette; **M:** Laurence Rosenthal.

A Home of Our Own 🦴🦴½ **1993 (PG-13)** Semi-autobiographical tearjerker based on screenwriter Duncan's childhood. Widowed and poor mother of six (Bates) is fired from her job at a Los Angeles potato chip factory, packs up the tribe and heads for a better life and a home to call their own. They end up in Idaho, in a ramshackle house owned by lonely Mr. Moon (Oh) and what follows is a winter of discontent. Bates provides an intense performance as a poor but proud woman with a tough exterior. Furlong provides the story's narration as the eldest son. A story of spiritual triumph, this one is sure to make your heart weep. **104m/C VHS, DVD.** Kathy Bates, Edward Furlong, Soon-Teck Oh, Amy Sakasitz, Tony Campisi; **D:** Tony Bill; **W:** Patrick Duncan; **C:** Jean Lepine; **M:** Michael Convertino.

Home of the Brave 🦴🦴🦴 **1949** A black soldier is sent on a top secret mission in the South Pacific, but finds that he must battle with his white comrades as he is subjected to subordinate treatment and constant racial slurs. Hollywood's first outstanding statement against racial prejudice. **86m/B VHS.** Lloyd Bridges, James Edwards, Frank Lovejoy, Jeff Corey, Douglas Dick, Steve Brodie, Cliff Clark; **D:** Mark Robson; **W:** Carl Foreman; **C:** Robert De Grasse; **M:** Dimitri Tiomkin.

Home of the Brave 🦴🦴 **2006 (R)** Iraqi war vets from the same National Guard unit return home to Spokane and have trouble readjusting to civilian life in Winkler's conventional drama. Medic Will Marsh (Jackson) turns to alcohol and lashing out at his wife (Rowell) and son (Jones). Single mom Vanessa (Biel) lost a hand and discovers her prosthesis makes everyone uncomfortable while Tommy (Presley) can't get past the death of his best friend. Actors do as well as can be expected with the cliched material. **105m/C DVD, Blu-ray Disc.** *US* Samuel L. Jackson, Jessica Biel, Curtis "50 Cent" Jackson, Sam Jones III, Victoria Rowell, Chad Michael Murray, Christina Ricci, Brian Presley; **D:** Irwin Winkler; **W:** Mark Friedman; **C:** Tony Pierce-Roberts; **M:** Stephen Endelman.

Home on the Range 🐾🐾½ 2004 (PG) Disney kicks this 2-D cartoon old-school style—which would be great if there was anything new, fresh, or very funny going on. Three gal cow pals (Barr, Dench, and Tilly) trying to save their farm from foreclosure go after the bounty on the evil rustler Alameda Slim (Quaid). Lots of hyped-up action and gags will keep the kids amused; however, it wants to mimic the classic Looney Tunes but, like Daffy to Bugs, it just doesn't measure up. Oscar winner Alan Menken produces some pleasant if not memorable music with singers k.d. lang, Bonnie Raitt. 76m/C **VHS, DVD.** Henry Fonda.

Home to Stay 🐾🐾 1979 A farmer who has suffered a stroke is fighting off repeated lapses into senility. His son and daughter have conflicting interests as to whether he should be committed to a nursing home. 74m/C VHS.

Home Remedy 🐾🐾 1988 An introverted New Jersey bachelor's isolated lifestyle is invaded by a flirtatious housewife and her zealous husband. 92m/C VHS. Seth Barrish, Maxine Albert. **D:** Maggie Greenwald.

Home Room 🐾🐾 2002 (R) Phillipps and Christensen shine in this riveting story of two girls on opposite end of the high school social spectrum who survive a Columbine-type massacre. Popular, affluent Deanna (Christensen) was seriously injured in the attack and is hospitalized. Alienated loner Alicia (Phillips) was near the perpetrator when he was killed, and is believed to be somehow involved. When Alicia is forced to visit Deanna in the hospital, the two eventually form a friendship and learn to cope with the aftermath of the incident. The two leads are excellent, with a breakout performance by Phillips, and the film wisely sticks to the story of their unlikely friendship, pushing other plotlines to the background. 133m/C VHS, DVD, Busy Philipps, Erika Christensen, Victor Garber, Raphael Sbarge, Ken Jenkins, Holland Taylor, Arthur Taxier, James Pickens Jr., Constance Zimmer, Richard Gilliland, Roxanne Hart, Agnes Bruckner, Nathan West, Ben Gould, Jeanette Goldstein, Vernee Watson-Johnson. **D:** Paul F. Ryan. **W:** Paul F. Ryan. **C:** Mike Shapiro. **M:** Rebecca Basher.

Home Sweet Home 🐾🐾 1914 Suggested by the life of John Howard Payne (actor, poet, dramatist, critic, and world-wanderer) who wrote the title song amid the bitterness of his sad life. Silent with musical score. 62m/B VHS. Lillian Gish, Dorothy Gish, Henry B. Walthall, Mae Marsh, Blanche Sweet, Donald Crisp, Robert "Bobbie" Harron. **D:** D.W. Griffith.

Home Sweet Home 🐾🐾½ 1982 Slasher in the House 1980 A murdering psychopath escapes from the local asylum, and rampages through a family's Thanksgiving dinner. 84m/C VHS. Jake Steinfeld, Sallee Elyse, Peter DePaula. **D:** Nettie Pena.

Home Team 🐾🐾½ 1998 (PG) Gambling addict and ex-con Henry Butler (Guttenberg) is required to perform community service as part of his parole. Since he's a former soccer coach, he finds a job at a boys' home where administer Karen (Lorain) figures a soccer team will teach the kids teamwork and sportsmanship. Familiar plot but that's not necessarily bad. 94m/C VHS, DVD. Steve Guttenberg, Sophie Lorain, Ryan Slater, Johnny Morina; **D:** Allen Goldstein. **C:** Barry Gravelle. **CABLE**

Homebodies 🐾🐾 1974 (PG) Six senior citizens, disgusted when they learn that they will be callously tossed out of their home, become violent murderers in their shocking attempt to solve their problem. An odd little film made in Cincinnati. 96m/C VHS. Ruth McDevitt, Linda Marsh, William Hansen, Peter Brocco, Frances Fuller. **D:** Larry Yust.

Homeboy 🐾🐾½ Black Fist 1975 "A Black boxer owes his career to the mob. When he tries to break free his wife is murdered—and he seeks revenge. 93m/C VHS, DVD. Richard Lawson, Dabney Coleman, Philip Michael Thomas. **D:** Timothy Galfas, Richard Kaye. **W:** Tim Kelly. **C:** William Larrabure. **M:** Ed Townsend.

Homeboy 🐾🐾 1988 (R) A small-time club boxer who dreams of becoming middleweight champ is offered his big break, but the opportunity is jeopardized by his dishonest manager's dealings. Never released theatrically. 118m/C VHS. Mickey Rourke, Christopher Walken, Debra Feuer, Kevin Conway, Antony Alda, Ruben Blades; **D:** Michael Seresin; **M:** Eric Clapton, Michael Kamen, Gustav Froehlich; **D:** Joe May.

Homeboys 🐾🐾 1992 Two East L.A. brothers find themselves on opposite sides of the law in this quickie designed to cash in on gang violence and ghetto dramas. 91m/C VHS. Todd Bridges, David Garrison, Ron Cdricoza, Ken Michaels; **D:** Lindsay Norgard.

Homecoming 🐾🐾 1928 Two German prisoners of war escape from a Siberian lead mine. One reaches home first and has an affair with his comrade's wife. Silent. 74m/B VHS. GE Dita Parlo, Lars Hanson.

Homecoming 🐾🐾 1948 Average soap opera starring Gable and Turner set amidst the trenches of WW II. Gable plays a selfish doctor who leaves behind his wife and colleague to enlist in the Medical Corps as a major. Turner is the battlefield nurse who forever changes his life. Film is hindered by a story which is far below the talents of the excellent cast. Although voted by the New York Critics as one of the ten worst movies of 1948, the public loved it. Based on the story "The Homecoming of Ulysses" by Sidney Kingsley. 113m/B VHS. Clark Gable, Lana Turner, Anne Baxter, John Hodiak, Ray Collins, Gladys Cooper, Cameron Mitchell, Art Baker, Lurene Tuttle; **D:** Mervyn LeRoy; **W:** Paul Osborn, Jan Lustig.

Homecoming 🐾🐾 1996 (PG) Mentally ill mother abandons her four children at a Connecticut shopping mall in the care of 13-year-old eldest daughter Dicey (Peterson). The children slowly make their way to a relative's (Bedelia) home in Bridgeport, but when she proves equally uncaring Dicey decides to continue the family trek to their maternal grandmother Ab's (Bancroft) house in Chrisfield, Maryland. No surprise when crazy grandma doesn't want them either but this time Dicey is determined to make them all a home. Based on the Newbery Medal-winning children's novel by Cynthia Voight. 105m/C VHS, DVD. Anne Bancroft, Kimberlee Peterson, Bonnie Bedelia, Trevor O'Brien, Hanna Hall, William Greenblatt; **D:** Mark Jean; **W:** Mark Jean, Christopher Carlson; **C:** Toyomichi Kurita; **M:** W.G. Snuffy Walden. **CABLE**

Homecoming: A Christmas Story 🐾🐾½ 1971 Hear-tugger that inspired the television series "The Waltons." A depression-era Virginia mountain family struggles to celebrate Christmas although the whereabouts and safety of their father are unknown. Adapted from the autobiographical novel by Earl Hamner Jr. 98m/C VHS, DVD. Richard Thomas, Patricia Neal, Edgar Bergen, Cleavon Little, Ellen Corby; **D:** Fielder Cook. **TV**

Homegrown 🐾🐾½ 1997 (R) Engaging comedy-noir has three dense Northern California pot growers (Thornton, Azaria, Phillipe) witness their Boss's (Lithgow) murder. Seeing this as a bad omen, they take off, with the crop, to the operation's packaging department (Lynch) and decide to carry on as if the boss is still alive. Amid many cameos (Danson, Curtis) they set up a big deal with a seemingly laid-back wholesaler (Bon Jovi). 101m/C VHS, DVD, Billy Bob Thornton, Hank Azaria, Ryan Phillippe, Kelly Lynch, Jon Bon Jovi, John Lithgow, Jon Tenney, Matt Clark, Graham Greene, Jamie _ee Curtis, Judge Reinhold; **D:** Stephen Gyllenhaal; **W:** Stephen Gyllenhaal, Nicholas Kazan; **C:** Greg Gardiner; **M:** Trevor Rabin.

Home Town Story 🐾🐾 1951 A politician is convinced big business is behind his election loss. Fair drama. Watch for Monroe in a bit part. 61m/B VHS, DVD. Jeffrey Lynn, Donald Crisp, Marjorie Reynolds, Alan Hale Jr., Marilyn Monroe, Barbara Brown, Melinda Plowman; **D:** Arthur Pierson.

Homer and Eddie 🐾🐾 1989 (R) A witless road comedy with Goldberg as a dying sociopath and a mentally retarded Belushi. They take off cross-country to make a little trouble, learn a little about life, and create a less than entertaining movie. 100m/C VHS, Whoopi Goldberg, James Belushi, Karen Black; **D:** Andrei Konchalovsky; **W:** Patrick Cirillo; **C:** Lajos Koltai; **M:** Eduard Artemyev.

Homesteaders of Paradise Valley 🐾🐾½ 1947 The Hume brothers oppose Red Ryder and a group of settlers building a dam in Paradise Valley. 54m/B VHS, DVD. Allan "Rocky" Lane, Robert (Bobby) Blake, Martha Wentworth, Ann E. Todd, Gene Roth, John James, George Chesebro, Edythe Elliott, Milton Kibbee, Tom London; **D:** R.G. Springsteen; **W:** Earle Snell; **C:** Alfred S. Keller.

Hometown Boy Makes Good 🐾🐾½ 1993 (R) Smalltown boy Boyd Geary moved to the big city to go to medical school. But what he never told his proud mom was that he dropped out and doesn't have the successful psychiatry practice she thinks he has, instead he's a barely surviving waiter. But when Boyd travels back home to confess to mom, the local mayor makes him an offer to set up his own practice and won't take no for an answer. 88m/C VHS, Anthony Edwards, Grace Zabriskie, Cynthia Bain; **D:** David Burton Morris; **W:** Barry Goldberg.

Hometown Legend 🐾🐾½ 2002 (PG) The local high school football team in Rachel Sawyer's (Chabert) Alabama hometown hasn't won a game in 12 years—ever since then-coach Buster Schuler's (O'Quinn) son died on the playing field. Rachel figures it wouldn't hurt to pray for a miracle and her prayers are answered when Coach Schuler returns and agrees to coach the team again. 106m/C VHS, DVD, Terry O'Quinn, Lacey Chabert, Nick Cornish, Kirk B.R. Woller, Ian Bohen; **D:** James Anderson; **W:** Shawn Hoffman, Michael Patwin; **C:** Mark Peterson; **M:** Dan Haseltine.

Hometown U.S.A. Woof! 1979 (R) Set in L.A. in the late '50s, this teenage cruising movie is the brainchild of director Baer, known as Jethro from the "The Beverly Hillbillies." 97m/C VHS, DVD, Brian Kerwin, Gary Springer, David Wilson, Cindy Fisher, Sally Kirkland; **D:** Max Baer Jr.

Homeward Bound 🐾 1980 (G) A dying teenager tries to reunite his long-estranged father and grandmother. 96m/C VHS, David Soul, Moosie Drier, Barnard Hughes; **D:** Richard Michaels. **TV**

Homeward Bound 2: Lost in San Francisco 🐾🐾½ 1996 (G) House pets Chance, the feisty bulldog (Fox), Sassy the sophisticated feline (Field), and Shadow the sage golden retriever (Waite) find themselves on the loose again, this time in the tough streets of San Francisco. The animals escape from the airport as the family departs for a Canadian holiday, and on their way back home, encounter some tough mutts—a gang of streetwise dogs, (most notably comedian Sinbad as Riley) and, of course, some dog nappers. Chance even finds romance along the way with Delilah (Gugino). Not too scary for the little ones, flick carries the same charm of the first adventure. 88m/C VHS, DVD, Robert Hays, Kim Greist, Veronica Lauren, Kevin Timothy Chevalia, Michael Rispoli, Chris Heidy; **C:** Jack Conroy; **V:** Michael J. Fox, Sally Field, Ralph Waite, Al Michaels, Tommy Lasorda, Bob Uecker, Jon Polito, Adam Goldberg, Sinbad, Carla Gugino.

Homicidal 🐾🐾 1961 Castle's "Psycho" imitation makes a belated debut on home video. He takes all the key elements of Hitchcock's original and reshuffles them: the big old house with the steep staircase, the creepy invalid older woman, a troubled young man, the blonde who's up to something, the cheap hotel, the vaguely threatening cops, the unexpectedly graphic knife violence, the young couple who investigates. And a central gimmick which is cheesily transparent; most viewers will tumble to it early on and that's part of the fun, too. With enthusiastic overacting from all the leads, the whole thing becomes a minor camp masterpiece. 87m/B DVD, Glenn Corbett, Patricia Breslin, Alan Bunce, James Westerfield; **D:** William Castle; **W:** Robb While; **C:** Burnett Guffey; **M:** Hugo Friedhofer.

Homicidal Impulse 🐾🐾½ Killer Instinct 1992 (R) When Assistant D.A. Tim Cansey has an affair with his boss' ambitious niece he doesn't realize the danger he's in. His lover discovers his lover's cold boyfriend Tim will get his job back. Some women will do anything for love. Also available in an unrated version. 84m/C VHS, Brian Cousins, Vanessa Angel, Talia Balsam, Scott Valentine; **D:** David Tausik; **C:** Janusz Kaminski; **M:** Nigel Holton.

Homicide 🐾🐾🐾 1991 (R) Terrific police thriller with as much thought as action; a driven detective faces his sudden merged Jewish identity while probing an anti-Semitic murder and a secret society. Playwright/filmmaker Mamet creates nail-biting suspense and shattering epiphanies without resorting to Hollywood glitz. Rich (often profane) dialogue includes a classic soliloquy mystically comparing a lawman's badge with a Star of David. 100m/C VHS, DVD, Joe Mantegna, William H. Macy, Natalija Nogulich, Ving Rhames, Rebecca Pidgeon; **D:** David Mamet; **W:** David Mamet; **C:** Roger Deakins.

Homicide: The Movie 🐾🐾 2000 (PG-13) Rather a disappointment for fans of the intelligent NBC cop series but at least the TV movie tied up some loose ends. Giardello (Kotto) is gunned down at a rally where he's campaigning for mayor of Baltimore. While G hovers between life and death, the tragedy brings Pembleton (Braugher) back to town and gets Giardello's old squad—most of whom have retired or been reassigned—back to work on his case. A somewhat surreal ending on this case by cast members from previ...

Homeward Bound: The Incredible Journey 🐾🐾🐾 1993 (G) Successful remake of the 1963 Disney release "The Incredible Journey." Two dogs and a cat once again try to find their way home after their family relocates, armed with greater depth of character than the original. Hard not to shed a tear for the brave animal trio who develop a trusting bond through assorted misadventures. Based on the novel by Sheila Burnford. Superior family fare. 85m/C VHS, DVD. Robert Hays, Kim Greist, Jean Smart, Benj Thall, Veronica Lauren, Kevin Timothy Chevalia; **D:** Duwayne Dunham; **W:** Linda Woolverton, Caroline Thompson; **C:** Reed Smoot; **M:** Bruce Broughton; **V:** Don Ameche, Michael J. Fox, Sally Field.

Homework 🐾 1982 (R) Young man's after-school lessons with a teacher are definitely not part of the curriculum. Yawn. 90m/C VHS, DVD. Joan Collins, Michael Morgan, Shell Kepler, Wings Hauser, Lee Purcell; **D:** Jaime Humberto Hermosillo; **W:** Joan Alonso; **W:** Eric Harlacher; **V:** Kate Jackson.

Homework 🐾🐾🐾 1992 La Tarea 1990 Film student Virginia (Rojo) decides to record her prearranged meeting with ex-lover Marcelo (Alonso). When Marcelo discovers that their sexual tryst has been videotaped, he eventually decides to help Virginia with her work. Spanish with subtitles. 85m/C VHS, DVD. MX Maria Rojo, Jose Alonso; **D:** Jaime Humberto Hermosillo; **W:** Jaime Humberto Hermosillo; **C:** Toni Kuhn.

Homewrecker 🐾🐾 1992 (PG-13) Benson stars as a scientist who invents a computer, with a female voice, as the ultimate domestic worker. Only the computer turns possessive and against Benson's estranged wife. 88m/C VHS, Robby Benson, Sydney Walsh, Sarah Rose Karr; **D:** Fred Walton; **W:** Eric Harlacher; **V:** Kate Jackson.

ous seasons. **89m/C VHS, DVD.** Yaphet Kotto, Andre Braugher, Kyle Secor, Richard Belzer, Giancarlo Esposito, Peter Gerety, Clark Johnson, Zeljko Ivanek, Michael Michele, Isabella Hofmann, Melissa Leo, Callie (Callipe) Thorne, Jon Seda, Max Perlich, Jason Priestley, Daniel Baldwin, Ned Beatty, Jon Polito, Toni Lewis; **D:** Jean De Segonzac; **W:** Eric Overmyer, Tom Fontana, James Yoshimura; **C:** Jean De Segonzac; **M:** Douglas J. Cuomo. **TV**

Hondo 🦴🦴🦴 *1953* In 1874, whites have broken their treaty with the Apache nation who are now preparing for war. Cavalry dispatch rider Hondo Lane (Wayne) encounters Angie (Page) and her young son at an isolated ranch and warns her of the danger but she refuses to leave. After various Indian attacks, Hondo persuades Angie (they've fallen in love) to leave for California with him. Based on the story "The Gift of Cochise" by Louis L'Amour. **84m/C VHS, DVD.** John Wayne, Geraldine Page, Ward Bond, Michael Pate, James Arness, Rodolfo Acosta, Leo Gordon, Lee Aaker, Paul Fix; **D:** John Farrow; **W:** James Edward Grant; **C:** Robert Burks, Archie Stout; **M:** Hugo Friedhofer, Emil Newman.

Honey 🦴½ *1981* Attractive writer pays an unusual visit to the home of a distinguished publisher. Brandishing a pistol, she demands that he read aloud from her manuscript. As he reads, a unique fantasy unfolds, a dreamlike erotic tale that may be the writer's own sexual awakening. Or maybe not. **89m/C VHS. IT SP** Clio Goldsmith, Fernando Rey, Catherine Spaak; **D:** Gianfranco Angelucci

Honey 🦴🦴 *2003 (PG-13)* Honey Daniels (Alba) shakes her tail feathers as a hip-hop dancer with a heart of gold. Honey is plucked out of clubland obscurity by slimy music director Michael Ellis (Moscow) and her career as a video choreographer skyrockets. Alba shines as Honey shows a lot of bare midriffs, romances the local good-guy barber (Phifer), and tries to prevent two local kids from falling in with the wrong crowd. Energetic dancing and hip-hop soundtrack couldn't prevent the formulaic cliches from popping up (does every dance movie need to put on a show to "Save the Last Electric Boogaloo Flashdance." Cameos by Jadakiss, Ginuwine and Missy Elliott. **94m/C VHS, DVD. US** Jessica Alba, Mekhi Phifer, Joy Bryant, Lil' Romeo, David Moscow, Lonette McKee, Zachary Isaiah Williams, Laurie Ann Gibson, Anthony Sherwood; **Cameos:** Missy Elliott; **D:** Billie Woodruff; **W:** Alonzo Brown, Kim Watson; **C:** John R. Leonetti; **M:** Mervyn Warren.

Honey & Ashes 🦴🦴 *Miel et Cendres 1996* Three women in Islamic Tunisia try to overcome their patriarchal society and control their own lives with bitter consequences. Leila flees to the city where her father disappoints the boy she loves; Naima may be a successful doctor but she still can't avoid a pre-arranged marriage; and Amina suffers constant abuse from her husband. French and Arabic with subtitles. **80m/C VHS, DVD. SI** Nozha Khouadra, Amel Hedhili, Samia Mzali, Lara Chaouachi, Naji Najeh; **D:** Nadia Fares; **W:** Nadia Fares, Yves Kropf; **C:** Ismael Ramirez; **M:** Slim Lamaouel, Jean-Francois Bovard, Mami Azalez.

Honey, I Blew Up the Kid 🦴🦴½ *1992 (PG)* Screwball suburban inventor Moranis reverses his shrinking process and this time manages to enlarge his two-year-old into a 112-foot giant who gets bigger every time he comes in contact with electricity. Yikes! Loaded with great special effects, this is a charming and funny film that's fit for the whole family. Sequel to "Honey I Shrunk the Kids." **89m/C VHS, DVD.** Rick Moranis, Daniel Shalikar, Joshua Shalikar, Lloyd Bridges, John Shea, Keri Russell, Gregory Sierra, Julia Sweeney, Kenneth Tobey, Peter Elbling; **D:** Randal Kleiser; **W:** Thom Ebenhardt, Garry Goodrow; **M:** Bruce Broughton.

Honey, I Shrunk the Kids 🦴🦴½ *1989 (G)* The popular Disney fantasy about a suburban inventor. His shrinking device accidentally reduces his kids to 1/4 inch tall, and the subsequently throws them out with the garbage.

Now they must journey back to the house through the jungle that was once the back lawn. Accompanied by "Tummy Trouble," the first of a projected series of Roger Rabbit Maroon Cartoons. Followed by "Honey, I Blew Up the Kids." **101m/C VHS, DVD.** Rick Moranis, Matt Frewer, Marcia Strassman, Kristine Sutherland, Thomas Wilson Brown, Jared Rushton, Amy O'Neill, Robert Oliveri; **D:** Joe Johnston, Rob Minkoff; **W:** Ed Naha, Tom Schulman, Stuart Gordon; **C:** Hiro Narita; **M:** James Horner; **V:** Charles Fleischer, Kathleen Turner, Lou Hirsch, April Winchell.

The Honey Pot 🦴🦴½ *It Comes Up Murder: Anyone for Venice?; Mr. Fox of Venice 1967* A millionaire feigns death to see the reaction of three of his former lovers. Amusing black comedy with their performances from all. Based on Moliere's "Volpone." **131m/C VHS.** Rex Harrison, Susan Hayward, Cliff Robertson, Capucine, Edie Adams, Maggie Smith, Adolfo Celi; **D:** Joseph L. Mankiewicz; **W:** Joseph L. Mankiewicz; **M:** John Addison.

Honey, We Shrunk Ourselves 🦴½ *1997 (PG)* Scientist Wayne Szalinsky (Moranis) manages to shrink himself, his wife, his brother, and his sister-in-law. The kids just think their parents are out of town for the weekend (so they go nuts). The third in the "Honey" series, this one was released directly to video. Though adults may find it dull, it was made with the kids in mind. **76m/C VHS.** Rick Moranis, Stuart Pankin, Robin Bartlett, Eve Gordon, Bug Hall; **D:** Dean Cundey; **W:** Karey Kirkpatrick, Nell Scovell, Joel Hodgson; **C:** Raymond N. Stella. **VIDEO**

Honeybaby 🦴🦴 *1974 (PG)* A smooth international soldier of fortune and a bright, sexy American interpreter are entangled in Middle-Eastern turbulence when they must rescue a politician kidnapped by terrorists. **94m/C VHS.** Calvin Lockhart, Diana Sands; **D:** Michael A. Schultz.

Honeyboy 🦴½ *1982* Estrada tries to win fame, fortune, and a ticket out of the barrio as an up-and-coming boxer. Outstanding fight scenes, but little else in this drama of the boxing scene. **100m/C VHS.** Erik Estrada, Morgan Fairchild, James McEachin, Robert Costanzo, Yvonne Wilder; **D:** John Berry. **TV**

Honeydripper 🦴🦴 *2007 (PG-13)* Sayles rarely is predictable, but this time the showbiz story seems all too familiar. In rural 1950s Alabama, Tyrone Purvis (Glover) is going to lose his debt-ridden roadhouse, the Honeydripper, unless he can come up with a surefire way to make money. He decides to advertise that local legend Guitar Sam will appear on Saturday night, though he hasn't actually booked the performer. Riding the rails into town to save the day is young blues upstart Sonny Blake (Clark), who brings along his solid wood-body electric guitar. **123m/C DVD. US** Danny Glover, Lisa Gay Hamilton, Yaya DaCosta, Charles S. Dutton, Gary Clark Jr., Vondie Curtis-Hall, Stacy Keach, Mable John; **D:** John Sayles; **W:** John Sayles; **C:** Dick Pope; **M:** Mason Daring.

Honeymoon 🦴🦴 *1987* A young French woman visiting New York learns she will be deported when her boyfriend is arrested for drug-smuggling. To stay, she is set up in a marriage of convenience and told her new husband will never see or bother her. But hubby has other plans! **96m/C VHS.** John Shea, Nathalie Baye, Richard Berry, Peter Donat; **D:** Patrick Jamain; **W:** Philippe Setbon.

Honeymoon Academy 🦴🦴 *For Better or For Worse 1990 (PG-13)* Newly married man has lots to learn in this comic outing. His new wife never told him about her unusual line of business—as an undercover agent! **94m/C VHS.** Robert Hays, Kim Cattrall, Leigh Taylor-Young, Charles Rocket, Doris Roberts, Gordon Jump, Jonathan Banks; **D:** Gene Quintano; **W:** Gene Quintano; **M:** Robert Folk.

Honeymoon Horror 🦴 *1982* Stranded on an island, three honeymooning couples soon realize their romantic retreat is a nightmare. A crazy man with an axe is tracking them down. Minimally effective. **90m/C VHS.** Cheryl Black, William F.

Pecchi, Bob Wagner; **D:** Harry Preston; **W:** Harry Preston; **C:** David Pinkston; **M:** Ron Di Lullo.

Honeymoon in Vegas 🦴🦴🦴 *1992 (PG-13)* Romantic comedy turns frantic after Cage loses his fiancee to Caan in a high stakes Vegas poker game. Cage displays lots of talent for manic comedy as the distraught young groom-to-be who encounters numerous obstacles on his way to the altar. Lightweight and funny, featuring a bevy of Elvis impersonators in every size, shape, and color and new versions of favorite Elvis tunes. Look for former UNLV basketball coach Jerry Tarkanian as one of Caan's gambling buddies. **95m/C VHS, DVD.** James Caan, Nicolas Cage, Sarah Jessica Parker, Noriyuki "Pat" Morita, John Capodice, Robert Costanzo, Anne Bancroft, Peter Boyle, Seymour Cassel, Tony Shalhoub, Ben Stein, Angela Pietropinto; **D:** Andrew Bergman; **W:** Andrew Bergman; **C:** William A. Fraker; **M:** David Newman.

Honeymoon Killers 🦴🦴🦴 *The Lonely Hearts Killers 1970 (R)* A grim, creepy dramatization of a true multiple-murder case wherein an overweight woman and a slimy gigolo living on Long Island seduce and murder one lonely woman after another. Independently made and frankly despairing. **103m/C VHS, DVD.** Tony LoBianco, Shirley Stoler, Mary Jane Higby, Dortha Duckworth, Doris Roberts, Marilyn Chris, Kip McArdle, Mary Breen, Barbara Cason, Ann Harris, Guy Sorel; **D:** Leonard Kastle; **W:** Leonard Kastle; **C:** Oliver Wood.

Honeymoon Lodge 🦴🦴 *1943* Bob (Bruce) and Carol (Vincent) make a last attempt to save their marriage by recreating their mountain resort honeymoon. Instead, they meet old flames Lorraine (Hilliard) and Big Boy (Cameron) and jealousy rears its ugly head. Hilliard also gets a chance to work with hubby Ozzie Nelson and his Orchestra. **63m/B VHS.** David Bruce, June Vincent, Rod Cameron, Franklin Pangborn, Harriet Hilliard Nelson; **D:** Edward Lilley; **W:** Clyde Bruckman; **C:** Paul Ivano.

The Honeymoon Machine 🦴🦴½ *1961* A lightweight comedy about two American sailors and a computer scam. McQueen and Mullaney hook up with computer expert Hutton to use their ship's computer to beat the gambling odds at an Italian casino. Their commander misinterprets the signals and thinks the ship is being attacked. Fast paced and the computer angle was new territory in '61. **87m/C VHS.** Steve McQueen, Jack Mullaney, Jim Hutton, Dean Jagger, Paula Prentiss, Brigid Bazlen, Jack Weston; **D:** Richard Thorpe; **W:** George Wells; **C:** Joseph LaShelle; **M:** Leigh Harline.

The Honeymooners 🦴🦴 *2003* Modest romantic comedy. When David is jilted at the altar, he gets drunk and decides to go on his honeymoon anyway. He meets Claire, who's just been fired and whose married lover keeps breaking his promises. She's anxious to get out of Dublin and David's too drunk to drive, so he pays her to take him to his brand-new cottage in Donegal where they can both recover from being betrayed. **86m/C DVD. IR GB** Jonathan Byren, Justine Mitchell, Alex Reid, Conor Mullen; **D:** Karl Golden; **W:** Karl Golden; **C:** Darran Tiernan; **M:** Niall Byrne.

The Honeymooners 🦴🦴 *2005 (PG-13)* The classic '50s TV series, which starred Jackie Gleason and Art Carney, is given an update—but why bother? Bus driver Ralph Kramden (Cedric the Entertainer) involves best pal, sewer worker Ed Norton (Epps), in various get-rich-quick schemes that always go awry, exasperating both Ralph's wife Alice (Union) and Ed's wife Trixie (Hall). At least this time Ralph wants to give Alice the moon instead of sending her there, but the story should have been left in the TV vault where it belonged. **90m/C DVD. US** Cedric the Entertainer, Mike Epps, Gabrielle Union, Regina Hall, John Leguizamo, Jon Polito, Eric Stoltz, Carol Woods, Ajay Naidu, Kim Schultz; **D:** John Schultz; **W:** Don Rhymer, Barry W. Blaustein, David Sheffield, Danny Jacobson; **C:** Shawn Maurer; **M:** Richard Gibbs.

Honeysuckle Rose 🦴🦴½ *1980 (PG)* On the Road Again 1980 (PG) A road-touring country-Western singer whose life is a series of one night stands, falls in love with an adoring young guitar player who has just joined his band. This nearly costs him his marriage when his wife, who while waiting patiently for him at home, decides she's had enough. Easygoing performance by Nelson, essentially playing himself. **120m/C VHS, DVD.** Willie Nelson, Dyan Cannon, Amy Irving, Slim Pickens, Joey Floyd, Charles Levin, Priscilla Pointer; **D:** Jerry Schatzberg; **W:** William D. Wittliff, John Binder, Carol Sobieski; **M:** Willie Nelson, Richard Baskin. Golden Raspberries '80: Worst Support. Actress (Irving).

Hong Kong Nights 🦴🦴½ *1935* Two agents attempt to break up a Chinese smuggling ring run by an unscrupulous madman. Good, action-packed low-budget film. **59m/B VHS.** Tom Keene, Wera Engels, Warren Hymer, Tetsu Komai, Cornelius Keefe; **D:** E. Mason Hopper.

Hong Kong 1941 🦴🦴½ *1984* Yip Kim Fay (Yun-Fat) arrives in Hong Kong on the eve of war in 1941 and befriends peasant Wong Hak Keung (Man). Fay and Keung plan to leave Hong Kong with Keung's girlfriend, Ah Nam (Yip), but fall victim to the Japanese invasion. An early role for Yun-Fat, who's the romantic hero here rather than the action star he later became. Chinese with subtitles. **118m/C VHS, DVD. HK** Cecilia Yip, Alex Man, Chow Yun-Fat; **D:** Po-Chih Leung; **W:** Koon-Chung Chan.

Hong Kong '97 🦴🦴 *1994 (R)* On the eve of China's takeover of Hong Kong from Great Britain, special agent Reg Cameron (Patrick) murders a Chinese general. With a $10 million bounty on his head, Cameron tries to escape with his partners and girlfriend in tow. Lots of action, good use of Hong Kong setting. **91m/C VHS.** Robert Patrick, Ming Na, Brion James, Tim Thomerson; **D:** Albert Pyun.

Honky 🦴½ *1971 (R)* An innocent friendship between a black woman and a white man develops into a passionate romance that has the whole town talking. **92m/C VHS.** Brenda Sykes, John Neilson, Maria Donzinger; **D:** William A. Graham; **M:** Quincy Jones.

Honky Tonk 🦴🦴🦴 *1941* A western soap opera in which ne'er do well Clark marries Lana and tries to live a respectable life. In this, the first of several MGM teamings between Gable and Turner, the chemistry between the two is evident. So much so in fact that Gable's then wife Carole Lombard let studio head Louis B. Mayer know that she was not at all thrilled. The public was pleased however, and made the film a hit. **106m/B VHS.** Clark Gable, Lana Turner, Frank Morgan, Claire Trevor, Marjorie Main, Albert Dekker, Chill Wills, Henry O'Neill, John Maxwell, Morgan Wallace, Betty Blythe, Francis X. Bushman, Veda Ann Borg; **D:** Jack Conway.

Honky Tonk Freeway 🦴 *1981 (PG)* An odd assortment of people become involved in a small town Mayor's scheme to turn a dying hamlet into a tourist wonderland. You can find better things to do with your evening than watch this accident. **107m/C VHS, DVD.** Teri Garr, Howard Hesseman, Beau Bridges, Hume Cronyn, William Devane, Beverly D'Angelo, Geraldine Page; **D:** John Schlesinger; **W:** Edward Clinton; **C:** John Bailey; **M:** Elmer Bernstein, Steve Dorff.

Honkytonk Man 🦴🦴 *1982 (PG)* Unsuccessful change-of-pace Eastwood vehicle set during the Depression. Aging alcoholic country singer tries one last time at the Grand Ole Opry. This time he takes his nephew (played by Eastwood's real-life son) with him. **123m/C VHS, DVD.** Clint Eastwood, Kyle Eastwood, John McIntire, Alexa Kenin, Verna Bloom; **D:** Clint Eastwood; **W:** Clancy Carlile; **C:** Bruce Surtees; **M:** Steve Dorff.

Honkytonk Nights 🦴 *1978 (R)* A honky-tonkin' romp through an evening in a country/western bar, featuring legendary topless dancer Carol Doda, Georgina ("Devil in Mrs. Jones") Spelvin, and the music of The Hot Licks (minus front man Dan Hicks). **90m/C VHS.** Carol Doda, Georgina

Honolulu 🎬🎬½ 1939 A screwball comedy with Powell providing the musical numbers. Young takes on the dual role of a Hollywood star who meets his exact double, a Hawaii plantation owner. They decide to switch identities to give their lives a little oomph. The star sails to Hawaii, falling for fellow passenger Powell, only to discover he's expected to get married upon his arrival in Honolulu, Anderson and Burns and Allen provide the comic relief. 🎬🎬🎬½ The Leader Doesn't Like Music; This Night Was Made For Dreaming; Honolulu; Hymn To The Sun. 83m/B VHS. Robert Young, Eleanor Powell, George Burns, Gracie Allen, Rita Johnson, Eddie Anderson, Clarence (C. William) Kolb; **D:** Edward Buzzell; **W:** Frank Partos, Herbert Fields; **M:** Franz Waxman.

Honor 🎬🎬 2006 (R) Staccard martial arts showdown between two neighborhood friends, Raymond (Wong) and Gabriel (Barry), who wind up on dueling gangs when a vicious police conflict sends Raymond to the slammer and Gabriel to the military and an overseas war. After returning home, it's a natural end game for the now more callous pair. 85m/C DVD. Jason Barry, Russell Wong, Roddy Piper, Remy Bonjasky, Linda Park; **D:** Davie Worth; **W:** Larry Felix Jr. VIDEO

Honor Among Thieves 🎬½ 1934 Farewell, Friend, Adieu, l'ami 1968 (R) Two former mercenaries reteam for a robbery that doesn't come off as planned. Not as fast paced as others in Bronson canon. 115m/C VHS, DVD. FR IT Charles Bronson, Alain Delon, Brigitte Fossey, Olga Georges-Picot, Bernard Fresson; **D:** Jean-Herman; **W:** Sebastien Japrisot; **C:** Jean-Jacques Tarbes; **M:** Francois de Roubaix.

Honor and Glory 🎬🎬 1992 (R) Tracy Pride, an FBI agent and martial arts expert, teams up with an Interpol agent, who doubles as a TV anchorwoman, to stop an international banker from getting his greedy hands on the key to a nuclear arsenal. These fighting gals are up against a team of assassins but they can more than hardle themselves. 90m/C VHS. Cynthia Rothrock, Donna Jason, Chuck Jeffreys, Gerald Klein, Robin Shou, Richard Yuen; **D:** Godfrey Ho; **W:** Herb Borkland.

Honor of the Range 🎬🎬 1934 The good sheriff's lady is whisked away by his evil twin brother and the sheriff must go undercover to get her back. Odd plot twists for a seemingly normal western. 60m/B VHS, DVD. Ken Maynard, Fred Kohler Sr.; **D:** Ken Maynard.

Honor Thy Father 🎬🎬 1973 The everyday life of a real-life Mafia family as seen through the eyes of Bill Bonanno, the son of mob chieftain Joe Bonanno. Adapted from the book by Gay Talese. 97m/C DVD. Raf Vallone, Richard S. Castellano, Brenda Vaccaro, Joseph Bologna; **D:** Paul Wendkos; **M:** George Duning. TV

Honor Thy Father and Mother: The True Story of the Menendez Brothers 🎬🎬½ 1994 First Amy Fisher won the true sleaze-on-TV award and now its the turn of Lyle and Erik Menendez. Accused of the gruesome 1989 shotgun murders of their wealthy parents, the trial provided numerous sordid details, including alleged sexual abuse of the brothers by both parents. (Both Menendez trials ended in hung juries and will be retried). Composite characters and compressed time sequences play fast and loose with the facts of the case. Based on public records and on the book "Blood Brothers," by reporters John Johnson and Ronald L. Soble. 90m/C VHS. Billy Warlock, David Beron, Jill Clayburgh, James Farentino, Susan Blakely, Erin Gray, Elaine Joyce, John Beck, John David Conti, Stanley Kamel; **D:** Paul Schneider; **W:** Michael J. Murray. TV

Hooch 🎬½ 1976 (PG) Comedy about three members of the New York Mafia who get some unexpected southern hospitality when they try to muscle in on a southern family's moonshine operation. 96m/C VHS. Gil Gerard, Erika Fox, Melody Rogers, Danny Aiello, Mike Allen, Raymond Serra; **D:** Edward Andrew (Santos A cocer) Mann.

Hoodlum 🎬🎬 1996 (R) Highly fictionalized tale of '30s gangster "Bumpy" Johnson (Fishburne, reprising his role from "The Cotton Club"), and Lucky Luciano (Garcia) to muscle into the Harlem numbers rackets. Duke makes the proceedings nice to look at, and does well by the eclectic cast, but the uneven screenplay occasionally lets everybody down, especially during the cheesy time-passage montage (complete with Tommy Gun fire and flipping calendar pages). Roth is ruthless as ever and Garcia is smooth as ever. But it's definitely Fishburne's show, as he explores Johnson's professional triumphs and the personal toll they take. Fishburne previously worked with director Duke on "Deep Cover," Singer Michael McCary from Boyz II Men makes his film debut as an explosives expert. 130m/C VHS, DVD. Laurence Fishburne, Tim Roth, Andy Garcia, Vanessa Lyonne] Williams, Cicely Tyson, Clarence Williams III, William Atherton, Chi McBride, Richard Bradford, Loretta Devine, Queen Latifah, Paul Benjamin', Mike Starr, Beau Starr, Joe Guzaldo, Ed O'Ross; **D:** Bill Duke; **W:** Chris Brancato; **C:** Frank Tidy; **M:** Elmer Bernstein.

Hoodlum & Son 🎬🎬 2003 (PG-13) Charlie's a 1930s gangster who neglects his ten-year-old trouble-prone son Archie. The kid then gets in dad's way when he's trying to do a job for mob boss Benny and collect on a debt. Stolen money and a beautiful widow also figure in to the good-natured plot. Shot (though not set) in South Africa. 92m/C DVD. GB T. W. (Ted) King, Ron Perlman, Myles Jeffrey, Mia Sara, Robert Vaughn; **D:** Ashley Way; **W:** Ashley Way; **C:** Buster Reynolds; **M:** Mark Thomas.

Hoodlum Empire 🎬🎬 1952 A senator enlists his ten-year-old trouble-prone son Archie. The kid then gets in dad's way, now a war hero, in his battle against the syndicate. Loosely based on the Kefauver investigations of 1950-51. 98m/B VHS. Brian Donlevy, Claire Trevor, Forrest Tucker, Vera Hruba Ralston, Luther Adler, John Russell, Gene ,ockhart Grant Withers, Taylor Holmes, Roy Barcroft, Richard Jaeckel; **D:** Joseph Kane.

The Hoodlum Priest 🎬🎬 1961 Biography of the Rev. Charles Dismas Clark (Murray), a Jesuit priest who dedicated his life to working with juvenile delinquents and ex-cons in St. Louis. Dullea made his screen debut as Billy Lee Jackson, a thief who finds the straight and narrow is a hard road with more detours than he can handle. Fine performances with Murray co-scripting under the pseudonym Don Deer. 101m/B VHS, DVD. Don Murray, Keir Dullea, Larry Gates, Logan Ramsey, Cindi Wood; **D:** Irvin Kershner; **W:** Don Murray, Joseph Landon; **C:** Haskell Wexler.

Hoodoo Ann 🎬🎬 1916 The story of Hoodoo Ann, from her days in the orphanage to her happy marriage. Silent. 27m/B VHS, DVD. Mae Marsh, Robert "Bobbie" Harron, Wilbur Higby, William H. Brown, Loyola O'Connor, Mildred Harris, Elmo Lincoln, Anne Dodge, Charles Lee, Carl Stockdale; **D:** Lloyd Ingraham; **W:** D.W. Griffith.

Hooded Angels 🎬🎬 2000 (R) Westvogen features six women out for revenge after enduring mistreatment by a gang of renegade soldiers shortly after the Civil War. Male posse, led by brothers Bauer and Johansson, don't realize their outlaws are female at first but they learn these ladies give as good as they get. 95m/C VHS, DVD. Amanda Donohoe, Steven Bauer, Paul Johansson, Chantell Stander, Gary Busey, Juliana Venter; **D:** Paul Matthews; **W:** Paul Matthews; **C:** Vincent Cox.

The Hooded Terror 🎬🎬 1938 Secon Blake and the Hooded Terror 1938 A merciless group of murderers take on a G-man. 70m/B VHS. GB George Curzon, Tony Sympson, Charles Oliver, David Farrar, Tod Slaughter, Greta Gynt; **D:** George King; **W:** A.R. Rawlinson; **C:** Hone Glendinning.

Hoods 🎬🎬½ 1998 (R) Mob comedy features a bunch of pros that make it worth watching. Smalltime mobster Martinelli (Mantegna) suffers a midlife crisis on his 50th birthday when he learns that his floozy girlfriend (Tilly) is cheating on him and his aging father wants him to whack someone named Carmine—who turns out to be a nine-year-old boy. 92m/C VHS, DVD. Joe Mantegna, Kevin Pollak, Joe Pantoliano, Jennifer Tilly; **D:** Mark Malone; **W:** Mark Malone; **C:** Tobias Schliessler; **M:** Anthony Marinelli.

Hoodwinked 🎬🎬 2005 (PG) "Rashamon" meets the brothers Grimm as the Weinsteins introduce the kiddies to police procedurals and action flicks by way of "The Thin Man" and extreme sports. Red Riding Hood (Hathaway), Granny (Close), the Wolf (Warburton), and the Woodsman (Belushi) all get to tell their side of the famous story when the cops bust in on the proceedings. Plenty of references to genres and movies and new and ensure that adults will enjoy this one as much, if not more than the kid's. Somewhat clunky animation is the only flaw. 80m/C DVD. US **D:** Cory Edwards; **W:** Cory Edwards, Todd Edwards, Tony Leech; **M:** Todd Edwards; **V:** Anne Hathaway, Glenn Close, James Belushi, Patrick Warburton, Anthony Anderson, David Ogden Stiers, Xzibit, Chazz Palminteri, Andy Dick, Cory Edwards, Benjy Gaither.

Hook 🎬🎬 1991 (PG) Although he said he was never gonna to do it, Peter Pan has grown up. Uptight Peter Banning has grown up. Uptight Peter Banning is all about Neverland and the evil Captain Hook, until Hook kidnaps the Banning kids and takes them to Neverland. With the help of Tinkerbell, her magic pixie dust, and happy thoughts, Peter rescues his kids and rediscovers his youth while visiting with the Lost Boys. The sets and special effects are spectacular, but the direction less so. Big-budget fantasy lacks the charm it needs to really fly. Still, kids seem to love it. You'll have to look hard to spot pirates Crosby and Close. Futurizes the J.M. Barrie classic. 142m/C VHS, DVD. Dustin Hoffman, Robin Williams, Julia Roberts, Bob Hoskins, Maggie Smith, Charlie Korsmo, Caroline Goodall, Amber Scott, Phil Collins, Arthur Malet, Dante Basco, Gwyneth Paltrow, Glenn Close, David Crosby; **D:** Steven Spielberg; **W:** Nick Castle; **C:** Dean Cundey; **M:** John Williams.

Hook, Line and Sinker 🎬🎬 1930 A couple of insurance investigators try to help a young woman restore a hotel, and they find romance and run-ins with crooks. Directed by Cline (who later directed W.C. Fields in "The Bank Dick," "My Little Chickadee," and "Never Give a Sucker an Even Break." 75m/B VHS, DVD. Bert Wheeler, Robert Woolsey, Dorothy Lee, Jobyna Howland, Ralf Harolde, Natalie Moorhead, George F. Marion Sr., Hugh Herbert; **D:** Edward F. (Eddie) Cline; **W:** Rod Amateau.

The Hooked Generation 🎬 1969 (R) A group of drug pushers kidnap defenseless victims, rape innocent girls, and even murder their own Cuban drug contacts (and all without the aid of a cohesive plot). Many gory events precede their untimely deaths; few will be entertained prepare to enter St. Joseph, a predominantly white Catholic school that has offered them partial athletic scholarships. The coach tabs Gates as the "next Isiah Thomas," alluding to the school's most famous alum. There's plenty of game footage, but the more telling and fascinating parts of the film deal with the kids' families and home life. Both players encounter the court, demonstrating the incredibly long odds they face. 169m/C VHS, DVD. Arthur Agee, William Gates; **C:** Peter Gilbert, Directors Guild '95: Feature Doc. (James) L.A. Film Critics '94: Feature Doc.; MTV Movie Awards '95: New Filmmaker (James), Natl. B.d. of Review '94: Feature Doc., Natl. Film Reg. '05; N.Y. Film Critics '94: Feature Doc.; Natl. Soc. Film Critics '94: Feature Doc.; Sundance '94: Aud. Award.

Hoop Dreams 🎬🎬🎬🎬 1994 Exceptional documentary follows two inner-city basketball phenoms' lives through high school as they chase their dreams of playing in the NBA. We meet Arthur Agee and William Gates as they prepare to enter St. Joseph, a predominantly white Catholic school.

Hooper 🎬🎬½ 1978 (PG) Lightweight behind-the-scenes satire about the world of movie stuntmen. Reynolds is a top stuntman who becomes involved in a rivalry with an up-and-coming young man out to surpass him. Dated good-ole-boy shenanigans. 94m/C VHS, DVD. Burt Reynolds, Jan-Michael Vincent, Robert Klein, Sally Field, Brian Keith, John Marley, Adam West; **D:** Hal Needham; **W:** Bill Kerby, Thomas (Tom) Rickman; **C:** Bobby Byrne; **M:** Bill Justis.

Hoopla 🎬🎬 1933 Bow's last film has her portraying the seductive older woman in a number of scanty outfits. Carnival femme Lou (Bow) seduces teen Chris (Cromwell) and makes him a man. Climax team gets a new, but surprisingly experienced coach. He makes the team, and (no: that kind') takes place at the Kenyon World's Fair. Adapted from the Chicago possible. Classic plot rings true because Nicholson play "The Barker." 85m/B VHS. Clara Bow, Richard Cromwell, Preston Foster, Herbert Mundin, James Gleason, Minna Gombell, Florence Roberts, Roger Imhof; **D:** Frank Lloyd; **W:** Joseph Moncure March, Bradley King; **C:** Ernest Palmer; **M:** Louis De Francesco.

Hoosiers 🎬🎬🎬 1986 (PG) In Indiana, where basketball is the sport of the gods, a small town high school basketball team gets a new, but surprisingly experienced coach. He makes the team, and each person in it, better than they thought possible. Classic plot rings true because of Hackman's complex and sensitive performance coupled with Hopper's touching portrait of an alcoholic basketball fanatic. 115m/C VHS, DVD, Blu-ray Disc, UMD. Gene Hackman, Barbara Hershey, Dennis Hopper, David Neidorf, Sheb Wooley, Fern Parsons, Brad Boyle, Steve Hollar, Brad Long; **D:** David Anspaugh; **W:** Angelo Pizzo; **C:** Fred Murphy; **M:** Jerry Goldsmith. L.A. Film Critics '86: Support. Actor (Hopper), Natl. Film Reg. '01.

Hoot 🎬🎬½ 2006 (PG) Mild eco-tale based on Carl Hiaasen's young-adult novel. Young teen Roy (Lerman) and cute kid at his Coconut Cove, Florida, school. After tangling with a bully, Roy is grateful to befriend tomboy Beatrice (Larson) and runaway Muller Fingers (Linley). Mullet spends his time sabotaging a construction site that is the habitat of the endangered burrowing owl (which is small and cute while the corporation destroying it is big and greedy). Naturally, Roy decides to help out (the owls of course). 90m/C DVD. US Luke Wilson, Logan Lerman, Tim Blake Nelson, Brie Larson, Cody Linley, Neil Flynn, Clark Gregg, Kiersten Warren, Jessica Cauffiel, Dean Collins, Robert Wagner, Eric Phillips, Jimmy Buffett, John Archie, Kin Shriner; **D:** Will Shriner; **W:** Will Shriner; **C:** Michael Chapman; **M:** Phil Marshall, Michael Utley, Mac McAnally.

Hootch Country Boys 🎬 1975 (PG) Redneck County; The Great Lester Boggs 1975 (PG) A film packed with moonshine, sheriffs, busty country girls, and chases. 90m/C VHS, DVD. Alex Karras, Scott MacKenzie, Dean Jagger, Willie Jones, Bob Ridgely, Susan Denbo, Bob Ginnaven, David Haney; **D:** Harry Z. Thomason.

Hopalong Cassidy 🎬🎬🎬 Hopalong Cassidy Enters 1935 In this first of a long series of "Hopalong Cassidy" films, Hoppy and his pals intervene in a brewing range war. A gang of rustlers is helped by a two-timing foreman who's playing both sides off each other. After a career in silent films, Boyd was pretty much washed up before taking on the role of Cassidy. He was originally asked to play the villain and declined, but agreed to be the good guy if the character was cleaned up. "Gabby" Hayes' stock character was killed off in this episode, but was brought back for later installments. 60m/B VHS, DVD. William Boyd, James Ellison, Paula Stone, Robert Warwick, Charles Middleton, Frank McGlynn, Kenneth Thomson, George "Gabby" Hayes, James Mason, Franklyn Farnum, Doris Schroeder; **D:** Howard Bretherton; **C:** Archie Stout.

Hopalong Cassidy: Borrowed Trouble 🦴🦴½ 1948 Hoppy must save a righteous teacher from the clutches of kidnappers out to place a saloon right next to the school. 61m/B VHS, DVD. William Boyd, Andy Clyde, Rand Brooks, Elaine Riley, John Kellogg, Helen Chapman; *D:* George Archainbaud.

Hopalong Cassidy: Dangerous Venture 🦴🦴 1948 "Dangerous Venture" was one of Hoppy's last ventures, produced the final year of the series' 13-year tenure. Hoppy and the gang hunt for Aztec ruins in the great Southwest, and have to deal with renegade Indians and a band of treacherous looters along the way. 55m/B VHS, DVD. William Boyd, Andy Clyde, Rand Brooks; *D:* George Archainbaud; *W:* Doris Schroeder; *C:* Mack Stengler; *M:* David Chudnow.

Hopalong Cassidy: False Paradise 🦴🦴 1948 Another late Hopalong has the noir-clad cowboy rushing to the aid of a girl and her dad when control of their ranch is threatened by swindlers with false mining claims. 59m/B VHS. William Boyd, Andy Clyde, Rand Brooks; *D:* George Archainbaud.

Hopalong Cassidy: Hoppy's Holiday 🦴🦴 1947 Boyd—the only celluloid incarnation of Clarence Mulford's pulp hero—plays the Hopster yet again. This time, the non-drinking, non-smoking (what does he do for kicks?) hero and a passel of Bar-20 cowboys visit Mesa City for some well-earned R and R, but find themselves caught in a web of corruption. 60m/B VHS, DVD. William Boyd, Andy Clyde, Rand Brooks, Jeff Corey; *D:* George Archainbaud.

Hopalong Cassidy: Renegade Trail 🦴🦴 1939 Hoppy comes to the aid of both a small town sheriff and a widow. 61m/B VHS. William Boyd, George "Gabby" Hayes, Russell Hayden, Charlotte Wynters, Russell Hopton, Sonny Bupp, Jack Rockwell, Roy Barcroft, John Merton, Robert F. (Bob) Kortman; *D:* Lesley Selander.

Hopalong Cassidy Returns 🦴🦴½ 1936 In the seventh entry in the "Hopalong Cassidy" series, Hoppy (Boyd) faces a lady outlaw, Lilli Marsh (Brent), who, of course, falls hard for our stalwart hero. If this is not one of the best in the series, it maintains the high production standards, and it contains the debut of series regular Morris Ankrum as a villain. 74m/B DVD. William Boyd, George "Gabby" Hayes, Evelyn Brent, Morris Ankrum, William Janney; *D:* Nate Watt; *W:* Doris Schroeder; *C:* Archie Stout.

Hopalong Cassidy: Riders of the Deadline 🦴🦴 1943 Hoppy turns into a baddie in this episode in order to infiltrate a treacherous gang and apprehend their leader. 70m/B VHS, DVD. William Boyd, Andy Clyde, Jimmy Rogers, Robert Mitchum; *D:* Lesley Selander.

Hopalong Cassidy: Silent Conflict 🦴🦴 1948 Lucky is tricked and hypnotized by a traveling medicine man who commands him to rob and kill Hoppy. 61m/B VHS, DVD. William Boyd, Andy Clyde, Rand Brooks, John Parrish; *D:* George Archainbaud.

Hopalong Cassidy: Sinister Journey 🦴🦴 1948 Mysterious accidents are plaguing a railroad where an old friend of Hoppy's works, so Hoppy, California, and Lucky take railroad jobs to find out what gives. 58m/B VHS, DVD. William Boyd, Andy Clyde, Rand Brooks; *D:* George Archainbaud.

Hopalong Cassidy: The Dead Don't Dream 🦴🦴 1948 Hoppy's sidekick Lucky decides to get married, but happily-ever-afterdom is threatened when the father of Mrs. Lucky-to-be is murdered. When Hoppy sets out to find the killer, he finds himself suspected of the dastardly deed. 55m/B VHS, DVD. William Boyd, Andy Clyde, Rand Brooks, John Parrish; *D:* George Archainbaud.

Hopalong Cassidy: The Devil's Playground 🦴🦴 1946 Strange things are afoot in a peaceful valley adjacent to a desolate, forbidding wasteland. When Hoppy and a young woman set out across the wasteland to make a gold delivery, they encounter a band of desperados and begin to unravel the secrets of a dishonest political ring. 65m/B VHS, DVD. William Boyd, Andy Clyde, Rand Brooks, Elaine Riley; *D:* George Archainbaud.

Hopalong Cassidy: The Marauders 🦴🦴 1947 After seeking shelter in an abandoned church one rainy night, Hoppy and the boys must defend the kirk when it is threatened by a marauder and his gang. 64m/B VHS, DVD. William Boyd, Andy Clyde, Rand Brooks; *D:* George Archainbaud.

Hopalong Cassidy: Unexpected Guest 🦴🦴½ 1947 When a small fortune is left to a California family, the head count starts to dwindle, and Hoppy aims to find out why. 54m/B VHS, DVD. William Boyd, Andy Clyde, Rand Brooks, Una O'Connor; *D:* George Archainbaud.

Hope 🦴🦴½ 1997 Thirteen-year-old Lily Kate Burns (Malone) is living in the small southern town of Hope in 1962. Her mother's had a severe stroke and the only family she has to turn to are racist Uncle Ray (Walsh) and fragile Aunt Emma (Lahti). Amidst the town's segregation and fears about the Cuban Missile Crisis, Lily Kate is also more open to befriending new town residents than her elders, including visiting black preacher Jediah (Sams). Hawn's directorial debut. 100m/C VHS. Mary Ellen Trainor, Christine Lahti, Jena Malone, J.T. Walsh, Jerry D. Sams, Catherine O'Hara; *D:* Goldie Hawn; *W:* Kerry Kennedy. CABLE

Hope and Glory 🦴🦴🦴½ 1987 (PG-13) Boorman turns his memories of WWII London into a complex and sensitive film. Father volunteers, and mother must deal with the awakening sexuality of her teenage daughter, keep her son in line, balance the ration books, and try to make it to the bomb shelter in the middle of the night. Seen through the boy's eyes, war creates a playground of shrapnel to collect and wild imaginings come true. Nice companion film to "Empire of the Sun" and "Au Revoir Les Enfants," two more 1987 releases that explore WWII from the recollections of young boys. 97m/C VHS, DVD. *GB* Sebastian Rice-Edwards, Geraldine Muir, Sarah Miles, Sammi Davis, David Hayman, Derrick O'Connor, Susan Wooldridge, Jean-Marc Barr, Ian Bannen, Jill Baker, Charley Boorman, Annie Leon, Katrine Boorman, Gerald James, Amelda Brown, Colin Higgins; *D:* John Boorman; *W:* John Boorman; *C:* Philippe Rousselot; *M:* Peter Martin. British Acad. '87: Film, Support. Actress (Wooldridge); Golden Globes '88: Film—Mus./Comedy; L.A. Film Critics '87: Director (Boorman), Film, Screenplay; Natl. Soc. Film Critics '87: Cinematog., Director (Boorman), Film, Screenplay.

Hope Floats 🦴🦴½ 1998 (PG-13) Former small town Texas beauty queen Birdee Pruitt (Bullock) finds out her husband Bill (Pare) is having an affair with her best friend (Arquette) live on TV, thanks to a tabloid talk show expose. Completely humiliated, she takes her daughter Bernice (Whitman) and heads home to her own rather spaced-out mom Ramona (Rowlands). She's trying to gain some perspective on her life—and maybe, slowly, find a new love with the help of handsome cowpoke Justin (Connick Jr.). Movie is sweet, sentimental, obvious, and has an appealing cast and a happy ending. Perfect girlfriend fare. 114m/C VHS, DVD. Sandra Bullock, Harry Connick Jr., Gena Rowlands, Mae Whitman, Cameron Finley, Michael Pare, Rosanna Arquette, Kathy Najimy, Bill Cobbs; *D:* Forest Whitaker; *W:* Steven Rogers; *C:* Caleb Deschanel; *M:* Dave Grusin.

Hope Ranch 🦴🦴 2002 (PG-13) J.T. Hope (Boxleitner), an ex-cop and Marine, runs a ranch designed to rehabilitate juvenile delinquents. When three street-wise but troubled kids arrive, J.T. and his staff are put to the test. Uplifting family fare blends action and message smoothly. Produced for the Animal Planet network. 100m/C VHS, DVD. Bruce Boxleitner, Lorenzo Lamas, Barry Corbin, Gail O'Grady, Laura Johnson, Richard Lee Jackson, Brian Gross, J.D. Pardo, Isabell Hovell, Brad Hawkins; *D:* Rex Piano; *W:* C. Thomas Howell, Jim Snider; *C:* Howard Wexler; *M:* Bruce Lynch. CABLE

Hoppity Goes to Town 🦴🦴 *Mr. Bug Goes to Town* 1941 Full-length animated feature from the Max Fleischer studios tells the story of the inhabitants of Bugville, who live in a weed patch in New York City. 77m/C VHS, DVD. *D:* Dave Fleischer; *M:* Frank Loesser, Hoagy Carmichael.

Hoppy Serves a Writ 🦴🦴 1943 In this last of the series to be based on the writings of the original author, Texas sheriff Cassidy tries to bring a gang of outlaws to justice. Look for a young Robert Mitchum as one of the villains. 67m/B VHS, DVD. William Boyd, Andy Clyde, Jay Kirby, Victor Jory, George Reeves, Hal Taliaferro, Robert Mitchum, Byron Foulger, Earle Hodgins, Roy Barcroft; *D:* George Archainbaud.

Hopscotch 🦴🦴🦴 1980 (R) A C.I.A. agent drops out when his overly zealous chief demotes him to a desk job. When he writes a book designed to expose the dirty deeds of the CIA, he leads his boss and KGB pal on a merry chase. Amiable comedy well-suited for Matthau's rumpled talents. 107m/C VHS, DVD. Walter Matthau, Glenda Jackson, Ned Beatty, Sam Waterston, Herbert Lom; *D:* Ronald Neame.

Horatio Hornblower 🦴🦴🦴 1999 Adventure on the high seas in these adaptations of C.S. Forester's popular novels, which are set in the late 18th-century. Hornblower (Gruffudd) is a young recruit who rises through the ranks of the King's Navy as the British battle the French. "The Duel" provides the introduction to Hornblower and his mentor, Captain Pellew (Lindsay). "The Fire Ships" has Hornblower preparing for his lieutenant's exam. "The Duchess and the Devil" finds Hornblower escorting the Duchess of Wharfedale (Lunghi) to England with important naval dispatches. "The Wrong War" finds the Brits preparing a coup against the French Republican government. 400m/C VHS, DVD. *GB* Ioan Gruffudd, Robert Lindsay, Denis Lawson, Chris Lunghi, Anthony Sher, Samuel West, Andrew Tiernan, Ronald Pickup; *D:* Andrew Grieve; *W:* Russell Lewis, Mike Cullen, Patrick Harbinson; *C:* Alec Curtis, Neve Cunningham. TV

Horatio Hornblower: The Adventure Continues 🦴🦴🦴 2001 The adventures of young British naval officer Hornblower (Gruffudd) continue with two linked stories: "Mutiny" and "The Retribution." Horatio recounts to his mentor, Captain Pellew (Lindsay), the reasons for his imprisonment on mutiny charges after confining his insane captain (Warner). But Hornblower must also lead a force to recapture an enemy fort. Based on C.S. Forester's novel, "Lieutenant Hornblower." 200m/C VHS, DVD. *GB* Ioan Gruffudd, Robert Lindsay, David Warner, Jamie Bamber, Paul McGann, Nicholas Jones, Philip Glenister, David Rintoul; *D:* Andrew Grieve; *C:* Chris O'Dell; *M:* John Keane. TV

Horizons West 🦴🦴½ 1952 Two brothers go their separate ways after the Civil War. One leads a peaceful life as a rancher but the other, corrupted by the war, engages in a violent campaign to build his own empire. Ryan's outstanding performance eclipses that of the young Hudson. 81m/C VHS, DVD. Robert Ryan, Julie Adams, Rock Hudson, Raymond Burr, James Arness, John McIntire, Dennis Weaver, Frances Bavier; *D:* Budd Boetticher; *M:* Henry Mancini.

The Horizontal Lieutenant 🦴🦴½ 1962 Hutton and Prentiss team up again in this moderately funny romantic-comedy about an officer's escapades during WWII. Based on the novel "The Bottletop Affair" by Gordon Cotler. 90m/C VHS, DVD. Jim Hutton, Paula Prentiss, Jack Carter, Jim Backus, Charles McGraw, Miyoshi Umeki; *D:* Richard Thorpe; *W:* George Wells.

The Horn Blows at Midnight 🦴🦴 1945 A band trumpeter falls asleep and dreams he's a bumbling archangel, on Earth to blow the note bringing the end of the world. But a pretty girl distracts him, and...A wild, high-gloss, well-cast fantasy farce, uniquely subversive in its lighthearted approach to biblical Doomsday. Benny made the film notorious by acting ashamed of it in his later broadcast routines. 78m/B VHS. Jack Benny, Alexis Smith, Dolores Moran, Allyn Joslyn, Reginald Gardiner, Guy Kibbee, John Alexander, Margaret Dumont; *D:* Raoul Walsh.

Hornet's Nest 🦴🦴½ 1970 Captain Turner (Hudson) is the lone survivor of an Army commando unit which parachuted into the Italian countryside in an effort to blow up a dam being held by the Nazis. He's rescued by a group of boys, the survivors of a German massacre of their nearby town. Turner wants the boys to help him blow up the dam—and they want his help in getting revenge on the Nazis who have occupied their homes. 110m/C VHS. Rock Hudson, Sylva Koscina, Sergio Fantoni, Jacques Sernas, Giacomo "Jack" Rossi-Stuart, Andrea Bosic, Gerard Herter, Tom Felleghi; *D:* Phil Karlson; *W:* S.S. Schweizer.

The Horrible Dr. Bones 🦴🦴 2000 (R) Dr. Bones (Igus) is a record producer who gives the young Urban Protectors band their big break, but it turns out that he's exploiting them in a supernatural scheme involving human sacrifice and zombies. The low-budget horror doesn't rise much above the studio's bare-bones production. 72m/C DVD. Darrow Igus, Larry Bates, Sarah Scott, Rhonda Claebaut, Nathaniel Lamar; *D:* Art Camage; *W:* Raymond Forchon; *C:* Adolfo Bartoli.

The Horrible Dr. Hichcock 🦴🦴🦴½ *L'Orribile Segreto del Dr. Hichcock* 1962 A sicko doctor, who accidentally killed his first wife while engaged in sexual antics, remarks to bring the first missus back from the dead using his new wife's blood. Genuinely creepy. Sequelled by "The Ghost." 76m/C VHS, DVD. *IT* Robert Flemyng, Barbara Steele, Silvano Tranquilli, Harriet Medin, Ernesto Gastaldi, Maria Teresa Vianello; *D:* Riccardo Freda; *W:* Perry (Ernesto Gastaldi) Julyan; *C:* Raffaele Masciocchi; *M:* Roman Vlad.

The Horror Chamber of Dr. Faustus 🦴🦴🦴½ *Panic in the Trans-Siberian Express; Panico en el Transiberiano; Panic in the Trans-Siberian Train* 1972 (R) A creature from prehistoric times, that was removed from its tomb, is transported on the Trans-Siberian railroad. Passengers suddenly discover strange things happening—such as having their souls sucked out of them. 88m/C VHS, DVD. *SP GB* Christopher Lee, Peter Cushing, Telly Savalas, Alberto De Mendoza, Silvia Tortosa, Julio Pena, Angel Del Pozo, Helga Line, Jorge (George) Rigaud, Jose Jaspe; *D:* Eugenio (Gene) Martin; *W:* Julian Zimet, Arnaud d'Usseau; *C:* Alejandro Ulloa.

Horror Express 🦴🦴🦴½ *Eyes without a Face; Les Yeux sans Visage; Occhi senza Volto* 1959 A wickedly intelligent, inventive piece of Grand Guignol about a mad doctor who kills young girls so he may graft their skin onto the face of his accidentally mutilated daughter. In French with English subtitles. 84m/B VHS, DVD. *FR* Alida Valli, Pierre Brasseur, Edith Scob, Francois Guerin, Juliette Mayniel, Alex(andre) Rignault, Claude Brasseur, Charles Blavette; *D:* Georges Franju; *W:* Jean Redon; *C:* Eugen Shuffan; *M:* Maurice Jarre.

Horror Hospital 🦴🦴½ *Computer Killers; Doctor Blood Bath* 1973 (R) Patients are turned into zombies by a mad doctor in this hospital where no anesthesia is used. Those who try to escape are taken care of by the doctor's guards. 91m/C VHS, DVD. *GB* Michael Gough, Robin Askwith, Vanessa Shaw, Ellen Pollock, Skip Martin, Dennis Price; *D:* Antony Balch; *W:* Antony Balch, Alan Watson; *C:* David McDonald.

Horror Hotel 🦴🦴🦴½ *The City of the Dead* 1960 A young witchcraft student visits a small Massachusetts town which has historic ties to witch burnings and discovers a new, and deadly, coven is now active. Well done and atmospheric. 76m/B VHS, DVD. *GB* Christopher Lee, Patricia Jessel, Betta St. John, Dennis Lotis, Venetia Stevenson, Valentine Dyall; *D:* John Llewellyn Moxey; *W:* George L. Baxt; *C:* Desmond Dickinson.

Horror House on Highway 5 WOOF! 1986 Someone in a Nixon mask kills people in this extremely cheap dud. 90m/C VHS, DVD. Phil Therrien, Max Manthey, Susan Leslie; *D:* Richard Casey; *W:* Richard Casey; *C:* David Golia.

The Horror of Dracula 🐾🐾½ *Dracula* 1958 The first Hammer Dracula film, in which the infamous vampire is given a new, elegant potential for both shock and arousal, which was probably the first time it was originally released in both "horror" and "girlie" versions. D'Arcy later admitted to 'taking over for director Bottger and adding all the horror sequences himself. Dubbed from the German. 82m/C VHS, DVD, GB Peter Cushing, Christopher Lee, Michael Gough, Melissa Stribling, Carol Marsh, John Van Eyssen, Valerie Gaunt; Charles Lloyd-Pack, Miles Malleson; D: Terence Fisher. W: Jimmy Sangster; C: Jack Asher; M: James Bernard.

The Horror of Frankenstein 🐾🐾 1970 Spoof of the standard Frankenstein story features philandering ex-med student Baron Frankenstein, whose interest in a weird and esoteric branch of science provides a shock-ing and up-to-date rendition of the age-old plot. Preceded by "Frankenstein Must Be Destroyed" and followed by "Frankenstein and the Monster from Hell." 93m/C VHS, DVD, GB Ralph Bates, Kate O'Mara, Dennis Price, David Prowse, Veronica Carlson, Joan Rice, Bernard Archard, Graham James; D: Jimmy Sangster; W: Jimmy Sangster, Jeremy Burnham; C: Moray Grant.

Horror of Party Beach WOOF! *Vampire Men of the Prehistoric Planet; Creatures of the Prehistoric Planet; Space Mission of the Lost Planet; The Flesh Creatures; Horror Creatures of the Red Planet; Flesh Creatures of the Red Planet* 1970 (PG) John Carradine made a career out of being in bad movies, and this one competes as one of the worst. This is an editor's nightmare, made up of black & white film spliced together in the "Blind dead" trilogy; see also "Tombs of the Blind Dead" and "Return of the Evil Dead." 90m/C VHS, DVD, SP Maria Perschy, Jack Taylor; D: Armando de Ossorio.

Horror of the Blood Monsters WOOF! *Invasion of the Zombies* 1964 Considered to be one of the all-time worst films. Features a mob of radioactive seaweed creatures who eat a slew of nubile, surf-minded teenagers. ↗Zombie Stomp. 71m/C VHS, DVD, John Scott, Alice Lyon, Allen Laurel, Marilyn Clarke, Augustin Mayer, Eulabelle Moore; D: Del Tenney; W: Richard Hilliard; C: Richard Hilliard; M: Bill Holmes.

Horror of the Zombies 🐾 *El Buque maldito* 1974 (R) Bikinied models are pursued by hooded zombies on board a pleasure yacht, starring the horror. Effete final installment in the "Blind dead" trilogy; see also "Tombs of the Blind Dead" and "Return of the Evil Dead." 90m/C VHS, DVD, SP Maria Perschy, Jack Taylor; D: Armando de Ossorio.

The Horror Show 🐾 *House 3* 1989 (R) Serial killer fries in electric chair, an event the cop who brought him in, Stanstays crazed guy who won't die and wants revenge flick. 95m/C VHS, DVD, Brion James, Lance Henriksen, Rita Taggart, Dedee Pfeiffer, Aron Eisenberg, Matt Clark, Thom Bray, Terry Alexander, David Oliver; D: James Isaac; W: Alan Smithee, Leslie Bohem; C: Mac Ahlberg.

Horrors of Burke & Hare 🐾 1971 A gory tale about the exploits of a bunch of 19th-century grave robbers. 94m/ C VHS, Derren Nesbitt, Harry Andrews, Yootha Joyce; D: Vernon Sewell.

Horrors of Spider Island 🐾 *It's Hot in Paradise; Ein Toter Hing im Netz; A Corpse Hangs in the Web* 1959 D'Arcy is a Hollywood talent scout who sniffs a goldmine in a team of young female dancers whom he schedules to perform for him in Singapore. Their transport plane crashes in the Pacific Ocean and he and the girls are forced to

take refuge on an uncharted isle. Upon landing there they discover it is infested with giant crab-sized spiders. Lots of potential for both shock and arousal, which was probably the first time it was originally released in both "horror" and "girlie" versions.

Horror Rises from the Tomb 🐾🐾 *El Espanto Surge de la Tumba* 1972 A 15th century knight and his assistant are beheaded for practicing witch-craft. Five hundred years later, they return to possess a group of vacationers and generally cause havoc. 89m/C VHS, DVD, SP Paul Nascry, Vic Winner, Emma Cohen, Helga Line, Cristina Suriani; D: Carlos Aured; W: Paul Nascry.

The Horse 🐾🐾½ *At* 1982 A moving, mature Turkish film about a father and son trying to overcome socio-economic obstacles and their own frailties in order to make enough money to send the boy to school. In Turkish with English subtitles. 116m/C VHS, DVD, TU Genco Erkal; D: Ali Ozgenturk; W: Isil Ozgenturk; C: Kenan Ormanlar; M: Okay Temiz.

Horse Feathers 🐾🐾🐾½ 1932 Huxley College has to beef up its football team to win the championship game which has been rigged by local gamblers in the opposition's favor, and the corrupt new college president (Groucho) knows just how to do it. Features some of the brothers' classic routines, and the songs "Whatever It Is, I'm Against It" and "Everyone Says I Love You." 67m/B VHS, DVD, Groucho Marx, Chico Marx, Harpo Marx, Zeppo Marx, Thelma Todd, David Landau, Nat Pendleton; D: Norman Z. McLeod; W: Bert Kalmar, S.J. Perelman, Harry Ruby; C: Ray June; M: Harry Ruby.

A Horse for Danny 🐾🐾½ 1995 (G) Horse trainer Eddie (Ulrich), clogged by bad luck, and his 11-year-old niece Danny (Sobieski), come across a thoroughbred named Tom Thumb, who may be their chance at racing's winners circle. TV movie. 92m/C VHS, DVD, Robert Urich, Leelee Sobieski, Ron Brice, Karen Carlson, Gary Basaraba; D: Dick Lowry; C: Steven Fierberg.

The Horse in the Gray Flannel Suit 🐾🐾½ 1968 (G) Disney comedy portrays an advertising executive who links his daughter's devotion to horses with a client's new ad campaign. There's lots of riding through the countryside and hiding out and not much actually happens. Nice scenery, attractive stars. Based on the 1951 novel by Jean Giono. French with subtitles; originally released at 135 minutes. 119m/C VHS, DVD, FR Olivier Martinez, Juliette Binoche, Francois Cluzet, Isabelle Carre, Jean Yanne, Claudio Amendola, Pierre Arditi; Cameos: Gerard Depardieu; D: Jean-Paul Rappeneau; W: Jean-Paul Rappeneau, Nina Companeez; C: Thierry Arbogast; M: Jean-Claude Petit. Cesar '96: Cinematog., Sound.

The Horse of Pride 🐾🐾½ *Le Cheval D'Orgeuil* 1980 Chabrol faces a telling look at the everyday life of the peasants of Breton—both their pleasures and their sorrows, in French with English subtitles. French script booklet available. 118m/C VHS, FR Jacques Dufilno, Francois Cluzet; D: Claude Chabrol.

The Horse Soldiers 🐾🐾½ 1959 An 1863 Union cavalry officer is sent 300 miles into Confederate territory to destroy a railroad junction and is accompanied by a fellow officer who's also a pacifist doctor. Based on a true Civil War incident. 114m/C VHS, DVD, John Wayne, William Holden, Hoot Gibson, Constance Towers, Russell Simpson, Strother Martin, Anna Lee, Judson Pratt, Denver Pyle, Jack Pennick, Althea Gibson, William Forrest, Willis Bouchey, Bing (Neil) Russell, Ken Curtis, O.Z. Whitehead, Walter Reec, Hank Worden, Carleton Young, Cliff Lyons; D: John Ford; W: John Lee Mahin, Martin Rackin; C: William Clothier; M: David Buttolph.

The Horse Thief 🐾🐾🐾 *Daoma Zei* 1987 Noted as the first movie from the People's Republic of China to be released on video, this epic tells the tale of Norbu, a man who, exiled from his people for horse thievery, is forced to wander the Tibetan countryside with his family in search of work. His son dies while he is in exile, and he, a devout Buddhist, is ultimately forced to accept tribal work in a ritual exorcism after which he pleads to be accepted back into his clan. Beautiful and image-driven, offering a rare glimpse into the Tibet you won't see in travel brochures. Filmed on location with locals as actors. In Mandarin with English subtitles. 88m/C VHS, CH Daiba, Jiji Dan, Diashi, Gaoba, Jamco Jayang, Riqzin Tseshang; D: Tian Zhuangzhuang; W: Rui Zhang; C: Fei Zhao, Hou Yong; M: Xiao-Song Qu.

The Horse's Mouth 🐾🐾🐾 *The Oracle* 1958 An obsessive painter discovers that he must rely upon his wits to survive in London. A hilarious adaptation of the

The Horse of the Red Planet 🐾 *The Wizard of Mars* 1964 Cheapo epic sees astronauts crash on Mars, meet its Wizard, and stumble into a few Oz-like creatures. Technically advised by Forrest J. Ackerman. 81m/C VHS, John Carradine, Roger Gentry, Vic McGee; D: David L. Hewitt.

The Horse 🐾🐾½ *Horse, My Horse* 1997 (PG-13) After her teenaged daughter Grace (Johansson) is injured in a riding accident, determined mom Annie (Thomas), believing that the girl's recovery is tied to the horse's, takes child and horse to Montana to seek the help of horse healer Tom (Redford) in the big-screen adaptation of the Nicholas Evans novel. While there, chilly New York editor Annie warms up to Tom and the possibility of love. Like "The Bridges of Madison County," this adaptation removes the overwrought syrupy melodrama of its source novel to concentrate on mature themes like fidelity, trust, and fate. Fine performances by all (although Redford could be seen as a bit self-indulgent at times) and the beautiful Montana backdrop make up for the lack of sustained dramatic impact, which is probably due to the almost three-hour run time and some dramatic changes from the book. 168m/C VHS, DVD, Robert Redford, Kristin Scott Thomas, Scarlett Johansson, Sam Neill, Chris Cooper, Dianne Wiest, Chery Jones, Jeanette Nolan, Don Edwards, Ty Hillman, Kate (Catherine) Bosworth, Steve Frye; D: Robert Redford; W: Eric Roth, Richard LaGravenese; C: Robert Richardson; M: Thomas Newman.

The Horse Without a Head 🐾🐾½ 1963 Stolen loot has been hidden in a discarded toy horse which is now the property of a group of poor children. The thieves, however, have different plans. Good family fare from the Disney TV show. 89m/C VHS, Jean-Pierre Aumont, Herbert Lom, Leo McKern, Pamela Franklin, Vincent Winter; D: Don Chaffey. TV

The Horseman on the Roof 🐾🐾½ *Le Hussard sur le Toit* 1995 (R) Lavish costume drama set in Provence in the 1830s, during a cholera epidemic. Italian officer/revolutionary Angelo (Martinez) is on the run and eventually meets up with beautiful Pauline de Theus (Binoche), who hides him in a quarantined French village. Pauline's in search of her husband and Angelo reluctantly agrees to help her. Together they manage to escape a military cordon and travel to another plague town. There's lots of riding through the countryside and hiding out and not much actually happens. Nice scenery, attractive stars. Based on the 1951 novel by Jean Giono. French with subtitles; originally released at 135 minutes. 119m/C VHS, DVD, FR Olivier Martinez, Juliette Binoche, Francois Cluzet, Isabelle Carre, Jean Yanne, Claudio Amendola, Pierre Arditi; Cameos: Gerard Depardieu; D: Jean-Paul Rappeneau; W: Jean-Paul Rappeneau, Nina Companeez; C: Thierry Arbogast; M: Jean-Claude Petit. Cesar '96: Cinematog., Sound.

Horsemasters 🐾🐾 1961 A group of young riders enter a special training program in England to achieve the ultimate equestrian title of horsemaster, with Annette having to overcome her fear of jumping. Originally a two-part Disney TV show, and released as a feature film in Europe. 85m/C VHS, Tommy Kirk, Annette Funicello, Janet Munro, Tony Britton, Donald Pleasence, Jean Marsh, John Fraser, Millicent Martin; D: William Fairchild. TV

The Horsemen 🐾🐾½ 1970 (PG) An Afghani youth enters the brutal buzkashi horse tournament to please his macho-minded father. Beautifully shot in Afghanistan and Spain by Claude Renoir. 109m/C VHS, DVD, Omar Sharif, Leigh Taylor-Young, Jack Palance, David De, Peter Jeffrey; D: John Frankenheimer; W: Dalton Trumbo; M: Georges Delerue.

The Horseplayer 🐾½ 1991 (R) A loner is drawn into a mysterious triangle of decadence and desire in this riveting psychothriller. 89m/C VHS, Brad Dourif, Sammi Davis, Michael (M.K.) Harris, Vic Tayback; D: Kurt Voss.

Horsey 🐾🐾 1999 Young Delilah makes no apologies for any of her passions—those of her art or of the men or women she chooses to love. Then she stars a relationship with volatile Ryland Yale, a rock 'n' roller with a heroin addiction who still manages to fill all Delilah's emotional and physical needs. But is Delilah ready to deal with what Ryland will cost her? 93m/C VHS, DVD, Holly Ferguson, Todd Kerns, Ryan Robbins, Victoria Descharnel; D: Kirsten Clarkson; W: Kirsten Clarkson; C: Glen Winter; M: Helen Keller.

Horton Foote's Alone 🐾🐾½ *Alone* 1997 John Webb (Cronyn) is an elderly Texas farmer, lost after the death of his wife of 52 years. His nephews (Forrest, Cooper) want him to sell his land to an interested oil company and his daughters (Miles, Hart) want to cry on his shoulder. Then Webb's former tenant farmer (Jones) comes back to visit and is the only one to ask the old man what he wants to do. 107m/C VHS, DVD, Hume Cronyn, James Earl Jones, Chris Cooper, Frederic Forrest, Joanna Miles, Roxanne Hart, Shelley Duvall, Halle Foote, Ed Begley, Jr., David Selby, Piper Laurie; D: Michael Lindsay-Hogg; W: Horton Foote; C: Jeffrey Jur; M: David Shire. CABLE

The Hospital 🐾🐾🐾½ 1971 (PG) Cult favorite providing savage, unrelentingly sarcastic look at the workings of a chaotic metropolitan hospital beset by murders, witchdoctors, madness, and plain ineptitude. Scott's suicidal chief surgeon Herbert Bock, who falls in love with free-spirited Barbara Drummond (Rigg), a patient's daughter. 101m/C VHS, DVD, George C. Scott, Diana Rigg, Barnard Hughes, Stockard Channing, Nancy Marchand, Richard Dysart, Stephen Elliott, Rena Scofield, Katherine Helmond, Roberts Blossom; D: Arthur Hiller; W: Paddy Chayefsky; C: Victor Kemper. Oscars '71: Story & Screenplay; Berlin Intl. Film Fest. '72: Silver Prize; British Acad. '72: Screenplay; Golden Globes '72: Screenplay, Natl. Film Reg. '95; Writers Guild '71: Orig. Screenplay.

Hospital Massacre 🐾🐾 *X-Ray; Be My Valentine, Or Else* 1981 (R) Psychopathic killer is loose in a hospital. Seems he holds a grudge against the woman who laughed as his valentine when they were children 20 years earlier, and too bad for her that she just checked in as a patient. Former "Playboy" and Hefner playmate Benton frolics in dangerous health care situation presented by the Cannon organization. 89m/C VHS, Barbi Benton, Jon Van Ness, Charles (Chip) Lucia; D: Boaz Davidson; W: Marc Behm.

Hospital of Terror 🐾🐾 *Nurse Sherri; Terror Hospital; Beyond the Living* 1978 (R) A transmigratory religious fanatic who died on the operating table manages to possess a nurse (Jacobson) before he kicks the bucket, and once in his candy-stripe incarnation, vents his spleen on the doctors who botched his operation. It's got a little more plasma than Adamson's "Astro-Zombies," considered by many to be a world-class boner. 89m/C VHS, DVD, Jill Jacobson, Geoffrey Land, Marilyn Joi, Mary Kay Pass, Prentiss Moulden, Clayton Foster; D: Al Adamson.

The Host 🐾🐾🐾 *Gwoemul* 2006 (R) An overgrown mutant tadpole is on a man-eating bender along the Han River in South Korea, but that's not the most peculiar thing going on in this genre-stomping thriller. The family of one of the monster's would-be victims, highschooler Park Hyeon-seo (Ko A-sung), is kookier than the monster. The story simultaneously lampoons and exploits the monster-on-the-loose genre to great effect. Fantastic visual effects, oddly juxtaposed humor and a super-style monster... it doesn't get much better. 119m/C DVD, Blu-ray Disc, HD DVD, KN Du-na Bae, Kang-ho Song, Hie-bon Byeon, Hae-il Park, Ah-sung Ko; D: Joon-ho Bong; W: Joon-ho Bong, Chul-hyun Baek; C: Hyung-ku Kim; M: Byung-woo Lee.

Hostage

The Hostage 🦴🦴½ **1967 (PG)** A young teenager is witness to a gruesome and clandestine burial. The two murderers responsible take it upon themselves to see that their secret is never told. 84m/C VHS. Don O'Kelly, Harry Dean Stanton, John Carradine, Danny Martins; *D:* Russell S. Doughten Jr.

Hostage 🦴½ **1987 (R)** Arab terrorists hijack a plane and the passengers start to fight back. Filmed in South Africa. 94m/C VHS. Karen Black, Kevin McCarthy, Wings Hauser; *D:* Hanro Mohr; *M:* Brad Fiedel.

Hostage 🦴🦴 **1992 (R)** British Secret Service agent John Rennie is fed up after a difficult mission in Argentina. He thinks he can walk away clean but his superiors beg to differ. He's marked for murder but Rennie has a dangerous plan that could guarantee his safety—only if he returns to Argentina to set things in motion. Based on the novel "No Place to Hide" by Ted Allbeury. 100m/C VHS. Sam Neill, Talisa Soto, James Fox; *D:* Robert W. Young.

Hostage 🦴🦴½ **2005 (R)** Burnt-out hostage negotiator (Willis) retreats to the suburbs hoping for calm, only to find himself pulled into the middle of a deadly crisis. Three delinquents take over the house of an underworld accountant (Pollack), whose shadowy employers then kidnap Willis's family, forcing him to retrieve their vital info hidden inside. Very violent, exciting, and grim melodrama with a dizzying number of twists and turns. Ben Foster is memorably sick as the psycho leader of the young thugs. 113m/C DVD. US Bruce Willis, Kevin Pollak, Ben Foster, Jonathan Tucker, Jimmy Bennett, Tina Lifford, Kim Coates, Serena Scott Thomas, Marshall Allman, Michelle Horn, Robert Knepper, Rumer Willis, Marjean Holden, Johnny Messner, Glenn Morshower, Chad Smith; *D:* Florent Emilio Siri; *W:* Doug Richardson; *C:* Giovanni Fiore Coltellacci; *M:* Alexandre Desplat.

Hostage for a Day 🦴🦴½ **1994** Married to a shrew, toiling for an overbearing father-in-law, and suffering a midlife crisis, Wendt decides to fake his own kidnapping, take the ransom money, and head off for a better life. A series of comedic complications abound. Candy's directorial debut. Made for TV. 92m/C VHS. George Wendt, John Vernon, Robin Duke, Peter Torokvei, Don Lake, Frank Moore, John Hemphill, Christopher Templeton; *Cameos:* John Candy; *D:* John Candy; *W:* Peter Torokvei, Robert Crane, Kari Hildebrand; *M:* Ian Thomas. TV

Hostage High 🦴🦴 *Detention: The Siege at Johnson High* **1997 (R)** Jason Copeland (Schroeder) returns to his former high school with a gun in order to take revenge on the teachers who failed him. The students, including Aaron (Prinze Jr.), he holds hostage inside the building have entirely different tactics for negotiation from the adults who are outside. Based on a true story. 93m/C VHS, DVD. Rick Schroder, Henry Winkler, Freddie Prinze Jr., Ren Woods, Katie Wright, Alexis Cruz, Patrick Malone; *D:* Michael W. Watkins; *W:* Larry Golin; *C:* Bill Roe; *M:* Brian Adler. TV

Hostage Hotel 🦴🦴 **2000 (R)** Ex-cop Logan McQueen (Reynolds) tries to outmaneuver a kidnapper who's holding a congressman's daughter and McQueen's old partner hostage in an abandoned old hotel. 95m/C VHS, DVD. Burt Reynolds, Charles Durning, Keith Carradine, David Rasche; *D:* Hal Needham; *W:* Nicholas Factor. CABLE

The Hostage Tower 🦴🦴 **1980 (PG)** In France, a group of international crime figures capture the visiting U.S. president's mother, hold her hostage in the Eiffel Tower and demand $30 million in ransom. 97m/C VHS. Peter Fonda, Maud Adams, Britt Ekland, Billy Dee Williams, Keir Dullea, Douglas Fairbanks Jr., Rachel Roberts, Celia Johnson; *D:* Claudio Guzman. TV

Hostages 🦴🦴 *Under Siege* **1980** A gang of criminals kidnap a family on vacation at a Caribbean island. 93m/C VHS. MX SP Hugo Stiglitz, Marisa Mell, Francesco Rabal, Stuart Whitman; *D:* Rene Cardona Jr.; *W:* Rene Cardona Jr.; *C:* Leopoldo Villasenor; *M:* Manuel De Sica.

1993 (R) Harrowing docudrama about the Beirut hostage crisis combines actual news footage with scenes of the prisoners and their families.

Under desperate conditions hostages John McCarthy, Brian Keenan, Terry Anderson, Thomas Sutherland, Frank Reed, and Terry Waite try to hold on to their sanity and humanity as their families struggle for their release. Filmed on location in England, Israel, and Lebanon. 90m/C VHS. Colin Firth, Ciaran Hinds, Jay O. Sanders, Josef Sommer, Harry Dean Stanton, Kathy Bates, Natasha Richardson, Conrad Asquith; *D:* David Wheatley; *W:* Bernard MacLaverty. CABLE

Hostel 🦴🦴 **2006 (R)** Just another brick in the faux-snuff genre wall. This time around some hot-to-trot American dudes are led to a Slovakian hostel after several splurges into red-light debauchery. (They probably got distracted on the way to the history museums.) Much to their chagrin, they find that the Russian mafia has converted their lodging quarters into a pleasuredome for sickos looking to get their sadism on. Since our heroes have been developed as mindless hornballs, we're expected to almost cheer their pain and agony. The creators try, rather unsuccessfully, to disguise the charade as a parody of the snuff and torture films it actually reproduces. 95m/C DVD, Blu-ray Disc, UMD. US Jay Hernandez, Derek Richardson, Jan Vlasak, Eythor Gudjonsson, Barbara Nedeljakova, Jana Kaderabkova, Jennifer Lim, Lubomir Bukovy, Petr Janis, Josef Bradna, Keiko Seiko, Rick Hoffman; *D:* Eli Roth; *W:* Eli Roth; *C:* Milan Chadima; *M:* Nathan Barr.

Hostel: Part 2 🦴 **2007 (R)** You can add (or subtract) your own bones to the rating, depending on your appetite for torture porn. Roth out-does the gross and gore of his original, and switches his victims to the female gender, also making them slightly more sympathetic. American tourists Beth (German), Whitney (Phillips), and Lorna (Matarazzo) wind up at a Slovakian hostel where scummy businessmen pay top dollar to torture snuff fantasies into reality, with Sasha (Knazko) the operational mastermind (and ripe for leading further sequels). 94m/C DVD, Blu-ray Disc. US Lauren German, Bijou Phillips, Heather Matarazzo, Vera Jordanova, Roger Bart, Richard Burgi, Stanislav Ianevski, Jay Hernandez, Jordan Ladd, Edwige Fenech, Milan Knazko; *D:* Eli Roth; *W:* Eli Roth; *C:* Milan Chadima; *M:* Nathan Barr.

Hostile Guns 🦴🦴½ **1967** A law man discovers a woman he once loved is now an inmate he's transporting across the Texas badlands. Routine with the exception of cameos by veteran actors. Based on a story by Sloan Nibley and James Edward Grant. 91m/C VHS. George Montgomery, Yvonne De Carlo, Tab Hunter, John Russell; *Cameos:* Brian Donlevy, Richard Arlen, Fuzzy Knight, Donald (Don "Red") Barry; *D:* R.G. Springsteen; *W:* Steve Fisher, Sloan Nibley.

Hostile Intent 🦴🦴 **1997 (R)** Computer whiz Mike Cleary (Lowe) has designed a new program to counter a computer chip that will allow the government access to everyone's computer. Naturally, this does not make the feds happy and when Mike and his team are off in the woods playing wargames for relaxation, someone is using real bullets to pick off the workers. 90m/C VHS, DVD. Rob Lowe, John Savage, Sofia Shinas, James Kidnie; *D:* Jonathan Heap; *W:* Manny Coto; *C:* Gerald R. Goozie; *M:* Marcos Loya.

Hostile Intentions 🦴½ **1994 (R)** Three girlfriends head for a weekend of fun in the sun in Tijuana and find themselves turned into fugitives through a series of misunderstandings. In order to get home, they must risk a night border crossing with a group of illegal immigrants. 90m/C VHS. Tia Carrere, Lisa Dean Ryan, Tricia Leigh Fisher, Carlos Gomez, Rigg Kennedy; *D:* Catherine Cyran; *W:* Catherine Cyran; *C:* Azusa Ohno; *M:* Marcos Loya.

Hostile Takeover 🦴🦴½ *Office Party* **1988 (R)** A mild-mannered accountant finally cracks and takes his co-workers hostage. He faces the police in a tense showdown. 93m/C VHS. David Warner, Michael Ironside, Kate Vernon, Jayne (Jane) Eastwood; *D:* George Mihalka.

Hostile Waters 🦴🦴½ **1997 (PG)** Based on Soviet accounts of an October 1986 incident that nearly set off a nuclear holocaust. A Russian and a U.S. sub play a game of cat-and-mouse 500 miles east of Bermuda. There's a collision and a fire aboard the Soviet sub threatens their cargo of thermonuclear missiles. Soviet captain Igor Britanov (Hauer) tries to control the situation while the U.S. skipper (Sheen) tries to figure out just what's going on. 92m/C VHS, DVD. Rutger Hauer, Martin Sheen, Colm Feore, Rob Campbell, Harris Yulin, Max von Sydow, Regina Taylor, John Rothman; *D:* David Drury; *M:* Troy Kennedy-Martin; *C:* Alec Curtis; *M:* David Ferguson. CABLE

Hot Blood **1989** Two bank robbers take an innocent woman hostage and thrust her in the midst of a huge family battle. Another lukewarm entry from the director of "The Arrogant." 89m/C VHS. Sylvia Kristel, Alicia Moro, Aldo Sambrel, Gaspar Cano; *D:* Philippe Blot.

Hot Blooded 🦴 *Hit & Run; Red Blooded American Girl 2* **1998 (R)** Trent Colbert (Winters) is a naive college freshman driving back to his family at Thanksgiving. Pulling into a truck stop he's makes the mistake of offering alluring hooker Miya (Wuhrer) a ride. But Miya's a twisted soul and all this means for the libidinous Trent is trouble. 95m/C VHS, DVD. Kari Wuhrer, Kristoffer Ryan Winters, David Keith, Burt Young; *D:* David Blyth; *W:* Nicolas Stiliadis; *C:* Edgar Egger; *M:* Paul Zaza. VIDEO

Hot Box woof! **1972 (R)** A Filipino-shot, low budget woofer. Prison flick about women who break out and foment a revolution. 85m/C VHS. Andrea Cagan, Margaret Markov, Rickey Richardson, Laurie Rose; *D:* Joe Viola; *W:* Joe Viola, Jonathan Demme.

Hot Bubblegum 🦴 *Shifshuf Naim* **1981 (R)** Three teenagers discover sex, the beach, rock 'n' roll, sex, drag racing, and sex. Hebrew with subtitles. 94m/C VHS. IS Jonathan Sagalla, Zachi Noy, Yftach Katzur; *D:* Boaz Davidson; *W:* Boaz Davidson, Eli Tavor; *C:* Amnon Salomon.

The Hot Chick 🦴🦴 **2002 (PG-13)** Snotty high school queen Jessica (MacAdams) magically switches bodies with 30-ish shlub Clive (Schneider) and finds the true meaning of "bad hair day." As you'd expect from a movie starring and co-written by Schneider and produced by Adam Sandler, it does take a few dips in the gutter, but manages to have heart, much like Sandler's surprising "Wedding Singer" a few years back. Strings together enough laughs to make you forget "Like Father, Like Son" ever happened. 101m/C VHS, DVD. US Rob Schneider, Anna Faris, Matthew Lawrence, Eric Christian Olsen, Robert Davi, Melora Hardin, Alexandra Holden, Rachel McAdams, Fay Hauser, Tamera Mowry, Tia Mowry, Lee Garlington, Michael O'Keefe; *Cameos:* Adam Sandler; *D:* Tom Brady; *W:* Tom Brady; *C:* Tim Suhrstedt; *M:* John Debney.

Hot Child in the City 🦴 **1987** A country girl goes to Los Angeles and searches through the city's fleshpots for her sister's killer. Music by Nick Glider, Lou Reed, Billy Idol, and Fun Boy Three. 85m/C VHS. Leah Ayres Hendrix, Shari Shattuck, Geof Pryssir; *D:* John Florea; *M:* W. Michael Lewis.

Hot Chocolate 🦴🦴½ **1992 (PG-13)** Derek is a sultry Texas tycoon who wants to buy out the French chocolate factory run by Hays. After getting a look at her, work isn't all that's on his mind. 93m/C VHS. Bo Derek, Robert Hays, Howard Hesseman, Vincent Cassel, Francois Marthouret, Amidou; *D:* Josee Dayan; *W:* Maryedith Burrell, Ginny Cerrella; *C:* Jean-Pierre Aliphat; *M:* John Goldstein.

Hot Dog... The Movie! 🦴½ **1983 (R)** There's an intense rivalry going on between an Austrian ski champ and his California challenger during the World Cup Freestyle competition in Squaw Valley. Snow movie strictly for teens or their equivalent. 96m/C VHS, DVD. David Naughton, Patrick Houser, Shannon Tweed, Tracy N. Smith; *D:* Peter Markle; *M:* Peter Bernstein.

Hot Fuzz 🦴🦴🦴 **1993 (R)** Wright and Pegg, the lads who revitalized the zombie genre with "Shaun of the Dead", offer this decidedly English take on the over-the-top Hollywood action genre. Constable Nick Angel (Pegg) is the best cop in London, but when his over-achieving starts making the force look bad, he's transferred to the quiet village of Sandford and saddled with a lump of a partner, Danny Butterman (Frost). However, once Angel discovers the secret behind Sandford's surprisingly high "accident" rate, he and Danny team up Riggs and Murtaugh-style to take down the town fathers, vicar and all. Such a smart premise, and Pegg sells every moment, but it veers off into parody occasionally due to some regrettably broad supporting players. 121m/C DVD, HD DVD, DVD. GB US Simon Pegg, Nick Frost, Jim Broadbent, Paddy Considine, Timothy Dalton, Billie Whitelaw, Edward Woodward, Rafe Spall, Olivia Colman, Paul Freeman, Martin Freeman, Bill Nighy, Steve Coogan, Cate Blanchett, Peter Jackson, Kevin Eldon, Stuart Wilson; *D:* Edgar Wright; *W:* Simon Pegg, Edgar Wright; *C:* Jess Hall; *M:* David Arnold.

Hot Lead 🦴🦴 **1951** Typical Holt oater which has the cowpoke and his sidekick Martin trying to avenge the death of a close friend who was killed by a gang of train robbers. 60m/B VHS. Tim Holt, Joan Dixon, Ross Elliott, John Dehner; *D:* Stuart Gilmore.

Hot Lead & Cold Feet 🦴🦴½ **1978 (G)** Twin brothers (one a gunfighter, the other meek and mild) compete in a train race where the winner will take ownership of a small western town. Dale not only plays both brothers, but also their tough father. Standard Disney fare. 89m/C VHS, DVD. Jim Dale, Don Knotts, Karen Valentine; *D:* Robert Butler; *W:* Arthur Alsberg; *M:* Buddy (Norman Dale) Baker.

The Hot Line 🦴½ *The Day the Hot Line Got Hot; Le Rouble a Deux Faces; El Rublo de las dos Caras* **1969** The world's two superpowers become befuddled when the hot line connecting Washington and Moscow breaks down. Taylor's final film. 87m/C VHS. Charles Boyer, George Chakiris, Dominique Fabre, Gerard Tichy; *D:* Etienne Perier.

Hot Millions 🦴🦴🦴 **1968** Hysterical comedy about high-class swindling operation with Ustinov as a refined embezzler. Excellent cast and sharp script. Although it didn't do well at the boxoffice, this amusing romp became one of the biggest sleepers of the year. 106m/C VHS. GB Peter Ustinov, Maggie Smith, Karl Malden, Bob Newhart, Robert Morley, Cesar Romero, Melinda May, Ann Lancaster, Margaret Courtenay, Lynda Baron, Billy Milton, Peter Jones, Raymond Huntley, Kynaston Reeves; *D:* Eric Till; *W:* Ira Wallach, Peter Ustinov; *C:* Ken Higgins.

Hot Money 🦴 **1979** A small-town drama about an ex-con who poses as an assistant sheriff and plots a million-dollar robbery during the town's 4th of July parade. Made shortly before Welles' death, and kept on the shelf for more than five years. 78m/C VHS. Orson Welles, Michael Murphy, Bobby "Boris" Pickett, Michelle Finney; *W:* Joel Cohen, Neil Cohen; *M:* Rob McConnell.

Hot Moves 🦴 **1984 (R)** Four high school boys make a pact to lose their virginity before the end of the summer. 89m/C VHS. Michael Zorek, Adam Silbar, Jill Schoelen, Deborah Richter, Monique Gabrielle, Tami Holbrook, Virgil Frye; *D:* Jim Sotos.

Hot Potato 🦴½ **1976 (PG)** Black Belt Jones rescues a senator's daughter from a megalomaniacal general by using skull-thwacking footwork. 87m/C VHS. Jim Kelly, George Memmoli, Geoffrey Binney; *D:* Oscar Williams.

Hot Pursuit 🦴½ **1987 (PG-13)** A prep-school bookworm resorts to Rambo-like tactics in tracking down his girlfriend and her family after being left behind for a trip to the tropics. 93m/C VHS, DVD. Monte Markham, Shelley Fabares, Ben Stiller, John Cusack, Robert Loggia, Jerry Stiller, Wendy Gazelle; *D:* Steven Lisberger; *W:* Steven W. Carabatsos; *C:* Frank Tidy; *M:* Joseph Conlan.

Hot Resort 🐾½ 1985 (R) Young American lacks mix work and play when they sign on as summer help at an island resort. Typical teen sex fantasy. 92m/C VHS, Bronson Pinchot, Tom Parsekian, Michael Berz, Linda Kenton, Frank Gorshin; **D:** John Robins, Boaz Davidson.

The Hot Rock 🐾🐾🐾 *Diamond in Four Easy Lessons; How to Steal a Diamond* 1970 (PG) A motley crew of bumbling thieves conspire to steal a huge, priceless diamond; a witty, gritty comedy that makes no moral excuses for its characters and plays like an early-'70s crime thriller gone awry. Adapted from the novel by Donald E. Westlake. The sequel, 1974's "Bank Shot," stars George C. Scott in the role created by Redford. 97m/C VHS, DVD, Robert Redford, George Segal, Ron Leibman, Zero Mostel, Moses Gunn, William Redfield, Charlotte Rae, Topo Swope; **M:** Quincy Jones.

Hot Rod 🐾🐾 1979 (PG) A young California hotrodder battles the evil sponsor of a drag race championship. 97m/C VHS, Gregg Henry, Robert Culp, Pernell Roberts, Robin Mattson, Grant Goodeve; **D:** George Armitage.

Hot Rod Girl 🐾 *Hot Car Girl* 1956 A seven year old moped-riding stuntman-wannabe Rod Kimble (Samberg) lives at home with mom Marie (Spacek) and stepdad Frank (McShane). Rod's real dad, now dead, is a legend as a former Evel Knievel second-hand man who is said to have performed all of Evel's stunts himself in order to test the bikes. Rod dreams of making his father proud; meanwhile he and stepdad go at it like archrivals, and Rod's always on the losing side of their jousts. Rod sees his chance when they raise the money by jumping over 15 buses on his moped, fix Frank's heart, and then beat him to a pulp. Loaded with goofy gags, and aimed at "Napoleon Dynamite," "Saturday Night Live" (several of the film's cast are from SNL, and Will Ferrell fans, but never nails the lancing. Has some moments, but that's about it. 88m/C VHS, HD DVD. *US* Isla Fisher, Andy Samberg, Jorma Taccone, Bill Hader, Sissy Spacek, Ian McShane, Will Arnett, Chris Parnell, Brittney Irvin, Danny McBride; **D:** Akiva Shaffer; **W:** Pam Brady; **C:** Andrew Dunn; **M:** Trevor Rabin.

Hot Shot 🐾½ 1986 (PG) An inspirational tale involving a young soccer player who goes to great lengths to take training from a soccer star, played—of course—by Pele. 90m/C VHS, DVD. Pele, Jim Youngs, Billy Warlock, Weyman Thompson, Mario Van Peebles, David Groh; **D:** Rick King.

Hot Shots! 🐾🐾🐾 1991 (PG-13) Another entry from "The Naked Gun" team of master movie parodists, this has lots of clever sight gags but the verbal humor of ten plummets to the ground. Spoofs "Top Gun" and similar gung-ho air corps adventures but doesn't forget other popular films including "Dances with Wolves" and "The Fabulous Baker Boys." Sheen is very funny as ace fighter pilot Sean "Topper" Harley who's to avenge the family honor. Great when you're in the mood for laughs that don't require much thought. 83m/C VHS, DVD. Charlie Sheen, Cary Elwes, Valeria Golino, Lloyd Bridges, Kevin Dunn, Jon Cryer, William O'Leary, Kristy Swanson, Efrem Zimbalist Jr., Bill Irwin, Heidi Swedberg, Judith Kahan, Pat Proft; **Cameos:** Charles Barkley, Bill Laimbeer; **D:** Jim Abrahams; **W:** Pat Proft, Jim Abrahams; **M:** Sylvester Levay.

Hot Shots! Part Deux 🐾🐾½ 1993 (PG-13) Second "Hot Shots" outing doesn't live up to the first, but it's not bad either. Admiral Tug Benson (Bridges) is elected President (yes, of the U.S.) and calls on Sheen's newly pumped-up Topper to take on Saddam Hussein Rambostyle. Love interest Ramada (Golino), returns but this time she's competing with

---

Michelle (Bakke), a sexy CIA agent. Crenna spoofs his role in the "Rambo" films as Sheen's mentor; look for real-life dad Martin in a take-off of "Apocalypse Now." Shtick flies as fast and furious as the bodies, with Bridges getting a chance to reprise his glory days of "Sea Hunt." Don't miss the credits. 89m/C VHS, DVD. Charlie Sheen, Lloyd Bridges, Valeria Golino, Brenda Bakke, Richard Crenna, Miguel Ferrer, Rowan Atkinson, Jerry Halova, Michael Ryan, Gregory Sierra, Ryan Stiles, Michael Colyar; **Cameos:** Martin Sheen, Bob Vila; **D:** Jim Abrahams; **W:** Pat Proft, Jim Abrahams; **M:** Basil Poledouris.

Hot Spell 🐾½ 1958 In an attempt to repair her marriage and unify her family, a mother plans a reunion-birthday party for her husband. Despair reigns in this sultry, Southern melodrama. 86m/B VHS. Shirley Booth, Anthony Quinn, Shirley MacLaire, Earl Holliman, Eileen Heckart; **D:** Daniel Mann; **C:** Loyal Griggs; **M:** Alex North.

The Hot Spot 🐾🐾½ 1990 (R) An amoral drifter arrives in a small Texas town and engages in affairs with two women, including his boss's over-sexed wife and a young woman with her own secrets. Things begin to heat up when he decides to plot a bank robbery. Based on Charles Williams' 1952 novel "Hell Hath No Fury." 120m/C VHS, DVD. Don Johnson, Virginia Madsen, Jennifer Connelly, Charles Martin Smith, William Sadler, Jerry Hardin, Barry Corbin, Leon Rippy, Jack Nance; **D:** Dennis Hopper; **W:** Charles Williams, Nona Tyson; **M:** Jack Nitzsche.

Hot Stuff 🐾 1980 (PG) Officers on a burglary task force decide the best way to obtain convictions is to go into the fencing business themselves. 91m/C VHS, Dom DeLuise, Jerry Reed, Suzanne Pleshette, Ossie Davis; **D:** Dom DeLuise; **W:** Donald E. Westlake.

Hot Summer 🐾🐾 *Heisser Sommer* 1968 A group of high school girls and boys meet on their way to a Baltic Sea vacation and begin their own version of the war between the sexes, especially since there's one more girl than boy. Then Kai (Schoel) and Brit (Doerk) decide they're in love, causing trouble for everyone else. Goofy teen romp starring pop stars Chris Doerk and Frank Schoebel and then German version of the '60s American beach movie. German with subtitles. 91m/C VHS, DVD. GE Frank Schoebel, Chris Doerk, Madeleine Lierck, Hanns-Michael Schmidt, Regine Albrecht; **D:** Joachim Hasler.

Hot Summer in Barefoot County 🐾 1974 (R) A state law enforcement officer on the search for illegal moonshiners finds more than he bargained for. 90m/C VHS, Sherry Robinson, Tonia Bryar, Dick Smith; **D:** Will Zens.

Hot T-Shirts WOOF! 1978 (R) A small town bar owner needs a boost for business, finding the answer in wet T-shirt contests. Softcore trash. 86m/C VHS. Ray Holland, Stephania Lawior, Pauline Rose, Corinne Alphen; **D:** Chuck Vincent.

Hot Tamale 🐾🐾½ 2005 (R) Amusing action-comedy finds naive musician Harlan Woodriff (Spelling) traveling from Wyoming to LA so he can play in a salsa band. Along the way, a con man (Priestley) hides some stolen diamonds in Harlan's car. In LA, Harlan meets sexy neighbor Tuesday (Baird) while unwittingly being targeted by thugs after the car. 90m/C VHS, DVD. Jason Priestley, Carmen Electra, Mike Starr, Beth Grant, Randy Spelling, Diora Baird, Matt Cerdeno; **D:** Michael Damian; **W:** Michael Damian, Janeen Damian; **C:** Fred Iannone; **M:** Mark Thomas.

Hot Target 🐾 1985 (R) An ideal mother becomes obsessed with the stranger who seduced her, even after she finds out he's a thief planning to rob her home. 93m/C VHS, DVD, NZ Simone Griffeth, Steve Marachuk; **D:** Denis Lewiston.

Hot Times 🐾 1974 (R) Low-budget comedy about a high school boy who, after striking out with the high school girls, decides to go to New York and decides out of his life. 80m/C VHS, Gail Lorber, Amy Farber, Henry Cory; **D:** Jim McBride; **W:** Jim McBride.

Hotel 🐾🐾 1967 (PG) A pale rehash of the "Grand Hotel" formula about an array of rich characters interacting in a New Orleans hotel. From the Arthur Hailey potboiler; basis for the TV series. 125m/C VHS, Rod Taylor, Catherine Spaak, Karl Malden, Melvyn Douglas, Merle Oberon, Michael Rennie, Richard Conte, Kevin McCarthy; **D:** Richard Quine; **W:** Wendell Mayes; **C:** Charles Bryant; Lang Jr.

Hotel 🐾🐾 2001 (R) Using a Dogma 95 approach, Director Figgis gathers a bunch of celebs and lets them aimlessly make things up as they go along. Follows the filming of John Webster's play "The Duchess of Malfi" by an English production crew at a hotel in Venice, Italy that has call staffers lurking about while the entire fiasco is caught on film by a brash documentarian. Fans of Figgis's work or the Dogme movement will want to check in on this one. 112m/C VHS, DVD. GB/IT Rhys Ifans, John Malkovich, Saffron Burrows, Salma Hayek, Max Beesley, Lucy Liu, Julian Sands, David Schwimmer, Jason Isaacs; **D:** Mike Figgis; **W:** Mike Figgis; **M:** Mike Figgis; Anthony Marinelli.

Hotel Colonial 🐾½ 1988 (R) A young Italian idealist ventures to Columbia to retrieve the body of his brother, who reportedly killed himself. Once there, he finds the dead man is not his brother, and decides to investigate. 103m/C VHS. IT Robert Duvall, John Savage, Rachel Ward, Massimo Troisi; **D:** Cinzia Torrini; **M:** Ira Barmak, Enzo Monteleone; **M:** Pino Donaggio.

Hotel de Love 🐾🐾½ 1996 (R) Seventeen-year-old fraternal twin brothers Rick (Young) and Stephen Dunne (Bosell) both fall for beautiful Melissa (Burrows) and she has a short-lived romance with the more-aggressive Rick. Ten years later, mopey stockbroker Stephen shows up at the tacky theme honeymoon hotel Rick now manages and who should show up (besides the twins bickering parents) but Melissa and her fiance Norman (O'Brien). So the twins renew their competition while Melissa decides if Norman is the right guy for her, Mrs. Dunne gets mash notes from a secret admirer, and fortuneteller Alison (Grandison), offers romantic advice to Stephen. 93m/C VHS, AU Aden Young, Simon Bossell, Saffron Burrows, Julia Blake, Ray Barrett, Pippa Grandison, Alan Hopgood, Peter O'Brien; **D:** Craig Rosenberg; **W:**

Hot Tip 🐾🐾 1935 Restaurant owner Jimmy McGill (James Gleason) is a sucker for the ponies but promises his wife Belle (Pitts) that he'll stop gambling. Until future son-in-law Ben (Gleason's real-life son Russell) gets into a jam after losing at the track and needs some quick cash. 70m/B VHS, James Gleason, Zasu Pitts, Russell Gleason, Margaret Callahan, J.M. Kerrigan; **D:** Ray McCarey; **W:** Olive Cooper, Hugh Cummings; **C:** Louis Stevens; **C:** Jack MacKenzie.

Hot to Trot! 🐾 1988 (PG) A babbling idiot links up with a talking horse in an updated version of the "Francis, the Talking Mule" comedies, by way of Mr. Ed. The equine voice is provided by Candy. Some real funny guys are wasted here. 90m/C VHS, Bob(cat) Goldthwait, Dabney Coleman, Virginia Madsen, Jim Metzler, Cindy Pickett, Tim Kazurinsky, Santos Morales, Barbara Whinnery, Garry Kluger; **D:** Michael Dinner; **W:** Charlie Peters; **M:** Danny Elfman; **V:** John Candy.

Hot Touch WOOF! 1982 An art forger with a large heist is besieged by a slashing maniac, and must discover the culprit. 92m/C VHS, Wayne Rogers, Samantha Eggar, Marie-France Pisier, Melvyn Douglas; **D:** Roger Vadim; **W:** Peter Dion; **C:** Francis Prolat; **M:** Andre Gagnon.

Hot Under the Collar 🐾½ 1991 (R) Jerry is a weasel who tries to seduce the luscious Monica by using hypnosis. But his plans backfire and instead Monica enters a convent and takes a vow of chastity. This isn't going to stop Jerry, he tries posing as a priest and even dressing as a nun in order to get her out. Things get even more complicated when a mobster, looking for a fortune in stolen diamonds, sneaks into the convent. 87m/C VHS, Richard Gabai, Angela Visser, Daniel Friedman, Melinda Clarke, Tane McClure; **D:** Richard Gabai.

Hotel Imperial 🐾🐾 1927 Set in 1917 Budapest, six Hungarian soldiers ride out on a frontier town and find it occupied by Russians. Hall plays Lieutenant Almasy, who takes refuge in the Hotel Imperial. Orchestra scored. 84m/B VHS, DVD. Pola Negri, James Hall, George Siegmann, Max Davidson; **D:** Mauritz Stiller.

Hotel du Lac 🐾🐾 1986 Adaptation of the Anita Brookner novel about a woman writer languishing at a Swiss lakefront hotel. 75m/C VHS, GB Anna Massey, Denholm Elliott, Googie Withers; **D:** Giles Foster; **M:** Carl Davis; TV

The Hotel New Hampshire 🐾🐾 1984 (R) The witless, amoral adaptation of John Irving's novel about a very strange family's adventures in New Hampshire, Vienna and New York City, which include gang rape, incest, and Kinski in a bear suit. 110m/C VHS, DVD. Jodie Foster, Rob Lowe, Beau Bridges, Nastassja Kinski, Wallace Shawn, Wilford Brimley, Amanda Plummer, Anita Morris, Matthew Modine, Lisa Banes, Seth Green, Jennifer (Jennie) Dundas, Lowe; **D:** Tony Richardson; **W:** Tony Richardson.

Hotel Paradiso 🐾🐾½ 1966 David Lynch's first feature film has timid Guinness trying to carry on an affair with Italian sexpot Lollobrigida. Guinness fans won't be disappointed, although it's not a top-rate production. Based on the play "L'Hotel du Libre Echange" by Georges Feydeau and Maurice Desvallieres. 100m/C VHS, GB Alec Guinness, Gina Lollobrigida, Akim Tamiroff, Marie Bell, Derek Fowlds; **D:** Peter Glenville; **W:** Peter Glenville, Jean-Claude Carriere.

Hotel Reserve 🐾🐾½ 1944 A Nazi spy is reportedly afoot in a French resort during WWII, and tension mounts as the guests attempt to flush him out. Critical response to this film is wildly split; some find it obvious, while others call it well-done and suspenseful. Based on the novel "Epitaph for a Spy" by Eric Ambler. 79m/B VHS, GB James Mason, Lucie Mannheim, Raymond Lovell, Julien Mitchell, Martin Miller, Herbert Lom, Frederick Valk, Valentine Dyall, Patricia Medina; **D:** Victor Hanbury, Lance Comfort, Max Greene.

Hotel Room 🐾🐾½ 1993 A trilogy of stories set in the same drab New York hotel room in three different time periods. "Getting Rid of Robert," ser. in 1992, has three girlfriends swilling champagne and discussing Sasha's slick, movie exec boyfriend whom she wants to dump. "Tricks," set in 1969, features Darlene, a bored, druggy prostitute; her client, Moe; and the sudden appearance of Moe's talkative friend, Lou. "Blackout" is set in 1936 and features a young husband trying to cope with the madness of his beautiful wife. Unfortunately, all three stories are rambling and lacking in energy. 100m/C VHS, Deborah Kara Unger, Mariska Hargitay, Chelsea Field, Griffin Dunne, Glenne Headly, Harry Dean Stanton, Freddie Jones, Crispin Glover, Alicia Witt, Clark Heathcliffe Brolly, Camilla Overbye Roos; **D:** James Signorelli, David Lynch; **W:** Barry Gifford, Jay Mcinerney; **M:** Angelo Badalamenti. CABLE

Hotel Rwanda 🐾🐾½ 2004 (PG-13) Cheadle gives a remarkable performance in a drama that covers a too-little-known episode in recent history. In 1994 Rwanda, a former Belgian colony, members of the Hutu tribe killed some 800,000 members of the once-dominant Tutsi tribe. Paul Rusesabagina (Cheadle) is a Hutu, who manages a four-star hotel in Kigali. When the genocide begins, he fears for his own family since his wife, Tatiana (Okonedo), is a Tutsi. Unacle to escape or to get any help, Paul decides his safety depends on business as usual (and bribing the military) even as he comes to shelter some 1,200 refugees within his hotel. Film focuses on Paul and not on what is happening in Rwanda in general. Without some historical background, the general viewer will likely be somewhat confused. 110m/C DVD. GB/IT/SA Don Cheadle, Sophie Okonedo, Nick Nolte, Desmond Dube, David O'Hara, Cara Seymour; **D:** Terry George; **W:** George, Keir Pearson.

C: Robert Fraisse, Naomi Geraghty; M: Andrea Guerra, Rupert Gregson-Williams.

Hothead 🐾🐾 *Coup de Tete* 1978 A heedless, impulsive soccer player's behavior gets him cut from the team, fired from his mill job, and booted out of his favorite bar. In French with English subtitles or dubbed. **98m/C VHS. FR** Patrick Dewaere, Jean Bouise, Michel Aumont, France Dougnac; **D:** Jean-Jacques Annaud; **W:** Francis Veber. Cesar '80: Support. Actor (Bouise).

Hotline 🐾🐾 1982 After taking a job answering phones at a crisis center, a woman becomes the next target of a psychotic killer. **96m/C VHS.** Lynda Carter, Steve Forrest, Granville Van Dusen, Monte Markham, James Booth; **D:** Jerry Jameson. **TV**

H.O.T.S. 🐾 *T & A Academy* 1979 (R) A sex-filled sorority rivalry film, starring a slew of ex-Playboy Playmates in wet shirts. Screenplay co-written by exploitation star Caffaro. **95m/C VHS, DVD.** Susan Kiger, Lisa London, Kimberly Cameron, Danny Bonaduce, Steve Bond; **D:** Gerald Seth Sindell; **W:** Cheri Caffaro, Joan Buchanan; **C:** Harvey Genkins; **M:** David Davis.

The Hottest State 🐾🐾 2006 (R) Sarah Garcia (Moreno), a young girl with dreams of the big city, sets out for New York to begin her singing career. Enter romantic William Harding (Webber), an aspiring actor transplanted from Texas. They fall in love, and then as often happens with young love, someone gets dumped. But Harding can't seem to move on, pining and yearning insufferably for his lost love, and in doing so annoys everyone around him. Mom Jesse (Linney) offers sympathy, but it's not until distant dad (Hawke) shows up that the lovesick puppy gets some clarity and maturity about his situation. Hawke serves as writer/director/actor in this self-indulgent and overly talky bit about young (and unrequited) love based on Hawke's own semi-biographical novel of the same name. **117m/C DVD. US** Mark Webber, Catalina Sandino Moreno, Laura Linney, Michelle Williams, Sonia Braga, Jesse Harris, Ethan Hawke; **D:** Ethan Hawke; **W:** Ethan Hawke; **C:** Christopher Norr; **M:** Jesse Harris.

Hotwire 🐾½ 1980 Tired comedy about the unscrupulous side of the car repossession racket. **92m/C VHS.** George Kennedy, Strother Martin, Lawrence (Larry) Dobkin; **D:** Frank Q. Dobbs; **W:** Frank Q. Dobbs; **C:** Robert Bethard; **M:** George Marshall; **W:** Philip Yordan.

Houdini 🐾🐾½ 1953 Historically inaccurate but entertaining biopic of the infamous magician and escapologist. Chronicles his rise to stardom, his efforts to contact his dearly departed mother through mediums (a prequel to "Ghost"?), and his heart-stopping logic-defying escapes. First screen teaming of Leigh and Curtis, who had already been married for two years. **107m/C VHS.** Tony Curtis, Janet Leigh, Torin Thatcher, Angela (Clark) Clarke, Stefan Schnabel, Ian Wolfe, Sig Rumann, Michael Pate, Connie Gilchrist, Mary Murphy, Tor Johnson; **D:** George Marshall; **W:** Philip Yordan.

Houdini 🐾🐾½ 1999 New York Jewish youth Erich Weiss transforms himself into vaudeville magician/illusionist Harry Houdini (Schaech) and marries Bess (Edwards), who becomes his assistant. Houdini soon becomes a famed escape artist, pushing himself into ever-more dangerous stunts. After his beloved mother's death, Houdini then goes on a crusade to expose fake spiritualists who had promised him contact with her. **94m/C VHS.** Johnathon Schaech, Stacy Edwards, Grace Zabriskie, Paul Sorvino, Rhea Perlman, George Segal, David Warner, Mark Ruffalo, Ron Perlman, Judy Geeson; **D:** Pen Densham; **W:** Pen Densham; **C:** Gordon C. Lonsdale; **M:** Don Harper. **CABLE**

The Hound of London 🐾🐾½ *Sherlock Holmes in The Hound of London* 1993 Inspector Lestrade brings Sherlock Holmes (Macnee) his latest case, a double murder that has taken place at the Strand Theatre. And among the suspects is the only woman Holmes has ever admired, the lovely Irene Adler. Eccentric characters, a sword duel, backstage mischief, and Holmes and Watson together once more. Based on the play by Craig Bowlsby. **72m/C VHS. CA** Patrick Macnee, Scott-Paget, Colin Skinner, Jack McCreath, Carolyn Wilkinson, Sophia Thornley, Drew Kemp, Ned Lemley, Craig Bowlsby; **D:** Gil Letourneau, Peter Reynolds-Long; **W:** Craig Bowlsby.

The Hound of the Baskervilles 🐾🐾🐾 1939 The curse of a demonic hound threatens descendants of an English noble family until Holmes and Watson solve the mystery. **80m/B VHS, DVD. GB** Basil Rathbone, Nigel Bruce, Richard Greene, John Carradine, Wendy Barrie, Lionel Atwill, E.E. Clive; **D:** Sidney Lanfield.

The Hound of the Baskervilles 🐾🐾½ 1959 Cushing's not half bad as Sherlock Holmes as he investigates the mystery of a supernatural hound threatening the life of a Dartmoor baronet. Dark and moody. **86m/C VHS, DVD. GB** Peter Cushing, Christopher Lee, Andre Morell; **D:** Terence Fisher; **W:** Peter Bryan; **C:** Jack Asher; **M:** James Bernard.

The Hound of the Baskervilles woof! 1977 Awful spoof of the Sherlock Holmes classic, with Cook as Holmes and Moore as Watson (and Holmes' mother). Even the cast can't save it. **84m/C VHS, DVD.** Dudley Moore, Peter Cook, Denholm Elliott, Joan Greenwood, Spike Milligan, Jessie Matthews, Roy Kinnear; **D:** Paul Morrissey; **W:** Dudley Moore, Peter Cook, Paul Morrissey; **C:** Dick Bush; **M:** Dudley Moore.

The Hound of the Baskervilles 🐾🐾 1983 Another remake of the Sherlock Holmes story which finds the great detective investigating the murder of Sir Charles Baskerville and a mysterious haunted moor. **100m/C VHS; DVD. GB** Ian Richardson, Donald Churchill, Martin Shaw, Nicholas Clay, Denholm Elliott, Brian Blessed, Ronald Lacey; **D:** Douglas Hickox; **W:** Charles Edward Pogue; **C:** Ronnie Taylor; **M:** Michael Lewis.

The Hound of the Baskervilles 🐾🐾½ 2000 Frewer takes on the role of Sherlock Holmes, emphasizing the character's cynical humor as well as his sometimes insufferable intelligence. Welsh ably backs him up as Watson and this version closely follows the Conan Doyle story. Sir Henry Baskerville (London) has inherited an estate with a curse and a devilish hound that terrorizes the moors. Holmes investigates. **90m/C VHS, DVD. CA** Matt Frewer, Kenneth Welsh, Jason London, Emma Campbell, Robin Wilcock, Arthur Holden, Leni Parker, Gordon Masten; **D:** Rodney Gibbons; **W:** Joe Wiesenfeld; **C:** Eric Cayla; **M:** Marc Ouellette. **CABLE**

The Hound of the Baskervilles 🐾🐾🐾 2002 The umpteenth version of the Sherlock Holmes story about an inheritance and a vicious dog out on the moors is distinguished by its cast with Roxburgh's Holmes and Hart's Watson ably playing off each other. **100m/C VHS, DVD. GB** Richard Roxburgh, Ian Hart, Matt(hew) Day, Richard E. Grant, Neve McIntosh, John Nettles, Geraldine James, Ron Cook, Danny (Daniel) Webb; **D:** David Attwood; **W:** Allan Cubitt; **C:** James Welland; **M:** Robert (Rob) Lane. **TV**

Hour of Decision 🐾½ 1957 When a newspaper columnist turns up dead, a reporter investigates the murder. Things get hairy when he finds the prime suspect is his own wife. **81m/B VHS. GB** Jeff Morrow, Hazel Court, Lionel Jeffries, Anthony Dawson, Mary Laura Wood; **D:** C.M. Pennington-Richards.

Hour of the Assassin 🐾½ 1986 (R) A mercenary is hired to assassinate a South American ruler, and a CIA operative is sent to stop him. Shot in Peru. **96m/C VHS.** Erik Estrada, Robert Vaughn; **D:** Luis Llosa.

Hour of the Gun 🐾🐾½ 1967 Western saga chronicles what happens after the gunfight at the OK Corral. Garner plays the grim Wyatt Earp on the trail of vengeance after his brothers are killed. Robards is excellent as the crusty Doc Holliday. **100m/C VHS, DVD.** James Garner, Jason Robards Jr., Robert Ryan, Albert Salmi, Charles Aidman, Steve Ihnat, Jon Voight, Robert Phillips; **D:** John Sturges; **W:** Edward Anhalt; **M:** Jerry Goldsmith.

The Hour of the Star 🐾🐾🐾½ *A Hora Da Estrela* 1985 The poignant, highly acclaimed feature debut by Amaral, about an innocent young woman moving to the city of Sao Paulo from the impoverished countryside of Brazil, and finding happiness despite her socioeconomic failures. Based on Clarice Lispector's novel. In Portuguese with English subtitles. **96m/C VHS, DVD. BR** Marcelia Cartaxo; **D:** Suzana Amaral. Berlin Intl. Film Fest. '85: Actress (Cartaxo).

Hour of the Wolf 🐾🐾🐾½ *Vargtimmen* 1968 An acclaimed, surreal view into the tormented inner life of a painter as he and his wife are isolated on a small northern island. In Swedish with English subtitles. **89m/B VHS, DVD. SW** Max von Sydow, Liv Ullmann, Ingrid Thulin, Erland Josephson, Gertrud Fridh, Gudrun Brost, Georg Rydeberg, Naima Wifstrand, Bertil Anderberg, Ulf Johansson; **D:** Ingmar Bergman; **W:** Ingmar Bergman; **C:** Sven Nykvist; **M:** Lars Johan Werle. Natl. Bd. of Review '68: Actress (Ullmann); Natl. Soc. Film Critics '68: Director (Bergman).

Hourglass 🐾🐾 1995 (R) Fashion industry honcho Michael Jardine (Howell) risks his reputation and his life when he becomes involved with deadly, revenge-minded seductress Dara (Shiras), who blames the Jardines for her father's suicide. Another in a long line of be careful who you sleep with movies. **91m/C VHS. C.** Thomas Howell, Sofia Shinas, Ed Begley Jr., Timothy Bottoms, Anthony Clark; **D:** C. Thomas Howell; **W:** C. Thomas Howell, Darren Dalton; **C:** John Lambert; **M:** Chris Saranec.

The Hours 🐾🐾🐾 2002 (PG-13) In 1923 Virginia Woolf (Kidman) is recovering from a mental collapse while writing her novel "Mrs. Dalloway." In the 1950s, Laura Brown (Moore) is reading said novel, and in 2001, Clarissa (Streep) eerily embodies Woolf's character Dalloway. All three are facing questions of fulfillment in their lives and examining whether it's worth living, and all have issues with their own sexuality and the current men in their lives. Parallel gestures and words from era to era wonderfully enhance the illusion the three are around one. Many felt Cunningham's Pulitzer Prize-winning novel would not translate well to the screen, but Hare's screenplay and Daldry's direction superbly present this quilt of tales. **114m/C VHS, DVD. US** Nicole Kidman, Julianne Moore, Meryl Streep, Stephen (Dillon) Dillane, Miranda Richardson, John C. Reilly, Ed Harris, Allison Janney, Claire Danes, Jeff Daniels, Toni Collette, Eileen Atkins, Jack Rovello, Margo Martindale, Linda Bassett; **D:** Stephen Daldry; **W:** David Hare; **C:** Seamus McGarvey; **M:** Philip Glass. Oscars '02: Actress (Kidman); British Acad. '02: Actress-Drama (Kidman), Film-Drama; L.A. Film Critics '02: Actress (Kidman); Score; Golden Globes '03: Actress-Drama (Kidman), Score; Natl. Bd. of Review '02: Film; Writers Guild '02: Adapt. Screenplay.

The Hours and Times 🐾🐾🐾 1992 A concise drama based on one point of fact used to quietly evoke differences in class, talent, sexual orientation, and unrequited love. The fact is that in the spring of 1963 Brian Epstein, the Beatles brilliant homosexual manager, shared a four-day Barcelona vacation with John Lennon. Director Munch speculates that the sophisticated Epstein was hopelessly in love with the younger, working-class Lennon who is friendly but unresponsive to the courtship. A tender and rueful depiction of friendship longing to be something more. **60m/B VHS, DVD.** David Angus, Ian Hart, Stephanie Pack, Robin McDonald, Sergio Moreno, Unity Grimwood; **D:** Christopher Munch; **W:** Christopher Munch. Sundance '92: Special Jury Prize.

House 🐾🐾 1986 (R) Horror novelist Roger Cobb (Katt) moves into his dead aunt's supposedly haunted house only to find that the monsters don't necessarily stay in the closets. His worst nightmares come to life as he writes about his Vietnam experiences and is forced to relive the tragic events, but these aren't the only visions that start springing to life. It sounds depressing, but is actually a funny, intelligent "horror" flick. Followed by several lesser sequels. **93m/C VHS, DVD.** William Katt, George Wendt, Richard Moll, Kay Lenz, Michael Ensign, Mary Stavin, Susan French; **D:** Steve Miner; **W:** Ethan Wiley; **C:** Mac Ahlberg; **M:** Harry Manfredini.

House 2: The Second Story 🐾 1987 (PG-13) The flaccid sequel to the haunted-house horror flick concerns two innocent guys who move into the family mansion and discover Aztec ghosts. Has none of the humor which helped the first movie along. **88m/C VHS, DVD.** John Ratzenberger, Arye Gross, Royal Dano, Bill Maher, Jonathan Stark, Lar Park-Lincoln, Amy Yasbeck, Devin Devasquez; **D:** Ethan Wiley; **W:** Ethan Wiley; **C:** Mac Ahlberg.

House 4: Home Deadly Home 🐾½ 1991 (R) Another bad real estate epic on a par with the other unusually inept "House" efforts. When her husband (Katt) is killed in an auto accident, a young woman and her daughter move into a mysterious old house. Terror begins to confront them at every turn, threatening to destroy them both. We can only hope. **93m/C VHS.** Terri Treas, Scott Burkholder, Melissa Clayton, William Katt, Ned Romero; **D:** Lewis Abernathy.

House Across the Bay 🐾🐾 1940 Raft, an imprisoned nightclub owner, finds that he is being duped by his attorney who's eager to get his hooks into the lingerie-clad prisoner's wife. But prison isn't going to stop the bitter husband from getting his revenge. **88m/B VHS.** George Raft, Walter Pidgeon, Joan Bennett, Lloyd Nolan, Gladys George; **D:** Archie Mayo.

House Arrest 🐾½ 1996 (PG) Another tired kids-think-they-know-best formula film. When Grover Beindorf (Howard) and his younger sister learn that their constantly fighting parents (Curtis and Pollak) are separating, they lock them in the basement so they'll be forced to sort things out. Word gets around and some school pals kidnap their problem parents and stash them in the basement with the Beindorfs. Most of the movie was actually shot in a basement; watch for Curtis hanging upside down in a laundry chute "True Lies" style. **107m/C VHS, DVD.** Jamie Lee Curtis, Kevin Pollak, Christopher McDonald, Jennifer Tilly, Caroline Aaron, Wallace Shawn, Sheila McCarthy, Ray Walston, Kyle Howard, Amy Sakasitz, Jennifer Love Hewitt; **D:** Harry Winer; **W:** Michael Hitchcock; **C:** Uel Steiger; **M:** Bruce Broughton.

House Calls 🐾🐾🐾 1978 (PG) A widowed surgeon turns into a swinging bachelor until he meets a witty but staid English divorcee. Wonderful change. Jackson is exceptional. Made into a short-lived TV series. **98m/C VHS, DVD.** Walter Matthau, Glenda Jackson, Art Carney, Richard Benjamin, Candice Azzara; **D:** Howard Zieff; **W:** Charles Shyer; **M:** Henry Mancini.

A House Divided 🐾🐾½ 2000 (R) Amanda (Beals) is the beloved only child of wealthy Georgia plantation owner David Dickson (Waterson) and is named as his heir when her father dies. But when Dickson's estranged brother (White) contests the will, family secrets come to light, including the devastating fact that Amanda's real mother is Julia (Hamilton), who was a slave of Dickson's slaves. And although it may be 1874, race is still definitely an issue. Based on a true court case described in the book "Woman of Color, Daughter of Privilege" by Kent Anderson Leslie. **99m/C VHS.** Sam Waterston, Jennifer Beals, Lisa Gay Hamilton, Timothy Daly, Ron White, Shirley Douglas, Sean McCann, Gerard Parkes, Colin Fox; **D:** John Kent Harrison; **W:** Paris Qualles; **C:** Kees Van Oostrum; **W:** Lawrence Shragge. **CABLE**

The House in Marsh Road 🐾🐾 1960 A faithless husband decides to rid himself of She Who Must Be Obeyed, but his wife's ghost-friend intervenes. **70m/B VHS. GB** Tony Wright, Patricia Dainton, Sandra Dorne, Derek Aylward, Sam Kydd; **D:** Montgomery Tully.

A House in the Hills 🦴🦴 1993 (R) A struggling actress is housesitting at a luxurious estate and innocently lets in the exterminator. Except he's an ex-con looking for revenge on the home's current occupant (whom the actress is pretending to be) and may just exterminate her instead. 91m/C VHS. Helen Slater, Michael Madsen, Jeffrey Tambor, James Laurenson, Elyssa Davalos, Terri Barry; *D:* Ken Wiederhorn; *W:* Ken Wiederhorn. *C:* Josep Civit. *M:* Richard Einhorn.

The House Next Door 🦴🦴 2001 Lori (Cook) and Tom (Harrison) Peterson move into their dream house, meeting next-door neighbors Helen and Carl (Russo) Schmidt. Carl seems rowdy but friendly but Lori comes to realize that he's a wife-beater and when Helen disappears she suspects the worse. Tom doesn't take his wife seriously and leaves on a business trip, with Lori's friend Monica (Young) coming to visit. So Lori persuades Monica to help her investigate Carl. 83m/C VHS. DVD. A.J. Cook, James Russo, Theresa Russell, Sean Young, Frederic Forrest, Matthew Harrison; *D:* Joey Travolta. *W:* John Benjamin Martz; *C:* Pieter Stathis; *M:* John Sereda. VIDEO

House of Angels 🦴🦴 *Änglagård; Colin Nutley's House of Angels* 1992 (R) Charming comedy, with some serious overtones, about what happens in a small Swedish village when two free-spirited newcomers come to stay. Fanny and her friend Zac, who are cabaret performers, show up at the funeral of the eccentric Erik, who turns out to be the grandfather Fanny never knew. With her comes information about her past, including who her father might be. What the generous Fanny wants is for Fanny and Zac to leave as quickly as possible. In Swedish with English subtitles. 119m/C VHS. SW Helena Bergstrom, Rikard Wolff, Sven Wollter, Jakob Eklund, Viveka Seldahl, Ernst Günther, Reine Brynolfsson, Per Oscarsson. *D:* Colin Nutley. *W:* Susanne Falck.

House of Bamboo 🦴🦴½ 1955 A ruthless gang in Tokyo is holding up U.S. ammunition trains and will stop at nothing to cover their tracks, including killing their own. Stack is an undercover cop who infiltrates the gang, led by Ryan's vicious crime boss. Although Ryan does not disappoint, Stack's not at his best, and love scenes between him and Shirley Yamaguchi are stilted and uncomfortable to watch. The real star in this remake of "The Street with No Name" (1948) is the Cinemascope view of post war Japan and the finale in a Tokyo amusement park. 102m/C DVD. Robert Ryan, Robert Stack, Yoshiko (Shirley) Yamaguchi, Cameron Mitchell, Brad Dexter, Sessue Hayakawa, Biff (Elliott) Elliot, Harry Carey Jr., John Doucette, Barry Coe, DeForest Kelley; *D:* Samuel Fuller; *W:* Harry Kleiner; *C:* Joe MacDonald; *M:* Leigh Harline.

House of Cards 🦴🦴🦴 1990 Depicts the political machinations of Machiavellian Tory whip Francis Urquhart (Richardson), who schemes to bring down the present government so that he can become the next Prime Minister. And there's absolutely nothing "F.U." (as he's appropriately known) won't do to achieve power. Followed by "To Play the King" and "The Final Cut," based on the novel by Michael Dobbs. On two cassettes. 200m/C VHS. DVD. GB Ian Richardson, Susannah Harker, Diane Fletcher, Nicholas Selby, James Villiers; *D:* Paul Seed; *W:* Andrew Davies; *C:* Ian Punter; *M:* Jim Parker.

House of Cards 🦴🦴½ 1992 (PG-13) Precocious six-year-old Sally (Menina) suddenly stops talking after her father is killed in an accident at an archeological site in Mexico. Mom Ruth (Turner) fights to bring her daughter out of her fantasy world and seeks medical advice from a psychiatrist (a sympathetic Jones) but ignores it when it clashes with her own theories. The ethereal Menina, in her acting debut, gives the best performance in this weakly plotted and confusing family saga. 109m/C VHS. DVD. Kathleen Turner, Asha Menina, Tommy Lee Jones, Shiloh Strong, Esther Rolle, Park Overall, Michael Horse, Anne Pitoniak; *D:* Michael Lessac. *W:* Michael Lessac; *C:* Victor Hammer.

House of D 🦴🦴 2004 (PG-13) First time writer/director Duchovny is Tom Warshaw. He recounts for his son the events of his own early adolescence that shaped his life. In the early '70s, young Tommy has recently lost his father, his mother is suffering from depression, his best friend is Pappas, the retarded janitor at his school, he gets life advice from an inmate at the nearby Women's House of Detention, and he is just now noticing girls, particularly neighbor Melissa. This last development leads a jealous Pappas to petty theft to win back Tommy's friendship. Cloying, overly sentimental, and shamelessly sappy, this tale works much better as nostalgia for the carefree Greenwich Village Duchovny grew up in than the coming of age fable he obviously intended. 96m/C DVD. US FR David Duchovny, Anton Yelchin, Erykah Badu, Robin Williams, Zelda Williams, Magali Amadei, Tea Leoni, Frank Langella, Harold Cartier, Orlando Jones, Alice Drummond; *D:* David Duchovny; *W:* David Duchovny; *C:* Michael Chapman; *M:* Geoff Zanelli.

House of Dark Shadows 🦴🦴 1970 (PG) Gory, intense feature-film version of the gothic TV daytime soap "Dark Shadows." Released from his coffin by a handyman seeking treasure, 150-year-old vampire Barnabas Collins (Frid) avails himself of the hospitality of his descendents and moves into a house on their property. As a series of vampire attacks plague the area, Barnabas finds himself involved with a love-smitten doctor who wants to cure him (Hall) and a young girl who resembles his lost love, Josette (Scott). A violent and exciting film, long on shocks but short on continuity and character development. 97m/C VHS. Jonathan Frid, Joan Bennett, Grayson Hall, Kathryn Leigh Scott, Roger Davis, Nancy Barret, John Karlen, Thayer David, Louis Edmonds; *D:* Dan Curtis; *W:* Sam Hall, Gordon Russell; *C:* Arthur Ornitz.

House of Death 🦴 *Death Screams* 1982 (R) The ex-Playmate of the Year runs in hysterical fear from a knife-wielding lunatic. 88m/C VHS. Susan Kiger, William T. Hicks, Jody Kay, Martin Tucker, Jennifer Chase; *D:* David Nelson; *W:* Paul Elliott; *C:* Darrell Cathcart; *M:* Dee Barton.

The House of Dies Drear 🦴🦴½ 1988 A modern-day African American family moves into an old house that turns out to be haunted by the ghost of a long dead abolitionist. The family is transported back to the days of slavery as they interact with the ghost. Based on the story by Virginia Hamilton. Aired on PBS as part of the "Wonderworks" family movie series. 107m/C VHS. DVD. Howard E. Rollins Jr., Moses Gunn, Shavar Ross, Gloria Foster, Clarence Williams III; *D:* Allan Goldstein.

House of Dracula 🦴🦴 1945 Sequel to "House of Frankenstein" features several of the Universal monsters. Overly ambitious story gets a bit hokey, but it's entertaining, nonetheless. 67m/B VHS. DVD. Lon Chaney Jr., Martha O'Driscoll, John Carradine, Lionel Atwill, Onslow Stevens, Glenn Strange, Jane Adams, Ludwig Stossel; *D:* Erle C. Kenton; *W:* Edward T. Lowe; *C:* George Robinson.

House of Dreams 🦴 1964 Berry is a blocked writer coping with domestic difficulties whose dreams reveal a disturbing future. Contains a bit part for Goodnow, now a CNN talking head. 80m/B VHS. Robert Berry, Pauline Elliott, Charlene Bradley, Lance Bird, David Goodnow; *D:* Robert Berry.

The House of Eliott 🦴🦴½ 1992 BBC miniseries set in 1920s London finds the orphaned Beatrice and Evangeline Eliott struggling to begin their fashion business as couturiers to the rich and influential, which eventually leads to their founding of the House of Eliott. Lots of romance and intrigue along the way. Boxed set of six cassettes. 300m/C DVD. GB Stella Gonet, Louise Lombard, Aden Gillett, Richard Lintern.

House of Fools 🦴🦴 2002 (R) Janna (Vysotsky) is a young psychiatric patient in an old mansion located near the border of Chechnya. The cheerful Janna believes herself to be the fiancee of Canadian singer Bryan Adams (who appears as himself in the young woman's fantasies). The everyday activities of the childlike patients are disrupted when the fighting between the Russians and the Chechens comes closer. The staff flees and the doctor (Bagdonas) leaves to find buses to evacuate his patients. Meanwhile, the inmates are left to fend for themselves—and are soon joined by a group of Chechen soldiers, including handsome Akhmed (Ssalmov) who Janna falls in love with. The film was inspired by an incident that happened in 1996. Russian with subtitles. 104m/C VHS. DVD. RU FR Julia Vysotsky, Sultan Iskamov, Bryan Adams, Vladas Bagdonas, Stanislav Varkki, Marina Pollsei-mako; *D:* Andrei Konchalovsky; *W:* Andrei Konchalovsky; *C:* Sergei Kozlov; *M:* Eduard Artemyev.

House of Flying Daggers 🦴🦴🦴 *Shimian Maifu* 2004 Zhang continues his interest in swordplay, following 2002's "Hero." Set in 859 A.D., during a period of unrest in the Tang Dynasty, the film follows three main characters. Police captains Leo (Lau) and Jin (Kaneshiro) are assigned to uncover the leader of the Flying Daggers, a secret anti-government rebel group. An elaborate set piece introduces beautiful blind dancer Mei (Zhang), the apex of the triangle. Jin poses as a sympathizer and hopes Mei will lead him to the rebel headquarters but doesn't expect to fall in love with her. A Bamboo forest scene is among the film's action highlights. Mandarin with subtitles. Film is dedicated to actress Anita Mui who died from cancer before filming her role. 120m/C VHS, DVD, Blu-ray Disc. CH HK Takeshi Kaneshiro, Andy Lau, Zhang Ziyi, Song Dandan; *D:* Yimou Zhang; *W:* Yimou Zhang, Feng Li, Bin Wang; *C:* Xiaoding Zhao; *M:* Shigeru Umebayashi.

House of Errors 🦴½ 1942 Two deliverymen pose as reporters to safeguard a prototype machine gun from the bad guys. Contrived plot consisting of outdated comic routines. This was Marsh's last film. 63m/B VHS. Roy Butler, Vernon Dent, Harry Langdon, Charles R. Rogers, Marian Marsh, Ray Walker, Betty Blythe, John Holland, Monte Montague; *C:* Guy Kingsford; *D:* Bernard B. Ray; *W:* Ewart Adamson, Eddie Davis; *M:* Lee Zahler.

House of Fear 🦴🦴½ 1945 Holmes and Watson investigate the murders of several members of the Good Comrades Club, men who were neither good nor comradely. 69m/B VHS. DVD. Basil Rathbone, Nigel Bruce, Dennis Hoey, Aubrey Mather, Paul Cavanagh, Gavin Muir; *D:* Roy William Neill.

House of Frankenstein 🦴🦴 1944 (R) An evil scientist (Karloff) escapes from prison and, along with his hunchback manservant, revives Dracula, Frankenstein's monster, and the Wolfman to carry out his dastardly deeds. An all-star cast helps this horror fest along. 71m/B VHS, DVD. Boris Karloff, J. Carrol Naish, Lon Chaney Jr., John Carradine, Elena Verdugo, Anne Gwynne, Lionel Atwill, Peter Coe, Glenn Strange, Sig Ruman; *D:* Erle C. Kenton; *W:* Edward T. Lowe; *C:* George Robinson.

House of Games 🦴🦴🦴 1987 (R) The directorial debut of playwright Mamet is a tale about an uptight female psychiatrist who investigates the secret underworld of con-artistry and becomes increasingly involved in an elaborate con game. She's led along her crooked path by smooth-talking con-master Mantegna. A taut, well plotted psychological suspense film with many twists and turns. Stylishly shot with dialogue which has that marked Mamet cadence. Most of the leads are from Mamet's theatre moving (including his wife, Crouse). 102m/C VHS, DVD, Blu-ray Disc. Joe Mantegna, Lindsay Crouse, Lilia Skala, J.T. Walsh, Mesach Taylor, Ricky Jay, Mike Nussbaum, Willo Hausman; *D:* David Mamet; *W:* David Mamet; *C:* Juan Ruiz-Anchia; *M:* Alaric Jans.

House of Horrors 🦴🦴½ 1946 Deformed murderer "The Creeper" (Hatton) is used by a mad sculptor in a twisted revenge plot. Marcel De Lange (Kosleck) believes his work has been vilely abused by art critics so he uses his friend's homicidal urges to get rid of anyone who stands in his way. 76m/B VHS. Martin Kosleck, Rondo Hatton, Robert Lowery, Virginia Grey, Bill Goodwin, Alan Napier, Joan Shawlee, Howard Freeman; *D:* Jean Yarbrough; *M:* George Bricker.

House of Mirth 🦴🦴🦴 2000 (PG-13) The treacherous world of high society is the backdrop for savvy social climber Lily Bart (Anderson), who seeks a shot at an eligible bachelor's money in early 20th-century N.Y.C. Stoltz plays friend Selden who is not quite up to snuff financially for Lily, and Aykroyd, a well-heeled and seemingly well-meaning married "friend" who offers her investment advice...but at a hefty price. To make matters worse, a high-profile social maven (Linney) uses Lily to distract her husband from her own infidelities which puts Lily's reputation in jeopardy. With powerful friends, finds her once promising social position compromised. Disturbing but involving story made all the more so by Anderson's performance. Based on the novel by Edith Wharton. 140m/C VHS, DVD. GB US Gillian Anderson, Eric Stoltz, Dan Aykroyd, Eleanor Bron, Terry Kinney, Anthony LaPaglia, Laura Linney, Jodhi May, Elizabeth McGovern; *D:* Terence Davies; *W:* Terence Davies; *C:* Remi Adefarasin.

House of Mystery 🦴🦴½ 1934 For a shot at some priceless jewels, several guests gather for a weekend in a spine-tingling mansion. A creepy curse keeps them looking over their shoulders. An old widow is killed for her jewels, but the murderers can't locate the goods. After they try a series of fiendish plans to retrieve them, the detective does stop the crooks. 61m/B VHS. Ed Lowry, Verna Hillie, Brandon Hurst, George "Gabby" Hayes; *D:* William Nigh.

House of Mystery 🦴🦴½ *At the Villa Rose* 1941 Splendid British remake of 1934 film in which the detective does some true sleuthing to catch the culprits. 62m/C VHS. DVD. GB Kenneth Kent, Judy Kelly, Peter Murray Hill, Walter Rilla, Ruth Maitland; *D:* Walter Summers.

House of 9 🦴🦴 2005 (R) So how familiar does this sound? Nine strangers wake up trapped in a creepy mansion without any idea how they got there. A voice tells them that only one will survive and that last person gets five million bucks for their trouble. Not as grisly as "Saw" or "Cube" but still nasty. 86m/C DVD. GB Dennis Hopper, Hippolyte Girardot, Peter Capaldi, Raffaello Degruttola, Kelly Brook, Ashley Walters, Susie Amy, Morven Christie, Julienne Davis; *D:* Stephen R. Monroe; *W:* Philippe Vidal; *C:* Damian Bromley; *M:* Mark Ryder.

House of 1000 Corpses 🦴 2003 (R) Disjointed and thoroughly confusing homage to horror films akin to "The Texas Chainsaw Massacre." Director/rocker Zombie has an honest affection for the films he references and recreates. Unfortunately, his movie is a hodge-podge of stories with no clear direction. It's stylish enough to be a popular cult film, but it lacks tangible scares or real drama. None of the episodes really fit together in this failure paved by good intentions. Hype may lead you to think this film is more than it is. 88m/C VHS, DVD, Blu-ray Disc. US Sid Haig, Bill Moseley, Karen Black, Sheri Moon, Chris Hardwick, Erin Daniels, Dennis Fimple, Jennifer Jostyn, Walton Goggins, Tom Towles, Michael J. Pollard, Harrison Young, Rob Zombie; *W:* Rob Zombie; *D:* Rob Zombie; *C:* Tom Richmond, Alex Poppas; *M:* Rob Zombie, Scott Humphrey.

The House of 1000 Dolls 🦴 *Haus Der Tausend Freuden* 1967 Doleful, not dollful, exploitation thriller as magician Price drugs young girls and sells them to slavery rings. An international production set in Tangiers; dialogue is dubbed. 79m/C VHS. GE SP GB Vincent Price, Martha Hyer, George Nader, Ann Smyrner, Maria Rohm; *D:* Jeremy Summers.

House of Psychotic Women woof!

Los Ojos Azules de la Muneca Rota; Blue Eyes of the Broken Doll 1973 (R) Naschy, Spain's premier horror movie star, plays a studly drifter who winds up in the home of three sisters, one with an artificial arm, one confined to a wheelchair and the other a nymphomaniac. No problemo thinks the hirsute Spaniard, until a series of bizarre murders—in which the victims eyes are ripped out—spoils his fun. Naschy, who usually sprouts fur and fangs, actually doesn't turn into a werewolf. Catchy but inappropriate score. A must for Naschy/bad movie fans. **87m/C VHS.** *SP* Paul Naschy, Maria Perschy, Diana Lorys, Eva Leon, Ines Morales, Tony Pica; *D:* Carlos Aured; *W:* Paul Naschy; *C:* Francisco Sanchez.

House of Sand 🐾🐾🐾

Casa de Areia 2005 (R) In 1910, Aurea (Torres) and her mother Maria (Montenegro, Torres' real-life mom) are transplanted to the oblivion of northern Brazil by Aurea's delusioned husband, who is intent on turning the barren land into a farm. She quickly finds her pregnant self widowed and stranded, but she is befriended by Massu (Moldia), a former slave from a nearby settlement who helps the women make their way. The story unfolds over three generations (Torres and Motenegro eventually shift roles, with Montenegro as Aurea and Torres as daughter Maria) as the house slowly fills with sand, symbolizing the effects of gradual but inevitable passage of time. Not much happens save the occasional opportunity for escape from the desolate desert life, but for those with patience, it's a visual and dramatic treat. Portuguese with English subtitles. **115m/C DVD, BR** Fernanda Montenegro, Fernanda Torres, Ruy Gerra, Luiz Melodia, Emiliano Queiroz, Enrique Diaz; *D:* Andrucha Waddington; *W:* Elena Soarez; *C:* Ricardo Della Rosa; *M:* Joao Barone.

House of Sand and Fog 🐾🐾½

2003 (R) Kathy (Connolly) is a recovering alcoholic whose husband recently left her. Because of a bureaucratic mix-up, she finds her house has been auctioned off from beneath her to Colonel Massoud Behrani (Kingsley), a former Iranian officer desperate to live the American dream. What follows is the conflict and struggle between the two, neither of which are evil or wrong in their viewpoints. Superb acting all around, combined with an interesting story. Based on the best-selling novel by Andre Dubus III. **126m/C VHS, DVD, US** Jennifer Connelly, Ben Kingsley, Ron Eldard, Shohreh Aghdashloo, Frances Fisher, Kim Dickens, Jonathan Ahdout, Navi Rawat, Carlos Gomez; *D:* Vadim Perelman; *W:* Vadim Perelman, Shawn Otto; *C:* Roger Deakins; *M:* James Horner. Ind. Spirit '04: Support. Actress (Aghdashloo); L.A. Film Critics '03: Support. Actress (Aghdashloo); N.Y. Film Critics '03: Support. Actress (Aghdashloo).

The House of Secrets 🐾🐾

1937 A Yank travels to Britain to collect an inheritance and stays in a dusty old mansion filled with an odd assortment of characters. **70m/B VHS, DVD.** Leslie Fenton, Muriel Evans, Noel Madison, Sidney Blackmer, Morgan Wallace, Holmes Herbert; *D:* Paul Harrison; *W:* Paul Harrison; *M:* Thomas J. Kelly.

The House of Seven Corpses 🐾🐾

1973 (PG) A crew attempts to film a horror movie in a Victorian manor where seven people died in a variety of gruesome manners. Things take a turn for the ghoulish when a crew member becomes possessed by the house's evil spirits. Good, low budget fun with a competent "B" cast. Filmed in what was the Utah governor's mansion. **90m/C VHS, DVD.** John Ireland, Faith Domergue, John Carradine, Carole Wells; *D:* Paul Harrison; *W:* Paul Harrison, Thomas J. Kelly.

House of Shadows 🐾½

1983 A 20-year-old murder comes back to haunt the victim's friends in this tale of mystery and terror. **90m/C VHS.** John Gavin, Yvonne De Carlo, Leonor Manso; *D:* Richard Wulicher.

House of Strangers 🐾🐾🐾½

1949 Conte, in a superb performance, swears vengeance on his brothers, whom he blames for his father's death. Robinson, in a smaller part than you'd expect from his billing, is nevertheless excellent as the ruthless banker father who sadly reaps a reward he didn't count on. Based on Philip Yordan's "I'll Never Go There Again." **101m/B VHS, DVD.** Edward G. Robinson, Susan Hayward, Richard Conte, Luther Adler, Efrem Zimbalist Jr., Debra Paget; *D:* Joseph L. Mankiewicz; *W:* Philip Yordan; *C:* Milton Krasner. Cannes '49: Actor (Robinson).

House of Terror 🐾

The Five at the Funeral; Scream Bloody Murder 1972 A woman and her boyfriend plot to kill her rich boss, while they too are being stalked by some undefined horror. **91m/C VHS.** Jennifer Bishop, Arell Blanton, Jacquelyn Hyde; *D:* Sergei Goncharoff.

The House of the Arrow 🐾🐾🐾

1953 Investigating the murder of a French widow, who was killed by a poisoned arrow, a detective must sort through a grab bag of potential suspects. Superior adaptation of the A.E.W. Mason thriller. **73m/B VHS.** *GB* Oscar Homolka, Yvonne Furneaux, Robert Urquhart; *D:* Michael Anderson Sr.

House of the Black Death 🐾½

Blood of the Man Devil; Night of the Beast 1965 Horror titans Chaney and Carradine manage to co-star in this warring warlocks, yet they share no scenes together! Chaney is the evil warlock (the horns are a giveaway) holding people hostage in the title edifice. **89m/B VHS.** Lon Chaney Jr., John Carradine, Katherine Victor, Tom Drake, Andrea King; *D:* Harold Daniels, Reginald LeBorg.

House of the Damned 🐾🐾

1971 A young woman, a mental hospital, a murdered father, a priceless gold statue—mix together and you get a mystery horror movie. A woman tries to solve her father's murder. **89m/C VHS.** Donald Pleasence, Michael Dunn; *D:* Gonzalo Suarez.

House of the Dead 🐾

Alien Zone 1978 Man is trapped inside a haunted house. Scary. **100m/C VHS.** John Ericson, Charles Aidman, Bernard Fox, Ivor Francis; *D:* Sharron Miller; *W:* David O'Malley; *C:* Ken Gibb; *M:* Stan Worth.

House of the Dead woof! 2003

(R) Cinematic trainwreck Uwe Boll attempts to make the filmmakers behind "Super Mario Brothers" feel better about themselves by directing one of the worst video game movies ever (and that's saying something). Four actors you could care less about travel to a remote island for the lamest rave ever captured on film (it has a baked goods tent... honestly) and, surprise, surprise, hordes of the undead start chomping on the extras. B-movie mainstays like Jurgen Prochnow and Clint Howard sleepwalk past the camera occasionally, but the real star is Boll's near-legendary technical ineptitude. Take a shot every time you notice a glaring gaffe and, trust us, you'll be dead long before the movie's over. **90m/C VHS, DVD, UMD.** *GE CA US* Jonathan Cherry, Tyron Leitso, Clint Howard, Ellie Cornell, Will Sanderson, Sonya Salomaa, Michael Eklund, David Palffy, Jurgen Prochnow, Erica Durance, Anthony Harrison, Ona Grauer, Enuka Okuma, Kira Clavell; *D:* Uwe Boll; *W:* Mark Altman, David Parker; *C:* Mathias Neumann; *M:* Reinhard Besser, Oliver Lieb.

House of the Dead 2: Dead Aim 🐾½

2005 (R) Tongue-in-cheek horror about a college prof (Haig) whose experiments unleash a zombie infestation on campus. A couple of scientists try to find a cure before the bomb-happy military decides to solve the problem by blowing up the area. **95m/C DVD.** Emmanuelle Vaugier, Edward Quinn, Kirk "Sticky Fingaz" Jones, Victoria Pratt, Sid Haig, Steve Monroe; *D:* Michael Hurst; *W:* Michael Roesch; *C:* Raymond N. Stella; *M:* Joe Kraemer. **VIDEO**

House of the Living Dead 🐾

Doctor Maniac 1973 (PG) Brattling Manor harbors a murderous and flesh-eating secret ready to lure the unsuspecting. Don't you be one. **87m/C VHS.** *SA* Mark Burns, Shirley Anne Field, David Oxley; *D:* Ray Austin.

House of the Long Shadows 🐾🐾½

1982 (PG) Comedy mixes with gore, as four of the horror screen's best leading men team up for the first time, although they have only minor roles. Might have been a contender, but Arnaz is miscast as author who stays in spooky house on a bet with Todd. Some wit but not enough. Based on the play "Seven Keys to Baldpate" by George M. Cohan (and novel by Earl Derr Biggers). **96m/C VHS, DVD.** *GB* Vincent Price, Christopher Lee, Peter Cushing, John Carradine, Desi Arnaz Jr., Sheila Keith, Richard Todd; *D:* Pete Walker; *W:* Michael Armstrong; *C:* Norman G. Langley.

House of the Rising Sun 🐾½

1987 A Los Angeles reporter goes under cover for a story on an exclusive brothel only to discover the owner is a psychopath who has very permanent ways of dealing with troublesome employees. **86m/C VHS.** John York, Bud Davis, Deborah Wakeham, Frank Annese; *D:* Greg Gold; *M:* Tina Turner, Bryan Ferry.

The House of the Seven Gables 🐾🐾½

1940 Nathaniel Hawthorne's brooding novel about greed and a family curse. Jaffrey Pyncheon (Sanders) frames his brother Clifford (Price) for the murder of their father so that he can search in peace for the fortune Jaffrey believes is hidden somewhere in the family mansion, Seven Gables. But, eventually, Clifford gets out of prison and returns to claim his birthright. The studio built an exact duplicate of the original Salem house. **89m/B VHS.** George Sanders, Vincent Price, Margaret Lindsay, Dick Foran, Nan Grey, Cecil Kellaway, Alan Napier; *D:* Joe May; *W:* Harold Greene; *C:* Milton Krasner.

The House of the Spirits 🐾🐾

1993 (R) Star-studded adaptation of the novel by Isabel Allende as a multi-generational saga following the fortunes of the powerful Trueba family. The ambitious Esteban (Irons) marries the clairvoyant Clara (Streep), exploits the peasants on his property, and becomes a conservative senator. Their rebellious daughter Blanca (Ryder) falls for rabble-rousing peasant Pedro (Banderas), and the country undergoes a bloody revolution. Magical realism of the novel is lost in screen melodrama, despite the international cast ill-served by tepid direction. The child Clara is played by Streep's daughter, Mary Willa (listed in the credits as Jane Gray). **109m/C VHS, DVD.** Meryl Streep, Jeremy Irons, Glenn Close, Winona Ryder, Antonio Banderas, Armin Mueller-Stahl, Vanessa Redgrave, Sarita Choudhury, Maria Conchita Alonso, Vincent Gallo, Miriam Colon, Jan Niklas, Teri Polo, Jane Gray; *D:* Billie August; *W:* Billie August; *C:* Jorgen Persson; *M:* Hans Zimmer.

House of the Yellow Carpet 🐾🐾

1984 A couple try to sell an ancient Persian carpet heirloom, and in doing so transgress some unwritten mystical law. Havoc ensues. **90m/C VHS.** Roland Josephson, Beatrice Romand; *D:* Carlo Lizzani.

The House of Usher 🐾

Edgar Allen Poe's House of Usher; The Fall of the House of Usher 1988 (R) Some serious overacting by Reed (as Roderick) and Pleasence (as his balmy brother) almost elevate this Poe retread to "so bad it's good" status, and there are a few admirably grisly moments. But, without other camp virtues, it's merely dreary. Adapted by Michael J. Murray and filmed in South Africa. **92m/C VHS, SA** Oliver Reed, Donald Pleasence, Romy Windsor, Rufus Swart, Norman Coombes, Anne Stradi; *D:* Alan Birkinshaw; *W:* Michael J. Murray; *C:* Yossi Wein; *M:* Gary Chang.

The House of Usher 🐾½

2006 (R) Jill arrives at Usher House, which comes complete with a sinister housekeeper, to attend the funeral of her friend Maddy. She also encounters Roderick, her former lover and Maddy's twin brother, who's suffering the same inherited illness that claimed his sister's life. Jill becomes drawn to Rick once again, despite menacing warnings and curiosity that could get her killed. Another very loose adaptation of the famed Poe story. **81m/C DVD.** Izabella Miko, Austin Nichols, Beth Grant, Danielle McCarthy, Stephen Fischer; *D:* Hayley Cloake; *W:* Colin Chang; *C:* Eric Trageser. **VIDEO**

House of Wax 🐾🐾

1953 (PG) A deranged sculptor (Price, who else?) builds a sinister wax museum which showcases creations that were once alive. A remake of the early horror flick "Mystery of the Wax Museum," and one of the '50s most popular 3-D films. This one still has the power to give the viewer the creeps, thanks to another chilling performance by Price. Look for a very young Charles Bronson, as well as Carolyn "Morticia Addams" Jones as a victim. **88m/C VHS, DVD.** Vincent Price, Frank Lovejoy, Carolyn Jones, Phyllis Kirk, Paul Cavanagh, Carolyn Jones, Paul Picerni, Angela (Clark) Clarke; *D:* Andre de Toth; *W:* Crane Wilbur; *C:* Bert Glennon; *M:* David Buttolph.

House of Wax 🐾½

2005 (R) Based on, but not very faithful to, the creepy 1953 3-D horror flick that starred Vincent Price. In this dismal dumbed-down remake, your usual gang of stupid college students are stranded by car trouble on their way to a football game. They wind up in the very small town of Ambrose and make the mistake of seeking help from the curator of a strange museum, Trudy's House of Wax, filled with wax figures that seem suspiciously lifelike. Said students include Hilton (making her legit film debut) who everyone will be happy to see encased in wax, which should actually make her more lifelike. **113m/C DVD, Blu-ray Disc, UMD, HD DVD.** *US AU* Elisha Cuthbert, Chad Michael Murray, Brian Van Holt, Jared Padalecki, Jon Abrahams, Robert Ri'chard, Paris Hilton; *D:* Jaume Collet-Serra; *W:* Carey Hayes, Chad Hayes; *C:* Stephen Windon; *M:* John Ottman. Golden Raspberries '05: Worst Support. Actress (Hilton).

House of Whipcord woof! 1975

Beautiful young women are kidnapped and tortured in this British gore-o-rama. Awful and degrading. **102m/C VHS, DVD.** *GB* Barbara Markham, Patrick Barr, Ray Brooks, Penny Irving, Anne Michelle, Ivor Salter, Robert Tayman; *D:* Pete Walker; *W:* Stanley Myers.

The House of Yes 🐾🐾

1997 (R) Thanksgiving certainly brings out the worst in families although the Pascal clan is dysfunction personified. Marty (Hamilton) brings home fiancee Lesley (Spelling) to meet his eccentric mom (Bujold) and siblings. Younger brother Anthony's (Prinze) a dropout with no direction and Marty's twin sister Jackie-O (Parker) is bonkers. She's recreated herself as Jacqueline Kennedy Onassis and has had a very intimate relationship with Marty that Lesley probably doesn't know about. **90m/C VHS, DVD.** Parker Posey, Josh Hamilton, Tori Spelling, Freddie Prinze Jr., Genevieve Bujold, Rachael Leigh Cook; *D:* Mark S. Waters; *W:* Mark S. Waters; *C:* Michael Spiller; *M:* Jeff Rona.

The House on Carroll Street 🐾🐾

1988 (PG) New York 1951, the middle of the McCarthy era. A young woman overhears a plot to smuggle Nazi war criminals into the U.S. She's already lost her job because of accusations of subversion, and it's not easy persuading FBI agent Daniels that she knows what she's talking about. Contrived plot and melodramatic finale help sink this period piece. **111m/C VHS, DVD.** Kelly McGillis, Jeff Daniels, Mandy Patinkin, Jessica Tandy; *D:* Peter Yates; *W:* Walter Bernstein; *C:* Michael Ballhaus; *M:* Georges Delerue.

The House on Chelouche Street 🐾🐾½

1973 In Tel-Aviv, during the summer of 1946, 15-year-old Sami, an Egyptian immigrant, tries to help support his mother and family during the upheavals of Palestine under the British mandate. A well thought-out story detailing the struggles of a North African Jewish family before the creation of the country of Israel. In Hebrew with English subtitles. **111m/C VHS.** *IS* Gila Almagor, Michal Bat-Adam, Shai K. Ophir; *D:* Moshe Mizrahi.

The House on Garibaldi Street 🐾🐾½

1979 Spy drama about the capture of Nazi war criminal Adolph Eichmann in Argentina and his extradition to Israel for trial. Based on the book by Isser Harel. **96m/C VHS.** Chaim Topol, Nick Mancuso, Martin Balsam, Janet Suzman, Leo McKern, Charles Gray, Alfred Burke; *D:* Peter Collinson; *M:* Charles Bernstein. **TV**

House on Haunted Hill 1958 A wealthy man throws a haunted house party and offers $10,000 to anyone who can survive the night there. Vintage cheap horror from the master of the macabre Castle. Remembered for Castle's in-theatre gimmick of dangling a skeleton over the audiences' heads in the film's initial release. 75m/B VHS, DVD, Vincent Price, Carol Ohmart, Richard Long, Alan Marshal, Carolyn Craig, Elisha Cook Jr., Julie Mitchum, Howard Hoffman; **D:** William Castle; **W:** Rob White; **C:** Carl Guthrie; **M:** Von Dexter.

House on Haunted Hill 1999 (R) This remake of William Castle's 1958 B-movie doesn't reach too far above its predecessor. In an homage to original star Vincent Price, Geoffrey Rush plays mincing amusement park tycoon Stephen Price, who invites a few friends over for his wife Evelyn's (Janssen) birthday. However, he invites them to a haunted "former insane asylum, and offers them a million bucks if they can stick it out for the entire night. Stephen and the scheming Evelyn have a few tricks rigged for the guests, who all end up having some connection to the horrors that went on in the house in the bad old days. Soon, however, actual supernatural creepiness starts thinning the ranks of the guests. Unashamedly bloody and cheesy. 96m/C VHS, DVD, Geoffrey Rush, Famke Janssen, Taye Diggs, Peter Gallagher, Chris Kattan, Ali Larter, Bridgette Wilson-Sampras, Max Perlich, Jeffrey Combs; **D:** William Malone; **W:** Dick Beebe; **C:** Rick Bota; **M:** Don Davis.

House on 92nd Street 1945 Documentary-style thriller finds federal investigator George Briggs (Nolan) contacted by German-American student Bill Dietrich (Eythe), who's been sought out by Nazi spies. Briggs encourages Dietrich to play along and report their nefarious activities to the feds. What Dietrich discovers is that a scientist, working on the atomic bomb project, is actually a Nazi agent. Los of atmosphere and action, with footage to highlight the true-to-life feel. Title refers the house where the head of the Nazi spies resides. 89m/B VHS, DVD, William Eythe, Lloyd Nolan, Signe Hasso, Gene Lockhart, Leo G. Carroll, William Post Jr., Harry Bellaver; **D:** Henry Hathaway; **W:** Barre Lyndon, John Monks Jr., Charles G. Booth; **C:** Norbert Brodine. **M:** David Buttolph. Oscars '45: Story.

The House on Skull Mountain 1974 (PG) The four surviving relatives of a deceased voodoo priestess are in for a bumpy night as they gather at the House on Skull Mountain for the reading of the will. 89m/C VHS, Victor French, Jeanne Michelle, Mike Evans, Jean Durand; **D:** Ron Honthaner.

The House on Sorority Row 1983 Less-than-harrowing story of what happens when seven sorority sisters have a last fling and get back at their housemother at the same time. 90m/C VHS, DVD, Eileen Davidson, Kate McNeil, Robin Meoy, Lois Kelso Hun, Christopher Lawrence, Janis Zido; **D:** Mark Rosman; **W:** Mark Rosman; **C:** Tim Suhrstedt; **M:** Richard Band.

The House on Straw Hill Expose; Trauma 1976 (R) A successful novelist is intrigued by an attractive woman who lives in an isolated farmhouse. Her presence inspires gory hallucinations, lust, and violence. 84m/C VHS, GB Udo Kier, Linda Hayden, Fiona Richmond, Karl Howman, Patsy Smart; **D:** James Kenelm Clarke; **W:** James Kenelm Clarke; **C:** Denis Lewiston.

House on the Edge of the Park 1985 (R) Fact-based story about a dangerous cult and its followers. 94m/C VHS, David Harrod, Terri Harrel, Lisa Marie Newmyer; **D:** Robert Burge; **C:** Eric Scott; **M:** David Connor.

House on the Edge of the Park Woof! La Casa Nel Parco 1984 A frustrated would-be womanizer takes revenge on a parade of women during an all-night party. 91m/C VHS, DVD, IT David Alexande(s) Hess, Lorraine (De Sette) De Selle; **D:** Ruggero Deodato.

The House on Todville Road 1995 (R)

House Party 1990 (R) Light-hearted, black hip-hop version of a '50s teen comedy with rap duo Kid 'n' Play. After his father grounds him for fighting, a high-schooler attempts all sorts of wacky schemes to get to his friend's party. Sleeper hit features real-life music rappers and some dynamite dance numbers. 100m/C VHS, DVD, Christopher Reid, Christopher Martin, Martin Lawrence, Tisha Campbell, Paul Anthony, A.J. (Anthony) Johnson, Robin Harris; **D:** Reginald Hudlin; **W:** Reginald Hudlin; **C:** Peter Deming; **M:** Marcus Miller. Sundance.

House Party 2: The Pajama Jam 1991 (R) Rap stars Kid 'N' Play are back in this hip-hop sequel to the original hit. At Harris University Kid 'N Play hustle up overdue tuition by holding a rap group (real life TLC). Strikes out early within spitting distance of first two flicks. 93m/C VHS, DVD, GB Christopher Reid, Christopher Martin, Tisha Campbell, Iman, Queen Latifah, Martin, Angela Means, Tisha Campbell, Bernie Mac, Barbara (Lee) Edwards, Michael Colyar, David Edwards, Betty Lester, Chris Tucker; **D:** Eric Meza; **W:** Takashi Bufford; **M:** Davis Allen Jones.

House Party 3 1994 (R) Kid is engaged to be married and Play tries to set up a blowout bachelor party. The duo are also working on their record producer careers by trying to sign a feisty female rap group (real life TLC). Strikes out early "jammie jam jam." A stellar cast shines in this rap-powered pajama bash. 94m/C VHS, DVD, Christopher Reid, Christopher Martin, Tisha Campbell, Iman, Queen Latifah, Georg Stanford Brown, Martin Lawrence, Eugene Allen, George Anthony Bell, Kannon, Tony Burton, Helen Martin, William Schallert; **D:** Eric Meza; **W:** Takashi Bufford; **M:** David Allen Jones.

The House that Bled to Death 1981 Strange things happen to a family when they move into a run-down house where a murder occurred years before. A part of the BBC's "Hammer House of Horror" TV series. 60m/C VHS, DVD, GB Nicholas Ball, Rachel Davies, Brian Croucher, Pat Maynard, Emma Ridley; **D:** Tom Clegg, Francis Megahy. TV

The House that Dripped Blood 1971 (PG) A Scotland Yard inspector discovers the history of an English country house while investigating an actor's disappearance. Four horror tales comprise the body of this omnibus creeper, following the successful "Tales from the Crypt" mold. Duffell's debut as director. 101m/C VHS, DVD, GB Christopher Lee, Peter Cushing, Jon Pertwee, Denholm Elliott, Ingrid Pitt, John Bennett, Tom Adams, Joss Ackland, Chloe Franks; **D:** Peter Duffell; **W:** Robert Bloch.

The House that Vanished Scream and Die; Psycho Sex Fiend 1973 (R) Semi-exploitative fare about a beautiful young model who witnesses a murder in a house but later can't find the place. Her boyfriend is skeptical. 84m/C VHS, GB Andrea Allan, Karl Lanchbury, Judy Matheson, Maggie Walker, Alex Leppard; **D:** Joseph (Jose Ramas) Larraz.

The House Where Evil Dwells 1982 (R) An American family is subjected to a reign of terror when they move into an old Japanese house possessed by three deadly samurai ghosts. The setting doesn't upgrade the creepiness of the plot. Based on a novel by James Hardiman. 88m/C VHS, DVD, Edward Albert, Susan George, Doug McClure, Amy Barrett, Mako Hattori, Toshiya Maruyama, Henry Mitowa, Tsuyako Okajima, Tsuyuki Sasaki; **D:** Kevin Connor; **W:** Robert Suboteyz; **C:** Jacques Haitkin.

A House without a Christmas Tree 1972 A frustrated middle-aged man denies his young daughter her one desire—a Christmas tree. Charming TV holiday fare. 90m/C VHS, Jason Robards Jr., Lisa Lucas, Mildred Natwick; **D:** Paul Bogart.

The House on Tombstone Hill 1992 An old, abandoned mansion seems like a good investment to

Houseboat 1958 Widower Grant with three precocious kids takes up residence on a houseboat with Italian maid Loren who is actually a socialite, incognito. Naturally, they fall in love. Light, fun Hollywood froth. 110m/C DVD Cary Grant, Sophia Loren, Martha Hyer, Eduardo Ciannelli, Murray Hamilton, Harry Guardino; **D:** Melville Shavelson; **W:** Melville Shavelson, Jack Rose; **M:** George Duning.

Houseguest 1994 (PG) Dumb comedy about mistaken identity finds hard luck dreamer Kevin Franklin (Sinbad) on the run from loan sharks. Fortunately, while trying to make a getaway at the airport, he's mistaken for the childhood buddy (who's also an eminent dentist prompt-ly) of family guy Gary Young (Hartman), who opens his suburban home to his long lost pal. Street smart Kevin naturally manages to solve every dysfunctional family problem that arises while avoiding some inept Mafia thugs. Everyone is oh-so-good-natured but there's nothing new to hold much interest. 109m/C VHS, DVD, Sinbad, Phil Hartman, Jeffrey Jones, Kim Greist, Stan Shaw, Tony Longo, Mason Adams, Paul Ben-Victor, Chauncey Leopaard, Ron Glass, Talia Seider, Kim Murphy; **D:** Randall Miller; **W:** Michael J. Di Gaetano, Lawrence Gay; **C:** Jerzy Zielinski; **M:** John Debney.

Household Saints 1993 (R) Chronicling one family from post-WWII Little Italy through the 1970s, this is a quirky little story about sausage, religion, womorder). Joseph (D'Onofrio) wins his bride (Ullman) in a pinochle game, much to his superstitious Catholic mother's (Malina) chagrin. The product of that union is a slightly obsessive girl (Taylor), who sees visions and wants to be a saint. Interesting study of Italian-American families, and the roles religion and food play in the culture of Little Italy. 124m/C VHS, Tracey Ullman, Vincent D'Onofrio, Lili Taylor, Judith Malina, Michael Rispoli, Victor Argo, Michael Imperioli, Rachael Bella, Illeana Douglas, Joe Grifasi, Sebastian Roche; **D:** Nancy Savoca; **W:** Nancy Savoca, Richard Guay; **C:** Bobby Bukowski; **M:** Stephen Endelman. Ind. Spirit '94: Support. Actress (Taylor).

The Housekeeper Screen and Die; A Judgement in Stone 1986 (R) Tushingham's portrayal of a deranged housekeeper brings this movie to life even as she kills off her employers. 97m/C VHS, CA Rita Tushingham, Ross Petty, Jackie Burroughs, Tom Kneebone, Shelly Peterson, Jessica Steen, Jonathan Crombie; **D:** Ousama Rawi.

The Householder Gharbar 1963 An early Merchant-Ivory collaboration featuring a young Indian schoolteacher whose widowed mother arranges his marriage to a woman he doesn't know. The immature couple find their adjustment to marriage fraught with, sometimes amusing, complications. 101m/B VHS, DVD, IN Shashi Kapoor, Leela Naidu, Durga Khote; **D:** James Ivory; **W:** Ruth Prawer Jhabvala.

How Come Nobody's On Our Side? 1973 (PG) Two out-of-work stuntmen try astrology to find the best time to make some easy money smuggling marijuana out of Mexico. 84m/C VHS, Adam Roarke, Larry Bishop, Alexandra Hay, Rob Reiner, Penny Marshall; **W:** Leigh Chapman.

How Funny Can Sex Be? 1976 (PG) Eight risqué sketches about love and marriage Italian style. 97m/C VHS, IT Giancarlo Giannini, Laura Antonelli, Duilio Del Prete; **D:** Dino Risi.

How Green Was My Valley 1941 Compelling story of the trials and tribulations of a Welsh mining family, from the youthful perspective of the youngest child (played by a 13-year-old McDowall). Spans 50 years, from the turn of the century, when coal mining was a difficult but fair-paying way of life, and ends, after unionization, strikes, deaths, and child abuse, with the demise of a town and its culture. Considered by many to be director Ford's finest work. When WWII prevented shooting on location, producer Zanuck built a facsimile Welsh valley in California (although Ford, who happens to be the town matchmaker. 118m/B VHS, DVD, Walter Pidgeon, Maureen O'Hara, Donald Crisp, Anna Lee, Roddy McDowall, John Loder, Sara Allgood, Barry Fitzgerald, Patric Knowles, Rhys Williams, Arthur Shields, Ann E. Todd, Mae Marsh; **D:** John Ford; **W:** Philip Dunne; **C:** Arthur C. Miller; **M:** Alfred Newman; **Nar:** Irving Pichel. Oscars '41: B&W Cinematog., Director (Ford), Picture, Support. Actor (Crisp), Natl. Film Reg. '90; N.Y. Film Critics '41: Director (Ford).

How Harry Became a Tree Bitter Harvest 2001 (R) Harry, an embittered farmer (Meany) declares war on the most powerful man in town, who happens to be the town matchmaker. In order to marry off his dim but handsome son, Harry finds himself again indebted to

Housekeeping 1987 (PG) A quiet but bizarre comedy by Forsyth (his first American film). A pair of orphaned sisters are cared for by their newly arrived eccentric, free-spirited aunt in a small and small-minded community in Oregon in the 1950s. Conventional townspeople attempt to intervene, but the sisters' relationship with their offbeat aunt has become strong enough to withstand the coercion of the townspeople. May move too slowly for some viewers. Based on novel by Marilynne Robinson. 117m/C VHS, Christine Lahti, Sarah Walker, Andrea Burchill; **D:** Bill Forsyth; **W:** Bill Forsyth; **C:** Michael Coulter; **M:** Michael Gibbs.

Housemaster 1938 In a British boys' school the housemaster is kind and understanding of his schoolboys charges. The stern new headmaster upsets all of that until the students conspire against him. An okay but dated comedy, featuring characters with names like Bimbo and Button. Based on 'Bachelor Born' by Ian Hay, a London stage hit at the time. 95m/B VHS, Otto Kruger, Diana Churchill, Phillips Holmes, Rene Ray, Walter Hudd, George L. Baxt, Cecil Parker, Michael Shepley, Jimmy Hanley, Rosamund Barnes; **D:** Herbert Brenon.

Housesitter 1992 (PG) Newton Davis (Martin), an architect/dreamer, builds his high school sweetheart (Delany) a beautiful house and surprises her with a marriage proposal. She says no, so he has a one-night stand with Gwen (Hawn), who moves into his empty house and assumes the position of Davis's wife, unbeknownst to him. Gwen spins whopper lies and soon has the entire town, including Davis's parents and ex-girlfriend, believing her wacky stories. This romantic screwball comedy is a delight, not only because of the array of other characters who complicate the stories they spin. 102m/C VHS, DVD, Steve Martin, Goldie Hawn, Dana Delany, Julie Harris, Donald McRae, Peter MacNicol, Richard B. Shull, Laurel Cronin, Christopher Durang; **D:** Frank Oz; **W:** Mark Stein, Brian Grazer; **C:** John A. Alonzo; **M:** Miles Goodman.

Housewife Bone, Beverly Hills Nightmare; Dial Pat for Terror 1972 (R) Bone (Kotto) is a vengeful black man, who holds an unhappily married Beverly Hills couple (Duggan and Van Patten) hostage in their home. 96m/C VHS, DVD, Yaphet Kotto, Andrew Duggan, Joyce Van Patten, Jeannie Berlin; **D:** Larry Cohen; **C:** George Folsey Jr.; **M:** Gil Melle.

his nemesis, which only fuels his anger and proves he is his own worst enemy. Engaging Irish drama with a dark comedic edge. 100m/C DVD. *IR IT GB FR* Colm Meaney, Adrian Dunbar, Cillian Murphy, Kerry Condon, Pat Laffan; *D:* Goran Paskaljevic; *W:* Goran Paskaljevic, Christine Walsh, Stephen Walsh; *C:* Milan Spasic; *M:* Stefano Arnaldi.

How High 2001 (R) Genial stoner comedy finds tokers Silas (Method Man) and Jamal (Redman) smoking some extra-potent "smart" ganja that magically gets them into Harvard. There the laid back homeboys clash with uptight Dean Cain (Babatunde) but find time for some fine chicks. 93m/C VHS, DVD. Method Man, Redman, Obba Babatunde, Chuck Davis, Anna Maria Horsford, Fred Willard, Lark Voorhies, Essence Atkins, Jeffrey Jones, Mike Epps, Hector Elizondo, Chris Elwood, Spalding Gray, Tracey Walter, Louis Freese, Al Shearer; *D:* Jesse Dylan; *W:* Dustin Lee Abraham; *C:* Francis Kenny; *M:* Rockwilder.

How I Got into College 1989 (PG-13) A slack, uninspired satire about doofus high school senior Marion Browne (Parker) who is eager to attend the same college as brainy Jessica (Boyle). But both run into problems from the snooty college recruiter (Rocket). More interesting for the cast went on to do in the nineties. 87m/C VHS, DVD. Corey Parker, Lara Flynn Boyle, Christopher Rydell, Anthony Edwards, Phil Hartman, Brian Doyle-Murray, Nora Dunn, Finn Carter, Charles Rocket; *D:* Savage Steve Holland; *W:* Terrel Seltzer; *C:* Robert Elswit; *M:* Joseph Vitarelli.

How I Killed My Father *Comment J'ai Tue Mon Pere* 2003 No fathers were actually killed in the making of this film. Grim, dry melodrama about a man whose life is upset when the father who deserted him as a boy reappears in his life. Jean-Luc (Berling) is an aloof doctor with a seemingly perfect life but very little passion for his work or his family, and he's afraid of having children. Enter his father, Maurice (Bouquet), who storms back in and starts to wear away at his son's appearance of perfection. The result is a metaphorical tug-of-war between the two men. Fontaine's direction is both effective and ruthless as she questions the nature of the relationship between father and son, but it's occasionally heavy-handed and predictable, giving the sense that the characters are doomed before they get a chance to start. 100m/C DVD. *FR SP* Michel Bouquet, Charles Berling, Natacha Regnier, Amira Casar, Hubert Kounde, Stephane Guillon; *D:* Anne Fontaine; *W:* Anne Fontaine, Jacques Fieschi; *C:* Jean-Marc Fabre; *M:* Jocelyn Pook.

How I Learned to Love Women 1966 A British comedy of errors involving a car-loving youth who learns about women and love. 95m/C VHS. *IT FR GE* Michele Mercier, Nadja Tiller, Romina Power, Robert Hoffman, Anita Ekberg; *D:* Luciano Salce; *C:* Erico Menczer; *M:* Ennio Morricone.

How I Spent My Summer Vacation 1997 Squabbling college sweethearts Perry (Lea) and Stephanie (Davis) have decided their battles have blighted their romance and they split up right before their senior year. Perry moves into an apartment with a couple of buddies and pines for his ex, who's independently getting on with her life, although the dating scene turns out to be trying for them both. Sweetly amusing debut for writer/director Fisher. 75m/C VHS, DVD. Ron-Reaco Lee, Deanna Davis, E. Roger Mitchell, Mike Ngaujah, Jade Janise Dixon; *D:* John Fisher; *W:* John Fisher; *C:* Charles Mills; *M:* Johnny Barrow.

How I Won the War 1967 (PG) An inept officer must lead his battalion out of England into the Egyptian desert to conquer a cricket field. Indulgent, scarcely amusing Richard Lester comedy, Lennon, in a bit part, provides the brightest moments. 111m/C VHS, DVD. *GB* Roy Kinnear, John Lennon, Michael Crawford, Michael Hordern; *D:* Richard Lester; *W:* Charles Wood; *C:* David Watkin; *M:* Ken Thorne.

How Many Miles to Babylon? 1982 During WWI, two young men become friends despite their different backgrounds. But one is court-martialed for desertion, and the other is supposed to oversee his execution. 106m/C VHS. *IR IT GB FR* Colm Meaney, Daniel Day-Lewis, Christopher Fairbank; *D:* Moira Armstrong. TV

How Much Do You Love Me? *Combien Tu M'Aimes?* 2005 Downtrodden, ordinary office worker Francois (Campan) tells gorgeous hooker Daniela (Bellucci) that he's won the lottery and invites her to live with him and help him spend his windfall. Naturally, she agrees despite her threatening gangster boyfriend Charly (Depardieu) and the fact that Francois' heart condition flairs up when he gets too, uh, stimulated. French with subtitles. 95m/C DVD. *FR* Monica Bellucci, Gerard Depardieu, Jean-Pierre Darroussin, Bernard Campan; *D:* Bernard Biler; *W:* Bernard Biler; *C:* Francois Catonne.

How She Move 2008 (PG-13) Talented dancer Raya (Wesley) returns to her inner-city Toronto neighborhood from private school after her sister dies of a drug overdose. Desperate for a new route out, she uses her dance talents to earn a spot in an all-male dance troupe, where she must constantly prove herself to be as good as the boys. Film's grit, depth, and excellent choreography make it a cut above the average hip-hop dance movie. 94m/C DVD. *CA* Melanie Nicholls-King, Rutina Wesley, Tre Armstrong, Dwain Murphy, Brennan Gademans, Shawn Desman, Kevin Duhaney; *D:* Ian Iqbal Rashid; *W:* Annmarie Morais; *C:* Andre Pienaar; *M:* Andrew Lockington.

How Stella Got Her Groove Back 1998 (R) Underneath the flawless physique and upscale way of life, fortyish single mom Stella (Bassett) is sad; too much work and no love life is to blame. Coaxed by her best friend Delilah (Goldberg), Stella takes a trip to Jamaica where she falls in love with 20-year-old islander Winston (Diggs in his film debut). A flipside to the May-December romance that is purely more gloss (picturesque shots of the Caribbean landscape) than grit. Bassett glows in a tailor-made role and muscular hunk Diggs is a find, but perfection in casting can't rescue this hollow romance that woefully missteps after a promising beginning. Based on the novel by Terry McMillan. 124m/C VHS, DVD. Angela Bassett, Whoopi Goldberg, Taye Diggs, Regina King, Suzzanne Douglass, Richard Lawson, Michael J. Pagan, Barry (Shabaka) Henley, Sicily; *D:* Kevin Rodney Sullivan; *W:* Ronald Bass, Terry McMillan; *C:* Jeffrey Jur; *M:* Michel Colombier.

How Sweet It Is! 1968 Typical American family takes a zany European vacation. Looks like a TV sitcom and is about as entertaining. National Lampoon's version is a lot more fun. 99m/C VHS. James Garner, Debbie Reynolds, Maurice Ronet, Paul Lynde, Erin Moran, Marcel Dalio, Terry-Thomas, Jenie Jackson; *D:* Jerry Paris; *W:* Jerry Belson; *C:* Lucien Ballard.

How Tasty Was My Little Frenchman *Meu Frances* 1971 French explorer is captured by a cannibal tribe in the jungles of Brazil. He's treated very well and attempts to learn tribal customs to avoid his fate—he's going to be the main course in a ceremonial dinner. French and Tupi with subtitles. 80m/C VHS, DVD. *BR* Arduino Colasanti, Ana Maria Magalhaes, Ital Natur, Eduardo Embassahy; *D:* Nelson Pereira dos Santos.

How the West Was Fun 1995 The Olsen gals are visiting great godmother Natty's dude ranch, which is in financial difficulty, and must outsmart her greedy son Bart (Mull), a land grabber who wants to turn the ranch into an environmentally unfriendly western theme park. Made for TV. 93m/C VHS, DVD. Mary-Kate Olsen, Ashley (Fuller) Olsen, Martin Mull, Michele Greene, Patrick Cassidy, Leon Pownall, Margaret "Peg" Phillips; *D:* Stuart Margolin; *M:* Richard Bellis. TV

How the West Was Won 1963 (G) A panoramic view of the American West, focusing on three generations of one family, set against the background of wars and historical events. Particularly notable for its impressive cast list and expansive western settings. 165m/C VHS, DVD. John Wayne, Carroll Baker, Lee J. Cobb, Spencer Tracy, Gregory Peck, Karl Malden, Robert Preston, Eli Wallach, Henry Fonda, George Peppard, Debbie Reynolds, Carolyn Jones, Richard Widmark, James Stewart, Walter Brennan, Andy Devine, Raymond Massey, Thelma Ritter, Russ Tamblyn; *D:* John Ford, Henry Hathaway, George Marshall; *W:* James R. Webb; *C:* Milton Krasner, Charles B(ryant) Lang Jr. Oscars '63: Film Editing, Sound, Story & Screenplay, Natl. Film Reg. '97.

How to Be a Woman and Not Die in the Attempt *Be a Woman and Not Die Trying; Como ser Mujer y No Morir en El* 1991 Carmen has just turned 42, is married to her third husband, and is raising three children. She's also very serious about her journalistic career on the local paper. So, she's a modern woman with too much to do and too little time, trying to juggle her home and her work and still keep a sense of humor. Based on the novel by Carmen Rico-Godoy. Spanish with subtitles. 96m/C VHS, DVD, *SP* Carmen Maura, Antonio Resines; *D:* Ana Belen; *W:* Carmen Rico Godoy; *C:* Juan Amoros.

How to Beat the High Cost of Living 1980 (PG) Three suburban housewives decide to beat inflation by taking up robbery, and they start by planning a heist at the local shopping mall. Comedic talent can't salvage whipped script and direction. 105m/C VHS, DVD. Jessica Lange, Susan St. James, Jane Curtin, Richard Benjamin, Eddie Albert, Dabney Coleman, Fred Willard, Cathryn Damon, Art Metrano; *D:* Robert Scheerer.

How to Break Up a Happy Divorce 1976 A divorced woman starts a vigorous campaign to win her ex-husband back by dating another man to make him jealous. Lightweight comedy. 74m/C VHS. Barbara Eden, Hal Linden, Peter Bonerz, Marcia Rodd, Harold Gould; *D:* Jerry Paris. TV

How to Commit Marriage 1969 (PG) Hope and Wyman have been married for 20 years when their daughter (Cameron) decides to marry her college boyfriend (Matheson). His father (Gleason) tries to stop the wedding, fails, but sticks around to cause more trouble. Subplots involve the divorced duo's new loves and the fact that they're about to become grandparents find the comedy is completely uninspired. 96m/C VHS, DVD. Bob Hope, Jane Wyman, Jackie Gleason, Joanna Cameron, Tim Matheson, Beatrice Arthur, Leslie Nielsen, Tina Louise, Paul Stewart, Prof. Irwin Corey; *D:* Norman Panama; *W:* Ben Starr, Michael Kanin; *C:* Charles B(ryant) Lang Jr.; *M:* Joseph J. Lilley.

How to Deal 2003 (PG-13) High schooler Halley (Moore) decides love bumps on the road of life. Her parents split when DJ dad Len (Gallagher) has a mid-life crisis and romances a younger woman. Bitter mom Lydia (Janney) copes by getting involved with the wedding plans of older daughter Ashley (Garrison), whose wealthy parents. Then Halley's best friend Scarlett (Holden) finds out she's preggers after her boyfriend is killed in an accident. So Halley is none too receptive to romance when sensitive hunk Macon (Ford) comes around. Adapted from the young adult novels "Someone Like You" and "That Summer" by Sarah Dessen. 101m/C VHS, DVD. *US* Mandy Moore, Allison Janney, Peter Gallagher, Trent Ford, Alexandra Holden, Dylan Baker, MacKenzie Astin, Connie Ray, Nina Foch, Sonja Smits, Mary Catherine Garrison; *D:* Clare Kilner; *W:* Neena Beber; *C:* Eric Alan Edwards; *M:* David Kitay.

How to Eat Fried Worms 2006 (PG) New kid in school tries to put the class bully in his place by meeting the challenge of eating 10 worms—each served up in increasingly creative but decidedly unappetizing ways—in one day without ralphing. The 1973 kid-lit classic of the same name by Thomas Rockwell is sliced and diced to fit its over-the-top big-screen rendering (really, what kids know their way around a kitchen like these do?). But with decent performances by the kiddie cast, it's big-time gross-out fun for the youngins, tied up with a positive (if equally barf-inducing) message about standing up for yourself—if you can get to the end without wretching, that is. 98m/C DVD. *US* Luke Benward, Hallie Kate Eisenberg, Alexander Gould, James Rebhorn, Adam Hicks, Austin Rogers, Tom Cavanagh, Kimberly Williams; *D:* Bob Dolman; *W:* Bob Dolman; *C:* Richard Rutkowski; *M:* Mark Mothersbaugh, Bob Mothersbaugh.

How to Eat Your Watermelon in White Company (and Enjoy It) 2005 Full-bodied documentary paying tribute to the life and times of Melvin Van Peebles, the famed black filmmaker most noted for 1971's "Sweet Sweetback's Baadasssss Song." Van Peebles was also an Air Force navigator, cable car operator, novelist in two languages, composer, recording artist, and floor trader at the American Stock Exchange. Title comes from an essay written by Van Peebles. 85m/C DVD. *US D:* Joe Angio; *C:* Michael Solomon, Joe Angio; *M:* Jeremy Parise.

How to Frame a Figg 1971 (G) Bookkeeper Hollis A. Figg (Knotts) is working at Dalton's corrupt city hall where he's setup to be the patsy in the fraudulent doings of the mayor and city council. But his best friends Prentiss (Welker) and Ema Letha (Joyce) set out to prove the bumbler's innocence. 103m/C VHS, DVD. Don Knotts, Elaine Joyce, Frank Welker, Joe Flynn, Edward Andrews, Yvonne Craig, Parker Fennelly, Fay DeWitt; *D:* Alan Rafkin; *W:* George Tibbles; *C:* William Margulies; *M:* Vic Mizzy.

How to Get Ahead in Advertising 1989 (R) A cynical, energetic satire about a manic advertising idea man who becomes so disgusted with trying to sell a pimple cream that he quits the business. Ultimately he grows a pimple of his own that talks and begins to take over his life. Acerbic and hilarious. 95m/C VHS, DVD. *GB* Richard E. Grant, Rachel Ward, Susan Wooldridge, Mick Ford, Richard Wilson, John Shrapnel, Jacqueline Tong; *D:* Bruce Robinson; *W:* Bruce Robinson; *C:* Peter Hannan; *M:* David Dundas, Rick Wentworth.

How to Go Out on a Date in Queens 2006 (R) Interesting cast, lame story involving three romantic crises set in a Queens restaurant called Mandatori's. Self-proclaimed dating expert Stan (Dritlinger) sets up a double date with his widowed friend Artie (Estes) that turns into a disaster. Bookie Johnny (Alexander) finds out that he owes a lot of money to the Russian mob and must blow town just as his gal Ann Marie (Dunford) tells him she's pregnant. And assistant manager Elizabeth (Lynn) is sure her boyfriend Frankie (Morales) is going to propose but he wants to use their life savings to bet on the Super Bowl. 90m/C DVD. Robert Estes, Jason Alexander, Esai Morales, Brian Dillinger, Jason Alexander, Christine Dunford, Meredith Scott Lynn, Ron Perlman, Alison Eastwood, Enrique Murciano, Bjorn Johnson, Michelle Danner; *D:* Michelle Danner; *W:* Richard Vetere; *C:* Jens Sturup; *M:* Shark.

How to Kill 400 Duponts *Arriva Dorellik* 1968 Bumbling Scotland Yard detective is off to France to stop a master criminal from trying to kill off the rich Dupont family. Why? So he'll be the only one left with any claim to the remaining family fortune. 90m/C VHS. *IT* Terry-Thomas, Johnny Dorelli, Margaret Lee, Rosella Como, Riccardo Garrone; *D:* Steno; *W:* Franco Castellano; *C:* Mario Capriotti; *M:* Franco Pisano.

How to Kill Your Neighbor's Dog 2001 (R) Critically acclaimed playwright Peter McGowen (Branagh) has fallen on hard times after a string of flops and is feeling the pressure from his sunny-natured wife Melanie (Wright Penn) to have kids. He's trying to fix his latest work with any claim to the remaining family fortune. The grouch also keeps him awake nights. The grouch also finds he must befriend a neighbor's daughter, Amy (Hofrichter), because he needs a model for the child role in his play, although Amy's presence does some not entirely unexpected reexamination of Peter and Melanie's marriage. Branagh is amusing/sharp-tongued but the film has a squishy, center. 108m/C VHS, DVD. Kenneth Branagh, Robin Wright Penn, Jared Harris, Suzi Hofrichter, Johnathon Schaech, Peter Riegert, Lynn Redgrave; D: Michael Kalesniko; W: Michael Kalesniko; C: Hubert Taczanowski; M: David Robbins.

How to Lose a Guy in 10 Days ♂♂ 2003 (PG-13)
(McConaughey), and then be so obnoxious that he will dump her in 10 days so she can write an article about it for Composure magazine. Ben has placed a bet with his colleagues that he can get any woman to fall in love with him in 10 days so he can get an account he wants. So while Andie is being the needy, clingy narcissic woman from hell, Ben patiently puts up with it for his own reasons. It's a universal rule that such contrivances in a romantic comedy guarantee that the two will genuinely fall in love. Unfortunately, the laughs are far too sparse and both characters too distasteful in their deceit for you to care. 112m/C VHS, DVD. US Kate Hudson, Matthew McConaughey, Adam Goldberg, Michael Michele, Shalom Harlow, Bebe Neuwirth, Robert Klein, Kathryn Hahn, Thomas Lennon, Annie Parisse; D: Donald Petrie; W: Kristen Buckley, Brian Regan, Burr Steers; C: John Bailey; M: David Newman.

How to Lose Your Lover
50 Ways to Leave Your Lover 2004 Owen (Schneider) lives in L.A. and writes trashy celebrity biographies. He decides to break free and move to New York to find intellectual fulfillment. So he won't be tempted to return, Owen crudely breaks all ties to friends and family. Of course, just as he's leaving, he meets the girl of his dreams, Val (Westfeldt), and decides to put her through various romantic trials to see if it could be true love. Val should personally put Owen on that plane instead. 95m/C DVD. Paul Schneider, Jennifer Westfeldt, Poppy Montgomery, Tori Spelling, Fred Willard; D: Joran Hawley; W: Joran Hawley; C: Dino Parks; M: Stephen Trask.

How to Make an American Quilt ♂♂½ 1995 (PG-13) Slow-moving take on female friendship and marriage revolves around perennial grad student Finn (the mopey Ryder), who is frantic to both finish her third attempted thesis and to answer a marriage proposal from practically perfect beau Sam (Mulroney). She takes a summer refuge with her grandmother (Burstyn), where a variety of family friends work on her wedding quilt as they tell stories of loves lost and won. Lots of (somewhat overextended) flashbacks some get the short end of the script. Based on the article by Whitney Otto. 109m/C VHS, DVD. Winona Ryder, Ellen Burstyn, Anne Bancroft, Lois Smith, Jean Simmons, Kate Nelligan, Maya Angelou, Alfre Woodard, Demot Mulroney, Kate Capshaw, Rip Torn, Derrick O'Connor, Loren Dean, Samantha Mathis, Joanna Going, Tim Guinee, Johnathon Schaech, Claire Danes, Jared Leto, Esther Rolle, Melinda Dillon, Alicia (Lecy) Goranson, Maria Celedonio, Mykelti Williamson; D: Jocelyn Moorhouse; W: Jane Anderson; C: Janusz Kaminski; M: Thomas Newman.

How to Make a Monster ♂♂ 2001 (R) Computer game company hires three ambitious programmers to finish a game and bring it to market in four weeks. A telemetry suit is used to render a 3-D version of the game's villain but a power surge brings the program to life. Now the game's killer cyborg 'AKA the telemetry suit) goes after the threesome, thinking they're players in the game. Basically takes only the title from the 1958 A.I.P. flick. 90m/C VHS, DVD. Steven Culp, Clea DuVall, Jason Marsden, Tyler Mane, Julie Strain, Karim Prince; D: George Huang; W: George Huang; C: Steven Firestone; M: David Reynolds. CABLE

How to Make a Monster ♂♂ 1958 In-joke from the creators of youth-oriented '50s AIP monster flicks: a mad makeup man's homebrew greasepaint brainwashes the actors. Disguised as famous monsters, they kill horror-hating movie execs. Mild fun if—and only if—you treasure the genre. Conway repeats his role as Teenage Frankenstein, but the studio couldn't get Michael Landon for the Teenage Werewolf. 73mB VHS. Robert H. Harris, Paul Brinegar, Gary Conway, Gary Clarke, Malcolm Atterbury, Dennis Cross, John Ashley, Morris Ankrum, Walter Reed, Heather Ames; D: Herbert L. Strock.

How to Make a Doll ♂ 1968 Lewis' sex farce about an extremely shy professor whose ineptness with women inspires him to invent android females to satisfy his sexual needs. 81m/C VHS. Robert S. Woods, Jim Vance, Patricia Rhea; D: Herschell Gordon Lewis; W: Herschell Gordon Lewis, Bert Ray.

How to Murder Your Wife ♂♂♂ 1964 While drunk, a cartoonist marries an unknown woman and then frantically tries to think of ways to get rid of her—even contemplating murder. Frantic comedy is tailored for Lemmon. 118m/C VHS, DVD. Jack Lemmon, Terry-Thomas, Virna Lisi, Eddie Mayehoff, Sidney Blackmer, Claire Trevor, Mary Wickes, Jack Albertson; D: Richard Quine; W: George Axelrod; C: Harry Stradling Sr.

How to Pick Up Girls ♂♂ 1978 Comic tale based on Eric Weber's bestseller follows the exploits of a small-town boy who moves to New York City and finds the secret to picking up women. Made for television. 93m/C VHS. Desi Arnaz Jr., Bess Armstrong, Fred McCarren, Polly Bergen, Richard Dawson, Alan King, Aba Vigoda, Deborah Raffin; D: Bill Persky. TV

How to Seduce a Woman Woof! 1974 A playboy attempts to bed five supposedly unattainable women. 108m/C VHS. Angus Duncan, Mary Ingels, Lillian Randolph; D: Charles Martin; W: Charles Martin; C: William Cronjager; M: Stu Phillips.

How to Steal a Million ♂♂♂ 1966 Sophisticated comedy-crime caper involving a million-dollar heist of a sculpture in a Paris art museum. Hepburn and O'Toole are perfectly cast as partners in crime and Griffith gives a good performance as Hepburn's art-forging father. A charming, lightweight script and various Parisian locales combine for fun, above-average fluff. Based on the story "Venus Rising" by George Bradshaw. 127m/C VHS, DVD. Audrey Hepburn, Peter O'Toole, Eli Wallach, Hugh Griffith, Charles Boyer, Fernand Gravey, Marcel Dalio, Jacques Marin; D: William Wyler; W: Harry Kurnitz; C: Charles B(yan) Lang Jr.; M: John Williams.

How to Stuff a Wild Bikini ♂♂ 1965 Tired next to last feature in the overlong tradition of Frankie and Annette doing the beach thing, featuring a pregnant Funicello (though this is hidden and not part of the plot). Avalon actually has only a small role as the jealous boyfriend trying to see if Annette will remain faithful while he's away on military duty. Keaton is the witch doctor who helps Frankie keep Annette true. "Playboy" playmates wander about in small swimsuits, garage band extraordinaire "The Kingsmen" play themselves, and Brian Wilson of the "Beach Boys" drops by. Followed by "Ghost in the Invisible Bikini," the only movie in the series that isn't on video. ♪After the Party; Better Be Ready; Follow Your Leader; Give Her Lovin'; How About Us?; How to Stuff a Wild Bikini; I'm the Boy Next Door; Madison Avenue; The

Howard the Duck ♂ 1986 (PG) Big-budget LucasFilm adaptation of the short-lived Marvel comic book about an alien, resembling a cigar-chomping duck, who gets sucked into a vortex, lands on Earth and saves it from the Dark Overlords. While he's at it, he befriends a nice young lady in a punk rock band and stars in one of the '80s' worst major films, although it seems to work well with children, given the simple storyline and good special effects. 111m/C VHS. Lea Thompson, Jeffrey Jones, Tim Robbins, Elizabeth Segal, Thomas Dolby, Paul Guilfoyle, Dominique Davalos, Holly Robinson, Tommy Swerdlow, Richard Edson, Mary Huyck; W: Willard Huyck, Gloria Katz; C: Richard H. Kline; M: John Barry, Sylvester Levay; V: Chip Zien, Richard Kiley. Golden Raspberries '86: Worst Picture, Worst Screenplay.

How to Marry a Millionaire ♂♂½ 1953 Three models pool their money and rent a lavish apartment in a campaign to trap millionaire 'husbands. Clever performances by three lead women salvage a vehicle intended primarily to bolster Monroe's career. The opening street scene, with the accompanying theme music, was a state-of-the-art achievement of screen and sound "for them." Remake of "The Greeks Had a Word for Them." 96m/C VHS, DVD. Charlotte Austin, Lauren Bacall, Marilyn Monroe, Betty Grable, William Powell, David Wayne, Cameron Mitchell; D: Jean Negulesco; W: Nunnally Johnson; C: Joe MacDonald; M: Alfred Newman.

How to Succeed with Girls ♂ 1964 Marginally funny comedy about pious wax salesman (Leder) who unwittingly enlists the aid of a secret fantasy life who unwittingly enlists the aid and fantasy wife who unwittingly enlists the aid and fantasy... 83m/C VHS. Marissa Mathes, Rue McClanahan, Paul Leder; C: Leon Schnier; D: Edward A. Biery.

How U Like Me Now? ♂♂♂ 1992 (R) Comedy set on Chicago's south side focuses on Thomas, an attractive but unmotivated guy with low earning potential, and his girl Valerie a pretentious over-achiever who wants much more than he's able to offer. Robert's second directorial effort offers a fresh look at African Americans on film with plenty of lively supporting characters and witty dialogue. Filmed on a $600,000 budget. 109m/C VHS, DVD. Darnell Williams, Salli Richardson, Daniel Gardner, Raymond Whitefield, Debra Crable, Jonelle Kennedy, Byron Stewart, Charnele Brown, Daryll Roberts; D: Darryl Roberts; W: Darryl Roberts; M: Kahil El Zabar; C: Chuck Webb.

How You Look to Me ♂♂ 2005 (R) William Marshall (Romans), the son of a wealthy Kentucky horse racing family, reluctantly heads back to graduate school to prevent being cut off financially by his family. Christopher Lee, Annie McEnroe, Marsha A. Hunt, Rob Brown, Ferdinand "Fer-dy" Mayne, Judd Omen, Jimmy Nail; D: Philippe Mora; W: Gary Brandner, Robert Sarno; C: Geoffrey Stephenson.

Howling 3: The Marsupials ♂♂ Howling 3: Marsupials; Howling 3 1987 (PG-13) Australians discover a pouch-laden form of lycanthrope. Third "Howling" (surprise), second from Mora and better than his first. 94m/C VHS, DVD. AU Barry Otto, Imogen Annesley, Dasha Blahova, Max Fairchild, Ralph Cotterill, Leigh Biclos, Frank Thring Jr., Michael Pate; D: Philippe Mora; W: Philippe Mora; C: Louis Irving; M: Allan Zavod.

Howling 4: The Original Nightmare ♂ 1988 (R) A woman novelist hears the call of the wild while taking a rest cure in the country. This werewolf tale has nothing to do with the other sequels and is a varied group of people stranded in a European castle are individually hunted down by evil 99m/C VHS. DVD. Philip Davis, Victoria Catlin, Elizabeth She,

Howling 5: The Rebirth ♂ 1989 (R) The fifth in the disconnected horror series, in which a varied group of people stranded in a European castle are individually hunted down by evil 99m/C VHS.

How to Succeed in Business without Really Trying ♂♂½ 1967 Classic musical comedy about a window-washer who charms his way to the top of a major company. Robert Morse repeats his Tony winning Broadway role. Loosely based on a non-fiction book of the same title by Shepherd Mead, which Morse purchases on his first day of work. Excellent transfer of stage to film, with choreography by Moreda expanding Bob Fosse's original plan. Dynamite from start to finish. ♪I Believe in You; The Company Way; Coffee Break; The Brotherhood of Man; A Secretary Is Not A Toy; Grand Old Ivy; Been A Long Day; Rosemary; Finch's Frolic; Love From a Heart of Gold. 121m/C VHS, DVD. Robert Morse, Michele Lee, Rudy Vallee, Anthony Teague, George David Swift, Abe Burrows; C: Burnett Guffey; M: Frank Loesser.

The Howards of Virginia ♂♂½ 1940 A lavish Hollywood historical epic, detailing one of the first film's victims) investigates a Transylvanian werewolf-ridden castle and gets mangled for his trouble. Followed by more sequels. 91m/C VHS, DVD. FR iT Sybil Danning, Christopher Lee, Annie McEnroe, the adventures of a backwoodsman and the rich Virginia girl he marries as their families become involved in the Revolutionary War. 117mB VHS, DVD. Cary Grant, Martha Scott, Cedric Hardwicke, Alan Marshal, Richard Carlson, Paul Kelly, Irving Bacon, Tom Drake, Anne Revere, Ralph Byrd, Alan Ladd; D: Frank Lloyd.

The Howling ♂♂♂ 1981 (R) A pretty TV reporter takes a rest at a clinic and discovers slowly that its denizens are actually werewolves. Crammed with inside jokes, this horror comedy pioneered the use of the body-altering prosthetic make-up (by Rob Bottin) now essential for on-screen man-to-wolf transformations. If last count, followed by six sequels. 91m/C VHS, DVD. Dee Wallace Stone, Patrick Macnee, Dennis Dugan, Christopher Stone, Belinca Balaski, Kevin McCarthy, John Carradine, Slim Pickens, Elisabeth Brooks, Robert Picardo, Dick Miller, Kenneth Tobey, Meshach Taylor; Cameos: John Sayles, Roger Corman, Forrest J Ackerman; D: Joe Dante; W: John Sayles, Terence H. Winkless; C: John Hora; M: Pino Donaggio.

Howling 2: Your Sister Is a Werewolf ♂♂ 1985 (R) A policeman (the brother of one of the first film's victims) investigates a Transylvanian werewolf-ridden castle and gets mangled for his trouble. Followed by more sequels. 91m/C VHS, DVD. FR iT Sybil Danning, Christopher Lee, Annie McEnroe, Marsha A. Hunt, Reb Brown, Ferdinand "Ferdy" Mayne, Judd Omen, Jimmy Nail; D: Philippe Mora; W: Gary Brandner, Robert Sarno; C: Geoffrey Stephenson.

Howard's End ♂♂♂♂ 1992 (PG) E.M. Forster's 1910 novel about property, privilege, class differences, and Edwardian society is brought to enchanting life by the Merchant Ivory team. A tragic series of events occurs after two impulsive middleclass sisters, Margaret (Thompson) and Helen (Bonham Carter), become involved with the working class Basts (West, Duffett), and the wealthy Wilcox family (Hopkins, Redgrave). Tragedy aside, this is a visually beautiful effort with subtle performances where a glance or a gesture says as much as any dialog. The winner of numerous awards and wide critical acclaim. Thompson is especially notable as the compassionate Margaret, while Hopkins plays the repressed English gentleman brilliantly. 143m/C VHS, DVD, GB Anthony Hopkins, Emma Thompson, Helena Bonham-Carter, Vanessa Redgrave, James Wilby, Samuel West, Jemma Redgrave, Nicola Duffett, Prunella Scales, Joseph Bennett; Cameos: Simon Callow; D: James Ivory; W: Ruth Prawer Jhabvala; C: Tony Pierce-Roberts; M: Richard Robbins. Oscars '92: Actress (Thompson), Adapt. Screenplay, Art Dir./ Set Dec.; British Acad. '92: Actress (Thompson); Golden Globes '92: Actress (Thompson); Natl Bd. of Review '92: Actress (Thompson), Director (Ivory); Film: N.Y. Film Critics '92: Actress (Thompson); Natl. Soc. Film Critics '92: Actress (Thompson).

Ben Cole, William Shockley; **D:** Neal Sundstrom; **C:** Arledge Armenaki.

Howling 6: The Freaks 🦴🦴½ **1990 (R)** Hideous werewolf suffers from multiple sequels, battles with vampire at freak show, and discovers that series won't die. Next up: "Howling 7: The Nightmare that Won't Go Away." **102m/C VHS.** Brendan Hughes, Michelle Matheson, Sean Gregory Sullivan, Antonio Fargas, Carol Lynley, Jared Barclay, Bruce Payne; **D:** Hope Perello.

The Howling: New Moon Rising 🦴½ *Howling 7* **1995 (R)** Small desert town is plagued by a series of terrifying murders believed to be the work of a werewolf, whose victims then join his vicious pack. **92m/C VHS.** Clive Turner, John Ramsden, Ernest Kester, Elizabeth She, Jacqueline Armitage, Romy Windsor; **D:** Clive Turner; **W:** Clive Turner.

Howl's Moving Castle 🦴🦴🦴½ *Hauru no ugoku shiro* **2004 (PG)** More eye-popping anime from Miyazaki. Young wizard Howl (Bale) and his moveable castle travel around the countryside to avoid his enemy, the Witch of the Waste (Bacall). When Howl rescues Sophie (Mortimer) from thugs, the jealous Witch turns her into an old woman (now voiced by Simmons). Sophie appoints herself the castle housekeeper and encounters various strange characters and many adventures. There's a lot of plot but it's the visuals that will keep attention riveted. Adapted from Diana Wynne Jones' 2000 fantasy novel. There is also a Japanese-language version. **120m/C DVD.** *JP* **D:** Hayao Miyazaki; **W:** Hayao Miyazaki; **C:** Atsushi Okui; **M:** Joe Hisaishi; **V:** Emily Mortimer, Jean Simmons, Christian Bale, Lauren Bacall, Blythe Danner, Josh Hutcherson, Billy Crystal, Jena Malone, Liliana Mumy. L.A. Film Critics '05: Orig. Score; N.Y. Film Critics '05: Animated Film.

H.P. Lovecraft's Necronomicon: Book of the Dead 🦴🦴 *Necronomicon* **1993 (R)** Trilogy of stories: Payne encounters a demon who resurrects his late wife and son in "The Drowning"; "The Cold" finds a reporter investigating a series of murders and uncovers crazed doctor Warner, who's discovered the secret to immortality; and a female cop discovers a subterranean alien in "Whispers." Combs serves as narrator, Lovecraft. **103m/C VHS, DVD.** Bruce Payne, Belinda Bauer, Bess Meyer, David Warner, Signy Coleman, Richard Lynch, Dennis Christopher, Jeffrey Combs, Maria Ford, Don Calfa; **D:** Brian Yuzna, Shusuke (Shu) Kaneko, Christophe Gans; **W:** Brian Yuzna, Christophe Gans, Brent Friedman, Kazunori Ito; **C:** Russ Brandt; **M:** Joseph LoDuca, Daniel Licht.

Huck and the King of Hearts 🦴🦴½ **1993 (PG)** When a cardshark and his young friend Huck travel the country searching for Huck's long-lost grandfather, they find adventure everywhere from Hannibal, Missouri to L.A. to Vegas. Loose, contemporary adaptation of Mark Twain's "The Adventures of Huckleberry Finn." **96m/C VHS.** Chauncey Leopardi, Graham Greene, Dee Wallace Stone, Joe Piscopo, John Astin, Gretchen Becker; **D:** Michael Keusch; **W:** Christopher Sturgeon; **M:** Chris Saranec.

Huckleberry Finn 🦴🦴 **1974 (G)** The musical version of the Mark Twain story about the adventures of a young boy and a runaway slave encounter along the Mississippi River. **114m/C VHS.** Jeff East, Paul Winfield, Harvey Korman, David Wayne, Arthur O'Connell, Gary Merrill, Natalie Trundy, Lucille Benson; **D:** J. Lee Thompson.

Huckleberry Finn 🦴🦴½ **1975 (G)** Whitewashed version of the Twain classic features post Opie Howard as the incredible Huck and Dano as the sharp witted short storyist. Made for TV. **74m/C VHS.** Ron Howard, Donny Most, Royal Dano, Antonio Fargas, Jack Elam, Merle Haggard, Rance Howard, Jean Howard, Clint Howard, Shug Fisher, Sarah Selby, Bill Erwin; **C:** Robert Totten. TV

Huckleberry Finn 🦴½ **1981** A version of the classic Mark Twain novel about the adventures of a young boy and a runaway slave encounter as they travel down the Mississippi River. **72m/C VHS.** **V:** Timothy Gibbs.

The Hucksters 🦴🦴🦴 **1947** Account of a man (Gable) looking for honesty and integrity in the radio advertising world and finding little to work with. All performances are excellent; but Greenstreet, as the tyrannical head of a soap company, is a stand out. Deborah Kerr's American debut. Based on the novel by Frederic Wakeman. **115m/B VHS.** Clark Gable, Deborah Kerr, Sydney Greenstreet, Adolphe Menjou, Ava Gardner, Keenan Wynn, Edward Arnold; **D:** Jack Conway; **W:** Edward Chodorov, Luther Davis, George Wells; **C:** Harold Rosson; **M:** Lennie Hayton.

Hud 🦴🦴🦴🦴 **1963** Newman is a hard-driving, hard-chasing, woman-chasing young man whose life is a revolt against the principles of stern father Douglas. Neal is outstanding as the family housekeeper. Excellent photography. Based on the Larry McMurtry novel "Horseman, Pass By." **112m/B VHS, DVD.** Paul Newman, Melvyn Douglas, Patricia Neal, Brandon de Wilde, John Ashley; **D:** Martin Ritt; **W:** Irving Ravetch, Harriet Frank Jr.; **C:** James Wong Howe; **M:** Elmer Bernstein. Oscars '63: Actress (Neal), B&W Cinematog., Support. Actor (Douglas); British Acad. '63: Actress (Neal); Natl. Bd. of Review '63: Actress (Neal), Support. Actor (Douglas); N.Y. Film Critics '63: Actress (Neal), Screenplay.

Hudson Hawk 🦴 **1991 (R)** A big-budget star vehicle with little else going for it. Willis plays a master burglar released from prison, only to find himself trapped by the CIA into one last theft. Everyone in the cast tries to be extra funny, resulting in a disjointed situation where no one is. Weakly plotted, poorly paced. **95m/C VHS, DVD.** Bruce Willis, Danny Aiello, Andie MacDowell, James Coburn, Sandra Bernhard, Richard E. Grant, Frank Stallone; **D:** Michael Lehmann; **W:** Steven E. de Souza, Daniel Waters; **C:** Dante Spinotti; **M:** Michael Kamen, Robert Kraft. Golden Raspberries '91: Worst Picture, Worst Director (Lehmann), Worst Screenplay.

The Hudsucker Proxy 🦴🦴🦴 **1993 (PG)** In an effort to scare off would-be investors in a public stock offering dim bulb mailboy Robbins is installed as the Prez of Hudsucker Industries (in 1958) by Board Director Newman after corporate magnate Hudsucker (Durning) takes a swan dive from the 44th floor. First truly mainstream effort from the maverick Coen brothers is peppered with obscure references to numerous points on the historical map of cinematic style, and trots out an equally old but instantly recognizable story. Will delight Coen fans, but may be too dark for others. Destined to scare but history profs busy for decades. **115m/C VHS, DVD.** Tim Robbins, Paul Newman, Jennifer Jason Leigh, Charles Durning, John Mahoney, Jim Truefrost, Bill Cobbs, Bruce Campbell, Steve Buscemi; **Cameos:** Peter Gallagher; **D:** Joel Coen; **W:** Ethan Coen, Joel Coen, Sam Raimi; **C:** Roger Deakins; **M:** Carter Burwell.

Hue and Cry 🦴🦴 **1947** Nobody believes a young boy when he discovers crooks are sending coded messages in a weekly children's magazine. A detective writer finally believes his story and they set off to capture the crooks. **82m/B VHS.** *GB* Alastair Sim, Jack Warner, Frederick Piper, Jack Lambert, Joan Dowling; **D:** Charles Crichton.

Hugh Hefner: Once Upon a Time 🦴🦴🦴 **1992 (R)** Fascinating look at the "Bunny" king and Playboy Enterprises. His celebrated life of isolation and excess at the Playboy mansion is portrayed as is the founding of "Playboy" (with their notorious Bunnies). Includes interviews, home movies, and photographs. Admiring yet not without a few sharp edges. **91m/C VHS, DVD.** Hugh Hefner; **D:** Robert Heath; **Nar:** James Coburn.

Hughes & Harlow: Angels in Hell 🦴 **1977 (R)** The story of the romance that occurred between Howard Hughes and Jean Harlow during the filming of "Hell's Angels" in 1930. **94m/C VHS.** Lindsay Bloom, Victor Holchak, David McLean, Royal Dano, Adam Roarke, Linda Cristal; **D:** Larry Buchanan.

Hugo Pool 🦴½ **1997 (R)** Pool cleaner Hugo Dugay (Milano) has to clean the pools of 44 backyard eccentrics. Reluctantly, she must enlist the aid of her gambler mom (Moriarty) and drug addict father (McDowell). Bizarre characters abound, including Downey Jr. overacting as Hungarian film director Franz Mazur, whose accent changes with each line. Most interesting is Dempsey as ALS-afflicted Floyd Galen. The romance between Floyd and Hugo supplies the most sensitive and well-acted sequences. Disappointing, long-anticipated outing from director Downey Sr. (this is his first directorial effort in six years) who shared writing duties with wife Laura, who also died of ALS in 1994. **92m/C VHS, DVD.** Alyssa Milano, Patrick Dempsey, Robert Downey Jr., Malcolm McDowell, Cathy Moriarty, Sean Penn, Richard Lewis, Chuck Barris; **D:** Robert Downey Sr.; **W:** Laura Downey; **C:** Joe Montgomery; **M:** Danilo Perez.

Hugo the Hippo 🦴🦴 **1976 (G)** Animated musical about a forlorn baby hippo who struggles to survive in the human jungle of old Zanzibar. **90m/C VHS.** **D:** William Feigenbaum; **W:** William Feigenbaum, Thomas Baum; **M:** Burt Keyes; **V:** Paul Lynde, Burt Yves, Robert Morley, Marie Osmond.

Hula 🦴🦴½ **1928** Unflappable flapper Bow and her gang frolic on a Pacific island. **64m/B VHS.** Clara Bow, Clive Brook, Patricia Dupont, Arnold Kent, Agostino Borgato; **D:** Victor Fleming.

Hulk 🦴🦴½ **2003 (PG-13)** Hulk SMASH! Hulk explore Oedipal relationship. Hulk confused! Scientist Bruce Banner (Bana) gets zapped by gamma rays during an experiment gone wrong, and finds out that it's harder than ever to control his temper. Ang Lee classes up the summer superhero blockbuster genre by going beyond the special effects and action (but he doesn't leave 'em behind, either) to explore Banner's troubled relationships with girlfriend/colleague Betty (Connolly) and wacked-out former scientist dad David (Nolte). The extra depth may be jarring for the target fan-boy audience, but it should play better to people looking for a little thought with their thrills. Solid performances by Bana, Connolly, and Elliot as Betty's aloof, gung-ho military man father help Lee pull off the more angst-ridden moments. **138m/C VHS, DVD, HD DVD.** *US* Eric Bana, Jennifer Connelly, Joshua Lucas, Sam Elliott, Nick Nolte, Paul Kersey, Cara Buono, Mike Erwin, Celia Weston; **Cameos:** Lou Ferrigno, Stan Lee; **D:** Ang Lee; **W:** James Schamus, Michael France, John Turman; **C:** Frederick Elmes; **M:** Danny Elfman.

Hullabaloo over Georgie & Bonnie's Pictures 🦴🦴½ **1978** A young maharajah has inherited a priceless collection of Indian miniature paintings he doesn't appreciate and which his greedy sister is anxious for him to sell. They're besieged by art dealers and collectors who learn about the treasure trove and will do anything to possess it. Among them are the British Ashcroft, who wants the art for the British Museum, and competing American collector Pine. **85m/C VHS, DVD.** *GB* Victor Banerjee, Aparna Sen, Larry Pine, Saeed Jaffrey, Peggy Ashcroft; **D:** James Ivory; **W:** Ruth Prawer Jhabvala; **C:** Walter Lassally. TV

Human Beasts 🦴 **1980** Jewel robbers face a tribe of hungry cannibals. **90m/C VHS.** *SP JP* Paul Naschy, Eiko Nagashima; **D:** Paul Naschy; **W:** Paul Naschy.

Human Bomb 🦴🦴½ **1997 (PG-13)** After her husband dies, Marcia Weller (Kensit) moves to Germany to be near her mother. Marcia's only been at her new teaching job a few days when she and her class of third-graders are taken hostage by a masked gunman. Captain Gerhardt (Prochnow) is brought in to resolve the crisis, but the terrorist won't negotiate, so before the bomber decides to carry out his threats. **93m/C VHS.** Patsy Kensit, Jurgen Prochnow, Bruce Greenwood, Dorian Healy, Richard Moore; **D:** Anthony Page.

The Human Comedy 🦴🦴🦴½ **1943** A small-town boy experiences love and loss and learns the meaning of true faith during WWII. Straight, unapologetically sentimental version of the William Saroyan novel. **117m/B VHS.** Mickey Rooney, Frank Morgan, James Craig, Fay Bainter, Ray Collins, Donna Reed, Van Johnson, Barry Nelson, Robert Mitchum, Jackie "Butch" Jenkins; **D:** Clarence Brown; **W:** William Saroyan; **C:** Harry Stradling Sr. Oscars '43: Story.

The Human Condition: A Soldier's Prayer 🦴🦴🦴 **1961** A Japanese pacifist escapes from his commanders and allows himself to be captured by Russian troops, hoping for better treatment as a P.O.W. The final part of the trilogy preceded by "The Human Condition: No Greater Love" and "The Human Condition: Road to Eternity." In Japanese with English subtitles. **190m/B VHS, DVD.** *JP* Tatsuya Nakadai, Michiyo Aratama, Yusuke Kawazu, Tamao Nakamura, Chishu Ryu, Taketoshi Naito, Reiko Hitomi, Kyoko Kishida, Keijiro Morozumi, Koji Kiyomura, Nobuo Kaneko, Fujio Suga; **D:** Masaki Kobayashi.

The Human Condition: No Greater Love 🦴🦴🦴 **1958** First of a three-part series of films. A pacifist is called into military service and subsequently sent to a run a military mining camp. A gripping look at one man's attempt to retain his humanity in the face of war. Followed by "The Human Condition: Road to Eternity" and "The Human Condition: A Soldier's Prayer." In Japanese with English subtitles. **200m/B VHS, DVD.** *JP* Tatsuya Nakadai, Michiyo Aratama, So Yamamura, Eitaro (Sakae, Saka Ozawa) Ozawa, Akira Ishihama, Chikage Awashima, Ineko Arima, Keiji Sada, Shinji Nambara, Seiji Miyaguchi, Toru Abe, Masao Mishima, Eijiro Tono, Yasushi Nagata, Yoshio Kosugi; **D:** Masaki Kobayashi; **W:** Masaki Kobayashi, Zenzo Matsuyama; **C:** Yoshio Miyajima; **M:** Chuji Kinoshita.

The Human Condition: Road to Eternity 🦴🦴🦴 *Ningen No Joken* **1959** A Japanese pacifist is on punishment duty in Manchuria where he is beaten by sadistic officers who try to destroy his humanity. The second part of the trilogy, preceded by "The Human Condition: No Greater Love" and followed by "The Human Condition: A Soldier's Prayer." In Japanese with English subtitles. **180m/B VHS, DVD.** *JP* Tatsuya Nakadai, Michiyo Aratama, Kokinji Katsura, Jun Tatara, Michio Minami, Keiji Sada, Minoru Chiaki, Ryohei Uchida, Kan Yanagidani, Kenjiro Uemura, Yusuke Kawazu, Susumu Fujita; **D:** Masaki Kobayashi; **W:** Masaki Kobayashi, Zenzo Matsuyama; **C:** Yoshio Miyajima; **M:** Chuji Kinoshita.

Human Desire 🦴🦴 **1954** Femme fatale Grahame and jealous husband Crawford turn out the lights on Crawford's boss (seems there's some confusion about how Miss Gloria managed to convince the guy to let her hubby have his job back). Ford's wise to them but plays see no evil because he's gone crackers for Grahame, who by now has decided she'd like a little help to rid herself of an unwanted husband. Bleak, melodramatic, full of big heat, its Lang through and through. Based on the Emile Zola novel "La Bete Humaine," which inspired Renoir's 1938 telling as well. **90m/B VHS.** Glenn Ford, Gloria Grahame, Broderick Crawford, Edgar Buchanan, Kathleen Case; **C:** Fritz Lang; **C:** Burnett Guffey.

Human Desires 🦴🦴 **1997 (R)** A lingerie beauty contest provides a bevy of beauties for P.I. Dean Thomas (Noble) to investigate when one of them turns up dead. The death is ruled a suicide but a fellow contestant thinks it was murder and Thomas is around to check things out—very closely. **95m/C VHS, DVD.** Shannon Tweed, Christian Noble, Dawn Ann Billings, Duke Stroud; **D:** Ellen Earnshaw; **W:** Todd Smith; **C:** Carl Oakwood; **M:** Ed Korvin.

The Human Duplicators 🦴🦴½ **1964** Kiel is an alien who has come to Earth to make androids out of important folk, thus allowing the "galaxy beings" to take over. Cheap stuff, but earnest performances make this more fun than it should be. **82m/C VHS.** George Nader, Barbara Nichols, George Macready, Dolores Faith, Hugh Beaumont, Richard Kiel, Richard Arlen; **D:** Hugo Grimaldi.

Human Experiments 🐾 1979 (R) Psychiatrist in a women's prison conducts a group of experiments in which he destroys the "criminal instinct" in the inmates through brute fear. 82m/C VHS, Linda Haynes, Jackie Coogan, Aldo Ray; **D:** Gregory Goodell.

The Human Factor 🐾🐾½ 1975 (R) Unexciting spy caper has a British Secret Service agent (Williamson) betraying his country in order to aid a friend. As a result of his actions an innocent man is killed and Williamson is forced to defect to technology. Bloody and violent. 96m/C VHS, DVD, GB **T** George Kennedy, John Mills, Rita Tushingham, Barry Sullivan, Arthur Franz; **D:** Edward Dmytryk; **M:** Ennio Morricone.

Human Gorilla 🐾 _Behind Locked Doors_ 1948 A thriller involving a mad scientist, an insane asylum, a reporter, and various other mysterious trappings. 58m/B VHS, DVD, Richard Carlson, Lucille Brener, Tor Johnson; **D:** Budd Boetticher, **W:** Eugene Ling.

Human Hearts 🐾 1922 A creaky old silent starring "Phantom of the Opera" leading lady Philbin. A family is torn apart by a con man and his femme fatale. 99m/B VHS, House Peters Sr., Russell Simpson, Mary Philbin; **D:** King Baggot; **W:** George C. Hull; **C:** Victor Milner, Oscar Day.

The Human Monster 🐾🐾½ _Dark Eyes of London_ 1939 Scotland Yard inspector investigates the drownings of the blind patients at a phony Dr. Orloff (Lugosi) is exploiting for insurance money. Superior Lugosi effort that's modestly violent and tasteless. Based on the Edgar Wallace novel. 73m/B VHS, DVD, GB Bela Lugosi, Hugh Williams, Greta Gynt; **D:** Walter Summers; **W:** Walter Summers.

Human Nature 🐾🐾½ 2002 (R) Offbeat and charming screwball comedy stars Arquette as Lila, a sweet kid with a hairy problem—extreme hirsutism—which forces her to become a reclusive nature writer living in the woods. Her sex drive finally forces her back to civilization, where she finds a sympathetic electrologist (Perez) who sets her up with repressed scientist Nathan (Robbins). As a result of his uber-repressed upbringing, Nathan is on a quest to teach mice good table manners, but when the couple finds a woods-dwelling wildman (Ifans), he has something new to experiment on and tries to teach nature-boy to be civilized, despite his raging libido. Eccentric feature debut of Gallic director Gondry, a quirky study of three characters at odds with their own true nature and trying to fit into a judgment-tal society. In keeping with the offbeat humor of writer/co-producer Kaufman's "Being John Malkovich". 96m/C VHS, DVD, US FR Tim Robbins, Rhys Ifans, Patricia Arquette, Miranda Otto, Rosie Perez, Mary Kay Place, Miguel (Michael) Sandoval, Toby Huss, Peter Dinklage, Rosie Perez; **D:** Michel Gondry; **W:** Charlie Kaufman; **C:** Tim Maurice-Jones; **M:** Graeme Revell. Nat. Bd. of Review '02: Screenplay.

The Human Shield 🐾🐾 1992 (R) A man risks his life on a mission to save his brother during the Persian Gulf War. 88m/C VHS, Michael Dudikoff, Tommy Hinkley, Steve Inwood; **D:** Ted Post.

The Human Stain 🐾🐾 2003 (R) Anthony Hopkins is a professor in the middle of a racial controversy wh'o's passing as a white Jew and Nicole Kidman is the sorrowful, down-on-her-luck janitor with whom he becomes involved in Benton's waterec-down adaptation of Philip Roth's 2000 novel. The book is an angry expose of America's struggles with issues of race, age, and sexuality, but the film falls short of conveying that anger. Excellent cast does what it can to compensate. 106m/C VHS, DVD, US Anthony Hopkins, Nicole Kidman, Ed Harris, Gary Sinise, Wentworth Miller, Harry J. Lennix, Anna Deavere Smith, Jacinda Barrett.

Phyllis Newman, Kerry Washington, Margo Martindale, Ron Canada, Mili Avital, Mimi Kuzyk; **D:** Robert Benton; **W:** Nicholas Meyer; **C:** Jean-Yves Escoffier **M:** Rachel Portman.

Human Traffic 🐾½ 1999 (R) It's kinda like "Groove" only these club kids are spending their oblivious weekend in Cardiff, Wales. They have various personal dilemmas that they try to overcome by taking E and dancing the hours away and they're all one step away from insufferable. Writer/director Kerrigan was just 25 when he recorded his debut film so he's just getting old. Or maybe the Hound got time to grow up. 84m/C VHS, DVD, GB John Simm, Lorraine Pilkington, Shaun Parkes, Nicola Reynolds, Danny Dyer, Dean Davies, Justin Kerrigan; **W:** Justin Kerrigan; **C:** David Bennett; **M:** Matthew Herbert, Rob Mello.

Human Trafficking 🐾🐾½ 2005 Kate Morozov (Sorvino) and Bill Meehan (Sutherland) are agents for Immigrations and Customs Enforcement. They're trying to bring down Russian gangster Sergei (Carlyle) who poses as the owner of a modeling agency while actually running a sex-slave ring, bringing in desperate young women from Eastern Europe to work for him. Tawdry and moralizing but still compelling. Montreal substitutes for Washington, D.C. 180m/C DVD, US CA Mira Sorvino, Donald Sutherland, Robert Carlyle, Remy Girard, Isabelle Blais, Vlasta Vrana, Celine Bonnier; **D:** Christian Duguay; **W:** Carol Doyle, Agatha Dominik; **C:** Christian Duguay; **M:** Normand Corbeil. C.A.B.L.E.

Humanity 🐾🐾 _L'Humanite_ 1999 Overly long and raw look at a few days in the life naïve cop Pharon De Winter (Schotté), who suffers from an overabundance of empathy for the pain of others. His latest assignment is certain to plunge Pharon into despair as he investigates the rape and murder of an 11-year-old girl. Pharon is also hopelessly attracted to his young neighbor Domino (Caneele), whose sexual interludes with boyfriend Joseph (Tullier) leave nothing to the viewer's imagination. French with subtitles. 142m/C VHS, DVD, FR Emmanuel Schotté, Severine Caneele, Philippe Tullier, Ghislain Ghesquiere, Ginette Allegre; **D:** Bruno Dumont; **W:** Bruno Dumont; **C:** Yves Cape; **M:** Richard Cuvillier. Cannes '99: Actor (Schotté), Actress (Caneele), Grand Jury Prize.

Humanoid Defender 🐾 1985 A scientist and an android rebel against the government that wants to use the android as a warfare prototype. 94m/C VHS. **M:** William Lucking. TV

Humanoids from the Deep WOOF! _Monster_ 1980 (R) Mutated salmon-like monsters rise from the depths of the ocean and decide to chomp on some b kinied babes. Violent and bloody. 81m/C VHS, DVD, Doug McClure, Ann Turkel, Vic Morrow, Cindy Weintraub, Anthony Penya, Denise Balik, Hoke Howell, Meegan King, Lynn Schureman; **D:** Barbara Peeters; **W:** Frank Arnold, Frederick James, Martin B. Cohen; **C:** Daniel Lacambre; **M:** James Homer.

Humanoids from the Deep 🐾🐾 _Roger Corman Presents: Humanoids from the Deep_ 1996 (R) Remake of the 1980 Corman cutie: finds fishery manager Wade Parker (Carradine) and researcher Dr. Drake (Samms) dealing with a coastal town's battle against killers whose DNA has been genetically combined with that of fish. When the fish' monsters escape the lab, their mutations are further altered by toxic waste and they go on a rampage. 90m/C VHS, DVD, Robert Carradine, Emma Samms, Mark Rolston, Clint Howard, Kaz Garas, et (Johnson) Julian, David Wallace, Jarit Baldwin, Joy Bousiel; **C:** Page Fletcher; **D:** Paul Lynch; **W:** Christopher Lofton.

Humongous WOOF! 1982 (R) Brain-dead bevy of teens shipwreck on an island where they encounter a deranged mutant giant who must kill to survive. You'll be rooting for the monster. 93m/C VHS, CA Janet (Johnson) Julian, David Wallace, Janit Baldwin, Joy Boushel; **C:** Brian R.R. Hebb; **D:** Paul Lynch; **W:** William Gray; **C:** Brian R.R. Hebb.

Humoresque 🐾🐾½ 1946 Talented but struggling young musician Paul Boray (Garfield) finds a patron in the married, wealthy, and older Helen Wright

The Hunchback of Notre Dame 🐾🐾½ 1997 Cable version of Victor Hugo's ever-popular "The Hunchback of Notre Dame." In 15th-century Paris, hunchbacked Quasimodo (Patrikin) loves spirited and kind gypsy Esmeralda (Hayek), who's the lustful obsession of evil archdeacon Frollo (Harris). Properly melodramatic, with Harris stealing the film as the cold cleric. 98m/C VHS, Mandy Patrikin, Richard Harris, Salma Hayek, Jim Dale, Edward Atterton; **D:** Peter Medak; **W:** John Fasano; **C:** Elemer Ragalyi; **M:** Ed Shearmur. C.A.B.L.E.

The Hunchback of Notre Dame 🐾🐾🐾 1939 Best Hollywood version of the Victor Hugo classic, infused with sweep, sadness, and an attempt at capturing a degree of spirited, Hugoesque detail. Laughton is Quasimodo, a deformed Parisian bellringer, who provides sanctuary to young gypsy Esmeralda (O'Hara) accused by church officials of being a witch. The final scene of the town-speople storming the cathedral remains a Hollywood classic. Great performances all around; the huge mock-up of the Notre Dame cathedral was constructed on a Hollywood set for this film. Remake of several earlier films, including 1923's Lon Chaney silent, and followed by several remakes for both the big screen (included an animated Disney version) and for TV. 117m/B VHS, DVD, Charles Laughton, Maureen O'Hara, Edmond O'Brien, Cedric Hardwicke, Thomas Mitchell, George Zucco, Alan Marshal, Walter Hampden, Harry Davenport, Curt Bois, George Tobias, Rod La Rocque; **D:** William Dieterle; **W:** Sonya Levien, Bruno Frank; **C:** Joseph August; **M:** Alfred Newman.

The Hunchback of Notre Dame 🐾🐾½ _Notre Dame de Paris_ 1957 (PG) Slow retelling of the Victor Hugo novel, filmed entirely in France in Cinema-Scope. Quinn's the tragic Quasimodo with bombshell Lollobrigida appropriately hot-blooded as gypsy Esmeralda. 104m/C VHS, DVD, FR Anthony Quinn, Gina Lollobrigida, Alain Cuny, Jean Danet, Robert Hirsch, Jean Tissier; **D:** Jean Delannoy; **W:** Jacques Prevert, Jean Aurenche; **C:** Michel Kelber; **M:** Georges Auric.

The Hunchback of Notre Dame 🐾🐾½ 1982 (PG) It's not often that a classic novel is remade into a classic movie that's remade into a made-for-TV reprise, and survives the multiple renderings. But it's not often a cast so rich in stage trained actors is assembled on the small screen. Hopkins gives a textured, pre-Hannibal Lecter interpretation of Quasimodo, the Hunchback in Hugo's eponymous novel. Impressive model of the cathedral by production designer John Stoll. 102m/C VHS, Anthony Hopkins, Derek Jacobi, Lesley-Anne Down, John Gielgud, Tim Pigott-Smith, Rosalie Crutchley, Robert Powell; **D:** Michael Tuchner.

The Hunchback of Notre Dame 🐾🐾🐾 1996 (G) Animated/musical version of Victor Hugo's story about deformed bellringer Quasimodo (Hulce) and his love for the beautiful gypsy Esmeralda (Moore). The original isn't exactly

(Crawford). His appreciation is not as romantic as she hoped. Stunning performance from Crawford, with excellent supporting cast. (Levant supplies the witty comebacks), including a young Robert Blake as a young Paul. Fine music sequences (Isaac Stern dubbed the violin), and lush production values. 123m/B VHS, DVD, Joan Crawford, John Garfield, Oscar Levant, J. Carol Naish, Joan Chandler, Tom D'Andrea, Peggy Knudsen, Ruth Nelson, Craig Stevens, Paul Cavanagh, Richard Gaines, John Abbott, Robert (Bobby) Blake; **D:** Jean Negulesco; **W:** Clifford Odets, Zachary Gold; **C:** Ernest Haller; **M:** Franz Waxman.

Hundra 🐾 1985 A warrior queen vows revenge when her all-female tribe is slain by men. Nothing can stop her fierce vendetta—except love. 96m/C VHS, DVD, IT Laurene Landon, John Gaffari, Ramiro Oliveros, Marissa Casel; **D:** Matt Cimber; **M:** Ennio Morricone.

A Hungarian Fairy Tale 🐾🐾 _Hol Volt, Hol Nem Volt_ 1987 Political satire meets fantasy in a magical tale of a fatherless young boy searching for a surrogate dad. Unusual characters as well as an homage to Mozart's "The Magic Flute." In Hungarian with English subtitles. 97m/B VHS, HU Gyorgy Csernami, Lajos Balazsovits, Gabor Koncz, Bertalan Solti; **D:** Miklos Jancso.

Hungarian Rhapsody 🐾🐾 1978 In 1911, a Hungarian nobleman joins the ranks of the rebelling peasants in order to oppose his brother, who represents aristocratic repression. One of Jancso's clearest political films, and one that continues the filmmaker's experiments with long, uncut sequences and dynamic mise-en-scene. In Hungarian with English subtitles. 101m/C VHS, HU Hungarian with English subtitles. 115m/B VHS, HU Arpad Vernes, Maria Varga, Franisek Husak, Eszter Csakanyi, Szilvia Toth, Judith Pogany, Geza Balkay; **D:** Gyula Gazdag.

The Hunger 🐾🐾 _Sult_ 1966 In the late 1800s, a starving Norwegian writer, unable to sell his work, rejects charity out of pride, and retains this faith in his talent. Based on a novel "Suit" by Knut Hamsun. In Danish with English subtitles. **D:** Henning Carlsen; **W:** Henning Carlsen, Peter Seeberg; Nat. Soc. Film Critics '68: Actor (Oscarsson).

The Hunger 🐾🐾 1983 (R) A beautiful 2000-year-old vampire needs new blood when she realizes that her current lover, Bowie, is aging fast. Visually sumptuous but sleepwalking modern vampire tale, complete with soft-focus lesbian love scenes between Deneuve and Sarandon. 100m/C VHS, DVD, Catherine Deneuve, David Bowie, Susan Sarandon, Cliff DeYoung, Ann Magnuson, Dan Hedaya, William Dafoe, Beth Ehlers, Suzanne Bertish, Rufus Collins, James Aubrey; **D:** Tony Scott; **W:** Michael Thomas, Ivan Davis; **C:** Stephen Goldblatt, Tom Mangravite; **M:** Denny Jaeger, Michel Rubini.

Hunk 🐾🐾 1987 (PG) A computer nerd sells his soul to the devil for a muscular, beach-blonde physique. Answers the question, "Was it worth it?" 102m/C VHS, John Allen Nelson, Steve Levitt, Deborah Shelton, Rebecca Bush, James Coco, Avery Schreiber; **D:** Lawrence Bassoff.

The Hunley 🐾🐾½ 1999 Based on the true story of the Confederate submarine that was used to defend Charleston harbor against Union forces in 1864. The experimental craft has already claimed the lives of two crews but General Beauregard blockade of the city and gives command to Lt. George E. Dixon (Assante), an engineer. As usual, Dixon's crew is a ragged bunch of misfits, but Dixon perseveres. 120m/C VHS, Armand Assante, Donald Sutherland, Alex Jennings, Sebastien Roche, Michael Dolan, Chris Bauer, Michael Stuhlbarg, Jack Baun, Kevin Robertson; **D:** John Gray; **W:** John Gray; **C:** John Dreyfuss. C.A.B.L.E.

The Hunt 🐾🐾🐾 _La Caza_ 1965 A teenage boy accompanies three Spanish Civil War veterans on what is supposed to be a friendly rabbit hunt. Things turn violent, however, when old rivalries and tensions

fun fare out you expect Disney to find a way to leave everybody humming (and happy). The sweeping music was provided by "Pocahontas" tunesmiths Menken and Schwartz. Comic relief is supplied by three gargoyles, companions to Quasimodo, who are voiced wonderfully by Alexander, Kimbrough and Wickes. 85, died six weeks after voicing her role. Looks like another boatload of boxoffice, making its way into old Walt's vaults. 91m/C VHS, DVD; **D:** Kirk Wise, Gary Trousdale; **W:** Irene Mecchi, Tab Murphy, Jonathan Roberts, Bob Tzudiker, Noni White; **M:** Stephen Schwartz, Alan Menken; **V:** Tom Hulce, Demi Moore, Kevin Kline, Tony Jay, Charles Kimbrough, Jason Alexander, Mary Wickes, David Ogden Stiers.

begin to surface. In Spanish with English subtitles. **87m/B VHS, DVD.** *SP* Alfredo Mayo, Ismael Merlo, Jose Maria Prada, Emilio Gutierrez-Caba, Fernando Sanchez Polack; *D:* Carlos Saura.

The Hunt for Eagle One: Crash Point ♂ 2006 (R)
Routine military action pic. The Strike Force team returns when terrorists steal an anti-hijack device. Lt. Matt Daniels (Dacascos) and his crew must get the device back and also prevent the bad guys from crashing a jetliner into a military base. **86m/C DVD.** Mark Dacascos, Theresa Randle, Gary Kasper, Rutger Hauer, Zach McGowan, Joe Suba, Jeff Fahey; *D:* Henry Crum; *W:* Michael Henry Carter; *C:* Andrea V. Rossotto; *M:* Mel Lewis. **VIDEO**

The Hunt for Red October ♂♂♂ 1990 (PG)
Based on Tom Clancy's blockbuster novel, a high-tech Cold War yarn about a Soviet nuclear sub (commanded by Connery) turning rogue and heading straight for U.S. waters, as both the U.S. and the U.S.S.R. try to stop it. Complicated, ill-plotted potboiler that succeeds breathlessly due to the cast and McTiernan's tommy-gun direction. Introduces the character of CIA analyst Jack Ryan (Baldwin) who returns in "Patriot Games," though in the guise of Harrison Ford. **137m/C VHS, DVD.** Sean Connery, Alec Baldwin, Richard Jordan, Scott Glenn, Joss Ackland, Sam Neill, James Earl Jones, Peter Firth, Tim Curry, Courtney B. Vance, Jeffrey Jones, Fred Dalton Thompson; *D:* John McTiernan; *W:* Larry Ferguson, Donald Stewart; *C:* Jan De Bont; *M:* Basil Poledouris. Oscars '90: Sound FX Editing.

The Hunt for the Night Stalker ♂♂ 1991 (PG-13)
Manhunt: The Search for the Night Stalker. Another one of those True-Detective quickies so beloved by network TV, following two hardworking L.A. cops who tracked down satanic serial killer Richard Ramirez in the mid-1980s. It originally aired (under the title "Manhunt: The Search for the Night Stalker") on the date of the killer's death-sentence verdict; the videotape lacks that particular timely sparkle. **95m/C VHS.** Richard Jordan, A. Martinez, Lisa Eilbacher, Julie Carmen, Alan Feinstein; *D:* Bruce Seth Green. **TV**

Hunt the Man Down ♂♂ 1/2 1950
An innocent man is charged with murder, and a public defender must find the real killer before time runs out. **68m/B VHS, DVD.** Gig Young, Lynne Roberts, Gerald Mohr; *D:* George Archainbaud.

Hunted ♂♂ 1988 (PG)
WWII prisoner attempts to escape from demented officer who seems to enjoy bugging him. Hunted by the MPs, he relies on unorthodox guide to sustain feature length footage. **75m/C VHS.** Andrew Buckland, Richard Carlson, Ron Smerczak, Mercia Van Wyk; *D:* David Lister.

The Hunted ♂ 1/2 1994 (R)
American businessman in Japan meets, beds, and witnesses the assassination of a mysterious woman and is forced on the run by the modern-day ninja clan that committed the crime. Only a notch above the low-budget, badly dubbed martial arts flicks of the '70s, this shameless bloodfest features unintentionally campy performances by Lambert and Lone and lots of silly dialogue. Beware, the cliches pile up as quickly as the bodies. **110m/C VHS, DVD.** Christopher Lambert, John Lone, Joan Chen, Yoshio Harada, Yoko Shimada, Mari Natsuki, Tak Kubota; *D:* J.F. Lawton; *W:* J.F. Lawton; *C:* Jack Conroy; *M:* Motofumi Yamaguchi. **VIDEO**

The Hunted ♂♂ 2003 (R)
"First Blood" meets "The Fugitive" in Friedkin's newest chase thriller. Ex-Special Forces member Hallam (Del Toro) comes back from Kosovo severely messed up and heads to the Oregon woods, fileting hunters who use high-powered scopes to stalk their prey. Apparently he's joined PETA's paramilitary wing. Jones is Bonham, the man who trained him in the arts of stalking, killing, and surviving, and must now stop him. He's teamed with female FBI agent Durrell (Nielsen), who doesn't realize she's brought a gun to knife fight. She (as well as plot) is basically window dressing, as Friedkin is clearly more concerned with the grunt-inducing mano-a-mano action scenes and car chases. It's a good thing they're well done, because the meditation of the good and evil that men do doesn't cut it. **94m/C VHS, DVD.** *US* Tommy Lee Jones, Benicio Del Toro, Connie Nielsen, Leslie Stefanson, John Finn, Jose Zuniga, Ron Canada, Mark Pellegrino, Lonny (Lonnie) Chapman, Rex Linn, Eddie Velez; *D:* William Friedkin; *W:* David Griffiths, Peter Griffiths, Art Montersatelli; *C:* Caleb Deschanel; *M:* Brian Tyler.

The Hunted Lady ♂ 1/2 1977
In this TV pilot, Mills is an undercover policewoman who is framed by the mob. Tired and predictable. **100m/C VHS.** Donna Mills, Robert Reed, Lawrence Casey, Andrew Duggan, Will Sampson, Alan Feinstein; *D:* Richard Lang. **TV**

Hunter ♂ 1/2 1973
Unsuccessful TV pilot in which a government agent uncovers an enemy brainwashing scam. **90m/C VHS.** John Vernon, Steve Ihnat, Fritz Weaver, Edward Binns, Sabrina Scharf, Barbara Rhoades; *D:* Leonard Horn. **TV**

Hunter ♂ 1976
An attorney is falsely accused of a crime and imprisoned. Released after eight years, he sets out to even the score with the mysterious millionaire who set him up. **120m/C VHS.** James Franciscus, Linda Evans, Broderick Crawford, Ned Beatty; *D:* Tom Gries. **TV**

The Hunter ♂♂ 1/2 1980 (PG)
Action drama based on the real life adventures of Ralph (Papa) Thorson, a modern day bounty hunter who makes his living by finding fugitives who have jumped bail. McQueen's last. **97m/C VHS, DVD.** Steve McQueen, Eli Wallach, Kathryn Harrold, LeVar Burton; *D:* Buzz Kulik; *W:* Peter Hyams; *C:* Fred W. Koenekamp; *M:* Charles Bernstein.

Hunter in the Dark ♂♂ 1/2 1980
Set in 18th-century Japan, where power, betrayal, and corruption are the dark side of the samurai world. Tanuma is a powerful bounty hunter who becomes involved with Gomyo, the leader of a secret underworld organization of thieves and murderers with a violent honor code. In Japanese with English subtitles. **138m/C VHS.** *JP* Tatsuya Nakadai, Tetsuro Tamba, Sonny Chiba; *D:* Hideo Gosha.

The Hunters ♂♂ 1/2 1958
A motley crew of pilots learn about each other and themselves in this melodrama set during Korean war. Incredible aerial photography sets this apart from other films of the genre. **108m/C VHS, DVD.** Robert Mitchum, Robert Wagner, Richard Egan, May Britt, Lee Philips, John Gabriel, Stacy Harris, John Doucette, Jay Jostyn, Leon Lontoc, Robert Reed, Victor Sen Yung, Candace Lee; *D:* Dick Powell; *W:* Wendell Mayes; *C:* Charles Clarke; *M:* Paul Sawtell. Natl. Film Reg. '03.

Hunter's Blood ♂ 1987 (R)
Five urbanites plunge into the Southern wilderness to hunt deer, and are stalked by maniacal hillbillies. **102m/C VHS.** Sam Bottoms, Kim Delaney, Clu Gulager, Mayf Nutter, Eugene Robert Glazer; *D:* Robert C. Hughes; *W:* Emmett Alston.

Hunter's Moon ♂♂ 1/2 1997 (R)
Reynolds plays a very bad guy (very well) as a Depression era, Kentucky backwoods moonshiner who has no intention of letting his lovely daughter, Flo (Du Mond), fall for a city boy (Carradine) who's trying to make a new life for himself. **104m/C VHS, DVD.** Burt Reynolds, Keith Carradine, Hayley Du Mond, Ann Wedgeworth, Pat Hingle, Brion James, Charles Napier; *D:* William Berman; *W:* Richard Weinman; L. Ford Neale, John Huff, William Kemper; *C:* Suki Medencevic.

Hunters of the Golden Cobra ♂ 1982 (R)
Two American soldiers plot to recover the priceless golden cobra from the Japanese general who stole the prized relic during the last days of WWII. **95m/C VHS.** David Warbeck, Almanta Suska, Alan Collins, John Steiner; *D:* Anthony M. Dawson.

The Hunting ♂♂ 1992 (R)
A married woman falls for a ruthless businessman and is drawn into a web of blackmail and murder in this low-budget erotic thriller. **97m/C VHS.** John Savage, Kerry Armstrong, Guy Pearce, Rebecca Rigg; *D:* Frank Howson; *W:* Frank Howson.

The Hunting of the President ♂♂ 2004
Documentary about the extreme Right's attempts to smear and destroy the presidency of Bill Clinton. Covers events from Whitewatergate to the impeachment proceedings. Partisan slam against Starr and company co-written and directed by Thomason, a close friend of the Clintons. In the year of partisan political docs, acceptance will depend on party affiliation and ideology. Techniques used are overly arch and comic at times. **88m/C VHS, DVD.** *D:* Nickolas Perry, Harry Z. Thomason; *W:* Nickolas Perry, Harry Z. Thomason; *C:* Jim Roberson; *M:* Bruce Miller.

The Hunting Party ♂ 1/2 2007 (R)
What could be funnier than a couple of journalists tromping through postwar Bosnia hunting a war criminal? Simon Hunt (Gere) is a former big-time television reporter, fallen from grace after an on-camera meltdown. Now a freelancer covering tragedies around the globe, he and his journalist buddies improbably find themselves mistaken as a hit squad on the lookout for a brutal war criminal, Radovan Karadzic (Kerekes). Based on Scott Anderson's 2000 article in "Esquire" magazine about five journalists who found themselves in just that situation, although sans the goofy and madcap tone. Doesn't work as a war comedy, as the story just doesn't translate, particularly with oddly-cast Gere. **104m/C DVD.** *US* Richard Gere, Terrence Howard, Jesse Eisenberg, Diane Kruger, James Brolin, Dylan Baker, Ljubomir Kerekes; *D:* Richard Shepard; *W:* Richard Shepard; *C:* David Tattersall; *M:* Rolfe Kent.

Hurlyburly ♂♂ 1998 (R)
Casting agents Eddie (Penn) and Mickey (Spacey) share a Hollywood apartment with out-of-work actor Phil (Palminteri). Eddie uses cocaine almost constantly, Phil has just been dumped by his wife, and Mickey (Spacey), although more low key, is himself ready to explode. They're all desperate to be huge "Hollywood" crap, particularly Bonnie (Ryan), a slutty exotic dancer traded between the boys. Snappy dialogue-happy script might have worked on the stage, but here, with the camera in close, the mean spirit becomes tiring very quickly. Paquin shows confidence in her first adult role, as a drifter girl-toy. **122m/C VHS, DVD.** Sean Penn, Kevin Spacey, Chazz Palminteri, Meg Ryan, Robin Wright Penn, Anna Paquin, Garry Shandling; *D:* Tony Drazan; *W:* David Rabe; *C:* Gu Changwei; *M:* David Baerwald.

The Hurricane ♂♂♂ 1937
A couple on the run from the law are aided by a hurricane and are able to build a new life for themselves on an idyllic island. Filmed two years before the Academy's "special effects" award came into being, but displaying some of the best effects of the decade. Boringly remade in 1979. **102m/B VHS, DVD.** Jon Hall, Dorothy Lamour, Mary Astor, Sir C. Aubrey Smith, Raymond Massey, Thomas Mitchell, John Carradine; *D:* John Ford; *W:* Oliver H.P. Garrett, Dudley Nichols; *C:* Bert Glennon, Paul Eagler, Archie Stout; *M:* Alfred Newman. Oscars '37: Sound.

Hurricane ♂ 1974
TV's answer to the disaster movie craze of the early 1970s. Realistic hurricane footage and an adequate cast cannot save this catastrophe. **78m/C VHS, DVD.** Larry Hagman, Martin Milner, Jessica Walter, Barry Sullivan, Will Geer, Frank Sutton; *D:* Jerry Jameson. **TV**

Hurricane woof! 1979 (PG)
And the wind cried, "turkey." Robards is the governor of a tropical island beset with environmental and personal concerns. Virginal daughter Farrow falls for hunky native, standard colonial power/indigenous people complications ensue, vital explanatory footage is cut, and over-acting reaches epidemic heights. Then too late the big wind blows in, leveling the place. Expensive (most of the $22 million must have gone to catering) and essentially misdirected remake of the 1937 semi-classic. **120m/C VHS.** Mia Farrow, Jason Robards Jr., Trevor Howard, Max von Sydow, Timothy Bottoms, James Keach; *D:* Jan Troell; *C:* Sven Nykvist; *M:* Nino Rota.

The Hurricane ♂♂♂ 1999 (R)
Lazarus and the Hurricane. Moving, albeit truncated account of the true story of middleweight boxing champ Rubin "Hurricane" Carter (Washington—in peak physical and professional form), who was falsely accused and convicted of murder and who spent 20 years in prison. Anchored by a transcendent performance by Washington, pic came under fire for its liberal rearrangement of the facts behind the case. If you want a full lowdown on the case, read one of several books written about this unique court battle by Carter himself ("The Sixteenth Round") or "Lazarus and the Hurricane," which served as the basis for the film; but if you want to see acting that can lift one to a higher spiritual plane, give "The Hurricane" a look. Carter was immortalized in Bob Dylan's 1976 protest song, "Hurricane." **125m/B VHS, DVD, HD DVD.** Denzel Washington, Vicellous Shannon, Deborah Kara Unger, Liev Schreiber, John Hannah, David Paymer, Dan Hedaya, Debbi (Deborah) Morgan, Clancy Brown, Harris Yulin, Vincent Pastore, Rod Steiger; *D:* Norman Jewison; *W:* Armyan Bernstein, Dan Gordon; *C:* Roger Deakins; *M:* Christopher Young. Golden Globes '00: Actor—Drama (Washington).

Hurricane Express ♂♂ 1932
Twelve episodes of the vintage serial, in which the Duke pits his courage against an unknown, powerful individual out to sabotage a railroad. **223m/B VHS, DVD.** John Wayne, Joseph Girard, Conway Tearle, Shirley Grey; *D:* J(ohn) P(aterson) McGowan, Armand Schaefer.

Hurricane Smith ♂♂ 1992 (R)
Weathers stars as a roughneck Texan who travels to Australia's Gold Coast in search of his missing sister. While in the land of Oz, he gets entangled in a Mafia-style drug and prostitution ring around the "Surfer's Paradise" section of the Gold Coast. Packed with mind-blowing stunts and a good performance from Weathers, this fast-paced action thriller won't disappoint fans of this genre. **86m/C VHS.** Carl Weathers, Jurgen Prochnow, Tony Bonner, Cassandra Delaney; *D:* Colin Budds.

Hurricane Streets ♂♂ 1/2 1996
Hurricane. Freeman's directorial debut centers on a group of young teenagers getting into trouble in lower Manhattan. 15-year-old Marcus (Sexton) is on the edge—his dad is dead, his mother's in jail, he's being ineffectually looked after by his working grandma, and the authorities are already eyeing this petty thief. He hangs with three buddies, one of whom, Chip (Frank), wants to start them stealing cars. Meanwhile, Marcus falls for 14-year-old Melena (Vega), whose father is both possessive and abusive, and tries to plan an escape for them both. **89m/C VHS.** Terry Alexander, Brendan Sexton III, Isidra Vega, David Roland Frank, L.M. Kit Carson, Jose Zuniga, Lynn Cohen, Edie Falco, Shawn Elliot, Heather Matarazzo; *D:* Morgan J. Freeman; *W:* Morgan J. Freeman; *C:* Enrique Chediak. Sundance '97: Cinematog, Director (Freeman), Aud. Award.

Hurry, Charlie, Hurry ♂ 1941
Husband gets in trouble when he bows out of a trip with his social-climber wife when he tells her he must travel to Washington to see the Vice President. **65m/B VHS.** Leon Errol, Mildred Coles, Kenneth Howell, Cecil Cunningham, George Watts, Noble Johnson; *D:* Charles E. Roberts; *W:* Paul Girard Smith; *C:* Nicholas Musuraca.

Hurry Up or I'll Be Thirty ♂♂ 1973
A Brooklyn bachelor celebrates his 30th birthday by becoming morose, depressed, and enraged. His friends try to help; they fail, but he finds love anyway. For those seeking a better life through celluloid. **87m/C VHS, DVD.** Danny DeVito, Ronald Lefkowitz, Steve Inwood, Linda DeCoff, Ronald Anton, Maureen Byrnes, Francis Gallagher; *D:* Joseph Jacoby.

Husbands 🐾🐾½ 1970 (PG-13) When Stuart (Rowlands) dies suddenly of a heart attack, his three equally middle-aged buddies—Harry (Gazzara), Archie (Falk), and Gus (Cassavetes)—are reluctantly confronted with their own mortality. These suburban married men decide to cut loose and go on a spree, with Harry even persuading his buddies they should carry their frantic merriment across the pond in a trip to London. Meanders on a bit too long, thanks to Cassavetes' usual reliance on improv and reluctance to edit. **140m/C** VHS, Ben Gazzara, Peter Falk, John Cassavetes; **W:** John Cassavetes; **C:** Victor Kemper.

Husbands and Lovers 🐾🐾 1991 (R) Controversial and confusing film focuses on a couple's untraditional marriage. Stephen (Sands) and Alina (Facula) have agreed to be totally honest with each other and when Alina decides to take a lover, Stephen agrees on the condition that she report back to him every intimate detail of her affair. In the confusion and excitement she starts losing control as sexual boundaries are pushed to the limit. Also available in an unrated version. **91m/C** VHS, Julian Sands, Joanna Pacula, Tcheky Karyo; **D:** Mauro Bolognini; **W:** Sergio Bazzini; **M:** Ennio Morricone.

Husbands and Wives 🐾🐾🐾½ 1992 (R) Art imitates life as Allen/Farrow relationship dissolves onscreen (and off) and Woody becomes involved with young student. Mature, penetrating look at modern pair bonding and loneliness offers more painful honesty and sadness than outright laughs, though still retains essential Allen charm. Stylistically burdened by experiment with pseudo-documentary telling of tale and spasmodic hand-held cameras that annoy more than entertain. Excellent, intriguing cast, notably Davis as the overwhelming, overbearing wife/friend. Trailers became unintentionally funny in light of the highly publicized personal problems of Allen and Farrow. **C** VHS, DVD, Woody Allen, Mia Farrow, Judy Davis, Sydney Pollack, Liam Neeson, Juliette Lewis, Lysette Anthony, Blythe Danner; **D:** Woody Allen; **W:** Woody Allen; **C:** Carlo Di Palma. British Acad. '92; Orig. Screenplay; L.A. Film Critics '92: Support. Actress (Davis); Natl. Bd. of Review '92: Support. Actress (Davis); Natl. Soc. Film Critics '92: Support. Actress (Davis).

Husbands, Wives, Money, and Murder 🐾 1986 A couple is pushed over the edge by a nosey census taker and then must dispose of the consequences. **92m/C** VHS, Meredith MacRae, Timothy Bottoms; **D:** Bruce Cook Jr.

Hush 🐾½ Kilroran; Bloodline 1998 (PG-13) Stinky thriller stars Paltrow as a working-class gal who marries wealthy dreamboat Jackson (Schaech) and moves to his family's Kentucky estate. Killronan, smother-in-law Lange camps it up (albeit unknowingly) as she turns psycho on the pregnant bride while coming on to her dim-witted son who doesn't have a clue. Apparently, neither did filmmaker Darby, whose film was held from release pending two years of pasting Band-Aids on this gaping wound of a movie. Foch's crusty grandmother is the sole highlight of this horror of a film. **96m/C** VHS, Gwyneth Paltrow, Jessica Lange, Johnathon Schaech, Nina Foch, Debi Mazar, Kaiulani Lee, David Thornton, Hal Holbrook; **D:** Jonathan Darby; **W:** Jonathan Darby, Jane Rusconi; **C:** Andrew Dunn; **M:** Christopher Young.

Hush, Hush, Sweet Charlotte 🐾🐾🐾 1965 A fading southern belle finds out the truth about her married lover's murder when the case is reopened 37 years later by her cousin in an elaborate plot to drive her crazy. Grisly, superbly entertaining Southern Gothic horror tale, with vivid performances from the aging leads. **134m/B** VHS, DVD, Bette Davis, Olivia de Havilland, Joseph Cotten, Agnes Moorehead, Mary Astor, Bruce Dern, Cecil Kellaway, Victor Buono; **D:** Robert Aldrich; **W:** Lukas Heller, Henry Farrell; **C:** Joseph Biroc. Golden Globes '65: Support. Actress (Moorehead).

Hush Little Baby 🐾½ 1993 Susan Nolan (Medrum), is shocked when the family of her own, is shocked when the it's racy, but it's also not as hardcore as biological mother she had thought was dead tries to contact her. Turns out the Edie Landers (Ladd) is another of those female psychos who were so popular in suspense films of the late '80s and '90s. This made-for-TV variation connects the dots competently enough. **91m/C** DVD, Diane Ladd, Wendel Meldrum, Geraint Wyn Davies, Ilya Woloshyn, Ingrid Veninger; **D:** Jorge Montesi. **TV**

The Hustle 🐾🐾 1980 (R) Hooker and her detective have an adventure with Reynolds as an L.A. detective investigating a young call girl's death, who becomes romantically entangled with high-priced call girl Deneuve. **120m/C** VHS, DVD, Burt Reynolds, Catherine Deneuve; **D:** Robert Aldrich; **C:** Joseph Biroc.

Hustle 🐾½ 2004 Slight, sometimes laughable, story of Pete Rose's banishment from Major League Baseball as a result of his gambling on games his team was playing. Traces the beginnings and escalation of his gambling problem and the investigation that brought him down. Sizemore's ridiculous portrayal of Rose makes nothing to light the situation. **90m/C** DVD, Tom Sizemore, Dash Mihok, Melissa Di Marco, George DiCenzo, Paul Fauteux; **D:** Peter Bogdanovich; **W:** Christian Darren; **C:** James Gardner; **M:** Lou Natale. **CABLE**

Hustle & Flow 🐾🐾🐾 2005 (R) After reuniting with an old buddy who's a sound engineer, Djay, an aging pimp (Howard), decides to go after a dream he let slide and use his talent as a wordsmith to make rap songs. The plan includes giving the demo to Skinny Black (Ludacris), a big-time rap star who Djay claims to know. The film's heart is in the second act where they create a makeshift recording studio and enlist a hooker to sing backup, daring to move beyond their current situations into one dreams are made of. Easy to see why this won the Audience Award at the 2005 Sundance Film Festival, earning Singleton and Allain a hefty distribution deal. **114m/C** DVD, Blu-ray Disc, UMD, HD DVD, US Terrence Howard, Taryn Manning, Taraji P. Henson, Paula Jai Parker, Elise Neal, Isaac Hayes, DJ Qualls, Ludacris, Anthony Anderson; **D:** Craig Brewer; **W:** Craig Brewer; **C:** Amy Vincent. Oscars '05; Song ("It's Hard Out Here for a Pimp"); Nat'l. Bd. of Review '05: Breakthrough Perf. (Howard); Broadcast Film Critics '05: Song ("Hustle and Flow").

The Hustler 🐾🐾🐾🐾 1961 The original story of Fast Eddie Felsen and his adventures in the seedy world of professional pool. Newman plays the naive, talented and self-destructive Felsen perfectly. Laurie is outstanding as his lover, and Gleason epitomizes the pool great Minnesota Fats. Rivetting atmospheric, and exquisitely photographed. Parent to the remake years later "The Color of Money," made 25 years later. **134m/B** VHS, DVD, Paul Newman, Jackie Gleason, Piper Laurie, George C. Scott, Myron McCormick, Murray Hamilton, Michael Constantine, Jake LaMotta, Vincent Gardenia; **D:** Robert Rossen; **W:** Robert Rossen; **C:** Eugen Shuftan. Oscars '61: Art Dir./Set Dec., B&W Cinematog.; British Acad. '61: Actor (Newman), Film; Nat'l. Film Reg. '97; N.Y. Film Critics '61: Director (Rossen).

Hustler Squad 🐾 1976 (R) U.S. Army major and Philippine guerrilla leader stage a major operation to help rid the Philippines of Japanese Occupation forces; they have four combat-trained prostitutes infiltrate a brothel patronized by top Japanese officers. Verrrry clever. **98m/C** VHS, DVD, John Ericson, Karen Ericson, Lynda Sinclaire, Nory Wright; **D:** Ted V. Mikels.

Hustler White 🐾 1996 Outrageous underground actor/filmmaker La-Bruce stars as pretentious German writer Jurgen Anger, who comes to Hollywood to research the gay scene for a book. Cruising Santa Monica Boulevard he becomes obsessively intrigued by local hustler Montgomery Ward (Ward), who serves as a tour guide to the city's sexual kinks. Yes, the subject matter might imply. Notable performance by Remick as the reporter and Clayburgh as a victimized hooker. Made for TV and based on a novel by Gail Sheehy. **80m/C** VHS, DVD, Tony Ward, Bruce La Bruce; **D:** Rick Castro, Bruce La Bruce.

Hybrid 🐾½ 1997 (R) Another bleak apocalyptic future flick, which finds a handful of survivors stumbling across a remote desert lab where they decide to take shelter. Big mistake since the lab still houses a living alien hybrid that's bent on reproduction and destruction. **87m/C** VHS, DVD, Ernie Stevens, Tim Abell, John Barrymore III; **D:** Fred Olen Ray; **W:** Sean O'Bannon; **C:** James Lawrence Spencer; **M:** Jeff Walton.

Hyena of London 🐾🐾 1962 A doctor steals the hyena of London's corpse and injects the rabid protoplasm into his own brain with deadly results. **7m/C** VHS, Sydney Penny, Keenan Wynn, Gail Strickland, Ricky Faull Goldin, Peter Jason, Talia Shire; **D:** Peter Hunt; **W:** Richard Adcock, Christopher Blue.

Hyper Space 🐾½ 1989 Black Forest; Rage in Space 1989 Six people awaken from cryogenic sleep to discover that their space-ship has become marooned lightyears from earth and only a single passenger shuttle is available to get someone home. Naturally, everyone wants that one chance. **90m/C** VHS, DVD, Richard Norton, Don Stroud, Lynn-Holly Johnson, James Van Patten, Ron O'Neal, Rebecca Cruz; **D:** David Huey; **W:** Richard Dominguez; **C:** Roger Olkowski.

Hyper-Sapien: People from Another Star 🐾½ 1986 (PG) Two cuddly aliens run away from home, are befriended by a lonely farmboy, and are chased all over the wilds of Wyoming. **93m/C** VHS, Sydney Penny, Keenan Wynn, Gail Strickland, Ricky Faull Goldin, Peter Jason, Talia Shire; **D:** Peter Hunt; **W:** Richard Adcock, Christopher Blue.

The Hypothesis of the Stolen Painting 🐾🐾 L'Hypothese du Tableau Vole 1978 An art collector guides an interviewer around six paintings by Frederic Tonnerre, an academic 19th century painter, in an attempt to solve the mysterious disappearance of a seventh painting. The film presents the paintings as tableaux vivants in which the actors hold poses as they are examined. Based on the novel "Baphomet" by Pierre Klossowski. In French with English subtitles. **87m/B** VHS. **D:** Raul Ruiz; **W:** Raul Ruiz.

Hysteria 🐾½ 1964 (PG) When an American becomes involved in an accident and has amnesia, a mysterious benefactor pays all his bills and gives the man a house to live in. But a series of murders could mean he's the murderer—or the next victim. **85m/B** VHS, GB Robert Webber, Sue Lloyd, Maurice Denham; **D:** Freddie Francis; **W:** Jimmy Sangster; **M:** Don Banks.

Hysterical 🐾🐾 1983 (PG) Odd little attempt at a horror flick parody features the Hudson Brothers and involves a haunted lighthouse occupied by the vengeful spirit of a spurned woman. Late-night fun. **86m/C** VHS, DVD, Brett Hudson, Bill Hudson, Mark Hudson, Cindy Pickett, Richard Kiel, Julie Newmar, Bud Cort; **D:** Chris Bearde; **W:** Trace Johnston, Brett Hudson, Bill Hudson, Mark Hudson; **C:** Thomas Del Ruth; **M:** Robert Alcivar.

Hysterical Blindness 🐾🐾🐾½ 2002 It's 1987 in Bayonne, New Jersey where Debby (Thurman) and her best friend Beth (Lewis) like to hang out at the local bar and pick up guys. Despite her looks, Debby, who lives with her waitress mom Virginia (Rowlands), comes off as so needy that she can't find anything more stable than a one-night stand. Meanwhile, Beth neglects her young daughter for noncommittal bartender Bobby (de Sando) and Virginia gets a second chance with nice-guy customer Nick (Gazzara). Overly familiar and somewhat shrill, the best reason to watch are veterans Rowlands and Gazzara. Cahill adapted from her play. **99m/C** VHS, DVD, Uma Thurman, Juliette Lewis, Gena Rowlands, Ben Gazzara, Justin Chambers, Anthony De Sando, Jolie Peters; **D:** Mira Nair; **W:** Laura Cahill; **C:** Declan Quinn; **M:** Lesley Barber. **CABLE**

I, a Woman 🐾🐾 Jag, en Kvinna 1966 Siv (Persson) is a seductive young nurse who likes to have sex with every man she meets—and the leave them after they fall in love with her. Based on the novel by Siv Holm. Dubbed. **90m/C** VHS, DVD, SW Essy Persson, Jorgen Reenberg, Preben Mahrt; **D:** Mac Ahlberg; **W:** Peer Guldbrandsen; **C:** Mac Ahlberg.

I Accidentally Domed Your Son 🐾½ 2004 (R) Uneven urban comedy has four friends trying to score some pot from the local kingpin's son. When the kid ends up dead the over-protective boss sends his killers after the guys, so they head underground to try to change their appearance and get away. Fans of the genre and star Kurupt may be the only ones pleased by this one. **89m/C** VHS, DVD, Ryan Combs, Tony Cox, Kurupt, Fredro (Pete) Pano; **D:** Ryan Combs; **W:** Ryan Combs.
VIDEO

I Am a Camera 🐾🐾🐾 1955 A young English writer develops a relationship with a reckless young English girl in Berlin during the 1930s. Based on the Berlin stories by Christopher Isherwood, later musicalized as "Cabaret." **99m/B** VHS, GB Julie Harris, Shelley Winters, Laurence Harvey, Patrick McGoohan; **D:** Henry Cornelius; **C:** Guy Green; **M:** Malcolm Arnold.

I Am a Fugitive from a Chain Gang 🐾🐾🐾🐾 1932 WWI veteran Muni returns home with dreams of travelling across America. After a brief stint as a clerk, he strikes out on his own. Near penniless, Muni meets up with a tramp who takes him to get a hamburger. He becomes an unwilling accomplice when the turn suddenly robs the place. Convicted and sentenced to a Georgia chain gang, he's brutalized and degraded, though he eventually escapes and lives the life of a criminal on the run. Based on the autobiography by Robert E. Burns. Brutal docu-details combine with powerhouse performances to create a classic. Timeless and thought-provoking. **93m/B** VHS, DVD, Paul Muni, Glenda Farrell, Helen Vinson, Preston Foster, Edward Ellis, Allen Jenkins; **D:** Mervyn LeRoy; **W:** Howard J. Green. Nat'l. Film Reg. '91.

I Am Cuba 🐾🐾 Soy Cuba; Ja Cuba 1964 Agitprop Russian-Cuban co-production illustrates different aspects of the Cuban revolution from the toppling of Batista and student revolutionaries. Lots of oratory and deliberate artificiality combined with cinematographer Urusevsky's stunning high-contrast photography. Spanish and Russian with subtitles. **141m/B** VHS, DVD, CU, RU Luz Maria Collazo, Jose Gallardo, Sergio Corrieri, Jean Bouise, Raul Garcia, Celia Rodriguez; **D:** Mikhail Kalatozov; **W:** Yevgeny Yevtushenko, Enrique Pineda Barnet; **C:** Sergei Urusevsky; **M:** Carlos Farinas.

I Am Curious (Yellow) 🐾🐾½ 1967 A woman sociologist is conducting a sexual survey on Swedish society, which leads her to buy a few numerous sexual encounters in all sorts of places. Very controversial upon its U.S. release because of the nudity and sexual content but it was today's standards. Followed by "I Am Curious (Blue)" which was filmed at the same time. In Swedish with English subtitles. **95m/B** VHS, DVD, SW Lena Nyman, Peter Lindgren, Borje Ahlstedt, Marie Goranzon, Magnus

Nilsson; *D:* Vilgot Sjoman; *M:* Bengt Ernyd.

I Am David 2004 (PG) Unlikely adventure story follows the travails of a 12-year-old orphan named David (Tibber), who escapes from a 1952 Stalinist labor camp in Bulgaria and makes his way across Greece, Italy, and Switzerland to safety in Denmark. He gets really lucky—first his nice camp friend Johannes (Caviezel) helps him, then nice Italian Roberto (De Vito), and then nice Swiss grandmother or Sophie (Plowright). Based on the novel "North to Freedom" by Anne Holm. **95m/C VHS, DVD.** *US* Ben Tibber, Joan Plowright, James (Jim) Caviezel, Maria Bonnevie, Paco Reconti, Hristo Naumov Shopov, Alessandro Sperduti, Viola Carinci, Silvia De Santis; *D:* Paul Feig; *M:* Stewart Copeland.

I Am Frigid... Why? *Je Suis Frigide...Pourquoi?; She Should Have Stayed in Bed; Comment le Desir Vient aux Filles* 1972 Eighteen-year-old Doris is the gardener's daughter. She is raped by Eric Chambon, the estate owner's son, and is then sent to boarding school to hush up the scandal. But Doris can't forget and befriends an older woman who runs an expensive call girl operation in Paris. Doris joins her other girls and one of her clients turns out to be Eric's father. French with subtitles. **90m/C VHS.** *FR* Joelle Coeur, Sandra Julien, Anne Kerylen, Stephane Machanovitch, Marie-Georges Pascal, Thierry Murzeau, Jean-Luc Terrade, Virginie Vignon; *D:* Max Pecas; *W:* Max Pecas; *C:* Robert Lefebvre; *M:* Derry Hall.

I Am Legend 2007 (PG-13) Third adaptation of Richard Matheson's 1954 classic novel, following "The Last Man on Earth" and "The Omega Man," about Robert Neville (Smith), a scientist who is the last man standing after a massive plague wipes out the entire world population. However, after three years of biological research and wandering the desolate streets of Manhattan with his dog, he discovers he may not be alone. Will Smith holds his own, with some big special effects carrying the rest. Entertaining as it is, apparently logic and coherency were lost in the plague as well. **100m/C DVD.** *US* Will Smith, Dash Mihok, Salli Richardson, Alice Braga, Charlie Tahan, Willow Smith; *D:* Francis Lawrence; *W:* Mark Protosevich, Akiva Goldsman; *C:* Andrew Lesnie; *M:* James Newton Howard.

I Am Sam 2001 (PG-13) Single father Penn with the mental capacity of a seven-year-old which makes authorities question his ability to raise young daughter Fanning. Pfeiffer's the hard-edged lawyer who comes to his aid and becomes a better person for it. Overly sentimental and sweet, with not much new to offer except the obvious talent of Fanning. **93m/C VHS, DVD.** *US* Sean Penn, Michelle Pfeiffer, Dakota Fanning, Dianne Wiest, Loretta Devine, Richard Schiff, Laura Dern, Brad Allan Silverman, Stanley DeSantis, Doug Hutchison, Joseph Rosenberg, Mary Steenburgen; *D:* Jessie Nelson; *W:* Jessie Nelson, Kristine Johnson; *C:* Elliot Davis; *M:* John Powell.

I Am the Cheese 1983 An institutionalized boy undergoes psychiatric treatment; with the aid of his therapist (Wagner) he relives his traumatic childhood and finds out the truth about the death of his parents. A bit muddled, but with its moments. Adapted from a Robert Cormier teen novel. **95m/C VHS, DVD.** Robert MacNaughton, Hope Lange, Don Murray, Robert Wagner, Sudie Bond, Cynthia Nixon, John Fiedler; *D:* Robert Jiras; *M:* Jonathan Tunick.

I Am the Law 1938 Robinson is given the task of stopping gangster activity in the city. Although regularly a law professor, he is made special prosecutor and starts canvassing for people to testify. His witnesses become murder victims as an enemy on the inside attempts to thwart the game plan. Robinson is dismissed from the case but continues to pursue justice in streetclothes. Fine performances but somewhat predictable. **83m/B VHS.** Edward G. Robinson, Otto Kruger, John Beal, Barbara O'Neil, Wendy Barrie, Arthur Loft, Marc Lawrence, Charles Halton; *D:* Alexander Hall; *W:* Jo Swerling.

I Beheld His Glory 1953 Story based on the experience of Cornelius, the Roman centurion who guarded Christ's tomb. **53m/C VHS, DVD.** George Macready, Robert Wilson, Virginia Wave; *D:* John T. Coyle; *W:* Arthur T. Horman; *C:* Frederick E. West; *M:* Irving Gertz.

I Bombed Pearl Harbor 1960 Mifune stars in this epic that shows events of WWII through Japanese eyes. Dramatic battle scenes boast the most ships destroyed per minute of film. Dubbed from Japanese. **98m/C VHS.** *JP* Toshiro Mifune, Yosuke Natsuki, Makoto Sato, Misa(ko) Uehara; *D:* Shue Matsubayashi; *W:* Shinobu Hashimoto, Takeo Kunihiro; *C:* Kazuo Yamada; *M:* Ikuma Dan.

I Bury the Living 1958 A cemetery manager sticks pins in his map of a graveyard and people mysteriously start to die. Well-done suspense film. **76m/B VHS, DVD.** Richard Boone, Theodore Bikel, Peggy Maurer, Herbert Anderson, Howard Smith, Robert Osterloh, Russ Bender, Matt Moore, Ken Drake, Glenn Vernon, Lynn Bernay, Cyril Delevanti; *D:* Albert Band; *W:* Louis Garfinkle; *C:* Frederick Gately; *M:* Gerald Fried.

I Can't Escape 1934 A man attempts to piece his life back together after serving time for a crime he didn't commit. To prove himself to his girlfriend, he tries to break up an illegal stock scam. **60m/B VHS.** Onslow Stevens, Lila Lee, Russell Gleason, Otis Harlan, Hooper Atchley, Clara Kimball Young; *D:* Otto Brower.

I Can't Sleep *Jai Pas Sommeil* 1993 Serial killers, French style. Gay, black Camille (Courcet), an immigrant from Martinique, and his white lover Raphael (Dupont) live in a Paris hotel and murder elderly women. Though they also rob them, the motive for their horrific crimes is vague (seemingly even to themselves). Not much actually happens—Camille visits his brother, who longs to return home, and their status as outsiders is juxtaposed against another immigrant, Daiga (Golubeva) from Lithuania, who takes little interest in the crimes but unwittingly crosses paths with Camille. Atmospheric if nothing else. Based on the 1987 "Granny Killer" slayings of 20 women. French with subtitles. **110m/C VHS, DVD.** *FR* Richard Courcet, Vincent Dupont, Yekaterina (Katia) Golubeva, Alex Descas, Beatrice Dalle, Laurent Grevill; *D:* Claire Denis; *W:* Claire Denis, Jean-Pol Fargeau; *C:* Agnes Godard; *M:* Jean Murat.

I Capture the Castle 2002 (R) First, the R rating is dumb—it's for a bit of nudity that wouldn't shock a country vicar. Second, the film is based on the book by Dodie Smith (who wrote "101 Dalmatians") and is a coming-of-age tale set in 1936 in the Suffolk countryside. The Mortmains rent a small crumbling castle and times are hard. Dad James (Nighy) ignores his family and hides away to "write," leaving flaky second wife Topaz (Fitzgerald) to cope. Cassandra (Garai) is 17, smart, and pretty but overshadowed by her ambitious, beautiful older sister Rose (Bryne) who is determined to marry well. She gets her chance when two wealthy American brothers, Simon (Thomas) and Neil (Blucas), arrive to claim their inheritance, which includes the castle. Quite a romantic tangle ensues. Fine acting, particularly by Garai who gives the story its point of view. **113m/C VHS, DVD.** *GB* Romola Garai, Rose Byrne, Henry Thomas, Marc Blucas, Bill Nighy, Tara Fitzgerald, Sinead Cusack, Henry Cavill, James Faulkner, Sarah Woodward; *D:* Tim Fywell; *W:* Heidi Thomas; *C:* Richard Greatrex; *M:* Dario Marianelli. L.A. Film Critics '03: Support. Actor (Nighy).

I Come in Peace *Dark Angel* 1990 (R) A tough, maverick Texas cop embarks on a one-way ride to Nosebleed City when he attempts to track down a malevolent alien drug czar who kills his victims by sucking their brains. Mindless thrills. **92m/C VHS.** Dolph Lundgren, Brian Benben, Betsy Brantley, Jesse Vint, Michael J. Pollard; *D:* Craig R. Baxley; *M:* Jan Hammer.

I Confess 1953 Interesting but overly serious mid-career Hitchcock, adapted from Paul Anthelme's 1902 play, "Our Two Consciences." Father Michael Logan (Clift) is a young curate in Quebec, who hears the murder confession of Otto Keller (Hasse). Keller knows Father Logan can tell no one because of the sanctity of the confessional, even when Logan himself comes under suspicion for the crime. Unfortunately, the resolution to the conflict is not up to the master's usual standards. **95m/B VHS, DVD.** Montgomery Clift, Anne Baxter, Karl Malden, Brian Aherne, O.E. Hasse, Dolly Haas, Roger Dann; *D:* Alfred Hitchcock; *W:* William Archibald, George Tabori; *C:* Robert Burks; *M:* Dimitri Tiomkin.

I Conquer the Sea 1936 Two brothers, who works as whalers, cast their affection on the same woman. Drowns in its own melodrama. **68m/B VHS.** Steffi Duna, Dennis Morgan, Douglas Walton, George Cleveland, Johnny Pirrone; *D:* Victor Halperin.

I Could Go on Singing 1963 An aging American songstress, on a tour in Britain, becomes reacquainted with her illegitimate son and his British father, but eventually goes back to the footlights. Garland's last film. Songs include "By Myself" and "It Never Was You." A must for Garland fans. Letterboxed. **99m/C VHS, DVD.** Judy Garland, Dirk Bogarde, Jack Klugman, Aline MacMahon; *D:* Ronald Neame.

I Could Never Be Your Woman 2006 (PG-13) Not terribly romantic or funny although Pfeiffer is as gorgeous as ever. Divorced and frazzled, 40-something TV sitcom producer Rosie (Pfeiffer) is shocked when she falls for the show's newest cast member, the years-younger Adam (Rudd). Meanwhile, Rosie's teen daughter Izzy (Ronan) is in the throes of first love. Thrown into the mix—and an uneasy addition—is Ullman's Mother Nature, who appears as Rosie's conscience, offering unsolicited and unwelcome romantic advice. **97m/C DVD.** Michelle Pfeiffer, Paul Rudd, Stacey Dash, Tracey Ullman, Fred Willard, Henry Winkler, Sally Kellerman, Jon Lovitz, Saoirse Ronan, Sarah Alexander, Brittany Benson, Jed Bernard; *D:* Amy Heckerling; *W:* Amy Heckerling; *C:* Brian Tufano.

I Cover the Waterfront 1933 A reporter is assigned to write about a boatman involved in a fishy scheme to smuggle Chinese immigrants into the country wrapped in shark skins. While trying to get the story, the journalist falls in love with the fisherman's daughter. Torrance passed away before its release. **70m/B VHS, DVD.** Claudette Colbert, Ben Lyon, Ernest Torrence, Hobart Cavanaugh; *D:* James Cruze.

I Died a Thousand Times 1955 Aging gangster Mad Dog Earle (pushup prince Palance) plans one last death-defying heist while hiding from police in the mountains. Meanwhile, the hard boiled gangster softens a bit thanks to surgery-needing girlfriend, but moll Winters doesn't seem to think that three's company. A low rent "High Sierra." From the novel by W.R. Burnett. **109m/C VHS.** Jack Palance, Shelley Winters, Lori Nelson, Lee Marvin, Earl Holliman, Lon Chaney Jr., Howard St. John; *D:* Stuart Heisler; *W:* W.R. Burnett.

I Dismember Mama WOOF! *Poor Albert and Little Annie* 1974 (R) Classless story of an asylum inmate who escapes to kill his mother. Although he hates women, he likes little girls as evidenced by his nine-year-old love interest. Notably lacking in bloody scenes. **81m/C VHS.** Zooey Hall, Joanne Moore Jordan, Greg Mullavey, Marlene Tracy, Geri Reischl, Frank Whiteman; *D:* Paul Leder; *W:* William W. Norton Sr.; *C:* Andreas Mannkopf; *M:* Herschel Burke Gilbert.

I Don't Buy Kisses Anymore 1992 (PG) Heartwarming story starring Alexander and Peeples as two mismatched lovers who each other, finally realizing that they're made for each other. Alexander plays Bernie Fishbine, an overweight Jewish shoe store owner who falls for a psychology graduate student (Peeples). Little does he know, but Peeples is studying him for her term paper, appropriately titled "The Psychological Study of an Obese Male." Alexander gives a great performance, as do Kazan and Jacobi who play Bernie's parents. **112m/C VHS, DVD.** Jason Alexander, Nia Peeples, Lainie Kazan, Lou Jacobi, Eileen Brennan, Larry Storch, Areen (Arlene) Sorkin; *D:* Robert Marcarelli; *W:* Jonnie Lindsell; *C:* Michael Ferris; *M:* Cobb Bussinger. TV

I Don't Give a Damn 1988 (R) An embittered wounded soldier returns home to his loved ones, rejects them, and becomes more and more uninterested in life itself. Subtitled. **94m/C VHS.** *IS* Ika Sohar, Anat Waxman; *D:* Shmuel Imberman.

I Don't Want to Be Born *The Devil Within Her* 1975 (R) It's got all the right ingredients for overnight pain: a spurned dwarf, a large, howling baby-thing, slice and dice murder and mayhem, and Collins. It could've been so bad. Instead, this "Rosemary's Baby" rehash is just stupid bad. **90m/C VHS.** *GB* Joan Collins, Eileen Atkins, Donald Pleasence, Ralph Bates, Caroline Munro; *D:* Peter Sasdy.

I Don't Want to Talk About It *De Eso No Se Habla* 1994 Fable set in a small South American town in the '30s. The widowed Leonor (Brando) is the community leader, a woman determined to see that her daughter Charlotte (Podesta) be as happy and accomplished as possible. Leonor refuses to acknowledge Charlotte is a dwarf and size is never permitted to be mentioned in her presence. Her zealous protectiveness is challenged by worldly and charming newcomer Ludovico (Mastroianni) who becomes entranced by Charlotte. Mastroianni is masterly as always but the moody film proves slight. Based on story by Julio Llinas. Spanish with subtitles. **102m/C VHS.** *AR* Marcello Mastroianni, Luisina Brando, Alejandra Podesta; *D:* Maria-Luisa Bemberg; *W:* Maria-Luisa Bemberg, Jorge Goldenberg.

I Dood It *By Hook or By Crook* 1943 Young tailor's assistant Skelton falls hard for young actress Powell working near his shop. She agrees to date, and eventually marry him, but only to spite her boyfriend who has just run off with another woman. All's well however, when Skelton stumbles across a spy ring, is hailed a hero and helps Powell realize she really loves him. ♫Star Eyes; Taking a Chance on Love; Jericho; One O'Clock Jump; So Long Sarah Jane; Hola E Pae; Swing the Jinx Away. **102m/B VHS.** Red Skelton, Eleanor Powell, Richard Ainley, Patricia Dane, Sam Levene, Thurston Hall, Lena Home, Butterfly McQueen; *D:* Vincente Minnelli.

I Dream of Jeannie 1952 The third and worst film of Stephen Foster has Foster as a bookkeeper-cum-songwriter alternating between writing tunes and chasing Lawrence. When she dumps him, he goes into a funk. Will he be able to complete the title song? The suspense will kill you. Lots of singing, but not much else. **90m/C VHS, DVD.** Ray Middleton, Bill (William) Shirley, Muriel Lawrence, Lynn Bari, Rex Allen; *D:* Allan Dwan.

I Dream Too Much 1935 A musical vehicle for opera star Pons, as a French singer who marries an American composer played by Fonda. Songwriter falls into wife's shadow after pushing her into a singing career; she then raises his spirits a couple of octaves by helping him sell a musical comedy. Went into production after a rival company, Columbia, launched opera singer Grace Moore's acting career. Ball later bought this studio, where she was given her second starring role. ♫The Jockey on the Carousel; I'm the Echo; I Got Love; I Dream Too Much; Bell Song; Caro Nome. **90m/B VHS.** Lily Pons, Henry Fonda, Eric Blore, Lucille Ball, Mischa Auer, Scotty Beckett; *D:* John Cromwell; *M:* Max Steiner.

I Dreamed of Africa 2000 (PG-13) Okay the scenery is beautiful (it was filmed in Kenya), she's a beautiful blonde (Basinger), but the story is predictable and trite despite being based on the autobiography of Italian socialite Kuki Gallmann. Gallmann (Basinger) trades in her designer duds for safari khaki when she, her young son, Emanuele (Aiken), and her second husband, Paolo (Perez), decide they need a fresh start. The somewhat irresponsible Paolo likes to go big game hunting with his friends, leaving Kuki alone, and she eventually becomes a conservationist after some personal tragedies. Most of the roles, except Basinger's, are one-dimensional. **114m/C VHS, DVD.** Kim Basinger, Vincent Perez, Eva Marie Saint, Daniel Craig, Lance Reddick, Liam Aiken, Garrett Strommen; *D:* Hugh Hudson; *W:* Paula Milne, Susan Shilliday; *C:* Bernard Lutic; *M:* Maurice Jarre.

I Drink Your Blood ♂️½ 1971 **(R)** Hippie satanists looking for kicks spike an old man's drink with LSD. To get revenge, the old codger's grandson sells the nasty flower children meat pies injected with the blood of a rabid dog. The hippies then turn into cannibalistic maniacs, infecting anyone they bite. From the man responsible for "I Spit on Your Grave", originally played on a double bill with "I Eat Your Skin." **83m/C VHS, DVD.** Bhasker, Jadee Wong, Ronda Fultz, Elizabeth Marner-Brooks, George Patterson, Riley Mills, Iris Brooks; *D:* David E. Durston; *W:* David E. Durston; *C:* Jacques Demarecaux; *M:* Clay Pitts.

I Eat Your Skin WOOF! *Voodoo Blood Bath; Zombie; Zombies* 1964 Cannibalistic zombies terrorize a novelist and his girlfriend on a Caribbean island. Blood and guts, usually shown on a gourmet double bill with "I Drink Your Blood." **82m/B VHS, DVD.** William Joyce, Heather Hewitt, Betty Hyatt Linton, Robert Stanton, Dan Stapleton; *D:* Del Tenney; *W:* Jel Tenney; *C:* Francois Farkas; *M:* Lon Norman.

I Got Five on It ♂️½ 2005 Absurd partying flick begins with Jimmy (Bridges) behind bars for buying dope, leaving his three spacey pals to fend for themselves. As they scavenge about town to score weed, trouble seems to be all they can find, even after Jimmy returns **76m/C DVD.** Todd Bridges, Jose Rosette, Chris Angelo, Carl Washington; *D:* Eduardo Quiroz, Jose Quiroz; *W:* Eduardo Quiroz, Jose Quiroz. **VIDEO**

I Got the Hook-Up ♂️½ 1998 **(R)** Inner-city hustlers Black (Master P) and Blue (Johnson) have their own "department store" in a vacant lot where they sell various goods of dubious quality and origin. When a truckload of cel phones is mistakenly delivered to them, it ushers them into a new business venture. All hell breaks loose when a thug (Lister) has a money pick-up go bad because of the defective phones. Sporadically amusing comedy plays gang violence and misogyny for laughs, while the leads do nothing to make their characters interesting or even likable. **93m/C VHS, DVD.** Mark Zwelcke, A.J. (Anthony) Johnson, Gretchen Palmer, Frantz Turner, Tommy (Tiny) Lister, Helen Martin, John Witherspoon, Harrison White, Ice Cube, Anthony Boswell, Lola Mae; *D:* Michael Martin; *W:* Mark Zwelcke; *C:* Antonio Calvache; *M:* Tommy Coster, Brad Farmar.

I Hate Blondes ♂️♂️½ *Odio le Bionde* 1983 A group of criminals use a ghostwriter's burglaring stories as instruction-al manuals. The writer becomes involved with the gang. Relies heavily on visual humor. Notable among the comedy scenes is the author's search for jewels at a get-together. **90m/C VHS, IT** *D:* Giorgio Capitani.

I Heard the Owl Call My Name ♂️♂️½ 1973 Poignant story of an Anglican priest who is relocated to an Indian fishing village on the outskirts of Vancouver, British Columbia. Based on a Margaret Craven book. **74m/C** Tom Courtenay, Dean Jagger, Paul Stanley; *D:* Daryl Duke. **TV**

I Heart Huckabees ♂️♂️ 2004 **(R)** Director Russell's existential comedy has a cast willing to take chances with material that is too clever for its own good—and viewers' enjoyment. Environmentalist/poet Albert (Schwartzman), fighting giant retail chain Huckabees, takes his search for enlightenment to the offices of existential detectives Bernard and Vivian Jaffe (Hoffman, Tomlin), who believe everything in life is connected. Albert thinks his nemesis is Huckabee's golden exec Brad Stand (Law), and Brad's gorgeous spokesmodel girlfriend Dawn (Watts) until they also become the Jaffes' clients. Then Albert becomes friends Tommy Corn (Wahlberg), a firefighter, who has become involved with French nihilist Caterine (Huppert), who believes everything is meaningless and...okay, things get even more convoluted, although Tomlin and Hoffman, at least, seem to be having a grand time. **105m/C VHS, DVD.** Jason Schwartzman, Isabelle Huppert, Dustin Hoffman, Lily Tomlin, Jude Law, Mark Wahlberg, Naomi Watts; *D:* David O. Russell; *W:* David O. Russell, Jeff Baena; *C:* Peter Deming.

I Killed That Man ♂️♂️½ 1942 A prisoner scheduled to die in the electric chair is given an early ticket out when he is found poisoned. Evidence points to an unusual group of suspects. Effective low-budget thriller offers a few unexpected surprises. **72m/B VHS, DVD.** Ricardo Cortez, Joan Woodbury, Iris Adrian, George Pembroke, Herbert Rawinson, Pat Gleason, Ralf Harolde, Jack Mulhall, Vince Barnett, Gavin Gordon, John Hamilton; *D:* Phil Rosen.

I Killed Rasputin ♂️♂️ 1967 The "Mad Monk" who rose to power before the Russian Revolution lost his life in a bizarre assassination by Felix Youssoupoff. Film deals with the friendship between the men that ended in betrayal. Well-mentioned and but overwrought. Dubbed. **95m/C VHS, FR IT.** Geraldine Chaplin, Gert Frobe, Peter McEnery; *D:* Robert Hossein; *M:* Don Banks.

I Know What You Did Last Summer ♂️♂️½ 1997 **(R)** Four teens get involved in a fatal hit-and-run accident and think they've managed to keep it a secret. Good girl Julie (Hewitt), beauty queen Helen (Gellar), arrogant jock Barry (Phillippe), and regular guy Ray (Prinze) make a pact to take the secret to their graves, which may be sooner than they thought. One year later, the quartet receive letters which give the movie its title and set them against each other. After a large fishing hooks, they band together to stop the bloodthirsty killer. Hint: it's not Mrs. Paul. Another quality slasher throwback written by Kevin Williamson, the man who made you "Scream." **100m/C VHS, DVD.** Jennifer Love Hewitt, Sarah Michelle Gellar, Ryan Phillippe, Freddie Prinze Jr., Muse Watson, Anne Heche, Bridgette Wilson-Sampras, Johnny Galecki, Dan Albright; *D:* Jim Gillespie; *W:* Kevin Williamson; *C:* Denis Crossan; *M:* John Debney.

I Know Where I'm Going ♂️♂️♂️ 1945 A young woman (Hiller), who believes that money brings happiness, is on the verge of marrying a rich old man, until she meets a handsome naval officer (Livesey) and finds a happy, simple life. Early on the female lead appears in a dream sequence filmed in the mode of surrealist painter Salvador Dali and avant garde director Luis Bunuel. Scottish setting and folk songs give a unique flavor. Brown provides a fine performance as a native Scot. **91m/B VHS, DVD, G9** Roger Livesey, Wendy Hiller, Finlay Currie, Pamela Brown, George Carney, Walter Huddart, Nancy Price; *D:* Michael Powell, Emeric Pressburger; *C:* Erwin Hillier; *W:* Allan Gray.

I Know Who Killed Me ♂️ 2007 **(R)** Upper middle class high school student Aubrey Fleming (Lohan) goes missing. Her distraught parents 'Ormond and McDonough) cooperate with the police but have little insight into the disappearance. When Aubrey's found beside a rural road near death and mutilated in the M.O. of a local serial killer, the case seems pretty simple, until Aubrey awakes and thinks she's actually stripper Dakota Moss, who she's the subject of a story Aubrey was writing for a class. Flashbacks, dream sequences and semi-plausible cinematic gimmicks bring this insight into the disappearance bles, this might be your last chance to see Lohan (outside a courthouse) for a while. Will Crawford, Neal McDonough, Garcelle Beauvais, Brian Geraghty, Spencer Garrett, Gregory Itzin, Rodney Rowland, Paula Marshall, Eddie Steeples, Kenya Moore, Donovan Scott, Bonnie Aarons, Thomas Tofel, David Figlioni, Michael (Mike) Papajohn, Michelle Page; *D:* Chris Sivertson; *W:* Jeffrey Hammond; *C:* John R. Leonetti; *M:* Joel McNeely; Golden Raspberries '07; Worst Actress (Lohan), Worst Director (Sivertson), Worst Screenplay, Worst Remake.

I Know Why the Caged Bird Sings ♂️♂️ 1979 A black writer's memories of growing up in the rural South during the 1930s. Strong performances from Rolle and Good. Based on the book by Maya Angelou. **100m/C VHS.** Diahann Carroll, Ruby Dee, Esther Rolle, Roger E. Mosley, Paul Benjamin, Constance Good; *D:* Fielder Cook.

I Like Bats 1985 Can a psychiatrist help a vampire become a human? Polish dialogue with English subtitles. **90m/C VHS.** Katarzyna Walter, Marek Barbasiewicz, Malgorzata Lorentowicz; *D:* Grzegorz Warchol; *W:* Grzegorz Warchol; *C:* Krzysztof Pakulski; *M:* Zbigniew Preisner.

I Like It Like That ♂️♂️♂️ 1994 Chaotic family life and loves in the Bronx are the setting for this tale of a Cinderella in the record industry. Strong-willed black-Latina Lisette (Velez) has been married for 10 years to macho Latin, Chino (Seda), who has a wandering eye. When Chino is jailed for looting during a blackout, Lisette, needing to support their three kids, talks her way into a job with WASP record promoter Stephen Price (Dunne). When local gossips make it seem Lisette is having an affair, the newly sprung Chino retaliates by turning to lusty Magdalena (Vidal). Lisette, meanwhile, gathers support from her transvestite brother and proves to have inner resources previously unnoticed. Great Latin no soundtrack illuminates the complications. Modest-budget sleeper quickly exits the theatre but proves to be a strong debut for director/writer Martin, reputed to be the first African-American woman to be given the reins by a major studio. **106m/C VHS, DVD.** Lauren Velez, Jon Seda, Lisa Vida, Jesse Borrego, Griffin Dunne, Rita Moreno, Tomas Melly, Desiree Casado, Isaiah Garcia, Darnell Martin; *W:* Darnell Martin; *C:* Alexander Gruszynski; *M:* Sergio Garcia.

I Like to Play Games ♂️½ 1995 **(R)** Michael is looking for a woman who enjoys playing sexual games—and he seems to find the perfect partner in Suzanne. But just how far will their kinks take them? Also available unrated **95m/C VHS, DVD.** Lisa Boyle, Ken Steadman; *D:* Kim Haun.

I Live in Fear ♂️♂️♂️ *Ikimono No Kiroku* 1955 Nakajima, an elderly, wealthy owner of a foundry, becomes increasingly fearful of atomic war and the threats to his family's safety. He tries to persuade them to leave Japan and move with him to Brazil but they fear his children to put instead they go to court and have him declared mentally incompetent. He is placed in an institution where he finds peace in the delusion that the Earth has indeed suffered a nuclear holocaust. Provocative look at the fear of atomic warfare and radiation. In Japanese with English subtitles. **105m/C VHS.** Toshiro Mifune, Takashi Shimura, Eiko Miyoshi, Haruko Togo; *D:* Akira Kurosawa; *W:* Akira Kurosawa, Shinobu Hashimoto, Hideo Oguni; *C:* Asakazu Nakai; *M:* Fumio Hayasaka.

I Live in Grosvenor Square ♂️♂️ A Yank in London 1946 An American soldier in Great Britain falls in love with a major's fiancee. Entertaining if a bit drawn out. **106m/B VHS, GB** Anna Neagle, Rex Harrison, Dean Jagger, Robert Morley, Jane Darwell; *D:* Herbert Wilcox.

I Live My Life ♂️½ 1935 Stylish glossy flick with Crawford playing a bored New York debutante who travels to Greece and meets a dedicated archaeologist (Aherne). A love/hate relationship ensues in this typical Crawford vehicle where she is witty and parades around in sophisticated fashions, but there is little substance here. **92m/B VHS.** Joan Crawford, Brian Aherne, Frank Morgan, Aline MacMahon, Eric Blore, Fred Keating, Jessie Ralph, Arthur Treacher, Hedda Hopper, Lionel Stander; *D:* Woodridge S. Van Dyke, *W:* Joseph L. Mankiewicz, Gottfried Reinhardt, Ethel B. Borden; *C:* George J. Folsey.

I Live with Me Dad ♂️½ 1986 A vagrant drunk and his son fight the authorities for the right to be together. **86m/C VHS.** AU Peter Hehir, Haydon Samuels; *D:* Paul Maloney.

I Love a Bandleader ♂️½ 1945 Housepainter Phil Burton (Harris) gets amnesia and imagines he's the leader of a swing band. He also falls in love with Ann (Brooks) who's determined to get him back on the bandstand when Phil's memory returns and he goes back to his old boring life. **70m/B VHS.** Phil Harris, Leslie Brooks, Eddie Anderson, Walter Catlett; *D:* Del Lord; *W:* Paul Yawitz; *C:* Franz Planer; *M:* Walter Kent.

I Love All of You ♂️♂️½ 1983 Deneuve relives experiences with three former lovers—a composer, a well-intentioned nobody, and a rock star—as she enters into a relationship with a widower, which will effect everyone's relationships. **103m/C VHS, FR** Catherine Deneuve, Jean-Louis Trintignant, Gerard Depardieu, Serge Gainsbourg; *D:* Claude Berri.

I Love Budapest ♂️♂️ 2001 Teenagers Aniko leaves her village to have a better life in Budapest. She gets a factory job and becomes smitten with security guard Miki. Aniko's new friend, the more sophisticated Moni, gets her boyfriend Krisztian to offer Miki a better job to impress Aniko. The problem is the job is part of Krisztian's underground criminal world. Hungarian with subtitles. **85m/C VHS, DVD.** HU Gabriella Hamor, Sandor Csanyi, Martina Kovacs, Tomas Lengyel; *D:* Agnes Incze; *W:* Agnes Incze; *C:* Gergely Pohárnok; *M:* Laszlo Fogaras.

I Love Melvin ♂️♂️½ 1953 Reynolds is a photographer's assistant for a little trouble on the "follow through. Choreographed by Robert Alton, it's got a least ever football player (with Reynolds as pigskin). A Lady Loves; Saturday Afternoon Before The Game; I Wanna Wander; We Have Never Met As Of Yet; Life Has Its Funny Little Ups And Downs; Where Did You Learn To Dance?; And There You Are. **77m/C VHS.** Donald O'Connor, Debbie Reynolds, Una Merkel, Richard Anderson, Jim Backus, Allyn Joslyn, Les Tremayne, Noreen Corcoran, Robert Taylor, Howard Keel, Helen Winston; *D:* Don Weis.

I Love My... Wife ♂️½ 1970 **(R)** A medical student plays doctor with hospital nurses when he and his wife stop having sex during her pregnancy. The marriage becomes more strained when their son is born and his mother-in-law moves in. A secretly exchange information on a big story, they find their lives threatened and their rivalry turning to romance. Some accolade. Written, produced and directed by husband/wife team Meyers and Shyer. **123m/C VHS, DVD.** Dan E. Butler, Kelly Rutherford, Olympia Dukakis, Marsha Mason, Eugene Levy, Charles Martin Smith, Paul Gleason, Jane Adams, Lisa Lu, Nora Dunn, Clark Gregg, Kevin Breznahan, Dorothy Lyman, Keith Gordon, Joseph (Joe) D'Onofrio, Barry Sobel, Frankie Faison, Stuart Pankin, Megan Cavanagh, Jessica Lundy, Nestor Serrano, Roon Duke, Julia Roberts, Nick Nolte.

I Love N.Y. ♂️ 1987 A young metropolitan couple struggles to find true love amidst disapproving parents and doubting friends. Choppy direction and poor writing contribute to its failure. **100m/C VHS, DVD.** Scott Baio, Kelley Van Der Velden, Christopher Plummer, Jennifer O'Neill, Jerry Orbach, Virna Lisi; *D:* Alan Smithee; *M:* Bill Conti.

I Love Trouble ♂️♂️½ 1994 **(PG)** Veteran reporter Peter Brackett (sexy veteran Nolte) and ambitious cub reporter Sabrina Petersen (young and sexy Roberts) are competitors working for rival Chicago newspapers. When they begin to contribute to its failure. **100m/C VHS, DVD.**

Saul Rubinek, Robert Loggia, James Rebhorn; **D:** Charles Shyer; **W:** Nancy Meyers, Charles Shyer; **C:** John Lindley; **M:** David Newman.

I Love You 1981 (R) Man down on his luck mistakenly assumes that a woman he meets is a hooker. She plays along, only to find that they are becoming emotionally involved. Pretentious cat-and-mouse game. 104m/C VHS. *BR* Sonia Braga, Paulo Cesar Pereio, Vera Fischer, Tarcisio Meira; **D:** Arnaldo Jabor.

I Love You Again 1940 A classic screwball comedy with Powell and Loy working together (wonderfully) in something other than their "Thin Man" series. Powell is a gloomy businessman who's about to be divorced by Loy. But after an accident it turns out Powell had been suffering from amnesia and has now regained his memory (which he keeps a secret). It seems Mr. Respectable used to be a con man and he decides to revert to his criminal ways. He also doesn't remember Loy but falls instantly in love with her and must decide what kind of life he wants. Witty dialog, amusing situations, fine direction. 97m/B VHS, DVD. William Powell, Myrna Loy, Frank McHugh, Edmund Lowe; **D:** Woodbridge S. Van Dyke.

I Love You, Alice B. Toklas! 1968 A straight uptight lawyer decides to join the peace and love generation in this somewhat maniacal satire of the hippie culture. Pretty dated now. Authored by Paul Mazursky and Larry Tucker. Incidentally, the title's Alice B. Toklas was actually the life-mate of "Lost Generation" author Gertrude Stein. 94m/C VHS, DVD. Peter Sellers, Jo Van Fleet, Leigh Taylor-Young, Joyce Van Patten, David Arkin, Herb Edelman, Salem Ludwig; **D:** Hy Averback; **W:** Paul Mazursky, Larry Tucker; **C:** Philip Lathrop; **M:** Elmer Bernstein.

I Love You Baby 2001 Absurd romantic comedy with an implausible premise (even for the genre) and a miscast leading actor in Sanz, who seems too old matched against his co-stars. Marcos (Sanz) has hooked up with Daniel (Magill). They're happy until a mirror ball falls on Marcos's head in a disco and he wakes up thinking he's straight. So he falls for Marisol (Scanda) and they settle down together to get his boyfriend back. Meanwhile Daniel will do anything to get his boyfriend back. Spanish with subtitles. 110m/C DVD. *SP* Jorge Sanz, Santiago Magill, Tiaré Scanda, Veronica Forque, Boy George; **D:** Alfonso Albacete, David Menkes; **W:** Alfonso Albacete, David Menkes, Lucia Etxeberria; **C:** Gonzalo Fernandez-Berridi; **M:** Paco Ortega, Miguel Angel Collado.

I Love You, Don't Touch Me! 1997 (R) Katie (Schafel) is a smart-mouthed, 25-year-old would-be singer in L.A., who also happens to be a virgin. She wants everything to be perfect her first time but all the guys she meets are just wrong. Her best friend Ben (Whitfield) would like to be the one, but Katie just can't see him in a romantic like. Then Katie finally gets involved with an older composer (Webber) who takes an interest in her career and all the romantic complications just get worse. 85m/C VHS, DVD. Marla Schafel, Mitchell Whitfield, Michael (M.K.) Harris, Nancy Sorel, Meredith Scott Lynn, Daryl Therse; **D:** Julie Davis; **W:** Julie Davis; **C:** Mark Putnam.

I Love You, Goodbye 1974 A frustrated housewife, fed up with the constant role of wife and mother, leaves her family in an effort to find a more challenging and fulfilling life. A good performance by Lange compensates for some of its muddledness. 74m/C VHS. Hope Lange, Earl Holliman, Michael Murphy, Patricia Smith, Mary Murphy; **D:** Sam O'Steen; **W:** Diana Gould; **C:** Andrew Jackson; **M:** Billy Goldenberg. TV

I Love You, I Love You Not 1997 (PG-13) The Holocaust becomes a metaphor for one teen's survival of her first painful romance. Daisy (Danes) is a Jewish student at a snobby and anti-Semitic Manhattan prep school, where she falls in love with the ultimate gentile, Ethan (Law) in a "Kids" meets "The Way We Were" spin. Moreau is a Holo-caust survivor, whom Daisy visits every weekend. The two share their painful stories (Danes also plays Nana as a young girl). Danes does what she does best as a misunderstood teen coming of age. Moreau shines in her role as the beloved grandmother. What misfires is the trite handling of the serious subject matter as Daisy's romance scores far more screen time than Nana's suffering. Hopkins, an established casting director, makes his feature debut. 92m/C VHS, DVD. *FR GE GB* Claire Danes, Jeanne Moreau, Jude Law, James Van Der Beek, Robert Sean Leonard, Kris Park, Lauren Fox, Emily Burkes-Nossiter, Carrie Slaza; **D:** Billy Hopkins; **W:** Wendy Kesselman; **C:** Maryse Alberti; **M:** Gil Goldstein.

I Love You Rosa 1972 Rosa, a young Jewish widow, wrestles big time with old world values. Required by custom to marry her dearly departed's eldest brother, she's not enamored with her newly betrothed. Not that he's not a nice guy; he seems to plan to take his marital duties very seriously. It's just that he's a tad youthful (11 years old, to be exact). Much rabbi consulting and soul searching. 90m/C VHS. Michal Bat-Adam, Gabi Oterman, Joseph Shiloah; **D:** Moshe Mizrahi; **W:** Moshe Mizrahi.

I Love You to Death 1990 (R) Dry comedy based on a true story, concerns a woman who tries to kill off her cheating husband. Lots of stars, but they never shine. Hurt and Reeves are somewhat amusing as drugged up hit men who struggle with the lyrics to the National Anthem. Watch for director Kasdan as Devo's lawyer. Cates, Kline's real-life wife, has an unbilled part as one of his one-night stands. 110m/C VHS, DVD. Kevin Kline, Tracey Ullman, Joan Plowright, River Phoenix, Keanu Reeves, James Gammon, Victoria Jackson, Miriam Margolyes, Heather Graham; *Cameos:* Phoebe Cates; **D:** Lawrence Kasdan; **W:** John Kostmayer; **C:** Owen Roizman; **M:** James Horner.

I Love Your Work 2003 (R) Goldberg tries to highlight the glamour and fake fabulousness of modern Hollywood celebrity, not always successfully, but at times interestingly. Loft-dwelling Gray Evans (Ribisi) and his wife Mia Lang (Potente) are famous, paparazzi-stalked actors living in Los Angeles. Gray's navel-gazing and paranoia turn into obsession with a young artist who reminds him of his pre-fame days. May be tedious for those not well-versed in the L.A. vibe. 111m/C DVD. *US* Marisa Coughlan, Judy Greer, Joshua Jackson, Nicky Katt, Jason Lee, Franka Potente, Giovanni Ribisi, Christina Ricci, Vince Vaughn; *Cameos:* Elvis Costello; **D:** Adam Goldberg; **W:** Adam Goldberg, Adrian Butchart; **C:** Mark Putnam; **M:** Adam Goldberg, Steven Drozd.

I, Madman 1989 (R) A novel-loving horror actress is stalked by the same mutilating madman that appears in the book she's presently reading. We call that bad luck. 90m/C VHS, DVD. Jenny Wright, Clayton Rohner, William Cook; **D:** Tibor Takacs; **W:** David Chaskin; **C:** Bryan England.

I Married a Centerfold 1984 Fluff about a young man's amorous pursuit of a model. 100m/C VHS, DVD. Teri Copley, Timothy Daly, Diane Ladd, Bert Remsen, Anson Williams; **D:** Peter Werner. TV

I Married a Dead Man 1982 *J'ai Epouse une Ombre; I Married a Shadow* When the train she's travelling on is involved in a terrible crash, abandoned, pregnant Helene (Baye) decides to assume the identity of a wealthy young woman who was killed in the wreck. But soon Helene is receiving anonymous threats from someone who knows who she really is. Based on a book by Cornell Woolrich and also filmed as "No Man of Her Own" (1950) and "Mrs. Winterbourne" (1996). French with subtitles. 110m/C VHS. *FR* Nathalie Baye, Richard Bohringer, Victoria Abril, Francis Huster, Madeleine Robinson; Guy Trejan, Humbert Balsan, Veronique Genest; **D:** Robin Davis; **W:** Patrick Laurent; **C:** Bernard Zitzermann; **M:** Philippe Sarde.

I Married a Monster 1998 (PG-13) Update of the 1958 sci-fi film "I Married a Monster from Outer Space." The title tells the story—small town newlywed (Walters) finds out her hubby (Burgi) has been possessed by an alien intent on procreating its dying race. 85m/C VHS. Susan Walters, Richard Burgi, Richard Herd, Barbara Niven; **D:** Nancy Malone; **W:** Duane Poole. TV

I Married a Monster from Outer Space 1958 The vintage thriller about a race of monster-like aliens from another planet who try to conquer earth. Despite its head-shaking title, an effective '50s sci-fi creeper. 78m/B VHS, DVD. Tom Tryon, Gloria Talbott, Maxie "Slapsie" Rosenbloom, Mary Treen, Ty Hardin, Ken Lynch, John Eldridge, Jean-Phillipe Casson, Alan Dexter; **D:** Gene Fowler Jr.; **W:** Louis Vittes; **C:** Haskell Boggs.

I Married a Vampire 1987 A country girl in the city is romanced and duped by a dashing vampire. Troma-produced hyper-camp. 85m/C VHS. Rachel Gorroll, Brendan Hickey, Ted Zalewski; Deborah Carroll, Temple Aaron; **D:** Jay Raskin; **W:** Jay Raskin; **C:** Oren Rudavsky.

I Married a Witch 1942 Jennifer (Lake) and her father Daniel (Kellaway) are burned at the stake during the Salem witch trials but not before cursing their persecutors, the Wooley family, vowing that no male of the line will ever find happiness. When Jennifer and Daniel are accidentally freed from their burial place centuries later, Jennifer locates Wallace Wooley (March) and tries to get him to fall in love with her so that she can remain on the mortal plane. Wonderfully played fantasy/comedy. 77m/B VHS. Veronica Lake, Fredric March, Susan Hayward, Robert Benchley, Cecil Kellaway, Elizabeth Patterson, Robert Warwick, Elly Malyon, Mary Field, Nora Cecil, Emory Parnell, Helen St. Rayer, Aldrich Bowker, Emma Dunn, Harry Tyler, Ralph Peters, Ann Carter; **D:** Rene Clair; **W:** Robert Pirosh, Marc Connelly; **C:** Ted Tetzlaff; **M:** Roy Webb.

I Married a Woman 1956 Advertising executive marries beautiful blonde woman, but finds it very difficult to balance his career and marriage. Low on laughs. Shot in black and white, but includes a fantasy scene in color that features John Wayne. Pay attention to see young Angie Dickinson. 84m/B VHS. George Gobel, Diana Dors, Adolphe Menjou, Nita Talbot, William Redfield, Jessie Royce Landis, Steve (Stephen) Dunne, Angie Dickinson; *Cameos:* John Wayne; **D:** Hal Kanter; **W:** Goodman Ace; **C:** Lucien Ballard; **M:** Cyril Mockridge.

I Married an Angel 1942 The last MacDonald/Eddy film. A playboy is lured away from his usual interests by a beautiful angel. Adapted from Rodgers and Hart Broadway play. Strange and less than compelling. Married An Angel; I'll Tell the Man in the Street; Spring is Here; Tira Lira La; A Twinkle in Your Eye; Aloha Oe; Caprice Viennoise; Chanson Boheme; Anges Purs. 84m/C VHS. Jeanette MacDonald, Nelson Eddy, Binnie Barnes, Edward Everett Horton, Reginald Owen, Mona Maris, Janis Carter, Inez Cooper, Douglass Dumbrille, Leonid Kinskey, Marion Rosamond, Anne Jeffreys, Marek Windheim, Veda Ann Borg; **D:** Woodbridge S. Van Dyke; **W:** Anita Loos; **M:** Richard Rodgers, Lorenz Hart.

I Met a Murderer 1939 A man kills his nagging wife after a bitter argument and flees from her vengeful brother. Fine fugitive drama with a number of interesting twists. 79m/B VHS. James Mason, Pamela Kellino, Sylvia Coleridge, William Devlin, Esma Cannon, James Harcourt; **D:** Roy Kellino; **W:** Roy Kellino; **C:** Roy Kellino.

I, Mobster 1958 Cochran tells a Senate Sub-Committee of his rise in the ranks of the Underworld—from his humble beginning as a bet collector for a bookie to his position as kingpin of the crime syndicate. 80m/B VHS, DVD. Steve Cochran, Lita Milan, Robert Strauss, Celia Lovsky; **D:** Roger Corman; **C:** Floyd Crosby.

I, Monster 1971 The character names may have changed but this is still Robert Louis Stevenson's "Dr. Jekyll and Mr. Hyde." Lee tackles the title char-acters with his usual sinister savoir faire as Dr. Marlowe, who is obsessed with the nature of the id, the ego, and the superego and whether they can be separated within an individual. He injects himself with his secret formula and is transformed into Mr. Blake, who prowls the seedy sections of Victorian London to satisfy his violent desires. Frequent co-star Cushing shows up as a suspicious colleague. 74m/C VHS, DVD. *GB* Christopher Lee, Peter Cushing, Mike Raven, George Merritt, Richard Hurndall, Kenneth J. Warren, Michael Des Barres, Susan Jameson; **D:** Stephen Weeks; **W:** Milton Subotsky; **C:** Moray Grant; **M:** Carl Davis.

I Never Promised You a Rose Garden 1977 (R) A disturbed 16-year-old girl spirals down into madness and despair during a hospital psychiatrist struggles to bring her back to life. Based on the Joanne Greenberg bestseller. Compelling and unyielding exploration of the clinical treatment of schizophrenia. 90m/C VHS, DVD. Kathleen Quinlan, Bibi Andersson, Sylvia Sidney, Diane Varsi, Dennis Quaid, Jeff Conaway; **D:** Anthony Page; **W:** Gavin Lambert, Lewis John Carlino; **C:** Bruce Logan; **M:** Paul Chihara.

I Never Sang for My Father 1970 (PG) A devoted son must choose between caring for his cantankerous but well-meaning father, and moving out West to marry the divorced doctor whom he loves. While his mother wants him to stay near home, his sister, who fell out of her father's favor by marrying out of the family faith, argues that he should do what he wants. An introspective, stirring story based on the Robert Anderson play. 90m/C VHS. Gene Hackman, Melvyn Douglas, Estelle Parsons, Dorothy Stickney; **D:** Gilbert Cates; **W:** Robert Anderson. Writers Guild '70: Adapt. Screenplay.

I Now Pronounce You Chuck and Larry 2007 (PG-13) In an effort to game the benefits system two Brooklyn firefighters pose as gay life partners. Larry's (James) spouse has died and he must name a new beneficiary, so of course he turns to his womanizing buddy Chuck (Sandler), who owes him one for saving his life. They have to make the whole gay couple thing believable, pulling out all of the cringe-worthy stereotypical gags while they're at it. Once their scam comes under suspicion they have to up the ante, which proves difficult while being represented by super hot (female) lawyer Alex (Biel). If you chuckle at bum jokes, or want to see Biel in a PVC catwoman costume, this is the movie to see. 115m/C DVD, HD DVD. *US* Adam Sandler, Kevin James, Jessica Biel, Ving Rhames, Steve Buscemi, Dan Aykroyd, Nicholas Turturro, Dennis Dugan, Allen Covert, Richard Chamberlain, Rob Schneider, Rachel Dratch, Mary Pat Gleason, Rob Corddry, Nick Swardson, Jonathan Loughran, Chandra West, Blake Clark, Richard Kline; **D:** Dennis Dugan; **W:** Barry Fanaro, Alexander Payne, Jim Taylor, Brooks Arthur; **C:** Dean Semler; **M:** Rupert Gregson-Williams.

I Only Want You to Love Me 1976 *Ich Will Doch Nur, Dass Ihr Mich Liebt* Peter's (Zeplichal) been denigrated by his family his entire life, so he decides to move with his wife (Aberle) to Munich and show them he can make something of himself. But his desires become compulsions and he falters under the strain of work and marriage, leading to a terrifying crackup. A true story, based on the book "Life Sentence" by Klaus Antes and Christine Eberhardt. Originally produced for TV; German with subtitles. 104m/C VHS. *GE* Vitus Zeplichal, Elke Aberle, Ernie Mangold, Joanna Hofe, Alexander Allerson; **D:** Rainer Werner Fassbinder; **W:** Rainer Werner Fassbinder; **C:** Michael Ballhaus; **M:** Peer Raben.

I Ought to Be in Pictures 1982 (PG) After hitchhiking from New York to Hollywood to break into the movies, a teenage actress finds her father, a screenwriter turned alcoholic-gambler. Late, desperately unfunny Neil Simon outing, adapted from a Simon play. 107m/C VHS. Walter Matthau, Ann-Margret, Dinah Manoff, Lance Guest, Michael Dudikoff; **D:** Herbert Ross; **W:** Neil Simon; **M:** Marvin Hamlisch.

Posed for Playboy 🎬 1991 (R) Three women—one a college co-ed, one a stockbroker, and one a 37-year-old mother—quench their private passions by posing for "Playboy" magazine. Made for TV with additional footage added to give it an "R" rating. **89m/C** VHS. Lynda Carter, Michele Greene, Amanda Peterson, Brittany York. **D:** Stephen Stafford. **TV**

Promise to Pay 🎬 1937 Working stiff Eddie Lang (Morris) borrows money from Richard Farra (Carrillo) to take his family on vacation. Apparently, Eddie didn't understand what a loan shark was and gets into serious trouble when he can't meet the payments. **68m/B** VHS. Chester Morris, Leo Carrillo, Helen Mack, Thomas Mitchell, Thurston Hall, John Gallaudet; **D:** David Ross Lederman; **W:** Lionel Houser, Mary C. McCall; **C:** Lucien Ballard.

Really Hate My Job 🎬½ 2007 Some days, don't we all. Five women all hold down mundane, low-paying jobs at the same London restaurant while dreaming of better opportunities ahead. They struggle through a somewhat atypical series of mishaps during their evening shift, with things going wrong at the worst possible times. **89m/C** DVD. GB Neve Campbell, Shirley Henderson, Alexandra Maria Lara, Oana Pellea, Danny Huston, Barry Morse; **D:** Oliver Parker; **W:** Jennifer Higgie; **C:** Tony Miller; **M:** Charlie Mole.

Remember Mama 🎬🎬🎬½ 1948 A true Hollywood heart tugger chronicling the life of a Norwegian immigrant family living in San Francisco during the early 1900s. Dunne triumphs as the mother, with a perfect Norwegian accent, and provides her family with wisdom and inspiration. A kindly father and four children round out the nuclear family. A host of oddball characters regularly pop in on the household—three high-strung aunts and an eccentric doctor who treats a live-in uncle. Adapted from John Van Druten's stage play, based on Kathryn Forbes memoirs, "Mama's Bank Account", a TV series ran from 1946-57. **95m/B** VHS, DVD. Irene Dunne, Barbara Bel Geddes, Oscar Homolka, Ellen Corby, Cedric Hardwicke, Edgar Bergen, Rudy Vallee, Barbara O'Neil, Florence Bates; **D:** George Stevens; **W:** DeWitt Bodeen. Golden Globes '49: Support. Actress (Corby).

Robot 🎬🎬 2004 (PG-13) Very loose adaptation of Asimov's seminal 1950 sci-fi collection of short stories has action-hero Smith as Chicago detective Del Spooner, who's investigating the murder of robotic pioneer Dr. Alfred Lanning (Cromwell). It's 2035, and robots are as common as household appliances and robots are as common as a toaster, and supposedly just as safe. But Spooner thinks those "bots have minds (and plans) of their own and that one of them offed the good doctor. When Spooner persists in his theory that a robot committed the crime, he gets bumped from the force, which doesn't stop his investigation. The robots are creepily cool but there's no shock of the new in this crime caper. **115m/C** DVD, UMD. *US* Will Smith, Bridget Moynahan, Bruce Greenwood, Chi McBride, Alan Tudyk, James Cromwell, Shia LaBeouf, Adrian L. Ricard; **D:** Alex Proyas; **W:** Akiva Goldsman, Jeff Vintar; **C:** Simon Duggan; **M:** Marco Beltrami.

See a Dark Stranger 🎬🎬🎬 *The Adventuress* 1946 Cynical yet whimsical postwar British spy thriller about an angry Irish lass who agrees to steal war plans for the Nazis in order to battle her native enemies, the British—then she falls in love with a British officer. A sharply performed, decidedly jaded view of nationalism and wartime "heroism." **112m/B** VHS, DVD, GB Deborah Kerr, Trevor Howard, Raymond Huntley; **D:** Frank Launder.

Sent a Letter to My Love 🎬🎬 1981 An aging spinster, faced with the lonely prospect of the death of her paralyzed brother, places a personal ad for a companion in a local newspaper, using a different name. Unknown to her, the brother is the one who answers it, and they begin a romantic correspondence. Well-acted, touching account of relationships that change lives, but it takes its time in telling the story. **102m/C** VHS. FR

Simone Signoret, Jean Rochefort, Delphine Seyrig; **D:** Moshe Mizrahi; **W:** Moshe Mizrahi, Gerard Brach; **C:** Ghislan Cloquet.

Shot a Man in Vegas 🎬½ 1996 (R) Low-budget variation of "Rashomon." Drinking buddies Johnny (Cubitt) and Grant (Stockwell) wind up in a back alley brawl and Johnny takes a bullet, supposedly shot dead by Grant. Only their friends, Gale (Garofalo), Martin (Drilling-er), and Amy (Lippman), know what happened at the bar, and each saw it differently. So they decide to stash the corpse in Grant's car trunk and head out across the desert to California. There's a last-minute revelation and a big finale but the strain shows. **84m/C** VHS. John Stockwell, Janeane Garofalo, Brian Dillinger, Noelle Lippman, David Cubitt; **D:** Keoni Waxman; **W:** Keoni Waxman, Mary C.

Shot Andy Warhol 🎬🎬 1996 (R) Based on a true story, this black comedy focuses on the 15 minutes of fame achieved by Valerie Solanas, the woman who shot pop artist Andy Warhol for ignoring her in 1968. Taylor manages to recreate the more unpleasant aspects of Solaras without making her completely unsympathetic. Writer/director Harron, with a perfect performance film debut, does a wonderful job of recreating the drugged-out world Warhol and his cohorts inhabited. Her script succeeds by attempting to understand Solanas's actions, while not excusing or sensationalizing them. Features music by former Velvet Underground member. John Cale. **100m/C** VHS, DVD. Lili Taylor, Jared Harris, Stephen Dorff, Martha Plimpton, Donovan Leitch, Tahnee Welch, Michael Imperioli, Lothaire Bluteau, Anna Thomson, Peter Friedman, Jill (Ian) Hennessey, Craig Chester, James Lyons, Reginald Rodgers, Jamie Harrold, Edoardo Ballerini, Lynn Cohen, Myriam Cyr, Isabel Gillies, Eric Mabius; **D:** Mary Harron; **W:** Mary Harron, Daniel Minahan; **C:** Ellen Kuras; **M:** John Cale.

Shot Billy the Kid 🎬½ 1950 Billy the Kid decides to turn over a new leaf and live a decent life. The cards are stacked against him though: He's killed a man for nearly every year of his life, and old habits are hard to break. **58m/B** VHS, DVD. Donald (Don "Red") Barry, Robert Lowery, Tom Neal, Jack Perrin; **D:** William Berke.

Shot Jesse James 🎬🎬🎬 1949 In this first film, director Fuller breathes characteristically feverish, maddened fire into the story of Bob Ford (Ireland) along the notorious outlaw. An essential moment in Fuller's unique, America-as-tabloid-nightmare canon, and one of the best anti-westerns ever made. **83m/B** VHS, DVD. John Ireland, Barbara Britton, Preston Foster, Reed Hadley; **D:** Samuel Fuller; **W:** Samuel Fuller.

Spit on Your Corpse woof! *Girls for Rent* 1974 (R) A vicious female hired killer engages in a series of terrorist activities. Stars Spelvin in a non-pornographic role. **90m/C** VHS, DVD. Georgina Spelvin, Susan McIver, Kent Taylor, Rosalind Miles, Preston Pierce, Robert "Bob" Livingston; **D:** Al Adamson.

Spit on Your Grave woof! *Day of the Woman* 1977 (R) New York vacationing at a Connecticut lake house (on the Housatonic River) is brutally attacked and raped by four men. Left for dead, she recovers and seeks revenge. Not to be confused with the 1962 film of the same title, this one is worth zero as a film; lots of violent terror and gory death, totally irresponsibly portrayed. Also available in a 102-minute version. **98m/C** VHS, DVD. Camille Keaton, Eron Tabor, Richard Pace, Anthony Nichols, Gunter Kleeman, Alexis Magnotti; **D:** Mier Zarchi; **W:** Mier Zarchi; **C:** Yuri Haviv.

Spy 🎬🎬 2002 (PG-13) Bland adaptation of the Robert Culp/Bill Cosby TV series falls short of the cool value of the original. Second-banana spy Alex Scott (Wilson) is teamed up with heavyweight boxer Kelly Robinson (Murphy) to catch illegal arms dealer Gundars (McDo-well), who has stolen a prototype stealth fighter from the U.S. government. Along the way, the duo engage in familiar buddy picture jokiness, and Kelly helps Alex woo mysterious spygirl Rachel (Janssen). Gary Cole is a scene stealer as "aux-Spanish supeagent Carlos.

---

the Jury 🎬🎬 1982 (R) A remake of the 1953 "Mike Hammer mystery in which the famed PI investigates the murder of his best friend. Assante tropes around as Hammer and looks out of place in this slowed-down version. **111m/C** VHS. Armand Assante, Barbara Carrera, Laurene Landon, Alan King, Geoffrey Lewis, Paul Sorvino, Jessica James, Leigh Anne Harris, Lynette Harris; **D:** Richard T. Heffron; **W:** Larry Cohen; **M:** Bill Conti.

Take This Oath 🎬 1940 A cop is shocked to discover that his uncle is a wanted mobster, responsible for the death of a man. Hackneyed plot. **64m/B** VHS, DVD. Gordon Jones, Joyce Compton, Craig Reynolds, J. Farrel MacDonald, Robert E. Homans, Veda Ann Borg. **D:** Sam Newfield.

Think I Do 🎬🎬 1997 Gay Bob (Arquette) has always had an unrequited crush on college roomie, Brendan (Maclen). Five years after graduation, the duo

---

die Murphy, Owen Wilson, Famke Janssen, Malcolm McDowell, Gary Cole, Phill Lewis, Viv Leacock; **D:** Betty Thomas; **W:** Cormac Wibberley, Marianne S. Wibberley, Jay Scherick, David Ronn; **C:** Oliver Wood; **M:** Richard Gibbs.

Stand Alone 🎬🎬 *Seul contre tous* 1998 (R) Loud and RE-PUL-SIVE drama about an unemployed butcher Chevalier (Na-hon) descending into madness at warp speed when he can't find work. The brutal approach Noe takes distracts, rather than intrigues, as the "hero" is such a low-life loser. His hate-filled narration is accompanied by wild camera moves and loud gunshot booms ending each scene. A 30-second warning plastered before the film's grisly climax is not only unique but warranted when the least of Chevalier's crimes is maliciously kicking his pregnant girlfriend in the stomach. Considered a continuation to Noe's 1991 short feature entitled "Carne." French with English subtitles. **93m/C** VHS, Philippe Nahon, Blandine Lenoir, Frankye Pain, Martine Audrain; **D:** Gaspar Noe. **W:** Gaspar Noe; **C:** Dominique Colin.

Stand Condemned 🎬🎬 *Moscow Nights* 1935 A Russian officer is tricked into borrowing money from a spy and is condemned for treason. He's saved when a girl who loves him gives herself to a profiteer. Worth seeing only for young Olivier's performance. **90m/B** VHS, GB Laurence Olivier, Penelope Dudley Ward, Robert Cochran; **D:** Anthony Asquith.

Still Know What You Did Last Summer 🎬🎬 1998 (R) You know what the real problem with teenagers is? It's that it's not the loud music or the messy room; it's that they can't finish off the psycho-killers who show up annually on a major holiday to wield the axe they've been grinding for the rest of the year. Perky survivor Julie James (Hewitt) and new best friend Karla (Brandy) win a vacation in the Bahamas, and take boyfriends Tyrell (Phifer) and Will (Settle) along for some fun in the monsoon. Along with the hurricane, the kids must cope with fish stick guy/killer Ben Willis, who's still pretty cranky. The scares come at such a regular interval, that the viewer becomes numb to them. The young cast, especially the wet t-shirt adorned Hewitt, help to keep it afloat, however. **100m/C** VHS, DVD, Jack Black, Jennifer Love Hewitt, Freddie Prinze Jr., Brandy Norwood, Mekhi Phifer, Muse Watson, Matthew Settle, Bill Cobbs, Jeffrey Combs, John Hawkes, Jennifer Esposito; **D:** Danny Cannon; **W:** Trey Callaway; **C:** Vernon Layton; **M:** John (Gianni) Frizzell.

VideoHound's Golden Movie Retriever

meet up at the wedding of mutual friends, Carol (Velez) and Matt (Harrold). Bob's brought along his boyfriend, Sterling (Watkins), and does't know that Brendan has come out and is anticipating their reunion. It seems no one's sure about any of their romantic entanglements and someone else's. There are some twists and turns before everyone can be disappointed or delighted. **92m/C** VHS, DVD. Alexis Arquette, Christian Maelen, Maddie Corman, Guillermo Diez, Lauren Vélez, Jamie Harrold, Marianne Hagan, Tuc Watkins, Marni Nixon, Brian Sloan; **D:** Brian Sloan; **W:** Brian Sloan; **C:** Milton Kam; **M:** Gerry Gershman.

Think I Love My Wife 🎬🎬 2007 (R) Redo of Eric Rohmer's 1972 French film "Chloe in the Afternoon." Rock directs and stars as bored, frustrated middle-class hubby Richard Cooper, who's not getting any play from his beautiful wife Brenda (Torres), leaving him vulnerable to the wanton charms of Nikki (Washington), the ex of an old pal. Richard's conscience won't quite let him actually indulge (all the guilt, none of the pleasure). Rock does manage some humorous takes on modern marriage and Washington is smokin' hot. **94m/C** DVD, US Chris Rock, Kerry Washington, Gina Torres, Steve Buscemi, Edward Herrmann, Michael K. Williams, Wendell Pierce, Cassandra Freeman, Welker White; **D:** Chris Rock; **W:** Louis CK; **C:** William Rexer; **M:** Marcus Miller.

Vampiri 🎬🎬 *The Devil's Commandment: Lust of the Vampires* 1956 Original vampire film which started the classic Italian horror cycle. A gorgeous Countess needs blood to stay young, otherwise she reverts to a 200-year-old vampire. **81m/B** VHS, DVD. *IT* Gianna Maria Canale, Carlo D'Angelo, Dario Michaelis, Wandisa Guida, Renato Tontini; **D:** Riccardo Freda; **M:** Riccardo Freda, Piero Regnoli; **C:** Mario Bava; **M:** Franco Mannino, Roman Vlad.

Vitelloni 🎬🎬🎬½ *The Young and the Passionate; Vitelloni; Spivs* 1953 Fellini's semi-autobiographical drama, argued by some to be his finest work. Five young men grow up in a small Italian town. As they mature, four of them remain in Romini and limit their opportunities by roping themselves off from the rest of the world. The characters are multi-dimensional, including a young stud who impregnates a local woman, a loafer who is supported by his sister and a young man who what's in between. **104m/B** VHS, DVD. *IT* Alberto Sordi, Franco Fabrizi, Leopoldo Trieste, Riccardo Fellini, Franco Interleghi; **C:** Otello Martelli; **M:** Nino Rota.

Wake Up Screaming 🎬🎬🎬 *Hot Spot* 1941 "An actress' promoter is accused of her murder. Entertaining mystery with a surprise ending. Remade as "Vicki." **82m/B** VHS, DVD. Betty Grable, Victor Mature, Carole Landis, Laird Cregar, William Gargan, Alan Mowbray, Allyn Joslyn, Elisha Cook Jr., Chick Chandler, Cyril Ring, Morris Ankrum, Charles Lane, May (Mae) Beatty, Frank Orth; **D:** H. Bruce Humberstone; **W:** Steve Fisher, Dwight Taylor; **C:** Edward Cronjager; **M:** Cyril Mockridge.

Walk the Line 🎬🎬🎬 1970 Tennessee sheriff Henry Tawes (Peck) is known for his inflexible upholding of the law and his moral character. But even the car't resist the lawdry charms of wild nymphet Alma (Jones), the daughter of local moonshiner Carl McCain (Meeker). Tawes crosses all lines to be with Alma, even leaving his family and ignoring McCain's crimes with tragic consequences. Johnny Cash sings the title track. **96m/C** DVD. Gregory Peck, Tuesday Weld, Ralph Meeker, Estelle Parsons, Charles Durning, Lonny (Lonnie) Chapman; **D:** John Frankenheimer; **W:** Alvin Sargent; **C:** David M. Walsh; **M:** Bobby Johnston.

Walked with a Zombie 🎬🎬🎬½ 1943 The definitive and eeriest of the famous Val Lewton/Jacques Tourneur horror films. Dee, a young American nurse, comes to Haiti to care for the catatonic matriarch of a troubled family. Local legend has brought themselves to bear when the nurse takes the ill woman to a local voodoo ceremony for "healing." Superb, startling images and atmosphere create a unique context for this serious

---

'Jane Eyre'-like story; its reputation has grown through the years. **69m/B VHS, DVD.** Frances Dee, Tom Conway, James Ellison, Christine Gordon, Edith Barrett, Darby Jones, Sir Lancelot; **W:** Jacques Tourneur; **C:** J. Roy Hunt; **M:** Roy Webb.

I Wanna Be a Beauty Queen 1985 Divine hosts the 'Alternative Miss World" pageant featuring all sorts of bizarre contestants. **81m/C VHS.** Divine, Neil Campbell, Andrew Logan; **D:** Richard Gayer; **M:** Peter Logan.

I Wanna Hold Your Hand 1978 (PG) Teenagers try to crash the Beatles' appearance on the Ed Sullivan show. **104m/C VHS, DVD.** Nancy Allen, Bobby DiCicco, Wendie Jo Sperber, Marc McClure, Susan Kendall Newman, Theresa Saldana, Eddie Deezen, William Jordan; **D:** Robert Zemeckis; **W:** Bob Gale.

I Want Someone to Eat Cheese With 2006 Garlin adapts his one-man stage show into a full-length movie about overeating comedian James (Garlin), who's trying to find love while still living at home with his mother (Kolb). His best options are a sweet but weird schoolteacher (Hunt) or a possibly crazy ice cream store worker (Silverman). Self-deprecating but sweet, Garlin's debut relies on the improvisation skills of his cast to flesh out a thin but charming story. **80m/C DVD.** US Jeff Garlin, Sarah Silverman, Bonnie Hunt, Amy Sedaris, Wallace (Wally) Langham, Joey Slotnick, Richard King, Gina Gershon, Mina Kolb, David Pasquesi; **D:** Jeff Garlin; **W:** Jeff Garlin; **C:** Pete Biagi; **M:** Rob Kolson.

I Want to Go Home 1989 *Je Veux Rentrer a la Maison* 1989 Crass comedy about culture shock and family ties. Cranky Cleveland cartoonist Joey Wellman (Green) agrees to attend an exhibition of his work in Paris in an effort to reunite with his estranged daughter Elsie (Benson), who's studying at the Sorbonne. Elsie is ashamed of her dad but the scholar she's trying to impress, Christian Gauthier (Depardieu), is a big fan of American comic books and is thrilled to befriend Joey, who can't adjust to French culture. Joey's cartoon cat characters pop up in animated thought balloons to offer their own comments. English and French with subtitles. **100m/C DVD.** FR Adolph Green, Gerard Depardieu, Linda Lavin, Geraldine Chaplin, Micheline Presle, John Aston, Laura Benson; **D:** Alain Resnais; **W:** Jules Feiffer; **C:** Charlie Van Damme.

I Want to Live! 1958 Based on a scandalous true story, Hayward gives a riveting, Oscar-winning performance as a prostitute framed for the murder of an elderly woman and sentenced to death in the gas chamber. Producer Walter Wanger's seething indictment of capital punishment. **120m/B VHS, DVD.** Susan Hayward, Simon Oakland, Theodore Bikel, Virginia Vincent, Wesley Lau; **D:** Robert Wise; **W:** Nelson Gidding, Don Mankiewicz; **C:** Lionel Lindon; **M:** Johnny Mandel. Oscars '58: Actress (Hayward); Golden Globes '59: Actress (Hayward); N.Y. Film Critics '58: Actress (Hayward).

I Want What I Want 1972 (R) A young Englishman wants a sex-change, lives as a woman, falls in love, complications ensue. Not as shocking to watch as it might seem, but more a melodramatic gender-bender. **91m/C VHS.** GB Anne Heywood, Harry Andrews, Jill Bennett; **D:** John Dexter.

I Want You 1951 Small-town life in Greenhill is disturbed by the gathering storm of the Korean War. WWII vet Martin Greer (Andrews) is uncertain about re-enlisting while his wife Nancy (McGuire) is totally against the idea. Young Jack (Granger) doesn't want to leave his girl and family while his dad (Keith) tries to instill some patriotic fervor in his son, while George's (Milner) father (Baldwin) doesn't want to let him go. Dated but not unaffecting. **102m/B VHS.** Dana Andrews, Dorothy McGuire, Farley Granger, Peggy Dow, Robert Keith, Mildred Dunnock, Martin Milner, Walter Baldwin, Jim Backus, Ray Collins; **D:** Mark Robson; **W:** Irwin Shaw; **C:** Harry Stradling Sr.; **M:** Leigh Harline.

I Want You 1998 (R) Smokey (Mitevska) and her mute brother Honda (Petrusic) are Central European refugees in the British seaside town of Haven. Honda is shyly entranced by Helen (Weisz), who is trying to deal with her old boyfriend, paroled con Martin (Nivola). Martin becomes increasingly violent towards Helen and Honda comes to her rescue, but there's more to her relationship with Martin than Helen wants to admit. Winterbottom often flirts with the darker side of human nature and does so again in this rather thinly plotted Brit noir. **87m/C VHS.** GB Rachel Weisz, Luka Petrusic, Alessandro Nivola, Labina Mitevska, Ben Daniels, Carmen Ejogo, Graham Crowden, Geraldine O'Rawe, Des McAleer, Phyllida Law, Mary MacLeod; **D:** Michael Winterbottom; **W:** Eoin McNamee; **C:** Slawomir Idziak; **M:** Adrian Johnston.

I Was a Male War Bride 1949 Hilarious WWII comedy. French officer Grant falls in love with and marries WAC lieutenant Sheridan in occupied Europe. Planning to leave the continent and settle down in the U.S., the couple hits a roadblock of red tape and Grant must cross-dress in order to accompany his bride on the troop ship taking her home. Worth watching for Grant's performance alone. Based on the novel by Henri Rochard. **105m/B VHS, DVD.** Cary Grant, Ann Sheridan, Randy Stuart, Kenneth Tobey, William Neff, Marion Marshall; **D:** Howard Hawks; **W:** Charles Lederer, Leonard Spigelgass, William Neff; **M:** Cyril Mockridge.

I Was a Teenage TV Terrorist WOOF! *Amateur Hour* 1987 Two teenagers pull on-the-air pranks at the local cable television, blaming it all on an imaginary terrorist group. Poorly acted, cheaply made, and pointless. **85m/C VHS.** Adam Nathan, Julie Hanlon, John MacKay; **D:** Stanford Singer, Kevin McDonough; **C:** Lisa Rinzler; **M:** Cengiz Yaltkaya.

I Was a Teenage Werewolf 1957 "Rebel Without a Cause" meets "The Curse of the Werewolf" in this drive-in rock 'n' roll horror. Troubled teen Tony (Landon in his first film appearance) suffers from teen angst and low production values, falling victim to shrink Dr. Brandon (Bissell). The doc's been exploring hypnosis and regression therapy that, when practiced on Tony, turn him positively prehistoric. Misconstrued and full of terrible longings, the hairy highschooler goes on a rampage despite the loyal love of girlfriend Arlene (Lime). Directorial debut of Fowler. **70m/B VHS.** Michael Landon, Yvonne Lime, Whit Bissell, Tony Marshall, Dawn Richard, Barney (Bernard) Phillips, Ken Miller, Cindy Robbins, Michael Rougas, Robert E. (Bob) Griffin, Joseph Mell, Malcolm Atterbury, Eddie Marr, Vladimir Sokoloff, Louise Lewis, S. John Launer, Guy Williams, Dorothy Crehan; **D:** Gene Fowler Jr.; **W:** Aben Kandel; **C:** Joseph LaShelle; **M:** Paul Dunlap.

I Was a Teenage Zombie 1987 Spoof of high school horror films features a good zombie against a drug-pushing zombie. Forget the story and listen to the music by Los Lobos, the Fleshtones, the Waitresses, Dream Syndicate, and Violent Femmes. **92m/C VHS, DVD.** Michael Rubin, Steve McCoy, Cassie Madden, Allen Rickman; **D:** John E. Michalakis; **W:** George Seminara, Steve McCoy; **C:** Peter Lewnes; **M:** Jonathan Roberts, Craig Seeman.

I Was a Zombie for the FBI 1982 Intelligence agency toughens its hiring criteria. Much McCarthyian mirth. **105m/B VHS, DVD.** James Raspberry, Larry, Raspberry, John Gillick, Christina Wellford, Anthony Isbell, Laurence Hall, Rick Crowe; **D:** Maurice Penczner; **W:** Maurice Penczner, John Gillick; **C:** Rick Dupree.

I Was Born But... *Umarete Wa Mita Keredo* 1932 Two young brothers (Sugahara and Tokkankozo) are the leaders of the neighborhood gang of kids. Their office clerk father (Saito), who is trying to advance his position by playing up to the boss, insists the boys accompany him to his boss' house for a visit. The sons are embarrassed by their father's ingratiating behavior, especially when they realize that the boss' son is a minor member of their gang. In retaliation, the brothers decide to go on a hunger strike. Charming social satire. Japanese with subtitles. **89m/B VHS.** JP Tatsuo Saito, Hideo Sugahara, Tokkankozo, Mitsuko Yoshikawa, Takeshi Sakamoto; **D:** Yasujiro Ozu; **W:** Akira Fushimi, Geibei Ibushiya; **C:** Hideo Shigehara.

I Was Nineteen *Ich War Neunzehn* 1968 Gregor Hecker left Germany with his parents as a eight-year-old. Now, at the end of WWII, he's returning at 19 in the uniform of a Russian Lieutenant and isn't sure of his identity anymore. Based on the diary kept by German filmmaker Wolf when he was in the Russian Army. German with subtitles. **115m/B VHS.** GE Jaeoki Schwarz, Wassili Liwanow, Alexej Ejboshenko; **D:** Konrad Wolf.

I Went Down 1997 (R) The title of this dark comedy about Irish gangsters has many meanings, including a quote from Plato. Not too many caper movies can boast of a plug from the father of Western philosophy, but luckily director Breathnach and writer McPherson don't take anything too seriously. Their heroes are hapless Git (McDonald) and hair-trigger Bunny (Gleeson), a duo who show you what Laurel and Hardy might look like if they were cast as the hit men in "Pulp Fiction." Ordered by big boss Tom French (Doyle) to bring in Frank Grogan (Caffrey), a man who swindled him out of big bucks and also slept with his wife, they fumble through bad directions and a missed meeting with a sinister fellow called "The Friendly Face," but manage to nab Grogan anyway. The two then attempt to deliver the extremely gabby Grogan to French, leading to a showdown between all four men. More character and dialogue driven than action oriented, this went down as the highest grossing independent Irish film after its theatrical release. **105m/C VHS.** IR GB Brendan Gleeson, Peter McDonald, Tony Doyle, Peter Caffrey, Donal O'Kelly, Antoine Byrne; **D:** Paddy Breathnach; **M:** Dario Marianelli.

I Will Fight No More Forever 1975 A vivid recounting of the epic true story of the legendary Chief Joseph who led the Nez Perce tribe on a 1600-mile trek to Canada in 1877. Disturbing and powerful. **100m/C VHS, DVD.** James Whitmore, Ned Romero, Sam Elliott; **D:** Richard T. Heffron. TV

I Will, I Will for Now 1976 (R) Tacky sex clinic comedy with Keaton and Gould trying to save their marriage through kinky therapy. **109m/C VHS.** Diane Keaton, Elliott Gould, Paul Sorvino, Victoria Principal, Robert Alda, Warren Bellinger; **D:** Norman Panama; **W:** Norman Panama; **C:** John A. Alonzo.

I Witness 2003 (R) Greed and corruption lead to a single culprit in three separate crimes: 27 people are found dead in a collapsed tunnel at a Mexican border town, two American college boys on holiday go missing and are later found murdered, and human rights observer James (Daniels) is monitoring a union election taking place at a chemical plant owned by a multinational corporation. Spader is typecast as an oily rep who keeps those third-world wheels greased and turning for the sake of the American economy. **95m/C DVD.** Jeff Daniels, James Spader, Portia de Rossi, Clifton (Gonzalez) Collins Jr., Wade Andrew Williams, Jordi Caballero; **D:** Rowdy Herrington; **W:** Colin Greene, Robert Orr; **C:** Michael G. Wojciechowski; **M:** David Kitay.

I Wonder Who's Killing Her Now? *Kill My Wife... Please!* 1976 (PG) Scuzzy husband pays to have his wife murdered for the insurance money, then changes his mind. On-again, off-again comedy. **87m/C VHS, DVD.** Bob (Robert) Dishy, Joanna Barnes, Bill Dana, Vito Scotti, Severn Darden, Harvey Jason, Richard Libertini, Noriyuki "Pat" Morita; **D:** Steven Hilliard Stern; **W:** Mickey Rose; **C:** Richard H. Kline; **M:** Patrick Williams.

Ibiza Dream *El Sueno de Ibiza* 2002 The island of Ibiza has the rep of being a party-time vacation resort but in this case the dreams of three friends go unfulfilled. Nacho (Collado) has returned from India determined to open a center for meditation. He enlists his childhood friends Chica (Dominguez), a nurse, and beach bum Cacho (Marin) to help him out, hoping it will strengthen their friendship. The center opens but the friends find themselves further apart than ever. Spanish with subtitles. **98m/C VHS, DVD.** SP Paco Marin, Adriana Dominguez, Adria Collado; **D:** Igor Fioravanti; **W:** Igor Fioravanti; **C:** Miguel Leal; **M:** Jose Padilla.

Ice 1993 (R) Charley and Ellen Reed are thieves whose latest heist is $60 million in diamonds from mob boss Vito Malta. There's trouble when they try to fence the goods and Ellen is left with the merchandise and on the run from Malta's henchmen. **91m/C VHS, DVD.** Traci Lords, Phillip Troy, Zach Galligan, Jorge (George) Rivero, Michael Bailey Smith, Jamie Alba, Jean Pflieger, Floyd Levine; **D:** Brook Yeaton; **W:** Sean Dash.

Ice Age 2002 (PG) Director Wedge (also the voice of Scrat the squirrel) crafts a smart, sophisticated and touching animated comedy/adventure about a group of prehistoric beasts who find a human baby and then try to restore the tyke to his tribe. During the long march south during an ice age, the cuddly Manfred the Mammoth (Romano) and Sid the Sloth (the already animated Leguizamo) are joined by Diego the scheming Sabertooth Tiger (Leary) whose bond is solidified after the two save Diego's life. Amazing computer-animation technology and artistry are top-notch. Characters are likeable but sometimes spew overly glib dialogue. Although not quite of the same caliber story-wise, this one fits right in with "Shrek," "Monsters, Inc." and "Toy Story." **81m/C VHS, DVD, Blu-ray Disc, UMD.** US **D:** Chris Wedge; **W:** Michael Berg, Michael J. Wilson, Peter Ackerman; **M:** David Newman; **V:** John Leguizamo, Denis Leary, Ray Romano, Goran Visnjic, Jack Black, Cedric the Entertainer, Stephen (Steve) Root, Tara Strong, Diedrich Bader, Alan Tudyk, Lorri Bagley, Jane Krakowski, Chris Wedge.

Ice Age: The Meltdown 2006 (PG) Okay, so global warming gets its licks in but this is hardly an environmental diatribe. Anyway, the glaciers are melting, the water is rising, and the animals are on the move to higher, drier ground. Manny (Romano) believes he's the last wooly mammoth left until he meets flirty Ellie (Queen Latifah), who thinks she's actually a possum like her two foster brothers (Scott & Peck). Fast-talking Sid (Leguizamo) and grumpy Diego (Leary) are part of the mix as acorn-chasing, scene-stealing Scrat the animation still rocks even if the adventures are a mild retread. **90m/C DVD, Blu-ray Disc.** US **D:** Carlos Saldanha; **W:** Peter Gaulke, Gerry Swallow, Jim Hecht; **C:** Harry Hitner; **M:** John Powell; **V:** Ray Romano, John Leguizamo, Denis Leary, Seann William Scott, Josh Peck, Queen Latifah, Will Arnett, Jay Leno, Joseph Bologna, Renee Taylor, Stephen (Steve) Root, Mindy Sterling, Alan Tudyk, Clea Lewis.

Ice Castles 1979 (PG) A young figure skater's Olympic dreams are dimmed when she is blinded in an accident, but her boyfriend gives her the strength, encouragement, and love necessary to perform a small miracle. Way too schmaltzy. **110m/C VHS, DVD.** Robby Benson, Lynn-Holly Johnson, Tom Skerritt, Colleen Dewhurst, Jennifer Warren, David Huffman; **D:** Donald Wrye, Gary L. Bain; **C:** Bill Butler; **M:** Marvin Hamlisch.

Ice Cream Man 1995 (R) Quite disgusting horror tale of a dweeby, demented ice cream man who delivers gore and death along with his frozen treats. **96m/C VHS, DVD.** Clint Howard, Sandahl Bergman, Olivia Hussey, Lee Majors II, David Naughton, Jan-Michael Vincent, David Warner, Steve Garvey; **D:** Norman Apstein.

The Ice Flood 1926 Silent family type comedy of a son who proves to the old man that he wrote the book on life, wagering the successful supervision of dad's lumberjacks. **63m/B VHS.** Kenneth Harlan, Viola Dana; **D:** George B. Seitz.

The Ice Harvest 2005 (R) It's Christmas Eve in Wichita, and mob lawyer Charlie (Cusack) still has a pretty long to-do list. But things got complicated when he and his partner Vic (Thornton) skimmed $2.2 million from crime lord Bill Guerrard (Quaid). Now, in the midst of an ice storm, Charlie has to dodge Bill's hit man Roy (Starr), withstand the dangerous charms of topless bar manager/femme fatale Renata (Nielson), baby-sit his drunken brother-in-law Pete (a hilariously over-the-top Platt), and finish his shopping. A lovely bit of screwball comedic film noir, but with a director like Ramis, things should have been funnier. **88m/C DVD. US** John Cusack, Billy Bob Thornton, Connie Nielsen, Randy Quaid, Oliver Platt; **D:** Harold Ramis; **W:** Richard Russo, Robert Benton; **C:** Alar Kivilo; **M:** David Kitay.

Ice House 🐾🐾 1989 A sophisticated young lady flees Texas for Hollywood, searching for a better life. When her ex-lover shows up and wants her to go back, the lackless turmoil begins. Pars real-life couple Gilbert and Brinkman. **88m/C VHS.** Melissa Gilbert, Eo Brinkman, Andreas Manoli-nell; **W:** Eo Brinkman.

Ice Men 🐾🐾 2004 Uptight Vaughn (Cummins) decides to throw a birthday party for buddy Bryan (Hewlett) at the lakeside cabin he's inherited. He also invites Jon (Spottiswood) and Steve (Thomas) for a weekend of hunting and drinking. Unfortunately, there's some uninvited guests as well. **M:** Michael Shields, Russell Broom.

Ice Palace 🐾🐾 1960 Two rugged adventurers maintain a lifelong rivalry in the primitive Alaskan wilderness, their relationship dramatizing the development of the 49th state. Silly but entertaining. Based on Edna Ferber's novel. **143m/C VHS.** Richard Burton, Robert Ryan, Carolyn Jones, Shirley Knight, Martha Hyer, Jim Backus, George Tavel; **D:** Vincent Sherman; **C:** Joseph Biroc; **M:** Max Steiner.

Ice Pawn 🐾🐾 1992 Alex Dalton may finally get to realize his dream of becoming a gold medal ice skater if he can beat Misha, his Russian rival. He soon finds out that Misha isn't his only problem, as he unknowingly becomes a pawn in a game of corruption and greed that could totally ruin his career. **102m/C VHS, DVD.** Paul Cross, Dan Haggerty, Robert Budasia, Chris Thomas; **D:** Barry Samson; **W:** Paul Cross.

Ice Pirates 🐾½ 1984 (PG) Space pirates in the far future steal blocks of ice to fill the needs of a thirsty galaxy. Cool plot has its moments. **91m/C VHS, DVD.** Robert Urich, Mary Crosby, Michael D. Roberts, John Matuszak, Anjelica Huston, Ron Perlman, John Carradine, Robert Symonds; **D:** Stewart Raffill; **W:** Stewart Raffill, Stanford Sherman.

Ice Princess 🐾🐾½ 2005 (G) Casey Carlyle (Trachtenberg) is a high school science whiz kid who needs a stellar science project to get into Harvard. She decides to analyze the science of figure skating by observing a bunch of local elite skaters at a nearby rink. Casey's not satisfied with simply observing, so she straps on a pair of skates and starts taking lessons. She soon realizes that she has a natural talent for it, but her feminist mother (Joan Cusack) disapproves. While the

movie holds no surprises, it's still enjoyable for the target audience. Go figure. **92m/C VHS, DVD.** US Michelle Tachtenberg, Joan Cusack, Kim Cattrall, Hayden Panettiere, Trevor Blumas, Kirsten Olson, Connie Ray, Juliana Cannarozzo; **Cameos:** Brian Boitano, Michelle Kwan; **D:** Tim Fywell; **W:** Hadley Davis, Meg Cabot; **C:** David Hennings; **M:** Christone Beck.

The Ice Rink 🐾🐾 La Patinoire 1999 A movie about the romance between an French-Canadian hockey player (Campbell) and an American French film crew that is making a movie. A generally playful look at the tribulations of making a movie. French with subtitles. **80m/C VHS, DVD. FR** Tom Novembre, Marie-France Pisier, Bruce Campbell, Dolores Chaplin, Mireille Perrier, Jean-Pierre Cassel; **D:** Jean-Philippe Toussaint; **C:** Jean-François Robin.

The Ice Runner 🐾🐾½ 1993 (R) Low-key Cold War thriller, filmed in 1991. Soviet gulag. Jeffrey West (Albert) gets caught in a botched payoff to a Soviet minister and when the diplomats wash their hands of him a rigged trial has West sentenced to 12 years hard labor. A convenient train wreck lets him assume a different prisoner's name which gets him to a minimum security camp under the eyes of a suspicious commander. Now, West needs to escape and cross 39 miles of icy tundra separating his Russian prison from American freedom. **116m/C VHS, DVD.** Edward Albert, Eugene (Yevgeny) Lazarev, Olga Kabo, Victor Wong, Alexander Kuznetsov, Basil Hoffman, Eilil Bordy, Sergei Ruban; **D:** Barry Samson; **W:** Joyce Warren, Clifford Coleman, Joshua Stallings.

Ice Spiders 🐾🐾½ 2007 (R) Pure camp and gore from the Sci-Fi Channel. Olympic ski hopefuls head to a remote resort in Utah where Cash (Muldoon) is the head instructor. He has the hots for Dr. April (Williams), who works at a secret government lab where they're doing military experiments on gigantic spiders with ravenous appetites who get close and don't mind the cold as they go looking for their next meal. **86m/C DVD.** Patrick Muldoon, Vanessa Williams, Thomas Calabro, Stephen J. Cannell, David Millbern, Noah Bastian, Carleigh King; **D:** Tibor Takacs; **W:** Eric Miller; **C:** Barry Gravelle. **CABLE**

Ice Station Zebra 🐾🐾½ 1968 (G) A nuclear submarine races Soviet seamen to find a downed Russian satellite under a polar ice cap. Suspenseful Cold War adventure based on the novel by Alistair Maclean. **148m/C VHS, DVD.** Rock Hudson, Ernest Borgnine, Patrick McGoohan, Jim Brown, Lloyd Nolan, Tony Bill; **D:** John Sturges; **M:** Douglas Heyes; **C:** Daniel F. Fapp; **M:** Michel Legrand.

The Ice Storm 🐾🐾🐾½ 1997 (R) Excellent family drama/period piece (the 1970s!) directed by Ang Lee and based on the book by Rick Moody. Kline plays a husband and father too self-absorbed to notice his marriage (to Allen) unraveling into crisis, and his children (Maguire and Ricci) mimicking the sordid behavior that surrounds them. Skillfully fuses together a frank, unsympathetic look at family psychology, while also making a comment on the social situation of the early 1970s. Flirts with being overpoweringly negative and moody, but is elevated by Lee's insight and direction. Excellent job by the entire cast, especially Weaver, frighteningly dead-on as an emotionally reckless wife and mother, and Hann-Byrd and Wood as her eerie sons. **113m/C VHS, DVD.** Kevin Kline, Tobey Maguire, Joan Allen, Christina Ricci, Sigourney Weaver, Elijah Wood, Katie Holmes, Henry Czerny, Adam Hann-Byrd, Kate Krumholtz, Jamey Sheridan, Maia Danziger, David Burton, John Benjamin Hickey, Allison Janney, Byron Jennings; **D:** Ang Lee; **W:** James Schamus; **C:** Frederick Elmes; **M:** Mychael Danna. British Acad. '97; Support.

I'd Climb the Highest Mountain 🐾🐾🐾 1951 Sincere, sentimental piece of Americana about a country preacher (Lundigan) and his city wife (Hayward) as they adjust to life in a small town in Southern hill county. Film was a big hit, especially in the South. Based on the novel by Corra Harris. **88m/C VHS.** Susan Hayward, William Lundigan, Roy Calhoun, Gene Lockhart, Ruth Donnelly, Barbara Bates, Lynn Bari, Alexander Knox; **D:** Henry King; **W:** Lamar Trotti.

I'd Give My Life 🐾½ 1936 On a mission to gangster's ex-wife is presently married to the governor. He tries to use their honest but framed son to blackmail her. **73m/B VHS.** Guy Standing, Frances Drake, Tom Brown, Janet Beecher; **D:** Edwin L. Marin.

Idaho 🐾½ 1943 On a mission to close down houses of ill repute, Rodgers teams up with Autry's old sidekick Burnette. **70m/B VHS, DVD.** Roy Rogers, Harry Shannon, Virginia Grey, Smiley Burnette, Ona Munson; **D:** Joseph Kane.

Idaho Transfer WOOF! Deranged 1973 (PG) Fonda's second directorial effort, Carradine's first screen appearance. An obnoxious group of teens travel through time to Idaho in the year 2044. Environmental waste and story is dull and confused. **90m/C VHS, DVD.** Keith Carradine, Kelley Bohanan; **D:** Peter Fonda.

An Ideal Husband 🐾🐾🐾 1999 (PG-13) Victorien comedy of manners adapted from the play by Oscar Wilde. The very proper Lady Gertrud Chiltern (Blanchett) discovers that her husband, Sir Robert (Northam), a member of Parliament, attained their fortune and position through questionable means. Robert is being blackmailed over a shady business deal by Gertrud's loathed ex-school mate, Laura Cheveley (Moore). Cynical social butterfly, Lord Arthur Goring (Everett), is drawn into the fray because of his friendship with Chiltern. It's rather exaggerated and very witty, as would expect of Wilde. **96m/C VHS, DVD. GB** Cate Blanchett, Jeremy Northam, Minnie Driver, Rupert Everett, Julianne Moore, Jeroen Krabbe, Lindsay Duncan, Peter Vaughan, John Wood, Marsha Fitzjean, Benjamin Pullen; **D:** Oliver Parker; **W:** Oliver Parker; **C:** David Cljark; Johnson; **M:** Charlie Mole. Natl. Bd. of Review '99; Support. Actress (Moore).

Identification of a Woman 🐾🐾 Identificazione di una Donna 1982 Niccolo (Millan) is a middle-aged film director who is searching for the perfect female image as the focus for his new movie. But his personal search allenates the flesh-and-blood women already in his life. Lots of visuals give the film a slow, dreamlike quality. Italian with subtitles. **131m/C VHS. IT** Tomas Millian, Christine Boisson, Daniela Silverio, Sandra Monteleonti; **D:** Michelangelo Antonion, Gerard Brach; **C:** Carlo Di Palma; **M:** John Foxx.

Identity 🐾🐾 2003 (R) See if this premise sounds familiar—ten strangers, an ex-cop turned chauffeur, his movie star passenger, a family with a wounded wife, a newlywed couple, a cop transporting a prisoner, and an ex-hooker are brought at a desolate motel run by a creepy clerk. One by one they start to die in various icky and/or disturbing ways. A possibly-connected subplot involves a man or death row getting a last-minute, late-night hearing. Well-executed, if unspectacular, suspenser provides a satisfyingly twisty thrill. **90m/C VHS, DVD. Blu-ray Disc. US** John Cusack, Rebecca De Mornay, Ray Liotta, Jake Busey, Amanda Peet, Clea Duvall, William Lee Scott, John C. McGinley, Leila Kenzie, Bret Loehr, John Hawkes, Pruitt Taylor Vince, Alfred Molina, Matt Letscher, Carmen Argenziano, Marshall Bell, Holmes Osborne, Frederick Coffin; **D:** James Mangold; **W:** Michael Cooney; **C:** Phedon Papamichael; **M:** Alan Silvestri.

Identity Crisis 🐾 1990 (R) Campy fashion maven and flamboyant rapper switch identities causing much tedious overacting. Lifeless murder comedy from father and son Van Peebles. **98m/C VHS, DVD.** Mario Van Peebles, Ilan Mitchell-Smith, Nicholas Kepros, Shelly Burch, Richard Clarke; **D:** Melvin Van Peebles.

Identity Unknown 🐾🐾½ 1945 Shell-shocked veteran goes AWOL to discover who he is, meeting grieving relatives along the way. Interesting premise is sometimes moving. **70m/B VHS, DVD.** Richard Arlen, Cheryl Walker, Roger Pryor, Bobby Driscoll; **D:** Walter Colmes.

The Iceberg 🐾½ L'iceberg 2005 Slight comedy features much physical humor, little dialogue, and is overly cute. Manager Fiona gets locked in the restaurant's walk-in freezer. Barely alive when she's rescued the next day, Fiona returns home to discover her husband and children didn't even notice her missing. She develops an obsession with everything frozen and cold, so she hides out in a frozen food delivery truck and leaves to make a new home for herself on an iceberg. French with subtitles. **84m/C DVD. BE** Fiona Gordon, Dominique Abel, Bruno Romy, Philippe Martz; **D:** Dominique Abel, Bruno Romy, Fiona Gordon, Dominique Abel, Bruno Romy; **C:** Sebastien Koeppel; **M:** Jacques Lutey.

Icebox Murders WOOF! 1982 A crazeo, motiveless, faceless killer hangs his victims in a walk-in freezer. Store this one. **90m/C VHS.** SP Jack Taylor, Mina Miller; **D:** Francisco Rodriguez Gordillo; **W:** Francisco Prosper; **C:** Raul P. Cupero; **M:** Gregorio Garcia Segura.

Iced 🐾 1988 Wild fun turns to horror on a ski trip as a group of college friends are hunted by a maniac on the loose. It's all downhill. **86m/C VHS.** Debra Deliso, Doug Stevenson, Ron Kobaje, Elizabeth Gorcey, Alan Johnson; **D:** Jeff Kwitny.

Iceland 🐾🐾 1942 Labored romance of an Iceland girl and a Marine with plenty of skating thrown in for good measure. Skating and singing interludes are the best part of an otherwise average film. ♫You Can't Say No to a Soldier. There Will Never Be Another You; Lover's Knot; Let's Bring New Glory to Old Glory; I Like a Military Tune. **79m/B VHS.** Sonja Henie, John Payne, Jack Oakie, Felix Bressart, Osa Massen, Fritz Feld; **D:** H. Bruce Humberstone; **W:** Robert Ellis, Helen Logan.

The Iceman Cometh 🐾🐾½ 1973 American Film Theater version of the Eugene O'Neill play with Marvin starring as salesman Hickey, who's found an unsettling peace of mind after—it's slowly revealed to the drunks of Harry Hope's bar—committing a terrible crime. However, it's Ryan who steals the picture as former anarchist Larry, a man simply waiting to die. Ryan was ill with terminal cancer, as was March (who plays Harry Hope); this would be the last appearance for both men. **239m/C DVD.** Lee Marvin, Fredric March, Robert Ryan, Jeff Bridges, Martyn Green, George Voskovec, Moses Gunn, Tom Pedi, Evans, Bradford Dillman, Sorrell Booke, John McLiam, Hilly Brooks, Clifton James; **D:** John Frankenheimer; **W:** Thomas Quinn Curtiss; **C:** Ralph Woolsey.

Iceman 🐾🐾🐾 1984 (PG) A frozen prehistoric man is brought back to life, after which severe culture shock takes hold. Underwritten but nicely acted, especially by Lore as the primal man. **101m/C VHS, DVD.** CA Timothy Hutton, Lindsay Crouse, John Lone, David Strathairn, Josef Sommer, Danny Glover; **D:** Fred Schepisi; **W:** Chip Proser; **C:** Ian Baker; **M:** Bruce Smeaton.

The Icicle Thief 🐾🐾🐾 Ladri di Saponette 1989 "The Naked Gun" for the arthouse crowd. As a stark, black-and-white neo-realist tragedy airs on TV, bright color commercials disrupt the narrative. Soon ads invade the movie itself, and the film's director jumps into his picture to fix the damage. Study up on your postwar Italian cinema and this'll seem hilarious; otherwise the real fun doesn't kick in until the halfway point. In Italian with English subtitles. **93m/C VHS. IT** Maurizio Nichetti, Caterina Sylos Labini, Giorgio G. Fava, Renato Scarpa, Heidi Komarek; **D:** Maurizio Nichetti; **C:** Mario Battistoni; **M:** Manuel De Sica.

Icy Breasts 🐾🐾 1975 A French psychiatrist tries to prevent his beautiful but psychotic patient from continuing her murdering spree. Dubbed. **105m/C VHS, DVD. FR** Alain Delon, Mireille Darc; **D:** Georges Lautner.

Idiocracy 🦴🦴 2006 (R) Mike Judge's "Office Space" became a cult hit after being rudely dumped during its studio release, and this satirical flick may obtain the same status. Everyman soldier Joe (Wilson) and hooker Rita (Rudolph) are selected by the Pentagon to take part in a hibernation experiment. Thanks to a snafu, they wake up 500 years later in an America so completely dumbed-down that they are now the smartest couple alive, with Joe given a presidential appointment to turn this mess around. The ultimate "what if" movie, with Wilson at his clueless, curious best. 84m/C DVD. *US* Luke Wilson, Maya Rudolph, Dax Shepard, Terry Crews, David Herman, Justin Long, Thomas Haden Church, Stephen (Steve) Root; *D:* Mike Judge; *W:* Mike Judge, Etan Cohen; *C:* Tim Suhrstedt; *V:* Earl Mann.

The Idiot 🦴🦴🦴🦴 1951 Dostoevski's Russian novel is transported by Kurosawa across two centuries to post-war Japan, where the madness and jealousy continue to rage. In Japanese with English subtitles. 166m/B VHS. Toshiro Mifune, Masayuki Mori, Setsuko Hara, Yoshiko Kuga, Takashi Shimura; *D:* Akira Kurosawa.

Idiot Box 🦴🦴 1997 Crazy youth comedy about lazy, brainless Kev (Mendelsohn) and Mick (Sims) who spend most of their unemployed time watching violent cop shows on TV and drinking beer. It's from the "idiot box" that the dim duo get the idea that they've learned enough to rob a bank, but it just so happens that a pair of crooks, who wear clown masks, are already on a bank crime spree. Naturally, both sets of robbers choose the same bank as their target and the cops just happen to be waiting. 83m/C VHS, DVD. *AU* Ben Mendelsohn, Jeremy Sims, John Polson, Robyn Loau, Graeme Blundell, Deborah Kennedy, Stephen Rae, Andrew S. Gilbert, Amanda Muggleton, Paul Gleeson, Susie Porter; *D:* David Caesar; *W:* David Caesar; *C:* Joseph Pickering; *M:* Tim Rogers, Nick Launay.

Idiot's Delight 🦴🦴🦴 1939 At an Alpine hotel, a song and dance man meets a gorgeous Russian countess who reminds him of a former lover. Incredibly, Gable sings and dances through "Puttin' on the Ritz," the film's big highlight. Based on the Pulitzer Prize-winning play by Robert Sherwood. 107m/B VHS. Clark Gable, Norma Shearer, Burgess Meredith, Edward Arnold, Charles Coburn, Joseph Schildkraut; *D:* Clarence Brown; *C:* William H. Daniels.

Idle Hands 🦴½ 1999 (R) Pothead slacker Anton (Sawa) finds that his very idle hand is possessed by a demon, making him do things he doesn't want to do, like get up off the couch and kill his friends Mick (Green) and Pnub (Henson). When Anton cuts off the offending appendage, it's free to terrorize his girlfriend Molly (Alba). With the help of a Druid priestess (Fox) and his now undead friends, Anton must stop the hand from taking Molly's soul to Hell. Even if the release hadn't coincided with the Littleton tragedy, this tasteless horror-comedy wouldn't be funny. Relentless overacting tries to cover up for a lame script filled with pot jokes and gory high school slasher conventions. Green and Henson are the only bright spots. 90m/C VHS, DVD. Devon Sawa, Seth Green, Elden (Ratliff) Henson, Jessica Alba, Christopher Hart, Vivica A. Fox, Jack Noseworthy, Sean M. Whalen, Nicholas Sadler, Fred Willard, Katie Wright, Connie Ray; *D:* Rodman Flender; *W:* Terri Hughes, Ron Milbauer; *C:* Christopher Baffa; *M:* Graeme Revell.

Idlewild 🦴🦴 2006 (R) OutKast bandmates star in a genre-bending tale of two buddies in 1930s Georgia, creating an anachronistic but entertaining jumble of eye- and ear-candy. Percival (Benjamin), a mortician by day, reserved piano player by night, and Rooster (Patton), a club-owning family man and musician in his own right, escape their ho-hum lives at Church, a lively speakeasy that encapsulates the flick's mash-up of jazz-era nostalgia with a contemporary vibe. Soon love and murder and lots of stars making cameos come to town for a mix of lavish production numbers and murder. It's all as gutsy and confusing as it sounds. 120m/C DVD. *US* Andre Benjamin, Antwan Andre Patton, Paula Patton, Terrence Howard, Malinda Williams, Macy Gray, Ben Vereen, Ving Rhames, Faizon Love; *D:* Bryan Barber; *W:* Bryan Barber; *C:* Pascal Rabaud; *M:* John Debney.

The Idol Dancer 🦴🦴½ 1920 Romance and adventure in the South Seas with a drunken American beachcomber. There's also a native uprising for added excitement. Minor Griffith but nice Nassau scenery. 93m/B VHS. Richard Barthelmess, Clarine Seymour, Creighton Hale, George MacQuarrie, Kate Bruce, Anders Randolf, Walter James, Thomas Carr; *D:* D.W. Griffith.

Idolmaker 🦴🦴½ 1980 (PG) A conniving agent can make a rock star out of anyone. Well-acted fluff with Sharkey taking a strong lead. The first film by hackmeister Hackford and somewhat based on true-life teen idol Fabian. 119m/C VHS, DVD. Ray Sharkey, Tovah Feldshuh, Peter Gallagher, Paul Land, Joe Pantoliano, Maureen McCormick, John Aprea, Richard Bright, Olympia Dukakis, Steven Apostlee Peck; *D:* Taylor Hackford; *C:* Adam Holender; *M:* Jeff Barry. Golden Globes '81: Actor—Mus./Comedy (Sharkey).

If... 🦴🦴🦴🦴 1969 (R) Three unruly seniors at a British boarding school refuse to conform. A popular, anarchic indictment of staid British society, using the same milieu as Vigo's "Zero de Conduite," with considerably more violence. The first of Anderson and McDowell's trilogy, culminating with "O Lucky Man!" and "Britannia Hospital." In color and black and white. 111m/C VHS, DVD. *GB* Malcolm McDowell, David Wood, Christine Noonan, Richard Warwick, Robert Swann, Arthur Lowe, Mona Washbourne, Graham Crowden, Hugh Thomas, Guy Ross, Peter Jeffrey, Geoffrey Chater, Mary MacLeod, Anthony Nicholls, Ben Aris, Charles Lloyd-Pack, Rupert Webster, Brian Pettifer, Sean Bury, Michael Cadman; *D:* Lindsay Anderson; *W:* David Sherwin; *C:* Miroslav Ondricek; *M:* Marc Wilkinson. Cannes '69: Film.

If Ever I See You Again 🦴 1978 (PG) The creator of "You Light Up My Life" stars in the sentimental melodrama. Two adolescent lovers meet again years later and try to rekindle old passions. Done with as much skill as "Light" minus a hit song. 105m/C VHS. Joseph Brooks, Shelley Hack, Jerry Keller, Jimmy Breslin; *D:* Joseph Brooks; *W:* Joseph Brooks; *M:* Joseph Brooks.

If I Die Before I Wake woof! 1998 (R) Suburban family become the grisly victims of three intruders who enjoy terrorizing, torturing, and killing until teenaged LoriBeth (Jones), who has been hiding from the bad guys, gets revenge. Ick, ick, ick. 77m/C VHS, DVD. Michael (Mick) McCleery, Muse Watson, Stephanie Jones, Anthony Nicosia; *D:* Brian Katkin; *W:* Brian Katkin; *C:* Zoran Hochstatter; *M:* Joseph Brooks. VIDEO

If I Had My Way 🦴🦴 1940 When their best friend Fred is killed in an accident, buddies Buzz (Crosby) and Axel (Brendel) vow to take his teenaged daughter Patricia (Jean) to find her relatives in New York. Joe (Dodd) and his wife Marian (Bryant) are a couple of kind-hearted but penniless vaudevillians and Buzz is horrified when Axel uses Patricia's inheritance to buy a failing restaurant. So he decides to make lemonade out of lemons and convert the eatery into a nightclub in hopes of providing for the family. 82m/B DVD. Bing Crosby, Gloria Jean, El Brendel, Claire Dodd, Nana Bryant, Charles Winninger, Allyn Joslyn, Donald Woods, William Conselman, James V. Kern; *D:* David Butler; *C:* George Robinson; *M:* Charles Previn.

If I Were King 🦴🦴🦴 1938 Colman, of the impeccable diction, stars as swashbuckling 15th-century French poet Francois Villon, who matches wits with King Louis XI (Rathbone), and falls in love with aristocratic Katherine de Vaucellos (Dee). He even manages to save Paris by leading a peasant army against the invading Burgundians. Probably the best scenes are the witty repartee between Colman and Rathbone, each trying to best the other. Also filmed as 1927's "The Beloved Rogue" (with John Barrymore) and the operetta "The Vagabond King." 102m/B VHS. Ronald Colman, Basil Rathbone, Frances Dee, Henry Wilcoxon, C.V. France, Ellen Drew, Sidney Toler, Heather Thatcher, Stanley Ridges; *D:* Frank Lloyd; *W:* Preston Sturges; *C:* Theodor Sparkuhl; *M:* Richard Hageman.

If I Were Rich 🦴🦴 *Cash; For Love or Money* 1933 Gwenn is arranging a meeting at his home for a group of financiers he hopes will back a scheme to save his ailing business. Meanwhile he has to dodge bill collectors and others determined to ruin his plans. 63m/B VHS. *GB* Edmund Gwenn, Wendy Barrie, Robert Donat, Clifford Heatherley; *D:* Zoltan Korda.

If I'm Lucky 🦴🦴 1946 Bandleader Earl Gordon (James) gets a gig working for a corrupt political campaign by playing concerts to lure in voters. The politicos decide that the band's squeaky clean singer, Allen Clark (Como), would be a better promoter than their own candidate. But when Allen doesn't want to go along, the politicians threaten to ruin everyone's reputations. A remake of 1935's "Thanks a Million." 80m/B DVD. Perry Como, Vivian Blaine, Harry James, Carmen Miranda, Phil Silvers, Edgar Buchanan, Reed Hadley; *D:* Lewis Seiler; *W:* Helen Logan, Snag Werris, Snag Werris; *C:* Glen MacWilliams; *M:* Emil Newman.

If It's a Man, Hang Up 🦴½ 1975 A model is terrified by harrowing telephone calls from a stranger. 71m/C VHS. Tom Conti, David Gwillim, Carol Lynley, Gerald Harper; *D:* Shaun O'Riordan; *W:* Brian Clemens.

If It's Tuesday, This Must Be Belgium 🦴🦴🦴 1969 (G) A fast-paced, frantic, and funny look at a group of Americans on a whirlwind European tour. The group does a nine-country, 18-day bus tour with clashing, comic personalities and lots of romantic possibilities. Remade in 1987 for TV. 99m/C VHS. Suzanne Pleshette, Ian McShane, Mildred Natwick, Norman Fell, Michael Constantine, Peggy Cass, Murray Hamilton, Marty Ingels, Sandy Baron, Pamela Britton, Luke Halpin; *D:* Mel Stuart.

If Looks Could Kill 🦴🦴 1986 (R) Would-be film noir about a man spying on a female assassin and falling in love. 90m/C VHS. Alan Fisler, Tim Gail, Kim Lambert, Jeanne Marie; *D:* Chuck Vincent.

If Looks Could Kill 🦴🦴½ 1991 (PG-13) TV stud Grieco makes film debut as a high school class cutup who travels to France with his class to parlez vous for extra credit. Mistaken for a CIA agent, he stumbles into a plot to take over all the money in the whole wide world, and much implausible action-and eyelash batting follows. Extra kibbles for supporting characterizations. Oh, and don't be put off by the fact that the Parisian scenes were shot in Montreal. 89m/C VHS. Richard Grieco, Linda Hunt, Roger Rees, Robin Bartlett, Gabrielle Anwar, Roger Daltrey, Geraldine James, Carole (Raphaelle) Davis; *D:* William Dear; *W:* Fred Dekker; *M:* David Foster.

If Lucy Fell 🦴½ 1995 (R) Schaeffer serves as writer/director/star of this predictable 90s-style romantic comedy. Ludicrous premise has psychotherapist Lucy (Parker) bent on realizing a 10-year-old pact with longtime friend Joe (Schaeffer) that stipulates they both jump off the Brooklyn Bridge if neither one has found true love by age 30. With the big birthday approaching, Lucy takes a desperate shot with eccentric painter Bwick (Stiller), while Joe finally goes for the object of his desire, asking beautiful neighbor Jane (MacPherson) to a showing of his paintings. Highlights come in the casting, with Parker a solid and energetic neurotic and MacPherson showing that there's something beyond her more obvious talents. 92m/C VHS, DVD. Sarah Jessica Parker, Eric Schaeffer, Ben Stiller, Elle Macpherson, James Rebhorn, Dominic Chianese; *D:* Eric Schaeffer; *W:* Eric Schaeffer, Tony Spiridakis; *C:* Ron Fortunato; *M:* Amanda Kravat, Charles Pettis.

If Only 🦴🦴½ 2004 (PG-13) Sappy romantic drama finds perky American Samantha Andrews (Hewitt) studying music in London. She and her British businessman boyfriend Ian (Nicholls) are constantly at odds and finally break up. Samantha is immediately killed in a car accident before Ian can come to his senses and reunite with her. But when Samantha appears the next morning, Ian realizes he's reliving their last day together. However, the more he tries to change the outcome, the more inevitable it seems. 92m/C DVD. *GB* Jennifer Love Hewitt, Paul Nicholls, Tom Wilkinson, Diana Hardcastle, Lucy Davenport; *D:* Gil Junger; *W:* Christian Welsh; *C:* Giles Nuttgens; *M:* Adrian Johnston.

If These Walls Could Talk 🦴🦴½ 1996 (R) Covers four decades, from the '50s to the present, telling the stories of three women and the different ways they deal with unexpected pregnancies. "1952" finds recently widowed nurse Claire (Moore) discovering she's pregnant—and it's not her late husband's. In some graphic scenes she tries to end the pregnancy herself with a knitting needle and later through a back-alley abortion. Happily married Barbara (Spacek) already has four children in "1974" and has just returned to college. Then she discovers she's pregnant again. Abortion's an option but does Barbara want one? Finally, college student Christine (Heche) gets pregnant by her married professor in "1996" and reluctantly opts for an abortion at a family planning clinic, which is besieged by pro-lifers and on the edge of some violent confrontations. 109m/C VHS, DVD. Demi Moore, Catherine Keener, Jason London, Shirley Knight, Kevin Cooney, CCH Pounder, Robin Gammell, Sissy Spacek, Xander Berkeley, Joanna Gleason, Harris Yulin, Anne Heche, Jada Pinkett Smith, Cher, Diana Scanwid, Lindsay Crouse, Lorraine Toussaint, Rita Wilson, Eileen Brennan, Craig T. Nelson; *D:* Cher, Nancy Savoca; *W:* Nancy Savoca, Susan Manus, I. Marlene King; *C:* Ellen Kuras, Bobby Bukowski, John Stanier; *M:* Cliff Eidelman.

If These Walls Could Talk 2 🦴🦴½ 2000 (R) Anthology features the stories of three lesbian couples in America. "1961" shows the sedate lives of retired schoolteachers Edith (Redgrave) and Abby (Seldes), who have lived together for decades. But when Abby suddenly dies, Edith discovers she will be disposed by Abby's greedy nephew. "1972" finds Linda (Williams) living with a group of lesbian feminists who disapprove of butch-femme couples. But Linda is still drawn to the butch Amy (Sevigny), who refuses to apologize for how she chooses to live. "2000" has thirtysomething couple Fran (Stone) and Kal (DeGeneres) deciding to have a baby and having some comical problems with the sperm issue. 96m/C VHS, DVD. Vanessa Redgrave, Marian Seldes, Paul Giamatti, Elizabeth Perkins, Michelle Williams, Chloe Sevigny, Nia Long, Natasha Lyonne, Heather McComb, Sharon Stone, Ellen DeGeneres, Regina King, Kathy Najimy, Mitchell Anderson, George Newbern, Amy Carlson; *D:* Jane Anderson, Martha Coolidge, Anne Heche, Alex Sichel; *W:* Jane Anderson, Sylvia Sichel, Anne Heche; *C:* Paul Elliott, Robbie Greenberg, Peter Deming; *M:* Basil Poledouris. CABLE

If They Tell You I Fell 🦴½ *Si Te Dicen Que Cai; Aventis* 1989 The corpse of a man famous from the Spanish Civil War and in local folk stories (called "aventis") is found by a doctor and nurse which spawns revelations that clash with the tall tales. Based on Juan Marse's 1976 novel, spans several decades in muddied flashbacks with actors taking on multiple roles. Spanish, with English subtitles. 120m/C VHS, DVD. Victoria Abril, Antonio Banderas, Juan Diego Botto, Maria Barranco, Javier Gurruchaga, Lluis Homar, Guillermo Montesinos, Margarita Calahorra, Jose Cerro, Pep Cruz, Tere-

If Things Were Different 🦴🦴½ *1979* Feisty woman struggles to hold her family together after her husband is hospitalized with a nervous breakdown. 96m/C VHS. Suzanne Pleshette, Tony Roberts, Arte Johnson, Chuck McCann, Don Murray; **D:** Robert Lewis.

If You Could See What I Hear 🦴½ *1982 (PG)* Irritatingly upbeat true-life story of blind singer-musician Tom Sullivan. Covers his life from college days to marriage. Sophomoric comedy centers around the hero's irresponsible, and often life-endangering, behavior. 103m/C VHS. **C:** Marc Singer, R.H. Thomson, Sarah Torgov, Shari Belafonte; **D:** Eric Till. Genie '83: Support. Actor (Thomson).

If You Don't Stop It... You'll Go Blind 🦴½ *1977 (R)* A series of gauche and tasteless vignettes from various little-known comedians. 80m/C VHS. **C:** Pat McCormick, George Spencer, Patrick Wright; **D:** I. Robert Levy, Keefe Brasselle.

If You Knew Susie 🦴🦴 *1948* Two retired vaudeville actors find a letter from George Washington which establishes them as descendants of a colonial patriot and the heirs to a $7 billion fortune. Song: What Do I Want With Money?; We're Living the Life We Love; My, How the Time Goes By. 90m/B VHS. Eddie Cantor, Joan Davis, Allyn Joslyn, Charles Dingle, Charles Halton; **D:** Gordon Douglas.

If You Only Knew 🦴 *2000* Struggling New York writer (are there any other kind?) Parker (Schaech) falls for painter Samantha (Eastwood) when he answers her ad for someone to share her loft. She has no problem rooming with a guy—as long as he's gay. So Parker moves in and finds the pretense an increasing struggle. Formulaic but Eastwood is a real charmer. 111m/C VHS, DVD. **C:** Johnathon Schaech, Alison Eastwood, Gabrielle Anwar, James LeGros, Lainie Kazan, Paul Sampson, Frank Vincent, Annie Corley, Miguel A. Nunez Jr., Gabrielle Anwar, David Snedeker; **D:** David Snedeker.

Igby Goes Down 🦴🦴🦴 *2002 (R)* Steers's directorial debut is a smart, dark comedy. Modern-day Holden Caulfield Igby (Culkin) rebels against his privileged upbringing, dropping out of countless prep schools, and, finally, military schools. Adrift, Igby heads to the boho pad of his 'rich godfather' (Goldblum) and his beautiful, drug-addled girlfriend (Peet) and is irritated into their degenerate "arty" scene. While in a questionable relationship with Peet, Igby falls for soulful college dropout Sookie Sapperstein (Danes) who's also the target of his sick older brother Oliver's (Phillippe) affection. The matriarch of Igby's dysfunctional family is Sarandon, in a humorously unlikable role. Thoughtful, satiric view of the emptiness of the American Dream. 98m/C VHS, DVD. US Kieran Culkin, Ryan Phillippe, Susan Sarandon, Claire Danes, Jeff Goldblum, Bill Pullman, Amanda Peet, Jared Harris, Rory Culkin, Cynthia Nixon, Eric Bogosian; **D:** Burr Steers. **M:** Uwe Peterson.

Ignition 🦴🦴½ *2001 (R)* The U.S. Army is preparing a major rocket launch just as 'Federal Judge Faith Matheson (Olin) begins a corruption and reason trial that involves the military. Is it any surprise that there are links between the launch and her case? When Faith is threatened, she turns to former Marine helicopter pilot Conor Gallagher (Pullman) for help. 95m/C VHS, DVD. US CA Lena Olin, Bill Pullman, Colm Feore, Nicholas Lea, Peter Kent, Michael Ironside, Roger Dunn, Scott Hylands, Benjamin Ratner; **D:** Yves Simoneau. **W:** William Davies, Benjamin Freeman.

Igor & the Lunatics 🦴 *1985 (R)* Tasteless tale of a cannibal cult leader released from prison who picks up where he left off. 75m/C VHS, DVD. Joseph Eero, Joe Niola, T.J. Michaels; **D:** Billy Parolini.

Iguana 🦴🦴 *1989* The videocassette box art makes this look like a horror movie, but it's really a stiff, solemn period drama about a deformed sailor with lizardlike features. After a life of mistreatment he reigns mercilessly over a handful of island castaways. An international coproduction with mostly English dialogue, done in Spanish and Portuguese with subtitles. 86m/C VHS, DVD. SI IT Everett McGill, Monte Hellman; **W:** Monte Hellman, Jaime Comas Gil, Steven Gaydos; **C:** Josep Civit.

Ike 🦴🦴 *Ike: The War Years 1979* Duvall is top brass in this epic biography tracing Eisenhower's career during WWII. Originally a six-hour miniseries. 291m/C VHS, DVD. Robert Duvall, Lee Remick, Dana Andrews, Laurence Luckinbill; **D:** Melville Shavelson. TV

Ike: Countdown to D-Day 🦴🦴½ *2004 (PG)* Selleck shaves off the signature mustache—and the rest of his hair—to star in this low-key (meaning no battle scenes) biopic of Gen. Dwight D. Eisenhower that gives a behind-the-scenes account of the war-room planning for the pivotal D-Day invasion. 85m/C VHS, DVD. Tom Selleck, James Remar, Timothy Bottoms, Gerald McRaney, Ian Mune, Bruce Phillips, John Bach, Nick Blake, Kevin J. Wilson, Christopher Baker, George Shevtsov, Gregor McLennan, Paul Gittins, Craig Hall, Stephen Brunton, Paul Barrett, Mickey Rose, Carole Sear; **D:** Robert Harmon; **M:** Lionel Chetwynd; **C:** David Gribble. TV

Ikiru 🦴🦴🦴🦴 *To Live; Doomed; Living 1952* When a clerk finds out he is dying of cancer, he decides to build a children's playground and give something of himself back to the world. Highly acclaimed, heartbreaking drama from the unusually restrained Kurosawa; possibly his most "eastern" film. In Japanese with English subtitles. 134m/B VHS, DVD. JP Takashi Shimura, Nobuo Kaneko, Kyoko Seki, Miki Odagari, Yunosuke Ito; **D:** Akira Kurosawa; **W:** Akira Kurosawa, Shinobu Hashimoto, Hideo Oguni; **C:** Asakazu Nakai; **M:** Fumio Hayasaka.

Il Bell'Antonio 🦴🦴½ *Handsome Antonio 1960* The boastful Antonio has a reputation as a womanizer but when he finally marries, to a lovely young woman, he faces the loss of his libido. Satire of machismo, marriage, and Catholicism. In Italian with English subtitles. 115m/C VHS. IT Marcello Mastroianni, Claudia Cardinale, Pierre Brasseur, Tomas Milian, Rina Morelli; **D:** Mauro Bolognini; **W:** Pier Paolo Pasolini, Gino Vissentini; **C:** Armando Nannuzzi; **M:** Piero Piccioni.

Il Bidone 🦴🦴 *The Swindle 1955* Three Italian conmen pull capers in Rome trying to make a better life for themselves. Dark overtones permeate one of Fellini's lesser efforts. Good cast can't bring up the level of this film. In Italian with English subtitles. 92m/C VHS, DVD. IT Broderick Crawford, Giulietta Masina, Richard Basehart, Franco Fabrizi, Federico Fellini; **D:** Federico Fellini; **W:** Federico Fellini, Tullio Pinelli, Ennio de Concini; **C:** Otello Martelli; **M:** Nino Rota.

Il Grido 🦴🦴 *The Cry; The Outcry 1957* A jilted husband takes his young daughter from village to village in search of the Italian woman who deserted them. Set in the desolate Po Valley of director Antonioni's childhood. In Italian with English subtitles. 115m/B VHS, DVD. IT Steve Cochran, Alida Valli, Dorian Gray, Betsy Blair, Gabriella Pallotta; **D:** Michelangelo Antonioni; **W:** Michelangelo Antonioni, Ennio de Concini; **C:** Gianni Di Venanzo; **M:** Giovanni Fusco.

Il Sorpasso 🦴🦴½ *1963* A braggart, who has failed at everything, spends all his time traveling around Italy in his sportscar. He takes a repressed law student under his wing and decides to teach him how to have fun. In Italian with English subtitles. 116m/B VHS. IT Vittorio Gassman, Jean-Louis Trintignant; **D:** Dino Risi.

I'll Be Home for Christmas 🦴½ *1998 (PG)* Snotty college kid Jake (Thomas) wants to teach his Dad a lesson by boycotting Christmas and stealing away to Mexico with his girlfriend (Biel). Jake thinks his Dad remarried too soon after his mother's death, but is bribed home with his Dad's prized Porsche (now there's a lesson for the kids) if he can arrive for Christmas Eve dinner. A series of absurd mishaps ensue (almost all of which occur because Jake is a lying, cheating jerk) as he makes his away cross-country while glued inside of a Santa suit. The characters are superficial and at times downright annoying. This run of the mill holiday stinker will likely only appeal to Thomas' legion of teenage groupies. 86m/C VHS, DVD. Jonathan Taylor Thomas, Jessica Biel, Adam LaVorgna, Gary Cole, Eve Gordon, Sean O'Bryan, Andrew Lauer; **D:** Arlene Sanford; **W:** Harris Goldberg, Tom Nursall; **C:** John Dabney.

I'll Be There 🦴½ *2003 (PG-13)* Aging pop idol (Ferguson) sobers up and discovers he has a teenage daughter (Church). The two start to develop a relationship in spite of Mother's reservations. Of course, the kid can sing and catches the attention of Dad's slimy manager. Church's acting has a way to go to catch up to her singing, but she's better than Britny or Mariah (at both). Scottish comic Ferguson seems to have taken on more currently handle, but still gets points for effort. 104m/C VHS, DVD. US Craig Ferguson, Jemma Redgrave, Joss Ackland, Charlotte Church, Ralph Brown, Ian McNeice, Imelda Staunton, Anthony Head; **D:** Craig Ferguson; **W:** Craig Ferguson, Philip McGrade; **C:** Ian Wilson; **M:** Trevor Jones.

I'll Be Yours 🦴🦴½ *1947* Small-town Louise Ginglebusher (Durbin) moves to New York and becomes an usher at the Buckingham Theatre (a fictional Radio City Music Hall). She gets involved with and struggling lawyer, George Prescott (Drake). She falls for George and tries to help him get a job with Nelson by telling Nelson that they have just gotten married. Bendix plays the sympathetic coffee shop owner. Remake of 1935's "The Good Fairy," which was also a play by Ferenc Molnar. Songs: Dreamtime; Cobbleskill; It's Dreamtime; Granada; Sari Waltz. 94m/B VHS. Deanna Durbin, Tom Drake, Adolphe Menjou, William Bendix, Walter Catlett, Franklin Pangborn; **D:** William A. Seiter; **W:** Preston Sturges; **C:** Hal Mohr; **M:** Frank Skinner.

I'll Bury You Tomorrow 🦴 *2002* Low-budget indie horror is a true creepfest. Beech Funeral Home attracts whack jobs, including new assistant mortician Delores (Chlanda), who keeps a big secret in a steamer trunk. This is discovered by fellow employee Jake (Murdock), who is into illegal organ donations. So he tries blackmailing Delores into helping him, which is a really bad idea. 119m/C DVD. Zoe Daelman Chlanda, Jerry Murdock, Bill Corry, Katherine O'Sullivan, Kristen Overdurf, Renee West, Alan Rowe Kelly, Tom Burns; **D:** Alan Rowe Kelly; **W:** Alan Rowe Kelly; **C:** Tom Cadawas Gary Mallok; **M:** Tom Burns.

I'll Cry Tomorrow 🦴🦴🦴 *1955* Hayward brilliantly portrays actress Lillian Roth as she descends into alcoholism and then tries to overcome her addiction. Based on Roth's memoirs. ♪Sing You Sinners; When The Red Red Robin Comes Bob Bop Bobbin' Along; Happiness Is Just a Thing Called Joe; Vagabond King Waltz. 119m/B VHS. Susan Hayward, Richard Conte, Eddie Albert, Jo Van Fleet, Margo, Don Taylor, Ray Danton, Veda Ann Borg; **D:** Daniel Mann; **M:** Alex North. Oscars '55: Costume Des. (B&W); Cannes '56: Actress (Hayward).

I'll Do Anything 🦴🦴 *1993 (PG-13)* Hollywood satire finds unemployed actor Matt (Nolte) suddenly forced to care for his six-year-old daughter Jeannie (Wright), whom he hasn't seen in three years. Matt also finally gets a job—as a chauffeur to an obnoxious producer (well played by Brooks) whose company winds up making the manipulative demon Jeannie into a hot child star. Great work by Kavner as the owner of a test-screening service who romances Brooks. Originally intended as a musical, the test screenings were so disastrous that the numbers were axed. What's left is less jerky than expected; Brooks reportedly based his character in part on mega-mogul Joel Silver. 115m/C VHS, DVD. Nick Nolte, Albert Brooks, Julie Kavner, Whittni Wright, Joely Richardson, Tracey Ullman; **D:** James L. Brooks; **W:** James L. Brooks; **M:** Hans Zimmer.

I'll Get You 🦴🦴 *Escape Route 1953* An FBI agent goes to England on the trail of a kidnapping ring. 78m/B VHS, DVD. George Raft, Sally Gray, Clifford Evans; **D:** Seymour Friedman.

I'll Name the Murderer 🦴🦴 *1936* Suspense film in which a gossip columnist starts his own investigation into the murder of a club singer. 66m/B VHS, DVD. Ralph Forbes, Marion Shilling; **D:** Bernard B. Ray.

I'll Never Forget What's 'isname 🦴🦴🦴 *1967* To some tastes, this overwrought and long-unseen comedy from the swinging '60s will seem dated with characters whose mindsets are totally alien. Protagonist Andrew Quint (Reed) is a piggish young ad executive who tries to leave his even more piggish boss (Welles), and his two mistresses his wife. Why? He wants to go back to do something meaningful with his life, something like working for a literary magazine. It's actually a long midlife crisis (though the phrase did not exist when the film was made) that set standards for frankness in its sexual material. 99m/C VHS, DVD. Oliver Reed, Orson Welles, Carol White, Marianne Faithfull, Michael Horden, Frank Finlay; **D:** Michael Winner; **W:** Peter Draper; **C:** Otto Heller; **M:** Francis Lai.

I'll Remember April 🦴🦴½ *1999* In the days following the bombing of Pearl Harbor rumors abound that Japanese submarines are patrolling the Pacific and four 10-year-old California boys like to pretend they are Marines in search of the enemy. Imagine their surprise when they discover a Japanese soldier who washed up on the beach and is hiding out in their clubhouse. They keep him there prisoner while trying to decide what to do but when the boys decide that they have to save him. 96m/C VHS, DVD. Haley Joel Osment, Trevor Morgan, Richard Taylor, Olson, Yuki Tokuhiro, Mark Harmon, Pam Dawber, Noriyuki "Pat" Morita, Yuji Okumoto, Troy Evans, Paul Dooley; **D:** Bob (Benjamin) Clark; **W:** Mark Sanderson; **C:** Stephen M. Katz; **M:** Paul Zaza.

I'll See You in My Dreams 🦴🦴½ *1951* Hokey but fun musical biography of songwriter Gus Kahn (Thomas) and his wife Grace LeBoy (Day). Kahn gets his start in Ziegfeld shows but loses both his career and wife after the 1929 crash. However, she soon returns and everything ends happily ever after. ♪The One I Love Belongs to Somebody Else; I'll See You in My Dreams; It Had To Be You; Swingin' Down the Lane; My Buddy; Makin' Whoopee!; Yes Sir, That's My Baby. 109m/B VHS, DVD. Danny Thomas, Doris Day, Frank Lovejoy, Patrice Wymore, James Gleason, Mary Wickes, Jim Backus, Minna Gombell, William Forrest; **D:** Michael Curtiz; **M:** Melville Shavelson, Jack Fose.

I'll Sleep When I'm Dead 🦴🦴 *2003 (R)* Will Graham (Owen) thinks he has escaped the horrors of urban life for the great outdoors. Unfortunately, his hipster drug-dealing younger brother (Rhys Meyers) has been found dead from an apparent suicide. Shady businessman Boad (McDowell) took a nasty fancy to him and, with the help of his stooges, raped him quite brutally. Now Will has to return to London and make the bad men pay. Extra dark and mean contemporary noir from Hodges who ably filling acts like a remake of this classic "Get Carter," with Clive Owen ably filling Michael Caine's shoes (unlike a certain American action star). Story is a bit muddled and confusing at times, but the onslaught of action makes up for it. The rape scene is one of the most agonizing sequences you'll see. Not for the faint of heart. 102m/C DVD. US GB Clive Owen, Charlotte Rampling, Malcolm McDowell, Jamie Foreman, Ken Stott, Sylvia Syms, Geoff Bell, Desmond Bayis, Kris O'Shea; **D:** Mike Hodges; **W:** Trevor Preston; **C:** Mike Garfath; **M:** Simon Fisher Turner.

I'll Take Sweden ♪♪½ 1965 (R) Overprotective father Hope disapproves of teenaged daughter Weld's guitar-playing boyfriend (Avalon). So to keep her out of harm's way he finagles a company transfer to Sweden. Dad falls for an interior decorator (Merrill) while Weld gets involved with a Swedish playboy (Slate). Deciding Avalon is the lesser of two evils, Hope schemes to get the two back together. 96m/C VHS, DVD. Bob Hope, Tuesday Weld, Frankie Avalon, Dina Merrill, Jeremy Slate, Walter Sande, John Qualen, Roy Roberts, Maudie Prickett; D: Fred de Cordova; W: Arthur Marx, Bob Fisher, Nat Perrin; C: Daniel F. Fapp.

I'll Take You There ♪♪ 1999 (R) Lightweight, somewhat schizophrenic romantic comedy-road flick-drama has despondent Bill (Rogers) trying to recover from a failed relationship. His sister sets him up with old school friend Bernice (Sheedy), but he viciously insults her on the date. She shows up a few days later, and kidnaps him on a road trip that begins with the heist of a prom dress. More outlandish events ensue, but the unbelievable plot almost sinks the whole enterprise. Solid work by a strong cast mostly save the day. 93m/C VHS, DVD. Ally Sheedy, Reg Rogers, Lara Harris, John Pyper-Ferguson, Alice Drummond, Alan North, Ben Vereen, Adrienne Shelly; D: Adrienne Shelly; W: Adrienne Shelly; C: Vanja Cernjul; M: Andrew Hollander.

Illegal ♪♪½ 1955 Crime melodrama stars Robinson as an attorney who risks all to acquit his assistant of murder. Early Mansfield appearance. Remake of "The Mouthpiece." 88m/B VHS, DVD. Edward G. Robinson, Nina Foch, Hugh Marlowe, Jayne Mansfield, Albert Dekker, Ellen Corby, DeForest Kelley, Howard St. John; D: Lewis Allen.

Illegal Affairs ♪ 1996 The kind of film that makes you feel sorry for lawyers. The sleazy firm of Grimes and Peterson specializes in divorce cases—and seem personally responsible for any number of them on account of adultery. 87m/C VHS, DVD. Jay Richardson, Monique Parent, Christian Noble; D: Michael Paul Girard; C: Michael Paul Girard; C: Denis Maloney; M: Miriam Cutler. VIDEO

Illegal Entry: Formula for Fear ♪½ 1993 Tracie's scientist father has invented a formula that could change the world. When he's murdered the formula falls into her unsuspecting hands. Tracie might not know what she has but that doesn't stop some very ruthless efforts to get the information others want. 88m/C VHS.

Illegal in Blue ♪♪ 1995 (R) Chris (Gauthier) the cop falls for sultry blues singer Kari (Dash) and then realizes she could be a suspect in the murder he's investigating. Will libido win out over loyalty to the job? Also available unrated. 94m/C VHS. Dan Gauthier, Stacey Dash, Louis Giambalvo, Michael Durrell, David Groh; D: Stu Segall; W: Noel Hynd; M: Stephen (Steve) Edwards.

Illegal Tender ♪♪½ 2007 (R) Twenty-one-year-old Wilson (Gonzalez) enjoys his upper-middle class lifestyle until his mother (De Jesus) informs him that his dead father was a drug dealer and hands him a gun. Turns out they need to defend themselves from his father's murderer, who's still after them and the money Dad stole. Wilson is mostly adequate as the reluctant heir to his father's legacy but is overshadowed by De Jesus's two-gun Pam Grier-style performance. You'll find yourself wishing you saw more of Mom and a lot less of Wilson. John Singleton produced what is, essentially, a blaxploitation film gone Latino (Laxploitation?). Nothing really distinguishes it from any other mediocre B-movie revenge flick. 107m/C DVD. US Wanda De Jesus, Rick Gonzalez, Dania Ramirez, Antonio Ortiz, Manny Perez, Tego Calderon; D: Franc Reyes; W: Franc Reyes; M: Heitor Pereira.

Illegally Yours ♪ 1987 (PG) Miscast comedy about a college student serving on the jury in trial of old girlfriend. Bring down the gavel on this one. 94m/C VHS, DVD. Rob Lowe, Colleen Camp, Kenneth Mars; D: Peter Bogdanovich.

Illicit ♪♪ 1931 In love, Stanwyck fears that marrying Rennie will only ruin their wonderful relationship. Two years after their marriage her fears are realized when each searches for happiness with a past lover. A melodramatic performance that doesn't quite hit its mark. Remade two years later as "Ex-Lady" with Bette Davis in the lead. Based on the play by Edith Fitzgerald and Robert Riskin. 76m/B VHS. Barbara Stanwyck, Ricardo Cortez, Natalie Moorhead, Charles Butterworth, Joan Blondell, Claude Gillingwater; D: Archie Mayo; W: Harvey Thew.

Illicit Behavior ♪♪½ 1991 (R) A dangerous manipulative woman (Severance) is out to claim a $2 million insurance in this intricate and seductive police thriller. Included among her victims are her husband; a Hollywood vice cop suspended for use of excessive force; his partner; and her own psychiatrist. Also available in an uncut, unrated version. 101m/C VHS. Joan Severance, Robert Davi, James Russo, Jack Scalia, Kent McCord; D: Worth Keeter.

Illicit Dreams ♪½ 1994 A lonely housewife fantasizes about a dream lover who then becomes real. Too bad her possessive and vicious tycoon hubby would rather kill than lose her. 93m/C VHS. Michelle Johnson, Stella Stevens, Joseph Cortese, Shannon Tweed, Andrew Stevens; D: Andrew Stevens; W: Karen Kelly; C: Christian Sebaldt; M: Claude Gaudette.

Illtown ♪♪½ 1996 A happy trio of yuppie-ish Florida drug dealers, led by Rapaport's Dante, land in their own inferno when Dante's former business partner Gabriel (Trese), emerges from jail hell-bent on revenge. Danza plays the evil, effeminate underworld boss while Hayes takes the high road as the saintly detective. Abundance of metaphors aside and amid all the violence, the sluggish narrative style, with everything thrown in from dream sequences and flashbacks to dissolves and slow motion, is more effective at setting a mood than telling a story. Effective score and powerful performances, beautifully filmed by Denault, make a stylish pic that sacrifices substance. 103m/C VHS. Michael Rapaport, Lili Taylor, Adam Trese, Kevin Corrigan, Paul Schulze, Angela Featherstone, Saul Stein, Tony Danza, Isaac Hayes; D: Nick Gomez; W: Nick Gomez; C: Jim Denault; M: Brian Keane.

Illuminata ♪♪ 1998 (R) Comedy-drama about a struggling theatre troupe in turn-of-the-century New York. Tuccio (Turturro) is the company's playwright—in love with manager/leading lady, Rachel (Turturro's wife Borowitz), and worried about the reception for his new work. Also involved are self-centered aging diva Celimene (Sarandon), theatre owner Astergourd (D'Angelo), foppish critic Bevalaqua (Walken) and the unlikely object of his affections, the troupe's clown, Marco (Irwin), among many others. Adapted from the play by Brandon Cole. 111m/C VHS, DVD. John Turturro, Katherine Borowitz, Christopher Walken, Susan Sarandon, Beverly D'Angelo, Bill Irwin, Rufus Sewell, Georgina Cates, Ben Gazzara, Donal McCann, Aida Turturro, Matthew Sussman, Leo Bassi; D: John Turturro; W: John Turturro, Brandon Cole; C: Harris Savides; M: William Bolcom, Arnold Black.

Illumination ♪♪ 1973 Illuminacja 1973 Cryptic drama about a young scientist who believes that rational analysis can solve every crisis. Until he must confront the accidental death of a close friend and his problematic affair with an older woman. Intercutting of documentary material can prove disconcerting. Polish with subtitles. 91m/C VHS. Pol. Stanislaw Latallo, Monika Dzienisiewicz-Olbrzychska, Malgorzata Pritulak, Edward Zebrowski; D: Krzysztof Zanussi; W: Krzysztof Zanussi; C: Edward Klosinski; M: Wojciech Kilar.

The Illusion Travels by Streetcar ♪♪♪ 1953 La Ilusión Viaja en Tranvia 1953 Odd but enchanting story of two men who restore a streetcar, only to find that it will not be used by the city. In a gesture of defiance, they steal the streetcar and take it for one last ride, picking up an interesting assortment of characters along the way. In Spanish with English subtitles. Not released in the U.S. until 1977. 90m/B VHS. MX Lilia Prado, Carlos Navarro, Domingo Soler, Fernando Soto Mantequilla, Agustin Isunza, Miguel Manzano; D: Luis Buñuel.

The Illusionist ♪♪½ 2006 (PG-13) Eisenheim (Norton) is a wildly popular magician in 1900 Vienna where he is reunited with his childhood love, the aristocratic Sophie (Biel). She's now engaged to suspicious Crown Prince Leopold (Sewell) who sics police chief Inspector Uhl (Giamatti) on Eisenheim in an effort to debunk his illusions. You won't find anyone pulling doves out of their sleeves to the tune of "Final Countdown" in Burger's icy turn-of-the-century romance, but there's still a lot to like, particularly the always-intriguing Norton and Giamatti. Unfortunately, no illusion can make the audience believe there's any spark between Eisenheim and Sophie, which is mostly the fault of the lovely, though vacant, Ms. Biel. 110m/C DVD. US Edward Norton, Jessica Biel, Rufus Sewell, Paul Giamatti, Eddie Marsan, Aaron Johnson; D: Neil Burger; W: Neil Burger; C: Dick Pope; M: Philip Glass.

Illusions ♪♪ 1991 (R) Jan (Locklear) is trying to recover from a nervous breakdown and improve her crumbling marriage when her husband's sexy sister arrives and things start to heat up. Jan thinks her husband and sister-in-law are just a little too close, but when she lets her landlord in on her suspicions, he reacts quite strangely. Will Jan have another nervous breakdown? Mysterious with lots of plot twists. Based on Colley's play "I'll Be Back Before Midnight." 95m/C VHS. Heather Locklear, Emma Samms, Ned Beatty; D: Victor Kulle; W: Peter Colley.

The Illustrated Man ♪♪♪ 1969 (PG) A young drifter meets a tattooed man. Each tattoo causes a fantastic story to unfold. A strange, interesting, but finally limited attempt at literary sci-fi. Based on the story collection by Ray Bradbury. 103m/C VHS, DVD. Rod Steiger, Claire Bloom, Robert Drivas, Don Dubbins; D: Jack Smight; M: Jerry Goldsmith.

Ilsa, Harem Keeper of the Oil Sheiks WOOF! 1976 (R) The naughty Ilsa works for an Arab sheik in the slave trade. More graphic violence and nudity. Plot makes an appearance. 90m/C VHS, DVD. Dyanne Thorne, Max (Michael) Thayer, Victor Alexander, Elke Von, Sharon Kelly, Haji, Tanya Boyd, Marilyn Joy, Bobby Woods; D: Don Edmonds; W: Langton Stafford; C: Dean Cundey, Glenn Roland.

Ilsa, She-Wolf of the SS WOOF! 1974 (R) The torture-loving Ilsa runs a medical camp for the Nazis. Plot is incidental to nudity and violence. 90m/C VHS, DVD. Dyanne Thorne, Gregory Knoph, Sharon Kelly, Sandy Richman; W: Jonah Royston.

Ilsa, the Tigress of Siberia WOOF! 1979 The Tigress 1979 Everyone's favorite torturer has been working her wiles on political prisoners in Russia. After escaping to Canada, her past threatens to catch up with her. As usual, no plot, no violence. 85m/C VHS. Dyanne Thorne, Michel Morin, Jean-Guy Latour, Michael Mallot, Tony Angelo, Terry Coady, Joe Mattia, Sonny Forbes, Greg Giants, Maura Maurer; D: Jean LaFleur; W: Marven McGara; C: Richard Ciupka.

Ilsa, the Wicked Warden WOOF! Ilsa, the Absolute Power; Greta the Mad Butcher 1978 Ilsa is now a warden of a woman's prison in South America, behaving just as badly as she always has, until the prisoners stage an uprising. Lots of skin, no violence, no acting. Also: no plot. 90m/C VHS, DVD. Dyanne Thorne, Lina Romay, Tania Busselier, Howard Maurer, Jess (Jesus) Franco; D: Jess (Jesus) Franco; W: Erwin C. Dietrich, Jess (Jesus) Franco; C: Ruedi Kuttel; M: Walter Baumgartner.

I'm All Right Jack ♪♪♪ 1959 Sellers plays a pompous communist union leader in this hilarious satire of worker-management relations. Based on Alan Hackney's novel "Private Life." 101m/B VHS, DVD. Peter Sellers, Ian Carmichael, Terry-Thomas, Victor Maddern; D: John Boulting. British Acad. '59: Actor (Sellers); Screenplay.

I'm Dancing as Fast as I Can ♪♪ 1982 (R) A successful TV producer hopelessly dependent on tranquilizers tries to stop cold turkey. Good story could be better; based on Barbara Gordon's memoirs. 107m/C VHS, DVD. Jill Clayburgh, Nicol Williamson, Dianne West, Joe Pesci, Geraldine Page, John Lithgow, Daniel Stern; D: Jack Hofsiss; W: David Rabe; C: Jan De Bont.

I'm Dangerous Tonight ♪♪½ 1990 (R) Wallflower Amick (Shelley the Waitress in "Twin Peaks") turns into party monster when she dons red dress made from evil ancient Aztec cloak. Many dead soldiers when this girl parties. Based on a Cornell Woolrich short story. It's another in a series of ever more disappointing entries from Hooper, whose cult fave "The Texas Chainsaw Massacre" had low as they come production values, but far better scares. 92m/C VHS, DVD. Madchen Amick, Corey Parker, R. Lee Ermey, Mary Frann, Dee Wallace Stone, Anthony Perkins, Natalie Schafer, William Berger; D: Tobe Hooper; W: Alice Wilson. CABLE

I'm from Arkansas ♪ 1944 The little town of Pitchfork, Arkansas, goes nuts when a pig gives birth to ten piglets. 68m/B VHS. El Brendel, Slim Summerville, Iris Adrian, Harry Harvey, Bruce Bennett; D: Lew Landers.

I'm Going Home ♪♪♪ a la Maison 2000 Je Rentre a la Maison 2000 Distinguished, elderly actor Gilbert Valence (Piccoli) is dealt a devastating blow when his wife, daughter, and son-in-law are killed in a car accident. Coping with dignity, he looks after his young grandson and works in the theatre (playing Prospero in "The Tempest"). His agent urges Valence to take his first role in an English-language film directed by an American (Malkovich) and he struggles mightily to cope with a simple statement when he realizes that this time is past. French with subtitles. 90m/C VHS, DVD. PT FR Michel Piccoli, Catherine Deneuve, John Malkovich, Leonor Silveira, Antoine Chappey, Leonor Baldaque, Jean Koeltgen; D: Manoel de Oliveira; W: Manoel de Oliveira; C: Sabine Lancelin.

I'm Gonna Git You Sucka ♪♪♪ 1988 (R) Parody of "blaxploitation" films popular during the '60s and '70s. Funny and laced with outright bellylaughs. A number of stars who made "blaxploitation" films, including Jim Brown, take part in the gags. 89m/C VHS, DVD. Keenen Ivory Wayans, Bernie Casey, Steve James, Isaac Hayes, Jim Brown, Ja'net DuBois, Dawnn Lewis, Anne-Marie Johnson, John Vernon, Antonio Fargas, Eve Plumb, Clu Gulager, Kadeem Hardison, Damon Wayans, Gary Owens, Clarence Williams III, David Alan Grier, Kim Wayans, Robin Harris, Chris Rock, Jester Hairston, Eugene Robert Glazer, Peggy Lipton, Robert Kevin Townsend; D: Keenen Ivory Wayans; W: Keenen Ivory Wayans; C: Tom Richmond; M: David Michael Frank.

I'm Losing You ♪♪ 1998 (R) Confusing story with too many shocks and no point of view, which wastes a good cast. TV producer Perry Krohn (Langella) learns that he's dying of cancer. His wife, Diantha (Jens), takes the news badly, as do his wayward children Bertie (McCarthy) and Rachel (Arquette). But it seems everyone has a doom-laden revelation to deal with. Wagner adapts from his own novel. 102m/C VHS, DVD. Frank Langella, Salome Jens, Rosanna Arquette, Andrew McCarthy, Amanda Donohoe, Elizabeth Perkins, Gina Gershon, Buck Henry, Ed Begley Jr.; D: Bruce Wagner; W: Bruce Wagner; C: Rob Sweeney; M: Daniel Catan.

I'm No Angel ♪♪♪ 1933 "Beulah, peel me a grape." "Well, you'd be hungry too if you spent your time eyeing playboy Grant as West does. She's a circus floozy who's prone to extorting money from her men (after hashing over their shortcomings with her seen-it-all-maid, the aforementioned Beulah). However, after wooing Grant, she sues for breach of promise. This leads to a comic courtroom scene with Grant bringing in all West's ex-lovers as witnesses. Grant's second film with West, following "She Done Him Wrong." 88m/B VHS, DVD. Mae West, Cary

I'm Not Rappaport 🐾🐾 1996

(PG-13) Matthau does some comic grump schtick as irascible, unrepentant 81-year-old New York Jewish radical Nat. He likes to vent his considerable opinions in Central Park and carries on a grumbling friendship with fellow octogenarian Midge (Davis), who still works as a building superintendent, tending an equally ancient boiler. But Nat's fed-up daughter Clara (Irving) is threatening to put him in a home and Midge seems likely to lose his job when the boiler is scheduled or replaced when Gardner's 1986 stage play tends to show its weaknesses on the big screen. 135m/C VHS, DVD. Walter Matthau, Ossie Davis, Amy Irving, Martha Plimpton, Craig T. Nelson, Boyd Gaines, Guillermo Diaz, Elina Lowensohn, Ron Rifkin; **D:** Herb Gardner; **W:** Herb Gardner; **C:** Adam Holender; **M:** Gerry Mulligan.

I'm Not Scared 🐾🐾 *Io Non Ho Paura* 2003 (R) 10-year-old Michele (Christiana) lives in a remote and poor village in southern Italy. As he pokes around an abandoned house one hot summer day, he discovers a trapdoor that leads to a pit where a traumatized kidnapped boy, Filippo (Di Pietro), is being held prisoner. Michele's afraid to tell his parents—mostly so as it becomes clear his father (Abbrescia) is involved—but he also can't abandon Filippo, returning to him again and again with food and water. Just what Michele does do to become the crux of this disturbing thriller. Based on the novel by co-screenwriter Ammaniti. **Italian** with subtitles. 110m/C DVD. **GB IT SP** Aitana Sanchez-Gijon, Diego Abatantuono, Dino Abbrescia, Giorgio Careccia, Giuseppe Cristiano, Mattia Di Pietro; **D:** Gabriele Salvatores; **W:** Francesca Marciano, Niccolo Ammaniti; **C:** Itao Pericione; **M:** Pepo Scherman, Ezio Bosso.

I'm Not There 🐾🐾🐾 2007 (R) Sort of a symbolist musical history, pic loaded with real-life clips and acted by no less than six separate actors and actresses representing different identities of poet/musician/revolutionary Bob Dylan. There's 11-year-old Woody (Franklin who hops trains and tells far-fetched stories; Jack Rollins (Bale) personifies Dylan's first look at fame in folk-song roots; Jude (Blanchett) represents Dylan's shift to electric rock, a divisive move that alienated many of his fans. Richard Gere shows up as Billy, a personification of Dylan exiled in Missouri. Arthur (Whishaw), yet another Dylan, narrates and brings the sequences somewhat into focus. It's long and rambling and creamlike, but Dylan fans will delight at the many references that their less-obsessed friends will miss. 135m/C DVD, GE US Christian Bale, Heath Ledger, Cate Blanchett, Ben Whishaw, Marcus Carl Franklin, Richard Gere, Charlotte Gainsbourg, Julianne Moore, Michelle Williams, David Cross, Bruce Greenwood, Lisa Bronwyn Moore; **D:** Todd Haynes; **W:** Todd Haynes, Oren Moverman; **C:** Edward Lachman; **Golden Globes '08:** Support. Actress (Blanchett); **Ind. Spirit '08:** Support. Actress (Blanchett).

I'm Reed Fish 🐾🐾 2006 (PG) Reed Fish (Baruchel), a talk jock on the small local radio station in Mud Meadows, is about to marry his high school sweetheart, Kate (Biedel). But Reed questions his carefully planned-out world when former school chum/aspiring musician Jill (Fisk) blows back into town. Feed decides to quit his job and make a movie about his life. Yeah, this quirky comedy is based on the life of screenwriter—wait for it—Reed Fish. 93m/C DVD. Jay Baruchel, Alexis Biedel, Schuyler Fisk, DJ Qualls, Shirl Appeby, Katey Sagal, Victor Rasuk, Chris Parnell, A.J. Cook; **D:** Zackary Adler; **W:** Reed Fish; **C:** Douglas Chamberlain; **M:** Fodty Bottum.

I'm the Girl He Wants to Kill 🐾½ 1974 A woman sees a murder committed and the murderer sees her. Now he's after her. 71m/C VHS. Robert Lang, Julie Sommars, Anthony Steel; **D:** Shaun O'Riordan.

I'm the One You're Looking For 🐾🐾½ 1988 A famous model obsessively combs Barcelona for the man who raped her. Suspenseful thriller based on a short story by Gabriel Garcia Marquez. In Spanish with English subtitles. 85m/C VHS. SP Patricia Adriani, Chus Lampreave, Ricard Borras, Frank Muro, Miriam Delmaz; **D:** Jaime Chavarri.

I'm with Lucy 🐾🐾½ 2002 (R) Courtesy romantic comedy. Lucy (Potter) gets publicly dumped by her boyfriend but still believes her soulmate is out there somewhere. So she goes on five blind dates (Hannah, Bernal, LaPaglia, Thomas, Boreanaz) but can only see her would-be suitors' flaws and not their good points. Still, it all comes out right in the end. 90m/C VHS, DVD. Monica Potter, John Hannah, Gael Garcia Bernal, Anthony LaPaglia, Henry Thomas, David Boreanaz, Julianne Nicholson, Harold Ramis, Julie Christie; **D:** Jon Sherman; **W:** Eric Pomerance; **C:** Tom Richmond; **M:** Stephen Endelman.

The Image 🐾 1989 Anchorman Finney, the unscrupulous czar of infotainment, does a little soul delving when a man he wrongly implicated in a savings and loan debacle decides to check into the hereafter ahead of schedule. Seems the newsmonger's cut a few corners in route to the bigtime, and his public is mad as hell and... oops, wrong movie (need we say there are not a few echoes of "Network"?). Finney's great. 91m/C VHS, DVD. Albert Finney, John Mahoney, Kathy Baker, Swoosie Kurtz, Marsha Mason, Spalding Gray; **D:** Peter Werner; **M:** James Newton Howard. CABLE

Image of Death 🐾 1977 Woman plots to take the life of an old school chum, assume her identity, and then love up the Capitol. 83m/C VHS, Cathy Paino, Cheryl Waters, Tony Banner, Barry Pierce, Sheila Helpmann, Penne Hackforth-Jones; **D:** Kevin James Dotson.

Image of Passion 🐾 1986 Weak account of male stripper/lovely advertising executive romance. 90m/C Edward Bell, Susan Darrante-Shaw, Edward Bell; **D:** Susan Orikoff-Simon.

Images 🐾 1972 (R) Minor Altman is a confusing mish-mash with the scenery more dramatic than the flick. Hugh (Auberjonois) has taken his ailing/batty wife Cathryn (York) for a weekend at their country retreat on the Irish coast. Cathryn is having hallucinations about dead lovers but Hugh doesn't seem to realize his wife is going nuts until it's too late. 101m/C DVD. Susannah York, Rene Auberjonois, Marcel Bozzuffi, Hugh Millais, Cathryn Harrison; **D:** Robert Altman; **W:** Robert Altman; **C:** Vilmos Zsigmond; **M:** John Williams.

Imaginary Crimes 🐾🐾 1994 (PG) Ray Weiler (Keitel) is a well-meaning salesman with dreams much bigger than his reach. After the death of his wife (Lynch), Ray tries to raise his two daughters, Sonya (Balk) and Greta (Moss). But gifted high school senior (in 1962) Sonya is resentful of being her father's scheme anchor and having her father's schemes come to nothing ever as she acknowledges how much Ray cares and how he wants to improve their lives. Remarkable performances by Keitel and Balk. From the novel by Sheila Ballantyne. 106m/C VHS, DVD. Harvey Keitel, Fairuza Balk, Kelly Lynch, Vincent D'Onofrio, Elissabeth Pena, Diane Baker, Christopher Penn, Seymour Cassel, Annette O'Toole; **D:** Tony Drazan; **W:** Kristine Johnson, Davia Nelson; **C:** John Campbell; **M:** Stephen Endelman.

Imaginary Heroes 🐾🐾 2005 (R) Painfully cliche-ridden story of a dysfunctional, angst-ridden suburban family. When her superjock son kills himself, Sandy (Weaver) descends into a weed-smoking haze while the rest of her family struggles to deal with Matt's death as well as their own problems. Drugs, anger, bisexual experimentation, eating disorders, and cancer scares ensue. Writer/director Harris piles on the plot twists and tragedies to remind you of how bad these people have it. Weaver and Hirsch (as younger son Tim) are convincing, but the film's combination of grief-stricken melodrama and wry irony is awkward and contrived, and the movie just ends up feeling like a cheap knock-off of many superior films. 112m/C DVD. US Sigourney Weaver, Emile Hirsch, Jeff Daniels, Michelle Williams, Kip Pardue, Deirdre O'Connell, Ryan Donowho, Jay Paulson, Suzanna Santo; **D:** Daniel P. "Dan" Harris; **W:** Daniel P. "Dan" Harris; **C:** Tim Orr; **M:** John Ottman, Deborah Lurie.

Imagine Me & You 🐾½ 2005 (R) In this London-set confection, Rachel (Perabo) is walking up the aisle to marry longtime sweetie Heck (Goode) when she catches the eye of attractive florist Luce (Headey). Newlywed Rachel and Luce then repeatedly thrown together and soon admit to their mutual attraction. Heck eventually realizes that something is amiss in his marriage even as Luce despairs at being the other woman. Bland and boring, despite, or maybe because of, the attractive cast. 93m/C DVD, US Piper Perabo, Lena Headey, Matthew Goode, Celia Imrie, Anthony Head, Darren Boyd, Eva Birthistle, Bo Jackson, Sue Johnston, Sharon Horgan; **D:** Ol Parker; **W:** Ol Parker; **C:** Benjamin Davis; **M:** Alex Heffes.

Imagining Argentina 🐾🐾 2004 (R) In 1970s Argentina, Banderas is Carlos Fueda, a childrens' theater director whose journalist wife (Thompson) has disappeared after trying to investigate the fate of thousands of people who have been taken away by government agents. He soon discovers psychic abilities and is able to tell the fates of many of the victims, but is only able to divine obscure clues to his wife's disappearance. The introduction of the psychic element is jarring to the political and personal story of the toll of totalitarian persecution, and derails the entire production. 108m/C DVD. Antonio Banderas, Emma Thompson, Ruben Blades, Mara Carreras, Claire Bloom, John Wood; **D:** Christopher Hampton; **W:** Christopher Hampton; **C:** Guillermo Navarro; **M:** George Fenton.

Imitation of Life 🐾🐾½ 1934 Fannie Hurst novel tells the story of widowed Beatrice Pullman (Colbert) who uses maid Delilah's (Beaver) recipe for pancakes in order to have the women open a restaurant, which becomes a success. Both mothers suffer at the hands of their willful teenaged daughters. Delilah's lightskinned daughter Peola (Washington) breaks away from her mother so she can continue to pass for white and Bea's daughter Jessie (Hudson) has a serious crush on her mother's beau, Stephen (William). Weepie was also successfully filmed in 1959. 106m/B VHS. Claudette Colbert, Louise Beevers, Rochelle Hudson, Fred Washington, Warren William, Ned Sparks, Alan Hale; **D:** John M. Stahl; **W:** Preston Sturges, William Hurlbut; **C:** Merritt B. Gerstad. Natl. Film Reg. '05.

Imitation of Life 🐾🐾🐾 1959 Remake of the successful 1934 Claudette Colbert outing of the same title, and based on Fanny Hurst's novel, with a few plot changes. Turner is a single mother, more determined to achieve acting fame and fortune than function as a parent. Her black maid Moore is devoted to her own girl discovers she can pass for white. When Turner discovers that she and her daughter are in love with the same men, she realizes how little she knows her daughter, and how much the two of them have missed by not having a stronger relationship. Highly successful at the box-office. 124m/C VHS, DVD. Lana Turner, John Gavin, Troy Donahue, Sandra Dee, Juanita Moore, Susan Kohner; **D:** Douglas Sirk; **C:** Russell Metty. Golden Globes '60: Support. Actress (Kohner).

Immediate Family 🐾🐾½ 1989 (PG-13) Childless couple contact a pregnant, unmarried girl and her boyfriend in hopes of adoption. As the pregnancy advances, the mother has doubts about giving up her baby. A bit sugar-coated in an effort to woo family trade. 112m/C VHS, DVD. Glenn Close, James Woods, Kevin Dillon, Mary Stuart Masterson, Linda Derlow, Jane Greer, Jessica James, Mimi Kennedy; **D:** Jonathan Kaplan; **W:** Barbara Benedek; **M:** Brad Fiedel. Natl. B1. of Review '89: Support. Actress (Masterson).

Immortal 🐾🐾 *Immortal Ad Vitam* 2004 (R) Writer/director Bilal uses CGI and blue screen to depict a devastated New York in 2095 in this visually arresting but completely confusing (and very loose) adaptation of two of his graphic novels. An interstellar pyramid invisibly hovers over the city, housing several Egyptian gods, including Horus (Kretschmann) and the blue-haired Jill (Hardy), only there are a lot of complications to overcome, including the fact that Jill isn't exactly human. 102m/C DVD, GB FR IT Linda Hardy, Thomas Pollard; **D:** Enki Bilal; **W:** Enki Bilal, Joe Sheridan, Serge Lehman; **C:** Pascal Gennesseaux; **M:** Goran Vejvoda.

Immortal Bachelor 🐾½ 1980 (PG) Good cast can't overcome the silliness of this one. A juror daydreams about the dead husband of a cleaning woman on trial for killing her adulterous spouse. She decides the dead man seems a lot more exciting than her own dull and tiresome husband. 94m/C VHS. IT Giancarlo Giannini, Monica Vitti, Claudia Cardinale, Vittorio Gassman; **D:** Marcello Fondaco; **C:** Pasqualino De Santis.

Immortal Battalion 🐾🐾🐾 *The Way Ahead* 1944 Entertaining wartime psuedo-documentary follows newly recruited soldiers as they are molded from an ordinary group of carping civilians into a hardened battalion of fighting men by a tough sergeant and officer. 89m/B VHS, DVD, GB David Niven, Stanley Holloway, Reginald Tate, Raymond Huntley, William Hartnell, James Donald, Peter Ustinov, John Laurie, Leslie Dwyer, Hugh Burden, Jimmy Hanley, Leo Genn, Renee Asherson; **D:** Carol Reed; **W:** Eric Ambler, Peter Ustinov; **C:** Guy Green; **M:** William Alwyn.

Immortal Beloved 🐾🐾 1994 (R) The death of Ludwig van Beethoven prompts his loyal secretary to unravel the identity of a mystery love to whom the composer has bequeathed his estate. While Beethoven's genius is awesome and his music breathtaking, his lovelife is neither, and the ensuing confessions of the maestro's former loves only get in the way of flashbacks that hint at his torment and triumph. Oldman is darkly intense, and a scene in which the aged Beethoven remembers his terrifying childhood amid the strains of "Ode to Joy" is simply stunning, but an unfocused script undoes what might have been a fine tribute to the master. The London Symphony Orchestra and soloists Murray Perahia, Emanuel Ax, and Yo Yo Ma contributed to the splendid soundtrack. 121m/C VHS, DVD, Blu-ray Disc. Gary Oldman, Jeroen Krabbe, Isabella Rossellini, Johanna Ter Steege, Marco Hofschneider, Miriam

---

cer scares ensue. Writer/director Harris piles on the plot twists and tragedies...

The Immigrant 🐾🐾🐾½ 1917 Chaplin portrays a newly arrived immigrant who falls in love with the first girl he meets. Silent with musical soundtrack added. 20m/B VHS, DVD. Charlie Chaplin, Edna Purviance, Eric Campbell, Kitty Bradbury; **D:** Charlie Chaplin; **W:** Charlie Chaplin.

The Immortal One 🐾 *sions of a Prostitute: L'Immorale* 1980 Lamo's suffering from amnesia. Fortunately she's apparently taped her life story for a book. And sordid they are since she was a prostitute in Paris, involved with both men and women, and with a blackmailing madam. 90m/C VHS, FR Sylvia Lamo, Yves Jouffroy, Isabelle Legentil; **D:** Claude Mulot; **W:** Claude Mulot.

The Immortal One 🐾🐾 2001 The pilot for a short-lived syndicated TV show that was more camp than action. Lamas is the title character who has a 400-year history of detecting and destroying demons who are plaguing the world. m/C VHS, DVD. Lorenzo Lamas, Steve Braun, April Telek. TV

Margolyes, Barry Humphries, Valeria Golino, Christopher Fulford; **D:** Bernard Rose; **W:** Bernard Rose; **C:** Peter Suschitzky.

Immortal Combat 🐾½ **1994 (R)** An army of men trained in ninja and guerilla warfare have seemingly immortal powers. Can our two violent heroes find an equally destructive way to stop the killing? **109m/C VHS, DVD.** Roddy Piper, Sonny Chiba, Tommy (Tiny) Lister, Meg Foster; **D:** Daniel Neira; **W:** Daniel Neira, Robert Crabtree; **C:** Henner Hofmann.

Immortal Sergeant 🐾🐾½ **1943** After the battle death of the squad leader, an inexperienced corporal takes command of North African troops during WWII. Fonda gives a strong performance. Based on a novel by John Brody. **91m/B VHS, DVD.** Henry Fonda, Thomas Mitchell, Maureen O'Hara, Allyn Joslyn, Reginald Gardiner, Melville Cooper, Morton Lowry, Peter Lawford, John Banner, Bud Geary, James Craven; **D:** John M. Stahl; **W:** Lamar Trotti; **C:** Clyde De Vinna, Arthur C. Miller; **M:** David Buttolph.

Immortal Sins 🐾 **1991 (R)** Michael and Susan inherited an old Spanish Castle, complete with its own curse, which comes in the form of a seductive woman that has haunted families for centuries. **80m/C VHS.** Cliff DeYoung, Maryam D'Abo; **W:** Thomas McKelvey Cleaver.

Immortality 🐾🐾 *The Wisdom of Crocodiles* **1998 (R)** The vampire myth undergoes yet another postmodern twist. Steven Griscz (Law) is a medical researcher, living in London, who stops Maria (Fox) from committing suicide and then sets out to seduce her. When he's convinced she's in love with him, he kills her and takes her blood. His next would-be victim is Anne (Lowensohn), but she's reluctant to commit to Steven and soon he becomes ill, which leads him to confess to Anne that his bloodsucking tendencies can only be satiated when he believes his victims love him. While Law is a charming seducer, he fails to chill as a vampire killer. **98m/C VHS, DVD. GB** Jude Law, Elina Lowensohn, Timothy Spall, Kerry Fox, Jack Davenport, Colin Salmon; **D:** Po-Chih Leung; **W:** Paul Hoffman; **C:** Oliver Curtis; **M:** John Lunn, Orlando Gough.

The Immortalizer 🐾 **1989 (R)** A mad doctor transfers people's brains into young bodies for a price, although it's not as simple as it sounds. **85m/C VHS.** Ron Kay, Chris Crone, Melody Patterson, Clarke Lindsley, Bekki Armstrong; **D:** Joel Bender.

The Immortals 🐾🐾 **1995 (R)** Nightclub owner Jack (Roberts) recruits eight terminally ill criminals in an elaborate heist that calls for simultaneously hitting targets citywide. But when they compare notes, they fear a double cross. **92m/C VHS, DVD.** Louis Lombardi, Eric Roberts, Tia Carrere, William Forsythe, Joe Pantoliano, Clarence Williams III, Tony Curtis, Chris Rock, Kieran Mulroney, Kevin Bernhardt; **D:** Brian Grant; **W:** Kevin Bernhardt; **C:** Anthony B. Richmond.

Impact 🐾🐾 **1949** A woman and her lover plan the murder of her rich industrialist husband, but the plan backfires. More twists and turns than a carnival ride. **111m/ B VHS.** Brian Donlevy, Ella Raines, Charles Coburn, Helen Walker, Anna May Wong, Philip Ahn, Art Baker, Tony Barrett, Harry Cheshire, Lucius Cooke, Joel Friedkin, Sheilah Graham, Tom Greenway, Hans Herbert, Linda Johnson, Joe (Joseph) Kirk, Clarence (C. William) Kolb, Mary Lan, da, Mae Marsh; **D:** Arthur Lubin; **W:** Dorothy Reid, Jay Dratler; **C:** Ernest Laszlo; **M:** Michel Michelet.

The Imperial Japanese Empire 🐾🐾 **1985** Epic of the WWII Pacific seen through Japanese eyes. **130m/C VHS. JP** Tetsuro Tamba, Tomokazu Miura, Teruhiko Saigo, Teruhiko Aoi, Saburo Shinoda; **D:** Toshio Masuda.

Imperial Venus 🐾🐾 **1971 (PG)** Biography of Napoleon's sister, Paolina Bonaparte—with particular focus on her many loves, lusts and tribulations. **121m/C VHS, DVD.** Gina Lollobrigida, Stephen Boyd, Raymond Pellegrin; **D:** Jean Delannoy.

Implicated 🐾🐾 **1998 (R)** Tom (McNamara) asks his new girlfriend Ann (Locane) to help him out by babysitting his boss' young daughter, Katie. But Ann soon realizes that Tom's kidnapped Katie and they're both pawns in an elaborate scheme that has gone out of control.

Based on the book "Wishful Thinking" by Frank Wyka. **95m/C VHS.** Amy Locane, William McNamara, Frederic Forrest, Priscilla Barnes; **D:** Irving Belateche; **W:** Webb Millsaps, Irving Belateche. **VIDEO**

Impolite 🐾½ **1992** After getting on the wrong side during a police corruption story, alcoholic reporter Jack (Wisden) has been demoted to writing obits. When he gets a tip that rich and powerful O'Rourke (an uncredited Plummer who also plays the character's twin brother, a priest) has died, Jack decides to investigate the rumor by interviewing the strange group who surrounded O'Rourke. **90m/C VHS, DVD.** CA Robert Wisden, Kevin McNulty, Stuart Margolin, Jill Teed, Susan Hogan, Christopher Plummer; **D:** David Hauka; **W:** Michael McKinley; **C:** David McLachlan; **M:** Braun Farnon, Robert Smart.

The Importance of Being Earnest 🐾🐾🐾 **1952** Fine production of classic Oscar Wilde comedy-of-manners. Cast couldn't be better or the story funnier. **95m/C VHS, DVD.** Michael Redgrave, Edith Evans, Margaret Rutherford, Michael Denison, Joan Greenwood, Dorothy Tutin; **D:** Anthony Asquith; **W:** Anthony Asquith; **C:** Desmond Dickinson; **M:** Benjamin Frankel.

The Importance of Being Earnest 🐾🐾 **2002 (PG)** Jack Worthing (Firth) has invented a brother, Earnest, in order to leave the dull country and visit lovely Gwendolyn (O'Connor), the daughter of the formidable Lady Bracknell (Dench), in London. His best friend Algernon Moncrieff (Everett), who is Gwendolyn's cousin, also has a make-believe chum named Bunbury to get Algy out of boring situations. Then Algy decides to pose as Earnest in order to woo Jack's country ward, Cecily (Witherspoon). But when everyone ends up together, chaos threatens. Based on the play by Oscar Wilde and filled with bon mots, director Parker felt compelled to "open up" the production, which only works some of the time. But the performances are all delightful and Witherspoon manages her English accent quite nicely. **100m/C VHS, DVD. US GB** Colin Firth, Rupert Everett, Frances O'Connor, Reese Witherspoon, Judi Dench, Tom Wilkinson, Anna Massey, Edward Fox, Patrick Godfrey, Charles Kay, Finty Williams; **D:** Oliver Parker; **W:** Oliver Parker; **C:** Tony Pierce-Roberts; **M:** Charlie Mole.

The Imported Bridegroom 🐾🐾 **1989** A comedy set at the turn of the century about a man who returns to Poland in order to find his daughter a proper husband. **93m/C VHS.** Eugene Troobnick, Avi Hoffman, Greta Cowan, Annette Miller; **D:** Pamela Berger; **W:** Pamela Berger.

The Impossible Spy 🐾🐾🐾 **1987** True story of Elie Cohen, an unassuming Israeli who doubled as a top level spy in Syria during the 1960s. Cohen became so close to Syria's president that he was nominated to become the Deputy Minister of Defense before his double life was exposed. Well-acted spy thriller and a look for espionage fans. **96m/C VHS, DVD. GB** John Shea, Eli Wallach, Michal Bat-Adam, Rami Danon, Sasson Gabray, Chaim Girafi; **D:** Jim Goddard; **M:** Richard Hartley. **CABLE**

The Impossible Years 🐾 **1968** Unattractive, leering sex farce about psychiatrist Nivens who has problems with his own young daughter. Dismal adaptation of the hit Broadway play by Bob Fisher and Arthur Marx. **97m/C VHS.** David Niven, Lola Albright, Chad Everett, Ozzie Nelson, Christina Ferrare, Jeff Cooper, John Harding; **D:** Michael Gordon; **W:** George Wells.

The Imposters 🐾🐾 *Ship of Fools* **1998 (R)** Its the 1930s, and third-rate actors Arthur and Maurice (Tucci and Platt, respectively) are out of work. Inadvertently forced into hiding on a cruise ship, they encounter a virtual ship of fools while slinking around in an array of costumes. The wacky story unfolds as the stowaways run into various characters: the Nazi-like, crop-wielding head steward (Scott), a gay Scottish wrestler (Connolly), an anarchist bomber from an unnamed Eastern European nation (Shalhoub), his country's deposed queen (Rossellini), and

a pair of murderous con artists posing as French tourists. Written and directed by Tucci, pic reunites much of the cast from Tucci and Scott's "Big Night." Unfortunately, they weren't as successful this time. Too much free-reign hamming by the big-name indie cast sinks this homage to Buster Keaton and the Marx Brothers. **101m/C VHS, DVD.** Stanley Tucci, Oliver Platt, Elizabeth Bracco, Steve Buscemi, Billy Connolly, Allan Corduner, Hope Davis, Dana Ivey, Allison Janney, Richard Jenkins, Matt McGrath, Alfred Molina, Isabella Rossellini, Campbell Scott, Tony Shalhoub, Lili Taylor, Lewis J. Stadlen, Woody Allen; **D:** Stanley Tucci; **W:** Stanley Tucci; **C:** Ken Kelsch; **M:** Gary DeMichele.

The Impostor 🐾🐾½ **1984** Improbable tale of a con artist/ex-con who impersonates a high school principal in order to regain his estranged girlfriend, who works as a teacher. Complications ensue when he tackles the school's drug problems. **95m/C VHS.** Anthony Geary, Billy Dee Williams, Lorna Patterson; **D:** Michael Pressman. **TV**

Impostor 🐾 **2002 (PG-13)** When a movie is shelved for a year and a half, there's usually a reason. Earth in 2079 is dystopian and paranoid, and the neon-blue cave lighting makes it difficult to see. Which is not a huge loss. Talented cast is reduced to a collection of archetypes, including the usually solid Sinise as an elite military scientist accused of fighting (as a replicant) for the wrong team, namely, the sinister aliens who are laying waste to our earth. Citizens are monitored via spinal identification chips, yet a hooded sweatshirt and sunglasses are enough to shield public enemy #1 from detection. Tired sci-fi themes of soul and identity are not enough to keep things interesting. Adapted (and yawningly stretched) from a short story by perennial sci-fi source Philip K. Dick. **96m/C VHS, DVD.** US Gary Sinise, Madeleine Stowe, Vincent D'Onofrio, Tony Shalhoub, Mekhi Phifer, Tim Guinee, Lindsay Crouse, Gary Dourdan, Erica Gimpel, Elizabeth Pena; **D:** Gary Fleder; **W:** Ehren Kruger, David N. Twohy, Caroline Case; **C:** Robert Elswit; **M:** Mark Isham.

Impostors 🐾🐾 **1980** A comedy centering on the romantic problems between a self-indulgent young man and the woman who cheats on him. **110m/C VHS.** Ellen McElduff, Charles Ludlam, Michael J. Burg, Peter Evans; **D:** Mark Rappaport; **W:** Mark Rappaport; **C:** Fred Murphy.

Impromptu 🐾🐾🐾 **1990 (PG-13)** A smart, sassy, romantic comedy set in 1830s Europe among the era's artistic greats—here depicted as scalawags, parasites and early beatniks. The film's ace is Davis in a lusty, dynamic role as mannish authoress George Sand, obsessively in love with the dismayed composer Chopin. Though he's too pallid a character for her attraction to be credible, a great cast and abundant wit make this a treat. Beautiful score featuring Chopin and Liszt. Film debut of stage director Lapine; screenplay written by his wife, Sarah Kernochan. **108m/C VHS, DVD.** Judy Davis, Hugh Grant, Mandy Patinkin, Bernadette Peters, Julian Sands, Ralph Brown, Georges Corraface, Anton Rodgers, Emma Thompson, Anna Massey, John Savident, Elizabeth Spriggs; **D:** James Lapine; **W:** Sarah Kernochan; **C:** Bruno de Keyzer. Ind. Spirit '92: Actress (Davis).

Improper Channels 🐾🐾 **1982 (PG)** Mediocre comedy about a couple trying to recover their daughter after being accused of child abuse. **91m/C VHS.** Monica Parker, Alan Arkin, Mariette Hartley; **D:** Eric Till; **W:** Adam Arkin.

Improper Conduct 🐾 **1994 (R)** Ad agency employee is sexually harassed by her boss but loses her court case. Her sister decides to get revenge by getting hired and setting the slimeball up for a fall. **95m/C VHS.** Steven Bauer, Lee Ann Beaman, John Laughlin, Kathy Shower, Tahnee Welch, Nia Peeples, Stuart Whitman, Adrian Zmed, Patsy Pease; **D:** Jag Mundhra; **W:** Carl Austin.

Impulse 🐾🐾½ **1955** When his wife leaves for a visit with her mother, a young man is thrust into cahoots with gangsters, and wrapped up in an affair with another woman. **81m/B VHS. GB** Arthur Kennedy, Constance Smith, Joy Shelton; **D:** Cy Endfield; **W:** Cy Endfield.

Impulse WOOF! *Want a Ride, Little Girl?; I Love to Kill* **1974 (PG)** Shatner, a crazed killer, is released from prison and starts to kill again in this low-budget, predictable, critically debased film about child-molesting. **85m/C VHS, DVD.** William Shatner, Ruth Roman, Harold Sakata, Kim Nicholas, Jennifer Bishop, James Dobson; **D:** William Grefe; **W:** Tony Crechales; **C:** Edwin Gibson; **M:** Lewis Perles.

Impulse 🐾🐾 **1984 (R)** Small town residents can't control their impulses, all because of government toxic waste in their milk. A woman worried about her mother's mental health returns to town with her doctor boyfriend to discover most of the inhabitants are quite mad. Starts strong but... **95m/C VHS, DVD.** Tim Matheson, Meg Tilly, Hume Cronyn, John Karlen, Bill Paxton, Amy Stryker, Claude Earl Jones, Sherri Stoner; **D:** Graham Baker; **W:** Don Carlos Dunaway, Nicholas Kazan; **C:** Thomas Del Ruth; **M:** Paul Chihara.

Impulse 🐾🐾 **1990 (R)** A beautiful undercover vice cop poses as a prostitute, and gives in to base desires. Russell gives a fine performance in this underrated sleeper. **109m/C VHS.** Theresa Russell, Nicholas Mele, Eli Danker, Charles McCaughan, Jeff Fahey, George Dzundza, Alan Rosenberg, Lynne Thigpen, Shawn Elliott; **D:** Sondra Locke; **W:** John DeMarco, Leigh Chapman; **M:** Michel Colombier.

Impure Thoughts 🐾🐾 **1986 (PG)** Four friends meet in the afterlife and discuss their Catholic school days. Odd premise never catches fire. **87m/C VHS.** Brad Dourif, Lane Davies, John Putch, Terry Beaver; **D:** Michael A. Simpson.

In a Class of His Own 🐾🐾½ **1999** School janitor Rich Donato (Phillips) is an ex-teen bad boy who has formed a close relationship with the teachers and the students at the high school where he works. However, in order to keep his job, he learns he must pass his GED and this isn't an easy task. When his wife appeals for help, Rich finds himself becoming a school project. Based on a true story. **94m/C VHS, DVD.** Lou Diamond Phillips, Cara Buono, Joan Chen, Nathaniel DeVeaux; **D:** Robert Munic; **W:** Robert Munic; **C:** Ron Stannett; **M:** Sharon Farber. **CABLE**

In a Glass Cage 🐾🐾½ *Tras el Cristal* **1986** A young boy who was tortured and sexually molested by a Nazi official seeks revenge. Years after the war, he shows up at the Nazi's residence in Spain and is immediately befriended by his tormentor's family. Confined to an iron lung, the official is at the mercy of the young man who tortuously acts out the incidents detailed in the Nazi's journal. Suspenseful and extremely graphic, it's well crafted and meaningful, but may be just too horrible to watch. Sexual and violent acts place it in the same league as Pasolini's infamous "Salo, or The 120 Days of Sodom." Definitely not for the faint of heart. In Spanish with English subtitles. **110m/C VHS, DVD. SP** Gunter Meisner, David Sust, Marisa Paredes, Gisela Echevarria; **D:** Agustin Villaronga; **W:** Agustin Villaronga.

In a Lonely Place 🐾🐾🐾½ **1950** Bogart is outstanding as Dixon Steele, a hard-drinking and volatile Hollywood screenwriter, who becomes the prime suspect in the murder of a hat-check girl, last seen alive leaving his apartment. New neighbor Laurel Gray (Grahame) alibis the guy because she doesn't think he's a killer and he's grateful. Enough to begin a romance with the cool beauty. But the investigating detectives still have the writer on their A-list and his paranoia kicks in,

In a Moment of Passion

1993 (R) A two-bit actor wants to be a star—it's a worst way possible. So he kills off the lead actor of a new film, takes his place, and proceeds to eliminate any obstacle that gets in his way. The problem comes in when an aspiring actress falls for the actor and then figures out what's going on. 100m/C VHS. Maxwell Caulfield, Chase Masterson, Vivian Schilling, Julie Araskog, Joe Estevez, Robert Z'Dar, Zbigniew Kaminski; Cameos: Jeff Conway; D: Charles Haigh.

In a Savage Land ♂♂½ 1999 Interesting premise gets a laughable execution. Prim married anthropologists Philip (Donovan) and Evelyn (Stange) Spence travel to the South Seas in the late 1930s to study native society and find their marriage quickly unraveling. Philip refuses to acknowledge the sexuality and importance of the tribe's women, so Evelyn decides to take advantage (in more than one way) of pearl merchant Mick (Sewell) to continue her studies in another village. Pretty scenery courtesy of the Trobriand Islands is the only high point. 116m/C VHS. AU: Martin Donovan, Rufus Sewell, Maya Stange; D: Bill Bennett; W: Bill Bennett, Jennifer Bennett; M: David Bridie. Australian Film Inst. '99; Sound, Score.

In a Shallow Grave ♂♂ 1988 (R) Shallow treatment of James Purdy's novel about a WWII veteran, badly disfigured in combat at Guadalcanal, who returns to Virginia in an attempt to return to the life he once had with the woman he still loves. Handsome Biehn plays the disfigured vet. Mueller's his ex-fiancee, and Dempsey's the drifter who adds a bisexual hypotenuse to the love triangle. Pokey. American Playhouse coproduction. 92m/C VHS. Michael Biehn, Maureen Mueller, Patrick Dempsey, Michael Beach, Thomas Boyd Mason; D: Kenneth Bowser; W: Kenneth Bowser.

In a Stranger's Hand ♂♂½ 1992 Uridi stars a respected businessman who happens to find a doll which belongs to a kidnapped young girl. The police have their suspicions, but Uridi teams up with the child's mother to find the girl and winds up uncovering a child-selling ring. 93m/C VHS, DVD. Robert Urich, Megan Gallagher, Brett Cullen, Vic-de Curtis-Hall, Dakin Matthews, Alan Rosenberg, Maria O'Brien; D: David Greene. TV

In a Year of 13 Moons ♂♂ In einem Jahr Mit 13 Monden 1978 Notorious Fassbinder tale of Erwin who becomes Elvira and is subjected to a series of humiliating relationships with men. Finally, with the aid of his/her ex-wife and a prostitute, Elvira looks into the past in an effort to resolve the present. Alternatingly depressing and pretentious. German with subtitles. 119m/C VHS, DVD. GE Volker Spengler, Ingrid Caven, Gottfried John, Elisabeth Trissenaar, Eva Mattes, Gunther Kaufmann; D: Rainer Werner Fassbinder; W: Rainer Werner Fassbinder. C: Rainer Werner Fassbinder; M: Peer Raben.

In America ♂♂♂ 2002 (PG-13) After their 2-year old son dies from a brain tumor, Johnny (Considine) and Sarah (Morton) Sheridan leave Ireland with their family and head for America. The family deals with poverty and personal struggles while trying to create a better life. Real life sisters Sarah and Emma Bolger steal every scene they're in as the young Sheridans, not an easy task with this top-notch group. Honsou stands out as a dying artist neighbor. Based on the experiences of director Jim Sheridan, who co-wrote with daughters Kirsten and Naomi. Well-paced and uplifting. 103m/C VHS, DVD, Ft GE Paddy Considine, Samantha Morton, Sarah Bolger, Emma Bolger, Djimon Hounsou; D: Jim Sheridan; W: Jim Sheridan, Naomi Sheridan, Kirsten Sheridan; C: Declan Quinn; M: Gavin Friday, Maurice Seezer. Ind. Spirit '04; Cinematog., Support. Actor (Hounsou).

In an Old Manor House ♂♂½ 1984 Residents of an old house are tormented by the vindictive murders of the four members of an family in Holcomb, Kansas by ex-cons Dick Hickock (Edwards) and Perry Smith (Roberts). The TV version covers more of the background of both the killers and the Holcombs, the relentless hunt by Al Dewey (Neill) of the Kansas Bureau of Investigation, and the duo's death row. 180m/C VHS, DVD. Anthony Edwards, Eric Roberts, Sam Neill, Kevin Tighe, Gillian Barber, Robbie Bowen, Margot Finley, Bethel Leslie, Gwen Verdon, Stella Stevens, L.Q. Jones, Louise Latham; W: Benedict Fitzgerald. TV

In Between ♂♂ 1992 (PG-13) When Margo, Jack, and Amy wake up, they expect it to be another average day. Instead, these three strangers find themselves together in a peculiar house. An angel informs them that the house is a way station between life and the hereafter. The three must look at their pasts, imagine their futures, and decide whether to return to the real lives or accept death and go on to an afterlife. 92m/C VHS. Robin Matson, Alexandra Paul, Robert Hauser, Wings Hauser, Robin Matson, Alexandra Paul, Robert Forster; D: Thomas Constantinides; C: Irv Goodnoff; M: Alfred Owens.

In Bruges ♂♂½ 2008 (R) Ray (Farrell) and Ken (Gleeson), two Irish hitmen, are sent to the picturesque medieval berg of Bruges, Belgium, to hide out following a partially botched job that targeted a priest but accidentally offed a young boy, hardly a premise for comedy. But writer/director McDonagh's debut mostly hits the mark with this pitch-black fish-out-of-water tale of tough guys laying low in the quaint town, a feat made impossible by their involvement with a local hottie and a film-making dwarf and the arrival of their cool boss (Fiennes). Snappy repartee and potscard scenery offset an abundance of inner torment and blood, and it's all almost too hip for its own good, but Farrell and Gleeson are terrific. 107m/C DVD, GB Colin Farrell, Brendan Gleeson, Ralph Fiennes, Clarence Posey, Jeremie Renier, Thekla Reuten, Jordan Prentice; D: Martin McDonagh; W: Martin McDonagh; C: Eigli Bryld; M: Carter Burwell.

In Celebration ♂♂♂½ 1975 (PG) Three successful brothers return to the old homestead for their parents' 40th wedding celebration. Intense drama but somewhat claustrophobic. Based on a play by David Storey. 131m/C VHS, DVD. GB CA Alan Bates, James Bolam, Brian Cox, Constance Chapman, Gabrielle Daye, Bill Owen; D: Lindsay Anderson.

In Cold Blood ♂♂♂½ 1967 Truman Capote's supposedly factual novel provided the basis for this hard-hitting docu-drama about two ex-cons who ruthlessly murder a Kansas family in 1959 in order to steal their non-existent stash of money. Blake is riveting as one of the killers. 133m/B VHS, DVD. Robert (Bobby) Blake, Scott Wilson, John Forsythe, Paul Stewart, Gerald S. O'Loughlin, Jeff Corey, Will Geer, James Flavin, John Gallaudet, John Collins, Charles McGraw, John McLam; D: Richard Brooks; W: Richard Brooks; C: Conrad L. Hall; M: Quincy Jones. Natl. Bd. of Review '67; Director (Brooks).

In and Out ♂♂♂ 1997 (PG-13) See what an Oscar can do? When Tom Hanks thanked, and outed, his high school drama teacher during his Academy Awards speech (for "Philadelphia"), it lead a serious hurtin' on Barbra Streisand). All-around excellent performances, especially by Kline and Cusack. 92m/C VHS, DVD. Kevin Kline and Cusack, Bob Newhart, Tom Selleck, Debbie Reynolds, Wilford Brimley, Bob Newhart, Tom Selleck, Debborah Rush, Lewis J. Stadlen, J. Smith-Cameron, Zak Orth, Gregory Jbara, Shalom Harlow, Kate McGregor-Stewart, Shawn Hatosy, Lauren Ambrose, Alexandra Holden; D: Frank Oz; W: Paul Rudnick; C: Rob Hahn; M: Marc Shaiman. N.Y. Film Critics '97; Support. Actress (Cusack); Broadcast Film Critics '97; Support. Actress (Cusack).

In Country ♂♂♂½ 1989 (R) Based on Bobbie Ann Mason's celebrated novel, the story of a young Kentucky high-school-er (perfectly played by Lloyd) and her search for her father, killed in Vietnam. Willis plays her uncle, a veteran still struggling to accept his own survival, and crippled with memories. Moving scene at the Vietnam Veterans Memorial. 116m/C VHS, DVD. Bruce Willis, Emily Lloyd, Joan Allen, Kevin Anderson, Richard Hamilton, Judith Ivey, Peggy Rea, John Terry, Patricia Richardson, Jim Beaver, Cic(re; D: Norman Jewison; W: Frank Pierson, Cynthia Cidre; C: Russell Boyd; M: James Horner.

The In Crowd ♂♂ 2000 (PG-13) Having been cured of her "erotomania," pretty, young Adrien (Heuring) is released from a psychiatric hospital, and, on the advice of her doctor, gains employment for the summer at a seaside country club. There Adrien is confronted by the in crowd, which is led by the ultra bitchy 'Ward), who, with clearly ulterior motives, befriends the lovely Adrien. As Adrien is introduced to the ways of the privileged, things become stranger and stranger as our heroine discovers some unpleasant things about her new acquaintance. 96m/C VHS, DVD. Susan Ward, Lori Heuring, Matthew Settle, Nathan Bexton, Tess Harper, Laurie Fortier, Kim Murphy; D: Mary Lambert; W: Mark Gibson, Philip Halprin; C: Tom Priestley; M: Jeff Rona.

The In Crowd ♂♂ 1988 (PG) A bright high school student gets involved with a local TV dance show circa 1965, and must choose between uncertain employment for his future, leitich, and an ivy League college. A fair nostalgic look at the period. Leitch is the son of psychedelic folk singer Donovan. 96m/C VHS, DVD. Donovan Leitch, Jennifer Runyon, Scott Plank, Joe Pantoliano; D: Mark Rosenthal; W: Mark Rosenthal.

In Custody ♂♂ Hifazaat 1994 (PG) Producer Merchant makes his feature debut rectorial debut with this dreamy tale of small-town time. It follows this dreamy tale of a small-town teacher Deven (Puri) who's urged by a publishing friend to interview Nur (Kapoor), the greatest living poet in the disappearing Urdu language. The wor-shipful Deven is dismayed to find his idol a wreck, surrounded by sycophants and a shrewish second wife who's plagiarizing her husband's work, and soon finds himself hopelessly entangled in the writer's life. Unabashedly literary (the poetry recited is by Faiz Ahmed Faiz) with a star cast. Based on the 1987 novel by Anita Desai. Urdu with English subtitles. 123m/C VHS, DVD. IN Shashi Kapoor, Om Puri, Shabana Azmi, Sushma Seth, Neena Gupta, Ajay Sahni, Tinnu Anand; D: Ismail Merchant; W: Anita Desai, Shahrukh Husain; C: Larry Pizer; M: Zakir Hussain, Ustad Sultan Khan.

In Cold Blood ♂♂ 1996 TV miniseries version of the Truman Capote true crime classic, which follows the 1959 murders of the four members of an family in Holcomb, Kansas by ex-cons survive with wits and courage. Based on a novel by Nobel prize-winning author Henryk Sienkiewicz, in Polish with English subtitles. 144m/C VHS, DVD. PL Monika Rosca, Tomasz Mędrzak, Emos Bango, Malija Mekki, Edmund Fetting; D: Władysław Ślesicki; W: Władysław Ślesicki; C: Bogusław Lambach; M: Andrzej Korzynski.

In Desert and Wilderness ♂♂½ 1973 Two kidnapped children escape and are thrust into the wilds of Africa, where they must survive with wits and courage. Based on a novel by Nobel prize-winning author Henryk Sienkiewicz, in Polish with English subtitles. 144m/C VHS, DVD. PL Monika Rosca, Tomasz Mędrzak, Emos Bango, Malija Mekki, Edmund Fetting; D: Władysław Ślesicki; W: Władysław Ślesicki; C: Bogusław Lambach; M: Andrzej Korzynski.

In Desert and Wilderness ♂♂ 2001 Children's adventure story has problems for what should be its target audience since it is in Polish with subtitles—maybe the stunning visuals will interest the kids. Set in North Africa at the end of the 19th century, Stas and Nel, who were slaves. Their journey is fraught with hardship and unexpected adventures. Based on the novel by Henryk Sienkiewicz. 111m/C VHS, DVD. PL Adam Fidusiewicz, Karolina Sawka, Lingiie Shongwe, Olivier Nguema, Krzysztof Kowalewski, Krzysztof Globisz; D: Gavin Hood; C: Paul Gilpin; M: Krzesimir Dębski.

In Dreams ♂♂½ 1999 (R) Bening is a small town wife and mother with a psychic connection to twisted child killer Downey, causing her to dream of his gruesome crimes before he commits them. After she dreams that her daughter is killed, her life begins to unravel, causing those around her to suspect her of insanity. Draws its chills from a more cerebral standpoint, so fans of big action may want to pass. The unnerving dream sequences are suitable murky and mysterious thanks to cinematographer Darius Khondji, who also filmed "Seven." 99m/C VHS, DVD. Annette Bening, Robert Downey Jr, Aidan Quinn, Stephen Rea, Paul Guilfoyle, Dennis Boutsikaris, Prudence Wright Holmes, Katie Sagona, Krystal Benn; D: Neil Jordan; W: Neil Jordan, Bruce Robinson; C: Darius Khondji; M: Elliot Goldenthal.

In Enemy Hands ♂♂ U-Boat 2004 Germans take an American submarine crew captive during WWII but the POWs face greater threats from a meningitis outbreak and a U.S. vessel posed to attack. 96m/C VHS, DVD. Til Schweiger, Thomas Kretschmann, Connor Donne, Matt Lindquist, Andy Gallen, Rene Heger, Alex Prusmack, Sascha Rosemann, Sven-Ole Thorsen, Scott Caan, Clark Gregg, A.J. Buckley, William H. Macy, Jeremy Sister, Ian Somerhalder, Carmine D. Giovinazzo, Sam Huntington, Lauren Holly, Xander Berkeley, Chris Ellis, James Burke, Roy Werner, Connor Donne, Matt Lindquist, Andy Gallen, Rene Heger, Alex Braden R. Morgen, Patrick Gallagher, Tom DeGreza, William Gregory Lee, Doug Bolchini; D: Tony Giglio; W: Tony Giglio, John Hartmann, John E. Deever; C: Gerry Lively; M: Steven Bremson. VIDEO

In for Treatment ♂♂♂ 1982 A terminally ill cancer patient, lost in the bureaucracy of the hospital, fights to rediscover the joy of life. Strong and disturbing story. In Dutch with English subtitles. 92m/C VHS. NL Helmut Woudenberg, Frank Groothof, Hans Man Int Veld; D: Eric Van Zuylen; M: John Morris.

In God We Trust woof! 1980 (PG) Dude! Check it out! Three surfers (Dorian, George, and Liu) travel the world looking for (what else?) the perfect wave. Disjointed, plot-deprived, but beautifully shot flick has the trio busting out of prison (why they're there is never explained) to begin raise money to save his monastery. He winds up getting involved with crooked TV evangelist Armageddon T. Thunderbird (Kaufman). Pryor plays G.O.D. Woof! 97m/C VHS. Marty Feldman, Andy Kaufman, Richard Pryor, Peter Boyle, Louise Lasser, Wilfrid Hyde-White, Severn Darden; D: Marty Feldman; W: Marty Feldman, Chris Allen; C: Charles Correll; M: John Morris.

In God's Hands ♂♂ 1998 (PG-13) Beautifully. Monumentally unfunny comedy about innocent monk, Brother Ambrose (Feldman), who travels to Hollywood to redistheir quest. Moving from Madagascar to Bali to Hawaii, one finds love with a girl from Ipanema (!), another contracts malaria, and the other succumbs to the surf. What happens to whom doesn't really matter, because as actors, they're really great surfers. Besides, the "story" is just connective tissue for the killer surfing scenes. Gnarly. **98m/C VHS, DVD.** Patrick Shane Dorian, Matt George, Matty Liu, Brion James, Shaun Thompson, Maylin Pultar, Bret Michaels, Brian L. Keaulana, Darrick Doerner; **D:** Zalman King, Matt George; **C:** John Aronson.

In Gold We Trust ♂️1/2 1991 Vincent leads an elite battalion of fighters against a group of rogue American MIAs (!) laying waste to the Vietnemese countryside. **89m/C VHS.** Jan-Michael Vincent, Sam Jones; **D:** P. (Philip) Chalong; **M:** Hummie Mann.

In Good Company ♂️♂️♂️ 2004 **(PG-13)** Writer-director Weitz scores with this wry commentary on the effect of corporate politics on the modern family. Seasoned ad-exec Dan Foreman (Quaid) arrives at work to discover he's been demoted to make room for his new boss, 26-year-old Carter Duryea (Grace). Carter is the golden boy of the office's new corporate owners, but his work success barely masks his unfulfilling personal life. Carter finds himself drawn to family-man Dan, particularly Dan's fetching daughter Alex (Johansson), and the two men reluctantly teach each other about the vagaries of workplace ethics. Lapses into sentimentality and the end comes a bit easy, but strong performances by Quaid and Grace save the day. **131m/C DVD, HD DVD.** *US* Dennis Quaid, Topher Grace, Scarlett Johansson, Marg Helgenberger, David Paymer, Clark Gregg, Philip Baker Hall, Selma Blair, Frankie Faison, Ty Burrell, Kevin Chapman, Amy Aquino, Zena Grey, Colleen Camp; **D:** Paul Weitz; **W:** Paul Weitz; **C:** Remi Adefarasin; **M:** Stephen Trask.

In Harm's Way ♂️♂️ 1965 Overdone story about two naval officers and their response to the Japanese attack at Pearl Harbor. Even the superb cast members (and there are plenty of them) can't overcome the incredible length and overly intricate plot. **165m/B VHS, DVD.** John Wayne, Kirk Douglas, Tom Tryon, Patricia Neal, Paula Prentiss, Brandon de Wilde, Burgess Meredith, Stanley Holloway, Henry Fonda, Dana Andrews, Franchot Tone, Jill Haworth, George Kennedy, Carroll O'Connor, Patrick O'Neal, Slim Pickens, Bruce Cabot, Larry Hagman, Hugh O'Brian, Jim Mitchum, Barbara Bouchet, Stewart Moss, Tod Andrews; **D:** Otto Preminger; **W:** Wendell Mayes; **C:** Loyal Griggs; **M:** Jerry Goldsmith. British Acad. '65: Actress (Neal).

In Hell ♂️♂️ *The Savage* 2003 **(R)** An American engineer working in Russia, Kyle LeBlanc (Van Damme) kills his wife's murderer and is convicted and sent to a remote prison run by corrupt officials. The warden likes to organize and run bets on fights between the prisoners and Kyle soon turns himself into a champion in order to survive. Now, he's pitted against his most vicious opponent—Valya (Smith). **98m/C VHS, DVD.** Jean-Claude Van Damme, Michael Bailey Smith, Lawrence Taylor, Marnie Alton, Malakai Davidson, Billy Reick; **D:** Ringo Lam; **W:** Eric James Virgels; **C:** John Aronson; **M:** Alexander Bubenheim. **VIDEO**

In Her Shoes ♂️♂️♂️ 2005 **(PG-13)** Despite its sometimes-embarrassing stereotypes and implausible situations, sappy but fun chick-flick works as a story of two very different sisters navigating the bonds of family. Rose (Collette) seemingly has life buttoned up, while Maggie (Diaz) is a mess who shows up homeless and drunk at Rose's door. Maggie manages to continually screw things up and Rose finally tosses her out. Maggie ends up at longlost grandma Ella's door, where she rather comically falls in with Ella's senior friends as relationships eventually get mended. Aaron earlier directed "The Miracle Worker," and you may recognize Ngor from "The Killing Fields." **66m/C VHS, DVD.** James Woods, Jane Alexander, Haing S. Ngor, Concetta Tomei, Richard McKenzie, James Pax; **D:** Paul Aaron; **M:** Carol Schreder.

In His Father's Shoes ♂️♂️1/2 1997 **(PG)** After his father (Gossett) dies, 15-year-old Clay (Ri'chard) takes a literal journey of self-discovery. Slipping on a pair of his dad's old wingtips, the teen is transported back to the '60s to revisit his father's past, and then further back to his grandfather's (Gossett again) day. Clay learns his granddad was a hard-working man who gave up his own dreams to support his family, which later caused a generational rift. Touching drama. **105m/C VHS, DVD.** Louis Gossett Jr., Robert Ri'chard, Rachael Crawford; **D:** Vic Sarin; **W:** Gary Gelt; **C:** Michael Storey; **M:** John Welsman. **CABLE**

In His Life: The John Lennon Story ♂️♂️1/2 2000 Focuses on seven years in the life of John Lennon—from the purchase of his first guitar to the Beatles' arrival in America. Flashbacks show a teenage John (McQuillan) in 1957 Liverpool teaming up with art school pal Stu Sutcliffe (Williams) and meeting Paul McCartney (McGowan) and George (Rice-Oxley). There's the trip to Hamburg, the group's meeting with eventual manager Brian Epstein (Ealey) becoming the band's drummer, and the first recordings. Skims the surface but, of course, the music is excellent. **87m/C VHS, DVD.** Philip McQuillan, Daniel McGowan, Mark Rice-Oxley, Lee Williams, Jamie Glover, Scot Williams, Blair Brown, Kristian Ealey, Christine Kavanagh, Gillian Kearney, Palina Jonsdottir; **D:** David Carson; **W:** Michael O'Hara; **C:** Lawrence Jones; **M:** Dennis McCarthy. **TV**

In Hot Pursuit ♂️1/2 *Polk County Pot Plane* 1977 Convicted for drug smuggling, two young men stage a daring but not too exciting escape from a southern prison. **90m/C VHS.** Bob Watson, Debbie Washington; **D:** Jim West.

The In-Laws ♂️♂️♂️ 1979 **(PG)** A wild comedy with Falk, who claims to be a CIA agent, and Arkin, a dentist whose daughter is marrying Falk's son. The farthers foil a South American dictator's counterfeiting scheme in a delightfully convoluted plot. **103m/C VHS, DVD.** Peter Falk, Alan Arkin, Richard Libertini, Nancy Dussault, Penny Peyser, Arlene Golonka, Michael Lembeck, Ed Begley Jr., Rosanna Desoto, Art Evans; **D:** Arthur Hiller; **W:** Andrew Bergman; **M:** John Morris.

The In-Laws ♂️1/2 2003 **(PG-13)** According to Douglas and Brooks this isn't really a remake of the 1979 Peter Falk/Alan Arkin comedy. They're right. That one was funny. Douglas is the groom's (Reynolds) dad, a CIA operative on the trail of a French weapons dealer and Brooks is the bride's neurotic podiatrist pop, who's shanghaied for the mission and becomes the object of the bad guy's affections. The tedious script avoids laughter at every turn, while Brooks and Douglas never seem to click as a comic duo. Bergen is amusing in her too few scenes as Douglas's New Age ex, while Reynolds does well with what little he's given to do. **98m/C VHS, DVD.** *US* Michael Douglas, Albert Brooks, Candice Bergen, Robin Tunney, Ryan Reynolds, Lindsay Sloane, David Suchet, Maria Ricossa, Russell Andrews; **D:** Andrew Fleming; **W:** Nat Mauldin, Edward Solomon; **C:** Alexander Gruysynski; **M:** Jocelyn Pook.

In Like Flint ♂️♂️ 1967 Sequel to "Our Man Flint" sees our dapper spy confronting an organization of women endeavoring to take over the world. Spy spoofery at its low-level best. **107m/C VHS, DVD.** James Coburn, Lee J. Cobb, Anna Lee, Andrew Duggan, Jean Hale; **D:** Gordon Douglas; **W:** Hal Fimberg; **C:** William H. Daniels; **M:** Jerry Goldsmith.

In Love and War ♂️♂️1/2 1991 **(R)** Woods plays Navy pilot Jim Stockdale, whose plane was grounded over hostile territory and who endured nearly eight years of torture as a POW. Meanwhile, wife Sybil is an organizer of POW wives back in the States. Low octane rendering of the US Navy Commander's true story. **96m/C VHS, DVD.** James Woods, Jane Alexander, Haing S. Ngor, Concetta Tomei, Richard McKenzie, James Pax; **D:** Paul Aaron; **M:** Carol Schreder.

In Love and War 1996 **(PG-13)** Tells the story of 19-year-old Ernest Hemingway's (O'Donnell) romance with 27-year-old Red Cross nurse Agnes (Bullock) while both were stationed in Italy during WWI. This romance later served as the basis for Hemingway's novel "A Farewell to Arms." Here's a thought. Read the book instead. The boyish O'Donnell is so miscast as testosterone-junkie Hemingway, the only analogy would be having Sylvester Stallone play Truman Capote. The lack of passion and chemistry between the two stars is unsetting, and the action is just plain clunky. Bullock looks great in a nurse's uniform, though. Adapted from "Hemingway in Love and War: The Lost Diary of Agnes Von Kurowsky" by Henry Villard and James Nagel. **115m/C VHS, DVD.** Chris O'Donnell, Sandra Bullock, MacKenzie Astin, Ingrid Lacey, Emilio Bonucci, Margot Steinberg, Colin Stinton, Ian Kelly, Richard Blackburn; **D:** Richard Attenborough; **W:** Allan Scott, Anna Hamilton Phelan, Clancy Sigal, Dimitri Villard; **C:** Roger Pratt; **M:** George Fenton.

In Love and War ♂️♂️1/2 2001 British commando Eric Newby (Blue) is captured by the Italian army in 1942 and held as a POW until the Italian Armistice in 1943. He is released just before the advancing German forces and is rescued by a group of anti-fascist farmers, including lovely Wanda (Bobulova). They fall in love but Eric is betrayed and Wanda risks her life to warn him so he can escape. But can he bear to leave her behind? Based on Newby's autobiography "Love and War in the Apennines." **98m/C VHS, DVD.** Callum Blue, Barbara Bobulova, Peter Bowles, Nick Reding, John Warnaby, Toby Jones, Robert Weathering, by, Nicholas Gallagher; **W:** John Kent Harrison; **W:** John Mortimer; **C:** Giovanni Fiore Coltellacci; **M:** Nicola Piovani. **TV**

In Love with an Older Woman ♂️♂️ 1982 Ritter takes fewer pratfalls than usual in this film; after all, it's a romantic comedy. Adapted from "Six Months with an Older Woman," the novel by David Kaufelt. **100m/C VHS.** John Ritter, Karen Carlson, Jamie Rose, Robert Mandan, Jeff Altman, George Murdock; **D:** Jack Bender. **TV**

In Memoriam ♂️♂️1/2 1976 Tragic and gripping drama about one man's ability, albeit too late, to come to terms with an unforgettable past. Based on a story by Adolfo Bioy Casares. In Spanish with English subtitles. **96m/C VHS.** *SP* Geraldine Chaplin, Jose Luis Gomez; **D:** Enrique Braso.

In My Country ♂️♂️ *Country of My Skull* 2004 **(R)** High-minded, well-intentioned, and oh-so-serious neocolonial drama. Based on the memoir "Country of My Skull" by Afrikaans poet Antjie Krog, a personal account of the 1996 Truth and Reconciliation Commission, investigating human rights abuses under apartheid. Washington Post reporter Langston Whitfield (Jackson) covers the hearings and meets poet/journalist Anna Malan (Binoche), who's doing daily radio broadcasts about the event. They each have their prejudices; they argue and, no surprise, find romance. The strongest moments are actually between Whitfield and his interviewee, Col. De Jager (Gleeson), a brutal cop who tries to explain his actions. Binoche seems merely bewildered. **100m/C DVD.** *US GB IR* Samuel L. Jackson, Juliette Binoche, Brendan Gleeson, Menzi "Ngubs" Ngubane, Sam Ngakane, Aletta Bezuidenhout, Lionel Newton, Langley Kirkwood, Owen Sejake, Harriet Manamela, Louis Van Niekirk, Jeremiah Ndlovu, Fiona Ramsay, Charley Boorman; **D:** John Boorman; **W:** Ann Peacock; **C:** Seamus Deasy.

In 'n Out ♂️1/2 1986 An American loser ventures to Mexico to recover a longlost inheritance, meeting with mildly comic obstacles along the way. **85m/C VHS, DVD.** Sam Bottoms, Pat Hingle; **D:** Ricardo Franco; **W:** Ricardo Franco; **C:** Juan Ruiz Anchia; **M:** T-Bone Burnett.

In Name Only ♂️♂️1/2 1939 Somber drama about a heartless woman who marries for wealth and prestige and holds her husband to a loveless marriage. Based on "Memory of Love" by Bessie Brewer. **102m/B VHS.** Carole Lombard, Cary Grant, Kay Francis, Charles Coburn; **D:** John Cromwell.

In Caliente ♂️1/2 1939 Rogers battles the bad guys in the frontier town of Caliente. **60m/B VHS, DVD.** Roy Rogers, Lynne Roberts, George "Gabby" Hayes, Jack La Rue, Katherine DeMille, Frank Puglia, Harry Woods; **D:** Joseph Kane; **W:** Gerald Geraghty, Norman Houston; **C:** William Nobles.

In Old California ♂️♂️1/2 1942 Plucky story of a young Boston pharmacist who searches for success in the California gold rush and runs into the local crime boss. Also available colorized. **88m/B VHS, DVD.** John Wayne, Patsy Kelly, Binnie Barnes, Albert Dekker, Charles Halton; **D:** William McGann.

In Old Cheyenne ♂️1/2 1941 Bank holdups, cattle rustling, fist fights, and even car crashes mix with some good ol' guitar plunking in this western. **60m/B VHS, DVD.** Roy Rogers, George "Gabby" Hayes, Joan Woodbury, J. Farrell MacDonald, Sally Payne, George Rosener, Wally Wales; **D:** Joseph Kane; **W:** Olive Cooper; **C:** William Nobles.

In Old Chicago ♂️♂️♂️ 1937 The O'Leary family travels to Chicago to seek their fortune, with mom working as a washerwoman to support her sons. Brothers Power and Ameche become power-broking rivals and when mom comes to break up a brawl between the two, she neglects to properly restrain the family cow. This leads to the great Chicago fire of 1871, supposedly started when the cow kicks over a latern and sets the barn ablaze. The city burns down in a spectacular 20-minute sequence. Based on the story "We the O'Learys" by Niven Busch. **115m/B VHS, DVD.** Tyrone Power, Alice Faye, Don Ameche, Alice Brady, Andy Devine, Brian Donlevy, Phyllis Brooks, Tom Brown, Sidney Blackmer, Gene Reynolds, Berton Churchill, Bobs Watson; **D:** Henry King; **W:** Lamar Trotti, Sonya Levien. Oscars '37: Support. Actress (Brady).

In Old Colorado ♂️♂️ 1941 Ankrum and his cronies try to stir up trouble over water rights, but Boyd and his pals ride to the rescue. **67m/B VHS, DVD.** William Boyd, Russell Hayden, Andy Clyde, Margaret (Maggie) Hayes, Morris Ankrum, Sarah Padden, Cliff Nazarro, Stanley Andrews, James Seay, Morgan Wallace; **D:** Howard Bretherton.

In Old Kentucky ♂️♂️1/2 1935 The Shattucks and the Martingales are fussing, feuding race horse owners. Steve Tapley (Rogers) is the Shattucks' trainer but gets fired for helping out crazy old coot Ezra Martingale (Sellon). So Steve decides to train the Martingale's horse Greyboy to run against the Shattucks' horse Emperor in a big race. Rogers' last released film. **86m/B DVD.** Will Rogers, Dorothy Wilson, Charles Sellon, Louise Henry, Russell Hardie, Charles Richman, Alan Dinehart, Esther Dale, Gladys Lehman; **D:** George Marshall; **W:** Sam Hellman; **C:** L.W. O'Connell; **M:** Arthur Lange.

In Old Montana ♂️ 1939 A Cavalry lieutenant tries to settle a cattleman vs. sheep-herding war. **60m/B VHS.** Fred Scott, Jeanne Carmen, Harry Harvey, John Merton; **D:** Bernard B. Ray.

In Old New Mexico ♂️ *The Cisco Kid in Old New Mexico* 1945 The Cisco Kid and Pancho reveal the murderer of an old woman—a mysterious doctor who was after her identity. **60m/B VHS.** Duncan Renaldo, Martin Garralaga, Gwen Kenyon, Norman Willis, Lee White, Ken Terrell; **D:** Phil Rosen; **M:** Betty Burbridge; **C:** Arthur Martinelli; **M:** David Chudnow.

In Old Santa Fe ♂️♂️1/2 1934 Cowboy star Maynard's best western, and the first film ever with Autry and Burnette. Maynard is framed for murder and his pals save him. **60m/B VHS.** Ken Maynard, Gene Autry, Smiley Burnette, Evalyn Knapp, George "Gabby" Hayes, Kenneth Thomson, Wheeler Oakman, George Chesebro; **D:** David Howard, Joseph Kane.

In Person ♂️♂️1/2 1935 Spry comedy about a movie star who disguises herself to take a vacation incognito and falls in love with a country doctor who is unaware of her identity. "Don't Mention: Got a New Lease on Life. **87m/B VHS.** Ginger Rogers, George Brent, Alan Mowbray, Grant Mitchell; **D:** William A. Seiter; **M:** Oscar Levant.

In Praise of Love *L'Amour Eloge de...* 2001 The aged New Wave pioneer has made a generally incomprehensible, didactic, visually interesting film that will be mostly of interest to Godard completists. Director Edgar (Putzulu) is in the process of casting his latest production (which is about the stages of love) but discovers the young woman, Berthe, he wants for the lead has committed suicide. The film then flashes back a couple of years to Edgar interviewing an elderly couple who are thinking of selling their story for an American film. Their granddaughter, who turns out to be Berthe, is present at the interview. French with subtitles. **98m/C VHS, DVD, FR** Sl'Bruno Putzulu, Cecile Camp, Jean Davy, Françoise Verney, Audrey Klebaner, Jeremy Lippman, Claude Baigneres; **D:** Jean-Luc Godard; **W:** Jean-Luc Godard; **C:** Christophe Pollock, Julien Hirsch.

In Praise of Older Women 1978 Berenger is just right as a young Hungarian who is corrupted by WWII and a large number of older women. Based on a novel by Stephen Vizinczey. **110m/C VHS, DVD, CA** Karen Black, Tom Berenger, Susan Strasberg, Helen Shaver, Alexandra Stewart; **D:** George Kaczender.

In Pursuit 2000 (R) Attorney Rick Alvarez (Baldwin) is accused of murdering his lover Katherine's (Schiffer) husband (Stockwell) and goes on the lam to Mexico. Routine thriller. **91m/C VHS, DVD,** Daniel Baldwin, Claudia Schiffer, Coolio, Sarah Lassez, Dean Stockwell; **D:** Peter Pistor; **W:** Peter Pistor, John Penney; **C:** Richard Crudo. **VIDEO**

In Pursuit of Honor 1995 (PG-13) Based on the true story of five American cavalry soldiers who find themselves being chased out in the 1935. Field's impressive... Army. Ordered by General Douglas MacArthur to destroy their horses, they instead try to outrun an elite tank division to get some 400 horses to safety in Canada. Rugged performances are aptly disturbing. Filmed on location in Australia and New Zealand. **110m/C VHS, DVD,** Don Johnson, Craig Sheffer, Gabrielle Anwar, Bob Gunton, Rod Steiger, James B. Sikking, John Dennis Johnston, Robert Coseby; **D:** Ken Olin; **W:** Dennis Lynton Clark; **C:** Stephen Windon; **M:** John Debney. **CABLE**

In Search of a Golden Sky 1984 (PG). Following their mother's death, a motley group of children move in with their secluded cabin-dwelling uncle, much to the righteous chagrin of the welfare department. **94m/C VHS,** Charles Napier, George "Buck" Flower, Cliff Osmond; **D:** Jefferson (Jeff) Richard.

In Search of Anna WOOF! 1979 When a convict is released from jail, he hits the road with a flighty model in search of the girlfriend who corresponded with him in prison. There auto be a law. **90m/C VHS, AU** Judy Morris, Richard Moir, Chris Haywood, Bill Hunter; **D:** Esben Storm.

In Search of the Castaways 1962 Stirring adventure tale of a teenage girl and her younger brother searching for their father, a ship's captain lost at sea years earlier. Powerful special effects and strong cast make for a winning Disney effort. Based on a story by Jules Verne. **98m/C VHS, DVD, GB** Hayley Mills, Maurice Chevalier, George Sanders, Wilfrid Hyde-White, Michael Anderson Jr.; **D:** Robert Stevenson.

In Self Defense 1983 (PG) Purl is supposed to be protected from the killer she testified against but it doesn't quite work out that way. **94m/C VHS,** Linda Purl, Yaphet Kotto, Billy Drago; **D:** Bruce Seth Green; **M:** Patrick Gleeson.

In Society 1944 The duo play dim-witted plumbers who are mistakenly invited to a high society party, where they promptly create catastrophe. **84m/B VHS, DVD,** Bud Abbott, Lou Costello, Marion Hutton, Kirby Grant, Ann Gillis, Arthur Treacher, Thomas Gomez, Steven Geray, Margaret Irving, Thurston Hall; **Cameos:** Sid Fields, Hal Finberg, Edmund Hartmann; **W:** Sid Fields, Hal Finberg, Edmund Hartmann, John Grant.

In the Aftermath: Angels Never Sleep 1987 Mix of animation and live-action in this post-nuclear wasteland tale never quite works. **85m/C VHS,** Tony Markes, Rainbow Dolan; **D:** Carl Colpaert.

In the Army Now 1994 (PG). Pauly dude gets his head shaved, man. Service comedy about a slacker who joins the Army hoping to cash in on military benefits but who winds up in combat instead. Shore drops the Valley Guy shtick he gets sent on a mission to the Sahara. Strictly for Shore's fans. **92m/C VHS, DVD,** Pauly Shore, Esai Morales, Lori Petty, David Alan Grier, Ernie Hudson, Andy Dick; **D:** Daniel Petrie Jr.; **W:** Daniel Petrie Jr., Ken Kaufman, Fax Bahr, Stu Krieger, Andy Small; **M:** Robert Folk.

In the Bedroom 2001 (R) Spacek and Wilkinson are a middle age couple who lose their son to violence. The numbing grief, paralyzing emotional swirl, and long-simmering marital resentments that follow combine to drastically alter their marriage and lives. Field's impressive, if gut-wrenching directorial debut shows trust for the script and the actors by not overplaying the obvious emotional moments, or the dramatic twists. This trust is rewarded with exceptional performances by Spacek, Wilkinson, and Tomei (in her best performance to date), and by a film that doesn't miss a chance to be subtle when it's called for, or explosive when it's needed. **131m/C VHS, DVD,** Sissy Spacek, Tom Wilkinson, Nick Stahl, Marisa Tomei, William Mapother, William Wise, Celia Weston, Karen Allen; **D:** Todd Field; **W:** Todd Field, Rob Festinger; **C:** Antonio Calvache; **M:** Thomas Newman. Golden Globes '02: Actress—Drama (Spacek); Ind. Spirit '02: Actor (Wilkinson); Actress (Spacek), First Feature, L.A. Film Critics '01: Actress (Spacek), Film; Natl. Bd. of Review '01: Actress (Spacek), Director (Field), Screenplay; N.Y. Film Critics '01: Director (Field), Actress (Spacek), First Feature; Broadcast Film Critics '01: Actress (Spacek).

In the Cold of the Night 1989 (R) Another drowsy entry into the "to sleep, perchance to have a nightmare genre." A photographer with a vivid imagination dreams he murders a woman he doesn't know, and when said dream girl rides into his life on the back of a Harley, Mr. Foto's faced with an etiquette quandary: haven't they met before? Cast includes Hedren (Hitchcock's Marnie and Melanie Griffith's mother). **112m/C VHS, DVD,** Jeff Lester, Adrienne Sachs, Shannon Tweed, David Soul, John Beck, Tippi Hedren, Marc Singer; **D:** Nico Mastorakis; **W:** Nico Mastorakis; **C:** Andreas Bellis.

In the Company of Men 1996 (R) A couple of dissatisfied Yuppies, Chad (Eckhart) and Howard (Malloy), are on a six-week job out of town by their home office. Grumbling about the lack of control in their lives (and blaming it on women), Chad formulates a nasty plan (to which Howard eventually agrees)—they'll deliberately get involved with the same girl, secretary Christine (Edwards), string her along, and then abandon her when their job is done. But Chad actually has his own agenda and bigger corporate ideas in mind. Think misogynistic satire. **93m/C VHS, DVD,** Matt Malloy, Aaron Eckhart, Stacy Edwards, Mark Rector, Jason Dixie, Emily Cline; **D:** Neil LaBute; **W:** Neil LaBute; **C:** Anthony P. Hettinger; **M:** Ken Williams. Ind. Spirit '98: Debut Perf. (Eckhart); Ind. Spirit '98: First Screenplay; Sundance '97: Filmmakers Trophy.

In the Company of Spies 1999 (PG-13) CIA operative Brown is captured and tortured by the North Koreans while his bosses back in Washington try to protect national security. Retired operative Berenger is called back to active service to retrieve the agent and the information in his possession. **102m/C VHS,** Tom Berenger, Clancy Brown, Elizabeth Arlen, Ron Silver, Alice Krige, Arye Gross, Al Waxman, Tom Lenoir, David McIlwraith; **D:** Tim Matheson; **W:** Roger Towne; **C:** Roy Wagner; **M:** Don Davis. **CABLE**

In the Country Where Nothing Happens *En el Pais de No Pasa Nada* 1999 Corrupt businessman Enrique is kidnapped but, thanks to a vidential escape, wife Elena discovers he has a young lover, Rita. Instead of getting angry, Elena befriends Rita and they both decide Enrique isn't worth the bother of rescuing, so he's left to deal with his inept kidnappers on his own. Spanish with subtitles. **92m/C VHS, DVD, MX** Fernando Lujan, Maria (Issai-Issamendi) Issai, Julieta Egurrola, Zaide Silvia Gutierrez; **D:** Maricarmen de Lara; **W:** Maricarmen de Lara, Laura Sosa; **C:** Arturo de la Rosa.

In the Custody of Strangers 1982 A teenager's parents refuse to help when he is arrested for being drunk and he ends up spending the night in jail. Realistic handling of a serious subject. Real-life father and son Sheen and Estevez play father and son. **113m/C VHS,** Martin Sheen, Jane Alexander, Emilio Estevez, Kenneth McMillan, Ed Lauter, Matt Clark, John Hancock; **D:** Robert Greenwald. **TV**

In the Cut 2003 (R) Meg Ryan, in an attempt to break out of her sweet, blond, comic romance roles takes on the part of a sexually repressed teacher who engages in an affair with a suspected serial killer. The sex scenes are appropriately steamy, but a weak plot and so-so acting conspire to undercut the suspense. Based on the Susanna Moore novel. **119m/C VHS, DVD, US AU** Meg Ryan, Mark Ruffalo, Jennifer Jason Leigh, Kevin Bacon, Nick Damici, Sharrieff Pugh; **D:** Jane Campion; **W:** Jane Campion, Susanna Moore; **C:** Dion Beebe; **M:** Hilmar Orn Hilmarsson.

In the Days of the Thundering Herd & the Law & the Outlaw 1914 In the first feature, a pony express rider sacrifices his job to accompany his sweetheart on a westward trek to meet her father. In the second show, a fugitive falls in love with a rancher's daughter and risks recognition. **76m/B VHS,** Tom Mix, Myrtle Stedman; **D:** Colin Campbell. **VIDEO**

In the Dead of Space 1999 (R) Confusing sci fier has the space station Tesla becoming the target of saboteurs, who are determined to crash the ship into Los Angeles. **85m/C VHS, DVD,** Michael Pare, Lisa Bingley, Tony Curtis Blondell; **D:** Eli Necakov. **VIDEO**

In the Deep Woods 1991 Children's author Joanna Warren (Arquette) gets too close to mayhem when a detective (Perkins) is on the killer's trail but when Joanna comes into the picture will she be a suspect or a victim? Based on the book by Nicholas Conde. **96m/C VHS, DVD,** Rosanna Arquette, Anthony Perkins, Will Patton, D.W. Moffett, Christopher Rydell, Harold Sylvester, Kimberly Beck; **D:** Charles Correll; **W:** Robert Nathan, Robert Rosenbaum; **C:** James Glennon.

In the Doghouse 1998 (PG) A valuable movie pooch is dognapped just before the start of his next film and his owners are out to discover whodunit. **90m/C VHS,** Matt Frewer, Rhea Perlman, Trevor Morgan; **D:** George Miller; **W:** Paul Bernbaum; **M:** Richard Band. **VIDEO**

In the Flesh 1997 Closeted Atlanta police detective Philip (Corbin) is working an undercover drug operation that puts him in a gay bar. Which is where he meets Oliver (Fitter), a student by day/hustler by night. When Oliver witnesses a murder, it's Philip who provides him with an alibi, a place to stay, and a new relationship, even though it nearly destroys his own career. But then it seems Philip and Oliver have other connections besides sex. **105m/C VHS, DVD,** Dane Ritter, Ed Corbin, Roxane T. Mims, Adrian Roberts; **D:** Ben Taylor; **W:** Ben Taylor; **C:** Brian Gurley; **M:** Eddie Horst.

In the Gloaming 1997 (PG) Twentysomething Danny (Leonard) bitterly returns home to his suburban, wealthy, emotionally cold family because he is dying of AIDS. He and mother Janet (Close) renew their strained family ties but his businessman dad (Strathairn) doesn't know how to cope except with distance, and his sullen sister Anne (Fonda) is resentful. Wrenching story with fine work by all, including Goldberg in the small role of a live-in nurse, Myrna. Based on a short story by Alice Elliott Dark. Reeve's directorial debut. **60m/C VHS, DVD,** Robert Sean Leonard, Glenn Close, David Strathairn, Bridget Fonda, Whoopi Goldberg; **D:** Christopher Reeve; **W:** Will Scheffer; **C:** Frederick Elmes; **M:** Dave Grusin. **CABLE**

In the Good Old Summertime 1949 This pleasant musical version of "The Shop Around the Corner" tells the story of two bickering co-workers who are also anonymous lovelorn pen pals. Minnelli made her second screen appearance at 18 months in the final scenes. I Don't Care; Meet Me Tonight In Dreamland; Play That Barbershop Chord; In the Good Old Summertime; Put Your Arms Around Me Honey; Wait Till the Sun Shines Nellie; Chicago; Merry Christmas. **104m/C VHS, DVD,** Judy Garland, Van Johnson, S.Z. Sakall, Buster Keaton, Spring Byington, Liza Minnelli, Clinton Sundberg; **D:** Robert Z. Leonard; **C:** Harry Stradling Sr.

In the Heat of Passion 1994 (R) Philip Donovan (Bostwick) is having an affair with his stepdaughter Casey (Hill) and the duo murder hapless wife/mother (Down) to get her money. But it seems someone else knows about their crime. **88m/C VHS,** Barry Bostwick, Teresa Hill, Lesley-Anne Down, Michael Gross; **D:** Catherine Cyran.

In the Heat of Passion 2: Unfaithful 1994 (R) A low-budget ripoff of "Body Heat" and "Fatal Attraction" starring Kirk...

In the Heat of the Night 1967 (R) A wealthy industrialist is murdered in a small Mississippi town. A black homicide expert is asked to help solve the murder, despite resentment on the part of the town's chief of police. Powerful script with underlying theme of racial prejudice is served well by taut direction and powerhouse performances. Poitier's memorable character Virgil Tibbs appeared in two more pictures, "They Call Me Mister Tibbs" and "The Organization." **109m/C VHS, DVD,** Sidney Poitier, Rod Steiger, Warren Oates, Lee Grant; **D:** Norman Jewison; **W:** Stirling Silliphant; **C:** Haskel Wexler; **M:** Quincy Jones. Oscars '67: Actor (Steiger); Adapt. Screenplay; Film Editing. Prima. Sound; British Acad. '67: Actor (Steiger); Golden Globes '68: Actor—Drama (Steiger), Film—Drama, Screenplay; Natl. Film Reg. '02; N.Y. Film Critics '67: Actor (Steiger), Film; Natl. Soc. Film Critics...

In the Kingdom of the Blind the Man with One Eye Is King 1994 (R) The title doesn't seem to mean anything and you may feel the same way about this standard crime drama, despite a strong cast. Mobster Tony (Petersen) gets police assistance from detective Al (Vallelonga) in discovering who murdered a mob boss' brother. **99m/C VHS,** Nick Vallelonga, William L. Petersen, Michael Biehn, Paul Winfield, James Quenter; **D:** Nick Vallelonga; **W:** Nick Vallelonga.

In the Lake of the Woods 1996 Senatorial candidate John Wayan (Strauss) finds his political campaign crashing down when a journalist reveals his part in a Vietnam massacre of civilians. He and wife Kathy (Quinlan) retire to a lakeside cottage to lick their wounds and repair their tattered marriage. But Kathy finds it difficult to reach her distant and increasingly disturbed husband, who's having wartime flashbacks. Then Kathy disappears and the local police, as well as Kathy's sister, suspect that John killed her. Very disturbing TV movie, adapted from the novel by Tim O'Brien. **90m/C VHS,** Peter Strauss, Kathleen Quinlan, Peter Boyle, Richard Anderson, Ken Pogue, Nancy Sorel; **D:** Carl Schenkel; **W:** Philip Rosenberg; **C:** Dietrich Lohmann; **M:** Don Davis.

In the Land of Women 🐾🐾 2006 (PG-13) Sensitive 26-year-old aspiring screenwriter Carter Webb (Brody) escapes a failed relationship and a nowhere career in L.A. to visit his grouchy ailing grandma, Phyllis (Dukakis), in Michigan. Carter then becomes involved in the lives of neighbors Sarah (Ryan) and Lucy (Stewart) Hardwicke. Sarah's just been diagnosed with breast cancer and has a troubled marriage, while 16-year-old Lucy is acting like an obnoxious brat. Carter becomes the confidante of each, which leads to some emotional fireworks, although the pic is so low-key and familiar it's hard to get involved. Kasdan, making his feature debut, is the son of director Lawrence and younger brother of writer Jake. 97m/C DVD. *US* Adam Brody, Kristen Stewart, Meg Ryan, Olympia Dukakis, Makenzie Vega, Elena Anaya, Gregg Henry, JoBeth Williams, Dustin Milligan, Ginnifer Goodwin, Clark Gregg, Gina Mantegna; *D:* Jonathan Kasdan; *W:* Jonathan Kasdan; *C:* Paul Cameron; *M:* Stephen Trask.

In the Line of Duty: A Cop for the Killing 🐾🐾 1990 (R) *A Cop for the Killing* Undercover L.A. narcotics squad is about to bust the city's biggest drug lord when their sting operation goes bad and one of the team is brutally murdered. So, squad leader Ray Wiltern (Farentino) decides to get even. One in a series of TV movies under the "In the Line of Duty" banner. 95m/C VHS. James Farentino, Steven Weber, Charles Haid, Tony Crane, Harold Sylvester, Dan Lauria, Tony Plana; *D:* Dick Lowry; *W:* Philip Rosenberg; *C:* Frank Beascoechea; *M:* Mark Snow. TV

In the Line of Duty: Ambush in Waco 🐾🐾½ 1993 (R) *Ambush in Waco* 1993 Insta-TV movie made by NBC even before the fire which engulfed the Texas compound and ended the standoff between self-proclaimed "prophet" David Koresh and the federal government. Daly does well as the manipulative, charasmatic Branch Davidian cult leader whose stockpiling of illegal weapons lead to an investigation by the Bureau of Alcohol, Tobacco and Firearms and a botched raid which caused the ultimately fatal siege. Filmed on location outside Tulsa, Oklahoma. 93m/C VHS, DVD. Timothy Daly, Dan Lauria, William O'Leary; *D:* Dick Lowry; *W:* Phil Penngroth. TV

In the Line of Duty: The FBI Murders 🐾🐾½ 1988 *The FBI Murders* 1988 A fact-based chiller about the bloody 1986 shootout between Miami FBI agents and a pair of violent killers (Soul and Gross playing against type). 95m/C VHS, DVD. David Soul, Michael Gross, Ronny Cox, Bruce Greenwood, Doug Sheehan, Teri Copley; *D:* Dick Lowry; *W:* Tracy Keenan Wynn. TV

In the Line of Fire 🐾🐾🐾½ 1993 (R) Aging Secret Service agent Frank Horrigan (Eastwood) meets his match in a spooky caller, ex-CIA assassin Mitch Leary (Malkovich), who threatens his honor and the president in an exciting, fast-paced cat and mouse game. Terrific performance by Eastwood includes lots of dry humor and an unscripted emotional moment, but is nearly overshadowed by Malkovich's menacing bad guy. Russo is agent Lily Raines, who begins a charmingly tentative romance with Horrigan. Eerie special effects add to the mood. The Secret Service cooperated and most scenes are believable, with a few Hollywood exceptions; the end result clearly pays homage to the agents who protect our presidents. 128m/C VHS, DVD. Clint Eastwood, John Malkovich, Rene Russo, Dylan McDermott, Gary Cole, Fred Dalton Thompson, John Mahoney, Gregory Alan Williams; *D:* Wolfgang Petersen; *W:* Jeff Maguire; *C:* John Bailey; *M:* Ennio Morricone.

In the Middle of Nowhere 🐾🐾 *En Medio de la Nada* 1993 Sounds vaguely like a Mexican version of "Petrified Forest." A quiet highway restaurant, run by a former union leader, his wife, and his son is invaded by three fugitives: a wounded criminal, his brother, and his mistress. They are being pursued by the woman's powerful husband. They hold the family as hostages until the inevitable confrontation but may be in for a surprise about who will

confront whom. Spanish with subtitles. 89m/C VHS, DVD. *MX* Gabriela Roel, Blanca Guerra, Manuel Ojeda, Alonso Echanove; *D:* Hugo Rodriguez; *W:* Hugo Rodriguez, Marina Stavenhagen; *C:* Guillermo Granillo.

In the Mix WOOF! 2005 (PG-13) This one's a straight-up vehicle for recording artist Usher. If that just made you wonder "Who?" stop here. Darrell (Usher) is a New York City DJ/chick magnet who, as a result of a family friendship, must step in as body guard to a Jersey mobster's daughter, Dolly (Chriqui). A romantic flame ignites between the two. With nowhere else to go, the film becomes a handful of mafia and racial jokes. 97m/C DVD. *US* Usher Raymond, Chazz Palminteri, Emmanuelle Chriqui, Robert Davi, Robert Costanzo, Geoff Stults, K.D. Aubert, Kevin Hart, Matt Gerald, Anthony Fazio; *D:* Ron Underwood; *W:* Jacqueline Zambrano; *C:* Clark Mathis; *M:* Aaron Zigman.

In the Money 🐾 1934 Veteran vaudevillian "Skeets" Gallagher introduces a muddled mass of acts, including a poor imitator of boxing great Gene Tunney, a mad scientist who talks to rabbits and writes rubber checks, and a limp-wristed lisper. 66m/B VHS. Lois Wilson, Warren Hymer, Arthur Hoyt, Frank "Junior" Coghlan, Louise Beavers; *D:* Frank Strayer.

In the Mood 🐾🐾½ 1987 (PG-13) Based on fact, this is the story of teenager Sonny Wisecarver, nicknamed "The Woo Woo Kid," who in 1944, seduced two older women and eventually landed in jail after marrying one of them. Look for Wisecarver in a cameo role as a mailman in the film. 98m/C VHS. Patrick Dempsey, Beverly D'Angelo, Talia Balsam, Michael Constantine, Betty Jinnette, Kathleen Freeman, Peter Hobbs, Edith Fellows; *Cameos:* Ellsworth Wisecarver; *D:* Phil Alden Robinson; *W:* Phil Alden Robinson; *M:* Ralph Burns.

In the Mood for Love 🐾🐾🐾½ 2000 (PG) Romantic melodrama set in the Shanghai community of Hong Kong in 1962. Newspaper editor Chow (Leung Chiu-Wai) and his wife have just moved into a new apartment across the hall from Li-zhen (Cheung) and her husband. Both their respective spouses are away from home a great deal, traveling on business, so the lonely duo begin a tentative friendship. Then Chow begins to suspect his wife is having an affair and it quickly becomes apparent that it's with Li-zhen's husband. Gorgeous to look at, melancholy in tone, if somewhat oblique. Chinese with subtitles. 98m/C VHS, DVD. *HK* Tony Leung Chiu-Wai, Maggie Cheung, Rebecca Pan, Lai Chen, Siu Ping-Lam; *D:* Wong Kar-Wai; *W:* Wong Kar-Wai; *C:* Christopher Doyle, Mark Lee Ping-Bin; *M:* Michael Galasso, Shingeru Umebayashi. Cannes '00: Actor (Leung Chiu-Wai); N.Y. Film Critics '01: Cinematog., Foreign Film.

In the Mouth of Madness 🐾🐾 1995 (R) Standard horror flick pays homage to or pokes fun at Stephen King (you decide) with story of successful horror novelist whose fans become a bit too engrossed in his stories—seems his readers tend to slip into dementia and carry out the grisly acts depicted within the pages. Neill plays an insurance investigator who must track down the missing author while combating the psychotic, axe-wielding residents of the seemingly quiet east coast hamlet where the author resides. Worth a look for the above-average special effects and makeup provided by Industrial Light and Magic (ILM). 95m/C VHS, DVD. Sam Neill, Julie Carmen, Charlton Heston, Jurgen Prochnow, Julie Carmen, Bernie Casey, Peter Jason, Frances Bay, Wilhelm von Homburg; *D:* John Carpenter; *W:* Michael De Luca; *C:* Gary B. Kibbe; *M:* John Carpenter, Jim Lang.

In the Name of the Father 🐾🐾🐾½ 1993 (R) Compelling true story of Gerry Conlon and the Guildford Four, illegally imprisoned in 1974 by British officials after a tragic IRA bombing near London. The British judicial system receives a black eye, but so does the horror and cruelty of IRA terrorism. Politics and family life in a prison cell share the focus, as Sheridan captures superior performances from Day-Lewis and Postlethwaite (beware the thick Belfast brogue). Thompson was accused of pro-IRA sym-

pathies in the British press for her role as the lawyer who believed in Conlon's innocence. Adapted from "Proved Innocent," Conlon's prison memoirs; reunites Sheridan and Day-Lewis after "My Left Foot." Includes original songs by U2's Bono, with a haunting theme sung by Sinead O'Connor. 127m/C VHS, DVD. *GB IR* Daniel Day-Lewis, Pete Postlethwaite, Emma Thompson, John Lynch, Corin Redgrave, Beatie Edney, John Benfield, Paterson Joseph, Marie Jones, Gerard McSorley, Frank Harper, Mark Sheppard, Don Baker, Britta Smith, Aidan Grennell, Daniel Massey, Bosco Hogan; *D:* Jim Sheridan; *W:* Jim Sheridan, Terry George; *C:* Peter Biziou; *M:* Trevor Jones, Bono, Sinead O'Connor. Berlin Intl. Film Fest. '94: Golden Berlin Bear.

In the Name of the King: A Dungeon Siege Tale WOOF! 2008 (PG-13) It's just like "Lord of the Rings"... only much, much worse. German schauenfreude-specialist Uwe Boll is at it again with yet another video game adaptation, this time with his biggest budget ever. But money doesn't mean a thing if you don't have the talent to spend it wisely, and Boll squanders his wad on unconvincing FX and Peter Jackson-esque helicopter shots. In ye olden times, a man named Farmer (Statham, who is, guess what... a farmer) rallies a nation to defend Burt Reynolds' kingdom (King Bandit the IV) against evil wizard and not-so-goodfella Ray Liotta. The rest is a mish-mash of boring battles, orc knock-offs, and inexplicable ninjas. What in the name of the king was Boll thinking? 124m/C DVD. *GE CA* Jason Statham, John Rhys-Davies, Ray Liotta, Leelee Sobieski; Matthew Lillard, Burt Reynolds, Ron Perlman, Claire Forlani, Kristanna Loken, Will Sanderson, Brian White, Mike Dopud; *D:* Uwe Boll; *W:* Doug Taylor; *C:* Mathias Neumann; *M:* Jessica de Rooij, Henning Lohner.

In the Name of the Pope-King 🐾🐾🐾 1985 An acclaimed historical epic about the politics and warfare raging around the 1867 Italian wars that made the Pope the sole ruler in Rome. In Italian with English subtitles. 115m/C VHS. *IT* Nino Manfredi, Danilo Mattei, Carmen Scarpitta, Giovannella Grifea, Carlo Bagno; *D:* Luigi Magni.

In the Navy 🐾🐾½ *Abbott and Costello in the Navy* 1941 Abbott and Costello join the Navy in one of four military-service comedies they cranked out in 1941 alone. The token narrative involves about a singing star (Powell) in uniform to escape his female fans, but that's just an excuse for classic A & C routines. With the Andrews Sisters. 🎵Starlight, Starbright; You're Off To See The World; Hula Ba Lua; Gimme Some Skin; A Sailor's Life For Me; We're In The Navy; Anchors Aweigh (instrumental); You're A Lucky Fellow, Mr. Smith (instrumental). 85m/B VHS, DVD. Lou Costello, Bud Abbott, Dick Powell, The Andrews Sisters; *D:* Arthur Lubin; *W:* Arthur T. Horman, John Grant; *C:* Joseph Valentine.

In the Pit 🐾🐾🐾 *En el Hoyo* 2006 Ruli-fo filmed a single crew, who were building the second level of Mexico City's Periferico freeway, from March 2003 to December 2005. He focuses primarily on the distinctly different attitudes of two workers: Shorty's live-and-let-live philosophy and El Grande's cynical, crude, constant assault on the working man. Spanish with subtitles. 84m/C DVD. *MX D:* Juan Carlos Rulfo; *C:* Juan Carlos Rulfo; *M:* Leonardo Heblum.

In the Presence of Mine Enemies 🐾🐾½ 1997 (PG-13) Re-working of Rod Serling's 1960 script for "Playhouse 90," Rabbi Adam Heller (Mueller-Stahl) and his daughter Rachel (Lowensöhn) are living in the Warsaw ghetto in 1942, trying to deal with Nazi oppression. But the Rabbi's faith is put the test when his son Paul (McKellar), who's escaped from the Treblinka labor camp, returns for vengeance and Rachel becomes the sexual victim of a vicious German officer (Dance). 100m/C VHS, DVD. Armin Mueller-Stahl, Elina Lowensohn, Don McKellar, Charles Dance, Chad Lowe; *D:* Joan Micklin Silver; *W:* Rod Serling. CABLE

In the Realm of the Senses 🐾🐾🐾 *Ai No Corrida* 1976 (NC-17) Taboo-breaking story of a woman and man who turn their backs on the militaristic rule of Japan in the mid-1930s by plunging into an erotic and sensual world all their own. Striking, graphic work that was seized by U.S. customs when it first entered the country. Violent with explicit sex, and considered by some critics as pretentious, while others call it Oshima's masterpiece. In Japanese with English subtitles. 105m/C VHS, DVD. *JP FR* Tatsuya Fuji, Eiko Matsuda, Aio Nakajima, Meika Seri; *D:* Nagisa Oshima; *W:* Nagisa Oshima; *C:* Hideo Ito; *M:* Minoru Miki.

In the Region of Ice 🐾🐾🐾 1976 Award-winning short reveals the complexities of the relationship between a nun and a disturbed student. 38m/B VHS. Fionnula Flanagan, Peter Lempert; *D:* Peter Werner.

In the Secret State 🐾🐾🐾 1985 Inspector Strange finds himself faced with the apparent suicide of a colleague on the day of his own retirement from the force. His private investigation into the case finds him mired in murder and espionage. 107m/C VHS. *GB* Frank Finlay, Matthew Marsh, Thorley Walters; *D:* Christopher Morahan; *W:* Brian Phelan; *C:* Nat Crosby; *M:* Richard Harvey. TV

In the Shadow of Kilimanjaro WOOF! 1986 (R) A pack of hungry baboons attacks innocent people in the wilderness of Kenya. Based on a true story but the characters are contrived and just plain stupid at times. Quite gory as well. Filmed on location in Kenya. 105m/C VHS. *GB* John Rhys-Davies, Timothy Bottoms, Michele Carey, Irene Miracle, Calvin Jung, Donald Blakely; *D:* Raju Patel.

In the Shadow of the Moon 🐾🐾🐾½ 2007 (PG) Using original (and some never-before-seen) footage, this exceptional documentary examines the triumphs and failures of America's race to the moon, from the beginnings of the Apollo program to its end in 1972. Movie focuses on the missions, capturing the wonder and unique perspective of the men who looked at Earth from the surface of another world. Notably absent is the legendary (and incredibly private) Neil Armstrong. Through interviews and remastered footage, Sington creates a compelling, moving film about a time when humanity reached for the skies and technology equaled hope for the future. 100m/C DVD. *D:* David Sington; *C:* Clive North; *M:* Philip Sheppard.

In the Shadows 🐾🐾½ *Under Heaven* 1998 (R) Modern update of Henry James' 1902 novel "The Wings of the Dove." Lonely, wealthy divorcee Eleanor (Richardson) is dying from cancer and needs a caregiver. Cynthia (Parker) moves in along with her weak-willed boyfriend Buck (Young), who passes himself off as Cynthia's brother and takes a job as a gardener. Avaricious Cynthia decides Buck should make Eleanor fall in love and marry him, so they can inherit her fortune. Of course this menage is made for misery. 115m/C VHS, DVD. Joely Richardson, Molly Parker, Aden Young; *D:* Meg Richman; *W:* Meg Richman; *C:* Claudio Rocha; *M:* Marc Olsen.

In the Shadows 🐾🐾 2001 (R) New York hitman Eric O'Byrne (Modine) is sent to Miami to kill veteran Hollywood stunt coordinator Lance Huston (Caan) in retaliation for an accident that killed stuntman Jimmy (Brancato), a mobster's nephew. But before he died, Jimmy managed to steal money and drugs from an undercover FBI agent (Gooding Jr.) who's posing as a dealer. So both the mob and the feds want to reclaim their property. And then Eric goes and falls for the doctor daughter (Adams) of his target just to complicate things further. 104m/C VHS, DVD. James Caan, Joey Lauren Adams, Matthew Modine, Cuba Gooding Jr., Lillo Brancato, Jeffrey Chase; *D:* Ric Roman Waugh; *W:* Ric Roman Waugh; *C:* Chuck Cohen; *M:* Adam Gorgoni.

In the Soup 🎬🎬1/2 1992 (R) Adolpho is a naive New York filmmaker barely scraping by. He decides to sell his script in a classified ad which is answered by the fast-talking Joe, a would-be film producer who's true profession is as a con artist. The two then try numerous (and humorous) ways to raise the money to begin filming. Also available colorized. 93m/B VHS, DVD. Steve Buscemi, Seymour Cassel, Jennifer Beals, Will Patton, Pat Moya, Stanley Tucci, Sully Boyar, Rockets Redgate, Elizabeth Bracco, Ruth Maleczech, Debi Mazar, Steven Randazzo, Francesco Messina; Cameos: Jim Jarmusch, Carol Kane; D: Alexandre Rockwell; W: Tim Kissell, Alexandre Rockwell; C: Phil Parmet; M: Mader. Sundance '92: Grand Jury Prize.

In the Spirit 🎬🎬1/2 1990 (R) New Age couple move from Beverly Hills to New York, where they meet an air-headed mystic and are forced to hide from a murderer. Felk gives solid performance in sometimes rocky production. Berlin is the real-life daughter of May. 94m/C VHS. Elaine May, Marlo Thomas, Jeannie Berlin, Peter Falk, Melanie Griffith, Olympia Dukakis, Chad Burton, Laurie Jones; D: Sandra Seacat; W: Jeannie Berlin, Laurie Jones; C: Dick Quinlan; M: Patrick Williams.

In the Steps of a Dead Man 🎬1/2 1974 A family grieving for a fallen soldier is earmarked for evil by a young man who bears an uncanny resemblance to the dead man. A friend of the family has her suspicions and must find out the truth before something terrible happens. 71m/C VHS. Skye Aubrey, John Nolan; D: Shaun O'Riordan; W: Brian Clemens.

In the Time of the Butterflies 🎬🎬1/2 2001 (PG-13) Based on the novel by Julia Alvarez, which was inspired by the true story of the three Mirabal sisters (collectively known as Las Mariposas) who fought against the Trujillo dictatorship in the Dominican Republic. After their father is murdered, Minerva (Hayek) persuades her sisters Mate (Maestro) and Patria (Cavazos) to join with the rebels in overthrowing the government to ultimately tragic consequences for the women. 92m/C VHS, DVD. Salma Hayek, Lumi Cavazos, Mia Maestro, Edward James Olmos, Marc Anthony, Pilar Padilla, Demián Bichir, Fernando Becerril; D: Mariano Barroso; W: Judy Klass, David Klass; C: Xavier Pérez Grobet; M: Van Dyke Parks. C.A.B.L.E.

In the Valley of Elah 🎬🎬🎬 2007 (R) Retired army sergeant and Vietnam vet Hank Deerfield (Jones) and wife Joan (Sarandon) learn that their soldier son is actually back from Iraq, but they haven't yet heard from him. Hank goes looking and finds that his son has been killed, not in the line of duty but stateside at his New Mexico base—and things may be involved. Army investigators and local police are anything but helpful, until Hank hooks up with detective Emily Sanders (Theron). Then the pieces begin to fall into place and Hank delves into his son's experience in the Middle East. Part exploration into the senselessness of war and part exploration into the depths of pain a family can encounter when losing a son to the terror and tragedy that comes with, and out of fighting. Gritty and raw, Jones' intensity makes it all work. 121m/C DVD. US Tommy Lee Jones, Charlize Theron, Susan Sarandon, Jason Patric, Jonathan Tucker, James Franco, Barry Corbin, Josh Brolin, Frances Fisher, Wes Chatham, Jake McLaughlin, Victor Wolf; D: Paul Haggis; W: Paul Haggis; C: Roger Deakins; M: Mark Isham.

In the White City 🎬🎬🎬 Dans la Ville Blanche 1983 A sailor jumps ship in Lisbon and uses a movie camera to record himself and his search through the twisted streets and alleys of the city for something or someone to connect to. In French, Portuguese, and German with English subtitles. 108m/C VHS. PT, SI Bruno Ganz, Teresa Madruga, Julia Vonderlinn, Jose Carvalho; D: Alain Tanner; W: Alain Tanner; C: Acacio De Almeida; M: Jean-Luc Barbier.

In the Winter Dark 🎬🎬 1998 The isolation of a remote valley community (filmed in Australia's Blue Mountains) is enhanced by the discovery of a woman's body and the slaughter of livestock. Maurice (Barrett) and Ida (Blethyn) have scratched out a life from living but personally never recovered from the death of their baby son long before. Outcast Laurie (Roxburgh) spends his time drifting through the countryside while pregnant Ronnie (Otto) has been abandoned by her lover. The four are brought together by death and what (or who) might be causing it. Based on the novel by Tim Winton. 92m/C VHS. AU Ray Barret, Brenda Blethyn, Richard Roxburgh, Pamela Brown, Gwen Watford, Denis Quilley, Judi Bowker; D: James Bogle; W: James Bogle, Peter Rasmussen; C: Martin McGrath; M: Peter Cobbin.

In This House of Brede 🎬🎬🎬 1975 A sophisticated London widow turns her back on her worldly life to become a cloistered Benedictine nun. Rigg is outstanding as the woman struggling to deal with the discipline of faith. Based on the novel by Rumer Godden. 105m/C VHS, DVD. Diana Rigg, Pamela Brown, Gwen Watford, Judi Bowker; D: George Schaefer; M: Peter Matz. TV

In This Our Life 🎬🎬1/2 1942 Histrionic melodrama handled effectively by Huston about a nutsy woman who steals her sister's husband, rejects him. Winterbottom's most political film in London. Winterbottom's most political film personal issues and travails of its characters with the larger issues it illustrates. The lack of a script (they used mostly outlines) hurts the film in the end, but the performances of the mostly non-professional cast balance that weakness. Shot in documentary style on digital video. 88m/C DVD. GB Jamal Udin Torabi, Enayatullah, Imran Paracha H. Idayatullah, Jamau, Wakeel Khan, Lai Zarin, Mirwais Torabi, Amanullah Torabi; D: Michael Winterbottom; W: Tony Grisoni; C: Marcel Zyskind; M: Dario Marianelli, British Acad. '03: Foreign Film.

In This World 🎬🎬🎬 M1187511 2003 (R) Torabi and Enayatullah star as themselves as the film recounts their journey as Afghan refugees from Pakistan to London. Winterbottom's most political film is powerful and effectively balances the personal issues and travails of its characters with the larger issues it illustrates. The lack of a script (they used mostly outlines) hurts the film in the end, but the performances of the mostly non-professional cast balance that weakness. Shot in documentary style on digital video. 88m/C DVD. GB Jamal Udin Torabi, Enayatullah, Imran Paracha, H. Idayatullah, Jamau, Wakeel Khan, Lai Zarin, Mirwais Torabi, Amanullah Torabi; D: Michael Winterbottom; W: Tony Grisoni; C: Marcel Zyskind; M: Dario Marianelli, British Acad. '03: Foreign Film.

In Too Deep 🎬1/2 1999 (R) A rock star and a beautiful woman are physically drawn to one another in spite of the fact that any contact between them could have disasterous results. 106m/C VHS. Hugo Race, Santha Press, Rebekah Elmaloglou, John Flaus, Dominic Sweeney; D: Colin South.

In Too Deep 🎬🎬 1999 (R) Omar Epps and LL Cool J rise above the tired formula in this by-the-book undercover cop/paranoid drug dealer crime drama. Young Cincinnati cop Jef Cole (Epps) is working undercover in a drug ring run by a none-too-humble crime lord who calls himself God (LL Cool J). As he tries to gain the confidence of God, Cole becomes so deeply mired in the gangster life that his commander Boyd (Tucci) begins to question his loyalty. Epps does an excellent job conveying the tension in his character's position, although the script is totally devoid of any kind of plot twist to help him out. Also shining in minor parts are Pam Grier as a veteran detective and Nia Long as the standard issue love interest. 104m/C VHS, DVD. Omar Epps, Stanley Tucci, LL Cool J, Pam Grier, Veronica Webb, Nia Long, David Patrick Kelly, Hill Harper, Kirk "Sticky Fingaz" Jones; D: Michael Rymer; W: Paul Aaron, Michael Henry Brown; C: Ellery Ryan; M: Christopher Young.

In Trouble WOOF! 1967 Hard-to-follow and frequently aimless story of a pregnant girl who invents a fake race story that her dull-witted brothers take seriously, embarking on a cross-country search for the culprit. 82m/C VHS. C.A. Julie LaChapelle, Katherine Mousseau; D: Gilles Carle.

In Which We Serve 🎬🎬🎬1/2 1943 Much stiff upper-lipping in this classic that captures the spirit of the British Navy during WWII. The sinking of the destroyer HMS Torrin during the Battle of Crete is told via flashbacks, with an emphasis on realism that was unusual in wartime flag-wavers. Features the film debuts of Johnson and Attenborough, and the first Lean directorial effort. Coward received a special Oscar for his "outstanding production achievement," having scripted, scored, codirected, and costarred. 114m/B VHS, DVD. GB Noel Coward, John Mills, Bernard Miles, Celia Johnson, Kay Walsh, James Donald, Richard Attenborough, Michael Wilding, George Carney, Gerald Case, John Varley; D: Ronald Neame; W: Noel Coward; C: Ronald Neame; M: Noel Coward N.Y. Film Critics '42: Film.

Incantato 🎬1/2 Il Cuore Altrove; The Heart is Elsewhere 2003 Meek Nello in Rome, he is sent to Bologna by his exasperated father in hopes that a change of scene will finally lead Nello into marriage. Nello meets society beauty Angela and thinks he has a chance because she has been recently blinded in an accident and hasn't resumed her wild ways. But Angela is just leading the poor schlub on. Italian with subtitles. 107m/C DVD. IT Neri Marcore, Vanessa Incontrada, Giulio Bosetti, Nino D'Angelo, Sandra Milo, Giancarlo Giannini; D: Pupi Avati; W: Pupi Avati; C: Pasquale Rachini; M: Riz Ortolani.

In Your Face 🎬1/2 1977 (R) Little known blaxploitation film about a black family harassed in a white suburb. A black motorcycle gang comes to their rescue. 90m/C VHS, DVD. J. Walter Smith, Tobar Mayo, Roxie Young, Tina James; D: Frank Packard.

The Incident 🎬🎬🎬 1967 A gritty, controversial (at-the-time) drama about two abusive thugs who take over a New York subway car late at night, humiliating and terrorizing each passenger in turn. Film debut for Sheen and Musante as the thugs. 99m/B VHS. Martin Sheen, Tony Musante, Beau Bridges, Ruby Dee, Jack Gilford, Thelma Ritter, Brock Peters, Ed McMahon, Gary Merrill, Donna Mills, Jan Sterling, Mike Kellin, Bob Bannard, Diana Van Der Vlis, Victor Arnold, Robert Fields; D: Larry Peerce; W: Charles Fox, Nicholas E. Baehr; C: Gerald Hirschfeld; M: Charles Fox.

The Incident 🎬🎬1/2 1989 Political thriller set during WWII in Lincoln Bluff, Colorado, as a small-town lawyer who must defend a German prisoner of war accused of murder at nearby Camp Bremen. An all-star cast lends powerful performances to this riveting made for TV drama. 95m/C VHS, DVD. Walter Matthau, Susan Blakely, Harry Hughes, Peter Firth, William Schallert; D: Joseph Sargent. TV

Incident at Channel Q 🎬1/2 1986 A heavy-metal rock musical about a suburban neighborhood declaring war on a chain-and-leather deejay. 85m/C VHS. Steve Mitchell, Joe Janus, David Dreisin, A Corey; D: Storm Thorgerson.

Incident at Deception Ridge 🎬🎬1/2 1994 (R) After five years in prison, Jack Bolder (O'Keefe) is finally a free man, and headed for Seattle by bus. Unfortunately, also aboard is weasely bank manager Jack Davis (Begley Jr.) who's bolted with the ransom money for his kidnapped wife, Helen (Purl). Now Helen is left at the mercy of her kidnappers, who've discovered where their money is and decide to go after it—no matter who gets in their way. Filmed in Vancouver, British Columbia. 94m/C VHS. Michael O'Keefe, Ed Begley Jr., Linda Purl, Miguel Ferrer, Colleen Flynn, Michelle Johnson, Ian Tracey; D: John McPherson; W: Ken Hixon, Randy Kornfield; C: David Geddes. C.A.B.L.E.

Incident at Loch Ness 🎬🎬1/2 2004 (PG-13) Famously difficult German director Werner Herzog is followed by a documentary crew aka "Burden of Dreams" as he tries to film his meditation on humanity's obsession with the Loch Ness monster. Whole production is wonderfully tongue-in-cheek mockumentary within a mockumentary. Game and lively cast pokes unrelenting fun at themselves and the task at hand in this humorous exploration of filmmaking and unmasking. Though nodding to such films as

---

Incident at Oglala: The Leonard Peltier Story 🎬🎬🎬 1992 (PG) Offers a detailed account of the violent events leading to the murder of two FBI agents in Oglala, South Dakota in 1975. American Indian activist Leonard Peltier was convicted of the murders and is presently serving two consecutive life sentences, but he's cited as a political prisoner by Amnesty International. This documentary examines the highly controversial trial and the tensions between the government and the Oglala Nation stemming back to the Indian occupation of Wounded Knee in 1973. Director Apted is sympathetic to Peltier and offers "reasons why he should be allowed a retrial; he examined similar incidents in his film "Thunderheart." 90m/C VHS, DVD. D: Michael Apted; Nar: Robert Redford.

Incognito 🎬1/2 1997 (R) Art forger Harry Donovan (Patric) is approached by a couple of British art dealers and a Japanese broker to forge a Rembrandt for a sympathetic client. He checks out the painter's style by traveling to Amsterdam and Paris, where he falls for art expert Marieke (Jacob). Harry forges the painting and then gets doublecrossed and caught up in murder. Convoluted plot; lots of cliches. Original director Peter Weller was replaced by Bacham after two weeks of filming. 107m/C VHS, DVD. Jason Patric, Irene Jacob, Rod Steiger, Thomas Lockyer, Simon Chandler, Michael Cochrane, Ian Richardson, Pip Torrens, Togo Igawa; D: John Badham; W: Jordan Katz; C: Denis Crossan; M: John Ottman.

An Inconvenient Truth 🎬🎬🎬1/2 2006 (PG) Former Vice President Al Gore speaks out on his personal cause—the dangers of global warming. Guggenheim follows Gore on the lecture circuit as he tries to raise awareness and state his case in an effective (and alarming) multimedia presentation that he has been giving, with a certain confident and professional charm, since 1989. 100m/C DVD. US D: Davis Guggenheim; D: Davis Guggenheim, Bob Richman; M: Michael Brook. Academy Awards '06: Feature Doc., Song ("I Need to Wake Up").

An Inconvenient Woman 🎬🎬 1991 When an older married man has an affair with a young seductress, there's suicide, murder, a nasty gossip columnist, a reporter, a knowing society wife, and a lot of cover-ups among the rich and famous. Miniseries from the novel by Dominick Dunne and based on the Alfred Bloomingdale scandal. 125m/C VHS. Rebeca De Mornay, Jason Robards Jr., Jill Eikenberry, Peter Gallagher, Roddy McDowall, Chad Lowe; D: Larry Elikann; M: John Pielmeier; M: Craig Safan. TV

The Incredible Hulk 🎬🎬1/2 1977 Bixby is a scientist who achieves superhuman strength after he is exposed to a massive dose of gamma rays. But his personal life suffers, as does this wardrobe. Ferrigno is the Hulkster. Pilot for a TV series; based on the Marvel Comics character. 94m/C VHS, DVD. Bill Bixby, Susan Sullivan, Lou Ferrigno, Jack Colvin; D: Kenneth Johnson. TV

The Incredible Hulk 🎬🎬 2008 Please don't let the Marvel hero suffer from a bland script he can't do in 2003's "Hulk." This time Nortor makes a believable (Roth). Leterrier is best-known for "The Transporter" flicks so he can move a story along, but the whispers are that he and Norton clashed over the film's focus and/or that they both clashed with Marvel over doing a commercial film. Not yet reviewed. ?m/C Edward Norton, Tim Roth, Liv Tyler, William Hurt, Tim Blake Nelson, Ty Burrell, Christina Cabot, Peter Mensah, Robert Downey Jr.; D: Louis

---

"Waiting for Guffman" and "Blair Witch Project," film is thoroughly and enjoyably one of a kind. 90m/C DVD. US D: Zak Penn; C: John Bailey; M: Henning Lohner.

Leiterier; **W:** Zak Penn; **C:** Peter Menzies Jr.; **M:** Craig Armstrong.

The Incredible Hulk Returns 🐶🐶½ 1988 The beefy green mutant is back and this time he wages war against a Viking named Thor. Very little substance in this made for TV flick, so be prepared to park your brain at the door. Followed by "The Trial of the Incredible Hulk." **100m/C VHS, DVD.** Bill Bixby, Lou Ferrigno, Jack Colvin, Lee Purcell, Charles Napier, Steve Levitt; **D:** Nicholas J. Corea. **TV**

The Incredible Journey 🐶🐶½ 1963 A labrador retriever, bull terrier and Siamese cat mistake their caretaker's intentions when he leaves for a hunting trip, believing he will never return. The three set out on a 250 mile adventure-filled trek across Canada's rugged terrain. Entertaining family adventure from Disney taken from Sheila Burnford's book. **80m/C VHS. D:** Fletcher Markle.

The Incredible Journey of Dr. Meg Laurel 🐶🐶🐶 1979 A young doctor returns to her roots to bring modern medicine to the 1930s. Features Wagner in a strong performance. **143m/C VHS.** Lindsay Wagner, Jane Wyman, Dorothy McGuire, James Woods, Gary Lockwood; **D:** Guy Green. **TV**

The Incredible Journey of Mary Bryant 🐶🐶½ *Mary Bryant* 2005 (R) Mary (Garai) is convicted of theft in 1786 and becomes one of the first British convicts transported to Australia's Botany Bay colony. She marries fellow convict Will Bryant (O'Loughlin) but when the colony faces starvation, Mary wants to save her family by escaping and reaching safety in the Dutch colony of Timor. True story was originally broadcast as an Australian miniseries. **185m/C DVD. AU** Romola Garai, Alex O'Loughlin, Jack Davenport, Sam Neill, Tony (Anthony) Martin; **D:** Peter Andrikidis; **W:** Peter Berry; **C:** Joseph Pickering; **M:** Iva Davies. **TV**

Incredible Melting Man woof! 1977 (R) Two transformations change an astronaut's life after his return to earth. First, his skin starts to melt, then he displays cannibalistic tendencies. Hard to swallow. Special effects by Rick Baker. Look for director Jonathan Demme in a bit part. Gross-out remake of 1958's "First Man Into Space." **85m/C VHS.** Alex Rebar, Burr de Benning, Cheryl "Rainbeaux" Smith; **Cameos:** Jonathan Demme; **D:** William Sachs.

The Incredible Mrs. Ritchie 🐶🐶 *L'Incroyable Mme. Ritchie* 2003 (PG-13) Sentimental "Afterschool-Special"influenced drama has troubled kid Charlie fall in with the wrong crowd, get in trouble, and find himself helping an eccentric old lady in her garden as punishment. This is one of those sappy dramas in which everyone who is not a part of Charlie's dysfunctional family is gentle, quirky, insightful, and always right. Of course, everyone in his family is none of these kinds of people to point out what they were doing wrong and help them mend their ways. As if that wasn't bad enough, there's a puppy drowning. **102m/C VHS, DVD. CA** Kevin Zegers, Gena Rowlands, James Caan, Brenda James, Leslie Hope, Justin Chatwin; **D:** Paul Johansson; **W:** Paul Johansson.

The Incredible Mr. Limpet 🐶🐶 1964 Limp comedy about a nebbish bookkeeper who's transformed into a fish, fulfilling his aquatic dreams. Eventually he falls in love with another fish, and helps the U.S. Navy find Nazi subs during WWII. Partially animated, beloved by some, particularly those under the age of seven. Based on Theodore Pratt's novel. **99m/C VHS, DVD.** Don Knotts, Jack Weston, Carole Cook, Andrew Duggan, Larry Keating, Elizabeth McRae; **D:** Arthur Lubin; **W:** Jameson Brewer.

The Incredible Petrified World woof! 1958 Divers are trapped in an underwater cave when volcanic eruptions begin. Suffocating nonsense. **78m/B VHS, DVD.** John Carradine, Allen Windsor, Phyllis Coates, Lloyd Nelson, George Skaff; **D:** Jerry Warren.

The Incredible Rocky Mountain Race 🐶🐶 1977 The townspeople of St. Joseph, fed up with Mark Twain's destructive feud with a neighbor, devise a shrewd scheme to rid the town of the troublemakers by sending them on a road race through the West. Comedy starring the F-Troop. **97m/C VHS.** Christopher Connelly, Forrest Tucker, Larry Storch, Mike Mazurki; **D:** James L. Conway. **TV**

The Incredible Sarah 🐶🐶 1976 (PG) A limp adapted stage biography from "Reader's Digest" of the great actress Sarah Bernhardt. Jackson chews scenery to no avail. **105m/C VHS.** Glenda Jackson, Daniel Massey, Yvonne Mitchell, Douglas Wilmer; **D:** Richard Fleischer; **M:** Elmer Bernstein.

The Incredible Shrinking Man 🐶🐶🐶½ 1957 Adapted by Richard Matheson from his own novel, the scifi classic is a philosophical thriller about a man who is doused with radioactive mist and begins to slowly shrink. His new size means that everyday objects take on sinister meaning and he must fight for his life in an increasingly hostile, absurd environment. A surreal, suspenseful allegory with impressive special effects. Endowed with the tension usually reserved for Hitchcock films. **81m/B VHS, DVD.** Grant Williams, Randy Stuart, April Kent, Paul Langton, Raymond Bailey, William Schallert, Frank Scanell, Billy Curtis; **D:** Jack Arnold; **W:** Richard Matheson; **C:** Ellis W. Carter.

The Incredible Shrinking Woman 🐶🐶½ 1981 (PG) "...Shrinking Man" spoof and inoffensive social satire finds household cleaners producing some strange side effects on model homemaker Tomlin, slowly shrinking her to doll-house size. She then encounters everyday happenings as big tasks and not so menial. Her advertising exec husband has a hand in the down-sizing. Sight gags abound but the cuteness wears thin by the end. **89m/C VHS.** Lily Tomlin, Charles Grodin, Ned Beatty, Henry Gibson; **D:** Joel Schumacher; **W:** Jane Wagner.

The Incredible Two-Headed Transplant woof! 1971 (PG) Mad scientist Dern has a criminal head transplanted on to the shoulder of big John Bloom and the critter runs amuck. Lowbudget special effects guaranteed to give you a headache or two. Watch for Pat "Marilyn Munster" Priest in a bikini. **88m/C VHS, DVD.** Bruce Dern, Pat Priest, Casey Kasem, Albert Cole, John Bloom, Berry Kroeger; **D:** Anthony M. Lanza; **W:** John Lawrence, James Gordon White; **C:** Glen Gano, Paul Hipp, Jack Steely; **M:** John Barber.

The Incredibles 🐶🐶🐶½ 2004 (PG) Pixar's final feature as a Disney partner ends the relationship on a high note with this story of a retired superhero family and their difficulties adjusting to "normal" life. Bob Parr (Nelson) is the former Mr. Incredible, who, because of multiple lawsuits, has been forced, along with all other costumed heroes, including wife Helen (Hunter) and best friend Lucius (Jackson), into the Hero Relocation Program. He's stuck in a soul-sucking corporate job where he can't save anyone, he misses the old crimefighting days, and his kids Dash and Violet aren't allowed to use their powers. That is, until someone from Mr. Incredible's past returns to endanger them all. Director/writer Bird's script is smart, funny, and insightful. There's plenty for the kids to enjoy, to be sure, but Bird makes some pointed and poignant observations about marriage, middle class values, and the rise of mediocrity in a self-esteem obsessed society. No wonder the screenplay was nominated for an Oscar. **115m/C VHS, DVD, Blu-ray Disc, UMD. US D:** Brad Bird; **W:** Brad Bird; **C:** Janet Lucroy, Patrick Lin, Andrew Jimenez; **M:** Michael Giacchino; **V:** Craig T. Nelson, Holly Hunter, Samuel L. Jackson, Jason Lee, Wallace Shawn, Sarah Vowell, Spencer Fox, Brad Bird, Elizabeth Pena, Dominique Louis. Oscars '04: Animated Film, Sound FX Editing.

Incredibly Strange Creatures Who Stopped Living and Became Mixed-Up Zombies woof! *The Teenage Psycho Meets Bloody Mary; The Incredibly Strange Crea-*

tures 1963 The infamous, super-cheap horror spoof that established Sheckler (for whom Cash Flagg is a pseudonym), about a carny side show riddled with ghouls and bad rock bands. Assistant cinematographers include the young Laszlo Kovacs and Vilmos Zsigmond. A must-see for connoisseurs of cult and camp. **90m/C VHS, DVD.** Ray Dennis Steckler, Carolyn Brandt, Brett O'Hara, Atlas King, Sharon Walsh, Toni Camel, Erina Enyc; **D:** Ray Dennis Steckler; **W:** Gene Pollock, Robert Silliphant; **C:** Laszlo Kovacs, Vilmos Zsigmond, Joseph Mascelli; **M:** Andre Brummer.

The Incredibly True Adventure of Two Girls in Love 🐶🐶½ 1995 (R) Gentle low-budget romantic comedy about first love between two high school girls. Tomboyish working-class Randy (Holloman) lives with her lesbian aunt and works part-time at the local gas station where she spots the rich and beautiful Evie (Parker), one of the popular girls in school. Some sparks fly but Evie's confused, though she's willing to be wooed and, later, defend her new relationship. The issue of race (Randy's white, Evie's black) is only briefly alluded to—more is made of the differences between the girls' social classes and their vulnerability. Directorial debut for Maggenti. **95m/C VHS, DVD.** Laurel Holloman, Nicole Ari Parker, Kate Stafford, Stephanie Berry; **D:** Maria Maggenti; **W:** Maria Maggenti.

Incubus 🐶🐶 1965 One of the very few films made in the artificial language of Esperanto (so it's subtitled in English). Beautiful Kia (Ames) and Amael (Hardt) are sisters who retain their youth and beauty by sucking the life out of the corrupted souls who visit a supposedly magic well. Then Kia discovers the uncorrupted soldier Mark (Shatner) and falls big time. But her succubis sisters doesn't like what's going on and casts a spell that calls an unspheric with striking cinematography by Hall. **76m/B VHS, DVD.** William Shatner, Allyson Ames, Eloise Hardt, Ann Atmar, Robert Fortier, Milos Milos; **D:** Leslie Stevens; **W:** Leslie Stevens; **C:** Conrad L. Hall; **M:** Dominic Frontiere.

Incubus 🐶 1982 (R) A doctor and his teenaged daughter settle in a quiet New England community, only to encounter the incubus, a terrifying, supernatural demon who enjoys sex murders. Offensive trash. **90m/C VHS, DVD. CA** John Cassavetes, Kerrie Keane, Helen Hughes, Erin Flannery, John Ireland, Duncan McIntosh; **D:** John Hough; **W:** George Franklin; **C:** Conrad L. Hall, Albert J. Dunk; **M:** Stanley Myers.

Incubus 🐶 2005 Getting stranded in the middle of nowhere never seems to end well. When Jay (Reid) and her college pals have a car accident, they find refuge in an ominous looking (for a reason!) building that is, indeed, filled with lots of dead folks and a killer in a coma who can enter people's minds as they sleep. No, he is NOT named Freddy but rather, um, cleverly "The Sleeper." Once in their dreams they themselves begin hunting one another so Jay tries really, really super-hard not to snooze, as does the unfortunate viewer. **86m/C VHS, DVD.** Tara Reid, Akemmji Ndifemyan, Alice O'Connell, Russell Carter II, Christian Brassington; **D:** Anya Camilleri; **W:** Gary Humphreys. **VIDEO**

Indecency 🐶🐶 1992 (PG-13) Ellie (Beals) is still recovering from a mental breakdown when she goes to work for Marie (Clarkson) at her ad agency. There Ellie must deal with manipulative associate Nia (Davis) and Marie's charming, estranged husband Mick (Remar), who draws the fragile Ellie into an affair. Then Marie commits suicide—or maybe it was murder. **88m/C VHS.** Jennifer Beals, James Remar, Sammi Davis, Barbara Williams, Christopher John Fields, Ray McKinnon; **D:** Marisa Silver; **W:** Amy Holden Jones, Holly Goldberg Sloan, Alan Ormsby.

Indecent Behavior 🐶🐶 1993 (R) Tweed is a sex therapist who's accused of murder when one of her clients overdose's on the latest designer drug. Hudson, who plays the genre's hard-boiled cop figure, gets very personally involved investigating the allegations, which really upsets

Tweed's hubby, Vincent. Also available in an unrated version. **93m/C VHS.** Shannon Tweed, Gary Hudson, Jan-Michael Vincent, Michelle Moffett, Lawrence-Hilton Jacobs, Penny Peyser; **D:** Lawrence Lanoff.

Indecent Behavior 2 🐶🐶½ 1994 (R) Sex therapist Rebecca is targeted for blackmail as she finds out all sorts of unhealthy things about her patients. Meanwhile, she's practicing her technique with a fellow therapist. Also available unrated. **96m/C VHS, DVD.** Shannon Tweed, James Brolin, Chad McQueen, Elizabeth Sandifer, Craig Stepp, Rochelle Swanson; **D:** Carlo Gustaff.

Indecent Behavior 3 🐶🐶 1995 (R) Sex therapist becomes the obsessed object of desire for a decidedly deadly client. Also available unrated. **90m/C VHS.** Shannon Tweed, Sam Hennings, Colleen T. Coffey, Doug Jeffery, Beau Billingslea, Laura Rogers; **D:** Kelley Cauthen; **W:** Hal Styverson.

An Indecent Obsession 🐶🐶 ½ 1985 Colleen McCullough's bestseller about WWII Australian soldiers recuperating in a field hospital mental ward. Hughes plays the nurse everyone's in love with. **100m/C VHS. AU** Wendy Hughes, Gary Sweet, Richard Moir, Jonathan Hyde, Bill Hunter, Bruno Lawrence; **D:** Lex Marinos; **W:** Denise Morgan.

Indecent Proposal 🐶🐶 ½ 1993 (R) High-gloss movie that had couples everywhere discussing the big question: Would you let your wife sleep with a billionaire in exchange for a million bucks? Probably, if all were as goodlooking as the weathered, yet ever gorgeous Redford. Moore and Harrelson are the financially down on their luck, but happy, couple who venture to Vegas on a last-ditch gambling effort. Surreally slick direction from Lyne, but an ultimately empty film that explores the values of marriage in a terribly angstridden fashion. Based on the novel by Jack Engelhard. Proof that average movies can make a killing at the boxoffice, landing in sixth place for 1993. **119m/C VHS, DVD.** Robert Redford, Demi Moore, Woody Harrelson, Seymour Cassel, Oliver Platt, Billy Bob Thornton, Rip Taylor, Billy Connolly, Joel Brooks, Sheena Easton, Herbie Hancock; **D:** Adrian Lyne; **W:** Amy Holden Jones; **C:** Howard Atherton; **M:** John Barry. MTV Movie Awards '94: Kiss (Demi Moore/Woody Harrelson); Golden Raspberries '93: Worst Support. Actor (Harrelson), Worst Screenplay.

Independence Day 🐶🐶 *Follow Your Dreams* 1983 (R) Uneven romantic drama about a small-town photographer, yearning for the big city, who falls in love with a racing car enthusiast, whose sister is a battered wife. Strong cast, particularly Wiest as the abused wife, is left occasionally stranded by a script reaching too hard for social significance. **110m/C VHS.** Kathleen Quinlan, David Keith, Frances Sternhagen, Dianne Wiest, Cliff DeYoung, Richard Farnsworth, Josef Sommer, Cheryl "Rainbeaux" Smith; **D:** Robert Mandel; **M:** Charles Bernstein.

Independence Day 🐶🐶🐶 1996 (PG-13) The biggest of the new wave of disaster flicks paying tribute to the Irwin Allen celebrity-fests of the '70s finds an alien armada descending on Earth to create some fireworks on the July 4th weekend. The fate of the world rests in the hands of an unlikely band of Earthlings led by President Whitmore (Pullman), a computer expert (Goldblum), and a Marine fighter pilot (Smith). Special effects, despite forgoing some of the more expensive newer technology, don't disappoint. Strong (if not A-list) cast and plenty of action. Devlin and Emmerich wrote the script while promoting "Stargate," after a reporter asked Emmerich if he believed in aliens. **135m/C VHS, DVD, UMD.** Bill Pullman, Will Smith, Jeff Goldblum, Judd Hirsch, Margaret Colin, Randy Quaid, Mary McDonnell, Robert Loggia, Brent Spiner, James Rebhorn, Vivica A. Fox, James Duval, Harry Connick Jr., Harvey Fierstein, Richard Speight Jr., Adam Baldwin, Bill Smitrovich, Mae Whitman, Kiersten Warren, Giuseppe Andrews, Devon Gummersall, Leland Orser, Raphael Sbarge, Bobby Hosea, Dan Lauria, Robert Pine, John Capodice, Lyman Ward; **D:** Roland Emmerich; **W:** Dean Devlin, Roland Emmerich; **C:** Karl Walter Lindenlaub; **M:** David Arnold. Oscars '96: Visual FX; MTV Movie Awards '97: Kiss (Vivica A. Fox/Will Smith).

The Independent 🐾🐾 2000 Affectionate spoof of low-budget, schlock cinema. Morty Fineman (Stiller) has directed more than 400 "B" movies, which has made him a legend in certain circles. His latest project has gone bust, leaving him facing bankruptcy once again, but he's sure he has a hit with his next idea—the rights to the life story of serial killer William Henry Ellis (Hankin). Now Morty just has to convince his exasperated, estranged daughter Paloma (Garofalo) to help him raise the cash for his new opus. Faux trailers from some of Morty's epics are interviews with various co-workers, admirers, and cast are among the inspired bits. 93m/C VHS, DVD, Jerry Stiller, Janeane Garofalo, Max Perlich, Larry Hankin, Ginger Lynn Allen, Billy Burke, Andy Dick, Fred (John F.) Dryer, Ethan (Randall) Embry, Jonathan Katz, John Lithgow, Ron (Randall) Lyon, Anne Meara. Cameos: Ben Stiller, Nick Cassavetes, Roger Corman, Fon Howard, Ted (Edward) Demme. D: Stephen Kessler. W: Stephen Kessler, Mike Wilkins. C: Amir Hamed. M: Ben Vaughn.

The Indian Scarf 🐾🐾 1963 Heirs to a dead man's fortune are being strangled one by one at the benefactor's country estate. An Edgar Wallace suspense

Indian Paint 🐾🐾 1964 A pleasant children's film about an Indian boy's love for his horse and his rite of passage. Stiverheels was Tonto or TV's "The Lone Ranger," while Crawford was the "Rifleman's" son. 90m/C VHS. Jay Silverheels, Jonny Crawford, Pat Hogan, Robert Crawford Jr., George Lewis; D: Norman Foster.

The Indian Runner 🐾🐾1/2 1991 (R) Penn's debut as a writer-director tells the story of two brothers in Nebraska during the late '60s, who are forced to change their lives with the loss of their family farm. Joe is a good cop and family man who can't deal with the rage of his brother Frank, who has just returned from Vietnam and is turning to a life of crime. Penn does a decent job of representing the struggle between the responsible versus the rebellious side of human nature. Quiet and very stark. Based on the song "Highway Patrolman" by Bruce Springsteen. 127m/C VHS, DVD. David Morse, Viggo Mortensen, Sandy Dennis, Charles Bronson, Valeria Golino, Patricia Arquette, Dennis Hopper, Benicio Del Toro; D: Sean Penn. W: Sean Penn.

The Indian in the Cupboard 🐾🐾1/2 1995 (PG) On his ninth birthday, Omri receives a three-inch plastic Indian named Little Bear and an old wooden medicine cabinet. (Guess they were out of Power Rangers.) When placed in the cabinet, Little Bear magically comes to life, taking Omri on adventures and teaching him important lessons. Blue screen technique allow them to appear together on-screen although they were actually shot together only once. Based on the best-selling children's book by Lynne Reid Banks. 97m/C VHS, DVD. Michael (Mike) Papajohn, Hal Scardino, Litefoot, Lindsay Crouse, Richard Jenkins, Rishi Bhat, David Keith; D: Frank Oz. W: Melissa Mathison. C: Russell Carpenter. M: Miles Goodman.

The Indian Fighter 🐾🐾🐾 1955 Exciting actioner has Douglas as a scout hired to lead a wagon train to Oregon in 1870. The train must pass through dangerous Sioux territory and Douglas tries to make peace with the Sioux leader but a secret Indian gold mine and romance cause friction and keep things lively. 88m/C VHS, DVD. Kirk Douglas, Elsa Martinelli, Walter Abel, Walter Matthau, Diana Douglas, Lon Chaney Jr., Eduard Franz, Alan Hale Jr., Elisha Cook Jr., Harry Landers; D: Andre de Toth; W: Frank Davis; C: John L. "Jack" Russell; M: Franz Waxman.

Indian Uprising 🐾🐾 1951 An army captain tries to keep local settlers from causing trouble with Geronimo and his people when gold is discovered on their territory. 75m/C VHS. George Montgomery, Audrey Long, Carl Benton Reid, John Baer, Joseph (Joe) Sawyer. D: Ray Nazarro.

Indiana Jones and the Kingdom of the Crystal Skull 2008 It's been a long wait since 1989's "Last Crusade" and time has marched on for our intrepid archaeologist, but Indy (Ford), along with his bullwhip, fedora, and leather jacket, just keeps rolling along while acknowledging the wear and tear. It's now 1957 and Indy is chasing after the mysterious title objects, with Soviet operative Irina Spalko (Blanchett) determined to outwit him (maybe after a little torture first). Indy's aided by ex-love Marion Ravenwood (Allen) and Mutt Williams (LeBeouf), who looks like a classic fifties juvenile delinquent. Is he also Indy's love child with Marion? That's just one of the mysteries to be solved. Not yet reviewed. 7m/C VHS, DVD. Cate Blanchett, Ray Winstone, Jim Broadbent, John Hurt, Andrew Divoff. D: Steven Spielberg. W: David Koepp. C: Janusz Kaminski. M: John Williams.

Indiana Jones and the Last Crusade 🐾🐾🐾 1989 (PG) In this, the third and last (?) Indiana Jones adventure, the fearless archaeologist is once again up against the Nazis in a race to find the Holy Grail. Connery is perfectly cast as Indy's father, opening sequence features Phoenix as a teenage Indy and explains his fear of snakes and the origins of the

The Indestructible Man 🐾 1956 Chaney, electrocuted for murder and bank robbery, is brought back to life by a scientist. Naturally, he seeks revenge on those who sentenced him to death. Chaney does the best he can with the material. 70m/B VHS, DVD. Ross Elliot, Ken Terrell, Robert Shayne, Lon Chaney Jr., Marian Carr, Max (Casey) Adams; Showalter; D: Jack Pollexfen; W: Sue Bradford; V. Russell; C: John L. "Jack" Russell; M: Albert Glasser.

Indian Summer 🐾🐾 1993 (PG-13) Yet another addition to the growing 30-something nostalgia genre. Delete the big house, add a crusty camp director (Arkin), change the characters' names (but not necessarily their lives) and you'll feel like you're experiencing deja vu. This time seven friends and the requisite outsider reconvene at Camp Tamakwa, the real-life summer camp to writer/director Binder. They save Camp Tamakwa and experience personal growth. A must see for those who appreciate listening to situational jokes that are followed by "I guess you had to be there." 108m/C VHS, DVD. Alan Arkin, Matt Craven, Diane Lane, Bill Paxton, Elizabeth Perkins, Kevin Pollak, Sam Raimi, Vincent Spano, Julie Warner, Kimberly Williams, Richard Chevolleau; D: Mike Binder; W: Mike Binder. M: Miles Goodman.

The Indian Tomb 🐾🐾🐾1/2 The Mission of the Yogi; The Tiger of Eschnapur 1921 Silent film fare in two parts. Ayan (Veidt) is the Maharajah of Eschnapur. But all his wealth and power has not prevented Ayan's wife, Princess Savitri, from falling in love with British officer MacAllan. Ayan plots to build a massive tomb but yogi Ramigani prophesizes that such revenge will destroy the prince's life. Huge budget (for the time) and lavish spectacle, which was all created at director May's German studio. Adapted from the novel by Thea von Harbou. 212m/B VHS, DVD. GE Conrad Veidt, Paul Richter, Olaf Fonss, Mia May, Bernhard Goetzke, Lya de Putti, Erna Morena; D: Joe May; W: Fritz Lang. C: Werner Brandes.

The Indian Tomb 🐾🐾 Das Indische Grabmal 1959 Sequel to "The Tiger of Eschnapur" finds Harald Berger (Hubschmid) and Seetha (Pagel) managing to elude Chandra's soldiers until Seetha's faith in her gods results in her capture and death. Berger's partner Dr. Rhode (Holm) and Berger's sister Irene (Bethmann) discover the evil that is afoot of a madman when Chandra lies about another knockout exotic dance (with Ms. Paget in an even more revealing costume), encounters with a horde of lepers locked away in the catacombs, and a full-scale palace revolt. 102m/C DVD, GE Debra Paget, Paul (Christian) Hubschmid, Walter Reyer, Sabine Bethmann; D: Fritz Lang. W: Werner Jorg Luddecke; C: Richard Angst. M: Michel Michelet.

Indio 🐾 1990 (R) A Marine-trained half-breed takes it on himself to save the Amazon rain forest. Not a peaceful demonstrator, his tactics are violent ones. 94m/C VHS. Marvin Hagler, Francesco Quinn, Brian Dennehy; D: Anthony M. Dawson.

Indio 2: The Revolt 🐾 1992 (R) Greedy developers are cutting a highway into the Amazon jungle, destroying everything in their path. All is not lost though, because U.S. Marine Sgt. Iron is on top of things, continuing his struggle to unite the Amazon tribes and save the rainforest, no matter what it takes. 104m/C VHS. Marvin Hagler, Charles Napier; M: Pino Donaggio.

Indiscreet 🐾🐾🐾 1958 A charming American diplomat in London falls in love with a stunning actress, but protects himself by saying he is married. Needless to say, she finds out. Stylish romp with Grant and Bergman at their sophisticated best. Adapted by Norman Krasna from his stage play "Kind Sir." 100m/C VHS, DVD. Cary Grant, Ingrid Bergman, Phyllis Calvert; D: Stanley Donen; W: Norman Krasna; C: Frederick A. (Freddie) Young; M: Richard Rodney Bennett.

Indiscreet 🐾🐾🐾 1931 Empty-headed romantic comedy about a fashion designer whose past catches up with her when her ex-lover starts romancing her sister. No relation to the classic 1958 film with Cary Grant and Ingrid Bergman. 81m/B To Me, If You Haven't Got Love, 🎵Come To Me, If You Haven't Got Love. 81m/B VHS, DVD. Gloria Swanson, Ben Lyon, Barbara Kent. D: Leo McCarey.

Indiscretion of an American Wife 🐾🐾 Indiscretion; Terminal Station; Stazione Termini. Set almost entirely in Rome's famous Terminal Station, Indiscretion 1954 Set almost entirely in Rome's famous Terminal Station, where an ill-fated couple say goodbye endlessly while the woman tries to decide whether to join her husband in the States. Trimmed down from 87 minutes upon U.S. release. 63m/C VHS, DVD. IT. Jennifer Jones, Montgomery Clift, Richard Beymer; D: Vittorio De Sica; W: Truman Capote; C: Oswald Morris.

Indictment: The McMartin Trial 🐾🐾🐾 1995 (R) Woods stars as daredevil attorney Danny Davis, who has the unenviable task of providing a defense in the notorious McMartin child molestation trial. In 1983, Manhattan Beach, California was rocked by reports that some 60 preschoolers had been abused at a day-care center. Seven defendants were accused thanks to lurid televised interviews with the children. The trial lasted six years (the longest and most expensive on record) and all charges were eventually dismissed. It's clear from this telepic that public hysteria and media hype lead to a grave miscarriage of justice that put the legal system on trial as well. 132m/C VHS, DVD. James Woods, Henry Thomas, Mercedes Ruehl, Shirley Knight, Sada Thompson, Mark Blum, Alison Elliott, Chelsea Field, Richard Bradford, Lolita (David) Davidovich; D: Mick Jackson; W: Abby Mann, Myra Mann; C: Rodrigo Garcia; M: Peter Melnick

Indiscreet 🐾🐾1/2 1998 (R) Private eye Michael Nash (Perry) is hired by a suspicious millionaire to follow his wife, Eve (Reuben). When Nash winds up saving the desperately unhappy Eve from suicide, the two begin an affair. Then her husband is murdered and the cops find Nash a very handy suspect. 101m/C VHS. Luke Perry, Gloria Reuben, Peter Coyote, Adam Baldwin; D: Marc Bienstock; W: Vladimir Nemirovsky.

Indiscreet 🐾🐾 1998 (R) denson, Robert McBain, Jeni Barnett; D: Richard Michaels. 'TV

Indochine 🐾🐾🐾 1992 (PG-13) Soapy melodrama follows the fortunes of Eliane (Deneuve), a "Frenchwoman born and reared in Indochina, then 1930 to the present. Naturally, Adam turns out to have more than a few screws loose herself and Lisa finds herself the object of his obsession. 104m/C VHS, Maxwell Caulfield, Stephanie Knights, Jennifer Nicholson, Tippi Hedren, Andrea King, Taylor Negron. Cameos: Samantha Eggar; D: Alex Cannawai; W: Alex Canawati; C: Christian Sebaldt; M: Christopher Whitten.

Infamous 🐾🐾 2006 (R) The other Truman Capote movie, which was filmed at the same time as the more successful (both financially and artistically) "Capote." Englishman Jones is at least physically more suited to the role of the fey author, who revels in his Gotham society milieu. Still, you've got Truman and his best friend Harper Lee (an understated Bullock, Daniel Craig, Lee Pace, Peter Bogdanovich, Jeff Daniels, Hope Davis, Sigourney Weaver, Isabella Rossellini, Juliet Stevenson, Gwyneth Paltrow, John Benjamin Hickey; D: Douglas McGrath; C: Bruno Delbonnel; M: Rachel Portman.

Infamous Crimes 🐾🐾 Philo Vance Returns 1947 Philo investigates the murders of a playboy and his girlfriends. One of the last of the series whose character was based on the S.S. Van Dine stories. 64m/B VHS. William Wright, Terry Austin, Leon Belasco, Clara Blandick, Iris Adrian, Frank Wilcox; D: William Beaudine.

Internal Affairs 🐾🐾🐾 Mogan Jou Wu jian dao 2002 (R) Claustrophobic cat-and-mouse, cops-and-robbers noir. Lau (Lau) is a Triad member who's sent by his boss

Indiana Jones and the Temple of Doom 🐾🐾🐾 1984 (PG) Daredevil archaeologist Indiana Jones is back. This time he's on the trail of the legendary Ankara Stone and a ruthless cult. More gore and violence than the original; Capshaw's whining character is an irritant, lacking the fresh quality that Karen Allen added to the original. Enough action for ten movies, special effects galore, and the usual booming Williams score make it a cinematic roller coaster ride, but with less regard for plot and pacing than the original. Through second in the series, it's actually a prequel to "Raiders of the Lost Ark." Followed by "Indiana Jones and the Last Crusade." 118m/C VHS, DVD. Harrison Ford, Kate Capshaw, Ke Huy Quan, Amrish Puri; D: Steven Spielberg; W: Willard Huyck, Gloria Katz; C: Douglas Slocombe; M: John Williams. Oscars '84:

infamous fedora. Returns to the look and feel of the original with more adventures, exotic places, dastardly villains, and daring escapes that ever before; a must for Indy fans. 125m/C VHS, DVD. Harrison Ford, Sean Connery, Denholm Elliott, Alison Doody, Julian Glover, John Rhys-Davies, River Phoenix, Michael Byrne, Alex Hyde-White; D: Steven Spielberg; W: Jeffrey Boam; C: Douglas Slocombe; M: John Williams.

tale. 85m/C VHS. GE Heinz Drache, Gisela Uhlen, Klaus Kinski; D: Alfred Vohrer.

Inevitable Grace 🐾🐾 1994 Strictly amateur attempt at neo-noir for fledgling director Canawati. Wealthy Adam Cestare (Caulfield) becomes enamoured with young psychiatrist Lisa Kelner (Knights), who's treating his hysterical wife, Veronica (Nicholson, daughter of Jack).

nique Blanc, Henri Marteau, Carlo Brandt, Gerard Lanigan; D: Regis Wargnier; M: Erik Orsenna, Louis Gardel, Catherine Cohen, Regis Wargnier. C: Francois Catonne. M: Patrick Doyle. Oscars '92: Foreign Film; Cesar '93. Actress (Deneuve), Art Dir/Set Dec., Cinematog., Sound, Support. Actress (Blanc); Golden Globes '93: Foreign Film; Natl. Bd. of Review '92: Foreign Film.

Hon Sam (Tsang) to the police academy so he can become a deep cover mole. Chan (Leung Chui-wai) is a cop whose boss, Supt. Wong (Wong), has sent him into the mob as a police informer. Each boss knows he has a mole and each mole knows it's only a matter of time before a slip-up will prove fatal. Lau is sent by Internal Affairs to investigate the Triad mole while Chan is told to find out who the police stoolie is. Talk about your identity crisis! Cantonese with subtitles. There's also a prequel and a sequel. **100m/C DVD.** Tony Leung Chiu-wai, Andy Lau, Anthony Wong, Eric Tsang, Lam Ka-tung, Ng Ting-yip, Wan Chi-keung, Sammi Cheng; **D:** Wai Keung (Andrew) Lau; **W:** Felix Chong; **C:** Lai Yui-fai Lang; **M:** Chan Kwong-wing.

The Infernal Trio *Le Trio Infernal* 1974 An attorney comes up with a plan involving two sisters (who are his lovers) which will make them both wealthy; but it will also make them both murderers. Sophisticated black comedy based on a true story. In French with English subtitles or dubbed. **100m/C VHS, FR IT** Romy Schneider, Michel Piccoli, Mascha Gonska; **D:** Francis Girod.

Inferno 1980 (R) Uneven occult horror tale about a young man who arrives in New York to investigate the mysterious circumstances surrounding his sister's death. Dubbed. **106m/C VHS, DVD.** *IT* Leigh McCloskey, Eleonora Giorgi, Irene Miracle, Sacha (Sascha) Pitoëff; **D:** Dario Argento; **W:** Dario Argento; **C:** Romano Albani; **M:** Keith Emerson.

Inferno 1998 (PG-13) A massive fireball is headed straight toward Earth. **90m/C VHS.** James Remar, Stephanie Niznik, Daniel von Bargen, Anthony Starke, Kathryn Morris, Frederic Lehne, Jonathan LaPaglia, Ian Barry; **W:** Bruce Taylor, Roderick Taylor; **C:** Jacques Haitkin; **M:** Joel Goldsmith, K. Alexander (Alex) Wilkinson.

Inferno 1999 (R) Jack Conley awakens in the middle of the desert with no idea who he is or what's happened to him. Taken in by a reclusive artist, Jack suffers violent flashbacks as he tries to piece together his identity, only remembering that he had a lot of money in his possession and it's gone. Then two of Jack's former associates track him down and he learns the dangerous truth about himself. **94m/C VHS, DVD.** Ray Liotta, Gloria Reuben, Armin Mueller-Stahl; **D:** Harley Cokliss; **C:** Stephen McNutt; **M:** Fred Mollin. VIDEO

Inferno 2001 Darcy Hamilton (Gunn) is an expert firejumper who leads her team in controlling a forest fire that Darcy suspects was arson. A second blaze erupts and heads for the nearest town and the local fire chief accuses Darcy's daughter and her boyfriend of being fire bugs. Now Darcy not only has to fight the fire but prove her daughter's innocence. **91m/C VHS, DVD.** Janet Gunn, Jeff Fahey, Dean Stockwell; **D:** Dusty Nelson; **M:** Jeff Marsh.

Inferno in Paradise 1988 Macho firefighter pal pal photographer get hot while trailing a murderous pyromaniac. More like purgatory in the living room (that is, unless you thought Forsyth's earlier "Chesty Anderson, US Navy" was divine comedy). **115m/C VHS.** Richard Young, Betty Ann Carr, Jim Davis, Andy Jarrell, Dennis Chun; **D:** Ed Forsyth.

Infested: Invasion of the Killer Bugs 2002 (R) It's a boomer reunion with bugs! Yuppie friends gather for a funeral and have their reminiscing disturbed by mutant flies that transform their victims into zombies. This one is meant to be cheesy. **84m/C VHS, DVD.** Zach Galligan, Amy Jo Johnson, Robert Duncan McNeill, Mark Margolis, Lisa Ann Hadley, Daniel H. Jenkins; **D:** Josh Olson; **W:** Josh Olson; **C:** M. David Mullen; **M:** Rodney Whittenberg. VIDEO

The Infiltrator 1995 (R) Based on the true story of Yaron Svoray (Platt), an Israeli journalist, whose latest assignment is to go to Berlin and investigate the rising Neo-Nazi movement. Eventually, Svoray manages to meet leaders of the rising Neo-Nazi movement. Eventually, Svoray manages to meet leaders of the Nationalist Front and then finds himself enmeshed in a worldwide political network. Based on the book "In Hitler's Shadow" by Yaron Svoray and Nick Taylor. **102m/C VHS.** Oliver Platt, Arliss Howard, Peter Riegert, Alan King, Tony Haygarth, Michael Byrne, Julian Glover, Alex Kingston; **D:** John MacKenzie; **W:** Guy Andrews; **M:** Hal Lindes. CABLE

Infinity 1996 (PG) Based on memoirs covering the early years of Nobel Prize-winning physicist Richard Feynman (Broderick) and his romance with aspiring artist Arline Greenbaum (Arquette). They marry despite the fact that Arline is diagnosed with tuberculosis, at this time in the '30s a contagious and incurable disease. Richard's recruited to work on the Manhattan Project at Los Alamos, New Mexico, and the narrative travels between his scientific endeavors and Arline's worsening illness in an Albuquerque hospital. Problem is it's neither a character study or a love story but a weak combo. Directing debut of Broderick; screenplay is written by his mother. **119m/C VHS, DVD.** Matthew Broderick, Patricia Arquette, James LeGros, Peter Riegert, Dori Brenner, Peter Michael Goetz, Zeljko Ivanek; **D:** Matthew Broderick; **W:** Patricia Broderick; **C:** Toyomichi Kurita; **M:** Bruce Broughton.

The Informant 1997 (R) In 1983, ex-IRA soldier Gingy McAnally (Brophy) has been tracked down by his cohorts and blackmailed (with threats to his family) into assassinating a Belfast judge. Recognized by British army officer Ferris (Elwes), Gingy is quickly arrested and interrogated by ruthless inspector Rennie (Dalton), who puts the pressure on Gingy to give up his comrades in exchange for immunity. Moved to a safe house, hapless Gingy has to live with being an informant and stay alive long enough to testify. Based on the novel "Field of Blood" by Gerald Seymour. **106m/C VHS.** *IR* Anthony Brophy, Timothy Dalton, Cary Elwes, Sean McGinley, Maria Lennon, John Kavanagh, Frankie McCafferty, Stuart Graham; **D:** Jim McBride; **W:** Nicholas Meyer; **C:** Alfonso Beato.

The Informer 1929 Hanson wants to flee Ireland's poverty for America, using the reward money he gets for turning in an IRA comrade. But things don't turn out as planned and instead he's haunted by the guilt of his betrayal. Based on the novel by Liam O'Flaherty and filmed to much greater effect by John Ford in 1935. **83m/B VHS.** *GB* Lars Hanson, Lya de Putti, Warwick Ward, Dennis Wynham; **D:** Arthur Robison; **W:** Benn W. Levy, Rolfe E. Vanlo.

The Informer 1935 Based on Liam O'Flaherty's novel about the Irish Sinn Fein Rebellion of 1922, it tells the story of a hard-drinking Dublin man (McLaglen) who informs on a friend (a member of the Irish Republican Army) in order to collect a 20-pound reward. When his "friend" is killed during capture, he goes on a drinking spree instead of using the money, as planned, for passage to America. Director Ford allowed McLaglen to improvise his lines during the trial scene in order to enhance the realism, leading to much excruciating suspense. Wonderful score. **91m/B VHS, DVD.** Victor McLaglen, Heather Angel, Wallace Ford, Margot Grahame, Joseph (Joe) Sawyer, Preston Foster, Una O'Connor, J.M. Kerrigan, Donald Meek; **D:** John Ford; **W:** Dudley Nichols; **M:** Max Steiner. Oscars '35: Actor (McLaglen), Director (Ford), Screenplay, Score; N.Y. Film Critics '35: Director (Ford), Film.

Infra-Man WOOF! *The Super Inframan; The Infra Superman* 1976 (PG) If you're looking for a truly bad, hokey flick, this could be it. Infra-man is a superhero who must rescue the galaxy from the clutches of the evil Princess Dragon Mom and her army of prehistoric monsters. Outlandish dialogue (delivered straight) combines with horrible special effects and costumes to create what may well be one of the best camp classics to date. Poorly dubbed in English. **92m/C VHS, DVD.** *HK* Li Hsiu-hsien, Wang Hsieh, Yuan Man-tzu, Terry Liu, Tsen Shu-yi, Huang Chien-lung, Lu Sheng; **D:** Hua-Shan; **W:** Kuang Ni.

Inherit the Wind 1960 Powerful courtroom drama, based on the Broadway play, is actually a fictionalized version of the infamous Scopes "Monkey Trial" of 1925. Tracy is the defense attorney for the schoolteacher on trial for teaching Darwin's Theory of Evolution to a group of students in a small town ruled by religion. March is the prosecutor seeking to put the teacher behind bars and restore religion to the schools. **128m/B VHS, DVD.** Spencer Tracy, Fredric March, Florence Eldridge, Gene Kelly, Dick York, Donna Anderson, Harry (Henry) Morgan, Elliott Reid, Philip Coolidge, Claude Akins, Noah Beery Jr., Norman Fell; **D:** Stanley Kramer; **W:** Nedrick Young, Harold Jacob Smith; **C:** Ernest Laszlo; **M:** Ernest Gold. Berlin Intl. Film Fest. '60: Actor (March).

Inherit the Wind 1999 (PG) Adaptation of the 1955 play by Jerome Lawrence and Robert E. Lee, previously filmed in 1960 and based on the 1925 Scopes Monkey Trial. Tennessee science teacher Bertram Cates (Tom Everett Scott) is being prosecuted for teaching evolution. Agnostic attorney Henry Drummond (Lemmon) comes to town to defend Cates against respected, conservative prosecutor Matthew Harrison Brady (George C. Scott) who wants to keep religious teachings in the school. **113m/C VHS.** Jack Lemmon, George C. Scott, Tom Everett Scott, Piper Laurie, Beau Bridges, John Cullum, Kathryn Morris, Lane Smith, Brad Greenquist, David Wells, Royce D. Applegate, Dirk Blocker, Russ Tamblyn, Steve Monroe; **D:** Daniel Petrie; **W:** Nedrick Young, Harold Jacob Smith; **C:** James Bartle; **M:** Laurence Rosenthal. CABLE

Inheritance *Uncle Silas* 1947 Victorian-era melodrama of a young heiress endangered by her guardian, who plots to murder his charge for her inheritance. Chilling and moody story based on a novel by Sheridan Le Fanu. **103m/B VHS.** *GB* Jean Simmons, Katina Paxinou, Derrick De Marney, Derek Bond; **D:** Charles Frank.

The Inheritance *L'Eredita Ferramonti* 1976 (R) Wealthy patriarch becomes sexually involved with scheming daughter-in-law. Tawdry tale is nonetheless engaging. **121m/C VHS, DVD.** *IT* Anthony Quinn, Fabio Testi, Dominique Sanda; **D:** Mauro Bolognini; **W:** Sergio Bazzini; **C:** Ennio Guarnieri; **M:** Ennio Morricone. Cannes '76: Actress (Sanda).

The Inheritance *Arven* 2003 Christoffer (Thomsen) is bullied by his manipulative mother Annelise (Norby) to take over the family's near-bankrupt steel company in Copenhagen after his father commits suicide. Doing this means making hard decisions, both personally and professionally, that torment Christoffer and cause serious problems within his family. Danish and Swedish with subtitles. **115m/C DVD.** *CZ* Ulrich Thomsen, Ghita Norby, Lisa Werlinder, Lars Brygmann, Karina Skands; **D:** Per Fly; **W:** Per Fly, Kim Leona; **C:** Harald Gunnar Paalgard.

The Inheritor 1990 (R) Set in a small New England town, this mystery centers on the death of a young woman and her sister's attempts to uncover the murderer. The local celebrity, a writer, seems to be at the heart of the mystery and the sister finds herself growing interested. Keeps you guessing. **83m/C VHS.** Dan Haggerty; **D:** Brian Savegar.

The Inheritors 1982 Not-too-subtle tale of a young German boy who becomes involved with a Nazi youth group as his home life deteriorates. Heavy-going anti-fascism creates more message than entertainment. In German with English subtitles or dubbed. **89m/C VHS, DVD.** *GE* Nikolas Vogel, Roger Schauer, Klaus Novak, Johanna Tomek; **D:** Walter Bannert; **W:** Walter Bannert.

The Inheritors *Die Siebtelbauern* 1998 (R) Seven peasants in 1930s rural Austria unexpectedly inherit the farm they've been working from its misanthropic owner, who was murdered by an elderly peasant woman. The foreman (Pruckner) tries to bully the others to sell the farm to the neighboring gentry, Danniger (Wildgruber). When they refuse, the twosome try to sabotage the property, which leads to the foreman's death and places the peasants in the murderous path of the intolerant locals. German with subtitles. **94m/C VHS, DVD.** *GE* Tito Pruckner, Ulrich Wildgruber, Simon Schwarz, Sophie Rois, Lars Rudolph, Julia Gschnitzer; **D:** Stefan Ruzowitzky; **W:** Stefan Ruzowitzky; **C:** Peter von Haller.

Inhibition 1976 A beautiful heiress has lots of sex with different people in exotic locales. Softcore soap. **90m/C VHS.** *IT* Claudine Beccaire, Ilona Staller; **D:** Paolo Poeti; **W:** Adriano Belli; **C:** Giancarlo Ferrando; **M:** Guido de Angelis, Maurizio de Angelis.

Inhumanity 2000 Serial killer thriller is indescribably inept. Though the lead performances are mostly all right, supporting work is amateur. The film is padded with shots of traffic and buildings in Dallas. Lighting, writing, and directing are substandard. **90m/C DVD.** Todd Bridges, Faizon Love, Carl Jackson, Georgia Foy, Billy Davis; **D:** Carl Jackson; **W:** Carl Jackson; **C:** Kurt Ugland; **M:** Damon Criswell.

Inhumanoid WOOF! *Roger Corman Presents: Inhumanoid; Circuit Breaker* 1996 (R) Violent sci-fier focusing on an android's unexpected obsession with his creator's wife. The lady doesn't share the passion (and the scientist isn't too happy either). Made for cable. **86m/C VHS.** Richard Grieco, Corbin Bernsen, Lara Harris, Edie McClurg, Robin Gammell; **D:** Victoria Muspratt; **W:** Victoria Muspratt; **C:** John Aronson; **M:** Marco Beltrami. CABLE

The Initiation 1984 (R) Trying to rid herself of a troublesome nightmare, a coed finds herself face-to-face with a psycho. Gory campus slaughterfest. **97m/C VHS, DVD.** Vera Miles, Clu Gulager, James Read, Daphne Zuniga; **D:** Larry Stewart.

Initiation of Sarah 1978 College freshman joins a sorority, undergoes abusive initiation, and gains a supernatural revenge. "Carrie" rip-off. **100m/C VHS.** Kay Lenz, Shelley Winters, Kathryn Crosby, Morgan Brittany, Tony Bill, Tisa Farrow, Robert Hays, Morgan Fairchild; **D:** Robert Day. TV

The Inkwell 1994 (R) Quiet teenager Drew Tate finds first love when his family spends their vacation with relatives on Martha's Vineyard. Drew is drawn into the party atmosphere of the Inkwell, the area where affluent black professionals have summered for decades. Meanwhile, political differences between Drew's former Black Panther father and his conservative uncle threaten family harmony. Everything about the film has a sugary aura, with conflicts handled tastefully. Rich directs broadly, leading to some overacting. Film is set in 1976. **112m/C VHS, DVD.** Larenz Tate, Joe Morton, Phyllis Stickney, Jada Pinkett Smith; **D:** Matty Rich; **W:** Paris Qualles, Trey Ellis; **C:** John L. (Ndiaga) Demps Jr.; **M:** Terence Blanchard.

Inland Empire 2006 (R) Lynch has taken his film experiments to a whole new level of weirdness with this digital-video effort. Nikki (Dern) is a married actress who is warned by her sinister new neighbor (Zabriskie), who may be a Polish Gypsy, that she shouldn't take the part in a new film because bad things will happen, but she doesn't listen. Nikki and married co-star Devon (Theroux) are playing characters (Sue and Billy) that have an affair, which leaks over into their real lives. And then they find out that their film is a remake of a Polish movie where the two leads were murdered. Giant talking rabbits and Polish hookers are also involved and there's something about an alternate reality—or maybe Lynch's. **172m/C DVD. US PL FR** Laura Dern, Justin Theroux, Jeremy Irons, Harry Dean Stanton, Grace Zabriskie, Peter J. Lucas, Diane Ladd, Julia Ormond, Ian Abercrombie, Laura Elena Harring; **D:** David Lynch; **W:** David Lynch; **C:** Odd Geir Saether; **V:** Scott Coffey, Naomi Watts.

Inn of Temptation *Hot Sex in Bangkok* 1973 A bunch of bowling buddies take off for Bangkok on an impulsive weekend, and meet lots of Oriental women. **72m/C VHS.** Michael Jacot, Claude Martin; **D:** Erwin C. Dietrich; **W:** Erwin C. Dietrich; **C:** Peter Baumgartner; **M:** Walter Baumgartner.

Inn of the Damned 1974 Detective looks into an inn where no one ever gets charged for an extra day; they simply die. Anderson is watchable. **92m/C VHS, DVD. AU** Alex Cord, Judith Anderson, Tony Bonner, Michael Craig, John Meillon; **D:** Terry Burke.

The Inn of the Sixth Happiness 🌑🌑🌑 1958 Inspiring story of Gladys Aylward, an English missionary in 1930's China, who leads a group of children through war-torn countryside. Donat's last film. **158m/C VHS, DVD.** Ingrid Bergman, Robert Donat, Curt Jurgens; **D:** Mark Robson; **C:** Frederick A. (Freddie) Young; **M:** Malcolm Arnold. Natl. Bd. of Review '58: Actress (Bergman).

Inn on the River 🌑🌑 1962 Scotland Yard investigates a series of murders taking place on the waterfront by the "Shark's" gang. Remake of "The Return of the Frog." **95m/C VHS, GE Klaus Kinski, Joachim Fuchsberger, Brigitte Grothum, Richard Much; D:** Alfred Vohrer.

The Inner Circle 🌑🌑 1946 A private detective, framed for murder by his secretary, has a limited amount of time to find the real murderer. Confusing. **57m/B VHS, DVD.** Adele Mara, Warren Douglas, William Frawley, Ricardo Cortez, Virginia Christine, Philip Ford.

The Inner Circle 🌑🌑🌑 1991 (PG-13) Ivan Sanshin is a meek, married man working as a movie projectionist for the KGB in 1935 Russia. Sanshin is taken by the KGB to the Kremlin to show movies, primarily Hollywood features, to leader Joseph Stalin, a job he cannot discuss with anyone, even his wife. Under the spell of Stalin's personality, Sanshin sees only what he's told and overlooks the oppression and persecution of the times. Based on the life of the projectionist who served from 1935 until Stalin's death in 1953. Filmed on location at the Kremlin. **122m/C VHS.** Tom Hulce, Lolita (David) Davidovich, Bob Hoskins, Alexandre Zbruev, Maria Baranova, Feodor Chaliapin Jr., Bess Meyer; **D:** Andrei Konchalovsky; **W:** Andrei Konchalovsky, Anatoli Usov; **M:** Eduard Artemyev.

Inner Sanctum 🌑🌑 1948 Adequate tale of a young girl accosted by a gypsy who claims that tragedy awaits her. Based on a radio show of the same name. **62m/B VHS, DVD.** Chuck Russell, Mary Beth Hughes, Lee Patrick, Nana Bryant; **D:** Lew Landers.

Inner Sanctum WOOF! 1991 (R) Cheating husband hires sensuous nurse to tend invalid wife. You can guess the rest; in fact, you have to because the plot ultimately makes no sense. Available in R-rated and sex-drenched unrated editions. **87m/C VHS, DVD.** Tanya Roberts, Margaux Hemingway, Joseph Bottoms, Valerie Wildman, William Butler, Brett (Baxter) Clark; **D:** Fred Olen Ray.

Inner Sanctum 2 🌑🌑½ 1994 (R) Jennifer Reed (Swope) had a breakdown and killed her husband in the first film. Now under a doctor's (Warner) care, Jennifer is under siege from her brother-in-law's (Nouri) evil plot to send her over the edge again and claim her fortune. As if that's not enough, Jennifer's also being stalked by a murderer. Also available in an unrated version. **90m/C VHS.** Michael Nouri, Tracy Brooks Swope, Sandahl Bergman, David Warner, Jennifer Ciesar, Margaux Hemingway; **D:** Fred Olen Ray; **W:** Sherman Scott; **M:** Chuck Cirino.

Innerspace 🌑🌑½ 1987 (PG) A space pilot, miniaturized for a journey through a lab rat in a "Fantastic Voyage," is accidentally injected into a nebbish supermarket clerk, and together they nab some bad guys and get the girl. Award-winning special effects support some funnerdy Short, with Ryan producing the confused romantic interest. **120m/C VHS, DVD.** Dennis Quaid, Martin Short, Meg Ryan, Kevin McCarthy, Fiona Lewis, Henry Gibson, Robert Picardo, John Hora, Wendy Schaal, Orson Bean, Chuck Jones, William Schallert, Dick Miller, Vernon Wells, Harold Sylvester, Kevin Hooks, Kathleen Freeman, Kenneth Tobey; **D:** Joe Dante; **W:** Jeffrey Boam, Chip Proser; **M:** Jerry Goldsmith. Oscars '87: Visual FX.

Innocence 🌑🌑🌑½ 2000 (R) Sweet tale of lasting love has postwar teenaged Belgian lovers meeting again 45 years later in Australia. Andreas is an affable widower who finds out his long-lost love, Claire, is living in his town and looks her up. Claire is still married, but soon the old feelings are rekindled between the two and they begin an affair. Film deals honestly and beautifully with the endurance of true love, and how the routinas and expectations of everyday life are affected by it. The role of Andreas was originally written for Kaye, but illness forced him to take a smaller, supporting role. **96m/C VHS, DVD.** AU AU Julia Blake, Charles "Bud" Tingwell, Terry Norris, Robert Menzies, Chris Haywood, Norman Kaye, Joey Kennedy, Marta Dusseldorp, Kristen Van Pellicom, Kenny Aernouts; **D:** Paul Cox; **W:** Paul Cox; **C:** Tony Clark; **M:** Paul Grabowsky.

Innocence Unprotected 🌑🌑🌑 1968 A film collage that contains footage from the 1942 film "Innocence Unprotected," the story of an acrobat trying to save an orphan from her wicked stepmother, via newsreels from Nazi-occupied Yugoslavia, and interviews from 1968 with people who were in the film. Confiscated by the Nazis during final production, "Innocence Unprotected" was discovered by director Makavejev, who worked it into the collage. Filmed in color and black and white, in Serbian with English subtitles. **78m/C VHS.** YU Dragoljub Aleksic, Ana Milosavlevic, Vera Jovanovic; **D:** Dusan Makavejev; **W:** Dusan Makavejev.

The Innocent 🌑🌑½ 1953 L'innocente; The Intruder 1976 (R) The setting: turn of the century Rome, ablaze with atheism and free love. The story: Giannini's a Sicilian aristocrat who ignores wife Antonelli and dallies with scheming mistress O'Neill. Discovering his wife's infidelity, he's profoundly disillusioned and his manly notion of self disintegrates. Visconti's last film, it was an art house fave and is considered by many to be his best. Lavishly photographed, well set and costumed, and true to the Gabriele D'Annunzio's novel, in Italian with English subtitles. **125m/C VHS, DVD.** IT Laura Antonelli, Jennifer O'Neill, Giancarlo Giannini, Didier Haudepin, Marc Porel; **D:** Luchino Visconti, Suso Cecchi D'Amico; **C:** Pasqualino De Santis.

The Innocent 🌑🌑½ 1993 (R) Cold War thriller has naive British engineer Leonard Markham (Scott) sent to Berlin in 1955 by Brits who are warily cooperating with the U.S. forces. He's turned over to CIA operator Bob Glass (Hopkins) and asked to intercept communications between East Germany and the Soviet Union. Glass continually warns Markham not to trust anyone, including Varia (Rossellini), the married German woman with whom he begins an affair. Failure to build necessary suspense and performances leads to disappointing one-note display. Based on the novel by McEwan. **97m/C VHS, DVD.** GE GB Anthony Hopkins, Campbell Scott, Isabella Rossellini, Hart Bochner, James Grant, Jeremy Sinden, Ronald Nitschke; **D:** John Schlesinger; **W:** Ian McEwan; **M:** Gerald Gouriet.

Innocent Blood 🌑🌑 1992 (R) A mediocre modern-day vampire/gangster combo with the beautiful (though red-eyed) Parillaud as the woman with a taste for someone "Italian." Unfortunately, she doesn't finish off her latest meal—mobster Loggia—who finds being undead very useful to his vicious work. LaPaglia plays the bewildered, love-struck cop involved with the vamp. Parillaud appears nude in several scenes and the gore and violence are stomach-turning. **112m/C VHS, DVD.** Anne Parillaud, Anthony LaPaglia, Robert Loggia, David Proval, Don Rickles, Rocco Sisto, Kim Coates, Chazz Palminteri, Angela Bassett, Tom Savini, Frank Oz, Forrest J Ackerman, Sam Raimi, Dario Argento, Linnea Quigley; **D:** John Landis; **W:** Michael Wolk; **C:** Mac Ahlberg; **M:** Ira Newborn.

Innocent Lies 🌑🌑½ 1995 (R) In 1938, British policeman Alan Cross (Dunbar) heads for an island off the French coast to look into the suicide of a colleague who was investigating the expatriate Graves family. There are family tensions, skeletons in the closet, and some old-fashioned but satisfying stew. **88m/C VHS, DVD.** FR GB Adrian Dunbar, Stephen Dorff, Gabrielle Anwar, Joanna Lumley; **D:** Patrick Dewolf; **W:** Kerry Crabbe, Patrick Dewolf; **C:** Patrick Blossier; **M:** Alexandre Desplat.

The Innocents 🌑🌑🌑½ 1961 In credibly creepy version of Henry James' "The Turn of the Screw." Minister's daughter, Miss Giddens (Kerr), is hired by Redgrave (known only as "The Uncle") as governess to young Flora (Franklin) and her brother Miles (Stephens) at his country estate. Miss Giddens begins to see the specters of a man and a woman and is told her descriptions match that of former estate manager Peter Quint and the last governess, his mistress, whose influence on the children was thought to be malevolent. Indeed, Miss Giddens believes the true evil is that the children are possessed by evil—but is it children are possessed by evil—but is it true or a product of her own hysteria? **85m/B VHS, DVD.** GB Deborah Kerr, Michael Redgrave, Pamela Franklin, Martin Stephens, Peter Wyngarde, Megs Jenkins, Clytie Jessop, Isla Cameron, Eric Woodburn; **D:** Jack Clayton; **W:** Truman Capote, William Archibald, John Mortimer; **C:** Freddie Francis; **M:** Georges Auric.

Innocents 🌑½ Dark Summer 2000 Boring thriller about French cellist Gerard Megan (Nielsen) and her disturbed your-ger sister, Dominique (Kirshner). After the

An Innocent Man 🌑🌑½ 1989 (R) Uneven story of Selleck, an ordinary family man and airline mechanic, framed as a drug dealer and sent to prison. **113m/C VHS, DVD.** Tom Selleck, F. Murray Abraham, Laila Robins, David Rasche, Richard Young, Badja (Medu) Djola; **D:** Peter Yates; **W:** Larry Brothers; **M:** Howard Shore.

Innocent Prey 🌑🌑 1988 (R) When a woman finally summons the courage to bid hasta la vista to her abusive husband, it turns out he's not so quick to say ciao. Definitely not a highlight in Balsam's career. **88m/C VHS, AU P.J. Soles, Martin Balsam, Kit Taylor, Grigor Taylor, John Warnock, Susan Stenmark, Richard Morgan; D:** Colin Eggleston.

The Innocent Sleep 🌑🌑 1995 (R) Adequate thriller that stays true to genre cliches. Homeless drunk Alan Terry (Graves) witnesses an execution (by hanging) from London's Tower Bridge, near where he's bedded down. He's spotted but manages to escape. When he tries to report the crime, Terry realizes that one of the killers is police investigator Matheson (Gambon). Terry then goes to tabloid journalist Billie Hayman (Sciorra) for help but her probing into the death leads to even more danger. **96m/C VHS, DVD. GB** Rupert Graves, Annabella Sciorra, Michael Gambon, Franco Nero, Graham Crowden, John Hannah; **D:** Scott Michell; **W:** Ray Villis; **C:** Alan Dunlop; **M:** Mark Ayres.

Innocent Sorcerers 🌑🌑 Niewinni czarodzieje 1960 Ironic comedy about aimless '60s Polish youth that finds a young doctor having trouble committing himself to his superficial girlfriend and coping with the problems of his cynical friends. Polish with subtitles. **86m/B VHS, DVD.** PL Tadeusz Lomnicki, Zbigniew Cybulski, Roman Polanski, Krystyna Stypulkowska, Jerzy Skolimowski; **D:** Andrzej Wajda; **W:** Jerzy Skolimowski, Andrzej Wajda; **M:** Krzysztof Komeda.

Innocent Victim 🌑 The Tree of Hands 1990 (R) Convoluted tale of revenge and madness. Bacall plays a mad grandmother who kidnaps a boy to take the place of her dead grandson. The kidnapped boy's stepfather then is accused of murdering him, and starts murdering others to get the boy back. **100m/C VHS.** Lauren Bacall, Helen Shaver, Paul McGann, Peter Firth; **D:** Giles Foster.

Innocent Voices 🌑🌑 Voces inocentes 2004 (R) In the 1980's Chava (Padilla) is the 11-year-old man of the family, trying to help his mother Kella (Varela) and his siblings survive during El Salvador's protracted civil war. Things are going to get worse since 12 is the legal age for conscription into the right-wing government's army. The horrifying and bewildering events are seen through Chava's eyes and are based on the experiences of co-writer Torres, Spanish with subtitles. **120m/C DVD.** Leonor Varela, Jose Maria Yazpik, Ofelia Medina, Daniel Gimenez Cacho, Jesus Ochoa, Carlos Padilla, Gustavo Munoz; **D:** Luis Mandoki; **W:** Oscar Torres; **C:** Juan Ruiz-Anchia; **M:** Andre Abujamra.

Insanity 🌑 Stripteese 1976 A film director becomes violently obsessed with a beautiful actress. **101m/C VHS. SP** Terence Stamp, Fernando Rey, Corinne Clery; **D:** German Lorente; **W:** German Lorente; **C:** Antonio Ballesteros; **M:** Francis Lai.

The Insatiable 🌑🌑 2006 Shy Harry (Flanery) witnesses a murder by beautiful vampire Tatiana (Ayanna). Since no one believes his story, Harry decides to track her down before she can strike again. But when he gets up close and personal, Harry can't kill Tatiana. Instead he puts her in a cage in his basement, trying to figure out what to do. But she'll die with out fresh blood so Harry has to find a way to keep her fed and satisfied. **103m/C DVD.** Sean Patrick Flanery, Charlotte Ayanna, Michael Biehn, Josh Hopkins, Boyd Kestner, Jon Huertas, Brad Rowe; **D:** Chuck Konzelman, Cary Solomon; **W:** Chuck Konzelman, Cary Solomon; **C:** Mike Washlesky; **M:** Christopher Tin.

The Insect Woman 🌑🌑 Nippon Konchuki 1963 Chronicles 45 years in the life of a woman who must work with the diligence of an ant in order to survive. Thoughtfully reflects the exploitation of women and the cruelty of human nature in Japanese society. Beautiful performance from Hidari, who ages from girlhood to middle age. In Japanese with English subtitles. **123m/B VHS. JP** Sachiko Hidari, Jitsuko Yoshimura, Hiroyuki Nagatos, Sumie Sasaki; **D:** Shohei Imamura.

Insecticidal 🌑 2005 (R) Oy. A science experiment in their scanties. Girls run around in their scanties house-bugged by really bad CGI. **81m/C DVD.** Megan (Nielsen) and her disturbed younger sister, Dominique (Kirshner). After the

sisters' father (Langella) dies, the trio head to Seattle to tell mom (Archer) she's now a widow. The road trip takes a turn for the worst when a judge (Culp) gets killed and Gerard gets blamed. Never does make much sense. **90m/C VHS, DVD.** CA Jean-Hugues Anglade, Connie Nielsen, Mia Kirshner, Robert Culp, Anne Archer, Keith David, Joseph Culp; **Cameos:** Frank Langella; **D:** Gregory Marquette; **W:** Gregory Marquette; **C:** Bruce Worrall; **M:** Michel Colombier.

The Innocents Abroad 🌑🌑½ 1984 Entertaining adaptation of Mark Twain's novel about a group of naive Americans cruising the Mediterranean. Ensemble cast offers some surprising performances. Originally produced for PBS. **116m/C VHS.** Craig Wasson, Brooke Adams, David Ogden Stiers; **D:** Luciano Salce; **W:** Alfredo Silveri; **C:** Eric Menczer; **M:** William Perry.

Innocents in Paris 🌑🌑½ 1953 A group of seven Britons visit Paris for the first time. A bit long but enough ooo-la-la to satisfy. **89m/B VHS. GB** Alastair Sim, Laurence Harvey, Jimmy Edwards, Claire Bloom, Margaret Rutherford; **D:** Gordon Parry.

Innocents with Dirty Hands 🌑🌑 Les Innocents aux Mains Sales; Dirty Hands 1976 A woman and her lover conspire to murder her husband. A lover conspire to murder her husband. A twist on the sexy Schneider. Cinematography provides enough moments that are both interesting and eerie. **102m/C VHS.** FR Rod Steiger, Romy Schneider, Paul(o) Giusti, Jean Rochefort, Hans-Christian Blech; **D:** Claude Chabrol.

The Inquiry 🌑🌑½ 1987 A new twist on the resurrection of Christ. Carradine senses a cover-up when he's sent from Rome to investigate the problem of Christ's missing corpse. He retraces Christ's final days to solve the case in this interesting, offbeat film. Dubbed. **107m/C VHS.** IT Keith Carradine, Harvey Keitel, Phyllis Logan, Angelo Infanti, Lina Sastri; **D:** Damiano Damiani.

Inquisition 🌑½ 1976 Naschy is a 16th century witch hunting judge who finds himself accused of witchcraft. **85m/C VHS. SP** Paul Naschy, Daniela Giordano, Juan Gallardo, Monica Randall; **D:** Paul Naschy; **W:** Paul Naschy.

Inseminoid WOOF! *Horror Planet* 1980 (R) Alien creature needs a chance to breed before moving on to spread its horror. When a group of explorers disturbs it, the years of waiting are over, and the unlucky mother-to-be will never be the same. Graphic and sensationalistic, capitalizing on the popularity of "Aliens." 93m/C VHS, DVD. *GB* Robin Clarke, Jennifer Ashley, Stephanie Beacham, Judy Geeson, Stephen Grives, Victoria Tennant; *D:* Norman J. Warren; *W:* Gloria Maley, Nick Maley; *C:* John Metcalfe; *M:* John Scott.

Inserts *♂* 1976 (R) A formerly successful director has been reduced to making porno films in this pretentious, long-winded effort set in a crumbling Hollywood mansion in the 1930s. Affected, windbaggish performances kill it. 99m/C VHS, DVD. *GB* Richard Dreyfuss, Jessica Harper, Veronica Cartwright, Bob Hoskins; *D:* John Byrum; *W:* John Byrum.

Inside *♂♂♂* 1996 (R) Harrowing antiapartheid drama finds university professor and white Afrikaaner Peter Martin Strydom (Stoltz) being held in a Johannesburg government prison. He's being interrogated by Col. Kruger (Hawthorne), head of the prison security force, supposedly for conspiracy against the South African regime. Tortured, Strydom's will begins to break as the drama flashes forward ten years, with Colonel Kruger now subjected to interrogation by a nameless black questioner (Gossett Jr.) investigating human rights crimes, including Strydom's fate. 94m/C VHS, DVD. Eric Stoltz, Nigel Hawthorne, Louis Gossett Jr.; *D:* Arthur Penn; *W:* Bima Stagg; *C:* Jan Weincke; *M:* Robert Levin. CABLE

Inside *♂½* 2006 Reclusive director (D'Agosto) likes to spy on people. He follows folks to observe their daily routines and becomes extremely interested in Alice (White) and Mark (Kilner) Smith because of the sadness they project. Alex goes too far and is caught in their home but the Smiths don't call the cops. Seems their only child—a son—has died and Alex looks like him. They start to bond (Alex's own parents are dead) and when he's in a car accident, the Smiths take him in to recover. Only the grieving Alice is now convinced that Alex IS her son returned from the grave and won't ever let him leave. Despite Meester's prominence on the box art, she only has a small role as a kleptomaniac, would-be friend of Alex's. 103m/C DVD. Nicholas D'Agosto, Kevin Kilner, Leighton Meester, Cheryl White; *D:* mahler Jeff; *W:* mahler Jeff; *C:* Michael Marius Pessah; *M:* Jason Brandt. VIDEO

Inside Daisy Clover *♂♂½* 1965 Wood is the self-sufficient, junior delinquent waif who becomes a teenage musical star and pays the price for fame in this Hollywood saga set in the 1930s. Discovered by tyrannical studio head Plummer, Daisy is given her big break and taken under his wing for grooming as Swan Studio's newest sensation. She falls for fellow performer, matinee idol Redford, who has some secrets of his own, and eventually has a breakdown from the career pressure. Glossy melodrama is filled with over-the-top performances but its sheer silliness makes it amusing. 128m/C VHS. Natalie Wood, Christopher Plummer, Robert Redford, Ruth Gordon, Roddy McDowall, Katharine Bard; *D:* Robert Mulligan; *W:* Gavin Lambert; *C:* Charles B(ryant) Lang Jr.; *M:* Andre Previn. Golden Globes '66: Support. Actress (Gordon).

Inside Deep Throat *♂♂♂* 2005 (NC-17) Respectable documentary about the landmark porno blockbuster "Deep Throat." Mixes old and new interviews, newsreel footage, and, yes, full-on, full-frontal clips to tell the story of an enterprising hairdresser, Gerard Damiano, who made for only $25,000, it went on to become the most profitable movie in history, grossing over $600 million. Since Universal produced the documentary, we're thankfully spared gratuitous reenactments. 90m/C *US* *D:* Fenton Bailey, Randy Barbato; *C:* Teodoro Maniaci; *M:* David Kempner.

Inside Edge *♂♂* 1992 (R) Urban crime thriller is a complex yet surprisingly uninteresting story of a police officer who falls for the girlfriend of the drug lord he is chasing. Filled with the standard genre violence. 84m/C VHS. Michael Madsen, Richard Lynch, Rosie Vela, Tony Peck, Conrad Dunn, Branscombe Richmond; *D:* Warren Clark; *W:* William Tannen.

Inside Information *♂* 1934 With Tarzan's (the Police Dog, not The Apeman) help, a cop searches out the leader of a ring of jewel thieves. 51m/B VHS. Rex Lease, Marion Shilling, Philo (Philip, P.H., P.M.) McCullough, Henry Hall, Charles "Blackie" King, Jean Porter, Victor Potel, Henry Roquemore, Robert F. "Bob" Hill; *D:* Robert F. "Bob" Hill; *W:* Victor Potel, Betty Laidlaw, Robert Lively; *C:* George Meehan Jr.

The Inside Man *♂♂½* 1984 Double agents struggle to find a submarine-detecting laser device. Based on true incidents in which a soviet sub ran aground in Sweden. Made in Sweden; dubbed. 90m/C VHS, DVD. *SW* Dennis Hopper, Hardy Kruger, Gosta Ekman Jr., David Wilson; *D:* Tom Clegg; *W:* Alan Plater; *C:* Jorgen Persson; *M:* Stefan Nilsson.

Inside Man *♂♂♂* 2006 (R) Lee spins the conventional in this over-extended, gabby but well-played crime thriller. Dalton Russell (Owen) and his gang enter a Manhattan bank, apparently to rob the vault. They take hostages but aren't in a hurry to negotiate with slick detective Keith Frazier (Washington). Frazier suspects more is up when icy fixer Madeline White appears, at nervous bank chairman Arthur Case's (Plummer) request, saying Russell must be prevented at any cost from obtaining the contents of a particular safety deposit box. Many twists and turns follow to a satisfying conclusion. 129m/C DVD, HD DVD. *US* Denzel Washington, Clive Owen, Jodie Foster, Christopher Plummer, Willem Dafoe, Chiwetel Ejiofor, Peter Gerety, Daryl (Chill) Mitchell, Kim Director, Marcia Jean Kurtz, Waris Ahluwalia, Amir Ali Said; *D:* Spike Lee; *W:* Russell Gewirtz; *C:* Matthew Libatique; *M:* Terence Blanchard.

Inside Monkey Zetterland *♂♂* 1993 (R) Monkey Zetterland (Antin) is a screenwriter and former actor with an eccentric family. His actress mother is neurotically insecure and a nag; his father is an aging hippie who only shows up at Thanksgiving; his lesbian sister Grace is trying to get over a failed relationship; and his brother Brent is totally self-absorbed. Add to this menage his equally lunatic friends: Imogene, the compulsive talker and exhibitionist; his vicious girlfriend Daphne; and frightening married couple Sophie and Sasha. Meanwhile, Monkey tries to survive amidst the chaos. Interesting cast but lots of camera tricks do not a successful film make and the effort to be hip is all too apparent. 92m/C VHS, DVD. Steve Antin, Patricia Arquette, Sandra Bernhard, Sofia Coppola, Tate Donovan, Katherine Helmond, Bo Hopkins, Debi Mazar, Martha Plimpton, Rupert Everett, Ricki Lake, Lance Loud, Frances Bay, Luca Bercovici; *D:* Jefery Levy; *W:* John Boskovich, Steve Antin; *C:* Christopher Taylor; *M:* Rick Cox, Jeff Elmassian.

Inside Moves *♂♂* 1980 (PG) A look at handicapped citizens trying to make it in everyday life, focusing on the relationship between an insecure, failed suicide and a volatile man who is only a knee operation away from a dreamed-about basketball career. 113m/C VHS. John Savage, Diana Scarwid, David Morse, Amy Wright; *D:* Richard Donner; *W:* Valerie Curtin, Barry Levinson; *M:* John Barry.

Inside Out *♂♂½* 1980 *The Golden Heist; Hitler's Gold* 1975 (PG) An ex-GI, a jewel thief and a German POW camp commandant band together to find a stolen shipment of Nazi gold behind the Iron Curtain. To find the gold, they help a Nazi prisoner who knows the secret to break out of prison. Good action caper. 97m/C VHS. Telly Savalas, Robert Culp, James Mason, Aldo Ray, Doris Kunstmann; *D:* Peter Duffell.

Inside Out *♂♂½* 1991 (R) Hiding in his apartment from a world which terrifies him, Jimmy doesn't feel he's missing much—since he has the necessary women and bookies come to him. He soon finds he's not quite as safe as he thought, and the only way out is "out there." Fine performance from Gould, suspenseful pacing. 87m/C VHS. Elliott Gould, Jennifer Tilly, Howard Hesseman, Beah Richards, Timothy Scott, Sandy McPeak, Diana Elcar, Meshach Taylor, Nicole Norman; *D:* Robert Taicher; *W:* Robert Taicher.

Inside Out *♂♂½* 2005 (R) Bored in the 'burbs. Neighbors suffer ennui until a mysterious single guy, shrink Dr. Peoples, moves in and antagonizes everyone with his peculiarities. Then the new guy gets suspected of murder. Dull, including the last-minute revelation. 95m/C DVD. Eriq La Salle, Steven Weber, Kate Walsh, Russell Wong, Nia Peeples, Tim Maculan, Tyler Posey; *D:* David Ogden; *W:* David Ogden; *C:* Steven Douglas Smith; *M:* Jamie Christopherson.

Inside Paris *♂♂½* *Dans Paris* 2006 Depressed, heartbroken Paul (Duris) moves into his father's apartment after a breakup and immediately confines himself to bed. His father (Marchand), himself divorced, worries that Paul's depression will have tragic results, while Paul's brother Jonathan (Garrel) goofs his way through life and his brother's trauma. All three men struggle to find common ground and understanding in light of Paul's ongoing depression. Tone alternates between fanciful and somber as characters break into song and jump into rivers. For fans of French cinema. 93m/C DVD. *FR* Louis Garrel, Guy Marchand, Joana Preiss, Romain Duris, Alice Butaud; *D:* Christophe Honore; *W:* Christophe Honore; *C:* Jean-Louis Vialard; *M:* Alexandre Beaupain.

Inside the Law *♂♂* 1942 A gang of crooks takes over a bank and must stay "inside the law" and resist their natural inclinations. Lots of comic situations. 65m/B VHS, DVD. Wallace Ford, Frank Sully, Harry Holman, Luana Walters, Late (Lafayette) McKee, Danny Duncan, Earle Hodgins; *D:* Hamilton MacFadden.

Inside the Lines *♂♂* 1930 A WWI tale of espionage and counter-espionage. 73m/B VHS, DVD. Betty Compson, Montagu Love, Mischa Auer, Ralph Forbes, Ivan Simpson, Wilhelm von Brinken, Reginald Sharland, Betty Carter, Evan Thomas; *D:* Roy Pomeroy; *W:* Ewart Adamson; *C:* Nicholas Musuraca; *M:* Roy Webb.

Inside the Third Reich *♂♂½* 1982 Miniseries detailing the rise to power within the Third Reich of Albert Speer, top advisor to Hitler. Based on Speer's rather self-serving memoirs. 250m/C VHS. Derek Jacobi, Rutger Hauer, John Gielgud, Blythe Danner, Maria Schell, Ian Holm, Trevor Howard, Randy Quaid, Viveca Lindfors, Robert Vaughn, Stephen Collins, Elke Sommer, Renee Soutendijk; *D:* Marvin J. Chomsky. TV

The Insider *♂♂♂½* 1999 (R) Riveting and controversial film that caused a real-life snit at "60 Minutes" over the facts and portrayals in the story. After Jeffrey Wigand (Crowe) is fired from his top-level tobacco company job, he turns whistle-blower, claiming his former employers lied about the dangers of cigarettes. Veteran "60 Minutes" producer Lowell Bergman (Pacino) and newsman Mike Wallace (Plummer) pursue the story—only to be shot down by their own network. The fallout causes ethical consequences for all involved. Performances are outstanding—from the chameleon Crowe to the relatively subdued Pacino and the slyly pompous Plummer. Based on a "Vanity Fair" magazine article. 157m/C VHS, DVD. Russell Crowe, Al Pacino, Christopher Plummer, Gina Gershon, Philip Baker Hall, Diane Venora, Lindsay Crouse, Debi Mazar, Stephen Tobolowsky, Colm Feore, Bruce McGill, Michael Gambon, Rip Torn, Lynne Thigpen, Hallie Kate Eisenberg, Michael Paul Chan, Wings Hauser, Pete Hamill, Nestor Serrano, Michael Moore; *D:* Michael Mann; *W:* Michael Mann, Eric Roth; *C:* Dante Spinotti; *M:* Graeme Revell. L.A. Film Critics '99: Actor (Crowe), Cinematog., Film, Support. Actor (Plummer); Natl. Bd. of Review '99: Actor (Crowe); Natl. Soc. Film Critics '99: Actor (Crowe), Support. Actor (Plummer); Broadcast Film Critics '99: Actor (Crowe).

Insignificance *♂♂♂* 1985 A film about an imaginary night spent in a New York hotel by characters who resemble Marilyn Monroe, Albert Einstein, Joe McCarthy, and Joe DiMaggio. Entertaining and often amusing as it follows the characters as they discuss theory and relativity, the Russians, and baseball among other things. 110m/C VHS, DVD. *GB* Gary Busey, Tony Curtis, Theresa Russell, Michael Emil, Will Sampson; *D:* Nicolas Roeg; *W:* Terry Johnson; *C:* Peter Hannan; *M:* Hans Zimmer.

Insomnia *♂♂♂* 1997 After a young girl is murdered in northern Norway, Oslo detective Jonas Engstrom (Skarsgard) and his partner Erik Vik (Armand) are called in to solve the crime, aided by local cop Hilde Hagen (Armand). Engstrom accidentally shoots and kills his partner during a stakeout in the fog and attempts to cover up one killing while uncovering another. He begins to unravel when his conscience and the unrelenting sun cause not only insomnia, but a moral breakdown. His nerves jangle as he comes under suspicion from Hilde. He's also forced into a face-to-face climax with the killer, who witnessed the shooting. Excellent feature debut for Norwegian director Erik Skjoldbjaerg. 97m/C VHS, DVD. *NO* Stellan Skarsgard, Sverre Anker Ousdal, Maria Bonnevie, Bjorn Floberg, Gisken Armand, Marianne O. Ulrichsen, Maria Mathiesen; *D:* Erik Skjoldbjaerg; *W:* Nikolaj Frobenius; *C:* Erling Thurmann-Andersen; *M:* Geir Jenssen.

Insomnia *♂♂♂½* 2002 (R) American remake of a 1997 Norwegian films finds veteran police detective Will Dormer (Pacino), under Internal Affairs investigation back home, sent to a small Alaskan town to investigate the murder of a 17-year-old girl. Primary suspect Walter Finch (Williams) plays a game of psychological chicken after witnessing a moment of Dormer's increasing weakness. Pacino, in service to an excellent script, gives an outstanding performance as the guilt-ridden, exhausted supercop, and Swank impresses (again) as the idol-worshipping but self-assured local deputy. "Memento" helmer Nolan proves there doesn't have to be a letdown after a breakout, ground-breaking hit. 116m/C VHS, DVD. *US* Al Pacino, Robin Williams, Hilary Swank, Maura Tierney, Marion Donovan, Nicky Katt, Paul Dooley, Jonathan Jackson, Katharine Isabelle, Larry Holden, Crystal Lowe, Tasha Simms; *D:* Christopher Nolan; *W:* Hillary Seitz; *C:* Wally Pfister; *M:* David Julyan.

Inspector Clouseau *♂♂* 1968 (G) The bumbling French detective (Arkin) goes to England to help break up a daring robbery ring that uses Clouseau masks to hide their identity. Arkin gives it a fine effort, but he's no Peter Sellers. This makes the absence of the usual band of comic foils like Cato, Dreyfus, and Hercule (as well as director Blake Edwards) that much more glaring. The same writing team reunites, but maybe they needed Sellers as their muse, because the entire script falls flat. 98m/C VHS, DVD. Alan Arkin, David Bauer, Patrick Cargill, Anthony Ainley, Delia Boccardo, Barbara Dana, Frank Finlay, Barry Foster, Beryl Reid, John Bindon, Tutte Lemkow, Bud Yorkin; *W:* Frank Waldman, Tom Waldman; *C:* Arthur Ibbetson; *M:* Ken Thorne.

Inspector Gadget *♂♂* 1999 (PG) Go-go gadget script rewrite! The popular cartoon character goes live-action with Broderick as a daring help break up a daring robbery ring by the evil Dr. Claw (Everett), a naive security guard is put back together by scientist Brenda Bradford (Fisher) with a vast array of grafted-on gizmos. Gadget becomes the world's top detective and discovers that Claw murdered Brenda's father. In his battle against Claw, he is forced to fight his evil robot twin in order to clear his own name. The computer generated effects are eye-catching but far too brief, and Broderick is forced to react lamely to them most of the time. 77m/C VHS, DVD. Matthew Broderick, Rupert Everett, Joely Fisher, Michelle Trachtenberg, Dabney Coleman, Andy Dick, Michael G. (Mike) Hagerty, Rene Auberjonois, Frances Bay; *D:* David Kellogg; *W:*

Inspector Gadget 2 🐾 2002 (G) A female agent called G2 is competing with Inspector Gadget (Stewart) to stop heart throb Cassidy; he suffers from a major bout of bad karma. 88m/C VHS, DVD. French Stewart, Elaine Hendrix, Caitlin Wachs, Tony (Anthony) Martin, Mark Mitchell, Sigrid Thornton, Bruce Spence. *D:* Alex Zamm; *W:* Alex Zamm.

Inspector Gadget's Biggest Caper Ever 🐾🐾½ 2005 Bionic detective Gadget must stop a flying dinosaur, under the control of the evil Dr. Claw, from destroying Metro City. Animated adventure has some slow patches but should still satisfy Gadget's kiddie fans. 70m/C VHS, DVD. *V:* Phil Hamage; *V:* Maurice LaMarche, Bernie Mac, Tegan Moss, Ezekiel Norton, Brian Drummond. VIDEO

The Inspector General 🐾🐾🐾 1949 Classic Kaye craziness of mistaken identities with the master comic portraying a carnival medicine man who is mistaken by the villagers for their feared Inspector General. If you like Kaye's manic performance, you'll enjoy this one. ♪The Gypsy Drinking Song; Onward Onward; The Medicine Show; The Inspector General; Lonely Heart; Soliloquy For Three Heads; Happy Times; Brodny. 103m/C VHS, DVD. Danny Kaye, Walter Slezak, Barbara Bates, Elsa Lanchester, Gene Lockhart, Walter Catlett, Alan Hale; *D:* Henry Koster; *W:* Harry Kurnitz, Philip Rapp; *C:* Elwood "Woody" Bredell; *M:* Johnny Green, Sylvia Fine.

The Inspector General 🐾🐾½ 1952 The filmed performance of Gogol's great play by the Moscow Art Theatre, wherein a bumbling detectives arrive on the scene when a Chancellor's fortune is stolen. Fine comedy, although the Scottish and British accents can be rather thick now and again. 76m/B VHS. *GB* Gordon Harker, Alastair Sim, Miki Hooc, Wally Patch, Steven Geray, Edward Underdown, Hugh Williams, Gibb McLaughlin; *D:* Eugene Forde.

Inspector Hornleigh 🐾🐾 1939 Inspector Thomas Lynley (Parker) just so happens to also be the eighth Earl of Asherton. His new partner is working-class Barbara Havers (Small), who deeply resents what she sees as Lynley's privileged life and again. 76m/B VHS. *GB* Gordon Harker, Alastair Sim, Miki Hooc, Wally Patch, Steven Geray, Edward Underdown, Hugh Williams, Gibb McLaughlin; *D:* Eugene Forde.

Inspector Lynley Mysteries: A Great Deliverance 🐾🐾½ 2001 Inspector Thomas Lynley (Parker) just so happens to also be the eighth Earl of Asherton. His new partner is working-class Barbara Havers (Small), who deeply resents what she sees as Lynley's privileged life and she's not the only one. Still, Lynley is very good at his job and their first case together is a rural murder where a farmer is found decapitated and his traumatized daughter is the primary suspect. Based on the mysteries by Elizabeth George. 160m/C VHS, DVD. *GB* Nathaniel Parker, Sharon Small, Anthony Calf, Amanda Ryan, Paul Brennan, Emma Fielding; *D:* Richard Laxton; *W:* Elizabeth (Lizzie) Mickery; *C:* Jonathan Bloom; *M:* Robert Lockhart. TV

The Inspectors 🐾🐾 1998 Remarkably dull thriller about postal inspectors Silverman and Gossett Jr., who are tracking a mail bomber. 91m/C VHS, DVD. Louis Gossett Jr., Jonathan Silverman; *D:* Brad Turner; *W:* Bruce Zimmerman; *C:* Albert J. Dunk; *M:* Terry Frewer. CABLE

The Inspectors 2: A Shred of Evidence 🐾🐾 2000 Con man is using the mail to assume other identities and must be stopped by our two intrepid postal inspectors. Standard made-for-TV suspense. 95m/C DVD. Louis Gossett Jr., Jonathan Silverman, Michael Madsen; *D:* Brad Turner; *W:* Bruce Zimmerman; *C:* Albert J. Dunk; *M:* Terry Frewer. CABLE

Instant Justice 🐾½ 1986 (R) A professional Marine jeopardizes his military career by avenging his sister's murder, vigilante style. Exclusive action. 101m/C VHS. *GB* Michael Pare, Tawny Kitaen, Charles Napier; *D:* Craig . Rumar.

Instant Karma 🐾½ 1990 Would be comedy depicts young man's far fetched attempts to score his erstwhile teen heart throb Cassidy; he suffers from a major bout of bad karma. 94m/C VHS. Craig Sheffer, Chelsea Noble, David Cassidy, Alan Blumenfeld, Glen Hirsch, Marty Ingels, Orson Bean; *D:* Roderick Taylor.

Instinct 🐾🐾 1999 (R) Primatologist Ethan Powell (Hopkins) has been in the African jungle studying gorillas a little too long, and has turned apeman, killing poachers threatening his primate friends. Since he's been returned to the U.S. and incarcerated in a Miami prison and the insane, he's taken a vow of silence. Theo Caulder (Gooding) is an ambitious shrink who's sent to see if Powell is still (or ever was) a clinical whacko. Hopkins mainly gets to chew the scenery and leave Gooding wide-eyed in his wake. "Suggested" by the novel "Ishmael" by Daniel Quinn. 123m/C VHS, DVD. Anthony Hopkins, Cuba Gooding Jr., Donald Sutherland, George Dzundza, Maura Tierney, John Ashton, Paul Bates, John Aylward; *D:* Jon Turteltaub; *W:* Gerald Di Pego; *C:* Philippe Rousselot; *M:* Danny Elfman.

Instinct to Kill 🐾🐾 2001 (R) Abused wife Tess (Crider) helps put her husband Jim (Abell) in prison after discovering he's a killer. But when he escapes, Tess hires martial arts expert J.T. Dillon (Dacascos) to teach her how to defend herself and waits for her hubby to come after her. Based on the novel "The Perfect Husband" by Lisa Gardner. 92m/C VHS, DVD. Missy Crider, Tim Abell, Mark Dacascos, Kadeem Hardison; *D:* Gustavo Graef-Marino; *W:* Randall Frakes. VIDEO

Institute Benjamenta or This Dream People Call Human Life 🐾🐾 1995 The Brothers Quay's first live-action feature is a surreal nightmareish fairytale based on the 1905 novel "Jakob von Gunten" by Robert Walser. "Jakob" (Rylance) arrives at a secluded institute Benjamenta, which is run by Lisa (Krige) and her brother Johannes (John), to train as a servant. He becomes a favorite of the enigmatic duo and tries to decide what is real and what isn't. Eccentric and wonderfully photographed by Knowland. 105m/B VHS, DVD. *GB* Mark Rylance, Alice Krige, Gottfried John; *D:* Stephen Quay, Timothy Quay; *W:* Stephen Quay, Timothy Quay; *C:* Nicholas D. Knowland; *M:* Lech Jankowski.

The Instructor 🐾 1983 The head of a karate school proves the value of his skill when threatened by the owner of a rival school. 91m/C VHS. Don Bendell, Bob Chaney, Bob Saal, Lynday Scharnot *D:* Don Bendell.

The Insurgents 🐾🐾½ 2006 (R) Thought-provoking look at post-9/11 paranoia and homegrown terrorism. A radical author persuades a small-time crook, an ex-hooker, and an angry Iraq War vet to become a terrorist cell, build a truck bomb, and detonate it on U.S. soil. 85m/C DVD. John Shea, Henry Simmons, Juliette Marquis, Michael Mosley, Mary Stuart Masterson; *D:* Scott Dacko; *W:* Scott Dacko; *M:* Ben Butler, Mario Grigorov, Learan Kahanov.

Intacto 🐾🐾 2001 (R) Samuel Berg (von Sydow) has survived the Nazi death camps and believes that it not only possesses good luck but runs a remote Spanish casino where the patrons bet their good luck against his own in a version of Russian roulette. When Sam steals the luck of his one-time confidante (and earthquake survivor) Federico (Poncela), the man goes looking for a privilege to pit against his former boss and eventually finds Tomas (Sbaraglia), the only person to survive a plane crash. But Tomas is also a bank robber trailed by police officer Sara (Lopez), who survived a car crash. So luck gets pitted against luck—winner takes all. English and Spanish with subtitles. 108m/C VHS, DVD. *SP* Max von Sydow, Leonardo Sbaraglia, Eusebio Poncela, Monica Lopez, Antonio Dechent, Paz Gomez; *C:* Juan Carlos Fresnadillo, Andrés M. Koppel; *C:* Xavier Jimenez; *M:* Lucio Godoy.

Interface 🐾🐾 1984 A computer game gets out of hand at a university, turning the turrets beneath the campus into a battleground of good and evil. 88m/C VHS. John Davies, Laura Lane, Matthew Sacks; *D:* Andy Anderson; *W:* Roger Pistole, John Hoey, Steven Jay Hoey.

Interiors 🐾🐾½ 1978 (R) Ultra serious, Bergmanesque drama about three neurotic adult sisters, coping with the dissolution of their family. When Father decides to leave mentally unbalanced mother for a divorcee, the daughters are shocked and bewildered. Depressing and humorless, but fine performances all the way around, supported by the elegant camera work at Gordon Willis. 95m/C VHS, DVD. Diane Keaton, Mary Beth Hurt, E.G. Marshall, Geraldine Page, Richard Jordan, Sam Waterston, Kristin Griffith, Maureen Stapleton; *D:* Woody Allen; *W:* Woody Allen; *C:* Gordon Willis. British Acad. '78: Support. Actress (Page); L.A. Film Critics '78: Support. Actress (Stapleton).

Interlocked 🐾½ 2006 (R) Another psycho-babe thriller. Pregnant Emily Anderson (Ferguson) and hubby Michael (Trachta) befriend Eva (Harrison), which turns into trouble. Harrison and Trachta previously worked together on TV soap "The Bold & the Beautiful." 94m/C VHS, DVD. Jeff Trachta, Sohae Harrison, Sandra Ferguson, George Alvarez, Bruce Kirby; *D:* Rick Jacobson; *W:* Al Sophianopoulos; *C:* Jesse Weatherston. VIDEO

Intermezzo 🐾🐾🐾 Interlude 1936 Married violinist Ekman meets pianist Bergman and they fall in love. He deserts his family to tour with Bergman, but the feelings for his wife and children become too much. When Bergman sees their love won't last, she leaves him. Shakily, he returns home and as his daughter runs to greet him, she is hit by a truck and he realizes that his family is his true love. One of the great grab-your-hanky melodramas. In Swedish with English subtitles. 1939 English re-make features Bergman's American film debut. 88m/B VHS, DVD, SW Gosta Ekman, Inga Tidblad, Ingrid Bergman, Erik "Bullen" Berglund, Anders Henrikson, Hasse Ekman, Britt Hagman, Hugo Bjorne; *D:* Gustaf Molander; *W:* Gustaf Molander, Gosta Stevens; *C:* Ake Dahlqvist; *M:* Heinz Provost.

International House 🐾🐾½ 1933 A wacky Dada-esque Hollywood farce about an incredible array of travelers quarantined in a Shanghai hotel where a mad doctor has perfected television. Essential ly a burlesque compilation of skits, gags, and routines. Guest stars Rudy Vallee, Baby Rose Marie, and Cab Calloway appear on the quaint "TV" device. ♪Tea Cup; Thank Heaven For You; My Bluebirds are Singing the Blues; Reefer Man. 72m/B VHS, DVD, W.C. Fields, Peggy Hopkins Joyce, Rudy Vallee, George Burns, Cab Calloway, Stuart Erwin, Bela Lugosi, Sterling Holloway, Baby Rose Marie; *D:* Edward Sutherland.

International Crime 🐾🐾 1937 Radio hero The Shadow solves a tough crime in this adventure film. 62m/B VHS. Rod La Rocque, Astrid Allwyn, Wilhelm von Brinken; *D:* Charles Lamont.

International Lady 🐾🐾½ 1941 Sexy musician Carla (Massey) travels the world performing and spying for the Germans in the early days of WWII. Brent and Rathbone are on the American and British agents sent to capture the spy. Things get complicated when Brent falls for her. Romantic spy thriller has its lighter moments. 102m/B VHS. Ilona Massey, George Brent, Basil Rathbone, George Zucco, Gene Lockhart, Clayton Moore, Charles D. Brown, Marjorie Gateson, Gordon DeMain, Leyland Hodgson, Martin Kosleck, Jack Mulhall, Frederick Worlock, William Forrest, Marten Lamont, Selmer Jackson; *D:* Tim Whelan; *W:* Howard Estabrook; *C:* Hal Mohr; *M:* Lucien Moraweck.

International Velvet 🐾½ 1978 (PG) Why did they bother? This dismal and long overdue sequel to "National Velvet" finds the adult Velvet, with live-in lover, grooming her orphaned niece (O'Neal) to become an Olympic champion horsewoman. O'Neal's way out of her league although Plummer and Hopkins give good performances and the sentiment is kept at a trot. 126m/C VHS, DVD. Tatum O'Neal, Anthony Hopkins, Christopher Plummer *D:* Bryan Forbes.

The Intended 🐾🐾 2002 (R) Period melodrama set in steamy 1920s Indochina. Ambitious young surveyor (Feild) heads upriver with his older fiancée (McTeer) in hopes of starting a new life at a colonial trading post. Of course, all is not right when they arrive. They find the post run by scary freakshow of family and hangers-on. Her son, a disgustingly oily slacker (Maudsley), is angry when mom decides to pass control over to a nephew instead of him and starts scheming. While Maudsley's unhinged nanny (Dukakis) creepily fawns over him, he casts a twisted over-the-top horror show reminds at times of Old Dark House thrillers at its good fun for fans of unintentional humor. Takes itself way too seriously, but it's good fun for fans of unintentional humor. 110m/C DVD, *GB* Janet McTeer, Ju-Feild, Olympia Dukakis, Brenda Fricker, Tony Maudsley, David Bradley, Philip Jackson, Robert Pugh; *D:* Kristian Levring; *W:* Kristian Levring; *C:* Jens Schlosser; *M:* Matthew Herbert.

Interceptor 🐾🐾 1992 (R) Hijackers attempt to steal a Stealth Bomber in this action-adventure saga which features virtual reality computer-generated imagery in its combat sequences. 92m/C VHS, DVD. Jurgen Prochnow, Andrew Divoff, Elizabeth Morehead; *D:* Michael Cohn; *W:* John Brancato, Michael Ferris; *M:* Richard (Rick) Marvin.

Interceptor Force 🐾🐾 1999 (R) The Interceptors are a top-secret group of soldier's trained for encounters with aliens. Their latest assignment involves a UFO in a remote community and a species that is capable of morphing into any form. And if they can't clean up the mess in 24 hours, the military will nuke the region. 91m/C VHS, DVD. Olivier Gruner, Brad Dourif, Glenn Plummer, Ernie Hudson, Ken Olandt, Angel Boris, Holly Fields; *D:* Phillip J. Roth; *W:* Phillip J. Roth; *M:* Martin Lazarus. VIDEO

Intermezzo: A Love Story 1939 Fine, though weepy, love story of a renowned, married violinist who has an affair with a stunningly beautiful protege (Bergman), but while on concert tour realizes that his wife and children hold his heart, and he returns to them. A re-make as Bergman's American debut. Howard's violin playing was dubbed by Toscha Seidel. 70m/B VHS, DVD, *I* Ingrid Bergman, Leslie Howard, Edna Best, Ann E. Todd; *D:* Gregory Ratoff; *C:* Gregg Toland; *M:* Max Steiner.

Intern 🐾½ 2000 Satire on the fashion industry is fillac with insider chit-chat and cameos from fashionistas and designers, takes a lot of well-placed digs, and is finally as superficial and throw away as the world it depicts. Naive Jocelyn (Swain) is an intern at fashion magazine Skirt who is desperate to fit in. But everyone is more paranoid and mean-spirited than usual because there's an insider giving the rag's best ideas to archrival Vogue. 93m/C VHS, DVD. Dominique Swain, Benjamin Pullen, Peggy Lipton, Joan Rivers, David Deblinger, Dwight Ewell, Billy Porter, Anna Thomson, Paulina Porizkova, Kathy Griffin *D:* Michael Lange; *W:* Caroline Doyle, Jill Kopelen; *C:* Rodney Charters; *M:* Jim Harry.

Internal Affairs 🐾🐾🐾 1990 (R) Wild, sexually charged action piece about an internal Affairs officer for the L.A.P.D. (Garcia) who becomes obsessed with exposing a sleazy corrupt street cop (Gere). Drama becomes illogical, but boasts excellent, strung out performances, especially Gere as the creepy degenerate you'd love to bust. 114m/C VHS, DVD. Richard Gere, Andy Garcia, Laurie Metcalf, Ron Vawner, Nancy Travis, William Baldwin, Richard Bradford, Annabella Sciorra, Michael Beach, Mike Figgis; *D:* Mike Figgis; *W:* Henry Bean; *C:* John A. Alonzo; *M:* Brian Banks, Mike Figgis.

Internecine Project 1973 (PG) Stylistic espionage tale with Coburn's English professor acting as the mastermind behind an unusual series of murders where industrial spies kill each other, so Coburn can garner a top government job in D.C. Unexpected ending is worth the viewing. Based on Mort Elkind's novel. 89m/C VHS, DVD. *GB* James Coburn, Lee Grant, Harry Andrews, Keenan Wynn; *D:* Ken Hughes; *W:* Barry Levinson. *C:* Geoffrey Unsworth.

Internes Can't Take Money 1937 With the help of McCrea and gangster Nolan, widow Stanwyck is desperately trying to find the daughter her bank robber husband hid before he died. Young doctor McCrea must save the life of another gangster who knows the whereabouts of the toddler. The first film featuring writer Max Brand's Dr. Kildare characters, which later became part of a series starring Lew Ayres and Laraine Day. 79m/B VHS. Barbara Stanwyck, Joel McCrea, Lloyd Nolan, Stanley Ridges, Lee Bowman, Irving Bacon; *D:* Alfred Santell; *W:* Rian James, Theodore Reeves; *C:* Theodor Sparkuhl; *M:* Gregory Stone.

The Interns 1962 Finessed hospital soaper about interns on the staff of a large city hospital, whose personal lives are fraught with trauma, drugs, birth, death, and abortion. Good performances and direction keep this medical melodrama moving in a gurney-like manner. Followed by the "The New Interns" and basis for a TV series. Adapted from a novel by Richard Frede. 120m/C VHS. Angela (Clark) Clarke, Cliff Robertson, James MacArthur, Michael Callan, Nick Adams, Stefanie Powers, Suzy Parker, Buddy Ebsen, Telly Savalas, Haya Harareet; *D:* David Swift; *W:* Walter Newman, David Swift; *C:* Russell Metty; *M:* Leith Stevens.

Interpol Connection 1992 International drug dealer Law Tak is being pursued by Hong Kong narcotics officer Ko Pang, international police officer Cynthia, and bumbling Philippine cop King-Kong. The cop trio reluctantly decide to work together to bring down the bad guy. Dubbed into English. 91m/C VHS. *HK* Robin Shou, Yukari Oshima, Philip Ko; *D:* Philip Ko.

The Interpreter 2005 (PG-13) White, native African U.N. interpreter Sylvia Broome (Kidman) accidentally overhears a plot to kill the corrupt and murderous president of a small African country, a man with whom her family has a past. Tobin Keller (Penn) is the level-headed partner. 128m/C DVD, HD DVD. *US* Nicole Kidman, Sean Penn, Catherine Keener, Jesper Christensen, Yvan Attal, Michael Wright, Earl Cameron, George Harris, Tsai Chin, Clyde Kusatsu, Hugo Speer, Maz Jobrani, Eric Keenleyside, Christopher Evan Welch, David Zayas, Sydney Pollack, Curtiss Cook, Byron Utley; *D:* Sydney Pollack; *W:* Charles Randolph, Scott Frank, Steven Zaillian; *C:* Darius Khondji; *M:* James Newton Howard.

The Interrogation 1982 *Przesluchanie* Grueling depiction of Stalin-era Poland proves that nobody makes anti-communist movies better than those who knew tyranny firsthand. A 1950s cabaret starlet is arrested on false charges and endures years of torment in custody. Banned under Polish martial law in 1982, it circulated illegally in the country until 1989. Janda won an award at Cannes for her transformation from showgirl floozy to defiant heroine. In Polish with English subtitles. 118m/C VHS. *PL* Krystyna Janda, Janusz Gajos, Adam Ferency, Agnieszka Holland, Anna Romantowska; *D:* Richard Bugajski; *W:* Richard Bugajski, Janusz Dymek; *C:* Jacek Petrycki.

Interrupted Journey 1949 A married man runs away to start a new life with another woman. When she is killed in a train accident, he becomes the prime suspect in her murder. Lots of action and speed, but a disappointing ending. 80m/B VHS. *GB* Richard Todd, Valerie Hobson; *D:* Daniel Birt.

Interrupted Melody 1955 True story of opera diva Marjorie Lawrence's courageous battle with polio and her right to appear once more at the Metropolitan Opera. Parker was nominated for an Oscar in her excellent portrayal of the Australian singer who continues her career despite her handicap. Vocals dubbed by opera star Eileen Farrell. Based on the book by Marjorie Lawrence. 106m/C VHS. Glenn Ford, Eleanor Parker, Roger Moore, Cecil Kellaway, Evelyn Ellis, Walter Baldwin; *D:* Curtis Bernhardt; *W:* William Ludwig, Sonya Levien; *C:* Paul Vogel. Oscars '55: Story & Screenplay.

Intersection 1993 (R) Successful architect Vincent (Gere) is torn between his aloof wife/partner, Sally (Stone), and a sexy journalist mistress, Olivia (Davidovitch). Whom to choose? Since he's a completely self-involved boor, you won't care either way. Another retooling of a French film ("Les Choses de la Vie") as a Hollywood star vehicle that doesn't work. Lousy dialogue doesn't help. Does boast some nice location shots of Vancouver, B.C. 98m/C VHS, DVD. Richard Gere, Sharon Stone, Lolita (David) Davidovich, Martin Landau, David Selby, Jenny (Jennifer) Morrison; *D:* Mark Rydell; *W:* Marshall Brickman, David Rayfiel; *C:* Vilmos Zsigmond; *M:* James Newton Howard. Golden Raspberries '94: Worst Actress (Stone).

Interstate 60 2002 (R) Weird road trip down a highway that doesn't exist. College grad Neil (Marsden) is being pressured to follow his dad into the law but thinks he may want to become an artist instead. After an accidental conk on the head, Neil's perceptions are skewed—his dream girl talks to him from billboards and he meets the oddball O.C. (Oldman), who persuades Neil to take a trip in his new convertible on (nonexistant) Interstate 60 to deliver a mysterious package. 112m/C VHS, DVD. James Marsden, Gary Oldman, Chris Cooper, Amy Smart, Christopher Lloyd, Ann-Margret; *Cameos:* Kurt Russell, Michael J. Fox; *D:* Bob Gale; *W:* Bob Gale; *C:* Denis Maloney; *M:* Christophe Beck.

Interval 1973 (PG) A middle-aged, globe-trotting woman becomes involved with a young American painter while running from her past. Oberon, 62 at the time, produced and played in this, her last film. Filmed in Mexico. 84m/C VHS. Merle Oberon, Robert Wolders; *D:* Daniel Mann.

The Interview 1998 Eddie Fleming (Weaving) is a seemingly ordinary bloke who is rudely awakened when armed police burst into his apartment and haul him off for questioning. His interrogators are tenacious Detective Steele (Martin) and his younger partner, Prior (Jeffery). It slowly becomes clear that the cops are interested in a serial killer and that Fleming isn't the only one under investigation. It seems the two detectives are being watched by an internal affairs unit who are suspicious of Steele himself. And maybe Fleming isn't quite as innocent as he protests. 101m/C VHS, DVD. *AU* Hugo Weaving, Tony (Anthony) Martin, Aaron Jeffery, Paul Sonkkila, Michael Caton, Peter McCauley; *D:* Craig Monahan; *W:* Craig Monahan, Gordon Davie; *C:* Simon Duggan; *M:* David Hirschfelder. Australian Film Inst. '98: Actor (Weaving), Film, Orig. Screenplay.

Interview 2007 (R) A White House scandal is breaking, but ace political reporter Pierre (Buscemi) is stuck in Manhattan profiling beautiful but vacuous starlet Katya (Miller). He waits an hour for the unapologetic diva, and once she shows up he's had enough and they arrive. Name-calling ensues and the interview ends with Katya running outside, Pierre on her heels. He's injured and she insists he come to her nearby loft for a cold compress. Here the two posture, drink, flirt and eventually reveal their darkest truths to each other. As in life, both characters are more complex than one initially assumes. Script, camera work and editing are top notch. 83m/C DVD. *US* Steve Buscemi, Sienna Miller; *D:* Steve Buscemi; *W:* Steve Buscemi, David Schechter; *C:* Thomas Kist; *M:* Evan Lurie.

Interview with the Assassin 2002 (R) Ron Kobeleski (Haggerty) is an unemployed video cameraman who needs cash, so Ron agrees when his loner neighbor Walter Ohlinger (Barry) wants to hire him to record a confession. What ex-Marine Walter confesses to is being the second gunman on the grassy knoll in Dallas and the one who actually fired the fatal shot killing President Kennedy. His story turns out to have enough truth that Ron accompanies Walter to Dallas for a re-enactment. But just what did the people who hired Walter want? Character actor Barry is formidable as the ambiguous assassin. 85m/C VHS, DVD. Raymond J. Barry, Dylan Haggerty, Darrell Sandeen, Kate Williamson; *D:* Neil Burger; *W:* Neil Burger; *C:* Richard Rutkowski.

Interview with the Vampire 1994 (R) Portrayal of the elegantly decadent world of vampires and their prey, which features the perverse 18th-century New Orleans aristocrat Louis (Pitt) his latest recruit. Only problem is Louis is horrified by his blood-sucking nature and whines about it for 200 years (it does get tedious). Lestat even makes a child-vampire, Claudia (Dunst), for their own very dysfunctional family but this doesn't turn out well. Director Jordan brings some much needed humor to the dark mix along with some overdone gore. The first book in Anne Rice's "The Vampire Chronicles" was a 17-year film project beset by controversy, including the casting of Cruise (who looks nothing like Rice's description of the character, although Pitt does), leading to an outcry among the cult book's fans though Rice finally came around. Slater replaced the late River Phoenix as the interviewer. 123m/C VHS, DVD. Tom Cruise, Brad Pitt, Kirsten Dunst, Christian Slater, Antonio Banderas, Stephen Rea, Domiziana Giordano; *D:* Neil Jordan; *W:* Anne Rice; *C:* Philippe Rousselot; *M:* Elliot Goldenthal. MTV Movie Awards '95: Male Perf. (Pitt), Breakthrough Perf. (Dunst), Most Desirable Male (Pitt).

Intervista 1987 *Federico Fellini's Intervista* A pseudo-documentary look at director Fellini's love of the movies. "Intervista" is a mixture of recollection, parody, memoir, satire, self-examination and fantasy. Fellini himself is the master of ceremonies in this joyous celebration of the studio community that features actors, actresses, bit players, make-up artists, scene painters, publicity agents, technicians, and gate-crashers. The high point of the film arrives with the stars of "La Dolce Vita" re-screening the Fellini masterpiece at Ekberg's country villa. It's a special moment of fantasy vs. reality in this glorious tribute to cinema history. In Italian with English subtitles. 108m/C VHS, DVD. *IT* Marcello Mastroianni, Anita Ekberg, Sergio Rubini, Lara Wendel, Antonio Cantafora, Antonella Ponziani, Maurizio Mein, Paola Liguori, Nadia Ottaviani, Federico Fellini; *D:* Federico Fellini; *W:* Federico Fellini, Gianfranco Angelucci; *C:* Tonino Delli Colli; *M:* Nicola Piovani.

Interzone 1988 Humans battle mutants in a post-holocaust world. 97m/C VHS. Beatrice Ring, Teagan Clive, John Armstead, Bruce Abbott; *D:* Deran Sarafian, Deran Sarafian; *W:* Deran Sarafian; *C:* Gianlorenzo Battaglia; *M:* Stefano Mainetti.

Intimacy 2000 Furtive and explicit. The English-language pic from director Chereau. Jay (Rylance), is walked away from his wife and kids, is managing a bar and living in a basement hovel. Unhappily married Claire (Fox) has sexual trysts with Jay every Wednesday afternoon, although neither seem interested in learning anything about one another. Then Jay decides to follow Claire and discovers she's married and an amateur actress; Jay then befriends Claire's taxi-driving husband, Andy (Spall). When Claire finds out, she skips her trysts and Jay becomes resentful, leading to more emotional upheavals. Based on two stories by Hanif Kureishi. 119m/C DVD. *FR* Mark Rylance, Kerry Fox, Timothy Spall, Alastair Galbraith, Marianne Faithfull, Susannah Harker, Philippe Calvario, Rebecca Palmer, Fraser Ayres; *D:* Patrice Chereau; *W:* Patrice Chereau, Anne-Louise Trividic; *C:* Eric Gautier; *M:* Eric Neveux.

Intimate Affairs 2001 (R) *Investigating Sex* 2001 (R) In 1929, academician Edgar (Mulroney) is determined to take a clinical, psychological approach to examining the heterosexual male libido. He hires two attractive women, Alice (Campbell) and Zoe (Tunney), as stenographers, but his approach soon goes awry as his subjects don't cooperate as expected. 101m/C DVD. Dermot Mulroney, Neve Campbell, Robin Tunney, Alan Cumming, Nick Nolte, Til Schweiger, John Light, Julie Delpy, Terrence Howard, Jeremy Davies, Tuesday Weld; *D:* Alan Rudolph; *W:* Alan Rudolph, Michael Henry Wilson; *C:* Florian Ballhaus; *M:* Ulf Skogsbergh.

Intimate Betrayal 1996 (R) Mack (Brown) is surprised when ex-friend Charlie (Edson) crashes his bachelor party. Charlie still wants the bride-to-be, Katie (Hecht), and has hired a hooker, Shelley (Conaway), to seduce Mack and then tell Katie all the dirty details. The wedding's off, Charlie makes his play, Shelley confesses the scam, blah, blah, blah. Neither of these guys is worth the time. 90m/C VHS. Dwier Brown, Richard Edson, Cristi Conaway, Jessica Hecht; *D:* Andrew Behar; *W:* Sara Sackner; *C:* Hamid Shams; *M:* Peter Fish.

Intimate Contact 1987 (PG) Top executive discovers he has AIDS after a business trip fling. Powerful drama as he and his wife try to cope. Excellent, understated performances from Massey and Bloom. 140m/C VHS. *GB* Claire Bloom, Daniel Massey, Abigail Cruttenden, Mark Kingston, Sylvia Syms, Sally Jane Jackson; *D:* Waris Hussein; *W:* Alma Cullen. CABLE

Intimate Deception 1996 Artist Charles Michaels is in a crumbling marriage and having dreams about a murder that took place in his past. Into his confused life comes new neighbor John and beautiful model Tina and neither meeting is a coincidence. 96m/C VHS. George Saunders, Lisa Boyle, Dan Frank, Nicole Gian; *D:* George Saunders; *W:* George Saunders.

Intimate Lighting 1965 *Intimni Osvetleni* Professional cello player takes his fiancee to a provincial town to meet his friend, the local orchestra director. Slice of life comedy enjoys the simple pleasures of sharing food, music, and reminiscences, all tinged with melancholy. 73m/B VHS. *CZ* Zdenek Bezusek, Vera Kresadlova, Jan Vostrcil, Karel Blazek, Jaroslava Stedra, Vlastimila Vlkova; *D:* Ivan Passer; *W:* Ivan Passer, Jaroslav Papousek, Vaclav Sasek; *C:* Miroslav Ondricek, Jan Strecha; *M:* Oldrich Korte.

Intimate Power 1989 (R) True story of French schoolgirl sold into slavery to an Ottoman sultan who becomes the harem queen. She bears an heir and begins to teach her son about his people's rights, in the hope that he will bring about reform in Turkey where he grows up to be a sultan. Good cast supports the exotic storytelling in this cable drama. 104m/C VHS, DVD. F. Murray Abraham, Maud Adams, Amber O'Shea; *D:* Jack Smight. CABLE

Intimate Relations 1995 (R) Fifties family dysfunction—British style. Harold Guppy (Graves) is an orphaned merchant marine who winds up in an English coastal town where he takes rooms with the seemingly respectable Beasleys. Stanley Beasley (Walker) is a quiet nonentity whose life is run by homemaker extraordinaire Marjorie (Walters), with 14-year-old daughter Joyce (Sadler) rounding out the family. The needy Harold fits in fine, especially to the sexually hungry Marjorie who's soon offering her boarder unexpected services. But young Joyce won't be left out and then there's a blackmailing tug of war between the threesome. Based on the true story of a crime of passion that shocked Great Britain. 105m/C VHS. *GB* Julie Walters, Rupert Graves, Laura Sadler, Matthew (Matt) Walker, Holly Aird, Les Dennis, Liz McKechnie; *D:* Philip Goodhew; *W:* Philip Goodhew; *C:* Andres Garretton; *M:* Lawrence Shragge. Montreal World Film Fest. '95: Actor (Graves).

Intimate Story ⅃⅃½ 1981 Intimate story of a husband and wife trying unsuccessfully to have a baby, amid the lack of privacy in a Kibbutz. Each blames the other for the problem and tries to escape the problems by focusing on person sex girl. This turns out to be an unwise career move, as she promptly finds herself as fantasies, in Hebrew with English subtitles. 95m/C VHS. *IS* Chava Alberstein, Alex Peleg; *D:* Israel Nadav Levitan.

Intimate Stranger ⅃½ 1991 (R) Sexy, would-be rock star by day, Harry sets out in search of a steadier source of income. Rather than wait on tables all day, she chooses instead to become a phone-sex girl. This turns out to be an unwise career move, as she promptly finds herself can't take "no" for an answer. Will Debbie be able to shake this loser, or will he put a permanent end to her life-long dreams? 96m/C VHS. Deborah Harry, James Russo, Tim Thomerson, Paige French, Grace Zabriskie; *D:* Allan Holzman.

Intimate Strangers ⅃⅃½ 1977 Taut expose on battering and its effects on the family. Weaver and Struthers outshine the material, but the finest performer is irascible aged father. 96m/C VHS. Dennis Weaver, Sally Struthers, Quinn Cummings, Tyne Daly, Larry Hagman, Rhea Perlman. *Cameos:* Melvyn Douglas; *D:* John Llewellyn Moxey. TV

Intimate Strangers ⅃⅃⅃½ *Confidences trop intimes* 2004 (R) French suspense thriller a mysterious Man in Black. his office by a beautiful woman named Anna (Bonnaire), who begins to unload her personal problems, mistaking him for a therapist. William, who is actually a tax consultant, is bewildered but also drawn into Anna's world. Stylish and sophisticated flick excellent makes use of two very talented and mesmerizing leads. 104m/C VHS, DVD. Sandrine Bonnaire, Fabrice Luchini, Michel Duchaussoy, Anne Brochet, Gilbert Melki, Helene Surgere, Urbain Cancellier, Laurent Gamelon; *D:* Patrice Leconte; *W:* Patrice Leconte, Jerome Tonnerre; *C:* Eduardo Serra; *M:* Pascal Esteve.

Into the Badlands ⅃⅃ 1992 (R) Mild thriller presents three suspense tales in "Twilight Zone" fashion, linked by the appearance of a mysterious Man in Black. It's not Johnny Cash, but Dern as a sinister bounty hunter in the old west, who inspires strange events on the trail. 89m/C VHS, DVD. Bruce Dern, Mariel Hemingway, Helen Hunt, Dylan McDermott, Lisa Pelikan, Andrew Robinson; *D:* Sam Pillsbury. *W:* Dick Beebe, Marjorie David, Gordon Dawson. CABLE

Into the Blue ⅃⅃ 2005 (PG-13) Sam (Alba) works for an entertainment venture, robbing aboard in a bikini and feeding sharks all day. Jared (Walker) has a similar affinity to water, earning his keep as a scuba instructor. Together they hunt for buried treasure, instead finding a cocaine stash buried at the bottom of the ocean in a crashed plane. Of course, the drug dealers aren't too happy to have them sniffing around the goods. Amazingly, there is a bit of a plot behind what first appears to be a video swimsuit catalog. Sure, attractive young people in bathing suits are the focus, but flick surprises with a decent dose of adventure, action, suspense, and some interesting underwater scenes. 110m/C VHS, Blu-ray Disc, UMD. *US* Paul Walker, Jessica Alba, Scott Caan, Ashley Scott, Josh Brolin, James Frain, Tyson Beckford.

Into the Blue ⅃⅃½ 1997 Harry Barnett (Thaw) is a bankrupt businessman now working as a caretaker at a friend's estate on the Greek isle of Rhodes. He has a one-nighter with young English woman Heather Mallender (Cruttenden) and when she mysteriously disappears, Harry becomes a suspect. Then he learns she was investigating the drowning death of her sister, which involves people Harry knows, and he returns to London to try and sort out the mess he's in. 112m/C VHS. GB John Thaw, Abigail Cruttenden, Celia Imrie; *D:* Jack Gold. TV

Into the Sun ⅃½ 1992 (R) Hall plays a Hollywood star who encounters real-life danger while hanging out with an Air Force pilot (Pare) to prepare for an upcoming role. Spectacular aerial scenes steal the show, which isn't bad for an otherwise lackluster movie. 101m/C VHS. Anthony Michael Hall, Michael Pare, Terry Kiser, Deborah Maria Moore; *D:* Fritz Kiersch; *M:* Patrick Doyle.

Into the West ⅃⅃⅃ 1992 (PG) Enchanting horse tale set amid the mystic isle of Eire. Brooding, drunken Riley (Byrne), once the leader of a band of travellers (the Irish version of gypsies), leaves the road after his wife's death and settles in a Dublin slum with his two boys. The boys are enraptured when their grandfather turns up with a beautiful white horse, but their happiness is shattered when the police take it away. Boys and horse eventually escape in a wild ride across Ireland and into the west. Spiritual and mythic, with an awe-inspiring performance by the horse. Fitzgerald and Conroy make a run at best performances by kids, while Byrne and Berkin shine in small parts as sibling travellers. 97m/C VHS, DVD. IR Gabriel Byrne, Ellen Barkin, Ciaran Fitzgerald, Ruaidhri Conroy, David Kelly, Colm Meaney; *D:* Mike Newell; *W:* Jim Sheridan; *M:* Patrick Doyle.

Into the Darkness ⅃⅃½ 1986 In the world of fashion models, a maniacal, demented killer stalks his prey. 90m/C VHS. John Saint Ryan, Donal Pleasence, Ronald Lacey; *D:* David Kent-Watson; *W:* John Saint Ryan.

Into the Fire ⅃ 1988 (R) Thriller about a young drifter who, against the backdrop of a Canadian winter, happens upon a roadside lodge and diner, where he gets involved in sex and murder. Title gives a good idea of what to do with this one. 88m/C VHS, DVD. *C4* Susan Anspach, Art Hindle, Olivia D'Abo, Lee Montgomery; *D:* Graeme Campbell.

Into the Homeland ⅃⅃ 1987 Seasoned ex-cop (Boothe) infiltrates a white supremacist group which had kidnapped his teenage daughter. Failed "message" about neo-nazi ethics, but good confrontation between Boothe and his son (Howell) make this so-so viewing. 95m/C VHS. Powers Boothe, C. Thomas Howell, Paul LeMat; *D:* Leslie Linka Glatter. CABLE

Into the Night ⅃⅃ 1985 (R) Cerebral, off-beat thriller about a middle-aged, jilted deadbeat (Goldblum), who meets a beautiful woman (Pfeiffer) when she suddenly drops onto the hood of his car, with a relentless gang of Iranians pursuing. During their search through L.A. and other parts of California for the one person who can help her out of this mess, a whole crew of Hollywood directors make cameo appearances, making this a delight for film buffs, but occasionally tedious for general audiences. B.B. King sings the title song. 115m/C VHS, DVD. Jeff Goldblum, Michelle Pfeiffer, David Bowie, Carl Perkins, Richard Farnsworth, Dan Aykroyd, Paul Mazursky, Roger Vadim, Irene Papas, Bruce McGill, Vera Miles, Clu Gulager, Don Steel, Kathryn Harrold; *Cameos:* Jim Henson, Paul Bartel, David Cronenberg, Jack Arnold, Jonathan Demme, Lawrence Kasdan, Amy Heckerling, Donald Siegel, Richard Franklin, Colin Higgins, Andrew Marton; *D:* John Landis; *W:* Ron Koslow; *M:* Ira Newborn.

Intolerable Cruelty ⅃⅃½ 2003 (PG-13) The Coens are back with another impeccably cast and written comedy. This time they tackle the genre of screwball comedy, with the formidable help of stars Clooney and Zeta-Jones. He is Miles Massey, an unbeatable divorce attorney, and she's Marilyn Rexroth, a gold-digging serial divorcee. They meet when Miles is hired by Marilyn's soon-to-be-ex, Rex, who's been caught cheating but doesn't want to pay up. When Miles beats her out of her settlement, they begin a dance of mutual attraction and escalating acts of...well, you know. In addition to the genuine movie-star spark of the leads, plenty of hilarious supporting characters inhabit the Coens' over-the-top L.A. landscape. Film's fascination with the characters' charming amorality results in great moments, but contributes to a weak ending by draining the warmth that the romance portion requires. 100m/C VHS, DVD. *US* George Clooney, Catherine Zeta-Jones, Geoffrey Rush, Cedric the Entertainer, Edward Herrmann, Richard Jenkins, Billy Bob Thornton, Paul Adelstein, Irwin Keyes, Julia Duffy, Tom Aldredge, Jonathan Hadary, Stacey Travis, Royce D. Applegate; *D:* Joel Coen; *W:* Joel Coen, Ethan Coen, Robert Ramsey, Matthew Stone; *C:* Roger Deakins; *M:* Carter Burwell.

Intolerance ⅃⅃⅃⅃ 1916 Griffith's largest film in every aspect. An interwoven, four-story epic about human intolerance, with segments set in Babylon, ancient Judea, and Paris. One of the cinema's grandest follies, and greatest achievements. Silent with music score; B&W with some restored color footage. 175m/B VHS, DVD. Lillian Gish, Mae Marsh, Constance Talmadge, Bessie Love, Elmer Clifton, Erich von Stroheim, Eugene Pallette, Seena Owen, Alfred Paget; *D:* D.W. Griffith; *W:* D.W. Griffith, Tod Browning; *C:* Billy (G.W.) Bitzer, Karl Brown. Natl. Film Reg. '89.

Intrigue ⅃⅃½ 1990 (PG) Former CIA agent (Loggia) defects to the KGB, but wants to return to the U.S. when he realizes he has a progressive illness. Underground agent and old buddy (Glenn) is recruited with orders to smuggle his former colleague out. Tension continues throughout as murder comes along with the orders. Loads of suspense and twist ending in this nail-biter. 96m/C VHS. Scott Glenn, Robert Loggia, William Atherton, Martin

Into the Wild ⅃⅃⅃ 2007 (R) Director Sean Penn tells the true story of Christopher McCandless' (Hirsch) heady journey from 22-year-old middle class college grad to a state of romanticized independence in wild and free Alaska, where McCandless finds the wilderness as brutally indifferent to his high-minded ideals as it is stunningly beautiful. Adapted from Jon Krakauer's book of the same name, the film follows McCandless from Virginia, through the American West, where he dons the moniker "Alexander Supertramp." Scenes cut between his journey, his last weeks in the wild, and his personal journal entries to effectively paint a picture of McCandless' thoughts and motivations as he tries to drop off the grid. Quintessential American film for adventurers and non-adventurers alike. 140m/C DVD, HD DVD. *US* Emile Hirsch, Marcia Gay Harden, William Hurt, Jena Malone, Catherine Keener, Vince Vaughn, Kristen Stewart, Hal Holbrook, Brian Dierker; *D:* Sean Penn; *W:* Sean Penn; *C:* Eric Gautier; *M:* Michael Brook, Edward Vedder, Kaki King. Golden Globes '08: Song ("Guaranteed").

Into Thin Air ⅃⅃⅃ 1985 A mother searches tirelessly for her college bound son who disappeared on a cross-country drive. Well-done TV drama with a good performance from Burstyn. 100m/C VHS, DVD. Ellen Burstyn, Robert Prosky, Sam Robards, Caroline McWilliams, Nicholas Pryor, John Dennis Johnston; *D:* Roger Young. *W:* George Rubio, Larry Cohen; *M:* Brad Fiedel. TV

Into Thin Air: Death on Everest ⅃⅃⅃ 1997 Based on the book by Jon Krakauer (played in the telepic by McDonald) about the tragic May, 1996 climbing expedition to Mount Everest that resulted in the deaths of eight climbers. 90m/C VHS, DVD. Peter Horton, Christopher McDonald, Nathaniel Parker, Richard Jenkins; *D:* Robert Markowitz; *W:* Robert J. Avrech. TV

Intruder ⅃⅃ 1988 (R) A psychotic killer stalks an all-night convenience store shopping for fresh meat (customers of course). Slasher movie fans should get a kick out of the plot twist at the end. 90m/C VHS, DVD. Elizabeth Cox, Renee Estevez, Alvy Moore; *D:* Scott Spiegel; *W:* Lawrence Bender.

Intruder ⅃⅃ *Les Passagers* 1976 A man and his stepson are terrorized by a stranger in a panel truck as they travel from Rome to Paris. Adapted from a novel by Dean R. Koontz. 89m/C VHS. FR Jean-Louis Trintignant, Mireille Darc, Adolfo Celi, Bernard Fresson; *D:* Serge Leroy; *W:* Christopher Frank; *M:* Claude Bolling.

Introducing the Dwights ⅃⅃ *Clubland* 2007 (R) Jean Dwight (Blethyn) and grown sons Tim (Chittenden) and Mark (Wilson) live in Sydney, Australia, where Jean laments her lost career as a comedienne, which she left behind in her native England after relocating with ex-husband and one-hit wonder musician John (Holden). Self-absorbed Jean works to in a cafeteria by day while attempting to resurrect her comedy career by night, leaving little room for help-ing the boys sort out adulthood. Mark, cocious, Tom, overcoming his shyness enough to pursue romance with blonde beauty Jill (Booth), sparks conflicts. Feel-good comedy drama strikes a good balance in her relationship with John. 105m/C DVD. *AU* Brenda Blethyn, Frankie J. Holden, Rebecca Gibney, Philip Quast, Russell Dykstra, Khan Chittenden, Emma Booth, Katie Wall; *D:* Cherie Nowlan; *M:* Keith Thompson; *C:* Mark Wareham; *M:* Martin Armiger.

Introducing Dorothy Dandridge ⅃⅃⅃⅃½ 1999 (R) Beautiful, sexy singer/actress Dorothy Dandridge (Berry) was the first African-American woman to be nominated for a best actress Oscar for her title role in 1955's "Carmen Jones." Ten years later, at the age of 42, she was dead from an overdose of antidepressants after suffering a lifetime of tragedies—an abusive childhood, two failed marriages, a brain-damaged child, tumultuous affairs, limited career choices, and bad financial decisions. Based on the book by Dandridge's loyal manager, Earl Mills. 115m/C VHS, DVD. Halle Berry, Brent Spiner, Obba Babatunde, Loretta Devine, Cynda Williams, LaTanya Richardson Jackson, Tamara Taylor, Klaus Maria Brandauer, D.B. Sweeney, William Atherton; *D:* Martha Coolidge; *W:* Scott Abbott, Shonda Rhimes; *C:* Robbie Greenberg; *M:* Elmer Bernstein. CABLE

Intrigue and Love ⅃⅃ *Kabale und Liebe* 1959 Luise, who's the daughter of the town musician, is in love with Ferdinand, the son of President von Walter, Von Walter wants his son to marry the Duke's mistress, in order to increase his own influence. Finding their romance impossible, the lovers come up with a drastic solution. Based on the drama by Friedrich Schiller. 109m/B VHS. *GE* Otto Mellies, Karola Ebeling, Wolf Kaiser, Marion Van de Kamp, Willi Schwabe; *D:* Martin Hellberg; *C:* Karl Plintzner; *M:* Wilhelm Neef.

Shaw, Cherie Lunghi, Eleanor Bron; *D:* David Drury. TV

Intruder in the Dust ✍✍½
1949 A small southern community develops a lynch mob mentality when a black man is accused of killing a white man. Powerful, but largely ignored portrait of race relations in the South. Solid performances from the whole cast; filmed in Mississippi. Adapted from a novel by William Faulkner. **87m/B VHS.** Chad Everett, Jr., David Brian, Claude Jarman Jr., Juano Hernandez, Porter Hall, Elizabeth Patterson; **D:** Clarence Brown; **C:** Robert L. Surtees.

Intruder Within ✍
1981 Half-baked thriller about crew on an isolated oil rig in Antarctica who, while drilling, unearth a nasty creature that goes around terrorizing the frost-bitten men and occasional stray woman. **91m/C VHS.** Chad Everett, Jo-seph Bottoms, Jennifer Warren; **D:** Peter Carter. **TV**

Intruders ✍✍
1992 Follows the story of three people who have unexplained lapses of time in their lives which they eventually believe are connected to visits by aliens. The three are brought together by a skeptical psychiatrist. The aliens are your typical bugged-eyed, white-faced spooks but part of the film is genuinely unsettling. **162m/C VHS.** Richard Crenna, Mare Winningham, Susan Blakely, Ben Vereen, Steven Berkoff, Daphne Ashbrook; **D:** Dan Curtis.

Intruso ✍✍½
Intruder 1993 Gloomy story set in a coastal city in northern Spain. Luisa (Abril) spots her destitute ex-husband Angel (Arias) and persuades him to stay with her and her new family, husband Ramiro (Valero)—once Angel's good friend—and their two young children. Angel turns out to be terminally ill and decides to wreak vengeance on Ramiro by reclaiming Luisa for himself. In Spanish with English subtitles. **85m/C VHS.** SP Victoria Abril, Imanol Arias, Antonio Valero; **D:** Vicente Aranda; **W:** Vicente Aranda, Alvaro del Amo.

Invader ✍✍
1991 (R) When a news reporter is sent to cover a mysterious massacre, he begins to realize that the culprits are vicious aliens thirsty for blood...and now they're after him! **95m/C VHS, DVD.** Sean Young, Ben Cross, Nick Mancuso, Daniel Baldwin; **D:** Mark Rosman; **W:** Mark Rosman; **M:** Gregory Middleton; **M:** Todd Hayen. **VIDEO**

The Invaders ✍✍
Erik the Conqueror; Gli Invasori; La Ruee Des Vikings; Fury of the Vikings 1963 Two Viking brothers battle each other and the Britons. **88m/C VHS.** FR IT Cameron Mitchell, George Ardisson, Andrea Checchi, Francoise Christophe, Joe Robinson; **D:** Mario Bava; **M:** Les Baxter.

The Invaders ✍✍½
1995 TV mini is an updated continuation of the 1967 sci-fi series that finds the pollution-loving aliens gradually conquering Earth by allowing humans to destroy their own ecosystem (which we're so good at anyway). Bewildered hero Nolan Wood (Bakula) is trying to get everyone to believe in the alien invasion but since he's just gotten out of prison, it's an uphill climb. Still, the aliens (lead by effectively evil Thomas) would like to permanently shut Nolan up. Thinnes, who starred in the original series, briefly reprises his role as David Vincent. **180m/C VHS.** Scott Bakula, Richard Thomas, DeLane Matthews, Terence Knox, Elizabeth Pena, Raoul Trujillo, Richard Belzer, Jon Polito, Roy Thinnes, Jon Cypher, Todd Susman, Jack Kehler, Elinor Donahue; **D:** Paul Shapiro; **W:** James Dott; **C:** Alar Kivilo; **M:** Joseph Vitarelli.

Invaders from Mars ✍✍½
1953 Young boy cries "martian" in this sci-fi cheapy classic. He can't convince the townspeople of this invasion because they've already been possessed by the alien beings. His parents are zapped by the little green things first, making this perhaps an allegory for the missing Eisenhower/Stepford years. Includes previews of coming attractions from classic science-fiction films. Remade in 1986 by Tobe Hooper. **78m/C VHS, DVD.** Helena Carter, Arthur Franz, Jimmy Hunt, Leif Erickson, Hillary Brooke, Morris Ankrum, Lock Martin; **D:** William Cameron Menzies; **W:** Richard Blake, John Tucker Battle; **C:** John Seitz; **M:** Raoul Kraushaar.

Invaders from Mars ✍✍½
1986 (PG) A high-tech remake of Menzies' 1953 semi-classic about a Martian invasion perceived only by one young boy and a sympathetic (though hysterical) school nurse, played by mother and son Black and Carson. Instant camp. **102m/C VHS, DVD.** Hunter Carson, Karen Black, Louise Fletcher, Laraine Newman, Timothy Bottoms, Bud Cort, Dale Dye; **D:** Tobe Hooper; **W:** Dan O'Bannon, Don Jakoby; **C:** Daniel Pearl; **M:** Sylvester Levay, David Storrs, Christopher Young.

Invasion ✍✍½
1965 A hospital opens its doors to an accident victim, and his attractive female visitors don't seem sympathetic to the idea of a long hospital stay. Turns out he's an escaped alien prisoner, and the alien babes, intent on intergalactic extradition, place a force field around the hospital and demand his return. Early effort of director Bridges, who later did "The Shooting Party." Interesting, creepy, atmospheric, with very cool camera moves. **82m/B VHS.** GB Edward Judd, Yoko Tani, Valerie Gearon, Lyndon Brook, Tsai Chin, Barrie Ingham; **D:** Alan Bridges.

Invasion! ✍✍½
Top of the Food Chain 1999 (PG-13) Deliberately tacky and frequently amusing spoof of alien invasion flicks. Atomic scientist Dr. Karel Lamonte (Scott) comes to the town of Exceptional Vista just after the local TV tower is hit by a big meteor. It's hard to tell if aliens have invaded since the townspeople are so weird to begin with, but they have. And they turn out to be the cannibalistic kind who take to munching on the locals. Oh, and it turns out that TV is the key to the aliens' destruction. **99m/C VHS, DVD.** CA Campbell Scott, Fiona Loewi, Tom Everett Scott, Hardee T. Lineham, Bernard Behrens, Nigel Bennett, Peter Donaldson, Robert Bockstael, Lorry Ayers, Ron Gabriel, James Allodi, Maggie Butterfield, Kathryn Kirkpatrick; **D:** John Paizs; **W:** Phil Bedard, Larry Lalonde; **C:** Bill Wong; **M:** David Krystal.

The Invasion ✍½
2007 (PG-13) In this "Body Snatchers" for the 21st century, Kidman and friends must fight infection by an alien species that takes hold while people are asleep, leaving zombies with no individual thought and no conflict. The only way to prevent the infection is to stay awake, which leads to sleep-deprived paranoia as they struggle to fight the alien menace. Never manages to settle on a consistent theme or tone, as director Hirschbiegel's original version was extensively reshot and recut by the Wachowski/McTeigue team. The end result is a movie that doesn't make any sense, switches from moody thriller to absurd high-impact actioner with no warning, and lacks any standout performances to redeem it. The worst of many versions of the "Invasion of the Body Snatchers" story. **93m/C DVD, Blu-ray Disc, HD DVD, UB** Nicole Kidman, Daniel Craig, Jeremy Northam, Jackson Bond, Jeffrey Wright, Veronica Cartwright, Malin Akerman, John M. Jackson, Josef Sommer, Celia Weston, Jeff Wincott, Alexis Raben, Roger Rees; **D:** Oliver Hirschbiegel; **W:** David Kajganich; **C:** Rainer Klausmann; **M:** John Ottman.

Invasion: Earth ✍✍½
1998 Britain's Royal Air Force and U.S. Air Force officers discover that two alien races have invaded earth and only one of them is amenable to letting the current inhabitants remain. British sci-fi miniseries on 3 cassettes. **270m/C VHS.** GB Fred Ward, Maggie O'Neill, Phyllis Logan, Vincent Regan; **D:** Richard Laxton, Patrick Lau. **TV**

Invasion Earth: The Aliens Are Here! ✍
1987 A cheap sci-fi projectionist takes over the minds of a movie audience. Clips of Godzilla, Mothra and other beasts are interpolated. **84m/C VHS,** DVD. Janice Fabian, Christian Lee; **D:** George Maitland.

Invasion Force ✍
1990 A terrorist army parachutes into a remote region where a film crew is preparing to set up for an action movie. The moviemakers must scare away the terrorists with their smokepots and blanks. Sounds promising, but proves to be as empty as the movie props used to scare the terrorists. **93m/C VHS.** Richard Lynch, David "Shark" Fralick, Renee Cline, Douglas Harter, Graham Times, Angie Synodis; **D:** David A. Prior.

The Invasion of Carol Enders ✍½
1974 A woman, almost killed by a prowler, awakens with an expanded consciousness, and tries to convince her husband that her near death wasn't an accident. **72m/C VHS.** Meredith Baxter, Christopher Connelly, Charles Aidman; **D:** Burt Brinckerhoff; **W:** Gene R. Kearney; **M:** Robert Colbert.

Invasion of Privacy ✍✍
1992 (R) Alex is a psycho prison inmate obsessed with high profile journalist, Hilary. When Hilary interviews Alex for a magazine cover story, his obsession only grows stronger. Then Alex gets paroled and goes to work for Hilary. When he discovers Hilary isn't interested in him, Alex turns his fantasies to her daughter, who has no notion what she's getting into. An unrated version is also available. **95m/C VHS.** Robby Benson, Jennifer O'Neill, Lydie Denier, Ian Ogilvy, John Agar; **D:** Kevin Meyer; **W:** Kevin Meyer. **CABLE**

Invasion of Privacy ✍✍
1996 (R) Some hot-button topics take the thriller route. When Theresa (Avital) becomes pregnant, she discovers her boyfriend Josh (Schaech) is seriously unbalanced. She decides on an abortion but retreats to an isolated lakeside cabin. Mistake—the expectant dad shows up and holds her prisoner until Theresa is too far along to terminate the pregnancy. When Josh finally releases her, Theresa heads for the cops and charges him with kidnapping. He gets a hot female lawyer (Rampling), who turns the media attention into making him a cause celebre for parental rights. Once the baby is born, Josh is also determined to gain custody—by whatever means necessary. **94m/C VHS.** Johnathon Schaech, Mili Avital, David Keith, Charlotte Rampling, Naomi Campbell, R.G. Armstrong; **D:** Anthony Hickox; **W:** Larry Cohen; **C:** Peter Wunstorf; **M:** Angelo Badalamenti.

Invasion of the Animal People WOOF!
Terror in the Midnight Sun; Space Invasion of Lapland; Horror in the Midnight Sun; Space Invasion from Lapland 1962 Hairy monster from outer space attacks Lapland. Narrated by Carradine, the only American in the cast. Pretty silly. **73m/B VHS, DVD. SW** Robert Burton, Barbara Wilson, John Carradine; **D:** Jerry Warren, Virgil W. Vogel; **W:** Arthur C. Pierce; **C:** Hilding Bladh; **M:** Harry Arnold, Allan Johansson.

Invasion of the Bee Girls ✍✍✍
Graveyard Tramps 1973 California girls are mysteriously transformed into deadly nymphomaniacs in this delightful campy science fiction romp. Written by Meyer who later directed "Star Trek II: The Wrath of Khan." **85m/C VHS, DVD.** William (Billy) Smith, Anitra Ford, Cliff Osmond, Victoria Vetri, Wright King, Ben Hammer, Cliff Emmich, Anna Aries, Tom Pittman; **D:** Denis Sanders; **W:** Nicholas Meyer; **C:** Gary Graver; **M:** Charles Bernstein.

Invasion of the Blood Farmers WOOF!
1972 (PG) In a small New York town, members of an ancient Druidic cult murder young women, taking their blood in the hope of finding the precise, rare blood type to keep their queen alive. A real woofer. **86m/C VHS, DVD.** Norman Kelley, Tanna Hunter, Bruce Detrick, Jack Neubeck, Cythia Fleming, Paul Craig Jennings; **D:** Ed Adlum; **W:** Ed Adlum, Ed Kelleher.

Invasion of the Body Snatchers ✍✍✍
Sleep No More 1956 The one and only anti-McCarthy paranoid sci-fi epic, where a small California town is infiltrated by pods from outer space that replicate and replace humans. A chilling, genuinely frightening exercise in nightmare dislocation. Based upon a novel by Jack Finney. Remade in 1978. **80m/B VHS, DVD.** Kevin McCarthy, Dana Wynter, Carolyn Jones, King Donovan, Larry Gates, Jean Willes, Whit Bissell, Richard Deacon, Pat O'Malley, Sam Peckinpah, Donald Siegel, Dabbs Greer, Whit Bissell; **D:** Donald Siegel; **W:** Daniel Mainwaring, Sam Peckinpah; **C:** Ellsworth Fredericks; **M:** Carmen Dragon. Natl. Film Reg. '94.

Invasion of the Body Snatchers ✍✍✍½
1978 (PG) One of the few instances where a remake is an improvement on the original, which was itself a classic. This time, the "pod people" are infesting San Francisco, with only a small group of people aware of the invasion. A ceaselessly inventive, creepy version of the alien-takeover paradigm, with an intense and winning performance by Sutherland. Features cameos by Don Siegel and Kevin McCarthy from the original, as well as an uncredited appearance by Robert Duvall. **115m/C VHS, DVD.** Donald Sutherland, Brooke Adams, Veronica Cartwright, Leonard Nimoy, Jeff Goldblum, Kevin McCarthy, Donald Siegel, Art Hindle, Robert Duvall; **D:** Philip Kaufman; **W:** W.D. Richter; **C:** Michael Chapman.

Invasion of the Body Stealers WOOF!
Thin Air; The Body Stealers 1969 (PG) Aliens are thought to be the captors when sky-divers begin vanishing for it. **115m/C VHS.** GB George Sanders, Maurice Evans, Patrick Allen; **D:** Gerry Levy.

Invasion of the Girl Snatchers WOOF!
1973 Aliens from another planet, in cahoots with a cult kingpin, subdue young earth girls and force them to undergo bizarre acts that may just rob them of their dignity. Save a bit of your own dignity by staying away. Cheap look, cheap feel, cheap thrills. **90m/C VHS.** Elizabeth Rush, Ele Grigsby, David Roster; **D:** Lee Jones.

Invasion of the Saucer Men ✍✍
Hell Creatures; Spacemen Saturday Night 1957 Suburban teenagers (Terrell, Castillo) are detained by a little green man at lovers lane. When they return with police to the scene, only the corpse of the town drunk (Gorshin) remains. Fortunately, the dead man's roommate (Osborn) believes them but the trio must convince authorities before the alien creatures multiply and take over the world. **69m/B VHS.** Steven Terrell, Gloria Castillo, Frank Gorshin, Lyn Osborn, Ed Nelson, Angelo Rossitto, Raymond Hatton, Russ Bender, Paul Blaisdell, Kelly Thordsen; **D:** Edward L. Cahn; **W:** Al Martin; **C:** Frederick E. West; **M:** Ronald Stein.

Invasion of the Space Preachers ✍✍
Strangest Dreams; Invasion of the Space Preachers 1990 Hideous creatures from outer space arrive on Earth with plans for conquest. Led by the seemingly human Reverend Lash, they prey on the innocent and trusting, fleecing God-fearing folk out of their hard earned cash! **100m/C VHS.** Jim Wolfe, Guy Nelson, Eliska Hahn, Gary Brown, Jesse Johnson, John Riggs, Jimmie Walker; **D:** Daniel Boyd; **W:** Daniel Boyd; **C:** Bill Hogan; **M:** Michael Lipton.

Invasion of the Vampires ✍
La Invasion de Los Vampiros 1961 Burrito batfest has Count Frankenhausen doing his vampire thing in a small, 16th century village. Atmospheric sets are highlight. Not a good substitute for No Doze. **78m/B VHS.** MX Carlos Agosti, Rafael Etienne, Bertha Moss, Tito Junco, Erna Martha Bauman, Fernando Soto Mantequilla, Enrique Garcia Alvarez, David Reynoso; **D:** Miguel Morayta; **W:** Miguel Morayta.

Invasion of the Zombies ✍
1961 Bare-fisted wrestler Santo faces off brace of zombies in order to prove that men with short necks can hug other men and still be mucho macho. **85m/B VHS.** MX Santo; **D:** Benito Alazraki.

Invasion U.S.A. ✍✍½
1952 Cheap Red Scare movie using tons of stock footage showing actual bombings and air battles. O'Herlihy is a stranger who visits a New York bar and convinces the patrons that the H-bomb has been unleashed on America, while Mohr romances Castle. Full of propaganda and overacting. Based on a story by Robert Smith and Franz Spencer. **73m/B VHS, DVD.** Gerald Mohr, Peggy

Castle, Dan O'Herlihy, Robert Bice, Tom Kennedy, Phyllis Coates, Erik Blythe, Wade Crosby, William Schallert, Noel Neill; **D:** Alfred E. Green; **W:** Robert Smith; **C:** John L. "Jack" Russell; **M:** Albert Glasser.

Invasion U.S.A. 1985 (R) A mercenary defends nothing less than an entire country against Russian terrorists landing in Florida and looking for condos. A record-setting amount of people killed. Count them—it's not like you'll miss anything important. Norris is a bit less animated than a wooden Indian, and the acting is more painful to endure than the violence. Glasnost saved the movie industry from additional paranoia movies of this kind. 108m/C VHS, DVD. Chuck Norris, Richard Lynch, Melissa Prophet, Alex Colon, Billy Drago; **D:** Joseph Zito; **W:** James Bruner; **C:** Joao Fernandes; **M:** Jay Chattaway.

Inventing the Abbotts 1997 (R) Appealing cast populates this sleepy, bittersweet coming-of-age story set in small town Illinois in 1957. Alice (Going), Eleanor (Connelly) and Pamela (Tyler) are the lovely daughters of wealthy Lloyd Abbot (Patton) who's determined that they'll marry well despite the temptations offered by the two working-class Holt boys. Surly stud Jacey (Crudup) holds a grudge against Lloyd for possibly cheating his deceased father in a business deal and causing whispers about his schoolteacher mother Helen's (Baker) reputation, while sweet-natured younger brother Doug (Phoenix) has his romantic ideals fixed on Pamela, who loves him in return. Not memorable, but not a complete waste of time, either. Based on the story by Sue Miller. 110m/C VHS, DVD. Billy Crudup, Joaquin Phoenix, Liv Tyler, Will Patton, Kathy Baker, Jennifer Connelly, Joanna Going, Barbara Williams; **D:** Pat O'Connor; **W:** Ken Hixon; **C:** Kenneth Macmillan; **M:** Michael Kamen.

Investigation 1979 A Frenchman plans to murder his wife so he can marry his pregnant mistress, guaranteeing an heir. Subtle study of small town people so concerned with their own welfare that the dirty deeds of the lead character might be overlooked. Fine performances and story development make this worth investigating. In French with English subtitles. 116m/C VHS. FF Victor Lanoux, Valerie Mairesse; **D:** Etienne Perier.

Invincible 2001 (PG-13) Herzog's stylized and operatic exploration of a true story is his first dramatic feature in 10 years. In 1932, naive Polish blacksmith Zishe (Ahola) is hired as a strongman to perform at the Palace of the Occult in Berlin, which is owned by showman Hanussen (Roth), who outfits Zishe to resemble German hero Siegfried. Hanussen wishes to be a significant player in the emerging Nazi party but when Zishe reveals himself to be Jewish, he takes it in stride and revels in Zishe's money-making abilities as a "new Samson." But politics and entertainment prove to be a volatile mix. 135m/C VHS, DVD. GB GE Tim Roth, Jouko Ahola, Anna Gourari, Max Raabe, Udo Kier, Jacob Weir, Gustav Peter Wohler; **D:** Werner Herzog; **W:** Werner Herzog; **C:** Peter Zeitlinger; **M:** Hans Zimmer, Klaus Badelt.

Invincible 2006 (PG) True-ish story of not-quite over-the-hill South Philly substitute teacher and part-time bartender Vince Papale (Wahlberg), who gives it a go when new Philadelphia Eagles coach Dick Vermeil (Kinnear) holds open tryouts. Of course the otherwise down-and-out Papale makes the team, much to the delight of his football-crazy buds and the dismay of other players. Papale's on-screen gridiron accomplishments and his real-life experience, but just try not to root for another underdog sports hero. Exceptional cinematography and cool soundtrack make up for any aggeration of his real-life experience, but schmaltz. Greg Kinnear, Elizabeth Banks, Kevin Conway, Michael Rispoli, Kirk Acevedo, Michael Nouri, Jack Kehler, Lola Glaudini, Paige Turco, Michael Kelly; **D:** Ericson Core; **W:** Brad Gann; **C:** Ericson Core; **M:** Mark Isham.

Invincible Barbarian Woof! 1983 A young man leads a tribe of amazing Amazon warriors in a sneak attack against the tribe that annihilated his native village. One of those movies that presumes "primitivism" can be recreated through bad activism. 92m/C VHS. IT Diana Roy, David Jenkins; **D:** Franco Prosperi; **W:** Piero Regnoli; **C:** Pasquale Fanetti; **M:** Roberto Pregadio.

The Invincible Gladiator Il Gladiatore Invincible 1963 A gladiator who saves the evil man ruling a land for a boy-king is given command of an army. He eventually leads the army in revolt when the evil man tries to take over the throne. Plodding with stock characters. 96m/C VHS, DVD. IT SP Richard Harrison, Isabel Corey, Livio Lorenzon; **D:** Frank Gregory.

Invincible Gladiators Woof! 1964 The sons of Hercules labor to aid a prince whose bride had been kidnapped by an evil queen. Laborious to watch. 87m/C VHS, DVD. Richard Lloyd, Claudie Lange; **D:** Robert (Roberto) Mauri.

Invincible Mr. Disraeli 1963 Presentation from "George Schaefer's Showcase Theatre" deals with the life and career of Benjamin Disraeli, novelist, philosopher, first Earl of Beaconsfield, statesman, and Prime Minister. Basically a tribute. 75m/C VHS. Trevor Howard, Greer Garson, Hurd Hatfield, Kate Reid; **D:** George Schaefer. TV

The Invincible Six The Heroes 1968 An unlikely band of thieves run up against the law winds up protecting a small village from marauding bandits. Plenty of action, as you would expect when thieves take on bandits, but with no scene-stealers or sympathetic characters the story lacks interest. Unremarkable. 96m/C VHS. Stuart Whitman, Elke Sommer, Curt Jurgens, Jim Mitchum, Ian Ogilvy; **D:** Jean Negulesco.

The Invisible 2007 (PG-13) Supernatural mystery of no particular distinction. Unhappy teen Nick Powell (Chatwin) is beaten by bad seed Annie (Levieva) and she dumps his body in the woods, but he's not dead. Now Nick's spirit is hovering around, hoping he's found before he does become a homicide case, although he can't do anything useful like spirit writing or move objects. Based on the 2002 Swedish film (and novel) "Den Osynlige." 97m/C DVD, Blu-ray Disc. US Justin Chatwin, Margarita Levieva, Christopher Marquette, Alex Neuberger, Callum Keith Rennie, Michelle Harrison, Ryan Kennedy, Serge Houde; **D:** David S. Goyer; **W:** Mick Davis, Christine Roum; **C:** Gabriel Beristain; **M:** Marco Beltrami.

Invisible Adversaries 1977 A photographer uncovers an extra-terrestrial plot to cause excessive aggression in humans. She and her lover attempt to hold on to their crumbling humanity. Moving around, hoping to make you mad enough to tear something up. Enjoyed a meek cult following. In German with English subtitles. 112m/C VHS. AT Susanne Wild, Peter Weibel; **D:** Valie Export.

Invisible Agent 1942 Hall outwit the Nazis in this third sequel to "The Invisible Man." Especially enjoyable for the kids. Based on characters suggested in H.G. Wells' "The Invisible Man." 83m/B VHS, DVD. Ilona Massey, Jon Hall, Peter Lorre, Cedric Hardwicke, J. Edward Bromberg, Albert Bassermann, John Litel, Holmes Herbert; **D:** Edwin L. Marin; **W:** Curt Siodmak.

The Invisible Avenger 1958 Based on the vintage radio character "The Shadow." A detective who can make himself invisible investigates the murder of a New Orleans jazz musician. The mysterious element successful on radio is lost on film, and only the Shadow knows why. 60m/B VHS, DVD. Richard Derr, Marc Daniels, Helen Westcott, Jeanne Neher; **D:** John Sledge, Ben Parker.

The Invisible Boy 1957 (G) Science fiction story about a young boy and his robot (Robby the Robot from "Forbidden Planet"). Kids will enjoy the adventure as told through the viewpoint of

Invisible Child 1999 Annie (Wilson) is a wife and mother who believes she has three children—only the third happens to be invisible. Her husband and kids go along with her delusions with the hope of keeping the family together but then Annie's delusions, this film is just silly. 93m/C VHS, DVD. Rita Wilson, Victor Garber, Tushka Bergen, Mae Whitman, David Dorfman; **D:** Joan Micklin Silver; **W:** David Field; **C:** Ken Kelsch; **M:** Victoria Rowell. CABLE

Invisible Circus 2000 (R) Coming-of-age drama set in 1976 of a young woman, Phoebe (Brewster), who treks through Europe in an attempt to solve the mystery of her older sister Faith (Diaz), a radical hippie who died three seven years ago. Her Nancy Drew-like sleuthing leads her to the big, bad Wolf (Eccleston) in Paris, Faith's old boho boyfriend, now a bourgeois married. Somewhat unlikely tales emerge about Faith's dealings with German terrorists gone bad and bring Phoebe closer to the truth and danger. Story to'd much like many a late 1960s memory, in confusing flashback. 92m/C VHS. Cameron Diaz, Jordana Brewster, Christopher Eccleston, Blythe Danner, Patrick Bergin, Moritz Bleibtreu, Isabelle Pasco; **D:** Adam Brooks; **W:** Adam Brooks; **C:** Henry Braham; **M:** Nick Laird-Clowes.

Invisible Dad 1997 (PG) Doug Bailly's dad invents a machine that makes him invisible and uses it to foil the evil designs of a co-worker. Unfortunately, the machine isn't perfect, and Mr. Bailly tends to reappear at inopportune moments. When Doug discovers his dad is in danger, he figures it's time to help out. 90m/C VHS, DVD. US Cameron Diaz, Jordana Brewster, Christopher Eccleston, Blythe Danner, Patrick Bergin; **D:** Fred Olen Ray; **W:** Steve Latshaw; **C:** Gary Graver; **M:** Adam Brooks.

The Invisible Dr. Mabuse Die Unsichtbaren Krallen des Dr. Mabuse 1962 Possibly the best of the Dr. Mabuse series sees the mad scientist using an invisibility agent in an attempt to take over the world. Preiss also played the title villain in Fritz Lang's "The Thousand Eyes of Dr. Mabuse." 89m/B VHS. GE Lex Barker, Karin Dor, Siegfried Lowitz, Wolfgang Preiss, Rudolf Fernau; **D:** Harald Reinl. VIDEO

Invisible Ghost 1941 A man carries out a series of grisly stranglings while under hypnosis by his insane wife. Typically bad low-budget exploiter about a fun-lovin' crazy couple bringing down property values in the neighborhood. 70m/B VHS, DVD. Bela Lugosi, Polly Ann Young, John McGuire, Clarence Muse, Betty Compson; **D:** Joseph H. Lewis; **W:** Helen Martin, Al Martin; **C:** Marcel Le Picard.

Invisible Invaders 1959 Short, cheap, and silly aliens-try-to-take-over-the-earth flick. This time they're moonmen who use the bodies of dead earthlings (ugh) to attack the living until Agar can save the day. Carradine has a brief role as a formerly dead scientist. 67m/B VHS, DVD. John Agar, Robert H. Hall, Hal Torey, Jean Byron, Philip Tonge, John Carradine; **D:** Edward L. Cahn; **W:** Samuel Newman; **C:** Maury Gertsman.

The Invisible Kid 1988 A shy teen manages to make himself invisible, a feat which ironically permits him to goad girls' locker rooms. For those who have dreamed about girls' locker rooms. 95m/C VHS. Karen Black, Jay Underwood, Chynna Phillips, Wallace (Wally) Langham, Brother Theodore; **D:** Avery Crounse; **W:** Avery Crounse.

the child. Based on a story by Edmund Cooper. 89m/B VHS, Richard Eyer, Diane Brewster, Philip Abbott, Harold J. Stone, Robert H. Harris; **D:** Herman Hoffman; **W:** Cyril Hume; **C:** Harold E. Wellman; **M:** Les Baxter.

The Invisible Killer 1940 Someone is killing folks by sending poison through telephone lines. A detective and a reporter team up to find the scoundrel by setting up an answering machine that automatically plays back messages to the caller. Bad correction of events leads to a static resolution. 61m/B VHS, DVD. Grace Bradley, Roland (Walter Goss) Drew, William "Blackie" Newell, David Oliver; **D:** Sam Newfield.

The Invisible Man 1933 The vintage horror-fest based on H.G. Wells' novella about scientist Jack Griffin (Rains) whose formula for invisibility slowly drives him insane. His mind definitely wandering, Jack plans to use his recipe to rule the world. Rains' first role; though his body doesn't appear until the final scene, his voice characterization is magnificent. The visual detail is excellent, setting standards that are imitated because they are difficult to surpass; with special effects by John P. Fulton and John Mescall. 71m/B VHS, DVD. Claude Rains, Gloria Stuart, Dudley Digges, William Harrigan, Una O'Connor, E.E. Clive, Dwight Frye, Henry Travers, Holmes Herbert; **D:** James Whale; **W:** R.C. Sheriff; **C:** Arthur Edeson; **M:** W. Franke Haring.

The Invisible Man Returns 1940 (R) A crazy voyeur perfects a serum for invisibility and promptly gets a job as a physics teacher in a high school. Using the same invisibility formula, Price tries to clear himself after being charged with murder. He reappears at the worst times. Get outta here, you maniac. Rifkin used the pseudonym Rif Coogan. 81m/B VHS, DVD. Vincent Price, Sir Cedric Hardwicke, Nan Grey, John Sutton, Cecil Kellaway, Alan Napier; **D:** Joe May; **W:** Lester Cole, Curt Siodmak; **C:** Milton Krasner.

The Invisible Man's Revenge 1944 Left for dead on a safari five years before, Robert Griffin (Hall) seeks revenge against wealthy English couple Lady Irene (Sondergaard) and Sir Jasper (Matthews) by taking over their estate and marrying their daughter, Julie (Akers). He's aided by scientist Peter Drury (Carradine) who renders Griffin invisible. Only problem is he doesn't stay that way. Fifth in Universal's "Invisible Man" film series. 78m/B VHS. Jon Hall, John Carradine, Gale Sondergaard, Lester Matthews, Evelyn Ankers, Alan Curtis, Leon Errol, Doris Lloyd; **D:** Ford Beebe; **W:** Bertram Millhauser; **C:** Milton Krasner; **M:** Hans J. Salter.

The Invisible Maniac Woof! 1990 (R) Price stars as the original invisible man's brother. Using his voyeuristic invisibility to spy on girls taking showers and slaughters students when he is caught. For voyeurs. 87m/C VHS. Noel Peters, Shannon Wilsey, Melissa Moore, Robert Ross, Rod Sweitzer, Eric Champnella, Kalei Shellabarger, Gail Lyon, Debra Lamb; **D:** Adam Rifkin; **W:** Adam Rifkin; **C:** James Bay; **M:** Marc David Decker.

Invisible Mom 1996 (PG) Newly adopted 12-year-old discovers his mom can literally disappear. 80m/C VHS. Dee Wallace Stone, Barry Livingston, Trenton Knight, Russ Tamblyn, Stella Stevens; **D:** Fred Olen Ray; **W:** William Martell, Sean O'Bannon; **C:** Gary Graver; **M:** Jeff Walton.

Invisible Mom 2 1999 (PG) Newly adopted 12-year-old's mom is still invisible. 76m/C VHS. Dee Wallace Stone, Barry Livingston, Trenton Knight, Russ Tamblyn, Stella Stevens; **D:** Fred Olen Ray; **W:** Jeff Walton.

The Invisible Monster Slaves of the Invisible Monster 1950 Special investigators Lane Carlson and Carol Richards battle a mad scientist ready to take over the world with his invisible army. Twelve episodes of the original serial edited onto two cassettes. 167m/B VHS. Richard Webb, Aline Towne, Lane Bradford, Stanley Price, John Crawford, George Meeker; **D:** Fred Brannon.

The Invisible Ray 1936 For a change, this horror film features Lugosi as the hero, fighting Karloff, a scientist who locates a meteor that contains a

Invisible

powerful substance. Karloff is poisoned and becomes a murdering megalomaniac. Watching Karloff and Lugosi interact, and the great special effects—including a hot scene where a scientist bursts into flames—helps you ignore a generally hokey script. **82m/B VHS, DVD. Boris Karloff, Bela Lugosi, Frances Drake, Frank Lawton, Beulah Bondi, Walter Kingsford;** *D:* **Lambert Hillyer;** *W:* John Colton; *C:* George Robinson.

The Invisible Strangler 𝄞½

The Astral Factor 1976 (PG) A death-row murderer can make himself invisible and rubs out witnesses who helped put him away, woman risks her life to expose him when the police fail to see the problem. Very violent collection of brutal scenes. Not released theatrically until 1984. **85m/C VHS, DVD. Robert Foxworth, Stefanie Powers, Elke Sommer, Sue Lyon, Leslie Parrish, Marianna Hill;** *D:* **John Florea;** *W:* **Arthur C. Pierce;** *C:* Alan Stensvold; *M:* Richard Hieronymous, Alan Oldfield.

The Invisible Terror 𝄞𝄞 1963 A

maniac steals a mad scientist's invisibility formula and uses it on a number of innocent victims. **102m/C VHS. GE Herbert Stass, Ellen Schwiers;** *D:* **Raphael Nussbaum;** *W:* Raphael Nussbaum.

Invisible: The Chronicles of Benjamin Knight 𝄞𝄞½ 1993 (R)

Scientist Benjamin Knight is rendered invisible during a terrible laboratory accident. His only hope of regaining his visible form is a desperate search by Knight and his fellow scientists for just the right chemical antidote. **80m/C VHS. Brian Cousins, Jennifer Nash, Michael DellaFemina, Curt Lowens, David Kaufman, Alan Oppenheimer, Aharon Ipale;** *D:* Joakim (Jack) Ersgard; *W:* Earl Kenton.

The Invisible Woman 𝄞𝄞𝄞

1940 Above average comedy about zany professor Gibbs (Barrymore) discovering the secret of invisibility and making luscious model Kitty (Bruce) transparent during his experiments. She tries some romance with Richard (Howard), the guy who financed the invention, and then gets involved with crooks who want to steal the machine for their own illicit gain. A very likeable movie with a good cast. Based on a story by Curt Siodmak and Joe May, the same team that wrote "The Invisible Man Returns." **73m/B VHS, DVD. John Barrymore, Virginia Bruce, John Howard, Charlie Ruggles, Oscar Homolka, Margaret Hamilton, Donald MacBride, Edward Brophy, Shemp Howard, Charles Lane, Thurston Hall;** *D:* **Edward Sutherland;** *W:* Robert Lees, Frederic Rinaldo, Gertrude Purcell; *C:* Elwood "Woody" Bredell.

The Invisibles 𝄞 1999 Likeable

actors in unlikeable roles and a rather pretentious script. Rock star Jude (Goorjian) and supermodel Joy (De Rossi) share more than a romance, they share a heroin habit. So they take off for a Paris flat to kick drugs (what's wrong with going into rehab?). They're spoiled and childish and not much happens that you'll care about. **86m/C VHS, DVD. Michael Goorjian, Portia de Rossi, Terry Camilleri, Jonathan Segel;** *D:* **Noah Stern;** *W:* Noah Stern; *C:* Robert Humphreys; *M:* Jonathan Segel.

The Invitation 𝄞 2003 (R) Clunky

thriller has wealthy writer Roland Levy (Henriksen) inviting six friends to his island for what turns out to be a deadly dinner invitation. Seems after a near-death experience, Roland poisons his guests so they can too can experience the bliss he felt. He promises the antidote—if they'll reveal their deepest, darkest secrets. **85m/C VHS, DVD. Lance Henriksen, Christopher Shyer, Sarah Jane Redmond, Stefanie von Pfetten, Doug O'Keefe, Fred Henderson;** *D:* **Patrick Bermel;** *W:* Patrick Bermel; *C:* Barney Donlevy; *M:* Michael Richard Plowman. **VIDEO**

Invitation au Voyage 𝄞𝄞½

1982 (R) Follows the journey of a twin who refuses to accept the death of his sister, a rock singer. The obsession is played fairly well, but it's a no-twin situation, even though the guy can't admit it. Perversity is played to the point of overkill. From the novel "Moi, Ma Soeur Images," by Jean Bany. In French with English subtitles. **90m/C VHS. FR Laurent Malet, Nina Scott, Aurore Clement, Mario Adorf;** *D:* Peter Del Monte.

Invitation to a Gunfighter 𝄞𝄞

1964 Small town politics change when a paid assassin ambles into town and creates a lot of talk among the neighbors. Like a long joke in which the teller keeps forgetting the important details, the plot grows confusing though it's not complicated. Brynner is interesting as an educated, half-black/half-creole, hired gun. **92m/C VHS, DVD. Yul Brynner, George Segal, Strother Martin, William Hickey, Janice Rule, Mike Kellin, Pat Hingle, John Alonzo;** *D:* Richard Wilson.

Invitation to Hell WOOF! 1982 Tor-

mented maiden has a devil of a time discovering a secret power that can enable her to gracefully decline a satanic summoning. The cliched evil is tormenting. **100m/C VHS, DVD. Becky Simpson, Joseph Sheahan, Colin Efford;** *D:* Michael J. Murphy; *W:* Carl Humphrey; *M:* Terence Mills.

Invitation to Hell 𝄞½ 1984

"Faust" meets "All My Children" in celluloid suburbia. Never Emmied Lucci is the devil's dirty worker, persuading upwardly mobile suburbanites to join a really exclusive country club in exchange for a little downward mobility. Urich, a space scientist, and family are new in town, and soul searching Lucci's got her devil vixen sights set on space jock and brood. Bound to disappoint both fans of Craven's early independent work ("Last House on the Left") and his later high gloss ("Nightmare on Elm Street") formulas. Made for TV on small screen. **100m/C VHS, DVD. Susan Lucci, Robert Urich, Joanna Cassidy, Kevin McCarthy, Patty McCormack, Joe Regalbuto, Soleil Moon Frye, Barret Oliver;** *D:* Wes Craven. TV

Invitation to the Dance 𝄞𝄞½

1956 Three classic dance sequences, "Circus," "Ring Around the Rosy," and "Sinbad the Sailor." For dance lovers, featuring excellent performances by Kelly. **93m/C VHS. Gene Kelly, Igor Youskevitch, Tamara Toumanova;** *D:* Gene Kelly. Berlin Intl. Film Fest. '56: Golden Berlin Bear.

The Ipcress File 𝄞𝄞𝄞 1965 The

first of the Harry Palmer spy mysteries that made Caine a star. Based upon the bestseller by Len Deighton, it features the flabby, nearsighted spy investigating the kidnapping of notable British scientists. Solid scenes, including a scary brainwashing session, and tongue-firmly-in-British-cheek humor. Lots of camera play to emphasize Caine's myopia. Two sequels: "Funeral in Berlin" and "Billion Dollar Brain." **108m/C VHS, DVD. GB Michael Caine, Nigel Green, Guy Doleman, Sue Lloyd, Gordon Jackson;** *D:* **Sidney J. Furie;** *W:* Bill Canaway, James Doran; *C:* Otto Heller; *M:* John Barry. British Acad. '65: Film.

Iphigenia 𝄞𝄞𝄞 1977 Based on the

classic Greek tragedy by Euripides, this story concerns the Greek leader Agamemnon, who plans to sacrifice his lovely daughter, Iphigenia, to please the gods. Mere mortals protest and start a save-the-babe movement, but Euripides' moral—you can't please 'em all—is devastatingly realized. Fine adaptation that becomes visually extravagant at times, with an equally fine musical score. In Greek with English subtitles. **130m/C VHS. GR Irene Papas, Costa Kazakos, Tatiana Papamoskou, Costas Carras, Christos Tsangas, Panos Michalopoulos;** *D:* Michael Cacoyannis; *W:* Michael Cacoyannis; *C:* Yorgos Arvanitis; *M:* Mikis Theodorakis.

I.Q. 𝄞𝄞½ 1994 (PG) Albert Einstein

(the irascible Matthau) thinks his co-ed niece (Ryan) is in need of a little romance, so he engineers a plan to get her into the arms of Robbins, a local auto mechanic. Robbins and Ryan are comfortable in their comic roles, although there's the famous physicist. Plot gets a little farfetched with its central contrivance of making Robbins look like a brilliant scientist, which

---

leaves second half of story flat. However, chemistry between leads is undeniable and you can't help but cheer on the inevitable. Visually pleasing with Ryan costumed in cool, elegant '50s fashions. Filmed in Princeton, New Jersey. **95m/C VHS, DVD. Tim Robbins, Meg Ryan, Walter Matthau, Lou Jacobi, Gene Saks, Joseph Maher, Stephen Fry, Tony Shalhoub, Frank Whaley;** *D:* Fred Schepisi; *W:* Michael Leeson, Andy Breckman; *C:* Ian Baker; *M:* Jerry Goldsmith.

Ira & Abby 𝄞𝄞 2006 (R) Jewish Ira

(Messina) is the neurotic, underachieving son of two analysts (Klein, Light) while shiksa Abby (Westfeldt) is a free spirit, thanks to her hipster parents (Willard, Conroy). They impulsively get married but discover exes and in-laws, affairs and insecurities, and too many therapists cause them lots of trouble. Manhattan looks great, the parents are great, but the whole is Woody Allen-lite via an episode of "Dharma & Greg" with swearing and overt sexual content. **105m/C DVD. Jennifer Westfeldt, Judith Light, Jason Alexander, Fred Willard, Chris Messina, Frances Conroy, Robert Klein, Darrell Hammond, Chris Parnell;** *D:* **Robert Cary;** *W:* Jennifer Westfeldt; *C:* Harlan Bosmajian; *M:* Marcelo Zarvos.

Iran: Days of Crisis 𝄞𝄞½

1991 An insightful cable miniseries recounts America's humiliation at the hands of Iranian radicals in 1979, told from the vantage of a U.S. embassy official married to a Tehran woman. Former Carter administration aides Hamilton Jordan and Gerald Rafshoon devised the docudrama, which spares neither them nor their president in showing how bungled and shortsighted policies led to 52 Americans held hostage for over a year. **185m/C VHS. Ariss Howard, Alice Krige, George Grizzard, Jeff Fahey, Tony Goldwyn, Ronald Guttman, Valerie Kaprisky, Daniel Gelin;** *D:* Kevin Connor. CABLE

Irezumi 𝄞𝄞𝄞 *Spirit of Tattoo* 1983 A

Japanese woman has her body elaborately tattooed to please her lover. Things start off well enough. He's an inept lover, so she has directions tattooed, but then he discovers a "Dear John" letter on her foot just as she gives him the boot. Actually proves an interesting study in obsession and eroticism, with the tattoos drawing the lovers deeper and deeper until they get under each other's skin. In Japanese with English subtitles. **88m/C VHS. JP Tomisaburo Wakayama, Yusuke Takita, Masayo Utsunomiya, Masaki Kyomoto, Taihi Tomoyama;** *D:* Yoichi Takabayashi; *W:* Chiho Katsura; *C:* Hideo Fujii; *M:* Masaru Sato.

Iris 𝄞𝄞 *Out of Time* 1989 Drama follows

the passionate and tragic life of New Zealand writer Iris Wilkinson, an international novelist, poet, and journalist. Wilkinson achieved a great deal of acclaim as a writer, but suffered many personal tragedies, and eventually took her own life at age 33. Well intentioned but clunky treatment of powerful subject matter. **90m/C VHS. NZ Philip Holder, John Bach, Donogh Rees, David Ashton, Helen Morse;** *D:* Tony Issac; *W:* Keith Aberdein; *C:* James Bartle; *M:* John Charles.

Iris 𝄞𝄞𝄞 2001 (R) Enduring love story

between novelist/philosopher Iris Murdoch and her husband John Bayley from their days at Oxford in the 1950s to Murdoch's long decline from Alzheimer's and death in 1999. Winslet and Bonneville play the young duo while Dench and Broadbent play the mature marrieds. The ladies have the showier roles, especially Winslet, since the young Iris was a sexual free-spirit and disdained conventional morality while John comes across as shy and rather awed by Murdoch's talents. Based on Bayley's memoirs "Iris: A Memoir" and "Elegy for Iris." **90m/C VHS, DVD. GB US Judi Dench, Jim Broadbent, Kate Winslet, Hugh Bonneville, Penelope Wilton, Juliet Aubrey, Timothy West, Samuel West, Eleanor Bron;** *D:* **Richard Eyre;** *W:* Richard Eyre, Charles Wood; *C:* Roger Pratt; *M:* James Horner. Oscars '01: Support. Actor (Broadbent); British Acad. '01: Actress (Dench); Golden Globes '02: Support. Actor (Broadbent); L.A. Film Critics '01: Support. Actor (Broadbent); Support. Actress (Winslet); Natl. Bd. of Review '01: Support. Actor (Broadbent).

Iris Blond 𝄞𝄞½ 1998 (R) Bitter-

sweet romantic comedy about a sadsack piano player named Romeo (Verdone) who's pushing 50 and is unlucky in love. Having been cuckholded by his girlfriend, Romeo asks a fortuneteller (Fumo) for some help. She tells him his future resides with a singer who has the name of a flower. Naturally, Romeo picks the wrong chick (Ferreroi), only to soon meet red-hot maneater, Iris (Gerini). Eventually things work out as they should. French and Italian with subtitles. **100m/C VHS. IT Carlo Verdone, Andrea Ferreol, Claudia Gerini, Nuccia Fumo;** *D:* **Carlo Verdone;** *W:* Carlo Verdone, Francesca Marciano, Pasquale Plastino; *C:* Giuseppe Di Biase.

The Iris Effect 𝄞𝄞 2004 (R) Con-

fusing thriller. Sarah Hathaway's (Archer) troubled son Thomas disappeared 10 years ago. Unexpectedly, Sarah sees an art catalog that contains paintings similar to those Thomas did, so she travels to St. Petersburg, Russia, to find the art gallery and the artist—which isn't Thomas. Or is it? Something strange is happening as Sarah is followed by a mute street kid (Alan) who seems to know a lot about her son. **90m/C DVD. Anne Archer, Agnes Bruckner, Mia Kirshner, Kip Pardue, Gregory Hlady, Devon Alan, Yuri Kolokol;** *D:* **Nikolai Lebedev;** *W:* Kam Miller; *C:* Irek Hartowicz; *M:* Alexey Rybnikov. **VIDEO**

Irish Cinderella 𝄞𝄞 1922 A silent

version of the Cinderella legend set in Ireland, with thematic stress on Irish politics and patriotism. **72m/B VHS. Pattie MacNamara.**

Irish Jam 𝄞𝄞 2005 Con man Jimmy

(Griffin) has a tough life in L.A. and sees a small Irish town's poetry contest as a way out. After lifting some rap lyrics he wins the grand prize and becomes the town's new pub owner, not knowing the locales concocted the whole thing to keep a filthy rich developer at bay. Usual "worlds colliding" confusion plus an unlikely romance with a lonely widowed mother. **90m/C DVD. Eddie Griffin, Anna Friel, Kevin McNally, Mo'Nique Imes;** *D:* John Eyres; *W:* Max Myers. **VIDEO**

Irish Luck 𝄞𝄞 1939 A bellhop turns

detective to figure out the mysterious happenings in his hotel. Becomes terminally cute by playing on a luck o' the Irish theme. **58m/B VHS, DVD. Frankie Darro, Dick Purcell, Sheila Darcy, Grant Withers;** *D:* Howard Bretherton.

The Irishman 𝄞𝄞½ 1978 Set in

1920s Australia, the tale of a proud North Queensland family and their struggles to stay together. The Irish immigrant father is a teamster whose horse-drawn wagons are threatened by progress. His fight to preserve old ways is impressive, but gives way to sentimentality. **108m/C VHS, DVD. AU Lou Brown, Michael Craig, Simon Burke, Robyn Nevin, Bryan Brown;** *D:* Donald Crombie; *W:* Donald Crombie; *C:* Peter James; *M:* Charles Marawood.

Irma La Douce 𝄞𝄞½ 1963 A

gendarme pulls a one-man raid on a back-street Parisian joint and falls in love with one of the hookers he arrests. Lemmon is great as a well-meaning, incompetent boob, and MacLaine gives her all as the hapless hooker. A plodding pace, however, robs it of the original's zip, though it was a boxoffice smash. Broadway musical is lost without the music. **144m/C VHS, DVD. Jack Lemmon, Shirley MacLaine, Herschel Bernardi;** *D:* **Billy Wilder;** *W:* Billy Wilder, I.A.L. Diamond; *M:* Andre Previn. Oscars '63: Adapt. Score; Golden Globes '64: Actress—Mus./Comedy (MacLaine).

Irma Vep 𝄞𝄞½ 1996 Satiric tweaking

of French filmmaking begins with has-been director Rene Vidal (Leaud) hiring Hong Kong star Maggie Cheung to take the lead role of Irma Vep in a remake of the 1915 silent French classic "Les Vampires." But from the moment the actress arrives in Paris, it's one disaster after another. Cheung has trouble with the language barrier, Vidal is having a breakdown, lesbian costumer Zoe (Richard) is instantly smitten by Cheung and has her interest humiliatingly conveyed to everyone on the production. Then there's Jose

Iron & Silk 🐾🐾½ **1991 (PG)** A young American searches for himself while he teaches English and learns martial arts in mainland China. Based on the true story of Salzman's travels. His studies of martial arts and Chinese culture provide a model for his students in their studies of American language and culture. Beautiful photography. Fine performances. **94m/C VHS, DVD.** Mark Salzman, Pan Qingfu, Jeanette Lin Tsui, Vivian Wu. **D:** Shirley Sun; **M:** Michael Gibbs.

Iron Angel 🐾½ **1964** During the Korean War a squadron sets out to silence North Korean guns. They do. Judging by their eternal bickering they must have put the enemy to sleep. **94m/B VHS.** Jim Davis, Margo Woode, Donald "Red" Barry, L.Q. Jones; **D:** Ken Kennedy.

Iron Cowboy 🐾🐾 **1968** Actor finds romance with film editor while audience stifles yawns. Filmed on the set of "Blue," this pre-"Deliverance" Reynolds comedy never made it to the theaters. (Smithee is actually director Jud Taylor) **85m/C VHS.** Burt Reynolds, Barbara Loden, Terence Stamp, Jane Hampton, Joseph V. Perry; **D:** Alan Smithee.

The Iron Crown 🐾🐾 **1941** A 13th-century legend inspired this sometime violent spectacle involving the title totem, a symbol of justice ignored by a powerful king at his peril. There's wonderful pageantry and a notable Tarzan imitator, but the pace is terribly slow. Italian dialogue with English subtitles. **100m/C VHS.** Massimo Girotti, Elisa Cegani, Rina Morelli, Osvaldo Valenti, Primo Camera, Gino Cervi, Luisa Ferida, Pietro Blasetti; **W:** Renato Castellani; **C:** Mario Craveri; **M:** Alessandro Cicognini.

The Iron Duke 🐾🐾½ **1934** Fair to middlin' historical account of the life of the Duke of Wellington, victor over Napoleon at Waterloo. **88m/B VHS, GB** George Arliss, Gladys Cooper, A.E. Matthews, Emlyn Williams, Felix Aylmer; **D:** Victor Saville.

Iron Eagle 🐾🐾 **1986 (PG-13)** A teenager teams with a renegade fighter pilot to rescue the youth's father from captivity in the Middle East. Predictable but often exciting. Followed by two sequels. **117m/C VHS, DVD, CA** Louis Gossett Jr., Jason Gedrick, Tim Thomerson, David Suchet, Larry B. Scott, Caroline Lagerfelt, Jerry Levine, Michael Bowen, Robbie (Reist) Rist, Bobby Jacoby, Melora Hardin; **D:** Sidney J. Furie; **W:** Kevin Elders, Sidney J. Furie; **M:** Basil Poledouris.

Iron Eagle 2 🐾🐾 **1988 (PG)** Lower-budget extended adventures of a maverick fighter pilot after he is reinstated in the Air Force. This time he links with an equally rebellious commie fighter and blasts away at nuke-happy Ivan. Yahoo fun for all over Yankees! Followed by "Aces: Iron Eagle 3." Available in Spanish. **102m/C VHS, DVD, CA** Louis Gossett Jr., Mark Humphrey, Stuart Margolin, Alan Scarfe, Maury Chaykin, Sharon H. Brandon; **D:** Sidney J. Furie; **C:** Alan Dostie; **M:** Amin Bhatia.

Iron Eagle 4 🐾 **1995 (PG-13)** Series has gotten old and tired though Gossett Jr. shows professionalism in his father-figure role of retired Air Force General "Chappy" Sinclair. He's running the Iron Eagle Flight School—a training center/ holding cell for troubled teens—along with pilot Doug Masters (Cadieux). Masters and his would-be pilots discover suspicious activities at a local air base, leading to biological weapons and an Air Force conspiracy. **95m/C VHS, DVD, CA** Louis Gossett Jr., Jason Cadieux, Al Waxman, Joanne Vannicola, Rachel Blanchard, Sean McCann, Ross Hill, Karen Gayle; **D:** Sidney J. Furie; **W:** Michael Stokes; **C:** Curtis Petersen; **M:** Paul Zaza.

Iron Giant 🐾🐾🐾 **1999 (PG)** After nesses are found bludgeoned, wit-ens a small town, only a young boy is willing to befriend the iron man. With his new friend, he teaches the townspeople a lesson about being afraid of what is different. Jennifer Aniston provides the voice for the boy's mother, and Harry Connick Jr. that of the town beatnik. Great animation and story propel this tale above the level of most kiddie fare. Based on the 1968 children's book by Ted Hughes, which was also used for a 1989 concept album by Pete Townshend. **86m/C VHS, DVD.** **V:** Vin Diesel, Eli Marienthal, Jennifer Aniston, Harry Connick Jr., John Mahoney, M. Emmet Walsh, Cloris Leachman, James Gammon, Christopher McDonald.

The Iron Horse 🐾🐾🐾 **1924** Davy learned about western trails from his surveyor father. His childhood sweetheart Miriam is traveling with her fiance Jesson, who is working on the route for the new transcontinental railway. Davy says he knows a shortcut but a jealous Jesson tries to kill him. There's lots more action (and Abraham Lincoln!) before the railroad is finished and the sweethearts reunited. Ford's epic western was filmed on location and was his first major studio success. **119m/B DVD.** George O'Brien, Madge Bellamy, Cyril Chadwick, Fred Kohler Jr., Charles Edward Bull, Gladys Hulette; **D:** John Ford; **W:** Charles Kenyon, John Russell, Charles Darton; **C:** George Schneiderman.

Iron Horsemen 🐾 **J.C 1971 (R)** A motorcycle gang leader has a prophetic vision while tripping on LSD, and returns to his former town to challenge its religious establishment. **97m/C VHS.** William F. McGaha, Hannibal Penny, Joanna Moore, Burr de Benning, Slim Pickens, Pat Delaney; **D:** William F. McGaha.

Iron Major 🐾🐾🐾 **1943** Frank Cavanaugh, a famous football coach, becomes a hero in WW I. Standard flag-waving biography to increase morale back home, but fairly well-made. **85m/B VHS.** Pat O'Brien, Ruth Warrick, Robert Ryan, Leon James, Russell Wade, Bruce Edwards; **D:** Ray Enright.

Iron Man 🐾🐾🐾 **2008 (PG-13)** Sadly not based on the Black Sabbath song, this big-screen version of Marvel Comics' B-list armored avenger is one of the better movies to emerge from the bloated, nerd-maker/media playboy Tony Stark (Downey) builds an amazing suit of armor to help him escape from terrorists and decides to make a go of it as a card-carrying hero, much to the confusion of his firm's assistant (Paltrow) and chagrin of his business partner (Bridges). There's some great FX and sharp dialogue, but 95 percent of the movie's appeal comes from Downey, who brings a ridiculous charm and energy to the whole affair. On the flip side, the plot is paper-thin and you saw all the best bits in the trailer. Not exactly iron, but solid summer fun, nonetheless. **126m/C VHS, DVD.** Robert Downey Jr., Gwyneth Paltrow, Terrence Howard, Jeff Bridges, Leslie Bibb, Bill Smitrovich, Clark Gregg, Shaun Toub, Faran Tahir, Ahmed Ahmed, Joshua Harto, Peter Billingsley, Jon Favreau; **D:** Jon Favreau; **W:** Mark Fergus, Art Marcum, Matt Holloway, Hawk Ostby; **C:** Matthew Libatique; **M:** Ramin Djawadi.

The Iron Mask 🐾🐾½ **1929** Early swashbuckling extravaganza with a master swordsman defending the French king young women at dance clubs, drug them, and sell them into slavery. But the trouble really starts when they kill a cop and former partner, John Keem (Lee), lashes out with his blazing martial arts skill to still the perpetrators. **92m/C VHS, DVD.** Jet Li, Virginia Madsen, Alex Hyde-White, Reed Edward Diamond, E.G. Marshall, Fritz Weaver, Philip Casnoff. **D:** Delbert Mann. against a scheme involving substitution by a lookalike. Still fairly exciting, thanks largely to director Dwan's flair. Based on Alexandre Dumas's "Three Musketeers" and "The Man in the Iron Mask" with talking sequences. **103m/B VHS, DVD.** Douglas Fairbanks Sr., Nigel de Brulier, Marguerite de la Motte, Ullrich Haupt, William "Billy" Bakewell; **D:** Allan Dwan; **W:** Douglas Fairbanks Sr.; **M:** Hugo Riesenfeld.

Iron Maze 🐾½ **1991 (R)** A fascinating notion forms the center of this dramatic scrapheap: the classic Japanese "Rashomon" plot shifted to a rustling Pennsylvania steel town. When a Tokyo businessman

---

Iron Monkey 🐾🐾🐾 **1993 (PG-13)** Historical fantasy martial arts is built around the Iron Monkey (Rongguang Yu), a Robin-Hood figure who defeats whole armies of opponents and can leap tall buildings in a single bound. The humor and outstanding choreography of the fight scenes put this one flick, a cut above the usual martial arts action flick, a cut above the usual martial arts action flick. **85m/C VHS, DVD, HK** Rongguang Yu, Donnie Yen, Yam Sai-Kun, Tsingying Wong; **D:** Yuen Woo-ping Yuen; **W:** Tseng Pik-Yin, Tsui Hark, Tai-Muk Lau, Cheung Tan, Pik-yin Tang; **C:** Arthur Wong Ngok Tai; **M:** James L. Venable.

Iron Mountain Trail 🐾 **1953** Postal inspector Allen is sent to California to see what's holding up mail delivery. He discovers a couple of nefarious types and he and his horse Koko put them in their place. **54m/B VHS.** Rex Allen, Slim Pickens, Roy Barcroft, Grant Withers, Nan Leslie, Forrest Taylor; **D:** William Witney; **W:** Gerald Geraghty; **C:** Bud Thackery; **M:** Stanley Wilson.

Iron Thunder 🐾½ **1989** Liberty is in peril and only much kicking and pec-flexing will make the world a kinder gentler place. A thundering bore. **85m/C VHS.** Anthony "Amp" Elmore, George M. Young, Julius Dorsey; **D:** Anthony "Amp" Elmore.

The Iron Triangle 🐾🐾 **1989 (R)** A U.S. officer taken prisoner by the Viet Cong forms a bond with one of his captors. Film lends the viewer an opportunity to see things from the other sides perspective. **94m/C VHS.** Beau Bridges, Haing S. Ngor, Liem Whatley; **D:** Eric Weston; **W:** John Bushelman.

Iron Warrior 🐾 **1987 (R)** A barbarian hacks his way through a fantastical world to get to a beautiful princess. **82m/C VHS.** Miles O'Keeffe, Savina Gersak, Tim Lane; **D:** Al (Alfonso Brescia) Bradley; **W:** Al (Alfonso Brescia) Bradley.

Iron Will 🐾🐾½ **1993 (PG)** Okay Disney family movie based on true story. Will Stoneman is a 17-year-old farm kid from South Dakota. It's 1917 and because of his father's death there's no money to send Will to college. So he decides to enter the 500 mile winner-take-all dog sled race, with its $10,000 prize. Lots of obstacles, several villains, and death from war. Virginia Madsen (Lee) perseveres. **109m/C VHS, DVD.** MacKenzie Astin, Kevin Spacey, David Ogden Stiers, August Schellenberg, George Gerdes, John Terry; **D:** Charles Haid; **W:** John Michael Hayes, Jeffrey Arch, Djordje Milicevic; **M:** Joel McNeely.

Ironclads 🐾🐾½ **1990** Memorable dramatization of the five-hour naval battle between the Confederate's Merrimac and the Union's Monitor during the Civil War. The special effects are the only thing worth watching in this overlong tale that includes standard subplots of loyalty, lost loves, and death from war. **94m/C VHS.** Virginia Madsen, Alex Hyde-White, Reed Edward Diamond, E.G. Marshall, Fritz Weaver, Philip Casnoff. **D:** Delbert Mann.

Ironheart 🐾½ **1992** Slimy Milverstead and his henchman meet lovely

Ironmaster 🐾 **1982** When a primitive tribesman is exiled from his tribe, he discovers a mysteriously power-filled iron staff on a mountainside. **98m/C VHS, IT FR** Jacques Herlin, Pamela Field, Danilo Mattei, George Eastman; **D:** Umberto Lenzi; **W:** Umberto Lenzi, Lea Martino; **C:** Giancarlo Ferrando; **M:** Guido de Angelis, Maurizio de Angelis.

---

businessman is found bludgeoned, witnesses (including his American-born wife) tell contradictory stories. It's too convoluted and contrived to work, with a hollow happy ending tacked on. Oliver Stone helped produce. **105m/C VHS, DVD.** Jeff Fahey, Bridget Fonda, Hiroaki Murakami, J.T. Walsh, Gabriel Damon, John Randolph, Peter Allas; **D:** Hiroaki Yoshida; **W:** Tim Metcalfe; **C:** Mono Saegusa; **M:** Stanley Myers.

Irreconcilable Differences 🐾🐾🐾 **1984 (PG)** When her Beverly Hills parents spend more time working and fretting than giving hugs and love, a ten-year-old girl sues them for divorce on the grounds of "irreconcilable differences." The media has a field day with the case, with well-developed characterizations. The script, by the creators of "Private Benjamin," is humanely comic rather than uproariously funny. **112m/C VHS.** Ryan O'Neal, Shelley Long, Drew Barrymore, Sam Wanamaker, Allen (Goober) Garfield, Sharon Stone, Luana Anders; **D:** Charles Shyer; **W:** Charles Shyer, Nancy Meyers.

Irresistible Impulse 🐾½ **1995** Sleazy real estate agent Jeffrey allows himself to become entangled in a wild scheme with bad girl Beaman. **107m/C VHS.** Doug Jeffrey, Lea Anne Beevan; **D:** Jag Mundhra.

Irreversible 🐾½ **2002** The rape scene is nine minutes long. If you're still willing to sit through this abrasive flick after knowing that, here's the story (which is told backwards). Marcus (Cassel) and Pierre (Dupontel) are being led away from a gay S&M club where a murder has occurred. They have sought revenge for what happened to Marcus's lover Alex (Bellucci). Earlier, Marcus tough with Alex at a party and she leaves alone—to be brutalized into a coma by a thug (Prestia) in an underground pedestrian tunnel. Then we see the trio, Pierre is an old friend of Alex's and is jealous of Marcus, going to the party and expecting to have fun. Everyone's destined to be disappointed. French with subtitles. **99m/C VHS, DVD.** Monica Bellucci, Vincent Cassel, Albert Dupontel, Jo Prestia, Philippe Nahon; **D:** Gaspar Noe; **W:** Gaspar Noe; **M:** Thomas Bangalter.

Irresistible 🐾🐾½ **2006** Sophie Harley (Sarandon) is convinced she's being stalked by her husband Craig's (Neill) beautiful co-worker Mara (Blunt) because she wants Sophie's life for herself. But the truth will shock Sophie even more. Formulaic psycho-thriller redeemed by expert cast. **109m/C VHS, AU** Susan Sarandon, Sam Neill, Emily Blunt, Charles "Bud" Tingwell, William McInnes; **D:** Ann Turner; **W:** Ann Turner; **C:** Martin McGrath; **M:** David Hirschfelder. **VIDEO**

Ironweed 🐾🐾🐾 **1987 (R)** Grim and gritty drama about bums living the hard life in Depression-era Albany. Nicholson excels as a former ballplayer turned drunk, bothered by visions of the past, and Streep is his equal in the lesser role of a tubercular boozer; Waits also shines. Another grim view from "Pixote" director Babenco. Kennedy scripted based on his Pulitzer Prize-winning tragedy. **135m/C VHS.** Jack Nicholson, Meryl Streep, Tom Waits, Carroll Baker, Michael O'Keefe, Fred Gwynne, Nathan Lane, James Gammon, Jake Dengel, Margaret Whitton, Diane Venora; **D:** Hector Babenco; **W:** William Kennedy; **M:** John Morris, L.A. Film Critics '87. Actor (Nicholson); N.Y. Film Critics '87. Actor (Nicholson).

Is Money Everything? 🐾🐾 **1923** Man goes to the big city, becomes a success, and then has an affair with a married woman. **38m/B VHS.** Norman Kerry, Miriam Cooper, Martha Mansfield, William Bailey, Andrew Hicks, John Sylvester, Lawrence Brooke; **D:** Glen Lyons; **W:** Glen Lyons.

Is Paris Burning? 🐾🐾🐾 **Paris Brule-t-il? 1966** A spectacularly star-studded but far too sprawling account of the liberation of Paris from Nazi occupation. The script, in which seven writers had a hand, is based on Larry Collins and Dominique Lapierre's best-seller. **173m/C VHS, DVD. FR** Jean-Paul Belmondo, Charles Boyer, Leslie Caron, Jean-Pierre Cassel, George Chakiris, Claude Dauphin, Alain Delon, Kirk Douglas, Glenn Ford, Gert Frobe, Daniel Gelin, E.G. Marshall, Yves Montand, Anthony Perkins, Claude Rich, Simone Signoret, Robert Stack, Jean-Louis Trintignant, Pierre Vaneck, Orson Welles, Bruno Cremer, Suzy Delair, Michel (Michel) Lonsdale; **D:** Rene Clement; **W:** Gore Vidal, Francis Ford Coppola; **C:** Marcel Grignon; **M:** Maurice Jarre.

Is

Is There Life Out There? 🦴🦴½ 1994

Wife, mother, and waitress Lily Marshall (McEntire) decides it's time to do something for herself—so she goes to work on her college degree. But there's her unexpected family resentments, a breast cancer scare, and the interest of a young teaching assistant to turn her head away from her studies. Filmed in Nashville, Tennessee. Based on a song by McEntire; made for TV. **92m/C VHS, DVD.** Reba McEntire, Keith Carradine, Mitchell Anderson, Donald Moffat, Genia Michaela; **D:** David Hugh Jones; **W:** Dalene Young. **TV**

Is There Sex After Death? 🦴🦴🦴 1971

Often funny satire on the sexual revolution is constructed as a behind-the-scenes view of the porn film world. Odd cast includes Henry and Warhol superstar Woodlawn. Originally rated "X." **97m/C VHS, DVD.** Buck Henry, Alan Abel, Marshall Efron, Holly Woodlawn, Earl Doud; **C:** Alan Abel, Jeanne Abel.

Isaac Asimov's Nightfall 🦴🦴

Nightfall 2000 (R) The planet Aeon has six suns and has never experienced night. But with an eclipse approaching, religious cultists are predicting catastrophe. Scientist Carradine tries to allay the population's fear. Low-budget and bland adaptation of Asimov's 1941 short story. **85m/C VHS, DVD.** David Carradine, Jennifer Burns, Joseph Hodge; **D:** Gwyneth Gibby; **W:** Gwyneth Gibby, John W. Corrington, Michael B. Druxman; **C:** Abhik Mukhopadhyay; **M:** Nicolas Tenbroek, Brad Segal.

Isadora 🦴🦴🦴

The Loves of Isadora 1968 A loose, imaginative biography of Isadora Duncan, the cause celebre dancer in the 1920s who became famous for her scandalous performances, outrageous behavior, public love affairs, and bizarre, early death. Redgrave is exceptional in the lead, and Fox provides fine support. Restored from its original 131-minute print length by the director. **138m/C VHS. GB** Vanessa Redgrave, Jason Robards Jr., James Fox, Ivan Tchenko, John Fraser, Bessie Love, Cynthia Harris, Libby Glenn, Tony Vogel, Wallace (Wallas) Eaton, John Quentin, Nicholas Pennell, Ronnie Gilbert, Alan Gifford, Christian Duvaleix; **D:** Karel Reisz; **W:** Melvyn Bragg, Clive Exton; **C:** Larry Pizer; **M:** Maurice Jarre. Cannes '69: Actress (Redgrave); Natl. Soc. Film Critics '69: Actress (Redgrave).

Ishtar 🦴🦴 1987 (PG-13)

Two astoundingly untalented performers have a gig in a fictional Middle Eastern country and become involved in foreign intrigue. A big-budget boxoffice bomb produced by Beatty offering few laughs, though it's not as bad as its reputation. Considering the talent involved, though, it's a disappointment, with Beatty and Hoffman laboring to create Hope and Crosby chemistry. Anyone for a slow night? **107m/C VHS.** Dustin Hoffman, Warren Beatty, Isabelle Adjani, Charles Grodin, Jack Weston, Tess Harper, Carol Kane, Matt Frewer; **D:** Elaine May; **W:** Elaine May; **C:** Vittorio Storaro; **M:** Dave Grusin, Bahjawa. Golden Raspberries '87: Worst Director (May).

The Island 🦴🦴½ 1987 (PG-13)

Hadaka No Shima; Naked Island 1961 Poetic examination of a peasant family's daily struggle for existence on a small island. No dialogue in this slow but absorbing work by one of Japan's master directors. **96m/B VHS. JP** Nobuko Otowa, Taiji Tonoyama, Shinji Tanaka, Masanori Horimoto; **D:** Kaneto Shindo.

The Island WOOF! 1980 (R)

New York reporter embarks on a Bermuda triangle investigation, only to meet with the murderous but sterile descendants of 17th century pirates on a deserted island. Caine is designated as stud service for the last remaining fertile woman. Almost surreal in its badness. Adapted by Benchley from his novel. **113m/C VHS.** Michael Caine, David Warner, Angela Punch McGregor, Frank Middlemass, Don Henderson; **D:** Michael Ritchie; **W:** Peter Benchley; **C:** Henri Decae; **M:** Ennio Morricone.

The Island 🦴🦴½ 2005 (PG-13)

In 2019, folks at the sterile, white-uniform-only, underground community believe that they've been spared from a cataclysmic disaster and await a lottery pick that's supposedly a ticket to "The Island," the last uncontaminated place on the planet. Among the placid group is troublemaker Lincoln Six Echo (McGregor), who discovers they're clones created by evil scientist Merrick (Bean) to serve as donors for their human counterparts. Lincoln flees with fellow resident Jordan Two Delta (Johansson) but Merrick's henchman Laurent (Hounsou) isn't far behind. Initially intriguing plot becomes a typical Bay blow'em up, kill'em all action fest. Interesting (at least to the original's producer) similarity to "Parts: The Clonus Horror" adds another dimension to all the cloning around, and became fodder for some controversy. Partially filmed in Detroit. **136m/C DVD, UMD. US** Ewan McGregor, Scarlett Johansson, Djimon Hounsou, Steve Buscemi, Michael Clarke Duncan, Shawnee Smith, Sean Bean, Ethan Phillips, Max Baker, Kim Coates; **D:** Michael Bay; **W:** Caspian Tredwell-Owen, Alex Kurtzman, Roberto Orci; **C:** Mauro Fiore; **M:** Steve Jablonsky.

The Island at the Top of the World 🦴🦴½ 1974 (G)

A rich English man, in search of his missing son, travels to the Arctic Circle in 1908. The rescue party includes an American archeologist, a French astronaut, and an Eskimo guide. Astonishingly, they discover an unknown, "lost" Viking kingdom. This Jules Verne-style adventure doesn't quite measure up, but kids will like it. **93m/C VHS, DVD.** David Hartman, Donald Sinden, Jacques Marin, Mako, David Gwillim; **D:** Robert Stevenson; **W:** John Whedon; **C:** Frank Phillips; **M:** Maurice Jarre.

Island Claw WOOF! *Night of the Claw*

1980 A group of marine biologists experimenting on a tropical island discover the result of toxic waste seeping into the ocean. A festering, oozing woofer. **91m/C VHS.** Barry Nelson, Robert Lansing; **D:** Herman Cardenas.

Island in the Sky 🦴🦴 1953

When a transport plane crashes in an isolated area of Labrador, the captain (Wayne) must keep his crew alive long enough for them to be rescued. Long-awaited release has all the rugged manliness you'd expect of a Wayne flick. Faithful adaptation successfully conveys the increasing desperation and sense of doom of the crew and the would-be rescuers. **109m/B DVD.** John Wayne, Lloyd Nolan, Walter Abel, James Arness, Andy Devine, Allyn Joslyn, Jimmy Lydon, Harry Carey Jr., Hal Baylor, Sean McClory, Wally Cassell, Gordon Jones, Frank Fenton, Regis Toomey, Paul Fix, George Chandler, Louis Jean Heydt, Darryl Hickman, Mike Connors, Carl "Alfalfa" Switzer, Ann Doran, Fess Parker; **D:** William A. Wellman; **W:** Ernest K. Gann; **C:** Archie Stout; **M:** Emil Newman.

Island in the Sun 🦴🦴 1957

Racial tension rips apart the lives of the residents of a Caribbean island. Good cast, but a very poor adaptation of Alec Waugh's novel. Marvelous location shots. **119m/C VHS, DVD.** James Mason, Joan Fontaine, Dorothy Dandridge, John Williams, Harry Belafonte; **D:** Robert Rossen; **C:** Frederick A. (Freddie) Young; **M:** Malcolm Arnold.

Island Monster 🦴🦴½ *Monster of the*

Island 1953 Deals with ruthless, kidnapping drug-smugglers led by "monster" Karloff, and the efforts to bring them to justice. **87m/B VHS, DVD. IT** Boris Karloff, Renata Vicario, Franca Marzi; **D:** Robert Bianchi Montero.

Island of Blood 🦴½ 1982

Buckets of blood abound on a remote island when a film crew's beset by berserk butcher. **84m/C VHS.** Gary Phillips, Rick Dean, Jim Williams, Dean Richards; **D:** William T. Naud; **W:** William T. Naud; **C:** Thomas E. Spalding; **M:** Joel Goldsmith.

Island of Desire 🦴 *Saturday Island*

1952 An Army nurse, a doctor, and a young Navy Adonis are trapped on a deserted island. Not surprisingly, a love triangle develops. **93m/C VHS.** *GB* Tab Hunter, Linda Darnell, Donald Gray; **D:** Stuart Heisler.

The Island of Dr. Moreau 🦴🦴½ 1977 (PG)

This remake of the "Island of the Lost Souls" (1933) is a bit disappointing but worth watching for Lancaster's solid performance as the scientist who has isolated himself on a Pacific island in order to continue his chromosome research—he can transform animals into near-humans and humans into animals. Neat-looking critters. Adaptation of the H.G. Wells novel of the same title. **99m/C VHS, DVD.** Burt Lancaster, Michael York, Nigel Davenport, Barbara Carrera, Richard Basehart, Nick Cravat; **D:** Don Taylor; **W:** John Herman Shaner, Al Ramrus; **C:** Gerry Fisher.

The Island of Dr. Moreau 🦴½ 1996 (PG-13)

What were they thinking? Not even the frightening "manimals" could prevent the unintentional laughs from this abomination of the horrifying 1896 H.G. Wells novel. Brando's enormous presence as the mad scientist Moreau walks a tight rope between puzzling and campy, especially as he explains his ghastly DNA experiments on a remote Pacific to a miscast Thewlis. A wasted Kilmer is the doctor's right-hand hybrid who often seems to be acting in a different movie. Filming hit some big rocks when "creative differences" caused original director Richard Stanley to be replaced and Rob Morrow (originally the lawyer) to ask for his release. Previously filmed under the same title in 1977 and (terrifically) as "Island of Lost Souls" in 1933. **91m/C VHS, DVD.** Marlon Brando, Val Kilmer, David Thewlis, Fairuza Balk, Marco Hofschneider, Temuera Morrison, Ron Perlman; **D:** John Frankenheimer; **W:** Richard Stanley, Ron Hutchinson; **C:** William A. Fraker; **M:** Gary Chang.

Island of Lost Girls WOOF! *Kommissar X - Drei Goldene Schlangen; Three Golden*

Serpents 1968 (R) Young women are taken from an unknown location in the Far East to be sold as part of a white slave ring. **85m/C VHS. IT** GE Brad Harris, Tony Kendall, Monica Pardo, Herbert (Fuchs) Fux; **D:** Robert (Roberto) Mauri; **W:** Manfred Kohler, Gianfranco Parolini; **C:** Francesco Izzarelli; **M:** Francesco De Masi.

Island of Lost Souls 🦴🦴🦴½ 1932

Horrifying adaptation of H.G. Wells's "The Island of Dr. Moreau" was initially banned in parts of the U.S. because of its disturbing contents. Dr. Moreau (Laughton) is a mad scientist who lives on a remote island and is obsessed with making men out of jungle animals. When shipwreck survivor Edward Parker (Arlen) gets stranded on the island, little does he know that Moreau wants to mate him with Lota (Burke), the Panther Woman, to produce the first human-animal child. As unsettling today as it was in the '30s. Lugosi has the notable role of the hybrid "Sayer of the Law" while Burke beat out more than 60,000 young women in a nationwide search to play the Panther Woman, winning the role because of her "feline" look. Remade as "The Island of Dr. Moreau" in both 1977 and 1996. **71m/B VHS, DVD.** Charles Laughton, Bela Lugosi, Richard Arlen, Leila Hyams, Kathleen Burke, Stanley Fields, Robert F. (Bob) Kortman, Arthur Hohl; *Cameos:* Alan Ladd, Randolph Scott, Buster Crabbe; **D:** Erle C. Kenton; **W:** Philip Wylie, Waldemar Young; **C:** Karl Struss.

Island of Terror 🦴🦴½ *Night of the*

Silicates; The Creepers 1966 First-rate science fiction chiller about an island overrun by shell-like creatures that suck the bones out of their living prey. Good performances and interesting twists make for prickles up the spine. **90m/C VHS. GB** Peter Cushing, Edward Judd, Carole Gray, Sam Kydd, Niall MacGinnis; **D:** Terence Fisher.

Island of the Blue Dolphins 🦴🦴½ 1964

Based on a popular children's book by Scott O'Dell, this is a true story of a young Native American girl who, with her brother, are stranded on a deserted island when their people accidentally leave them. When the boy is killed, the girl learns to survive by her skills and by befriending the leader of a pack of wild dogs. Good family fare. **99m/C VHS.** Celia Kaye, Larry Domasin, Ann Daniel, George Kennedy; **D:** James B. Clark; **W:** Ted Sherdeman; **C:** Leo Tover; **M:** Paul Sawtell.

Island of the Burning Doomed 🦴🦴 *Night of the Big Heat; Island of the Burning*

Damned; Night of the Big Heat 1967 A brutal heat wave accompanies invading aliens in this British-made outing. Lee and Cushing carry the picture. **94m/C VHS, DVD. GB** Christopher Lee, Peter Cushing, Patrick Allen, Sarah Lawson, Jane Merrow; **D:** Terence Fisher.

Island of the Dead 🦴🦴 2000 (R)

Now here's a storyline sure to be entertaining. One business tycoon, one policewoman, one prison warden, and three convicts are all trapped on an island burial ground. Just when they become shipwrecked on a mysterious island, things start to rise up and strike a little terror. **91m/C VHS, DVD.** Malcolm McDowell, Talisa Soto, Bruce Ramsay, Mos Def; **D:** Tim Southam; **W:** Peter Koper, Tim Southam. **VIDEO**

Island of the Lost 🦴½ 1968

An anthropologist's family must fight for survival when they become shipwrecked on a mysterious island. **92m/C VHS, DVD. GB** Richard Greene, Luke Halpin, Mart Hulswit, Jose De Vega, Robin Mattson, Irene Tsu, Sheilah Wells; **D:** John Florea, Ricou Browning; **W:** Richard Carlson, Ivan Tors; **C:** Howard Winner; **M:** George Bruns.

The Island on Bird Street 🦴🦴½ 1997 (PG-13)

Eleven-year-old Jewish Alex (Kiziuk) is forced to live in the Warsaw ghetto with his father Stefan (Bergin) and great-uncle Boruch (Warden). When the Gestapo round up the inhabitants to send them to concentration camps, Alex manages to elude capture. Inspired by his favorite book, "The Adventures of Robinson Crusoe," he hides out in an abandoned building on Bird Street with only his pet mouse Snow for company. Alex struggles with daily survival as he awaits his father's promised return. Based on the autobiographical children's book by Uri Orlev. **102m/C DVD. GB DK GE** Patrick Bergin, Jack Warden, Soeren Kragh-Jacobsen, Jordan Kiziuk; **W:** John Goldsmith, Tony Grisoni; **C:** Ian Wilson; **M:** Zbigniew Preisner.

Island Trader 🦴 1971

Young lad battles pirates and a crooked tug captain who seek hidden gold that he knows about. **95m/C VHS.** John Ewart, Ruth Cracknell, Eric Oldfield; **D:** Harold Rubie.

The Islander 🦴 1988

Sixteen-year-old Inga comes of age among the commercial fishermen of Lake Michigan. **99m/C VHS.** Kit Wholihan, Jeff Weborg, Celia Klehr, Jacob Mills, Julie Johnson, Mary Ann McHugh, Michael Rock, Sheri Parish; **D:** Phyllis Berg-Pigorsch.

Islands 🦴🦴 1987

Drama about a middle-aged ex-hippie and a young rebellious punk who clash during a summer together on a secluded island. **55m/C VHS.** Louise Fletcher; **D:** Rene Bonniere. **TV**

Islands in the Stream 🦴🦴½ 1977 (PG)

Based on Ernest Hemingway's novel, this film is actually two movies in one. An American painter/sculptor, Thomas Hudson, lives a reclusive life on the island of Bimini shortly before the outbreak of WWII. The first part is a sensitive story of a broken family and the coming of the artist's three sons to live with their father after a four-year separation. The second part is a second rate action-adventure. **105m/C VHS, DVD.** George C. Scott, David Hemmings, Claire Bloom, Susan Tyrrell, Gilbert Roland; **D:** Franklin J. Schaffner; **C:** Fred W. Koenekamp; **M:** Jerry Goldsmith.

The Isle 🦴🦴 1½

Seom 2001 For those who like their arthouse features on the kinky side. The isle is a series of small huts anchored in a river that's part of a remote fishing area. But the male guests don't just come for the fishing—they bring their own female company or take what's offered by mute manager Hee-Jin. She becomes obsessed with Hyun-Shik, an ex-cop who murdered his unfaithful lover and who's hiding out while contemplating suicide. She saves him, protects him from the police, and shares a very intimate relationship with the unstable man. Korean with subtitles. **89m/C VHS, DVD. KV** Suh Jung, Yoo-Suk Kim, Sung-Hee Park; **D:** Ki-Duk Kim; **W:** Ki-Duk Kim; **C:** Seo-Shik Hwang; **M:** Sang-Yun Jeon.

Isle of Forgotten Sins 🦴🦴

Monsoon 1943 Deep sea divers and an evil ship's captain vie for treasure. Good cast and direction but unremarkable material. **82m/B VHS, DVD.** John Carradine, Gale Sondergaard, Sidney Toler, Frank Fenton, Veda Ann Borg; **D:** Edgar G. Ulmer.

Isle of Secret Passion 🐾 1982
A romance novel comes to video life as two lovers thrash out their problems on a plague-infested island in the early 1900s. The fear is that vampires walk among them. Characteristically spooky Val Lewton production with some original twists. **72m/C VHS, DVD.** Boris Karloff, Ellen Drew, Marc Cramer, Katherine Emery, Helen Thimig, Alan Napier, Jason Robards Sr., Skelton Knaggs; **D:** Mark Robson; **W:** Josef Mischel, Ardel Wray; **C:** Jack MacKenzie; **M:** Leigh Harline.

Isle of the Dead 🐾🐾½ 1945 A Greek general is quarantined with seemingly all manner of social vermin on a Greek island. While on location, Michael MacRae, Zohra Lampert. **D:** Herbert Stein.

Istanbul 🐾 1957 Adventurer Jim Brennan (Flynn) finds a fortune in smuggled diamonds, which he hides in a hotel room. Unfortunately, he's deported before he can retrieve the gems and it takes him five years to make it back to Istanbul. Then he's hounded by the original smugglers who want their gems back and discovers his lost love Stephanie (Borchers). Cole croons a couple of songs in his role as a lounge singer. Remake of 1947's "Singapore." 🎵 "When I Fall in Love; I Was a Little Too Lonely. **85m/C VHS.** Errol Flynn, Cornell Borchers, John Bentley, Torin Thatcher, Leif Erickson, Peggy Knudsen, Martin Benson, Nat King Cole, Werner Klemperer; **D:** Joseph Pevney; **W:** Seton I. Miller, Barbara Gray; **C:** William H. Daniels.

Istanbul 🐾 1985 (R) An American charms a Belgian student into taking part in a kidnap scheme. **30m/C VHS, FR** Brad Dourif, Dominique Deruddere, Ingrid De Vos, Francois Beukelaers; **D:** Marc Didden.

Istanbul, Keep Your Eyes Open 1990 (PG-13) Believing he has stumbled upon the best story of his career, a journalist soon discovers that he has been pulled into a world of guns and violence. **88m/C VHS.** Til SW Robert Morley, Timothy Bottoms, Twiggy. **D:** Mats Arehn.

The Ister 🐾 2004 Fookie writers/directors Barison and Ross document in a thought-provoking five-year trek up the 2,000-mile-long Danube River (ancient Greek name "The Ister") from its mouth in the Black Sea to its origin in Germany's Black Forest. Along the way, the Austrian philosophy students visit with prominent European philosophers who discuss the 1942 lecture of German existentialist Martin Heidegger (their inspiration and author of "Time and Being") while capturing such images as an ancient Greek city, war-torn Serbian towns, and the Mauthausen-Gusen concentration camp. **189m/C DVD.** **D:** Daniel Ross, David Barison; **C:** Daniel Ross, David Barison.

Isn't Life Wonderful 🐾🐾🐾 1924 Inga's (Dempster) a Polish war orphan who struggles to provide for her family in post-WWI Germany. It means giving up her dream to marry former soldier, Paul (Hamilton), but he has a secret plan to reunite them. Filmed on location. **118m/B VHS.** Carol Dempster, Neil Hamilton, Lupino Lane, Hans von Schlettow; **D:** D.W. Griffith; **W:** D.W. Griffith.

Isn't She Great 🐾🐾½ 2000 (R) Irreverant biopic about the queen of '60s trash novels, Jacqueline Susann (Midler), and her hungry quest for flashy fame. Lane plays her ever-loyal husband and manager, Irving Mansfield. Susann's life was no bed of roses as she fought a long battle with breast cancer and had an autistic child, although she never let her personal tragedies become public fodder. Midler gives an overripe performance while Channing (as best friend Florence) proves to be the true scene-stealer. Unfortunately, the film is even more shallow than a memoir by Susann's editor, Michael Korda. **96m/C VHS, DVD.** Bette Midler, Nathan Lane, Stockard Channing, David Hyde Pierce, John Cleese, John Larroquette, Amanda Peet, Lisa Bronwyn Moore, Dina Spybey; **D:** Andrew Bergman; **W:** Paul Rudnick; **C:** Karl Walter Lindenlaub; **M:** Burt Bacharach.

It 🐾🐾½ 1927 The film that established Bow as a prominent screen siren. Betty Lou (Bow) is a saucy lingerie sales clerk who sets her sights on department store owner Cyrus (Moreno), despite the fact that he has a fiancee. Adapted by Elinor Glyn from her own story; Glyn also makes an appearance. **71m/B VHS, DVD.** Clara Bow, Antonio Moreno, Jacqueline Gadston, William Austin, Gary Cooper, Julia Swayne Gordon; **D:** Clarence Badger, Josef von Sternberg; **W:** Hope Loring, Louis D. Lighton; **C:** Kinley Martin. Natl. Film Reg. '01.

It Ain't Hay 🐾🐾½ 1943 Grover (Abbott) and buddy Wilbur (Costello) accidentally kill their friend King O'Hara's (Kellaway) horse, so they steal a horse named Teabiscuit. Only the new horse turns out to be a champion racer. Remake of the 1935 film "Princess O'Hara" and based on a Damon Runyon story. **79m/B VHS.** Bud Abbott, Lou Costello, Cecil Kellaway, Grace McDonald, Eugene Pallette, Shemp Howard, Eddie Quillan; **D:** Erie C. Kenton; **W:** Allen Boretz, John Grant; **C:** Charles Van Enger.

It Came from Beneath the Sea 🐾🐾🐾 1955 A giant octopus arises from the depths of the sea to scour San Francisco for human food. Ray Harryhausen effects are special. **80m/B VHS, DVD.** Kenneth Tobey, Faith Domergue, Ian Keith, Donald Curtis; **D:** Robert Gordon.

It Came from Outer Space 🐾🐾🐾 1953 Aliens take on the form of local humans to repair their spacecraft in a small Arizona town. Good performances and outstanding direction add up to a fine science fiction film. Based on the story "The Meteor" by Ray Bradbury, who also wrote the script. Originally filmed in 3-D. **81m/B VHS, DVD.** Richard Carlson, Barbara Rush, Charles Drake, Russell Johnson, Kathleen Hughes; **D:** Jack Arnold; **W:** Harry Essex, Ray Bradbury; **C:** Clifford Stine; **M:** Henry Mancini, Herman Stein, Irving Gertz.

It Came from Outer Space 2 🐾½ 1995 (PG-13) Poorly updated cable version of the sci-fi film finds photographer Jack Putnam (Kerwin) heading home to his isolated desert community. A freakish blue lightning storm causes big charges amongst the desert dwellers who are sucked into a glowing ground mass and re-emerge possessed by shape-shifting aliens, who need the human bodies to rebuild their crashed space ship. Based on a story by Ray Bradbury and the 1953 screenplay by Harry Essex. **85m/C VHS.** Brian Kerwin, Elizabeth Pena, Bill McKinney, Jonathan Carrasco, Adrian Sparks, Howard Morris, Mickey Jones, Lauren Tewes; **D:** Roger Duchowny; **W:** Jim Wheat, Ken Wheat; **M:** Shirley Walker. CABLE.

It Came from the Sky 🐾🐾 1998 (R) Eccentric strangers Jarvis Moody (Lloyd) and his girlfriend Pepper (Bleeth) invade the lives of bitter Donald (Ritter), his long-suffering wife Alice (Williams), and their brain-damaged teenage son (Zegers). Has fate sent the strange duo to intervene for good or is disaster about to strike? **92m/C VHS.** John Ritter, Christopher Lloyd, Yasmine Bleeth, JoBeth Williams, Kevin Zegers; **D:** Jack Bender.

It Came Upon a Midnight Clear 🐾½ 1984 A heavenly miracle enables a retired (and dead) New York policeman to keep a Christmas promise to his grandson. **96m/C VHS, DVD.** Mickey Rooney, Scott Grimes, George Gaynes, Annie Potts, Lloyd Nolan, Barrie Youngfellow; **D:** Peter H. Hunt; **C:** Dean Cundey. TV

It Conquered the World 🐾🐾½ 1956 Vegetable critters from Venus follow a probe satellite back to Earth and drop in on scientist Van Cleef, who'd been their intergalactic pen pal (seems he thought a Venusian invasion would improve the neighborhood). Their turn earth dwellers into murderous zombies, and it starts to look like the Venusians are trying to make earth their planetary exurbia. Early vintage zero-budget Corman, for schlock connoisseurs. Remade for TV as "Zontar, the Thing from Venus." **66m/C VHS.** Peter Graves, Beverly Garland, Lee Van Cleef, Sally Fraser, Charles B. Griffith, Russ Bender, Jonathan Haze, Dick Miller, Karen Kadler, Paul Blaisdell; **D:** Roger Corman; **W:** Lou Rusoff, Charles B. Griffith; **C:** Frederick E. West; **M:** Ronald Stein.

It Could Happen to You 🐾🐾 1937 Stepbrothers raised by a gentle immigrant take different paths in life. When one ends up killing someone during a botched robbery, the other—a lawyer—defends him. Standard '30s morality play. **64m/B VHS.** Alan Baxter, Andrea Leeds, Owen Davis Jr., Astrid Allwyn, Walter Kingsford, Al Shean; **D:** Phil Rosen.

It Could Happen to You 🐾🐾 1994 (PG) Cop Tips Waitress $2 Million, cried the real-life tabloid headline that inspired this feel-good romantic comedy. NYC cop Charlie Lang (Cage) doesn't have any change to leave coffee shop waitress Yvonne (Fonda) a tip, so he promises to split his lottery ticket with her. When he nets $4 million, he makes good on the promise, much to the chagrin of his upwardly mobile wife (Perez). Capra-corn for the X-crowd is pleasant dinner-time diversion as Cage and Perez shine as henpecked nice guy and the wife committed to making him miserable. Don't look for the diner on your next trip to NYC; it was specially built in TriBeCa and dismantled after the shoot. **101m/C VHS, DVD.** Bridget Fonda, Nicolas Cage, Rosie Perez, Red Buttons, Isaac Hayes, Seymour Cassel, Stanley Tucci, J.E. Freeman, Richard Jenkins, Ann Dowd, Wendell Pierce, Angela Pietropinto, Vincent Pastore, Peter Jacobson; **D:** Andrew Bergman; **W:** Andrew Bergman, Jane Anderson; **C:** Caleb Deschanel; **M:** Carter Burwell.

It Couldn't Happen Here 🐾 1988 (PG-13) Fans of the techno-pop duo The Pet Shop Boys can test their loyalty by enduring this feature music-video that actually during a few theatres. The four pair journey across a surreal England, encountering a sinister blind priest, a philosophical ventriloquist's dummy, and incidental music, include the title track, "West End Girls," "It's a Sin," and "Always on My Mind." **87m/C VHS, GB** Neil Tennant, Chris Lowe, Joss Ackland, Neil Dickson, Carmen (De Sautoy) Du Sautoy, Gareth Hunt; **D:** Jack Bond.

It Had to Be You 🐾 2000 (PG) Elementary school teacher Anna (Henstridge) is engaged to busy editor Claire (Vartan). Both find themselves staying at the Plaza Hotel—without their fiancees who have opted to work-planning their mutual weddings. As Charlie and Anna discuss flowers and entertainment, it becomes clear that the duo are marrying the wrong people. But what will they do about it? Charming and lightweight romantic comedy. **95m/C VHS, DVD.** Natasha Henstridge, Michael Vartan, Joelle Carter, David Healy, Frankie Muniz, Phyllis Newman, Faith Prince, Olivia D'Abo; **D:** Steven Feder; **C:** Steven Feder; **C:** Ken Kelsch; **M:** Luis Bacalov.

It Happened at Nightmare Inn 🐾🐾 A Candle for the Devil; Nightmare Hotel 1970 Average thriller in which Geeson travels to Spanish inn and confronts two mad sisters who run the hotel. **95m/C VHS, DVD, SP** Judy Geeson, Aurora Bautista, Esperanza Roy, Victor Alcocer, Lone Fleming; **D:** Eugenio (Gene) Martin.

It Happened at the World's Fair 🐾🐾½ 1963 Fun and light romance comedy has Elvis and a companion (O'Brien) being escorted through the Seattle World's Fair by a fetching Chinese girl. 🎵 I'm Falling in Love Tonight; They Remind Me Too Much Of You; Take Me To The Fair; Relax; How Would You Like To Be; Beyond the Bend; One Broken Heart For Sale; Cotton Candy Land; A World Of Our Own. **105m/C VHS, DVD.** Elvis Presley, Joan O'Brien, Gary Lockwood, Kurt Russell, Edith Atwater, Yvonne Craig; **D:** Norman Taurog.

It Happened in Brooklyn 🐾🐾 1947 Former sailor with blue eyes bunks with janitor witt big nose in Brooklyn. Sailor and cronies encounter many musical opportunities. Lots of songs and falling in love, little entertainment. **104m/B VHS.** Frank Sinatra, Kathryn Grayson, Jimmy Durante, Peter Lawford, Gloria Grahame; **D:** Richard Whorf.

It Happened in New Orleans 🐾½ Rainbow on the River 1936 A young boy is cared for by a former slave in post-Civil War New Orleans until his Yankee grandmother claims him and takes him to New York. The boy is resented by his family but manages to overcome their hostilities. **88m/B VHS.** Bobby Breen, May Robson, Alan Mowbray, Benita Hume, Charles Butterworth, Louise Beavers, Henry O'Neill, Marilyn Knowlden; **D:** Kurt Neumann; **W:** Harry Chandlee, William Hurlbut; **C:** Charles E. Schoenbaum; **M:** Karl Hajos, Hugo Riesenfeld.

It Happened in the Park 🐾🐾½ 1956 A rare film exercise for De Sica, wherein the patrons of the Villa Borghese parks are surveyed for a 24-hour period. In French with English dialogue. **72m/B VHS, FR** Vittorio De Sica.

It Happened One Night 🐾🐾🐾🐾 1934 Classic Capra comedy about an antagonistic couple determined to teach each other about life. Colbert is an unhappy heiress who runs away from her affluent home in search of contentment. On a bus she meets newspaper reporter Gable, who teaches her how "real" people live. She returns the favor in this first of the 1930s screwball comedies. The plot is a framework for an amusing examination of war between the sexes. Colbert and Gable are superb as affectionate foes. Remade as the musicals "Eve Knew Her Apples" and "You Can't Run Away From It." **105m/B VHS, DVD.** Clark Gable, Claudette Colbert, Roscoe Karns, Walter Connolly, Alan Hale, Ward Bond; **D:** Frank Capra; **W:** Robert Riskin; **C:** Joseph Walker. Oscars '34: Actor (Gable), Actress (Colbert), Adapt. Screenplay, Director (Capra), Picture; AFI '98: Top 100, Natl. Film Reg. '93.

It Happened Tomorrow 🐾🐾🐾 1944 Now-familiar plotline will remind TV viewers of "Early Edition." Whimsical fantasy finds obituary writer Larry Stevens (Powell) receiving the next day's newspaper from his paper's librarian (Philliber). Stevens uses this knowledge of coming events to get some major scoops, win at the track, and impress beautiful spiritualist Sylvia (Darnell). Then he reads his own obituary and tries to avoid his fate. **84m/B VHS.** Dick Powell, Linda Darnell, Jack Oakie, John Philliber, Edgar Kennedy, Edward Brophy, Sig Ruman, George Cleveland, Paul Guilfoyle, Eddie Acuff; **D:** Rene Clair; **W:** Dudley Nichols; **C:** Archie Stout.

It Happens Every Spring 🐾🐾🐾½ 1949 Chemistry professor Vernon Simpson (Milland) is working on a bug repellant for trees and accidentally invents a potion that repels any kind of wood that it comes in contact with. Since he needs some big bucks to pop the question to his sweetie Deborah (Peters), Vernon, who also loves baseball, gets a tryout as a pitcher with a major league team and uses the solution on the baseballs he pitches. Naturally, it's strikeout time and the prof becomes a pitching phenom. Now, if he can only keep his little secret. Wacky baseball footage is a highlight. **87m/B VHS.** Ray Milland, Jean Peters, Paul Douglas, Ed Begley Sr., Ted de Corsia, Ray Collins, Jessie Royce Landis, Alan Hale Jr., Gene Evans; **D:** Lloyd Bacon; **W:** Valentine Davies; **M:** Leigh Harline.

It Means That to Me 🐾🐾 Me Faire ça à Moi 1960 Espionage thriller in which Constantine plays a reporter who's hired by the government to transport top secret micro-film. **88m/B VHS.** Eddie Constantine, Jean-Louis Richard, Rita Cadillac, Henri Cogan, Bernadette LaFont; **D:** Pierre Grimblat; **W:** Pierre Grimblat; **C:** Michel Kelber; **M:** Michel Legrand.

It Rained All Night the Day I Left 🦴🦴 1978 (R) Two drifters find their fortunes change when they are hired by a wealthy widow. Interesting romance adventure. 100m/C VHS. Louis Gossett Jr., Sally Kellerman, Tony Curtis; D: Nicolas Gessner.

It Runs in the Family 🦴🦴½ 2003 (PG-13) The curiosity factor is at least high, even if the family drama seems familiar. Michael Douglas co-stars with father Kirk, as well as mom Diana (Kirk's first wife), and Cameron, the son from his first marriage. They're the Grombergs, a Jewish upper-middle class professional family living in Manhattan. Alex (Michael) is a lawyer; dad Mitchell (Kirk) founded the firm. Alex's marriage to Rebecca (Peters) is strained and their older son Asher (Cameron) is troubled. Only Mitchell and wife Evelyn (Diana) seem to have found a measure of peace despite Mitchell's still recovering from a stroke. There's a lot of bickering until the true meaning of family comes through. 101m/C VHS, DVD. US Michael Douglas, Kirk Douglas, Diana Douglas, Cameron Douglas, Rory Culkin, Bernadette Peters, Michelle Monaghan, Geoffrey Arend, Sarita Choudhury, Annie Golden, Irene Gorovaia, Mark Hammer, Audra McDonald; D: Fred Schepisi; W: Jesse Wigutow; C: Ian Baker; M: Paul Grabowsky.

It Seemed Like a Good Idea at the Time 🦴🦴 Good Idea 1975 Newley is an artist whose gold-digging wife leaves him for a dim rich guy. Of course he embarks on a convoluted scheme to get her back. Canadian production wastes a decent cast and premise with underveiped writing. Candy's feature premiere, which got him a sequel, "Find the Lady." 106m/C VHS, DVD. CA Anthony Newley, Stefanie Powers, Isaac Hayes, Lloyd Bochner, John Candy, Yvonne De Carlo, Henry Ramer, Lawrence Dane; D: John Trent; W: David Main, Claude Harz; M: William McCauley.

It Should Happen to You 🦴🦴🦴 1954 An aspiring model attempts to boost her career by promoting herself on a New York City billboard. 87m/B VHS, DVD. Judy Holliday, Jack Lemmon, Peter Lawford; D: George Cukor; W: Ruth Gordon, Garson Kanin; C: Charles B(ryant) Lang Jr.

It Started in Naples 🦴🦴🦴 1960 Good performances by both Gable and Loren in this comedy-drama about an American lawyer in Italy who, upon preparing his late brother's estate, finds that his brother's nephew is living with a stripper. A custody battle ensues, but love wins out in the end. Loren is incredible in nightclub scenes. 104m/C VHS, DVD. Clark Gable, Sophia Loren, Marietto, Vittorio De Sica, Paolo Carlini, Claudio Ermelli, Giovanni Filidoro; D: Melville Shavelson; W: Melville Shavelson, Jack Rose.

It Started with a Kiss 🦴🦴½ 1959 Reynolds plays a showgirl who impulsively marries an Air Force sergeant (Ford). When he's transferred to Spain they try to make a go of their hasty marriage among numerous comic complications. Flimsy farce with likeable leads. 104m/C VHS. Debbie Reynolds, Glenn Ford, Eva Gabor, Gustavo Rojo, Fred Clark, Edgar Buchanan, Robert Warwick, Harry (Henry) Morgan, Frances Bavier; D: George Marshall.

It Started with Eve 🦴🦴🦴 1941 Funny comedy about grumpy old millionaire Jonathan Reynolds (Laughton) whose dying wish is to meet the young lady his son Johnny (Cummings) is to wed. Unfortunately, the bride-to-be is unavailable, so Johnny finds a replacement in hatcheck girl Anne (Durbin). Of course, Anne steals the old man's heart and he miraculously makes a full-blown recovery, which means big trouble for Johnny. Remade in 1964 as "I'd Rather Be Rich." Based on the story "Almost An Angel" by Hans Kraly. ♪Clavelitos; Going Home. 92m/B VHS, DVD. Deanna Durbin, Charles Laughton, Robert Cummings, Guy Kibbee, Margaret Tallichet, Catherine Doucet, Walter Catlett, Charles Coleman, Clara Blandick; D: Henry Koster; W: Norman Krasna, Leo Townsend; C: Rudolph Mate; M: Hans J. Salter.

It Takes a Thief 🦴🦴 The Challenge 1959 Tough cookie Jayne's a buxom gangstress who does the hokey pokey with her criminal minions. A former lover who's been released from the big house seems to think she's been minding the mint for him. Au contraire. 93m/B VHS, DVD. GB Jayne Mansfield, Anthony Quayle, Carl Mohner, Peter Reynolds, John Bennett, Barbara Mullen, Robert Brown, Dermot Walsh, Patrick Holt; D: John Gilling; W: John Gilling; C: Gordon Dines; M: Bill McGuffie.

It Takes Two 🦴🦴 1988 (PG-13) A young man spends his last ten days of bachelorhood cruising down Texas highways with a beautiful car saleswoman. Meanwhile, back at the altar, his bride waits patiently. Upbeat with some genuinely funny moments. From the director of "Pass the Ammo." 79m/C VHS. George Newbern, Leslie Hope, Kimberly Foster, Barry Corbin, Anthony Geary; D: David Beaird; W: Thomas Szollosi, Richard Christian Matheson; C: Peter Deming; M: Carter Burwell.

It Takes Two 🦴🦴½ 1995 (PG) Vapid sugary comedy finds the nine-year-old Olsen twins playing a duo from opposite sides of the tracks who change identities in an effort to get their respective adults (Guttenberg and Alley) together. See "The Parent Trap" instead. 100m/C VHS, DVD. Ashley (Fuller) Olsen, Mary-Kate Olsen, Kirstie Alley, Steve Guttenberg, Philip Bosco, Jane Sibbett, Lawrence Dane, Gerard Parkes; D: Andy Tennant; W: Deborah Dean Davis; C: Kenneth Zunder; M: Sherman Foote, Ray Foote.

It! The Terror from Beyond Space 🦴🦴½ It! The Vampire from Beyond Space 1958 The sole survivor of a Martian expedition is believed to have murdered his colleagues. He's arrested and brought back to Earth via space ship. En route, a vicious alien, the actual culprit, is discovered on board and begins killing the crew members. A fun science fiction thriller which, 20 years later, would provide Ridley Scott with the plot for "Alien." 68m/B VHS, DVD. Marshall Thompson, Shawn Smith, Kim Spalding, Ann Doran, Dabbs Greer, Paul Langton, Ray Corrigan; D: Edward L. Cahn; W: Jerome Bixby; C: Kenneth Peach Sr.; M: Paul Sawtell, Bert Shefter.

It Waits WOOF! 2005 And you'll wish it hadn't. Silly spooker finds alcoholic forest ranger Danielle (Vincent, she of the bouncy breasts and tight tank tops) goes into the woods after the creature that has ripped apart her boyfriend. It turns out to be a Native American spirit that was entombed in a cave until some stupid college kids released it. 88m/C DVD. Cerina Vincent, Dominic Zamprogna, Eric Schweig; D: Stephen R. Monroe; W: Richard Christian Matheson, Thomas Szollosi, Stephen J. Cannell; C: Jon Joffin; M: A. Jackson. VIDEO

The Italian 1915 The story of an Italian immigrant family living in the slums of New York during the turn of the century. 78m/B VHS. George Beban, Clara Williams, Leo Willis, J. Frank Burke, Fanny Midgley; D: Reginald Barker; W: Thomas Ince. Natl. Film Reg. '91.

The Italian 🦴🦴 Italianez 2005 (PG-13) Tough story based on a true incident and best seen by adults despite its MPAA rating. Six-year-old Vanya (solemnly appealing Spiridonov) has been deposited in a bleak Russian orphanage by his mother. His luck is apparently changing when a rich Italian couple offer to buy him from the home's corrupt adoption broker, known only as Madam (Kuznetsova). While waiting for the red tape to untangle, Vanya decides he wants to find his birth mom and, armed with an old address from his stolen files, he hits the road pursued by Madam and her lackey, who don't want to lose a sale. 99m/C DVD. RU Kolya Spiridonov, Denis Moiseenko, Sasha Syrotkin, Olga Shuvalova, Dima Zemlyanko, Maria Kuznetsova, Yuri Itskov; D: Andrei Kravchuk; W: Andrei Romanov; C: Alexander Burov; M: Alexander Kneifel.

Italian for Beginners 🦴🦴½ Italiensk for Begyndere 2001 (R) Director Scherfig is the first woman to use the strict Dogma 95 filmmaking rules (hand-held cameras, natural light, live music, no studios scenes, no costumes, and no special effects) of her Danish colleagues. She's also the first to try to do a romantic comedy in the Dogma style, and she pulls it off nicely. Her tale brings six quirky lonelyhearts: Andreas (Berthlesen), newly widowed minister; Hall-Finn (Kaalund), a soccer-obsessed restaurant manager; his best friend Jorgen (Gantzler), who's convinced he's impotent; Olympia (Stovelbaek), who likes Andreas and cares for her abusive, ill father; Karen (Jorgensen) who cuts Hal-Finn's hair and cares for her alcoholic shrew of a mother; and Giulia (Jensen), an Italian waitress with a crush on Jorgen, in a Conversational Italian class. The seemingly lightweight plot is anchored by insight into everyday misery and hurt amid the giddy matchmaking and likeable characters. 112m/C VHS, DVD. DK Anders W. Berthelsen, Peter Gantzler, Anette Stovelbaek, Ann Eleonora Jorgensen, Lars Kaalund, Sara Indrio Jensen; D: Lone Scherfig; W: Lone Scherfig; C: Jorgen Johansson.

The Italian Job 🦴🦴½ 1969 (G) Caine and Coward pair up to steal $4 million in gold by causing a major traffic jam in Turin, Italy. During the jam, the pair steals the gold from an armored car. Silliness and chases through the Swiss mountains ensue, culminating in a hilarious ending. 99m/C VHS, DVD. GB Michael Caine, Noel Coward, Benny Hill, Raf Vallone, Tony Beckley, Rossano Brazzi, Margaret Blye; D: Peter Collinson; M: Quincy Jones.

The Italian Job 🦴🦴🦴 2003 (PG-13) Typically cool crew of expert theives, led by Charlie (Wahlberg), pulls off a heist of $35 million worth of gold bars in Venice, only to be doublecrossed by crewmember Steve (Norton), who kills Charlie's mentor John (Sutherland) and leaves the rest for dead. When the group find Steve a year later in L.A., John's daughter Stella (Theron), an exceptional safecracker in her own right, joins the gang for revenge. Amiable caper flick succeeds on the multiple strengths of understated cool, superbly orchestrated action, pitch-perfect humor, and an excellent cast doing a great job. Green, as computer geek Lyle, stands out, while Wahlberg boosts his leading man appeal. Remake of the 1969 Michael Caine vehicle copies original's use of Mini Coopers, but not much else. 111m/C VHS, DVD, Blu-ray Disc, UMD, HD DVD. US Mark Wahlberg, Edward Norton, Charlize Theron, Mos Def, Seth Green, Jason Statham, Donald Sutherland, Christina Cabot, Franky G., Olek Krupa; D: F. Gary Gray; W: Wayne Powers, Donna Powers; C: Wally Pfister; M: John Powell.

Italian Movie 🦴🦴 1993 First-generation Italian immigrant Leonardo decides to become a male escort to pay off his gambling debts and support his large family but things get quite complicated. 95m/C VHS, DVD. Michael Della Femina, Rita Moreno, James Gandolfini, Caprice Benedetti; D: Roberto Monticello.

The Italian Stallion 🦴 The Party at Kitty and Stud's 1973 Stallone plays a man with only one thing on his mind...sex! 90m/C VHS, DVD. Sylvester Stallone, Henrietta Holm; D: Morton Lewis; W: Morton Lewis; C: Rolph Laube; M: Kay Leodel.

Italian Straw Hat 🦴🦴🦴 Un Chapeau de Paille d'Italie 1927 Classic silent about a man's horse eats a woman's hat. His vast, unending struggle to replace the hat is the source of continual comedy. From Eugene Labiche's play. 114m/B VHS. FR Albert Prejean, Olga Tschekowa; D: Rene Clair.

It's a Date 🦴🦴🦴 1940 A mother and daughter, both actresses, continually get their professional and romantic lives intertwined. It begins when Durbin (the daughter) is offered Kay's (the mother) Broadway role. It continues in Hawaii where the mother Kay is in love with tries to court Durbin. As if it's a comedy, of course, all is put right in the end. ♪Musetta's Waltz; Ave Maria; Loch Lomond; Love Is All; It Happened in Kaloha; Rhythm of the Islands; Hawaiian War Chant. 103m/B VHS. Deanna Durbin, Kay Francis, Walter Pidgeon, Samuel S. Hinds, S.Z. Sakall, Henry Stephenson, Charles Lane, Leon Belasco; D: William A. Seiter; W: Norman Krasna; C: Joseph Valentine.

It's a Dog's Life 🦴🦴½ The Bar Sinister 1955 The hero and narrator of this story is a wily bull terrier called Wildfire. Wildfire is a tough dog on the mean streets of the Bowery in turn-of-the-century New York. His master has him in dog fights. Wildfire is then taken in by the kindly employee of the rich and dog-hating Jagger but naturally manages to win the codger over. Based on the short story "The Bar Sinister" by Richard Harding Davis. 87m/C VHS. Jeff Richards, Edmund Gwenn, Dean Jagger; D: Herman Hoffman; W: John Michael Hayes; M: Elmer Bernstein.

It's a Gift 🦴🦴🦴 1934 A grocery clerk moves his family to the West to manage orange groves in this classic Fields comedy. Several inspired sequences. The supporting cast shines too. A real find for the discriminating comedy buff. Remake of the silent "It's the Old Army Game." 71m/B VHS, DVD. W.C. Fields, Baby LeRoy, Kathleen Howard, Jean Rouveral, Julian Madison, Tammany Young, Tommy Bupp; D: Norman Z. McLeod; W: Jack Cunningham; C: Henry Sharp.

It's a Great Feeling 🦴🦴½ 1949 Another Carson and Day team-up where Carson plays a camera-hogging show-off whom no one wants to direct. He's such an industry piranha that he ends up directing himself! He cons Day, a waitress and would-be actress, by promising her a part in his new film. Some executives hear her singing before she heads back home to Wisconsin, fed up with Hollywood. They make Carson track her down to star in the new picture, but when he arrives she is at the altar with her high school sweetheart. 85m/C VHS. Dennis Morgan, Doris Day, Jack Carson, Bill Goodwin, Errol Flynn, Gary Cooper, Joan Crawford, Ronald Reagan, Sydney Greenstreet, Danny Kaye, Eleanor Parker, Edward G. Robinson, Jane Wyman; D: David Butler.

It's a Great Life 🦴🦴½ 1943 Blondie wants Dagwood to buy a house but instead he buys a horse. He's scheming to impress a client of Mr. Dither's by participating in a fox hunt. Blondie comes to the rescue. 13th entry in series. 75m/B VHS, DVD. Penny Singleton, Arthur Lake, Larry Simms, Hugh Herbert, Jonathan Hale, Danny Mummert, Alan Dinehart, Irving Bacon, Douglas Leavitt, Marjorie Ann Mutchie; D: Frank Strayer; W: Karen De Wolf, Connie Lee.

It's a Joke, Son! 🦴🦴 1947 Follows the fictional politician, Senator Claghorn from the Fred Allen radio show, during his first run for the U.S. Senate. 67m/C VHS, DVD. Kenny Delmar, Una Merkel; D: Ben Stoloff.

It's a Mad, Mad, Mad, Mad World 🦴🦴 1963 Overblown epic comedy with a cast of notables desperately seeking the whereabouts of stolen money. Ultimately exhausting film undone by its length and overbearing performances. 155m/C VHS, DVD. Spencer Tracy, Sid Caesar, Milton Berle, Ethel Merman, Jonathan Winters, Jimmy Durante, Buddy Hackett, Mickey Rooney, Phil Silvers, Dick Shawn, Edie Adams, Dorothy Provine, Buster Keaton, Terry-Thomas, Moe Howard, Larry Fine, Joe DeRita, Jim Backus, William Demarest, Peter Falk, Leo Gorcey, Edward Everett Horton, Joe E. Brown, Carl Reiner, Zasu Pitts, Eddie Anderson, Jack Benny, Jerry Lewis, Norman Fell, Stan Freberg, Don Knotts; D: Stanley Kramer; M: Ernest Gold. Oscars '63: Sound FX Editing.

It's a Wonderful Life 🦴🦴🦴🦴 1946 American classic about a man saved from suicide by a considerate angel, who then shows the hero how important he's been to the lives of loved ones. Corny but inspirational and heartwarming, with an endearing performance by Travers as an angel Clarence. Stewart and Reed are typically wholesome. Perfect film for people who want to feel good, joyfully teetering on the border between Hollywood schmaltz and genuine heartbreak. Available colorized. Also available in a 160-minute Collector's Edition with original preview trailer, "The Making of 'It's a Wonderful Life,'" and a new digital transfer of the "original" negative. 125m/B VHS, DVD. Carl "Alfalfa" Switzer, James Stewart, Donna Reed, Henry Travers, Thomas Mitchell, Lionel Barrymore, Samuel S. Hinds, Frank Faylen, Gloria Grahame, H.B. Warner, Ellen Corby, Sheldon Leonard, Beulah Bondi, Ward Bond, Frank Albertson, Todd Karns, Mary Treen, Charles Halton; **D:** Frank Capra; **W:** Frances Goodrich, Albert Hackett, Jo Swerling; **C:** Joseph Biroc, Joseph Walker; **M:** Dimitri Tiomkin. *AFI '98: Top 100; Golden Globes '47: Director (Capra). Nat. Film Reg. '90.*

It's Alive! *🐾* 1966. Slow-moving dud about a farmer feeding passersby to the area's cave-dwelling lizard man. It's the ping-pong ball-eyed monster puts in a belated appearance that's not worth the wait. **80m/C VHS, DVD.** Tommy Kirk, Shirley Bonne, Bill (Billemouse) Thurman, Annabelle MacAdams, Corveth Ostherhen; **D:** Larry Buchanan; **W:** Larry Buchanan; **C:** Robert Alcott.

It's Alive *🐾🐾* 1974 (PG) Cult film about a mutated baby, born to a normal Los Angeles couple, who escapes and goes on a bloodthirsty, murderous rampage. It's a sight to behold. Fantastic score by Bernard Herrmann makes this chilling film a memorable one. **91m/C VHS, DVD.** John P. Ryan, Sharon Farrell, Andrew Duggan, Guy Stockwell, James Dixon, Michael Ansara, Ramsen; **D:** Larry Cohen; **W:** Larry Cohen; **C:** Fenton Hamilton.

It's Alive 2: It Lives Again *🐾🐾* this sequel to "It's Alive," the original horror film, in which the infant mutant of the previous films has been left with other murdering everyone they can find. Truly horrendous. **94m/C VHS, DVD.** Michael Moriarty, Karen Black, Laurene Landon, Gerrit Graham, James Dixon, Neal Israel, MacDonald Carey; **D:** Larry Cohen; **W:** Larry Cohen; **C:** Daniel Pearl; **M:** Laurie Johnson.

It's Alive 3: Island of the Alive *🐾* *Island of the Alive* 1987 (R) The second sequel to the tongue-in-cheek horror film, one of the found-ers of Dogme 95, tries on a futuristic romantic thriller with dismal results. John (Phoenix) arrives in New York to sign final divorce papers with his estranged wife Elena (Danes), an ice-skating superstar. Elena is in some kind of mysterious trouble and the twosome elude her funkes to be together, later learning that Elena has been cloned for insurance purposes. They then go on the run. And Penn is around as John's brother who muses while constantly flying around the world (and no, it doesn't make any sense). Both American accents and (in any sense). Both American accents and although it's supposed to be New York it was filmed in a Swedish movie studio. **104m/C DVD, US** Joaquin Rafael Phoenix, Claire Danes, Sean Penn, Douglas Henshall, Alun Armstrong, Margo Martindale, Mark Strong, Geoffrey Hutchings; **D:** Thomas Vinterberg; **C:** Anthony Dod Mantle; **M:** Zbigniew Preisner.

It's All Gone, Pete Tong *🐾🐾* 2004 (R) "Pete Tong" is a Cockney rhyming slang for 'wrong.' Frankie Wilde (Kaye) is a DJ with a major coke habit and the club world at his feet when, after years of audio at excessive levels, he loses his hearing. Dropping out or sight he hires a beautiful deaf woman to teach him lip-reading and learns the properties of vibration from a flamenco dancer, and he eventually reclaim his King of the Club DJ status. Too little hilarity and an unfocused script. **88m/C DVD, GB CA** Paul Kaye, Beatriz Batarda, Mia Wilmot, Paul J. Spence, Kate Magowan, Dave Lawrence; **D:** Michael Dowse; **C:** Balasz Bolygo; **M:** Graham Massey.

It's All True *🐾🐾* 1993 (G) A look at auteur Welles' ill-fated WWII filmmaking project. Welles served as a special cultural ambassador to South America and, in 1942, began a documentary covering the area's complex political and social issues. Includes "footage from "Four Men on a

Raft." Welles' recreation about the peasant fishermen of Brazil; surviving excerpts from "The Story of Samba," a Technicolor musical about Carnaval in Rio de Janeiro; and "footage from "My Friend Bonito," set against a backdrop of bullfighting in Mexico. **85m/C VHS, DVD.** D: Richard Wilson, Bill Krohn, Myron Meise, Orson Welles; **W:** Richard Wilson, Bill Krohn, Myron Meise; **C:** Gary Graver, George Fanto; **M:** Jorge Arriagada; **Narr:** Miguel Ferrer.

It's Always Fair Weather *🐾🐾* 1955 Three WWII buddies meet again at a 10-year reunion and find that they can't like each other very much. A surprisingly cynical film. Director Donen produced "Seven Brides for Seven Brothers" the previous year. *♫Stillman's Gym; March, March; Why Are We Here?; Blue, Da-nube; Music Is Better Than Words; Once Upon A Time; The Time For Parting; I Like Myself; Baby You Knock Me Cut; Thanks A Lot; But No Thanks.* **102m/C VHS, DVD.** Gene Kelly, Cyd Charisse, Dan Dailey, Michael Kidd; **D:** Stanley Donen; **W:** Betty Comden, Adolph Green; **M:** Betty Comden, Adolph Green, Andre Previn.

It's Called Murder, Baby *🐾* 1982 (R) The famed porn star gives the viewer a lesson in English vocabulary in this tale of a blackmailed movie queen. **94m/C VHS.** John Leslie, Cameron Mitchell, Lisa Trego; **D:** Sam Weston.

It's Good to Be Alive *🐾🐾🐾* 1974 The true story of how Brooklyn Dodgers' catcher Roy Campanella learned to face life after an automobile accident left him a quadriplegic. Good performances all around. **100m/C VHS, DVD.** Ramon Bieri, Joe De Santis, Paul Winfield, Ruby Dee, Louis Gossett Jr.; **D:** Michael Landon; **M:** Michel Legrand.

It's in the Bag *🐾🐾½* The *Fifth Chair* 1945 A shiftless flea circus owner learns that a fortune is hidden in one of them. **87m/B VHS.** Fred Allen, Don Ameche, Jack Benny, William Bendix, Binnie Barnes, Robert Benchley; **D:** Richard Wallace.

It's in the Water *🐾🐾* 1996 Small, conservative Azalea Springs, Texas is rocked by the opening of an AIDS hospice. The homophobia outrages society until Alex, who begins working at the hospice alongside best friend (soon to be more) Grace. Then a rumor starts that the local drinking water turns you gay and things really get wild. Fast-moving and funny. **108m/C VHS, DVD.** Keri Jo Chapman, Teresa Garrett, Barbara Lasater, Larry Randolph; **D:** Kelli Herd.

It's Love Again *🐾🐾½* 1936 A streetwise chorus girl poses as a fictional socialite in a light music-hall comedy. It's Love Again; Heaven In Your Arms. **83m/B VHS, GB** Jessie Matthews, Robert Young, Sonnie Hale; **D:** Victor Saville.

It's My Party *🐾🐾½* 1995 (R) When L.A. architect Nick Stark (Roberts) learns that he's developed untreatable brain lesions from AIDS that will essentially leave him helpless, he decides to throw himself a monumental farewell bash before taking a drug overdose. Friends and family all turn up as does, awkwardly enough, Brandon Theis (Harrison), Nick's former live-in who couldn't handle his HIV-positive diagnosis but would like a last reapproachment. Fine, sympathetic, performances, especially by the two leads, and yes, it's a weepie. Based on a true story that Kleiser himself experienced. **120m/C VHS, DVD.** Eric Roberts, Gregory Harrison, Marlee Matlin, Lee Grant, George Segal, Bronson Pinchot, Bruce Davison, Devon Gummersall, Roddy McDowall, Margaret Cho, Paul Regina, Olivia Newton-John, Christopher Atkins, Dennis Christopher, Ron Glass, Eugene Robert Glazer; **D:** Randal Kleiser; **W:** Randal Kleiser; **C:** Bernd Heinl; **M:** Basil Poledouris.

It's My Turn *🐾🐾* 1980 (R) A mathematics professor (Clayburgh) struggles in her relationship with live-in lover (Grodin) who sells real-estate in Chicago. She meets retired baseball player (Douglas) and falls in love. "Ho-hum" just about describes the rest. **91m/C VHS.** Jill Clayburgh, Charles Grodin, Beverly Garland, Steven Hill, Dianne Wiest, Daniel Stern; **D:** Claudia Weill; **W:** Eleanor Bergstein; **C:** Bill Butler.

It's My Turn, Laura Cadieux *🐾🐾* *C'ta Ton Tour, Laura Cadieux* 1998 One a week several women meet at the same doctor's office as they've done for the past 15 years. The social aspects 'far outweigh the medical benefits for the women as they gossip and talk about their restricted lives. But one week a series of misunderstandings un-fold when Madame Therrien believes her friend Laura Cadieux's has gone missing. Based on the novel by Michel Tremblay. French with subtitles. **92m/C VHS, C4** Ginette Reno, Donald Pilon, Pierrette Rocaille, Denise Dubois, Samuel Landry, Adele Reinhardt; **D:** Denise Filatrault; **W:** Denise Filatrault; **C:** Daniel Jobin; **M:** Francois Dompierre.

It's Not the Size That Counts woof! *Percy's Progress* 1974 After the Earth's drinking water is contaminated, Lawson is the only man on Earth not to be struck by impotency. Limp sequel to "Percy," the British comedy about the first man to receive a penis transplant. Promising comedy doesn't deliver. **90m/C VHS.** Leigh Lawson, Elke Sommer, Denholm Elliott, Vincent Price, Judy Geeson, Milo O'Shea, Julie Ege, George Coulouris, Bernard Lee; **D:** Ralph Thomas; **W:** Harry H. Corbett, Sid Colin, Ian La Frenais; **C:** Tony Imi; **M:** Tony Macaulay.

It's Pat: The Movie woof! 1994 (PG-13) This movie is so bad, let's pray it sounds the death knell to big-screen versions of "Saturday Night Live" sketch characters—who possessed little humor to begin with. For what it's worth, the androgynous Pat (Sweeney) falls for the equally gender-suspect Chris (Foley, from Canada's version of SNL. "Kids in the Hall") and all sorts of embarrassing situations arise. Pat's quest to find Pat's self is sketch material stretched see-through thin. **78m/C VHS, DVD.** Julia Sweeney, Dave Foley, Charles Rocket, Kathy Griffin, Julie Haydon, Tim Meadows, Arleen (Arlene) Sorkin, Cameos: Sally Jesse Raphael, Kathy Najimy; **D:** Adam Bernstein; **W:** Julia Sweeney, Jim Emerson, Stephen Hibbert.

It's the Old Army Game *🐾🐾* 1926 Classic Fields gags in three of his best Ziegfeld Follies sketches: "The Drug Store," "A Peaceful Morning," and "The Family Flivver." The beautiful Brooks serves as his comic foil. **75m/B VHS.** W.C. Fields, Louise Brooks, Blanche Ring, William Gaxton; **D:** Edward Sutherland.

It's the Rage *🐾🐾½* *All the Rage* 1999 (R) Glib ensemble comedy about the best collision of guns and anger, with an interesting cast. Warren (Daniels) shoots an intruder who turns out to be his business partner, and around with Warren's prim wife, Helen (Allen). His lawyer, Tim (Braugher), has just been given a gun by his boyfriend (Schwimmer) whose brother (Ribisi) is trigger-happy. Meanwhile, Helen takes a job with paranoid billionaire, Mr. Morgan (Sinise), while Warren's being investigated by a couple of detectives (Forster, Woodbine) for whom guns are job accessories. Red-din scripted from this play. **97m/C VHS, DVD.** Jeff Daniels, Joan Allen, Andre Braugher, David Schwimmer, Anna Paquin, Giovanni Ribisi, Gary Sinise, Josh Brolin, Robert Forster, Bokeem Woodbine; **D:** James D. Stern; **W:** Keith Reddin; **C:** Yoande Zauberman; **M:** Mark Mothersbaugh.

Ivan and Abraham *🐾🐾* 1994 Abraham (Alexandrovitch) is a nine-year-old Jewish boy, living on a shtetl in 1930s eastern Poland, with his best friend being the family's 14-year-old Christian apprentice Ivan (Iakovlev). The boys sense the increasing family tensions and escape into the nearby forest, only to find politics and prejudice sweeping over them all. In Yiddish, Russian, Polish, and Romany, with English subtitles. **105m/B VHS.** Roma Aleksandrovitch, Sacha Iakovlev, Vladimir Machkov, Meria Lipkina, Rolan Bykov, Daniel Olbrychski; **D:** Yoande Zauberman; **W:** Yolande Zauberman; **C:** Jean-Marc Fabre.

Ivan the Terrible, Part 1 *🐾🐾🐾🐾* *Ivan Grozny* 1944 Contemplative epic of Russia's first czar is a classic, innovative film from cinema genius Eisenstein. Visually stunning, with a fine perfor-

mance by Cherkassov. Ivan's struggles to preserve his country is the main concern of the first half of Eisenstein's masterwork (which he originally planned as a trilogy). In Russian with English subtitles. **100m/B VHS, DVD, RU** Nikolai Cherkassov, Lyudmila Tselikovskaya, Serafina Birman, Piotr Kadochnikov; **D:** Sergei Eisenstein; **W:** Sergei Eisenstein; **C:** Eduard Tisse; **M:** Sergei Prokofiev.

Ivan the Terrible, Part 2 *🐾🐾🐾½* *Ivan the Terrible, Part 2; The Boyars' Plot; Ivan Grozny 2* 1946 Landed gentry conspire to dethrone the czar in this continuation of the innovative epic. More stunning imagery from master Eisenstein, who makes no false moves in this one. Slow going, but immensely rewarding. Russian dialogue with English subtitles; contains color sequences. **87m/B VHS, DVD, RU** Nikolai Cherkassov, Lyudmila Tselikovskaya, Serafina Birman, Piotr Kadochnikov; **D:** Sergei Eisenstein; **C:** Eduard Tisse, Andrei Moskvin; **M:** Sergei Prokofiev.

Ivanhoe *🐾🐾🐾* 1952 Knights fight each other and woo maidens in this chivalrous romance derived from the Sir Walter Scott classic. Taylor is suitably noble, while Sanders is familiarly serpentine. Remade in 1982. **107m/C VHS, DVD.** Robert Taylor, Elizabeth Taylor, Joan Fontaine, George Sanders, Finlay Currie, Felix Aylmer; **D:** Richard Thorpe; **W:** Marguerite Roberts, Noel Langley; **C:** Frederick A. (Freddie) Young; **M:** Miklos Rozsa.

Ivanhoe *🐾🐾½* 1982 A version of Sir Walter Scott's classic novel of chivalry and knighthood in 12th-century England. Remake of the 1953 film classic. **142m/C VHS, DVD.** Anthony Andrews, James Mason, Lysette Anthony, Sam Neill, Olivia Hussey, Michael Hordern, Julian Glover, George Innes, Ronald Pickup, John Rhys-Davies, Chloe Franks; **D:** Douglas Camfield. **TV**

Ivanhoe *🐾🐾* 1997 TV miniseries version of Sir Walter Scott's epic tale of knights, chivalry, romance, and daring. Saxon knight Wilfred of Ivanhoe (Wadington), having fought for Richard the Lionheart (Edwards) during the Crusades, returns to England to battle the scheming Prince John (Brown) and sinister Grand Master of the Templars, Lucas De Beaumanoir (Lee) in order to regain his honor. His childhood sweetheart, Saxon heiress Rowena (Smurfit), is betrothed to another but Ivanhoe's also drawn to Jewish healer Rebecca (Lynch) as is scheming Knight Templar (Edwards). Lots of action. On six cassettes. **292m/C VHS, DVD.** Steven Waddington, Susan Lynch, Ciaran Hinds, Victoria Smurfit, Ralph Brown, Roy Edwards, Ronald Pickup, David Horovitch, Trevor Cooper, Valentine Pelka, Nick Brimble, Jimmy Chisholm, Christopher Lee, Aden (John) Gillett, James Cosmo, Siar Phillips, Ciaran Madden; **D:** Stuart Orme; **W:** Deborah Cook; **C:** Colin Towns. **TV**

I've Always Loved You *🐾🐾½* *Concerto* 1946 The drama of love and jealousy explored in an extravagant production filled with classical music. **117m/C VHS.** Philip Dorn, Catherine McLeod; **D:** Frank Borzage; **C:** Gaetano Antonio "Tony" Gaudio.

I've Been Waiting for You *🐾🐾* 1998 (PG-13) California teen Sarah Zoltanne (Chalke), who has an interest in the occult, moves with her family to a New England town. Her fellow teens begin to believe that she's a witch out for revenge on the descendents of the townspeople who burned another witch, who had the same name. Then on Hallloween, Sarah begins to see events beyond her knowledge of a crush. Good-natured tone helped considerably by McCarthy's winning performance. **88m/C VHS, DVD.** Sarah Chalke, Soleil Moon Frye, Markie Post, Christian Campbell, Tom Dugan; **D:** Christopher Leitch; **W:** Duane Poole. **TV**

I've Heard the Mermaids Singing *🐾🐾🐾* 1987 Independent Canadian semi-satiric romantic comedy details the misadventures of a klutzy woman who suddenly obtains a desirable job in an art gallery run by a lesbian on whom she develops a crush. Good-natured fun

VideoHound's Golden Movie Retriever **495**

The Ivory Handled Gun 🎬🎬
1935 The Wolverine Kid wants Buck Ward (Jones) dead because the Kid's father, John Plunkett, was rejected by Buck's mother in favor of Buck's dad, Bill, who killed the interloper in a fight. Bill also happens to be in possession of one of Plunkett's ivory-handed guns and the Kid wants that back as well. In chapter 2 of "Gordon of Ghost City," Gordon and Mary Gray are observed by a mysterious, threatening figure and Mary gets caught in a stampede. **81m/B VHS.** Buck Jones, Charlotte Wynters, Walter Miller, Frank Rice, Carl Stockdale, Joseph Girard, Madge Bellamy; **D:** Ray Taylor.

Ivory Hunters 🎬🎬1/2 *The Last Elephant* **1990** Conservationists team up to thwart a massacre of elephants by poachers. Predictable made-for-cable entertainment co-produced by the National Audubon Society. **94m/C VHS.** John Lithgow, Isabella Rossellini, James Earl Jones, Tony Todd, Olek Krupa; **D:** Joseph Sargent; **W:** Richard Guttman, Bill Bozzone; **M:** Charles Bernstein. **CABLE**

Ivory Tower 🎬🎬 **1997** Anthony Daytona (Van Horn) is a hotshot marketing exec in charge of launching a new computer product. But then his new boss arrives and suddenly not only the project but Anthony's career and the company itself is in jeopardy. **107m/C VHS, DVD.** Patrick Van Horn, James Wilder, Kari Wuhrer, Michael Ironside, Donna Pescow, Keith Coogan, Ian Buchanan; **D:** Darin Ferriola; **W:** Darin Ferriola; **C:** Maida Sussman.

Izzy & Moe 🎬🎬1/2 **1985** Carney and The Great One are reunited for the last time on screen as former vaudevillians who become federal agents and create havoc amid speak-easies and bathtub gin during Prohibition. Based on true stories. **92m/C VHS, DVD.** Jackie Gleason, Art Carney, Cynthia Harris, Zohra Lampert, Drew Snyder, Dick Latessa; **D:** Jackie Cooper. **TV**

J. Edgar Hoover 🎬🎬 **1987** Cable adaptation from "My 30 years in Hoover's FBI" by William G. Sullivan and William S. Brown. Biographical drama deals with Hoover's 55-year career with the government. Included are his FBI days. **110m/C VHS.** Treat Williams, Rip Torn, David Ogden Stiers, Andrew Duggan, Art Hindle, Louise Fletcher; **D:** Robert E. Collins. **CABLE**

J-Men Forever! 🎬🎬1/2 **1979 (PG)** A spoof on early sci-fi/spy serials in which an alien takeover is attempted via rock-n-roll (your parents warned you). Employs an amusing technique of dubbing footage from dozens of Republic dramas intercut with new film featuring the "Firesign Theater" crew. **73m/B VHS, DVD.** Peter Bergman, Phil(ip) Proctor; **D:** Richard Patterson.

J'Accuse 🎬🎬🎬1/2 *I Accuse; That They May Live* **1937** A Frenchman creates a device he believes will stop the war but it is confiscated by the government and used as part of the national defense. Subsequently, he goes mad. Gance (known for his 1927 "Napoleon"), remade this 1919 silent film, retelling the powerful anti-war message with great sensitivity. Banned in Nazi Germany. **125m/B VHS.** Victor Francen, Jean Max, Delaire, Renee Devillers; **D:** Abel Gance.

Jabberwocky 🎬🎬1/2 **1977 (PG)** Pythonesque chaos prevails in the medieval cartoon kingdom of King Bruno the Questionable, who rules with cruelty, stupidity, lust and dust. Jabberwocky is the big dragon mowing everything down in its path until hero Palin decides to take it on. Uneven, but real funny at times. **104m/C VHS, DVD.** Michael Palin, Eric Idle, Max Wall, Deborah Fallender, Terry Jones, John Le Mesurier, Annette Badland, Warren Mitchell, Harry H. Corbett, David Prowse, Neil Innes; **D:** Terry Gilliam; **W:** Charles Alverson, Terry Gilliam; **C:** Terry Bedford; **M:** De Wolfe.

Jack 🎬🎬1/2 **1996 (PG-13)** Ten-year-old Jack Powell (Williams) suffers from a rare genetic disorder that causes him to age at four times the normal rate so he looks like a 40-year-old. His family, fearing ridicule, has kept him isolated but since Jack's so lonely, they finally agree to let him attend school. This new fourth grader isn't the only one with a lot to learn. **111m/C VHS, DVD.** Robin Williams, Bill Cosby, Diane Lane, Bri-

---

an Kerwin, Fran Drescher, Michael McKean, Jennifer Lopez, Don Novello, Todd Bosley; **D:** Francis Ford Coppola; **W:** James DeMonaco, Gary Nadeau; **C:** John Toll; **M:** Michael Kamen.

Jack Ahoy 🎬1/2 **1934** Jack Hulbert plays an incompetent sailor set on impressing his country and the admiral's daughter by finding the British submarine that was stolen by the Chinese. Froth with song and dance for the jaunty at heart. **70m/B VHS.** Jack Hulbert, Nancy O'Neil, Alfred Drayton; **D:** Leslie Arliss, Walter Ford; **W:** Gerald Fairlie. **VIDEO**

Jack and His Friends 🎬🎬
1992 (R) Comic satire of the tribulations of Jack the shoe salesman (Garfield), who is shown the front door by his unfaithful wife. Beset by grief, he drives the streets aimlessly until he is kidnapped by a young couple (Rockwell and Reyes) on the run from the law, who force Jack to take them to his summer house where they all try to decide what to do with their lives. **93m/C VHS.** Allen (Goorwitz) Garfield, Sam Rockwell, Judy Reyes; **D:** Bruce Ornstein.

Jack and Sarah 🎬🎬1/2 **1995 (R)** Widowed London lawyer (Grant) hires American waitress (Mathis), to help raise his infant daughter Sarah. Complications arise because Amy has no child rearing skills and Jack's parents and in-laws disapprove of the whole situation. Performances are nice (especially the scene-stealing infants), and there's some fine moments combining tragedy with romance, but the plot is a little thin and the whole film is slow moving (it takes more than half the movie to get the three protagonists in place). An edited version is rated PG. **110m/C VHS, DVD.** *GB* Richard E. Grant, Samantha Mathis, Ian McKellen, Judi Dench, Cherie Lunghi, Eileen Atkins, Imogen Stubbs; **D:** Tim Sullivan; **W:** Tim Sullivan; **C:** Jean-Yves Escoffier; **M:** Simon Boswell.

Jack & the Beanstalk 🎬🎬 **1952** While baby-sitting, Lou falls asleep and dreams he's Jack in this spoof of the classic fairy tale. **78m/C VHS, DVD.** Bud Abbott, Lou Costello, Buddy Baer, Dorothy Ford, Barbara Brown, William Farnum; **D:** Jean Yarbrough; **W:** Nathaniel Curtis; **C:** George Robinson; **M:** Heinz Roemheld.

Jack & the Beanstalk: The Real Story 🎬🎬1/2 *Jim Henson's Jack and the Beanstalk* **2001** Attenuated and dull take on the familiar fairytale finds Modine's Jack a modern-day descendant of the Jack who stole the golden goose. That's how his family built an empire but it's payback time and Jack needs to climb that beanstalk and make reparations for his ancestor's crimes. **184m/C VHS, DVD.** *NZ* Alexis Arquette, Sarah Smuts-Kennedy, Bruno Lawrence; **D:** Garth Maxwell; **W:** Garth Maxwell; **C:** Donald Duncan; **M:** Chris Neal.

The Jack Bull 🎬🎬1/2 **1999 (R)** Cusack's father adapted a 19th-century German novel, "Michael Kohlhaas" by Heinrich Von Kleist, into a 19th-century American western, set in Wyoming. Myrl Redding (Cusack) is a peaceful horse trader who demands justice when wealthy landowner Henry Ballard (Jones) beats two of

---

Redding's horses and their Indian caretaker. Since Ballard has the local law in his pocket, Redding gets no satisfaction. Becoming obsessed, he decides to form a vigilante posse to get Ballard to pay for his actions. **120m/C VHS, DVD.** John Cusack, L.Q. Jones, John Goodman, Rodney A. Grant, Miranda Otto, John C. McGinley, John Savage, Jay O. Sanders, Scott Wilson, Drake Bell, Glenn Morshower, Ken Pogue; **D:** John Badham; **W:** Richard (Dick) Cusack; **C:** Gale Tattersall; **M:** Lennie Niehaus. **CABLE**

Jack Frost 🎬 **1997 (R)** Convicted serial killer Jack Frost (McDonald) mutates after accidental exposure to an experimental liquid DNA, becomes a killer snowman, and terrorizes a town preparing for the annual Snowman Festival. Snickering seasonal gore with a killer who uses icicles and a carrot nose to dispatch some of his latest victims. **89m/C VHS, DVD.** Scott MacDonald, Christopher Allport, F. William Parker; **D:** Michael Cooney; **W:** Michael Cooney; **C:** Dean Lent. **VIDEO**

Jack Frost 🎬 **1998 (PG)** As emotionally realistic and cool as soap flake snow, alleged family feature has Keaton playing Jack Frost, a struggling musician who spends too much time away from wife Gabby (Preston) and son Charlie (Cross). He decides to blow off a Christmas Day gig to spend more time with the family, only to be killed on his way to their mountain cabin. One year later, forlorn Charlie makes a snowman, dresses it in his dead dad's duds, and blows a note on Jack's harmonica. Bingo! Now his dead father is back to life as a creepy-looking talking snowman! Keaton tries his best with the lame material; but with the use of four confused screenwriters, he didn't have a snowball's chance. Additional warning: Keaton sings. Not to be confused with the straight-to-video release of the same name about a murderous deranged talking snowman. **95m/C VHS, DVD.** Michael Keaton, Kelly Preston, Joseph Cross, Mark Addy, Eli Marienthal, Dweezil Zappa, Henry Rollins, Andy Lawrence, Ahmet Zappa, Jeff Cesario; **D:** Troy Miller; **W:** Mark Steven Johnson, Steven L. Bloom, Jonathan Roberts, Jeff Cesario; **C:** Laszlo Kovacs; **M:** Trevor Rabin.

Jack Frost 2: Revenge of the Mutant Killer Snowman woof! **2000 (R)** Snowy horror is returned to his evil ways by a lab accident that also makes him impervious to heat, bullets, and antifreeze. So Jack decides to get revenge on Sheriff Sam (who defeated him previously), who just happens to be on vacation in a tropical paradise. But Chilly Boy doesn't have to worry about that. **91m/ C VHS, DVD.** Christopher Allport, David Allan Brooks, Chip Heller, Eileen Seeley, Adrienne Barbeau; **D:** Michael Cooney; **W:** Michael Cooney. **VIDEO**

Jack Higgins' Midnight Man 🎬1/2 *Midnight Man* **1996 (R)** Ex-terrorist Sean Dillon (Lowe) is reluctantly recruited by British intelligence to thwart a plot to kill Princes Harry and William in a scheme to overthrow the monarchy. Only Dillon soon realizes his target is a dangerous ex-colleague and a band of fanatics. Based on the Higgins novel "Eye of the Storm." **104m/C VHS.** Rob Lowe, Kenneth Cranham, Deborah Maria Moore, Michael Sarrazin, Hannes Jaenicke, Daphne Cheung, Jim Duggan; **D:** Lawrence Gordon-Clark; **W:** Jurgen Wolff; **C:** Ken Westbury; **M:** Leon Aronson. **CABLE**

Jack Higgins' On Dangerous Ground 🎬 *On Dangerous Ground* **1995 (R)** A major miscast ruins thriller writer Higgins's chances in this cable movie. Ex-IRA assassin and all-around terrorist Sean Dillon (Lowe) now works for a British intelligence agency, headed by Brigadier Ferguson (Cranham). A secret agreement documenting a WWII deal between Lord Mountbatten and Mao Tse-tung has come to murky light and could exacerbate the tensions between China and Britain over Hong Kong. Dillon not only is expected to retrieve the document but also prevent an assassination attempt while the U.S. prez visits England. Lowe's way too lightweight for the Dillon role and manages to throw what should have been a good action yarn completely off-balance. **105m/C VHS. CA GB**

Jack Higgins' The Windsor Protocol 🎬1/2 *The Windsor Protocol* **1997 (R)** The sequel to "Jack Higgins' Thunder Point" finds ex-terrorist Sean Dillon (MacLachlan), now working for British Intelligence, still trying to recover The Windsor Protocol, a Nazi-era document that has recently come to light and involves present-day Nazi sympathizers, money, power, and both the U.S. and British governments. **96m/C VHS.** Kyle MacLachlan, Alan Thicke, Macha Grenon, John Colicos, Chris Wiggins; **D:** George Mihalka; **W:** David Preston, Stephen Zoller; **C:** Peter Benison; **M:** Stanislas Syrewicz. **CABLE**

Jack Higgins' Thunder Point 🎬1/2 *Thunder Point* **1997 (R)** MacLachlan takes over from Dillon and the casting still stinks. (Doesn't anybody read Higgins' books!) A treasure diver finds The Windsor Protocol, a Hitler directive that also contains info on hidden funds that neo-Nazis hope to use to resurrect the Reich. Dillon's hired to find the document but it eventually does winds up in the hands of Nazi sympathizers, leading to the sequel "Jack Higgins' The Windsor Protocol." **95m/C VHS.** Kyle MacLachlan, Michael Sarrazin, Kenneth Welsh, Pascale Bussieres, Chris Wiggins, John Colicos, Cedric Smith; **D:** George Mihalka; **W:** Morrie Ruvinsky; **C:** Peter Benison; **M:** Stanislas Syrewicz. **CABLE**

The Jack Knife Man 🎬🎬
1920 Sentimental silent treatment of the relationship between a boy and a man. A new mother close to death hands over her bundle of joy to a kindly old river man, and the two bond in a familial way despite incessant adversity. Made the year following Vidor's debut as a feature film director. **70m/B VHS.** Fred Turner, Harry Todd, Bobby Kelso, Willis Marks, Lillian (Lillianne, Lyllian) Leighton, James Corrigan; **D:** King Vidor; **W:** William Parker.

Jack London 🎬🎬1/2 *The Adventures of Jack London; The Life of Jack London* **1944** Dramatizes London's most creative years during his careers as oyster pirate, prospector, war correspondent and author. Based on "The Book of Jack London" by Charmian London. **94m/B VHS, DVD.** Michael O'Shea, Susan Hayward, Harry Davenport, Virginia Mayo, Frank Craven; **D:** Alfred Santell.

Jack London's The Call of the Wild 🎬🎬1/2 *The Call of the Wild: Dog of the Yukon* **1997 (PG)** Adaptation of Jack London's 1903 adventure story is told from the view of Buck, an intelligent St. Bernard-Labrador mix who's kidnapped from his California home. He's sold in the Yukon and eventually winds up with prospector John Thornton (Hauer) but Buck is increasingly drawn to running free. **90m/C VHS, DVD.** Rutger Hauer, Luc Morissette, Bronwyn Booth; **D:** Peter Svatek; **W:** Graham Ludlow; **C:** Sylvain Brault; **M:** Alan Reeves; **Nar:** Richard Dreyfuss.

Jack-O 🎬1/2 **1995 (R)** Halloween nightmares in the small town of Oakmoor Crossing. When warlock Walter Machen (Carradine) was hung 100 years before, he invoked a demon creature to take his revenge. Now partyers, fooling around in the local cemetery, have stumbled onto horrific Jack-O's remains and manage to once again unleash the evil within. Cheesy grade-Z horror features old footage of deceased actors Carradine and Mitchell incorporated into what little plot there is. **90m/C VHS, DVD.** Linnea Quigley, Ryan Latshaw, Cameron Mitchell, John Carradine, Dawn Wildsmith, Brinke Stevens; **D:** Steve Latshaw; **W:** Patrick Moran; **C:** Maxwell J. Beck; **M:** Walton.

Jack O'Lantern 🎬 **2004 (R)** Inept, miniscule-budgeted horror flick finds Jack (Watkins) still suffering nightmares a year after a deadly car crash. Only his nightmares are now resulting in murder. Oh, and the monster has a jack o'lantern for a head. **94m/C VHS, DVD.** David R. Watkins, Kevin L. Powers, Tracy Yarkoni, Justice Leak, Brian Avenet-Bradley, Ron McLellen, Sacha A. Dzuba;

Jack the Bear ♂♂½ 1993 (PG-13)
Exercise in misery centers on a father and
his two sons, trying to pick up the pieces
after the death of wife and mother. Marcovicci, Dad DeVito is the host of a late-night
horror show who's cuddly as a bear—
when he's not drinking. While the talent
and circumstances might have been
enough to create a sensitive study, the
emotion is completely overwrought by
contrived pict twists, including a kidnapping by the local Nazi. TV's "thirtysomething" director Herskovitz creates an effecting "director" Herskovitz creates an effective, not unlike a cement block being dropped
on a card house. Point made, but so much
for subtlety. Based on a novel by Dan
McCall. **98m/C VHS, DVD.** Danny DeVito, Robert
J. Steinmiller Jr., Miko Hughes, Gary Sinise, Art
LaFleur, Andrea Marcovicci, Julia Louis-Dreyfus,
Reese Witherspoon; **D:** Marshall Herskovitz; **W:**
Steven Zaillian; **C:** Fred Murphy; **M:** James Horner.

Jack the Giant Killer ♂♂♂ 1962 (G) A young farmer joins a medieval
princess on a journey to a distant convent.
Along the way, they combat an evil wizard, dragons, sea monsters, and other
mystical creatures, and are assisted by leprechauns, a dog, and a chimp. Generally
considered a blatant rip-off of "The Seventh Voyage of Sinbad", the film nonetheless delivers plenty of fun and excitement.
Jim Danforth of "Gumby" fame provided
the stop-motion animation. **95m/C VHS,
DVD.** Kerwin Mathews, Judi Meredith, Torin
Thatcher, Walter Burke, Roger Mobley, Barry Kelley, Don Beddoe, Anna Lee, Robert Gist; **D:** Nathan "Jerry" Juran; **W:** Nathan "Jerry" Juran, Orville H. Hampton; **C:** David S. Horsley; **M:** Paul
Sawtell, Bert Shefter.

Jack the Ripper ♂♂ 1960 An
American detective joins Scotland Yard in
tracking down the legendary and elusive
Jack the Ripper. More gory than most.
The last scene is in color. **88m/B VHS, DVD.
GB** Lee Patterson, Betty McDowall, Barbara
Burke, John Le Mesurier, George Rose; **D:** Monty
Berman, Robert S. Baker; **M:** Stanley Black.

Jack the Ripper ♂♂♂ 1988 Der Dimen-
moerder von London 1976 (R) The inimitable
Kinski assumes the role of the most hei-
nous criminal of modern history—Jack the
Ripper. **82m/C VHS, DVD.** *SI GE* Klaus Kinski,
Josephine Chaplin, Herbert (Fuchs) Fux, Ursula
von Wiese, Lina Romay, Andreas Mannkopff; **D:**
Jess (Jesus) Franco; **W:** Jess (Jesus) Franco; **C:**
Peter Baumgartner.

Jack the Ripper ♂♂½ 1997 (R) The plot
has more holes than Swiss cheese but
thanks to a pro cast this film manages to
be at least a workmanlike thriller. Willis
stars as a killer-for-hire known only as
"The Jackal." His latest employer, a Russian gangster, wants revenge for FBI interference in his business, and the Jackal's target is apparently the FBI's Director.
Few know what the Jackal looks like and
the most available is Declan Mulqueen
(Gere), an IRA gunman imprisoned in the
U.S. He's given a deal by good FBI guy
Preston (Poitier) and the hunt is on. Unfortunately, the Jackal's elaborate preparations don't raise the tension, though they
do provide some gross-out moments. The
end game "in the D.C. subway) between
the Jackal and Mulqueen provides a satisfying conclusion and Willis does excel as
the ice-cold killer. Started off as a heavily
reworked version of the 1973 assassination thriller "The Day of the Jackal" but
most of the associations have been cut.
124m/C VHS, DVD. Bruce Willis, Richard Gere,
Sidney Poitier, Diane Venora, Mathilda May,
Stephen Spinella, John Cunningham, J.K. Simmons, Tess Harper, Richard Lineback, Jack Black,
David Hayman, Steve Bassett; **D:** Michael Caton-
Jones; **W:** Chuck Pfarrer; **C:** Karl Walter Lindenlaub; **M:** Carter Burwell.

Jack the Ripper ♂♂ 1988 An-
other retelling of the life of the legendary
serial killer. Caine is the Scotland Yard inspector who tracks down the murderer.
Ending is based on recent evidence found
by director/co-writer Wickes. Extremely
well done TV film. **200m/C VHS.** Michael
Caine, Armand Assante, Ray McAnally, Susan
George, Jane Seymour, Lewis Collins, Ken Bones;
D: David Wickes; **W:** David Wickes. **TV**

The Jackals ♂♂ 1967 Six bandits
threaten miner Price and his granddaugh-
ter in order to get his gold. Set in South
Africa. **105m/C VHS, DVD.** Vincent Price, Diana
Ivarson, Robert Gunner, Bob Courtney, Patrick
Mynhardt; **D:** Robert D. Webb.

Jackass Number Two ♂♂ 2006 (R) With the TV series iced, the Jackass posse is back with four years' worth
of new gags, stunts, and bad ideas.
There's less talk, more shock and if you're
familiar with the curiously charismatic
Knoxville, you'll know what to expect—
body parts in even more insane contests.
By the way, the title is not just an indication that it's a sequel, it's a literal warning
of what to expect. **95m/C DVD.** Johnny
Knoxville, Bam Margera, Chris Pontius, Ryan
Dunn, Steve-O, Dave England, Preston Lacy, Ehren McGhehey; **D:** Jeff Tremaine; **W:** Preston
Lacy, Sean Cliver; **C:** Dimitry Elyashkevich, Lance
Bangs, Rick Kosick.

Jackass: The Movie ♂♂ 2002 (R) The ultimate critic-proof movie. Those
who love the TV show will also love the
gross as they wanna be, and indulge in
even bigger, dumber, if not always more
elaborate stunts. Those who think the
drill, Johnny Knoxville and his crew continue to think so, in case you don't know
perform homemade or made-up stunts to
a) get laughs, b) get a reaction out of people, c) gross out bystanders, d) see if they
can be done, and e) all your of the above.
Watch it to bring out your inner 12-year-
old with ADHD. **87m/C VHS, DVD.** Johnny
Knoxville, Bam Margera, Steve "Steve-O" Glover,
Chris Pontius, Ryan Dunn, Jason "Wee Man" Acuna; **D:** Jeff Tremaine; **C:** Dimitry Elyashkevich.

The Jacket ♂♂½ 2005 (R) A gulf
vet (Brody) is falsely convicted of murder.
Having no memory of the crime, he's sentenced to a mental institution instead of
prison. The chief psychiatrist's therapy
consists of drugs, a straitjacket, and sensory deprivation in a morgue drawer. Vet's
reaction to this is, of course, to time-travel,
allowing him to confront the ghosts of his
present in the future and effect changes
for the general good of all. Interesting
premise, but handled with a lead foot and
little originality. Think "Jacob's Ladder"
meets "Twelve Monkeys" meets "One
Flew Over the Cuckoo's Nest." Fairly entertaining with good performances by solid
cast. **102m/C DVD.** *US* Adrien Brody, Keira
Knightley, Kris Kristofferson, Jennifer Jason Leigh,
Kelly Lynch, Brad Renfro, Daniel Craig, MacKenzie
Phillips; **D:** John Maybury; **W:** Massy Tadjedin; **C:**
Peter Deming; **M:** Brian Eno.

Jackie Brown ♂♂♂ 1997 (R) Tarantino finally climbs back into the director's chair with his leisurely but satisfying
adaptation of Elmore Leonard's "Rum
Punch." No, it's not "Pulp Fiction," but it
could do for Pam Grier what "Pulp" did for
John Travolta. Grier stars as out-of-luck
and-options stewardess Jackie Brown,
who runs money to Mexico for ruthless
arms dealer Ordell (Jackson). Busted on
an intricate plan to get out from under, hopefully with the money and without getting
caught or killed. Slower and less bloody
than Quentin's films are used to, but as usual, he gets killer performances from everybody. Cool dialogue and chronological
shifts are again key ingredients, along with
a heightened sense of character development. Fonda and De Niro make the most
of small (but crucial) roles, but it's Forster
(another '70s whatever-happened-to refugee) who provides the standout performance. The look and feel of the movie
reflects the dingy world it inhabits, as well
as Tarantino's love of '70s blaxploitation
flicks. **155m/C VHS, DVD.** Pam Grier, Robert Forster, Samuel L. Jackson, Robert De Niro, Bridget
Fonda, Michael Keaton, Michael Bowen, Chris
Tucker, Lisa Gay Hamilton, Tommy (Tiny) Lister,
Hattie Winston, Aimee Graham, Sid Haig; **D:**
Quentin Tarantino; **W:** Quentin Tarantino; **C:** Guillermo Navarro; **M:** Mary Ramos, Michelle Kuznet-
sky.

**Jackie Chan's First
Strike** ♂♂½ *Police Story 4*
1996 (PG-13) Plot, schmot. The human hurricane that is Jackie Chan is once again
amazing in this kung-fu comedy homage
to '60s James Bond movies. Half Bruce
Lee and half Charlie Chaplin, Chan reprises the role of the Hong Kong super-
named Jackie, who is this time loaned out
by his superior officer "Uncle Bill" (Tung)
to the CIA. He is sent to the Ukraine to spy
on a beautiful young woman involved in
smuggling nuclear weapons along with rogue CIA agent Tsui (Lou). He follows the
villains to Australia, where he secures justice, peace, and sharp blows to the head.
Enough about the plot. Listen to this! He
holds bad guys at bay by whirling an aluminum stepladder like it was a drum, major's baton! He kicks somebody off his
second story ledge while on stilts! He
sings and dances while wearing koala
bear underwear! Dubbed in English. **87m/C
VHS, DVD.** *HK* Jackie Chan, Bill Tung, Jackson
Lou, Annie (Chen Chun) Wu, Jouri (Yuri) Petrov
Grishaieva Nonna; **D:** Stanley Tong; **W:** Stanley
Tong, Greg Mellott, Nick Tramontane, Elliot Tong;
C: Jingle Ma; **M:** J. Peter Robinson.

**Jackie Chan's Who Am
I** ♂♂½ *Who Am I; Ngo Hai Sui* 1998 (PG-13) Jackie (Chan) is recruited by the
CIA to join a team of commandos leading
a raid on a secret weapons research lab in
South Africa. The team hijack a piece of
highly explosive experimental material
and are betrayed by their leader. Only
Jackie survives, but he's got amnesia.
When he finally returns home, he's still
wondering who he is—an important ques-
tion since he's being pursued by the bad
guys who want him to stay dead. **108m/C
VHS.** *HK* Jackie Chan, Ed Nelson, Ron
Smerczak, Michelle Ferre, Mirai Yamamoto; **D:**
Jackie Chan, Benny Chan, Lee
Reynolds, Susan Chan; **C:** Hang-Seng Poon; **M:**
Nathan Wang.

**Jackie, Ethel, Joan: The
Kennedy Women** ♂♂½ 2001 TV mini-
series focuses on the Kennedy wives:
Jackie (Hennessy), Ethel (Holly), and
Joan (Stefanson) rather than on their husbands and the toll that politics and the
spotlight took on them as individuals. Sud-
ser follows the period from 1960 to 1980,
based on the bestseller by J. Randy Tara-
borelli. **172m/C VHS, DVD.** Jillian) Hennessey
Lauren Holly, Leslie Stefanson, Daniel Hugh-Kelly,
Robert Knepper, Matt Letscher, Harve Presnell,
Charmion King, Thom Christopher; **D:** Larry Shaw;
W: Barry Byers; **M:** Martin Da-
vich. **TV**

**The Jackie Robinson
Story** ♂♂♂ 1950 Chronicles Robinson's rise from UCLA to his breakthrough
as the first black man to play baseball in
the major league. Robinson plays himself,
the film deals honestly with the racial issues of the time. **76m/B VHS, DVD.** Jackie
Robinson, Ruby Dee, Minor Watson, Louise Beavers, Richard Lane, Harry Shannon, Joel Fluellen,
Ben Lessy; **D:** Alfred E. Green; **W:** Arthur Mann,
Lawrence Taylor; **C:** Ernest Laszlo; **M:** David
Chudnow.

Jackie's Back ♂♂½ 1999 (R)
Mockumentary follows the stumbling
comeback of forgotten pop diva, Jackie
Washington (Lewis). Spoiled and temper-
amental, Jackie is followed by a supersilli-
cious British documentary filmmaker, Ed-
ward Whatsett St. John (Curry), as she
prepares for a big concert as everything is
in chaos around her. Flashbacks reflect on
Jackie's early career, Faced on
her Lewis, Tim Curry, Tangie Ambrose, Whoopi
Goldberg, David Hyde Pierce, Tom Arnold, Julie
Hagerty, JoBeth Williams, Dolly Parton, Grace
Slick, Liza Minnelli; **D:** Robert Kevin Townsend; **W:**
Marc Brown, Dee La Duke; **C:** Charles Mills; **M:**
Arthur. **TV**

Jacknife ♂♂♂ 1989 (R) The well-
crafted story of a Vietnam veteran who
visits his old war buddy and tries to piece
together what's happened to their lives
since their homecoming. During his visit
he encounters anger and hostility from his
other veteran, and tenderness from his
friend's sister. A masterfully acted, small-
scale drama, adapted by Stephen Mes-

Jack's Back ♂♂♂ 1987 (R) When
a lunatic is killing Los Angeles prostitutes
Jack-the-Ripper style, twin brothers get
mistakenly involved (Spader in both roles).
One of the brothers is accused of the
murders and it is up to the other either to
clear his name and turn the final evidence of guilt. A well-thought out story
with enough twists and turns for any suspense buff. **97m/C VHS, DVD.** James Spader, Cynthia
Gibb, Rod Loomis, Rex Ryon, Robert Picardo, Jim
Haynie, Chris Mulkey, Danitza Kingsley, Wendell
Wright; **C:** Rowdy Herrington; **W:** Rowdy Herrington; **C:** Shelly Johnson.

Jackson County Jail ♂♂½ 1976 (R) While driving cross-country, a
young woman is robbed, imprisoned, and
raped by a deputy, whom she kills. Faced
law in hot pursuit. Also known by its later
remade-for-TV name, "Outside Chance."
84m/C VHS, DVD. Yvette Mimieux, Tommy Lee Jones, Robert Carradine, Severn Darden, Howard Hesseman, Mary
Woronov, Ed Marshall, Cliff Emmich, Betty
Thomas; **D:** Michael Miller; **W:** Donald Stewart; **C:**
Bruce Logan; **M:** Loren Newkirk.

**The Jacksons: An American
Dream** ♂♂½ 1992 Miniseries covering the career of the Jackson 5, the working-class family from Gary, Indiana, who
became a celebrated show business success. The series begins with the courtship
of Joseph and Katherine Jackson and
ends with the group's farewell tour in
1984, covering both family and career tur-
moils. Simplistic, glossy biography. **225m/C
VHS, DVD.** Lawrence-Hilton Jacobs, Angela Bassett, Wylie Draper, Angel Vargas, Jason Weaver, Jermaine
Jackson II, Billy Dee Williams, Vanessa Llynne)
Williams, Holly Robinson, Margaret Avery; **D:** Kar-
en Arthur. **TV**

Jacko & Lise ♂♂ 1982 (R) A
French lad falls in love with a young girl
and abandons his previously decadent
lifestyle to win her. Available with English
subtitles or dubbed. **92m/C VHS,** FR Laurent
Malet, Annie Girardot; **D:** Walter Bal.

The Jackpot ♂♂ 1950 An average
Joe wins a bushel of money from a radio
quiz show but can't pay the taxes. Maybe
doesn't deliver on its promise. Lang, noted
for mostly mediocre efforts, went on to
direct "The King and I." With an all-star cast.
87m/C VHS, DVD. James
Stewart, Natalie Wood, Barbara Hale, James Gleason, Fred Clark, Patricia Medina; **D:** Walter Lang;
C: Joseph LaShelle.

The Jackpot ♂♂ 2001 (R) Brothers Mark
and Michael Polish follow up their critically
lauded debut "Twin Falls Idaho" with this
road tale of karaoke and crackpots. Sunny
Holiday (Gries) is an aspiring country singer riding the back roads of the remote
West with his manager Les (Morris), trying
to break into Nashville via the untraveled
karaoke route. Neither one seems to realize the futility of his dreams, but Bobbi
(Hannah), the wife he's abandoned with
their young child, does. The "Jackpot" of
the title is his dream of making it big, the
way he hopes to support his family (the
sends them a lottery ticket each week in
Nevada town where he hopes to be discovered. Tries way too hard to be artful and
folksy "look at these eccentric characters"
way, but it's not without its own weird
charm. **100m/C VHS, DVD.** *US* Jon(athan) Gries,
Garrett Morris, Daryl Hannah, Peggy Lipton, Adam
Baldwin, Mac Davis, Crystal Bernard, Anthony Edwards; **D:** Michael Polish; **W:** Michael Polish, Mark
Polish; **C:** M. David Mullen; **M:** Stuart Matthewman; **V:** Patrick Bauchau.

Leah (Aubrey), before allowing his marriage to Rachel. Finally, Jacob settles on his own land with his wives and children (who will become the tribes of Israel). Dignified retelling of the biblical story; filmed on location in Morocco. 120m/C VHS, DVD. Matthew Modine, Lara Flynn Boyle, Sean Bean, Juliet Aubrey, Giancarlo Giannini, Joss Ackland, Irene Papas, Christoph Waltz; *D:* Peter Hall; *W:* Lionel Chetwynd; *M:* Marco Frisina. CABLE

Jacob Have I Loved 1988 A teenage girl struggles to overcome her jealousy of her twin sister and find her own place in life as she comes of age on a Chesapeake Island. Based on the book by Katherine Paterson. Part of the "Wonderworks" family movie series from PBS. 57m/C VHS, DVD. Bridget Fonda, Jenny Robertson, John Kellogg; *D:* Victoria Hochberg.

Jacob the Liar 🦴🦴 *Jakob der Lugner* 1974 (PG-13) When Jacob Heim is stopped for being out of the Jewish ghetto after curfew, he is sent to see the ghetto commander. On the police radio, he hears that the Red Army is advancing and he returns to the ghetto to pass along the news, pretending that he heard it on his own hidden radio. Soon, Jacob is inventing news reports to give his fellow Jews hope. German with subtitles. A sentimental American remake came out in 1999. 101m/C VHS, DVD. GE Armin Mueller-Stahl, Vlastimil Brodsky, Erwin Geschonneck, Henry Hubchen, Blanche Kommerell, Manuela Simon; *D:* Frank Beyer; *C:* Gunter Marcinkowski.

Jacob Two Two Meets the Hooded Fang 🦴🦴½ 1999 Edgy kids fantasy based on the book by Mordecai Richler. Jacob (Morrow) is nicknamed Jacob Two Two because he repeats everything since no one every listens to him the first time he says something. Because of this Jacob gets into unexpected trouble when shopping at the corner store, runs into the store basement, and knocks himself out in the darkness. Jacob dreams he's now on trial and is sentenced to Slimers' Island, which is run by a bizarre creature called the Hooded Fang (Busey) and his equally strange henchmen. 96m/C VHS, DVD. CA Max Morrow, Gary Busey, Miranda Richardson, Ice-T, Mark McKinney, Maury Chaykin; *D:* George Bloomfield; *W:* Tim Burns; *C:* Gerald Packer; *M:* Jono Grant.

Jacqueline Bouvier Kennedy 🦴½ 1981 Biography of the former First Lady, from her childhood to "Camelot," the glorious years with JFK in the White House. Smith bears a physical resemblance to her husband's childhood as a boy shopping with movies, try to help him before he's lost forever. too glossy. 150m/C VHS. Jaclyn Smith, James Franciscus, Rod Taylor, Donald Moffat, Dolph Sweet, Stephen Elliott, Claudette Nevins; *D:* Steven Gethers; *M:* Billy Goldenberg. TV

Jacob's Ladder 🦴🦴½ 1990 (R) A man struggles with events he experienced while serving in Vietnam. Gradually, he becomes unable to separate reality from the strange, psychotic world into which he increasingly lapses. His friends and family try to help him before he's lost forever. Great story potential is flawed by too many flashbacks, leaving the viewer more confused than the characters. 116m/C VHS, DVD. Tim Robbins, Elizabeth Pena, Danny Aiello, Matt Craven, Pruitt Taylor Vince, Jason Alexander, Patricia Kalember, Eriq La Salle, Ving Rhames, Macaulay Culkin; *D:* Adrian Lyne; *W:* Bruce Joel Rubin; *C:* Jeffrey L. Kimball; *M:* Maurice Jarre.

Jacqueline Bouvier

Jacquot 🦴🦴 *Jacquot de Nantes* 1991 (PG) Director Varda offers a loving tribute to her husband, filmmaker Jacques Demy. Based on the memoirs of her husband's childhood as a boy shopping with movies, Varda re-stages scenes and also uses clips from various Demy films to illustrate her points. In French with English subtitles. 118m/C VHS, DVD. FR Philippe Maron, Edouard Joubeaud, Laurent Monnier, Brigitte de Villepoix, Daniel Dublet; *D:* Agnes Varda; *W:* Agnes Varda; *C:* Patrick Blossier; *M:* Joanne Bruzdowicz.

Jade 🦴½ 1995 (R) Sleazy whodunit scraped from the bottom of the Eszterhas barrel (and it's a deep one) has hot-shot San Francisco Assistant D.A. David Corelli (Caruso) tracking a trail of pubic hairs across San Francisco. Seems he's caught up in the murder of a millionaire that points to his ex-lover, psychologist Katrina Gavin (Fiorentino), as the killer. Oh yeah, she's also a kinky call girl of choice to California's rich and famous, and happens to be married to Corelli's best friend (Palminteri). Psycho-thriller with little of either interest and lots of lurid details (and a car chase scene that Friedkin has done much better elsewhere) in an attempt to curtail boredom; it doesn't work. Combine it with "Showgirls" for the No Self-Respect Film Festival, then go to confession. 94m/C VHS, DVD. David Caruso, Linda Fiorentino, Chazz Palminteri, Michael Biehn, Richard Crenna, Kenneth King, Angie Everhart; *D:* William Friedkin; *W:* Joe Eszterhas; *C:* Andrzej Bartkowiak; *M:* James Horner.

The Jade Mask 🦴½ 1945 Chan discovers a murderer and his wife use puppets and masks to make it appear their victims are still alive. Another in the detective series with nothing noteworthy about it. Luke, the brother of actor Keye Luke, takes on the role of Chan's Number Four son. 66m/B VHS, DVD. Sidney Toler, Mantan Moreland, Edwin Luke, Janet Warren, Hardie Albright, Edith Evanson; *D:* Phil Rosen.

Jaded 🦴🦴½ 1996 (R) Seemingly innocent Meg (Gugino) is befriended by a couple of uninhibited babes (Kihlstedt, Thompson) at the local bar and goes with them to a party where she's sexually assaulted. The two women are accused of rape and the case goes to trial but Meg's past secrets come to light and things don't seem so cut-and-dried anymore. The box art is the real tease since the film isn't the erotic thriller it might appear to be. 95m/C VHS, DVD. Carla Gugino, Anna Thomson, Rya Kihlstedt, Christopher McDonald, Lorraine Toussaint; *D:* Caryn Krooth. VIDEO

JAG 🦴🦴½ 1995 TV pilot episode features Navy pilot-turned-lawyer Lt. Harmon Rabb, Jr. (Elliott) assigned to investigate the case of a young female pilot who disappears from an aircraft carrier. Seems some of her fellow sailors resented having women on board so was it an accident or murder? JAG stands for the office of the Judge Advocate General, whose Navy lawyers serve as investigators, prosecutors, and defense attorneys. 94m/C VHS, DVD. David James Elliott, Andrea Parker, Terry O'Quinn, John Roselius, Katie Rich, Scott Jaeck, Patrick Labonteaux, Cliff DeYoung, Kevin Dunn; *D:* Donald P. Bellisario; *C:* Thomas Del Ruth; *M:* Bruce Broughton. TV

The Jagged Edge 🦴🦴½ 1985 (R) The beautiful wife of successful newspaper editor, Jack Forester, is killed and the police want to point the guilty finger at Jack. Attorney Teddy Barnes is brought in to defend him and accidentally falls in love. Taut murder mystery will keep you guessing "whodunit" until the very end. 108m/C VHS, DVD. Jeff Bridges, Glenn Close, Robert Loggia, Peter Coyote, John Dehner, Leigh Taylor-Young, Lance Henriksen, James Karen, Karen Austin, Michael Dorn, Guy Boyd, Marshall Colt, Louis Giambalvo; *D:* Richard Marquand; *W:* Joe Eszterhas; *C:* Matthew F. Leonetti; *M:* John Barry.

Jaguar 1956 Three men leave their homes in Niger in order to find jobs in the cities. When they return to their village, they bring back with them their experiences. 93m/C VHS. Sabu, Mike Connors, Jay Novello, Barton MacLane; *D:* George Blair; *W:* John Fenton Murray, Benedict Freedman; *C:* Bud Thackery; *M:* Van Alexander.

Jaguar Lives 🦴 1979 (PG) A high-kicking secret agent tracks down bad boy drug kings around the world. 91m/C VHS. Joe Lewis, Barbara Bach, Christopher Lee, Woody Strode, Donald Pleasence, Joseph Wiseman, John Huston, Capucine; *D:* Ernest Pintoff.

Jail Bait 🦴½ *Hidden Face* 1954 Early Wood film about a group of small-time crooks who are always in trouble with the law; they blackmail a plastic surgeon into using his talents to help them ditch the cops. Not as "bad" as Wood's "Plan 9 From Outer Space," but still bad enough for camp fans to love (check the cheesy score leftover from an equally cheesy Mexican mad-scientist flick). 80m/B VHS, DVD. Timothy Farrell, Clancy Malone, Lyle Talbot, Steve Reeves, Herbert Rawlinson, Dolores Fuller, Theodora Thurman, Conrad Brooks, Mona McKinnon; *D:* Edward D. Wood Jr.; *W:* Edward D. Wood Jr., Alex Gordon; *C:* William C. Thompson.

Jail Party 🦴🦴 2004 Urban spoof tries to put the funny into ex-con Yusef Porter's (Sharp) desire to flee his Atlanta 'hood in search of a better life with girlfriend Elise (Terry) after his prison time wraps up. Things go expectedly sour at his homecoming party here, his past, naturally, catches up to him. 90m/C DVD. Shane Sharp, Rashaun Murdaugh, Tina Braxton, Antonette Terry, Rashaun Murdaugh; *D:* Bernie Calloway; *W:* Redd Claiborne, Donnie Leapheart, Jason Upson; VIDEO

Jailbait! 🦴🦴 *Streetwise* 1993 (R) A cop gets involved with an alleged murder witness, a teenaged runaway named Kyle. What they discover is an international crime syndicate that kidnaps runaways to exploit as sex slaves. Now they know too much. An unrated version is also available. 100m/C VHS. C. Thomas Howell, Renee Humphrey; *D:* Rafal Zielinski; *W:* Robert Vincent O'Neil.

Jailbait! 🦴🦴 2000 (R) Popular high school jock Adam (Mundy), who's 18, cheats on his girlfriend and gets wrong side of the tracks 16-year-old Gynger (Purrott) preggers leading to a charge of statutory rape. Satire on teen sex, political platforms, and society. First original movie made for MTV. 94m/C VHS, DVD. Kevin Mundy, Mo Gaffney, Alycia Purrott, Melody Johnson; Matt Frewer, Mary Gross, Reagan Pasternak; *D:* Allan Moyle. CABLE

Jailbait: Betrayed By Innocence 🦴½ 1986 (R) A man is on trial for statutory rape. 90m/C VHS. Barry Bostwick, Lee Purcell, Paul Sorvino, Cristen Kauffman, Isaac Hayes; *D:* Elliot Silverstein. TV

Jailbird Rock 🦴½ 1988 We'd like to tell you that this isn't really a sweet young-thing-in-prison musical, but it is. When Antin shoots her stepfather (he told her to turn that damn noise down?) she tries to bring down the Big House with song and dance. No kidding. 90m/C VHS. Robin Antin, Valchie Gene Richards, Robin Cleavon Antin, Rhonda Aldrich, Jacquelyn Houston, Debra Laws, Erica Jordan, Perry Lang, Ronald Lacey; *D:* Phillip Schuman; *W:* Edward Kovach, Carole Stanley; *C:* Leonardo Solis; *M:* Rick Nowecs.

Jailbird's Vacation 🦴🦴½ *Les Grandes Gueules* 1965 From the director of the classic "An Encounter at Owl Creek Bridge," comes this comedy-drama about a sawmill owner dealing with two ex-convicts hired as lumberjacks. They want to get revenge on the bum who put them away. French with subtitles. 125m/C VHS. FR Lino Ventura, Andre Bourvil, Marie DuBois; *D:* Robert Enrico.

Jailbreakers 🦴 1994 Another remake from Showtime's "Rebel Highway" series that takes little but the title from the 1960 A.I.P. flick. Cheerleader Angel (Doherty) falls for bad boy Tony (Sabato Jr.) and gets busted by the cops while they're out on a little crime spree. He goes to prison, she and her family must leave town. But boy can't get girl out of his head and he busts out of the big house to reunite with his true love. Then the crazy kids hit the road for the Mexican border. 76m/C VHS, DVD. Shannen Doherty, Antonio Sabato Jr., Adrienne Barbeau, Adrien Brody, Vince Edwards, George Gerdes; *D:* William Friedkin; *W:* Debra Hill, Gigi Vorgan; *C:* Cary Fisher; *M:* Hummie Mann. CABLE

Jailbreakin' 🦴 *The Ballad of Billie Blue* 1972 A faded country singer and a rebellious youth team up to break out of jail. 90m/C VHS. Jason Ledger, Marty Allen, Ray Danton, Sherry Bain, Sherry Miles, Erik Estrada; *D:* Ken Osborne.

Jailhouse Rock 🦴🦴🦴 1957 (G) While in jail for manslaughter, teenager Vince Everett (Presley) learns to play the guitar. After his release, he slowly develops into a top recording star. Probably the only film that captured the magnetic power of the young Elvis Presley; an absolute must for fans. Also available in a colorized version. ♫Jailhouse Rock; Treat Me Nice; Baby, I Don't Care; Young and Beautiful; Don't Leave Me Now; I Wanna Be Free; One More Day. 96m/B VHS, DVD. Blu-ray Disc, HD DVD. Elvis Presley, Judy Tyler, Vaughn Taylor, Dean Jones, Mickey Shaughnessy, William Forrest, Glenn Strange, Jennifer Holden, Anne Neyland; *D:* Richard Thorpe; *W:* Guy Trosper; *C:* Robert J. Bronner; *M:* Jeff Alexander. Natl. Film Reg. '04.

Jakarta 🦴🦴 1988 (R) Before gaining fame on the popular t.v. series "Law and Order," actor Chris Noth was action hero material. Sadly without much success in this dud. A love-hardened CIA operative (Noth) is whisked away to Jakarta for reasons unknown, only to find his thought-to-be-dead lover still alive and caught in a deadly game of espionage. 94m/C VHS. Christopher Noth, Sue Francis Pai, Ronald Hunter; *D:* Charles Kaufman.

Jake Speed 🦴½ 1986 (PG) Comic-book mercenary Jake and his loyal associate Remo rescue a beautiful girl from white slave traders. Supposedly a parody of the action adventure genre. 93m/C VHS, DVD. Wayne Crawford, John Hurt, Karen Kopins, Dennis Christopher; *D:* Andrew Lane; *W:* Wayne Crawford; *C:* Bryan Loftus; *M:* Mark Snow.

Jakob the Liar 🦴🦴½ 1999 (PG-13) Robin Williams reins in his usual manic personality in this touching tale set during the Holocaust. Jakob (Williams) is a Jew confined to the Polish ghetto by the Nazis. After he hears a radio broadcast describing German defeats while in a Nazi commandant's office, he relates the news to his friend Mischa (Schreiber). This leads to rumors that he owns a contraband radio, which is an offense punishable by death. He sees the excitement and hope that his news has brought and begins to make up new stories to encourage his oppressed community. Finally, the men become courageous enough to start a resistance movement, with Jakob as the leader. The realities of the Holocaust are shown with no attempt to sugarcoat them, and the performances are excellent all around. 114m/C VHS, DVD. Robin Williams, Armin Mueller-Stahl, Alan Arkin, Bob Balaban, Michael Jeter, Liev Schreiber, Hannah Taylor Gordon, Nina Siemaszko, Mathieu Kassovitz, Mark Margolis; *D:* Peter Kassovitz; *W:* Peter Kassovitz, Didier Decoin; *C:* Elemer Ragalyi; *M:* Ed Shearmur.

Jalsaghar 🦴🦴 *The Music Room* 1958 Bisambhar Roy is the last in his aristocratic line and has inherited nothing but debts. But his position in society demands a certain style and he pawns family heirlooms in order to host expensive private concerts, even after tragedy strikes his family. Bengali with subtitles. 100m/B VHS, DVD. IN Chhabi Biswas, Padma Devi, Tulsi Lahiri, Pinaki Sen Gupta, Kali Sarkar; *D:* Satyajit Ray; *W:* Satyajit Ray; *C:* Subrata Mitra; *M:* Satyajit Ray.

Jam 🦴 2006 That's jam in traffic, not food product, or Phish concert. Sitcom characters and situations abound as 15 weary souls are trapped in their cars after an accident on a mountain road. It's Father's Day--so everyone can exchange trite stories. A woman goes into labor (ah, that old chestnut). There's a couple of bumbling crooks and even a kitchen sink 'cause someone's driving a camper. 91m/C DVD. Jeffrey Dean Morgan, William Forsythe, Gina Torres, Amanda Detmer, Jonathan Silverman, Marianne Jean-Baptiste, Dan Byrd, David DeLuise, Elizabeth Rodriguez, Tess Harper, Alex Rocco, Christopher Amitrano, Christopher Amitrano, Julie Claire, Amanda Foreman; *D:* Craig Sterling; *W:* Craig Sterling, Nicole Lonner; *C:* Jeff Venditti; *M:* Andy Kubiszewski. VIDEO

Jamaica Inn 🦴🦴 1939 In old Cornwall, an orphan girl becomes involved with smugglers. Remade in 1982; based on the story by Daphne Du Maurier. 98m/B VHS, DVD. GB Charles Laughton, Maureen O'Hara, Leslie Banks, Robert Newton; *D:* Alfred Hitchcock; *W:* Sidney Gilliat, Joan Harrison; *C:* Harry Stradling Sr.; *M:* Eric Fenby.

Jamaica Inn 🦴🦴½ 1982 Miniseries based on the old Daphne Du Maurier adventure about highwaymen and moor-lurking thieves in Cornwall. Remake of the 1939 Hitchcock film. 192m/C VHS, DVD. Patrick McGoohan, Jane Seymour; *D:* Lawrence Gordon-Clark. TV

James and the Giant Peach 1996 (PG) Terrific combo of live action and stop-motion animation highlights this adaptation of Roald Dahl's 1961 children's book. Orphaned James is sent to live with his wicked aunts. When magic "crocodile tongues," given to James by a hobo, spill at the base of a peach tree, one fruit grows to such a tremendous size that James crawls inside, meets six insect friends, and goes on numerous adventures, all the while trying to face his fears. Dahl's books are creepy and since the people who brought you "Nightmare Before Christmas" are also doing "James," expect the visuals to be astonishing but too scary for the little ones. 80m/C VHS, DVD, D: Henry Selick; C: Pete Postlethwaite, Joanna Lumley, Miriam Margolyes, Richard Dreyfuss, Susan Sarandon, David Thewlis, Simon Callow, Jane Leeves.

James Dean 1976 *The Legend* Dean's friend Bast wrote this behind-the-scenes look at the short life of the enigmatic movie star. 99m/C VHS, DVD, Stephen McHattie, Michael Brandon, Candy Clark, Amy Irving, Brooke Adams, Dane Clark, Jayne Meadows, Meg Foster; D: William Bast, Robert Butler; W: William Bast; M: Billy Goldenberg. TV

James Dean 1/2 200: The original rebel without a cause gets a superficial biopic treatment that doesn't have much time to explore the appeal of the young legend who died at the age of 24. Dean's (Franco) troubles stem from his unhappy relationship with his distant father (McriJarty) and even his impressive acting talents can't save him from self-destruction. Film focuses on the making of "East of Eden" and Dean's romance with fragile actress Pier Angeli (Cervi). Franco does well in the title role. 95m/C VHS, DVD. James Franco, Michael Moriarty, Valentina Cervi, Enrico Colantoni, Edward Herrmann, Barry Primus, Mark Rydel, Joanne Linville, John Pleshette; D: Mark Rydel; W: Israel Horovitz; C: Robbie Greenberg. CABLE

James Dean: Live Fast, Die Young 1997 (PG-13) Lightweight biopic of legendary acting rebel with a cause Dean (Van Dien). Film finds Dean troubled when girlfriend Pier Angeli (Carrie Mitchum) does well in the title role. Robert's granddaughter; marries another, and in trouble with studio boss Jack Warner (Connors), and director George Stevens (Mitchum), Mike Connors, Carrie Mitchum, Diane Ladd, Connie Stevens, Monique Parent, Casey Kasem, Joseph Camanella; D: Mark Rustam; W: Dan Sefton; C: Gary Graver, Ivan Goodhoff. TV

James' Journey to Jerusalem *Massa'ot James Be'eretz Hakodash* 2003 Idealistic James (Shibe) is a young African Christian who is sent on a pilgrimage to the promised land of Zion. Only the promise starts out tarnished when the innocent is thrown into a Tel Aviv jail by a cynical immigration official who thinks he's just another illegal. James gets bailed out by shady businessman Shimi (Daw) to be used as cheap labor and he begins to learn—and work—the system, which leads James into some very secular temptation. English, Zulu, and Hebrew with subtitles. 87m/C DVD. Siyabonga Melongisi Shibe, Salim Dau, Arie Elias, Sandra Schonwald, Hugh Masebenza, Gregory Tai; D: Ra'anan Alexandrowicz; W: Ra'anan Alexandrowicz, Sami Duenias; C: Shark (Sharon) De Mayo; M: Ehud Banay.

James Joyce's A Portrait of the Artist as a Young Man 1977 A moving, lyrical adaptation of the author's autobiography, told through the character of Stephen Dedalus. Joyce's characterizations, words, and scenes are beautifully translated to the medium of film. Excellent casting. 93m/C VHS. John Gielgud, T.P. McKenna, Bosco Hogan; D: Joseph Strick.

James Joyce's Women 1985 (R) Adapted from her one-woman stage show as produced by Fionnula Flanagan, this acclaimed film features enacted portraits of three real-life Joyce associates, including his wife (Nora Barnacle) and three of his famous characters. 91m/C VHS. Fionnula Flanagan, Timothy E. O'Grady, Chris O'Neill; D: Michael Pearce; W: Fionnula Flanagan.

Jamon, Jamon *Ham Ham* 1993 Comedic melodrama satirizing various aspects of the Spanish character, including machismo, sex, and food. A small Spanish town is dominated by two businesses—an underwear factory and a brothel—both run by strong-minded women. The brothel's Carmen and the factory's Conchita clash when Carmen's daughter, Silvia, becomes pregnant by Conchita's son, Manuel. Conchita's appalled and hires stud Raul to seduce Silvia—only to fall for him herself. Oh yes, Raul attributes his sexual prowess to a steady diet of ham and garlic. In Spanish with English subtitles. 95m/C VHS, SP Penelope Cruz, Anna Galiena, Javier Bardem, Stefania Sandrelli, Juan Diego, Jordi Molla; D: Bigas Luna; W: Cuca Canals; C: Jose Luis Alcaine; M: Nicola Piovani.

Jane & the Lost City 1987 (PG) A British farce based on the age-old, barely dressed comic-strip character, Jane, as she stumbles on ancient cities, treasures, villains, and blond/blue-eyed heroes. Low-budget camp fun. 94m/C VHS, DVD. GB Kristen Hughes, Maud Adams, Sam Jones; D: Terry Marcel; W: Mervyn Haisman; C: Paul Beeson; M: Harry Robertson.

The Jane Austen Book Club 2007 (PG-13) Why yes, this is a chick flick, and proudly so. A group of Jane Austen devotees gather monthly to discuss six Jane Austen books, but end up revealing themselves in the process. The characters are not unlike Austen's, albeit living in the dizzying pace of the modern world. There's Bernadette (Baker), a wise and carefree divorcee; Sylvia (Brenneman), whose 20-plus-year marriage has abruptly ended, and her lesbian daughter (Grace); uptight teacher Prudie (Blunt); and a token man, software geek Grigg (Dancy). Austen's spirit floats (figuratively) in and out of the clubber's lives, losses, and romances as they navigate the passages Austen penned two centuries ago. 106m/C DVD, Blu-ray Disc. US DVD, GB Kathy Baker, Maria Bello, Emily Blunt, Amy Brenneman, Maggie Grace, Hugh Dancy, Lynn Redgrave, Jimmy Smits, Marc Blucas, Kevin Zegers, Nancy Travis, Parisa Fitz-Henley; D: Robin Swicord; C: John Toon; M: Aaron Zigman.

Jane Austen in Manhattan 1980 Two acting teachers vie to stage a long-lost play written by a youthful Jane Austen. Dreary, despite the cast. Hodlak is the real-life daughter of Baxter. 108m/C VHS, DVD. Anne Baxter, Robert Powell, Michael Wager, Sean Young, Kurt Johnson, Katrina Hodiak; D: James Ivory; W: Ruth Prawer Jhabvala.

Jane Doe 1983 Valentine plays a young amnesia victim who is linked to a series of brutal slayings. Quite suspenseful for a TV movie. 100m/C VHS, DVD. Karen Valentine, William Devane, Eva Marie Saint, Stephen E. Miller, Jackson Davies; D: Ivan Nagy. TV

Jane Doe 1996 (R) Jane Doe (Flockhart) is a drug addict who's getting seriously involved with shy writer Horace (Peditto). Only her addictions begin to cause some serious trouble for this odd couple. Adapted from a play. 92m/C VHS, DVD. Calista Flockhart, Elina Lowensohn, Joe Ragno, Christopher Peditto; D: Paul Peditto; W: Paul Peditto.

Jane Eyre 1934 Stiff, early version of Charlotte Bronte's classic gothic romance. English orphan grows up to become the governess of a mysterious man-o'. Notable as the first talkie version. Remade several times. 67m/B VHS, DVD. Virginia Bruce, Colin Clive, Beryl Mercer, Jameson Thomas, Aileen Pringle, David Torrence, Clarissa Selwynne, Anne Howard; D: Christy Cabanne; W: Adele Comandini; C: Robert Planck; M: Mischa Bakaleinikoff.

Jane Eyre 1944 Excellent adaptation of the Charlotte Bronte novel about the plain governess with the noble heart and her love for the mysterious and tragic Mr. Rochester. Fontaine has the proper backbone and yearning in the title role but to accommodate Welles' emerging popularity in the role of Rochester was enlarged. Excellent bleak romantic-Gothic look. Taylor, in her third film role, is seen briefly in the early orphanage scenes. 97m/B VHS, DVD. Joan Fontaine, Orson Welles, Margaret O'Brien, Peggy Ann Garner, John Sutton, Sara Allgood, Henry Daniell, Agnes Moorehead, Aubrey Mather, Edith Barrett, Barbara Everest, Hillary Brooke, Elizabeth Taylor; D: Robert Stevenson; C: George Barnes; M: Bernard Herrmann.

Jane Eyre 1983 Miniseries based on the famed Charlotte Bronte novel about the maturation of a homeless English waif, her love for the tormented English Rochester, and her quest for permanent peace. 239m/C VHS, DVD. GB Timothy Dalton, Zelah Clarke; D: Julian Amyes.

Jane Eyre 1996 (PG) Zeffirelli creates an eloquent, yet spare interpretation of Charlotte Bronte's 1847 masterpiece, about a meek governess and her love for the tormented-yet-dashing Englishman Rochester, and her quest for permanent peace. 116m/C VHS, DVD. William Hurt, Anna Paquin, Charlotte Gainsbourg, Joan Plowright, Elle Macpherson, Geraldine Chaplin, Fiona Shaw, John Wood, Amanda Root, Maria Schneider, Josephine Serre, Billie Whitelaw; D: Franco Zeffirelli; W: Franco Zeffirelli, Hugh Whitemore; C: David Watkin; M: Alessio Vlad, Claudio Capponi.

Jane Eyre 1997 Charlotte Bronte's dark romance between meek-yet-strong-willed governess Jane (Morton) and her tormented-yet-dashing employer, Mr. Rochester (Hinds). This version disappoints quickly with many of the subjects to concentrate on the main duo. 108m/C VHS, DVD. GB Samantha Morton, Ciaran Hinds, Gemma Jones, Abigail Cruttenden, Richard Hawley; D: Robert M. Young; W: Kay Mellor; M: Richard Harvey. CABLE

Jane Eyre 2006 (from the BBC) Yet another version of Charlotte Bronte's novel, unique with gothic romance, naive but undaunted governess Jane (Wilson, properly plain), and secretive aristocrat Edward Rochester (Stephens), more grumpy than brooding. Well done but unnecessary; didn't Charlotte write anything else worth filming? 247m/C DVD. GB Toby Stephens, Ruth Wilson, Christina Cole, Tara Fitzgerald, Francesca Annis, Christopher Benjamin, Pam Ferris, Andrew Buchan; D: Susanna White; W: Sandy Welch; C: Mike Eley; M: Robert Lane. TV

Janice Beard 1999 Eccentric comedy about a social misfit that's overwhelmed by whimsey. Janice (Walsh) moves from her Scottish town to London in hopes of making enough money to help her agoraphobic mother Mimi (Voe). Lively, office assistant Sean (Hans) sneaky office antics get tedious. 80m/C DVD, GB Eileen Walsh, Rhys Ifans, Patsy Kensit, Sandra Voe, David Kilner, Ben Hopkins; C: Richard Greatrex, Peter Thwaites; M: Paul Carr.

The January Man 1989 (R) An unorthodox cop, previously exiled by a corrupt local government to the fire department, is brought back to track down a serial killer. Written by the "Moonstruck" guy, Shanley, who apparently peaked with the earlier movie. 97m/C VHS, DVD. Kevin Kline, Susan Sarandon, Mary Elizabeth Mastrantonio, Harvey Keitel, Rod Steiger, Alan Rickman, Danny Aiello; D: Pat O'Connor; W: Pat O'Connor, John Patrick Shanley; C: Jerzy Zielinski; M: Marvin Hamlisch.

Japanese Story 2003 (R) Headstrong Sandy (Collette) is a geologist by trade and part owner of a software firm who is obliged to entertain a potential client, Hiromitsu (Tsunashima), an uptight Japanese businessman looking to experience the Australian landscape. Despite her objections he insists that they drive into the desert where they end up stranded for a night amid the harsh elements. Their struggle to endure brings them closer, until a dramatic plot twist midstream that shakes Sandy to her core. Gorgeous scenery provides a striking backdrop for Brooks' passionate piece while Collette displays great depth as a woman challenged by a gamut of emotions. 105m/C DVD, AU Toni Collette, Gotaro Tsunashima, Yukimo Tanaka, Kate Atkinson, Bill Young, George Shevtsov, Justine Clarke; D: Sue Brooks; W: Alison Tilson; C: Ian Baker; M: Elizabeth Drake.

Jarhead 2005 (R) Solid adaptation of Anthony Swofford's memoir is not so much an anti-war film as an absence-of-war film. Gyllenhaal is excellent as "Swoff," a Marine recruit trained as a sniper and sent to fight in the first Gulf War. Only when he gets there, there's no fighting, just waiting and preparing. Mendes's deft touch is put to good use in showing the frustration and boredom of the Marines, using other war movies as touchstones and keeping politics in the background while focusing on the characters. The drawback of this approach is that the audience becomes just as frustrated as the soldiers with all the inaction. 122m/C DVD, UMD, HD DVD, US Jake Gyllenhaal, Peter Sarsgaard, Lucas Black, Brian Geraghty, Jacob Vargas, Laz Alonso, Evan Jones, Ivan Fenyo, Chris Cooper, Dennis Haysbert, Scott MacDonald, Jamie Foxx, Jamie Martz, Kareem Grimes, Peter Gail, Jocko Sims, John Krasinski; D: Sam Mendes; W: William Broyles Jr.; C: Roger Deakins; M: Thomas Newman.

The Jar 1984 A recluse discovers a disgusting creature in a jar. He keeps it, only to discover that it is out to kill him. Only when he gets home is there no fright. 90m/C VHS, Gary Wallace, Karen Sjoberg; D: Bruce Toscano; W: George Bradley.

Jason and the Argonauts 1963 (G) Jason, son of the King of Thessaly, sails on the Argo to the land of Colchis, where the Golden Fleece is kept. Superb special effects and multitudes of mythological creatures; fun for the whole family. 104m/C VHS, DVD. GB Todd Armstrong, Nancy Kovack, Gary Raymond, Laurence Naismith, Nigel Green, Douglas Wilmer, Jack (Gwyllyn) Gwillim; D: Don Chaffey; W: Jan Read, Beverley Cross; C: Wilkie Cooper; M: Bernard Herrmann.

Jason and the Argonauts 2000 Elaborate retelling of the Greek myth of Jason and his quest for the golden fleece. Young Prince Jason (London) has had his heritage usurped by his evil Uncle Pelias (Hopper in braids), who has killed Jason's father and taken his throne. In order to reclaim it, Jason must retrieve the magical golden fleece from distant Colchis and bring it to Pelias. So Jason assembles the usual motley crew of would-be heroes and sets sail on the Argos for uncharted waters and numerous adventures. TV saga with lots of action and some good special effects. 179m/C VHS, DVD. Jason London, Dennis Hopper, Angus MacFadyen, Olivia Williams, Brian Thompson, Adrian Lester, Derek Jacobi, Jolene Blalock, Frank Langella, Natasha Henstridge, Ciaran Hinds, Kieran O'Brien, Charles Cartmell; D: Nick Willing; M: Matthew Faulk, Mark Skeet; C: Sergei Kozlov; M: Simon Boswell. TV

Jason Goes to Hell: The Final Friday 1993 (R) The supposed last, at least so far, in the "Friday the 13th" gore series. Only through the bodies—dead or alive—of his various kin can supernatural killer Jason be reborn, and only at their hands can he truly die. One can only hope that this is finally true. An unrated, even gorier, version is also available. **89m/C VHS, DVD.** Kane Hodder, John D. LeMay, Kari Keegan, Steven Williams, Steven Culp, Erin Gray, Richard Gant, Leslie Jordan, Billy Green Bush, Rusty Schwimmer, Allison Smith, Julie Michaels; *D:* Adam Marcus; *W:* Dean Lorey, Jay Huguely-Cass; *M:* Harry Manfredini.

Jason X 🦴 **2001 (R)** This time it's Jason in space. The tenth installment of the "Friday the 13th" franchise is set in 2455, when Earth has been abandoned because of toxic damage. An archeological expedition discovers the cryogenically frozen Jason and a young woman and brings them back to their spaceship. Of course, if they'd just leave him on Earth with no one to kill, he'd die a horrible existential death that'd be really cool to see. Unfortunately, there's a passel of horny med students that needs killin' so here we go again. The space setting does give the series a bunch of new franchises to rip off, but that doesn't really help. **93m/C VHS, DVD.** *US* Lexa Doig, Lisa Ryder, Kane Hodder, Jonathan Potts, Chuck Campbell, Peter Mensah, Melyssa Ade, Melody Johnson, Dov Tiefenbach, David Cronenberg, Derwin Jordan; *D:* James Isaac; *W:* Todd Farmer; *C:* Derick Underschultz; *M:* Harry Manfredini.

Jason's Lyric 🦴🦴 **1994 (R)** A romantic triangle, sibling rivalry, family bonds, and neighborhood violence all set on the wrong side of the Houston tracks. Jason (Payne) is the responsible young man who works hard and helps out his mom; younger brother Joshua (Woodbine) has just gotten out of jail and is headed straight for more trouble. Between the two is Lyric (Pinkett), a soul-food waitress whose bad news half-brother Alonzo (Treach) is naturally one of Joshua's homies. Good-looking but ultimately empty storytelling. **119m/C VHS, DVD.** Allen Payne, Bokeem Woodbine, Jada Pinkett Smith, Suzzanne Douglass, Forest Whitaker, Treach; *D:* Doug McHenry; *W:* Bobby Smith Jr.; *M:* Matt Noble.

Jasper, Texas 🦴🦴½ **2003** Dramatization of the 1998 hate crime that shook the small Texas town. When black James Byrd Jr. dies after being chained to the back of a pickup truck and dragged for three miles, the town's citizens find themselves at the center of a nationwide political and media frenzy. It's up to Sheriff Billy Rowles (Voight) and Jasper's first black mayor, R.C. Horn (Gossett Jr.) to portray the murder as an isolated incident, but the subsequent trial force the townsfolk to take a hard look at their community. Some is neither white-washed nor sensationalized. **120m/C DVD.** Jon Voight, Louis Gossett Jr., Joe Morton, Emily Yancy, Bokeem Woodbine, Blu Mankuma, Karen Robinson, Ron White, Eugene Clark; *D:* Jeff Byrd; *W:* Jonathan Estrin; *C:* Ousama Rawi. **CABLE**

Java Head 🦴🦴🦴 **1935** Young Chinese wife commits suicide so her husband can marry an English girl. Set in mid-1800s England. Based on the novel by Joseph Hergesheimer. **70m/B VHS.** *GB* Anna May Wong, Elizabeth Allan, John Loder, Edmund Gwenn, Ralph Richardson, George Curzon; *D:* J. Walter Ruben.

Jawbreaker 🦴🦴 **1998 (R)** Writer-director Darren Stein steals the plot from "Heathers" and adds a dash of S&M for this black comedy about high school clique queens. Courtney (McGowan) is the leader of a group of glam princesses who accidentally kill one of their own during a mock kidnapping. Fellow beautiful people Julie (Greer) and Marcie (Benz) help her cover up, but class nerd Fern (Greer) is a witness. Further complicating things are nosy detective Vera Cruz (Grier) and the upcoming prom, which provides a "Carrie" style finale. Although the movie treads familiar ground, McGowan's performance keeps it interesting. Cameo by rocker Marilyn Manson, billed as Brian Warner. **87m/C VHS, DVD.** Rose McGowan, Rebecca Gayheart, Julie Benz, Charlotte Roldan, Judy Greer, Chad Christ, Carol Kane, Pam Grier, William Katt, P.J. Soles, Jeff Conaway, Ethan Er-ickson; *D:* Darren Stein; *W:* Darren Stein; *C:* Amy Vincent.

Jaws 🦴🦴🦴½ **1975 (PG)** Early directorial effort by Spielberg from the Peter Benchley potboiler. A tight, very scary, and sometimes hilarious film about the struggle to kill a giant great white shark that is terrorizing an eastern beach community's waters. The characterizations by Dreyfuss, Scheider, and Shaw are much more enduring than the shock effects. Memorable score. Sequeled by "Jaws 2" in 1978, "Jaws 3" in 1983, and "Jaws: The Revenge" in 1987. Look for Benchley as a TV reporter. **124m/C VHS, DVD.** Roy Scheider, Robert Shaw, Richard Dreyfuss, Lorraine Gary, Murray Hamilton, Carl Gottlieb, Peter Benchley; *C:* Bill Butler; *W:* Carl Gottlieb, Peter Benchley; *D:* Steven Spielberg; *M:* John Williams. Oscars '75: Film Editing, Sound, Orig. Score; AFI '98: Top 100; Golden Globes '76: Score, Natl. Film Reg. '01.

Jaws 2 🦴🦴½ **1978 (PG)** Unsatisfactory sequel to "Jaws." It's been four years since the man-eating shark feasted on the resort town of Amity; suddenly a second shark stalks the waters and the terror returns. Scheider—who must by now wonder at his tendency to attract large aquatic carnivores with lunch on their minds—battles without his compatriots from the original. And we haven't seen the last of the mechanical dorsal fin yet; two more sequels follow. **116m/C VHS, DVD.** Roy Scheider, Lorraine Gary, Murray Hamilton, Joseph Mascolo, Jeffrey Kramer, Collin Wilcox-Paxton, Keith Gordon; *D:* Jeannot Szwarc; *W:* Carl Gottlieb, Howard Sackler; *C:* Michael C. Butler; *M:* John Williams.

Jaws 3 🦴🦴 *Jaws 3-D* **1983 (PG)** Same monster, new setting: in a Sea World-type amusement park, a great white shark escapes from its tank and proceeds to cause terror and chaos. Little connection to the previous "Jaws" sagas. Followed by one more sequel, "Jaws: The Revenge." **98m/C VHS, DVD.** Dennis Quaid, Bess Armstrong, Louis Gossett Jr., Simon MacCorkindale, Lea Thompson, John Putch; *D:* Joe Alves; *W:* Richard Matheson, Carl Gottlieb; *C:* James A. Contner; *M:* John Williams.

Jaws of Death 🦴🦴 *Mako: The Jaws of Death* **1976** "Jaws"-like saga of shark terror. Jaeckel illogically strikes out to protect his "friends," the sharks. **91m/C VHS, DVD.** Richard Jaeckel, Harold Sakata, Jennifer Bishop, John Chandler, Buffy Dee; *D:* William Grefe.

Jaws of Justice 🦴🦴½ **1933** A Canadian Mountie and his trusty German shepherd track down outlaws in the Canadian Northwest. **55m/B VHS.** Richard Terry, Lafe (Lafayette) McKee; *D:* Spencer Gordon Bennett; *W:* Joseph Anthony Roach; *C:* Edward Snyder.

Jaws of Satan woof! *King Cobra* **1981** Weaver is terrorized by a slimy snake who is, in actuality, the Devil. Not released for two years after it was filmed, and generally considered a bomb of the first caliber. Unfortunate work for usually worthwhile Weaver. **92m/C VHS.** Fritz Weaver, Gretchen Corbett, Jon Korkes, Norman Lloyd, Christina Applegate; *D:* Bob Claver; *C:* Dean Cundey.

Jaws: The Revenge 🦴 **1987 (PG-13)** The third sequel, in which Mrs. Brody is pursued the world over by a seemingly personally motivated Great White Shark. Includes footage not seen in the theatrical release. Each sequel in this series is progressively inferior to the original. **87m/C VHS, DVD.** Lorraine Gary, Lance Guest, Karen Young, Mario Van Peebles, Michael Caine, Judith Barsi, Lynn Whitfield; *D:* Joseph Sargent; *W:* Michael deGuzman; *C:* John McPherson; *M:* Michael Small.

Jay and Silent Bob Strike Back 🦴🦴 **2001 (R)** The fifth in Smith's series of movies with ties to Red Bank, New Jersey, is a road movie as the boys go after Miramax studio (which produced the film) when it makes a movie based on the comic book characters that are based on them without their permission. It makes more sense (and is probably more enjoyable) if you've seen Smith's entire ouvre. Besides Jay (Mewes) and Silent Bob (Smith himself), many of the characters and jokes are from Smith's previous movies. Subplots and detours abound for our heroes, allowing Smith to effectively parody and lampoon recent summer blockbusters, his own stars, and Hollywood in general. **95m/C VHS, DVD, Blu-ray Disc.** *US* Kevin Smith, Jason Mewes, Jason Lee, Ben Affleck, Jennifer Schwalbach Smith, Chris Rock, Will Ferrell, Brian O'Halloran, Seann William Scott, George Carlin, Carrie Fisher, Judd Nelson, Jon Stewart, Mark Hamill, Diedrich Bader, Renee Humphrey, Joey Lauren Adams, Dwight Ewell, Eli Marienthal, Marc Blucas; *Cameos:* Wes Craven, Gus Van Sant, Matt Damon, Shannen Doherty, Jason Biggs, James Van Der Beek, Alanis Morissette; *D:* Kevin Smith; *W:* Kevin Smith; *C:* Jamie Anderson; *M:* James L. Venable.

The Jayhawkers 🦴🦴 **1959** Chandler and Parker battle for power and women in pre-Civil War Kansas. **100m/C VHS.** Jeff Chandler, Fess Parker, Nicole Maurey, Henry Silva, Herbert Rudley, Frank De Kova, Don McGowan, Leo Gordon; *D:* Melvin Frank.

The Jayne Mansfield Story 🦴🦴½ **1980** Recounts the blond bombshell's career from her first career exposure, through her marriage to a bodybuilder, to the famous car crash that beheaded her. **97m/C VHS, DVD.** Loni Anderson, Arnold Schwarzenegger, Raymond Buktenica, Kathleen Lloyd, G.D. Spradlin, Dave Shelley; *D:* Dick Lowry. **TV**

The Jazz Singer 🦴🦴🦴½ **1927** A Jewish cantor's son breaks with his family to become a singer of popular music. Of historical importance as the first successful part-talkie; a very early Loy performance. Stick with the classic line "You ain't heard nothing yet!" Remade several times. ♫ Toot, Toot, Tootsie Goodbye; Blue Skies; My Gal Sal; Waiting for the Robert E. Lee; Dirty Hands, Dirty Face; Mother; I Still Have You; Kol Nidre; Yahrzeit; My Mammy. **89m/B VHS, DVD.** Al Jolson, May McAvoy, Warner Oland, William Demarest, Eugenie Besserer, Myrna Loy; *D:* Alan Crosland; *C:* Hal Mohr. AFI '98: Top 100, Natl. Film Reg. '96.

The Jazz Singer woof! **1980 (PG)** Flat and uninteresting (if not unintentionally funny) remake of the 1927 classic about a Jewish boy who rebels against his father and family tradition to become a popular entertainer. Stick with the original, this is little more than a vehicle for Diamond to sing. ♫ America; You Baby Baby; Jerusalem; Love on the Rocks; Summer Love; On the Robert E. Lee; Louise; Songs of Life; Hello Again. **115m/C VHS, DVD.** Neil Diamond, Laurence Olivier, Lucie Arnaz, Caitlin Adams, Franklin Ajaye, Ernie Hudson; *D:* Richard Fleischer; *W:* Herbert Baker, Stephen H. Foreman; *C:* Isidore Mankofsky; *M:* Leonard Roseman, Neil Diamond. Golden Raspberries '80: Worst Support. Actor (Olivier).

Jazzman 🦴🦴🦴 **1984** A comedy set in the late 1920s with a young musician forming a jazz band with two street musicians and a saxophonist who played in the czar's marching band. Their music is condemned as a product of bourgeois society but that doesn't stop them. In Russian with English subtitles. **80m/C VHS.** *RU* Igor Sklyar, Alexander Chorny; *D:* Karen Chakhnazarov.

J.D.'s Revenge 🦴🦴½ **1976 (R)** Attorney in training Glynn Turman is possessed by the spirit of a gangster who was murdered on Bourbon Street in the early 1940s and grisly blaxploitation results. Ever so slightly better than others of the genre. Shot in New Orleans, with a soundtrack by a then-unknown Prince. **95m/C VHS, DVD.** Louis Gossett Jr., Glynn Turman, Joan Pringle, David McKnight, James L. Watkins; *D:* Arthur Marks; *W:* Jaison Starkes; *C:* Harry J. May; *M:* Prince.

Je Tu Il Elle 🦴🦴½ *I You She He* **1974** A hyperactive young woman desperately seeking the answers to life gradually gains experience and maturity as she travels around France. The directorial debut of Ackerman. In French with English subtitles. **90m/B VHS.** *FR* Niels Arestrup, Claire Wauthion, Chantal Akerman; *D:* Chantal Akerman.

Jealousy 🦴🦴 **1984** Three dramatic episodes dealing with jealousy. Made for TV. **95m/C VHS.** Angie Dickinson, Paul Michael Glaser, David Carradine, Bo Svenson; *D:* Jeffrey Bloom. **TV**

Jealousy 🦴🦴 *Celos* **1999** Antonio Sanchez (Giménez Cacho) and Carmen (Sanchez-Gijón) seem to be happily engaged and making wedding plans when Antonio finds an old photo of Carmen with another man. Although he has no reason to be suspicious, he begins to investigate Carmen's past and becomes consumed by a jealous obsession that threatens to tear the couple apart. Spanish with subtitles. **105m/C VHS, DVD.** *SP* Daniel Giménez Cacho, Aitana Sanchez-Gijon, Maria Botto, Luis Tosar; *D:* Vicente Aranda; *W:* Vicente Aranda, Alvaro del Amo; *C:* Jose Luis Alcaine; *M:* Jose Nieto.

Jean de Florette 🦴🦴🦴½ **1987 (PG)** The first of two films (with "Manon of the Spring") based on Marcel Pagnol's novel. A single spring in drought-ridden Provence, France is blocked by two scheming countrymen (Montand and Auteuil). They await the imminent failure of the farm nearby, inherited by a city-born hunchback, whose chances for survival fade without water for his crops. A devastating story with a heartrending performance by Depardieu as the hunchback. Lauded and awarded; in French with English subtitles. **122m/C VHS, DVD.** *FR* Gerard Depardieu, Yves Montand, Daniel Auteuil, Elisabeth Depardieu, Ernestine Mazurowna, Margarita Lozano, Armand Meffre; *D:* Claude Berri; *W:* Claude Berri, Gerard Brach; *C:* Bruno Nuytten; *M:* Jean-Claude Petit. British Acad. '87: Adapt. Screenplay, Film, Support. Actor (Auteuil); Cesar '87: Actor (Auteuil), Support. Actress (Béart).

Jeanne and the Perfect Guy 🦴🦴 *Jeanne et le Garcon Formidable* **1998** Jeanne (Ledoyen) is a hopeless romantic looking for her perfect love and having a lot of sex as she "auditions" her would-be Romeos. Then she meets Olivier (Demy) in the subway and decides he's the one. Only Olivier tells Jeanne that he has AIDS. Oh yeah, and it's a musical, with everyone breaking into song and dancing through the Parisian streets. It's gawky romanticism is strangely appealing and Ledoyen has a lot of charisma. French with subtitles. **98m/C VHS, DVD.** *FR* Virginie Ledoyen, Mathieu Demy, Frederic Gorny, Jacques Bonnaffe, Valerie Bonneton; *D:* Olivier Ducastel, Jacques Martineau; *W:* Olivier Ducastel, Jacques Martineau; *C:* Mathieu Poirot-Delpech; *M:* Philippe Miller.

Jeanne la Pucelle 🦴🦴 *Joan the Maid: The Battles; Joan the Maid: The Prisons; Jeanne la Pucelle: Les Batailles; Jeanne la Pucelle: Les Prisons* **1994** Rivette's ambitious two-part production on the life of Joan of Arc. The first section, "The Battles," follows Joan (Bonnaire) as she becomes convinced that God has spoken to her, and that only she can lead the Dauphin's soldiers and end the English siege of Orleans. "The Prisons" finds the Dauphin crowned King Charles VII and no longer needing Joan's aid—in fact she becomes a hindrance to his plans and is sold to the English for trial and execution. French with subtitles. **241m/C VHS, DVD.** *FR* Sandrine Bonnaire, Andre Marcon, Jean-Louis Richard, Jean-Pierre Lorit; *D:* Jacques Rivette; *W:* Christine Laurent, Pascal Bonitzer; *C:* William Lubtchansky; *M:* Jordi Savall.

Jeepers Creepers 🦴🦴½ **1939** Rogers is strictly sidekick material in this story. Hall discovers coal on the Weaver's property and proceeds to, underhandedly, acquire the land for himself. **69m/B VHS.** Thurston Hall, Leon Weaver, Frank Weaver, June "Elviry" Weaver, Loretta Weaver, Roy Rogers, Lucien Littlefield; *D:* Frank McDonald; *W:* Dorrell McGowan, Stuart E. McGowan; *C:* Ernest Miller.

Jeepers Creepers 🦴🦴 **2001 (R)** Uneven horror entry that slips from mocking trite slasher flicks to becoming a trite slasher flick itself. Trish (Phillips) and her brother Darry (Long) are driving home from college during spring break when they're almost run down by a dilapidated cargo hauler. Further on down the abandoned desolate road, they see the driver of the van dumping what looks to be squirming human bodies into a drain pipe near a creepy church. They turn around to see if anyone needs help. Well, no one needs help, but a horror movie needs victims and they've just volunteered. The storyline then degrades into demonic, prophecy-laden voodoo nonsense while trying to keep its tongue firmly in cheek. Creature effects and make-up take over in no time. **89m/C VHS, DVD. US** Gina Philips, Justin Long, Jonathan Breck, Patricia Belcher, Brandon Smith, Eileen Brennan; **D:** Victor Salva; **W:** Victor Salva. **C:** Don E. Fauntleroy; **M:** Bennett Salvay.

Jeepers Creepers 2 ♫♫ 2003 **(R)** Sequel finds teen football players and cheerleaders stranded on a bus sometime. Looking like this next batch of victims, looking like this next batch of victims, the stereotypical, cardboard cast crews on the doomed bus, grizzled local farmer Jack Taggart (Wise) prepares to do battle with the thing that ate his son on amping up the monster came out of the wardrobe budget, as a host of well-developed football players frequently, and inexplicably, walk around shirtless. **103m/C VHS, DVD.** US Ray Wise, Jonathan Breck, Deaunde "Double D" Davis, Eric Nenninger, Nicki Aycox, Travis Schiffner, Lena Cardwell, Billy Aaron Brown, Drew Tyler Bell, Marieh Delfino; **D:** Victor Salva; **W:** Victor Salva; **C:** Don E. Fauntleroy; **M:** Bennett Salvay.

Jefferson in Paris ♫♫½ 1994 **(PG-13)** Costume drama explores the impact Thomas Jefferson's (Nolte) five years in pre-revolutionary Paris (as American ambassador to Versailles) had on his private life. Jefferson confronts the personal and political issues of slavery in America, as well as his feelings for Sally Hemings (Newton), a Monticello slave brought to Paris by Jefferson's daughter. The Jefferson-Hemings legend may or may not be true (more likely not, according to many historians), but it seems to be the central theme here. Merchant Ivory's trademark tasteful production values and earnest characters can't camouflage the fact that they're playing fast and loose with the historical facts. **139m/C VHS, DVD.** Nick Nolte, Greta Scacchi, Gwyneth Paltrow, Thandie Newton, Jean-Pierre Aumont, Seth Gilliam, Todd Boyce, James Earl Jones; **D:** James Ivory; **W:** Ruth Prawer Jhabvala; **M:** Richard Robbins.

Jeffrey ♫♫½ 1995 **(R)** AIDS-fearing Jeffrey (Weber) decides to give celibacy a try until a trip to the gym brings Mr. Right into the picture. Steve (Weiss) is a hunk, but he happens to be HIV-positive, which prompts Jeffrey to do some serious soul-searching. Hence the message: AIDS sucks, but don't let it destroy life's joys. Musical "fantasy numbers, phallic fireworks, and a game show are a bit crass and the high theatrics can get annoying, but wicked barbs and one-liners score lots of laughs. Scene-stealer Stewart is caustically funny as Jeffrey's flamboyantly effeminate best friend Sterling, who works as an interior decorator and dates a "Cats" chorus boy. Adapted from the Paul Rudnick play. **92m/C VHS, DVD.** Steven Weber, Patrick Stewart, Michael T. Weiss, Bryan Batt, Sigourney Weaver, Olympia Dukakis, Kathy Najimy, Nathan Lane; **Cameos:** Olympia Dukakis, Kathy Najimy, Nathan Lane; **Cameos:** Christine Baranski; **D:** Christopher Ashley; **W:** Paul Rudnick; **C:** Jeffrey Tufano; **M:** Stephen Endelman.

Jekyll 2007 A modern retelling of the Robert Louis Stevenson tale of the ultimate split personality. Using modern technology, Dr. Tom Jackson (Nesbitt), the last descendent of Jekyl/Hyde, is determined to keep his dangerous alter ego under control. But he doesn't realize that someone else is monitoring him (or them, as the case may be). As usual, Hyde has a great deal more fun than his responsible other half. **300m/C DVD. GB** James Nesbitt, Gina Bellman, Denis Lawson, Michelle Ryan, Meera Syal, Fenella Woolgar; **D:** Douglas Mackinnon, Matt Lipsey; **W:** Steven Moffat; **C:** Adam Suschitzky; **M:** Debbie Wiseman. **TV**

Jekyll and Hyde ♫♫½ 1990 Unmemorable remake of the Robert Louis Stevenson tale of a doctor whose scientific experiments lead to a horrifyingly violent split personality. Caine does have a good time with his dual role. Made for TV.

C VHS, DVD. Michael Caine, Cheryl Ladd, Joss Ackland, Ronald Pickup, Kim Thomson, Lionel Jeffries, Kevin McNally, Lee Montague, Diane Keen, David Schofield; **D:** David Wickes; **W:** David Wickes; **C:** Norman G. Langley. **TV**

Jennifer ♫♫ 1978 **(R)** New Wave comic version of the classic story. This time, a serious young surgeon turns into a drug-crazed punk rocker after sniffing a mysterious powder. Mad scientist Blankfield fires and misfires, occasionally eliciting a few laughs. **87m/C VHS, DVD.** Mark Blankfield, Bess Armstrong, Krista Errickson, Tim Thomerson; **D:** Jerry Belson; **W:** Monica Johnson, Michael Leeson, Harvey Miller, Jerry Belson.

Jennifer (The Snake Goddess) 1978 **(PG)** Elaboration of that old "Carrie" theme: a teenage girl outcast who likes snakes wreaks havoc on her catty classmates in this supernatural thriller. **90m/C VHS.** Lisa Pelikan, Bert Convy, Nina Foch, John Gavin, Wesley Eure, Jeff Corey; **D:** Jerry Brice Mack; **W:** Kay Cousins Johnson, Steve Krantz.

Jennifer 8 ♫♫ 1992 **(R)** Mix of family drama and thriller isn't as successful as the sum of its parts. Garcia's results in a film about a burned-out cop moving to the suburbs where he finds the eighth victim of a serial killer and falls in love with the chief witness. Garcia is John Berlin, the cop who discovers the hand of the blind female victim, which leads him to her school and Helena Robertson (Thurman), another blind woman who may have the information he needs. Dark and mysterious atmosphere is dramatic, but plot lacks logic and sense of thrill. **127m/C VHS, DVD.** Andy Garcia, Uma Thurman, Lance Henriksen, Kathy Baker, Graham Beckel, Kevin Conway, John Malkovich; **D:** Bruce Robinson; **W:** Bruce Robinson.

Jenny Lamour ♫♫ Quai des Orfevres 1947 A dark mystery thriller about a singer accused of murdering a man he thought was stealing his woman. Acclaimed genre piece, dubbed into English. **95m/B VHS, DVD. FR** Louis Jouvet, Suzy Delair, Bernard Blier, Simone Renant; **D:** Henri-Georges Clouzot.

Jenny's War ♫♫½ 1985 **(PG)** An unbelievable WWII adventure story of an American teacher (Cannon) who outwits the Gestapo and infiltrates a Nazi POW camp in search of her missing soldier son. Actually based on a true story. From the book by Jack Stoneley. **192m/C VHS.** Dyan Cannon, Elke Sommer, Robert Hardy, Nigel Hawthorne, Christopher Cazenove, Patrick Ryecart, Hartmut Becker; **D:** Steven Gethers; **W:** Steven Gethers. **TV**

Jeopardy ♫♫½ 1953 Sunlit noirish thriller with an intriguingly crazed performance by Meeker and Stanwyck doing some vamping. While vacationing on a remote beach spot in Baja, Mexico, Doug Stilwin (Sullivan) gets trapped by a piling on a rotted pier with the tide coming in. Leaving their young son (Aaker) to comfort dad, mom Barb (Stanwyck) takes off in the car to get help. She's thankful to run into an American along the deserted road, except Lawson (Meeker) turns out to be a dangerous escaped con who takes her hostage and steals the car. Barb eventually persuades Lawson that she'll run away with him if only he'll rescue her husband first. Ya know, sometimes crime does pay. **69m/C VHS, DVD.** Barbara Stanwyck, Ralph Meeker, Barry Sullivan, Lee Aaker; **D:** John Sturges; **W:** Mel Dinelli; **C:** Victor Milner; **M:** Dimitri Tiomkin.

Jeremiah ♫♫½ 1998 The prophet Jeremiah abandons his family and the woman he loves in order to proclaim God's message that the people of Judah must change their ways or be overcome by the Babylonians. He's deemed a traitor but the prophecy is fulfilled when Jerusalem is destroyed. **96m/C VHS, DVD.** Patrick Dempsey, Oliver Reed, Klaus Maria Brandauer; **D:** Harry Winer. **CABLE**

Jeremiah Johnson ♫♫♫ 1972 **(PG)** The story of a man (Redford) who turns his back on civilization, circa 1830, and learns a new code of survival (thanks to a trapper, played by Geer) in a brutal land of isolated mountains and hostile Indians. In the process, Jeremiah becomes part of the wilderness, eventually taking an Indian wife and adopting a son. When hostile Crow warriors kill them, he begins a one-man revenge mission, gaining legendary status as a warrior. Based on the novel "Mountain Man" by Vardis Fisher and the story "Crow Killer" by Raymond W. Thorp and Robert Bunker. A notable and picturesque movie, filmed in Utah. **107m/C VHS, DVD.** Robert Redford, Will Geer, Stefan Gierasch, Allyn Ann McLerie, Joaquin Martinez, Charles Tyner, Paul Benedict, Josh Albee, Delle Bolton; **D:** Sydney Pollack; **W:** Edward Anhalt, John Milius; **C:** Duke Callaghan; **M:** John Rubinstein. **VIDEO**

Jeremy's Family Reunion ♫ 2004 Jeremy is a young, successful, African American attorney in New York City. He and his attractive white fiancee, Lisa, attend Jeremy's annual family reunion in New Orleans, where his colorful kin embarrass Jeremy. The family shows their disapproval of Jeremy's relationship and his city lifestyle, and Lisa flirts with the relatives—ultimately ending up in the bathroom with one. Unapologetically urban farce with unapologetically cheap story line and production values. **88m/C DVD.** Abel Jones, Gavin Lewis, Chauvon Higgins, Nolan Powell; **D:** Abel Garcia; **W:** Abel Garcia.

Jericho ♫♫ Dark Sands 1938 Jericho Jackson (Robeson) is a corporal in the black unit of the U.S.'s Expeditionary Forces in WWI France. After a fight with his sergeant leads to the man's accidental death, Jackson is court-martialed and sentenced to die. He manages to escape to North Africa and begin a new life but military authorities eventually discover his whereabouts. Despite the military drama, Robeson's vocal talents are still showcased. **77m/ B&W. GB** Paul Robeson, Henry Wilcoxon, Wallace Ford; **D:** Thornton Freeland.

Jericho ♫♫½ 2001 **(PG-13)** When a robbery goes wrong in the town of Jericho, the three bandits—one of whom has suffered a serious head wound—leave a dead sheriff behind as they head out of town. The wounded thief is soon left to die but is found and nursed back to health by freed slave turned preacher Joshua (Coffee), who names the amnesiac "Jericho." As the two travel the countryside, bits and pieces of Jericho's past surface and he's drawn to the town's namesake town, where his past is finally revealed. The surprise ending feels tacked on rather than a part of the ordinary script but the two men's friendship is a bonus as is Coffee's affecting performance. **102m/C VHS, DVD.** Mark Valley, R. Lee Ermey, Leon Coffee, Lisa Stewart, Buck Taylor, Mark Collie; **D:** Merlin Miller; **W:** Robert Avard Miller; **C:** Jerry Folway; **M:** Mark Haffner. **VIDEO**

Jericho Fever ♫♫½ 1993 **(PG-13)** A group of terrorists assassinate Palestinian and Israeli negotiators engaged in peace talks in Mexico. Infected with a deadly disease they escape to the U.S., tracked by Israeli Mossad agents, a border patrolman, an American along and two investigators from the Centers for Disease Control who want to stop the spread of the plague. **88m/C VHS.** Stephanie Zimbalist, Perry King, Branssombe Richmond, Alan Scarfe, Perry King, Branssombe Richmond, Alan Scarfe; **D:** Sandor Stern; **W:** I.C. Rappoport; **M:** Cameron Allan.

Jericho Mansions ♫♫½ 2003 **(R)** Longtime apartment building super Leonard (Caan) becomes involved in a murder investigation when a tenant turns up dead. He's already having a rough time, with complaints from other tenants and a theft accusation. Director Sciamma takes a much cooler, smarter path to the surprise ending than most mystery/thriller tales these days. Caan is in fine form. **98m/C VHS, DVD.** James Caan, Jennifer Tilly, Genevieve Bujold, Maribel Verdu, Peter Keleghan, Bruce Ramsay, Susan Glover, Mark Camacho; **D:** Alberto Sciamma; **W:** Alberto Sciamma, Harriet Sand; **C:** Alastair Meux; **M:** Dan (Daniel) Jones.

The Jericho Mile ♫♫ 1979 Drama about a track-obsessed convicted murderer who is given a chance at the Olympics. Powerful lead performance by Strauss. **97m/C VHS.** Peter Strauss, Roger E. Mosley, Brian Dennehy; **D:** Michael Mann. **TV**

The Jerk ♫♫½ 1979 **(R)** A jerk tells his rags-to-riches-to-rags story in history flashbacks, from "I was born a poor Black child," through his entrepreneurial success in his invention of the "Optigrab," to his inevitable decline. Only Martin's first starring role, back in his wild and crazy days; his ridiculous misadventures pay tribute to Jerry Lewis movies of the late '60s. Followed by a TV version released in 1984 as "The Jerk Too." **94m/C VHS, DVD. HD DVD.** Steve Martin, Bernadette Peters, Catlin Adams, Bill Macy, Jackie Mason, Mabel King, Richard Ward, M. Emmet Walsh, Dick O'Neill, Maurice Evans, Pepe Serna, Trinidad Silva, Carl Gottlieb; **Cameos:** Carl Reiner, Rob Reiner; **D:** Carl Reiner; **W:** Michael Elias, Steve Martin, Carl Gottlieb; **M:** Jack Elliott.

The Jerky Boys WOOF! 1995 **(R)** Quick! Let's make a Jerky Boys movie and exploit their popularity before everyone realizes what a lame, one-joke act it is! Too late, guys. In what passes for a plot, Johnny and Kamal prank call an irritable mob boss (Arkin), pretending to be Chicago hitmen in need of a hideout. The wiseguys soon figure out the truth, but the requisite dumb cop (Sullivan) packs the film by not catching on. All these "twists" serve only one purpose—to get our heroes to their next phone. Don't expect the charges for this one. **82m/C VHS.** Johnny Brennan, Kamal Ahmed, Alan Arkin, William Hickey, Alan North, James Lorinz, Brad Sullivan, Vincent Pastore, Ozzy Osbourne, Paul Bartel, Suzanne Shepherd; **Cameos:** Tom Jones; **D:** James Melkonian; **W:** Johnny Brennan, Kamal Ahmed, Rich Wilkes, James Melkonian.

Jerome ♫♫♫ 1998 Well-acted indie with a compelling story that deserves a wider audience. After 15 soul-sucking years as a factory welder in California, Wade Hampton (Pillsbury) decides to just walk away from his life. He picks Jerome, Arizona as his destination because he's heard it has an artists' colony and Wade has secretly been making miniature metal sculptures. So Wade heads out on the highway and encounters restless hitchhiker Jane (Malick), who has no destination in mind at all. The film is interspersed with interviews with people from Wade's past, so the viewer also anticipates trouble coming for the travelers as well. **91m/C VHS, DVD.** Wendle Malick, Drew Pillsbury, Drew McKenna, Beth Kennedy, James Keeley; **D:** Thomas Johnston, David Elton, Eric Tignini; **W:** Thomas Johnston, David Elton, Eric Tignini; **C:** Gina DeGirolamo.

Jerry and Tom ♫♫ 1998 **(R)** Tom (Mantegna) is a veteran hitman breaking in an impatient protege, Jerry (Rockwell), in an used-car dealership business he's in—nothing personal—but that kind of emotional vacuum isn't easy to maintain. Familiar story but it has the advantage of a talented cast and good direction. **97m/C VHS, DVD.** Joe Mantegna, Sam Rockwell, Maury Chaykin, Charles Durning, Peter Riegert, William H. Macy, Ted Danson; **D:** Saul Rubinek; **W:** Rick Cleveland; **C:** Paul Sarossy; **M:** David Buchbinder.

Jerry Maguire ♫♫½ 1996 **(R)** Romantic sports comedy focuses on the off-field action and makes an agent the good guy. Risky business in an era of strikes, lockouts, and astronomical salaries, but writer/director Crowe manages to pull it off. Cruise is well-used as the title character in the story of a shark-like sports agent who sees the error of his ways and transforms into...a more moral sports agent who gets him fired from his ultra-huge agency), he allies himself

self with his obnoxious and least important client Rod Tidwell (Gooding Jr.), as well as Dorothy, an adoring young accountant (Zellweger) making a strong bid for Culkin-like stardom). Famously well-researched, film sports great dialogue, talented leads, great supporting cast and a mega-star currently riding a wave of $100-million-plus films (talk about "Show me the money!"). Pop culture bonus points for coining 1996's most memorable catch phrase, which Crowe took from real life ex-Phoenix Cardinal Tim McDonald, and is now being used to sell everything from magazines to t-shirts. **135m/C VHS, DVD, UMD, Blu-Ray.** Tom Cruise, Cuba Gooding Jr., Renee Zellweger, Kelly Preston, Bonnie Hunt, Jerry O'Connell, Jay Mohr, Regina King, Glenn Frey, Jonathan Lipnicki, Todd Louiso, Mark Pellington; *Cameos:* Eric Stoltz; *D:* Cameron Crowe; *W:* Cameron Crowe; *M:* Nancy Wilson. Oscars '96: Support. Actor (Gooding); Golden Globes '97: Actor—Mus./Comedy (Cruise); MTV Movie Awards '97: Male Perf.; Natl. Bd. of Review '96: Support. Actor (Gooding); Screen Actors Guild '96: Support. Actor (Gooding); Broadcast Film Critics '96: Breakthrough Perf. (Zellweger), Support. Actor (Gooding).

Jersey Girl 🦴🦴 **1992 (PG-13)** Toby Mastellone (Gertz) is a bright single gal from the Jersey shore who wants something better in her life. Her hard-working dad (Bologna) has fixed her up with an apprentice plumber but she wants a Manhattan guy. And then Toby meets cute with Sal (McDermott), who seems just the ticket, but can you really take the Jersey out of the girl? **95m/C VHS, DVD.** Jami Gertz, Dylan McDermott, Joseph Bologna, Aida Turturro, Star Jasper, Sheryl Lee, Joseph Mazzello, Molly Price; *D:* David Burton Morris; *M:* Stephen Bedell.

Jersey Girl 🦴🦴½ **2004 (PG-13)** Big shot music PR man Ollie (Affleck) is widowed when wife Gertrude (Lopez) dies in childbirth and must raise his daughter Gertie (Castro) on his own. But this proves too challenging as he loses his job and is forced to crash with dear old dad (Carlin) in New Jersey. After seven years, he's still struggling with his loss. Celibate, he frequents the video shop for porno flicks where he meets the shoot-from-the-hip clerk, Maya (Tyler). Ah, and there the romance begins, along with the "should I be a good parent or have a great career" dilemma. Writer-director Smith's considerable comedic talents emerge unevenly in his foray into the dramatic-comedy genre. Granted, it's probably not what Smith's fans are used to, but it's still enjoyable. Castro is a fresh, sassy presence in her feature cebut. **102m/C VHS, DVD.** *US* Ben Affleck, Jennifer Lopez, George Carlin, Liv Tyler, Raquel Castro, Stephen (Steve) Root, Mike Starr, Jason Biggs, S. Epatha Merkerson, Jennifer Schwalbach Smith, Jason Lee, Matt Damon, Paulie (Litowsky) Litt; *Cameos:* Will Smith; *D:* Kevin Smith; *W:* Kevin Smith; *C:* Vilmos Zsigmond; *M:* James L. Venable.

Jerusalem 🦴🦴 **1996 (PG-13)** Charismatic fundamentalist preacher Helgum (Taube) travels to a small turn-of-the-century Swedish village preaching the end of the world and encouraging the people in his belief that all Christians should move to the Holy Land in order to build the new Jerusalem. He manages to convince the wealthy Karin (August) and to tempt young Gertrud (Bonnevie), whose fiance Ingmar (Friberg) is away trying to earn money so they can get married. Based on the novel by Selma Lagerlof who was inspired by Swedes who made a move to Palestine in 1900. Swedish with subtitles. **166m/C VHS.** *SW* Maria Bonnevie, Ulf Friberg, Lena Endre, Pernilla August, Olympia Dukakis, Max von Sydow, Sven-Bertil Taube; *D:* Bille August; *W:* Bille August; *C:* Jorgen Persson; *M:* Stefan Nilsson.

Jesse 🦴🦴 **1988 (PG)** A heroic nurse ministers to remote Death Valley residents, and state bureaucats hound her for practicing medicine without a license. Although based on a true case and well-acted, this made-for-TV drama just lacks import and impact. **94m/C VHS.** Lee Remick, Scott Wilson, Leon Rippy, Priscilla Lopez, Albert Salmi; *D:* Glenn Jordan; *M:* David Shire.

Jesse James 🦴🦴🦴 **1939** One of director King's best efforts is this Hollywood biography of the notorious outlaw. 24-year-old Power showed he was more than just good looks in the title role but Fonda truly became a star in the role of brother Frank James. Screenwriter Johnson also focused more on the legend than the reality of the outlaw's career in post-Civil War Missouri. **105m/C VHS, DVD.** Henry Fonda, Tyrone Power, Randolph Scott, Henry Hull, Jane Darwell, Brian Donlevy, Charles Halton, John Carradine, Donald Meek, Slim Summerville; *D:* Henry King; *W:* Nunnally Johnson; *C:* George Barnes, William Howard Greene; *M:* Louis Silvers.

Jesse James at Bay 🦴🦴 **1941** Rogers is the do-good Jesse who's warring against some crooked railroad execs. Interesting perspective. **54m/B VHS, DVD.** Roy Rogers, George "Gabby" Hayes, Sally Payne; *D:* Joseph Kane.

Jesse James Meets Frankenstein's Daughter 🦴½ **1965** The gunslinger and Frankenstein's granddaughter, Maria, meet up in the Old West in this wacky combination of western and horror genres. **95m/C VHS, DVD.** John Lupton, Cal Bolder, Narda Onyx, Steven Geray, Estelita, Jim Davis, William "Bill" Fawcett, Nestor Paiva, Rayford Barnes, Roger Creed; *D:* William Beaudine; *W:* Carl K. Hittleman; *C:* Lothrop Worth; *M:* Raoul Kraushaar.

Jesse James Rides Again **1947** Originally a serial, this feature depicts the further adventures of the West's most notorious outlaw. **181m/B VHS, DVD.** Clayton Moore, Linda Stirling, Roy Barcroft, Tristram Coffin; *D:* Fred Brannon, Thomas Carr.

Jesse James Under the Black Flag 🦴🦴½ **1921** An interesting western/pseudo biography/flashback in which Coates and James Jr. (the outlaw's son) play themselves. As Coates attempts to gather information from Jesse's descendants, a stranger appears and falls for Jesse's granddaughter, who shuns him. He proceeds to read the Coates biography and the flashback begins, in the Jesse was really a good guy format. Off the straight and narrow vein. **59m/B VHS.** Jesse James Jr., Franklin Coates, Diana Reed, Marguerite Hungerford; *D:* Franklin Coates.

The Jesse Owens Story 🦴🦴 **1984** The moving story of the four-time Olympic Gold medal winner's triumphs and misfortunes. **174m/C VHS, DVD.** Dorian Harewood, Debbi (Deborah) Morgan, Georg Stanford Brown, LeVar Burton, George Kennedy, Tom Bosley, Ben Vereen; *D:* Richard Irving; *W:* Harold Gast. **TV**

Jesse Stone: Death in Paradise 🦴🦴½ *Robert B. Parker's Jesse Stone: Death in Paradise* **2006** Jesse (Selleck) is reluctantly seeing a shrink (Devane) to help him with his drinking problem but his bad habits don't interfere with his investigating skills. When the body of a pregnant teenage girl is found floating in a lake, he wants to know why no one reported her missing. Jesse's investigation soon leads him to a best-selling local author (Basaraba) and a Boston mob boss (Flynn). The third in the series of TV movies. Based on a novel by Robert B. Parker. **87m/C DVD.** Tom Selleck, Viola Davis, Koh1 Sudduth, Stephen McHattie, William Devane, Edward Edwards, Gary Basaraba, Matthew F. Bar, Steve Flynn, John Diehl, Debra Christofferson, Orla Brady, Mae Whitman; *D:* Robert Harmon; *W:* J.T. Allen, Michael Brandman; *C:* David Gribble; *M:* Jeff Beal. **TV**

Jesse Stone: Night Passage 🦴🦴½ *Jesse Stone: Night Passage; Robert B. Parker's Jesse Stone: Night Passage* **2006** In this prequel, we see how Jesse Stone (Selleck), a former L.A. homicide detective with a drinking problem and an ex-wife he still loves, gets his last chance by taking on the job of police chief of Paradise. Town councilor Hasty Hardaway (Rubinek) thinks Stone will be easy to push around but he learns differently. Jesse is soon investigating the suspicious death of his recently retired predecessor, which leads to a money laundering scheme and mob ties. Second in the series of TV movies. Based on the book by Robert B. Parker. **89m/C DVD.** Tom Selleck, Viola Davis, Koh1 Sudduth, Polly Shannon, Stephen McHattie, Saul Rubinek, Stephanie March, Stephen Baldwin, Mike Starr; *D:* Robert Harmon; *W:* Tom Epperson; *C:* David Gribble; *M:* Jeff Beal. **TV**

Jesse Stone: Sea Change 🦴🦴½ *Sea Change* **2007** In this fourth TV movie (based on the novel by Robert B. Parker), Paradise sheriff Jesse Stone (Selleck) is bored, brooding, and drinking too much. So bored that he recruits deputy Rose (Baker) and reopens a cold case—a bank robbery, shooting, and missing teller from 15 years ago. Then things heat up when a young local woman claims to have been raped aboard a visitor's yacht and some Boston thug is tailing Jesse with bad intent. **87m/C DVD.** Tom Selleck, Kathy Baker, William Devane, Rebecca Pidgeon, Sean Young, Saul Rubinek, Viola Davis, Koh1 Sudduth, Nigel Bennett; *D:* Robert Harmon; *W:* Ronni Kern; *C:* Rene Ohashi; *M:* Jeff Beal. **TV**

Jesse Stone: Stone Cold 🦴🦴½ *Jesse Stone: Stone Cold; Robert B. Parker's Jesse Stone: Stone Cold* **2005** Jesse (Selleck) is settling into his life as police chief of Paradise, a small New England fishing/tourist community. But his quiet, which is usually spent with a bottle of scotch, is disturbed by a series of murders—one of which hits too close to home. The first in a series of TV movies. Based on the book by Robert B. Parker. **87m/C DVD.** Tom Selleck, Viola Davis, Koh1 Sudduth, Polly Shannon, Stephen McHattie, Jane Adams, Mimi Rogers; *D:* Robert Harmon; *W:* John Fasano, Michael Brandman; *C:* Rene Ohashi; *M:* Jeff Beal. **TV**

The Jesse Ventura Story 🦴½ **1999** Cheap quickie TV movie capitalizes on Ventura's unlikely career path. Small-town boy Ventura becomes a Navy SEAL, a professional wrestler known as "The Body" (among other jobs), and eventually winds up in an upset victory as the governor of Minnesota. A dull, unauthorized whitewash that would probably bore even Ventura himself. **95m/C VHS, DVD.** Nils Allen Stewart, Nancy Sakovich, Thomas Brandise, Christopher Bondy, Nola Augustion; *D:* David S. Jackson; *W:* Patricia Jones, Donald Reiker; *C:* John Holosko; *M:* Richard Gibbs. **TV**

Jessi's Girls 🦴½ **1975** In retaliation for the murder of her husband, an angry young woman frees three female prisoners, and they embark on a bloody course of revenge. Together, they track down the killers, and one by one, they fight to even the score. **86m/C VHS.** Sondra Currie, Regina Carrol, Jennifer Bishop, Rigg Kennedy; *D:* Al Adamson.

Jesus 🦴🦴½ **2000** Not completely reverential look at the life and teachings of Jesus (Sisto) from a historical, political, and religious viewpoint. Jesus is kind of a fun-loving 30-year-old who knows he has a destiny to fulfill. He and his parents (Bissett and Mueller-Stahl) struggle to deal with that as his followers seek the best course of resistance to Roman oppression, embodied by the political savvy Pontius Pilate (Oldman). The only truly disconcerting note is a slick Satan (Krabbe), who dresses like a contemporary wiseguy, and his temptation of Jesus in the wilderness. **174m/C VHS, DVD.** Jeremy Sisto, Jacqueline Bisset, Armin Mueller-Stahl, Debra Messing, Gary Oldman, Jeroen Krabbe, David O'Hara, G.W. Bailey, Thomas Lockyer, Luca Zingaretti, Stefania Rocca, Claudio Amendola; *D:* Roger Young; *W:* Suzette Couture; *C:* Raffaele Mertes; *M:* Patrick Williams. **TV**

Jesus Christ, Superstar 🦴🦴🦴 **1973 (G)** A rock opera that portrays, in music, the last seven days in the earthly life of Christ, as reenacted by young tourists in Israel. Outstanding musical score was the key to the success of the film, although Elliman and Anderson are standouts as, respectively, Mary Magdalene and Judas. Based on the stage play by Tim Rice and Andrew Lloyd Webber stirring while exhibiting the usual heavy-handed Jewison approach. ♪Jesus Christ, Superstar; I Don't Know How To Love Him; What's The Buzz?; Herod's Song; Heaven On Their Minds; Strange Thing; Mystifying; Then We Are Decided; Everything's Alright; This Jesus Must Die. **108m/C VHS, DVD.** Ted Neeley, Carl Anderson, Yvonne Elliman, Josh Mostel, Barry Dennen, Bob Bingham, Larry T. Marshall; *D:* Norman Jewison; *W:* Melvyn Bragg; *C:* Douglas Slocombe; *M:* Andrew Lloyd Webber, Andre Previn, Herbert W. Spencer.

Jesus Christ Superstar 🦴🦴½ **2000** This new version updates the Tim Rice-Andrew Lloyd Webber rock opera for the MTV generation. The musical numbers have a rock video look and feel. The production is based on a stage version and so it doesn't feel or look like a real film. **112m/C VHS, DVD.** Glenn Carter, Jerome Pradon, Renee Castle, Rik Mayall; *D:* Nick Morris, Gale Edwards; *W:* Tim Rice, Andrew Lloyd Webber; *C:* Nicholas D. Knowland, Anthony Van Laast; *M:* Simon Lee, Tim Rice, Andrew Lloyd Webber.

Jesus of Montreal 🦴🦴🦴½ *Jesus de Montreal* **1989 (R)** A vagrant young actor (stage-trained Canadian star Bluteau) is hired by a Montreal priest to produce a fresh interpretation of an Easter passion play. Taking the good book at its word, he produces a contemporized literal telling that captivates audiences, inflames the men of the cloth, and eventually wins the players' faith. Quebecois director Arcand (keep an eye out for him as the judge) tells a compelling, acerbically satirical and haunting story that never forces its Biblical parallels. In French with English subtitles. **119m/C VHS, DVD.** *FR CA* Gilles Pelletier, Lothaire Bluteau, Catherine Wilkening, Robert Lepage, Johanne-Marie Tremblay, Remy Girard, Marie-Christine Barrault; *D:* Denys Arcand; *W:* Denys Arcand; *C:* Guy Dufaux; *M:* Jean-Marie Benoit, Francois Dompierre, Yves Laferriere. Cannes '89: Special Jury Prize; Genie '90: Actor (Girard), Director (Arcand), Film. Support. Actor (Girard).

Jesus of Nazareth 🦴🦴½ **1928** A dramatic recreation of the life of Christ from the Annunciation through the Ascension. The film titles are taken from description. **85m/B VHS.** Philip Van Loan, Anna Lehr, Charles McCaffrey; *W:* Jean Conover.

Jesus of Nazareth 🦴🦴🦴 **1977** An all-star cast lavishly portrays the life of Christ in this miniseries. Wonderfully directed and sensitively acted. **371m/C VHS, DVD.** Robert Powell, Anne Bancroft, Ernest Borgnine, Claudia Cardinale, James Mason, Laurence Olivier, Anthony Quinn; *D:* Franco Zeffirelli; *W:* Franco Zeffirelli, Anthony Burgess, Suso Cecchi D'Amico; *M:* Maurice Jarre. **TV**

Jesus' Son 🦴🦴🦴 **1999 (R)** Crudup gives a fine performance as a sweet, passive, bungling druggie known only as FH (which stands for F*** head). He falls for reckless heroin-addict Michelle (Morton), ODs, gets saved, gets dumped, gets in a car wreck, and eventually cleans up and finds some kind of peace working in an Arizona nursing home. There's really not much plot; it's the characters that carry things along. Film is set in the '70s and based on Dennis Johnson's 1992 collection of short stories. **109m/C VHS, DVD.** Billy Crudup, Samantha Morton, Denis Leary, Holly Hunter, Dennis Hopper, Jack Black, Will Patton, Greg Germann; *D:* Alison Maclean; *W:* Elizabeth Cuthrel, David Urrutia, Oren Moverman; *C:* Adam Kimmel; *M:* Joe Henry.

The Jesus Trip 🦴½ **1971** Hunted motorcyclists take a young nun hostage in the desert. **86m/C VHS.** Robert Porter, Tippy Walker; *D:* Russ Mayberry.

Jet Benny Show **1986** A Buck Rogers/Star Wars-style spoof of Jack Benny's classic TV show. **76m/C VHS.** Steve Norman, Kevin Dees, Polly MacIntyre, Ted Luedemann; *D:* Roger Evans.

Jet Lag 🦴🦴 *Decalage Horaire* **2002 (R)** Lightweight romance finds beautician Rose (Binoche) stuck at Charles de Gaulle airport thanks to an unexpected strike. She is heading on a solo holiday away from her abusive boyfriend Sergio (Lopez). Also stuck is Felix (Reno), a former chef turned frozen-food businessman on his way to Munich. Rose loses her cell

Jet Li's Fearless 🐾🐾 *Huo Yuan Jia* 2006 (PG-13) Touted as Jet Li's final go at traditional Chinese martial arts (wushu) cinema, Li plays famed mainland fighter Huo Yuanjia in this elaborate bio, which begins in 1910, with flashbacks and flashforwards that document Yuanjia's childhood and gradual ascent to martial arts stardom. Yuanjia's initial arrogance costs him much and he must learn humility in order to achieve true harmony (or something like that). Director Yu wisely avoids wasting much time in-between fight scenes and takes an almost purist approach with every little CGI and cable work. English and Chinese with subtitles. 103m/C VHS, DVD, CH, HK Jet Li, Shido Nakamura, Betty Sun, Yong Dong, Collin Chou, Nathar Jones, Yun Qu; D: Ronny Yu; W: Wang Bin, Chris Chow, Christine To, Li Feng; C: Hang-Sheng Poon; M: Mei Linmao.

Jet Over the Atlantic 🐾1/2 1959 Dangerous situation arises as a bomb is discovered aboard a plane en route from Spain to New York. 92m/B VHS Guy Madison, George Raft, Virginia Mayo, Brett Halsey; D: Byron Haskin.

Jet Pilot 🐾🐾 1957 An American Air Force colonel (Wayne) in charge of an Alaskan Air Force base falls in love with a detecting Russian jet pilot (Leigh). They marry, but Wayne suspects Leigh is a spy planted to find out top U.S. secrets. He pretends to defect with her back to Russia to see what he can find out, but they again flee. Ludicrous plot is saved only by spectacular flying scenes, some performed by Chuck Yeager. Although this was filmed in 1950, it took seven more years to be released because producer Hughes couldn't keep his hands off it. 112m/B VHS, DVD John Wayne, Janet Leigh, Jay C. Flippen, Paul Fix, Richard Rober, Roland Winters, Hans Conried, Ivan Triesault; D: Josef von Sternberg; C: Winton C. Hoch.

Jets: The Movie 🐾🐾 1990 (G) The famous outer space family of '60s TV is given a new silver-screened life. George gets a promotion that puts him in charge of an asteroid populated by furry creatures. Ecological concerns are expressed; while this is rare for a cartoon, the story is overall typical. 82m/C VHS, D: William Hanna, Joseph Barbera; M: John Debney; V: George O'Hanlon, Mel Blanc, Penny Singleton, Tiffany, Patric Zimmerman, Donald E. Messick, Jean Vander Pyl, Ronnie Schell, Pat Deutsch, Dana Hill, Russi Taylor, Paul Kreppel, Rick Dees.

The Jew 🐾🐾 1996 Portrait of 18th century playwright Antonio Jose da Silva (Pinheiro), whose family was forcibly converted from their Jewish faith by the Catholic Church. Living in Lisbon, da Silva founded a puppet theatre for which he wrote comic operas. Eventually condemned for heresy, he was executed by the Inquisition in 1739. Explicit torture scenes. Portuguese with subtitles. 85m/C VHS, PT Felipe Pinheiro, Dina Stat, Mario Viegas, Edwin Luisi, Jose Netz; D: Jom Tob Azulay; W: Milbir Fernendes, Billy Eckstine, Gilvan Pereira; C: Eduardo Serra.

phone and asks to borrow Felix's. They wind up sharing the last available room in an airport hotel and compare lives. Felix bar and is romanced by cattle trader Levi (Cathoras) each year when he passes through town. Only this year, a Nazi engineer and his men are in town to repair a tunnel and gradually the peace of the community is shattered by unreasoning hatred and is turned dead. German with subtitles. 90m/C VHS, DVD, GE Bruno Ganz, Bernd-Michael Lade, Eva Mattes, Caroline Ebner, Georg Olschewski, Martina Gedeck; D: Didi Danquart; W: Didi Danquart, Martina Docker; C: Johann Feindt; M: Cornelius Schwehr.

Jew-Boy Levi 🐾🐾 *Viehjud Levi* 1999 The Enforcer: My Father Is a Hero; Letter to Dad-

Jet Li's The Enforcer 🐾🐾1/2

The Jewel in the Crown 🐾🐾🐾 1984 Epic saga of the last years of British rule in India from 1942-47 concentrating on a controversial love affair between the Indian Hari Kumar and the English Daphne Manners, which profoundly affects the lives of many. Based on "The Raj Quartet" by Paul Scott. Originally shown on British TV, it aired in the U.S. on the PBS series "Masterpiece Theatre." An excellent miniseries that was shown in 14 segments. 750m/C VHS, DVD, GB Charles Dance, Susan Wooldridge, Art Malik, Tim Pigott-Smith, Geraldine James, Peggy Ashcroft, Judy Parfitt; D: Christopher Morahan, Jim O'Brien; M: George Fenton. **TV**

The Jewel of the Nile 🐾🐾1/2 1985 (PG) Sequel to "Romancing the Stone" with the same cast but new director. Romance novelist Joan thought she found her true love in Jack but finds that life doesn't always end happily ever. After they part ways, Jack realizes that she may be in trouble and endeavors to rescue her from the criminal hands of a charming North African president. Of course, he can check out this "jewel" at the same time. Chemistry is still there, but the rest of the film isn't quite up to the "Stone's" charm. 106m/C VHS, DVD, Michael Douglas, Kathleen Turner, Danny DeVito, Avner Eisenberg, Spiros Focas, The Flying Karamazov Brothers, Holland Taylor; D: Lewis Teague; W: Mark Rosenthal, Larry Konner; C: Jan De Bont; M: Jack Nitzsche.

The Jeweller's Shop 🐾🐾 1990 A highly spiritual tale of two married couples in Poland whose children meet and fall in love much later in Canada. Based on a play by Karol Wojtyla—who later became Pope Jean-Paul II. Adapted under strict Vatican supervision. 90m/C VHS, Burt Lancaster, Ben Cross, Olivia Hussey, Andrea Occhipinti; W: Jeff Andrus; C: Franco D Giacomo; M: Michel Legrand.

Jewels 🐾🐾🐾 *Danielle Steel's Jewels* 1992 Sarah and her second husband the Duke of Whitfield—as a goodwill gesture after WWI—start buying jewelry from war survivors, which eventually leads to a successful jewelry store business. After William dies, Sarah struggles to keep control of her children and the family business. Classic soap-opera mini-series drama. 228m/C DVD, Annette O'Toole, Robert Wagner, Ursula Howells, Geoffrey Whitehead, Corinne Touzet; D: Roger Young; W: Jonathan Estrin; M: Patrick Williams.

Jezebel 🐾🐾🐾 1938 Davis is a willful Southern belle who loses fiance Fonda through her selfish and spiteful ways in this pre-Civil War drama. When she becomes ill, she realizes her cruelty and rushes to nurse him back to health. Davis' role won her an Oscar for Best Actress, and certainly provided Scarlett O'Hara with a rival for most memorable female character of all time. 105m/B VHS, DVD, Bette Davis, George Brent, Henry Fonda, Margaret Lindsay, Fay Bainter, Donald Crisp, Spring Byington, Eddie Anderson; D: William Wyler; W: Clements Ripley, Abem Finkel, John Huston, Robert Buckner; C: Ernest Haller; M: Max Steiner; Oscars '38: Actress (Davis), Support. Actress (Bainter).

Jezebel's Kiss 🐾🐾 1990 (R) A sizzling young beauty returns to the town where she grew up and proceeds to destroy any man she pleases. 96m/C VHS, DVD, Meg Foster, Malcolm McDowell, Meredith Baxter, Everett McGill, Katherine Barrese; D: Harvey Keith; W: Harvey Keith.

Jigsaw 🐾🐾 *Man on the Move* 1971 Missing persons lawman is lured into a cover-up more complex than he had bargained for. A tense drama originated as the pilot for a series. 100m/C VHS, James Wainwright, Vera Miles, Richard Kiley, Andrew Duggan, Edmond O'Brien; D: William A. Graham. **TV**

Jigsaw 🐾🐾 1990 A developer is found dead the night before his wedding. His widow and a cop team up to find out who, what, where, and why. Lukewarm Australian mystery export. 85m/C VHS, Rebecca Gibney, Dominic Sweeney, Michael Coard; D: Marc Gracie; W: Marc Gracie; C: Jaems Grant; M: Dalmazio Bebare.

The Jigsaw Man 🐾🐾 1984 (PG) A British-Russian double agent is sent back to England to retrieve a list of Soviet agents which he hid there many years before. 90m/C VHS, GB Michael Caine, Laurence Olivier, Susan George, Robert Powell, Charles Gray; David Patrick Kelly, Michael Medwin; D: Terence Young.

Jigsaw 🐾1/2 1999 (R) Convential neo-noir is weak in both plot and performances. Vicky (Ehm) asks her boyfriend, Jules (Como), to pick up $5000 that's owed her. Vicky winds up dead and Jules is on the lam from both cops and drug dealers. 83m/C VHS, DVD, CA William Como, Erica Ehm, Edgar George; D: Paul Shoebridge. **VIDEO**

JFK 🐾🐾🐾1/2 1991 (R) Highly controversial examination of President John F. Kennedy's 1963 assassination, from the viewpoint of New Orleans district attorney Jim Garrison. Hotly debated because of Stone's conspiracy theory, it sparked new calls to open the sealed government records from the 1977 House Select Committee on Assassinations investigation. Outstanding performances from all-star principal and supporting casts, stunning cinematography, and excellent editing. Even Garrison himself shows up as Chief Justice Earl Warren. Considered by some to be a cinematic masterpiece, others see it as revisionist history that should be taken with a grain of salt. Extended version adds 17 minutes. 188m/C VHS, DVD, Dae Dye, Kevin Costner, Sissy Spacek, Kevin Bacon, Tommy Lee Jones, Laurie Metcalf, Gary Oldman, Michael Rooker, Jay O. Sanders, Beata Pozniak, Joe Pesci, Donald Sutherland, John Candy, Jack Lemmon, Walter Matthau, Ed Asner, Vincent D'Onofrio, Sally Kirkland, Brian Doyle-Murray, Wayne Knight, Tony Plana, Tomas Millian, Sean Stone, Cameos: Lolita (David) Davidovic, Frank Whaley, Jim Garrison; D: Oliver Stone; W: Oliver Stone, Zachary Sklar; C: Robert Richardson; M: John Williams Oscars '91: Cinematog., Film Editing; Golden Globe '92; Director (Stone).

The JFK Conspiracy 1991 Did Lee Harvey Oswald act alone? Opinions of government officials, eyewitnesses, and director Oliver Stone, in addition to testimony, photographs, documents, and other evidence, address the perennial American question. Includes footage from the House Select Committee on Assassination. 98m/C VHS. **TV**

JFK: Reckless Youth 🐾🐾1/2 1993 Dempsey does a fine job as the young John F. Kennedy Jr. TV flick covers the first 30 years of his life and the family lies and influences that shape him up to his 1946 election to Congress. Based on the book by Nigel Hamilton. 183m/C DVD, US Patrick Dempsey, Terry Kinney, Loren Dean, Robin Tunney, Diana Scarwid, Malachy McCourt, Claire Forlani, Yolanda Jilot, James Rebhorn, Natalie Radford, Star Cahill, Andrew Lowery, Cedric Smith, Greg Spottiswood, Nikki de Boer, Barry Morse; D: Harry Winer; W: William Broyles Jr.; C: Jean Lepine; M: Cameron Allan. **TV**

Jigsaw 🐾🐾🐾 *Gun Moll* 1949 Crime drama with a smattering of cameos by Hollywood favorites. The dead man's friend an assistant district attorney, seeks the punks responsible. They send in a seductress to keep the D.A. busy, but she too is murdered. Action and tension in a well-made flick. Based on a story by John Roeburt. 70m/B VHS, DVD, Franchot Tone, Jean Wallace, Myron McCormick, Marc Lawrence, Winifred Lenihan, Betty Harper, Robert Gist; Cameos: Marlene Dietrich, Henry Fonda, Burgess Meredith, John Garfield; D: Fletcher Markle.

Jigsaw Murders 1989 A macho detective is out to solve a grisly murder, but the only available leads are a jigsaw puzzle and the victim's severed, tattooed lower limb. 98m/C VHS, Chad Everett, Michelle Johnson, Yaphet Kotto; D: Jag Mundhra.

Jill the Ripper 🐾 2000 (R) Alcoholic ex-cop Matt Wilson launches his own investigation into the murder of his brother is murdered. This takes him into a world of political corruption and kinky sex, circa 1977 in Boston. 94m/C VHS, Dolph Lundgren, Danielle Brett; D: Anthony Hickox; W: Kevin Bernhardt; Gareth Wardell; C: David Pelletier; M: Steve Gurevitch, Thomas Barquee. **VIDEO**

Jim Thorpe: All American 🐾🐾🐾1/2 1951 *Man of Bronze* 1951 The life story of Thorpe, a Native American athlete who gained international recognition for his excellence in many different sports. A must for sports fans. 105m/B VHS, Burt Lancaster, Phyllis Thaxter, Charles Bickford, Steve Cochran, Dick Wesson; D: Michael Curtiz; W: Douglas S. Morrow; M: Max Steiner.

Jimmy Glick in LaLa Wood 🐾1/2 2005 (R) Obsequious smalltime entertainment critic Jimmy Glick (Short) and his clueless wife Dixie (Hooks) are in showbiz heaven at the Toronto Film Festival. Granted an exclusive interview with rising young star Ben DiCarlo (Pearson), Jimmy is wired and and catches the eye of fading diva Miranda Coolidge (Perkins). When Miranda is murdered, Jimmy inexplicably investigates. Derivative drivel trying way too hard. 100m/C DVD, Edward Furlong, Rachael Bella, William Sadler, James Eckhouse, A.J. Buckley; D: Randal K. Rubin, Jon Schroder; W: Jon Schroder; C: Ben Kurfin; M: Benoit Lowe; C: Mike J. Fox; M: David Lawrence.

Jimmy & Judy 🐾🐾 2006 (R) Social misfits Jimmy (Furlong) and Judy (Bella) turn into lovers, gone the later inter setting out from suburbia on one wild ride—all which is naturally documented by video camera. Derivative drivel trying way too comes a community vigilante. Burned-out sidekick Slater helps create the videotapes that will bring Jimmy his 15 minutes of fame. Although appropriately desperate, Pesci's role comes off as mostly shtick; two dogs in a row for the talented Levinson (after "Toys"). 118m/C VHS, DVD, Joe Pesci, Christian Slater, Victoria Abril; Cameos: Barry Levinson, Rob Weiss; D: Barry Levinson; W: Barry Levinson; C: Peter Sova; M: Robbie Robertson.

Jimmy Hollywood 🐾🐾1/2 1994 (R) Wanna-be Hollywood actor Pesci has never acted in his life but longs for stardom—which he gets after he accidentally becomes a community vigilante.

Jimmy Neutron: Boy Genius 🐾🐾1/2 2001 (G) Huge-brained and grease-haired Jimmy Neutron is a retro-geek hero for the new millennium in this bright and flashy computer animated feature. The child-inventor is young enough to think a sugar rush is the ultimate taboo but smart enough to have created a toaster-satellite that makes contact with an alien race. When said alien race respond by stealing all the parents in Retroville, Jimmy and his band of nerds targeted at adults, it prefers gags to pop culture reference; even the new-wave songs are covered by kiddie bands. Frenetic pacing and onslaught of images may tire older (than teenage) viewers, although there are some inventive lines that will go over the young-uns' heads. Short and

Stewart are amusing as a pair of egg-shaped space invaders. **90m/C VHS, DVD.** *US* **D:** John A. Davis; **W:** David N. Weiss, J. David Stern, Steve Oedekerk, John A. Davis; **M:** John Debney; **V:** Debi Derryberry, Carolyn Lawrence, Rob Paulsen, Martin Short, Patrick Stewart, Megan Cavanagh, Mark DeCarlo, Jeff Garcia, Candi Milo, Andrea Martin.

The Jimmy Show 🦴🦴½ **2001 (R)** Average Jimmy O'Brien (Whaley) vents the frustrations of his humble daily life at open mike night at a comedy club. But his routine isn't about jokes—his monologues are painful confessions about thwarted dreams, which only get worse when his fed-up wife Annie (Gugino) leaves. Whaley's at his best in the club scenes but they tend to overwhelm the rest of film. **93m/C VHS, DVD.** Frank Whaley, Carla Gugino, Ethan Hawke, Lynn Cohen; **D:** Frank Whaley; **C:** Mike Mayers; **M:** Robert Whaley, Anthony Grimaldi.

Jimmy, the Boy Wonder 🦴🦴½ **1966** Goremeister Lewis' attempt at a "family" film turns out just as weird as expected. A young boy goes on a magical trip to find out who stopped time and meets an absent-minded astronomer, the evil Mr. Fig, and then discovers what happens at world's end. **?m/C VHS.** Dennis Jones, David Blight Jr., Nancy Jo Berg; **D:** Herschell Gordon Lewis; **W:** Hal Berg; **C:** Andy Romanoff.

Jimmy the Kid 🦴🦴 **1982 (PG)** A young boy becomes the unlikely target for an improbable gang of would-be crooks on a crazy, "fool-proof" crime caper. Kiddie comic caper. **95m/C VHS.** Gary Coleman, Cleavon Little, Fay Hauser, Ruth Gordon, Dee Wallace Stone, Paul LeMat, Don Adams; **D:** Gary Nelson; **W:** Sam Bobrick.

Jimmy Zip 🦴🦴 **2000 (R)** Jimmy (Fletcher) is a pyromaniac abused runaway who gets a job working for drug dealing pimp Rick (Mulkey). He goes on a fireworks spree, which is how Jimmy meets down-and-out sculptor Horace (Gossett), who encourages him to channel his energies in more productive directions. But Jimmy fuels his new interests by stealing money from Rick, which puts him and girlfriend Sheila (Frantz) in a very dangerous position. **112m/C VHS, DVD.** *CA* Brendan Fletcher, Chris Mulkey, Robert Gossett, Adrienne Frantz, James Russo, Kim (Kimberly Dawn) Dawson; **D:** Robert McGinley; **W:** Robert McGinley; **C:** Christopher Tufty; **M:** Geoff Levin.

Jindabyne 🦴🦴½ **2006 (R)** Director Lawrence transports this Raymond Carver story from the Pacific Northwest to the mountainous southwest of Australia. Working-class buddies Stewart (Byrne), Carl (Howard), Rocco (Yiakmis), and Billy (Stone) go off for a weekend fishing trip. They quickly find a dead Aboriginal girl floating in the river and tie the body to a tree while they continue with their plans. When they finally report their discovery, all hell breaks loose: Stewart's wife Claire (Linney) is appalled at their callousness, there's the racial aspect (would they have left the body if she had been white?), and it turns out that the girl was murdered. Despite some strong performances, pic tends to be sluggish and underdeveloped. **123m/C DVD.** *AU* Gabriel Byrne, Laura Linney, John Howard, Stelios Yiakmis, Deborra-Lee Furness, Leah Purcell, Chris Haywood, Alice Garner, Simon Stone, Sean Rees-Memyes, Eva Lazzaro, Tatea Reilly; **D:** Ray Lawrence; **W:** Beatrix Christian; **C:** David Williamson; **M:** Paul Kelly, Dan Luscombe.

Jingle All the Way 🦴🦴 **1996 (PG)** Producer Chris Columbus grabs the reins of the slapstick and sentiment sleigh from mentor John Hughes in this farce of holiday capitalism. Any parent who has searched frantically for that Mighty Morphin' Cabbage Elmo will understand hapless Howard Langston (Schwarzenegger), a workaholic dad who was supposed to secure the coveted Turbo Man action figure for his son Jamie (Lloyd). Unfortunately, it slips his mind until Christmas Eve and all the Turbo Men have blasted off with more mindful parents. In his panic-stricken quest for the toy, he is confronted by a crazed postman (Sinbad) hunting Turbo Man, a pack of sleazy Santas, and a vicious reindeer attack. Meanwhile, Howard's slimy neighbor Ted (Hartman) is attempting to get into his wife Liz's (Wilson) stockings with great care. Although aimed at a younger audience, there's a definite lack of kids; which leaves it too grown-up for the kids and too childish for the adults. There is some satisfaction in seeing the Mall of America torn to shreds, however. Ho ho hum. **88m/C VHS, DVD.** Arnold Schwarzenegger, Phil Hartman, Sinbad, Rita Wilson, James Belushi, Robert Conrad, Martin Mull, Jake Lloyd, Harvey Korman, Laraine Newman; **D:** Brian Levant; **W:** Randy Kornfield; **C:** Victor Kemper; **M:** David Newman.

Jinxed 🦴🦴 **1982 (R)** Las Vegas nightclub singer tries to convince a gullible blackjack dealer to murder her crooked boyfriend, but the plan backfires when the gangster electrocutes himself while taking a shower. Offscreen cast disputes were probably much more interesting than onscreen comedy. **104m/C VHS, DVD.** Bette Midler, Ken Wahl, Rip Torn; **D:** Donald Siegel; **W:** David Newman, Frank D. Gilroy; **M:** Miles Goodman.

Jit 🦴🦴 **1994** Unpretentious romantic comedy finds the easy-going U.K., who runs errands for his uncle in a Zimbabwe town, falling in love with the beautiful Sofi, who already has a boyfriend. But U.K. won't be stopped by his or Sofi's greedy father. "Jit" refers to the infectious local music, a fusion of traditional African rhythms and reggae-pop. **98m/C VHS.** Dominic Makuvachuma, Sibongile Nene, Faria Sevenzo, Winnie Ndemera; **D:** Michael Raeburn.

The Jitters 🦴 **1988 (R)** The Chinese hopping vampire comes to America to make a bad movie on a different continent. The murdered dead turn into zombies and seek revenge on their killers. Maybe they should've sought revenge on the producers. **80m/C VHS.** Sal Viviano, Marilyn Tokuda, James Hong, Frank Dietz; **D:** John Fasano.

Jive Junction 🦴 **1943** A group of patriotic teenagers convert a barn into a canteen for servicemen and name it "Jive Junction." **62m/B VHS.** Dickie Moore, Tina Thayer, Gerra Young, Johnny Michaels, Jan Wiley, Beverly Boyd, William (Billy) Halligan; **D:** Edgar G. Ulmer.

Jo Jo Dancer, Your Life Is Calling 🦴🦴½ **1986 (R)** Pryor directed and starred in this semi-autobiographical price-of-fame story of a comic, hospitalized for a drug-related accident, who must re-evaluate his life. A serious departure from Pryor's slapstick comedies that doesn't quite make it as a drama; Pryor nevertheless deserves credit for the honesty he demonstrates in dealing with his real-life problems. **97m/C VHS, DVD.** Richard Pryor, Debbie Allen, Art Evans, Fay Hauser, Barbara Williams, Paula Kelly, Wings Hauser, Carmen McRae, Diahnne Abbott, Scoey Mitchell, Billy Eckstine, Virginia Capers, Dennis Farina; **D:** Richard Pryor; **W:** Richard Pryor, Rocco Urbisci; **C:** John A. Alonzo; **M:** Herbie Hancock.

Joan of Arc 🦴🦴½ **1948** A touching and devout look at the life of Joan of Arc. Perhaps unfortunately, the film is accurately based on the play by Maxwell Anderson, and adds up too much talk and too little action. **100m/C VHS, DVD.** Ingrid Bergman, Jose Ferrer, John Ireland, Leif Erickson; **D:** Victor Fleming; **C:** Joseph Valentine. Oscars '48: Color Cinematog., Costume Des. **C:**

Joan of Arc 🦴🦴½ **1999** Earnest biopic of legendary 15th-century French heroine, Joan of Arc (Sobieski). Joan is a peasant girl, born during France's Hundred Years War with England. She hears saints' voices telling her to help the Dauphin Charles (Harris) claim the French throne and drive out the English. Charles persuades Joan to proclaim herself the legendary Maid of Lorraine and raise an army to battle the Brits. But after her success, Joan is betrayed by the King, sold to the English, and put on trial for heresy. **240m/C VHS, DVD.** Leelee Sobieski, Neil Patrick Harris, Peter O'Toole, Robert Loggia, Jacqueline Bisset, Powers Boothe, Shirley MacLaine, Olympia Dukakis, Maury Chaykin, Jonathan Hyde, Maximilian Schell, Peter Strauss; **D:** Christian Duguay; **W:** Ronald Parker, Michael Miller; **C:** Pierre Gill; **M:** Asher Ettinger, Tony Kosinec. **TV**

Joan of Paris 🦴🦴½ **1942** A French resistance leader dies so that Allied pilots can escape from the Nazis. A well done, but obviously dated propaganda feature. **91m/B VHS.** Michele Morgan, Paul Henreid, Thomas Mitchell, Laird Cregar, May Robson, Alexander Granach, Alan Ladd; **D:** Robert Stevenson; **W:** Charles Bennett.

The Job 🦴🦴 **2003 (R)** Hitwoman CJ (Hannah) has agreed to one last job before she leaves her violent life behind her. Only she has a crisis of conscience and finds it difficult to pull the trigger on the target—young wannabe gangster Troy (Renfro), who stole a drug shipment from the wrong people. However, if CJ doesn't follow through, it'll be her life on the line. **86m/C VHS, DVD.** Daryl Hannah, Brad Renfro, Dominique Swain, Eric Mabius, Alex Rocco; **D:** Kenny Golde; **W:** Kenny Golde; **C:** Scott Kevan. **VIDEO**

Jock Petersen 🦴 *Petersen* **1974 (R)** A light-hearted story about a blonde hunk who enrolls in college, cavorting and seducing his way to questionable fame and fortune. **97m/C VHS.** Jack Thompson, Wendy Hughes; **D:** Tim Burstall.

Jocks 🦴🦴½ **1987 (R)** A whiz-kid tennis team competes in a pro meet in Las Vegas, and paints the town red. **90m/C VHS, DVD.** Christopher Lee, Perry Lang, Richard Roundtree, Scott Strader; **D:** Steve Carver; **W:** Jeff Buhai.

Joe 🦴🦴½ **1970 (R)** An odd friendship grows between a businessman and a blue-collar worker as they search together for the executive's runaway daughter. Thrust into the midst of the counter-culture, they react with an orgy of violence. **107m/C VHS, DVD.** Peter Boyle, Susan Sarandon, Dennis Patrick; **D:** John G. Avildsen; **W:** Norman Wexler; **C:** John G. Avildsen, Henri Decae; **M:** Bobby Scott.

Joe and Max 🦴🦴 **2002 (PG-13)** That would be heavyweight boxing champs Joe "the Brown Bomber" Louis and Max Schmeling. In 1936, Max defeats Joe in a title match, although the two become friends. Joe has to put up with his country's racism (the whites in the audience cheer for Schmeling) while Max has to endure the Nazi's using him as a symbol of Aryan superiority. In 1938, the tables are turned in a rematch at Yankee Stadium—this time it's Louis that's the people's choice and the victor. Not only does the film relate the duo's celebrity (and symbolism) but their alternating fortunes after WWII. Both leads do fine work, although Schweiger seems more comfortable in his role. **113m/C VHS, DVD.** *US GE* Til Schweiger, Leonard Roberts, Peta Wilson, Richard Roundtree, David Paymer, John Toles-Bey, Bruce Weitz; **D:** Steve James; **W:** Jason Horwitch; **C:** Bill Butler; **M:** Jeff Beal. **CABLE**

Joe Dirt 🦴🦴 **2001 (PG-13)** Spade plays the hapless, trailer-trash joke you've ever heard or told. He sports a robo-mullet, earns his keep with degrading, subminimum wage jobs, drives a beat-up muscle car, and grooves to '70s arena-rock. He's also searching for his parents, who bailed on him during a trip to the Grand Canyon when he was eight. Too bad he isn't funny. Co-writers Spade and Wolf spend too much time on the heart strings and not enough on the funny bone, which results in an unholy hybrid of Jerry Springer and the Lifetime Network. Miller's shock-jock and Walken's crazed janitor add some genuine laughs to the proceedings, but not enough. **91m/C VHS, DVD, UMD.** *US* David Spade, Dennis Miller, Adam Beach, Christopher Walken, Jaime Pressly, Caroline Aaron, Fred Ward, Brittany Daniel, Kid Rock, Erik Per Sullivan, Megan Taylor Harvey; **D:** Dennis Gordon; **W:** David Spade, Fred Wolf; **C:** John R. Leonetti; **M:** Waddy Wachtel.

Joe Gould's Secret 🦴🦴½ **2000 (R)** Tucci directed, co-wrote, and stars as Joe Mitchell, famed "New Yorker" columnist who chronicled, among many others, the peculiar life of Greenwich Village eccentric Joe Gould in the 1940s. Gould (Holm) lived on the streets of New York for 26 years, regaling the intelligentsia with wild stories and behavior while claiming to be writing the "Oral History of Our Time," which he said was two million words long and contained the fruits of 20,000 overheard conversations. The film quietly (except when Holm's Gould is onscreen) and effectively explores the relationship between Mitchell and Gould, and the reasons for Mitchell's fascination with his subject. **108m/C VHS, DVD.** Stanley Tucci, Ian Holm, Hope Davis, Patricia Clarkson, Steve Martin, Susan Sarandon, Celia Weston, Allan Corduner, Alice Drummond, Julie Halston, Hallee Hirsh, Ben Jones, John Tormey, David Wohl, Patrick Tovatt, Sarah Hyland; **D:** Stanley Tucci; **W:** Howard A. Rodman, Stanley Tucci; **C:** Maryse Alberti; **M:** Evan Lurie.

Joe Kidd 🦴🦴½ **1972 (PG)** A land war breaks out in New Mexico between Mexican natives and American land barons. Eastwood, once again portraying the "mysterious stranger," must decide with whom he should side, all the while falling in love with Garcia. Lackluster direction results in a surprisingly tedious western, in spite of Eastwood's lowest money grossers. **88m/C VHS, DVD.** Clint Eastwood, Robert Duvall, John Saxon, Don Stroud, Stella Garcia, James Wainwright, Paul Koslo, Gregory Walcott, Dick Van Patten, Lynn(e) Maria; **D:** John Sturges; **W:** Elmore Leonard; **C:** Bruce Surtees; **M:** Lalo Schifrin.

The Joe Louis Story 🦴🦴 **1953** The story of Joe Louis' rise to fame as boxing's Heavyweight Champion of the world. **88m/B VHS, DVD.** Coley Wallace, Paul Stewart, Hilda Simms, Albert "Poppy" Popwell; **D:** Robert Gordon; **W:** Robert Sylvester; **C:** Joseph Brun; **M:** George Bassman.

Joe Panther 🦴🦴🦴 **1976 (G)** Family drama about a young Seminole Indian who stakes his claim in the Anglo world by wrestling alligators. Montalban plays a wise old chieftain who helps the youth handle the conflict between Indian and white societies. **110m/C VHS, DVD.** Brian Keith, Ricardo Montalban, Alan Feinstein, Cliff Osmond, A. Martinez, Robert Hoffman; **D:** Paul Krasny.

Joe Somebody 🦴 **2001 (PG)** By-the-numbers dud feels like an after-school special with ten times the budget and half the brains or heart. Tim Allen again plays the allegedly likable Average Joe, only this time, his name is actually Joe. Trouble is, he doesn't look nerdy or ineffectual, even if he's wearing glasses and getting beat up in the parking lot. After Joe's daughter (Panettiere) witnesses his turn as punching bag for the office bully (Warburton), he slides into a depression. But after a visit from sure-to-be romantic interest Meg (Bowen), Joe decides he wants a rematch. He enlists the help of a faded martial arts guru (Belushi) and becomes popular, but his daughter and love interest like the old Joe better. Tries to have a moral message about rejecting violence while also giving a good dose of it. Joe's precocious, sage-like daughter makes the Olsen twins pleasant by comparison. **97m/C VHS, DVD.** *US* Tim Allen, Julie Bowen, Hayden Panettiere, Kelly Lynch, James Belushi, Patrick Warburton, Greg Germann, Robert Joy, Ken Marino; **D:** John Pasquin; **W:** John Scott Shepherd; **C:** Daryn Okada; **M:** George S. Clinton.

Joe the King 🦴🦴 **1999 (R)** Undistinguished coming of age pic, set in the mid-'70s, about a boy caught up in violence. Fourteen-year-old Joe (Fleiss) is subjected to the constant drunken abuse of their father Bob (Henry), and the indifference of their overworked mother Theresa (Young). Joe begins stealing to get by but his crimes gradually becomes less than petty. A troubled student as well, Joe is befriended by guidance counselor Len (Hawke), whose attempts to help only result in a stint for Joe in a juvie center. Slow-paced and developmentally challenged. **101m/C VHS, DVD.** Noah Fleiss, Val Kilmer, Karen Young, John Leguizamo, Austin Pendleton, Max Ligosh, James Costa; **D:** Frank Whaley; **W:** Frank Whaley; **C:** Mike Mayers; **M:** Robert Whaley, Anthony Grimaldi. Sundance '99: Screenplay.

Joe Torre: Curveballs Along the Way ✓✓½ 1997 Bio of manager Torre (Sorvino), who's hired by George Steinbrenner (Welsh) in 1996 to coach the New York Yankees. The Yanks actually start winning and Torre takes them all the way to the World Series (they win), but his triumph is marred by family heartbreak, as his brother Frank (Loggia) is in the hospital awaiting a heart transplant. Not bad for a quickie cable biopic, but only because the cast is outstanding. **90m/C VHS.** Paul Sorvino, Robert Loggia, Barbara Williams, Isaiah Washington IV, Gaillard Sartain, Kenneth Welsh, Marilyn Chris; **D:** Sturla Gunnarsson; **W:** Philip Rosenberg; **C:** Mark Irwin. **CABLE**

Joe Versus the Volcano ✓✓ 1990 (PG) Expressionistic goofball comedy about a dopey guy who, after finding out he has only months to live, contracts with a millionaire to leap into a volcano alive. Imaginative farce with great "Metropolis"-ish visuals that eventually fizzle out. Watch for Ryan in not one, but three roles, and mysterious symbolism throughout. Special effects courtesy of Industrial Light and Magic. **106m/C VHS, DVD.** Tom Hanks, Meg Ryan, Lloyd Bridges, Robert Stack, Amanda Plummer, Abe Vigoda, Dan Hedaya, Barry McGovern, Ossie Davis; **D:** John Patrick Shanley; **W:** John Patrick Shanley; **C:** Stephen Goldblatt; **M:** Georges Delerue.

Joe's Apartment ✓✓ 1996 (PG-13) Fresh-from-Iowa Joe (O'Connell) comes to New York, finds a squalid apartment, and then discovers its other occupants are hordes of singing, joking cockroaches. Lucky for Joe, his unwelcome roommates are on his side, even helping out with his love life, when necessary. Gross but interesting, throw in Vaughn as a panty-wearing politician and you've got yourself a potential cult-movie favorite. Neat freaks probably won't enjoy it much. Flick took three years to finish as computer-animated roaches had to do all the cancing and singing. Feature directorial debut for writer Payson, who created the original 1992 live-action/animation MTV short. **82m/C VHS, DVD.** Jerry O'Connell, Megan Ward, Robert Vaughn, Jim Turner, Don Ho, Sandra "Pepa" Denton, Shiek Mahmud-Bey; **D:** John Payson; **W:** John Payson; **C:** Peter Deming; **V:** Billy West, Reginald (Reggie) Hudlin.

Joe's Bed-Stuy Barbershop: We Cut Heads ✓½ 1983 Lee's first film takes place inside a neighborhood landmark, the corner barbershop. Lee displays the social awareness and urban humor that he honed in his later, bigger films. Features multi-generational rock songs. **90m/C VHS, DVD.** Neill 3arry, James Quinn, Ellen Hammill, Dan Grimaldi; **D:** Joseph Ellison; **W:** Ellen Hammill, Joseph Ellison; **C:** Oliver Wood; **M:** Jim Roberge.

Joey ✓✓ 1986 (PG) Young Billy (Croft) rescues a baby kangaroo (known as a joey) who was left behind when an evil hunter captures a group of kangaroos and hauls them off to Sydney for nefarious purposes. So Billy puts Joey in his backpack and heads off to the city to reunite the little family—aided by the rebellious daughter (McKenna) of the newly appointed U.S. ambassador (Begley). **96m/C VHS, DVD.** Alli Jamie Croft, Alex McKenna, Ed Begley Jr., Rebecca Gibney, Ruth Cracknell, Harold Hopkins; **D:** an Barry; **W:** Stuart Beattie; **C:** David Burr; **M:** Roger Mason.

Joey Breaker ✓✓✓ 1993 (R) Joey (cult-fave Edson) is a hot-shot Manhattan talent agent who's consumed by his job. A series of encounters (romantic and otherwise) expands his outlook, first among them with Cyan (Marley), a young Jamaican waitress. On his journey to possible enlightenment Joey also meets AIDS-stricken Alfred Moore (Wise), who also helps Joey see another side of life. Quirky with a reggae beat, small pic works large message with sense of humor and sincere performances. Dedicated to Fondran, who died of AIDS in 1992. Marley, daughter of late reggae superstar Bob, shares a tune on the soundtrack with brother Ziggy. Filmed in da Big Apple and St. Lucia, West Indies. **92m/C VHS.** Richard Edson, Cedella Marley, Erik King, Gina Gershon, Philip Seymour Hoffman, Fred Fondren; **D:** Steven Starr; **W:** Steven Starr; **C:** Joe DeSalvo; **M:** Paul Aston.

John Adams ✓✓✓ 2008 Enjoyment rests on whether you can buy Giamatti as the titular founding father and second president of the U.S. Eased on the best-selling bio by David McCullough, Adams is intelligent, impatient, irascible, resentful, and deeply devoted to both his country and his wife, the equally resourceful Abigail (Linney). Most of the familiar historical figures are present and accounted for—George Washington, Benjamin Franklin (Wilkinson), Thomas Jefferson (Dillane)—as well as such events as the Continental Congress and the Declaration of Independence, but probably find out more than you could ever want to know. **560m/C DVD.** Paul Giamatti, Laura Linney, David Morse, Tom Wilkinson, Stephen Dillon, Dillane, Zeljko Ivanek, Danny Huston, Sarah Polley, Rufus Sewell, Justin Theroux; **D:** Tom Hooper; **W:** Kirk Ellis; **C:** Tak Fujimoto; **M:** Robert (Rob) Lane, Joseph Vitarelli. **CABLE**

John and the Missus ✓✓½ 1987 (PG) After the discovery of a copper mine threatens to destroy a nearby town, the Canadian government begins a relocation process. Pinsent, cre man refuses to give up his generations-old home. Canadian Pinsent's directorial debut, adapting his own 1973 novel. **98m/C VHS.** McGann, Kim Miyori, Kenneth Price, Peter Capaldi, Richard Morant, Philip Walsh; **D:** Gordon Pinsent. **TV**

John and Julie ✓½ 1955 Sweet story about two young friends, living in the English countryside in 1953, who decide to run away to London in order to witness the coronation of Queen Elizabeth II. They're hoping John's Uncle, a Royal Escort guard, will help them but first they have to get to the city, which involves a lot of complicated travelling plans. **82m/C VHS, GB.** Colin Gibson, Lesley Dudley, Noelle Middleton, Moira Lister, Constance Cummings, Wilfrid Hyde-White, Sidney James, Joseph Tomelty, Megs Jenkins, Patric Doonan, Peter Sellers, John Stuart, Vincent Ball, Colin Gordon, Peter Jones, Katie Johnson, Cyril Smith, Andrew Cruikshank, Winifred Shotter, Richard Dimbleby, Wynford Vaughn Thomas; **D:** William Fairchild; **W:** William Fairchild; **C:** Arthur Grant.

John & Yoko: A Love Story ✓ 1985 Appalling TV version of the rock legend's life and marriage. With original Beatles tunes. **146m/C VHS.** Mark McGann, Kim Miyori, Kenneth Price, Peter Capaldi, Richard Morant, Philip Walsh; **D:** Sandor Stern. **TV**

John Carpenter Presents Vampires: Los Muertos ✓½ Vampires: Los Muertos 2002 (R) It's mostly a yawner because it's so predictable. Vamp hunter Derek (Bon Jovi) sets his team to the bloodsuckers but hooks up with a rag tag crew, including Father Rodrigo (De La Fuente), to go a-hunting in Mexico. This time the head biter is a vampire babe (Jover). Pretty tame even in comparison to the first flick. **94m/C VHS, DVD.** Jon Bon Jovi, Christian de la Fuente, Arly Jover, Darius McCrary, Natasha Gregson Wagner, Diego Luna; **D:** Tommy Lee Wallace; **W:** Tommy Lee Wallace; **C:** Jack Lorenz; **M:** Brian Tyler.

John Carpenter's Ghosts of Mars ✓✓ Ghosts of Mars 2001 (R) John Carpenter unashamedly fires up his B-movie machine to maximum cheese factor in this tale of space babes and zombies. On a 22nd century matriarchal Mars colony in 2225 sent to retrieve murderer "Desolation" Williams (Ice Cube). The job turns from get the bad guy to simple survival when long-dormant Martian warriors begin taking over the bodies of the Earth intruders, turning them into zombies. So do you think the bad guys and the good guys have to team up to win one for the humans? At its best, during the action sequences, but probably a bad choice to follow "A Room with a View" for a Saturday night double feature. **98m/C VHS, DVD.** US Natasha Henstridge, Ice Cube, Clea DuVall, Pam Grier, Jason Statham, Joanna Cassidy, Rosemary Forsyth, Liam Waite, Richard Cetrone; **D:** John Carpenter; **W:** John Carpenter, Larry Sulkis; **C:** Gary B. Kibbe; **M:** John Carpenter.

John John in the Sky ✓✓ 2000 (PG-13) Ten-year-old John John (Craft) is living with a lot of tension in his father's household. His dad (Travis) is abusive and angry at the changes going on around him, especially the fact that his wife (Rosemont) wants to take her kid and flee to San Francisco to join a commune. And John John also doesn't know how to deal with the unwanted friendship of the disabled Zeola (Schwimmer). Title comes from the boy's dream to build his own airplane. Sometimes confusing story with its series of flashbacks and flash-forwards. **101m/C VHS, DVD.** Randy Travis, Christian Craft, Romy Rosemont, Rusty Schwimmer, Matt Leitscher; **D:** Jefferson Davis; **W:** Ket Skogland, Jefferson Davis; **C:** Joel David; **M:** Christopher Ward.

John Carpenter's Vampires ✓✓½ Vampires 1997 (R) Vatican-sponsored vampire hunter Jack Crow (Woods) leads his team of mercenaries into the American Southwest to battle and destroy the inevitable showdown from his usual bug-eyed crazy to merely borderline disturbed here. Based on the novel "Vampires" by John Steakley. **108m/C VHS, DVD.** James Woods, Thomas Ian Griffith, Sheryl Lee, Daniel Baldwin, Tim Guinee, Maximilian Schell, Cary-Hiroyuki Tagawa, Mark Boone Jr., Tom Rosales; **D:** John Carpenter; **W:** Don Jacoby; **C:** Gary B. Kibbe.

John Cleese on How to Irritate People ✓✓✓ How to Irritate People 1968 Cleese, a master of irritation, demonstrates how to take care of all those annoying people who irritate you, including job interviewers, bank clerks, waiters, and salesmen. Monty Python alumni Palin and Chapman also join Cleese in the "Airline Pilots" sketch about bored pilots deliberately trying to terrify their passengers. **65m/C VHS, DVD.** John Cleese, Michael Palin, Graham Chapman, Connie Booth.

John Grisham's The Rainmaker ✓✓✓½ The Rainmaker 1997 (PG-13) Yet another legal drama from the successful pen of John Grisham. Baylor (Damon) is a young lawyer whose job disappears when his firm is absorbed by a giant company. He fills his first time giving legal advice to indigents and mooning over Kelly (Danes), a young abused wife. Then he takes on the case of a couple whose leukemia-stricken son was denied treatment by their insurance company, coincidentally represented by the firm that booted Baylor. Pre-"Jack," Coppola probably wouldn't have gone anywhere near such formulaic franchise fare, and if he did, he could've directed it in his sleep. As it is he creates a serviceable, if not spectacular, piece of entertainment. His main allies are Voight's insurance company mouthpiece and DeVito's ambulance chaser. Damon plays the hero with much less bravado than previous Grisham protagonists. **137m/C VHS, DVD.** Matt Damon, Claire Danes, Danny DeVito, Jon Voight, Danny Glover, Virginia Madsen, Mary Kay Place, Mickey Rourke, Johnny Whitworth, Teresa Wright, Dean Stockwell, Red West, Roy Scheider, Randy Travis, Andrew Shue; **D:** Francis Ford Coppola; **W:** Francis Ford Coppola; **C:** John Toll; **M:** Elmer Bernstein.

John Q ✓✓ 2002 (PG-13) "Dog Day Afternoon" lite is essentially a two hour tirade against the U.S. health system (who can blame them?) which casts Washington as the title's everyman hero who's desperate and gutsy enough to bypass medical bureaucracy altogether to get his 10-year old son Mike (Smith) the heart transplant he desperately needs to live. Unable to come up with $75,000 for his son's operation, with the run-around, John takes over the ER and demands his son be placed at the top of the transplant list. Talented cast, including Duvall as the sympathetic police negotiator, Woods as the cynical doctor, and Liotta, as the boldly drawn police chief, is generally wasted on the sentimental and melodramatic one-note premise. **118m/C VHS, DVD.** US Denzel Washington, Robert Duvall, James Woods, Anne Heche, Eddie Griffin, Kimberly Elise, Shawn Hatosy, Ray Liotta, Daniel E. Smith, David Thornton, Ethan Suplee, Obba Babatunde, Laura Elena Harring, Troy Beyer, Olbe Babatunde, Laura Elena Harring; **D:** Nick Cassavetes; **W:** James Kearns; **C:** Rogier Stoffers; **M:** Aaron Zigman.

John Tucker Must Die ✓✓ 2006 (PG-13) The character (Metcalfe) is the resident B.M.O.C. who uses his looks and status to triple-time the three hottest girls in school, who end up learning about his cheating ways. The hotties plot unsuccessfully for revenge until they enlist the help of the ugly-duckling new girl, Kate (Snow), and the requisite makeover-to-lure-the-jerk ensues. Pic backfires in its girl-power message by resorting to cliches and female sexuality, self-image, and estrogen side-effects and never gets as mean as "Mean Girls" or as darkly original as "Heathers." **82m/C DVD.** US Jesse Metcalfe, Ashanti, Arielle Kebbel, Brittany Snow, Sophia Bush, Jenny McCarthy, Fulvio Cecere, Penn Badgley; **D:** Betty Thomas; **W:** Jeff Lowell; **C:** Anthony B. Richmond; **M:** Richard Gibbs.

Johnny Angel ✓✓✓ 1945 Merchant Marine captain unravels mystery of his father's murder aboard a ship. Tense film noir. **79m/B VHS.** George Raft, Claire Trevor, Signe Hasso, Lowell Gilmore, Hoagy Carmichael; **D:** Edwin L. Marin.

Johnny Apollo ✓✓½ 1940 Upright college student Power keeps his nose clean until Dad's sent to jail for playing with numbers. Scheming to free his old man (Arnold) from the big house, he decides crime will pay for the stiff price tag of freedom. Predictable and melodramatic, but well directed. **93m/B VHS.** Tyrone Power, Dorothy Lamour, Lloyd Nolan, Edward Arnold, Charley Grapewin, Lionel Atwill, Marc Lawrence, Jonathan Hale, Russell Hicks, Selmer Jackson, Charles Trowbridge; **D:** Yves Allegret; **W:** Rowland Brown, Philip Dunne, Samuel G. Engel; **C:** Arthur C. Miller; **M:** Cyril Mockridge, Alfred Newman.

John Paul Jones ✓✓½ 1959 Big bio of the Revolutionary War naval hero ("I have not yet begun to fight!") who wins a lot of battles but can't convince Congress to maintain a strong navy at war's end. He's sent to win sea battles for the Empress Catherine the Great of Russia and then spends his last years in France. Great action scenes, otherwise tedious. **126m/C VHS.** Robert Stack, Charles Coburn, MacDonald Carey, Marisa Pavan, Jean-Pierre Aumont, Peter Cushing, Erin O'Brien, Bruce Cabot, David Farrar, Basil Sydney, John Crawford, Farrow, Jesse Lasky Jr.; **M:** Max Steiner. **Cameos:** Bette Davis; **D:** John Farrow; **M:** Max Steiner.

Johnnie Gibson F.B.I. ✓✓ 1986 Johnnie Mae Gibson; **TV** 1987 FBI agent unravels mystery of a beautiful, black FBI agent who falls in love with a man she's investigating. **96m/C VHS, DVD.** Howard E. Rollins Jr., Lynn Whitfield, William Allen Young, Richard Lawson; **D:** Bill Duke; **M:** Billy Goldenberg.

Johnny Appleseed 1986 True story of the legendary American who spent his life planting apple trees across the country. Comedy the entire family will enjoy from Shelly Duval's "Tall Tales and Legends" cable series. **60m/C VHS.** Martin Short, Rob Reiner, Molly Ringwald. **CABLE**

Johnny

505 VideoHound's Golden Movie Retriever

Johnny B. 🦴🦴½ 2000 (R) College dropout Johnny B. has become a small-time hustler with no ambitions since the murder of his older brother. Then he learns his ex-girlfriend, who's also the mother of his young daughter, has gotten engaged to a successful lawyer. Now, Johnny has some tough decisions to make. 98m/C VHS, DVD. Richard Brooks, Vonetta McGee, Richard Gant, Kent Masters King, Tempestt Bledsoe; *D:* Richard Brooks; *W:* Gwendolyn J. Lester; *C:* Pancho Gonzales.

Johnny Be Good 🦴 1988 (R) A too-talented high school quarterback is torn between loyalty to his best friend and to his girlfriend amid bribery and schemings by colleges eager to sign him up. 91m/C VHS, DVD. Anthony Michael Hall, Robert Downey Jr., Paul Gleason, Uma Thurman, John Pankow, Steve James, Seymour Cassel, Michael Greene, Marshall Bell, Deborah May; *D:* Bud Smith; *W:* Jeff Buhai; *M:* Jay Ferguson.

Johnny Belinda 🦴🦴🦴 1948 A compassionate physician cares for a young deaf mute woman and her illegitimate child. Tension builds as the baby's father returns to claim the boy. 103m/B VHS, DVD. Jane Wyman, Lew Ayres, Charles Bickford, Agnes Moorehead, Jan Sterling; *D:* Jean Negulesco; *M:* Max Steiner. Oscars '48: Actress (Wyman); Golden Globes '49: Actress—Drama (Wyman), Film—Drama.

Johnny Belinda 🦴🦴½ 1982 TV adaptation of the Elmer Harris weepie about a small town doctor who befriends an abused deaf girl. Remake of the 1948 film. 95m/C VHS. Richard Thomas, Rosanna Arquette, Dennis Quaid, Candy Clark, Roberts Blossom, Fran Ryan; *D:* Anthony Page. TV

Johnny Come Lately 🦴🦴½ *Johnny Vagabond* 1943 An elderly editor helps out an ex-newspaperman with a police charge. The two then team up to expose political corruption despite threats from a rival newspaperman. 97m/B VHS. James Cagney, Grace George, Marjorie Main, Marjorie Lord, Hattie McDaniel, Edward McNamara; *D:* William K. Howard.

Johnny Dangerously 🦴🦴 1984 (PG-13) A gangster spoof about Johnny Dangerously, who turned to crime in order to pay his mother's medical bills. Now, Dangerously wants to go straight, but competitive crooks would rather see him dead than law-abiding and his mother requires more and more expensive operations. Crime pays in comic ways. 90m/C VHS, DVD. Michael Keaton, Joe Piscopo, Danny DeVito, Maureen Stapleton, Marilu Henner, Peter Boyle, Griffin Dunne, Glynnis O'Connor, Dom DeLuise, Richard Dimitri, Ray Walston, Dick Butkus, Alan Hale Jr., Bob Eubanks; *D:* Amy Heckerling; *W:* Norman Steinberg, Harry Colomby.

Johnny Eager 🦴🦴🦴 1942 Glossy crime melodrama starring Taylor as an unscrupulous racketeer and Turner as the daughter of D.A. Arnold who falls for him and ends up becoming a pawn in his schemes. Heflin won an Oscar for his outstanding performance as Taylor's alcoholic confidant. Excellent direction by LeRoy makes this a top-rate gangster film. Based on a story by James Edward Grant. 107m/B VHS. Robert Taylor, Lana Turner, Edward Arnold, Van Heflin, Robert Sterling, Patricia Dane, Glenda Farrell, Barry Nelson, Henry O'Neill, Charles Dingle, Cy Kendall; *D:* Mervyn LeRoy; *W:* James Edward Grant, John Lee Mahin. Oscars 42: Support. Actor (Heflin).

Johnny English 🦴🦴½ 2003 (PG) Johnny English (Atkinson) is a deskbound member of the espionage community who's promoted to active status due to some unfortunate circumstances that he caused. The klutz must then prevent an evil French businessman (Malkovich) from dethroning the Queen and taking over. Anglophiles, fans of Rowan Atkinson, and toilet/slapstick humor lovers will enjoy this stale crumpet, but there's just not much here for anyone else Stateside. Atkinson manages to squeeze some laughs from a poor script with his supreme gift for physical comedy, however, and Malkovich gleefully throws himself over the top. Imbruglia, making her feature debut, is game, but doesn't have much to do. 86m/C VHS, DVD. *GB US* Rowan Atkinson, John Malkovich, Natalie Imbruglia, Ben Miller, Kevin McNally, Tim Pigott-Smith, Douglas McFerran, Greg Wise, Oliver Ford Davies; *D:* Peter Howitt; *W:* Neal Purvis, Robert Wade, William Davies; *M:* Ed Shearmur.

Johnny Firecloud 🦴 1975 A modern Indian goes on the warpath when the persecution of his people reawakens his sense of identity. 94m/C VHS, DVD. Victor Mohica, Ralph Meeker, Frank De Kova, Sacheen Littlefeather, David Canary, Christina Hart; *D:* William Allen Castleman; *W:* Wilton Denmark; *M:* William Loose.

Johnny Frenchman 🦴🦴 1946 Rival fishing groups battle it out, complicated by a romance across the water, but when World War II breaks out they join together. Featured in the cast are real fishermen and villagers from Cornwall, as well as authentic Free French Resistance fighters from WWII. 104m/B VHS. *GB* Françoise Rosay, Tom Walls, Patricia Roc, Ralph Michael, Frederick Piper, Pierre Richard, Bill Blewitt, Carroll O'Connor, Paul Dupuis, James Harcourt, Richard George; *D:* Charles Frend; *W:* T.E.B. Clarke; *C:* Roy Kellino; *M:* Clifton Parker.

Johnny Got His Gun 🦴🦴🦴 1971 (R) Dalton Trumbo's story of a young WWI veteran (Bottoms) who meets a bomb with his name on it and is rendered armless, legless, and more or less faceless, as well as deaf, dumb, and blind. Regarded as a vegetable and stuck in a lightless hospital utility room, he dreams and fantasizes about life before and after the bomb, and tries vainly to communicate with the staff. Wrenching and bleak antiwar diatribe made at the climax of the Vietnam War. 111m/C VHS. Timothy Bottoms, Jason Robards Jr., Donald Sutherland, Diane Varsi, Kathy Fields, Donald (Don "Red") Barry, Peter Brocco, Judy Chaikin, Eric Christmas, Maurice Dallimore, Robert Easton, Eduard Franz, Anthony Geary, Edmund Gilbert, Ben Hammer, Wayne Heffley, Marsha Hunt, Joseph Kaufmann, Charles McGraw, Byron Morrow, David Soul; *D:* Dalton Trumbo; *W:* Dalton Trumbo; *C:* Jules Brenner; *M:* Jerry Fielding. Cannes '71: Grand Jury Prize.

Johnny Guitar 🦴🦴🦴 1953 Women strap on six-guns in Nicholas Ray's unintentionally hilarious, gender-bending western. A guitar-playing loner wanders into a small town feud between lovelorn saloon owner Crawford and McCambridge, the town's resident lynch mob-leading harpy. This fascinating cult favorite has had film theorists arguing for decades: is it a parody, a political McCarthy-era allegory, or Freudian exercise? The off-screen battles of the two female stars are equally legendary. Stick around for the end credits to hear Peggy Lee sing the title song. 116m/C VHS, DVD. Joan Crawford, Ernest Borgnine, Sterling Hayden, Mercedes McCambridge, Scott Brady, Ward Bond, Royal Dano, John Carradine, Ben Cooper, Frank Ferguson, Paul Fix, Denver Pyle; *D:* Nicholas Ray; *W:* Philip Yordan; *C:* Harry Stradling Sr; *M:* Victor Young.

Johnny Handsome 🦴🦴🦴 1989 (R) An ugly, deformed hood, after he's been double-crossed and sent to prison, volunteers for a reconstructive surgery experiment and is released with a new face, determined to hunt down the scum that set him up. A terrific modern B-picture based on John Godey's "The Three Worlds of Johnny Handsome". 96m/C VHS, DVD. Mickey Rourke, Ellen Barkin, Lance Henriksen, Elizabeth McGovern, Morgan Freeman, Forest Whitaker, Scott Wilson, Blake Clark; *D:* Walter Hill; *W:* Ken Friedman; *M:* Ry Cooder.

Johnny Holiday 🦴🦴½ 1949 A heart-warming story about a fatherless boy, Johnny, who is dumped into reform school to prevent him from pursuing a life of crime with his small-time hood buddies. While there, he is befriended by Sargeant Walker, an ex-Calvary man who teaches him about life and becomes the father Johnny never had. 94m/B VHS. Allen Martin Jr., William Bendix, Stanley Clements; *D:* Willis Goldbeck.

Johnny Mnemonic 🦴🦴 1995 (R) Robo-yuppie data courier Johnny (Reeves), has over extended the storage capacity in his head and must download his latest job before his brain turns to applesauce. Aided by an implant-enhanced bodyguard (Meyer), underground hacker rebels called LoTeks, and a former doctor (Rollins) battling a technology-induced epidemic, Johnny is on the run from the corporation that wants his head (literally). Freshman director Longo can't seem to get a handle on the plot and doesn't get much help from Gibson, who combined characters and scenarios from his other books. Action sequences are appropriately spiffy, preventing a total system crash. 98m/C VHS, DVD. Keanu Reeves, Dina Meyer, Ice-T, Takeshi "Beat" Kitano, Dolph Lundgren, Henry Rollins, Udo Kier, Barbara Sukowa, Denis Akayama; *D:* Robert Longo; *W:* William Gibson; *C:* François Protat; *M:* Brad Fiedel.

Johnny Nobody 🦴🦴½ 1961 A mysterious stranger murders a writer who has been taunting the residents of a quaint Irish town. A sleeper of a thriller, especially in the treatment of the town's reaction to this murder. 88m/B VHS. *GB* William Bendix, Aldo Ray, Nigel Patrick, Yvonne Mitchell, Cyril Cusack; *D:* Nigel Patrick.

Johnny 100 Pesos 🦴🦴 1993 Seventeen-year-old Johnny (Araiza) walks into a video store that is a front for an illegal currency exchange operation. He's been planning to rob the place but before they can escape with the cash, the police show up and the crooks take the store's inhabitants hostage. Now there's a standoff, with the media shamelessly broadcasting all events and the Chilean authorities struggling to control the escalating situation. Based on a true 1990 incident. Spanish with subtitles. 90m/C VHS, DVD. Armando Araiza, Patricia Rivera, Willy Semler, Sergio Hernandez; *D:* Gustavo Graef-Marino; *W:* Gustavo Graef-Marino; *C:* Jose Luis Arredondo; *M:* Andres Pollak.

Johnny Reno 🦴🦴½ 1966 Laughable western that has U.S. Marshal Andrews trying to save an accused killer from lynching. Of interest for star-watching only. Based on a story by Steve Fisher. 83m/C VHS, DVD. Dana Andrews, Jane Russell, Lon Chaney Jr., John Agar, Lyle Bettger, Tom Drake, Richard Arlen, Robert Lowery; *D:* R.G. Springsteen; *W:* Steve Fisher.

Johnny Shiloh 🦴🦴 1963 An underage youth becomes a heroic drummer during the Civil War. Originally a two-part Disney TV show. 90m/C VHS. Kevin Corcoran, Brian Keith, Darryl Hickman, Skip Homeier; *D:* James Neilson. TV

Johnny Skidmarks 🦴🦴 1997 (R) Johnny (Gallagher) is a burned-out freelance crime-scene photographer who moonlights for blackmailers by shooting incriminating pics of prominent citizens in seedy motels. Then the blackmailers start winding up dead and Johnny checks out his photos to see if he can figure out who's doing the crime before he becomes the next target. 96m/C VHS, DVD. Peter Gallagher, Frances McDormand, John Lithgow, Jack Black, Charlie Spradling; *D:* John Raffo; *W:* John Raffo, William Preston Robinson; *C:* Bernd Heinl; *M:* Brian Langsbard.

Johnny Stecchino 🦴🦴 1992 (R) A breathless, charming comedy about mistaken identity, with Benigni starring as both Dante, a mild-mannered Roman bus driver, and his double, a notorious Mafioso known as "Johnny Toothpick." Dante happens to meet a lovely woman who takes exceptional interest in him, even inviting him to visit her home in Palermo. The reason she's interested is that Dante is the exact double of her husband, who has ratted on his fellow mobsters and needs a patsy to take the fall. Benigni's expressive body language and sweetness of character is well-showcased. In Italian with English subtitles. 100m/C VHS. *IT* Roberto Benigni, Nicoletta Braschi, Paolo Bonacelli, Ignazio Pappalardo, Franco Volpi; *D:* Roberto Benigni; *W:* Roberto Benigni, Vincenzo Cerami; *C:* Giuseppe Lanci; *M:* Evan Lurie.

Johnny Suede 🦴🦴½ 1992 (R) Hip kid with big hair wanders the city seeking an identity via retro black suede elevator shoes. Sleepy surreal comedy walks Pitt through two romantic entanglements and a rendezvous with his own rock idol in his quest for musical talent and pop singer nirvana (not necessarily in that order). Candidate for induction into the David Lynch Movie Museum of the Weird. 97m/C VHS, DVD. Brad Pitt, Calvin Levels, Nick Cave, Wilfredo Giovanni Clark, Alison Moir, Peter McRobbie, Tina Louise, Michael Mulheren, Catherine Keener, Samuel L. Jackson; *D:* Tom DiCillo; *W:* Tom DiCillo; *M:* Jim Farmer.

Johnny Tiger 🦴🦴½ 1966 A teacher has his hands full when he arrives at the Seminole Reservation in Florida to instruct the Indian children. 100m/C VHS. Robert Taylor, Geraldine Brooks, Chad Everett, Brenda Scott; *D:* Paul Wendkos.

Johnny Tremain & the Sons of Liberty 🦴🦴 1958 The story of the gallant American patriots who participated in the Boston Tea Party. 85m/C VHS, DVD. Sebastian Cabot, Hal Stalmaster, Luana Patten, Richard Beymer; *D:* Robert Stevenson.

Johnny 2.0 🦴🦴½ (PG-13) Contrived thriller about a genetic scientist, Johnny Dalton (Fahey), who awakens from a 15-year coma and discovers his memory has been transplanted into a clone, Johnny 2.0. Now Dalton has six days to find his duplicate before the Corporation, the group behind the procedure, decides on termination. 95m/C VHS, DVD. Jeff Fahey, Michael Ironside, Tahnee Welch; *D:* Neill Fearnley. CABLE

Johnny Was 🦴½ 2005 (R) Johnny Doyle (Jones) escapes his IRA past by hiding out in London's tough Brixton neighborhood, trapped between a pirate reggae radio station and a crack-dealing gangster. His life gets tougher when former mentor Flynn (Bergin) escapes from prison and is determined to derail the Irish peace process with a new bombing campaign. Good soundtrack but inept thriller. 90m/C DVD. *GB IR* Vinnie Jones, Patrick Bergin, Roger Daltrey, Samantha Mumba, Lennox Lewis, Eriq La Salle; *D:* Mark Hammond; *W:* Brendan Foley; *C:* Mark Moriaty.

Johnny We Hardly Knew Ye 🦴🦴½ 1977 Well-made biographical drama recounts John F. Kennedy's first political campaign for local office in Boston in 1946. 90m/C VHS. Paul Rudd, Kevin Conway, William Prince, Burgess Meredith, Tom Berenger, Brian Dennehy, Kenneth McMillan; *D:* Gilbert Cates. TV

Johnny's Girl 🦴🦴½ 1995 After her mom's death, a 16-year-old (Kirshner) moves to Anchorage, Alaska to live with her wayward dad (Williams). He's a kinda con man involved in shady deals, who tries to go legit in order to give his daughter a proper home. TV movie based on the novel by Kim Rich. 92m/C VHS. Mia Kirshner, Treat Williams, Ron White, Gloria Reuben, Shirley Douglas, Janne Mortil; *D:* John Kent Harrison.

Johns 🦴🦴½ 1996 (R) A gritty, unpredictable tale of street hustling in L.A. Predeemed by intense performances by its two lead actors. It's Christmas Eve and John (Arquette) has only one thing in mind: recover his stolen money and celebrate his birthday in style. On the way, he mentors crony Donnor (Haas), who's love for John blinds him to the rules of hustling, which can only lead to tragedy. Arquette's controlled performance is on target for the cynical male lead and Haas's doe-eyed look is perfect for the slightly dim-witted naivete his character revels in. Downfall comes when first-time director Silver fails to maintain actors' intensity with uneven editing and out of place symbolism. Still, not a bad first try. 96m/C VHS, DVD. David Arquette, Lukas Haas, Arliss Howard, Keith David, Elliott Gould, Christopher Gartin, Joshua Schaefer, Wilson Cruz, Terrence Howard, Nicky Katt, Alanna Ubach; *D:* Scott Silver; *W:* Scott Silver; *C:* Tom Richmond; *M:* Charles D. Brown.

Johnson County War 🦴🦴 2002 The Hammett brothers, Cain (Berenger), Harry (Perry), and Dale (Storke) struggle to protect their ranch against greedy cattle barons after their property and that of other homesteaders. And in this case, the "law" in the guise of trigger-happy Hunt Lawton (Reynolds) is on the side of the bad guys. Based on the novel "Riders of Judgment" by Frederic Manfred. The story of this 1890s Wyoming range war was also covered in the film "Heaven's Gate." 178m/C VHS, DVD... Tom Berenger; Luke Perry; Adam Storke; Burt Reynolds; Rachel Ward; Michelle Forbes; Christopher Cazenove; Jack Conley; Fay Masterson; Blu Mankuma; Silas Weir Mitchell; Ken Pogue; **D:** David S. Cass Sr.; **W:** Larry McMurtry; Diana Ossana; **C:** Doug Milsome; **M:** Sheldon Mirowitz. CABLE

The Jolson Story 1946 A smash Hollywood bio of Jolson, from his childhood to super-stardom. Features dozens of vintage songs from Jolson's parade of hits. Jolson himself dubbed the vocals for Parks, rejuvenating his own career in the process. ♪ Swanee; You Made Me Love You; I'm Looking Over a Four-Leaf Clover; ...Say About: Dixie?; Ma Blushin' Rose. 96m/C VHS, DVD, Larry Parks, William Demarest, Barbara Hale, Bill Goodwin; **D:** George Duning.

Jolson Sings Again 1949 This sequel to "The Jolson Story" brings back Larry Parks as the ebullient entertainer, with Jolson himself dubbing Parks's voice for the songs. Picking up where the other film ended, the movie chronicles Jolson's comeback in the 1940s and his tireless work with the USO overseas during WWII and the Korean War. ♪ After You've Gone; Chinatown, My Chinatown; Give My Regards to Broadway; I Only Have Eyes For You; I'm Just Wild About Harry. 96m/C VHS, DVD, Larry Parks, Barbara Hale, William Demarest, Bill Goodwin; **D:** Henry Levin; **M:** George Duning.

Johnson Family Vacation 2004 (PG-13) Slapstick road comedy will have viewers whining miles before the end. "Are we there yet?" At a crisp 97 minutes, that is no easy feat but one managed with uninspired, corny dialogue, and not one ounce of originality in the Johnson family, headed by patriarch Nate (Cedric the Entertainer) hit the road in search of a decent premise...er, family reunion in Missouri. Recently separated from wife Dorothy (Williams), Nate hopes the trip with their three children (Bow Wow, Knowles, and Soleil) will bring them closer together and hopefully snatch the coveted reunion "family of the year" trophy from regular winner Mack (Harvey), Nate's older bro. Cedric's natural charisma somewhat elevates this washed-out "Vacation." 97m/C DVD, Cedric the Entertainer, Vanessa Lynn Williams, Bow Wow, Steve Harvey, Solange Knowles, Shannon Elizabeth, Aloma Wright, Shari Headley, Jennifer Freeman, Lea Garlington, Gabby Soleil, Philip Daniel Bolden, Rodney B. Perry, Christopher Erskin; **W:** Todd R. Jones, Earl Richey Jones; **C:** Shawn Maurer, Shawn Maurer; **M:** Richard Gibbs.

A Joke of Destiny, Lying in Wait Around the Corner Like a Bandit A Joke of Destiny 1984 (PG) A irreverent satire about a Minister of the Interior (Tognazzi) of "La Cage aux Folles" fame) who becomes trapped in his high-tech limousine before a vital press conference. An exaggerated vision of Italian bureaucracy. With English subtitles. 105m/C VHS, /T: Ugo Tognazzi, Piera Degli Esposti, Gastone Moschin, Renzo Montegnani, Valeria Golino; **D:** Lina Wertmuller; **W:** Lina Wertmuller.

The Jolly Boys' Last Stand 2000 Spider (Serkis) is leaving behind his loutish, hard-drinking friends, known as the Jolly Boys after proposing to girlfriend Annie (Craig). His best man Des (Twomey) decides to make a pre-wedding video for the groom as a gift. Then Vinnie (Baron Cohen) also goes domestic, which throws the rest of the gang into a tizzy and the video turns into a group effort with unexpected results. Ragged (and amiable) debut for writer/director Payne that was shot in 1998. 88m/C DVD, GB Andy Serkis, Sacha Baron Cohen, Milo Twomey, Rebecca Craig, Jo Martin; **D:** Christopher Payne; **W:** Christopher Payne; **C:** Will Jacob, Robin Cox; **M:** Jeremy Parufhik.

The Jolly Paupers Freylekhe Katsonim 1938 A pre-war comedy made in Warsaw about two smalltown Jews who try to achieve fame and fortune in the face of setbacks, community quarrels, and insanity. In Yiddish with English subtitles. 62m/B VHS, Shimon Dzigan, Yisroel Shumacher, Max Bozyk, Menasha Oppenheim; **D:** Zygmund Turkow.

Me Love You; By the Light of the Silvery Moon; I'm Sitting On Top of the World; There's a Rainbow Round My Shoulder; My Mammy; Rock-A-Bye Your Baby With a Dixie Melody; Liza; Waiting for the Robert E. Lee. 128m/C VHS, DVD, Larry Parks, Evelyn Keyes, William Demarest, Bill Goodwin, Tamara Shayne, John Alexander, Jimmy Lloyd, Ludwig Donath, Myron McCormick, Alfred E. Green; **M:** Morris Stoloff. Oscars '46: Sound, Scoring/Musical.

Jon Jost's Frameup Frame-up 1993 Cocky ex-con Ricky Lee hooks up with dizzy waitress Beth Ann and they head out on a 3000-mile nightmare road trip to California. Free-form story shot in 10 days. 91m/C VHS, Howard Swain, Nancy Carlin; **D:** Jon Jost; **W:** Jon Jost.

Jonah Who Will Be 25 in the Year 2000 Jonas—Qui Aura 25 Ans en l'An 2000 1976 A group of eight friends, former 60s radicals, try to adjust to growing older and coping with life in the 70s. The eccentric octet include a disillusioned journalist turned gambler, an unorthodox teacher, and a grocery store cashier who gives away food to the elderly. Wonderful performances highlight this social comedy. In French with English subtitles. 110m/C VHS, Si Jean-Luc Bideau, Myriam Meziere, Miou-Miou, Jacques Denis, Rufus, Dominique Labourier, Roger Jendly, Miriam Boyer, Raymond Bussieres; **D:** Alain Tanner; **W:** Alain Tanner; **C:** Renato Berta; **M:** Jean-Marie Senia. Natl. Soc. Film Critics '76: Screenplay.

Jonathan Livingston Seagull 1973 (G) Based on the best-selling novella by Richard Bach, this film quietly envisions a world of love, understanding, achievement, hope and individuality. 99m/C VHS, James Franciscus, Juliet Mills; **D:** Hall Bartlett; **M:** Neil Diamond. Golden Globes '74: Score.

Joni 1979 (G) An inspirational story based on the real life of Tada (playing herself) who was seriously injured in a diving accident, and her conquering of the odds. A born-again feature film based on the book by Tada. 75m/C VHS, Joni Eareckson Tada, Bert Remsen, Katherine De Terre, Cooper Huckabee; **D:** James F. Collier.

Jory 1972 (PG) A young man's father is killed in a saloon fight, and he must grow up quickly to survive. 96m/C VHS, Robby Benson, B.J. Thomas, John Marley; **D:** Jorge Fons.

Joseph 1995 Following "Abraham" and "Jacob" comes the Old Testament story of young Joseph (Mercurio), beloved son of Jacob, who's sold into slavery by his envious older brothers. Joseph is bought by the Pharoah's chief steward, Potiphar (Kingsley), and, after a long series of tribulations, rises to become a power in Egypt, which unexpectedly leads Joseph to hold the fate of his long-lost family in his hands. Filmed in Morocco. 240m/C VHS, DVD, Paul Mercurio, Ben Kingsley, Martin Landau, Lesley Ann Warren, Warren Clarke, Alice Krige, Dominique Sanda, Stefano Dionisi, Valeria Cavalli, Peter Eyre, Timothy Bateson, Jamie Glover, Michael Attwell; **D:** Roger Young; **W:** Lionel Chetwynd, James Carrington; **C:** Raffaele Mertes; **M:** Marco Frisina.

Joseph Andrews 1977 (R) This adaptation of a 1742 Henry Fielding novel chronicles the rise of Joseph Andrews from servant to personal footman (and fancy) of Lady Booby. 99m/C VHS, DVD, GB Ann-Margret, Peter Firth, Jim Dale, Michael Horden, Beryl Reid; **D:** Tony Richardson.

Joseph and the Amazing Technicolor Dreamcoat 2000 Something more than a filmed stage presentation of the Webber-Rice musical, but something less than a real movie. It begins with a school assembly hall where the narrator (Friedman) bursts into song and tells the biblical story of Joseph (Osmond). Then the scene shifts to soundstages. The catchy songs often seem to be on the verge of morphing into "Cats" or "Phantom of the Opera." Overal, the production values are good and the sound is excellent. 78m/C VHS, DVD, Donny Osmond, Richard Attenborough, Joan Collins, Maria Friedman; **D:** David Mallet, Steven Pimlott; **C:** Nicholas D. Knowland; **M:** Andrew Lloyd Webber, Tim Rice. VIDEO

Josepha 1982 (R) A husband and wife, both actors, are forced to re-examine their relationship when the wife finds a new love while on a film location. In French with English subtitles. 114m/C VHS, DVD, FR Miou-Miou, Claude Brasseur, Bruno Cremer; **D:** Christopher Frank.

The Josephine Baker Story 1990 (R) Biopic of exotic entertainer/activist Josephine Baker, an Afro-American woman from St. Louis who found superstardom in pre-WWII Europe, but repeated racism and rejection in the U.S. At times trite treatment turns her eventful life into a standard rise-and-fall showbiz tale, but a great cast and lavish scope pull it through. Whitfield recreates Baker's (sometimes topless) dance routines; Carol Dennis dubs her singing. Filmed on location in Budapest. 129m/C VHS, DVD, Lynn Whitfield, Ruben Blades, David Dukes, Craig T. Nelson, Louis Gossett Jr., Kene Holiday, Vivian Bonnell; **D:** Brian Gibson; **M:** Ralph Burns, Vivian Bonnell. CABLE

Josh Kirby...Time Warrior: Chapter 1, Planet of the Dino-Knights 1995 (PG) Time-traveling 14-year-old Josh Kirby is accidently pulled out of his own time where fierce warriors ride dinosaurs and a madman is out to destroy the universe. The first tale in a fantasy series designed as an old-fashioned movie serial, complete with cliff-hanger ending. 88m/C VHS, DVD, Corbin Allred, Jennifer Burns, Derek Webster, John De Mita; **D:** Ernest Farino; **W:** Ethan Reiff, Cyrus Voris; **M:** Paul Callisi.

Josh Kirby...Time Warrior: Chapter 2, The Human Pets 1995 (PG) Josh and his friends now find themselves in the year 70,370—held hostage by the enormous Fatlings, who regard their human finds as pet-like action toys. 90m/C VHS, DVD, Corbin Allred, Jennifer Burns; **D:** Frank Arnold; **W:** Ethan Reiff, Cyrus Voris; **M:** Paul Callisi.

Josh Kirby...Time Warrior: Chapter 3, Trapped on Toyworld 1995 (PG) Josh is stranded away from his friends on the strange planet of Toyworld and must rely on the lifelike creations of a toy magnate to defend himself from the villainous Dr. Zoetrope. 90m/C VHS, DVD, Corbin Allred, Jennifer Burns, Derek Webster, Sharon Lee Jones, Buck Kartalian, Barrie Ingham; **D:** Frank Arnold; **W:** Nick Paine.

Josh Kirby...Time Warrior: Chapter 4, Eggs from 70 Million B.C. 1995 (PG) Josh and his pals finds themselves in a military compound that is under attack and encounter some very hungry alien worms. 93m/C VHS, DVD, Corbin Allred, Jennifer Burns, Michael Hagwara, Barrie Ingham; **D:** Ernest Farino; **W:** Ethan Reiff, Cyrus Voris.

Josh Kirby...Time Warrior: Chapter 5, Journey to the Magic Cavern 1996 (PG) Josh and pals find themselves in the center of a planet where they are befriended by the weird Mushroom People who live under siege by a monster known as "the Muncher." 93m/C VHS, DVD, Corbin Allred, Jennifer Burns, Derek Webster, Michael Hagwara, Barrie Ingham; **D:** Ernest Farino; **M:** Cyrus Voris.

Josh Kirby...Time Warrior: Chapter 6, Last Battle for the Universe 1996 (PG) Josh is ready to get back to his own time but first he must survive a battle between longfeuding rivals of the timebelt. 90m/C VHS, DVD, Corbin Allred, Jennifer Burns, Derek Webster, Barrie Ingham; **D:** Frank Arnold; **W:** Ethan Reiff, Cyrus Voris.

W: Chris Bryant, Alan Scott; **C:** David Watkin; **M:** John Addison.

Josh and S.A.M. 1993 (PG-13) Road movie for youngsters with a twist: the driver can barely see over the dashboard, Josh and Sam are brothers whose parents are splitting. They cope by taking off on their own. Sam, meanwhile has been convinced by Josh that he's not really a boy at all but rather a S.A.M.: Strategically Altered Mutant. Weber's directional debut will appeal to young kids, but adults will see over the dashboard and through the transparent plot. 97m/C VHS, Jacob Tierney, Noah Fleiss, Martha Plimpton, Stephen Tobolowsky, Ronald Guttman; **D:** Billy Weber; **M:** Frank Deese; **C:** Don Burgess; **M:** Thomas Newman.

Joshua 2007 (R) New twist on the creepy-kid movie trades demon possession for subtle psychological twists and turns. Joshua (Kogan) is a tidy, disconnected child prodigy who goes from simply odd to creepy after the birth of his sister. Meanwhile, his mother Abby (Farmiga) descends into post-partum depression and dad Brad (Rockwell) struggles to hold his family together as pets die and Granny has an accident. Director Ratliff maintains suspense by never showing all his cards, but it leaves you with a question: is there a method to the madness, or is this just a series of events in the lives of some screwed-up people? 105m/C DVD, US Sam Rockwell, Vera Farmiga, Dallas Roberts, Celia Weston, Michael Mickeas, Jacob Kogan; **D:** George Ratliff; **W:** George Ratliff, David Gilbert; **C:** Benoit Debie; **M:** Nico Muhly.

Joshua Black Rider 1976 (R) Wes'ern drama about a vigilante who tracks down the group of outlaws that killed his mother. 75m/C VHS, DVD, Fred Williamson, Isela Vega; **D:** Larry Spangler.

Joshua 2002 (G) Joshua (Goldwyn) is a stranger to the 19th-century midwestern community of Auburn. He rents a barn and sets himself up as a woodworker and all-around helpful guy. Seeing that the black community's church is damaged, Joshua sets out to rebuild it help. But traditional priest Father Tardone (Abraham) is askance when townsfolk begin to think Joshua has miraculous powers. Spiritually uplifting without being preachy, based on the novel by Father Joseph Girzone. 90m/C VHS, DVD, Tony Goldwyn, F. Murray Abraham, Kurt Fuller, Giancarlo Giannini, Stacy Edwards, Colleen Camp; **D:** Jon Purdy; **W:** Brad Mirman, Keith Giglio; **C:** Bruce Surtees; **M:** Michael W. Smith.

Joshua Then and Now 1985 (R) When a Jewish-Canadian novelist (Woods) is threatened by the breakup of his marriage to his gangster father (Arkin) A stirring story that is enhanced by a strong performance by Woods, as well as a picturesque Canadian backdrop. Adapted by Mordecai Richler from his own novel. 102m/C VHS, CA James Woods, Gabrielle Lazure, Alan Arkin, Michael Sarrazin, Chuck Shamata, Linda Sorensen, Alan Scarfe, Alexander Knox, Robert Joy, Ken Campbell; **D:** Ted Kotcheff; **W:** Mordecai Richler; **M:** Philippe Sarde. Genie '86: Support. Actor (Arkin), Support. Actress (Sorensen).

Josie and the Pussycats 2001 (PG-13) This Josie and company have almost as many dimensions as the cartoon from whence they came. Simple plot has Josie's band looking for their big break when record company exec Wyatt Frame, looking for a new sound, spots our heroines and remakes them as teen sensations. Wyatt is partnered with Fiona (Posey, chewing scenery like a starving dog in an Alpo factory) in a scheme to use pop music to control the minds of teens. Basically harmless parody of the pop music biz-risy, but gets by on the obvious charms of leads Cook, Reid, and Dawson. 98m/C VHS, DVD, US Rachael Leigh Cook, Tara Reid, Rosario Dawson, Parker Posey, Alan Cumming, Gabriel Mann, Paulo Costanzo, Tom Butler, Missi Pyle, Carson Daly; Cameos: Seth Green, Breckin Meyer, Donald Adeosun Faison; **D:** Deborah Kaplan, Harry Elfont; **W:** Deborah Kaplan, Harry Elfont; **C:** Matthew Libatique; **M:** John Frizzell.

Jour de Fete The Big Day; Holiday 1948 Tati's first film, dealing with a French postman's accelerated efforts at efficiency after viewing a motivational film of the American post service. Wonderful slapstick moments. In French with English subtitles. 79m/B VHS. FR Jacques Tati, Guy Decomble, Paul Fankeur, Santa Relli; D: Jacques Tati; W: Henri Marquet, Jacques Tati; C: Jacques Mercanton; M: Jean Yatove.

Journey 1977 (PG) Violent story of a girl who is rescued from the Saguenay River and falls in love with her rescuer. Choosing to remain in the remote pioneer community of this "hero," she brings everyone bad luck and misery. 87m/C VHS. CA Genevieve Bujold, John Vernon; D: Paul Almond.

Journey 1995 (PG) Eleven-year-old Journey (Pomeranc) and his teenaged sister Cat (Dushku) are abandoned by their unhappy, restless mother Min (Tilly) at the home of her parents. Marcus (Robards) and Lottie (Fricker). Marcus is an amateur photographer and Journey searches through the family photos to albums to find reasons for his mother's leaving as he and his grandfather slowly build their relationship. Based on the book by Patricia MacLachlan. 98m/C VHS. Max Pomeranc, Jason Robards Jr., Brenda Fricker, Eliza Dushku, Meg Tilly; D: Tom McLoughlin; W: Patricia MacLachlan; C: Kees Van Oostrum. TV

Journey Back to Oz 1971 Animated special features Dorothy and Toto returning to visit their friends in the magical land of Oz. 90m/C VHS. D: Hal Sutherland; W: Fred Ladd, Norm Prescott; M: Walter Scharf, James Van Heusen; V: Liza Minnelli, Ethel Merman, Paul Lynde, Milton Berle, Mickey Rooney, Danny Thomas, Herschel Bernardi, Margaret Hamilton.

Journey Beneath the Desert Antinea, l'Amante Della Citta Sepolta 1961 Three engineers discover the lost-but-always-found-in-the-movies kingdom of Atlantis when their helicopter is forced down in the sunny Sahara. A poor hostess with a rotten disposition, the mean sub-saharan queen doesn't roll out the welcome mat for her grounded guests, so a beautiful slave babe helps them make a hasty exit. Dawdling Euro production with adequate visuals. 105m/C VHS. IT Haya Harareet, Jean-Louis Trintignant, James Westmoreland, Amedeo Nazzari, George Riviere, Giulia Rubini, Gabriele Tinti, Gian Marie Volonte; D: Edgar G. Ulmer, Giuseppe Masini, Frank Borzage.

Journey for Margaret 1942 Young and Day star as an expectant American couple living in London during WWII so Young can cover the war for a newspaper back home. After she loses her baby during an air raid, Day heads back to the States. Young stays in London where he meets two young orphans and takes them under his wing. He decides to take them back to the United States and adopt them, but problems arise. A real tearjerker and a good story that shows the war through the eyes of children. O'Brien's first film. Based on the book by William L. White. 81m/B VHS. Robert Young, Laraine Day, Fay Bainter, Signe Hasso, Margaret O'Brien, Nigel Bruce, G.P. (Tim) Huntley Jr., William Severn, Doris Lloyd, Halliwell Hobbes, Jill Esmond; D: Woodbridge S. Van Dyke.

Journey into Fear 1942 During WWII, an American armaments expert is smuggled out of Istanbul, but Axis agents are close behind. From the novel by Eric Ambler. 71m/B VHS. Joseph Cotten, Dolores Del Rio, Orson Welles, Agnes Moorehead, Norman Foster; C: Karl Struss.

Journey into Fear 1974 A remake of the 1942 Orson Welles classic about a geologist ensnared in Turkish intrigue and murder. 96m/C VHS. CA Sam Waterston, Vincent Price, Shelley Winters, Donald Pleasence, Zero Mostel, Yvette Mimieux, Ian McShane; D: Daniel Mann; M: Alex North.

The Journey of August King 1995 (PG-13) Adapted by Ehle from his own 1971 novel, set in 1815, about a runaway slave (Newton) protected by a lonely farmer against the landowner and posse tracking her down. August King (Patric), a widower on his way home from town, comes upon Annalees (Newton), prize possession of powerful slaveowner Olaf Singletary (Drake). August, a highly principled man, resists helping her at first, for fear of breaking the law and losing his farm and only remaining possessions. But he rises to higher moral ground, deciding to help her find freedom, whatever the consequences. Director Duigan ("Sirens") crafts a thoughtful, but not particularly suspenseful, period piece of early American history. Patric/Newton relationship reflects the gradual feel of the story. Drake booms as slaveowner. Includes brief brutal scene of slave torture. 91m/C VHS, DVD. Jason Patric, Thandie Newton, Larry Drake, Sam Waterston; D: John Duigan; W: John Ehle; C: Slawomir Idziak; M: Stephen Endelman.

Journey of Honor 1991 (PG-13) During a civil war in 17th century Japan, a nearly defeated Shogun sends his son, Lord Mayeda, to Spain to buy guns from King Phillip III. Along the way he must fight shipboard spies and fierce storms, and once Mayeda arrives in Spain, he is confronted by the evil Duke Don Pedro. In defeating Don Pedro, Mayeda saves King Phillip, gets his guns, and wins the love of Lady Cecilia. To get revenge, Don Pedro plots to capture the Japanese ship and enslave everyone on board. Lots of action and fine acting. 107m/C VHS. Sho Kosugi, David Essex, Kane (Takeshi) Kosugi, Christopher Lee, Norman Lloyd, Ronald Pickup, John Rhys-Davies, Dylan Kussman, Toshiro Mifune; D: Gordon Hessler.

Journey of Hope 1990 (PG) Powerful drama about Kurdish family that sells its material possessions in hopes of emigrating legally to Switzerland, where life will surely be better. During the perilous journey, smugglers take their money and the family must attempt crossing the formidable slopes of the Swiss Mountains on foot. Based on a true story. In Turkish with English subtitles. 111m/C VHS. SI Necmettin Cobanoglu, Nur Surer, Emin Sivas, Yaman Okay, Mathias Gnaedinger, Dietmar Schoenherr; D: Xavier Koller; W: Xavier Koller. Oscars '90: Foreign Film.

The Journey of Jared Price 2000 Sweet-natured but predictable gay coming of age tale. 19-year-old Jared (Spears) leaves Georgia for California and self-discovery, winding up in a youth hostel where he's befriended by Robert (Jacobson), who wants to be more than buddies. Jared eventually gets a job as a caretaker to elderly, blind Mrs. Haines (Craigg) and is soon pulled into a destructive relationship with the older Matthew (Tyler), Mrs. Haines son. 96m/C VHS, DVD. Corey Spears, Josh Jacobson, Steve Tyler, Rocki Craigg; D: Dustin Lance Black; W: Dustin Lance Black; C: Tony Croll; M: Damon Intrabartolo.

The Journey of Natty Gann 1985 (PG) With the help of a wolf (brilliantly portrayed by a dog) and a drifter, a 14-year-old girl travels across the country in search of her father in this warm and touching film. Excellent Disney representation of life during the Great Depression. 101m/C VHS, DVD. Meredith Salenger, John Cusack, Ray Wise, Scatman Crothers, Lainie Kazan, Verna Bloom; D: Jeremy Paul Kagan; W: Jeanne Rosenberg; C: Dick Bush; M: James Horner.

Journey Through Rosebud 1972 A re-enactment of the 1970s protest at Wounded Knee by Native Americans. 93m/C VHS. Robert Forster, Eddie Little Sky; D: Tom Giles.

The Journey to Kafiristan Die Reise nach Kafiristan 2001 In 1939, Zurich writer Annemarie Schwarzenbach (Hain) and Geneva ethnologist Ella Maillart (Petri) drive from Switzerland to a remote valley in Afghanistan. Ella's on a scientific expedition but Annemarie, just out of a drug rehab clinic, is out to test her emotional and sexual limits. Based on a true story. German with subtitles. 100m/C VHS, DVD. GE SI NL Jeanette Hain, Nina Petri, Matthew Burton, Ozlen Soydani; D: Donatello Dubini, Fosco Dubini; W: Donatello Dubini, Fosco Dubini; C: Matthias Kaelin.

Journey to Spirit Island 1992 (PG) A young Native American girl dreams of her ancestors who are buried on Spirit Island, an ancient burial ground. However, the island is now scheduled to be developed into a resort. But With the help of three friends the girl tries to protect the land. Filmed in the Pacific Northwest. 93m/C VHS. Brandon Douglas, Gabriel Damon, Tony Acierto, Nick Ramus, Marie Antoinette Rodgers, Tarek McCarthy; D: Laszlo Pal.

Journey to the Center of the Earth 1959 A scientist and student undergo a hazardous journey to find the center of the earth and along the way they find the lost city of Atlantis. Based upon the Jules Verne novel. 132m/C VHS, DVD. James Mason, Pat Boone, Arlene Dahl, Diane Baker, Thayer David, Alan Napier, Peter Ronson; D: Henry Levin; W: Charles Brackett, Robert Gunter, Walter Reisch; C: Leo Tover; M: Bernard Herrmann.

Journey to the Center of the Earth 1988 (PG) A young nanny and two teenage boys discover Atlantis while exploring a volcano. 83m/C VHS, DVD. Nicola Cowper, Paul Carafotes, Ilan Mitchell-Smith; D: Rusty Lemorande; W: Rusty Lemorande, Kitty Chalmers.

Journey to the Center of the Earth 1999 Jules Verne's 1864 fantasy made its way to cable in this adventurous journey. Geologist Theodore Lytton (Williams) is hired by wealthy Alice Hastings (Bergen) to find her husband, Casper (Brown), who disappeared seven years earlier during an expedition to a volcano in New Zealand. Lytton and his compatriots descend into deep caverns and discover a tunnel system leading to the planet's center and a new civilization that Hastings has usurped for his own greedy purposes. There's derring-do and some babes in animal-hide bikinis. 139m/C VHS, DVD. Treat Williams, Jeremy London, Tushka Bergen, Hugh Keays-Byrne, Bryan Brown, Sarah Chadwick, Petra Yared, Tessa Wells; D: George Miller; W: Thomas Baum; C: John Stokes; M: Bruce Rowland. CABLE

Journey to the Center of the Earth 3D 2008 (PG) Science professor Trevor (Fraser) is an academic laughingstock because of his unorthodox theories. But on a journey to Iceland to find his missing brother, he and nephew Sean (Hutcherson) stumble across a discovery that leads them to adventure far beneath Earth's surface. Based on the Jules Verne novel and the first film to be shot in digital 3D. Not yet reviewed. ?m/C Brendan Fraser, Josh Hutcherson, Anita Briem, Eric Brevig; W: Michael D. Weiss, Jennifer Flackett, Marc Levin; C: Chuck Shuman; M: Andrew Lockington.

Journey to the Center of Time 1967 A scientist and his crew are hurled into a time trap when a giant reactor explodes. 83m/C VHS, DVD. Lyle Waggoner, Scott Brady, Gigi Perreau, Anthony Eisley; D: David L. Hewitt.

Journey to the Far Side of the Sun Doppelganger 1969 (G) Chaos erupts in the Earth's scientific community when it is discovered that a second, identical Earth is on the other side of the Sun. Both planets end up sending out identical exploratory missions. The denouement is worth the journey. 92m/C VHS, DVD. GB Roy Thinnes, Ian Hendry, Lynn Loring, Patrick Wymark, Loni von Friedl, Herbert Lom, Ed Bishop; D: Robert Parrish; W: Gerry Anderson; C: John Read; M: Barry Gray.

Journey to the Lost City Tiger of Bengal 1958 Architect living in India happens upon a lost city, the rulership of which is being contested by two brothers. In the midst of fighting snakes and tigers, he falls in love with Paget, a beautiful dancer. This feature is actually a poorly edited hybrid of two Lang German adventures, "Der Tiger von Eschnapur" and "Das Indische Grabmal" merged for U.S. release. 95m/C VHS, DVD. FR IT GE Debra Paget, Paul (Christian) Hubschmid, Walter Reyer, Claus Holm, Sabine Bethmann, Valeri Inkizhinov, Rene Deltgen, Luciana Paluzzi; D: Fritz Lang.

Journeys with George 2002 On the road with George W. Bush's 2000 presidential campaign, NBC News producer Alexandra Pelosi—daughter of California congresswoman Nancy Pelosi—offers a day-in-the-grinding-life view of a pool reporter captured via camcorder yet stops short of any meaty behind-the-scenes strategy sessions. Allows W to show off his easy-going manner while sidestepping any heavy topics. 76m/C VHS, DVD. Cameos: George W. Bush, Tom Brokaw, Barbara Bush, George Bush, Howard Dean, Alexandra Pelosi, Erin Brockovich-Ellis, Jeb Bush, Laura Bush, Dick Cheney, Al Gore, John McCain; To: Alexandra Pelosi; W: Alexandra Pelosi; C: Alexandra Pelosi. TV

Joy House The Love Cage; Les Felins 1964 French playboy Marc (Delon) seduces the wife of an American mobster who sends his goons after him. Marc hides out by becoming the chauffeur to Barbara (Albright) at her chateau, which is also where he meets his employer's niece, Melinda (Fonda). Soon, Marc is part of a romantic triangle—or is it quartet since Barbara's lover, Vincent (Oumansky), is also living there. And don't forget the gangsters, who certainly haven't forgotten Marc. Complicated plot with no particular payoff. 98m/B VHS, DVD. Jane Fonda, Alain Delon, Lola Albright, Andre Oumansky, Sorrel Booke; D: Rene Clement; W: Rene Clement; C: Henri Decae; M: Lalo Schifrin.

The Joy Luck Club 1993 (R) Universal themes in mother/daughter relationships are explored in a context Hollywood first rejected as too narrow, but which proved to be a modest sleeper hit. Tan skillfully weaves the plot of her 1989 best-seller into a screenplay which centers around young June's (Ming-Na) going-away party. Slowly the stories of four Chinese women, who meet weekly to play mah-jongg, are unraveled. Each vignette reveals life in China for the four women and the tragedies they survived, before reaching into the present to capture the relationships between the mothers and their daughters. Powerful, relevant, and moving. 136m/C VHS, DVD. Tsai Chin, Kieu Chinh, France Nuyen, Rosalind Chao, Tamlyn Tomita, Lisa Lu, Lauren Tom, Ming Na, Michael Paul Chan, Andrew McCarthy, Christopher Rich, Russell Wong, Victor Wong, Vivian Wu, Jack Ford, Diane Baker; D: Wayne Wang; W: Amy Tan, Ronald Bass.

The Joy of Knowledge Le Gai Savoir 1965 Godard's experimental use of language and image in a plotless narrative. Berto and Leaud sit together on a bare sound stage and are exposed to popular culture through images, word association, and conversation. In French with English subtitles. 96m/C VHS. FR Juliet Berto, Jean-Pierre Leaud; D: Jean-Luc Godard; W: Jean-Luc Godard.

Joy of Living 1938 Vintage screwball farce finds successful songstress Maggie (Dunne) the sole support of her n'er-do-well family. Maggie's aggressively courted by playboy Dan Brewster (Fairbanks Jr.) and finally (after numerous silly complications) they fall in love. ♪You Couldn't Be Cuter; A Heavenly Party; What's Good About Goodnight; Just Let Me Look At You. 90m/B VHS. Irene Dunne, Douglas Fairbanks Jr., Alice Brady, Guy Kibbee, Jean Dixon, Eric Blore, Lucille Ball, Warren Hymer, Billy Gilbert, Frank Milan; D: Tay Garnett; W: Graham Baker, Allan Scott, Gene Towne; C: Joseph Walker; M: Jerome Kern, Dorothy Fields.

Joy of Sex 1984 (R) An undercover narcotics agent is sent to Southern California's Richard M. Nixon High School to investigate the school's extracurricular activities. Typical teen sex flick; no relation to the book. 93m/C VHS. Cameron Dye, Michelle Meyrink, Colleen Camp, Christopher Lloyd, Ernie Deltgen, Lisa Langlois; D: Martha Coolidge; W: Kathleen Rowell.

Joy Ride 2001 (R) Released about the same time as fellow road thriller/horror entry "Jeepers Creepers," this superior outing benefits from better humor, pacing, and performances. Nice guy Lewis (Walker), a college freshman, drive to drive friend/potential squeeze Venna (Sobieski) back home from Colorado for the holidays. Unfortunately for Lewis, roguish brother Fuller (Zahn) calls Lewis to bail him out of jail in Utah and sticks around for the ride. Fuller instigates a CB radio prank in which Lewis, imitating a woman's voice, invites a trucker with the handle Rusty Nail to the hotel room next to theirs. The next day, the man in the room

Joy Ride to Nowhere ✗ 1978 (PG) Two young women steal a Cadillac with $2 million in the trunk and ride away with the owner 'not on their tail. 88m/C VHS. Leslie Ackerman, Sandy Serrano, Len Lesser, Ron Ross, Speed Stearns; **D:** Mel Welles; **W:** Mel Welles; **C:** Bill Davies.

Joyeux Noel ✗✗✗ 2005 (PG-13) On Christmas Eve, during World War I, in France, troops on both sides of the battlefield laid down their weapons in unified holiday spirit for a performance of "Silent Night" by a German soldier, and famed tenor named Sprink, along with his wife. Drinking, cheering, and even some soccer followed, right there in the trenches. This really happened, and it makes for the perfect centerpiece in this postmodern French Christmas miracle movie. WWI is a backdrop to the human turmoil faced by German, French, and Scottish troops at war. An almost ironically surreal melodrama that's just as sad as it is joyous. Nominated for Best Foreign Film Oscar. 110m/C DVD. FR GE GB BE RO Diane Kruger, Benno Fürmann, Guillaume Canet, Gary Lewis, Daniel Brühl, Steven Robertson, Lucas Belvaux, Bernard Le Coq, Christian Carion; **C:** Walther Vanden Ende; **M:** Philippe Rombi.

Joyful Laughter ✗✗✗½ Risate di Gioia 1960 The dreary life of an Italian movie bit player draws strength from Magnani's powerful emotions as she repeatedly comes near to success only to find disappointment. Lovely piano score accompanies the film. 106m/B VHS. IT Anna Magnani, Ben Gazzara, Carlo Pisacane, Fred Clark; **D:** Mario Monicelli; **W:** Suso Cecchi D'Amico, Agenore Incrocci; **C:** Leonida Barboni; **M:** Lelio Luttazzi.

Joyless Street ✗✗✗½ Street of Sorrow; Die Freudlosse Gasse 1925 Silent film focuses on the dismal life of the middle class in Austria during an economic crisis. With English subtitles. 96m/B VHS. GE Greta Garbo, Werner Krauss, Asta Nielson, Jaro Fürth, Loni Nest, Max Kohlhase, Silva Torf, Karl Ettlinger, Ilka Grüning, Agnes Esterhazy, Alexander Mursky, Valeska Gert; **D:** G.W. Pabst; **W:** Willi Haas; **C:** Guido Seeber, Curt Oertel, Walter Robert Lach.

Joyride ✗✗ 1977 (R) Mistreated by a union official, three friends steal a car for a joy ride and plummet into a life of crime. 91m/C VHS, DVD. Desi Arnaz Jr., Robert Carradine, Melanie Griffin, Anne Lockhart; **D:** Joseph Ruben.

Joyride ✗✗ 1997 (R) Three friends make the mistake of stealing a car that belongs to a beautiful blonde assassin, who'll stop at nothing to get her wheels back (her latest victim is stashed in the trunk). 92m/C VHS, DVD. Tobey Maguire, Wilson Cruz, Amy Hathaway, Christina Nally, James Karen, Adam West, Benicio Del Toro, Judson Mills; **D:** Quinton Peeples; **W:** Quinton Peeples; **C:** Douglas Smith. VIDEO

Ju Dou ✗✗✗ 1990 (PG-13) Breath-taking story of an aging factory owner in search of an heir. He takes a third wife, but she finds caring in the arms of another man, when her husband's brutality proves too much. Beautiful color cinematography, excellent acting, and epic story. Oscar nominee for Best Foreign Film. In Chinese with English subtitles. 98m/C VHS, DVD. CH Gong Li, Baotian Li, Li Wei, Zhang Yi, Zheng Jian; **D:** Yimou Zhang; **W:** Liu

Joy Sticks WOOF! 1983 (R) Merry Christmas Joy sticks in question are down at the arcade. Businessman wants to shut down local video game palace. Inhabitants just say no. 88m/C VHS, DVD. Joe Don Baker, Leif Green, Jim Greenleaf, Scott McGinnis, Jonathan Gries; **D:** Greydon Clark.

Juarez ✗✗ 1939 A revolutionary leader overthrows the Mexican government and then becomes President of the country. Based on the true story of Benito Pablo Juarez. 132m/B VHS. Paul Muni, John Garfield, Bette Davis, Claude Rains, Gale Sondergaard, Brian Aherne, Donald Crisp; **D:** William Dieterle; **C:** Gaetano Antonio "Tony" Gaudio.

Jubal ✗✗ 1956 A rancher (Borgnine) seeks advice from a cowhand (Ford) about pleasing his wife, but another cowhand (Steiger) implies that Ford is "advising" Borgnine's wife, as well. A western take on "Othello." 101m/C VHS, DVD. Glenn Ford, Rod Steiger, Ernest Borgnine, Felicia Farr, Charles Bronson, Valerie Francis, Noah Beery Jr.; **D:** Delmer Daves.

Jubilee Trail ✗✗½ 1954 Wagon trail western follows the lives of a group of pioneers from New Orleans to California. A woman goes through a marriage, a baby, and her husband's death. Ralston has some good tunes in this lush picture. 103m/C VHS. Vera Hruba Ralston, Joan Leslie, Forrest Tucker, John Russell, Ray Middleton, Pat O'Brien; **D:** Joseph Kane.

Jud ✗✗½ 1971 (PG) Society's refusal to understand a young soldier returning from the Vietnam conflict leads him to violence and tragedy. Jennings' first film; music by Phillips of Creedence Clearwater Revival. 80m/C VHS. Joseph Kaufmann, Robert Deman, Alix Wyeth, Norman Burton, Claudia Jennings, Maurice Sherbanee, Vic Dunlop, Bonnie Bittner; **D:** Gunther Collins; **M:** Stu Phillips.

Jud Suess ✗✗✗ 1940 Classic, scandalous Nazi anti-Semitic tract about a Jew who rises to power under the duchy of Wuerttemberg by stepping on, abusing, and raping Aryans. A film that caused riots at its screenings and tragedy for its cast and crew, and the Third Reich's most notorious fictional expression of policy. In German with English subtitles. 100m/B VHS. GE Ferdinand Marian, Werner Krauss, Heinrich George, Kristina Soderbaum, Eugene Klopfer; **D:** Veit Harlan.

Judas Kiss ✗✗½ 1998 (R) Coco (Gugino) and her lover Junior (Baker-Denny) kidnap New Orleans exec Ben Dyson (Wise), but during the transaction a woman who turns out to be Patty Hornbeck (Penberthy), the wife of a powerful Senator (Holbrook). Assigned to the case are detective David Friedman (Rickman) and FBI agent Sadie Hawkins (Thompson) and their investigation uncovers some secrets, including the fact that Patty and the kidnapped Dyson were having an affair. Uneven crime drama with an interesting cast. 108m/C VHS, Emma Thompson, Alan Rickman, Carla Gugino, Simon Baker, Hal Holbrook, Gil Bellows, Til Schweiger, Greg Wise, Lisa Eichhorn, Beverly Penberthy; **D:** Sebastian Gutierrez; **W:** Sebastian Gutierrez; **C:** James Chressanthis; **M:** Christopher Young.

The Judas Project: The Ultimate Encounter ✗½ 1994 (PG-13) Religious fantasy finds Jesse better fitting corruption and pseudo-religious figures in a fight to save a violent and decaying world. But Jesse's destroyed by his

Ju-On: The Grudge ✗✗ The Grudge 2003 This is the third in the Shimizu's Japanese horror series, following "Ju-On: The Grudge" and "Jun-On 2: The Curse 2," which all revolve around (in a convoluted manner) a horrific event occurring in the same house. Social worker Rika (Okina) discovers her elderly patient mute, terrified, and alone. Then Rika finds a ghostly boy hiding in a closet—the victim of previous violence. Premise is that great rage leaves an evil presence behind, which drives new inhabitants mad and causes them to commit more acts of violence, leaving more evil behind. Or something like that. Lots of interlocking flashbacks and intermittent shocks that great subtitles. The 2004 American remake, "The Grudge," holds no surprises. 92m/C VHS, DVD. JP Megumi Okina, Misaki Ito, Yuya Ozeki, Takako Fuji; **D:** Takashi Shimizu; **W:** Takashi Shimizu; **C:** Tokusho Kikumura; **M:** Shiro Sato.

Jude ✗✗✗ Jude the Obscure 1996 (R) Engrossing retelling of Thomas Hardy's depressing 1896 novel "Jude the Obscure," set in his fictional Wessex. Country stonemason Jude (Eccleston) hopes to improve his impoverished lot in life by becoming a student at Christminster University. But first he's distracted into an unwise marriage with lively Arabella (Griffiths), who soon leaves him, and then into an ill-fated romance with his capricious cousin Sue Bridesehead (Winslet). Class and societal barriers prove impossible for the couple to overcome and lead to a shocking tragedy. Hardy's book was so badly received by critics that he never wrote another novel and stuck to poetry for the rest of his life. 123m/C VHS, DVD. GB Christopher Eccleston, Kate Winslet, Liam Cunningham, Rachel Griffiths; **D:** Michael Winterbottom; **W:** Hossain Amini; **C:** Eduardo Serra; **M:** Adrian Johnston.

Jude the Obscure ✗✗½ 1971 Thomas Hardy's last novel is a tragic, bleak story of mismatched lovers and blighted ambitions. Jude is a poor stonemason whose dream is to get a proper education and marry his beloved cousin. Failing to get into Oxford he is seduced by a farm girl, whom he marries and fathers a child by (a gnome-like creature named "Father Time"). Meanwhile, his cousin marries a schoolteacher who disgusts her. Finally, the two thwarted lovers marry, only to find themselves living in poverty and hopelessness. After this novel (said to be Hardy's favorite), he devoted the rest of his long life to poetry. On three cassettes. 262m/C VHS, DVD. GB Robert Powell, Daphne Heard, Alex Marshall, John Franklyn-Robbins, Fiona Walker; **D:** Hugh David; **W:** Harry Green. TV

Judex ✗✗½ 1964 Judex, a sensitive cloaked hero-avenger, fights master criminal gangs. In French with English subtitles. Remake of the silent French serial. 103m/B VHS. FR IT Channing Pollock, Francine Berge, Jacques Jouanneau; **D:** Georges Franju; **M:** Maurice Jarre.

The Judge ✗✗ 1949 A courtroom crime-drama cloaked about the consequences of infidelity. A lawyer sends an acquitted hit man to kill his wife and her lover. Things go amiss and the lawyer winds up dead? 69m/B VHS. Milburn Stone, Katherine DeMille, Paul Guilfoyle, Jonathan Hale; **D:** Elmer Clifton.

Judge & Jury ✗✗½ 1996 (R) Convicted killer Joseph Miller (Keith) dies in the electric chair but then manages to return from the dead to get revenge. So how do you kill someone who's already dead? Well, Michael Silvana (Kove) will have to find a way to send Miller back where he belongs. 98m/C VHS, DVD. David Keith, Martin Kove, Laura Johnson, Thomas Ian Nicholas, Paul Koslo; **D:** John Eyres; **W:** John Eyres, John Clarke-t, Amanda I. Kirpaur; **C:** Bob Paone; **M:** Johnathon Flood. VIDEO

The Judge and the Assassin ✗✗✗½ Le Juge et L'assassin 1975 Intriguing courtroom drama. A prejudiced judge has his values chal- lenged when he must decide if a child-kill- er is insane or not. The relationship that develops between the judge and the killer is the film's focus. Excellent direction by Tavernier. In French with English subtitles. 130m/C VHS. FR Philippe Noiret, Michel Galabru, Isabelle Huppert, Jean-Claude Brialy, Yves Robert, Renee Faure; **D:** Bertrand Tavernier; **W:** Bertrand Tavernier, Jean Aurenche, Pierre Bost; **C:** Pierre William Glenn; **M:** Philippe Sarde. Cesar '77: Writing, Score.

Judge Dredd ✗✗ 1995 (R) Futuris- tic lawman Dredd (Stallone) acts as cop, judge, jury, and executioner; is framed for murder by his "brother" Rico (Assante), a renegade misfit. With the help of a female Judge (Lane) and an ex- con (Schneider), Dredd fights to clear his name and save the people of Mega City One. Big names, big bangs, big budget— big disappointment. Dialogue makes "Rambo" sound like Shakespeare, and the choppy, convoluted plot doesn't help.

own disciple, Jude. Sound familiar? (There's even a crucifixion scene.) 93m/C VHS, DVD. John O'Bannon, Ramy Zada, Richard Herd; **D:** James H. Barden; **C:** Bryan England

Jude the Obscure The source comic book has been a cult favorite in England for 20 years. 96m/C Diane Lane, Rob Schneider, Joan Chen, Jurgen Prochnow, Max von Sydow; **D:** Danny Cannon; **W:** Steven E. de Souza, William Wisher; **C:** Adrian Biddle; **M:** Alan Silvestri.

Judge Horton and the Scottsboro Boys ✗✗✗½ 1976 A courtroom drama focusing on a famous 1931 trial. A courageous judge must battle the South in the case of nine black men charged with gang-raping two white women. 100m/C VHS, Arthur Hill, Vera Miles, Ken Kercheval, Suzanne Lederer, Tom Ligon; **D:** Fielder Cook. TV

Judge Priest ✗✗✗ 1934 Small- town judge in the old South stirs up the place with stinging humor and common- sense observances as he tangles with prejudices and civil injustices. Funny, warm slice-of-life is occasionally defeated by racist characterizations. Ford remade it later as "The Sun Shines Bright." Taken from the Irvin S. Cobb stories. 80m/B VHS, DVD. Will Rogers, Stepin Fetchit, Anita Louise, Henry B. Walthall; **D:** John Ford.

The Judge Steps Out ✗✗½ 1949 Pleasant, light comedy about a hen- pecked, Bostonian judge who decides he's had enough and heads for balmy Ca- lifornia. There he finds a job in a restau- rant and, more importantly, a sympathetic friend in its female owner. He soon finds himself falling for the woman, and realizes he faces an important decision. 91m/B VHS. Alexander Knox, Ann Sothern, George Tobias, Sharyn Moffett, Florence Bates, Frieda Inescort, Myrna Dell, Ian Wolfe, H.B. Warner; **D:** Boris Ing- ster.

The Judgement ✗✗ / Fak Al-Fak 2004 Slow-moving, Thai Buddhist story from first-time director Thongsang is likely to appeal to cinephiles only. Novice monk Fak (Yaowananon) returns to his isolated village for his ailing father, whom the flick turns from a dark road after dad dies and the self-righteous villagers get increasingly suspicious over the relation- ship between Fak and his female in-laws. Far from being the comedy it first seems, the discovers has married young and a beautiful Somson (Kongmalai). The villag- ers all think she's crazy and Somson doesn't help matters by promptly flirting with Fak, whose vows include chastity. Louisiana parish. When they find out their son is not the first victim, and other fami- lies have been coerced into silence, they vow to fight back. Tasteful treatment of a real court case. 89m/C VHS, DVD. TH Pitisak Yaowananon, Theedisak Yaemniyon; **D:** Pant- ham Thongsang; **W:** Somkiat Withuranich; **C:** Wi- san Jiraaungkoonsakun; **M:** Hualampong Riddim.

Judgment ✗✗✗ 1990 (PG-13) A devout Catholic couple are shocked to learn that their young son has been mo- lested by the popular priest of their small town. Excellent performances throughout, especially by Dietrich and Garland. Considers to what extent an inci- dividual may be held accountable for ac- tions committed under orders of a superior officer. Consuming account of the Holo- caust and WWII; deeply moving and pow- erful. Based on a "Playhouse 90" TV pro- gram. 178m/B VHS, DVD. Spencer Tracy, Burt Lancaster, Montgomery Clift, Maximilian Schell, Judy Garland, Marlene Dietrich, William Shatner, Edward Binns, Werner Klemper- er, Torben Meyer, Alan Baxter, Ray Teal, Karl Swenson; **D:** Stanley Kramer; **W:** Abby Mann; **C:** Ernest Laszlo; **M:** Ernest Gold. Oscars '61: Actor (Schell), Adapt. Screenplay; Golden Globes '62: Actor—Drama

Judgment at Nuremberg ✗✗✗ 1961 It's 1948 and a group of high-level Nazis are on trial for war crimes. Chief Justice Tracy must resist political pressures as he presides over the trials.

Heng **C:** Gu Changwei, Yang Lun; **M:** Xia Ru-jin, Jiping Zhao.

Schneider provides a rare, bright spot while acting circles around Sly, who hoped (in vain) that the project would provide him

(Schell), Director (Kramer); N.Y. Film Critics '61: Actor (Schell), Screenplay.

Judgment Day 🦴 1988 (PG-13) Four college buddies pick the wrong New England town for their vacation. It seems that the town made a deal with the Devil in 1689 to save themselves from the plague, and now the Dark Master is here to collect. 93m/C VHS. Kenneth McLeod, David Anthony Smith, Monte Markham, Gloria Hayes, Peter Mark Richman, Cesar Romero; **D:** Ferde Grofe Jr.

Judgment Day 🦴🦴 1999 (R) A meteor collides with an asteroid in deep space and if fragments from the mishap should hit Earth, it's goodbye planet. One scientist has an idea how to prevent disaster but he's kidnapped by a cult leader who thinks the planet's doom is foretold. Now the government has to get the scientist back before it's too late. 90m/C VHS, DVD. Mario Van Peebles, Ice-T, Suzy Amis, Tommy (Tiny) Lister, Coolio; **D:** John Terlesky; **W:** William Carson; **C:** Maximo Munzi; **M:** Joseph Williams. **VIDEO**

Judgment in Berlin 🦴🦴 *Escape to Freedom* 1988 (PG) East German family hijacks a U.S. airliner into West Germany, and then must stand trial in Berlin before a troubled American judge. Based on a true 1978 incident and the book by Herbert J. Stern. 92m/C VHS, DVD. Martin Sheen, Sam Wanamaker, Max Gail, Sean Penn, Heinz Hoenig, Carl Lumbly, Max Volkert Martens, Harris Yulin, Jutta Speidel, Juerger Heimich; **D:** Leo Penn; **W:** Joshua Sinclair; **M:** Peter Goldtool.

Judgment Night 🦴🦴 1993 (R) Four macho buddies on their way to a boxing match detour a highway traffic jam via surface streets and find themselves witnesses to a murder. The rest of their guys'-night-out is spent trying to escape a gloomy ghetto and determined killer (played convincingly by Leary). All of the action takes place after dark on the streets and in the sewers and, subsequently, the scenes are extremely dark with only a burnt orange lighting. Lots of action and a little oomph. Based on a story by Lewis Collick and Jere Cunningham. 109m/C VHS, DVD. Emilio Estevez, Cuba Gooding Jr., Stephen Dorff, Denis Leary, Jeremy Piven, Peter Greene; **D:** Stephen Hopkins; **W:** Lewis Collick; **C:** Peter Levy; **M:** Alan Silvestri.

Judicial Consent 🦴🦴 1/2 1994 Gwen Warwick (Bedelia) is an accomplished criminal court judge with a bland husband (Patton) and a lot of unfulfilled desires. At least one desire is taken care of when Gwen succumbs to the charms of handsome law clerk Martin (Wirth). Then her colleague Charles (Coleman) is murdered and all the evidence points to Gwen. She knows she's been set up but can Gwen prove her innocence? Familiar plot, good performances although Patton gets stuck in an underwritten role. 101m/C VHS. Bonnie Bedelia, Dabney Coleman, Billy Wirth, Will Patton, Lisa Blount; **D:** William Bindley; **W:** William Bindley; **M:** Christopher Young.

Judith of Bethulia 🦴🦴🦴 1914 A young widow uses her charm and wits to save her city from attack by the Assyrians. Based on the Apocrypha, this is the last film Griffith directed for Biograph. It was re-released as "Her Condoned Sin" in 1971, including two reels of Griffith's outtakes. 65m/B VHS. Blanche Sweet, Henry B. Walthall, Mae Marsh, Robert "Bobbie" Harron, Lillian Gish, Dorothy Gish, Kate Bruce, Harry Carey Sr.; **D:** D.W. Griffith; **W:** D.W. Griffith.

Judy Berlin 🦴🦴 1/2 1999 It's a school day in the placid suburb of Babylon, Long Island. Teacher Sue (Barrie) likes to flirt with weary principal Arthur (Dishy) who has a high-maintenance wife, Alice (Kahn), and a mopey grown son, David (Harnick), whose homecoming visit has gone on too long. Sue has her own offspring problems with sunnily ditsy, aspiring actress daughter Judy (Falco). Then Judy and David meet cute and a solar eclipse seems to inspire strange behavior. 97m/B VHS. Barbara Barrie, Bob (Robert) Dishy, Edie Falco, Aaron Harnick, Madeline Kahn, Carlin Glynn, Julie Kavner, Anne Meara; **D:** Eric Mendelsohn; **W:** Eric Mendelsohn; **C:** Jeffrey Seckendorf; **M:** Michael Nicholas. Sundance '99: Director (Mendelsohn).

...er, filmed in high-definition video and then transferred to film stock, it has a very different look and feel from other films of the genre. Intriguing and engaging mystery of the time, slow moving and confusing some of the time, it ultimately challenges but fails adequately to reward the viewer. 98m/C VHS. Kathleen Turner, Sting, Gabriel Byrne, Gabriele Ferzetti, Angela Goodwin; **D:** Peter Del Monte; **W:** Joe Minion, Sandro Petraglia, Silvia Napolitano; **C:** Giuseppe Rotunno; **M:** Maurice Jarre.

Julia Has Two Lovers 🦴🦴 1991 (R) Minimalist comedy-drama about a woman torn between two men—her dull fiance and a mysterious phone caller. Mostly a long phone conversation; don't expect blistering action. 87m/C VHS. Daphna Kastner, David Duchovny, David Charles; **D:** Bashar Shbib.

Julia Misbehaves 🦴🦴🦴 1948 Charming comedy that has Garson returning to ex-husband Pidgeon and daughter Taylor after an 18-year absence. Taylor is about to be married at a chateau in France and wants Garson to be there. While traveling to France from England, Garson encounters a bunch of colorful circus characters who are taking their act to Paris. Wonderful slapstick scenes give the stars a chance to have some real fun. Based on the novel "The Nutmeg Tree" by Margery Sharp. 99m/B VHS. Greer Garson, Walter Pidgeon, Peter Lawford, Cesar Romero, Elizabeth Taylor, Lucile Watson, Nigel Bruce, Mary Boland, Reginald Owen, Veda Ann Borg, Joi Lansing; **D:** Jack Conway.

Julian Po 🦴🦴 1/2 *The Tears of Julian Po* 1997 (PG-13) Nondescript bookkeeper Julian Po (Slater) has his car break down near an isolated mountain community and immediately comes under suspicion when he checks into the local boarding house, which never gets any guests. And the next day Julian's car has vanished, stranding him in nowherestown. The locals become convinced he's a hit man and demand explanations. Julian unexpectedly blurts out that the only person he's planning to kill is himself. Immediately the center of attention, Julian becomes confessor to everyone's darkest secrets and a recipient of their constant kindnesses but since he really doesn't intend to off himself, he's also got some unexpected problems. 82m/C VHS, DVD. Christian Slater, Robin Tunney, Michael Parks, Frankie Faison, Harve Presnell, Allison Janney, Cherry Jones, LaTanya Richardson Jackson, Dina Spybey, Zeljko Ivanek; **D:** Alan Wade; **W:** Alan Wade; **C:** Bernd Heinl; **M:** Patrick Williams.

Julien Donkey-boy 🦴🦴 1999 (R) Harmony Korine's story of a schizophrenic young man and his disturbed family is the first American movie to be filmed using the principles of the restrictive Danish filmmaking method known as Dogma '95. Apparently, there must be some kind of restriction on the plot and narrative as well, because the audience is merely shown disturbing images of the mentally ill Julien (Bremner), his pregnant sister Pearl (Sevigny), his jock brother Chris (Neumann) and their abusive father (Herzog). Largely improvised and shot using hand-held digital video cameras, this unsettling project is for the cinematically adventurous only. 101m/C VHS, DVD. Ewen Bremner, Chloe Sevigny, Werner Herzog, Evan Neumann, Joyce Korine, Chrissy Kobylak, Alvin Law; **D:** Harmony Korine; **W:** Harmony Korine; **C:** Anthony Dod Mantle.

Juliet of the Spirits 🦴🦴🦴 *Giulietta Degli Spiriti* 1965 Fellini uses the sparse story of a woman (Fellini's real-life wife) deliberating over her husband's possible infidelity to create a wild, often senseless surrealistic film. With a highly symbolic interplay of fantasy and reality, Fellini's fantasy logic and complex imagery elucidates the inner life of a modern woman. In Italian with English subtitles. 142m/C VHS, DVD. IT Giulietta Masina, Valentina Cortese, Sylva Koscina, Mario Pisu, Sandra Milo, Caterina Boratto, Valeska Gert; **D:** Federico Fellini; **W:** Federico Fellini, Tullio Pinelli, Ennio Flaiano, Brunello Rondi; **C:** Gianni Di Venanzo; **M:** Nino Rota. N.Y. Film Critics '65: Foreign Film.

Juggernaut 🦴 1937 Not the classic disaster film of the '70s. A young woman hires a sinister doctor (Karloff) to murder her wealthy husband. The doctor, who happens to be insane, does away with the husband and then goes on a poisoning spree. Seems to drag on forever. 64m/B VHS, DVD. Boris Karloff, Mona Goya, Arthur Margetson, Joan Wyndham, Anthony Ireland; **D:** Henry Edwards; **W:** Cyril Campion; **C:** Sydney Blythe, William Luff; **M:** W.L. Trytel.

Juggernaut 🦴🦴🦴 1974 (PG-13) Well-done drama about a doomed luxury liner. A madman plants bombs aboard a cruise ship and mocks the crew about his plan over the wireless. The countdown ensues, while the bomb experts struggle to find the explosives. Suspenseful with good direction. 109m/C VHS, DVD. GB Richard Harris, Omar Sharif, David Hemmings, Anthony Hopkins, Shirley Knight, Ian Holm, Roy Kinnear, Freddie Jones; **D:** Richard Lester; **W:** Richard De Koker; **C:** Gerry Fisher; **M:** Ken Thorne.

Juice 🦴🦴 1/2 1992 (R) Day-to-day street life of four Harlem youths as they try to earn respect ("juice") in their neighborhood. Q, an aspiring deejay, is talked into a robbery by his friends but everything takes a turn for the worse when one of the others, Bishop, gets hold of a gun. The gritty look and feel of the drama comes naturally to Dickerson in his directorial debut. Prior to his first film, Dickerson served as cinematographer for Spike Lee's "Do the Right Thing" and "Jungle Fever." 95m/C VHS, DVD. Omar Epps, Jermaine "Huggy" Hopkins, Tupac Shakur, Khalil Kain, Cindy Herron, Vincent Laresca, Samuel L. Jackson; **D:** Ernest R. Dickerson; **W:** Gerard Brown, Ernest R. Dickerson; **C:** Larry Banks.

Juke Joint 🦴🦴 1/2 1947 "Amos 'n Andy" star Spencer Williams acted in and directed this tale of two men who arrive in Hollywood with only 25 cents between them. Features an all-black cast and musical numbers. 60m/B VHS, DVD. Spencer Williams Jr., Judy Jones, Mantan Moreland; **D:** Spencer Williams Jr.

Jules and Jim 🦴🦴🦴🦴 *Jules et Jim* 1962 Beautiful film with perfect casting, particularly Moreau. Spanning from 1912 to 1932, it is the story of a friendship between two men and their 20-year love for the same woman. Werner is the shy German Jew and Serre the fun-loving Frenchman, who meet as students. The two men discover and woo the bohemian, destructive Moreau, although it is Werner she marries. After WWI, the friends are reunited but the marriage of Moreau and Werner is in trouble and she has an affair with Serre, which leads to tragedy for all three. Adapted from the novel by Henri-Pierre Roche. In French with English subtitles. 104m/B VHS, DVD. FR Jeanne Moreau, Oskar Werner, Henri Serre, Marie DuBois, Vanna Urbino; **D:** Francois Truffaut; **W:** Jean Gruault, Francois Truffaut; **C:** Raoul Coutard; **M:** Georges Delerue.

Julia 🦴🦴🦴 1/2 1977 (PG) The story recounted in Lillian Hellman's fictional memoir "Pentimento." Fonda plays Hellman as she risks her life smuggling money into Germany during WWII for the sake of Julia, her beloved childhood friend (Redgrave), who is working in the Resistance. All cast members shine in their performances; watch for Streep in her screen debut. 118m/C VHS, DVD. Jane Fonda, Jason Robards Jr., Vanessa Redgrave, Maximilian Schell, Hal Holbrook, Rosemary Murphy, Meryl Streep, Lisa Pelikan, John Glover, Mark Metcalf, Lambert Wilson; **D:** Fred Zinnemann; **W:** Alvin Sargent; **C:** Douglas Slocombe; **M:** Georges Delerue. Oscars '77: Adapt. Screenplay, Support. Actor (Robards), Support. Actress (Redgrave); British Acad. '78: Actress (Fonda), Film, Screenplay, Support. Actress—Drama (Fonda), Support. Actress (Redgrave); Golden Globes '78: Actress—Drama (Fonda), Support. Actress (Redgrave); L.A. Film Critics '77: Cinematog., Support. Actor (Robards), Support. Actress (Redgrave); N.Y. Film Critics '77: Support. Actress (Redgrave); Writers Guild '77: Adapt. Screenplay.

Julia and Julia 🦴🦴 1/2 1987 (R) A beautiful American woman in Trieste is tossed between two seemingly parallel dimensions, one in which her husband died six years earlier in a car crash, and the other in which he didn't. A purposefully obscure Italian-made psychological thrill-

Julius Caesar 🦴🦴 1/2 1953 All-star version of the Shakespearean tragedy, heavily acclaimed and deservedly so. Working directly from the original Shakespeare, director Mankiewicz produced a lifelike, yet poetic production. 121m/B VHS, DVD. James Mason, Marlon Brando, John Gielgud, Greer Garson, Deborah Kerr, Louis Calhern, Edmond O'Brien, George Macready, John Hoyt, Michael Pate; **D:** Joseph L. Mankiewicz; **W:** Joseph L. Mankiewicz; **C:** Joseph Ruttenberg; **M:** Miklos Rozsa. Oscars '53: Art Dir./Set Dec., B&W; Natl. Bd. of Review '53: Actor (Mason).

Julius Caesar 🦴🦴 1970 Subpar adaptation of the Shakespeare play about political greed and corruption within the Roman Empire. 116m/C VHS, DVD. GB Charlton Heston, John Gielgud, Jason Robards Jr., Richard Chamberlain, Diana Rigg; **D:** Stuart Burge.

July Group 🦴 1/2 1981 A Quaker family's peaceful existence is threatened when kidnappers invade their home and hold them for ransom. 75m/C VHS. CA Nicholas (Nick) Campbell, Maury Chaykin, Ken Pogue, Tom Butler; **D:** George McCowan; **C:** Brian R.R. Hebb; **M:** Samuel Matlovsky. **TV**

Jumanji 🦴🦴 1/2 1995 (PG) For the past 26 years Alan Parish (Williams) has been stuck in the netherworld of Jumanji, a jungle-themed board game that sucks players into its alternate universe. When unsuspecting youngsters Judy (Dunst) and Peter (Pierce) happen upon the game and begin to play, they release Williams and a jungle full of rampaging beasts from the game and into the present. Loosely based on Chris Van Allsburg's children's book, the film version relies too heavily on cutting-edge special effects to make up for a thin story. Many of the creatures and effects are utterly too bizarre and unsettling for younger audiences. With a $65 million pricetag, Jumanji is definitely a roll of the dice. 104m/C VHS, DVD, UMD. Robin Williams, Kirsten Dunst, Bonnie Hunt, Bradley Michael Pierce, Bebe Neuwirth, Jonathan Hyde, David Alan Grier, Adam Hann-Byrd; **D:** Joe Johnston; **W:** Jonathan Hensleigh; **C:** Thomas Ackerman; **M:** James Horner.

Jump In! 🦴🦴 1/2 2007 Relentlessly chipper Disney Channel movie finds Izzy (Bleu) taking up boxing to please his dad, a former Golden Gloves champ. When his sister takes Izzy to a double-dutch competition, he's surprised to see cute girl-next-door Mary (Palmer) on a team. Mary convinces Izzy to take his moves to her sport when they need a replacement jumper, but the guy's worried about not appearing cool at school. But he soon learns, of course, that first you have to be true to yourself. 85m/C DVD. Corbin Bleu, Keke Palmer, David Reivers, Shanica Knowles, Patrick Johnson Jr.; **D:** Paul Hoen; **W:** Doreen Spicer, Regina Hicks, Karin Gist; **C:** David Makin; **M:** Frank Fitzpatrick. **CABLE**

Jumper 🦴 1/2 2008 (PG-13) Picked-on kid David (Christensen) discovers that he has the ability to teleport at will, and he uses his gift to flit around the world, rob banks, and basically do what he pleases, including pursuing his childhood crush Millie (Bilson). Enter Roland (Jackson), a member of a mysterious group that hunts and kills "jumpers" like David. Heavy action fails to cover up the weak plot and David's brattiness. Loosely based on a series of young adult novels by Steven Gould. 88m/C DVD. US Hayden Christensen, Jamie Bell, Samuel L. Jackson, Rachel Bilson, Diane Lane, Michael Rooker, AnnaSophia Robb, Max Thieriot; **D:** Doug Liman; **W:** David S. Goyer, Simon Kinberg, Jim Uhls; **C:** Barry Peterson; **M:** John Powell.

Jumpin' at the Boneyard 🦴🦴 1992 Gritty family drama about the trials of two dispossessed brothers, set on the streets of New York. Deeply depressed, out-of-work, divorced Manny hates his recently deceased father, adores his mother, and is estranged from his younger brother, Danny. Danny is a scared crack addict who's supported by a hooker/girlfriend. The two brothers reunite for a trip to their scarred past when Danny tries to rob his brother's apartment to get dope money. Manny starts to believe that the only way to redeem his own life is to get his brother into a rehab program. Good acting helps to overcome some script weaknesses but this is one depressing movie. **107m/C VHS, DVD.** Tim Roth, Alexis Arquette, Danira Vance, Samuel L. Jackson, Kathleen Chesterd, Luis Guzman; **D:** Jeff Stanzler; **W:** Jeff Stanzler.

Jumpin' Jack Flash 🐾🐾½
1986 (R) A bank worker is humorously embroiled in international espionage when her computer terminal picks up distress signals from a British agent in Russia. Marshall's directing debut. Good performances from a fun cast and a particularly energetic effort by Goldberg are held back by an average and predictable script. **98m/C VHS, DVD.** Whoopi Goldberg, Stephen Collins, Carol Kane, Annie Potts, Jonathan Pryce, James Belushi, Jon Lovitz, Jon Wood, Roscoe Lee Browne, Tracey Ullman, Phil Hartman, Tracy Reiner, Paxton Whitehead, Jane Sheridan, Garry Marshall, Peter Michael Goetz; **D:** Penny Marshall; **W:** David Franzoni; **C:** Jan De Bont; **M:** Thomas Newman.

The Junction Boys 🐾🐾
2002 A look at one phase in the career of legendary tough-guy college football coach Paul "Bear" Bryant (well-played by Berenger). Film star's in 1954 with Bryant's arrival at Texas A&M as he drives his players, eventually known as the Junction Boys, to make the team. (Drama sticks to football practice not competition.) The focus is on three key players (who, of course, have personal problems to overcome)—Skeet, Keeler (Humphrys), Claude Gearheart (Kwanten), and Johnny Haynes (Curry). **93m/C VHS, DVD.** Tom Berenger, Bernard Curry, Fletcher Humphrys, Ryan Kwanten, Nick Nicholas; Tate, Mark Lee, Andy Anderson; **D:** Mike Robe; **W:** Mike Robe; **C:** Stephen F. Andrich; **M:** Steve Dorff.

Junction 88 🐾
1947 Early all-black musical. Shock full of great dancing and hot music. **60m/B VHS.** Noble Sissie, Bob Howard, Dewey "Pigmeat" Markham, J. Augustus Smith; **D:** George P. Quigley; **C:** John Visconti; **M:** J. Augustus Smith.

June Bride 🐾🐾🐾
1948 Fast-paced and entertaining comedy in which Davis and Montgomery are teamed up as magazine writers. A hilarious battle of the sexes erupts as they're sent to Indiana to do a feature story on June brides. Look for Debbie Reynolds in her film debut. **97m/B VHS.** Bette Davis, Robert Montgomery, Fay Bainter, Betty Lynn, Tom Tully, Barbara Bates, Jerome Cowan, Mary Wickes, Debbie Reynolds; **D:** Bretaigne Windust; **W:** Ranald MacDougall.

June Night 🐾🐾
1940 A woman who was victimized by a shooting incident cannot escape the public eye due to her former promiscuous behavior. In Swedish with English subtitles. **90m/C VHS, DVD, SW.** Ingrid Bergman, Marianne Lofgren, Gunnar Sjoberg, Olof Widgren; **D:** Per Lindberg; **W:** Ragnar Hylten-Cavallius; **C:** Ake Dahlquist; **M:** Jules Sylvain.

Junebug 🐾🐾🐾
2005 (R) Sophisticated Chicago art dealer Madeleine (Davidtz) has impulsively married enigmatic, ex-small town North Carolinian George (Nivola) and is finally about to meet her in-laws. George's homecoming is reluctant at best; his mom Peg (Weston), is a busybody who immediately dislikes her new daughter-in-law; dad Eugene (Wilson) lives in his own quiet world; younger brother Johnny (McKenzie) is moody and resentful; and only his young and very pregnant bride Ashley (Adams) is happy and welcoming. It's a cultural and familial clash without being condescending. Pic is stolen by the delightful Adams as a sweetly wise chatterbox. **107m/C VHS, DVD.** Embeth Davidtz, Alessandro Nivola, Amy Adams, Celia Weston, Benjamin McKenzie, Scott Wilson, Frank Hoyt Taylor, Joanne Pankow; **D:** Phil Morrison; **W:** Angus MacLachlan; **C:** Peter Donahue; **M:** Yo La Tengo; Ind. Spirit '06: Support. Actress (Adams); Natl. Soc. Film Critics '05: Support. Actress (Adams); Broadcast Film Critics '06: Support. Actress (Adams).

Jungle 🐾
1952 A princess and an American adventurer lead an expedition into the Indian wilds to discover the source of recent elephant attacks. **74m/B VHS.** Rod Cameron, Cesar Romero, Marie Windsor; **D:** William Berke; **C:** Clyde De Vinna.

Jungle Assault 🐾
1989 Two Vietnam vets with nothing left to lose are called back into the bloodiest action of their lives. Their assignment is to locate and destroy a terrorist base and bring back an American general's brainwashed daughter. **86m/C VHS.** William (Bill) Smith, Ted Prior, William Zipp; **D:** David A. Prior.

The Jungle Book 🐾🐾 Rudyard Kipling's *Jungle Book* 1942 A lavish version of Rudyard Kipling's stories about Mowgli, the boy raised by wolves in the jungles of India. **109m/C VHS, DVD.** Sabu, Joseph Calleia, Rosemary DeCamp, Ralph Byrd, John Qualen; **D:** Zoltan Korda; **W:** Laurence Stallings; **C:** Lee Garmes; **M:** Miklos Rozsa.

The Jungle Book 🐾🐾🐾
1967 Based on Kipling's classic, a young boy raised by wolves must choose between his jungle friends and human "civilization." Along the way he meets a variety of jungle characters including zany King Louie, kind-hearted Baloo, wise Baghera and the evil Shere Khan. Great, classic songs including "Trust in Me," "I Wanna Be Like You," and Oscar-nominated "Bare Necessities." Last Disney feature overseen by Uncle Walt himself and a must for kids of all ages. **78m/C VHS, DVD.** **D:** Wolfgang Reitherman; **V:** Phil Harris, Sebastian Cabot, Louis Prima, George Sanders, Sterling Holloway, J. Pat O'Malley, Verna Felton, Darlene Carr.

The Jungle Book 2 🐾🐾
2003 (G) Sequel to the classic Disney version, it picks up where the original left off. Mowgli (voice by Osment) is now living in the village with a warm-hearted human family. He misses the excitement of the jungle and sneaks back to his old pal, Baloo the Bear (a decent enough Goodman, but the original voice of Phil Harris is a tough act to follow). Two of the village children follow him and many adventures ensue. Although the animation is quite good, the plot merely recycles old material, even going so far as reprising the classic song "Bare Necessities" three times. Adults will find the movie tiresome, but the younger set won't be as picky. **72m/C VHS, DVD.** **D:** Steve Trenbirth; **W:** Karl Geurs; **M:** Joel McNeely; **V:** John Goodman, Haley Joel Osment, Mae Whitman, Tony Jay, Connor Funk, Bob Joles, John Rhys-Davies, Phil Collins.

Jungle Boy 🐾🐾
1996 (PG) After being lost in the jungles of India, Manling (Seth) is raised by a monkey and an elephant. Able to communicate with the animals, Manling uses his talents to defeat the evil poacher, Hook (Roberts), who's out to steal a sacred statue. **88m/C VHS, DVD.** Asif Mohammed Seth, Jeremy Roberts, Lea Moreno; **D:** Allan Goldstein; **W:** Allen Goldstein, John Lawson, Damian Lee; **C:** Nicholas Josef von Sternberg.

Jungle Bride 🐾🐾½
1933 Three people are shipwrecked and one of them is a suspected murderer. **66m/B VHS, DVD.** Anita Page, Charles Starrett, Kenneth Thomson, Clarence Geldart; **D:** Harry Hoyt, Albert Kelley; **C:** Harry Jackson.

Jungle Captive 🐾½
1945 Second campy sequel to "Captive Wild Woman" following "Jungle Woman." Mad scientist Dr. Stendahl (Kruger) has been experimenting on bringing dead animals back to life and then attempting to make them human. He steals the body of an female ape (Lane) to practice on and kidnaps his human assistant, Ann (Ward), so she can "donate" her blood. The ape becomes a woman but still has the brain of an animal. This leads to violence. **64m/B VHS, DVD.** Vicky Lane, Amelita Ward, Rondo Hatton, Phil Brown, Jerome Cowan; **D:** Harold Young; **C:** Maury Gertsman.

Jungle Drums of Africa 🐾 *Jungle Drums* 1953 Jungle adventures abound as Moore and Coates encounter the *Witch Doctor* 1953 and **Jungle Drums of Africa** and the *Witch Doctor* 1953 Jungle adventures abound as Moore and Coates encounter lions, wind tunnels, voodoo and enemy agents in deepest Africa. A 12-episode serial re-edited onto two cassettes. **167m/B VHS.** Clayton Moore, Phyllis Coates, Roy Glenn, John Cason; **D:** Fred Brannon.

Jungle Fever 🐾🐾🐾
1991 (R) Married black architect's affair with his white secretary provides the backdrop for a cold look at interracial love. Focuses more on the discomfort of friends and families than the intense world created by the lovers for themselves. Provides the quota of humor and fresh insight we expect from Lee, but none of the joyous sexuality experienced by the lovers in "She's Gotta Have It." In fact, Lee tells viewers that in interracial love is unnatural, never more than skin deep, never more than a blind obsession with the allure of the opposite race. Very fine cast but if you don't agree with Lee, a real disappointment in spite of his prodigious skills as a filmmaker. **131m/C VHS, DVD.** Michael Imperioli, Nicholas Turturro, Steven Randazzo, Joseph (Joe) D'Onofrio, Michael Badalucco, Debi Mazar, Gina Mastrogiacomo, Phyllis Stickney, Theresa Randle, Pamela Tyson, Rick Aiello, Miguel (Michael) Sandoval, Doug E. Doug, Queen Latifah, Wesley Snipes, Annabella Sciorra, John Turturro, Samuel L. Jackson, Ossie Davis, Ruby Dee, Lonette McKee, Anthony Quinn, Spike Lee, Halle Berry, Tyra Ferrell, Veronica Webb, Frank Vincent, Tim Robbins, Brad Dourif, Richard Edson; **D:** Spike Lee; **W:** Spike Lee; **C:** Ernest R. Dickerson; **M:** Terence Blanchard; N.Y. Film Critics '91: Support. Actor (Jackson).

Jungle Goddess 🐾½
1949 Two mercenaries set out for the reward offered for finding a wealthy heiress last seen in the jungles of Africa. **61m/B VHS, DVD.** George Reeves, Wanda McKay, Ralph Byrd, Armida; **D:** Lewis D. Collins.

Jungle Heat 🐾🐾½ *Dance of the Dwarfs* 1984 (PG) While searching for a pygmy tribe, an anthropologist and her pilot run into a pack of anthropoid mutants. **93m/C VHS.** Peter Fonda, Deborah Raffin; **D:** Gus Trikonis.

Jungle Hell 🐾🐾
1955 Sabu comes to the rescue of an Indian tribe being harassed by flying saucers, death rays and radioactive debris. **78m/B VHS.** Sabu, David Bruce, George E. Stone, K.T. Stevens; **D:** Norman A. Cerf.

Jungle Inferno 🐾 *Zamba, King of the Jungle* 1972 Nature boy, a fugitive from the government, fights lions, tigers and pursuing feds in this story of escape and survival. **90m/C VHS.** Daniele Vargas, Anthony Steffen, Brad Harris; **D:** Al Bitto Albertini; **W:** Bitto Albertini; **M:** Marcello Giombini.

Jungle Master 🐾 **1956** Noble British types hunt for Karzan, the jungle's number one guy, with the aid of a tribal priestess and a lovely photo-journalist. Must see for trash movie fans. **90m/C VHS.** John Kitzmiler, Simone Blondell; **D:** Mike Deem.

Jungle Patrol 🐾½ **1948** In 1943 New Guinea, a squadron of entrapped fliers are confronted with a beautiful USO entertainer. Romance and show tunes follow. **72m/B VHS.** Kristine Miller, Arthur Franz, Richard Jaeckel, Ross Ford, Tommy Noonan, Gene Reynolds; **D:** Joseph M. Newman.

Jungle Raiders 🐾½ *Leggenda Del Rubio Malese; Captain Yankee* 1985 (PG-13) An Indiana Jones-esque mercenary searches the steamy jungles of Malaysia for a valuable jewel, the Ruby of Gloom. **102m/C VHS.** Lee Van Cleef, Christopher Connelly, Marina Costa; **D:** Anthony M. Dawson.

Jungle Siren 🐾 **1942** Nazis in Africa try to foment rebellion amongst the black natives against the white residents. Crabbe and a white woman raised in the jungle set things right. **68m/B VHS, DVD.** Buster Crabbe, Evelyn Wahl, Milton Kibbee; **D:** Sam Newfield.

Jungle 2 Jungle 🐾🐾½ **1996 (PG)** Remake of French farce released as "Little Indian, Big City," changes little of the "wild child" premise. Workaholic Wall Streeter Michael Cromwell (Allen) decides to finalize the divorce from his long-estranged doctor wife, Patricia (Williams),

Junior 🐾🐾 **1994 (PG-13)** Out of the way women! Schwarzenegger trades the war room for a delivery room to experience the miracle of birth. As scientists, he and DeVito take a dip in the gene pool once again to test an anti-miscarriage drug. Thompson provides the egg and some surprisingly good physical comedy as the klutzy cryogenics expert who moves into their university digs. Every pregnancy cliche is explored as Schwarzenegger and DeVito bring the concept to term. Sorry, action fans...nothing blows up except Arnold. **109m/C VHS, DVD.** Arnold Schwarzenegger, Danny DeVito, Emma Thompson, Frank Langella, Pamela Reed, Judy Collins, James Eckhouse, Aida Turturro; **D:** Ivan Reitman; **W:** Kevin Wade, Chris Conrad; **C:** Adam Greenberg; **M:** James Newton Howard.

Junior woof! **1986** A raving, drooling lunatic cuts up girls with a chainsaw. **80m/C VHS.** Suzanne Delaurentis, Linda Singer, Jeremy Ruhford, Michael McKeever; **D:** Jim Hanley; **W:** Don Carmody, John Maxwell; **C:** Jean-Maurice de Ernsted; **M:** Allan Gerber.

Junior Army 🐾½ **1942** English refugee Freddie Hewlett (Bartholomew) saves brash Jimmie Fletcher (Halop) from juvenile delinquent Bushy Thomas (Hall) and the two wind up at the same military academy. Jimmie wants to become a pilot but doesn't take the grades and gets kicked out. Bushy reappears, in the company of a Nazi saboteur, and Freddie and Jimmie save the day. **70m/B VHS.** Freddie Bartholomew, Billy Halop, Huntz Hall, Bobby Jordan, Joseph Crehan, Don Beddoe, Peter Lawford, Rudolph Anders **L:** Lew Landers; **W:** Paul Gangelin; **C:** Charles E. Schoenbaum.

Junior Bonner 🐾🐾🐾 **1972 (PG)** A rowdy modern-day western about a young drifting rodeo star who decides to raise money for his father's new ranch by challenging a formidable bull. **100m/C VHS, DVD.** Steve McQueen, Robert Preston, Ida Lupino, Ben

who happens to have been ministering to a tribe in the Amazon rain forest for many years. He gets more than the divorce when he meets the 13-year-old son, Mimi-Siku (Huntington), he never knew he had. Although the boy speaks English, he's been raised as a tribal native, which causes quite a culture shock when he returns with Michael to the jungles of Manhattan. Of course the kid's more than a match for any situation. **105m/C VHS, DVD.** Tim Allen, Sam Huntington, Martin Short, JoBeth Williams, Lolita (David) Davidovich, David Ogden Stiers, Bob (Robert) Disny, Valerie Mahaffey, Leelee Sobieski, Luis Avalos, Frankie J. Galasso; **D:** John Pasquin; **W:** Bruce A. Evans, Raynold Gideon; **C:** Tony Pierce-Roberts; **M:** Michael Convertino.

Jungle Warriors 🐾½ **1984 (R)** Seven fashion models are abducted by a Peruvian cocaine dealer. To escape him, they must become Jungle Warriors, and does research on apes and has a female simian currently in his lab. The ape disappears and a young woman, Paula (Acquanetta), mysteriously appears. As you might guess, Paula and the ape are the same creature and a dangerous one at that. Follows by "Jungle Wild Woman" and is followed by "Captive Wild Woman" and that. Follows by "Jungle Captive" and no. **90m/C VHS.** J. Carol Naish, Acquanetta, Evelyn Ankers, Samuel S. Hinds, Lois Collier, Milburn Stone, Douglass Dumbrille; **D:** Reginald Le Borg; **W:** Bernard Schubert, Henry Sucher, Edward Dein; **C:** Jack Mackenzie.

Jungleground 🐾½ **1995 (R)** Jungleground is a urban wasteland controlled by rival gangs. Lt. Jake Cornel (Piper) gets caught in a shot-out when a sting operation goes bad and winds up before psychotic gang leader Odin. Odin offers him one chance—Cornel's going to be hunted in Jungleground's abandoned streets and if he can escape before dawn, he gets to live. **90m/C VHS, DVD.** CA Roddy Piper, Torri Higginson, Peter Williams; **D:** Don Allan; **W:** Michael Stokes; **C:** Gilles Corbeil; **M:** Varouje.

Jungle Woman 🐾½ **1944 (R)** Scientist Dr. Fletcher (Naish) is being tried for murder and relates his story in court. He

Junior 511

Johnson, Joe Don Baker, Barbara Leigh; *D:* Sam Peckinpah; *W:* Jeb Rosebrook; *C:* Lucien Ballard; *M:* Jerry Fielding.

Junior G-Men 1940 The Dead End Kids fight Fifth Columnists who are trying to sabotage America's war effort. Twelve episodes. 237m/B VHS, DVD: Billy Halop, Huntz Hall, Gabriel Dell, Bernard Punsley, Harris Berger, Hal E. Chester, Kenneth Howell, Kenneth Lundy; *D:* Ford Beebe, John Rawlins; *W:* Basil Dickey, George Plympton, Rex Taylor; *C:* Jerome Ash; *M:* Charles Previn.

Junior G-Men of the Air 1942 The Dead End Kids become teenage flyboys in this 12-episode serial adventure. 215m/B VHS, DVD: Billy Halop, Huntz Hall, Gene Reynolds, Lionel Atwill, Frank Albertson, Richard Lane, Gabriel Dell, Bernard Punsley, Frankie Darro, David Gorcey, Turhan Bey, Vinton (Hayworth) Haworth; *D:* Lewis D. Collins, Ray Taylor; *W:* George Plympton, Griffin Jay, Paul Huston; *C:* William Sickner.

Junior's Groove *The Planet of Junior Brown* 1997 (R) Young piano prodigy grows up in a tough neighbor with a caring mom, eccentric piano teacher, and a group of street-smart friends. Based on the novel by Virginia Hamilton. 91m/C VHS, DVD. Lynn Whitfield, Clark Johnson, Margot Kidder, Sarah Polley, Martin Villafana; *D:* Clement Virgo; *W:* Clement Virgo, Cameron Bailey; *C:* Jonathan Freeman; *M:* Christopher Dedrick. VIDEO

The Juniper Tree 1987 Based on a tale by the Brothers Grimm, this Icelandic curio finds sisters Margit (Bjork) and Katla (Bragadottir) fleeing across the remote countryside after their mother is burned at the stake for witchcraft. The sisters have their own special powers, which they turn on each other when they become romantic rivals over a young widower (Flygenring). 78m/B VHS, DVD. ⓘC Björk, Bryndis Petra Bragadottir, Vladimir Om Flygenring; *D:* Nietzchka Keene.

Junk Mail *Budbringeren* 1997 Grimy Oslo postman Roy (Skjaerstad) enjoys reading other people's mail, stalking Line, a deaf girl (Saether) on his route, and not washing. One day the girl leaves her keys in the mailbox, so Roy decides to have a look around, later saving her from a suicide attempt. During another of his "visits," Roy learns that Line is involved in a violent crime, along with a thug named Georg (Aske). Through a series of mistaken identities and coincidences, he becomes deeply involved in the proceedings. Skjaerstad's promising debut is quirky and painstaking in its attention to detail. 83m/C VHS. NO Robert Skjaerstad, Andrine Saether, Per Egil Aske, Eli Anne Linnestad; *D:* Pal Sletaune; *W:* Pal Sletaune, Jonny Halberg; *C:* Kjell Vassdal; *M:* Joachim Holbek.

The Junkman 1982 (R) Movie maker whose new film is about to be premiered is being chased by a mysterious killer. Promoted as "the ultimate car chase film" since the production used and destroyed over 150 automobiles. From the makers of "Gone in 60 Seconds." 97m/C VHS, DVD. H.B. Halicki, Christopher Stone, Susan Shaw, Hoyt Axton, Lynda Day George; *D:* H.B. Halicki.

Juno 2007 (PG-13) Ultra-sassy Juno (Page) realizes she may not know it all after she finds herself facing teenage motherhood, but has trouble following through after she's met with the childless yuppie couple Venessa (Garner) and Mark (Bateman) who are first in line to snatch up her baby. Note-perfect performances all around, especially by Page as the girl unwillingly rocketing into womanhood. Director Jason Reitman retains expert balance for this very smart, funny, offbeat, and touching story, which easily could've come out as lame teen comedy. 92m/C DVD. US Ellen Page, Michael Cera, Jennifer Garner, Jason Bateman, Allison Janney, J.K. Simmons, Olivia Thirlby; *D:* Jason Reitman; *W:* Diablo Cody; *C:* Eric Steelberg; *M:* Mateo Messina. Oscars '07: Orig. Screenplay; British Acad. '07: Orig. Screenplay; Ind. Spirit '08: Actress, Film, First Film, First Screenplay. Writers Guild '07: Orig. Screenplay.

Juno and the Paycock 1930 Perhaps if Hitchcock hadn't been so faithful to O'Casey this early effort would have been less stagey and more entertaining. In Dublin during the civil uprising, a poor family is torn apart when they receive news of an imminent fortune. Hitchcock's reported to have said that "drama is life with the dull bits left out," though here too many dull bits remain. 96m/B VHS, DVD. Sara Allgood, Edward Chapman, John Longden, John Laurie, Maire O'Neill; *D:* Alfred Hitchcock; *W:* Alfred Hitchcock; *Nar:* Barry Fitzgerald.

Jupiter's Darling 1955 This spoof of Hannibal (Keel) and Amytis (Williams) gravely misses the mark in making funny the world of the Roman Empire. Amytis has the job of distracting Hannibal from attacking the Eternal City, and does so through musical interludes and unfunny jokes. ♫ I Have A Dream; If This Be Slav'ry; I Never Trust A Woman; Hannibal's Victory March; Don't Let This Night Get Away; The Life Of An Elephant; Horatio's Narration. 96m/C Esther Williams, Howard Keel, George Sanders, Gower Champion, Marge Champion, Norma Varden, Richard Haydn, William Demarest, Douglass Dumbrille, Michael Ansara, Martha Wentworth, Chris Alcaide, William Tannen; *D:* George Sidney; *C:* Charles Rosher.

Jupiter's Thigh 1981 A madcap married pair of treasure-hunters honeymoon in Greece in search of an ancient statue's lost thigh. Available in French with English subtitles, or dubbed into English. 96m/C VHS. FR Annie Girardot, Philippe Noiret, Francis Perrin, Catherine Alric, Marc Dudicourt, Paulette Dubost; *D:* Philippe de Broca; *W:* Philippe de Broca, Michel Audiard.

Jurassic Park 1993 (PG-13) Crichton's spine-tingling thriller translates well (but not faithfully) due to its main attraction: realistic, rampaging dinosaurs. Genetically cloned from prehistoric DNA, all is well until they escape from their pens—smarter and less predictable than expected. Contrived plot and thin characters (except Goldblum), but who cares? The true stars are the dinos, an incredible combination of models and computer animation. Violent, suspenseful, and realistic with gory attack scenes. Not for small kids, though much of the marketing was aimed at them. At the time, Spielberg knocked his own "E.T." out of the box office top spot, making "JP" the highest grossing movie ever. The T-Rex has since been bested by an iceberg and Celine Dion. 127m/C VHS, DVD. Sam Neill, Laura Dern, Jeff Goldblum, Richard Attenborough, Bob Peck, Martin Ferrero, B.D. Wong, Joseph Mazzello, Ariana Richards, Samuel L. Jackson, Wayne Knight; *D:* Steven Spielberg; *W:* David Koepp, Michael Crichton; *C:* Dean Cundey; *M:* John Williams; *V:* Richard Kiley. Oscars '93: Sound, Sound FX Editing, Visual FX.

Jurassic Park 3 2001 (PG-13) Neill (who skipped JP2) is back as Dr. Alan Grant, reluctantly leading a search-and-rescue mission when a plane crashlands on an island populated by his old nemeses, the dinos. Another new dinosaur species, the Spinosaurus, shows up and to make some more humans into snack food. The talented, and probably over-qualified, group of writers mercifully makes this trip a short one, making sure that any dialogue is mostly expository or in-joke amusing while glossing over the dumb-as-a-box-of-fossils plot and characters. The dinosaurs are, once again, impressive; if you haven't gotten enough of the computer-generated ferocity in the first two outings. Warning: Just because this franchise is getting progressively worse doesn't mean they didn't set up JP4. 90m/C VHS, DVD. US Sam Neill, William H. Macy, Tea Leoni, Alessandro Nivola, Michael Jeter, Trevor Morgan, John Diehl, Bruce A. Young, Taylor Nichols, Mark Harelik, Julio Oscar Mechoso, Laura Dern; *D:* Joe Johnston; *W:* Peter Buchman, Alexander Payne, Jim Taylor; *C:* Shelly Johnson; *M:* Don Davis.

The Juror 1996 (R) Plucky single mom (Moore) ends up on the jury in the trial of a powerful mobster and draws the attention of the smooth enforcer (Baldwin) who muscles her into providing a certain verdict. The usual good-vs.-evil, family-in-danger action ensues. Despite boasting a fine cast and impressive attention to detail, flick is guilty of ludicrous situations, a mechanical plot and a dopey ending. Based on the novel by George Dawes Green. 107m/C VHS, DVD: Demi Moore, Alec Baldwin, Joseph Gordon-Levitt, Anne Heche, James Gandolfini, Lindsay Crouse, Tony LoBianco, Michael Constantine, Matt Craven, Polly Adams; *D:* Brian Gibson; *W:* Ted Tally; *C:* Jamie Anderson; *M:* James Newton Howard.

Jury Duty 1995 (PG-13) Mama's boy loser Tommy Collins (Shore) gets jury duty on a serial-killer case and tries to keep what seems to be an open-and-shut case going so he can continue to get free room and board. He falls for babe juror Monica (Carrere) and really drags the trial (and the film) out in a pathetic attempt to woo her. Shore is even more annoying and unfunny than ever. Low-rent bastardization of "Twelve Angry Men" tries to pass off lame O.J. references and Shore falling out of chairs as humor. Creates reasonable doubt as to Shore's talent and movie execs' judgment. 88m/C VHS, DVD. Pauly Shore, Tia Carrere, Shelley Winters, Brian Doyle-Murray, Abe Vigoda, Stanley Tucci, Charles Napier, Richard Edson; *Cameos:* Andrew (Dice Clay) Silverstein; *D:* John Fortenberry; *W:* Neil Tolkin, Barbara Williams. Golden Raspberries '95: Worst Actor (Shore).

The Jury's Secret 1938 Bill Sheldon (Blake) is tried for the murder of a newspaper publisher. The story is covered by reporter Linda Ware (Wray), who discovers that her old beau and fellow writer, Walter Russell (Taylor), is part of the jury and has something to hide. 65m/B VHS. Kent Taylor, Fay Wray, Larry J. Blake, Jane Darwell, Nan Grey, Leonard Mudie, Samuel S. Hinds, Granville Bates; *D:* Edward Sloman; *W:* Lester Cole, Newman Levy; *C:* Milton Krasner.

Just a Gigolo 1979 (R) Bowie stars in this unusual melodrama about a Prussian war vet turned male prostitute. He spends most of his time working for the sexiest of women. Splendid cast, but a bit incoherent. 105m/C VHS. GE David Bowie, Sydne Rome, Kim Novak, David Hemmings, Maria Schell, Curt Jurgens, Marlene Dietrich; *D:* David Hemmings.

Just a Kiss 2002 (R) Actor Stevens' clever directorial debut shows the dark side of 30-something NYC hipsters whose infidelity and jealousy rival any low-brow talk show fodder. Chain of perilous events is set off by Dag (Eldard), who cheats on his live-in Halley (Sedgwick) with suicidal ballerina Rebecca (Shelton), the girlfriend of Dag's best friend Peter (Breen). When the secret is revealed, more cheating takes place with newcomers Diggs, Choudhury, and Tomei—who plays a hilarious bowling alley waitress. A quirky singles mixer/romantic comedy with a twist, characters are given the chance to go back in time and change their actions. Good performances and writing keep this a few notches above melodramatic send-up, even with somewhat gimmicky use of an animation technique called rotomation. 89m/C VHS, DVD. US Ron Eldard, Kyra Sedgwick, Patrick Breen, Marisa Tomei, Marley Shelton, Taye Diggs, Sarita Choudhury, Zoe Caldwell; *D:* Fisher Stevens; *W:* Patrick Breen; *C:* Terry Stacey; *M:* Sean Dinsmore.

Just a Little Harmless Sex 1999 (R) Alan (Mailhouse) has spent the evening with his buddies, Danny (Silverman) and Brent (Ragsdale), at a topless bar. Driving home, he offers help to a stranded motorist (who turns out to be a hooker) and winds up getting arrested. Alan's wife, Laura (Eastwood), is, naturally, not happy about the situation and discusses her plight with her gal pals while Alan and his buddies discuss his fractured marriage. Angsty but not particularly novel. 98m/C VHS, DVD. Robert Mailhouse, Alison Eastwood, Jonathan Silverman, William Ragsdale, Lauren Hutton, Kimberly Williams, Jessica Lundy, Rachel Hunter, Michael Ontkean, Tito Larriva; *D:* Rick Rosenthal; *W:* Roger Miller, Marti Noxon; *C:* Bruce Surtees; *M:* Tito Larriva.

Just Another Girl on the I.R.T. 1993 (R) Double debut from two African American women, writer/director Harris, and actress Johnson, captures the sass and wit of a girl from the projects. Seventeen-year-old Chantal has a plan for her life and challenges authority with assurance, even after an unexpected pregnancy puts a twist into her plan. Strong initial statement tends to become weak and cloudy as Chantal loses her focus. This doesn't dismiss the remarkable realism and raw talent portrayed in a picture filmed in just seventeen days for $130,000. Winner of a special jury prize at the Sundance Film Festival. 96m/C VHS, DVD. Ariyan Johnson, Kevin Thigpen, Ebony Jendo, Jerard Washington, Chequita Jackson, William Badget; *D:* Leslie Harris; *W:* Leslie Harris; *C:* Richard Conners. Sundance '93: Special Jury Prize.

Just Another Pretty Face *Be Beautiful but Shut Up* 1958 An aging detective catches a gang of jewel smugglers, and gets involved with their young moll. In French with English subtitles. 110m/B VHS. FR Henri Vidal, Mylene Demongeot, Isa Miranda; *D:* Henri Verneuil.

Just Around the Corner 1938 (G) Temple helps her Depression-poor father get a job after she befriends a cantankerous millionaire. Temple duets with Bill "Bojangles" Robinson with the fourth time. Also available colorized. ♫ This Is A Happy Little Ditty; I'm Not Myself Today; I'll Be Lucky With You; Just Around the Corner; I Love To Walk in the Rain; Brass Buttons and Epaulets. 71m/B VHS, DVD. Shirley Temple, Charles Farrell, Bert Lahr, Joan Davis, Bill Robinson, Cora Witherspoon, Franklin Pangborn; *D:* Irving Cummings.

Just Before Dawn 1980 (R) Another murderers stalk campers story; humans resort to their animal instincts in their struggle for survival. Not to be confused with the William Castle film (1946) from the "Crime Doctor" series. 90m/C VHS, DVD. Chris Lemmon, Deborah Benson, Gregg Henry, George Kennedy; *D:* Jeff Lieberman; *M:* Brad Fiedel.

Just Between Friends 1986 (PG-13) Two women become friends, not knowing that one is having an affair with the husband of the other. Allan Burns directorial debut. 110m/C VHS, DVD. Mary Tyler Moore, Christine Lahti, Sam Waterston, Ted Danson, Jim MacKrell, Jane Greer; *D:* Allan Burns; *W:* Allan Burns; *C:* Jordan Cronenweth.

Just Cause 1994 (R) Incoherent mystery/thriller set in the Florida Everglades. Retired attorney, Paul Armstrong, now a Harvard law professor, decides to defend Bobby Earl (Underwood), on death row for the murder of a white girl. As Armstrong investigates the case, he discovers that the arresting officer Tanny Brown, (Fishburne) is corrupt and tortured the confession out of Bobby. Starts off promisingly with the electricity of Connery's and Fishburne's presence and a frightening cameo by Ed Harris as an incarcerated serial killer, but once the barrage of plot twists start, creating gator size holes in the plot, the movie drifts into a murkey swamp of absurdity. Adapted from the legal thriller by John Katzenbach. 102m/C VHS, DVD. Sean Connery, Laurence Fishburne, Kate Capshaw, Blair Underwood, Ruby Dee, Daniel J. Travanti, Ned Beatty, Lynne Thigpen, George Plimpton, Chris Sarandon, Kevin McCarthy, Ed Harris; *D:* Arne Glimcher; *W:* Jeb Stuart, Robert Stone; *C:* Lajos Koltai; *M:* James Newton Howard.

Just for the Hell of It woof! *Destruction, Inc* 1968 A quartet of teenage punks ruthlessly terrorize their suburban Miami 'hood while an innocent kid gets blamed. More exploitation from schlock king Lewis, who also wrote the theme song, "Destruction, Inc." (pic's alternate title). Essentially the same cast as the director's "She Devils on Wheels," filmed simultaneously. 85m/C VHS, DVD. Rodney Bender, Ray Sager, Nancy Lee Noble, Agi Gyenes, Steve White; *D:* Herschell Gordon Lewis; *W:* Allison Louise Downe; *C:* Roy Collodi; *M:* Larry Wellington.

Just for You ♂♂½ 1952 Entertaining musical about producer Crosby who doesn't have time for his kids until Wyman steps in and shows him the way. Based on Stephen Vincent Benet's novel "Famous." ♫ 🎵 Zing A Little Zong; Crazy For Me; The Live Oak Tree; A Flight of Fancy; I'll Si-Si Ya In Bahia; On the 10:10; Just for You. **95m/C VHS, DVD, Bing Crosby, Jane Wyman, Ethel Barrymore, Robert Arthur, Natalie Wood, Cora Witherspoon; D: Elliott Nugent; W: Robert Carson.

Just Friends ♂ 2005 (PG-13) No surprises in this romantic comedy, but it's sweet enough anyway. Chris (Reynolds) is the chubby Jersey kid, but with his high school crush Jamie "Smart" but he's overweight, shy, and in the "friend zone." Chris moves to L.A., where he transforms into a super hot So-Cal babe collector before returning to his hometown 10 years later. **94m/C DVD, US Ryan Reynolds, Amy Smart, Anna Faris, Julie Hagerty, Christopher Marquette, Stephen (Steve) Root, Chris Klein, Fred Ewanuick; D: Roger Kumble; W: Adam "Tex" Davis; C: Anthony B. Richmond.

Just Like a Woman ♂♂ 1995 (R) Sweet-natured film about an unlikely romance with some decided quirks. Young American Gerald (Pasdar) is working for a London bank and renting a flat from lonely older divorcee Monica (Walters). Ideal tenant Gerald is also recently divorced and a mutual attraction develops, in fact Gerald trusts Monica enough to confess his darkest secret—seems his marriage broke up over women's lingerie—the ones Gerald likes to wear when he cross-dresses in his female persona of Geraldine. Does this put Monica off? Well, she turns out to be very understanding indeed. Based on the memoir "Geraldine" by Monica Jay. **102m/C VHS, DVD, Julie Walters, Adrian Pasdar, Paul Freeman, Ian Redford, Susan Wooldridge, Gordon Kennedy, Shelley Thompson; D: Christopher Monger; W: Nick Evans; C: Alan Fume; M: William Goldstein.

Just like Heaven ♂♂ 2005 (PG-13) David Abbott (Buffalo) tragically loses his wife, sending him into a tailspin of depression. Looking to start anew, Abbott moves into a new apartment, which just happens to be occupied—by a ghost, Elizabeth (Witherspoon), who doesn't know she's dead. Actually she's only mostly dead—she's in limbo, in a coma after a car accident. Mindless 'romantic fluff worth it for fans of that sort of thing, or for those of you with a crush on one of the attractive leads. **101m/C VHS, DVD, US Reese Witherspoon, Mark Ruffalo, Dina Spybey, Donal Logue, Ben Shenkman, Jon Heder, Ivana Milicevic, Rosalind Chao, Ron Canada; D: Mark S. Waters; W: Peter Tolan, Leslie Dixon; C: Daryn Okada; M: Rolfe Kent.

Just Looking ♂♂½ 1999 (R) A comedy about teenaged voyeurism set in 1955. 14-year-old Lanny (Merriman) has only one thing on his mind for summer vacation in his Bronx neighborhood. He's determined to figure out what sex is all about by watching some adults "do it." Well, Lenny's mom decides to send him to stay in suburban Queens with her sister but that doesn't change his plans. Predictable coming of age comedy but... **97m/C VHS, DVD, US Ryan Merriman, Gretchen Mo, Patti LuPone, Peter Onorati, Ilana Levine, Richard V. Licata, John Bolger, Joey Franqui-

Just Like Weather ♂♂♂ 1986 Contemporary Hong Kong and the city's looming return to control by mainland China provide the backdrop for the troubled marriage of a young couple. Couple endure abortion, arrest, and veterinarian episodes before departing for an U.S. trip with high hopes. **98m/C VHS, DVD, -K Christine Lee, Lee Chi-Keung, Allen Fong; D: Allen Fong.

Just Like Dad ♂♂ 1995 (PG) Nerdy kid with an equally nerdy dad wants to actually win some of the Father,Son Picnic contests. Even if he has to hire a heroic dad substitute to do help him out. **102m/C VHS, Wallace Shawn, Nick Cassavetes, Laura Innes, Ben (Dillon; D: Blair Treu; W: Wayne Rice; C: Brian Sullivan; M: William Olvis.

Just One Night ♂ 1993 (R) College professor Isaac Adler (Hutton) is spending the night before his wedding in San Francisco. His taxi collides with a beautiful, married Aurora (Cucinotta) and maybe the collision shook them up more than they thought, since they decide to spend the evening getting to know each other better. **90m/C VHS, DVD, W. Alan Jacobs; C: John Campbell; M: Anthony Marinelli.

Just One of the Guys ♂♂ 1985 (PG-13) When the school newspaper refuses to accept the work of an attractive young girl, she goes undercover as a boy to prove that her work is good. She goes on to befriend the school's toughest gang whom he has unwittingly enraged. Falling around with Egbert becomes one of his costume's unexpected perks. Is it Hot" and "90210." **94m/C VHS, DVD, Corey Haim, Nicole Eggert, Cameron Bancroft; D: Michael Keusch; M: Arnin Bhatia.

Just One Time ♂♂ 2000 (R) New York-set romantic comedy about fulfilling fantasies. Fireman Anthony (Langen) is about to marry lawyer Amy (Carter) but can't resist telling her about his sexual dream to see her make out with another woman—just once—before the wedding. Distraught, Amy confides in her gay neighbor, Victor (Diaz), who admits to a crush on Anthony. So she offers a quid pro quo or her beau—she'll indulge him with sultry lesbian Michelle (Esposito) if

Just One of the Girls ♂♂½ 2000

Just Married ♂½ 2003 (PG-13) Mismatched newlyweds Tom (Kutcher) and Sarah (Murphy) find slapstick situations and jealousy instead of romantic bliss on their European honeymoon. Tom's a sports-lovin' regular guy, and Sarah's the well-educated daughter of a Beverly Hills tycoon. In Europe, they must deal with that, along with every ugly American and snooty European stereotype in the book, er, script. Kutcher plays his usual pretty-boy doofus, but Murphy is wasted in a stupid movie seemingly designed to give Kutcher pin-up status. **94m/C DVD, US Ashton Kutcher, Brittany Murphy, Christian Kane, David Moscow, Monet Mazur, David Rasche, Veronica Cartwright, Raymond J. Barry, Thad Luckinbill, David Agranov, Jonathan Brown; D: Shawn Levy; W: Sam Harper; C: Jonathan Brown; M: Christophe Beck.

Just Me & You ♂♂ 1978 An "It Happened One Night" tale of an unlikely couple who fall in love with each other during a cross-country drive. **100m/C VHS, Louise Lasser, Charles Grodin; D: Charles Erman; W: Louise Lasser. TV

Just My Luck ♂♂½ 2006 (PG-13) Bland romantic fantasy finds Ashley growing up and trying to escape the teenqueen ghetto. Ashley, as a junior exec in Manhattan, is just the luckiest gal ever. Her opposite is cute-pie Jake (Pine), whose life is one continuous calamity. They meet at a costume party, kiss, and their worlds turn—Jake can do no wrong and Ashley, well, life is just so not fair! Now she needs to kiss Jake again and find another switcheroo. Lohan's game for slapstick humiliation, but this one's just another rung up the acting ladder. **106m/C DVD, US Lindsay Lohan, Chris Pine, Samaire Armstrong, Bree Turner, Faizon Love, Missi Pyle, Makenzie Vega, Tovah Feldshuh, Jaqueline Fleming, Carlos Ponce; D: Donald Petrie; W: I. Marlene King, Amy Harris; C: Dean Semler; M: Teddy Castellucci.

Just Suppose ♂♂½ 1926 Prince in waiting decides he'd prefer the simple life, travels to the land of the free in search of honest work and is felled by cupid's arrow. All's well 'til duty calls, and his princely presence is expected back in the royal fold. Features beautiful boy Barthelmess, whom Lillian Gish described as having "the most beautiful face of any man who ever went before a camera." Silent. **90m/B VHS, Richard Barthelmess, Lois Moran, Geoffrey Kerr, Henry Vibart, George Spelvin; D: Kenneth Webb.

Just Tell Me What You Want ♂♂♂ 1980 (R) A wealthy, self-made married man finally drives his longtime mistress away when he refuses to let her take over the operation of a failing movie studio he has acquired. After she falls for another man, the tycoon does everything he can to win her back. The department store battle between MacGraw and King is priceless. **112m/C VHS, DVD, Alan King, Ali MacGraw, Myrna Loy, Keenan Wynn, Tony Roberts; D: Sidney Lumet; W: Jay Presson Allen; C: Oswald Morris.

Just Tell Me You Love Me ♂ 1980 (PG) Three budding con artists plot to make easy money in the Hawaiian romp. **90m/C VHS, Robert Hegyes, Debralee Scott, Lisa Harman Black, Ricci Martin, June Lockhart; D: Tony Mordente.

Just the Ticket ♂♂ 1998 (R) Romantic comedy set in the seedy world of ticket scalpers should have skipped the title love story and centered on the ducat slingers. Gary (Garcia) is a fast talking huckster trying to win back ex-girlfriend Linda (MacDowell). He's also hoping for the ever-popular last big score before he goes legit. His opportunity arrives when the Pope announces a visit to Yankee Stadium, but he must out-hustle competitor Casino (Blake). Garcia wrote many of the Salsa-flavored songs used in the movie. **107m/C VHS, DVD, Lenny Venito, Andy Garcia, Andie MacDowell, Richard Bradford, Laura Harris, Andre B. Blake, Elizabeth Ashley, Patrick Breen, Ron Leibman, Chris Lemmon, Don Novello, Abe Vigoda, Bill Irwin, Ronald Guttman, Donna Hanover, Irene Worth, Fred Asparagus, Louis Mustillo, Paunita Nichols, Joe Frazier; D: Richard Wenk; W: Richard Wenk; C: Ellen Kuras; M: Rick Marotta.

Just the Way You Are ♂ 1984 (PG) An attractive musician struggles to overcome a physical handicap and winds up falling in love while on vacation in the French Alps. **96m/C VHS, Kristy McNichol, Robert Carradine, Kaki Hunter, Michael Ontkean, Alexandra Paul, Lance Guest, Timothy Daly, Patrick Cassidy; D: Edouard Molinaro; W: Allan Burns; M: Vladimir Cosma.

Just Visiting ♂♂ 2001 (PG-13) Remake of the 1993 French flick "Les Visiteurs" has Reno and Clavier reprising their roles as a medieval knight and his servant who find themselves in modern-day Chicago. Original was a huge hit in France, but bombed here. This one should do much better here, since there's much less "reading" of subtitles involved, and this one makes good use of the excellent leads and the transplanted Chicago locales. **88m/C VHS, DVD, US Jean Reno, Christian Clavier, Christina Applegate, Tara Reid, Matt Ross, Bridgette Wilson-Sampras, John Aylward, George Plimpton, Malcolm McDowell, Sarah Badel; D: Jean-Marie Poire; W: Christian Clavier, Jean-Marie Poire, John Hughes; C: Ueli Steiger; M: John Powell.

Just William's Luck ♂♂ 1947 A precocious English brat sneaks into an old mansion, which just happens to be the headquarters for a gang of thieves. Based on British series of children's books. **87m/B VHS, GB William A. Graham, Gary Marsh; D: Val Guest.

Just Write ♂♂ 1997 (PG-13) Sweet and slight romantic comedy about making your dreams come true. Harold "Piven) is a Hollywood tour bus driver who

Anthony will do the same for her with Victor, and he has to go first. **94m/C VHS, DVD, US Lane Janger, Joelle Carter, Guillermo Diaz, Jennifer Esposito, Vincent Laresca, David Lee Russell, Domenick Lombardozzi; D: Lane Janger; W: Jennifer Vandever, Lane Janger; C: Michael S. Hilaire; M: Edward Bilcus.

Mismatched newlyweds Tom (Kutcher)

nha; D: Jason Alexander; W: Marshall Karp; C: Fred Schuler; M: Michael Skloff.

works for his well-meaning but overbearing father (Rocco). He meets cute with rising star Amanda (Fenn), who is mistakenly led to believe Harold is a screenwriter. And Amanda just happens to be a script that needs some work. They begin to fall in love but sooner or later the truth is bound to come out. Leads play well together and the supporting cast is fine, especially Williams as a hard-charging agent. **95m/C VHS, DVD, Jeremy Piven, Sherilyn Fenn, JoBeth Williams, Alex Rocco, Jeffrey D. Sams, Wallace Shawn, Costas Mandylor, Yeardley Smith, Holland Taylor; C: Cameras; Nancy Mason, Ed McMahon; D: Andrew Gallerani; W: Stan Williamson; C: Michael Brown; M: Leland Bond.

Justice Rides Again ♂♂ 1961 The New Sudka Cafe II, owned by the high strung Nick (Pcllto), is the setting for one wild night. An old man promptly keels over dead upon learning that his lottery ticket is a $6 million pre-winner. Customer Kim (Madsen) tries to convince Nick and her fellow diners that they should keep the ticket and split the winnings. **86m/C VHS, Virginia Madsen, Sean Patrick Flanery, Francis Ford, George Ernest, Earle Foxe; D: Alan James, Ben Stoloff; W: Richard Schayer; C: Daniel B. Clark.

Justice of the West ♂ 1961 The Lone Ranger and his sidekick, Tonto, perform good deeds in the Old West, including helping to retrieve stolen gold, helping to build an Incian school, and giving a blind man a fresh perspective on life. **71m/ C VHS, Clayton Moore, Jay Silverheels; D: Earl Bellamy.

Justin Morgan Had a Horse ♂♂ 1981 The true story of a colonial school teacher in post-Revolutionary War Vermont who first bred the Morgan horse, the first and most versatile American breed. **91m/C VHS, Don Murray, Lana Wood, Gary Crosby; D: Hollingsworth Morse.

Justine ♂ 1969 (R) A high-class prostitute who marries an Egyptian banker becomes involved with a variety of men and a plot to arm Palestinian rebels in their revolt against English rule. A condensed film version of Lawrence Durrell's "The Alexandria Quartet." **115m/C VHS, US Anouk Aimee, Michael York, Dirk Bogarde, Philippe Noiret, Michael Constantine, John Vernon, Jack Albertson; D: George Cukor; W: Lawrence B. Marcus; C: Leon Shamroy; M: Jerry Goldsmith.

Juwanna Mann ♂♂ 2002 (PG-13) Cross-dressing comedy plays like a "Tootsie" retread in sneakers. Jamal (Nunez) is an obnoxious pro basketball player booted out of the league after mooning a ref while protesting a call. Facing total bankruptcy and realizing his only skills are on the basketball court, Jamal dons make-up and falsies and joins a pro women's league as Juwanna Mann. Predictable situations occur, including Jamal falling for beautiful teammate Michelle (Fox) and being hit on by clueless suitor Puff Smokey Smoke (Davidson), but performances save what could have been a complete disaster. **91m/ C VHS, DVD, US Miguel A. Nunez Jr., Vivica A. Fox, Kevin Pollak, Tommy Davidson, Kim Wayans, Ginuwine, Jenifer Lewis, Kimberly 'Lil' Kim) Jones, Annie Corley, Ginuwine; D: Jesse Vaughan; W: Bradley Allenstein; C: Reynaldo Villalobos; M: Wendy Melvoin, Lisa Coleman.

K-9 ♂♂½ 1989 (PG-13) After having his car destroyed by a drug dealer, "I work alone" Belushi is forced to take on a partner—a German Shepherd. Together they work to round up the bad guys and maybe chew on their shoes a little. Sometimes amusing one-joke comedy done in by a paper-thin script. Both the dog and Belushi are good, however. **111m/C VHS, DVD, James Belushi, Mel Harris, Kevin Tighe, Ed O'Neill, Cotter Smith, James Handy, Jerry Lee; D: Rod Daniel; W: Steven Siegel, Scott Myers; C: Dean Semler; M: Miles Goodman.

K-9 3: P.I. ♂♂½ 2001 (PG-13) Detective Dooley (Belushi) and Jerry Lee are heading for retirement and new careers as private eyes. But when they try stopping a crime in progress, they wind up as the prime suspects and now must try to find the real culprits. Oh, and Dooley thinks he can earn some extra cash by having Jerry Lee serve as a German Shepard stud for a dog breeder. Family friendly fun. **95m/C VHS, DVD.** James Belushi, Gary Basaraba, Kimberley Huffman, Christopher Shyer; **D:** Richard J. Lewis; **W:** Gary Scott Thompson, Ed Horowitz. **VIDEO**

K-911 ♂♂½ 1999 (PG-13) Ten years after the original Pitt, Belushi returns to his role of LAPD Detective Dooley, along with his German Shepard partner, Jerry Lee. The aging duo are now reluctantly partnered with a younger K-9 unit—no-nonsense detective Welles (Tucci) and her partner, a Doberman named Zeus. But Dooley has some other things on his mind—some kook is trying to kill him. **91m/C VHS, DVD.** James Belushi, James Handy, Christine Tucci, Wade Andrew Williams, J.J. Johnston, Vincent Castellanos; **D:** Charles Kanganis; **W:** Gary Scott Thompson; **C:** George Mooradian; **M:** Stephen (Steve) Edwards. **VIDEO**

K-9000 ♂♂ 1989 The Hound salutes the idea behind this standard sci-fi crimefighter; a cyberdog fights the forces of evil with the aid of a cop, a lady reporter, and the usual cliches. **96m/C VHS, DVD.** Catherine Oxenberg; **D:** Kim Manners; **M:** Jan Hammer. **TV**

K-19: The Widowmaker ♂♂ 2002 (PG-13) Cold War tensions abound in this aptly claustrophobic submarine suspenser involving the Soviet Union's first nuclear ballistic sub, which suffers a reactor malfunction during a test voyage in the North Atlantic. Ford plays the tough Russian captain, who takes command from the more-popular Neeson, and must deal with rebellion in the ranks in order to save his sub and crew, and prevent an all out World War. Sarsgaard is the panicky, inexperienced reactor officer who's every nuke sub captain's nightmare. Strong performances by the lead actors almost overshadows their flimsy Russian accents. Bigelow shot on a set built to scale, with parts salvaged from an old diesel sub. Loosely based on a military incident that happened in 1961 but wasn't publicly revealed until the 1990s. **138m/C VHS, DVD.** US Harrison Ford, Liam Neeson, Peter Sarsgaard, Joss Ackland, John Shrapnel, Donald (Don) Sumpter, Tim Woodward, Ravil Isyanov, Christian Camargo, Steve Nicholson; **D:** Kathryn Bigelow; **W:** Christopher Kyle; **C:** Jeff Cronenweth; **M:** Klaus Badelt.

K-PAX ♂♂½ 2001 (PG-13) Spacey plays his patented "smirky guy with a secret" again in this tale of aliens and the humans who love them. Prot (Spacey) is admitted to a psychiatric hospital when he claims to be from outer space. Dr. Powell (Bridges) is assigned his case and soon finds himself intrigued by Prot. It seems that he's going around helping the patients in the hospital to actually get better. His other quirks include an astounding knowledge of astrophysics and an amazing tolerance to Thorazine. After Powell hypnotizes Prot, a deeply hidden personality is unmasked, but the actual truth about his identity is left open to interpretation. Bridges and Spacey work well together, and they save this sentimental E.T. tale from turning to schmaltzy mush. **120m/C VHS, DVD.** US Kevin Spacey, Jeff Bridges, Mary McCormack, Alfre Woodard, David Patrick Kelly, Saul Williams, Peter Gerety, Celia Weston, Ajay Naidu, John Toles-Bey, Kimberly Scott, Mary Mara, Aaron Paul, William Lucking; **D:** Iain Softley; **W:** Charles Leavitt; **C:** John Mathieson; **M:** Ed Shearmur.

Kaaterskill Falls ♂ 2001 Indie horror flick suffers from its obvious low budget and stilted improvisations. Yuppie couple Mitchell (Riggs) and Ren (Howard) are driving to a cabin in upstate New York where they hope to rekindle their disintegrating marriage. Ren decides to offer monosyllabic hitchhiker Lyle (Leslie) a ride to a nearby motel. But Lyle soon makes an appearance at their cabin and they decide

to extend their hospitality to inviting him in for dinner. This is the first of many mistakes. **87m/C VHS, DVD.** Mitchel Riggs, Hilary Howard, Anthony Leslie; **D:** Josh Apter, Peter Olsen; **W:** Mitchel Riggs, Hilary Howard, Anthony Leslie, Josh Apter, Peter Olsen; **C:** Peter Olsen.

Kadosh ♂♂½ 1999 Meir (Hattab) and his wife Rivka (Abecassis) are ultra-Orthodox Jews living in the Mea Shearim quarter of Jerusalem. They have been married for 10 years and are still childless, so Meir is being pressured by his rabbi father to divorce his wife (though they love each other) and remarry. Rivka learns the fertility problem is with her husband but can do nothing because of religious tenets and she leaves their home. Meanwhile, Rivka's younger sister, Malka (Barda), contemplates abandoning her unhappy arranged marriage to be with the man she loves. Hebrew with subtitles. **110m/C VHS, DVD.** IS Yael Abecassis, Yoram Hattab, Meital Barda, Sami Hori, Uri Klauzner, Yussef Abu-Warda; **D:** Amos Gitai; **W:** Amos Gitai, Eliette Abecassis; **C:** Renato Berta; **M:** Louis Sclavis.

Kaena: The Prophecy ♂♂½ 2003 (PG-13) Sci-fi fantasy epic about a brave young humanoid girl (Dunst) who resists her society's groveling submission to its tyrannical "gods." Once cast out, she discovers many hidden secrets about her world. She meets an old astronaut/scientist (Harris) who is the last survivor of the ancient spaceship-wreck that formed her world, and who may possess the power to revive or destroy it as well. Visually stunning movie is France's first entry into full-length CGI animation. Texture is so rich and intricate, it should hold up well to multiple viewings. Characters are a bit thin, and the dubbed dialogue is annoyingly flat and unnatural. It would be interesting to see the French version. One of Richard Harris' last performances. **91m/C DVD.** FR CA FR D: Chris Delaporte, Pascal Pinon; **W:** Chris Delaporte, Tarik Hamdine; **M:** Farid Russlan; **V:** Kirsten Dunst, Richard Harris, Anjelica Huston, Michael McShane, Greg Proops, Keith David.

Kafka ♂½ 1991 (PG-13) Disappointing and gloomy Soderbergh film that serves no purpose whatsoever. Irons plays Kafka, an insurance workers by day and a writer by night. The movie exists largely without interest until Kafka uncovers an office conspiracy and makes his way to the enemy's castle headquarters. From then on, "Kafka" is nothing but a conventional horror film. Irons is wasted in a role that requires nothing but an impeccable British accent. On the plus side, the film is exquisitely shot in black and white until the castle scenes, when the cinematography is switched to color. **100m/C VHS.** Jeremy Irons, Theresa Russell, Joel Grey, Ian Holm, Jeroen Krabbe, Armin Mueller-Stahl, Alec Guinness, Brian Glover, Robert Flemyng, Keith Allen, Simon McBurney; **D:** Steven Soderbergh; **W:** Lem Dobbs; **C:** Walt Lloyd; **M:** Cliff Martinez. Ind. Spirit '92: Cinematog.

Kagemusha ♂♂½ 1980 (PG) *The Shadow Warrior; The Double* A thief is rescued from the gallows because of his striking resemblance to a warlord in 16th Century Japan. When the ambitious warlord is fatally wounded, the thief is required to pose as the warlord. In Japanese with English subtitles. **160m/C VHS, DVD.** JP Tatsuya Nakadai, Tsutomu Yamazaki, Kenichi Hagiwara, Hideji Otaki; **D:** Akira Kurosawa; **W:** Akira Kurosawa, Masato Ide; **C:** Kazuo Miyagawa, Masaharu Ueda; **M:** Shinichiro Ikebe. British Acad. '80: Director (Kurosawa); Cannes '80: Film; Cesar '81: Foreign Film.

The Kaiser's Lackey ♂♂ 1951 *Der Untertan* Cowardly but ambitious Diedrich Hessling has learned his lesson—in order to gain power, you must bow to those who have it and ignore those who don't. Diedrich thinks he's finally achieved his goal when he's chosen to give the keynote speech at the dedication of an Emperor's monument. Based on the novel by Heinrich Mann. German with subtitles. **105m/B VHS.** GE Werner Peters, Paul Esser; **D:** Wolfgang Staudte; **W:** Wolfgang Staudte.

Kalifornia ♂♂½ 1993 (R) "Badlands" meets the '90s in a road trip with the hitchhikers from hell. Early Grayce (Pitt) is your average slimeball who murders his landlord and hops a ride with his waifish girlfriend Adele (Lewis) from Kentucky to California with Brian (Duchovny), a yuppie writer interested in mass murderers, and his sultry photographer girlfriend Carrie (Forbes). Pitt and Lewis were still an item when they made this. Pitt reportedly wanted to play against type, and as pretty boy gone homicidal, he succeeds. Extremely violent and disturbing. Also available in an unrated version. **117m/C VHS, DVD, UMD.** Brad Pitt, Juliette Lewis, David Duchovny, Michelle Forbes, Sierra Pecheur, Lois Hall, Gregory Mars Martin; **D:** Dominic Sena; **W:** Tim Metcalfe; **C:** Bojan Bazelli; **M:** Carter Burwell.

Kama Sutra: A Tale of Love ♂♂ 1996 Erotic but flawed fantasy covering the sexual and political wiles of palace life in 16th-century India. Princess Tara (Choudhury) and girlhood friend/servant Maya (Varma) are close until the Princess becomes jealous of the even-more beautiful Maya. In revenge for a public humiliation, Maya seduces Tara's dissolute fiance, Raj Singh (Andrews), and is banished from the palace after the wedding. She becomes involved with handsome royal sculptor Jai Kumar (Tikaram) and later learns the sexual arts of the Kama Sutra, becoming the chief courtesan to the Raj. Messy, somewhat overwrought plot, extremely attractive cast. Also available in an R-rated version. **117m/C VHS, DVD.** IN Indira Varma, Sarita Choudhury, Ramon Tikaram, Naveen Andrews, Devi Rekha; **D:** Mira Nair; **W:** Mira Nair, Helena Kriel; **C:** Declan Quinn; **M:** Mychael Danna. Ind. Spirit '98: Cinematog.

Kameradschaft ♂♂♂½ 1931 *La Tragedie de la Mine; Comradeship* A great, early German sound film about Germans struggling to free themselves and French miners trapped underground on the countries' border. In German and French with English subtitles. **80m/B VHS.** GE Ernst Busch, Alexander Granach, Fritz Kampers, Gustav Puttjer, Daniel Mendaille, Elizabeth Wenst; **D:** G.W. Pabst; **W:** Laszlo Wajda, Karl Otten, Peter Martin Lampel; **C:** Fritz Arno Wagner, Robert Baberske.

Kamikaze '89 ♂♂♂ 1983 German director Fassbinder has the lead acting role (his last) in this offbeat story of a police lieutenant (Sharon the actress and Tina the director/producer) making underground X-rated movies. **80m/C VHS.** Sharon Mitchell, Tina "Tigr" Mennet; **D:** Juliet Bashore; **W:** Tina "Tigr" Mennet.

Kamikaze Hearts ♂♂ 1991 A quasi-documentary set in the world of two lesbian-junkies (Sharon the actress and Tina the director/producer) making underground X-rated movies. **80m/C VHS.** Sharon Mitchell, Tina "Tigr" Mennet; **D:** Juliet Bashore; **W:** Tina "Tigr" Mennet.

Kanal ♂♂♂½ 1956 *They Loved Life* Wajda's first major success, a grueling account of Warsaw patriots, upon the onset of the Nazis toward the end of the war, fleeing through the ruined city's sewers. Highly acclaimed. Part 2 of Wajda's "War Trilogy," preceded by "A Generation" and followed by "Ashes and Diamonds." In Polish with English subtitles or dubbed. **96m/B VHS, DVD.** PL Teresa Izewska, Tadeusz Janczar, Vladek Sheybal, Emil Kariewicz, Wienczyslaw Glinski; **D:** Andrzej Wajda; **W:** Jerzy Stefan Stawinski; **C:** Jerzy Lipman; **M:** Jan Krenz. Cannes '57: Grand Jury Prize.

Kandahar ♂♂♂ 2001 Nafas (Pazira) and her family emigrated to Canda from Afghanistan, although they were forced to leave behind Nafas's crippled sister. Now, the sister has vowed to commit suicide rather than live any long under Taliban rule and Nafas returns to try and save her. But journeying to Kandahar is a maze of obstacles and restrictions. Farsi and English. **85m/C VHS, DVD.** IA Nelofer Pazira, Hassan Tantai, Sadou Teymouri; **D:** Mohsen Makhmalbaf; **W:** Mohsen Makhmalbaf; **C:** Ebraheem Ghafouri; **M:** Mohammad Reza Darvishi.

Kandyland ♂ 1987 (R) An over-the-hill stripper takes a young innocent stripper under her wing. **94m/C VHS.** Sandahl Bergman, Kimberly Evenson, Charles Laulette, Bruce Baum; **D:** Robert Allen Schnitzer; **C:** Robert Brinkmann.

Kangaroo ♂♂♂ 1986 (R) An Australian adaptation of the semi-autobiographical D.H. Lawrence novel. A controversial English novelist and his wife move to the Outback in 1922, and are confronted with all manner of prejudice and temptation. **115m/C VHS.** AU Judy Davis, Colin Friels, John Walton, Hugh Keays-Byrne, Julie Nihill; **D:** Tim Burstall; **W:** Evan Jones; **C:** Dan Burstall; **M:** Nathan Waks. Australian Film Inst. '86: Actress (Davis).

Kangaroo Jack ♂ 2002 (PG) Pals O'Connell and Anderson are forced to deliver mob money to Australia, but it's accidentally stolen from them by a kangaroo. If this sounds like a sad excuse for a movie, it is. Aside from some beautiful shots of the Australian landscape, there's little redeeming value. Jokes are lowbrow and (even worse) not funny, script is bland and mainly uninspired. Walken must've owed producer Jerry Bruckheimer a favor. The kangaroo was computer-generated, but still had more charisma than any of the leading actors. **88m/C VHS, DVD.** US Jerry O'Connell, Anthony Anderson, Estella Warren, Michael Shannon, Christopher Walken, Bill Hunter, Marton Csokas, David Ngoombujara; **D:** David McNally; **W:** Steve Bing, Scott Rosenberg; **C:** Peter Menzies Jr.

The Kansan ♂ 1943 The marshall in a Kansas town won't rest until he's stamped out all traces of corruption. **79m/B VHS, DVD.** Richard Dix, Jane Wyatt, Eugene Pallette, Albert Dekker, Robert Armstrong, Beryl Wallace, Clem Bevans, Hobart Cavanaugh, Francis McDonald, George Reeves, Willie Best; **D:** George Archainbaud; **W:** Harold Shumate; **C:** Russell Harlan; **M:** Gerard Carbonara.

Kansas ♂ 1988 (R) Two young men, one a lawless rebel, the other a rational loner, stage a bank heist, and then go on the lam. Lame plot and very weak acting combine to make this film a dud. **111m/C VHS, DVD.** Matt Dillon, Andrew McCarthy, Leslie Hope, Kyra Sedgwick; **D:** David Stevens; **W:** Spencer Eastman; **C:** David Eggby; **M:** Pino Donaggio.

Kansas City ♂♂♂ 1995 (R) Altman mixes music, politics, crime and the movies in this bittersweet homage to his hometown, set in the jazz-driven 1930s. Star-struck, tough-talking Blondie (Leigh) kidnaps Carolyn Stilton (Richardson), a self-sedating wife of a political shaker (Murphy), in a hair-brained scheme to save her husband from a local mobster (Belafonte). Styled to imitate the brilliant jazz scores played by the likes of Joshua Redman and James Carter, the action can become a bit confusing and Leigh is beyond irritating with her derivative dame routine. Belafonte, however, is brilliant, relishing the part of the legendary Seldom Seen, a real-life K.C. gangster. **110m/C VHS, DVD.** Jennifer Jason Leigh, Miranda Richardson, Harry Belafonte, Michael Murphy, Dermot Mulroney, Steve Buscemi, Brooke Smith, Jane Adams; **D:** Robert Altman; **W:** Frank Barhydt, Robert Altman; **C:** Oliver Stapleton; **M:** Hal Willner. N.Y. Film Critics '96: Support. Actor (Belafonte).

Kansas City Confidential ♂♂♂ 1952 An ex-cop on the wrong side of the law launches a sophisticated armored car heist. A disgruntled ex-con gets arrested for the crime on circumstantial evidence. When released, he scours the underworld for the real thieves. **98m/B VHS, DVD.** John Payne, Coleen Gray, Preston Foster, Neville Brand, Lee Van Cleef, Jack Elam, Carleton Young; **D:** Phil Karlson; **W:** Rowland Brown, George Bruce, Harry Essex, Harold Greene; **C:** George E. Diskant; **M:** Paul Sawtell.

Kansas Pacific ♂♂ 1953 A group of Confederate sympathizers try to stop the Kansas Pacific Railroad from reaching the West Coast in the 1860s. **73m/C VHS, DVD.** Sterling Hayden, Eve Miller, Barton MacLane, Reed Hadley, Douglas Hadley; **D:** Ray Nazarro.

The Kansas Terrors 🏃🏃 1939 The "Three Mesquiteers" head for the Caribbean to deliver a herd of horses and wind up in a battle against local despot. 57m/B VHS. Robert "Bob" Livingston, Raymond Hatton, Duncan Renaldo, Julie Bishop, Yakima Canutt, Richard Alexander, Merrill McCormic; D: George Sherman.

Kaos 🏃🏃🏃 Chaos 1985 (R) The Taviani brothers adaptation of four stories by Luigi Pirandelic ("The Other Son," "Moonstruck," "The Jar," and "Requiem"), which look at peasant life in Sicily, ranging from the comic to the tragic. A fictional epilog, "Conversing with Mother," has Pirandello talking with the spirit of his dead mother. As with any anthology, some stories are stronger than others but all possess the Taviani's great visual style and some fine acting. In Italian with English subtitles. 188m/C VHS, 7T Margarita Lozano, Claudio Bigagli, Massimo Bonetti, Omero Antonutti, Enrica Maria Modugno, Ciccio Ingrassia, Franco Franchi, Biagio Barone, Salvatore Rossi, Franco Scaldati, Pasquale Spaoca, Regina Bianchi; D: Paolo Taviani, Vittorio Taviani; W: Paolo Taviani, Vittorio Taviani; C: Giuseppe Lanci; M: Nicola Piovani.

Kapo 🏃🏃🏃 1959 A 14-year-old Jewish girl and her family are imprisoned by the Nazis in a concentration camp. There, the girl changes identities with the help of the camp doctor, and rises to the position of camp guard. She proceeds to become taken with her power until a friend commits suicide and jolts the girl back into harsh reality. An Academy Award nominee for Best Foreign Film (lost to "The Virgin Spring"). Primarily English dialogue, with subtitles for foreign language. 116m/B VHS, 7T FR YU Susan Strasberg, Laurent Terzieff, Emmanuelle Riva, Gianni "John" Garko; D: Gillo Pontecorvo; W: Gillo Pontecorvo.

Karate Cop 🏃¹/₂ 1991 (R) In a future without law or order John Travis (Marchini) is the last cop on earth. He saves Rachel, a beautiful scientist, from a band of scavengers and together they hunt for a hidden crystal with mysterious powers. Only firs John has to defeat a gladiator in a martial arts fight to the death. 90m/C VHS, DVD. Ron Marchini, Carrie Chambers, David Carradine, Michael Bristow, D.W. Landingham, Michael Foley, Dana Bentley; D: Alan Roberts.

Karate Dog WOOF! 2004 (PG) Totally inept comedy finds wisecracking dog Cho-Cho (voiced by Chase) teaming up with a geeky detective (Rex) to investigate the murder of his Zen karate master (Morita). Presumably everyone involved had bills to pay. 7m/C DVD. Simon Rex, Jon Voight, Jaime Pressly, Noriyuki "Pat" Morita, Thomas Kretschmann; D: Bob (Benjamin) Clark; W: Steven Paul; C: Brian Fearson; V: Chevy Chase, Lori Petty, Nicolette Sheridan.

The Karate Kid 🏃🏃¹/₂ 1984 (PG) A teenage boy finds out that Karate involves using more than your fists when a handyman agrees to teach him martial arts. The friendship that they develop is deep and sincere; the Karate is only an afterthought. From the director of the original "Rocky," this movie is easy to like. 126m/C VHS, DVD. Ralph Macchio, Noriyuki "Pat" Morita, Elisabeth Shue, Randee Heller, Martin Kove, Chad McQueen, William Zabka; D: John G. Avildsen; W: Robert Mark Kamen; M: Bill Conti.

The Karate Kid: Part 2 🏃🏃¹/₂ 1986 (PG) Sequel to the first film wherein our high-kicking hero tests his mettle in real-life karate exchanges in Okinawa, and settles a long-standing score. Followed by a second sequel. 95m/C VHS, DVD. Ralph Macchio, Noriyuki "Pat" Morita, Danny Kamekona, Martin Kove, Tamlyn Tomita, Nobu McCarthy, Yuji Okumoto, William Zabka; D: John G. Avildsen; W: Robert Mark Kamen; C: James A. Crabe; M: Bill Conti.

The Karate Kid: Part 3 🏃¹/₂ 1989 (PG) Second sequel takes a tired plot and doesn't do much to perk it up. Macchio again battles an evil nemesis and learns about honor, but this time Morita refuses to be a part of his training until, of course, Macchio desperately needs his help. Followed by "The Next Karate Kid," which introduces a new kid—a girl. 105m/C VHS, DVD. Ralph Macchio, Noriyuki "Pat" Morita, Robin (Robyn) Lively, Gabe Jarret, Frances Bay, Thomas Ian Griffith, Martin Kove, Sean Kanan, Robin (Robyn) Lively, Gabe Jarret, Frances Bay.

Karate Warrior 🏃¹/₂ The Boy in the Golden Kimono 1988 Young martial artist is beaten and left for dead by Filipino crime syndicate. Bones mended, he prescribes a dose of their medicine. Plenty of rest and retaliation. 90m/C VHS. 7T Janet Agren, Enrico Turralba, Jared Martin, Kenjsaku Watanabe; D: Fabrizio de Angelis; W: Fabrizio de Angelis; C: Alberto Pinori; M: Simon Boswell.

Karla 🏃¹/₂ 2006 (R) Routine true crime saga based on the story of Canadian serial killers Paul Bernardo and Karla Homolka. Told in flashback as Karla talks to her shrink in an effort to mitigate her part in the crimes. 101m/C DVD. Laura Prepon, Misha Collins, Tess Harper, Patrick Bauchau, Alexandra Boyd, Shawn Hoffman, Emilie Jacobs, Cherilyn Hayes, Adam Lieberman; D: Joel Bender; W: Joel Bender, Michael D. Sellers, Manette Beth Rosen; C: Charles Mills; M: Tim Jones.

Karmina 🏃🏃 1996 Unusual French-Canadian vampire parody finds 140-year-old vamp Karmina (Cyr) fighting with her Transylvanian parents over their insistence that she marry nerdy Vlad (Pelletier). Karmina flees her home and heads to Montreal, in search of her aunt, Esmeralda (Castel), who has managed to 'egain her humanity and now runs a dating service. A magic potion also makes Karmina human (it's a difficult transition) and she falls in love with Philippe (Brouillette) but Vlad's not out of the picture. He also turns up in Montreal, and begins adding to the vampire population. 109m/C VHS. CA Isabelle Cyr, Yves Pelletier, Robert Brouillette, France Castel, Gildor Roy, Raymond Cloutier, Sylvie Potvin; D: Gabriel Pelletier, Andrée Pelletier, Ann Burke, Yves Pelletier; C: Eric Cayla; M: Patrick Bourgeois, Genie '97; Art. Dir/Set. Dec., Costume. Des.

Kashmiri Run 🏃🏃 1969 (R) Action adventure about trio on the lam from Chinese communists chasing them through Tibet. 101m/C VHS. SP Pernell Roberts, Alexandra Bastedo, Julian Mateos, Gloria Gamata; D: John Peyser.

Kaspar Hauser 🏃🏃 1993 Historical epic based on the true story of Kaspar Hauser (Eisenmann), a 16-year-old found abandoned in Nuremberg, Germany in 1828, who was unable to walk, write, or speak. Entrusted to the scientific concerns of Professor Daumer (Samel), rumors begin to circulate that the boy is actually the Crown Prince of Baden. Supposedly, Kaspar was abducted as a baby and substituted for a child who died so his Uncle Ludwig (Ocssenknecht) could become Grand Duke. Court intrigue and threats abound as Kaspar struggles to survive. German with subtitles. 137m/C VHS. GE Andre Eisenmann, Jeremy Clyde, Katharina Thalbach, Uto Samel, Uwe Ochsenknecht; D: Peter Sehr; W: Peter Sehr; C: Gernot Roll; M: Nikos Mamangakis.

Kate & Leopold 🏃🏃 2001 (PG-13) Cute but underwhelming romantic comedy involving time travel. Eccentric scientist Stuart (Schreiber) finds a portal that allows him to visit New York City in 1876. But his presence is noticed by dashing Leopold, the Duke of Albany (Jackman), who unwittingly follows Stuart to present-day Manhattan. The Duke manages the adjustment quite well, especially after meeting business exec Kate (Ryan), Stuart's ex-girlfriend. Kate's more interested in a big promotion than romance, though she finds Leopold can't help being if strange. Too bad Leopold can't hang around, he has to go back to 1876 but can be persuaded to go with him? This is familiar territory for Ryan (who's more brittle than perky) but Jackman does chivalry with the best of them. 121m/C VHS, DVD. US Meg Ryan, Hugh Jackman, Liev Schreiber, Breckin Meyer, Natasha Lyonne, Bradley Whitford, Paxton Whitehead, Spalding Gray, Philip Bosco, David Aaron Baker; D: James Mangold; W: Steven Rogers; C: Stuart Dryburgh; M: Rolfe Kent. Golden Globes '02: Song ("Until").

Keane 🏃🏃 2004 (R) Unflinching, unsettling, and intense portrait of grief, and one man's struggle to regain his sanity. William Keane (Lewis), a wanderer an NYC bus terminal, searching for his daughter, who may or may not have disappeared from there a year earlier while in his care. He struggles to hold himself together to continue his search when he meets, and helps, a fellow lost soul, Lynn (Ryan) who trusts him enough to ask him to watch her seven year old daughter Kira. Lewis's performance more than stands up to the constant scrutiny director/writer keeps on his character, as the tension in the film just mounts. 100m/C DVD. US Damian Lewis, Abigail Breslin, Amy Ryan; D: Lodge Kerrigan; W: Lodge Kerrigan; C: John Foster.

Keaton's Cop 🏃 1990 (R) Another cheap cop comedy involving the mistaken identity of an important mob witness. 95m/C VHS. Lee Majors, Abe Vigoda, Don Rickles; D: Robert Burge.

The Keep 🏃🏃 1983 (R) At the height of the Nazi onslaught, several German soldiers unleash an unknown power from a medieval stone fortress. Technically impressive but lacking in all other aspects. From a novel by F. Paul Wilson. 96m/C VHS. Scott Glenn, Alberta Watson, Jurgen Prochnow, Robert Prosky, Gabriel Byrne, Ian McKellen, William Morgan Sheppard; D: Michael Mann; W: Michael Mann, Dennis Lynton Clark; C: Alex Thomson; M: Tangerine Dream.

Keep 'Em Flying 🏃🏃 1941 Bud and Lou star in the this wartime morale-booster that hasn't aged well. The duo follow their barnstorming friend into flight academy; a not-too-taxing plot includes five musical numbers and two Martha Rayes (she plays twins). 86m/B VHS. Bud Abbott, Lou Costello, Martha Raye, Dick Foran, William Gargan, Carol Bruce, Martha Raye; D: Arthur Lubin.

Katherine 🏃 The Radical 1975 A young heiress rejects her pampered lifestyle and becomes a violent revolutionary, rebelling against social injustices and the system that spawned them. 98m/C VHS, DVD. Sissy Spacek, Art Carney, Jane Wyatt, Henry Winkler, Julie Kavner, Hector Elizondo, Jenny Sullivan; D: Jeremy Paul Kagan. TV

Katie Tippel 🏃🏃 Katie's Passion; Cathy Tippel; Hot Sweat; Keetje Tippel 1975 (R) In 1881 Amsterdam, a young Dutch prostitute works her way out of poverty and enters a world of education and wealth. A Victorian tale of exploitation with a tough, intelligent Cinderella heroine. In Dutch with English subtitles. 104m/C VHS, DVD. NL Monique Van De Leeuwe, Rutger Hauer, Eddie Brugman, Hannah De Leeuwe, Andrea Domburg; D: Paul Verhoeven; W: Gerard Soeteman; C: Jan De Bont; M: Roger van Otterloo.

Kavik the Wolf Dog 🏃¹/₂ The Courage of Kavik, the Wolf Dog 1980 Heartwarming story of a courageous dog's love and suffering for the boy he loves. 99m/C VHS, DVD. Ronny Cox, Linda Sorensen, Andrew Ian McMillan, Chris Wiggins, John Ireland; D: Peter Carter. TV

Kazaam 🏃¹/₂ 1996 (PG) Twelve-year-old Max (Capra) is having problems—but lies are chasing him and his single mom's just found a new boyfriend. But his luck seems ready to change when a battered boombox reveals a seven-foot rappin' genie named Kazaam (O'Neal). The kid's beyond obnoxious and Shaq shouldn't plan to give up b-ball anytime soon (at least for an acting career), even though director Glaser did think up the part for the tall guy just before he met him at an NBA All-Star Game. 93m/C VHS, DVD. Francis Capra, Shaquille O'Neal, Ally Walker, John A. Coste-Ioe, Marshall Manesh, James Acheson; D: Paul Michael Glaser; W: Christian Ford, Roger Soffer; C: Charles Minsky; M: Christopher Tyng.

Kate's Addiction 🏃🏃 1999 (R) Kate (Wuhrer) comes to L.A. in search of an old friend (Forke) but she's really interested in more than hanging around. And anyone who gets in her way may not live to regret it. 95m/C VHS, DVD. Kari Wuhrer, Farrah Forke, Matt Borlenghi; D: Eric De La Barre. VIDEO

Keep My Grave Open 🏃🏃 The House Where Hell Froze Over 1980 (R) A woman lives in an isolated house where a series of strange murders take place. She attributes them to her brother, but does he really exist? Made cheaply, but not without style; filmed in Harrison County, Texas. 85m/C VHS, DVD. Camilla Carr, Gene Ross, Stephen Tobolowsky, Ann Stafford, Sharon Bunn, Chelcie Ross; D: S.F. Brownrigg. Cameos: Cameos: Caneca Lee; D: John Clein.

Keep Punching 🏃🏃 1939 A gambler/boxer is almost destroyed by life in the fast lane, as well as by a seductive woman. 80m/C VHS. Henry Armstrong, Mae Johnson.

Keep Talking Baby 🏃🏃 Cause Toujours, Mon Lapin 1961 Action-packed thriller's block, living in California with his girlfriend Astrid. He decides to revisit the family ranch in Deadrock, Montana, and his crackpot Uncle Smitty and saintly Aunt Lureen. The family ranch is coveted by Joe, evil Overstreet (typecasting for Palance), whose daughter was once loved by Joe but is now married to his ex-best friend. Character more than plot rules this moody, low-key story based on a novel by Thomas McCuane. 95m/C VHS. William L. Petersen, Lolita (David) Davidovich, Rachel Ticotin, Buck Henry, Jack Palance, Fred Dalton Thompson, Jeff Kober, Los Smith; D: Andy Tennant. CABLE.

The Keeper 🏃🏃¹/₂ 1996 Disillusioned Paul Lamott (Esposito) is a corrections officer at the King's County House of Detention in Brooklyn. Nevertheless, Paul, who's earning a law degree, is moved by the pleas of Haitian prisoner Jean Baptiste (de Bankole), who swears he's been wrongly accused of rape. Paul, who's far from an ideal fellow himself, manages to help Jean make bail and then invites him home—to the strong dismay of Paul's teacher wife Angela (Taylor). However, Angela begins warming to Jean's charm—but beware the stranger. 97m/C VHS, DVD. Giancarlo Esposito, Regina Taylor, Isaach de Bankole; D: Joe Brewster; C: Igor Sunara; M: John Petersen.

Keeper of the City 🏃🏃¹/₂ 1992 (R) Gossett stars as a tough detective out to get a vigilante (LaPaglia) who is roaming the streets of Chicago. LaPaglia turns in an effective portrayal of a hit man with a conscience who targets crime bosses. Peretti plays the crusading newspaper journalist tags him "The Gangster Killer." Coyote plays the crusading journalist who is always interfering in Gossett's business. Good performances and an intriguing storyline combine to make this action-packed thriller worthwhile, although the script isn't as good as Di Pega's novel, which he adapted himself. 95m/C VHS. Louis Gossett Jr., Peter Coyote, Anthony LaPaglia, Renee Soutendijk, Aeryk Egan, Tony Todd; D: Bobby Roth; M: Gerald Di Pego.

Keeper of the Flame 🏃🏃¹/₂ 1942 Tracy and Hepburn manage to keep the murk of this story at bay as war correspondent Steven O'Malley (Tracy) is assigned to write about super patriot Robert V. Forrest, who's just died in an accident. Reclusive widow Christine Forrest (Hepburn) finally agrees to help O'Malley out but what our intrepid reporter discovers is that the hero was really a heel—something Christine still doesn't want known.

Keep the Change 🏃🏃 1992 Wealthy patients at Underwood Asylum suffer unspeakable horrors while under the care of Lee. Detective Dick Driver investigates. Obscure horror spoof. 96m/C VHS, DVD. CA Christopher Lee, Tell Schreiber, Sally Gray; D: Tom Drake; M: Tom Drake.

Keeper 🏃🏃 1984 Wealthy patients at Underwood Asylum suffer unspeakable horrors while under the care of Lee.

Based on the novel by I.A.R. Wylie. **100m/ B** VHS. *D:* Spencer Tracy, Katharine Hepburn, Richard Whorf, Margaret Wycherly, Donald Meek, Stephen McNally, Audrey Christie, Frank Craven, Forrest Tucker, Percy Kilbride, Howard da Silva, Darryl Hickman; *D:* George Cukor; *W:* Donald Ogden Stewart; *C:* William H. Daniels; *M:* Bronislau Kaper.

The Keeper: The Legend of Omar Khayyam 🐾🐾 2005 (PG) Account of 11th century poet-astronomer Omar Khayyam and his love triangle in 11th century Persia. First-time director Mashayekh intercuts an autobiographical tale of 12-year-old Kkayyam descendent Kamran (Echahly) in modern Houston. Respectable labor of love is an indie that looks quite epic. Unfortunately, the movie comes off more like an after-school special with a flair for bright costumes. Surprise cameo from Vanessa Redgrave sparks things only for as long as she's on the screen. **95m/C** DVD. *US* Bruno Lastra, Moritz Bleibtreu, Rade Serbedzija, Vanessa Redgrave, C. Thomas Howell, Diane Baker, Christopher Simpson, Adam Echahly, Marie Espinosa; *D:* Kayvan Mashayekh; *W:* Kayvan Mashayekh, Belle Avery; *C:* Dusan Joksimovic, Matt Cantrell; *M:* Elton Ahi.

Keeping Mum 🐾🐾½ 2005 (R) Smith steals the show in this black comedy as homicidal housekeeper Grace. She's just taken a job with harried, oblivious vicar Walter Goodfellow (Atkinson) and his neglected family. Bored wife Gloria (Scott Thomas) is flirting with her brash American golf pro Lance (Swayze); teen daughter Holly is a nympho; and younger son Petey (Parkes) is beset by bullies. But tart-tongued Grace will make everything all right since her lurid past (a stint in a prison for the criminally insane) has not made her squeamish about getting things done. **103m/C** DVD. *GB* Maggie Smith, Rowan Atkinson, Patrick Swayze, Kristin Scott Thomas, Emilia Fox, James Booth, Liz Smith, Tamsin Egerton, Toby Parkes; *D:* Niall Johnson; *W:* Niall Johnson, Richard Russo; *C:* Gavin Finney; *M:* Dickon Hinchliffe.

Keeping On 🐾🐾½ 1981 TV movie with a pro-union stance. A preacher, who is also a millworker, teams up with an organizer to try to unionize the mill. Originally produced for the PBS "American Playhouse" series. **75m/C** VHS. Dick Anthony Williams, Carol Kane, James Broderick, Marcia Rodd, Rosalind Cash, Carl Lee, Danny Glover, Guy Boyd; *D:* Barbara Kopple. TV

Keeping the Faith 🐾🐾½ 2000 (PG-13) Norton's directorial debut sounds like a bad bar joke but turns out to be a slick, if meandering, romantic comedy. He's a priest, Brian, whose longtime best friend Jake (Stiller) is a rabbi with a congregation that wants him married to a nice Jewish girl. As kids, their mutual best pal was Anna, who returns to New York as a workaholic corporate exec (Elfman). The friendship is re-established but so is something more—both men fall for the lady and, unbeknownst to Brian, Anna and Jake begin an affair. More than sparks fly, **127m/C** VHS, DVD. Edward Norton, Ben Stiller, Jenna Elfman, Anne Bancroft, Eli Wallach, Milos Forman, Ron Rifkin, Holland Taylor, Rena Sofer, Lisa Edelstein, Bodhi (Pine) Elfman; *D:* Edward Norton; *W:* Stuart Blumberg; *C:* Anastas Michos; *M:* Elmer Bernstein.

Keeping Up with the Steins 🐾 2006 (PG-13) Benjamin Fiedler (Sabara) finds his bar mitzvah being turned into a chance for his Hollywood agent dad Adam (Piven) to one-up rival find the stolen $5 million on a New York-bound train. The two are relentlessly pursued by everyone, including the CIA and Russian spies. **102m/C** VHS, DVD. Michael Sarrazin, Margot Kidder, Alan Scarfe, Ken Pogue, Vlasta Vrana, Robin Pilon; *D:* Robin Spry.

Keeping Track 🐾 1986 (R) Two tourists witness a murder and robbery and find the stolen $5 million on a New York-bound train. The two are relentlessly pursued by everyone, including the CIA and Russian spies. **102m/C** VHS, DVD. Michael Sarrazin, Margot Kidder, Alan Scarfe, Ken Pogue, Vlasta Vrana, Robin Pilon; *D:* Robin Spry.

special sitcom" way. Subtract at least a bone for the sight of Garry Marshall's naked backside. **95m/C** DVD. *US* Daryl Sabara, Jeremy Piven, Garry Marshall, Jami Gertz, Cheryl Hines, Daryl Hannah, Doris Roberts, Larry Miller, Carter Jenkins, Richard Benjamin, Miranda Cosgrove, Adam Goldberg, Sandra Taylor; *Cameos:* Neil Diamond; *D:* Scott Marshall; *W:* Mark Zakarin; *C:* Charles Minsky; *M:* John Debney.

Keillers Park 🐾🐾 2005 A true hate crime story told in flashbacks. Peter sits in jail accused of a murder in Gothenburg's Keillers Park. Engaged and involved in the family business, Peter catches the eye of young street vendor Nassim and soon the two are lovers. Peter becomes obsessive and his life unravels with devastating consequences. Swedish with subtitles. **87m/C** DVD. *SW* Marten Klingberg, Piotr Giro, Karin Bergquist, Gosta Bredefeldt; *D:* Susanna Edwards; *W:* Pia Gradvall; *C:* Robert Nordstrom; *M:* Peter Adolfsson.

Kelly of the Secret Service 🐾 1936 Agent tries to find out who stole the plans for a guided missile system. Fast-pace rides over the silliness of the plot. **69m/B** VHS. Lloyd Hughes, Sheila (Manors) Manors, Fuzzy Knight, Syd Saylor; *D:* Jack Muhall; Forrest Taylor; *D:* Robert F. "Bob" Hill; *W:* Al Martin.

Kelly the Second 🐾½ 1936 Slow-moving boxing comedy about a punch-drunk fighter trying to win again with the encouragement of his trainer and manager. **70m/B** VHS. Guinn "Big Boy" Williams, Patsy Kelly, Charley Chase, Pert Kelton, Edward Brophy, Maxie "Slapsie" Rosenbloom, Harold Huber, DeWitt Jennings, Billy Gilbert, Syd Saylor; *D:* Gus Meins.

Kelly's Heroes 🐾🐾½ 1970 (PG) A misfit band of crooks are led by Eastwood on a daring mission: to steal a fortune in gold from behind enemy lines. In the process, they almost win WWII. Sutherland is superb, as is McLeod, in his pre-Love Boat days. **145m/C** VHS, DVD. Clint Eastwood, Donald Sutherland, Telly Savalas, Gavin MacLeod, Don Rickles, Carroll O'Connor, Stuart Margolin, Harry Dean Stanton, Jeff Morris, Richard (Dick) Davalos, Perry Lopez, Tom Troupe, Len Lesser, David Hurst, George Savalas, Tom Signorelli; *C:* Gabriel Figueroa; *M:* Lalo Schifrin.

Kemek 🐾 1970 (R) An eccentric chemical company owner has his mistress push a new mind-control drug on an American writer, and has them killed after discovering their subsequent affair. Unfortunately, he didn't count on the woman's ex-husband seeking revenge. **82m/C** VHS. David Hedison, Helmut Snider, Mary Woronov, Alexandra Stewart, Cal Haynes; *D:* Theodore Gershuny; *W:* Theodore Gershuny; *C:* Enzo Barboni; *M:* John Lewis.

Kennedy 🐾🐾 1983 Miniseries biography of JFK from his inauguration to his assassination. **278m/C** VHS, DVD. Martin Sheen, Blair Brown, Vincent Gardenia, Geraldine Fitzgerald, E.G. Marshall, John Shea; *D:* Richard Hartley. TV

The Kennedys of Massachusetts 🐾🐾½ 1995 Three cassette TV miniseries chronicles six decades of Kennedy life, from Joe Kennedy's (Petersen) courtship of Rose (O'Toole) to the presidential election of JFK and all the various scandals and tragedies. Adapted from the book "The Fitzgeralds and the Kennedys" by Doris Kearns Godwin. Remade as "Calling Philo Vance" in 1940. **73m/B** VHS, DVD. William Petersen, Annette O'Toole, Charles Durning, Steven Weber, Tracy Pollan, Campbell Scott; *D:* Lamont Johnson; *W:* William Hanley; *M:* David Shire. TV

The Kennel Murder Case 🐾🐾 1933 Debonair detective Philo Vance suspects that a clear-cut case of suicide is actually murder. Fourth Vance mystery starring Powell. **73m/B** VHS, DVD. William Powell, Mary Astor, Jack La Rue, Ralph Morgan, Eugene Pallette; *D:* Michael Curtiz; *W:* Robert Presnell Sr., Robert N. Lee, Peter Milne; *C:* William Rees; *M:* Bernhard Kaun.

Kenny Rogers as the Gambler 🐾½ 1980 Rogers stars as Brady Hawkes, debonair gambler searching for a son he never knew he had. Based on the Rogers song of the same name. One of the highest rated TV movies

ever. Followed by several sequels. **94m/C** VHS, DVD. Kenny Rogers, Christine Belford, Bruce Boxleitner, Harold Gould, Clu Gulager, Lance LeGault, Lee Purcell, Noble Willingham; *D:* Dick Lowry. TV

Kenny Rogers as the Gambler, Part 2: The Adventure Continues 🐾½ 1983 The surprise success of the made-for-TV western based on the popular Kenny Rogers' song spawned this equally popular sequel. Rogers returns as Brady Hawkes, this time searching for his kidnapped son. Followed by two more sequels. **195m/C** VHS, DVD. Kenny Rogers, Bruce Boxleitner, Linda Evans, Harold Gould, David Hedison, Clu Gulager, Johnny Crawford; *D:* Dick Lowry. TV

Kenny Rogers as the Gambler, Part 3: The Legend Continues 🐾½ 1987 Roger's third attempt at humanizing the gambler from his hit '70s song. This time, the Gambler gives a hand with the mediating between the warring U.S. government and the Sioux nation. Sitting Bull and Buffalo Bill add credibility to this average undertaking. Made for TV. **190m/C** VHS. Kenny Rogers, Bruce Boxleitner, Linda Gray, Melanie Chartoff, Matt Clark, George Kennedy, Dean Stockwell, Charles Durning, Jeffrey Jones, George American Horse; *D:* Dick Lowry. TV

Kent State 🐾🐾 1981 Recounts the tragic events that took place at Kent State University in 1970, when student demonstrators faced National Guardsmen. Goldstone won an Emmy for Outstanding Direction. **120m/C** VHS. Talia Balsam, Ellen Barkin, Jane Fleiss, John Getz, Keith Gordon; *D:* James Goldstone. TV

The Kentuckian 🐾🐾½ 1955 Burt Lancaster stars as a rugged frontiersman who leaves with his son to go to Texas. On their journey the two are harassed by fighting mountaineers. **104m/C** VHS, DVD. Burt Lancaster, Walter Matthau, Diana Lynn, John McIntire, Dianne Foster, Una Merkel, John Carradine; *D:* Burt Lancaster; *C:* Ernest Laszlo.

Kentucky Blue Streak 🐾½ 1935 Young jockey is framed for murder while riding at an "illegal" racetrack. Later, almost eligible for parole, he escapes from jail to ride "Blue Streak" in the Kentucky Derby. **61m/B** VHS. Eddie Nugent, Frank "Junior" Coghlan, Patricia Scott, Cornelius Keefe, Margaret Mann, Roy D'Arcy, Joseph Girard, Roy Watson; *D:* Bernard B. Ray; *W:* Rose Gordon.

Kentucky Fried Movie 🐾🐾½ 1977 (R) A zany potpourri of satire about movies, TV, commercials, and contemporary society. Written by Abrahams and the Zuckers, who later gave us "Airplane!" **85m/C** VHS, DVD. Bill Bixby, Jerry Zucker, Jim Abrahams, David Zucker, Donald Sutherland, Henry Gibson, George Lazenby, Tony Dow, Uschi Digart, Rick Baker, Marilyn Joi, Forrest J Ackerman; *D:* Jon Landis; *W:* Jerry Zucker, Jim Abrahams, David Zucker; *C:* Stephen M. Katz.

Kentucky Jubilee 🐾½ 1951 At the jubilee, a movie director is kidnapped and the master of ceremonies, among others, decides to find him. **67m/B** VHS. Jerry Colonna, Jean Porter, James Ellison, Raymond Hatton, Fritz Feld, Vince Barnett, Michael Whalen, Archie Twitchell, Russell Hicks, Margia Dean, Si Jenks, Ralph Sanford, Jack Reitzen; *D:* Ron Ormond; *W:* Ron Ormond, Maurice Tombragel; *C:* Carl K.

Kentucky Kernels 🐾🐾 *Triple Trouble* 1934 A pair of down and out magicians ('30s comic duo Wheeler and Woolsey) happen upon a young boy (Little Rascal Spanky) who happens to be heir to a fortune. The three head for the rascal's Kentucky home, where they're welcomed with southern inhospitality. Much feuding and slapsticking. **75m/B** VHS. Bert Wheeler, Robert Woolsey, Mary Carlisle, George "Spanky" McFarland, Noah Beery Sr., Lucille LaVerne, Willie Best; *D:* George Stevens; *M:* Max Steiner.

Kentucky Rifle 🐾½ 1955 A Comanche Indian tribe will let a group of stranded pioneers through their territory only if they agree to sell the Kentucky rifles aboard their wagon. **80m/C** VHS, DVD. Chill Wills, Lance Fuller, Cathy Downs, Jess Barker, Sterling Holloway, Jeanne Cagney; *D:* Carl K. Hittleman.

Kept 🐾🐾 2001 (R) Struggling architectural student Kyle Griffin thinks his worries are over when he lands a job at the firm owned by Barbara Weldon and her husband. But Barbara is a very hands-on employer and soon Kyle is involved in an affair and a suspect in a murder. Now he has to save himself from being the fall guy. **98m/C** VHS, DVD. Ice-T, Yvette Nipar, Christian Oliver, Paul Michael Robinson, Michelle Von Flotow, Laura Rose, Art Hingle; *D:* Fred Olen Ray; *W:* Richard Uhlig, Kimberly A. Ray; *C:* Theo Angell; *M:* Herman Jackson, Michael van Blum, Barry Taylor. VIDEO

Kept Husbands 🐾🐾 1931 A factory worker saves two lives in an industrial accident, and the boss invites him home to dinner. When he meets the boss' daughter, romance blooms. But their different backgrounds cause difficulties. A bit dull, and dated by its chauvinism. **76m/B** VHS, DVD. Dorothy Mackaill, Joel McCrea, Robert McWade, Florence Roberts, Clara Kimball Young, Mary Carr, Ned Sparks, Bryant Washburn; *D:* Lloyd Bacon; *M:* Max Steiner.

Kettle of Fish 🐾🐾 2006 (R) Jazz sax man Mel (Modine) decides it's time to act like an adult and he moves in with his girlfriend—subletting his apartment to nerdy biologist Ginger (Gershon). But when Mel becomes obsessed with another woman, he gets tossed out on his ear, and is forced to beg Ginger to allow him to share the apartment. Romantic complications follow. Familiar story, rather engaging performances. **97m/C** DVD. Matthew Modine, Gina Gershon, Fisher Stevens, Isiah Whitlock Jr., Christy Scott Cashman, Kevin J. O'Connor; *D:* Claudia Myers; *W:* Claudia Myers; *C:* Neil Lisk; *M:* David Tobocman.

The Kettles in the Ozarks 🐾🐾½ 1956 Since Kilbride retired after the seventh comedy, Uncle Huntcutt played a new male character, Uncle Sledge, in the eighth film. Ma (Main) takes the young'uns to visit their uncle in the Ozarks and finds she must help him and fiancee Bedelia (Merkel) save the failing farm from bootleggers. **81m/B** VHS. Marjorie Main, Arthur Hunnicutt, Una Merkel, Ted de Corsia, Richard Eyer, Joseph (Joe) Sawyer, Richard Deacon; *D:* Charles Lamont; *W:* Kay Lenard.

The Kettles on Old MacDonald's Farm 🐾🐾½ 1957 The ninth and last in the series finds Ma (Main in her final film) and Pa (Kennelly replacing the retired Kilbride) playing matchmakers for humble lumberman Brad (Smith). Seems he wants to marry the boss' spoiled daughter, Sally (Talbott), whom Ma decides needs a little backwoods seasoning before she'll make the proper wife. **82m/B** VHS. Marjorie Main, Parker Fennelly, John Smith, Gloria Talbott, Claude Akins, Roy Barcroft, Patricia Morrow, George Dunn; *D:* Virgil W. Vogel; *W:* Herbert Margolis, William Raynor.

Kevin & Perry Go Large 🐾½ 2000 (R) The Brits can make bad teen sex comedies adapted from TV shows just as easily as Americans can. Kevin (Enfield) and Perry (Burka in drag) are a couple of gormless teenage boys who have only one thing on their teeny brains. And since the Brits all seem to go to Spain to be naughty, the boys decide to take their summer holidays in party capital Ibiza and get some chicks. Only problem is Kevin's parents decide to accompany them. Bummer (or whatever the Brit equivalent would be). May make more sense if you've seen the characters on TV. **83m/C** VHS, DVD. *GB* Harry Enfield, Kathy Burke, Rhys Ifans, Laura Fraser, Tabitha Wady, James Fleet, Louisa Rix; *D:* Ed Bye; *W:* David Cummings, Harry Enfield; *C:* Alan Almond.

The Key 🐾🐾½ 1958 A long, slow WWII drama about the key to an Italian girl's apartment that gets passed from tugboat skipper to tugboat skipper before dangerous missions. Ultimately she finds true love, or does she? Based on the novel "Stella" by Jan de Hartog. **134m/B** VHS. *GB* William Holden, Sophia Loren, Trevor Howard, Oscar Homolka, Kieron Moore; *D:* Carol Reed; *W:* Carl Foreman; *C:* Oswald Morris; *M:* Malcolm Arnold. '58: Actor (Howard).

Key Exchange ⅋⅋½ **1985 (R)** Kevin Scott and Paul Kurta based this contemporary look at love and commitments on a play by Kevin Wade's popular play. Two New York City "yuppies" have reached an ex-point in their relationship where an excchange of apartment keys commonly occurs—but they are hesitant. **96m/C** VHS. Brooke Adams, Ben Masters, Daniel Stern, Tony Roberts, Danny Aiello, Annie Golden, Nancy Mette. **D:** Barnet Kellman. **W:** Jonathan Elias.

Key Largo ⅋⅋⅋½ **1948** WWII vet Bogart travels to the run-down Florida hotel owned by Barrymore and Bacall who are, respectively, the father and widow of a war buddy. Bogart notes the other guests are a decidedly criminal bent, but as a hurricane threatens, no one can leave. One-time mob kingpin Robinson lords it over the others while Bogart keeps his usual cynical cool. Trevor, who plays Robinson's alcoholic ex-singer moll, deservedly won an Oscar for her role. Based on a play by Maxwell Anderson. **101m/B** VHS, DVD. Humphrey Bogart, Lauren Bacall, Claire Trevor, Edward G. Robinson, Lionel Barrymore, Thomas Gomez, Dan Seymour; **Cameos:** John Huston; **W:** Richard Brooks, John Huston; **C:** Karl Freund; **M:** Max Steiner. Oscars '48: Support. Actress (Trevor).

The Key Man ⅋½ *Life at Stake* **1957** A radio show host manages to get mixed up with gangsters after recreating a crime on the air. He uses his knowledge of a crime to thwart the crooks. **63m/B** VHS. GB Lee Patterson, Hy Hazell, Colin Gordon, Philip Leaver, Paula Byrne. **D:** Montgomery Tully, Lira Raymond.

The Key to Rebecca ⅋⅋½ **1985** The Nazis and the British go head-to-head in war torn North Africa. As the Germans push their way across Egypt, they find an unexpected ally in a half-German/half-Arab killer behind the British lines. Tense, well-made thriller, originally a miniseries. **190m/C** VHS. David Soul, Cliff Robertson, Robert Culp, Season Hubley, Lira Raymond, Anthony Quayle, David Hemmings. **TV**

The Keys of the Kingdom ⅋⅋½ **1944** An earnest adaptation of A.J. Cronin's novel about a young Scottish missionary spreading God's word in 19th Century China. **137m/B** VHS, DVD. Gregory Peck, Thomas Mitchell, Edmund Gwenn, Vincent Price, Roddy McDowall, Cedric Hardwicke, Peggy Ann Garner, James Gleason, Anne Revere, Rose Stradner, Sara Allgood, Abner Biberman, Arthur Shields; **D:** John M. Stahl; **W:** Joseph L. Mankiewicz, Nunnally Johnson; **C:** Arthur C. Miller.

Keys to Tulsa ⅋⅋½ **1996 (R)** After losing his job as a lowly movie reviewer (gasp!), Richter Bourdreau (Stoltz), the young wastrel son of a wealthy Tulsa family, is lured into a blackmail scheme by his exflame Vicky (Unger) and her perpetually stoned husband Ronnie (Spader). When the tables are turned on him, Richter finally gets up off his slacker butt for some revenge. Excellent cast includes Moore as his flinty mother and Coburn as a wealthy redneck patriarch. Stoltz's performance holds the spiraling story of class distinction, murder and deceit together, and back together and enter a hip-hop dance Spader's Elvis-helmeted loser is fun to watch. Based on the novel by Brian Fair Berkey. **112m/C** VHS, DVD. Eric Stoltz, James Spader, Mary Tyler Moore, Joanna Going, Cameron Diaz, James Coburn, Michael Rooker, Peter Strauss, Deborah Kara Unger; **D:** Leslie Greif. **M:** Stephen Endelman.

The KGB: The Secret War ⅋½ *Lethal* **1986 (PG-13)** Reheated Cold War fare. **90m/C** VHS. Sally Kellerman, Michael Ansara, Michael Billington; **W:** Sandra K. Bailey. **C:** Peter Lyons Collister.

Khartoum ⅋⅋½ **1966** A sweeping but talky adventure epic detailing the last days of General "Chinese" Gordon as the title city is besieged by Arab tribes in 1884. **134m/C** VHS, DVD. Charlton Heston, Laurence Olivier, Ralph Richardson, Richard Johnson, Alexander Knox, Hugh Williams, Nigel Green, Michael Hordern, Johnny Sekka; **D:** Basil Dearden; **W:** Robert Ardrey; **C:** Edward Scaife; **M:** Frank Cordell.

The Kick Fighter ⅋ **1991** Would you believe the hero has to kickbox to finance his kid sister's operation? Grungy, Bangkok-set chopsocky cheapie leaves no cliche untouched, but fights are wellstaged. A strange and credit lauds real-life champ Jirquidez, here a bad guy. **92m/C** VHS, DVD. Richard Norton, Benny "the Jet" Urquidez, Glen Ruehland, Franco Guerrero, Erica Van Wagener, Steve Rackman; **D:** Anthony Maharaj.

Kick of Death: The Prodigal Boxer ⅋ *The Prodigal Boxer: Fang Shi Yu; Kung Fu: The Punch of Death* **1973 (R)** A young boxer is accused of a murder he didn't commit, and fights a battle to the death to prove it. **90m/C** VHS, DVD. Marg Sei, Suma Wah Lung, Pa Hung; **D:** Chai Yang Min.

Kickboxer ⅋⅋½ **1989 (R)** The brother of a permanently crippled kickboxing champ trains for a revenge match. **97m/C** VHS, DVD. Jean-Claude Van Damme, Rochelle Ashara, Dennis Chan, Dennis Alexio; **D:** Mark DiSalle. **W:** Jean-Claude Van Damme. **M:** Paul Hertzog.

Kickboxer 2: The Road Back ⅋½ **1990 (R)** Mitchell takes over for Van Damme in this action sequel which finds our kickboxer who murdered his brother. **90m/C** VHS. GB Sasha Mitchell, Peter Boyle, John Diehl; **D:** Albert Pyun.

Kickboxer 3: The Art of War ⅋½ **1992 (R)** Mitchell returns in this second sequel. This time the American kickboxer who murdered his brother. For a little more fun our hero saves a kidnapped girl and fights a hired killer. **92m/C** VHS, DVD. Sasha Mitchell, Dennis Chan, Richard Comar, Noah Verduzco, Alethea Miranda, Ian Jacklin; **D:** Rick Jang.

Kickboxer 4: The Aggressor ⅋⅋½ **1994 (R)** Martial arts expert David Sloan (Mitchell) was framed by sworn enemy Tong Po but now he's back and looking for revenge. **90m/C** VHS, DVD. Sasha Mitchell, Kamal Krifla, Nicholas Guest, Deborah Mansy, Brad Thornton; **D:** Albert Pyun.

Kickboxer the Champion ⅋ **1991** The opium trade is in for a kick to the stomach when Archer challenges the big man in charge to a deathly duel. **?m/C** VHS. Don Murray, Wayne Archer; **D:** Allen Cheung.

Kicked in the Head ⅋⅋ **1997 (R)** Redmond, a loser who dreams of the Hindenburg disaster, is newly jobless, homeless and loveless. He decides to go on a "spiritual quest", which unfortunately consists of bad poetry and worse trouble. Uncle Sam (Woods) wants him to deliver a package, his buddy Stretch (Rapaport) wants him to work for his shady (and sometimes violent) beer business and stewardess Megan (Fiorentino) wants him to leave her alone. It's all settled in a hail of gunfire and car chases, because that's how things are solved in the movies. Directorial debut "Rhythm Thief." **97m/C** VHS, DVD. Kevin Corrigan, Linda Fiorentino, James Woods, Lili Taylor, Michael Rapaport, Burt Young, Clerk Krupa; **D:** Matthew Harrison; **W:** Matthew Harrison, Kevin Corrigan; **C:** John Thomas, Howard Krupa; **M:** Stephen Endelman.

Kickin' It Old Skool ⅋ **2007 (PG-13)** Lame comedy has breakdancing schooler Jimmy Albright (Saunier) is secretly taking boxing lessons from trainer Harry Sloan (Steiger) since his parents don't approve. Jimmy is a natural and is ready to compete in the amateur championship match. Then Harry dies and fellow boxer Trey (Brochu) schemes to have Jimmy's parents find out about his secret life and forbid him to box. **89m/C** VHS, DVD. Jamie Kennedy, Maria Menounos, Bobb'e J. Thompson, Miguel A. Nunez Jr., Vivica A. Fox; **D:** Harvey Glazer; **M:** Richard Glasser.

Kicking and Screaming ⅋⅋⅋ **1995 (R)** Baumbach's deft, though slightly self-conscious directorial debut examines the post-college angst of Grover (Hamilton) and his three other slacker roommies. In denial of their recently achieved non-student status, the four bond together in pursuit of the inane and trivial, while their various girlfriends slip more easily into adulthood. Funny and tender flashback scenes of Grover and girlfriend Jane (D'Abo) add depth without all the dialogue. And it's to its sole credit that a movie this derivative works as well as it does. Midwell-written though it is. Hilarious highlight occurs as roommate Otis interviews for that most popular of low-budget, Gen-X movie jobs—video store clerk. **96m/C** VHS, DVD. Josh Hamilton, Olivia D'Abo, Carlos Jacott, Christopher Eigeman, Eric Stoltz, Jason Wiles, Parker Posey, Cara Buono, Elliott Gould; **D:** Noah Baumbach; **W:** Oliver Berkman, Noah Baumbach; **C:** Steven Bernstein; **M:** Phil Marshall.

Kicking & Screaming ⅋⅋½ **2005 (PG)** Anemic family sports comedy has mild-mannered Phil (Ferrell) in the anxiety-prone son of Buck (Duvall), a ridiculously competitive junior soccer coach who traded his own grandson, Phil's son Sam (McLaughlin), to another team. Determined to prove himself to Buck, Phil takes over coaching Sam's new soccer team filled with losers and misfits, with the help of Buck's arch-rival Mike Ditka, that is. Ferrell screaming at kids never stops being funny, but there's not an original moment in the entire film. **95m/C** DVD. US Will Ferrell, Robert Duvall, Steven Anthony Lawrence, Musetta Vander, Elliot Cho, Josh Hutcheson, Dylan McLaughlin, Eric Walker, Dallas McKinney, Jeremy Bergman, Kate Walsh, Francesco Lotti, Alessandro Ruggiero, Laura Kightling-er, Rachael Harris; **Cameos:** Mike Ditka; **D:** Jesse Dylan; **W:** Leo Benvenuti, Steve Rudnick; **C:** Lloyd Ahern I; **M:** Mark sham.

Kicks ⅋½ **1985** Two well-off San Francisco professionals play high-risk games with each other, culminating in a life-or-death hunt. **97m/C** VHS. Anthony Geary, Shelley Hack, Tom Mason, Ian Abercrombie, James Avery; **D:** William Wiard; **M:** Peter Bernstein. **TV**

The Kid ⅋⅋⅋ **1921** Sensitive and sassy film about a tramp who takes home an orphan. Chaplin's first feature. Also launched Coogan as the first child superstar. **60m/B** VHS, DVD. Charlie Chaplin, Jackie Coogan, Edna Purviance; **C:** Charlie Chaplin.

The Kid ⅋⅋½ **1997 (PG)** High schooler Jimmy Albright (Saunier) is secretly taking boxing lessons from trainer Harry Sloan (Steiger) since his parents don't approve. Jimmy is a natural and is ready to compete in the amateur championship match. **89m/C** VHS, DVD. Green, Sarah Trigger, Dale Dye; **D:** Charlie Chaplin.

The Kid and I ⅋⅋ **2005 (PG-13)** A film about the making of a film, built around Aaron Roman (Gores) who, although born with cerebral palsy, dreams of starring in action movies like his favor-ite. "True Lies." Since his father (Martegna) is a wealthy and powerful Los Angeles business mogul, Aaron gets his chance. Bill Williams (Arnold), whose acting career is floundering, is hired to write and co-star with Aaron, Actor Gores, who actually has cerebral palsy, is great as Aaron. Uplifting and fun. If you have a high schmaltz tolerance. **93m/C** DVD. US Tom Arnold, Linda Hamilton, Henry Winkler, Richard Edson, Joe Mantegna, Shannon Elizabeth, Arielle Kebbel, Brenda Strong, Eric Gores; **Cameos:** Penelope Spheeris; **W:** Tom Arnold. **C:** Robert E. Seaman.

Kid and the Killers ⅋ **1974 (PG)** Young orphan and a hardened criminal band together to pursue a villain. **90m/C** VHS. Jon Cypher, John Garces, Ralph Bluemke; **D:** Ralph Bluemke.

The Kid Brother ⅋⅋⅋ ½ **1927** The shy, weak son of a tough sheriff. Harold fantasizes about being a hero like his father and big brothers, falls in love with a carnival lady, and somehow saves the day. Classic silent comedy. **84m/B** VHS. Harold Lloyd, Walter James, Jobyna Ralston; **D:** Ted Wilde.

Kid Colter ⅋½ **1985** The young weak son of a city kid who goes to visit his dad in a remote wilderness area of the Pacific Northwest. While there he is abducted by two grizzly mountain men and left for dead, but survives and pursues his abductors relentlessly. Received the Award of Merit from the Film Advisory Board. **101m/C** VHS, DVD. Jim Stafford, Jeremy Shannos, Hal Terrace, Greg Ward, Jim Turner; **D:** David O'Malley; **W:** Jobyna Ralston.

Kid Courageous ⅋ **1935** An athlete goes west, tracks one mine thieves and prevents a hot-blooded spitfire from marrying the wrong man. **53m/B** VHS. Bob Steele, Late (Lafayette) McKee, Rene Borden, Bob Steele; **D:** Robert North Bradbury; **M:** Robert North Bradbury.

Kid Dynamite ⅋½ *Queen of Broadway* **1943** A Bowery Boys series episode. Gorcey is a boxer who is kidnapped to prevent his participation in a major fight. The real fighting occurs when his brother is substituted. **73m/B** VHS, DVD. Leo Gorcey, Huntz Hall, Bobby Jordan, Gabriel Dell, Pamela Blake; **D:** Wallace Fox.

A Kid for Two Farthings ⅋⅋½ **1955** An episodic, sentimental portrait of the Jewish quarter in London's East End, centered on a boy with a malformed goat he thinks is a magic unicorn capable of granting wishes and bringing happiness to his impoverished 'hood. Acclaimed adaptation of a novel by screenwriter Wolf Mankowitz. **96m/C** VHS, DVD. GB Diana Dors, David Kossoff, Celia Johnson, Jonathan Ashmore, Joe Robinson, Brenda de Banzie, Primo Carnera, Lou Jacobi, Irene Handl; **D:** Carol Reed; **W:** Wolf Mankowitz; **C:** Edward Scaife; **M:** Benjamin Frankel.

Kid from Brooklyn ⅋⅋ **1946** A shy, musically inclined milkman becomes a middleweight boxing champ in a street brawl. Remake of "The Milky Way" by Harold Lloyd. Available with a malformed goat he thinks is a magic colorized. **114m/C** VHS, DVD. Danny Kaye, Virginia Mayo, Eve Arden, Fay Bainter, Walter Abel; **D:** Norman Z. McLeod; **C:** Gregg Toland.

Kid from Gower Gulch ⅋ **1950** A singing, non-horse-riding cowboy enters a rodeo through a clever ruse. **56m/B** VHS, DVD. Jack Baxley, Joe Hiser, Wanda Cantlon, Spade Cooley; **D:** Oliver Drake; **M:** Elmer Clifton; **C:** Harvey Hines.

The Kid from Left Field ⅋⅋ **1979** Bat boy for the San Diego Padres transforms the team from losers to champions when he passes on the advice of his father, a "has-been" ballplayer, to the team members. TV remake of the 1953 classic. **80m/C** VHS. Gary Coleman, Robert Guillaume, Ed McMahon, Tab Hunter; **D:** Adell Aldrich. **TV**

Kid from Not-So-Big 🦴🦴 1978 (G) A family film that tells the story of Jenny, a young girl left to carry on her grandfather's frontier-town newspaper. When two con-men come to town, Jenny sets out to expose them. 87m/C VHS. Jennifer McAllister, Veronica Cartwright, Robert Viharo, Paul Tulley; D: William Crain.

Kid from Spain 🦴🦴1/2 1932 Early Busby Berkeley choreography highlights this fun, if nonsensical, musical. Thanks to the usual mixups, college boy Eddie (Cantor) witnesses a bank robbery and flees to his friend Ricardo's (Young) home in Mexico, with the crooks on his trail. Then he gets mistaken for a famous bullfighter and is even forced into the ring. Oh, and there's some romantic complications as well. ♪What You've Done; In the Moonlight; Look What I Got Lucky; A Perfect Combination. 96m/B VHS. Eddie Cantor, Robert Young, Lyda Roberti, Ruth Hall, John Miljan, Noah Beery Sr., J. Carrol Naish, Robert Emmett O'Connor; D: Leo McCarey; W: William Anthony McGuire, Bert Kalmar, Harry Ruby; C: Gregg Toland.

Kid Galahad 🦴🦴🦴 (The Battling Bellhop) 1937 Well-acted boxing drama with Robinson playing an honest promoter who wants to make Morris into a prize fighter. Davis plays the girl they both want. Remade as "The Wagons Roll at Night" and then made again as an Elvis Presley vehicle. 101m/B VHS. Edward G. Robinson, Bette Davis, Humphrey Bogart, Wayne Morris, Jane Bryan, Harry Carey Sr., Veda Ann Borg; D: Michael Curtiz; W: Seton I. Miller; C: Gaetano Antonio "Tony" Gaudio; M: Max Steiner.

A Kid in Aladdin's Palace 🦴🦴1/2 1997 (PG) Burger flipper Calvin (Nicholas) time travels to animated... thanks to a mischief-making genie (Negron). He meets Princess Scheherazade (Mitra), who wants Calvin's help in fighting evil Luxor (Faulkner), who's overthrown her father, King Aladdin (Ipale). 89m/C VHS, DVD. Thomas Ian Nicholas, Rhona Mitra, Taylor Negron, James Faulkner, Aharon Ipale; D: Robert L. Levy; W: Michael Part, Robert L. Levy; M: J.A.C. Redford.

A Kid in King Arthur's Court 🦴🦴1/2 1995 (PG) Lame adaptation of Mark Twain's "A Connecticut Yankee in King Arthur's Court" finds insecure California teen Calvin Fuller (Nicholas), falling down a hole created by an earthquake and landing in Camelot. Arthur's (Ackland) a doddering old man with a cute teen daughter, Princess Katey (Baeza), who needs some help in defeating the evil Lord Belasco (Malik). Naturally, Calvin helps out and gains confidence in himself. Okay time-waster for the kids. 91m/C VHS, DVD. Thomas Ian Nicholas, Joss Ackland, Art Malik, Paloma Baeza, Kate Winslet, Ron Moody, Daniel Craig; D: Michael Gottlieb; W: Michael Part, Robert L. Levy; C: Elemer Ragalyi; M: J.A.C. Redford.

Kid Millions 🦴🦴1/2 1934 Vintage musical comedy in which a dull-witted Brooklyn boy must travel to exotic Egypt to collect an inherited fortune. The finale is filmed in early three-strip Technicolor. Lucille Ball appears as a Goldwyn Girl. ♪Your Head on My Shoulder; Ice Cream Fantasy; An Earful of Music; When My Ship Comes In; Okay Toots; I Want to be a Minstrel Man; Mandy. 90m/B VHS. Eddie Cantor, Ethel Merman, Ann Sothern, George Murphy; D: Roy Del Ruth.

Kid Monk Baroni 🦴🦴1/2 1952 Street punk Baroni (Nimoy) leaves his gang behind when a good-guy priest (Rober) introduces him to boxing. The kid rises to success thanks to a cagey manager (Cabot) and despite the presence of organized crime. Typical B-movie melodrama. 80m/B VHS, DVD. Leonard Nimoy, Bruce Cabot, Richard Rober, Kathleen Freeman; D: Harold Schuster.

Kid 'n' Hollywood and Polly Tix in Washington 🦴🦴 1933 These two "Baby Burlesks" shorts star a cast of toddlers, featuring the most famous moppet of all time, Shirley Temple, in her earliest screen appearances. 20m/B VHS, DVD. Shirley Temple; D: Charles Lamont; C: Dwight Warren.

Kid Ranger 🦴 1936 A ranger shoots an innocent man, but later sets things straight by bringing the real culprit to justice. 57m/B VHS, DVD. Bob Steele, William Farnum; D: Robert North Bradbury.

Kid Sister 🦴1/2 1945 A young girl is determined to grab her sister's boyfriend for herself, and enlists the aid of a burglar to do it. 56m/B VHS. Roger Pryor, Judy Clark, Frank Jenks, Constance Worth, Tom Dugan, Minerva Urecal; D: Sam Newfield; W: Fred Myton; C: James S. Brown Jr.

The Kid Stays in the Picture 🦴🦴🦴 2002 (R) Documentary covers the up-and-down career and life of one-time actor and '70s-super film producer Robert Evans. Evans narrates the film memoir that is taken from his 1994 autobiography—so don't expect objectivity (or, necessarily, accuracy). Evans discusses not only his career but his marriages, romances, drug problems, involvement in a murder investigation, and his rise-and-fall-rise life. 93m/C VHS, DVD. US D: Brett Morgen, Nanette Burstein; W: Brett Morgen; C: John Bailey; M: Jeff Danna; Nar: Robert Evans.

Kid Vengeance 🦴1/2 1975 (R) After witnessing the brutal slaying of his family, a boy carries out a personal vendetta against the outlaws. 90m/C VHS, DVD. Leif Garrett, Jim Brown, Lee Van Cleef, John Marley, Glynnis O'Connor; D: Joseph Manduke.

The Kid Who Loved Christmas 🦴🦴 1990 After his adoptive mother is killed in a car accident, a young boy is taken from his adoptive father. The boy, upset about being removed from his new family, writes to Santa Claus for help. A touching yuletide drama. This was Sammy Davis Jr.'s last film. 118m/C VHS. Cicely Tyson, Michael Warren, Sammy Davis Jr., Gilbert Lewis, Ken Page, Della Reese, Esther Rolle, Ben Vereen, Vanessa Lynne Williams, John Beal, Trent Cameron; D: Arthur Allan Seidelman; C: Hanania Baer. TV

The Kid with the Broken Halo 🦴🦴 1982 Coleman and Guillaume are paired again in this unsuccessful pilot for a TV series. A young angel, out to earn his wings, must try to help three desperate families, with the help of an experienced angel. 96m/C VHS. Gary Coleman, Robert Guillaume, Harriet Hilliard Nelson, Dean Butler, Karl Michaelson, Christina Murrull, Mel Stewart; D: Leslie Martinson. TV

The Kid with the 200 I.Q. 🦴🦴 1983 When an earnest boy genius enters college at age 13, predictable comic situations arise that involve his attempts at impressing his idolized astronomy professor (Guillaume), as well as finally getting a girl. Harmless comedy, one of a series of squeaky-clean family fare starring Coleman. 96m/C VHS. Gary Coleman, Robert Guillaume, Mel Stewart; D: Leslie Martinson. TV

The Kid with the X-Ray Eyes 🦴🦴 1999 (PG) Twelve-year-old Bobby wants to be a spy when he grows up. Then he finds a strange pair of glasses that allow him to see through anything. He attracts the attentions of the C.I.A., the police, and a pair of thieves who all want his special specs. 84m/C VHS, DVD. Justin Berfield, Keith Carradine, Mark Collie, Diane Salinger, Griffin (Griffen) Drew, Brinke Stevens; D: Fred Olen Ray; W: Sean O'Bannon; C: Theo Angell; M: Jay Bolton. VIDEO

Kidco 🦴🦴 1983 (PG) The true story of a money-making corporation headed and run by a group of children ranging in age from 9 to 16. 104m/C VHS. Scott Schwartz, Elizabeth Gorcey, Cinnamon Idles, Tristen Skylar; D: Ronald F. Maxwell.

Kidnap Syndicate 🦴1/2 1976 (R) Kidnappers swipe two boys, releasing one—the son of a wealthy industrialist who meets their ransom demands. When they kill the other boy, a mechanic's son, the father goes on a revengeful killing spree. 105m/C VHS. IT:James Mason, Valentina Cortese; D: Fernando Di Leo.

Kidnapped 🦴🦴1/2 1960 A young boy is sold by his wicked uncle as a slave, and is helped by an outlaw. A Disney film based on the Robert Louis Stevenson classic. 94m/C VHS. Peter Finch, James MacArthur, Peter O'Toole; D: Robert Stevenson.

Kidnapped woof! 1987 (R) When a pregnant teenage girl is kidnapped by pornographers, her sister seeks help from a tough cop and together they go undercover to find her. Plot is flimsy cover for what is actually an exploitative piece. 100m/C VHS. David Naughton, Barbara Crampton, Lance LeGault, Chick Vennera, Charles Napier; D: Howard (Hikmet) Avedis; W: Howard (Hikmet) Avedis.

Kidnapped 🦴🦴1/2 1995 Cable adaptation of Robert Louis Stevenson's 1886 novel. In 1751 shanghaied young David Balfour (McCardie) and Highland patriot Ain Breck Stewart (Assante) escape from a slave ship and return to Scotland to battle the British. 142m/C VHS, DVD. Armand Assante, Brian McCardie, Michael Kitchen, Brian Blessed, Patrick Malahide; D: Ivan Passer; W: John Goldsmith. CABLE

Kidnapped 🦴🦴 2005 This BBC version of the Robert Louis Stevenson adventure tale finds orphaned Davie Balfour (Pearson) trying to claim his inheritance from his eccentric Uncle Ebeneezer (Dunbar). Instead, Davie gets kidnapped and imprisoned on a slave ship. Fortunately, he joins forces with exiled rebel Alan Breck (Glen) and the two wind up shipwrecked and running from evil English soldier Colonel McNabb (McGann) and his bounty hunters in the Scottish Highlands circa the 1750s. Exciting swashbuckling abounds. 150m/C VHS, DVD. GB Iain Glen, Adrian Dunbar, Paul McGann, Gregor Fisher, John Bach, John Leigh, James Anthony Pearson, Kirstin Coulter Smith; D: Brendan Maher; W: Bev Doyle, Richard Kurti; C: Geoffrey Hall; M: David Hirschfelder. TV

Kidnapped in Paradise 🦴🦴 1999 (PG-13) Spoiled beauty Megan (Ross), her fiance Jack, and her practical sister, Beth (Fisher), are sailing in the Caribbean when their yacht is boarded by Renard, who's obsessed with Megan. He kills Jack, kidnaps Megan, and leaves Beth in the sinking vessel. She's rescued by Matt, who agrees to help her find her sister, which leads them to Renard's private island. 91m/C VHS. Joely Fisher, Charlotte Ross, Robert Knepper, David Beecroft; D: Rob Hedden; W: David Chisholm. CABLE

Kidnapping of Baby John Doe 1988 Tragedy strikes a family's newborn, and they must make the terrifying decision between life and death. A doctor and nurse, however, take matters into their own hands to save the baby. 90m/C VHS. Helen Hughes, Jayne (Jane) Eastwood, Janet-Laine Green, Geoffrey Bowes, Peter Gerretsen; D: Peter Gerretsen; C: Douglas Koch; M: Heather Conkie.

Kids 🦴🦴 1995 Very controversial docudrama about 24 hours in the lives of some aimless New York teenagers. The sullen Telly (Fitzpatrick) enjoys bragging about his skill in deflowering virgins but his promiscuity has lead Jennie (Sevigny) to test H.I.V. positive—something Telly is as yet unaware of. Telly'd rather hang around with best friend Casper (Pierce) anyway, out on the streets, being generally profane and obnoxious. Can either be regarded as a brutally realistic look at teen life today or a lot of fuss about nothing. Korine was 19 when he wrote the screenplay. The MPAA rated the film NC-17, after a protest the distributors chose to release it unrated. 90m/C VHS, DVD. Jon Abrahams, Leo Fitzpatrick, Justin Pierce, Chloe Sevigny, Rosario Dawson, Sarah Henderson, Harold Hunter, Yakira Peguero, Joseph Knafelmacher; D: Larry Clark; W: Harmony Korine; C: Eric Alan Edwards; M: Louis Barlow. Ind. Spirit '96: Debut Perf. (Pierce).

The Kids Are Alright 🦴🦴🦴1/2 1979 (PG) A feature-length compilation of performances and interviews spanning the first 15 years of the rock group, The Who. Includes rare footage from the "Rolling Stones Rock and Roll Circus" film. Songs include: "My Generation," "I Can't Explain," "Young Man's Blues," "Won't Get Fooled Again," "Baba O' Reilly," and excerpts from "Tommy." 106m/C VHS, DVD. Roger Daltrey, Pete Townshend, Keith Moon, John Entwhistle, Ringo Starr, Keith Richards, Steve Martin, Tom Smothers, Rick Danko; D: Jeff Stein; W: Jeff Stein; C: Anthony B. Richmond, Norman Wexler; M: Roger Daltrey, Pete Townshend, Keith Moon, John Entwhistle.

Kids in America 🦴1/2 2005 (PG-13) Self-satisfied satire finds ambitious, control-freak high school principal Donna Weller (Bowen) clamping down on various activities organized by her mildly-rebellious suburban students. They finally get fed up by her dictatorial policies and decide to fight back. Richie makes her film debut as a (what else?) bimbette cheerleader. 91m/C DVD. US Andrew Shalfer, Gregory Edward Smith, Caitlin Wachs, Crystal Grant, Stephanie Sherrin, Chris Morris, Emy Colgado, Julie Bowen, Malik Yoba, George Wendt, Adam Arkin, Jeffrey Chase, Nicole Richie, Rosanna Arquette, Elizabeth Perkins, Charles Shaughnessy, Samantha Mathis, Rain Phoenix, Amy Hill, Michelle Phillips; D: Josh Stolberg; W: Josh Stolberg, Andrew Shalfer; C: Guy Livneh; M: B.C. Smith.

Kids in the Hall: Brain Candy 🦴🦴 1996 (R) The Canadian Kids bring their Monty Python-meets-SCTV humor to the big screen with moderate success. Dr. Cooper (McDonald), facing corporate downsizing, allows his new, untested anti-depressant to be released to the public after it shows promise. The drug, Gleeomex, sweeps the country by forcing the user's mind to focus on a favorite memory. As befits the troupe's twisted vision, these happy memories aren't always pleasant to the "Family Values" crowd. The easily offended should be warned—there's a character named "Cancer Boy." The story wanders a bit, giving everyone a chance to show their versatility (these Kids collectively play 32 different roles). Sophomore director Makin served the same duty on many of the TV episodes. 88m/C VHS, DVD. Dave Foley, Bruce McCulloch, Kevin McDonald, Scott Thompson, Mark McKinney, Janeane Garofalo; D: Kelly Makin; W: Bruce McCulloch, Kevin McDonald, Scott Thompson, Mark McKinney, Norm Hiscock; C: David Makin; M: Craig Northey.

Kid's Last Ride 🦴 1941 Three tough guys come into town to settle a feud. 55m/B VHS, DVD. Ray Corrigan, John "Dusty" King, Max Terhune, Luana Walters, Edwin Brian; D: S. Roy Luby.

Kids of the Round Table 🦴🦴1/2 1996 Eleven-year-old Alex (Morina) and his buddies like to have mock sword battles, pretending to be King Arthur and his knights. When their games are broken up by the local bully, Alex takes off into the woods where he discovers a sword in a stone. It's the legendary Excalibur and when Alex removes it, Merlin (McDowell) appears, explaining the sword will give the boy special powers. Of course, Alex abuses his newfound strength until he comes to the rescue of his friends. 89m/C VHS, DVD. C4 Johnny Morina, Michael Ironside, Malcolm McDowell, Peter Aykroyd, Rene Simard; D: Robert Tinnell; W: David Sherman; C: Roxanne Di Santo; M: Normand Corbeil.

Kika 🦴🦴 1994 Another flamboyant comedy from Almodovar finds irrepressible beautician Kika (Forque) involved with kinky photographer Ramon (Casanovas) and his stepfather Nicholas (Coyote), a sinister American pulp novelist. There's also Andrea Scarface (Jean-Paul Gaultier-costumed April), the host of a vile tabloid TV show called "Today's Worst," and Kika's lesbian maid Juana (de Palma) whose brother happens to be an escaped con/porn star, leading to an outlandish rape and...well, it's all pretty nonsensical, anyway. Spanish with subtitles. **115mC VHS, DVD.** *SP* Veronica Forque, Peter Coyote, Victoria Abril, Alex Casanovas, Rossy de Palma, fredo Mayo. *M:* Enrique Granados.

Kiki's Delivery Service 🐾🐾½ **1998 (G)** Young witch Kiki, accompanied by her outspoken cat Jiji, tries to find her place in the world. She becomes the resident witch in a small town due to her job. Bored on his summer vacation, the boy decides to visit his mother—accompanied by the tough-guy husband, Kikujiro (Kitano), of a neighbor. Only this guy doesn't have much of an idea about kids and their travels lead to some unpredictable adventures. Clumsy and protracted; Japanese with subtitles. **116mC VHS, DVD.** *JP* Takeshi "Beat" Kitano, Yusuke Sekiguchi; *D:* Takeshi "Beat" Kitano. **VIDEO**

The Kill 🐾🐾½ **1973** A rough, cynical, hard-boiled, womanizing detective tracks down stolen cash in downtown Macac. **81mC VHS.** Richard Jaeckel, Henry Duval, Judy Washington; *D:* Rolf Bayer; *W:* Noel Quinan.

Kill Alex Kill woof! **1976** A Vietnam PCW returns to find his family murdered, and uses the crime underworld to take revenge. **86mC VHS.** Tony Zarindast; *C:* Tina Bowmann, Chris Ponti; *D:* Tai Krige. Nicholas Josef von Sternberg.

Kill and Kill Again 🐾🐾½ **1981 (PG)** A martial arts champion attempts to rescue a kidnapped Nobel Prize-winning chemist who has developed a high-yield synthetic fuel. Colorful, tongue-in-cheek, and fun even for those unfamiliar with the genre. **100mC VHS.** James Ryan, Anneline Kriel, Stan Schmidt, Bill Flynn, Norman Robinson, Ken Gampu, John Ramsbottom; *D:* Ivan Hall; *W:* John Crowther; *C:* Tai Krige.

Kill, Baby, Kill 🐾🐾½ **1966** A small Transylvania town is haunted by the ghost of a seven-year-old witchcraft victim, and the town's suicide victims all seem to have hearts of gold (coins, that is). Lots of style and atmosphere in this Transylvanian tale from horror tongue-in-cheek. Considered by many genre connoisseurs to be the B man's finest, except that it bears early symptoms of the director's late onset infatuation with the zoom shot. **83mC VHS, DVD.** *IT* Erika Blanc, Giacomo si-Stuart, Fabienne Dali, Giana Vivaldi; *D:* Mario Bava; *W:* Mario Bava; *C:* Antonio Rinaldi; *M:* Carlo Rustichelli.

Kill Bill Vol. 1 🐾🐾🐾 **2003 (R)** Tarantino is back with a vengeance, in the first of two volumes of what originally was supposed to be a single film. Uma Thurman is spectacular as The Bride, a former assassin, betrayed and left for cead at her wedding by her associates and mysterious boss, Bill. When she awakens from a coma four years later she begins a mission of revenge that takes her from suburban L.A. to Okinawa, to Tokyo. Tarantino joyfully immerses the audience in the different styles and ultraviolence of the Asian cinema he loves so much, even using anime for one backstory sequence, with some spaghetti western and '70s TV added for spice. His trademark sharp dialogue is not as plentiful as in the past, but what's here is layered,

sometimes moving, and often humorous. Tarantino fave Chiba delivers as a master samurai swordmaker. **110mC VHS, DVD, Blu-ray Disc, UMD.** *US* Uma Thurman, Lucy Liu, Vivica A. Fox, Michael Madsen, Daryl Hannah, Gordon (Chia Hui) Liu, Sonny Chiba, Michael Parks, Chiaki Kuriyama, Jun Kunimura, Julie Dreyfus, Larry Bishop, Michael Bowen; *D:* Quentin Tarantino; *W:* Quentin Tarantino; *C:* Robert Richardson; *M:* The RZA; *V:* David Carradine.

Kill Bill Vol. 2 🐾🐾🐾½ **2004 (R)** The Bride continues to work her way through her former associates on the way to the big showdown with Bill, where she discovers some unexpected developments. This volume is less action than the first, but it is just as intense. All that was hidden in Vol. 1 is revealed, and it's done with more of the character development and dialogue-driven scenes that were thought were lacking in the first installment. The two volumes are so vastly different in tone and style that it seems odd that they were intended as one (very) long movie, but the idea of seeing them gives what might be the finest performance of his career as the enigmatic Bill. Thurman proves that her work on set was more than just physical, and that she can carry a movie even when she isn't carrying a sword. **137mC DVD, UMD.** *US* Uma Thurman, David Carradine, Lucy Liu, Michael Madsen, Vivica A. Fox, Daryl Hannah, Michael Parks, Julie Dreyfus, Chiaki Kuriyama, Sonny Chiba, Gordon (Chia Hui) Liu, LaTanya Richardson Jackson, Bo Svenson, Samuel L. Jackson, Jeannie Epper, Perla Haney-Jardine, Caitlin Keats, Christopher Allen Nelson, Steve Poly, Venessia Valentino; *D:* Quentin Tarantino; *W:* Quentin Tarantino; *C:* Robert Richardson; *M:* The RZA, Robert Rodriguez.

Kill by Inches 🐾🐾 **1999** Strange and stylized story follows traumatized tailor Thomas Klamm (Salinger) who, as a child, was forced to carry on his authoritarian father (Powell) to literally eat a tape measure as punishment for a dispute with his sister. Since then, Tom finds a sexual thrill in the measurement of human bodies. Sister Vera (Cyr), also a tailor, suddenly shows up at Thomas Brooklyn shop with her own special gifts and they play out their odd sibling rivalry. **85mC VHS, DVD, FR** Emmanuel Salinger, Myriam Cyr, Marcus Powell, Peter McRobbie; *D:* Diane Doniol-Valcroze, Arthur Flam; *C:* Richard Rutkowski; *M:* Geir Jenssen.

Kill Castro 🐾 **1980 (R)** Ever hear the one about the exploding cigar? Key West boat skipper is forced to carry a CIA agent to Cuba on a mission to assassinate Castro. Low-budget adventure that's deadly dull. **90mC VHS.** Sybil Danning, Albert Salmi, Michael V. Gazzo, Raymond St. Jacques, Woody Strode, Stuart Whitman, Robert Vaughn, Caren Kaye; *D:* Chuck Workman.

Kill Cruise 🐾🐾 **1990 (R)** The depressed and alcoholic skipper of the yacht Bella Donna gives up sailing until he meets two beautiful young women who want to sail to Bermuda for a taste of the good life. The calm of the Atlantic is disturbed when they are plagued by bad weather and fierce storms, and tensions rise as the two women's jealousies erupt. Will it set the climate for murder? **99mC VHS, DVD.** Jurgen Prochnow, Patsy Kensit, Elizabeth Hurley; *D:* Peter Keglevic; *W:* Peter Keglevic; *C:* Edward Klosinski; *M:* Brynmor Jones.

Kill Factor woof! *Death Dimension; The Freeze Bomb* **1978 (R)** Something stupid about a killer bomb tht could freeze the planet. So inept your brain cells will also be frozen if you watch it. **91mC VHS, DVD.** Jim Kelly, George Lazenby, Aldo Ray, Harold Sakata, Terry Moore; *D:* Al Adamson.

Kill Line 🐾🐾 **1991 (R)** Kim stars as Joe, a street fighter who seeks to clear his name after serving a 10-year prison sentence for a crime he didn't commit. When he finds his brother's family has been murdered by criminals looking for the millions he supposedly stole, Joe wages a corrupt police force and the gang of thugs who are looking for the money. **93mC VHS, DVD.** Bobby Kim, Michael Parker, Marlene Zimmerman,

Kill Later 🐾🐾🐾½ **2001 (R)** Loan officer Shawn (Blair) has just broken up with her married lover/boss (Moffet) and decides to kill herself by jumping off the bank's roof. However, she's just in time to become the hostage of British thief Charlie (Beesley) whose robbery of the bank has gone wrong. Shawn agrees to help Charlie escape if he will agree to kill her later. An unlikely romance blossoms as the on the lam duo are tracked by a couple of FBI agents. **89mC VHS, DVD.** *US* Selma Blair, Max Beesley, Lochlyn Munro, O'Neal Compton, Brendan Fehr, D.W. Moffett; *D:* Dana Lustig; *W:* Annette Goliti Gutierrez; *C:* David Ferrara; *M:* Tal Bergman, Renata Neto.

Kill Me Later 🐾🐾🐾 **1990 (R)** Bedridden Luanne (Gross), married to janitor Ralph (Monroe), manages to cause dissension in her isolated New Jersey community with her vicious gossip. But when Luanne learns Ralph's involved with a stripper (Haase), it puts her own life in danger. Based on a story by Jim Thompson. **100mC VHS.** Loretta Gross, Steve Monroe, Cathy Haase, Jackson Sims; *D:* Maggie Greenwald.

The Kill-Off 🐾🐾 **1990 (R)** Bedridden Luanne (Gross), married to janitor Ralph (Monroe), manages to cause dissension in her isolated New Jersey community with her vicious gossip. But when Luanne learns Ralph's involved with a stripper (Haase), it puts her own life in danger. Based on a story by Jim Thompson. **100mC VHS.** Loretta Gross, Steve Monroe, Cathy Haase, Jackson Sims; *D:* Maggie Greenwald. **VIDEO**

Kill Me Tomorrow 🐾½ **1999** Teenaged witch Holly (Varnshon) sets her sights on hunk Russell (Sheppard), which doesn't sit well with his present girlfriend Tricia (Shafra). So Holly decides to get even by stealing his soul. The inexperienced of the cast shows up bigtime but they're very earnest. **80mC VHS, DVD.** sa Shalla, Gregory Sheppard, Lyndse Yamshon; *D:* Patrick McGuinn; *W:* Patrick McGuinn.

Kill or Be Killed 🐾 **1993** Michael Julian just spent eight years in jail for saving his brother Charlie's life. He must wonder why he bothered since Charlie has stolen his girl Beth and set up a drug empire. Michael ambushes Charlie's men and steals $1 million to use as leverage but Charlie thinks rival drug lords are out to get him and starts a street war. **97mC VHS, DVD.** David Heavener, Joseph Nuzzolo, Paulo Tocha, Lynn Levrand; *D:* Joe Straw; *W:* Joseph Nuzzolo.

Kill or Be Killed 🐾 **1980 (PG)** Martial arts champion is lured to a phony martial arts contest by a madman bent on revenge. **90mC VHS.** James Ryan, Charlotte Michelle, Norman Coombes; *D:* Ivan Hall.

The Kill Reflex 🐾 **1989 (R)** A tough black cop and his beautiful rookie partner battle the mob and corruption. **90mC VHS.** Maud Adams, Fred Williamson, Bo Svenson, Phyllis Hyman; *D:* Fred Williamson.

Kill Slade 🐾 **1989 (PG-13)** When a United Nations food-aid diversion conspiracy is uncovered by a beautiful journalist, a plan to kidnap her is put into action. Romance follows. **90mC VHS, SA** Patrick Dollaghan, Lisa Brady, Anthony Fridjhon, Danny Keogh, Alfred Nowke; *D:* Bruce McFarlane.

Kill Squad 🐾 **1981 (R)** Squad of martial arts masters follow a trail of violence and bloodshed to a vengeful, deadly battle of skills. **85mC VHS.** Jean Claude, Jeff Risk, Jerry Johnson, Bill Cambra, Cameron Mitchell; *D:* Patrick G. Donahue; *W:* Patrick G. Donahue; *C:* Christopher W. Strattan; *M:* Joseph Conlan.

Kill the Golden Goose 🐾 **1979 (R)** Two martial arts masters work on opposite sides of a government corruption and corporate influence peddling case. **91mC VHS, DVD.** Brad von Beltz, Ed Parker, Master Bong Soo Han; *D:* Elliot Hong.

H. Wayne Lowery, C.R. Valdez, Mark Williams Ben Pfeifer; *D:* Richard H. Kim; *W:* Richard H. Kim

Kill Me Again 🐾🐾 **1989 (R)** Director Dahl does the contemporary noir better grow up, right now. Rather than moving out of their New York squatter building in the Lower East Side, Joe decides to become the co-op president, fighting off crackheads with a baseball bat and sleeping in the lobby as night security. Dark comedies normally only work if the comedy part is exercised. This one needs to lighten up...abor of love for director Alan Taylor, who struggled to adapt Joel Rose's tragicomic novel for 15 years. **84mC DVD.** *US* David Krumholtz, Clara Bellar, Paul Calderon, Larry (Lawrence) Gilliard Jr., Jon Budinoff, Cliff Gorman, Damian Young, Heather Burns, Otto Sanchez, Zak Orth; *D:* Alan Taylor; *W:* Daniel Handler; *C:* Hallam Bosmajian; *M:* Michal Deony, Anna Domino.

Kill the Poor 🐾🐾 **2006** When Joe's wife becomes pregnant, it's clear that their marriage of convenience will suddenly take emotional root and they'd...

Kill the Umpire 🐾🐾½ **1950** Baseball comedy with much stillck and sight gags. Bill Johnson (Bendix) keeps losing jobs because he's always skipping work to go to baseball games. With his wife (Merkel) threatening to take the kids and leave, Bill's father-in-law Jonah (Collins) and sends him to umpire school despite Bill's contempt for the guy the fans love to hate. After graduation, Bill is assigned to the Texas Interstate League where he discovers a couple of gamblers are trying to fix the pennant race. **78mB DVD.** William Bendix, Una Merkel, Jeff Richards, Ray Collins, Gloria Henry, Connie Marshall, William Frawley, Tom D'Andrea, Jeff York, Robert J. Wilke; *D:* Lloyd Bacon; *W:* Frank Tashlin; *C:* Charles Lawton Jr.; *M:* Heinz Roemheld.

Kill Your Darlings 🐾🐾 **2006 (R)** Swede Erik (Wilson) is a failed Hollywood screenwriter. In an attempt to jump-start his life, Erik allows crazy free spirit Lola (Davidovich) to talk him into a road trip into the desert but she has ulterior motives. Meanwhile, celebrity shrink Dr. Bagley (Larroquette) has arranged for some of his suicidal patients to attend his book signing in Vegas. Think the two parallel plots will combine? **94mC DVD.** *US SW* Andreas Wilson, Lolita (David) Davidovich, John Larroquette, Julie Benz, Alexander Skarsgard, Greg Germann, Skye McCole Bartusiak, Benito Martinez, Fares Fares, John Savage, Stellan Skarsgard, Terry Moore; *D:* Bjorne Larson; *W:* Bjorne Larsson, Johan Sandstrom, Lisa Taube; *C:* Irek Hartowicz; *M:* Jon Rekdal.

Killcrazy 🐾 **1989 (R)** On the way to a weekend camping trip, five Vietnam vets released from a mental hospital are slowly messacred by a group of dangerous killers until one of the vets decides to fight back. **94mC VHS.** David Heavener, Danielle Brisebois, Burt Ward, Lawrence-Hilton Jacobs, Bruce Glover, Gary Owens, Rachelle Carson, Robert Dalton; *D:* David Heavener.

Killer 🐾 *The Insolent* **1973** An ex-convict sets up an ingenious bank robbery, and gets double-crossed himself. **87mC VHS.** FR Andre Pousse, Georges Geret, Robert Dalban, Philippe Clay, Henry Silva; *D:* Jean-Claude Roy; *C:* Claude Saunier; *M:* Bernard Gerard.

The Killer 🐾🐾🐾½ *Die Xue Shuang Xiong* **1990 (R)** Jeffrey Chow is a gangster gunman who wants out. He's hired by his best friend to perform one last killing, but it doesn't go as smoothly as he wanted. He's almost caught by "Eagle" Lee, a detective who vows to hunt him down using good introduction to the Chinese gangster-flick genre. Available with subtitles or dubbed in English. **110mC VHS, DVD.** *HK* Chow Yun-Fat, Sally Yen, Danny Lee, Kenneth Tsang, Chu Kong, Fui-On Shing, Kenneth John Woo; *C:* Wing-Hung Wong, Peter Pau; *M:* Lowell Lo.

Killer: A Journal of Murder 🐾🐾½ **1995 (R)** Young, idealistic Jewish guard Henry Lesser (Leonard) befriends prisoner Carl Panzram (Woods) and encourages the man to write his life story. Then he must deal with the consequences of discovering the brutality behind Panzram's murderous crimes. The leads do fine but there's nothing new here. Inspired by true events and set in the 1920s. **91m/C VHS, DVD.** James Woods, Robert Sean Leonard, Ellen Greene, Cara Buono, Robert John Burke, Steve Forrest, John Bedford Lloyd, Harold Gould; **D:** Tim Metcalfe; **W:** Tim Metcalfe; **C:** Ken Kelsch; **M:** Graeme Revell.

Killer Bud ♂️ ½ **2000 (R)** Best buds Waylon (Nemec) and Buzz (Faustino) get fired and decide to to go on a road trip to score babes and marijuana. They're incredibly dumb—as is the movie—but it's funny in a stupid, I can't believe I'm watching this, kinda way. **92m/C VHS, DVD.** Conin "Corky" Nemec, David Faustino, Robert Stack, Danielle Harris, Caroline Keenan; **D:** Karl T. Hirsch; **W:** Greg DePaul, Hank Nelken; **C:** David Lewis; **M:** Russ Landau.

Killer Condom ♂️ ♂️ *Kondom des Grauens* **1995** Deadpan humor, gore, and severed flesh—all based on a Ralf Konig comic book that's definitely for adults. The killer condoms are jellyfish-like creatures with piranha-like teeth who have taken to feeding on the male sexual organs of the unfortunates who frequent Times Square's sleazy Hotel Quickie. Gay cop Luigi Macaroni (Semel) is determined to prevent any more emasculations. German with subtitles. **108m/C VHS, DVD. GE** Udo Samel, Peter Lohmeyer, Marc Richter, Leonard Lansink, Iris Berben, Hella Von Sinnen; **D:** Martin Walz, Ralf Walz, Ralf Konig; **C:** Alexander Honisch; **M:** Emil Vikicky.

Killer Dill ♂️ **1947** Also killer dull. A meek salesman is misidentified as a death-dealing gangster, and the comic mixups begin. **71m/B VHS, DVD.** Stuart Erwin, Anne Gwynne, Frank Albertson, Mike Mazurki, Milburn Stone, Dorothy Granger; **D:** Lewis D. Collins.

Killer Diller ♂️ ½ **1948** All-black musical revue featuring Nat King Cole and his Trio. **70m/B VHS, DVD.** Dusty Fletcher, Nat King Cole, Butterfly McQueen, Moms (Jackie) Mabley, George Wiltshire; **D:** Josh Binney.

The Killer Elite ♂️ ♂️ ½ **1975 (PG)** Straight-ahead Peckinpah fare examining friendship and betrayal. Two professional assassins begin as friends but end up stalking each other when they are double-crossed. This minor Peckinpah effort is murky and doesn't have a clear resolution, but is plenty bloody. Lots of Dobermans roam through this picture too. **120m/C VHS, DVD.** James Caan, Robert Duvall, Arthur Hill, Gig Young, Burt Young, Mako, Bo Hopkins, Helmut Dantine; **D:** Sam Peckinpah; **W:** Marc Norman, Stirling Silliphant; **C:** Peter Lathrop; **M:** Jerry Fielding.

Killer Fish ♂️ *Deadly Treasure of the Piranha* **1979 (PG)** A scheme to steal and then hide a fortune in emeralds at the bottom of a tank full of piranhas backfires as the criminals find it impossible to retrieve them...as if that took a lot of foresight. Directed Dawson is AKA Antonio Margheriti. Filmed in Brazil. **101m/C VHS, BR GB** Lee Majors, James Franciscus, Margaux Hemingway, Karen Black, Roy Brocksmith, Marisa Berenson; **D:** Anthony M. Dawson.

Killer Force ♂️ ½ **1975 (R)** Predictable adventure involving international diamond smuggling. **100m/C VHS, DVD.** Telly Savalas, Peter Fonda, Maud Adams, Hugh O'Brian; **D:** Val Guest.

Killer Image ♂️ **1992 (R)** A photographer unwittingly sees more than he should and becomes involved in a lethal political coverup. At the same time a wealthy senator targets him and he must fight for his life. Viewers might feel they have to fight their boredom. **97m/C VHS.** John Pyper-Ferguson, Michael Ironside, M. Emmet Walsh, Krista Errickson; **D:** David Winning.

A Killer in Every Corner ♂️ **1974** Three psychology students visit a loony professor and succumb to his hairraising shenanigans. **80m/C VHS.** Joanna Pettet, Patrick Magee, Max Wall, Eric Flynn; **D:** Malcolm Taylor; **W:** Brian Clemens.

The Killer Inside Me ♂️ ♂️ **1976 (R)** The inhabitants of a small Western town are unaware that their mild-mannered deputy sheriff is actually becoming a crazed psychotic murderer. From the novel by Jim Thompson. **99m/C VHS, DVD.** Stacy Keach, Susan Tyrrell, Tisha Sterling, Keenan Wynn, John Dehner, John Carradine, Don Stroud, Charles McGraw, Julie Adams, Royal Dano; **D:** Burt Kennedy; **W:** Robert Chandlee; **C:** William A. Fraker; **M:** Tim McIntire, John Rubinstein.

Killer Instinct ♂️ ♂️ **1992 (R)** Two brothers do bloody warfare with notorious mobster kingpins in prohibition-era New York City. **101m/C VHS.** Christopher Bradley, Bruce Nozick, Rachel York; **D:** Greydon Clark, Ken Stein.

Killer Instinct ♂️ ♂️ **2000 (R)** A bunch of teens attempt to spend the night in a creepy abandoned mental hospital, with predictably bloody results. Meanwhile, an outsider trying to broker the sale of a factory, the small town's main employer, finds out deadly secrets about the place. Somehow, the two stories are related and tied up nicely. **87m/C DVD.** Corbin Bernsen, Peg Moss, Jeannie Meyers, Brigitte Brooks, Dee Wallace Stone; **D:** Ken Barbet; **W:** Christopher Stone, Bruce Cameron; **C:** Richard Ashbury; **M:** Timothy S. (Tim) Jones.

Killer Klowns from Outer Space ♂️ ♂️ ½ **1988 (PG-13)** Bozo-like aliens resembling demented clowns land on earth and set up circus tents to lure Earthlings in. Visually striking, campy but slick horror flick that'll make you think twice about your next visit to the big top. Mood is heightened by a cool title tune by the Dickies. Definitely has cult potential. **90m/C VHS, DVD.** Grant Cramer, Suzanne Snyder, John Allen Nelson, Royal Dano, John Vernon, Peter Licassi, Michael Siegel, Charles Chiodo; **D:** Stephen Chiodo; **W:** Stephen Chiodo, Charles Chiodo; **C:** Alfred Taylor; **M:** John Massari.

Killer Likes Candy ♂️ **1978** An assassin stalks the King of Kafristan, and a CIA operative tries to stop him. **86m/C VHS.** Kerwin Mathews, Marilu Tolo; **D:** Richard Owens.

Killer Looks ♂️ ½ **1994 (R)** Phil likes to watch his wife Diane seduce strangers. Then they meet Mickey, a charmer with ideas of his own. Soon Diane and Phil find their kinky world threatened. Unrated version contains 13 minutes of additional footage. **87m/C VHS.** Michael Artura, Sara Suzanne Brown, Len Donato; **D:** Paul Thomas.

Killer Me ♂️ ♂️ **2001** George (Foster) is a college student who takes criminology classes and works in the library—the kind of quiet kid nobody notices. Except for fellow loner Anna (Kew), who practically stalks George in order to befriend him. Perhaps not the best of ideas since George had an abusive childhood and suffers from hallucinations in which he kills people with a straight-edged razor. Of course, they might not be just delusions at all. **80m/C VHS, DVD.** George Foster, Kirk B.R. Woller, Christina Kew; **D:** Zachary Hansen; **W:** Zachary Hansen; **C:** Neal Fredericks; **M:** Zachary Hansen.

The Killer Must Kill Again ♂️ ♂️ *Il Ragno; The Spider* **1975** After cheating hubby Giorgio Mainardi (Hilton) witnesses nameless killer (at the joyrid-

---

ing teen thieves while Giorgio tries to convince the cops that his wife's been kidnapped. Italian with subtitles or dubbed. **90m/C DVD. IT FR** Teresa Velazquez, Eduardo Fajardo; **D:** Luigi Cozzi; **W:** Luigi Cozzi; **C:** Riccardo Del Giudice; **D:** Riccardo (Pallton) Pallottini; **M:** Nand De Luca.

Killer of Sheep ♂️ ♂️ ♂️ ♂️ **1977** Age does nothing to date this seminal examination of urban poverty and race in 1970's Watts. Stan (Sanders) is a slaughterhouse worker plagued by insomnia who becomes increasingly disconnected from the rest of the world, including his wife (Moore). Nothing seems to help as a series of events just serves to compound Stan's sense of futility. Burnett wrote and directed as a student on a budget of $10,000. A popular part of the festival circuit that took 30 years to be released theatrically, in part because of the time and expense in licensing the music used in the soundtrack. **80m/B DVD. US** Henry Sanders, Kaycee Moore, Eugene Cherry, Charles Bracy; **D:** Charles Burnett; **W:** Charles Burnett; **C:** Charles Burnett. Natl. Film Reg. '90.

Killer on Board ♂️ ♂️ **1977** Folks spending their holiday on a cruise ship are afflicted by a fatal virus and subsequently quarantined. Typical made-for-TV disaster flick. **100m/C VHS.** Claude Akins, Beatrice Straight, George Hamilton, Patty Duke, Frank Converse, Jane Seymour, William Daniels; **D:** Philip Leacock.

Killer Pad ♂️ ½ **2006 (R)** Silly horror comedy about three not-too-bright buddies who don't bother to question their luck when they get an exceptional deal on a Hollywood Hills mansion. But their dream pad is a nightmare since it's also a direct portal to Hell. **84m/C DVD.** Daniel Franzese, Eric Jungmann, Andy Milonakis, Hector Jimenez, Shane McRae, Joey Lawrence, Jennifer Lyons; **D:** Robert Englund; **W:** Dan Stoller; **C:** David G. Stump; **M:** Timothy Andrew Edwards. **VIDEO**

Killer Party woof! **1986 (R)** Three coeds pledge a sorority and are subjected to a hazing that involves a haunted fraternity house. Standard horror plot; Paul Bartel ("Eating Raoul"; "Lust in the Dust") is the only significant element. **91m/C VHS.** Elaine Wilkes, Sherry Willis-Burch, Joanna Johnson, Paul Bartel, Martin Hewitt, Ralph Seymour, Woody Brown, Alicia Fleer; **D:** William Fruet; **W:** Barney Cohen; **C:** John Lindley; **M:** John Beal.

The Killer Shrews ♂️ ♂️ *Attack of the Killer Shrews* **1959** Lumet (Sidney's father) creates a serum that causes the humble shrew to take on killer proportions. The creatures are actually dogs in makeup. Goude was 1957's Miss Universe. **70m/B VHS, DVD.** James Best, Ingrid Goude, Baruch Lumet, Ken Curtis, Alfredo DeSoto, Gordon McLendon; **D:** Ray Kellogg; **W:** Jay Simms; **C:** Wilfrid M. Cline; **M:** Emil Cadkin, Harry Bluestone.

Killer Tomatoes Eat France ♂️ ½ **1991** Professor Gangrene takes his tomato fetish to France, where the giant vegetables try to take over the streets. The fourth in the killer-vegetable series. **94m/C VHS, DVD.** John Astin, Marc Price, Steve Lundquist, Kevin West, Tom Ashworth, Angela Visser, Kevin West, Debra Fares, Amie Miller, J.R. Morley; **D:** John DeBello; **W:** John DeBello, Steve Peace, Constantine Dillon; **C:** Kevin Morrisey.

Killer Tomatoes Strike Back ♂️ ½ **1990** The third "Killer Tomatoes" movie isn't in the league of "The Naked Gun" satires, but it's still bright parody for the Mad Magazine crowd, as tomatoes of trash-TV in a planned vegetable invasion. Perhaps due to a 'Killer Tomatoes' cartoon series at the time, this isn't as saucy as its predecessors and is acceptable for family audiences. Followed by "Killer Tomatoes Eat France." **87m/C VHS, DVD.** John Astin, Rick Rockwell, Crystal Carson, Steve Lundquist, John Witherspoon, John DeBello, Tom Ashworth, Frank Davis, Debra Fares, Rock Peace, Constantine Dillon, Kevin West, Spike Sorrentino, D.J. Sullivan; **D:** John DeBello; **W:** Rick Rockwell, John DeBello, Constantine Dillon; **C:** Stephen F. Andrich; **M:** Neal Fox.

Killer Tongue ♂️ *La Lengua Asesina* **1996 (R)** Okay, now here's a story (but not a good story, mind): Candy (Clarke) and Johnny (Durr) pull off a heist but Johnny winds up in jail while Candy hides out with the loot. She winds up in a desert hotel, near where a meteorite has landed. Somehow, Candy ingests a piece of the meteorite and an alien parasite (in the form of the titular killer tongue) takes over. The tongue is big on human sacrifices and Candy can't seem to do anything to stop it. Oh, and Candy's four poodles also get a meteorite taste and turn into drag queens. Just as gross as you may imagine it to be. **98m/C VHS, DVD. GB SP** Melinda (Mindy) Clarke, Jason Durr, Robert Englund, Mapi Galan, Doug Bradley, Jonathan Rhys Meyers; **D:** Alberto Sciamma; **C:** Denis Crossan.

Killer with Two Faces ♂️ **1974** A woman is terrorized by the evil twin of her boyfriend. **70m/C VHS.** Donna Mills, Ian Hendry, David Lodge, Roddy McMillan; **D:** John Scholz-Conway; **W:** Brian Clemens. **TV**

Killer Workout ♂️ *Aerobicide* **1986 (R)** A murderer stalks the clients of a sweat/sex/muscle-filled gym. **89m/C VHS.** David James Campbell, Ted Prior; **D:** David A. Prior.

The Killers ♂️ ♂️ **1946** Classic film noir based on a Hemingway story. Lancaster's film debut comes as an exboxer, "The Swede," who's murdered in a contract hit. Insurance investigator Jim Reardon (O'Brien) reconstructs the young man's life, discovering his involvement with crime boss Big Jim Colfax (Dekker) and double-crossing femme fatale Kitty Collins (Gardner). So Reardon sets out to set up Colfax and Kitty. Rosza's musical score may sound familiar—it was later used on the TV series "Dragnet." **105m/B VHS, DVD.** Edmond O'Brien, Albert Dekker, Ava Gardner, Burt Lancaster, Sam Levene, William Conrad, Charles McGraw, Virginia Christine; **D:** Robert Siodmak; **W:** Anthony Veiller, John Huston; **C:** Elwood "Woody" Bredell; **M:** Miklos Rozsa.

The Killers ♂️ ♂️ *the Killers* **1964** After two hired assassins kill a teacher, they look into his past and try to find leads to a $1,000,000 robbery. Reagan's last film. Remake of 1946 film of the same name, which was loosely based on a short story by Ernest Hemingway. Originally intended for TV, but released to theatres instead due to it's violence. **95m/C VHS, DVD.** Lee Marvin, Angie Dickinson, John Cassavetes, Ronald Reagan, Clu Gulager, Claude Akins, Norman Fell, Don Haggerty, Seymour Cassel, Robert Phillips; **D:** Donald Siegel; **W:** Gene L. Coon; **C:** Richard L. Rawlings; **M:** John Williams.

Killers ♂️ ♂️ **1988** Remote jungles of southern Africa are the scene of a military coup. **83m/C VHS, DVD.** Cameron Mitchell, Alicia Hammond, Kevin Dix; **D:** Ewing Miles Brown.

The Killer's Edge ♂️ ½ *Blood Money* **1990 (R)** Cop is caught between rock and a hard place in L.A. when he's forced to confront criminal who once saved his life in 'Nam. Plenty of gut busting and soul wrenching. **90m/C VHS, DVD.** Wings Hauser, Robert Z'Dar, Karen Black.

Killers from Space woof! **1954** Cheap sci-fi flick in which big-eyed men from beyond Earth bring scientist Graves back to life to assist them with their evil plan for world domination. **80m/B VHS, DVD.** Peter Graves, Barbara Bestar, James Scay; **D:** W. Lee Wilder.

Killer's Kiss ♂️ ♂️ ½ **1955** A boxer and a dancer set out to start a new life together when he saves the woman from an attempted rape. Gritty, second feature from Kubrick and shows signs of his budding talent. **67m/C VHS, DVD.** Frank Silvera, Jamie Smith, Irene Kane, Jerry Jarrett; **D:** Stanley Kubrick; **W:** Stanley Kubrick; **C:** Stanley Kubrick; **M:** Gerald Fried.

The Killing ♂️ ♂️ ½ **1956** The dirty, harsh, street-level big heist epic that established Kubrick and presented its genre with a new and vivid existentialist aura, as an ex-con engineers the rip-off of a racetrack with disastrous results. Displays characteristic nonsentimental sharpedged Kubrick vision. Based on the novel "Clean Break" by Lionel White. **83m/B VHS, DVD.** Sterling Hayden, Marie Windsor, Elisha

A Killing Affair ✗ 1986 (R) Set in West Virginia, 1943, this is the story of a widow who takes in a drifter who she believes is the man who killed her husband. She begins to "fall for him, but cannot be sure if she should trust him. Vague and melodramatic. "From the novel "Monday, Tuesday, Wednesday" by Robert Houston. Saperstein's directorial debut. 100m/C VHS, DVD. Peter Weller, Kathy Baker, John Glover, Bill Smitrovich; D: David Saperstein; M: Gerald Fried.

Killing at Hell's Gate ✗ 1981 A group of white-water rafters are being picked off by snipers as they travel down river. 96m/C VHS. Robert Urich, Deborah Raffin, Lee Purcell; D: Jerry Jameson; M: David Shire.

The Killing Beach ✗✗ Turtle Beach 1992 (R) Australian photojournalist Judith Wikes (Scacchi) travels to Malaysia in the late 1970s to report on the plight of Vietnamese boat people seeking refuge there. She befriends the wife of an Australian ambassador, a former callgirl from Saigon, who hopes to find her own children among the refugees. But the natives (Maxey) resent the foreign intrusion and are determined to stop the boat people—no matter what the cost in blood. Based on the novel "Turtle Beach" by Blanche D'Alpuget. 105m/C VHS, DVD. Greta Scacchi, Joan Chen, Jack Thompson, Art Malik, Norman Kaye; D: Stephen Wallace; W: Ann Turner; C: Russell Boyd. VIDEO

The Killing Club ✗✗½ You're Killing Me 2001 (R) When timid Jamie (Bowen) accidentally kills her controlling boyfriend, her tough best friend Laura (Lords) decides they should dispose of the body and give themselves an alibi. When this works, the ladies decide there's lots of users who need disposing of—starting with the leering boss (McDonough) of another pal, Arlene (Maxey). There's neither enough black comedy nor suspense to make this anything but ordinary. 86m/C DVD. Julie Bowen, Traci Lords, Dawn Maxey, Neal McDonough, David Packer; D: Antoni Stutz; W: Amy Kiehl; C: James Lawrence Spencer; M: Tom Hiel. VIDEO

The Killing Device ✗½ 1992 Two government scientists lose their funding on a covert political assassination project and decide to eliminate the government officials responsible. When two journalists attempt to solve the murders they become the next targets. 93m/C VHS, DVD. Clu Gulager, Antony Alda, Gig Rauch; D: Paul MacFarlane; W: Kliff Keuhl; C: Paul MacFarlane.

The Killing Edge ✗½ 1986 In post-nuclear holocaust Earth, a one warrior seeks justice, and his family, in a lawless land. 85m/C VHS. Bill French, Marv Spencer; D: Lindsay Shonteff.

Killing 'Em Softly ✗ 1985 Segal portrays a down-on-his-luck musician who accidentally murders a music manager during an argument. Cara's boyfriend is accused and to clear his name, the singer moonlights as a detective. She and Segal end up falling in love. Disappointing. 90m/C VHS, CA George Segal, Irene Cara; D: Max Fischer.

Killing Emmett Young ✗✗ Emmett's Mark 2002 (R) Homicide detective Emmett Young (Wolf) has been told by his doctor that he has a terminal illness and only a short time to live. To avoid the disease's debilitating effects, Emmett takes up the offer of a mysterious stranger (Byrne) to arrange for a hit man (Roth) to do the job quickly. Of course, Emmett discovers he's not really dying (ALWAYS get a second opinion about a terminal disease) and tries to call the hit off. 104m/C VHS, DVD. Scott Wolf, Tim Roth, Gabriel Byrne, Khandi Alexander, John Doman, Wayne Duvall; D: Keith Snyder; W: Keith Snyder; C: Lawrence Sher.

The Killing Fields ✗✗✗½ 1984 (R) Based on the New York Times' Sydney Schanberg's account of his friendship with Cambodian interpreter Dith Pran. They separated during the fall of Saigon, when Western journalists fled, leaving behind countless assistants who were later accused of collusion with the enemy by the Khmer Rouge and killed or sent to reeducation camps during the bloodbath known as "Year Zero." Schanberg searched for Pran through the Red Cross and U.S. government, while Pran struggled to survive, finally escaping and walking miles to freedom. Ngor's own experiences echoed those of his character Pran. Malkovich's debut is intense. Joffe's directorial debut shows a generally sure hand, with only a bit of melodrama at the end. 142m/C VHS, DVD. GB Sam Waterston, Haing S. Ngor, John Malkovich, Athol Fugard, Craig T. Nelson, Julian Sands, Spalding Gray, Bill Paterson; D: Roland Joffe; W: Bruce Robinson; C: Chris Menges. Oscars '84: Cinematog., Film Editing, Support. Actor (Ngor); British Acad. '84: Actor (Ngor), Adapt. Screenplay, Film; Golden Globes '85: Support. Actor (Ngor); L.A. Film Critics '84: Cinematog.; N.Y. Film Critics '84: Cinematog.; Natl. Soc. Film Critics '84: Cinematog.; Writers Guild '84: Adapt. Screenplay.

Killing Floor ✗✗ 1985 (PG) During WWI, black sharecropper Frank Custer (Leake) travels to Chicago to get work in the stockyards and becomes a voice in the growing labor movement. The tensions in the factories lead to to bloody race riots of 1919. 118m/C VHS. Damien Leake, Alfre Woodard, Moses Gunn, Clarence Felder, Mary Alice; Cameos: Peter J. DiNoto; D: Bill Duke; W: Leslie Lee; M: Elizabeth Swados. TV

Killing for Love ✗½ 2006 (R) David Lamont (Bucas), a literary agent who specializes in horror writers, has just moved into a lavish Manhattan penthouse, but weird things start happening. A young man turns up, claiming he inherited the place from his father. David is sent bloody crime scene photos that show his apartment, only the police have no record of any crimes, and the receives videotapes showing him sleeping. Obsessed, David will go to any length to find his stalker. 98m/C DVD. Marc Blucas, Shin Appleby, Peiko Aylesworth, Jeff Carlson; D: Gideon Raft; W: Andrew Weems, Jeff Carlson; D: Gideon Raft; W: Gideon Raft, Ryan Swanson; C: Merlina Radwan; M: Michael Wandmacher. VIDEO

The Killing Game ✗✗½ 1987 A slew of Californians kill and betray each other for lustful reasons. 90m/C VHS, Chard Hayward, Cynthia Killion, Geoffrey Sadwith; D: Joseph Merhi.

The Killing Game ✗✗½ Jeu de Massacre 1967 A husband-wife cartoonist team link up with an unhinged playboy and act out a murder-mystery comic they created. Amusing French with subtitles. 95m/C VHS. FR Jean-Pierre Cassel, Claudine Auger, Michel Duchaussoy, Anna Gaylor; D: Alain Jessua.

Killing Grandpa ✗✗ Matar al Abuelito 1991 Wealthy family patriarch Don Mariano Aguero (Luppi) has lost the will to live and attempted suicide, which has left him comatose. His three greedy children are anxious for their inheritance but the Don's loyal handyman enlists the aid of his half-sister Rosita (Esteves), who possesses healing powers, to give his aged employer the strength to recover. Spanish with subtitles. 114m/C VHS. SP AR Federico Luppi, Ines Estevez; D: Luis Cesar D'Angiolillo; W: Luis Cesar D'Angiolillo, Ariel Sienra; C: Miguel Abal.

Killing Me Softly ✗ 2001 (R) Chinese director Kaige's English-language debut turned out to be an unfortunate choice—a turgid, sexual melodrama based on the novel by the pseudonymous Nicci French. American Alice (Graham) is living in London, seemingly content with boyfriend Jake (Hughes). Then she meets mysterious Adam (Fiennes) and intense mountaineer Adam (Fiennes) and she's soon agreeing to marry him despite evidence of his violent temper and how little she knows about him. Bouts of S&M sex follow but it's when Alice learns that her new hubby's previous lover disappeared that she decides maybe she's made a mistake. An unrated version is also available. 100m/C VHS, DVD. Heather Graham, Joseph Fiennes, Jason Hughes, Natasha (Natasha) McElhone, Ulrich Thomsen, Ian Hart; D: Chen Kaige; W: Kara Lindstrom; C: Michael Coulter; M: Patrick Doyle.

The Killing Mind 1990 A young girl witnesses a grisly murder that is never solved. Twenty years later she (Zimbalist) becomes a cop who specializes in trapping psychos. Haunted by her memories, she and a reporter (Bill) team up to find the killer, never suspecting that she is his next victim. 95m/C VHS, DVD. Stephanie Zimbalist, Tony Bill, Daniel Roebuck; D: Michael Rhodes. CABLE

Killing Mr. Griffin ✗✗½ 1997 If this sounds suspiciously akin to the plot for 1999's "Teaching Mrs. Tingle," it's not just your imagination. However, this TV movie is based on the novel by Lois Duncan. Evil high school teacher Mr. Griffin antagonizes all his students, who wind up kidnapping and humiliating him—leaving him tied up in the woods. But when Mr. G turns up dead, the students are all suspects unless they can point the cops in another direction. 108m/C VHS, DVD. Scott Bairstow, Amy Jo Johnson, Mario Lopez, Chris Young, Michelle Williams, Jay Thomas, Scott Jaeck, Denise Dowse; D: Jack Bender; W: Michael Angeli, Kathleen Rowell; C: David Geddes; M: Christophe Beck. TV

Killing Moon Woof! 2000 Abysmal air disaster flick features an airborne (on a plane!) virus that makes it's victims bleed to death in its mind she's always responsible. Annie's mother, Annie is Albert's obsession and in his mind she's always responsible... [text obscured] 109m/C VHS. DVD. Bobby Di-Cicco, John Savage, Kimberly Chase, John Saxon, Joe Hugh, Robert Phillips, Timothy Carey, Morgan Woodward; D: John Cassavetes; W: John Cassavetes; C: Frederic Elmes.

Killing Obsession ✗✗ 1994 Albert (Savage) has been locked in the Parkview State Psychiatric Facility for 20 years, ever since he murdered 11-year-old Annie's mother. When he can't come up with the cash, he's offered a deal—get rid of troublesome Chinese bookie and all debts will be forgiven. But it turns out the bookie is highly connected in the Asian mob and nothing goes as planned. Cassavette's improv technique makes for a self-indulgent and endless film. 109m/C VHS, DVD. Ben Gazzara, Jean-Pierre Cassel, Zizi Johari, Soto Joe Hugh, Robert Phillips, Timothy Carey, Morgan Woodward; D: John Cassavetes; W: John Cassavetes; C: Frederic Elmes.

The Killing of a Chinese Bookie ✗✗ 1976 (R) Hustler Cosmo Vitelli (Gazzara) runs a Sunset Strip nightclub and is in hock to loan sharks. When he can't come up with the cash, he's offered a deal—get rid of a troublesome Chinese bookie and all debts will be forgiven. But it turns out the bookie is highly connected in the Asian mob and nothing goes as planned. Cassavette's improv technique makes for a self-indulgent and endless film. 109m/C VHS, DVD. Ben Gazzara, Jean-Pierre Cassel, Zizi Johari, Soto Joe Hugh, Robert Phillips, Timothy Carey, Morgan Woodward; D: John Cassavetes; W: John Cassavetes; C: Frederic Elmes.

Killing of Angel Street ✗✗ 1981 (PG) A courageous young woman unwittingly becomes the central character in an escalating nightmare about saving a community from corrupt politicians and organized crime. 131m/C VHS, AU Elizabeth (Liz) Alexander, John Hargreaves; D: Donald Crombie; W: Evan Jones; M: Brian May.

The Killing of John Lennon ✗✗½ 2007 Stylized pseudo-documentary examination of what led Mark David Chapman (Ball) to kill John Lennon. Using information from interviews and legal documents, movie charts Chapman's descent from married security guard in Hawaii to obsessed stalker who believed himself to be the Holden Caulfield from "The Catcher in the Rye." Dark and disturbing, the movie never leaves Chapman's head as he loses touch with reality. Well made but too focused on Chapman's madness to give the viewer much perspective. 114m/C DVD. GB Robert Kirk, Jonas Ball, Mie Omori, Krisha Fairchild, Ulrich Michael Heinzfeld; D: Andrew Piddington; C: Roger Eaton; M: Makana.

Killing of Randy Webster ✗½ 1981 A father attempts to prove that his son did not die as a criminal when Texas policemen shot him after transporting a ...

Killing Heat ✗½ The Grass is Singing 1984 (R) An independent career woman living in South Africa decides to abandon her career to marry a struggling jungle farmer. Based on Doris Lessing's novel "The Grass is Singing." 104m/C VHS, DVD. GB SW Karen Black, John Thaw, John Kani, John Moulder-Brown; D: Michael Raeburn.

Killing Hour ✗✗ The Clairvoyant 1984 (R) A psychic painter finds that the visions she paints come true in a string of grisly murders. Her ability interests a TV reporter and a homicide detective. 97m/C VHS, DVD. Elizabeth Kemp, Perry King, Norman Parker, Kenneth McMillan; D: Armand Mastroianni; M: Alexander Peskanov.

A Killing in a Small Town ✗✗✗ Evidence of Love 1990 (R) Candy Morrison seems like the perfect member of her small Texas community—but appearances can be deceiving, particularly after she's charged with killing a fellow church-goer by striking her 41 times with an axe (shades of Lizzie Borden). Dennehy is her skeptical lawyer who isn't sure it it was self-defense or a peculiar sort of revenge. Good performances by Hershey and Dennehy lift this above the usual tawdry made-for-TV level. Based on a true story. 95m/C VHS, Barbara Hershey, Brian Dennehy, Hal Holbrook, Richard Gilliland, John Terry, Lee Garlington; D: Stephen Gyllenhaal; C: Robert Elswit; M: Richard Gibbs. TV

Killing in the Sun ✗✗ The Men 1973 (R) Gripping struggle for prosperous mobsters from three countries, smuggling in the Mediterranean consume. 90m/C VHS. FR IT Henry Silva, Michael Constantine; D: Daniel Vigne; W: Leo Carrier; C: Jean Charveln; M: Francis Lai.

The Killing Jar ✗✗½ 1996 (R) Michael Sanford (Cullen) has taken his pregnant wife Diane (Tomita) back to the California wine country to take over the family vineyard. A series of vicious murders occur in the area, one of which Michael may have witnessed. Hypnosis brings up a lot of Michael's repressed childhood memories, he begins to unravel, and becomes the prime suspect in the killings. 101m/C VHS, DVD. Brett Cullen, Tamlyn Tomita, Wes Studi, Brion James, M. Emmet Walsh, Tom Bower, Xander Berkeley; D: Evan Crooke; W: Mark Mullin; C: Michael G. Wojciechowski; M: Andrew Beling.

The Killing Kind ✗✗½ 1973 (R) Former mobster tries going legit by changing his identity and working for the government. 91m/C VHS, DVD. John Savage, Ruth Roman, Luana Anders, Cindy Williams; D: Curtis Harrington; M: Andrew Beling.

The Killing Man ✗✗ 1994 (R) Former mobster tries going legit by changing his identity and working for the government. 91m/C VHS, DVD. John Savage, Ruth Roman, Luana Anders, Cindy Williams; D: Curtis Harrington; M: Andrew Beling.

The Killing Mind 1990 A young girl witnesses a grisly murder...

Cook Jr., Jay C. Flippen, Vince Edwards, Timothy Carey, Coleen Gray, Joseph (Joe) Sawyer, Ted de Corsia, James Edwards, Jay Adler, Kola Kwarian, Joe Turkel; D: Stanley Kubrick; W: Stanley Kubrick, Jim Thompson; C: Lucien Ballard; M: Gerald Fried.

The Killing of Sister George 1969 (R) Racy, sensationalized film based on the Frank Marcus black comedy/melodrama about a lesbian love triangle between a television executive, the soap opera star she's about to fire, and the soap star's girlfriend. 138m/C VHS, DVD. Beryl Reid, Susannah York, Coral Browne, Ronald Fraser, Patricia Medina, Hugh Paddick, Cyril Delevanti, Brandan Dillon, Sivi Aberg, William Beckley, Elaine Church, Mike Freeman, Maggie Paige, Jack Raine, Dolly Taylor; **D:** Robert Aldrich; **W:** Lukas Heller, Frank Marcus; **C:** Joseph Biroc; **M:** Gerald Fried.

(continued from previous) stolen van across state lines. 90m/C VHS. Hal Holbrook, Dixie Carter, Sean Penn, Jennifer Jason Leigh; **D:** Sam Wanamaker.

A Killing Spring 2002 (R) Former cop turned reporter, Joanne Kilbourn (Crewson), who once taught at Saskholme College, is pulled into the investigation of the suspicious death of the disliked dean of the School of Journalism. Ambition, jealousy, and corruption run rampant in academia. 85m/C VHS, DVD. CA Wendy Crewson, Shawn Doyle, Michael Ontkean, Zachery Ty Bryan, Sherry Miller, John Furey, Bruce Gray; **D:** Stephen Williams; **W:** Joe Wiesenfeld, Andrew Hole; **C:** David Herrington; **M:** Robert Carli. **TV**

Killing Stone 1978 A freelance writer uncovers a small town sheriff's plot to cover up a scandalous homicide. 120m/C VHS. Gil Gerard, J.D. Cannon, Jim Davis, Nehemiah Persoff; **D:** Michael Landon; **W:** Michael Landon. **TV**

Killing Streets 1991 A commando learns that his twin brother is being held hostage in Lebanon and plans a rescue mission. A standard farfetched actioner; noteworthy for a real sense of despair over the endless carnage in the Mideast. Some dialogue in Arabic with subtitles. 109m/C VHS. Michael Pare, Lorenzo Lamas; **D:** Stephen Cornwell; **W:** Stephen Cornwell.

The Killing Time 1987 (R) A minor, effective murder thriller about a quiet small resort town suddenly beset by a web of murder, double-crossings, blackmail, and infidelity. They seem to coincide with the appearance of a mysterious stranger posing as the town's deputy sheriff just as the new sheriff is about to take up the badge. 94m/C VHS. Kiefer Sutherland, Beau Bridges, Joe Don Baker, Wayne Rogers; **D:** Rick King; **W:** Don Bohlinger.

Killing Time 1997 (R) Twisted little English thriller about a day in the life of Italian hitwoman Maria (Torgan), who's working in Northern England. Gangland boss Reilly (Leach) has killed a police officer and revenge is wanted by the cop's mate, fellow officer Bryant (Fairbass). Only Bryant can't really afford Maria so after she does the job, Bryant wants her killed by a cheaper hitman, Charlie (Thirkeld). But Reilly won't be back in town until the evening train—so Maria decides to take out a few of Reilly's henchmen to kill some time, leading to a police investigation (by Bryant), and leaving Charlie itching to carry out his part of the killing spree. 91m/C VHS. GB Kendra Torgan, Craig Fairbrass, Nigel Leach, Stephen D. Thirkeld; **D:** Bharat Nalluri; **W:** Neal Marshall, Fleur Costello, Caspar Berry.

The Killing Yard 2001 (R) Based on the true story of the 1971 Attica prison riots in New York State where nearly 50 people were killed and the state tried to avoid accountability for its role in the massacre. Civil rights attorney Ernie Goodman (Alda) defends inmate Shango (Chestnut) who's been wrongly accused of a double homicide during the melee. 110m/C VHS, DVD. Alan Alda, Morris Chestnut, Rose McGowan; **D:** Euzhan Palcy; **W:** Benita Garvin; **C:** Johnny (John W.) Simmons; **M:** Patrice Rushen. **CABLE**

Killing Zoe 1994 (R) American safecracker travels to Paris for a little rest, recreation, and robbery. At the request of a childhood friend, he involves himself in an ill-conceived daytime bank heist, but not before enjoying a night with a local call girl and participating in some good ol' fashioned heroin-induced debauchery with the other bank robbers on the night before the job. Surprising no one (except maybe the still-stoned crooks), things don't go exactly as planned. Visually impressive debut for Tarantino collaborator Avary, who had his actors read "Beowulf" for its portrayal of Viking excess. 97m/C VHS, DVD. Eric Stoltz, Julie Delpy, Jean-Hugues Anglade, Gary Kemp, Bruce Ramsay, Kario Salem, Carlo Scanduzzi; **D:** Roger Avary; **W:** Roger Avary; **C:** Tom Richmond.

The Killing Zone 1990 Convict nephew of onetime Drug Enforcement agent rewrites zoning ordinances to hunt for Mexican drug lord south of the border. 90m/C VHS, DVD. Daron McBee, James Dalesandro, Melissa Moore, Armando Silvestre, Augustine Beral, Sydne Squire, Debra (Deborah Dutch) Dare; **D:** Addison Randall.

Killings at Outpost Zeta 1980 Earthmen investigate a barren planet where previous expeditions have disappeared, and find hordes of aliens. 92m/C VHS. Gordon Devol, Jackie Ray, James A. Watson Jr.; **D:** Bob Emenegger, Allan Sandler; **W:** Peter Dawson; **M:** Bob Emenegger.

Killjoy *Who Murdered Joy Morgan?* 1981 A sleazy surgeon's daughter is the prey in this TV thriller. The plot twists are led by the array of people who become involved. A clever suspense mystery. 100m/C VHS, DVD. Kim Basinger, Robert Culp, Stephen Macht, Nancy Marchand, John Rubinstein, Ann Dusenberry, Ann Wedgeworth, Helene Winston; **D:** John Llewellyn Moxey; **M:** Bruce Broughton. **TV**

Killpoint 1984 (R) Special task force is assembled to catch the criminals who robbed a National Guard armory for its weapons. 89m/C VHS. Leo Fong, Richard Roundtree, Cameron Mitchell; **D:** Frank Harris.

Killzone 1985 A brainwashed Vietnam vet becomes involved during a training exercise and embarks on a psychotic killing spree. 86m/C VHS. Ted Prior, David James Campbell, Richard Massey; **D:** David A. Prior.

Kilma, Queen of the Amazons woof! 1975 A shipwrecked sailor finds himself on an island populated by man-hating Amazons. When a shipload of lusty sailors arrive to rescue him, carnage ensues. 90m/C VHS, DVD. SP Francisco (Frank) Brana, Eva Miller, Claudia Gravy; **D:** Miguel Iglesias; **W:** Miguel Iglesias; **C:** Francisco Sanchez.

Kim 1950 A colorful Hollywood adaptation of the Rudyard Kipling classic about an English boy disguised as a native in 19th Century India, and his various adventures. 113m/C VHS, DVD. Errol Flynn, Dean Stockwell, Paul Lukas, Cecil Kellaway; **D:** Victor Saville; **M:** Andre Previn.

Kim 1984 Kim (Sheth) is a 15-year-old boy living by his wits on the streets of 1890s India. Trying to discover his true identity, Kim's befriended by a Buddhist monk who wishes the boy to be his disciple and a British spy, who trains him for a daring mission against the Russians. Rousing TV adaptation of the Rudyard Kipling novel. 135m/C VHS, DVD. Ravi Sheth, Peter O'Toole, Bryan Brown, John Rhys-Davies, Julian Glover; **D:** John Davies.

Kind Hearts and Coronets 1949 Black comedy, set in 1900, in which ambitious young Louis (Price) sets out to bump off eight relatives in an effort to claim a family title. Guinness is wonderful in his role as all eight (male and female) of the fated relations. There are a number of clever twists and turns and it proves that writing one's memoirs can be fatal. Very loosely based on Roy Horniman's novel "Israel Rank." 104m/B VHS, DVD. GB Alec Guinness, Dennis Price, Valerie Hobson, Joan Greenwood, Audrey Fildes, Miles Malleson, Clive Morton, Cecil Ramage, John Penrose, Hugh Griffith, John Salew, Eric Messiter, Anne Valery, Arthur Lowe, Jeremy Spenser; **D:** Robert Hamer; **W:** Robert Hamer, John Dighton; **C:** Douglas Slocombe; **M:** Ernest Irving.

A Kind of Loving 1962 Two North English young people marry rashly as a result of pregnancy, find they really didn't like each other all that much, but manage to adjust. 107m/B VHS, DVD. GB Alan Bates, Thora Hird, June Ritchie, Pat Keen, James Bolam; **D:** John Schlesinger; **W:** Willis Hall, Keith Waterhouse; **C:** Denys Coop; **M:** Ron Grainer.

Kindergarten 1984 Endearing tale based on a true story of a young Russian street violinist. During WWII, the boy meets a variety of interesting people as he travels throughout the Soviet Union. In Russian with English subtitles. 143m/C VHS. RU Sergei Gusak, Sergei Bobrovsky, Galina Stakhanova, Klaus Maria Brandauer; **D:** Yevgeny Yevtushenko; **W:** Yevgeny Yevtushenko; **C:** Vladimir Papyan; **M:** Gleb Mai.

Kindergarten Cop 1990 (PG-13) Pectoral perfect cop Kimble (Schwarzenegger) stalks mama's boy/criminal Crisp (Tyson) by locating the drug lord's ex and his six-year-old son. When the pec man's female partner succumbs to a nasty bout of food poisoning, he's forced to take her place as an undercover kindergarten teacher in the drowsy Pacific northwest community where mother and son reside incognito. A cover all the bases Christmas release, it's got romance, action, comedy and cute. And boxoffice earnings to match Arnie's chest measurements. A bit violent for the milk and cookie set. 111m/C VHS, DVD. Arnold Schwarzenegger, Penelope Ann Miller, Pamela Reed, Linda Hunt, Richard Tyson, Carroll Baker, Cathy Moriarty, Park Overall, Richard Portnow, Jayne Brook; **D:** Ivan Reitman; **W:** Murray Salem, Herschel Weingrod, Timothy Harris; **C:** Michael Chapman; **M:** Randy Edelman.

Kindergarten Ninja 1994 Football star is sentenced to community service after a drunk-driving arrest and is guided by a kung fu angel into helping a group of children. 80m/C VHS, DVD. Dwight Clark; **D:** Anthony Chan.

The Kindred 1987 (R) A young student discovers that his mother the biologist has created a hybrid creature using his body tissue. Naturally, he is horrified and begins to search for his testtube brother; the problem is, this brother likes eating people. Not too bad; boasts some good acting. 92m/C VHS. Rod Steiger, Kim Hunter, David Allan Brooks, Timothy Gibbs, Amanda Pays, Talia Balsam, Jeffrey Obrow, Peter Frechette, Julia Montgomery; **D:** Stephen Carpenter, Jeffrey Obrow; **W:** Stephen Carpenter, Joseph Stefano, Earl Ghaffari, Jeffrey Obrow; **M:** David Newman.

King 1978 Docudrama with terrific cast follows the life and career of one of the greatest non-violent civil rights leaders of all time, Martin Luther King. 272m/C VHS, DVD. Paul Winfield, Cicely Tyson, Roscoe Lee Browne, Ossie Davis, Art Evans, Ernie Banks, Howard E. Rollins Jr., William Jordan, Cliff DeYoung; **D:** Abby Mann; **W:** Abby Mann; **M:** Billy Goldenberg. **TV**

King and Country 1964 Aristocratic army officer, Capt. Hargreaves (Bogarde), serves as the defense lawyer for troubled Private Arthur Hamp (Courtenay), whose wartime experiences have caused him to desert. Hargreaves at first ignores the uneducated Hamp's obvious shell-shock but soon begins to feel sympathy for his confused client. Director Losey shows the effects of war rather than the war itself and provides a sincere and bitter condemnation of military mentality. Based on the play "Hamp" by John Wilson. 86m/B VHS, DVD. GB Dirk Bogarde, Tom Courtenay, Leo McKern, Barry Foster, James Villiers, Peter Copley; **D:** Joseph Losey; **W:** Evan Jones; **C:** Denys Coop; **M:** Larry Adler. British Acad. '64: Film.

The King and Four Queens 1956 Gable, on the run from the law, happens upon a deserted town, deserted, that is, except for a woman and her three daughters. Clark soon discovers that the women are looking for $100,000 in gold that one of their missing husbands had stolen. True to form, conniving Clark wastes no time putting the moves on each of them to find the whereabouts of the loot. 86m/C VHS, DVD. Clark Gable, Eleanor Parker, Jo Van Fleet, Jean Willes, Barbara Nichols, Sara Shane, Roy Roberts, Arthur Shields, Jay C. Flippen; **D:** Raoul Walsh; **M:** Alex North.

The King and I 1956 Wonderful adaptation of Rodgers and Hammerstein's Broadway play based on the novel "Anna and the King of Siam" by Margaret Landon. English governess Kerr is hired to teach the King of Siam's many children and bring them into the 20th century. She has more of a job than she realizes, for this is a king, a country, and a people who value tradition above all else. Features one of Rodgers and Hammerstein's best-loved scores. Brynner made this role his, playing it over 4,000 times on stage and screen before his death. Kerr's voice was dubbed when she sang; the voice you hear is Marni Nixon, who also dubbed the star's singing voices in "West Side Story" and "My Fair Lady." ♫Shall We Dance?; Getting To Know You; Hello, Young Lovers; We Kiss in a Shadow; I Whistle a Happy Tune; March of the Siamese Children; Something Wonderful. 133m/C VHS, DVD. Deborah Kerr, Yul Brynner, Rita Moreno, Martin Benson, Terry Saunders, Rex Thompson, Alan Mowbray, Carlos Rivas, Patrick Adiate; **D:** Walter Lang; **W:** Ernest Lehman; **C:** Leon Shamroy; **M:** Richard Rodgers, Oscar Hammerstein. Oscars '56: Actor (Brynner), Art Dir/Set Dec., Color, Costume Des. (C), Sound, Scoring/Musical; Golden Globes '57: Actress—Mus./Comedy (Kerr), Film—Mus./Comedy.

The King and I 1999 (G) Animated musical tries, but fails, to split the difference between faithfulness to the Broadway version and the action needed to entertain kids. Tells the story of Anna (Richardson), an English woman who travels to Siam in order to tutor the children of the King (Vidnovic). The evil Kralahome and stereotypical comic relief sidekick Master Little (Hammond) plan to use Anna to capture the throne. The ending is given a kid-friendly twist, but eight of the original 20 Broadway songs were slashed to keep it brief for the short attention span set. 87m/C VHS, DVD. **D:** Richard Rich; **W:** Jacqueline Feather, David Seidler, Peter Bakalian; **V:** Miranda Richardson, Martin Vidnovic, Ian Richardson, Darrell Hammond, Allen D. Hong, Armi Arabe, Adam Wylie, Sean Smith.

King Arthur 2004 (PG-13) The noble knights are recast as centurions fighting for Rome in Britain circa 500 A.D. Arthur is Artorius, a mercenary from a backwater colony fighting to earn back his freedom by pacifying Celts. He and his men don't like this one bit, especially when sent to rescue a rich brat favored by the Pope from encroaching Saxon invaders. The filmmakers claim historical accuracy. Well...maybe, but it's still just an excuse to recycle a classic western/war story: corrupt command sends band of hardened roughnecks on suicide mission. Nothing feels very novel about this novel idea, but it is a fun ride. Owen is a terrific Arthur, all brooding and steely. Knightley is perhaps the sexiest (and most proactive) Guinevere ever. Skaargard hams it up as a nasty proto-fascist villain. 130m/C DVD, Blu-ray Disc, UMD. GB IR Clive Owen, Stephen (Dillon) Dillane, Keira Knightley, Ioan Gruffudd, Stellan Skarsgard, Ray Winstone, Hugh Dancy, Ray Stevenson, Charlie Creed-Miles, Joel Edgerton, Ken Stott, Til Schweiger, Mads Mikkelsen, Sean Gilder, Ivano Marescotti, Lorenzo De Angelis; **D:** Antoine Fuqua; **W:** David Franzoni; **C:** Slawomir Idziak; **M:** Hans Zimmer.

King Arthur, the Young Warlord 1975 (PG) The struggle that was the other side of Camelot—the campaign against the Saxon hordes. The early, somewhat violent years of King Art. 90m/C VHS, DVD. Oliver Tobias, Michael Gothard, Jack Watson, Brian Blessed, Peter Firth; **D:** Sidney Hayers, Pat Jackson, Peter Sasdy.

King Cobra 1998 (PG-13) If you like big snakes, this low-budgeter is for you! A mutant cobra/rattlesnake hybrid, having escaped its lab environment, threatens the populace of a small California town. 93m/C VHS, DVD. Noriyuki "Pat" Morita, Hoyt Axton, Kasey Fallo, Scott Brandon, Joseph Ruskin, Courtney Gains; **D:** David Hillenbrand, Scott Hillenbrand; **W:** David Hillenbrand, Scott Hillenbrand; **C:** Philip D. Schwartz. **VIDEO**

King Creole 1958 (PG) The King goes film noir as a teenager with a criminal record who becomes a successful pop singer in New Orleans but is threatened by his ties to crime, represented by Walter Matthau. One of the better Elvis films, based on Harold Robbins' "A Stone for Danny Fisher." Features Elvis's last film appearance before his service in the Army. ♪♪King Creole; Banana; New Orleans; Turtles, Berries and Gumbo; Crawfish; Don't Ask Me Why; As Long As I Have You; Trouble; Hard-Headed Woman. 115m/B VHS, DVD. Elvis Presley, Carolyn Jones, Walter Matthau, Dean Jagger, Dolores Hart, Vic Morrow, Paul Stewart, Brian G. Hutton, Liliane Montevecchi, Jan Shepard, Jack Grinnage; **D:** Michael Curtiz; **W:** Herbert Baker, Michael V. Gazzo; **M:** Walter Schaf1.

King David ⋆⋆½ 1985 (PG-13) The story of David, the legendary Biblical hero whose acts of bravery paved the way for him to become king of Israel. 114m/C VHS, DVD. Richard Gere, Alice Krige, Cherie Lunghi, Hurd Hatfield, Edward Woodward; **D:** Bruce Beresford; **W:** Andrew Birkin, James Costigan; **M:** Carl Davis.

A King in New York ⋆⋆ 1957 Chaplin plays the deposed king of a European mini-monarchy who comes to the United States in hope of making a new life. Looks critically at 1950s-era America, including Cold War paranoia and over-reliance on technology. Containing Chaplin's last starring performance, this film wasn't released in the U.S. until 1973. Uneven but interesting. 105m/B VHS, DVD. Charlie Chaplin, Dawn Addams, Michael Chaplin, Oliver Johnston, Maxine Audley, Harry Green; **D:** Charlie Chaplin; **W:** Charlie Chaplin; **C:** Georges Perinal; **M:** Charlie Chaplin.

The King Is Alive ⋆⋆½ 2000 (R) A tourist bus traveling in Namibia strays off-course and runs out of gas. The passengers stumble into a deserted mining town with little food or water and only a small chance at survival. Retired actor Henry (Bradley) begins to think their situation resembles that of "King Lear" and he gradually begins to convince the others to rehearse the play as a way to pass the time. Much lunacy ensues. 118m/C VHS, DVD. **DK** Miles Anderson, Romane Bohringer, David Bradley, David Calder, Brion James, Lisi Kunena, Peter Kubheka, Janet McTeer, Lia Williams, Chris Walker; **D:** Kristian Levring; **W:** Anders Thomas Jensen, Kristian Levring; **C:** Jens Schlosser.

King Kelly of the U.S.A. ⋆ 1934 Robertson carries on a forgettable romance with a princess aboard a trans-Atlantic liner. 64m/B VHS. Guy Robertson, Irene Ware, Edgar Kennedy, Franklin Pangborn, Joyce Compton, Ferdinand Gottschalk, Wilhelm von Brinken, Otis Harlan; **D:** Leonard Fields.

King Kong ⋆⋆⋆ 1933 The original beauty and the beast film classic tells the story of Kong, a giant ape captured in Africa by filmmaker Carl Denham (Armstrong) and brought to New York as a sideshow attraction. Kong falls for starlet Ann (Wray), escapes from his captors, and rampages through the city, ending up on top of the newly built Empire State Building. Moody Steiner score adds color, and Willis O'Brien's stop-motion animation still holds up well. Scenes were cut during the 1938 re-release because of the Hays production code, including one where a curious Kong strips Wray of her clothes. Remade numerous times with various theme derivations. 105m/B VHS, DVD. Fay Wray, Bruce Cabot, Robert Armstrong, Frank Reicher, Noble Johnson, Sam Hardy, James Flavin, Ernest B. Schoedsack, Merian C. Cooper; **D:** Ernest B. Schoedsack, Merian C. Cooper; **W:** James A. Creelman, Ruth Rose, Edgar Wallace; **C:** Edward Linden, J.O. Taylor, Vernon Walker; **M:** Max Steiner. AFI '98: Top 100, Nat. Film Reg. '91.

King Kong ⋆⋆ 1976 (PG) Oil company official travels to a remote island to discover oil inhabited by a huge gorilla. The transplanted beast suffers unrequited love in classic fashion: monkey meets girl, monkey gets girl and brandishes her while atop the World Trade Center. An updated remake of the 1933 movie classic that also marks the screen debut of Lange. Im-pressive sets and a believable King Kong romp around New York City in this film. Watch for Joe Piscopo, and quickly for Corbin Bernsen as a reporter. 135m/C VHS, DVD. Jeff Bridges, Charles Grodin, Jessica Lange, Rene Auberjonois, John Randolph, Ed Lauter, Jack O'Halloran, Dennis Fimple, John Agar, Rick Baker, Joe Piscopo, Corbin Bernsen; **D:** John Guillermin; **W:** Lorenzo Semple Jr.; **C:** Richard H. Kline; **M:** John Barry. Oscars '76: Visual FX.

King Kong ⋆⋆⋆½ 2005 (PG-13) In this remake of the 1933 classic, Depression-era filmmaker Carl Denham (Black) lures starving ingenue Ann Darrow (Watts) and screenwriter Jack Driscoll (Brody) to the uncharted Skull Island to shoot his masterpiece. However, once they arrive, the crew meets angry natives, rampaging dinosaurs, and a massive, menacing monkey named Kong. We all know where the story goes from there, but Jackson enlivens the familiar with thrilling action sequences (Kong vs. T. Rexes equals awesome) and the most expressive simian ever put to film [WETA deserves an acting Oscar for Kong's face alone]. Regrettably, the three-hour flick drags whenever Kong isn't on-screen, and Jackson spends way too much time with his so-so supporting cast. But, as always, Kong remains king. 187m/C DVD, HD DVD. Naomi Watts, Jack Black, Adrien Brody, Thomas Kretschmann, Colin Hanks, Jamie Bell, Evan Dexter Parke, Kyle Chandler, Andy Serkis, Lobo Chen; **D:** Peter Jackson; **W:** Peter Jackson, Fran Walsh, Philippa Boyers; **C:** Andrew Lesnie; **M:** James Newton Howard. Oscars '05: Sound, Visual FX; British Acad. '05: Visual FX.

King Kong Lives ⋆ 1986 (PG-13) Unnecessary sequel to the 1976 remake of "King Kong," in which two scientists get the big ape, now restored after his assault-upsetting fall, together with a lady ape his size and type. 105m/C VHS, DVD. Brian Kerwin, Linda Hamilton, John Ashton, Peter Michael Goetz; **D:** John Guillermin; **W:** Steven Pressfield, Ronald Shusett.

King Kong vs. Godzilla ⋆⋆½ 1963 King Kong tai Gojira; Kinkongu tai Gojira The plot issues a collective shudder as the two mightiest monsters slug it out for reasons known only to themselves. Humankind can only stand by and watch in impotent horror as the tide of the battle sways to and fro, until one monster stands alone and victorious. 105m/C VHS, DVD, **JP** Michael Keith, Tadao Takashima, Mie Hama, Kenji Sahara, Yu Fujiki, Akihiko Hirata, Jun Tazaki, Akiko Wakabayashi, Ichiro Arishima, Tauno Nakajima, Katsumi Tezuka; **D:** Inoshiro Honda; **W:** Shinichi Sekizawa; **C:** Hajime Koizumi; **M:** Akira Ifukube.

King Kung Fu ⋆ 1987 (G) A karate master raises a gorilla, and sends it from Asia to the U.S. There, two out-of-work reporters decide to release it from captivity and then recapture it so they can get the story and some needed recognition. The background they can't have on the gorilla is that its master taught it kung fu. 90m/C VHS. Tim McGowan, Bill Schwartz; **D:** Bill Hayes.

King Lear ⋆⋆⋆ 1971 Brook's version of Shakespeare's tragedy. The king finds a battle-torn French town evacuated of all occupants except a colorful collection of escaped lunatics from a nearby asylum. The lunatics want to make him their king, which is not a bad alternative to the insanity of war. Bujold is cute as ballerina wanna-be look for Serrault ("La Cage aux Folles") as, not surprisingly, a effeminate would-be hairdresser. Light-hearted comedy with a serious message; definitely worthwhile. 101m/C VHS, DVD, **FR GB IT** Alan Bates, Genevieve Bujold, Adolfo Celi, Francoise Christophe, Micheline Presle, Michel Serrault, Julien Guiomar, Pierre Brasseur, Jean-Claude Brialy, Pier Paolo Capponi, Jacques Balutin, Marc Dudicourt, Daniel Boulanger; **D:** Philippe de Broca; **W:** Daniel Boulanger; **C:** Pierre Lhomme; **M:** Georges Delerue.

King Lear ⋆⋆⋆ 1987 Loosely adapted from Shakespeare's tragedy of a king who oses everything. A fragmented French existential reading with gangster undercurrent. This updated version is dark, ominous, wandering, strange, and quite unlike the other 1984 remake. Or any other remake, for that matter. 91m/C VHS. Sf Peter Sellars, Burgess Meredith, Molly Ringwald, Jean-Luc Godard, Woody Allen; **D:** Jean-Luc Godard; **W:** Norman Mailer.

King Lear ⋆⋆⋆½ 1998 Holm gives a powerful performance as the deluded monarch. The King comes to rue tte day he banished faithful daughter Cordelia (Hamilton) in favor of dividing his kingdom between her manipulative siblings Goneril (Flynn) and Regan (Redman). As war engulfs his country, Lear descends into despair and madness. 150m/C VHS. Ian Holm, Victoria Hamilton, Barbara Flynn, Amanda Redman, Michael Bryan, Paul Rhys, Timothy West, Finbar Lynch, David Burke; **D:** Richard Eyre; **W:** Richard Eyre; **C:** Roger Pratt; **M:** Dominic Muldowney. TV

The King Murder ⋆⋆ 1932 High-society sleuth Tearle tries to solve the mysterious death of a beautiful, yet dangerous exortionist. Looks a lot like r-urd-head, Marceline Day, Dorothy Revier; **D:** Richard Thorpe; **W:** Charles Reed Jones.

King of Alcatraz ⋆⋆ 1938 Alcatraz escapee takes over a passenger ship, but the ship's crew won't be going down without a fight. Two brave crewmates create a plan to overtake the convict and rescue the passengers. 68m/B VHS. Gail Patrick, Lloyd Nolan, Harry Carey Jr., J. Carrol Naish, Robert Preston; **D:** Robert Florey; **W:** Irving Reis.

King of America ⋆ 1980 A Greek sailor and a local labor agent battle over who will become King of America. 90m/C VHS. Larry Atlas, David Canary, Philip Casnoff, Michael Walden, Olympia Dukakis, Stephen Lang; **D:** Dezso Magyar; **W:** E.J. Merholz; **C:** Mike Fash; **M:** Elizabeth Swados.

King of California ⋆⋆½ 2007 (PG-13) Charlie (Douglas), a bipolar jazz musician, leaves his hospital in order to find the horde of Spanish treasure he's convinced is buried in his old neighborhood. His teenage daughter Miranda (Wood), abandoned by her mother, reluctantly joins him on his quest, and the two must seek clues as to the treasure's location amongst a sea of box stores and chain restaurants. Douglas is excellent as the erratic, Quixote-like Charlie in search of meaning in an alienated world, but the movie fails to dig much deeper than the superficial word it satirizes. 93m/C DVD, Blu-ray Disc, HD DVD. US Michael Douglas, Evan Rachel Wood, Willis Burke; **D:** Mike Cahill; **W:** Mike Cahill; **C:** James Whitaker; **M:** Mike Robbins.

King of Comedy ⋆⋆⋆ 1982 (PG) An unhinged would-be comedian haunts and eventually kidnaps a massively popular Johnny Carson-type TV personality. A cold, cynical farce delivered by Scorsese seemingly in reaction to John Hinckley's obsession with his film "Taxi Driver." Controlled, hard-hitting performances, especially by De Niro and Lewis. 101m/C VHS, DVD. Robert De Niro, Jerry Lewis, Sandra Bernhard, Tony Randall, Dianne Abbott, Shelley Hack, Liza Minnelli; **D:** Martin Scorsese; **W:** Paul Zimmerman; **C:** Fred Schuler; **M:** Robbie Robertson. British Acad. '83: Orig. Screenplay; Natl. Soc. Film Critics '83: Support. Actress (Bernhard).

The King of Hearts ⋆⋆⋆ Le Roi de Coeur 1966 In WWI, a Scottish soldier

King of Jazz ⋆⋆½ 1930 A lavish revue built around the Paul Whiteman Orchestra with comedy sketches and songs by the stars on Universal Pictures' talent roster. (Though billed as the King of Jazz, Whiteman was never as good as jazz's real royalty.) Filmed in two-color Technicolor with a cartoon segment by Walter Lantz. ♪♪Rhapsody in Blue; So the Bluebirds and the Blackbirds Got Together; Mississippi Mud; It Happened in Monterey; Ragamuffin Romeo; Happy Feet; Song of the Dawn; A Bench in the Park. 93m/C VHS. Paul Whiteman, John Boles, Jeanette Loff, Bing Crosby; **D:** John Murray Anderson.

King of Kings ⋆⋆ 1927 DeMille depicts the life of Jesus Christ in this highly regarded silent epic. The resurrection scene appears in color. Remade by DeMille's Nicholas Ray in 1961. 115m/B VHS, DVD. H.B. Warner, Dorothy (Dorothy G. Cummings) Cumming, Ernest Torrence, Joseph Schildkraut, Jacqueline Logan, Victor Varconi, William Boyd, James Neill, Robert Edeson, Charles Belcher, Montagu Love, Monte (Monty) Collins; **D:** Cecil B. DeMille; **C:** J. Peverell Marley.

The King of Kings ⋆⋆⋆ 1961 An attractive visual sense and a memorable score. Remake of Cecil B. DeMille's silent film, released in 1927. 170m/C VHS. Jeffrey Hunter, Siobhan McKenna, Hurd Hatfield, Robert Ryan, Rita Gam, Viveca Lindfors, Rip Torn; **D:** Nicholas Ray; **W:** Philip Yordan; **C:** Milton Krasner; **M:** Miklós Rózsa; **Narr:** Orson Welles.

The King of Kong: A Fistful of Quarters ⋆⋆⋆ 2007 (PG-13) Documentary follows the intense rivalry of two men battling to be declared the undisputed King of Donkey Kong, and you couldn't ask for two more intriguing characters. Hot-sauce tycoon and jolly rich Billy Mitchell is at the top of the arcade champ heap, holding the high score in Donkey Kong for over 25 years until lowly, humble high school teacher Steve Wiebe appears on the scene with an even higher score. A battle on multiple fronts ensues as Mitchell challenges the validity of Wiebe's score to us inside a competition few people (even acters, enthusiasts) care about and turns it into an exploration of egoism, rivalry, and what it means to be a champion. The movie clearly roots for underdog Wiebe, but the obvious slant is half the fun. 79m/C DVD. US **D:** Seth Gordon; **C:** Seth Gordon; **M:** Craig Richey.

King of Kong Island woof! 1968 Intent on world domination, a group of mad scientists implant receptors in the brains of gorillas on Kong Island, and the monster apes run amok. 92m/C VHS, DVD. SF Brad Harris, Marc Lawrence, Adriana Alben; **D:** Robert Morris.

The King of Marvin Gardens ⋆⋆⋆ 1972 (R) Nicholson stars as a radio personality who prefers to reminisce about his life and family back in Manhattan's chic Plaza hotel. When Nicholson returns for a visit he finds brother Dern, king of the get-rich-quick schemers, working for a black crime syndicate. Dern is involved in another scheme which means embezzling money from his boss—not a smart idea although Nicholson can't dissuade him. Talky drama also features Burstyn as Dern's neglected girlfriend. 104m/C VHS, DVD. Jack Nicholson, Bruce Dern, Ellen Burstyn, Scatman Crothers, Julia Anne Robinson, Charles Lavine, Arnold Williams, Josh Mostel; **D:** Bob Rafelson; **W:** Jacob Brackman.

The King of Masks ⋆⋆⋆ 1999 The King (Xu) is an elderly street performer in 1930s China who practices the ancient art of face-changing with masks. Tradition holds that he pass his secrets to a male heir, which Wang doesn't have. So, he decides to purchase a boy child on the black market, only to later discover that his clever protege (Ren-ying) is actually a little girl. Chinese with subtitles. 101m/C VHS, DVD. CH Zhu Xu, Zhou Ren-ying; **D:** Wu Tianming; **W:** Wei Minglung; **C:** Mu Dayuan; **M:** Jiping Zhao.

King of New York ⋆⋆⋆ 1990 (R) Drug czar Frank White (Walken), recently returned from a prison sabbatical, regains control of his New York drug empire with the aid of a loyal network of black dealers. How? Call it dangerous charisma. Headquartered in Manhattan's chic Plaza hotel, he ruthlessly orchestrates the profits into a Bronx hospital for the poor. As inscrutable to the drug czar's power tangible, believable, yet never fathomable. **106m/C VHS, DVD, Blu-ray Disc, UMD.** Christopher Walken, Laurence Fishburne, David Caruso, Victor Argo, Wesley Snipes, Janet (Johnson) Julian, Joey Chin, Giancarlo Esposito, Steve Buscemi; **D:** Abel Ferrara; **W:** Nicholas St. John; **C:** Bojan Bazelli; **M:** Joe Delia.

King of Texas ✓✓✓ 2002 Shakespeare's "King Lear" set in 1840s Texas with Stewart as John Lear, the patriarch rancher who gives his property to greedy daughters Susannah (Harden) and Rebecca (Holly) and is forced to sweet daughter Claudia (Cox). Then the bad girls kick him out into the wilderness. Powerful performance by Stewart does the Bard proud. **120m/C DVD.** Patrick Stewart, Marcia Gay Harden, Lauren Holly, Julie Cox, David Alan Grier, Roy Scheider, Colm Meaney, Matt Letscher, Steven Bauer, Patrick Bergin, Liam Waite; **D:** Uli Edel; **W:** Stephen Harrigan; **C:** Paul Elliott; **M:** John Altman. **C A B L E.**

King of the Airwaves ✓✓
Louis 19, le Roi des Ondes 1994 Louis (Drainville) is a dull salesman who spends his days working in front of an electronics store and his nights in front of the TV. This leads Louis to enter (and win) a contest sponsored by the local TV station, which promises to provide 24-hour-a-day coverage of the winner's every move. Now, ordinary Louis is a media celebrity who must deal with constant intrusion and the soap opera-ish changes wrought upon his life. **93m/C VHS.** *CA FR* Martin Drainville, Agathe de la Fontaine, Dominique Michel, Patricia Tulasne, Gilbert Lachance; **D:** Michel Poulette; **W:** Michael Michaud, Emile Gaudreault, Sylvie Bouchard; **M:** Jean-Marie Benoit.

King of the Ants ✓✓½ 2003 Handyman Sean (McKenna) could stand a little excitement but he gets more than he bargained for when Duke (Wendt, convincing in quite the anti-"Norm" role) steers him to crooked businessman Ray (Baldwin) who wants Sean to clip a city accountant who's getting too close for comfort. He jumps at the chance but the feel-good ends there when Ray and Duke cut him loose and have his face rearranged. Whereupon, it becomes a standard revenge tale. Screenwriter Charlie Higson adapted from his 1992 novel of the same name. **103m/C VHS, DVD.** Kari Wuhrer, Daniel Baldwin, George Wendt, Ron Livingston, Christopher McKenna, Timm Sharp, Vernon Wells, Lionel Mark Smith, Carlie Westerman; **D:** Stuart Gordon; **W:** Charles Higson; **C:** Mac Ahlberg. **V I D E O**

King of the Bullwhip ✓½ 1951 Crabbe, in his last serial, as a pilot who is frantically searching for an important piece of film, in 15 parts. **?m/B VHS.** Buster Crabbe, Gloria Dee; **D:** Spencer Gordon Bennet, Wallace Grissell.

King of the Congo ✓✓ 1952 Two undercover U.S. Marshals are sent to Tioga City to stop the killing and looting of a masked bandit, whose whip is as dangerous as his gun. **59m/B VHS.** Lash LaRue, Al "Fuzzy" St. John, Anne Gwynne, Tom Neal, Jack Holt, Dennis Moore, Michael Whalen, George Lewis; **D:** Ron Ormond.

King of the Corner ✓✓✓ 2004 (R) Leo (Riegert) has hit the middle-age wall and can hardly hold back his angst. He abhors his lifelong VP status at a Manhattan marketing job, wife Rachel (Rosselini) appears mentally unstable, and teenage daughter Elena (Johnson) just started dating. Adding to the stress are every-other-weekend treks to Arizona to visit his dying father Sol, whose sage advice for Leo teaches him the real meaning about being a "good Jew." Adapted from the short-story collection "Bad Jews and Other Stories" by Gerald Shapiro, who co-wrote the screenplay along with actor/director Riegert. **93m/C VHS, DVD.** *US* Peter Riegert, Isabella Rossellini, Beverly D'Angelo, Eli Wallach, Ashley Johnson, Eric Bogosian, Dominic Chianese, Rita Moreno, Peter Friedman, Harris Yulin, Frank Wood; **D:** Peter Riegert; **W:** Peter Riegert; **C:** Mauricio Rubinstein.

King of the Cowboys ✓✓ 1943 Roy fights a gang of saboteurs and saves a defense installation. **54m/B VHS, DVD.** Roy Rogers, Smiley Burnette, James Bush, Bob Nolan, Peggy Moran, Gerald Mohr, Dorothea Kent, Lloyd

---

Corrigan, Russell Hicks; **D:** Joseph Kane; **W:** J. Benton Cheney; **C:** Reggie Lanning.

King of the Damned ✓ 1936 On an island prison Veidt leads a convict's revolt against the cruel administrator (Hallard), who gets killed. Before he dies, Hallard alerts a convenient warship, which begins shelling the island. Hallard's daughter, who has fallen for Veidt, pleads for the men and everyone is given a fair trial. Miscast and ineptly performed, although Veidt retains some dignity. **81m/B VHS.** *GB* Conrad Veidt, Helen Vinson, C.M. Hallard, Noah Beery Sr., Percy Walsh, Raymond Lovell, Cecil Ramage, Peter Croft; **D:** Walter Forde; **W:** Charles Bennett, Sidney Gilliat, Noel Langley.

King of the Forest Rangers 1946 Ranger Steve King must stop an evil archaeologist from finding a treasure whose secret lies within an ancient Indian rug pattern. Edited from an original, 12 episode serial on two cassettes. **167m/B VHS.** Larry Thompson, Helen Talbot, Stuart Hamblen, Anthony Warde, Scott Elliott; **D:** Spencer Gordon Bennet, Fred Brannon; **W:** Albert DeMond, Ronald Davidson, Basil Dickey, Jesse Duffy, Lynn Perkins; **C:** Bud Thackery.

King of the Grizzlies ✓½ 1969 (G) The mystical relationship between a Cree Indian and a grizzly cub is put to the test when the full grown bear attacks a ranch at which the Indian is foreman. **93m/C VHS, DVD.** Chris Wiggins, John Yesno; **D:** Ron Kelly.

King of the Gypsies ✓✓✓½ 1978 (R) Interesting drama. A young man, scornful of his gypsy heritage, runs away from the tribe and tries to make a life of his own. He is summoned home to his grandfather's deathbed where he is proclaimed the new king of the gypsies, thus incurring the wrath of the gypsies. From Peter Maas's best-selling novel. **112m/C VHS.** Sterling Hayden, Eric Roberts, Susan Sarandon, Brooke Shields, Shelley Winters, Annie Potts, Annette O'Toole, Judd Hirsch, Michael V. Gazzo, Roy Brocksmith, Anthony Holland; **D:** Frank Pierson; **W:** Frank Pierson; **C:** Sven Nykvist.

King of the Hill ✓✓✓½ 1993 (PG-13) Quiet depression-era drama focuses on Aaron, a 12-year-old who lives in a seedy hotel in St. Louis. The family is barely scraping by; his mother is in a tuberculosis sanitarium, his younger brother has been sent away to live with relatives, and Aaron must fend for himself when his father gets work as a traveling salesman. Aaron excels at school and his efforts there, as well as his hotel friends, manage to provide him with some semblance of a regular life. Soderbergh's third directorial effort is unsentimental but admiring of his character's resourcefulness and imagination during difficult times. Based on the book by A.E. Hochner describing his own childhood. **102m/C VHS.** Jesse Bradford, Jeroen Krabbe, Lisa Eichhorn, Karen Allen, Spalding Gray, Elizabeth McGovern, Joseph Chrest, Adrien Brody, Cameron Boyd, Chris Samples, Katherine Heigl, Amber Benson, John McConnell, Ron Vawter, John Durbin, Lauryn Hill, David Jensen; **D:** Steven Soderbergh; **W:** Steven Soderbergh; **M:** Cliff Martinez.

King of the Jungle ✓✓ 1933 Paramount's answer to Tarzan stars Crabbe as Kaspa the Lion Man. This jungle boy, raised by animals, is captured on safari and displayed (attired in a skimpy loincloth) as a circus attraction. Dee is the babe helping to soothe Kaspa's savage breast, or beast, or something. Big finale includes a circus fire and an elephant stampede. **73m/B VHS.** Buster Crabbe, Frances Dee, Sidney Toler, Nydia Westman, Douglass Dumbrille, Robert Barrat; **D:** H. Bruce Humberstone, Max Marcin; **W:** Max Marcin; **C:** Ernest Haller.

King of the Jungle ✓✓ 2001 (R) Contrived story with an energized performance by Leguizamo. He's Seymour, a mentally challenged man with the intellectual and emotional capacity of a preadolescent. He lives with his long-divorced Puerto Rican mother Mona (Carmen) and her lover Joanne (Perez). His dad, Jack (Gorman), is a deadbeat poet who has never accepted his son's limitations. Seymour spends his time on the streets

---

playing basketball until his mother is fatally shot and he wants revenge. **87m/C VHS, DVD.** John Leguizamo, Cliff Gorman, Julie Carmen, Rosie Perez, Michael Rapaport, Rosario Dawson, Marisa Tomei, Annabella Sciorra; **D:** Seth Zvi Rosenfeld; **W:** Seth Zvi Rosenfeld; **C:** Fortunato Procopio; **M:** Harry Gregson-Williams.

King of the Kickboxers Woof! 1991 (R) The villains make kung-fu snuff movies with unwitting actors killed on camera. Otherwise, same old junk about a karate cop back in Bangkok to get the dude who squashed his brother. Pretty racist at times. **90m/C VHS.** Loren Avedon, Richard Jaeckel, Billy Blanks, Don Stroud, Keith Cooke; **D:** Lucas Lowe.

King of the Kongo ✓✓ 1929 A handsome young man is sent by the government to Nuhalla, deep in the jungle, to break up a gang of ivory thieves. Serial was made in silent and sound versions. **213m/B VHS.** Jacqueline Logan, Boris Karloff, Richard Tucker; **D:** Richard Thorpe.

King of the Mountain ✓✓½ 1981 (PG) The "Old King" and the "New King" must square off in this tale of daredevil road racers who zoom through the streets of Hollywood. Interesting cast trapped by tired script. **92m/C VHS.** Richard Cox, Harry Hamlin, Dennis Hopper, Joseph Bottoms, Deborah Van Valkenburgh, Dan Haggerty; **D:** Noel Nosseck; **W:** Roger Christian.

King of the Pecos ✓✓½ 1936 A young lawyer (who's also adept at the shootin' iron) exacts revenge on his parents' killers in the courtroom. Well made early Wayne outing, with good character development, taut pacing and beautiful photography. **54m/B VHS, DVD.** John Wayne, Muriel Evans, Cy Kendall, Jack Clifford, John (Jack) Beck, Yakima Canutt; **D:** Joseph Kane; **W:** Dorrell McGowan, Stuart E. McGowan, Bernard McConville; **C:** Jack Marta.

The King of the Roaring '20s: The Story of Arnold Rothstein ✓✓ 1961 *The Big Bankroll* "True" story of infamous gangster, Arnold Rothstein, a brilliant and ruthless gambler who practically ran New York in the '20s. This version of his rise focuses on his rise to power, the dealings with his enemies, and his crumbling personal life. Superficial due mostly to the weak screenplay. Adapted from the book "The Big Bankroll" by Leo Katcher. **106m/B VHS.** David Janssen, Dianne Foster, Mickey Rooney, Jack Carson, Diana Dors, Dan O'Herlihy, Mickey Shaughnessy, Keenan Wynn; **D:** Joseph M. Newman.

King of the Rocketmen ✓✓ 1928 *Lost Planet Airmen* 1949 Jeff King thwarts an attempt by traitors to steal government scientific secrets. Serial in 12 episodes. Later released as a feature titled "Lost Planet Airmen." **156m/B VHS, DVD.** Tristram Coffin, Mae Clarke, I. Stanford Jolley; **D:** Fred Brannon.

King of the Rodeo ✓✓ 1928 Cowpoke Hoot wins a rodeo and catches a thief in the Windy City. Hoot's final silent ride into the sunset. **54m/B VHS.** Hoot Gibson, Kathryn Crawford, Slim Summerville, Charles French, Monte Montague, Joseph Girard; **D:** Henry MacRae.

King of the Sierras ✓½ 1938 Bosworth tells his nephew the story of a white horse that protected his mares from a black stallion. The acting of the horses is better than that of the humans. **58m/B VHS.** Hobart Bosworth, Harry Harvey, Harry Harvey Jr., Jim Campeau; **D:** Samuel Diege; **W:** Scott Darling.

King of the Stallions ✓½ 1942 A dangerous stallion is a menacing threat to the herd and the cowboys and Indians and other scattered wildlife. Chief Thundercloud is the only one capable of tackling the matter. Largely Indian cast, including Iron Eyes Cody, famed for the anti-litter campaign. **63m/B VHS.** Chief Thundercloud, Princess Bluebird, Chief Yowlachie, Rick Vallin, Dave O'Brien, Barbara Felker, Iron Eyes Cody; **D:** Edward Finney.

King of the Texas Rangers ✓✓ 1941 Tom King, Texas Ranger, finds that his father's killers are a group of saboteurs who have destroyed American oil fields. This 12-episode serial comes on two tapes. **195m/B VHS.** Sammy

---

Baugh, Neil Hamilton; **D:** William Witney, John English.

King of the Wild Horses ✓✓✓ 1924 Engaging children's story about a wild stallion that comes to the rescue. Terrific action photography of Rex going through his paces. Look for Chase in a rare dramatic role. Silent. **50m/B VHS.** Rex, Edna Murphy, Leon Bary, Pat Hartigan, Frank Butler, Charley Chase; **D:** Fred W. Jackman.

King of the Wind ✓✓½ 1993 (PG) An epic adventure featuring the true story of a legendary Arabian horse and a poor stable boy who gave the most precious gift of all: love. **101m/C VHS.** Richard Harris, Glenda Jackson.

King of the Zombies Woof! 1941 Mad scientist creates his own zombies without souls, to be used as the evil tools of a foreign government. Zombie nonsense. **67m/B VHS, DVD.** John Archer, Dick Purcell, Mantan Moreland, Henry Victor, Joan Woodbury; **D:** Jean Yarbrough; **W:** Edmond Kelso; **C:** Mack Stengler; **M:** Edward Kay.

King of Thieves ✓✓ *Konig der Diebe* 2004 Poor Ukrainian circus kids, 10-year-old Barbu and his 13-year-old sister Mimma, are sold to one-time circus performer Caruso who makes a lot of promises about a better life. After smuggling them into Berlin, the siblings are separated and Barbu learns to be a pickpocket. But when he discovers that Mimma is forced to work in a brothel, he tries to free her. German with subtitles. **101m/C DVD.** *GE* Lazar Ristovski, Paulus Manker, Katharina Thalbach, Iakov Kultiasov, Julia Khanverdieva; **D:** Ivan Fila; **W:** Ivan Fila; **C:** Vladimir Smutny; **M:** Michael Kocab.

The King on Main Street ✓✓½ 1925 *Konig der* Molvania (Menjou) comes to America to get a loan for his country and falls for Gladys (Love), who returns his interest. But duty calls in the end. Based on the play "The King" by Leo Ditrichstein. **68m/B VHS.** Adolphe Menjou, Bessie Love, Greta Nissen, Joseph Kilgour, Oscar Shaw, Edgar Norton; **D:** Monta Bell; **W:** Monta Bell, Douglas Z. Doty; **C:** James Wong Howe.

King, Queen, Knave ✓✓ *Herzbube* 1972 Sexy black comedy about a shy, awkward 19-year-old boy, keenly aware that his interest in girls is not reciprocated. He has to go live with his prosperous uncle and his much younger wife is the long-suffering valet who tries to coax him for the job. Funny in spots and Goodman is the quintessential good sport, making the whole outing pleasant. Sometimes too forced. **96m/C VHS, DVD.** John Goodman, Peter O'Toole, Camille Coduri, Joely Richardson, John Hurt; **D:** David S. Ward; **W:** David S. Ward; **C:** Kenneth Macmillan; **M:** James Newton Howard.

King Ralph ✓✓ 1991 (PG) When the rest of the royal family passes away in a freak accident, lounge lizard Ralph finds himself the only heir to the throne. O'Toole is the long-suffering valet who tries to train him for the job. Based on James Clavell's novel. **134m/B VHS, DVD.** George Segal, Tom Courtenay, James Fox, James Donald, Denholm Elliott, Patrick O'Neal, John Mills, Todd Armstrong, Gerald Sim, Leonard Rossiter, John Standing, Alan Webb, Sam Reese, Wright King, Joe Turkel, Geoffrey Bayldon, Reg Lye, Arthur Malet, Richard Dawson, William "Bill" Fawcett, John Warburton, John Ronane, Michael Lees, Hamilton Dyce, Hedley Mattingly, Dale Ishimoto; **D:** Bryan Forbes; **W:** Bryan Forbes, James Clavell; **C:** Burnett Guffey; **M:** John Barry.

King Rat ✓✓✓ 1965 Drama set in a WWII Japanese prisoner-of-war camp. Focuses on the effect of captivity on the English, Australian, and American prisoners. An American officer bribes his Japanese captors to live more comfortably than the rest. Based on James Clavell's novel.

King Richard and the Crusaders ✓½ 1954 Laughable costume epic with Sanders as Richard the Lionheart, who survives an assassination attempt during the Crusades. Harvey is a loyal knight sworn to find the traitors with Harrison as the noble leader of the Arab

King Solomon's Mines 🎬🎬🎬 1937 The search for King Solomon's Mines leads a safari through treacherous terrain of the desert, fending off sandstorms, Zulus, and a volcanic eruption. Adapted from the novel by H. Rider Haggard and remade twice. **80m/B VHS, DVD.** *GB* Cedric Hardwicke, Paul Robeson, Roland Young, John Loder, Anna Lee; *D:* Robert Stevenson; *W:* Michael Hogan, Roland Pertwee; *C:* Cyril Knowles, Glen MacWilliams; *M:* Mischa Spoliansky.

King Solomon's Mines 🎬🎬🎬 1950 Hunter Allan Quatermain (Granger) is hired by Elizabeth Curtis (Kerr) and her brother John (Carlson) to find Elizabeth's missing husband who was searching for the legendary diamond mines of King Solomon. Naturally, there are numerous adventures during their expedition. Filmed on location in Nairobi, Tanganyika and the Belgian Congo. A lavish version of the classic H. Rider Haggard novel; remake of the 1937 classic and remade again in 1985. **102m/C VHS, DVD.** Stewart Granger, Deborah Kerr, Richard Carlson, Hugo Haas, Lowell Gilmore; *D:* Compton Bennett, Andrew Marton; *W:* Helen Deutsch; *C:* Robert L. Surtees. Oscars '50: Color Cinematog., Film Editing.

King Solomon's Mines 🎬🎬½ 1985 (PG-13) The third remake of the classic H. Rider Haggard novel about a safari deep into Africa in search of an explorer who disappeared while searching for the legendary diamond mines of King Solomon. Updated but lacking the style of the previous two films. Somewhat imperialistic, racist point of view. **101m/C VHS, DVD.** Richard Chamberlain, John Rhys-Davies, Sharon Stone, Herbert Lom; *D:* J. Lee Thompson; *W:* Gene Quintano; *M:* Jerry Goldsmith.

King Solomon's Treasure 🎬 1976 The great white adventurer takes on the African jungle, hunting for hidden treasure in the Forbidden City. Ekland stars as a Phoenician Queen—need we say more?? **90m/C VHS, CA GB David McCallum, Britt Ekland, Patrick Macnee, Wilfrid Hyde-White; *D:* Alvin Rakoff.

The Kingdom 🎬🎬🎬½ Riget 1995 Danish director von Trier serves up what must be the first four-and-a-half-hour long hospital soap opera/ghost story/comedy/satire. El dusty Mrs. Drusse checks herself into a hospital known as the Kingdom, which is inhabited by the usual medical suspects. Pompous surgeons, incompetent bureaucrats, and quirky residents. She hears the ghostly call of a child from an elevator shaft and sticks around to investigate. Made for Danish TV but released theatrically, there and in the States, film owes a great deal to "Twin Peaks" and B-movie honor flicks. Doesn't take itself too seriously, but probably can't be watched all in one sitting. Danish and Swedish with subtitles. **279m/C VHS, DVD.** *DK* Kirsten Rolffes, Ernst-Hugo Järegård, Søren Pilmark, Holger Juul Hansen, Baard Owe, Birgitte Raaberg, Peter Mygind, Solbjørg Højfeldt; *D:* Lars von Trier, Tomas Gislason, Niels Vørsel; *C:* Eric Kress; *M:* Joachim Holbek.

The Kingdom 🎬🎬 2007 (R) After a suicide bombing in Saudi Arabia kills over 100 Americans, FBI agent Ronald Fleury (Foxx) leads a hotshot team (Cooper, Garner, and a particularly obnoxious Bateman) to investigate, although officials from both governments aren't exactly happy about the situation. Fleury and company arrive on Saudi soil ready to open a can of American whoop-ass, but not everything is as simple as it seems for the trio of Saudi hardliner Col. at Ghazi (Barhom). Culture clashes, personal agendas, and political intrigue prove complicated while they track the terrorist suspected of planning the bombing. Big-budget actioner strives for relevance with its true-life backdrop, but too often settles for exploitation, and director Berg never seems at ease with his subject until the movie's final explosion-fest. **110m/C DVD, HD DVD, US** Jamie Foxx, Chris Cooper, Jennifer Garner, Jason Bateman, Ashraf Barhoum, Ali Suliman, Jeremy Piven; *D:* Peter Berg; *W:* Matthew Carnahan; *C:* Mauro Fiore; *M:* Danny Elfman.

The Kingdom 2 🎬🎬🎬½ Riget II 1997 In the continuation of Von Trier's hospital soap/supernatural/satire, madness runs rampant through Copenhagen's Kingdom hospital. Spiritualist Mrs. Drosse comes back to life after dying during surgery. A baby, sired by a demon, grows at a monstrous rate. Pompous Swedish neurosurgeon Helmer returns from Haiti with voodoo potions and is besieged by his unbalanced lover and on and on it goes in this quirky, bizarre way. Swedish and Danish with subtitles. **286m/C VHS, DVD.** *DK* Kirsten Rolffes, Ghita Nørby, Udo Kier, Ernst-Hugo Järegård, Søren Pilmark, Holger Juul Hansen, Baard Owe, Birgitte Raaberg, Peter Mygind, Solbjørg Højfeldt; *D:* Lars von Trier, Niels Vørsel; *C:* Eric Kress; *M:* Joachim Holbek.

Kingdom Come 🎬🎬 2001 (PG) The death of an African-American family's patriarch brings archetypical relatives from near and far for the funeral. There's the wise, saintly widow (Goldberg) and his eager-to-please wife (Fox), the ne'er-do-well son (Anderson) and his shrewish wife (Pinkett-Smith), the Bible-thumper (Devine), and the gold-digger (Braxton). Throw in an over-officious aunt, a lazy, unfortunately flatulent preacher (Cedric), let simmer, and bring to a boil. Most of the humor comes from the over-the-top renditions of the characters, as well as the aforementioned gastrointestinal distress, but it keeps getting in the way of the serious, well-done drama between the at-odds family members. The swings in tone and mood are jarring, but the ride is made easier by the stellar performances, highlighted by LL Cool J's breakout as the eldest son. **89m/C VHS, DVD.** *US* LL Cool J, Jada Pinkett Smith, Vivica A. Fox, Loretta Devine, Anthony Anderson, Cedric the Entertainer, Darius McCrary, Whoopi Goldberg, Toni Braxton, Masasa, Clifton Davis, Richard Gant, Doug McHenry; *D:* Doug McHenry; *W:* Jessie Jones, David Bicknell; *C:* Francis Kenny; *M:* Tyler Bates.

Kingdom of Heaven 🎬🎬🎬 2005 (R) Scott successfully moves from Roman epic "Gladiator" to the 12th century in the service of dying King Baldwin IV (Norton) of Jerusalem. He returns to France to recruit for a crusade and to seek out his legitimate son, black-smith Balian (Bloom). During his quest, Balian becomes a knight, falls in love with Baldwin's sister, Princess Sibylla (Green), and tries to protect Jerusalem from the conspirators within the city and the amassing forces of Saladin (Massoud) without. Of course, as the smart screenplay deftly points out, it's the self-interested extremists on both sides that cause most of the trouble. Despite the epic scale, Scott pays ample attention to the human aspect of poor judgment. These characters talk for real, and walk right past the emotional traps that any Hollywood screenplay might fall into. Stunning conclusion leaves an ambiguous taste in the mouth. **150m/C DVD, Blu-ray D sc.** *US GB* Orlando Bloom, Eva Green, Liam Neeson, Jeremy Irons, David Thewlis, Brendan Gleeson, Marton Csokas, Michael Sheen, Edward Norton, Alexander Siddig, Kevin McKidd, Jon Finch, Ghassan Massoud, Velibor Topi, Ulrich Thomsen, Nikolaj Coster-Waldau, Iain Glen; *D:* Ridley Scott; *W:* William Monahan; *C:* John Mathieson; *M:* Harry Gregson-Williams.

Kingdom of the Spiders 🎬🎬½ 1977 (PG) A desert town is invaded by swarms of killer tarantulas, which begin to consume townspeople. **90m/C VHS, DVD.** William Shatner, Tiffany Bolling, Woody Strode; *D:* John Cardos; *W:* Alan Caillou, Richard Robinson; *C:* John Morrill.

Kingfish: A Story of Huey P. Long 🎬🎬½ 1995 Charismatic political kingpin of Louisiana, Huey P. Long is brought to vivid life with Goodman's swaggering portrayal. Story is told in flashback, beginning with Long's assassination in 1935. A champion of the working man, Long parlayed charm and corruption into a Depression-era political career as governor and U.S. Senator. But naturally, the hard-drinking, hard-loving Long makes a lot of enemies along the way. Long's life was also memorably recreated in Robert Penn Warren's "All the King's Men," as was that of his younger brother, Governor Earl Long, in the film "Blaze." **97m/C DVD, US** John Goodman, Matt Craven, Anne Heche, Ann Dowd, Jeffrey Perry, Bob Gunton, Hoyt Axton, Kirk Baltz, Bill Cobbs; *D:* Thomas Schlamme; *W:* Paul Monash; *M:* Patrick Williams.

Kingfisher Caper 🎬🎬 1976 (PG) A power struggle between a businessman, his brother, and a divorced sister is threatening to rip a family-owned diamond empire apart. **90m/C VHS.** Hayley Mills, David McCallum; *D:* Dirk Devilliers.

Kingfisher the Killer 🎬 1981 Charles, the Raging Titan of Ninja skill, stalks the bad gang that killed his mother and his them with nunchakos. **90m/C VHS.** HK Sho Kosugi.

Kingpin 🎬🎬½ 1996 (PG-13) Bowling epic saves up social satire while showcasing some of the worst hair ever seen at the cinema. Roy Munson (a very bald Harrelson, reasonably subdued in relation to the rest of cast) is a former bowling champ who, thanks to his sleazy ways, lost a hand and is reduced to selling bowling equipment while wearing a crude rubber prosthetic (on his hand). That is until Roy can confront an old nemesis (Murray) and compare shampoos, while Ish attempts to win enough money to save the family farm. Claudia (Angel) is around as the highly decorative love interest of Roy, whom he persuades to hit the road to a big money tournament in Reno, where he meets innocent Amish phenom Ishmael (Quaid), resplendent in a dutch boy wig. Co-written by "Dumb & Dumber" writers the brothers Farrelly. Look for Amish sensations Blues Traveler at the credit roll. **107m/C VHS, DVD.** Woody Harrelson, Randy Quaid, Vanessa Angel, Bill Murray, Chris Elliott, Mike Cerrone, William Jordan, Richard Tyson, Lin Shaye, Zen Gesner, Prudence Wright Holmes, Rob Moran; *D:* Peter Farrelly, Bobby Farrelly; *W:* Bobby Farrelly, Mort Nathan; *C:* Mark Irwin; *M:* Freedy Johnston.

Kings and Desperate Men 🎬🎬½ 1983 Apprentice terrorists plea their case at a public forum when they take a rakish talk show host hostage. **118m/C VHS, GB** Patrick McGoohan, Alexis Kanner, Andrea Marcovicci, Robin Spry, Frank Moore; *D:* Alexis Kanner.

Kings and Queen 🎬🎬🎬 Rois et reine 2004 French portrait of seemingly ordinary life, steeped with hints at a dark reality that refuses to admit the truth. Nora is a divorced-divorced, hip, intelligent art gallery owner, and mother to an 11-year-old boy. She's now engaged to a very rich man, and has a father dying of stomach cancer. A standard set-up to any Hollywood melodrama, but Hollywood doesn't exist in France. Therefore, Nora may not care about any of them the way we think she should. Ismael is Nora's most recent lover, stuck in a mental institution only because of poor judgment. **150m/C DVD.** *FR* Emmanuelle Devos, Mathieu Amalric, Catherine Deneuve, Magali Woch, Olivier Rabourdin, Maurice Garrel, Nathalie Boutefeu, Hippolyte Girardot, Joachim Salinger; *D:* Arnaud Desplechin, Roger Bohbot; *C:* Eric Gautier.

Kings Go Forth 🎬🎬½ 1958 Hormones and war rage in this love triangle set against the backdrop of WWII France. Sinatra loves Wood who loves Curtis. When Sinatra asks for her hand in marriage she refuses because she is mixed—half black, half white. He says it doesn't matter, but she still declines because she's in love with Curtis. When Sinatra tells Curtis that Wood is mixed, Curtis says that it doesn't matter to him either because he'd never planned on marrying her. Meanwhile, the war continues. Not particularly satisfying on either the war or race front. Based on a novel by Joe David Brown. **109m/B VHS, DVD.** Frank Sinatra, Tony Curtis, Natalie Wood, Leora Dana; *D:* Delmer Daves; *W:* Merle Miller; *C:* Daniel F. Fapp; *M:* Elmer Bernstein.

The King's Guard 🎬🎬½ 2001 (PG-13) Captain Reynolds (St. John) and his men must accompany betrothed Princess Gwendolyn (Jones)—and her dowry of gold—to her intended's kingdom. But the fast-paced action helps keep things interesting. **94m/C VHS, DVD.** Ashley Jones, Eric Roberts, Ron Perlman, Trevor St. John, Lesley-Anne Down; *D:* Joshua Wexler; *W:* Joshua Wexler; *M:* Jonathan Tydor. VIDEO

Kings in Grass Castles 🎬🎬½ 1997 Aussie miniseries based on the memoirs of Dame Mary Durack and her immigrant family who leave famine-stricken Ireland in the 1850s for Australia. After dealing with an eight-year internment, the family become Queensland cattle barons. **200m/C VHS.** *AU* Stephen (Dillon) Dillane, Essie Davis, Fionnula Flanagan, David Ngcombujarra, Susan Lynch, Ernie Dingo, James Fox, Max Cullen, Des McAleer; *D:* John Woods; *W:* Tony Morphett; *C:* Roger Lanser; TV

Kings of the Road—In the Course of Time 🎬🎬½ Im Lauf der Zeit 1976 A writer and a film projectionist travel by truck across Germany. The film stands out for its simple and expressive direction, and truly captures the sense of physical and ideological freedom of being on the road. A landmark Wenders epic. In German with English subtitles. **176m/B VHS, GE Rüdiger Vogler, Hanns Zischler, Elisabeth (Lisa) Kreuzer; *D:* Wim Wenders; *W:* Wim Wenders; *C:* Robby Müller, Martin Schäfer; *M:* Axel Linstädt.

Kings of the Sun 🎬🎬 1963 Balian (Chakiris), the newly crowned king of the Mayans, decides to resettle his people in another area of Mexico, thus angering the locals who are led by Black Eagle (Brynner). But the two make peace when a greater threat emerges. Brynner always has presence but Chakiris is solemn and lightweight and this story is more foolish than fact. **108m/C DVD.** Yul Brynner, George Chakiris, Shirley Anne Field, Richard Basehart, Brad Dexter, Barry Morse, Leo Gordon; *D:* J. Lee Thompson; *W:* Elliott Arnold, James R. Webb; *C:* Joe MacDonald; *M:* Elmer Bernstein.

King's Ransom 🎬 Woo!! 1991 When the Japanese Emperor's Pearl is stolen, the underworld is abuzz with excitement. But only the wealthiest individuals are invited to bid for the jewel at Cameron King's secret casino. There, untold pleasures, and dangers, await them. **7m/C VHS, GB** Miles O'Keeffe, Debbie Pfeiffer, Christopher Atkins; *D:* Hugh Parks.

King's Ransom 🎬🎬 2005 (PG-13) Perennial comic sidekick Anderson proves that some actors are only funny in small doses when he's first leading role as obnoxious self-obsessed billionaire Malcolm King. The deceitful mogul ignores his gold-digging wife (Smith), harasses his good-natured secretary (Devine), and makes life a living hell for the employees at his Chicago-based marketing firm. His enemies all get the same idea—kidnap King and teach him a lesson—and painful King and help gets good-dig-ging wife (Smith), harasses his unfunny hijinks ensue. Even King gets involved with faking his own kidnapping, which was amusing back when it was originally done in "Ruthless People." The cast features an ensemble of legitimately funny actors who are cast adrift in this pointless, humorless wreck. **97m/C DVD, US** Anthony Anderson, Jay Mohr, Kellita Smith, Nicole Ari Parker, Regina Hall, Loretta Devine, Donald Adeosun Faison, Charlie (Charles Q.) Murphy, Lisa Marcos, Brooke D'Orsay, Leila Arcieri, Jackie Burroughs; *D:* Jeff Byrd; *W:* Wayne Conley; *C:* Robert McLachlan.

The King's Rhapsody 🎬🎬 1955 Flynn is an heir who abdicates his throne in order to be with the woman he loves. But when the king dies, Flynn sacrifices love for honor and goes back to marry a princess. Very dated and Flynn is long past his swashbuckling-romantic days. **93m/C VHS, GB** Errol Flynn, Anna Neagle, Patrice...

Wymore, Martita Hunt, Finlay Currie, Frank Wolff, Joan Benham, Reginald Tate, Miles Malleson; *D:* Herbert Wilcox.

Kings Row ✶✶✶ **1941** The Harry Bellamann best-selling Middle American potboiler comes to life. Childhood friends grow up with varying degrees of success, in a decidedly macabre town. All are continually dependent on and inspired by Parris (Cummings) a psychiatric doctor and genuine gentleman. Many cast members worked against type with unusual success. Warner held the film for a year after its completion, in concern for its dark subject matter, but it received wide acclaim. Shot completely within studio settings—excellent scenic design by William Cameron Menzies, and wonderful score. **127m/B VHS, DVD.** Ann Sheridan, Robert Cummings, Ronald Reagan, Betty Field, Charles Coburn, Claude Rains, Judith Anderson, Nancy Coleman, Karen Verne, Maria Ouspenskaya, Harry Davenport, Ernest Cossart, Pat Moriarty, Scotty Beckett; *D:* Sam Wood; *C:* James Wong Howe; *M:* Erich Wolfgang Korngold.

The King's Thief ✶✶½ **1955** Costume swashbuckler with Niven as the bad guy. He's a duke at the court of 17th-century English King Charles II and is involved in a plot to steal the crown jewels. **78m/C VHS.** David Niven, Edmund Purdom, George Sanders, Ann Blyth, Roger Moore, John Dehner, Sean McClory, Melville Cooper, Alan Mowbray; *D:* Robert Z. Leonard; *W:* Christopher Knopf; *M:* Miklos Rozsa.

The King's Whore ✶✶ **1990 (R)** Dalton stars as a 17th-century king who falls obsessively in love with the wife of one of his courtiers. His passions lead him to make a decision between the woman and the throne. Good-looking costume epic with obligatory sword fights. **111m/C VHS, DVD.** Timothy Dalton, Valeria Golino, Feodor Chaliapin Jr., Margaret Tyzack; *W:* Daniel Vigne, Frederic Raphael.

Kinjite: Forbidden Subjects ✶✶ **1989 (R)** A cop takes on a sleazy pimp whose specialty is recruiting teenage girls, including the daughter of a Japanese business man. Slimy, standard Bronson fare. **97m/C VHS, DVD.** Charles Bronson, Juan Fernandez, Peggy Lipton; *D:* J. Lee Thompson.

A Kink in the Picasso ✶✶ **1990** MTV personality Daddo joins a cast of criminals who chase after a Picasso artwork and a counterfeit. Artless Australian production. **84m/C VHS.** Peter O'Brien, Jon Finlayson, Jane Clifton, Andrew Daddo; *D:* Marc Gracie.

Kinky Boots ✶✶½ **2006 (PG-13)** Title says it all in this slight Brit comedy that's based on a true story. Charlie Price (Edgerton) reluctantly takes over the failing family shoe factory after his dad dies. They need a specialty product to save the day, and Charlie receives unexpected inspiration when he comes to the aid of big black drag queen Lola (a sweet Ejiofor), who bemoans that the average stiletto wasn't made to support someone of his size. With Lola offering expertise, Charlie and his workers find their new market in cross-dressers. A big fashion show finale adds to the feel-good fantasy. **106m/C DVD.** *GB* Joel Edgerton, Chiwetel Ejiofor, Sarah-Jane Potts, Jemima Rooper, Linda Bassett, Nick Frost, Ewan Hooper, Robert Pugh, Geoffrey Streatfeild; *D:* Julian Jarrold; *W:* Tim Firth, Geoff Deane; *C:* Eigil Bryld; *M:* Adrian Johnston.

Kinsey ✶✶✶ **2004 (R)** Well-written, well-acted, and provocative biopic on the life of still-controversial sex researcher Alfred Kinsey. Trained as a zoologist, Kinsey (Neeson) found his true calling when his own sexual ignorance and that of his equally inexperienced bride Clara (Linney) caused them marital problems. The Indiana U professor began by offering his students factual and explicit information on human sexuality and then embarked on a massive research project that involved interviewing thousands about their sexual histories. Rumpled but charismatic, Kinsey's own complicated sexual feelings, especially towards young associate Clyde Martin (Sarsgaard), offer emotional consequences Kinsey is unprepared for. Nor is he prepared for the increasingly shrill notoriety his published works bring him. Lynn Redgrave offers a striking cameo. **118m/C DVD.** *US* Liam Neeson, Laura Linney, Chris O'Donnell, Peter Sarsgaard, Timothy Hutton, John Lithgow, Tim Curry, Oliver Platt, Dylan Baker, Julianne Nicholson, William Sadler, Heather Goldenhersch, John McMartin, Veronica Cartwright, Kathleen Chalfant, Dagmara Dominczyk, Lynn Redgrave, John Krasinski; *D:* Bill Condon; *W:* Bill Condon; *C:* Joe Dunton; *M:* Carter Burwell.

Kipperbang ✶✶ *Pfang, Kipperbang* **1982 (PG)** During the summer of 1948, a 13-year-old boy wishes he could kiss the girl of his dreams. He finally gets the chance in a school play. Not unsatisfying, but falls short of being the bittersweet coming-of-age drama it could have been. **85m/C VHS.** *GB* John Albasiny, Abigail Cruttenden, Alison Steadman; *D:* Michael Apted.

Kipps ✶✶✶ *The Remarkable Mr. Kipps* **1941** Based on H.G. Wells's satirical novel. A young British shopkeeper inherits a fortune and tries to join high society while neglecting his working-class girlfriend. Set the stage for the musical "Half a Sixpence." **95m/B VHS.** *GB* Michael Redgrave, Phyllis Calvert, Michael Wilding; *D:* Carol Reed.

Kippur ✶✶✶ **2000** Set during Israel's 1973 Yom Kippur War—named after the Jewish holiday on which Egypt and Syria launched a surprise attack. Director Gitai's (a veteran himself) war drama concerns friends Weinraub (Levo) and Ruso (Ruso), who are in a rush to join their reserve unit. But their unit has already left, so they wind up in the company of Klauzner (Klauzner), a medic, and join a helicopter rescue squad in evacuating the dead and wounded. It's a searing combination of commitment, tedium, frustration, fear, and disillusionment. Hebrew with subtitles. **117m/C VHS, DVD.** *IS* Liron Levo, Tomer Ruso, Uri Klauzner; *D:* Amos Gitai; *W:* Amos Gitai, Marie-Jose Sanselme; *C:* Renato Berta; *M:* Jan Garbarek.

Kira's Reason—A Love Story ✶✶ *En Kaerlighedshistorie* **2001** Uneven depiction of mental illness and a marriage in crisis. Thirtysomethings Kira (Stenegade) and Mads (Mikkelsen) have a seemingly comfortable life with a happy marriage and kids—until Kira has a breakdown and is committed to an institution. Even after returning to her family, Kira's behavior is erratic, disruptive, and sometimes publicly humiliating. Mads continues to stand by his troubled wife but though their love survives, can their lives together? Danish with subtitles. **94m/C VHS, DVD.** *DK* Stine Stengade, Lars Mikkelsen, Sven Wollter; *D:* Ole Christian Madsen; *W:* Ole Christian Madsen; *C:* Jorgen Johansson; *M:* Oyvind Ougaard, Cesar Berti.

The Kirlian Witness ✶ *The Plants Are Watching* **1978 (PG)** A woman uses the power of telepathic communication with house plants to solve her sister's murder. **88m/C VHS.** Nancy Snyder, Joel Colodner, Ted Leplat; *D:* Jonathan Sarno.

Kismet ✶✶✶ **1920** Original screen version of the much filmed lavish Arabian Nights saga (remade in '30, '44 and '55). A beggar is drawn into deception and intrigue among Bagdad upper-crusters. Glorious sets and costumes; silent with original organ score. **88m/C VHS.** Otis Skinner, Elinor Fair, Herschel Mayall; *D:* Louis Gasnier; *C:* Gaetano Antonio "Tony" Gaudio.

Kismet ✶✶✶ **1955** A big-budget Arabian Nights musical drama of a Baghdad street poet who manages to infiltrate himself into the Wazir's harem. The music was adapted from Borodin by Robert Wright and George Forrest. ♪Fate; Not Since Ninevah; Baubles, Bangles, and Beads; Stranger in Paradise; Bored; Night of My Nights; The Olive Tree; and This Is My Beloved; Sands of Time. **113m/C VHS.** Howard Keel, Ann Blyth, Dolores Gray, Vic Damone; *D:* Vincente Minnelli; *W:* Charles Lederer, Luther Davis; *C:* Joseph Ruttenberg; *M:* Andre Previn.

The Kiss ✶✶✶ **1929** Garbo, the married object of earnest young Ayres' lovelorn affection, innocently kisses him nightly night since a kiss is just a kiss. Or so she thought. Utterly misconstrued, the platonic peck sets the stage for disaster, murder and courtroom anguish follow. French Feyder's direction is stylized and artsy. Garbo's last silent and Ayres' first film. **89m/B VHS.** Greta Garbo, Conrad Nagel, Holmes Herbert, Lew Ayres, Anders Randolf; *D:* Jacques Feyder; *C:* William H. Daniels.

The Kiss ✶ **1988 (R)** A kind of "Auntie Mame from Hell" story in which a mysterious aunt visits her teenage niece in New York, and tries to apprentice her to the family business of sorcery, demon possession, and murder. Aunt Felicity's kiss will make you appreciate the harmless cheek-pinching of your own aunt; your evening would be better spent with her, rather than this movie. **98m/C VHS, DVD.** Pamela Collyer, Peter Dvorsky, Joanna Pacula, Meredith Salenger, Mimi Kuzyk, Nicholas Kilbertus, Jan Rubes; *D:* Pen Densham; *W:* Tom Ropelewski.

Kiss and Be Killed ✶½ **1991 (R)** Crazy guy with knife cuts short couple's wedding night. Shortchanged widow is mighty miffed. Will she have to return the wedding gifts? **89m/C VHS.** Caroline Ludvik, Crystal Carson, Tom Reilly, Chip Hall, Ken Norton, Jimmy Baio; *D:* Tom Milo.

Kiss and Kill ✶✶ *Blood of Fu Manchu; Against All Odds* **1968 (R)** Lee returns in his fourth outing as Fu Manchu. This time the evil one has injected beautiful girls with a deadly poison that reacts upon kissing. They are then sent out to seduce world leaders. Not on par with the previous movies, but still enjoyable. Sequel to "Castle of Fu Manchu." **91m/C VHS, DVD.** Christopher Lee, Richard Greene, Shirley Eaton, Tsai Chin, Maria Rohm, Howard Marion-Crawford; *D:* Jess (Jesus) Franco.

Kiss and Make Up ✶✶½ **1934** Grants stars as suave Dr. Maurice Lamar—a purveyor of beauty creams, fad diets, and cosmetic surgery. He marries his best patient—Eve (Tobin)—without realizing that her beauty really is only skin deep since she's shallow and selfish. Meanwhile, Eve's sweet ex-husband Marcel (Horton) is charmed by the natural beauty of Lamar's loyal secretary Ann (Mack). Still a remarkably prescient, offbeat comedy where Grant winds up with "a" girl but not the "right" girl for a change. **78m/B DVD.** Cary Grant, Helen Mack, Genevieve Tobin, Edward Everett Horton, Lucien Littlefield, Mona Maris; *D:* Harlan Thompson; *W:* Harlan Thompson, Jane Hinton, George Marion Jr.; *C:* Leon Shamroy; *M:* Ralph Rainger.

Kiss and Tell ✶✶ **1996** Lonely undercover policewoman Jude (Rowell) tries to get a confession from a man suspected of murdering his wife. Becoming attracted to her quarry, Jude's previous murder (by carrot) of performance artist Bateman. Naturally, the suspects are as weird as the crime. **90m/C VHS.** Richmond Arquette, Justine Bateman, Heather Graham, Pamela Gidley; *D:* Jordan Alan.

A Kiss Before Dying ✶✶ **1991 (R)** Botched adaptation of Ira Levin's cunning thriller novel (filmed before in 1956). This flick serves up an exploded head in the first few minutes. So much for subtlety. The highlight is Dillon's chilly role as a murderous opportunist bent on marrying into a wealthy family. Young plays two roles (not very well) as lookalike sisters on his agenda. The ending was hastily reshot and it shows. **93m/C VHS, DVD.** Matt Dillon, Sean Young, Max von Sydow, Diane Ladd, James Russo, Martha Gehman, Ben Browder, Joy Lee, Adam Horovitz; *D:* James Dearden; *W:* James Dearden. Golden Raspberries '91: Worst Actress (Young), Worst Support. Actress (Young).

Kiss Daddy Goodbye ✶½ *Revenge of the Zombie; The Vengeful Dead* **1981 (R)** A widower keeps his two children isolated in order to protect their secret telekinetic powers. When he is killed by bikers, the kids attempt to raise him from the dead. **81m/C VHS, DVD.** Fabian, Marilyn Burns, Jon Cedar, Marvin Miller; *D:* Patrick Regan.

Kiss Daddy Goodnight ✶ **1987** A Danish-made thriller about a beautiful young girl who seduces men, drugs them and takes their money. One man turns the tables on her, however, and decides that she will only belong to him. **89m/C VHS, DVD.** *DK* Uma Thurman, Paul Dillon, Paul Richards, David Brisbin; *D:* P.I. Huemer; *C:* Bobby Bukowski.

A Kiss for Mary Pickford ✶✶½ **1927** A rare, hilarious cinematic oddity, a film formulated from Kuleshov montage techniques from footage of the famous American couple's visit to Russia in 1926, wherein a regular guy tries to win a girl through friendship with the stars. Fairbanks and Pickford didn't know of their role in this film, being spliced in later according to montage theory. **70m/B VHS.** Mary Pickford, Douglas Fairbanks Sr., Igor Ilyinsky; *D:* Sergei Komarov.

A Kiss Goodnight ✶✶½ **1994 (R)** Natalie (Trickey) has a romp in the sheets with ad exec Kurt (Corley) when regular beau Michael (Moses) ignores her for work. But when Natalie decides to break things off, Kurt won't take no for an answer. **86m/C VHS.** Paula Trickey, Al Corley, Mark Moses, Lawrence Tierney, Brett Cullen, James Karen, Roger Wuhl, Sydney Walsh; *D:* Daniel Raskov; *W:* Daniel Raskov; *C:* Glenn Kershaw.

Kiss Kiss Bang Bang ✶✶½ **2005 (R)** Making his directorial debut, Black—the screenwriter responsible for such explosive cinematic machismo as "Lethal Weapon" and "Last Boy Scout"—reinvents crime noir with this hilarious riff on hardboiled detective fiction and vapid LA culture. Harry Lockhart (Downey Jr.) is a two-bit thief who stumbles into an acting audition after a robbery gone wrong. The producers fly him to Hollywood where he takes private eye lessons from a gay PI named Perry (Kilmer) and gets embroiled in a complicated conspiracy involving a dead body and a femme fatale from his past (Monaghan). Kilmer and Downey have never been funnier, thanks to Black's sharp-as-a-laser dialogue, and Monaghan is insanely easy on the eyes. Sam Spade never had it this good. **103m/C DVD, Blu-ray Disc. HD DVD.** *US* Robert Downey Jr., Val Kilmer, Michelle Monaghan, Corbin Bernsen, Dash Mihok, Larry Miller, Shannyn Sossamon, Angela Lindvall, Rockmond Dunbar; *D:* Shane Black; *W:* Shane Black; *C:* Michael Barrett; *M:* John Ottman.

Kiss Me a Killer ✶✶ **1991 (R)** The ancient thriller plot about a young wife and her lover who scheme to kill her middle-aged husband. It's set in L.A.'s Latino community, but extensive shots of salsa music and ethnic cooking hardly raise this above the mediocre. **91m/C VHS.** Julie Carmen, Robert Beltran, Guy Boyd, Ramon Franco, Charles Boswell; *D:* Marcus De Leon; *W:* Marcus De Leon.

Kiss Me Deadly ✶✶✶½ **1955** Aldrich's adaptation of Mickey Spillane's private eye tale takes pulp literature high concept. Meeker, as Mike Hammer, is a self-interested rough-and-tumble all-American dick (detective, that is). When a woman to whom he happened to give a ride is found murdered, he follows the mystery straight into a nuclear conspiracy. Aldrich, with tongue deftly in cheek, styles a message through the medium; topsy-turvy camera work and rat-a-tat-tat pacing tell volumes about Hammer, the world he orbits, and that special '50s kind of paranoia. Now a cult fave, it's considered to be the American grandaddy to French New Wave. **105m/B VHS, DVD.** Ralph Meeker, Albert Dekker, Paul Stewart, Wesley Addy, Cloris Leachman, Strother Martin, Marjorie Bennett, Jack Elam, Maxine Cooper, Gaby Rodgers, Nick Dennis, Jack Lambert, Percy Helton; *D:* Robert Aldrich; *W:* A(lbert) I(saac) Bezzerides; *C:* Ernest Laszlo; *M:* Frank DeVol. Natl. Film Reg. '99.

Kiss Me Goodbye ✶✶ **1982 (PG)** Young widow Fields can't shake the memory of her first husband, a charismatic but philandering Broadway choreographer,

Kiss Me, Guido 🐾🐾½ 1997 (R) Heterosexual and handsome Frankie (Scott) is a Bronx-born and -raised pizza maker and De Niro wanna-be who's not too bright. Apartment hunting in Manhattan, he thinks an ad listing "GWM" stands for "guy with money and Italian-American and moves in with gay stereotypes without offending or canonizing either group. Vitale and an excellent, if largely unknown, cast inject enough energy and humor to rise above the often predictable story. Low-budget independent sex farce that offers a promising start for first-time filmmaker Vitale. 90m/C VHS, DVD. Nick Scotti, Anthony Barrile, Craig Chester, Anthony De Sando, Christopher Lawford, Molly Price; D: Tony Vitale; W: Tony Vitale; C: Claudia Raschke; M: Randall Poster.

Kiss My Kate 🐾🐾🐾 1953 A married couple can't separate their real lives from their stage roles in this musical comedy screen adaptation of Shakespeare's "Taming of the Shrew" based on Cole Porter's Broadway show. Bob Fosse may have murdered someone, see the 3-D version—when he does his dance number. "Out of This World; From This Moment On; Wunderbar; So in Love; I Hate Men; We're Thine That Special Face; I've Come To Wive It Wealthily In Padua; Where Is The Life That Late I Led?; Always True To You Darling In My Fashion. 110m/C VHS, DVD. Kathryn Grayson, Howard Keel, Ann Miller, Tommy (Thomas) Rall, Bob Fosse, Bobby Van, Keenan Wynn, James Whitmore; D: George Sidney; C: Charles Rosher; M: Andre Previn.

Kiss Me, Kill Me 🐾🐾½ 1964 Devil's Witch; Baba Yaga, So Sweet, So Perverse; Cosi Dolce, Cosi Perverse; Baba Yaga-Devil Witch 1969 (R) Confused woman is on the run after she may have murdered someone. 91m/C VHS. Carroll Baker, George Eastman, Isabelle DeFunes, Ely Galio; D: Corrado Farina; W: Corrado Farina.

Kiss Me, Stupid! 🐾🐾 1964 (PG-13) Once condemned as smut, this lesser Billy Wilder effort now seems no worse than an average TV sitcom. Martin basically plays himself as a horny Vegas crooner stranded in the boondocks. A local songwriter wants Dino to hear his tunes but knows the cad will seduce his pretty wife so he hires a floozy to pose as the tempting spouse. It gets better as it goes along, but the whole thing suffers from staginess, being an adaptation of an Italian play, "L'Ora Della Fantasia" by Anna Bonacci. 126m/B VHS, DVD. Dean Martin, Kim Novak, Ray Walston, Felicia Farr, Cliff Osmond, Barbara Pepper, Doro Merande, Howard McNear, Henry Gibson, John Fiedler, Mel Blanc; D: Billy Wilder; W: Billy Wilder, I.A.L. Diamond; C: Joseph LaSelle; M: Andre Previn.

KISS Meets the Phantom of the Park 🐾 1978 (PG) Attack of the Phantoms 1978 The popular '70s rock band is featured in this Dr. Jekyll-esque Halloween horror tale, interspersed with musical numbers. 96m/C VHS. Peter Criss, Ace Frehley, Gene Simmons, Paul Stanley, Anthony Zerbe, Carmine Caridi, Deborah Ryan, John Dennis Johnston, John Lisbon Wood, Lisa Jane Persky, Brion James, Bill Hudson; D: Gordon Hessler; W: J. Michael Sherman, Albert (Don) Buday; C: Robert Caramico; M: Hoyt Curtin, Fred Karlin.

Kiss My Grits 🐾 1982 (PG) A good ole boy hightails it to Mexico with his girlfriend and son, chased by mobsters and the law. 101m/C VHS. Bruce Davison, Anthony (Tony) Franciosa, Susan George, Bruno Kirby; D: Jack Starrett.

Kiss of a Killer 🐾🐾½ 1993 O'Toole is a mousy miss living a dead-end life with her nagging mother. But she has a secret—she spends weekends in a hotel, dressed to entice and picking up strangers. Involved in an auto mishap, she's aided by a handsome mechanic, who turns out to be a rapist. When he accidentally kills his latest victim, he realizes our mystery woman can identify him and tries to find her. Based on the novel "The Point of Murder" by Margaret Yorke. 93m/C VHS. Annette O'Toole, Brian Wimmer, Eva Marie Saint, Gregg Henry, Vic Polizos; D: Larry Elikann; W: David Warfield. TV

Kiss of Death 🐾🐾🐾 1947 Paroled when he turns state's evidence, Mature must now watch his back constantly. Widmark, in his film debut, seeks to destroy him. Police chief Donlevy tries to help. Filmed on location in New York, this gripping and gritty film is a vision of the most terrifying sort of existence, one where nothing is certain, and everything is dangerous. Excellent, and one of the first-rate film noir efforts. 98m/B VHS, DVD. Victor Mature, Richard Widmark, Coleen Gray, Brian Donlevy, Karl Malden, Coleen Gray; D: Henry Hathaway.

Kiss of Death 🐾🐾 1977 Weird comedy about a shy undertaker's assistant and his attempts at first romance. 80m/C VHS, DVD. GB David Threlfall, John Wheatley, Kay Adshead, Angela Curran; D: Mike Leigh; W: Mike Leigh. TV

Kiss of Death 🐾🐾½ 1994 (R) Very loose contemporary remake of the 1947 film noir classic of the same name. Jimmy Kilmartin (Caruso) is a paroled car thief turned informant. He soon finds himself trapped in a web of deceit involving corrupt district attorneys and ruthless hoodlums like Little Junior (Cage, pumped up and paying against type), with no one to trust. Crime drama keeps the "arfetched genre conventions in check until the end. Caruso makes the transition from TV cop on "NYPD Blue" by not straying far from his small screen persona. Cage's standout performance as a villain is worth the original, but he's able to convey a level of mercilessness and depth that it'll make you wince. 100m/C VHS, DVD. David Caruso, Nicolas Cage, Samuel L. Jackson, Helen Hunt, Stanley Tucci, Michael Rapaport, Ving Rhames, Anthony Heald, Anne Meara, Hope Davis, Kathryn Erbe, Philip Baker Hall, Kevin Corrigan, Michael Artura, Jay O. Sanders, Joe Lisi; D: Barbet Schroeder; W: Richard Price; M: Trevor Jones.

Kiss of Fire 🐾🐾 🐾 Claudine's Return 1998 (R) Stefano (Dionisi) gets a job as the handyman at a Georgia motel and gets involved with laundress/stripper Claudine (Applegate) in what proves to be a dangerous relationship. And despite her role, Applegate does not get naked. 92m/C VHS, DVD. Stefano Dionisi, Christina Applegate, Matt Clark, Gabriel Mann, Perry Anzilotti, Tom Nowicki, Hall; C: Antonio Tibaldi; W: Antonio Tibaldi, Heidi A. Hall; C: Luca Bigazzi; M: Trevor Jones. VIDEO

Kiss of the Dragon 🐾🐾½ 2001 (R) Li is Chinese super-cop Liu who is sent to Paris to help stop a Chinese drug lord. Once there, he learns that the cop, Richard (Karyo), he was sent to help is actually running the crug ring, and has set Liu up for the dealer's murder. Fonda is the hooker/addict who helps Lu in order to free herself and her daughter from Richard. Spectacular action sequences, as well as Li's martial art skills and charisma more than make up for a pretty lame script which is little more than connective tissue anyway. Besson and Li co-produced the feature debut of director Nahon, who comes from the video/commercials world. 98m/C VHS, DVD. Blu-ray Disc. UMD. FR US-Jet Li, Bridget Fonda, Tcheky Karyo, Burt Kwouk; D: Chris Nahon; W: Luc Besson, Robert Mark Kamen; C: Thierry Arbogast; M: Craig Armstrong.

Kiss of the Spider Woman 🐾🐾🐾 1985 (R) From the novel by Manuel Puig, an acclaimed drama concerning two cell mates in a South American prison, one a revolutionary, the other a homosexual. Literate, haunting, powerful. 119m/C VHS, BR

Kiss of the Tarantula 🐾 1975 (PG) Teen girl who lives with her family in a mortuary battles inner torment and vents anxiety by releasing her deadly pet spiders on those whom she despises. Eightlegged "Carrie" rip-off. 85m/C VHS, DVD. Eric Mason; D: Chris Munger; W: Warren Hamilton.

Kiss of the Vampire 🐾🐾½ Kiss of Evil 1962 Newlywed couple is stranded in Bavaria near a villa of vampires and are invited in by its charmingly evil owner. Fortunately, hubby manages to escape and finds a knowledgeable professor who unleashes a horde of bats to rout the bloodsuckers. Properly creepy; producer Hinds used the pseudonym John Elder for his screenplay. 88m/C VHS, DVD. GB Clifford Evans, Noel Willman, Edward De Souza, Jennifer Daniel, Barry Warren, Jacqueline Wallis, Peter Madden, Isobel Black, Vera Cook, Olga Dickie; D: Don Sharp; W: John (Anthony Hinds) Elder; C: Alan Hume; M: James Bernard.

Kiss or Kill 🐾🐾🐾 1997 (R) Thieves/con artists and lovers Nikki (O'Connor) and Al (Day) head out across the Australian desert towards Perth when one of their schemes results in death. Since they've also got a videotape showing football player Zipper Doyle (Langrishe) in a pedophile activity, he's on their trail as are a couple of cops. But trouble also seems to follow them—everywhere they begin wondering about each other. Quirky characters and fine performances from all concerned, even if the emotional core of the film is somewhat cold. 95m/C Au Frances O'Connor, Matthew Day, Chris Haywood, Barry Otto, Max Cullen, Andrew S. Gilbert, Barry Langrishe, Jennifer Cluff; D: Bill Bennett; W: Bill Bennett; C: Malcolm McCulloch; M: World Film Fest. '97: Director (Bennett), Film, Film Editing, Sound, Support. Actor (Gilbert), Montreal World Film Fest. '97: Actress (O'Connor)

Kiss Shot 🐾🐾 1989 Goldberg is a struggling single mother who loses her job but still must make the mortgage payments. She takes a job as a waitress but realizes it isn't going to pay the bills so she tries her hand as a pool hustler. Frantz is the promoter who finances her bets and Harewood, the pool-shooting playboy whose romantic advances are destroying her concentration. 88m/C VHS, DVD. Whoopi Goldberg, Dennis Franz, Dorian Harewood, David Marciano, Teddy Wilson; D: Jerry London; C: Chuy Elizondo; M: Steve Dorff.

Kiss the Girls 🐾🐾 1997 (R) After his niece is abducted, forensic psychologist Alex Cross (Freeman) joins the hunt for a lunatic who's kidnapping and collecting successful young women. After doctor Kate McTiernan (Judd), who also happens to be a kickboxer, escapes the sicko's love dungeon, she helps Cross track him down. Borrowing heavily from "Silence of the Lambs" and "Seven," this psycho-killer thriller falls far short of both. Adapted from the novel by James Patterson. 117m/C VHS, DVD. Morgan Freeman, Ashley Judd, Cary Elwes, Tony Goldwyn, Jay O. Sanders, Bill Nunn, Brian Cox, Alex MacArthur Richard T. Jones, Jeremy Piven, William Converse-Roberts, Gina Ravera, Roma Maffia; D: Gary Fleder; W: David Klass; C: Aaron Schneider; M: Mark Isham.

Kiss the Sky 🐾🐾 1998 (R) Suffering from midlife crises, Jeff (Petersen) and Marty (Cole) head off on a business trip to the Philippines. Once there, they decide to abandon their settled lives and families in order to experiment with recapturing their lost youth. In their case, it's by becoming a manage a trois with sexy Oxford grad, Andy (Lee). Provocative but hardly gratuitous. 105m/C VHS, DVD. William L. Petersen, Gary Cole, Sheryl Lee, Terence Stamp, Patricia Charbonneau, Season Hubley; D: Roger Young; W: Eric Lerner; C: Donald M. Morgan; M: Patrick Williams.

Kisses for My President 🐾🐾½ 1964 Silly comedy about the first woman elected President and her trials and tribulations. MacMurray is the husband who has to adjust to the protocol of being "First Man." Bergen is miscast, but the other performances are just fine. 113m/C VHS. Fred MacMurray, Polly Bergen, Arlene Dahl, Edward Andrews, Eli Wallach, Donald May; D: Curtis Bernhardt.

Kisses in the Dark 🐾🐾 1997 Four short award-winning films. "Coriolis Effect" finds two daredevil tornado-chasers falling in love. "Solly's Diner" has a

---

William Hurt, Raul Julia, Sonia Braga, Jose Lewgoy, Milton Gonçalves, Nuno Leal Maia, Denise Dumont, Antonio Petrim, Miriam Pires, Fernando Torres; D: Hector Babenco; W: Leonard Schrader; C: Rodolfo Sanchez; M: John Neschling, Wally Badarou, Oscars '85: Actor (Hurt); British Acad. '85: Actor (Hurt); Cannes '85: Actor (Hurt); Ind. Spirit '86: Foreign Film; L.A. Film Critics '85: Actor (Hurt); Natl. Bd. of Review '85: Actor (Hurt), Actor (Julia); Williams.

Kiss of Evil 1962 Newlywed couple is stranded

Kiss Tomorrow Goodbye 🐾🐾 1950 A brutal, murderous escaped convict rises to crime-lord status before his inevitable downfall. Based on a novel by Horace McCoy. 102m/B VHS, DVD. James Cagney, Barbara Payton, Ward Bond, Luther Adler, Helena Carter, Steve Brodie, Rhys Williams; D: Gordon Douglas.

Kiss Tomorrow Goodbye 🐾🐾 El Beso Que Me Diste 2000 Set in 2006, Angela is the star reporter of Telecigital TV Network in Puerto Rico. When her marriage to Armando falls apart, he kidnaps their eight-year-old son Ivan and takes the boy to the U.S. Angela enlists lawyer (and old flame) Pedro to go to the States with her and get the boy back. Based on the novel by Stella Soto. Spanish with subtitles. 90m/C VHS, DVD. Mercarmen Aviles, Jimmy Navarro, Rene Mondova, Carola Garcia, Ernesto Concepcion, Humberto Gonzales; D: Sonia Fritz; W: Sonia Fritz; C: Augustin Cubano; M: Miguel Cubano.

The Kiss You Gave Me 🐾🐾 1996 (R) The subject matter (necrophilia) is sure to give one pause though debut director Stopkewich hardly dwells on the prurient. Sandra Larson (Parker) has been obsessed with death and its rituals since childhood. So as a young adult it seems natural when she gets a job in a funeral home, preparing the bodies for embalming. Only Sandra's obsession leads her to begin making love (shown through a gauzy white light) to the corpses. She does attract the attentions of a very alive medical student, Matt (Outerbridge), who becomes fascinated by Sandra's fetish and determined to cure himself as appealing to her as the dead. Adapted from Barbara Gowdy's short story "We So Seldom Look on Love." 78m/C VHS, DVD. CA Molly Parker, Peter Outerbridge, Jay Brazeau; D: Lynne Stopkewich; W: Lynne Stopkewich, Angus Fraser; C: Gregory Middleton; M: Don MacDonald Genie '97: Actress (Parker).

Kissed 🐾🐾 1996 (R) The subject matter (necrophilia) is sure to give one pause

---

vagrant becoming a hero during a diner hold-up. "Looping" finds an egotistic Italian director deciding in the middle of shooting this big-budget Mafia musical that the material isn't worthy of him. "Joe" finds solace in his daily routine in a psych ward when an interloper disturbs his refuge. **75m/C VHS, DVD.** Jennifer Rubin, James Wilder, Dana Ashbrook, Corinne Bohrer, Katherine Wallach, Ronald Guttman, Quentin Tarantino; **D:** Larry Hankin, Louis Venosta, Roger Paradiso, Sasha Wolf; **W:** Louis Venosta, Roger Paradiso, Sasha Wolf.

Kissin' Cousins ⭐½ 1964 Air Force officer on a secluded base in the South discovers a local hillbilly is his double. Presley quickie that includes country tunes such as "Smokey Mountain Boy" and "Barefoot Ballad" as well as the title song. **96m/C VHS, DVD.** Elvis Presley, Arthur O'Connell, Jack Albertson, Glenda Farrell, Pam(ela) Austin, Yvonne Craig, Cynthia Pepper, Donald Woods, Tommy Farrell, Beverly (Hills) Powers; **D:** Gene Nelson.

Kissing a Fool ⭐½ 1998 (R) Movie asks the titillating question: Who will smart, pretty Sam marry? The unctuous Schwimmer character, Max, or the sensitive writer guy Max sets up with Sam to test her fidelity? Who cares. Hunt sets up the utterly lame opening premise as Sam's boss, who is throwing her a wedding and explains to guests how Sam and her intended met while the rote triangle scenario plays out in flashback. Schwimmer, as a Chicago sportscaster with a roving eye, plays nicely and wisely against type while Lee's novelist Jay, a supposedly close friend of Max, occupies a less gratifying role. Avital has little to do but does is well. **93m/C VHS, DVD.** David Schwimmer, Jason Lee, Mili Avital, Bonnie Hunt, Vanessa Angel, Kari Wuhrer, Frank Medrano, Bitty Schram, Judy Greer; **D:** Doug Ellin; **W:** Doug Ellin, James Frey; **C:** Thomas Del Ruth; **M:** Joseph Vitarelli.

The Kissing Bandit ⭐½ 1948 A misbegotten MGM musical that's minor Sinatra. Mild-mannered, Boston-bred Ricardo inherits his father's inn in California. When he decides to take it over, he learns that dad was also a thief whose trademark was kissing his female victims. Dad's old gang wants Ricardo to carry on but he's more interested in Theresa (Grayson), the governor's daughter. Ricardo Montalban, Cyd Charisse, and Ann Miller are the dancers performing the number "Dance of Fury," which is the most exciting thing in the flick. **102m/B DVD.** Frank Sinatra, Kathryn Grayson, J. Carrol Naish, Mildred Natwick, Mikhail Rasumny, Billy Gilbert; **D:** Laszlo Benedek; **W:** Isobel Lennart, John Harding; **C:** Robert L. Surtees.

Kissing Jessica Stein ⭐½ 2002 (R) Neurotic, Jewish, and straight Jessica (Westfeldt) is tired of blind dates with loser guys so she decides to respond to a personal ad that was placed by Helen (Jurgensen). Much to Jessica's surprise, the two have a lot in common and awkwardly begin a relationship, even though Jessica is skittish when it comes to sex. However, Jessica can't fess up to her family about Helen so they have some other issues to work out. Feldshuh, who plays Westfeldt's doting Jewish mama steals the film. **96m/C VHS, DVD.** US Jennifer Westfeldt, Heather Juergensen, Tovah Feldshuh, Scott Cohen, Jackie Hoffman, Michael Mastro, Carson Elrod, David Aaron Baker; **D:** Charles Herman-Wurmfeld; **W:** Jennifer Westfeldt, Heather Juergensen; **C:** Lawrence Sher; **M:** Marcelo Zarvos.

The Kissing Place ⭐½ 1990 A woman who abducted her "son" years ago tracks the boy to New York City to prevent him from finding his biological family. **90m/C VHS.** Meredith Baxter, David Ogden Stiers; **D:** Tony Wharmby; **W:** Richard Altabef, Cynthia A. Cherbak.

Kissinger and Nixon ⭐½ 1996 Intrigue, ambition, and backbiting politics consume the 18 weeks leading up to the signing of the Vietnam peace accords in Paris in January, 1973. Egotistical Kissinger (Silver) is prepared to sacrifice South Vietnam for the sake of his own ambitions (and an end to the conflict) while a distrustful Nixon (Bridges) lurks uneasily in the background. TV docudrama offers little insight; based on Walter Isaacson's biography "Kissinger." **94m/C VHS.** Ron Silver, Beau Bridges, Matt Frewer, Ron White, George Takei, Kenneth Welsh; **D:** Daniel Petrie; **W:** Lionel Chetwynd; **M:** Jonathan Goldsmith.

Kit Carson ⭐⭐ 1940 Frontiersman Kit Carson leads a wagon train to California, fighting off marauding Indians all the way. **97m/B VHS.** Jon Hall, Dana Andrews, Ward Bond, Lynn Bari; **D:** George B. Seitz.

Kitchen Stories ⭐⭐ *Salmer fra Kjokkenet* 2003 Subversive Scandinavian comedy set in the 1950s. A number of scientific observers from Sweden's Home Research Institute are sent to collect data from the homes of confirmed bachelors living in the rural community of Landstad, Norway. The idea is to track domestic habits and then standardize the average household kitchen for maximum efficiency. Folke (Norstrom) is sent to the tiny home of codger Isak (Calmeyer), who initially makes things as difficult as possible. The men slowly begin to bond even as the study begins to fall apart. Swedish and Norwegian with subtitles. **95m/C DVD.** *NO SW Bjorn Floberg, Reine Brynolfsson, Joachim Calmeyer, Tomas Norstrom; **D:** Bent Hamer; **W:** Bent Hamer, Jorgen Bergmark; **C:** Philip Ogaard; **M:** Hans Mathisen.

The Kitchen Toto ⭐⭐⭐ 1987 (PG-13) Set in 1950 Kenya as British rule was being threatened by Mau Mau terrorists. A young black boy is torn between the British for whom he works and the terrorists who want him to join them. Complex and powerful story of the Kenyan freedom crusade. **96m/C VHS.** GB Bob Peck, Phyllis Logan, Robert Urquhart, Edward Judd, Edwin Mahinda, Kirsten Hughes; **D:** Harry Hook; **W:** Harry Hook; **C:** Roger Deakins; **M:** John Keane.

The Kite Runner ⭐⭐½ 2007 (PG-13) Amir and Hassan spend their days flying kites in a safe and peaceful Afghanistan, before it descended into war and terror. But after secretly witnessing Hussan's brutal assault from neighborhood bullies, Amir turns to shame and eventual resentment. Hussan and his father leave the country, and the two friends never reconcile. Over the next twenty years Afghanistan is torn apart by war, and Amir, now living in the U.S., continues to struggle with his past, until an urgent phone call opens a window for his redemption. Majority of the story focuses on the boys, with each showing incredible range and emotion. A realistic and moving experience, based on the popular novel by Khaled Hosseini. **122m/C DVD.** US Khalid Abdalla, Homayon Ershadi, Shaun Toub, Zekiria Ebrahimi, Ahmad Khan Mahmoodzada; **D:** Marc Foster; **W:** David Benioff; **C:** Roberto Schaefer; **M:** Alberto Iglesias.

Kitten with a Whip ⭐⭐½ 1964 Whatever the film's original intentions, it's now become pure camp. Jody (Ann-Margret) is a juvenile delinquent who's broken out of a girls reformatory and breaks into the home of wannabe politician David Patton (Forsythe), who's separated from his wife. Jody works her considerable wiles and soon Patton's life is filled with wild parties, rampant teen lust, and violence. Too bad it wasn't filmed in the lurid color it deserved. Based on the book by Wade Miller. **84m/B VHS.** Ann-Margret, John Forsythe, Peter Brown, Patricia Barry, Richard Anderson, Diane Sayer, Ann Doran, Patrick Whyte, Audrey Dalton, Leo Gordon; **D:** Douglas Heyes; **W:** Douglas Heyes; **C:** Joseph Biroc.

Kitty and the Bagman ⭐⭐ 1982 A comedy about two rival madames who ruled Australia in the 1920s. **95m/C VHS.** AU Liddy Clark; **D:** Donald Crombie.

Kitty Foyle ⭐⭐⭐ 1940 From the novel by Christopher Morley, Rogers portrays the white-collar working girl whose involvement with a married man presents her with both romantic and social conflicts. **108m/B VHS, DVD.** Ginger Rogers, Dennis Morgan, James Craig, Gladys Cooper, Ernest Cossart, Eduardo Ciannelli; **D:** Sam Wood. Oscars '40: Actress (Rogers).

The Klansman ⭐ *Burning Cross; KKK* 1974 (R) Race relations come out on the short end in this film about a sheriff trying to keep the lid on racial tensions in a southern town. Even the big-name cast can't save what comes off as a nighttime soaper rather than a serious drama. **112m/C VHS, DVD.** Lee Marvin, Richard Burton, Cameron Mitchell, Lola Falana, Luciana Paluzzi, Linda Evans, O.J. Simpson; **D:** Terence Young; **W:** Samuel Fuller.

Klepto ⭐⭐ 2003 Emily (Bishop) is a kleptomaniac. When ex-con/department store security guard Nick (Garcia) catches her stealing on camera, he decides to use Emily's talents to further a drug deal so that he can get enough money together to open his own private security business. Naturally, things don't go as planned. Okay crime thriller that's rough around the edges. **82m/C DVD.** US Jsu Garcia, Leigh Taylor-Young, Henry Czerny, Michael Nouri, Meredith Bishop; **D:** Thomas Trail; **W:** Thomas Trail, Ethan Gross; **C:** Peter Rievesch; **M:** David DeLaski.

Kleptomania ⭐½ 1994 (R) Socialite meets a runaway and discoers they're both kleptomaniacs. **90m/C VHS.** Amy Irving, Patsy Kensit, Victor Garber; **D:** Don Boyd; **W:** Don Boyd.

Klimt ⭐½ 2006 Unwieldy and unenlightening biopic of Austrian artist Gustav Klimt (Malkovich) that starts with him on his deathbed (in 1918), hallucinating as he's dying from syphilis. Jumps back to 1900 where Klimt scandalizes proper Viennese society with his fin-de-siecle style. Klimt also has a lot of mistresses, including Parisian muse Lea (Burrows), who highlight the eroticism of his work. English, German, and French with subtitles. **97m/C DVD.** AT GB FR GE John Malkovich, Saffron Burrows, Stephen (Dillon) Dillane, Nikolai Kinski, Veronica Ferres; **D:** Raul Ruiz; **C:** Ricardo Aronovich; **M:** Jorge Arriagada.

Klondike Annie ⭐⭐½ 1936 West stars as a woman on the lam for a murder (self-defense) who heads out for the Yukon aboard McLaglen's ship. He falls for her, finds out about her problems, and helps her with a scam to pass herself off as a missionary, only she begins to take her saving souls seriously (although in her own risque style). **77m/B VHS, DVD.** Mae West, Victor McLaglen, Philip Reed, Helen Jerome Eddy, Harry Beresford, Harold Huber, Conway Tearle, Esther Howard; **D:** Raoul Walsh; **W:** Mae West; **C:** George T. Clemens.

Klondike Fever ⭐½ *Jack London's Klondike Fever* 1979 (PG) Join the young Jack London as he travels from San Francisco to the Klondike fields during the Great Gold Rush of 1898. **118m/C VHS, DVD.** Rod Steiger, Angie Dickinson, Lorne Greene; **D:** Peter Carter; **M:** Hagood Hardy.

Klute ⭐⭐⭐ 1971 (R) A small-town policeman (Sutherland) comes to New York in search of a missing friend and gets involved with a prostitute/would-be actress (Fonda) being stalked by a killer. Intelligent, gripping drama. **114m/C VHS, DVD.** Jane Fonda, Donald Sutherland, Charles Cioffi, Roy Scheider, Rita Gam, Jean Stapleton; **D:** Alan J. Pakula; **M:** Andy Lewis, Dave Lewis; **C:** Gordon Willis; **M:** Michael Small. Oscars '71: Actress (Fonda); Golden Globes '72: Actress—Drama (Fonda); N.Y. Film Critics '71: Actress (Fonda); Natl. Soc. Film Critics '71: Actress (Fonda).

The Klutz ⭐⭐ 1973 A bumbling fool, on the way to visit his girlfriend, becomes accidentally embroiled in a bank robbery and other ridiculous mishaps. Light French comedy; dubbed. **87m/C VHS.** FR Claude Michaud, Louise Portal, Guy Provost; **D:** Pierre Rose.

Km. 0 ⭐½ *Kilometer Zero* 2000 (R) Good-natured romantic comedy takes its title from the marker in Madrid's Puerta del Sol plaza that designates the spot from which all road travel is measured. It's a popular meeting place as this mixed bag of stories show. Actress Silvia (Pons) forgets she's to meet her sister's friend, Pedro (Fuentes), and Pedro mistakes hooker Tatiana (Matilla) for Silvia. Tatiana thinks Pedro is her new client, but that's actually virginal Sergio (San Juan), who's comforted instead by kindly gay Maximo (del Rio). Lonely Benjamin (Garcia) is mistaken for the Internet date of hottie Bruno (Ullate) and neglected wife Marga (Velasco) finds her meeting with escort Miguel (Cabrero) doesn't go as planned. Amor in all its follies. Spanish with subtitles. **108m/C DVD.** SP Carlos Fuentes, Merce Pons, Georges Corraface, Elisa Matilla, Armando Del Rio, Jesus Cabrero, Tristan Ullate, Alberto San Juan, Concha Velasco, Victor Ullate Jr., Miguel Garcia; **D:** Juan Luis Iborra, Yolanda Garcia Serrano; **W:** Juan Luis Iborra, Yolanda Garcia Serrano; **C:** Angel Luis Fernandez; **M:** Joan Bibiloni.

The Knack ⭐⭐⭐ *The Knack...and How to Get It* 1965 Amusing, fast-paced adaptation of the play by Ann Jellicoe. Schoolteacher Crawford is baffled by his tenant Brooks' extreme luck with the ladies so Brooks decides to teach him the "knack" of picking up women. Crawford promptly falls for the first woman (Tushingham) he meets. Swinging London at its most mod. **84m/B VHS, DVD.** GB Michael Crawford, Ray Brooks, Rita Tushingham, Donal Donnelly; **D:** Richard Lester; **W:** Charles Wood; **C:** David Watkin; **M:** John Barry.

Knife in the Head ⭐⭐ *Messer Im Kopf* 1978 Biogeneticist Berthold Hoffman (Ganz) is meeting his wife (Winkler) at the left-wing youth centre where she works when there's a police raid and Berthold is shot in the head. He awakens in the hospital having lost both his memory and all physical co-ordination. Determined to battle his disabilities, Berthold also becomes the pawn in a political game between the police and political dissidents. In German with English subtitles. **108m/C VHS.** GE Bruno Ganz, Angela Winkler, Hans Honig, Hans Brenner, Udo Samel, Carla Egerer; **D:** Reinhard Hauff; **W:** Peter Schneider.

Knife in the Water ⭐⭐⭐ *Noz w Wodzie* 1962 A journalist, his wife and a hitchhiker spend a day aboard a sailboat. Sex and violence can't be far off. Tense psychological drama. Served as director Polanski's debut. In Polish with English subtitles. **94m/B VHS, DVD.** PL Leon Niemczyk, Jolanta Umecka, Zygmunt Malandowicz; **D:** Roman Polanski; **W:** Jakub Goldberg, Jerzy Skolimowski, Roman Polanski; **C:** Jerzy Lipman; **M:** Krzysztof Komeda.

A Knight in Camelot ⭐⭐½ 1998 Oft told Mark Twain tale this time finds computer expert Vivien (Goldberg) conducting an experiment that transports her back to medieval England and the court of King Arthur (York). Lucky for Viv, she's travelling with her laptop, unluckily the kingly court think she's the tart-tongued woman is a witch. Bossy Vivien makes Merlin (Richardson) jealous and antagonizes everyone until lessons are learned by all. Engaging fluff. **88m/C VHS.** Whoopi Goldberg, James Coombes; **D:** Roger Young; **W:** Joe Wiesenfeld; **C:** Elemer Ragalyi; **M:** Patrick Williams. TV

Knight Moves ⭐⭐ 1993 (R) Suspenseful thriller about a series of murders which take place at an international resort where a championship chess match is underway. The prime suspect is a chess master who has an unlikely affair with a beautiful police psychologist called in to decipher the mind of the murderer. Filmed in the Pacific Northwest. **105m/C VHS, DVD.** Christopher Lambert, Diane Lane, Tom Skerritt, Daniel Baldwin; **D:** Carl Schenkel; **W:** Brad Mirman; **C:** Dietrich Lohmann; **M:** Anne Dudley.

Knight Without Armour ⭐⭐⭐ 1937 A journalist opposed to the Russian monarchy falls in love with the daughter of a czarist minister in this classic romantic drama. **107m/B VHS.** GB Marlene Dietrich, Robert Donat; **D:** Jacques Feyder; **C:** Harry Stradling Sr.; **M:** Miklos Rozsa.

Knightriders ⭐⭐½ 1981 (R) The story of a troupe of motorcyclists who are members of a traveling Renaissance Fair and look and act like modern-day Knights of the Round Table. Their battles center around who is to be king. **145m/C VHS, DVD.** Ed Harris, Gary Lahti, Tom Savini, Amy Ingersoll; **D:** George A. Romero; **W:** George A. Romero; **C:** Michael Gornick; **M:** Donald Rubinstein.

Knights ♂♂½ 1993 (R) In a futuristic wasteland a young martial-arts warrior (Long) and a cyborg (Kristofferson) team up to battle rebel cyborgs that have discovered a new source of fuel—human blood. **89m/C** VHS. Kathy Long, Kris Kristofferson, Lance Henriksen, Scott Paulin, Gary Daniels; **D:** Albert Pyun; **W:** Albert Pyun.

Knights & Emeralds ♂♂½ 1987 (PG) Cross-cultural rivalries and romances develop between members of two high school marching bands in a British factory town near. **90m/C** VHS. Christopher Wild, Beverly (-Hills) Powers, Warren Mitchell; **D:** Ian Emes; **M:** Colin Towns.

Knights of the City ♂ 1985 (R) Miami street gangs fight each other over their "turf." One leader decides to opt out, using music. "Let the Music Play, Cry of the City, Jailhouse Rap; T.K. and Jessie Rap; Kurtis Blow Rap; Bounce; My Part of Town; Can You Feel It; Love Goes Up and Down. **87m/C** VHS. Nicholas (Nic) Campbell, John Mengatti, Wendy Barry, Stoney Jackson, Janine Turner, Michael Ansara; **D:** Leon Isaac Kennedy, Dominic Orlando.

Knights of the Range ♂♂½ 1940 Vintage western. **66m/B** VHS. Russell Hayden, Victor Jory, Jean Parker, Britt Wood, J. Farrell MacDonald, Eddie Dean; **D:** Lesley Selander.

Knights of the Round Table ♂♂½ 1953 The story of the romantic triangle between King Arthur, Sir Lancelot, and Guinevere during the civil wars of 6th-century England. **106m/C** VHS, DVD. Robert Taylor, Ava Gardner, Mel Ferrer, Anne Crawford, Felix Aylmer, Stanley Baker; **D:** Richard Thorpe; **C:** Frederick A. (Freddie) Young; **M:** Miklos Rozsa.

Knights of the South Bronx ♂♂½ 2005 (PG) Middle-aged and recently unemployed Richard Mason (Danson) decides to return to teaching and works at an inner-city school with fourth-graders. He begins using chess to motivate his students and finds them responding—and becoming champions. Based on a true story and an ongoing project that uses chess as an educational tool. **90m/C** DVD. Ted Danson, Keke Palmer, Antonio Ortiz, Malcolm David Kelly, Yucimi Diaz; **D:** Allen Hughes; **W:** Dianne Houston, Jamal Joseph; **C:** Derick Underschultz; **M:** Stephen Endelman. CABLE

A Knight's Tale ♂♂½ 2001 (PG-13) Peasant squire William Thatcher (hunky Ledger) takes the identity of his recently deceased master in 14th-century France so that he may enter the jousting tournaments, which are only open to nobility. He also falls in love with Jocelyn (newcomer Sossamon), a noble lady who would be out of his league given his lowly birth. Count Adhemar (Sewell) is tte bad guy rival and a young Geoffrey Chaucer (Bettany), pre-"Canterbury Teles," aids William. The movie's strictly popcorn entertainment for the teen set. **132m/C** VHS, DVD. US Heath Ledger, Mark Addy, Rufus Sewell, Shannyn Sossamon, Paul Bettany, Laura Fraser, Christopher Cazenove, Alan Tudyk, James Purefoy; **D:** Brian Helgeland; **W:** Brian Helgeland; **C:** Richard Greatrex; **M:** Carter Burwel.

Knives of the Avenger ♂♂½ Brutal ax-bearing Vikings ruin the days of hundreds in this primitive story of courage and desperation. John Hold is the pseudonym for director Maric Bava. **85m/C** VHS, DVD. I" Coltelli Del Vendicatore 1965 Cameron Mitchell, Elissa Pichelli, Luciano Pollentin, Fausto Tozzi, Giacomo "Jack" Rossi-Stuart; **D:** Mario Bava; **W:** Mario Bava, Alberto Liberati, Giorgio Simonelli; **M:** Marcello Giombini.

Knock Off ♂♂ 1998 (R) As if anyone really cares whether the plot makes any sense (no) but a lot of booty is certainly kicked. Marcus Ray (Van Damme) and Tommy Hendricks (Schneider) are partners in a Hong Kong business that manufactures designer jeans Marcus was once involved in the shady fashion 'knock-off' business and still knows people in low

---

places, where he hears about a Russian mob plot to sell bombs to terrorists. Oh yeah, seems Tommy has a little secret too—he's actually working undercover for the CIA. It's action schlock and you won't own life (Ana must sign a paper claiming the young man threatened her with a gun but will her religious faith transcend political expediencies? Adapted from a play by Gene; Spanish with subtitles. **105m/C** VHS. VZ Veronica Oddo, Elba Escobar; **D:** Alejandro Saderman; **M:** Juan Carlos Gene; **C:** Adriano Moreno; **M:** Julio D'Escrivan.

Knocking on Death's Door ♂♂ 1999 (R) Newlyweds Blicom and Rowe are students of the supernatural and head to a Maine town in order to document the ghosts haunting creepy Hillside House. Their investigation leads them to even more creepy doctor Caradine. Actually filmed in Ireland. **92m/C** VHS, DVD. David Carradine, Brian Blicom, Kimberly Rowe, John Doe; **D:** Mitch Marcus. VIDEO

Knocks at My Door ♂♂ A small Latin American town is in political turmoil, with military patrols making a brutal search for a rebel fugitive. The fugitive seeks refuge in the home of two Catholic nuns, Sister Ana (Oddo), and Sister Ursula (Escobar), who theoretically are protected by the Church.

Knocked Up ♂♂½ 2007 (R) Alison Scott (Heigl) is an ambitious blonde entertainment show producer who celebrates her promotion by getting drunk. This makes teddy-bearish chronic slacker Ben (Rogen) look appealing and they hook up—much to his amazement. And hers, when she winds up pregnant. Een's initially horrified when she decides to have the baby and expects some type of commitment from him. They bond cute, although the situation remains uncertain, with Ben's equally clueless stoner buds and Alison's control-freak married sister Debbie (Mem) offering opinions and running commentary. Apatow has an ear for just the right how to cast his flicks to have quirky appeal. **132m/C** DVD, HD DVD. US Katherine Heigl, Seth Rogen, Leslie Mann, Paul Rudd, Tim Bagley, Jay Baruchel, Jonah Hill, Alan Tudyk, J.P. Manoux, B.J. Novak, Kristen Wiig, Harold Ramis, Martin Starr; **D:** Judd Apatow; **W:** Judd Apatow; **C:** Eric Alan Edwards; **M:** Loudon Wainwright III, Joe Henry.

Knockaround Guys ♂♂½ 2001 (R) Matty (Pepper), the son of mobster Benny Chains (Hopper), finds it difficult to find normal work due to his notorious heritage. He pesters his dad to give him a chance, and with the backing of his uncle Teddy (Malkovich) is given an assignment to pick up a bag of cash in Spokane. His unreliable pal Johnny Marbles (Green) botches the job by losing the loot in a rural Wyoming town. Matty is forced to call in friends Chris (Davoli) and Taylor (Diesel) as muscle to deal with a couple of skate punks and a crooked sheriff (Noonan). Collected dust on the shelf for two years at New Line until executives noticed the cash that Diesel's "XXX" was making. **93m/C** VHS, DVD. US Barry Pepper, Seth Green, Dennis Hopper, Vin Diesel, Andrew Davoli, John Malkovich, Tom Noonan; **D:** Brian Koppelman, David Levier; **W:** Brian Koppelman, David Levier; **C:** Tom Richmond; **M:** Clint Mansell.

Knock on Any Door ♂♂ 1949 A young hoodlum from the slums is tried for murdering a cop. He is defended by a prominent attorney who has known him from childhood. **100m/B** VHS. Humphrey Bogart, John Derek, George Macready; **D:** Nicholas Ray; **W:** Daniel Taradash, John Monks Jr.; **C:** Burnett Guffey.

Knock Outs ♂ 1992 Samantha not only loses her shirt at a sorority strip poker marathon but she loses her tuition money too and has a reaction. Then Samantha and a bevy of biker chicks, Ther Samantha pose for a swimsuit calendar to earn some cash but are secretly videotaped in the nude by some local sleaze promoters. Tired of being taken advantage of these lovelies take up martial arts and challenge their nefarious girl biker rivals to a winner-take-all wrestling match, not forgetting the purveyors of the not-so-secret videotape. **90m/C** VHS, DVD. Chona Jeson, Cindy Rome, Brad Zutaut; **D:** John Bowen.

Knots ♂ 2005 (R) Troubled married couple calls it quits when they turn to a seductive lawyer to sort things out. Meanwhile, one of the hubby's friends loses his girlfriend, while another can't even get anything going. A fizzling comedy that can't drive home the punchlines, so it turns to absurd "shocks" to Kicks-a reaction. **93m/C** VHS, DVD, Scott Cohen, Annabeth Gish, Tara Reid, KaDee Strickland, Paulina Porizkova; **D:** Guy Lombardo; **W:** Guy Lombardo; **C:** Michael Firnogmair; **M:** Joseph Saba. VIDEO

Knute Rockne: All American ♂♂♂ A Modern Hero 1940 Life story of Notre Dame football coach Knute Rockne, who inspired many victories with his powerful speeches. Reagan, in a dashing rogue's bid for power in feudal times. With English subtitles. **152m/C** VHS. JP Kikunosuke Onoe, Tatsuya Nakagai; **D:** Hiroshi Inagaki

Kojak: The Belarus File ♂♂ 1985 The bald-headed detective of prime-time TV fame searches for a neo-Nazi who is killing Holocaust survivors in New York. **95m/C** VHS. Telly Savalas, Suzanne Pleshette, Max von Sycow, George Savalas; **D:** Robert Markowitz. TV

Kojiro ♂♂♂ 1967 A sprawling epic by prolific Japanese director Inagaki about the Gipper." **96m/B** VHS, DVD. Ronald Reagan, Pat O'Brien, Gale Page, Donald Criso, John Qualen; **D:** Lloyd Bacon. Natl. Film Reg. '97.

Kolberg ♂♂ Burning Hears 1945 The story of a Prussian town heroically withstanding Napoleon. Produced by Joseph Goebbels in the last days of the Third Reich, it is best remembered as the film whose expensive production and momentous use of real German soldiers, supplies, and ammunition eventually helped to fell the Axis war machine. In German with English subtitles. **118m/C** VHS. GE Kristina Soderbaum, Heinrich George, Horst Caspar, Paul Wegener; **D:** Veit Harlan.

Kolobos ♂ 1999 Kyra and her fellow actors report to a remote filming location only to discover it's all a setup. They've been lured into a fight for survival by a mutilated man-ac—or have they? Low-budget hard-core gore. **87m/C** VHS, DVD. Amy Weber, Promise LeMarco, Linnea Quigley; **D:** Daniel Liatowitsch, David Todd Ocvirk. VIDEO

Kolya ♂♂♂ 1996 (PG-13) Set in the late '80s, just before the Velvet Revolution ended Soviet domination of Czechoslovakia, womanizing Prague cellist Louka (Sverak) agrees to marry (for money) the Russian Klara (Safrankova) who wants Czech papers. She soon clears out to join her lover in Berlin and Louka finds himself saddled with her five-year-old son, Kolya (Chalimon). Grumpy Louka isn't obvious dad material and they don't even speak the same language but the kid (who's adorable without being cloying) manages to worm his way into his new life. Czech CZ Zdenek Sverak, Andrej Chalimon, Libuse Safrankova; **D:** Jan Sverak; **W:** Zdenek Sverak; **C:** Vladimir Smutny; **M:** Ondrej Soukup. Oscars '96: Foreign Film. Golden Globes '97: Foreign Film.

Komodo ♂½ 1999 (PG-13) Komodo dragons are pretty impressive in the wild but are they really scary? This low-budget animatronic/computer-generated versions are tries to assure you that at east these are breeding on an island off the North Carolina coast where teen Patrick (Zegers) and his aunt (Landis) have unwisely ventured. **85m/C** VHS, DVD. AU Kevin Zegers, Nina Landis, Jillian Hennessey, Paul Gleeson, Billy Burke; **D:** Michael

---

Ana knows the young man will be tortured and executed but when a neighbor betrays his presence, not only is he captured but D Sister Ana is arrested. To save her

Konrad ♂♂½ 1985 Konrad, an "instant" child made in a factory, is accidentally delivered to an eccentric woman. The factory wants him back when the mistake is discovered, but Konrad stands up against it, includes a viewers' guide. Part of the "Wonderworks" series. **110m/C** VHS, Ned Beatty, Polly Holliday, Max Wright, Huckleberry Fox; **D:** Nell Cox; **M:** Malcolm Mammorstein.

Kontroll ♂♂♂ Control 2003 (R) Hungary's claustrophobic, dimly fluorescent lit subways employ "Kontrollers"—ticket inspectors roaming train to train checking the fare is real. **106m/C** DVD. HU Sandor Csanyi, Laps Kovacs, Sandor Badar, Csaba Fundrich, Zsolt Nagy, Eszter Balla, Bence Matyasi, Szabo Gyozo, Balazs Mihalyfi; **D:** Nimrod Antal; **W:** Nimrod Antal; **C:** Gyula Pados; **M:** NEO.

Korczak ♂♂♂ 1990 Based on the life of Dr. Janusz Korczak, an outspoken critic of the Nazis, who ran the Jewish orphanage in Warsaw, Poland, and accompanied 200 orphans actually entering the gas chambers, he used this allegory to imply that their souls were freed. In Polish with English subtitles. **118m/C** VHS. PL Wojciech Pszoniak, Ewa Dalkowska, Piotr Kozlowski, Marzena Tryxala Wojciech Klata Adam Siemion; **D:** Andrzej Wajda. **W:** Agnieszka Holland.

Koroshi ♂♂ 1967 Secret Agent John Drake is dispatched to Hong Kong to disband a secret society who is killing off international political figures. **100m/C** VHS. Patrick McGoohan, Kenneth Griffith, Yoko Tani; **D:** Michael Truman, Peter Yates.

Kostas ♂♂ 1979 (R) A migrant Greek taxi driver romantically pursues a wealthy Australian divorcee in England. **88m/C** VHS. Takis Emmanuel, Wendy Hughes; **D:** Paul Cox.

Kotch ♂♂ 1971 (PG) An elderly man resists his children's attempts to retire him. Warm detailing of old age with a splendid performance by Matthau. Lemmon's directorial debut. **113m/C** VHS, DVD. Walter Matthau, Deborah Winters, Felicia Farr; **D:** Jack Lemmon; **M:** Marvin Hamlisch. Golden Globes '72: Song ("Life is What You Make It").

Kounterfeit ♂♂ 1996 (R) Hopscotch (Hawkes) finds three million in counterfeit cash and tries to get some real cash for the fake stuff with his toolass-bar owner buddy Frankie (Payne) serving as muscle. But things go bad. Bernsen has little more than a cameo rcle as Hopscotch's brother. **87m/C** VHS, DVD. Andrew Hawkes, Bruce Payne, Hilary Swank, Michael Gross, Mark Paul Gosselaar, Corbin Bernsen; **D:** John Mallory Asher; **W:** Jay Irwin, David Chase; **C:** Karl Herrmann.

The Kovak Box ♂ 2006 (R) Best-selling sci-fi author David Norton (Hutton) arrives on a Mediterranean island for a conference, his fiancee receives a mysterious phone call and inexplicably commits suicide. That's only the beginning as David's fictional world and his real world overlap, with a government conspiracy thrown in. Dull and confusing, with Hutton's acting consisting of a furrowed brow and grimaces. **102m/C** DVD. Timothy Hutton, Lucia Jimenez, David Kelly, Georgia Mackenzie, Gary Piquer, Annette Bacland; **D:** Daniel Monzon; **W:** Daniel Monzon; **C:** Carlos Gusi; **M:** Roque Banos.

Lantieri; **W:** Hans Bauer, Craig Mitchell; **C:** David Burr; **M:** John Debney.

Koyaanisqatsi ✶✶✶ 1983 A mesmerizing film that takes an intense look at modern life (the movie's title is the Hopi word for "life out of balance"). Without dialogue or narration, it brings traditional background elements, landscapes and cityscapes, up front to produce a unique view of the structure and mechanics of our daily lives. Riveting and immensely powerful. A critically acclaimed score by Glass, and Reggio's cinematography prove to be the perfect match to this brilliant film. Followed by "Powaqqatsi." **87m/C VHS, DVD**; *D:* Godfrey Reggio; *W:* Godfrey Reggio, Ron Fricke, Michael Hoenig; *C:* Ron Fricke; *M:* Philip Glass, Michael Hoenig. L.A. Film Reg. '83: Score, Natl. Film Reg. '00.

Kraken: Tentacles of the Deep ✶ 2006 (R) Cheap CGI and an over-familiar story make this big beastie tale mostly a yawn. Ray (O'Connell) wants revenge on the multi-tentacled creature that killed his parents so he tracks it down with the help of underwater archeologist Nicole (Pratt, looking very—uh—fit in her scanty attire). But the creature is guarding a treasure that mobster Maxwell (Scalia) is determined to have. **87m/C DVD**. Charlie O'Connell, Victoria Pratt, Jack Scalia, Kristi Angus, Cory Monteith; *D:* Tibor Takacs; *W:* Sean Keller; *C:* George Campbell; *M:* Rich Walters. **C A B L E**

Kramer vs. Kramer ✶✶✶½ 1979 (PG) Highly acclaimed family drama about an advertising executive husband and child left behind when their wife and mother leaves on a quest to find herself, and the subsequent courtroom battle for custody when she returns. Hoffman and Streep give exacting performances as does young Henry. Successfully moves you from tears to laughter and back again. Based on the novel by Avery Corman. **105m/C VHS, DVD**. Dustin Hoffman, Meryl Streep, Jane Alexander, Justin Henry, Howard Duff, Jo-Beth Williams; *D:* Robert Benton; *W:* Robert Benton; *C:* Nestor Almendros. Oscars '79: Actor (Hoffman), Adapt. Screenplay, Director (Benton), Picture, Support. Actress (Streep); Directors Guild '79: Director (Benton); Golden Globes '80: Actor—Drama (Hoffman), Film—Drama, Screenplay, Support. Actress (Streep); L.A. Film Critics '79: Actor (Hoffman), Director (Benton), Film, Screenplay, Support. Actress (Streep); N.Y. Film Critics '79: Actor (Hoffman), Film, Support. Actress (Streep); Natl. Soc. Film Critics '79: Actor (Hoffman), Director (Benton), Support. Actress (Streep); Writers Guild '79: Adapt. Screenplay.

The Krays ✶✶✶½ 1990 (R) An account of British gangsters Reggie and Ronnie Kray, the brothers who ruled London's East End with brutality and violence, making them bizarre celebrities of the '60s. The leads are portrayed by Gary and Martin Kemp, founders of the British pop group Spandau Ballet. **119m/C VHS**. *GB* Gary Kemp, Martin Kemp, Billie Whitelaw, Steven Berkoff, Susan Fleetwood, Charlotte Cornwell, Jimmy Jewel, Avis Bunnage, Kate Hardie, Alfred Lynch, Tom Bell, Victor Spinetti, Barbara Ferris, Julia Migenes, John McEnery, Sadie Frost, Norman Rossington, Murray Melvin; *D:* Peter Medak; *W:* Philip Ridley; *C:* Alex Thomson; *M:* Michael Kamen.

Kriemhilde's Revenge ✶✶✶✶ *Die Nibelungen* 1924 The second film, following "Siegfried," of Lang's "Die Nibelungen," a lavish silent version of the Teutonic legends Wagner's "Ring of the Nibelungen" was based upon. In this episode, Kriemhilde avenges Siegfried's death by her marriage to the Kings of the Huns, thus fulfilling a prophecy of destruction. **95m/B VHS, DVD**. *GE* Paul Richter, Margareta Schoen, Theodore Loos, Hanna Ralph, Rudolf Klein-Rogge; *D:* Fritz Lang.

Krippendorf's Tribe ✶✶✶ 1998 (PG-13) James Krippendorf (Dreyfuss), a widowed anthropology professor, returns from an expedition to New Guinea after squandering all his grant money on his kids. Since he didn't find the rare tribe he was sent there for, he makes up tribal stories based on his own kids. When skeptic Tomlin demands proof of his amazing discoveries, the Krippendorf clan and an over-eager colleague (Elfman) go native in front of the camera. Works best when at its silliest, and in fact, could have been a fun family film. Unfortunately, most of the humor is of the smutty variety, involving mating rituals, tribal sex toys, circumcision jokes, and so on. **94m/C VHS, DVD**. Richard Dreyfuss, Jenna Elfman, Natasha Lyonne, Gregory Edward Smith, Stephen (Steve) Root, Elaine Stritch, Tom Poston, David Ogden Stiers, Lily Tomlin, Doris Belack, Julio Oscar Mechoso, Barbara Williams, Zakes Mokae, Carl Michael Lindner, Siobhan Fallon; *D:* Todd Holland; *W:* Charlie Peters; *C:* Dean Cundey; *M:* Bruce Broughton.

Kristin Lavransdatter ✶✶½ 1995 Slow and tedious romance, set in 14th-century Norway, and based on the novel "Kransen" by Sigrid Undset. Teenaged Kristin causes much grief for her family when she rejects an arranged marriage to a decent man her father has chosen for the more exciting but morally dubious nobleman Erland. Norwegian with subtitles. **144m/C VHS**. *NO* Elisabeth Matheson, Bjørn Skagestad, Henny Moan, Rut Tellefsen, Sverre Anker Ousdal; *W:* Liv Ullmann; *C:* Sven Nykvist; *M:* Henryk Nikolai Gorecki.

Kronos ✶✶½ 1957 A giant robot from space drains the Earth of all its energy resources. A good example of this genre from the 50s. Includes previews of coming attractions from classic science fiction films. **78m/B VHS, DVD**. Jeff Morrow, Barbara Lawrence; John Emery; *D:* Kurt Neumann; *W:* Lawrence Louis Goldman; *C:* Karl Struss; *M:* Paul Sawtell, Bert Shefter.

Krull ✶✶ 1983 (PG) Likeable fantasy adventure set in a world peopled by creatures of myth and magic. A prince embarks on a quest to find the Glaive (a magical weapon) and then rescues his young bride, taken by the Beast of the Black Fortress. **121m/C VHS, DVD**. *GB* Ken Marshall, Lysette Anthony, Freddie Jones, Francesca Annis, Liam Neeson; *D:* Peter Yates; *W:* Stafford Sherman; *C:* Peter Suschitzky; *M:* James Horner.

Krush Groove ✶ 1985 (R) The world of rap music is highlighted in this movie, the first all-rap musical. ♪"King of Rock; Don't You Dog Me; A Love Bizarre; Pick Up the Pace; if I Ruled the World; Holly Rock; It's Like That; Feel the Spirit; I Can't Live Without My Radio. **95m/C VHS, DVD**. Blair Underwood, Lisa Gay Hamilton, Kurtis Blow, Sheila E. John MacKay, Richard Gant, LL Cool J; *D:* Michael A. Schultz.

K2: The Ultimate High ✶✶ 1992 (R) Two men, one a skirt-chasing lawyer, the other a happily married physicist, tackle the world's second largest mountain—the K-2 in Kashmir, northern Pakistan. They encounter a number of dangers, including an ascent of sheer rock face, an avalanche, and a fall down perpendicular mountain ice, but even the exciting mountain-climbing scenes can't hold up this watered down movie. The film was actually shot on Canada's Mount Waddington. Based on the play by Patrick Meyers. **104m/C VHS**. Michael Biehn, Matt Craven, Raymond J. Barry, Luca Bercovici, Patricia Charbonneau, Julia Nickson-Soul, Hiroshi Fujioka, Jamal Shah; *D:* Franc Roddam; *W:* Patrick Meyers, Scott Roberts.

Kuffs ✶✶ 1992 (PG-13) Slater stars as George Kuffs, a young guy who reluctantly joins his brother's highly respected private security team in this original action comedy. After his brother is gunned down in the line of duty, George finds himself the new owner of the business. Out to avenge his brother, George pursues a crooked art dealer as he battles crime on the streets of San Francisco. Worthwhile premise is hampered by a predictable plot and mediocre acting. **102m/C VHS, DVD**. Christian Slater, Tony Goldwyn, Milla Jovovich, Bruce Boxleitner, Troy Evans, George de la Pena, Leon Rippy; *D:* Bruce A. Evans; *W:* Bruce A. Evans, Raynold Gideon; *M:* Harold Faltermeyer.

Kull the Conqueror ✶✶ 1997 (PG-13) Sorbo goes from TV's heroic Hercules to action-fantasy hero Kull, a slave who becomes the warrior king of a mythic land. Overthrown by a corrupt nobility, Kull begins a perilous journey to find the one weapon that will destroy the she-demon Akivasha (Carrere) and save the land of Valusia. Lots of action, although the PG-13 rating keeps some of the mayhem less bloody than might be expected for this genre. Based on the '30s character created by pulp writer Robert E. Howard, who also originated "Conan the Barbarian." **96m/C VHS, DVD**. Kevin Sorbo, Tia Carrere, Thomas Ian Griffith, Karina Lombard, Litefoot, Harvey Fierstein, Roy Brocksmith, Douglas Henshall, Sven-Ole Thorsen, Terry O'Neill; *D:* John Nicolella; *W:* Charles Edward Pogue; *C:* Rodney Charters; *M:* Joel Goldsmith.

The Kumite ✶ *Star Runner* 2003 (PG-13) So it takes 40 minutes to get to any martial arts competition, as the first part of the flick is taken up by the romance between Hong Kong student Bond (Wu) and his young Korean-born teacher Mei (Kim). Bond wants to enter the Star Runner competition but has trouble finding the right mentor and then lets love get in the way of his training. Wu and Kim are both popular Asian pop stars but that doesn't mean they can act (not that it seems to be a requirement). Korean and Cantonese with subtitles. **104m/C DVD**. *HK KN* Hyung-koo Kim, David Chiang, Vanessa Wu, Andy On, Shawn Tam; *D:* Daniel Lee; *W:* Daniel Lee; *M:* Henry Lai.

Kundun ✶✶✶ 1997 (PG-13) Scorsese's cinematic portrait of the life of the young 14th Dalai Lama from 1937 through 1959, when he was forced to flee Chinese-occupied Tibet and live in exile in India. The incredibly detailed and sumptuous Tibetan journey begins with the discovery of the young boy as the Buddha reborn and uses different actors to portray him through young adulthood. Dramatic depiction of the Chairman Mao-ordered slaughter of Tibetan nuns and monks around the young Kundun illustrates theme of an increasingly violent world. The adult Dalai Lama's (Tsarong) meeting with cartoonishly evil incarnate Chairman Mao Zedong (Lin) mars an otherwise realistic and honest portrayal. Made with the cooperation of the 14th Dalai Lama, the story reflects the director's yen for accuracy and integrity. Scorsese's gamble on using a cast of non-professional Tibetan refugees pays off. Beautiful scenery and dreamy Philip Glass score set the proper mood. **134m/C DVD**. Tanzin Thuthob Tsarong, Robert Lin; *D:* Martin Scorsese; *W:* Melissa Mathison; *C:* Roger Deakins; *M:* Philip Glass. N.Y. Film Critics '97: Cinematog.; Natl. Soc. Film Critics '97: Cinematog.

Kung Fu ✶✶½ 1972 A fugitive Buddhist quasi-Asian martial arts master accused of murder in his native land, roams across the Old West fighting injustice. Pilot for the successful TV series; was reincarnated 14 years later in the sequel, "Kung Fu: The Movie." **75m/C VHS**. Keith Carradine, David Carradine, Barry Sullivan, Keye Luke; *D:* Jerry Thorpe; *C:* Richard L. Rawlings. **TV**

Kung Fu Hustle ✶✶ *Gong fu* 2004 (R) Writer/director Chow casts himself as the lead in this goofy kung-fu comedy. Sing (Chow), a good-natured con man, desperately wants to join the evil Axe Gang. Posing as a gangster, Sing tries to shake down the poor residents of Pig Sty Alley, but a number of hapless martial arts masters have retired to the slum. Sing's scam starts an all-out war between the Axe Gang and Pig Sty Alley, resulting in a series of larger-than-life, CGI-enhanced battles that more closely resemble Looney Tunes than Bruce Lee. While the unrelenting action might cross cultural borders, Chow's sense of humor doesn't seem to. In Cantonese and Mandarin with English subtitles. **99m/C DVD, Blu-ray Disc, UMD**. Stephen (Chiau) Chow, Yuen Wah, Kwok-Kwan Chan, Feng Xiao Gang, Lam Suet, Leung Siu Lung, Dong Zhi Hua, Chiu Chi Ling, Yuen Qui, Xing Yu, Huang Sheng Yi, Lam Tze Chung; *D:* Stephen (Chiau) Chow; *W:* Stephen (Chiau) Chow, Kan-Cheung (Sammy) Tsang, Chan Man-keung, Lola Huo; *C:* Hang-Seng Poon; *M:* Raymond Wong.

Kung Fu Panda ✶✶ 2008 Animated panda-monium. Po Panda (Black) is a kung fu fanatic who works as a waiter in his family's noodle shop. The clumsy rotund slacker has to get his game together when a group of martial art masters discover that Po is the chosen one named in a prophecy to save China from its enemies, but who's gonna save them from

Po? And everybody's kung fu fighting! Not yet reviewed. **?m/C** *D:* John Stevenson, Mark Osborne; *W:* Jonathan Aibel, Glenn Berger; *C:* Yong Duk Jhun; *M:* Hans Zimmer; *V:* Jack Black, Dustin Hoffman, Jackie Chan, Angelina Jolie, Lucy Liu, Ian McShane, Seth Rogen, David Cross, Michael Clarke Duncan, James Hong, Dan Fogler, Randall Duk Kim.

Kung Fu: The Movie ✶✶½ 1986 Carradine reprises his role as Kwai Chang Caine from the TV show of the early '70s. Now, he's hunted by evil warlord Mako, who's involved in the California opium trade. Mako sends assassin Lee (son of martial-arts star Bruce) after Caine. Luke appears in flashbacks as the young Grasshopper's blind mentor, Master Po. **93m/C VHS**. David Carradine, Mako, Brandon Lee, Keye Luke, Kerrie Keane, Martin Landau, William Lucking, Luke Askew, Benson Fong; *D:* Richard Lang. **TV**

Kung Pow! Enter the Fist ✶✶½ 2002 (PG-13) Oedekerk, the "mind" behind such comedies as "Ace Ventura: When Nature Calls" and "Patch Adams," opts to put himself in front of the camera in this painfully boring kung-fu spoof. He splices new footage into a 1970s martial arts movie, making himself the lead character and adding in a liberal helping of scatological humor. It's "What's Up, Tiger Lily" meets "Dead Men Don't Wear Plaid," only without the comedic genius or even an elementary grasp of basic filmmaking. Leave this fist closed, grasshopper. **81m/C VHS, DVD**. Steve Oedekerk, Tad Horino, Simon Rhee, Lin Yan, Jennifer Tung, Lo Ming; *D:* Steve Oedekerk; *W:* Steve Oedekerk; *C:* John J. Connor; *M:* Robert Folk.

Kuni Lemel in Tel Aviv ✶✶½ 1977 The bungling folk-hero of the shtetl of 100 years ago is updated to the present. Grandpa Kuni is now 80 and living in Brooklyn. Anxious to see the family line continue, he offers $5 million to the first of his twin grandsons to marry a nice Jewish girl and settle in Israel. However, the grandsons have plans of their own which conflict with Grandpa's. In Hebrew with English subtitles. **90m/C VHS, DVD**. *IS* Mike Burstyn, Mandy Rice-Davies; *D:* Joel Silberg.

Kurt Vonnegut's Harrison Bergeron ✶✶½ *Harrison Bergeron* 1995 (R) In the year 2053 the American government has gone to absurd lengths to ensure equality. Mediocrity is championed and everyone is forced to wear metallic headbands that stifle intellect through electronic impulses. Too bad for Harrison Bergeron (Astin), a smart young man being punished for his intelligence. But there's a secret underground elite offering Harrison the chance to think freely, though this power comes with a price. Adapted from Vonnegut's 1961 short story. **99m/C VHS**. Sean Astin, Christopher Plummer, Miranda de Pencier, Nigel Bennett, Buck Henry, Eugene Levy, Howie Mandel, Andrea Martin; *D:* Bruce Pittman; *W:* Arthur Crimm. **C A B L E**

Kurt Vonnegut's Monkey House ✶✶ 1991 Dramatization of four short stories from Vonnegut's "Welcome to the Monkey House" collection, including a twist on the familiar Frankenstein tale. **100m/C VHS**. Frank Langella, Madeline Kahn, Kaj-Erik Eriksen, Donnelly Rhodes, Len Cariou, Gordon Clapp; *D:* Allan King, Paul Shapiro; *W:* Jeff B. Cohen, Stan Daniels. **C A B L E**

Kwaidan ✶✶✶ 1964 A haunting, stylized quartet of supernatural stories, each with a surprise ending. Adapted from the stories of Lafcadio Hearn, an American author who lived in Japan just before the turn of the century. The visual effects are splendid. In Japanese with English subtitles. **164m/C VHS, DVD**. *JP* Michiyo Aratama, Rentaro Mikuni, Katsuo Nakamura, Keiko Kishi, Tatsuya Nakadai, Takashi Shimura; *D:* Masaki Kobayashi; *W:* Yoko Mizuki; *C:* Yoshio Miyajima; *M:* Toru Takemitsu. Cannes '65: Grand Jury Prize.

The L-Shaped Room ✶✶✶ 1962 Young Frenchwoman Jane (Caron) is living in London and has an affair that leaves her pregnant. She winds up moving to a tacky boarding house, into the small room of the title. Soon, Jane has fallen for fellow tenant, out-of-work writer Toby (Bell), without disclosing her situa-

L.627 ♂♂ 1992 Melancholy police procedural about dedicated veteran narcotics cop Lulu (Bezace) who works with a small and ill-equipped Parisian drug squad prone to taking the law into their own hands. Lulu constantly finds himself thwarted by obtuse bureaucrats while his life is disrupted by an informant—a young drug-addicted prostitute who has disappeared and whom Lulu desires to protect. Film title refers to the French anti-drug statute. French with subtitles. **145m/C VHS.** *FR* Didier Bezace, Jean-Paul Comart, Cecile Garcia-Fogel, Lara Guirao, Charlotte Kady, Jean-Roger Milo, Philippe Torreton, Nils (Niels) Tavernier; *D:* Bertrand Tavernier; *W:* Bertrand Tavernier, Michel Alexandre; *C:* Alain Choquart; *M:* Philippe Sarde.

L.A. Bad ♂ 1985 (R) A Puerto Rican street thug learns he has cancer, and must come to terms with his own impending death. **101m/C VHS.** Esai Morales, Janice Rule, John Phillip Law, Charlotte Kady, Carmie Snodgrass; *D:* Gary Kent; *W:* Gary Kent; *M:* Jimmie Haskell.

La Balance ♂♂♂ 1982 (R) An underworld stool pigeon is recruited by the Parisian police to blow the whistle on a murderous mob. Baye, as a prostitute in love with the pimp-stoolie, is a standout. Critically acclaimed French film. **103m/C VHS, DVD.** *FR* Philippe Leotard, Nathalie Baye, Bob Swaim; *D:* Raymond Leotard; *M:* Roland Bocquet. Cesar '83: Actor (Leotard), Actress (Baye). Film.

La Bamba ♂♂♂ 1987 (PG-13) A romantic biography of the late '50s pop idol Ritchie Valens, concentrating on his stormy relationship with his half-brother Bob (Morales), his love for his WASP girlfriend Donna (Von Zerneck) to whom he wrote a hit song, and his tragic, sudden death in the famed plane crash that also took the lives of Buddy Holly and the Big Bopper. Soundtrack features Setzer, Huntsberry, Crenshaw, and Los Lobos as, respectively, Eddie Cochran, the Big Bopper, Buddy Holly, and a Mexican bordello band. **99m/C VHS, DVD.** Lou Diamond Phillips, Esai Morales, Danielle von Zerneck, Joe Pantoliano, Brian Setzer, Marshall Crenshaw, Howard Huntsberry, Rosana Desoto, Elizabeth Pena, Rick Dees; *D:* Luis Valdez; *W:* Luis Valdez; *C:* Adam Greenberg; *M:* Miles Goodman, Carlos Santana.

La Belle Noiseuse ♂♂♂½ *Divertimento, The Beautiful Troublemaker* 1990 The connections between art and life are explored in this beautiful (and long) drama. Creatively crippled, an aging painter has left unfinished a masterpiece work, entitled "La Belle Noiseuse," for ten years. When an admiring younger artist and his beautiful lover arrive for a visit, the painter is newly inspired by the young woman and makes her the model and muse for his masterwork. The film details every nuance of the work from the first to the last brushstroke and the battle of wills between artist and model over the symbolic creative process. Based on a novella by Honore Balzac. French with subtitles. "Divertimento" is actually a recut and shortened version (126 minutes) of the original film. **240m/C VHS, DVD.** *FR* Michel Piccoli, Emmanuelle Beart, Jane Birkin, David Bursztein, Marianne (Ciau), Denicourt; *D:* Jacques Rivette; *W:* Pascal Bonitzer, Christine Laurent, Pascal Bonitzer; *C:* William Lubtchansky. Cannes '91: Grand Jury Prize; L.A. Film Critics '91: Foreign Film.

La Bete Humaine ♂♂♂½ *The Human Beast* 1938 A dark, psychological melodrama about human passion and duplicity, as an unhinged trainman plots with a married woman to kill her husband. Wonderful performances and stunning photography. Based on the Emile Zola novel. In French with English subtitles.

tion. However, when Toby's jealous best friend, jazz musician Johnny (Peters), learns of Jane's pregnancy, he uses his knowledge to break the twosome up. In the kitchen-sink tradition of British films that doesn't expect a happy ending. Based on the novel by Lynne Feild Banks. **88m/B VHS.** *GB* Leslie Caron, Tom Bell, Brock Peters, Mark Eden, Cicely Courtnidge, Emlyn Williams, Bernard Lee, Avis Bunnage; *D:* Bryan Forbes; *W:* Bryan Forbes; *C:* Douglas Slocombe; *M:* John Barry.

1954 Hollywood remake, "Human Desire," was directed by Fritz Lang. **90m/B VHS, DVD.** *FR* Jean Gabin, Simone Simon, Julien Carette, Fernand Ledoux; *D:* Jean Renoir; *W:* Jean Renoir; *C:* Curt Courant; *M:* Joseph Cosma.

La Boca del Lobo ♂♂ *The Lion's Den* 1989 Peru's civil strife inspired this sluggish drama about government troops occupying a jungle village. Tormented by unseen communist guerillas, the stressed-out soldiers reach the breaking point. Spanish with subtitles. **111m/C VHS.** *AR* Gustavo Eueno, Tono Vega, Jose Tejada; *D:* Francisco J. Lombardi.

La Boum ♂♂½ 1981 (R) A teenager's adjustment to the changes brought about by a move to Paris is compounded by her parents' marital problems. Followed by "La Boum 2." **90m/C VHS, DVD.** *FR* Sophie Marceau, Claude Brasseur, Brigitte Fossey, Denise Grey, Bernard Giraudeau; *D:* Claude Pinoteau; *W:* Danielle Thompson.

La Buche ♂♂½ 2000 The title refers to a special Christmas cake, fashioned in the shape of a yule log. The holiday season is proving to be particularly tiresome for three sisters: nightclub singer Louba (Azema) who's pregnant with her married lover's child; homemaker Sonia (Beart) whose husband is leaving her for a younger woman; and career-driven Milla (Gainsbourg) who becomes intrigued by a (melancholy) Joseph (Thompson, the director's son). Family crises start with the funeral of the sisters' stepfather, leading to a reunion between their parents, who haven't spoken in 25 years, and get more complicated from there. French with subtitles. **106m/C VHS, DVD.** *FR* Sabine Azema, Emmanuelle Beart, Charlotte Gainsbourg, Francoise Fabian, Claude Rich, Christopher Thompson, Jean-Pierre Darroussin; *D:* Daniele Thompson; *W:* Christopher Thompson, Daniele Thompson; *C:* Robert Fraisse; *M:* Michel Legrand.

La Cage aux Folles ♂♂♂½ *Birds of a Feather* 1978 (R) Adaption of the popular French play. Gay Saint-Tropez nightclub owner Renato (Tognazzi) and his drag queen lover Albin (Serrault) try to play it straight when Renato's son (Laurent) from a long-ago liaison brings his fiancee and her conservative parents home for dinner. Charming music and lots of fun. So successful, it was followed by two sequels in 1980 and 1985, a Broadway musical, and a 1995 American remake, "The Birdcage." French with subtitles. **91m/C VHS, DVD.** *FR* Ugo Tognazzi, Michel Serrault, Michel Galabru, Claire Maurier, Remy Laurent, Benny Luke, Carmen Scarpitta, Luisa Maneri; *D:* Edouard Molinaro; *W:* Edouard Molinaro, Francis Veber, Jean Poiret, Marcello Danon; *C:* Armando Nannuzzi; *M:* Ennio Morricone. Cesar '79: Actor (Serrault); Golden Globes '80: Foreign Film.

La Cage aux Folles 2 ♂♂½ 1981 (R) Albin sets out to prove to his companion that he still has sex appeal, and gets mixed up in some espionage antics. This sequel to the highly successful "La Cage aux Folles" loses some steam, but is still worth seeing. Followed by "La Cage Aux Folles 3: The Wedding." **101m/C VHS, DVD.** *FR* Ugo Tognazzi, Michel Serrault, Michel Galabru, Benny Luke, Marcel Bozzuffi, Michel Galabru, Benny Luke; *D:* Edouard Molinaro; *W:* Francis Veber; *C:* Armando Nannuzzi; *M:* Ennio Morricone.

La Cage aux Folles 3: The Wedding ♂♂½ 1986 (PG-13) The flamboyant drag queen Albin must feign normalcy by marrying and fathering a child in order to collect a weighty inheritance. Final segment of the trilogy; inferior to the previous films. In French with English subtitles. **88m/C VHS.** *FR* Michel Serrault, Ugo Tognazzi, Michel Galabru, Benny Luke, Stephane Audran; *D:* Georges Lautner; *M:* Ennio Morricone.

La Ceremonie ♂♂♂ *A Judgment in Stone* 1995 Sullen maid Sophie (Bonnaire) is hired by the rich Lelievre family to work at their country estate. She's befriended

by independent postmistress Jeanne (Huppert), who's disliked by Sophie's employers, and who encourages Sophie into small defiant actions. Something's off about the entire situation and there's violence beneath the seemingly calm surface. Based on Ruth Rendell's chiller novel. Released in the U.S. as "Judgment in Stone." French with subtitles. **109m/C VHS, DVD.** *FR* GE Sandrine Bonnaire, Isabelle Huppert, Jacqueline Bisset, Jean-Pierre Cassel, Virginie Ledoyen, Valentine Merlet, Julien Rochefort, Dominique Frot, Jean-Francois Perrier; *D:* Claude Chabrol; *W:* Claude Chabrol, Caroline Eliacheff; *C:* Bernard Zitzermann; *M:* Matthieu Chabrol. Cesar '96: Actress (Huppert); L.A. Film Critics '96; Natl. Soc. Film Critics '96: Foreign Film.

L.A. Bounty ♂♂ 1989 (R) A beautiful cop and a bounty hunter go after the same murderer. Hauser steals the show as a psychopath who has completely blown a gasket. **85m/C VHS.** Sybil Danning, Wings Hauser, Henry Darrow, Lenore Kasdorf, Robert Hanley; *D:* Worth Keeter.

La Chartreuse de Parme ♂♂½ *Charterhouse at Parma* 1948 Nineteenth century period piece featuring an Archbishop willing to break his vows for the woman he loves, and the aunt who will make sure that if she can't have him only God will. French adaptation of the novel by Stendahl. Available dubbed. **170m/B VHS, DVD.** *FR* Gerard Philipe, Maria Casares, Renee Faure; *D:* Christian-Jaque; *W:* Christian-Jaque.

La Chevre ♂♂♂½ *The Goat* 1981 A screwball French comedy about two policemen (Richard and Depardieu—picture Gene Wilder and Nick Nolte with accents) stumbling along the path of a missing heiress who suffers from chronic bad luck. Contains a hilarious scene with chairs used to test the luck of the investigative team; based on one partner's ability to sit down on the only broken chair in a rather large collection, he is judged to be sufficiently jinxed to allow them to re-create the same outrageous misfortunes that befell the heiress in her plight. In French with English subtitles. **91m/C VHS, DVD.** *FR* Gerard Depardieu, Pierre Richard, Corynne Charbit, Michel Robin, Pedro Armendariz Jr.; *D:* Francis Veber; *M:* Vladimir Cosma.

La Chienne ♂♂♂ *Isn't Life A Bitch?; The Bitch* 1931 Dark, troubling tale of a betrayed husband whose only excitement is his painting hobby until he becomes consumed by the ever-tempting prostitute Lulu. Director Renoir broke ground with his use of direct sound and Paris shooting locations, and the experiment was a hit. Portrays marriage broke up as a result of this film's casting. Mareze died shortly after the filming was complete in a car crash. Based on the novel by Georges de la Fouchardiere. Produced in 1931, but didn't reach American theatres until 1975. In French with English subtitles. Remade in 1945 as "Scarlet Street." **93m/B VHS.** *FR* Michel Simon, Janie Mareze, Georges Flament, Madeleine Berubet; *D:* Jean Renoir; *W:* Andre Girard, Jean Renoir.

La Chute de la Maison Usher ♂♂ *The Fall of the House of Usher* 1928 An expressionistic, abstracted adaptation of the Poe story "The Fall of the House of Usher" about an evil mansion and its ruined denizens. Epstein used slow motion, superimpressions, and weird camera angles to obtain the proper atmosphere. **48m/B VHS, DVD.** *FR* Marguerite Gance, Jean Debucourt, Charles Lamy; *D:* Jean Epstein; *W:* Jean Epstein; *C:* Georges Lucas. Jean Lucas. Natl. Film Reg. '00.

La Cicada ♂½ *The Cricket* 1983 The sparks fly when a woman and her 17-year-old daughter become rivals for the affections of the same man. **90m/C VHS.** *IT* Clio Goldsmith, Virna Lisi, Anthony (Tony) Franciosa, Renato Salvatori; *D:* Alberto Lattuada.

La Collectionneuse ♂♂ *The Gentleman Tramp* 1967 The third of Rohmer's "Moral Tales" finds an artist and an antiques dealer (Pommereulle) vacationing in St. Tropez and sharing a villa with a young woman (Politoff) who picks a different man to sleep with each night. Both try to resist the sexual temptations of being added to her collection of lovers. French with subtitles. **88m/C VHS, DVD.** *FR* Patrick Bauchau, Daniel Pommereulle, Haydee Politoff; *D:* Eric Rohmer; *W:* Eric Rohmer; *C:* Nestor Almendros.

L.A. Confidential ♂♂♂♂ 1997 Hard-boiled, complicated crime drama based on James Ellroy's even more complex novel. Fifties Hollywood is ripe with corruption in many forms—politics, police, journalistic sleaze in the persona of Sid Hudgens (DeVito), editor of tabloid rag Hush-Hush, Sid's police contact is celebrity Sgt. Jack Vincennes (Spacey), who serves as an advisor to a TV cop show (think "Dragnet"). There's a bloodbath murder case that involves brutal-yet-tender cop Bud White (Crowe); the ruthlessly ambitious, college-educated neophyte Ed Exley (Pearce); and their veteran boss, Capt. Dudley Smith (Cromwell). There's also wealthy pimp/businessman Pierce Patchett (Strathairn) and his movie-star look-alike hookers, including world-weary Lynn (Basinger), who gets involved with Bud, who... Well, let's just say that Hanson does a masterful job tying up all the loose ends and still leaving you wanting more. **136m/C VHS, DVD.** Kevin Spacey, Russell Crowe, Guy Pearce, Danny DeVito, Kim Basinger, James Cromwell, David Strathairn, Ron Rifkin, Graham Beckel, Matt McCoy, Simon Baker, Paul Guilfoyle, Amber Smith, John Mahon, Paolo Seganti, Gwenda Deacon; *D:* Curtis Hanson; *W:* Curtis Hanson, Brian Helgeland; *C:* Dante Spinotti; *M:* Jerry Goldsmith. Oscars '97: Adapt. Screenplay, Support. Actress (Basinger); Australian Film Inst. '98: Foreign Film; British Acad. '97: Film Editing, Sound; Golden Globes '98: Support. Actress (Basinger); L.A. Film Critics '97: Cinematog., Director (Hanson), Film, Screenplay; Natl. Bd. of Review '97: Director (Hanson), Film; N.Y. Film Critics '97: Director (Hanson), Screenplay; Natl. Soc. Film Critics '97: Director (Hanson), Film, Screenplay; Screen Actors Guild '97: Support. Actor (Basinger); Writers Guild '97: Adapt. Screenplay; Broadcast Film Critics '97: Adapt. Screenplay, Film.

La Cucaracha ♂♂ 1998 Joe Aiello has made a successful life for himself and his family since emigrating from Sicily to Canada 30 years before. Since his son Nuccio is mentally handicapped, Joe rests his hopes on his 23-year-old daughter Bennie, who only wants freedom from the possessive father. And she takes it by impulsively marrying Diego, a South American refugee about to be deported. Feeling rejected and betrayed, Joe finds himself falling into despair. French with subtitles. **111m/C VHS.** *CA* Tony Nardi, Michelle-Barbara Pelletier, Hugolin Chevrette, John Dunn-Hill, Richard Lemire; *D:* Paul Tana; *W:* Tony Nardi, Paul Tana, Bruno Ramirez; *C:* Michel Caron; *M:* Pierre Desrochers.

La Deroute ♂♂ 1998 Two private eyes fall victim to predictions about their own futures before the current job involves tracking a psychic while they also compete with some of L.A.'s finest to drum up Hollywood interest in their cases. **90m/C DVD.** Anthony Guicera, Michael Madsen, Sarah Wynter, Erik Palladino, Dean Alioto, Kym E. Whitley; *D:* Dean Alioto; *W:* Dean Alioto; *C:* Tim Gibbons; *M:* Ryan Beveridge. **VIDEO**

L.A. Crackdown ♂ 1988 A woman cop goes undercover as a dancer in a dance hall to catch a psychotic killer who stalks hookers in this silly sequel to "L.A. Crackdown." **90m/C VHS.** Pamela Dixon, Anthony Gates, Joe Vance, Cynthia Miguel, Bo Sabato; *D:* Joseph Merhi.

L.A. Crackdown 2 ♂ 1988 Ex-office worker Walter (Roberts) has high-tailed it to Mexico to become a writer—or so he says. Instead, he's a drunk practically immobilized by night terrors. Then Things don't go as expected. **95m/C VHS.** Eric Roberts, Joaquin de Almeida, Tara Crespo, James McManus; *D:* Jack Perez; *W:* Shawn Maurer; *M:* Martin Davich.

L.A. Dicks ♂½ 2005 Two private eyes fall victim to predictions about their futures... [*see L.A. Deroute*]

La

La Discrete ✓✓✓ *The Discreet* 1990 Antoine (Luchini) is a cocky writer who is not the lothario he imagines himself to be—in fact his publisher plan a sexist revenge with Antoine advertising for a young female typist whom he will seduce and abandon—all the while keeping a diary of the experience which will be published. The self-possessed Catherine (Henry) answers the ad and even though Antoine protests that she is not his type he finds himself falling in love. Then Catherine discovers Antoine's original scheme. In French with English subtitles. 95m/C VHS. FR Fabrice Luchini, Judith Henry, Maurice Garrel, Marie Bunel, Francois Toumarkine; D: Christian Vincent; W: Jean-Pierre Ronssin, Christian Vincent; M: Jay Gottlieb. Cesar '91: Writing.

La Dolce Vita ✓✓✓✓ 1960 In this influential and popular work a successful, sensationalistic Italian journalist covers the show-biz life in Rome, and alternately covets and disdains its glitzy shallowness. The film follows his dealings with the "sweet life" over a pivotal week. A surreal, comic tableaux with award-winning costuming; one of Fellini's most acclaimed films. In this film Fellini called his hungry celebrity photographers the Paparazzo—and it is as the paparazzi they have been ever since. In Italian with English subtitles. 174m/B VHS, DVD. IT Marcello Mastroianni, Anita Ekberg, Anouk Aimee, Alain Cuny, Lex Barker, Yvonne Furneaux, Barbara Steele, Nadia Gray, Magali Noel, Walter Santesso, Jacques Sernas, Annibale Ninchi; D: Federico Fellini; W: Tullio Pinelli, Ennio Flaiano, Brunello Rondi, Federico Fellini; M: Nino Rota. Oscars '61: Costume Des. (B&W); Cannes '60: Film; N.Y. Film Critics '61: Film.

La Femme Infidele ✓✓✓½ *The Unfaithful Wife* 1969 When Charles (Bouquet) learns that his wife (Audran) has found the passion that their marriage now lacks in the arms of another man (Ronet), he confronts and kills him. This rekindles his wife's interest in him. Chabrol at his best. 98m/C VHS. FR Stephane Audran, Michel Bouquet, Michel Duchaussoy, Henri Marteau, Maurice Ronet, Dominique Zardi; D: Claude Chabrol; W: Claude Chabrol; C: Jean Rabier; M: Pierre Jansen.

La Femme Nikita ✓✓✓ 1991 (R) Stylish French noir version of Pygmalion. Having killed a cop during a drugstore theft gone awry, young French sociopath Nikita (Parillaud) is reprieved from a death sentence in order to enroll in a government finishing school, of sorts. Trained in etiquette (by Moreau) and the assassination (by Karyo), she's released after three years, and starts a new life with a new beau (Anglade), all the while carrying out agency-mandated assassinations. Parillaud is excellent as the once-amoral street urchin transformed into a woman of depth and sensitivity—a bitterly ironic-moral evolution for a contract killer. Remade as "Point of No Return." 117m/C VHS, DVD. FR Anne Parillaud, Jean-Hugues Anglade, Tcheky Karyo, Jeanne Moreau, Jean Reno, Jean Bouise; D: Luc Besson; W: Luc Besson; C: Thierry Arbogast; M: Eric Serra. Cesar '91: Actress (Parillaud).

L.A. Gangs Rising ✓✓ 1989 The streets of Los Angeles run red with blood as a gang war explodes into bloody fury. 87m/C VHS. David Kyle, Steve Bond, John Ashton; D: John Bushelman.

L.A. Goddess ✓½ 1992 (R) A hard-living, and drinking, movie star and her beautiful stunt double both fall for a studio head. Both of these women know what they want and the man in the middle hasn't got a clue. Also available in an unrated version. 92m/C VHS. Kathy Shower, Jeff Conaway, David Heavener, Wendy McDonald, Joe Estevez, James Hong; D: Jag Mundhra; W: Jerry Davis.

La Grande Bouffe ✓✓✓ *The Blow-Out* 1973 Four middle-aged men, bored with life, meet at a secluded mansion for one last excessive fling and literally eat themselves to death. Four very fine actors in a vulgar feast. French with subtitles. 125m/C VHS, DVD. FR Marcello Mastroianni, Philippe Noiret, Michel Piccoli, Ugo Tognazzi, Andrea Ferreol; D: Marco Ferreri; W: Marco Ferreri, Rafael Azcona; C: Mario Vulpiani; M: Philippe Sarde.

La Grande Bourgeoise ✓✓½ *The Murri Affair* 1974 Historical romance about the clash of aristocratic society and the new bourgeoisie in 1897 Italy. Great cast tries to save the true tale of romance and political intrigue from film's slow pacing, but in the end it's the movie's visual polish that shines forth. In Italian with subtitles. 115m/C VHS. IT Catherine Deneuve, Giancarlo Giannini, Fernando Rey, Tina Aumont; D: Mauro Bolognini; M: Ennio Morricone.

La Grande Vadrouille ✓✓✓ *Don't Look Now, We've Been Shot At* 1966 In 1943 German-occupied France, three Allied parachutists join forces on a Paris Opera conductor and a house painter. If the pair wish to find some peace, they must help the trio get to the free zone. France's number one boxoffice hit for almost 30 years. Also available dubbed. 122m/C VHS. FR Louis de Funes, Andre Bourvil, Terry-Thomas; D: Gerard Oury.

La Guerre Est Finie ✓✓✓ *The War Is Over; Kriget ar Slut* 1966 Alain Resnais's understated suspense film makes a belated debut on home video. It's the story of Diego (Montand), a revolutionary who comes to wonder if he can still fight the good fight against the fascists who control Spain. Montand, one of the most deceptively effortless actors ever to appear on screen, is a commanding presence in this low-keyed exercise. 121m/C VHS. FR SW Yves Montand, Michel Piccoli, Ingrid Thulin, Genevieve Bujold, Jean Daste, Dominique Rozan, Jean-Francois Remi; D: Alain Resnais; W: Jorge Semprun; C: Sacha Vierny; M: Giovanni Fusco; Nar: Jorge Semprun.

L.A. Heat ✓½ 1988 When a vice cop's partner is killed, he seeks revenge on the murderers, only to find that his own department may have been involved. Followed by "L.A. Vice." 90m/C VHS, DVD. Jim Brown, Lawrence-Hilton Jacobs; D: Joseph Merhi.

L.A. Law ✓✓½ 1986 The pilot episode of the acclaimed dramatic series, in which the staff of a Los Angeles law firm tries a variety of cases. 97m/C VHS. Michael Tucker, Jill Eikenberry, Harry Hamlin, Richard Dysart, Jimmy Smits, Alan Rachins, Susan Ruttan, Susan Dey, Corbin Bernsen; D: Gregory Hoblit. TV

La Lectrice ✓✓½ *The Reader* 1988 (R) Artesian landscapes, Beethoven sonatas, and a Raymond Jean novel titled "La Lectrice" provide the backdrop for Constance (Miou-Miou) to read aloud to her boyfriend in bed, and from there she imagines herself the novel's heroine, who hires out her services as a reader to various odd characters. She reads from "L'Amant," "Alice," "War and Peace," and "Les Fleurs du Mal." Richly textured and not overly intellectual. In French with English subtitles. 98m/C VHS. FR Miou-Miou, Christian Ruche, Sylvie Laporte, Michael Raskine, Brigitte Catillon, Regis Royer, Maria Casares, Pierre Dux, Patrick Chesnais; D: Michel Deville; W: Rosalinde Deville, Michel Deville. Cesar '89: Support. Actor (Chesnais); Montreal World Film Fest. '88: Film.

La Marseillaise ✓✓✓½ 1937 Sweeping epic by Renoir made before he hit his stride with "Grand Illusion." It details the events of the French Revolution in the summer of 1789 using a cast of thousands. The opulent lifestyle of the French nobility is starkly contrasted with the peasant lifestyle of poverty and despair. The focus is on two new recruits who have joined the Marseilles division of the revolutionary army as they begin their long march to Paris, the heart of France. As they travel, they adopt a stirring and passionate song that embodies the spirit and ideals of the revolution known as "La Marseillaise," now France's national anthem. In French with English subtitles. 130m/B VHS. FR Pierre Renoir, Lisa (Lise) Delamare, Louis Jouvet, Aime Clariond, Andrex Andrisson, Paul Dullac; D: Jean Renoir; W: Jean Renoir; C: Jean (Yves, Georges) Bourgoin.

La Merveilleuse Visite ✓✓½ *The Marvelous Visit* 1974 Bittersweet fantasy about an angel that falls from the sky and is found unconcious by a priest. He's nursed back to health but causes problems for his host when he wanders into the nearby village and his curiosity is misunderstood. Adapted from a short story by H.G. Wells. In French with English subtitles. 102m/C VHS. FR Gilles Kohler, Deborah Berger, Jean-Pierre Castaldi; D: Marcel Carne; W: Marcel Carne.

La Moustache ✓✓ *The Moustache* 2005 Carree adapts and directs his 1986 novel in which architect Marc (Lindon) decides to shave off the moustache he's had most of his life. He's taken aback when his wife Agnes (Devos) doesn't notice. Nor does anyone else. Marc first thinks it's an elaborate practical joke but then suspects everyone of more sinister motives. His marriage unravels as, perhaps, does Marc's sanity. French with subtitles. 86m/C DVD. FR Vincent Lindon, Emmanuelle Devos, Mathieu Amalric, Hippolyte Girardot, Cylia Malki, Macha Polikarpova; D: Emmanuel Carrere; W: Jerome Beaujour, Emmanuel Carrere; C: Patrick Blossier.

La Mujer de Mi Hermano ✓✓ *My Brother's Wife* 2006 (R) Glossy, romantic melodrama set in Mexico City. Beautiful Zoe (Mori) is bored as well as childless in her marriage to rich, uptight Ignacio (Meier). Is it any wonder she's so very attracted to Ignacio's hot-blooded younger brother Gonzalo (Cardona)? Soon they're tearing up the sheets with Gonzalo making insinuations about his brother's manhood and revealing some family secrets while Zoe feels guilty. Screenwriter Bayly adapted his own novel. Spanish with subtitles. 93m/C DVD. MX Christian Meier, Bruno Bichir, Angelica Aragon, Barbara Mori, Manolo Cardona, Beto Cuevas; D: Ricardo de Montreuil; W: Jaime Bayly. C: Andres E. Sanchez; M: Angelo Milli.

La Nuit de Varennes ✓✓✓ 1982 (R) This semi-historical romp is based on an actual chapter in French history when King Louis XVI and Marie Antoinette fled from revolutionary Paris to Varennes in 1791. On the way they meet an unlikely group of characters, including Cassanova and Thomas Paine. At times witty and charming, the melange of history and fiction is full of talk, sometimes profane, punctuated by sex and nudity. Director Scola's imagination stretches to light up this night. In French with English subtitles. 133m/C VHS. IT Marcello Mastroianni, Harvey Keitel, Jean-Louis Barrault, Hanna Schygulla, Jean-Claude Brialy, Michel Piccoli, Jean-Louis Trintignant; D: Ettore Scola; W: Ettore Scola.

La Passante ✓✓✓ *La Passante du Sans Souci; The Passerby* 1983 An otherwise peace-loving man murders the Paraguayan ambassador to France. In somewhat clumsy flashback style the murderer's orphaned childhood and other memories provide motives for the murder. Though posed more slowly than typical intrigue plots, the movie blends love and the legacy of Nazism, passion and politics in an engaging way, spiced with nudity and some violence. In her last screen appearance Schneider movingly portrays dual roles. In French with English subtitles. 106m/C VHS. FR GE Romy Schneider, Michel Piccoli, Helmut Griem, Gerard Klein, Matthieu Carriere, Maria Schell; D: Jacques Rouffio; M: Georges Delerue. Cesar '83: Sound.

La Petite Lili ✓✓½ *Little Lili* 2003 Miller develops a freeform adaptation of Chekhov's 1895 "The Seagull," moving it from 19th-century Russia to 21st-century rural France and shifting the literature/theater emphasis to filmmaking. What transpires is much unrequited love, geriatric loathing, and opinions about making art. In French with English subtitles. 104m/C DVD. FR CA Nicole Garcia, Bernard Giraudeau, Jean-Pierre Marielle, Ludivine Sagnier, Robinson Stevenin, Julie Depardieu, Yves Jacques; Anne LeNy, Marc Betton; D: Claude Miller; C: Gerard de Battista.

La Petite Sirene ✓✓ *The Little Mermaid* 1980 Isabelle is a 14-year-old schoolgirl, obsessed with the story of the Little Mermaid, who tries to ingratiate herself to Georges, a 40-year-old garage mechanic. Seeing him as her prince charming, she persists in trying to make him a part of her life, in spite of his resistance. In French with English subtitles. 104m/C VHS. FR Laura Alexis, Philippe Leotard, Evelyne Dress, Marie Dubois; D: Roger Andrieux; W: Roger Andrieux.

La Piscine ✓✓ *The Swimming Pool; The Sinners* 1969 Jean-Paul (Delon) and his wife Marianne (Schneider) are on vacation at a villa near St. Tropez. Marianne invites her ex-lover Harry (Ronet) and his teenaged daughter Penelope (Birkin) to join them and the foursome spend most of their time lounging around the pool. But tensions develop and the consequences are dramatic when Jean-Paul decides to seduce the nubile Penelope. French with subtitles. 120m/C DVD. FR Alain Delon, Romy Schneider, Maurice Ronet, Jane Birkin; D: Jacques Deray; W: Jacques Deray, Jean-Claude Carriere; C: Jean-Jacques Tarbes; M: Michel Legrand.

La Promesse ✓✓ *The Promise* 1996 Fifteen-year-old Igor (Renier) helps his disreputable father Roger (Gourmet) run an illegal immigrant operation in the Belgian town of Liege. African immigrant Amidou (Quedraogo) has just been joined by his wife Assita (Quedraogo) and their baby. When Amidou dies in an accident, Roger forces Igor to help him bury the body secretly and tells the bewildered wife that her husband has left her. But Igor is caught in the middle—he'd promised the dying Amidou to look after Assita and he still has enough conscience to want to help—but it also puts Igor into a dangerous conflict with his father. French with subtitles. 93m/C VHS, DVD. FR BE Jeremie Renier, Olivier Gourmet, Assita Quedraogo, Rasmane Quedraogo; D: Jean-Pierre Dardenne, Luc Dardenne; W: Jean-Pierre Dardenne, Luc Dardenne; C: Alain Marcoen; M: Jean-Marie Billy. L.A. Film Critics '97; Natl. Soc. Film Critics '97; Foreign Film.

La Puritaine ✓✓½ 1986 Before his planned reconciliation with his daughter, the artistic manager of a theatre has young actresses portray different sides of the daughter's personality. In French with English subtitles. 90m/C VHS, DVD. FR Michel Piccoli, Sandrine Bonnaire; D: Lou Doillon.

La Ronde ✓✓½ 1951 A classic comedy of manners and sharply witty tour-de-farce in which a group of people in 1900 Vienna keep changing romantic partners until things wind up where they started. Ophuls' swirling direction creates a fast-paced farce of desire and regret with wicked yet subtle style. Based on Arthur Schnitzler's play and remade as "Circle of Love." In French with English subtitles. 97m/B VHS, DVD. FR Simone Signoret, Anton Walbrook, Simone Simon, Serge Reggiani, Daniel Gelin, Danielle Darrieux, Jean-Louis Barrault, Fernand Gravey, Odette Joyeux, Isa Miranda, Gerard Philipe; D: Max Ophuls. British Acad. '51: Film.

L.A. Rules: The Pros and Cons of Breathing ✓½ 1994

Four friends meet regularly at the same trendy L.A. bar, discussing their travails as they try to make it in Hollywood. 92m/C VHS. Joey Lauren Adams, Phil Brock, Noelle Parker, Barry Sobel, Joey Dedeo, Ira Heiden, Philip Tanzini; D: Robert Munic; W: Robert Munic; C: Steve Adcock.

La Rupture ✓✓ *The Breakup* 1970 Thriller about a wife trying to protect her child from her husband's unsavory family. Audran and her son are attacked by her husband (Drouot), who's high on drugs. She fights back and he winds up in the hospital. Her father-in-law (Bouquet), who wants his grandson to live with him, then hires a seedy investigator (Cassel) to spy on Audran. Based on the Charlotte Armstrong novel. In French with English subtitles. 124m/C VHS. FR Stephane Audran, Jean-Claude Drouot, Michel Bouquet, Jean-Pierre Cassel, Catherine Rouvel, Jean Carmet, Annie Cordy; D: Claude Chabrol; W: Claude Chabrol; M: Pierre Jansen.

La Salamandre ✓✓ *The Salamander* 1971 Non-conformist Rosemonde, suspected of shooting her guardian, is being interviewed by a novelist and a journalist trying to write a television script about the incident. The more they supposedly learn, the more they are both intimately drawn towards her. French with subtitles. 119m/B VHS. SI Bulle Ogier, Jean-Luc Bideau, Jacques

Denis; **D:** Alain Tanner; **W:** Alain Tanner; John Berger; **M:** Patrick Moraz.

La Scorta 🦴🦴½ *The Bodyguards; The Escort's* 1994 Slick, fact-based political thriller focuses on four carabinieri (state police officers) who struggle to maintain some semblance of their normal lives after they are assigned to protect a judge investigating government corruption and a related murder in a Sicilian town. A cracking alternative to Americanized mobster melodrama, marked by taut direction, meaty characters, and coolly understated performances that seamlessly portray brotherhood, heroism, suspicion, and betrayal amid the battle for power between the Italian state and the Mafia. In Italian with English subtitles. 92m/C VHS, DVD. *IT* Claudio Amendola, Enrico Lo Verso, Tony Sperandeo, Ricky Memphis, Caro Cecchi, Leo Gullotta; **D:** Ricky Tognazzi; **W:** Graziano Diana, Simona Izzo; **M:** Ennio Morricone.

La Sentinelle 🦴🦴 *The Sentinel* 1992 Morose Mathias (Salinger) is traveling by train from Germany to France to attend medical school. The sinister Bleicher (Richard), who seems to be a customs official, grills Mathias but lets him go. In his hotel, Mathias finds a strange package in his luggage and discovers it contains the shrunken head of a man. He keeps his discovery a secret but tests samples of the head in the school laboratory on a quest to figure out who the man was. May sound like a thriller but it's toc talky and paced too slowly to hold complete interest. French with subtitles. 139m/C VHS. *FR* Emmanuel Salinger, Jean-Louis Richard, Thibault de Montalembert, Valerie Dreville, Marianne (Quau) Denicourt, Bruno Todeschini, Jean-Luc Boute; **C:** Caroline Champetier; **M:** Marc Oliver Sommer.

La Separation 🦴🦴½ 1998 Pierre (Auteuil) and Anne (Huppert) share a long-term relationship and a 15-month-old son. What they no longer seer to have is any passion for each other as they go through their daily routine. Anne decides to have an affair—but she doesn't share any reason it should break up her household. However, the increasingly miserable Pierre can't share her belief. Based on the 1991 novel "Separation" by Franck. French with subtitles. 85m/C VHS, DVD. *FR* Daniel Auteuil, Isabelle Huppert, Karin Viard, Jerome Deschamps; **D:** Christian Vincent; **W:** Christian Vincent, Dan Franck; **C:** Denis Lenoir.

La Signora di Tutti 🦴🦴🦴 1934 An early Italian biography of Gaby Doriot, a movie star whose professional success is paired by personal misery. Prestigious director Ophuls, working in exile from his native Germany, was unable to complete many projects in the years leading up to and during WWII. This is one of te few. Watch for innovative camera work intended to underscore the film's mood. In Italian with English subtitles. 92m/B VHS. *IT* Isa Miranda. **D:** Max Ophuls.

La Silence de la Mer 🦴🦴🦴 *The Silence of the Sea* 1947 An old French farmer (Robian) and his niece (Stephane) are forced to billet a German officer (Vernon) in their home during the Occupation. They've vowed never to speak to him but the German continues to pour out his thoughts on music, war, and his love of France into their silence. Melville's first feature. French with subtitles. 86m/B VHS. *FR* Howard Vernon, Jean-Marie Robian, Nicole Stephane; **D:** Jean-Pierre Melville; **W:** Jean-Pierre Melville; **C:** Henri Decae; **M:** Edgar Bischoff.

L.A. Story 🦴🦴🦴 1991 (PG-13) Livin' ain't easy in the city of angels. Harris K. Telemacher (Martin), a weatherman in a city where the weather never changes, wrestles with the meaning of if'e and love while consoring with beautiful people, distancing from significant other Henner, cavorting with valley girl Parker, and falling for newswoman Tennant (Martin's real life wife). Written by the comedian, the story's full of keen insights on living in the everyday problems and ironies of living in the Big Tangerine. It's no wonder the script's full of so much thoughtful detail; Martin is said to have worked on it intermittertly for several years. Charming, fault forgiving but not fault ignoring portrait. 98m/C VHS, DVD. Steve Martin, Victoria Tennant, Richard E. Grant, Marilu Henner, Sarah Jessica Parker, Sam McMurray, Patrick Stewart, Iman; **C:** Andrew Dunn; **M:** Peter Melnick.

La Strada 🦴🦴🦴 *The Road* 1954 Simple-minded girl, played by, Fellini's circus strong-man and is sold to a brutal, coarse circus strong-man and she tells to join with him despite his abuse. They tour the countryside and eventually meet up with a gentle acrobat, played by Basehart, who alters their fate. Fellini masterwork was the director's first internationally acclaimed film, and is, by turns, somber and amusing as it demonstrates the filmmaker's sensitivity to the underprivileged and the world and his belief in spiritual redemption. Subtitled in English. 107m/B VHS, DVD. *IT* Giulietta Masina, Anthony Quinn, Richard Basehart, Aldo Silvani; **D:** Federico Fellini; **W:** Ennio Flaiano, Brunello Rondi, Tullio Pinelli, Federico Fellini; **M:** Nino Rota, Carlo Savina; Film; N.Y. Film Critics '56: Foreign Film.

La Symphonie Pastorale 🦴🦴🦴½ 1946 A Swiss pastor takes in an orphan blind girl who grows up to be beautiful. The pastor then competes for her affections with his son. Quiet drama based on the Andre Gide novel, with breathtaking mountain scenery as the backdrop for this tragedy rife with symbolism. 105m/B VHS, *FR* Pierre Blanchar, Michele Morgan, Jean Desailly, Line Noro, Andree Clement; **D:** Jean Delannoy; **M:** Georges (Morgan).

La Terra Trema 🦴🦴🦴½ *Episoda Del Mare; The Earth Will Tremble* 1948 The classic example of Italian neo-realism, about a poor Sicilian fisherman, his family and poor village. A spare, slow-moving, profound and ultimately 'lyrical tragedy, this semi-documentary explores the economic exploitation on location with the villagers playing themselves; highly acclaimed though not commercially successful. In Sicilian with English subtitles. Some radically cut versions may be available, but are to be avoided. Franco Zeffirelli was one of the assistant directors. 161m/B VHS, DVD. *IT* Antonio Pierangeli; **D:** Luchino Visconti.

La Truite 🦴🦴🦴 *The Trout* 1983 (R) A young woman leaves her family's rural trout farm and a loveless marriage to seek her fortune in high finance and corporate mayhem. The complicated plot, full of intrigue and sexual encounters, sometimes lacks focus. Slickly filmed. 80m/C VHS, DVD. *FR* Isabelle Huppert, Jean-Pierre Cassel, Daniel Olbrychski, Jeanne Moreau, Jacques Spiesser, Ruggero Raimondi, Alexis Smith, Craig Stevens; **D:** Joseph Losey; **C:** Henri Alekan.

La Vengeance d'une Femme 🦴🦴 *A Woman's Revenge* 1989 Retired Cecile and sultry Suzy are two sides of a love triangle whose third member, Cecile's husband, has just died. Cecile decides to get to know his mistress better, which naturally has Suzy worried. Does she befriend the 'other woman.' Based on Dostoyevski's 'The Eternal Husband.' In French with English subtitles. 133m/C VHS. *FR* Isabelle Huppert, Beatrice Dalle; **D:** Jacques Doillon; **W:** Jean-Francois Goyet, Jacques Doillon.

La Vice 🦴🦴½ 1989 A detective is transferred to the vice squad, where he must investigate a series of murders. Sequel to 'L.A. Heat.' 90m/C VHS, DVD. Jim Brown, Lawrence-Hilton Jacobs, William (Bill) Smith; **D:** Joseph Merhi.

La Vie Continue 🦴🦴½ 1982 A middle-aged woman suddenly finds herself widowed after 20 years of marriage and tries to build a new life for herself and her children. Girardot's performance can't quite dispel melodramatic suds. Loosely and more effectively remade as "Men Don't Leave." In French with English subtitles or dubbed 93m/C VHS. *IT* Annie Girardot, Jean-Pierre Cassel, Emmanuel Goyet, Pierre Dux, Giulia Salvatori, Emmanuel Goyet, Rivera Andres; **D:** Moshe Mizrahi; **W:** Moshe Mizrahi; **M:** Georges Delerue.

La Vie de Boheme 🦴🦴🦴 *Bohemien Life* 1993 Comedy takes a mocking look at art and 'romantic love. A trio of hapless, but dedicated comrades, Rodolfo (Pellonpaa) the painter, Marcel (Vaananen) the poet, and Schaunard (Vaananan) must scrounge around the mealy edge of modern Paris because their art isn't filling their stomachs. Meanwhile, they experience the pangs of love like everyone else, although each is devoutly committed to his art as well. Starkly different from the lush operatic version by Puccini, but based on the same source, a 19th century novel by Henri Mullet. French with subtitles. 100m/C VHS, Matti Pellonpaa, Andre Wilms, Kari Vaananen, Jean-Pierre Leaud, Samuel Fuller, Louis Malle Evelyne Didi, Christine Murillo, Laika, Carlos Salgado, Alexis Nitzer, Sylvie van den Elsen, Gilles Charmant, Dominique Marcas; **D:** Aki Kaurismaki; **W:** Aki Kaurismaki.

La Vie en Rose 🦴🦴 *La Mome; The Kid* 2007 (PG-13) Think Judy Garland—only French. Somewhat old-fashioned, non-chronological biopic follows the triumphs and tragedies of Edith Piaf (Cotillard), France's famous "little sparrow." Dirt-poor, little Edith grows up in a brothel, sings on street corners, gets discovered (by Depardieu's only impresario), and finds success in cabaret with her astonishing voice. She also finds alcohol and drug addiction, ill health and a tragic love with married boxer Marcel Cerdan (Martins). Cotillard is amazing in the lead, getting both Piaf's gestures and attitude just right (she lip-synchs her vocals). French with subtitles. 140m/C DVD, *FR GB CZ* Marion Cotillard, Gerard Depardieu, Emmanuelle Seigner, Pascal Greggory, Sylvie Testud, Clotilde Courau, Jean-Paul Rouve, Catherine Allegret, Jean-Pierre Martins; **D:** Olivier Dahan; **W:** Olivier Dahan, Isabelle Sobelman; **C:** Tetsuo Nagata; **M:** Christopher Gunning. Oscars '07: Actress (Cotillard), Makeup; British Acad. '07: Actress (Cotillard), Costume Des., Makeup, Orig. Score; Golden Globes '08: Actress—Mus./Comedy (Cotillard).

La Vie Est Belle 🦴🦴 *Life is Rosy* 1987 The rags to riches story of a poor rural musician from Zaire who goes to the city to break into radio and TV. He uses a beautiful wife, and make himself a singing sensation. French with subtitles. 85m/C VHS. **D:** Naganguna Mweze, Bernard Lamy.

La Vie Promise 🦴🦴½ *The Promised Life* 2002 Cold, aging French prostitute reevaluates her life after meeting the daughter she abandoned years ago. Pic turns into a road movie as the decidedly unmaternal Sylvia (Huppert) and her stubborn 14-year-old Laurence (Forgel) go on the lam after Laurence rashly murders Sylvia's abusive pimp. They separately meet up with the mysterious Joshua (Gerlgory) who joins them on their journey which has now become Sylvia's quest to reunite with her former husband (Marcon) and 8-year-old son she abandoned which drove her into a mental asylum. In an otherwise mediocre film, Huppert turns in a stunning performance as the street-walker who must face a past she's trying to forget. Haunting soundtrack and lush French scenery are highlights. 94m/C DVD. *FR* Isabelle Huppert, Pascal Greggory, Maud Forget, Fabienne Babe, Andre Marcon; **D:** Olivier Dehan; **W:** Agnes Fustier-Dahan; **C:** Alex Lamarque.

L.A. Wars 🦴½ 1994 (R) A Latin American drug dealer moves into the territory of an Italian mobster, causing a turf war. When a cop rescues the scuzzball, his boss forces him to infiltrate the mobster's organization. Aburcpant body count, lots of dialogue. 94m/C VHS. Vince Murdocco, Mary Zilba, A.J. Stevens, Rodrigo Obregon; **D:** Martin Morris, Tony Kandah.

Labor Pains 🦴🦴½ 1999 (R) Sedgwick gets preggers by artist Morrow who disappears for eight months. When he returns, she's in labor and both her parents (Klein and Moore) and her best friend (Rochon) are trying to convince Sedgwick not to give the baby up for adoption. Meanwhile, the new parents decide to get reacquainted. 89m/C VHS. Kyra Sedgwick, Rob Morrow, Lela Rochon, Mary Tyler Moore, Robert Klein, Dann Fink; **D:** Tracy Alexsor; **W:** Tracy Alexson.

Laboratory 🦴 1980 Things go awry when the earthling subjects of an alien experiment revolt against their captors. 93m/C VHS. Camille Mitchell, Martin Kove, Ken Washington, Corinne Michel; **D:** Allan Sandler, Bob Emenegger; **W:** Steve Marshall, Allan Sandler.

Labyrinth 🦴🦴🦴 1986 (PG) While baby-sitting her baby brother Froud, Connelly is so frustrated she asks the goblins to take him away. When the Goblin King, played by Bowie, comes to answer her idle wish, she must try to rescue Froud by solving the fantastic labyrinth. If she does not find him in time, Froud will become one of the goblins forever. During her journey, Connelly is befriended by all sorts of odd creatures created by Henson, and she grows up a little along the way. A fascinating adventure movie for the whole family. 90m/C VHS, DVD. David Bowie Jennifer Connelly, Toby Froud, Shelley Thompson, Dave Goelz, Karen Prell, Steve Whitmire; **D:** Jim Henson; **W:** Jim Henson, Terry Jones; **C:** Alex Thomson; **M:** Trevor Jones, David Bowie.

Labyrinth of Passion 🦴🦴½ *Laberinto de Pasiones* 1982 A screwball farce, directed by Almodovar, featuring a host of strange characters running around Madrid in search of sex and laughter. They find plenty of both. An early film by an influential director. In Spanish with English subtitles. 100m/C VHS, *SP* Antonio Banderas, Imanol Arias, Cecilia (Cela) Roth; **D:** Pedro Almodovar, **W:** Pedro Almodovar.

The Lacemaker 🦴🦴🦴 *La Dentellière* 1977 Huppert's first shot at stardom, on videodisc with digital sound and a letterboxed print. A young beautician and a university student fall in love on vacation but soon begin to realize the differences in their lives. Adapted from the novel by Pascal Laine. In French with English subtitles. 107m/C FR SI GE Isabelle Huppert, Yves Beneyton, Florence Giorgetti, Anna Marie Duringer; **D:** Claude Goretta.

Ladder 49 🦴🦴½ 2004 (PG-13) An old-fashioned homage to firefighters begins when Jack Morrison (Phoenix) is injured and trapped in a burning warehouse. While his chief and mentor, Mike Kennedy (Travolta), coo ordinates a rescue effort, Jack remembers his first day as a rookie. The movie will continue alternating between Jack's career as a firefighter and his current predicament as well as his personal life, which includes his supportive, loving wife Linda (Barrett). That's pretty much it; you watch pros doing a job that can be very dangerous and how firehouse camaraderie helps them cope. The actors are earnest and the action convincing; it's not ground-breaking but it's not boring either. 115m/C VHS, DVD, Blu-ray Disc. US Joaquin Rafael (Leaf) Phoenix, John Travolta, Jacinda Barrett, Robert Patrick, Morris Chestnut, Billy Burke, Balthazar Getty, Tim Guinee; **D:** Jay Russell; **W:** Lewis Colick, Scott B. Smith; **C:** James L. Carter; **M:** William Ross.

L'Addition 🦴🦴½ *The Patsy; Caged Heart* 1985 (R) According to some cinematic code, the male lead always gets in lots of trouble whenever he tries to help a beautiful stranger. This time, Berry, as Bruno Windler, winds up arrested for shoplifting when he attempts to help Abril. Jailed and on the verge of parole, Windler unwittingly becomes involved in a prison break and is accused cf helping a crime con mastermind the escape and of shooting a guard. That's where the gallic flair for capturing the sado-masochistic underbelly of humanity comes in, as Windler is viciously pursued by the malevolent guard. 86m/C VHS. Richard Berry, Victoria Abril, Richard Bohringer, Farid Chopel, Fabrice Eberhard; **D:** Denis

Amar; *W:* Jean Curtelin; *C:* Robert Fraisse; *M:* Jean-Claude Petit.

The Ladies Club 1986 (R) A group of rape victims get together and begin to victimize rapists. 86m/C VHS. Bruce Davison, Karen Austin, Diana Scarwid, Shera Danese, Beverly Todd; *D:* A.K. Allen.

Ladies in Lavender 2004 (PG-13) Sisters Janet (Smith) and Ursula (Dench) Widdington have their routine Cornwall cottage life turned about when a handsome, half-drowned young man (Bruhl), who washes up on their pebbled beach. How, we never find out. Passions and jealousies ignite in the sisters as they nurse him back to health and intercept the advances of a pretty young artist who is attracted to their patient's musical talents. The dames' performances do not disappoint, but the same cannot be said for Bruhl, who lacks depth in comparison. Gallant effort by Dance in reworking William J. Locke's short story, although a bit overreaching. 103m/C DVD. GB Judi Dench, Maggie Smith, Daniel Bruhl, Miriam Margolyes, David Warner, Natascha (Natasha) McElhone, Freddie Jones, Clive Russell; *D:* Charles Dance; *W:* Charles Dance; *C:* Peter Biziou; *M:* Nigel Hess.

The Ladies' Man 1961 Piecemeal Lewis farce, with Jerry playing a clutzy handyman working at a girls' boarding house. Some riotous routines balanced by slow pacing. 106m/C VHS, DVD. Jerry Lewis, Helen Traubel, Jack Kruschen, Doodles Weaver, Gloria Jean; *D:* Jerry Lewis; *W:* Jerry Lewis.

The Ladies Man 2000 (R) Producer Lorne Michaels was allegedly the model for Mike Myers' Dr. Evil. It's becoming clear that his repeated abduction of SNL skits in order to stretch them out on the rack and loose them on the public is part of some nefarious plan. The victim this time is Leon Phelps (Meadows), a stuck-in-the-'70s late-night talk show host who dispenses inappropriate romantic advice. Raised by Hugh Hefner but banished for sleeping with the wrong bunny, Leon soon becomes banished from his radio gig, too. He eases the pain by seducing other men's wives, leading to the formation of an anti-Leon posse. Meanwhile, his faithful ex-producer Julie (Parsons) inexplicably sticks by his side hoping to tame Leon's wild ways. In the end, Leon is converted to a one-lady man, and the comic possibilities of this lame flick are squandered. 84m/C VHS, DVD. Tim Meadows, Will Ferrell, Tiffani(-Amber) Thiessen, Billy Dee Williams, Karyn Parsons, Lee Evans, John Witherspoon, Eugene Levy, Tamala Jones, Julianne Moore, Sean Thibodeau; *D:* Reginald (Reggie) Hudlin; *W:* Tim Meadows, Dennis McNicholas, Andrew Steele; *C:* Johnny E. Jensen; *M:* Marcus Miller.

Ladies of the Bois de Bologne 1945 *Les Dames du Bois de Bologne; Ladies of the Park* 1944 Beware the woman scorned—as Jean (Bernard) learns. He ends his longtime relationship with Helene (Casares), although they vow to stay friends, but she secretly plots revenge and finds it in the person of Agnes (Labourdette), a former prostitute. Helene introduces Agnes to Jean, hoping they'll be attracted to one another. They are that after the wedding ceremony Helene reveals the truth about Agnes' sordid past. Updated adaptation of a story in Diderot's "Jacques Le Fatalist." French with subtitles. 83m/B VHS, DVD. FR Maria Casares, Paul Bernard, Elina Labourdette; *D:* Robert Bresson; *W:* Robert Bresson, Jean Cocteau.

Ladies of the Chorus 1949 Monroe stars as a burlesque chorus girl who shares the stage with her mom (Jergens) and a handful of other beauties. She meets and falls in love with a wealthy socialite (Brooks), but her mother completely disapproves of the relationship. Monroe later learns that her mother was in the same circumstances several years before. Although only her second film appearance, Monroe's talents are already quite apparent in this low-budget musical romance. ♫Every Baby Nees a Da Da Daddy; Anyone Can Tell I Love You; Crazy For You; You're Never Too Old; Ladies of the Chorus. 61m/B VHS. Adele Jergens, Marilyn Monroe, Rand Brooks, Nana Bryant, Steven Geray, Bill Edwards; *D:* Phil Karlson.

Ladies of the Lotus 1987 Bloodthirsty Vancouver gangsters raid Lotus, Inc., a modeling agency, and sell beautiful young women into slavery. As bad as it sounds. 120m/C VHS. CA Richard Dale, Angela Read, Patrick Bermel, Darcia Camie; *D:* Lloyd A. Simandl, Douglas C. Nicolle.

Ladies on the Rocks 1983 Aspiring comediennes *Koks I Kulissen* 1983 Micha and Laura pack up their van and take their bizarre cabaret act on the road through rural Denmark. They find their private lives disintegrating but turn each disaster into new material for their act. In Danish with English subtitles. 100m/C VHS. DK Helle Ryslinge, Anne Marie Helger, Flemming Quist Moller; *D:* Christian Braad Thomsen.

Ladies They Talk About 1933 *Women in Prison* 1933 Stanwyck stars as a tough-talking gun moll who belongs to a gang of bank robbers. They get caught and Stanwyck is sent to the female division of San Quentin. The acting is great in this pre-Code prison movie, but the film gets a bit punchy at times. Based on the true-life experiences of actress Dorothy Mackaye, who went to jail after her husband was killed in a fight with actor Paul Kelley, who was also sent to prison. Adapted from the play "Women in Prison" by Dorothy Mackaye and Carlton Miles. 69m/B VHS. Barbara Stanwyck, Preston Foster, Lyle Talbot, Dorothy Burgess, Lillian Roth, Maude Eburne, Harold Huber, Ruth Donnelly; *D:* Howard Bretherton, William Keighley.

Ladies Who Do 1963 A group of cleaning ladies band together against the unscrupulous businessman who wants to tear down their homes in order to build an office tower. Along with a retired colonel, they use the stock market secrets gleaned from the rubbish they toss away to make a killing in the market and save the day. 90m/B VHS. GB Peggy Mount, Robert Morley, Harry H. Corbett, Miriam Karlin, Avril Elgar, Dandy Nichols, Jon Pertwee, Nigel Davenport; *D:* C.M. Pennington-Richards; *W:* Michael Pertwee.

The Lady and the Duke 2001 *L'Anglaise et le Duc* (PG-13) Based on the memoirs of English-woman Grace Elliott (Russell), who lived in Paris during the French Revolution and remained a loyal supporter of King Louis XVI. The Duke in question is her former lover, Philippe, Duc d'Orleans (Dreyfus), with whom Grace has remained friends. A moderate revolutionary and encourages Grace to return to England for her own safety, which she refuses to do. 81-year-old Rohmer commissioned a series of painted backdrops depicting 18th-century France rather than build sets and then superimposed his actors upon the backdrops, offering remarkably effective visuals. French with subtitles. 129m/C VHS, DVD. FR Lucy Russell, Jean-Claude Dreyfus, Francois Marthouret, Leonard Cobiant, Caroline Morin, Alain Libolt, Marie Riviere, Helena Dubeil; *D:* Eric Rohmer; *W:* Eric Rohmer; *C:* Diane Baratier.

The Lady and the Highwayman 1989 TV adaptation of the Barbara Cartland historical romance finds a rogue falling for the lady he's sworn to protect. Naturally, there's a happy ending. 100m/C VHS, DVD. GB Hugh Grant, Emma Samms, Oliver Reed, Michael York, Robert Morley, John Mills, Lysette Anthony; *D:* John Hough; *W:* Terence Feely; *M:* Laurie Johnson.

Lady and the Tramp 1955 (G) The animated Disney classic about two dogs who fall in love. Tramp is wild and carefree; Lady is a spoiled pedigree who runs away from home after her owners have a baby. They just don't make dog romances like this anymore. ♫He's a Tramp; La La Lu; Siamese Cat Song; Peace on Earth; Bella Notte. 76m/C VHS, DVD. *D:* Hamilton Luske, Clyde Geronimi, Wilfred Jackson; *W:* Erdman Penner, Ralph Wright, Don DaGradi; *M:* Sonny Burke, Peggy Lee; *V:* Larry Roberts, Peggy Lee, Barbara Luddy, Stan Freberg, Alan Reed, Bill Thompson, Bill Baucon, Verna Felton, George Givot, Dallas McKennon, Lee Millar.

Lady Audley's Secret 2000 Old-fashioned and rather dull potboiler based on the 1862 novel by Mary Elizabeth Braddon. Governess Lucy (McIntosh) marries her employer, Sir Michael Audley (Cranham). But Lucy has a shady past, including a previous husband, George (Bamber), who turns out to be a friend of Sir Michael's nephew, Robert (Mackintosh). Then George disappears and Robert wonders just how dangerous the new Lady Audley is. 120m/C VHS, DVD. Neve McIntosh, Steven Mackintosh, Kenneth Cranham, Jamie Bamber, Juliette Caton, Melanie Clark Pullen; *D:* Betsan Morris-Evans; *W:* Donal Hounam; *C:* Julian Court; *M:* Paul Carr. TV

Lady Avenger 1989 (R) A woman is bent on getting revenge on her brother's killers. 90m/C VHS. Peggie Sanders, Michelle (McClellan) Bauer, Daniel Hirsch; *D:* David DeCoteau; *C:* Thomas Callaway.

Lady Be Good 1941 Adapted from the 1924 Gershwin Broadway hit, the plot's been revamped, much to the critics' distaste ("Variety" called it "molasses paced"). Sothern and Young play a tunesmith duo who excel at musical harmony and marital strife. Applauded for its music (the critics loved Hammerstein's and the Gershwins' tunes), the show's Academy Award-winning song was, ironically, written by Jerome Kern. And if that's not enough, levity man Skelton and hoofer Powell are thrown in for good measure. ♫The Last Time I Saw Paris; So Am I; Oh Lady Be Good; Fascinating Rhythm; Hang On To Me; You'll Never Know; You're Words, My Music; Saudades. 111m/B VHS. Eleanor Powell, Ann Sothern, Robert Young, Lionel Barrymore, John Carroll, Red Skelton, Dan Dailey, Virginia O'Brien, Tom Conway, Phil Silvers, Doris Day; *D:* Norman Z. McLeod; *C:* George J. Folsey; *M:* Oscar Hammerstein, Ira Gershwin, Jerome Kern, George Bassman. Oscars '41: Song ("The Last Time I Saw Paris").

Lady Beware 1987 (R) A psychotic doctor becomes obsessed with a beautiful store-window dresser who specializes in steamy, erotic fantasies. When he wages a campaign of terror against her, she realizes that she must stop him before he kills her. 108m/C VHS. Diane Lane, Michael Woods, Cotter Smith, Viveca Lindfors, Tyra Ferrell, Peter Nevargic, Edward Penn; *D:* Karen Arthur; *W:* Charles Zev Cohen.

Lady By Choice 1934 Lombard stars as a beautiful young fan dancer who is arrested for a lewd public performance. Taking the advice of her press agent, she hires an old bag lady to pose as her mother on Mother's Day. Robson portrays her "mother" and comes to think of Lombard as her own daughter. Robson encourages Lombard to give up fan dancing and to strive for greater things in life. She also pushes her into romance with a wealthy young man (Pryor). Robson is excellent in her role as "mother" and Lombard shows great comic talent in this charming film. 78m/C VHS. Carole Lombard, May Robson, Roger Pryor, Walter Connolly, Raymond Walburn, James Burke; *D:* David Burton; *W:* Jo Swerling.

Lady Caroline Lamb 1973 Lady Caroline is a passionate young lady in 19th-century England, who, although the wife of a member of Parliament, has an affair with Lord Byron and brings about her own downfall. Costume drama that never quite goes anywhere. 123m/C GB IT Sarah Miles, Richard Chamberlain, Jon Finch, Laurence Olivier, John Mills, Ralph Richardson; *D:* Robert Bolt; *W:* Robert Bolt; *C:* Oswald Morris; *M:* Richard Rodney Bennett.

Lady Chatterley 1992 Oh my, Russell takes his provocative ways to D.H. Lawrence's scandalous novel about the adulterous affair between aristocratic Lady Connie Chatterley (Richardson) and her husband's gamekeeper, Oliver Mellors (Bean). Also includes material taken from two early drafts of the book "The First Lady Chatterley" and "John Thomas and Lady Jane." 210m/C VHS, DVD. GB Joely Richardson, Sean Bean; James Wilby, Shirley Anne Field, Roger Hammond; *D:* Ken Russell; *W:* Ken Russell; *C:* Robin Vidgeon; *M:* Jean-Claude Petit. TV

Lady Chatterley 2006 Lady Chatterley (Hinds) spends her days collecting flowers after her husband (Giradot) is paralyzed in World War I. She encounters gamekeeper Parkin (Coullo'ch) and the two begin an affair that brings about her sexual awakening. Stunningly shot, and director Ferran manages to maintain a high level of eroticism and character development. French adaptation of the second version of the D.H. Lawrence novel. 168m/C DVD. BE FR Marina Hands, Hippolyte Girardot, Jean-Louis Coullo'ch, Helene Alexandridis; *D:* Pascal Ferran; *W:* Roger Bohbot, Pierre Trividic, Pascal Ferran; *C:* Julien Hirsch; *M:* Beatrice Thiriet.

Lady Chatterley's Lover 1955 *L'Amant de Lady Chatterley* 1955 Englishwoman has bad luck to have husband shot up during WWI and sent home paralyzed. In her quest for sexual fulfillment, she takes a new lover, the estate's earthy gamekeeper. Limp adaptation of D.H. Lawrence's novel. In French with English subtitles. 102m/B VHS. FR Danielle Darrieux, Erno Crisa, Leo Genn; *D:* Marc Allegret.

Lady Chatterley's Lover 1981 (R) Remake of the 1955 film version of D.H. Lawrence's classic novel of an English lady who has an affair with the gamekeeper of her husband's estate. Basically soft-focus soft porn. 107m/C VHS, DVD. GB FR Sylvia Kristel, Nicholas Clay, Shane Briant; *D:* Just Jaeckin; *C:* Robert Fraisse.

Lady Cocoa 1975 (R) Routine story of a young woman who gets released from jail for 24 hours and sets out for Las Vegas to find the man who framed her. 93m/C VHS, DVD. Lola Falana, Joe "Mean Joe" Greene, Gene Washington, Alex Dreier; *D:* Matt Cimber.

The Lady Confesses 1945 Average mystery that involves Hughes trying to clear her boyfriend of murder. Independently produced. "Leave it to Beaver" fans will want to watch for "Ward Cleaver" Beaumont. 66m/B VHS, DVD. Mary Beth Hughes, Hugh Beaumont, Edmund MacDonald, Claudia Drake, Emmett Vogan, Barbara Slater, Edward Howard, Dewey Robinson, Carol Andrews; *D:* Sam Newfield; *W:* Helen Martin, Irwin H. Franklyn; *C:* Jack Greenhalgh; *M:* Lee Zahler.

Lady Dragon 1992 (R) A woman and her husband are viciously attacked and only she survives. Found by an old man, she learns a number of martial arts tricks and goes out to get her revenge. 89m/C VHS, DVD. Cynthia Rothrock, Billy Drago, Sam Jones, Greg Stuart, Bella Esperance, George Rudy, Adisoerya Abdi; *D:* David Worth; *W:* Clifford Mohr; *C:* David Worth; *M:* Jim West.

Lady Dragon 2 1993 (R) Martial arts queen Rothrock returns in another saga of kickboxing vengeance. Susan Morgan seeks revenge on the three killers who terrorized her family. When she unleashes the power of the dragon they don't stand a chance. 92m/C VHS. Cynthia Rothrock, Nicholas Clay, Bella Esperance; *D:* David Worth; *C:* David Worth; *M:* Jim West.

The Lady Eve 1941 Father/daughter (Coburn, Stanwyck) con artists, out to trip up wealthy beer tycoon Charles Pike (Fonda), instead find themselves tripped up when Jean falls in love with the mark. Ridiculous situations, but Sturges manages to keep them believable and funny. With a train scene that's every man's nightmare. Perhaps the best Sturges ever. Based on the story "The Faithful Heart" by Monckton Hoffe. Later remade as "The Birds and the Bees." 93m/B VHS, DVD. Barbara Stanwyck, Henry Fonda, Charles Coburn, Eugene Pallette, William Demarest, Eric Blore, Melville Cooper; *D:* Preston Sturges; *W:* Preston Sturges; *C:* Victor Milner. Natl. Film Reg. '94.

Lady for a Day 1933 Delightful telling of the Damon Runyon story, "Madame La Gimp," about an apple peddler (Robson) down on her luck, who is transformed into a lady by a criminal with a heart. "Lady By Choice" is the sequel. 96m/B VHS, DVD. May Robson, Warren

Lady for a Night 🎬 **1942** The female owner of a gambling riverboat does her best to break into high society, when murder threatens to spoil her plans. Cast and costumes burdened by pacing. **88m/B VHS.** John Wayne, Joan Blondell, Ray Middleton, Philip Merivale, Blanche Yurka, Edith Barrett, Leonid Kinskey, Montagu Love; **D:** Leigh Jason.

Lady Frankenstein 🎬½ **1972 (R)** _La Figlia di Frankenstein; The Daughter of Frankenstein; Madame Frankenstein 1972 (R)_ Frankenstein's lovely daughter graduates from medical school and returns home. When she sees what her father's been up to she gets some ideas of her own. Good fun for fans of the genre. **84m/C VHS, DVD.** Rosalba Neri, Mickey Hargitay, Paul Muller, Herbert (Fuchs) Fux, Renate Kasche, Ada Pometti, Lorenzo Terzon, Paul Whiteman; **D:** Mel Welles; **W:** Edward Di Lorenzo; **C:** Riccardo (Pallton) Pallottini.

Lady from Louisiana 🎬 **1942** A lawyer in old New Orleans out to rid the city of corruption falls in love with the daughter of a big-time gambler. Great storm scene. **84m/B VHS.** John Wayne, Ona Munson, Dorothy Dandridge, Ray Middleton, Henry Stephenson, Helen Westley, Jack Pennick; **D:** Bernard Vorhaus.

Lady from Nowhere 🎬 **1936** A woman is the only witness to a gangland rub-out and is subsequently pursued by both the mob and the police. Unfortunately for her, the gangsters catch up with her first. **60m/B VHS.** Mary Astor, Charles Quigley, Thurston Hall, Victor Kilian, Spencer Charters; **D:** Gordon Wiles.

The Lady from Shanghai 🎬🎬½ **1948** An unsuspecting seaman becomes involved in a web of intrigue when a woman hires him to work on her husband's yacht. Hayworth (a one-time Mrs. Orson Welles) in her only role as a villainess, plays a manipulative, sensual schemer. Wonderful and innovative cinematic techniques from Welles, as usual, including a tense scene in a hall of mirrors. Filmed on a yacht belonging to Errol Flynn. **87m/B VHS, DVD.** Orson Welles, Rita Hayworth, Everett Sloane, Glenn Anders, Ted de Corsia, Erskine Sanford, Gus Schilling; **D:** Orson Welles; **W:** Orson Welles; **C:** Charles Lawton Jr.; **M:** Heinz Roemheld.

Lady Godiva 🎬½ **1955** The lovely O'Hara is wasted in the title role as a Saxon noblewoman married to Leofric (Nader). They're trying to stem Norman influence and Godiva vows to ride naked through the streets of Canterbury to prove the Saxon people's loyalty to King Edward (Franz). Cardboard costumer. Clint Eastwood has a bit as a Saxon soldier. **89m/C VHS.** Maureen O'Hara, George Nader, Eduard Franz, Leslie Bradley, Victor McLaglen, Torin Thatcher, Rex Reason; **D:** Arthur Lubin; **W:** Oscar Brodney, Harry Ruskin; **C:** Carl Guthrie.

Lady Godiva Rides 🎬½ **1968** _Lady Godiva Meets Tom Jones 1968_ A bad, campy version of the story of Lady Godiva. Godiva comes to the United States with a bevy of scantily clad maidens and winds up in the Old West. When the town villain threatens to compromise her, Tom Jones comes to the rescue. The film (or course) features Godiva's naked ride on horseback through the town. **88m/C VHS, DVD.** Marsha Jordan, Forman Shane, Deborah Downey, Elizabeth Knowles, James E. Myers, Jennie Jackson, Liz Renay, Vincent Barbi; **D:** A.C. (Stephen Apostolof) Stephen; **W:** A.C. (Stephen Apostolof) Stephen; **C:** R.C. Ruben; **M:** Jay Colonna, Robert E. Lee.

Lady Grey 🎬 **1982** A poor farmer's daughter rises to the top of the country music charts, but at a price. **111m/C VHS.** Ginger Alden, David Allan Coe; **D:** Worth Keeter.

Lady Ice 🎬 **1973 (PG)** Sutherland, as an insurance investigator on the trail of jewel thieves, follows them to Miami Beach and the Bahamas. After stealing a diamond he enters into partnership with a crook's daughter. Worth seeing for the cast. **93m/C VHS, DVD.** Donald Sutherland, Jennifer O'Neill, Robert Duvall, Eric (Hans Gudegast) Braeden; **D:** Tom Gries; **W:** Alan R. Trustman; **M:** Perry Botkin.

Lady in a Cage 🎬🎬 **1964** A wealthy widow is trapped in her home elevator during a power failure and becomes desperate when hoodlums break in. Shocking violence ahead of its time probably plays better than when first released. Young Caan is a standout among the star-studded cast. **95m/B VHS, DVD.** Olivia de Havilland, Ann Sothern, James Caan, Jennifer Billingsley, Jeff Corey, Scatman Crothers, Rafael Campos; **D:** Walter Grauman; **W:** Luther Davis.

Lady in Cement 🎬½ **1968 (R)** The second Tony Rome mystery, in which the seedy Miami dick finds a corpse with cement shoes while swimming. **93m/C VHS, DVD.** Frank Sinatra, Raquel Welch, Richard Conte, Martin Gabel, Lainie Kazan, Pat Henry, Steve Peck, Joe E. Lewis, Dan Blocker; **D:** Gordon Douglas; **C:** Joseph Biroc.

The Lady in Question 🎬🎬 **1999** Sequel to "Murder in a Small Town" finds Broadway director Larry "Gesh" Carter (Wilder) pursuing his amateur gumshoe sideline once again. This time it's the poisoning death of his wealthy friend, Emma Sachs (Bloom). And there are lots of suspects. Everyone seems to be enjoying themselves in this stylish period mystery, especially Wilder. **100m/C VHS, DVD.** Gene Wilder, Mike Starr, Cherry Jones, Clare Bloom, Barbara Sukowa, John Benjamin Hickey, Michael Cumpsty, Dixie Seatle, Kerry McPherson; **D:** Joyce Chopra; **W:** Gilbert Pearlman; **C:** Bruce Surtees; **M:** John Morris; **C:** C.A.B.L.E.

The Lady in Question 🎬½ **It Happened in Paris 1940** A Parisian shopkeeper, played by Arleme, sits on a jury that finds Hayworth of murder. His interest doesn't end with the trial, however, and comes involved. Fun to see Hayworth and Ford in an early, pre-"Gilda" dramatic French release. **81m/B VHS.** Rita Hayworth, Glenn Ford, Brian Aherne, Irene Rich, Lloyd Corrigan, George Coulouris, Evelyn Keyes, Curt Bois, Edward Norris; **D:** Charles Vidor; **W:** Ben Barzman.

Lady in Distress 🎬🎬½ **1940** _A Window in London 1939_ A British drama about an unhappily married man who witnesses an apparent murder. He discovers, however, it was actually the prank of an illusionist and his flirtatious wife. He soon finds himself becoming increasingly involved with their lives. **71m/B VHS.** Sally Gray; **D:** Herbert Mason.

Lady in Red 🎬🎬½ _Guns, Sin and Bathtub Gin 1979_ A story of America in the '30s, and the progress through the underworld of the woman who was Dillinger's last lover. **90m/C VHS, DVD.** Pamela Sue Martin, Louse Fletcher, Robert Conrad, Christopher Lloyd, Dick Miller, Laurie Heineman, Glenn Withrow, Rod Gist, Mary Woronov; **D:** Lewis Teague; **W:** John Sayles; **C:** Daniel Lacambre; **M:** James Horner.

Lady in the Death House 🎬 **1944** A framed woman is set to walk the last mile, as a scientist struggles to find the real killer in time. **57m/B VHS.** Jean Parker, Lionel Atwill, Marcia Mae Jones; **D:** Steve Sekely; **W:** Harry Hoyt; **C:** Gus Peterson; **M:** Jan Gray.

Lady in the Lake 🎬🎬 **1946** Why is it everyone wants to get artsy with pulp fiction? Actor Montgomery directs himself in this Philip Marlowe go-round, using a subjective camera style (c imitate Chandler's first-person narrative (that means she the only time we get to see Marlowe/Montgomery's mug is in a mirror. That pretty well says it all). Having decided to give up eyeing privately, Marlowe turns tc the pen to tell the tangled tale of a detective who was hired to find the wicked wife of a paying client. Some find the direction clever. Others consider MGM chief Louis B. Mayer, who made sure this was Montgomery's last project with MGM, to be a wise man. **103m/B VHS.** Robert Montgomery, Lloyd Nolan, Audrey Totter, Tom Tully, Leon Ames, Jayne Meadows; **D:** Robert Montgomery; **C:** Paul Vogel.

Lady in the Water 🎬🎬 **2006 (PG-13)** Another Shyamalan vehicle full of darkness, mysterious creatures that go bump in the night, and himself (literally this time) in the apartment pool after hours. He tries to rescue the nymph (or "narf" in Shyamalan's unoriginal world), the apartment's residents, and himself from a variety of evil forces, only some of which are actually shown. More of the same heavy-handed symbolism and convoluted storyline that passed 'or plot twists in his earlier work. Shyamalan wrote, directed, and, as always, gave himself a role in this fairy tale, which he states is based on a real-time story he made up for his daughters. **106m/C DVD, Blu-ray Disc, HD DVD, US Bryce Dallas Howard, Paul Giamatti, Jeffrey Wright, Bob Balaban, Freddy Rodriguez, Sarita Choudhury, Jared Harris, Bill Irwin, Mary Beth Hurt, Tovah Feldshuh, M. Night Shyamalan, Cindy Cheung, Noah Gray-Cabey; D:** M. Night Shyamalan; **W:** M. Night Shyamalan; **C:** Christopher Doyle; **M:** James Newton Howard; **Narr:** David Ogden Stiers. Raspberries '06: Worst Director (Shyamalan), Worst Support. Actor (Shyamalan).

Lady in Waiting 🎬🎬 **1994 (R)** Detective Jimmy Scavetti (Nouri) is hunting down a serial killer preying on call girls when he meets the seductive Lori (Whirry). Then he discovers his ex-wife's new hubby was the lawyer 'or each of the victims—only three turns up dead and Jimmy becomes a suspect. Also available in an unrated version. **85m/C VHS, Michael Nouri, Shannon Whirry, William Devane, Karen Kopins, Crystal Chappell, Robert Costanzo, Meg Foster, Charles Grant; D:** Fred Gallo.

The Lady in White 🎬🎬 **1988 (PG-13)** Small-town ghost story about murder and revenge. When young Haas is locked in school one night, he's visited by the ghost of a little girl who wants his help in discovering who murdered her. Well-developed characters, interesting style, and suspenseful plot make for a sometimes scary but overall exceptional film. **92m/C VHS, DVD.** Lukas Haas, Len Cariou, Alex Rocco, Katherine Helmond, Jason Presson, Renata Vanni, Angelo Bertolini, Jared Rushton, Joelle Jacob; **D:** Frank Laloggia; **W:** Frank Laloggia; **C:** Russell Carpenter; **M:** Frank Laloggia.

The Lady Is Willing 🎬🎬½ **1942** Dietrich is a Broadway star who longs for a baby and when an abandoned infant comes her way she decides to keep the child. Only she hasn't a clue about any of the practical aspects. Lucky for her MacMurray is a friendly pediatrician who gives her some advice. Dietrich finds out she can't adopt as a single parent and persuades MacMurray to marry her, in name only, but since this is a romantic comedy the two eventually fall in love. **91m/B VHS.** Marlene Dietrich, Fred MacMurray, Aline MacMahon, Stanley Ridges, Arline Judge, Roger Clark, Ruth Ford, Sterling Holloway, Harvey Stephens, Harry Shannon, Elisabeth Risdon, Charles Halton; **D:** Mitchell Leisen; **W:** James Edward Grant, Albert McCleery.

Lady Jane 🎬🎬½ **1985 (PG-13)** An accurate account of the life of 15-year-old Lady Jane Grey, who secured the throne of England for nine days in 1553 as a result of political maneuvering by noblemen and the Church of England. A wonderful film even for non-history buffs. Carter's first film. **140m/C VHS, DVD, GB Helena Bonham-Carter, Cary Elwes, Sara Kestelman, Michael Hordern, Joss Ackland, Richard Johnson, Patrick Stewart; D:** Trevor Nunn.

Lady Jayne Killer 🎬🎬 _Betrayal 2003 (R)_ Jayne Ferre (Du Page) is an L.A. hitwoman for mobster Frank Bianchi (Mandylor) from whom she has just stolen a million bucks. So she needs revenge against the mob. **100m/** ey to get to Texas. When Jayne and Emily meet, she offers to foot the bill if she can hitch a ride. Then Kerry discovers the cash, steals it from Jayne, and heads back to L.A. Naturally, Jayne and Emily are soon behind him. And then FBI agent Alex Tyler (Remar) comes into the picture. **90m/C VHS, DVD.** Julie Du Page, Erika Eleniak, Jeremy Lelliott, James Remar, Louis Mandylor, Adam Baldwin, Demian Chepa, Don Swayze, Peter Dobson; **D:** Mark L. Lester; **W:** C. Courtney Joyner; **C:** Joao Fernandes.

Lady Killer 🎬🎬 **1933** Racy, pre-Code comedy with mobster Cagney hiding out in Hollywood. He gets discovered and becomes a big star, but his old gang turns up to blackmail him. Lots of movie "in" jokes and Clark (or "Public Enemy" fame) is great as a wisecracking moll. Based on the story "The Finger Man" by Rosalind Keating Shaffer. **74m/B VHS.** James Cagney, Mae Clarke, Leslie Fenton, Margaret Lindsay, Henry O'Neill, Raymond Hatton, George Chandler; **D:** Roy Del Ruth; **M:** Ben Markson, Lillie Hayward. **VIDEO**

Lady Killer 🎬🎬 **1997 (R)** A serial killer called the PiggyBack Murderer is terrorizing a college campus. Police Lt. Jack Lasky (Gazzara) is particularly anxious since his daughter Jennifer (Allman) is a student at the school. When her new boyfriend, aspiring actor Richard Darling (McArthur), keeps turning up at the murder scenes, guess who becomes dad's prime suspect. **90m/C VHS.** Ben Gazzara, Alex McArthur, Terri Treas, Renée Allman; **D:** Peter Ustinov; **W:** Peter Ustinov; **C:** Christopher Baffa.

Lady L 🎬½ **1965** Silly turn-of-the-century farce about a sexy laundress (Loren), married to a French anarchist (Newman), who also marries the aristocratic Paris and London backgrounds couldn't overcome the odd casting and weak script. Adapted from the novel by Romain Gary. **107m/C VHS, FR IT** Sophia Loren, Paul Newman, David Niven, Cecil Parker, Claude Dauphin, Marcel Dalio, Philippe Noiret, Michie Piccoli, Daniel Emilfork, Eugene Deckers; **Cameos:** Peter Ustinov; **D:** Peter Ustinov; **W:** Peter Ustinov.

Lady Mobster 🎬 **1988 (PG-13)** _Lease Lady 1943_ Strangled with her own G-String by Gypsy Rose Lee. **91m/B VHS, DVD.** Barbara Stanwyck, Michael O'Shea, Janis Carter, Pinky Lee; **D:** William A. Wellman.

Lady of Burlesque 🎬🎬½ _Strip-tease Lady 1943_ Burlesque cancer is found dead, strangled with her own G-String by Gypsy Rose Lee. **91m/B VHS, DVD.** Barbara Stanwyck, Michael O'Shea, Janis Carter, Pinky Lee; **D:** William A. Wellman.

Lady of the Evening 🎬🎬 _Gun Moll; Get Rita, Oopsie Poopsie; La Gangster del Papa 1975 (R)_ A prostitute and a crook team up to seek revenge against the mob. **110m/ C VHS, IT** Sophia Loren, Marcello Mastroianni, Pierre Brice, Dalila d Lazzaro, Aldo Maccione; **D:** Giorgio Capitani; **W:** Ernesto Gastaldi; **C:** Alberto Spagnoli; **M:** Piero Umiliani.

Lady of the House 🎬🎬 **1978** A true story about a madame who rose from true story about a madame who rose from operator of a brothel to become a political force in San Francisco. **100m/C VHS.** Dyan Cannon, Susan Tyrell, Colleen Camp, Armand Assante; **D:** Ralph Nelson.

Lady of the Lake 🎬🎬 **1928** Rare silent adventure film in which an exiled girl saves the king from outlaws in 1553. Orchestra score. **47m/B VHS, DVD, GB Percy Marmont, Benita Hume, Haddon Mason, Lawson Butt; D:** James A. FitzPatrick.

Lady on a Train 🎬🎬 **1945** Traveling at Christmas, wealthy young Nicky Collins (Durbin) thinks she sees a murder from her train window but when she arrives in New York she can't get anyone to believe her. But not willing to give up, Nicky turns to Wayne Morgan (Bruce), a mystery writer for help. Recognizing the

---

victim from a newspaper photo, Nicky checks out his family and gets mistaken for a nightclub singer (so Durbin can vamp a torch song). Lots of comedy amidst the mystery and romance, and some surprizes as well. Based on a story by Leslie Charteris. ♪Gimme a Little Kiss, Will You, Huh?; Night and Day; Silent Night. **95m/C VHS, DVD.** Deanna Durbin, David Bruce, Ralph Bellamy, Dan Duryea, Edward Everett Horton, Allen Jenkins, Elizabeth Patterson, William Frawley, Jacqueline DeWit, George Coulouris; **D:** Charles David; **W:** Robert O'Brien, Edmund Beloin; **C:** Elwood "Woody" Bredell; **M:** Miklos Rozsa.

Lady on the Bus ♪♪ 1978 (R) Sexually frustrated newlywed bride rides the city buses looking for men to satisfy her. This bothers her husband. Shot in Rio de Janeiro. In Portuguese with English subtitles. **102m/C VHS.** BR Sonia Braga; **D:** Neville D'Almeida.

The Lady Refuses ♪♪ 1931 A stuffy Victorian father is disappointed in his wastrel son and decides a poor but honest young woman could be the making of him. Problems arise when the girl falls for the father instead. **70m/B VHS, DVD.** Betty Compson, John Darrow, Margaret Livingston, Gilbert Emery, Ivan Lebedeff, Edgar Norton, Daphne Pollard, Halliwell Hobbes; **D:** George Archainbaud; **W:** Wallace Smith; **C:** Leo Tover.

The Lady Says No ♪♪ 1951 A photographer must photograph an attractive author who has written a book uncomplimentary toward the male sex. **80m/B VHS, DVD.** Joan Caulfield, David Niven, James Robertson Justice, Frances Bavier, Henry Jones, Jeff York; **D:** Frank Ross.

Lady Scarface ♪♪ 1941 Murderous mobster queen breaks the law, bats men around, and takes the cops on a merry chase. Cheap, fast-paced action. **66m/B VHS.** Mildred Coles, Dennis O'Keefe, Frances Neal, Judith Anderson, Eric Blore, Charles Halton; **D:** Frank Woodruff.

Lady Sings the Blues ♪♪♪½ 1972 (R) Jazz artist Billie Holiday's life becomes a musical drama depicting her struggle against racism and drug addiction in her pursuit of fame and romance. What could be a typical price-of-fame story is saved by Ross' inspired performance as the tragic singer. ♪My Man; Strange Fruit; God Bless the Child; Don't Explain; T'Ain't Nobody's Business If I Do; Lady Sings the Blues; All Of Me; The Man I Love; Our Love Is Here to Stay. **144m/C VHS, DVD.** Diana Ross, Billy Dee Williams, Richard Pryor, James Callahan, Paul Hampton, Sid Melton; **D:** Sidney J. Furie; **C:** John A. Alonzo.

Lady Street Fighter ♪ 1986 A well-armed female combat fighter battles an organization of assassins to avenge her sister's murder. **73m/C VHS.** Renee Harmon, Joel McCrea Jr.; **D:** James Bryan; **C:** Max Reed.

Lady Takes a Chance ♪♪♪ 1943 A romantic comedy about a New York working girl with matrimonial ideas and a wide-open spaces. Fine fun on the range. **86m/B VHS, DVD.** John Wayne, Jean Arthur, Phil Silvers, Charles Winninger; **D:** William A. Seiter.

Lady Terminator ♪½ 1989 (R) A student on an anthropology expedition digs up more than she bargained for when she is possessed by an evil spirit and goes on a rampage. **83m/C VHS, DVD.** Barbara Constable, Christopher J. Hart, Joseph McGlynn, Claudia Rademaker; **D:** Jalil Jackson.

The Lady Vanishes ♪♪♪♪ 1938 Kindly old lady, Miss Froy (Witty) seemingly disappears from a fast-moving train bound for England. But when her young friend Iris (Lockwood) investigates, she finds no one appears to believe her and she has a spiraling mystery to solve. Of course, Irish has music scholar Gilbert (Redgrave) eager to help her out. Hitchcock's first real winner, a smarmy, witdrenched British mystery that precipitated his move to Hollywood. Along with "39 Steps," considered the novel "The Wheel Spins," by Ethel Lina White. Remade in 1979. **99m/B VHS, DVD.** GB Margaret Lockwood, Paul Lukas, Michael Redgrave, May Whitty, Googie Withers, Basil Radford, Naunton Wayne, Cecil Parker, Linden Travers, Catherine Lacey, Alfred Hitchcock; **D:** Alfred Hitchcock; **W:** Sidney Gilliat, Frank Launder; **C:** Jack Cox; **M:** Louis Levy. N.Y. Film Critics '38: Director. (Hitchcock).

The Lady Vanishes ♪♪ 1979 In this reworking of the '38 Alfred Hitchcock film, a woman on a Swiss bound train awakens from a nap to find that the elderly woman seated next to her has kidnapped. Falls short of the original movie due to the "screwball" nature of the main characters, Gould and Shepherd. Based on Ethel Lina White's novel "The Wheel Spins." **95m/C VHS, DVD.** GB Elliott Gould, Cybill Shepherd, Angela Lansbury, Herbert Lom; **D:** Anthony Page; **W:** George Axelrod.

Lady Vengeance ♪½ 2005 (R) Violent and bloody revenge saga. Geum-ja (Lee) spent 13 years in prison after being forced to help her former teacher, Mr Baek (Choi), abduct and murder a young boy and was then being betrayed by him. (Baek kidnapped her own baby as leverage.) Now out of prison, Geum-ja is also out for a grisly payback. Korean with subtitles. **112m/C DVD.** KN Min-Sik Choi, Yeong-ae Lee; **D:** Chan-wook Park; **W:** Chan-wook Park, Seo-gyeong Jeong; **C:** Jeong-hun Jeong; **M:** Seung-hyun Choi.

Lady Windermere's Fan ♪♪½ 1925 The silent, Lubitsch adaptation of the Oscar Wilde tale concerning an upper-class couple's marriage being almost destroyed by suspected adultery. **66m/B VHS, DVD.** Ronald Colman, May McAvoy, Bert Lytell; **D:** Ernst Lubitsch. Natl. Film Reg. '02.

The Lady with the Dog ♪♪♪ 1959 A bittersweet love story based on the Anton Chekhov story, about two married Russians who meet by chance in a park, fall in love, and realize they are fated to a haphazard, clandestine affair. In Russian with English titles. **86m/B VHS, DVD.** RU Iya Savvina, Alexei Batalov, Ala Chostakova, N. Alisova; **D:** Yosif Heifitz.

The Lady Without Camelias ♪♪♪½ 1953 La Signora Senza Camelie A young woman is discovered by a film producer who casts her in a successful movie and eventually marries her. Convinced that she can sustain a career as a serious actress, the producer is dismayed by the job offers that come her way, usually of a sexually exploitive nature. What follows is a tragic decline for both. **106m/B VHS.** IT Lucia Bose, Gino Cervi, Andrea Checchi, Ivan Desny, Alain Cuny; **D:** Michelangelo Antonioni; **W:** Michelangelo Antonioni, Suso Cecchi D'Amico; **C:** Enzo Serafin; **M:** Giovanni Fusco.

Ladybird, Ladybird ♪♪♪ 1993 (R) Loach's emotionally bruising look at working-class life and family in the '90s. Maggie (Rock) is a tough unmarried mother of four who's been battered by her lovers and has come under the over-watchful eye of Britain's social services. She meets Jorge (Vega), a gentle Paraguayan, and just when things are looking up, Jorge gets immigration heat, Maggie's insecurities surface, and her baby daughter is taken into care by child welfare. Rock has a no-nonsense manner and acerbic wit that precludes any hand-wringing for her character, even as you hope she'll win out over circumstance. Based on a true story. **102m/C VHS.** GB Crissy Rock, Vladimir Vega, Ray Winstone, Sandie Lavelle, Mauricio Venegas, Clare Perkins, Jason Stracey, Luke Brown, Lily Farrell; **D:** Ken Loach; **W:** Rona Munro; **C:** Barry Ackroyd; **M:** George Fenton. Berlin Intl. Film Fest. '94: Actress (Rock).

Ladybugs ♪½ 1992 (PG-13) Hangdog salesman Dangerfield would like to move up the corporate ladder, but must first turn the company-sponsored girl's soccer team into winners. Routine Dangerfield vehicle exploits nearly everything for laughs, including dressing an athletic boy as a girl so he can play on the team. Obvious fluff. **91m/C VHS, DVD.** Rodney Dangerfield, Jackee, Jonathan Brandis, Ilene Graff, Vinessa Shaw, Tom Parks, Jeanetta Arnette, Nancy Parsons, Blake Clark, Tommy Lasorda; **D:** Sidney J. Furie; **W:** Curtis Burch; **C:** Dan Burstall; **M:** Richard Gibbs.

Ladyhawke ♪♪½ 1985 (PG-13) In medieval times, a youthful pickpocket befriends a strange knight who is on a mysterious quest. This unlikely duo, accompanied by a watchful hawk, are enveloped in a magical adventure. **121m/C VHS, DVD.** Matthew Broderick, Rutger Hauer, Michelle Pfeiffer, John Wood, Leo McKern, Alfred Molina, Ken Hutchison; **D:** Richard Donner; **W:** Edward Khmara, Michael Thomas, Tom Mankiewicz; **C:** Vittorio Storaro; **M:** Andrew Powell.

Ladykiller ♪♪ 1992 (R) Rogers stars as a burned-out cop who goes to a dating service to find a man who'll give her the attention she craves. When she meets wealthy professional Shea she thinks he's the one but her cop's curiosity about her lover's past may cost her her life. **92m/C VHS.** Mimi Rogers, John Shea, Alice Krige, Tom Irwin; **D:** Michael Scott; **W:** Shelley Evans.

The Ladykillers ♪♪♪½ 1955 The Lady Killers 1955 A gang of bumbling bank robbers is foiled by a little old lady. Hilarious antics follow, especially on the part of Guinness, who plays the slightly demented-looking leader of the gang. **87m/C VHS, DVD.** GB Alec Guinness, Cecil Parker, Katie Johnson, Herbert Lom, Peter Sellers, Danny Green, Jack Warner, Kenneth Connor, Edie Martin, Jack Melford; **D:** Alexander MacKendrick; **W:** William Rose; **C:** Otto Heller; **M:** Tristram Cary. British Acad. '55: Actress (Johnson), Screenplay.

Ladykillers ♪♪ 1988 At the glitzy L.A. club Ladykillers, men strip as the women cheer. At the climax of the performance, one of the dancers is brutally murdered, live on stage. In this decadent world of glitter and sex, the women are the hunters and the men are the reward. **97m/C VHS.** Marilu Henner, Susan Blakely, Lesley-Anne Down, Thomas Calabro; **D:** Robert Lewis; **W:** Greg Dinallo.

The Ladykillers ♪♪½ 2004 (R) It takes an actor with a lot of gumption to take on a classic role that was played by the classiest of thespians, Alec Guinness, but Hanks (as G.H. Dorr, Ph.D.) takes to the task with gusto and mostly positive results. This quirky remake of the 1955 British offering, the setting shifts to Mississippi, where the robbers attempt to burrow from little old lady Mrs. Munson's (Hall) basement to the nearby casino's money room. While Hall is superb and Hanks is often dynamic as he plows through ornate speeches with a wicked laugh, it will depend on your tolerance for flowery language and a mannered Southern drawl whether you think it's melodious or annoying. Overall enjoyable, if uneven effort by the Coen brothers falls a bit short of the original. **104m/C DVD.** US Tom Hanks, Irma P. Hall, Marlon Wayans, J.K. Simmons, Tzi Ma, Ryan Hurst, Diane Delano, George Wallace, John McConnell, Stephen (Steve) Root, Jason Weaver, Greg Grunberg, Blake Clark, Jeremy Suarez; **D:** Ethan Coen, Joel Coen; **W:** Ethan Coen, Joel Coen; **C:** Roger Deakins; **M:** Carter Burwell.

The Lady's Not for Burning ♪♪½ 1987 Romantic comedy, set in a medieval English village, finds ex-soldier Thomas Mendip (Branagh) invading the home of querulous Mayor Hebble Tyson (Hepton), demanding to be hanged. He says he's murdered the local rag and bone merchant but the townspeople insist Jennet Jourdemayne (Lunghi), who's seeking refuge at the mayor's, has turned him into a dog. They demand she be burned as a witch (hence the title, since Thomas, unwillingly but strongly, objects to this action). Adapted by Fry from his play; made for TV. **90m/C VHS.** Kenneth Branagh, Cherie Lunghi, Bernard Hepton, Tim Watson, Susannah Harker, Angela Thorne, Shaun Scott; **D:** Julian Amyes; **W:** Christopher Fry. TV

Lafayette Escadrille ♪♪ 1958 Hell Bent for Glory 1958 Action and romance in WWI via the famed flying unit manned by American volunteers. Hunter is banal in the lead role as his romance with a reformed prostitute (Choreau). Director Wellman actually was a member of the squadron and his son plays him in the film but the director regarded the film as a failure because of studio interference. **92m/B VHS.** Tab Hunter, Etchika Choureau, William Wellman Jr., Joel McCrea, Dennis Devine, Marcel Dalio, David Janssen, Paul Fix, Will Hutchins, Clint Eastwood, Tom Watson; **D:** William A. Wellman; **W:** A.S. Fleischman; **C:** William Clothier; **M:** Leonard Rosenman.

Lagaan: Once upon a Time in India ♪♪ 2001 (PG) Bollywood musical set in 1893, in the drought-stricken village of Champaner. The lagaan is a tax levied by the occupying British on the local rajahs, which the village can't pay. The region's nasty British commander, Captain Russell (Blackthorne), states that if the villagers can beat his soldiers at cricket, the lagaan will be cancelled for three years; if they lose, the lagaan will be tripled. Heroic Bhuvan (Khan) persuades the locals that even if they don't understand the game, they can certainly show those arrogant Brits a thing or two! English, Hindi and Bhojpuri with subtitles. **225m/C DVD.** IN Aamir Khan, Gracy Singh, Rachel Shelley, Paul Blackthorne, Suhasini Mulay, Kulbashan Kharbanda, Raghuvir Yadav; **D:** Ashutosh Gowariker; **W:** Ashutosh Gowariker, Kumar Dave, Sanjay Dayma, K.P. Saxena; **C:** Anil Mehta; **M:** A.R. Rahman.

L'Age D'Or ♪♪♪ 1930 Age of Gold; The Golden Age 1930 Bunuel's first full-length film and his masterpiece of sex, repression, and of course, death. A hapless man is prevented from reaching his beloved by middle-class morality, forces of the establishment, the Church, government and every bastion of modern values. Banned for years because of its anti-religious stance. Co-scripted by Dali. A mercilessly savage, surreal satire, the purest expression of Bunuel's wry misanthropy. In French with English subtitles. **62m/B VHS, DVD.** FR Gaston Modot, Lya Lys, Max Ernst, Pierre Prevert, Marie Berthe Ernst, Paul Eluard; **D:** Luis Bunuel; **W:** Salvador Dali, Luis Bunuel; **C:** Albert Duverger.

Laguna Heat ♪♪½ 1987 A tired LA cop investigates a series of murders that are related to an old friend of his father's. Based on a novel by T. Jefferson Parker. **110m/C VHS.** Harry Hamlin, Jason Robards Jr., Catherine Hicks, Rip Torn, Anne Francis; **D:** Simon Langton. TV

The Lair of the White Worm ♪♪♪ 1988 (R) Scottish archaeologist uncovers a strange skull, and then a bizarre religion to go with it, and then a very big worm. An unusual look at the effects of Christianity and paganism on each other, colored with sexual innuendo and, of course, giant worms. A cross between a morality play and a horror film. Adapted from Bram Stoker's last writings, done while he was going mad from Bright's disease. Everything you'd expect from Russell. **93m/C VHS, DVD.** GB Amanda Donohoe, Sammi Davis, Catherine Oxenberg, Hugh Grant, Peter Capaldi, Stratford Johns, Paul Brooke, Christopher Gable; **D:** Ken Russell; **W:** Ken Russell; **C:** Dick Bush; **M:** Stanislas Syrewicz.

Lake Consequence ♪♪ 1992 (R) Severance plays a suburban housewife who accidentally gets locked in the camper of the tree-trimmer stud (Zane) she's been eyeing while he's been working in her neighborhood. Next thing she knows they wind up at a distant lake where the bored housewife is more than willing to give into her growing sexual fantasies. An unrated version at 90 minutes is also available. **85m/C VHS, DVD.** Joan Severance, Billy Zane, May Karasun; **D:** Rafael Eisenman; **W:** Zalman King, Melanie Finn, Henry Cobbold; **M:** George S. Clinton.

The Lake House ♪♪½ 2006 (PG) Confusing time-travel romance that appeals because of its leads, who haven't worked together since 1994's "Speed." Chicago doctor Kate (Bullock) leaves a note for the next renter of her glass box lakeside house. Only architect Alex (Reeves) insists that no one has lived in the rundown property for years before him. Hmmm, somehow the attractive twosome communicates with each other despite a two-year time gap. They fall in love, but trying to meet face-to-face is a complicated business. A remake of the 2000 South Korean film "Siworae." **108m/C DVD, Blu-ray Disc, HD DVD.** US Keanu Reeves, Sandra Bullock, Shohreh Aghdashloo, Dylan Walsh, Christopher Plummer, Ebon Moss-Bachrach, Willeke Van Ammelrooy, Lynn Collins; **D:** Alejandro Agresti; **W:** David Auburn; **C:** Alar Kivilo; **M:** Rachel Portman.

Lake Placid 🐾½ 1999 (R) Hotshot TV producer David E. Kelley lures some acting careers into deadly peril in this lame comedy-horror ripoff of "Jaws." Paleontologist (Fonda) is sent to examine a tooth after a grisly death occurs in rural Maine. She discovers that the tooth is prehistoric, but she decides to stick around with game warden Pullman, sheriff Gleeson and ec-centric professor Platt anyway. You know, just in case the crocodile that escaped through a hole in the plot is still hungry (after eating the fatter (and therefore more buttery) cast members. Betty White is the lone bright spot as a foul-mouthed old woman who is rooting for the crocodile. You'll be rooting for it too, but you'll be rooting for it to devour the movie exec who green-lighted this crock. 83m/C VHS, DVD. Bridget Fonda, Bill Pullman, Oliver Platt, Brendan Gleeson, Mariska Hargitay, Meredith Salenger, Betty White, David Lewis; C: Steve Miner; W: David E. Kelley; C: Daryn Okada; M: John Ottman.

Lake Placid 2 woof! 2007 (R) A hunter track three hungry 30-foot prehistoric crocodiles munching on the local populace. Sci-Fi Channel sequel-in-name-only with really bad CGI and possibly worse acting and script. 84m/C VHS, DVD. John Schneider, Sam McMurray, Cloris Leachman, Sarah Lafleur, Chad Collins, Alicia Ziegler; D: David Flores; W: Todd Hurvitz, Howie Miller; C: Lorenzo Senator; M: Nathan Furst. C A B L E

Lakeboat 🐾🐾½ 2000 (R) Longtime Mamet collaborator Mantegna makes his directorial debut adapting one of Mamet's earliest (and most autobiographical) plays. Grad student Dale (Mamet's younger brother Tony) signs on a Great Lakes ore freighter as the cook. Plot consists of Can-turbury Tales-esque storytelling by the crew, along with differing opinion is on what happened to the previous cook, ala "Rashomon." The thrust of the film is Dale's observations and gleanings from the crew, especially Joe (Forster), who once had artistic and educational ambi-tions which he gave up for a regular pay-check. Excellent, understated perfor-mances by all help mask the film's inability to escape its stage limitations and Man-tegna's uneven first-time direction. Dia-logue shows the promise, as well as the themes, realized in Mamet's later work. 98m/C VHS, DVD. Charles Durning, Peter Falk, Robert Forster, J... Johnston, Denis Leary, Jack Wallace, George Wendt, Saul Rubinek, Tony Mamet, Andy Garcia; Cameos: Joe Mantegna; D: Joe Mantegna; W: David Mamet; C: Paul Sarossy; M: Bob Mamet.

Lakota Woman: Siege at Wounded Knee 🐾🐾½ 1994 Au-tobiography of Mary Crow Dog (Bedard) and her coming of age during the Ameri-can Indian Movement's 1973 occupation of Wounded Knee. Tangled loyalties and the battle between Native Americans and U.S. troops make for strong drama. Based on the book by Mary Crow Dog and is remarkable in her film debut. Based on the book by Mary Crow Dog and Richard Erdoes. Filmed on location in South Dakota. 113m/C VHS. Irene Bedard, August Schellenberg, Joseph Runningfox, Floyd "Red Crow" Westerman, Tantoo Cardinal, Michael Horse, Lawrence Bayne, Nancy Parsons; D: Frank Pierson; W: Bill Kerby; C: Toyomichi Kurita; M: Richard Horowitz.

The Lamb 🐾🐾½ 1915 Intent on proving to his sweetheart that he's not the coward people say he is, a guy heads west to engage in various manly activities, including fisticuffs, karate and Indian kid-napping. Fairbanks' debut on film (he was already in an established Broadway star) set the mold for the American leading man: moral, cheerful, physical, and not hard to look at. A popular guy with the public, Fair-banks formed his own film company the following year. Story's based on D.W. Grif-fith's book, "The Man and the Test." 60m/B VHS. Douglas Fairbanks Sr., Seena Owen, Lillian Langdon, Monroe Salisbury, Kate Toncray, Alfred Paget, William E. (W.E.) William A., W.A.) Lowery; D: Christy Cabanne.

Lamb 🐾🐾 1985 Troubled 13-year-old epileptic Owen Kane (Kane) has been dumped by his abusive mother et a Catho-lic-run institutor for wayward boys in Ire-land, run by self-righteous headmaster Brother Benedict (Bannen). Owen be-comes Benedict's scapegoat—much to the dismay of Brother Michael Lamb (Nee-son). When Lamb claims a small family inheritance, he decides to take Owen and head to London, posing as father and son, where they live in increasingly depressed surroundings while Michael tries painfully to make them live in a real family. Based on the novel by Bernard MacLaverty, who also wrote the screenplay. 110m/C VHS, DVD. Liam Neeson, Hugh O'Conor, Ian Bannen, Frances To-melty; D: Colin Gregg; W: Bernard MacLaverty; C: Mike Garfath; M: Van Morrison.

Lambada 🐾 1989 (PG) By day, he's a high school teacher in Beverly Hills; by night, a Latin dirty dancer cum tutor of ghetto teens. The very first of several films based on the short-lived dance craze. Spiro (Di Mazzarelli), who's spent most of his life in prison camps, and stash him in an orphanage for safe keeping. Only when Spiro gets away Gino heads for the coun-tryside to find him and discovers some se-crets about Spiro's past and just how the wily Albanians have been surviving. Italian with subtitles. 116m/C VHS, DVD. IT Enrico Lo Verso, Michele Placido, Carmelo Di Mazzarelli, Piro Milkani; D: Gianni Amelio; W: Gianni Amelio, Andrea Porporati, Alessandro Sermoneta; C: Luca Bigazzi; M: Franco Piersanti.

L'Amour en Herbe 🐾🐾 Budding Love; Tender Love 1977 His parents realize Pascal (Placido) and his younger partner Gino (Lo Verso), head for poverty-stricken Albania in 1991, the first year af-ter the collapse of the Communist dictator-ship. They intend to set up a phony corpo-ration and scam money from government grants but they need an Albanian figure-head. The duo find simple-minded, elderly Spiro (Di Mazzarelli), who's spent most of his life in prison camps, and stash him in an orphanage for safe keeping. Only when Spiro gets away Gino heads for the coun-tryside to find him and discovers some se-crets about Spiro's past and just how the wily Albanians have been surviving. Try-ed. In French with subtitles. 100m/C VHS. FR Fascal Meynier, Guillaine Dubos, Bruno Raffaeli, Michel Galabru, Francoise Prevost, Alix Mahieux; D: Roger Andrieux; W: Roger Andrieux, Jean-Marie Benard; C: Ramon Suarez; M: Maxime Le Forestier.

Lamp at Midnight 🐾🐾½ 1966 Presentation from "George Schaefer's Showcase Theatre" deals with three criti-cal periods in the life of Italian astronomer Galileo Galilei, from his invention of the telescope, through his appearance at the Holy Office of the Inquisition, to the publi-cation of his "Dialogue on the Two Sys-tems of the World." For those in a plane-tary state of mind. 76m/C VHS. Melvyn Doug-las, David Wayne, Michael Hordern, Hurd Hatfield, Kim Hunter; D: George Schaefer. TV

Lan Yu 🐾🐾 2001 Lan Yu (Ye) is a young architecture student, newly arrived in Beijing in 1988. He's introduced to a businessman Hangdong (Jun) and the two become lovers, though Hangdong is chronically unfaithful and they become es-tranged. When Lan Yu participates in the demonstrations in Tiananmen Square, Hangdong goes looking for him and the two resume their affair which continues to be rocky. Based on the anonymous novel "Beijing Story," published only on the In-ternet in 1997 in order to avoid Chinese censorship. Chinese with subtitles. 86m/C VHS, DVD. HK Hu Jun, Liu Ye; D: Stanley Kwan; W: Jimmy Ngai; C: Yang Tao; M: Zhang Yadong.

Lana in Love 🐾🐾 1992 A lonely woman places an ad in the personal sec-tion in hopes of finding her Mr. Right. 9m/C VHS. Daphna Kastner, Clark Gregg; D: Bashar Shbib; W: Bashar Shbib; C: Stepher Reizes; M: Harry Mayronne Jr.

Lancelot of the Lake 🐾🐾 Lan-celot du Lac; The Grail; Le Graal 1974 The Knights of the Round Table return to the court of King Arthur after a long, bloody, and fruitless quest for the Holy Grail. Ri-valries and jealousies debase the heroes as Lancelot struggles with his feelings for

Lamerica 🐾🐾 1995 Two Italian hustlers, Fiore (Placido) and his younger partner Gino (Lo Verso), head for poverty-stricken Albania in 1991, the first year af-ter the collapse of the Communist dictator-ship. They intend to set up a phony corpo-ration and scam money from government grants but they need an Albanian figure-head. The duo find simple-minded, elderly Spiro (Di Mazzarelli), who's spent most of his life in prison camps, and stash him in an orphanage for safe keeping. Only when Spiro gets away Gino heads for the coun-tryside to find him and discovers some se-crets about Spiro's past and just how the wily Albanians have been surviving. Italian with subtitles. 116m/C VHS, DVD. IT Enrico Lo Verso, Michele Placido, Carmelo Di Mazzarelli, Piro Milkani; D: Gianni Amelio; W: Gianni Amelio, Andrea Porporati, Alessandro Sermoneta; C: Luca Bigazzi; M: Franco Piersanti.

The Land Before Time 2: The Great Valley Adventure 🐾🐾½ 1994 (G) Sequel to 1988's animated ad-venture finds dinosaur pals Littlefoot, Cera, Ducky, Petrie, and Spike happily settled in the Great Valley. But their ad-ventures don't stop as they chase two egg-stealing Struthiomimuses and retrieve an egg of unknown origin from the Myste-rious Beyond. 75m/C VHS, DVD. D: Don Bluth; W: Stu Krieger; M: James Horner; V: Pat Hingle, Helen Shaver, Gabriel Damon, Candace Hutson, Burke Barnes, Judith Barsi, Will Ryan.

The Land Before Time 3: The Time of the Great Giving 🐾🐾½ 1995 (G) Littlefoot and his pals try to find a new source of water when the Great Valley experiences a se-vere water shortage. 71m/C VHS, DVD. D: Roy Allen Smith; W: John Loy, Dev Ross, John Ludin; M: Michael Tavera; V: Scott McAfee, Candy Hutson, Heather Hogan, Jeff Glenn Bennett, Ken-neth Mars, John Ingle, Rob Paulsen, Linda Gary.

The Land Before Time 4: Journey Through the Mists 🐾🐾½ 1996 The little dinosaurs travel through the land of the mists in search of a rejuvenation flower that can save the life of Littlefoot's sick grandpa. 74m/C VHS, DVD. D: Roy Allen Smith; W: Dev Ross; M: Michael Tavera; V: Scott McAfee, Candy Hutson, Heather Hogan, Jeff Glenn Bennett, Ken-neth Mars, John Ingle, Rob Paulsen, Linda Gary.

The Land Before Time 5: The Mysterious Island 🐾🐾½ 1997 (G) When a swarm of insects devour all the plants in the Great Valley, the herds are forced to move. But with the adults fighting, Littlefoot and his pals go off on their own. They cross the Big Water to a mysterious island, which just happens to be the home of that old friend, the baby T-Rex, Chomper. And it's up to Chomper to protect his plant-eating friends from the island's meat-eaters, who look on the little band as dinner. 74m/C VHS, DVD. D: Charles Grosvenor; W: John Loy; M: Michael Tavera; V: Jeff Glenn Bennett, Kenneth Mars, John Ingle, Rob Paulsen, Thomas Dekker, Aria Noelle Curzon, Miriam Flynn, Anndi McAfee, Brandon Lacroix.

The Land Before Time 6: The Secret of Saurus Rock 🐾🐾½ 1998 (G) Children's animated tale takes place in the age of the dinosaurs. In this sequel, Littlefoot and the rest of his dino-saur pals explore the myth of a mysterious

Land and Freedom 🐾🐾🐾 1995 Earnestly talky drama focusing on idealist Liverpudlian communist David Carr (Hart), who heads to Spain in 1937 to fight against Franco's fascists. What David learns is that the Republican forces, made up of independent militia, are bitterly divid-ed, with much infighting and betrayal from the Stalinist forces within David's own par-ty. He falls for socialist Blanca (Pastori) and learns how terrifying and haphazard war can be (with timeout for ideological discussions), the inevitable figure-sweeping action help to compensate for the political polemics. 109m/C VHS, DVD. GB SP Ian Hart, Rosana Pastor, Iciar Bollain, Tom Gilroy, Frederic Pierrot, Marc Martinez, Angela Clarke, Dave Allen; D: Ken Loach; W: Jim Allen; C: Barry Ackroyd; M: George Fenton, Cesar '96: For-eign Film.

The Land Before Time 🐾🐾🐾 1988 (G). Lushly animated children's film about five orphaned baby dinosaurs who band together and try to find the Great Valley, a paradise where they might live safely. Works same parental separation theme as Bluth's "American Tail." Charm-ing, coy, and shamelessly tearjerking; pro-ducers included Steven Spielberg and George Lucas. 67m/C VHS, DVD. D: Don Bluth; W: Stu Krieger; M: James Horner; V: Pat Hingle, Helen Shaver, Gabriel Damon, Candace Hutson, Burke Barnes, Judith Barsi, Will Ryan.

Land of Doom 🐾 1984 An amazon and a warrior struggle for survival in a post-holocaust fantasy setting. 87m/C VHS. Deborah Rennard, Garrick Dowhen; D: Peter Maris.

The Land of Faraway 🐾🐾 1987 (G) A Swedish boy is whisked off to a magical land where he does battle with the evil knights and flies on winged horses. Dubbed; based on a novel by Astrid Lindgren. 95m/C VHS, DVD. Timothy Bottoms, Christian Bale, Susannah York, Christo-pher Lee, Nicholas Rickard; D: Vladimir Grammati-kov.

Land of Fury 🐾🐾 The Seekers 1955 British naval officer Hawkins steps on New Zealand's shore and into trouble when he accidentally walks on sacred Maori burial ground. Very British, vary dated colonial saga, based on the novel "The Seekers" by John Guthrie. 90m/C VHS. GB Jack Haw-kins, Glynis Johns, Noel Purcell, Ian Fleming; D: Ken Annakin.

Land of Hunted Men 🐾 1943 The Range Busters are on the case as they track down the hideout of terrorizing gunmen. 59m/B VHS. Ray Corrigan, Dennis Moore, Max Terhune, Phyllis Adair, Charles "Blackie" King, John Merton, Forrest Taylor, Steve Clark; D: S. Roy Luby; W: Elizabeth Beecher; C: James S. Brown Jr.

Land of Plenty 🐾🐾 2004 Director Wenders takes on some post-9/11 angst in this well-meaning digital video feature. Lana (Williams), the daughter of mission-aries, arrives in LA after living in the Mid-dle East. She takes a job at a homeless shelter while she searches for her long-es-tranged Uncle Paul (Diehl). Paul is a trou-bled Vietnam vet who has become a self-appointed homeland security expert—traveling the streets in a van filled with sur-veillance equipment. The two finally meet, and bond, over their mutual sense of help-lessness and confusion. 119m/C DVD. US Michelle Williams, John Diehl, Shaun Toub, Wen-dell Pierce, Richard Edson, Burt Young, Gloria Stu-art, Bernie (Bernard) White; D: Wim Wenders; W: Wim Wenders, Michael Meredith; C: Franz Lustig; M: Thomas Hanreich.

Land Before Time 7: The Stone of Cold Fire 🐾🐾½ 2000 (G) In the seventh installment of the popular kid's series, the young dinosaurs Little-foot, Cera, Spike, Ducky, and Petrie go off saw, Petrie's disreputable uncle Pterano eggs them on. The moral lessons are sim-ple; the animation is bright; the story moves quickly, in short, the movie delivers exactly what its young fans want to see. The pidgin English dialog will be hard for adults to take. 75m/C DVD. D: Charles Grosve-nor; W: Len Uhley; V: Jeff Glenn Bennett, Anndi McAfee, Rob Paulsen, Thomas Dekker, Aria Noelle Curzon.

The Land Girls 🐾🐾½ 1998 (R) Based on the real life Women's Land Army in England, which consisted of fe-male volunteers who helped take over the duties of farmers who were fighting WWII. Stella (McCormack), Ag (Weisz) and Prue (Friel) are three city girls who come to Dorset in rural Britain to work on the farm of crusty Mr. Lawrence (Georgeson). Since the war started he has had only his son Joe (Mackintosh) to help him. Joe, who dreams of being a fighter pilot, ends up in bed with each of the women but on their terms, no his own. The movie is more concerned with the hard work these women did and the historical context than the shared sacrifice and camaraderie overshadow the romantic subplots. Shot on location in western England. 110m/C VHS. GB Catherine McCormack, Rachel Weisz, Anna Friel, Steven Mackintosh, Tom Georgeson, Maureen O'Brien, Paul Bettany, Lucy Akhurst; D: David Leland; W: David Leland, Keith Dewhurst; C: Henry Braham; M: Brian Lock.

Land of Promise *Ziemia Obiecana* 1974 At the turn of the century three men build a textile factory in Lodz, Poland. They each represent a particular ethnic group: a Pole (Olbrychski), a German (Seweryn), and a Jew (Pszoniak). Class conflicts threaten to overwhelm as their overworked and underpaid workers plan a revolt. Based on the novel by Wladyslav Reymont. In Polish with English subtitles. 178m/C VHS, DVD, PL Daniel Olbrychski, Wojciech Pszoniak, Andrzej Seweryn, Anna Nehrebecka; D: Andrzej Wajda; W: Andrzej Wajda; M: Wojciech Kilar.

Land of the Blind 2006 (R) Failed political satire about a revolution set in an unknown time and a nameless country. Thorne (Sutherland) is a leftist rebel leader who's imprisoned and tortured for his beliefs. But once the dictatorship is overthrown and Thorne assumes power, he becomes just as repressive as the old regime. Former jailer turned second-in-command Joe (Fiennes) realizes what a mistake he's made. Edwards' first feature is also an all-around mistake that even professionals like Fiennes and Sutherland can't salvage. 101m/C DVD, GB Ralph Fiennes, Donald Sutherland, Tom Hollander, Lara Flynn Boyle, Mark Warren, Camilla Rutherford, Mackenzie Crook, Jodhi May; D: Robert Edwards; W: Robert Edwards; C: Barbara Parkins; M: Guy Farley, Simon White, Doug Edwards.

Land of the Free 1998 (R) Frank Jennings (Speakman) is the campaign manager for super-patriot Senate hopeful Aidan Carvell (a deliberately hammy Shatner). Then Jennings discovers his boss has big ambitions—he wants to take over the government as the head of a terrorist organization. 96m/C VHS, DVD. Jeff Speakman, William Shatner, Chris Lemmon, Charles Robinson; D: Jerry Jameson; W: Terry Cunningham; C: Ken Blakey. VIDEO

Land of the Lawless 1947 A group of outlaws rule over a barren wasteland. What's the point? 54m/B VHS. Rachel Brown, Raymond Hatton, Christine McIntyre, Tristram Coffin; D: Lambert Hillyer.

Land of the Minotaur 1977 (PG) *The Devil's Men* Small village is the setting for horrifying ritual murders, demons, and disappearances of young tourists. Fans of Pleasence and Cushing won't want to miss this. 88m/C VHS, DVD. Jack Pleasence, Peter Cushing, Luan Peters; D: Costa Carayiannis; M: Brian Eno.

Land Raiders 1969 Savalas plays a man who hates Apaches and wants their land, but is distracted when his brother arrives on the scene, igniting an old feud. 101m/C VHS, DVD. Telly Savalas, George Maharis, Arlene Dahl, Janet Landgard; D: Nathan "Jerry" Juran.

Land of the Pharaohs 1955 Epic about the building of Egypt's Great Pyramid. Hawkins is the extremely talkative pharaoh and Collins plays his sugary-sweet yet villainous wife. Sort of campy, but worth watching for the great surprise ending. 106m/C VHS, DVD. Jack Hawkins, Joan Collins, James Robertson Justice, Dewey Martin, Alexis Minotis, Sydney Chaplin; D: Howard Hawks; W: Harold Jack Bloom; C: Lee Garmes.

The Land That Time Forgot 1975 (PG) A WWI veteran, a beautiful woman, and their German enemies are stranded in a land outside time filled with prehistoric creatures. Based on the 1918 novel by Edgar Rice Burroughs. Followed in 1977 by "The People that Time Forgot." 90m/C VHS, DVD, GB Doug McClure, John McEnery, Susan Penhaligon, Keith Barren, Anthony Ainley, Godfrey James, Bobby Parr, Declan Mulholland, Colin Farrell, Ben Howard, Roy Holder, Andrew McCulloch, Ron Pember, Steve James; D: Kevin Connor; W: James Cawthorn, Michael Moorcock; C: Alan Hume; M: Douglas Gamley.

The Land Unknown 1957 A Naval helicopter is forced down in a tropical land of prehistoric terror, complete with ferocious creatures from the Mesozoic Era. While trying to make repairs, the crew discovers the sole survivor of a previous expedition who was driven to madness by life in the primordial jungle. Good performances from cast, although monsters aren't that believable. Based on a story by Charles Palmer. 78m/B VHS. Jock Mahoney, Shawn Smith, William Reynolds, Henry (Kleinbach) Brandon, Douglas Kennedy; D: Virgil W. Vogel; W: Laszlo Gorog; M: Henry Mancini.

The Landlady 1998 (R) Melanie Leroy (Shire) kills her hubby after discovering him cheating on her. When she becomes the landlady of an apartment house, she decides one of her tenants, nice-guy Patrick (Coleman), would be ideal husband material. And Melanie intends to get rid of any obstacles in her way. 98m/C VHS, DVD. Talia Shire, Jack Coleman, Bruce Weitz, Melissa Behr, Susie Singer, Bette Ford; D: Rob Malenfant; W: Frank Rehwaldt, George Saunders; C: Darko Suvak; M: Eric Lundmark.

Landlord Blues 1987 A trashy slumlord without morals or a conscience goes one step too far, and a tenant retaliates with munitions. 96m/C VHS. Mark Boone Jr., Raye Dowell, Richard Litt, Bill Rice, Mary Schultz, Gigi Williams; D: Jacob Burckhardt.

Landscape After Battle 1970 *Krajobraz Po Bitwie* A group of concentration camp survivors are awaiting repatriation in a disused barracks in a German stalag in 1945. Among them are young Poles, Nina and Tadeusz, who fall in love. But tragedy continues when Nina is accidentally killed by an American guard. Based on the stories of Tadeusz Borowski, an Auschwitz survivor who later committed suicide. Polish with subtitles. 101m/C DVD, PL Daniel Olbrychski, Stanislawa Celinska, Tadeusz Janczar; D: Andrzej Wajda; W: Andrzej Wajda, Andrzej Brzozowski; C: Zygmunt Samosiuk; M: Zygmunt Konieczny.

Landscape in the Mist 1988 *Topio Stin Omichli* A stark Greek landscape in a rainy winter sets the scene for the tragic search by two children for their unknown father. Relies heavily on symbolism to make its point about unfulfilled desire (including the film's imaginary German-Greek border). In Greek with English subtitles. 126m/C VHS, DVD, GR FR IT Tania Palaiologou, Michalis Zeke, Stratos Tzortzoglou, Eva Kotamanidou, Aliki Georgouli; D: Theo Angelopoulos; W: Thanassis Valtinos, Tonino Guerra, Theo Angelopoulos; C: Yorgos Arvanitis; M: Eleni Karaindrou.

Landslide 1992 (PG-13) As a geologist, suffering from memory loss, comes closer to discovering his identity his life is endangered by a sinister plot. 95m/C VHS. Anthony Edwards, Tom Burlinson, Joanna Cassidy, Melody Anderson, Ronald Lacey, Ken James, Lloyd Bochner; D: Jean-Claude Lord.

L'Annee des Meduses *The Year of the Jellyfish* 1986 (R) An 18-year-old girl tries to seduce the local Monsieur Beefcake she meets on her vacation. When he doesn't return her interest, she decides to teach him a lesson. In French with English subtitles, or dubbed. 110m/C VHS. FR Valerie Kaprisky, Bernard Giraudeau; D: Christopher Frank; C: Renato Berta.

L'Annee Sainte *Pilgrimage to Rome; Holy Year* 1976 In his last film, Gabin is an escaped convict returning to his hidden loot in Rome when his plane is hijacked by international terrorists. Available dubbed. 85m/C VHS, DVD. FR Jean Gabin, Jean-Claude Brialy, Paul(o) Giusti, Jean-Claude Darrieux; D: Jean Girault; W: Louis-Emile Galey, Jacques Vilfrid; C: Guy Suzuki; M: Claude Bolling.

Lansdown 2001 Flat attempt at a neo-noir/crime comedy. Jake (Sheilds) is a bland criminal defense attorney in the fictitious New Jersey title town. His wife Lexi (Carlson) is bored and has been fooling around with roofer Pat (Stewart). When Jake finds out, he decides he wants the lover dead but can't get his former client Gustav (Warren)—who provided the info on the infidelity—to do the hit himself. Instead, Gustav subcontracts to a couple of doofus hit men, who both it. So Jake is forced to get more personally involved. 80m/C VHS, DVD. Adam Fidusiewicz, Jennifer Carlson, Chris Stewart, D.W. Warren, Patrick Louis, Chris Baran, Marc Krinsky; D: Tom Zuber; W: Tom Zuber; C: Ty Bolia; M: Atli Ovarsson.

Lansky 1999 (R) Traces some 70 years in the life of Jewish mobster Meyer Lansky (Dreyfuss), which, surprisingly, doesn't make for exciting drama. Lansky grew up on New York's Lower East Side with Benjamin "Bugsy" Siegel (Roberts) and Charlie "Lucky" Luciano (LaPaglia). Th trio would mastermind a crime syndicate, with Lansky basically serving as the Mob accountant. Story is told in flashbacks as the aged Lansky awaits federal trial in Miami. 120m/C VHS, DVD. Richard Dreyfuss, Eric Roberts, Anthony LaPaglia, Illeana Douglas, Beverly D'Angelo, Ryan Merriman, Francis Guinan, Stanley DeSantis, Nick(y) Corello; D: John McNaughton; W: David Mamet; C: John A. Alonzo; M: George S. Clinton. CABLE

Lantana 2001 (R) This impressive Aussie thriller starts off as a seemingly straightforward murder mystery, but that's only the jumping-off point. The burned-out cop, Leon (LaPaglia) investigating the murder, is cheating on his wife with a woman, Jane (Blke), who may know something about the case. His wife is consulting a psychiatrist, Valerie (Hershey), whose marriage to John (Rush) has been damaged by the murder of their 11-year-old daughter. John may also be having a homosexual affair with one of his wife's patients. Jane's neighbors, Nik (Colosimo) and Paula (Farinacci) seem like the only happy ones in the mix, but they, too, are touched by the mystery. LaPaglia stands out in a brilliant cast, and the deep character studies and attention to detail add dimension to what could have been a standard whodunit. 120m/C VHS, DVD. AU Anthony LaPaglia, Kerry Armstrong, Geoffrey Rush, Barbara Hershey, Rachael Blake, Vince Colosimo, Peter Phelps, Daniela Farinacci, Leah Purcell, Glenn Robbins; D: Ray Lawrence; W: Andrew Bovell; C: Mandy Walker; M: Paul Kelly. Australian Film Inst. '01: Actor (LaPaglia), Actress (Armstrong), Adapt. Screenplay, Director (Lawrence), Film, Support. Actor (Colosimo), Support. Actress (Blake).

Lantern Hill 1990 (G) During the Depression, a 12-year-old girl attempts to fan the embers between her estranged parents. A Wonderworks production, filmed partly on Canada's Prince Edward Island. Based on a story by Lucy Maud Montgomery, whose "Anne of Green Gables" is also part of the Wonderworks series. 112m/C VHS. CA Sam Waterston, Colleen Dewhurst, Sarah Polley, Marion Bennett, Zoe Caldwell; D: Kevin Sullivan. CABLE

Lap Dancing Woof! 1995 (R) What hath "Showgirls" wrought? Small town gal Angie Parker moves to Hollywood to become an actress and, when the money runs out, winds up as an exotic dancer. Also available unrated. 90m/C VHS, DVD. Lorissa McComas, Tane McClure, C.T. Miller; D: Mike Sedan; W: K.C. Martin; C: Carlos Montaner; M: Ron Allen, Todd Schroeder. VIDEO

L.A.P.D.: To Protect and Serve 2001 Hey, Hopper is actually a good guy in this police corruption drama! He's a captain determined to weed out a group of bad apples in the department. 96m/C VHS, DVD. Dennis Hopper, Michael Madsen, Charles Durning, Mace Singer; D: Ed Anders; W: Rob Neighbors; C: Michael Balery. VIDEO

L'Appat *Fresh Bait; Live Bait; The Bait* 1994 Deglamourizing, if familiar, look at amoral teens and violence. 18-year-old salesgirl Nathalie (Gillain) supports her unemployed boyfriend Eric (Sitruk) and his dim-bulb buddy Bruno (Putzulu). The guys hang out, watch too many gangster videos, and try to be tough, deciding to get rich by dangling Nathalie as bait. She goes to a man's home (presumably for sex) but Eric and Bruno will break in and rob the mark instead. Plan goes awry when their first victim is killed. What's truly disturbing is the trio's blase attitude that anything would happen to them should they be caught. Based on the book by Morgan Sportes, which recounted the 1984 crime. In French with subtitles. 117m/C VHS. FR Marie Gillain, Olivier Sitruk, Bruno Putzulu, Philippe Duclos, Richard Berry; D: Bertrand Tavernier; W: Bertrand Tavernier; C: Colo Tavernier O'Hagan; M: Philippe Haim. Berlin Intl. Film Fest. '94: Film.

Lara Croft: Tomb Raider *Tomb Raider* 2001 (PG-13) Laura Croft (Jolie), the daughter of a British aristocrat/adventurer (Jolie's real-life dad Voight), gives up her upper-crusty life to hunt down ancient treasures that hold the key to controlling time before they fall into the wrong hands. Sounds straightforward enough, right? Maybe it once was but too much tinkering results in a muddled story and foggy details that do, however, divert your attention away from the cheesy dialogue and flimsy characters. Stunning sets and visuals, along with Jolie's "let's have some fun" attitude go a long way toward making this disappointment more entertaining than it probably should be. 96m/C VHS, DVD, Blu-ray Disc, UMD. US Angelina Jolie, Iain Glen, Daniel Craig, Leslie Phillips, Jon Voight, Noah Taylor, Richard Johnson, Julian Rhind-Tutt, Chris (Christopher) Barrie; D: Simon West; W: Patrick Massett, John Zinman; C: Peter Menzies Jr.; M: Graeme Revell.

Lara Croft Tomb Raider: The Cradle of Life 2003 (PG-13) Arguably better than its predecessor, sequel has Croft (Jolie) searching for Pandora's box: a mythical container which is supposed to contain unfathomable evils. Our intrepid hero must outsmart the diabolical Dr. Reiss (Hinds) who wants to use it to wipe out all humanity save a lucky few over which he would, naturally, rule. With her hunky Scottish ex (Butler) in tow, the quest takes the pillow-lipped raider of the lost box on an undersea adventure in Greece and other exotic locales, including Shanghai and Mt. Kilimanjaro. Jolie injects Lara with more character, while the plethora of action scenes and special effects are deftly directed by De Bont, MIA since 1999's "The Haunting." Less noisy scenes, however, lack luster. 116m/C VHS, DVD, UMD. US Angelina Jolie, Gerard Butler, Ciaran Hinds, Til Schweiger, Djimon Hounsou, Noah Taylor, Chris (Christopher) Barrie, Simon Yam; D: Jan De Bont; W: Dean Georgaris; C: David Tattersall; M: Alan Silvestri.

Laramie Kid 1935 A vintage Tyler sagebrush saga. 60m/B VHS. Tom Tyler, Alberta Vaughn, Al Ferguson, Murdock MacQuarrie, George Chesebro; D: Harry S. Webb.

The Laramie Project 2002 (R) A docudrama that explores the 1998 gay-bashing death of Matthew Shepard in Laramie, Wyoming. Shortly after the crime, Moises Kaufman (here played by Carbonell) and members of his New York Tectonic Theater Project arrived in Laramie to interview residents and others associated with the crime. Kaufman then adapted the transcripts into a stage piece, which debuted in Denver. Kaufman himself directs the film adaptation, which includes actual news footage interspersed with actor re-creations. 87m/C VHS, DVD. Nestor Carbonell, Peter Fonda, Amy Madigan, Janeane Garofalo, Jeremy Davies, Steve Buscemi, Christina Ricci, Mark Webber, Laura Linney, Terry Kinney; D: Moises Kaufman; W: Moises Kaufman; C: Terry Stacey; M: Peter Golub. CABLE

Larceny On the Air 1937 Righteous Dr. Lawrence Baxter (Livingston) is appalled by quacks selling their patent cures on the radio and is determined to force them out of business, even when he falls for the daughter (Bradley) of one scammer. 67m/B VHS. Robert "Bob" Livingston, Grace Bradley, Willard Robertson, Pierre Watkin, Smiley Burnette, Granville Bates; D: Irving Pichel; W: Richard English; C: Jack Marta.

L'Argent *Money* 1983 When a young man's parents refuse to lend him any money a friend helps out by giving him a counterfeit 500-franc note. This sets off a chain of events, with every passing of the money leading to another lie, betrayal, and increasingly violent crime. Austere and stylized vision is not for all tastes. In French with English subtitles. 82m/C VHS, DVD. FR Christian Patey, Sylvie van den Elsen, Michel Briguet, Caroline Lang; D: Robert Bresson; W: Robert Bresson; C: Pasqualino. De Santis. Cannes '83: Director (Bresson); Natl. Soc. Film Critics '84: Director (Bresson).

Larger Than Life 𝒹½ *Nickel and Dime*; *Large as Life* 1996 (PG) The pitch for this movie (Murray takes an elephant on a cross-country trip) must have sounded terrific. Unfortunately, the actual movie falls off. Murray is his usual smarmy self as a cut-rate motivational speaker Jack Corcoran, who inherits the pachyderm and a pile of bills after his circus clown father dies. Following the "road movie" formula, he encounters wacky characters along the way, including a speed-freak trucker (McConaughey), a sexy animal trainer (Florentino) and a strait-laced zookeeper (Garofalo). In a piece of brilliant casting, Tai, the star of "Operation Dumbo Drop" appears as the elephant. 93m/C VHS, DVD. Bill Murray, Janeane Garofalo, Linda Fiorentino, Matthew McConaughey, Keith David, Pat Hingle, Jeremy Piven, Lois Smith, Anita Gillette, Maureen Mueller, Harve Presnell, Tracey Walter; **D:** Howard Franklin; **W:** Roy Blount Jr.; **C:** Elliot Davis; **M:** Miles Goodman.

Larks on a String 𝒹𝒹½ 1968 Banned for 23 years, this wonderful film is Menzel's masterpiece, even better than his Oscar winning "Closely Watched Trains." Portrays the story of life in labor camps where men and women are re-educated at the whim of the government. No matter what the hardships, these people find humor, hope and love. Their individuality will not be lost, nor their humanity dissolved. Excellent performances, tellingly directed with a beautiful sense of compassion and tone. Screenplay written by Menzel and Bohumil Hrabil, author of the short story on which it is based. In Czech with English subtitles. 96m/C VHS. CZ Vaclav Neckar, Jitka Zelenohorska, Jaroslav Satoransky, Rudolf Hrusinsky; **D:** Jiri Menzel; **W:** Jiri Menzel.

Larry 𝒹𝒹 1974 Based on the Nevada State Hospital case history of a 26-year-old man, institutionalized since infancy, who is discovered to be of normal intelligence and must learn to live the life he has always been capable of living. 80m/C VHS. Frederic Forrest, Tyne Daly, Katherine Helmond, Michael McGuire, Robert Walden; **D:** William A. Graham. TV

Larry McMurtry's Dead Man's Walk 𝒹𝒹½ *Dead Man's Walk* 1996 (PG-13) McMurtry's prequel to "Lonesome Dove" focuses on the teenaged Gus McCrae (Arquette) and Woodrow Call (Miller) and their first adventures as Texas Rangers in the 1840s. They're involved in the ill-fated Texas-Santa Fe Expedition, led by parrot-owning former seafarer Caleb Cobb (Abraham), to take Santa Fe and make New Mexico part of the Texas Republic. Instead, a Mexican Army detachment led by Capt. Salazar (Olmos) captures the rag-tag group, which is then forced to march across a deadly stretch of desert that few survive. Likeable leads but the supporting actors, including Carradine and Stanton as scouts, steal the show. 271m/C VHS, DVD. Jonny Lee Miller, David Arquette, Keith Carradine, Harry Dean Stanton, F. Murray Abraham, Edward James Olmos, Eric Schweig, Patricia Childress, Jennifer Garner, Haviland (Haylie Morris, Brian Dennehy, Joaquim de Almeida, Ray McKinnon, Akosua Busia; **D:** Yves Simoneau; **W:** Larry McMurtry, Diana Ossana; **C:** Edward Pei; **M:** David Bell. TV

Larry McMurtry's Streets of Laredo 𝒹𝒹𝒹 *Lonesome Dove: Streets of Laredo* 1995 Texas Ranger-turned-bounty hunter Woodrow F. Call (a splendid Garner) is hired by the railroad to track down ruthless Mexican bandit Joey Garza (Cruz), pitting an old man's skills against a young man's daring, and driving both men across Texas, deep into Mexican territory, reluctantly comes along, with ex-prostitute Lorena (Spacek), who's Parker's wife, and Maria (Braga), Joey's tough-but-deluded mom, providing strong support. Casual cruelty and violence are the norm in the sunset days of both Call's life and that of the west itself. Third in the TV sagas, following "Return to Lonesome Dove." 227m/C VHS, DVD. James Garner, Alexis Cruz, Sam Shepard, Sissy Spacek, Sonia Braga, Wes Studi, Randy Quaid, Charles Martin Smith, Kevin Conway, George Carlin, Ned Beatty, James Gammon, Tristan Tait, Anjanette Comer; **D:** Joseph Sargent.

Larry the Cable Guy: Health Inspector woof! 2006 (PG-13) Gross-out comedy appealing to those who like flatulence, vomiting, and other sorts of intestinal distress. Blue-collar comedian Larry the Cable Guy is Larry, the Florida health inspector guy who suspects someone is deliberately causing the food poisoning epidemic that's hitting a number of upscale restaurants. So he goes undercover, along with his uptight partner Amy (Bahn), to find the culprit. Hilarity doesn't ensue. Who let the guys who greenlit "Chairman of the Board" back on the lot? 89m/C DVD. US Larry the Cable Guy, Joanna Cassidy, David Koechner, Thomas F. Wilson, Joe Pantoliano, Iris Bahr, Bruce Bruce, Brooke Dillman, Tony Hale, Lisa Lampanelli, Megyn Price; **D:** Trent Cooper; **W:** Jon Bernstein, James Greer; **C:** Kim Marks; **M:** Steven R. Phillips, Tim P

Lars and the Real Girl 𝒹𝒹½ 2007 (PG-13) Lars (Gosling) is one of those sweetly awkward small-town loonies that movies are so fond of. He's a damaged soul who tries to avoid too much human contact, including that of his well-meaning brother Gus (Schneider) and sister-in-law Karin (Mortimer). Then Lars buys a customized life-size sex doll (no, he's not a perv) online and begins introducing his girlfriend, Bianca. Family doctor Dagmar (Clarkson) persuades everyone to go along with Lars' delusion for the time being and Bianca is quickly integrated into the community. Fortunately, Gosling et al manage to sell this story without too much ick or schmaltz. 106m/C DVD. US Ryan Gosling, Paul Schneider, Emily Mortimer, Patricia Clarkson, Kelli Garner, Nancy Beatty, Karen Robinson; **D:** Nancy Oliver; **W:** Gerri Gillan; **C:** Adam Kimmel; **M:** David Torn.

Las Vegas Hillbillys 𝒹 *Country Music* 1966 A pair of country-singing hillbillies inherit a saloon in Las Vegas and enjoy wine, moonshine, and song. These two make the Clampetts look like high society. Followed, believe it or not, by "Hillbillys in a Haunted House." 𝒹 *Money* Greases the Wheel. 85m/C VHS, DVD. Mamie Van Doren, Jayne Mansfield, Ferlin Husky, Sonny James; **D:** Arthur C. Pierce.

Las Vegas Lady 𝒹 1976 (PG) Three shrewd casino hostesses plot a multi-million dollar heist in the nation's gambling capital. Non-captivating caper. 90m/C VHS, DVD. Stella Stevens, Stuart Whitman, George DiCenzo, Andrew Stevens, Lynne Moody, Linda Scruggs; **D:** Noel Nosseck; **W:** Walter Dallenbach; **C:** Stephen M. Katz; **M:** Alan Silvestri.

The Las Vegas Story woof! 1952 Gambling, colorful sights, and a murder provide the framework for this non-compelling fictional guided-tour of the city. Save your money for the sights. 88m/B VHS. Victor Mature, Jane Russell, Vincent Price, Hoagy Carmichael, Brad Dexter; **D:** Robert Stevenson; **W:** Paul Jarrico.

Las Vegas Serial Killer woof! 1986 A serial killer, let out of prison on a technicality, starts killing again. 90m/C VHS, DVD. Pierre Agostino, Ron Jason, Tara MacGowran, Kathryn Downey; **D:** Ray Dennis Steckler; **W:** Ray Dennis Steckler. VIDEO

Laser Mission 𝒹𝒹½ 1990 When it is discovered that the Soviets have laser weapon capabilities, an agent is given the task of destroying the weapon and kidnapping the scientist who developed it. 83m/C VHS, DVD. Brandon Lee, Debi Monahan, Ernest Borgnine, Werner Pochath, Graham Clarke, Maureen Lahoud, Pierre Knoessen; **D:** Beau Davis; **M:** David Knopfler.

Laser Moon 𝒹𝒹 1992 A serial killer uses a surgical laser beam to kill his beautiful victims, and he strikes at every full moon. When he announces his next attack on a late-night radio talk show the police call in a beautiful rookie cop (Lords) to use as bait. 90m/C VHS, DVD. Traci Lords,

Laser Vegas Weekend 𝒹 1985 A computer nerd goes to Las Vegas and discovers fun. 83m/C VHS. Barry Hickey, Macka Foley, Ray Dennis Steckler; **D:** Dale Trevillion.

Laserblast woof! 1978 (PG) Standard wimp-gets-revenge story in which a frustrated young man finds a powerful and deadly laser which was left near his home by aliens; upon learning of its devastating capabilities, his personality changes and he seeks revenge against all who have taken advantage of him. 87m/C VHS, DVD. Kim Milford, Cheryl "Rainbeaux" Smith, Keenan Wynn, Roddy McDowall; **D:** Michael Raeburn; **W:** Frank Ray Perilli, Franne Schacht; **C:** Terry Bowers; **M:** Richard Band, Joel Goldsmith.

Laserhawk 𝒹½ 1999 (PG-13) Now here's an interesting take on the origin of species—millions of years ago carnivorous aliens planted humans as a crop on earth. Now they've returned to harvest their goods and only a band of misfits may have a chance to save humanity if they can find one of the aliens' crashed spacecraft/weapons called a Laserhawk to use against them. 102m/C VHS, DVD, Mark Hamill, Jason James Richter; Gordon Currie, Melissa Gallianos; **D:** Jean Pellerin; **W:** John A. Curtis. VIDEO

The Laserman 𝒹𝒹 1990 (R) Exotic black comedy about a Chinese-American scientist who, when not fending off an overbearing Jewish mother or having telepathic orgasms, is contending with a band of political terrorists. 92m/C VHS. Marc Hayashi, Peter Wang, Tony Leung Ka-Fai, Sally Yeh, Maryann Urbano, Joan Copeland; **D:** Peter Wang; **W:** Peter Wang; **M:** Mason Daring.

Lassie 𝒹𝒹½ 1994 (PG) Everyone's favorite collie returns as the Turner family moves to Virginia's Shenandoah Valley to take up sheep ranching. However, because this is the '90s, Dad meets financial disaster, and junior can't stand this step-mom. Can Lassie meet the challenges of dysfunctional family living? "What is it girl? Call a therapist?" This Lassie is a direct descendant of Pal, the original 1943 star. 92m/C VHS, DVD. Helen Slater, Jon Tenney, Tom Guiry, Brittany Boyd, Richard Farnsworth, Frederic Forrest, Michelle Williams; **D:** Daniel Petrie; **W:** Matthew Jacobs, Gary Ross, Elizabeth Anderson; **C:** Kenneth Macmillan; **M:** Basil Poledouris.

Lassie 𝒹𝒹½ 2005 (PG) Lassie goes back to her British roots (based on Eric Knight's 1938 novel) in this sentimental adventure. Young Joe (Mason) is heartbroken when Lassie must be sold because his miner father has lost his job. Lassie's new owner, the Duke of Rudling (O'Toole), has bought the photogenic collie for his granddaughter Cilla (Odgers), and both dog and girl are soon sent up to Scotland. Lassie's having none of it and escapes to start a 500-mile trek back to Yorkshire, surviving a number of trials along the way. Sweet yet realistic, with great performances throughout. 100m/C DVD. US GB IR FR Peter O'Toole, Samantha Morton, John Lynch, Peter Dinklage, Jonathan Mason, Steve Pemberton, Jemma Redgrave, Edward Fox, John Standing, Kelly Macdonald, Robert Hardy, Hester Odgers; **D:** Charles Sturridge; **W:** Charles Sturridge; **C:** Howard Atherton; **M:** Adrian Johnston.

Lassie: Adventures of Neeka 1968 America's best friend joins her Native American buddy, Neeka, for a journey through a forest in the Pacific Northwest. They camp out in a deserted settlement, pull an elderly gentleman out of a frigid pond, and risk their lives to release horses from a stable during a raging wildfire. 75m/ B VHS. Jed Allan, Mark Miranda, Robert Rockwell; **D:** Richard (Dick) Moder, Jack B. Hively.

Lassie, Come Home 𝒹𝒹½ 1943 (G) In first of the Lassie series, the famed collie is reluctantly sold and makes a treacherous cross-country journey back to her original family. 90m/C VHS, DVD, Roddy McDowall, Elizabeth Taylor, Donald Crisp, Edmund Gwenn, May Whitty, Nigel Bruce, Elsa Lanchester. J. Pat O'Malley; **D:** Fred M. Wilcox. Natl. Film Reg. '93.

Lassie from Lancashire 𝒹𝒹 1938 Not the famous Collie—but here, a Colleen. A pair of struggling lovebirds try to make it in show biz against all odds, including the girl's lunatic aunt, who locks her away before an audition. 67m/B VHS.

The Last American Hero 𝒹𝒹𝒹 *Hard Driver* 1973 (PG) The true story of how former moonshine runner Junior Johnson became one of the fastest race car drivers in the history of the sport. Entertaining slice of life chronicling whiskey running and stock car racing, with Bridges superb in the lead. Based on a series of articles written by Tom Wolfe. 95m/C VHS, DVD. Jeff Bridges, Valerie Perrine, Geraldine Fitzgerald, Ned Beatty, Ed Lauter, Jane Smith, Gregory Walcott; **D:** Lamont Johnson; **W:** William Roberts; **M:** Charles Fox.

Last American Virgin 𝒹𝒹 1982 (R) Usual brainless teen sex comedy about three school buddies who must search for girls who are willing. Music by Blondie, The Cars, The Police, The Waitresses, Devo, U2, Human League, and Quincy Jones. 92m/C VHS, DVD. Lawrence Monoson, Diane Franklin, Steve Antin, Louisa Moritz; **D:**

Lassie: Well of Love 1970 Various installments of the heroic collie are combined to create a movie-length presentation for home video. Lassie takes two young pups under her paw and, in the process, loses her way. As she tries to get home, she brings joy back into the lives of two despondent children. Finally, the old girl faces death when she tumbles into an abandoned well and must depend on humans for rescue. 76m/C VHS. Mary Gregory, Robert Donner, Robert Sampson, Bruce Bennett, Sean Kelly; **D:** James B. Clark, Jack B. Hively; **W:** Eric Freiwald, Robert Schaefer; **C:** Robert Sparks; **M:** Nathan Scott. TV

Lassie's Great Adventure 𝒹𝒹½ 1962 Lassie and her master Timmy are swept away from home by a runaway balloon. After they land in the Canadian wilderness, they learn to rely on each other through peril and adventure. 104m/C VHS, DVD. June Lockhart, Jon(athan) Provost, Hugh Reilly; **D:** William Beaudine; **W:** Charles "Blackie" O'Neal. TV

Lassiter 𝒹𝒹½ 1984 (R) Selleck plays a jewel thief who is asked to steal diamonds from the Nazis for the FBI. Supporting cast adds value to what is otherwise a fairly ordinary adventure drama. 100m/C VHS. Tom Selleck, Jane Seymour, Lauren Hutton, Bob Hoskins, Joe Regalbuto, Ed Lauter, Warren Clarke, William Morgan Sheppard; **D:** Roger Young.

Last Action Hero 𝒹𝒹 1993 (PG-13) Newcomer O'Brien finds himself in a movie starring his idol Jack Slater, the kind of guy who never loses a fight and is impervious to gunfire and explosions (and he has a really cool car and a really big gun.) Disappointing action/spoof of movies within a movie (rumored to have cost $80 million) was critically maimed and never recovered. The concept isn't new and has been done better before, though Ah-nold possesses his usual self-mocking charm, which is more than can be said for the movie. Look for lots of big stars in small roles and cameos. Cluttered with inside Hollywood gags, the script was given uncredited assistance from William Goldman. 131m/C VHS, DVD. Arnold Schwarzenegger, Austin O'Brien, Mercedes Ruehl, F. Murray Abraham, Charles Dance, Anthony Quinn, Robert Prosky, Tom Noonan, Frank McRae, Art Carney, Bridgette Wilson-Sampras; **Cameos:** Sharon Stone, Hammer, Chevy Chase, Jean-Claude Van Damme, Tori Spelling, Joan Plowright, Adam Ant, James Belushi, James Cameron, Tony Curtis, Timothy Dalton, Tony Danza, Edward Furlong, Little Richard, Damon Wayans, Robert Patrick; **D:** John McTiernan; **W:** David Arnott, Shane Black; **C:** Dean Semler; **M:** Michael Kamen.

The Last Adventure 𝒹𝒹½ *Les Aventuriers* 1967 Two friends find themselves swindled in an insurance scam and set out after the perpetrator who sent them off to Africa in search of a treasure. Available dubbed. 112m/C VHS. FR Alain Delon, Lino Ventura, Joanna Shimkus; **D:** Robert Enrico; **W:** Robert Enrico, Jose Giovanni, Pierre Pelegri; **C:** Jean Boffety; **M:** François de Roubaix.

The Last Angry Man 🐾🐾🐾½ 1959 An old, idealistic Brooklyn doctor attracts a TV producer wanting to make a documentary about his life and career, and the two conflict. Muni was Oscar-nominated for this, his last film. 100m/B VHS. Paul Muni, David Wayne, Betsy Palmer, Luther Adler, Dan Tobin; **D:** Daniel Mann; **c:** James Wong Howe.

The Last Assassins 🐾🐾 *Dusting Cliff Seven* 1996 (R) Ex-CIA agent Anne Bishop (Allen) is persuaded to reunite with former commander McBride (Henriksen) for another mission. Then she discovers he has his own agenda, but when Anne tries to get out, McBride kidnaps her husband to ensure her cooperation. 90m/C VHS, DVD. Lance Henriksen, Nancy Allen, Floyd "Red Crow" Westerman, Dean Scofield; **D:** William H. Molina; **w:** William H. Molina, Jim Menza, Charles Philip Moore, Justin Stanley; **c:** William H. Molina; **M:** David Wurst, Eric Wurst. VIDEO

The Last Bastion 🐾🐾 1984 A WWII drama emphasizing the political struggle between Churchill, MacArthur, Roosevelt, and Australia's John Curtin. 160m/C VHS. *AU* Michael Blakemore, John Wood, Warren Mitchell, Ray Barrett, Robert Vaughn, Timothy West; **D:** Chris Thomson; **w:** Denis Whitburn, David Williamson; **c:** Louis Irving; **M:** Colin Stead. VIDEO

The Last Best Sunday 🐾🐾 1998 Mexican-American Joseph (Spain) kills the two racist thugs who beat him and hides out in the isolated home of religiously brought up classmate Lolly (Bettis), whose parents are away for the weekend. Naturally, the teens bond and then they fall in love. Not quite as obvious as it all sounds. 101m/C VHS, DVD. Douglas Spain, Angela Bettis, Kim Darby, William Lucking, Marion Ross, Craig Wasson, Daniel Beer; **D:** Donny Most; **w:** Karen Kelly; **c:** Zoran Hochstatter; **M:** Tim Westergren.

The Last Best Year 🐾🐾½ 1990 (PG) Basic TV tearjerker has lonely psychologist Wendy (Moore) befriending patient Jane (Peters), who has a terminal illness. 88m/C VHS, DVD. Mary Tyler Moore, Bernadette Peters, Brian Bedford, Dorothy McGuire, Kate Reid, Kenneth Welsh; **D:** Tony Scott; **w:** Shane Black; **c:** Ward Russell; **M:** Michael Kamen.

The Last Boy Scout 🐾🐾 1991 (R) Are you ready for some gunplay? Formula thriller stars Willis as a private eye and Wayans as an ex-quarterback teaming up against a football team owner who will stop at nothing to get political backing for a bill promoting legalized gambling on sports. Another variation of the violent buddy-picture by "Lethal Weapon" screenwriter Black. 105m/C VHS, DVD. Bruce Willis, Damon Wayans, Halle Berry, Chelsea Field, Noble Willingham, Taylor Negron, Danielle Harris, Chelcie Ross, Bruce McGill, Morris Chestnut, Eddie Griffin, Kim Coates, Joe Santos, Tony Longo, Billy Blanks, Jack Kehler, Michael (Mike) Papajohn; **D:** Tony Scott; **w:** Shane Black; **c:** Ward Russell; **M:** Michael Kamen.

Last Breath 🐾🐾 *Lifebreath* 1996 (R) Martin (Perry) is obsessively devoted to his dying wife, Chrystie (Swift), who needs a double lung transplant to survive. So Martin decides to romance lovely Gail (Carides)—with murder on his mind. Twisted ending. 90m/C VHS, DVD. Luke Perry, Gia Carides, Francie Swift, David Margulies, Lisa Gay Hamilton, Jack Gilpin, Matt McGrath, Hillary Bailey Smith; **D:** P.J. Posner; **w:** P.J. Posner, Jon Posner; **c:** Fred Kollhanek; **M:** Carol De Groot. Cannes '54: Special Jury Prize, Actress (Schell).

The Last Bridge 🐾🐾 *Die Letzte Brucke* 1954 German doctor Schell is captured by Yugoslavian partisans during WWII and forced to tend to their wounded, gradually realizing that suffering is universal. German with subtitles. 104m/B VHS. AT Maria Schell, Bernhard Wicki, Barbara Rutting, Carl Mohner; **D:** Helmut Kautner; **w:** Helmut Kautner, Norbert Kunze; **c:** P.J. Posner. VIDEO

The Last Broadcast 🐾🐾🐾 1998 Festival hit—and the first film to be digitally distributed to theatres—predates "The Blair Witch Project" in telling the story of a group of young people who go into the woods with video cameras and meet a grisly fate. But this one is much more complicated and ambitious. Directors Steven

Avalos and Lance Weiler play public access cable TV show hosts who take a sound man (Clabbers) and a psychic (Seward) into the Pine Barrens for a live broadcast of their search for the legendary Jersey Devil. Only one comes out. A year later, a documentary filmmaker (Beard) and a video editor (Pulaski) try to find the truth of the matter. 87m/C DVD. Stefan Avalos, Lance Weiler, David Beard, Rein Clabbers, Michele Pulaski; **D:** Stefan Avalos, Lance Weiler; **w:** Stefan Avalos, Lance Weiler; **c:** Lance Weiler; **M:** Stefan Avalos.

Last Bullet 🐾🐾 *Crooked River* 1950 A young westerner chases after a band of outlaws to avenge the cold-blooded murder of his parents. 55m/B VHS. James Ellison, Russell Hayden, John Cason, Raymond Hatton, Fuzzy Knight, Julie Adams, Tom Tyler; **D:** Thomas Carr; **w:** Ron Ormond, Maurice Tombragel; **c:** Ernest Miller; **M:** Walter Greene.

The Last Butterfly 🐾🐾 1992 Quiet Holocaust movie set in Theresienstadt, the Czechoslovak ghetto city used by the Nazis to persuade the outside world of their humane treatment of the Jews. Noted French mime Antoine Moreau (Courtenay) has fallen under suspicion by the Gestapo. He's "persuaded" to give a performance in Theresienstadt for the benefit of the visiting Red Cross but decides to subvert Nazi propaganda with his own version of "Hansel and Gretel." This time the witch feeds the children into her oven. Muted performances and screenplay (adapted from the Michael Jacot novel) heightened the film's surreal calmness. 106m/C VHS, DVD. *CZ* Tom Courtenay, Brigitte Fossey, Freddie Jones, Ingrid Held, Linda Jablonska; **D:** Karel Kachyna; **w:** Karel Kachyna, Ota Hofman; **M:** Alex North.

Last Call 🐾 1990 (R) Clearly, Joe Sixpack won't rent this bimbo fest for its subtle plot. Katt, a mafiosi-cheated real estate guy, decides to even the score with the assistance of gal pal/playmate of the year Tweed, who's more than willing to compromise her position. Also features the talents of playboy emerita Stevens. Available in rated and unrated versions. 90m/C VHS, DVD. William Katt, Shannon Tweed, Joseph Campanella, Stella Stevens, Matt Roe; **D:** Jag Mundhra. VIDEO

Last Call: The Final Chapter of F. Scott Fitzgerald 🐾🐾½ 2002 In 1939, aspiring writer Frances Kroll (Campbell) interviews for a secretarial position with F. Scott Fitzgerald (Irons). Alcoholic, in declining health, and haunted by images of his institutionalized wife Zelda (Spacek), Fitzgerald hasn't published in years. She becomes his confidante and begin work on his new novel—a scathing indictment of Hollywood (which will become the unfinished "The Last Tycoon"). Based on the memoir by Kroll Ring. 108m/ C VHS, DVD. Jeremy Irons, Neve Campbell, Sissy Spacek, Natalie Radford, Shannon Lawson; **D:** Henry Bromell; **w:** Henry Bromell; **c:** Jeffrey Jur; **M:** Brian Tyler. CABLE

The Last Castle 🐾🐾½ 2001 (R) Redford is Gen. Irwin, a legendary army officer sent to prison on a charge that isn't clear until well into the film. The warden of the prison, Col. Winter (Gandolfini), is a dictatorial collector of military memorabilia who clearly admires his new inmate. After overhearing a remark by Irwin disparaging his collection, Winter begins to resent him. Irwin witnesses the cruelty administered by the warden and begins to win over his fellow inmates' loyalty by restoring their pride. As Winter notices control of the men slipping away, his punishments grow worse, until finally Irwin leads the inmates in an insurrection. Although driven by powerhouse performances by Redford and Gandolfini, the plot spends too much time on the background of the other inmates, while a storyline about Irwin's daughter is dropped altogether. 133m/C VHS, DVD. *US* Robert Redford, James Gandolfini, Mark Ruffalo, Delroy Lindo, Steve (Stephen) Burton, Paul Calderon, Samuel Ball, Clifton (Gonzalez) Collins Jr., Frank Military, George W. Scott, Brian Goodman, Michael Irby, Maurice Bullard, Jeremy Childs, Robin Wright Penn; **D:** Rod Lurie; **w:** Graham Yost,

David Scarpa; **c:** Shelly Johnson; **M:** Jerry Goldsmith.

The Last Chance 🐾🐾🐾 1945 A realistic look at the efforts of three WWII Allied officers to help a group of refugees escape across the Alps from Italy to Switzerland. The officers are played by former pilots who were shot down over Switzerland. In spite of this—or perhaps because of it—the acting is superb. Watch for inspirational scene of refugees singing. 105m/B VHS, DVD. E.G. Morrison, John Hoy, Ray Reagan, Odeardo Mosini, Sigfrit Steiner, Emil Gerber; **D:** Leopold Lindtberg.

Last Chase 🐾½ 1981 (PG) Famed race car driver becomes a vocal dissenter against the sterile society that has emerged, in this drama set in the near future. Screenplay written by Christopher Crowe under the pseudonym C.R. O'Cristopher. 106m/C VHS. *CA* Lee Majors, Burgess Meredith, Chris Makepeace, Alexandra Stewart; **D:** Martyn Burke; **w:** Martyn Burke, Christopher Crowe. TV

Last Command 🐾🐾🐾 1928 Famous powerful silent film by Sternberg about an expatriate Czarist general forging out a pitiful living as a silent Hollywood extra, where he is hired by his former adversary to reenact the revolution he just left. Next to "The Last Laugh," this is considered Jannings' most acclaimed performance. Deeply ironic, visually compelling film with a new score by Gaylord Carter. 88m/B VHS. Emil Jannings, William Powell, Evelyn Brent, Nicholas Soussanin, Michael Visaroff, Jack Raymond, Fritz Feld; **D:** Josef von Sternberg; **M:** Max Steiner, Gaylord Carter. Oscars '28: Actor (Jannings). Natl. Film Reg. '06.

The Last Command 🐾🐾½ 1955 Jim Bowie and his followers sacrifice their lives in defending the Alamo. A good cast holds its own against a mediocre script; battle scenes are terrific. 110m/C VHS. Sterling Hayden, Richard Carlson, Ernest Borgnine, J. Carrol Naish, Virginia Grey, Anna Maria Alberghetti; **D:** Frank Lloyd.

The Last Confederate: The Story of Robert Adams 🐾🐾 *Strike the Tent* 2005 (R) Adams portrays his own great-great grandfather Robert, a South Carolina native who becomes a captain in the Confederacy. He falls in love with northern belle Evilyn McCord (Edwards), the sister of best friend Nelson (Lindsey), who also joins the southern cause. When both men are captured and sent to a Union prison camp, Robert plans an escape that will eventually bring him back to Evilyn. 96m/C DVD. Amy Redford, Tippi Hedren, Mickey Rooney, Julian Adams, Gwendolyn Edwards, Joshua Lindsey, Eric Holloway, Tim Sherrill; **D:** Julian Adams, A. Blaine Miller; **w:** Julian Adams, Gwendolyn Edwards, Joshua Lindsey; **c:** Shawn Lewallen; **M:** Alli Onvarsson.

The Last Contract 🐾🐾 1986 (R) An artist who pays his bills by working as a hitman, kills the wrong man. As a result, he must fear for his life since a counterhit is inevitable. 85m/C VHS. Jack Palance, Rod Steiger, Bo Svenson, Richard Roundtree, Ann Turkel; **D:** Allan A. Buckhantz.

Last Cry for Help 🐾½ 1979 A psychiatrist helps a 17-year-old high school coed who, fearing she has disappointed her parents, attempts suicide. Typical melodrama that attempts to make a statement, but falls short. Definitely not the "Partridge Family." 98m/C VHS. Linda Purl, Shirley Jones, Tony LoBianco, Murray Hamilton, Grant Goodeve; **D:** Hal Sitowitz; **M:** Miles Goodman. TV

Last Dance 🐾🐾 1991 Five scantily clad exotic dancers are ready to compete for the title of Miss Dance-TV, but trouble ensues when the dancers start turning up dead. 86m/C VHS, DVD. Cynthia Bassinet, Elaine Hendrix, Kurt T. Williams, Allison Rhea, Erica Ringston; **D:** Anthony Markes.

The Last Dance 🐾🐾 *Sista Darsen* 1993 Two couples, Claus and Tove (Brynolfsson, Bergstrom) and best friends Lennart and Liselott (Andersson, Froling), have a shared obsession with ballroom dance competitions and some secret desires. Seems Claus and Tove have a rocky marriage and think their friends have the perfect union. Instead, Lennart is

tired of his overbearing wife and longs for Tove, to whom he was once engaged. Then Liselott's body is found beneath the pier after a competition. Swedish with subtitles. 109m/C VHS. *SW* Helena Bergstrom, Reine Brynolfsson, Ewa Froling, Peter Andersson; **D:** Colin Nutley; **w:** Colin Nutley; **c:** Jens Fischer.

Last Dance 🐾🐾 1996 (R) Following closely on the heels of "Dead Man Walking," this death-row drama suffered from bad timing and was dubbed by some as "Bad Hair Walking." Stone plays a convicted murderess condemned to die in an unnamed Southern state. Morrow's the rookie attorney for the state's clemency office assigned to her case. As a bond grows between the two, he uncovers errors in her trial that his bosses would rather have him ignore. The movie makes its big mistake by centering on Morrow's callow lawyer instead of Stone's embittered con. The clock-ticking countdown to the execution (which will amuse fans of "The Player") even fails to hold attention. 103m/ C VHS. Sharon Stone, Rob Morrow, Randy Quaid, Peter Gallagher, Jack Thompson, Jayne Brook, Pamela Tyson, Skeet Ulrich, Don Harvey, Diane Sellers; **D:** Bruce Beresford; **w:** Ron Koslow; **c:** Peter James; **M:** Mark Isham.

Last Day of the War 🐾½ 1969 (PG) A German scientist is chased by Americans and Germans as WWII winds to its conclusion. Filmed in Spain. 96m/C VHS. *SP* George Maharis, Maria Perschy, James Philbrook, Gerard Herter; **D:** Juan Antonio Bardem.

Last Days 🐾🐾½ 2005 (R) A reclusive rock star (Pitt) lives an increasingly bizarre existence, barely interacting with the trail of hangers-on and band members that frequent his stone mansion until he finally lives his own life. Loosely based on the Kurt Cobain tragedy but emphatically denied as any type of biography. 97m/C DVD. *US* Michael Pitt, Lukas Haas, Asia Argento, Ricky Jay, Harmony Korine, Scott Green, Nicole Vicius, Ryan Orion, Kim Gordon, Adam Friberg, Andy Friberg, Thadeus A. Thomas, Chip Marks; **D:** Gus Van Sant; **w:** Gus Van Sant; **c:** Harris Savides.

The Last Days of Chez Nous 🐾🐾½ 1992 (R) Armstrong's dramatic comedy about a family falling apart has Ganz as a homesick Frenchman married to controlling, successful Australian writer Harrow. Trouble starts when his wayward sister-in-law Fox returns home to live with them and his wife decides to take an extended holiday with her father. Ganz suddenly finds himself only too involved in Fox's complicated life. Self-involved characters with messy emotional lives leave viewers feeling rather distant, though cast, and particularly Ganz, strive for intimacy. 96m/C VHS. *AU* Bruno Ganz, Lisa Harrow, Kerry Fox, Kiri Paramore, Bill Hunter, Miranda Otto; **D:** Gillian Armstrong; **w:** Helen Garner; **M:** Paul Grabowsky. Australian Film Inst. '92: Actress (Harrow).

The Last Days of Disco 🐾🐾🐾 1998 (R) It's the early 80s and the disco scene is still alive, although it's beginning to develop a wet, hacking cough. Oblivious to this fact are brash Charlotte (Beckinsale) and reserved Alice (Sevigny), recent college grads who work as low-level corporate drones by day and party at an exclusive Studio 54-like club by night. The girls mingle with a group of Harvard educated proto-yuppie clones that include hot shot assistant D.A. Josh (Keeslar), environmental lawyer Tom (Leonard) and ad man Jimmy (Astin). Also populating the club are assistant club manager Des (Eigeman) and shady club owner Bernie (Thornton). Sharp, funny dialogue (and plenty of it) help ease the fact that the characters are merely poor little rich kids who need to shut up and dance. 113m/C VHS, DVD. Chloe Sevigny, Kate Beckinsale, Christopher Eigeman, MacKenzie Astin, Robert Sean Leonard, Matt Keeslar, Tara Subkoff, Jennifer Beals, David Thornton, Michael Weatherly, Burr Steers; **D:** Whit Stillman; **w:** Whit Stillman; **c:** John Thomas; **M:** Mark Suozzo.

The Last Days of Dolwyn 🐾🐾½ *Woman of Dolwyn; Dolwyn* 1949 A man banned for thievery from his Welsh village returns bent upon revenge, he plans to buy the entire district when it is designated part of a water reservoir project, but finds plans thwarted by a dowager. And her stepson, Nicholson shines in an act of compassion, they attempt to show the prisoner a final good time. Nicholson shines in both the complexity and completeness of his character. Adapted from a Daryl Ponicsan novel. **95m/B VHS.** Anthony James, Emlyn Williams, Richard Burton, worth, Hugh Griffith, Roddy McDowall, Tom Jones; *D:* Emlyn Williams; *W:* Emlyn Williams. TV

The Last Detail 🐾🐾🐾 1973 (R) Two hard-boiled career petty officers (Nicholson and Young) are commissioned to transfer a young sailor facing an eight-

year sentence for petty theft from one brig to another, in an act of compassion, they attempt to show the prisoner a final good time. Nicholson shines in both the complexity and completeness of his character. Adapted from a Daryl Ponicsan novel. **104m/C VHS, DVD.** Jack Nicholson, Otis Young, Randy Quaid, Clifton James, Michael Moriarty, Carol Kane, Nancy Allen, Gilda Radner; *D:* Hal Ashby; *W:* Robert Towne; *C:* Michael Chapman; *M:* Johnny Mandel. British Acad. '74; Actor (Nicholson), Screenplay; Cannes '74; Actor (Nicholson); Natl. Soc. Film Critics '74; Actor (Nicholson).

The Last Days of Frank & Jesse James 🐾½ 1986 A tired TV rehash of the well-known western legend in which the famous brothers try to be like others after their personal war against society ends. **100m/C VHS, DVD.** Johnny Cash, Kris Kristofferson, June Carter Cash, Willie Nelson, Margaret Gibson, Gail Youngs; *D:* William A. Graham. TV

The Last Days of Frankie the Fly 🐾½ 1996 (R) It's gonna seem familiar because it's yet another criminal lowlife story set in L.A. but at least Hopper's presence makes this slightly more than routine. He's Frankie, a semi-pathetic petty thief with big dreams and not much talent. He works for vicious gangster Sal (Madsen) and becomes smitten with ex-junkie Margaret (Hannah), who would like to be a legit actress but is instead working in porn. When Frankie decides to impress Margaret, he naturally gets into trouble. **96m/C VHS, DVD.** Dennis Hopper, Daryl Hannah, Michael Madsen, Kiefer Sutherland, Dayton Callie, Jack McGee; *D:* Peter Markle; *W:* Dayton Callie; *C:* Phil Parmet; *M:* George S. Clinton.

The Last Days of Patton 🐾½ 1986 Depicts the aging general's autumn years as a controversial ex-Nazi defender and desk-bound WWII historian Scott reprises his feature-film role. **146m/C VHS.** George C. Scott, Ed Lauter, Eva Marie Saint, Richard Dysart, Murray Hamilton, Kathryn Leigh Scott; *D:* Delbert Mann. TV

Last Days of Planet Earth WOOf! *Prophecies of Nostradamus; Catastrophe 1999; Nostradamus No Daiyogen* 1974 Really stinky Japanese doomsday movie about a scientist who charges that a build-up of pollution is responsible for giant mutant sea slugs and other environmental disasters. Dubbed. **88m/C VHS. JP** Tetsuro Tamba, So Yamamura, Takashi Shimura; *D:* Toshio Masuda.

The Last Days of Pompeii 🐾🐾 *Ultima Giorni di Pompeii* 1960 Superman Reeves plays a gladiator trying to clean up the doomed town of Pompeii in this remake of the 1935 classic. Some spectacular scenes, including the explosive climax when the mountain blows its top. **105m/C VHS.** Steve Reeves, Christine Kaufmann, Barbara Carroll, Anne Marie Baumann, Mimmo Palmara; *D:* Mario Bonnard; *W:* Sergio Leone.

Last Days of Pompeii 🐾🐾🐾 1935 Vintage DeMille-style epic loosely based on Lord Lytton's book, where the eruption of Vesuvius threatens noblemen and slaves alike. State-of-the-art special effects still look fantastic today. Remade in 1960, available colorized. **96m/B VHS, DVD.** Preston Foster, Alan Hale, Basil Rathbone, George L. Baxt, Louis Calhern, David Holt, Dorothy Wilson, Wyrley Birch, Gloria Shea; *D:* Ernest B. Schoedsack; *C:* Jack Cardiff.

The Last Debate 🐾🐾 2000 Presidential candidates Richard Meredith (Young) and Paul Greene (Gray) are having only one televised debate in their tight race, which is being moderated by political columnist Mike Howley (Garner) and three fellow journalists (McDonald, Murphy, Sanchez). Just before the debate, Howley is given camaging info that could Americanize Meredith. Then investigative journalist Tom Chapman (Gallagher) comes in with a lot of questions about the leak and its source. Based on the novel by Jim Lehrer. **90m/C VHS, DVD.** James Garner, Peter Gallagher, Audra McDonald, Dorian Harewood; *D:* John Badham; *W:* Noray Kasser. CABLE.

The Last Dragon 🐾½ *Berry Gordy's The Last Dragon* 1985 (PG-13) It's time for a Motown kung fu showdown on the streets of Harlem, for there is scarcely enough room for even one dragon. **108m/C VHS, DVD.** Taimak, Vanity, Christopher Murney, Julius J. Carry III, Faith Prince; *D:* Michael A. Schultz; *W:* Louis Venosta; *C:* James A. Contner; *M:* Misha Segal.

The Last Drop 🐾🐾 2005 (R) Over-stuffed WWII adventure that takes place during Operation Market Drop, a failed mission that parachuted British troops into German-occupied Holland. One unit has a separate agenda—they are to rendezvous with Dutch resistance to prevent the Nazis from sending some looted national treasures to Berlin. Only a trio of Nazi deserters are after the same goods. Zane is supposed to be a Canadian pilot and Madsen briefly wanders through as a crusty American officer. **110m/C DVD. GB** Billy Zane, Karel Roden, Michael Madsen, Tommy Flanagan, Alexander Skarsgard, Sean Pertwee, Laurence Fox, Neil Newbon; *D:* Colin Teague; *W:* Colin Teague, Gary Young; *C:* Maxime Alexandre; *M:* David Julyan.

Last Embrace 🐾🐾 1979 (R) A feverish thriller in the Hitchcock style dealing with an ex-secret serviceman who is convinced someone is trying to kill him. **102m/C VHS.** Roy Scheider, Janet Margolin, Christopher Walken, John Glover, Charles Napier, Mandy Patinkin; *D:* Jonathan Demme; *M:* Miklos Rozsa.

The Last Don 🐾🐾 1997 (R) Re-edited version of the TV miniseries finds author Puzo, of "Godfather" fame, sticking to what he knows best. The Don in question is Domenico Clericuzio (Aiello), a ruthless patriarch who wipes out the rival family who into (and doesn't spare her hubby). Carrying out the Don's orders is nephew Pippi (Mantegna), an enforcer who weds Vegas showgirl Nalene (Miller) and who gets involved with the casino business. The years pass with the Don manipulating the next generation, as bloodthirsty grandchild Dante (Cochrane) fights for control with Pippi's cool-headed son Cross (Gedrick). Divided loyalties abound. A complete five-hour version of the saga is also available. **150m/C VHS, DVD.** Nick(y) Corello, Danny Aiello, Joe Mantegna, Jason Gedrick, Rory Cochrane, Penelope Ann Miller, Daryl Hannah, Kirstie Alley, Michelle Rene Thomas, David Marciano, Robert Wuhl, k.d. lang, John Colicos, Cliff DeYoung, Michael Massee; *D:* Graeme Clifford; *W:* Joyce Eliason; *M:* Angelo Badalamenti.

The Last Don 2 🐾🐾½ 1998 (R) Since Don *Puzo's The Last Don 2* 1998 (R) Since Don Clericuzio (Aiello) has died there's a power vacuum that forces widower Cross De Lena (Gedrick) back into the family business. The family is besieged by traitors, even as Cross gets involved in a tentative romance with his autistic stepdaughter's teacher, Josie (Kensit). Then there's crazy, vindictive Aunt Rose Marie (Alley) who falls in love with her conflicted priest (Isaacs), problems with the Hollywood studio headed by Cross's sister Claudia (Thomas), and ambitious mobster Billy D'Angelo (Wilder) for Cross to deal with. Unwittingly campy but slower moving than the first installment. **127m/C VHS, DVD.** Jason Gedrick, Kirstie Alley, Patsy Kensit, James Wilder, David Marciano, Jason Isaacs, Michelle Rene Thomas, Conrad Dunn, Robert Wuhl, Andrew Jackson, Joe Mantegna; *Cameos:* Danny Aiello; *D:* Graeme Clifford; *W:* Joyce Eliason; *C:* David Franco; *M:* Roger Bellon. TV

The Last Fight 🐾 1982 (R) Boxer risks his life and his girlfriend for a shot at the championship title. Watch and see if he could've been a contender. **85m/C VHS.** Fred Williamson, Willie Colon, Ruben Blades, Joe Spinell, Darlanne Fluegel; *D:* Fred Williamson.

The Last Five Days 🐾🐾 1982 Based on the true story of a girl and her brother who, in 1943 Munich, were arrested for distributing anti-Nazi propaganda. The film covers the five days between their capture and execution. In German with English subtitles. **112m/C VHS. GE** Lena Stoize, Irm Hermann; *D:* Percy Adlon.

The Last Flight of Noah's Ark 🐾🐾½ 1980 (G) Disney adventure concerns a high-living pilot, a prim missionary, and two stowaway orphans who must pilot their way off a deserted island following the crash landing of their broken-down plane. **97m/C VHS, DVD.** Elliott Gould, Genevieve Bujold, Rick Schroder, Vincent Gardenia, Tammy Lauren; *D:* Charles Jarrott; *W:* Steven W. Carabatsos, George Arthur Bloom; *C:* Charles F. Wheeler; *M:* Maurice Jarre.

Last Flight Out: A True Story 🐾🐾 1990 100 Hours before Saigon fell to the Vietcong in 1975, Vietnamese and Americans rushed to board the last commercial flight out of Vietnam. Luke-warm account of a true story. **99m/C VHS.** James Earl Jones, Richard Crenna, Haing S. Ngor, Eric Bogosian; *D:* Larry Elikann; *W:* Walter Halsey Davis; *C:* Laszlo George; *M:* Christopher Young.

Last Flight to Hell 🐾 1991 When a drug lord is kidnapped, Brown is sent to South America to rescue the slimeball. His interest in the job picks up when the drug lord's 11-on-a-scale-of-ten daughter joins him for the chase. **94m/C VHS.** Reb Brown, Chuck Connors; *D:* Paul D. Robinson.

The Last Emperor 🐾🐾🐾 1987 (PG-13) Deeply ironic epic detailing life of Pu Yi, crowned at the age of three as the last emperor of China before the onset of communism. Follows Pu Yi from childhood to manhood (sequestered away in the Forbidden City) to fugitive to puppet-ruler to party proletariat. O'Toole portrays the sympathetic Scot tutor who educates the adult Pu Yi (Lone) in the ways of the western world after Pu Yi abdicates power in 1912. Shot on location inside the People's Republic of China with a cast of thousands; authentic costumes. Rich, visually stunning movie. The Talking Heads' David Byrne contributed to the score. **140m/C VHS, DVD.** John Lone, Peter O'Toole, Joan Chen, Victor Wong, Ryuichi Sakamoto, Dennis Dun, Maggie Han, Ying Ruocheng, Ric Young; *D:* Bernardo Bertolucci; *W:* Mark Peploe, Bernardo Bertolucci; *C:* Vittorio Storaro; *M:* Ryuichi Sakamoto, David Byrne, Cong Su. Oscars '87; Adapt. Screenplay, Art Dir./Set Dec., Cinematog., Costume Des., Director (Bertolucci), Film Editing, Picture, Sound, Orig. Score; British Acad. '88; Film, Costume Des., Director; Directors Guild '87; Director (Bertolucci); Golden Globes '88; Director (Bertolucci), Film—Drama, Screenplay, Score; L.A. Film Critics '87; Cinematog.; N.Y. Film Critics '87.

Last Exit to Brooklyn 🐾🐾🐾½ 1990 (R) Hubert Selby Jr.'s shocking book comes to vivid life in a vivid film. Leigh gives a stunning performance as a young Brooklyn girl caught between the Mafia, union men, and friends struggling for something better. Set in the 1950s. Fine supporting cast; excellent pacing. **102m/C VHS.** Jennifer Jason Leigh, Burt Young, Stephen Lang, Ricki Lake, Jerry Orbach, Maia Danziger, Stephen Baldwin; *D:* Uli Edel; *C:* Stefan Czapsky. N.Y. Film Critics '89; Support. Actress (Leigh).

Last Exit to Earth 🐾🐾 1996 (R) Your basic male fantasy. Lusty alien babes from dying world need to find some fertile males, since the men of their home planet shoot blanks. They plan to hijack a male-inhabited spaceship that's stuck in a time-warp and has (unbeknownst to the femmes) already been taken over by hijackers. Anyway, the guys get to the planet and being aggressive male pigs decide they want to run things. **86m/C VHS.** Costas Mandylor, Kim Greist, David Groh, Hilary Shepard Turner; *D:* Katt Shea. CABLE

Last Four Days 🐾🐾 1977 (PG) A chronicle of the final days of Benito Mussolini. **91m/C VHS, DVD.** Rod Steiger, Henry Fonda, Franco Nero; *D:* Carlo Lizzani.

Last Frontier 🐾🐾½ 1932 Serial of 12 chapters contains shades of spectacular figures in Western history: Custer, Hickok, and others in a background of grazing buffalo, boom towns, and covered wagon trails. **216m/B VHS, DVD.** Lon Chaney Jr., Yakima Canutt, Francis X. Bushman; *D:* Spencer Gordon Bennet, Thomas L. Story.

Last Game 🐾🐾 1980 A college student is torn between his devotion to his blind father and going out for the college's football team. **107m/C VHS, DVD.** Howard Segal, Ed L. Grady, Terry Alden; *D:* Martin Beck.

The Last Good Time 🐾🐾½ 1994 (R) Old-world violinist Joseph Kopple (Mueller-Stahl), retired and living in a small Brooklyn apartment, has his world turned upside down when his street-smart neighbor Charlotte (d'Abo) seeks refuge from her abusive boyfriend Eddie (PassDur). An unsentimental friendship develops between the two in spite of the differences in their ages, educations, and lifestyles. Terrific performance from Mueller-Stahl as the lonely but dignified old man. Based on the novel by Richard Bausch. **90m/C VHS.** Armin Mueller-Stahl, Olivia D'Abo, Maureen Stapleton, Lionel Stander, Adrian Pasdar; *D:* Bob Balaban; *W:* Bob Balaban, John McLaughlin; *C:* Claudia Raschke.

Last Gun 🐾🐾 1964 A legendary gunman on the verge of retirement has to save his town from a reign of terror before turning his gun in. **98m/C VHS.** Carl Mohner, Livio Lorenzon, Celina Cely, Kitty Carver, Cameron Mitchell; *D:* Sergio Bergonzelli; *W:* Ambrogio Molteni; *C:* Romolo Garroni; *M:* Marcello Gigante.

The Last Gasp 🐾½ 1994 (R) Contractor Patrick murders the Mexican Indian who's interfering with his project and is cursed. He turns into a wild killer who must satisfy his blood lust every 20 days. Only Pacula tries to save him. Gory and predictable. **90m/C VHS.** Robert Patrick, Joanna Pacula, Vyto Ruginis, Mimi (Meyer) Craven; *D:* Scott McGinnis.

The Last Hard Men 🐾🐾½ 1976 Retired sheriff Sam Burgade (Heston) must save his daughter (Hershey) from escaped convict Provo (Coburn) who kidnapped her as revenge for jailing him and accidentally killing his wife. Provo and his gang force a showdown with the reluctant former lawman by threatening bodily harm and worse to the daughter if he doesn't show. Solid work by the leads raises this one above the usual genre fare. **103m/C VHS.** Charlton Heston, James Coburn, Barbara Hershey, Michael Parks, Jorge (George) Rivero, Larry Wilcox, Thalmus Rasulala, Chris Mitchum, Morgan Paull, John Quade, Robert Donner; *D:* Andrew V. McLaglen; *W:* Guerdon (Gordon) Trueblood; *C:* Duke Callaghan; *M:* Jerry Goldsmith.

The Last Hit 🐾🐾½ 1993 (R) Michael Grant (Brown) is a professional assassin, working for the CIA, who's very good at his job. But now he's burned out and ready to retire to New Mexico for some peace and quiet. He buys a house from the widowed Anna (Adams), naturally falling in love with her. Then one last assignment comes along and, wouldn't you know, his target turns out to be Anna's father (Yulin). Based on the novel "The Large Kill" by Patrick Ruell. **93m/C VHS.** Bryan Brown, Brooke Adams, Harris Yulin; *D:* Jan Egleson; *W:* Walter Klenhard, Alan Sharp; *M:* Gary Chang.

Last Holiday 🐾🐾🐾 1950 A man who is told he has a few weeks to live decides to spend them in a posh resort where people assume he is important.

The Last Fling 🐾½ 1986 When Seleca has her mind set on a romantic fling, Ritter is headed for trouble. She wants love for one night, he wants it forever. Will they solve this difference of opinion? Will true love prevail? Will Ritter consent to being used as a one-night stand? Weakly plotted and poorly acted comedy. **95m/C VHS.** John Ritter, Connie Selecca, Scott Bakula, Shannon Tweed, Paul Sand, John Bennett Perry; *D:* Corey Allen; *M:* Charles Bernstein. TV

89m/B VHS. *GB* Alec Guinness, Kay Walsh, Beatrice Campbell, Wilfrid Hyde-White, Bernard Lee; *D:* Henry Cass; *W:* J.B. Priestley.

Last Holiday ♂♂½ 2006 (PG-13) Georgia Byrd (Queen Latifah) is a shy New Orleans salesclerk with a passion for gourmet cooking and a habit of setting her dreams aside. This changes when Georgia is (mis)diagnosed with a fatal disease that gives her only weeks to live. She decides to make the most of her time by giving herself a makeover and a holiday at the ritzy Czech Grandhotel Pupp so she can enjoy the gastronomical delights of her favorite chef, Didier (the charming Depardieu). The Queen is as appealing as ever, even in this warmed-over comedy, which is a remake of the 1950 Alec Guinness comedy. 112m/C DVD. *US* Queen Latifah, LL Cool J, Timothy Hutton, Giancarlo Esposito, Alicia Witt, Gerard Depardieu, Jane Adams, Susan Kellerman, Jascha Washington, Matt Ross, Ranjit (Chadha) Chowdhry, Mike Estime, Michael Nouri, Julia Lashae, Richmond Werner, Emeril Lagasse, Shirl Cleutat; *D:* Wayne Wang; *W:* Jeffrey Price, Peter S. Seaman; *C:* Geoffrey Simpson; *M:* George Fenton.

The Last Hour ♂ 1991 (R) A Wall Street crook crosses a Mafia punk, so the latter holds the former's wife hostage in an unfinished skyscraper. Fortunately the lady's first husband is a gung-ho cop eager to commence the DIE HARD-esque action. Undistinguished fare that gives away the climax in an opening flash-forward. 85m/C VHS. Michael Pare, Shannon Tweed, Bobby DiCicco, Robert Pucci; *D:* William Sachs.

Last House on Dead End Street WOOF! *The Fun House* 1977 (R) Gore galore as actors die for their art in this splatter flick about snuff films. 90m/C VHS, DVD. Steven Morrison, Dennis Crawford, Lawrence Bornman, Janet Sorley; *D:* Victor Janos.

Last House on the Left ♂♂ *Krug and Company; Sex Crime of the Century* 1972 (R) Two girls are kidnapped from a rock concert by a gang of escaped convicts; the girls' parents exact bloody revenge when the guilty parties pay an intended housecall. Controversial and grim low-budget shocker; loosely based on Bergman's "The Virgin Spring." 83m/C VHS, DVD. David A(lexander) Hess, Lucy Grantham, Sandra Cassel, Mark Sheffler, Fred J. Lincoln, Jeramie Rain, Gaylord St. James, Cynthia Carr, Ada Washington, Martin Kove; *D:* Wes Craven; *W:* Wes Craven; *C:* Victor Hurwitz; *M:* A(lexander) Hess.

The Last Hunt ♂♂½ 1956 Well-performed western starring Taylor as a seedy buffalo hunter who gains his identity from senseless acts of murder. When personalities clash, he seeks revenge on fellow buffalo hunter Granger. Shot in Custer National Park, the buffalo scenes were real-life attempts at keeping the animals controlled. Based on the novel by Milton Lott. 108m/C VHS. Robert Taylor, Stewart Granger, Lloyd Nolan, Debra Paget, Russ Tamblyn, Constance Ford, Ainslie Pryor, Ralph Moody, Fred Graham, Dan(iel) White, Bill Phillips, Roy Barcroft; *D:* Richard Brooks; *W:* Richard Brooks; *M:* Daniele Amfitheatrof.

The Last Hunter ♂ *Hunter of the Apocalypse* 1980 (R) A soldier fights for his life behind enemy lines during the Vietnam War. 97m/C VHS. *IT* Tisa Farrow, David Warbeck, Tony King, Bobby Rhodes, Margit Evelyn Newton, John Steiner, Alan Collins; *D:* Anthony M. Dawson.

Last Hurrah ♂♂½ 1958 An aging Irish-American mayor battles corruption and political backbiting in his effort to get re-elected one last time. Semi-acclaimed heart warmer, based on the novel by Edwin O'Connor. 121m/B VHS, DVD. Spencer Tracy, Basil Rathbone, John Carradine, Jeffrey Hunter, Dianne Foster, Pat O'Brien, Edward Brophy, James Gleason, Donald Crisp, Ricardo Cortez, Wallace Ford, Frank McHugh, Jane Darwell, Arthur Walsh; *D:* John Ford; *W:* Frank Nugent; *C:* Charles Lawton Jr. Natl. Bd. of Review '58: Actor (Tracy), Director (Ford).

Last Hurrah for Chivalry ♂♂ *Hao xia* 1978 An honorable man cannot defend his family from a ruthless enemy and turns to two swordsmen-for-hire for help. Chinese with subtitles or dubbed. 108m/C VHS, DVD. *HK* Damian Lau, Wei Pai, San Lee Hoi;

D: John Woo; *W:* John Woo; *C:* Ching Yu, Yao Chu Chang.

The Last Innocent Man ♂♂½ 1987 An attorney who quit law due to a guilty conscience is lured into defending a suspected murderer. Things become even more complicated when he begins having an affair with his client's seductive wife. A well-acted and suspense-filled flick. 113m/C VHS. Ed Harris, Roxanne Hart, Bruce McGill, Clarence Williams III, Rose Gregorio, David Suchet, Darrell Larson; *D:* Roger Spottiswoode; *W:* Dan Bronson; *M:* Brad Fiedel. C A B L E

The Last King of Scotland ♂♂♂ 2006 (R) Raging biopic recounts the Ugandan dictatorship of Idi Amin, which lasted from 1971-1979 and devastated the country. Whitaker's performance captures the leader's charisma and savagery without flinching. A fictionalized composite character, Scotsman Nicholas Garrigan (McAvoy), enters Amin's camp in 1971 as a doctor determined to help, but slowly finds himself in the unenviable position of being Amin's right-hand man. Title refers to Amin's obsession with British imperialism and his belief that the Scots, whom he admired as fierce fighters, were equally ill-treated. Based on Giles Foden's 1998 novel. 121m/C DVD. *GB GE* Forest Whitaker, James McAvoy, Kerry Washington, Gillian Anderson, Simon McBurney, Kevin MacDonald; *W:* Peter Morgan, Jeremy Brock; *C:* Anthony Dod Mantle; *M:* Alex Heffes. Oscars '06: Actor (Whitaker); British Acad. '06: Actor (Whitaker), Adapt. Screenplay; Golden Globes '07: Actor—Drama (Whitaker); Screen Actors Guild '06: Actor (Whitaker).

The Last Kiss ♂♂½ *L'Ultimo Bacio* 2001 (R) Responsibility and middle crisis and romantic complications. Carlo (Accorsi) is living with his longtime girlfriend Giulia (Mezzogiorno), who tells him she's pregnant. This throws him into a tizzy since he doesn't really want to be a grown-up. Carlo's fading beauty mother, Anna (Sandrelli), also reacts badly to the news since she doesn't want to be a grandma; she abruptly decides to leave her boring hubby for some new romantic possibilities. Both mother and son use their angst to justify affairs as they try to figure out what they really want from their lives. A generally sophisticated melodrama that doesn't take itself too seriously. Italian with subtitles. 115m/C DVD. *IT* Stefano Accorsi, Stefania Stella, Claudio Santamaria, Marco Cocci, Pierfrancesco Favino, Regina Orioli, Giorgio Pasotti; *D:* Gabriele Muccino; *W:* Gabriele Muccino; *C:* Marcello Montarsi; *M:* Paolo Buonino.

The Last Kiss ♂♂½ 2006 (R) Botched remake of the Italian hit "L'Ultimo Bacio," now taking place in Madison, WI. About to hit 30, Michael (Braff, with a constant hangdog expression) finds his life spinning out of control after meeting sexy undergrad Kim (Bilson), while trying to balance the revelation that his live-in girlfriend Jenna (Barrett) is pregnant. Self-conscious dramedy about men unwilling to accept adult responsibility (yawn) and the exasperated women around them. How did Ed Burns not make this? 105m/C DVD. *US* Zach Braff, Jacinda Barrett, Casey Affleck, Michael Weston, Blythe Danner, Tom Wilkinson, Lauren Lee Smith, Marley Shelton, Rachel Bilson, Eric Christian, Harold Ramis; *D:* Tony Goldwyn; *W:* Paul Haggis; *C:* Tom Stern; *M:* Michael Penn.

The Last Laugh ♂♂♂ *Der Letzte Mann* 1924 An elderly man, who as the doorman of a great hotel was looked on as a symbol of "upper class," is demoted to washroom attendant due to his age. Important due to camera technique and consuming performance by Jannings. Silent with music score. A 91-minute version is also available. 88m/B VHS, DVD. *GE* Emil Jannings, Maly Delshaft, Max Hiller; *D:* F.W. Murnau; *W:* Carl Mayer; *C:* Karl Freund; *M:* Giuseppe Becce.

The Last Legion ♂ 2007 (PG-13) Barbarians have taken Rome, and Britain's heroes haven't even been born in this revision of the Arthurian legend. Romulus (Sangster), last of the Caesars, flees to Britain under the protection of General Aurelius (Firth), wise-man Ambrosinus

(Kingsley), and a rag-tag group of cohorts. Seeking the Roman 9th Legion for protection, they find a group of men who have become farmers and avoid conflict with evil warlord Vortigern. Bloody battles for control of Britain ensue, although they're reduced to cheap CGI sequences worthy only as a distraction from the unlikeable characters and weak plot. Sangster is adequate as the boy emperor, Firth is desperately miscast as an action hero and cannot muster any chemistry with token female warrior Mira (Rai), while Kingsley chews scenery throughout in what's best described as an imitation of Obi-Wan Kenobi. 110m/C DVD. *FR GB IT* Colin Firth, Ben Kingsley, Thomas Sangster, Kevin McKidd, John Hannah, Iain Glen, Aishwarya Rai, Rupert Friend, Peter Mullan, Alexander Siddig, Robert Pugh, James Cosmo, Owen Teale; *D:* Doug Lefler; *W:* Jez Butterworth, Tom Butterworth; *C:* Marco Pontecorvo; *M:* Patrick Doyle.

The Last Letter ♂♂ 2004 (R) A twist ending somewhat redeems the slow pace of this courtroom thriller. Forceful jury foreman Griffith (Forsythe) leads the other jurors in deciding the verdict for a serial killer (writer/director Gannon) accused of 14 gory murders (shown in flashbacks). But their deliberations aren't as clear-cut as you might imagine since the foreman seems determined to raise more than a reasonable doubt that the right man is on trial. 80m/C DVD. William Forsythe, Yancy Butler, Grace Zabriskie, Leo Rossi, Russell Gannon; *D:* Russell Gannon; *W:* Russell Gannon; *C:* Sean Dinwoodie; *M:* Terry Plumeri. V I D E O

The Last Lieutenant ♂♂½ *The Second Lieutenant; Secondløitnanten* 1994 Aging Thor Espedal (Skjonberg) is a one-time second lieutenant who has just retired from the Merchant Marines and returned home to his beloved wife, Anna (Tellefsen). But since the year is 1940, his retirement is interrupted by the German Army invading his country. Espedal enlists in the resistance effort but finds the army in complete disarray. Still the old man and a group of volunteers become determined to hold a key mountain pass. Norwegian with subtitles. 102m/C VHS, DVD. *NO* Espen Skjonberg, Bjorn Sundquist, Rut Tellefsen, Gard B. Eidsvold, Lars Andreas Larssen; *D:* Hans Petter Moland; *W:* Hans Petter Moland, Axel Hellstenius; *C:* Harald Gunnar Paalgard; *M:* Randall Meyers.

Last Life in the Universe ♂♂½ *Ruang rak noi nid mahasan* 2003 Kenji (Tadanobu) is a suicidal ex-yakuza living in exile in Bangkok where he works as a librarian at the Japan Cultural Center. He meets Noi (Boonyasak), an equally suicidal hooker and is soon living with her at her family's derelict beach house. The opposites (he has OCD, she lives in filth) attract and various magical realism sequences take place until the past comes to haunt them both. English, Thai, and Japanese with subtitles. 112m/C DVD. Tadanobu Asano, Sinitta Boonyasak, Laila Boonyasak, Yutaka Matsushige, Takeuchi Riki, Takashi Miike, Yohji Tanaka, Sakichi Sato, Thitt Phum-Om; *D:* Pen-ek Ratanaruang; *C:* Christopher Doyle; *M:* Hualampong Riddim.

Last Light ♂♂ 1993 (R) A prison guard (Whitaker) on death row forms a tenuous bond with an incorrigible inmate (Sutherland) who's about to be executed. Disturbing, especially the execution scene. Filmed on location at California's Soledad Prison. Sutherland's directorial debut. 95m/C VHS, DVD. Kiefer Sutherland, Forest Whitaker, Clancy Brown, Lynne Moody, Kathleen Quinlan, Amanda Plummer; *D:* Kiefer Sutherland. C A B L E

Last Lives ♂♂ 1998 (R) Confusing parallel universe story has Malakai (Wirth) traveling to an alternate world to search for his lost wife. He discovers Adrienne (Rubin) about to marry Aaron (Howell) and Malakai kidnaps her to take her back to his world. 99m/C VHS. C. Thomas Howell, Jennifer Rubin, Billy Wirth, Judge Reinhold; *D:* Worth Keeter; *W:* Dan Duling; *C:* Kent Wakeford; *M:* Greg Edmonson. V I D E O

The Last Man ♂♂ 2000 (R) Overweight, balding, neurotic graduate student Alan (Arnott), who believes he's the last man alive on earth, is thrilled to discover

Sarah (Ryan), a babe who would never have even looked at him pre-apocalypse. But a snake appears in Alan's paradise in the form of hitchhiker Raphael (Montgomery), who's as dumb as he is good-looking (and he's very good looking). Naturally, Sarah is attracted to him—much to Alan's jealous dismay. So if you were the last three people alive, just how would you handle the situation? 93m/C VHS, DVD. David Arnott, Jeri Ryan, Dan Montgomery Jr.; *D:* Harry Ralston; *W:* Harry Ralston; *C:* Michael Grady; *M:* Woody Jackson, Ivan Knight.

The Last Man on Earth ♂♂ *L'Ultimo Uomo Della Terra* 1964 Price is the sole survivor of a plague which has turned the rest of the world into vampires, who constantly harass him. Uneven U.S./Italian production manages to convey a creepy atmosphere of dismay. 86m/B VHS, DVD. *IT* Vincent Price, Franca Bettoya, Giacomo "Jack" Rossi-Stuart, Emma Danieli; *D:* Ubaldo Ragona, Sidney Salkow; *W:* Richard Matheson, William P. Leicester, Furio M. Menotti; *C:* Franco Delli Colli; *M:* Paul Sawtell, Bert Shefter.

Last Man Standing ♂ 1987 (R) A cheap, gritty drama about bare-knuckle fist fighting. Wells stars as a down-on-his-luck prizefighter trying to find work that doesn't involve pugilism. 89m/C VHS. William Sanderson, Vernon Wells, Franco (Columbo) Columbu; *D:* Damian Lee.

Last Man Standing ♂♂ 1995 (R) L.A. police officer Wincott discovers corruption after his partner Banks is murdered. 96m/C VHS, DVD. Jeff Wincott, Jillian McWhirter, Jonathan Banks, Steve Eastin, Jonathan Fuller, Michael Greene, Ava Fabian; *D:* Joseph Merhi; *M:* Louis Febre.

Last Man Standing ♂♂½ 1996 (R) *Welcome to Jericho* Engaging, but not terribly original gangster/western features a plot taken from Clint Eastwood's career-making "Fistful of Dollars" (in turn, an adaptation of Akira Kurosawa's "Yojimbo"). The producers and credits claim lineage directly from the Kurosawa film, but this story's been around for a while, folks. In the small 1930s border town of Jericho Texas, Willis, under the pseudonym John Smith, hires himself out to both sides of a bootlegging war in an effort to make some quick cash. Bigger roles for Walken, the flinty trigger man for Irish boss Doyle (Kelly), and Dern, the town sheriff on the mob payroll, could have perked things up a little. Willis nicely injects his smirking brand of wit into a film that may have benefited from more of the dark "Yojimbo" humor. Hill provides his trademark visually exciting action sequences. 101m/C VHS, DVD. Bruce Willis, Bruce Dern, Christopher Walken, Karina Lombard, William Sanderson, David Patrick Kelly, Alexandra Powers, Leslie Mann, Michael Imperioli, R.D. Call, Ken Jenkins, Ned Eisenberg; *D:* Walter Hill; *W:* Walter Hill; *C:* Lloyd Ahern II; *M:* Ry Cooder.

The Last Married Couple in America ♂♂ 1980 (R) A couple fight to stay happily married amidst the rampant divorce epidemic engulfing their friends. 103m/C VHS. George Segal, Natalie Wood, Richard Benjamin, Valerie Harper, Dom DeLuise, Priscilla Barnes; *D:* Gilbert Cates; *M:* Charles Fox.

The Last Marshal ♂♂ 1999 (R) Tough Texas lawman Glenn is mighty riled when some no-account prisoners manage to escape from his jail. So he trails them to Miami to get them back. 102m/C VHS, DVD. Scott Glenn, Constance Marie, Randall Batinkoff, Vincent Castellanos, John Ortiz, Raymond Cruz, William Forsythe, Lisa Boyle; *D:* Mike Kirton. V I D E O

Last Mercenary WOOF! 1984 An angry ex-soldier kills everyone who makes him mad. 90m/C VHS. *IT* Tony Marsina, Malcolm Duff, Kitty Nichols, Louis Walser; *D:* Mario Siciliano; *C:* Mario Siciliano; *C:* Louis Smith; *M:* Fabio Frizzi.

The Last Metro ♂♂♂ *Le Dernier Metro* 1980 (PG) Truffaut's alternately gripping and touching drama about a theatre company in Nazi-occupied Paris. In 1942, Lucas Steiner (Bennent) is a successful Jewish theatre director who is forced into hiding. He turns the running of the theatre over to his wife, Marion (the always exquisite Deneuve, who must contend with a pro-Nazi theatre critic (Richard) and her growing attraction to the company's leading man (Depardieu), who is secretly working with the Resistance. In French with English subtitles. **135m/C VHS, DVD, FR** *Catherine Deneuve, Gerard Depardieu, Heinz Bennent, Jean-Louis Richard, Jean-Pierre Ferrol, Paulette Dubost, Sabine Haudepin, Maurice Risch, Jean-Pierre Klein, Martine Simonet, Franck Pasquier, Jean-Jose Richer, Laszlo Szabo, Jessica Zucman; D: Francois Truffaut; W: Francois Truffaut, Suzanne Schiffman, Jean-Claude Gruenberg; C: Nestor Almendros; M: Georges Delerue. Cesar '81: Actor (Depardieu), Actress (Deneuve), Art Dir/Set Dec., Cinematog., Director (Truffaut), Film, Score, Writing, Score.*

The Last Mile 🎬🎬 **1932** The staff of a prison prepares for the execution of a celebrated murderer. Dated. **70m/B VHS.** *Preston Foster, Howard Phillips, George E. Stone; D: Sam Bischoff.*

Last Night 🎬🎬 **1993 (R)** It's 6 p.m. in the city of Toronto and the world will come to an end in six hours. And no one's going to save the day. So all the characters are deciding how they'd like to spend their last few hours. Patrick (McKellar) is attending a family dinner and then wants to spend his last hours alone—instead he's drawn into Sandra's (Oh) dilemma. She's stuck in traffic across town from her husband and Patrick tries to help her

get to her rendezvous. Meanwhile, his best friend Craig (Rennie) has a few sexual conquests he still wants to make, including one with their high school French teacher, Mrs. Carlton (Bujold). Mordant humor, appealing performances. **94m/C VHS, DVD, CA** *Don McKellar, Sandra Oh, Callum Keith Rennie, Sarah Polley, David Cronenberg, Genevieve Bujold, Tracy Wright, Roberta Maxwell, Robin Gammell, Karen Glave, Jackie Burroughs; D: Don McKellar; W: Don McKellar; C: Douglas Koch; M: Alexina Louie, Alex Pauk. Genie '98: Actor (McKellar), Director (McKellar).*

Last Night at the Alamo 🎬🎬 **1983** Patrons fight to stop the destruction of their Houston bar, the Alamo, which is about to be razed to make room for a modern skyscraper. Insightful comedy written by the author of "The Texas Chainsaw Massacre." **80m/B VHS.** *Sonny Carl Davis, Lou Perry, Steve Matila, Tina Hubbard, Doris Hargrave; D: Eagle Pennell.*

The Last of England 🎬🎬½ **1987** A furious non-narrative film by avant-garde filmmaker Jarman, depicting the modern British landscape as a funereal, waste-filled, rubble-heap—as depleted morally as it is environmentally. **87m/C VHS, DVD, GB** *Tilda Swinton, Spencer Leigh, Spring, Gerard McArthur; D: Derek Jarman; W: Derek Jarman; C: Derek Jarman, Richard Heslop, Christopher Hughes; M: Simon Fisher Turner.*

The Last of His Tribe 🎬🎬 **1992 (PG-13)** In 1911 an anthropologist befriends an Indian and discovers that Ishi is the last surviving member of California's Yahi tribe. Ishi then becomes a media and scientific society darling, spending the remainder of his remaining life in captivity to academia. A good portrayal of the Native American plight. Based on a true story. **90m/C VHS, DVD.** *Jon Voight, Graham Greene, David Ogden Stiers, Jack Blessing, Anne Archer, Daniel Benzali; D: Harry Hook. CABLE.*

The Last of Mrs. Cheyney 🎬🎬🎬 **1937** Remake of Norma Shearer's 1929 hit, based on the play by Frederick Lonsdale, about a sophisticated jewel thief in England. Crawford stars as the jewel thief who poses as a wealthy woman to get into parties hosting some of London's bluebloods. Dripping with charm, she works her way into Lord Drilling's mansion where she pars a huge heist. The film is handled well, and the cast gives solid performances throughout. This chic comedy of high society proved to be one of Crawford's most popular films of the '30s. **98m/B VHS.** *Joan Crawford, Robert Montgomery, William Powell, Frank Morgan, Nigel Bruce, Jessie Ralph; D: Richard Boleslawski, George Fitzmaurice; C: George J. Folsey.*

The Last of Philip Banter 🎬🎬½ **1987 (R)** An alcoholic writer is terrified to learn events in his life exactly match a mysterious manuscript. **105m/C VHS.** *Tony Curtis, Gregg Henry, Irene Miracle, Scott Paulin, Kate Vernon; D: Herve Hachuel.*

The Last of Sheila 🎬🎬½ **1973 (PG)** A movie producer invites six big-star friends for a cruise aboard his yacht, the "Sheila." He then stages an elaborate "Whodunnit" parlor game to discover three months. **75m/B VHS, DVD.** *Wallace Beery, Barbara Bedford, Albert Roscoe, Lillian Hall-Davis, Henry Woodward, James Gordon; D: Maurice Tourneur, Clarence Brown; W: Robert A.(R.A.) Dillon; C: Charles Van Enger. Natl. Film Reg. '95.*

The Last of the Mohicans 🎬🎬 **1932** Serial based on James Fenimore Cooper's novel of the Mohican Indian War. Twelve chapters, 13 minutes each. Remade as a movie in 1936 and 1992 and as a TV movie in 1977. **230m/B VHS, DVD.** *Edwina Booth, "Harry Carey Sr., Hobart Bosworth, Frank Coghlan, D: Ford Beebe, B. Reeves Eason.*

The Last of the Mohicans 🎬🎬½ **1936** James Fenimore Cooper's classic about the French and Indian War in colonial America is brought to the screen. Remake of the 1932 serial. **91m/B VHS.** *Randolph Scott, Binnie Barnes, Bruce Cabot, Henry Wilcoxon, Heather Angel, Hugh Buckler; D: George B. Seitz.*

The Last of the Mohicans 🎬🎬 **1965** The classic novel by James Fenimore Cooper. **TV**

The Last of the Mohicans 🎬🎬🎬 **1992 (R)** It's 1757, at the height of the French and English war in the American colonies, with various Native American tribes allied to each side. Hawkeye (Day-Lewis), a white frontiersman raised by the Mohicans, wants nothing to do with either "civilized" side, until he rescues the beautiful Cora (Stowe) from the revenge-minded Huron Magua (Studi) in a powerful performance). Graphically violent battle scenes are realistic, but not gratuitous. The real pleasure in this adaptation, which draws from both the 1936 film, is in its lush look and attractive stars. Means is terrific in his film debut as Hawkeye's foster-father. Released in a letterbox format to preserve the original integrity of the film. **114m/C VHS, DVD.** *Daniel Day-Lewis, Madeleine Stowe, Wes Studi, Russell Means, Eric Schweig, Jodhi May, Steven Waddington, Maurice Roeeves, Colm Meaney, Patrice Chereau, Pete Postlethwaite, Terry Kinney, Tracey Ellis, Dennis Banks, Dylan Baker; D: Michael Mann; W: Christopher Crowe, Michael Mann; C: Dante Spinotti; M: Trevor Jones, Randy Edelman. Oscars '92: Sound.*

The Last of the Pony Riders 🎬½ **1953** When the telegraph lines linking the East and West Coasts are geared toward youngsters; Hall must lead three children of a British general through dangerous Indian territory. They have a number of adventures including meeting up with Uncas the last of the Mohicans, who's a villain in this mangled version. **79m/B VHS.** *Jon Hall, Michael O'Shea, Evelyn Ankers, Julie Bishop, Buster Crabbe, Rick Vallin, Frederick Worlock, Guy Hedlund; D: George Sherman; W: Herbert Dalmas.*

Last of the Clintons 🎬½ **1935** A range detective tracks an outlaw gang amid spur jinglin', sharp shootin' and cow punchin'. **64m/B VHS.** *Betty Mack, Del Gordon, Harry Fraser, Harry Carey Sr.; D: Slim Whitaker; W: Slim Whitaker; C: Robert E. Cline.*

Last of the Comanches 🎬🎬 **1952** Cavalry and Indians fight for water when both are dying of thirst in the desert. **85m/C VHS, Broderick Crawford, Barbara Hale, John Stewart, Lloyd Bridges, Mickey Shaughnessy, George Mathews; D: Andre de Toth.*

The Last of the Dogmen 🎬🎬½ **1995 (PG)** Cliched modern western with an intriguing premise and good actors. Montana bounty hunter Lewis Gates (Berenger) is recruited to nab three escaped cons but finds them dead and a Cheyenne arrow nearby. Gates does some investigating (in a library no less) and discovers that maybe some descendants of the 1864 Sand Creek massacre are existing in the woods. He gets involved, discovers a tribe of modern-day Indians, and finds a very angry sheriff (Smith) on their trail. Alberta, Canada passes for Big Sky country. **117m/C VHS, DVD.** *Tom Berenger, Barbara Hershey, Kurtwood Smith, Steve Reevs, Andrew Miller, Gregory Scott Cummins; D: Tab Murphy; W: Tab Murphy; C: Karl Walter Lindenlaub; M: David Arnold; Narr: Wilford Brimley.*

The Last of the Finest 🎬½ **1990 (R)** Overzealous *Street Legal; Blue Heat* anti-drug task force cops break the rules in trying to put dealer-drug lords in prison, ostensibly a parallel on the Iran-Contra affair. **106m/C VHS.** *Brian Dennehy, Joe Pantoliano, Jeff Fahey, Bill Paxton, Deborah-Lee Furness, Guy Boyd, Henry Darrow, Lisa Jane Persky, Michael C. Gwynne; D: John MacKenzie; W: George Armitage, Jere P. Cunningham; M: Jack Nitzsche.*

The Last of the High Kings 🎬🎬½ **1996 (R)** Un- *Summer Fling* deracievieng Irish Frankie (Leto) decides to forget about his university entrance exams and enjoy his summer (it's 1977) by cutting loose and fantasizing about various girls he knows. What he doesn't realize is that young American Erin (Ricci), who's staying with his crazy family, has fallen for him. Pleasant romance with a talented cast. Based on the novel "The Last of the High Kings" by Ferdia Mac Anna. **103m/C VHS, DVD, IR GB DK** *Catherine O'Hara, Jared Leto, Christina Ricci, Gabriel Byrne, Stephen Rea, Colm Meaney, Lorraine Pilkington, Jason Barry, Emily Morimer, Karl Hayden, Ciaran Fitzgerald, Darren Monks, Peter Keating, Alexandra Haughey; Renee Weldon, Amanda Shur; D: David Keating; W: David Keating, Gabriel Byrne; C: Bernd Heinl; M: Michael Convenino.*

The Last of the Mohicans 🎬🎬🎬 **1920** Color tints enhance this silent version of the James Fenimore Cooper rouser. Beery is the villainous Magua, with Bedford memorable as the lovely Cora and Roscoe as the brave Uncas. Fine action sequences, including the Huron massacre at Fort Henry. Director credit was shared when Tourneur suffered an on-set injury and was off for three months. **75m/B VHS, DVD.** *Wallace Beery, Barbara Bedford, Albert Roscoe, Lillian Hall-Davis, Henry Woodward, James Gordon; D: Maurice Tourneur, Clarence Brown; W: Robert A.(R.A.) Dillon; C: Charles Van Enger. Natl. Film Reg. '95.*

Last of the Redmen 🎬½ **1947** An adaptation of James Fenimore Cooper's "The Last of the Mohicans" geared toward youngsters; Hall must lead three children of a British general through dangerous Indian territory. They have a number of adventures including meeting up with Uncas the last of the Mohicans, who's a villain in this mangled version. **79m/B VHS.** *Jon Hall, Michael O'Shea, Evelyn Ankers, Julie Bishop, Buster Crabbe, Rick Vallin, Frederick Worlock, Guy Hedlund; D: George Sherman; W: Herbert Dalmas.*

Last of the Red Hot Lovers 🎬½ **1972 (PG)** Not so funny adaptation of Neil Simon's Broadway hit. Middle-aged man decides to have a fling and uses his mother's apartment to seduce three very strange women. **98m/C VHS, DVD.** *Alan Arkin, Paula Prentiss, Sally Kellerman, Renee Taylor; D: Gene Saks; W: Neil Simon.*

The Last of the Warrens 🎬½ **1936** A cowboy returns home after WWI to discover that an unscrupulous storekeeper has stolen his property. **56m/C VHS.** *Bob Steele, Margaret Marquis, Horace Murphy; D: Robert North Bradbury.*

Last of the Wild Horses 🎬½ **2001 (R)** Based on Graham Swift's award-winning 1996 novel, which covers some 50 years in the lives of four London friends. Vic (Courtenay), Ray (Hoskins), and Lenny (Hemmings) all meet in their favorite East London pub to toast their recently deceased

Last Orders 🎬🎬 **1949** Range war almost starts when ranch owner is accused of trying to force the small ranchers out of business. **86m/B VHS.** *Mary Beth Hughes, James Ellison, Jane Frazee, Douglas Dumbrille, James Millican, Reed Hedley, Olin Howlin, Grady Sutton; D: Robert L. Lippert; W: Jack Harvey; C: Benjamin (Ben H.) Kline.*

members. If they can find them and get them to agree. Good cast but the charm is on the low-burner and rather than swinging, it's more a sedate fox-trot. **80m/C VHS, DVD.** *Judi Dench, Ian Holm, Olympia Dukakis, Leslie Caron, Cleo Laine, Joan Sims, Billie Whitelaw, Helen Whitfield, Felicity Dean, Valentine Pelka, Millie Findlay; D: Gilles Mackinnon; W: Alan Plater; C: Richard Greatrex; M: John Keane. CABLE.

"Junior" Coghlan; D: Ford Beebe, B. Reeves Eason.

The Last Minute 🎬🎬 **1971 (R)** A movie stunt man stays in a small *Chinchero* Peruvian town after his filming stint is over. Hopper's confused, pretentious follow-up to "Easy Rider" has a multitude of cameos but little else. Given an award by the Italians; nobody else understood it. Kristofferson's film debut; he also wrote the music. Based on a story by Hopper and Stern. **108m/C VHS.** *Dennis Hopper, Julie Adams, Peter Fonda, Kris Kristofferson, Sylvia Miles, John Phillip Law, Russ Tamblyn, Rod Cameron; D: Dennis Hopper; W: Stewart Stern; M: Kris Kristofferson.*

The Last Musketeer 🎬🎬½ **2000** Gifted fencer Steve McTaer (Green) wants to get away from his past and his family's criminal activities. So when he's falsely accused of a crime, he decides to hide out in the Scottish Highlands, taking an instructor position at a girls' boarding school. But he can't really escape. **85m/C DVD, GB** *Robson Green, Arkie Whiteley; Maureen Beattie, John McGlynn; D: Bill Britten; W: Sebastian Secker Walker; C: Tony Miller; M: John Rea. TV*

The Last Minzy 🎬🎬 **2007 (PG)** Loose adaptation of Lewis Padgett's short story "All Mimzy Were the Borogroves" (yeah, it's from Lewis Carroll's "Jabberwocky"). Noah (O'Neil) and his sister Emma (Wynn) find a box that's filled with odd objects, including a cute stuffed rabbit named Mimzy, who is actually a spokesuh-rabbit, from the future, where things are bad because of pollution and disease. The objects give the kids extraordinary powers that they are expected to use to solve these eco problems. Noah's spiritually-minded science teacher Larry (Wilson) is thrilled with ideas but not condescending. Overstuffed with ideas this is very cool, while the kids' parents seem to be the most clued—but not so. **90m/C VHS, DVD. US** *Joely Richardson, Timothy Hutton, Rainn Wilson, Kathryn Hahn, Noah Wyle, Rhiannon Leigh Wryn, Michael Clarke Duncan; D: Robert Shaye; M: James Newton Howard Shore.*

The Last Movie 🎬🎬 **1971 (R)** Bill-y Byrne "Beesley) is the "next big thing" and subjected to an incredible amount of media hype. But when his latest project is considered a dud, he falls just as fast. Jobless, friendless, and hopeless, Billy is taken in by Anna (Corrie), a young ruffian living with a group of adolescents under the thrall of Fagin-like drug dealer Grimm shanks (3ell). Billy gets sucked into this new world as easily as he was manipulated in the old one. **104m/C VHS, DVD, GB** *Emily Corrie, Ciaran McMenamin, Jasmin Isaacs, Kate Ashfield, Anthony Corlan; Higgins, Leo Ker, Stephen Dorff; D: Stephen Norrington; W: Stephen Norrington; C: J(James) Michael Muro; M: Paul Rabjohns.*

friend Jack (Caine), along with Jack's son, Vince (Winstone). Jack's last request was to have his ashes scattered in the sea at Margate, where he spent his honeymoon with wife Amy (Mirren) in 1939. Amy, however, will not make the trip as she has is going to visit their severely handicapped daughter June (Morelli), whom Jack could never accept, at the institution where June lives. Flashbacks fill out the storylines and the cast is stellar. **109m/C VHS, DVD, GB** Michael Caine, Bob Hoskins, Tom Courtenay, David Hemmings, Ray Winstone, Helen Mirren, J.J. Feild, Cameron Fitch, Nolan Hemmings, Anatol Yusef, Kelly Reilly, Laura Morelli; **D:** Fred Schepisi; **W:** Fred Schepisi; **C:** Brian Tufano; **M:** Paul Grabowsky.

The Last Outlaw ♂♂ 1984
SCTV vets Candy and Levy are Yosh and Stan Schmenge, polka kings interviewed for a "documentary" on their years in the spotlight and on the road. Hilarious spoof on Martin Scorsese's "The Last Waltz," about The Band's last concert. Several fellow Second City-ers keep the laughs coming. If you liked this, **54m/C VHS**, John Candy, Eugene Levy, Rick Moranis, Robin Duke, Catherine O'Hara; **D:** John Blanchard. **CABLE**

The Last Porno Flick ♂ 1974
(PG) A pornographic movie script winds up in the hands of a couple of goofy cab drivers. The twosome sneak the movie's genre past the producers, families, and police. **90m/C VHS**, Michael Pataki, Marianna Hill, Carmen Zapata, Mike Kellin, Colleen Camp, Tom Signorelli, Antony Carbone; **D:** Ray Marsh.

The Last Prostitute ♂♂ 1991
(PG-13) Two teenage boys search for a legendary prostitute to initiate them into manhood, only to discover that she has retired. They hire on as laborers on her horse farm, and one of them discovers the meaning of love. **93m/C VHS**, Sonia Braga, Wil Wheaton, David Kaufman, Woody Watson, Dennis Letts, Cotter Smith; **D:** Lou Antonio; **W:** Carmen Culver. **CABLE**

The Last Remake of Beau Geste ♂♂ 1977 (PG) A slapstick parody of the familiar Foreign Legion story from the Mel Brooks-ish school of loud genre farce. Gary Cooper makes an appearance by way of inserted footage from the 1939 straight version. **85m/C VHS**, Marty Feldman, Ann-Margret, Michael York, Peter Ustinov, James Earl Jones; **D:** Marty Feldman; **W:** Marty Feldman, Chris Allen.

Last Resort ♂♂ 1986 **She Knew No Other**
Way 1986 (R) A married furniture executive unknowingly takes his family on vacation to a sex-saturated, Club Med-type holiday spot, and gets more than the anticipated **80m/C VHS, DVD**, Charles Grodin, Robin Pearson Rose, John Aston, Ellen Blake, Megan Mullally, Christopher Ames, Jon Lovitz, Scott Nemes, Gerrit Graham, Mario Van Peebles, Phil Hartman, Mimi Lieber, Steve Levitt; **D:** Zane Buzby; **W:** Jeff Buhai; **C:** Stephen M. Katz, Alex Nepomniaschy; **W:** Steven Nelson, Thom Sharp.

The Last Picture Show ♂♂♂♂ 1971 (R) Slice of life/ nostalgic 'farewell to an innocent age, based on Larry McMurtry's novel. Set in Archer City, a backwater Texas town, most of the story plays out at the local hangout run by ex-cowboy Sam the Lion (Johnson). Duane (Bridges) is hooked up with spoiled pretty girl Jacy (Shepherd), while Sonny (Bottoms), a sensitive guy, is having an affair with the coach's neglected wife, Ruth (Leachman). Loss of innocence, disillusionment and confusion are played out against the backdrop of a town about to close its cinema. Shepherd's and Bottoms' film debut. Stunningly photographed in black and white (Bogdanovich claimed he didn't want to "prettify" the picture by shooting in color) by Robert Surtees. Followed by a weak sequel, "Texasville." **118m/B VHS, DVD**, Jeff Bridges, Timothy Bottoms, Ben Johnson, Cloris Leachman, Cybill Shepherd, Ellen Burstyn, Eileen Brennan, Clu Gulager, Sharon Taggart, Randy Quaid, Sam Bottoms, Bill(Billy) Thurman, John Hillerman; **D:** Peter Bogdanovich; **W:** Peter Bogdanovich, Larry McMurtry; **C:** Robert L. Surtees. Oscars '71: Support. Actor (Johnson), Support. Actress (Leachman); British Acad. '72: Screenplay, Support. Actor (Johnson); Golden Globes '72: Support. Actor (Johnson); Natl. Bd. of Review '71: Support. Actor, Support. Actress (Leachman), Natl. Film Reg. '98; N.Y. Film Critics '71: Screenplay, Support. Actor (Johnson), Support. Actress (Burstyn); Natl. Soc. Film Critics '71: Support. Actress (Burstyn).

The Last Place on Earth ♂♂♂ 1985 Saga of bitter hardship and ambition depicting the 1911 race between the British Antarctic Expedition, led by Captain Robert Falcon (Shaw), and his Norwegian rival Roald Amundsen (Ousdal) to conquer the South Pole. On seven cassettes. **385m/C VHS, DVD, CA** Martin Shaw, Sverre Anker Ousdal, Max von Sydow, Susan Wooldridge; **D:** Ferdinand Fairfax; **W:** Trevor Griffiths; **C:** John Coquillon; **M:** Trevor Jones. **TV**

Last Plane Out ♂½ 1983 (R) A Texas journalist sent out on assignment to Nicaragua falls in love with a Sandanista rebel. Based on producer Jack Cox's real-life experiences as a journalist during the last days of the Samosa regime. Low-budget propaganda. **90m/C VHS**, Jan-Michael Vincent, Lloyd Battista, Julie Carmen, Mary Crosby, David Huffman, William Windom; **D:** David Nelson.

Smith, Armando Silvestre, Kathrin Lautner; **D:** Joseph Merhi.

Last Rites ♂♂ 1988 (R) A priest at St. Patrick's Cathedral in New York allows a young Mexican woman to seek sanctuary from the Mob, who soon come after both of them. **103m/C VHS, DVD**, Tom Berenger, Daphne Zuniga, Chick Vennera, Dane Clark, Carlo Pacchi, Anne Twomey, Paul Dooley, Vassili Lambrinos; **D:** Donald P. Bellisario; **W:** Donald P. Bellisario; **C:** David Watkin; **M:** Bruce Broughton.

Last Rites ♂♂ 1998 (R) Dillon (Quaid) is a Florida Death Row serial killer, whose execution goes awry when the electric chair blows the generator and Dillon is left with amnesia. Oh, and he's suddenly gained psychic powers that allow him to solve crimes. A shrink (Davidtz) is brought in to see if he's faking, while the warden just wants to try tying Dillon again. **88m/C VHS**, Randy Quaid, Embeth Davidtz, A. Martinez; **D:** Kevin Dowling; **W:** Richard Outten, Tim Frost. **CABLE**

Last Run ♂½ 2001 (R) Frank (Assante) is a former top-secret op who specialized in rescuing Russian defectors. His last assignment got his lover killed and now Frank is after the assassin who caused his life to go wrong. **84m/C VHS, DVD**, Armand Assante, Jurgen Prochnow, Ornella Muti, David Lipper, Corey Johnson; **D:** Anthony Hickox; **W:** Anthony Hickox. **VIDEO**

The Last Safari ♂♂½ 1967 A young man on safari in Africa befriends a bitter professional guide in a drama hampered by a poor script. Granger and Garas set out to hunt the rampaging elephant which killed Granger's friend. Granger thinks killing the beast will restore his courage and help him overcome the guilt he feels. Based on the novel "Gilligan's Last Elephant" by Gerald Hanley. **111m/C VHS**, Stewart Granger, Kaz Garas, Gabriella Licudi, Johnny Sekka, Liam Redmond; **D:** Henry Hathaway; **W:** John Gay; **C:** Ted Moore.

The Last Samurai ♂ 1990 (R) Arab arms dealer Saxon arranges a fake kidnapping by rebel military leader Cele in order to keep the other hostages a secret. But among the other hostages is mercenary Hendricksen, who escapes and wrecks havoc on their plotting. **94m/C VHS**, Lance Henriksen, John Saxon, Henry Cele, Arabella Holzbog, John Fujioka, James Ryan, Duncan Regehr, Lisa Eilbacher; **D:** Paul Mayersberg.

The Last Samurai ♂♂♂½ 2003 (R) Embittered ex-Army Captain Nathan Algren (Cruise) is hired to train Japanese soldiers in modern warfare in order to quell a rebellion led by samurai Katsumoto (Watanabe). The inexperienced soldiers are forced to go into battle too early and, despite the superior firepower of their American rifles, are quickly defeated. Algren is taken prisoner and brought to a remote mountain village, where he learns the Japanese, swordplay, and the samurai's ancient code of honor(all in one winter). While Cruise is certainly the big name of the film, Watanabe is the one to watch as the magnetic and charismatic samurai leader. A bit over-romanticized, but the intricate battle sequences and spectacular cinematography make up for it. **150m/C VHS, DVD, Blu-ray Disc, HD DVD, US** Tom Cruise, Ken(saku) Watanabe, Timothy Spall, Billy Connolly, Tony Goldwyn, Masato Harada, Hiroyuki (Henry) Sanada, Koyuki, William Atherton, Scott Wilson, Togo gawa, Shun Sugata, Shin Koyamada, Shichinosuke Nakamura; **D:** Edward Zwick; **W:** Edward Zwick, John Logan, Marshall Herskovitz; **C:** John Toll; **M:** Hans Zimmer.

The Last Season WOOF! 1987 Shoot 'em up involving a bunch of hunters. Their aimless destruction provokes the good guy to save the forest they are demolishing. A battle ensues. **90m/C VHS**, Christopher Gosch, Louise Dorsey, David Cox; **D:** Raja Zahr.

The Last Seduction ♂♂♂♂ 1994 (R) Dahl, the master of modern noir, delivers another stylish hit exploring the darker side of urban life. Fiorentino gives the performance of her life as the most evil, rotten femme fatale to ever hit the big screen. Bridget (Fiorentino) rips off the money her husband Clay (Pullman) made in a pharmaceutical drug deal and leaves

Manhattan for a small town in Upstate New York. Once there, she takes nice, naive Mike (Berg) as her lover, while Clay tries to ferret her out and get his money back. Lots of dry humor and a wickedly amusing heroine make for a devilishly entertaining film. **110m/C VHS, DVD**, Linda Fiorentino, Peter Berg, J.T. Walsh, Bill Nunn, Bill Pullman; **D:** John Dahl; **W:** Steve Barancik; **C:** Jeffrey Jur; **M:** Joseph Vitarelli. Ind. Spirit '95: Actress (Fiorentino); N.Y. Film Critics '94: Actress (Fiorentino).

The Last Seduction 2 ♂ 1998 (R) Low-rent sequel finds Bridget Gregory (Severance) enjoying her spoils in Barcelona where she runs a scam on a phone sex service to get even more cash. But a detective, Murphy (Goddard), has been hired to track Bridget down—only the femme fatale has no intention of getting caught. Severance looks sexy but can't match predecessor Fiorentino's cold-blooded wiles. **96m/C VHS**, Joan Severance, Beth Goddard, Con O'Neill, Rocky Taylor, Dave Atkins; **D:** Terry Marcel; **W:** David Cummings; **C:** Geza Sinkovics; **M:** Jon Mellor. **VIDEO**

The Last Sentinel ♂ 2007 (R) Loner Tallis (Wilson) is a scarred, part bionic super soldier battling cloned drones that have exceeded their protective purpose and are now exterminating humans. Together with an unnamed freedom fighter (Sackhoff), Tallis is out to destroy the drone police command center. If you like either of the leads, you may be able to sit through this crappy Sci-Fi Channel original. **94m/C DVD**, Don Wilson, Katee Sackhoff, Bokeem Woodbine, Keith David; **D:** Jesse Johnson; **W:** Jesse Johnson; **C:** Robert Hayes; **M:** Marcello De Francisci. **CABLE**

The Last September ♂♂ 1999 (R) Danielstown is an Anglo-Irish estate located in County Cork in 1920—just four years after the Irish rebellion of 1916. Sir Richard (Gambon) and his wife, Lady Myra (Smith), have a houseful of guests, including Richard's overly romantic young niece Lois (Hawes), who's flirting with British officer, Gerald Colthurst (Tennant). But Lois has also taken to frequently visiting an old mill—where Irish guerilla fighter Peter (Lydon) is hiding out. Based on the novel by Elizabeth Bowen; first-time film director Warner is best known for her long career in the theatre. **103m/C VHS, DVD, IR GB FR** Maggie Smith, Michael Gambon, Keeley Hawes, David Tennant, Gary Lydon, Fiona Shaw, Lambert Wilson, Jane Birkin, Jonathan Slinger, Richard Roxburgh; **D:** Deborah Warner; **W:** John Banville; **C:** Slawomir Idziak; **M:** Zbigniew Preisner.

The Last Shot ♂♂ 2004 (R) Negligible comedy is an exaggeration of a true story about the FBI, mobsters, and an eager beaver filmmaker. Set in 1985, undercover agent Joe Devine (Baldwin) is bent on ensnaring minor mobster Tommy Sanz (Shalhoub) who's taking bribes to keep teamsters in line on film shoots. So Joe poses as a producer and gets a script and director in one package with nebbish Steven Schats (Broderick), who doesn't know the whole thing is a hoax. The fantasy begins to take over as the production rolls along. Joan Cusack has an unbilled cameo as a movie exec. Too-crowded story collapses under the weight after a promising set-up. **93m/C DVD, US** Matthew Broderick, Alec Baldwin, Toni Collette, Tony Shalhoub, Calista Flockhart, Tim Blake Nelson, Ray Liotta, James Rebhorn, Buck Henry, Ian Gomez, Troy Winbush, Evan Jones, Glenn Morshower, Michael (Mike) Papajohn, Jon Polito, Joan Cusack, Sean M. Whalen; **D:** Jeff Nathanson; **W:** Jeff Nathanson; **C:** John Lindley; **M:** Rolfe Kent.

The Last Slumber Party WOOF! 1987 A slumber party is beset by a homicidal maniac. Heavy metal soundtrack. **89m/C VHS, DVD**, Jan Jensen, Nancy Meyer; **D:** Stephen Tyler; **C:** Georges Cardona; **M:** John Brennan.

Last Song ♂½ 1980 (PG) A singer's husband discovers a plot to cover up a fatal toxic-waste accident, and is killed because of it. It's up to her to warn the authorities before becoming the next victim. **96m/C VHS, DVD**, Lynda Carter, Ronny Cox, Nicholas Pryor, Paul Rudd, Jenny O'Hara; **D:** Alan J. Levi.

Last Outlaw ♂♂ 1936 The last of the famous badmen of the old West is released from jail and returns home to find that times have changed. The action climaxes in an old-time blazing shoot-out. **79m/B VHS**, Harry Carey Sr., Hoot Gibson, Henry B. Walthall, Tom Tyler, Russell Hopton, Alan Curtis, Harry Woods, Barbara Pepper; **D:** Christy Cabanne.

The Last Outlaw ♂♂½ 1993 (R) Rourke stars as an ex-Confederate officer who leads a gang of outlaws until his violent excesses leave even them disgusted. The gang shoots Rourke but of course he doesn't die and then he sets out for revenge. **90m/C VHS, DVD**, Mickey Rourke, Dermot Mulroney, Ted Levine, John C. McGinley, Steve Buscemi, Keith David; **D:** Geoff Murphy; **W:** Eric Red. **CABLE**

The Last Reunion ♂♂ 1980 The only witness to a brutal killing of a Japanese official and his wife during WWII seeks revenge on the guilty American platoon, 33 years later. Violent. **98m/C VHS**, Cameron Mitchell, Leo Fong, Chanda Romero, Vic Silayan, Hal Bokar, Philip Baker Hall; **D:** Jay Wertz.

The Last Ride ♂♂ 1991 Another movie probing the dark side of hitchhiking. This time our hero thumbs a ride with a truck driver who plans to bypass the next city...for hell. **84m/C VHS**, Dan Ranger, Michael Hilow; **D:** Karl Krogstad; **W:** Ted Prior; **C:** David Crowther; **M:** Tony Capelli, Charles Shepard.

The Last Ride ♂♂ F.T.W 1994 (R) Frank T. Wells (Rourke) is out of prison after 10 years and free to try to recapture his former rodeo glory. Hellcat Scarlett Stuart's on the run from a botched bank job/murder perpetrated by her vicious brother Clem (Berg). Scarlett manages to hook up with Frank and decides to help him out financially by robbing convenience stores. Frank's not too happy when he finds out. Rourke is surprisingly subdued and Singer's properly unsympathetic but they don't seem to be working in the same movie. Nice Montana scenery though. **102m/C VHS, DVD**, Mickey Rourke, Lori Singer, Brion James, Peter Berg, Rodney A. Grant, Aaron Neville; **D:** Michael Karbelnikoff; **W:** Mari Kornhauser; **C:** James L. Carter; **M:** Gary Chang.

The Last, Ride of the Dalton Gang ♂♂ 1979 A long-winded retelling of the wild adventures that made the Dalton gang legendary among outlaws. **146m/C VHS, DVD**, Larry Wilcox, Jack Palance, Randy Quaid, Cliff (Potter) Potts, Dale Robertson, Don Collier; **D:** Dan Curtis.

The Last Riders ♂ 1990 (R) Motorcycle centaur Estrada revs a few motors fleeing from cycle club cronies and crooked cops. Full throttle foolishness. **90m/C VHS, DVD**, Erik Estrada, William (Bill)

Last Stand at Saber River ✍✍½ 1996 Adaptation of Elmore Leonard's 1959 western novel finds Confederate Civil War vet Paul Cable (Selleck) coming home to his wife Martha's (Arnis) family in Texas, having been wounded in the fighting. However, Martha was informed he was dead, so imagine her surprise. What Cable wants to do now is return to his pre-war life—a horse ranch in Arizona—but after making the journey the family discovers their ranch has been taken over by Union sympathizer Duane Kidston (Carradine) and he's not intending to let it go. Selleck was born to ride tall in the saddle. **95m/C VHS, DVD. D:** Dick Lowry. **W:** Ronald M. Cohen. **C:** Ric Waite. **M:** David Shire. **CABLE**

The Last Starfighter ✍✍ 1984 (PG) A young man who becomes an expert at a video game is recruited to fight in an inter-galactic war. Listless adventure which explains where all those video games come from. Watch for O'Herlihy disguised as a lizard. **100m/C VHS, DVD, HD DVD.** Lance Guest, Robert Preston, Barbara Bosson, Dan O'Herlihy, Catherine Mary Stewart, Cameron Dye, Kimberly Ross, Wil Wheaton; **D:** Nick Castle. **W:** Jonathan Betuel. **C:** King Baggot. **M:** Craig Safan.

The Last Stop ✍✍½ 1999 (R) Colorado State Trooper Jason (Beach) gets stranded because of a snowstorm at the remote "The Last Stop Cafe and Motel." He greets the other stranded souls who include his ex-girlfriend Nancy (McGowan) and soon finds out that owner Fritz (Prochnow) has stumbled on a murderer and a bag of cash that's probably the loot from a recent bank robbery. So just who's guilty? **94m/C VHS, DVD. CA** Adam Beach, Jürgen Prochnow, Rose McGowan, Callum Keith Rennie, Winston Rekert; **D:** Mark Malone. **W:** Bart Sumner. **C:** Tony Westman. **M:** Terry Frewer.

Last Summer ✍✍ 1969 (R) Three teenagers discover love, sex, and friendship on the write sands of Fire Island, N.Y. The summer vacation fantasy world they create shatters when a sweet but homely female teenager joins their group. Based on a novel by Evan Hunter. **97m/C VHS.** Barbara Hershey, Richard Thomas, Bruce Davison, Cathy Burns; **D:** Frank Perry.

Last Summer in the Hamptons ✍✍ 1996 (R) In her last film, Lindfors stars as Helena Mora, the matriarch of a charming three generation theatrical clan that gets together one weekend a year at her spacious, slightly run-down estate to participate in drama workshops and perform plays. When Helena is forced to sell the estate, the family reunites for one last weekend of bickering and performing. Featuring fine performances from the entire ensemble (including Lindfors son and Jaglom's wife), Jaglom's touching and engaging tribute to his family gives nepotism a good name. **105m/C VHS, DVD.** Victoria Foyt, Viveca Lindfors, Jon Robin Baitz, Andre Gregory, Melissa Leo, Martha Plimpton, Roddy McDowall, Nick Gregory, Savannah Smith Boucher, Roscoe Lee Browne, Ron Rifkin, Diane Salinger, Brooke Smith, Kristopher Tabori, Holland Taylor, Henry Jaglom; **D:** Henry Jaglom; **W:** Victoria Foyt, Henry Jaglom; **C:** Hania Baer.

The Last Supper ✍✍½ 1976 A repentant Cuban slave-owner in the 18th-century decides to cleanse his soul and convert his slaves to Christianity by having 12 of them reenact the Last Supper. Based on a true story. In Spanish with English subtitles. **110m/C VHS. CU** Nelson Villagra, Silvano Rey, Lamberto Garcia, Jose Antonio Rodriguez, Samuel Claxton, Mario Balmaseda; **D:** Tomas Gutierrez Alea.

The Last Supper ✍✍½ 1996 (R) First-time feature director Title dishes out an extremely black comedy about a group of liberal roommates who accidentally kill a racist marine they've invited to dinner. This leads to the devious plan of inviting more right wingers over, baiting them into arguments about controversial topics, then killing and burying them into the garden. Somehow manages to avoid excessive preachiness despite taking on political corners. Not exactly a great feast, but there's enough tasty snacks to be satisfying. Performances are good and the victims (led by Penn's Limbaugh turn) really shine. Too bad their characters aren't on screen very long before they become tomato fertilizer. **91m/C VHS, DVD.** Cameron Diaz, Annabeth Gish, Ron Eldard, Jonathan Penner, Courtney B. Vance, Nora Dunn, Ron Perlman, Jason Alexander, Charles Durning, Mark Harmon, Bill Paxton; **D:** Stacy Title; **W:** Dan Rosen; **C:** Paul Cameron; **M:** Mark Mothersbaugh.

Last Tango in Paris ✍✍✍½ 1973 (R) Brando plays a middle-aged American who meets a French girl and tries to forget his wife's suicide with a short, extremely steamy affair. Bertolucci proves to be a master; Brando gives one of his best performances. Very controversial when made, still quite explicit. Visually stunning. The X-rated version, at 130 minutes, is also available. **126m/C VHS, DVD. FR** L'Ultimo Tango a Parigi; Le Dernier Tango a Paris IT Marlon Brando, Maria Schneider, Jean-Pierre Leaud, Maria Michi, Massimo Girotti, Catherine Allegret; **D:** Bernardo Bertolucci; **W:** Bernardo Bertolucci; **C:** Vittorio Storaro; **M:** Gato Barbieri. N.Y. Film Critics '73: Actor (Brando); Natl. Soc. Film Critics '73: Actor (Brando).

The Last Temptation of Christ ✍✍✍½ 1988 (R) Scorsese's controversial adaptation of the Nikos Kazantzakis novel, portraying Christ in his last year as an ordinary Israelite tormented by divine doubt, human desires and the voice of God. The controversy engulfing the film, as it was heavily protested and widely banned, tended to divert attention from what is an exceptional statement of religious and artistic vision. Excellent score by Peter Gabriel. **164m/C VHS, DVD.** Willem Dafoe, Harvey Keitel, Barbara Hershey, Harry Dean Stanton, Andre Gregory, David Bowie, Verna Bloom, Juliette Caton, John Lurie, Roberts Blossom, Irvin Kershner, Barry Miller, Tomas Arana, Nehemiah Persoff, Paul Herman, Illeana Douglas; **D:** Martin Scorsese; **W:** Paul Schrader; **C:** Michael Ballhaus; **M:** Peter Gabriel.

The Last Time ✍✍ 2006 (R) Ted's (Keaton) a cynical middle-aged salesman in New York who decides to go after new partner Jamie's (Fraser) beautiful fiancee Belisa (Valletta). Belisa is bored with her boyish Midwesterner and ready to move on but the two guys' mental stability seems to short-circuit as they battle in boardroom and bedroom. Keaton's good but Fraser overplays the idiot role; Valletta slinks and pouts convincingly. **97m/C DVD.** Michael Keaton, Brendan Fraser, Amber Valletta, Daniel Stern, Neal McDonough, Michael Lerner; **D:** Michael Caleo; **W:** Michael Caleo; **C:** Tim Suhrstedt; **M:** Randy Edelman.

The Last Time I Committed Suicide ✍✍ 1996 (R) Based on a Beat-era letter from Neal Cassady to Jack Kerouac and set in the late '40s, this independent pic follows a 20-year-old Cassady (Jane) as he drifts into Denver's substantial underbelly. Although a bit farfetched, film is made watchable because of fine performances and excellent camera work. **91m/C VHS, DVD.** Robert Stack, Dorothy Malone, George Sanders, Edmond O'Brien, Woody Strode, Jack Kruschen; **D:** Andrew L. Stone; **W:** Andrew L. Stone; **C:** Hal Mohr; **M:** Rudolph (Rudy) Schrager.

The Last Voyage ✍✍ 1960 Suspenseful disaster film in which Stack and Malone play a married couple in jeopardy while on an ocean cruise. To make the film more realistic, the French liner Ile de France was actually used in the sinking scenes. Although a bit farfetched, film is made watchable because of fine performances and excellent camera work. **91m/C VHS, DVD.** Robert Stack, Dorothy Malone, George Sanders, Edmond O'Brien, Woody Strode, Jack Kruschen; **D:** Andrew L. Stone; **W:** Andrew L. Stone; **C:** Hal Mohr; **M:** Rudolph (Rudy) Schrager.

The Last Waltz ✍✍✍½ 1973 (PG) Martin Scorsese filmed this rock documentary featuring the farewell performance of The Band, joined by a host of musical guests that they have been associated with over the years. Songs include: "Up On Cripple Creek," "Don't Do It," "Stage Fright" (The Band), "Helpless," "The Night They Drove Old Dixie Down," "Caravan" (Van Morrison), "Further On Up the Road" (Eric Clapton), "Who Do You Love" (Ronnie Hawkins), "Mannish Boy" (Muddy Waters), "Evangeline" (Emmylou Harris), "Baby, Let Me Follow You Down" (Bob Dylan). **117m/C VHS, DVD, Blu-ray Disc. D:** Martin Scorsese; **C:** Michael Chapman.

The Last Train ✍✍ 1974 Romance most hopeless in the heart of France during zee beeg war. During the 1940 invasion of Paris a man and woman turn to each other for comfort when separate from their families while trying to escape the city. French, very French. **101m/C VHS, DVD. FR** Rmy Schneider, Jean-Louis Trintignant, Maurice Biraud; **D:** Pierre Granier-Deferre; **W:** Pierre Granier-Deferre; **C:** Walter Wottitz; **M:** Philippe Sarde.

The Last Tomahawk ✍✍ 1965 Colorful and action packed reworking of Cooper's "Last of the Mohicans." **92m/C VHS. GE** IT Anthony Steffen, Karin Dor, Dan (Harald) Reinl; **D:** Danny Martin, Joachim Fuchsberger; **D:** Harald Reinl.

The Last Train from Gun Hill ✍✍✍ 1959 An all-star cast highlights this suspenseful tale of a U.S. marshall determined to catch the man who raped and murdered his wife. Excellent action packed western. **94m/C VHS, DVD.** Kirk Douglas, Anthony Quinn, Carolyn Jones, Earl Holliman, Brad Dexter, Brian Hutton, Ziva Rodann; **D:** John Sturges; **C:** Charles B(ryant) Lang Jr.

The Last Tycoon ✍✍½ 1976 An adaptation of the unfinished F. Scott Fitzgerald novel about the life and times of a Hollywood movie executive of the 1920s. Confusing and slow moving despite a blockbuster conglomeration of talent. Joan Collins introduces the film. **123m/C VHS, DVD.** Robert De Niro, Tony Curtis, Ingrid Boulting, Jack Nicholson, Jeanne Moreau, Peter Strauss, Robert Mitchum, Theresa Russell, Donald Pleasence, Ray Milland, Dana Andrews, John Carradine, Anjelica Huston; **D:** Elia Kazan; **W:** Harold Pinter; **M:** Maurice Jarre.

The Last Unicorn ✍✍ 1982 (G) Peter Beagle's popular tale of a beautiful unicorn who goes in search of her lost, mythical "family." **95m/C VHS, DVD. D:** Jules Bass; **W:** Peter S. Beagle; **M:** Jimmy Webb; **V:** Alan Arkin, Jeff Bridges, Tammy Grimes, Angela Lansbury, Mia Farrow, Robert Klein, Christopher Lee, Keenan Wynn.

The Last Valley ✍✍ 1971 (PG) A scholar tries to protect a pristine 17th century Swiss valley, untouched by the Thirty Years War, from marauding soldiers. Historical action with an intellectual twist. **128m/C VHS, DVD.** Michael Caine, Omar Sharif, Florinda Bolkan, Nigel Davenport, Per Oscarsson, Arthur O'Connell; **D:** James Clavell; **W:** James Clavell; **C:** John Wilcox; **M:** John Barry.

The Last Winter ✍✍½ 1989 (PG) Ten-year-old Will (Murray) has always lived in the country and finds it hard to accept his parents' decision to move to the city. But with the help of his grandfather (Parkes), Will begins to understand about change and growing up. **103m/C VHS. CA** Joshua Murray, Gerard Parkes, David Ferry, Wanda Cannon, Marsha Moreau, Nathaniel Moreau, Katie Murray; **D:** Aaron Kim Johnston; **W:** Aaron Kim Johnston; **C:** Ian Elkin; **M:** Victor Davies.

The Last Winter ✍✍ 1984 (R) An American woman fights to find her Israeli husband who has disappeared in the 1973 Yom Kippur War. Trouble is, an Israeli really her husband too. **92m/C VHS, IS Kathleen Quinlan, Yona Elian, Zipora Peled, Michael Schneider; **D:** Riki Shelach.

The Last Wave ✍✍✍ 1977 (PG) An Australian attorney takes on a murder case involving an aborigine and finds himself becoming distracted by apocalyptic visions concerning tidal waves and drowings that seem to foretell the future. Weir's masterful creation and communication of time and place are married by a somewhat pat ending. **109m/C VHS, DVD. AU** Richard Chamberlain, Olivia Hamnett, David Gulpilil, Frederick Parslow, Vivean Gray, Nadjiwarra Amagula, Roy Bara, Walter Amagula, Cedric Lalara, Morris Lalara, Peter Carroll; **D:** Peter Weir; **W:** Peter Weir, Tony Morphett, Petru Popescu; **C:** Russell Boyd.

The Last Warrior ✍✍ 1999 (PG-13) A devastating earthquake has turned Southern California into an island and Green Beret Nick Preston (Lundgren) takes it upon himself to help a group of survivors finds civilization. Of course there's a villain—a murderer (Mer) who has taken over a maximum security prison and has his own ideas. **95m/C VHS, DVD.** Dolph Lundgren, Rebecca Cross, Julio Mer-Lenittin; **W:** Stephen J. Blackely, Pamela K. Long; **C:** David Garfinkel; **M:** David Michael Frank. **VIDEO**

The Last Warrior ✍ 1989 (R) Coast-watcher 1989 (R) A good-looking but exploitive "Hell in the Pacific" rip-off, as an American and a Japanese soldier battle it out alone on a remote island during WWII. **94m/C VHS, DVD.** Gary (Rand) Graham, Cary-Hiroyuki Tagawa, Maria Holvoe; **D:** Martin Wragge.

The Last Woman on Earth WOOF! 1961 Two men vie for the affections of the sole surviving woman after a vague and unexplained disaster afflicts vast proportions. Robert Towne, who appears herein under the pseudonym Edward Wain, wrote the script (his first screenwriting effort). You might want to watch this if it were the last movie on earth, although Corman fans will probably love it. **71m/C VHS, DVD.** Antony Carbone, Edward Wain, Betsy Jones-Moreland; **D:** Roger Corman; **W:** Robert Towne.

The Last Word ✍✍ 1980 (PG) Comedy drama about struggling inventor Harris fighting to protect his home, family, and neighbors from a corrupt real estate deal involving shady politicians, angry policeman, and a beautiful TV reporter. **103m/C VHS, DVD.** Richard Harris, Karen Black, Martin Landau, Dennis Christopher, Bill McGuire, Christopher Guest, Penelope Milford, Michael Pataki; **W:** Michael Varhol, L.M. Kit Carson.

The Last Word ✍✍ 1995 (R) Journalist Martin (Hutton) writes a newspaper column, often featuring characters based on hometown Detroit mob figures, with terback career cut short by a drinking problem and he's worried his son will follow low in his unsteady footsteps. **92m/C VHS. D:** John Beck, Christian Conrad, Lori Wiener, Gail Strickland, Betty Buckley; **D:** Don Fox Greene.

Last Witness ✍ 1988 A man on the run from the government claims that he is innocent and was unjustly persecuted, but the government sees him as a dangerous threat. Nothing will stop the hunt for the escaped man, no matter what it costs. **85m/C VHS.** Mike Schuster, Jeff Henderson; **D:** E. Bruce Weiss.

Last Winters ✍ 1971 From Jean Charles Tacchella, writer-producer-director of "Cousin, Cousine," comes this first short film about an old couple's bittersweet romance. In French with English subtitles. **23m/C VHS. FR** Charles Tacchella.

Last War ✍ 1968 A nuclear war begins between the United States and Russia triggers Armageecon. **79m/C VHS, DVD.** Nobuko Otowa, Akira Takarada, Yuriko Hoshi; **D:** Shue Matsubayashi.

info supplied to him by his friend, Doc (Pantoliano), who owes the gangsters Martin to his latest column subject—stripper Caprice (Burke)—and, thanks again to Doc, a Hollywood studio gets interested in filming her story but wants more sex and violence, which means Martin will be betraying her deepest secrets. Now, he must choose between love, success, or friendship. **95m/C VHS, DVD.** Timothy Hutton, Joe Pantoliano, Michelle Rene Thomas, Chazz Palminteri, Tony Goldwyn, Richard Dreyfuss, Cybill Shepherd, Jimmy Smits; **D:** Tony Spiridakis; **W:** Tony Spiridakis; **C:** Zoltan David; **M:** Paul Buckmaster.

Last Year at Marienbad 🐾🐾🐾½ *L'Anee Derniere a Marienbad* 1961 A young man tries to lure a mysterious woman to run away with him from a hotel in France. Once a hit on the artsy circuit, it's most interesting for its beautiful photography. In French with English subtitles. **93m/B VHS, DVD.** *FR IT* Delphine Seyrig, Giorgio Albertazzi, Sacha (Sascha) Pitoeff, Luce Garcia-Ville; **D:** Alain Resnais; **W:** Alain Robbe-Grillet; **C:** Sacha Vierny; **M:** Francis Seyrig.

L'Atalante 🐾🐾🐾½ *Le Chaland qui Passe* 1934 Vigo's great masterpiece, a slight story about a husband and wife quarreling, splitting, and reuniting around which has been fashioned one of the cinema's greatest poetic films. In French with English subtitles. **82m/B VHS, DVD.** *FR* Dita Parlo, Jean Daste, Michel Simon; **D:** Jean Vigo; **W:** Jean Vigo, Jean Guinee, Albert Riera; **C:** Boris Kaufman, Louis Berger; **M:** Maurice Jaubert.

Late August, Early September 🐾🐾½ *Fin Aout Debut Septembre* 1998 Self-absorbed group of friends and lovers find their relationships in flux and their mortality in question over the course of a year (from August of one year to the September of the next). Adrien (Cluzet) is a serious writer whose work elicits critical but not commercial acclaim. His indecisive friend Gabriel (Amalric) is an editor at a publishing house who has split with long-time love, Jenny (Balibar), for the young Anne (Ledoyen). Meanwhile, Adrien, who's learned he has a terminal illness, plunges into a reckless affair with the teenaged Vera (Hansen-Love). French with subtitles. **112m/C VHS, DVD.** *FR* Mathieu Amalric, Virginie Ledoyen, Francois Cluzet, Jeanne Balibar, Alex Descas, Arsinee Khanjian, Mia Hansen-Love; **D:** Olivier Assayas; **W:** Olivier Assayas; **C:** Denis Lenoir; **M:** Ali Sarka Toure.

Late Bloomers 🐾🐾 1995 Romantic comedy focuses on what happens when two Midwestern women fall in love. Math teacher/basketball coach Dinah (Nelson) is friendly with fellow teacher Rom (Carter) and his wife, Carly (Hennigan), the high school secretary. A misinterpreted note, an impulsive kiss, and Carly's soon out of door and living with Dinah, which leads to a community uproar. The two leads are likeable but the other characters and the situation are heavily cliched. **105m/C VHS, DVD.** Connie Nelson, Dee Hennigan, Gary Carter, Lisa Peterson; **D:** Julia Dyer; **W:** Gretchen Dyer; **C:** Bill Schwarz; **M:** Ted Pine.

Late Chrysanthemums 🐾🐾 *Bangiku* 1954 A middle-aged geisha has settled into comfortable retirement as a monkey lender. When she hears a former lover wants to visit her, she tries to recapture her old glamour only to be disillusioned. Based on a short story by Fumiko Hayashi. In Japanese with English subtitles. **101m/B VHS.** *JP* Haruko Sugimura, Chikako Hosokawa, Sadako Sawamura; **D:** Mikio Naruse.

Late Extra 🐾🐾 1935 A novice reporter attempts to track down a notorious bank robber and gets some help from a savvy female journalist. Mason's first role of substance. **69m/B VHS.** *GB* Virginia Cherrill, James Mason, Alastair Sim, Ian Colin, Clifford McLaglen, Cyril Cusack, David Horne, Antoinette Cellier, Donald Wolfit, Michael Wilding; **D:** Albert Parker.

Late for Dinner 🐾🐾 1991 (PG) In 1962 Willie, a young, married man, and his best friend Frank are framed by a sleazy land developer. On the run, the two decide to become guinea pigs in a cryonics experiment and wind up frozen for 29 years. It's now 1991 and Willie wants to find his family—only his wife is middle-aged and his daughter is all grown-up. Can he make a life with them again or has time indeed passed him by? **93m/C VHS, DVD.** Brian Wimmer, Peter Berg, Marcia Gay Harden, Peter Gallagher, Ross Malinger; **D:** W.D. Richter; **W:** Mark Andrus.

Late Last Night 🐾🐾 1999 (R) After a big bash with his wife, Dan (Estevez) hooks up with best pal, Jeff (Weber), who proposes they cut loose for the evening. So they pick up a couple of women and proceed to party, which eventually lands them in the slammer. **90m/C VHS, DVD.** Emilio Estevez, Steven Weber, Carlene O'Hara, Leah Lail, Lisa Robin Kelly; **D:** Steven Brill.

Late Marriage 🐾🐾🐾½ *Hatouna Meuherer1* 2001 Thirty-one-year-old Zaza (Ashkenazi) is an Israeli of Georgian descent who lives in a very close-knit and traditional community. His parents are appalled that he's still single and keep setting him up with virginal likely prospects. They don't know that he's devoted to Judith (Elkabetz), who's not only slightly older (she's 34) but a divorced single mom and Moroccan! When they do find out, they barge into her apartment—humiliating both. But is Zaza strong enough to defy conventions and stay with his true love? In Georgian and Hebrew with English subtitles. **100m/C VHS, DVD.** *IS FR* Lior Loui Ashkenazi, Ronit Elkabetz, Moni Moshonov, Lili Kosashvili, Sapir Kugman, Aya Steinovits Laor; **D:** Dover Kosashvili; **W:** Dover Kosashvili; **M:** Joseph Bardanashvili.

The Late Shift 🐾🐾½ 1996 (R) Cable adaptation of Bill Carter's book chronicling the follies surrounding NBC's "The Tonight Show" succession battle between Jay Leno (Roebuck) and Dave Letterman (Higgins). It's the behind-the-scenes dealmakers that really steal the show, however, including Jay's profane manager Helen Kushnick (Bates) and superagent Michael Ovitz (Williams), who ultimately orchestrated Dave's move to rival CBS. Both Letterman and Leno made the movie/book fodder for their opening monologues. **96m/C VHS, DVD.** Daniel Roebuck, John Michael Higgins, Kathy Bates, Treat Williams, Bob Balaban, Ed Begley Jr., Rich Little, Sandra Bernhard, Peter Jurasik, Reni Santoni, John Kapelos, John Getz, Lawrence Pressman; **D:** Betty Thomas; **W:** Bill Carter, George Armitage; **C:** Mac Ahlberg; **M:** Ira Newborn. **CABLE**

The Late Show 🐾🐾🐾 1977 (PG) A veteran private detective finds his world turned upside down when his ex-partner comes to visit and winds up dead, and a flaky woman whose cat is missing decides to become his sidekick. Carney and Tomlin are fun to watch in this sleeper, a tribute to the classic detective film noirs. **93m/C VHS, DVD.** Art Carney, Lily Tomlin, Bill Macy, Eugene Roche, Joanna Cassidy, John Considine; **D:** Robert Benton; **W:** Robert Benton. Natl. Soc. Film Critics '77: Actor (Carney).

Late Spring 🐾🐾🐾 1949 An exquisite Ozu masterpiece. A young woman lives with her widowed father for years. He decides to remarry so that she can begin life for herself. Highly acclaimed, in Japanese with English subtitles. Reworked in 1960 as "Late Autumn." **107m/B VHS, DVD.** *JP* Setsuko Hara, Chishu Ryu, Jun Usami, Haruko Sugimura; **D:** Yasujiro Ozu.

Late Summer Blues 🐾🐾 *Blues La-Chofesh Ha-Gadol* 1987 Experience the life and death decisions of seven teenagers who have finished their finals and face now a more difficult test: serving in the Israeli Armed Forces in the Suez Canal. In Hebrew with English subtitles. **101m/C VHS.** *IS* Dor Zweigenbom, Shahar Segal, Yoav Zafrir; **D:** Renen Schorr.

The Lathe of Heaven 🐾🐾🐾 1980 In a late 20th century world suffocating from pollution, George Orr (Davison) visits a dream specialist because he can dream things into being. The specialist wants George to dream of a world free from war, pestilence, and overpopulation, but these dreams have disastrous side effects. Based on the futuristic novel by Ursula K. LeGuin. **100m/C VHS, DVD.** Bruce Davison, Kevin Conway, Margaret Avery, Peyton E. Park; **D:** David Loxton, Fred Barzyk; **W:** Roger E. Swaybill, Diane English; **C:** Robbie Greenberg; **M:** Michael Small. **TV**

The Lathe of Heaven 🐾🐾 2002 Remake of the 1980 PBS pic based on the 1971 novel by Ursula LeGuin. George Orr (Haas) refuses to sleep because when he does, his dreams alter reality. Or at least George thinks so, which is why he's forced to see a court-appointed shrink, Dr. William Haber (Caan), after a drug overdose. But when Haber discovers George's ability is real, he uses it for his own purpose. **100m/C VHS, DVD.** Lukas Haas, James Caan, Lisa Bonet, David Strathairn, Sheila McCarthy, Serge Houde; **D:** Philip Haas; **W:** Alan Sharp; **C:** Pierre Mignot; **M:** Angelo Badalamenti. **CABLE**

The Lather Effect 🐾🐾 2006 High school friends from the '80s reunite for a wild weekend and find they're older but no wiser. They face the morning after cleaning up after their shindig, reminiscing, and revealing various issues and disappointments. Situations are predictable, but if you lived through the era they'll be familiar (as will the music). **95m/C DVD.** Connie Britton, Sarah Clarke, Tate Donovan, David Herman, Peter Facinelli, Caitlin Keats, William Mapother, Ione Skye, Eric Stoltz, Kevin Heffernan, Monica Keena; **D:** Sarah Kelly; **W:** Sarah Kelly, Tim Talbott; **C:** Eric Haase; **M:** Dominic Kelly.

Latin Dragon 🐾🐾½ 2003 (R) Home sweet home is in ruins when Danny Silva returns from war duty to find gangs in charge of his L.A. 'hood. Disgusted, he takes it upon himself to hunt down the rotten head honchos behind the chaos. Typical war-hero-turned-vigilante fare. **101m/C VHS, DVD.** Gary Busey, Lorenzo Lamas, Robert LaSardo, Pepe Serna, Fabian Carrillo, Joyce Giraud, Luis Antonio Ramos, James Hong; **D:** Scott Thomas; **W:** Fabian Carrillo, James Becket; **C:** Mark Eberle; **M:** H. Scott Salinas. **VIDEO**

Latin Lovers 🐾🐾½ 1953 Turner plays a wealthy heiress who can't decide if men love her for herself or her money. Had To Kiss You. **104m/C VHS.** Lana Turner, Ricardo Montalban, John Lund, Louis Calhern, Jean Hagen, Eduard Franz, Beulah Bondi, Rita Moreno; **D:** Mervyn LeRoy; **M:** Isobel Lennart. **CABLE**

Latino 🐾🐾½ 1985 The self-tortured adventures of a Chicano Green Beret who, while fighting a covert U.S. military action in war-torn Nicaragua, begins to rebel against the senselessness of... **108m/C VHS.** Robert Beltran, Annette Cardona, Tony Plana, James Karen, Ricardo Lopez, Luis Torrentes, Juan Carlos Ortiz, Julio Medina; **D:** Haskell Wexler; **W:** Haskell Wexler; **M:** Diane Louie.

Latter Days 🐾🐾½ 2004 Melodramatic gay romance finds wide-eyed young Aaron Davis (Sandvoss), an earnest Mormon missionary from Idaho, sent to bring the good word to the heathens of West Hollywood. This would include his new neighbor, handsome, heedless gay waiter Christian (Ramsey), who sets out to seduce the virgin on a bet. Seeing as how this is a really big religious no-no for Aaron, you know there's trouble ahead, even as the hot twosome find themselves falling in love. Bisset adds some class as sardonic restaurant owner and surrogate mother figure Lila. Writer-director Cox (directing his first film) is a former Mormon and has some definite issues to air but he manages to offer a certain sweetness along with all the overwrought angst. **108m/C DVD.** *US* Steve Sandvoss, Wes Ramsey, Rebekah Jordan, Khary Payton, Amber Benson, Jacqueline Bisset, Joseph Gordon-Levitt, Erik Palladino, Mary Kay Place, Rob McElhenney; **D:** C. Jay Cox; **W:** C. Jay Cox; **C:** Carl F. Bartels; **M:** Eric Allaman.

L'Auberge Espagnole 🐾🐾🐾 2002 (R) *The Spanish Apartment; Euro Pudding* 2002 (R) Exuberant comedy that follows a French student during an eventful year in Barcelona. Xavier (Duris) is advised to study Spanish and Spanish economics in order to secure a government job. So he signs up for a European exchange program, bids goodbye to girlfriend Martine (Tautou), and heads to Spain where he eventually moves into a lively rooming house filled with fellow students. Xavier is a title bit of a rogue who is soon squiring around (at her husband's request), the shy wife (Godreche) of an obnoxious countryman and developing a crush on a Belgian exchange student (de France), who is interested in Xavier only as a friend. Barcelona's baroque charms are also another character in Klapisch's light-hearted production. English, French, and Spanish with subtitles. **117m/C VHS, DVD. FR SP** Romain Duris, Audrey Tautou, Judith Godreche, Cecile De France, Kelly Reilly, Kevin Bishop, Xavier De Guillebon; **D:** Cedric Klapisch; **W:** Cedric Klapisch; **C:** Dominique Colin.

Lauderdale woof! *Spring Fever USA; Spring Break USA* 1989 (R) Two college schmoes hit the beach looking for beer and babes. Few laughs for the sober and mature. Surf's down in this woofer. **91m/C VHS, DVD.** Darrel Guilbeau, Michelle Kemp, Jeff Greenman, Lara Belmonte; **D:** Bill Milling; **W:** Bill Milling.

Laughing at Danger 🐾🐾 1924 Talmadge is the supposedly playboy son of a Washington politician. In reality, he's the dashing "Mr. Pep" who comes to the rescue of a scientist who has invented a death ray and is being stalked by agents of a sinister foreign power. Talmadge was a fine silent-screen action star, though his heavy German action proved a barrier with sound films. **45m/B VHS.** Richard Talmadge, Joseph Girard, Eva Novak, Joe Harrington, Stanhope Wheatcroft; **D:** James W. Home.

Laughing at Life 🐾🐾 1933 A mercenary leaves his family to fight in South America. Years later, when he is the leader of said country, he meets a man who turns out to be his son. Rehashed plot has been done better. **72m/B VHS, DVD.** Victor McLaglen, William "Stage" Boyd, Lois Wilson, Henry B. Walthall, Regis Toomey; **D:** Ford Beebe.

The Laughing Policeman 🐾🐾½ *An Investigation of Murder* 1974 (R) Two antagonistic cops embark on a vengeful hunt for a mass murderer through the seamy underbelly of San Francisco. Adapted from the Swedish novel by Per Wahloo and Maj Sjowallo. **111m/C VHS, DVD.** Walter Matthau, Bruce Dern, Louis Gossett Jr.; **D:** Stuart Rosenberg; **M:** Charles Fox.

Laughing Sinners 🐾🐾 1931 Society girl Crawford attempts suicide after Hamilton dumps her and is rescued by Gable—a Salvation Army worker! Predictable drama with some unintentionally funny moments. Gable and Crawford were having an off-screen romance at the time which accounts for the sparks generated on-screen. Based on the play "Torch Song" by Kenyon Nicholson. **71m/B VHS.** Joan Crawford, Neil Hamilton, Clark Gable, Marjorie Rambeau, Guy Kibbee, Cliff Edwards, Roscoe Karns; **D:** Harry Beaumont; **C:** Charles Rosher.

Laura 🐾🐾🐾🐾 1944 Detective Mark McPherson (Andrews) assigned to the murder investigation of the late Laura Hunt (Tierney) finds himself falling in love with her painted portrait and discovering some surprising facts. Superb collaboration by excellent cast and fine director. Superior suspense yarn, enhanced by a love story. Based on the novel by Vera Caspary. Rouben Mamoulian was the original director, then Preminger finished the film. **85m/B VHS, DVD.** Gene Tierney, Dana Andrews, Clifton Webb, Lane Chandler, Vincent Price, Judith Anderson, Grant Mitchell, Dorothy Adams, Ron Dunn, Clyde Fillmore, James Flavin; **D:** Otto Preminger; **W:** Elizabeth Reinhardt, Jay Dratler, Samuel Hoffenstein, Ring Lardner Jr.; **C:** Joseph LaShelle; **M:** David Raksin. Oscars '44: B&W Cinematog.; Natl. Film Reg. '99.

Laurel & Hardy and the Family 1933 Four zany comedies seeing the boys in all kinds of trouble involving home or family life. Includes "Brats," "Perfect Day," "Their First Mistake" and "Twice Two." **85m/B VHS.** Stan Laurel, Oliver Hardy.

Laurel & Hardy: Another Fine Mess ☝☝½ 1930 The boys find themselves the owners of a magnificent Beverly Hills mansion. Yeah right. Lots of physical comedy and hilarious dialogue with a "special appearance" by Laurel in drag as a maid. Based on a sketch written by Laurel's father. Colorized. 25mC VHS, DVD, Stan Laurel, Oliver Hardy, Thelma Todd *D:* James Parrott. *W:* H.M. Walker, *C:* Jack Stevens; *M:* Leroy Shield.

Laurel & Hardy: At Work 1932 Three short films collected here. Includes "Towed in a Hole," "Busy Bodies," and "The Music Box." 70m/B VHS, Oliver Hardy, Stan Laurel.

Laurel & Hardy: Be Big ☝☝½ 1931 Stan and Ollie ditch their wives to go to a swinging stag party at their club. Of course everything goes wrong in their quest for lascivious fun. Filled with tons of sight gags. Colorized. 25mC VHS, DVD, Stan Laurel, Oliver Hardy; *D:* James Parrott. *W:* H.M. Walker, *C:* George Stevens.

Laurel & Hardy: Below Zero ☝☝½ 1930 It's the Great Depression of 1929, and Laurel and Hardy are about as depressed as you can get, working for pennies as street musicians. Their luck changes when they find a full wallet lying in the snow. But, as the saying goes, a fool and his money are soon parted. Colorized. 25mC VHS, Stan Laurel, Oliver Hardy; *D:* James Parrott. *W:* H.M. Walker, *C:* George Stevens.

Laurel & Hardy: Berth Marks 1929 Laurel and Ollie take a hilarious train trip to Pottsville for a vaudeville performance. Colorized. 25mC VHS, Stan Laurel, Oliver Hardy; *D:* Lewis R. Foster; *W:* H.M. Walker, *C:* Len Powers.

Laurel & Hardy: Blotto 1930 Laurel and Hardy want to get drunk, but they can't get any alcohol and their wives won't let them get away. When they finally do escape, they wind up at the swanky Rainbow Club, where they're drastically out of their element. Colorized. 25mC VHS, Stan Laurel, Oliver Hardy; *D:* James Parrott. *W:* H.M. Walker, Leo McCarey, *C:* George Stevens.

Laurel & Hardy: Brats ☝☝½ 1930 Stan and Ollie play not only their children but also their children when their wives go away. When they finally get away it only gets worse as the children, of course, wreak havoc wherever they go, playing on this hilarious few films in which only Laurel and Hardy appear. Colorized. 25mC VHS, Stan Laurel, Oliver Hardy; *D:* James W. Horne; *W:* H.M. Walker, *C:* George Stevens.

Laurel & Hardy: Chickens Come Home ☝☝½ 1931 Hilarity ensues when Laurel and Hardy try to fix the radio antenna on Hardy's roof. It may sound easy, but come on, this is Laurel and Hardy. Colorized. 25mC VHS, Stan Laurel, Oliver Hardy; *D:* James Parrott. *W:* H.M. Walker, *C:* Jack Stevens.

Laurel & Hardy: Hog Wild ☝☝½ 1930 Ollie is running for mayor, but things go crazy when an ex-girlfriend shows up and blackmails him with a compromising photo. Stan, acting as Ollie's campaign manager, tries to help, but things just get worse. A remake of their own film "Love 'Em and Weep." Colorized. 25mC VHS, DVD, Stan Laurel, Oliver Hardy, James Finlayson; *D:* James W. Horne; *W:* H.M. Walker, *C:* Jack Stevens.

Laurel & Hardy: Laughing Gravy ☝☝½ 1931 The boys pet dog, oddly named Laughing Gravy, gets them into trouble with their landlord who keeps trying to evict them. So funny even the mashed potatoes will laugh. Colorized. 25mC VHS, Stan Laurel, Oliver Hardy; *D:* James Parrott. *W:* H.M. Walker, *C:* Jack Stevens. *M:* William Axt.

Laurel & Hardy: Men O'War 1929 Laurel & Hardy star as two sailors on shore leave trying to impress the ladies. Things go from bad to worse when they take two ladies out on a date. Features the memorable soda fountain and canoe scenes. Colorized. 25mC VHS, Stan Laurel, Oliver Hardy, Gloria Greer, Anne Cornwall; *D:*

Laurel & Hardy: Night Owls 1930 When a cop needs to capture some crooks to save his job, he sets up a fake break-in and catches two bungling burglars—Laurel and Hardy. Lots of sight gags and slapstick. Colorized. 25mC VHS, Stan Laurel, Oliver Hardy, Edgar Kennedy; *D:* James Parrott. *W:* H.M. Walker, Edgar Kennedy; *C:* James Parrott, *W:* H.M. Walker, *C:* George Stevens. *M:* Marvin Hatley, Harry von Tilzer.

Laurel & Hardy On the Lam 1930 Four Laurel & Hardy classics are collected, including "Scram," "Another Fine Mess," "One Good Turn," and "Going Bye-Bye." 90m/B VHS, Oliver Hardy, Stan Laurel.

Laurel & Hardy: Perfect Day 1929 Laurel and Hardy plan a quiet picnic with their wives, but car trouble turns their day into a disaster. Colorized. 25mC VHS, Stan Laurel, Oliver Hardy, Edgar Kennedy; *D:* James Parrott. *W:* H.M. Walker; *M:* Nathaniel Shilkret.

Laurel & Hardy Spooktacular 1934 Stan and Ollie scream through four spooky comedies, including "The Live Ghost," "The Laurel-Hardy Murder Case," "Oliver the Eighth" and "Dirty Work." 95m/ B VHS, Stan Laurel, Oliver Hardy.

Laurel & Hardy: Stan "Helps" Ollie 1933 Four Stan and Ollie classics including "County Hospital," "Me and My Pal," "Hog Wild" and "Helpmates." 85m/B VHS, Stan Laurel, Oliver Hardy.

Laurel & Hardy: The Hoose-Gow 1929 Laurel and Hardy are mistakenly picked up at a political demonstration and sent to prison to do hard labor. Hilarity ensues when they try to convince the warden that they're innocent. Colorized. 25mC VHS, Stan Laurel, Oliver Hardy; *D:* James Parrott. *W:* H.M. Walker; *C:* George Stevens.

Laurel Avenue ☝☝½ 1993 Looks at the life of an extended working-class black family in St. Paul, Minnesota, over a busy weekend. Large cast includes family heads Jake and Maggie who live with their basketball coach son, teenage daughter, and elderly uncle. Other children include fraternal twin Yolanda, a cop married to a white man, who knows sister Rolanda's (a recovering drug addict) son is a dealer. Their brother Marcus manages a Mafia-controlled clothing store and is involved in some shady deals while brother Woody is an aspiring musician. The four households are all united at a disastrous Sunday afternoon party. 156m/C VHS, Mary Alice, Mel Winkler, Scott Lawrence, Malinda Williams, Jay Brooks, Juanita Jennings, Rhonda Stubbins White, Monte Russell, Vonte Sweet; *D:* Carl Franklin. *W:* Michael Henry Brown, Paul Aaron. C.A.B.L.E.

Laurel Canyon ☝☝ 2002 (R) Aspiring shrink Sam (Bale) brings fiance and fellow doctor Alex (Beckinsale) home to meet mom Jane (McDormand), a bohemian record producer with a very non-maternal view of sex and drugs—she likes 'em, a lot. Sam still resents her for the way he was brought up, and she hasn't changed much, as she's currently sleeping with the young musician (Nivola) whose album she's producing. Alex is soon drawn into the care-free world around her as Sam is tempted by a colleague at work. Choloden-ko tries to recreate the insight and verve of her debut, "High Art," but falls short by making the story predictable and the characters flat. The only one who comes alive is Jane, and that's due more to McDormand's performance than anything she's given to work with. Nivola has a nice turn as her beau of the month. 101m/C VHS, DVD, US Frances McDormand, Christian Bale, Kate Beckinsale, Alessandro Nivola, Natascha McElhone; *D:* Lisa Cholodenko. *W:* Lisa Cholodenko; *C:* Wally Pfister. *M:* Craig (Shudder to Think) Wedren.

The Lavender Hill Mob ☝☝☝☝ 1951 A prim and prissy bank clerk schemes to melt the bank's gold down and re-mold it into miniature Eiffel Tower paper-weights for later resale. The foolproof plan appears to succeed, but then develops a snag. An excellent comedy that is still a delight to watch. 78m/

B VHS, DVD, GB Alec Guinness, Stanley Holloway, Sidney James, Alfie Bass, Marjorie Fielding, John Gregson; *Cameos:* Audrey Hepburn; *D:* Charles Crichton. *W:* T.E.B. Clarke, Oscars 52; *Story & Screenplay;* British Acad. '51: Film.

L'Avventura ☝☝☝½ 1960 A stark, dry and minimalist exercise in narrative by Antonioni, dealing with the search for a girl on an Italian island by her lethargic socialite friends who eventually forget her in favor of their own preoccupations. A highly acclaimed, innovative treatment of many film treatments of angst and anomie, somewhat less effective now, in the wake of many film treatments of angst and anomie, rally. Subtitled in English. Laser edition an features the original trailer, commentary and a collection of still photographs from Antonioni's work. 145m/C VHS, DVD, IT Monica Vitti, Gabriele Ferzetti, Lea Massari, Dominique Blanchar, James Addams; *D:* Michelangelo Antonioni; *W:* Tonino Guerra, Michelangelo Antonioni, Elio Bartolini; *C:* Aldo Scavarda; *M:* Giovanni Fusco, Cannes '60: Special Jury Prize.

Law and Disorder ☝☝☝ 1974 (R) Two average Joes, fed up with the rate of rising crime, start their own auxiliary police group. Alternately funny and serious turns up and forces Taylor to lead them to buried loot. 86m/C VHS, Robert Taylor, Richard Widmark, Patricia Owens, Robert Middleton, Henry Silva, DeForest Kelley, Burt Douglas, Eddie Firestone; *D:* Oliver Drake; *C:* William Nobles.

Law and Lawless ☝☝ 1933 A roving cowboy brings justice to a gang of cattle thieves in this film. 58m/B VHS, Julian Rivero, Yakima Canutt, Jack Mower, Wally Wales, Hilda Moreno, Jack Hoxie; *D:* Armand Schaefer.

Law and Order 1942 Billy the Kid's nemesis a Cavalry lieutenant in order to swindle his aunt out of her money. 58m/B VHS, Dave O'Brien, Sarah Padden, Wanda McKay, Charles King, Buster Crabbe, Al "Fuzzy" St. John; *D:* Sam Newfield; *W:* Sam Robins; *C:* Jack Greenhalgh.

Law for Tombstone ☝☝ 1935 Alamo Bowie (Jones) must protect the Wells Fargo stagecoach from outlaw Twin Gun Jack. Includes chapter 1 of the serial "Gordon of Ghost City," which features Jones as retired ranch hand Buck Gordon who's on the trail of rustlers and meets a mysterious girl. 81m/B VHS, Buck Jones, Muriel Evans, Harvey Clark, Carl Stockdale, Earle Hodgins, Margaret Gray; *D:* Ray Taylor, Buck Jones.

Law of Desire ☝☝☝½ 1986 La Ley del Deseo 1986 A wicked, Almodovarian attack-on-decency farce about a promiscuous gay filmmaker, Pablo (Pancela), who becomes the object of desire for obsessive Antonio (Banderas), whom Pablo treats too casually for his own safety. Also in the mix is Pablo's sister, the transsexual Tina (Maura), and his current lover Juan (Molina). Romantic complications and violence abound. Unlike the work of any other director. Spanish with subtitles. 100m/C VHS, DVD, SP Carmen Maura, Eusebio Poncela, Antonio Banderas, Bibi Andersson, Miguel Molina, Manuela Velasco, Nacho Martinez; *D:* Pedro Almodovar; *W:* Pedro Almodovar; *C:* Angel Luis Fernandez.

Law of the Jungle ☝½ 1942 A lady scientist and a fugitive team up to uncover a secret Nazi radio base in the jungle. 61m/B VHS, DVD, Arline Judge, John "Dusty" King, Mantan Moreland, Martin Wilkins, Arthur O'Connell; *D:* Jean Yarbrough.

Law of the Land ☝ 1976 Sagebrush epic with the author/artist of "Garfield" portraying an accused but innocent man searching for a murderer. 100m/C VHS, Jim Davis, Don Johnson, Barbara Parkins Rolfe, John Wilder; *C:* William Spencer Jr.; *M:* John Parker, TV.

Lawless

Law of the Lash ☝ 1947 Cowboys and rustlers battle it out. 54m/B VHS, DVD, Lee Roberts, Charles "Blackie" King, Lash LaRue, Al "Fuzzy" St. John, Betty Miles; *D:* Ray Taylor; *C:* Robert E. Cline; *M:* Albert Glasser.

Law of the Pampas ☝☝ 1939 Boyd and Hayden ride off to South America to deliver some cattle, but the bad guys intervene. This is Toler's first outing as "Hoppy's sidekick, briefly replacing "Gabby" Hayes. 72m/B VHS, William Boyd, Russell Hayden, Steffi Duna, Sidney Toler, Sidney Blackmer, Pedro de Cordoba, Eddie Dean, Glenn Strange; *D:* Nate Watt.

Law of the Saddle ☝½ 1943 A family on a sinking ship is rescued by a lecherous sea captain who makes advances on the wife and binds the husband in a fight. Twenty years later, the husband meets him again, recognizes his laugh, and exacts revenge. 63m/B VHS, Priscilla Dean, Sally Blane, Ralph Ince, Rex Bell, William Farnum, Sally Albright, Jack Clifford, Frank LaRue, Syd Saylor, Eve Southern; *D:* Otto Brower; *C:* Archie Stout.

Law of the Sea ☝ 1932 A family on a sinking ship is rescued by a lecherous sea captain who makes advances on the wife. 58m/B VHS, Priscilla Dean, Sally Blane, Ralph Ince, Rex Bell, William Farnum.

Law of the Texan ☝ 1938 Jones goes undercover to stop Harlan and his gang from stealing a town's store of silver bullion. 54m/B VHS, Buck Jones, Dorothy Fay, Kenneth Harlan, Don Douglas, Matty Kemp, Robert F. (Bob) Kortman, Dave O'Brien; *D:* Elmer Clifton.

Law of the Underworld ☝½ 1938 An innocent couple is framed for the robbery of a jewelry store which resulted in the death of a clerk. When they are arrested, their fate lies in the hands of a gangster responsible for the crime. Will he let them fry in the electric chair, or will his conscience get the better of him? 58m/B VHS, Chester Morris, Anne Shirley, Eduardo Ciannelli, Walter Abel, Richard Bond, Lee Patrick, Paul Guilfoyle, Frank M. Thomas Sr., Eddie Acuff, Vinton (Hayworth) Haworth; *D:* Lew Landers.

Law of the Wild ☝ 1934 The search for a magnificent stallion that was hijacked by race racketeers before a big sweepstakes race is shown in this 12 chapter serial. 230m/B VHS, DVD, Bob Custer, Ben Turpin, Lucile Browne, Late (Lafayette) McKee; *D:* B. Reeves Eason, Armand Schaefer.

The Law Rides ☝ 1936 Rush of gold claims causes an outbreak of murder and robbery. 57m/B VHS, Bob Steele, Charles "Blackie" King, Buck Connors, Harlene Wood, Margaret Mann, Jack Rockwell; *D:* Robert North Bradbury. *W:* A. Martin.

The Law Rides Again ☝ 1943 Prairie lawmen bring a cheating Indian agent to justice. 56m/B VHS, DVD, Ken Maynard, Hoot Gibson, Betty Miles, Jack La Rue *D:* William Castle.

Law West of Tombstone ☝☝ 1938 A former outlaw moves to a dangerous frontier town in order to restore the peace. 73m/B VHS, Tim Holt, Harry Carey Sr., Evelyn Brent; *D:* Glenn Tryon.

The Lawless Breed ☝☝☝ 1952 Episodic saga based on the autobiography of outlaw John Wesley Hardin, published after his release from prison in 1896. Hardin's (Hudson) life of crime begins with a killing in self-defense that escalates into further bloodshed and flights from the law. Along the way Hardin marries (Adams) and has a son, whom he fears will follow in his violent footsteps. Walsh directs with plenty of brio. 83m/C VHS, DVD, Rock Hudson, Julie Adams, John McIntire, Hugh O'Brian, Lee Van Cleef, Dennis Weaver, Glenn Strange, Michael Ansara; *D:* Raoul Walsh; *W:* Bernard Gordon; *C:* Irving Glassberg; *M:* Joseph Gershenson.

Lawless Frontier ☝½ 1935 In the early West, the Duke fights for law and order. 53m/B VHS, DVD, John Wayne, George "Gabby" Hayes, Sheila Terry, Earl Dwire; *D:* Robert North Bradbury.

Lawless Heart ♂♂½ 2001 (R) Divided into three sections, with the characters seen from different perspectives. We start out with the funeral of Stuart, a local restaurateur with his partner, Nick (Hollander). Stuart died without a will so his sister (Haddington) becomes his unexpected heir and has to decide whether to share with Nick or not. Meanwhile, her husband, Dan (Nighy), thinking life has passed him by, is having a flirtation with florist, Corinne (Celarie). Nick is also having some unexpected feelings towards Charlie (Smith), a fun-loving party girl who helps with the loneliness (and more). Finally, there's Tim (Henshall) a feckless boyhood chum of Stuart's who's just returned home and who suddenly falls in love with shop owner Leah (Butler). **81m/C VHS, DVD.** *GB* Tom Hollander, Douglas Henshall, Bill Nighy, Clementine Celarie, Josephine Butler, Ellie Haddington, Stuart Laing, Sukie Smith, David Coffey, Dominic Hall, June Barrie, Peter Symonds; *D:* Neil Hunter, Tom Hunsinger; *W:* Neil Hunter, Tom Hunsinger; *C:* Sean Bobbitt; *M:* Adrian Johnston. L.A. Film Critics '03: Support. Actor (Nighy).

The Lawless Land ♂♂ 1988 (R) Post-holocaust America is ruled by a tyrant. Two young lovers who can't take it anymore go on the lam to escape the despotic rule. **56m/B VHS, DVD.** Leon Berkeley, Xander Berkeley, Jsu Garcia, Amanda Peterson; *D:* Jon Hess; *W:* Tony Cinciripini, Larry Leahy.

The Lawless Nineties ♂♂ 1936 Wayne plays a government agent sent to guarantee honest elections in the Wyoming territory. Hayes is exceptional as the newspaper editor who backs him up. Remade in 1940 as "The Dark Command." **55m/B VHS.** John Wayne, Ann Rutherford, Lane Chandler, Harry Woods, George "Gabby" Hayes, Charles "Blackie" King, Sam Flint; *D:* Joseph Kane.

Lawless Range ♂½ 1935 Wayne and the marshal's posse save the ranchers from trouble. **56m/B VHS, DVD.** John Wayne, Sheila (Manors) Mannors, Jack Curtis, Earl Dwire; *D:* Robert North Bradbury.

A Lawless Street ♂♂½ 1955 Scott portrays a she[riff who rides the Colorado Territory clean]ing up lawless towns. His dedication to dut[y has] caused his wife to leave him and s[he] won't come back until he lays dow[n] his guns forever, which may come [soon]er than they think after he rides int[o a corru]pt town of Medicine Bend. Ba[sed on the] novel "Marshal of Medicine [...] Ward. **78m/B VHS, DVD.** R[andolph Scott, A]ngela Lansbury, [...] [Lan]caster [...] fron[...] after Cobb and his si[...] ch fills up cowboys have accidenta[ll]y kille[...]on and are [...] caster is determined t[o bring] them to justice no matter w[hat] the cost. Though the entire town is [grateful to] him that doesn't stop his missio[n...]. Brooding and relentless with fine performances, particularly by Ryan as the local marshall living on past glories. **95m/C VHS, DVD.** Burt Lancaster, Robert Ryan, Lee J. Cobb, Sheree North, Joseph Wiseman, Robert Duvall, Albert Salmi, J.D. Cannon, John McGiver, Richard Jordan, John Beck, Ralph Waite, John Hillerman, Richard Bull; *D:* Michael Winner; *W:* Gerald Wilson; *C:* Robert Paynter; *M:* Jerry Fielding.

A Lawman Is Born ♂♂ 1937 A tough-as-nails marshal goes gunning for a pack of no-good, land-stealing varmits in this installment of the Johnny Mack Brown movie serials. Be sure to count the number of bullets each cowboy can fire from a six-shooter before being forced to reload; you may be surprised. **58m/B VHS.** Johnny Mack Brown, Iris Meredith, Warner Richmond, Mary MacLaren, Dick Curtis, Earle Hodgins, Charles "Blackie" King, Frank LaRue; *D:* Sam Newfield.

Lawmen ♂½ 1944 Government agents fight to enforce the law in the badlands. **55m/B VHS, DVD.** Johnny Mack Brown, Raymond Hatton, Jan Wiley, Kirby Grant, Robert Frazer, Edmund Cobb, Hal Price, Marshall Reed;

D: Lambert Hillyer; *W:* Glenn Tryon; *C:* Harry Neumann.

Lawn Dogs ♂♂½ 1996 After moving into an overly manicured suburban complex for the financially secure but morally bankrupt, Morton (McDonald) and Clare (Quinlan) want their daughter to mix with the social elite. Instead, the imaginative Devon (Barton) strikes up a friendship with Trent (Rockwell), an outsider who cuts lawns in the sterile burb. At first Trent, fearing the repercussions of such a friendship, pushes Devon away. The two eventually bond over their mutual dislike for the lifeless complex. After a conflict with a couple of dim college boys, events take a turn for the worse, and Trent is forced to escape from the community with Devon's help. Interweaved with the Russian fairy tale of Baba Yaga, the climax is visually stunning. Excellent performances from both Rockwell and Barton as the unlikely friends. **101m/C VHS, DVD.** *GB* Sam Rockwell, Mischa Barton, Kathleen Quinlan, Christopher McDonald, Bruce McGill, David Barry Gray, Eric Mabius, Tom Aldredge, Beth Grant; *D:* John Duigan; *W:* Naomi Wallace; *C:* Elliot Davis; *M:* Trevor Jones.

The Lawnmower Man ♂♂ 1992 (R) Brosnan is a scientist who uses Fahey, a dim-witted gardener, as a guinea pig to test his experiments in "virtual reality," an artificial computer environment. With the use of drugs and high-tech equipment, Brosnan is able to increase Fahey's mental powers—but not necessarily for the better. Fantastic special effects and a memorable "virtual reality" sex scene. Available in an unrated version which contains 32 more minutes of footage. So minimally based on a short story by Stephen King that the author sued (and won) to have his name removed from the film. **108m/C VHS, DVD.** Jeff Fahey, Pierce Brosnan, Jenny Wright, Mark Bringleson, Geoffrey Lewis, Jeremy Slate, Dean Norris, Troy Evans, John Laughlin; *D:* Brett Leonard; *W:* Brett Leonard, Gimel Everett; *M:* Russell Carpenter; *M:* Danny Wyman.

Lawnmower Man 2: Beyond Cyberspace ♂♂ 1995 (PG-13) Resurrecting Jobe (the title character from number one) was easy. So was blowing off his face to explain the new actor (Frewer in for Fahey) playing him. The hard part was trying to make an original movie with a decent script and believable characters. Better luck next time. Corporate baddie Walker (Conway) enlists Jobe to (what else?) take over the world using Virtual Reality. To the rescue comes one burned-out computer expert (Bergin) and a group of VR-addicted kids living in an abandoned subway. Techno-babble abounds but nothing interesting ever happens. Mann and Frewer must've raided their old "Max Headroom" set for the dreary near-future L.A. landscape scenes. **93m/C VHS, DVD.** Patrick Bergin, Matt Frewer, Austin O'Brien, Kevin Conway, Ely Pouget, Camille (Cami) Cooper; *D:* Farhad Mann; *W:* Farhad Mann; *C:* Ward Russell; *M:* Robert Folk.

Lawrence of Arabia ♂♂♂♂ 1962 (PG) Exceptional biography of T.E. Lawrence, a British military "observer" who strategically aids the Bedouins battle the Turks during WWI. Lawrence, played masterfully by O'Toole in his first major film, is a hero consumed more by a need to reject British tradition than to save the Arab population. He takes on Arab costume and a larger-than-life persona. Stunning photography of the desert in all its harsh reality. Blacklisted co-writer Wilson had his screen credit restored by the Writers Guild of America in 1995. Laser edition contains 20 minutes of restored footage and a short documentary about the making of the film. Available in letterboxed format. **221m/C VHS, DVD.** *GB* Peter O'Toole, Omar Sharif, Anthony Quinn, Alec Guinness, Jack Hawkins, Claude Rains, Anthony Quayle, Arthur Kennedy, Jose Ferrer, Michel Ray, Norman Rossington, John Ruddock, Donald Wolfit; *D:* David Lean; *W:* Robert Bolt, Michael Wilson; *C:* Frederick A. (Freddie) Young; *M:* Maurice Jarre. Oscars '62: Art Dir/Set Dec. Color, Color Cinematog., Director (Lean), Film Editing, Picture, Sound, Orig. Score;

AFI '98: Top 100; British Acad. '62: Actor (O'Toole), Film, Screenplay; Directors Guild '62: Director (Lean); Golden Globes '63: Director (Lean), Film—Drama, Support. Actor (Sharif); Natl. Bd. of Review '62: Director (Lean), Natl. Film Reg. '91.

The Lawrenceville Stories ♂♂½ 1988 Chronicles the life and times of a group of young men at the prestigious Lawrenceville prep school in 1905. Galligan plays William Hicks, alias "The Prodigious Hickey," the ringleader of their obnoxious stunts. Based on the stories of Owen Johnson, which originally ran in the Saturday Evening Post. Shown on "American Playhouse" and The Disney Channel. Tapes are available separately or as a set. **180m/C VHS.** Zach Galligan, Edward Herrmann, Nicholas (Nick) Rowe, Allan Goldstein, Robert Joy, Stephen Baldwin; *D:* Robert Iscove.

Laws of Attraction ♂♂ 2004 (PG-13) Powerhouse New York divorce lawyers Daniel (Brosnan) and Audrey (Moore) fight for their opposing clients and against their growing attraction to each other in this formulaic romantic comedy that attempts to recall classic Hollywood screwballs. The case between fashion designer Posey and rock star Sheen allows them to engage in the kind of witty banter, bickering, and heated sparring that everyone knows will eventually lead to the bedroom. The brief, drunken romp leaves them both in emotional denial until one of the disputed assets in the case, an Irish castle, forces the two to travel to the quaint country where they proceed to get drunk (again) and married. The two leads provide plenty of chemistry and charm despite a wafer thin premise, stale scripting and characterization, and weak direction. **89m/C DVD.** Pierce Brosnan, Julianne Moore, Michael Sheen, Parker Posey, Frances Fisher, Nora Dunn, Alan Houston, Vincent Marzello, Mina (Badiyi) Badie; *D:* Peter Howitt; *W:* Aline Brosh McKenna, Robert Harling; *C:* Adrian Biddle; *M:* Ed Shearmur.

Laws of Deception ♂½ 1997 As a child, Evan Marino (Howell) witnessed the murder of his parents by mobster Gino Carlucci (Russo). After becoming a ruthlessly successful criminal attorney in Miami, Evan gets drawn back into the life of former flame Elise (Smith), who happens to be Mrs. Carlucci and is accused of murdering her scummy husband. She says she didn't do it. You'll figure out all the would-be twists in this wanna-be thriller without any problem. **98m/C VHS.** C. Thomas Howell, Amber Smith, Brian Austin Green, James Russo, Nick Mancuso, Robert Miano; *Cameos:* John Landis; *D:* Joey Travolta; *W:* Rollin Jarrett; *C:* Dan Heigh; *M:* Jeff Lass. **VIDEO**

Laws of Gravity ♂♂♂ 1992 (R) Critically acclaimed debut film from 29-year-old writer/director Gomez is a three day slice of life set in Brooklyn. Hotheaded Jon (Trese) and married friend Jimmy (Greene) channel violent energy into their relationships and illegal activities. Camera follows "cinema verite" style and captures urban tension as it trails them through a gun heist and subsequent arrest. **100m/C VHS.** Peter Greene, Edie Falco, Adam Trese, Arabella Field, Paul Schulze; *D:* Nick Gomez; *W:* Nick Gomez; *C:* Jean De Segonzac.

Layer Cake ♂♂♂ 2005 (R) The unnamed protagonist (Craig), referred to only as "XXXX" in the closing credits, is a too-cool-for-you cocaine dealer trying to leave the business. But, just as we all could've guessed, somehow he's convinced to pull "one last job," searching out the daughter of a fellow crime-boss and, oh yeah, coordinate the sale of a million stolen tablets of Ecstasy along the way. And, of course, a few things go wrong. Guy Ritchie's buddy and producer Matthew Vaughn's directorial debut. Vaughn successfully negotiates the cockney-chocked, bass-thumping, and humorously violent British crime genre his colleague defined so well with just as much pizzazz and twists. **105m/C DVD, Blu-ray Disc, UMD, HD DVD.** *GB* Daniel Craig, Colm Meaney, Kenneth Cranham, George Harris, Jamie Foreman, Michael Gambon, Tamer Hassan, Ben Whishaw, Burn Gorman, Sally

Hawkins, Sienna Miller, Stephen Walters, Jason Flemyng, Dragan Micanovic, Dexter Fletcher, Steve John Shepherd, Marvin Benoit, Marcel Iures; *D:* Matthew Vaughn; *W:* J.J. Connolly; *C:* Benjamin Davis; *M:* Lisa Gerrard, Ilan Eshkeri.

Lazarillo ♂♂ *El Lazarillo de Tormes* 1959 In 17th-century Castille, a fatherless boy, abandoned by his mother, finds work with a strange succession of employers, including a blind beggar, fake nobleman, and traveling band of performers. They all teach him lessons in survival as well as cunning and deception. Spanish with subtitles. **109m/B VHS.** *SP* Marco Paoletti, Juan Jose Menendez, Carlos Casaravilla, Margarita Lozano; *D:* Cesar Ardavin; *W:* Cesar Ardavin; *M:* Ruiz De Luna. Berlin Intl. Film Fest. '60: Film.

The Lazarus Man ♂♂ 1996 Pilot episode of the TV series finds the amnesiac Urich discovering he's linked to the assassination of President Lincoln. In 1865 Texas he literally claws his way out of the grave and is taken in by a farming family. This back from the dead Lazarus may not remember who he is but a trip to town demonstrates his gunslinger skills and images from his dreams may provide clues to his past. Now, he has to stay alive long enough to figure them out. **90m/C VHS.** Robert Urich, Elizabeth Dennehy, David Marshall Grant, John Diehl, Wayne Grace, Brion James; *D:* Johnny E. Jensen; *W:* Dick Beebe; *C:* Gary Holt; *M:* John Debney. **TV**

The Lazarus Syndrome 1979 Astute doctor teams up with an ex-patient of the chief of surgery in an effort to expose the chief's unethical surgical procedures. **90m/C VHS.** Ronald Hunter, Sheila Frazier, Lara Parker, Louis Gossett Jr., E.G. Marshall; *D:* Michael Firth; *W:* William Blinn; *C:* Chuck (Charles G.) Arnold; *M:* John Rubenstein.

LBJ: A Biography 1991 Produced for the PBS series "The American Experience," this four-hour revisionist look at LBJ is one of the most critically acclaimed political documentaries of our time. Divided into four segments. "Beautiful Texas" chronicles Johnson's rise to power. "My Fellow Americans" focuses on his years as an unelected president. The Great Society and and the escalation of war in Vietnam are covered in "We Shall Overcome." "The Last Believer" highlights events leading to Johnson's withdrawal from politics. **240m/C VHS, DVD.** *D:* David Grubin.

LBJ: The Early Years ♂♂♂ 1988 The early years of President Lyndon Baines Johnson's political career are dramatized. Winning performances hoist this above other biographies. **144m/C VHS.** Randy Quaid, Patti LuPone, Morgan Brittany, Pat Hingle, Kevin McCarthy, Barry Corbin, Charles Frank; *D:* Peter Werner. **TV**

Le Bal ♂♂♂ 1982 You won't find many films with the music of Paul McCartney and Chopin in the credits, and even fewer without dialogue. With only music and dancing the film uses a French dance hall to illustrate the changes in French society over a 50-year period. Based on a French play. ♪La Vie en Rose; In the Mood; Michelle; Top Hat White Tie and Tails; Let's Face the Music and Dance; Harlem Nocturne; Shuffle Blues; Tutti Frutti; Only You. **112m/C VHS.** *IT FR* *D:* Ettore Scola; *M:* Irving Berlin, Paul McCartney, John Lennon, Vladimir Cosma. Cesar '84: Director (Scola), Film, Score.

Le Beau Mariage ♂♂♂ *A Good Marriage; The Well-Made Marriage* 1982 (R) An award-winning comedy from the great French director about a zealous woman trying to find a husband and the unsuspecting man she chooses to marry. The second in Rohmer's Comedies and Proverbs series. French with subtitles. **97m/C VHS, DVD.** *FR* Beatrice Romand, Arielle Dombasle, Andre Dussollier, Feodor Atkine, Pascal Greggory, Sophie Renoir; *D:* Eric Rohmer; *W:* Eric Rohmer; *C:* Bernard Lutic; *M:* Ronan Girre, Simon des Innocents. Venice Film Fest. '82: Actress (Romand).

Le Beau Serge ♂♂♂ *Handsome Serge* 1958 Young theology student Francois returns to his home village and discovers his friend Serge, in despair of ever changing his life, has become a hopeless drunk. So Francis meddles in his life (with the best of intentions) and only causes Serge further disaster. Chabrol's first film, and a major forerunner of the nouvelle vague. In French with English subtitles. **97m/B VHS. FR** Gerard Blain, Jean-Claude Brialy, Michele Meritz, Bernadette LaFont. **D:** Claude Chabrol.

Le Bonheur ♦♦½ *Happiness* 1965 A seemingly happily married carpenter (Drouot) takes a vacation with his wife and children where he meets the local postal clerk and the two begin a passionate affair. Unwilling to leave his family, Drouot believes the two women can share him but when his wife discovers his infidelity she kills herself. His grief does not cause Drouot to stop the affair, instead he moves in with his mistress. An uninvolving, unbelievable tale with a lovely Mozart score. In French with English subtitles. **87m/C VHS. FR** Jean-Claude Drouot, Claire Drouot, Marie-France Boyer, **C:** Jean Rabier, Claude Beausoleil.

Le Bonheur Est Dans le Pre ♦♦ *Happiness Is In the Fields; Happiness* 1995 Francis (Serrault) is the harried owner of a toilet brush-making business that is about to undergo a tax audit and is threatened by a workers strike. His wife and daughter are never happy and Francis' one relief is to have lunch with his macho, easy-going friend, Gerard (Mitchell). One day, he watches a TV show about missing persons and sees that a woman who disappeared 28 years before—a man who looks suspiciously like Francis. The plot's convoluted and the comedy's flat. French with subtitles. **105m/C VHS. FR** Michel Serrault, Sabine Azema, Eddy Mitchel, Carmen Maura, Alexandra London; **D:** Etienne Chatiliez; **W:** Florence Quentin. **C:** Philippe Welt; **M:** Pascal Andreacchio. Cesar '95: Support. Actor (Mitchell).

Le Boucher ♦♦♦ *The Butcher* 1969 In a provincial French town a sophisticated schoolmistress is courted by the shy local butcher—who turns out to be a sex murderer. A well-played thriller that looks at sexual frustration. French with subtitles. **94m/C VHS. DVD. FR** Stephane Audran, Jean Yanne, Antonio Passalia, **D:** Claude Chabrol.

Le Cas du Dr. Laurent ♦♦♦ 1957 A country doctor in a small French town tries to introduce methods of natural childbirth to the native women, but meets opposition from the superstitious villagers. Fine performance by Gabin. **88m/B VHS, FR** Jean Gabin, Nicole Courcel. **D:** Jean-Paul LeChanois.

Le Cavaleur ♦♦ *Practice Makes Perfect* 1978 A light hearted comedy about a philandering concert pianist. **90m/C VHS. FR** Jean Rochefort, Lila Kedrova, Nicole Garcia, Annie Girardot, Danielle Darrieux. **D:** Philippe de Broca; **M:** Georges Delerue.

Le Cercle Rouge ♦♦♦ *The Red Circle* 1971 An ex-con, an escaped prisoner, a diamond heist, a police manhunt, and mob vengeance—all set during a wet Paris winter. Ex-con Corey (Delon) planning to rob a jewelry store; Vogel (Volonte) escapes from his police guard, Mattei (Bourvil) during a train trip; fate brings the two together. Corey is in trouble for stealing from the mob and Vogel helps him out. They seek the help of ex-con Jansen (Montand) for their heist (which isn't even the most important part of the movie), while Mattei is out to re-capture Vogel to salvage his reputation. It's trench coats and fedoras and the ever-present smoldering cigarette—and it's all very, very cool. French with subtitles. **140m/C DVD. FR** Alain Delon, Gian Maria Volonte, Yves Montand, Andre Bourvil, Francois Perier, **D:** Jean-Pierre Melville, **W:** Jean-Pierre Melville. **C:** Henri Decae. **M:** Eric Demasen.

Le Chat ♦♦½ *The Cat* 1975 A middle-aged couple's marriage dissolves into a hate-filled battle of wits, centering around the husband's love for their cat. In French with English subtitles. **88m/C VHS. FR** Jean Gabin, Simone Signoret, Annie Cordy. Berlin Intl. Film Fest '71: Actor (Gabin).

Le Complot ♦♦ *The Conspiracy* 1973 When de Gaulle announces his intention to abandon Algeria, several army officers, feeling that their service has been in vain, stage a coup. There's suspense aplenty as the Gaulists, the leftists, and the police spy and are spied upon. In French with English subtitles. **120m/C VHS. FR** Michel Bouquet, Jean Rochefort. **D:** Rene Gainville.

Le Corbeau ♦♦♦ *The Raven* 1943 A great, notorious drama about a small French village whose everyday serenity is ruptured by a series of poison pen letters that lead to suicide and despair. The film was made within Nazi-occupied France, sponsored by the Nazis, and has been subjected to much misdirected malice because of it. In French with English subtitles. **92m/B VHS, DVD. FR** Pierre Fresnay, Noel Roquevert, Ginette LeClerc, Pierre Larquey, Antoine Belpierre, **D:** Henri-Georges Clouzot.

Le Crabe Tambour ♦♦♦ 1977 Rochefort plays a dying naval captain remembering his relationship with his first officer. Revealed via flashbacks, the recollections concern the adventures which transpired on a North Atlantic supply ship. Great performances from all and award-winning cinematography by Raoul Coutard. Winner of several French Cesars. A French script booklet is available. **120m/C VHS. FR** Jean Rochefort, Claude Rich, Jacques Dufilho, Jacques Perrin, Odile Versois, Aurore Clement. **D:** Pierre Schoendoerffer. **C:** Raoul Courand, Cinemabog. Support. Actor (Dufilho).

Le Dernier Combat ♦♦ *The Last Battle* 1984 (R) A stark film about life after a devastating nuclear war marks the directorial debut of Besson. The characters fight to survive in a now speechless world by staking territorial claims and vors. An original and expressive film made without dialogue. French with subtitles. **93m/B VHS, DVD. FR** Pierre Jolivet, Fritz Wepper, Jean Reno, Jean Bouise, Christiane Kruger. **D:** Luc Besson; **W:** Luc Besson; **C:** Carlo Varini; **M:** Eric Serra.

Le Divorce ♦♦ 2003 (PG-13) Cutie blonde American Isabel Walker (Hudson) heads to Paris to support her equally blonde but depressed pregnant sister Roxeanne (Watts) whose French husband Charles-Henri (Poupard) has walked out because of an obsessive affair. Hubby insists on a quick divorce but Roxy is refusing. Meanwhile, Isabel becomes involved with Charles-Henri's worldly uncle, Edgar (Lhermitte), who knows how to begin and end an affair with aplomb (and gifts). A culture clash comedy of manners that's brittle with artifice. Based on the 1997 novel by Diane Johnson. **115m/C VHS, DVD. US** Kate Hudson, Naomi Watts, Thierry Lhermitte, Melvil Poupaud, Leslie Caron, Glenn Close, Stockard Channing, Sam Waterston, Thomas Lennon, Matthew Modine, Rona Harmer, Jean-Marc Barr, Stephen Fry, Bebe Neuwirth, Samuel Labarthe, Nathalie Richard, Romain Duris, Daniel Mesguich; **D:** James Ivory; **W:** Ruth Prawer Jhabvala; **C:** Pierre Lhomme; **M:** Richard Robbins.

Le Doulos ♦♦♦ *Doulos—The Finger Man* 1961 Compelling story of an ex-convict and his buddy, a man who may be a police informant. Chronicles the efforts of the snitch (the "doulos" of the title) to bring the criminal element before the law. Melville blends in several plot twists and breathes a new-French life into the cliche-ridden genre. **108m/B VHS. FR** Serge Reggiani, Jean-Paul Belmondo, Michel Piccoli; **D:** Jean-Pierre Melville.

Le Gentleman D'Epsom ♦♦ 1962 A French comedy about a breezy con man who scams everyone around him in order to keep up his upwardly mobile appearance and to put his bets down at the racetrack. Subtitled in English. **83m/B VHS. FR** Jean Gabin, Paul Frankeur.

Le Gitan ♦♦ *The Gypsy* 1975 Gypsy Hugo (Delon) steals from the rich to provide for his fellows, who are poverty-stricken outcasts in French society. But no good deed goes unpunished. French with subtitles. **102m/C VHS. FR** Alain Delon, Paul Meurisse, Annie Girardot, Marcel Bozzuffi, Bernard

Le Jour Se Leve ♦♦♦ *Daybreak* 1939 The dark, expressionist film that put Carne and Gabin on the cinematic map. Highly acclaimed. French with subtitles. Remade in 1947 as "The Long Night". **89m/B VHS. FR** Jean Gabin, Jules Berry, Arletty, Jacqueline Laurent; **D:** Marcel Carne.

Le Jupon Rouge ♦♦ *Manuela's Loves* 1987 Bacha (Valli) is a human rights activist and concentration camp survivor who is involved with younger fashion designer Manuela (Barrault). But when Manuela becomes drawn to the even younger Claude (Grobon), Bracha's overwhelmed with jealousy and Manuela is torn by her feelings for both women. French with subtitles. **90m/C VHS. FR** Alida Valli, Marie-Christine Barrault, Guillemette Grobon; **D:** Genevieve Lefebvre.

Le Magnifique ♦♦ *The Magnificent One* 1976 Belmondo is a master spy and novelist who mixes fantasy with reality in his own mind. The film chases women and solves cases. **84m/C VHS, DVD. FR** Jean-Paul Belmondo, Jacqueline Bisset, Hans Meyer, Vittorio Caprioli; **D:** Philippe de Broca; **W:** Francis Veber, Philippe de Broca; **C:** Rene Mathelin; **M:** Claude Bolling.

Le Mans ♦♦♦ 1971 (G) The famous 24-hour sports car race sets the stage for this tale of love and speed. McQueen (who did his own driving) is the leading race driver, a man who battles competition, fear of death by accident, and emotional involvement. Excellent documentary-style race footage almost makes up for weak plot and minimal acting. **106m/C VHS, DVD.** Steve McQueen, Elga Andersen, Ronald Leigh-Hunt, Luc Merenda; **D:** Lee H. Katzin; **W:** Harry Kleiner; **C:** Robert B. Hause.

Le Million ♦♦♦½ 1931 A comedy/musical masterpiece of the early sound era which centers on an artist's adventures in searching for a winning lottery ticket throughout Paris. Highly acclaimed member of the Clair school of subtle French farce. In French with English subtitles. **85m/B VHS. FR** Rene Lefevre, Paul Olivier, Louis Allibert; **D:** Rene Clair.

Le Petit Amour ♦♦♦ *Kung Fu Master* 1987 (R) Popular French comedy about the fateful romance between a 40-year-old divorced woman and a 15-year-old boy obsessed with a kung fu video game. In French with English subtitles. **80m/C VHS. FR** Jane Birkin, Mathieu Demy, Charlotte Gainsbourg, Lou Doillon, David Birkin; **D:** Agnes Varda.

Le Petit Lieutenant ♦♦ *The Young Lieutenant* 2005 Rookie detective Antoine (Lespert) leaves his wife in Normandy so he can find some action in Paris by working in homicide. His commander is Catherine (Baye), a recovering alcoholic who has just returned to the job, and she takes the new guy under her wing. A homeless man is the latest victim of a robbery and murder crew that Antoine investigates, with unexpectedly devastat-

Giraudeau; **D:** Jose Giovanni; **W:** Jose Giovanni; **C:** Jean-Jacques Tarbes; **M:** Claude Bolling.

Le Grand Chemin ♦♦♦ *The Grand Highway* 1987 A sweet, slice-of-life French film about a young boy's idyllic summer on a family friend's farm while his mother is having a baby. Hubert's son plays the boy Louis in this retelling of the director's own childhood. In French with English subtitles. Remade with an American setting in 1991 as "Paradise." **107m/C VHS. FR** Anemone, Richard Bohringer, Antoine Hubert, Vanessa Guedj, Christine Pascal, Raoul Billerey, Pascale Roberts; **D:** Jean-Loup Hubert; **C:** Claude Lecomte; **M:** Georges Granier, Cesar '88: Actor (Bohringer), Actress (Anemone).

Le Joli Mai ♦♦♦ 1962 A famous documentary that established Marker, depicting the everyday life of Paris denizens on the occasion of the end of the Algerian War, May 1962, when France was at peace for the first time since 1939. In French with English subtitles. **180m/B VHS. FR D:** Chris Marker. **Nar:** Yves Montand, Simone Signoret.

Le Plaisir ♦♦½ *House of Pleasure* 1952 An anthology of three Guy de Maupassant stories. "Le Masque," and "La Maison Teillier," about the **88m/B VHS, DVD. FR** Claude Dauphin, Simone Simon, Jean Gabin, Danielle Darrieux, Madeleine Renaud, Gaby Morlay; **D:** Max Ophuls; **Nar:** Peter Ustinov.

Le Polygraphe ♦♦ *The Lie Detector* 1996 Francois (Goyette) is still a suspect in the murder of his girlfriend, Marie-Claire, two years after her death. The murder has so affected her friend Judith (Descenes) that she's written a screenplay about the murder/love triangle that starts with a police stance-off and evolves into a series of flashbacks. French with subtitles. **97m/C VHS. CA** Patrick Goyette, Jose Descenes, Marie Brassard, Peter Stormare, Maria Da Medeiros; **D:** Robert Lepage; **C:** Georges Dufeux.

Le Petit Soldat ♦♦♦ 1960 The passage of time has softened the controversy that swirled about Godard's second film (after "Breathless") in the initial release. It's the story of photographer Bruno Forestier (Subor), who joins the French nationalist movement against Algeria. While he tries to decide whether to follow orders to kill one of the opposition, he falls in love with a model (the lovely Karina, in her debut), unaware of her political beliefs. Godard's once-revolutionary or-the-fly filmmaking techniques seem completely contemporary and natural now. For serious students of film, this one makes a long-overdue debut on home video. **88m/B VHS, DVD. FR** Michel Subor, Anna Karina, Henri-Jacques Huet, Paul Beauvais, Georges De Beauregard, Jean-Luc Godard, Laszlo Szabo; **D:** Jean-Luc Godard; **W:** Jean-Luc Godard; **C:** Raoul Coutard; **M:** Maurice Leroux.

Le Professionnel ♦♦½ *The Professional* 1981 French assassin Joss Beaumont (Belmondo) returns from the African republic of Malagasy, where he's been imprisoned for two years because his own superiors turned him in to the authorities when they decided to abort his mission. Instantly his old department is mobilized to eliminate him, but Beaumont is faster and smarter than all of them put together. Fast, clever, and beholden to nothing done before, the film is a slick package, a spy thriller that relies on brains instead of guns. There's a constant flow of fistfights and combat encounters in the picture, none of which are hyped with cutting or music. Belmondo makes them all credible. A surprise picture for people who like intelligent thrillers. **109m/C DVD. FR** Jean-Paul Belmondo, Jean Desailly, Robert Hossein, Michel Beaune, Cyrielle Claire, Jean-Louis Richard, Sidiki Bakaba; **D:** Georges Lautner; **W:** Georges Lautner, Michel Audiard; **C:** Henri Decae; **M:** Ennio Morricone.

Le Repos du Guerrier ♦♦ *Warrior's Rest* 1962 Star vehicle for Bardot in which she plays a respectable woman who abandons societal norms to pursue an unbalanced lover. In French with English subtitles. **100m/C VHS, DVD. FR** Brigitte Bardot, Robert Hossein, James Robertson Justice, Jean-Mark Bory; **D:** Roger Vadim.

Le Samourai ♦♦♦½ *The Samurai Godson* 1967 Cool, precise professional killer Jef Costello (Delon) lives by his version of the code of the Japanese samurai. Hired to kill a nightclub owner, he establishes an alibi with the help of his lover Jane (Nathalie Delon, Alain's then-wife) and, unexpectedly, by Valerie (Rosier), the club's black piano-player. Jef finds Valerie's aid suspicious and begins to dig deeper, finding himself betrayed by his employers, and the subject of a police chase throughout Paris. The icy Delon was perfect for the anti-hero role and Mel-

ing consequences to all. French with subtitles. **110m/C DVD. FR** Nathalie Baye, Jalil Lespert, Roschdy Zem, Antoine Chappey, Jacques Perrin, Berangere Allaux; **D:** Xavier Beauvois; **W:** Xavier Beauvois, Guillaume Breaud, Jean-Eric Troubat; **C:** Caroline Champetier.

ville's stylized filming heightens the tension and inevitable tragedy. A film much-admired and copied, by contemporary filmmakers. French with subtitles. **95m/C VHS, DVD.** *FR* Alain Delon, Francois Perier, Cathy Rosier, Nathalie Delon, Jacques Leroy, Jean-Pierre Posier; *D:* Jean-Pierre Melville; *M:* Francois de Roubaix.

Le Schpountz ✓✓ *Heartbeat* **1938** Satire on filmmaking and film-loving fans finds a small town grocer (Fernandel) in southern France becoming the victim of a practical joke when a visiting film crew promises to make him a star (signing him to a phony contract) if he'll come to Paris. Naturally, the joke's on them when the naive grocer arrives in the City of Light and becomes a successful movie comic. French with subtitles. **135m/B VHS.** *FR* Fernandel, Charpin, Orane Demazis, Odette Roger, Jean Castan, Leon Belieres; *D:* Marcel Pagnol; *M:* Casimir Oberfeld.

Le Secret ✓✓✓ **1974** This classic French thriller with a shocking ending finds an escaped convict seeking shelter with a reclusive couple in the mountains. His tales of abuse and torture create tension for the pair as one believes the woeful story and the other doesn't. Dubbed in English. **103m/C VHS.** *FR* Jean-Louis Trintignant, Philippe Noiret, Jean-Francois Adam; *D:* Robert Enrico; *M:* Ennio Morricone.

Le Sex Shop ✓✓✓ **1973 (R)** A man turns his little book store into a porn equipment palace, to make ends meet. When his relationship with his wife gets boring, they begin to use their erotic merchandise and adopt a swinging lifestyle. **92m/C VHS.** *FR* Claude Berri, Juliet Berto, Daniel Auteuil, Nathalie Delon; *D:* Claude Berri; *M:* Serge Gainsbourg.

Le Sexe des Etoiles ✓✓✓ *The Sex of the Stars* **1993** Curiously uninvolving film about 12-year-old Camille who discovers that the father who abandoned her is now a transsexual. Pierre walked out years before and Camille has always dreamed of his return but though they reach a tentative relationship, it's not what Camille hoped for. Title refers to Camille's obsession with astronomy because stars have no sex. Based on the novel by Proulx (who also wrote the screenplay). In French with English subtitles. **100m/C VHS.** *CA* Marianne-Coquelicot Mercier, Denis Mercier, Tobie Pelletier, Sylvie Drapeau; *D:* Paule Baillargeon; *W:* Monique Proulx; *C:* Eric Cayla. Genie '93: Sound.

Le Trou ✓✓✓ *The Night Watch; Il Buco* **1959** Four long-term convicts in a Paris prison cell are planning to escape by tunneling to freedom. Then, a fifth prisoner joins them—is he going to betray them? Or is there already a Judas amongst the men? Based on a true story, the film has no musical score in order to heighten the tension and the actors were all nonprofessionals. Becker died in 1960; this is his final film. French with subtitles. **123m/B VHS, DVD.** *FR* Phillipe LeRoy, Marc Michel, Catherine Spaak, Andre Bervil, Michel Constantin, Jean-Paul Coquelin, Jean Keraudy, Raymond Meunier, Eddy Rasimi, Dominique Zardi; *D:* Jacques Becker; *W:* Jacques Becker, Jose Giovanni, Jean Aurel; *C:* Ghislan Cloquet.

Lea ✓✓ **1996** Lea (Vlasakova) becomes mute after witnessing her abusive father kill her mother but writes the dead woman poems and letters to express her emotions. However, Lea becomes even more withdrawn from the world when she's given in an arranged marriage to the much-older Herbert (Redl). Herbert marries Lea because she resembles his dead wife but Lea finds he has disturbing similarities to her father. German with subtitles. **100m/C VHS, DVD.** *GE* Lenka Vlasakov, Christian Redl, Hanna Schygulla; *D:* Ivan Fila; *W:* Ivan Fila.

Leader of the Band ✓✓ **1987 (PG)** An out-of-work musician tries to train the world's worst high school band. Landesberg helps this attempted comedy along. **90m/C VHS.** Steve Landesberg, Gailard Sartain, Mercedes Ruehl, James Martinez, Calvert Deforest; *D:* Nessa Hyams; *M:* Dick Hyman.

The Leading Man ✓✓½ **1996 (R)** Bon Jovi's charming in the title role as American movie star Robin Grange. Grange has come to London to work in the prestige stage production by playwright Felix Webb (Wilson) and he's also become aware of Webb's complex romantic situation. Although married to Elena (Galiena), Felix is having an affair with young leading lady, Hilary Rule (Newton). So the studly Robin proposes that he seduce Elena, thus leaving Felix free to carry on with his own affair. Except Felix gets jealous when Robin succeeds and soon realizes that the actor has his own agenda. **96m/C VHS, DVD.** *GB* Lambert Wilson, Jon Bon Jovi, Anna Galiena, Thandie Newton, David Warner, Barry Humphries, Patricia Hodge, Diana Quick, Nicole Kidman; *D:* John Duigan; *W:* John Duigan; *C:* Jean-Francois Robin; *M:* Ed Shearmur.

The League of Extraordinary Gentlemen ✓✓ **2003 (PG-13)** There's little left of the "League" featured in the 1999 comic book by Alan Moore and Kevin O'Neill. Instead, there's overblown action and a lack of heart. Aging adventurer Allan Quartermain (Connery) is but one of the literary characters called to defeat a madman bent on starting a world war for profit in 1899. He's somewhat reluctantly teamed with Captain Nemo (Shah) and his Nautilus submarine, vampiric scientist Mina Harker (Wilson), the ageless Dorian Gray (Townsend), the invisible man Rodney Skinner (Curran), Dr. Jekyll and his hulkish alter ego Mr. Hyde (Flemyng), and Tom Sawyer (West), who's grown up to be a member of the American secret service. Clumsily telegraphs many plot twists, but the well-read should get a kick out of the many literary references. **110m/C VHS, DVD, Blu-ray Disc, UMD.** *US* Sean Connery, Stuart Townsend, Peta Wilson, Shane West, Tony Curran, Richard Roxburgh, Jason Flemyng, Naseeruddin Shah, David Hemmings, Terry O'Neill, Max Ryan, Tom Goodman-Hill; *D:* Stephen Norrington; *W:* James Robinson; *C:* Dan Laustsen; *M:* Trevor Jones.

The League of Gentlemen ✓✓✓½ **1960** An ex-Army officer plots a daring bank robbery using specially skilled military personnel and irreproachable panache. Hilarious British humor fills the screen. **115m/B VHS, DVD.** *GB* Jack Hawkins, Nigel Patrick, Richard Attenborough, Roger Livesey, Bryan Forbes; *D:* Basil Dearden.

League of Ordinary Gentlemen ✓✓✓ **2004** Three former Microsoft execs purchased the Pro Bowlers Association for $5 million and hired Steve Miller from Nike to help revive and make it more exciting and media friendly. Film documents the 2003 nationwide tour, which culminated in a tense world championship in Detroit. We witness the tour through the fortunes of four pros, Pete Weber, a flamboyant player, Walter Ray Williams Jr., a low-key guy who can be a bit imposing, Chris Barnes, a clean-cut but moody fellow, and Wayne Webb, who knows after his past broken marriages and bankruptcies that will make or break his bowling career. An endearing film touching on American life and the eccentricities and hardships of competition. **100m/C DVD.** *US D:* Christopher Browne; *C:* Ken Seng.

A League of Their Own ✓✓✓ **1992 (PG)** Charming look at sports history and the Rockford Peaches, one of the teams in the real-life All American Girls Professional Baseball League, formed in the 40s when the men were off at war. Main focus is on sibling rivalry between Dottie Hinson (Davis), the beautiful, crackerjack catcher, and Kit Keller (Petty), her younger, insecure sister and team pitcher. Boozy coach Jimmy Dugan (Hanks) is wonderful as he reluctantly leads the team; he also gets credit for the classic "There's no crying in baseball" scene. Great cast of supporting characters, including sarcastic talent scout Ernie (Lovitz), opinionated, sleazy taxi dancer Mae (Madonna), loud-mouthed Doris (O'Donnell), and shy, homely Marla (Cavanagh). Lots of baseball for the sports fan. **127m/C VHS, DVD.** Geena Davis, Tom Hanks, Lori Petty, Madonna, Rosie O'Donnell, Megan Cavanagh, Tracy Reiner, Bitty Schram, Jon Lovitz, David Strathairn, Garry Marshall, Bill Pullman, Ann Cusack, Anne Elizabeth Ramsey, Freddie Simpson, Renee Coleman, Tea Leoni, Joey Slotnick, Mark Holton, Gregory Sporleder, David Lander; *D:* Penny Marshall; *W:* Lowell Ganz, Babaloo Mandel; *C:* Miroslav Ondricek; *M:* Hans Zimmer; *V:* Harry Shearer.

Lean on Me ✓✓✓ **1989 (PG-13)** The romanticized version of the career of Joe Clark, a tough New Jersey teacher who became the principal of the state's toughest, worst school and, through controversial hard-line tactics, turned it around. **109m/C VHS, DVD.** Morgan Freeman, Robert Guillaume, Beverly Todd, Alan North, Lynne Thigpen, Robin Bartlett, Michael Beach, Ethan Phillips, Regina Taylor; *D:* John G. Avildsen; *W:* Michael Schiffer; *C:* Victor Hammer; *M:* Bill Conti.

Leap of Faith ✓✓½ **1992 (PG-13)** Jonas Nightengale (Martin) is a traveling evangelist/scam artist whose tour bus is stranded in an impoverished farm town. Nevertheless he sets up his show and goes to work, aided by the technology utilized by accomplice Winger. Both Martin and Winger begin to have a change of heart after experiencing love—Winger with local sheriff Neeson and Martin after befriending a waitress (Davidovich) and her crippled brother (Haas). Martin is in his element as the slick revivalist with the hidden heart but the film is soft-headed as well as soft-hearted. **110m/C VHS, DVD.** Steve Martin, Debra Winger, Lolita (David) Davidovich, Liam Neeson, Lukas Haas, Meat Loaf Aday, Philip Seymour Hoffman, M.C. Gainey, La Chanze, Delores Hall, John Toles-Bey, Albertina Walker, Ricky Dillard; *D:* Richard Pearce; *W:* Janus Cercone; *M:* Cliff Eidelman.

Leap Year ✓✓½ **1921** Made at the apex of the 300-pound comedian's career, "Leap Year" wasn't released in the States until the '60s. Tried for manslaughter in 1921 (with two hung juries), Fatty was forced off camera and his films were taken out of circulation (although he did return to cinema behind the camera using the pseudonym William Goodrich). **60m/B VHS, DVD.** Mary Thurman, Lucien Littlefield, Clarence Geldart, Harriet Hammond, Fatty Arbuckle; *D:* James Cruze; *W:* Walter Woods; *C:* Karl Brown.

Leapin' Leprechauns ✓✓ **1995 (PG)** John Dennehy's dad Michael has arrived from Ireland for a visit, accompanied by some "wee folk" who are invisible to all non-believers. Seems the little leprechauns are just in time to rescue their ancestral home from a plot by John to turn their Irish land into a theme park and make believers out of a family of skeptics. **84m/C VHS.** Grant Cramer, John Bluthal, Sharon Lee Jones, Gregory Edward Smith, Sylvester McCoy, James Ellis, Godfrey James, Tina Martin, Erica Nicole Hess; *D:* Ted Nicolaou; *W:* Ted Nicolaou, Michael McGann.

The Learning Curve ✓✓ **2001 (R)** Hospital orderly Paul (Giovinazzo) comes to the rescue of Georgia (Mazur) and gets involved in a shady sex scam. These small-timers are in for trouble when they target Marshall (Ventresca) who turns out to be a ruthless L.A. record producer with a lot of clout. Marshall's amused by their chutzpah and decides to bring them into his own shady deals where they are in over their heads. **97m/C VHS, DVD.** Carmine D. Giovinazzo, Monet Mazur, Vincent Ventresca, Steven Bauer, Majandra Delfino, Richard Erdman, Jack Lauder; *D:* Eric Schwab; *W:* Eric Schwab; *C:* Michael Hofstein; *M:* Zoran Boris.

The Learning Tree ✓✓ **1969 (PG)** A beautifully photographed adaptation of Parks' biographical novel about a 14-year-old black boy in the 1920s South, living on the verge of manhood, maturity, love, and wisdom. **107m/C VHS.** Kyle Johnson, Alex Clarke, Estelle Evans, Dana Elcar; *D:* Gordon Parks; *C:* Burnett Guffey. Natl. Film Reg. '89.

The Leather Boys ✓✓ **1963** *The Leatherboys* **1963** Teenaged Dot (Tushingham) marries mechanic Reggie (Campbell) and soon both begin to look beyond the boundaries of marriage. Dot enjoys her freedom from parental supervision by staying out and coming home drunk while Reggie takes up his friendship with biker pal, Pete (Sutton). Then Dot begins wondering just how close her husband and his best pal really are. Considered very controversial in the '60s, but looks staid now. **110m/B VHS, DVD.** *GB* Rita Tushingham, Colin Campbell, Dudley Sutton, Gladys Henson, Avice Landon, Betty Marsden, Dandy Nichols, Johnny Briggs, Geoffrey Dunn, Lockwood West, Denholm Elliott; *D:* Sidney J. Furie; *W:* Gillian Freeman; *C:* Gerald Gibbs.

Leather Burners ✓✓ **1943** Hoppy goes under cover to get the goods on a suspected rustler. When his cover is blown, the bad guys frame him for murder. Look for Robert Mitchum in his third bit part in this series. **66m/B VHS, DVD.** William Boyd, Andy Clyde, Jay Kirby, Victor Jory, George Givot, Bobby Larson, George Reeves, Hal Taliaferro, Forbes Murray, Robert Mitchum; *D:* Joseph Henabery.

Leather Jacket Love Story ✓✓ **1998** Remarkably sweet, campy, and raunchy romance finds 18-year-old Valley boy Kyle (Tataryn) taking a summer rental in bohemian Silver Lake in order to get the proper inspiration for his poetry. The local coffee shop is the preferred hangout and that's where Kyle spots leather-jacketed motorcycle man Mike (Bradley). Some 12 years older than Kyle, easygoing carpenter Mike is not adverse to some sexual fun, but both men are surprised when their feelings for each other start turning serious. **85m/B VHS.** Sean Tataryn, Christopher Bradley, Hector Mercado, Geoffrey Moody; *Cameos:* Mink Stole; *D:* David DeCoteau; *W:* Rondo Mieczkowski; *C:* Howard Wexler; *M:* Jeremy Jordan.

Leather Jackets ✓✓ **1990 (R)** Sweeney plays a nice guy who lets involvement with a childhood pal destroy his life. Elwes is the friend, now gang member, in trouble with both the cops and members of a rival gang, who needs Sweeney's help to escape. Fonda plays Sweeney's girlfriend caught between the two men. Essentially a routine fugitive pic with an attractive cast. **90m/C VHS.** D.B. Sweeney, Bridget Fonda, Cary Elwes, Christopher Penn, Marshall Bell, James LeGros, Jon Polito, Craig Ng, Ginger Lynn Allen; *D:* Lee Drysdale; *W:* Lee Drysdale.

Leatherface: The Texas Chainsaw Massacre 3 ✓ *Texas Chainsaw Massacre 3: Leatherface* **1989 (R)** The human-skin-wearing cannibal is at it again in this, the second sequel to the Tobe Hooper original and it's worth seeing for that more humor and it's worth seeing for that reason. **81m/C VHS, DVD.** Kate Hodge, William Butler, Ken Foree, Tom Hudson, R.A. Mihailoff, Miriam Byrd-Nethery, Tom Everett, Joe Unger, Viggo Mortensen, David Cloud, Beth de Patie; *D:* Jeff Burr; *W:* David J. Schow; *C:* James L. Carter; *M:* Jim Manzie.

Leatherheads ✓✓½ **2008 (PG-13)** The 1925 Duluth Bulldogs, led by star player and all-around charmer Dodge Connelly (Clooney), are an upstart professional football team during a time when the pros lack the polish and respect of the college game. In a top-notch marketing move, Connelly adds well-known war hero Carter "The Bullet" Rutherford (Krasinski) to the roster in an effort to turn the tide of popular opinion. Unfortunately for the Bulldogs, Rutherford's war-hero credentials may have a few holes in them, which draw the attention of cute and sassy newspaper reporter Lexie Littleton (Zellweger). A kooky romantic triangle ensues as Connelly, the reporter and "The Bullet" ride the train between games and speakeasies through the season. Handsome threesome never quite pulls us in and the script's a clunker, but the chuckles are good and the period details are spot on. **113m/C DVD.** *US* George Clooney, Renee Zellweger, John Krasinski, Jonathan Pryce, Peter Gerety, Jack Thompson, Stephen (Steve) Root, Wayne Duvall, Keith Loneker; *W:* Duncan Brantley, Rick Reilly; *C:* Newton Thomas (Tom) Sigel; *M:* Randy Newman.

The Leatherneck ✓✓ **1928** Love unrequited in a faraway place starring soon to be cowboy (Hopalong Cassidy) matinee idol Boyd and Hale, the real life dad of Gilligan Island's skipper. **65m/B VHS**

Leave 'Em Laughing ✗ 1981 Rooney plays Chicago clown Jack Thum in this based-on-real-life TV movie. Thum takes in orphans even though he cannot find steady work, and then discovers he has cancer. Clichés, but excellent as the pathologically possessive creature. Oscar-winning usual roles, is excellent as the pathologically possessive creature. Oscar-winner Leon Shamroy's photography (in Technicolor) is breathtaking. 103mC VHS. **D:** Jackie Cooper. **C:** John Mescall. **W:** Elliot J. Clawson. **C:** John Mescall. William Boyd, Diane Ellis; **D:** Howard Higgin. **W:** Elliot J. Clawson. **C:** John Mescall.

Leave Her to Heaven ✗✗✗ 1945 Beautiful neurotic Tierney takes drastic measures to keep hubby all to herself and will do anything to get what she wants. Tierney, in a departure from her usual roles, is excellent as the pathologically possessive creature. Oscar-winner Leon Shamroy's photography (in Technicolor) is breathtaking. 110mC VHS, DVD. Gene Tierney, Cornel Wilde, Jeanne Crain, Vincent Price, Mary Phillips, Ray Collins, Darryl Hickman, Gene Lockhart; **D:** John M. Stahl; **W:** Jo Swerling; **C:** Leon Shamroy; **M:** Alfred Newman. Oscars '45: Color Cinematog.

Leave It to Beaver ✗✗ 1997 Gee, Mrs. Cleaver, that's an awful nice updating of an old TV favorite, you have there. Cut the crap, Eddie. The "let's plop a lovable sitcom family into the dysfunctional 90s" bit has had its run. This time the victims are the Cleavers: wise dad Ward (McDonald), perfect mom June (Turner), popular older brother Wally (von Detten), and newcomer Cameron Finley as the Beaver. Unlike the Bradys, the modern world has made some impact here. Beav has an African American friend while Mom wears jeans and owns a business. Gosh Wally, do you really think America was anxiously awaiting the return of the impossible-to-live-up-to clan? Don't be such a little dope. 88mC VHS, DVD. Christopher McDonald, Janine Turner, Erik von Detten, Cameron Finley, Barbara Billingsley, Ken Osmond, Adam Zolotin, Alan Rachins; **D:** Andy Cadiff; **W:** Brian Levant; **C:** Thomas Del Ruth; **M:** Randy Edelman.

Leave It to the Marines ✗½ 1951 A jerky guy wanders into a recruiting office instead of a marriage license bureau and unwittingly signs on for military service. 66m/B VHS, Sid Melton, Mara Lynn, Gregg Martell, Lia Moore, Sam Flint, Douglas Evans, Margia Dean; **D:** Sam Newfield; **W:** Orville H. Hampton.

Leaves from Satan's Book ✗✗½ 1919 Impressionistic episodes of Satan's fiddling with man through the ages, from Christ to the Russian Revolution. An early cinematic film by Dreyer, with ample indications of his later brilliance. Silent. 165m/B VHS, DVD. JK Helge Nilsen, Hallor Hoff, Jacob Texiere; **D:** Carl Theodor Dreyer.

Leaving Las Vegas ✗✗✗½ 1995 (R) Ben Sanderson (Cage) is a hopeless alcoholic who goes to Vegas to drink himself to death, which is where he meets Sera (Shue), a lonely hooker who loves him enough not to stop him. Definitely as depressing as it sounds, but still manages to have both a subtle sense of humor and compassion. Cage tops his best work and Shue proves she deserves better than the lightweight roles she's had in the past. Not for everyone, but worth the effort for people who like to see honest emotion and rate Hollywood's insistence on happy endings. Based on the semi-autobiographical novel by John O'Brien, who committed suicide shortly before pre-production on the film began. 120mC VHS, DVD. N:Olas Cage, Elisabeth Shue, Julian Sands, Laurie Metcalf, David Brisbin, Richard Lewis, Valeria Golino, Steven Weber, Mariska Hargitay, Julian Lennon, Carey Lowell, Lucinda Jenney, Ed Lauter, R. Lee Ermey; **D:** Mike Figgis; **W:** Mike Figgis; **C:** Declan Quinn; **M:** Mike Figgis. Oscars '95: Actor (Cage); Golden Globes '96: Actor—Drama (Cage); Ind. Spir '96: Actress (Shue), Cinematog., Director (Figgis). Film: L.A. Film Critic's '95: Actor (Cage), Actress (Shue), Director (Figgis). Film: Natl. Bd. of Review '95: Actor (Cage); N.Y. Film Critics '95: Actor (Cage), Film; Natl. Soc. Film Critics '95; Actor (Cage), Actress (Shue), Director (Figgis); Screen Actors Guild '95: Actor (Cage), Actress (Shue).

Leaving Metropolis ✗✗ 2002 Successful Winnipeg artist David (Raptash) is creatively blocked so he decides to get some inspiration by rejoining the real world as a waiter for married diner owners Violet (Taylor) and Matt (Corrazza). David's keeping his past quiet, but (Fraser) is the daughter of Holocaust survivors (Sagebrecht and Schell), but has never sought to understand their ordeal or her religion. But that doesn't prevent her from taking a job as a nanny to a strict Hasidic family, the Kalmans. Carefree Chaja even manages to coax her mute four-year-old charge into speaking. She learns some lessons, the families learn some lessons, there's the prerequisite tragedy), and it's all so much unfortunate overkill. 100mC VHS, DVD. Laura Fraser, Isabella Rossellini, Jeroen Krabbé, Maximilian Schell, Marianne Saegebrecht, Chaim Topol; **D:** Jeroen Krabbé; **W:** Edwin de Vries; **C:** Walther Vanden Ende; **M:** Henny Vrienten.

Leaving Normal ✗½ 1992 (R) Darly, a fed-up waitress, and Marianne, an abused housewife, meet at a bus stop in Normal, Wyoming and decide to blow town. They travel across the American West, where Lahti's ex-boyfriend has left her a house. Because both women have made bad choices all their lives, they decide to leave their futures to chance, and end up finding their nirvana. Plot is similar to "Thelma & Louise," but "Leaving Normal" doesn't come close to the innovativeness of the former. Snappy and sentimental to the point of annoyance at times. 110mC VHS, Christine Lahti, Meg Tilly, Lenny Von Dohlen, Maury Chaykin, James Eakhouse, Patrika Darbo, Eve Gordon, James Eckhouse, Brett Cullen, Rutanya Alda; **D:** Edward Zwick; **W:** Edward Solomon; **C:** Ralf Bode.

The Leech Woman ✗✗ 1959 While in Africa, an older woman (Gray) discovers how to restore her youth through a tribal ritual. The only problem is it requires the pineal gland of males, which causes her to go on a killing spree to keep that youthful look. Based on a story by Ben Pivar and Francis Rosenwald. 77m/B VHS. Coleen Gray, Grant Williams, Gloria Talbot, Phillip Terry; **D:** Edward Dein; **W:** David Duncan.

Left Behind: The Movie ✗ 2000 Ace TV newsman Buck Williams (Cameron) is on hand for a sneak attack on Israel. Right after it, devout Christians and innocent children mysteriously vanish. The film is a dramatization of the novels based on a conservative Christian interpretation of the Book of Revelation. As entertainment, it's heavy handed at every level—plotting, acting, writing, directing. 95mC VHS, DVD. Kirk Cameron, Brad Johnson, Chelsea Noble, Clarence Gilyard Jr., Colin Fox, Gordon Currie, Daniel Pilon, Jack Langediik; **D:** Vic Sarin; **W:** Alan B. McElroy, Joe Goodman; **C:** Jiri (George) Tirl.

Left for Dead ✗½ 1978 A millionaire is accused of brutally killing his wife, and discovers in his search for an alibi that he is the victim of a conspiracy. 82mC VHS. Elke Sommer, Donald Pilon; **D:** Murray Markowitz.

The Left Hand of God ✗✗ 1955 After an American pilot escapes into a Chinese warlord in post-WWII, he disguises himself as a Catholic priest and takes refuge in a missionary hospital. Bogie is great as the flyboy/cleric. 87mC VHS. Humphrey Bogart, Gene Tierney, E.G. Marshall, Agnes Moorehead, Gene Tierney; **D:** Edward Dmytryk.

The Left-Handed Gun ✗✗✗ 1958 An offbeat version of the exploits of Billy the Kid, which portrays film as a 19th-century Wild West juvenile delinquent. Newman's role, which he method-acted, was originally intended for James Dean. Based on a 1955 Philco teleplay by Gore Vidal. 102m/B VHS, DVD. Paul Newman, Lita Milan, John Dehner; **D:** Arthur Penn.

Left in Darkness ✗✗ 2006 Well-done creepfest. Celia (Keena) goes to a frat party on her 21st birthday and dies after being given a date rape drug. She winds up in an otherworld, battling soul eaters, while her guard/an/guide Donovan (Anders) tries to help Celia complete her journey to heaven. 88mC DVD.

Left Luggage ✗½ 1998 Sticky family saga set in Antwerp, Belgium in 1972. Nonreligious college student Chaja (Fraser) is the daughter of Holocaust survivors (Sagebrecht and Schell), but has never sought to understand their ordeal or her religion. But that doesn't prevent her from taking a job as a nanny to a strict Hasidic family, the Kalmans. Carefree Chaja even manages to coax her mute four-year-old charge into speaking. She learns some lessons, the families learn some lessons, there's the prerequisite tragedy), and it's all so much unfortunate overkill. 100mC VHS, DVD. Laura Fraser, Isabella Rossellini, Jeroen Krabbé, Maximilian Schell, Marianne Saegebrecht, Chaim Topol; **D:** Jeroen Krabbé. **VIDEO**

Legacy of Horror Woof! 1978 (R) An American couple brought to video. 90mC Loyita Chapel, Michael Anderson Jr.; **D:** Jim Drake.

A Legacy for Leonette woof! 1985 A girl is led into a web of murder and gie Wash 1979 (R) An American couple become privy to the dark secrets of an English family gathering in a creepy mansion to inherit an eccentric millionaire's fortune. Death and demons abound. 100mC VHS, DVD. Gß Katharine Ross, Sam Elliot, John Standing, Roger Daltrey, Ian Hogg; **D:** Richard Marquand; **C:** Dick Bush.

The Legacy ✗✗ The Legacy of Maggie Wash 1979 (R) An American couple become privy to the dark secrets of an English family gathering in a creepy mansion to inherit an eccentric millionaire's fortune. Death and demons abound. 100mC VHS, DVD. Gß Katharine Ross, Sam Elliot, John Standing, Roger Daltrey, Ian Hogg; **D:** Richard Marquand; **C:** Dick Bush. **CABLE**

Legacy of Lies ✗✗½ 1992 (R) Zack Resnick is a serious, honest Chicago cop assigned to a murder investigation. He first discovers the killers got the wrong man and then finds out a lot of family secrets he wishes he didn't know. His copfather is on the take to the Mob, which is really no surprise since Zack's grandfather turns out to be a retired gangland boss, all of which leaves Zack wondering where his loyalties lie. Too intricate plot hampers the cast performances are well worth watching. 94mC VHS. Michael Ontkean, Martin Landau, Joe Morton, Patricia Clarkson, Gerry Becker, Chelcie Ross, Ron Dean; **D:** Jason Meshover-Iorg; **W:** David Black. **CABLE**

Legacy of Rage ✗✗ 1986 Brandon (Lee), a waiter, befriends young mobster Michael (Wong), who turns out to be in love with Brandon's fiancee, May (Kent). In fact, Michael frames Brandon on a murder charge and gets him thrown in prison in order to get the girl. And what's Brandon's first thought when he gets out of the slammer? Revenge. Lee's first feature film, Chinese with subtitles or dubbed. 86mC VHS, DVD. HK Brandon Lee, Michael Wong, Bolo Yeung, Regina Kent; **D:** Ronny Yu.

Legal Deceit ✗✗½ 1986 (PG) An assistant D.A. faces murder, mayhem, and romance while prosecuting a girl accused of stealing a portrait painted by her father. Redford sparkles in this convoluted tale from Reitman, while Hannah lacks depth as the daffy thief. 116mC VHS, DVD. Robert Redford, Debra Winger, Daryl Hannah, Brian Dennehy, Terence Stamp, Steven Hill, David Clennon, Roscoe Lee Browne, John McMartin, Jennifer (Jennie) Dundas Lowe, Ivan Reitman; **D:** Ivan Reitman; **W:** Jack Epps Jr., Jim Cash; **C:** Laszlo Kovacs; **M:** Elmer Bernstein.

Legal Eagles ✗✗½ 1986 (PG) An assistant D.A. faces murder, mayhem, and romance while prosecuting a girl accused of stealing a portrait painted by her father. Redford sparkles in this convoluted tale from Reitman, while Hannah lacks depth as the daffy thief. 116mC VHS, DVD. Robert Redford, Debra Winger, Daryl Hannah, Brian Dennehy, Terence Stamp, Steven Hill, David Clennon, Roscoe Lee Browne, John Stockwell, Jeffrey Dean Morgan, Phil Morris, John Stockwell, Cheryl Francis Harrington, Jeff Marcus; **M:** Michael Giacchino.

Legal Tender ✗✗ 1990 (R) Rude talk-show host Cowney as a corrupt S & L chief? Big menacing Davi as a romantic hero? Give this often-inept thriller credit for creative casting, if little else. Roberts adds steamy sex appeal as a lovely saloon-keeper imperiled by deadly bank fraud. 93mC VHS. Robert Davi, Tanya Roberts, Morton Downey Jr.; **D:** Jag Mundhra.

Legalese ✗✗½ 1998 (R) Solid cast provides solid enjoyment in this skewering of tabloid journalists and the legal system. Celeb lawyer Norman Keane (Garner) doesn't take the case of actress Angela Beale (Gershon) who's accused of killing her brother-in-law. But he does recommend new kid attorney, Roy Guyton (Kerr), to take the heat while Keane works behind the scenes. This raises the antennae of of tabloid TV anchorwoman Brenda Whitlass (Turner) who winds up with a video of Guyton getting up close and personal with fellow lawyer Rica Martin (Parker). Needless to say, ethics have very little to do with anything. 105mC VHS. James Garner, Gina Gershon, Kathleen Turner, Mary-Louise Parker, Edward Kerr, James Garner; **D:** Glenn Jordan; **W:** Tobias Schliessler; **M:** Stewart Copeland. **CABLE**

Legally Blonde ✗✗½ 2001 (PG-13) Beverly Hills blonde Elle Woods (Witherspoon) is a sorority babe who dresses in pink and has her Chihuahua, Bruiser as a constant companion. After getting dumped by frat boyfriend Warner (Davis), who's on his way to Harvard Law School, Elle wallows in chocolate-fueled misery. But determined to show him that's she more than the sum of her pretty parts, Elle also gets accepted and shows all those pasty-faced easterners, including Warner's new fiancee, brunette Vivian (Blair), that she has brains as well as big murder case. Witherspoon is a delight in a very lightweight comedy. 95mC VHS, DVD. US Reese Witherspoon, Matthew Davis, Selma Blair, Luke Wilson, Ali Larter, Holland Taylor, Victor Garber, Jessica Cauffiel, Jennifer Coolidge, Oz (Osgood) Perkins II, Alanna Ubach, Raquel Welch, Linda Cardellini, Meredith Scott Lynn; **D:** Robert Luketic; **W:** Karen McCullah Lutz, Kirsten Smith; **C:** Anthony B. Richmond; **M:** Rolfe Kent.

Legally Blonde 2: Red, White & Blonde ✗✗ 2003 (PG-13) In the sequel to the 2001 surprise hit, Boston lawyer Elle Woods (Witherspoon) heads to D.C. and becomes the aide to congresswoman Rudd (Field) and joins up the cause of animal rights. Witherspoon's zest and charm are the only things to recommend about this mostly unfunny clichefest that traps some real talent in ridiculously cardboard roles. Other than Witherspoon, the only bright spots are Coolidge as Elle's manicurist friend, and the dog whose family provides the main plot push. 95mC VHS, DVD. US Reese Witherspoon, Sally Field, Bob Newhart, Luke Wilson, Jennifer Coolidge, Regina King, Bruce McGill, Dana Ivey, Mary Lynn Rajskub, Jessica Cauffiel, Alanna Ubach, J Barton; **D:** Charles Herman-Wurmfeld; **W:** Kate Kondell; **C:** Elliot Davis; **M:** Rolfe Kent.

Legend ✗✗ 1986 (PG) A colorful, unabashedly Tolkien-esque fantasy about the struggle to save an innocent waif from the Prince of Darkness. Set in a land packed with unicorns, magic swamps, bumbling dwarves and rainbows. Produced in Great Britain. 89mC VHS, DVD. GB Tom Cruise, Mia Sara, Tim Curry, David Bennent, Billy Barty, Alice Playten; **D:** Ridley Scott; **M:** Jerry Goldsmith.

Legend of Alfred Packer ✗✗½ 1980 The true story of how a guide taking five men searching for gold in Colorado managed to be the sole survivor of a blizzard. 87mC VHS. Patrick Dray, Ron Haines, Bo Damon, Dave Ellingson; **D:** Jim Roberson.

The Legend of Bagger Vance ✗✗½ 2000 (PG-13) Director Redford misses the cut by presenting got as a mystical experience instead of a bunch of guys in funny pants tortuting a lawn. Rannulph Junuh (Damon) returns

Legend

from WWI a vastly changed man. The former golf golden boy seems content to squander the rest of his life drinking at the 19th hole. His former girlfriend Adele (Theron), facing a pile of debts, convinces him to participate in an exhibition against golf giants Bobby Jones (Gretsch) and Walter Hagen (McGill) to showcase her new course. As he's shanking practice shots in every direction, the mysterious Bagger (Smith) appears, offering him guidance about golf and life in Eastern philosophy sound bites. Junuh finds his "Authentic Swing" with the help of Bagger, but it may be too late to catch his competition. Beautiful scenery, but the pace is a little too slow (just like golf). Fits in well with the flawed American hero theme that has run through Redford's work since his turn as Jay Gatsby. Based on the novel by Steven Pressfield. Once upon a time director Redford wanted to star himself before deciding he was too mature for the part. **127m/C VHS, DVD.** Matt Damon, Will Smith, Charlize Theron, Jack Lemmon, Bruce McGill, Lane Smith, Harve Presnell, Peter Gerety, Michael O'Neill, Thomas Jay Ryan, Joel Gretsch, J. Michael Moncrief; **D:** Robert Redford; **W:** Jeremy Leven; **C:** Michael Ballhaus; **M:** Rachel Portman.

Legend of Billie Jean
1985 (PG-13) Billie Jean believed in justice for all. When the law and its bureaucracy landed hard on her, she took her cause to the masses and inspired a generation. **92m/C VHS.** Helen Slater, Peter Coyote, Keith Gordon, Christian Slater, Richard Bradford, Yeardley Smith, Dean Stockwell; **D:** Matthew Robbins; **W:** Mark Rosenthal.

The Legend of Black Thunder Mountain
1979 (G). A children's adventure in the mold of "Grizzly Adams" and "The Wilderness Family." **90m/C VHS, DVD.** Holly Beeman, Steve Beeman, Ron Brown, F.A. Milovich; **D:** Tom Beeman.

The Legend of Blood Castle
The Female Butcher; Blood Ceremory; Ceremonia Sangrienta 1972 (R) Another version of the Countess of Bathory legend, in which an evil woman bathes in the blood of virgins in an attempt to keep the wrinkles away. Released hot on the heels of Hammer's "Countess Dracula." **87m/C VHS. IT SP** Lucia Bose, Ewa Aulin; **D:** Jorge Grau.

Legend of Boggy Creek
1975 (G) A dramatized version of various Arkansas Bigfoot sightings. **87m/C VHS, DVD.** Willie E. Smith, John P. Nixon, John W. Gates, Jeff Crabtree, Buddy Crabtree; **D:** Charles B. Pierce; **W:** Earl E. Smith; **C:** Charles B. Pierce; **Nar:** Vern Stierman. TV

The Legend of Butch & Sundance
2004 (PG-13) This unsold NBC TV pilot is a generally lively western that finds Butch Parker (Rogers) going from easy-going cowboy to bank robber alongside his best friend, gunslinger Harry "Sundance Kid" Longabaugh (Browning). Both become part of Mike Cassidy's (Biehn) "Wild Bunch" gang, targeting banks that are controlled by greedy railroad barons. The two men are also equally attached to schoolteacher Etta Place (Lefevre). When Pinkerton Charlie Durango (Gibbons) kills Cassidy, Butch takes his last name out of respect and vows vengeance. **120m/C DVD.** Ryan Browning, Rachel Lefevre, Michael Biehn, Susan Ruttan, David Clayton Rogers, Blake Gibbons; **D:** Sergio Mimica-Gezzan; **W:** John Fasano; **C:** Igor Meglic; **M:** Basil Poledouris. TV

The Legend of Cryin' Ryan
1998 (PG) After leveling the tombstone of a long-dead school bully, teenager Kris freaks out when his ghost is set loose. But when the boy, who died at age 13 of unknown causes, tells her about his abusive father she's bent on setting the record straight so that his soul can move along. **90m/C VHS, DVD.** Harrison Myers, Rhelda Mortensen, Rob Lunn, Christian LeBrun, Charlie Foster Fulkerson, Anne Marie Fulkerson; **D:** Julie St. Claire; **C:** Mark Foggetti; **M:** Sean Murray. VIDEO

The Legend of Drunken Master
Drunken Master 2; Jui Kun 2 1994 (R) Jackie Chan shows the moves that made him the Charlie Chaplin of chopsocky in this sequel to the original "Drunken Master," the movie that made him a star in Hong Kong. Chan plays legendary Chinese folk hero Wong Fei-hong as a rowdy young man (although Chan was nearly 40 when it was filmed) whose martial arts moves get better as he gets drunker. While traveling by train with his father Wong Kei-ying (Lung), he mistakenly takes a package that contains a priceless imperial Chinese artifact that is in the process of being smuggled out of the country by a corrupt British official. Evil henchmen are then sent to be pummeled by Fei-hong's inebriated fists. Director Lau Kar-leung performs double duty by playing Fu Min-chi, a grizzled old man also on the trail of the stolen artifact. If you're a fan of the kung-fu genre, the finale between Chan and Low Houi-kang (also known as Ken Lo, Chan's bodyguard) is not to be missed. Re-released in America six years after its original Asian release complete with classic "bad Chinese accent" dubbing. **102m/C VHS, DVD. HK** Jackie Chan, Lau Kar Leung, Anita (Yim-Fong) Mui, Ti Lung, Andy Lau; **D:** Lau Kar Leung; **W:** Edward Tang; **C:** Yiutsou Cheung, Tong-Leung Cheung, Jingle Ma, Man-Wan Wong; **M:** Michael Wandmacher.

Legend of Earl Durand
1974 In Wyoming 1939, a man spends his life searching for freedom and justice. His Robin Hood actions cause a manhunt of massive proportions. **90m/C VHS.** Martin Sheen, Peter Haskell, Keenan Wynn, Slim Pickens, Anthony Caruso; **D:** John D. Patterson.

The Legend of Frank Woods
1977 Gunslinger returns to the land of the free after an extended holiday south of the border. Mistaken for an expected preacher in a small town, he poses as the padre and signs on the dotted line to take out a new lease on life. **88m/C VHS, DVD.** Troy Donahue, Brad Steward, Kitty Vallacher, Michael Christian; **D:** Deno Paoli.

Legend of Frenchie King
Petroleum Girls 1971 When prospectors discover oil on disputed land, two families feud over their conflicting claims to the property. Adult western still working out the kinks has Bardot heading a band of female outlaws. **96m/C VHS.** Brigitte Bardot, Claudia Cardinale, Michael J. Pollard, Micheline Presle; **D:** Christian-Jaque.

The Legend of Gator Face
1996 (PG) Hermit Winfield fills three youngsters in on their small community's legend of Gator Face—halfman, half-alligator. Kids being kids, they decide to wade through the swamps in search of the creature, which they find and also realize is harmless. Too bad the local folk don't believe the same thing and call out the national guard to destroy it. **100m/C VHS, DVD.** Paul Winfield, John White, Dan Warryvett; **D:** Vic Sarin.

The Legend of Hell House
1973 (PG) A multi-millionaire hires a team of scientists and mediums to investigate his newly acquired haunted mansion. It seems that the creepy house has been the site of a number of deaths and may hold clues to the afterlife. A suspenseful, scary screamfest. Matheson wrote the screenplay from his novel "Hell House." **94m/C VHS, DVD.** Roddy McDowall, Pamela Franklin, Clive Revill, Gayle Hunnicutt, Peter Bowles, Roland Culver, Michael Gough; **D:** John Hough; **W:** Richard Matheson; **C:** Alan Hume; **M:** Brian Hodgson, Delia Derbyshire.

The Legend of Hillbilly John
Who Fears the Devil; My Name is John 1973 (G). Hillbilly John holds off the devil with a strum of his six-string. While demons plague the residents of rural America, the hayseed messiah wanders about, saving the day. **86m/C VHS.** Severn Darden, Denver Pyle, Susan Strasberg, Hedge Capers; **D:** John Newland.

The Legend of Jedediah Carver
1976 A rancher battles desert elements and hostile Indians in a desperate bid for survival. **90m/C VHS.** DeWitt Lee, Joshua Hoffman, Val Chapman, Richard Montgomery, David Terril; **D:** DeWitt Lee.

The Legend of Johnny Lingo
2003 (G) Orphaned as an infant, Tama winds up on a remote South Pacific island where he is initially revered as a god but ultimately is cast aside. He befriends Mahana, and when he decides to sail away in search of a better life he assures her that he'll come back for her. Washing up on another island, he meets a well-to-do trader, Johnny Lingo, who becomes his life mentor and aides him in fulfilling his promise. Drawing from Patricia McGerr's "Johnny Lingo's Eight-Cow Wife" and the 1969 film short "Johnny Lingo" by Wezel O. Whitaker, rookie director Ramirez holds to the tale's feel-good essence but drifts astray in the execution. **95m/C VHS, DVD.** George Henare, Joe Folau, Rawiri Paratene, Kayte Ferguson; **D:** Steve Ramirez; **M:** Kevin Kiner. VIDEO

Legend of Lobo
1962 The story of Lobo, a crafty wolf who seeks to free his mate from the clutches of greedy hunters. A Disney wildlife adventure. **67m/C VHS, DVD. D:** James Nelson Algar; **W:** James Nelson Algar; **Nar:** Rex Allen.

The Legend of Lucy Keyes
2006 (R) The Cooley family moves into the old Keyes house in Massachusetts, which is reputed to be haunted. In 1755, young Lucy Keyes disappeared while in the nearby woods and her mother Martha went mad searching for her daughter. Now, mom Jeanne (Delpy) begins to have nightmares and fears for her own daughter Lucy (Hinkle), especially when ghostly visions seem to want Jeanne to solve the mystery and let Lucy Keyes finally rest. **93m/C VHS, DVD.** Julie Delpy, Justin Theroux, Brooke Adams, Mark Boone Jr., Cassidy Hinkle, Anna Friedman; **D:** John Stimpson; **W:** John Stimpson; **C:** Gary Henoch; **M:** Ed Grenga.

The Legend of 1900
The Legend of the Pianist on the Ocean; La Leggenda del Pianista Sull'Oceano 1998 (R) Originally released under a different title and at 170 minutes, this re-cut English-language debut feature for Italian director Tornatore still has its problems. An abandoned infant is discovered aboard the luxury liner Virginian in 1900 and reared by the engine crew. As an adult, the nicknamed 1900 (Roth), has become a virtuoso pianist in the ship's orchestra and has superstitiously never set foot off the boat. His best friend is trumpet player Max (Vince), who tells the story in flashback after learning the ship has been condemned. But since 1900 remains an enigma, you won't really care what happens to him. **116m/C VHS, DVD.** Tim Roth, Pruitt Taylor Vince, Clarence Williams III, Bill Nunn, Melanie Thierry; **D:** Giuseppe Tornatore; **W:** Giuseppe Tornatore; **C:** Lajos Koltai; **M:** Ennio Morricone. Golden Globes '00: Score.

The Legend of Paul and Paula
Die Legende von Paul und Paula 1973 East German censors tried to ban Carow's film, which focuses on personal freedoms, but it proved to be so popular with audiences that the ban never worked. Paula (Domrose) is a free-spirited unmarried saleclerk with two children while Paul (Glatzeder) is a conservative bureaucrat in a loveless marriage. They met by accident and fall in love while Paula tries to liberate Paul from his dull existence. But Paul finds it difficult to let go—until tragedy beset them. German with subtitles. **106m/C VHS, DVD. GE** Angelica Domröse, Winifred Glatzeder; **D:** Heiner Carow; **W:** Heiner Carow, Ulrich Plenzdorf; **C:** Jürgen Brauer; **M:** Peter Gotthardt.

The Legend of Rita
Die Stille Nach dem Schuss; The Silence After the Shot 1999 Rita (Beglau) is part of a West German left-wing terrorist group in the 1970s. She's caught attempting to enter East Germany by Stasi officer Erwin Hull (Wuttke), who lets her go but slyly offers to come to her aid when needed. After some trouble, Rita agrees to Hull's offer to assume a new identity and live a worker's life in East Germany. Then Rita discovers that her political ideals are at odds with the ordinary, everyday life and people disenchanted by socialism. But she faces a greater change when the Berlin Wall comes down and Rita's terrorist past is exposed. German with subtitles. **101m/C VHS, DVD. GE** Bibiana Beglau, Martin Wuttke, Nadja Uhl, Harald Schrott, Alexander Beyer, Jenny Schily; **D:** Volker Schlondorff; **W:** Volker Schlondorff, Wolfgang Kohlhaase; **C:** Andreas Hofer.

The Legend of Sea Wolf
Wolf Larsen 1975 (PG) A sadistic sea captain forcefully rules his crew in this weak version of Jack London's novel. **90m/C VHS, DVD. IT** Chuck Connors, Barbara Bach, Joseph Palmer; **D:** Giuseppe Vari; **W:** Marcello Ciorciolini; **C:** Sergio Rubini; **M:** Guido de Angelis, Maurizio de Angelis.

The Legend of Sleepy Hollow
1949 The story of Ichabod Crane and the legendary ride of the headless horseman by Washington Irving; narrated by Crosby. Also includes two classic short cartoons, "Lonesome Ghosts" (1932) with Mickey Mouse and "Trick or Treat" (1952) with Donald Duck. **45m/C VHS. D:** Jack Kinney, Clyde Geronimi, James Nelson Algar; **Nar:** Bing Crosby.

The Legend of Sleepy Hollow
1979 (G) Washington Irving's classic tale of the Headless Horseman of Sleepy Hollow is brought to life on the screen. **100m/C VHS.** Jeff Goldblum, Dick Butkus, Paul Sand, Meg Foster, James J. Griffith, John S. White; **D:** Henning Schellerup; **W:** Malvin Wald. TV

The Legend of Sleepy Hollow
1986 Classic Washington Irving tale is given the Shelly Duvall treatment in her "Tall Tales and Legends" series. When a snooty teacher goes too far, the town blacksmith decides to play the ultimate Halloween trick on him. **51m/C VHS.** Ed Begley Jr., Beverly D'Angelo, Charles Durning, Tim Thomerson. CABLE

The Legend of Suram Fortress
Legenda Suramskoi Kreposti 1985 Based on a Georgian folktale about a medieval fortress that collapses as soon as it is built. The village soothsayer tells a young man he must sacrifice himself by bricking himself up alive within the fortress walls, if the building is every to stand. In Russian with English subtitles. **89m/C VHS, DVD. RU** Levani Outchanechvili, Zourab Kipchidze; **D:** Sergei Paradjanov; **W:** Vaja Gigashivili; **C:** Yuri Klimenko.

Legend of the Lone Ranger
1981 (PG) The fabled Lone Ranger (whose voice is dubbed throughout the entire movie) and the story of his first meeting with his Indian companion, Tonto, are brought to life in this weak and vapid version of the famous legend. The narration by Merle Haggard leaves something to be desired as do most of the performances. **98m/C VHS.** Klinton Spilsbury, Michael Horse, Jason Robards Jr., Richard Farnsworth, Christopher Lloyd, Matt Clark; **D:** William A. Fraker; **W:** William Roberts, Ivan Goff. Golden Raspberries '81: Worst Actor (Spilsbury), Worst New Star (Spilsbury).

Legend of the Lost
1957 Two men vie for desert treasure and desert women. Interesting only because of Wayne, but certainly not one of his more memorable films. **109m/C VHS, DVD.** John Wayne, Sophia Loren, Rossano Brazzi, Kurt Kasznar, Sonia Moser; **D:** Henry Hathaway; **C:** Jack Cardiff.

Legend of the Lost Tomb
1997 (PG) Adventure finds Egyptologist Dr. Leonhardt (Rossovich) discovering half of an ancient papyrus that could lead to the riches of the desert tomb of pharaoh Ramses II. But Leonhardt is ambushed by his rival Dr. Bent (Keach), who demands the rest of the document, which just happens to be in the hands of Leonhardt's son (Pierce) and his archaeologist associate Karen (Peterson). **90m/C VHS.** Rick Rossovich, Stacy Keach, Kimberlee Peterson, Brook Pierce; **D:** Jonathan Winfrey. CABLE

The Legend of the Sea Wolf
Wolf Larsen; Larsen, Wolf of the Seven Seas 1958 Adaptation of Jack London's dramatic adventure novel, "The Sea Wolf." A slave driving ship captain rescues a shipwreck victim and sets to abus-

The Legend of the 7 Golden Vampires *The Seven Brothers Meet Dracula, Dracula and the Seven Golden Vampires* 1973 It's kung-fu meets horror as Van Helsing pursues Dracula to 19th-century China and is assisted by martial artists. One of the last Hammer coproductions. The Anchor Bay release also contains the 75-minute "Seven Brothers Meet Dracula," which was the U.S. version of the movie. 89m/C VHS, DVD, GB Peter Cushing, David Chiang, Robin Stewart, Julie Ege, John Forbes-Robertson; D: Roy Ward Baker; W: Don Houghton; C: Roy Ford, John Wilcox; M: Renee Houston.

The Legend of the Werewolf *Legend of the Werewolf, Werewolf Woman, She-Wolf* 1977 (R) The beautiful Daniella assumes the personality of the legendary wolfwoman, leaving a trail of gruesome killings across the countryside. Genre fans will find the country entertaining. Also on video as "Werewolf Woman." 84m/C VHS, DVD, IT Annik Borel, Frederick Stafford, Tino Carey, Elliot Zamuto, Olle Reynolds, Andrea Scotti, Karen Carter, Howard (Red) Ross; D: Rino Di Silvestro; W: Rino Di Silvestro, Howard (Red) Ross.

The Legend of the Wolf Woman *Daughter of the Werewolf* 1975 (R) A child who once ran with the wolves has forgotten his past, except when the moon is full. 90m/C VHS, GB Peter Cushing, Hugh Griffith, Ron Moody, David Rimoul, Lynn Dalby, Stefan Gryff, Renee Houston, Norman Mitchell, Marjorie Yates, Roy Castle; D: Freddie Francis; W: Renee Houston.

Legend of Tom Dooley 1959 Somber western about three Confederate soldiers who rob a Union stagecoach and kill two soldiers, not knowing that the Civil War has ended. Landon turns in a good performance as the Rebel soldier turned outlaw. Based on the hit song by the Kingston trio. 79m/B VHS, DVD, Michael Landon, Jo Morrow, Jack Hogan, Richard Rust, Dee Pollock, Ken Lynch; D: Ted Post; M: Ronald Stein.

Legend of Valentino 1975 Docudrama traces the legendary exploits of one of the silver screen's greatest lovers, Rudolph Valentino. Typical TV-movie fare that lacks the substance and excitement of the real star's life. 96m/C VHS, DVD, Franco Nero, Suzanne Pleshette, Lesley Ann Warren, Yvette Mimieux, Judd Hirsch, Milton Berle, Harold J. Stone; D: Melville Shavelson. TV

Legend of Walks Far Woman 1982 A proud Sioux woman fights for survival and her tribe during the American-Indian Wars. Welch is miscast. From Colin Stuart's novel. 120m/C VHS, Raquel Welch, Nick Mancuso, Bradford Dillman; D: Mel Damski. TV

The Legend of Wolf Mountain 1992 (PG) Three children are held hostage by two prison escapees in the Utah mountains. They are aided in their escape by a Native American "wolf spirit." With the criminals on their trail will the three be able to survive in the wilderness until a search party can find them? 91m/C VHS, Mickey Rooney, Bo Hopkins, Don Shanks, Vivian Schilling, Robert Z'Dar, David "Shark" Fralick, Nicole Lund, Natalie Lund, Matthew Lewis, Jonathan Best; D: Craig Clyde; W: Craig Clyde.

The Legend of Zorro 2005 (PG) Noisy sequel to "The Mask of Zorro" finds Banderas returning as our swashbuckling masked hero, along with Zeta-Jones as his equally hot-blooded spouse, Elena. They are now the parents of impetuous 10-year-old Joaquin (Alonso), but the marriage has enough cracks that Elena kicks Zorro out of his cape. There's also a couple of bad guys—sneering aristocrat Armand (Sewell) and scurvy McGivens (Chinlund)—and a plot that has California becoming part of the United States. The leads are having a lot of fun and there's enough ridiculous action to make the pic speed by. 129m/C DVD, Blu-ray Disc, UMD, US Antonio Banderas, Catherine Zeta-Jones, Rufus Sewell, Nicholas Chinlund, Julio Oscar Mechoso, Shuler Hensley, Michael Emerson, Adrian Alonso; D: Martin Campbell; W: Roberto Orci, Alex Kurtzman; C: Phil Meheux; M: James Horner.

Legends of the Fall 1994 Sweeping, meandering, melodramatic family saga set in Montana (though filmed in Alberta, Canada). Patriarch William Ludlow (Hopkins), a retired Army colonel, is raising three sons: reserved Alfred (Quinn), idealist Samuel (Thomas), and wild middle son Tristan (Pitt, in 1913. Samuel returns from Boston with a fiancee, the lovely and refined Susannah (Ormond). Only problem is Alfred and Tristan take one look and also desire her—a passion that will carry them through some 20 years of heartbreak. Pitt is a visual feast (and not just because the camera seems to drool over the Pitt appears on screen.) 134m/C VHS, DVD, Blu-ray Disc, Brad Pitt, Aidan Quinn, Julia Ormond, Anthony Hopkins, Henry Thomas, Gordon Tootoosis, Tantoo Cardinal, Karina Lombard, Paul Desmond, Kenneth Welsh; D: Edward Zwick; W: Susan Shilliday, William D. Wittliff; C: John Toll; M: James Horner. Oscars '94: Cinematog.

Legends of the North *Adventures of the Great North* 1995 (PG) Crusty prospector Whip Gorman (Quaid) and partner Paul Bel Air are searching for a mythical lake of gold when Paul takes a fall off a mountain. Whip sends for Paul's son Charles so that he can translate his father's diary (it's in French) and get the clues to the gold's whereabouts. Naturally, some rival prospectors, some Indians, and some feisty gal or two help or hinder our treasure seekers. Based on a story by Jack London. 95m/C VHS, CA FR Georges Corralace, Sandrine Holt, Serge Houde, Macha Grenon, Randy Quaid; D: Rene Manzor; W: Rene Manzor; C: Pal Gyulay; M: Milan Kymlicka.

Legion 1998 (R) Major Agatha Doyle (Farrell) is given a group of convicts to lead on a mission to destroy The Legion, a genetically engineered killing machine. But first she has to keep them from killing each other—or her. 97m/C VHS, DVD, Terry Farrell, Corey Feldman, Rick Springfield, Parker Stevenson, Audie England; D: Jon Hess. CABLE

Legion of Iron 1990 (R) Adventures in a computer-run, neo-Roman civilization where men and women battle for supremacy. 85m/C VHS, Kevin T. Walsh, Erica Nann, Reggie De Morton, Camille Carrigan; D: Yakov Bentsvi.

Legion of Missing Men 1937 Professional soldiers of fortune, the French Foreign Legion, fight the evil sheik Ahmed in the Sahara. 62m/B VHS, DVD, Ralph Forbes, Ben Alexander, Hala Linda, Roy D'Arcy, Paul Hurst, Jimmy Aubrey; D: Hamilton MacFadden.

Legion of the Lawless 1940 Group of outlaws band together in order to spread terror and confusion among the populace. 59m/B VHS, George O'Brien, Virginia Vale, Norman Willis, Herbert Heywood, Hugh Sothern, William Benedict, Eddy (Eddie, Ed) Waller; D: David Howard; W: Doris Schroeder; C: Harry Wild.

Legionnaire 1998 (R) In the 1920s, Alain Lefevre (Van Damme) enlists in the French Foreign Legion and is stationed in Morocco after other new recruits. After rigorous training, the men find themselves being sent into battle at a remote outpost, where they'll learn about war and survival. 99m/C VHS, DVD, Jean-Claude Van Damme, Nicholas Farrell, Steven Berkoff, Jim Carter, Adewale Akinnuoye-Agbaje; D: Peter Macdonald; W: Sheldon Lettich, Rebecca Morrison; C: Doug Milsome; M: John Altman.

Legs 1983 Backstage story of three girls who are competing for a job with Radio City Music Hall's Rockettes. 91m/C VHS, Gwen Verdon, John Heard, Sheree North, Shanna Reed, Maureen Teefy; D: Jerrold Freedman; C: Alen Daviau. TV

Leila 1997 Leila, an Iranian woman, finds that she cannot have children shortly after she is married. Although her husband does not mind, Leila's mother-in-law convinces her to let her son take another wife in order to produce an heir. Farsi with subtitles. 129m/C VHS, DVD, IA Leila Hatami, Ali Mosaffa, Jamileh Sheikhi; D: Dariush Mehrjui.

L'Elève *The Pupil* 1995 In 1897 Europe, an aristocratic family hires inexperienced 25-year-old Julien (Cassel) to tutor their precocious teenaged son, Morgan (Salmon). After a tentative battle for control, the two establish a strong emotional rapport and Julien learns that the family is not only in financial difficulty but is part of an empty, amoral social class only concerned with appearance. Based on a story by Henry James; French with subtitles. 92m/C VHS, FR Vincent Cassel, Caspar Salomon, Caroline Cellier, Jean-Pierre Marielle, Sabine Dessailleur, Sandrine Le Berre, Olivier Schatzky; D: Olivier Schatzky; W: Eva Deboise, Olivier Schatzky; C: Carlo Varini; M: Romano Musumarra. Montreal World Film Fest. '95: Director (Schatzky).

Lemming 2005 Moll's French puzzler involves the construction of the title—a Scandinavian lemming that somehow finds itself clogging up the French plumbing of computer gadget designer Alain (Lucas) and his wife Benedicte (Gainsbourg). Naturally this happens during a dinner party for Alain's boss, Richard (Dussollier), and his very difficult wife, Alice (Rampling). Alain's life goes from ordinary and pleasant to sinister and unsettled the flick offers more questions than solutions. French with subtitles. 129m/C DVD, FR FR Laurent Lucas, Charlotte Gainsbourg, Charlotte Rampling, Andre Dussollier, Jacques Bonnafe, Veronique Affholder; D: Dominik Moll; W: Dominik Moll, Gilles Marchand; C: Jean-Marc Fabre; M: David Whitaker.

The Lemon Drop Kid 1951 Second version of the Damon Runyon chestnut about a racetrack bookie who must recover the gangster's money he lost on a bet. As the fast-talking bookie Hope sparkles. It Doesn't Cost a Dime to Dream; They Obviously Want Me to Sing. 91m/B VHS, DVD, Bob Hope, Lloyd Nolan, Fred Clark, Marilyn Maxwell, Jane Darwell, Andrea King, William Frawley, Jay C. Flippen, Harry Bellaver; D: Sidney Lanfield; W: Frank Tashlin, Edmund Hartmann, Robert O'Brien; C: Daniel F. Fapp; M: Ray Evans, Jay Livingston; M: Victor Young.

The Lemon Sisters 1990 (PG-13) Three women, friends and performance partners since childhood, struggle to buy their own club. They juggle the men in their lives with less success. Great actresses like these should have done more excellent male cast has much more potential. 93m/C VHS, DVD, Diane Keaton, Carol Kane, Kathryn Grody, Elliot Gould, Ruben Blades, Aidan Quinn; D: Joyce Chopra; W: Jeremy Pikser; C: Bobby Byrne; M: Dick Hyman.

Lemonade Joe *Limonadovy Joe aneb Konska Opera* 1964 The Czech New Wave does a broad spoof of the American western complete with good guys in white hats, bad guys in black hats, and a saloon gal with a heart of gold. Doug Badman (Kopecky) runs the Trigger Whiskey Saloon, along with his hotsie singer Tornado Lou (Fialova). The hard-drinking bar flies harass sweet temperance worker Winifred (Schoberova) until clean-living soft drink salesman Lemonade Joe (Fiala) shows up to save the day. Czech with subtitles. 87m/B VHS, DVD, CZ Milos Kopecky, Karel Fiala, Kveta Fialova, Olga Schoberova; D: Oldrich Lipsky; W: Oldrich Lipsky, Jiri Brdecka; C: Vladimir Novotny; M: Vladimir Hala, Jan Rychlik.

Lemony Snicket's A Series of Unfortunate Events 2004 (PG) Visually splendid Burtonesque Victorian Gothic adaptation of three books from the series by Snicket (aka Daniel Handler) is playfully gruesome yet not quite subversive enough. Violet (Browning), Klaus (Aiken), and Sunny Baudelaire are wealthy orphans shuttled from one peculiar, distant relative to another. These include sinister Count Olaf (Carrey), who is determined to obtain the family fortune, snake-loving Uncle Monty (Connolly), and phobic Aunt Josephine (Streep). The siblings survive every calamity through pluck, brains, and the fact that toddler Sunny is a ferocious biter. Much hammy villainy and episodic adventure abounds, to enjoyable effect, a silhouetted Law (as Snicket himself) supplies ominous narration. 107m/C VHS, DVD, UMD, US Jim Carrey, Liam Aiken, Emily Browning, Kara Hoffman, Shelby Hoffman, Jude Law, Timothy Spall, Catherine O'Hara, Billy Connolly, Meryl Street; D: Brad Silberling; W: Robert Gordon; C: Emmanuel Lubezki; M: Thomas Newman. Oscars '04: Makeup.

Lemora, Lady Dracula *Lady Dracula; The Legendary Curse of Lemora; Lemora: A Child's Tale of the Supernatural* 1973 (PG) A pretty young church singer is drawn into the lair of the evil Lady Dracula, whose desires include her blood. Horror fans will enjoy some excellent atmosphere, particularly in a scene where the girl's church bus is attacked by zombie-like creatures; Smith remains a '70s "B" movie favorite. Perhaps a double feature with "Lady Frankenstein"...? 80m/C VHS, DVD, Leslie Gib, Cheryl "Rainbeaux" Smith, William Whitton, Steve Johnson, Hy Pyke, Maxine Ballantyne, Parker West, Richard Blackburn, Richard Blackburn; D: Richard Fern, Richard Blackburn; C: Robert Caramico.

Leningrad Cowboys Go America 1989 (PG-13) An outlandish Finnish band, the Leningrad Cowboys, pack up their electric accordions and their one dead member and go on tour in America. With matching front-swept pompadours and pointy shoes, the group's appearance is the picture's best joke—and one of its only jokes, as the road trip plods in deadpan fashion that may bore viewers. It's best appreciated by fans of comic minimalist; Jim Jarmusch (who has a guest role), in Finnish with English subtitles. 78m/C VHS, FR Matti Pellonpaa, Kari Vaananen, Sakke Jarvenpaa, Silu Seppala, Mauri Sumen, Mato Valtonen, Nicky Tesco, Jim Jarmusch; D: Aki Kaurismaki; W: Aki Kaurismaki; C: Timo Salminen; M: Mauri Sumen.

L'Ennui 1998 Detached rather than titillating look at sexual obsession. Middleaged, middle-class philosophy prof Martin (Berling) has recently separated from his wife and is dealing (or rather not dealing) with his midlife crisis. He meets teenaged artist's model Cecilia (Guillemin) and the two begin a very carnal affair, though Martin thinks his paramour is shallow and stupid. Then he discovers Cecilia also has a lover her own age and she wants to keep them both. In French with subtitles. Martin turns obsessively jealous. Based on the novel "La Noia" by Al-

L'Enfer *Jealousy; Torment* 1993 Claustrophobic thriller chronicles the descent into madness of an unstable hotel owner (Cluzet) convinced that his beautiful wife (Beart) is having an affair. Intriguing plot points that blur appearances and reality lead to ambiguous and unsettling ending. Clouzot himself began filming the screenplay in 1964, but a heart attack forced him to abandon the project. So this version uses the same script. In French with English subtitles. 103m/C VHS, DVD, FR Emmanuelle Beart, Francois Cluzet, Nathalie Cardone, Andre Wilms, Marc Lavoine; D: Claude Chabrol; W: Claude Chabrol, Henri-Georges Clouzot; C: Bernard Zitzermann; M: Matthieu Chabrol.

Lena's Holiday 1990 (PG-13) *Water Child; Behind the Blue* 1995 Mentally handicapped twentysomething Ernie (La Haye) and precocious 12-year-old Cedrine (Monette) must learn to work together to survive after a plane crash strands them on an island in the Bahamas. Familiar story of characters that ensues. Sharp script and performances. 97m/C VHS, Marie Monta, Susan Anton, Michael Sarrazin, Nick Mancuso, Bill Dana, Liz Torres; D: Michael Keusch; W: Michael Keusch, Deborah Tilton; C: Louis DiCesare.

L'Ennui

berto Moravia. French with subtitles. **120m/C VHS, DVD.** *FR* Charles Berling, Sophie Guillemin, Arielle Dombasle, Robert Kramer, Tom Ouedraoge; *D:* Cedric Kahn; *W:* Cedric Kahn, Laurence Ferreira Barbosa; *C:* Pascal Marti.

Lenny 🦴🦴🦴 **1974 (R)** Smoky nightclubs, drug abuse, and obscenities abound in Hoffman's portrayal of the controversial comedian Lenny Bruce, whose use of street language led to his eventual blacklisting. Perrine is a gem as his stripper wife. Adapted from the Julian Barry play, this is a visually compelling piece that sharply divided critics upon release. **111m/B VHS, DVD.** Dustin Hoffman, Valerie Perrine, Jan Miner, Stanley Beck; *D:* Bob Fosse; *W:* Julian Barry; *C:* Bruce Surtees; *M:* Ralph Burns. Cannes '75: Support. Actress (Perrine); Natl. Bd. of Review '74: Support. Actress (Perrine); N.Y. Film Critics '74: Support. Actress (Perrine).

Lensman 🦴🦴 **1984** In the 25th century space pirates known as the Boskande are threatening the civilized universe. Young Kimall Kenison is chosen by a higher power to become a lensman—and live or die for freedom. Based on the E.E. "Doc" Smith novels, this production is a combination of animation and computer graphics. Dubbed in English. **107m/C VHS.** *JP D:* Kazuyuki Hirokawa, Yoshiaki Kawajiri; *W:* Soji Yoshikawa; *M:* Akira Inoue; *V:* Robert Axelrod, Richard Barnes, Michael Forest, Michael Kenworthy.

Leo 🦴🦴 **2002 (R)** Craving love from his dispirited mom who sees him as all that went wrong in her past, Leo connects with incarcerated Stephen during a class writing project. Through their letters they become each other's lifeline and upon his release Stephen is determined to find him. Wants to give an twisty ending and boasts lots of acting talent but payoff doesn't deliver. **103m/C VHS, DVD.** Mary Stuart Masterson, Joseph Fiennes, Sam Shepard, Elisabeth Shue, Davis Sweat, Dennis Hopper, Deborah Kara Unger, Jake Weber, Justin Chambers; *D:* Mehdi Norowzian; *W:* Massy Tadjedin, Amir Tadjedin; *C:* Zubin Mistry; *M:* Mark Adler. **VIDEO**

Leo Tolstoy's Anna Karenina 🦴🦴1/2 **1996 (PG-13)** *Leo Tolstoy's Anna Karenina*, the third film version of Tolstoy's tempestuous, tragic romance certainly looks good, even if the performances don't engender the passion the story demands. Beautiful married Anna (Marceau) leaves stuffy husband Karenin (Fox) and their son to travel to 1880 Moscow and mend the marriage of her philandering brother Stiva (Huston). But she meets dashing soldier, Count Alexei Vronsky (Bean), who immediately decides to pursue the beauty and the two begin an all-encompassing affair that leads to tragedy. This version also includes the secondary, contrasting romance between young Kitty (Kirshner) and Tolstoy's alter ego, questioning aristo Levin (Molina). Filmed on location in St. Petersburg, Russia. The classical score includes selections from Tschaikovsky, Rachmaninoff and Prokofiev, under the direction of Georg Solti. **120m/C VHS, DVD.** Sophie Marceau, Sean Bean, Alfred Molina, Mia Kirshner, James Fox, Danny Huston, Fiona Shaw, Phyllida Law, David Schofield, Saskia Wickham; *D:* Bernard Rose; *W:* Bernard Rose; *C:* Daryn Okada.

Leolo 🦴🦴🦴 **1992** Deeply disturbing black comedy about one of the screen's most dysfunctional families. Leo is a 12-year-old French Canadian from Montreal who is determined to remake himself. He's decided to be a Sicilian lad named Leolo, escaping from his horrific family into his fantasies (and potential madness). "I dream, therefore I am not," he thinks. His parents are obsessed with toilet training, his sisters are demented, and his grandfather is a sadistic, dirty old man. Striking cinematography and great soundtrack, but not for the faint of heart (or stomach). In French with English subtitles. **107m/C VHS, DVD.** *CA* Maxime Collin, Julien Guiomar, Ginette Reno, Pierre Bourgault, Yves Montmarquette, Roland Biouin, Giuditta del Vecchio; *D:* Jean-Claude Lauzon; *W:* Jean-Claude Lauzon. Genie '92: Costume Des., Film Editing, Orig. Screenplay.

Leon Morin, Priest 🦴🦴1/2 **1961** A young priest and a widow, who happens to be a Communist, fall in love during the WWII German occupation of France. Based on the novel by Beatrix Beck. In French with English subtitles. **118m/B VHS.** *IT FR* Jean-Paul Belmondo, Emmanuelle Riva; *D:* Jean-Pierre Melville.

Leon the Pig Farmer 🦴🦴1/2 **1993** Dry comedic satire about identity. Leon Geller has never quite fitted into his parents' comfortable Jewish society and no wonder—Leon accidentally discovers he is the product of artificial insemination. And what's more, the lab made a mistake and Leon isn't a true Geller after all. His father is actually a genial (and Gentile) Yorkshire pig farmer named Brian Chadwick, who cheerfully welcomes Leon as his long-lost son. All four parents try to cope while Leon moves bewilderedly amongst them. Film tends to be too timid in its satire but still has its witty moments. **98m/C VHS.** *GB* Mark Frankel, Janet Suzman, Brian Glover, Connie Booth, David de Keyser, Maryam D'Abo, Gina Bellman; *D:* Vadim Jean, Gary Sinyor; *W:* Gary Sinyor, Michael Normand.

Leonard Part 6 🦴 **1987 (PG)** A former secret agent comes out of retirement to save the world from a crime queen using animals to kill agents. In the meantime, he tries to patch up his collapsing personal life. Wooden and disappointing; produced and co-written by Cosby, who himself panned the film. **83m/C VHS, DVD.** Bill Cosby, Gloria Foster, Tom Courtenay, Joe Don Baker; *D:* Paul Weiland; *W:* Bill Cosby, Jonathan Reynolds; *C:* Jan De Bont; *M:* Elmer Bernstein. Golden Raspberries '87: Worst Picture, Worst Actor (Cosby), Worst Screenplay.

Leonor 🦴 **1975** Idiotic medieval drivel with Ullmann rising from the dead after husband Piccoli seals her in a tomb. Directed by the son of Luis Bunuel. **90m/C VHS.** *FR SP IT* Liv Ullmann, Michel Piccoli, Ornella Muti; *D:* Juan Bunuel; *M:* Ennio Morricone.

The Leopard 🦴🦴🦴1/2 *Il Gattopardo* **1963** American Lancaster (allegedly foisted on the movie by the studio to help bring in box office cash for the sumptuous production) holds his own in meeting the style of master director Visconti in this adaptation of Guiseppe di Lampedusa's 1958 bestseller. Sicilian nobility, Prince Don Fabrizio Salina realizes his privileged way of life is doomed as revolution overthrows the old order in the 1860s. Ever practical, he looks for ways for his family to survive, including marrying his ambitious nephew Tancredi (Delon) to Angelica (Cardinale), the daughter of a buffoonish local bureaucrat (Stoppa) who's suddenly gained power with the new regime. The beautiful ending ballroom sequence, lasts some 45 minutes. Italian with subtitles or dubbed. There are many butchered versions of this film but the Criterion release was meticulously restored and is the closest available to Visconti's original (now lost), which was 205 minutes. **185m/C DVD.** *IT* Burt Lancaster, Alain Delon, Claudia Cardinale, Paolo Stoppa, Rina Morelli; *D:* Luchino Visconti; *W:* Luchino Visconti, Enrico Medioli, Romolo Valli, Terence Hill, Pierre Clementi; *D:* Suso Cecchi D'Amico, Pasquale Festa Campanile; *C:* Giuseppe Rotunno; *M:* Nino Rota.

Leopard in the Snow 🦴🦴 **1978 (PG)** The romance between a race car driver allegedly killed in a crash and a young woman is the premise of this film. **89m/C VHS, DVD.** Keir Dullea, Susan Penhaligon, Kenneth More, Billie Whitelaw; *D:* Gerry O'Hara.

The Leopard Man 🦴🦴1/2 **1943** An escaped leopard terrorizes a small town in New Mexico. After a search, the big cat is found dead, but the killings continue. Minor but effective Jacques Tourneur creepie. Based on Cornell Woolrich's novel "Black Alibi." Another Val Lewton Horror production. **66m/B VHS, DVD.** Jean Brooks, Isabel Jewell, James Bell, Margaret Landry, Dennis O'Keefe, Margo, Rita (Paula) Corday, Abner Biberman; *D:* Jacques Tourneur; *W:* Ardel Wray; *C:* Robert De Grasse; *M:* Roy Webb.

The Leopard Son 🦴🦴🦴 **1996 (G)** Beautiful documentary follows the birth and first two years of life for a leopard cub born on Africa's Serengeti plain. Mom leopard shows him how to survive and then he's out into the harsh world on his own. Parents should be forewarned that the hunt-and-kill scenes may upset the little ones. **87m/C VHS.** *D:* Hugo Van Lawick; *W:* Michael Olmert; *C:* Hugo Van Lawick, Matthew Aeberhardt; *M:* Stewart Copeland; *Nar:* John Gielgud.

The Leopard Woman 🦴🦴 **1920** Long before the cat lady cut her first claws, there was the Leopard woman. Vamp Glaum finds much trouble to meow about on the Equator. **66m/B VHS.** House Peters Sr., Noble Johnson, Louise Glaum; *D:* Wesley Ruggles.

Leper 🦴🦴 *Tredowata* **1976** A melodrama of forbidden love between a wealthy nobleman and a beautiful high school teacher. The townspeople try to destroy the love between the two because of their different social classes. In Polish with English subtitles. **100m/C VHS, DVD.** *PL* Elzbieta Starostecka, Leszek Teleszynski; *D:* Jerzy Hoffman.

Lepke 🦴🦴1/2 **1975 (R)** The life and fast times of Louis "Lepke" Buchalter from his days in reform school to his days as head of Murder, Inc. and his execution in 1944. **110m/C VHS.** Tony Curtis, Milton Berle, Gianni Russo, Vic Tayback, Michael Callan; *D:* Menahem Golan.

Leprechaun WOOF! **1993 (R)** A sadistic 600-year-old leprechaun winds up wreaking havoc in North Dakota. If this makes no particular sense, neither does the film which is basic horror story excess. A man goes to Ireland for his mother's funeral, steals the gold belonging to the leprechaun, locks the creature up, and winds up accidentally taking the evil imp back to the States with him. When the leprechaun gets free, he wants a bloodthirsty revenge—and his shoes. One of the so-called humorous bits is the leprechaun's shoe fetish. Irish eyes will not be smiling watching this mess. **92m/C VHS, DVD.** Warwick Davis, Jennifer Aniston, Ken Olandt, Mark Holton, John Sanderford, Robert Gorman, Shay Duffin, John Voldstad; *D:* Mark Jones; *W:* Mark Jones; *C:* Levie Isaacks. **VIDEO**

Leprechaun 2 🦴🦴 **1994 (R)** Sequel to the horror flick about a malevolent Irish gnome. It seems one of his fairy entitlements is that he can possess any woman he wants if she sneezes three times. Thwarted in his attempt to snare a comely lass one thousand years earlier, he returns to present-day California to exact revenge on her descendant Durkin. Contrary to the popular legend that leprechauns are benign kind-hearted sprites, this nasty combines the treachery of a Gestapo officer with the firepower of Rambo in his attempt to harass the unimpressed Durkin into his clutches. **85m/C VHS, DVD.** Warwick Davis, Sandy Baron, Adam Biesk, James Lancaster, Clint Howard, Kimmy Robertson, Charlie Heath, Shevonne Durkin; *D:* Rodman Flender; *W:* Turi Meyer, Al Septien; *C:* Jane Castle; *M:* Jonathan Elias.

Leprechaun 3 🦴 **1995 (R)** A student steals the nasty little beastie's gold and he's off to Las Vegas to get it back and to kill the gamblers, also after his magic money, in decidedly disgusting ways. **93m/C VHS, DVD.** Warwick Davis, John Gatins, Michael Callan, Caroline Williams, Lee Armstrong; *D:* Brian Trenchard-Smith; *W:* Brian Dubos; *C:* David Lewis; *M:* Dennis Michael Tenney.

Leprechaun 4: In Space WOOF! **1996 (R)** Who knows how the little imp got there but now our old friend the Leprechaun (Davis) is busy terrorizing an alien princess (Carlton) on a distant planet. He wants to marry the babe and rule the universe but its the Marines to the rescue! Yes, an Earth platoon arrives to foil his plans. **98m/C VHS, DVD.** Warwick Davis, Rebekah Carlton, Brent Jasmer, Debbe Dunning, Rebecca Cross, Tim Colceri; *D:* Brian Trenchard-Smith; *W:* Dennis Pratt; *C:* David Lewis; *M:* Dennis Michael Tenney.

Leprechaun 5: In the Hood WOOF! **1999 (R)** This time around the bloodthirsty leprechaun wants revenge on a group of wannabe rap artists who use his magic (and steal his gold) in order to become successful. If you've seen any of the others in this series, you know what to expect. **91m/C VHS, DVD.** Warwick Davis, Ice-T, Coolio; *D:* Robert Spera. **VIDEO**

Leprechaun 6: Back 2 Tha Hood WOOF! **2003 (R)** This series becomes campier horror with each new installment. Beautician Emily and her friends find the Leprechaun's gold and foolishly spend it, which earns the little imp's wrath. **87m/C VHS, DVD.** Warwick Davis, Tangi Miller, Kirk "Sticky Fingaz" Jones, Shiek Mahmud-Bey; *D:* Steven Ayromlooi; *W:* Steven Ayromlooi; *C:* David Daniel. **VIDEO**

Les Apprentis 🦴🦴🦴 *The Apprentices* **1995** Womanizing deadbeat Fred (Depardieu) winds up sharing an apartment with antisocial journalist Antoine (Cluzet) and the mismatched duo eventually form an uneasy (though comic) bond. In need of cash, they decide to rob Antoine's office, but bungle the job, which leads to disturbing consequences. Watchable leads, intelligent script. French with subtitles. **95m/C VHS.** *FR* Guillaume Depardieu, Francois Cluzet; *D:* Pierre Salvadori; *W:* Pierre Salvadori, Philippe Harel.

Les Assassins de L'Ordre 🦴🦴 *Law Breakers* **1971** A righteous French judge faces the case of an innocent man killed by police brutality. Subtitled in English. **100m/C VHS.** *FR* Jacques Brel, Catherine Rouvel, Michael (Michel) Lonsdale, Charles Denner; *D:* Marcel Carne; *M:* Michel Colombier.

Les Biches 🦴🦴🦴1/2 *The Heterosexuals* **1968 (R)** An exquisite film that became a landmark in film history with its theme of bisexuality and upper class decadence. A rich socialite picks up a young artist drawing on the streets of Paris, seduces her, and then takes her to St. Tropez. Conflict arises when a suave architect shows up and threatens to come between the two lovers. In French with English subtitles. **95m/C VHS, DVD.** *FR* Stephane Audran, Jean-Louis Trintignant, Jacqueline Sassard; *D:* Claude Chabrol; *W:* Claude Chabrol.

Les Bonnes Femmes 🦴🦴🦴 *The Girls* **1960** Four Paris shopgirls dream of escaping the monotony of their lives and finding romance but instead discover broken dreams and danger. Chabrol's New Wave thriller focuses more on character and irony than suspense. French with subtitles. **105m/B VHS, DVD.** *FR* Bernadette LaFont, Stephane Audran, Clothilde Joano, Lucile Saint-Simon; *D:* Claude Chabrol; *W:* Paul Gegauff; *C:* Henri Decae; *M:* Pierre Jansen, Paul Misraki.

Les Bons Debarras 🦴🦴🦴1/2 **1981** In French with English subtitles, this Canadian film follows a lonely 13-year-old's effort to win her mother's exclusive love. **114m/C VHS.** *CA* Marie Tifo, Charlotte Laurier, Germain Houde; *D:* Francis Mankiewicz. Genie '81: Actress (Tifo), Director (Mankiewicz), Film, Support. Actor (Houde).

Les Carabiniers 🦴🦴🦴 *The Soldiers* **1963** A cynical, grim anti-war tract, detailing the pathetic adventures of two young bums lured into enlisting with promises of rape, looting, torture and battle without justification. Controversial in its day, and typically elliptical and non-narrative. In French with English subtitles. **80m/B VHS, DVD.** *GB IT FR* Albert Juross, Marino (Martin) Mase, Catherine Ribeiro, Genevieve Galea, Anna Karina; *D:* Jean-Luc Godard; *W:* Jean-Luc Godard; *C:* Raoul Coutard; *M:* Philippe Arthuys.

Les Comperes 🦴🦴1/2 **1983** A woman suckers two former lovers into finding her wayward son by secretly telling each ex he is the natural father of the punk. Depardieu is a streetwise journalist who teams up with a suicidal hypochondriac/wimp (Richard) to find the little brat. Humorous story full of bumbling misadventures. In French with English subtitles. **92m/C VHS, DVD.** *FR* Pierre Richard, Gerard Depardieu, Anny (Annie Legras) Duperey, Michel Aumont; *D:* Francis Veber; *W:* Francis Veber; *M:* Vladimir Cosma.

Les Destinees 🦴🦴1/2 *Les Destinees Sentimentales; Sentimental Destinies* **2000** Lavish, sprawling, but emotionally flat costume drama follows forty years in the life of Jean Barnery, Jean, a Protestant minister, finds that his wife, Nathalie, has been unfaithful and sends her, along with their daughter Aline away. After he meets, and falls in love with the independent Pauline, he has re-entered his family's World War I, the call to return to the Wall Street crash impose themselves into Jean and Pauline's life. Film is technically and visually impressive, but a lack of any real spark (except when Huppert is onscreen) blunt its impact. Based on the novel by Jacques Charonne. 2 **DVD, FR** *St* Charles Berling, Emmanuelle Beart, Isabelle Huppert, Olivier Perrier, Dominique Reymond, Andre Marcon, Alexandra London, Julie Depardieu; *D:* Olivier Assayas; *W:* Olivier Assayas, Jacques Fieschi; *C:* Eric Gautier; *M:* Guillaume Lekeu.

Les Enfants Terrible 🐾🐾🐾 *Strange Ones* 1950 The classic, lyrical treatment of adolescent deviance adapted by Cocteau from his own play, wherein a seductive soldier (Philipe) and a divorcee (Morgan) in a pre-WWI garrison town. Gentle comedy has Philipe falling in love but his reputation as a Don Juan comes between them. French with English subtitles. 106m/C VHS, FR GE **DVD, FR** *St* Jacques Perrin, Jean Gielgud, Cyril Cusack, Jean-Pierre Melville.

Les Girls 🐾🐾½ 1957 When one memoirs, the other girls sue for libel. Told through a series of flashbacks, this story traces the girls' recollections of their relationships to American dancer Kelly. Cole Porter wrote the score for this enjoyable "Rashomon"-styled musical. ♫Les Girls; C'est L'Amour; Ladies in Waiting; La Habanera; Why Am I So Gone (About That Gal?) 114m/C VHS, DVD, Gene Kelly, Mitzi Gaynor, Kay Kendall, Taina Elg, Henry Daniell, Patrick Macnee; *D:* George Cukor; *C:* Robert L. Surtees. Oscars '57: Costume Des.; Golden Globes '58: Actress—Mus./Comedy (Kendall). Film—Mus/Comedy.

Les Grandes Manoeuvres 🐾🐾🐾 *Summer Maneuvers: The Grand Maneuvers* 1955 Clair's first film in color depicts the romance between a seductive soldier (Philipe) and a divorcee (Morgan) in a pre-WWI garrison town. Gentle comedy has Philipe falling in love but his reputation as a Don Juan comes between them. French with subtitles. 106m/C VHS, FR **St** Gerard Philipe, Michele Morgan, Yves Robert, Brigitte Bardot, Jean Desailly, Pierre Dux; *D:* Rene Clair; *W:* Rene Clair; *M:* Georges Van Parys.

Les Miserables 🐾🐾🐾 1935 Victor Hugo's classic novel about small-time criminal Jean Valjean and 18th-century France. After facing poverty and prison, escape and torture, Valjean is redeemed by the kindness of a bishop. As he tries to mend his ways, he is continually hounded by the policeman Javert, who is determined to lock him away. The final act is set during a student uprising in the 1730s. This version is the best of many, finely detailed and well-paced with excellent cinematography by Gregg Toland. 108m/B VHS, Fredric March, Charles Laughton, Cedric Hardwicke, Rochelle Hudson, John Beal, Frances Drake, Florence Eldridge, John Carradine, Jessie Ralph, Leonid Kinskey; *D:* Richard Boleslawski; *W:* W.P. Lipscomb; *C:* Gregg Toland; *M:* Alfred Newman.

Les Miserables 🐾🐾½ 1952 Hugo's classic novel done up in Italian style with lavish sets and spectacle. Dubbed in English. 119m/B VHS, IT Charlotte Austin, Gino Cervi, Valentina Cortese; *D:* Riccaro Freda; *C:* Joseph LaShelle; *M:* Alex North.

Les Miserables 🐾🐾🐾 1957 An epic French adaptation of the Victor Hugo standard about Valjean, Javert, and injustice. Although this doesn't reach the level of the 1935 classic, it is still worth watching. Dubbed in English. 210m/C VHS, FR GE Jean Gabin, Daniele Delorme, Bernard Blier, Andre Bourvil, Gianni Esposito, Serge Reggiani; *D:* Jean-Paul LeCanois.

Les Miserables 🐾🐾½ 1978 An excellent made-for-TV version of the Victor Hugo classic about the criminal Valjean and the policeman Javert playing cat-and-mouse in 18th-century France. Dau-

phin's last film role. 150m/C VHS Richard Jordan, Anthony Perkins, John Gielgud, Cyril Cusack, Flora Robson, Celia Johnson, Claude Dauphin; *D:* Glenn Jordan. **TV**

Les Miserables 🐾🐾 1995 (R) Clever, modern rendering of the famous furniture mover Fortin (Belmondo), nicknamed Valjean for displaying the same brutish strength as his Hugo counterpart, helps a Jewish family escape German occupation. The family becomes separated in the attempt, with lawyer Monsieur Ziman (Boujenah) being hidden by farmers in the country, Madame Ziman (Martines) relegated to a Polish concentration camp, and their daughter Salome (Lelouch, the daughter of the director) protected by a nun at a Catholic school. Gump-like, the story becomes involved with the French resistance and joins in D-Day. Events, though obviously updated, mirror experiences of Hugo's characters. In one sequence, Ziman's even teach Fortin to read Hugo's "Les Miserables," with actors playing their counterparts in dramatizations. Reported by France's most expensive film ever. 174m/C VHS, Jean-Paul Belmondo, Michel Boujenah, Annie Girardot, Philippe Leotard, Clementine Celarie, Rufus, Alessandra Martines, Salome, Philippe Khorsand; *D:* Claude Lelouch; *W:* Claude Lelouch; *C:* Claude Lelouch; *M:* Francis Lai, Cesar '96: Support. Actress (Girardot); Golden Globes '96: Foreign Film.

Les Miserables 🐾🐾🐾 1997 (PG-13) Yet another adaptation of the Victor Hugo novel. Parceled convict Jean Valjean (Neeson) gets chased by police inspector Javert (Rush) while factory worker Fantine (Thurman) turns to prostitution to survive. August chose to begin this tale after Valjean's trial and imprisonment for petty theft, and until the final third of the film, doesn't really deal with the political upheaval of the time. Not as sweeping or grand as other versions, but what this adaptation lacks in scope, it makes up for by Neeson and Rush) and more careful study of the characters themselves. 134m/C DVD, Liam Neeson, Geoffrey Rush, Uma Thurman, Claire Danes, Paris Vaughan, Reine Brynolfsson, Hans Matheson, Mimi Newman; *D:* Bille August; *W:* Rafael Yglesias; *C:* Jorgen Persson; *M:* Basil Poledouris.

Les Mistons 🐾🐾🐾 1957 *The Mischief Makers; The Kids* 1957 This study of male adolescence finds five teenage boys worshiping a beautiful girl from afar, following her everywhere, spoiling her dates, and finally reaching maturity in light of their mistakes. 18m/C VHS, DVD, FR Gerard Blain, Bernadette LaFont, Michel Francois; *D:* Francois Truffaut; *W:* Francois Truffaut; *C:* Jean Malige; *M:* Maurice Leroux.

Les Nuits Fauves 🐾🐾🐾 *Savage Nights* 1992 Collard's semi-autobiographical film about the emotional and physical havoc an H.I.V.-positive filmmaker visits on the two objects of his violent affections—an innocent 18-year-old girl and a sadomasochistic 20-year-old boy. As Jean displays increasing desperation with his situation, the life around him shows an equally arbitrary violence and humor. In French with English subtitles. Collard died of AIDS shortly before his film won both best first film and best French film at the 1993 Cesars—a first in the ceremony's history. 129m/C VHS, FR Cyril Collard, Romane Bohringer, Carlos Lopez, Maria Schneider; *D:* Cyril Collard; Cesars '93: Film.

Les Patterson Saves the World 🐾½ 1990 (R) An obnoxious ambassador to an anonymous Middle Eastern country teams up with the singularly distastefully named Dr. Herpes to stop a new killer disease about to engulf the world. 105m/C VHS, Barry Humphries, Pamela Stephenson, Thaao Penghlis, Andrew Clarke, Joan Rivers; *D:* George Miller; *C:* David Connell.

Les Rendez-vous D'Anna 🐾🐾 *The Meetings of Anna* 1978 An independent woman travels through Europe and comes face to face with its post-war modernism. In French with English subtitles. 120m/C VHS, FR BE GE Aurore Clement, Helmut Griem,

Magali Noel, Hans Zischler, Lea Massari, Jean-Pierre Cassel; *D:* Chantal Akerman; *W:* Chantal Akerman.

Les Vampires 🐾🐾 1915 Irma Vep (an anagram for vampire) leads a bloodthirsty gang of thieves in Paris. She and her cohorts will use kidnapping, gas, sexual domination, and murder to gain power over the city's elite. Feuillade's 10-part serial has been restored with color tinting and title cards in English. 420m/B VHS, DVD, FR Musidora, Jean Ayme, Marcel Levesque, Edouard Mathe; *D:* Louis Feuillade; *W:* Louis Feuillade.

Les Violons du Bal 🐾🐾 1974 Follows the story of a young Jewish boy during his family's attempted escape from Nazi-occupied France during WWII. The boy grows up to be a filmmaker obsessed with making a film about his childhood experiences. In French with English subtitles. 110m/C VHS, FR Marie-Jose Nat, Jean-Louis Trintignant; *D:* Michael Drach, Cannes '74: Actress (Nat).

Les Visiteurs du Soir 🐾🐾🐾 *The Devil's Envoys* 1942 A beautiful, charming fairy tale about the devil's intrepid interference with a particular love affair in 15th-century France, which he cannot squelch. Purportedly a parable about Hitler's invasion of France. Interestingly, this was in France, so one assumes that the Germans didn't make the connection. In French with English subtitles. 120m/B VHS, FR Arletty, Jules Barry, Marie Dea, Alain Cuny, Fernand Ledoux, Marcel Herrand; *D:* Marcel Carne; *M:* Jacques Prevert, Pierre Laroche.

Les Voleurs 🐾🐾 *Thieves* 1996 (R) Unexpected romantic triangle among desperate, lonely people, set against a crime backdrop and told from a variety of viewpoints. Edgy cop Alex (Auteuil) is from a family of thieves, including his older brother Ivan (Bezace) who's been murdered. Marie and Alex over the unstable Juliette (the scenes between Auteuil and Deneuve being the most interesting in the film). French with subtitles. 116m/C VHS, FR Catherine Deneuve, Daniel Auteuil, Laurence Cote, Benoit Magimel, Didier Bezace, Fabienne Babe, Ivan Desny, Julien Riviere; *D:* Andre Techine; *W:* Andre Techine; *C:* Jeanne Lapoirie; *M:* Philippe Sarde.

L'Escorte 🐾🐾 *The Escort* 1996 Thirty-years-old and long-term lovers, Jean-Marc and Philippe find their relationship in crisis thanks to both the stress caused by their failing Montreal restaurant and the intrusion of a third party. Free-spirited Steve works as an escort and soon becomes an object of desire for both men as well as catalyst for the revelation of long-held secrets. French with subtitles. 91m/C VHS, CA Eric Cabana, Paul-Antoine Taillefer, Robin Aubert, Marie Lefebvre; *D:* Denis Langlois; *W:* Denis Langlois, Bertrand Lachance; *C:* Yves Beaudoin; *M:* Bertrand Chenier.

Less Than Zero 🐾 1987 (R) An adaptation of Bret Easton Ellis' popular, controversial novel about a group of affluent, drug-abusing youth in Los Angeles. McCarthy and Gertz play friends of Downey, who try to get him off his self-destructive path—to no avail. Although it tries, the film fails to inspire any sort of sympathy for this self-absorbed and hedonistic group. Mirrors the shallowness of the characters although Downey manages to rise above this somewhat. Music by the Bangles, David Lee Roth, Poison, Roy Orbison, Aerosmith and more. 98m/C VHS, DVD, Andrew McCarthy, Jami Gertz, Robert Downey Jr., James Spader; *D:* Marek Kanievska; *W:* Harley Peyton; *C:* Edward Lachman; *M:* Thomas Newman.

The Lesser Evil 🐾🐾½ 1997 (R) Derek (Feore), the struggling owner of a lumber business, has invited three former high school buddies to his cabin in the Missouri woods. Ivan (Howard) is now a priest, Frank (Goldwyn) is a police officer, and George 'Paymer) is a big-shot attor-

ney. As teens they got mixed up with two deaths and a coverup that has now come back to haunt them. Now, just what kind of justice will prevail? Good cast, nice mix of flashbacks, and a satisfying final twist. 97m/C VHS, Com Feore, Tony Goldwyn, Arliss Howard, David Paymer, Jonathan Scarfe, Petracca, Adam Scott, Marc Worden, Jack Kehler, Richard Riehle, Mason Adams, Anne Haney; *D:* David Mackay; *W:* David Mackay, Jeremy Levine; *C:* Stephan Schultze; *M:* Don Davis.

A Lesson Before Dying 🐾🐾🐾 1999 (PG-13) Cheadle's impressive as idealistic teacher Grant Wiggins, who has a one-room school for black children in 1948 Louisiana. He's reluctantly pressed into service by his formidable Aunt Lou (Tyson) and her friend Miss Emma (Hall), who want him to bring some dignity to the life of Jefferson (Phifer). This is no easy task since the young man is awaiting execution for a crime he didn't commit. Based on the 1993 novel by Ernest J. Gaines. 100m/C VHS, Don Cheadle, Cicely Tyson, Mekhi Phifer, Irma P. Hall, Brent Jennings, Lisa Arndall Anderson, Frank Hoyt Taylor; *D:* Joseph Sargent; *W:* Ann Peacock; *C:* Donald M. Morgan; *M:* Ernest Troost. **C.A.B.L.E.**

Lesson in Love 🐾🐾½ *En Lektion i Kärlek* 1954 A gynecologist's philandering is discovered by his wife, who then starts an affair of her own. Change of pace for Bergman as he does this modest comedy. In Swedish with English subtitles. 95m/B VHS, SW Gunnar Bjornstrand, Eva Dahlbeck, Harriet Andersson; *D:* Ingmar Bergman; *W:* Ingmar Bergman.

Let 'Em Have It 🐾🐾½ *False Faces* 1935 Exciting action saga loosely based on the newly formed FBI and its bouts with John Dillinger. Car chases and tommy guns abound in this fairly ordinary film. 90m/B VHS, DVD, Richard Arlen, Virginia Bruce, Bruce Cabot, Harvey Stephens, Eric Linden, Joyce Compton, Gordon Jones; *D:* Sam Wood.

Let 'er Go Gallegher 🐾🐾 1928 A youngster sees a murder, tells his newspaper buddy about it, and the guy writes an article about the crime. It's a big hit, the guy's ego starts to overinflate, and his life starts to head downwind until he decides its time for him and his lug to rope themselves as a miscreant. 57m/B VHS, Frank "Junior" Coghlan, Elinor Fair, Wade Boteler; *D:* Elmer Clifton.

Let Freedom Ring 🐾🐾½ 1939 Sappy, yet enjoyable patriotism that has lawyer Eddy returning to small hometown and fighting corruption. Hokey, but it works largely due to Hecht's fine script. ♫Dusty Road; Love Serenade; Home Sweet Home; When Irish Eyes Are Smiling; America; Pat Sez He; Where Else But Here; Funiculi Funicula; Ten Thousand Cattle Straying. 100m/B VHS, Nelson Eddy, Virginia Bruce, Victor McLaglen, Lionel Barrymore, Edward Arnold, Guy Kibbee, Charles Butterworth, H.B.Warner, Raymond Walburn; *D:* Jack Conway; *W:* Ben Hecht.

Let Him Have It 🐾🐾🐾 1991 (R) Compelling, controversial film about a miscarriage of British justice. In 1952 Christopher Craig, 16, and Derek Bentley, 19, climbed onto the roof of a warehouse in an apparent burglary attempt. The police arrived and captured Bentley; Craig shot and wounded one policeman and killed another. According to testimony Bentley shouted "Let him have it" but did he mean shoot or give the officer the gun? Bentley, whose Q was 66, was sentenced to death by the British courts—though he didn't commit this murder. The uproar over the sentence was reignited by this review, leading to a request for a reexamination of evidence and sentencing by the British Home Office. 115m/C VHS, DVD, GB Christopher Eccleston, Paul Reynolds, Tom Bell, Eileen Atkins, Clare Holman, Michael Elphick, Mark McGann, Tom Courtenay, Ronald Fraser, Michael Gough, Murray Melvin, Clive Revill, Norman Rossington, James Villiers, Peter Medak; *W:* Oliver Stapleton, Neal Purvis, Robert Wade.

Let It Be 🐾🐾 1970 Documentary look at a Beatles recording session, giving glimpses of the conflicts which led to their breakup. Features appearances by Yoko

Ono and Billy Preston. 80m/C VHS, DVD. John Lennon, Paul McCartney, George Harrison, Ringo Starr, Billy Preston, Yoko Ono; *D:* Michael Lindsay-Hogg; *M:* John Lennon, Paul McCartney, George Harrison, Ringo Starr. Oscars '70: Orig. Song Score and/or Adapt.

Let It Ride 🐾🐾 1989 (PG-13) Dreyfuss is a small-time gambler who finally hits it big at the track. Some funny moments but generally a lame script cripples the cast, although the horses seem unaffected. Garr is okay as his wife who slips further into alcoholism with each race. 91m/C VHS, DVD. Richard Dreyfuss, Teri Garr, David Johansen, Jennifer Tilly, Allen (Goodwin) Garfield, Ed Walsh, Michelle Phillips, Mary Woronov, Robbie Coltrane, Richard Edson, Cynthia Nixon; *D:* Joe Pytka; *W:* Nancy Dowd; *C:* Curtis J. Wehr; *M:* Giorgio Moroder.

Let It Rock 🐾 1986 A maniacal promoter makes superstars out of his new band by staging publicity stunts. Not one of Hopper's better efforts. Filmed in Germany, but Roger Corman bought the U.S. rights and added clips from other movies before it was released here. 75m/C VHS. GE Dennis Hopper, David Alexander) Hess; *D:* Roland Klick.

Let It Snow 🐾🐾½ Snow Days 1999 (R) Appealing romantic comedy centers on the emotional insecurity of James Ellis (scripter Marcus), whose brother, Adam, directs), who witnessed his mother Elise's (Peters) post-divorce series of loser boyfriends. His best friend is Sarah (Dylan) and the two dance around the romantic possibilities until a sudden kiss throws their relationship into turmoil. Some miscommunication has Sarah leaving to study in England and James becoming determined to win her love. 90m/C VHS, DVD. Kipp Marcus, Alice Dylan, Bernadette Peters, Judith Malina, Henry Simmons, Miriam Shor, Larry Pine, Debra Sullivan; *D:* Adam Marcus; *W:* Kipp Marcus; *C:* Ben Weinstein; *M:* Sean McCourt.

Let No Man Write My Epitaph 🐾🐾 1960 Winters emotes theatrically as Nellie, a southside Chicago junkie mom who is trying to raise her son, Nick (Darren), to live a better life. Based on the novel by Willard Motley. 105m/B VHS. Shelley Winters, James Darren, Burl Ives, Ricardo Montalban, Jean Seberg, Ella Fitzgerald, Rodolfo Acosta, Jeanne Cooper, Michael Davis; *D:* Philip Leacock; *W:* Robert Presnell Jr.; *C:* Burnett Guffey; *M:* George Duning.

Let the Devil Wear Black 🐾🐾½ 1999 (R) A "Hamlet" update gets the noir treatment. Jack (Penner) is suspicious about his dad's murder, especially when his mom (Bisset) suddenly marries his uncle (Sheridan). Jack becomes obsessed with linking his uncle to some shady business dealings also involving dear old dad, while his girlfriend, Julia (Parker), goes a little crazy from Jack's neglect. Cleverly done. 89m/C VHS, DVD. Jonathan Penner, Jacqueline Bisset, Jamey Sheridan, Mary-Louise Parker, Philip Baker Hall, Jonathan Banks, Maury Chaykin, Chris Sarandon, Randall Batinkoff, Norman Reedus; *D:* Stacy Title; *W:* Jonathan Penner, Stacy Title; *C:* James Whitaker.

L'Etat Sauvage 🐾🐾½ The Savage State 1978 This French political thriller finds its heart in the middle of racism. The story unfolds around a newly independent African republic and a love affair between a black cabinet minister and a white Frenchwoman. Corruption abounds in this film based on George Conchon's award-winning novel. In French with English subtitles. 111m/C VHS. FR Marie-Christine Barrault, Claude Brasseur, Jacques Dutronc, Doura Mane, Michel Piccoli; *D:* Francis Girod. Cesar '79: Sound.

Lethal woof! 🐾🐾 2004 (R) Bounty hunter Sara (Marsden) teams up with an FBI agent (Zagarino) to bring down Russian mobster/weapons smuggler Federov (Lamas), he of the wandering accent). Lethally inept. 90m/C DVD. Lorenzo Lamas, Frank Zagarino, Heather Marie Marsden, Mark Mortimer, John Colton; *D:* Dustin Rikert; *W:* Jeff Wright, Robert Yap; *C:* John Muscatine. VIDEO

Lethal Charm 🐾 Her Wicked Ways 1990 Two power-hungry journalists go head-to-head in the high stakes arena of Washington D.C. 92m/C VHS. Stuart Wilson, David James Elliott, Julie Fulton, Jed Allan, Barbara Eden, Heather Locklear; *D:* Richard Michaels; *C:* Steve (Steven) Shaw; *M:* Fred Karlin.

Lethal Dose 🐾½ LD 50 Lethal Dose 2003 (R) Extremist animal activist group ditches team member Gary during a botched rescue mission and wants to make it up to him a year later by springing him from the slammer. Instead, a freaky e-mail directs them to a long-deserted lab where grisly torture awaits. 97m/C VHS, DVD. Katharine Towne, Melanie (Scary Spice) Brown, Thomas (Tom) Hardy, Ross McCall, Philip Winchester, Stephen Lord, Toby Fisher, Leo Bill, Tania Emery, Alan Talbot, Antony Zaki, Xanthe Elbrick; *D:* Simon DeSelva; *W:* Matthew McGuchan; *C:* Robin Vidgeon; *M:* Michael Price. VIDEO

Lethal Force 🐾🐾½ Cottonmouth 2000 Houston cop Carruth (Tyson) turns vigilante on criminals with the backing of a judge (Vaughn) and some powerful businessmen. Unfortunately, there are innocent victims, including the family of former D.A. Thornton (Owsley), who is persuaded by noisy lawyer Rene (Stafford) to investigate and bring the rogue cop to justice. 95m/C VHS, DVD. Richard Tyson, Robert Vaughn, Michelle Stafford, Steven Owsley; *D:* James Dalthorp; *W:* Steven Owsley. VIDEO

Lethal Games 🐾 1990 Stallone and Vaccaro lead a small community against a blood-thirsty band of criminals. 83m/C VHS. Frank Stallone, Brenda Vaccaro, Dave Adams, Christopher Whalley, Heidi Paine, Karen Russell; *D:* John Bowen.

Lethal Lolita—Amy Fisher: My Story 🐾🐾 Amy Fisher: My Story 1992 The only made-for-TV Amy Fisher story out of three whose cast members even remotely resemble the real people—except of course actress Parker is actually pretty. Minor details aside, this account is Amy's story, purchased by NBC for an undisclosed amount, portraying her as an incest victim who gets involved with an opportunistic married jerk who drags her into prostitution, leading her to take out her frustration on his wife. If this is true, the obvious question is "why?"...to which she answers, "He loves me. We have great sex. And he fixes my car." Oh. See also: "The Amy Fisher Story" and "Casualties of Love: The 'Long Island Lolita' Story." 93m/C VHS, DVD. Noelle Parker, Ed Marinaro, Lawrence Dane, Kathleen Lasky, Boyd Kestner, Mary Ann Pascal; *D:* Bradford May. TV

Lethal Ninja 🐾 1993 (R) Kickboxers Joe and Pete set out to rescue Joe's wife from some third-world country overrun by ninjas. Hackneyed but lots of action for martial arts fans. 97m/C VHS, DVD. Ross Kettle, David Webb, Karyn Hill, Frank Notaro; *D:* Yossi Wein; *W:* Chris Dresser; *C:* Yossi Wein.

Lethal Obsession 🐾🐾½ Der Joker 1987 (R) Two cops battle street crime and a powerful drug ring. Filmed in Germany. 100m/C VHS, DVD. GE Michael York, Elliott Gould, Tahnee Welch, Peter Maffay, Armin Mueller-Stahl; *D:* Peter Patzak; *M:* Tony Carey.

Lethal Panther 🐾🐾 1990 A film where the female is indeed deadlier than the male. Japanese hit woman Ling (Miyamoto) gets involved with drug-smuggling gangsters operating out of the Philippines and is opposed by CIA agent Betty Lee (Hu). Dubbed. 120m/C VHS, DVD. HK Yoko Miyamoto, Sibelle Hu, Lawrence Ng; *D:* Godfrey Ho.

Lethal Pursuit 🐾 1988 A popular singer who returns to the town where she grew up is tormented by her ex-boyfriend, a criminal. 90m/C VHS. Mitzi Donahue, Blake Gahner, John Wildman; *D:* Donald M. Jones.

Lethal Seduction 🐾🐾 1997 Local crime boss Gus Gruman (Estevez) is rapidly losing friends and associates to a sexually oriented serial killer. And there's obsessed cop Trent Jacobson (Mitchum) who's determined to solve the crimes. The one clue is a mystery brunette seen leaving a crime scene. 110m/C VHS, DVD. Julie Strain, Chris Mitchum, Joe Estevez; *D:* Frederick P. Watkins; *C:* Robert Dracup.

Lethal Tender 🐾🐾 1996 (R) A tour group is held hostage by a gang of terrorists as part of a plot to steal $400 million and it's up to a lone Chicago cop to save the day. Fahey does equally well in both bad and good guy roles and here he's in hero mode. 93m/C VHS. Jeff Fahey, Kim Coates, Gary Busey, Carrie-Anne Moss; *D:* John Bradshaw.

Lethal Weapon 🐾🐾🐾 1987 (R) In Los Angeles, a cop nearing retirement (Glover) unwillingly begins work with a new partner (Gibson), a suicidal, semi-crazed risk-taker who seems determined to get the duo killed. Both Vietnam vets, the pair uncover a vicious heroin smuggling ring run by ruthless ex-Special Forces personnel. Packed with plenty of action, violence, and humorous undertones. Clapton's contributions to the musical score are an added bonus. Gibson and Glover work well together and give this movie extra punch. Followed by three sequels. 110m/C VHS, DVD, Blu-ray Disc, HD DVD. Mel Gibson, Danny Glover, Gary Busey, Mitchell Ryan, Tom Atkins, Darlene Love, Traci Wolfe, Steve Kahan, Jackie Swanson, Damon Hines, Lycia Naff, Mary Ellen Trainor, Jack Thibeau, Ed O'Ross, Gustav Vintas, Al Leong, Joan Severance; *D:* Richard Donner; *W:* Shane Black; *C:* Stephen Goldblatt; *M:* Michael Kamen, Eric Clapton.

Lethal Weapon 2 🐾🐾🐾 1989 (R) This sequel to the popular cop adventure finds Gibson and Glover taking on a variety of blond South African "diplomats" who try to use their diplomatic immunity status to thwart the duo's efforts to crack their smuggling ring. Gibson finally finds romance, and viewers learn the truth about his late wife's accident. Also features the introduction of obnoxious, fast-talking con artist Leo ("OK", OK") Getz, adeptly played by Pesci, who becomes a third wheel to the crime-fighting team. 114m/C VHS, DVD, Blu-ray Disc, HD DVD. Mel Gibson, Danny Glover, Joe Pesci, Joss Ackland, Derrick O'Connor, Patsy Kensit, Darlene Love, Traci Wolfe, Steve Kahan, Mary Ellen Trainor, Damon Hines, Jenette Goldstein, Mark Rolston, Dean Norris, Nestor Serrano, Grand L. Bush; *D:* Richard Donner; *W:* Jeffrey Boam; *C:* Stephen Goldblatt; *M:* Michael Kamen, Eric Clapton, David Sanborn.

Lethal Weapon 3 🐾🐾½ 1992 (R) Murtaugh and Riggs return for more action in another slam-bang adventure. Murtaugh hopes his last week before retirement will be a peaceful one, but partner Riggs isn't about to let him go quietly. Not many changes from the successful formula with bickering buddies, lots of action, exploding buildings, a little comic relief from Pesci, and the addition of Russo as an Internal Affairs cop who proves to be more than a match for Riggs. 118m/C VHS, DVD. Mel Gibson, Danny Glover, Joe Pesci, Rene Russo, Stuart Wilson, Steve Kahan, Darlene Love, Traci Wolfe, Gregory Millar, Jason Meshover-Iorg, Delores Hall, Mary Ellen Trainor, Nicholas Chinlund, Damon Hines, Miguel A. Nunez Jr.; *D:* Richard Donner; *W:* Jeffrey Boam, Robert Mark Kamen; *C:* Jan De Bont; *M:* Eric Clapton, David Sanborn, Michael Kamen. MTV Movie Awards '93: On-Screen Duo (Mel Gibson/Danny Glover), Action Seq.

Lethal Weapon 4 🐾🐾½ 1998 (R) It's old home week as Gibson, Glover, Pesci, and Russo all reunite for one more escapade, six years after 1992's "Lethal Weapon 3." Rock joins the veterans as junior detective Lee Butters, who has some unexpected ties to Murtaugh. They're investigating Asian crimelord Wah Sing Ku (Chinese action star Li) who's involved in smuggling and counterfeiting and has no problem with violence, including kicking the bejeezus out of Riggs on more than one occasion. Russo had to do her action sequences with a prosthetic belly since her character, Lorna Cole, and Riggs are about to become parents. It's the same old-same old but it's still a good time. 125m/C VHS, DVD. Mel Gibson, Danny Glover, Joe Pesci, Rene Russo, Chris Rock, Jet Li, Steve Kahan, Darlene Love, Mary Ellen Trainor, Jack Kehler, Damon Hines, Traci Wolfe, Richard Libertini, Richard Riehle; *D:* Richard Donner; *W:* Channing Gibson; *C:* Andrzej Bartkowiak; *M:* Michael Kamen, Eric Clapton; David Sanborn.

Lethal Woman 🐾🐾 1988 A group of beautiful women, all once victimized by rapes, is recruited to an island by the "Lethal Woman," who plots revenge on any man who dares to vacation on the island. 96m/C VHS. Robert Lipton, James Luisi, Shannon Tweed, Merete Van Kamp; *D:* Christian Marnham; *W:* Gabe Ellis; *C:* Vincent Cox; *M:* Meir Eshel.

Lethal Dance 🐾🐾½ 1950 A young widow tries to protect her son from his wealthy, paternal grandmother, while Fred dances his way into her heart. More obscure Astaire vehicle, but as charming as the rest. Needless to say, great dancing. ♪Tunnel of Love; The Hyacinth; Piano Dance; Jack and the Beanstalk; Can't Stop Talking; Oh, Them Dudes; Why Fight the Feeling?. 112m/C VHS. Betty Hutton, Fred Astaire, Roland Young, Ruth Warrick, Shepperd Strudwick, Lucile Watson, Barton MacLane, Gregory Moffett, Melville Cooper; *D:* Norman Z. McLeod.

Let's Do It Again 🐾½ 1975 (PG) Atlanta milkman and his pal, a factory worker, milk two big-time gamblers out of a large sum of money in order to build a meeting hall for their fraternal lodge. Lesser sequel to "'Uptown Saturday Night." 113m/C VHS. Sidney Poitier, Bill Cosby, John Amos, Jimmie Walker, Ossie Davis, Denise Nicholas, Calvin Lockhart; *D:* Sidney Poitier; *W:* Richard Wesley.

Let's Get Harry 🐾½ The Rescue 1987 (R) Americans led by mercenaries mix it up with a Columbian cocaine franchise in an attempt to rescue their friend, Harry. Never released theatrically, for good reason. 107m/C VHS. Robert Duvall, Gary Busey, Michael Schoeffling, Thomas F. Wilson, Glenn Frey, Rick Rossovich, Ben Johnson, Matt Clark, Mark Harmon, Gregory Sierra, Elpidia Carrillo; *D:* Alan Smithee; *W:* Samuel Fuller, Charles Robert Carner; *M:* Brad Fiedel.

Let's Get Lost 🐾🐾 1988 Absorbing documentary of Chet Baker, the prominent '50s "cool" jazz trumpeter (and occasional vocalist) who succumbed, like many of his peers, to drug addiction. Weber's black-and-white, fashion photography style well suits his subject. Downbeat, but rarely less than worthy. 125m/B VHS. Chet Baker; *D:* Bruce Weber.

Let's Get Married 🐾 1960 A young doctor's weakness under pressure brings him to the brink of babbling idiocy when his wife goes into early labor. 90m/B VHS. Hermione Baddeley, Bernie Winters, Anthony Newley, Ann Aubrey; *D:* Peter Graham Scott; *W:* Kent Taylor; *C:* Ted Moore; *M:* Edwin Astley.

Let's Get Tough 🐾 1942 The East Side Kids, unable to enlist because of their age, harass local Oriental shopkeepers and eventually get involved with a murder. 62m/B VHS, DVD. Leo Gorcey, Bobby Jordan, Huntz Hall, Gabriel Dell, Sammy (Earnest) Morrison; *D:* Wallace Fox.

Let's Go! 🐾½ 1923 The son of a cement company president sets out to prove his worth to the firm by landing a contract with the town of Hillsboro. For some unknown reason, he sets off on an amazing set of stunts. Silent with original organ music. 79m/B VHS. Richard Talmadge, Hal Clements, Eileen (Elaine Persey) Percy, Tully Marshall; *D:* William K. Howard.

Let's Go Collegiate 🐾½ 1941 Two college rowers promise their girlfriends that they'll win the big race, but their plans are almost frustrated when their best oarsman is drafted. Their only hope lies in replacing him with a truck driver. ♪Look What You've Done To Me;

Sweet 16; Let's Do A Little Dreaming. **62m/ B** VHS, DVD. Frankie Darro, Marcia Mae Jones, Jackie Moran, Kaye Luke, Mantan Moreland, Gale Storm; **D:** Jean Yarbrough.

Let's Go to Prison 🐾½ **2006 (R)** What we have here is a failure to entertain. John Lyshtski (Shepard) is a bitter ex-con who plots revenge on the judge who sent him up the river three times. John sets up the judge's preppy son Nelson (Arnatt), then gets himself thrown back in the pokey so he can give Nelson terrible advice on prison survival. Standard jokes about bad food, soap-dropping and license plates ensue. Eventually, situations involving a psycho white supremacist (Shannon) and an amorous black prisoner (McBride) turn the tables on John. It's not very funny considering the comedy pedigree of director Odenkirk and the majority of the cast. **84m/C** VHS, DVD. **US** Dax Shepard, Will Arnett, Chi McBride, David Koechner, Dylan Baker, Michael Shannon; **D:** Bob Odenkirk; **W:** Robert Ben Garant, Thomas Lennon, Michael Patrick Jann; **C:** Ramsay Nickell; **M:** Alan Elliott.

Let's Kill All the Lawyers 🐾½ **1993 (R)** Low-budget satire about one man's angst over whether to become a lawyer is witty, entertaining, and not just for legal eagles. Law-firm intern Foster Merkul (Frederick) is apprenticed to a sleezeball (Vezina) who teaches him the finer points of the law biz. Growing in creasingly disillusioned, Foster sets out to reform the system with the help of Satori, a beautiful and mysterious creature of his imagination. Shot at sites in and around Detroit, this independent production features lots of cameos by local media celebrities. **103m/C** VHS, Rick Frederick, James Vezina, Michelle Da Vuono, Maggie Patton, Marty Smith; **D:** Ron Senkowski; **W:** Ron Senkowski.

Let's Make It Legal 🐾½ **1951** Amusing comedy of a married couple who decide to get a divorce after 20 years of marriage. Colbert stars as the woman who decides to leave her husband, Carey, because he's a chronic gambler. They part as friends, but soon Colbert's old flame, Scott, is back in town and things get rather complicated. A solid cast serves as the main strength in this film. **77m/B** VHS, DVD. Claudette Colbert, MacDonald Carey, Zachary Scott, Barbara Bates, Robert Wagner, Marilyn Monroe, Frank Cady, Kathleen Freeman; **D:** Richard Sale; **W:** F. Hugh Herbert, I.A.L. Diamond; **C:** Lucien Balard; **M:** Cyril Mockridge.

Let's Make Love 🐾🐾 **1960** An urbane millionaire discovers he is to be parodied in an off-Broadway play, and vows to stop it—until he falls in love with the star of the show. He then ends up acting in the play. ♫My Heart Belongs to Daddy; Let's Make Love; Specialization; Incurably Romantic; Sing Me a Song That Sells; You With the Crazy Eyes; Give Me the Simple Life. **118m/C** VHS, DVD. Yves Montand, Marilyn Monroe, Tony Randall, Frankie Vaughan, Bing Crosby, Gene Kelly, Milton Berle; **D:** George C. kor; **W:** Norman Krasna; **C:** George Cukor; **M:** Lionel Newman.

Let's Make Up 🐾🐾 _Lilacs in the Spring_ 1955 When it comes to giving her heart, Neagle can't decide between two dashing men. **94m/C** VHS, Anna Neagle, David Farrar, Kathleen Harrison, Peter Graves; **D:** Herbert Wilcox.

Let's Scare Jessica to Death 🐾🐾 **1971 (PG)** A young woman who was recently released from a mental hospital is subjected to unspeakable happenings at a country home with her friends. She encounters murder, vampires, and corpses coming out of nowhere. A supernatural thriller with quite a few genuine scares. **89m/C** VHS, DVD. Zohra Lampert, Barton Heyman, Kevin J. O'Connor, Gretchen Corbett; **D:** John Harcourt.

Let's Sing Again 🐾🐾 **1936** Eight-year-old singing sensation Bobby Breen made his debut in this dusty musical vehicle, as a runaway orphan who becomes the pal of a washed-up opera star in a traveling show. ♫Let's Sing Again; La Donna e Mobile. **70m/B** VHS, Bobby Breen, Henry Armetta, George

---

Houston, Vivienne Osborne, Grant Withers, Inez Courtney, Lucien Littlefield; **D:** Kurt Neumann.

Let's Talk About Sex 🐾½ **1998 (R)** Miami magazine columnist Jazz (Beyer) pitches her idea for a TV program about women who candidly discuss sex (more accurately, their complaints about men), but is told she has the weekend to create a sample video. Jazz enlists the help of her equally frustrated and unhappy friends, Michelle and Lena (Brewster and Ingerman), and armed with a video camera, the three comb the steamy streets of Miami asking random women personal questions about their sex lives and bailing them into complaining about men. Tries to comes across as a soft-core sex farce/soap opera. Beyer also wrote and directed. **82m/C** VHS, Troy Beyer, Randi Ingerman, Joseph C. Phillips, Paget Brewster, Victhaine Bebich, Tina Nguyen; **D:** Troy Beyer; **W:** Troy Beyer; **C:** Kely Evans; **M:** Michael Carpenter.

The Letter 🐾🐾🐾 **1940** When a man s shot and killed on a Malaysian plantation, the woman who committed the murder pleads self-defense. Her husband and her lawyer attempt to free her, but find more than they expected in this tightly paced film noir. Based on the novel by W. Somerset Maugham. Davis emulated the originator of her role, Jeanne Eagels, in her mannerisms and line readings, although Eagels later went mad from drug abuse and overwork. **96m/B** VHS, DVD. Bette Davis, Herbert Marshall, James Stephenson, Gale Sondergaard, Bruce Lester, Cecil Kellaway, Victor Sen Yung, Frieda Inesort; **D:** William Wyler; **W:** Howard Koch; **C:** Gaetano Antonio "Tony" Gaudio; **M:** Max Steiner.

Letter from an Unknown Woman 🐾🐾🐾 **1948** A woman falls in love with a concert pianist on the eve of his departure. He promises to return but never does. The story is told in flashbacks as the pianist reads a letter from the woman. A great romantic melodrama. **90m/B** VHS, DVD. Joan Fontaine, Louis Jourdan, Mady Christians, Marcel Journet, Art Smith; **D:** Max Ophuls; Natl. Film Reg. '92.

Letter of Introduction 🐾🐾½ **1938** A struggling young actress learns that her father is 'really a well known screen star and agrees not to reveal the news to the public. **104m/B** VHS, DVD. Adolphe Menjou, Edgar Bergen, George Murphy, Eve Arden, Ann Sheridan, Andrea Leeds; **D:** John M. Stehi; **C:** Karl Freund.

Letter to Brezhnev 🐾🐾🐾 **1986 (R)** Acclaimed independent film about two working-class Liverpool girls who fall in love with two furloughed Russian sailors. When the men eventually return to the USSR, one of the girls contacts the Russian Secretary General in an effort to rejoin her lover. Amusing tale of different relationships. **94m/C** VHS, **GB** Margi Clarke, Alexandra "Igg; Peter Firth, Ken Campbel, Tracy Lea, Alfred Molina, Angela Clarke; **D:** Chris Bernard; **W:** Frank Clarke; **M:** Alan Gill.

A Letter to Three Wives 🐾🐾🐾 **1949** Crain, Darnell, and Sothern star as three friends who, shortly before embarking on a Hudson River boat trip, each receive a letter from once... **92m/C** VHS, Marie Winningham, Nicholas Chimlund, Rip Torn, Josef Sommer, Eddie Jones, Dey Young; **D:** Jared Meyers; **W:** Norman Strum; **C:** Stephen M. Katz; **M:** Mason Daring. CABLE

Letter to My Killer 🐾½ **1995 (PG-13)** Construction worker Nick Parma (Chinlund) finds an unmailed letter in a demolished building, which he and wife Judy (Winningham) discover is 30 years old. The woman letter writer is describing major fraud and when Judy learns that she was murdered, she and Nick decide to blackmail the probable suspects—a powerful business cartel. But if they killed once... **92m/C** VHS, Mare Winningham, Nicholas Chinlund, Rip Torn, Josef Sommer, Eddie Jones, Dey Young; **D:** Jared Meyers; **W:** Norman Strum; **C:** Stephen M. Katz; **M:** Mason Daring. CABLE

---

most caustic scenes, including Douglas (as Sothern's husband) ranting against the advertising business which supports his wife's radio soap opera. Sharp dialogue, moving performances. Based on the novel by John Klempner. Remade for TV in 1985. **103m/B** VHS, DVD. Jeanne Crain, Linda Darnell, Ann Sothern, Kirk Douglas, Paul Douglas, Jeffrey Lynn, Thelma Ritter, Barbara Lawrence, Connie Gilchrist, Florence Bates; **D:** Joseph L. Mankiewicz; **W:** Joseph L. Mankiewicz; **C:** Arthur C. Miller; **M:** Alfred Newman; **V:** Celeste Holm. Oscars '49: Director, Adapt. Screenplay; Directors Guild '48: Director (Mankiewicz).

Letters from a Killer 🐾🐾 **1998 (R)** Death-row con Race Darnell (Swayze) has been corresponding with four women every since writing a best-seller about his conviction and sets him free. Race discovers that one of his correspondents—who believed she was his only love—is framing him for murder in revenge for his "betrayal" of her. **103m/C** VHS, DVD. Patrick Swayze, Gia Carides, Kim Myers, Olivia Birkelund, Tina Lifford, Elizabeth Ruscio, Roger E. Mosley, Bruce McGill, Mark Rolston; **D:** David Carson; **W:** Nicholas Hicks-Beach; **C:** John A. Alonzo; **M:** Dennis McCarthy.

Letters from Alou 🐾🐾 _Las Cartas de Alou_ **1990** African immigrant Alou is trying to get to Barcelona to meet up with a friend but faces much exploitation and discrimination along the way. Spanish with subtitles. **95m/C** VHS, **SP** Mulie Jarju, Eulalia Ramon; **D:** Montxo Armendariz; **W:** Montxo Armendariz.

Letters from Iwo Jima 🐾🐾🐾🐾 **2006 (R)** Recounts the dramatic 36 days of battle on Iwo Jima that began in February 1945, as told from the Japanese viewpoint. Serves as a companion to director Eastwood's "Flags of Our Fathers." Facing a completely lopsided confrontation, the 22,000 Japanese military men kept about 110,000 American troops in combat far longer than anticipated under the guidance of the gifted Lt. Gen. Tadamichi Kuribayashi (Watanabe), whose letters to his wife provide the story's narrative. Setting a somber tone for the horrific losses incurred by both sides—nearly 21,000 Japanese and 7,000 Americans—are the muted colors used by Eastwood, who admirably captures the humanity of the Japanese men as they confront the impossible mission ahead. In direct comparison to "Flags," the ending has the Japanese viewing the raising of the American flag in the distance rather than close-up. First screenplay by Yamashita after being a research assistant on "Flags" in Japanese with subtitles. **145m/C** DVD, Blu-ray Disc, HD DVD. **US** Ken(saku) Watanabe, Tsuyoki Ihara, Shido Nakamura, Kazunari Ninomiya, Ryo Kase; **D:** Clint Eastwood; **W:** Iris Yamashita, Paul Haggis; **C:** Tom Stern; **M:** Kyle Eastwood, Michael Stevens. Oscars '06: Sound FX Editing; Golden Globes '07: Foreign Film.

Letters from My Windmill 🐾🐾½ **1954** A series of three short stories: "The Three Low Masses," "The Elixir of Father Gaucher," and "The Secret of Master Cornille" from respected director Pagnol. The unique for dramatic only enhances this film. In French with English subtitles. **116m/B** VHS, FR Henri Velbert, Yvonne Gamy, Robert Vattier, Roger Crouzet; **D:** Marcel Pagnol.

Letters from the Park 🐾🐾🐾 _Cartas del Parque_ **1988** In Cuba, 1913, two tacitiurn would-be lovers hire a poet Victor La Place, to write love letters to each other. Normal probolosis aside, the poet follows the tale of Cyrano, and finds himself the unhappy hypotenuse in a triangular romance. Based on an original story by Marquez; made for Spanish TV. Subtitled. **85m/C** VHS, CU Victor Laplace, Ivonne Lopez, Miguel Paneque; **D:** Tomas Gutierrez Alea; **W:** Tomas Gutierrez Alea, Gabriel Garcia Marquez; **C:** Mario Garcia Joya. TV

Letters to an Unknown Lover 🐾🐾½ _Les Louves_ **1984** During WWII, a man and woman engage in sexual and emotional combat. **101m/C** VHS, **GB** Cherie Lunghi, Mathilda May, Yves Beneyton, Ralph Bates; **D:** Peter Duffel.

Letting Go 🐾🐾 **1985 (PG)** Comedy-drama about a broken-hearted career woman and a young widower who fall in love. **94m/C** VHS, DVD. John Ritter, Sharon Gless, Joe Cortese; **D:** Jack Bender. TV

Letting the Birds Go Free **1986** When a stranger is caught stealing from a farmer's barn, the farmer and his son decide to let the villain work off his crime. Some very interesting relationships develop from this arrangement. **60m/C** VHS, Lionel Jeffries.

Leviathan 🐾🐾 **1989 (R)** A motley crew of ocean-floor miners are trapped when they are accidentally exposed to a failed Soviet experiment that turns humans into insatiable, regenerating fish-creatures. **98m/C** VHS, DVD. Peter Weller, Ernie Hudson, Hector Elizondo, Amanda Pays, Richard Crenna, Daniel Stern, Lisa Eilbacher, Michael Carmine, Meg Foster; **D:** George P. Cosmatos; **W:** David Peoples, Jeb Stuart; **C:** Alex Thomson; **M:** Jerry Goldsmith.

Levitation 🐾½ **1997** Pregnant teenager Acey (Paulson), decides to leave her unhappy adoptive parents and search for her birth mother. She has an imaginary friend (possibly her guardian angel) she calls Bob (London) and a real friend, DJ Downtime (Hudson), to help her but her quest doesn't end in happiness. Title refers to Acey's weird uncontrollable ability to levitate, unfortunately the film doesn't—it's a muddled mess. **99m/C** VHS, DVD. Sarah Paulson, Jeremy London, Ann Magnuson, Brett Cullen, Christopher Boyer; **D:** Scott Goldstein; **W:** Scott Goldstein; **C:** Michael G. Wojciechowski; **M:** Leonard Rosenman.

Levity 🐾🐾 **2003 (R)** Manuel Jordan (Thornton) has just been released from prison after serving 22 years of a life sentence for killing a clerk during a botched robbery. He returns to his neighborhood, looking for, but not expecting to find redemption. What he finds is a job working at a community center run by a fire-and-brimstone preacher, possible romance with the sister (Hunter) of his victim, her troubled son, and a self-destructive club kid, along with the wish to protect them all from contrived coincidences and over-wrought sentimentality. Soloman was going for mood and atmospheric, and while it is moody (and crushingly boring), it's not very atmospheric. What it is is a complete waste of a talented cast. **100m/C** VHS, DVD. **US** Billy Bob Thornton, Morgan Freeman, Holly Hunter, Kirsten Dunst, Dorian Harewood, Geoff Wigdor, Catherine Colvey, Manuel Aranguiz, Luke Robertson, Billoah Greene; **D:** Edward Solomon; **W:** Edward Solomon; **C:** Roger Deakins; **M:** Mark Oliver Everett.

Lewis and Clark and George 🐾🐾🐾 **1997 (R)** Lewis (Xuereb) is a dim-witted killer and Clark (Gunther) is a computer nerd. Both are prison escapees in possession of what is supposed to be a map to a gold mine. Lewis happens to be illiterate and needs Clark, who's afraid of Lewis's trigger-happy ways. George (McGowan) is a sexy mute thief who takes both men for quite a wild ride. Filmed in rural New Mexico. **84m/C** VHS, DVD. Salvator Xuereb, Dan Gunther, Rose McGowan, Art LaFleur, Aki Aleong, James Brolin, Paul Bartel; **D:** Rod McCall; **W:** Rod McCall; **C:** Mike Mayers; **M:** Ben Vaughn.

L'Homme Blesse 🐾🐾🐾 _The Wounded Man_ **1983** The serious erotic film about 18-year-old Henri (Anglade), cloistered by an overbearing family, and his sudden awakening to his own homosexuality. Anglade's film debut. In French with English subtitles. **90m/C** VHS, DVD. FR Jean-Hugues Anglade, Roland Bertin, Vittorio Mezzogiorno; **D:** Patrice Chereau; **C:** Renato Berta. Cesar '84: Writing.

Liam 🐾🐾 **2000 (R)** Stuttering, 7-year-old Liam (Borrows) is an Irish Catholic living in Liverpool in the 1930s. His hard-working mother is determined that Liam will look presentable for his first Communion no matter what the sacrifice as the family's struggles worsen when his father (Hart) loses his job and becomes increasingly bitter, blaming his woes on others and turning to violence as a solution.

c VHS, DVD. *GE GB* Ian Hart, Claire Hackett, David Hart, Anthony Borrows, Megan Burns, Anne Reid, Russell Dixon, Julia Deakin, Andrew Schofield, Bernadette Short, Colin Patrick Lynch; **D:** Jeff Frears; **W:** Jimmy McGovern; **C:** Andrew Dunn; **M:** John Murphy.

Liane, Jungle Goddess 🐾🐾
1956 A variation on the Greystoke legend featuring a beautiful (and topless) jungle goddess who is discovered living in the wilds of Africa. Thinking that she may be the lost granddaughter of a wealthy English nobleman, she's brought back to London for a reunion. Will civilization prove to be as dangerous as the jungle? **88m/C VHS, DVD.** *GE* Marion Michael, Hardy Kruger, Irene Galter, Peter Mosbacher; **D:** Eduard von Borsody; **C:** Bruno Timm; **M:** Erwin Halletz.

Lianna 🐾🐾🐾
1983 (R) Acclaimed screenwriter/director John Sayles wrote and directed this story of a woman's romantic involvement with another woman. Chronicles an unhappy homemaker's awakening to the feelings of love that she develops for a female professor. Sayles makes an appearance as a family friend. **110m/C VHS, DVD.** Jon (John) DeVries, Linda Griffiths, Jane Hallaren, Jo Henderson, Jessica Wight MacDonald; **Cameos:** John Sayles; **D:** John Sayles; **W:** John Sayles; **M:** Mason Daring.

Liar Liar 🐾🐾½ **1997 (PG-13)** Carrey takes on one of his less manic but still appealing personas as compulsive liar and attorney Fletcher Reid. A constant disappointment to his ex-wife Audrey (Tierney) and young son Max (Cooper), Fletcher is forced to tell nothing but the truth for 24 hours, thanks to his son's supernatural birthday wish. This puts a crimp in his legal practice, especially as he tries to defend brazen would-be divorcee Samantha Cole (Tilly). Gets kinda sappy but Carrey can carry almost any situation. **87m/C VHS, DVD, HD DVD.** Jim Carrey, Jennifer Tilly, Maura Tierney, Amanda Donohoe, Swoosie Kurtz, Justin Cooper, Jason Bernard, Mitchell Ryan, Anne Haney, Chip (Christopher) Mayer, Randall "Tex" Cobb, Cary Elwes, Eric Pierpoint, Cheri Oteri; **D:** Tom Shadyac; **W:** Paul Guay, Stephen Mazur; **C:** Russell Boyd; **M:** John Debney. MTV Movie Awards '98: Comedic Perf. (Carrey).

The Liar's Club 🐾🐾 **1993 (R)** High-school football teammates try to cover up a rape and wind up involved in murder. **100m/C VHS.** Wil. Wheaton, Brian Krause, Soleil Moon Frye, Jennifer Burns, Michael Cudlitz, Bruce Weitz; **D:** Jeffrey Porter.

Liar's Edge 🐾🐾 **1992 (R)** Tweed portrays a single mother whose teenaged son, Mark, is plagued by violent fantasies. When she remarries and her new husband and sleazy brother-in-law move in, Mark's hallucinations become stronger until he believes he's witnessed a murder. The murder turns out to be a fact and his new stepfather is involved but can Mark prove it. Filmed on location in Niagra Falls. **97m/C VHS.** Shannon Tweed, Nicholas Shields, David Keith, Joseph Bottoms, Christopher Plummer; **D:** Ron Oliver; **W:** Ron Oliver.

Liar's Moon 🐾🐾 **1982 (PG)** A local boy woos and weds the town's wealthiest young lady, only to be trapped in family intrigue. **106m/C VHS, DVD.** Cindy Fisher, Matt Dillon, Christopher Connelly, Susan Tyrrell; **D:** David Fisher.

Liar's Poker 🐾½ **1999** Car salesman Jack (Tyson) has invested a quarter-million bucks in friend Vic's (Blondell) club to silence Jack is beginning to silence. Married Jack is also competing with bud, Niko (Luisi), for the affections of young babe, Rebecca (Heinle) while his own wife, Linda (Gridley), plays around. And fourth buddy Freddie (Flea) enjoys knowing too much about everybody else's business. It finally comes down to a deadly confrontation between the male foursome. Unfortunately, bland acting and a lack of plot details detract from this macho crime drama's twisty ending. **93m/C VHS, DVD.** Richard Tyson, Flea, Jimmy Blondell, Caesar Luisi, Pamela Gidley, Amelia Heinle, Neith Adriana, Colin Patrick Lynch; **D:** Jeff Santo; **W:** Jeff Santo; **C:** Giles M.I. Dunning; **M:** Peter Himmelman.

Libeled Lady 🐾🐾🐾½ **1936** A fast, complicated screwball masterwork. Newspaper editor Warren Haggerty (Tracy) prints an erroneous story that heiress Connie Allenbury (Loy) is after a married man. Connie sues and in order to defuse the lawsuit, Warren comes up with an elaborate scheme (certain to backfire) that involves his own fiancee Gladys (Harlow) and recently fired reporter Bill (Powell). Remade in 1946 as "Easy to Wed." **98m/B VHS, DVD.** Myrna Loy, Spencer Tracy, Jean Harlow, William Powell, Walter Connolly, Charley Grapewin, Cora Witherspoon, E.E. Clive, Charles Trowbridge, Dennis O'Keefe, Hattie McDaniel; **D:** Jack Conway; **W:** George Oppenheimer, Howard Emmett Rogers, Maurine Watkins; **C:** Norbert Brodine; **M:** William Axt.

The Liberation of L.B. Jones 🐾🐾 **1970 (R)** A wealthy black undertaker wants a divorce from his wife, who is having an affair with a white policeman. Wyler's final film. **101m/C VHS.** Lee J. Cobb, Lola Falana, Barbara Hershey, Anthony Zerbe, Roscoe Lee Browne; **D:** William Wyler; **M:** Elmer Bernstein.

Liberators 🐾 **1969** Kinski stars as a criminal soldier battling with the American authorities, German troops, and his fugitive partner. **91m/C VHS, DVD.** *IT* George Hilton, Ray Saunders, Betsy Bell, Klaus Kinski; **D:** Tonino Ricci; **W:** Tonino Ricci; **C:** Sandro Mancori; **M:** Riz Ortolani.

The Libertine 🐾🐾 *La Matriaca* **1969** Mimi (Spaak) is a young widow who's just discovered her late husband kept a separate apartment equipped to satisfy his more unusual sexual desires. Intrigued, Mimi decides to keep the apartment and do her own sexual exploring. Dubbed. **90m/C VHS, DVD.** *IT* Catherine Spaak, Jean-Louis Trintignant, Luigi Pistilli, Luigi Proietti, Renzo Montagnani; **D:** Pasquale Festa Campanile; **C:** Alfio Contini; **M:** Armando Trovajoli.

The Libertine 🐾½ **2005 (R)** Covering a portion of the life of the 17th century's famous degenerate the 2nd Earl of Rochester, John Wilmot (Depp). Depp's portrayal is well done, but the story eventually collapses under its own weight. A little taste of Wilmot's naughtiness might be interesting, even fun, but watching him destroy himself with dreadful behavior over and over begins to feel tiresome. Like watching a heavyweight prize fight, eventually you hope the fallen fighter just stays down, relieving everyone's pain. **130m/C DVD.** Johnny Depp, Samantha Morton, John Malkovich, Rosamund Pike, Tom Hollander, Kelly Reilly, Jack Davenport, Richard Coyle, Francesca Annis, Rupert Friend, Clare Higgins, Johnny Vegas; **D:** Laurence Dunmore; **W:** Stephen Jeffreys; **C:** Alexander Melman; **M:** Michael Nyman.

Liberty & Bash 🐾 **1990 (R)** Two boyhood friends who served together in Vietnam reunite to rid their neighborhood of drug pushers and save the life of a friend. **92m/C VHS.** Miles O'Keeffe, Lou Ferrigno, Mitzi Kapture, Richard Eden, Cheryl Paris, Gary Conway; **D:** Myrl A. Schreibman.

Liberty Heights 🐾🐾½ **1999 (R)** Levinson heads back to Baltimore (for the fourth time) for his 1954 coming of age/family drama with his focus on the city's Jewish community and the Kurtzman family in particular. Nate (Mantegna) has a two-bit numbers racket and a family burlesque house, college son Van (Brody) falls for a shiksa (Murphy), while high schooler Ben (Foster) is captivated by Sylvia (Johnson), the first black student in his class. It may be too early for Bob Dylan but the times were a-changin' indeed and Levinson takes an unsentimental, if heartfelt, look at his past. **127m/C VHS, DVD.** Adrien Brody, Joe Mantegna, Ben Foster, Bebe Neuwirth, Rebekah Johnson, Orlando Jones, Frania Rubinek, David Krumholtz, Richard Kline, Vincent Guastaferro, Carolyn Murphy, Justin Chambers, James Pickens Jr., Anthony Anderson, Kiersten Warren; **D:** Barry Levinson; **W:** Barry Levinson; **C:** Christopher Doyle; **M:** Andrea Morricone.

Liberty Stands Still 🐾🐾 **2002 (R)** Title lends itself to several interpretations, one of which is literal. If Liberty Wallace (Fiorentino) doesn't stand still, she's a dead woman. Liberty is the wife of gun manufacturer Victor (Platt). She takes a cell call while walking in downtown L.A. and is informed if she doesn't handcuff herself to a nearby hotdog cart and keep talking that she will immediately be shot. Joe (Snipes), the sniper/caller, then informs Liberty that he has placed a bomb in the cart itself. His daughter was murdered by a gun and this is his way to bring attention to the situation. Good cast but the points are belabored—guns bad, we get it. **96m/C VHS, DVD.** Wesley Snipes, Linda Fiorentino, Oliver Platt, Martin Cummins, Hart Bochner, Jonathan Scarfe, Ian Tracey; **D:** Kari Skogland; **W:** Kari Skogland; **C:** Denis Maloney; **M:** Michael Convertino.

License to Drive 🐾🐾 **1988 (PG-13)** When teen Haim fails the road test for his all-important driver's license, he steals the family car for a hot date with the girl of his dreams. The evening starts out quietly enough, but things soon go awry. If Haim survives the weekend, he'll definitely be able to pass his driving test on Monday morning. Semi-funny in a demolition derby sort of way. **90m/C VHS, DVD.** Corey Feldman, Corey Haim, Carol Kane, Richard Masur, Michael Manasseri; **D:** Greg Beeman; **C:** Bruce Surtees; **M:** Jay Ferguson.

License to Kill 🐾🐾 **1964** Constantine stars as Agent Nick Carter involved with Oriental spies and a new secret weapon. **100m/C VHS.** *FR* Eddie Constantine, Yvonne Monlaur, Paul Frankeur; **D:** Henri Decoin.

License to Kill 🐾🐾 **1984** A young girl is killed by a drunk driver, devastating both families. Offers a strong message against drinking and driving. **96m/C VHS, DVD.** James Farentino, Don Murray, Penny Fuller, Millie Perkins, Donald Moffat, Denzel Washington, Ari Meyers; **D:** Jud Taylor. *TV*

License to Kill 🐾🐾🐾 **1989 (PG-13)** Dalton's second Bond effort, in which drug lords try to kill 007's best friend and former CIA agent. Disobeying orders for the first time and operating without his infamous "license to kill," Bond goes after the fiends. Fine outing for Dalton (and Bond, too). **133m/C VHS, DVD.** *GB* Timothy Dalton, Carey Lowell, Robert Davi, Frank McRae, Talisa Soto, David Hedison, Anthony Zerbe, Everett McGill, Wayne Newton, Benicio Del Toro, Desmond Llewelyn, Priscilla Barnes, Robert Brown, Tom Adams; **D:** John Glen; **W:** Michael G. Wilson, Richard Maibaum; **C:** Alec Mills; **M:** Michael Kamen.

License to Wed 🐾 **2007 (PG-13)** Nothing redeems this dull, obnoxious comedy that mostly serves as a vehicle for Williams to do the same ad-libbed characters he's been doing for years. Newly engaged couple Ben and Sadie (Krasinski and Moore) must undergo Rev. Frank's (Williams) premarital counseling, but what they get is an endless series of laugh-free, sadism-lite tests of endurance. Nothing, from Ben and Sadie's cliche personality mismatch, to Frank's junior sadist sidekick Choir Boy (Flitter), saves this movie from being a big "I don't" for all involved. **91m/C DVD, Blu-ray Disc, HD DVD.** John Krasinski, Mandy Moore, John Krasinski, Eric Christian Olsen, Christine Taylor, Peter Strauss, Rachael Harris, DeRay Davis, Angela Kinsey, Mindy Kaling, Brian Baumgartner, Josh Flitter; **D:** Ken Kwapis; **C:** John Bailey; **M:** Christophe Beck.

The Lickerish Quartet 🐾🐾 **1970 (R)** A bored, aristocratic couple live with their teenaged son in a secluded castle in Italy's Abruzzi mountains. Traveling to a nearby carnival, they think they recognize the female daredevil as the same actress they've just seen in a home-viewed porno film. So they invite her back to the castle for a little family fun—only she may not be the same woman at all. **90m/C VHS, DVD.** Silvana Venturelli, Frank Wolff, Erika Remberg, Paolo Turco; **D:** Radley Metzger; **W:** Michael DeForrest; **C:** Hans Jura.

L'Idiot 🐾🐾 *The Idiot* **1946** Smooth adaptation of Dostoevsky's novel about noble Prince Mishkin's (Philipe) attempts to bring peace to the life of tormented Nastasia Filipovna (Feuillere). First feature for Lampin; French with subtitles. **98m/B VHS.** *FR* Gerard Philipe, Edwige Feuillere, Lucien Coedel, Nathalie Nattier, Marguerite Moreno; **D:** Georges Lampin; **W:** Charles Spaak; **C:** Christian Matras; **M:** Maurice Thiriet.

L.I.E. 🐾🐾 **2001 (NC-17)** Can you say "controversial"? 15-year-old Howie's (Dano) mother has recently died in a car accident on the Long Island Expressway (hence the title) and his world is falling apart. His dad, Marty, (Blitzer), brings his bimbo girlfriend to stay and has some very shady business dealings. Meanwhile, Howie is hanging out with teen troublemaker Gary (Kay), who is both a thief and a hustler. Gary and Howie break into the home of ex-Marine, Big John Harrigan (Cox), who as it turns out, is a pedophile who discovers and confronts the boys and takes a purient interest in Howie's charms. At least at first, since the complex Harrigan realizes Howie really needs some friendly guidance and not a sex partner. Cuesta offers no apologies or explanations for the behavior he depicts and Cox is both commanding and subtle. **97m/C VHS, DVD.** *US* Brian Cox, Paul Franklin Dano, Billy Kay, Bruce Altman, James Costa, Tony Donnelly, Walter Masterson, Marcia DeBonis, Adam LeFevre; **D:** Michael Cuesta; **W:** Michael Cuesta, Stephen M. Ryder, Gerald Cuesta; **C:** Romeo Tirone; **M:** Pierre Foldes. Ind. Spirit '02: Debut Perf. (Dano).

Lie Down with Dogs 🐾 **1995 (R)** You will wake up with fleas if you watch this dull, very low-budget comedy about young Tommie (White), who heads out of New York for some summer fun in the gay-friendly resort of Provincetown, Massachusetts. There's lots of temporary (discreetly filmed) encounters but no lasting romance and Tommie heads back to the Big Apple at season's end satisfied but no wiser. White's debut film. **85m/C VHS, DVD.** Wally White, Randy Becker, Darren Dryden; **D:** Wally White; **W:** Wally White; **C:** George Mitas.

Lie Down with Lions 🐾🐾 **1994** Long and dull TV adaptation of the Ken Follett spy novel. American nurse Kate Neeson (Helgenberger) is aghast when she discovers her lover, Jack Carver (Dalton), is a CIA agent. She marries Czech doctor Peter Husak (Havers) on the rebound and the newlyweds travel to Azerbijan to run a clinic, where Kate has a baby. But Jack's not out of the picture since his current assignment takes him into Kate's life, especially when he discovers Peter is not what he seems. On three cassettes. **136m/C VHS.** Timothy Dalton, Marg Helgenberger, Nigel Havers, Omar Sharif, Kabir Bedi, Jurgen Prochnow; **D:** Jim Goddard; **W:** Guy Andrews, Julian Bond; **C:** Eddy van der Enden.

Liebelei 🐾🐾 **1932** Fritz (Liebeneiner), a handsome lieutenant, has broken off his romance with a married baroness and fallen for young opera singer Christine (Schneider) in turn-of-the-century Vienna. However, when the jealous baron (Grundgens) learns of his wife's infidelity, he challenges Fritz to a duel. Remade as "Christine" in 1967, with Romy Schneider in her mother's role. In German with English subtitles. **82m/B VHS.** *GE* Magda Schneider, Wolfgang Liebeneiner, Gustav Grundgens; **D:** Max Ophuls.

Liebestraum 🐾🐾 **1991 (R)** An architectural expert, his old college friend, and the friend's wife form a dangerous triangle of passion and lust that strangely duplicates a situation that led to a double murder 40 years earlier. The unrated version clocks in at 116 minutes. **109m/C VHS, DVD.** Kevin Anderson, Bill Pullman, Pamela Gidley, Kim Novak; **D:** Mike Figgis; **W:** Mike Figgis; **C:** Juan Ruiz-Anchia; **M:** Mike Figgis.

Lies 🐾🐾½ **1983 (PG)** Complicated mystery about a murder/thriller movie plot becoming reality as it is being filmed, revolving around a scam to collect an inheritance from a rich guy in a mental hospital. **93m/C VHS.** *GB* Ann Dusenberry, Gail Strickland,

Lies & Alibis 🐾🐾½ *The Alibi* 2006 (R) Ray Elliot (Coogan) runs a successful L.A. service that offers alibis to cheating spouses. But he doesn't expect Wendell (Marsden), the screw-up son of Ray's best client, tycoon Robert Hatch (Broin), to accidentally kill his fling Heather (King) during some kinky sex play. So Ray and his new assistant Lola (Romijn), she of the cool head and hot bod, have to really come up with a good alibi, especially when a police detective (Mazer) comes around. Clever crime comedy with Coogan a capable leading man and all pros. Broin and Elliot (as an unhappy Mormon with a cheating wife) obviously enjoying their roles. 90m/C DVD. Steve Coogan, Rebecca Romijn, James Broin, John Leguizamo, James Marsden, Sam Elliott, Debi Mazar, Selma Blair, Deborah Kara Unger, Henry Rollins, Sharon Lawrence, Jaime (James) King; **D:** Matt Checkowski; **W:** Noah Hawley; **C:** Enrique Chediak; **M:** Alexandre Desplat.

Lies and Whispers 🐾🐾 *Prague Duet* 1998 (R) American child psychologist Dr. Lauren Granger (Gershon) is attending a medical convention in Prague, meets dissident Czech writer Jiri Kolnar (Serbedzija), falls instantly in love and becomes engaged. Lauren decides to explore her own family's ties to the country and discovers a very embarrassing revelation for Jiri, who's about to be appointed to a government post. 99m/C VHS, DVD. Gina Gershon, Rade Serbedzija, Patricia Hodge, Otakar Brousek, Gordon Lovitt, Stuart Milligan; **D:** Roger L. Simon; **W:** Roger L. Simon, Sherry Lonjin; **C:** Ivan Slapeta; **M:** Boris Zelkin.

Lies Before Kisses 🐾🐾 1992 A woman finds out her loving husband has been spending time with a beautiful call girl. When the call girl is murdered, the husband is accused. His wife decides to help him clear his name but she just may have her own type of revenge in mind. 93m/C VHS. Jaclyn Smith, Ben Gazzara, Nick Mancuso, Greg Evigan, Penny Fuller, James Karen; **D:** Lou Antonio; **W:** Ellen Weston.

Lies of the Twins 🐾🐾 1991 A beautiful model becomes involved with her therapist and his identical and irresponsible, twin brother. 93m/C VHS. Isabella Rossellini, Aidan Quinn, Imen, John Pleshette; **D:** Tim Hunter.

Lies My Father Told Me 🐾🐾🐾 1975 (PG) Simple drama about growing up in the 1920s in a Jewish ghetto. The story revolves around a young boy's relationship with his immigrant grandfather. Quiet and moving. 102m/C VHS. Yossi Yadin, Len Birman, Marilyn Lightstone, Jeffry Lynas; **D:** Jan Kadar; **W:** Ted Allan. Golden Globes '76: Foreign Film.

Life 🐾🐾½ 1995 Explores the relationships between a group of prisoners doing time in a prison unit for HIV-positive inmates and what it means to be a man. Stylized production was developed from Brumpton's 1991 play "Containment." Feature film debut for director Johnston. 85m/C VHS. At John Brumpton, David Tredinnick, Dick Van Dyke, Nancy Kwan, Akim Tamiroff; **D:** Byron Peul; **M:** Robert F. Brunner.

Lt. Robin Crusoe, U.S.N. 🐾 1966 (G) A lighthearted navy pilot crash lands amusingly on a tropical island, falls hard for an island babe and schemes intensely against the local evil ruler. Lackluster Disney debacle. 113m/C VHS, DVD. Dick Van Dyke, Nancy Kwan, Akim Tamiroff; **D:** Byron Paul; **M:** Robert F. Brunner.

Life 🐾🐾½ 1999 (R) New Yorkers Ray (Murphy) and Claude (Lawrence) head south on a moonshine run to pay off a debt to a bootlegger (Jarreau). Along the way, they're framed for murder and sentenced to life at a Mississippi prison farm. Through the years, the two develop a deep, but insult-filled friendship while adjusting to prison life and harboring dreams of freedom. Murphy and Lawrence click well as a comic team, and the movie is best when it stays out of their way. The institutionalized racism of the setting is treated superficially, with the prison appearing to be, despite the slave-like work and gun-toting guards, not an entirely horrible place to live. 108m/C VHS, DVD. Eddie Murphy, Martin Lawrence, Ned Beatty, Cicely Tyson, Clarence Williams III, Obba Babatunde, Bernie Mac, Michael "Bear" Taliferro, Miguel A. Nunez Jr., Bokeem Woodbine, Barry (Shadeka) Henley, Brent Jennings, Guy Torry, Lisa Nicole Carson, Ned Vaughn, R. Lee Ermey, Nick Cassavetes, Noah Emmerich, Anthony Anderson, Rick James; **D:** Ted Demme; **W:** Robert Ramsey, Matthew Stone; **C:** Geoffrey Simpson; **M:** Nelust Wyclef Jean.

The Life and Death of Colonel Blimp 🐾🐾🐾 *Colonel Blimp* 1943 Chronicles the life of a British soldier who survives three wars (Boer, WWI, and WWII), falls in love with three women (all portrayed by Kerr), and dances a fine waltz. Fine direction and performance abound. 115m/C VHS, DVD. GB Roger Livesey, Deborah Kerr, Anton Walbrook, Ursula Jeans, Albert Lieven, John Varley; **D:** Michael Powell, Emeric Pressburger; **C:** Georges Perinal.

The Life and Loves of Mozart 🐾🐾½ 1959 Despite the title, this is really about the great composer's life later in life at the time of the premiere of "Die Zauberlfoere" ("The Magic Flute"). This is only partly saved by a stellar performance from Werner, as well as the music. Other than that it gets bogged down in titillation about W.A.M.'s romantic life. In German with English subtitles. 87m/C VHS, DVD. GR Oskar Werner, Johanna (Hanner) Matz, Angelika Hauff; **D:** Karl Hartl; **V:** Anton Dermota.

The Life and Assassination of the Kingfish 1976 Recommended by the NEA, this story of Louisiana politician Huey Long is riveting. Asner gives a profound performance. 96m/C VHS, Ed Asner, Nicholas Pryor, Diane Kagan; **D:** Robert E. Collins.

The Life and Adventures of Nicholas Nickleby 🐾🐾🐾🐾 *Nicholas Nickleby* 1981 Nine-hour performance of the 1836 Dickens' tale by the Royal Shakespeare Company, featuring the outstanding talents of 39 actors portraying 150 characters. Wonderful performances are characterized by frantic action and smoothly meshing interlinking plots, focusing on the trials and tribulations of the Nickleby family, amidst wealth, poverty, and injustice in Victorian England. Nine cassettes. 540m/C VHS, DVD. GB Roger Rees, David Threlfall; **W:** David Edgar; **M:** Stephen Oliver.

Life According to Muriel 🐾🐾 *La Vida Segun Muriel* 1997 After her husband abandons her, Laura takes 9-year-old daughter Muriel and leaves Buenos Aires for the peace of the countryside. Only they lose all their stuff in an accident and are forced to rely on Mirta—another single mom who owns a run-down hotel. The women bond and start to fix up the place when Muriel's dad shows up wanting a second chance. Spanish with subtitles. 97m/C VHS, DVD. AR Ines Estevez, Jorge Perugorria, Florencia Camiletti, Federico Olivera, Soledad Villamil; **D:** Eduardo Milewicz; **W:** Eduardo Milewicz, Susana Silvestre; **C:** Esteban Sapir; **M:** Bob Telson.

Life & Times of Grizzly Adams 🐾🐾 1974 (G) Lightweight family adventure film based on the rugged life of legendary frontiersman, Grizzly Adams, that served as the launching pad for his TV series. Grizzly is mistakenly chased for a crime he didn't commit and along the way befriends a big bear. 93m/C VHS. Dan Haggerty, Denver Pyle, Lisa Jones, Marjorie Harper, Don Shanks; **D:** Richard Friedenberg.

The Life and Times of Hank Greenberg 🐾🐾🐾 1999 (PG) Excellent documentary tells the career of legendary frontiersman, Grizzly Adams, that served as the launching pad for his TV series.

Life & Times of Judge Roy Bean 🐾🐾½ 1972 (PG) Based on the life of the famed Texas "hanging judge," the film features Newman as the legendary Bean who dispenses frontier justice in the settings (New York and Detroit during the '20s and '30s) in which Greenberg grew up and rose to stardom. 95m/C VHS, DVD. **D:** Aviva Kempner; **W:** Aviva Kempner.

Life & Times of the Chocolate Killer 🐾½ 1988 Police turn against the hand that's helped them save property and lives, by framing a good samaritan with deeds done by the "Chocolate Killer." 75m/C VHS, Michael Adrian, Rod Browning, Tabi Cooper.

The Life Aquatic with Steve Zissou 🐾🐾 2004 (R) Director Anderson's muddled comedy follows the career of oceanographer Steve Zissou (Murray), famed for his series of pop-culture documentaries (think Jacques Cousteau). Zissou's latest mission is to take revenge on the shark that ate his longtime partner (Cassel). Besides his motley crew (including Dafoe and Gambon), there is Zissou's business partner/wife Eleanor (Huston), nosy reporter Jane (Blanchett), and amiable newcomer Ned (Wilson), who may be Steve's illegitimate son, as well as his archival slick Alistair Hennessey (Goldblum). **D:** Wes Anderson; **W:** Wes Anderson, Noah Baumbach; **C:** Robert Yeoman; **M:** Mark Mothersbaugh. Randall Poster.

The Life and Times of Hank Greenberg 🐾🐾🐾 1999 (PG) Excellent documentary tells the life of Detroit Tiger Hall of Fame first baseman Hank Greenberg through interviews with sportswriters, teammates, other players of the era, and fans (many of which were young Jewish boys who later became famous themselves), and archival footage from on and off the field. Details Greenberg's struggles as a high-profile Jew in a very anti-Semitic era and as a hero and source of inspiration to the Jewish community. Also does a fine job of exploring the era. 95m/C VHS. Lily Langtry; **D:** John Milius; **W:** John Milius; **M:** Maurice Jarre.

Life as a House 🐾🐾½ 2001 (R) George (Kline) is an architect who lives in a broken down shack surrounded by ritzy homes on California's Pacific shore. His ex-wife, Robin (Thomas) is raising their drugged-out Goth son Sam (Christensen) with her emotionally unavailable husband Peter (Sheridan). In quick succession, George is fired from his job and learns he has a fatal disease. He examines his life and decides to use his remaining time to tear down the old house and build a new one. He forces Sam to help him, intending to use the project as a means to repair his relationship with his son. Robin's feelings for George also rekindle, and they become more than friends once again. The performances of the excellent ensemble cast, especially Kline and Thomas, save this from being called "Sappy Symbolism" ... **W:** Mark Andrus; **C:** Vilmos Zsigmond; **M:** Mark Isham. Natl. Bd. of Review '01; Breakthrough Perf. (Christensen).

The Life Before This 🐾🐾 1999 Complicated tale has six overlapping stories and 44 characters that follow the lives of a group of Torontonians for 12 hours and ends in a casino heist and a related cafe shootout. Film begins and ends with the shooting and takes place in flashbacks that show how each person came to be in the wrong place at the wrong time. Very loosely based on a true incident. 92m/C VHS, DVD. CA Leslie Hope, David Hewlett, Joel S. Keller, Jacob Tierney, Alberta Watson, Jennifer Dale, Dan Lett, Catherine O'Hara, Martha Burns, Joe Pantoliano, Sarah Polley, Stephen Seibel, Cas Chellas; **C:** Norayr Kasper; **M:** Ron Suares, Genie '99: Support. Actress (O'Hara).

A Life in the Theater 🐾🐾½ 1993 Life in the theatre as a hammy stage veteran (Lemmon) shares his experiences (and his dressing room) with a callow newcomer (Broderick). Petty squabbles, missed cues, and rare candor are dispensed as the two stage scenes from their various repertory. Gentle, slight Mamet play, written when he was 25. 78m/C VHS. Jack Lemmon, Matthew Broderick; **D:** Gregory Mosher; **W:** David Mamet.

Life in the Fast Lane 🐾🐾 2000 (R) Mona has accidentally killed her boyfriend. And when his ghost starts to follow her everywhere, Mona realizes how much she still loves him. So just how do you make a romance between a live girl and a dead guy work? 92m/C VHS, DVD. Fairuza Balk, Patrick Dempsey, Tea Leoni, Debi Mazar, Noah Taylor, Udo Kier.

Life Is a Bed of Roses 🐾🐾 *La Vie est un Roman: Life is a Fairy Tale* 1983 Three intertwined stories from Resnais. Count Forbeck is building a castle in Ardennes, planning to start a utopian society before WWI interferes. After the war, Forbeck tries again, offering his friends a drug that will make them forget the past, although his former love Livia refuses the offer. By the 1980s, the castle has been transformed into a progressive school that allows children's imaginations to roam free, although not all the educators are comfortable with the idea. While the adults fuss over their methods, the children play a fairytale game of knights and dragons. In French with subtitles. 110m/C DVD. FR Ruggero Raimondi, Fanny Ardant, Andre Dussollier, Geraldine Chaplin, Pierre Arditi; **D:** Alain Resnais; **W:** Jean Gruault; **C:** Sabine Azema, Geraldine Chaplin, Pierre Arditi, Veronique Silver, Robert Manuel, Vittorio Gassman, Sabine Azema, Geraldine Chaplin; **D:** Alain Resnais; **W:** Jean Gruault; **M:** M. Philippe-Gerard.

Life Is a Long Quiet River 🐾🐾🐾 *La Vie Est Une Longue Fleuve Tranquille* 1988 Social comedy about a nurse who, infuriated with her married doctor employer/lover, switches two babies...

bies at birth. Twelve years later, after her lover's wife has died and he still refuses to marry her, she reveals the swap. The children are returned to their rightful families causing a multitude of confusion and adjustment. Directorial debut of Chatilliez. In French with English subtitles. **89m/C VHS.** *FR* Benoit Magimel, Helene Vincent, Andre Wilms, Daniel Gelin, Catherine Hiegel, Christine Pignet, Patrick Bouchitey, Valerie Lalande, Tara Romer, Jerome Floch, Sylvie Cubertafon; *D:* Etienne Chatiliez; *W:* Florence Quentin, Etienne Chatiliez; *M:* Gerard Kawczynski. Cesar '89: Support. Actress (Vincent), Writing.

Life Is Beautiful ✓✓½ 1979

A politically neutral man is arrested and tortured in pre-revolutionary Lisbon, and forced to make, and act on, a political commitment. Dubbed. **102m/C VHS.** *PT* Giancarlo Giannini, Ornella Muti; *D:* Grigori Chukhrai.

Life Is Beautiful (PG-13)

La Vita E Bella 1998 (PG-13) The notion of a "feel-good Holocaust comedy" shouldn't work. But Benigni's stunning epic is not, at its core, a Holocaust movie, but rather a story of endurance of family love. Benigni's Guido is so intent on *believing* that life is—and should be—beautiful, he goes to great lengths to ensure that vision for his wife and, particularly, his son. The first half is an amusing boy-meets-girl Italian comedy, with Benigni chasing his real-life wife (Braschi). The second half shifts to the concentration camps where Guido, his son, and—because she would not be parted from him—his wife are imprisoned. Guido invents an elaborate game to convince his son that the whole ordeal—the "trip"—is an endurance test to be won, with prizes forthcoming. If Benigni depicts the concentration camps as less than horrifying, he should be forgiven; his focus is on the love between father, son, and wife. Italian with subtitles. **122m/C VHS, DVD.** *IT* Roberto Benigni, Nicoletta Braschi, Giustino Durano, Sergio Bustric, Horst Buchholz, Giorgio Cantarini, Marisa Paredes, Lidia Alfonsi, Giuliana Lojodice; *D:* Roberto Benigni; *W:* Vincenzo Cerami, Roberto Benigni; *C:* Tonino Delli Colli; *M:* Nicola Piovani. Oscars '98: Actor (Benigni), Foreign Film, Orig. Dramatic Score; Australian Film Inst. '99: Foreign Film; British Acad. '98: Actor (Benigni); Cannes '98: Grand Jury Prize; Cesar '99: Foreign Film; Screen Actors Guild '98: Actor (Benigni); Broadcast Film Critics '98: Foreign Film.

Life Is Sweet ✓✓✓½ 1990 (R)

The consuming passions of food and drink focus the lives of an oddball English working-class family. Mother is always fixing family meals—in between helping her friend open a gourmet restaurant which features such revolting dishes as pork cyst and prune quiche. Dad is a chef who buys a snack truck and dreams of life on the road. Natalie and Nicola, the grown twins, are their meals in front of the television but Nicola is also a bulimic who binges and purges on chocolate bars behind her bedroom door. (Note the chocolate scene between Nicola and her boyfriend.) An affectionate, if sometimes unattractive, look at a chaotic family. **103m/C VHS.** *GB* Alison Steadman, Jane Horrocks, Jim Broadbent, Claire Skinner, Timothy Spall, Stephen Rea, David Thewlis; *D:* Mike Leigh; *W:* Mike Leigh. L.A. Film Critics '91: Support. Actress (Horrocks); Natl. Soc. Film Critics '91: Actress (Steadman), Film, Support. Actress (Horrocks).

A Life Less Ordinary ✓✓½ 1997 (R)

Third outing from U.K. team of Boyle/Hodge/Macdonald, who made "Shallow Grave" and "Trainspotting," has hapless janitor Robert (MacGregor) lose his job, girlfriend, and home. He reacts by kidnapping the boss's daughter Celine (Diaz); who's more upset at Robert's ineptness than anything else. Meanwhile two angels (Hunter and Lindo) are sent to make these two kids fall in love. Confused? You should be. Hodge's script looks like someone threw "It Happened One Night," "Stairway to Heaven," outtakes from a Tarantino movie, and a Road Runner cartoon into a blender and hit frappe. Some of the surreal set pieces work, and the MacGregor/Diaz chemistry clicks sporadically, but the overall effect is overkill. Producer MacDonald is the grandson of Emeric Pressburger, co-director of "Stairway to Heaven." **103m/C VHS, DVD.** Ewan McGregor, Cameron Diaz, Holly Hunter, Delroy Lindo, Ian Holm, Ian McNeice, Stanley Tucci, Dan Hedaya, Tony Shalhoub, Maury Chaykin, Judith Ivey, K.K. Dodds; *D:* Danny Boyle; *W:* John Hodge; *C:* Brian Tufano; *M:* David Arnold.

The Life of David Gale ✓✓ 2003 (R)

David Gale (Spacey) is an anti-death penalty activist awaiting his execution after being convicted for the rape and murder of his colleague Constance (Linney, in the film's only worthy performance). Told in flashback to hard-boiled reporter Bitsey (Winslet), his story plays out from his fall from respected philosophy professor to boorish drunk after an ill-advised dalliance with a student turns into a rape accusation. Pick your poison with this one. If you want social commentary, the heavy-handed diatribes and speechifying will assault you while you wait for the murder mystery-thriller elements to insult your intelligence with their telegraphed clues and convoluted, implausible plots and red herrings. Even more of a spectacular failure at blending the two genres than "Mississippi Burning." **130m/C VHS, DVD.** *US* Kevin Spacey, Kate Winslet, Laura Linney, Gabriel Mann, Matt Craven, Rhona Mitra, Leon Rippy, Jim Beaver; *D:* Alan Parker; *W:* Charles Randolph; *C:* Michael Seresin; *M:* Alex Parker, Jake Parker.

The Life of Emile Zola ✓✓✓½ 1937

Writer Emile Zola intervenes in the case of Alfred Dreyfus who was sent to Devil's Island for a crime he did not commit. Well-crafted production featuring a handsome performance from Muni. **117m/B VHS, DVD.** Paul Muni, Gale Sondergaard, Gloria Holden, Joseph Schildkraut; *D:* William Dieterle; *W:* Norman Reilly Raine; *C:* Gaetano Antonio "Tony" Gaudio; *M:* Max Steiner. Oscars '37: Picture, Screenplay, Support. Actor (Schildkraut), Natl. Film Reg. '00;; N.Y. Film Critics '37: Actor (Muni), Film.

A Life of Her Own ✓✓½ 1950

Turner stars as a farm girl who takes her dream of becoming a top model to the Big Apple. She signs with an agency and is befriended by Dvorak, an aging model, who acts as her mentor. Turner finds success and is soon the toast of the town until she gets involved with a married man (Milland) and her life starts to crumble. Average soap opera with flimsy script. Turner is good, but Dvorak steals the show in her role as an over-the-hill fashion plate. **108m/B VHS.** Lana Turner, Ray Milland, Tom Ewell, Louis Calhern, Ann Dvorak, Barry Sullivan, Jean Hagen, Phyllis Kirk, Sara Haden; *D:* George Cukor; *W:* Isobel Lennart; *C:* George J. Folsey.

The Life of Jesus ✓✓½ 1996

La Vie de Jesus 1996 Small town boredom and despair—French style. Twenty-year-old Freddy (Douche) is an unemployed epileptic, who lives with his mother. He spends his time with girlfriend Marie (Cottreel) or riding his moped with his equally disenfranchised buddies. When a young Arab, Kader (Chaatouf), shows an interest in Marie (that's reciprocated), Freddy and his friends beat him up. Apparently the title is a reference to the spiritual suffering Freddy feels, even if he doesn't know exactly how to articulate his emotions. French with subtitles. **96m/C VHS, DVD.** *FR* David Douche, Marjorie Cottreel, Kader Chaatouf, Samuel Boldin, Genevieve Cottreel; *D:* Bruno Dumont; *W:* Bruno Dumont; *C:* Philippe Van Leeuw; *M:* Richard Cuvillier.

Life of Oharu ✓✓✓½

Oharu; Saikaku Ichidai Onna 1952 A near masterpiece rivaled only by "Ugetsu" in the Mizoguchi canon, this film details the slow and agonizing moral decline of a woman in feudal Japan, from wife to concubine to prostitute. A scathing portrait of social destination based on a novel by Ibara Saikaku. In Japanese with English subtitles. **136m/B VHS.** *JP* Kinuyo Tanaka, Toshiro Mifune; *D:* Kenji Mizoguchi.

A Life of Sin ✓✓ 1992 (R)

Scandalous drama about an impoverished Caribbean girl who rises to wealth and power as the beautiful Isabel, who is betrayed by her childhood friend Paulo (Julia) and rejected by the Catholic bishop (Ferrer) in this tragic story of passion and greed. **112m/C VHS.** Raul Julia, Miriam Colon, Jose Ferrer; *D:* Efrain Lopez Neris; *W:* Emilio Diaz Valcarcel.

Life of the Party ✓✓ 2005 (R)

Michael (Bailey), an ex-golden boy turned alcoholic, goes into a panic when his wife Phoebe (Pompeo) finally leaves him. With Michael in the hospital after a car crash, everyone close to him decides its past time to hold an intervention, which turns into chaos. Refrains from pomposity while showing the consequences alcoholic behavior has on not just the drinker but those around him. **87m/C DVD.** Eion Bailey, Ellen Pompeo, John Ales, Clifton (Gonzalez) Collins Jr., Gabriel Olds, David Clennon, Pamela Reed, Rosalind Chao, Larry Miller; *D:* Barra Grant; *W:* Barra Grant; *C:* Lawrence Sher; *M:* Mark Adler.

Life of Verdi ✓✓ 1982

Epic miniseries biography of the famous composer, with many excerpts of his music sung by Luciano Pavarotti, Renata Tebaldi, and Maria Callas. **600m/B VHS, DVD.** *IT* Ronald Pickup, Carla Fracci, Daria Nicolodi; Omero Antonutti, Giampiero Albertini; *D:* Renato Castellani; *W:* Renato Castellani; *C:* Giuseppe Ruzzolini. **TV**

Life on a String ✓✓ 1990

Set in the distant past, this is a lyrical story of a young boy searching for a cure for his blindness. His possible cure involves a myth which requires him to devote his life to music and the breaking of 1000 strings on a banjo. Adapted from a story by Shi Tiesheng. In Chinese with English subtitles. **110m/C VHS, DVD.** *CH* Xu Qing; *D:* Chen Kaige; *W:* Chen Kaige; *C:* Gu Changwei; *M:* Xiao-Song Qu.

Life 101 ✓✓½ 1995

Innocent freshman Haim tries to adjust to college life in the '60s, aided by his hippie roommate Coogan, who introduces Haim to the pleasures of life. Innocuous coming-of-age comedy. **95m/C VHS.** Corey Haim, Keith Coogan, Ami Dolenz; *D:* Redge Mahaffey; *W:* Redge Mahaffey.

Life or Something Like It ✓½ 2002 (PG-13)

Disappointing fluff bunny blonde role for Jolie, who's best when she's playing for Jolie. Instead, she plays shallow Seattle newscaster Lanie Kerigan who has a fab life and a fab famous boyfriend in Seattle Mariners player Cal (Kane). Then she interviews street prophet Jack (Shalhoub), who tells Lanie that she's going to die next week—and since all his other predictions have come true, Lanie gets stressed and decides she needs to get in touch with her regular-gal roots again. Of course it doesn't hurt that her cameraman, sexy Pete (Burns), is willing to do all he can to make things better. **104m/C VHS, DVD.** *US* Angelina Jolie, Edward Burns, Tony Shalhoub, Christian Kane, Melissa Errico, Stockard Channing, James Gammon, Gregory Itzin; *D:* Stephen Herek; *W:* John Scott Shepherd, Dana Stevens; *C:* Stephen Burum; *M:* David Newman.

Life-Size ✓✓½ 2000

Twelve-year-old tomboy, Casey (Lohan), desperately misses her recently deceased mother but her dad, Ben (Burns), is dealing with his own grief by becoming a workaholic. Casey tries out a magic spell to resurrect her mom and instead makes her beauty pageant doll, Eve (Banks), come to life. Casey's horrified and wants to send Eve back to her doll world but Eve loves becoming a human and wants to stay. **89m/C VHS, DVD.** Lindsay Lohan, Tyra Banks, Jere Burns, Anne Marie Loder, Garwin Sanford, Tom Butler; *D:* Mark Rosman; *W:* Mark Rosman, Stephanie Moore; *C:* Philip Linzey; *M:* Eric Colvin. **TV**

Life Stinks ✓ 1991 (PG-13)

So does the film. A grasping tycoon bets he can spend a month living on the street without money, resulting in cheap laughs, heavy-handed sentiment and one musical number. Those expecting the innovative, hilarious Brooks of "Young Frankenstein" or "Blazing Saddles" will be very disappointed—these jokes are stale and the timing is tedious. Those looking for a Chaplinesque tale for modern times should stick with Chaplin. **93m/C VHS, DVD.** Mel Brooks, Jeffrey Tambor, Lesley Ann Warren, Stuart Pankin, Howard Morris, Teddy Wilson, Michael Ensign, Billy Barty, Carmine Caridi, Rudy DeLuca; *D:* Mel Brooks; *W:* Mel Brooks, Rudy DeLuca; *C:* Steven Poster.

Life Support ✓✓✓ 2007

Ana Williams (Queen Latifah) is an HIV-positive, recovering junkie, trying to win back the affections of her estranged daughter Kelly (Nicks), who elects to live with her grandmother (Smith). The story begins to unravel when Kelly ask her mother to help her find her best friend Omari (Ross—as in Diana's son), who is gay and very sick from AIDS. As the two search the city talking with Omari's friends and lovers, Ana's heartfelt activism for the community is seen and her daughter's guard begins to let down. Nelson George's portrayal of his sister's real life battle could have come off as sap, but instead it is a solid effort with equally substantial performances. **88m/C DVD.** Queen Latifah, Anna Deavere Smith, Wendell Pierce, Evan Ross, Rachel Nicks, Gloria Reuben, Tracee Ellis Ross, Darrin Dewitt Henson, Tony Rock; *D:* Nelson George; *W:* Nelson George, Jim McKay, Hannah Weyer; *C:* Uta Briesewitz; *M:* Stuart Matthewman. **C A B L E**

Life Tastes Good ✓✓ 1999

San Franciscan Harry has been laundering money for the mob and skimming some off the top. He wants to leave a suitcase of cash to his abandoned kids but the wise-guys he stole from want their money back and send a hitman after Harry. Told in beyond-the-grave flashbacks. Gotanda adapted his own play. **88m/C DVD.** Sab Shimono, Tamlyn Tomita, Julia Nickson-Soul, Kelvin Han Yee, Bob Todd, Tim Lounibos; *D:* Sue Upton; *W:* Sue Upton; *C:* Michael G. Chin; *M:* Dan Kuramato.

Life Upside Down ✓✓

La Vie a L'Envers 1964 Ordinary Paris worker (Denner) decides to withdraw from his seemingly perfect life, including his wife and friends. He ends staring at a blank wall in a mental institution. French with subtitles. **115m/B VHS.** *FR* Charles Denner, Anna Gaylor, Jean Yanne; *D:* Alain Jessua; *W:* Alain Jessua; *C:* Jacques Robin; *M:* Jacques Loussier.

Life with Father ✓✓✓½ 1947

Based on the writings of the late Clarence Day Jr., this is the story of his childhood in NYC during the 1880s. A delightful saga about a stern but loving father and his relationship with his knowing wife and four red-headed sons. **118m/C VHS, DVD.** William Powell, Irene Dunne, Elizabeth Taylor, Edmund Gwenn, Zasu Pitts, Jimmy Lydon, Martin Milner; *D:* Michael Curtiz; *W:* Donald Ogden Stewart; *C:* William V. Skall, J. Peverell Marley; *M:* Max Steiner. Golden Globes '48: Score; N.Y. Film Critics '47: Actor (Powell).

Life with Judy Garland—Me and My Shadows ✓✓✓½ 2001 (PG)

Sharp direction, a solid script that goes beyond the cliches, plus excellent performances (especially by Davis and Blanchard) prevent this telling of the tortured life of Judy Garland from slipping into made-for-TV docudrama hell. Garland's life is followed, from her insecure early teens, through the movie success and the many marriages and the drug addiction that brought her downfall. Based on the book "Me and My Shadows: A Family Memoir" by daughter Lorna Luft, who participated in the production. **107m/C VHS, DVD.** Judy Davis, Victor Garber, Hugh Laurie, Tammy Blanchard, Stewart Bick, John Benjamin Hickey, Sonja Smits, Dwayne Adams, Al Waxman, Jayne (Jane) Eastwood, Marsha Mason, Daniel Kash, Aidan Devine; *Cameos:* Lorna Luft; *D:* Robert Allan Ackerman; *W:* Robert Freedman; *C:* James Chressanthis; *M:* William Ross; *Nar:* Cynthia Gibb. **TV**

Life with Mikey ✓✓½ 1993 (PG-13)

Michael "Mikey" Chapman (Fox) is a washed-up former child star who now half-heartedly runs a minor talent agency for other pint-sized would-be thespians. Ever mindful of his previous glory, he believes he is doomed to obscurity when a 10-year-old Brooklyn pickpocket reanimates his taste for life. Light, sweet comedy is generally predictable, a typical Fox effort. Unbilled cameo from Reuben Blades as Vidal's father. **92m/C VHS, DVD.** Michael J. Fox, Christina Vidal, Cyndi Lauper, Nathan Lane, David Huddleston, Victor Garber, David Krumholtz, Tony Hendra; *Cameos:* Ruben Blades;

Life Without Dick 🐶🐶½ 2001 (PG-13) Would-be romantic comedy that does passably on the romance and fails completely at the comedy. Ditzy Colleen (Parker) is devastated when she discovers sleazy boyfriend Dick (Knoxville) is cheating on her. She threatens him with a gun and accidentally kills him. Then Daniel (Connick Jr.) shows up. He works for the Irish mob as a hitman only he can't actually kill anyone. (He really wants to be a professional singer.) Dick was his assignment and he's pleased that everything is already taken care of. Colleen thinks Daniel is just grand and decides she will help him out by taking on his hitman duties herself. 96m/C VHS, DVD. Sarah Jessica Parker, Harry Connick Jr., Teri Garr, Johnny Knoxville, Craig Ferguson, Geoffrey Blake, Brigid Brannah, Ever Carradine, Erik Palladino, Claudia Schiffer; D: Bix Skahill; W: Bix Skahill; C: James Glennon; M: David Lawrence.

Lifeboat 🐶🐶🐶½ 1944 When a German U-boat sinks a freighter during WWII, the eight survivors seek refuge in a tiny lifeboat. Tension peaks after the drifting passengers take in a stranded Nazi. Hitchcock thriller. Sex was never stranger. Screenwriters O'Bannon and Jakoby adapted the story from Colin Wilson's novel, "The Space Vampires." 100m/C VHS, DVD. Tallulah Bankhead, John Hodiak, William Bendix, Canada Lee, Walter Slezak, Hume Cronyn, Henry Hull, Mary Anderson, Heather Angel, William Yetter Jr.; D: Alfred Hitchcock; W: Jo Swerling; C: Glen MacWilliams; M: Hugo Friedhofer. N.Y. Film Critics '44: Actress (Bankhead).

Paul Hogan, Cuba Gooding Jr., Beverly D'Angelo, Kamala Dawson, Pat Hingle, Richard Riehle, Frank McRae, Roger Daltrey, L.Q. Jones, Max Cullen; *D:* Simon Wincer; *W:* Paul Hogan; *C:* David Eggby; *M:* Bruce Rowland.

Lightning Raiders 🐾🐾 1945
When a stage coach filled with mail gets robbed, Billy Carson (Crabbe) and Fuzzy (St. John) set off to avenge the postal system. One of the last Crabbe/St. John efforts; perhaps they should have called it quits a few films earlier. 61m/C VHS. Buster Crabbe, Al "Fuzzy" St. John, Mady Lawrence, Henry Hall, Steve Darrell, I. Stanford Jolley, Karl Hackett, Roy Brent, Marin Sais, Al Ferguson; *D:* Sam Newfield; *W:* Elmer Clifton.

Lightning Range 🐾 1933 Roosevelt stars as a U.S. Deputy Marshal who continually foils the nefarious plots of a gang of outlaws. 50m/B VHS. Buddy Roosevelt, Lale (Lafayette) McKee, Patsy Bellamy, Olin Francis; *D:* Victor Adamson; *W:* L.V. Jefferson; *C:* Brydon Baker.

Lightning Strikes West 🐾½ 1940 U.S. Marshal trails an escaped convict, eventually catches him, and brings him in to finish paying his debt to society. 57m/B VHS, DVD. Ken Maynard, Claire Rochelle, Bob Terry, Charles "Blackie" King, Michael Vallon, Reed Howes, George Chesebro, William (Bill) Gould; *D:* Harry Fraser; *W:* Martha Chapin, Monro Talbot; *C:* Elmer Dyer; *M:* Lew Porter.

Lightning: The White Stallion 🐾½ 1986 (PG) An old gambler and his two young friends enter a horse race in order to win their beloved white stallion back from thieves. 93m/C VHS, DVD. Mickey Rooney, Susan George, Isabel Lorca; *D:* William A. Levey.

Lightning Warrior 🐾🐾 1931 Western suspense about pioneer life and the unraveling of a baffling mystery. Twelve chapters, 13 minutes each. 156m/B VHS, DVD. George Brent, Frankie Darro; *D:* Armand Schaefer, Benjamin (Ben H.) Kline.

Lights! Camera! Murder! 🐾🐾 *Death Force* 1989 When a 12-year-old boy witnesses a filmed murder, he becomes the next target. 89m/C VHS. Graham Clarke, Robin Smith, John Barrett; *D:* Frans Nel; *W:* Emil Kolbe; *C:* Paul Morkel.

Lights in the Dusk 🐾🐾½ *Laitakaupungin Valot* 2006 Limp noir finds lonely shopping mall security guard Koiskinen (Hyytiainen) falling for the charms of bombshell Mirja (Jarvenhelmi), who works for sleazy businessman Lindholm (Koviula). Koiskinen becomes the patsy in a jewel robbery and goes to prison, not even ratting out Mirja. Things don't improve from there. Finnish with subtitles. 80m/C VHS, DVD. Fi Janne Hyytiainen, Maria Jarvenhelmi, Ilkka Koivula, Maria Heiskanen; *D:* Aki Kaurismaki; *W:* Aki Kaurismaki; *C:* Timo Salminen.

Lights of Old Santa Fe 🐾½ 1947 A cowboy rescues a beautiful rodeo owner from bankruptcy. The original, unedited version of the film. 78m/B VHS, DVD. Roy Rogers, Dale Evans, George "Gabby" Hayes, Lloyd Corrigan, Tom Keene, Arthur Loft, Roy Barcroft, Lucien Littlefield, Sam Flint, Bob Nolan; *D:* Frank McDonald; *W:* Gordon Kahn; *C:* Reggie Lanning.

The Lightship 🐾🐾 1986 (PG-13) On a stationary lightship off the Carolina coast, the crew rescues three men from a disabled boat, only to find they are murderous criminals. Duvall as a flamboyant homosexual psychopath is memorable, but the tale is pretentious, overdone, and hackneyed. Based on Siegfried Lenz's story. 87m/C VHS, DVD. Robert Duvall, Klaus Maria Brandauer, Tom Bower, William Forsythe, Arliss Howard; *D:* Jerzy Skolimowski.

Like A Bride 🐾🐾 *Novia Que Te Vea* 1994 Two teenage Jewish girls grapple with their families' expectations and cultural norms during the 1960s in Mexico City when one resists marriage to be an artist while the other falls in love with a Gentile. In Spanish, with subtitles. 115m/C VHS, DVD. MX Claudette Maille, Maya Michalska, Angelica Aragon, Ernesto Laguardia, Pedro Armendariz Jr.; *D:* Guita Schyfter; *W:* Guita Schyfter, Hugo Hiriart, John Gorrie, David Butler; *C:* Toni Kuhn; *M:* Joaquin Gutierrez Heras, Joseph Horovitz.
VIDEO

Like a Brother 🐾🐾½ *Comme un Frère* 2005 Eighteen-year-old Sebastian moves to Paris to get away from his unrequited crush on Romain. He decides a new life deserves a new name—Zack—as he explores the gay clubs, especially when Romain says he's coming for a visit. Short run time and abrupt ending makes you wonder if this indie ran out of money before completion. French with subtitles. 55m/C DVD. *FR* Bill Hays, Don Shaw, Rebecca Hall; *D:* Guy Henry, Cyril Legann; *W:* Guy Henry, Cyril Legann; *C:* Joachim Villain.

Like a Fish Out of Water 🐾🐾 *Comme un Poisson Hors de l'eau* 1999 Michael is an average loveless, middle-aged nobody with a tropical fish hobby. This is how he's set up by a trio of con artists who need his help in stealing a very rare and valuable tropical fish, which they will hold for ransom until the eccentric owner pays up. Bellucci's the femme who entices Muller while Karyo is the alleged brains of the operation and Pinon the crazy muscle. French with subtitles. 90m/C VHS, DVD. *FR* Michel Muller, Monica Bellucci, Tcheky Karyo, Dominique Pinon; *D:* Herve Hadmar; *W:* Michel Muller, Herve Hadmar, Christopher Bergeronneau; *C:* Jacques Boumendil.

Like a Puppet Out of Strings 🐾½ 2005 Brothers Tom and Felipe watch out for each other as they gain more power in the local gangs. Cop Luis, a former gangbanger whose life was turned around by police officer Angelica, goes after the brothers when she's murdered. Tom gets accused although Felipe did the crime, and Felipe does a deal with Luis to save his brother. Eventually, the siblings wind up confronting each other in a situation that calls their loyalty into question. 83m/C DVD. CA Tom Rodriguez, Ed Casagrande, Leslie Hibberd, Catherine Braund, Felipe Rodriguez; *D:* Felipe Rodriguez; *W:* Felipe Rodriguez; *C:* Felipe Rodriguez, Dylan Harrison; *M:* Louis Marc Vautour.

Like Father, Like Son 🐾 1987 (PG-13) First and worst of a barrage of interchangeable switcheroo movies that came out in '87-'88. Moore is in top form, but the plot is contrived. 101m/C VHS, DVD. Dudley Moore, Kirk Cameron, Catherine Hicks, Margaret Colin, Sean Astin; *D:* Rod Daniel; *W:* Steven L. Bloom, Lorne Cameron; *M:* Miles Goodman.

Like Father Like Son 🐾🐾½ 2005 When teacher Dominic Milne gets engaged to Dee Stanton, she finally admits that she isn't a widow but that her exhusband, Paul, is imprisoned as a serial killer. Her 15-year-old son Jamie overhears Dee's confession and demands to see the father he was told was dead and Dee is frightened that Jamie will become fascinated by the manipulative monster. Then Morag, a pupil whom Jamie was accused of stalking, is strangled and he falls under suspicion. Is Jamie following in his father's footsteps or is someone else close to Dee actually the killer? 137m/C DVD. GB Robson Green, Jemma Redgrave, Somerset Prew, Philip Davis, Tara Fitzgerald, Francesca Fowler, Georgia Moffett, Florence Bell; *D:* Nicholas Laughland; *W:* Shaun McKenna; *C:* Dominic Clemence; *M:* John Lunn. TV

Like It Is 🐾🐾🐾 1998 Young Craig (Bell) makes his living in illegal bareknuckles fighting matches in the old British beach resort town of Blackpool. After one win, he heads for a local disco where he meets ambitious London record producer, Matt (Rose), who's accompanying his roommate, singer Paula (Behr), to a gig. Uncertain of his sexual feelings, Craig can't follow through on his attraction to the willing Matt but does soon turn up on his London doorstep. However, not only is jealous Paula a problem for their budding romance but so is Kelvin (Daltry), Matt's manipulative gay boss. Appealing lead performances but vet Daltry steals scenes with smarmy charm. Accents and slang will be a challenge to American ears. 95m/C VHS, DVD. GB Steve Bell, Ian Rose, Dani Behr, Roger Daltrey; *D:* Paul Oremland; *W:* Robert Cray; *C:* Alistair Cameron; *M:* Don McGlashan.

Like It Never Was Before 🐾🐾 *Pensionat Oskar* 1995 Conventional, middle-aged married Rune (Falkman) and Gunnel (Ekblad) Runeberg travel to a seaside hotel for their annual vacation with their three children. Ordinary family man Rune, though dissatisfied, is expecting little until he meets, and falls in love with, young handyman Petrus (Norrthon), and suddenly decides to break free. Swedish with subtitles. 108m/B VHS. SW Loa Falkman, Stina Ekblad, Simon Norrthon, Philip Zanden, Sif Ruud, Ghita Norby; *D:* Suzanne (Susanne) Bier; *W:* Jonas Gardell; *C:* Kjell Lagerros; *M:* Johan Soderqvist.

Like Mike 🐾🐾½ 2002 (PG) That's "Mike" as in basketball legend Michael Jordan—or at least his basketball shoes. A pair of old shoes, supposedly once belonging to Jordan, is donated to an orphanage and ending up the property of teen Calvin (Bow Wow). The shoes give him super skills on the basketball court, and he wins a chance to play spoiled star Tracey (Chestnutt) during halftime of a game. Impressed, the coach (Forster) signs Calvin to the fictional L.A. Knights. The hoops story is merely window dressing, however, because most of the story revolves around the efforts of Calvin and fellow orphans Murph (Lipnicki) and Reg (Song) to get adopted. NBA players Gary Payton, Alonzo Mourning, Rasheed Wallace, and Jason Kidd make appearances. 100m/C VHS, DVD, UMD. US Bow Wow, Jonathan Lipnicki, Morris Chestnut, Eugene Levy, Crispin Glover, Robert Forster, Brenda Song, Jesse Plemons, Julius Charles Ritter, Anne Meara; *D:* John Schultz; *W:* Jordan Moffet, Mike Elliot; *C:* Shawn Maurer; *M:* Richard Gibbs.

Like Water for Chocolate 🐾🐾🐾½ *Como Agua para Chocolate* 1993 (R) Magical Mexican fairytale set in the early 1900s about family, love, and the power of food. Formidable Mama Elena is left a widow with three daughters. The youngest, Tita, grows up in the kitchen surrounded by all the magic. Nacha, the housekeeper, can impart to her about food. Doomed by tradition to spend her days caring for her mother, Tita escapes by cooking, releasing her sorrows and longings into the food, infecting all who eat it. Wonderfully sensuous and slyly exaggerated. Based on the novel by Esquival, who also wrote the screenplay and whose husband, Arau, directed. In Spanish with English subtitles; also available dubbed. 105m/C VHS, DVD, DVD. MX Lumi Cavazos, Marco Leonardi, Regina Torne, Mario Ivan Martinez, Ada Carrasco, Yareli Arizmendi, Caludette Maille, Pilar Aranda; *D:* Alfonso Arau; *W:* Laura Esquivel; *C:* Steven Bernstein; *M:* Leo Brouwer.

Li'l Abner 🐾½ *Trouble Chaser* 1940 Al Capp's famed comic strip comes somewhat to life in this low-budget comedy featuring all of the Dogpatch favorites. 78m/C VHS. Granville Owen, Martha Driscoll, Buster Keaton; *D:* Albert Rogell.

Li'l Abner 🐾🐾½ 1959 High color Dogpatch drama adapted from the Broadway play (with most of the original cast) based on the Al Capp comic strip. When Abner's berg is considered as a site for atomic bomb testing, the natives have to come up with a reason why they should be allowed to exist. Choreography by Michael Kidd and Dee Dee Wood. Jubilation T. Cornpone; Don't Take That Rag Offn the Bush; A Typical Day; If I Had My Druthers; Room Enuff for Us; Namely You; The Country's in the Very Best of Hands; Unnecessary Town; I'm Past My Prime. 114m/C VHS, DVD. Peter Palmer, Leslie Parrish, Stubby Kaye, Julie Newmar, Howard St. John, Stella Stevens, Billie Hayes, Joe E. Marks; *D:* Melvin Frank; *W:* Norman Panama; *C:* Daniel F. Fapp; *M:* Johnny Mercer, Jean De Paul.

Lila Says 🐾🐾 *Lila Dit Ca* 2004 Chimo (Khouas) is a handsome 19-year-old Arab boy in Marseilles who, rather than further his writing talent, hangs out with his layabout friends and dabbles in petty crime. Along comes Lila (Giocante), a beautiful blond 16-year-old, who ensnares Chimo with her teasing talk. His friends blatantly disapprove of her and as he clings to his

chivalrous demeanor, her antics become more annoying. 89m/C DVD. FR GB Vahina Giocante, Mohammed Khouas, Karim Ben Haddou, Carmen Lebbos, Hamid Dkhissi, Lotfi Chakri, Edmonde Franchi, Stephanie Fatout; *D:* Ziad Doueiri; *W:* Ziad Doueiri, Joelle Touma; *C:* John Daly.

Lili 🐾🐾🐾 1953 Delightful musical romance about a 16-year-old orphan who joins a traveling carnival and falls in love with a crippled, embittered puppeteer. Heartwarming and charming, if occasionally cloying. Leslie Caron sings the film's song hit, "Hi-Lili, Hi-Lo." 81m/C VHS. Leslie Caron, Jean-Pierre Aumont, Mel Ferrer, Kurt Kasznar, Zsa Zsa Gabor; *D:* Charles Walters; *M:* Bronislau Kaper. Oscars '53: Orig. Dramatic Score; British Acad. '53: Actress (Caron); Golden Globes '54: Screenplay.

Lilian's Story 🐾🐾½ 1995 Aging Lilian (Cracknell) has just been released after spending 40 years in a mental institution, placed there as an adolescent by her controlling, possessive father. The haunted Lilian is given a room at a residential hotel in Sydney's red-light district where the local prostitutes look out for her and she spends her days wandering the streets. Flashbacks reveal what lead the high-strung young Lilian (Collette) to her incarceration. Based on Kate Greville's 1984 novel, which was a fictional account of real-life Sydney eccentric Bea Miles. 94m/C VHS, DVD. AU Ruth Cracknell, Barry Otto, Toni Collette, John Flaus, Essie Davis, Susie Lindemann, Anne Louise Lambert, Iris Shand; *D:* Jerzy Domaradzki; *W:* Steve Wright; *C:* Slawomir Idziak; *M:* Cezary Skubiszewski. Australian Film Inst. '95: Support. Actress (Collette).

Lilies 🐾🐾🐾 *Les Feluettes* 1996 (R) Strange revenge fantasy set in a northern Quebec men's prison in 1952. A bishop (Sabourin) goes to the prison to hear the confession of a dying convict and is taken hostage in the chapel by the prison's homosexual population. There, he's forced to watch a play that recreates a 40-year-old incident in his own life. As the prison walls fade away, the actor/prisoners turn into students Simon (Cadieux) and Vallier (Gilmore), who take the lovers' roles in a pageant about the martyrdom of St. Sebastien too seriously for comfort. The female roles in the flashbacks (which include Vallier's crazy mother and Simon's would-be fiance) are played by men. Adapted from Bouchard's play "Les Feluettes out La Repetition d'un Drame Romantique." 95m/C VHS, DVD. CA Marcel Sabourin, Jason Cadieux, Danny Gilmore, Brent Carver, Matthew Ferguson, Alexander Chapman, Aubert Pallascio; *D:* John Greyson; *W:* Michel Marc Bouchard; *C:* Daniel Jobin; *M:* Mychael Danna. Genie '96: Art Dir./Set Dec., Costume Des., Film, Sound.

Lilies of the Field 🐾🐾🐾 1963 Five former East German nuns, living on a small farm in the Southwest U.S., enlist the aid of a free-spirited Army veteran (Poitier) to build a chapel for them and teach them English. Poitier is excellent as the itinerant laborer, holding the saccharine to an acceptable level, bringing honesty and strength to his role. Actress Skala, as Mother Maria, had been struggling to make ends meet in a variety of day jobs until this opportunity. Poitier was the first African American man to win an Oscar, and the first African American nominated since Hattie MacDaniel in 1939. Followed by "Christmas Lilies of the Field" (1979). 94m/B VHS, DVD. Sidney Poitier, Lilia Skala, Lisa Mann, Isa Crino, Stanley Adams, Francesca Jarvis, Pamela Branch, Dan Frazer, Ralph Nelson; *D:* Ralph Nelson; *W:* James Poe; *C:* Ernest Haller; *M:* Jerry Goldsmith. Oscars '63: Actor (Poitier); Berlin Intl. Film Fest. '63: Actor (Poitier); Golden Globes '64: Actor—Drama (Poitier).

Liliom 🐾🐾🐾 1935 Boyer goes to heaven and is put on trial to see if he is deserving of his wings. Lang's first film after leaving Nazi Germany is filled with wonderful ethereal imagery, surprising coming from the man responsible for such grim visions as "Metropolis." In French only. 85m/B VHS. FR Charles Boyer, Madeleine Ozeray, Florelle, Roland Toutain; *D:* Fritz Lang.

Lilith 1964 Therapist-in-training Beatty falls in love with beautiful mental patient Seberg and approaches madness himself. A look at the doctor-patient relationship among the mentally ill and at the nature of madness and love. Doesn't always satisfy, but intrigues. Rossen's swan song. 114m/B VHS, DVD. Warren Beatty, Jean Seberg, Peter Fonda, Gene Hackman, Kim Hunter, Anne Meacham, Olympia Dukakis, James Patterson; D: Robert Rossen; W: Robert Rossen; C: Eugen Shuftan; M: Kenyon Hopkins.

Lillian Russell 1940 Often draggy biopic of the theatrical legend. In the 1890s, Helen Leonard (Faye) is taking singing lessons when she's heard by impresario Tony Pastor (Carrillo). He changes her name and hires her to sing in his theater, where Lillian becomes the toast of New York and has numerous suitors. She decides to marry musician Edward So-omon ('Ameche) and is aided in her continued success by the flattering articles written by old friend Alexander Moore (Fonda). But it wouldn't be showbiz if there wasn't some sorrow to dim the bright lights. 127m/B DVD. Alice Faye, Don Ameche, Henry Fonda, Lynn Bari, Nigel Bruce, Claude Allister, Helen Wesley; D: Irving Cummings Jr.; W: William Anthony McGuire; C: Leon Shamroy; M: Alfred Newman.

Lily Dale 1996 (PG) Nineteen-year-old Horace Robedaux (Guinee) is in Houston to visit his estranged mother Corella (Channing) and sister Lily Dale (Masterson) while his taciturn stepfather Pete Davenport (Shepard) is supposed to be away. Pete dislikes Horace and left the boy behind with relatives when he married Corella and they moved away. Self-centered Lily Dale resents Horace taking away attention from herself and matters only get worse when Pete comes home early and Horace becomes so ill that he can't leave. Set in 1910; Foote wrote the play as a memoir to his father, Horace. Made for TV. 95m/C VHS, DVD. Tim Guinee,

Lillie 1979 The life of Edwardian beauty Lillie Langtry, known as "The Jersey Lily," is portrayed in this British drama. Defying the morals of the times, Lillie was the first publicly acknowledged mistress of the Prince of Wales, only one of her numerous lovers. Shown on "Masterpiece Theatre" on PBS. 660m/C VHS, DVD. GB Francesca Annis, Cheryl Campbell, John Castle, Dennis (Denis) Lill, Peter Egan, Anton Rodgers, Anne(i) Firbank. TV

Lilo & Stitch 2002 (PG) Modern and entertaining animated tale of problem child Lilo, a Hawaiian orphan being raised by her sister, who finds an unlikely soulmate when she adopts Stitch, a strange little alien banished from his home planet, who hides out in an animal shelter. Stitch is rife with socially unacceptable behavior (including naughty words, drooling, and spitting food) and creates chaos everywhere they go, which worse is Lilo's situation with a concerned social worker investigating her upbringing. Kiddies will love the sassy humor and gross-cut behavior while parents will love the Elvis references (and songs), and the message of ohana—the Hawaiian word for family. Disney resurrected the appealing hand drawn and watercolored animation, unused since 1942's "Bambi." 85m/C VHS, DVD. US D: Dean DeBois, Christopher Sanders; W: Dean DeBlois, Christopher Sanders; M: Alan Silvestri; V: Daveigh Chase, Tia Carrere, Jason Scott Lee, David Ogden Stiers, Christopher Sanders, Kevin McDonald, Ving Rhames, Zoe Caldwell, Kevin McDonald, David Ogden Stiers, Liliana Mumy, Holliston Coleman, Jillian Henry, Susan Hegary.

The Limbic Region 1996 Terminally ill police detective Jon Lucca (Olmos) has spent 20 years tracking a serial killer known as "The Scorekeeper," who likes to shotgun the young inhabitants of small-town lovers' lanes. His most likely suspect is Lloyd Warden (Dzundza) and the duo engage in a deadly cat-and-mouse battle that may destroy them both. 96m/C VHS. Edward James Olmos, George Dzundza, Gwynyth Walsh; D: Michael Pattinson; W: Patrick Ranahan, Todd Johnson; C: Tobias Schliessler. CABLE

Limbo 1999 (R) Ambivalent family saga that leaves the viewers deliberately in limbo for good or ill. Alaskan Joe Gastineau (Strathairn) is a former fisherman traumatized by an accident at sea years before. Into his life comes small-time singer Donna de Angelo (Mastrantonio) and her depressed teen daughter Noelle (Martinez). Joe and Donna start a tentative romance and Joe even goes back to fishing. Then Joe's fast-talking half-brother Bobby (Siemaszko) shows up, precipitating a crisis that leaves Bobby dead and Joe, Donna, and Noelle stranded on a deserted island. 126m/C VHS, DVD. David Strathairn, Mary Elizabeth Mastrantonio, Vanessa Martinez, Casey Siemaszko, Kris Kristofferson Kathryn Grody, Rita Taggart, Leo Burmester, Michael Laskin; D: John Sayles; W: John Sayles; C: Haskell Wexler; M: Mason Daring.

Limelight 1952 A nearly washed-up music hall comedian is stimulated by a young ballerina to a final hour of glory. A subtle if self-indulgent portrait of Chaplin's own life, featuring an historic pairing of Chaplin and Keaton. 120m/B VHS, DVD. Charlie Chaplin, Claire Bloom, Buster Keaton, Nigel Bruce, Sydney Chaplin; D: Charlie Chaplin; W: Charlie Chaplin; C: Karl Struss; M: Charlie Chaplin.

Lily in Love Playing for Keeps: Jatszani Kell 1985 (PG-13) An aging stage star disguises himself as a suave Italian to star in his playwright wife's new play, and woos her to test her fidelity. Charming, warm, and sophisticated. Loosely based on Molnar's "The Guardsman." 100m/C VHS. HU Maggie Smith, Christopher Plummer, Elke Sommer, Adolph Green. D: Karoly Makk; M: Frank Cucci. TV

Lily Was Here 1989 (R) After her fiancee is senselessly murdered, a young woman named Lily is forced to turn to a life of crime in order to survive. A series of petty thefts evolves into a huge crime wave and Lily soon finds herself the object of a massive manhunt. Lily must make the ultimate choice between freedom and motherhood in this shocking thriller. Soundtrack by Dave Stewart features hit instrumental "Lily was Here" by saxophonist Candy Dulfur. 110m/C VHS. Marion Van Thijn, Thom Hoffman, Adrian Brine, Dennis Rudge; D: Ben Verbong; W: Ben Verbong, Syrze Van Der Laan, Willem Jan Otten.

The Lindbergh Kidnapping Case 1976 The famous Lindbergh baby kidnapping in 1932 and the trial and execution of Bruno Hauptmann, convincingly portrayed by Hopkins. DeYoung as Lindbergh is blah, but the script is quite good. Made for TV. 150m/C VHS. Anthony Hopkins, Joseph Cotten, Cliff DeYoung, Walter Pidgeon, Dean Jagger, Martin Balsam, Laurence Lucknhill, Tony Roberts; D: Buzz Kulik; W: (James) P(Jmckrey) Miller; M: Billy Goldenberg. TV

The Line 1980 (R) Not-so-hot anti-war drama about a sit-down strike at a military installation by Vietnam veteran prison inmates. Leans heavily on recycled footage from other films. 94m/C VHS. Russ Thacker, David Doyle, Erik Estrada; D: Robert Siegel.

The Line of Beauty 2006 Middle-class Nick Guest (Stevens) is befriended at Oxford by wealthy Toby Fedden (Coleman), whose father Gerald (McInerney) is a rising Tory politician in Thatcher's Britain of the 1980s. Guest moves into the family's London home—in part to keep an eye on Toby's trouble-prone sister Catherine (Atwell). The gay Nick also starts exploring his sexuality; first with working-class Leo (Gilet) and then with Wani (Wyndham), the closeted druggie son of a Lebanese tycoon. Scandals eventually catch up with both Nick and the Feddens. Based on the novel by Alan Hollinghurst. 180m/C DVD. Tim (Mohrney) nny) McInerney, Alice Krige, Dan Stevens, Oliver Coleman, Hayley Atwell, Alex Wyndham, Don Gil-

Lily of Killarney The Bride of the Lake 1934 A musical comedy romance about a British lord who arranges to pay his debts via horse-races, arranged marriages and inheritances. 82m/B VHS. GB Gina Malc, John Garrick, Stanley Holloway; C: Charles Mills; D: Delbert Mann; W: Robert Eisele; M: David Shire. CABLE

Linda 1993 (PG-13) Madsen in her femme fatale mode as treacherous wife Linda who wants to frame her schlump husband (Thomas) for murder. Whose murder? Why the inconvenient wife (Harrington) of her boyfriend (McGinley), two homicidal lovebirds want to take the insurance money and run—leaving the hubby to face the consequences. Based on the novella "Linda" by John D. MacDonald. 88m/C VHS. Virginia Madsen, Richard Thomas, Ted McGinley, Laura Harrington; D: Nathaniel Gutman; W: Nevin Schreiner; M: David Michael Frank.

Linda 1929 Linda, a young mountain girl, is forced to marry a much older man though her heart belongs to a young doctor. Her kind husband tries to make the best of the situation. 75m/B VHS. Helen Foster, Warner Baxter, Noah Beery Sr., Mitchell Lewis, Kate Price, Alan Connor; D: Dorothy Davenport Reid.

The Limping Man 1953 Bridges returns to post-WWII London to renew a wartime romance. On the way, he gets caught up in solving a murder. Unexceptional of-its-era thriller. 76m/B VHS, DVD. GB Lloyd Bridges, Moira Lister, Leslie Phillips, Helene Cordet, Alan Wheatley; D: Charles De Latour.

Limit Up 1989 (PG-13) An ambitious Chicago Trade Exchange employee makes a deal with the devil to corner the market in soybeans. Turgid attempt at supernatural comedy, featuring Charles as God. Catch Sally Kellerman in a cameo as a nightclub singer. 88m/C VHS, DVD. Nancy Allen, Dean Stockwell, Brad Hall, Danitra Vance, Ray Charles, Luena Anders; Cameos: Sally Kellerman; D: Richard Martini; M: Cliff Martinez.

The Limey 1999 (R) Sixties icons Stamp and Fonda show that age has not withered their acting chops in Soderbergh's revenge thriller. Wilson (Stamp) is a Cockney career criminal who gets out of a Brit prison and immediately flies to L.A. to investigate the death of his daughter Jenny. She was involved with self-important record producer Valentine (Fonda), who has an obvious fondness for young women. Wilson may be out-of-touch with California culture but he's definitely in control of any situation. Soderbergh's flashback sequences meld the footage from Ken Loach's 1967 film "Poor Cow," which featured Stamp as a young thief named Wilson. 90m/C VHS, DVD. Terence Stamp, Peter Fonda, Lesley Ann Warren, Luis Guzman, Barry Newman, Joe Dallesandro, Nicky Katt, Amelia Heinle, Melissa George, Bill Duke; D: Steven Soderbergh; W: Lem Dobbs; C: Edward Lachman; M: Cliff Martinez.

Link WOOF! 1986 (R) A primatologist and his nubile assistant find that their experiment has gone—you guessed it—awry, and their hairy charges are running—yep, amok. Run for your life! 103m/C VHS, DVD. GB Elisabeth Shue, Terence Stamp, Steven Pinner, Richard Garnett; D: Richard Franklin; W: Everett DeRoche; C: Mike Molloy; M: Jerry Goldsmith.

The Lion Has Wings 1940 The story of how Britain's Air Defense was set up to meet the challenge of Hitler's Luftwaffe during their "finest hour." Dated, now-quaint but stirring wartime period piece. "Docudrama" style was original at the time. 76m/B VHS. Merle Oberon, Ralph Richardson, Flora Robson, June Duprez, John Robinson; D: Brian Desmond Hurst, Michael Powell; C: Harry Stradling Sr.

The Lion in Winter 1968 (PG) Medieval monarch Henry II and his wife, Eleanor of Aquitaine, match wits over the succession to the English throne and much else in this fast-paced film version of James Goldman's play. The family, including three grown sons, and visiting royalty are united for the Christmas holidays fraught with tension, rapidly shifting allegiances, and layers of psychological manipulation. Superb dialogue and perfectly realized characterizations. O'Toole's Hepburn are triumphant. Screen debuts for Hopkins and Dalton. Shot on location, this literate costume drama surprised the experts with its boxoffice success. 134m/C VHS, DVD. Peter O'Toole, Katharine Hepburn, Jane Merrow, Nigel Terry, Timothy Dalton, Anthony Hopkins, John Castle, Nigel Stock; D: Anthony Harvey; W: James Goldman; M: John Barry. Oscars '68: Actress (Hepburn), Adapt. Screenplay, Orig Score; Directors Guild '68: Director (Harvey), Golden Globes '39: Actor—Drama (O'Toole), Film—Drama. N.Y. Film Critics '68: Film.

The Lion in Winter 2003 In this Showtime miniseries remake of the 1968 masterpiece, Close and Stewart gracefully, if not quite as joyously, inhabit the lead roles made classic by Hepburn and O'Toole. Using Goldman's screenplay, Konchalovsky's presentation is admirably true to its source, and the scenery in Hungary anc Slovakia splendidly suits the subject. Certainly an excellent effort by a talented cast and crew, but it won't dethrone its predecessor. 167m/C VHS, DVD. Patrick Stewart, Glenn Close, John Light, Jonathan Rhys Meyers, Ralph Spall, Yuliya Vysotskaya, Andrew Howard, Clive Wood; D: Andrei Konchalovsky; W: James Goldman; C: Sergei Kozlov; M: Richard Hartley. CABLE

A Lion Is in the Streets 1953 Cagney stars as a backwoods politician in a southern state who fights on the side of the sharecroppers and wins their support when he exposes the corrupt business practices of a powerful businessman. On his way up the political ladder, however, Cagney betrays and then plots the very people who support him. Although this is a familiar storyline, Cagney is riveting as the corrupt politician, and Hale is wonderful as his patient wife. 88m/C VHS. James Cagney, Barbara Hale, Anne Francis, Warner Anderson, John McIntire, Jeanne Cagney, Lon Chaney Jr., Frank McHugh, Larry Keating, Onslow Stevens; D: Raoul Walsh.

The Lion King 1994 (G) Highest grossing film in Disney history (likely a temporary title) is a winner for kids and their folks. Like his dad Mufasa (Jones), lion cub Simba (Taylor) is destined to be king of the beasts. Growing up in his dad Mufasa... uncle Scar (Irons) plots against him and makes him an outcast. Growing up in the

et: D: Saul Dibb; W: Andrew Davies; C: David Odd; M: Martin Phipps. TV

The Linguini Incident 1992 (R) An inept escape artist, a pathological liar, a lingerie designer, and a dead restaurant hostess who throws out one-liners in sign language, and two sinister, yet chic, restaurant owners get together in this marginal comedy about magic and adventure. 99m/C VHS. Rosanna Arquette, David Bowie, Eszter Balint, Andre Gregory, Buck Henry, Viveca Lindfors, Marlee Matlin, Lewis Arquette, Andrea King; Cameos: Julian Lennon, Iman; D: Richard Shepard; C: Robert Yeoman; M: Thomas Newman.

jungles of Africa, Simba (now Broderick) learns about life and responsibility, before facing his uncle once again. Supporting characters frequently steal the show, with Sabella's Pumba the warthog and Lane's Timon the meerkat heading the procession (though Chong and Goldberg as hyenas give them a run). Disney epic features heartwarming combo of crowd-pleasing songs, a story with depth, emotion, and politically correct multiculturalism, and stunning animation. The sound quality is equally spectacular; during the two and a half-minute wildebeest stampede scene, you'll swear the animals are running amuck in the house. Thirty-second Disney animated feature is the first without human characters, and the first to use the voices of a well known, ethnically diverse cast. Scenes of violence in the animal kingdom may be too much for younger viewers. ♪Can You Feel the Love Tonight; The Circle of Life; I Just Can't Wait to Be King; Be Prepared; Hakuna Matata. **88m/C VHS, DVD. D:** Rob Minkoff; Roger Allers; **W:** Jonathan Roberts, Irene Mecchi; **M:** Elton John, Hans Zimmer, Tim Rice; **V:** Matthew Broderick, Jeremy Irons, James Earl Jones, Madge Sinclair, Robert Guillaume, Jonathan Taylor Thomas, Richard "Cheech" Marin, Whoopi Goldberg, Rowan Atkinson, Nathan Lane, Ernie Sabella, Niketa Calame, Moira Kelly, Jim (Jonah) Cummings. Oscars '94: Song ("Can You Feel the Love Tonight"), Orig. Score; Golden Globes '95: Film—Mus./Comedy, Song ("Can You Feel the Love Tonight?"), Score; Blockbuster '95: Family Movie, T., Soundtrack.

The Lion King 1 1/2 ♪♪♪ 2004 (G) Timon and Pumbaa tell the story of the original from their point of view, so we get to see what happened to Simba and how he grew up between the time he ran away and when he returned. Sort of a "Rosencrantz and Guildenstern are Dead" for the pre-teen set. Offers up the original cast (with some new additions), and a new song. Doesn't disappoint fans of the franchise, with plenty of enjoyment for every age group. **77m/C VHS, DVD. W:** Tom Rogers; **M:** Don Harper; **V:** Nathan Lane, Ernie Sabella, Matthew Broderick, Robert Guillaume, Moira Kelly, Whoopi Goldberg, Richard "Cheech" Marin, Julie Kavner, Jerry Stiller, Jim (Jonah) Cummings, Edward Hibbert, Bradley Raymond, Matt Weinberg, Jason Marsden. VIDEO

The Lion King: Simba's Pride ♪♪ 1998 Simba's heir comes of age and must be prepared to assume the responsibility of leadership. **75m/C VHS, DVD. D:** Darrell Rooney, Rob LaDuca; **W:** Flip Kobler, Cindy Marcus; **V:** Matthew Broderick, James Earl Jones, Nathan Lane, Ernie Sabella, Robert Guillaume, Andy Dick, Neve Campbell, Suzanne Pleshette, Jason Marsden. VIDEO

The Lion Man ♪♪ 1936 Arabian tale of a boy raised by lions. **67m/B VHS, DVD.** Jon Hall, Ted Adams, Kathleen Burke, Richard Carlyle; **D:** John P. McCarthy; **W:** Richard Gordon; **C:** Robert E. Cline.

Lion Man ♪ Aslan Adam 1975 Raised by wild animals, the son of King Solomon returns to his father's kingdom and roars his way to the throne. **91m/C VHS. TU** Barbara Lake, Charles Garrett, Alison Soames, Steve Arkin; **D:** Natuk Baytan.

The Lion of Africa ♪♪ 1987 A down-to-earth woman doctor and an abrasive diamond dealer share a truck ride across Kenya. Filmed on location in East Africa. Fine lead performances in otherwise nothing-special adventure. **115m/C VHS.** Brian Dennehy, Brooke Adams, Joseph Shiloah; **D:** Kevin Connor; **M:** George S. Clinton. CABLE

Lion of the Desert ♪♪ Omar Mukhtar 1981 (PG) Bedouin horse militias face-off against Mussolini's armored terror in this epic historical drama. Omar Muktar (Quinn as the "Desert Lion") and his Libyan guerrilla patriots kept the Italian troops of Mussolini (Steiger) at bay for 20 years. Outstanding performances enhanced by the desert backdrop. A British-Libyan co-production. **162m/C VHS, DVD. GB** Anthony Quinn, Oliver Reed, Irene Papas, Rod Steiger, Raf Vallone, John Gielgud; **D:** Moustapha Akkad; **W:** H.A.L. Craig; **C:** Jack Hildyard; **M:** Maurice Jarre.

The Lion of Thebes ♪♪♪ 1964 A muscleman unhesitatingly jumps into the thick of things when Helen of Troy is kidnapped. A superior sword and sandal entry. **87m/C VHS, DVD. IT** Massimo Serato, Pierre Cressoy, Alberto Lupo, Rosalba Neri, Mark Forest, Yvonne Furneaux; **D:** Giorgio Ferroni; **W:** Giorgio Ferroni, Andrei De Coligny; **C:** Angelo Lotti; **M:** Francesco De Masi.

Lionheart ♪♪½ 1987 (PG) A romantic portrayal of the famous English King Richard the Lionheart's early years. Meant for kids, but no Ninja turtles herein—and this is just as silly, and slow to boot. **105m/C VHS,** Eric Stoltz, Talia Shire, Nicola Cowper, Dexter Fletcher, Nicholas Clay, Deborah Maria Moore, Gabriel Byrne; **D:** Franklin J. Schaffner; **W:** Richard Outten; **M:** Jerry Goldsmith.

Lionheart ♪♪ A.W.O.L.; Wrong Bet 1990 (R) Van Damme deserts the foreign legion and hits the streets when he learns his brother has been hassled. Many fights ensue, until you fall asleep. **105m/C VHS, DVD.** Jean-Claude Van Damme, Harrison Page, Deborah Rennard, Lisa Pelikan, Brian Thompson, Ashley Johnson; **D:** Sheldon Lettich; **W:** Sheldon Lettich, Jean-Claude Van Damme; **C:** Robert New; **M:** John Scott.

Lion's Den ♪♪½ 1936 A night club performer and a detective head west to fight crime in this film. **59m/B VHS.** Joan Woodbury, Don Barclay, J. Frank Glendon, John Merton, Tim McCoy, Dave O'Brien; **D:** Sam Newfield; **W:** John Thomas "Jack" Neville; **C:** Jack Greenhalgh.

Lions for Lambs ♪♪ 2007 (R) Three interrelated stories of those affected by the Iraq war, including a hawkish politician, an anti-war professor, and the soldiers stuck in between. Senator Irving (Cruise) pushes a war strategy destined for failure in Iraq and Afghanistan while Professor Malley (Redford) debates with his students and worries about two in particular (Pena and Luke) who, as soldiers, are part of Irving's strategy. Director Redford boldly strives to say something meaningful about the war on terror but fails to give his characters any depth. Instead, they all function as flat representations of different viewpoints, spouting talking points rather than actually interacting. Co-stars Cruise and Streep (as the skeptical journalist Roth) do their best, but a bunch of A-list actors making speeches is less a drama than a series of lectures. **92m/C DVD. US** Robert Redford, Meryl Streep, Tom Cruise, Michael Pena, Peter Berg, Kevin Dunn, Derek Luke, Andrew Garfield; **D:** Robert Redford; **W:** Matthew Carnahan; **C:** Philippe Rousselot; **M:** Mark Isham.

The Lion's Share ♪ 1979 A gang of bank robbers have their loot stolen and go after the guy who ripped them off. **105m/C VHS. SP** Julio de Grazia, Luisina Brando, Fernanda Mistral, Ulises Dumont, Julio Chavez; **D:** Adolfo Aristarain; **W:** Adolfo Aristarain; **C:** Horacio Maira; **M:** Anibal Gruart, Jorge Navarro.

Lip Service ♪♪♪ 1988 Satirical comedy-drama about the TV news industry. An ambitious young newscaster befriends a veteran reporter. He then manipulates his way to replace him on the reporter's morning program. Dooley as the veteran and Dunne as the upstart are fun to watch in this well-done cable rip-off of "Broadcast News." **67m/C VHS.** Griffin Dunne, Paul Dooley; **D:** William H. Macy. CABLE

Lip Service ♪♪½ Out of Synch 2000 2000 (R) Allison (Temchen) is a conservative, successful, furniture designer with a successful lawyer boyfriend, Stuart (Camargo). She reunites with her old college roommate, Kat (Gertz), a high-strung free spirit who moves into Allison's home. Then Kat discovers that Allison's success is predicated on selling copies of a chair that Kat herself designed and gave to Allison as a gift. So Kat decides to get revenge. **95m/C VHS, DVD.** Jami Gertz, Sybil Temchen, Jonathan Silverman, Christian Camargo, Adewale Akinnuoye-Agbaje, Jenna Byrne; **D:** Shawn Schepps; **W:** Shawn Schepps; **C:** Feliks Parnell.

Lips of Blood ♪♪½ Levres de Sang 1975 Rollin whips up a typically festive mix of sex, horror, and hallucination in what some have dubbed his best film. A young man (Philippe) has visions of a woman (Briand, AKA Annie Belle) he met as a child in an abandoned castle. When he sees her again, she persuades him to unleash a couple of female vampires. Do not expect anything more in the way of narrative, but it is a well-made low-budget French horror movie. French with subtitles. **88m/C DVD. FR** Jean-Loup Philippe, Annie Belle; **D:** Jean Rollin.

Lipstick woof! 1976 (R) Fashion model Margaux seeks revenge on the man who brutally attacked and raped her, after he preys on her kid sister (real-life sis Mariel, in her debut). Exquisitely exploitative excuse for entertainment. **90m/C VHS, DVD.** Margaux Hemingway, Anne Bancroft, Perry King, Chris Sarandon, Mariel Hemingway; **D:** Lamont Johnson; **W:** David Rayfiel; **C:** Bill Butler, William A. Fraker.

Lipstick Camera ♪♪ 1993 (R) Keats wants a career in TV news and seeks out a successful freelance cameraman (Wimmer) to help her out. She also asks to borrow her techno-friend Feldman's mini-camera and then goes after a story on an ex-spy and his sexy companion. Only no one expects what the camera captures. Weak plot but strong cast and high-end production. **93m/C VHS, DVD.** Ele Keats, Brian Wimmer, Corey Feldman, Sandahl Bergman, Terry O'Quinn; **D:** Mike Bonifer; **W:** Mike Bonifer; **C:** M. David Mullen; **M:** Jeff Rona.

Lipstick on Your Collar ♪♪½ 1994 British TV fantasy/drama set in the stuffy confines of the British War Offices during the Suez Crisis of 1956. Two army clerks fantasize about the world outside through daydreams set to original tunes. Last series for the innovative Potter; on three cassettes. **360m/C VHS. GB** Ewan McGregor, Giles Thomas, Louise Germaine, Bernard Hill; **D:** Remy Rye; **W:** Dennis Potter. TV

Liquid Dreams ♪♪ 1992 (R) In this fast-paced, futuristic thriller, Daly goes undercover as an erotic dancer in a glitzy strip joint to try and solve her sister's murder. She finds that the owner and clientele deal not only in sexual thrills, but also in a strange brain-sucking ritual that provides the ultimate rush. Also available in an unrated version. **92m/C VHS, DVD.** Richard Steinmetz, Candice Daly, Barry Dennen, Juan Fernandez, Tracey Walter, Frankie Thorn, Paul Bartel, Mink Stole, John Doe, Mark Manos; **D:** Mark Manos; **W:** Zach Davis, Mark Manos; **C:** Ed Tomney, Alexandre Magno.

Liquid Sky ♪♪♪ 1983 (R) An androgynous bisexual model living in Manhattan is the primary attraction for a UFO, which lands atop her penthouse in search of the chemical nourishment that her sexual encounters provide. Low-budget, highly creative film may not be for everyone, but the audience for which it was made will love it. Look for Carlisle also playing a gay male. **112m/C VHS, DVD.** Anne Carlisle, Paula Sheppard, Bob Brady, Susan Doukas, Otto von Wemherr, Elaine C. Grove, Stanley Knap, Jack Adalist, Lloyd Ziff; **D:** Slava Tsukerman; **W:** Slava Tsukerman, Anne Carlisle; **C:** Yuri Neyman; **M:** Slava Tsukerman, Brenda Hutchinson.

Lisa ♪♪ 1990 (PG-13) A young girl develops a crush on the new guy in town and arranges a meeting with him in which she pretends to be her mother. Little does she realize he's a psychotic serial killer. Lock your doors! Don't let anyone in if they have this video! **95m/C VHS.** Staci Keanan, Cheryl Ladd, D.W. Moffett, Tanya Fenmore, Jeffrey Tambor, Julie Cobb; **D:** Gary Sherman; **W:** Karen Clark; **C:** Alex Nepomniaschy.

Lisa and the Devil woof! The House of Exorcism; La Casa Dell'Exorcismo; The Devil and the Dead; The Devil in the House of Exorcism; El Diablo se Lleva a los Muertos; Il Diavolo e i Morti; Lisa e il Diavolo 1975 (R) An unfortunate outing for Savalas and Sommer, about devil worship. Poor quality leaves little room for redemption. Just like on the telly, Telly's sucking on a sucker. A shortened version of the director's original 1972 release, re-edited and with additional footage added by producer Alfred Leone. **93m/C VHS, DVD. IT SP** Telly Savalas, Elke Sommer, Sylva Kosina, Robert Alda, Alessio Orano, Gabriele Tinti, Eduardo Fajardo, Espartaco (Spartaco) Santoni, Alida Valli; **D:** Mario Bava; **W:** Mario Bava, Alfred Leone; **C:** Cecilio Paniagua; **M:** Carlo Savina.

Lisa Picard Is Famous ♪♪½ 2001 Well, New Yorker Lisa (Wolf) would like to be famous but right now, she's best known for a cereal commercial. Neurotic, self-absorbed Lisa just can't catch that one big break—unlike her gay pal Tate (DeWolf) whose one-man confessional show becomes a hit. So Lisa agrees to let a filmmaker (Dunne) document her struggling career in the hopes it will help her would-be career. **87m/C VHS, DVD.** Laura Kirk, Nat DeWolf, Griffin Dunne; **Cameos:** Sandra Bullock, Charlie Sheen, Spike Lee; **D:** Griffin Dunne; **W:** Laura Kirk, Nat DeWolf; **C:** William Rexer; **M:** Evan Lurie.

Lisboa ♪♪ Lisbon 1999 (Joao (Lopez) is a salesman who travels between Portugal and Spain. One day he picks up Berta (Maura) who is on her way to Lisbon and who refuses to tell him anything about herself. If he knew what was good for him, Joao would have made Berta get out of the car since her nasty husband Jose Luis (Luppi) and psychotic family are soon after them. Spanish with subtitles. **100m/C VHS, DVD. SP** Sergi Lopez, Carmen Maura, Federico Luppi; **D:** Antonio Hernandez; **W:** Antonio Hernandez, Enrique Braso; **C:** Alter Mantxola; **M:** Victor Reyes.

Lisbon ♪♪ 1956 First film directed by Milland, shot in Portugal, details the adventures of a sea captain entangled in international espionage and crime while attempting to rescue damsel O'Hara's husband from communist doings. A familiar plot told with less-than-average panache. **90m/C VHS,** Ray Milland, Claude Rains, Maureen O'Hara, Francis Lederer, Percy Marmont; **D:** Ray Milland.

Lisbon Story ♪♪ 1994 Director Friedrich Monroe (Bauchau) calls his friend, sound engineer Phillip Winter (Vogler), to come to Lisbon to help him finish his film on the city. By the time Winter arrives in Portugal, Monroe has vanished, leaving the unfinished silent film behind. While waiting for his friend to return, Winter starts work, wandering through the city streets in search of inspiring sounds. English, German, and Portuguese with subtitles. **100m/C VHS. GE** Ruediger Vogler, Patrick Bauchau; **D:** Wim Wenders; **W:** Wim Wenders; **C:** Lisa Renzler.

The List ♪♪ 1999 (R) When prostitute Gabrielle (Amick) gets herself arrested and tried for solicitation, she attempts to use her client book to barter for her freedom. Judge Miller (O'Neal) has to decide whether to make the list public and embarrass many of his wealthy and powerful friends, but when Gabrielle's clients start turning up dead, the judge is forced to take action. **93m/C VHS, DVD.** Madchen Amick, Ryan O'Neal, Roc Lafortune, Ben Gazzara; **D:** Sylvain Guy; **W:** Sylvain Guy; **C:** Yves Belanger; **M:** Louis Babin. VIDEO

The List of Adrian Messenger ♪♪♪ 1963 A crafty murderer resorts to a variety of disguises to eliminate potential heirs to a family fortune. Solid Huston-directed thriller with a 'twist' you won't recognize any of the name stars. **98m/B VHS.** Kirk Douglas, George C. Scott, Robert Mitchum, Dana Wynter, Burt Lancaster, Frank Sinatra; **D:** John Huston; **M:** Jerry Goldsmith. VIDEO

Listen ♪♪½ 1996 (R) Sex and violence and a faulty cordless telephone. Krista's (Buxton) suffered a nervous breakdown after her breakup with Sarah (Langton).

But now they're friends again and Krista's even encouraging Sarah's new romance with weirdo boyfriend Jake (Currie) who likes phone sex. Then there's the obscene phone caller who seems to live in Sarah's apartment building and a serial killer who preys on women. Lots of nastiness and it's easy to figure out who the real killer is. **104m/C VHS.** Brooke Langton, Sarah Buxton, Gavin Wilding; **W:** Jonas Quastel, Michael Bafaro; **C:** Brian Pearson; **M:** David Davidson.

Listen, Darling 🐱🐱½ 1938 Garland is appealing in her first big screen role as Pinky Wingate, who decides to find the perfect husband for her widowed mother (Astor). Pinky and her friend Buzz (Bartholomew) manage to find Pidgeon and have him become the engaging object of everyone's affections. 🐱Zing! Went the Strings of My Heart; Ten Pins in the Sky; On the Bumpy Road to Love. **70m/C VHS.** Judy Garland, Freddie Bartholomew, Mary Astor, Walter Pidgeon, Alan Hale, Scotty Beckett; **D:** Edwin L. Marin.

Listen to Me 🐱½ 1989 (PG-13) A small-town college debate team heads for the big time when they go to a national debate tournament. The usual mutual-distrust-turns-to-romance thing. Cheesy-as-all-get-out climactic abortion debate, in front of supposed real-life Supreme Court justices—yeah, right. And Kirk Cameron: get an accent, will ya? **109m/C VHS.** Kirk Cameron, Jami Gertz, Roy Scheider, Amanda Peterson, Tim Quill, Christopher Atkins; **D:** Douglas Day Stewart; **C:** Fred W. Koenekamp; **M:** David Foster, Maribeth Derwent '89. Worst Support.

The Listening 🐱½ 2006 (R) 1983 Office romance in the '80s! Sounds like a mediocre, forgettable made-for-TV comedy-drama—which is exactly what it is. If Jackson was the brainy one on "Charlie's Angels," why wasn't she smart enough to avoid this one? **90m/C VHS.** Tim Matheson.

Lisztomania woof! 1975 (R) Russell's excessive vision of what it must have been like to be classical composer/musician Franz Liszt, who is depicted as the first pop star. Rock opera in the tradition of "Tommy," with none of the sense or music. **106m/C VHS.** GB Roger Daltrey, Sara Kestelman, Paul Nicholas, Fiona Lewis, Ringo Starr, Veronica Quilligan, Nell Campbell, John Justin, Andrew Reilly, Anulka Dziubinska, Rick Wakeman, Rikki Howard, Felicity Devonshire, Aubrey Morris, Kenneth Colley, Ken Parry, Otto Diamont, Murray Melvin, Andrew Faulds, Oliver Reed; **D:** Ken Russell; **W:** Ken Russell; **C:** Peter Suschitzky; **M:** Christian Kusche-Tomasini.

The Little American 🐱🐱 1917 German-American Karl Von Austrein leaves sweetheart Angela Moore, returning to Germany to fight in WWI. Angela travels to France to care for her dying aunt and discovers her aunt's chateau has been turned into a hospital. She remains in the face of a German advance and is naturally reunited with her much-changed beau. **80m/B VHS.** Mary Pickford, Jack Holt, Raymond Hatton, Walter Long, Hobart Bosworth, Ben Alexander, DeWitt Jennings; **D:** Cecil B. DeMille; **W:** Jeanie Macpherson; **C:** Alvin Wyckoff.

Little Annie Rooney 🐱🐱 1925 A policeman's tomboy daughter spends her time mothering her father and brother while getting into mischief with street punks. Minor melodrama. Silent. **60m/B VHS, D.** Mary Pickford, William Haines, Walter James, Gordon Griffith, Vola Vale; **D:** William Beaudine; **C:** Charles Rosher.

Little Athens 🐱 2005 (R) A day in the life of a multitude of annoying characters who live in Little Athens, Arizona. Drug dealer Jimmy is a bookie; Heather's paranoid that her boyfriend is cheating on her; self-involved Jessica is a certain age (in this case Hunter) when they are reduced to playing eccentric mentors to the pouty blonde flavor of the moment. That would be Murphy as Stacy, who wants to be a broadcast journalist but is slaving away at a lousy daytime talk show hosted by Kippie Kann (a slumming Bates). Maybe things will go better in her romance with sports agent Derek (Living-ston). Oops, shouldn't have peeked at his Palm Pilot, which lists his glamorous, maybe-not-so-ex-girlfriends. Since Derek doesn't talk about his past relationships, Stacy sets up "interviews," none of which ends well. There's a fitting description of the one big mess—a fitting description of the movie. **95m/C DVD.** US Kate Winslet, Cathy Moriarty, Kathy Bates, Ron Livingston, Julianne Nicholson, Stephen Tobolowsky, Kevin Sussman, Josie Maren, Rashida Jones, Jason Antoon, Nick Kurran; **W:** Elissa Bell, Melissa Carter; **C:** Theo van de Sande; **M:** Christophe Beck.

Little Ballerina 🐱½ 1947 A young dancer struggles against misfortune and jealousy to succeed in the world of ballet. **62m/B VHS.** Yvonne Marsh; **D:** Lewis Gilbert; **W:** Lewis Gilbert.

Little Big Horn 🐱🐱½ The Fighting Seventh 1951 Low-budget depiction of Custer et al. at Little Big Horn actually has its gripping moments; solid acting all around helps. **88m/B VHS, DVD.** Marie Windsor, John Ireland, Lloyd Bridges, Reed Hadley, Hugh O'Brian, Jim Davis; **D:** Charles Marquis Warren.

Little Big League 🐱🐱½ 1994 (PG) 12-year-old inherits the Minnesota Twins baseball team from his grandfather, appoints himself manager when everyone else declines, and becomes the youngest owner-manager in history. Nothing new about the premise, but kids and America's favorite pastime add up to good clean family fun. Features real-life baseball players, including the Ken Griffey, Jr. and Paul O'Neill. Good cast features TV's Busfield at first base. Screenwriting debut from Pincus, and directorial debut from the executive producer of "Seinfeld" and "The Animal" later. **120m/C VHS, DVD.** Luke Edwards, Jason Robards Jr., Kevin Dunn, Dennis Farina, John Ashton, Jonathan Silverman, Wolfgang Bodison, Timothy Busfield, Ashley Crow, Scott Patterson, Billy L. Sullivan, Miles Feulner, Kevin Elster, **Cameos:** Don Mattingly, Ken Griffey Jr., Paul O'Neill; **D:** Andrew Scheinman; **W:** Gregory Pincus, Adam Scheinman.

Little Big Man 🐱🐱🐱½ 1970 (PG) Based on Thomas Berger's picaresque novel, this is the story of 121-year-old Jack Crabb and his quixotic life as gunslinger, charlatan, Indian, ally to George Custer, and the only white survivor of Little Big Horn. Told mainly through flashbacks, Hoffman provides a classic portrayal of Crabb, as fact and myth are jumbled and reshaped. **135m/C VHS, DVD.** Dustin Hoffman, Faye Dunaway, Chief Dan George, Richard Mulligan, Martin Balsam, Jeff Corey, Aimee (Amy) Eccles; **D:** Arthur Penn; **W:** Calder Willingham; **C:** Harry Stradling Jr. N.Y. Film Critics '70: Support. Actor (George).

Little Bigfoot 🐱🐱 1996 (PG) The Shoemaker family are taking a camping vacation when the kids discover a baby bigfoot in the wilderness. They find out the hairy little guy and his mom are threatened by the owner of a logging company, who's hired a group of hunters to get rid of the critters. **99m/C VHS, DVD.** Ross Malinger, P.J. Soles, Ken Tigar, Kelly Packard, Don Stroud, Matt McCoy; **D:** Art Camacho; **W:** Richard Preston Jr.; **C:** Ken Blakey; **M:** Louis Febre. **VIDEO**

A Little Bit of Soul 🐱🐱½ 1997 (R) Godfrey Usher (Rush) is an ambitious politician whose present position is that of federal treasurer, a job he has no clue about. Usher is married to Grace Michael (Mitchell) the head of a philanthropic foundation. Scientist Richard Shorking-Haslett (O'Connor), have both applied for funding from the foundation and are invited to the Usher/Michael home for a weekend. Surprises abound for Richard and Kate when they discover their kinky hosts are Satanists. Amusing comedy does falter but its not the fault of the performers. **83m/C VHS, DVD.** AU Geoffrey Rush, David Wenham, Frances O'Connor, Heather Mitchell, John Gaden, Kerry Walker; **D:** Peter Duncan; **W:** Peter Duncan; **C:** Martin McGrath; **M:** Nigel Westlake.

Little Black Book 🐱 2004 (PG-13) You know there are tough for actresses of a certain age Hunter) when to rid the neighborhood of ex-con Ronald (Haley) who's living with his doting mom (Somerville). Field drags things out too long but the performances are strong. **130m/C DVD.** US Kate Winslet, Patrick Wilson, Jennifer Connelly, Jackie Earle Haley, Noah Emmerich, Gregg Edelman, Phyllis Somerville, Sadie Goolsbein; **D:** Todd Field; **W:** Todd Field, Tom Perrotta; **C:** Antonio Calvache; **M:** Thomas Newman. **Nar:** Will Lyman.

Little Boy Blue 🐱🐱 1997 You want dysfunction? This movie has got it. Controlling husbands, impotence, uncontrollable rage, incest, family secrets, alcoholics... Southern Gothic family drama focuses on Jimmy (Phillippe) with three of the gals (Maran, Jones, Nicholson) to check out her possible rivals. Eventually, her snooping and her job converge into ano\pated and impotent Vietnam vet Ray West (Savage). He decides not to go to college because he's afraid to leave his younger brothers with dear ol' abusive alcoholic Dad, Ray runs a bar with his timid wife Kate (Kinski), who he also forces to sleep with son Jimmy to satisfy his own twisted sexual kicks. After a man comes snooping around and ends up dead in the bathroom of the bar, secrets from the past are dredged up. A mysterious woman (Knight) arrives bringing revenge on Ray for ruining her life and the possibility of freedom for the tormented family. Excellent performances (especially Kinski and Phillippe) save the twisted ball of loose strings that make up the farfetched plot. **107m/C VHS.** Ryan Phillippe, John Savage, Nastassja Kinski, Shirley Knight, Jenny Lewis, Tyrin Turner; **D:** Antonio Tibaldi; **W:** Michael Boston; **C:** Ron Hagen; **M:** Stewart Copeland.

Little Boy Lost 🐱🐱 1978 (G) The true story of the disappearance of a young boy in Australia. **92m/C VHS.** AU John Hargreaves, Tony Barry, Lorna Lesley; **D:** Alan Syres.

Little Buddha 🐱🐱 1993 (PG) Tibetan Lama Norbu informs the Seattle Konsleman that their 10-year-old son Jesse may be the reincarnation of a respected monk. He wants to take the boy back to Tibet to find out and, with some apparently minor doubts, the family head off on their spiritual quest. In an effort to instruct Jesse in Buddhism, this journey is interspersed with the story of Prince Siddhartha, who will leave behind his worldly ways to follow the path towards enlightenment and become the Buddha. The two stories are an ill-fit, the acting awkward (with the exception of Ruocheng as the wise Norbu), but boy, does the film look good (from cinematographer Vittorio Storaro). Filmed on location in Nepal and Bhutan. **123m/C VHS, DVD.** Keanu Reeves, Alex Wiesendanger, Ying Ruocheng, Chris Isaak, Bridget Fonda; **D:** Bernardo Bertolucci; **W:** Mark Peploe, Rudy Wurlitzer; **C:** Vittorio Storaro; **M:** Ryuichi Sakamoto.

Little Caesar 🐱🐱🐱 1930 A small-time hood rises to become a gangland czar, but his downfall is as rapid as his rise. Still thrilling. The role of Rico made Robinson a star and typecast him as a crook for all time. **80m/B VHS, DVD.** Edward G. Robinson, Glenda Farrell, Sidney Blackmer, Douglas Fairbanks Jr.; **D:** Mervyn LeRoy; **C:** Gaetano Antonio "Tony" Gaudio; Natl. Film Reg. '00.

Little Children 🐱🐱🐱 2006 (R) 1997 (R) Adultery in the 'burbs and a vulnerable sex offender on parole collide in Perrotta's adaptation of his 2004 novel. Bored outsider Sarah (Winslet) is with the other moms at the playground where handsome house husband Brad (Wilson) also plays with his son. A brief first meeting slowly leads to an affair, eventually discovered by Brad's successful wife Kathy (Connelly). Meanwhile, Brad's tightly wound, ex-cop buddy Larry (Emmerich) is on a mission to rid the neighborhood of ex-con Ronald (Haley) who's living with his doting mom (Somerville). Field drags things out too long but the performances are strong. **130m/C DVD.** US Kate Winslet, Patrick Wilson, Jennifer Connelly, Jackie Earle Haley, Noah Emmerich, Gregg Edelman, Phyllis Somerville, Sadie Goolsbein; **D:** Todd Field; **W:** Todd Field, Tom Perrotta; **C:** Antonio Calvache; **M:** Thomas Newman. **Nar:** Will Lyman.

Little Church Around the Corner 🐱🐱🐱 1923 Silent small town melodrama about a preacher who falls in love with a mine owner's daughter, but finds he isn't dad's favorite fella when he confronts him about poor mining conditions. When the mine caves in, the preacher man's caught between a rock and hard place when his sweetie's family needs protection from an angry mob. **70m/B VHS.** Kenneth Harlan, Hobart Bosworth, Walter Long, Pauline Starke, Alec B. Francis, Margaret Seddon, George Cooper; **D:** William A. Seiter.

Little City 🐱🐱½ 1997 (R) Best friends Kevin (Bon Jovi) and Adam (Charles) discover sex can screw up the best relationship. Adam's current girlfriend Nina (Sciorra) is having an affair with Kevin, while his ex-girlfriend Kate (Going) is having problems with her girlfriend Ann (Williams), who broke up Adam and Kate. Now Kate is having a fling with Rebecca (Miller), who's just flirting with lesbianism and Rebecca then gets involved with Adam. Meanwhile, Kevin decides he's in love with Nina, she's not reciprocating that emotion and instead she begins thinking about going back to Adam. San Francisco turns out to be a very small town. **90m/C DVD.** Jon Bon Jovi, Penelope Ann Miller, Annabella Sciorra, Josh Charles, Joanna Going, JoBeth Williams, Suzy Amis; **W:** Roberto Benabib; **D:** Roberto Benabib; **M:** Randal Love.

The Little Colonel 🐱🐱🐱 1935 tasteful premise has summer campers Kristy and Tatum in a race to lose their virginity. Kristy is better (at acting, that is) but who cares? And just who is meant to be the market for this movie, anyway? **95m/C VHS.** Tatum O'Neal, Kristy McNichol, Matt Dillon, Armand Assante, Margaret Blye; **D:** Ronald F. Maxwell; **M:** Charles Fox.

Little Darlings woof! 1980 (R) Distasteful premise has summer campers Kristy and Tatum in a race to lose their virginity. Kristy is better (at acting, that is) but who cares? And just who is meant to be the market for this movie, anyway? **95m/C VHS.** Tatum O'Neal, Kristy McNichol, Matt Dillon, Armand Assante, Margaret Blye; **D:** Ronald F. Maxwell; **M:** Charles Fox.

The Little Death 🐱🐱 1995 Struggling musician Nick Hannon (Fraser) is forced to work for wealthy dad Ted (Walsh), who's married to young trophy wife Kelly (Gidley). She's being stalked by weirdo Bobby (Yoakam), who kills Ted but weirdo Bobby (Yoakam), who kills Ted but the good samaritan who works to free them. Told in two parts (on four tapes), "Nobody's Fault," and "Little Dorrit's Story." **180m/C VHS.** GB Alec Guinness, Derek Jacobi, Cyril Cusack, Sarah Pickering, Joan Greenwood, Max Wall, Amelia Brown, Daniel Chatto, Miriam Margolyes, Bill Fraser, Roshan Seth, Michael Elphick, Eleanor Bron, Patricia Hayes, Robert Morley, Sophie Ward; **D:** Christine Edzard; **W:**

Little Dorrit, Film 1: Nobody's Fault 🐱🐱🐱 1988 The mammoth version of the Dickens tome, about a father and daughter trapped interminably in life dreaded Marshalsea debtors' prison, and the good samaritan who works to free them. Told in two parts (on four tapes), "Nobody's Fault," and "Little Dorrit's Story." **180m/C VHS.** GB Alec Guinness, Derek Jacobi, Cyril Cusack, Sarah Pickering, Joan Greenwood, Max Wall, Amelia Brown, Daniel Chatto, Miriam Margolyes, Bill Fraser, Roshan Seth, Michael Elphick, Eleanor Bron, Patricia Hayes, Robert Morley, Sophie Ward; **D:** Christine Edzard; **W:**

Christine Edzard; **C:** Bruno de Keyzer. L.A. Film Critics '88: Film, Support. Actor (Guinness). **TV**

Little Dorrit, Film 2: Little Dorrit's Story 🐾🐾🐾 1988 The second half of the monumental adaptation of Dickens' most popular novel during his lifetime tells of Amy Dorrit's rise from debtor's prison to happiness. **189m/C VHS.** *GB* Alec Guinness, Derek Jacobi, Cyril Cusack, Sarah Pickering, Joan Greenwood, Max Wall, Amelda Brown, Daniel Chatto, Miriam Margolyes, Bill Fraser, Roshan Seth, Michael Elphick, Patricia Hayes, Robert Morley, Sophie Ward, Eleanor Bron; **D:** Christine Edzard; **W:** Christine Edzard; **C:** Bruno de Keyzer. L.A. Film Critics '88: Film, Support. Actor (Guinness). **TV**

Little Dragons 🐾 1980 A grandfather and two young karate students rescue a family held captive by a backwoods gang. **90m/C VHS.** Ann Sothern, Joe Spinell, Charles Lane, Chris Petersen, Pat Petersen, Sally Boyden, Rick Lenz, Sharon Weber, Tony Bill; **D:** Curtis Hanson; **W:** Alan Ormsby.

The Little Drummer Girl 🐾🐾🐾 1984 (R) An Israeli counterintelligence agent recruits an actress sympathetic to the Palestinian cause to trap a fanatical terrorist leader. Solid performances from Keaton is at or near her very best. Based on the bestselling novel by John Le Carre. **130m/C VHS.** Diane Keaton, Klaus Kinski, Yorgo Voyagis, Sami Frey, Michael Cristofer, Anna Massey, Thorley Walters; **D:** George Roy Hill; **M:** Dave Grusin.

Little Fish 🐾🐾🐾 2005 (R) As an Asian video store manager in the tough "Little Saigon" suburb of Sydney, Australia, Tracy Heart (Blanchett) has bigger dreams of starting her own business, although she's a recovering junkie is having trouble securing the funds—a fact she often fibs about in conversation. Her protective mother Janelle (Hazlehurst) labors to keep her daughter away from the bad influences that surround her, including the return of her old boyfriend and her estranged stepfather Lionel (Weaving), a user who Janelle accuses of influencing Tracy's addiction. Vivid storyline focuses on living life as a post-addict. Blanchett deftly delivers (as usual). **114m/C DVD.** Cate Blanchett, Sam Neill, Hugo Weaving, Martin Henderson, Noni Hazlehurst, Dustin Nguyen, Joel Tobeck; **D:** Rowan Woods; **W:** Jacquelin Perske; **C:** Danny Ruhlmann; **M:** Nathan Larson.

The Little Foxes 🐾🐾🐾 1941 A vicious southern woman will destroy everyone around her to satisfy her desire for wealth and power. Filled with corrupt characters who commit numerous revolting deeds. The vicious matriarch is a part made to fit for Davis, and she makes the most of it. Script by Lillian Hellman from her own play. **116m/B VHS, DVD.** Bette Davis, Herbert Marshall, Dan Duryea, Teresa Wright, Charles Dingle, Richard Carlson, Carl Benton Reid; **D:** William Wyler; **W:** Lillian Hellman; **C:** Gregg Toland; **M:** Meredith Willson.

Little Fugitive 🐾🐾🐾½ 1953 Seven-year-old Joey (Andrusco) is convinced by his Brooklyn pals that he's murdered his brother. So the tyke takes off and winds up wandering lost around Coney Island. Independent feature made on a miniscule budget features endearing performances from non-pros. **80m/C VHS, DVD.** Richie Andrusco, Ricky Brewster, Winnifred Cushing, Jay Williams; **D:** Morris Engel, Ruth Orkin, Ray Ashley; **W:** Ray Ashley; **C:** Morris Engel; **M:** Eddy Manson. Natl. Film Reg. '97.

Little Giant 🐾🐾½ 1946 The duo fly separately in this entry, which highlights Costello's comic talents and leaves Abbott in the supporting role. Costello is a country bumpkin come to the big city to get enough money to marry his sweetheart. He's hired to sell vacuum cleaners by Abbott and becomes the butt of everyone's jokes but the joke's on them when Lou becomes the company's top-selling salesman. **92m/B VHS, DVD.** Bud Abbott, Lou Costello, Brenda Joyce, Jacqueline DeWit, George Cleveland, Elena Verdugo, Mary Gordon, Pierre Watkin; **D:** William A. Seiter; **W:** Walter DeLeon.

Little Giants 🐾🐾½ (PG) 1994 Familiar kids/sport movie about the klutzy coach (Moranis) of an equally woeful pee-wee football team. Coach Danny is up against his overbearing big brother Kevin (O'Neill), former local football hero and the coach of the best team in town. Naturally, there's the big game between the misfit underdogs and the stars. Predictable, of course, but not without some amusing moments. **106m/C VHS, DVD.** Rick Moranis, Ed O'Neill, Shawna Waldron, Mary Ellen Trainor, Devon Sawa, Susanna Thompson, Todd Bosley, Alexa Vega, Joey Simmrin, Sam Horrigan, Brian Haley, Mathew McCurley, Harry Shearer, Dabbs Greer; *Cameos:* John Madden; **D:** Duwayne Dunham; **W:** Tommy Swerdlow, Michael Goldberg, James Ferguson, Robert Shallcross; **C:** Janusz Kaminski; **M:** John Debney.

Little Girl... Big Tease 🐾 1975 (R) Teen society girl is kidnapped and exploited (along with the viewer) by a group which includes her teacher. **86m/C VHS.** Jody Ray, Rebecca Brooke; **D:** Roberto Mitrotti.

The Little Girl Who Lives down the Lane 🐾🐾½ 1976 (PG) Engrossing, offbeat thriller about a strange 13-year-old girl whose father is never home, and who hides something—we won't say what—in her basement. Very young Foster is excellent, as are her supporters, including Sheen as the child molester who knows what she's hiding. Based on the novel by Koenig, who also penned the script. **90m/C VHS, DVD.** *CA FR* Jodie Foster, Martin Sheen, Alexis Smith, Scott Jacoby, Mort Shuman, Dorothy Davis, Hubert Noel, Jacques Famery, Mary Morter, Judie Wildman; **D:** Nicolas Gessner; **W:** Laird Koenig; **C:** Rene Verzier, **M:** Christian Gaubert.

Little Gloria... Happy at Last 🐾🐾 1984 Miniseries about the custody battle over child heiress Gloria Vanderbilt, and her tumultuous youth. Lansbury leads a fine cast as the poor little rich girl's aunt Gertrude, the matriarchal family power broker. **180m/C VHS.** Bette Davis, Angela Lansbury, Christopher Plummer, Maureen Stapleton, Martin Balsam, Barnard Hughes, John Hillerman; **D:** Waris Hussein. **TV**

Little Heroes 🐾🐾 1991 (G) An impoverished little girl gets through hard times with the aid of her loyal dog (the Hound can relate). A low-budget family tearjerker that nonetheless works, if claims to be based on a true story. **78m/C VHS, DVD.** Raeanin Simpson, Katherine Willis, Keith Christensen; **D:** Craig Clyde; **W:** Craig Clyde; **M:** Jon McCallum.

Little House on the Prairie 🐾🐾🐾 1974 Pilot for the TV series based on the life of Laura Ingalls Wilder and her family's struggles on the American plains in the 1860s. Other episodes are also available on tape, including one in which Patricia Neal guest stars as a terminally ill widow seeking a home for her children. Neal's performance earned her a best actress Emmy in 1975. **98m/C VHS, DVD.** Michael Landon, Karen Grassle, Victor French, Melissa Gilbert, Melissa Sue Anderson; **D:** Michael Landon. **TV**

Little Indian, Big City 🐾🐾½ *An Indian in the City; Un Indien dans la Ville* 1995 (PG) French blockbuster dubbed over with "Americanized" feature made on a miniscule budget features endearing performances this charming story as loin cloth meets Eiffel Tower, but Lhermitte, Briand and Miou-Miou (as estranged wife Patricia) shine through. Subplot of Russian mobsters who cut the fingers off their victims gives an indication of the French definition of "family fare." **90m/C VHS.** *FR* Thierry Lhermitte, Miou-Miou, Patrick Timsit, Arielle Dombasle, Ludwig Briand; **D:** Herve Palud; **W:** Thierry Lhermitte, Herve Palud, Philippe Bruneau, Igor Aptekman; **C:** Pierre Lorraine; **M:** Manu Katche.

A Little Inside 🐾🐾½ 2001 (PG) Ed Mills (King) is a promising minor-league baseball player who quits the game when his wife dies so he can care for their daughter. Five years later, Ed is still struggling with this parenting gig, especially since Abby (Eisenberg) is growing up and getting into girlier things than Ed can cope with. So, since Abby does like baseball, Ed decides to take a second shot at rejoining his old team and regaining Abby's attention. The pint-sized Eisenberg is a scene-stealer par excellence. **95m/C VHS, DVD.** Benjamin King, Hallie Kate Eisenberg, Kathy Baker, Frankie Faison, Amanda Detmer, Jay Harrington, Sean Michael Arthur, Jared Padalecki; **D:** Kara Harshbarger; **W:** Kara James Levine. **VIDEO**

Little John 🐾🐾½ 2002 Natalie Britain (Reuben) is a Family Court judge with a secret of her own. Twelve years ago, she gave birth to a baby boy that she thought was put up for adoption. Instead, Little John (Bailey Jr.), known as L.J., was raised on a Texas farm by Natalie's estranged father John (Rhames). When John's health begins to fail, it's time for his daughter to learn the truth and for L.J. to get to know his mom. **99m/C VHS, DVD.** Gloria Reuben, Ving Rhames, Robert Bailey Jr., Patty Duke; **D:** Dick Lowry. **TV**

The Little Kidnappers 🐾🐾½ 1990 (G) Embittered man (Heston) is forced to take in his Scottish grandsons when the two boys are orphaned. They settle in with gramps in Nova Scotia but doned baby they've found, they are accused of being kidnappers. Cable remake of 1953 British film. **100m/C VHS.** *CA* Charlton Heston, Bruce Greenwood, Leah K. Pinsent, Charles Miller, Leo Wheatley, Patricia Gage; **D:** Donald Shebib. **CABLE**

Little Ladies of the Night 🐾 *Diamond Alley* 1977 Former pimp tries to save Purl and other teenagers from the world of prostitution. Exploitation posing as "significant drama." **96m/C VHS, DVD.** Linda Purl, David Soul, Clifton Davis, Carolyn Jones, Louis Gossett Jr.; **D:** Marvin J. Chomsky.

Little Laura & Big John 🐾🐾 1973 The true-life exploits of the small-time Ashley Gang in the Florida everglades around the turn of the century. Fabian's comeback vehicle, for what it's worth. **82m/C VHS, DVD.** Fabian, Karen Black; **D:** Luke Moberly.

Little Lord Fauntleroy 🐾🐾🐾½ 1936 Frances Hodgson Burnett story of a fatherless American boy who discovers he's heir to a British dukedom. Also available in computer-colorized version. Well cast, charming, remade for TV in 1980. Smith is loveable as the noble tyke's crusty old guardian. **102m/B VHS, DVD.** Freddie Bartholomew, Sir C. Aubrey Smith, Mickey Rooney, Dolores Costello, Jessie Ralph, Guy Kibbee; **D:** John Cromwell; **W:** Hugh Walpole; **C:** Charles Rosher; **M:** Max Steiner.

Little Lord Fauntleroy 🐾🐾½ 1980 A poor boy in New York suddenly finds himself the heir to his grandfather's estate in England. Lavish remake of the Frances Hodgson Burnett classic finds Cedric Erroll's life changing forever when he's discovered to be the Earl of Dorincourt. But the Earl turns out to be a bitter miser and it's up to the innocent boy to discover his joy in life. **100m/C VHS, DVD.** *GB* Ricky Schroder, Alec Guinness, Victoria Tennant, Eric Porter, Colin Blakely, Connie Booth, Rachel Kempson; **D:** Jack Gold. **TV**

Little Lord Fauntleroy 🐾🐾 1995 (G) British TV adaptation of the Frances Hodgson Burnett classic finds Cedric Erroll's life changing forever when he's discovered to be the Earl of Dorincourt. **100m/C VHS, DVD.** *GB* Michael Benz, Betsy Brantley, George Baker, Bernice Stegers; **D:** Andrew Morgan.

Little Man 🐾 2006 (PG-13) Another Wayans family vehicle, probably the worst yet, attempts to make a film about a dwarf jewel thief who poses as a baby in order to retrieve a stolen diamond he stashed with an unsuspecting couple. CGI-manipulation puts Wayans' face on a pint-sized body, while the "humor" seems to have been lifted directly from old Bugs Bunny cartoons and the crotch-shots of "America's Funniest Home Videos," either of which are better than this clunker. Directed by elder Wayans sib, Keenen Ivory. **97m/C DVD, Blu-ray Disc.** *US* Marlon Wayans, Shawn Wayans, Kerry Washington, Tracy Morgan, John Witherspoon, Lochlyn Munro, Chazz Palminteri, Linden Porco, Molly Shannon, Gabe Pimental, Paul DeMeliche, Alex Borstein, Brittany Daniel; **D:** Keenen Ivory Wayans; **W:** Marlon Wayans, Shawn Wayans, Keenen Ivory Wayans; **C:** Steven Bernstein; **M:** Teddy Castellucci. Golden Raspberries '06: Worst Actor (Wayans), Worst Actor (Wayans), Worst Remake.

Little Man Tate 🐾🐾🐾 1991 (PG) A seven-year-old genius is the prize in a tug of war between his mother, who wants him to lead a normal life, and a domineering school director who loves him for his intellect. An acclaimed directorial debut for Foster, with overtones of her own extraordinary life as a child prodigy. **99m/C VHS, DVD.** Jodie Foster, Dianne Wiest, Harry Connick Jr., Adam Hann-Byrd, George Plimpton, Debi Mazar, Celia Weston, David Hyde Pierce, Danitra Vance, Josh Mostel, P.J. Ochlan; **D:** Jodie Foster; **W:** Scott Frank; **C:** Mike Southon; **M:** Mark Isham.

Little Manhattan 🐾🐾 2005 (PG) Puppy love. Average 11-year-old Gabe (Hutcherson) likes to hang out with his pals and play hoops. Then, in karate class, he meets Rosemary (Ray) and Gabe is instantly smitten. But handling all these new emotions makes for some awkward moments. The overly-adult narration by Gabe is jarring but the outlook is sunny. **90m/C DVD.** Bradley Whitford, Cynthia Nixon, Josh Hutcherson, Willie Garson, Charlie Ray; **C:** Marc Levin; **W:** Jennifer Flackett; **C:** Tim Orr; **M:** Chad Fischer.

Little Marines 1990 Three young boys journey into the wilderness for three days of fun and instead embark on an incredible adventure. **90m/C VHS, DVD.** Stephen Baker, Steve Landers Jr., Noah Williams; **D:** A.J. Hixon.

The Little Match Girl 🐾🐾 1984 A musical version of the Hans Christian Andersen classic about a girl whose dying grandmother sells her of the magic in the matches she sells. **54m/C VHS.** Monica McSwain, Nancy Duncan, Matt McKim, Don Hays; **D:** Mark Hoeger.

The Little Match Girl 🐾🐾 1987 The Hans Christian Andersen Yuletide classic about an orphan selling magical matches, this time set in the 1920s, with the littlest "Cosby" kid in the title role. Ain't she cute? **96m/C VHS.** *GB* Keisha Knight Pulliam, Maryedith Burrell, William Daniels, Hallie Foote, Bill Davis, Rue McClanahan, John Rhys-Davies, Jim Metzler; **D:** Michael Lindsay-Hogg; **W:** Maryedith Burrell.

Little Men 🐾🐾½ 1940 A modern version of the classic juvenile story by Louisa May Alcott as too cute for words. **86m/B VHS, DVD.** Jack Oakie, Jimmy Lydon, Kay Francis, George Bancroft, Anne Howard; **D:** Norman Z. McLeod.

Little Men 🐾🐾½ 1998 (PG) Louisa May Alcott's sequel to "Little Women" hits the screen with a lot less hoopla than its 1994 predecessor. Jo March (Hemingway) has grown up, married Fritz Bhaer (Sarandon), and opened an idyllic, wholesome school for troubled boys. The house is immaculate, the grounds are beautiful, and the boys are little angels. That is, until streetwise 14-year-old Dan (Cook) shows up. He soon has the boys smoking, drinking, and stealing, until they almost burn the place down. Since this is a family movie, with moral lessons to be learned, all's well by the end. Adults may find the syrupy sweetness too much to take, and the characters are barely two-dimensional, but young kids should enjoy it. **98m/C VHS.** Mariel Hemingway, Chris Sarandon, Michael Caloz, Ben Cook, Michael Yarmush, Gabrielle Boni, Ricky Mabe, Julia Garland, B.J. McLellan, Tyler Hines, Kathleen Fee; **D:** Rodney Gibbons; **W:** Mark Evan Schwartz; **C:** Arch Archambault; **M:** Milan Kymlicka.

The Little Mermaid ✍✍½ 1975
(G) An animated version of Hans Christian Andersen's tale about a little mermaid who rescues a prince whose boat has capsized. She immediately falls in love and wishes that she could become a human girl. Not to be confused with the 1989 Disney version. 71m/C VHS, JP **D:** Tim Reid; **M:** Ronald Goodwin; **V:** Kirsten Bishop, Ian Finley, Thor Bishopric.

Little Miss Marker ✍✍½ 1980 (PG)
Mediocre remake of the often retold story of a bookie who accepts a little girl as a security marker for a $10 bet. Disappointing performance from Curtis adds to an already dull film. 103m/C VHS, DVD, Walter Matthau, Julie Andrews, Tony Curtis, Bob Newhart, Lee Grant, Sara Stimson, Brian Dennehy; **D:** Walter Bernstein; **W:** Walter Bernstein; **M:** Henry Mancini.

Little Miss Sunshine ✍✍✍ 2006 (R) A quirky, dysfunctional family piles into their VW bus and road trips to California so little sis, Olive (Breslin), can compete (as an alternate from the Albu-

querque region) in the titular pre-teen pageant, her young life's ambition. Along for the ride are her hugely unsuccessful motivational speaker dad (Kinnear), ready-to-snap mom (Collette), crass drug-snorting grandpa (Arkin), mute-by-choice Nietzschean brother (Dano), and suicidal despondent uncle (Carell). Smart script in the hands of top-notch cast results in original, enjoyable movie. 101m/C DVD, US Greg Kinnear, Toni Collette, Abigail Breslin, Steven Carell, Alan Arkin, Paul Franklin Dano, Bryan Cranston, Wallace (Wally) Langham, Mary Lynn Rajskub, Beth Grant; **D:** Jonathan Dayton, Valerie Faris; **W:** Michael Arndt; **C:** Tim Suristedt; **M:** Mychael Danna. Oscars '06: Orig. Screenplay, Supp. Actor (Arkin); British Acad. '06: Orig. Screenplay, Support. Actor (Arkin); Ind. Spirit '07: Director (Dayton), Director (Faris), Film, Support. Actor (Arkin), First Screenplay; Screen Actors Guild '06: Cast; First Screenplay; Screen Actors Guild '06: Orig. Screenplay.

Little Minister ✍✍ 1934 An adaptation of the James Barrie novel about a prissy Scottish pastor who falls in love with a free-spirited gypsy...he thinks she is, in fact, the local earl's daughter, played to perfection by the young Hepburn. 101m/B VHS, Katharine Hepburn, John Beal, Alan Hale, Donald Crisp; **D:** Richard Wallace; **W:** Victor Heerman; **M:** Max Steiner.

Little Miss Broadway ✍✍ 1938
Orphan Temple brings the residents of a theatrical boarding house together in hopes of getting them into show business. She and Durante give worthwhile performances. Also available in computer-colorized version. ♪Be Optimistic; How Can I Thank You; I'll Build a Broadway For You; If All the World Were Paper; Thank You For the Use of the Hall; We Should Be Together; Swing Me an Old-Fashioned Song; When You Were Sweet Sixteen; Happy Birthday to You. 70m/B VHS, DVD, Shirley Temple, George Murphy, Jimmy Durante, Phyllis Brooks, Edna May Oliver, George Barbier, Donald Meek, Jane Darwell; **D:** Irving Cummings; **C:** Artur C. Miller.

Little Miss Innocence ✍ 1973
Recording executives tries to survive the amorous advances of the two attractive female hitchhikers that he drove home. 79m/C VHS, Judy Medford; **D:** Chris Warfield.

Little Miss Marker ✍✍✍ 1934 Heartwarming story starring Temple as the little character, who is left with bookie Sorrowful Jones (Menjou) as father as a gambling debt. But when her father doesn't return, it's up to Jones and his racetrack friends to make little Marky a home. Naturally, Temple steals her way into everyone's heart. Based on a story by Damon Runyon; remade three times as "Sorrowful Jones," as "40 Pounds of Trouble," and in 1980 with the original title. 83m/B VHS, DVD, Adolphe Menjou, Shirley Temple, Dorothy Dell, Charles Bickford, Lynne Overman; **D:** Alexander Hall; **W:** Sam Hellman, Gladys Lehman, William R. Lipman; **M:** Ralph Rainger; Natl Film Reg. '98.

Little Nellie Kelly ✍✍½ 1940
Garland plays both mother and daughter in a film based on a musical comedy by George M. Cohan. Garland is married to Irish cop Murphy but dies in childbirth. The film then advances 20 years to daughter Garland who is trying to make good on the stage and have a romance with a young man her father disapproves of. ♪Nellie Kelly I Love You; Nellie is a Darling; It's a Great Day For the Irish; A Pretty Girl Milking Her Cow; Danny Boy; Singing in the Rain. 100m/B VHS, Judy Garland, George Murphy, Charles Winninger, Douglas McPhail; **D:** Norman Taurog.

Little Nemo: Adventures in Slumberland ✍✍½ 1992 (G) A bland animated tale of a young boy whose dreams take him to Slumberland. There, Nemo unwittingly unleashes a monster from Nightmare Land who kidnaps Slumberland's king. Nemo must then rescue the king—aided by the king's daughter, a comic squirrel sidekick, and a mischievous con-frog. Based on Winsor McCay's 1900 comic strip. Has some cute comic moments for the kiddies and while the animation is better than Saturday-morning cartoon quality, it's not Disney. 85m/C VHS, DVD. **D:** William T. Hurtz, Masami Hata; **W:** Chris Columbus, Richard Outten; **M:** Tom Chase, Steve Rucker; **V:** Gabriel Damon, Mickey Rooney, Rene Auberjonois, Daniel Mann, Laura Mooney, Bernard Erhard, William E. Martin.

Little Monsters ✍✍ 1989 (PG) A young boy (Savage) discovers a monster (Mandel) under his bed and eventually befriends it. The pair embark on adventures that land them in trouble. Hardworking, talented cast hurdles the weak script, but can't save the film. 100m/C VHS, DVD, Fred Savage, Howie Mandel, Margaret Whitton, Ben Savage, Daniel Stern, Rick) Ducommun, Frank Whaley; **D:** Richard Alan Greenberg; **W:** Ted Elliott, Terry Rossio; **C:** Dick Bush; **M:** David Newman.

Little Mother ✍✍ 1971 Metzger's take on Argentina's Eva Peron highlights her sexual powers (of course) as it tells of Eva's climb out of poverty, and into the heights of political power. Filmed in Yugoslavia. 95m/C VHS, DVD, Christiane Kruger, Ivan Desny, Anton Diffring; **D:** Radley Metzger; **W:** Brian Phelan; **C:** Hans Jura.

Little Murders ✍✍✍ 1971 (PG) Black comedy set in NYC. A woman convinces a passive photographer to marry her. Gardenia gives an excellent performance as the woman's father. A shadow of crime, depression, and strife seem to hangs over the funny parts of this film; more often than depressing than anything else. Adapted by Jules Feiffer from his own play. 108m/C VHS, DVD, Elliott Gould, Marcia Rodd, Vincent Gardenia, Elizabeth Wilson, Jon Korkes, Donald Sutherland, Alan Arkin, Lou Jacobi; **D:** Alan Arkin; **W:** Jules Feiffer; **C:** Gordon Willis.

Little Moon & Jud McGraw ✍✍ 1978 A wronged Indian woman and a framed cowpoke take their revenge on a small, corrupt town, razing it overnight. Already-weak plot is disabled by too many flashbacks. 92m/C VHS, DVD, James Caan, Sammy Davis Jr., Stefanie Powers, Aldo Ray; **D:** Bernard Girard.

Little Nicky ✍✍ 2000 (PG-13) All hail Adam Sandler, King of the Idiot Boys! Notoriously bashed by critics, Sandler doesn't seem too worried about their opinions as he rolls around on the giant pile of money his crude but funny movies make. This time his underdog hero is Nicky (Sandler), the son of Satan (Keitel) and an angel (Witherspoon), who hangs out in a very cartoony hell. When Satan calls his sons together to name his heir, he instead declares that he will rule for another 10,000 years, causing brothers Adrian (Rhys Ifans, Tommy (Tiny) Lister, Harvey Keitel, and Cassius to stage a rebellion by being let loose to New York City. Nicky and his talking dog sidekick Mr. Beefy (voice of Smigel) are then sent to capture them. Along the way, he gains the standard Hollywood-issued love interest (Arquette). Broader and more satirical than the standard Sandler's work, it's also the first that has him surrounded by top-line talent (not that it helps any). 90m/C VHS, DVD, Adam Sandler, Patricia Arquette, Allen Covert, Blake Clark, Rodney Dangerfield, Kevin Nealon, Reese Witherspoon, Lewis Arquette, Dana Carvey, Jon Lovitz, Michael McKean, Quentin Tarantino, Carl Weathers, Rob Schneider, Clint Howard, Ellen Cleghorne, Fred Wolf Cameos: Dan Marino, Henry Winkler, Regis Philbin, Ozzy Osbourne, Bill Walton; **D:** Steven Brill; **W:** Adam Sandler, Steven Brill, Tim Herzlihy; **C:** Theo van de Sande; **M:** Teddy Castellucci; **V:** Robert Smigel.

A Little Night Music ✍✍½ 1977
(PG) Features four interwoven, contemporary love stories adapted from the Broadway play, and based loosely on Bergman's "Smiles of a Summer Night." Taylor's pathetic rendition of "Send in the Clowns" should be banned. Filmed on location in Austria. 110m/C VHS, DVD, Elizabeth Taylor, Diana Rigg, Hermione Gingold, Len Cariou, Lesley-Anne Down; **D:** Harold Prince. Oscars '77: Orig. Song Score and/or Adapt.

Little Nikita ✍✍ 1988 (PG) A California boy (Phoenix) discovers that his parents are actually Soviet spies planted as American citizens for eventual call to duty. Poitier's performance as the FBI agent tracking the spies is about the only spark in this somewhat incoherent thriller. 98m/C VHS, DVD, River Phoenix, Sidney Poitier, Richard Bradford, Richard Lynch, Caroline Kava, Lucy Deakins; **D:** Richard Benjamin; **W:** Bo Goldman, John Hill; **M:** Marvin Hamlisch.

Little Ninjas ✍✍½ 1992 Three topnotch ninja kids go up against the Samurai to rescue their friend who is being held hostage. 85m/C VHS, Steven Nelson, Jon Anzaldo, Alan Godshaw; **D:** Emmett Alston.

Little Noises ✍✍ 1991 Glover stars as an artist who seeks not only fame and fortune, but also the love of his best friend (O'Neal). He finally creates a piece that his agent loves, but problems arise. 91m/C VHS, Crispin Glover, Tatum O'Neal, Rik Mayall, Tate Donovan, John C. McGinley; **D:** Jane Spencer; **W:** Jane Spencer.

Little Odessa ✍✍½ 1994 (R) Working for an organized crime family, hitman Joshua Shapira (Roth) returns to his childhood neighborhood to carry out his next assignment. Set in the Russian-Jewish emigre community of Brooklyn's Brighton Beach, Gray's directorial debut explores Joshua's relationship with his family—especially kid brother Reuben (Furlong). Not your typical mob opera, this one focuses more on characters than killing. Relationships between family members are explored to the hilt, but the audience is left with too many unanswered questions. Dimly lit and entirely too ambiguous, this family tragedy could spawn a serious case of depression. 98m/C VHS, DVD, Tim Roth, Edward Furlong, Moira Kelly, Vanessa Redgrave, Maximilian Schell, Paul Guilfoyle, Natasha Andrejchenko, David Vadim, Mina Bern, Boris McGiver, Mohammed Ghaffari, Michael Khumov, Dmitry Preyers, David Ross, Ron Brice, Jace Kant, Marianna Lead, Gene Ruffini; **D:** James Gray; **W:** James Gray; **C:** Tom Richmond; **M:** Dana Sano.

Little Orphan Annie ✍✍ 1918
Surrounded by a group of children, poet James Whitcomb Riley narrates the story of Little Orphant Annie, who loses her mother at an early age and is sent to an

orphanage where she charms the other children with her stories of ghosts and elves. 57m/B VHS, Thomas Santschi, Eugenie Besserer, Ben Alexander, Lillie Hayward, Lafe (Lafayette) McKee, Colleen Moore, Harry Lonsdale, Doris Baker, Lillian Wade, Billy Jacobs, James Whitcomb Riley; **D:** Colin Campbell.

The Little Prince ✍✍ 1974 (G) Disappointing adaptation of the classic children's story by Antoine de Saint-Exupery, about a little boy from asteroid B-612. Lousy Lerner and Loewe score underscores a general lack of magic or spontaneity. ♪It's a Hat; I Need Air; I'm On Your Side; Be Happy; You're a Child; I Never Met a Rose; Why is the Desert (Lovely to See)?; Closer and Closer and Closer; Little Prince (From Who Knows Where). 88m/C VHS, DVD, *B* Richard Kiley, Bob Fosse, Steven Warner, Gene Wilder, Joss Ackland, Clive Revill, Victor Spinetti, Graham Crowden, Donna McKechnie; **D:** Stanley Donen; **W:** Alan Jay Lerner; **C:** Christopher Challis; **M:** Frederick Loewe, Alan Jay Lerner; Golden Globes '75: Score.

Little Orphan Annie ✍✍½ 1932 The unjustly forgotten first sound adaptation of the comic strip. Fun score adds a lot, as does the good cast. 60m/B VHS, May Robson, Buster Phelps, Mitzie Green, Edgar Kennedy; **D:** John S. Robertson; **M:** Max Steiner.

The Little Princess ✍✍✍½ 1995
(G) Compelling fantasy, based on the children's book by Frances Hodgson Burnett, and previously best known for the 1939 Shirley Temple incarnation. Sara (Matthews) has been raised in India by her widowed father (Cunningham). When he's called up to fight in WWI, Sara is forced into stern Miss Michin's (Bron) school, where her money makes her a favored boarder. However, the irrepressible Sara suffers a severe reversal of fortune when her father is reported killed and Miss Michin promptly makes charm has made her some true friends who become her allies under trying circumstances. Lively script, dazzling visuals, and a welcome lack of sappiness create a classic-in-the-making. 97m/C VHS, DVD, Liesl Matthews, Eleanor Bron, Liam Cunningham, Rusty Schwimmer, Heather DeLoach, Vanessa Lee Chester, Errol Sitahal, Heather Ashton Holmes, Bug Hall, Zachary Mabry, Kevin Jamal Woods, Ross Bagley, Sam Saletta, Blake Collins, Jordan Warkol, Blake Ewing, Juliette Brewer, Heather Karasek; Cameos: Whoopi Goldberg; **D:** Alfonso Cuaron; **W:** Richard La-Gravenese, Elizabeth Chandler; **C:** Emmanuel Lubezki; **M:** Patrick Doyle.

The Little Rascals ✍✍½ 1994
(PG) Alfalfa runs afoul of the membership requirements for the "He-Man Woman Haters Club" when he starts to fall for Darla. Charming remake of the short film series, now set in suburban L.A., from Spheeris, who also recast another TV favorite, the Beverly Hillbillies. 83m/C VHS, DVD, Daryl Hannah, Courtland Mead, Travis Tedford, Brittany Ashton Holmes, Bug Hall, Zachary Mabry, Kevin Jamal Woods, Ross Bagley, Sam Saletta, Blake Collins, Jordan Warkol, Blake Ewing, Juliette Brewer, Heather Karasek; Cameos: Whoopi Goldberg, Donald Trump, Mel Brooks, Daryl Hannah, Reba McEntire; **D:** Penelope Spheeris; **W:** Penelope Spheeris, Paul Guay, Stephen Mazur; **C:** Richard Bowen; **M:** David Foster, Linda Thompson.

The Little Princess ✍✍✍½ 1939 (G) Based on the Frances Hodgson Burnett children's classic, perhaps the best of the moppet's films. Shirley is a young schoolgirl in Victorian London sent to a harsh boarding school when her Army officer father is posted abroad. When her father is declared missing, the penniless girl must work as a servant at the school to pay her keep, all the while haunting the hospitals, never believing her father has died. A classic tearjerker. 91m/B VHS, DVD, Shirley Temple, Richard Greene, Anita Louise, Ian Hunter, Cesar Romero, Arthur Treacher, Sybil Jason, Miles Mander, Marcia Mae Jones, E.E. Clive; **D:** Walter Lang; **W:** Ethel Hill, Walter Ferris; **C:** Arthur C. Miller; **M:** Walter Bullock.

The Little Princess ✍✍ 1987 A three-cassette adaptation of Frances Hodgson Burnett's book. In Victorian England, kind-hearted Sara is forced into poverty when her father suddenly dies. Can his longtime friend find her and restore her happiness? Originally aired on PBS as part of the "Wonderworks" family movie series. 180m/C VHS, *B* Amelia Shankley, Nigel Havers, Maureen Lipman; **D:** Carol Wiseman. **TV**

Little Red Riding Hood 🟊🟊🟊 1983 From "Faerie Tale Theatre" comes the retelling of the story about a girl (Mary Steenburgen) who is sent over her grandmother a picnic basket, only to get stopped by a wicked wolf McDowell. Not particularly faithful, but fun and scary. 60m/C VHS, DVD. Mary Steenburgen, Malcolm McDowell; **D:** Graeme Clifford. **CABLE**

Little Red Schoolhouse 🟊🟊 1936 A hard-nosed schoolteacher hunts for a truant lad and both of them land in jail. 64m/C VHS. Frank "Junior" Coghlan, Dickie Moore, Ann Doran, Lloyd Hughes, Richard Carle, Ralf Harolde, Matthew Betz, Kenneth Howell, Sidney Miller, Lafe (Lafayette) McKee; **D:** Charles Lamont; **W:** Paul Perez; **C:** M.A. Anderson.

Little Richard 🟊🟊½ 2000 The struggle between rock 'n' roll and religion is the story behind this biography of the legendary Little Richard Penniman (well-played by Leon). Born in Georgia in 1943, the boy is too much of a sissy for his stern father (Lumbly) although his mother (Lewis) and local minister Preacher Rainey (Morris) encourage his singing in the choir. But soon Little Richard has succumbed to the secular and found success, although he comes to realize the inequities of the music business for a black man. But he also sees signs from God to leave show business for life in the ministry and continues to struggle between the two. 120m/C VHS, DVD. Leon, Jenifer Lewis, Carl Lumbly, Tamala Jones, Mel Jackson, Garrett Morris; **D:** Robert Kevin Townsend; **W:** Daniel Taplitz; **C:** Edward Pei. **TV**

A Little Romance 🟊🟊🟊 1979 (PG) An American girl living in Paris falls in love with a French boy; eventually the two run away, to seal their love with a kiss beneath a bridge. Olivier gives a wonderful, if not hammy, performance as the old pickpocket who encourages her. Gentle, agile comedy based on the novel by Patrick Cauvin. 110m/C VHS, DVD. Laurence Olivier, Diane Lane, Thelonious Bernard, Sally Kellerman, Broderick Crawford; **D:** George Roy Hill; **W:** Allan Burns; **M:** Georges Delerue. Oscars '79: Orig. Score.

Little Secrets 🟊🟊½ 2002 (PG) Fourteen-year-old Emily (Wood) is spending the summer practicing her violin in hopes of auditioning for a place in the local orchestra. As a sideline, she runs a service in her backyard for the neighbor kids, where they can reveal their secrets, which Emily writes down and locks away for safekeeping. The film reassures that it's better to tell the truth than keep secrets and that even big problems are able to be solved if you talk about them. It may not be the real world but it's a nice one to visit. 107m/C VHS, DVD. US Evan Rachel Wood, David Gallagher, Vivica A. Fox, Michael Angarano, Jan Gardner; **D:** Blair Treu; **W:** Jessica Barondes; **C:** Brian Sullivan; **M:** Sam Cardon.

A Little Sex 🟊🟊 1982 (R) Capshaw, in her screen debut, finds herself the wife of womanizer Matheson. Harmless, but pointless, with a TV-style plot. 94m/C VHS, DVD. Tim Matheson, Kate Capshaw, Edward Herrmann, Wallace Shawn, John Glover; **D:** Bruce Paltrow; **W:** Robert De Laurentiis; **M:** Georges Delerue.

Little Shop of Horrors 🟊🟊🟊 1986 (PG-13) During a solar eclipse, Seymour buys an unusual plant and takes it back to the flower shop where he works. The plant, Audrey 2, becomes a town at-

traction as it grows at an unusual rate, but Seymour learns that he must feed Audrey fresh human blood to keep her growing. Soon, Audrey is giving the orders ("Feed me") and timid Seymour must find "deserving" victims. Martin's performance as the masochistic dentist is alone worth the price. Song, dance, gore, and more prevail in this outrageous musical comedy. Four Tops Levi Stubbs is the commanding voice of Audrey 2. Based on the Off-Broadway play, which was based on Roger Corman's 1960 horror spoof. 🎵 Mean Green Mother From Outer Space; Some Fun Now; Your Day Begins Tonight. 94m/C VHS, DVD. Rick Moranis, Ellen Greene, Vincent Gardenia, Steve Martin, James Belushi, Christopher Guest, Bill Murray, John Candy, Tisha Campbell, Tichina Arnold, Michelle Weeks; **D:** Frank Oz; **W:** Howard Ashman; **C:** Robert Paynter; **M:** Miles Goodman, Alan Menken, Howard Ashman; **V:** Levi Stubbs Jr.

Little Shots of Happiness 🟊🟊 1997 (R) Prim Frances leaves her unstable husband and, unbeknownst to her co-workers, is living out of her office. In the evenings, she creates a wild new identity for herself and finds the Boston nightclubs where she picks up a different man each night. Of course, Frances discovers there's a price to pay for her new liberation. 85m/C VHS, DVD. Bonnie Dickenson, Todd Verow, Linda Ekolian, Rita Gavelis, P.J. Marino, Castalia Jason, Leanne Whitney, Bill Dwyer, Eric Sapp, Maureen Picard, Eric Romley; **D:** Todd Verow; **W:** Jim Dwyer, Todd Verow; **C:** Todd Verow.

Little Sister 🟊🟊½ 1992 (PG-13) Prankster Silverman, on a dare, dresses up as a girl and joins a sorority. Problems arise when he falls in love with his "big sister" (Milano) in the sorority. What will happen when she finds out the truth? Will we care? 94m/C VHS. Jonathan Silverman, Alyssa Milano; **W:** Sergio D. Altieri.

A Little Stiff 🟊🟊 1991 Slacker romantic comedy about the unrequited romance between filmmaker Caveh and fellow UCLA student McKim from first meeting, through angst, and grand final gestures. 85m/C VHS. Erin McKim, Caveh Zahedi; **D:** Caveh Zahedi, Greg Watkins; **M:** Kath Bloom.

Little Sweetheart 🟊🟊½ 1990 (R) A reworking of "The Bad Seed," with a nine-year-old girl engaging in murder, burglary, and blackmail, ruining the adults around her. Based on "The Naughty Girls" by Arthur Wise. 93m/C VHS. John Hurt, Karen Young, Barbara Bosson, John McMartin, Cassie Barasch; **D:** Anthony Simmons.

The Little Theatre of Jean Renoir 🟊🟊🟊 1971 A farewell by director Jean Renoir featuring three short films. In the first, Renoir's humanist beliefs are apparent in "The Last Christmas Dinner," a Hans Christian Andersen-inspired story. Next, "The Electric Floor Waxer" is a comic opera. The third piece is called "A Tribute to Tolerance." Slight but important late statement by a great director. In French with English subtitles. 100m/C VHS. Jean Amoul, Fernand Sardou, Jean Carmet, Francoise Amoul, Jeanne Moreau; **D:** Jean Renoir; **W:** Jean Renoir.

The Little Thief 🟊🟊🟊 1989 (PG-13) Touted as Francois Truffaut's final legacy, this trite minidrama is actually based on a story he co-wrote with Claude de Givray about a post-WWII adolescent girl who reacts to the world around her by stealing and petty crime. Truffaut's hand is markedly absent, but this film is a testament to his abruptly and sadly truncated career. Director Miller was Truffaut's long-time assistant. French with subtitles. 108m/C VHS. FR Charlotte Gainsbourg, Simon de la Brosse, Didier Bezace, Raoul Billerey, Nathalie Cardone; **D:** Claude Miller; **W:** Annie Miller, Claude Miller; **C:** Dominique Chapuis; **M:** Alain Jomy.

Little Tough Guys 🟊🟊 1938 The Little Tough Guys (a.k.a. Dead End Kids) come to the rescue of Halop, a young tough guy gone bad to avenge his father's unjust imprisonment. First of the "Little Tough Guys" series for the former Dead End Kids, who later became the East Side Kids before eventually evolving into the Bowery Boys. 84m/B VHS. Helen Parrish, Billy

Halop, Leo Gorcey, Marjorie Main, Gabriel Dell, Huntz Hall; **D:** Harold Young.

Little Treasure 🟊🟊½ 1985 (R) A stripper heads for Mexico to search for her long-lost father, but ends up looking for treasure with an American guy. Disappointing effort of director Sharp. 95m/C VHS. Burt Lancaster, Margot Kidder, Ted Danson, Joseph Hacker, Malena Doria; **D:** Alan Sharp; **W:** Alan Sharp.

The Little Valentino 🟊🟊 1979 One day in the aimless life of a young punk who gets by on his wits and petty theft. Jeles' directorial debut. In Hungarian with English subtitles. 102m/B VHS. HU Janos Opoczki, Denes Ladanyi, Sandome Arpa, Phyllis Fraser; **D:** Andras Jeles; **W:** Andras Jeles; **C:** Sandor Kavdos; **M:** Kamillo Lendvay.

The Little Vampire 🟊🟊 2000 (PG) A cluttered storyline and wandering direction help put a stake in the heart of this tale of a lonely boy and a family of vegetarian vampires. Tony (Lipnicki) is forced to move from sunny California to gloomy Scotland when his father gets a job building a golf course for crusty Lord Ashton (Wood). After being bullied by the local kids at school, Tony starts daydreaming about vampires to take his mind off his loneliness. As if summoned by magic, soon a young vampire named Rudolph (Weeks) appears at his window, befriending Tony and taking him on a flight through the countryside. After he introduces Rudolph to American slang and Nintendo, Tony is introduced to Rudolph's family. Rudolph's father Frederick (Grant) and mother Freda (Krige) explain to Tony that they are trying to become human once again, but need the other half of a magic amulet held by Lord Ashton to complete the spell. Meanwhile, crazed vampire hunter Rookery (Carter) stalks the family. Some scenes are visually stunning (especially those vampire cows) but the convoluted plot puts this one six feet under. 91m/C VHS, DVD. Jonathan Lipnicki, Richard E. Grant, Alice Krige, Jim Carter, John Wood, Pamela Gidley, Tommy Hinkley, Rollo Weeks, Anna Popplewell, Dean Cook; **D:** Uli Edel; **W:** Karey Kirkpatrick, Larry Wilson; **C:** Bernd Heinl; **M:** Nigel Clarke, Michael Csanyi-Wills.

Little Vegas 🟊🟊½ 1990 (R) Looks like easy street for a young man who inherits a bundle from his girlfriend, but he's forced to wake up and smell the cappuccino when her family and the other residents of the tiny desert berg think there's a gigolo in the woodpile. Much strife with siblings as he wages a battle for the bucks with the son while wooing the woman's daughter, who has a measure of mob inflicted plot twists. Mildly amusing, cut from vein of you can't get rich quick and get away with it. 90m/C VHS. Michael Nouri, Jerry Stiller, John Sayles, Anthony John (Tony) Denison, Catherine O'Hara, Bruce McGill, Anne Francis, Bob(cat) Goldthwait, Jay Thomas, Perry Lang; **D:** Perry Lang; **W:** Perry Lang; **M:** Mason Daring.

Little Vera 🟊🟊 1988 Extremely well-done Soviet film chronicles the life of a young working-class woman who loves rock music and who has been profoundly affected by Western civilization. Post-glasnost Soviet production gives Westerners a glimpse into the Russian way of life. A boxoffice bonanza back home. Russian with subtitles. 130m/C VHS, DVD. RU Natalia (Natalya) Negoda, Andrei Sokolov, Yuri Nazarov, Ludmila Zaisova, Alexander Niegreva; **D:** Vassili Pitchul.

Little Voice 🟊🟊🟊 1998 (R) Little Voice (Horrocks) misses her dead father so much that she withdraws from the world, communicating only by singing along with the records Dad loved. Whether it's Judy Garland, Shirley Bassey, or Edith Piaf, "LV" can match the voice exactly. When her mom's (Blethyn) sleazy talent-agent boyfriend (Caine) hears her, he knows she's the ticket to fame and fortune. Little Voice has no desire to be a star, so she clams up whenever there's an audience. Club owner and weasel Mr. Boo (Broadbent) books her for several shows, including one with a London talent scout on hand, and everyone wonders if she'll sing. Caine and Broadbent do their best to

out-slime each other and deliver most of the comedy. Horrocks gives a showcase performance, re-creating her role from the stage play "The Rise and Fall of Little Voice." The play was written specifically to take advantage of her spectacular impersonation talents. 97m/C VHS, DVD. GB Jane Horrocks, Michael Caine, Ewan McGregor, Brenda Blethyn, Jim Broadbent, Annette Badland, Philip Jackson; **D:** Mark Herman; **W:** Mark Herman; **C:** Andy Collins; **M:** John Altman. Golden Globes '99: Actor—Mus./Comedy (Caine).

Little White Lies 🟊🟊 1989 Jillian and Matheson meet and fall in love during an exotic vacation. But both are traveling under assumed identities—she's a police-woman tracking a jewel thief and he's an incognito doctor. When they reunite stateside they try to stick to their ruses in humdrum comedic fashion. Made for network TV. 88m/C VHS. Ann Jillian, Tim Matheson; **D:** Anson Williams. **TV**

Little Witches 🟊🟊 1996 (R) Rejected group of seniors at Catholic girls' high school are transformed into a witches coven, thanks to a book of spells. A rip-off of "The Craft." 91m/C VHS, DVD. Mimi Reichmeister, Jack Nance, Jennifer Rubin, Sheeri Rappaport, Melissa Taub, Zoe Alexander, Zelda Rubinstein, Eric Pierpoint; **D:** Jane Simpson; **W:** Brian DiMuccio, Dino Vindeni; **C:** Ron Turowski; **M:** Nicholas Rivera.

Little Women 🟊🟊 1933 Louisa May Alcott's Civil War story of the four March sisters—Jo, Beth, Amy, and Meg—who share their loves, their joys, and their sorrows. Everything about this classic film is wonderful, from the lavish period costumes to the excellent script, and particularly the captivating performances by the cast. A must-see for fans of Alcott and Hepburn, and others will find it enjoyable. 107m/B VHS, DVD. Katharine Hepburn, Joan Bennett, Paul Lukas, Edna May Oliver, Frances Dee, Spring Byington, Jean Parker, Douglass Montgomery; **D:** George Cukor; **W:** Victor Heerman, Sarah Y. Mason; **C:** Henry W. Gerrard; **M:** Max Steiner. Oscars '33: Adapt. Screenplay; Venice Film Fest. '34: Actress (Hepburn).

Little Women 🟊🟊 1949 Stylized color remake of the George Cukor 1933 classic. Top-notch if too obvious cast portrays Louisa May Alcott's story of teenage girls growing up against the backdrop of the Civil War. 121m/C VHS, DVD. June Allyson, Peter Lawford, Margaret O'Brien, Elizabeth Taylor, Janet Leigh, Mary Astor; **D:** Mervyn LeRoy; **W:** Andrew Solt; **M:** Adolph Deutsch. Oscars '49: Art Dir./Set Dec., Color.

Little Women 🟊🟊 1978 The third screen version of Louisa May Alcott's classic story. Lackluster compared to the previous attempts, particularly the sterling 1933 film, but still worthwhile. During the Civil War, four sisters share their lives as they grow up and find romance. Garson's TV debut. Followed by a TV series. 200m/C VHS. Meredith Baxter, Susan Dey, Ann Dusenberry, Eve Plumb, Dorothy McGuire, Robert Young, Greer Garson, Cliff (Potter) Potts, William Shatner; **D:** David Lowell Rich; **M:** Elmer Bernstein. **TV**

Little Women 🟊🟊🟊 1994 (PG) Beloved story of the March women is beautifully portrayed in a solid production that blends a seamless screenplay with an excellent cast, authentic period costumes, and lovely cinematography and music. Ryder, perfectly cast as the unconventional Jo, is also the strongest of the sisters: domestically inclined Meg (Alvarado), the fragile Beth (Danes), and the youngest, mischievous Amy (the delightful Dunst) who grows up into a sedate young lady (Mathis). Charming adaptation remains faithful to the spirit of the Alcott classic while adding contemporary touches. Fitting prelude to the big screen by producer/director Armstrong. 118m/C VHS, DVD. Winona Ryder, Gabriel Byrne, Trini Alvarado, Samantha Mathis, Kirsten Dunst, Claire Danes, Christian Bale, Eric Stoltz, John Newville, Mary Wickes, Susan Sarandon; **D:** Gillian Armstrong; **W:** Robin Swicord; **C:** Geoffrey Simpson; **M:** Thomas Newman.

Little World of Don Camillo 🟊🟊 1951 *Le Petit Monde de Don Camillo* 1951 A French-made farce based on the beloved novels of Giovanni

Guareschi. Earthy, priest Don Camillo clashes repeatedly with his friendly enemy, the communist mayor of a tiny Italian village. The hero talks directly to God, whose voice is provided by Orson Welles. Charming, good-natured approach. 106m/ B VHS, *FR* Ifernandel, Gino Cervi, Sylvia, Vera Talchi; *D:* Julien Duvivier. *Mar:* Orson Welles.

The Littlest Angel ♪♪ 1969 Musical about a shepherd boy who dies falling off a cliff and wants to become an angel. He learns a valuable lesson in the spirit of giving. Made for TV. 77m/C VHS, DVD. Johnny Whitaker, Fred Gwynne, E.G. Marshall, Cab Calloway, Connie Stevens, Tony Randall; *D:* Joe Layton; *W:* Patricia Gray, Lan O'Kun; *M:* Joseph Howard. TV

The Littlest Horse Thieves ♪♪ 1976 (G) *Escape from the Dark* Good Disney film about three children and their efforts to save some ponies who work in mines. The children take it upon themselves to see that the animals escape the abuse and neglect they are put through. Filmed on location in England with excellent photography. 109m/C VHS, DVD. Maurice Colbourne, Susan Tebbs, Andrew Harrison, Chloe Franks, Alastair Sim, Peter Barkworth; *D:* Charles Jarrott; *W:* Rosemary Anne Sisson; *C:* Paul Beeson; *M:* Ronald Goodwin.

The Littlest Outlaw ♪♪½ 1954 A Mexican peasant boy steals a beautiful stallion to save it from being destroyed. She befriends a Union officer while protecting her father at the same time. She even goes to Washington to talk with President Lincoln. Nice dance sequences by Temple and Robinson. Available in computer-colored version. 75m/C VHS, DVD. Shirley Temple, John Boles, Jack Holt, Bill Robinson, Karen Morley, Willie Best; *D:* David Butler.

The Littlest Viking ♪♪½ 1994 (PG) Twelve-year-old Sigurd finds archery practice and mock battles an exciting way to learn to be a Viking. But when his older brother is killed in battle, Sigurd's father expects him to avenge the death, and Sigurd must decide just what being a Viking prince means. Scenic Scandinavian settings; obvious dubbing. 85m/C VHS. Kristian Tonby, Per Jansen, Terje Strömdahl; *D:* Knut W. Jorfald, Lars Rasmussen, Paul Trevor Bale.

Live a Little, Love a Little ♪♪ 1968 (PG) Itinerant photographer Elvis juggles two different jobs by running around a lot. Sexually more frank than earlier King vehicles. ♪Almost in Love; A Little Less Conversation; Edge of Reality; Wonderful World. 90m/C VHS, DVD. Elvis Presley, Michele Carey, Rudy Vallee, Don Porter, Dick Sargent, Sterling Holloway, Eddie Hodges; *D:* Norman Taurog.

Live and Let Die ♪♪ 1973 (PG) Agent 007 (Moore) is out to thwart the villainous Dr. Kananga (Kotto), a black mastermind who plans to control western powers with voodoo and hard drugs. He's aided by psychic tarot-reading virgin Solitaire (Seymour), who falls prey to Bond's charms. Moore's first appearance as Bond in the 8th film in the series. Can't we have the real Bond back? Title song by Paul McCartney and Wings. 131m/C VHS, DVD. GB Roger Moore, Jane Seymour, Yaphet Kotto, Clifton James, Julius W. Harris, Geoffrey Holder, David Hedison, Gloria Hendry, Bernard Lee, Lois Maxwell, Madeline Smith; *C:* Ted Moore; *W:* Tom Mankewicz; *D:* Guy Hamilton; *M:* George Martin.

Live Bait ♪♪½ 1995 Canadian-flavored Gen-X comedy features suburban 23-year-old virgin Trevor MacIntosh (Scholte) trying for a little romance (or at least sex) but seemingly doomed to failure. At least until he meets much older artist Charlotte (Maunsell). Sweeney handles his debut writing, directing, and producing skills with equal aplomb. 84m/B VHS, CA Tom Scholte, Micki Maunsell, Kevin McNulty, Babz Chula, David Lovgrer, Laara Sadiq, Michelle Beaudoin, Kelly Aisenstat; *D:* Bruce Sweeney; *W:* Bruce Sweeney; *C:* David Pelletier. Toronto-City '95; Canadian Feature Film.

Live from Baghdad ♪♪♪ 2003 In 1991, veteran CNN producer Robert Wiener (Keaton) and his longtime partner Ingrid Formanek (Bonham Carter) find themselves in Baghdad at the start of the first Gulf War. The other networks have pulled out for safety reasons and CNN is the only game around with Wiener and Formanek risking their lives to get the story. Adapted from the book by Wiener. 108m/C VHS, DVD. Michael Keaton, Helena Bonham-Carter, Lili Taylor, Bruce McGill, David Suchet, Joshua Leonard, Michael Cudlitz, Matt Keeslar, Robert Wisdom, Michael Murphy, Paul Guilfoyle, John Carroll Lynch, Tom Amandes, Murphy Dunne; *D:* Mick Jackson; *W:* Chapman, John Patrick Shanley, Timothy J. Sexton; *C:* Ivan Strasburg. CABLE

Live! From Death Row ♪♪ 1992 Cassidy plays a tabloid TV host who'll do anything to get ratings. She's set to do a live interview with a condemned serial killer (Davison) shortly before his execution. But Davison and his fellow death-row inmates take Cassidy and her crew hostage as he decides to use the show for his own media message. 94m/C VHS. Bruce Davison, At La'Fleur, Calvin Levels, Michael D. Roberts; *D:* Patrick Sheane Duncan; *W:* Patrick Sheane Duncan.

Live-In Maid ♪♪ *Cama Adentro* 2004 Witt Argentina in the midst of an economic meltdown, once-privileged divorcee Beba can't afford to pay her longtime maid Dora and she continues working, despite spending nearly 30 years together, despite class and other differences, the women find it tough to let go. Spanish with subtitles. 87m/C DVD, AR SP Norma Aleandro, Norma Argentina, Marcus Mundstock, Raul Pantin.

Live Flesh ♪♪♪½ *Carne Trémula* 1997 (R) The courses of five lives in Madrid are forever altered when naive, young Victor (Rabal) accidentally shoots cop David (Bardem) and is sent to prison after an argument with Elena (Neri), a one-night stand he falls for. When he gets out he discovers Elena has transformed from junkie to model wife who runs a home for paraplegic. Still, Victor both wants and resents Elena, who he blames for the accident. While apparently stalking Elena, Victor enters into a relationship with Clara, the wife of David's former partner, Sancho (Sancho) which dramatically draws all five back together. Complex, noirish drama shows a new, more serious side for director Almodovar, who still manages some of his patented brand of humor. Highly original plot and unexpected twists delivered by a talented and attractive cast. Adapted from a British novel by Ruth Rendell. 100m/C VHS, DVD, FR SP Javier Bardem, Francesca Neri, Angela Molina, Liberto Rabal, Jose Sancho, Penelope Cruz, Pilar Bardem, Alex Angulo; *D:* Pedro Almodovar; *W:* Pedro Almodovar, Ray Loriga, Jorge Guerricaechevarria; *C:* Affonso Beato; *M:* Alberto Iglesias.

Live Free or Die Hard ♪♪½ 2007 (PG-13) The last "Die Hard" was released in 1995 and director Wiseman plays to the fact that times have changed, even if John McClane (Willis) has not. His analog cop in a digital world first thinks he's going to be stuck babysitting smart-mouthed twenty-something computer hacker Matt (Long), who's wanted for questioning when the government's computers go wonky. Ah, but it's really supercilious disaffected techie Thomas Gabriel (Olyphant) showing off what happens when you ignore his warnings. Well, you really shouldn't ignore McClane either, Willis acknowledges his years while still kicking bad-guy butt in some ludicrous but amazing action sequences. 129m/C DVD, Blu-ray Disc, *US* Bruce Willis, Justin Long, Mary Elizabeth Winstead, Timothy Olyphant, Maggie Q, Jeffry Wright, Kevin Smith, Yancey Arias, Tim Russ, Cyril Raffaelli, Clifford Curtis, Yorgo Constantine, Andrew Friedman; *D:* Len Wiseman; *W:* Mark Bomback; *C:* Simon Duggart; *M:* Marco Beltrami.

The Lives of Others ♪♪♪ *Das Leben der Anderen* 2006 (R) Oscar-winning drama is set in East Berlin in 1984. The population is controlled by the Stasi (the secret police) and its informers. Strict bureaucrat Wiesler (Muehe) doesn't believe that successful playwright Dreyman (Koch) is a true socialist so he wires the man's apartment and becomes intrigued with his life and lover, actress Christa-Maria (Gedeck). Wiesler's loyalty (and belief in the system) is shaken when a superior orders him to pin something on Dreyman; instead, he decides to protect him. Immersive debut for writer/director von Donnersmarck. German with subtitles. 137m/C DVD, Blu-ray Disc, GE Martina Gedeck, Ulrich Tukur, Ulrich Muehe, Sebastian Koch, Ulrich Kleiner; *D:* Florian Henskel von Donnersmarck; *W:* Florian Henkel von Donnersmarck; *C:* Hagen Bogdianski; *M:* Gabriel Yared, Stephane Moucha. Oscars '06; Foreign Film; British Acad. '07; Foreign Film.

Livin' for Love: The Natalie Cole Story ♪♪ 2000 Singer Natalie Cole plays herself (at least in her adult years), telling the harrowing story of her slide into drug addiction after growing up the adored daughter of the legendary Nat King Cole. Based on her autobiography. 120m/C VHS, Natalie Cole, Theresa Randle, guitar; *D:* Jorge Gaggero; *W:* Jorge Gaggero; *C:* Javier Julia.

Live Nude Girls ♪♪ 1995 (R) Group of 30-something girlfriends get together to throw a bachelorette party for one of their number and sit around gossiping about sex, relationships, family, and friends. Not much plot but nice ensemble work. 92m/C VHS, DVD. Dana Delany, Kim Cattrall, Cynthia Stevenson, Laila Robins, Olivia D'Abo, Lora Zane, Glenn Quinn, Tim Choate; *D:* Julianna Lavin; *W:* Julianna Lavin; *C:* Christophe Taylor; *M:* Anton Sanko.

The Live Wire ♪♪ 1934 Stunt-ridden action fare featuring Talmadge at his most daring. This adventure is complete with desert island, lost treasure, stowaways, evil-doers, and a race against the clock. 57m/B VHS, DVD. Richard Talmadge, Alberta Vaughn.

Live Wire ♪♪½ 1992 (R) Brosnan is an FBI bomb expert who needs a new line of work. He's up against a terrorist psychopath who has his greedy hands on a new type of explosive. It's liquid, undetectable, looks as innocent as a glass of water, and is capable of blowing up Washington, D.C. Also available in an unrated version. 85m/C VHS, DVD. Pierce Brosnan, Ben Cross, Ron Silver, Lisa Eilbacher; *D:* Christian Duguay; *W:* Bart Baker. CABLE

Live Wire: Human Timebomb ♪♪½ 1995 (R) FBI agent Jim Parker is captured by a Cuban general who implants a computer chip into his neck—turning Parker into a human time-bomb. 99m/C VHS, DVD. Bryan Genesse, Joe Lara, Frantz Dobrowsky, J. Cynthia Brooks; *D:* Mark Roper; *W:* Jeff Albert; *C:* Rod Stewart; *M:* Ita Haber.

The Lives of a Bengal Lancer ♪♪♪ 1935 One of Hollywood's greatest rousing adventures. Based in northwest India, Lt. McGregor (Cooper) is a seasoned frontier fighter in the Bengals Lancers who befriends new officer Lt. Forsythe (Tone). Also new to the regiment is Donald Stone (Cromwell), the son of the current commanding officer (Standing). All three will test their courage when the Brits encounter a vicious local revolution against colonial rule. Swell plot, lotsa action, great comraderie. Based on the novel by Major Francis Yeats-Brown, and remade in 1939 as "Geronimo". 110m/B VHS, DVD. Gary Cooper, Franchot Tone, Richard Cromwell, Guy Standing, Sir C. Aubrey Smith, Douglass Dumbrille, Kathleen Burke, Noble Johnson, Jumsden Hare, Akim Tamiroff, J. Carrol Naish, Monte Blue, Ray Cooper, Leonic Kinskey, George Regas, Reginald (Reggie, Reggy) Sheffield, Mischa Auer, Charles Stevens, James Warwick, Clive Morgan, Colin Tapley, Rollo Lloyd, Maj. Sam Harris; *D:* Henry Hathaway; *W:* Waldemar Young, John Lloyd Balderston, Grover Jones, William Slavens McNutt; *C:* Charles Biryani Lang Jr.; *M:* Milan Roder.

Living & Dying ♪ 2007 (R) An African-American delivery boy gets the break of his life when a nearby newscaster is shot dead. Grabbing the microphone and continuing the story, he soon finds himself hired by an Atlanta news station as an anchorman, fulfilling a life-long dream. But problems arise when he finds himself losing touch with his friends, his neighborhood and his roots. Comedy "deals" with the compelling issue of blacks finding success in a white world by trivializing the issue at every turn and resorting to racial stereotypes. 96m/C VHS, DVD. Terrence "T.C." Carson, Lisa Arimdell Anderson, Blandine Baker, Nathanie 'Afrika' Hall, Julia Campbell; *D:* Michael A. Schultz; *C:* Peter Lyons Collister; *M:* Herbie Hancock.

The Living Coffin ♪½ *El Grito de la Muerte* 1958 Woman has alarm rigged on her coffin in case she's buried alive. And they called her paranoid. Loosely based on Poe's "Premature Burial". 72m/C VHS, MX Gaston Santos, Maria Duval, Pedro de Aguillon; *D:* Fernando Mendez.

The Living Daylights ♪♪♪ 1987 (PG) After being used as a pawn in a fake Russian defector plot, our intrepid spy tracks down an international arms and opium smuggling ring. Fine debut by Dalton, who takes his role as 007 in a more serious vein, in a rousing, refreshing cosmopolitan shoot-em-up. Let's be frank we were all getting a little fatigued by Roger Moore. The 15th film in the series. 130m/C VHS, DVD. Timothy Dalton, Maryam D'Abo, Jeroen Krabbe, John Rhys-Davies, Robert Brown, Joe Don Baker, Desmond Llewelyn, Art Malik, Geoffrey Keen, Walter Gotell, Andreas Wisniewski; *D:* John Glen; *W:* Richard Maibaum, Michael G. Wilson; *C:* Alec Mills; *M:* John Barry.

The Living Dead ♪♪ 1933 The Scotland Yard Mystery 1933 An English film about a mad, re-animating scientist. 76m/B VHS, GB Gerald du Maurier, George Curzon; *D:* Thomas Bentley; *W:* Frank Miller; *C:* James Wilson.

The Living Dead Girl ♪♪½ *La Morte Vivante* 1982 Workers illegally trying to dispose of hazardous chemical wastes in a cellar make the mistake of indulging in a bit of grave robbing at the next-door crypt. A 55-gallon drum cracks open; the stuff hits an open coffin and a blonde (Blanchard) with long sharp fingernails and a taste for blood is 'reanimated. It's another sex-and-gore fest from the prolific Rollin, though this is one of his more polished productions. French with subtitles. 91m/C DVD, FR Marina Pierro, Françoise Blanchard, Mike Marshall, Carina Barone, Fanny Magier; *D:* Jean Rollin; *W:* Jean Rollin.

The Living Dead Girl (see Living Doll)

Living Doll ♪½ 1990 (R) A mentally unbalanced med student abducts a cadaver and brings it to his apartment. The beautiful female corpse takes to telling him to seek revenge on those that killed her. 95m/C DVD, GB Mark Jax, Eartha Kitt, Katie Orgill; *D:* George Dugdale, Peter Mackenzie Litten, Mark Ezra. VIDEO

The Living End ♪♪ 1992 Director Araki's radical lovers-on-the-lam story concerns freelance L.A. writer Jon (Gilmore) who has just learned he is H.I.V.-positive. He meets a handsome, violent, hustler named Luke (Dytri) and the two begin a desperate road trip along the California coast which can only end in tragedy. Araki not only wrote and directed the film but also served as cinematographer and editor—all on a $23,000 budget. Stylish, tragic, and filled with black humor and frank homoeroticism. 92m/C VHS, DVD. Craig

Livin' Large ♪♪ 1991 (R) An African-American delivery boy gets the break of his life.

James McDaniel, Dishann Carroll; *D:* Robert Kevin Townsend. TV

Gilmore, Mike Dytri, Darcy Marta; **D:** Dick Lowry; **W:** Gregg Araki; **C:** Gregg Araki;

Living Free 🦴🦴½ **1972 (G)** Sequel to "Born Free," based on the nonfictional books by Joy and George Adamson are called in to take charge of her three cubs, who are causing havoc on nearby villages. Nice and pleasant, but could you pick up the pace? **91m/C VHS, DVD.** Susan Hampshire, Nigel Davenport; **D:** Jack Couffer; **W:** Millard Kaufman; **C:** Jack Couffer.

The Living Head 🦴🦴½ *La Cabeza Viviente* **1959** Archaeologists discover the ancient sepulcher of the great Aztec warrior, Acatl. Ignoring a curse, they steal his severed head and incur the fury of Xitsila-poli. They should have known better. Dubbed in English. **75m/B VHS, DVD. MX** Mauricio Garces, Ana Luisa Peluffo, German Robles, Abel Salazar; **D:** Chano Urueto.

Living in Oblivion 🦴🦴🦴 **1994 (R)** Humorous tri-part story is an insiders joke on the problems of low-budget filmmaking, including talent, libido, ego, and pervasive chaos. First, director Nick Reve (Buscemi) tries to film an emotional scene with leading lady Nicole (Keener) only to have everything go wrong; then star Chad (LeGros), a dimwit but a "name," arrives to throw his weight around (and seduce Nicole); and finally the leading lady must deal with an overly sensitive dwarf and Nick's mother. A sleeper. **92m/C VHS, DVD.** Steve Buscemi, Catherine Keener, James LeGros, Dermot Mulroney, Danielle von Zerneck, Robert Wightman, Rica Martens, Hilary Gilford, Peter Dinklage, Kevin Corrigan, Matthew Grace, Michael Griffiths, Ryna Bowker, Francesca DiMauro; **D:** Tom DiCillo; **C:** Frank Prinzi; **M:** Jim Farmer. Sundance '95: Screenplay.

Living in Peril 🦴🦴 **1997 (R)** Ambitious architect Walter Woods (Lowe) is in L.A. to design a mansion for an eccentric client (Belushi). But a series of accidents threaten to ruin his reputation, if not provoke something more deadly. **95m/C VHS, DVD.** Rob Lowe, James Belushi, Dean Stockwell, Dana Wheeler-Nicholson, Richard Moll, Alex Meneses, Patrick Esrgard; **D:** Joakim (Jack) Esrgard; **W:** Joakim (Jack) Esrgard, Patrick Esrgard; **C:** Ross Berryman; **M:** Randy Miller. VIDEO

Living on Tokyo Time 🦴🦴½ **1987** Interesting but often dull, low budget independent comedy about a young Japanese woman who hitches up with a boorish Japanese-American man in order to stay in the United States. An Asian view of Asian-America, filmed on location in San Francisco. **83m/C VHS.** Minako Ohashi, Ken Nakagawa, Kate Connell, Mitzi Abe, Bill Bonham, Brenda Acki; **D:** Steven Okazaki; **W:** Steven Okazaki, John McCormick.

Living Out Loud 🦴🦴 **1998 (R)** Judith (Hunter) is dumped by her cardiologist husband for a younger woman and spirals downward into depression. Of course, this leads to dramatic self-discovery, and Judith opens her eyes to the world around her, including the nice-guy elevator operator (DeVito) in her building. The two wallow in their respective personal loss and form an unlikely friendship, which teeters on becoming something more. Screenwriter LaGravanese tries his hand at directing but delivers a choppy, hard-to-believe tale of female independence and self-fulfillment. The reliable Hunter seems miscast; she's just too intense and jittery to appear sullen and reflective. DeVito gives his usual excellent performance, but also appears miscast as the debt-ridden gambler who catches Judith's refined eye. Significant events take place off-screen and the audience is left to fill in the blanks. **102m/C VHS, DVD.** Holly Hunter, Danny DeVito, Queen Latifah, Martin Donovan, Elias Koteas, Richard LaGravenese; **D:** Richard LaGravenese; **W:** John Bailey; **M:** George Fenton.

Living Proof: The Hank Williams Jr. Story 🦴🦴½ **1983** TV biopic focusing on the country singer's hell-raising ways as he seeks to get out from under the shadow of his famous father and into the spotlight on his own right. Based on Williams Jr.'s autobiography; includes 10 songs by Sr. and Jr. **97m/C VHS.** Richard Thomas, Clu Gulager, Allyn Ann McLerie, Naomi Judd, Christian Slater; **D:** Dick Lowry; **W:** I.C. Rapoport, Stephen Kandel. TV

Living to Die 🦴🦴½ **1991 (R)** Vegas gumshoe is assigned to investigate a blackmailed official, and discovers a woman believed to be dead is alive and beautiful and living incognito. This mystifies him. **84m/C VHS, DVD.** Wings Hauser, Darcy Demoss, Asher Brauner, Arnold Vosloo, Jim Williams; **D:** Wings Hauser.

A Lizard in a Woman's Skin 🦴🦴 *Una Lucertola con la Pelle di Donna* **1971** Carol (Bolkan) tells her shrink about dreams in which she kills her party girl neighbor Julia (Strindberg, in her film debut). Of course, Julia winds up dead in exactly the manner Carol has described. Cop Corvin (Baker) thinks Carol is being set up by her two-timing husband Frank (Sorel). Then other people from Carol's dreams begin to die as well. There's some freaky-deaky druggie hippie stuff included, too. Italian with subtitles. **98m/C DVD. IT** Florinda Bolkan, Stanley Baker, Jean Sorel, Alberto De Mendoza, Leo Genn, Silvia Monti, Anita Strindberg; **D:** Lucio Fulci; **C:** Luigi Kuveiller; **M:** Ennio Morricone.

The Lizzie McGuire Movie 🦴🦴½ **2003 (PG)** Let's just call this "Lizzie Goes to Rome." Tweenie heroine Lizzie (an endearingly klutzy Duff) celebrates her graduation from junior high with a two-week trip to Italy with some classmates. In real life, Lizzie meets the slightly older teen Europop star Paolo (Gelman), whose singing partner Isabella has just left him. Lizzie looks like her (Duff plays both roles), and agrees to put on a dark wig and impersonate the Italian diva for an awards show. Some sightseeing and a little romance follow. An adaptation of the Disney Channel series. **90m/C VHS, DVD. US** Hilary Duff, Robert Carradine, Hallie Todd, Jake Thomas, Yani Gellman, Adam Lamberg, Brendan Kelly, Ashlie Brillault, Clayton Snyder, Alex Borstein, Carly Schroeder; **D:** Jim Fall; **W:** Edward Decter, John J. Strauss, Susan Estelle Jansen; **C:** Jerzy Zielinski; **M:** Cliff Eidelman.

Lloyd 🦴🦴 **2000 (PG)** Goofy 11-year-old Lloyd is the class clown always getting in trouble in school. In fact, he gets demoted to a class of losers where Lloyd gets a crush on pretty Tracy. But how can he compare with junior high rebel Storm for her affections? **72m/C VHS, DVD.** Todd Bosley, Brendon Ryan Barrett, Mary Mara, Taylor Negron, Tom Arnold, Kristen Parker; **D:** Hector Barron; **W:** Hector Barron; **C:** Michael Orefice; **M:** Conrad Pope. VIDEO

Lloyds of London 🦴🦴🦴 **1936** If you wonder how the story of a British insurance company can be exciting, just watch this lavish spectacular (which, of course, lacks historical accuracy). Jonathan Blake (Power) has risen in the ranks of the firm, thanks in part to his lifelong friendship with Lord Horatio Nelson (Burton), much to the disgust of haughty Lord Everett Stacy (an ever-supercilious Sanders). As Bonaparte comes to power, Blake travels to France to rescue some friends and saves Elizabeth (Carroll), who turns out to be Stacy's wife. Stacy is also spreading rumors about Lloyds' solvency and Nelson's heroics at Trafalgar and his machinations lead to further trouble with Blake. **115m/B VHS.** Tyrone Power, George Sanders, Madeleine Carroll, John Burton, Guy Standing, Sir C. Aubrey Smith, Freddie Bartholomew, Virginia Field, Montagu Love, Una O'Connor, Anne Howard; **D:** Henry King; **W:** Ernest Pascal, Walter Ferris; **C:** Bert Glennon.

Loaded 🦴🦴 *Bloody Weekend* **1994 (R)** Writer-director Campion (sister of director Jane) follows a group of teens to an abandoned English mansion as they try to film an amateur horror movie. While there, the group decides to have some fun, with the help of LSD. This leads to some therapeutic and angst-ridden discussions about each of their problems, as well as a tragic accident, which changes the lives of all involved. There's some nice character sketches, unfortunately they're more interesting than the loose plot, which leaves too many questions unanswered. Retitled and recut since its original '94 release. **95m/C VHS, DVD. NZ GB** Thandie Newton, Catherine McCormack, Oliver Milburn, Nick Patrick, Danny Cunningham, Mathew Eggleton, Biddy Hodson; **D:** Anna Campion; **W:** Anna Campion; **C:** Alan Almond; **M:** Simon Fisher Turner.

Loaded 🦴🦴½ **2008 (R)** Tristan Price (Metcalfe) is a handsome young law student from a wealthy family who goes looking for some extra excitement. Then he meets upscale coke dealer Sebastian Cole (Large) and gets more than he bargained for. As Tristan descends deeper into addiction, he's pulled into Sebastian's drug deals, which lead to murder and even more plot twists. **100m/C DVD.** Jesse Metcalfe, Corey Large, Monica Keena, Nathalie Kelley, Johnny Messner, Jimmy Jean-Louis, Chace Crawford, Vinnie Jones, Erin Gray, John Bennett Perry; **D:** Alan Pao; **W:** Corey Large, Alan Pao; **C:** Roger Chingirian; **M:** Ralph Rieckermann. VIDEO

Loaded Guns woof! **1975** Airline stewardess-cum-double agent must totally immobilize a top drug trafficking ring. Pathetic spy tale with plenty of unintended laughs. **90m/C VHS.** Ursula Andress, Woody Strode; **D:** Fernando Di Leo.

Loaded Pistols 🦴🦴 **1948** Story set in the old West starring Gene Autry. **80m/B VHS, DVD.** Gene Autry, Jack Holt, Barbara Britton; **D:** John English.

Loan Shark 🦴🦴 **1952** An ex-convict gets a job at a tire company, working undercover to expose a loan shark ring. Hackneyed plot moves quickly. **79m/B VHS, DVD.** George Raft, John Hoyt, Dorothy Hart, Paul Stewart, Robert Bice, Russell Johnson, Benny Baker, Lawrence (Larry) Dobkin, Harlan Warde, Margia Dean, William Phipps; **D:** Seymour Friedman; **W:** Martin Rackin, Eugene Ling; **C:** Joseph Biroc; **M:** Heinz Roemheld.

Lobster for Breakfast 🦴🦴½ **1982 (R)** An Italian gag-fest about a toilet salesman infiltrating his friend's confused marital existence just to make a sale. With English subtitles; also available in a dubbed version. **96m/C VHS. IT** Enrico Montesano, Claude Brasseur, Claudine Auger; **D:** Giorgio Capitani.

Lobster Man from Mars 🦴🦴½ **1989 (PG)** When rich movie producer (Curtis) learns from his accountant that he must produce a flop or be taken to the cleaners by the IRS, he buys a home-made horror movie from a young filmmaker. The film is an ultra-low budget production featuring a kooky lobster man and a screaming damsel. The premise peters out about halfway through, but there are enough yuks to keep you going. **84m/C VHS, DVD.** Tony Curtis, Deborah Foreman, Patrick Macnee, Tommy Sledge, Billy Barty, Phillip Proctor, Anthony Hickox, Bobby "Boris" Pickett, Stanley Sheff; **D:** Stanley Sheff; **W:** Bob Greenberg; **C:** Gerry Lively; **M:** Sasha Matson.

Local Badman 🦴 **1932** A dim-witted cowhand saves the day in this rip-roaring tale of the old west. **60m/B VHS.** Sally Blane, Hooper Atchley, Edward Hearn, Edward Peil Sr., Hoot Gibson; **D:** Otto Brower; **W:** Philip Graham White; **C:** Tom Galligan, Harry Neumann.

Local Boys 🦴🦴 **2002 (PG-13)** California surf dude Randy (Olsen) buys his brother Skeet (Sumpter) his first board for his 12th birthday. But Randy gets jealous when Skeet turns to surfing legend Jim Wesley (Harmon) to be his mentor. Things get even more complicated when Wesley begins romancing the boys' widowed mom (Edwards). **103m/C VHS, DVD.** Mark Harmon, Eric Christian Olsen, Jeremy Sumpter, Stacy Edwards, Giuseppe Andrews, Travis Aaron, Shelby Fenner, Lukas Behnken; **D:** Ron Moler; **C:** James Glennon. VIDEO

Local Hero 🦴🦴🦴 **1983 (PG)** Riegert is a yuppie representative of a huge oil company who endeavors to buy a sleepy Scottish fishing village for excavation, and finds himself hypnotized by the place and its crusty denizens. Back in Texas at company headquarters, tycoon Lancaster deals with a psycho therapist and gazes at the stars looking for clues. A low-key, charmingly offbeat Scottish comedy with its own sense of logic and quiet humor, poetic landscapes, and unique characters, epitomizing Forsyth's original style. **112m/C VHS, DVD. GB** Peter Riegert, Denis Lawson, Burt Lancaster, Fulton Mackay, Jenny Seagrove, Peter Capaldi, Norman Chancer; **D:** Bill Forsyth; **W:** Bill Forsyth; **C:** Chris Menges; **M:** Mark Knopfler. British Acad. '83: Director (Forsyth); N.Y. Film Critics '83: Screenplay; Natl. Soc. Film Critics '83: Screenplay.

Loch Ness 🦴🦴½ **1995 (PG)** American zoologist Jonathan Dempsey (Danson) specializes in hunting legendary animals and this latest assignment is to head for the Scottish highlands and take on the Nessie legend. He gets an assistant (Frain), a potential romance with single mom Laura (Richardson), and a lot of grief from some hostile locals before Laura's young daughter Isabel (Graham) decides to help him out. Jim Henson's Creature Shop takes care of the monster's animatronics. **101m/C VHS, DVD. GB** Ted Danson, Ian Holm, Joely Richardson, Kirsty Graham, James Frain, Harris Yulin, Keith Allen, Nick Brimble; **D:** John Henderson; **W:** John Fusco; **C:** Clive Tickner; **M:** Trevor Jones.

The Loch Ness Horror woof! **1982** The famed monster surfaces and chomps on the local poachers—and with good reason. Would that it had munched this movie's producer in, say, 1981. **93m/C VHS.** Barry Buchanan, Miki McKenzie, Sandy Kenyon; **D:** Larry Buchanan.

Lock 'n' Load 🦴🦴 **1990 (R)** Why are all the soldiers in the 82nd Airborne stealing vast sums, then committing suicide? One of the guys involved wants to know. **89m/C VHS.** Renee Cline, Jeffrey Smith, Greg E. Russell, Jack Vogel; **D:** David A. Prior, David A. Prior; **C:** Brian Veatch; **M:** Tony Cappelli.

Lock, Stock and 2 Smoking Barrels 🦴🦴🦴 **1998 (R)** Plot twist-laden British caper comedy plays like Tarantino and crumpets. Four dim hoods, Bacon (Statham), Soap (Fletcher), Eddy (Moran) and Tom (Flemyng), pool their ill-gotten gains so that Eddy can play in a high stakes card game. They don't know that the game is fixed, however, and they end up owing gambler Hatchet Harry (Moriarty) 500,000 pounds. The bumbling band plan to rob their drug dealing neighbor Dog (Harper), who's planning on robbing an upper class rival of his own. Throw in a wandering pair of antique shotguns and you have the recipe for a cap-poppin' good time. Rock star Sting appears as the pub-owning father of one of the lads. **105m/C VHS, DVD. GB** Jason Flemyng, Dexter Fletcher, Nick Moran, Jason Statham, Steven Mackintosh, Vinnie Jones, Sting, Lenny McLean, P. H. Moriarty, Stephen Marcus; **D:** Guy Ritchie; **W:** Guy Ritchie; **C:** Tim Maurice-Jones; **M:** David A. Hughes, John Murphy. MTV Movie Awards '99: New Filmmaker (Ritchie).

Lock Up 🦴🦴½ **1989 (R)** Peaceful con Stallone, with only six months to go, is harassed and tortured by vicious prison warden Sutherland in retribution for an unexplained past conflict. Lackluster and moronic; semi-color; surely Sutherland can find better roles. **115m/C VHS, DVD.** Sylvester Stallone, Donald Sutherland, Sonny Landham, John Amos, Darlanne Fluegel, Frank McRae; **D:** John Flynn; **W:** Jeb Stuart; **C:** Donald E. Thorin; **M:** Bill Conti.

Lockdown 🦴🦴½ **1990** Charged with his partner's murder, a detective is forced to ponder the perennial puzzle of life. Not a pretty sight. **90m/C VHS, DVD.** Joe Estevez, Mike Farrell, Richard Lynch; **D:** Frank Harris. VIDEO

Lockdown 🦴🦴 **2000 (R)** Brutal men in the big house pic follows the fortunes of three friends who wind up doing time in New Mexico. Violent drug dealer Cashmere (Casseus) is framed by another player and manages to take two right-living buddies—Avery (Jones) and Dre (Bonds)—down with him. Cashmere joins the in-house crew of black boss Clean Up (Master P) while Avery is lucky enough to be taken under the wing of a self-educated cellmate who passes on wise advice in situations familiar to viewers of the cable series "Oz." Grim watching. **105m/C VHS, DVD.** Richard T. Jones, De'Aundre Bonds, Gabriel Casseus, Master P, Bill Nunn, Clifton Powell, Joe Torry, Anna Maria Horsford, Melissa De Sousa, Kirk "Sticky Fingaz" Jones; **D:** John Lues-

Locked in Silence ✍✍ 1999 Young boy becomes electively mute after believing he saw his older brother kill another boy. His farm family nearly goes bankrupt trying to find a cure until a psychologist is able to help the child deal with reality. Based on a true story. 94m/C VHS. W: Preston A. Whitmore II; C: Chris Chomyr; M: Gary Chang. CABLE.

The Locket ✍✍ 2002 After his mother dies, Michael Keddington (Willett) takes a job at a health-care facility to pay off debts. There he meets Esther Huish (Redgrave), a lonely widow who encourages Michael not to give up his dreams. But when he's supportive girlfriend Faye (Moreau) goes off to college and a jealous co-worker (Heuring) accuses Michael of a crime, he needs Esther's strength to see him through. Based on the novel by Richard Paul Evans. 100m/C VHS, DVD. C: Chad Willet, Vanessa Redgrave, Marguerite Moreau, Lori Heuring, Mary (Elizabeth) McDonough, Brock Peters, Terry O'Quinn; D: Karen Arthur. W: Ron Raley; C: Thomas Neuwirth; M: Bruce Broughton. TV.

Loco Love ✍½ *Mi Casa, Su Casa* 2003 (PG) Flat and hopelessly dumb romantic comedy. Gardener Miguel (Mejia) wins big in the lottery and makes a deal with former client Donald (Werner); if Donald will make a green card marriage with his sister Catalina (Harring) so she can come to the U.S. Miguel will give Donald a big chunk of change. Donald wants to open a restaurant so he agrees, not realizing that this means Catalina's entire family will be joining them. And (for no apparent reason) Donald's ex-wife Barbara (Scarcides she wants Donald back. 94m/C VHS, DVD. Laura Elena Harring, Gerardo Mejia, Roy Werner, Margaret Scarborough, Barbara Eden; D: Bryan Lewis; W: Steven Bear; C: Thaddeus Wadleigh; M: Jon McCallum.

The Locusts ✍½ 1997 (R) Backwater beefcake Clay Hewitt (Vaughn) swaggers into a small Kansas town where everyone has a lit cigarette and a secret and no one is safe from first-time director Kelley. Any high school freshman with an English lit class under his belt won't miss the not-so-subtle metaphors at play—Delilah has workers castrating bulls a lot. 123m/C VHS, DVD. Kate Capshaw, Jeremy Davies, Vince Vaughn, Ashley Judd, Paul Rudd, Danie Meyer, Jessica Capshaw; D: John Patrick Kelley; W: John Patrick Kelley; C: Phedon Papamichael; M: Carter Burwell.

The Lodger ✍✍ *The Case of Jonathan Drew; A Case of London Fog* 1926 A mysterious lodger is thought to be a rampaging mass murderer of young women. First Hitchcock film to explore the themes and ideas that would become his trademarks. Remade three times. Silent. Climactic chase is memorable. Look closely for the Master in his first cameo. 91m/B VHS. DVD. GB Ivor Novello, Marie Ault, Arthur Chesney, Malcolm Keen, June. Cameos: Alfred Hitchcock; D: Alfred Hitchcock; W: Alfred Hitchcock, Eliot Stannard.

L'Odeur des Fauves ✍ 1966 One of a cynical reporter's scandalous stories gets an innocent man killed, compelling the reporter somehow to make restitution. Subtitled in English. 86m/C VHS. FR Maurice Ronet, Josephine Chaplin, Vittorio De Sica; D: Richard Balducci.

Logan's Run ✍✍½ 1976 In the 23rd century, a hedonistic society exists in a huge bubble and people are only allowed to live to the age of 30. Intriguing

concepts and great futuristic sets prevail here. Based on the novel by William Nolan and George Clayton Johnson. 120m/C VHS, DVD. Michael York, Jenny Agutter, Richard Jordan, Roscoe Lee Browne, Farrah Fawcett, Peter Ustinov, Camilla Carr, Ann Ford; D: Michael Anderson Sr.; W: David Zelag Goodman; C: Ernest Laszlo; M: Jerry Goldsmith. Oscars '76: Visual FX.

Loggerheads ✍✍ 2005 Families and the ties that bind. Drifter Mark (Pardue) heads to Kure Beach, North Carolina to help rescue the endangered loggerhead turtle. Mark ran away from his adoptive parents, well-meaning religious conservatives Robert (Sarandon) and Elizabeth (Harper), whom they learned he was gay. Also living in NC is Mark's birth mother, Grace (Hunt), who's recovering from a breakdown and has decided to find the baby she gave up as a teenager. Meanwhile, Mark is bonding with gentle George (Kelly), whose male lover has died. More enjoyable for fans of the sincere and sentimental, it's well worth a look, especially for the strong performances of Harper and Hunt. 93m/C DVD. US Bonnie Hunt, Kip Pardue, Tess Harper, Chris Sarandon, Michael Learned, Michael Kelly, Robin Weigert; D: Tim Kirkman; W: Tim Kirkman; D: Glenn Jorden. TV.

Lois Gibbs and the Love Canal ✍✍ 1982 Mason's TV movie debut as Lois Gibbs, a housewife turned activist, fighting the authorities over chemical-dumping in the Love Canal area of Niagara Falls, New York. The script doesn't convey the seriousness of developments in that region. 100m/C VHS. Marsha Mason, Bob Gunton, Penny Fuller, Roberta Maxwell, Jeremy Licht, Louise Latham; D: Glenn Jordan.

Lola ✍✍ 1961 A wonderful tale of a nightclub dancer and her amorous adventures. Innovative film that marked the beginning of French New Wave, in French with English subtitles. 90m/B VHS, DVD. FR Anouk Aimee, Marc Michel, Elina Labourdette, Jacques Harden; D: Jacques Demy.

Lola ✍✍ *The Statutory Affair; Twinky* 1969 (PG) A teenaged girl links up romantically with a considerably older writer of pornographic books. One would expect more from such a good cast, but the film never follows through. British release was originally 98 minutes. 88m/C VHS, DVD, GB IT Charles Bronson, Susan George, Trevor Howard, Michael Craig, Honor Blackman, Lionel Jeffries, Robert Morley, Jack Hawkins, Orson Bean, Kay Medford, Paul Ford; D: Richard Donner.

Lola and Billy the Kid ✍✍ *Lola + Bilikid* 1998 Murat (Davrat) is a closeted gay Turkish teenager livng in Berlin with his widowed mother and homophobic brother Osman (Mete). Lola (Mukli) is a travestite dancer at a nightclub who lives with hustler Bili (Yildiz). When Lola tries to contact Murat's family, the boy discovers that Lola is his brother, who was thrown out by Osman. Murat meets Lola, who is later killed—apparently by neo-Nazi thugs. Bili vows revenge but Murat learns that the situation isn't as clear as it seems. German and Turkish with subtitles. 95m/C VHS, DVD. GE Baki Darrak, Gandi Mukli, Erdal Yildiz, Hasan Ali Mete, Michael Gerber, Murat Yilmaz, Inge Keller; D: Kutlug Ataman; W: Kutlug Ataman; C: Chris Squires; M: Arpad Bondy.

Lola Montes ✍✍✍ 1955 Ophuls' final masterpiece (and his only film in color) recounts the life and sins of the famous courtesan, mistress of Franz Liszt and the King of Bavaria. Ignored upon release, but hailed later by the French as a cinematic landmark. Adapted from an unpublished novel by Cecil Saint-Laurent. French with subtitles. The original widescreen release clocked in at 140 minutes. 110m/C DVD. FR Martine Carol, Peter Ustinov, Anton Walbrook, Ivan Desny, Oskar Werner; D: Max Ophuls; W: Max Ophuls; C: Christian Matras; M: Georges Auric.

Lolita ✍✍ 1997 In the future all sexual activity is prohibited (bummer). Lolita's working for an organization that destroys sexual material but her that she just has to act on. 90m/C VHS, D: Cybil (Sybil) Richards.

Lolita ✍✍✍ 1962 A middle-aged professor is consumed by his lust for a teenage nymphet in this strange film considered daring in its time. Based on Vladimir Nabokov's novel. Watch for Winters' terrific portrayal as Lolita's sex-starved mother. 152m/B VHS, DVD. GB James Mason, Shelley Winters, Peter Sellers, Sue Lyon, Gary Cockrell, Jerry Sovin, Diana Decker, Lois Maxwell, Cec Linder, Bill Greene, Shirley Douglas, Marianne Stone, Marion Mathie, James Dyrenforth, C. Denier Warren, Terence (Terry) Kilburn, John Harrison; D: Stanley Kubrick; W: Vladimir Nabokov; C: Oswald Morris; M: Nelson Riddle.

Lolita ✍✍ 1997 (R) Middle-aged college professor Humbert Humbert (Irons) becomes obsessed with nymphet Lolita (Swain), even to the point of marrying her mother Charlotte (Griffith) so he can always be close by. Then Charlotte dies, and the unlikely duo begin an aimless road trip that eventually leads Lolita to a fateful meeting with yet another older man, Quilty (Langella). Director Lyne's no stranger to controversy but his reverential take on the Vladimir Nabokov novel turns out to be much ado about nothing. Then 14-year-old Swain (in a fetchingly flirty performance) debuts as Lolita (along with a body-double). 137m/C VHS, DVD. Jeremy Irons, Melanie Griffith, Frank Langella, Dominique Swain, Suzanne Shephard, Keith Reddin, Erin J. Dean, Ben Silverstone; D: Adrian Lyne; W: Stephen Schiff; C: Howard Atherton; M: Ennio Morricone.

Lolo ✍✍ 1992 Outcast Lolo loses his job in Mexico City and then accidentally kills the local moneylender. The only one who will help him is his girlfriend Sonia, who gets the money for them to flee the city by prostituting herself. Spanish with subtitles. 88m/C VHS, DVD, MX Roberto Sosa, Lucha Villa; D: Francisco Athie; W: Francisco Athie; C: Jorge Medina; M: Juan Cristobal Perez.

London ✍✍ 2005 (R) Syd (Evans) is a pathetic drunk and druggie whose girlfriend London (Biel) has unsurprisingly left him for a new guy. She is also leaving New York, and Syd decides to crash her going-away party, accompanied by dealer Bateman (Statham) from whom Syd has just scored a lot of coke. The two guys spend most of their time in the bathroom doing blow and yapping. They are tiresome and misogynistic and so is the entire enterprise. 92m/C DVD. US Chris Evans, Jessica Biel, Jason Statham, Isla Fisher, Joy Bryant, Kelli Garner, Dana Cook; D: Hunter Richards; W: Hunter Richards; C: Jo Willems.

London Kills Me ✍ 1991 (R) A slice-of-life story London-style. Set at the end of the Thatcher era, Clint is a homeless drifter dealing drugs to get by. He's trying to get enough money for a new pair of shoes which will enable him to get a job in a fancy restaurant and away from his aimless life. His friend Muffdiver leads the group of drug pushers and is obsessed with money and drugs. Sylvie is the sultry junkie who drifts between Clint, Muffdiver, and her drug needs. The directorial debut of Kureishi is more a collection of characters and situations than a complete film but there are moments of disturbing intensity and odd sweetness. 105m/C VHS. GB Justin Chadwick, Steven Mackintosh, Emer McCourt, Roshar Seth, Fiona Shaw, Brad Dourif, Gordon Warnecke, Dave Atkins; D: Hanif Kureishi; W: Hanif Kureishi; C: Edward Lachman.

London Melody ✍½ *Girl in the Street* 1937 Neagle is a spirited Cockney busker who meets a kindly Italian diplomat who decides to finance her musical education. He promptly also falls in love with her. 71m/B VHS. GB Anna Neagle, Tullio Carminati, Robert Douglas, Horace Hodgers; D: Herbert Wilcox.

London Voodoo ✍½ 2004 Workaholic Lincoln (Cockle) and wife Sarah (Stewart) are Yanks in London who, while renovating their new digs, discover a grave in their cellar. It's that of a voodoo priestess who then possesses Sarah. Sex and exorcism are involved. 90m/C DVD. GB Doug Cockle, Vonda Barnes, Michael Nyquist; D: Robert Pratten; W: Robert Pratten; C: Patrick Jackson; M: Steven Severin.

The Lone Avenger ✍✍ 1933 Average oater centers around a bank panic, with two-gun Maynard clearing up the trouble. 60m/B VHS. Ken Maynard, Muriel Gordon, James A. Marcus, Charles "Blackie" King, Jack Rockwell, Alan Bridge, Niles Welch, William Bailey; D: Alan James; W: Alan James, Betty Burbridge, Forrest Sheldon; C: William Nobles.

Lone Bandit ✍½ 1933 Vintage western starring Chandler. 57m/B VHS, Lane Chandler, Doris Erook, Wally Wales; D: (John) Paterson) McGowan.

The Lone Defender 1932 A dozen episodes of the western serial starring the canine crusade, Rin Tin Tin. 225m/B VHS. Walter Miller, June Marlowe, Buzz Barton, Josef Swickard, Frank Lanning, Robert F. (Bob) Kortman; D: Richard Thorpe.

Lone Hero ✍✍ 2002 (R) You can tell by the video box that Phillips is not the titular hero—in fact, he's Bart (Phillips), a psycho biker gang leader who terrorizes a small town. Flanery is the somewhat goofball hero, John, who plays a gunfighter in the local Wild West show and gets the girl, only one willing to stand up to the violent menace. 91m/C VHS, DVD. Lou Diamond Phillips, Sean Patrick Flanery, Robert Forster, Tanya Allen, Gary Chalk; D: Ken Sanzel; W: Ken Sanzel; C: David Pelletier; M: Anthony Marinelli.

Lone Justice ✍✍½ 1993 (R) Cowboy Ned Blessing has seen and done it all (from outlaw to sheriff), but his wild ways have caught up with him. Now, he's relaxing his exploits from a jail cell as he awaits his fate at the end of a rope. Beware—this looks like the first chapter of a series and there's no real ending. 94m/C VHS. Daniel Baldwin, Luis Avalos, Chris Cooper, Sean Baca, Taylor Fry, Julia Campbell, Rene Auberjonois, Timothy Scott, Eot Gunton, Miguel (Michael) Sandoval, Jeff Kober; D: Peter Werner; W: William D. Wittliff; M: Basil Poledouris.

Lone Justice 2 ✍✍ 1993 *Ned Blessing: The Story of My Life and Times* 1993 (PG-13) Laconic hero Ned Blessing (Johnson), along with Mexican sidekick Crecencio (A-valos), return to Blessing's hometown after a six-year absence and find it ruled by six-shooters and fists. The despicable Borgers clan has murdered the local sheriff (who happens to be Blessing's daddy) and rules by intimidation—until Ned gets involved. Clichéd but amusing. 90m/C VHS. Brad Johnson, Luis Avalos, Wes Studi, Bill McKinney, Brenda Bakke, Julius Tennon, Richard Riehle, Gregory Scott Cummins, Rob Campbell, Rusty Schwimmer; D: Jack Bender; W: William D. Wittliff; C: Neil Roach; M: William D. Roach. TV.

The Lone Ranger ✍½ 1938 Western serial about the masked man and his faithful Indian sidekick. From a long-sought print found in Mexico, this program is burdened by a noisy sound track, two completely missing chapters, an abridged episode 15, and Spanish subtitles. 234m/B VHS. Lee Powell; D: William Witney, John English.

The Lone Ranger ✍✍½ 1956 Tonto and that strange masked man must prevent a war between ranchers and Indians in the first of the "Lone Ranger" series. 86m/C VHS. Clayton Moore, Jay Silverheels, Lyle Bettger, Bonita Granville; D: Stuart Heisler; W: Herb Meadow; C: Edwin DuPar; M: David Buttolph.

The Lone Rider in Cheyenne ✍½ 1942 One of the last in the "Lone Rider" series. The Lone Rider is out to clear the name of an innocent man accused of murder. 59m/B VHS. George Houston, Al "Fuzzy" St. John; D: Sam Newfield.

Lone Justice 3: Showdown at Plum Creek ✍✍½ 1996 (PG) Ex-outlaw-turned-sheriff Ned Blessing (Johnson) discovers the body of the previous sheriff has disappeared from its grave. Big Emma has taken over the saloon and wants Blessing out of the way, and Oscar Wilde comes to town. Three re-edited stories from the TV miniseries. 94m/C VHS. Brad Johnson, Wes Studi, Brenda Bakke, William Sanderson, Luis Avalos, Rusty Schwimmer, Stephen Fry; D: Jack Bender, Dan Lerner, David Hemmings; W: Stephen Harrigan; C: Neil Roach. TV.

Lone

The Lone Rider in Frontier Fury 🦴½ 1941 The Lone Rider (Houston) has been wrongly accused of murdering a rancher and must clear his name. 60m/B VHS. George Houston, Hillary Brooke, Al "Fuzzy" St. John, Karl Hackett, Ted Adams, Arch (Archie) Hall Sr., Budd Buster; Edward Pell Sr., Tom London; D: Sam Newfield; W: Fred Myton.

The Lone Rider in Ghost Town 🦴½ 1941 Outlaws "haunt" a ghost town to protect their hidden mine and the Lone Rider and his pal, Fuzzy, are out to solve the mystery. Installment in the short-lived "Lone Rider" series. 64m/B VHS, DVD. George Houston, Al "Fuzzy" St. John, Budd Buster; D: Sam Newfield.

The Lone Runner WOOF! 1988 (PG) An adventurer rescues a beautiful heiress from Arab kidnappers in this dud. 90m/C VHS. Miles O'Keeffe, Ronald Lacey, Michael J. Aronin, John Steiner, Hal Yamanouchi; D: Ruggero Deodato.

Lone Star 🦴🦴½ 1952 Big stars, big budget western in which Texas fights for independence as good guy Gable and badman Crawford fight each other. Gardner plays a fiery newspaper editor as well as Gable's love interest. Script is chock full of holes, but great action scenes make up for it. Based on the story by Borden Chase. 94m/B VHS. Clark Gable, Ava Gardner, Broderick Crawford, Lionel Barrymore, Beulah Bondi, Ed Begley Sr., William Farnum, Lowell Gilmore; D: Vincent Sherman; W: Howard Estabrook, Borden Chase.

Lone Star 🦴🦴🦴½ 1995 (R) Terrific contemporary western set in the border town Frontera, Texas. Sheriff Sam Deeds (Cooper) is still dealing with the legacy of his father, legendary lawman Buddy Deeds (McConaughey) who, 40 years before, wrestled control of the town from his racist, corrupt predecessor Charlie Wade (Kristofferson) and supposedly sent him packing. But when skeletal remains and a sheriff's badge turn up on an abandoned Army rifle range, guess whose bones they turn out to be. Buddy's friends would like Sam to just leave the past like he can't, and learns some hard home truths. This is only one of the town's stories that Sayles gracefully tells and, as always, his ensemble cast all offer outstanding performances. 137m/C VHS, DVD. Gabriel Casseus, Chris Cooper, Matthew McConaughey, Kris Kristofferson, Elizabeth Pena, Joe Morton, Ron Canada, Clifton James, Miriam Colon, Frances McDormand, Richard Jones; D: John Sayles; W: John Sayles; C: Stuart Dryburgh; M: Mason Daring. Ind. Spirit '97: Support. Actress (Pena).

Lone Star Kid 1988 11-year-old Brian Zimmerman lives in Crabb, Texas—population 400. After he witnesses a car accident death because there's no adequate emergency service, he decides to run for mayor and help modernize the town. Based on a true story. Includes a viewers' guide. Presented as part of the "Wonderworks" series. 55m/C VHS. James Earl Jones, Chad Sheets; M: Charlie Daniels.

Lone Star Law Men 🦴 1942 A U.S. marshal has his hands full in a border town overrun with bandits. Keene stars as the deputy marshal who goes undercover and joins the gang in an attempt to foil their crooked plans. 58m/B VHS. Tom Keene, Frank Yaconelli, Sugar Dawn, Betty Miles; D: Robert Emmet Tansey.

The Lone Star Ranger 🦴½ 1930 Former outlaw O'Brien is trying to go straight by helping to bring a gang of russlers to justice. Interesting plot twist in the link between his girlfriend and the head of the gang. 64m/B VHS. George O'Brien, Sue Carol, Walter McGrail, Warren Hymer, Russell Simpson; D: A.F. Erickson.

Lone Star State of Mind 🦴½ 2002 (PG-13) That state seems to be perplexed if not downright idiotic. Good-hearted Earl (Jackson) has promised his ditsy girlfriend Baby (King) that he will take her to L.A. so that she can fulfill her dream of becoming a soap opera actress. Only before they can leave their redneck community, Baby's doofus cousin Junior (Qualls) lands in a whole heap 'o trouble and Earl promises to set things right. 88m/C VHS, DVD. Joshua Jackson, Jaime (James) King, DJ Qualls, Matthew Davis, Ryan Hurst, John Cougar Mellencamp, Thomas Haden Church, Sam McMurray; D: David Semel; W: Trevor Munson; C: Michael Barrett; M: Tyler Bates.

Lone Wolf 🦴 1988 A werewolf terrorizes a high school, and a few computerniks track it down. 97m/C VHS. Dyann Brown, Kevin Hart, Jamie Newcomb, Ann Douglas; D: John Callas.

Lone Wolf and Cub 🦴 *Baby Cart 1: Lend a Child...Lend an Arm* 1972 First in a series of six from the sword-wielding samurai genre. Chronicles the events leading up to a samurai warrior's (Wakayama) expulsion from his native village along with his infant son (Tomikawa). Father's intense rivalry with the evil Shogun whom he was ousted by becomes an epic struggle of good vs. evil. The adorable little "Lone Cub" provides an effective counterpoint for Dad's sideline excursion into a local brothel. In Japanese with English subtitles in a letterbox format. 83m/C VHS. JP Tomisaburo Wakayama, Akihiro Tomikawa; D: Kenji Misumi.

Lone Wolf and Cub 4 🦴 1972 Fourth in a series of six. A man (Wakayama) pushes his son (Tomikawa) across Japan in a baby cart loaded with deadly accessories including built-in guns and switchblades. Copious amounts of bloodshed. In Japanese with English subtitles in a letterbox format. 80m/C VHS. JP Tomisaburo Wakayama, Akihiro Tomikawa; D: Buichi Saito.

Lone Wolf and Cub: Baby Cart at the River Styx 🦴 *Baby Cart at the River Styx; Baby Cart 2* 1972 Second of six parts in the "Kozure Ohkami" ("Sword of Vengeance") series about a man who wheels his motherless infant through the Chinese countryside in a baby cart armed with secret weapons, plotting his revenge on the warlord who expelled him. This one features the intro of Sayka and her fellow female assassins. Subtitled in English. 80m/C VHS, DVD. JP Tomisaburo Wakayama, Akihiro Tomikawa; D: Kenji Misumi.

Lone Wolf and Cub: Baby Cart to Hades 🦴 *Baby Cart to Hades* 1972 The third "Kozure Ohkami" ("Sword of Vengeance") film once again finds samurai Itto Ogami and his son Diagoro embroiled in a power struggle between a regional landlord and a governor in feudal Japan. Subtitled in English. 88m/C VHS. JP Tomisaburo Wakayama, Akihiro Tomikawa; D: Kenji Misumi.

Lone Wolf McQuade 🦴🦴½ 1983 Martial arts action abounds in this modern-day Western which pits unorthodox Texas Ranger Norris against a band of gun-running mercenaries led by Carradine. Oh, and there's a conflict-ridden love interest as well. Violent and not particularly literary) but worthy entry in chop-socky genre. 107m/C VHS, DVD. Chuck Norris, Leon Isaac Kennedy, David Carradine, L.Q. Jones, Barbara Carrera; D: Steve Carver; W: H. Kaye Dyal; C: Roger Shearman; M: Francesco De Masi.

The Loneliest Runner 🦴🦴 1976 Based on the true story of an Olympic track star who, as a teenager, suffered humiliation as a bed-wetter. The real-life experiences of producer-director Landon are presented in a touching and sensitive manner. 74m/C VHS. Michael Landon, Lance Kerwin, DeAnn Mears, Brian Keith, Melissa Sue Anderson; D: Michael Landon. TV

The Loneliness of the Long Distance Runner 🦴🦴🦴 *Rebel with a Cause* 1962 Courtenay, in his film debut, turns in a powerful performance as an angry young man infected by the poverty and hopelessness of the British slums. His first attempt at crime is a bust and lands him in a boys reformatory where he is recruited for the running team. While training for the big event with a rival school, Redgrave's obsession with winning the race and Courtenay's continued indifference to the outcome lock the two in an intriguing, seemingly one-sided power struggle. Though widely overlooked when first released, it has since been praised as one of the finest teenage angst films of the '60s. Riveting depiction on a boy's rite of passage into manhood. 104m/B VHS, DVD. GB Tom Courtenay, Michael Redgrave, Avis Bunnage, Peter Madden, James Bolam, Julia Foster, Topsy Jane, Frank Finlay, Christopher Parker; D: Tony Richardson; C: Walter Lassally; M: John Addison.

Lonely Are the Brave 🦴🦴🦴 1962 A free-spirited cowboy out of sync with the modern age tries to rescue a buddy from a local jail, and in his eventual escape is tracked relentlessly by modern law enforcement. A compelling, sorrowful essay on civilized progress and exploitation of nature. Adapted from the novel "Brave Cowboy" by Edward Abbey. 107m/B VHS. Kirk Douglas, Walter Matthau, Gena Rowlands, Carroll O'Connor, George Kennedy, Michael Kane, Karl Swenson, William Schallert, Bill Bixby; D: David Miller; W: Dalton Trumbo; C: Philip Lathrop; M: Jerry Goldsmith.

The Lonely Guy 🦴🦴½ 1984 (R) Romantic comedy as a jilted writer who writes a best-selling book about being a lonely guy and finds stardom does have its rewards. Based on "The Lonely Guy's Book of Life" by Bruce Jay Friedman. 91m/C VHS, DVD. Steve Martin, Charles Grodin, Judith Ivey, Steve Lawrence, Robyn Douglass, Merv Griffin, Dr. Joyce Brothers; D: Arthur Hiller; W: Stan Daniels; C: Victor Kemper; M: Jerry Goldsmith.

Lonely Hearts 🦴🦴🦴 1982 (R) An endearing Australian romantic comedy about a piano tuner, who at 50 finds himself alone after years of caring for his mother, and a sexually insecure spinster, whom he meets through a dating service. Wonderful performances and a good script make this a delightful film that touches the human heart. 95m/C VHS, DVD. AU Wendy Hughes, Norman Kaye, Jon Finlayson, Julia Blake, Jonathan Hardy; D: Paul Cox; W: Paul Cox, John Clarke; C: Yuri Sokol; M: Norman Kaye. Australian Film Inst. '82: Film.

Lonely Hearts 🦴½ 1991 (R) A handsome con man works his wiles on a lonely woman in this erotic thriller. Standard plot wastes a good cast. 109m/C VHS. Eric Roberts, Beverly D'Angelo, Joanna Cassidy; W: R.E. Daniels.

Lonely Hearts 🦴🦴 2006 (R) True crime thriller based on the 1940s Lonely Hearts Killers, previously filmed as "The Honeymoon Killers" (1970). Raymond (Leto) is a smalltime con artist who's overwhelmed by possessive—and homicidal—partner Martha (Hayek), who decides it's best to off their detective Elmer Robinson (Travolta) and partner Hildebrandt (Gandolfini) are assigned to the case. Director Robinson (the grandson of the real-life detective) is matter-of-fact about the violence, which makes it more shocking, and Hayek is the ultimate fatal beauty. 107m/C DVD. US John Travolta, James Gandolfini, Salma Hayek, Jared Leto, Laura Dern, Scott Caan, Alice Krige; D: Todd Robinson; W: Todd Robinson; C: Peter Levy; M: Mychael Danna.

Lonely in America 🦴🦴½ 1990 Charming romantic comedy of a newcomer in New York City. Arun (Chowdhry) has just arrived from India and has quite a few things to learn about life in the Big Apple. 96m/C VHS. Ranjit (Chaudry) Chowdhry, Adelaide Miller, Robert Kessler, Melissa Christopher, David Toney, Tirlok Malik; D: Barry Alexander Brown; W: Barry Alexander Brown, Satyajit Joy Palit.

The Lonely Lady WOOF! 1983 (R) Young writer comes to Hollywood with dreams of success, gets involved with the seamy side of movie-making, and is driven to a nervous breakdown. Pia needs acting lessons, yet it probably wouldn't have helped this trash. Adapted from the novel by Harold Robbins. 92m/C VHS. Pia Zadora, Lloyd Bochner, Bibi Besch, Joseph Cali, Ray Liotta, Jared Martin, Anthony Holland, Carla Romanelli, Olivier Pierre, Craig G. Kelly; D: Peter Sasdy; W: John Kershaw, Shawn Randall; C: Brian West; M: Charlie Calello. Golden Raspberries '83: Worst Picture, Worst Actress (Zadora), Worst Director (Sasdy), Worst Screenplay, Worst Song ("The Way You Do It").

Lonely Man 🦴🦴½ 1957 A gunfighter tries to end his career, but is urged into one last battle. Strong performances and tight direction make up for weak plot. 87m/B VHS, DVD. Jack Palance, Anthony Perkins, Neville Brand, Elaine Aiken; D: Henry Levin; C: Lionel Lindon.

The Lonely Passion of Judith Hearne 🦴🦴🦴 1987 (R) A self-effacing Dublin spinster meets a man who gives her his attention, but she must overcome her own self-doubt and crisis of faith. Adapted from Brian Moore's 1955 novel. Excellent performances from both Hoskins and Smith. 116m/C VHS. GB Maggie Smith, Bob Hoskins, Wendy Hiller, Marie Kean, Ian McNeice, Alan Devlin, Rudi Davies, Prunella Scales; D: Jack Clayton; W: Peter Nelson; C: Peter Hannan; M: Georges Delerue. British Acad. '88: Actress (Smith).

The Lonely Sex 🦴½ 1959 Creepy and bizarre film in which a maniac kidnaps a young girl and is then harassed by her psychotic housemate. ?m/C VHS, DVD. Jean Evans, Karl Light, Mary Gonzales; D: Richard Hilliard; W: Richard Hilliard; C: Richard Hilliard.

Lonely Wives 🦴🦴 1931 A lawyer hires an entertainer to serve as his double because of his marital problems. 86m/B VHS, DVD. Edward Everett Horton, Patsy Ruth Miller, Laura La Plante, Esther Ralston; D: Russell Mack; W: Walter DeLeon; C: Edward Snyder.

Lonelyhearts 🦴🦴½ 1958 Clift plays a reporter who is assigned the lovelorn column of his paper and gets too immersed in the problems of its readers. Given the superior cast and excellent material, this is a somewhat disappointing adaptation of the brilliant Nathanael West novel "Miss Lonelyhearts." Film debuts of both Stapleton and director Donehue. 101m/B VHS. Montgomery Clift, Robert Ryan, Myrna Loy, Dolores Hart, Maureen Stapleton, Frank Maxwell, Jackie Coogan, Mike Kellin; D: Vincent J. Donehue.

Loners 🦴🦴 1972 (R) Three teenagers run from the Southwest police after they are accused of murdering a highway patrolman. 80m/C VHS. Dean Stockwell, Gloria Grahame, Scott Brady, Alex Dreier, Pat Stich; D: Sutton Roley; W: Barry Sandler.

Lonesome Dove 🦴🦴🦴½ 1989 Classic western saga with Duvall and Jones in outstanding roles as two aging ex-Texas Rangers who decide to leave their quiet lives for a last adventure—a cattle drive from Texas to Montana. Along the way they encounter a new love (Lane), a lost love (Huston), and a savage renegade Indian (well-played by Forrest). Based on Pulitzer prize-winner Larry McMurtry's novel, this handsome TV miniseries is a finely detailed evocation of the Old West, with a wonderful cast and an equally fine production. Followed by "Return to Lonesome Dove." 480m/C VHS, DVD. Robert Duvall, Tommy Lee Jones, Anjelica Huston, Danny Glover, Diane Lane, Rick Schroder, Robert Urich, D.B. Sweeney, Frederic Forrest; D: Simon Wincer; W: William D. Wittliff; M: Basil Poledouris. TV

Lonesome Jim 🦴🦴 2006 (R) Jim (Affleck) is an aimless, melancholic 27-year-old returning to his dull hometown in Indiana after a spirit-crushing stint in New York. Low-key, with mildly eccentric characters, it paints a nice little picture of Midwestern alienation, soaked with dry humor. Buscemi is subtle and meticulous with his direction, working in familiar territory. 91m/C DVD. US Casey Affleck, Liv Tyler, Mary Kay Place, Seymour Cassel, Kevin Corrigan, Jack Rovello, Mark Boone Jr.; D: Steve Buscemi; W: James C. Strouse; C: Phil Parmet.

Lonesome Trail 🦴½ 1955 Routine Western that differs from the average oater by having the good guys use bows and arrows to fight their battles. 73m/B VHS, DVD. John Agar, Margia Dean, Edgar Buchanan, Wayne Morris, Adele Jergens, Douglas Fowley, Earle Lyon, Richard Bartlett; D: Richard Bartlett; W: Richard Bartlett; M: Leo Klatzkin.

Long Ago Tomorrow 🦴🦴 1971 (PG) *The Raging Moon* 1971 A paralyzed athlete enters a church-run home for the disabled rather than return to his family as the object of their pity. A love affair with a woman, who shares the same disability, helps the athlete to adjust. 90m/C VHS. GB Malcolm McDowell, Nanette Newman, Bernard Lee, Georgia Brown, Gerald Sim; D: Bryan Forbes.

The Long Dark Hall 🎬🎬½ 1951 Courtroom drama in which an innocent man is brought to trial when his showgirl mistress is found dead. 86mB VHS, GB Rex Harrison, Lilli Palmer, Denis O'Dea, Raymond Huntley, Patricia Wayne, Anthony Dawson. D: Anthony Bushell, Reginald Beck.

The Long Day Closes 🎬🎬½ 1992 (PG). It's 1956 Liverpool and 11-year-old Bud (McCormack) is part of a working class Catholic family who longs to escape from his humdrum life. And how? By going to the movies, of course and filling his head with pop songs. Nostalgic view of family life filled with sweet, small everyday moments set in a dreary postwar England. Depicts a day in the life of a family. Hepburn's performance is outstanding... Sequel to Davies's also autobiographical film "Distant Voices, Still Lives." 84mC video. 17mB VHS, DVD, Ralph Richardson, Katharine Hepburn, Dean Stockwell, Jeanne Barr, Jason Edwards Jr.; D: Sidney Lumet; C: Boris Kaufman; M: A. Andre Previn. Cannes '62. Actress (Hepburn). Natl. Bd. of Review '62. Support. Actor (Richards).

Long Day's Journey into Night 🎬🎬🎬 1962 A brooding, devastating film based on Eugene O'Neill's most powerful and autobiographical play. Depicts a day in the life of a family deteriorating under the weight of terminal illness, alcoholism and drug abuse. Hepburn's performance is outstanding. This version was taped and released on video. 174mB VHS, DVD, Katharine Hepburn, Ralph Richardson, Jason Robards Jr.; D: Sidney Lumet; C: Boris Kaufman; M: A. Andre Previn. Cannes '62. Actress (Hepburn). Natl. Bd. of Review '62. Support. Actor (Richards).

Long Day's Journey into Night 🎬🎬🎬 1988 A taped version of the Broadway production of the epic Eugene O'Neill play about a Southern family deteriorating under the weight of terminal illness, alcoholism and drug abuse. This is the inspiring story of this rising movie adaptation of outstanding performances from its cast. 169mC VHS, DVD, Jack Lemmon, Bethe Leslie, Peter Gallagher, Kevin Spacey, Jodie Lynne McLintock; D: Jonathan Miller.

Long Day's Journey Into Night 🎬🎬🎬 1996 Eugene O'Neill's autobiographical play about his family is adapted from Canada's Stratford Festival production. The Tyrones are a troubled Irish-American family: bullying James (Hutt) was a once-great Shakespearean actor who has been typecast in a popular stage potboiler; wife Mary (Henry) is a morphine addict; elder son James Jr. (Donaldson) is an alcoholic; and O'Neill's alter-ego is Edmund (McCamus), an overly sensitive, consumptive writer. Fine performances, excellent production. 174mC VHS, CA William Hutt, Martha Henry, Tom McCamus, Peter Donaldson, Martha Burns; D: David Wellington; C: David Franz; M: Ron Sures. Genie '96. Actor (Hutt), Actress (Henry). Support. Actress (Burns); Toronto-City '96: Canadian Feature Film.

The Long Days of Summer 🎬🎬 1980 Set in America, this film portrays a Jewish attorney's struggle against the prejudices of the New England town where he lives. Sequel to "When Every Day is the Fourth of July." 105mC VHS, Dean Jones, Joan Hackett, Louanne, Donald Moffat, Andrew Duggan, Michael McGuire; D: Dan Curtis. TV

The Long Good Friday 🎬🎬🎬½ 1980 Set in London's dockland, this is a violent story of a crime boss who meets his match. Hoskin's world crumbles over an Easter weekend when his buildings are bombed and his men murdered. He thinks its the work of rival gangsters only to discover an even deadlier threat is behind his troubles. One of the best of the crime genre, with an exquisitely charismatic performance by Hoskins. 109mC VHS, DVD, GB Bob Hoskins, Helen Mirren, Dave King, Bryan Marshall, George Coulouris, Pierce Brosnan, Derek Thompson, Eddie

The Long Gone 🎬🎬½ 1987 In the '50s, an over-the-hill minor-league player/manager is given a last lease on life and the pennant with two talented rookies and a sexy baseball groupie. 113mC VHS, William L. Petersen, Henry Gibson, Katy Boyer, Virginia Madsen, Dermot Mulroney, Larry Riley, Teller; D: Martin Davidson. CABLE

The Long Goodnight 🎬🎬½ 1996 (R) Audience-pleasing, blood-soaked, foul-mouthed, and action-packed. Davis obviously has a career as a '90s action star (female division), displaying the proper bravado, and muscles, necessary for her role. As mild-mannered, brown-haired Samantha Caine, she's a school-teacher with an eight-year-old daughter, Caitlin (Zima), a nice boyfriend, Hal (Aaron; D: John MacKenzie; W: Barrie Keefe; C: Phil Meheux; M: Francis Monkman.

The Long Goodbye 🎬🎬🎬 1973 with the unmistakable Altman touch—which is to say that some of the charges to the story have pushed purist noses out of joint. Gould is cast as an insouciant anti-Marlowe, the film noir atmosphere has been transmuted into a Hollywood then neon, garish jibing abounds, and the ending has been rewritten. But the revamping serves a purpose, which is to make Marlowe a viable character in a contemporary world. Handsomely photographed by Vilmos Zsigmond, Don't miss this bulky boy Arnold's cameo (his second film appearance). 112mC VHS, DVD, Elliott Gould, Nina Van Pallandt, Sterling Hayden, Henry Gibson, Mark Rydell, David Arkin, Warren Berlinger; Cameos: Arnold Schwarzenegger, David Carradine; D: Robert Altman; W: Leigh Brackett; C: Vilmos Zsigmond; M: John Williams. Natl. Soc. Film Critics '73: Cinematog.

The Long Gray Line 🎬🎬🎬 1955 Power gives an outstanding performance as Marty Maher, a humble Irish immigrant who became an institution at West Point in this affectionate drama. Director Ford gracefully captures the spirit and honor associated with West Point. This is the inspiring story of this rise from an unruly cadet to one of the academy's most beloved instructors. O'Hara does a fine job of playing his wife, who like her husband, adopts the young cadets as her own. 138mC VHS, DVD, Tyrone Power, Maureen O'Hara, Robert Francis, Donald Crisp, Ward Bond, Betsy Palmer, Phil Carey; D: John Ford; W: Edward Hope; C: Charles Lawton Jr.

The Long Haul 🎬🎬 1957 A truck driver becomes involved with crooks as his marriage sours. 88mC VHS, Victor Mature, Diana Dors, Patrick Allen, Gene Anderson; D: Ken Hughes.

The Long, Hot Summer 🎬🎬½ 1958 A tense, well-played adaptation of the William Faulkner story about drifter Ben Quick (Newman), who latches himself onto a tyrannical Mississippi family. The first on-screen pairing of Newman and Woodward (who plays spinster daughter Clara), and one of the best. Remade for TV in 1986. 117mC VHS, DVD, Paul Newman, Orson Welles, Joanne Woodward, Lee Remick, Anthony (Tony) Franciosa, Angela Lansbury, Richard Anderson; D: Martin Ritt; W: Harriet Frank Jr., Irving Ravetch; C: Joseph LaShelle; M: Alex North. Cannes '58: Actor (Newman).

The Long, Hot Summer 🎬🎬½ 1986 TV version of the William Faulkner story, "The Hamlet," about a drifter taken under a Southern patriarch's wing. He's bribed into courting the man's unmarried daughter. Wonderful performances from the entire cast, especially Ivey and surprisingly, Johnson. Remake of the 1958 film with Paul Newman and Joanne Woodward that is on par with the original. 172mC VHS, Don Johnson, Cybill Shepherd, Judith Ivey, Jason Robards Jr., Ava Gardner, William Russ, Wings Hauser, William Forsythe, Albert Hall; D: Stuart Cooper; M: Charles Bernstein. TV

Long John Silver 🎬🎬½ 1954 Famed pirate John Silver plans a return trip to Treasure Island to search for the elusive treasure; unofficial sequel to "Treasure Island" by Disney. 103mC VHS, DVD, AU Robert Newton, Connie Gilchrist, Kit Taylor, Grant Taylor, Rod Taylor; D: Byron Haskin; M: Martin Rackin; C: Carl Guthrie; M: David Buttolph.

Long Journey Back 🎬🎬½ 1978 The biographical story of a young woman's rehabilitation after her injury in a school bus accident. 100mC VHS, Mike Connors, Cloris Leachman, Stephanie Zimbalist, Katy Kurtzman; D: Mel Damski. TV

The Long Kiss Goodnight 🎬🎬½ 1996 (R) Audience-pleasing, blood-soaked, foul-mouthed, and action-packed. Davis obviously has a career as a '90s action star (female division), displaying the proper bravado, and muscles, necessary for her role. As mild-mannered, brown-haired Samantha Caine, she's a schoolteacher with an eight-year-old daughter, Caitlin (Zima), a nice boyfriend, Hal (A-)... Geena Davis, Samuel L. Jackson, Craig Bierko, Patrick Malahide, Brian Cox, David Morse, Yvonne Zima, Tom Amandes, Melina Kanakaredes, G.D. Spradlin; C: Guillermo Navarro; M: Alan Silvestri.

The Long, Long Trailer 🎬🎬½ 1954 A couple on their honeymoon find that trailer life is more than they bargained for. Lots of fun with charming direction from Minnelli, and Ball's incredible slapstick style. 97mC VHS, DVD, Desi Arnaz Sr., Lucille Ball, Marjorie Main, Keenan Wynn, Gladys Hurlbut, Moroni Olsen, Bert Freed, Madge Blake, Walter Baldwin; D: Vincente Minnelli; W: Albert Hackett, Frances Goodrich; C: Robert L. Surtees; M: Adolph Deutsch.

Long, Long Night 🎬🎬½ 1947 Remake of Marcel Carné's "Le Jour se Lève/Daybreak" (1939). WWII vet Joe Adams (Fonda) is having a hard time with his life. In fact, he's just killed con man/magician Maximilian (Price) and has barricaded himself from the cops in his apartment. Flashbacks serve o show how Joe got into his present situation (women are involved, naturally). Not too involving. 101mB VHS, DVD, Henry Fonda, Vincent Price, Barbara Bel Geddes, Ann Dvorak, Howard Freeman, Moroni Olsen, Elisha Cook Jr.; D: Anatole Litvak; W: John Wexley; C: Sol Polito; M: Dimitri Tiomkin.

Long Pants 🎬🎬🎬 1927 Langdon, in a typical man/child role, plays a naive young man who gets his first pair of long pants, which certainly ushers him into adulthood. He immediately falls for the wrong gal (Bonner), a drug runner who winds up in jail. So he breaks her out and they go on the lam. 58mB VHS, DVD, Harry Langdon, Priscilla Bonner, Alma Bennett; D: Frank Capra.

The Long Ride Home 🎬🎬 2001 (PG-13) After being accused of being a gunslinger, Jack Cole (Travis) has spent eight years running from the law and various vigilantes. He finally decides it's time to clear his name and be reunited with his family so he heads home for the final showdown. Plot's more convoluted that it may seem and it's a cliched story to begin with. 7mC VHS, DVD, Randy Travis, Eric Roberts, Ernest Borgnine, Stella Stevens; D: Marcari; C: Gary Graver.

The Long Riders 🎬🎬🎬 1980 (R) Excellent mythic western in which the Jesse James and Cole Younger gangs raid banks, trains, and stagecoaches in post-Civil War Missouri. Stylish, meticulous and a violent look back, with one of the better slow-motion shootouts in Hollywood history. Notable for the portrayal of four sets of outlaw brothers (James, Younger, Miller, Ford) by four Hollywood brother sets (Keach, Carradine, Quaid, Guest) sets. Complimented by excellent Cooder score. 100mC VHS, DVD, Stacy Keach, James Keach, Randy Quaid, Dennis Quaid, David Carradine, Keith Carradine, Robert Carradine, Christopher Guest, Nicholas Guest, Pamela Reed, Savannah Smith, James Whitmore Jr., Harry Carey Jr.; D: Walter Hill; W: Stacy Keach, James Keach, Bill Bryden; C: Ric Waite; M: Ry Cooder.

Long Road Home 🎬🎬½ 1991 (PG) Migrant family must decide between working under inhumane conditions or risk losing everything by joining the labor movement during the depression. TV

The Long Walk Home 🎬🎬🎬 1989 (PG) In Montgomery, Alabama, in the mid-1950s, sometime after Rosa Parks refused to sit in the black-designated back of the bus, Martin Luther King Jr. led a bus boycott. Spacek is the affluent wife of a white businessman who is trying to get home and stay out of trouble as he and the other seaman get shore leave. 105mB VHS, Whoopi Goldberg, Sissy Spacek, Dwight Schultz, Ving Rhames, Dylan Baker, Erika Alexander, Richard Habersham, Lonny Chapman, Dan Butler; D: Richard Pearce; W: John Cork; C: Roger Deakins; M: George Fenton.

The Long Voyage Home 🎬🎬🎬 1940 A talented cast performs this must-see screen adaptation of Eugene O'Neill's play about a merchant crew members aboard a merchant steamer in 1939. Wayne plays a young lad from Sweden who is trying to get home and stay out of trouble as he and the other seaman get shore leave. 105mB VHS, DVD, John Wayne, Thomas Mitchell, Ian Hunter, Barry Fitzgerald, Mildred Natwick, John Qualen; D: John Ford; C: Gregg Toland. N.Y. Film Critics '40: Director (Ford)

Long Time Gone 🎬🎬 1986 An over-the-hill detective tries to solve a murder while dealing with his bratty, alien-together leads her to the solitary Michael (Sands), whose wife and baby daughter, when missing around the same time as Diane's accident. 89mC VHS, DVD, Paulina Porizkova, Julian Sands, Julianne Nicholson, Jeff Webster; D: Jay Anania; W: Jay Anania; C: Oliver Bokelberg; M: Judy Kuhn.

Long Time Since 🎬½ 1997 A bit too remote and artsy to be involving. On New Year's Eve in 1971, Diane (Porizkova) hit something (or someone) with her car while driving on a remote country road. The repressed Diane has blocked all memories for some 24 years—until she hears "Auld Lang Syne" on the radio and fragments begin to come by. Putting these bits together leads her to the personals—traditional southern charmer Adam (Beach). Only their differences may make a long-term relationship an impossibility. Low-budget romantic comedy (the debut for writer-director Williams) offers a compelling performance from Montgomery but shoves conflicts out of the way to get to a forced happy ending. 97mC DVD, Matthew Montgomery, Windham Beach, Artie O'Daly, Jeremy Lucas; D: Rob Williams; W: Rob Williams; C: Shawn Grice; M: Ben Holbrook.

Long-Term Relationship 🎬🎬 2006 Glenn's (Montgomery) been a long-time player on L.A.'s gay single scene when he finds his would-be soulmate in the personals—traditional southern charmer Adam (Beach). Only their differences may make a long-term relationship an impossibility. Low-budget romantic comedy (the debut for writer-director Williams) offers a compelling performance from Montgomery but shoves conflicts out of the way to get to a forced happy ending. 97mC DVD, Matthew Montgomery, Windham Beach, Artie O'Daly, Jeremy Lucas; D: Rob Williams; W: Rob Williams; C: Shawn Grice; M: Ben Holbrook.

Long Shot Kids 🎬 Longshot 1981 Two foosball enthusiasts work their way through local tournaments to make enough money to make it to the World Championships in Tahoe. 100mC VHS, Wil Wheaton, Ann Dusenberry, Barbara Stock; D: Robert Butler. TV

The Long Ships 🎬🎬 1964 Silly Viking saga finds brothers Rolfe (Widmark) and Orm (Tamblyn) stealing a ship and heading off in search of a solid-gold bell. Among their trials as a mutinous crew and battling Moorish Prince El Mansuh (Poitier). Something to be left off the resume. 125mC VHS, DVD, Richard Widmark, Russ Tamblyn, Sidney Poitier, Oscar Homolka, Rosanna Schiaffino, Beba Loncar, Lionel Jeffries, Edward Judd; D: Jack Cardiff; W: Beverley Cross, Berkely Mather; C: Christopher Challis; M: Dusan Radic.

Long Shadows 🎬½ 1986 An analysis of how the resonating effects of the Civil War can still be felt on society, via interviews with a number of noted writers, historians, civil rights activists and politicians. 88mC VHS, Mark Harmon, John Evans, Adam Horovitz, Lee Purcell, Leon Russom, Donald Sutherland, Morgan Weisser; D: John Korty; C: Kees Van Oostrum.

exploring gender equality between the women. Outstanding performances by Spacek and Goldberg, and a great 50s feel. **95m/C VHS, DVD.** Dan E. Butler, Sissy Spacek, Whoopi Goldberg, Dwight Schultz, Ving Rhames, Dylan Baker; **D:** Richard Pearce; **W:** John Cork; **C:** Roger Deakins; **M:** George Fenton; **Nar:** Mary Steenburgen.

A Long Way Home 🐾🐾🐾 1981 A grown man searches for his long-lost siblings, after the three of them were given up for adoption after birth. **97m/C VHS.** Timothy Hutton, Brenda Vaccaro, Rosanna Arquette, Paul Regina, George Dzundza, John Lehne, Bonnie Bartlett; **D:** Robert Markowitz; **C:** Ralf Bode; **M:** William Goldstein. **TV**

The Long Weekend Woof! 2005 (R) Dismal, crude sex comedy. Ad exec Ed (Fehr) needs to come up with a new campaign to save his job but his sleazy horndog older brother Cooper (Klein) is just interested in getting them laid. Ed is a porn watcher and the (deemed too raunchy for TV) clips actually come from "America's Funniest Home Videos." **85m/C DVD. GB CA** Chris Klein, Brendan Fehr, Chandra West, Craig Fairbrass, Cobie Smulders, Paul Campbell; **D:** Pat Holden; **W:** Tad Safran; **C:** Brian Pearson; **M:** David A. Hughes. **VIDEO**

The Longest Day 🐾🐾🐾½ 1962 The complete story of the D-Day landings at Normandy on June 6, 1944, as seen through the eyes of American, French, British, and German participants. Exhaustively accurate details and extremely talented cast make this one of the all-time great Hollywood epic productions. The first of the big budget, all-star war productions; based on the book by Cornelius Ryan. Three directors share credit. Also available on video as "The Captive: The Longest Drive 2." **92m/C VHS, DVD.** Kurt Russell, Richard Burton, Red Buttons, Henry Fonda, Robert Ryan, Paul Anka, Mel Ferrer, Edmond O'Brien, Fabian, Sean Connery, Roddy McDowall, Arletty, Curt Jurgens, Rod Steiger, Jean-Louis Barrault, Peter Lawford, Robert Wagner, Sal Mineo, Leo Genn, Richard Beymer, Jeffrey Hunter, Stuart Whitman, Eddie Albert, Tom Tryon, Alexander Knox, Ray Danton, Kenneth More, Richard Todd, Gert Frobe, Christopher Lee, John Robinson; **D:** Bernhard Wicki, Ken Annakin, Andrew Marton; **W:** James Jones, David Pursall, Jack Seddon, Romain Gary; **C:** Jean (Yves, Georges) Bourgoin, Pierre Levent, Henri Persin, Walter Wottitz; **M:** Maurice Jarre. Oscars '62: B&W Cinematog.

The Longest Drive 🐾🐾 1976 *The Quest* 1976 Two brothers comb the wildest parts of the West for their sister, whom they believe is living with Indians. TV movie originally titled "The Quest," which became a brief television series. Highlights include colorful performances from the veteran actors and a unique horse/camel race. A continuation of the series is available on video as "The Captive: The Longest Drive 2." **92m/C VHS, DVD.** Kurt Russell, Brian Keith, Keenan Wynn, Neville Brand, Cameron Mitchell, Morgan Woodward, Iron Eyes Cody, Luke Askew; **D:** Lee H. Katzin. **TV**

The Longest Yard 🐾🐾🐾 1974 (R) A one-time pro football quarterback, now an inmate, organizes his fellow convicts into a football team to play against the prison guards. Of course, he's being pressured by the evil warden to throw the game. One of the all-time classic football movies. Filmed on location at Georgia State Prison. **121m/C VHS, DVD.** Sonny Shroyer, Michael Conrad, James Hampton, Harry Caesar, Charles Tyner, Mike Henry, Anitra Ford, Michael Fox, Joe Kapp, Pepper Martin, Robert Tessier, Burt Reynolds, Eddie Albert, Bernadette Peters, Ed Lauter, Richard Kiel; **D:** Robert Aldrich; **W:** Tracy Keenan Wynn; **C:** Joseph Biroc; **M:** Frank De Vol. Golden Globes '75: Film—Mus./Comedy.

The Longest Yard 🐾🐾 2005 (PG-13) Does anyone really believe Sandler as a QB? Well, in this remake of the more brutal 1974 original, Sandler is expro Paul 'Wrecking' Crewe, who's stuck in a Texas federal pen that also houses onetime college football legend Nate Scarborough (Reynolds), who formerly played the QB). The football-obsessed warden (Cromwell) okays a televised game that pits Paul and his woeful cons against the bone-crunching guards (many cameos by ex-jocks). Motor-mouthed Rock makes a

relatively brief appearance as a prison fixer and game day takes up a big part of the movie's running time. The comedy's been amped up, the pace is brisk, and Sandler is actually tolerable, but none of that makes up for doing it in the first place. **113m/C DVD, UMD. US** Adam Sandler, Burt Reynolds, Chris Rock, James Cromwell, Nelly, David Patrick Kelly, Nicholas Turturro, William Fichtner, Tracy Morgan, Brian Bosworth, Ed Lauter, Cloris Leachman, Steve Austin, Bob Sapp, Dalip Singh, Lobo Sebastian, Rob Schneider, Courteney Cox, Edward (Eddie) Bunker, Terry Crews; **D:** Peter Segal; **W:** Sheldon Turner; **C:** Dean Semler; **M:** Teddy Castellucci.

Longford 🐾🐾 2006 In 1967, Lord Frank Aungier Pakenham (Broadbent), 7th Earl of Longford, is the respected leader of the House of Lords and a tireless worker for prison rehabilitation. He stakes his name and career when he befriends notorious convicted child murderess, Myra Hindley (Morton), and campaigns for her parole (over a 30-year period), believing his fellow Catholic convert is truly redemptive. But few share his belief. **90m/C DVD. GB** Jim Broadbent, Samantha Morton, Tam Dean Burn, Lindsay Duncan, Lee Boardman, Andy Serkis, Robert Pugh, Anton Rodgers, Kate Miles, Kika Markham; **D:** Tom Hooper; **W:** Peter Morgan; **C:** Danny Cohen; **M:** Robert (Rob) Lane. **TV**

Longitude 🐾🐾🐾 2000 In 1714, England's Parliament offered a large reward to anyone who could discover a way to accurately measure longitude at sea to prevent nautical disasters. Carpenter John Harrison (Gambon) decided on a mechanical solution in the form of a clock (now known as the marine chronometer) and strove to have his ideas excepted (for 40 years). His story is paralleled with that of shellshocked ex-WWI soldier Rupert Gould (Irons), who discovered Harrison's neglected originals and became equally obsessed with restoring them to working order. The performances carry the somewhat diffuse plot. Based on the book by Dava Sobel. **200m/C VHS, DVD. GB** Jeremy Irons, Michael Gambon, Anna Chancellor, Ian Hart, Peter Vaughan, Gemma Jones, John Wood, Stephen Fry, Alec McCowen, Frank Finlay, Sam Standing, Samuel West, Bill Nighy, Brian Cox, Barbara Leigh-Hunt, Clive Francis, Daragh O'Malley, Tim (McInnerny) McInnery, Nicholas (Nick) Rowe; **D:** Charles Sturridge; **W:** Charles Sturridge; **C:** Peter Hannan; **M:** Geoffrey Burgon. **TV**

The Longshot Woof! 1986 (PG-13) Four bumblers try to raise cash to put on a sure-bet racetrack tip in this sorry comedy. Mike Nichols is the executive producer. **89m/C VHS, DVD.** Tim Conway, Harvey Korman, Jack Weston, Ted Wass, Jonathan Winters, Stella Stevens, Anne Meara; **D:** Paul Bartel; **W:** Tim Conway, John Myhers; **M:** Charles Fox.

The Longshots 2008 Yet another inspirational sports true story. The citizens of Wallace, a struggling small town in Illinois, come together behind their Pop Warner football team and its history-making first female quarterback, 11-year-old Jasmine Plummer. Coached by her Uncle Curtis, a former high school star, Jasmine leads the Harvey Colts to the Pop Warner Super Bowl. Not yet reviewed. **?m/C** Ice Cube, Tasha Smith, Keke Palmer, Matt Craven, Jill Marie Jones, Glenn Plummer, Malcolm Goodwin; **D:** Fred Durst; **W:** Doug Atchison, Nick Santora; **C:** Conrad W. Hall; **M:** John Swihart.

Longtime Companion 🐾🐾🐾½ 1990 (R) Critically acclaimed film follows a group of gay men and their friends during the 1980s. The closely knit group monitors the progression of the AIDS virus from early news reports until it finally hits home and begins to take the lives of their loved ones. One of the first films to look at the situation in an intelligent and touching manner. Produced by the PBS "American Playhouse" company. **100m/C VHS, DVD.** Dan E. Butler, Stephen Caffrey, Patrick Cassidy, Brian Cousins, Bruce Davison, John Dossett, Mark Lamos, Dermot Mulroney, Mary-Louise Parker, Michael Schoeffling, Campbell Scott, Robert Joy, Brad O'Hara; **D:** Norman Rene; **W:** Craig Lucas; **C:** Tony Jennelli. Golden Globes '91: Support. Actor (Davison); Ind. Spirit '91: Support. Actor (Davison); N.Y. Film Critics '90: Support. Actor (Davison); Natl. Soc. Film Critics '90: Support. Actor (Davison); Sundance '90: Aud. Award.

Look at Me 🐾🐾½ *Comme une image* 2004 (PG-13) Unhappy Parisian tale of gigantically egotistical father (Bacri) jetsetting his way around town and his plump daughter (Berry) unsuccessfully vying for his attention. She is a gifted singer, constantly tuning her voice. He is an acclaimed novelist, constantly tuning her out. He's also got a young trophy wife (Desarnauts) who gets nothing from her husband but ridicule and indifference. He wants his wife to look perfect, he wants his daughter to look like her voice sounds. French co-writers and co-stars Agnes Jaoui and Jean-Pierre Bacri craft a poignant, unpredictable film defying stereotype. Awarded best screenplay at Cannes. **110m/C FR** Agnès Jaoui, Jean-Pierre Bacri, Laurent Grevill, Marilou Berry, Virginie Desamauts, Keine Bouhiza, Grégoire Oestermann; **D:** Agnès Jaoui; **W:** Agnes Jaoui, Jean-Pierre Bacri; **C:** Stephane Fontaine; **M:** Philippe Rombi.

Look Back in Anger 🐾🐾🐾½ 1958 Based on John Osbourne's famous play, the first British "angry young man" film, in which a squalor-living lad takes out his anger on the world by seducing his friend's wife. **99m/B VHS, DVD. GB** Richard Burton, Claire Bloom, Mary Ure, Edith Evans, Gary Raymond, Glen Byam Shaw, George Devine, Donald Pleasence, Phyllis Neilson-Terry; **D:** Tony Richardson; **W:** John Osborne, Nigel Kneale; **C:** Oswald Morris; **M:** John Addison.

Look Back in Anger 🐾🐾 1980 A working class man angered by society's hypocrisy lashes out at his upper class wife, his mistress, and the world. Inferior remake of 1958 film version starring Richard Burton, based on '50s stage hit. **100m/ C VHS. GB** Malcolm McDowell, Lisa Banes, Fran Brill, Raymond Hardie, Robert Burr; **D:** Lindsay Anderson; **W:** John Osborne.

Look Back in Anger 🐾🐾🐾 1989 There's something about John Osborne's play that brings out the angry young man in British leads. Richard Burton played Osborne's irascible guy in 1958, Malcom McDowell looked back angrily in '80, and now Branagh convincingly vents his spleen on wife and mistress in this made for British TV production. Director Jones earlier filmed "84 Charing Cross Road" and "Jacknife." **114m/C VHS, DVD.** Kenneth Branagh, Emma Thompson, Gerard Horan, Siobhan Redmond; **D:** David Hugh Jones. **TV**

Look Both Ways 🐾🐾 2005 (PG-13) In Watt's first feature-length film, she examines our fears of dying and death. Artist Meryl (Clarke) is constantly imagining disasters (depicted in animated sequences), but then she witnesses a real tragedy—a man getting killed by a train. Local photographer Nick (McInnes), who's just been told he has cancer, takes a picture of the man's anguished widow, which is printed on the newspaper's front page along with reporter Andy's (Hayes) somewhat brutal story. Nick and Meryl make a tentative connection while struggling with fear, loneliness, hope, and forgiveness. The secondary characters and their problems (including an unplanned pregnancy) are a distraction but the film's overall quirkiness tends to work well. **100m/C DVD. AU** Justine Clarke, Anthony Hayes, Andrew S. Gilbert, Daniela Farinacci, William McInnes, Lisa Flanagan, Maggie Dence, Sacha Horler, Edwin Hodgeman; **D:** Sarah Watt; **W:** Sarah Watt; **C:** Ray Argall; **M:** Amanda Brown.

Look for the Silver Lining 🐾🐾 1949 Insipid musical biography of Broadway star Marilyn Miller (Haver). Bolger is the highlight as Miller's mentor in vaudeville to the Great White Way. ♪♫Look for the Silver Lining; Whip-Poor-Will; A Kiss in the Dark; Pirouette; Sunny; Shine On Harvest Moon; Back, Back, Back to Baltimore. **100m/C VHS.** June Haver, Ray Bolger, Gordon MacRae, Charlie Ruggles, Rosemary DeCamp, S.Z. Sakall; **D:** David Butler; **W:** Phoebe Ephron, Henry Ephron, Marian Spitzer.

Look Out Sister 🐾🐾🐾 1948 Jordan and an all-black cast star in this musical satire of westerns. "Two Gun" Jordan saves a dude ranch from foreclosure and

wins the girl. Lots of black culture, slang and music from the '40s. Broad but enjoyable humor. ♪♫Caldonia; Don't Burn the Candle at Both Ends. **64m/B VHS, DVD.** Louis Jordan, Suzette Harbin, Monte Hawley, Maceo B. Sheffield; **D:** Bud Pollard.

Look Who's Laughing 🐾🐾 1941 Bergen's plane lands in a town conveniently populated by radio stars. Not much plot here, but it might be worth a look to fans of the stars including Jim and Marion Jordan, better known as Fibber McGee and Molly. **79m/B VHS.** Edgar Bergen, Jim Jordan, Marian Jordan, Lucille Ball, Harold (Hal) Peary, Lee Bonnell, Charles Halton; **D:** Allan Dwan.

Look Who's Talking 🐾🐾🐾 1989 (PG-13) When Alley bears the child of a married, and quite fickle man, she sets her sights elsewhere in search of the perfect father; Travolta is the cabbie with more on his mind than driving Alley around and babysitting. All the while, the baby gives us his views via the voice of Bruce Willis. A very light comedy with laughs for the whole family. **90m/C VHS, DVD.** John Travolta, Kirstie Alley, Olympia Dukakis, George Segal, Abe Vigoda; **D:** Amy Heckerling; **W:** Amy Heckerling; **C:** David Kitay; **V:** Bruce Willis.

Look Who's Talking Now 🐾🐾½ 1993 (PG-13) Continuing to wring revenue from a tired premise, the family dogs throw in their two cents in the second sequel to "Look Who's Talking." For anyone who thinks Diane Keaton's hair makes her look a little like a hound dog, here's a chance to visualize her as a similarly long-eared poodle with an attitude. DeVito is also cast in character as the voice of a rough street-smart mutt, who happens to get thrown into the same household as the bosses' pure-bred poodle. Sparks, Alpo, and butt jokes fly as the dogs mark their territory. Meanwhile, dimwit wife Alley is worried that husband Travolta is having an affair, and is determined to get him back. **95m/C VHS, DVD.** John Travolta, Kirstie Alley, Olympia Dukakis, George Segal, Lysette Anthony; **D:** Tom Ropelewski; **W:** Leslie Dixon, Tom Ropelewski; **C:** Oliver Stapleton; **M:** William Ross; **V:** Diane Keaton, Danny DeVito.

Look Who's Talking, Too 🐾 1990 (PG-13) If Academy Awards for Stupidest Sequel and Lamest Dialogue existed, this diaper drama would have cleaned up. The second go-round throws the now married accountant-cabbie duo into a marital tailspin when Alley's babysitting brother moves in and the Saturday Night dancer moves out. Meanwhile, Willis cum baby smartasses incessantly. A once-clever gimmick now unencumbered by plot; not advised for linear thinkers. The **81m/C VHS, DVD.** Kirstie Alley, John Travolta, Olympia Dukakis, Elias Koteas; **D:** Amy Heckerling; **W:** Amy Heckerling, Neal Israeli; **C:** Thomas Del Ruth; **M:** David Kitay; **V:** Bruce Willis, Mel Brooks, Damon Wayans, Roseanne.

The Lookalike 🐾🐾 1990 (PG-13) Stunning models are made even more beautiful by a plastic surgeon, but one by one begin to die. Finney plays the Beverly Hills surgeon who decides to investigate when he starts losing all his clients. **94m/C VHS, DVD.** Melissa Gilbert, Diane Ladd, Frances Lee McCain, Jason Scott Lee, Thaao Penghlis; **D:** Gary Nelson; **W:** Linda J. Bergman. **CABLE**

Looker 🐾½ 1981 (PG) Comedy about two gamblers running the MGM Grand in Las Vegas trying to get out of a mess. **70m/C VHS.** Ann-Margret, Jon Voight, Burt Young; **D:** Hal Ashby; **M:** John Beal, Miles Goodman.

Lookin' to Get Out 🐾🐾½ 1982 (R) Comedy about two gamblers running the MGM Grand in Las Vegas trying to get out of his debts. They wind up at the

Looking for an Echo ♂♂½ 1999 (R) Vince (Assante) is a widower pushing 50 who had some teen success in a do-wop group and but his singing aside to marry and raise his kids. His middle son, Anthony (Balerini), is now bringing up dad's old dreams (and some regrets) by being in his own rock band. But Vince's main concerns are for youngest child, Tina (Romano), who's in the hospital battling leukemia. This puts Vince in a flirty orbit of brassy nurse Joanne (Venora), who would like to offer the guy some personal care. Assante supplies lots of charm in a glossy, sentimenta tearjerker. **97m/C VHS, DVD.** Armand Assante, Diane Venora, Joe Grifasi, Tom Mason, Anthony John (Tony) Denison, Edoarco Ballerini, David Margulies, Christy Carlson Romano. **D:** Martin Davidson. **W:** Martin Davidson, Jeffrey Goldenberg Robert Heldt; **C:** Charles Minsky.

Looking for Comedy in the Muslim World ♂♂½ 2006 (PG-13) Lame conceit has comedian Brooks play himself, more or less. He's asked by the State Department to spend a month traveling in India and Pakistan in order to figure out what Muslims find funny and write a government-sized (500 pages) report. Why this would matter is best left to the bureaucrats. There are some funny moments but not enough to carry the film, and Brooks' mild-mannered neuotic is something of an acquired taste. **98m/C DVD. US:** Albert Brooks, Sheetal Sheth, John Carroll Lynch, Jon Tenney, Fred Dalton Thompson, Amy Ryan, Homie Doroodian, Penny Marshall; **D:** Albert Brooks; **W:** Albert Brooks; **C:** Thomas Ackerman; **M:** Michael Giacchino.

Looking for Kitty ♂♂ 2004 (R) Upstate New York high school baseball coach Abe (Krumholtz in a bad mustache) comes to Manhattan to look for his missing wife Kitty, who supposedly ran off and is now shacked up with a rock star. Abe hires a wizowed PI Jack (Burns) and decides to tag along as the two lonely guys begin to bond while looking for Abe's missus. Low-key, low-budget. **95m/C DVD. US:** Elliott Burns, Max Baker, Connie Britton; **D:** Edward Burns; **W:** Edward Burns; **C:** William Rexer; **M:** Robert Gary, P. Walkley.

Looking for Miracles ♂♂½ 1990 (G) Two brothers, separated during the Depression because of poverty, get a chance to cultivate brotherly love when they're reunited in 1935. A Wonderworks production based on the bestseller novel. **104m/C VHS, CA** Zachary Bennett, Greg Spottswood, Joe Flaherty; **D:** Kevin Sullivan; **W:** Kevin Sullivan, Stuart McLean; **M:** John Welsman.

Looking for Mr. Goodbar ♂♂ 1977 (R) Young teacher Keaton seeks companionship and love by frequenting single's bars and furthers her self-destruction by her aimless intake of drugs and alcohol, in need of a father figure, she makes herself available to numerous men and eventually regrets her hedonistic behavior. Unpleasant, aimless characters do little for this dreary film, whose sexual theme sparked a bit of public conversation when first released. Based on the bestselling novel by Judith Rossner. Oscar nominations for supporting actress Weld, and cinematography. **136m/C VHS.** Diane Keaton, Tuesday Weld, Richard Gere, Tom Berenger, William Atherton, Richard Kiley; **D:** Richard Brooks; **W:** Richard Brooks; **C:** William A. Fraker.

Looking for Richard ♂♂♂ 1996 (PG-13) A Shakespearean "Vanya on 42nd Street." "Richard" is the first semi-documentary, addition to the barrage of Bard adaptations. Pacino's protracted pic dwells on a filmmaker's struggles to understand the play. Punctuated with comic relief, Pacino makes a pilgrimage to the Globe Theatre, taps Brit theatre heavyweights Gielgud and Redgrave for thoughts on interpreting Shakespeare, and combs New York for candid "man in the street impressions in a quest to bring his subject to a wider public. Over the course of four years, Pacino, in various stages of facial hair growth, plays the de-formed usurper with a cast of worthy

Looking for Trouble ♂ 1996 (PG) Lame 'kid-friendly movie finds young Jaime (Butler) befriending a baby circus elephant she names Trouble, who has an abusive owner. Jaime follows along, worried when the circus leaves town. **108m/C VHS. DVD.** Billy Butler, Shawn McAllister, Art Tutk; **D:** Peter Tors, Jay Aubrey; **W:** Peter Tors, Jay Aubrey.

The Looking Glass War ♂♂ 1996 (PG) 1969 (PG) Polish defector is sent behind the Iron Curtain on a final mission to photograph a rocket in East Berlin. He's guided by frustrated British security officers Rogers and Richardson, who both offer tation of John Le Carre's bestselling spy novel. **108m/C VHS. GB** Christopher Jones, Ralph Richardson, Pia Degermark, Anthony Hopkins, Susan George, Paul Rogers; **D:** Frank Pierson.

The Lookout ♂♂♂ 2007 (R) Crime thriller with a stellar performance by Gordon–Levitt as former golden boy jock Chris. After a car accident that left him with severe brain trauma, Chris struggles with emotional outbursts, memory gaps, and everyday tasks. He lives with sardonic blind roommate Lewis (Daniels, offering superb support) in a small Kansas town and works as a janitor at the bank, giving Chris the perfect in when con man/criminal Gary (Goode) shows up to entice him into a heist to restore some self-esteem. Gary dangles luscious Luviee (Fisher) as a prize but Chris isn't as dumb as everyone supposes. Screenwriter Frank uses his knowledge of neo-noir territory in his directorial debut. **99m/C DVD. Blu-ray Disc. US** Joseph Gordon-Levitt, Jeff Daniels, Matthew Goode, Isla Fisher, Carla Gugino, Bruce McGill, Alberta Watson, Alex Borstein, Sergio Di Zio, Greg Dunham; **D:** Scott Frank; **W:** Scott Frank; **C:** Alar Kivilo; **M:** James Newton Howard. Ind. Spirit '08:

Looney Tunes: Back in Action ♂ 2003 (PG) Mixing live action with animation, the familiar cast of Looney Toon characters participate in a series of hi-jinx with a selection of normally funny human actors. Sure there's a plot somewhere, as Daffy Duck teams up with human buddy D.J. (Fraser) to find a Blue Monkey Diamond before the bad guys, but that's secondary to pushing out as many pop culture references and corny jokes as possible in a 90 minute span. Since the people who actually knew how to do that best did it right 50 (or so) years ago, your time and money are better spent on seeking out and viewing the original cartoons. **91m/C VHS, DVD. US** Brendan Fraser, Jenna Elfman, Steve Martin, Timothy Dalton, Heather Locklear, Joan Cusack, Bill Goldberg; **D:** Joe Dante; **W:** Larry Doyle; **C:** Dean Cundey; **M:** Jerry Goldsmith; **V:** Joe Alaskey, Billy West, Jeff Glenn Bennett, Eric Goldberg.

Looney Looney Looney Bugs Bunny Movie ♂♂½ Friz Freleng's Looney Looney Looney Bugs Bunny Movie 1981 Warner Bros. cartoons tied together with new animation. Cartoon stars featured include Bugs Bunny, Elmer Fudd, Porky Pig, Yosemite Sam, Duffy Duck, and Foghorn Leghorn. **80m/C VHS. D:** Isadore 'Friz' Freleng, Chuck Jones, Bob Clampett; **V:** Mel Blanc, June Foray.

Loophole ♂♂ Break in 1983 An out-of-work architect, hard pressed for money, joins forces with an elite team of expert criminals, in a scheme to make off with millions from the most established holding bank's vault. **105m/C VHS, DVD, GB** Albert Finney, Martin Sheen, Susannah York, Robert Morley, Colin Blakely, Jonathan Pryce; **D:** John Quested.

Lord of Illusions ♂♂½ 1995 (R) New York P.I. Harry D'Amour (Bakula), who has an affinity for the occult, becomes involved with Dorothea (Janssen), the supposed widow of magician Philip Swann (O'Connor). As Harry investigates he discovers some terrifying secrets, including resurrected cult leader Nix (Von Bargen). Gruesome effects rather than excessive gore but you'll feel like you've been dropped in the middle of a plot without a clear idea what's happening. Bakula's Harry obviously has more stories to tell but just around to cower. Barker directs from his own short story. The unrated director's cut clocks in at 120 minutes. **109m/C VHS, DVD.** Scott Bakula, Famke Janssen, Kevin J. O'Connor, Daniel von Bargen, Joel Swetow, Barry Sherman, Jordan Marder, Joseph Latimore, Vincent Schiavelli; **D:** Clive Barker; **W:** Clive Barker; **C:** Ronn Schmidt; **M:** Simon Boswell.

Lord of the Flies ♂♂♂½ 1963 Proper English schoolboys stranded on a desert island during a nuclear war are transformed into savages. A study in greed power, and the innate animalistic survivalistic instincts of human nature. Based on William Golding's novel, which he described as a "journey to the darkness of the human heart." made with **91m/B VHS. DVD. GB** James Aubrey, Tom Chapin, Hugh Edwards, Roger Elwin, Tom Gaman; **D:** Peter Brook; **W:** Peter Brook; **M:** Raymond Leppard.

Loose Cannons ♂ 1990 (R) Yet another mismatched-cop-partner comedy, wherein a mystery is ostensibly solved by a veteran cop and a schizophrenic detective. **95m/C VHS. DVD.** Gene Hackman, Dan Aykroyd, Dom DeLuise, Ronny Cox, Nancy Travis, David Alan Grier, Richard Christian Matheson, (Benjamin) Clark, Richard Christian Clark; **D:** Bob (Benjamin) Clark; **W:** Bob (Benjamin) Clark, Richard Christian Matheson.

Loose Connections ♂♂ 1987 A feminist driving to a convention in Europe advertises for a travelmate, and gets a hopeless chauvinist who is masquerading as a gay man in this offbeat cult comedy. **90m/C VHS. GB** Lindsay Duncan, Stephen Rea, Robbie Coltrane; **D:** Richard Eyre.

Loose in New York ♂♂ Fiscina II sesso 1974 Much to her surprise, a cynical socialite begins to fall for her computer-arranged mate. **91m/C VHS. IT** Rita Tushingham, Aldo Maccione, George Dzundza, Leopoldo Trieste; **D:** Gian Luigi Polidoro.

Loose Screws ♂ 1985 (R) Four perverted teenagers are sent to a restrictive academy where they continue their ways in this stupid sequel to "Screwballs." **75m/C VHS, DVD. CA** Bryan Genesse, Karen Wood, Alan Deveau, Jason Warren; **D:** Rafal Zielinski; **W:** Michael Cory.

Loot... Give Me Money, Honey! ♂♂½ 1970 Black comedy about a motley crew of greed-driven gold-diggers who chase after a heisted fortune in jewels, which is hidden in a coffin belonging to one of the thieves' mother. From Joe Orton's play. **101m/C VHS. GB** Richard Attenborough, Lee Remick, Hywel Bennett, Milo O'Shea, Roy Holder; **D:** Silvio Narizzano.

Lord Jim ♂♂♂ 1965 A ship officer (O'Toole) commits an act of cowardice that results in his dismissal and disgrace, which leads him to the Far East in search of self-respect. Excellent supporting cast. Based on Joseph Conrad's novel. **154m/C VHS, DVD.** Peter O'Toole, James Mason, Curt Jurgens, Eli Wallach, Jack Hawkins, Paul Lukas, Akim Tamiroff, Daliah Lavi, Andrew Keir, Jack MacGowran, Walter Gotell; **D:** Richard Brooks; **W:** Richard Brooks; **C:** Frederick A. (Freddie) Young; **M:** Bronislau Kaper.

Lord Love a Duck ♂♂½ 1966 McDowall plays a high school nerd who grants the wishes of classmate Weld, even as they get increasingly complicated. Excellent '60s satire of society in and around high school. **105m/C VHS.** Roddy McDowall, Tuesday Weld, Lola Albright, Martin West, Ruth Gordon, Harvey Korman, Sarah Marshall, Max (Casey Adams) Showalter, Donald Murphy, Joseph Mell, Dan Frazer, Martine Bartlett; **D:** George Axelrod; **W:** George Axelrod; **C:** Neal Hefti.

Lord of the Rings: The Fellowship of the Ring ♂♂♂½ 2001 (PG-13) The first in Jackson's trilogy of films based on the books by J.R.R. Tolkien. Young hobbit Frodo Baggins, after inheriting a mysterious ring from his uncle Bilbo, must leave his home in order to keep it from falling into the hands of its evil creator. Along the way, a fellowship is formed to protect the ringbearer and make sure that the ring arrives at its final destination: Mt. Doom, the only place where it can be destroyed. The three and a half hour pic stays closer to the original novel than any of the previous efforts (all animated), while still managing to keep a quick enough pace for those unfamiliar with the lengthy literary work. Should get repeated viewing in parents' basements for years to come. **178m/C VHS, DVD.** Elijah Wood, Ian McKellen, Liv Tyler, Viggo Mortensen, Sean Astin, Cate Blanchett, John Rhys-Davies, Dominic Monaghan, Billy Boyd, Orlando Bloom, Christopher Lee, Hugo Weaving, Sean Bean, Ian Holm, Andy Serkis, Marton Csokas; **D:** Peter Jackson; **W:** Peter Jackson, Fran Walsh, Philippa Boyens; **C:** Andrew Lesnie; **M:** Howard Shore. Oscars '01: Cinematog.; British Film Critics '01: Director (Jackson), Film, Visual FX; LA. Film Critics '01: Score; Natl. Bd. of Review '01: Support. Actress (Blanchett); Screen Actors Guild '01: Support. Actor (McKellen); Broadcast Film Critics '01: Song, "May It Be") Score.

Lord of the Rings: The Two Towers ♂♂♂½ 2002 (PG-13) The second installment of the "Rings" trilogy does not disappoint. Picking up shortly after the first one left off, Frodo and Samwise are still heading toward Mordor, with Gollum following/abetting their progress. Aragorn, Legolas, and Gimli join together with the denizens of Rohan to fight Saruman's army of Orcs. Gandalf is back to Plenty of action (the battle scenes are incredible) and plot twists (Frodo's battle of wills with himself and Gollum add yet more depth to both characters), provide enough entertainment to keep the chat rooms humming until the last chapter comes out. Speaking of final chapters, George Lucas must be sweating bullets right about now. **179m/C VHS, DVD.** US Elijah Wood, Sean Astin, Viggo Mortensen, Orlando Bloom, John Rhys-Davies, Ian McKellen, Christopher Lee, Billy Boyd, Dominic Monaghan, Liv Tyler, Bernard Hill, Miranda Otto, David Wenham, Karl Urban, Brad Dourif, Cate Blanchett, Hugo Weaving; **D:** Peter Jackson; **W:** Peter Jackson, Fran Walsh, Philippa Boyens; **C:** Andrew Lesnie; **M:** Howard Shore. Oscars '02: Sound FX Ed., Visual FX.

Lord of the Rings: The Return of the King ♂♂♂ 2003 (PG-13) Jackson's triumphant last chapter of the superb Tolkien trilogy brings the story to a satisfying close. After the climactic battle for Helm's Deep in "The Two Towers," Rohan's forces, along with most of the original members of the Fellowship, must come to the aid of Minas Tirith, the capital city of Gondor, and Sauron's next target. They also attempt to distract Sauron from Frodo and Sam, who

The Lord of the Rings ♂♂ 1978 (PG) An animated interpretation of Tolkien's classic tale of the hobbits, wizards, elves, and dwarfs who inhabit Middle Earth. Animator Ralph Bakshi used live motion animation (roto-scoping) to give his characters more life-like and human motion. Well done in spite of the difficulty of adapting from Tolkien's highly detailed and lengthy works. **128m/C VHS, DVD.** Ralph Bakshi; **V:** J.C. (Chris) Conkling Peter S. Beagle; **V:** Christopher Guard, John Hurt.

Lord of the Flies ♂♂ 1990 (R) Inferior second filming of the famed William Golding novel about schoolboys marooned on a desert island who gradually degenerate into savages. Lushly photographed, yet redundant and poorly acted. **90m/C VHS, DVD** Balthazar Getty, Daniel Pipoly, Chris Furrh, Badgett Dale, Edward Taft, Andrew Taft; **D:** Harry Hook; **W:** Sara Schiff; **C:** Martin Furrer; **M:** Philippe Sarde.

encounter even worse hardships, including misplaced trust, deceit, and giant spiders, on their way to Mt. Doom to destroy the ring. Although the two main plots are very different in scope and dynamics, each is equally adept at maintaining depth and character development, while keeping the plot moving along. As with the first two installments, the photography is breathtaking. **200m/C VHS, DVD.** *US* Elijah Wood, Sean Astin, Viggo Mortensen, Orlando Bloom, John Rhys-Davies, Ian McKellen, Billy Boyd, Dominic Monaghan, Liv Tyler, Bernard Hill, Miranda Otto, David Wenham, Karl Urban, Hugo Weaving, Andy Serkis, Cate Blanchett, John Noble, Ian Holm, Sean Bean, Lawrence Makoare, Marton Csokas; *D:* Peter Jackson; *W:* Peter Jackson, Fran Walsh, Philippa Boyens; *C:* Andrew Lesnie; *M:* Howard Shore. Oscars '03: Adapt. Screenplay, Art Dir./Set Dec., Costume Des., Director (Jackson), Film, Film Editing, Makeup, Song ("Into the West"), Sound, Visual FX; Orig. Score; British Acad. '03: Adapt. Screenplay, Cinematog., Film, Visual FX; Directors Guild '03: Director (Jackson); Golden Globes '04: Director (Jackson), Film—Drama, Song ("Into the West"), Orig. Score; L.A. Film Critics '03: Director (Jackson); N.Y. Film Critics '03: Film; Screen Actors Guild '03: Cast.

Lord of War 🦴🦴🦴 **2005 (R)** Niccol's look into the dark world of international weapons trade says guns are evil but its vivid imagery suggests something very different. Yuri Orlov (Cage), a Ukrainian immigrant living in Manhattan, would like to put a gun in the hand of every person on the planet. Aided in business by his brother Vitaly (Leto) and pursued by Interpol agent Valentine (Hawke), Yuri slickly operates in his frightening underworld of bloody regional conflict. His fabulous life is fueled by profits extracted from the ever-growing stack of dead bodies. Cage's performance is at the center of a satisfying movie experience. **122m/C DVD, Blu-ray Disc, UMD.** *US* Nicolas Cage, Jared Leto, Bridget Moynahan, Ian Holm, Ethan Hawke, Eamonn Walker, Sammi Rotibi, Eugene (Yevgeny) Lazarev; *D:* Andrew Niccol; *W:* Andrew Niccol; *C:* Amir M. Mokri; *M:* Antonio Pinto.

The Lords of Discipline 🦴🦴½ **1983 (R)** A military academy cadet is given the unenviable task of protecting a black freshman from racist factions at a southern school circa 1964. Based on Pat Conroy's autobiographical novel. **103m/C VHS, DVD.** David Keith, Robert Prosky, Barbara Babcock, Judge Reinhold, G.D. Spradlin, Rick Rossovich, Michael Biehn, Bill Paxton, Matt Frewer; *D:* Franc Roddam; *C:* Brian Tufano; *M:* Howard Blake.

Lords of Dogtown 🦴🦴 **2005 (PG-13)** Another ego-trip down memory lane for writer and original Z-Boy Stacy Peralta, serving as a dramatic reenactment to his documentary "Dogtown and Z-Boys." A motley crew of surfer-turned-skater kids in 1975's Venice, CA, turn skateboarding into a pop-culture revolution. The movie version of their story, however, is a bit of a wipe out. The skating looks great, but some botched acting and poor pacing confuses everything. Ledger does his best with the clumsy role of Zephyr founder Skip Englom, but others, mostly real life skater kids, aren't as convincing. Stick to click in the second-half, but still riddled with bad dialogue and rushed storytelling. Loaded with cameos, mostly by pro skate veterans, and one by the late great, cult stand-up comic Mitch Hedberg. **107m/C DVD, UMD.** *US* Heath Ledger, Emile Hirsch, Victor Rasuk, John Robinson, Nikki Reed, Michael Angarano, Rebecca De Mornay, Johnny Knoxville; *D:* Catherine Hardwicke; *W:* Stacy Peralta; *C:* Elliot Davis; *M:* Mark Mothersbaugh.

The Lords of Flatbush 🦴🦴½ **1974 (PG)** Four street toughs battle against their own maturation and responsibilities in 1950s Brooklyn. Winkler introduces the leather-clad hood he's made a career of unlike Rocky. Interesting slice of life. **88m/C VHS, DVD.** Sylvester Stallone, Perry King, Henry Winkler, Susan Blakely, Armand Assante, Paul Mace; *D:* Stephen Verona, Martin Davidson; *W:* Sylvester Stallone, Stephen Verona, Martin Davidson; *M:* Joseph Brooks.

Lords of Magick 🦴 **1988 (PG-13)** WOOF! Two warriors chase an evil sorcerer and the princess he's kidnapped across time to the 20th century. **98m/C VHS.** Jarrett Parker, Matt Gauthier, Brendan Dillon Jr.; *D:* David Marsh.

Lords of the Deep WOOF! **1989 (PG-13)** A Roger Corman cheapie about underwater technicians trapped on the ocean floor with a race of aliens. A film rushed out to capitalize on the undersea sci-fi subgenre highlighted by "The Abyss." **95m/C VHS.** Bradford Dillman, Priscilla Barnes, Melody Ryane, Eb Lottimer, Daryl Haney; *Cameos:* Roger Corman; *D:* Mary Ann Fisher; *W:* Howard R. Cohen, Daryl Haney.

Lorenzo's Oil 🦴🦴🦴 **1992 (PG-13)** Based on the true story of Augusto and Michaela Odone's efforts to find a cure for their five-year-old, Lorenzo, diagnosed with the rare and incurable disease ALD (Adrenoleukodystrophy). Confronted by a slow-moving and clinically cold medical community, the Odones embark on their own quest for a cure. Sarandon delivers an outstanding and emotionally charged performance as Lorenzo's determined mother. Nolte is his equally devoted Italian father, complete with black hair and hand gestures. They are a powerful presence in a film which could have easily degenerated into a made-for-TV movie, but is instead a tribute to what love and hope can accomplish. **135m/C VHS, DVD.** Nick Nolte, Susan Sarandon, Zach O'Malley-Greenberg, Peter Ustinov, Kathleen Wilhoite, Gerry Bamman, Margo Martindale, James Rebhorn, Ann Hearn, Elizabeth (E.G. Dailey) Daily; *D:* George Miller; *W:* George Miller, Nick Enright; *C:* John Seale.

The Loretta Claiborne Story 🦴🦴½ **2000** Your basic inspirational TV movie based on a true story. Loretta (Elise) is black, poor, partially blind, and mildly retarded. She's mercilessly teased until a grade-school teacher (Palk) interests the young Loretta in running. But it's not until she's a teenager that Loretta finds her own cheerleader—social worker Janet McFarland (Manheim) who signs the girl up to participate in the Special Olympics. **90m/C VHS.** Kimberly Elise, Camryn Manheim, Tina Lifford, Nancy Palk, Damon Gupton, Nicole Ari Parker; *D:* Lee Grant; *W:* Grace McKeaney; *C:* Laszlo George; *M:* Stanley Clarke. TV

Lorna Doone 🦴🦴½ **1922** A young girl of royal descent is kidnapped and raised by the bandit Doone family in the highlands of Scotland. Adapted from the novel by R.D. Blackmore. **79m/B VHS, DVD.** Madge Bellamy, John Bowers; *D:* Maurice Tourneur.

Lorna Doone 🦴🦴½ **1934** Early version of the R.D. Blackmore novel about an English farmer who falls in love with the daughter of an outlaw family. Set in rural England in the 1600s; remade in 1951 and 1990. **90m/B VHS.** Victoria Hopper, John Loder, Margaret Lockwood, Roy Emerton, Mary Clare, Edward Rigby, Roger Livesey; *D:* Basil Dean; *M:* Miles Malleson.

Lorna Doone 🦴🦴 **1990 (PG)** Classic romance set in 17th-century England and based on the novel by R.D. Blackmore. John Ridd (Bean) vows to destroy the land-grabbing Doone family, whom he blames for the death of his parents. Then he meets, and immediately falls in love with, the beautiful and innocent Lorna Doone (Walker). **90m/C VHS.** *GB* Sean Bean, Polly Walker, Clive Owen, Billie Whitelaw; *D:* Andrew Grieve; *W:* Matthew Jacobs. TV

Lorna Doone 🦴🦴½ **2001** Based on R.D. Blackmore's novel, which is set in the west country of 17th-century Britain, this swashbuckler is a star-crossed romance with an ultimately happy ending. John Ridd (Coyle) is a common farmer who discovers that Lorna (Warner), the young beauty he loves, is a member of the infamous Doone clan—a once aristocratic family that has turned outlaw. To make things worse for John, Lorna is already betrothed to the violent Carver Doone (Gillen) who will do anything to keep her. **150m/C VHS, DVD.** *GB* Richard Coyle, Amelia Warner, Aidan Gillen, Martin Clunes, Michael Kitchen, Martin Jarvis, Barbara Flynn, Peter Vaughan, Anton Lesser, Jack Shepherd; *D:* Mike Barker; *W:* Adrian Hodges; *C:* Chris Seager; *M:* John Lunn. TV

Los Locos Posse 🦴🦴 **1997 (R)** Uneven would-be sequel to 1993's "Posse." Chance (Van Peebles) is a black military scout who is found, injured, by one of the unhinged denizens of a nearby mission. The Mother Superior enlists Chance to lead the nuns and their "Los Locos" charges to another mission some hundred miles away. The trip doesn't go smoothly and their arrival only leads to more problems. First English-language feature for Montreal director Vallee. **100m/C VHS.** Mario Van Peebles, Rene Auberjonois, Kathryn Witt, Danny Trejo, Melora Walters, Rusty Schwimmer; *D:* Jean-Marc Vallee; *W:* Mario Van Peebles; *C:* Pierre Gill; *M:* Lesley Barber.

Los Olvidados 🦴🦴🦴½ *The Young and the Damned* **1950** From surrealist Bunuel, a powerful story of the poverty and violence of young people's lives in Mexico's slums. In Spanish with English subtitles. **88m/B VHS, DVD.** *MX* Alfonso Mejias, Roberto Cobo; *D:* Luis Bunuel. Cannes '51: Director (Bunuel), Film.

Loser 🦴½ **1997 (R)** Very low-budget street drama concerns young small-time drug dealer James Dean Ray (Harris) and his self-destruction slide towards oblivion. **90m/C VHS, DVD.** Kirk Harris, Jonathon Chaus, Peta Wilson, Norman Salect, Jack Rubio; *D:* Kirk Harris; *W:* Kirk Harris; *C:* Kent Wakeford.

Loser 🦴🦴 **2000 (PG-13)** College comedy finds nerdy midwesterner Biggs branded a loser by his dorm mates at New York University. He's also pining over beauty Suvari, who's having an affair with heartless prof Kinnear. Writer-director Heckerling's trademark sympathy for the adolescent outcast is intact, but this outing is missing the insight, subtlety, and (most importantly) the fun of her earlier efforts. Biggs and Suvari give passable performances, but Kinnear is the bright spot. **95m/C VHS, DVD.** Jason Biggs, Mena Suvari, Greg Kinnear, Zak Orth, Dan Aykroyd, Tom Sadoski, Jimmi Simpson, Colleen Camp, Robert Miano, Andy Dick, David Spade, Steven Wright, Taylor Negron, Andrea Martin, Scott Thompson; *D:* Amy Heckerling; *W:* Amy Heckerling; *C:* Rob Hahn; *M:* David Kitay.

The Losers 🦴½ *Nam's Angels* **1970 (R)** Four motorcyclists are hired by the U.S. Army to rescue a presidential advisor who is being held captive by Asian bad guys. **96m/C VHS.** William (Bill) Smith, Bernie Hamilton, Adam Roarke, Houston Savage, Paul Koslo, John Garwood, Jack Starrett, Alan Caillou; *D:* Jack Starrett; *W:* Alan Caillou; *C:* Nonong Rasca; *M:* Stu Phillips.

Losin' It 🦴🦴 **1982 (R)** Four teens travel across the Mexican border to Tijuana on a journey to lose their virginity. Cruise meets a married woman who says she is in town for a divorce, while the others become caught up in frenzied undertakings of their own. **104m/C VHS, DVD.** Tom Cruise, John Stockwell, Shelley Long, Jackie Earle Haley, John P. Navin Jr., Timothy Brown, Rick Rossovich; *D:* Curtis Hanson; *W:* Bill W.L. Norton; *C:* Gilbert Taylor; *M:* Kenneth Wannberg.

Losing Chase 🦴🦴½ **1996 (R)** Bacon makes his directorial debut in this drama that features wife Sedgwick as Elizabeth, mother's helper to Chase (Mirren) and Richard Philips (Bridges) at their summer home on Martha's Vineyard. Chase is still recovering from a mental breakdown, having spent several months in an institution, and she resents Elizabeth's presence, constantly criticizing her. But when the two women are alone together a confusing and emotional bond gradually begins to form between them. **95m/C VHS, DVD.** Helen Mirren, Kyra Sedgwick, Beau Bridges; *D:* Kevin Bacon; *W:* Anne Meredith; *C:* Dick Quinlan; *M:* Michael Bacon. CABLE

Losing Isaiah 🦴🦴 **1994 (R)** "Kramer vs. Kramer" meets the movie-of-the-week in this controversial and emotionally moving story of a social worker (Lange) who adopts the title character, an African American baby abandoned by his drug-addicted mother (Berry). Courtroom battle ensues when four years later mom, now clean and sober, discovers Isaiah is alive. She enlists the aid of a lawyer (Jackson) known for his high-profile, racially charged cases. Lange and Berry lead the parade of fine performances. Taking on some volatile issues, director Gyllenhaal manages (for the most part) to refrain from melodrama. Based on the novel by Seth Margolis. **108m/C VHS, DVD.** Jessica Lange, Halle Berry, David Strathairn, Samuel L. Jackson, Cuba Gooding Jr., LaTanya Richardson Jackson; *D:* Stephen Gyllenhaal; *W:* Naomi Foner; *C:* Andrzej Bartkowiak; *M:* Mark Isham.

The Loss of Sexual Innocence 🦴🦴½ **1998 (R)** Figgis' ambitious film follows the fall from grace (literally of Adam and Eve), and the nature of sex, love, jealousy, and violence. Unfortunately, this turns out to be less than scintillating material. Interspered with scenes from the Garden of Eden story is that of dissatisfied filmmaker Nic (Sands), as he relives his past and ponders his unhappy present. **101m/C VHS, DVD.** Julian Sands, Saffron Burrows, Stefano Dionisi, Jonathan Rhys Meyers, Kelly Macdonald, Femi Ogumbanjo, Hanne Klintoe, Johanna Torrel, George Moktar, John Cowey; *D:* Mike Figgis; *W:* Mike Figgis; *C:* Benoit Delhomme; *M:* Mike Figgis.

Lost 🦴½ **1983** A young girl runs away into the wilderness because of the resentment she feels toward her new stepfather. **92m/C VHS.** Sandra Dee, Don Stewart, Ken Curtis, Jack Elam, Sheila Newhouse; *D:* Al Adamson; *W:* Don Buday; *C:* Gary Graver.

Lost 🦴🦴 **1986** When their boat capsizes in the Pacific, three sailors desperately cling to life, drifting aimlessly for 74 days. Based on a true story, this film is adult-fare. **93m/C VHS.** *CA* Michael Hogan, Helen Shaver, Kenneth Welsh; *D:* Peter Rowe.

Lost 🦴🦴 **2005** Former L.A. resident Jeremy Stanton (Cain) gets lost on a Mojave highway while driving to meet his family at their new Nevada home. His nightmare journey turns into a maze of detours on flood-closed roads, while he gets bad directions from clueless road-service operator Judy (voiced by Scott). A tight thriller in the best B-movie tradition and the debut feature for Lemke. **86m/C DVD.** *US* Dean Cain, Ashley Scott, Danny Trejo, Irina Bjorklund, Justin Henry, Griffin Armstoff; *D:* Darren Lemke; *W:* Darren Lemke; *C:* Paul Emami; *M:* Russ Landau.

Lost and Delirious 🦴🦴 **2001** Teen angst, romance, and sexuality taken to extremes. Shy Mouse (Barton) is trying to settle in at her exclusive girls' boarding school with new roomies, wealthy Tory (Pare) and wild Paulie (Perabo). When Mouse realizes that the girls are lovers she takes it in stride but Tory gets anxious and denies the relationship. Mouse watches helplessly as Paulie gets increasingly desperate to win Tory back and matters take a turn for the baroque. Based on the novel "The Wives of Bath" by Susan Swan. **100m/C VHS.** *CA* Mischa Barton, Piper Perabo, Jessica Pare, Jackie Burroughs, Graham Greene, Mimi Kuzyk, Luke Kirby; *D:* Lea Pool; *W:* Judith Thompson; *C:* Pierre Gill; *M:* Yves Chamberland. Genie '01: Cinematog.

Lost and Found 🦴🦴½ **1979 (PG)** An American professor of English and an English film production secretary fall in love on a skiing vacation. Good cast but Segal and Jackson did romance better in "A Touch of Class." **104m/C VHS.** George Segal, Glenda Jackson, Maureen Stapleton, Hollis McLaren, John Cunningham, Paul Sorvino, John Candy, Martin Short; *D:* Melvin Frank; *W:* Jack Rose.

Lost and Found 🦴 **1999 (PG-13)** The only, repeat ONLY, reason to see this movie is Sophie Marceau. Spade, in a bold bit of casting, plays Dylan, a sniveling pipsqueak taken with his French neighbor Lila (the aforementioned Marceau). In a sick attempt to win her love, he kidnaps her dog in order to "find" him a few days later. When the dog swallows an anniversary ring Dylan's holding for a friend, many tasteless dog poo jokes ensue. Wants to be "There's Something About

The Lost Angel 🎬🎬 2004

Plagued by the memory of her mother's death and facing an internal investigation, a police inspector (Eastwood) must overcome her own demons along with intense media scrutiny to track down a serial killer. **97m/C VHS, DVD.** David Spade, Sophie Marceau, Arlie Lange, Martin Sheen, Patrick Shiel, Jon Lovitz, Mitchell Whitfield, Carole Cook, Estelle Harris, Maria Gibbs, Natalie Barish, Phil Leeds, Christian Clemenson, Daphne Lynn Dupsik; **D:** Jeff Pollack; **W:** J.B. Cook, Marc Meeks, David Spade; **C:** Paul Elliott; **M:** John Debney.

Lost Angels 🎬🎬½ 1989 (R) A glossy "Rebel Without a Cause" '80s reprise providing a no-holds-barred portrait of life in the fast lane. A wealthy, disaffected San Fernando Valley youth immerses himself in sex, drugs and rock 'n' roll. Ultimately he is arrested and sent by his parents to a youth home, where a dedicated therapist assists his tortuous road back to reality. **116m/C VHS.** Donald Sutherland, Adam Horovitz, Amy Locane, Kevin Tighe, John C. McGinley, Graham Becke, Park Overall, Don Bloomfield, Celia Weston; **D:** Hugh Hudson; **W:** Michael Weller; **M:** Philippe Sarde.

Lost Battalion 🎬🎬½ 2001 True story based on the heroism of U.S. Major Charles Whittlesey (Schroder), who won the Congressional Medal of Honor during the closing days of WWI. Part of the Army's 77th Division, Whittlesey and his troops find themselves separated from their allies and surrounded by German forces in the Argonne Forest. Whittlesey led his men on a five-day defensive march back to Allied lines despite limited supplies and constant battle. **100m/C VHS, DVD.** Rick Schroder, Jamie Harris, Phil McKee, Jay Rodan, Adam James; **D:** Russell Mulcahy; **W:** James (Jim) Carabatsos; **C:** Jonathan Freeman; **M:** (Rick) Marvin. **CABLE**

Lost Boundaries 🎬🎬 1949 Respected physician Scott Carter (debut role for Ferrar) and his family live and work in a small New Hampshire town, hiding the fact that they are black, passing for white, in their segregated society. But then the truth becomes known. Strong, if slow-moving, and based on a true story; the use of white leads for black roles was common casting. **99m/B VHS.** Mel Ferrer, Beatrice Pearson, Richard Hylton, Susan Douglas, Canada Lee, Carleton Carpenter, Seth Arnold, Wendell Holmes; **D:** Alfred Werker; **W:** Virginia Shaler, Eugene Ling, Charles A. Palmer, Furland de Kay; **C:** William J. Miller; **M:** Louis Applebaum.

The Lost Boys 🎬🎬 1978 Holm gives a brilliant performance as writer J.M. Barrie, whose friendship with young George Llewellyn-Davies and his four brothers will lead to the story of Peter Pan. But as the depressed Barrie's marriage falls apart and tragedy strikes the Llewellyn-Davies family, the relationship grows ever more complex. **270m/C DVD. GB** Ian Holm, Tim Pigott-Smith, Anna Cropper, Maureen O'Brien, Ann Bell; **D:** Rodney Bennett; **W:** Andrew Birkin; **M:** Dudley Simpson. **TV**

The Lost Boys 🎬🎬 1987 (R) Santa Cruz seems like a dull town when Michael, his younger brother, and their divorced mom move into their eccentric grandfather's home. But when Michael falls for a pretty girl with some hard-living friends he takes on more than he imagines—these partying teens are actually a group of vampires. Some humor, some bloodletting violence, and an attractive cast help out this updated vampire tale. Rock-filled soundtrack. **97m/C VHS, DVD.** Jason Patric, Kiefer Sutherland, Corey Haim, Jami Gertz, Dianne Wiest, Corey Feldman, Barnard Hughes, Edward Herrmann, Billy Wirth, Jamison Newlander, Brooke McCarter, Alex Winter; **D:** Joel Schumacher; **W:** Jeffrey Boam, Janice Fischer, James Jeremias; **C:** Michael Chapman; **M:** Thomas Newman.

Mary," but doesn't have its winking sense of absurdity. Spade should stick to the snarky sidekick roles and Marceau should fire whoever told her that this would be a good career move. **97m/C VHS, DVD.**

Lost Canyon 🎬 1943 Hoppy tries to help a fugitive who's been framed for bank robbery. This is the second installment distributed by United Artists. The song "Jingle, Jangle, Jingle" is sung by the Sportsman Quartet. **61m/B VHS, DVD.** William Boyd, Jay Kirby, Andy Clyde, Lola Lane, Douglas Fowley, Herbert Rawlinson; **D:** Lesley Selander.

The Lost Capone 🎬🎬🎬 1990 Cable TV version of the story of Al Capone's youngest brother, a clean living small town sheriff who struggles with his sibling's reputation at every turn. **95m/C VHS.** Dominic Chianese, Ally Sheedy, Eric Roberts, Adrian Pasdar, Titus Welliver, Jimmie F. Skaggs, Maria Pitillo, Anthony Crivello; **D:** John Gray; **W:** John Gray; **C:** Paul Elliot. **CABLE**

The Lost Child 🎬🎬½ 2000 Remarkable true story about a search for identity. Rebecca (Ruehl) always knew she was adopted, being raised Jewish in Pennsylvania. After her adoptive parents are both dead, Rebecca decides to search for her birth parents and discovers that she is a full-blooded Navaho who was taken from her family on the reservation. She immediately decides to take her children to meet her relatives in Arizona, where they are welcomed into the community. But it isn't so simple for Rebecca's husband, Jack (Sheridan), to deal with his outsider status. Based on the autobiography "Looking for Lost Bird" by Yvette Melanson and Claire Safran. **100m/C VHS, DVD.** Mercedes Ruehl, Jamey Sheridan, Irene Bedard, Dinah Manoff, Ned Romero, Taimdo Cardinal, Michael Greyeyes, Julia McIlvaine; **D:** Karen Arthur; **W:** Sally Robinson; **C:** Thomas Neuwirth; **M:** Mark McKenzie. **TV**

The Lost City 🎬🎬 1934 A feature version of the rollicking vintage movie serial about a lost jungle city, adventurers and mad scientists. **74m/B VHS, DVD.** William "Stage" Boyd, Kane Richmond, George "Gabby" Hayes, Claudia Dell; **D:** Harry Revier.

The Lost City 🎬🎬 2005 (R) Garcia's directorial debut is a 20-year, overextended labor of love. Set in 1958 Havana, the old-fashioned saga focuses on the three Fellove brothers and their reactions to the Batista dictatorship and Castro's revolution. Fico (Garcia), the eldest, is an apolitical nightclub owner who wants life to go on as it always has, while his two younger brothers, Luis (Carbonell) and Rico (Murcian), believe in violent change. Politics not only divides the family but soon shatters their comfortable existence, leading Fico into exile from his beloved home (as it did for Garcia's own family). The numerous musical interludes are only in Spanish. **143m/C DVD, HD DVD.** Andy Garcia, Nestor Carbonell, Enrique Murciano, Richard Bradford, Steven Bauer, Dustin Hoffman, Julio Oscar Mechoso, Tomas Milian, William Marquez, Bill Murray, Elizabeth Pena, Millie Perkins, Tony Plana, Ines Sastre, Juan Fernandez, Gorzalo Menendez, Jsu Garcia, Ruben Rabasa; **D:** Andy Garcia; **W:** G. Cabrera Infante; **C:** Emmanue (Manu) Kadosh; **M:** Andy Garcia.

The Lost Command 🎬🎬½ 1966 A French colonel, relieved of his command and, endeavors to regain power by battling a powerful Arab terrorist with his own specially trained platoon of soldiers. Crisp adventure set in post-WWII North Africa. Based on "The Centurions" by Jean Larreguy. **129m/C DVD.** Anthony Quinn, Michele Morgan, George Segal, Alain Delon, Maurice Ronet, Claudia Cardinale; **D:** Ray Taylor, Lewis D. Collins.

The Lost Continent 🎬½ 1951 An expedition searching for a lost rocket on a jungle island discovers dinosaurs and other extinct creatures. **82m/B VHS, DVD.** Cesar Romero, Hillary Brooke, Chick Chandler, John Hoyt, Acquanetta, Sid Melton, Whit Bissell, Hugh Beaumont; **D:** Sam Newfield; **W:** Richard H. Landau; **C:** Jack Greenhalgh; **M:** Paul Dunlap.

Lost City of the Jungle 🎬🎬½ 1945 13-chapter serial focusing on a crazed Anwill, in his last screen role, believing that he can rule the world from the heart of a deep, dark jungle by utilizing a special mineral. The final Universal serial. **169m/B VHS, DVD.** Russell Hayden, Lionel Atwill, Jane Adams; **D:** Ray Taylor, Lewis D. Collins.

Lost Highway 🎬🎬 1996 (R) Well-parallel universe understood only by master David. Jazz musician Fred Madison (Pullman) is on Death Row—supposedly for the murder of his wife Renee (Arquette). Only why does young mechanic Pete Dayton (Getty) wind up in Fred's cell (with Fred missing)? Oh, and why does gangster Mr. Eddy (Loggia) have a girl-friend named Alice (Arquette again) who looks just like Renee? And is she real—or did Fred conjure her up? Who's the Mystery Man (Blake), who literally looks like the idea. Or maybe you're not supposed to. **135m/C VHS, DVD.** Bill Pullman, Patricia Arquette, Balthazar Getty, Robert Loggia, Robert Blake, Gary Busey, Jack Nance, Richard Pryor, Natasha Gregson Wagner, Lisa Boyle, Michael Massee, Jack Kehler, Henry Rollins, Gene Ross, Scott Coffey; **D:** David Lynch; **W:** David Lynch, Barry Gifford; **C:** Peter Deming; **M:** Angelo Badalamenti.

Lost Honeymoon 🎬🎬 1947 Monkeyshines abound as a soldier marries a girl while in a state of amnesia, and then wakes up to find twin daughters. **70m/B VHS, DVD.** Franchot Tone, Ann Richards, Tom Conway; **C:** Leigh Jeson.

Lost for Words 🎬🎬 1999 Aging and the parent/child bond has never been more bittersweet and amusing as in this British production, which is based on the memoirs of Deric Longden (he also wrote the teleplay). Elderly Annie (88-year-old Hird in a touchingly tart performance) lives alone, with her middleaged son Deric (Postlethwaite) and his blind wife Aileen (Downie) popping in to offer support and company. But then a series of strokes rob Annie of her ability to speak coherently and of her cherished independence. **90m/C VHS, DVD.** Thora Hird, Pete Postlethwaite, Penny Downie, Tom Higgins; **D:** Alan J.W. Bell; **W:** Deric Longden. **TV**

Lost Diamond 🎬 1986 Bumbling spies search for a smuggled gem. **83m/C VHS. AR** Juan Ramon, Sonia Rivas, Ricardo Bauleo; **D:** Sergio Mottola; **W:** Gustavo Ghirardi; **C:** Jorge Pizzi; **M:** Emilio Kauderer.

Lost Embrace 🎬🎬 El Abrazo Partido 2004 Aimless Ariel (Hendler), the son of Jewish immigrants, lives in Buenos Aires and helps his mother (Aizenberg) at her lingerie store in a downscale shopping mall. Ariel asks his Polish emigrant grandma (Londner) to help him claim Polish citizenship in order to get a Polish passport so he can move to Europe and start over (he wants to feel "European"). Since grams fled Poland during WWII, she's past ize that Ariel needs to change his inner self and not merely his outer surroundings. Spanish with subtitles. **99m/C VHS, DVD. AR** Daniel Hendler, Jorge d'Elia, Sergio Boris, Adriana Aizenberg, Rosita Londner; **D:** Daniel Burman, Marcelo Bromiajer; **C:** Ramiro Civita; **M:** Cesar Lerner.

The Lost Empire 🎬 2001 Lavish but muddled (and ultimately dull) story originally broadcast as a four-hour miniseries. American businessman Nicholas Orton (Gibson), who once studied Chinese literature and history, meets cute with a mystery woman who turns out to be Kwan Ying (Ling), the Goddess of Mercy. She tells Nick he has 3 days to save the classic Chinese manuscript "The Journey to the West" from falling into the wrong hands. Helping Nick are characters from the story, including the anarchic Monkey King (Wong). **134m/C VHS, DVD.** Thomas Gibson, Bai Ling, Russell Wong, Ric Young, Kabir Bedi, Henry O; **D:** Peter Macdonald; **W:** David Henry Hwang; **C:** David Connell; **M:** Jim Wynorski.

The Lost Empire 🎬 1983 (R) Three bountiful and powerful women team up to battle the evil Dr. Syn Do, who with a mystery woman... Angela Aames, Melanie Vincz, Raven De La Croix, Angela Aames, Paul Coufos, Robert Tessier, Angus Scrimm, Angelique Pettyjohn, Kenneth Tobey; **D:** Jim Wynorski; **M:** Jim Wynorski.

Lost in a Harem 🎬🎬½ 1944 Abbott & Costello play magicians in a theatrical troupe stranded in a desert kingdom ruled by an evil sheik. The sheik's nephew (and rightful heir) hires the two to steal some magic rings and the pretty Maxwell to play footsie with his susceptible uncle in an attempt to regain his kingdom. Average comedy with musical numbers by Jimmy Dorsey and His Orchestra. **89m/B VHS, DVD.** Bud Abbott, Lou Costello, Marilyn Maxwell, John Conte, Douglass Dumbrille, Lottie Harrison; **D:** Charles Reisner.

Lost in Alaska 🎬½ 1952 Up in the Alaskan wilderness, Abbott & Costello save Ewell from a greedy saloon owner and his cohorts who are trying to get their hands on Ewell's fortune. **76m/B VHS, DVD.** Bud Abbott, Lou Costello, Tom Ewell, Mitzie Green, Bruce Cabot, Emory Parnell, Jack Ingram, Rex Lease; **D:** Jean Yarbrough; **W:** Martin Ragaway, Leonard Stern; **M:** Henry Mancini.

Lost in America 🎬🎬🎬 1985 (R) After deciding that he can't "find himself" at his current job, ad exec David Howard and his wife sell everything they own and buy a Winnebago to travel across the country. This Albert Brooks comedy is a must-see for everyone who thinks that there is more in life than pushing papers at your desk and sitting on "Mercedes leather." **91m/C VHS, DVD.** Albert Brooks, Julie Hagerty, Michael Greene, Tom Tarpey, Garry Marshall, Art Frankel; **D:** Albert Brooks; **W:** Albert Brooks, Monica Johnson; **M:** Arthur B. Rubinstein. Natl. Soc. Film Critics '85. Screenplay.

Lost in La Mancha 🎬🎬½ 2003 (R) Once upon a time, director Terry Gilliam set out to make a film about Don Quixote, called "The Man Who Killed Don Quixote," starring Jean Rochefort and Johnny Depp. In August, 2000, Gilliam arrived in Spain to start filming and watched one disaster (illness, weather, budget problems) after another unfold until the project had to be abandoned. Gilliam provided the filmmakers with complete access, even after the misfortunes piled up enough to make the cancellation inevitable. The result is a fascinating inside look at the derailment of the creative process. **93m/C VHS, DVD. GB** Keith Fulton, Louis Pepe; **W:** Keith Fulton, Louis Pepe; **C:** Louis Pepe; **Nar:** Jeff Bridges.

Lost in Space 🎬🎬½ 1998 (PG-13) Big-screen remake of the cheesy '60s sci-fi TV show retains the basic plot and premise, but jettisons the camp. In 2058, the Robinsons and pilot Don West (Le-Blanc) are chosen to pioneer the colonization of a far-off world because Earth has become nearly uninhabitable. The evil Dr. Smith (Oldman) sabotages the mission

---

Lost Horizon 🎬🎬🎬 1937 A group of strangers fleeing revolution in China are lost in the Tibetan Himalayas and stumble across the valley of Shangri-La. The inhabitants of this Utopian community have lived for hundreds of years in kindness and peace—but what will the internal prize-winning novel. In German with English subtitles. Remade for TV as "The Lost Honor of Katharina Blum." **97m/C VHS, DVD. GE** Angela Winkler, Mario Adorf, Dieter Laser, Jurgen Prochnow; **D:** Volker Schlondorff, Margarethe von Trotta.

The Lost Honor of Katharina Blum 🎬🎬🎬 1975 (R) Die Verlorene Ehre Der Katharina Blum A woman becomes involved with a man who's under police surveillance and finds her life open to public scrutiny and abuse from the media and the government. Based on Heinrich Böll's prize-winning novel. In German with English subtitles.

but gets stuck on board. Once the family is appropriately lost, the story veers into familiar sci-fi territory of apparently deserted spaceships, marauding aliens, and time warps. It's visually impressive, but writer Goldsman can't resist turning the Robinsons into an annoying collection of 1990s dysfunction. The plot pretty much hinges on Dad's lousy parenting skills, and the kids are disaffected and resentful. Eye-candy effects, the occasionally witty inside joke for fans of the show, and Oldman's deliciously oily Smith provide plenty of fun, but where's the giant carrot? **131m/C VHS, DVD.** William Hurt, Mimi Rogers, Gary Oldman, Heather Graham, Matt LeBlanc, Lacey Chabert, Jack Johnson, Lennie James, Jared Harris, Mark Goddard, Edward Fox, Adam Sims; *Cameos:* June Lockhart, Marta Kristen, Angela Cartwright; *D:* Stephen Hopkins; *W:* Akiva Goldsman; *C:* Peter Levy; *M:* Bruce Broughton; *V:* Dick Tufeld.

Lost in the Barrens 🦴🦴 **1991** Two young boys, one a Canadian Indian and the other a rich white boy, get lost in the wilderness of the Canadian north. Out of necessity and common need they become close and form a lifelong friendship. Based on the book by Farley Mowat. **95m/C VHS, DVD.** *CA* Evan Adams, Lee J. Campbell, Graham Greene, Nicholas Shields; *D:* Michael Scott; *W:* Keith Ross Leckie; *C:* Ina Elkin; *M:* Randolph Peters.

Lost in the Bermuda Triangle 🦴½ **1998 (PG)** Brian (Haag, ca) searches for his wife Mary (Haag), who was lost at sea, and gets sucked into the same parallel universe she was transported to after they entered the Bermuda Triangle. Dumb and dull. **88m/C VHS.** Tom Verica, Graham Beckel, Ron Canada, Charlotte d'Amboise, Christina Haag; *D:* Norberto Barba; *M:* Christopher Franke. **TV**

Lost in Translation 🦴🦴🦴½ **2003 (R)** Coppola's pitch-perfect moody dramedy of mannerisms and loneliness stars Murray as Bob, a washed-up action star in Japan to shoot a lucrative liquor commercial. Homesick, displaced and jet-lagged, Bob heads to the hotel bar and meets fellow Yank Charlotte (Johansson). Also married and lonely, Charlotte is accompanying her photographer husband (Ribisi), whose glamorous job takes him away to far-flung locations and beautiful people that she can't understand. Despite their age difference, the two bond over cocktails and karaoke (a memorable scene), discussing the difficulties of marriage and life while steering clear of the formulaic May/December romance trappings. Murray's restrained performance speaks volumes, conveying a weary acceptance of his life. Johansson deftly displays a suitably discontented air. **105m/C VHS, DVD, HD DVD.** *US* Bill Murray, Scarlett Johansson, Giovanni Ribisi, Anna Faris, Yutaka Tadokoro, Catherine Lambert, Fumihiro Hayashi; *D:* Sofia Coppola; *W:* Sofia Coppola; *C:* Lance Acord. Oscars '03: Orig. Screenplay; British Acad. '03: Actor (Murray), Actress (Johansson), Film Editing; Golden Globes '04: Actor—Mus./Comedy (Murray), Film—Mus./Comedy; Ind. Spirit '04: Actor (Murray), Director (Coppola), Screenplay; L.A. Film Critics '03: Actor (Murray); N.Y. Film Critics '03: Actor (Murray); Writers Guild '03: Orig. Screenplay.

Lost in Yonkers 🦴🦴½ 1993 (PG) *Neil Simon's Lost in Yonkers* 1993 Arty and Jay are two teenage brothers who, while their widowed father looks for work, are sent to live with their stern grandmother, small-time gangster uncle, and childlike aunt in 1942 New York. Ruehl reprises her Tony award-winning performance as Aunt Bella, who loses herself in the movies while trying to find a love of her own, out from under the oppressive thumb of her domineering mother (Worth). Performances by the adults are more theatrical than necessary but the teenagers do well in their observer roles. Based on the play by Neil Simon, which again chronicles his boyhood. **114m/C VHS, DVD.** Mercedes Ruehl, Irene Worth, Richard Dreyfuss, Brad Stoll, Mike Damus, David Strathairn, Robert Miranda, Jack Laufer, Susan Merson; *D:* Martha Coolidge; *W:* Neil Simon; *M:* Elmer Bernstein.

Lost Junction 🦴🦴 **2003 (R)** Jimmy bums a ride from Missy not knowing she's got extra cargo in the trunk—her murdered husband. Unsure of her guilt but totally smitten, Jimmy is game to dumping the body for her but the plan gets mucked up when her crazy boyfriend shows up on their tail. **95m/C VHS, DVD.** Neve Campbell, Billy Burke, Jake Busey, Charles Powell, Michel Perron, David Gow, Norman Mikeal Berketa, Mariah Inger, Dawn Ford, Matt O'Toole; *D:* Peter Masterson; *W:* Jeff Cole; *C:* Thomas Burstyn; *M:* Normand Corbell. **VIDEO**

The Lost Jungle 🦴🦴 **1934** Circus legend Beatty searches for his girl and her dad in the jungle. Animal stunts keep it interesting. Serial in 12 chapters, 13 minutes each. **156m/B VHS, DVD.** Clyde Beatty, Cecilia Parker, Syd Saylor, Warner Richmond, Wheeler Oakman; *D:* Armand Schaefer, David Howard.

The Lost Language of Cranes 🦴🦴🦴 **1992** David Leavitt's novel is transported from New York to present-day London but the wrenching emotional drama remains the same. A family is in crisis as long-hidden secrets concerning homosexuality and infidelity are finally revealed. The title refers to one character's social worker's thesis on a young boy from a dysfunctional family who imitates the movements of the building cranes he sees. Fine performances by all. Adult sexual situations. **90m/C VHS, DVD.** *GB* Brian Cox, Eileen Atkins, Angus MacFadyen, Corey Parker, Cathy Tyson; *Cameos:* John Schlesinger, Rene Auberjonois; *D:* Nigel Finch; *C:* Remi Adefarasin.

Lost Legacy: A Girl Called Hatter Fox 🦴🦴½ **1977** Tradition and technology are at odds in the life of a young Indian girl. Strong cast makes this work. **100m/C VHS.** Ronny Cox, Joanelle Romero, Conchata Ferrell; *D:* George Schaefer. **TV**

Lost, Lonely, and Vicious 🦴 **1959** Clayton is a suicidal Hollywood actor who spends much of his time indulging his penchant for women, figuring he may as well enjoy what little time he has left. Then he meets Wilson, a drugstore clerk who moves him to reconsider his self-destructive ways. **73m/B VHS, DVD.** Ken Clayton, Barbara Wilson, Lilyan Chauvin, Richard Gilden, Carole Nugent, Sandra Giles, Allen File, Frank Stallworth, Johnny Erben, Clint Quigley, T. Earl Johnson; *D:* Frank Myers; *W:* Norman Graham; *C:* Ted Saizis, Vincent Saizis; *M:* Frederick Gold.

The Lost Man 🦴🦴½ **1969 (PG-13)** Odd, updated remake of 1947's "Odd Man Out," which was based on the novel by F.L. Green. Jason (Poitier) leads a group of black militants in robbing a factory in order to provide money for some civil rights organizations. Two are killed during the crime, which leads to various police shootouts. Meanwhile, Jason enlists the help of white social worker Cathy (Shimkus) to help him escape the country. **122m/C VHS.** Sidney Poitier, Joanna Shimkus, Al Freeman Jr., Michael (Lawrence) Tolan, Richard Dysart, Paul Winfield, Bernie Hamilton, Dolph Sweet, David Steinberg; *D:* Robert Arthur; *W:* Robert Arthur; *C:* Gerald Perry Finnerman; *M:* Quincy Jones.

The Lost Missile 🦴🦴 **1958** A lost, alien missile circles the Earth, causing overheating and destruction on the planet's surface. A scientist works to find a way to save the planet before it explodes into a gigantic fireball. Director Burke's last film. **70m/B VHS.** Robert Loggia, Ellen Parker, Larry Kerr, Phillip Pine, Marilee Earle; *D:* William Berke.

Lost Moment 🦴🦴 **1947** A publisher travels to Italy to search for a valuable collection of a celebrated author's love letters, but finds a neurotic woman in his way. Based on Henry James' "Aspern Papers." **89m/B VHS.** Robert Cummings, Agnes Moorehead, Susan Hayward; *D:* Martin Gabel; *C:* Hal Mohr.

The Lost One 🦴🦴 *Der Verlone* **1951** A German scientist's lover is suspected of selling his findings to England during WWII. Based on a true story; Lorre's only directorial outing. **97m/B VHS.** *GE* Peter Lorre, Karl John, Renate Mannhardt; *D:* Peter Lorre.

The Lost Patrol 🦴🦴🦴½ **1934** WWI British soldiers lost in the desert are shot down one by one by Arab marauders as Karloff portrays a religious soldier convinced he's going to die. The usual spiffy Ford exteriors peopled by great characters with a stirring score. Based on the story "Patrol" by Philip MacDonald. **66m/B VHS, DVD.** Victor McLaglen, Boris Karloff, Reginald Denny, Wallace Ford, Alan Hale, J.M. Kerrigan, Billy Bevan, Brandon Hurst, Douglas Walton; *D:* John Ford; *W:* Dudley Nichols, Garrett Fort; *C:* Harold Wenstrom; *M:* Max Steiner.

Lost Planet Airmen 🦴🦴½ **1949** A feature-length condensation of the 12-part sci-fi serial "King of the Rocket Men." Rocket Man is pitted against the sinister Dr. Vulcan in this intergalactic battle of good and evil. **65m/B VHS.** Tristram Coffin, Mae Clarke, Dale Van Sickel; *D:* Fred Brannon.

The Lost Platoon 🦴🦴½ **1989 (R)** A troop of soldiers are transformed into vampires. **120m/C VHS.** David Parry, William Knight, Sean Heyman; *D:* David A. Prior.

The Lost Son 🦴🦴 **1998 (R)** Former French narcotics cop Xavier Lombard (Auteuil) has relocated to London where he works as a P.I. An ex-colleague, Carlos (Hinds), asks Lombard to locate his wife Deborah's (Kinski) missing brother Leon, a photographer who has somehow gotten involved with a pedophile ring. Lombard eventually tracks the supposed leader of the ring to Mexico but finds his ultimate answer lies closer to home. A serious topic undone by a one-dimensional script. **102m/C VHS, DVD.** *GB FR* Daniel Auteuil, Katrin Cartlidge, Ciaran Hinds, Nastassja Kinski, Bruce Greenwood, Marianne (Cuau) Denicourt, Billie Whitelaw; *D:* Chris Menges; *W:* Eric Leclere, Margaret Leclere, Mark Mills; *C:* Barry Ackroyd; *M:* Goran Bregovic.

Lost Souls 🦴½ **2000 (R)** If the devil keeps showing up in second-rate horror flicks like this, he should get himself an agent. Although in all likelihood he probably is an agent. At any rate, he's back and trying to take over the world again by possessing the body of atheistic New York crime journalist Peter Kelson (Chaplin). Maya (Ryder), a former possession victim herself, is one of a group of New York exorcists who become aware of the conspiracy. She tries to convince the cynical Peter, but he scoffs at the idea until he begins to experience creepy hallucinations. Rent "The Exorcist" instead. Directorial debut of "Saving Private Ryan" and "Schindler's List" cinematographer Kaminski, who offers up some beautiful scenes in the midst of an ugly movie. **98m/C VHS, DVD.** Winona Ryder, Ben Chaplin, John Hurt, Elias Koteas, John Diehl, W. Earl Brown, Sarah Wynter, Philip Baker Hall, Brad Greenquist; *D:* Janusz Kaminski; *W:* Pierce Gardner, Betsy Stahl; *C:* Mauro Fiore; *M:* Jan A.P. Kaczmarek.

Lost Squadron 🦴🦴½ **1932** World War I vet pilots chafe under an autocratic director as they act as stuntmen for a war picture. Pre-Code actioner depicts vets' adjustment upon returning home. **79m/B VHS.** Richard Dix, Erich von Stroheim, Mary Astor, Robert Armstrong, Joel McCrea, Dorothy Jordan, Hugh Herbert, Ralph Ince; *D:* George Archainbaud; *W:* Herman J. Mankiewicz, Wallace Smith, Humphrey Pearson; *C:* Leo Tover, Edward Cronjager; *M:* Max Steiner.

The Lost Stooges 🦴🦴½ **1933** From the trio's one year at MGM, rare slapstick gags. In black and white and color. **68m/B VHS.** Moe Howard, Curly Howard, Larry Fine, Clark Gable, Joan Crawford, Jimmy Durante, Robert Montgomery; *Nar:* Leonard Maltin.

The Lost Tribe 🦴🦴 **1989** A man takes his wife on a trek through the jungle to find his lost brother. **96m/C VHS.** John Bach, Darien Teakle; *D:* John Laing.

Lost Voyage 🦴🦴 **2001 (R)** The cruise ship Corona Queen disappears in the Bermuda Triangle in the early seventies. Aaron Roberts (Nelson) grew up obsessed by the event since his father and stepmother were aboard. Then the ship mysteriously reappears. Roberts, TV reporter Dana Elway (Gunn) and salvager David Shaw (Henriksen) helicopter aboard and unsettling things begin to happen. **95m/C VHS, DVD.** Judd Nelson, Lance Henriksen, Janet Gunn, Jeff Kober, Mark Sheppard, Robert Pine, Scarlet Chorvat; *D:* Christian McIntire; *W:* Christian McIntire; *C:* Todd Baron; *M:* Rich McHugh. **CABLE**

The Lost Weekend 🦴🦴🦴🦴 **1945** The heartrending Hollywood masterpiece about alcoholism, depicting a single weekend in the life of struggling writer Don Birnam (Milland), who cannot believe he's addicted until he finally hits bottom. Except for its pat ending, it is an uncompromising, startlingly harsh treatment, with Milland giving one of the industry's bravest lead performances ever. Acclaimed then and now. **100m/B VHS, DVD.** Ray Milland, Jane Wyman, Phillip Terry, Howard da Silva, Doris Dowling, Frank Faylen, Mary (Marsden) Young; *D:* Billy Wilder; *W:* Charles Brackett, Billy Wilder; *C:* John Seitz; *M:* Miklos Rozsa. Oscars '45: Actor (Milland), Director (Wilder), Picture, Screenplay; Cannes '46: Actor (Milland), Film; Golden Globes '46: Actor—Drama (Milland), Director (Wilder); N.Y. Film Critics '45: Actor (Milland); Director (Wilder), Film.

The Lost World 🦴🦴🦴 **1925** A zoology professor leads a group on a South American expedition in search of the "lost world" where dinosaurs roam in this silent film. Based on a story by Sir Arthur Conan Doyle. A 90-minute version includes the film's original trailer and a re-creation of some of the missing footage (the film was released at 108 minutes). **93m/B VHS, DVD.** Wallace Beery, Lewis Stone, Bessie Love, Lloyd Hughes; *D:* Harry Hoyt; *W:* Marion Fairfax; *C:* Arthur Edeson. Natl. Film Reg. '98.

The Lost World 🦴🦴½ **1992** "Land of the Lost"/"Jurassic Park" themes, based on the story by Sir Arthur Conan Doyle. A scientific team ventures deep into uncharted African jungles where they find themselves confronted by dinosaurs and other dangers. **99m/C VHS, DVD.** John Rhys-Davies, David Warner; *D:* Timothy Bond.

The Lost World 🦴🦴½ **2002** Another version of the Arthur Conan Doyle story about a British expedition to the Amazon in 1912. Eccentric Professor George Challenger (Hoskins) leads a mixed group of characters in search of a remote plateau where he believes dinosaurs still exist. And he turns out to be right. **200m/C VHS, DVD.** Bob Hoskins, Peter Falk, James Fox, Tom Ward, Matthew Rhys, Elaine Cassidy; *D:* Stuart Orme; *W:* Adrian Hodges, Tony Mulholland; *C:* David Odd; *M:* Robert (Rob) Lane. **CABLE**

The Lost World: Jurassic Park 2 🦴🦴½ *Jurassic Park 2* **1997 (PG-13)** Sequel to "Jurassic Park," proves only that Spielberg has tapped this well one too many times. It's four years after the first adventure and the surviving dinos have escaped and set up house on a deserted island near Costa Rica. Mathematician Ian Malcolm (Goldblum, reprising his role) reluctantly becomes part of an expedition to monitor the beasts, only because his paleontologist girlfriend (Moore) is so gung-ho. Other characters exist, but are reduced to the role of entrees. More dinos (two T-Rexs, a clan of Raptors, and bite-sized newcomers Compsognathus), thrilling special effects, and more gore make up for thin subplots involving a rich businessman who wants to use the dinosaurs for a new zoo and another who hunts them for sport. Ironically, Spielberg's predilection owes much to better films such as "King Kong," "Aliens" and "Godzilla." Still, T-Rex and buddies, the true stars, rise to the occasion to entertain in an otherwise lackluster sequel. Based on Michael Crichton's book. **129m/C VHS, DVD.** Jeff Goldblum, Julianne Moore, Vince Vaughn, Richard Attenborough, Arliss Howard, Pete Postlethwaite, Peter Stormare, Vanessa Lee Chester, Richard Schiff, Harvey Jason, Thomas F. Duffy, Ariana Richards, Joseph Mazzello; *D:* Steven Spielberg; *W:* David Koepp; *C:* Janusz Kaminski; *M:* John Williams.

A Lost Year 🐾🐾 1993 It's 1976 and Matilde and Yolanda are best friends struggling to follow their own dreams against parental authority, difficult boyfriends, and their coming-of-age from girls to women. Spanish with subtitles. **91m/C VHS, DVD, MX** Vanessa Bauche, Bruno Bichir, Tiaré Scanda; **D:** Gerardo Lara; **W:** Gerardo Lara; **C:** Luis Manuel Serrano.

Lost Zeppelin 🐾🐾 1929 A dirigible becomes lost in the wastes of Antarctica, forcing its passengers to combat the elements. Impressive special effects and miniatures for the day. **73m/B VHS, DVD,** Conway Tearle, Virginia Valli, Ricardo Cortez, Duke Martin, Kathryn McGuire; **D:** Edward Sloman.

The Lotus Eaters 🐾🐾 1993 Sensitive family drama set in British Columbia in the 1960s about a wife who discovers her husband has fallen in love with their childrens' new teacher. Domestic angst done with naturalism and not without humor. **100m/C VHS, CA** Sheila McCarthy, R.H. Thomson, Michelle-Barbara Pelletier, Frances Hyland, Paul Soles; **D:** Paul Shapiro; **W:** Peggy Thompson. Genie '93: Actress (McCarthy). Orig. Screenplay, Sound.

Louder than Bombs 🐾🐾 2001 Twenty-or-a-year-old Marcin is making his father's funeral arrangements, which means he must also deal with his out-of-town relatives who disparage his life as a small-town mechanic. If this wasn't enough stress, Marcin learns his girlfriend Kaska is going to America to attend college. Can he convince her to change her mind by asking him to start a better life he give her the chance to lead a better life than their small town can offer? Polish with subtitles. **92m/C VHS, DVD, PL** Rafal Maćkowiak, Sylwia Juszczak, Magdalena Schejbal; **D:** Przemysław Wojcieszek; **W:** Przemysław Wojcieszek; **C:** Jolanta Dylewska; **M:** Bartek Straburzyński.

Lottery Bride 🐾🐾½ 1930 In this charming musical, Jeanette MacDonald is slapping comedy about a family that wins the million-dollar lottery and sees that money doesn't solve all problems. **88m/C VHS,** Martin Mull, Annette Funicello, Fred Willard, Polly Holliday, Hamilton Camp, Vincent Schiavelli, Carol Nye. **89m/** Jerzy Moes, Adam Pawlikowski; **D:** Andrzej Wajda; **W:** Andrzej Wajda, Wojciech Żukrowski; **C:** Jerzy Lipman; **M:** Tadeusz Baird.

Lots of Luck 🐾🐾 1985 A knee-slapping comedy about a family that wins the lottery; the college-bound Joy (Gonzalez). The neighbor-hood's-at-jazz when someone in their area holds the winning ticket for a $27 million lottery, which was sold from Flo's store, but just who it is and what happens when the money is claimed leads to a dramatic twist. Debut for Rubino, who shows real affection for his characters. **90m/C VHS, DVD,** Larry (Lawrence) Gilliard Jr., Barbara Gonzalez, Suzanne Costallos, Wendell Holmes, Jamie Tirelli, Luis Guzman, Paul Calderon; **D:** John Rubino; **W:** John Rubino; **C:** Rufus Standefer; **M:** Sherman Holmes, Wendell Holmes.

Lotto Land 🐾🐾½ 1995 Looks at the lives of black and Hispanic characters from the same Brooklyn neighborhood. Ambitious high school grad Hank (Gilliard, Jr.) works stocking shelves at the local liquor store for manager Flo (Costallos).

Love 🐾🐾 1971 Szerelem 1971 Torocsik, touted as Hungary's leading actress in the '70s, plays a young woman whose husband has been imprisoned for political crimes. Living in a cramped apartment with her mother-in-law, she keeps the news from the aged and dying woman (Darvas) by reading letters she's fabricated to keep alive the woman's belief that her son is a successful movie director in America. The story is punctuated by the older woman's dreamy remembrances of things past. Exceptional performances by Toth women, it was Darvas' final film. Based on two novellas by Tibor Dery. Hungarian with subtitles. **92m/B VHS, DVD, PU** Lili Darvas, Mari Torocsik, Ivan Darvas; **D:** Karoly Makk.

Love 🐾🐾½ 2005 Dreary thriller set in New York City about Yugoslav hitman Vanya (Trifunovic) who runs into his ex-wife Anna (Lechner) while performing one last job for his old crime boss as repay-ment for his escape to the United States. Caught in a drug deal gone fatally wrong, Vanya takes Anna as his hostage while her new boyfriend—a police officer—scours the city in search of the pair. Things get mucked up a bit when Anna and Vanya find out that they still have feelings for one another. **90m/C VHS, DVD,** isser, Mario Padula, Al Naz, Eric Frandsen, Liat G.lick, Kerry Rossi, Vija Vetra, Marianc Mederos; **D:** Vladan Nikolic; **W:** Vladan Nikolic; **C:** Vladimir Subotic.

The Lovable Cheat 🐾🐾 1949 "Pretty lame adaptation of Balzac's play "Mercadet Le Faiseur," about a father who cons money from his friends in order to line up a marriage suitable for his daughter. **75m/B VHS,** Charlie Ruggles, Peggy Ann Garner, Richard Ney, Alan Mowbray, Iris Adrian, Ludwig Donath, Fritz Feld; **D:** Richard Oswald.

The Love Affair, or The Case of the Missing Switchboard Operator 🐾🐾🐾 Switchboard Operator; Love Case of the Missing Switchboard Operator; Ljubavni Slucaj: An Affair of the Heart 1967 Makavejev's second film, a dissertation on the relationship between sex and politics, inter-viewing an affair between a switchboard operator and a middle-aged ex-revolutionary, is told in the director's unique, farci-cally disjointed manner. In Serbian with English subtitles. **73m/B VHS, YU** Eva Ras, Slobodan Aligrudic, Ruzica Sokic; **D:** Dusan Makavejev; **W:** Dusan Makavejev.

Love Affair: The Eleanor & Lou Gehrig Story 🐾🐾🐾 1977 The true story, told from Mrs. Gehrig's point of view, of the love affair between baseball great Lou Gehrig and his wife El-Yenkee, to his glory days as a New York Yankee, to his battle with an incurable dis-ease. Drama supported by Herrmann and Denner's convincing portrayals. **96m/C VHS,** Blythe Danner, Edward Herrmann, Patricia

---

Lotna 🐾🐾½ 1964 Wadja's first color film serves as a tribute to the Polish cavalry who fought against the Germans in WWII. The story is told through the trials of a horse that passes to various military officials until it breaks a leg and must be shot. Wadja himself is the son of a cavalryman killed in the war. Polish with subtitles. **89m/C VHS, DVD,** Pt. Bozena Kurowska, Jerzy Pichelski, Jerzy Moes, Adam Pawlikowski; **D:** Andrzej Wajda; **W:** Andrzej Wajda, Wojciech Żukrowski; **C:** Jerzy Lipman; **M:** Tadeusz Baird.

Louisiana 🐾 1987 A belle of the Old South tries to get back the family planta-tion by romancing the new owner, even though she loves someone else. Oh, and then the Civil War breaks out. **130m/C VHS,** Ian Charleson, Margot Kidder, Victor Lanoux, Len Cariou, Lloyd Bochner; **D:** Philippe de Broca. **TV**

Louisiana Hayride 🐾🐾½ 1944 A couple of con men dupe a country girl into forking over all her money with the prom-ise of Hollywood stardom in her future. But the crooks disappear with the cash, and the would-be starlet and her family (still clueless that they've been taken) track them down in Hollywood, where the villains enlist others to keep the farce going. **67m/B VHS,** Judy Canova, Ross Hunter, Richard Lane, Lloyd Bridges; **D:** Charles T. Barton; **W:** Manuel Seff.

Louisiana Purchase 🐾🐾½ 1941 Successful screen adaptation of the Broadway musical features several per-formers from the original cast, lavish cos-tumes, and great musical numbers. As usual, Hope's comedy is extremely funny, especially his famous filibuster scene in Congress. Based on the stage musical by Morrie Ryskind and B. G. DeSylva. **95m/C VHS, DVD,** Bob Hope, Vera Zorina, Victor Moore, Dona Drake, Irene Bordoni, Raymond Walburn, Maxie "Slapsie" Rosenbloom, Frank Albertson, Barbara Britton; **D:** Irving Cummings; **W:** Jerome Chodorov, Joseph Fields; **C:** Harry Hallenberger; **M:** Virgil Thomson, Nat. Film Reg. '94.

Louisiana Story 🐾🐾🐾 1948 The final effort by the master filmmaker, de-picting the effects of oil industrialization on the southern Bayou country as seen through the eyes of a young boy. One of Flaherty's greatest, widely considered a premiere achievement. **77m/B VHS, DVD, D:** Robert Flaherty; **M:** Virgil Thomson. Nat. Film Reg. '94.

Loulou 🐾🐾🐾½ 1980 (R) A woman leaves her middle-class husband for a leather-clad, uneducated jock who is more attentive. Romantic and erotic. In French with English subtitles. **110m/C VHS, DVD, FR** Isabelle Huppert, Gerard Depardieu, Guy Marchand; **D:** Maurice Pialat; **W:** Maurice Fialat, Arlette Langmann; **C:** Pierre William Glenn; **M:** Philippe Sarde.

Love Actually 🐾🐾½ 2003 (R) One movie, ten love stories, and like any epi-sodic multi-character, intertwining story-line romance, some work and some don't. The most engaging are those involving the bachelor Prime Minister (Grant), his sister (Thompson) with the wandering husband, a Richard Curtis, already established as a worthy romantic comedy writer, crams in a sweet-enough story would help, but, but if he may never direct again. The good is absolutely every possible love situation as a less-crowded story would help, but, but if he may never direct again. The good is absolutely every possible love situation as ghly. **129m/C VHS, DVD, GB** Hugh Grant, Colin Firth, Liam Neeson, Laura Linney, Emma Thompson, Alan Rickman, Keira Knightley, Martine McCutcheon, Bill Nighy, Rodrigo Santoro, Chiwetel Ejiofor, An-drew Lincoln, Kris Marshall, Heike Makatsch, Joanna Page, Martin Freeman, Billy Bob Thornton, Rowan Atkinson, Claudia Schiffer, Shannon Elizabeth, Denise Richards, Sienna Guillory, Gregor Fisher; **D:** Richard Curtis; **W:** Richard Curtis; **C:** Michael Coulter; **M:** Craig Armstrong. British Acad. '03: Support. Actor (Nighy); L.A. Film Critics '03: Support. Actor (Ni-ghly).

Love Affair 🐾🐾½ 1939 Multi-kleenex weepie inspired countless roman-tic dreams of true love atop the Empire State Building. Dunn and Boyer fall in love on a ship bound for NYC, but they're both involved. They agree to meet later at. Look for fleeting glimpses of the original. Leslie, Beckett, and Mohr. Ignore the pub-lic domain video, which replaces the origi-nal music. Remade again in 1994 as "Love Affair." **87m/B VHS, DVD,** Irene Dunne, Charles Boyer, Maria Ouspenskaya, Lee Bowman, Astrid Allwyn, Maurice (Moscovitch) Moscovich, Scotty Beckett, Joan Leslie, Gerald Mohr, Dell Henderson, Carol Hughes; **D:** Leo McCarey; **W:** Leo McCarey, Delmer Daves, Donald Ogden Stewart; **C:** Rudolph Mate; **M:** Roy Webb.

Love Affair 🐾🐾 1994 (PG-13) Sec-ond remake of the timeless classic has a contemporary look and feel but doesn't justify a new version. The photogenic leads may meet on a plane, but never fear, the Empire State Building and a trag-edy are still the main plot devices. They are all real, but their lives. Hepburn has a small but mov-ing role as Beatty's aunt. Superb cinema-tography makes it easy on the eyes and easy on the mind, but ultimately, it's all gloss with little substance. Watch this one, but then set aside time to see the superior original (made in 1939) or the better known '1957 attempt "An Affair to Remem-ber." **103m/C VHS, DVD,** Warren Beatty, Annette Bening, Katharine Hepburn, Gary Shandling, Chloe Webb, Pierce Brosnan, Kate Capshaw, Paul Mazursky, Brenda Vaccaro, Glenn Shadix, Barry Miller, Harold Ramis; **D:** Glenn Gordon Caron; **W:** Warren Beatty, Robert Towne; **M:** Ennio Morricone.

Love and Anarchy 🐾🐾🐾 Film d'Amore et d'Anarchia 1973 An oppressed peasant vows to assassinate Mussolini af-ter a close friend is murdered. Powerful drama about the rise of Italian fascism. In Italian with English subtitles. **108m/C VHS, DVD, IT** Giancarlo Giannini, Mariangela Melato; **D:** Lina Wertmuller; **W:** Lina Wertmuller; **C:** Giuseppe Rotunno; **M:** Nino Rota. Cannes '73: Actor (Gianni-ni).

Love and Basketball 🐾🐾🐾 2000 (R) Childhood friends and high school sweethearts Monica (Lathan) and Quincy (Epps) pursue their dreams of pro basket-ball careers and try to sort out their feel-ings for each other over a 12-year period. First-time director Prince-Bythewood avoids the cliches of both sports movies by removing it the Big Game climax and re-placing it with thoughtful character study and the understanding of the sacrifices athletes make to excel at their chosen pro-fession. Leads Lathan and Epps are im-pressive. **124m/C VHS, DVD,** Omar Epps, Sa-naa Lathan, Alfre Woodard, Dennis Haysbert, Deb-bi (Deborah) Morgan, Harry J. Lennix, Kyla Pratt, Glendon Chatman; **D:** Gina Prince-Bythewood; **W:** Gina Prince-Bythewood; **C:** Reynaldo Villalo-bos; **M:** Terence Blanchard.

Love and Bullets 🐾🐾 1979 (PG) An Arizona hom:cde detective is sent on a special assignment to Switzerland to bring a mobster's girlfriend back to the United States to testify against him in court. **95m/C VHS, GB** Charles Bronson, Jill Ireland, Rod Steig-

---

Love Among the Ruins 🐾🐾🐾 1975 Romance about an aging, wealthy widow who, after being scandalously sued for breach of promise by her very young lover, turns for aid to an old lawyer friend who has loved her silently for more than 40 years. **100m/C VHS,** Laurence Olivier, Katha-rine Hepburn, Leigh Lawson, Colin Blakely; **D:** George Cukor. ACE '75. **TV**

Love and a.45 🐾🐾 1994 (R) Satiri-cal and violent: 'oad movie finds petty ca-reer criminal Watty Watts (Bellows) living in a Texas trailer park with gal Starlene (Zellweger), for whom he's just purchased dead bodies behind them and the media are on the run to Mexico with a trail of pressing him to take one more job. And if action, this one is of the black comedy variety with a few particularly good as the doesn't, he could become number one reluctant hitman. **97m/C VHS, DVD,** Courtney B. Vance, Regina King, Jason Alexander, Kathleen Turner, Ed Asner; **D:** Dwayne Johnson-Cochran; **W:** C.M. Talkington; **C:** Phil Parmet; **M:** Tom Richmond; **M:** Tom Verlaine.

Love and Action in Chicago 🐾🐾 1999 (R) Eddie Jones (Vance) works for the State Department's Eliminator Corps, getting rid of anyone the government doesn't want around. Eddie wants to leave and make a new life with girlfriend Lois (King) but his bosses are pressing him to take one more job. And if he doesn't, he could become number one on the Corps hit parade. Although there's action, this one is of the black comedy variety with a few particularly good as the reluctant hitman. **97m/C VHS, DVD,** Courtney B. Vance, Regina King, Jason Alexander, Kathleen Turner, Ed Asner; **D:** Dwayne Johnson-Cochran; **W:** C.M. Talkington; **C:** Phil Parmet; **M:** George Landau.

Love After Love 🐾🐾 Apres l'Amour 1994 A look at sex and relationships among 30-something professionals in Paris. Lola (Huppert), a successful ro-mance novelist is suffering a crisis in both her career and, ironically, in her love life. She is involved with two men who, in turn, are involved with different women who happen to have borne them children. The movie starts off with so much mate switch-ing and secret sexual randezvous, that by the second half, you really don't care who Lola ends up with. French with English subtitles. **104m/C VHS, DVD, FR** Isabelle Hup-pert, Hippolyte Girardot, Lio; **D:** Diane Kurys; **W:** Diane Kurys, Antoine Lacomblez; **C:** Fabio Con-versi; **M:** Yves Simon, Serge Perathone. Jannick Top.

Neal, Ramon Bieri, Lainie Kazan; **D:** Fielder Cook. **TV** er, Strother Martin, Bradford Dillman, Henry Silva, Michael V. Gazzo; *D:* Stuart Rosenberg; *W:* Wendell Mayes; *C:* Fred W. Koenekamp; *M:* Lalo Schifrin.

Love and Death ♦♦♦ 1975 (PG) In 1812 Russia, a condemned man reviews the follies of his life. Woody Allen's satire on "War and Peace," and every other major Russian novel. 88m/C VHS, DVD. Woody Allen, Diane Keaton, Georges Adel, Despo Diamantidou, Frank Adu, Harold Gould; *D:* Woody Allen; *W:* Woody Allen; *C:* Ghislan Cloquet.

Love and Death on Long Island ♦♦½ 1997 (PG-13) Stuffy English author Giles De'Ath (Hurt), barely on speaking terms with the 20th century, wanders into the wrong theatre, encounters a teen exploitation flick and becomes obsessed with Ronnie Bostock (Priestley), one of the movie's "stars." De'Ath's obsession leads to his discovery of fan magazines, TV, and video, which provide some moments of amusement as he comes to grips with the technology. It also leads Giles to seek out Bostock at his home on Long Island, where Hurt shines as Giles tries to reconcile his dignity and increasingly irrational behavior. Priestley does a fine job lampooning his own image (while not exactly dispelling it), and the supporting characters (especially Chaykin's diner owner) are appropriately quirky. Subtle reworking of "Death in Venice," based on a novel by Gilbert Adair, has its moments, but is probably best enjoyed by the same type of people who would like De'Ath's work. 93m/C VHS, DVD. *GB CA* John Hurt, Jason Priestley, Fiona Loewi, Sheila Hancock, Maury Chaykin, Gawn Grainger, Elizabeth Quinn, Danny (Daniel) Webb; *D:* Richard Kwietniowski; *W:* Richard Kwietniowski; *C:* Oliver Curtis; *M:* Richard Grassby-Lewis.

Love and Faith ♦♦ 1978 Two lovers are torn between their love for each other and their faiths during 16th-century Japan. English subtitles. 154m/C VHS. *JP* Toshiro Mifune, Takashi Shimura, Yoshiko Nakana; *D:* Kei Kumai.

Love and Hate: A Marriage Made in Hell ♦♦½ *Love and Hate: The Story of Colin and Joanne Thatcher* 1990 Marital murder mystery based on a true Canadian case. Joanne (Nelligan), the wife of wealthy rancher-politico Colin (Walsh), leaves her publicly charismatic and privately abusive husband and two thirds of their brood. A bitter battle for custody is waged, and Joanne is soon found savagely slain. The number one suspect: philandering ex-spouse Colin. Based on Maggie Siggins' "A Canadian Tragedy," the faux biography originally aired in two parts on Canadian TV. 156m/C VHS. Kate Nelligan, Kenneth Welsh, Leon Pownall, John Collicos, Noam Zylberman, Victoria Snow, Cedric Smith, R.H. Thomson, Victoria Wauchope, Doris Petrie, Duncan Ollerenshaw; *D:* Francis Mankiewicz; *M:* Suzette Couture.

Love and Human Remains ♦♦♦ 1993 (R) Director Arcand's first English-language film features a group of late 20ish urbanites trying to come to grips with their place in the world (and their sexuality). David (Gibson) is an amoral Lothario who doesn't believe in love and can only manage casual gay relationships. He hangs out with a variety of friends, all of whom are trying to cope with their varying sexual natures. Melodramatic framing story about a serial murderer who may, or may not, be one of the principal characters proves somewhat of a distraction. Lots of caustically witty dialogue and some fine performances (particularly Gibson's); filmed in Montreal. Adaptation of the play "Unidentified Human Remains and the True Nature of Love" by Fraser, who also did the screenplay. 100m/C VHS, DVD. *CA* Thomas Gibson, Ruth Marshall, Cameron Bancroft, Mia Kirshner, Joanne Vannicola, Matthew Ferguson, Rick Roberts; *D:* Denys Arcand; *W:* Brad Fraser; *C:* Paul Sarossy. Genie '94: Adapt. Screenplay.

Love & Murder ♦♦½ 1991 (R) Poorly developed tale of a photographer and his bevy of beautiful models involved with murder and love, not necessarily in that order. 87m/C VHS. Todd Waring, Kathleen Lasky, Ron White, Wayne Robson; *D:* Steven Hillard Stern.

Love and Other Catastrophes ♦♦ 1995 (R) Short, low-budget first feature from 23-year-old Croghan engagingly focuses on 24 hours in the lives of five confused college students. Film students Alice (Garner) and Mia (O'Connor) need a third roommate for their new apartment. Danni (Mitchell), Mia's girlfriend, is upset that Mia doesn't want them living together, while Alice is eyeing potential boyfriends, including shy med student Michael (Day) and womanizing Ari (Dyktynski). Meanwhile, both Alice and Mia try to cope with various academic frustrations. 76m/C VHS. *AU* Frances O'Connor, Alice Garner, Matthew Day, Radha Mitchell, Matthew Dyktynski, Suzi Dougherty, Kim Gyngell; *D:* Emma-Kate Croghan; *W:* Emma-Kate Croghan, Yael Bergman, Helen Bandis; *C:* Justin Brickle; *M:* Oleh Witer.

Love and Rage ♦♦ 1999 (R) James Lynchehaun (Craig) turns up on the remote island of Achill in 1896 and soon sets a job looking after the estate of wealthy widow Agnes MacDonnell (Scacchi). He also becomes her lover and the two engage in some unnerving psychosexual games that lead to Agnes' being brutalized by James. Based on a true story; adapted from the novel "The Playboy and the Yellow Lady" by James Carney. 100m/C VHS, DVD. *IR GE GB* Daniel Craig, Greta Scacchi, Stephen (Dillon) Dillane, Donal Donnelly, Valerie Edmond; *D:* Cathal Black; *W:* Brian Lynch; *C:* Slawomir Idziak; *M:* Ralf Wienrich.

Love & Sex ♦♦½ 2000 Famke Janssen shines in her role as Kate, a manic L.A. magazine writer who nearly gets fired due to her inability to write about good relationships because she hasn't had many. She begins to remember fondly her relationship with Adam (Favreau), a doughy artist whose fast talk made up for his slow looks. Their relationship is traced from its initial spark to its last gasp, when Adam breaks up with Kate due to a feeling of complacency. Kate then attempts to make Adam jealous by dating a string of pretty-boy losers, including his favorite actor. Kate becomes increasingly depressed and Adam becomes increasingly obsessed, setting the stage for the inevitable happy ending. Good performances and chemistry between the lead actors saves this indie effort from feeling like a really long sitcom episode. 82m/C VHS, DVD. Famke Janssen, Jon Favreau, Noah Emmerich, Ann Magnuson, Cheri Oteri, Josh Hopkins, Robert Knepper, Vincent Ventresca; *D:* Valerie Breiman; *W:* Valerie Breiman; *C:* Adam Kane.

Love and the Frenchwoman ♦♦♦ *La Francaise et L'Amour* 1960 A French tale tracing the nature of love through various stages. Deals with a story about where babies come from, puppy love, saving sex for marriage, and the way some men treat women. 135m/B VHS, DVD. *FR* Jean-Paul Belmondo, Pierre-Jean Vaillard, Marie-Jose Nat, Annie Girardot; *D:* Jean Delannoy; *M:* Georges Delerue.

Love at First Bite ♦♦½ 1979 (PG) Intentionally campy spoof of the vampire film. Dracula is forced to leave his Transylvanian home as the Rumanian government has designated his castle a training center for young gymnasts. Once in New York, the Count takes in the night life and falls in love with a woman whose boyfriend embarks on a campaign to warn the city of Dracula's presence. Hamilton of the never-failing tan is appropriately tongue-in-cheek in a role which resurrected his career. 93m/C VHS, DVD. George Hamilton, Susan St. James, Richard Benjamin, Dick Shawn, Arte Johnson, Sherman Hemsley, Isabel Sanford, Barry J. Gordon, Michael Pataki, Basil Hoffman, Eric Laneuville; *D:* Stan Dragoti; *W:* Robert Kaufman; *M:* Charles Bernstein.

Love at First Sight ♦♦ *Love is Blind; At First Sight* 1976 A pre-"Saturday Night Live" hack job for Aykroyd, playing a blind man who falls in love with a girl he bumps into. ♫Love at First Sight. 86m/C VHS. Dan Aykroyd, Mary Ann McDonald, George Murray, Barry Morse; *D:* Rex Bromfield.

Love at Large ♦♦♦ 1989 (R) Hired by a beautiful woman, a private detective accidentally follows the wrong man and winds up being followed himself. He vies with a female detective in solving this case of mistaken identity. 90m/C VHS, DVD. Tom Berenger, Elizabeth Perkins, Anne Archer, Ann Magnuson, Annette O'Toole, Kate Capshaw, Ted Levine, Kevin J. O'Connor, Ruby Dee, Neil Young, Barry Miller; *D:* Alan Rudolph; *W:* Alan Rudolph; *C:* Elliot Davis.

Love at Stake ♦♦½ 1987 (R) It's condo owners versus the witches in this charming parody that features a hilarious sexy performance from Carrera. 83m/C VHS, DVD. Patrick Cassidy, Kelly Preston, Bud Cort, Barbara Carrera, Stuart Pankin, Dave Thomas, Georgia Brown, Annie Golden; *Cameos:* Dr. Joyce Brothers; *D:* John Moffitt; *M:* Charles Fox.

Love at the Top ♦♦½ 1986 Ladies' foundation designer falls in love with her boss's son-in-law, jeopardizing her career. 90m/C VHS. Janis Paige, Richard Young, Jim MacKrell; *D:* John Bowab.

Love Beat the Hell Outta Me ♦♦ 2000 (R) Four friends get together for what's supposed to be a friendly game of dominos, only to find some serious rivalries surfacing. 89m/C VHS, DVD. Glenn Plummer, Terrence Howard, Clyde Jones, Charles R. Penland; *D:* Kennedy Goldsby; *W:* Kennedy Goldsby.

The Love Bug ♦♦♦ 1968 (G) A race car driver (Jones) is followed home by Herbie, a white Volkswagen with a mind of its own. Eventually, Jones follows the "Love Bug" to a life of madcap fun. Followed by several sequels. 110m/C VHS, DVD. Dean Jones, Michele Lee, Hope Lange, Robert Reed, Bert Convy; *D:* Robert Stevenson; *C:* Edward Colman; *M:* George Bruns.

The Love Bug ♦♦ 1997 Herbie, the magical Volkswagen Beetle, is now owned by egotistical English nobleman Simon Moore III (Hannah), who junks him after he loses a race. Then Herbie gets a new owner, down-on-his-luck mechanic Hank (Campbell), who decides the little guy can make a comeback. And when Herbie sees Hank and his ex-girlfriend Alex (Wentworth) together, the car decides he should live up to his nickname and get the two back together. 88m/C VHS. Bruce Campbell, John Hannah, Alexandra Wentworth, Kevin J. O'Connor, Mickey Dolenz, Dean Jones, Clarence Williams III, Harold Gould; *C:* Peyton Reed. TV

Love Butcher ♦♦ 1982 (R) A crippled old gardener kills his female employers with his garden tools and cleans up neatly afterward. 84m/C VHS, DVD. Erik Stern, Kay Neer, Robin Sherwood; *D:* Mikel Angel, Donald M. Jones.

Love by Appointment ♦ 1976 An unlikely romantic comedy with a very unlikely cast has two businessmen meeting up with European prostitutes. 96m/C VHS, DVD. *IT* Ernest Borgnine, Robert Alda, Francoise Fabian, Corinne Clery; *D:* Armando Nannuzzi; *M:* Riz Ortolani. TV

Love Camp ♦ *Divine Emmanuelle* 1981 A woman is invited to a swinger's holiday camp, frolics for a while, then is told she can never leave. Suspenseful hijinks ensue. 100m/C VHS. *GE* Laura Gemser, Christian Anders, Gabriele Tinti; *C:* Vassilis Christomoglou; *M:* Christian Anders.

Love Can Seriously Damage Your Health ♦♦½ *Amor Perjudica Seriamente la Salud* 1996 At a gala dinner Santi (Puigcorbe) and Diana (Belen) are reunited. Thirty years before, young Beatles fan Diana (Cruz) hides out in John Lennon's room when the group comes to Madrid, reluctantly aided by young hotel bellman Santi (Diego). It's love at first sight and they spend the intervening years falling in and out of a crazy romance. Spanish with subtitles. 118m/C VHS, DVD. *SP* Ana Belen, Penelope Cruz, Gabino Diego, Juanjo Puigcorbe, Carles Sans, Lola Herrera; *D:* Manuel Gomez Pereira; *W:* Manuel Gomez Pereira; *C:* Juan Amoros.

Love, Cheat & Steal ♦♦ 1993 (R) Convicted murderer Reno Adams (Roberts) breaks out of prison when he hears that his luscious ex (Amick) has just married another man (Lithgow). He turns up on her door, threatening to destroy her new life, but things aren't exactly what they seem. Faux noir. 95m/C VHS. Eric Roberts, Madchen Amick, John Lithgow, Richard Edson, Donald Moffat, David Ackroyd, Dan O'Herlihy; *D:* William Curran; *W:* William Curran.

Love Child ♦♦ 1982 (R) The story of a young woman in prison who becomes pregnant by a guard and fights to have and keep her baby. 97m/C VHS. Amy Madigan, Beau Bridges, MacKenzie Phillips, Albert Salmi; *D:* Larry Peerce; *M:* Charles Fox.

Love Come Down ♦♦ 2000 (R) Matthew (Cummins) is white, his half-brother Neville (Tate) is black. Their mother is in prison for killing Neville's abusive father but there's a definite question about her guilt. Both boys have been hugely affected by their pasts—Matthew puts his anger into his boxing career while Neville has become a drug addicted stand-up comic. Neville tries to stay clean when he falls for a singer (Cox) with her own family issues but the brothers also have to lay their traumatic past to rest. 102m/C VHS, DVD. *CA* Larenz Tate, Martin Cummins, Sarah Polley, Deborah Cox, Travis Davis, Jake LeDoux, Rainbow Sun Francks, Barbara Williams, Peter Williams, Clark Johnson, Kenneth Welsh, Jennifer Dale, Naomi Gaskin; *D:* Clement Virgo; *W:* Clement Virgo; *C:* Dylan Mcleod; *M:* Aaron Davis, John Lang. Genie '01: Sound, Support. Actor (Cummins).

Love Comes Softly ♦♦♦ 2003 Marty Claridge (Heigl) has just moved west with her husband when he suddenly dies. Alone and afraid, she accepts the offer of widowed neighbor Clark Davis (Midkiff) to becomes his housekeeper and look after his tomboy daughter Missie (Bartusiak). Naturally as Marty and Missie slowly bond, Clark and the pretty widow gradually find themselves growing closer. Adapted from the first book in inspirational author Janette Oke's series. 88m/C DVD. Katherine Heigl, Dale Midkiff, Skye McCole Bartusiak, Corbin Bemsen, Theresa Russell; *D:* Michael Landon Jr.; *W:* Michael Landon Jr., Cindy Kelley; *C:* James W. Wrenn; *M:* Ken Thorne, William Ashford. CABLE

Love Crazy ♦♦♦½ 1941 Powell and Loy team once again for a non-"Thin Man" romp through a married-people farce. Via a nosy mother-in-law and a series of misunderstandings, Powell and Loy squabble almost to the point of divorce. Not the wry wit the team was known for, but zany, high-action comedy at its best. 99m/B VHS, DVD. William Powell, Myrna Loy, Gail Patrick, Jack Carson, Florence Bates, Sidney Blackmer, Sig Rumann; *D:* Jack Conway.

Love Crimes ♦ 1992 (R) A con man (Bergin) poses as a photographer who sexually intimidates women while playing into their erotic fantasies. Young is the Atlanta district attorney who sets out to nail him when none of his victims will testify against him, only she may be enjoying her undercover work more than she realizes. Implausible and sleazy. Also available in an unrated version. 84m/C VHS. Sonny Shroyer, Sean Young, Patrick Bergin, Arnetia Walker, James Read; *D:* Lizzie Borden; *W:* Laurie Frank, Allan Moyle; *C:* Phedon Papamichael; *M:* Graeme Revell.

Love Desperados ♦ *The Hot Spur* 1968 Cowboys and ranchers' wives mix it up in a lot of softcore hay. 99m/C VHS. James Arena, Virginia Gordon, John Alderman, Joseph Mascolo, Wes Bishop; *D:* Lee Frost; *W:* Lee Frost.

A Love Divided ♦♦ 2001 In 1950s Ireland, Protestant Sheila Kelly (Brady) marries Catholic Sean Cloney (Cunningham) and signs an agreement to raise their children Catholic to appease the mostly Catholic farming community, County Wexford. When it comes time for their daughter Eileen (Bolger) to attend school, however, a battle emerges over religion between headstrong Sheila and Milquetoast Sean. When things begin escalating into an all-out war that divides the villagers, Sheila flees with her two daughters to Scotland. Heavy-handed, melodramatic script displays a movie-of-the-week lack of subtlety, while one-dimensional characters offer little in the way of sympathy for anyone involved. Based on a true story. **98m/C VHS, DVD.** Ona Bracy, Liam Cunningham, Brian McGrath, Sarah Bolger, Nicole Burnham, Peter Caffrey, Tony Doyle, Ali White; *D:* Syd Macartney; *C:* Cedric Culliton; *M:* Fiachra French.

Love Don't Cost a Thing ✶✶½ **2003 (PG-13)** Amusing remake of the 1987 movie "Can't Buy Me Love". Alvin Johnson (Cannon) pays the most popular girl in high school, Paris Morgan (Milian), to pretend to be his girlfriend for two weeks in order to be popular. Charming leads make this one a touch better than the original. **101m/C VHS, DVD.** *US* Nick Cannon, Christina Milian, Kenan Thompson, Kal Penn, Steve Harvey, Vanessa Bell Calloway, Al Thompson; *D:* Troy Beyer; *W:* Troy Beyer, Michael Swerdlick; *C:* Chuck Cohen; *M:* Richard Gibbs.

Love Finds Andy Hardy ✶✶✶ **1938** Young Andy Hardy finds himself torn between three girls before returning to the girl next door. Garland's first appearance in the acclaimed Andy Hardy series fea- tures her singing "In Between" and "Meet the Best of my Heart". **90m/B VHS, DVD.** Mickey Rooney, Judy Garland, Lana Turner, Ann Rutherford, Fay Holden, Lewis Stone, Marie Blake, Cecilia Parker, Gene Reynolds; *D:* George B. Seitz. *Natl. Film Reg. '00.*

Love 'Em and Leave 'Em ✶✶½ **1926** Two sister's, with opposite personalities, are department store sales clerks. Both are the "good" girl and "bad" flirt who, under the influence of Perkins, bets the store's welfare benefit money on the horses and loses it all. Brent manages to make things right, while keeping boyfriend Gray from her sister's clutches. Brooks' baby va rip (the actress was 19) stole the picture. Introduced the "Black Bottom" shimmy dance to the screen. Remade in 1929 as 'The Saturday Night Kid' with Clara Bow and Jean Arthur. **70m/B VHS.** Louise Brooks, Evelyn Brent, Lawrence Gray, Osgood Perkins; *D:* Frank Tuttle.

Love, etc. ✶✶ **1996** Another messy romantic triangle played for both comedy and tragedy. Shy, thirtysomething bank employee Benoit (Attal) takes out a personal ad, but supplies a photo of his egocentric best friend Pierre (Berling) instead of his own. He meets twentysomething art restorer Marie (Gainsbourg) and, despite traveling with his young daughter, Pierre thinks he's in love with Marie and has decided to win her away—and she's torn by the attention. Based on the novel "Taking it Over" by Julian Barnes. French with subtitles. **105m/C VHS, DVD.** *FR* Charlotte Gainsbourg, Yvan Attal, Charles Berling; *D:* Marion Vernoux; *W:* Marion Vernoux, Dodine Harry; *C:* Eric Gautier; *M:* Leonard Cohen, Alexandra Desplat.

Love Field ✶✶½ **1991 (PG-13)** Pfeiffer is a Jackie Kennedy-obsessed hairdresser who decides to travel by bus to D.C. when she hears about President Kennedy's assassination. Along the way she gets involved in an interracial friendship with the secretive Haysbert, who's traveling with his young daughter. Pfeiffer's Lurene is basically a sweet dim bulb and Haysbert has an unfortunately written one-note character (mainly exasperation). The six-year-old McFadden (in her debut) makes the most impact. **104m/C VHS, DVD.** Michelle Pfeiffer, Dennis Haysbert, Stephanie McFadden, Brian Kerwin, Louise Latham, Peggy Rea, Beth Grant, Cooper Huckabee, Mark Miller, Johnny Rae McGhee; *D:* Jonathan Kaplan; *W:* Don Roos; *C:* Ralf Bode; *M:* Jerry Goldsmith.

Love Film ✶✶✶ *Szerelmesfilm: A Film about Love* **1970** A train trip from Budapest, Hungary to Lyon, France leads a young man to recall his past as he journeys to visit a childhood sweetheart. Jancsi and Kata's friendship has been disrupted by the 1956 uprising and Jancsi wonders if the love once developing between them has been broken by distance and time. In Hungarian with English subtitles. **123m/C VHS, DVD.** *HU* Andras Balint, Judit Halasz, Edit Kelemen, Andras Szamosfalvi; *D:* Istvan Szabo; *C:* Josef Lorinc.

The Love Flower ✶✶½ **1920** A woman kills his second wife's lover and escapes with his daughter to a tropical island, pursued by a detective and a young adventurer. Interesting ending wraps things up nicely. Silent. **70m/B VHS.** Carol Dempster, Richard Barthelmess, George MacQuarrie, Anders Randolf, Florence Short; *D:* D.W. Griffith; *W:* D.W. Griffith.

Love for Lydia ✶✶½ **1979** British TV miniseries follows wayward beauty Lydia, orphaned heiress to a manufacturing fortune, through the high-spirited 1920s. Set in the industrial Midlands and farming communities of England, Lydia dazzles every man she meets, often to an unhappy end. Based on the novel by H.E. Bates. Available as a boxed set. **657m/C VHS, DVD,** *GB* Mel Martin, Christopher Blake, Peter Davison, Jeremy Irons, Michael Aldridge, Rachel Kempson, Beatrix _ehmann; *D:* Tony Wharmby; *W:* Julian Bond; *C:* Tony Mayne; *M:* Carl Davis. **TV**

Love for Rent ✶✶½ **2005 (R).** Slight romantic comedy finds Colombian immigrant Sofia's (Cepeda) life falling apart when her green card hubby (Rowe) steals their money. Sofia buy big dreams, so rather than return home she becomes a surrogate mother for a wealthy, eccentric couple (Piddock, Dunn). But how will Sofia explain the situation to her new doctor boyfriend Neil (Marino)? **90m/C DVD.** *US* Ken Marino, Nora Dunn, Jim Piddock, Brad Rowe, Angie Cepeda, Richard Speight Jr., Martha Roca, Max Burkholder; *D:* Shane Edelman; *W:* Andrew Miles; *C:* David Rush Morrison; *M:* Jeff Cardoni.

Love from a Stranger ✶✶ **1937** Thriller about a working woman who wins a lottery. Soon she is charmed by and marries a man whom she later suspects may be trying to kill her. Remade in 1947. **90m/B VHS, DVD.** *GB* Ann Harding, Basil Rathbone, Binnie Hale, Bruce Seton, Bryan Powley, Jean Cadell; *D:* Rowland V. Lee.

Love from a Stranger ✶✶½ *A Stranger Walked in* **1947** In this remake of the 1937 film, a young newlywed bride fears that the honeymoon is over when she suspects that her husband is a notorious killer. Good thriller that she will be his next victim. **81m/B VHS.** Sylvia Sidney, John Hodiak, John Howard, Ann Richards, Isobel Elsom, Ernest Cossart, Philip Tonge, Frederick Worlock; *D:* Gaetano Antonio "Tony" Gaudio; *M:* Hans J. Salter.

The Love God? ✶✶ **1970 (PG-13)** Very silly comedy finds mild-mannered Abner Peacock (Knotts) trying on Hugh Hefner's mantle. With his bird-watcher's magazine in financial trouble, Abner takes it into a couple of shifty partners who change magazine (the nude female kind) that gets Abner charged with pornography and finds him becoming a (very) unlikely sex symbol. **103m/C VHS, DVD.** Don Knotts, Edmond O'Brien, Anne Francis, Maureen Arthur, James Gregory, Margaret (Maggie) Peterson, Marjorie Bennett; *D:* Nat Hiken; *W:* Nat Hiken; *C:* William Margulies; *M:* Vic Mizzy.

The Love Goddesses ✶✶✶ **1965** A 60-year examination of some of the most beautiful women on the silver screen, reflecting with extraordinary accuracy the customs, manners and mores of the times. Released theatrically in 1972. **83m/B VHS, DVD.** Marlene Dietrich, Greta Garbo, Jean Harlow, Gloria Swanson, Mae West, Betty Grable, Rita Hayworth, Elizabeth _aylor, Marilyn Monroe, Theda Bara, Claudette Colbert, Dorothy Lamour, Lillian Gish, Sophia Loren; *D:* Saul J. Turell; *W:* Saul J. Turell, Graeme Ferguson; *Nar:* Carl King.

(Campbell). However, if he follows Top-cat's misogynistic views, Ollie isn't going to have to worry about Mona sticking around. But then those 'love goggles' or winds up falling in love with him. Cooper's heart are focusing all Ollie's thoughts on romance. **106m/C DVD.** Trevor David, Ruby Campbell, Steven Peacock Jacoby, Q-Tip, Kirk "Sticky Fingaz" Jones; *D:* Anthony Travis.

Love Happy ✶✶½ **1950** A group of impoverished actors accidentally gain possession of valuable diamonds. Unfortunately for them, detective Groucho is assigned to recover them! **85m/B VHS, DVD.** Groucho Marx, Harpo Marx, Chico Marx, Vera-Ellen, Ilona Massey, Marion Hutton, Raymond Burr, Marilyn Monroe, Eric Blore; *D:* David Miller; *W:* Frank _ashlin, Mac Benoff; *C:* William Mellor; *M:* Ann Ronell.

Love Has Many Faces ✶✶½ **1965** Judith Crist was too kind when she said this was for connoisseurs of truly awful movies. Playgal Turner marries beach-boy Robertson and many faces come between them. Much melodrama. Filmed on location. **104m/C VHS,** Lana Turner, Cliff Robertson, Hugh O'Brian, Ruth Roman, Stefanie Powers, Virginia Grey, Ron Husmann; *D:* Alexander Singer.

Love, Honour & Obey ✶✶ **2000** Lowlife London bad boys and a karaoke bar. Jonny (Miller) wants his best bud Jude (Law) to get him a job with Jude's gangster uncle, Ray (Winstone), who loves to croon a tune at the local karaoke club. But Jonny loves his new life too much and can't resist stirring up local gangland rivalries—to the grief of everyone. Low-budget, sometime puerile comedy. **95m/C VHS, DVD,** *GB* Jonny Lee Miller, Jude Law, Ray Winstone, Sadie Frost, Sean Pertwee, Kathy Burke, Rhys Ifans, Lalla Morse, Dominic Anciano, Ray Burdis; *D:* Dominic Anciano, Ray Burdis; *C:* John Ward.

Love Hurts ✶✶ **1991 (R)** A guy looking for romance finds his hands full with a number of romantic women. Will he find the love he craves, or will the pain be too much to bear? **110m/C VHS, DVD.** Jeff Daniels, Judith Ivey, John Mahoney, Cynthia Sikes, Amy Wright; *D:* Bud Yorkin; *W:* Ron Nyswaner.

Love in Bloom ✶✶ **1935** Predictable romance, with Burns and Allen providing some much-needed comic relief. Carnival gal Vi.olet Downey (Lee) falls for struggling songwriter Larry Deane (Morrison) but thinks her tawdry background will ruin his chances and takes off. After Larry becomes successful he searches for Violet, still determined to marry her. **75m/B VHS, DVD.** George Burns, Gracie Allen, Joe Morrison, Dixie Lee, Lee Kohlmar, Richard Carle; *D:* Elliott Nugent; *W:* J.P. McEvoy, Keene Thompson; *C:* Leo Tover.

A Love in Germany ✶✶½ *Amour En Allemagne; Eine Liebe in Deutschland* **1984 (R)** A tragic love affair develops between a German shopkeeper's wife and a Polish prisoner-of-war in a small German village during WWII. In German with English subtitles. **110m/C VHS.** *FR GE* Hanna Schygulla, Piotr Lysak, Elisabeth Trissenaar, Armin Mueller-Stahl; *D:* Andrzej Wajda; *W:* Andrzej Wajda, Agnieszka Holland, Boleslaw Michalek.

Love Is a Many-Splendored Thing ✶✶½ **1955** A married American war correspondent and a beautiful Eurasian doctor fall in love in post-WWII Hong Kong. They struggle with racism and unhappiness, until he's sent to Korea to observe the Army's activities there. Based on the novel by Han Suyin. The extensive L.A. Asian acting community got some work out of this film, although the leads are played by Caucasians. Oscar-winning song was a very big popular hit. ♪Love is a Many-Splendored Thing. **102m/C VHS, DVD.** William Holden, Jennifer Jones, Torin Thatcher, Isobel Elsom, Jorja Curtright, Virginia Gregg, Richard Loo; *D:* Henry King; *W:* John Patrick; *C:* Leon Shamroy; *M:* Alfred Newman. Oscars '55: Costume Des, (C), Song ("Love Is a Many-Splendored Thing"), Orig. Dramatic Score.

Love Is All There Is ✶✶ **1996 (R)** It's a kind of comedic (happy-ending) version of "Romeo and Juliet," set in the Bronx, about rival restaurant families. Beautiful Gina's (Jolie) a finishing-school grad and Rosario's (Marston) the local boy too handsome for his own good. Both sets

The Love Guru ✶ **2008** A lame trailer and cliches galore don't bode well for this limp Myers comedy. American Pitka was abandoned at an ashram in India as a child and raised by gurus. As an adult, he heads back to the states to cash in on the self-help/spirituality craze. Pitka's unorthodox methods (his mantra is "Mariska Hargitay") are put to the test when he must solve the marital problems of Toronto hockey star Darren Roanoke (Malco), whose wife has left him for rival Jacques Grande (Timberlake). Team owner Jane Bullard (Alba) is counting on the love guru to come through in time for the playoffs. Not yet reviewed. **?m/C** Mike Myers, Jessica Alba, Romany Malco, Justin Timberlake, Meagan Good, Verne Troyer, Ben Kingsley, Telma Hopkins, Omid Djalili; *D:* Marco Schnabel; *W:* Mike Myers, Graham Gordy; *C:* Peter Deming; *M:* George S. Clinton.

Love in the City ✶✶✶ *Amore in Citta* **1953** Five stories of life, love and tears in Rome. In Italian with English subtitles. **90m/B VHS.** *IT* Ugo Tognazzi, Maresa Gallo, Caterina Rigoglioso, Silvia Lillo; *D:* Carlo Lizzani, Alberto Lattuada, Francesco Maselli, Michelangelo Antonioni, Federico Fellini, Dino Risi, Cesare Zavattini; *W:* Aldo Buzzi, Luigi Malerba, Luigi Chiarini, Tullio Pinelli, Vittorio Veltroni; *C:* Gianni Di Venanzo; *M:* Mario Nascimbene.

Love in the Afternoon ✶✶½ **1957** A Parisian private eye's daughter (Hepburn) decides to investigate a philanderer/American millionaire (Cooper) and winds up falling in love with him. Cooper's a little old for the Casanova role but Hepburn is always enchanting. **126m/B VHS, DVD** Gary Cooper, Audrey Hepburn, John McGiver, Maurice Chevalier; *D:* Billy Wilder; *W:* Billy Wilder, I.A.L. Diamond; *C:* William Mellor.

Love in the Time of Cholera ✶✶ **2007 (R)** In 19th century Columbia, Florentino (Bardem), a low-born young man who falls madly in love with neighbor Fermina (Mezzogiorno), but cannot have her. Constrained by social rules, Fermina marries a doctor instead of meaningless sexual relationships, but his love for Fermina never truly wanes, even over decades. Based on the novel by Nobel Prize winner G.G. Marquez, the movie loses much of its magic in a straightforward, somewhat dull romantic tragicomedy, a soap opera disguised under layers of age-enhancing makeup. **138m/C DVD.** *US* Javier Bardem, Giovanna Mezzogiorno, Benjamin Bratt, Catalina Sandino Moreno, Hector Elizondo, Liev Schreiber, Ana Claudia Talancon, John Leguizamo, Laura Elena Harring; *D:* Mike Newell; *W:* Ronald Harwood; *C:* Alfonso Beato; *M:* Antonio Pinto.

Love in the Time of Money ✶✶½ **2002 (R)** Overly-familiar story about a group of lonely and/or opportunistic New Yorkers and their various encounters, beginning with a femme fatale model (P'eston) enters the picture. **92m/C VHS,** Jack Kehler, Eric Roberts, Kelly Preston, Eliza (Simone) Garrett R, Lee Ermey; *D:* David Hartwell.

Love Is a Gun ✶✶½ **1994 (R)** A police photographer (Roberts) begins having violent and erotic hallucinations that begin to affect his fiancee (Garrett). Things get even's weirder when a femme fatale (Greniel) enters the picture. With a couple of more people on the daisy chain, the bored viewer eventually finds themselves back with Greta. **90m/C DVD.** *US* Vera Farmiga, Domenick Lombardozzi, Jillian Hennessey, Malcolm Gets, Steve Buscemi, Rosario Dawson, Adrian Grenier, Carol Kane, Michael Imperioli; *D:* Peter Mattei; *W:* Peter Mattei; *C:* Stephen Kazmierski; *M:* Theodore Shapiro.

of parents are crazy. Oddly enough, Sorvino also plays the heroine's dad in the '96 "William Shakespeare's Romeo & Juliet." **98m/C VHS, DVD.** Dominic Chianese, Angelina Jolie, Nathaniel Marston, Paul Sorvino, Renee Taylor, Joseph Bologna, Lainie Kazan, Barbara Carrera, William Hickey, Abe Vigoda, Dick Van Patten, Connie Stevens; **D:** Renee Taylor, Joseph Bologna; **W:** Renee Taylor, Joseph Bologna; **C:** Alan Jones; **M:** Jeff Beal.

Love Is Better Than Ever ♂♂½ *The Light Fantastic* **1952** Lightweight romantic-comedy casts Taylor as a dancing instructor who travels to the Big Apple for a convention. Once there, she meets and falls for talent agent Parks. Carefree, bachelor Parks is too busy to be bothered by small town Taylor, but Liz is determined to land her man. Release of this picture was held back because of Parks' blacklisting by the McCarthy committee. **81m/B VHS.** Larry Parks, Elizabeth Taylor, Josephine Hutchinson, Tom Tully, Ann Doran, Elinor Donahue, Kathleen Freeman; *Cameos:* Gene Kelly; **D:** Stanley Donen; **W:** Ruth Brooks Flippen.

Love Is Colder Than Death ♂♂ *Liebe Ist Kalter Als Der Tod* **1969** Fassbinder's first feature film has a smalltime pimp hooking up with another lowlife to go on a crime spree that ends in a botched bank robbery. German with subtitles. **85m/B VHS, DVD.** *GE* Ulli Lommel, Hanna Schygulla, Katrin Schaake, Liz Scellner; **D:** Rainer Werner Fassbinder; **W:** Rainer Werner Fassbinder; **C:** Dietrich Lohmann; **M:** Peer Raben, Holger Munzer.

Love Is the Devil ♂♂♂½ **1998 1996 (R)** A contemporary Chicago nightclub, the Sanctuary, is the gathering spot for middle-class black urbanites looking for romance. Would-be writer/poet Darius (Tate) spouts provocative verse to beautiful photographer Nina (Long), who's not too happy with men at the moment (she's just been dumped). But they make a connection, with both protesting a little too much that's it just a "sex thing." Funny what happens when love clearly enters the picture. Witcher's directorial debut features fine lead performances. **105m/C VHS, DVD.** Larenz Tate, Nia Long, Isaiah Washington IV, Lisa Nicole Carson, Khalil Kain, Bill Bellamy, Leonard Roberts, Bernadette L. Clarke; **D:** Theodore Witcher; **W:** Theodore Witcher; **C:** Ernest Holzman; **M:** Daryl Jones. Sundance '97: Aud. Award.

Love Jones ♂♂♂ **1996 (R)** A contemporary Chicago nightclub, the Sanctuary, is the gathering spot for middle-class black urbanites looking for romance. Would-be writer/poet Darius (Tate) spouts provocative verse to beautiful photographer Nina (Long), who's not too happy with men at the moment (she's just been dumped). But they make a connection, with both protesting a little too much that's it just a "sex thing." Funny what happens when love clearly enters the picture. Witcher's directorial debut features fine lead performances. **105m/C VHS, DVD.** Larenz Tate, Nia Long, Isaiah Washington IV, Lisa Nicole Carson, Khalil Kain, Bill Bellamy, Leonard Roberts, Bernadette L. Clarke; **D:** Theodore Witcher; **W:** Theodore Witcher; **C:** Ernest Holzman; **M:** Daryl Jones. Sundance '97: Aud. Award.

Love Kills ♂½ **1991 (PG-13)** Is the man a beautiful heiress falls in love with actually an assassin hired by her husband to kill her? Find out in this steamy suspenser. **92m/C VHS.** Virginia Madsen, Lenny Von Dohlen, Erich Anderson, Kate Hodge, Jim Metzler; **D:** Brian Grant.

Love Kills ♂½ **1998 (R)** Good cast can't hold this messy film together. New Age masseur Poe Finklestein (Van Peebles) arrives at the Beverly Hills estate of wealthy widow Evelyn Heiss (Warren). Also living with Evelyn are her no-account, gay stepson Dominique (Leitch) and her voyeuristic sister-in-law Alena (Fletcher). There's shots fired, and drugs, and a cop (Baldwin) and various other hijinks but not

much of it makes sense. **97m/C VHS, DVD.** Mario Van Peebles, Lesley Ann Warren, Daniel Baldwin, Donovan Leitch, Louise Fletcher, Loretta Devine, Melvin Van Peebles, Susan Ruttan, Alexis Arquette; **D:** Mario Van Peebles, Daniel Baldwin; **W:** Mario Van Peebles; **C:** George Mooradian.

Love Laughs at Andy Hardy ♂♂ **1946** Andy Hardy, college boy, is in love and in trouble. Financial and romantic problems come to a head when Andy is paired with a six-foot tall blind date. One in the series. **93m/B VHS, DVD.** Mickey Rooney, Lewis Stone, Sara Haden, Lina Romay, Bonita Granville, Fay Holden; **D:** Willis Goldbeck.

Love Leads the Way ♂♂ **1984** The true story of how Morris Frank established the seeing-eye dog system in the 1930s. **99m/C VHS.** Richard Speight Jr., Timothy Bottoms, Eva Marie Saint, Arthur Hill, Susan Dey, Ralph Bellamy, Ernest Borgnine, Patricia Neal; **D:** Delbert Mann.

The Love Letter ♂♂♂½ **1998** Scotty Corrigan (Scott) discovers a love letter in the antique desk he's purchased, written by Lizzie Whitcomb (Leigh) who lived during the Civil War. Haunted, Scotty decides to reply to the missive and, magically, Lizzie receives his letter. Soon, they not only have a regular correspondence but a romance that transcends time. Based on a story by Jack Finney. **99m/C VHS, DVD.** Campbell Scott, Jennifer Jason Leigh, David Dukes, Estelle Parsons, Daphne Ashbrook, Gerrit Graham, Irma P. Hall; **D:** Dan Curtis; **W:** James Henerson; **M:** Robert Cobert. TV

The Love Letter ♂♂½ **1999 (PG-13)** Disappointingly loose adaptation of the novel by Cathleen Schine feels the need to take the focus off the unexpected love story developing between fortysomething bookstore owner Helen MacFarquhar (Capshaw) and college student Johnny (Scott), who too many peripheral characters. (Yeah, Tom Selleck's charming but his character's a goofy distraction.) Anyway, the love letter in question is an anonymous missive Helen receives at her bookstore. She's not certain it's meant for her, and if it is, just who the secret admirer might be. Then Johnny finds the letter and thinks it's meant for him—or maybe it was for Helen's cynical partner, Janet (DeGeneres). The biggest mystery is why the lovely Danner is playing Capshaw's MOTHER (can a ton of rubber makeup) for heaven's sake! **88m/C VHS, DVD.** Kate Capshaw, Tom Everett Scott, Tom Selleck, Ellen DeGeneres, Blythe Danner, Gloria Stuart, Geraldine McEwan, Alice Drummond, Jack Black; **D:** Peter Chan; **W:** Maria Maggenti; **C:** Tami Reiker; **M:** Luis Bacalov.

Love Letters ♂♂½ **1945** Typical '40s weepie finds Victoria (Jones) marrying soldier Roger Morland (Sully) because of the beautiful letters he wrote her. Only he didn't write them, his best, bud Alan Quinton (Cotten) did. Roger's actually a wife-beater and winds up dead. Victoria becomes an amnesiac from the shock but when Alan comes to check out the situation he falls immediately in love with her double life. She, in turn, begins an affair with a married man. Thoughtful treatment of the psychology of infidelity. **102m/C VHS, DVD.** Jamie Lee Curtis, Amy Madigan, Bud Cort, Matt Clark, Bonnie Bartlett, Sally Kirkland, James Keach; **D:** Amy Hirschfeld; **M:** Ralph Jones.

Love Letters **1983 (R)** A young disc jockey falls under the spell of a box of love letters that her mother left behind which detailed her double life. She, in turn, begins an affair with a married man. Thoughtful treatment of the psychology of infidelity. **102m/C VHS, DVD.** Jamie Lee Curtis, Amy Madigan, Bud Cort, Matt Clark, Bonnie Bartlett, Sally Kirkland, James Keach; **D:** Amy Hirschfeld; **M:** Ralph Jones.

Love Letters ♂♂♂ **1999 (PG-13)** Andy (Weber) and Melissa's (Linney) tender friendship began as children and their attraction continued throughout their lives, as Andy recounts after Melissa's death via many years worth of letters between them. Despite the intense feelings, their careers took them in opposite directions as Andy flourished as a lawyer-turned-senator and

Melissa toiled as an artist. Directed by the legendary Dohen and based on A.R. Guerney's smash play. **90m/C VHS, DVD.** Steven Weber, Laura Linney, Emily Hampshire, Chas Lawther, Marcia Diamond; **D:** Stanley Donen; **W:** A.R. Gurney; **C:** Mike Fash; **M:** Lee Holdridge. TV

Love, Lies and Murder ♂♂½ **1991 (PG-13)** Shocking psychological thriller in which a businessman convinces his daughter and sister-in-law to murder his wife and then sends his daughter to prison for the crime. The "perfect murder" is not so perfect, however, when the daughter learns that her father has remarried and is now living an insurance-rich lifestyle. She decides to fight back in this true story of bizarre murder and deception. **190m/C VHS.** Clancy Brown, John Ashton, Sheryl Lee, Moira Kelly, Ramon Bieri, Kenneth Welsh, Tom Bower, John M. Jackson, Kate McGregor-Stewart; **D:** Robert Markowitz. TV

Love Lies Bleeding ♂♂½ **2007 (R)** Hapless Duke (Geraghty) stumbles across a duffel bag full of money from a drug deal gone bad, grabs it and wife Amber (Dewan), and they head out on the road to start a new life. But they are soon pursued by very ticked-off (and corrupt) DEA agent Pollen (Slater), who wants that money gone for good. There's a lot more tragedy before Angela finds happiness. One of Pickford's rare adult roles. **75m/B VHS, DVD.** Mary Pickford, Raymond Bloomer, Jean De Briac, Evelyn Dumo, Eddie (Edward) Phillips, Albert Priscoe, George Regas, Fred Thomson; **D:** Frances Marion; **W:** Frances Marion; **C:** Henry Cronjager, Charles Rosher.

The Love Light ♂♂½ **1921** Angela (Pickford) is a lighthouse keeper in Italy who's awaiting her soldier brother's return from war. Instead, she learns of his death. When a wounded soldier is washed ashore, Angela rescues him and nurses him back to health, thinking he's an American sailor. They fall in love and marry before she learns that he's really a German spy and may have killed her brother. There's a lot more tragedy before Angela finds happiness. One of Pickford's rare adult roles. **75m/B VHS, DVD.** Mary Pickford, Raymond Bloomer, Jean De Briac, Evelyn Dumo, Eddie (Edward) Phillips, Albert Priscoe, George Regas, Fred Thomson; **D:** Frances Marion; **W:** Frances Marion; **C:** Henry Cronjager, Charles Rosher.

Love Liza ♂♂ **2002 (R)** An acquired taste of a film that rests firmly on the slumped shoulders of Hoffman. He's Wilson Joel, whose wife Liza has just committed suicide (by carbon-monoxide poisoning in her car). He can't read the note she left him, can't deal with her sympathetic mother Mary Ann (Bates), can't—in fact—do much of anything except mope. Oh, and huff. Yes, Wilson decides to cope with his trauma by inhaling gasoline fumes (the fuel used in his model airplane hobby). Soon, his addiction is all there is to his sad sack existence. **90m/C VHS, DVD.** Philip Seymour Hoffman, Kathy Bates, Jack Kehler, Stephen Tobolowsky, Sarah Koskoff, Erika Alexander; **D:** Todd Louiso; **W:** Gordy Hoffman; **C:** Lisa Rinzler; **M:** Jim O'Rourke. Sundance '02: Screenplay.

Love, Ludlow ♂½ **2005 (R)** Bipolar painter Ludlow (Sexton) has been cared for by his single older sister Myra (Goransson) since their mother's death. So he feels especially threatened when Myra agrees to date shy co-worker Reggie (Eigenberg) and it turns into something more than casual. Modest romantic comedy that Paterson adapted from his play "Finger Painting in a Murphy Bed." **86m/C DVD.** Alicia (Lecy) Goranson, Brendan Sexton III, David Eigenberg; **D:** Adrienne J. Weiss; **W:** David Paterson; **C:** Ruben O'Malley; **M:** Tomandandy, James Kole.

The Love Machine ♂½ **1971 (R)** A power-hungry newscaster climbs the corporate ladder by sleeping with many, including the president's wife. An adaptation of Jacqueline Susann's novel. **108m/C VHS.** John Phillip Law, Dyan Cannon, Robert Ryan, Jackie Cooper, David Hemmings, Jodi West, William Roerick, Maureen Arthur, Shecky Greene, Clinton Greyn, Sharon Farrell, Alexandra Hay, Eve Bruce, Greg Mullavey, Edith Atwater, Gene Baylos, Claudia Jennings, Mary Collinson, Madeleine Collinson, Ann Ford, Gayle Hunnicutt; **D:** Jack Haley Jr.; **W:** Samuel A. Taylor; **C:** Charles B(ryant) Lang Jr.; **M:** Artie Butler.

Love Matters ♂♂ **1993 (R)** Tom and Julie's fast-track marriage is hovering on the brink when Tom's best friend Geoff, who's also married, shows up on their doorstep with his sexy mistress and announces he's getting a divorce. Reluctantly, Tom and Julie allow the X-rated lovebirds to stay the night but all that heat only shows up the flaws in their own marriage even more. An unrated version at 103 minutes is also available. **97m/C VHS.** Griffin Dunne, Tony Goldwyn, Annette O'Toole, Gina Gershon, Kate Burton; **D:** Eb Lottimer; **W:** Eb Lottimer; **M:** Simon Boswell.

Love Me Deadly ♂ **1973 (R)** A young woman tries to get her husband interested in her new hobby—necrophilia. **95m/C VHS, DVD.** Mary Wilcox, Lyle Waggoner, Christopher Stone, Timothy Scott; **D:** Jacques Lacerte; **W:** Jacques Lacerte; **C:** David Aaron; **M:** Phil Moody.

Love Me if You Dare ♂ *Jeux D'Enfants; Child's Play* **2003 (R)** Overwrought romance-French style. Julien (Canet) and Sophie (Cotillard) have played a game of dare since childhood-no matter how embarrassing or dangerous the challenge. Obsessed with each other, they are unable to admit their devotion in any conventional way and perpetuate their play for the excitement it brings them even as they risk self-destruction. Unfortunately for the viewer, the duo are mainly exasperating. French with subtitles. **95m/C DVD.** *FR BE* Guillaume Canet, Marion Cotillard, Thibault Verhaeghe, Josephine Lebas Joly, Emmanuelle Gronvold, Gerard Watkins; **D:** Yann Samuell; **W:** Yann Samuell, Jacky Cuckier; **C:** Antoine Roch; **M:** Philippe Rombi.

Love Me or Leave Me ♂♂♂ **1955** A hard-hitting biography of '20s torch singer Ruth Etting and her rise and fall at the hand of her abusive, gangster husband, a part just made for Cagney. Day emotes and sings expressively in one of the best performances of her career. ♫I'll Never Stop Loving You; Never Look Back; Shaking the Blues Away; Mean to Me; Love Me or Leave Me; Sam, the Old Accordian Man; At Sundown; Everybody Loves My Baby; Five Foot Two. **122m/C VHS, DVD.** Doris Day, James Cagney, Cameron Mitchell, Robert Keith, Tom Tully, Veda Ann Borg; **D:** Charles Vidor. Oscars '55: Story.

Love Me Tender ♂♂ **1956** A Civil War-torn family is divided by in-fighting between two brothers who both seek the affections of the same woman. Presley's first film. Songs include "Poor Boy," "We're Gonna Move," and the title tune. **89m/B VHS, DVD.** Richard Egan, Debra Paget, Elvis Presley, Neville Brand, Mildred Dunnock, James Drury, Barry Coe, Robert Middleton, William Campbell, Russ Conway, L.Q. Jones; **D:** Robert D. Webb; **W:** Robert Buckner; **C:** Leo Tover; **M:** Lionel Newman.

Love Meetings *Comizi d'Amore* **1964** Pasolini acts as director and interviewer to query a wide-range of individuals on their experiences at love, including homosexuality, prostitution, marital and non-marital interludes. In Italian with English subtitles. **90m/B VHS, DVD.** *IT* Pier Paolo Pasolini; **W:** Pier Paolo Pasolini; **C:** Tonino Delli Colli, Mario Bernardo.

Love Nest ♂♂ **1951** Lundigan stars as Jim Scott, the landlord of an apartment building brimming with wacky tenants, including Monroe, Paar, and Fay. He dreams of becoming a famous writer, but his time is always filled with fixing up the building and trying to pay the mortgage. When one of the tenants ends up in jail because he was living off wealthy widows, Scott's luck changes. This moderately funny film is a good look at the early careers of Monroe and Paar. **84m/B VHS, DVD.** William Lundigan, June Haver, Frank Fay, Marilyn Monroe, Jack Paar; **D:** Joseph M. Newman; **W:** I.A.L. Diamond; **M:** Cyril Mockridge.

Love Notes **1988** Three short vignettes of soft core fantasy, in the life of an ordinary guy. **60m/C VHS.** Jeff Daniels, Christine Veronica.

The Love of Jeanne Ney ♂♂½ **1927** Wildly convoluted silent film begins in Russia where Jeanne's (Jehanne) Bolshevik lover (Henning) kills her father for betraying the cause, and then shifts to Paris where the pair face even more daunting obstacles. The new score by Timrothy Brock is engaging and effective. **113m B VHS, DVD, GE** *Edith Jehanne, Brigitte Helm, Uno Henning, Eugen Jenson, Fritz Rasp;* **D:** *G.W. Pabst;* **W:** *Ilya Ehrenburg, Ladislaus Vajda.*

Love on a Pillow ✶✶ 1954 The loves, on and off stage, of a beautiful actress in a European traveling theatre group. The new score... **80m C VHS.** *Gerard Oury, Massimo Serato, Robert Beatty, Ca...;* **D:** *Marc Allegret.*

Love on the Dole ✶✶✶ 1941 In a gloomy industrial section of England during the early '30s a family struggles to survive and maintain dignity. Grim Depression drama salvaged by great acting. **89m B VHS, G3** *Deborah Kerr, Clifford Evans, George Carney;* **D:** *John Baxter.*

Love on the Run ✶✶✶ 1979 (PG) The further amorous adventures of Antoine Doinel, hero of "The 400 Blows," "Stolen Kisses," and "Bed and Board." Doine is now in his 30s and newly divorced. He renews affairs with several women from his past but, after his mother's death, must contend with his emotional immaturity and his inability to sustain a relationship. In French with English subtitles. **95m C VHS, DVD, FR** *Jean-Pierre Leaud, Marie-France Pisier, Claude Jade, S. Van Dyke;* **W:** *John Lee Mahin, Manuel Seff, Gladys Hurlbut;* **D:** *Francois Truffaut.* Cesar '80: Score.

Love on the Run ✶✶✶ 1985 A beautiful lawyer helps a wrongly accused convict escape from prison, then they both evade the law. **102m C VHS.** *Stephanie Zimbalist, Alec Baldwin, Constance McCashin, Howard Duff;* **D:** *Gus Trikonis;* **M:** *Billy Goldenberg.* TV

Love on the Side ✶✶ Deluxe Combo Platter 2004 (R) Quirky small town comedy. When tall, blonde, gorgeous Linda (Schnarre), suddenly turns up in Squamish, British Columbia, she brings trouble to the would-be romance of waitress Eve (Sokoloff), and local dumb hunk Jeff (Watson). But Linda is keeping secrets—such as the fact that she's romantically attracted to Eve and has some interest in the local real estate too. **102m C DVD, CA** *Monica Schnarre, Marla Sokoloff, Jennifer Tilly;* **D:** *Vic Sarin;* **M:** *Brigitte Taievski;* **C:** *Vic Sarin;* **M:** *Dave Thomas, Jennifer Tilly.*

Love or Money ✶✶ 2001 Daniel (Duffy) and Samantha (Cunniffe) are strangers to each other when they become contestants on a reality TV show

The Love of Three Queens ✶½ 1954 The loves of a beautiful actress in a European traveling theatre group. **du Guernier, The Rest of the Warrior** 1962 *Beautiful Genevieve (Bardot) accidentally prevents the suicide of alcoholic Renaud (Hossein) and decides she must redeem him. They fall in love but Genevieve finally tires of his cynical abuse and leaves, which serves as a wake-up call to Renaud. Bardot's a looker but her character is a masochist for sticking with such a loser. French with subtitles.* **112m C DVD, FR17/Brigitte Bardot, Robert Hossein, Jean-Mark Bory, Michel Serrault;** **D:** *Roger Vadim;* **W:** *Roger Vadim, Claude Choublier;* **C:** *Armand Thirard, Edmond Sechan;* **M:** *Michel Magne.*

The Love Parade ✶✶½ 1929 Lubitsch's first sound film takes place in Sylvania, one of those mythic, musical, mitt-European countries with a royal ruler. In this case, it's unmarried and lonely Queen Louise (MacDonald) in her film debut. Recalling her randy ambassador, Count Alfred Renard (Chevalier), from Paris for his indiscretions, Louise is nonetheless entranced by his charms and they quickly marry. But Count Alfred soon discovers that being a royal consort is not to his liking. **107m B DVD.** *Jeanette MacDonald, Maurice Chevalier, Lupino Lane, Lillian Roth, Edgar Norton, Lionel Belmore, Eugene Pallette, E.H. Calvert;* **D:** *Ernst Lubitsch;* **W:** *Ernest Vajda, Guy Bolton;* **C:** *Victor Milner;* **M:** *Victor Schertzinger.*

Love Play Playtime; La Recreation 1960 Debut film for Moreuil, who was married to leading lady Seberg at the time, is a bland drama based on a story by Francoise Sagan (who also wrote the much better "Bonjour Tristesse" that Seberg starred in.) Young American Kate Hudson (Seberg), enrolled in a Paris school, becomes obsessed with her next-door neighbors—sculptor Philippe (Marquand) and his wealthy older mistress and patron (Prevost). Soon Kate's involved in a triangle that's even more complicated than it first appears. **87m B VHS, FR** *Jean Seberg, Christian Marquand, Francoise Prevost, Evelyne Ker;* **D:** *Francois Moreuil;* **W:** *Daniel Boulanger;* **C:** *Jean Penzer;* **M:** *Georges Delerue.*

Love Potion #9 ✶✶ 1992 (PG-13) Two nerdy biochemists procure a love potion that they test on animals. Meeting with success they agree to test it on themselves. Predictably, the scientists are transformed and fall in love with each other. Features a talented young cast, with an amusing cameo by Bancroft, but the script is a real disappointment because of its shallow characters and lame gags. Inspired by the song by Jerry Leiber and Mike Stoller. **96m C VHS, DVD.** *Tate Donovan, Sandra Bullock, Mary Mara, Dale Midkiff, Hillary Bailey Smith, Dylan Baker, Anne Bancroft, Rebecca Staab;* **D:** *Dale Launer;* **W:** *Dale Launer;* **C:** *William Wages;* **M:** *Jed Leiber.*

Love Serenade ✶✶ 1996 (R) Former big-time Brisbane DJ and 70s refugee Ken Sherry (Shevtsov) arrives in a sleepy Australian backwater town, setting off a rivalry between two bored sisters, Dimity (Otto) and Vicki-Ann (Frith). Fishing is one of their hobbies and metaphorically, Ken is the big fish in a very little pond. To them, his pretentious disco-era schmooze comes off as sophistication, mostly because he uses Barry White lyrics and his pillow-talk DJ voice to sell it. Critically speaking, director/writer Barrett's debut demonstrates a keen ear for dialogue and comic timing. To the average viewer though, this one's a dog, boring and very strange. If you're looking for a good Aussie comedy rent "Strictly Ballroom" instead. **101m C VHS, DVD, AU** *Miranda Otto, Rebecca Frith, George Shevtsov, John Alansu, Jessica Napier;* **D:** *Shirley Barrett;* **W:** *Shirley Barrett;* **C:** *Mandy Walker.*

Love Song ✶✶½ 2000 Camille (Arnold) is a college student from an upper-crust African-American family whose surgeon father expects her to follow him into the medical field. She's also expected to marry earnest but dull Calvin (Francks). Then Camille meets white blues musician/singer Billy Ryan (Kane) and begins to question just whose dreams she's following as she discovers unexpected romance. Appealing story with sexy leads. **120m C VHS.** *Monica Arnold, Christian Kane, Rainbow Sun Francks, Peter Francis James, Vanessa Bell Calloway, Rachel True, Essence Atkins, Teck Holmes, Tyrese Gibson;* **D:** *Julie Dash.*

Love Stinks ✶½ 1999 (R) Apparently designed as an "unromantic" comedy movie, this joyless "unromantic" comedy gives off a few rank fumes of its own. Writer Seth Winnick (Stewart) meets Chelsea (Wilson) at the wedding of his pals Larry (Bellamy) and Holly (Banks). After he's lured into Chelsea's clutches, she begins to take over his life while dropping hints that he should pop the big question. After he promises to marry her in a year but doesn't follow through, Chelsea decides to sue him for palimony. The non-couple then inexplicably live together until the trial be inflicted on the audience. Stewart attempts to rise above the material with his excellent comedic timing, but he's unable to escape this misogynistic mess. **94m C VHS, DVD.** *French Stewart, Bridgette Wilson-Sampras, Tyra Banks, Bill Bellamy, Steve Hytner, Jason Bateman, Tiffani-Amber Thiessen;* **D:** *Jeff Franklin;* **C:** *Uta Briesewitz;* **M:** *Bennett Salvay.*

where they are chosen by the audience to get married. If they can form a relationship and stay together for six months, they win $1 million. But between media scrutiny, family interference, and personal difficulties, the pressure may be too much. **90m C DVD, GB** *Emma Cunniffe, George Costigan, Sheila Hancock, David Calder, Steven Duffy, Nicky Henson, Pippa Heywood, Toby Jones;* **D:** *Martyn Friend;* **W:** *Elizabeth (Lizzie) Mickery;* **C:** *Sean Van Hales;* **M:** *Nigel Hess.* TV

Love Songs ✶✶ d'Amour 2007 Ismael (Garel) lives with long-time girlfriend Julie (Sagnier) and has just persuaded her (reluctantly) into a three-way with his co-worker Alice (Hesme). Julie's sudden death plunges the immature Ismael into a series of complicated emotional situations that involve Julie's sister Jeanne (Mastroianni), Alice taking on a new beau Gwendal (Renier), and Gwendal's teenaged brother Erwann (Leprince-Ringuet) developing a serious crush on Ismael. And every so often the cast bursts out singing pop songs, which sometimes works (and sometimes doesn't) but at least writer/director Honore is trying for something out of the ordinary. French with subtitles. **95m C DVD, FR** *Ludivine Sagnier, Yannick Renier, Louis Garrel, Brigitte Rouan; D: Christophe Honore, Chiara Mastroianni, Gregoire Leprince-Ringuet, Clotilde Hesme;* **C:** *Remy Chevrin;* **M:** *Alexandre Beaupain.*

Love Songs ✶✶ Les Chansons d'Amour 2007

A Love Song for Bobby Long ✶✶ 2004 (R) Bobby Long (Travolta) and protege Lawson Pines (Macht) are alcoholic literary has-beens who escape a shady past by relocating to a notorious singer's house in New Orleans. When the singer dies, her 18-year-old daughter (Johansson) shows up to claim the house, but must share it with the shabby twosome. Heartwarming misunderstandings and bonding moments ensue. Very over-the-top story actually manages to charm, saved by the relaxed performances of talented cast. Neither Travolta gets to sing again. **119m C VHS, DVD, US** *John Travolta, Scarlett Johansson, Gabriel Macht, Deborah Kara Unger, Sonny Shroyer, Dane Rhodes;* **D:** *Shainee Gabel;* **C:** *Elliot Davis;* **M:** *Nathan Larson.*

Love Songs ✶✶½ 1999 Trilogy of stories all set in the same black neighborhood. "A Love Song for a Champ" concerns boxer Townsend who agrees to throw a fight. "A Love Song for Jean and Ellis" concerns the would-be romance between grocer Braugher and the haughty Whitfield. "A Love Song for Dad" follows bartender Grossett who comes to the aid of his abused sister-in-law. **101m C VHS, DVD.** *Robert Kevin Townsend, Andre Braugher, Louis Gossett Jr., Fachael Crawford, Carl Gordon, Lynn Whitfield, Brent Jennings, Dule Hill, Sandra Caldwell;* **D:** *Robert Kevin Townsend, Andre Braugher, Louis Gossett Jr.;* **W:** *Charles Fuller;* **C:** *James R. Bagdonas;* **M:** *Pete Anthony, Rornie Laws.* CABLE

Love Songs ✶✶ 1985 (R) A mother of two is confronted with her husband's abandonment and a subsequent romance with a younger man in French (and dubbed). "Leave It to Me; Psychic Flash; I Am With You Now; Human Race; We Can Dance; One More Moment. From the heart; This Must Be Heaven. **107m C VHS, DVD, FR CA** *Catherine Deneuve, Christopher Lambert;* **D:** *Elie Chouraqui;* **C:** *Robert Alazraki.*

Love the Hard Way ✶✶ 2001 Would-be hipster writer Jack Grace (Brody) runs smalltime scams with his friend Charlie (Seda). Grad student Claire (Ayanna) falls for the romeo, even though she can see he's a loser. Though Jack cheats on her, Claire hangs around, even dedicating that the best way to keep him is to join in Jack's con games. The characters are tedious as is the story; Grier shows up to give the film some spark in the small role of a cop out to oust Jack. "Inspired" by the Chinese novel "Fire and Ice" by Wang Shuo. **104m C VHS, DVD, US** *Adrien Brody, Charlotte Ayanna, Jon Seda, Pam Grier, August Diehl, David W. Ross;* **D:** *Peter Sehr;* **W:** *Sehr, Marie Noelle;* **C:** *Guy Dufaux;* **M:** *Jeff Barry.*

Love Thrill Murders WOOF! Sweet Savior 1971 (R) A film about a Manson-esque lunatic who is worshipped and obeyed by a mob of runaways and dropouts. **89m C VHS.** *Fran Middleton, Tele Cochrane, Matt Greene, Tobi Maxton, Troy Donahue;* **D:** *Robert L. Roberts;* **M:** *Nick Gregory;* **C:** *Victor Petrashevich;* **M:** *Jeff Barry.* VIDEO

Love Thy Neighbor ✶½ 2002 Two married neighbors, Jack (Gwaltney) and Molly (Overbey), decide to hook up, and ultimately facilitate the date lured into Chelsea's clutches, she begins to hook up. The simple affair leads to potentially disastrous fallout when Molly's husband admits to Jack that he might have AIDS. The resulting juxtaposition of emotions—marital boredom, betrayal among friends, and threat of disease—is awkward at best and ultimately picturesque. **87m C VHS, DVD.** *Jack Gwaltney, Kellie Overbey, John Enos, Jennifer Brensford, Roy Scheider, Wallace Shawn, Jake Weber;* **D:** *Nick Gregory;* **W:** *Nick Gregory, Kirk Aanes;* **C:** *Dejan Georgevich;* **M:** *Stephen Cohan.* VIDEO

Love to Kill ✶✶ The Girl Gets Moe 1997 (R) Moe (Danza) is a low-level arms dealer who falls for Elizabeth (Barondes), a gal who happens to like guns. But things go wrong thanks to dead bodies, double-crosses, and dirty cops. **102m C VHS, DVD.** *Tony Danza, Michael Madsen, James Russo, Elizabeth Barondes, Louise Fletcher, Amy Locane, Richmond Arquette, Rustam Branaman;* **D:** *James Bruce;* **W:** *Monica Clemens, Rustam Branaman;* **C:** *Keith L. Smith;* **M:** *Barry Coffing.* CABLE

The Love Trap ✶✶½ 1929 Early partial talkie (the film starts off as a silent with captions) is your basic Cinderella story. Chorus girl Laura Todd (La Plante) loses her job and gets tooted out of her appartment. Cabbie Peter Cadwallader (Hamilton) offers his taxi as shelter and

Love Story ✶✶✶ 1970 (PG) Melodrama had enormous popular appeal. O'Neal is the son of Boston's upper crust at Harvard; McGraw's the daughter of a poor Italian on scholarship to study music at Radcliffe. They find happiness, but only for a brief period. Timeless story, simply told, with artful direction from the young exceptional performances from the young duo (who have never done one as well since). The end result is perhaps better than Segal's simplistic novel, which was produced after he sold the screenplay and became a best-seller before the picture's release—"Love means never having to say you're sorry." Remember. **100m C VHS, DVD, Ryan O'Neal, Ali MacGraw, Ray Milland, John Marley, Tommy Lee Jones;** **D:** *Arthur Hiller;* **W:** *Erich Segal;* **C:** *Richard Kratina;* **M:** *Francis Lai.* Oscars '70: Orig. Score; Golden Globes '71: Actress—Drama (MacGraw), Director (Hiller), Film—Drama, Screenplay, Score.

Love Streams ✶✶ 1984 (PG-13) A quirky character drama about a writer who works in a luxurious bordello. Also available in an unedited 120-minute version. **97m C VHS, BR** *Vera Fischer, Mauro Mendonca, Tarcisio Meira;* **D:** *Walter Hugo Khouri;* **W:** *Gena Rowlands, John Cassavetes, Diahnne Abbott, Seymour Cassel;* **D:** *John Cassavetes.*

Love Strange Love ✶✶ 1982 (R) Amorous young boy develops a bizarre relationship with his mother and his sister who struggle to find love. **97m C VHS, BR** *Vera Fischer, Mauro Mendonca, Tarcisio Meira;* **D:** *Walter Hugo Khouri;* **C:** *Antonio Meliande;* **M:** *Rogerio Duprat.*

the two fall in love and marry—much to the displeasure of his snooty (and wealthy) family. The DVD includes the documentary "Directed by William Wyler." 71m/B VHS, DVD. Laura La Plante, Neil Hamilton, Robert Ellis, Rita La Roy, Jocelyn Lee, Norman Trevor, Clarissa Selwynne; D: William Wyler; W: Clarence Marks, John B. Clymer, Albert DeMond, Clarence Thompson; C: Gilbert Warrenton.

Love Under Pressure ♂♂ *Because He's My Friend 1978* Man and woman's marriage starts to evaporate when they realize their son is seriously disturbed. 92m/C VHS. AU Jack Thompson, Tom Oliver, Barbara Stephens, Don Reid, Karen Black, Keir Dullea; D: Ralph Nelson; W: Peter Schreck; C: Peter Hendry; M: Pete Jones.

Love Unto Death ♂♂ *L'Amour a Mort 1984* Simon (Arditi) and Elisabeth (Azema) are still working out their romantic relationship when he suddenly dies—and is quickly revived. His near-death experience has Simon becoming obsessed with mortality and he starts to withdraw from daily life. Friends Judith (Ardant) and Jerome (Dussollier), who are also Protestant ministers, offer their guidance but the idea of a love beyond death is all Simon can think about. French with subtitles. 92m/C DVD. FR Jean Daste, Pierre Arditi, Sabine Azema, Fanny Ardant, Andre Dussollier, Alain Resnais; W: Jean Gruault; C: Sacha Vierny; M: Hans Werner Henze.

Love! Valour! Compassion! ♂♂½ *1996* (R) Follows eight gay men, longtime friends, who spend summer holiday weekends together at a beach house. Excellent cast features Alexander as Buzz, who has a severe show tune fixation, and Glover playing a pair of twins with very different personalities (and they're actually named Jeckyll). Together they wander through the turmoil of AIDS, infidelity, rage and impromptu ballet practice. Excellent cast only occasionally swerves from humor and genuine pathos into maudlin. Intermittent periods of stagy claustrophobia betray pic's Broadway origin. Based on the play by Terrence McNally. 120m/C VHS, DVD. Jason Alexander, John Glover, Randy Becker, John Benjamin Hickey, Stephen Bogardus, Stephen Spinella, Justin Kirk; D: Joe Mantello; W: Terrance McNally; C: Alik Sakharov; M: Harold Wheeler.

Love Walked In ♂♂ *The Bitter End 1997* (R) Hardly an original story but this B-movie has a standout performance from the edgy Leary. He's Jack Hanaway, a P.I. friend Eddie (Badalucco). Jack's old P.I. friend Eddie (Badalucco) shows up with a scheme to make them all rich. He's been hired by a wealthy woman (Dusay) who adores her husband Fred (Stamp) of infidelity. Fred's faithful (he likes his wife's money) but he's a patron of Jack's and is naturally appreciative of Vicky's charms. So they try to set Fred up. Scenes of would-be writer Jack's pulp novel intrude into the action and provide an unneeded distraction. Adapted from the novel by Jose Pablo Feinmann. 90m/C VHS. J.K. Simmons, Denis Leary, Aitana Sanchez-Gijon, Terence Stamp, Michael Badalucco, Marj Dusay, Danny Nucci, Moira Kelly, Neal Huff; D: Juan J. Campanella; W: Larry Golin, Juan J. Campanella; C: Daniel Shulman; M: Wendy Blackstone.

Love with the Proper Stranger ♂♂½ *1963* A quiet, gritty romance about an itinerant musician and a young working girl in Manhattan awkwardly living through the consequences of their one-night stand. Moved? Wood well into the realm of adult roles, after years playing teenagers and innocents. Although the story is about an Italian neighborhood and family, an exceptional number of the cast members were Jewish, as was the screenwriter. Story does not conclude strongly, although this did not hamper the boxoffice returns. 102m/B VHS. Nata-

lie Wood, Steve McQueen, Edie Adams, Herschel Bernardi, Tom Bosley, Harvey Lembeck, Penny Santon, Virginia Vincent, Nick Alexander, Augusta Ciolli; D: Robert Mulligan; W: Arnold Schulman; C: Milton Krasner; M: Elmer Bernstein.

Love Without Pity ♂♂½ *1991* Rochant's theatrical debut is a modern romance, with more distance and alienation than joy. A lovely, successful grad student loses her heart to a jobless, unambitious layabout who wants total commitment from her. Untypical, sardonic love story may be too cynical for sentimental types. In French with English subtitles. 95m/C VHS. FR Hippolyte Girardot, Mireille Perrier, Jean Marie Rollin; D: Eric Rochant; W: Eric Rochant; M: Gerard Torikian.

Love Your Mama ♂♂½ *1989* (PG-13) An urban black drama about the strong Dorothy whose faith helps her cope with her many family complications, including her drunken husband, car thief son, and pregnant teenage daughter. Believable role models and good performances help out this amateur filmmaking effort. 93m/C VHS. Audrey Morgan, Carol E. Hall, Andre Robinson, Ernest Rayford, Kearo Johnson, Jacqueline Williams; D: Ruby L. Oliver; W: Ruby L. Oliver.

Loved ♂♂ *1997* (PG-13) Hedda's (Wright Penn) obsessively and destructively in love with the nameless ex-boyfriend (Lucero) who left her scarred after a suspicious fall out a window. The loser's being arraigned for the murder of his latest girlfriend and prosecutor Dietrickson (Hurt) wants Hedda to testify. But what no one counts on, and what no one can understand, is Hedda's justification for her ex's abuse. Pic and performances are vague. 109m/C VHS. Robin Wright Penn, William Hurt, Amy Madigan, Anthony Lucero, Lucinda Jenney, Joanna Cassidy, Paul Dooley, Jennifer Rubin; Cameos: Sean Penn; D: Erin Dignam; W: Erin Dignam; C: Reynaldo Villalobos; M: David Baerwald.

The Loved One ♂♂½ *1965* A famously outlandish, death-mocking farce based on Evelyn Waugh's satire about a particularly horrendous California funeral parlor/cemetery and how its denizens do business. A shrill, protracted spearing of American capitalism. 118m/B VHS, DVD. Robert Morse, John Gielgud, Rod Steiger, Liberace, Anjanette Comer, Jonathan Winters, James Coburn, Dana Andrews, Milton Berle, Tab Hunter, Robert Morley, Lionel Stander, Margaret Leighton, Roddy McDowall, Bernie Kopell, Alan Napier, Paul Williams, Barbara Nichols, James Farr; D: Tony Richardson; W: Terry Southern, Christopher Isherwood; C: Haskell Wexler; M: John Addison.

Loveless ♂ *1983* (R) A menacing glance into the exploits of an outcast motorcycle gang. In the 50s, a group of bikers on their way to the Florida Cycle Races stop for lunch in a small-town diner. While repairs are being made on their motorcycles, they decide to take full advantage of their situation. 85m/C VHS, DVD. Robert Gordon, Willem Dafoe, J. Don Ferguson; D: Kathryn Bigelow; W: Kathryn Bigelow.

Loveless in Los Angeles ♂ *1983* (R) Dave (Mihok) has a good job producing a reality TV dating show but he strenuously avoids commitment. That is until he bumps into now-divorced Kelly (Daniel), the girl he crushed on in college. But Dave's sleazy womanizing drives Kelly up the wall and he needs her to find his inner nice guy once again. Standard romance isn't really worth the effort. 95m/C DVD. Dash Mihok, Brittany Daniel, James Lesure, Navi Rawat, Christopher Coppola, Stephen Tobolowsky, Geoffrey Arend; D: Archie Gip; W: Archie Gip; C: Michael Marius Passai; M: Gregg Lehrman. VIDEO

Lovelife ♂♂½ *1997* (R) Yet another romantic saga about a group of disenchanted boomer friends who can't seem to make that love connection work. Maybe they should stop serial dating within their same small circle and take advantage of the outside world. 97m/C VHS, DVD, Sherilyn Fenn, Bruce Davison, Saffron Burrows, Jon Tenney, Carla Gugino, Matt Letscher, Tushka Bergen, Peter Krause; D: John Harmon Feldman; W: John Harmon Feldman; C: Anthony C. "Tony" Jannelli; M: Adam Fields. VIDEO

Lovelines ♂ *1984* (R) Two rock singers from rival high schools meet and fall in love during a panty raid. Laughs uncounted ensue. 93m/C VHS. Greg Bradford, Michael Winslow, Mary Beth Evans, Don Michael Paul, Tammy Taylor, Stacey Toten, Miguel Ferrer, Shecky Greene, Jamie (Amy) Eccles, Sherri Stoner; D: Rod Amateau.

Lovely & Amazing ♂♂♂ *2002* (R) Mom Blethyn watches over her three dysfunctional daughters: Michelle (Keener), who's bored by her marriage; insecure wannabe actress Elizabeth (Mortimer) and adopted eight-year-old African-American Annie (Goodwin), who's preoccupied with her looks. Unstable Michelle begins a hopeless affair with a teenager (Gyllenhaal), while a post-coital scene between Elizabeth and lover Mulroney shows the extent of the neurotic actresses' body image problem. Annie is the least disturbed of the three sisters, who just wants to look like everyone else in the family. Led by Blethyn, the cast expertly embody their complicated, quirky characters. Skillfully written and directed study in character flaws and family by Holofcener. 91m/C VHS, DVD. US Brenda Blethyn, Catherine Keener, Emily Mortimer, Raven Goodwin, Dermot Mulroney, Jake Gyllenhaal, Aunjanue Ellis, Clark Gregg, James LeGros, Michael Nouri; D: Nicole Holofcener; W: Nicole Holofcener; C: Harlan Bosmajian; M: Craig Richey. Ind. Spirit '03: Support. Actress (Mortimer).

Lovely... But Deadly ♂♂½ *1982* (R) Young girl wages a war against the drug dealers in her school after her brother dies of an overdose. 95m/C VHS. Lucinda Dooling, John Randolph, Richard Herd, Susan Mechsner, Mel Novak; D: David Sheldon.

Lovely to Look At ♂♂♂ *1952* Three wanna-be Broadway producers (Skelton, Keel, Champion) go to gay Paree to peddle Skelton's half interest in Madame Roberta's, a chi chi dress shop. There, they meet the shop's other half interest, two sisters (Champion and Miller), and together they stage a fashion show to finance the floundering hospice of haute couture. Lavish production, light plot. Filmed in Technicolor based on Kern's 1933 Broadway hit (inspired by Alice Duer Miller's "Gowns by Roberta"). Vincent Minnelli staged the fashion show, with gowns by Adrian (watch for cop-beater Zsa Zsa as a model). ♫Opening Night; Smoke Gets in Your Eyes; Lovely to Look At; The Touch of Your Hand; Yesterdays; I Won't Dance; You're Devastating; The Most Exciting Night; I'll Be Hard to Handle. 105m/C VHS. Kathryn Grayson, Red Skelton, Howard Keel, Gower Champion, Marge Champion, Ann Miller, Zsa Zsa Gabor, Kurt Kasznar, Marcel Dalio, Diane Cassidy; D: Mervyn LeRoy; C: George J. Folsey.

The Lover ♂♂ *L'Amant 1992* (R) Portrays the sexual awakening of a French teenager and her older Chinese lover in Indochina in 1929. The characters, who remain nameless, meet on a ferry where the man is smitten by the girl's beauty. Detached, determined, and unromantic, she's the opposite of her indolent lover), she allows herself to be seduced for the experience, and money, he offers. The film is equally detached, including the beautifully photographed but uninvolving sex scenes. Moreau narrates as an adult looking back on her life. March's debut; filmed on location in Vietnam. Based on the semi-autobiographical novel by Marguerite Duras who reputated director Annuaud's film when it was released in France. Also available in an unrated, letterbox version at 115 minutes. 103m/C VHS, DVD. FR Jane March, Tony Leung Ka-Fai, Frederique Meininger, Arnaud Giovaninetti, Melvil Poupaud, Lisa Faulkner, Xiem Mang; D: Jean-Jacques Annaud; W: Gerard Brach, Jean-Jacques Annaud; C: Robert Fraisse; M: Gabriel Yared; Nar: Jeanne Moreau. Cesar '93: Score.

Lover Come Back ♂♂½ *1961* More Day-Hudson antics in which an advertising executive falls in love with his competitor but that doesn't stop him from stealing her clients. Is there no shame? 107m/C VHS, DVD. Rock Hudson, Doris Day, Tony Randall, Edie Adams, Joe Flynn, Ann B. Davis, Jack Oakie, Jack Albertson, Jack Kruschen, Howard St. John; D: Delbert Mann.

Lover Girl ♂♂♂ *1997* (R) When teenager Jake Ferrari (Subkoff) is abandoned by her mother, she decides to track down long-gone sister, Darlene (Swanson). But when Darlene doesn't want her either, Jake is at a loss until she's reluctantly befriended by Marci (Bernhard), manager of a massage parlor. Underage Jake even badgers tough Marci into giving her a job, although the film is skittish about just how far Jake goes with her clients. Still, given the sleazy and potentially exploitative premise, the film is surprizing cheerful and light. 87m/C VHS. Tara Subkoff, Sandra Bernhard, Kristy Swanson, Loretta Devine, Renee Humphrey, Susan Barnes, Sahara Lotti, Tim Griffin; D: Lisa Addario, Joe Syracuse; W: Lisa Addario, Joe Syracuse; C: Dean Lent; M: Mark Killian.

Loverboy ♂ *1989* (PG-13) A college schnook takes a summer job as a Beverly Hills pizza delivery boy and is preyed upon by many rich and sex-hungry housewives. 105m/C VHS, DVD. Patrick Dempsey, Kate Jackson, Barbara Carrera, Kirstie Alley, Carrie Fisher, Robert Ginty, Elizabeth (E.G. Dailey) Daily; D: Joan Micklin Silver; W: Tom Ropelewski, Leslie Dixon; C: Michael Colombier.

Loverboy ♂♂ *2005* (R) Obsessive mom love. Bacon directs wife Sedgwick in this adaptation of Victoria Redel's novel. Young Emily (played by daughter Sosie Bacon) always felt like an outsider because her parents (Tomei, Bacon) were so wrapped up in each other. So when she's an adult, Emily ruthlessly decides to become a single mom and give son Paul all the love she missed out on. But Emily freaks out at the slightest hint of independence from the growing Paul (Kay), who she still insists on calling "Loverboy." Really creepy pic is spent waiting for Emily to go completely off the rails. 86m/C DVD. US Kyra Sedgwick, Kevin Bacon, Blair Brown, Matt Dillon, Oliver Platt, Campbell Scott, Marisa Tomei, John Lafayette, Dominic Scott, Sosie Bacon, Jessica Stone, Melissa Errico, Nancy Giles, Sandra Bullock; D: Kevin Bacon; W: Hannah Shakespeare; C: Nancy Schreiber; M: Michael Bacon.

The Lovers ♂♂♂ *1959* Chic tale of French adultery with Moreau starring as a provincial wife whose shallow life changes overnight when she meets a young man. Had a controversial American debut because of the film's tender eroticism and innocent view of adultery. In French with English subtitles. 90m/B VHS, DVD. FR Jeanne Moreau, Alain Cuny, Jose-Luis De Villalonga, Jean-Mark Bory; D: Louis Malle; W: Louis Malle. Venice Fest. '59: Special Jury Prize.

Lovers: A True Story ♂♂ *Amantes 1990* (R) Erotic love triangle in 1950s Madrid, while Spain is under the suffocating dictatorship of Franco. Naive, young Paco has a virginal, hardworking fiancee named Trini. Things would seem to be headed for an average life until Paco rents a room from young widow Luisa and they embark on a sexual affair bordering on obsession. When Trini discovers what's going on she turns out to have a more passionate, and violent, nature than even Paco could imagine. Steamy and highly dramatic with excellent performances. Based on a true story. In Spanish with English subtitles. An unrated version is also available. 105m/C VHS. SP Victoria Abril, Jorge Sanz, Maribel Verdu; D: Vicente Aranda; W: Vicente Aranda, Alvaro del Amo; C: Jose Luis Alcaine; M: Jose Nieto. Berlin Int. Film Fest. '91: Actress (Abril).

Lovers and Liars ♂♂ *Travels with Anita; A Trip with Anita 1981* (R) A romantic adventure in Rome turns into a symphony of zany mishaps when the man forgets to tell the woman that he is married!! 93m/C VHS, DVD. IT Goldie Hawn, Giancarlo Giannini, Laura Betti; D: Mario Monicelli; W: Mario Monicelli, Paul Zimmerman; C: Tonino Delli Colli; M: Ennio Morricone.

Lovers and Other Strangers ♂♂♂ *1970* (R) Two young people decide to marry after living together for a year and a half. Various tensions surface between them and among their families as the wedding day approaches. Good comedy features some charming performances. Keaton's first film. ♫For All We Know, 106m/C VHS, DVD. Gig Young, Beatrice Arthur, Bonnie Bedelia, Anne

Lover's Knot 🌭🌭½ 1996 (R) Cutesy romantic comedy has Curry as an angel whose heavenly mission is to get the proper romantic couples together. His current pair are poetic college English prof Steve (Campbell) and practical pediatrician Megan (Grey). Steve's imaginative courtship wins Megan but the duo separate, leaving their angelic guide to get them back together. 82m/C VHS, DVD. Billy Campbell, Jennifer Grey, Tim Curry, Adam Baldwin; Cameos: Adam Ant, Anne Francis; D: Peter Shaner, C: Garet Griffin; M: Laura Karpman.

Lovers Like Us 🌭🌭½ 1975 Two people each leave their spouses, meet one another, and fall in love. 103m/C VHS. FR Catherine Deneuve, Yves Montand, Luigi Vannucchi, Tony Roberts, Dana Wynter; D: Jean-Paul Rappeneau.

Lovers' Lovers 🌭 1944 All sorts of bizarre and erotic adventures ensue when Blaire and jilted narcissist meets Michael, who doesn't want to commit to girl-friend Teri. Michael plans an affair with Blaire without realizing that Teri is already having a fling with Ray, Blaire's ex. Some funny situations but too many ta ky scenes stop the film cold. 90m/C VHS, Serge Rodnunsky, Serge Rodnunsky; D: Serge Rodnunsky; M: Pierre Rodnunsky.

Lovers of the Arctic Circle 🌭🌭🌭 1998. (R) Complex romantic drama set in Spain and Finland. Otto and Ana meet as children and instantly recognized each other as soul mates—their first kiss occurring over a geography book describing the Arctic Circle. When Otto's divorced father takes up with Ana's widowed mother, the now-adolescent pair wind up sharing the same house, and secretly become lovers. When Otto's mother dies, he blames himself for abandoning her and leaves Ana to become a pilot. She, in turn, becomes obsessed with being where the Arctic sun never sets, and fate, eventually, brings the adult duo together in Finland. Spanish with subtitles. 112m/C VHS, SP Fele Martinez, Najwa Nimri, Nancho Novo, Maru Valdivielso, Beate Jensen; D: Julio Medem; C: Gonzalo F. Berrdi; M: Alberto Iglesias.

Lovers of Their Time 🌭 1985 A romantic novel on tape, about forbidden love and other problems. 60m/C VHS. Edward Petherbridge, Cheryl Prime, Lynn Farleigh; D: Robert Knights.

The Lovers on the Bridge 🌭🌭 1991 (R) Les Amants du Pont-Neuf. Overblown, extravagant romantic drama about two homeless lovers who live on Paris' Pont-Neuf bridge, which is closed for repairs. Michele (Binoche) is a disoriented artist losing her eyesight to a degenerative eye disease. She has left her home and stumbles upon the bridge squatters who include Alex (Lavant), a disturbed and alcoholic street performer. Alex rescues her and becomes Michele's protector and lover. He also becomes obsessive—fearing Michele will leave him and desperate to stop her. Set in 1989, the bicentennial of the French Revolution. The Alex character also appears in the Carax films "Boy Meets Girl" (1984) and "Bad Blood" (1986). French with subtitles. 125m/C VHS, DVD. FR Juliette Binoche, Denis Lavant, Klaus-Michael Gruber, Marion Stalens; D: Leos Carax; W: Leos Carax; C: Jean-Yves Escoffier.

Lover's Prayer 🌭🌭½ All Forgotten 1999 (PG-13) Wealthy, innocent young man (Stahl) becomes infatuated with a mysterious young woman (Dunst) who has moved next door for the summer. Then he learns that romance isn't what he had fantasized it to be. 106m/C VHS, DVD. Nick Stahl, Kirsten Dunst, Julie Walters, Geraldine James, Nathaniel Parker, James Fox; D: Reverge Anselmo.

Lovers Like Us ... Jackson, Harry Guardino, Michael Brandon, Richard S. Castellano, Bob (Robert Dishy) Maran Hatley, Cloris Leachman, Anne Meara, Diane Keaton; D: Cy Howard; W: Renee Taylor, Joseph Bologna, David Zelag Goodman, Oscars '70: Song ("For All We Know").

Loves & Times of Scaramouche 🌭½ Scaramouche 1976 Eighteenth-century rogue becomes involved in a plot to assassinate Napoleon and winds up seducing Josephine in the process. Dubbed. 92m/C VHS. IT Michael Sarrazin, Ursula Andress, Aldo Maccione; D: Enzo G. Castellari.

Love's Enduring Promise 🌭🌭½ 2004. In this follow-up to "Love Comes Softly," it's 10 years later and Marty and Clark are happily married and raising their young children while the now-grown Missie (Jones) has become a teacher. She is also being courted by both the wealthy Grant (Astin) and poor Willie (Bartholomew). But romance will have to wait when Clark has an accident and Missie must help out on the farm. From the novel by Janette Oke. 88m/C DVD. Katherine Heigl, Dale Midkiff, January Jones, MacKenzie Astin, Logan Bartholomew, Cliff De Young; D: Michael Landon Jr.; M: Kevin Kiner. CABLE

Love's Labour's Lost 🌭🌭 2000 (PG) Branagh's latest dip into the Bard is moved into the 1930s and accompanied by the music of Cole Porter, the Gershwins, and Jerome Kern. Just as four men vow to swear off women and concentrate on their studies along comes a French princess and her three companions. Guess what happens. As with the 1996 Woody Allen film, "Everyone Says I Love You," the actors try their best to be singing/dancing fools but most just end up looking foolish. As for Shakespeare, well about two-thirds of the text is actually gone and even lesser Will shouldn't be treated like that. 93m/C VHS, DVD, GB Kenneth Branagh, Alicia Silverstone, Natascha (Natasha) McElhone, Alessandro Nivola, Matthew Lillard, Nathan Lane, Timothy Spall, Geraldine McEwan, Carmen Ejogo, Adrian Lester, Emily Mortimer, Richard Briers, Stefania Rocca, Jimmy Yuill; D: Kenneth Branagh; W: Kenneth Branagh; C: Alex Thomson; M: Patrick Doyle.

Love's Long Journey 🌭🌭½ 2005 The third in the series, following "Love's Enduring Promise." Missie (Cottrell) has married Willie LaHaye (Bartholomew) and the two have left their families and community to begin a new life together on a cattle ranch. A pregnant Missie befriends their Native American neighbor Miriam (Bedard) but there's trouble when three strangers show up, looking for money that's supposedly hidden on the property. From the novel by Janette Oke. 88m/C DVD. Irene Bedard, William Morgan Sheppard, Richard Lee Jackson, Erin Cottrell, Logan Bartholomew, James Tupper, Cindy Keller; D: Michael Landon Jr.; W: Michael Landon Jr., Douglas Lloyd McIntosh; C: Brian Shanley; M: Kevin Kiner. CABLE

Loves of a Blonde 🌭🌭🌭½ 1965 A shy teenage factory girl falls in love with a visiting piano player when the reservist army comes to her small town. But when she goes to visit his family, she discovers things aren't as she imagined. Touching look at the complications of love and our expectations. Czech with subtitles. 88m/B VHS, DVD. CZ Hana Brejchova, Josef Sebanek, Vladimir Pucholt, Milada Jezkova; D: Milos Forman; W: Jaroslav Papousek; C: Miroslav Ondricek; M: Evsen Illin.

The Loves of Carmen 🌭🌭 1948 Film version of the classic Prosper Merrimee novel about a tempestuous Spanish gypsy and the soldier who loves her. Hayworth is great to look at and the film's main selling point. 98m/C VHS, DVD. Rita Hayworth, Glenn Ford, Ron Randell, Victor Jory, Arnold Moss, Luther Adler, Joseph Buloff; D: Charles Vidor; W: Helen Deutsch; C: William E. Snyder; M: Mario Castelnuovo-Tedesco.

The Loves of Edgar Allen Poe 🌭🌭 1942 A bland biographical drama about young Poe's adoption, his treatment at the hands of his foster father, his rejection by a woman for a more well-off man, his marriage to his first cousin, and his early death from alcoholism. 67m/B VHS. Linda Darnell, Shepperd Strudwick, Virginia Gilmore, Jane Darwell, Mary Howard; D: Harry Lachman.

The Loves of Hercules 🌭 Gli Amori di Ercole 1960 The mythic morph fields a mate with equiponderant chest measurements, and must save her from an evil queen. Somehow it eludes him that both queen and maiden are Miss Jayne in red and black wigs. Kudos for worst dubbing and special effects; a must-see for connoisseurs of kitsch. 94m/C VHS. IT FR Jayne Mansfield, Mickey Hargitay; D: Carlo L. Bragaglia; W: Alessandro Continenza. CABLE

Love's Savage Fury WOOF! 1979 Two escapees from a Union prison camp seek out a hidden treasure that could determine the outcome of the Civil War. Bad ripoff of "Gone with the Wind." 100m/C VHS. Jennifer O'Neill, Perry King, Robert Reed, Raymond Burr, Connie Stevens, Ed Lauter; D: Joseph Hardy; M: John Addison. TV

Love's Unending Legacy 🌭🌭 2007 The fifth film in author Janette Oke's bestselling series. After Willie LaHaye's death, Missie (Cottrell) returns to her father's ranch, aged girl. As Missie becomes romantically interested in town sheriff Zach Tyler (Browne), she discovers that her new daughter's brother is being mistreated by the family who adopted him. 84m/C DVD. Erin Cottrell, Dale Midkiff, Victor Browne, Samantha Smith, Holliston Coleman, Brett Coker, Frank Stratton, Braeden Lemasters; D: Mark Griffiths W: Pamela Wallace; C: Brian Shanley; M: Kevin Kiner. CABLE

Lovesick 🌭🌭 1983 (PG) A very-married New York psychiatrist goes against his own best judgment when he falls in love with one of his patients. 98m/C VHS, DVD. Dudley Moore, Elizabeth McGovern, Alec Guinness, John Huston, Ron Silver; D: Marshall Brickman; C: Gerry Fisher; M: Philippe Sarde.

Lovespell 🌭 Tristan and Isolde 1979 A retelling of the legend of Isolde and Tristan. Stilted direction and writing, but another chance to reminisce on Richard Burton. 91m/C VHS, DVD. Richard Burton, Kate Mulgrew, Nicholas Clay, Cyril Cusack, Geraldine Fitzgerald, Niall Toibin, Diana Van Der Vlis, Niall O'Brien; D: Tom Donovan.

Loving 🌭🌭 1970 (R) Nondescript dramedy has Segal as a commercial artist whose midlife crisis comes to a head when his wife, mistress, and neighborhood witness his drunken foray with a neighbor's wife via closed-circuit TV. Saint is very good as the wronged wife, but the whole thing is much duller than it should be. 89m/C DVD. George Segal, Eva Marie Saint, Sterling Hayden, Keenan Wynn, David Doyle, Paul Sparer, Nancie Phillips, Sherry Lansing, Janis Young, Roy Scheider, Sab Shimono, D: Irvin Kershner; W: Don Devlin; C: Gordon Willis; M: Bernardo Segall.

Loving Annabelle 🌭🌭½ 2006 Senator's daughter Annabelle (Kelly) attends school where her rebelliousness gives the Mother Superior (Graff) fits. So she instructs Annabelle's favorite teacher, Simone Bradley (Gairty), to help the girl cope. But what teacher and student soon realize is that there's a romantic attraction between them, which Annabelle is determined to pursue. A modern update of the 1931 German film "Maedchen in Uniform." 79m/C DVD. Ilene Graff, Kevin McCarthy, would-be cool guy to do? 96m/C VHS, DVD.

Loving 🌭🌭 1984 The full-length, snot-on-video pilot for the daytime TV soap opera, with various guest stars. Exteriors shot at C.W. Post Center on Long Island. 120m/C VHS. Lloyd Bridges, Geraldine Page. TV

Loving Couples 🌭🌭 1980 (PG) Two happily married couples meet at a weekend resort...and switch partners. Tired and predictable but it has its moments. 120m/C VHS, DVD. Shirley MacLaine, James Coburn, Susan Sarandon, Stephen Collins, Sally Kellerman; D: Jack Smight.

A Loving Father 🌭🌭 Aime ton pere 2002 Leo spent one time with his writing then with his son, Paul, but Paul's making up for lost time by kidnapping his father, interrupting his trip to pick up his Nobel Prize. Schmaltzy effort but Gerard Depardieu does as well enough opposite his real-life son, Guillaume. 100m/C VHS, DVD. Gerard Depardieu, Guillaume Depardieu, Sylvie Testud, Hiam Abbass, Julien Boisselier, Noemie Kocher; D: Jacob Berger; W: Edward A. Radtke, Jacob Berger, Pascal Bardiler; C: Pascal Marti; M: Jean-Claude Petit. VIDEO

Loving Jezebel 🌭🌭 1999 (R) If anything, writer/director Kwyn Bader's "Loving Jezebel" proves that Hill Harper ("The Skulls", "in Too Deep," etc.) is a terrific talent. The problem is, even at a mere 88 minutes, Bader's film seems long and even Harper can't act his way out of a weak and contrived script. The gist of the story is that he, Hill Harper, has a track record for falling in love with his friends' many a sit-com—with consistently bad results. Of course you have to give Harper credit for one thing, he has excellent taste in women as all of his "girlfriends" are "eye-candy" super models. 88m/C VHS, DVD. Hill Harper, Laurel Holloman, Nicole Ari Parker, Sandrine Holt, David Moscow, Elisa Donovan, Phylicia Rashad; D: Kwyn Bader; M: Kwyn Bader; C: Horacio Marquinez; M: Tony Prandatt.

Loving You 🌭🌭 1957 A small town boy with a musical style all his own becomes a big success thanks to the help of a female press agent. Features many early Elvis hits. 🌭Loving You, Teddy Bear, Lonesome Cowboy, Got a Lot of Livin' To Do; Party; Mean Woman Blues; Hot Dog, Lonesome Cowboy. 101m/C VHS, DVD. Elvis Presley, Wendell Corey, Lizabeth Scott, Dolores Hart, James Gleason, Paul Smith, Jana Lund, Grace Hayle; D: Hal Kanter; C: Charles Boyland; Lang Jr.; M: Walter Scharf.

The Low Down 🌭🌭 2000 Not much happens in this sketchy tale of London gameshow worker Frank (Gillen), who dreams of maybe becoming a sculptor while running the prop business with his less-than-eager roommates. Tiring of their layabout ways, he moves out, facilitating this hook-up with Ruby (Ashfield), the real estate agent. Film then follows, but not too closely or attentively, their budding romance and its passive-aggressiveness and growing dissatisfaction with his own life. Thewes's directorial debut is laid-back to the point of being comatose, but some interesting scenes do occur between Gillen and Ashfield. 96m/C VHS, GB Aidan Gillen, Kate Ashfield, Dean Lennox Kelly, Tobias Menzies, Rupert Proctor Samantha Powers; D: Jamie Thrawes; W: Jamie Thrawes; C: Igor Jadue-Lillo; M: Nick Currie, Fred Thomas.

The Low Life 🌭🌭½ 1995 (R) A "day in the life" sort of story about aspiring writer John (Cochrane) who comes to L.A. with high hopes but instead gets stuck in with a vicious drug lord, a sultry ex-girlfriend, and $20 million. Lots of fun stunts and one iners can't make up for major plot holes. 100m/C VHS, DVD. Keenan Ivory Wayans, Jada Pinkett Smith, Salli Richardson, Charles S. Dutton, Andrew Divoff, Corwin Hawkins; D: Keenen Ivory Wayans; W: Keenen Ivory Wayans.

A Low Down Dirty Shame 🌭🌭 1994 (R) Shame (Wayans) is a down-on-his-luck private eye, stuck with the obligatory wisecracking secretary, Peaches (Pinkett), who's hired by an old friend to find a vicious drug lord, a sultry landlord (LeGros), and row, his newly arrived loser cousin Andrew (Astin). He tries to cozy up to looker Sedgwick but she doesn't seem too interested—so what's a

---

Rory Cochrane, Kyra Sedgwick, Sean Astin, James LeGros, Christian Meoli, Shawnee Smith, J.T. Walsh, Renee Zellweger; *D:* George Hickenlooper; *W:* George Hickenlooper, John Enbom; *C:* Richard Crudo; *M:* Bill Boll.

The Lower Depths 🐾🐾½ 1978
Bas Fonds: Underground 1936 Renoir's adaptation of the Maxim Gorky play about a thief and a financially ruined baron learning about life from one another. In French with English subtitles. 92m/B VHS, DVD. *FR* Jean Gabin, Louis Jouvet, Vladimir Sokoloff, Robert Le Vigan, Suzy Prim; *D:* Jean Renoir; *W:* Jean Renoir, Charles Spaak; *C:* Jean Bachelet; *M:* Jean Wiener.

The Lower Depths 🐾🐾🐾½
Donzoko 1957 Kurosawa sets the Maxim Gorky play in Edo during the final Tokugawa period, using Noh theatre elements in depicting the lowly denizens of a low-rent hovel. In Japanese with English subtitles. 125m/B VHS, DVD. *JP* Toshiro Mifune, Isuzu Yamada, Ganjiro Nakamura, Kyoko Kagawa, Bokuzo Hidari; *D:* Akira Kurosawa; *W:* Akira Kurosawa, Hideo Oguni; *C:* Kazuo Yamazaki; *M:* Masaru Sato.

Lower Level 🐾 1991 (R) While working late, an attractive business woman becomes trapped in an office building by her psychotic secret admirer. 88m/C VHS, DVD. David Bradley, Elizabeth (Ward) Gracen, Jeff Yagher; *D:* Kristine Peterson; *W:* Joel Soisson; *C:* Wally Pfister; *M:* Terry Plumeri.

Loyalties 🐾🐾½ 1986 (R) A strong treatment of the issue of sexual abuse of girls by men, and of an upper-class woman's willingness to establish a true friendship with a woman of a so-called lower economic class. 98m/C VHS. *CA* Kenneth Welsh, Tantoo Cardinal, Susan Wooldridge, Vera Martin, Christopher Barrington-Leigh; *D:* Anne Wheeler; *W:* Sharon Riis; *M:* Michael Conway Baker.

Loyola, the Soldier Saint 1952
A biography of the founder of the Jesuits from his years as a page in the Spanish court to his daring exploits on the battle field and, finally, his spiritual awakening at the University of Paris. Narrated by Father Alfred J. Barrett. 93m/B VHS. Rafael Duran, Maria Rosa Jiménez; *D:* Jose Diaz Morales.

Lucas 🐾🐾🐾 1986 (PG-13) A high school brain falls in love with the new girl in town, and tries to win her by trying out for the football team. Genuine film about the perils of coming of age. Thoughtful, non-condescending, and humorous. 100m/C VHS, DVD. Corey Haim, Kerri Green, Charlie Sheen, Winona Ryder, Courtney Thorne-Smith, Tom (Thomas E.) Hodges; *D:* David Seltzer; *W:* David Seltzer; *M:* Dave Grusin.

Lucía, Lucía 🐾🐾🐾 2003 (R) *La Hija del Caníbal: The Cannibal's Daughter* 2003 (R) Middle-aged Lucia (Roth) is the unreliable narrator of this Mexican fable. Lucia's husband, Ramon (Moreno), disappears in the Mexico City airport. Since their marriage was unhappy, maybe she decided to abandon her, or maybe Ramon was kidnapped. Since the police are no help, Lucia turns to two neighbors for assistance—Felix (Alvarez-Novoa), an elderly Spanish Civil War veteran, and young and handsome Adrian (Becker). There's a botched ransom drop and Ramon's exposure as an embezzler and Lucia's tryst with Adrian and many, many red herrings. Maybe Lucia is just spinning one big tale (she turns out to be a writer). And maybe it just doesn't matter. Adapted from the novel "La Hija del Caníbal" by Rosa Montero. Spanish with subtitles. 113m/C VHS, DVD. *MX SP* Cecilia (Celia) Roth, Carlos Alvarez-Novoa, Kuno Becker, Jose Elias Moreno Jr., Margarita Isabel, Javier Diaz Duenas, Hector Ortega; *D:* Antonio Serrano; *W:* Antonio Serrano; *C:* Xavier Perez Grobet; *M:* Nacho Mastretta.

Lucie Aubrac 🐾🐾 1998 (R) In 1943, having freed her Resistance fighter husband, Raymond Samuel (Auteuil), from the Vichy police, Lucie Aubrac (Bouquet), is not about to let the Germans execute him. Even if it means using her pregnancy and tricking Gestapo commander Klaus Barbie (Ferch). Noble but rather emotionless. Based on a true story and Aubrac's novel "Ils Partiront Dans l'Ivresse." French with subtitles. 116m/C

VHS. *FR* Daniel Auteuil, Carole Bouquet, Patrice Chereau, Heino Ferch, Jean-Roger Milo, Jean Martin, Bernard Verley, Andrzej Seweryn, Hubert Saint Macary, Eric Boucher, Gregoire Oestermann; *D:* Claude Berri; *W:* Claude Berri; *C:* Vincenzo Marano; *M:* Philippe Sarde.

The Lucifer Complex 🐾 1978
Nazi doctors are cloning exact duplicates of such world leaders as the Pope and the President of the United States on a remote South American island in the year 1996. 91m/C VHS, DVD. Robert Vaughn, Merrie Lynn Ross, Keenan Wynn, Aldo Ray; *D:* David L. Hewitt, Kenneth Hartford.

Luck of the Draw 🐾🐾 2000 (R)
Ex-con Marshall, who finds going straight to be very dull, finds some unexpected excitement when a couple of counterfeit printing plates come into his possession. He soon realizes that a lot of unsavory types are after the plates, including mob boss Hopper. Run-of-the-mill. 108m/C VHS, DVD. James Marshall, Michael Madsen, Ice-T, Frank Gorshin, Eric Roberts, Dennis Hopper, Wendy Benson, William Forsythe, Sasha Mitchell, Richard Riccolo; *D:* Luca Bercovici; *W:* Namon Ami, Rick Bloggs, Kandice King; *C:* Keith L. Smith; *M:* Stephen (Steve) Edwards.

Lucky Break 🐾🐾 2001 (PG-13)
Smalltime crooks Jimmy (Nesbitt) and Rudy (James) wind up in the same prison after a bank job gone wrong. Eccentric prison governor Mortimer (Plummer) loves musicals and has written one of his own. Jimmy encourages Mortimer to let the prisoners stage his opus and plans an escape attempt during the performance. Film gets schzoid with comic rehearsals, a tentative romance between Jimmy and support worker Annabel (Williams), a suicide, and the confusing prison break. 109m/C VHS, DVD. *GB* James Nesbitt, Lennie James, Christopher Plummer, Olivia Williams, Timothy Spall, Bill Nighy, Ron Cook, Frank Harper, Peter Wight, Celia Imrie, Raymond Waring, Julian Barratt; *D:* Peter Cattaneo; *W:* Ronan Bennett; *C:* Alwin Kuchler; *M:* Anne Dudley.

Lucky Cisco Kid 🐾🐾½ 1940
Romero takes over from Warner Baxter in the fourth entry in the series, with Martin as his loyal sidekick. This time a rustler and his gang are stealing cattle and trying to place the blame on the Kid's name to place the blame. Fast-paced with Romero appropriately debonair. Andrews' screen debut. 67m/B VHS. Cesar Romero, Chris-Pin (Ethier Crispin Martin) Martin, Mary Beth Hughes, Dana Andrews, Evelyn Venable, Joseph (Joe) Sawyer, Francis Ford; *D:* H. Bruce Humberstone; *W:* Robert Ellis, Helen Logan; *C:* Lucien N. Andriot; *M:* Cyril Mockridge.

Lucky Devil 🐾½ 1925 Lucky devil wins car and motors around the country to the tune of organ music. 63m/B VHS. Richard Dix, Esther Ralston, Edna May Oliver, Tom Findley; *D:* Frank Tuttle.

Lucky Devils 🐾🐾½ 1933 A group of Hollywood stuntmen call themselves the "Lucky Devils" and live by the motto "a stuntman makes a bad stuntman." This proves to be true when Slugger Jones (Bakewell) dies on a stunt shortly after his marriage. When Skipper (Boyd) marries an extra he quickly loses his edge but tries again to pull off one last stunt when he needs the money to cover his wife's hospital bill. 64m/B VHS. William Boyd, Dorothy Wilson, William Gargan, Roscoe Ates, William "Billy" Bakewell; *D:* Ralph Ince; *W:* Agnes Christine Johnston, Ben Markson. VIDEO

Lucky Jim 🐾🐾½ 1958 A junior lecturer in history at a small university tries to get himself in good graces with the head of his department, but is doomed from the start by doing the wrong things at the worst possible times. Minus the social satire of the Kingsley Amis novel on which it was based; what's left is a cheerful comedy. 91m/B VHS. *GB* Ian Carmichael, Terry-Thomas, Hugh Griffith, Sharon Acker, Jean Anderson, Maureen Connell, Clive Morton, John Welsh, Reginald Beckwith, Kenneth Griffith, Jeremy Hawk, Harry Fowler; *D:* John Boulting, Roy Boulting; *W:* Jeffrey Dell, Patrick Campbell; *C:* Mutz Greenbaum; *M:* John Addison.

Lucky Luciano 1974 (R) *A Proposito Luciano; RE: Lucky Luciano* 1974 (R) A violent depiction of the final years of Lucky Luciano, gangster kingpin. 108m/C VHS, DVD. *IT*

FR Edmond O'Brien, Rod Steiger, Vincent Gardenia, Gian Marie Volonte; *D:* Francesco Rosi; *C:* Pasqualino De Santis.

Lucky Luke 🐾🐾½ 1994 (PG) Fastest gun in the west brings the law to Daisy Town, aided by his horse, Jolly Jumper—material but amusing. 91m/C VHS, DVD. Terence Hill, Nancy Morgan, Ron Carey; *D:* Terence Hill; *W:* Rene Goscinny; *C:* Carlo Tafani, Gianfranco Transunto; *M:* David Grover, Aaron Schroeder; *V:* Roger Miller.

Lucky Me 🐾🐾 1954 A group of theatre entertainers are stranded in Miami and are forced to work in a hotel kitchen. They soon acquire the support of a wealthy oilman (Goodwin) who invests in their show, but not before his spoiled daughter tries to thwart all plans. ♪Lucky Me; Superstition Song; I Speak to the Stars; Take a Memo to the Moon; Love You Dearly; Bluebells of Broadway; Parisian Pretties; Wanna Sing Like an Angel; High Hopes. 100m/C VHS, DVD. Doris Day, Robert Cummings, Phil Silvers, Eddie Foy Jr., Nancy Walker, Martha Hyer, Bill Goodwin, Marcel Dalio, James Burke, Jack Shea, William "Billy" Bakewell, Charles Cane, Ray Teal, Tom Powers, Angie Dickinson, Dolores Dorn; *D:* Jack Donohue.

Lucky Number Slevin 🐾🐾🐾 2006 (R) This too-twisty thriller owes a lot to "Pulp Fiction" and "The Usual Suspects," although it doesn't come close to their league. What it does have is the wicked gravitas of Freeman and Kingsley as rival New York mobsters (known respectively as "The Boss" and "The Rabbi") who both mistake sweet-faced Slevin (Hartnett) for his missing friend Nick, who owes big money to both men. The Boss will forgive the debt if Slevin will kill someone, while the Rabbi just wants the cash. Meanwhile, sexy neighbor Lindsey (Liu), who's a coroner, is romancing the hunk and trying to help him avoid certain death—maybe at the hands of hitman Mr. Goodkat (Willis). Except, nothing is really as it appears to be. 110m/C DVD, HD DVD. *US* Josh Hartnett, Morgan Freeman, Ben Kingsley, Lucy Liu, Stanley Tucci, Bruce Willis, Peter Outerbridge, Mykelti Williamson, Danny Aiello, Robert Forster, Dorian Missick, Jennifer Miller, Kevin Chamberlin, Oliver Davis, Michael Rubenfeld; *D:* Paul McGuigan; *W:* Jason Smilovic; *C:* Peter Sova; *M:* J. Ralph.

Lucky Numbers 🐾🐾 2000 (R)
Here's a lucky number for you: Zero. That's the amount of time you should spend on this unfortunate comedy. TV weatherman Russ (Travolta) is caught up in a lavish lifestyle he can't afford because unseasonably warm weather is ruining his on-the-side snowmobile business. He schemes with the station's morally lax lotto ball girl Crystal (Kudrow) to fix a jackpot lottery, with her oafish cousin Walter (Moore) as the front man with the ticket. Their plan slips out, so they're hounded by a host of greedy dimwits hoping to get in on the action. Resnick, who hails from Harrisburg PA, where the movie is set, apparently has no qualms painting his fellow townspeople as amoral losers. Loosely based on a 1980 attempt to fix the Pennsylvania State lottery. 105m/C VHS, DVD. John Travolta, Lisa Kudrow, Tim Roth, Ed O'Neill, Michael Rapaport, Daryl (Chill) Mitchell, Bill Pullman, Richard Schiff, Michael Moore, Michael Weston, Sam McMurray; *D:* Nora Ephron; *W:* Adam Resnick; *C:* John Lindley; *M:* George Fenton.

Lucky Partners 🐾🐾 1940 When an artist and an errand girl share a winning lottery ticket, funny complications arise as they embark on a fantasy honeymoon. Although Rogers' innocence and Coleman's savoir faire provide an interesting contrast, the script isn't equal to the status of its stars. 101m/B VHS. Ronald Colman, Ginger Rogers, Jack Carson, Spring Byington, Harry Davenport, Cecilia Loftus; *D:* Lewis Milestone; *W:* Lewis Milestone, Allan Scott, John Van Druten; *C:* Robert De Grasse; *M:* Dimitri Tiomkin.

Lucky Seven 🐾🐾 2003 (PG-13)
Amy's dying mother (O'Grady) informs her seven-year-old daughter that she has drawn a timeline for her life, including the fact that Amy will marry her seventh boyfriend. Amy (Williams) has always fol-

lowed her mother's advice, but the successful lawyer now has a problem—she's fallen for boyfriend #6, Peter (Dempsey). So should she follow her heart or wait for #7, who's the equally handsome and charming Daniel (Rowe). Amusing romantic comedy with a very attractive cast. 90m/C VHS, DVD. Kimberly Williams, Patrick Dempsey, Brad Rowe, Gail O'Grady; *D:* Harry Winer; *W:* Jessica Barondes; *C:* Jon Joffin; *M:* Danny Lux. CABLE

Lucky Stiff 🐾🐾 1988 (PG) A fat, unpopular dweeb has the shock of his life when a radiant woman falls in love with him, the strangeness of which becomes evident when he meets her very weird family. 83m/C VHS, DVD. Donna Dixon, Joe Alaskey, Jeff Kober, Elizabeth Arlen, Charles Frank, Barbara Howard; *D:* Anthony Perkins; *W:* Pat Proft.

Lucky Terror 🐾 1936 Routine Hoot cowboy drama. 60m/B VHS. Hoot Gibson, Lona Andre, Charles "Blackie" King; *D:* Alan James.

Lucky Texan 🐾½ 1934 Wayne plays a tough easterner who goes West and finds himself involved with miners and claim jumpers. 61m/B VHS, DVD. John Wayne, George "Gabby" Hayes, Yakima Canutt, Lloyd Whitlock, Eddie (Ed, Eddy, Edwin) Parker, Gordon DeMain; *D:* Robert North Bradbury; *W:* Robert North Bradbury; *C:* Archie Stout.

Lucky You 🐾🐾 2007 (PG-13) Huck Cheever (Bana) is a talented poker player who makes his living fleecing tourists in Las Vegas but dreams of making it big in the World Championship (Series) of Poker. Unfortunately, his emotions usually get in the way, especially when it comes to dealing with his deadbeat father, L.C. (Duvall), who becomes his poker arch-nemesis. On his way to a showdown with Dad, Huck alternately romances and rips off struggling lounge singer Billie (Barrymore). Hansen obviously loves his characters, poker, and the eccentrics that make up Las Vegas's underbelly, but it's not enough to help this movie's desperate identity crisis. Had it not sat on the shelf through the boom of the poker craze this would have been a better-than-standard poker movie; instead, it's a weak romantic drama with a cast and director who should have created something much better. 123m/C DVD. *US* Eric Bana, Drew Barrymore, Debra Messing, Horatio Sanz, Jean Smart, Charles Martin Smith, Robert Downey Jr., Kelvin Han Yee, Evan Jones, Michael Shannon; *D:* Curtis Hanson; *W:* Curtis Hanson, Eric Roth; *C:* Peter Deming; *M:* Christopher Young.

Luckytown 🐾🐾 2000 (R) Part road movie, part Vegas movie, part family ties, and none of the parts turn out to fit together. Oklahoman Lidda (Dusnt) gets a check on her 18th birthday from her long-gone dad, gambler Charlie (Caan), so she decides to track him down in Vegas. Along for the ride is store clerk and potential beau Colonel (Kartheiser), who happens to know his way around the cards himself. Only it turns out dad is in big trouble with club owner Tony (Miano) and the kids are soon caught in the middle. 101m/C VHS, DVD. Kirsten Dunst, Vincent Kartheiser, James Caan, Robert Miano, Luis Guzman, Jennifer Garels, Theresa Russell; *D:* Paul Nicholas; *W:* Brendon Beseth; *C:* Denis Maloney; *M:* Greg Edmonson.

Lucy and Desi: Before the Laughter 🐾🐾½ 1991 (PG-13) The meeting and early married life of actress/comedian Lucille Ball and Cuban bandleader Desi Arnaz is depicted in this routine biopic. Film depicts Desi's womanizing, their struggles with fame, and their efforts to get their show on the air. Fisher does well as TV's favorite redhead but this effort is melodramatic. Daughter Lucy Arnaz vehemently opposed this depiction of her parents life. 95m/C VHS. Frances Fisher, Maurice Benard, John Wheeler, Robin Pearson Rose; *D:* Charles Jarrott; *W:* William Luce. TV

L'Udienza 🐾🐾½ 1971 A bizarre black comedy about a guy who does anything he can, at any criminal cost, to obtain an audience with the Pope. In Italian with subtitles. 111m/C VHS. *IT* Claudia Cardinale, Ugo Tognazzi; *D:* Marco Ferreri.

Ludwig 1972 (PG) Lavish-but-slow epic bio of Bavaria's mad monarch, Ludwig II (Berger), who built extravagant fantasy castles and sponsored composer Richard Wagner (Howard), whom the king became obsessed with. Italian with subtitles. 231m/C VHS, TT GE Helmut Berger, Trevor Howard, Romy Schneider, Silvana Mangano, Helmut Griem, Gert Frobe; **D:** Luchino Visconti. **C:** Armando Nannuzzi.

Lullaby of Broadway 1951 Many songs highlight this flimsy musical about a girl (Day) who ventures from England to the Big Apple in search of an acting career. She soon discovers that her mom has become a has-been actress now performing in a Greenwich Village dive. Day struggles to gain her own success while coping with her mother's downfall. ♪Lullaby of Broadway; You're Getting to Be a Habit With Me; Just One of Those Things; Somebody Loves Me; I Love the Way You Say Goodnight; Fine and Dandy; Please Don't Talk About Me When I'm Gone; A Shanty in Old Shanty Town; We'd Like to Go On A Trip. 92m/C VHS, DVD. Doris Day, Gene Nelson, S.Z. Sakall, Billy DeWolfe, Gladys George, Florence Bates; **D:** David Butler.

Luggage of the Gods 1987 (G) A lost tribe of cave people are confronted with civilization when suitcases fall from an airplane. Low-budget comedy reminiscent of "The Gods Must Be Crazy." 78m/C VHS, Mark Stolzenberg, Gabriel Barre, Gwen Ellison; **D:** David Kendall.

Luminous Motion 2000 Philip (Lloyd) is an introspective 10-year-old who spends his life on the road travelling in a red impala with his mother (Unger), a beautiful, depressed lush who drifts from man to man. But the only male she's really close to is her son—until Philip's father (Sheridan) finds them and wants to reclaim his family. Except the boundaries between Philip's reality and his imagination aren't very clear at all. Based on Bradfield's novel "The History of Luminous Motion." 94m/C VHS, DVD. Eric Lloyd, Deborah Kara Unger, Jamey Sheridan, Terry Kinney, Paz de la Huerta, James Berland; **D:** Bette Gordon; **W:** Scott Bradfield, Robert Roth; **C:** Teodoro Maniaci; **M:** Lesley Barber.

Luminarias 1999 (R) Romantic comedy about four Hispanic friends looking for love in East L.A. and meeting to console each other at the Luminarias restaurant. Lawyer Andrea (Fernandez), who's divorcing her philandering husband (Beltran), finds herself attracted to anglo Joseph (Bakula). Therapist Sofia (DuBois) has always tried to distance herself from her roots but gets is surprised by her feelings for cute Mexican waiter Pablo (Lopez). Artist Lilly (Moya) is hoping to change her luck in love with Korean Lu (Lim) only to run into prejudice from his parents and sexy designer Irene (Ortelli) who's sworn off sex for Lent and is trying to accept her cross-dressing gay brother (Rivas). The friendships are believable even if there's too much going on with the plot. 101m/C VHS, DVD. Evelina Fernandez, Marta DuBois, Dyana Ortelli, Angela Moya, Scott Bakula, Robert Beltran, Sal Lopez, Andrew Lim, Luis Valenzuela; **W:** Evelina Fernandez; **C:** Alex Phillips Jr.; **M:** Eric Allaman.

Lumiere 1976 (R) An acclaimed drama about four actresses who, during the course of one night together, make pivotal decisions about their lives and relationships. Moreau's first directorial effort; dubbed. 104m/C VHS, DVD. Harvey Keitel, Lucia Bose, Francine Racette, Caroline Cartier, Bruno Ganz, Rene Feret, Niels A'restrup, Jeanne Moreau; **C:** Alik Sakharov; **M:** Graeme Revell.

Lulu on the Bridge 1998 (PG-13) Jazz saxman Izzy Maurer (Keitel) sinks into depression when he can no longer perform. Walking one night, Izzy stumbles across a dead body and finds no ID—only a phone number and a mysterious stone that emits a blue light. Izzy calls the number, which belongs to actress/waitress Celia (Sorvino), and their first meeting finds them instantly in love (or some variation). Meanwhile, the mysterious Dr. Van Horn (Dafoe) questions Izzy about finding the stone. And things don't get much clearer. First solo directorial effort for Auster, who co-directed Keitel in "Blue in the Face," the spinoff to his screenplay "Smoke." 104m/C VHS, DVD. Harvey Keitel, Mira Sorvino, Willem Dafoe, Gina Gershon, Mandy Patinkin, Vanessa Redgrave, Victor Argo, Kevin Corrigan, Richard Edson; **D:** Paul Auster; **W:** Paul Auster; **C:** Alik Sakharov; **M:** Astor Piazzolla.

Luna: Spirit of the Whale 2007 (PG) A young orphaned killer whale has taken up residence in a small Canadian coastal town bay and government official Priestley has been hired to capture the whale and try to return it to its pod. Only the local native peoples would rather that the whale was left alone. Based on a true story. 93m/C DVD. C4 Jason Priestley, Adam Beach, Graham Greene, Tantoo Cardinal, Michelle Harrison, Aaron Miko; **D:** Don McBrearty; **W:** Elizabeth Stewart. **C:** Jan Kiesser. TV

Lunatic, The 1991 "Some minds should be wasted" according to the film promo and if you're in the mood for an amateur mind (and time) waster, this is for you. High schoolers in the woods encounter mayhem in the best horror tradition as the innocents are slaughtered by an escapee from the local lunatic asylum. The Jamaican scenery, a few bawdy laughs, and a great reggae soundtrack make this one worthwhile. 93m/C VHS. GB Julie Wallace, Paul Campbell, Reggie Carter, Carl Bradshaw; **D:** Lol Creme; **M:** Wally Badarou.

Lumumba 2000 Powerful biopic of Patrice Lumumba, the first elected Prime Minister of the Congo, who was assassinated mere months after the country gained its independence from Belgium. Director-writer Peck, who also filmed the documentary "Lumumba—Death of a Prophet" uses flashbacks to show Lumumba's ascent from beer salesman to prominence in the independence movement and his eventual rise to, and violent removal from power. Peck neccesarily omits some details of Lumumba's early life, but in the process glosses over his early work in the Congolese National Movement. French actor Ebouaney gives a masterful performance, finding the humanity behind the icon. Filmed in Zimbabwe and Mozambique because the Congo was suffering through yet another civil war. 115m/C VHS, DVD, FR EE GE Eriq Ebouaney, Alex Descas, Theophile Moussa Sowie, Maka Kotto, Dieudonne Kabongo, Pascal Nzonzi, Mariam Kaba; **D:** Raoul Peck; **W:** Raoul Peck, Pascal Bonitzer; **C:** Bernard Lutic; **M:** Jean-Claude Petit.

Luna e L'Altra 1996 Dizzy schoolteacher Luna (Forte) is 'the butt of practical jokes by her students and ignored by the other faculty. Dutiful and self-effacing, she's also the secret crush of school custodian Angelo (Nichetti). But Luna has a hidden side that comes to the surface thanks to magician Igor's magic lantern and it turns out to be a sexy one. Italian with subtitles. 92m/C VHS. 'Tiaia Forte, Maurizio Nichetti, Aurelio Fierro, Luigi Burruano; **D:** Maurizio Nichetti; **M:** Carlo Siliotto.

Luna Park 1991 In contemporary Russia, Andrei (Gouttine) is the leader of a gang of body-builder, right-wing skinheads who beat up Jews, foreigners, and anyone else they dislike. Then the anti-Semitic Andrei learns his father is Jewish and he frantically searches through Moscow to find him and discover his past. In Russian with subtitles. 105m/C VHS, RU Oleg Borisov, Andrei Gouttine, Natalya Yegorova; **D:** Pavel Lungin; **W:** Pavel Lungin; Lounguine.

Lunatics: A Love Story 1992 (PG-13) Hank (Raimi) is an ex-mental patient poet suffering from hallucinations and afraid to leave his Los Angeles apartment. For companionship he dials a party-line until, one day, he misdials and insteads gets the number of a local pay telephone, which is answered by a naive woman dumped by her boyfriend. When Nancy (Foreman) decides to visit Hank you learn she's as crazy as he is—so it only makes sense they would fall in love. A well-acted fable of how love fragilely connects even the most unlikely of people. 87m/C VHS. Theodore (Ted) Raimi, Deborah Foreman, Bruce Campbell, Brian McCree, Eddie Rosmaya, Michele Stacey, George Aguilar; **D:** Josh Becker; **W:** Josh Becker; **C:** Jeffrey Dougherty; **M:** Joseph LoDuca.

Lunatics & Lovers 1976 (PG) Musician meets a bizarre nobleman who is in love with an imaginary woman. 92m/C VHS. IT Marcello Mastroianni, Lino Toffalo; **D:** Flavo Mogherin.

Lunch Wagon Come 'n' Get It; Lunch Wagon Girls 1981 (R) Two co-eds are given a restaurant to manage during summer vacation and wind up involved in a hilarious diamond chase and sex romp. 88m/C VHS. Rick Podell, Candy Moore, Pamela Bryant, Rosanne Katon; **D:** Ernest Pintoff.

Lupo 1970 (G) When threatened with the loss of his home and the separation of his family, an exuberant Greek man challenges the modern world. 99m/C VHS. Yehuda Barkan, Gabi Armoni, Esther Greenberg; **D:** Menahem Golan.

Lure of the Islands 1942 Federal agents track wanted criminals to an island retreat in this highly predictable low-budget thriller. 61m/B VHS. Margie Hart, Robert Lowery, Guinn 'Big Boy' Williams, Warren Hymer, Gale Storm; **D:** Jean Yarbrough.

Lure of the Sila 1949 Italian melodrama about a young peasant girl infiltrating a landowner's home in order to avenge the death of her brother and mother. Dubbed and more interesting than it sounds. 72m/B VHS. IT Silvana Mangano, Vittorio Gassman; **D:** Duilio Coletti.

Lured 1947 Ball gives a fine dramatic performance in Sirk's glossy thriller. Sandra (Ball) is an American dancer in London whose friend falls victim to a lonelyhearts killer. She agrees to act as a decoy for Scotland Yard even while getting involved with nightclub owner Robert Fleming (Sanders), who turns out to be one of the suspects. 103m/B VHS, DVD. Lucille Ball, George Sanders, Charles Coburn, Cedric Hardwicke, Boris Karloff, Alan Mowbray, George Zucco, Joseph Calleia, Tanis Chandler, Alan Napier, Robert Coote; **D:** Douglas Sirk; **W:** Leo Rosten; **C:** William H. Daniels; **M:** Michel Michelet.

Lured Innocence 1997 (R) Steamy romance in a small town leads to murderous impulses. Elsie (Shelton) is having an affair with older, married Rick (Hopper). Then his ailing wife (Shire) finds out and threatens the twosome. The lovers aren't pleased and there's an eventual murder trial where one of the key witnesses is a newspaper reporter (Gummersall), who was also Elsie's lover. 97m/C VHS, DVD. Dennis Hopper, Marley Shelton, Devon Gummersall, Talia Shire; **D:** Kikuo Kawasaki; **W:** Kikuo Kawasaki; **C:** Irek Hartowicz.

Lurkers WOOf! 1988 (R) An unappealing metaphysical morass about a woman who has been haunted throughout her life by...something. 90m/C VHS, DVD. Christine Moore, Gary Warner, Marina Taylor, Carissa Channing, Tom Billett; **D:** Roberta Findlay; **W:** Ed Kelleher, Harriette Vidal; **C:** Roberta Findlay.

Lurking Fear 1994 (R) The town of Lefferts Corner has suffered from generations of horror thanks to man-eating ghouls that dwell beneath the local graveyard and arise whenever a storm breaks out. The inhabitants prepare to fight back but their plan is hindered by the arrival of a group of criminals who are after a fortune supposedly hidden in one of the graves. ...Lovecraft. 78m/C VHS. Jon Finch, Blake Bailey, Ashley Laurence, Jeffrey Combs, Paul Mantee, Allison Mackie, Joe Leavengood, Vincent Schiavelli; **D:** C. Courtney Joyner; **W:** C. Courtney Joyner; **M:** Jim Manzie.

Luscious Vivid 1997 (R) It's about sex. Cole (Shelan) is a painter having inspiration problems. Then he splashes girlfriend Billie (Wuhrer) with paint and they have sex on the canvas. Suddenly his art is selling like hotcakes but Billie gets a little tired being a literal paint brush. An unrated version has three more minutes of sex and nudity. 83m/C VHS, DVD. Stephen Shellen, Karl Wahrer; **D:** Evan Georgiades.

Lush 2001 (R) The New Orleans setting is the best thing about this limp drama. Alcoholic golf pro Lionel (Scott) is friends with alcoholic lawyer Carter (Harris), who names his buddy beneficiary in an insurance policy. The lawyer promptly gets murdered and Exley decides to go on the lam from the suspicious cops, winding up taking refuge with two women. 96m/C VHS, DVD. Campbell Scott, Jared Harris, Laura Linney, Laurel Holloman; **D:** Mark Gibson; **W:** Mark Gibson; **C:** Caroline Champetier; **M:** Barrett Martin. VIDEO

Lush Life 1994 (R) New York jazz session musicians Al (Goldblum) and Buddy (Whitaker) roam the city's musical scene until dawn, on the prowl for food, women, and ever more music. When trumpeter Buddy is diagnosed with an operable brain tumor, saxophonist Al decides on a grand final gesture—a Park Avenue farewell bash, though no one is told. Great jazz soundtrack, fine acting, and atmospheric use of the Big Apple. 96m/C VHS. Jeff Goldblum, Forest Whitaker, Kathy Baker, Lois Chiles, Don Cheadle; **D:** Michael Elias; **W:** Michael Elias. CABLE

Lust, Caution Se, Jie 2007 (NC-17) Director Lee extensively expanded Eileen Chang's short story to create this broad epic of intrigue and lust in Japanese-occupied China during World War II. Wong (Wei) is a Chinese patriot involved in a plot to assassinate Mr. Yee (Leung), a collaborator with the Japanese. Once she seduces him, however, she begins to realize that she's in way over her head. Wei and Leung are both excellent, but Lee's adaptation goes beyond the original short story, and much of the early portion of the film seems unfocused, with lots of filler. Earned an NC-17 rating and a great deal of attention because of its extremely erotic and explicit sex scenes. 158m/C DVD. US HK CH Tony Leung Chiu-Wai, Tang Wei, Joan Chen, Wang Leehom, Chu Tsz-ying; **D:** Ang Lee; **W:** James Schamus, Wang Hui-ling; **C:** Rodrigo Prieto; **M:** Alexandre Desplat.

Lust and Revenge 1995 When wealthy George Oliphant (Haywood) needs a tax break, he commissions a statue (to be donated to the National Gallery) and gets daughter Georgina (Karvan) to choose the subject and artist. Flirty Georgina hires lesbian sculptress Lily (Eagger) and decides on the creation of a male nude, for which Karl-Heinz Applebaum (Hope) is hired to pose. Appleabaum's religious wife Cecilia (Dobrowolska) is not pleased, especially when hubby begins an affair. But she's also not above plotting a suitable revenge. Last role for Hargreaves (a cameo as a gallery habitue) while Hughes, who also worked for director Cox in "My First Wife," plays a male financial adviser. 95m/C VHS. AU Claudia Karvan, Chris Haywood, Nicholas Hope, Gosia Dobrowolska, Victoria Eagger, Norman Kaye; **Cameos:** Wendy Hughes, John Hargreaves; **D:** Paul Cox; **W:** Paul Cox, John Clarke; **C:** Nino Martinetti; **M:** Paul Grabowsky.

Lust for a Vampire To Love a Vampire 1971 (R) The sanguine tale of a deadly vampire who indiscriminately preys on pupils and teachers when she enrolls at a British finishing school. Moody and erotically charged, with an impressive ending. Quasi-sequel to "The Vampire

"Lovers." 95m/C VHS, DVD. *GB* Ralph Bates, Barbara Jefford, Suzanna Leigh, Michael Johnson, Yutte Stensgaard, Pippa Steele, Helen Christie, David Healy, Mike Raven; *D:* Jimmy Sangster; *W:* Tudor Gates; *C:* David Muir.

Lust for Dracula woof! 2004 (R) Softcore Dracula story has Mina Harker (Mundae) kept in a drugged stupor by husband Jonathan (Wells)—so drugged that she apparently doesn't realize her husband is a woman. But then, so is Dracula (Caine) and all the vamp minions. Mina's sister Abigail (Shelly Jones) wants to destroy Dracula and get Jonathan for herself. Let's face it, no one's watching this for the plot but for skin and girl-on-girl action. 90m/C DVD. Darian Caine, Misty Mundae, Shelly Jones, Julian Wells, Andrea Davis; *D:* Anthony Marsiglia; *W:* Anthony Marsiglia; *C:* Dang Lenaewaz; *M:* Don Mike. **VIDEO**

Lust for Freedom 1987 An undercover cop decides to hit the road after she sees her partner gunned down. She winds up near the California-Mexico border, where she is wrongly imprisoned with a number of other young women in a white slavery business. This low-budget film includes lots of steamy women-behind-bars sex scenes. 92m/C VHS, DVD. Melanie Coll, William J. Kulzer; *D:* Eric Louizi.

Lust for Gold 1949 Ford battles against greedy former lover Lupino and her husband for control of the Lost Dutchman gold mine. 90m/B VHS, DVD. Ida Lupino, Glenn Ford, Gig Young, William Prince, Edgar Buchanan, Will Geer, Paul Ford, Jay Silverheels; *D:* S. Sylvan Simon; *M:* George Duning.

Lust for Life 1956 Absorbing, serious biography of Vincent Van Gogh, from his first paintings to his death. Remarkable for Douglas' furiously convincing portrayal. Featuring dozens of actual Van Gogh works from private collections. Based on an Irving Stone novel, produced by John Houseman. 122m/C VHS, DVD. Kirk Douglas, Anthony Quinn, James Donald, Pamela Brown, Everett Sloane, Henry Daniell, Niall MacGinnis, Noel Purcell, Lionel Jeffries, Jill Bennett; *D:* Vincente Minnelli; *M:* Miklos Rozsa. Oscars '56: Support. Actor (Quinn); Golden Globes '57: Actor—Drama (Douglas); N.Y. Film Critics '56: Actor (Douglas).

Luster 1985 (R) A look at the L.A. gay/punk scene that coasts by on its own oddball charms. Skateboarding, blue-haired Jackson (Herwick) works at a record store while aspiring to be a poet. After too many drunken, druggy sexual encounters, he decides he needs a real romance—maybe with crush Billy (Blechman) who'd rather just be friends. Meanwhile, preppie customer Derek (Thibodeau) thinks Jackson is swell. Then add to the mix naive newcomer Jed (Wyatt), willing to try anything, and closeted rock star Sonny Spike (Garson), who has an unsavory past with Billy, as well as Jackson's chic lesbian pals, Alyssa (Gidley) and Sandra (Melvoin). 90m/C DVD. Justin Herwick, Shane Powers, B. Wyatt, Jonah Blechman, Pamela Gidley, Sean Thibodeau, Willie Garson, Susan Melvoin; *D:* Everet Lewis; *W:* Everet Lewis; *C:* Humberto Deluna; *M:* Michael Leon.

The Lusty Men 1952 Two rival rodeo champions, both in love with the same woman, work the rodeo circuit until a tragic accident occurs. Mitchum turns in a fine performance as the has-been rodeo star trying to make it big again. 113m/B VHS. Robert Mitchum, Susan Hayward, Arthur Kennedy, Arthur Hunnicutt; *D:* Nicholas Ray; *C:* Lee Garmes.

Luther 1974 (G) A well-acted characterization of Martin Luther's development from a young seminarian to his leadership of the Reformation Movement. 112m/C VHS, DVD. Stacy Keach, Patrick Magee, Hugh Griffith, Robert Stephens, Alan Badel, Julian Glover, Judi Dench, Leonard Rossiter, Maurice Denham, Peter Cellier, Thomas Heathcote, Malcolm Stoddard, Bruce Carstairs; *D:* Guy Green; *W:* Edward Anhalt, John Osborne; *C:* Frederick A. (Freddie) Young; *M:* John Addison.

Luther 2003 (PG-13) Tame religious biopic follows the 16th century law student turned young monk who started the Protestant religious movement. Despite depicting a plethora of the remarkable moments that made up Luther's life, pic lacks focus that might have illuminated this important historical figure. Refusing to recant his beliefs, including the famous 95 Theses questioning Catholic Church practices, Luther was excommunicated, which sparked the Reformation and Protestantism. Fiennes gives an able but diluted performance in the title role while Ustinov as Prince Frederick is at his scene-stealing best. 112m/C VHS, DVD. *GE* Joseph Fiennes, Alfred Molina, Jonathan Firth, Claire Cox, Peter Ustinov, Bruno Ganz, Uwe Ochsenknecht, Matthieu Carriere, Jochen Horst; *D:* Eric Till; *W:* Camille Thomasson, Bart Gavigan; *C:* Robert Fraisse; *M:* Richard Harvey.

Luther the Geek woof! 1990 Little Luther's visit to the circus is dramatically changed when he sees the geek, a sideshow freak. Since then Luther has taken to biting off chicken's heads and drinking their blood in his small Illinois town; the town will never be the same. (And neither will you if you watch this stupid film.) 90m/C VHS, DVD. Edward Terry, Joan Roth, J. Jerome Clarke, Tom Mills, Stacy Haiduk; *D:* Carlton J. Albright; *W:* Whitey Styles; *C:* David Knox.

Luv 1967 (PG) Although good cast tries hard, they can't do much with this comic farce. Three intellectuals, including one that's suicidal, discuss the trials and tribulations of their middle-class New York existence. 95m/C VHS. Jack Lemmon, Peter Falk, Elaine May; *D:* Clive Donner; *W:* Murray Schisgal; *C:* Ernest Laszlo.

The Luzhin Defence 2000 (PG-13) Luzhin (Turturro) is an eccentric Russian chess genius who is staying at an Italian lakeside resort in 1929 preparing for an important match. Also preparing for a match—the marital kind—is Russian emigre Natalia (Watson) and her aristocratic mother Vera (James). And Luzhin is not the man Vera has in mind for her daughter, no matter what Natalia thinks. But as the stress of the match takes its toll on Luzhin, he believes he cannot have both love and the game. Based on the 1930 novel by Vladimir Nabokov. 106m/C VHS, DVD. *FR GB* John Turturro, Emily Watson, Geraldine James, Stuart Wilson, Christopher Thompson, Peter Blythe, Orla Brady, Fabio Santor; *D:* Marleen Gorris; *W:* Peter Berry; *C:* Bernard Lutic; *M:* Alexandre Desplat.

Luzia 1988 (PG) Ohana stars as a tough and sexy Brazilian cowgirl who is caught in the middle of a class struggle where the personal is definitely political. Her horseriding skills and beauty give her options in both lifestyles. Will she choose to side with the squatters or the wealthy landowners? In Portuguese with English subtitles. 112m/C VHS. *BR* Claudia Ohana, Thales Pan Chacon, Jose de Abreu, Luiza Falcao; *D:* Fabio Barreto.

Lydia 1941 Sentimental drama in which an elderly lady (Oberon) gets to relive her romantic past when she has a reunion with four of her lost loves. Well acted and directed, Oberon gives one of her best performances ever. Adapted from the highly regarded French film "Un Carnet de Bal." 98m/B VHS. Merle Oberon, Joseph Cotten, Alan Marshal, George Reeves; *D:* Julien Duvivier; *C:* Lee Garmes; *M:* Miklos Rozsa.

Lying Lips 1939 All-black detective mystery about a young nightclub singer framed for murder. Her boyfriend then turns detective to clear her name. 60m/B VHS. Edna Mae Harris, Carmen Newsome, Earl Jones, Amanda Randolph; *D:* Oscar Micheaux.

M 1931 The great Lang dissection of criminal deviance, following the tortured last days of a child murderer, and the efforts of both the police and the underground to bring him to justice. Poetic, compassionate, and chilling. Inspired by real-life serial killer Peter Kurten, known as "Vampire of Dusseldorf," Lang also borrowed story elements from Jack the Ripper's killing spree. Lorre's screen debut. Lang's personal favorite among his own films. In German with English subtitles. Remade in 1951. 111m/B VHS, DVD. *GE* Peter Lorre, Ellen Widmann, Inge Landgut, Gustav Grundgens, Otto Wernicke, Ernst Stahl-Nachbaur, Franz Stein, Theodore Loos, Fritz Gnass, Fritz Odemar, Paul Kemp, Theo Lingen, Georg John, Karl Platen, Rosa Valetti, Hertha von Walther, Rudolf Blumner; *D:* Fritz Lang; *W:* Fritz Lang, Thea von Harbou; *C:* Fritz Arno Wagner, Gustav Rathje; *M:* Edvard Grieg.

M. Butterfly 1993 (R) Disappointing adaptation of Hwang's award-winning play, which was based on a true story. Irons is Rene Gallimard, a minor French diplomat sent to China in 1964. Taken in by the exoticism of the mysterious east, he falls for a Chinese opera performer, Song Liling (Lone). Only she's no lady and the oblivious diplomat turns out to be a patsy as Song Liling uses him to gather information. The story only works if the passion, however deceptive, between Gallimard and Song Liling is believable, passion which is noticeably lacking between Irons and Lone. Irons comes across as too intelligent to be gullible and the usually excellent Lone does not make his role believable. 101m/C VHS. Jeremy Irons, John Lone, Ian Richardson, Barbara Sukowa, Vernon Dobtcheff, Annabel Leventon, Shizuko Hoshi, Richard McMillan; *D:* David Cronenberg; *W:* David Henry Hwang; *M:* Howard Shore.

Ma and Pa Kettle 1949 *The Further Adventures of Ma and Pa Kettle* 1949 The hillbilly couple were supporting characters in "The Egg and I" but their popularity found them spun off into their own comfortably couple and their 15 children about to be evicted only to have Pa win a tobacco slogan contest. The prize is a brand-new fully automated house whose futuristic contraptions get the better of Pa. 76m/B VHS. Marjorie Main, Percy Kilbride, Richard Long, Meg Randall, Esther Dale, Barry Kelley, Patricia Alphin; *D:* Charles Lamont; *W:* Al Lewis, Herbert Margolis, Louis Morheim.

Ma and Pa Kettle at Home 1954 Elwin, one of the Kettle's 15 children, is a finalist in an essay contest that could win him a college scholarship. Then Pa Kettle hears the two judges plan to visit each of the finalists' homes so he tries to spruce-up the family's tumbled-down farm. 80m/B VHS, DVD. Marjorie Main, Percy Kilbride, Lori Nelson, James Best, Esther Dale, Russell Simpson, Emory Parnell; *D:* Charles T. Barton; *W:* John Grant, Richard Morris.

Ma and Pa Kettle at the Fair 1952 The Kettle's eldest daughter Rosie wants to go to college so Ma enters the county fair baking contest to win some money and Pa buys a decrepit old nag to enter in the fair's horse race. Somehow things just have a way of working out for the Kettles. 79m/B VHS, DVD. Marjorie Main, Percy Kilbride, Lori Nelson, Loring Smith, Russell Johnson, Byron Palmer, Mabel Albertson, Hilo Hattie, Fay Roope, Oliver Blake, Lowell Gilmore, Teddy Hart; *D:* Lee Sholem; *W:* Jack Henley, Harry Clork, Elwood Ullman.

Ma and Pa Kettle Back On the Farm 1951 First-time grandparents, the Kettles have to deal with their daughter-in-law's snobby Bostonian parents and their parenting ideas. The family's also moved back to their ramshackle farm where Pa thinks he's found uranium, leading to all sorts of problems. 81m/B VHS, DVD. Marjorie Main, Percy Kilbride, Richard Long, Meg Randall, Ray Collins, Barbara Brown, Emory Parnell; *D:* Edward Sedgwick; *W:* Jack Henley.

Ma and Pa Kettle Go to Town 1950 Ma and Pa head off for New York City when Pa wins a jingle-writing contest, unknowingly leaving their brood in the care of on the lam mobster Mike, who asks the Kettles to deliver a package to his brother. This gets both the crooks and the cops trailing the hillbilly couple, whose backwoods ways are more than a match for any city slicker. 80m/B VHS, DVD. Marjorie Main, Percy Kilbride, Richard Long, Meg Randall, Charles McGraw, Ray Collins, Esther Dale, Ellen Corby, Barbara Brown; *D:* Charles Lamont; *W:* Martin Ragaway, Leonard Stern.

Ma and Pa Kettle on Vacation Go to Paris 1953 Ma and Pa visit Paris as guests of their son's wealthy in-laws and Pa unwittingly gets involved with spies and shady ladies. 79m/B VHS, DVD. Marjorie Main, Percy Kilbride, Ray Collins, Sig Rumann, Bodil Miller, Barbara Brown, Peter Brocco, Jay Novello; *D:* Charles Lamont; *W:* Jack Henley.

Ma Barker's Killer Brood 1960 Biography of the infamous American criminal and her four sons, edited together from a TV serial. The shoot-'em-up scenes and Tuttle's performance keep the pace from slackening. 82m/B VHS, DVD. Lurene Tuttle, Tristram Coffin, Paul Dubov, Nelson Leigh, Myrna Dell, Vic Lundin, Donald Spruance; *D:* Bill Karn.

Ma Saison Preferee 1993 *My Favorite Season* 1993 Focuses on the intense relationship between a middleaged brother (Auteuil) and sister (Deneuve). When the elderly Berthe (Villalonga) collapses, she goes to stay with daughter Emilie and her family, which provides Emilie with an excuse to invite her estranged brother Antoine for Christmas. It's a disaster with numerous family fights, that leads Emilie to declare her marriage over and to an eventual reapproachment with Antoine. Film is divided into four parts, to coincide with the four seasons, beginning with autumn and ending with summer. French with subtitles. Deneuve and Auteuil reteamed for Techine's "Les Voleurs." 124m/C VHS, DVD. *FR* Daniel Auteuil, Catherine Deneuve, Marthe Villalonga, Jean-Pierre Bouvier, Chiara Mastroianni, Anthony Prada, Carmen Chaplin; *D:* Andre Techine; *W:* Andre Techine; *C:* Thierry Arbogast; *M:* Philippe Sarde.

Ma Vie en Rose 1997 (R) *My Life in Pink* 1997 (R) Berliner's debut portrays seven-year-old misfit Ludovic (du Fresne), who is convinced he's really a girl and likes to dress in girls' clothes. His close-knit family merely regards this as a childhood eccentricity Ludovic will grow out of. But when the child decides he's going to marry Jerome (Rivere), the boy next door, and stages a mock wedding ceremony, things get a bit dicey. Jerome's father is the straitlaced Albert (Hanssens), who happens to be the boss of Ludovic's father, Pierre (Ecoffey), and he's not nearly so understanding (neither are the other neighbors in the conservative Parisian suburb). Poignant and funny look at a child's search for identity. Convincing turn by pre-pubescent performer du Fresne. 90m/C VHS, DVD. *BE FR GB* Georges DuFresne, Jean-Philippe Ecoffey, Michele Laroque, Daniel Hanssens, Julien Riviere, Helene Vincent, Laurence Bibot, Jean-Francois Galotte, Caroline Baehr, Marie Bunel, Jean-Marie Berliner; *W:* Alain Berliner, Chris Vander Stappen; *C:* Yves Cape; *M:* Dominique Dalcan. Golden Globes '98: Foreign Film.

Mabel & Fatty 1916 Three silent shorts featuring the two stars, made with Mack Sennett: "He Did and He Didn't," "Mabel and Fatty Viewing The World's Fair at San Francisco" (with scenes of the actual 1914 World's Fair) and "Mabel's Blunder." *61m/B VHS.* Mabel Normand, Fatty Arbuckle, Al "Fuzzy" St. John.

Maborosi *ⅉⅉⅉ* *Hikari* 1995 Yumiko (Esumi) has a content-ed life in Osaka with her husband Ikuo (Asano) and their newborn son. Yet, inex-plicably, her husband commits suicide one night. Later, a neighbor of Yumiko's helps her with an arranged marriage to prosper-ous widower Tamio (Naitoh), who lives in a remote fishing village, and once again things seem to be happy. But her first hus-band's death still haunts her and Yumiko seeks an explanation that will allow her to have some peace in her life. Adapted from a story by Teru Miyamoto. Japanese with subtitles. *110m/C VHS, DVD. JP* Makiko Esumi, Takashi Naito, Tadanobu Asano, Go-ki Kashiya-ma; *D:* Hirokazu Kore-eda; *W:* Yoshihisa Ogita; *C:* Masao Nakaboni; *M:* Chen Ming-Cheng.

Mac *ⅉⅉⅉ* 1993 (R) It's a family affair. Immigrant carpenter's funeral is the start-ing point for the story of his three sons, construction workers who live in Queens, New York in the 1950s. The passionate bros battle, bitch, and build, with Turturro as the best summing up the prevailing philosophy: "It's the doing, that's the thing." Turturro's directorial debut is a la-bor of love and a tribute to his own dad. Filmed on location in New York City. Fine performances from newcomers Badalucco and Capotorto are complemented by smaller roles from Amos, Barkin, and Tur-turro's real-life wife Borowitz and brother potoro. Michael Badalucco, Katherine Bor-owitz, John Amos, Olek Krupa, Ellen Barkin, Joe Papar-one; Nicholas Turturro, Dennis Farina, Steven Randazzo; *D:* Stewart Raffill; *M:* Alan Sil-vestri; *C:* Fon Fortunato.

Mac and Me *ⅉ* 1988 (PG) Lost E.T.-like alien stranded on Earth befriends a wheelchair-bound boy. Aimed at young kids, it's full of continual product plugs, most notably for McDonald's. Make the kids happy and stick to the real thing. *94m/C VHS, DVD.* Christine Ebersole, Jonathan Ward, Katrina Caspary, Lauren Stanley, Jade Calegory; *D:* Stewart Raffill.

Macabre *ⅉ* *Frozen Terror* 1980 A mad-man resembling both Jack Frost and Jack the Ripper claims victims at random. *90m/C VHS, DVD.* Bernice Stegers, Stanko Molnar, Ve-ronica Zinny, Roberto Posse; *D:* Lamberto Bava; *W:* Lamberto Bava, Antonio Avati; *C:* Franco Delli Colli.

Macao *ⅉⅉ* 1952 On the lam for a crime he didn't commit, an adventurer sails to the exotic Far East, meets a bux-om cafe singer, and helps Interpol catch a notorious crime boss. A strong film noir entry. Russell sneers, Mitchum wise cracks. Director von Sternberg's last film for RKO. *81m/B VHS, DVD.* Robert Mitchum, Jane Russell, William Bendix, Gloria Grahame; *D:* Josef von Sternberg.

Macaroni *ⅉ½* *Maccheroni* 1985 (PG) An uptight American businessman returns to Naples 40 years after being stationed there in WWII. Comedic situations abound when he is reunited with his Italian war buddy, brother of his lover. Pleasant act-ing can't save irritating script. *104m/C VHS.* *IT* Jack Lemmon, Marcello Mastroianni, Dania Ni-colodi, Isa Danieli; *D:* Ettore Scola; *W:* Ettore Sco-la.

MacArthur *ⅉⅉ* 1977 (PG) General Douglas MacArthur's life from Corregidor in 1942 to his dismissal a decade later in the midst of the Korean conflict. Episodic saga with forceful Peck but weak support-ing characters. Fourteen minutes were cut

from the original version; intended to be Peck's "Patton," it falls short of the mark. *130m/C VHS, DVD.* Gregory Peck, Ivan Bonar, Ward (Edward) Costello, Nicolas Coster, Dan O'Herlihy; *C:* Joseph Sargent; *M:* Hal Barwood, Matthew Robbins; *C:* Mario Tosi; *M:* Jerry Gold-smith.

MacArthur Park *ⅉⅉ½* 2001 (R) A group of L.A. crack addicts try to escape the despair of their lives by duping a ce-lebrity junkie. Cody (Byrd), a middle-aged former musician, is the de facto leader of the group, whose estranged son brings news that his ex-wife has died. Actor-turned-director Wirth turns in a fine film which includes excellent performances and a rare insight into the inner lives of the "crackheads" that are often just part of the periphery of most urban dramas. *86m/C DVD.* Thomas Jefferson Byrd, Louis Freese, Ellen Cleghorne, Brandon Adams, Lori Petty, Julie Del-py, Bathazar Getty, David Faustino, Rachel Hun-Tamie Potter, Sydney Walsh, Cynda Williams, Kirk "Sticky Fingaz" Jones, Bad Azz; *D:* Billy Wirth; *W:* Billy Wirth, Tyrone Atkins, Aaron Courseault, Sheri Sussman; *C:* Kristian Bernier; *M:* Stephen Perkins. *VIDEO*

MacArthur's Children *ⅉⅉⅉ* 1985 A poignant evocation of life in a Jap-anese fishing village as it faces the end of WWII and American occupation. Not as good as some of the other Japanese films, but it is an interesting look at the changes in culture caused by their defeat in the war. In Japanese with English subtitles. *115m/C VHS. JP* Masako Natsume, Shiori Saku-ra, Ken'saku) Watanabe, Juzo Itami, Yoshiyuka Omori; *D:* Masahiro Shinoda; *W:* Takeshi Tamura.

Macbeth *ⅉⅉⅉ* 1948 Shake-speare's classic tragedy is performed with a celebrated lead performance by Welles, who plays the tragic king as a demonic leader of a barbaric society. A low budget adaptation with cheap sets, a three-week shooting schedule, lots of mood, and an attempt at Scottish accents. After making this film, Welles took a 10-year break from Hollywood. *111m/B VHS.* Orson Welles, Jean-ette Nolan, Dan O'Herlihy, Roddy McDowall, Rob-ert Coote; *D:* Orson Welles.

Macbeth *ⅉⅉ* *Play of the Month: Mac-Beth* 1970 An extraordinary version of Shakespeare's "Macbeth" in which all the fire, ambition and doom of his text come brilliantly to life. *137m/C DVD.* Eric Porter, Jan-et Suzman, John Alderton, Michael Goodliffe, John Thaw, Daphne Heard, Hilary Mason; *D:* Alan Gor-rie. *TV*

Macbeth *ⅉⅉⅉ* 1971 (R) Polanski's notorious adaptation of the Shakespeare-an classic, marked by realistic design, un-flinching violence, and fatalistic atmo-sphere. Finch and Annis star as Macbeth and his equally murderous lady (who ap-pears nude in the sleepwalking scene), murder of his pregnant wife, actress Shar-on Tate, was torn apart by critics but it contains stunning fight scenes and fine acting. It is in fact a worthy continuation of his work in the horror genre. Very well made. First film made by PlayToy Enter-prises Originally rated X. *139m/C VHS, DVD.* Jon Finch, Nicholas Selby, Martin Shaw, Frances-za Annis, Terence Baylor, John Stride, Stephan Chase, Noelle Rimmington, Maisie Farquhar, Elsie Taylor; *D:* Roman Polanski; *W:* Roman Polanski, Kenneth Tynan; *C:* Gilbert Taylor.

Macbeth *ⅉⅉ½* 1988 Another produc-tion of the classic tragedy by Shake-speare. Produced as part of HBO's Thames Collection. *110m/C VHS.* Michael Jayston, Leigh Hunt; *D:* Charles Marquis Warren.

Macbeth *ⅉ½* 2006 MacBeth as gangster tale? Interesting idea but it loses much in translation. Director Wright moves the action to modern day Melbourne, where MacBeth (Worthington) whacks his boss Duncan (Sweet), as well as anyone who thinks is a threat. Lacking in subtley, the film is the victim of a conspir-acy and bewiled by unseen tormentors and that his only solace is kindly waitress Marie (Sanchez-Gijon). It's creepy and stylistic (there's a kind of cold blue tinge to the photography) and Anderson provides

oria Hill, Geoffrey Wright; C: William Gibson; *M:* John Clifford White.

Mach 2 *ⅉⅉ½* 2000 (R) A senator, who's running for president, has gotten nold of a computer disk that reveals treachery by the current vice president White House Secret Service agents are sent to retrieve the disk from the Senator who's boarded the Concorde, and set it up so that the plane will be destroyed. Bosworth is the Air Force hero who must let that happen. *94m/C VHS, DVD. M:* Brian Bos-worth, Michael Dorn, Shannon Whirry, Cliff Robert-son, Lance Guest, Bruce Weitz; *D:* Fred Olen Ray; *W:* Steve Latshaw; *C:* Thomas Callaway; *M:* Eric Wurst, David Wurst. *VIDEO*

The Machine *ⅉⅉ* 1996 Psychiatrist and inventor Marc Lacroix (Depardieu) is obsessed with the brain. He develops a brain transfer machine and decides to test it on himself (naturally) by fusing his psy-che with that of his patient, cold-blooded killer Michael Zyto (does this sound like a good idea to you?). Naturally, the experi-ment causes terrifying consequences for Lacroix and his family. *96m/C VHS.* Gerard Depardieu, Nathalie Baye, Didier Boundon, Natalia Woemer, Erwan Baynaud; *D:* Francois Dupeyron; *W:* Francois Dupeyron; *C:* Dietrich Lohmann; *M:* Michel Portal.

Machine Gun Blues *ⅉⅉ* *Black Rose of Harlem; Fistol Blues* 1995 (R) 1930s jazz singer Georgia (Williams) sings at a black-owned club that mobster Constanza (Vilerelli) wants to take over. Right-hand man Johnny Verona (Cassavettes) is sent to help things along and makes the mis-take of falling for the chanteuse amidst a scene of moonshine, gunrunning and racketeering. *80m/C VHS.* Cynda Williams, Nick Cassavetes, Joe (Johnny) Vilerelli, Maria Ford, Lawrence Monsson, Garrett Morris, Richard Erooks; *D:* Fred Gallo; *W:* Charles Philip Moore; *C:* Jan Aronson; *M:* David Wurst, Eric Wurst.

Machine Gun Kelly *ⅉⅉ½* 1958 Corman found Euro-appeal with this '30s style gangster bio. Bronson, who was just gaining a reputation as an action lead, stars as criminal Kelly, who's convinced by his moll to give up bank robbery for kidnapping. *80m/B VHS.* Charles Bronson, Susan Cabot, Morey Amster-dam, Barboura Morris, Frank De Kova, Jack Lam-bert, Wally Campo, Richard Devon, Bob Griffin; *D:* Roger Corman; *W:* Mike Weib, Robert W(right) Campbell; *C:* Floyd Crosby; *M:* Gerald Fried.

Machine to Kill Bad People *ⅉⅉ* *La Macchina Ammazzacativi* 1948 In a small Italian village, a photogra-pher receives a magical camera that has the power to terrify and kill anyone it pho-tographs. The photographer decides to get rid of all the village's evil people but soon learns the difficulty of distinguishing between the grey areas of good and bad. Italian with subtitles. *80m/B VHS. IT* Gennaro Pisano, Giovanni Amato, Marilyn Buferd; *D:* Ro-berto Rossellini; *W:* Roberto Rossellini.

Machined *WOOF!* 2006 (R) Sicko Mo-tor Man Dan accidentally runs over Ryan, so he takes him back to his shack to "fix" him. Which means Dan robocops him into a half-man/half-machine, all serial killer freak. Then the two go on a murder spree. As nasty as it sounds. *92m/C DVD. US* David C. Hayes, Jose Rosete, Patti Tindall; *D:* Craig McMahon; *W:* Craig McMahon; *M:* Maurice Jarre.

The Machinist *ⅉⅉ* 2006 (R) *El Maquinista 2004* (R) Best-known as the film in which Bale dropped more than 60 pounds to por-tray the cadaverous title role. Trevor (Bale) is a lonely, disturbed insomniac whose inattention causes a co-worker (Ironside) to lose an arm. Trevor comes to believe that his fellow workers want re-venge, including the sinister Ivan (Sheri-dan), who may actually be a figment of Tre-vor's paranoid imagination; that his hooker girlfriend Stevie (Leigh) may be playing

Macho Callahan *ⅉⅉ* 1970 (R) A Civil War convict escapes from a frontier jail bent on tracking down the man who imprisoned him. (The escaped prisoner bit is a recurring theme in Janssen's oeuvre.) Confused script even has a one-armed Carradine! *99m/C VHS, DVD.* David Janssen, Jean Seberg, David Carradine, Lee J. Cobb; *D:* Bernard L. Kowalski.

Maciste in Hell *ⅉ½* 1973 (R) A pimp who comes out of retirement to reclaim a piece of the action in Oakland, California. Violent blaxploitation flick was boxoffice dynamite at time of release. Ear-ly Pryor appearance. *110m/C VHS, DVD. M:* Max Julien, Richard Pryor, Don Gordon, Roger E. Mos-ley, Carol Speed; *D:* Michael Campus.

Mack & Carole *ⅉⅉ½* 1923 Lom-bard began her screen career, in earnest, as a Mack Sennett comedienne. These three shorts represent her earliest screen swims nude. A must for all earthquake buffs. *128m/C VHS, DVD.* Gregory Peck, Omar Sharif, Telly Savalas, Julie Newmar, Edward G. Robinson, Keenan Wynn, Ted Cassidy, Eduardo Ciannelli, Eli Wallach, Raymond Massey, Lee J. Cobb, Burgess Meredith, Anthony Quayle, John David Garfield, Robert Phillips; *D: J.* Lee Thomp-son; *W:* Carl Foreman; *C:* Joe MacDorald; *M:* Quincy Jones.

Mack the Knife *ⅉⅉ* 1989 (PG-13) The Threep-enny Opera 1989 (PG-13) Terrible adaptation of Brecht and Weill's "Threepenny Op-era", detailing the adventures of a master thief in love with an innocent girl. Too much music, too much dancing, too much emoting. *121m/C VHS.* Raul Julia, Roger Dal-trey, Richard Harris, Julie Walters, Clive Revill, Erin Donovan, Rachel Robertson, Julia Migenes; *D:* Menahem Golan.

Mackintosh Man *ⅉⅉ* 1973 (PG) An intelligence agent must undo a com-munist who has infiltrated the free world's network in this solid but somewhat sub-dued thriller. Good cast keeps narrative rolling, but don't look here for nudity-pro-"anity-violence fix. *100m/C VHS, DVD.* Paul Newman, Dominique Sanda, James Mason, Ian Bannen, Nigel Patrick, Harry Andrews, Lee Genn, Peter Vaughan, Michael Hordern; *D:* John Huston; *W:* Walter Hill; *M:* Maurice Jarre.

MacKenna's Gold *ⅉⅉ½* 1969 (PG) Grim desperados trek through Apache territory to uncover legendary cache of gold in this somewhat legendary epic. Subdued stars Peck and Shariff vie for attention here with such overacrors as Cobb, Meredith, and Wallach. Meanwhile, Newmar (Catwoman of TV's Batman)

Macumba Love *ⅉ* 1960 An author journeys to Brazil to prove a connection between mysterious murders and voodoo. A tedious suspense exploitation travel-ogue with generous servings of cheese-cake and calypso music. *86m/C VHS.* Walter Reed, Ziva Rodann, William Wellman Jr., June Wil-kinson, Ruth de Souza; *D:* Douglas Fowley.

Macon County Line *ⅉⅉ½* 1974 (R) A series of deadly mistakes and misfortunes lead to a sudden turn-around in the lives of three young people when they enter a small Georgia town and find themselves accused of brutally slaying the sheriff's wife. Sequelled by "Return to Macon County" in 1975, starring Don John-son and Nick Nolte. *89m/C VHS, DVD.* Alan Vint, Jesse Vint, Cheryl Waters, Geoffrey Lewis, Joan Blackman, Max Baer Jr.; *D:* Richard Comp-

a quasi-believable conclusion as a payoff for all the misery endured. *102m/C DVD. US* Christian Bale, Jennifer Jason Leigh, Michael Iron-side, Reg E. Cathey, Anna Massey, Aitana San-chez-Gijon, John Sharian, Larry (Lawrence) Gilli-ard Jr., Matthew Romero Moore; *D:* Brad Ander-son; *W:* Scott Kosar; *C:* Xavi Gimenez; *M:* Roque Banos.

Mad

Mad About Mambo ✓✓½ 2000 (PG-13) Lucy McLoughlin (Russell) is an upper-class student in Belfast who's determined to prove herself as a Latin dancer. So she teams up with a working-class athlete, Danny Mitchell (Ash), who wants to play pro soccer and who needs to improve his timing, and the duo polish their moves on the dance floor. Appealing romance that doesn't ignore its setting but doesn't dwell on religious differences and soldiers either. 92m/C VHS. Keri Russell, William Ash, Brian Cox, Rosaleen Linehan, Theo Fraser Steele; **D:** John Forte; **C:** Ashley Rowe; **M:** Richard Hartley.

Mad About Money ✓✓ *He Loved an Actress; Stardust* 1937 Comedy about a bespectacled mild-mannered fellow who runs up against a Mexican spitfire. ♫Oh So Beautiful; Perpetual Motion; Little Lost Tune; Dustin' The Stars. 80m/B VHS. *GB* Lupe Velez, Wallace Ford, Ben Lyon, Harry Langdon, Jean Colin; **D:** Melville Brown.

Mad About Music ✓✓✓ 1938 On the advice of her publicist, film star Gwen Taylor (Patrick) sends her teenaged daughter Gloria (Durbin) off to a Swiss boarding school and keeps her identity a secret. So Gloria invents an exciting world-traveler father that envious schoolmate Felice (Parrish) insists upon meeting. Gloria manages to persuade a complete stranger, composer Richard Todd (Marshall), into playing the role (he's charmed by her singing). Naturally, there's lots of confusion, especially when mother and "father" finally meet. ♫I Love to Whistle; Chapel Bells; Serenade to the Stars; There Isn't a Day Goes By. 92m/B VHS. Deanna Durbin, Herbert Marshall, Gail Patrick, Arthur Treacher, Helen Parrish, William Frawley, Marcia Mae Jones, Jackie Moran; **D:** Norman Taurog; **W:** Bruce Manning, Felix Jackson; **C:** Joseph Valentine.

Mad About You WOOF! 1990 (PG) Millionaire helps his daughter measure prospective suitors. Adam West is not the fourth man in the Montgomery Clift-James Dean-Marlon Brando chain of American acting greats. 92m/C VHS. Claudia Christian, Joseph Gian, Adam West, Shari Shattuck; **D:** Lorenzo Doumani.

The Mad Adventures of Rabbi Jacob ✓✓✓ *Les Adventures de Rabbi Jacob* 1973 (G) In order to hide out from Arab revolutionaries and the police, bigoted businessman Victor Pivert borrows the identity of a beloved Rabbi returning to France after 30 years. Much French slapstick hilarity and some musings on racism and tolerance ensues. One of the most popular comedies of all time in France (even though Jerry Lewis is nowhere to be seen!), it's also one of the most-requested video releases here in the States. Suitable for children, it might serve as a good way to introduce them to foreign films. 100m/C VHS, DVD. *FR* Louis de Funes, Suzy Delair, Marcel Dalio, Claude Giraud, Renzo Montagnani, Andre Falcon, Henri Guybet, Miou-Miou; **W:** Josy Eisenberg; **M:** Vladimir Cosma.

The Mad Bomber WOOF! *Police Connection; Detective Geronimo* 1972 Grim lawman Edwards tracks deranged bomber Connors, who is determined to blow up anyone who ever offended him. A must for all connoisseurs of acting that is simultaneously, overblown and flat. 80m/C VHS, DVD. Vince Edwards, Chuck Connors, Neville Brand; **D:** Bert I. Gordon.

Mad Bull ✓ 1977 Sensitive wrestler finds meaning in life when he falls in love. If you ever cared about Karras, then you probably already saw this. If you never

cared about Karras, then you probably never heard of this. If you ever cared about Anspach, rent "Five Easy Pieces" instead. 96m/C VHS. Alex Karras, Susan Anspach, Nicholas Colasanto, Tracey Walter; **D:** Walter Doniger.

The Mad Butcher ✓ *The Mad Butcher of Vienna; The Strangler of Vienna; Der Wurger kommt auf leisen Socken; Lo Strangolatore di Vienna; Meat Is Meat* 1972 (R) Typically unhinged mental patient seeks teenage flesh for his various instruments of torture and death. Buono has never been more imposing. 82m/C VHS, DVD. *IT* Victor Buono, Karin (Karen) Field, Brad Harris; **D:** Guido Zurli.

Mad City ✓✓½ 1997 (PG-13) Out-of-work security guard Sam Bailly (Travolta) goes postal, taking hostages in a museum while has-been journalist Max Brackett (Hoffman) manages to exploit Bailly and hype the situation into a massive broadcast news event. The media circus that ensues provides social commentary on the questionable state of journalism. Drawing from famously explored material in numerous older films ("Network" and "All the President's Men") the subject is also enjoying a revival in current films ("Primary Colors" and "Wag the Dog"). Relationship between Max and Sam carries most interest in Costa-Gavras' intense drama, while uneven tone and script inadequacies hold back satisfying story development. Talented supporting cast (Alda, Danner, Kirshner, Prosky) have little to do. 114m/C VHS, DVD. John Travolta, Dustin Hoffman, Mia Kirshner, Alan Alda, Blythe Danner, Robert Prosky, William Atherton, Ted Levine, Bill Nunn; **D:** Constantin Costa-Gavras; **W:** Tom Matthews; **C:** Patrick Blossier, **M:** Thomas Newman.

Mad Cowgirl ✓✓ 2006 Probably the first mad cow disease movie. Meat inspector Therese (Lassez) goes off the rails when she's diagnosed with brain cancer, possibly caused by tainted beef. She revels in various surreal sex and splatter scenarios, including assuming the identity of her favorite kung-fu TV heroine and having a torrid liaison with her brother (Duval). Designed to turn watchers into vegetarians, if not vegans. 89m/C DVD. Sarah Lassez, James Duval, Devon Odessa, Walter Koenig, Vic Chao, Chris Dimassio; **D:** Gregory Hatanka; **W:** Gregory Hatanka, North Soth; **C:** Gregory Hatanka.

Mad Death of Blood

Mad Doctor of Blood Island WOOF! *Tomb of the Living Dead; Blood Doctor* 1968 Dull band of travelers arrives on mysterious tropical island and encounter bloodthirsty creature. Warning: This film is not recognized for outstanding achievements in acting, dialogue, or cinematography. 110m/C VHS, DVD, PH John Ashley, Angelique Pettyjohn, Ronald Remy, Alicia Alonzo, Alfonso Carvajal, Johnny Long, Nadja, Bruno Romero; **W:** Gerardo (Gerry) De Leon, Eddie Romero; **M:** Reuben Candy; **C:** Justo Paulino; **M:** Tito Arevalo.

Mad Dog WOOF! 1984 An escaped convict seeks revenge on the cop responsible for his imprisonment. 90m/C VHS, DVD. Helmut Berger, Marisa Mell; **D:** Sergio Grieco.

Mad Dog and Glory ✓✓ 1993 (R) Cast against type, Murray and De Niro play each other's straight man in this (De Niro) is an off-duty police photographer who happens upon a convenience store robbery and manages to save the life of Frank (Murray), obnoxious gangster by day, obnoxious stand-up comic by night. To settle up, Frank offers him Glory (Thurman), for a week. Eventually, Frank wants Glory back, forcing wimpy Mad Dog to either confront or surrender. Directed by

McNaughton, who established himself with "Henry: Portrait of a Serial Killer." Uneven and not of the knee-slapper ilk, but the performances are tight, including Caruso as a cop buddy of De Niro's. 97m/C VHS, DVD. Robert De Niro, Uma Thurman, Bill Murray, David Caruso, Mike Starr, Tom Towles, Kathy Baker, Derek Anunciation, J.J. Johnston, Richard Belzer; **D:** John McNaughton; **W:** Richard Price; **C:** Robby Muller; **M:** Elmer Bernstein.

Mad Dog Morgan ✓✓½ *Mad Dog* 1976 (R) Hopper delivers as engaging outlaw roaming outlands of 19th-century Australia. Quirky and violent G'day man. Based on a true story. 93m/C VHS, DVD. *AU* Dennis Hopper, David Gulpilil; **D:** Philippe Mora.

The Mad Executioners ✓✓ *Der Henker Von London* 1965 Scotland Yard inspector searches for a sex maniac who decapitates women. In the meantime, a group of vigilantes capture criminals and sentence them without a trial. Confusing film with a predictable ending. Based on the book "White Carpet" by Bryan Edgar Wallace. 92m/B VHS. *GE* Hansjorg Felmy, Maria Perschy, Dieter Borsche, Rudolph Forster, Chris Howland, Wolfgang Preiss; **D:** Edwin Zbonek.

The Mad Ghoul ✓✓½ 1943 Mad scientist (is there any other kind?) Dr. Morris (Zucco) is researching an ancient Egyptian gas that causes paralysis, turning victims into obedient zombies. Morris exposes his innocent assistant Ted (Bruce) to the gas, making Ted dependent on the antidote serum made from newly dead hearts. Poor Ted's fiance Isabel (Ankers) just can't understand what's the matter; 66m/B VHS. George Zucco, David Bruce, Evelyn Ankers, Turhan Bey, Robert Armstrong, Milburn Stone, Charles McGraw, Rose Hobart; **D:** James Hogan; **W:** Brenda Weisberg, Paul Gangelin.

Mad Hot Ballroom ✓✓✓ 2005 (PG) Sweet documentary about ballroom dancing. Only the participants are New York City fifth graders participating in a 10-week program organized by the American Ballroom Theater. The doc follows students from Bensonhurst, Tribeca, and Washington Heights (a mixture of races, ethnicities, and incomes) as they learn the fox trot, meringue, rumba, swing, and tango (and how to deal with the opposite sex) in order to take part in an annual citywide competition. 105m/C DVD. *US* **D:** Marilyn Agrelo; **W:** Amy Sewell; **C:** Claudia Raschke; **M:** Steven Lutvak, Joseph Baker.

Mad Love ✓✓✓ *The Hands of Orlac* 1935 Brilliant surgeon Gogol (Lorre) falls madly in love with actress Yvonne Orlac (Drake), but she rebuffs him. When her pianist husband Stephen's (Clive) hands are cut off in a train accident, Gogol agrees to attach new hands, using those of a recently executed knife-wielding murderer, Reagan (Brophy). Gogol then kills Stephen's stepfather and uses psychological terror to make the pianist think he killed him. There's also an appearance by the supposedly dead murderer who shows up to reclaim his hands. A real chiller about obsessive love and psychological fear. The only downfall to this one is the unnecessary comic relief by Healy. Lorre's first American film. 70m/B VHS. Peter Lorre, Colin Clive, Frances Drake, Ted Healy, Edward Brophy, Sara Haden, Henry Kolker, Keye Luke, May (Mai) Beatty; **D:** Karl Freund; **W:** P.J. Wolfson, John Lloyd Balderston, Guy Endore; **C:** Gregg Toland, Chester Lyons; **M:** Dimitri Tiomkin.

Mad Love ✓✓½ 1995 (PG-13) Teen love has rarely been so insipid. Impulsive, fragile, and annoyingly melodramatic Casey (Barrymore) bewitches responsible, straightlaced Matt (O'Donnell) with her kewpie-doll charm and penchant for mischief. When Casey's bipolar ways land her in a mental hospital, Matt breaks her out and the unconvincing duo hit the road, where their supposedly free-spirited, passion-filled escapades grow increasingly inconsistent and silly, eventually halted by Casey's clinical crash. Slightly redeemed by a cool soundtrack and decent acting, but otherwise dull and insignificant, with an ending that may induce involuntary eyerolling. You've been warned. 95m/C VHS, DVD. Chris O'Donnell, Drew Barrymore,

Joan Allen, Kevin Dunn, Jude Ciccolella, Amy Sakasitz, T.J. Lowther; **D:** Antonia Bird; **W:** Paula Milne; **C:** Fred Tammes.

Mad Love ✓✓½ *Madness of Love; Juana la Loca; Joan the Mad* 2001 (R) Peculiar costume drama is base on the life of Spanish queen Joan (known as "Joan the Mad" or "Juana La Loca"), daughter of King Ferdinand and Queen Isabella. In 1496, she is sent to marry Prince Philip of Flanders (known as "Philip the Handsome"). Although the marriage is arranged, the two are instantly smitten, Joan exceedingly so. As the passion wears thin her intense love is enhanced by jealousy, which Philip uses to ascend to the throne by having Joan declared insane in comparison to Aranda's previous work (especially considering the passionate subject matter), pic does well on his attention to subtle detail and the standout performance of Lopez de Ayala as the lusty queen. 117m/C VHS, DVD. *SP IT PT* Pilar Lopez de Ayala, Daniele Liotti, Manuela Arcuri, Eloy Azorin, Rosana Pastor, Giuliano Gemma; **D:** Vicente Aranda; **W:** Vicente Aranda; **C:** Paco Femenia; **M:** Jose Nieto.

Mad Max ✓✓✓½ 1980 (R) Set on the stark highways of the post-nuclear future, an ex-cop seeks personal revenge against a rovin' band of vicious outlaw bikers who killed his wife and child. Futuristic scenery and excellent stunt work make for an exceptionally entertaining action-packed adventure. Followed by "The Road Warrior" (also known as "Mad Max 2") in 1981 and "Mad Max Beyond Thunderdome" in 1985. 93m/C VHS, DVD, UMD. *AU* Mel Gibson, Joanne Samuel, Hugh Keays-Byrne, Steve Bisley, Tim Burns, Roger Ward, Vincent (Vince Gill) Gil; **D:** George Miller; **W:** George Miller; **C:** David Eggby; **M:** Brian May.

Mad Max: Beyond Thunderdome ✓✓✓½ 1985 (PG-13) Max drifts into evil town ruled by Turner and becomes gladiator, then gets dumped in desert and is rescued by band of feral orphans. Third in a bleak, extremely violent, often exhilirating series. 107m/C VHS, DVD. *AU* Mel Gibson, Tina Turner, Helen Buday, Frank Thring Jr., Bruce Spence, Robert Grubb, Angelo Rossitto, Angry Anderson, George Spartels, Rod Zuanic; **D:** George Miller, George Ogilvie; **W:** Terry Hayes, George Miller; **C:** Dean Semler; **M:** Maurice Jarre.

Mad Miss Manton ✓✓½ 1938 A socialite turns detective to solve murder. Pleasant comedy-mystery provides occasional laughs and suspense. 80m/B VHS. Barbara Stanwyck, Henry Fonda, Hattie McDaniel, Sam Levene, Miles Mander, Charles Halton; **D:** Leigh Jason.

Mad Mission 3 ✓½ *Aces Go Places 3: Our Man From Bond Street* 1984 Chinese man vacationing in Paris becomes involved in plot to recover precious jewels stolen from England's royal crown. Has there already been "Mad Mission" and "Mad Mission 2"? 81m/C VHS, DVD. *HK* Richard Kiel, Sam Hui, Peter Graves, Sylvia Chang; **Cameos:** Tsui Hark; **W:** Raymond Wong; **C:** Henry Chan; **M:** Lynsey De Paul, Terry Britten.

Mad Money ✓½ 2008 (PG-13) Bridget (Keaton), a middle-class wife and mother, is in trouble when her husband (Danson) is downsized and her comfortable home and lifestyle are threatened. The only job she can find is as a janitor at the Federal Reserve Bank, where she forges unlikely friendships with single mom Nina (Queen Latifah) and young dreamer Jackie (Holmes). Of course, the women aren't content in their menial positions and find, ahem, an opportunity to even the score. Reluctant at first, Nina and Jackie end up following Bridget's lead, and the gals hatch a scheme to "recycle" (i.e., steal) old, out-of-circulation bills that are about to be destroyed anyway. What can it hurt? Bridget gets greedy and the plan starts to fall apart, but no matter, the fizzling silliness continues in this madcap caper that's just a little too mad. 104m/C DVD. *US GB* Diane Keaton, Queen Latifah, Katie Holmes, Ted Danson, Stephen (Steve) Root, Christopher McDonald, Adam Rothenberg, Barry; **D:** Callie Khouri; **W:** Glen Gers; **C:**

The Mad Monster *M:* Martin Davich, James Newton Howard.

The Mad Monster 𝒹𝒹 1942 This "Wolf Man"-inspired creepie looks like a war relic today. A mad scientist furthers retire from the responsibilities of being senior monster, so he calls a convention of creepy creatures to decide who should take his place—The Wolfman, Dracula, the Mummy, Dr. Jekyll and Mr. Hyde, the Invisible Man, or Dr. Acula and the Creature. It, at the boxoffice. 115m/B VHS, Kay Johnson, Reginald Denny, Lillian Roth, Roland Young, Boyd Irwin, Elsa Peterson; *D:* Cecil B. DeMille.

Mad Monster Party 𝒹𝒹 1968 Frankenstein is getting older and wants to retire from the responsibilities of being senior monster, so he calls a convention of creepy creatures to decide who should take his place. The Wolfman, Dracula, the Mummy, Dr. Jekyll and Mr. Hyde, the Invisible Man, or Dr. Acula and the Creature. It, 77m/B VHS, DVD. Johnny, Downs, George Zucco, Anne Nagel, Sarah Padden, Glenn Strange, Gordon DeMain, Mae Busch; *D:* Sam Newfield.

Mad Wax: The Surf Movie 𝒹 1990 A flimsy plot about a window-cleaner who discovers a magical surfing wax serves as a framework for lots and lots of scenes of surfin' dudes. 45m/C VHS, Richard Cram, Marvin Foster, Aaron Napolean, Tom Carroll, Bryce Andrews, Ross Clarke-Jones; *D:* Michael Hohnsee.

Mad Youth *Woof!* 1940 A teenage girl falls in love with a man whom her slutty, alcoholic mother had been chasing. Bottom of the barrel production provides many unintentional laughs. Extraneous South American dance sequences included as character development. 61m/C VHS, DVD. Mary Ainslee, Betty Atkinson, Willy Castello, Betty Compson, Tommy Wonder; *D:* Mi-chael Shyer; *W:* Willis Kent.

The Mad Whirl 𝒹½ 1925 The Roarin' '20s are a mad mad whirl in this silent silent period piece. 80m/B VHS, Myrtle Stedman, Barbara Bedford, Alec 3. Francis, George Fawcett, Joseph Singleton; *C:* William A. Seiter; *W:* Harvey Thew; *C:* Merritt 3. Gerstad.

Madagascar 𝒹𝒹½ 2005 (PG) Marty the Zebra (Rock) just turned ' 0 and he wants to escape the comfortable confines of New York's Central Park Zoo and head off into "the wild" (okay, Connecticut). Aided by a group of sassy penguins, he makes his break, but his zoo buddies—Alex the Lion (Stiller), Gloria the Hippo (Pinkett Smith), and Melman the Giraffe (Schwimmer)—escape to stop him. Things go more awry and the group ends up on the shores of Madagascar. A romp for the kids with lots of pizzazz but not much substance. Adults will find some "Shrek"-type jokes to enjoy, but this one's mainly for the kiddies. 80m/C DVD US *D:* Eric Darnell, Tom McGrath; *W:* Eric Darnell, Tom McGrath, Billy Frolick, Mark Burton; *M:* Hans Zimmer; *V:* Ben Stiller, Chris Rock, Jada Pinkett Smith, David Schwimmer, Cedric the Entertainer, Andy Richter, Sacha Baron Cohen.

Madagascar Skin 𝒹𝒹 1995 (R) Harry (Hannah) is a young gay man who's distigured by a large port-wine birthmark on one side of his face (in the shape of Madagascar). Suicidally depressed he drives to a deserted beach on the Welsh coast, but before making any final decisions, he picks up an overturned bucket lying on the sand. To his shock, it's covering the head of the very much alive middle-aged Flint (Hill), who's been buried up to his neck in sand and left to drown by some fellow crooks. Flint knows of a deserted beach shack, the oddly matched duo move in, and Harry falls in love. Deliberately dreamlike in some respects the leads provide a bittersweet, adult romance. 96m/C VHS, GB John Hannah, Bernard Hill, *D:* Chris Newby; *W:* Chris Newby; *C:* Oliver Curtis.

Madam Satan 𝒹𝒹½ 1930 Extremely bizarre DeMille film highlighted by lavish musical numbers and outrageous costumes. Wealthy socialite realizes she's losing her husband so she disguises herself as a sultry French tramp and entices herself to a young showgirl, so she disguises herself to a zeppelin-surely one of the wildest party scenes ever captured on film. Chorus girls perform several exotic dance numbers inside the airship that are nothing short of fantastic. A storm breaks out and the floating dirigible is struck by lightning—leading viewers to wonder if the mad party-goers will make it to safety or crash and burn like this pic did at the boxoffice. 115m/B VHS, Kay Johnson, Reginald Denny, Lillian Roth, Roland Young, Boyd Irwin, Elsa Peterson; *D:* Cecil B. DeMille.

Madame Bovary 𝒹𝒹 1934 A young adultress with delusions of romantic love finds only despair in this offbeat adaptation of Flaubert's masterpiece. In French with English subtitles. 102m/B VHS, FR Pierre Renoir, Valentine Tessier, Max Dearly; *D:* Jean Renoir.

Madame Bovary 𝒹𝒹 1949 Young adultress with delusions of romantic love finds only despair, even in this Hollywood version of Flaubert's classic. Mason/Flaubert is put on trial for indecency following publication of the novel, with the story told from the witness stand. While this device occasionally slows the narrative, astute direction helps the plot along. Minnelli's handling of the celebrated ball sequence is superb. 115m/B VHS, DVD. Jennifer Jones, Van Heflin, Louis Jourdan, James Mason, Gene Lockhart, Gladys Cooper, George Zucco; *D:* Vincente Minnelli; *M:* Miklos Rozsa.

Madame Bovary 𝒹𝒹½ 1991 (PG-13) Provincial 19th century France is the setting for the tragedy of a romantic woman. Emma Bovary is bored by her marriage to an unsuccessful country doctor and longs for passion and excitement. She allows herself to be seduced (and abandoned) by a local aristocrat and herself seduces a young banker. She also struggles with an increasing burden of debt as she continues her quest for luxury. Realizing she will never find the pass on she desires, Emma takes drastic, and tragic, measures. Sumptuous-looking film, with an extraordinary performance by Huppert. In French with English subtitles. Based on the novel by Gustave Flaubert. 130m/C VHS, DVD. FR Isabelle Huppert, Jean-Francois Balmer, Christophe McLavoy, Jean-Yanne; *D:* Claude Chabrol; *W:* Claude Chabrol; *M:* Matthieu Chabrol.

Madame Bovary 𝒹𝒹½ 2000 British adaptation of Gustave Flaubert's scandalous novel, which is set in rural Normandy in the 1830s and '40s. Emma Bovary (Bonneville), whom she doesn't love. Indeed, Emma has some overly romantic notions about love that lead to infidelity and despair. But it's Emma's extravagance and her borrowing from the usurious Lheureux (Barron) that bring her to "death" in order to prevent a scandal. None of the characters are particularly bright (or likeable) so you sympathy is at a minimum. 140m/C VHS, GB Hugh Dancy, Keith Barron, Trevor Peacock; *D:* Tim Fywell; *W:* Heidi Thomas. **TV**

Madame Butterfly 𝒹𝒹 1995 A French production, filmed in Tunisia, with a Chinese soprano, and Italian subtitles. Mitterand takes on Puccini's opera, setting it in 1904 Nagasaki, but playing most of the story straight (the adds some documentary footage of old Japan between the acts). 15-year-old Butterfly (Huang) is a geisha who makes the mistake of falling in love and marrying deceitful American naval officer Pinkerton (Troxell). She's disowned by her family, he eventually sails away, and when he does return, it's with an American bride. Tragedy ensues. Newcomer Huang's fine but the handsome Troxell's a little stiff. 129m/C VHS, DVD. FR Ying Huang, Richard Troxell, Ning Liang, Richard Cowan; *D:* Frederic Mitterand; *W:* Frederic Mitterand; *C:* Philippe Welt.

Madame Curie 𝒹𝒹½ 1943 The film biography of Madame Marie Curie, the woman who discovered Radium. A deft portrayal by Garson, who is reteamed with her "Mrs. Miniver" co-star, Pidgeon. Certainly better than most biographies from this time period and more truthful as

Madame Rosa 𝒹𝒹 *La Vie Devant Soi* 1977 (PG) An aging Jewish prostitute tends prostitutes' offspring in this warmhearted work. A survivor of the Holocaust, the old woman finds her spirit revived by one of her charges—an abandoned Arab boy. In French with English subtitles. 105m/C VHS, FR /S Simone Signoret, Claude Dauphin, Samy Ben Youb, Michal Bar-Adam; *D:* Moshe Mizrahi; *W:* Moshe Mizrahi; *C:* Nestor Almendros; *M:* Karim Anouz; *A:* Luke Film Crit-ics '78: Actress (Signoret). **Foreign Film.**

Madame Sata 𝒹𝒹 2002 Frist feature for director Karim Ainouz is a stylized portrait of Joao Francisco dos Santos, who became a legend in the slums and prisons of Brazil as both a criminal and the cabaret performer Madame Sata. The film covers a period in 1930s Rio showcasing Joao's (Ramos) life at the Blue Danube club where he performs and the boarding house where he lives with his ready-made family-hooker Laurita (Carfaxo) and her baby daughter and flamboyant hustler Taboo (Baureqi). Ramos gives a compelling performance of a sometimes violent character who lives his life without apologies. Portuguese with subtitles. 105m/C VHS, DVD. BR FR Lazaro Ramos, Marcelia Cartaxa, Flavio Bauraqui, Felippe Marques; *D:* Karim Ainouz; *W:* Karim Ainouz; *C:* Walter Carvalho; *M:* Marcos Suzano, Sacha Ambak.

Madame Sin 𝒹𝒹½ 1971 Aspiring world dominator enlists former CIA agent in scheme to obtain nuclear submarine. MacLaine is perfectly cast in this powerful, winning film. 113m/C VHS, DVD. Shirley MacLaine, Peggy Ashcroft, Shabana Azmi, Twiggy, Leigh Lawson, Geoffrey Bayldon, Navin Chowdhry, Lee Montague; *D:* John Schlesinger; *W:* Ruth Prawer Jhabvala, John Schlesinger; *M:* Gerald Gouriet, Golden Globes '89: Actress-Drama (MacLaine), Venice Film Fest. '88: Actress (MacLaine).

Madame Sousatzka 𝒹𝒹½ 1988 (PG-13). Eccentric, extroverted piano teacher helps students develop spiritually as well as musically. When she engages a teenage Indian student, however, she finds herself considerably challenged. 113m/C VHS, DVD. Shirley MacLaine, Peggy Ashcroft, Shabana Azmi, Twiggy, Leigh Lawson, Geoffrey Bayldon, Navin Chowdhry, Lee Montague; *D:* John Schlesinger; *W:* Ruth Prawer Jhabvala, John Schlesinger; *M:* Gerald Gouriet, Golden Globes '89: Actress-Drama (MacLaine), Venice Film Fest. '88: Actress (MacLaine). **TV**

Madame X 𝒹𝒹½ 1937 Fourth version of this classic tearjerker finds diplomat's wife George having a fling with a playboy. There's a murder and she turns to "death" in order to prevent a scandal. Then George is on the slippery path to alcoholism and prostitution. Adapted from the play by Alexandre Bisson. Run-of-the-mill. Lana Turner's 1966 version is still the one to watch. 96m/B VHS, Gladys George, John Beal, Warren William, Reginald Owen, William Henry, Henry Daniell, Philip Reed, Lynne Carver, Emma Dunn, Ruth Hussey; *D:* John Meehan.

Madame X 𝒹𝒹 *Absinthe* 1966 Lonely diplomat's wife Holly (Turner) has a fling with playboy Phil (Montalban) who dies in her presence. Her nasty mother-in-law (Bennett in her last role) advises her to skedaddle or ruin hubby Clay's (Forsythe) career. She leaves her young son and eventually winds up a prostitute in Mexico where she falls in with slimy crook Sullivan (Meredith). Holly winds up killing him and goes on trial as Madame X. Off-filmed melodrama works because of Turner's heartfelt and affecting performance. 100m/C VHS, Lana Turner, John Forsythe, Ricardo Montalban, Burgess Meredith, Virginia Grey, Constance Bennett, Keir Dullea; *D:* David Lowell Rich; *W:* Jean Holloway; *C:* Russell Metty; *M:* Frank Skinner.

M.A.D.D.: Mothers Against Drunk Driving 𝒹𝒹½ 1983 Emotionally gripping movie recounts the story of Candy Lightner, who, after her daughter was killed in a drunk driving accident, well. 124m/B VHS, DVD. Greer Garson, Walter Pidgeon, Robert Walker, May Whitty, Henry Travers, Sir C. Aubrey Smith, Albert Bassermann, Victor Francen, Reginald Owen, Van Johnson; *D:* Mervyn LeRoy; *C:* Joseph Ruttenberg.

Made 𝒹𝒹½ 2001 (R) Favreau, who also wrote and directed, teams up again with "Swingers" buddy Vaughn in this tale of two-bit losers trying to weasel their way into the mob. Bobby (Favreau), a past-his-prime boxer and construction worker, chauffeurs his stripper girlfriend Jessica (Dickinson), At least Cassie thought it was a refuge—until she reaches the Scudders are crazy killers. 97m/C VHS, Burt Reynolds, Angie Dickinson, Mia Sara, Brian Wimmer, Josh Mostel, William Hickey; *D:* Danny Huston; *W:* Leslie Greif.

The Maddening 𝒹½ 1995 (R) When their car breaks down in a remote area, Cassie (Sara) and daughter Samantha find refuge at the home of Roy Scudder (Reynolds) and his wife Georgina (Dickinson). At least Cassie thought it was a refuge—until she reaches the Scudders are crazy killers. 97m/C VHS, Burt Reynolds, Angie Dickinson, Mia Sara, Brian Wimmer, Josh Mostel, William Hickey; *D:* Danny Huston; *W:* Leslie Greif.

Made for Each Other 𝒹𝒹𝒹 1939 Newlyweds John (Stewart) and Jane get out. 65m/B VHS. Leatrice Joy, Edmund Burns, Ethel Wales, Brandon Hurst, Frank Butler; *D:* Paul Sloane.

Made for Love 𝒹𝒹 1926 Couple journeys romantically to Egypt until disaster strikes: they fall into a tomb and can't get out. 65m/B VHS. Leatrice Joy, Edmund Burns, Ethel Wales, Brandon Hurst, Frank Butler; *D:* Paul Sloane.

Made in America 𝒹𝒹 1993 (PG-13). High-energy, lightweight comedy stars Whoopi as a single mom whose daughter Long discovers her birth was the result of artificial insemination. More surprising is her biological dad: white, obnoxious, country-western car dealer Danson. Overwrought with obvious gags, basically a one-joke movie. Nonetheless, Goldberg and Danson chemically connect onscreen (and for a short time offscreen as well) while supporting actor Smith grabs comedic attention as Teacake, Goldberg's best friend. Both Goldberg and Danson deserve better material. 111m/C VHS, DVD. Whoopi Goldberg, Ted Danson, Will Smith, Nia Long, Paul Rodriguez, Jennifer Tilly, Peggy Rea, Clyde Kusatsu; *D:* Richard Benjamin; *W:* Holly Goldberg Sloan; *C:* Ralf Bode; *M:* Mark Isham.

Made in Argentina 𝒹𝒹 1986 An Argentinean couple living in New York decide to return for a visit. Having left for political reasons they still harbor bitterness. 90m/C VHS, AR Luis Brandoni, Marta Bianchi, Leonor Manso; *D:* Juan Jose Jusid.

Made in Heaven 𝒹𝒹½ 1952 Arid comedy in which British newlyweds try to sustain honeymoon for entire year. The husband, however, eventually suspects her of shenanigans with the maid. 90m/C VHS. GB Petula Clark, David Tomlinson, Sonja Ziemann, A.E. Matthews, Charles Victor,

founded M.A.D.D. and built it into a nationwide organization. Similar to "License to Kill," which dramatized the effect that a drunk driving accident can have on the families of those involved. 97m/C VHS. Mariette Hartley, Paula Prentiss, Bert Remsen; *D:* William A. Graham; *C:* Dean Cundey; *M:* Bruce Broughton. **TV**

Sophie Stewart, John Stanton, Ferdinand "Ferdy" Mayne, Richard Wattis, Alfie Bass, Dora Bryan; **D:** Jack Paddy Carstairs; **W:** George H. Brown, William Douglas-Home; **C:** Geoffrey Unsworth.

Made in Heaven 🦴🦴½ **1987 (PG)** Two souls in heaven fall in love and must find each other after being reborn on Earth if they are to remain eternal lovers. Contains ethereal interpretations of heaven and several cameo appearances by famous actors and musicians. **105m/C VHS.** Timothy Hutton, Kelly McGillis, Maureen Stapleton, Mare Winningham, Ann Wedgeworth, Don Murray, Amanda Plummer, Timothy Daly, Marj Dusay; **Cameos:** Ellen Barkin, Neil Young, Tom Petty, Ric Ocasek, Tom Robbins, Debra Winger, Gary Larsen, David Rasche; **D:** Alan Rudolph; **W:** Raynold Gideon, Bruce A. Evans; **M:** Mark Isham.

Made in USA 🦴🦴 **1988 (R)** Wayward dudes engage vixen while cruising Midwest. Trouble, however, awaits. Note: This is not Godard's mid-'60s classic. **82m/C VHS.** Adrian Pasdar, Lori Singer, Christopher Penn; **D:** Ken Friedman; **W:** Ken Friedman.

Made Men 🦴🦴 **1999 (R)** Former hitman, now in the witness protection program, gets caught stealing 12 million from the mob. If he wants to save his life, he's got to outwit four mobsters sent to get the money. **90m/C VHS, DVD.** James Belushi, Michael Beach, Timothy Dalton, Vanessa Angel, Steve Railsback; **D:** Louis Morneau; **C:** George Mooradian; **M:** Stewart Copeland. VIDEO

Made of Honor 2008 (PG-13) Single man-about-town (Dempsey) can always depend on his platonic best friend Hannah (Monaghan). Then she goes to Scotland on an extended business trip and Tom finally realizes that she's "the one" when he misses her so much he can barely function. Too bad Hannah comes home engaged to Colin (McKidd) and wants Tom to be her maid of honor. Tom agrees, but just so he can go to Scotland and stop the wedding. Why does this sound like a distaff version of "My Best Friend's Wedding" with some "Four Weddings and a Funeral" tossed in? Not yet reviewed. **101m/C DVD.** US Patrick Dempsey, Michelle Monaghan, Kevin McKidd, Kathleen Quinlan, Sydney Pollack, Kadeem Hardison, Chris Messina, Busy Philipps, Kelly Carlson, James B. Sikking, Richmond Arquette, Beau Garrett, Whitney Cummings, Emily Nelson; **D:** Paul Weiland; **W:** Deborah Kaplan, Harry Elfont; **C:** Tony Pierce-Roberts; **M:** Rupert Gregson-Williams.

Madea's Family Reunion 🦴½ **2006 (PG-13)** Director/writer/actor Perry

a little flat, even for kids. McDormand and Hawthorne as Lord "Cucuface" Covington are unable to act to their fullest, and the child actors are mostly forgettable. If you liked the books as a kid, you may be disappointed; but it's a good way to introduce your own children to the series. **90m/C VHS, DVD.** Hatty Jones, Frances McDormand, Nigel Hawthorne, Ben Daniels, Arturo Venegas, Stephane Audran, Katia Caballero; **D:** Daisy von Scherler Mayer; **W:** Marc Levin, Jennifer Flackett, Chris Weitz, Paul Weitz; **C:** Pierre Aim; **M:** Michel Legrand.

Mademoiselle 🦴🦴 **1966** Moreau is a psychotic, sexually repressed schoolteacher in a small village who manages to keep herself under control until studly woodcutter Manni and his son take up residence. The locals distrust the stranger but Moreau can't wait to get her hands on him. Suddenly, the village is battered by a rash of poisonings, fires, and floods, all of which are blamed on Manni, leading the locals to exact a terrible vengeance. In French with English subtitles. **105m/B VHS, DVD. FR GB** Jeanne Moreau, Ettore Manni, Umberto Orsini, Keith Skinner, Jane Beretta, Mony Rey; **D:** Tony Richardson; **W:** Jean Genet; **C:** David Watkin.

Mademoiselle Fifi 🦴½ **1944** Simone stars as a French laundress in 1870 France who refuses to give in to her small town's Prussian oppressors. The film title is the nickname of the most brutal of the Prussian officers, played by Kreuger. An unsuccessful attempt at political allegory for the devastation of WWII. **69m/B VHS.** Simone Simon, John Emery, Kurt Kreuger, Alan Napier, Jason Robards Sr.; **D:** Robert Wise.

Madhouse 🦴🦴 **1974** A troubled horror film star tries to bring his "Dr. Death" character to TV, but during production people begin dying in ways remarkably similar to the script. A strong genre cast should hold the fans' attention during this mild adaptation of Angus Hall's novel "Devilday." **92m/C VHS, DVD. GB** Vincent Price, Peter Cushing, Robert Quarry, Adrienne Corri, Natasha Pyne, Linda Hayden, Michael Parkinson; **D:** Jim Clark.

Madhouse 🦴🦴 **1987** A woman has bizarre recollections of her twin sister whom she finally meets when she escapes from a mental hospital. Lots of violence and gore, has definite cult potential. **90m/C VHS.** Trish Everly, Michael MacRae, Dennis Robertson, Morgan Hart; **D:** Ovidio G. Assonitis.

Madhouse 🦴🦴 **1990 (PG-13)** New homeowners find themselves unable to expel loathsome, boorish guests. Presumably, a comedy cashing in on two of sitcom's brightest lights. **90m/C VHS.** John Larroquette, Kirstie Alley, Alison La Placa, John Diehl, Jessica Lundy, Bradley Gregg, Dennis Miller, Robert Ginty; **D:** Tom Ropelewski; **W:** Tom Ropelewski; **M:** David Newman.

Madhouse 🦴🦴 **2004 (R)** Clark Stevens (Leonard) accepts a psychiatric internship at a dilapidated asylum where murders begin to occur, and he's haunted by the figure of a young boy. He teams up with sympathetic nurse Sara (Ladd) to find out what's going on. **91m/C DVD.** Joshua Leonard, Jordan Ladd, Natasha Lyonne, Lance Henriksen, Leslie Jordan, Patrika Darbo, Christian Leffler, Dendrie Taylor, Aaron Strongoni; **D:** William Butler; **W:** William Butler, Aaron Strongoni; **C:** Viorel Sergovici Jr.; **M:** Alberto Caruso.

Madhouse Mansion 🦴🦴 *Ghost Story* **1974 (PG)** A horror actor revives his career and becomes embroiled in murder. Plenty of in-jokes and clips from older movies. **86m/C VHS. GB** Marianne Faithfull, Leigh Lawson, Anthony Bate, Larry Dann, Sally Grace, Penelope Keith, Vivian Mackerell, Murray Melvin, Barbara Shelley; **D:** Stephen Weeks; **C:** Peter Hurst.

Madigan 🦴🦴🦴 **1968** Realistic and exciting and among the best of the behind-the-scenes urban police thrillers. Hardened NYC detectives (Widmark and Guardino) lose their guns to a sadistic killer and are given 72 hours to track him down. Fonda is the police chief none too pleased with their performance. Adapted by Howard Rodman, Abraham Polonsky, and Harry Kleiner from Richard Dougher-ty's "The Commissioner." **101m/C VHS, DVD.** Richard Widmark, Henry Fonda, Inger Stevens, Harry Guardino, James Whitmore, Susan Clark, Michael Dunn, Don Stroud; **D:** Donald Siegel; **W:** Abraham Polonsky; **C:** Russell Metty; **M:** Don Costa.

Madigan's Millions WOOF! **1967 (G)** Incompetent Treasury agent treks to Italy to recover funds swiped from deceased gangster. This is Hoffman's first film, and is to his career what "The Last Chalice" was to Paul Newman's and "Studs and Kitty" was Sylvester Stallone. Recommended only to the terminally foolhardy. **89m/C VHS, DVD.** Dustin Hoffman, Elsa Martinelli, Cesar Romero; **D:** Stanley Prager.

Madison 🦴🦴½ **2001 (PG)** Predictably cliched sports drama based on a true story. Title refers to Madison, Indiana, a hard-luck community that, by 1971, has little going for it but a tradition of hydroplane racing and a chance to host the Gold Cup tournament. It also has allaround great guy Jim McCormick (Caviezel), a former pilot of the community-owned race boat, the Miss Madison. Both McCormick and Miss Madison have seen better days but golly, Jim just has to make his son Mike (Lloyd) proud. There's nothing actually wrong with the film (which sat on the shelf since 2001) but, boy, have you seen this story before. **94m/C DVD. US** James (Jim) Caviezel, Jake Lloyd, Mary McCormack, Bruce Dern, Brent Briscoe, Paul Dooley, Reed Edward Diamond, Chelcie Ross, Frank Knapp, Byrne Piven, William Shockley, Matt Letscher, Richard Lee Jackson, Kristina Anapau, Vincent Ventresca, Cody McMains; **D:** William Bindley; **W:** William Bindley, Scott Bindley; **C:** James Glennon; **M:** Kevin Kiner.

Madman 🦴 **1979 (R)** Deranged Soviet Jew joins Israeli army to more effectively fulfill his desire to kill loathsome Soviets. Good date movie for those nights when you're home alone. Weaver's first starring role. **95m/C VHS, DVD. IS** Sigourney Weaver, Michael Beck, F. Murray Abraham; **D:** Dan Cohen.

Madman 🦴 **1982 (R)** Camp leader prompts terror when he revives legend regarding ax murderer. Seems that when you call his name, he appears. Buffoon does not believe story and calls out madman's name. Madman hears the call and emerges from forest, says hi, and hacks everyone to death. Lesson learned, case closed. Filmed on Long Island. **89m/C VHS, DVD.** Carl Fredericks, Alexis Dubin, Tony Fish, Paul Ehlers; **D:** Joe Giannone; **W:** Joe Giannone, Gary Sales; **C:** James (Momel) Lemmo; **M:** Gary Sales, Stephen Horelick.

The Madness of King George 🦴🦴🦴½ **1994 (R)** Poor King George is a monarch with problems—his 30 years of royal authority are being usurped by Parliament, his American colonies have been lost, and, in 1788, he's begun to periodically lose his mind. So what do you do when a ruler becomes irrational? The royal physicians are baffled, his loving Queen Charlotte (Mirren) is in despair, but the noxious Prince of Wales (Everett) can barely contain his glee at finally having a chance at the throne. A last resort is offered by Dr. Willis (Holm), a former clergyman with some unusual and sadistic ideas about treating the mentally ill (even if they do have royal blood). Brilliant performance by Hawthorne (who originated the stage role in Bennett's 1991 play "The Madness of George III"). Screen note explains that King George suffered from the metabolic disorder known as porphyria. A Tony Award-winner for its Broadway productions of "Miss Saigon" and "Carousel," Hytner makes his feature-film directing debut. **110m/C VHS, DVD. GB** Nigel Hawthorne, Helen Mirren, Ian Holm, Rupert Everett, Amanda Donohoe, Rupert Graves, Julian Wadham, John Wood, Julian Rhind-Tutt, Jim Carter; **D:** Nicholas Hytner; **W:** Alan Bennett; **C:** Andrew Dunn; **M:** George Fenton. Oscars '94: Art Dir/Set Dec; British Acad. '95: Actor (Hawthorne); Cannes '95: Actress (Mirren).

Mado 🦴🦴 **1976** A middle-aged businessman's life is undone when he falls for a mysterious woman. Piccoli and Schneider are, as usual, convincing. Another of underrated director Sautet's effective, low-key works. In French with subtitles. **130m/C VHS.** Romy Schneider, Michel Piccoli, Charles Denner; **D:** Claude Sautet. Cesar '77: Sound.

Madonna: Innocence Lost 🦴½ **1995** Tacky TV movie focusing on the ambitious singer and would-be actress who made wearing underwear as outerwear almost acceptable. Tawdry gossip highlights this laughfest as the trash talker hustles her way to the top of the heap, uncaring of whom she steps on along the way. Toronto substitutes for New York City grit. **90m/C VHS.** Terumi Matthews, Wendie Malick, Jeff Yagher, Dean Stockwell, Nigel Bennett, Don Francks, Rod Wilson, Tom Melissis; **D:** Bradford May; **W:** Michael J. Murray.

Madron 🦴½ **1970 (PG)** Road western filmed in the Israeli desert, complete with menacing Apaches, wagon train massacre, a nun and a gunslinger. **93m/C VHS, DVD.** Richard Boone, Leslie Caron, Paul Smith; **D:** Jerry Hopper; **W:** Edward Chappell, Lee McMahon; **C:** Marcel Grignon, Adam Greenberg; **M:** Riz Ortolani.

The Madwoman of Chaillot 🦴🦴½ **1969 (G)** Four men conspire to drill for oil which they believe lurks under Paris. Hepburn finds out about their plot and tells each man that oil is bubbling up through her basement. Before the men can arrive at her house to confirm this, she and her three cronies hold a mock trial and sentence the men to death. Features a stellar cast, but this modern-day adaptation of Jean Giraudoux's play "La Folle de Chaillot" falls flat. **142m/C VHS.** Katharine Hepburn, Charles Boyer, Claude Dauphin, Edith Evans, John Gavin, Paul Henreid, Oscar Homolka, Margaret Leighton, Giulietta Masina, Nanette Newman, Richard Chamberlain, Yul Brynner, Donald Pleasence, Danny Kaye, Fernand Gravey; **D:** Bryan Forbes; **W:** Edward Anhalt.

Mae West 🦴🦴½ **1984** Details West's life from her humble beginnings to her racy film stardom. Jillian does a good job bringing the buxom legend back to life. **97m/C VHS.** Ann Jillian, James Brolin, Piper Laurie, Roddy McDowall; **D:** Lee Philips; **M:** Brad Fiedel. TV

Maedchen in Uniform 🦴🦴1½ *Girls in Uniform* **1931** A scandalous early German talkie about a rebellious schoolgirl who falls in love with a female teacher and attempts suicide when the teacher is punished for the relationship. A controversial criticism of lesbianism and militarism that impelled the Nazis, rising to power two years later, to exile its director. It was also banned in the United States. In German with English subtitles; edited versions are also in circulation. Remade in 1965. **90m/B VHS. GE** Dorothea Wieck, Ellen Schwanneke, Hertha Thiele; **D:** Leontine Sagan.

Maelstrom 🦴🦴 **2000** Offbeat mixture of the surreal, the whimsical, and the melodramatic. A drunken Bibiliane (Croze) commits a hit-and-run and reads in the next day's newspaper that the man, a fishmonger, has died. Guilt-stricken, she meets the man's son, a deep sea diver named Evian (Verrault), at the funeral home and he mistakes her for a concerned neighbor. Bibiliane's friendship with Evian leads to an affair but she becomes compelled to tell him the truth and accept whatever punishment he decrees. There's lots of water and fish imagery. French with subtitles. **86m/C VHS, DVD. CA** Marie-Josee Croze, Jean-Nicholas Verreault, Stephanie Morgenstern, Bobby Beshro; **D:** Andre Turpin; **W:** Denis Villeneuve; **C:** Andre Turpin; **M:** Pierre Desrochers. Genie '00: Actress (Croze), Cinematog, Director (Villeneuve), Film, Screenplay.

Mafia! 🦴🦴 *Jane Austen's Mafia!* **1998 (PG-13)** Director Abrahams returns to the "Airplane" well once again as he takes aim at the Mafia movies of Coppola and Scorsese. As usual, the results are hit and miss, with the joke machine gun set on full automatic. Plot follows that of the Godfather trilogy most closely, with Bridges (in his last film) as klutzy patriarch Vincenzo Cortino. His sons, sensitive war hero Anthony (Mohr) and hot tempered Joey (Burke), wrestle for control of the keystone kriminal empire after pop takes the dirt

[The following is a sidebar from the "Madeline" entry area, lower-left column:]

Madeleine 🦴🦴½ *The Strange Case of Madeline* **1950** Courtroom drama of woman charged with poisoning her French lover in 1850s Scotland. Directed by the same David Lean who made "Bridge on the River Kwai" and "Lawrence of Arabia". Here, though, he was merely trying to provide a vehicle for his wife, actress Todd. Intrigued? **114m/B VHS, DVD.** Ann Todd, Leslie Banks, Ivan Desny, Norman Wooland, Barbara Everest, Susan Stranks, Patricia Raine, Elizabeth Sellars, Edward Chapman, Jean Cadell, Eugene Deckers, Amy Veness, John Laurie, Henry Edwards, Ivor Barnard, Barry Jones, David Horne, Andre Morell; **D:** David Lean; **W:** Nicholas Phipps, Stanley Haynes; **C:** Guy Green; **M:** William Alwyn.

Madeline 🦴🦴 **1998 (PG)** Adaptation of Ludwig Bemelmans' classic 1939 children's book about the trouble-finding orphan Madeline (Jones), her schoolmates, and their patient teacher Miss Clavel (McDormand). As the credits open, Bemelmans' familiar paintings are animated. After the live action starts, you'll wish that the producers had animated the entire film. Travelling through the plots of four of the six Madeline books, the acting seems nap. Basically, the actors' jobs are to remain deadpan while all manner of shenanigans and hijinks take place and hilarity allegedly ensues. This genre is quickly running out of ammo. It's time for someone to administer the kiss of death, pronto. **VHS, DVD.** Olympia Dukakis, Christina Applegate, Pamela Gidley, Tony LoSianco, Joe (Johnny) Viterelli, Vincent Pastore, Jason Fuchs, Gregory Sierra, Louis Mandylor; **D:** Jim Abrahams; **W:** Jim Abrahams, Michael McManus, Greg Norberg; **C:** Pierre Letarte; **M:** John (Gianni) Frizzell.

Magenta 🐾🐾½ **1996 (R)** Don't mess around with your teenaged sister-in-law! You'd think guys would've learned that lesson by now. Handsome Dr. Michael Walsh (McMahon) and his lovely wife, Helen (Storry), have a seemingly happy life with their daughter Brittany. Then Helen's sister Magenta (Atkins) comes to stay and she and Michael are soon exchanging more than eye contact. Naturally, all this leads to betrayal, lies, and even more problems. 94mC VHS. Julian McMahon, Crystal Atkins, Alison Storry, Marklen Kennedy; **D:** Gregory C. Haynes; **W:** Gregory C. Haynes; **C:** Mark Anthony Galuzzo; **M:** Harold Kloser. **VIDEO**

Magee and the Lady 🐾🐾 **Shell Be Sweet 1978 (PG)** The crusty captain of a rusty ship must warm up to a spoiled debutante or lose his ship to a foreclosure. Could be better. Made for TV. 92mC VHS. **AU** Tony LoSianco, Sally Kellerman; **D:** Gene Levitt. **TV**

The Magdalene Sisters 🐾🐾½ **2002 (R)** Semifictionalized stories of four young Irish women sentenced to life in a religious labor camp run by the Sisters of the Magdalene Order from 1964 to 1969. Their "crimes" include overt flirtatiousness, having been raped, bearing a child out of wedlock, and other perceived sexual offenses. They're treated cruelly by the ogre in authority, Sister Bridget (McEwan) and any attempt at escape is met with more brutality. Grim, powerful film captures the atrocities of 1960s-era Irish Catholicism with frightful clarity. 119mC VHS, DVD, GB IR Geraldine McEwan, Anne-Marie Duff, Nora-Jane Noone, Dorothy Duffy, Eileen Walsh, Mary Murray, Britta Smith, Frances Healy, Eithne McGuinness, Daniel Costello; **D:** Peter Mullan; **W:** Peter Mullan; **C:** Nigel Willoughby; **M:** Craig Armstrong. Venice Film Fest. '02: Film.

Magdalene 🐾🐾 **1988 (R)** Violent baron seeks revenge in medieval Europe, where a beautiful whore that spurned him... **C** VHS. Steve Bond, Nastassja Kinski, David Warner, Gunter Meisner, Ferdinand "Ferdy" Mayne, Anthony Quayle, Franco Nero, Janet Agren; **D:** Monica Teuber.

Mafioso 🐾🐾½ **1962** Black comedy from Lattuada that was revolutionary for its depiction of everyday Mafia life in Sicily. Nino (Sordi) is a longtime foreman at the Fiat plant in Milan. He decides to use his vacation time and take his wife (Conti) and daughters to visit his small hometown of Calabro. It's Nino's culture shock for his wife) but that doesn't mean he's forgotten where to pay his respects. But town boss Don Vincenzo (Attanasio) is quick to remind Nino he still owes him a favor and the Don now wants to collect. Italian with subtitles. 106m/B/B IT Alberto Sordi, Norma Bengell, Cinzia Bruno, Ugo Attanasio, Gabriella Conti, Armando Tine, Francesco Lo Briglio, Katiusca Pretti; **D:** Alberto Lattuada; **W:** Rafael Azzona, Marco Ferreri, Agenore Incrocci, Furio Scarpelli; **C:** Armando Nannuzzi; **M:** Piero Piccioni.

Mafia vs. Ninja 🐾 **1984** The mob wants to control the city, but the Ninja has other ideas. 90mC VHS. Alexander Lou, Wang Hsia, Charlena Hsu, Eugene Trammel; **D:** Robert Tai.

Mafia Princess 🐾🐾 **1986** The daughter of a Mafia boss tries to discover her own identity despite her father's involvement in crime. Based on a best-selling autobiography by a real-life member of a Mob family. Antoinette Giancana. 100mC VHS. Tony Curtis, Susan Lucci, Kathleen Widdoes, Chuck Shamata, Louie Dibianco; **D:** Robert E. Collins. **TV**

Magic 🐾🐾 **1978 (R)** Ventriloquist Hopkins and his dummy, an all-too-human counterpart, get involved with a beautiful woman lost between reality and the irresistible world of illusion. Spine-chilling psycho-drama with a less-than-believable premise. Screenplay by Anthony Hopkins, Ann-Margret, Burgess Meredith, Ed Lauter, Jerry Houser, David Ogden Stiers, Lillian Randolph; **D:** Richard Attenborough; **W:** William Goldman; **C:** Victor Kemper; **M:** Jerry Goldsmith.

The Magic Bow 🐾½ **1947** Typically ridiculous musical bio—this time of violinist Nicolo Paganini (Granger). He's the talented poor boy who falls for the wealthy Jeanne (Calvert) but his one true love is for his Stradivarius. Yehudi Menuhin plays the solos. Based on the novel by Manuel Komroff. 105m/B VHS GB Stewart Granger, Phyllis Calvert, Jean Kent, Dennis Price, Cecil Parker, Felix Aylmer, Frank Cellier, Marie Lohr; **D:** Bernard Knowles; **W:** Roland Pertwee, Norman Ginsburg; **C:** Jack Asher, Jack Cox.

The Magic Bubble 🐾🐾½ **1993** (PG-13) On her 40th birthday, Julia Cole finds the fountain of youth...inside a bottle of enchanted bubbles. Ageless and timeless, she begins to know the meaning of true happiness. Raucous, now somewhat dated comedy; music by Badfinger, including Paul McCartney's "Come and Get It." 90mC VHS, DVD, Diane Salinger, John Calvin, Priscilla Porter, Coleen Camp, Tony Peck, Wallace Shawn, George Cooney; **D:** Alfredo Ringel, Mark Harmon; **W:** Meridth Beer, Geof Prysiri.

The Magic Christian 🐾🐾🐾 **1969 (PG)** A series of related skits about a rich m'an (Sellers) and his son (Starr) who try to prove that anyone can be bought. Raucous, uneven dated comedy. 92mC VHS, DVD, GB Peter Sellers, Ringo Starr, Isabel Jeans, Wilfrid Hyde-White, Graham Chapman, John Cleese, Peter Graves, John Lennon, Yoko Ono, Richard Attenborough, Leonard Frey, Laurence Harvey, Christopher Lee, Spike Milligan, Yul Brynner, Roman Polanski, Raquel Welch, Caroline Blakiston, Ferdinand "Ferdy" Mayne; **D:** Joseph McGrath; **W:** Terry Southern, Peter Sellers, Graham Chapman, John Cleese; **C:** Geoffrey Unsworth; **M:** Ken Thorne.

The Magic Flute 🐾🐾🐾½ **1973 (G)** Bergman's acclaimed version of Mozart's famous comic opera, universally considered one of the greatest adaptations of opera to film ever made. Staged before a live audience for Swedish TV. Subtitled. 134mC VHS, DVD, SW Josef Kostlinger, Irma Urrila, Hakan Hagegard, Elisabeth Erikson; **D:** Ingmar Bergman.

The Magic Fountain 🐾🐾 **1961** Three princes search for a magic fountain whose waters will cure their ailing father. Two of them, however, take the wrong course and are turned into ravens by a wicked dwarf. Based on the fairy tale "Das Wasser des Lebens" by the Brothers Grimm. 82mC VHS. Peter Nestler, Helmo Kindermann, Josef Marz, Catherine Hansen, Cecric Hardwicke; **D:** Alan David.

Magic Hunter 🐾🐾 **1996** Max (Kemp) is supposed to be the best sharpshooter on the Budapest police force, but his skill deserts him and he accidentally shoots the woman he was assigned to protect. A sinister colleague gives him seven magic bullets guaranteed to hit their target but what Max doesn't realize is that he's made a bargain with the Devil, and the Devil gets to choose the seventh target. Hungarian with subtitles. 106mC VHS, HU Gary Kemp, Alexander Kaidanovsky, Sadie Frost; **D:** Ildiko Enyedi.

Magic in the Mirror: Fowl Play 🐾🐾½ **1996 (G)** Young Mary Margaret (Smith) does an "Alice Through the Looking Glass" when she steps through an antique mirror bequeathed to her by her grandmother and discovers an enchanted kingdom run by giant ducks. But just how will MM find her way back? 86mC VHS. Jamie Renee Smith, Kevin Wixted, Saxon Trainor, David Brooks, Godfrey James; **D:** Ted Nicolaou; **W:** Frank Dietz, Ken Carter Jr.; **D:** Adolfo Bartoli; **M:** Richard Kosinski.

Magic Island 🐾🐾½ **1995 (PG)** Thirteen-year-old Jack (Bryan) gets sucked into the pages of a pirate book and finds himself with Blackbeard and his scurvy crew. They're on a treasure hunt and figure Jack's book contains some missing clues. Naturally, Jack finds himself in lots of trouble. 88mC VHS, DVD, Zachary TV art, Abraham Benrubi, Jessie-Ann Friend, Oscar Dillon, Sean O'Kane, Schae Harrison, Janet DuBois, Andrew Divoff; **D:** Sam Irvin; **W:** Neil Ruttenberg, Brent Friedman; **C:** James Lawrence Spencer; **M:** Richard Band.

Magic Kid 2 🐾🐾½ **1994 (PG)** The young star of a popular martial arts program wants to quit and go to high school like a normal teenager. But the studio execs have other ideas. 90mC VHS, DVD. Ted Jan Roberts, Stephen Furst, Donald Gibb, Jennifer Savidge; **D:** Stephen Furst.

Magic Kid 🐾🐾½ **Ninja Dragons 1992 (PG)** Thirteen-year-old martial-arts champ (Roberts) visits his older sister vacation in L.A., which puts the "little person" in his martial arts movie idol and his sister her favorite soap opera hunk. But they wind up being chased by the mobsters Uncle Bob owes money to. 91mC VHS, DVD. Ted Jan Roberts, Shonda Whipple, Stephen Furst, Joseph Campanella, Billy Hufsey, Sondra Kerns, Pamela Dixon, Lauren Tewes, Don "The Dragon" Wilson; **D:** Joseph Merhi; **W:** Stephen Smoke; **M:** Jim Halfpenny.

Magic Moments 🐾🐾½ **1989** Ambitious British TV exec Melanie James (Seagrove) is about to score the coup of her career. She's persuaded charismatic American illusionist Troy Gardner (Shea) to recreate his death-defying act on TV—but only if Melanie will produce the show herself. Too bad her power-hungry boss is out to cause trouble. Made for British TV. 103mC VHS, GB Jenny Seagrove, John Shea; **D:** Lawrence Gordon-Clark; **W:** Charlotte Bingham, Terence Brady; **C:** Alan Hawkshaw. **TV**

Magic of Lassie 🐾🐾 **1976 (G)** Romantic misadventures ensue when Stewart is engaging as the nice grandpa who refuses to sell his land to mean rich guy Roberts. Innocuous, pleasant remake of "Lassie Come Home." Stewart sings. 100mC VHS. James Stewart, Mickey Rooney, Stephanie Zimbalist, Alice Faye, Pernel Roberts; **D:** Don Chaffey.

Magic on Love Island 🐾 **1980** Romantic misadventures ensue when eight ladies go on vacation to Love Island, a tropical paradise. 96mC VHS, Adrienne Barbeau, Bill Daily, Howard Duff, Dody Goodman, Dominique Dunne, Lisa Hartman Black, Janis Paige; **D:** Earl Bellamy.

Magic Serpent 🐾🐾 **1966** Fantasy set in medieval Japan features a grand duel in magic between a good hero and evil sorcerer who transform into a giant dragon and a giant frog to do battle. 86mC VHS, DVD. Hiroki Matsukata, Tomoko Ogawa, Ryutaro Otomo, Bin Amatsu; **D:** Tetsuya Yamauchi.

Magic in the Water 🐾🐾 **1995 (PG)** Divorced, obnoxious radio shrink and neglectful dad Dr. Jack Black (Harmon) takes the kiddies on a summer jaunt to a Canadian lake, where they hope to explore the legend of Orky, Canada's answer to the Loch Ness monster. Dad becomes a believer when Orky possesses his body and (New Age Alert!) releases his inner child. Harmless fun for the kids, but parents will gag at the attempt to provide a meaningful and symbolic message when arrives with all the subtlety of an Oliver Stone history lesson. Sort of an "E.T." meets "Free Willy" with Orky shilling for the EPA. Beautiful cinematography showcasing the British Columbia landscape helps, but not enough. 100mC VHS, DVD. Mark Harmon, Joshua Jackson, Harley Jane Kozak, Sarah Wayne, Willie Nark-Orn, Frank S. Salsedo; **D:** Rick Stevenson; **W:** Icel Dobell Massey, Rick Stevenson; **C:** Thomas Burstyn; **M:** David Schwartz. Genie '95: Cinematog., Sound.

Magic Town 🐾🐾½ **1947** An opinion pollster investigates a small town which exactly reflects the views of the entire nation, making his job a cinch. The publicity causes much ado in the town with ensuing laughs. Uneven but entertaining. 103mC VHS. Jane Wyman, James Stewart, Kent Smith Regis Toomey, Donald Meek; **D:** William A. Wellman; **C:** Joseph Biroc.

The Magic Voyage 🐾🐾 **1993** (G) Animated tale of a friendly woodworm named Pico who voyages with Columbus to the new world and convinces him that the world is indeed round. He then comes to the aid of a magical firefly named Marilyn who helps Columbus find gold to bring back to Spain. 82mC VHS, DVD. Mickey Rooney, Corey Feldman, Irene Cara, Dan Haggerty, Samantha Eggar.

The Magical Legend of the Leprechauns 🐾🐾½ **1999** Goofy fantasy finds American businessman Jack Woods (Quaid) sent to a remote part of Ireland where he happens to save the life of a young leprechaun, Seamus Muldoon (Meaney), which puts him the life of leprechaun. While Jack tries to romance neighbor Kathleen (Brody), the leprechauns are getting into a fracas with their enemies, the Trooping Fairies, leading to a battle and Jack's involvement. 139mC VHS, DVD. Randy Quaid, Colm Meaney, Orla Brady, Whoopi Goldberg, Roger Daltrey, Daniel Betts, Zoe Wanamaker, Caroline Carver, Kieran Culkin, Frank Finlay, Phyllida Law; **D:** John Henderson; **W:** Peter Barnes; **C:** Clive Tickner; **M:** Richard Harvey. **TV**

Magical Mystery Tour 🐾🐾½ **1967** On the road with an oddball assortment of people, the Beatles experience a number of strange incidents around the English countryside. ♪ Magical Mystery Tour; Blue Jay Way; Your Mother Should Know; The Fool on the Hill. 55mC VHS, DVD, GB John Lennon, George Harrison, Ringo Starr, Paul McCartney; **D:** John Lennon, George Harrison, Ringo Starr, Paul McCartney. **TV**

The Magician 🐾🐾🐾 **1958** A master magician in 19th century Sweden (von Sydow) wreaks ill in this darkly comical, supernatural parable. Dark, well photographed early Bergman effort. In Swedish with English subtitles. 101m/B VHS, SW Max von Sydow, Ingrid Thulin, Gunnar Bjornstrand, Bibi Andersson, Naima Wifstrand; **D:** Ingmar Bergman; **W:** Ingmar Bergman. Venice Film Fest. '59: Special Jury Prize.

The Magic Stone 🐾🐾 **Killian's Chronicle 1995** Kilian is the 10th-century Irish slave of brutish Viking Ivar, who decides to sacrifice him to the Norse god Thor when the Vikings become lost while sailing off the North American coast. Kilian manages to escape and make it to shore where he's rescued by a Native American tribe and falls in love with local beauty Turtle. But Ivar goes after Kilian to steal his magic stone, which can navigate a ship through the worst weather, and be captive by an evil sorcerer and his dragon. 80mC VHS, DVD, Basil Rathbone, Estelle Winwood, Gary Lockwood; **D:** Bert I. Gordon.

The Magic Sword 🐾🐾 **St. George and the Seven Curses; St. George and the Dragon 1962** A family-oriented adventure film about a young knight who sets out to rescue a beautiful princess who is being held captive by an evil sorcerer and his dragon. 80mC VHS, DVD, Basil Rathbone, Estelle Winwood, Gary Lockwood, Gary Lockwood; **D:** Bert I. Gordon.

The Magic Voyage of Sinbad 🐾🐾 **Sadko 1952** Sinbad embarks on a fantastic journey after promising the people of his Covasian home that he will find the elusive Phoenix, the bird of happiness. Unreleased in the U.S. until 1962; rewritten for the American screen by a young Coppola. 79mC VHS, DVD, RU Sergey Stolyarov, Alla Larionova, Mark Troyanovsky; **D:** Alexander Ptushko; **W:** Francis Ford Coppola.

The Magician 🐾🐾½ 1993 In the early 1980s, Scotland Yard detective George Byrne (Owen) partners with shady American businessman David Katz (Accovone) to bring down a counterfeiting ring. Katz goes undercover to try and meet the mysterious head of the ring (the title character) but risks his family by getting too involved. Meanwhile, the IRA also wants the counterfeiter so they can destabilize the British economy by flooding the country with fake currency. Based on a true story. 99m/C **DVD.** *GB* Jay Acovone, Clive Owen; Jeremy Kemp, Peter Howitt, Jennifer Calvert; **D:** Terry Winsor; **W:** Jeff Pope. **TV**

The Magician of Lublin 🐾🐾½ 1979 (R) Based on an unusual story by Issac Bashevis Singer. Follows the exploits of a magician/con man in turn-of-the-century Poland whose personal flaws kill his career, until a chance emerges for one last trick. A good example of movie not as good as book; this rendering is superficial, badly acted and unsatisfying. Made soon after Singer won the Nobel Prize for literature in 1978. 105m/C **VHS.** Alan Arkin, Valerie Perrine, Louise Fletcher, Lou Jacobi, Shelley Winters, Elspeth March, Lisa Whelchel; **D:** Menahem Golan; **M:** Maurice Jarre.

Magma: Volcanic Disaster 🐾 2006 (PG-13) Silly cable disaster flick with cheesy CGI. Dr. Peter Shepard (Berkley) believes that volcanic eruptions in Iceland are the precursor to global catastrophe. Naturally, the bureaucrats don't believe him until there's more explosions. Now it's up to Peter to test out his theory that deep sea ventilation will relieve the pressure build-up and save the planet! 87m/C **DVD.** Xander Berkeley, Amy Jo Johnson, Michael Durell, Reiko Aylesworth, Doug Death, David O'Donnell; **D:** Ian Gilmore; **W:** Rebecca Rian; **M:** Nathan Furst. **CABLE**

Magnificent Adventurer 🐾 1963 Ostensibly a biography of Benvenuto Cellini, the Florentine sculptor, with a concentration on his love life and swordplay. 94m/C **VHS.** *IT* Claudia Mori, Francoise Fabian, Jose Nieto, Felix Defauce, Brett Halsey; **D:** Riccardo Fredo; **W:** Filippo Sanjust; **C:** Raffaele Masciocchi; **M:** Francesco De Masi.

The Magnificent Ambersons 🐾🐾🐾½ 1942 Welles's second film. A fascinating, inventive translation of the Booth Tarkington novel about a wealthy turn of the century family collapsing under the changing currents of progress. Pure Welles, except the glaring ly bad tacked-on ending that the studio shot (under the direction of the great Robert Wise and Fred Fleck), after taking the film from him. It seems they wanted the proverbial happy ending. 88m/B **VHS.** Joseph Cotten, Anne Baxter, Tim Holt, Richard Bennett, Dolores Costello, Erskine Sanford, Ray Collins, Agnes Moorehead; **D:** Freddie Fleck, Robert Wise, Orson Welles; **W:** Orson Welles; **M:** Bernard Herrmann, Roy Webb. Natl. Film Reg. '91;; N.Y. Film Critics '42: Actress (Moorehead).

The Magnificent Ambersons 🐾🐾½ 2002 George Amberson (Rhys Meyers) is the spoiled son of an upper-class, turn-of-the-century Midwestern family. When his widowed mother Isabel (Stowe) is reunited with old flame Eugene Morgan (Greenwood), George becomes obsessively jealous and schemes to break up the match even as he romances Eugene's daughter, Lucy (Mol). Stowe looks beautiful but Rhys Meyers over-emphasizes George's lessthan-filial response to his mother. Adaptation of Booth Tarkington's novel that reportedly used Orson Welles original script for his 1942 film. 139m/C **VHS, DVD.** Madeleine Stowe, Bruce Greenwood, Jonathan Rhys Meyers, Jennifer Tilly, Gretchen Mol, James Cromwell, William Hookins; **D:** Alfonso Arau. **CABLE**

Magnificent Doll 🐾🐾 1946 Boring Hollywood bio of first lady Dolly Madison (Rogers) who is wooed by dynamic Aaron Burr (Niven) before she decides on marrying quiet James Madison (Meredith) and pushing his political career to the office of the presidency. 93m/B **VHS.** Ginger Rogers, David Niven, Burgess Meredith, Stephen McNally, Peggy Wood, Grandon Rhodes, Arthur Space,

Robert Barrat; **D:** Frank Borzage; **W:** Irving Stone; **C:** Joseph Valentine; **M:** Hans J. Salter.

The Magnificent Dope 🐾🐾½ 1942 Fonda is likeable, as usual, as the hapless yokel in the big city. A trip to New York to take a course on being successful is his prize for winning a "laziest man" contest. He falls for his teacher; she uses his crush to motivate him. Funny and entertaining. 83m/B **VHS.** Henry Fonda, Lynn Bari, Don Ameche, Edward Everett Horton, Hobart Cavanaugh, Pierre Watkin; **D:** Walter Lang.

The Magnificent Matador 🐾🐾½ The Brave and the Beautiful 1955 The story of an aging matador who faces death in the bullring to win the love of a woman. Quinn is the bullfighter on the horns of a dilemma. Lots of bull in script carried by harried bull in ring. 94m/C **VHS.** Anthony Quinn, Maureen O'Hara, Thomas Gomez; **D:** Budd Boetticher.

Magnificent Obsession 🐾🐾½ 1954 A drunken playboy (Hudson) kills a man and blinds his wife in an automobile accident. Plagued by guilt, he devotes his life to studying medicine in order to restore the widow's sight. Well-acted melodrama lifted Hudson to stardom. Faithful to the 1935 original, based on a novel by Lloyd C. Douglas. 108m/C **VHS.** Jane Wyman, Rock Hudson, Barbara Rush, Agnes Moorehead; **D:** Douglas Sirk; **W:** Robert Blees; **C:** Russell Metty.

The Magnificent Seven 🐾🐾🐾 1960 Western remake of Akira Kurosawa's classic "The Seven Samurai." Mexican villagers hire gunmen to protect them from the bandits who are destroying their town. Most of the actors were relative unknowns, though not for long. Sequelled by "Return of the Seven" in 1966, "Guns of the Magnificent Seven" in 1969, and "The Magnificent Seven Ride" in 1972. Excellent score. Uncredited writing by Walter Newman and Walter Bernstein. 126m/C **VHS. DVD.** Yul Brynner, Steve McQueen, Robert Vaughn, James Coburn, Charles Bronson, Horst Buchholz, Eli Wallach, Brad Dexter; **D:** John Sturges; **W:** William Roberts; **C:** Charles B(ryant) Lang Jr.; **M:** Elmer Bernstein.

The Magnificent Seven 🐾🐾½ 1998 Pilot movie for the brief TV series that was loosely based on the 1960 film. An indian chief hires seven gunslingers to help defend tribal land from a gang of greedy outlaws who want the tribe's gold mine. 90m/C **VHS.** Michael Biehn, Ron Perlman, Dale Midkiff, Eric Close, Anthony Starke, Laurie Holden, Andrew Kavovit, Rick Worthy, Kurtwood Smith, Ned Romero, Daragh O'Malley, Michael Greyeyes, Tony Burton; **D:** Geoff Murphy; **W:** Frank Q. Dobbs, Chris Black; **C:** Jack Conroy; **M:** Don Harper. **TV**

The Magnificent Yankee 🐾🐾🐾 The Man with Thirty Sons 1950 Adaptation of Emmet Lavery's Broadway play on the life of Supreme Court Justice Oliver Wendell Holmes, starring Calhern (who also did the stage version). America's foremost legal mind was well-served by Calhern, with Harding as his ever-patient wife. 80m/B **VHS.** Louis Calhern, Ann Harding, Eduard Franz, Philip Ober, Ian Wolfe, Edith Evanson, Richard Anderson, Jimmy Lydon, Robert Sherwood, Hugh Sanders; **D:** John Sturges; **W:** Emmet Lavery.

Magnolia 🐾🐾🐾 1999 (R) It's a really long, frantic, and surreal look into a 24-hour series of interlocking stories, with a fine ensemble cast. Bad dads Jimmy Gator (Hall) and Earl Partridge (Robards) are both dying and estranged from their children—Jimmy's coke-addicted daughter, Claudia (Walters), and Earl's flashy motivational speaker son, Frank (Cruise). Earl's trophy wife Linda (Moore) is having a breakdown but he's being cared for by kind-hearted nurse Phil (Hoffman). And then there's a popular game show (of which Jimmy is the host) and its current newcomer Posey, who plays her 10-year-old son, and loud-mouthed best friend Matrone. 105m/C **VHS, DVD.** US Jennifer Lopez, Ralph Fiennes, Natasha Richardson, Stanley Tucci, Tyler Garcia Posey, Marissa Matrone, Bob Hoskins, Frances Conroy, Christopher Eigeman, Priscilla Lopez, Amy Sedaris; **D:** Wayne Wang; **W:** Kevin Wade; **C:** Karl Walter Lindenlaub; **M:** Alan Silvestri.

Aimee Mann. Golden Globes '00: Support. Actor (Cruise); Natl. Bd. of Review '99: Support. Actor (Hoffman), Support. Actress (Moore).

Magnum Force 🐾🐾½ 1973 (R) Eastwood's second "Dirty Harry" movie. Harry finds a trail leading from a series of gangland killings straight back to the P.D. Less gripping than "Dirty Harry" (1971), but still effective. Holbrook is cast intriguingly against type. 124m/C **VHS, DVD.** Clint Eastwood, Hal Holbrook, Mitchell Ryan, David Soul, Robert Urich, Tim Matheson, Kip Niven, Albert "Poppy" Popwell; **D:** Ted Post; **W:** Michael Cimino, John Milius; **C:** Frank Stanley; **M:** Lalo Schifrin.

Magnum Killers 🐾 1976 A young man becomes involved in a web of deadly intrigue when he sets out to find who cheated him out of a small fortune during a card game. 92m/C **VHS.** Sombat Methance, Prichela Lee.

Magnum P.I.: Don't Eat the Snow in Hawaii 🐾🐾½ 1980 Series pilot finds Vietnam-vet-turned-private-eye Thomas Sullivan Magnum (Selleck) living in Hawaii (in the guest house of never-seen mystery writer Robin Masters) and investigating the death of a wartime buddy. Hillerman excels as autocratic major domo Higgins. 99m/C **VHS, DVD.** Tom Selleck, John Hillerman, Roger E. Mosley, Larry Manetti; **D:** Roger Young; **W:** Donald P. Belisario, Glen Larson. **TV**

The Mahabharata 1989 Adapted from the myths and folklore of ancient India, the screen version of the original nine-hour stage play is the story of a devastating war between two powerful clans. Initially broadcast on public TV, the six-hour movie is divided into three two-hour segments: "The Game of Dice," "Exile in the Forest," and "The War." 318m/C **VHS, DVD.** *GB FR* Robert Langton-Lloyd, Antonin Stahly-Vishwanadan, Bruce Myers; **D:** Peter Brook; **W:** Jean-Claude Carriere; **M:** Toshi Tsuchitori. **TV**

Mahler 🐾🐾🐾 1974 (PG) Strange Russell effort on the life of the great composer Gustav Mahler. Imperfect script is rescued by fine acting. 110m/C **VHS, DVD.** Robert Powell, Georgina Hale, Richard Morant, Lee Montague, Terry O'Quinn; **D:** Ken Russell; **W:** Ken Russell; **C:** Dick Bush.

Mahogany 🐾🐾½ 1975 (PG) Poor girl becomes world-famous high fashion model and designer, ditches boyfriend in the old neighborhood, gets a career boost when she daringly appears in a dress of her own creation at a Roman fashion show, and still yearns for the boy back home. Motown attempt to make mainstream hit that's glossy and predictable. 109m/C **VHS, DVD.** Diana Ross, Billy Dee Williams, Jean-Pierre Aumont, Anthony Perkins, Nina Foch; **D:** Berry Gordy; **W:** John Byrum; **C:** David Watkin.

The Maid 🐾🐾½ 1990 (PG) An offbeat comedy romance with Sheen as the house husband to Bisset's female executive character. Nice acting; charming, if unoriginal, premise. 91m/C **VHS.** Martin Sheen, Jacqueline Bisset, Jean-Pierre Cassel, James Faulkner, Victoria Shalet; **D:** Ian Toynton.

Maid in Manhattan 🐾🐾½ 2002 (PG-13) Ralph Fiennes smiles! Okay, so it's not Greta Garbo laughs but the serious-minded Brit is not known for romantic comedies—in fact, this bit of fluff is his first. He's wealthy political scion Christopher Marshall, who's running for a New York Senate seat when he meets cute with Marisa (Lopez). She's the ambitious Latina single mom who's working as a maid in a posh NYC hotel but the mistakes in a room for a guest. Much angst and tabloid gossip) when the truth is revealed until the prerequisite happy ending. Lopez is tenacious but her best scenes are with cutie

Maid to Order 🐾½ 1987 (PG) Rich girl Sheedy's fairy godmother puts her in her place by turning her into a maid for a snooty Malibu couple. Good-natured and well-acted if rather mindless Cinderella story. 92m/C **VHS, DVD.** Ally Sheedy, Beverly D'Angelo, Michael Ontkean, Dick Shawn, Tom Skerritt, Valerie Perrine, Rigg Kennedy; **D:** Amy Holden Jones; **W:** Perry Howze; **M:** Georges Delerue.

Maid's Night Out 🐾🐾 1938 Pleasant, simple-minded mistaken-identity comedy. Fontaine as an heiress; rich-guy posing-as-milkman Lane thinks she is a maid. They fall in love, of course. 64m/B **VHS.** Joan Fontaine, Allan "Rocky" Lane, Hedda Hopper, George Irving, William Brisbane, Billy Gilbert, Cecil Kellaway; **D:** Ben Holmes.

Maids of Wilko 🐾🐾 The Young Ladies of Wilko; Panny z Wilka; The Young Girls of Wilko 1979 Wajda's adaptation of Jaroslav Iwaszkiewicz's memoirs set in the late '20s. Viktor Ruben (Olbrychski) reexamines his life following the death of a friend. He returns to the home of his aunt and uncle in Wilko where he renews friendships with five sisters on a neighboring estate in an attempt to resurrect a happier past. Lots of fruitless romantic yearning. In French and Polish with English subtitles. 118m/C **VHS, DVD. PL FR** Daniel Olbrychski, Christine Pascal, Maja Komorowska, Anna Seniuk, Krystyna Zachwatowicz, Stanislawa Celinska, Zofia Jaroszewska, Tadeusz Bialoszczynski; **D:** Andrzej Wajda; **W:** Zbigniew Kaminski.

Mail Order Wife 🐾🐾 2004 (R) Making a documentary parody really only works if the subject is funny and the characters are caricatures (see "This is Spinal Tap"). Abusive men who order wives through the mail doesn't quite have the same wink-wink-nudge-nudge appeal. Director Andrew Gurland, playing himself, is a documentary filmmaker getting wrapped up in a mail-order marriage gone bad, who then offers the overseas newlywed a place to stay (i.e. his bed) and helps her find a job. The camera bobs and weaves, trying to focus the entire time. It's almost like it doesn't want to watch, either. An unlikable cast of fictional characters is trumped by a cameo from unlikable non-fictional caricature Jose Canseco. 92m/C **DVD.** US Andrew Gurland, Eugenia Yuan, Adrian Martinez, Deborah Teng; **D:** Huck Botko, Andrew Gurland; **W:** Huck Botko, Andrew Gurland; **C:** Luke Geissbuhler.

Mail to the Chief 🐾🐾 2000 Junior high schooler Kenny has a school assignment on the upcoming presidential election. So he goes to a chat room and starts dissing the incumbent's gaffes, only to discover his online chat buddy is actually the President himself. The eighth-grader gives the prez some advice and when he starts to follow it, the President's popularity starts to rise in the polls. 89m/C **VHS.** Randy Quaid, Holland Taylor, Bill Switzer, Ashley Gorrell, Martin Doyle; **D:** Eric Champnella; **C:** Albert J. Dunk; **M:** Peter Bernstein. **VIDEO**

The Main Event 🐾🐾 1979 (PG) Streisand plays a wacky—and bankrupt—cosmetic executive who must depend on the career of washed-up boxer O'Neal to rebuild her fortune. Desperate (and more than a little smitten), she badgers and bullies him back into the ring. Lame, derivative screwball comedy desperate to suggest chemistry of Streisand and O'Neal's "What's Up, Doc?" (1972). Streisand sings the title song. 109m/C **VHS, DVD.** Barbra Streisand, Ryan O'Neal; **D:** Howard Zieff.

Main Street to Broadway 🐾🐾 1953 Superficial story of a struggling playwright. Interesting mainly for abundant big-name cameos. Based on a story by Robert E. Sherwood. 102m/B **VHS.** Tom Morton, Mary Murphy, Agnes Moorehead, Herb Shriner, Rosemary DeCamp, Clinton Sundberg; **Cameos:** Lionel Barrymore, Ethel Barrymore, Tallulah Bankhead, Shirley Booth, Cornel Wilde, Rex Harrison, Joshua Logan, Helen Hayes, Mary Martin; **D:** Tay Garnett.

Mainline Run 🐾½ 1998 Smalltime drug runner Taro (Speer) gets out of prison and immediately goes back to work for crime boss Mr. Fletcher (Ward). Taro sets up a deal, which goes bad, the drugs are lost, and one of his men is killed. Now Taro and his buddy Sean (Joseph) are looking to get out, but 'Mr. Fletcher has something else in mind. **96m/C VHS, DVD.** *Hugo Speer, Andrew Joseph, Nelson E. Ward, Kei-ly Marcel; **D:** Howard Ford.*

Maitresse ♂♂1/2 **1976** An examination of the sexual underworld in the same vein as "Blue Velvet" and "Crimes of Passion" as a man falls for a high-priced dominatrix. Director Schroeder also created "Reversal of Fortune." In French with English subtitles. **112m/C VHS, DVD, FR** *Gerard Depardieu, Bulle Ogier; **D:** Barbet Schroeder; **C:** Nestor Almendros.*

The Majestic ♂♂1/2 **2001 (PG)** Carrey is a blacklisted writer who suffers from amnesia after a car crash. He winds up in a small town where he's mistaken for a presumed MIA soldier, who was the son of Landau, the local movie theatre owner. Darabont's self-admitted ode to Frank Capra evokes the All-American innocence and decency that Capra's films reveled in, but doesn't quite match the charm. Cynics will think it's too sentimental and tries too hard, romantics and others not quick to sneer at nostalgia should enjoy themselves. Carrey does a fine job with the lead role. **152m/C VHS, DVD.** *US Jim Carrey, Martin Landau, Laurie Holden, David Ogden Stiers, Jame Whitmore, Jeffrey DeMunn, Ron Rifkin, Hal Holbrook, Bob Balaban, Brent Briscoe, Gerry Black, Susan Willis, Catherine Dent, Cricice Ross, Amanda Detmer, Allen (Goorwitz) Garfield, Daniel von Bargen, Shawn Doyle, Bruce Campbell, Clifford Curtis; **D:** Frank Darabont; **W:** Michael Sloane; **C:** David Tattersall; **M:** Mark Isham.*

The Major and the Minor ♂♂1/2 **1942** Very funny comedy that marked Wilder's directorial debut. Susan Applegate (Rogers) decides she's had it with New York and wants to head home to Iowa, but she only has enough money for a child's half-price train ticket. So she passes herself off as a 12-year-old (!) and then runs into problems when Army major Kirby (Milland), who's traveling to a boys military school, decides to take the child under his protective wing. Soon he's insisting Susan stay at the school until her mother (played by Rogers' mother Lela) can collect her. Potentially risque situations never cross the line into sleaze but remain bright and breezy. **101m/B VHS.** *Ginger Rogers, Ray Milland, Rita Johnson, Robert Benchley, Diana Lynn, Frankie Thomas Jr.; **D:** Billy Wilder; **W:** Billy Wilder, Charles Brackett; **C:** Leo Tover; **M:** Robert Emmett Dolan.*

Major Barbara ♂♂♂1/2 **1941** A wealthy, idealistic girl joins the Salvation Army against her father's wishes. Based on the play by George Bernard Shaw. The excellent adaptation of the original and the cast make this film a winner. Deborah Kerr's film debut. **90m/B VHS, GB** *Wendy Hiller, Rex Harrison, Robert Morley, Sybil Thorndike, Deborah Kerr; **D:** Gabriel Pascal.*

Major Dundee ♂♂1/2 **1965** A Union army officer (Heston) chases Apaches into Mexico with a motley collection of prisoner volunteers. Too long and flawed; would have been better had Peckinpah been allowed to finish the project. Excellent cast. **124m/C VHS, DVD.** *Charlton Heston, Richard Harris, James Coburn, Jim Hutton, Ben Johnson, Slim Pickens; **D:** Sam Peckinpah; **C:** Sam Leavitt.*

Major League ♂♂1/2 **1989 (R)** Comedy about the Cleveland Indians, a pathetic major league baseball team whose new owner, ex-showgirl Rachel (Wilton) who inherited from her late hubby, schemes to lose the season and relocate the team to Miami. Sheen is okay as pitcher Ricky "Wild Thing" Vaughan, who suffers with control problems (both on and off the field), while Bernsen (as third baseman Roger Dorn) seems to be gazing affectionately at "LA Law" from a distance. Predictable sports spoof is good for a few laughs, particularly those scenes involving Haysbert as slugger Pedro Cerano with voodoo on his mind (and in his locker and Snipes as base stealer Willie Mays Hayes, whose onry problem is getting on base. Followed by two sequels. **107m/C VHS, DVD.** *Tom Berenger, Charlie Sheen, Corbin Bernsen, James Gammon, Margaret Whitton, Bob Uecker, Rene Russo, Wesley Snipes, Dennis Haysbert, Charles Cyphers, Chelcie Ross; **D:** David S. Ward; **C:** Reynaldo Villalobos; **M:** James Newton Howard.*

Major League 2 ♂♂1/2 **1994 (PG)** It's been five years since they won the series, and this plodding sequel finds the wacky championship Cleveland Indians ruined by success and once again situation comedy. Limited charm of original is lost; dull and filled with so many lame jokes that you won't care if they manage to make it to the top again. Cast returns, with the exception of Wesley Snipes as Willie Mays Hays (now played by Epps). **105m/C VHS, DVD.** *Charlie Sheen, Tom Berenger, Corbin Bernsen, James Gammon, Tom Berenger, Omar Epps, David Keith, Bob Uecker, Alison Doody, Michelle Rene Thomas, Margaret Whitton, Eric Bruskotter, Takaaki Ishibashi, Randy Quaid; **D:** David S. Ward; **W:** R.J. Stewart; **C:** Victor Hammer; **M:** Michel Colombier.*

Major League 3: Back to the Minors ♂1/2 **1998 (PG-13)** Three strikes and this franchise is out. Gus Cantrell (Bakula) is a burned-out pitcher who's offered the chance to manage the Minnesota Twins' Triple A team and finds a bunch of central casting misfits. Just when you thought they'd run out of baseball cliches, in comes a young prospect who won't take advice (Goggins), an arrogant manager (McGinley), and the "big game" showdown (twice). We've seen this stuff done (not much better) in the first two "Major Leagues" and (very much better) elsewhere. Bakula's always sad, but it's not enough to get the save. Take an intentional pass on this one. **90m/C VHS, DVD.** *Scott Bakula, Corbin Bernsen, Dennis Haysbert, Takaaki Ishibashi, Jensen (Jennifer) Daggett, Eric Bruskotter, Walton Goggins, Ted McGinley, Kenneth Johnson, Peter M. MacKenzie, Bob Uecker, Steve Yeager, Larry Brandenburg, Judson Mills, Lobo Sebastian, Thom Barry, Tim DiFilippo, Tom DiFilippo, Ted DiFilippo; **D:** John Warren; **W:** John Warren; **C:** Tim Suhrstedt; **M:** Robert Folk.*

Major Payne ♂ **1995 (PG-13)** When the marines have no more use for killing-machine Major Payne (Wayans), he reluctantly agrees to train the inept junior ROTC cadets at academically challenged Madison Academy. The misfit brigade contains the usual assortment of stock loser-types who follow the predictable "outcasts get even" plot to the letter. Wayans shows flashes of comic genius, but not nearly enough to make up for the one-dimensional characters and indifferent writing. Most of the showcase jokes involve the humiliation and degradation of the kids, always a laugh-riot. Sub-moronic remake of 1955's "The Private War of Major Benson." **97m/C VHS, DVD.** *Damon Wayans, Karyn Parsons, William Hickey, Albert Hall, Steven Martini, Andrew Harrison Leeds, Scott Bigelow; **D:** Nick Castle; **W:** Dean Lorey, Gary Rosen, Damon Wayans; **C:** Richard Bowen; **M:** Craig Safan.*

The Majorettes ♂ **1987 (R)** Eek! Someone is lurking around a high school murdering the majorettes with their own batons. A bare-bones plot lurks within this otherwise worthless pic. **93m/C VHS, DVD.** *Kevin Kindlin, Terrie Godfrey, Mark V. Jevicky, Sueanne Seamans, John A. Russo, Bill (William Heinzman) Hinzman, Russell Streiner; **D:** Bill (William Heinzman) Hinzman; **W:** John A. Russo.*

A Majority of One ♂♂ **1956** Dated comedy about late-in-life romance and prejudice. Russell stars as Jewish Brooklyn widow Mrs. Jacoby, who tags along with her daughter and diplomat son-in-law on their shipboard trip to Japan. She meets the charming Koichi Asano (Guinness), who's surprisingly effective Guinness), runs into problems with her family, and decides she must give up her chance at romance, when Alicia suddenly raises the stakes. Adapted from the play by Leonard Spigelgass. **149m/C VHS.** *Rosalind Russell, Alec Guinness, Ray Danton, Madlyn Rhue, Mae Questel, Frank Wilcox, Alan Mowbray; **D:** Mervyn LeRoy; **W:** Leonard Spigelgass.*

Makin' Baby ♂ **2002 (R)** New-lyweds Michael and Alicia are having a tough time coping with the married life itself, when Alicia suddenly raises the stakes, deciding she wants a baby. If that isn't enough to push hip-hop-hopeful Michael over the edge, the temptation of a

Make a Million ♂♂ **1935** The Depression is played (successfully) for yuks in this tale of an economics professor fired from his post for advocating radical income redistribution. He doesn't get mad, he gets even: he makes a million by advertising for money; he makes a million by ad... **66m/B VHS, DVD.** *Charles Starrett, Pauline Brooks, George E. Stone, James Burke, Guy Usher, Norman Houston; **D:** Lewis D. Collins; **W:** Charles Logue; **C:** Milton Krasner.*

Make a Wish ♂♂ **1937** A noted composer goes stale in this colorful musical about backstage life. The comic relief provides the films best moments. ♫Music McGuire is good as the terrorized wife. **80m/B VHS, DVD.** *Basil Rathbone, Leon Errol, Bobby Breen, Ralph Forbes; **D:** Kurt Neumann; **M:** Oscar Straus.*

Make Haste to Live ♂♂1/2 **1954** Good, scary thriller. A woman survives attempted murder by her husband; moves far away to raise their infant daughter. He does time, then returns for revenge. **90m/B VHS, DVD.** *Dorothy McGuire, Stephen McNally, Edgar Buchanan, John Howard; **D:** William A. Seiter.*

Make Me an Offer ♂♂ **1955** Somewhat slow-moving comedy centering on an antique dealer who attempts to buy an expensive vase from an old man. From the novel by Wolf Mankowitz. **88m/B VHS, GB** *Peter Finch, Adrienne Corri, Rosalie Crutchley, Finlay Currie; **D:** Cyril Frankel.*

Make Me an Offer ♂♂1/2 **1980** Made-for-TV movie about selling real estate in Hollywood. Better than similar efforts. **97m/C VHS.** *Susan Blakely, Stella Stevens, Patrick O'Neal; **D:** Jerry Paris; **M:** Ralph Burns.*

Make Mine Mink ♂♂1/2 **1960** Offhilarious British comedy about guests at an elegant but run-down mansion who become unlikely thieves, stealing furs for charity. Good cast headed by Terry-Thomas. **100m/C VHS, DVD, GB** *Terry-Thomas, Hattie Jacques; **D:** Robert Asher.*

Make Room for Tomorrow ♂♂ **1981 (R)** Subtle, somewhat funny French comedy about generations in a family. A man in mid-life crisis has to cope with his father, son, and grandfather on the grandfather's 90th birthday. **106m/C VHS.** *FR Victor Lanoux, Jane Birkin, Georges Wilson; **D:** Peter Kassovitz.*

Make-Up ♂♂ **1937** A doctor turned circus clown uses his medical skills when an elephant renders a society girl unconscious. After she awakens the two become involved. The clown's daughter obsesses, but is soon caught up in an accusation that she murdered the lion tamer. Her father the clown tries to save the day. Predictable doctor/clown relationship. **72m/B VHS, Nils Asther, June Clyde, Judy Kelly, Kenne Duncan, John Turnbull; **D:** Alfred Zeisler.*

The Maker ♂♂1/2 **1998 (R)** Restless SoCal high-schooler Josh (Rhys Myers) indulges in petty crime with lesbian friend Bella (Balk) but isn't really in trouble until his long-missing older brother Walter (Modine) hits town. Walter soon pulls Josh into this shady schemes that turn into some very dangerous games. **98m/C VHS, DVD.** *Jonathan Rhys Meyers, Matthew Modine, Mary-Louise Parker, Fairuza Balk, Michael Madsen, Jesse Borrego, Kate McGregor-Stewart, Lawrence Pressman, Jeff Kober; **D:** Tim Hunter; **W:** Rand Ravich; **C:** Hubert Taczanowski; **M:** Paul Buckmaster.*

Maker of Men ♂ **1931** Melodrama finds tough college football coach Dudley pushing son Bob to play. Only the kid's inexperience causes the team's defeat in the big game. Humiliated, Bob transfers to a rival school and gives football another try, going up against this old man. **71m/B VHS.** *Jack Holt, Richard Cromwell, Joan Marsh, John Wayne, Walter Catlett; **D:** Edward Sedgwick; **W:** Howard J. Green; **C:** L.W. O'Connell.*

Malaya ♂♂1/2 **1949** Hokey adventure tale set in WWII that's based on a true story. Stewart and Tracy are hired to smuggle a huge shipment of rubber out of Malaya to waiting U.S. ships without the Japanese finding out. Greenstreet does his usual shifty role in that city's teen detention center in his book "Hey, Malarek." Compelling lead performance from Kcteas in decent though not great screen adaptation. **95m/C VHS, Michael Sarrazin, Elias Koteas, Al Waxman, Kerrie Keane; **D:** Roger Cardinal.*

Malcolm ♂♂1/2 **1986 (PG-13)** An off-beat comedy about a slightly retarded young man who is mechanically inclined and his unusual entry into a life of crime. Directorial debut for actress Tass, whose husband Parker wrote the screenplay out. Greenstreet does his usual shifty role. **86m/C VHS.** *AU Colin Friels, John Hargreaves, Lindy Davies, Chris Heywood, Charles "Bud" Tingwell, Beverly Phillips, Judith Stratford; **D:** Nadia Tass; **C:** David Parker.*

Malarek ♂♂ **1989 (R)** Tough Montreal journalist Victor Malarek exposed abuse in that city's teen detention center in his book "Hey, Malarek." Compelling lead performance from Kcteas in decent though not great screen adaptation. **95m/C VHS, Michael Sarrazin, Elias Koteas, Al Waxman, Kerrie Keane; **D:** Roger Cardinal.*

The Makioka Sisters ♂♂♂ **1983** Much praised drama centering around the lives of four Japanese sisters who are heiresses to the family fortune and, hence, must be found proper husbands. The efforts of the older sisters to "match" their younger siblings are entwined with a gradual realization on the part of the elders that the quiet way of life representative of their own formative years is passing away with the advent of WWII. The movie is as visually stunning as it is poignant. In Japanese with English subtitles. **140m/C VHS.** *JP Keiko Kishi, Yoshiko Sakuma, Sayuri Yoshinaga; **D:** Kon Ichikawa.*

Making Mr. Right ♂♂1/2 **1986 (PG-13)** Under-rated satire about a high-powered marketing and image consultant who falls in love with the android that she's supposed to be promoting. Unbelievable comedy is shaky at times, but Magnuson and Malkovich create some magic. **95m/C VHS, DVD.** *John Malkovich, Ann Magnuson, Glenne Headly, Ben Masters, Laurie Metcalf, Polly Bergen, Hart Bochner, Polly Draper, Susan Anton; **D:** Susan Seidelman; **W:** Laurie Frank, Floyd Byars.*

Making the Grade ♂♂ **1984 (PG)** Jersey tough kid owes the mob; attends prep school in place of a rich kid who can't be bothered. Better than similar '80s teen flicks, but not by much. **105m/C VHS, DVD.** *Judd Nelson, Joanna Lee, Dana Olsen, Ronald Lacey, Scott McGinnis, Gordon Jump, Carey Scott, Andrew (Dice Clay) Silverstein; **D:** Dorian Walker; **W:** Gene Quintano; **C:** Jacques Haitkin; **M:** Basil Poledouris.*

Making Love ♂♂ **1982 (R)** A closet homosexual risks his eight-year marriage by getting involved with a carefree writer. What could be a powerful subject gets only bland treatment. **112m/C VHS, DVD.** *Kate Jackson, Harry Hamlin, Michael Ontkean, Wendy Hiller, Arthur Hill, Nancy Olson, Terry Kiser, Camilla Carr, Michael Dudikoff; **D:** Arthur Hiller; **W:**

Making Contact ♂ **1986 (PG)** A small boy's telekinetic powers enable him to bring to life his favorite toys. The ridicule he endures because of this leads him to set off on terrifying adventures with only his toys and a friend for company. **83m/C VHS, DVD.** *Joshua Morrell, Eve Kryll; **D:** Roland Emmerich.*

slimy music exec (Mystikal, in his feature debut) offering to take him under his wing and transform him into a full-time rhymin' thug puts the sweethearts in danger. Mean-spirited jokes fall flat and come at the worst times. Fans of Mystikal will be severely dissed by his limited screen time. And, nope, he doesn't even rap. **94m/C VHS, DVD.** *Ponta Realer, Aaron Spears, Mystikal, Sheila Lussier, Kim Hill; **D:** Paul Wynne; **W:** Michael Jones. **VIDEO**

Malcolm

vid Parker; **M:** Simon Jeffes. Australian Film Inst. '86: Actor (Fries). Film.

Malcolm X 🦴🦴🦴 **1992 (PG-13)** Stirring tribute to the controversial black activist, a leader in the struggle for black liberation. Hitting bottom during his imprisonment in the '50s, he became a Black Muslim and then a leader in the Nation of Islam. His assassination in 1965 left a legacy of black nationalism, self-determination, and racial pride. Marked by strong direction from Lee and good performances (notably Freeman Jr. as Elijah Muhammad), it's Washington's convincing performance in the title role that truly brings the film alive. Based on "The Autobiography of Malcolm X" by Malcolm X and Alex Haley. **201m/C VHS, DVD.** Denzel Washington, Angela Bassett, Albert Hall, Al Freeman Jr., Delroy Lindo, Spike Lee, Theresa Randle, Kate Vernon, Lonette McKee, Tommy Hollis, James McDaniel, Ernest Thompson, Jean LaMarre, Giancarlo Esposito, Craig Wasson, John Ottavino, David Patrick Kelly, Shirley Stoler; **Cameos:** Christopher Plummer, Karen Allen, Peter Boyle, William Kunstler, Bobby Seale, Al Sharpton; **D:** Spike Lee. **W:** Spike Lee, Arnold Perl, James Baldwin; **M:** Terence Blanchard. MTV Movie Awards '93: Male Perf. (Washington); N.Y. Film Critics '92: Actor (Washington).

Malcolm X: Make It Plain 🦴🦴🦴 **1995** In-depth portrait of the life of Malcolm X as told through the memories of many of Malcolm's close personal friends and individuals who had worked closely with him. Contains footage of Malcolm X speaking at rallies, meetings, and interviews with Maya Angelou, Ossie Davis, Alex Haley, Mike Wallace, and his family. **136m/C VHS. Nar:** Alfre Woodard.

The Maldonado Miracle 🦴🦴½ **2003 (PG)** The small desert border town of San Ramos is slowly dying until the church's Jesus statue is found to be crying tears of blood. This development brings pilgrims, media, and curiosity seekers at the same time a Mexican boy arrives looking for his father and on the run from immigration. Hayek's directorial debut is uplifting and earnest, if a bit predictable, and she gets solid performances from an excellent cast. **100m/C DVD.** Peter Fonda, Mare Winningham, Ruben Blades, Bill Sage, Eddy Martin, Soledad St. Hilaire, Scott Michael Campbell, Jesse Borrego, Christina Cabot; **D:** Salma Hayek; **W:** Paul Cooper; **C:** Claudio Rocha; **M:** Leonardo Heiblum, Jacobo Lieberman. **CABLE**

Male and Female 🦴🦴🦴½ **1919** A group of British aristocrats is shipwrecked on an island and must allow their efficient butler (Meighan) to take command for their survival. Swanson is the spoiled rich girl who falls for her social inferior. Their rescue provides a return to the rigid British class system. Based on the play "The Admirable Crichton" by James M. Barrie. **110m/B VHS, DVD.** Gloria Swanson, Thomas Meighan, Lila Lee, Raymond Hatton, Bebe Daniels; **D:** Cecil B. DeMille; **W:** Jeanie Macpherson; **C:** Alvin Wyckoff.

The Male Animal 🦴🦴½ **1942** Fonda uses his penchant for playing principled men to uneven comedic effect as stuffy English professor Tommy Turner. He gets into trouble with university trustees over his views about free speech and it threatens his job, which worries wife Ellen (de Havilland). Tommy gets jealous when Ellen's college beau, ex-football star Joe Ferguson (Carson), suddenly shows up on campus and seems to want to rekindle the flame. The men behave like idiots while Ellen deals with their male posturing. Based on the play by James Thurber and director Nugent. Fonda later played the same role in a Broadway revival. **101m/B VHS.** Henry Fonda, Olivia de Havilland, Jack Carson, Joan Leslie, Eugene Pallette, Herbert Anderson, Hattie McDaniel, Don DeFore; **D:** Elliott Nugent; **W:** Julius J. Epstein, Philip G. Epstein, Stephen Morehouse Avery; **C:** Arthur Edeson; **M:** Heinz Roemheld.

Malena 🦴🦴 **2000** Nostalgic coming of age story centered on a fantasy woman. The beautiful Malena (Bellucci) inspires lust in the men and jealousy in the women of her Sicilian village in 1940. Her husband is away fighting and, because of unjustified gossip, Malena loses her teaching job and eventually turns to prostitution to support herself. Only puberty-struck 13-year-old Renato (Sulfaro) shows any interest in her plight, which becomes worse as the war drags on. Italian with subtitles. **106m/C VHS, DVD. IT** Monica Bellucci, Giuseppe Sulfaro, Luciano Federico, Matilde Piana, Pietro Notarianni, Gaetano Aronica; **D:** Giuseppe Tornatore; **W:** Giuseppe Tornatore; **C:** Lajos Koltai; **M:** Ennio Morricone.

Malevolence 🦴🦴 **1995 (R)** Billy Bob Jones (Cortese) was unjustly imprisoned as a boy and has now spent half his life in jail. Shortly after his release, he drifts into petty crime and is suddenly the prime suspect in the murder of a black politician. The only thing is, Billy Bob is being framed. **95m/C VHS.** Joe Cortese, Michael McGrady, Tom Bower, Lou Rawls; **D:** Belle Avery; **W:** Belle Avery; **C:** Joe C. Maxwell.

Malevolence 🦴 **2004 (R)** Debut for writer/director Mena is a basic slasher film. There's something about a serial killer, an abducted single mom, a bank heist gone wrong, and lots of blood. Mena had to start somewhere but this effort is unmemorable at best. **90m/C DVD. US** Samantha Dark, Brandon Johnson, Heather Magee, Richard Glover, Courtney Bertolone, John Richard Ingram; **D:** Stevan Mena; **W:** Stevan Mena; **C:** Tsuyashi Kimoto; **M:** Stevan Mena.

Malibu Beach 🦴½ **1978 (R)** The California beach scene is the setting for this movie filled with bikini clad girls, tanned young men, and instant romances. For connoisseurs of the empty-headed teen beach movie. **93m/C VHS, DVD.** Kim Lankford, James Daughton; **D:** Robert J. Rosenthal; **C:** Jamie Anderson.

The Malibu Beach Vampires **1991 (R)** Three unscrupulous yuppies: Congressman Teri Upstart, Col. Ollie West and Rev. Timmy Fakker, keep beautiful mistresses in their Malibu beach house. What they don't know is, the girls are all really vampires who have injected them with a serum that compels them to tell the truth! Will our "heroes" continue to dupe the American Public, or will the sexy blood suckers cause their downfall? **90m/C VHS, DVD.** Angelyne, Becky LeBeau, Joan Rudelstein, Marcus A. Frishman, Rod Sweitzer, Francis Creighton, Anet Anatelle, Yvette Buchanan, Cherie Romaoro, Kelly Galindo; **D:** Francis Creighton.

Malibu Bikini Shop 🦴 **1986 (R)** Two brothers manage a beachfront bikini shop in Malibu, and spend their time ogling the customers and arguing about running the "business." Just another excuse for parading babes in bathing suits across the naked screen. **90m/C VHS.** Michael David Wright, Bruce Greenwood, Barbara Horan, Debra Blee, Jay Robinson, Galyn Gorg, Ami Julius, Frank Nelson, Kathleen Freeman, Rita Jenrette; **D:** David Wechter; **W:** David Wechter.

Malibu Express 🦴 **1985 (R)** Mystery/adventure plot about a P.I. is the excuse; babes in swimsuits is the reason for this waste of time. **101m/C VHS, DVD.** Darby Hinton, Sybil Danning, Art Metrano, Shelley Taylor Morgan, Niki Dantine, Barbara (Lee) Edwards; **D:** Andy Sidaris.

Malibu High 🦴 **1979 (R)** The accidental death of a young prostitute's client leads her to a new series of illegal activities of the "sex and hit" variety. Dark, sleazy and antisocial; belies Beach Boys-esque title. **92m/C VHS, DVD.** Jill Lansing, Stuart Taylor; **D:** Irvin Berwick.

Malibu's Most Wanted 🦴🦴 **2003 (PG-13)** Kennedy brings his TV character Brad "B-Rad" Gluckman to the big screen with minimal success. "B-Rad" is a rich white wannabe rapper from Malibu, whose dad (O'Neal) is running for governor. When he embarrasses pop at a campaign stop, dad takes drastic action. He hires classically trained black actors Sean and PJ to kidnap Brad to South Central for a little "Scared White" therapy. Since the middle class actors have no idea how to be "gangsta" they enlist the help of Sean's cousin Shondra, who promptly falls for Brad, angering her ex boyfriend Tec (yet another Wayans), who lives the thug life. Shows flashes of the clever, biting satire it could've been, but fades in the end by backing off on some of the wry observations it makes early on. Diggs and Anderson click, and O'Neal is amusingly smarmy. **86m/C VHS, DVD. US** Jamie Kennedy, Taye Diggs, Anthony Anderson, Blair Underwood, Regina Hall, Ryan O'Neal, Bo Derek, Damien Dante Wayans, Jeffrey Tambor, Kal Penn, Snoop Whitesell; **W:** Jamie Kennedy, Fax Bahr, Adam Small, Nick Swardson; **C:** Mark Irwin; **M:** John Van Tongeren, Damon Elliott; **V:** Snoop Dogg.

Malice 🦴🦴½ **1993 (R)** In a sleepy little college town, strange things sure do happen. Too bad rumpled college dean Andy Safian (Pullman) didn't see "Pacific Heights." If he did, he would know that sometimes roommates are more trouble than they're worth, even if renovation on that 'old' Victorian is getting expensive. Routine thriller throws out an inventive twist to keep things moving, but manages to be fairly predictable anyway. **107m/C VHS, DVD.** Alec Baldwin, Nicole Kidman, Bill Pullman, Bebe Neuwirth, Anne Bancroft, George C. Scott, Peter Gallagher, Josef Sommer, Gwyneth Paltrow; **D:** Harold Becker; **W:** Aaron Sorkin, Scott Frank; **C:** Gordon Willis; **M:** Jerry Goldsmith.

Malicious **1974 (R)** A housekeeper hired for a widower and his three sons becomes the object of lusty affection of all four men. As Papa makes plans to court and marry her, his 14-year-old son plots to have her as a companion on his road to sensual maturity. Dubbed in English. **98m/C VHS. IT** Laura Antonelli, Turi Ferro, Alessandro Momo, Tina Aumont; **D:** Salvatore Samperi.

Malicious 🦴🦴 **1995 (R)** College athlete Doug Gordon (McGaw) impulsively has what he thinks is a one-nighter with mystery lady, Melissa (Ringwald). Only she's not willing to give him up and his rejection sends her on the road to revenge. **92m/C VHS.** Molly Ringwald, Patrick McGaw, Sarah Lassez, John Vernon, Mimi Kuzyk, Rick Henrickson; **D:** Ian Corson; **W:** George Saunders; **C:** Michael Slovis; **M:** Graeme Coleman.

Malicious Intent 🦴½ *Civility* **1999** Young man returns home for his father's funeral and learns that he was murdered. So he gets together with some of his father's buddies on a plan for revenge—and money. **86m/C VHS, DVD.** Zack (Zach) Ward, Tom Arnold, William Forsythe, Rachel Ticotin, Clarence Williams III, Ed Lauter, Liam Waite, Christopher Atkins; **D:** Caesar Cavaricci; **W:** Caesar Cavaricci. **VIDEO**

Mallrats 🦴🦴½ **1995 (R)** Smith's better-financed follow-up to the legendary "Clerks" follows Jersey slackers T.S. (London) and Brodie (Lee) to the mall, where they intend to wallow in food-court cookies and reclaim their girlfriends, who recently dumped them. While wandering the mall in low-key and confused pursuit of their women and self respect, they encounter the usual band of bizarre inhabitants, including Ivannah, the topless psychic, Silent Bob (Smith) and stoner Jay (Mewes). Dialogue and sightgags are director/writer Smith's strong point; moving the plot forward is not high on the priority list. The ensemble cast, featuring Doherty as the bored babe who spurns Brodie, is up to the often funny sidebits and gen-x references. **95m/C VHS, DVD, HD DVD.** Jeremy London, Jason Lee, Shannen Doherty, Claire Forlani, Kevin Smith, Michael Rooker, Priscilla Barnes, Renee Humphrey, Ben Affleck, Joey Lauren Adams, Jason Mewes, Brian O'Halloran, David Brinkley, Art James, Ethan Suplee, Sven-Ole Thorsen; **Cameos:** Stan Lee; **D:** Kevin Smith; **W:** Kevin Smith; **C:** David Klein; **M:** Ira Newborn.

Malone 🦴🦴 **1987 (R)** A burnt-out secret agent stumbles into a real-estate swindle/murder plot in Oregon and sets out to stop it. Film tries hard but doesn't succeed in being believable. **92m/C VHS, DVD.** Burt Reynolds, Lauren Hutton, Cliff Robertson, Kenneth McMillan, Scott Wilson, Cynthia Gibb; **D:** Harley Cokliss; **M:** David Newman.

Malou 🦴🦴 **1983 (R)** A young French woman tries to uncover the truth about her late mother's life, sifting through wildly contradictory evidence in the desire to discover her own identity and avoid her mother's mistakes. A feminist story. In German with English subtitles. **95m/C VHS. GE** Grischa Huber, Ingrid Caven, Helmut Griem; **D:** Jeanine Meerapfel; **C:** Michael Ballhaus.

Malta Story 🦴🦴½ **1953** A British WWII flier becomes involved with the defense of Malta. **103m/B VHS.** Alec Guinness, Jack Hawkins, Anthony Steel, Flora Robson, Muriel Pavlow; **D:** Brian Desmond Hurst.

The Maltese Falcon 🦴🦴 *Dangerous Female* **1931** A good first screen version of the Dashiell Hammett story about private detective Sam Spade's search for the elusive Black Bird. Remade five years later as "Satan Met a Lady" with Bette Davis. Its most famous remake, however, occurred in 1941 with Humphrey Bogart in the lead. **80m/B VHS.** Bebe Daniels, Ricardo Cortez, Dudley Digges, Thelma Todd, Una Merkel, Dwight Frye, Robert Elliott; **D:** Roy Del Ruth.

The Maltese Falcon 🦴🦴🦴 **1941** After the death of his partner, detective Sam Spade (Bogart) finds himself enmeshed in a complicated, intriguing search for a priceless statuette. "It's the stuff dreams are made of," says Bogart of the Falcon. Excellent, fast-paced film noir with outstanding performances, great dialogue, and concentrated attention to details. Director Huston's first film and Greenstreet's talky debut. First of several films starring Bogart and Astor. Based on the novel by Dashiell Hammett. Also available colorized. **101m/B VHS, DVD.** Humphrey Bogart, Mary Astor, Peter Lorre, Sydney Greenstreet, Ward Bond, Barton MacLane, Gladys George, Lee Patrick, Elisha Cook Jr., Jerome Cowan, Walter Huston; **C:** Arthur Edeson; **M:** Adolph Deutsch. AFI '98: Top 100, Natl. Film Reg. '89.

Mama Africa 🦴🦴½ **2002** Three segments, directed by three different African filmmakers are tied together by the authoritative introductions of Queen Latifah. Stylistically plain but emotionally charged, all three tales involve young, poverty-stricken but promising Africans facing difficult moral choices for a better life. In two of the stories young, single mothers Raya (Abrahams) and Uno (David) take up with questionable men for love or money and find themselves tempted to enter their world of crime. Director Onwurah's modern-day fable, the best of the three, focuses on young Nigerian Kwame, who desperately needs $100 to buy a pair of basketball sneakers for a tryout with an American scout. As the day approaches, Kwame is enticed by a slimy gangster to join up with his crew as a way to get what he desperately needs. Fine performances and a refreshing lack of melodrama or moralizing. **89m/C VHS, DVD.** Rehane Abrahams, Damien Chamley, Ivan Lucas, Oscar Petersen, Denise Newman, Hyppolite Ouangrawa, Alima Salouka, Cindy Sampson, Graham Weir; **D:** Fanta Regina Nacro, Zulfar Otto-Sallies, Ingrid Sinclair.

Mama Dracula WOOF! **1980** Fletcher stars in this poor satire of the horror genre. She's a vampire who needs the blood of virgins to stay young. Her son helps out—what good son wouldn't? **90m/C VHS, DVD. FR** Louise Fletcher, Bonnie Schneider, Maria Schneider, Marc-Henri Wajnberg, Alexander Wajnberg, Jess Hahn; **D:** Boris Szulzinger.

Mama Flora's Family 🦴🦴½ **1998** Based on the novel by Alex Haley, which was finished by co-author Stevens after Haley's 1992 death. Loosely based on Haley's mother, Mama Flora (Tyson) endures one tragedy after another while raising her family. First, as a teenaged servant, Flora gets pregnant and is forced to give the child up. Then when she does marry, her husband is killed and their property burned. Meanwhile, her other children and grandchildren struggle with discrimination and grow angry and resentful. Holds together because of the force of Tyson's portrayal. **175m/C VHS, DVD.** Cicely Tyson, Mario Van Peebles, Blair Underwood, Queen Latifah, Hill Harper, Shemar Moore, Della Reese; **D:** Peter Werner; **W:** David Stevens, Carol Schreder; **C:** Neil Roach. **TV**

Mama, There's a Man in Your Bed 🦴🦴🦴 *Romauld et Juliet* **1989 (PG)** When a powerful executive is framed for insider trading, the only witness to the crime and his only hope is an earthy cleaning woman named Juliette. Together they plot revenge and takeovers in her tiny

Mama Turns a Hundred ⅊⅊⅊ 1979 (R) A baronial family (a bizarre set of characters) is celebrating their mother's 100th birthday at her estate. One of the daughter's seduces her brother-in-law, another has a uniform fetish, a religious zealot is desperate to hang-glide, and several of them are trying to kill poor Mama. But of course she prevails, although sick and ailing. Slow-paced yet uproarious film full of inept characters who bumble along in Spanish with English subtitles. 100m/C VHS, SP Geraldine Chaplin, Fernando Fernan-Gomez, Amparo Munoz; **D:** Carlos Saura.

Mama's Dirty Girls 1974 (R) A gangster mom's daughters take over where their mother left off and have the time of their lives. 82m/C VHS, Gloria Grahame, Paul Lambert, Sondra Currie, Candice Rialson, Mary Stoddard; **D:** John Hayes; **M:** Don Bagley.

Mambo ⅊⅊½ 1955 A poor young dancer inspires patronage and lust by dancing the Mambo. Although attracted to Gassman, she marries Rennie for his money. Technically weak but artistically interesting, though Rennie and Mangano have done their roles somewhat better elsewhere. 94m/B VHS, Silvana Mangano, Michael Rennie, Vittorio Gassman, Shelley Winters, Katherine Dunham, Mary Clare, Eduardo Ciannelli; **D:** Robert Rossen; **M:** Nino Rota.

Mambo Cafe 2000 (PG-13) Low-budget mob comedy with a quirky premise. The Mambo Cafe is a Spanish Harlem restaurant in dire need of some business. So the owners invite a local mobster to dine at their establishment in hopes he'll be murdered and they'll get a boost from the publicity. He is, business improves, but the unwelcome Mob scrutiny may also draw unwelcome attention elsewhere. 94m/C VHS, DVD, Paul Rodriguez, Rosanna DeSoto, Danny Aiello, Thalia, Kamar De Los Reyes; **D:** Reuben Gonzalez. VIDEO

Mambo Italiano ⅊⅊ 2003 (R) Broad, ethnic romantic comedy that could be titled "My Big Gay Italian/Canadian Wedding." Kirby plays Angelo Barberini, a 30-year-old nice Italian boy still living with his parents in Montreal's version of Little Italy when he falls for childhood bully Nino (Miller), now a cop and secretly also gay. The two begin a clandestine relationship and move in together while both families unsuccessfully begin a whirlwind of last-ditch matchmaking activities. A pleasant turn by lead Kirby highlights this good-natured yet technically simple comedy where most of the performances, and accents, are uneven. 99m/C VHS, DVD, CA Luke Kirby, Ginette Reno, Paul Sorvino, Claudia Ferri, Peter Miller, Mary Walsh, Sophie Lorain, Tim Post, Lisa Bronwyn Moore; **D:** Emile Gaudreault; **W:** Emile Gaudreault, Steve Galluccio; **C:** Serge Ladouceur.

The Mambo Kings ⅊⅊⅊ 1992 (R) Armand and Banderas (in his first English speaking role) are Cesar and Nestor Castillo, two brothers who flee Cuba for New York City with dreams of hitting it big with their mambo music. Desi Arnaz Jr. gets to play his own dad in a funny and technical scene that leads to a climactic confrontation between the brothers. Good cast and great music make this one worthwhile. Based on the Pulitzer prizewinning novel "The Mambo Kings Play Songs of Love" by Oscar Hijuelos. 100m/C VHS, DVD, Armand Assante, Antonio Banderas, Cathy Moriarty, Maruschka Detmers, Desi Arnaz Jr., Celia Cruz, Roscoe Lee Browne, Vondie Curtis-Hall, Tito Puente, Talisa Soto; **D:** Arne Glimcher; **W:** Cynthia Cidre; **C:** Michael Ballhaus; **M:** Robert Kraft, Carlos Franzetti.

Mame ⅊⅊ 1974 (PG) In an adaptation of the Broadway musical "Auntie Mame" by Jerry Herman, Ball plays a dynamic woman who takes it upon herself to teach

apartment, filled with children. Soon, he regains his former position of power but realizes his life isn't complete without his co-conspirator. In French with English subtitles. 111m/C VHS, FR Daniel Auteuil, Firmine Richard, Pierre Vernier, Maxime LeRoux, Gilles Privat, Muriel Combeau, Catherine Salviat, Sambou Tati; **D:** Coline Serreau; **W:** Coline Serreau.

Mamele ⅊½ *Little Mother* 1938 Picon prematurely becomes the "mother" of her seven siblings when their mother dies. Quintessential Yiddish musical with the usual shimmering performance from Picon. In Yiddish with English subtitles. 95m/B VHS, PL Molly Picon, Max Bozyk, Edmund Zayenda; **D:** Joseph Green.

Mamma Mia! 2008 Mamma Meryl gets down to ABBA! Single mom Donna (Streep) is the owner of a small hotel in Greece (filmed on Skopelos). She's thrilled when her daughter Sophie (Seyfried) gets engaged until she learns that the property that once belonged to his family. When the newly married sister is found dead, her sibling sets out to solve the murder. 83m/B VHS, GB Kieron Moore, Margaret Johnston, Dulcie Gray, Guy Middleton, Felix Aylmer; **D:** Leslie Arliss.

Mamma Roma ⅊⅊⅊½ 1962 Pasolini's second film is a heartbreaking story of family ties, escaping the past, and dreams of the future. The title character (Magnani) is a former prostitute who attempts respectability for herself and her teenaged son (Garofolo). But her ex-pimp (Citti) threatens her new life and Rome's big-city temptations prove to be a pathway to crime and tragedy for the boy. Magnani gives one of her finest performances. Italian with subtitles. 110m/B VHS, DVD, IT Anna Magnani, Ettore Garofolo, Franco Citti, Silvana Corsini, Luisa Loiano; **C:** Tonino Delli Colli; **D:** Pier Paolo Pasolini; **W:** Pier Paolo Pasolini.

Mammoth ⅊ 2006 Frank Abernathy (Ventresca) is the curator of a natural history museum in Blackwood, Louisiana. When a meteor hits the building, it thaws the ice-encased star attractor. That would be a mammoth that can suck the life out of people with its trunk when it's not stomping on 'em. Unfortunately, the pic's tone varies from goofy to banal to gross, which diminishes it's cheese factor. A Sci-Fi Channel original. 90m/C DVD, Vincent Ventresca, Summer Glau, Leila Arcieri, Tom Skerritt, Cole Williams, Marcus Lyle Brown, Charles Carroll; **D:** Tim Cox; **W:** Sean Keller, Tim Dickson; **C:** Bing Sokolsky; **M:** John Dickson. CABLE

Mam'zelle Pigalle ⅊½ *Naughty Girl* 1958 Bardot portrays a songstress involved with criminals. French with subtitles. 77m/C VHS, DVD, FR Brigitte Bardot, Jean Bretonniere, Francoise Fabian, Bernard Lancret; **D:** Michel Boisrond.

The Man ⅊ 2005 (PG-13) Andy Fiedler (Levy) an eccentrically nerdy dental-supply salesman from Milwaukee, travels to Detroit for a convention where some illegal arms-dealing crooks mistake him for hard-boiled ATF agent, Derrick Vann (Jackson). Andy gets drawn into the crime-busting plot. Jackson and Levy deliver exactly what you expect in this old-school kooky crime buster, but nothing more in this seen-it-done-better-elsewhere attempt at mismatched buddy comedy. 79m/C DVD, US Samuel L. Jackson, Eugene Levy, Luke Goss, Miguel Ferrer, Anthony Mackie, Horatio Sanz, Rachael Crawford, Susie Essman, Tomorrow Baldwin; **D:** Les Mayfield; **W:** Jim Piddock, Margaret Grieco Oberman, Stephen Carpenter; **C:** Adam Kane; **M:** John Murphy, Deria Sana.

a group of eccentrics how to live life to the fullest: Arthur plays Mame's friend just as splendidly as she did in the Broadway version, but Ball in her last feature film is a lame Mame. Overly ambitious production avoids reaching goal. ♪"Mame; We Need a Little Christmas; It's Today; Loving You; My Best Girl; What Do I Do Now?" (Gooch's Song); Open a New Window; Bosom Buddies; If He Walked Into My Life. 132m/C VHS, DVD, Lucille Ball, Beatrice Arthur, Robert Preston, Joyce Van Patten, Bruce Davison, Jane Connell, Don Cook, Don Porter, Audrey Christie, John McGiver, Patrick Labyorteaux, Lucille Benson, Burt Mustin, Barbara Bosson; **D:** Gene Saks; **W:** Paul Zindel; **C:** Philip Lathrop; **M:** Jerry Herman.

A Man About the House ⅊⅊ 1947 Two unmarried English sisters move into the Italian villa they have inherited. There, one marries the caretaker, who secretly plans to regain the property that once belonged to his ... 95m/C VHS, GB Kieron Moore, Margaret Johnston, Dulcie Gray, Guy Middleton, Felix Aylmer; **D:** Leslie Arliss.

Man About Town ⅊⅊½ 1939 Bob Templeton (Benny), an American producing a play in London, falls for a beautiful actress who won't give him the time of day. As a ploy to make her jealous and gain her affections, he woos Lady Arlington who is all for making her inattentive husband jealous as well. Music and dance enchant as our playboy barely escapes alive. 85m/B VHS, Jack Benny, Dorothy Lamour, Edward Arnold, Binnie Barnes, Monty Woolley, Phil Harris, Betty Grable; **D:** Mark Sandrich.

A Man Alone ⅊⅊ 1955 Man falsely accused of robbing a stagecoach hides out, not alone but with comedy sheriff's daughter. Milland's debut behind the camera. 96m/C VHS, Ray Milland, Ward Bond, Mary Murphy, Raymond Burr, Lee Van Cleef; **D:** Ray Milland; **C:** Lionel Lindon.

A Man and a Woman ⅊⅊⅊ *Un Homme et Une Femme* 1966 When a man and a woman, both widowed, meet and become interested in one another but experience difficulties in putting their past loves behind them. Intelligently handled emotional conflicts within a well-acted romantic drama, acclaimed for excellent visual detail. Remade in 1977 as "Another Man, Another Chance." Followed in 1986 with "A Man and A Woman: 20 Years Later." Dubbed. 102m/C VHS, DVD, FR Anouk Aimee, Jean-Louis Trintignant, Pierre Barouh, Valerie Lagrange; **D:** Claude Lelouch; **W:** Claude Lelouch, Pierre Uytterhoeven; **C:** Claude Lelouch; Francis Lai. Oscars '66: Foreign Film, Story & Screenplay; British Acad. '67: Actress (Aimee). Cannes '66: Film; Golden Globes '67: Actress-Drama (Aimee), Foreign Film.

A Man and a Woman: 20 Years Later ⅊½ *Un Homme Et Une Femme: Vingt Ans Deja* 1986 (PG) Slouchy sequel to the highly praised "A Man and a Woman" that catches up with a couple after a long separation. The sad romantic complications of the original are more mundane in this sequel, which is burdened by a film-within-a-film script as well as shots from the original. In French with English subtitles. 112m/C VHS, FR Jean-Louis Trintignant, Anouk Aimee, Richard Berry; **D:** Claude Lelouch; **W:** Claude Lelouch.

A Man, a Woman, and a Bank ⅊⅊½ *A Very Big Weekend* 1979 (PG) Two con-men plan to rob a bank by posing as workers during the bank's construction. An advertising agency woman snaps their picture for a billboard to show how nice the builders have been, then becomes romantically involved with one of the would-be thieves. Nice performances, but wacky touches aren't plentiful enough or well timed to sustain comedy. 100m/C VHS, DVD, Donald Sutherland, Brooke Adams, Paul Mazursky; **D:** Noel Black; **W:** Bruce A. Evans, Raynold Gideon; **C:** Jack Cardiff; **M:** Bill Conti.

A Man Apart ⅊⅊ 2003 (R) As action buddy cop movies go, this is one, Sean Vetter (Diesel) is a DEA agent, who, along with his partner and childhood pal Hicks (Tate), has just closed a seven-year case by busting cartel head Lucero (Silva). Before the cartel can catch its breath, Vetter's plot device wife is killed on the orders of the supposedly-defunct cartel's new ruler, El Diablo. Vetter goes into full revenge mode, and all semblence of restraint is eliminated, from Sean and the rotechic equipment) goes unused as Vetter and Diablo career toward the inevitable showdown with Hicks and many other characters. 114m/C VHS, DVD, US Vin Diesel, Larenz Tate, Timothy Olyphant, Geno Silva, Jacqueline Obradors, Steve Eastin, Juan Fernandez, Jeff Kober, George Sharperson; **D:** F. Gary Gray; **W:** Christian Gudegast, Paul Scheuring; **C:** Jack N. Green; **M:** Anne Dudley.

Man Bait ⅊⅊½ *The Last Page* 1952 A complex web of intrigue and mystery surrounds a blackmailed book dealer when he allows a blonde woman to catch his eye. A competently made film. 78m/B VHS, DVD, GB George Brent, Marguerite Chapman, Diana Dors; **D:** Terence Fisher.

Man Beast ⅊ 1955 The abominable snowman is sought and found in this grade-Z '50s monster movie. 65m/B VHS, Virginia Maynor, George Skaff, Lloyd Nelson, Tom Maruzzi; **D:** Jerry Warren.

Man Bites Dog ⅊⅊½ *C'est Arrive pres de Chez Vous* 1991 (NC-17) A pseudo-documentary about a serial killer, filled with ever-mounting violence. Ben is the film crew's subject as they interview and follow him. The sat-ire on film violence, as well as reality-based TV shows, is both appalling and humorous in a sick way. French with English subtitles. Also available in an unrated edited version. 95m/B VHS, DVD, BE Benoit Poelvoorde, Remy Belvaux, Andre Bonzel, Vincent Tavier, Jean-Marc Chenut; **D:** Benoit Poelvoorde, Remy Belvaux, Andre Bonzel, Vincent Tavier; **C:** Andre Bonzel; **M:** Laurence Dufrene, Jean-Marc Chenut.

A Man Called Adam ⅊½ 1966 A jazz musician is tortured by prejudice and the guilt created by his having accidentally killed his wife and baby years before. Davis is appropriately haunted, but the film is poorly produced. 103m/B VHS, DVD, Sammy Davis Jr., Louis Armstrong, Ossie Davis, Cicely Tyson, Frank Sinatra Jr., Lola Falana, Mel Torme, Peter Lawford; **D:** Leo Penn; **C:** Jack Priestley.

A Man Called Horse ⅊⅊⅊ 1970 (PG) After a wealthy Britisher is captured and tortured by the Sioux Indians in the Dakotas, he abandons his formal ways and discovers his own strength. As he passes their torture tests, he is embraced by the tribe. In this very realistic and gripping portrayal of American Indian life, Harris provides a strong performance. Sequelled by "Return of a Man Called Horse" (1983). 114m/C VHS, DVD, Richard Harris, Judith Anderson, Jean Gascon, Manu Tupou, Dub Taylor; **D:** Elliot Silverstein; **W:** Jack DeWitt; **C:** Robert B. Hauser.

A Man Called Peter ⅊⅊⅊ 1955 A biographical epic about Peter Marshall, a Scottish chaplain who served the U.S. Senate. Todd does his subject justice by sensitively showing all that was human in a man capable of great inspiration. 119m/C VHS, DVD, Richard Todd, Jean Peters, Marjorie Rambeau, Jill Esmond, Les Tremayne, Robert Burton; **D:** Henry Koster.

A Man Called Rage WOOF! 1984 Rage is the leader of a group of safely escorting a group of pioneers through a nuclear wasteland infested with mutants.

and cannibals. **90m/C VHS.** *IT* Stelio Candelli, Conrad Nichols. *D:* Anthony Richmond.

A Man Called Sarge 🐾½ **1990** (PG-13) Sophomoric comedy about a daffy WWII sergeant leading his squad against the Germans at Tobruk. **88m/C VHS.** Bobby DiCicco, Gary Kroeger, Marc Singer, Gretchen German, Jennifer Runyon; *D:* Stuart Gillard.

A Man Called Sledge 🐾🐾 **1971** Garner fans might be surprised to see the star play a villain in this violent story of a gang of outlaws who wind up fighting each over a cache of gold. This is mainstream Western entertainment. **93m/C VHS, DVD.** James Garner, Dennis Weaver, Claude Akins, John Marley, Laura Antonelli; *D:* Vic Morrow.

A Man Escaped 🐾🐾🐾½ *Un Condamne a Mort s'est Echappe, Ou le Vent Souffle ou il Vent; A Man Escaped, or the Wind Bloweth Where It Listeth; A Condemned Man Has Escaped* **1957** There's an excruciating realism about Bresson's account of a WWII Resistance fighter's escape from a Nazi prison just before he was to be executed by the Gestapo. It's the sounds and lingering camera shots, not the wham bam variety of action, that create and sustain the film's suspense. Bresson, who had been a Nazi prisoner, solicited the supervision of Andre Devigny, whose true story the film tells. Contributing to the realistic feel was the use of non professional actors. An award-wining film that fellow director Truffaut lauded as the most crucial French film of the previous ten years. In French with English subtitles. **102m/B VHS, DVD.** Francois Leterrier, Charles Le Clainche, Roland Monod, Maurice Beerblock, Jacques Ertaud, Jean-Paul Delhumeau, Roger Treheme, Jean-Philippe Delamarre, Cesar Gattegno, Jacques Oerfmans, Klaus Detlef Grevenhorst, Leonard Schmidt; *D:* Robert Bresson; *W:* Robert Bresson; *C:* Leonce-Henri Burel. Cannes '57: Director (Bresson).

Man Facing Southeast 🐾🐾🐾½ *Hombre Mirando Al Sudeste; Man Looking Southeast* **1986** (R) The acclaimed Argentinean film about the sudden appearance of a strange man in an asylum who claims to be an extraterrestrial, and a psychologist's attempts to discover his true identity. The sense of mystery intensifies when the new patient indeed seems to have some remarkable powers. Although the pace at times lags, the story intriguingly keeps one guessing about the stranger right to the end. In Spanish, with English subtitles. **105m/C VHS.** *AR* Lorenzo Quinteros, Hugo Soto, Ines Vernengo; *D:* Eliseo Subiela; *C:* Ricardo De Angelis; *M:* Pedro Aznar.

A Man for All Seasons 🐾🐾🐾🐾 **1966** (G) Sterling, heavily Oscar-honored biographical drama concerning the life and subsequent martyrdom of 16th-century Chancellor of England, Sir Thomas More (Scofield). Story revolves around his personal conflict when King Henry VIII (Shaw) seeks a divorce from his wife, Catherine of Aragon, so he can wed his mistress, Anne Boleyn—events that ultimately lead the King to bolt from the Pope and declare himself head of the Church of England. Remade for TV in 1988 with Charlton Heston in the lead role. **120m/C VHS, DVD.** *GB* Paul Scofield, Robert Shaw, Orson Welles, Wendy Hiller, Susannah York, John Hurt, Nigel Davenport, Vanessa Redgrave; *D:* Fred Zinnemann; *W:* Constance Willis, Robert Bolt; *C:* Ted Moore; *M:* Georges Delerue. Oscars '66: Actor (Scofield), Adapt. Screenplay, Color Cinematog., Costume Des. (C), Director (Zinnemann), Picture; British Acad. '67: Actor (Scofield), Film, Screenplay; Directors Guild '66: Director (Zinnemann); Golden Globes '67: Actor—Drama (Scofield), Director (Zinnemann), Film—Drama, Screenplay; Natl. Bd. of Review '66: Actor (Scofield), Director (Zinnemann); Support. Actor (Shaw); N.Y. Film Critics '66: Actor (Scofield), Director (Zinnemann), Film, Screenplay.

A Man for All Seasons 🐾🐾 **1988** Fresh from the London stage, Heston directs and stars in this version of Robert Bolt's play depicting the conflict between Henry VIII and his chief advisor, Sir Thomas More. Strong supporting cast. **150m/C VHS.** Charlton Heston, Vanessa Redgrave, John Gielgud, Richard Johnson, Roy Kinnear, Martin Chamberlain; *D:* Charlton Heston. CABLE

Man Friday 🐾🐾 **1975** (PG) Stranded on a deserted island, a man forces a native from a neighboring island to be his slave. Based on the classic story "Robinson Crusoe" by Daniel Defoe, this adaptation charts the often-brutal treatment the native receives as his captor tries to civilize him. Through his intelligence, the enslaved man regains his freedom and returns home with his former captor, who then seeks acceptance from the native's tribe. A sometimes confusing storyline and excessive blood and guts detract from this message-laden effort. **115m/C VHS, DVD.** *GB* Peter O'Toole, Richard Roundtree, Peter Cellier, Christopher Cabot, Joel Fluellen; *D:* Jack Gold; *M:* Carl Davis.

The Man from Atlantis 🐾🐾 **1977** Patrick Duffy stars as the water-breathing alien who emerges from his undersea home, the Lost City of Atlantis. Led to a brief TV series. **60m/C VHS.** Patrick Duffy, Belinda J. Montgomery, Victor Buono; *D:* Lee H. Katzin. TV

The Man from Beyond 🐾🐾½ **1922** Frozen alive, a man returns 100 years later to try and find his lost love. Silent. **50m/B VHS, DVD.** Harry Houdini, Arthur Maude, Nita Naldi; *D:* Burton King.

Man from Button Willow 🐾🐾 **1965** (G) Classic animated adventure is the story of Justin Eagle, a man who leads a double life. He is a respected rancher and a shrewd secret agent for the government, but in 1869 he suddenly finds himself the guardian of a four-year-old Oriental girl, leading him into a whole new series of adventures. Strictly for younger audiences. **79m/C VHS, DVD.** *M:* George Bruns; *V:* Dale Robertson, Edgar Buchanan, Barbara Jean Wong, Howard Keel.

Man from Cairo 🐾🐾 **1954** An American in Algiers is mistaken for a detective in search of gold lost during WWII and decides to play along. **82m/B VHS, DVD.** *IT* George Raft, Gianna Maria Canale; *D:* Ray Enright.

Man from Cheyenne 🐾 **1942** Cowboy comes home to find his town under a siege of terror from a lawless gang of cattle rustlers. He gets mad and seeks some frontier justice. **54m/B VHS.** Roy Rogers, Gale Storm, George "Gabby" Hayes, Sally Payne, Lynne Carver; *D:* Joseph Kane; *W:* Winston Miller; *C:* Reggie Lanning.

Man from Colorado 🐾🐾½ **1949** An odd Technicolor western about two Civil War vets at odds, one an honest marshall, the other a sadistic judge. Solid Western fare with a quirky performance by Ford. **99m/C VHS, DVD.** William Holden, Glenn Ford, Ellen Drew, Ray Collins, Edgar Buchanan, Jerome Courtland, Gianna Maria Canale, Jim Bannon; *D:* Henry Levin; *M:* George Duning.

Man from Deep River woof! **1977** (R) A photographer is captured by a savage tribe in Thailand and forced to undergo a series of grueling initiation rites. Full of very violent and sickening tortures inflicted on both human and animal victims. **90m/C VHS, DVD.** *IT* Ivan Rassimov; *D:* Umberto Lenzi.

The Man from Earth 🐾🐾½ **2007** College professor John Oldman (Smith) gathers his most trusted colleagues at a remote cabin to inform them that he's actual an immortal who has been evolving since the Cro-Magnon age. So is he telling the truth or just nuts? Low-key, speculative fiction from classic sci-fi writer Bixby. Falls apart at the end but until then it's an interesting look at belief. **90m/C DVD.** David Lee Smith, John Billingsley, Richard Riehle, Tony Todd, William Katt, Ellen Crawford, Annika Peterson, Alexis Thorpe; *D:* Richard Schenkman; *W:* Jerome Bixby; *C:* Afshin Shahidi. VIDEO

The Man from Elysian Fields 🐾🐾🐾 **2001** (R) Byron (Garcia) is a failing novelist who's having trouble supporting his wife (Margulies) and family. At his lowest point Byron meets dapper escort service operator Luther (Jagger), who offers him a job as a highly paid gigolo. Hiding his new job from his wife, Byron begins seeing Andrea (Williams), who happens to be the wife of his literary hero Tobias Alcott (Coburn). Tobias, who is agreeable to the arrangement, soon begins to ask Byron for help on his novel, which he believes will be his swan song. Meanwhile, Luther is having his own complications with a client (Huston) with whom he has fallen in love. An offbeat, satisfying look at seduction, betrayal and forgiveness of all kinds. **106m/C VHS, DVD.** *US* Andy Garcia, Mick Jagger, Julianna Margulies, Olivia Williams, James Coburn, Anjelica Huston, Michael Des Barres, Richard Bradford; *D:* George Hickenlooper; *W:* Jayson Philip Lasker; *C:* Kramer Morgenthau; *M:* Anthony Marinelli.

The Man from Gun Town 🐾🐾½ **1936** McCoy comes to the rescue of a woman who has been framed by an evil gang for the murder of her brother. **68m/B VHS.** Tim McCoy, Billie Seward, Rex Lease, Jack Clifford, Wheeler Oakman, Bob McKenzie; *D:* Ford Beebe.

The Man from Headquarters 🐾🐾 **1928** Good silent mystery in which a U.S. agent takes on a gang of foreign operatives. **7m/B VHS.** Cornelius Keefe, Edith Roberts, Charles West, Lloyd Whitlock; *D:* Duke Worne; *W:* Arthur Hoerl; *C:* Hap Depew.

The Man from Hell 🐾 **1934** Sheriff Russell goes undercover to expose the head of a gang of outlaws. Low-budget fare. **55m/B VHS.** Reb Russell, Fred Kohler Jr., Ann Darcy, George "Gabby" Hayes, Jack Rockwell, Charles French, Charles "Slim" Whitaker, Yakima Canutt; *D:* Lewis D. Collins.

Man from Hell's Edges 🐾🐾½ **1932** An innocent cowpoke escapes from jail and brings the real baddy to justice. **63m/B VHS, DVD.** Bob Steele, Nancy Drexel, Julian Rivero, Robert E. Homans, George "Gabby" Hayes; *D:* Robert North Bradbury.

The Man from Laramie 🐾🐾🐾½ **1955** Aging ranch baron Alec Waggoman (Crisp), who is going blind, worries about which of his two sons he will leave the ranch to. Into this tension-filled familial atmosphere rides Lockhart (Stewart), a cow-herder obsessed with hunting down the men who sold guns to the Indians that killed his brother. Needless to say, the tension increases. Tough, surprisingly brutal western, the best of the classic Stewart-Mann films. **104m/B VHS, DVD.** James Stewart, Arthur Kennedy, Donald Crisp, Alex Nicol, Cathy O'Donnell, Aline MacMahon, Wallace Ford, Jack Elam; *D:* Anthony Mann; *W:* Philip Yordan; *C:* Charles B(ryant) Lang Jr.; *M:* George Duning.

The Man from Left Field 🐾🐾 **1993** Homeless man winds up coaching a little league baseball team, inspiring the kids, and turning his life around. Made for TV. **96m/C VHS, DVD.** Burt Reynolds, Reba McEntire; *D:* Burt Reynolds; *M:* Bobby Goldsboro. TV

Man from Mallorca 🐾🐾½ *Mannen fran Mallorca* **1984** Sgts. Jarnebring (Wollter) and Johansson (von Bromssen) are in pursuit of a gunman who robbed a Stockholm post office. The robber gets away and the investigation stalls until two witnesses are murdered. The detectives begin to suspect an official cover-up and think that senior police officer Hedberg (Hellberg) has something to hide. When they're taken off the case, the duo forge ahead on their own time with some disturbing results. Swedish with subtitles. **104m/C VHS.** *SW* Sven Wollter, Tomas von Bromssen, Thomas Hellberg; *D:* Bo Widerberg; *W:* Bo Widerberg; *C:* Thomas Wahlberg.

Man from Montana 🐾🐾½ *Montana Justice* **1941** Brown is a sheriff who battles outlaws trying to stir up trouble between ranchers and farmers. **56m/B VHS.** Johnny Mack Brown, Fuzzy Knight, William (Bill) Gould, Kermit Maynard, Nell O'Day, Billy Lenhart, Murdock MacQuarrie; *D:* Ray Taylor; *W:* Bennett Cohen; *C:* Charles Van Enger.

Man from Monterey 🐾🐾 **1933** South-of-the-border Western has U.S. Army captain Wayne trying to get Mexican landowners to register their property under the Spanish land grants or lose them to public domain. Wayne's last series western for Warner Bros. **59m/B VHS, DVD.** John Wayne, Ruth Hall, Luis Alberni, Francis Ford, Lafe (Lafayette) McKee, Lillian (Lilliane, Lyllian) Leighton, Charles "Slim" Whitaker; *D:* Mack V. Wright; *W:* Lesley Mason.

The Man from Music Mountain 🐾🐾 **1938** Worthless mining stock is sold in a desert mining town, but Gene and Smiley clear that up, with a little singing as well. **54m/B VHS.** Gene Autry, Smiley Burnette, Carol Hughes, Polly Jenkins.

Man from Nowhere 🐾🐾½ **1937** A henpecked man gets the break of his life when his domineering wife and mother-in-law believe he's dead. Based on the novel by Luigi Pirandello. In French with English subtitles. **98m/B VHS.** *FR* Pierre Blanchar, Ginette LeClerc; *D:* Pierre Chenal.

The Man from Painted Post 🐾 **1917** Fairbanks plays a Cattlemen's Association detective who comes to the range to stop the cattle rustlers as well as to find the man who murdered his sister. **7m/B VHS.** Douglas Fairbanks Sr., Eileen (Elaine Persey) Percy, Frank Campeau, Monte Blue; *D:* Joseph Henabery.

The Man from Planet X 🐾🐾 **1951** Making a belated arrival on home video is this prototypical low-budget first-contact tale. All the elements are there—reporter, aging scientist, his nubile daughter, crafty associate—but the setting is Scotland. Not that it matters, because virtually all of the action takes place on sets. **71m/B DVD.** Robert Clarke, Margaret Field, William Schallert; *D:* Edgar G. Ulmer; *W:* Aubrey Wisberg, Jack Pollexfen; *C:* John L. "Jack" Russell; *M:* Charles Koff.

The Man from Snowy River 🐾🐾½ **1982** (PG) Stunning cinematography highlights this otherwise fairly ordinary adventure story set in 1880s Australia. Jim Craig (Burlinson) is an orphaned young man coming of age in the mountains while seeking a life of his own and falling in love with the well-brought up Jessica (Thornton). In a dual role, Douglas portrays battling brothers, one a rich land-owner and the other a one-legged prospector. A wild horse roundup is a stunning highlight. Based on the epic poem by A.B. "Banjo" Paterson and followed by "Return to Snowy River." A big hit in Australia and not directed by "Mad Max's" Miller, but another Miller named George. **104m/C VHS, DVD.** *AU* Kirk Douglas, Tom Burlinson, Sigrid Thornton, Terence Donovan, Tommy Dysart, Jack Thompson, Bruce Kerr; *D:* George Miller; *W:* Fred Cullen, John Dixon; *C:* Keith Wagstaff; *M:* Bruce Rowland.

Man from Texas 🐾🐾 **1939** Singing and gun-slinging Tex defends a kid accused of horse thieving until the kid turns bad and Tex must bring him in. **55m/B VHS, DVD.** Tex Ritter, Hal Price, Charles B. Wood, Vic Demourelle Sr.; *D:* Albert Herman.

Man from the Alamo 🐾🐾½ **1953** A soldier sent from the Alamo during its last hours to get help is branded as a deserter, and struggles to clear his name. Well acted, this film will satisfy those with a taste for action. **79m/C VHS, DVD.** Glenn Ford, Julie Adams, Chill Wills, Victor Joy, Hugh O'Brian; *D:* Budd Boetticher.

The Man from the Pru 🐾🐾½ **1989** Shocking 1931 murder case follows insurance agent William Wallace (Pryce) who was sentenced to hang for the murder of his wife, Julia. Wallace insisted he was called from home on a possible insurance sale and returned home to find his wife dead. His case made British history when the case's appeal overturned the verdict. Made for TV. **90m/C VHS.** *GB* Jonathan Pryce, Anna Massey, Susannah York; *D:* Rob Rohrer. TV

Man from Thunder River 🐾🐾 **1943** A group of cowboys uncover a plot to steal gold ore and wind up saving a young girl's life in the process. Standard western with lots of action. **55m/B VHS.** William (Wild Bill) Elliott, George "Gabby" Hayes, Anne Jeffreys, Ian Keith, John James; *D:* John English.

Man from Utah 🐾½ **1934** The Duke tangles with the crooked sponsor of some rodeo events who has killed several of the participants. **55m/B VHS, DVD.** John Wayne, George "Gabby" Hayes, Polly Ann Young, Yakima Canutt, Lafe (Lafayette) McKee; Robert North Bradbury; *W:* Lindsley Parsons; *C:* Archie Stout.

The Man I Love 🐾🐾🐾 1945
Slick drama about nightclub singer Lupino falling for no-good mobster Alda. Enjoyable and well-acted, although script doesn't make sense. Great selection of tunes. This film inspired Scorsese's "New York, New York." Based on the novel "Night Shift" by Maritta Wolff. 🎵 Body and Soul; Why Was I Born; Bill; The Man I Love; Liza; If I Could Be With You. **96m/B VHS.** Ida Lupino, Robert Alda, Andrea King, Martha Vickers, Bruce Bennett, Alan Hale, Dolores Moran, Don McGuire, Warren Douglas, Craig Stevens; **D:** Raoul Walsh, John Maxwell; **W:** Catherine Turney, Jo Pagano; **M:** Max Steiner.

The Man I Love 🐾🐾 1997
J'aime 1997 Heart-on-its-sleeve romance originally made for French TV. Martin (Di Fonzo Bo) is hired to work at a Marseilles municipal swimming pool and falls immediately for golden boy lifeguard Lucas (Seigner), who has a live-in girlfriend, Lise (Seigner). Lise thinks Lucas's new buddy Martin is after the hunk. Of course, Lucas isn't as straight as he seems and eventually switches partners. But there's another problem. Martin, who's HIV-positive, decides to take a break from this onerous treatment despite the consequences. French with subtitles. **87m/C VHS, DVD, FR** Marcial Di Fonzo Bo, Jean-Michel Portal, Mathilde Seigner, Victoria Scongamigo, Jacques Hansen; **D:** Stéphane Giusti; **W:** Stéphane Giusti; **C:** Jacques Bouquin; **M:** Lazare Boghossian.

The Man in Grey 🐾🐾🐾 1945
In a story of romantic intrigue set in 19th-century England, a Marquis's wife is betrayed by her vile husband and the schoolmate she once befriended who has an affair with him. Stunning costumes and fine performances compensate for the overly extravagant production values in a work that helped bring stardom to Mason. **B VHS, GB** James Mason, Margaret Lockwood, Stewart Granger, Phyllis Calvert; **D:** Leslie Arliss.

A Man in Love 🐾🐾½ *Un Homme Amoureux* 1987 (R) An international romantic melodrama set during the Italian filming of a biography of suicidal author Cesar Pavese. The self-important lead actor and a beautiful supporting actress (Coyote and Scacchi) become immersed in the roles that Coyote is married and Scacchi's engaged. The two make a steamy pair, to the detriment of friends, family, and the movie they're making. Kurys' first English-language film is visually appealing in a lush, romantic score, seamlessly weaving the storylines among vivid characters. **110m/C VHS. FP** Peter Coyote, Greta Scacchi, Jamie Lee Curtis, Peter Riegert, Jean Pigozzi, John Berry, Claudia Cardinale, Vincent Lindon; **D:** Diane Kurys; **W:** Diane Kurys, Olivier Schatzky; Israel Horovtz; **M:** Georges Delerue.

Man in the Attic 🐾🐾 1953
Mild but creepy pathologist Slade (Palance) rents an attic room from Mrs. Harley and moons over her actress daughter Lily (Smith) in late 1880s London. About the same time Lily starts finding Slade attractive and interesting, Mrs. Harvey starts suspecting him of being Jack the Ripper. Satisfying suspenser keeps the audience guessing thanks largely to Palance's ambiguous performance. **82m/B VHS, DVD.** Jack Palance, Constance Smith, Byron Palmer, Frances Bavier, Rhys Williams, Sean McClory, Leslie Bradley, Lester Matthews, Harry Cording, Lillian Bond, Isabel Jewell; **D:** Hugo Fregonese; **W:** Earrle Lynisabel, Robert Presnall Jr.; **C:** Leo Tover; **M:** Hugo Friedhofer.

The Man in the Attic 🐾½ 1994 (R) Harris certainly leaves his "Doogie Howser" past behind as he takes a grownup turn in an erotic thriller based on a true case history from the early 20th century, garnered from the book "Sex and the Criminal Mind." Teenaged Edward (Harris) has a blazing affair with married, mature Krista (Archer), who does indeed hide her young lover in the family attic when her clueless husband (Carou) returns home at night. But such consuming passion can hardly be kept a secret for long—and takes a decidedly deadly turn. **87m/C VHS.** Anne Archer, Neil Patrick Harris, Len Cariou, Alex Carter; **D:** Graeme Campbell; **W:** Duane Poole, Tom Swale; **C:** Dick Bush; **M:** Lou Natale. **C.A.B.L.E.**

The Man in the Glass Booth 🐾🐾🐾 1975 (PG) In this adaptation of a play featuring actor Robert Shaw, a successful Jewish businessman is suspected of being a Nazi war criminal. Loosely based on the life of death camp commandant Otto Adolf Eichmann, the film depicts the arrest and subsequent trial of the former Nazi by the Israelis. The film's title is derived from the fact that Eichmann sat in a glass booth during his trial. Schell's performance is outstanding, nerving this treatment despite the low-budget. **117m/C VHS, DVD, Maximilian Schell, Lois Nettleton, Luther Adler, Lawrence Pressman, Henry Brown, Richard Rasof; **D:** Arthur Hiller; **W:** Edward Anhalt; **C:** Sam Leavitt.

The Man in the Gray Flannel Suit 🐾🐾🐾½ 1956 A very long and serious adaptation of the Sloan Wilson novel about a Madison Avenue advertising exec trying to balance his life between work and family. The Hollywood treatment falls short of the adaptation potential of the original story. **152m/C VHS, DVD.** Gregory Peck, Fredric March, Jennifer Jones, Ann Harding, Arthur O'Connell, Henry Daniell, Lee J. Cobb, Marisa Pavan, Gene Lockhart, Keenan Wynn, Gigi Perreau, Joseph Sweeney, Kenneth Tobey, DeForest Kelley; **D:** Nunnally Johnson.

The Man in the Iron Mask 🐾🐾🐾 1939 Swashbuckling tale about twin brothers (played by Hayward) separated at birth. One turns out to be King Louis XIV of France, and the other his imprisoned and forced to wear an iron mask that hides his identity. Philippe is eventually rescued by musketeer D'Artagnan (William) and the musketeers join forces for action-packed adventure and royal revenge. Remake of the "The Iron Mask" (1929) with Douglas Fairbanks and subsequently remade several times for both TV and the big screen. **110m/B VHS, DVD.** Louis Hayward, Alan Hale, Joan Bennett, Warren William, Joseph Schildkraut, Walter Kingsford, Marion Martin; **D:** James Whale; **W:** George Bruce; **C:** Robert Planck; **M:** Lucien Moraweck.

The Man in the Iron Mask 🐾🐾 1977 A tyrannical French king kidnaps his twin brother and imprisons him on a remote island. Chamberlain, the king of the miniseries, is excellent in a dual role in this big production swashbuckler. Adapted from the Dumas classic. **105m/C VHS.** Richard Chamberlain, Patrick McGoohan, Louis Jourdan, Jenny Agutter, Ian Holm, Ralph Richardson; **D:** Mike Newell. **TV**

The Man in the Iron Mask 🐾½ 1997 Low-budget personalized version of the Dumas swashbuckler from director Richert, which he filmed at the historic Mission Inn in Riverside, CA. Prologue establishes the birth of twin royals to the French Queen (Foster) and the fate of Philippe (Richert's own Nick) as the man in the iron mask. A deathbed confession to Count Aramis (the director himself) alerts the Musketeers, who decide to set things right. Well-intentioned but not a lot of fun. **35m/C VHS, DVD.** William Richert, Edward Albert, Rex Ryon, Timothy Bottoms, Dana Barron, Brigid Brannagh, Fannie Brett, **D:** William Richert; **C:** William Barber; **M:** Jim Ervin.

The Man in the Iron Mask 🐾🐾🐾 1998 (PG-13) Lavish retelling of Alexandre Dumas's classic story boasts a stellar cast with teen heartthrob DiCaprio in a dual role. Snotty tyrant King Louis XIV's (DiCaprio) lust for women inadvertently leads to the reunion of the retired Musketeers, bent on replacing cold Louis with his more sensitive twin brother Phillippe (DiCaprio, again), an inmate of the Bastille and hidden behind a ghastly mask. Irons, Malkovich, Depardieu, and Byrne bring a welcome seriousness and style to the often-told story as the older, jaded Musketeers, while DiCaprio holds his own in the presence of such formidable company. Although first-time director Wallace doesn't balance the star power-and enough swordplay, the high gloss production provides old-fashioned escapism with enough swordplay, the high gloss production provides old-fashioned escapism. **132m/C VHS, DVD.** Leonardo DiCaprio, Gabriel Byrne, Jeremy Irons, John Malkovich, Gérard Depardieu, Anne Parillaud, Edward Atterton, Peter Sarsgaard, Hugh Laurie; **D:** Randall Wallace; **W:** Randall Wallace; **C:** Peter Suschitzky; **M:** Nick Glennie-Smith.

Man in the Silk Hat 🐾🐾🐾 1983 Gabriel-Maximilien Leuvielle, known in film's as Max Linder, is now credited with developing the style of silent-movie slapstick comedy that Mack Sennett, Charlie Chaplin, and others became more famous for in their time. Here, Linder's daughter has done a fine job writing and directing a film full of historic footage of her father's work. **96m/B VHS, FR** Max Linder; **D:** Maud Linder.

Man in the Silk Hat 🐾🐾🐾 1915 A collection of the nearly forgotten French comic's early silent comedy shorts, made in France before his resettlement in America. **96m/B VHS.** Max Linder; **D:** Maud Linder; **C:** Arthur E. Arling; **M:** Gene L. Coon; **C:** Arthur E. Arling.

Man in the Mirror: The Michael Jackson Story 🐾 2004
Like rubber-necking at a car wreck. Poorly-dramatized showbiz bio of the pop star (Alexander) in all his legendary weirdness. It takes us from Jackson's musical success to his career slide, unplagued him. Listen to the music instead. **87m/C DVD.** Flex Alexander, Eugene Clark, Jason Griffith, April Telek, Krista Rae; **D:** Allan Moyle; **W:** Claudia Salter; **C:** David (Robert) A. Greene; **M:** Bruce Leitl. **C.A.B.L.E.**

The Man in the Moon 🐾🐾🐾½ 1991 (PG-13) Beautifully rendered coming-of-age tale. On a farm outside a small Louisiana town in the 1950s, 14-year-old Dani wonders as her 17-year-old sister Maureen. This becomes especially important, as Dani is beginning to notice boys, particularly Court, the 17-year-old young man she meets when swimming. Although Dani and Maureen have always been especially close, a rift develops between the sisters after Court meets Maureen. Intelligently written, excellent direction, lovely cinematography, and exceptional acting make this a particularly worthwhile and entertaining film. **100m/C VHS, DVD.** Reese Witherspoon, Emily Warfield, Jason London, Tess Harper, Sam Waterston, Gail Strickland; **D:** Robert Mulligan.

The Man in the Raincoat 🐾🐾 1957 French film about a bumbling clarinet player who is erroneously tracked down as a murderer. Strenuous efforts to evoke laughter usually fail. Dubbed. **97m/B VHS, FR** Fernandel, John McGiver, Bernard Blier; **D:** Julian Duvivier.

Man in the Saddle 🐾🐾½ The *Outcast* 1951 Western star Scott gets roped in a romantic triangle out on the range, leading to some exciting gunplay. As usual, justice triumphs in this above average oater. Based on the novel by Ernest Haycox. **87m/C VHS, DVD.** Randolph Scott, Joan Leslie, Ellen Drew, Alexander Knox, Richard Rober, John Russell; **D:** Andre de Toth; **W:** Kenneth Gamet.

Man in the Santa Claus Suit 🐾🐾 1979 A costume shop owner has an effect on three people who rent Santa Claus costumes from him. Astaire plays seven different roles in this average holiday feel-good movie. **96m/C VHS.** Fred Astaire, Gary Burghoff, John Byner, Nanette Fabray, Bert Convy; **D:** Corey Allen. **TV**

Man in the Shadow 🐾🐾 1957 *Pay the Devil; Seeds of Wrath* 1957 Sheriff Ben Sadler (Chandler) is the only man in the county (Chandler) to stand up to wealthy Texas rancher Virgil Renchler (Welles). Sadler suspects Renchler is behind the brutal death of a Mexican laborer but gets no support when he tries to find justice. **80m/C VHS.** Jeff Chandler, Orson Welles, Ben Alexander, Colleen Miller, John Larch, James Gleason, Barbara Lawrence, Royal Dano, Paul Fix, William Schallert; **D:** Jack Arnold; **W:** Gene L. Coon; **C:** Arthur E. Arling.

A Man Like Eva 🐾🐾🐾 1983 *Ein Mann wie Eva* 1983 A weird, morbid homage to and portrait of Rainer Werner Fassbinder after his inevitable death, detailing his work-obsessed self-destruction. Mattes, one of Fassbinder's favorite actresses, plays him in drag in an eerie gender-crossing transformation. In German with English subtitles. **92m/C VHS.** Eva Mattes, Lisabeth (Lisa) Kreuzer, Charles Regnier, Werner Stocker; **D:** Radu Gabrea.

Man Is Not a Bird 🐾🐾 1965 *Covek Nije Tica* 1965 Follows the destructive love of a factory engineer and a hairdresser in a small Yugoslavian mining town. In Serbian with English subtitles. **80m/B VHS, YU** Eva Ras, Milena Dravic, Janez Urhovec; **D:** Dusan Makavejev; **W:** Dusan Makavejev; **C:** Aleksandar Petkovic; **M:** Petar Bergamo.

Man Made Monster 🐾🐾🐾 *Atomic Monster; The Electric Man* 1941 Chaney stars as carnival performer "Dynamo" Dan McCormick, whose act has caused Dan to build up an immunity to electrical charges. Dan falls prey to the mad Dr. Rigas (Atwill) who seeks to create a race of electro-men who'll do his bidding. Experiments on the hapless Dan turn him into a glowing monster whose very touch can kill. Chaney's first role in the horror genre led to Universal's casting him in "The Wolf Man" and "The Ghost of Frankenstein." **61m/B VHS.** Lon Chaney Jr., Lionel Atwill, Anne Nagel, Frank Albertson, Samuel S. Hinds; **D:** George Waggner; **W:** Joseph West; **C:** Elwood "Woody" Bredell.

Man of a Thousand Faces 🐾🐾🐾½ 1957 A tasteful and touching portrayal of Lon Chaney, from his childhood with his deaf and mute parents to his success as a screen star. Recreates the Phantom of the Opera and Quasimodo in "Notre Dame." Cagney is magnificent as the long-suffering film star who was a genius with makeup and mime.

The Man in the White Suit 🐾🐾🐾½ 1951 A humble laboratory assistant in a textile mill invents a white cloth that won't stain, tear, or wear out, and can't be dyed. The panicked garment industry sets out to destroy him and the fabric, resulting in some sublimely comic situations and a variety of inventive chases. **82m/B VHS, DVD, GB** Alec Guinness, Joan Greenwood; **D:** Alexander Mackendrick.

A Man in Uniform 🐾🐾 / *Love a Man in Uniform* 1993 (R) A look at the making of a sociopath. Henry (McCamus) is a quiet bank employee who moonlights as an actor. Then he gets his big break in the role of a self-righteous cop in a TV series. Only the lines between his make-believe cop and the real world begin to blur and Henry's intensity turns to violence. Fine performances lead to an unsatisfying film conclusion. **99m/C VHS, DVD, CA** Tom McCamus, Brigitte Bako, Kevin Tighe, David Hemblen, Alex Karzis, Graham McPherson, Richard Blackburn; **D:** David Wellington; **W:** David Wellington; **C:** David Franco; **M:** Ron Sures. Genie '93: Actor (Tighe).

Man in the Wilderness 🐾🐾½ 1971 (PG) Harris is part of an expedition traveling through the Northwest Territory. He's mauled by a grizzly and left for dead by leader Huston, who leads his fights for survival, he also plots revenge. Blood and violence is somewhat offset by good lead performances. **105m/C VHS.** Richard Harris, John Huston, Henry Wilcoxon, Percy Herbert, Dennis Waterman, Prunella Ransome, Norman Rossington, James Doolan; **D:** Richard Sarafian; **W:** Jack DeWitt; **M:** Johnny Harris.

The Man Inside 🐾🐾 1990 (PG) Lukewarm Cold War saga based on the true story of Guntner Wallraff, a West German journalist who risked all to expose the corruption behind a large European newspaper. **93m/C VHS.** NL GE Jürgen Prochnow, Peter Coyote, Nathalie Baye, Dieter Laser, Monique Van De Ven, Sylvie Granotier; **D:** Bobby Roth; **W:** Bobby Roth.

122m/B VHS, DVD. James Cagney, Dorothy Malone, Jane Greer, Marjorie Rambeau, Jim Backus, Roger Smith, Robert Evans; **D:** Joseph Pevney. **W:** Ivan Goff; **C:** Russell Metty; **M:** Frank Skinner.

Man of Action 🐾½ 1933 Texas Ranger McCoy is out to solve the mystery of what happened to money, recovered from a robbery, which has vanished once again. 56m/B VHS. Tim McCoy, Wheeler Oakman, Walter Brennan, Stanley Blystone, Charles French; **D:** George Melford.

Man of Aran 🐾🐾🐾 1934 Celebrated account of a fisherman's struggle for survival on a barren island near the west coast of Ireland, featuring amateur actors. Three years in the making, it's the last word in man against nature cinema, and a visual marvel. A former explorer, Flaherty became an influential documentarian. Having first gained fame with "Nanook of the North," he compiled an opus of documentaries made for commercial release. 132m/B VHS, DVD. **D:** Robert Flaherty. **TV**

Man of Ashes 🐾🐾 1986 *Rih Essed* 1986 Hachemi is terrified of women though he is a bridegroom-to-be. He and his friend Farfat have kept hidden the fact that they were molested by their male employer. They try to overcome their insecurities by visiting a prostitute but this experience is only successful for one of the men, leading the other to more torment. Arabic with subtitles. 109m/C VHS, DVD. Imad Maalal, Khalid Ksouri; **D:** Nouri Bouzid; **W:** Nouri Bouzid; **C:** Youssef Ben Youssef; **M:** Salah Mahdi.

Man of Destiny 🐾🐾½ 1973 Bonaparte (Keach) and a mysterious woman battle good-humoredly over a collection of love letters. From a Bernard Shaw story. Charming and well-acted. 60m/C VHS. Stacy Keach, Samantha Eggar; **D:** Joseph Hardy; **M:** Robert Prince.

Man of Evil 🐾🐾 1948 *Fanny by Gaslight* 1948 The hard times of the illegitimate daughter of a member of the British Parliament in the early 1900s, told with an astonishing number of plot twists and a plodding melodramatic style. Based on the novel "Fanny by Gaslight." 108m/B VHS, DVD. **GB** Phyllis Calvert, James Mason, Wilfred Lawson, Stewart Granger, Margaretta Scott, Jean Kent, John Laurie, Stuart Lindsell, Nora Swinburne, Amy Veness, Ann Wilton, Helen Haye, Cathleen Nesbitt, Guy Le Feuvre, John Turnbull, Peter Jones; **D:** Anthony Asquith.

Man of Flowers 🐾🐾½ 1984 Because of his puritan upbringing, a reclusive art collector has trouble coping with his feelings of sexuality. He pays a woman to disrobe in front of him, but is never able to bring himself to see her naked. A moody piece with overtones of black humor, this work has limited audience appeal. 91m/C VHS, DVD. **AU** Norman Kaye, Alyson Best, Chris Haywood, Sarah Walker, Julia Blake, Bob Ellis, Werner Herzog; **D:** Paul Cox; **W:** Bob Ellis, Paul Cox; **C:** Yuri Sokol; **M:** Gaetano Donizetti. Australian Film Inst. '83: Actor (Kaye).

Man of Iron 🐾🐾🐾 *Wajda: Czlowiek Z Zelaza* 1981 (PG) Director Wajda's follow-up to "Man of Marble" deals with a reporter (Odania) who is expected to tow the government line when writing about the Gdansk shipyard strike of 1980. He meets the harassed laborer son (Radziwilowicz) of worker-hero Birkut, against whom Odania is expected to conduct a smear campaign, and finds his loyalties tested. In Polish with English subtitles. 116m/C VHS, DVD. **PL** Jerzy Radziwilowicz, Marian Opania, Krystyna Janda; **D:** Andrzej Wajda; **W:** Aleksander Scibor-Rylski; **C:** Edward Klosinski; **M:** Andrzej Korzynski. Cannes '81: Film.

Man of La Mancha 🐾🐾½ 1972 (PG) Arrested by the Inquisition and thrown into prison, Miguel de Cervantes relates the story of Don Quixote. Not nearly as good as the Broadway musical it's based on. ♪It's All the Same; The Impossible Dream; Dulcinea; I'm Only Thinking of Him; Little Bird, Little Bird; Life as It Really Is; The Dubbing. 132m/C VHS, DVD. Peter O'Toole, Sophia Loren, James Coco, Harry Andrews, John Castle, Brian Blessed; **D:** Arthur Hiller. Natl. Bd. of Review '72: Actor (O'Toole).

Man of Legend 🐾🐾 1971 (PG) An adventure-romance filmed in Morocco; a WWI German soldier flees to the Foreign Legion and fights with nomadic rebels, ultimately falling in love with their chief's beautiful daughter. An unoriginal desert saga. 95m/C VHS. *IT SP* Peter Strauss, Tina Aumont, Pier Paolo Capponi; **D:** Sergio Grieco.

Man of Marble 🐾🐾🐾 1976 A satire on life in post-WWII Poland. A young filmmaker sets out to tell the story of a bricklayer who, because of his exceptional skill, once gained popularity with other workers. He became a champion for workers' rights, only to then find himself being persecuted by the government. The conclusion was censored by the Polish government. Highly acclaimed and followed by "Man of Iron" in 1981. In Polish with English subtitles. 160m/C VHS, DVD. **PL** Krystyna Janda, Jerzy Radziwilowicz, Tadeusz Lomnicki, Jacek Lomnicki, Krystyna Zachwatowicz; **D:** Andrzej Wajda; **W:** Aleksander Scibor-Rylski; **M:** Andrzej Korzynski.

The Man of My Life 🐾🐾🐾 *L'Homme de Sa Vie* 2006 Frederic (Campan) is on holiday with his wife (Drucker) at his family's home in the Provencale countryside. They invite their new neighbor, cynical gay Hugo (Berling), to a party and he and Frederic wind up talking for hours. An unexpected bond develops between the two middle-aged men and starts disrupting Frederic's marriage. French with subtitles. 111m/C DVD. *FR IT* Bernard Campan, Charles Berling, Lea Drucker; **D:** Zabou Breitman; **W:** Zabou Breitman, Agnes de Sacy; **C:** Michel Amathieu; **M:** Liviu Beda, Laurent Korcia.

A Man of No Importance 🐾🐾🐾 1994 (R) Touching and entertaining saga of lovable Alfie Byrne (Finney), a 1960s Dublin bus conductor with a passion for the work of Oscar Wilde, who successfully represses his own homosexuality. He also moonlights as director of a community theatre, where he sets out to produce Wilde's controversial play "Salome" starring fetching new bus passenger Adele (Fitzgerald), who further confuses Alfie's take on his identity. Finney is both delightful and heartbreaking in this character study of an innocent soul whose life is tested by the social code of his day. Equally affecting and charming supporting performances round out this witty but sad tale. 98m/C VHS. GB Albert Finney, Brenda Fricker, Michael Gambon, Tara Fitzgerald, Rufus Sewell, Patrick Malahide, David Kelly, Mick (Michael) Lally; **D:** Suri Krishnamma; **W:** Barry Devlin; **M:** Julian Nott.

A Man of Passion 🐾🐾 1988 (R) Quinn plays an aging artist living comfortably on a Mediterranean isle. His summer is led by his former partners in crime (who are led by his wacko uncle) he's forced to revert to his wanton ways in order to survive and save innocent hostages. There's a raging debate among Cooper fans whether the tale effort has been unduly overlooked or duly ignored. A number of things conspire to give it a bad rap: Cooper does little but look mournful until the very end; there's no hiding the fact that he's older than Cobb, who plays his uncle; and the acting is in general more befitting of a B-grade slice and dicer. You be the judge. 100m/C VHS. Gary Cooper, Julie London, Lee J. Cobb, Arthur O'Connell, Jack Lord, John Dehner, Royal Dano, Guy Wilkerson, Emory Parnell; **D:** Anthony Mann; **W:** Reginald Rose.

Man of the Century 🐾🐾½ 1999 (R) Journalist Johnny Twennies (Frazier) is an anachronism living in 1990s Manhattan. He dresses, talks, and acts as if it were the 1920s. But Johnny doesn't seem to find anything strange in this, nor does anyone else. 77m/C VHS, DVD. Gibson Frazier, Susan Egan, Anthony Rapp, Cara Buono, Dwight Ewell, Brian Davies, Frank Gorshin; **D:** Adam Abraham; **W:** Adam Abraham, Gibson Frazier; **C:** Matthew Jensen; **M:** Michael Weiner.

Man of the Forest 🐾🐾 1933 A cowboy goes to the aid of a damsel in distress and he winds up being framed for murder by bad guys. Based on Zane Grey's novel. 59m/B VHS, DVD. Randolph Scott, Verna Hillie, Harry Carey Sr., Noah Beery Sr., Barton MacLane; **D:** Henry Hathaway.

Man of the House 🐾 1995 (PG) Kids' comedy about a boy's scheme to sabotage his mother's new love interest. Ben (Thomas) concocts a plan to join the YMCA Indian Guides to discourage daddy wanna-be Jack (Chase), while mom (Fawcett) stands idly by tolerating her son's

bratty behavior. Subplot involves a screwy gangster theme that deteriorates into a "Home Alone-ish" ending. Film attempts to play off of Chase's knack for physical comedy, but falls short. And what's with the mime? Wendt is amusing as the Indian Guide leader. Will probably appeal more to younger crowds as Thomas's scheming teen upstages Chase's deadpan dad-to-be. 97m/C VHS, DVD. Chevy Chase, Farrah Fawcett, Jonathan Taylor Thomas, George Wendt, David Shiner, Art LaFleur, Richard Portnow, Richard Foronjy, Spencer Vrooman, John Disanti, Chief Leonard George, Peter Appel, George Gosdin, Chris Miranda, Ron Canada, Zachary Browne, Nicholas Garrett; **D:** James Orr; **W:** James Orr, Jim Cruickshank; **C:** Jamie Anderson; **M:** Mark Mancina.

Man of the House 🐾🐾 2005 (PG-13) Jones, with his weathered face and deadpan grumpiness, goes slumming in this silly comedy about cheerleaders who witness a murder. Roland Sharp is a stoic Texas Ranger assigned to protect five giggly (and jiggly) members (Millian, Keena, Garces, Ferrito, Garner) of the University of Texas Longhorns' cheerleading squad. He moves into their sorority house and offers fatherly advice while trying to awkwardly woo an age-appropriate professor (Archer) and find the bad guy. For some reason Cedric the Entertainer turns up briefly as an ex-con preacher with his own pep squad moves. 99m/C VHS, DVD, UMD. US Tommy Lee Jones, Cedric the Entertainer, Christina Milian, Paula Garces, Monica Keena, Vanessa Ferlito, Kelli Garner, Anne Archer, Brian Van Holt, Shea Whigham, R. Lee Ermey, Paget Brewster, Liz Vassey, Curtis Armstrong; *Cameos:* James Richard Perry; **D:** Stephen Herek; **W:** Robert Ramsey, Matthew Stone, John McLaughlin; **C:** Peter Menzies Jr.; **M:** David Newman.

Man of the West 🐾🐾½ 1958 Reformed bad guy Cooper is asked to deliver a tidy hunk of cash to another city to recruit a school marm. Ambushed en route by his former partners in crime (who are led by his wacko uncle) he's forced to revert to his wanton ways in order to survive and save innocent hostages. There's a raging debate among Cooper fans whether the tale effort has been unduly overlooked or duly ignored. A number of things conspire to give it a bad rap: Cooper does little but look mournful until the very end; there's no hiding the fact that he's older than Cobb, who plays his uncle; and the acting is in general more befitting of a B-grade slice and dicer. You be the judge. 100m/C VHS. Gary Cooper, Julie London, Lee J. Cobb, Arthur O'Connell, Jack Lord, John Dehner, Royal Dano, Guy Wilkerson, Emory Parnell; **D:** Anthony Mann; **W:** Reginald Rose.

Man of the World 🐾🐾 1931 Outcast journalist Michael Trevor (Powell) lives in Paris and blackmails wealthy Americans, aided by girlfriend Irene (Gibson). He wants to go straight when he falls for debutante Mary Kendall (Lombard) but tables are turned when Irene threatens to expose Michael's schemes. Pre-Production Code flick says crime may not pay but you still can get away. 74m/B VHS, DVD. William Powell, Carole Lombard, Wynne Gibson, Guy Kibbee, Lawrence Gray; **D:** Richard Wallace, Edward Goodman; **W:** Herbert J. Mankiewicz; **C:** Victor Milner.

Man of the Year 🐾🐾 2006 (PG-13) Schizoid blend of comedy and political thriller that features a subdued Williams as Tom Dobbs, a late-night talk show host whose joke about running for president turns into the real thing. But when he wins, it's thanks to a voting machine glitch that computer nerd Eleanor (Linney) warned her company about. When Eleanor tries to turn whistleblower, things really turn ridiculous, with the lady on the run from corporate hit men. Levinson should have stuck with a political satire about a well-intentioned guy taking on the biggest job in the land, which he is totally unequipped to handle. 108m/C DVD. US Robin Williams, Laura Linney, Christopher Walken, Lewis Black, Jeff Goldblum, Rick Roberts; **D:** Barry Levinson; **W:** Barry Levinson; **M:** Graeme Revell.

Man of Violence 🐾 *The Sex Racketeers* 1971 A vulgar, tasteless man spends the worthless hours of his wasted life lurking about the more wretched entranceways of his native land. 107m/C VHS. Michael Latimer, Luan Peters; **D:** Pete Walker.

Man on a String 🐾🐾½ 1971 (PG) In order to bring down a Mob boss the feds first frame cop Peter King and send him to the pen. When he gets out, King uses his prison contacts to get in with the Mob and winds up pitting two rival gangs against each other in order to destroy them both. 73m/C VHS. Christopher George, Jack Warden, Keith Carradine, Joel Grey, William Schallert, Kitty Winn; **D:** Joseph Sargent. **TV**

Man on Fire 🐾 1987 (R) Told via flashback, a cynical ex-CIA man is hired as a bodyguard for the daughter of a wealthy Italian couple, who is soon thereafter kidnapped by terrorists. He goes to her rescue with all the subtlety of a wrecking ball. Decent cast goes down the tubes in this botched thriller. 92m/C VHS. *FR* Scott Glenn, Brooke Adams, Danny Aiello, Joe Pesci, Paul Shenar, Jonathan Pryce, Jade Malle; **D:** Elie Chouraqui.

Man on Fire 🐾🐾½ 2004 (R) Slick actioner deploys the effective Washington as a world-weary anti-hero whose mission is to find a kidnapped young girl in Mexico City. Problem is, Creasy (Washington), a former government assassin who admittedly drinks too much, was hired as the bodyguard for nine-year-old Pita (Fanning) and her Mexican businessman father Samuel Ramos (Anthony) and American mother Lisa (Mitchell). The plot thickens as Creasy's investigation into the kidnapping reveals Mexican police involvement (surprise) and government ties. A botched ransom drop sets Creasy off on a rage-fueled rampage through the city. Vet Walken shows up to help goose the plot along as an old military buddy of Creasy's. Though plot comes up lacking, pic is full of non-stop action and gritty style highlighted by an excellent Washington. 145m/C DVD, Blu-ray Disc, UMD. US Denzel Washington, Christopher Walken, Dakota Fanning, Radha Mitchell, Marc Anthony, Giancarlo Giannini, Rachel Ticotin, Mickey Rourke, Jesus Ochoa; **D:** Tony Scott; **W:** Brian Helgeland; **C:** Paul Cameron; **M:** Harry Gregson-Williams.

The Man on the Box 🐾🐾½ 1925 Chaplin is a wealthy bachelor who takes a job as a gardener to be near his girl. He overhears a plot by the butler, who's an enemy agent, to steal the secret plans for a helicopter from his sweetie's father. In order to thwart the dastardedly scheme Chaplin dresses as a maid to infiltrate the household. 58m/B VHS. Sydney Chaplin, David Butler, Alice Calhoun, Kathleen Calhoun, Helene Costello, Theodore Lorch; **D:** Charles Reisner.

Man on the Eiffel Tower 🐾🐾 1948 Laughton plays Inspector Maigret, the detective created by novelist Georges Simenon, in a highly suspenseful and cerebral mystery about a crazed killer who defies the police to discover his identity. This is the first film Meredith directed. 82m/C VHS, DVD. Charles Laughton, Burgess Meredith, Franchot Tone, Patricia Roc; **D:** Burgess Meredith.

Man on the Moon 🐾🐾 1999 (R) Clunky bio of bizarro comedian Andy Kaufman (Carrey) who died of cancer at age 35 in 1984. The problem is that Kaufman was opaque—he doesn't seem to have a true personality that assumes bizarre alter-egos, including obnoxious lounge singer Tony Clifton. Kaufman turned out to be most appealing as innocent Latka on the sitcom "Taxi," which he professes to despise. For all Carrey's expertise, you won't care too much about what's onscreen. Title comes from R.E.M.'s song about Kaufman; they also supplied the film's music. 118m/C VHS, DVD. Jim Carrey, Courtney Love, Danny DeVito, Paul Giamatti, Vincent Schiavelli, Peter Bonerz, Marilu Henner, Judd Hirsch; **D:** Milos Forman; **W:** Scott M. Alexander, Larry Karaszewski; **C:** Terry Michos. Golden Globes '00: Actor—Mus./Comedy (Carrey).

The Men on the Roof *Manen Pa Taket* 1976 A police officer, who's been accused of brutality, is murdered and Martin Beck (Lindstedt) and his colleagues are called in to investigate. Then someone climbs a roof in central Stockholm and begins killing policemen with a rifle. Turns out the cases are related and involve an ex-cop named Eriksson (Hirdwall). Based on the novel "The Abominable Man" by Maj Sjowall and Per Wahloo. Swedish with subtitles. 110m/C VHS, *SW* Carl Gustav Lindstedt, Ingvar Hirdwall, Sven Wollter, Thomas Hellberg; *D:* Bo Widerberg. *C:* Ood Geir Saether Per Kallberg.

Man on the Run 1949 (R) A robbery takes place in the store where an Army deserter is trying to sell his gun and he ends up taking the rap. It's up to a lovely lacy lawyer to prove his innocence. Efficiently told. "B" crime drama. 82m/B VHS, *GB* Derek Farr, Joan Hopkins, Edward Chapman, Laurence Harvey, Howard Marion-Crawford, Alfie Bass, John Bailey, John Stuart, Edward Underdown, Leslie Perrins, Kenneth More, Martin Miller; *D:* Lawrence Huntington.

Man on the Run 1974 (R) After an unwitting involvement with a small robbery, a teenager finds himself the object of a police manhunt for a murder suspect. 90m/C VHS, Kyle Johnson, James B. Sikking, Terry Carter; *D:* Herbert L. Strock.

The Man on the Train 2002 (R) *L'Homme du Train* A chance encounter between two very different men offers viewers subtle pleasures. Elderly retired teacher Manesculier (Rochefort) is intrigued when weary, leather-jacketed stranger Milan (Halliday) turns up in his small provincial town. Since the only hotel is closed, the bored Manesquier offers Milan hospitality. He enjoys each other as an odd friendship develops. Old-pro Rochefort, in his seventh film with Leconte, is engaging while French pop icon Halliday offers a surprisingly strong performance that is a mixture of machismo and sensitivity. French with subtitles. 90m/C VHS, DVD, *FR* Jean Rochefort, Johnny Halliday, Jean-Francois Stevenin, Charlie Nelson, Isabelle Petit-Jacques, Edith Scob, Pascal Parmentier; *D:* Patrice Leconte; *W:* Claude Klotz; *C:* Jean-Marie Dreujou; *M:* Pascal Esteve. L.A. Film Critics '03: Foreign Film.

Man or Gun 1958 Standard western yarn involving a drifter who rides into a town operated by a powerful family and liberates the cowardly townsfolk. 79m/B VHS, MacDonald Carey, Audrey Totter, James Craig, James Gleeson, Warran Stevens, Harry Shannon; *D:* Albert C. Gannaway; *W:* Vance Skarstedt. James C. Cassity.

The Man Outside 1968 (R) After a CIA agent is fired for allegedly assisting another agent in defecting to the East, he becomes involved in further intrigue. A Russian spy is looking to defect in the process, the ex-agent is framed for murder. Straightforward espionage tale taken from Gene Stackleborg's novel "Double Agent." 98m/C VHS, DVD, *GB* Van Heflin, Heidelinde Weis, Pinkas Braun, Peter Vaughan, Charles Gray, Ronnie Barker; *D:* Samuel Gallu.

Man Outside 1988 (PG-13) Logan is an ex-lawyer who takes to the Arkansas outback after his wife dies. Anthropologist/teacher Quinlan takes a shine to him. He seems like an okay guy, but bad guy Dillman has made it look like he's a child snatcher. Slick on the outside but empty inside independent effort. Look for former members of "The Band in supporting roles. 109m/C VHS, DVD, Robert F. Logan, Kathleen Quinlan, Bradford Dillman, Rick Danko, Levon Helm; *D:* Mark Stouffer.

The Man They Could Not Hang 1939 A good doctor tinkering with artificial hearts is caught by police while experimenting on a willing student. When the doctor is convicted and hanged for a murder, his assistant uses the heart to bring him back to life. No longer a nice guy, he vows revenge against the jurors that sentenced him. Karloff repeated the same story line in several films, and this one is representative of the type. 70m/B VHS, DVD, Boris Karloff, Adrian Booth, Roger Pryor; *D:* Nick Grinde.

Man Trouble 1992 (PG-13) A divorcing opera singer (Barkin) seeks the help of a sleazy attack-dog trainer (Nicholson) when she becomes the victim of a stalker. Nicholson hits on her, first he becomes that's one of his habits, and then because he is being paid to by a billionaire who wants him to steal the manuscript of a tell-all book about her written by Barkin's sister. Although both Nicholson and Barkin are excellent actors, they lack the electricity to make the romance credible, and the jokes are weak. Supporting cast, including D'Angelo, Stanton, and McKean, provide the funny parts in this otherwise dull film. 100m/C VHS, DVD, Jack Nicholson, Ellen Barkin, Harry Dean Stanton, Beverly D'Angelo, Michael McKean, Saul Rubinek, Viveka Davis, Veronica Cartwright, David Clennon, John Kapelos, Paul Mazursky; *D:* Bob Rafelson; *W:* Carole Eastman) Joyce; *C:* Stephen Burum; *M:* Georges Delerue.

The Man Upstairs 1993 Escaped con "Moony" Polaski (O'Neal) hides out in the home of crotchety spinster Victoria Brown (Hepburn). When she finds the crook in her attic, instead of turning him in, Victoria befriends the slob and soon the two are sharing dinner and secrets. Meanwhile, the manhunt for Moony is intensifying and, oh yes, Christmas is coming as well. TV compone barely saved by some professional performances. Executive producer Burt Reynolds was hoping for a part until scheduling made it impossible. 95m/C VHS, Katharine Hepburn, Ryan O'Neal, Henry Beckman, Helen Carroll, Brenda Forbes; *D:* George Schaefer; *W:* James Prideaux. TV.

The Man Who Broke 1,000 Chains 1987 Tells the story of a man who is committed to a chain gang for a petty crime, and his efforts, after escaping, in making a new life for himself. An unimaginative plot is occasionally highlighted by a good scene or two. 113m/C VHS, Val Kilmer, Charles Durning, Sonia Braga; *D:* Daniel Mann; *M:* Charles Bernstein. TV.

The Man Who Came to Dinner 1941 Based on the Moss Hart-George S. Kaufman play, this comedy is about a bitter radio celebrity (Woolley) on a lecture tour (a character based on Alexander Woolcott). He breaks his hip and must stay in a quiet suburban home for the winter. While there, he occupies his time by barking orders, being obnoxious and generally just driving the other residents nuts. Woolley reprises his Broadway role in this film that succeeds at every turn, loaded with plenty of satiric jabs at the Algonquin Hotel Roundtable regulars. 112m/B VHS, DVD, Monty Woolley, Bette Davis, Ann Sheridan, Jimmy Durante, Reginald Gardiner, Richard Travis, Billie Burke, Grant Mitchell, Mary Wickes, George Barbier, Ruth Vivian, Elisabeth Fraser; *D:* William Keighley; *W:* Julius J. Epstein, Philip G. Epstein; *C:* Gaetano Antonio "Tony" Gaudio.

The Man Who Captured Eichmann 1996 In 1960 Israeli Mossad agents prepare to capture Adolf Eichmann (Duvall), who organized the transport of millions of Jews to the concentration camps, from his home in Argentina. Peter Malkin (Howard), the agent responsible for the kidnapping, holds Eichmann in a Buenos Aires safe house before smuggling him into Israel as Eichmann tries to ingratiate himself with Malkin, refusing to accept responsibility and constantly maintaining his innocence. Based on the book "Eichmann in My Hands" by Peter Z. Malkin and Harry Stein. 96m/C VHS, Robert Duvall, Arliss Howard, Jeffrey Tambor, Jack Laufer, Nicolas Surovy, Joel Brooks, Sam Robards, Michael Tucci; *D:* William A. Graham; *M:* Laurence Rosenthal. CABLE.

The Man Who Cried 2000 (R) ... er a young man. In 1927 Russia, young Jewish Fegele is separated from her father (who manages to emigrate to America and instead winds up in England, where she's adopted and renamed Suzie. An adult Suzie (Ricci) heads to Paris in the late '30s and finds bit work in an opera company, sharing a garret with gold-digging Russian Lola (a lively Blanchett) and a romance with gypsy Cesar (Depp). Lola has set her sights on nanny opera singer, Dante (Turturro). Then the Nazis invade Paris. The film's 97m/C VHS, DVD, *GB* *FR* Christina Ricci, Johnny Depp, Cate Blanchett, John Turturro, Harry Dean Stanton, Oleg Yankovsky; *D:* Sally Potter; *W:* Sally Potter; *C:* Sacha Vierny; *M:* Osvaldo Golijov. Natl. Bd. of Review '01: Support. Actress (Blanchett).

The Man Who Envied Women 1985 The non-narrative feminist story of a smug womanizer; the man "who knows almost too much about women." 125m/C VHS, Bill Raymond, Larry Loomis, Trisha Brown; *D:* Yvonne Rainer, *W:* Yvonne Rainer.

The Man Who Fell to Earth 1976 (R) Entertaining hopes of finding water to save his family and drought-stricken planet. Instead he becomes a successful inventor and businessman, along the way discovering the human vices of booze, sex, and television. Also available in a restored version at 138 minutes. Remade for TV in 1987 and based on Walter Tevis's novel. 118m/C VHS, DVD, *GB* David Bowie, Candy Clark, Rip Torn, Buck Henry, Bernie Casey, Jackson D. Kane, Rick Riccardo, Tony Mascia; *D:* Nicolas Roeg; *W:* Paul Mayersberg; *C:* Anthony B. Richmond; *M:* John Phillips.

The Man Who Guards the Greenhouse 1988 Tracy must come to terms with her attraction for Jeff as well as once again trying to write a meaningful novel. 150m/C VHS, *CA* Christopher Cazenove, Rebeca Dewey; *D:* Marc Boizard; *W:* George Arthur Bloom; *C:* Karol Ike.

Man Who Had Power Over Women 1970 (R) Disappointing sex farce about the exploits of a carnally insatiable (and married) talent executive (Taylor) who has an affair with every woman he meets and creates problems aplenty. Adapted from a novel by Gordon Williams. 89m/C VHS, Rod Taylor, James Booth, Carol White, Penelope Homer, Clive Francis; *D:* John Krish; *W:* Chris Bryant, Allan Scott.

The Man Who Haunted Himself 1970 While a man lies in critical condition on the operating table after a car accident, his alter-ego emerges fascinated by "Hitchcock" or "The Twilight Zone"—where mystery matters most. Filmed in London. 94m/C VHS, DVD, *GB* Roger Moore, Hildegard(e) Neil, Olga Georges-Picot; *D:* Basil Dearden; *W:* Bryan Forbes; *C:* Tony Spratling; *M:* Michael Lewis.

The Man Who Knew Too Little 1997 (PG) Wallace (Murray), a video store clerk from Iowa, travels to London in order to surprise his yuppie brother James (Gallagher) on his birthday. James is hosting an important dinner party, however, so he sends his less than upper-crusty brother to the Theater of Life, where the patrons take part in scenes with actors in real-life settings. Underknowing to Wallace, the designated call to start the play is intended for a real hit man, and fine personated call for his wishes. Great personalities result in a classic piece of science fiction.

The Man Who Could Work Miracles 1937 A mild-mannered draper's assistant becomes suddenly endowed with supernatural powers to perform any feat he wishes. Great personalities result in a classic piece of science fiction. 84m/B VHS, Ralph Richardson, Joan Gardner, Roland Young; *D:* Lothar Mendes.

The Man Who Knew Too Much 1934 Hitchcock's first international success. A British family man stumbles onto an assassination plot by a dying agent. His daughter is kidnapped to force his silence. In typical Hitchcock fashion, the innocent person becomes caught in a web of intrigue; the sticky situation culminates with a shootout in the final scenes. Remade by Hitchcock in 1956. 75m/B VHS, DVD, *GB* Leslie Banks, Edna Best, Peter Lorre, Nova Pilbeam, Pierre Fresnay, Frank Vosper, Hugh Wakefield, Cicely Oates, D. A. Clarke-Smith, George Curzon, Henry Oscar, Wilfrid Hyde-White; *D:* Alfred Hitchcock; *W:* Emlyn Williams, Charles Bennett, A.R. Rawlinson, Edwin Greenwood, D. B. Wyndham-Lewis; *C:* Curt Courant.

The Man Who Knew Too Much 1956 (PG) Hitchcock's remake of his 1934 film, this time about an American doctor and his family vacationing in Marrakech. They become involved in a complicated international plot involving kidnapping and murder. While Doris tries to save the day by singing "Que Sera, Sera." Stewart tries to locate his abducted son. More lavish settings and forms of intrigue make this a less focused and, to some, inferior version. 120m/C VHS, DVD, James Stewart, Doris Day, Brenda de Banze, Bernard Miles, Ralph Truman, Daniel Gelin, Alan Mowbray, Carolyn Jones, Hillary Brooke; *D:* Alfred Hitchcock; *W:* John Michael Hayes; *C:* Robert Burks; *M:* Bernard Herrmann. Oscars '56: Song ("Que Sera, Sera").

The Man Who Laughs 1927 Veidt's sensitive performance highlights this silent classic. He plays a young man whose features are surgically altered into a permanent smile because his father, who defied the king, is executed. The man is be-friended by the owner of a sideshow who first exhibits him as a freak but later finds Veidt gaining fame as a clown. A beautiful blind girl in the show loves Veidt for who he is and the two find happiness. 110m/B VHS, DVD, Conrad Veidt, Mary Philbin, Olga Baclanova, Josephine Crowell, George Siegmann, Brandon Hurst; *D:* Paul Leni.

The Man Who Lived Again 1936 *Man!, The Brainsnatchers; The Man Who Changed His Mind; Dr. Maniac* 1936 Boris strives to be a brain-switcher, and suspense builds around the question of whether or not he will change his mind. Shot in England with fine sets and a definite Anglo feel to the proceedings, with Karloff doing one of his better mad scientist routines. 61m/B VHS, DVD, *GB* Boris Karloff, Anna Lee, John Loder, Frank Cellier, Lyn Harding, Cecil Parker; *D:* Robert Stevenson.

Man Who Loved Cat Dancing 1973 (PG) Reynolds is an outlaw on the run after avenging his wife's murder and robbing a safe with pals Hopkins and Warden, and Miles has recently escaped from her abusive husband. It's love on the run as Burt and Sarah are pursued by bounty hunters and their tragic pasts—coming close to making us care, but close doesn't mean as much in movies as it does in dancing. Based on Marilyn Durham's novel. 114m/C VHS, Burt Reynolds,

Sarah Miles, Jack Warden, Lee J. Cobb, Jay Silverheels, Robert Donner, Bo Hopkins, Nancy Malone; **D:** Richard Sarafian; **W:** Eleanor Perry; **C:** Harry Stradling Jr.; **M:** John Williams.

The Man Who Loved Women
L'Homme Qui Aimait les Femmes 1977 An intelligent, sensitive bachelor writes his memoirs and recalls the many, many, many women he has loved. Truffaut couples sophistication and lightheartedness, the thrill of the chase and, when it leads to an accidental death, the wondering what-it's-all-about in mourning. In French with English subtitles. Remade in 1983. **119m/C** VHS, DVD. *FR* Charles Denner, Brigitte Fossey, Leslie Caron, Nelly Borgeaud, Genevieve Fontanel, Nathalie Baye, Sabine Glaser; **D:** Francois Truffaut; **W:** Francois Truffaut, Suzanne Schiffman, Michel Fermaud; **C:** Nestor Almendros; **M:** Maurice Jaubert.

The Man Who Loved Women
1983 (R) A remake of the 1977 French film, this is slower, tries to be funnier, and is less subtle than the original. Reynolds is a Los Angeles sculptor whose reputation as a playboy leads him to a psychoanalyst's couch, where a lot of talk slows the action—though Burt & Julie (the shrink) do share the couch. **110m/C** VHS, DVD. Burt Reynolds, Julie Andrews, Kim Basinger, Marilu Henner, Cynthia Sikes, Jennifer Edwards; **D:** Blake Edwards; **W:** Blake Edwards; **C:** Haskell Wexler; **M:** Henry Mancini.

The Man Who Made Husbands Jealous
Jilly Cooper's The Man Who Made Husbands Jealous 1998 Young, handsome ne'er-do-well Lysander (Billington) is broke. He has few prospects but one undeniable talent—women love him. So his friend Ferdie (Bonneville) looks around at the unhappily married women he knows and their cheating spouses) and comes up with a plan. The wives will hire Lysander to make their neglectful husbands jealous. And the plan is very enjoyable for both Lysander and the ladies, until he falls in love. Based on the naughty novel by Jilly Cooper. **150m/C** VHS. *GB* Stephen Billington, Hugh Bonneville, Kate Byers, Gilly Coman, Kim Criswell, Derek de Lint; **D:** Robert Knights; **W:** Andrew Maclear, Harvey Bamburg. TV

The Man Who Never Was
1955 Tense true story (with melodramatic embroidery) from WWII shows in step-by-step detail how Britain duped the Axis by letting them find an Allied corpse bearing phony invasion plans. Based on the book by the scheme's mastermind Ewen Montagu, played by Webb; Peter Sellers provides the voice of an offscreen Winston Churchill. **102m/C** VHS, DVD. *GB* Clifton Webb, Gloria Grahame, Robert Flemyng, Josephine Griffin, Stephen Boyd, Andre Morell, Laurence Naismith, Geoffrey Keen, Michael Hordern; **D:** Ronald Neame; **C:** Oswald Morris. '56: Screenplay.

The Man Who Shot Liberty Valance
1962 Tough cowboy Wayne and idealistic lawyer Stewart join forces against dreaded gunfighter Liberty Valance, played leatherly by Marvin. While Stewart rides to Senatorial success on his reputation as the man who shot the villain, he suffers moral crises about the act, but is toughened up by Wayne. Wayne's use of the word "pilgrim" became a standard for his impersonators. Strong character acting, great Western scenes, and value judgments to ponder over make this last of Ford's black-and-white westerns among his best. **123m/B** VHS, DVD. James Stewart, John Wayne, Vera Miles, Lee Marvin, Edmond O'Brien, Andy Devine, Woody Strode, Ken Murray, Jeanette Nolan, John Qualen, Strother Martin, Lee Van Cleef, John Carradine, Carleton Young, Willis Bouchey, Denver Pyle, Robert F. Simon, O.Z. Whitehead, Paul Birch, Joseph Hoover, Earle Hodgins, Jack Pennick; **D:** John Ford; **W:** James Warner Bellah, Willis Goldbeck; **C:** William Clothier; **M:** Cyril Mockridge, Alfred Newman. Natl. Film. Reg. '07.

The Man Who Wagged His Tail
An Angel Passed Over Brooklyn; Un Angelo e Sceso a Brooklyn 1957 A mean slumlord is turned into a dog as the result of a curse cast upon him. In order to return to his human form, he must be loved by someone. Despite his attempts to be loved, the dog alienates his only friend and must try to redeem himself. Played for fun, this is a mildly amusing fantasy filmed in Spain and Brooklyn. Not released in the U.S. until 1961. **91m/B** VHS. *IT SP* Peter Ustinov, Pablito Calvo, Aroldo Tieri, Silvia Marco; **D:** Ladislao Vajda.

The Man Who Wasn't There
1983 (R) A member of the State department receives a formula from a dying spy that can render him invisible, see? He has to use the formula to protect himself from the police and other spies, becoming a comic "Invisible Man," see? Generally chaotic tale that's bad, but not so bad that it's worth seeing, though you might want to see what invisibility looks like in 3-D. **111m/C** VHS. Steve Guttenberg, Jeffrey Tambor, Art Hindle, Lisa Langlois; **D:** Bruce Malmuth; **M:** Miles Goodman.

The Man Who Wasn't There
2001 (R) Ed Crane (Thornton, in a masterfully underplayed performance) is a small-town barber who goes unnoticed by many. He suspects that his wife Doris (McDormand) is cheating on him with Dave (Gandolfini), who owns the store where she works. When Ed decides that he wants to invest in the new "dry cleaning" process that a stranger tells him about, he decides to try blackmail. What follows is a series of stately paced twists and complications. **116m/B** VHS, DVD. *US* Billy Bob Thornton, Frances McDormand, Michael Badalucco, James Gandolfini, Katherine Borowitz, Jon Polito, Scarlett Johansson, Richard Jenkins, Tony Shalhoub; **D:** Joel Coen; **W:** Joel Coen, Ethan Coen; **C:** Roger Deakins; **M:** Carter Burwell. L.A. Film Critics '01: Cinematog.; Natl. Bd. of Review '01: Actor (Thornton).

The Man Who Would Be King
1975 (PG) A grand, old-fashioned adventure based on the classic story by Rudyard Kipling about two mercenary soldiers who travel from India to Kafiristan in order to conquer it and set themselves up as kings. Splendid characterizations by Connery and Caine, and Huston's royal directorial treatment provides it with adventure, majestic sweep, and well-developed characters. **129m/C** VHS, DVD. Sean Connery, Michael Caine, Christopher Plummer, Saeed Jaffrey, Shakira Caine; **D:** John Huston; **W:** Gladys Hill, John Huston; **C:** Oswald Morris; **M:** Maurice Jarre.

The Man Who Would Not Die
Target in the Sun 1975 (PG) During his investigation of several deaths, a man discovers that all of the deceased were actually the same man. It seems the deaths were part of a intricate scheme to cover up a $1 million heist. Two of the top three actors are killed early on; it's not very suspenseful. It's more like the mystery that would not die. From Charles Williams's novel "The Sailcloth Shroud." **83m/C** VHS. Dorothy Malone, Keenan Wynn, Aldo Ray; **D:** Robert Arkless.

The Man Who Wouldn't Die
1942 Shayne (Nolan) masquerades as the new and unknown hubby of wealthy Catherine Wolff (Weaver), who brings her spouse home to meet her rich daddy Dudley (Harvey). He's under investigation by the U.S. Senate for shady deals, which may be the reason someone is trying to kill him. But why would anyone take potshots at Catherine? Then there's that body that just doesn't want to stay dead and buried. **65m/B** DVD. Lloyd Nolan, Marjorie Weaver, Paul Harvey, Henry Emmett Keane, Henry Wilcoxon, Richard Derr, Jeff Corey, Billy Bevan, Helene Reynolds, Olin Howland, Leroy Mason; **D:** Herbert I. Leeds; **W:** Arnaud d'Usseau; **C:** Joe MacDonald; **M:** David Raskin.

Man with a Cross
1943 Archaeologists of the cinema may want to unearth this early Rossellini, made by the future father of neo-realist cinema as a propaganda piece for the fascist war effort. A heroic Italian chaplain on the Russian front ministers to foe and friend alike, and even converts a few commies to Christ. Not as awful as it sounds—but never forget where this came from. **88m/B** VHS. *IT* Alberto Tavazzi, Roswita Schmidt, Attilio Dottesio; **D:** Roberto Rossellini; **W:** Roberto Rossellini; **C:** Gugliemo Lombardi; **M:** Renzo Rossellini.

Man with a Gun
1995 (R) Hitman John Hardin (Madsen) is asked by mobster employer Jack Rushton (Busey) to kill his ex-girlfriend Rena (Tilly) and get a CD-ROM filled with info he doesn't want to get out. Rena now happens to be John's gal pal but isn't too upset since she figures they'll substitute Rena's goody two-shoes twin sister Kathy for the needed intended victim, leaving the plan to unravel. It's a connect-the-dots plot with a creditable cast. Based on the novel "The Shroud Society" by Hugh C. Rae. **100m/C** VHS, DVD. Michael Madsen, Jennifer Tilly, Gary Busey, Robert Loggia, Ian Tracey, Bill Cobbs; **D:** David Wyles; **W:** Laurie Finstad-Knizhik; **C:** Jan Kiesser; **M:** George Blondheim.

A Man with a Maid
The Groove Room; What the Swedish Butler Saw; Swedish Wildcats 1973 A bizarre British exploitation pic mixes spookhouse cliches and sex, as a young man found by Jack the Ripper, bachelor pad haunted by Jack the Ripper. Originally shot in 3-D. **83m/C** VHS, DVD. Sue Longhurst, Martin Long, Diana Dors; **D:** Vernon Becker.

The Man with Bogart's Face
Sam Marlowe, Private Eye 1980 (PG) Sacchi is no Bogart, but he does imitate him well. Bogart fans will enjoy this fond tribute to the late great actor, but the story uncertainly wavers between genuine detective story and detective spoof. **106m/C** VHS, DVD. Robert Sacchi, Misty Rowe, Sybil Danning, Franco Nero, Herbert Lom, Victor Buono, Olivia Hussey; **D:** Robert Day; **W:** Andrew J. Fenady; **M:** John Beal. George Duning. Golden Raspberries '80: Worst Song (The Man with Bogart's Face").

The Man with One Red Shoe
1985 (PG) Hanks is a lovable clod of a violinist who ensnares himself in a web of intrigue when CIA agents, both good and evil, mistake him for a contact by his wearing one red shoe. Sporadically funny remake of the French "The Tall Blond Man with One Black Shoe." **92m/C** VHS, DVD. Tom Hanks, Dabney Coleman, Lori Singer, Carrie Fisher, James Belushi, Charles Durning, Edward Herrmann, Tom Noonan, Gerrit Graham, David Lander, David Ogden Stiers; **D:** Stan Dragoti; **M:** Thomas Newman.

The Man with the Golden Arm
1955 A gripping film version of the Nelson Algren junkie melodrama, about an ex-addict who returns to town only to get mixed up with Frankie Machine (Sinatra in a standout performance) returns after a stint in rehab, hoping to pursue new dreams. But his crippled wife Zosch (Parker) wants him to stick with what he knows while drug dealer Louie (McGavin) makes Frankie offers he finds harder and harder to refuse, even with blonde beauty Molly (Novak) to offer Frankie comfort. Considered controversial in its depiction of addiction when released. **119m/B** VHS, DVD. Frank Sinatra, Kim Novak, Eleanor Parker, Arnold Stang, Darren McGavin, Robert Strauss, George Mathews, John Conte, Doro Merande; **D:** Otto Preminger; **W:** Lewis Meltzer, Walter Newman; **C:** Sam Leavitt; **M:** Elmer Bernstein.

The Man with the Golden Gun
1974 (PG) Roger Moore is the debonair secret agent 007 in this ninth James Bond flick. Assigned to recover a small piece of equipment which can be utilized to harness the sun's energy, Bond engages the usual bevy of villains and beauties. **134m/C** VHS, DVD. Roger Moore, Christopher Lee, Britt Ekland, Maud Adams, Herve Villechaize, Clifton James, Soon-Teck Oh, Richard Loo, Marc Lawrence, Bernard Lee, Lois Maxwell, Desmond Llewelyn; **D:** Guy Hamilton; **W:** Tom Mankiewicz; **C:** Ted Moore; **M:** John Barry.

The Man with the Movie Camera
Chelovek s Kinoaparatom 1929 A plotless, experimental view of Moscow through the creative eye of the cameraman Dziga Vertov, founder of the Kino Eye. The editing methods and camera techniques used in this silent film were very influential and still stand up to scrutiny today. **68m/B** VHS, DVD. *RU* **D:** Dziga Vertov; **C:** Mikhail Kaufman; **M:** Pierre Henry.

The Man with the Perfect Swing
1995 Middle-aged ex-baseball player-turned-business entrepreneur Anthony "Babe" Lombardo (Black) is deep in debt and having trouble with the IRS even as he schemes to find success with his latest endeavor—designing specialty golf equipment. But Babe's woeful record, the money just doesn't seem to be coming his way. **94m/C** VHS, DVD. James Black, Suzanne Savoy, Marco Perella, James Belcher, Richard Bradshaw; **D:** Michael Hovis; **W:** Michael Hovis; **C:** Jim Barham; **M:** Paul English.

The Man with Two Brains
1983 (R) Did you hear the one about the brilliant neurosurgeon who falls in love with a woman's disembodied brain in his laboratory? Dr. Michael Hfuhruhurr (Martin) only has two problems: dealing with his frigid, covetous wife (Turner) and finding a body for his cerebral lover. Isn't it nice that a serial murderer, known as the Elevator Killer, is on the loose. Plenty of laughs, most of it spoof of mad scientist movies that is redeemed from potential idiocy by the cast's titillating performances. Listen closely and you'll recognize the voice of Spacek as the brain-in-the-jar of Martin's dreams. **91m/C** VHS, DVD. Steve Martin, Kathleen Turner, David Warner, Paul Benedict, James Cromwell, Francis X. (Frank) McCarthy, George Furth, Randi Brooks, Bernard Behrens, Stephanie Kramer; *Cameos:* Merv Griffin; **D:** Carl Reiner; **W:** Carl Reiner, George Gipe, Steve Martin; **C:** Michael Chapman; **M:** Joel Goldsmith; **V:** Sissy Spacek.

Man with Two Heads
1972 (R) Doctor Jekyll gets in touch with his innermost feelings when his muffed experiments turn him into, gasp, Mr. Blood. Another forlorn addition to the Dr. Jekyll retread collection. **80m/C** VHS. Denis DeMarne, Gay Feld, Julia Stratton, Jaqueline Lawrence; **D:** Andy Milligan; **C:** Andy Milligan.

The Man Without a Lives
1942 Well done horror thriller about a wealthy young man who's killed in a car accident, then brought back to life by a mad scientist. At precisely the moment his life is restored, a murderous gangster is executed and his soul enters the young man's body. **65m/B** VHS, DVD. Edward Norris, Addison Richards, Mario Dwyer, Eleanor Lawson; **D:** Phil Rosen; **W:** Joseph Hoffman; **C:** Harry Neumann.

The Man Without a Country
1973 Faithful adaptation of Everett Edward Hale's short story features a sparkling performance by Robertson as Lt. Philip Nolan, who is court-martialed for treason and denounces his country, proclaiming that he never wishes to see or hear of the United States again. He gets his wish when his sentence is to spend the rest of his life aboard a ship sailing the U.S. coast but never docking. The crew of the ship is forbidden from giving him news of America. Beautifully illustrates the old warning "Be careful what you wish for." **90m/C** VHS. Cliff Robertson, Beau Bridges, Peter Strauss, Robert Ryan, Walter Abel, Geoffrey Holder, Shepperd Strudwick, John Cullum, Peter Coffield, Addison Powell, Peter Weller; **D:** Delbert Mann; **W:** Sidney Carroll; **C:** Andrew Laszlo; **M:** Jack Elliott, Allyn Ferguson. TV

The Man Without a Face
1993 (PG-13) Gibson plays a badly scarred recluse in Maine who develops a mentor relationship with a lonely, fatherless boy. Chuck (Stahl) wants to go away to military school, but flunks the entrance exam, and enlists former teacher McLeod as a tutor. First foray for Gibson into the director's chair tends to be overly melodramatic. Adapted from a novel by Isabelle Holland. **115m/C** VHS, DVD. Mel Gibson, Nick Stahl, Margaret Whitton, Fay Masterson, Richard Masur, Gaby Hoffman, Geoffrey Lewis, Jack DeMave; **D:** Mel Gibson; **W:** Malcolm MacRury; **M:** James Horner.

The Man Without a Past 🐾🐾 *Mies Vailla Menneisyytta* 2002 Deadpan comedy/drama takes place on the outskirts of Helsinki and the fringes of society. A man (Peltola) is robbed and left for dead; he stumbles out of the hospital with amnesia and is found by two young brothers who take him home to their shantytown existence in a shipping container. He gets housing in his own container, does odd jobs to make some money, and finds romance with Salvation Army worker Irma (Outinen). When his identity is finally discovered, it doesn't matter, as he has made a new life and decides to let go of his past. Finnish with subtitles. **97m/C VHS, DVD, Fi GE FR** Markku Peltola, Kati Outinen, Juhani Niemela, Kaija Pakarinen, Sakari Kuosmanen; **C:** Timo Salminen. Nat. Soc. Film Critics '03. Foreign Film.

Man Without a Star 🐾🐾🐾 1955 A cowboy helps ranchers stop a ruthless cattle owner from taking over their land. The conflict between freedom in the wild west and the need for order and settlements is powerfully internalized in Douglas, whose fight for justice will tame the cowboy code he lives by. You'll shed a tear for the fading frontier. **89m/C VHS, DVD.** Kirk Douglas, Jeanne Crain, Claire Trevor, William Campbell; **D:** King Vidor.

Man, Woman & Child 🐾🐾🐾 1983 (PG) A close, upscale California family is shocked when a child from the husband's long-ago affair with a Frenchwoman appears at their door. Pure sentimentalism, as the family confronts this unexpected development. Two hankies—one each for fine performances by Sheen and Danner. Based on a sentimental novel by Erich Segal of "Love Story" fame, who co-wrote the script. **99m/C VHS.** Martin Sheen, Blythe Danner, Craig T. Nelson, David Hemmings, Assumpta Serna, John Savage, Robert Beltran, Michael Moriarty, John Diehl; **D:** Michele Taverna.

Manchurian Avenger 🐾 1984 (R) Desperados have wrested control of a Colorado gold rush town from Joe Kim's family, but he'll put an end to that, chop, chop. **87m/C VHS.** Bobby Kim, Bill Wallace; **D:** Ed Warnick.

The Manchurian Candidate 🐾🐾🐾 2004 (R) Political cynicism is at its most sinister in this updated take on the 1962 John Frankenheimer classic. Remake changes Ben Marco (Washington) and Raymond Shaw (Schreiber) from Korean War to Gulf War I vets. Shaw is now a New York congressman, with mom, Sen. Eleanor Shaw (Streep) pulling his strings. Marco comes to believe that his men were brainwashed by mega-corporation Manchurian Global Shaw to be a vice-presidential candidate who they can control via microchip. Washington is properly heroic and tormented while Schreiber is tormented and forlorn. Streep has fun with her power-hungry, mother-knows-best viper. Based on the novel by Richard Condon. 129m/C DVD, Blu-ray Disc, UMD, HD DVD. Denzel Washington, Liev Schreiber, Meryl Streep, Kimberly Elise, Vera Farmiga, Jon Voight, Jeffrey Wright, Sakina Jaffrey, Simon McBurney, Pablo Schreiber, Ted Levine, Bruno Ganz, Dean Stockwell, Miguel Ferrer, Jude Ciccolella, Zeljko Ivanek, Obba Babatunde, Charles Napier, Roger Corman, Robert Castle, John Bedford Lloyd, Anthony Mackie, Paul Lazar, Tom Stechschulte, Be Be Winans, Robyn Hitchcock, David Keeley, Dean Olmstead, Walter Mosley; **D:** Jonathan Demme; **W:** Dean Georgaris, Daniel Pyne; **C:** Tak Fujimoto; **M:** Rachel Portman, Neust Wyclef Jean.

The Manchurian Candidate 🐾🐾🐾 1962 Political thriller about an American Korean War vet who suspects that he and his platoon may have been brainwashed during the war, with his highly decorated, heroic friend programmed by commies to be an operational assassin. Loaded with shocks, conspiracy, inventive visual imagery, and bitter political satire of naivete and machinations of the left and right. Excellent performances by an all-star cast, with Lansbury and Gregory particularly frightening. Based on the Richard Condon novel. Featuring a special interview with Sinatra and Frankenheimer in which Sinatra is deified. **126m/B VHS, DVD.** Frank Sinatra, Laurence Harvey, Angela Lansbury, Janet Leigh, James Gregory, Leslie Parrish, John McGiver, Henry Silva, Khigh Dhiegh (Kale Deei), James Edwards, Douglas Henderson, Albert Paulsen, Barry Kelley, Lloyd Corrigan, Whit Bissell, Joe Adams, Madame Spivy, Mimi Dillard, John Lawrence, Tom Lowell; **D:** John Frankenheimer; **W:** John Frankenheimer; **C:** Lionel Lindon; **M:** David Amram. AFI '98: Top 100; Golden Globes '63. Support. Actress (Lansbury); Natl. Bd. of Review '62: Support. Actress (Lansbury); Natl. Film Reg. '94.

Managua 🐾🐾 1997 (R) Paul Gleason (Gossett Jr.) goes to Nicaragua to claim the body of old friend Dennis Rice (Savage) but gets stonewalled by the authorities. Rice was working undercover, going after drug cartels and supposedly crossed over to the bad guys. Gleason decides to find out the truth and, of course, discovers Rice is alive. **108m/C VHS.** Louis Gossett Jr., John Savage, Robert Beltran, Michael Moriarty, John Diehl; **D:** Dick Richards; **W:** Erich Segal; **M:** Georges Delerue.

Manderlay 🐾🐾 2005 Yet another tiresome screed from Danish director Von Trier, following 2003's "Dogville." In 1933, Grace (now played by Howard instead of Nicole Kidman) comes across the titular Alabama plantation where slavery still exists. Grace self-righteously decides to medle, against her gangster father's (Dafoe) warnings, and finds out that, despite appearances, everyone else is okay with the status quo and it's Grace who must change. Deliberately artificial and of interest only to the director's devotees. **139m/C DVD.** Bryce Dallas Howard, Isaach de Bankole, Danny Glover, Willem Dafoe, Lauren Bacall, Jean-Marc Barr, Geoffrey Bateman, Jeremy Davies, Michael Abiteboul, Virgile Bramly, Ruben Birkman, Dona Croll, John Hurt, Zeljko Ivanek, Udo Kier, Rik Launspach, Llewella Gideon, Mona Hammond, Ginny Holder, Emmanuel Idowu, Teddy Kempner, Suzette Llewellyn, Chloe Sevigny, Cheres Marquignon, Joseph Mydell, Javone Prince, Clive Rowe, Nina Sosanya; **D:** Lars von Trier; **W:** Lars von Trier; **C:** Anthony Dod Mantle.

Mandinga 🐾 1977 A plantation owner develops an obsession for one of his female slaves. Made to cash in on the already exploitive "Mandingo"; two wrongs don't make a right. **100m/C VHS.** /T Paul Marie Pinzauti, Anthony Gismond; **D:** Mario Pinzauti; **W:** Tecla Romanelli; **C:** Maurizio Centini; **M:** Anthony Dod Mantle.

Mandela 🐾🐾🐾 1987 A gripping, powerful drama about human rights and dignity, tracing the real-life trials of Nelson and Winnie Mandela. The story focuses on the couple's early opposition to South African apartheid, as well as the events leading up to Nelson's life-imprisonment sentencing in 1964. Excellent, restrained performances from Glover and Woodard. **135m/C VHS, DVD.** Danny Glover, Alfre Woodard, John Matshikiza, Warren Clarke, Allan Cordner, Julian Glover; **D:** Philip Saville. **CABLE**

Mandela and de Klerk 🐾🐾½ 1997 (PG) Docudrama about the two men who changed South Africa. White African president F.W. de Klerk (Caine) declared an end to apartheid in 1992 and two years later was succeeded as the country's president by Nelson Mandela (Poitier), a black activist imprisoned on treason charges for 27 years before his release. Both men shared the Nobel Peace Prize for their efforts to unite South Africa. **114m/C VHS, DVD.** Sidney Poitier, Michael Caine, Tina Lifford, Ian Roberts, Gary Maritz, Jerry Mofokeng; **D:** Joseph Sargent; **M:** Cedric Gradus-Samson. **CABLE**

Mandragora 🐾🐾🐾 1997 Marek (Caslavka) is a 16-year-old small town boy who takes off for the bright lights of post-Communist Prague. He's soon selling his body on the streets and makes friends with fellow hustler, David (Svec), but the duo sink into the usual morass of drugs and self-destruction. Czech with subtitles. **133m/C VHS, DVD.** CZ Miroslav Caslavka, David Svec, Miroslav Breu, Pavel Skripac; **D:** Wiktor Grodecki; **W:** Wiktor Grodecki, Pavel Skripac; **C:** Vladimir Holomek; **M:** Wolfgang Hammerschmid.

The Mandarin Mystery 🐾½ 1937 In the process of trying to retrieve a stolen Mandarin stamp, detective Ellery Queen uncovers a counterfeiting ring. Some fine performances, but a muddled script creates a mystery as to whether or not the murder is played for laughs. **65m/B VHS, DVD.** Eddie Quillan, Charlotte Henry, Rita La Roy, Wade Boteler, Franklin Pangborn, George Irving, Kay Hughes, William "Billy" Newell; **D:** Ralph Staub.

Mandingo 🐾🐾 1975 (R) Overheated Southern-fried tale of slavery in the Deep South, circa 1840, dealing with the tangled loves and hates of a family on the slave trade. Heavyweight boxer Norton made his screen debut in the title role as the slave who makes his master money with his boxing prowess. King is the wastrel son, who makes Norton's wife, another son, his mistress. Followed by 1975's "Drum." Based on the novel by Kyle Onstott. **127m/C VHS.** James Mason, Susan George, Perry King, Richard Ward, Ken Norton, Ben Masters, Brenda Sykes, Paul Benedict, Ji-Tu Cumbuka; **D:** Richard Fleischer; **W:** Richard H. Kline, Norman Wexler; **M:** Maurice Jarre.

Mandroid 🐾🐾½ 1993 (R) Two scientists design a high-tech robot, Mandroid, to handle a powerful new element they've discovered. Dr. Zimmer and daughter Zanna want to use their creation to help mankind while mad scientist Dr. Drago wants the power Mandroid can give him. When a laboratory accident leaves Drago horribly disfigured it also gives him the chance to steal Mandroid and put his evil plan into action. Filmed on location in Romania. **81m/C VHS.** Brian Cousins, Jane Caldwell, Michael DellaFemina, Curt Lowens, Patrick Ersgard, Robert Symonds; **D:** Jack Ersgard; **W:** Jackson Barr, Earl Kenton.

Mandy 🐾🐾🐾 1983 Crash of Silence 1953 Poignant drama of a deaf child and the family who must come to terms with her deafness. Well-developed plot and well performed; an intelligent treatment in all. **93m/B VHS.** GB Phyllis Calvert, Jack Hawkins, Mandy Miller; **D:** Alexander Mackendrick.

Manfish 🐾½ 1956 Two men venture out in a boat, the Manfish, to hunt for sunken treasure in the Caribbean. Only one survives the trip, as his greed destroys the other. The scenes off the Jamaican coast are lovely, but the story fails to take hold. Though there's a star aboard in Chaney, you'll look astern and bow out with a sinking feeling. Derived from two Edgar Allan Poe stories, "The Gold Bug" and "The Tell-Tale Heart." **76m/C VHS.** John Bromfield, Lon Chaney Jr., Victor Jory, Barbara Nichols; **D:** W. Lee Wilder.

The Mangler 🐾 1994 (R) Laundry machine munches workers in a small-town Maine industrial plant. Bossman Englund's only concern (besides huge workman's comp premiums) is keeping the machine well-fed. Weak attempt at horror by veteran Tobe "If it's worth doing, it's worth overdoing" Hooper that tries to capitalize on the popularity of story originator Stephen King. Offers little in plot or scare, but fans of the gore genre will enjoy the overuse of chunky-style blood and guts spewed from the monstrous steam ironer and folder that is apparently possessed by the devil. About 45 minutes too long for anybody to suspend their disbelief. **106m/C VHS, DVD.** Robert Englund, Ted Levine, Daniel Matmor, Vanessa Pike, Demetre Phillips, Lisa Morris, Ashley Hayden, Vera Blacker; **D:** Tobe Hooper; **W:** Tobe Hooper, Harry Alan Towers, Stephen Brooks; **C:** Armon Salomon; **M:** Barrington Pheloung.

The Mango Tree 🐾🐾½ 1977 A young man comes of age in a small Australian town during the 1920s. Everything is well done, if not dramatic or fascinating. **93m/C VHS.** AU Geraldine Fitzgerald, Robert Helpmann, Diane Craig, Gerad Kennedy, Christopher Pate; **D:** Kevin James Dobson.

Mango Yellow 🐾🐾 Amarelo Manga 2002 A volatile brew of conniving characters in the seedy underbelly of a swelter-ing, poor Brazilian neighborhood. A slaughterhouse butcher is having an affair behind the back of his devout church-going wife. He delivers meat to a rickety hotel with a kitchen run by a flamboyantly gay cook, who is plotting to win over the heart of the butcher. Somewhere around the corner a sultry barkeep pours her customer while still fighting off every dirtbag advances. As expected, paths cross and things get sticky in this steambath of a Brazilian dramedy. Dirty hodgepodge character piece is at best an entertaining glimpse into a very deranged subculture, but too often feels cheap and easy. **100m/C DVD.** Chico Diaz, Dira Paes, Matheus Nachtergaele, Leona Cavali; **D:** Claudio Assis.

Manhandled 🐾🐾 1924 Department store clerk Swanson is the hit of an artist's party with her impersonations and is asked by Morgan to impersonate a Russian countess to lend some class to his store. She winds up with lots of suitors. **67m/B VHS.** Gloria Swanson, Frank Morgan, Tom Moore, Lillyan Tashman, Ian Keith, Arthur Housman; **D:** Allan Dwan.

The Manhandlers 🐾½ 1973 (R) After the uncle of a young woman is killed by the mob, she goes after them for revenge. For your entertainment pleasure, best stick with the soup commercial of the same name. **87m/C VHS.** Cara Burgess, Judy (Judith) Brown, Vince Cannon, Rosalind Miles; **D:** Lee Madden.

Manhattan 🐾🐾🐾 1979 (R) Successful TV writer Isaac Davis (Allen) yearns to be a serious writer. He struggles through a series of ill-fated romances, including one with high school senior Tracy (Hemingway) and another with Mary (Keaton), who's also having an on-again, off-again affair with Yale (Murphy). Isaac's best friend. Streep does very well with her role of Jill, Isaac's ex-wife who's come out as a lesbian and written a withering (and successful) account of their marriage. Scathingly serious and comic view of modern relationships in urban America and of the modern intellectual neuroses. Shot in black-and-white to capture the mood of Manhattan and mated with an excellent Gershwin soundtrack. **96m/B VHS, DVD.** Woody Allen, Diane Keaton, Meryl Streep, Mariel Hemingway, Michael Murphy, Wallace Shawn, Anne Byrne, Tisa Farrow, Mark Linn-Baker, David Rasche, Karen Allen; **D:** Woody Allen; **W:** Woody Allen, Marshall Brickman; **C:** Gordon Willis. British Acad. '79: Film, Screenplay; Cesar '80: Foreign Film; L.A. Film Critics '79: Support. Actress (Streep); Natl. Film Reg. '01; N.Y. Film Critics '79: Director (Allen), Support. Actress (Streep); Natl. Soc. Film Critics '79: Director (Allen), Support. Actress (Streep).

Manhattan Baby 🐾 1982 Unscary horror film about an archaeologist who digs up a relic that draws evil into the world and infects an American girl with powers that lead to many deaths. Advice to you that might have saved the archaeologist: don't dig this. **90m/C VHS, DVD.** IT Christopher Connelly, Martha Taylor, Brigitta Boccoli, Giovanni Frezza, Lucio Fulci; **D:** Lucio Fulci; **W:** Elisa Briganti, Dardano Sacchetti; **C:** Guglielmo Mancori; **M:** Fabio Frizzi.

Manhattan Melodrama 🐾🐾🐾½ 1934 Powell and Gable are best friends from childhood, growing up together in an orphanage. Their adult lives take different paths, however, as Powell becomes a respected prosecuting attorney while Gable becomes a notorious gambler/racketeer. Lovely Loy is Gable's girl who comes between the two. Eventually, Powell must prosecute his life-long friend for murder in order to win the governorship. One of Gable's toughest roles; Powell's character, however, is a bit unbelievable as his ethics seem to extend beyond love and friendship. This is the first film to team Powell and Loy, who would go on to make 13 more films together including the "Thin Man" series. **93m/B VHS, DVD.** Clark Gable, William Powell, Myrna Loy, Leo Carrillo, Nat Pendleton, George Sidney, Isabel Jewell, Muriel Evans, Claudelle Kaye, Frank Conroy, Jimmy Butler, Mickey Rooney, Edward Van Sloan; **D:** W.S. Van Dyke; **W:** Joseph L. Mankiewicz, Oliver H.P. Garrett; **C:** James Wong Howe. Oscars '34: Story.

Manhattan Merengue! 🐾🐾½
Rice, Beans and Ketchup 1995 (R) Young mambo dancer Miguel (Perez) has been unable to get a visa to come to the U.S. from the Dominican Republic so he stows away with new friend Carmello (Leonardi), who's searching for an old girlfriend and their son. While Miguel tries for dance work on Broadway, he makes a friend in dance instructor Susan (Reed) and locates long-lost girlfriend Rosita (Cavazos). Too bad Carmello's luck isn't as good. Sweetly comball and romantic. **100m/C VHS, DVD.** George Perez, Lumi Cavazos, Marco Leonardi, Alyson Reed; *D:* Joseph B. Vasquez; *W:* Joseph B. Vasquez, Rue Kent Wildman; *C:* David Castillo; *M:* Lalo Schifrin.

Manhattan Merry-Go-Round 🐾🐾 1937 One of the movies where a corrupt boss—in this case a record producer—threatens a bunch of good people as a pretense for a plot when the movie simply serves as a showcase for stars. Features many singing stars of the '30s ("where have you gone Cab Calloway?") plus Joltin' Joe, who ended up having a hit-streak in another genre. ♪Mama I Wanna Make Rhythm; Manhattan Merry-Go-Round; Heaven?; I Owe You; It's Round Up Time in Reno. **88m/B VHS, DVD.** Cab Calloway, Louis Prima, Ted Lewis, Ann Dvorak, Phil Regan, Kay Thompson, Gene Autry, Joe DiMaggio; *D:* Charles Reisner.

Manhattan Murder Mystery 🐾🐾🐾 1993 (PG) Keaton and Allen team up again as two New Yorkers who get involved in a mystery when their neighbor dies under strange circumstances. Light, entertaining comedy steers clear of some of Allen's heavier themes and should keep audiences laughing till the end. Allen, writing with Brickman for the first time since "Annie Hall" and "Manhattan," makes viewers fall in love with the magic of NYC all over again. **105m/C VHS, DVD.** Woody Allen, Diane Keaton, Anjelica Huston, Alan Alda, Jerry Adler, Ron Rifkin, Joy Behar, Lynn Cohen, Melanie Norris, Zach Braff; *D:* Woody Allen; *W:* Marshall Brickman, Woody Allen; *C:* Carlo Di Palma.

The Manhattan Project 🐾🐾
Manhattan Project: The Deadly Game 1986 (PG-13) An exceptionally bright teenager decides to build a nuclear bomb for his project at the New York City science fair. He's out to prove how dangerously easy it is to build big bombs. When he steals plutonium from a local government installation, the feds attempt to nab the precocious youngster. Light moral overtones abound. Director Brickman co-wrote similarly titled "Manhattan." **112m/C VHS, DVD.** Dan E. Butler, Robert Sean Leonard, John David (J.D.) Cullum, Richard Jenkins, Timothy Carhart, Sully Boyar, Jimmie Ray Weeks, John Lithgow, Christopher Collet, Cynthia Nixon, Jill Eikenberry, John Mahoney, Richard Council, Robert Schenkkan, Paul Austin; *D:* Marshall Brickman; *W:* Marshall Brickman, Thomas Baum; *C:* Billy Williams.

Manhunt 🐾🐾 *The Italian Connection; La Mala Ordina* 1973 (R) A man marked for execution by the mob launches his own assault on the organization's headquarters. Action and Italian food, but not much else. Dubbed. **93m/C VHS.** *IT* Henry Silva, Mario Adorf, Woody Strode, Luciana Paluzzi; *D:* Fernando Di Leo.

The Manhunt 🐾🐾 1986 A framed cowhand escapes from prison to prove his innocence. De Angelis used the pseudonym Larry Ludman. **89m/C VHS, DVD.** Ernest Borgnine, Bo Svenson, John Ethan Wayne; *D:* Fabrizio de Angelis. **TV**

Manhunt 🐾🐾 *Caceria* 2001 Daniel used to work for a gangster named Lucas but he betrayed him and now Lucas wants revenge. Daniel has returned to his hometown of Redemption and re-establishes his friendship with boyhood chum Miguel and long-lost love Elisa, even though he knows his chance of happiness is fleeting. And soon enough Lucas and his men show up to hunt Daniel down. Spanish with subtitles. **90m/C VHS, DVD. AR** Luis Luque, Claribel Medina, Juan Palomino, Matias Sansone, Carlos Leyes; *D:* Ezio Massa; *W:* Ezio

sa, Jorge Bechara; *C:* Mariano Cuneo, Ada Frontini; *M:* Mariano Nunez West.

Manhunt for Claude Dallas 🐾🐾 1986 Mountain man uses game wardens for firing practice, ticks off local sheriff Torn, is tossed behind bars, checks out ahead of schedule and becomes a legend in his own time. Mediocre made-for-TV macho man melodrama. From the novel "Outlaw" by Jeff Long. **93m/C VHS.** Matt Salinger, Rip Torn, Claude Akins, Pat Hingle, Lois Nettleton, Beau Starr, Frederick Coffin; *D:* Jerry London; *W:* John Gay; *M:* Steve Dorff.

Manhunt in the African Jungles 🐾🐾 *Secret Service in Darkest Africa* 1943 An American undercover agent battles Nazi forces in Africa. A serial in 15 episodes. **240m/B VHS.** Rod Cameron, Joan Marsh, Duncan Renaldo, Lionel Royce, Kurt Krueger, Georges Renavent, Ralf Harolde; *D:* Spencer Gordon Bennet; *W:* Ronald Davidson, Basil Dickey, Joseph O'Donnell, Joseph Poland; *C:* William Bradford; *M:* Paul Sawtell, Mort Glickman.

Manhunt of Mystery Island *Captain Mephisto and the Transformation Machine* 1945 Serial about the super-powered Captain Mephisto. **100m/C VHS.** Linda Stirling, Roy Barcroft, Richard Bailey, Kenne Duncan; *D:* Spencer Gordon Bennet, Yakima Canutt, Wallace Grissell; *W:* Albert DeMond, Basil Dickey, Jesse Duffy, Joseph Poland; *C:* Bud Thackery.

Manhunter 🐾 1974 A WWI Marine returns home from China in 1933 to track down a bunch of gangsters headed by his sister. **78m/C VHS.** Ken Howard, Stefanie Powers, Gary Lockwood, Tim O'Connor, L.Q. Jones; *D:* Walter Grauman. **TV**

Manhunter 🐾🐾½ 1983 A mercenary sets out to disengage organized crime from high-level politics. Produced by Owensby. **92m/C VHS.** Earl Owensby, Johnny Popwell, Doug Hale, Elizabeth Upton; *D:* Earl Owensby.

Manhunter 🐾🐾🐾 1986 (R) Will Graham (Petersen) was the FBI's top guy in their Behavioral Science Unit who retired after a harrowing pursuit of a serial killer. Now, he's called back to duty to find a psychotic family killer. Will's technique: to match the thought processes of serial killers and thus anticipate their moves. Intense thriller, based on the Thomas Harris novel "Red Dragon." Harris also wrote "The Silence of the Lambs," whose most notorious character Hannibal ("The Cannibal") Lecter, appears in this movie as well (spelled Lektor and played by Cox). Graham visits the prisoner to get fresh insights into his new case and Lektor plays his usual nasty mind games. Director Mann applies the slick techniques he introduced in the popular TV series "Miami Vice," creating a quiet, moody intensity broken by sudden onslaughts of violence. **100m/C VHS, DVD.** William L. Petersen, Kim Greist, Joan Allen, Brian Cox, Dennis Farina, Stephen Lang, Tom Noonan, Benjamin Hendrickson, David Seaman, Dan E. Butler, Michael Talbott, Michele Shay, Paul Perri, Patricia Charbonneau, Joanne Camp, David Allan Brooks, Chris Elliott, Kim Shriner, Bill Smitrovich, Kristin Holby; *D:* Michael Mann; *W:* Michael Mann; *C:* Dante Spinotti; *M:* Michel Rubini.

Maniac WOOF! 1934 A scientist has designs on raising the dead and searches for victims on which to experiment. Bizarre "adults only" exploitation feature was considered very risque for its time, and includes eaten eyeballs, a cat fight with syringes, and a rapist who thinks he's an orangutan. A must for genre aficionados. **67m/B VHS, DVD.** Bill Woods, Horace Carpenter, Ted Edwards, Thea Ramsey, Jennie Dark, Marcel Andre, Celia McGann; *D:* Dwain Esper; *W:* Hildegarde Stadie; *C:* William C. Thompson.

Maniac 🐾🐾 1963 An American artist living in France becomes involved with the daughter of a cafe owner, not suspecting that murder will follow. Seems that her old man is locked up in an insane asylum for torching the daughter's rapist several years earlier. **86m/B VHS. GB** Kerwin Mathews, Nadia Gray, Donald Houston, Liliane Brousse; *D:* Michael Carreras; *W:* Jimmy Sangster; *C:* Wilkie Cooper; *M:* Stanley Black.

Maniac 🐾 *Ransom; Assault on Paradise; The Town That Cried Terror* 1977 (PG) A New York cop hunts down an arrow-shooting and obviously crazed Vietnam veteran who endeavors to hold an entire Arizona town for ransom. Which is entirely appropriate, since the cast is in it only for the money. **87m/C VHS.** Bill Allen, Oliver Reed, Deborah Raffin, Stuart Whitman, Jim Mitchum, Edward Brett, John Ireland, Paul Koslo; *D:* Richard Compton.

Maniac WOOF! 1980 A psycho murderer slaughters and scalps his victims, adding the "trophies" to his collection. Carries a self-imposed equivalent "X" rating due to its highly graphic gore content. For extremely strong stomachs only. **91m/C VHS, DVD.** Joe Spinell, Caroline Munro, Gail Lawrence, Kelly Piper, Tom Savini, Rita Montone, Hyla Marrow, William Lustig, Sharon Mitchell; *D:* William Lustig; *W:* C.A. Rosenberg, Joe Spinell; *C:* Robert Lindsay; *M:* Jay Chattaway.

Maniac Cop 🐾 1988 (R) In New York city, a cop goes beyond the realm of sanity and turns vigilante. Low-budget slasher/thriller that too often sags. **92m/C VHS, DVD.** Tom Atkins, Bruce Campbell, Laurene Landon, Richard Roundtree, William (Bill) Smith, Robert Z'Dar, Sheree North, Sam Raimi; *D:* William Lustig; *W:* Larry Cohen; *C:* Vincent Rabe, James (Momel) Lemmo; *M:* Jay Chattaway.

Maniac Cop 2 🐾 1990 (R) Everyone thought he was dead but you can't keep a bad guy down so this grossly disfigured policeman forms a one-man vigilante squad, seeking revenge (why never matters—just the body count). Blood and guts fly as any plot shortcomings are cleverly disguised by an array of violent video deaths. Sequel to "Maniac Cop." **90m/C VHS.** Robert Davi, Claudia Christian, Michael Lerner, Bruce Campbell, Laurene Landon, Robert Z'Dar, Clarence Williams III, Leo Rossi, James Dixon, Robert Earl Jones; *D:* William Lustig; *W:* Larry Cohen; *C:* James (Momel) Lemmo.

Maniac Cop 3: Badge of Silence 🐾 1993 (R) The grossly disfigured policeman returns to exact gory vengeance as the good guys try to get rid of him once and for all. **85m/C VHS, DVD.** Bobby DiCicco, Robert Z'Dar, Caitlin Dulany, Jackie Earle Haley, Robert Forster; *D:* William Lustig, Joel Soisson; *W:* Larry Cohen; *M:* Andrew Menzies.

Maniac Nurses Find Ecstasy WOOF! 1994 Even by Troma standards, this one's scraping the bottom of the barrel. The nearly non-existent plot is an excuse to present several young women dressed in nurse uniforms and underwear while holding various weapons. The sense of energy that's needed for good exploitation is lacking. **86m/C VHS, DVD.** Susanna Makay, Hajni Brown, Nicole A. Gyony, Csilla Farago; *D:* Harry M. (Leon P. Howard) Love.

Maniac Warriors 🐾 *Empire of Ash* 1988 A nuclear apocalypse has caused some strange changes in the population—and not for the better. Blood-crazed mutants attack the heavily armed inhabitants of New State Idaho and there's lots of mayhem in store. **91m/C VHS.** *CA* Tom Schioler, John Wood, Melanie Kilgour; *D:* Michael Mazo, Lloyd A. Simandl; *W:* John Ogis; *C:* Danny Nowak; *M:* Jerry Goldsmith.

Manic 🐾🐾🐾 2001 (R) Lyle (Gordon-Levitt), prone to fits of violent rage, is sent to a juvenile psychiatric hospital to control his temper. There he meets, but doesn't exactly warm up to, a variety of other mentally and emotionally troubled teens. Led by patient counselor David (Cheadle), they endure group sessions that do little but introduce the audience to the varied, if stereotypical problems of the other patients. These scenes do point out the reality that there are rarely any quick fixes in this area. Lyle eventually is drawn to shy Tracy, who suffers from crushingly low self-esteem. Excellent performances and script keep the situations and emotions realistic, mostly avoiding cliche, but the affected Dogme-style jittery hand-held digital camera work is a distraction that's not needed. **100m/C VHS, DVD.** Joseph Gordon-Levitt, Don Cheadle, Zooey Deschanel, Cody Lightning, Sara Rivas, Michael Bacall, William Ric-

her, Elden (Ratliff) Henson, Blayne Weaver; *D:* Jordan Melamed; *W:* Michael Bacall, Blayne Weaver; *C:* Nick Hay.

1981 The long and sometimes interesting rags-to-riches tale of Rory O'Manion, a feisty Irish patriot who leaves his native land during the potato famine of 1845 to settle in America. Originally a TV miniseries. **290m/C VHS.** Pierce Brosnan, Kate Mulgrew, Linda Purl, David Soul, Kathleen Beller, Simon MacCorkindale; *D:* Joseph Sargent, Charles S. Dubin. **TV**

Manipulator 🐾 1971 (R) A deranged ex-movie makeup man (Rooney, playing to type) kidnaps a young actress and holds her prisoner in a deserted Hollywood sound stage. **91m/C VHS.** Mickey Rooney, Luana Anders, Keenan Wynn; *D:* Yabo Yablonsky.

Manito 🐾🐾🐾 2003 Slice of life family drama set in New York City's largely Hispanic Washington Heights neighborhood. Manny Moreno (Minaya) is about to graduate from high school and has been accepted to college on a full scholarship. His older brother, Junior (Franky G), is an ex-con who was busted for working with their drug-dealer dad (Cabral). Junior is trying to go straight and keep Manny away from trouble as well by refusing to allow their father any contact with the family. But it's just not that simple. Debut film for Eason is somewhat limited by being shot on digital video, but the performances are powerful. **77m/C DVD.** *US* Franky G., Leo Minaya, Manny Cabral, Hector Gonzalez, Julissa Lopez, Jessica Morales; *D:* Eric Eason; *W:* Eric Eason; *C:* Didier Gertsch; *M:* Saundi Wilson.

The Manitou 🐾🐾 1978 (PG) A San Francisco woman suffers from a rapidly growing neck tumor which eventually grows into a 400-year-old Indian witch doctor. (I hate when that happens.) Redeemed only by good special effects, especially those that kept Curtis, Strasberg, and Meredith from laughing. **104m/C VHS, DVD.** Susan Strasberg, Tony Curtis, Stella Stevens, Ann Sothern, Burgess Meredith, Michael Ansara, Jon Cedar, Paul Mantee, Lurene Tuttle, Jeanette Nolan; *D:* William Girdler; *W:* William Girdler, Tom Pope, Jon Cedar; *C:* Michael Hugo; *M:* Lalo Schifrin.

Manna from Heaven 🐾🐾 2002 (PG) A cash-strapped extended family, living in a working-class Buffalo neighborhood, receive an unexpected windfall when a passing truck with a faulty door dumps a load of $20 bills. A pious young girl thinks the money was a gift from God but, 30 years later, Sister Teresa (Burton) has now decided the money was just a loan and God must be repaid. However, the money's long spent and the rest of those involved are reluctant (at first) to go along with the nun's fund-raising efforts. **119m/C DVD.** Shirley Jones, Cloris Leachman, Harry Groener, Jill Eikenberry, Ursula Burton, Faye Grant, Wendie Malick, Seymour Cassel; *D:* Gabrielle C. Burton, Maria Burton; *W:* Gabrielle B. Burton; *C:* Ed Slattery.

Mankillers 🐾 1987 A group of tough female convicts are enlisted to hunt down and rub out a psycho drug dealer, all the while displaying their feminine charms. **90m/C VHS.** Edd Byrnes, Gail Fisher, Edy Williams, Lynda Aldon, William Zipp, Christopher Lunde, Susanne Tegman, Marilyn Stafford, Paul Bruno, Byron Clark; *D:* David A. Prior.

Mannequin 🐾🐾½ 1937 Tracy and Crawford star in this romantic story of a poor girl who finds temporary happiness by marrying a wealthy man after ditching her con-artist husband. Somewhat predictable, the movie reads like a "People" magazine story on The Donald and Ivana. Tracy and Crawford keep the story afloat (in their only film together), with an able assist from Curtis. **95m/B VHS.** Joan Crawford, Spencer Tracy, Alan Curtis, Ralph Morgan, Leo Gorcey, Elisabeth Risdon, Paul Fix; *D:* Frank Borzage; *W:* Lawrence Hazard; *C:* George J. Folsey.

Mannequin 🐾🐾 1987 (PG) A young artist creates a store window display using various mannequins, one of which contains the spirit of an ancient Egyptian woman. She comes to life when he is around, and naturally none of his co-workers believe him. Very light comedy, featuring two pretty stars and music by Jefferson Starship. **90m/C VHS, DVD.** Andrew McCarthy, Kim Catrall, Estelle Getty, James Spader, G.W. Bailey; **C:** Meshach Taylor, Carole (Raphaelle) Davis, G.W. Bailey; **D:** Michael Gottlieb; **W:** Ed Rugoff, Tim Suhrstedt; **M:** Sylvester Levay.

Man's Best Friend 🐾½ 1993 (R) A guard dog is the object of a genetic experiment that has given him the aggressiveness of other creatures, including a co-bra and a leopard. Since Max is an enormous Tibetan mastiff this means big trouble for everyone but the reporter (Sheedy) who rescued him—and even she better watch out. **87m/C VHS, DVD.** Ally Sheedy, Lance Henriksen, Fredric Lehne, Robert Costanzo, John Cassini, J.D. Daniels; **D:** John Lafia; **W:** John Lafia; **M:** Joel Goldsmith.

Man's Country 🐾½ 1938 A rip-roarin' western saga filled with the usual action and danger, as ranger Randall leads the fight against a band of nasties headed by Long, in a dual role as twin brothers. **55m/B VHS, DVD.** Jack Randall, Ralph Peters, Marjorie Reynolds, Water Long; **D:** Robert F. "Bob" Hill.

Man's Favorite Sport? 🐾🐾½ 1963 A slapstick comedy about a re-nowned fishing expert author who actually hates fishing, but is forced to compete in a major tournament by a romantically inclined publicity agent. Very funny in spots. **121m/C VHS, DVD.** Rock Hudson, Paula Prentiss, Charlene Holt, Maria Perschy, John McGiver; **D:** Howard Hawks; **M:** Henry Mancini.

Man's Land 🐾½ 1932 A ranch needs savin', and Hoot's the guy to do it in this formulaic Gibson epic. **65m/B VHS.** Hoot Gibson, Marion Shilling, Skeeter Bill Robbins, Alan Bridge; **D:** Phil Rosen.

Mansfield Park 🐾🐾½ 1985 Fanny is an impoverished young woman, snubbed by society, who earns the respect and love of her cousin in a BBC miniseries adaptation of the Jane Austen classic set in 19th-century England. **261m/C VHS, DVD. GB** Sylvestra Le Touzel, Bernard Hepton, Anna Massey, Donald Pleasence; **D:** David Giles. **TV**

Mansfield Park 🐾🐾½ 1999 (PG-13) Fanny Price (O'Connor) is a poor relation, who has grown up with her wealthy cousins at their elegant home, Mansfield Park. While some of the Bertrams have been civil, others have treated Fanny as little better than a servant. However, as she breaks into Jane Austen's 3rd novel and indeed and Fanny develops very warm feelings towards him. Then the entire family is thrown into chaos by the arrival of Henry Crawford (Nivola) and his sister Mary (Davidtz) and scandal seer's cousin Edmund (Miller) has been very belabored relevancy by Rozema. **110m/C VHS, DVD.** Frances O'Connor, Jonny Lee Miller, Alessandro Nivola, Embeth Davidtz, Harold Pinter, Lindsay Duncan, Sheila Gish, Justine Waddel, Victoria Hamilton, James Purefoy, Hugh Bonneville; **D:** Patricia Rozema; **W:** Patricia Rozema; **M:** Lesley Barber.

The Manster 🐾 Man, Half Monster; The Split; The Manster—Half Monster 1959 Another masterpiece from the director who brought us "Monster from Green Hell." Womanizing, whiskey-swilling American journalist receives mysterious injection from crazed scientist. Al sprouts unsightly hair and extra head. Although shot in the land of the rising sun, lips move in sync with dialogue. **72m/B VHS, DVD. JP** Peter Dyneley, Jane Hylton, Satoshi Nakamura, Terri Zimmern, Tetsu Nakamura, Jerry Ito, Toyoko Takechi; **D:** Kenneth Crane, George Breakston; **W:** William J. Sheldon; **C:** David Williams. **CABLE**

Manticore 🐾 2005 Usual low-budget cheesefest from the Sci-Fi Channel. American soldiers patrolling an Iraqi town check a bombed-out museum and are attacked by insurgents. An ancient medallion was stolen from the museum and the megalomaniac Umari wants to use it to unleash the power of the manticore, only to figure out too late that he can't control it. **88m/C VHS, DVD.** Robert Beltran, Jeff Fahey, Chase Masterson, Faran Tahir, Heather Donahue, A.J. Buckley; **D:** Tripp Reed; **W:** John Werner; **C:** Lorenzo Senatore; **M:** Mark McCarty.

Mantrap 🐾🐾½ 1926 Early silent go-go dancer slaughters men while tripping on LSD. Watch it for the "hep" dialogue. **66m/C VHS, DVD.** Susan Stewart, Steve Vincent, M.K. Evans, Vic Lance, Pat (Barringer) Barrington, Janu Wine, Stuart Lancaster, John Carol, Judith Crane, Cheryl Trepton; **D:** William Rotsler; **W:** Sanford White; **C:** Laszlo Kovacs; **M:** Frank A. Coe.

The Manxman 🐾🐾½ 1929 Hitchcock's last silent film, a romantic melodrama about ambition and infidelity in the beloved characters and their adventures in the Hundred Acre Wood. Includes a behind-the-scenes featurette with the original creators, animators, and voices. **83m/C VHS, DVD.** Anny Ondra, Malcolm Keen, Randle Ayrton; **D:** Alfred Hitchcock; **W:** Hall Caine, Eliot Stannard; **C:** Jack Cox.

The Many Adventures of Winnie the Pooh 🐾🐾 1977 (G) Disney's 22nd animated feature offers A.A. Milne's beloved characters and their adventures. **74m/C VHS, DVD.** Sterling Holloway, Paul Winchell, John Fiedler, Junius Matthews, Howard Morris; **Nar:** Sebastian Cabot.

Many Faces of Sherlock Holmes 1986 A documentary look at the various incarnations of the famous sleuth from A. Conan Doyle's stories to various film portrayals. **55m/C VHS, DVD.** Christopher Plummer, Basil Rathbone, Christopher Lee.

Map of the Human Heart 🐾🐾 1993 (R) Thirty-year saga told in flashback. Young Eskimo Avik (Lee) and his Metis love interest Albertine (Parillaud) struggle with racism in a white world. They meet and become friends as children and years later meet again in Dresden during WWII, but now Albertine is married to Avik's love close friend, denying her heritage and living in the white world that he has been fighting for so long. Mediocre movie with extraordinary Arctic scenery. Cusack has a small role as a mapmaker. **109m/C VHS, DVD.** Jason Scott Lee, Anne Parillaud, Patrick Bergin, Robert Joamie, Arnie Galipeau, John Cusack, Jeanne Moreau; **D:** Vincent Ward; **W:** Vincent Ward, Louis Nowra.

A Map of the World 🐾🐾 1999 (R) Excellent cast; tough story, based on the novel by Jane Hamilton. Flinty would-be farm wife/mom Alice Goodwin (Weaver) hasn't endeared herself to her Wisconsin community. But she's a good deal more vulnerable than anyone suspects as Alice finds her life falling apart. Her neighbor Theresa's (Moore) daughter accidentally drowns while in Alice's care and soon after Alice is shockingly accused of sexual abuse in her role as school nurse, which go to propagate their species—endless marching drama, part prison drama, part courtroom drama, part melodrama, and all the drama doesn't really make for a coherent movie. **125m/C VHS, DVD.** Sigourney Weaver,

David Strathairn, Julianne Moore, Ron Lea, Arliss Howard, Chloe Sevigny, Louise Fletcher; **D:** Scott Elliott; **W:** Peter Hedges, Polly Platt; **C:** Seamus McGarvey; **M:** Pat Metheny. Natl. Bd. of Review '99. **Support. Actress (Moore).**

The Mapmaker 🐾🐾½ 2001 Engineer Richard Markey is hired to map out some land in a rural border town in Northern Ireland. Only he uncovers the body of an alleged informer tied to the IRA and puts his own life in danger when the hostilities surface. **89m/C DVD. IR** Brian F. O'Byrne, Susan Lynch, Brendan Coyle, Ian McElhinney, Oisín Kearney; **D:** Johnny Gogan; **C:** Owen McPolin; **M:** Brian Coughlan. **TV**

Mapp & Lucia 🐾🐾½ 1985 British TV adaptation of H.E. Benson's stories of provincial English society in the fictional village of Tilling-on-Sea in the 1920s. Miss Mapp (Scales) holds local court but with a potential usurper when elegant widow Lucia (McEwan) comes to town. Battle lines are formed between the two women in this sharp-tongued satire. On five cassettes; followed by a second series of five episodes. **270m/C VHS, DVD. GB** Prunella Scales, Geraldine McEwan, Nigel Hawthorne; **D:** Donald McWhinnie; **W:** Gerald Savory; **C:** Lisle Middleditch; **M:** Jim Parker.

Mararia 🐾🐾 1998 Romantic triangle set amidst the heat and beauty of 1940s island life on Lanzarote in the Canary Islands. The newly arrived Dr. Fermin with subtitles. **109m/C VHS, DVD. SP** Goya Toledo, Carmelo Gomez, Iain Glen, Mirta Ibarra; **D:** Antonio J. Betancor; **W:** Antonio J. Betancor, Carlos Alvarez; **C:** Juan Ruiz-Anchía; **M:** Pedro Guerra.

Marathon 🐾🐾 1980 When a middle-aged jogger's ego gets a boost through the attention of a beautiful young woman, he takes up marathon running. Light comedy. **100m/C VHS, DVD.** Bob Newhart, Leigh Taylor-Young, Herb Edelman, Dick Gautier, Anita Gillette, John Hillerman; **D:** Jackie Cooper. **TV**

Marathon Man 🐾🐾 1976 (R) Nightmarish chase-thriller in which a graduate student becomes entangled in a plot involving a murderous Nazi fugitive. As student Hoffman is preparing for the Olympic marathon he is reunited with his secret-agent brother, setting the intricate plot in motion. Courtesy of his brother, Hoffman becomes involved with Olivier, an old crazed Nazi seeking jewels taken from concentration camp victims. Non-stop action throughout, including a torture scene sure to set your teeth on edge. Goldman adapted the screenplay from his novel. **125m/C VHS, DVD.** Dustin Hoffman, Laurence Olivier, Roy Scheider, William Devane, Fritz Weaver, Richard Bright, Marc Lawrence, Fritz Weaver, Richard Bright, Marc Lawrence; **D:** John Schlesinger; **W:** William Goldman; **C:** Conrad L. Hall; **M:** Michael Small. Golden Globes '77. **Suppor. Actor (Olivier).**

Marauder 🐾🐾 1965 The prince of Venice leads a sea-faring onslaught against ransacking pirates and enemy fleets. **90m/C VHS, IT** Gordon Scott, Gianna Maria Canale, Franca Bettoya; **D:** Luigi Capuano.

Marbella 🐾½ 1985 A luxury resort in Spain is the setting for a big caper heist of $3 million from a monarchical tycoon. **90m/C VHS.** Rod Taylor, Britt Ekland; **D:** Miguel Hermoso.

March of the Penguins 🐾🐾🐾 2005 (G) Oscar winner for Best Documentary proves that animals can be movie stars even if they aren't animated by Pixar or Dreamworks. Director Jacquet traveled to Antarctica to film the mating rituals of the Emperor penguin and walked away with pure Animal Planet gold. You'll marvel at how ridiculously far the penguins will go to propagate their species—endless marching such over frozen wastelands, working daily to escape predators, cutely ignoring the French camera crew. It's "Booty Call" meets National Geographic, all brought together by the smooth vocal stylings of nar-

---

Mannequin 2: On the Move WOOF! 1991 (PG) Less of a sequel, more of a lame rehash proving that the first "Mannequin" could have been even dumber. At this rate part three will be off the scale. Now it's a lovesick Teutonic princess frozen for 1,000 years who revives in a department store. Taylor reprises his grotesque gay role. **55m/C VHS.** Kristy Swanson, William Ragsdale, Meshach Taylor, Terry Kiser, Stuart Pankin; **D:** Stewart Raffill; **W:** Ed Rugoff.

Manny & Lo 🐾🐾🐾 1996 (R) Krueger's directorial debut features fine performances in a story about three misfits forming a unique family bond. Surly 16-year-old Lo (Palladino) and her serious 11-year-old sister Manny (Johansson) have run away from their foster homes and hit the road together. Living hand-to-mouth, it's Manny who persuades her irresponsible pregnant sister that they need a home and they settle into an isolated cabin. When the sisters visit a baby store, eccentric clerk Elaine (Place) seems such a font of wisdom that the girls kidnap her and hold her as a hostage to help with the pregnancy. But Elaine's not trying to escape and has an agenda of her own. **90m/C VHS, DVD.** Mary Kay Place, Scarlett Johansson, Aleksa Palladino, Paul Guilfoyle, Angie Phillips; **D:** Lisa Krueger; **W:** Lisa Krueger; **C:** Tom Krueger; **M:** John Lurie.

Manny's Orphans 🐾 Here Come the Tigers 1978 (PG) An out-of-work teacher takes on a lovable home for orphaned boys. Dull remake of "Bad News Bears." **92m/C VHS.** Richard Lincoln Malachy McCourt, Sel Skolnick; **D:** Sean S. Cunningham.

Manon 🐾🐾 1950 Tragic tale of a French woman condemned for her affair with a Resistance fighter. They flee to Paris, where her brother forces her into prostitution. Based on the novel "Manon Lescaut" by Abbe Antoine-Francois Prevost, in French with English subtitles. **91m/B VHS.** Cecile Aubry, Michel Auclair, Serge Reggiani, Henri Vilbert, Daniel Ivernel; **D:** Henri-Georges Clouzot.

Manon of the Spring 🐾🐾🐾½ Manon des Sources; Jean de Florette 2 1987 (PG) In this excellent sequel to "Jean de Florette," the adult daughter of the dead hunchback Jean, discovers who blocked up the spring on her father's land. She plots her revenge, which proves greater than she could ever imagine. Montand is astonishing. Based on a Marcel Pagnol novel. In French with English subtitles. **113m/C VHS, DVD. FR** Yves Montand, Daniel Auteuil, Emmanuelle Beart, Hippolyte Girardot, Margarita Lozano, Elisabeth Depardieu, Yvonne Gamy, Armand Meffre, Gabriel Bacquier; **D:** Claude Berri; **W:** Claude Berri, Gerard Brach; **C:** Bruno Nuytten; **M:** Jean-Claude Petit, Roger Legri.

Manos, the Hands of Fate WOOF! 1966 Horrible acting and laughable special effects elevate this story of a family ensnared by a satanic cult a notch above your average bad horror film. Highlights include a Satan-like character who can't stop laughing, the dreaded "hounds of hell" (or are those mangy dogs with big ears glued on?); and Torgo the monstrous henchman, who you know is evil because he has giant kneecaps (a sure sign of the devil's work). Notable as the one of the most often requested movies on Comedy Central's satire, "Mystery Science Theatre 3000," ths one is good for a laugh. **74m/C VHS, DVD.** Tom Neyman, Dane Manhee, Hal P. Warren, John Reynolds; **D:** Hal P. Warren; **W:** Hal P. Warren.

The Manson Family 🐾½ 2004 A graphic depiction of Charlie (Games), his followers, and their crimes, which took director Van Bebber something like 15 years to finance and complete. You can admire his dedication without admiring the results, which intentionally look like exploitation schlock. A framing device has a TV reporter (Day) working on a documentary of the Family that leads to flashbacks of the sex, drugs, and violence that consume them. **95m/C DVD. US D:** Jim Van Bebber; **C:** Mike King.

rator Morgan Freeman. Tries a bit too hard to imbue the birds with human personalities, but for astounding footage wins in the end. **80m/C DVD, Blu-ray Disc, HD DVD.** *US* **D:** Luc Jacquet; **W:** Jordan Roberts; **C:** Laurent Chalet, Jerome Maison; **Nar:** Morgan Freeman. Oscars '05: Feature Doc.; Natl. Bd. of Review '05: Feature Doc.; Broadcast Film Critics '05: Feature Doc.

March of the Wooden Soldiers 🦴🦴🦴 *Babes in Toyland* 1934 The classic Mother Goose tale about the secret life of Christmas toys, with Laurel and Hardy as Santa's helpers who must save Toyland from the wicked Barnaby. A Yuletide "must see." Also available in a colorized version. **73m/B VHS, DVD.** Stan Laurel, Oliver Hardy, Charlotte Henry, Henry (Kleinbach) Brandon, Felix Knight, Jean Darling, Johnny Downs, Marie Wilson; **D:** Charles R. Rogers, Gus Meins; **W:** Frank Butler, Nick Grinde; **C:** Art Lloyd, Francis Corby.

March or Die 🦴🦴½ 1977 (PG) Great potential, unrealized. An American joins the French Foreign Legion during WWI after his dismissal from West Point. Following the brutality of training, he is assigned to guard an archeological expedition in Morocco, where he pulls together a rag-tag outfit for the mission. Hackman proves once again the wide range of his acting abilities, surmounting the cliched and fairly sadistic plot. Shot on location in the Sahara Desert. **104m/C VHS, DVD.** *GB* Gene Hackman, Terence Hill, Max von Sydow, Catherine Deneuve, Ian Holm; **D:** Dick Richards; **W:** David Zelag Goodman; **M:** Maurice Jarre.

Marci X 🦴 2003 (R) Ill-begotten social satire stars Kudrow as the title character, who takes over for dad Ben (director Benjamin) at his record company after he suffers a heart attack. When the target of Dr. S (Wayans), the label's top rapper, provoke conservative U.S. Senator Spinkle (Baranski) to attempt to ban the rapper's songs, the uptown, Jewish Marci tries to smooth things over and ends up falling for the Dr.'s downtown charms. Culture clash comedy has its moments, but is ultimately too predictable and the characters too one-dimensional to care about. Rap soundtrack is similarly uninspired, except a hilarious number by the fictitious boy band, Boyz 'R' Us. **97m/C VHS, DVD.** *US* Lisa Kudrow, Damon Wayans, Richard Benjamin, Christine Baranski, Paula Garces, Jane Krakowski, Veanne Cox; **D:** Richard Benjamin; **W:** Paul Rudnick; **C:** Robbie Greenberg; **M:** Mervyn Warren.

Marciano 🦴🦴 1979 Average fight movie chronicling the great boxer's life. **97m/C VHS.** Tony LoBianco, Vincent Gardenia; **D:** Bernard L. Kowalski; **M:** Ernest Gold. TV

Marco 🦴🦴 1973 Entertaining musical adventure of Marco Polo's life casts Amaz as Marco Polo and Mostel as Kublai Khan. A couple of cut-ups, right? One of the first films to combine animation with live action. Shot partially on location in the Orient. ♫By Damn; Walls; A Family Man; Spaghetti. **109m/C VHS, DVD.** Desi Arnaz Jr., Zero Mostel, Jack Weston, Cie Cie Win; **D:** Seymour Robbie.

Marco Polo, Jr. 🦴½ 2007 *Marco Polo Junior Versus the Red Dragon* 1972 Marco Polo Jr., the daring descendant of the legendary explorer, travels the world in search of his destiny in this song-filled, feature-length, but poorly animated, fantasy. **82m/C VHS, DVD.** Ian Somerhalder, Brian Dennehy, B.D. Wong, Desiree Slahaan; **D:** Kevin Connor; **W:** Ron Hutchinson; **C:** Thomas Burstyn. CABLE

Mardi Gras for the Devil 🦴🦴 *Night Trap* 1993 (R) Black magic and the occult combine as a New Orleans cop tries to catch a killer who strikes only at Mardi Gras. The cop's got his work cut out for him since the killer is no mere mortal but a demon who believes in human sacrifice. **95m/C VHS.** Robert Davi, Michael Ironside, Les-

ley-Anne Down, Lydie Denier, Mike Starr, Margaret Avery, John Amos; **D:** David A. Prior; **W:** David A. Prior.

Mardi Gras Massacre 🦴 WOOF! *Crypt of Dark Secrets* 1978 Aztec priest arrives in New Orleans during Mardi Gras to revive the blood ritual of human sacrifice to an Aztec god. A police detective relentlessly pursues him. Much gore and gut-slicing, with no redeeming social value. **92m/C VHS, DVD.** Curt Dawson, Gwen Arment, Wayne Mack, Laura Misch; **D:** Jack Weis.

Marebito 🦴🦴 *The Stranger from Afar* 2004 (R) In his quest to capture the ultimate moment of fear, Masuoka (Tsukamoto), a freelance cameraman, becomes engrossed by video he films of a seemingly-possessed man as he violently commits suicide in a Tokyo subway. While searching for more clues in the macabre underground, he happens upon a naked, mute girl who he calls "F" (Miyashita) and decides taking her home would be a good idea. He soon find her behavior distressing and her means of survival alarming. Very dark, though much of the scary stuff isn't shown. In Japanese with subtitles. **92m/C DVD.** *JP* Shinya Tsukamoto, Shun Sugata, Tomomi Miyashita, Kazuhiro Nakahara, Miho Ninagawa; **D:** Takashi Shimizu; **W:** Chiaki Konaka. VIDEO

Margaret's Museum 🦴🦴🦴½ 1995 (R) The museum of the title is the bizarre shrine Margaret (Bonham Carter) dedicates to the family members who have been killed in the coal mines that dominate her small (1940s) Cape Breton, Nova Scotia town. Both Margaret and her mother, Catherine (Nelligan), are embittered by their tragedies and when Margaret finds romance with eccentric bagpiper Neil (Russell), she makes him promise he'll never return to mine work. But with a bad economy, Neil is forced back to the pits and inevitable disaster. It's Bonham Carter's picture all the way and she shows a wide (and welcome) range of emotions and strength. Adapted from a story by Sheldon Currie. **114m/C VHS.** *CA GB* Helena Bonham-Carter, Clive Russell, Kate Nelligan, Kenneth Welsh, Craig Olejnik; **D:** Mort Ransen; **W:** Mort Ransen, Gerald Wexler; **C:** Vic Sarin; **M:** Milan Kymlicka. Genie '95: Actress (Bonham-Carter), Adapt. Screenplay, Costume Des., Support. Actor (Welsh), Support. Actress (Nelligan), Score.

Margarita Happy Hour 🦴🦴🦴½ 2001 Zelda (Hutchins) is a hard-partying New York single mom who makes a living (barely) as an illustrator and lives with her toddler daughter's unemployed, passive father Max (Fessenden), who has a drinking problem. Zelda's support group are her single mom friends who regularly meets at a local bar for happy hour. Zelda's life gets more complicated when her recovering junkie friend Natali (Ramos) moves in, needing to get her act together although she hasn't a clue how to do it. She's in good company. **98m/C DVD.** *US* Eleanor Hutchins, Larry Fessenden, Holly Ramos, Barbara Sicuranza, Amanda Vogel, Macha Ross, Kristen Dispatro, Will Keenan; **D:** Ilya Chaiken; **W:** Ilya Chaiken; **C:** Gordon Chou; **M:** Max Lichtenstein.

Margin for Murder 🦴🦴 *Mickey Spillane's Margin for Murder* 1981 Mike Hammer investigates a mysterious accident that killed his best friend. **98m/C VHS.** Kevin Dobson, Cindy Pickett, Donna Dixon, Charles Hallahan; **D:** Daniel Haller. TV

Margot at the Wedding 🦴🦴 2007 (R) Writer Margot (Kidman) returns to her family's home for her sister Pauline's (Leigh) wedding to "artist" Malcolm (Black), but years of contempt, ego, and neuroses boil over among the sisters, their children, and anyone else who happens to be around. Writer/director Baumbach specializes in finding biting humor and poignancy in the struggles of flawed, overly educated East Coasters, but the nasty, petty characters he's created here are so hard to relate to that anything funny or moving is buried under an avalanche of meanness. **92m/C DVD.** *US* Nicole Kidman, Jennifer Jason Leigh, Jack Black, John Turturro, Ciaran Hinds, Flora Cross, Halley Feiffer, Zane

Pais; **D:** Noah Baumbach; **W:** Noah Baumbach; **C:** Harris Savides.

Maria Candelaria 🦴🦴 *Portrait of Maria; Xochimilco* 1946 Society rejects a woman because people don't like her mother. (She posed nude for an artist, and the town responds by stoning her to death, proving that going against small-town morals can be lethal). Eventually, time and circumstance push daughter onto mother's path in this tragic soaper. Del Rio portrays the scorned young woman, although she was 40 years old. **96m/B VHS.** *MX* Dolores Del Rio, Pedro Armendariz Sr., Margarita Cortes; **D:** Emilio Fernandez.

Maria Chapdelaine 🦴🦴🦴 1934 An early film from the renowned French director, in which a brutish trapper and a sophisticate battle for the love of a girl in the Canadian wilderness. English subtitles. Remade in 1984. **75m/B VHS.** *FR* Jean Gabin, Jean-Pierre Aumont, Madeleine Renaud; **D:** Julien Duvivier.

Maria Chapdelaine 🦴🦴½ 1984 Around the turn of the century, a young girl in the Northern Canadian wilderness endures a year of passion, doomed love, and tragedy. In French with subtitles. Remake of a 1935 French film. **108m/C VHS.** *FR CA* Nick Mancuso, Carole Laure, Claude Rich, Pierre Curzi; **D:** Gilles Carle.

Maria Full of Grace 🦴🦴🦴 *Maria, llena eres de gracia* 2004 (R) Moreno (in her film debut) gives a graceful performance in the title role of also-debuting director Marston's all-too-human look at desperation and heroin trafficking in Colombia. Maria is a 17-year-old working for a pittance at a flower factory in her rural hometown. She realizes she's pregnant just as she impulsively quits her job and is ripe for the sweet talk of Franklin (Toro), who tells Maria about all the money to be made if she'll only become a drug mule. After swallowing heroin-filled pellets, Maria boards a plane for New York along with her best friend Blanca (Vega) and fellow courier Lucy (Lopez). Problems arise when Lucy becomes ill, thugs threaten the girls if any of the drugs come up missing, and Maria flees into the city's Colombian immigrant community for safety. Spanish with subtitles. **101m/C VHS, DVD.** *US* Catalina Sandino Moreno, Yenny Paola Vega, Giuiled Lorenzo, John Alex Toro, Patricia Rae, Wilson Guerrero, Jaime Osorio Gomez, Johanna Andrea Mora, Orlando Tobon, Fernando Velasquez; **D:** Joshua Marston; **W:** Joshua Marston; **C:** Jim Denault; **M:** Jacobo Lieberman, Leonardo Heiblum. Ind. Spirit '05: Actress (Moreno), First Screenplay.

Marianne and Juliane 🦴🦴🦴½ *The German Sisters; Die Bleierne Zeit* 1982 Powerful combination of relationships and politics in West Germany as experienced through the lives of two sisters—Juliane, a feminist editor, and Marianne, a political terrorist. Based on the lives of Gudrun and Christiane Ensslin. German with subtitles. **106m/C VHS.** *GE* Jutta Lampe, Barbara Sukowa, Ruediger Vogler, Doris Schade, Franz Rudnick; **D:** Margarethe von Trotta; **W:** Margarethe von Trotta; **C:** Franz Rath; **M:** Nicolas Economou.

Maria's Child 🦴🦴🦴½ 1993 Light comedy about a dancer who becomes pregnant and must decide whether or not to keep the baby. When her live-in boyfriend (not the father) admits he cheated on her, she kicks him out. Unable to make up her mind, she imagines a dialogue with the fetus. Second of a trilogy by British TV screenwriter Malcolm McKay on the subject of forgiveness. **97m/C VHS.** *GB* Yolanda Vasquez, David O'Hara, Fiona Shaw, Alec McCowen, Sophie Okonedo, Linda Davidson, Rudi Davies, Nicholas Woodeson, Anita Zagaria; **D:** Malcolm McKay; **W:** Malcolm McKay; **M:** Philip Appleby.

Maria's Day 🦴🦴🦴 *Maria-nap* 1984 Chronicles the plague-riddled downfall of a formerly aristocratic and wealthy Hungarian family in the years following the failed 1849 Revolution. In Hungarian with English subtitles. **113m/C VHS.** Sandor Szabo, Lajos Kovacs, Edit Handel, Eva Igo, Imre Csiszar, Tamas Fodor; **D:** Judit Elek; **W:** Luca Karall, Gyorgy Petho; **C:** Emil Novak; **M:** Gabor Csalog.

Maria's Lovers 🦴🦴½ 1984 (R) The wife (Kinski) of an impotent WWII veteran (Savage) succumbs to the charms of a rakish lady-killer (Spano). Savage turns to the charms of an older woman, finds love again with Kinski, but is still impotent; she gets pregnant by a wandering minstrel (Carradine) and on we go to film climax. Offbeat and uneven, representing Russian director Konchalovsky's first American film and one of Kinski's better roles. **103m/C VHS, DVD.** Nastassja Kinski, John Savage, Robert Mitchum, Keith Carradine, Anita Morris, Bud Cort, Karen Young, Tracy Nelson, John Goodman, Vincent Spano; **D:** Andrei Konchalovsky; **W:** Andrei Konchalovsky, Marjorie David, Gerard Brach, Paul Zindel; **C:** Juan Ruiz-Anchia; **M:** Gary S. Remal.

Maricela 🦴🦴🦴 1988 Young Maricela Flores and her mother have come to the U.S. from El Salvador to escape the fighting. Living with a Southern Californian family, Maricela has a hard time adjusting to American life and, in particular, dealing with prejudice. An entry in the PBS "Wonderworks" series. **55m/C VHS, DVD.** Linda Lavin, Carlina Cruz.

Marie 🦴🦴 1985 (PG-13) In this true story, a divorced (and battered) mother works her way through school and the system to become the first woman to head the Parole Board in Tennessee. Finding rampant corruption, she blows the whistle on her bosses, who put her life in jeopardy. Spacek gives a powerful performance, as does first-time actor Thompson, portraying himself as the abused woman's attorney. Based on the book by Peter Maas. **113m/C VHS, DVD.** Sissy Spacek, Jeff Daniels, Keith Szarabajka, John Cullum, Morgan Freeman, Fred Dalton Thompson, Don Hood, Lisa Banes, Vincent Irizarry; **D:** Roger Donaldson; **W:** John Briley; **C:** Chris Menges; **M:** Francis Lai.

Marie Antoinette 🦴🦴½ 1938 An elephantine costume drama chronicling the French queen's life from princesshood to her final days before the Revolution. A Shearer festival all the way, and a late example of MGM's overstuffed period style and star-power. Overlong, but engrossing for the wrong reasons. Morley, in his first film, plays Louis XVI. Power's only MGM loan-out casts him as a Swedish count and Marie's romantic dalliance. Based on a book by Stephan Zweig, with script assistance from (among others) F. Scott Fitzgerald. **160m/B VHS, DVD.** Norma Shearer, Tyrone Power, John Barrymore, Robert Morley, Gladys George, Anita Louise, Joseph Schildkraut, Henry Stephenson, Reginald Gardiner, Peter Bull, Albert Dekker, Joseph Calleia, George Zucco, Cora Witherspoon, Barry Fitzgerald, Mae Busch, Harry Davenport, Scotty Beckett; **D:** Woodbridge S. Van Dyke; **W:** F. Scott Fitzgerald; **C:** William H. Daniels.

Marie Antoinette 🦴🦴 2006 (PG-13) Coppola goes her own anachronistic way in this revisionist biopic. Pink-and-white Dunst dimples her way through as the teenaged Marie Antoinette, an Austrian princess who is married off at 14 to bumptious French prince (and eventual king) Louis (Schwartzman), who can't even bed her properly. So what's a bored and lonely young woman, stuck in a hostile royal court, to do? Why, party, party, party (extravagantly) of course. It's all pop tunes and lavish costumes and splendid isolation at Versailles while the rabble rouses. Fortunately, Coppola ends her confection before tragedy befalls the delectable Marie. **123m/C DVD.** *US* Kirsten Dunst, Jason Schwartzman, Judy Davis, Rip Torn, Rose Byrne, Asia Argento, Molly Shannon, Shirley Henderson, Danny Huston, Marianne Faithfull, Jamie Dornan, Mary Nighy, Steve Coogan, Lauriane Mascaro, Florrie Betts; **D:** Sofia Coppola; **W:** Sofia Coppola; **C:** Lance Acord. Oscars '06: Costume Des.

Marie Baie des Anges 🦴🦴 *Angel Sharks; Marie Bay of Angels* 1997 (R) Although Nice's feature film is in a sort of mythic French port, filled with French teens, gang members, American sailors, and tourists. Pretty gypsy Marie (Giocante) likes to flirt with the Americans but after getting dumped goes back to the local toughs, including petty criminal Orso (Malgras). They manage a brief idyll, then Orso begins pressuring Marie to steal a

Marie Galante ✍✍ 1934 Fine spy drama with Tracy running into Gallian in Panama (years earlier she had been left there after a kidnapping). He finds her most helpful in his attempt to thwart the bombing of the Panama Canal. It's the standard thriller up a few notches. 88m/B VHS, DVD. Spencer Tracy, Ketti Gallian, Ned Sparks, Helen Morgan, Sig Rumann, Leslie Fenton, Jay C. Flippen. **D:** Roland Price.

Marilyn & Bobby: Her Final Affair ✍ 1994 Sordid account of the alleged romance between movie star Monroe (Anderson) and Attorney General Robert Kennedy (Kelly). Culminates in a silly scene at Marilyn's home, on the night of her death, where various men all try to find her tell-all diary while keeping out of sight of each other. 95m/C VHS. Melody Anderson, James F. Kelly, Richard Dysart, Thomas Wagner, Raymond Serra, Kristopher Tabori, Jonathan Banks, Geoffrey Blake, Ian Buchanan; **D:** Bradford May. **M:** CABLE.

Marilyn Hotchkiss' Ballroom Dancing & Charm School ✍½ 2006 (PG-13) When he promised his sweetheart Lisa that in five years they would meet again at their dance school's class reunion. Now here we are, five years later, trying to believe that this is all going down and that Steve is still passionately fixated on this historic moment. Not buying it. Everything goes wrong and Steve wonders if he'll ever get to see his long-lost love again. Silly sideling but bittersweet sentiment all over the place. Somehow snagged an incredible cast. Based on the director's own short film made 15 years earlier. 103m/C DVD. Robert Carlyle, Marisa Tomei, Mary Steenburgen, John Goodman, Donnie Wahlberg, Sonia Braga, Sean Astin, Danny DeVito, David Payne; **Cameo:** Camryn Manheim, Adam Arkin, Elden (Ratliff) Henson, Ernie Hudson, Miguel (Michael) Sandoval, Ian Abercrombie, Mary Pat Gleason; **D:** Randall Miller. **W:** Randall Miller, Jody Savin; **C:** Jonathan Sea; **M:** Mark Adler.

The Marine ✍½ 2006 (PG-13) A frozen slab of grade-A beef, wrestler Cena makes his movie debut as action director Bonito) in this slam-bang actioner. When John Triton is shipped back to South Carolina from Iraq, he decides to take his hottie wife (Carlson) on vacation. But they wind up in the wrong place just when a violent gang of jewel thieves need a hostage and take Kate. This pisses off John and you don't want anybody that big angry at you. Cartoonish mayhem follows (it's PG-13, remember). Patrick has fun with his villainous ringleader role but you know he's slumming. 93m/C DVD, Blu-ray Disc. *US* Robert Patrick, Kelly Carlson, Anthony Ray Parker, Jerome Ehlers, John Cena, Abigail Bianca; **D:** David Eggby. **M:** Don Davis.

Marihuana ✍ *Marijuana, Weed with Roots in Hell* 1936 An unintentionally hilarious, "Reefer Madness"-type cautionary film about the exaggerated evils of pot smoking. A real dopey filter favored by right-winger zealots. 57m/B VHS, DVD. Harley Wood, Hugh McArthur, Pat Carlyle, Dorothy Dehn, Paul Ellis, Richard Erskine. **D:** Dwan Esper. **W:** Rex Elgin, Hildegarde Stadie. **C:** Roland Price.

Marius ✍✍ 1931 This is the first of Marcel Pagnol's trilogy ("Fanny" and "César" followed), about the lives and adventures of the people of Provence, France. Marius is a young man who dreams of going away to sea. When he acts on those dreams, he leaves behind his girlfriend, Fanny. Realistic dialogue and vivid characterizations. Adapted by Pagnol from his play. The musical play "Fanny" (1961) were adapted from this trilogy. 125m/B VHS, DVD. *FR* Raimu, Pierre Fresnay, Orane Demazis; **D:** Alexander Korda. **W:** Marcel Pagnol. **M:** Francis Gromon.

Marius and Jeannette ✍✍½ *Marius et Jeannette: Un Conte de L'Estaque* 1997 Single mother of two, Jeannette (Ascaride), works as a checkout clerk in a poor Marseilles neighborhood. Marius (Meylan) works as a security guard at a closed cement factory and meets Jeannette when he catches her stealing paint cans from the property. He offers to help her paint her apartment and the two begin a tentative romance. But something spooks Marius and he begins to drink heavily, abandoning Jeannette. Two of Jeannette's male neighbors decide to find out what Marius' problem is and get the 'wosome back together. Very sweet and sentimental. 101m/C VHS, DVD. *FR* Ariane Ascaride, Gerard Meylan, Pascale Roberts, Jacques Boudet, Jean-Pierre Darroussin, Frederique Bonnal; **D:** Robert Guediguian; **W:** Robert Guediguian, Jean-Louis Milesi; **C:** Bernard Cavile, Cesar '98: Actress (Ascaride).

Marjoe ✍✍ 1972 (PG) Documentary follows the career of rock-style evangelist Marjoe Gortner, who spent 25 years of his life touring the country as a professional preacher. Marjoe later went on to become an actor and professional fundraiser. 88m/C VHS, DVD. Marjoe Gortner; **D:** Howard Smith, Sarah Kernochan. Oscars '72: Feature Doc.

Marjorie Morningstar ✍✍ 1958 A temperate Hollywood adaptation of the Herman Wouk story of a young actress who fails to achieve stardom and settles on being a housewife. Wood slipped a bit on this film. 123m/C VHS, DVD. Natalie Wood, Gene Kelly, Martin Balsam, Claire Trevor, Ed Wynn, Everett Sloane, Carolyn Jones; **D:** Irving Rapper; **C:** Harry Stradling Sr.; **M:** Max Steiner.

The Mark ✍✍½ 1961 Story of a convicted child molester who cannot escape his past upon his release from prison. Whitman gives a riveting performance as the convict. 127m/B VHS, DVD. *GB* Stuart Whitman, Maria Schell, Rod Steiger, Brenda de Banzie, Maurice Denham, Donald Wolfit, Paul Rogers, Donald Houston, Amanda Black, Russell Napier, Maire Devereux; **D:** Guy Green; **W:** Sidney Buchman, Raymond Stross; **C:** Dudley Lovell; **M:** Richard Rodney Bennett.

Mark of Cain ✍✍½ 1984 Twin brothers, one normal, the other a raving lunatic with murderous tendencies, confuse the authorities who imprison the nice guy, allowing the nutcase to chase after his beautiful sister-in-law. 90m/C VHS. Robin

---

Marine Raiders ✍✍ 1943 Marines train and then fight at Guadalcanal. A typical flag-waver, watchable but not particularly engaging. 90m/B VHS. Pat O'Brien, Robert Ryan, Ruth Hussey, Frank McHugh, Barton MacLane; **D:** Harold Schuster.

Marion Bridge ✍✍ 2002 Chain-smoking alcoholic Rose (McNeil) is dying, which brings her three daughters back together with all their past family traumas unresolved. Former wild child Agnes (Parker) was sexually abused by their father, which resulted in the birth of a child whom she gave up. Now that child is a sullen teen living nearby with her adoptive mother and Agnes would like to befriend her. Eldest sister Theresa (Jenkins) is a bitter divorcee who can't let go of her ex and middle sister Louise (Smith) is a couch potato who is slowly working up the courage to admit she's a lesbian. Much angst ensues for all. Screenwriter McIvor adapted from his play. 90m/C DVD. *CA* Molly Parker, Rebecca Jenkins, Stacy Smith, Marguerite McNeil; **D:** Wiebke von Carolsfeld; **W:** Daniel McIvor. **C:** Stefan Ivanov; **M:** Lesley Barber.

Mark of the Devil ✍ *Burn, Witch, Burn; Brenn, Brenn: Austria 1700; Satan, Heren bei aufs Blut Gequael!* 1969 (R) Witchcraft and romance don't mix, as a Medieval witch hunter and a sexy girl accused of witchery discover. Notoriously graphic torture scenes acid to the mayhem but the weird part is that this is based on true stories. 96m/C VHS, DVD. *GB GE* Herbert Lom, Oliviera Vuco, Udo Kier, Reggie Nalder, Herbert (Fuchs) Fux, Michael Maien, Ingeborg (Urge) Schoener, Johannes Buzalski, Gaby Fuchs, Adrian Hoven; **D:** Michael Armstrong; **W:** Sergio Casstner, Adrian Hoven; **C:** Ernst W. Kalinke; **M:** Michael Holm.

Mark of the Devil 2 ✍ 1972 (R) Sadistic witchhunters torture satan's servants and torch sisters of mercy, whilst trying to horn in on a nobleman's fortune. It's just not as gross as the vomit bags. 90m/C VHS, DVD. *GE* Erika Blanc, Anton Diffring, Reggie Nalder; **D:** Adrian Hoven.

The Mark of the Hawk ✍✍ *The Accused* 1957 A uniquely told story of African nations struggling to achieve racial equality after gaining independence. Songs include "This Man Is Mine," sung by Kitt. 83m/C VHS. *GB* Sidney Poitier, Eartha Kitt, Juano Hemandez, John McIntire; **D:** Michael Audley.

Mark of the Spur ✍½ 1932 The track down his attacker. 60m/B VHS. Bob Custer, Lillian Rich, Franklyn Farnum, Bud Osborne, Reginald Barlow; **D:** J. Parkerson)(McGowan.

Mark of the Vampire ✍✍ 1935 A murder in a small town is solved through the use of vaudeville actors who pose as vampires. Great cast, surprise ending. 61m/B VHS, DVD. Lionel Barrymore, Bela Lugosi, Elizabeth Allan, Lionel Atwill, Jean Hersholt, Donald Meek, Carroll Borland; **D:** Tod Browning; **W:** Tod Browning, Guy Endore, Bernard Schubert; **C:** James Wong Howe.

Mark of Zorro ✍✍½ 1920 Fairbanks plays a dual role as the hapless Don Diego and his dashing counterpart, Zorro, the hero of the oppressed. Silent film. 80m/B VHS, DVD. Douglas Fairbanks Sr., Marguerite de la Motte, Noah Beery Sr., Mary Astor, Noah Beery Jr., Milton Berle, Charles Stevens; **D:** Fred Niblo; **W:** Douglas Fairbanks Sr.; **C:** James Wong Howe.

The Mark of Zorro ✍✍✍ 1940 The dashing Power swashbuckles his way through this wonderfully acted and directed romp. A 19th-century California aristocrat who is secretly the masked avenger of the oppressed peons. Bromberg plays the wicked governor, with the beautiful niece (Darnell) beloved by Power, and Rathbone is supremely evil as his cruel minion. Lots of swordplay with a particularly excit-ing duel to the death between Power and Power. Based on the novel "The Curse of Capistrano" by Johnston McCulley. Remake of the 1921 silent film, followed by a number of other Zorro incarnations. 93m/B VHS, DVD. Tyrone Power, Linda Darnell, Basil Rathbone, Gale Sondergaard, Eugene Pallette, J. Edward Bromberg, Montagu Love, Janet Beecher; **D:** Rouben Mamoulian; **W:** John Taintor Foote; **C:** Arthur C. Miller; **M:** Alfred Newman.

Mark Twain and Me ✍✍½ 1991 Robards portrays the aging and irascible Mark Twain, attended by a neglected but devoted daughter, and befriended by 11-year-old Dorothy Quick, as they travel on the same ship. Based on a true story. 93m/C VHS, Jason Robards Jr., Talia Shire, Amy Stewart, Chris Wiggins, R.H. Thomson, Fione Reid; **D:** Daniel Petrie. TV.

Marked for Death ✍✍½ *Screwface* 1990 (R) Having killed a prostitute, DEA agent Seagal decides it's time to roll out the white picket fence in the 'burbs with the little woman and brood. Trouble is, a bunch of guys with dreadlocks don't approve of his early retirement, and the Ja-

---

Ward, Wendy Crewson, August Schellenberg; **D:** Bruce Pittman; **W:** Peter Colley.

Mark of the Beast ✍ 1987 Two students inadvertently videotape an assassination and are then relentlessly pursued by the killer. 90m/C VHS, Carolyn Guillet, David Smulen; **D:** Robert Stewart.

Marked for Murder ✍½ 1945 Another in the Texas Ranger series. In this entry, the Rangers come to the rescue when a rancher war appears inevitable. 58m/B VHS. Tex Ritter, Dave O'Brien, Guy Wilkerson; **D:** Elmer Clifton; **W:** Elmer Clifton.

Marked for Murder ✍½ 1989 (R) Two TV station employees are framed for murder after being sent out to find a missing videocassette. Renee Estevez is part of the Sheen/Estevez dynasty. 88m/C VHS. Renee Estevez, Wings Hauser, Jim Mitchum, Ross Hagen, Ken Abraham; **D:** Rick Sloane.

Marked Man ✍✍ 1996 (R) After auto mechanic Frank Stanton (Piper) witnesses a murder he finds himself accused of the crime and on the run, trying to prove his innocence. 94m/C VHS, Roddy Piper, Jane Wheeler, Alina Thompson, Miles O'Keeffe, Marc Volzard; **W:** Thomas Ritz; **C:** Stephen Reza. **M:** Marty Simon.

Marked Money ✍½ 1928 Amiable captain takes in toy whelz'll soon roll in the dough and swindlers show up on the joint hostesses to testify against their gangster boss. A gritty studio melodrama loosely based on a true story. 97m/B VHS, DVD. Bette Davis, Humphrey Bogart, Eduardo Ciamelli, Isabel Jewell, Allen Jenkins, Lola Lane; **D:** Lloyd Bacon; **C:** George Barnes, Venice Film Fest. '37: Actress

Marked Trails ✍ 1944 One clue telling the guilty parties in this wild west saga. 59m/B VHS. Hoot Gibson, Bob Steele, Veda Ann 3org; **D:** John P. McCarthy; **C:** Harry Neumann.

Marlowe ✍✍½ 1969 (PG) Updated telling by Stirling Silliphant of Chandler's "The Little Sister" sports retro guy Garner as Philip Marlowe, gumshoe. Hired by a mystery blonde to find her misplaced brother, rumpled sleuth Marlowe encounters kicking Bruce Lee in his first film. Slick looking, but the story's a bit slippery. 95m/C VHS. James Garner, Gayle Hunnicutt, Carroll O'Connor, Rita Moreno, Sharon Farrell, William Daniels, Bruce Lee; **D:** Paul Bogart; **W:** Stirling Silliphant; **C:** William H. Daniels.

Marnie ✍✍ 1964 A lovely blonde with a mysterious past robs her employers and then changes her identity. When her current boss catches her in the act and forces her to marry him, he soon learns the puzzling aspects of Marnie's background. Critic zed at the time of its release, the move has since been accepted as a Hitchcock classic. 130m/C VHS, DVD. Tippi Hedren, Sean Connery, Diane Baker, Bruce Dern, Louise Latham, Martin Gabel, Henry Beckman, Mariette Hartley, Alan Napier; **D:** Alfred Hitchcock; **W:** Jay Presson Allen; **C:** Robert Burks; **M:** Bernard Herrmann.

Maroc 7 ✍ 1967 Slow story of a secret agent after a thief suffering from a split personality. 92m/C VHS. Gene Barry, Elsa Martinelli, Cyd Charisse, Leslie Phillips; **D:** Gerry O'Hara.

Marooned ✍½ *Space Travelers* 1969 (G) Tense thriller casts Crenna, Hackman, and Franciscus as astronauts stranded in space after a retro-rocket mistfires and their craft is unable to return to earth. Amazingly inept despite an Academy Award for effects and an excellent cast. Story. Seems a striking resemblance to 1995's "Apollo 13." 134m/C VHS, DVD. Gregory Peck, David Janssen, Richard Crenna, James

---

maican gangsters plan to send him and his family to the great Rasta playground in the sky. Whereupon the Steventer kicks and punches and wags his ponytail. Much blood flows, mcn. Tunes by Jimmy Cliff. 93m/C VHS, DVD. Steven Seagal, Joanna Pacula, Basil Wallace, Keith David, Danielle Harris, Arlen Dean Snyder, Tari Weigel; **D:** Dwight Little; **W:** Mark Victor, Michael Grais; **C:** Ric Waite; **M:** James Newton Howard.

Franciscus, Gene Hackman, Lee Grant; **D:** John Sturges; **C:** Daniel F. Fapp. **Oscars '69:** Visual FX.

Marooned in Iraq ♂♂ *The Songs of My Homeland; Avazhaye Sarzamine Madaryam* **2002** Set between 1989 and 1991, this is a road movie about family and survival. Victimized by Suddam Hussein, Iraqi Kurds fled towards the Iranian border and an uncertain future in refugee camps. One such family is led by the aged Mirza (Ebrahim), a locally famous singer who has summoned his two sons, Barat (Mohammadi) and Audeh (Rashtiani), to accompany him back to Iraq in order to find his wife, Hanareh (Ghobadi), whom he has learned is in trouble and needs him. Armed robbers steal all their possessions on their journey and they are forced to walk, eventually coming to orphaned children, other contains only women). Folk music and comic bits help break up the admittedly bleak story. Kurdish with subtitles. **97m/C VHS, DVD.** *IA* Shahab Ebrahimi, Faegh Mohammadi, Allahmorad Rashtiani, Iran Ghobadi; **D:** Bahman Ghobadi; **W:** Bahman Ghobadi; **C:** Saed Nikzat, Shahriar Assadi; **M:** Arsalan Komkar.

Marquis ♂ **1990** A bizarre satire combining sex, lust, and the French Revolution, based on the writings of the Marquis de Sade. Amusing, decadent, and not for the prudish. In French with English subtitles. **88m/C VHS, DVD.** **FR D:** Henri Xhonneux; **W:** Henri Xhonneux, Roland Topor; **C:** Etienne Fauduet; **M:** Reinhardt Wagner; **V:** Francois Marthouret, Michel Robin, Valerie King, Isabella Wolfe.

Marquis de Sade ♂½ *Dark Prince: Intimate Tales of Marquis de Sade* **1996** (R) Justine searches for her sister Juliette in 17th-century Paris and is drawn into the sexually deviant world of the Marquis de Sade. Also available unrated. **88m/C VHS, DVD.** Nick Mancuso, Janet Gunn, John Rhys-Davies; **D:** Gwyneth Gibby; **W:** Craig J. Nevius; **C:** Eugeny Guslinsky. **CABLE**

The Marquise of O ♂ *Die Marquise Von O* **1976 (PG)** In the early 18th century, the widowed Marquise (Clever) is drugged and raped by Count F (Ganz), an officer with the Russians. When the Marquise discovers she's pregnant, she forces the Count to marry her, although they separate immediately after the ceremony. Adaptation of Heinrich Von Kleist's novella. German with English subtitles. **102m/C VHS, DVD.** **FR GE** Edith Clever, Bruno Ganz, Peter Lühr, Edda Seipel, Otto Sander, Ruth Drexel; **D:** Eric Rohmer; **W:** Eric Rohmer; **C:** Nestor Almendros.

The Marriage Circle ♂♂♂ **1924** A pivotal silent comedy depicting the infidelity of several married couples in Vienna. Director Lubitsch's first American comedy. Remade as a musical, "One Hour With You," in 1932. Silent. **90m/B VHS, DVD.** Florence Vidor, Monte Blue, Marie Prevost, Creighton Hale, Adolphe Menjou, Harry C. (Henry) Myers, Dale Fuller; **D:** Ernst Lubitsch; **W:** Paul Bern; **C:** Charles Van Enger.

Marriage Is Alive and Well ♂ **1980** A wedding photographer reflects on the institution of marriage from his unique perspective. **100m/C VHS.** Joe Namath, Jack Albertson, Melinda Dillon, Judd Hirsch, Susan Sullivan, Fred McCarren, Swoosie Kurtz; **D:** Russ Mayberry. **TV**

Marriage Italian Style ♂♂♂ **1964** When an engaged man hears that his mistress is on her death bed, he goes to her side and, in an emotional gesture, promises to marry her if she survives. She does, and holds him to his promise. After they're married, however, she gives him a big surprise—three grown sons. A silly film, but DeSica's direction keeps it from being too fluffy. Lots of fun. Based on the play "Filumena Marfurano" by Eduardo De Filippo. **102m/C VHS, DVD.** *IT* Sophia Loren, Marcello Mastroianni, Aldo Puglisi, Tecla Scarano, Marilu Tolo; **D:** Vittorio De Sica. Golden Globes '65: Foreign Film.

The Marriage of Figaro ♂♂ *Figaros Hochzeit* **1949** DEFA studio's lavish adaptation of Mozart's opera. Count Almaviva's valet, Figaro, plans to marry the Countess's chambermaid, Susanna. But since the Count also fancies Susanna, he

keeps coming up with plans to postpone the wedding and the lovestuck duo must use their own trickery to forge ahead. German with subtitles. **108m/B VHS.** **GE** Angelika Hauff, Willi Domgraf-Fassbaender, Sabine Peters, Mathieu Ahlersmeyer; **D:** Georg Wildhagen; **W:** Georg Wildhagen; **C:** Eugen Klagemann, Karl Plintzner.

The Marriage of Maria Braun ♂♂♂♂ *Die Ehe Der Maria Braun* **1979 (R)** In post-WWII Germany, a young woman uses guile and sexuality to survive as the nation rebuilds itself into an industrial power. The first movie in Fassbinder's trilogy about German women in Germany during the post war years, it is considered one of the director's finest films, and an indispensable example of the New German Cinema. In German with English subtitles. **120m/C VHS, DVD.** **GE** Hanna Schygulla, Klaus Lowitsch, Ivan Desny, Gottfried John, Gisela Uhlen; **D:** Rainer Werner Fassbinder; **W:** Rainer Werner Fassbinder, Peter Marthesheimer, Pea Frolich; **C:** Michael Ballhaus; **M:** Peer Raben. Berlin Intl. Film Fest. '79: Actress (Schygulla).

Marriage on the Rocks ♂♂ **1965** Mildly amusing marital comedy finds Valerie (Kerr) bored by her 20-year marriage to Dan (Sinatra) so she decides to divorce him. The family lawyer (McGiver) persuades them to take a would-be second honeymoon to Mexico instead, which is cut short for Dan by business. Meanwhile, a mix-up with Mexican lawyer Santos (Romero) actually has the couple divorced. Then, when Dan's womanizing best buddy Ernie (Martin) shows up, he accidentally marries Valerie. More complications ensue but not much comes of all the havoc. **109m/C VHS.** Frank Sinatra, Deborah Kerr, Dean Martin, Cesar Romero, John McGiver, Hermione Baddeley, Tony Bill, Nancy Sinatra; **D:** Jack Donohue; **C:** William H. Daniels; **M:** Nelson Riddle.

Married? ♂½ **1926** Couple endures 365 days of marital bliss in order to inherit big bucks. Some do it for less. **65m/B VHS.** Owen Moore, Constance Bennett; **D:** George Terwilliger.

Married Life ♂♂♂ **2007 (PG-13)** Set in 1949 and steeped in the style, mood, and sensibilities of the time, this is the story of Harry Allen (Cooper), a buttoned-down married man who falls in love with young and gorgeous widow Kay (McAdams). Burdened with guilt and hoping for understanding, Harry confides in his womanizing pal Richard (Brosnan), who then becomes fascinated with Kay, too. Harry's marriage to Pat (Clarkson) is functional if not entirely satisfying and Pat appears to know nothing of the affair. Harry decides to end his marriage but is so duty bound to Pat that he plans to murder her rather than subject her to the pain of a divorce (hmm, wonder if that's the option she'd pick). Several big surprises both together this intriguing, smart drama. **90m/C DVD.** *US* Chris Cooper, Patricia Clarkson, Rachel McAdams, Pierce Brosnan, David Wenham; **D:** Ira Sachs; **W:** Ira Sachs, Oren Moverman; **C:** Peter Deming; **M:** Dickon Hinchliffe.

A Married Man ♂ **1984** Story focusing on a bored British lawyer who begins cheating on his wife. Amid the affair, someone gets murdered. **200m/C VHS, DVD.** **GB** Anthony Hopkins, Ciaran Madden, Lise Hilboldt, Yvonne Coulette, John Le Mesurier, Sophie Ashton; **D:** John Davies. **TV**

Married People, Single Sex ♂♂½ **1993 (R)** Three couples decide to spread their sexual wings. Shelly takes a new lover; Artie makes obscene phone calls; and Beth and Mike, who end their relationship, still can't keep out of bed. An unrated version is also available. **110m/C VHS, DVD.** Chase Masterson, Joe Pilato, Darla Haun, Shelley Michelle, Wendi Westbrook, Robert Zachar, Samuel Mongiello, Teri Thompson; **D:** Mike Sedan; **W:** Catherine Tavel.

Married People, Single Sex 2: For Better or Worse ♂♂½ **1994** (R) Three women are faced with sexual unhappiness: Carol's hubby had her affair, Valerie wants a baby but her spouse doesn't, and Karen's husband is just too darn nice (she wants some spice in her life). So, there's lots of sexual encounters

to solve their problems. Also available unrated. **93m/C VHS.** Kathy Shower, Monique Parent, Liza Smith, Craig Stepp, Doug Jeffery; **D:** Mike Sedan.

Married to It ♂♂ **1993 (R)** Three vastly different couples work together to plan a pageant at a private school. The oil and water group includes struggling hippie leftovers Bridges and Channing, '80s-era corporate cutthroats Shepherd and Leonard. Contrived plot offers few humourous moments, with the main focus revolving around coping rather than comedy. And the coping is slow business, done with problems that don't really matter. **112m/C VHS, DVD.** Beau Bridges, Stockard Channing, Robert Sean Leonard, Mary Stuart Masterson, Cybill Shepherd, Ron Silver; **D:** Arthur Hiller; **W:** Janet Kovalcik; **M:** Henry Mancini.

Married to the Mob ♂♂♂ **1988** After the murder of her husband, an attractive Mafia widow tries to escape "mob" life, but ends up fighting off amorous advances from the current mob boss while being wooed by an undercover cop. A snappy script and a spry performance by Pfeiffer pepper this easy-to-watch film. **102m/C VHS, DVD.** Michelle Pfeiffer, Dean Stockwell, Alec Baldwin, Matthew Modine, Mercedes Ruehl, Anthony J. Nici, Joan Cusack, Ellen Foley, Chris Isaak, Trey Wilson, Charles Napier, Tracey Walter, Al Lewis, Nancy Travis, David Johansen, Jonathan Demme; **D:** Jonathan Demme; **W:** Mark Burns, Barry Strugatz; **C:** Tak Fujimoto; **M:** David Byrne. N.Y. Film Critics '88: Support. Actor (Stockwell); Nat. Soc. Film Critics '88: Support. Actor (Stockwell), Support. Actress (Ruehl).

Married Too Young ♂ *I Married Too Young* **1962** High school honeys elope, despite disapproval from the parental units. When the boy groom trades his med school plans for a monkey wrench in order to support the little missus, he finds much trouble with the hot rod heavies. **76m/B VHS.** Harold Lloyd Jr., Jana Lund, Anthony Dexter, Marianna Hill, Trudy Marshall, Brian O'Hara, Nita Loveless; **D:** George Moskov; **W:** Nat Tanchuck; **C:** Ernest Haller.

A Married Woman ♂♂♂ *La Femme Mariee* **1965** Dramatizes a day in the life of a woman who has both a husband and a lover. One of Godard's more mainstream efforts. **94m/B VHS.** **FR** Macha Meril, Phillippe LeRoy, Bernard Noel; **D:** Jean-Luc Godard; **W:** Jean-Luc Godard; **C:** Raoul Coutard.

Marrionnier ♂ *Marrionnier: Doll Horror Movie* **2005 (R)** Wigged-out Japanese horror flick with a confused, convoluted plot involving a psycho stalker, his sadistically violent method of turning girls into wax dolls, and the kidnapping of his obsession so she can meet the demonic creations. Subtitled. **79m/C DVD.** *JP* Mayu, Hime, Yuriko Arijho, Masakazu Yoshida, Haruna Hoshino, Miyako Ojima, Takanori Kagami, Hideyuki Kobayashi, Hiroto Nakayama, Tetsuya Shibata, Miki Yoshida; **D:** Akira Kobayashi.

Marry Me, Marry Me ♂♂ *Mazel Tov Ou le Mariage* **1969** (R) While in Paris, a Jewish encyclopedia salesman falls in love with a pregnant Belgian woman. A sensitive story about European Jewish families. Berri wrote, produced, directed, and starred in this romantic comedy. **87m/C VHS.** **FR** Elisabeth Wiener, Regine, Claude Berri, Louisa Colpeyn; **D:** Claude Berri; **C:** Ghislain Cloquet.

The Marrying Kind ♂♂♂½ **1952** Marrieds Florence (Holliday) and Chet (Ray) Keefer are in the chambers of Judge Carroll (Kennedy) talking about why they want a divorce. They flashback to their courtship and marriage and the bumps they've endured along the way, and then realize they still love each other. Holliday reunited with Cukor and scriptwriters Gordon and Kanin after their triumph with "Born Yesterday." **92m/B VHS, DVD.** Judy Holliday, Aldo Ray, Madge Kennedy, Sheila Bond, John Alexander, Peggy Cass, Rex Williams; **D:** George Cukor; **W:** Ruth Gordon, Garson Kanin; **C:** Joseph Walker; **M:** Hugo Friedhofer.

The Marrying Man ♂½ **1991 (R)** Young man meets his match when his buddies take him to Las Vegas for his bachelor party. He falls like a ton of bricks for the singer, not knowing she belongs to the local crime lord, who catches them together and forces them to marry. They immediately divorce, can't forget each other and eventually re-marry, again and again and again. Silly story supposedly based on the story of Harry Karl (eventual husband of Debbie Reynolds) and Marie MacDonald. Basinger and Baldwin's off-stage romance created quite a stir but their chemistry onscreen is zilch. Ineffective, not funny, poorly paced and acted: a good example of what happens when egotistical stars get their way. **116m/C VHS, DVD.** Alec Baldwin, Kim Basinger, Robert Loggia, Armand Assante, Elisabeth Shue, Paul Reiser, Fisher Stevens, Peter Dobson, Gretchen Wyler; **D:** Jerry Rees; **W:** Neil Simon; **M:** David Newman.

Mars ♂½ **1996** Fast-paced space western finds independent lawman Caution Templar (Gruner) receiving a frantic message from his brother to return to the wild mining town of Alpha City, Mars. Only by the time he arrives his brother is dead and Templar is determined to find out what happened along the way. **92m/C VHS, DVD.** Olivier Gruner, Shari Belafonte, Scott Valentine, Amber Smith, Alex Hyde-White, Lee DeBroux, Gabriel Dell; **D:** Jon Hess; **W:** Patrick Highsmith, Steven Hartov. **VIDEO**

Mars Attacks! ♂♂½ **1996 (PG-13)** Only director Burton could make a movie based on a series of 1960s trading cards. Intentionally tacky, this huge scale epic spoof of monster, sci-fi, and disaster flicks finds moronic President Dale (Nicholson), his frigid wife (Close) and a cast of thousands battling the green-skinned invaders. Jack's back for a second role as Vegas hotel developer Art Land, who tries to cash in on the opportunities the invasion brings. Plot is relatively nonexistent and zig-zags wildly throughout, but the gist is that the aliens are bent on destroying the population, and have little trouble battling the bumbling humans. Brosnan is the hilariously deluded alien-hugger, Professor Kessler. A semi-lampoon of fellow alien flick competitor "Independence Day," this film goes all out for the camp laugh, but its big budget effects, way over-the-top style and all-star cast can't conquer the audience. **106m/C VHS, DVD.** Jack Black, Jack Nicholson, Glenn Close, Martin Short, Pierce Brosnan, Lukas Haas, Sarah Jessica Parker, Michael J. Fox, Natalie Portman, Rod Steiger, Paul Winfield, Annette Bening, Sylvia Sidney, Danny DeVito, Joe Don Baker, Pam Grier, Jim Brown, Lisa Marie; *Cameos:* Tom Jones; **C:** Peter Suschitzky; **M:** Danny Elfman.

Mars Needs Women ♂ **1966** When the Martian singles scene starts to drag, Mars boys cross the galaxy in search of fertile earth babes to help them repopulate the planet. Seems Batgirl Craig, the go-go dancing lady scientist, is at the top of their dance cards. **80m/C VHS, DVD.** Tommy Kirk, Yvonne Craig, Warren Hammack, Tony Houston, Larry Tanner, Cal Duggan; **W:** Larry Buchanan; **C:** Robert C. Jessup.

Marshal Law ♂♂ **1996 (R)** Highland and Glen is a gated community in L.A. that seems very secure, especially to ex-Texas Marshal Jack Coleman (Smits) and his family. But an earthquake leaves the neighborhood prey to a vicious gang unless Coleman can find a way to outwit them. **95m/C VHS.** Jimmy Smits, James LeGros, Vonte Sweet, Scott Plank, Kristy Swanson, Chan-

Marsha of Cedar Rock ✗
1953 Marshal Rocky Lane sets a prisoner free, thinking the guy will lead him to a stash of stolen bank funds. Seems he miscalculates, but by way of consolation, he routs a rotten railroad agent who's rooking innocent people. Features the equire talent of Black Jack. **54mnB VHS, DVD, Allan** "Rocky" Lane, Phyllis Coates, Roy Barcroft, William Henry, Robert Shayne, Eddy (Eddie, Ed) Waller; *D:* Harry Keller; *M:* Albert DeMond.

Marshal of Heldorado ✗ **1950**
An outlaw-infested town needs an injection of law and order. **53mnB VHS, James Ellison, Russel Hayden, Raymond Hatton, Fuzzy Knight; *D:* Thomas Carr.

The Marshal's Daughter ✗ **1953** A father and daughter team up to outwit an outlaw. Features many cowboy songs, including the title track by Tex Ritter. **71mnB VHS, Tex Ritter, Ken Murray, Laurie Anders, Preston Foster, Hoot Gibson; *D:* William Berke.

Martha and I ✗✗✗ **1991** In 1934 Czechoslovakia, a distinguished Jewish doctor Ernest Paul Fuchs (Piccoli), having divorced his unfaithful wife, impulsively marries the lower-class gentile German maid Martha (Sagebrecht). What turns out to be a true love match is witnessed through the adolescent eyes of nephew Emil (Chalupa), who comes to live with the couple. With the rise of Nazism and increased Jewish persecution in the devoted Martha begins to fear for her husband and makes a futile attempt to find a safe haven. Stirring drama based on the director's childhood (he's the semi-fictionalized Emil) German with subtitles. **90mnC VHS, GE Marianne Saegebrecht, Michel Piccoli, Vaclav Chalupa, Ondrej Vetchy; *D:* Jiri Weiss; *W:* Jiri Stivin. Weiss; *C:* Viktor Ruzicka; *M:* Jiri Stivin.

Martial Law ✗✗½ **1990 (R)** A film solely for martial arts fans. Two cops use their hands, feet, and other body parts to fight crime. **90mnC VHS, Chad McQueen, Cynthia Rothrock, David Carradine, Andy McCutcheon; *D: S.E. Cohen; *W:* Richard Brandes.

Martial Law 2: Undercover ✗½ **1991 (R)** Two cops, martial arts experts and part of an elite police force called Martial Law, go undercover to investigate the murder of a colleague. They uncover a fast-growing crime ring headed by a bad cop and a nightclub owner. The nightclub is host to the city's rich and powerful, who are treated to a bevy of beautiful women, protected by martial arts experts, and entertained by high-kicking action. **92mnC VHS, Jeff Wincott, Cynthia Rothrock, Paul Johansson, Evan Lurie, Charles Taylor Sherrie Rose, Billy Drago; *D:* Kurt Anderson; *W:* Richard Brandes, Jules Fitzgerald.

Martial Outlaw ✗✗ **1993 (R)** DEA man Kevin White (Wincott) has been following a drug-dealing ex-KGB kingpin from Moscow to San Francisco. The Russian's latest move takes him to Los Angeles where Kevin meets up with his older brother Jack (Hudson), a maverick LA cop. Jack persuades Kevin to let him in on the action. Jack is playing both sides and their sibling rivalry could lead to death. While Jack is starting to suspect Wincott, Gary Hudson, Richard Jaeckel, Krista Errickson, Vladimir Skomarovsky, Liliana Komorowska, Gary Wooc; *D:* Kurt Anderson; *W:* Thomas Ritz, John Bryant.

Martian Child ✗✗ **2007 (PG)** Who better to adopt orphan Dennis (Co zeman), who believes he is from Mars, than a successful science fiction writer? A two-year widower, David (Cusack) lives a relatively lonely life with his dog, a frenetic agent who's on his back to write the sequel to his successful novel, the cute friend (Peet) who could adopt a child when the kid (reality sib ng Joan Cusack). David and Dennis form the cute friend, he's drawn to Dennis's now certain that the timing is wrong, he's about to adopt a child when she died; although David's now certain that the timing is wrong, he's drawn to Dennis and patience never packs...

The Martian Chronicles: Part 1 ✗ **1979** Series episode "The Explorers." Adapted from Ray Bradbury's critically acclaimed novel. Futuristic explorations of the planet Mars. Strange tales of the discovery teams make everything more curious. **120mnC VHS, DVD, Rock Hudson, Roy Thinnes, Darren McGavin, Bernadette Peters; *D:* Michael Anderson Sr. TV

The Martian Chronicles: Part 2 ✗½ **1979** Episode following the television movie. This part is called "The Settlers." The planet Mars meets with its first Earth explode. **97mnC VHS, Rock Hudson, Fritz Weaver, Roddy McDowall, Bernie Casey, Darren McGavin, Gayle Hunnicutt, Barry Morse, Bernadette Peters; *D:* Michael Anderson Sr. TV

The Martian Chronicles: Part 3 ✗✗½ **1979** In the final chapter of this space saga, the Martian's secrets become known and will forever change man's destiny. Adapted from Ray Bradbury's classic novel. **97mnC VHS, DVD, Rock Hudson, Bernadette Peters, Christopher Connelly, Fritz Weaver, Roddy McDowall, Bernie Casey, Nicholas Hammond, Darren McGavin, Gayle Hunnicutt, Barry Morse; *D:* Michael Anderson Sr. TV

Martians Go Home! ✗½ **1990 (PG-13)** Joke-loving Martians come to earth and pester a nerdy composer. **89mnC VHS, Randy Quaid, Margaret Colin, Anita Morris, John Philbin, Ronny Cox, Gerrit Graham, Barry Sobel, Vic Dunlop; *D:* David Odell.

Martin ✗✗✗ **1977 (R)** Martin is a charming young man, though slightly mad. He freely admits the need to drink blood. Contemporary vampire has found a new abhorrent means of killing his victims. **96mnC VHS, DVD, John Amplas, Lincoln Maazel, Christine Forrest, Elayne Nadeau, Tom Savini, Sarah Venable, George A. Romero, Fran Middleton; *D:* George A. Romero; *C:* Michael Gornick; *M:* Donald Rubinstein.

Martin Chuzzlewit ✗✗½ **1994** Martin Chuzzlewit (Scofield) is a rich and elderly man with a lot of greedy relatives just waiting for him to die so they can get their hands on his money. The only exception is his grandson and his young orphaned nurse, Mary Graham. Adapted from the Charles Dickens novel. On three cassettes. **288mnC VHS, DVD, Paul Scofield, John Mills, Pete Postlethwaite, Tom Wilkinson, Julia Sawalha, David Bradley; *D:* Pedr James. TV

Martin (Hache) ✗✗✗ **1997** "Hache" means Junior, and 19-year-old Martin is named after his estranged film director-father. When the teenager accidentally overdoses after a bad break-up, his remarried mother insists her ex finally take responsibility and sends Martin to live with his dad in Madrid. Alicia, his dad's lover, and flamboyant best friend Dante try to make the boy feel welcome, but Martin Sr. is not doing his part. Spanish with subtitles. **123mnC VHS, AR SP Federico Luppi, Juan Diego Botto, Cecilia (Chela) Roth, Eusebio Poncela; *D:* Adolfo Aristarain; *W:* Adolfo Aristarain, Kathy Saavedra; *C:* Porfirio Enriquez; *M:* Eric Paez.

Martin's Day ✗✗ **1985 (PG)** An unusual friendship develops between an escaped convict and the young boy he kidnaps. **99mnC VHS, CA Richard Harris, Lindsay Wagner, James Coburn, Justin Henry, Karen Black, John Ireland; *D:* Alan Gibson; *W:* Chris Bryant, Allan Scott.

Martin Luther ✗½ **1953** French-made biography of the 16th century reformer who began the Protestant Reformation. **105mnB VHS, DVD, FR Niall MacGinnis John Ruddock, Pierre Lefevre, Guy Verney; *D:* Irving Pichel; *W:* Allan Sloane, Lothar Wolff; *C:* Joseph Brun; *M:* Mark Lothar.

Marty ✗✗½ **1955** Marty is a painfully shy bachelor who feels trapped in a pointless life of family squabbles. When he finds love, he also finds the strength to break out of what he feels is a meaningless existence. A sensitive and poignant look at the bourgeoisie to magic realism and terror—may confuse. Spanish with much of a punch, but this suitable-for-the-entire-family film is relatively charming and generally unoffending. **106mnC DVD, US John Okonedo, Oliver Platt, Joan Cusack, Anjelica Huston; *D:* Menno Meyjes; *W:* Seth Bass, Jonathan Tolins; *C:* Robert Yeoman; *M:* Aaron Zigman.

The Marx Brothers in a Nutshell ✗✗✗ **1990** A tribute to the Marx Brothers, narrated by Gene Kelly. Contains clips from "Duck Soup," "Horse Feathers," "Animal Crackers," "Cocoanuts," and "Room Service." Also contains rare outtakes and interviews with the brothers, plus guest appearances by Dick Cavett, Robert Klein, David Steinberg, and others. Indispensable. **100mnC VHS, Groucho Marx, Chico Marx, Harpo Marx, Zeppo Marx, Robert Klein, David Steinberg, Dick Cavett; *D:* Richard Patterson; *W:* Joseph Adamson; *Nar:* Gene Kelly.

Mary and Joseph: A Story of Faith ✗½ **1979** A speculative look at the experiences and courtship of Mary and Joseph before the birth of Jesus. When even her friends become victims, her father steps in to end the bloodbath. **85mnC VHS, Christina Ferrare, David Young, Helen Hughes, Colleen Dewhurst, Stephen McHattie, Lloyd Bochner, Paul Hecht; *D:* Eric Till. TV

Mary, Mary, Bloody Mary ✗ **1976 (R)** Young, beautiful artist ravages Mexico with her penchant for drinking blood. Turns out she's a bisexual vampire. **100mnC VHS, Blanche Baker, Jeff East, Colleen Dewhurst, Stephen McHattie, Lloyd Bochner, Paul Hecht; *D:* Eric Till. TV

Mary, Mother of Jesus ✗✗ **1999** The life of Jesus (Bale) is retold through the eyes of his mother (August) as her faith is tested by her son's ultimate sacrifice. The production stays close to the Biblical scripts of Matthew, Mark, Luke, and John and the characters are pretty much reverential cardboard. **94mnC VHS, DVD, Christian Bale, Pernilla August, Geraldine Chaplin, David Threlfall, Hywel Bennett, Christopher Lawford; *D:* Kevin Connor; *W:* Albert Ross; *C:* Elemer Ragalyi; *M:* Maria Klemens. TV

Mary, My Dearest ✗✗ **1983** María (Rojo) persuades her smalltime crook boyfriend Hector (Bonilla) to join her in a traveling magic show. When the van breaks down while they're touring, Maria goes in search of a telephone and winds up in a mental institution. Mixture of styles—from an everyday look at the bourgeoisie to magic realism and terror—may confuse. Spanish with

Marvin & Tige ✗✗ **1984 (PG)** A deep friendship develops between an old, alcoholic and a street-wise 11-year-old boy after they meet one night in an Atlanta park. **104mnC VHS, John Cassavetes, Gibran Brown, Billy Dee Williams, Fay Hauser, Denise Nicholas-Hill; *D:* Eric Weston; *W:* Eric Weston.

Marvin's Room ✗✗✗ **1996 (PG-13)** Guaranteed sobfest with a gifted set of performers. Sensitive spinster Bessie (Keaton) is living in Orlando where she's been caring for her bedridden father, Marvin (Cronyn), who's been dying for the last 20 years, and her eccentric aunt Ruth (Verdon). When she's stricken with leukemia and needs a bone marrow donor, Bessie must rely on tough, estranged sister Lee (Streep) to help out. But divorcee Lee's got her hands full with rebellious teenaged son Hank (DiCaprio) and his geeky younger bro Charlie (Scardino) and is none too eager to renew the family ties. Based on Scott McPherson's 1991 Off-Broadway play. **98mnC VHS, DVD, Diane Keaton, Meryl Streep, Leonardo DiCaprio, Hume Cronyn, Gwen Verdon, Hal Scardino, Robert De Niro, Dan Hedaya, Margo Martindale, Cynthia Nixon; *D:* Jerry Zaks; *W:* Scott McPherson; *C:* Piotr Sobocinski; *M:* Rachel Portman.

film from the writer of "Altered States." Remake of a TV version that originally aired in 1953. Notable for Borgnine's sensitive portrayal, one of his last quality jobs before sinking into the B-movie sludge pit. **91mnB VHS, DVD, Ernest Borgnine, Betsy Blair, Joe Mantell, Esther Minciotti, Jerry Paris, Karen Steele, Augusta Ciolli, Frank Sutton, Walter Kelley, Robin Morse; *D:* Delbert Mann; *W:* Paddy Chayefsky; *C:* Joseph LaShelle; *M:* Roy Webb, Harry Warren. Oscars '55: Actor (Borgnine), Director (Mann), Picture, Screenplay; British Acad. '55: Actor (Borgnine); Golden Globes '56: Actor—Drama (Borgnine); Natl. Bd. of Review '55: Actor (Borgnine); Natl. Film Reg. '94;; N.Y. Film Critics '55: Actor (Borgnine), Film.

Mary Poppins ✗✗✗½ **1964** Magical English nanny arrives one day on the East Wind and takes over the household of a very proper London banker. She introduces her two charges to her friends and family, including Bert, the chimney sweep (Van Dyke), and eccentric Uncle Albert (Wynn). She also changes the lives of everyone in the family. From her they learn that life can always be happy and joyous if you take the proper perspective. Film debut of Andrews. Based on the books by P.L. Travers. A Disney classic that hasn't lost any of its magic. Look for the wonderful sequence where Van Dyke dances with animated penguins. ♪Chim Chim Cheree; A Spoonful of Sugar; The Perfect Nanny; Sister Suffragette; The Life I Lead; Stay Awake; Feed the Birds; Fidelity Feduciary Bank; Let's Go Fly a Kite. **139mnC VHS, DVD, Julie Andrews, Dick Van Dyke, Ed Wynn, Hermione Baddeley, David Tomlinson, Glynis Johns, Karen Dotrice, Matthew Garber; *D:* Robert Stevenson; *M:* Richard M. Sherman, Robert B. Sherman. Oscars '64: Actress (Andrews), Film Editing, Song ("Chim Chim Cheree"), Visual FX, Orig. Score; Golden Globes '65: Actress—Mus./Comedy (Andrews).

Mary, Queen of Scots ✗✗ **1971 (PG-13)** Redgrave does a spirited job in the title role as the headstrong and romantic queen who came to an unfortunate end. Mary is raised in France by her mother's Catholic family, from whom she inherits the Scottish title after her mother's death. She claims the throne much to the dismay of her Protestant half-brother James Stuart (McGoohan) and England's equally Protestant Queen Elizabeth (Jackson), who does not want her own Catholic subjects to get any ideas. Mary makes two unfortunate marriages and winds up being betrayed, eventually forcing Elizabeth to eliminate her dangerous cousin. **128mnC VHS, Vanessa Redgrave, Glenda Jackson, Patrick McGoohan, Timothy Dalton, Nigel Davenport, Trevor Howard, Daniel Massey, Ian Holm; *D:* Charles Jarrott; *W:* John Hale; *C:* Christopher Challis; *M:* John Barry.

Mary Reilly ✗✗ **1995 (R)** Mary (Roberts) is an innocent maid whose employer happens to be the infamous Dr. Jekyll (Malkovich). They both seem to be employed by Dr. Freud in this dank, dreary psychosexual thriller. Mary is torn between the repressed affection of the doctor and the oily sexuality of his alter ego, who conjures up images of her abusive father. Reuniting the crew and cast of "Dangerous Liaisons" (Glenn Close also appears as a bawdy brothel owner), they fail to reach their previous heights. Most of the gloomy sets will make you wish you were wearing galoshes. Release date was bumped several times as the ending of the film was reshot (more than once). Based on the novel by Valerie Martin. **108mnC VHS, DVD, Julia Roberts, John Malkovich, George Cole, Michael Gambon, Kathy Staff, Glenn Close, Michael Sheen, Bronagh Gallagher, Linda Bassett, Henry Goodman, Ciaran Hinds, Sasha Hanau, David Ross; *D:* Stephen Frears; *W:* Christopher Hampton; *C:* Philippe Rousselot; *M:* George Fenton.

Mary Shelley's Frankenstein ✗✗½ **1994 (R)** Branagh turns from Shakespeare to another form of literary classic with this operatic (and loose) adaptation of the Shelley novel. He also plays Victor, the overwrought medical student who decides

Mary of Scotland ✗✗✗ **1936** The historical tragedy of Mary, Queen of Scots and her cousin, Queen Elizabeth I of England is enacted in this classic film. Traces Mary's claims to the throne of England which ultimately end in her execution. Based on the Maxwell Anderson play. **123mnB VHS, DVD, Katharine Hepburn, Fredric March, Florence Eldridge, Douglas Walton, John Carradine, Robert Barrat, Gavin Muir, Ian Keith, Moroni Olsen, William Stack, Alan Mowbray; *D:* John Ford.

Mary of Scotland subtitles. **100mnC VHS, MX Maria Rojo, Hector Bonilla, Salvador Sanchez; *D:* Jaime Humberto Hermosillo; *W:* Gabriel Garcia Marquez, Jaime Humberto Hermosillo; *C:* Angel Goded; *M:* Joaquin Gutierrez Heras.

Mary

that death can be vanquished and sets out to prove his theories by making a man. De Niro is sufficiently gristy (though lacking in pathos) as the reanimated corpse with Bonham Carter alternately suffering and excitable as Victor's fiancee Elizabeth. Visually arresting—particularly the Creature's birth scene—pic doesn't engender audience sympathy for the characters' trials and final fates. **123m/C VHS, DVD.** Kenneth Branagh, Robert De Niro, Helena Bonham-Carter, Tom Hulce, Aidan Quinn, John Cleese, Ian Holm, Richard Briers, Robert Hardy, Cherie Lunghi, Celia Imrie, Trevyn McDowell; **D:** Kenneth Branagh; **W:** Frank Darabont, Steph Lady; **C:** Roger Pratt; **M:** Patrick Doyle.

Mary White ♂♂ 1977 The true story of Mary White, the 16-year-old daughter of a newspaper editor who rejects her life of wealth and sets out to find her own identity. **102m/C VHS, DVD.** Ed Flanders, Kathleen Beller, Tim Matheson, Donald Moffat, Fionnula Flanagan; **D:** Jud Taylor; **C:** Bill Butler.

Maryam ♂♂½ 2000 High school senior Maryam (Parris) considers herself a typical New Jersey teen, circa 1979. She doesn't think much about her Iranian or Muslim heritage and works her way around some of her father's cultural strictures. But then the Iran hostage crisis provokes knee-jerk hostility from her classmates and Maryam's fundamentalist cousin in Ali (Ackert) arrives from Tehran to pursue his college studies. Maryam's father feels compelled to take in the orphaned Ali for unhappy family reasons Maryam is only learning. Ali causes tensions to rise within while Maryam and her family also try to cope with the tensions they experience in their community as the hostage crisis continues. **90m/C VHS, DVD.** Mariam Parris, David Ackert, Shaun Toub, Shohreh Aghdashloo; **D:** Ramin Serry; **W:** Ramin Serry; **M:** Ahrin Mishram.

Masada ♂♂ 1981 Based on Ernest K. Gann's novel "The Antagonists," this dramatization re-creates the 1st-century A.D. Roman siege of the fortress Masada, headquarters for a group of Jewish freedom fighters. Abridged from the original TV presentation. **131m/C VHS.** Peter O'Toole, Peter Strauss, Barbara Carrera, Anthony Quayle, Giulia Pagano, David Warner; **D:** Boris Sagal; **M:** Jerry Goldsmith.

Masala ♂½ 1991 An experiment in a variety of genres, including glitzy musical-comedy numbers, erotic fantasy sequences, and all manner of kitsch. Krishna (who both stars and directs in his feature film debut) is a violence-prone, ex-junkie still trying to recover from the deaths of his family in a plane crash as they travelled from their home in Toronto to a vacation in India. Jaffrey has multi-roles as Krishna's unscrupulous uncle and cousin as well as the blue-skinned Indian deity, Lord Krishna, who appears to an Indian grandmother on her TV set. Multicultural confusion. **105m/C VHS, DVD.** CA Srinivas Krishna, Saeed Jaffrey, Zohra Sehgal, Sakina Jaffrey; **D:** Srinivas Krishna; **W:** Srinivas Krishna.

Mascara ♂♂ 1987 (R) A group inspecting a transvestite's death are led into the seedy underground world of Belgian nightlife. **99m/C VHS.** BE Derek de Lint, Charlotte Rampling, Michael Sarrazin; **D:** Patrick Conrad.

Masculine Feminine ♂♂♂½ *Masculin Feminin* 1966 A young Parisian just out of the Army engages in some anarchistic activities when he has an affair with a radical woman singer. Hailed as one of the best French New Wave films. In French with English subtitles. **103m/B VHS, DVD.** FR Jean-Pierre Leaud, Chantal Goya, Marlene Jobert; **D:** Jean-Luc Godard. Berlin Intl. Film Fest. '66: Actor (Leaud).

M*A*S*H ♂♂♂♂ 1970 (R) Hilarious, irreverent, and well-cast black comedy about a group of surgeons and nurses at a Mobile Army Surgical Hospital in Korea. The horror of war is set in counterpoint to their need to create havoc with episodic late-night parties, practical jokes, and sexual antics. An all-out anti-war festival, highlighted by scenes that starkly uncover the chaos and irony of war, and establish Altman's influential style. Watch for

real-life football players Fran Tarkenton, Ben Davidson, and Buck Buchanan in the game. Loosely adapted from the novel by the pseudonymous Richard Hooker (Dr. H. Richard Hornberger and William Heinz). Subsequent hit TV series moved even further from the source novel. **116m/C VHS, DVD.** Carl Gottlieb, Donald Sutherland, Elliott Gould, Tom Skerritt, Sally Kellerman, JoAnn Pflug, Robert Duvall, Rene Auberjonois, Roger Bowen, Gary Burghoff, Fred Williamson, John Schuck, Bud Cort, G(eorge) Wood, David Arkin, Michael Murphy, Indus Arthur, Ken Prymus, Bobby Troup, Kim Atwood, Timothy Brown; **D:** Robert Altman; **W:** Ring Lardner Jr.; **C:** Harold E. Stine; **M:** Johnny Mandel; **V:** Sal Viscuso. Oscars '70: Adapt. Screenplay; AFI '98: Top 100; Cannes '70: Film; Golden Globes '71: Film—Mus./Comedy; Natl. Film Reg. '96; Natl. Soc. Film Critics '70: Film; Writers Guild '70: Adapt. Screenplay.

M*A*S*H: Goodbye, Farewell & Amen ♂♂♂½ 1983 The final two-hour special episode of the TV series "M*A*S*H" follows Hawkeye, B.J., Colonel Potter, Charles, Margaret, Klinger, Father Mulcahy, and the rest of the men and women of the 4077th through the last days of the Korean War, the declaration of peace, the dismantling of the camp, and the fond and tearful farewells. **120m/C VHS.** Alan Alda, Mike Farrell, Harry (Henry) Morgan, David Ogden Stiers, Loretta Swit, Jamie Farr, William (Bill) Christopher, Allan Arbus, G.W. Bailey, Rosalind Chao; **D:** Alan Alda; **W:** Alan Alda. TV

The Mask ♂♂♂ *Eyes of Hell; The Spooky Movie Show* 1961 A deservedly obscure gory horror film about a masked killer, filmed mostly in 3-D. With special 3-D packaging and limited edition 3-D glasses. **85m/B VHS.** CA Paul Stevens, Claudette Nevins, Bill Walker, Anne Collings, Martin Lavut, Leo Leyden, Bill Bryden, Eleanor Beecroft, Steven Appleby; **D:** Julian Roffman; **W:** Slavko Vorkapich, Franklin Delessert, Sandy Haver, Frank Taubes; **C:** Herbert S. Alpert; **M:** Louis Applebaum.

The Mask ♂♂♂ 1985 (PG-13) A dramatization of the true story of a young boy afflicted with craniodiaphyseal dysplasia (elephantiasis). The boy overcomes his appearance and revels in the joys of life in the California bikers' community. Well acted, particularly the performances of Stoltz and Cher. A touching film, well-directed by Bogdanovich, that only occasionally slips into maudlin territory. **120m/C VHS, DVD.** Cher, Sam Elliott, Eric Stoltz, Estelle Getty, Richard Dysart, Laura Dern, Harry Carey Jr., Lawrence Monoson, Marsha Warfield, Barry Tubb, Andrew (Andy) Robinson, Alexandra Powers; **D:** Peter Bogdanovich; **W:** Anna Hamilton Phelan; **C:** Laszlo Kovacs. Oscars '85: Makeup; Cannes '85: Actress (Cher).

The Mask ♂♂♂ 1994 (PG-13) Adolescent supernatural comedy with lollapalooza special effects is Carrey's follow-up to "Ace Ventura." Mild-mannered bank clerk Carrey discovers an ancient mask that has supernatural powers. Upon putting on the mask, he turns into one truly animated guy. He falls for a dame mixed up with gangsters and from there on, our hero deals not only with the incredible powers of the mask, but with hormones and bad guys as well. Based on the Dark Horse comic book series and originally conceived as a horror flick, director Russell, who gave Freddy Krueger a sense of humor, recast this one as a hellzapoppin' cartoon-action black comedy. Carrey's rubber face is an asset magnified by the breakthrough special effects courtesy of Industrial Light and Magic. **100m/C VHS, DVD.** Jim Carrey, Cameron Diaz, Peter Greene, Peter Riegert, Amy Yasbeck, Orestes Matacena, Richard Jeni, Ben Stein; **D:** Chuck Russell; **W:** Mike Werb; **C:** John R. Leonetti; **M:** Randy Edelman. Blockbuster '95: Comedy Actor, T. (Carrey), Female Newcomer, T. (Diaz); Blockbuster '96: Comedy Actor, V. (Carrey).

Mask of Death ♂♂♂ 1997 (R) Detective Dan McKenna's (Lamas) daughter is killed by Frank Dallio (Dunn) during the criminal's escape from the FBI and he's shot in the face by Dallio's buddy Mason, who happens to be a ringer for McKenna and conveniently dies in a car crash. Since the FBI want Dallio, Agent Jeffries (Williams) persuades McKenna to pose as Mason, which he does in order to get revenge. **125m/C VHS, DVD.** Lorenzo Lamas, Billy

Dee Williams, Rae Dawn Chong, Conrad Dunn; **D:** David Mitchell; **C:** David Pelletier; **M:** Norman Orenstein.

The Mask of Diijon ♂♂½ 1946 A mad magician suspects that his wife is cheating on him and tries to hypnotize her into killing her supposed paramour. Von Stroheim's performance makes it worthwhile. **73m/B VHS, DVD.** Erich von Stroheim, Jeanne Bates, William Wright, Edward Van Sloan, Denise Vernac; **D:** Lew Landers; **W:** Griffin Jay, Arthur St. Claire; **C:** Jack Greenhalgh; **M:** Lee Zahler.

The Mask of Dimitrios ♂♂♂ 1944 Dutch mystery writer Leyden (Lorre) is vacationing in Instanbul, where he meets a fan, Col. Haki (Katch), at a party. Haki, the head of the secret police, informs Leyden that the body of arch criminal Dimitrios Makropoulous (Scott) has washed ashore and the man was stabbed to death. Leyden decides to write a novel about the criminal and delves into a dark world of intrigue and danger. Adapted from Eric Ambler's novel "A Coffin for Dimitrios." **96m/B VHS.** Peter Lorre, Kurt Katch, Zachary Scott, Sydney Greenstreet, Faye Emerson, George Tobias, Victor Francen, Steven Geray, Florence Bates, Eduardo Ciannelli, George Metaxa, Monte Blue; **D:** Jean Negulesco; **W:** Frank Gruber; **C:** Arthur Edeson; **M:** Adolph Deutsch.

The Mask of Fu Manchu ♂♂½ 1932 The evil Dr. Fu Manchu and his equally evil daughter set out to capture the scimitar and golden mask of Genghis Khan. With them, they will be able to destroy all white men and rule the world. Although a detective from Scotland Yard tries to stop them, the pair obtain the treasures and begin sadistically torturing their victims to death. Can they be stopped before they destroy the earth? One of the creepiest entries in the Fu Manchu series, and Loy's last oriental role. Based on the novel by Sam Rohmer. **72m/B VHS.** Boris Karloff, Lewis Stone, Karen Morley, Charles Starrett, Myrna Loy, Jean Hersholt, Lawrence Grant, David Torrence; **D:** Charles Brabin; **C:** Gaetano Antonio "Tony" Gaudio.

Mask of the Dragon ♂ 1951 A soldier's friend and girlfriend track down his killer after he delivers a golden curio to a shop in Los Angeles. **54m/B VHS, DVD.** Richard Travis, Sheila Ryan, Richard Emory, Jack Reitzen, Sid Melton, Michael Whalen, Lyle Talbot; **W:** Orville H. Hampton; **C:** Jack Greenhalgh.

The Mask of Zorro ♂♂♂ *Zorro* 1998 (PG-13) The dashing masked swordsman, who first made an appearance in a 1919 newspaper comic, returns to the big screen. Aging Zorro (Hopkins) escapes from 20 years in prison when he discovers his mortal enemy, Montero (Wilson) is looking to establish an independent republic of California. But he needs some help and picks bandit Alejandro (Banderas), who needs a lot of training. Caught in the middle is Elena (Zeta Jones), a spirited beauty who was raised by Montero (Wilson) and doesn't know she's really Zorro's daughter. She wields quite a mean sword herself as Alejandro learns before any romancing can begin. A little long but offering swashbuckling fun. **136m/C VHS, DVD, UMD.** Antonio Banderas, Anthony Hopkins, Catherine Zeta-Jones, Stuart Wilson, Matt Letscher, Maury Chaykin, Tony Amendola, Pedro Armendariz Jr., L.Q. Jones; **D:** Martin Campbell; **W:** Ted Elliott, Terry Rossio, John Eskow; **C:** Phil Meheux; **M:** James Horner.

Masked and Anonymous ♂ 2003 (PG-13) For hard-core Dylan fans only. He may be the only reason to see this one. The abundant, muddled meanderings about fame, life, politics and the like sure aren't. Co-written and starring the enigmatic folk legend, the tenuous threads of a plot have Dylan as a has-been musical legend who's been sprung from jail by rock promoter Uncle Sweetheart (Goodman) and partner Nina Veronica (Lange) for a dubious benefit concert in a post-revolutionary, America-like country. Dylan is then given a chance to croon, and his fans. A host of big-names drop in for walk-ons and seeming improv performances. **113m/C VHS, DVD.** US GB Bob Dylan, Jeff Bridges, Penelope Cruz, John Goodman, Jessica

Lange, Luke Wilson, Angela Bassett, Bruce Dern, Ed Harris; **D:** Larry Charles; **W:** Rene Fontaine, Sergei Perov; **C:** Rogier Stoffers; **M:** Bob Dylan.

The Masked Marvel ♂♂ 1943 *The Masked and the Masked Marvel* The Masked Marvel saves America's war industries from sabotage. Serial in 12 episodes. **195m/B VHS.** William Forrest, Louise Currie, Johnny Arthur; **D:** Spencer Gordon Bennet.

The Masked Rider ♂♂½ 1941 Drifters Brown and Knight head south of the border and find themselves trying to solve crimes committed by a mysterious masked rider. Latin American dancers and singers provide a nice change of pace from the usual cowpoke musical relief. Based on a story by Sam Robins. **57m/B VHS.** Johnny Mack Brown, Fuzzy Knight, Nell O'Day, Grant Withers; **D:** Ford Beebe; **W:** Sherman Lowe, Victor McLeod.

Masks of Death ♂♂ 1986 New adventure for Sherlock Holmes, as he is pulled from retirement to find the murderer of three unidentified corpses found in London's East End. **80m/C VHS.** Peter Cushing, John Mills, Anne Baxter, Ray Milland; **D:** Roy Ward Baker.

Maslin Beach WOOF! 1997 Hmmm, if this flick was intended as some sort of romantic comedy, it failed. Of course, probably having a coherent script and a cast who could do more than appear comfortable nude (or in minimal beach attire) would have helped too. Yep, the titular beach is a real nudist beach in South Australia where these characters bare their bodies as they look for love or sex or friendship or something. The Hound hopes they used lots of sunscreen. **80m/C VHS, DVD.** AU Garry Waddell, Bonnie-Jaye Lawrence, Michael Allen, Eliza Lovell; **D:** Wayne Groom; **W:** Wayne Groom; **C:** Rodney Bolton; **M:** Robert Kral.

Mason of the Mounted ♂♂ 1932 Harmless enough western in which a Canadian Mountie tracks down a murderer in the U.S. **58m/B VHS.** Bill Cody, Nancy Drexel, Art Mix, Nelson McDowell; **D:** Harry Fraser.

Masque of the Red Death ♂♂♂ 1965 An integral selection in the famous Edgar Allan Poe/Roger Corman canon, it deals with an evil prince who traffics with the devil and playfully murders any of his subjects not already dead of the plague. Remade in 1989 with Corman as producer. **88m/C VHS, DVD.** GB Vincent Price, Hazel Court, Jane Asher, Patrick Magee, David Weston, Nigel Green, Julian Burton, Skip Martin, Gaye Brown, John Westbrook; **D:** Roger Corman; **W:** Charles Beaumont, Robert W(right) Campbell; **C:** Nicolas Roeg; **M:** David Lee.

Masque of the Red Death ♂½ 1989 (R) Roger Corman's second attempt at Edgar Allan Poe's horror tale pales compared to his Vincent Price version made 25 years earlier. Under-aged cast adds youth appeal but subtracts credibility from the fable of a sadistic prince and his sycophants trying to ignore the plague outside castle walls. Only late in the plot does veteran actor Macnee add proper note of doom. **90m/C VHS.** Patrick Macnee, Jeffery Osterhage, Adrian Paul, Tracy Reiner, Maria Ford, Clare Hoak; **D:** Larry Brand; **W:** Larry Brand, Daryl Haney; **C:** Edward Pei; **M:** Mark Governor.

Masque of the Red Death ♂♂♂ 1990 (R) Unrecognizable Poe mutation has guests invited to be murdered by an unknown stalker. One scene features a pendulum, and that's it for literary faithfulness. **94m/C VHS.** Frank Stallone, Brenda Vaccaro, Herbert Lom, Michelle McBride, Christine Lunde; **D:** Alan Birkinshaw.

Masquerade ♂♂♂ 1988 (R) A lonely young heiress meets a handsome "nobody" with a mysterious background and it is love at first sight. The romance distresses everyone in the circle of the elite because they assume she's after her money and not her love. At first it seems decidedly so, then definitely not, and then nothing is certain. A real romantic thriller, with wonderful scenes of the Hamptons. **91m/C VHS, DVD.** Rob Lowe, Meg Tilly, John Glover, Kim Cattrall, Doug Savant, Dana Delany,

Mass Appeal ♂♂ 1984 (PG) An adaptation of the Bill C. Davis play about the ideological debate between a young seminarian and a complacent but successful parish pastor. Lemmon has had better roles and done better acting. **99m/C VHS.** *D:* Glenn Jordan; *W:* Bill Davis; *M:* Bill Conti.

Massacre ♂½ 1934 That would be what the cavalry frequently did to the Indians. Joe Thunder Horse (miscast Barthelmess) is a Sioux who has been appearing in a Wild West show. He learns his father is dying and returns to the reservation, only to see how his people have been mistreated by the corrupt agents of the Bureau of Indian Affairs. So he goes to Washington to protest. **70m/B VHS.** Richard Barthelmess, Ann Dvorak, Dudley Digges, Sidney Toler, Claire Dodd, Henry O'Neill, Robert Barrat, Arthur Hohl; *D:* Alan Crosland; *W:* Ralph Block, Sheridan Gibney; *C:* George Barnes.

Massacre at Central High ♂♂½ 1976 (R) A new student takes matters into his own hands when gang members harass other students at a local high school. Other than some silly dialogue, this low-budget production is a bit above average. **85m/C VHS, DVD.** Derrel Maury, Andrew Stevens, Kimberly Beck, Robert Carradine, Roy Underwood, Steve Bond, Steve Sikes, Lani O'Grady, Damon Douglas, Cheryl "Rainbeaux" Smith; *D:* Renee Daalder; *W:* Renee Daalder; *C:* Bert Van Munster.

Massacre in Dinosaur Valley ♂½ 1985 A dashing young paleontologist and his fellow explorers go on a perilous journey down the Amazon on a search of the Valley of the Dinosaur. **98m/C VHS, DVD.** /T Milton Morris, Marta Anderson, Michael Sopkiw, Suzanne Carvali; *D:* Michael Tarantini; *W:* Michael Tarantini; *C:* Edson Batista.

Massacre in Rome ♂♂½ 1973 (PG) A priest opposes a Nazi colonel's plan to execute Italian civilians in retaliation for the deaths of 33 German soldiers. Strong drama based on a real event. **110m/C VHS, DVD.** Richard Burton, Marcello Mastroianni, Leo McKern, John Steiner, Anthony Steel; *D:* Gary Graver; *W:* George P. Cosmatos; *M:* Ennio Morricone.

Massive Retaliation ♂ 1985 Hordes of pesky villagers seek refuge within the secluded safety of a family's country house as WWIII approaches. **90m/C VHS, DVD.** Tom Bower, Peter Donat, Karlene Crockett, Jason Gedrick, Michael Pritchard; *D:* Thomas A. Cohen.

Masseuse ♂ 1995 (R) Kristy (Drew) decides to get back at cheating fiance Jack (Abell), who's out of town on a business trip by turning their house into a massage parlor. **90m/C VHS, DVD.** Griffin (Griffen) Drew, Monique Parent, Tim Abell, Brinke Stevens; *D:* Daniel Peters; *M:* Paul Di Franco.

Master and Commander: The Far Side of the World ♂♂♂♂ 2003 (PG-13) Captain Jack Aubrey (Crowe) is the relentless commander of the HMS Surprise of the British navy, whose mission is to capture and destroy the Acheron, a much superior and larger French ship. Among the crew is best friend Maturin (Bettany), the ship's surgeon who serves as a quiet balance to Aubrey's fiery man of action. Epic contains some of the most spectacular naval battles ever filmed, but pays close attention to the relationships and respect that are forged in such extreme living conditions. Crowe does a brilliant job showcasing Aubrey's leadership and poise in battle, while Bettany takes a back seat to no one. Based on ries by Patrick O'Brien. **139m/C VHS, DVD.** Blu-ray Disc. US Russell Crowe, Paul Bettany, Billy Boyd, Max Pirkis, James D'Arcy, Mark Lewis Jones, Chris Larkin, Richard Woodall, Ian Mercer, Max Benitz; *D:* Peter Weir; *W:* Peter Weir, John Collee; *C:* Russell Boyd; *M:* Christopher Gordon, Iva Davies, Richard Tognetti. Oscars '03: Cinematog., Sound FX Editing.

Master Blaster ♂♂ 1985 (R) Friendly game of survival with paintball guns goes awry when one of the contestants exchanges the play guns for deadly weapons. **94m/C VHS.** Jeff Moldovan, Donna Rosae, Joe Hess, Peter Lunblad, Robert Goodman, Richard St. George, George Gill; *D:* Glenn R. Wilder; *W:* Glenn R. Wilder, Randy Ginter Jr., Jeff Moldovan; *C:-F.* Pershing Flynn; *M:* Alain Salvati.

Master of Disguise ♂½ 2002 (PG) This disjointed patchwork of lame comedy routines tries to masquerade as "family friendly" entertainment, but is revealed to be a mess that kids may tolerate by flatulent criminal Devlin Bowman (Spiner) who kidnaps Fabbrizio. So Pistachio (Carvey) is a waiter at his father Fabbrizio's (Brolin) restaurant, where he displays a talent for mimicking all the customers. Turns out this is a family legacy, coveted and parents will hate. Pistachio Disguisey has to get together, rescue dad, and defeat Devlin. There is no saving the movie, however. Running time is actually padded with 15 minutes of credits and outtakes. **80m/C VHS, DVD.** US Dana Carvey, Jennifer Esposito, Brent Spiner, James Brolin, Edie McClurg, Harold Gould, Maria Canals, Austin Wolf; *D:* Perry Andelin Blake; *W:* Dana Carvey, Harris Goldberg; *C:* Peter Lyons Collister; *M:* Marc Ellis.

Master of Dragonard Hill ♂½ 1989 A low-rent swashbuckling romance-novel pastiche. **92m/C VHS.** Oliver Reed, Eartha Kitt; *W:* R.J. Marx.

Master of the House ♂♂♂ 1925 Story of a spoiled husband, a type extinct in this country but still in existence abroad. Silent with titles in English. **107m/B VHS. CZ** Johannes Meyer, Astrid Holm, Mathilde Nielsen, Karin Nellemose; *D:* Carl Theodor Dreyer; *W:* Carl Theodor Dreyer; *C:* George Schneevoigt.

Master of the World ♂♂½ 1961 Visionary tale of a fanatical 19th century inventor who uses his wondrous flying fortress as an antiwar weapon. Adapted from "Robur, the Conqueror" and "Master of the World," both by Jules Verne. **95m/C VHS, DVD.** Vincent Price, Charles Bronson, Henry Hull; *D:* William Witney; *W:* Richard Matheson; *M:* Les Baxter.

Master Harold and the Boys ♂♂♂ 1984 Stagey cable presentation of South African Athol Fugard's play about relationship between white man and two black servants. Occasionally provocative. **90m/C VHS.** John Kani, Zakes Mokae, Matthew Broderick; *D:* Michael Lindsay-Hogg; *W:* Athol Fugard.

Master Key ♂♂½ 1944 Federal agents battle Nazis in this action-packed 12-chapter serial. **169m/B VHS, DVD.** Milburn Stone, Lash LaRue, Dennis Moore; *D:* Ray Taylor, Lewis D. Collins.

Master Mind ♂♂ 1973 A renowned Japanese super sleuth attempts to solve the theft of a sophisticated midget android. **86m/C VHS.** Zero Mostel, Keiko Kishi, Bradford Dillman, Frankie Sakai; *D:* Alex March.

Master Minds ♂½ 1949 The Bowery Boys run into trouble when Hall gets a toothache and can suddenly predict the future. He takes a job at a carnival where a mad scientist wants to transplant his brain into that of a monster ape man. **64m/ B VHS.** Leo Gorcey, Huntz Hall, Glenn Strange, Gabriel Dell, Alan Napier, William Benedict, Bennie Bartlett, David Gorcey; *D:* Jean Yarbrough.

The Master of Ballantrae ♂♂ 1953 Flynn plays James Durrisdear, the heir to a Scottish title, who gets involved in a rebellion with Bonnie Prince Charlie against the English crown. When the rebellion fails, Flynn heads for the West Indies where he and his partner amass quite a fortune through piracy. Flynn eventually returns to Scotland to claim the fate that his brother has taken over his title as well as his longtime love. Based on the novel by Robert Louis Stevenson. Flynn's riotous buckling days, as this film unfortunately demonstrates. **89m/C VHS, DVD.** Errol Flynn, Roger Livesey, Anthony Steel, Beatrice Campbell, Yvonne Furneaux, Jacques Berthier, Felix Aylmer, Mervyn Johns; *D:* William Keighley; *C:* Jack Cardiff.

Master Race ♂♂½ 1944 Absorbing cautionary tale of a German officer who escapes retribution when the Nazis collapse, continuing to hold control over the inhabitants of a small town through intimidation. **98m/B VHS.** George Coulouris, Lloyd Bridges, Osa Massen, Nancy Gates, Stanley Ridges; *D:* Herbert Biberman; *W:* Herbert Biberman.

Master Spy: The Robert Hanssen Story ♂½ 2002 (R) Drawn-out drama that finds FBI agent Robert Hanssen (Hurt), deeply in debt and frustrated by his lack of career advancement, selling documents to the KGB. Hanssen's so low-key he would be completely uninteresting if not for a couple of personal quirks: he likes to take naughty photos of his deeply devoted wife Bonnie (Parker) and pass them along to best buddy Jack (Strathairn) and he has a platonic relationship with stripper Priscilla (Pace), who becomes Hanssen's confidante. **122m/C VHS, DVD.** William Hurt, Mary-Louise Parker, David Strathairn, Hill Pace, Ron Silver, Wayne Knight, Peter Boyle; *D:* Lawrence Schiller; *W:* Norman Mailer; *C:* Alan Caso; *M:* Laurence Rosenthal. TV.

Master Touch ♂½ 1974 (PG) When Minds: Un Uomo da Rispettare 1974 (PG) When a legendary safecracker is released from prison, he attempts one last heist at a deadly 'snake fist' technique against the bad guys. Chan's first feature is an abominable low-budget flick which, reportedly, sat on a shelf until he became a star. Then it was re-edited and footage of a double was inserted. **83m/C VHS, DVD. HK** Jackie Chan; *D:* Chin Hsin.

Mastergate ♂♂♂½ 1992 Satire on mass media and the government features in one of the highest-grossing martial arts movies of all time, Jackie Chan uses the secret arms deal with Central American revolutionaries. Masterful dialogue fuels this thinly-veiled spoof of the Iran-Contra hearings. **90m/C VHS.** Richard Kiley, David Ogden Stiers, Ed Begley Jr., Bruno Kirby, Tim Reid, Marcia Strassman, Ken Howard, Dennis McGavin, James Coburn, Burgess Meredith, Buck Henry, Noriyuki "Pat" Morita, Ron Vawter, Louis Giambalvo; *D:* Michael Engler; *M:* Larry Gelbart.

Master with Cracked Fingers *Snake Fist Fighter* 1971 (R) In one of the highest-grossing martial arts movies of all time, Jackie Chan uses the deadly 'snake fist' technique against the bad guys. Chan's first feature is an abominable low-budget flick which, reportedly, sat on a shelf until he became a star. Then it was re-edited and footage of a double was inserted. **83m/C VHS, DVD. HK** Jackie Chan; *D:* Chin Hsin.

Masterminds ♂♂½ 1996 (PG-13) Mildly diverting actioner has teen troublemaker Ozzie (Kartheiser) once again on security analyst Ralph Bentley (Stewart) puts his plan in motion, taking control of the school and asking a ransom for a group of the wealthiest children. But the ingenious Ozzie's lurking about to get the best of the adults. **105m/C VHS.** Vincent Kartheiser, Patrick Stewart, Brenda Fricker, Matt Craven, Bradley Whitford, Annabelle Gurwitch, Katie Stuart, Callum Keith Rennie, Michael MacRae, Earl Pastko, Michael Sirrns, Jon Abrahams; *D:* Roger Christian; *W:* Floyd Byars; *C:* Nic Morris; *M:* Anthony Marinelli.

Masters of Horror: Cigarette Burns 2005 Repertory theater owner Kirby Sweetman searches for "Le Fin Absolue du Monde," the rare film collector. The film is believed to be destroyed after its only showing caused viewers to become homicidal, cannibalistic maniacs. As Kirby Sweetman searches for "Le Fin Absolue du Monde," a type extinct in this country but still in existence abroad. Silent 1989 A low-rent swashbuckling romance-novel pastiche. As Reeves and violent depravities. Star and writer Stephen Weber adapted the script from a short story by Bruce Jones. **59m/C DVD.** Steven Weber, Brenda James, Harris Allan, Beau Starr, Carrie Fleming; *D:* Dario Argento; *W:* Steven Weber; *M:* Claudio Simonetti.

Masters of Horror: Homecoming 2005 In an attempt to finally bring the Iraq war to an end, veteran zombie soldiers rise up to vote the president out of office. Unable to say the zombies die on their own after casting their ballots in this satire of the war on terrorism. **59m/C DVD.** Jon Tenney, Thea Gill, Wanda Cannon, Terry David Mulligan, Robert Picardo; *D:* Joe Dante.

Masters of Horror: Imprint 2005 An American returns to an eerie Japanese island bordello in search of a girl he lost long ago. The prostitute he meets there has many stories to share, laced with incest, abortion, murder, and torture in one of the most grisly "Masters of Horror" productions. **63m/C DVD.** Billy Drago, Youki Kudoh, Toshie Negishi, Michie Ito, Shino Marumi; *D:* Takashi Miike.

Masters of Horror: Jenifer 2005 One of the most eerily stomach-flipping installments of the "Masters of Horror" centers on a police detective who saves a young girl with a luscious body but face that has been horribly disfigured by homicidal lunatic. He takes responsibility for the mentally challenged orphan and begins to 'realize she is a creature of secret carnal pleasures and violent depravities. **59m/C DVD.** Steven Weber, Carrie Fleming; *D:* Dario Argento; *W:* Bruce Jones.

Masters of Horror: Pelts 2006 A sleazy furrier obsessed with a lesbian stripper sets out to make her a coat from the finest furs he can obtain. His trapper comes through with some beautiful raccoon skins that unbeknownst to him are magical guardians of a lost raccoon city whereby all associated with their deaths effects. **59m/C DVD.** Norman Reedus, Udo Kier; *D:* John Carpenter.

Masters of Horror: Deer Woman 2006 Detective Dwight Faraday is seduced into a case involving the murder of several men killed while at the height of sexual arousal and found trampled into hamburger by what appear to be hoof marks. Each of the men was last seen in the company of a mysteriously sexy Native American woman. **59m/C DVD.** Anthony Griffith, Brian Benben, Cinthia Moura; *D:* John Landis.

Masters of Horror: Dream Cruise 2007 An American businessman working in Japan is having an affair with Eiji Saito. When the three embark on a cruise together, it turns into terror on the high seas. **87m/C DVD.** Daniel Gillies, Ryo Ishibashi, Yoshino Kimura; *D:* Norio Tsuruta.

Masters of Horror: Dreams in the Witch House 2005 A stressed-out graduate student rents a room in an old boarding house and starts to experience nightmares about a rapacious 'rat thinks he's being seduced by a she-devil. Based on a short story by H.P. Lovecraft. **59m/C DVD.** Jay Brazeau, Ezra Godden, Chelah Horsdal; *D:* Stuart Gordon.

Masters of Horror: Fair Haired Child 2006 A psychotic couple kidnap the virgin Tara and hold her in an old basement for a sacrifice to their locked basement for a sacrifice to bring their drowned son back from the dead. Child Johnny is mute and communicates through scribbling in the dirt his guilt over living at the expense of others. **59m/C DVD.** Lori Petty, Lindsay Pulsipher, Jesse Haddock; *D:* William Malone; *W:* Matt Greenberg.

Masters of Horror: Family 2005 George Wendt plays a groomed-lawn, sweater-vest-wearing suburbanite who is by true nature a bloodthirsty serial killer, kidnapping and mutilating strangers in order to put together his own perfect nuclear family. **58m/C DVD.** George Wendt, Meredith Monroe, Matt Keeslar, Haley Guiel, Kerry Sandomirsky; *D:* John Landis; *W:* Brent Hanley.

are cursed with the desire to commit gory suicides. **55m/C DVD.** John Saxon, Meat Loaf Aday, Ellen Ewusie, Link Baker, Brenda McDonald; **D:** Dario Argento.

Masters of Horror: Pro-Life 2005 After being raped by the Devil, 15-year old Angelique seeks an abortion at a local clinic. Believing his daughter is about to birth God's child, the right wing Christian father guns his way into the operating room as doctors discover they are unable to exterminate the evil spawn. **57m/C DVD.** Caitlin Wachs, Ron Perlman, Emmanuelle Vaugier, Mark Feuerstein, John Carpenter.

Masters of Horror: Right to Die 2007 A couple is involved in a fiery car wreck late one night, leaving her hideously burned and comatose, while he remains unscathed. The family enters into great debate about whether to pull the plug while her spirit goes on a vengeful rampage against her philandering husband, the heartless money-grubbing lawyer, and others looking to profit from her plight. **58m/C DVD.** Martin Donovan, Anna Galvin, Corbin Bernsen, Julie Anderson, Robin Sydney; **D:** Rob Schmidt.

Masters of Horror: Sick Girl 2006 The life of a shy entomologist changes dramatically after the arrival of a large, mysterious bug and the beginning of a steamy affair with a sexy lesbian. As the women enters into their relationship one of them is bitten by the bug and begins to undergo a metamorphosis that is emotional at first but then escalates to horrific mutation and eventually murder. **60m/C DVD.** Angela Bettis, Jesse Hlubik, Misty Mundae, Marcia Bennett, Mike McKee; **D:** Lucky McKee.

Masters of Horror: Sounds Like 2006 Office drone Larry Pearce is suffering after the loss of his young son. This excruciating grief triggers his acute sense of hearing allowing him to hear whispered conversations from hundreds of feet away, leading to the slow and tragic decline of his sanity. **58m/C DVD.** Chris Bauer, Laura Margolis, David Pearson, Richard Kahan, Michael Daingerfield; **D:** Brad Anderson.

Masters of Horror: The Screwfly Solution 2006 Adaptation of the 1977 short story written by James Tiptree wherein men are suddenly brutally attacking women when they become sexually aroused. As scientists Jason Priestley and Elliott Gould work to remedy the situation it quickly escalates into a global epidemic, leaving women and children to fend for their lives in a world that wants to eliminate them. **60m/C DVD.** Jason Priestley, Elliott Gould, Kerry Norton, Linda Darlow, Brenna O'Brien, Steve Lawlor; **D:** Joe Dante; **W:** Sam Hamm.

Masters of Horror: The V Word 2005 Two college students enter a mortuary in the middle of the night to view the body of a dead bully. The bully awakens and attacks one boy, turning him into a semi-vampire who then goes after his friend. The friends then band together against their collective foe. **59m/C DVD.** Michael Ironside, Jodelle Ferland, Arjay Smith, Branden Nadon; **D:** Ernest R. Dickerson.

Masters of Horror: The Washingtonians 2007 Based on Bentley Little's short story, this black humor-ish tale presents the exploits of a group of cannibals that have existed since the beginning of America. **58m/C DVD.** Johnathon Schaech, Venus Terzo, Myron Natwick, Duncan Fraser, Julia Tortolano; **D:** Peter Medak.

Masters of Horror: Valerie on the Stairs 2006 A haunted writer moves into a community that houses a crazed creature who is holding a beautiful young woman as his sexual prisoner in this tale based on a Clive Barker story. **60m/C DVD.** Tyron Leitso, Christopher Lloyd, Nicola Lipman, Jonathan Watton, Christine Barrie; **D:** Mick Garris.

Masters of Horror: We All Scream for Ice Cream 2007 A group of ill-reputed youths play a prank on a mentally-challenged ice cream truck driver that results in his accidental death. Years later the maniac zombie clown returns to take revenge on the now grown-up pranksters. **57m/C DVD.** William Forsythe, Colin Cunningham, Tim Henry, Ingrid Tesch, Spencer Achtymichuk; **D:** Tom Holland.

The Masters of Menace 🐾🐾1/2 1990 (PG-13) The men in blue are mighty miffed when a bunch of bikers break parole to pay their last respects to a comrade in leather. Comic bits by Candy, Belushi, Aykroyd and Wendt provide little relief. **97m/C VHS.** David Rasche, Catherine Bach, Dan Aykroyd, James Belushi, John Candy, George Wendt, Tino Insana; **D:** Daniel Raskov; **W:** Tino Insana.

Masters of the Universe 🐾🐾1/2 1987 (PG) A big-budget live-action version of the cartoon character's adventures, with He-Man battling Skeletor for the sake of the universe. **109m/C VHS, DVD.** Dolph Lundgren, Frank Langella, Billy Barty, Courteney Cox, Meg Foster; **D:** Gary Goddard; **W:** David Odell; **C:** Hanania Baer; **M:** Bill Conti.

Masters of Venus 🐾🐾1/2 1962 Eight-part serial about spaceships, space maidens and the like. **121m/B VHS.** GB Norman Woolland, Robin Stewart, Mandy Harper, Ferdinand "Ferdy" Mayne; **D:** Ernest Morris; **W:** Michael Barnes; **C:** Reg Wyer; **M:** Eric Rogers.

Master's Revenge 🐾1/2 1971 When a girl is kidnapped by a violent motorcycle gang, martial artists are called in to rescue her. Originally released as "Devil Rider." **78m/C VHS.** Sharon Mahon, Ridgely Abele, Johnny Pacheco; **D:** Brad Grinter; **W:** Brad Grinter; **C:** Barry Mahon; **M:** Gil Wood.

Mata Hari 🐾🐾🐾 1932 During WWI, a lovely German spy steals secrets from the French through her involvement with two military officers. Lavish production and exquisite direction truly make this one of Garbo's best. Watch for the exotic pseudo-strip tease. **90m/B VHS, DVD.** Greta Garbo, Ramon Novarro, Lionel Barrymore, Lewis Stone, C. Henry Gordon, Karen Morley, Alec B. Francis; **D:** George Fitzmaurice; **C:** William H. Daniels.

Mata Hari 🐾🐾 1985 (R) Racy, adventure-prone story of WWI's most notorious spy, Mata Hari, who uses her seductive beauty to seduce the leaders of Europe. Stars "Emmanuelle" Kristel. **105m/C VHS, DVD.** Sylvia Kristel, Christopher Cazenove, Oliver Tobias, Gaye Brown, Gottfried John; **D:** Curtis Cunningham.

Matador 🐾🐾1/2 1986 Bizarre, entertaining black comedy about a retired matador who finds a new way to satiate his desire to kill. He meets his match in an equally deadly woman and the two are drawn closer together by a young bullfighting student who confesses to a series of murders. Not for all tastes, but fine for those who like the outrageous. In Spanish with English subtitles. **90m/C VHS.** SP Assumpta Serna, Antonio Banderas, Nacho Martinez, Eva Cobo, Carmen Maura, Julieta Serrano, Chus (Maria Jesus) Lampreave, Julia Ponce; **D:** Pedro Almodovar; **W:** Pedro Almodovar, Jesus Ferrere; **C:** Angel Luis Fernandez; **M:** Bernardo Bonezzi.

The Matador 🐾🐾🐾 2006 (R) Quirky black comedy stars Brosnan as a veteran hitman with a case of the yips. Boorish, drunken Julian Noble meets desperate businessman Danny Wright (Kinnear) in a Mexico City bar and the unlikely duo become increasingly simpatico. After botching two assignments, Julian needs his only friend Danny's help in fulfilling his last-chance contract. The men are complemented by Davis' portrayal of Danny's devoted wife, Carolyn, who's titillated by Julian's fatal attractions. **96m/C DVD, HD DVD.** US Pierce Brosnan, Greg Kinnear, Hope Davis, Philip Baker Hall, Dylan Baker, Adam Scott; **D:** Richard Shepard; **W:** Richard Shepard; **C:** David Tattersall; **M:** Rolfe Kent.

The Match 🐾🐾1/2 1999 (PG-13) The small Scottish Highland village of Inverdoune has a very important soccer match on its collective minds. It's the annual grudge match with Le Bistro against rival pub Benny's Bar. Benny's has lost all previous 99 matches and, according to an ancient wager, if they lose the 100th match, Le Bisto can shut them down for good. So it's up to eccentric milkman Wullie (Beesley) to save the day. Predictable but filled with eccentric characters and a lot of heart. **96m/C VHS.** GB Max Beesley, James Cosmo, Laura Fraser, Isla Blair, Richard E. Grant, Ian Holm, Neil Morrissey, David Hayman, Bill Paterson, David O'Hara, Iain Robertson, Tom Sizemore; Cameos: Pierce Brosnan; **D:** Mick Davis; **W:** Mick Davis; **C:** Witold Stok; **M:** Harry Gregson-Williams.

The Match Factory Girl 🐾🐾🐾 Tulitikkutehtaan Tytto 1990 Kaurismak's final segment of his "working class" trilogy. Iris, a plain, shy outsider shares a drab dwelling with her one-dimensional mother and stepfather, works in a match factory, and hopes desperately for romantic love. Her world is transformed when the extraordinary occurs—she spots a brightly colored party dress in a shop window, buys it, wears it to a bar, and meets the Scandinavian creep who will soon get her pregnant and dump her. Angry at the world, Iris seeks revenge, and in so doing the audience learns that she has become very real and human. Kaurismaki makes his point that beauty can exist in ugly places. In Finnish with English subtitles. **70m/C VHS.** SW FI Kati Outinen, Elina Salo, Esko Nikkari, Vesa Vierikko; **D:** Aki Kaurismaki; **W:** Aki Kaurismaki.

Match Point 🐾🐾1/2 2005 (R) Brilliantly Allen-esque—full of layers and complexities—but with a new setting, new scenery, and some new players too. Allen ventures far from his usual cinematic haunts, all the way to London, where gorgeous, tortured social-climbers find themselves torn apart by lust, morality, and class divisions. Chris Wilton (Rhys-Meyers), a former tennis pro of modest means, is introduced to high society through the wealthy family of his pal Tom Hewett (Goode). He soon hooks up with Tom's sister Chloe (Mortimer), but Chris' tryst with Tom's smoldering American girlfriend (Johansson) sets the scene for good old-fashioned murder. Light on the laughs, but hasn't been this thrilling in years. **124m/C DVD.** Scarlett Johansson, Jonathan Rhys Meyers, Emily Mortimer, Matthew Goode, Brian Cox, Penelope Wilton, Ewen Bremner, James Nesbitt, Rupert Penry-Jones, Margaret Tyzack; **D:** Woody Allen; **W:** Woody Allen; **C:** Remi Adefarasin.

The Matchmaker 🐾🐾🐾 1958 An adaptation of the Thornton Wilder play concerning two young men in search of romance in 1884 New York. Later adapted as "Hello Dolly." An amusing diversion. **101m/B VHS, DVD.** Shirley Booth, Anthony Perkins, Shirley MacLaine, Paul Ford, Robert Morse, Perry Wilson, Wallace Ford, Russell Collins, Rex Evans, Gavin Gordon, Torben Meyer; **D:** Joseph Anthony; **W:** John Michael Hayes; **C:** Charles B(ryant) Lang Jr.

The Matchmaker 🐾🐾1/2 1997 (R) Big city girl Marcy (Garofalo) heads to a wee quaint Ireland burgh where she finds love and humanity amid the beer-guzzling, blarney-slinging locals. Jaded aide to a politico spin doctor (Leary), Marcy is there to track down some McGlory's, the Irish relatives of an American senator, in order to help his re-election campaign but hits town during the annual matchmaking festival and becomes the target of Irish marriage broker O'Shea. O'Hara is Sean, Marcy's laconic and appealing local suitor. Entertaining enough, with Garofalo and O'Hara more than filling the bill in a romantic comedy that heavily flirts with cliche. Sweeping vistas and a soundtrack appropriately filled with Irish favorites, old and new. Filmed in the village of Roundstone, Ireland. **97m/C VHS, DVD.** Janeane Garofalo, Milo O'Shea, David O'Hara, Denis Leary, Jay O. Sanders, Rosaleen Linehan, Maria Doyle Kennedy, Saffron Burrows, Paul Hickey, Jimmy Keogh; **D:** Mark Joffe; **W:** Louis Nowra, Karen Janszen, Graham Linehan, Greg Dinner; **C:** Ellery Ryan; **M:** John Altman.

Matchstick Men 🐾🐾🐾1/2 2003 (PG-13) Roy (Cage) is a small time con man suffering from a host of psychological tics, including obsessive-compulsive disorder, who's urged by his longtime partner (Rockwell) into a "really big score." Enter a teenage daughter, Angela (Lohman), he never knew. While Roy occasionally displays a kind of smug pride in his work as a con "artist," being with the ever-more-present Angela causes Roy to admit that he actually has little to be truly proud of. Cage is at the top of his game, and he and Rockwell play off each other perfectly, while Lohman proves a worthy co-star as well. Director Scott mixes just the right amounts of comedy, drama, and suspense. Adapted from the novel by Eric Garcia. **120m/C VHS, DVD.** US Nicolas Cage, Alison Lohman, Sam Rockwell, Bruce Altman, Bruce McGill, Sheila Kelley, Beth Grant, Steve Eastin; **D:** Ridley Scott; **W:** Ted Griffin, Nicholas Griffin; **C:** John Mathieson; **M:** Hans Zimmer.

Material Girls WOOF! 2006 (PG) And we are living in a material world, which explains why movies like this get made. Two snotty, vapid cosmetic-heir sisters (Hilary and Haylie Duff) find themselves suddenly penniless when their company faces scandal. They spend much of the running time yelling at each other as they primp and mug and fuss over the indignities of being poor (or at least at the same economic level as the wanna-be teen queens to whom the flick might possibly appeal). By the time they make their obligatory transformation to girls with hearts of gold, they're so unlikable it's impossible to give a dam. Huston's appearance as the menacing Fabiella is hardly a consolation. And the Duffs' limp cover of the title song sounds like it was performed by automatons on karaoke night. **100m/C DVD.** US Hilary Duff, Haylie Duff, Anjelica Huston, Brent Spiner, Lukas Haas, Judy Tenuta, Maria Conchita Alonso, Obba Babatunde, Marcus Coloma; **D:** Martha Coolidge; **W:** Amy Rardin, John Quaintance, Jessica O'Toole; **C:** Johnny E. Jensen; **M:** Jennie Muskett.

Maternal Instincts 🐾🐾 1996 (PG-13) Tracy (Burke) is a childless woman who undergoes an emergency hysterectomy without her consent. But she badly wants a baby and decides to get revenge on anyone thwarting her plans. **92m/C VHS.** Delta Burke, Beth Broderick, Garwin Sanford, Sandra Nelson, Gillian Barber, Kevin McNulty, Tom Butler, Tom Mason; **D:** George Kaczender.

C A B L E

Matewan 🐾🐾🐾 1987 (PG-13) An acclaimed dramatization of the famous Matewan massacre in the 1920s, in which coal miners in West Virginia, reluctantly influenced by union organizer Joe Kenehan (Cooper), rebelled against terrible working conditions. Complex and imbued with myth, the film is gritty, moving, and powerful drama with typically superb Sayles dialogue and Haskell Wexler's beautiful and poetic cinematography. Jones delivers an economical yet intense portrayal of the black leader of the miners. Sayles makes his usual onscreen appearance, this time as an establishment-backed reactionary minister. Partially based on the Sayles novel "Union Dues." **130m/C VHS, DVD.** John Sayles, Chris Cooper, James Earl Jones, Mary McDonnell, William Oldham, Kevin Tighe, David Strathairn, Jace Alexander, Gordon Clapp, Mason Daring, Joe Gritasi, Bob Gunton, Jo Henderson, Jason Jenkins, Ken Jenkins, Nancy Mette, Josh Mostel, Michael B. Preston, Maggie Renzi, Frank Hoyt Taylor; **D:** John Sayles; **W:** John Sayles; **C:** Haskell Wexler; **M:** Mason Daring. Ind. Spirit '88: Cinematog.

Matilda 🐾🐾 1978 (PG) Family fare about a entrepreneur who decides to manage a boxing kangaroo, which nearly succeeds in defeating the world heavyweight champion. Uneven and occasionally engaging. Based on Paul Gallico's novel. **103m/C VHS.** Elliott Gould, Robert Mitchum, Harry Guardino, Clive Revill; **D:** Daniel Mann.

Matilda 🐾🐾🐾 1996 (PG) Intelligent child Matilda Wormwood (Wilson) is oppressed by both her monstrous parents (DeVito and Perlman) and awful school principal, Trunchbull (Ferris). However, her first grade teacher, appropriately named Miss Honey (Davidtz), believes in her, which is enough to make Matilda plot an appropriate fate for the miserable people in her life. Excellent adaptation of a typically subversive book by Roald Dahl. Director DeVito, who wanted to create the illusion of a live-action cartoon, built among other things a "Carrot-cam" to capture the flying food of a food fight. **93m/ C VHS, DVD.** Mara Wilson, Danny DeVito, Rhea Perlman, Embeth Davidtz, Pam Ferris, Paul (Pee-wee Herman) Reubens, Tracey Walter; **D:** Danny

DeVito; **W:** Robin Swicord, Nicholas Kazan; **C:** Stefan Czapsky; **M:** David Newman.

Matinee ✦✦½ 1992 (PG) "MANT: Half-man, Half-ant, All Terror!" screams from the movie marquee after Lawrence Woolsey, promoter extraordinaire, attempts to bring his B-movie horror to Key West circa 1962. Meanwhile, teen Gene Loomis listens to his health teacher push the benefits of 'red meat and his girlfriend question life, while worrying about its dad, stationed in Cuba. Builds sly parallels between real life and movie horror by juxtaposing Woolsey (modeled after B-movie king William Castle) hyping his schlock, shown in "Atomo-Vision," against JFK solemnly announcing the Russian's approach. Fun, nostalgic look at days gone by—and the matinees that died with them. **98m/C VHS, DVD.** John Goodman, Cathy Moriarty, Omri Katz, Lisa Jakub, Lucinda Jenney, James Villemaire, Robert Picardo, Dick Miller, John Sayles, Charles S. Haas, Mark McCracken, Simon Fenton, Kellie Martin, Jesse Lee, Jesse White, David Clennon, Luke Halpin, Robert Cornthwaite, Kevin McCarthy, William Schallert; **D:** Joe Dante; **W:** Charles S. Haas, Jerico Stone; **C:** John Hora; **M:** Jerry Goldsmith.

The Mating Game ✦✦✦ 1959 A fast-paced comedy about a tax collector, a beautiful girl, and a wily farm couple. Randall is the straitlaced IRS agent who finds out that the farming Larkins have never paid taxes and use a complicated barter system to get along. Randall falls for farm daughter Reynolds, gets drunk with her Pa, and decides to help the family out of their government dilemma—to the dismay of his superiors. Randall has a terrific drunk scene among his many comedic capers and Reynolds is a highlight. **96m/C VHS.** Tony Randall, Debbie Reynolds, Paul Douglas, Una Merkel, Fred Clark, Philip Ober, Charles Lane; **D:** George Marshall; **W:** Anita Loos.

The Mating Habits of the Earthbound Human ✦½ 1999 (R) One-joke premise has an alien narrator (Pierce) making a nature documentary about humans, focusing on the mating habits of nebbishy accountant Bill (Astin) and babe Jenny (Electra). The actors do what they can but the humor and situations are predictable. **96m/C VHS.** MacKenzie Astin, Carmen Electra, Markus Redmond, Lucy Liu, Jack Kehler; **D:** Jeff Abugov; **W:** Jeff Abugov; **C:** Michael Bucher; **M:** Michael McCarty; **Nar:** David Hyde Pierce.

Mating Season ✦✦½ 1981 Successful female attorney Arnaz meets good-natured laundromat owner Luckinbill at a bird-watching retreat. Romance ensues. **96m/C VHS.** Lucie Arnaz, Laurence Luckinbill; **D:** John Llewellyn Moxey. TV

Matrimaniac ✦✦ 1916 A man goes to great lengths to marry a woman against her father's wishes. Silent with music score. **45m/B VHS.** Douglas Fairbanks Sr., Constance Talmadge, Wilbur Higby, Fred Warren; **D:** Paul Powell; **W:** Anita Loos.

The Matrix ✦✦✦½ 1999 (R) Visually wild ride (and rather complicated plot), courtesy of the brothers Wachowski. Mild-mannered computer programmer Thomas Anderson (Reeves) turns into hacker Neo by night. Neo thinks something is off about his world and he's right. Seems everything around him is just a computer-generated illusion, fostered by machines who use human beings as an electrical energy source. Neo is shown the truth by the mysterious Morpheus (Fishburne) and his renegade team, including capable and beautiful Trinity (Moss). Is Neo the chosen one, who'll make the world safe for humanity once again? Spectacular action sequences, a hssably evil villain (Weaving), a magisterial mentor, and a reluctant hero. What more could you ask for? **136m/C VHS, DVD, Blu-ray Disc, UMD.** Keanu Reeves, Carrie-Anne Moss, Laurence Fishburne, Joe Pantoliano, Hugo Weaving, Gloria Foster, Marcus Chong, Paul Goddard, Robert Taylor, Julian (Sonny) Arahanga, Matt Doran, Belinda McClory, Anthony Ray Parker; **D:** Andy Wachowski, Larry Wachowski; **W:** Andy Wachowski, Larry Wachowski; **C:** Bill Pope; **M:** Don Davis. Visual FX; MTV Movie Awards '00: Film, Male Perf.

(Reeves), Fight (Keanu Reeves/Laurence Fishburne).

The Matrix Reloaded ✦✦½ 2003 (R) Neo, Morpheus, Trinity, and the denizens of Zion brace for the machines' attempt to find and destroy the last human stronghold. Neo also discovers more about his destiny as he deals with the ubiquitous and even more powerful Agent Smith. The Wachowski brothers have gone all-out to top the original, and at least visually, they have succeeded. But this one suffers from the attempt to mix navel-gazing ponderings on such topics as choice, destiny, and fate with the visceral thrills, all while trying to move the story forward. A daunting task, which "Reloaded" almost fulfills, providing a complicated twist on the story created in the original, but not mixing it as smoothly with the action set-pieces that, out of necessity, had to be (and definitely are) show-stopping. By no means a failure, it's just not the overwhelming success many hoped it would be. **138m/C VHS, DVD, Blu-ray Disc.** US Keanu Reeves, Carrie-Anne Moss, Laurence Fishburne, Hugo Weaving, Jada Pinkett Smith, Monica Bellucci, Gloria Foster, Nona Gaye, Randall Duk Kim, Lambert Wilson, Harold Perrineau Jr., Harry J. Lennix, Helmut Bakaitis, Anthony Zerbe, Neil Rayment, Adrian Rayment, Matt McColm, Daniel Bernhardt, Gina Torres, Collin Chou; **W:** Andy Wachowski, Larry Wachowski; **C:** Bill Pope; **M:** Don Davis.

The Matrix Revolutions ✦✦✦ 2003 (R) The battle for the last human stronghold continues, as Zion itself comes under attack. Meanwhile Neo continues his battle with Agent Smith and the machines in his own way, in and out of the Matrix. Better blending of action (there's plenty), philosophy, and narrative helps this one surpass the somewhat disappointing previous installment. It also helps that the effects are more smoothly integrated and less obvious. Add a half-bone if you think the Wachowski boys can do no wrong, subtract one if you thought the whole thing was ridiculous to begin with. You must choose. **130m/C VHS, DVD.** US Keanu Reeves, Laurence Fishburne, Carrie-Anne Moss, Hugo Weaving, Mary Alice, Monica Bellucci, Jada Pinkett Smith, Harold Perrineau Jr., Nona Gaye, Anthony Zerbe, Lambert Wilson, Harry J. Lennix, Collin Chou, Ian Bliss, Bruce Spence, Gina Torres, Helmut Bakaitis, Lachy Hulme, Robyn Nevin, Essie Davis, Anthony Wong, Kevin M. Richardson; **D:** Andy Wachowski, Larry Wachowski; **C:** Bill Pope; **M:** Don Davis.

A Matter of Degrees ✦✦ 1990 A week before his graduation, a beatnik-type college senior finally acquires a goal: romancing a mystery DJ...or maybe saving the student radio station...or not. The hero's aimlessness permeates in its exploration of campus ennui. Good photography and a great stratum of alternative music groups on the soundtrack: Dream Syndicate, Pere Ubu, Schoolly D, Pixies, Poi Dog Pondering, Minutemen, and Throwing Muses. **89m/C VHS.** Arye Gross, Judith Hoag, Tom Sizemore, John Doe; Cameos: Poi Dog Pondering, Minutemen, and Throwing Muses; **D:** W.T. Morgan.

A Matter of Dignity ✦✦ 1957 Chloe (Lambetti), whose family is on the brink of financial ruin, agrees to marriage with an incredibly boring millionaire to try and save them. She has to make a painful journey of self-discovery in order to escape the shallowness of how she was raised and the life she doesn't want to lead. Greek with subtitles. **104m/B VHS, DVD, GR** Georges Pappas, Ellie Lambetti, Athena Michaelidou, Eleni Zafiriou; **D:** Michael Cacoyannis; **W:** Michael Cacoyannis; **C:** Walter Lassally; **M:** Manos Hadjidakis.

A Matter of Honor ✦✦ 1995 (PG) Rugby player is killed during match and his coach gets blamed. So, to clear his name, said coach takes up an unusual challenge with the captain of the opposing team. **95m/C VHS.** Rebecca Gray, David Michie; **D:** Frederick P. Watkins.

Matters of the Heart ✦✦ 1990 Young pianist searches for an opportunity to display his talents, much to the disapproval of his veteran father. He meets a successful but embittered musician who takes him under her wing and passion between the two soon flares. Based on "The Country of the Heart" by Barbara Wersh. **94m/C VHS.** Jane Seymour, Christopher Gartin, James Stacy, Geoffrey Lewis, Nan Martin, Allan Rich, Clifford David, Katherine (Kathy) Cannon; **D:** Michael Rhodes; **W:** Linda J. Bergman. CABLE

Maurice ✦✦✦ 1987 (R) Based on E.M. Forster's novel about a pair of Edwardian-era Cambridge undergraduates who fall in love, but must deny their affection and abide by British society's strict norms regarding homosexuality. Maurice finds, however, that he cannot deny his nature, and must come to a decision regarding family, friends, and social structures. A beautiful and stately film of struggle and courage. **140m/C VHS, DVD, GB** James Wilby, Hugh Grant, Rupert Graves, Mark Tandy, Ben Kingsley, Denholm Elliott, Simon Callow, Judy Parfitt, Helena Bonham-Carter, Billie Whitelaw, Phoebe Nicholls, Barry Foster; **D:** James Ivory; **W:** James Ivory, Kit Hesketh-Harvey; **C:** Pierre Lhomme; **M:** Richard Robbins.

Mausoleum ✦✦ 1983 (R) Only one man can save a woman from eternal damnation. **96m/C VHS, DVD.** Marjoe Gortner, Bobbie Bresse, Norman Burton, LaWanda Page, Shari Mann, Julie Christy Murray, Laura Hippe, Maurice Sherbanee; **D:** Michael Dugan; **M:** Robert Madero, Robert Barich; **C:** Robert Barich.

Max ✦✦ 1979 A night watchman watches an aspiring actress who is working on her performance in a Broadway play. He tells her the details of marrying a doctor. **20m/C VHS.** Jack Gifford, Jennifer Lax.

Max ✦✦ 2002 (R) Historical fantasy has an interesting premise: what would have happened if Adolf Hitler had been successful as an artist? In 1919, Hitler (Taylor) is a starving, embittered (but ambitious) war veteran in Munich who is befriended by Max Rothman (Cusack), a Jewish art dealer and fellow veteran who has just opened his own avant-garde gallery. Hitler's art is kitsch but Max encourages him along and shrugs off his rantings, which draw more attention from fellow Army officer Mayr (Thomsen). Mayr thinks Adolf would make a good political spokesman. Guess who was proved right? Rothman is a fictional character, but the film drew a lot of protest for "humanizing" Hitler. The movie is flawed but not for that reason. **106m/C VHS, DVD, HU CA GB** John Cusack, Noah Taylor, Leelee Sobieski, Molly Parker, David Horovitch, Janet Suzman, Peter Capaldi, Kevin McKidd, John Grillo, Ulrich Thomsen; **D:** Menno Meyjes; **W:** Menno Meyjes; **C:** Lajos Koltai; **M:** Dan (Daniel) Jones.

The Matrix Reloaded — see above.

A Matter of Life and Death ✦ 1981 True story follows the real-life experiences of nurse Joy Ufema who has devoted her life to helping terminally ill patients. Exceptional work from Lavin. **98m/C VHS.** Linda Lavin, Salome Jens, Gail Strickland, Gerald S. O'Loughlin, Ramon Bieri, Tyne Daly, Larry Breeding, John Bennett Perry; **D:** Russ Mayberry. TV

A Matter of Love ✦ 1978 (R) Two couples indulge in spouse swapping while vacationing at the beach. **89m/C VHS.** Michelle Harris, Mark Anderson, Christy Neal, Jeff Alvin; **D:** Chuck Vincent.

A Matter of Principle ✦ 1983 The perennial Christmas special about a Scrooge-like character's yuletide change of heart. He decides it's time to shape up when he realizes he may lose his family permanently. **60m/C VHS.** Alan Arkin, Barbara Dana, Tony Arkin; **D:** Gwen Arner.

A Matter of Time woof! 1976 (PG) Maid is taught to enjoy life by an eccentric, flamboyant contessa, then finds the determination to become an aspiring actress. Often depressing and uneven, arguably Minnelli's worst directing job and his last film. Also Boyer's last appearance and first bit for Bergman's daughter Rossellini, in a small part as a nun. **97m/C VHS.** Liza Minnelli, Ingrid Bergman, Charles Boyer, Tina Aumont, Spiros Andros, Anna Proclemer, Isabella Rossellini; **D:** Vincente Minnelli; **C:** Geoffrey Unsworth.

A Matter of Trust ✦✦ 1998 (R) Mike D'Angelo (Howell) is an alcoholic L.A. cop barely hanging onto his job. The woman he loves, Theresa (Severance), is not only an Assistant D.A. but is married to a prominent doctor, Peter (Mancuso). But their paths aren't as separate as Mike might believe. **90m/C VHS, DVD.** C. Thomas Howell, Joan Severance, Nick Mancuso, Robert Milano, Jennifer Leigh Warren, Randee Heller; **D:** Joey Travolta. VIDEO

A Matter of WHO ✦✦ 1962 A detective for the World Health Organization, or WHO, investigates the disease related deaths of several oil men. Travelling to the Middle East, he uncovers a plot by an unscrupulous businessman to control the oil industry by killing off its most powerful members. Although intended as a comedy, the subject matter is too grim to be taken lightly. **92m/B VHS, GB** Terry-Thomas, Alex Nicol, Sonja Ziemann, Richard Briers, Clive Morton, Vincent Ball, Honor Blackman, Carol White, Martin Benson, Geoffrey Keen; **D:** Don Chaffey; **M:** Edwin Astley.

Mauvais Sang ✦✦ 1986 Bad Blood Carax's second film tells the story of rival gangsters who are searching for a serum that cures a devastating disease. Street-wise Alex (Lavant) from "Boy Meets Girl" (1984) also returns as the thief who is supposed to steal the serum (his character is again seen in 1991's "The Lovers on the Bridge"). French with subtitles. **125m/C VHS, DVD, FR** Michel Piccoli, Denis Lavant, Juliette Binoche, Hans Meyer, Julie Delpy, Carroll Brooks, Serge Reggiani, Hugo Pratt, Mireille Perrier; **D:** Leos Carax; **W:** Leos Carax; **C:** Jean-Yves Escoffier; **M:** Serge Reggiani, Charles Aznavour.

Mauvaise Graine ✦✦ 1933 Wilder (in his debut) filmed this comedy-drama (along with Esway) before heading off to Hollywood. Parisian wastrel Henri Pasquier (Mingand) impulsively steals a car when his disgusted wealthy father cuts him off. This lands Henri in with a professional gang of thieves, headed by Jean (Gaile), who uses his pretty teenaged sister Jeannette (Darrieux) as a decoy. Henri enjoys his new career (and Jeannette) until jealousy gets in the way. French with subtitles. **76m/B VHS, DVD, FR** Pierre Mingand, Danielle Darrieux, Raymond Gale, Jean Wall; **D:** Billy Wilder, Alexander Esway; **W:** Billy Wilder, Alexander Esway; **C:** Paul Cotteret, Maurice Delattre; **M:** Franz Waxman, Walter Gray.

Maverick ✦✦✦ 1994 (PG) Entertaining remake of the popular ABC series is fresh and funny, with sharp dialogue and a good cast. Everybody looks like they're having a great time, not difficult for the charming Gibson, but a refreshing change of pace for the usually serious Foster and Greene. In a fun bit of casting, Garner, the original Maverick, shows up as Marshal Zane Cooper. Lightweight, fast-paced comedy was reportedly highly improvised, though Donner retained enough control to keep it coherent. The end is left wide open so a sequel seems likely. Keep your eyes peeled for cameos from country stars, old time Western actors, and an unbilled appearance from Glover. **127m/C VHS, DVD.** Mel Gibson, Jodie Foster, James Garner, Graham Greene, James Coburn, Alfred Molina, Paul Smith, Geoffrey Lewis, Max Perlich; Cameos: Dub Taylor, Dan Hedaya, James Garner, Will Hutchins, Waylon Jennings, Kathy Mattea, Danny Glover, Clint Black; **D:** Richard Donner; **W:** William Goldman; **C:** Vilmos Zsigmond; **M:** Randy Newman. Blockbuster '95: Comedy Actress.

The Maverick Queen ✦✦½ 1956 Barbara Stanwyck, owner of a gambling casino and a member of the "Wild Bunch" outlaw gang, is torn between going straight for the love of a lawman or sticking with the criminals. Stanwyck is perfectly cast in this interesting though flawed Western. **90m/C VHS.** Barbara Stanwyck, Barry Sullivan, Wallace Ford, Scott Brady, Jim Davis, Mary Murphy; **D:** Joseph Kane.

Max and Helen 🦴🦴½ 1990 Uneven, but sensitive and at times highly moving made for TV story of two lovers who are victims of the holocaust. Max (Williams) survives both Nazi and Stalinist camps out of both love for his fiancee and guilt for having lived while she did not. 94m/C VHS. GB Treat Williams, Alice Krige, Martin Landau, Jodhi May, John Phillips, Adam Kotz; D: Philip Saville; W: Corey Blechman. TV

Max Dugan Returns 🦴🦴 1983 (PG) A Simon comedy about an ex-con trying to make up with his daughter by showering her with presents bought with stolen money. Sweet and light, with a good cast. 98m/C VHS, DVD. Jason Robards Jr., Marsha Mason, Donald Sutherland, Matthew Broderick, Kiefer Sutherland; D: Herbert Ross; W: Neil Simon; M: David Shire.

Max Is Missing 🦴🦴½ 1995 (PG) Twelve-year-old Max (Caudell) gets separated from his father, is given a priceless Incan artifact by a dying man, and joins with a local lad to guard it from fortune hunters. Set in the ruins of Machu Picchu in the Peruvian Andes. 95m/C VHS. Toran Caudell, Victor Rojas, Matthew Sullivan, Rick Dean, Charles Napier; D: Mark Griffiths. CABLE

Max Keeble's Big Move 🦴🦴 2001 (PG) Max (Linz), a kid on the verge of entering seventh grade, decides that he must change his image to be a little cooler, much to the dismay of his pals Megan (Grey) and Robe (Peck). On the first day of school, however, he is confronted with two bullies, a fussy principal (Miller) who wants to tear down an animal shelter that Max loves, and a renegade ice cream man. Max's dad comes home and announces that the family is moving to Chicago. Thinking that the family is moving out of town, Max hatches numerous messy plots to get back at everyone who's tormenting him. After Max has taken revenge, dad reveals that the family is staying put after all, leaving Max to face the music. Not very original, but the kids will get a kick out of the food fight scene. 101m/C VHS, DVD. US Alex D. Linz, Larry Miller, Jamie Kennedy, Zena Grey, Josh Peck, Orlando Brown, Noel Fisher, Nora Dunn, Robert Carradine, Clifton Davis, Amy Hill; W: Jon Bernstein; Mark Blackwell, James Greer; C: Arthur Albert; M: Michael Wandmacher.

Max, Mon Amour 🦴🦴 Max, My Love 1986 A very refined British diplomat in Paris discovers his bored wife has become involved with Max, who happens to be a chimpanzee. Instead of being upset, the husband decides Max should live with them. Very strange menage a trois manages to avoid the obvious vulgarities. In French with English subtitles. 97m/C VHS. FR Anthony (Cotran) Higgins, Charlotte Rampling, Victoria Abril, Christopher Hovik, Anne-Marie Besse, Pierre Etaix; D: Nagisa Oshima; W: Jean-Claude Carriere, Nagisa Oshima; C: Raoul Coutard; M: Michel Portal.

Maxie 🦴🦴 1985 (PG) Highly predictable, and forgettable, comedy where a ghost of a flamboyant flapper inhabits the body of a modern-day secretary, and her husband is both delighted and befuddled with the transformations in his spouse. Close is okay, but the film is pretty flaky. 98m/C VHS, DVD. Glenn Close, Ruth Gordon, Mandy Patinkin, Barnard Hughes, Valerie Curtin, Harry Hamlin; D: Paul Aaron; W: Patricia Resnick; M: Georges Delerue.

Maxed Out: Hard Times, Easy Credit and the Era Of Predatory Lenders 🦴🦴½ 2006 Scurlock tries to explain the wheeling and dealing of the financial community by focusing on the worst case scenarios of the consumer-lending industry, involving massive consumer debt, too easy credit, ill-advised loans, and bankruptcy and foreclosures. Basically most people are dumb about money and even dumber when it comes to borrowing and getting into (and less likely out of) debt. 86m/C DVD. US D: James D. Scurlock; W: James D. Scurlock; C: Jon Aaron Aaseng; M: Benoit Vharest.

Maxim Xul WOOF! 1991 A professor of the occult is forced to tangle with a beast from Hell that possesses enormous strength and an insatiable appetite for human blood. 90m/C VHS. Adam West, Jefferson Leinberger, Hal Strieb, Mary Schaefer; D: Arthur Egeli.

Maximum Breakout 🦴½ 1991 A beautiful and wealthy girl is kidnapped, her boyfriend left for dead. But he recovers and leads a posse of mercenaries to the rescue. 93m/C VHS. Sydney Coale Phillips; D: Tracy Lynch Britton.

Maximum Force 🦴½ 1992 (R) Three renegade cops join together to infiltrate the underworld and bring to justice both the city's leading crime king and their own corrupt chief of police. 90m/C VHS. Sam Jones, Sherrie Rose, Jason Lively, John Saxon, Richard Lynch, Mickey Rooney, Jeff Langton; D: Joseph Merhi.

Maximum Overdrive 🦴 1986 (R) Based upon King's story "Trucks," recounts what happens when a meteor hits Earth and machines run by themselves, wanting only to kill people. Score by AC/DC. King shows that as a director, he's an excellent horror writer. 97m/C VHS, DVD. Emilio Estevez, Pat Hingle, Laura Harrington, Christopher Murney, Yeardley Smith, Stephen King; D: Stephen King; W: Stephen King; C: Armando Nannuzzi; M: AC/DC.

Maximum Risk 🦴🦴½ 1996 (R) Like we need two of them? Van Damme, in a deja vu storyline (see "Double Impact") plays identical twins—a good French guy and a bad Russian guy—and when the bad guy gets killed, his brother takes over his life to find out whodunit. Risk and danger aside, the ruse is not all that bad, what with Henstridge as his sib's squeeze, unaware that the man she has in a lip lock is not her beloved. Has all the action you'd expect from a pic with "The Muscles from Brussels" and more guns, fists, and car chases is, of course, the major reason to invest your entertainment dollars here. Hong Kong action auteur Lam's stateside debut ensures that fast-paced chases and full-throttle combat is well done and visually appealing. 100m/C VHS, DVD. Jean-Claude Van Damme, Natasha Henstridge, Jean-Claude Anglade, Stephane Audran, Paul Ben-Victor, Zach Grenier, Frank Senger; D: Ringo Lam; W: Larry Ferguson; C: Alexander Grusynski; M: Robert Folk.

Maximum Security 🦴 1987 A small-budget prison film detailing the tribulations of a model prisoner struggling to resist mental collapse. 113m/C VHS, DVD. Geoffrey Lewis, Jean Smart, Robert Desiderio; D: Bill Duke.

Maximum Thrust WOOF! Waldo Warren: Private Dick Without a Brain 1988 A few white men confront a deadly Caribbean voodoo tribe. 80m/C Rick Gianasi, Joe Derrig, Jennifer Kanter, Mizan Nunes; D: Tim Kincaid.

May 🦴🦴 2002 (R) May's (Bettis) motto is "If you can't find a friend, make one." Thanks to a disturbed childhood (where her only companion was a doll), May is one messed-up chick. She works at an animal hospital with lesbian Polly (Faris), sews as a hobby, and falls for Adam (Sisto), who thinks he likes weird girls. He doesn't know from weird. When Adam finally rejects May, she looks around and decides to make her own best friend—using only the choicest body parts. 95m/C VHS, DVD. Angela Bettis, Jeremy Sisto, Anna Faris, James Duval, Nichole Hiltz, Kevin Gage, Merle Kennedy; D: Lucky McKee; W: Lucky McKee; M: Jaye Barnes-Luckett.

May Fools 🦴🦴½ Milou en Mai; Milou in May 1990 (R) Malle portrays individuals collectively experiencing personal upheaval against the backdrop of unrelated social upheaval. An upper-crust family gathers at a country estate for the funeral of the clan's matriarch, while the May of '68 Parisian riots unfold. Few among the family members mourn the woman's passing, save her son Milou (Piccoli) who leads a pastoral existence tending grapes on the estate. Milou's daughter (Miou-Miou), like the others, is more concerned with her personal gain, suggesting, to her father's horror, that they divide the estate in three. Touching, slow, keenly observed. In French with English subtitles. 105m/C VHS. FR Michel Piccoli, Miou-Miou, Michel Duchaussoy, Dominique Blanc, Harriet Walter, Francois Berleand, Paulette Dubost, Bruno Carette, Martine Gautier; D: Louis Malle; W: Jean-Claude Carriere, Louis Malle; C: Renato Berta; M: Stephane Grappelli. Cesar '91: Support. Actress (Blanc).

May Wine 🦴🦴 1990 (R) A sexy, romantic comedy starring "Twin Peaks" alumna, Boyle. 85m/C VHS. Paul Freeman, Guy Marchand, Lara Flynn Boyle, Joanna Cassidy; D: Carol Wiseman; W: Peter Lefcourt; C: Yves Dahan; M: Andre Georgel.

Maya 🦴½ 1966 After the death of his mother, young Terry (North) goes to join his big-game hunting father in India. After a quarrel Terry runs off and meets an Indian boy who has promised his dying father he will deliver a sacred white elephant to a jungle temple. The two lads join forces for the trek and have all sorts of adventures along the way. Basis for a short-lived TV series. 91m/C VHS. Jay North, Clint Walker, Sajid Khan, I.S. Johar; D: John Berry; W: John Fante.

Maya WOOF! 1982 A teacher of fashion in a high school moves the object of a student's devotion and another teacher's insane jealousy. 114m/C VHS. Berta Dominguez, Joseph D. Rosevich; D: Agust Agustsson.

Mayalunta Bad Company 1986 A young artist is emotionally tortured by a dying older couple. 90m/C VHS. SP Federico Luppi, Miguel Angel Sola, Barbara Mujica; D: Jose Santiso; W: Jose Santiso; C: Eduardo Legaria; M: Litto Nebbia.

Maybe Baby 🦴🦴 1999 (R) Sam (Laurie) and Lucy (Richardson) Bell are a happily married couple trying to have a baby. She's a talent agent and he works for the BBC. Dissatisfied at work, Sam tries his hand at scriptwriting and decides his subject will be a comic look at the couple's infertility problems. Naturally, he keeps this a secret from Lucy, although she finds out when his script is accepted and walks out on Sam. Tends towards the smug and the leads don't particularly click as a couple, which makes the supporting players the most interesting to watch on-screen. 93m/C VHS, DVD. GB FR Hugh Laurie, Joely Richardson, Adrian Lester, James Purefoy, Tom Hollander, Joanna Lumley, Rowan Atkinson, Dawn French, Emma Thompson, Rachael Stirling; D: Ben Elton; W: Ben Elton; C: Roger Lanser; M: Colin Towns.

Maybe I'll Be Home in the Spring 🦴🦴 Deadly Desire 1970 (PG) Denise (Field) is estranged from her family and decides to leave home for life on a commune where she becomes involved with drugs. When she decides to return home everyone finds it hard to adjust. 90m/C VHS, DVD. Sally Field, Jackie Cooper, Eleanor Parker, David Carradine, Lane Bradbury; D: Joseph Sargent. TV

Maybe... Maybe Not 🦴🦴 Der Bewegte Mann; The Most Desired Man 1994 (R) The German title refers to a man who moves between both sexual preferences although the film takes a straighter line. Hunky-but-dumb Axel (Schweiger) has cheated on girlfriend Dorothy (Riemann) once too often and she kicks him out. Axel winds up staying with gay pal Norbert (Krol), who would like to go from friendship to lovers, which Axel doesn't pick up on. Dorothy does, however, and wonders if Axel is really gay, but when she discovers she's pregnant, Dorothy decides to marry him anyway. Warm-hearted and campy, with some blatantly sexual dialogue. Based on two gay comic books by Ralf Koenig. German with subtitles or dubbed. 93m/C VHS. GE Til Schweiger, Katja Riemann, Joachim Krol, Rufus Beck; D: Soenke Wortmann; W: Soenke Wortmann; C: Gernot Roll; M: Torsten Breuer.

Mayerling 🦴🦴🦴½ 1936 Considered one of the greatest films about doomed love. Story of the tragic and hopeless affair between Crown Prince Rudolf of Hapsburg and young Baroness Marie Vetsera. Heart wrenching and beautiful, with stupendous acting. Remade in 1968. In French with English subtitles. 95m/B VHS. Charles Boyer, Danielle Darrieux; D: Anatole Litvak. N.Y. Film Critics '37: Foreign Film.

Mayerling 🦴🦴½ 1968 (PG-13) Based on the tragic romance between Crown Prince Rudolf of Hapsburg (Sharif) and the teenaged Baroness Maria Vetsera (Deneuve). Set in 1888, the royal Rudolf defies his father, the Emperor Franz Josef (Mason), to take part in a student revolt for the liberation of Hungary and to fall for the common-born Maria (despite his political marriage). No doubt meant to be a sweeping combo of politics and love ala "Doctor Zhivago," it's mostly tedious; see the 1936 version instead. 140m/C VHS, DVD. GB FR Omar Sharif, Catherine Deneuve, James Mason, Ava Gardner, James Robertson Justice, Genevieve Page, Ivan Desny, Fabienne Dali; D: Terence Young; W: Terence Young; C: Henri Alekan; M: Francis Lai.

Mayflower Madam 🦴🦴 1987 (R) Fairly unsexy and uninteresting TV movie recounting the business dealings and court battles of the real-life Sydney Biddle Barrows. Barrows/Bergen is a prominent New York socialite and madam of an exclusive escort service whose clientele includes businessmen and dignitaries. 93m/C VHS, DVD. Candice Bergen, Chris Sarandon, Chita Rivera; D: Lou Antonio; M: David Shire. TV

Mayflower: The Pilgrims' Adventure 🦴🦴½ 1979 The Pilgrims flee religious persecution in England in 1620 and sail to America on the Mayflower, which is captained by Hopkins. Crenna plays the leader of the Puritans, the Rev. William Brewster. 96m/C VHS. Anthony Hopkins, Richard Crenna, Jenny Agutter, Michael Beck, David Dukes, Trish Van Devere, Guy Sorel, Paul Sparer; D: George Schaefer; W: James Lee Barrett. TV

Mayhem 🦴 1987 Two loners in Hollywood confront all types of urban low-life murderers, drug pushers, and child molesters. 90m/C VHS. Raymond Martino, Pamela Dixon, Robert Gallo, Wendy MacDonald; D: Joseph Merhi; W: Joseph Merhi; C: Richard Pepin; M: John Gonzalez.

The Mayor of Casterbridge 🦴🦴½ 2003 Appropriately brooding adaptation of Thomas Hardy's dark novel of regret. Farm worker Michael Henchard (Hinds) gets drunk and sells his wife Susan (Aubrey) and their baby daughter at a country fair. Since her husband is an abusive drunk and the buyer (Russell) is a good-natured sailor, Susan decides to take her chances. Suffering from a drunkard's remorse, Henchard searches fruitlessly for his family. He eventually settles in Casterbridge where, through sobriety and hard work, Henchard becomes the town's mayor. Then his past returns to haunt him when Susan and his now-grown daughter, Elizabeth-Jane (May), seek him out. But when young rival Farfrae (Purefoy) romances his daughter, Henchard's darker nature resurfaces. 200m/C DVD. GB Ciaran Hinds, James Purefoy, Jodhi May, Juliet Aubrey, Polly Walker, Clive Russell; D: David Thacker; W: Ted Whitehead; C: Ivan Strasburg; M: Adrian Johnston. CABLE

The Mayor of Hell 🦴🦴½ 1933 Gangster Patsy Gargan (Cagney) has his political cronies appoint him the titular head of a state reformatory. But when he sees the brutal conditions, Gargan makes improvements and tries to get the teen-aged criminal inmates to see the error of their ways. However, when Gargan is forced into hiding after killing a rival, things get bad again until he finally decides to step up. Remade as 1938's "Crime School." 85m/B DVD. James Cagney, Madge Evans, Allen Jenkins, Dudley Digges, Frankie Darro, Carolyn Farina; D: Archie Mayo; W: Edward Chodorov; C: Barney McGill.

Mayor of the Sunset Strip 🦴🦴🦴 2003 (R) As a popular Los Angeles disc jockey, Rodney Bingenheimer pushed new musical acts into the limelight—including the Sex Pistols, Blondie, and Nirvana—meanwhile living as the greatest groupie, befriending The Beatles, Elton John, Elvis, and the Doors. But in his documentary, director-writer Hickenlooper poignantly reveals how this man rose up from a lonely childhood to unexpectedly become all of the "get to know me" guy on the music scene, only to learn that life inside all of the glittering lights can be just as harsh and emotionally isolating as was his youth. Music industry cameos and interviews abound. **94m/C VHS, DVD.** *D:* George Hickenlooper; *C:* Kramer Morgenthau, Igor Meglic; *M:* Anthony Marinelli.

Maytime ♫♫ **1937** Lovely story of an opera star (MacDonald) and penniless singer (Eddy) who fall in love in Paris, but her husband/teacher (Barrymore) interferes. One of the best films the singing duo ever made. "Maytime Finale; Virginia Ham and Eggs; Student Drinking Song; Carry Me Back to Old Virginia; Reverie; Page's Aria. **132m/B VHS.** Jeanette MacDonald, Nelson Eddy, John Barrymore, Herman Bing Tom Brown, Lynne Carver; *D:* Robert Z. Leonard; *W:* Noel Langley.

Maytime in Mayfair ♫♫ **1949** A dress shop owner's rival is getting all the goodies first. When he takes the heat from his partner. When he finds out how the rival is doing it, the partners up and head for a vacation in the south of France. Overly simplistic but charming kitsch, helped along by Technicolor shots of the fashions and sets. **94m/C VHS.** Anna Neagle, Michael Wilding, Peter Graves, Nicholas Phipps, Tom Walls, Tom Walls Jr.; *D:* Herbert Wilcox.

The Maze ♫♫ **1985** Mystery about a young girl who meets the ghost of her mother's first love in her garden estate. **60m/C VHS, GB** Francesca Annis, James Bolam, Sky McCaskill; *D:* Peter Hammond; *W:* Kenneth Taylor; *C:* Ken Morgan; *D:* Robert Z. **TV.**

Maze ♫♫½ **2001 (R)** Introverted New York artist Lyle Maze (Morrow) is a sculptor afflicted with Tourette's syndrome, which makes him romantically hesitant. Lyle's best friend is a doctor named Mike (Sheffer), whose devotion is to his career rather than his girlfriend Callie (Linney). Mike leaves Callie for a month-long tour with Doctors Without Borders in Africa and when Callie discovers she is pregnant, she turns to Lyle for emotional support. Unsurprisingly, the needy duo fall in love before they have to explain what's happened on Mike's return. **98m/C VHS, DVD.** Rob Morrow, Laura Linney, Craig Sheffer, Gia Carides, Rose Gregorio, Robert Hogan; *D:* Rob Morrow; *W:* Rob Morrow, Bradley White; *C:* Wolfgang Held; *M:* Bobby Previte.

Mazes and Monsters ♫♫½ *Rona Jaffe's Mazes and Monsters; Dungeons and Dragons* **1982** A group of university students becomes obsessed with playing a real life version of the fantasy role-playing game, Dungeons and Dragons (known in the film as Mazes & Monsters since D&D is trademarked). Early Hanks appearance is among the film's assets. Adapted from the book by Rona Jaffe. **100m/C VHS, DVD, CA** Tom Hanks, Wendy Crewson, David Wallace, Chris Makepeace, Lloyd Bochner, Peter Donat, Murray Hamilton, Vera Miles, Louise Sorel, Susan Strasberg, Anne Francis; *D:* Steven Hilliard Stern; *M:* Hagood Hardy. **TV.**

McBain ♫♫ **1991 (R)** In this exciting fast-paced action-thriller, POW Robert McBain (Walken) leads a group of veterans into battle against the Columbian drug cartel. Stunning cinematography and superb performances combine to make this a riveting action film you won't soon forget. **104m/C VHS.** Christopher Walken, Maria Conchita Alonso, Michael Ironside, Steve James, Jay Patterson, Thomas G. Waites; *D:* James Glickenhaus; *W:* James Glickenhaus.

McCabe & Mrs. Miller ♫♫♫ **1971 (R)** Altman's characteristically quirky take on the Western casts Beatty as a self-initiated entrepreneur who opens a brothel in the Great North. Christie is the madame who helps stabilize the operation. Unfortunately, success comes at a high price, and when gunmen arrive to enforce a business proposition, Beatty must become the man he has, presumably, merely pretended to be. A poetic, moving work, and a likely classic of the genre. Based on the novel by Edmund Naughton. **121m/C VHS.** Warren Beatty, Julie Christie, William Devane, Keith Carradine.

McHale's Navy ♫♫½ **1997 (PG)** Yet TV sitcom and let it loose on the big screen. Retired Navy skipper McHale (Arnold) has set up his old gambling ways on the Caribbean island of San Ysidro, where he can be a thorn in the side of Capt. Binghampton (Stockwell), the newly transferred commanding officer of the island's sleepy naval base. McHale's former cronies aid their leader when he's reluctantly reunited with the Navy in order to prevent the terrorist threats of his former Soviet nemesis Vladakov (Curry). A shining example of "why bother?" moviemaking. **108m/C VHS, DVD.** Tom Arnold, Tim Curry, Dean Stockwell, David Alan Grier, Dayra Messing, Thomas Chong, Bruce Campbell, French Stewart, Brian Haley, Danton Stone; *Cameos:* Ernest Borgnine; *D:* Bryan Spicer; *W:* Peter Crabbe; *C:* Buzz Feitshans IV; *M:* Dennis McCarthy.

McHale's Navy Joins the Air Force ♫♫½ **1965** McHale is conspicuously missing from this sequel (Borgnine had a contract dispute) so second-banana Conway, as Ensign Charles Parker, gets to shine in slapstick gags. A drunken Parker winds up in an Air Force uniform and is mistaken for a hot-shot flier, gets involved with some Russians, and is even cited for bravery by President Franklin D. Roosevelt. **91m/C VHS.** Tim Conway, Joe Flynn, Tom Tully, Ted Bessell, Bob Hastings, Gavin MacLeod, Billy (Billie) Sands; *D:* Edward Montagne; *W:* John Fenton Murray; *C:* Lionel Lindon.

McKenzie Break ♫♫♫ **1970** Irish intelligence agent John Connor (Keith) is sent to Scotland to Camp McKenzie, a prison for German POWs during WWII. Captured U-boat commander Schluetter (Griem) is suspected of planning a mass escape and Connor is supposed to stop the action. The battle of wills between the hard-headed Connor and wily Schluetter provides taut, suspenseful drama. Adapted from "The Bowmanville Break" by Sidney Shelley. **106m/C VHS, DVD.** Brian Keith, Helmut Griem, Ian Hendry, Jack Watson, Horst Janson, Patrick O'Connell; *D:* Lamont Johnson; *W:* William W. Norton Sr.; *C:* Michael Reed; *M:* Riz Ortolani.

McKenzie Break ♫♫½ **1970** (continued)

The McConnell Story ♫♫½ *Tiger in the Sky* **1955** True story of ace flyer McConnell, his heroism during the Korean conflict, and his postwar aviation pioneer efforts. Fine acting from Ally son and Ladd, with good support from Whitmore and Faylen. **107m/C VHS.** Alan Ladd, June Allyson, James Whitmore, Frank Faylen; *D:* Gordon Douglas; *M:* Max Steiner.

The McCullochs ♫♫½ *The Wild McCullochs* **1975 (PG)** Texas millionaire J.J. McCulloch (Tucker) is the kind of domineering patriarch whose kids won't end up being him and destroying their own lives. Stereotypical family saga set in 1949. **93m/C VHS, DVD.** Forrest Tucker, Julie Adams, Janice Heiden, Max Baer Jr., Don Grady, Chip Hand, Dennis Redfield, William Demarest, Harold J. Stone, Vito Scotti, James Gammon, Mike Mazurki; *D:* Max Baer Jr.; *W:* Max Baer Jr.; *C:* Fred W. Koenekamp; *M:* Ernest Gold.

The McGuffin ♫♫ **1985** A film critic's inquisitiveness about the activities of his neighbors gets him caught up in murder and a host of other problems. A takeoff of Alfred Hitchcock's 1954 classic "Rear Window." **95m/C VHS, GB** Charlie Dance, Ritza Brown, Francis Matthews, Brian Glover, Phyllis Logan, Jerry Stiller, Anna Massey; *D:* Colin Bucksey.

McLintock! ♫♫♫ **1963** Rowdy western starring Wayne as a tough cattle baron whose refined wife (O'Hara) returns from the east after a two-year separation. She wants a divorce and custody of their 17-year-old daughter (Powers), who's been away at school. In the meantime, he's hired a housekeeper (De Carlo), whose teenage son (real-life son Patrick) promptly falls for Powers. It's a battle royal between the feisty wife and cantankerous husband but no one out-dukes the Duke. Other Wayne family members involved in the production include daughter Aissa (as the housekeeper's daughter) and son Michael who produced the film. **127m/C VHS, DVD.** John Wayne, Maureen O'Hara, Yvonne De Carlo, Patrick Wayne, Stefanie Powers, Jack Kruschen, Chill Wills, Jerry Van Dyke, Edgar Buchanan, Bruce Cabot, Perry Lopez, Michael Pate, Strother Martin, Gordon Jones; *D:* Andrew V. McLaglen; *W:* James Edward Grant; *C:* William Clothier.

McQ ♫♫½ **1974 (PG)** After several big dope dealers kill two police officers, a lieutenant resigns to track them down. Dirty Harry done with an aging Big Duke. **116m/C VHS, DVD.** John Wayne, Eddie Albert, Diana Muldaur, Clu Gulager, Colleen Dewhurst, Al Lettieri, Julie Adams, David Huddleston; *D:* John Sturges; *C:* Harry Stradling Jr.; *M:* Elmer Bernstein.

McVicar ♫♫½ **1980 (R)** A brutish and realistic depiction of crime and punishment based on the life of John McVicar, who plotted to escape from prison. From the book by McVicar. **90m/C VHS, GB** Roger Daltrey, Adam Faith, Cheryl Campbell; *D:* Tom Clegg; *W:* Tom Clegg.

Me and Him ♫½ *Ich und Er* **1989 (R)** An unsuspecting New Yorker finds himself jockeying for position with his own instincts when his libido decides it wants a life of its own. **94m/C VHS, GE** Griffin Dunne, Carey Lowell, Ellen Greene, Craig T. Nelson; *D:* Doris Dorrie; *M:* Klaus Doldinger; *V:* Mark Linn-Baker.

Me & Mrs. Jones ♫♫½ **2002** Unhappy divorced tabloid reporter Liam under the nom de plume "Mrs. Jones." He reviews nothing about politics but his ex-wife Jane (Hawes), who's also his boss, wants dirt on female prime minister Laura Bowden (Goodall), who is in the middle of an election campaign. Liam manages to pangs of conscience when they unexpectedly fall in love. **100m/C VHS, DVD, GB** Robson Green, Caroline Goodall, Philip Quast, Keeley Hawes, Michael Maloney, Peter Firth, Aisling O'Sullivan; *D:* Catherine Morshead; *W:* Caleb Ranson; *C:* John Daly; *M:* Simon Lacey. **TV.**

Me and the Colonel ♫♫½ **1958** Average satire finds Jewish refugee S.L. Jacobowsky (Kaye) trying to get out of Paris to Spain before the Nazis occupy the city. He gets stuck travelling with anti-Semitic Polish colonel Prokoszny (Jurgens), who's also not eager to fall into German hands. If the trip went smoothly, there wouldn't be a story, so naturally the men are forced to put aside their differences to survive. Adapted from Franz Werfel's play "Jacobowsky and the Colonel." **110m/B VHS.** Danny Kaye, Curt Jurgens, Martita Hunt, Alexander Scourby, Liliane Montevecchi; *D:* Peter Glenville; *W:* S.N. Behrman.

The McMasters ♫♫ *The Blood Crowd; The McMasters... Tougher Than the West Itself* **1970 (R)** Set shortly after the Civil War, the film tells the story of the prejudice faced by a black soldier who returns to the southern ranch on which he was raised. Once there, the rancher gives him half of the property, but the ex-soldier has difficulty finding men who will work for him. When a group of Native Americans assist him, a band of bigoted men do their best to stop it. The movie was released in two versions with different endings: in one, prejudice prevails; in the other, bigotry is defeated. **89m/C VHS, DVD.** Burl Ives, Brock Peters, David Carradine, Nancy Kwan, Jack Palance, Dane Clark, L.Q. Jones, Alan Vint, John Carradine; *D:* Alf Kjellin.

McLintock! (continued)

Me and the Kid ♫♫½ **1993 (PG)** Minor career criminals Aiello and Pantoliani try a robbery on a ruthless financier's (Dukes) home and wind up kidnapping his 10-year-old son instead. But dad doesn't want to pay the ransom and Aiello dumps his partner (who wants to kill the kid) and heads out on the road with the boy. **97m/C VHS, DVD.** Danny Aiello, Joe Pantoliano, Alex Zuckerman, Cathy Moriarty, David Dukes, Anita Morris; *D:* Dan Curtis.

Me and the Mob ♫♫ *We Do I Gotta Kill?* **1994 (R)** Writer Jimmy Corona (Lorinz) thinks the way to get some colorful stories is to join up with his mobster uncle (Darrow). But Jimmy's no tough guy and (Darrow). But Jimmy's no tough guy and the feds coerce him into wearing a wire to bust the local godfather. Low-budget comedy is a lesson in tedium. **85m/C VHS, DVD.** James Lorinz, Tony Darrow, John A. Costello, Sandra Bullock, Anthony Michael Hall, Stephen Lee. Ted (Theodore) Sorel; *Cameos:* Steve Buscemi; *D:* Frank Rainone; *M:* Frank Rainone.

Me & Veronica ♫♫ **1993 (R)** Two estranged sisters try to come to terms with each other and their dead end lives. Good sister Fanny (McGovern) is a divorced waitress living in a run-down seaside town in New Jersey. One day bad sister Veronica (Wettig) shows up, announcing she's about to be sent to jail for welfare fraud. Veronica asks Fanny to look after her two kids while she's in jail and it's while visiting Veronica in prison that Fanny comes to realize her seemingly flamboyant sister is actually mentally ill and possibly suicidal. Grim little film with good lead performances. **97m/C VHS.** Elizabeth McGovern, Patricia Wettig, Michael O'Keefe, John Heard; *D:* Don Scardino; *W:* Leslie Lyles; *M:* David Mansfield.

Me & Will ♫½ **1999 (R)** Babes on bikes take to the road. Aspiring writer Jane (Rose) and artist Will (Behr) both have bad luck with men and drug problems, as well as a liking for chopper-riding. They meet in rehab and decide a road trip in search of the cycle ridden by Peter Fonda in "Easy Rider" is just the kind of quest they need. Uneven quality but a lot of recognizable faces in supporting roles. **93m/C VHS, DVD.** Sherrie Rose, Melissa Behr, Patrick Dempsey, Seymour Cassel, Grace Zabriskie, M. Emmet Walsh, Steve Railsback, Traci Lords, Billy Wirth; *D:* Sherrie Rose, Melissa Behr; *W:* Sherrie Rose, Melissa Behr; *C:* Joey Forsyte. **VIDEO**

Me and You and Everyone We Know ♫♫♫ **2005 (R)** Debut feature from conceptual artist July finds her playing wistful, struggling video artist Christine, who supports herself by chauffeuring senior citizens. She becomes unexpectedly involved with Richard (Hawkes), a shoe salesman with a raw heart from his recent divorce and two precocious sons with their own problems. Seven-year-old Robby (Ratcliff) unwittingly starts an online sex chat room, where he's mistaken for an adult with kinky sexuality at ideas. Meanwhile, his older brother Peter (Thompson) is tormented by two classmates who want to practice their oral sex techniques on 'im while he is more interested in a domestically-inclined neighbor. Saves itself from just being quirky and precious with winning performances. **90m/C DVD, US GB US** John Hawkes, Carlie Westerman, Miranda July, Miles Thompson, Brandon Ratcliff, Natasha Slayton, Najarra Townsend; *D:* Miranda July; *W:* Miranda July; *C:* Chuy Chavez; *M:* Michael Andrews.

Me, Myself & I ♫♫½ **1992 (R)** Segal is a successful New York writer who falls in love with next-door neighbor who S.L. Jacobowsky... turns out to be a multiple personality disorder. Fun leads, dumb movie. **97m/C VHS.** George Segal, JoBeth Williams, Shelley Hack, Don McNicOl, Bill Macy, Betsey Lynn George, Sharon Barry.

Me, Myself, and Irene ♫♫♫ **2000 (R)** Carrey is Charlie, a Rhode Island state trooper whose split personality (one meek and mild-mannered, the other an out-of-control sociopath) is controlled by medication, which he loses when transporting crime suspect Irene (Zellweger). Both sides fall for the girl and declare war on each other. Carrey's verbal and physical acrobatics, along with the Farrellys' patented gross-out scenes are as hilarious, and joyfully disgusting, as you'd imagine. And if you're into that kind of thing, you'll not be disappointed, but the movie shares the lead character's ailment: it has another side. The romance between Charlie and Irene can't keep up with the energy of the comedic scenes, especially the ones involving Charlie's three Mensacandidate, African-American sons, who almost steal the movie right out from under him (who'd a thunk it?) 117m/C VHS, DVD, Blu-ray Disc. Jim Carrey, Renee Zellweger, Robert Forster, Chris Cooper, Richard Jenkins, Traylor Howard, Daniel Greene, Zen Gesner, Tony Cox, Anthony Anderson, Lenny Clarke, Shannon Whirry, Rob Moran, Mongo Brownlee, Jerod Mixon, Michael Bowman, Mike Cerrone; *Cameos:* Anna Kournikova, Cam Neely, Brendan Shanahan; *D:* Bobby Farrelly, Peter Farrelly; *W:* Bobby Farrelly, Peter Farrelly, Mike Cerrone; *C:* Mark Irwin; *M:* Peter Yorn; *V:* Rex Allen.

Me Myself I ✓✓ 1999 (R) Pamela Drury (Griffiths) is a successful Sydney journalist who's also single, in her late 30s, and depressed by both situations. She moans about not marrying her longago beau Robert Dickson (Roberts) and, lo and behold, Pam's whisked into the life she could have had—marriage and mother of three in the suburbs. Of course, this Pam doesn't have a clue as to how her new life runs, which makes for some comic mileage. But it's the appealing Griffiths that holds all the unlikely yet cliched situations together. 104m/C VHS, DVD. *AU* Rachel Griffiths, David Roberts, Sandy Winton; *D:* Pip Karmel; *W:* Pip Karmel; *C:* Graeme Lind; *M:* Charlie Chan.

Me Without You ✓✓ 2001 (R) Marina (Friel) and Holly (Williams) are adolescent friends in London in 1974, whose changing relationship is seen over a 20-year period. Holly fancies Marina's brother Nat (Milburn) but Marina's jealousy prevents anything serious from developing. In college, Holly studies, Marina parties, and both become rivals for American lecturer Daniel (MacLachlan). Holly becomes increasingly dissatisfied with Marina's selfishness and eventually decides to pursue a relationship with Nat after all. Friel plays a brat whose vulnerability is occasionally revealed, while Williams works on her English accent as the idealistic nice girl. 107m/C VHS, DVD. *GB* Anna Friel, Michelle Williams, Oliver Milburn, Kyle MacLachlan, Trudie Styler, Nicky Henson, Allan Corduner, Deborah Findlay, Marianne (Cuau) Denicourt, Steve John Shepherd; *D:* Sandra Goldbacher; *W:* Sandra Goldbacher, Laurence Coriat; *C:* Denis Crossan; *M:* Adrian Johnston.

Me You Them ✓✓ 2000 *Eu Tu Eles* (PG-13) Hard-working Darlene (Case) returns to her dusty Brazilian village with a young son (and no husband) upon the death of her mother. She marries elderly Osias (Duarte) basically because he has a new house and has another son, whose father is probably not Osias. Then Osias's younger cousin Zezinho (Garcia) moves in and takes over household management while Darlene works in the fields. Yep, there's another baby. Finally, Darlene meets younger Ciro (Vasconcelos), a migrant worker, and invites him to stay around. You can guess what happens next. There's a little squabbling but soon everyone settles into a big, contented family. Portuguese with subtitles. 107m/C VHS, DVD. *BR PT* Regina Case, Lima Duarte, Stenio Garcia, Luiz Carlos Vasconcelos, Nilda Spencer; *D:* Andrucha Waddington; *W:* Elena Soarez; *C:* Breno Silveira; *M:* Gilberto Gil.

The Meal ✓✓ *Deadly Encounter* 1975 (R) During a dinner party held by a wealthy woman, the rich and powerful guests divulge each others' secrets with reckless disregard for the consequences. 90m/C VHS. Dina Merrill, Carl Betz, Leon Ames, Susan Logan, Vicki Powers, Steve Potter; *D:* R. John Hugh.

Mean Creek ✓✓✓ 2004 (R) The feature debut of Estes goes beyond teen coming-of-age clichés to tell a hard tale of moral choices. Shy, slight 13-year-old Sam (Culkin) is the favorite target of school bully George (Peck). Tough older bro Rocky (Morgan) decides to get even by inviting George on a boat trip and then humiliating and stranding him. Along for the ride are Rocky's friends, Marty (Mechowicz) and Clyde (Kelley), and Sam's potential girlfriend Millie (Schroeder). Of course, the plan goes awry as the characters prove to be multi-dimensional: the bully is lonely and vulnerable, the macho kid hides deep insecurities. Unexpected consequences reveal that the taste of revenge isn't sweet at all. The rating isn't primarily for language but isn't likely to shock the film's peer group. 89m/C DVD. *US* Rory Culkin, Ryan Kelly, Scott Mechowicz, Trevor Morgan, Josh Peck, Carly Schroeder; *D:* Jacob Aaron Estes; *W:* Jacob Aaron Estes; *C:* Sharon Meir; *M:* Tomandandy.

Mean Dog Blues ✓✓½ 1978 (PG) A musician is convicted of hit-and-run driving after hitching a ride with an inebriated politician. 108m/C VHS. George Kennedy, Kay Lenz, Scatman Crothers, Gregory Sierra, Tina Louise, William Windom; *D:* Mel Stuart; *C:* Robert B. Hauser.

Mean Frank and Crazy Tony ✓✓ 1975 (R) A mobster and the man who idolizes him attempt a prison breakout in this fun, action-packed production. 92m/C VHS, DVD. *IT* Lee Van Cleef, Tony LoBianco, Jean Rochefort, Jess Hahn; *D:* Michele Lupo.

Mean Girls ✓✓✓ 2004 (PG-13) "SNL" head writer/performer Fey successfully takes her sassy wit to the big screen with this clever teen comedy. Cady (Lohan) is a home-schooled kid raised in Africa attending school for the first time at 16 who uses jungle animals as her frame of reference. The popular girls are The Plastics, Barbie-esque divas led by Regina (McAdams), who take in the brainy Cady for sport. When Cady stupidly reveals her crush on Regina's ex, she quickly becomes a target. Familiar but updated, edgy portrayal of the high school social caste system is probably the smartest teen comedy since the heyday of John Hughes. Based on the non-fiction book "Queen Bees and Wannabees" by Rosalind Wiseman. 97m/C DVD. *US* Lindsay Lohan, Rachel McAdams, Lacey Chabert, Amanda Seyfried, Tina Fey, Lizzy Caplan, Tim Meadows, Amy Poehler, Ana Gasteyer, Daniel Franzese, Courtney Chase, Neil Flynn, Jonathan Bennett; *D:* Mark S. Waters; *W:* Tina Fey; *C:* Daryn Okada; *M:* Rolfe Kent.

Mean Guns ✓½ 1997 (R) Lots of mayhem will redeem this silly plot for the action fan. Moon (Ice-T) lures 100 assassins to an abandoned prison with the promise of $10 million for the last three men standing. Lou (Lambert) and Marcus (Halsey) are Moon's rivals. 90m/C VHS, DVD. Ice-T, Christopher Lambert, Michael Halsey, Deborah Van Valkenburgh, Tina Cote, Yuji Okumoto; *D:* Albert Pyun; *W:* Andrew Witham, Nat Whitcomb; *C:* George Mooradian; *M:* Tony Riparetti. VIDEO

Mean Johnny Barrows ✓½ 1975 When Johnny Barrows returns to his home town after being dishonorably discharged from the Army he is offered a job as a gang hitman. 83m/C VHS, DVD. Fred Williamson, Roddy McDowall, Stuart Whitman, Luther Adler, Jenny Sherman, Elliott Gould; *D:* Fred Williamson.

Mean Machine ✓✓ *Un Tipo con Una Faccia Strana ti Cerca per Uccideri; Cauldron of Death; Gangland; The Dirty Mob; Ricco* 1973 (R) British mob and his beautiful cohort plot revenge on organized crime for the murder of his father. 89m/C VHS, DVD. *IT SP* Chris Mitchum, Barbara Bouchet, Arthur Kennedy, Eduardo Fajardo, Paola Senatore; *D:* Tulio Demicheli; *W:* Mario di Nardo, Santiago Moncada; *C:* Francisco Fraile; *M:* Nando De Luca.

Mean Machine ✓✓ 2001 (R) British remake of Robert Aldrich's 1974 film, "The Longest Yard," that stresses comedy and crazies. Danny Meechan (former soccer star Jones) is a disgraced pro player who winds up in prison on assault charges. The warden (Hemmings) wants Danny to coach the guards' soccer team instead of chief guard Burton (Brown), who will make Danny's life very difficult if he accepts. So Danny proposes a compromise—he'll train and coach an inmate team in a match against the guards. You can guess where this one is going but Jones and Statham (who plays a violent con) are worth watching. 98m/C VHS, DVD. *US GB* Vinnie Jones, Jason Statham, David Hemmings, Ralph Brown, David Kelly, Jason Flemyng, Danny Dyer, Vas Blackwood, John Forgeham, Robbie Gee; *D:* Barry Skolnick; *W:* Charlie Fletcher, Chris Baker, Andrew Day; *C:* John Murphy; *M:* Alex Barber.

Mean Season ✓ 1985 (R) A vicious mass murderer makes a Miami crime reporter his confidante in his quest for publicity during his killing spree. In time, the madman's intentions become clear as the tensions and headlines grow clear as the tensions and headlines grow clear at each gruesome slaying. Then the reporter must come to terms with the idea that he is letting himself be used due to the success that the association is bringing him. Suspenseful story with a tense ending. Good performance from Russell as the reporter. Screenplay written by Christopher Crowe under the pseudonym Leon Piedmont. 106m/C VHS, DVD. Kurt Russell, Mariel Hemingway, Richard Jordan, Richard Masur, Andy Garcia, Joe Pantoliano, Richard Bradford, William (Bill) Smith; *D:* Phillip Borsos; *W:* Christopher Crowe; *M:* Lalo Schifrin.

Mean Streak ✓✓ 1999 (R) White supremacist serial killer goes after black baseball player Cash Manley (Dell), who's about to break Joe DiMaggio's hitting streak record of 56 baseball games. White cop Lou Mattoni (Bakula) and black FBI agent Altman Rogers (Leon) are out to stop him if their own prejudices don't derail the investigation. 97m/C VHS. Scott Bakula, Leon, Howard G.H. Dell, Wayne Best, Ron McLarty, Beau Starr, Brigid Coulter, Michael Filipowich; *D:* Tim Hunter; *W:* David Ryan, John Fasano; *C:* Denis Lenoir; *M:* Paul Buckmaster. CABLE

Mean Streets ✓✓✓✓ 1973 (R) A grimy slice of street life in Little Italy among lower echelon Mafiosos, unbalanced punks, and petty criminals. Charlie (Keitel), the nephew of mob boss Giovanni (Danova), struggles to keep his crazy friend Johnny Boy (De Niro) out of serious trouble. A riveting, free-form feature film, marking the formal debut by Scorsese (five years earlier he had completed a student film, "Who's That Knocking At My Door?"). Unorthodox camera movement and gritty performances by De Niro and Keitel, with underlying Catholic guilt providing the moral conflict. Excellent early '60s soundtrack. 112m/C VHS, DVD. Harvey Keitel, Robert De Niro, David Proval, Amy Robinson, Richard Romanus, David Carradine, Robert Carradine, Cesare Danova, George Memmoli, Victor Argo; *D:* Martin Scorsese; *W:* Martin Scorsese, Mardik Martin; *C:* Kent Wakeford. Natl. Film Reg. '97; Natl. Soc. Film Critics '73: Support. Actor (De Niro).

The Meanest Men in the West ✓ 1967 (PG) Two criminal halfbrothers battle frontier law and each other. 92m/C VHS, DVD. Charles Bronson, Lee Marvin, Lee J. Cobb, James Drury, Albert Salmi, Charles Grodin; *D:* Samuel Fuller; *W:* Charles S. Dubin; *C:* Lionel London, Alric Edens; *M:* Hal Mooney. TV

Meantime ✓✓ 1981 British TV comedy/drama about the working class finds brothers Mark (Daniels) and Colin (Roth) living with their unemployed dad in a depressing East London flat. Colin, who's looking to escape his dreary life, befriends skinhead Coxy (Oldman) to the dismay of the rest of the family. 90m/C VHS, DVD. *GB* Tim Roth, Gary Oldman, Phil Daniels, Alfred Molina, Pam Ferris; *D:* Mike Leigh; *C:* Roger Pratt; *M:* Andrew Dickson.

Meat Loaf: To Hell and Back ✓✓ 2000 (PG-13) Saga of rock singer Meat Loaf (Brown), born Marvin Lee Aday, from his dysfunctional family life to his early musical start and his first success in the '70s with the Top 10 hits from "Bat Out of Hell." Of course, there's also the inevitable decline and resurrection. Brown's a Meat Loaf lookalike and Pfeiffer is good as his loyal wife, Leslie, but this is a very familiar story. 90m/C VHS. W. Earl Brown, Dedee Pfeiffer, Zachary Throne, Jesse Lenat, Lisa Jane Persky; *D:* Jim McBride; *W:* Ron McGee; *C:* Denis Lenoir; *M:* Hummie Mann. CABLE

Meatballs ✓✓ 1979 (PG) The Activities Director at a summer camp who is supposed to organize fun for everyone prefers his own style of "fun." If you enjoy watching Murray blow through a movie, you'll like this one even as it lapses into boxoffice sentimentality. 92m/C VHS, DVD. *CA* Bill Murray, Harvey Atkin, Kate Lynch; *D:* Ivan Reitman; *W:* Len Blum, Harold Ramis, Janis Allen; *C:* Donald Wilder; *M:* Elmer Bernstein. Genie '80: Actress (Lynch).

Meatballs 2 ✓✓ 1984 (PG) The future of Camp Sasquatch is in danger unless the camp's best fighter can beat Camp Patton's champ in a boxing match. The saving grace of Bill Murray is absent in this one. 87m/C VHS. Archie Hahn, John Mengatti, Tammy Taylor, Kim Richards, Ralph Seymour, Richard Mulligan, Hamilton Camp, John Larroquette, Paul (Pee-wee Herman) Reubens, Misty Rowe, Elayne Boosler; *D:* Ken Wiederhorn.

Meatballs 3 ✓ WOOF! 1987 (R) Second sequel to the teenage sex/summer camp comedy. Enough is enough! 95m/C VHS. Sally Kellerman, Shannon Tweed, George Buza, Isabelle Mejias, Al Waxman, Patrick Dempsey; *D:* George Mendeluk.

Meatballs 4 ✓½ 1992 (R) Feldman stars as a water skier hired to serve as recreation director of Lakeside Water Ski Camp. His enemy is Monica (Douglas) of a nearby rival camp who wants to buy out Lakeside's owner and use the land for real estate development. Lame plot only serves to showcase some good water skiing stunts. 87m/C VHS, DVD. Corey Feldman, Jack Nance, Sarah Douglas, Bojesse Christopher; *D:* Bob Logan.

The Meateater WOOF! 1979 Disgusting horror flick of a disfigured hermit who inhabits a closed-up movie house. When it is reopened he turns into a stereotypical slasher. Vegetarians beware: references throughout about eating meat. 84m/C VHS. Arch Jaboulian, Diane Davis, Emily Spencer; *D:* Derek Savage.

The Mechanic ✓✓½ *Killer of Killers* 1972 (R) Bronson stars as Arthur Bishop, a wealthy professional killer for a powerful organization. When old friend "Big Harry" comes to him for help against the organization, he becomes Bishop's next job. Harry's son then shows up, wanting Bishop to mentor him in the ways of a hit man. A little slow but well done. One of Bronson's better action outings. 100m/C VHS, DVD. Charles Bronson, Jan-Michael Vincent, Keenan Wynn, Jill Ireland, Linda Ridgeway; *D:* Michael Winner; *W:* Lewis John Carlino; *C:* Richard H. Kline; *M:* Jerry Fielding.

The Medallion ✓✓ *Highbinders* 2003 (PG-13) So-so actioner has Hong Kong cop Eddie (Chan) transformed into an immortal warrior with superhuman powers thanks to a mysterious medallion. Eddie teams up with British Interpol agents Watson (Evans) and the beautiful Nicole (Forlani) and travels to Dublin to learn the medallion's secrets, rescue a kidnapped holy child, and fight the evil Snakehead (Sands), who wants the medallion for his own nefarious purposes (no doubt, world domination is involved). Nothing special in the way of plot but pic is watchable due to Chan's usual skills and considerable charm. Though still impressively doing much of his own stunt work, Chan's signature brand of gymnastic-style martial-arts is slightly undercut here by digital enhancement and an unnecessary array of special effect, fast-motion sequences. 90m/C VHS, DVD. *US HK* Jackie Chan, Claire Forlani, Julian Sands, Lee Evans, John Rhys-Davies, Anthony Wong, Christy Chung, Julian Myers; *D:* Gordon Chan; *W:* Gordon Chan, Bey Logan; *C:* Arthur Wong Ngok Tai; *M:* Adrian Lee.

Medea ✓✓½ 1970 Cinema poet Pasolini directs opera diva Callas in this straightforward adaptation of Euripides's classic about a sorceress whose escapades range from assisting in the theft of

Medea ✗✗ 1988 Director von Trier's adaptation of the classic Greek play by Euripides was filmed for Danish TV from a script originally co-written by Carl-Theodor Dreyer. Jason (Kier) betrays his lover Medea (Oleson) and their two sons when he agrees to a marriage with the daughter (Glinska) of King Creon (Jensen). Medea enacts a very bloody revenge. Danish with subtitles. 76m/C VHS, DVD, DK Udo Kier, Kirsten Olesen, Henning Jensen, Ludmilla Glinska, Baard Owe. D: Lars von Trier. W: Lars von Trier, Carl Theodor Dreyer, Preben Thomsen. C: Sejr Brockmann. M: Joachim Holbek. TV

Medicine Man ✗✗ 1992 (PG-13) Connery's usual commanding presence and the beautiful scenery are the only things to recommend in this lame effort. Dr. Robert Campbell (Connery) is a biochemist working in the Amazon rain forest on a cancer cure. Bracco is Dr. Rae Crane, a fellow researcher sent by the institute sponsoring Campbell to see how things are going. Although Crane is uptight and Campbell is gruff, they fall in love (supposedly), but they're sorely lacking in chemistry. Oh, Campbell's cancer cure is made from a rare flower being eradicated by the destruction of the rain forest. This politically correct cause meets romance falls short of ever being truly entertaining. 105m/C VHS, DVD, Sean Connery, Lorraine Bracco, Jose Wilker, Rodolfo de Alexandra, Francisco Tsirene Tsere Rereme, Elias Monteiro da Silva; D: John McTiernan; W: Tom Schulman; C: Donald McAlpine. M: Jerry Goldsmith.

The Medicine Show ✗✗½ 2001 (R) Dark comedy in which sarcastic cartoon writer Taylor (Silverman) is diagnosed with colon cancer. As the disease and treatment, progresses, he views the reactions of co-workers and family, the absurdity of the hospital experience, and impending surgery with sardonic wit. This is a welcome departure from the treacly, disease-of-the-week approach most filmmakers take to the subject. The proceedings begin to lose their edge, however, when Taylor meets, and begins a romance when cute, quirky leukemia patient Lynn. Silverman does an excellent job in the lead role. Based on the experiences of writer-director Morris. 100m/C DVD. Jonathan Silverman, Natasha Gregson Wagner, Greg Grunberg, Karl Wührer, Annabella Gurwitch, Maz Jobrani, Dennis Libscomb; D: Wendell Morris; W: Wendell Morris; C: Ramsey Nickell. CABLE

The Mediterranean in Flames ✗✗½ 1972 In Nazi-occupied Greece, a small but brave resistance is formed to fight its captors. One of the women within the group is forced to seduce a Nazi officer in an attempt to learn enemy secrets. 85m/C VHS, GR Costas Karras, Costas Precas. D: Dimis Dadras.

Mediterraneo ✗✗✗ 1991 (R) Languid, charming comedy based on the premise that love does make the world go 'round—especially in wartime. In 1941, eight misfit Italian soldiers are stranded on a tiny Greek island and are absorbed into the life of the island, finding love and liberty in the idyllic setting. Lighthearted fun. In Italian with English subtitles. 90m/C VHS, IT Diego Abatantuono, Giuseppe Cederna, Claudio Bigagli, Vanna Barba, Giuseppe Bisio, Luigi Ugo Conti, Memo Dini, Vasco Mirandola, Luigi

the Golden Fleece to murdering her own children. Not Pasolini at his best, but still better than most if what you're looking for is something arty. In Italian with English subtitles. 118m/C VHS, DVD, IT Maria Callas, Giuseppe Gentile, Laurent Terzieff; D: Pier Paolo Pasolini.

Medicine Man ✗½ 1930 Benny stars as a con-man who fronts a medicine show in this early talkie comedy. 57m/B VHS, DVD. Jack Benny, Betty Bronson, E. Alyn Warren, George E. Stone, Tom Dugan; D: Scott Pembroke.

Medicine River ✗✗½ 1994 (PG) A Native American photojournalist returns to his hometown after a 20-year absence and winds up in hot water with newfound friend Harlen Bigbear. 96m/C VHS, CA Graham Greene, Tom Jackson, Sheila Tousey, Jimmy Herman, Fisou Trujillo, Byron Chief-Moon, Janet-Laine Green; D: Stuart Margolin.

Medium Cool ✗✗½ 1969 Commentary on life in the '60s focuses on a TV news cameraman and his growing apathy with the events around him. His involvement with a Appalachian woman and her young son reawakens his conscience, leading to the three getting caught up in the turbulence of the 1968 Chicago Democratic convention. A frightening depiction of detachment in modern society. 111m/C VHS, DVD, Robert Forster, Verna Bloom, Peter Bonerz, Marianna Hill, Peter Boyle, Harold Blankenship, Charles Geary, Sid McCoy, Christine Bergstrom, William Sickinger; D: Haskell Wexler; W: Haskell Wexler; C: Haskell Wexler; M: Michael Bloomfield. Natl. Film Reg. '03.

Medusa ✗ Twisted 1974 A bizarre series of events occur when an abandoned yacht, containing two lifeless bodies is found on the Aegean Sea. 103m/C VHS, George Hamilton, Cameron Mitchell, Luciana Paluzzi, Theodore Roubanis; D: Gordon Hessler.

Medusa Against the Son of Hercules ✗ Perseo l'invincibile; Medusa vs. the Son of Hercules 1962 This time the strongman takes on the evil Medusa and her deadly army of rock men. 90m/C VHS, DVD, IT Richard Harrison, Elisa Cegani, Anna Ranalli, Angel Jordan; D: Alberto De Martino; W: Mario Caiano; C: Eloy Mella; M: Carlo Franci.

The Medusa Touch ✗ 1978 (R) A man is struck over the head and is admitted to a hospital. Meanwhile, strange disasters befall the surrounding city. It seems that despite his unconscious state, the man is using his telekinetic powers to will things to happen... 110m/C VHS, GB Richard Burton, Lino Ventura, Lee Remick, Harry Andrews, Alan Badel, Marie-Christine Barrault, Michael Hordern, Derek Jacobi, Jeremy Brett; D: Jack Gold; W: Jack Gold, John Briley.

The Medium ✗✗ 1951 A phony medium is done in by her own trickery in this filmed version of the Menotti opera. 80m/B VHS, DVD, Marie Powers, Anna Maria Alberghetti, Leo Coleman; D: Gian-Carlo Menotti; W: Gian-Carlo Menotti.

Meet Danny Wilson ✗✗½ 1952 Talented New York singer Wilson (Sinatra) and his pianist buddy Mike Ryan (Nicol) head out to Hollywood to try their luck. Danny meets club singer Joy Carroll (Winters) who introduces him to gangster owner Nick Driscoll (Burr). Nick manages Danny for a hefty percentage and makes him a star at his club but Danny's lovelife goes south when Joy picks Mike over him. Then Driscoll demands his money, Sinatra gets to croon some great tunes. I've Got a Crush on You; How Deep Is the Ocean; When You're Smiling; All of Me; She's Funny That Way; That Old Black Magic. You're a Sweetheart; Lonesome Man Blues; A Good Man Is Hard to Find. 88m/B VHS. Frank Sinatra, Alex Nicol, Shelley Winters, Raymond Burr, Tommy Farrell, Vaughn Taylor, Jack Kruschen, Donald MacBride; D: Joseph Pevney; W: Don McGuire.

Meet Dave 2008 Another question-able Murphy sci-fi comedy (did he learn nothing from "Pluto Nash"?). There's something not quite right about Dave—probably because he's actually a space ship staffed by 100 teeny aliens, that's been designed in the image of the ship's captain. The aliens have come to Earth in this disguise looking for help to save their own planet. All sorts of slapstick confusion follows as Dave interacts with the human population of the Big Apple. Not yet reviewed. 77m/C Eddie Murphy, Elizabeth Banks, Gabrielle Union, Ed Helms, Judah Friedlander, Shawn Christian, Scott Caan, Marc Blucas, Pat Kilbane, Michael O'Malley; D: Brian Robbins; W: Bill Corbett, Rob Greenberg; C: Clark Mathis; M:

Meet John Doe ✗✗✗ 1941 A social commentary about an unemployed, down-and-out man selected to be the face of a political goodwill campaign. Honest and trusting, he eventually realizes that he is being used to further the careers of corrupt politicians. Available in colorized version. 123m/B VHS, DVD, Gary Cooper, Barbara Stanwyck, Edward Arnold, James Gleason, Walter Brennan, Spring Byington, Gene Lockhart, Regis Toomey, Ann Doran, Rod La Rocque; D: Frank Capra; W: Robert Riskin, Robert Presnell Sr.; C: George Barnes; M: Dimitri Tiomkin.

Meet Me in Las Vegas ✗✗ 1956 Compulsive gambler/cowboy Dailey betters his luck when he hooks up with hoofer girlfriend Charisse. Much frolicking and dancing and cameo appearances by a truckload of stars. A little more entertaining than a game of solitaire. The Girl With the Yaller Shoes; If You Can Dream; Hell Hath No Fury; Lucky Charm; I Refuse to Rock 'n Roll; Rehearsal Ballet; Sleeping Beauty Ballet; Frankie and Johnny. 112m/C VHS. Dan Dailey, Cyd Charisse, Agnes Moorehead, Lili Darvas, Jim Backus, Cara Williams, Betty Lynn, Oscar Karlweis, Liliane Montevecchi, Jerry Colonna, Frankie Laine; Cameos: Debbie Reynolds, Frank Sinatra, Peter Lorre, Vic Damone, Tony Martin, Elaine Stewart; D: Roy Rowland; W: Isobel Lennart.

Meet Me in St. Louis ✗✗✗½ 1944 Wonderful music in this charming tale of a St. Louis family during the 1903 World's Fair. One of Garland's better movies. You and I; Skip to My Lou; Over the Banister; Meet Me in St. Louis; Brighten the Corner; Summer in St. Louis; All Hallow's Eve; Ah, Love; The Horrible One. 113m/C VHS, DVD, Judy Garland, Margaret O'Brien, Mary Astor, Lucille Bremer, Tom Drake, June Lockhart, Harry Davenport; D: Vincente Minnelli; C: George J. Folsey. Natl. Film Reg. '94.

Meet Sexton Blake ✗✗ 1944 A detective is hired to find a ring and some secret papers that were stolen from the corpse of a man killed in an air raid. He discovers that the papers contained the plans for a new metal alloy to be used in planes. Entertaining for its melodramatic elements. 80m/B VHS, GB David Farrar, John Varley, Magda Kun, Gordon McLeod, Manning Whiley, Charles Farrell; D: John Harlow; W: John Harlow.

Meet Joe Black ✗✗ 1998 (PG-13) "Death Takes a Holiday," Pitt plays a not-so-Grim Reaper who decides to see what living is all about by inhabiting the body of a recently deceased man. He grants some extra time to wealthy businessman William Parrish (Hopkins), if he'll serve as Death's guide. Now named Joe Black, Death takes to his new life but causes problems in Parrish's household, especially when he falls in love with Parrish's doctor daughter, Susan (a weak Forlani). 180m/C VHS, DVD, HD DVD, Brad Pitt, Anthony Hopkins, Claire Forlani, Marcia Gay Harden, Jeffrey Tambor, Jake Weber; D: Martin Brest; W: Ron Osborn, Jeff Reno, Kevin Wade, Bo Goldman; C: Emmanuel Lubezki; M: Thomas Newman.

Meet the Fockers ✗✗½ 2004 (PG-13) Free-spirited Jews meet uptight WASPs in this long-awaited sequel to 2000's "Meet the Parents." Nervous Greg Focker (Stiller) and fiancee Pam (Polo) take Dina and Jack (De Niro) to finally meet his folks: lawyer turned house hubby Bernie (Hoffman) and senior citizen sex therapist Roz (Streisand). The duo extravagantly adores each other, much to Greg's embarrassment, and of course, there's more problems for poor Greg. Cultural clashes follow predictably and everyone seems to be coasting comfortably on their talent. 116m/C VHS, DVD, HD DVD, US Robert De Niro, Ben Stiller, Dustin Hoffman, Barbra Streisand, Blythe Danner, Teri Polo, Tim Blake Nelson, Alanna Ubach, Ray Santiago, Kali Rocha, Shelley Berman, Owen Wilson, Spencer Pickren, Bradley Pickren; D: Jay Roach; W: Jim Herzfeld, John Hamburg; C: John Schwartzman; M: Randy Newman.

Meet the Mob ✗✗ So's Your Aunt Emma 1942 A country spinster visits her son in the big city and is mistaken for a notorious murderess. Complications arise when she tries to keep the boy honest. Could have worked better. 62m/B VHS, DVD, Zasu Pitts, Roger Pryor, Warren Hymer, Gwen Kenyon, Douglas Fowley, Elizabeth Russell, Tristram Coffin, Lester Dorr, Wheeler Oakman, Malcolm "Bud" McTaggart; D: Jean Yarbrough.

Meet the Navy ✗✗ 1946 Post-war musical revue about a pianist and a dancer. 81m/B VHS, Lionel Murton, Margaret Hurst, John Pratt, Robert Goodier; D: Alfred Travers; W: Lester Cooper; C: Ernest Palmer, Geoffrey Unsworth; M: Louis Silvers.

Meet the Deedles ✗✗ 1998 (PG) The answer to the question, "What would happen if Bill and Ted or Wayne and Garth were even dumber?" Hard to believe? No, just hard to watch. Phil and Stew Deedle (Walker and Van Wormer) are two rich surfer airheads who just wanna have fun, so under circumstances we have no time to explain here, they're mistaken for new rangers at a Yellowstone national park, where a mounting prairie dog problem. It seems that critter ex-ranger Slater (Hopper, phoning in his patented mondo-weirdo) has enslaved the rodents and is trying to redirect the geyser Old Faithful. Features heinous dialogue and stunts filled from Mountain Dew commercials. 94m/C VHS, Steve Van Wormer, Paul Walker, A.J. (Allison Joy) Langer, John Ashton, Dennis Hopper, Eric (Hans Gudegast) Braeden, Richard Lineback, Robert Englund, Megan Cavanagh; D: Steve Boyum; W: Jim Herzfeld, Dale Pollock; C: David Hennings.

Meet the Parents ✗✗ 1991 A young man visits his fiance's parents and every nightmare, every tragedy that can possibly happen, does. From the minds of "National Lampoon," with an appearance by beyond-bizarre comedian Emo Phillips. 72m/C VHS, Greg Glienna, Jacqueline Cahill, Dick Galoway, Carol Wheeler, Mary Ruth Clarke, Emo Phillips; D: Greg Glienna; W: Mary Ruth Clarke.

Meet the Parents ✗✗✗ 2000 (PG-13) If you have any sense of empathy at all, you'll be squirming uncomfortably for Greg (Stiller), a nice Jewish boy who suffers an extended brainlock when he meets his girlfriend Pam's parents and parents during her sister's wedding weekend. It doesn't help that one of those parents is Jack (De Niro), an ex-CIA psychological profiler who takes an immediate dislike to his prospective son-in-law. Greg smashing off on the wrong foot by accidentally smashing the urn holding the ashes of Jack's mother with a champagne cork, and his luck goes down from there. The rest of the cast performs well, especially Danner as Pam's mother, and De Niro plays off of his tough guy image for a brilliant comedic performance. 108m/C VHS, DVD, HD DVD, Ben Stiller, Robert De Niro, Teri Polo, Blythe Danner, James Rebhorn, Jon Abrahams, Owen Wilson, Phyllis George, Kali Rocha, Thomas (Tom) McCarthy, Nicole DeHuff; D: Jay Roach; W: Jim Herzfeld, John Hamburg; C: Peter James; M: Randy Newman.

Meet the Feebles ✗✗ 1989 Sex and violence gorefest perpetuated by puppets—and the dementia of director Jackson. A TV variety show, populated by animal puppets and humans in costume, is enough for you already. Among the characters are a sleazy walrus producer, his slinky Siamese cat mistress, a junkie frog, and a manic-depressive elephant. There's also several musical production numbers, if things aren't strange enough for you already. 94m/C VHS, DVD, NZ D: Peter Jackson; W: Peter Jackson, Danny Mulheron, Fran Walsh, Stephen Sinclair; C: Murray Milne; M: Peter Dasent; V: Peter Vere-Jones, Mark Hadlow, Stuart Devine, Donna Akinson, Mark Wright, Brian Sergent.

Meet the Hollowheads ✗½ 1989 (PG-13) Family situation comedy set in a futuristic society. 88m/C VHS, DVD, John Glover, Nancy Mette, Richard Portnow, Matt Shakman, Juliette Lewis, Anne Ramsey; D: Tom Burman; W: Tom Burman.

Meet the Robinsons ♂♂ ½

2007 (G) Based on William Joyce's book "A Day With Wilbur Robinson," which finds young science geek Lewis despairing of ever being adopted. But his luck changes thanks to teenager Wilbur Robinson and his time machine. Wilbur takes Lewis into the future to meet his eccentric family, but everyone's dreams are threatened by the sinister man in the bowler hat, who's got it out for Lewis. The jovial T-Rex, who's meant to aid the bad guy, is a scene-stealer. Hyperactive animated comedy is the first release by Disney in its Digital 3-D process. **102m/C DVD, Blu-ray Disc.** *US* **D:** Stephen John Anderson; **W:** Jon Bernstein, Donald Hall, Stephen John Anderson, Michelle Spitz, Nathan Greno, Aurian Redson, Joe Mateo; **M:** Danny Elfman; **V:** Jordan Fry, Angela Bassett, Tom Selleck, Harland Williams, Daniel Hansen, Wesley Singerman, Laurie Metcalf, Adam West, Nicole Sullivan, Stephen John Anderson.

Meet the Spartans woof! 2008

(PG-13) Brain-dead spoof of the hardly cerebral but ripe for parody "300" swords-and-sandals epic hangs on the story of Leonidas (Maguire) leading his fierce army of 13 into battle against the invading hordes of Xerxes (Davitian), supported by his Queen Margo (Electra). But plot hardly matters as Seltzer and Friedberg once again scrape the bottom of the pop-culture barrel for a make-it-stop string of lazy swipes at movies and celebs buoyed by body-function gags and gay jokes that barely bother to be funny, let alone subversive. Way too long and way too dumb. **83m/C DVD.** *US* Carmen Electra, Ken Davitian, Kevin Sorbo, Diedrich Bader, Sean Maguire, Method Man, Phil Morris, Travis Van Winkle, Jareb Dauplaise; **D:** Aaron Seltzer, Jason Friedberg; **W:** Aaron Seltzer, Jason Friedberg.

Meet Wally Sparks ♂♂ 1997 (R)

No-brow. "Man Who Came to Dinner." Smutty TV shock-talk host Sparks (Dangerfield) is given one week to save his failing show when producer Reynolds (with a noticeably bad rug) puts him on notice. Opportunity knocks when he is invited to a party at the governor's mansion to interview the conservative head honcho (Stiers). Once there, a freak accident with a drunken horse prevents Sparks from leaving, and the new guest makes himself right at home by turning the fancy digs into a broadcast studio. Dangerfield's machine gun spray of one liners occasionally hits, as do his sometimes lengthy and elaborately set up jokes that do little to propel the plot along but are pure Dangerfield. Not much beyond Rodney makes lackluster "Sparks" fly. **107m/C VHS, DVD.** Rodney Dangerfield, David Ogden Stiers, Burt Reynolds, Debi Mazar, Cindy Williams, Alan Rachins; **D:** Peter Baldwin; **W:** Rodney Dangerfield, Harry Basil; **C:** Richard H. Kline; **M:** Michel Colombier.

Meeting at Midnight ♂♂ 1944

Charlie Chan is invited to a seance to solve a perplexing mystery. Chan discovers that they use mechanical figures and from there on solving the murder is easy. **67m/B VHS, DVD.** Sidney Toler, Joseph Crehan, Mantan Moreland, Frances Chan, Ralph Peters, Helen Beverly; **D:** Phil Rosen.

Meeting Daddy ♂♂ ½ 1998 (R)

Neurotic New Yorker Peter (Charles) falls in love with Georgia peach Melanie (Wentworth) and then he travels to Savannah to meet her southern-fried family, including her eccentric, irascible father, the Colonel (Bridges). **91m/C VHS, DVD.** Lloyd Bridges, Josh Charles, Alexandra Wentworth, Beau Bridges, Walter Olkewicz, Kristy Swanson; **D:** Peter Gould; **C:** Mike Mayers; **M:** Adam Fields. **VIDEO**

Meeting Venus ♂♂ ½ 1991

(PG-13) Backstage drama featuring Close as Karin Andersson, a world-famous Swedish opera diva. An international cast of characters adds to this sophisticated fiction set amidst a newly unified Europe. Josephson, Johanna Ter Steege, Maria De Medeiros, Ildiko Bansagi, Macha Meril, Dorottya Udvaros, Jay O. Sanders, Victor Poletti; **D:** Istvan Szabo; **W:** Istvan Szabo, Michael Hirst; **C:** Lajos Koltai; **V:** Kiri Te Kanawa.

---

and rarefied an atmosphere to take much interest. **99m/C DVD.** *US* Radha Mitchell, Chloe Sevigny, Jonny Lee Miller, Will Ferrell, Amanda Peet, Chiwetel Ejiofor, Wallace Shawn; **D:** Woody Allen; **W:** Woody Allen; **C:** Vilmos Zsigmond.

Meetings with Remarkable Men ♂♂ ½ 1979

An acclaimed, visually awesome film version of the memoir by Gurdjieff, about his wanderings through Asia and the Middle East searching for answers and developing his own spiritual code. Mildly entertaining but only of true interest to those familiar with the subject. **108m/C VHS.** Terence Stamp, Dragan Maksimovic, Mikica Dmitrijevic; **D:** Peter Brook.

Megaforce woof! 1982 (PG)

Futuristic thriller directed by stuntman Needham follows the adventures of the military task force, Megaforce, on its mission to save a small democratic nation from attack. Bostwick leads the attack. 'Nuff said. **99m/C VHS.** Barry Bostwick, Persis Khambatta, Edward Mulhare, Henry Silva, Michael Beck, Ralph Wilcox; **D:** Hal Needham.

Megalodon ♂♂ 2003 (PG-13)

Prehistoric 11-ton shark, Carchardodon Megalodon, is rudely awakened by unsuspecting deep-sea oil diggers and he's not in the mood to make nice with the trespassers. **91m/C VHS, DVD.** Robin Sachs, Al Sapienza, Leighanne Littrell, Mark Sheppard, Jennifer Sommerfield, Evan Mirand, Steve Scionti, Gary J. Tunnicliffe, Fred Belford, Yasmine Delawari, Stanley Isaacs, Will Boroers, John Michael Mauer; **D:** Pat Corbitt; **W:** Gary J. Tunnicliffe, Stanley Isaacs; **C:** Timothy Housel; **M:** Tony Fennell, Billy T. James, Brian Randazzo. **VIDEO**

Megasnake ♂♂ ½ *Mega Snake 2007 (R)*

Ah yes, another Sci-Fi Channel creation (with some decent CGI). In a backwater town filled with snakes and snake handlers, dimwit Duff steals a very rare snake to add to his collection. It must be super-snake because, given the chance, it grows and grows and grows until it can swallow a man in a single gulp. Having escaped Duff, Megasnake heads off to have some fun at the county fair (and we don't mean elephant ears and ring toss). **90m/C DVD.** Michael Shanks, Siri Baruc, Mick Harvey, Ben Cardinal, John T. Woods, Michele Atherton; **D:** Tibor Takacs; **W:** Rob Robinson, Alexander Volz; **C:** Emil Topuzov; **M:** Guy Zerafa, Dave Klotz. **CABLE**

Megaville ♂♂ 1991 (R)

Set in the not too distant future, corrupt politician Travanti struggles to corner the market on the evil technology "Dream-a-Life," which aims to control the rebellious "riff-raff" of Megaville. He does all of his dealings while up against a hitman who has a defective memory chip in his brain. **96m/C VHS.** Billy Zane, Daniel J. Travanti, J.C. Quinn, Grace Zabriskie; **D:** Peter Lehner; **W:** Peter Lehner.

Melanie ♂♂ ½ 1982 (PG)

Drama tells the tale of one poor woman's courage, determination, and optimism, as she tries to regain her child from her ex-husband. She befriends musician Cummings (a founding member of "Guess Who" rock band) who helps. Usual cliches balanced: by good performances. **109m/C VHS.** *CA* Glynnis O'Connor, Paul Sorvino, Don Johnson, Burton Cummings; **D:** Rex Bromfield.

Melanie Darrow ♂♂ ½ 1997 (PG-13)

Routine drama finds relentless attorney Melanie Darrow (Burke) defending the younger husband of a socialite friend for the woman's murder, much to the dismay of Melanie's homicide cop brother (Bloom). **88m/C VHS.** Delta Burke, Brian Bloom, Daniel Birt, Jonathan Banks, Bruce Abbott, Shawn Ashmore, Wendel Meldrum; **D:** Gary Nelson.

Melinda and Melinda ♂♂ 2005

(PG-13) Allen sticks to the familiar in a talky tale of Manhattanites debating the tragic and comic. Over dinner, playwright Sy (Shawn), who writes comedies, and tragedienne Max (Pine) entertain themselves with an urban anecdote about an unhappy, neurotic woman named Melinda (Mitchell). In both stories she crashes the dinner party of friends with her tale of disaster, causing marital misunderstandings and emotional dramas. The leading males in the story are both ineffectual, unemployed actors (Miller, Ferrell) while their wives (Sevigny, Peet) are successful. And what does that say, we wonder. Or maybe we don't because, despite the talent involved, it all seems rather too precious

---

Melody Time ♂♂ 1948

Seven animated/musical tales from the Disney studios, including "Blame It On the Samba" with Donald Duck; "Once Upon a Wintertime;" "Bumble Boogie;" "Johnny Appleseed;" "Little Toot" with musical narration provided by the Andrews Sisters; Fred Waring and the Pennsylvanians singing "Trees;" the Joyce Kilmer poem; and Roy Rogers narrating the story of "Pecos Bill." **75m/C VHS, DVD.** Roy Rogers; **D:** Clyde Geronimi, Wilfred Jackson, Jack Kinney, Hamilton Luske; **C:** Winton C. Hoch; **V:** Dennis Day, Ethel Smith, Buddy Clark, Bob Nolan, The Andrews Sisters, Frances Langford.

Melody Trail ♂ 1935

Autry wins $1000 in a rodeo, loses the money to a gypsy, gets a job, falls for his employer's daughter...and in the end captures a kidnapper and cattle rustlers. ♫ Hold On, Little Doggie, Hold On; On the Prairie; Lookin for the Lost Chord; The Hurdy Gurdy Man; My Prayer For Tonight; End of the Trail; I'd Love a Home in the Mountains. **60m/B VHS.** Gene Autry, Smiley Burnette, Ann Rutherford; **D:** Joseph Kane.

Meltdown ♂♂ *High Risk; Shu Dan Long Wei* 1995

Apparently producer/director Wong Jing has a score to settle with Jackie Chan. This action/comedy revolves around a drunken action star called Frankie (Cheung) who claims to do all of his own stunts but uses a team of stuntmen, including former cop Kit Li (Li), whose wife and son were killed (in a particularly ridiculous opening sequence) by an evil criminal mastermind (Wong). Who, with his gang, turns up to steal the Russian crown jewels that are being exhibited in a Hong Kong hotel. Think slapstick "Die Hard," although it's virtually impossible for western audiences to figure out where the action ends and the comedy begins. **100m/C VHS, DVD.** *HK* Jet Li, Jacky Cheung, Chingmy Yau, Valerie Chow, Charlie Yeoh, Kelvin Wong; **D:** Wong Jing; **W:** Wong Jing.

Meltdown woof! 2006

Which is what you'll want to do to the DVD after you've wasted your time on this lame "Armageddon-is-a-comin'" flick. Scientist blows up an asteroid endangering earth, but its fragments push our planet's orbit closer to the sun, causing intense global warming and evacuations to the Arctic. Uh, isn't all that ice supposed to melt? What do these people have—an ark? Maybe the hungry polar bears will get to them first. **93m/C DVD.** Casper Van Dien, Stefanie von Pfetten, Venus Terzo, Amanda Crew, Vincent Gale, Ryan McDonell; **D:** J.P. Howell; **W:** Rick Drew; **C:** Adam Sliwinski; **M:** Ron Ramin. **CABLE**

Melvin and Howard ♂♂♂ ½

1980 (R) Story of Melvin Dummar, who once gave Howard Hughes a ride. Dummar later claimed a share of Hughes's will. Significant for Demme's direction and fine acting from Steenburgen/LeMat, and Robards in a small role as Hughes. Offbeat and very funny. **95m/C VHS, DVD.** Paul LeMat, Jason Robards Jr., Mary Steenburgen, Michael J. Pollard, Dabney Coleman, Elizabeth Cheshire, Pamela Reed, Cheryl "Rainbeaux" Smith; **D:** Jonathan Demme; **W:** Bo Goldman; **C:** Tak Fujimoto; **M:** Bruce Langhorne. Oscars '80: Orig. Screenplay, Support. Actress (Steenburgen); Golden Globes '81: Support. Actress (Steenburgen); L.A. Film Critics '80: Support. Actress (Steenburgen); N.Y. Film Critics '80: Director (Demme), Screenplay, Support. Actress (Steenburgen); Natl. Soc. Film Critics '80: Film. Screenplay, Support. Actress (Steenburgen); Writers Guild '80: Orig. Screenplay.

Melvin Goes to Dinner ♂♂

2003 (R) Joey (Price) invites Melvin (Blieden) and Alex (Courtney) to dinner as a way of catching up; they are also unexpectedly joined by Alex's friend Sarah (Gurwitch). Since each person at the table is determined to drive him out of there's a one other person at the table, there's a certain awkwardness at first, but then the conversation (often confessional) starts to flow. Oh, and despite the title, the characters are not actually shown dining, so at least you won't get hungry, although all the talking may make you sleepy. **83m/C VHS, DVD.** Annabelle Blieden, Stephanie Courtney, Matt Price, Annabelle Gurwitch, Maura Tierney; **D:** Bob Odenkirk; **W:** Michael Blieden; **C:** Alex Vendler; **M:** Michael Penn.

Melissa ♂♂ 1997

Unemployed reporter Guy Foster (Dutton) is trying to make a new career as a novelist. But when his wife Melissa (Ehle) is murdered, all the evidence points to Guy and he has to find the real killer to prove his innocence. Based on the novel by Francis Durbridge. **150m/C DVD.** *GB* Tim Dutton, Jemifer Ehle, Adrian Dunbar, Julie Walters, Faith Edwards, Hugh Quarshie, Diana Weston; **D:** Bill Anderson; **W:** Alan Bleasdale; **C:** Dick Dodd; **M:** Richard Harvey. **TV**

Melo ♂♂ 1986

The title is short for "melodrama" so you know exactly when sort of story you're in for. Discontented Romaine begins an affair with womanizing concert violinist Marcel, an old friend of her boring husband Pierre's. While Marcel is away on tour, Pierre becomes seriously (and suspiciously) ill. When Romaine's perfidy is discovered, she commits suicide. However, years later, Pierre demands the truth from Marcel. French with subtitles. **112m/C DVD.** *FR* Sabine Azema, Pierre Arditi, Andre Dussollier, Fanny Ardant, Jacques Dacqmine; **D:** Alain Resnais; **W:** Alain Resnais; **C:** Charlie Van Damme, Michel Philippe-Gerard.

Melody ♂♂ 1971 (G)

Sensitive but slow study of a special friendship which enables two pre-teens to survive in a regimented and impersonal world. Features music by the Bee Gees. **106m/C VHS.** *GB* Tracy Hyde, Jack Wild, Mark Lester, Colin Barrie, Roy Kinnear; **D:** Waris Hussein; **W:** Alan Parker.

Melody Cruise ♂♂ 1932

Boring musical romantic comedy that can't stay with any one of three things for more than a minute without careening into one of the other two. ♫ I Met Her at a Party; He's Not the Marrying Kind; Isn't This a Night For Love; This is the Hour. **75m/B VHS.** Phil Harris, Charlie Ruggles, Greta Nissen, Helen Mack, Chick Chandler; **D:** Mark Sandrich; **M:** Max Steiner.

Melody for Three ♂♂ 1941

In the tradition of matchmaker, Doctor Christian aids in the reuniting of music-teacher mother and great-conductor father, who have been divorced for years, in order to help the couple's son, a violin prodigy. **69m/B VHS, DVD.** Jean Hersholt, Fay Wray; **D:** Erle C. Kenton.

Melody in Love ♂ 1978

A young girl visits her cousin and her swinging friends on a tropical island. Dubbed. **90m/C VHS.** Melody O'Bryan, Sasha Hehn; **D:** Hubert Frank.

Melody Master ♂♂ *New Wine 1941*

Romanticized biography of composer Franz Schubert, chronicling his personal life and loves, along with performances of his compositions. If you just have to know what drove the composer of "Ave Maria" it may hold your interest, but otherwise not very compelling. **80m/B VHS.** Alan Curtis, Ilona Massey, Binnie Barnes, Albert Bassermann, Billy Gilbert, Sterling Holloway; **M:** Miklos Rozsa.

Melody of the Plains ♂ 1937

Singing cowpoke teams up with a young girl for some cattle-rustlin' adventure. Substandard horse opry due to poor direction and haphazard lensing. **53m/B VHS.** Fred Scott, Louise Small, Al "Fuzzy" St. John, David Sharpe, Lafe (Lafayette) McKee, Charles "Slim" Whitaker; **D:** Sam Newfield; **W:** Bennett Cohen.

Melody Ranch ♂♂ ½ 1940

Gene returns to his home town as an honored guest and appointed sheriff. But gangster MacLane is determined to drive him out of town. ♫ Melody Ranch; Call of the Canyon; Vote for Autry; My Gal Sal; Torpedo Joe; What Are Cowboys Made Of?; Rodeo Rose; Back in the Saddle Again. **84m/C VHS, DVD.** Gene Autry, Jimmy Durante, George "Gabby" Hayes, Ann Miller, Barton MacLane, Joseph (Joe) Sawyer, Horace Mahoney, Veda Ann Borg; **D:** Joseph Santley; Natl. Film Reg. '02.

Melvin Purvis: G-Man *The Legend of Machine Gun Kelly; Kansas City Massacre* 1974 Mediocre action film has dedicated federal agent tracking killer Machine Gun Kelly across American Midwest during Depression. 78m/C VHS, Dale Robertson, Harris Yulin, Margaret Blye, Matt Clark, Ellie Street, Dick Sargent, John Karlen, David Canary; *D:* Dan Curtis. TV

The Member of the Wedding 1952 While struggling through her adolescence, 12-year-old tomboy Frankie (played by 26-year-old Harris) is growing up in 1945 Georgia and seeking solace from her family's cook, Berenice (Waters) and her cousin, John Henry (de Wilde). Based on Carson McCuller's play, this story of family, longing, and growth is well acted and touching. 90m/C VHS, Ethel Waters, Julie Harris, Brandon de Wilde, Arthur Franz, William Hansen, Nancy Gates, James Edwards, Harry Bolden; *D:* Fred Zinnemann; *W:* Edward Anhalt; *C:* Hal Mohr; *M:* Alex North.

The Member of the Wedding 1997 (PG) TV rehash of Carson McCuller's play about a young girl who finds she's got some growing up to do when big brother marries. No match for Zinnemann's '52 version, nor Mann's earlier "All Quiet on the Western Front" and "Marty." 90m/C VHS, Dana Hill, Pearl Bailey, Howard E. Rollins Jr.; *D:* Delbert Mann.

Memento 2000 (R) Twisty and engaging noir thriller of a man searching for his wife's killer in Los Angeles. Only problem is, Leonard Shelby (Pearce) lost his short-term memory after the attack and forgets all current events every 15 minutes, or so. Problem solved as Shelby tattoos the most vital info all over his body and leaves less permanent "clues" for family's gentle but no-nonsense housekeeper Berenice. Shelby meets Natalie (Moss) and Teddy (Pantoliano) who may want to help him, but like his own memory, definitely can't be trusted. Ingeniously constructed story is told backwards, from Pearce's shooting of the killer to his puzzle-like construction of events and renders the audience as clueless as the impaired hero. Clever use of flashbacks and black-and-white segs help define events in time. More than normally required mental exercise is more than worth the effort. Director Nolan adapted the film from short story by brother Jonathan. 116m/C VHS, DVD, Blu-ray Disc. US Guy Pearce, Carrie-Anne Moss, Joe Pantoliano, Mark Boone Jr., Stephen Tobolowsky, Callum Keith Rennie, Harriet Sansom Harris, Jorja Fox; *D:* Christopher Nolan; *W:* Christopher Nolan; *C:* Wally Pfister; *M:* David Julyan. Ir'd. Spirit '01: Director (Nolan); Screenplay; Ind. Spirit '02: Film, Support. Actress (Moss); L.A. Film Critics '01: Screenplay; Broadcast Film Critics '01: Screenplay.

Memoirs of a Geisha 2005 (PG-13) This look into the world of Japan's "Geisha" escorts in the 1930s flounders thanks to Marshall's bizarre decision to cast the film with Chinese actors and shoot it in the U.S., but cultural insensitivity isn't this melodrama's only sin. Sayuri (Zhang) is sold into a geisha household, where her companionship skills are refined by Mameha (Yeoh), the chief rival of the household's "Mother" (Momoi). Sayuri is ambivalent about being a geisha until she realizes that it can get her closer to The Chairman (Watanabe), a kindly businessman she once met. Sayuri begins relishing her role as a renowned geisha. The predictable plot grows in both heft and velocity, straining audience patience with its two and a half hour running time. 137m/C DVD, Blu-ray Disc. UMD. US Ken(saku) Watanabe, Michelle Yeoh, Koji Yakusho, Youki Kudoh, Tsai Chin, Cary-Hiroyuki Tagawa, Gong Li, Randall Duk Kim, Mako, Kenneth Tsang, Shizuko Hoshi, Zhang Ziyi, Kaori Momoi, Suzuka Ohgo, Thomas Ikeda, Eugenia Yuan; *D:* Rob Marshall; *W:* Robin Swicord; *C:* Dion Beebe; *M:* John Williams. Oscars '05: Art Dir./Set Dec., Cinematog., Costume Des.; British Acad. '05: Cinematog., Costume Des., Orig. Score; Golden Globes '06: Orig. Score; Natl. Bd. of Review '05: Support. Actress (Li); Broadcast Film Critics '05: Orig. Score.

Memoirs of Murder 2003 Effective South Korean thriller based on a true incident. In 1986, the body of a young woman is found raped and murdered in a backwater town near Seoul. The two local detectives, Park ('Song) and Jo (Rwe-ha Kim), are ill-equipped to deal with what turns into bizarre serial killings in a country where multiple homicides are a rarity. An experienced big city cop, Seo (Sang-kyung Kim), shows up and clashes with the others. Frustration mounts as bodies continue to be found (until 1991, in fact) and the investigation drags on. A coda is set in 2003. Korean with subtitles. 132m/C DVD, Kn Song Kang-ho, Kim Sang-gyeong, Kim Roi-ha, Song Jae-ho, Byeon Heui-bong, Ryu Tae-ho, Park Noh-shik, Park Hae-il; *D:* Bong Joon-ho; *W:* Bong Joon-ho, Shim Seong-bo; *C:* Kim Hyeong-gu; *M:* Taro Iwashiro.

Memories of an Invisible Man 1992 (PG-13) Nick Halloway, a slick and shallow stock analyst, is rendered invisible by a freak accident. When he is pursued by a CIA agent-hit man who wants to exploit him, Nick turns for help to Alice, a documentary filmmaker he has just met. Naturally, they fall in love along the way. Effective sight gags, hardworking cast can't overcome pitfalls in script, which indecisively meanders between comedy and thrills. 99m/C VHS, DVD, Chevy Chase, Daryl Hannah, Sam Neill, Michael McKean, Stephen Tobolowsky, Jim Norton, Patricia Heaton, Rosalind Chao; *D:* John Carpenter; *W:* Robert Collector.

Memorial Day 1983 Good cast highlights this TV outing covering a Vietnam veterans reunion. With the old memories coming new problems for the men and their families. 120m/C VHS, Mike Farrell, Shelley Fabares, Keith Mitchell, Bonnie Beceila, Robert Walden, Edward Herrmann, Danny Glover; *D:* Joseph Sargent; *M:* Billy Goldenberg. TV

Memorial Day 1998 (R) Routine to the point of boredom. Downey (Speakman) is an ex-Marine/government operative who's just been released from a mental ward. He's needed to get into a terrorist group that's stolen a Russian satellite. Hmmmm. 95m/C VHS, Jeff Speakman, Bruce Weitz, Paul Mones, Stephanie Niznik; *D:* Worth Keeter. VIDEO

Memorial Valley Massacre 1988 (R) When campers settle for a weekend in a new, unfinished campground, they're slaughtered in turn by a nutty hermit. 93m/C VHS, DVD, Cameron Mitchell, William (Bill) Smith, John Kerry, Mark Mears, Lesa Lee, John Caso; *D:* Robert C. Hughes.

Memories of a Marriage 1990 A nostalgic look at a couple's many years of marriage, from the husband's point of view, as they face their most trying times. Touchingly reminiscent as it spans the youthful years of new love and marriage to the more quiet, solid years of marriage and life. Filmed with English subtitles. 90m/C VHS, DK Ghita Norby, Frits Helmuth, Rikke Bendsen, Henning Moritzen; *D:* Kaspar Rostrup.

Memory of a Killer 1974 (PG) Still-relevant story of a married, middle-aged woman who starts to question her happiness as a wife and mother. Written by its star Geer, whose father, Will, plays a bit part. 93m/C VHS, Ellen Geer, Jon Cypher, Barbara Colby, Peter Brown, Robert Hogan, Rose Marie, Will Geer; *D:* H. Kaye Dyal.

Memory of Us 1974 (PG) Still-relevant story of a married, middle-aged woman who starts to question her happiness as a wife and mother. Written by its star Geer, whose father, Will, plays a bit part. 93m/C VHS, Ellen Geer, Jon Cypher, Barbara Colby, Peter Brown, Robert Hogan, Rose Marie, Will Geer; *D:* H. Kaye Dyal.

Memories of Hell 1987 Examines the special bonds of friendship that have been maintained among the New Mexicans who survived one of WWII's most brutal battles and subsequent prisoner experiences. 57m/C VHS.

Memories of Me 1988 (PG-13) A distraught doctor travels to L.A. to see his ailing father and make up for lost time. Both the doctor and his father learn about themselves and each other. Story of child/parent relationships attempts to pull at the heartstrings but only gets as far as the liver. Co-written and co-produced by Crystal, this film never quite reaches the potential of its cast. 103m/C VHS, DVD, Angela Clarke, Billy Crystal, Alan King, JoBeth Williams, David Ackroyd, Sean Connery, Janet Carroll; *D:* Henry Winkler; *W:* Billy Crystal, Eric Roth; *M:* Georges Delerue.

Memories of Murder 1990 A woman suffering from amnesia is stalked by a merciless killer, apparently seeking revenge. Can she regain her memory and understand why she is being hunted, before it's too late? 104m/C VHS, Nancy Allen, Robin Thomas, Olivia Brown; *D:* Robert Lewis; *W:* John Kent Harrison, Nevin Schreiner.

Memphis 1991 (PG-13) In 1957 three white drifters (two men and a woman) decide to secure some easy money by kidnapping the young grandson of the richest black businessman in Memphis. They think it's an easy job since, given the prejudice of the times, the police will do little or nothing but they reckon without the resources of the black community itself. Based on the novel "September" by Shelby Foote. 92m/C VHS, Cybill Shepherd, John Laughlin, J.E. Freeman, Richard Brooks, Moses Gunn, Vanessa Bell Calloway, Martin C. Gardner; *D:* Yves Simoneau; *W:* Cybill Shepherd, Larry McMurtry; *M:* David Bell. CABLE

Memphis Belle 1990 (PG-13) Satisfying Hollywood version of the documentary of the same name captures the true story of the final mission of a WWII bomber crew stationed in England. The boys of the Memphis Belle were the first group of B-17 crewmen to complete a 25 mission tour—no small feat in an air war that claimed many lives. Good ensemble cast of up and coming young actors. Lithgow has a nice turn as an army PR guy determined to exploit their boyish good looks on the homefront. Caton-Jones effectively uses 1940s film techniques and some original footage, making up for a rather hokey script. Film debut of singer Connick. Produced by Catherine Wyler, whose father made the original. 107m/C VHS, DVD, Matthew Modine, John Lithgow, Eric Stoltz, Sean Astin, Harry Connick Jr., Reed Edward Diamond, Tate Donovan, D.B. Sweeney, Billy Zane, David Stratharin, Jane Horrocks, Courtney Gains, Neil Giuntoli; *D:* Michael Caton-Jones; *M:* George Fenton.

Memories of Underdevelopment *Memorias del Subdesarrollo* 1968 Set in the early 1960s. An anti-revolutionary, European-ized intellectual takes a stand against the new government in Cuba. In Spanish with English subtitles. 97m/B VHS, CU Sergio Corrieri, Daisy Granados, Eslinda Nunez, Beatriz Ponchora; *D:* Tomas Gutierrez Alea; *W:* Tomas Gutierrez Alea, Edmundo Desnoes; *C:* Ramon Suarez; *M:* Leo Bower.

Memory 2006 (R) Nonsensical story with Zane chewing scenery. While in Brazil, Dr. Taylor Briggs (Zane) accidentally ingests a hallucinogen that a local tribe uses in rituals that bestow memories of the user's ancestors. But Taylor has visions of little girls being kidnapped and killed and hopes to discover who's behind the crimes. Hmmmm, could it be someone close to him? 98m/C DVD, Billy Zane, Tricia Helfer, Ann-Margret, Dennis Hopper, Terry Chen; *D:* Bennett Davlin; *W:* Bennett Davlin, Anthony Badalucco; *C:* Peter Benison; *M:* Anthony Marinelli, Clint Bennett.

The Memory of a Killer *The Alzheimer Affair; De Zaak Alzheimer* 2003 (R) Kinky crime thriller takes places in 1995 when tough, aging hitman Angelo (Declair) travels to Antwerp for a job. But when he won't fulfill his contract, his employers turn on him. Angelo may be in the early stages of Alzheimer's (which he realizes) but he's still not a guy you mess with. There's a nasty tie-in to a child prostitution ring and blackmail that has local cop Vincke (De Bouw) working the case and Angelo soon cross paths. In Flemish and French with English subtitles. 120m/C DVD, Jan Decleir, Werner De Smedt, Gene Bervoets, Koen de Bouw, Jo de Meyere, Erik van Looy; *W:* Erik van Looy, Carl Joos; *M:* Stephen Warbeck.

Memron woof! 2004 Thoroughly unfunny attempt at a mockumentary of the Enron scandal. The bankrupt company's CEO (McShane) is locked away at a country club prison where he spends his time, greedy wife (Fo'lan) spends what cash is left, and the company's former employees (all of whom seem to be mentally challenged) scramble to find new jobs. 79m/C DVD, Michael McShane, Claire Forlani, Mary Pat Gleeson, Tim Bagley, John Lehr, David Walter, Joey Slotnik; *D:* Nancy Hower; *W:* Nancy Hower, Robert Stark Hickey; *C:* Nancy Hower; *M:* Steven Argila. CABLE

The Men *Battle Stripe* 1950 A paraplegic WWII veteran sinks into depression until his former girlfriend convinces him to marry her. Film debut of Brando. 85m/B VHS, Marlon Brando, Teresa Wright, Everett Sloane, Jack Webb; *D:* Fred Zinnemann.

Men 1997 (R) Aspiring chef Stella James (Young) is encouraged by best friend Teo (Dylan Walsh) to move from New York to L.A. in search of romance. Stella promptly lands a job and gets involved with George (Heard), the restaurant's owner. However, a new man, photographer Frank (Hillman), comes onto the scene and Stella decides she likes him too. But what she thinks will be another casual encounter becomes unexpectedly serious. Based on the novel by Margaret Diehl. 93m/C VHS, DVD, Sean Young, John Heard, Dylan Walsh, Richard Hillman, Karen Black; *D:* Zoe Clarke-Williams; *W:* Zoe Clarke-Williams, Karen Black; *C:* Susan Emerson; *M:* Mark Mothersbaugh.

Men... 1985 A funny and insightful satire about a man who discovers his loving wife has been having an affair with a young artist. In a unique course of revenge, the husband ingratiates himself with the artist and gradually turns him into a carbon copy of himself. In German with English subtitles or dubbed. 99m/C VHS, GE Heiner Lauterbach, Uwe Ochsenknecht, Ulrike Kriener, Janna Marangosoff; *D:* Doris Dorrie.

Men at Work 1990 (PG-13) Garbage collectors Sheen and Estevez may not love their work, but at least it's consistent from day to day. That is, until they get wrapped up in a very dirty politically motivated murder. And who will clean up the mess when the politicians are through trashing each other? A semi-thrilling semi-comedy that may leave you semi-satisfied. 98m/C VHS, DVD, Charlie Sheen, Emilio Estevez, Leslie Hope, Keith David; *D:* Emilio Estevez; *W:* Emilio Estevez; *C:* Tim Suhrstedt; *M:* Stewart Copeland.

Men Are Not Gods 1937 Verbose film (precursor to "A Double Life") about an actor playing Othello who nearly kills his wife during Desdemona's death scene. 9m/B VHS, GB Rex Harrison, Miriam Hopkins, Gertruce Lawrence; *D:* Walter Reisch.

Men Cry Bullets 2000 Low-budget weird comedy has midnight movie potential. Billy (Nelson) is a naive performance artist who falls for hard-drinking writer Gloria (Lauren) who introduces him to the world of rough sex. And Gloria's unhappy when her debutante cousin Lydia (Ryan) comes for a pay a visit and Billy starts looking her way. 106m/C VHS, Steven Nelson, Jeri Ryan, Honey Lauren; *D:* Tamara Hernandez; *W:* Tamara Hernandez.

Men Don't Leave 1989 (PG-13) A recent widow tries to raise her kids single-handedly, suffers big city life, and takes a chance at a second love. Good performances by all, especially Cusack as the sweet seducer of teenaged O'Donnell. By the director of "Risky Business." 115m/C VHS. Jessica Lange, Ariss Howard, Joan Cusack, Kathy Bates, Charlie Korsmo, Corey Carrier, Chris O'Donnell, Tom Mason, Jim Haynie; *D:* Paul Brickman; *W:* Barbara Benedek, Paul Brickman; *C:* Bruce Surtees; *M:* Thomas Newman.

Men in Black ✓✓✓ **(PG-13)** *MIB* **1997** Charm, wit and some outrageous insect-type aliens make a winning cosmic combination. K (Jones) and J (Smith) are top-secret government operatives, investigating alien visitations on Earth, who must stop terrorist extraterrestrial D'Onofrio from causing a galactic disaster. Excellent chemistry between deadpan Jones and hip-hop Smith is strengthened by a very funny script. Director Sonnenfeld tops off with just enough detail and human element to keep the special effects from stealing the show, and with Rick Baker around, that's not easy to do. Boxoffice hit that should spawn a sequel or two. Adapted from the Marvel comic book. 98m/C VHS, DVD, UMD. Tommy Lee Jones, Will Smith, Linda Fiorentino, Rip Torn, Vincent D'Onofrio, Tony Shalhoub, Carel Struycken, Sergio Calderon, Siobhan Fallon; *D:* Barry Sonnenfeld; *W:* Edward Solomon; *C:* Don Peterman; *M:* Danny Elfman. Oscars '97: Makeup; MTV Movie Awards '98: Song ("Men in Black"), Fight (Will Smith/alien).

Men in Black 2 ✓✓ **2002 (PG-13)** Kay (Jones) had returned to civilian life at the end of the first film (with no memory of his past life), while Jay (Smith) went on with the men in black. When evil alien Serleena (Boyle) takes the entire MIB hostage, lone escapee Kay must convince Kay to help him save the galaxy. So-so effort suffers from lackluster script and doesn't have the spark of the original, but is helped along by solid performances all around. There are plenty of amusing scenes, mostly provided by the supporting players. Warburton is funny as an early MiB washout, Shalhoub provides some instant energy, and the talking dog does yeoman's work. Should hold up better on the small screen. 88m/C VHS, DVD. US Tommy Lee Jones, Will Smith, Lara Flynn Boyle, Johnny Knoxville, Rosario Dawson, Rip Torn, Tony Shalhoub, Patrick Warburton, Jack Kehler, David Cross, Colombe Jacobsen, Peter Spellos, Lenny Venito; *Cameos:* Michael Jackson, Martha Stewart, Peter Graves; *D:* Barry Sonnenfeld; *W:* Robert Gordon, Barry Fanaro; *C:* Greg Gardiner; *M:* Danny Elfman; *V:* Tim Blaney.

Men in Love ✓✓ **1990** A young San Francisco travels to Hawaii with the cremated remains of his lover, who has succumbed to AIDS. There he encounters a supportive group of men who nurse him back to sexual and spiritual wholeness. 93m/C VHS. Doug Self, Joe Tolbe, Emerald Starr, Kutira Decosterd, Scott Catamas; *D:* Marc Huestis; *W:* Emerald Starr, Scott Catamas; *C:* Fawn Yacker.

Men in War ✓✓½ **1957** Korean War drama about a small platoon trying to take an enemy hill by themselves. A worthwhile effort with some good action sequences. 100m/B VHS, DVD. Robert Ryan, Robert Keith, Aldo Ray, Vic Morrow, Phillip Pine, Nehemiah Persoff, James Edwards, L.Q. Jones, Scott Marlowe, Adam Kennedy, Race Gentry, Walter Kelley, Anthony Ray, Robert Normand, Michael Miller, Victor Sen Yung; *D:* Anthony Mann; *W:* Philip Yordan, Ben Maddow; *C:* Ernest Haller; *M:* Elmer Bernstein.

Men Men Men ✓✓ *Uomini Uomini Uomini* **1995** Quartet of gay friends are permanent Peter Pans. Never having grown up, they extend their adolescence in a series of increasingly vicious pranks at the expense of both strangers and friends. But eventually they're forced to re-examine their behavior. Very funny, if certainly non-pc, comedy. Italian with subtitles. 84m/C VHS, DVD. IT Christian de Sica, Massimo Ghini, Leo Gullotta, Alessandro Haber, Monica Scattini, Paco Reconti; *D:* Christian de Sica; *W:* Christian de Sica, Gianlorenzo Battaglia; *M:* Manuel De Sica.

Men of America ✓✓ *The Great Decision* **1932** A group of not-so-bright criminals is hiding out after robbing a bank of $50,000 in $1000 bills they cannot spend. When they murder a farmhand who's

to them, an innocent townsman is suspected but sets out to set the record straight and capture the true villains. 58m/B VHS. William Boyd, Charles "Chic" Sale, Dorothy Wilson, Ralph Ince; *D:* Ralph Ince; *W:* Humphrey Pearson, Jack Jungmeyer, Henry McCarty, Samuel Ornitz. VIDEO

Men of Boys Town ✓✓½ **1941** Sequel to 1938's "Boys Town" has the same sentimentality, even more if that's possible. Father Flanagan's reformatory faces closure, while the kids reach out to an embittered new inmate. Worth seeing for the ace cast reprising their roles. 106m/B VHS. Spencer Tracy, Mickey Rooney, Darryl Hickman, Henry O'Neil, Lee J. Cobb, Sidney Miller; *D:* Norman Taurog.

Men of Honor ✓✓½ *Navy Diver* **2000 (R)** Based on the true story of Carl Brashear, the first African-American to break the color barrier in the U.S. Navy's diving program, this biography is a straightforward no-frills tribute. Played by Gooding, Brashear comes across as the very embodiment of perseverance, as shown in his rise from sharecropper's son to military man. De Niro plays Billy Sunday, a racist training officer whose discrimination nearly kills Brashear on several occasions before Brashear earns Sunday's respect. As Brashear's career advances, Sunday's declines due to drunkenness and insubordination. When Brashear loses his leg in the line of duty, the now-recovered Sunday helps him retrain using a prosthetic leg. The character of Billy Sunday is actually a composite drawn from many men in Carl Brashear's military career. 129m/C VHS, DVD, Blu-ray Disc. Cuba Gooding Jr., Robert De Niro, Charlize Theron, David Keith, Michael Rapaport, Hal Holbrook, Powers Boothe, Aunjanue Ellis, Joshua Leonard, David Conrad, Glynn Turman, Holt McCallany, Lonette McKee, Carl Lumbly; *D:* George Tillman Jr.; *W:* Scott Marshall Smith; *C:* Anthony B. Richmond; *M:* Mark Isham.

Men of Ireland ✓✓ **1938** A Dublin medical student cavorts with islanders off the Irish coast. Uninspired programmer with authentic native folk of the Blasket Islands, plus their songs and dances. 62m/ B VHS. IR Cecil Ford, Eileen Curran, Brian O'Sullivan, Gabriel Fallon; *D:* Richard Bird.

Men of Means ✓✓ **1999 (R)** Mob goon Rico Burke (Pare) decides it's time to get out when he sees his boss (Serra) becoming increasingly psychotic. Only he gets doublecrossed. Lots of action and avoids most mob movie clichés. 80m/C VHS, DVD. John Turturro, Katherine Borowitz, Peter Boyle, Dennis Farina, Chris Stein, Steven Wright, Stanley Tucci; *D:* William Reilly; *W:* William Reilly; *C:* Bobby Bukowski.

Men of Sherwood Forest ✓✓½ **1957** Robin Hood and his band take it to the sheriff et al in this colorful Hammer version of the timeless legend. 77m/C VHS. GB Don Taylor, Reginald Beckwith, Eileen Moore, David King-Wood, Patrick Holt, John Van Eyssen, Douglas Wilmer; *D:* Val Guest.

Men of Steel ✓ **1988 (PG)** Two Canadian military officers, one French and one English, must struggle to survive when their plane crashes in the wilderness. Besides contending with the surroundings, they must deal with one another's instilled bitterness and underlying prejudices. 91m/C VHS. Allan Royal, Robert Lalonde, David Ferry, Mavor Moore, Yvan Ponton; *D:* Donald Shebib.

Men of the Fighting Lady ✓✓½ *Panther Squadron* **1954** Action-adventure offers plenty of exciting battle footage. Features the stories of selected pilots stationed on a U.S. aircraft carrier in the Pacific during the Korean War. The stories, told to Calhern as writer

James A. Michener, center around the lead pilot Johnson. Dramatic airfights include a scene in which Johnson helps a blinded Martin land his plane safely on the carrier deck. Gene Ruggerio's editing of the war footage was so expertly done that he was questioned by the Pentagon when they had a hard time believing the scenes were achieved by skillful editing and painted backdrops. Look for "Beaver" Mathers as one of Wynn's sons. 81m/C VHS. Van Johnson, Walter Pidgeon, Louis Calhern, Dewey Martin, Keenan Wynn, Frank Lovejoy, Robert Horton, Bert Freed, Lewis Martin, Dick Simmons, Paul Smith, George Cooper, Ann Baker, Jonathan Hale, Dorothy Patrick, Jerry Mathers, Sarah Selby; *D:* Andrew Marton; *W:* Art Cohn; *C:* George J. Folsey; *M:* Miklos Rozsa.

Men of Two Worlds ✓✓ *Witch Doctor; Kisenga, Man of Africa* **1946** Classical musician raised in Africa is the toast of Europe until he finds out he's got a voodoo curse, and suddenly he's got the heebie jeebies too bad to play chopsticks. 90m/C VHS. GB Robert Adams, Eric Portman, Orlando Martins, Phyllis Calvert, Arnold Marle, Cathleen Nesbitt, David Horne, Cyril Raymond; *D:* Thorold Dickinson.

Men of War ✓½ **1994 (R)** Ex-Special Forces mercenaries decide to defend, rather than destroy, the inhabitants of an exotic island, whose land is wanted by a suspicious company interested in mining rights. 102m/C VHS, DVD. Dolph Lundgren, Charlotte Lewis, B.D. Wong, Anthony John (Tony) Denison, Tim Guinee, Don Harvey, Tommy (Tiny) Lister, Trevor Goddard, Kevin Tighe, Perry Lang; *W:* John Sayles, Ethan Reiff, Cyrus Voris; *C:* Ronn Schmidt; *M:* Gerald Gouriet.

The Men Who Tread on the Tiger's Tail ✓✓½ *Tora No O Wo Fumu Otokotachi; They Who Step on the Tiger's Tail* **1945** Twelfth-century Japan is the setting for this struggle of power between two brothers, one a reigning shogun, the other on the run. English subtitles. 60m/B VHS. JP Denjiro Okochi, Susumu Fujita, Masayuki Mori, Takashi Shimura, Yoshio Kosugi; *D:* Akira Kurosawa; *W:* Akira Kurosawa; *C:* Takeo Ito; *M:* Tadashi Hattori.

Men with Brooms ✓✓½ **2002** Goofy Canadian comedy about curling. In the small mining town of Long Bay, curling player/coach Donald Foley (Douglas) has just died (although his narration continues throughout the pic). At his funeral, members of his last team reunite and decide to reform the team and compete for the Golden Broom curling championship trophy in Foley's honor. Among them are oil roughneck Chris (Gross), who convinces his eccentric dad Gordon (Nielsen) to coach the team. 102m/C VHS, DVD. CA Paul Gross, Molly Parker, Peter Outerbridge, Leslie Nielsen, James Allodi, James B. Douglas, Polly Shannon, Jed Rees, Michelle Nolden, Barbara Gordon, Kari Matchett, Jane Spidell; *D:* Paul Gross; *W:* Paul Gross, John Krizanc; *C:* Thom Best; *M:* Paul Gross, Jack Lenz.

Menace on the Mountain ✓✓ **1970 (G)** Family-oriented drama about a family. A father and son who battle carpetbagging Confederate deserters during the Civil War. 89m/C VHS. Pat(ricia) Crowley, Albert Salmi, Charles Aidman; *D:* Vincent McVeety.

Menace II Society ✓✓✓½ **1993 (R)** Portrayal of black teens lost in inner-city hell is realistically captured by 21-year-old twin directors, in their big-screen debut. Caine (Turner) lives with his grandparents and peddles drugs for spending money, from the eve of his high school graduation to his decision to escape south-central Los Angeles for Atlanta. Bleak and haunting, with some of the most unsettling, bloodiest violence ever shown in a commercial film. Disturbing to watch, but critically acclaimed. The Hughes' make their mark on contemporary black cinema with intensity, enhanced by an action-comics visual flair. Based on a story by the Hughes' and Tyger Williams. 104m/C VHS, DVD. Tyrin Turner, Larenz Tate, Samuel L. Jackson, Glenn Plummer, Julian Roy Doster, Bill Duke, Charles S. Dutton, Jada Pinkett Smith, Vonte Sweet, Ryan Williams; *W:* Tyger Williams; *C:* Lisa Rinzler. Ind. Spirit '94: Cinematog.; MTV Movie Awards '94: Film.

Menage ✓✓ *Tenue de Soiree* **1986** Depardieu is the homosexual crook who breaks into the home of an impoverished couple—the dominating Miou-Miou and her submissive husband, Blanc. An unrepentant thief, he begins to take over their lives, introducing them to the wonderful world of crime, among other, more kinky, pastimes. Gender-bending farce that doesn't hold up to the end but is worth watching for sheer outrageousness. In French with English subtitles. 84m/C VHS. FR Gerard Depardieu, Michel Blanc, Miou-Miou, Bruno Cremer, Jean-Pierre Marielle; *D:* Bertrand Blier; *W:* Bertrand Blier; *M:* Serge Gainsbourg. Cannes '86: Actor (Blanc).

Mendel ✓✓✓ **1998** Mendel (Sorenson) is the nine-year-old son of German-Jewish concentration camp survivors and displaced persons, who are relocated to Norway in 1954. Mendal is too young to know about the horrors that befell his family and that still cause them all nightmares. His parents are determined to shield him from their past while Mendel is equally determined to discover the family secrets. German and Norwegian with subtitles. 98m/C VHS. NO Thomas Jungling Sorensen, Teresa Harder, Hans Kremer, Martin Meingast; *D:* Alexander Rosler; *W:* Alexander Rosler; *C:* Helge Sembe; *M:* Geir Bohren, Bent Aserud.

Menno's Mind ✓✓½ **1996** Rebel leader Bruce Campbell downloads his brain into a computer before being killed. Now his associates force computer techie Menno (Bill Campbell) to upload his memorial into his own mind in order to thwart presidential candidate Bensen, who wants to use his online skills to influence the outcome of the election. 95m/C VHS, DVD. Billy Campbell, Corbin Bernsen, Bruce Campbell, Michael Dorn, Robert Picardo, Robert Vaughn, Richard Speight Jr.; *D:* Jon Kroll; *W:* Mark Valenti; *C:* Gary Tieche; *M:* Christopher Franke. CABLE

The Men's Club ✓½ **1986 (R)** Seven middle-aged buddies get together for a single night, and bare their respective souls and personal traumas, talking about women and eating and drinking. Based on novel by Leonard Michael. 100m/C VHS. Harvey Keitel, Roy Scheider, Craig Wasson, Frank Langella, David Dukes, Richard Jordan, Treat Williams, Stockard Channing, Jennifer Jason Leigh, Ann Dusenberry, Cindy Pickett, Gwen Welles; *D:* Peter Medak.

Mephisto ✓✓✓½ **1981** Egomaniacal stage actor Hendrik Hofgren (compellingly played by Brandauer) sides with the Nazis to further his career, with disastrous results. An updated version of the Faust legend and the first of three brilliant films by Szabo and Brandauer exploring the price of power and personal sublimation in German history. Klaus Mann based his 1936 novel on the career of German stage actor Gustaf Grundgens who became the director and star of Berlin's Prussian State Theater during WWII. German with subtitles. Followed by "Colonel Redl" and "Hanussen." 144m/C VHS, DVD. HU Klaus Maria Brandauer, Krystyna Janda, Ildiko Bansagi, Karin Boyd, Rolf Hoppe, Christine Harbort, Gyorgy Cserhalmi, Christiane Graskoff, Peter Andorai, Ildiko Kishonti; *D:* Istvan Szabo; *W:* Istvan Szabo, Peter Dobai; *C:* Lajos Koltai; *M:* Zdenko Tamassy. Oscars '81: Foreign Film.

The Mephisto Waltz ✓✓½ **1971 (R)** Journalist gets more than a story when he is granted an interview with a dying pianist. It turns out that he is a satanist and the cult he is a part of wants the journalist. Chilling adaptation of the Fred Mustard Stewart novel features a haunting musical score. 108m/C VHS. Alan Alda, Jacqueline Bisset, Barbara Parkins, Curt Jurgens, Bradford Dillman, William Windom, Kathleen Widdoes; *D:* Paul Wendkos; *M:* Jerry Goldsmith.

The Mercenaries ✓✓½ *I Mascadieri* **1962** Romantic warrior fights to save the lives and honor of his people who are under attack from mercenaries murdering and raping their way across Europe. 98m/C VHS. IT Daniela Rocca, Antonio Cifariello, Folco Lulli, Debra Paget, Salvo Randone; *D:* Mario Bonnard; *W:* Mario Bonnard, Nino Minuto; *C:* Marco Scarpelli; *M:* Giulio Bonnard.

The Mercenaries *♂*
Kill Castro; Assignment: Kill Castro; Key West Crossing; Sweet Dirty Tony 1980 A tough guy, given the assignment to kill Fidel Castro, encounters all sorts of adversity along the way. Key West scenery is the only thing of interest. **82m/C VHS, DVD.** Stuart Whitman, Robert Vaughn, Caren Kaye, Raymond St. Jacques, Woody Strode, Sybil Danning, Albert Salmi, Michael V. Gazzo; **D:** Chuck Workman.

Mercenary *♂♂* 1996 Ex-Commando-turned-mercenary Alex Hawks (Grunger) is hired by wealthy businessman Jonas Ambler (Ritter) to avenge his wife's death at the hands of terrorists. Only Ambler's desk jockey doesn't want to stay on the sidelines and watch—he wants to do. So, Hawks is forced to take him along to Iraq when he goes after the bad guys. **97m/C VHS.** Olivier Gruner, John Ritter, Robert Culp, Ed Lauter, Martin Kove; **D:** Avi Nesher; **W:** Roger Neill.

Mercenary 2: Thick and Thin *♂½* 1997 (R) Mercenaries Hawk (Gruner) and Ray (Turturro) are hired to rescue a businessman (Townsend) who's apparently been kidnapped by a druglord and who's being held in a Central America jungle. Turns out it's all a set-up. Shot in South Africa. **90m/C VHS.** Peter Fonda, Reb Brown, Ron O'Neal, Jim Mitchum; **D:** Riki Shelach.

Mercenary Fighters *♂* 1988 (R) An American soldier-of-fortune fights for both sides of an African revolution. Shot in South Africa. **90m/C VHS.** Peter Fonda, Reb Brown, Ron O'Neal, Jim Mitchum; **D:** Riki Shelach.

The Merchant of Four Seasons *♂♂♂* 1971 Story focuses on the depression and unfulfilled dreams of an average street merchant. Direction from Fassbinder is slow, deliberate, and mesmerizing. In German with English subtitles. **88m/C VHS, DVD.** Hans Hirschmuller, Irm Hermann, Hana Schygulla, Andrea Schober, Gusti Kriesel; **D:** Rainer Werner Fassbinder. **W:** Rainer Werner Fassbinder.

The Merchant of Venice *♂♂♂* 1973 Shakespeare's tragedy of prejudice, vengeance, and sacrifice stars Olivier as the persecuted money lender Shylock, who demands his payment of a pound of flesh for a defaulted loan. **131m/C VHS, GB** Laurence Olivier, Joan Plowright, Jeremy Brett; **D:** John Sichel.

The Merchant of Venice *♂♂♂* 2004 (R) Antonio (Irons) makes a deal with calculating moneylender Shylock (Pacino) to help his friend Bassanio (Fiennes) gain the hand of fair Portia (Collins). When the deal goes south, Shylock demands a pound of flesh from Antonio's breast and it's up to Portia, disguised as a young lawyer, to save him. Lavish, but subtle, take on Shakespeare's classic comedy. Pacino takes care to make Shylock as sympathetic as possible and director Radford places the play's overt racism in historical context, making the play feel less viciously anti-semitic than usual. **138m/C DVD, US** AI Pacino, Jeremy Irons, Joseph Fiennes, Zuleikha Robinson, Kris Marshall, Heather Goldenhersch, John Sessions, Mackenzie Crook, Gregor Fisher, Ron Cook, Allan Corduner, Anton Rodgers, Lynn Collins, Charlie Cox; **D:** Michael Radford; **W:** Michael Radford; **C:** Benoit Delhomme.

Merchants of Death *♂* 1999 Fairly perverse schlock about an aspiring actress lured into an audition at a mysterious mansion. Soon enough she's bound and gagged by some raw dog dudes who toss her in a room with another woman, also tied up, who came to avenge her sister's death. With the audition still underway and the cameras set to roll, they realize they're about to become reluctant (to say the least) stars in a snuff film. A maniacal priest is thrown into the mix for some reason, too. Only the sight campy smirk saves it from complete disaster. **81m/C VHS.** Christine Lydon, Jason Robert Stephens, Raquel Maldonado, Raymond Scott; **D:** Jason Robert Stephens; **W:** Jason Robert Stephens; **C:** Dennis Devine.

Merchants of War *♂* 1990 (R) Sent out by the CIA on a mission, two best friends are soon the target of one of the most dangerous terrorists in the world. The fanatical Islamic terrorist soon casts his wrath upon the two men. **100m/C VHS, DVD.** Asher Brauner, Jesse Vint, Bonnie Beck; **D:** Peter M. MacKenzie.

Merci Docteur Rey *♂♂♂* 2004 (R) Odd choice for a Merchant-Ivory production. Enjoyable French farce mixes questionable sexual orientation, mistaken identity, murder, and an estranged father for a rousing ride. Wiest's opera diva visits her closeted gay son, who witnesses a murder on a blind date with a chat room hook-up. Complimented by an eclectic soundtrack ranging from pop to opera. **91m/C DVD, FR** Dianne Wiest, Jane Birkin, Stanislas Merhar, Bulle Ogier, Jerry Hall, Simon Callow; **W:** Andrew Litvack; **C:** Laurent Machuel; **M:** Geoffrey Alexander. **VIDEO**

Merci pour le Chocolat *♂♂♂* Nightcap 2000 This is Huppert's movie all the way. She's Mika Muller, a chocolate company manager in Switzerland who has just re-married widowed concert pianist Andre (Dutronc) after 18 years, the romantic reunion of young love. Andre married and had son Guillaume (Pauly) who was nearly switched at birth for Jeanne (Mouglalis), an 18-year-old with musical talent (unlike Guillaume). Jeanne impulsively decides to meet Andre and they bond over music, which causes the polite but pathologically jealous Mika to pour hot chocolate and plot. Based on the novel "The Chocolate Cobweb" by Charlotte Armstrong. French with subtitles. **99m/C VHS, DVD, FR** Isabelle Huppert, Jacques Dutronc, Anna Mouglalis, Rodolphe Pauly, Michel Robin, Brigitte Catillon, Mathieu Simonet; **D:** Claude Chabrol; **W:** Claude Chabrol, Caroline Eliacheff; **C:** Renato Berta; **M:** Matthieu Chabrol.

Mercury Rising *♂♂½* 1998 (R) Renegade FBI agent Art Jeffries (Willis) must protect an autistic child who has inadvertently cracked a secret government code. Together, they dodge bullets from evil government forces headed by Nicholas Kudrow (Baldwin), who insist on having the innocent boy killed rather than change the code. That glaring logic aside, Willis does more than grunt here showing moments of tenderness as he bonds with the orphaned boy in between the nailing bad guys and amassing an assortment of cuts and bruises. Baldwin is effective as the snake who truly believes killing a child will benefit national security. When action time isn't being sacrificed for Jeffries' paternal aspirations, film rises slightly above tepid to provide substantial thrills. **112m/C VHS, DVD.** Bruce Willis, Alec Baldwin, Miko Hughes, Kim Dickens, Chi McBride, Robert Stanton, Peter Stormare, Kevin Conway; **D:** Harold Becker; **W:** Lawrence Konner, Mark Rosenthal; **C:** Michael Seresin; **M:** John Barry, Golden Raspberries '98: Worst Actor (Willis).

Mercy *♂♂* 1996 (R) When New York lawyer Frank Kramer's (Rubenstein) daughter is kidnapped he comes to realize it was'1 for ransom but for revenge. **82m/C VHS, DVD, DVD.** John Rubinstein, Sam Rockwell, Phil Brock, Novella Nelson, Amber Kain, Jane Lanier; **D:** Richard Shepard; **W:** Richard Shepard; **C:** Sarah Cawley.

Mercy *♂♂* 2000 (R) Glossy sleaze based on the book by David L. Lindsey. Catherine Barker (Barkin) is a hard-drinking homicide detective investigating a serial killer with sexual kinks. Bombshell Vickie Kittie (Wilson) reveals that each female victim belonged to an exclusive club that liked to experiment with the wilder side of life. All the victims also turn out to be patients of psychotherapist Dominick Broussard (Sands), who may be no psycho but anyone knows. **94m/C VHS, DVD.** Ellen Barkin, Peta Wilson, Julian Sands, Wendy Crewson, Karen Young, Marshall Bell, Stephen Baldwin, Bru Starr, Bill MacDonald, Stewart Bick; **D:** Damian Harris; **C:** Manuel Teran; **M:** B.C. Smith.

Mercy Mission *♂♂½* 1993 Young pilot Bakula runs into trouble over the Pacific with his small plane and it's upto Air New Zealand airline pilot Loggia, who risks the lives of his passengers and crew, to come to his rescue. **92m/C VHS.** Scott Bakula, Robert Loggia; **D:** Roger Young.

Meridian: Kiss of the Beast *♂½* 1990 (R) A beautiful heiress is courted, kidnapped and loved by a demonic man-beast. **90m/C VHS, Sherilyn Fenn, Malcolm Jamieson, Hilary Mason, Alex Daniels, Phil Fondacaro, Charlie Spradling; D: Charles Band; W: Dennis Paoli; M: Pino Donaggio.

Merlin *♂♂♂* 1998 Legend of Camelot and Arthur's mentor is brought to the small screen with fine performances and equally impressive special effects. Merlin is conceived through the magic of evil Queen Mab (Richardson) to bring Britain back to its pagan roots. But Merlin doesn't really like magic and grows up to be (in the commanding persona of Neil), not reluctant sorcerer. Still, he mentors Arthur (Curran) and continues to battle Mab, who works with Arthur's half sister Morgan Le Fey (Bonham Carter) to destroy Camelot. Merlin also pursues a long-time romance with Nimue (Rossellini), who falls victim to Mab's treachery. **140m/C VHS, DVD. Sam Neill, Miranda Richardson, Isabella Rossellini, Martin Short, Helena Bonham-Carter, Rutger Hauer, Paul Curran, Billie White an, Lena Headey, Jason Done, Mark Jax, John McEnery, Nicholas Clay, Sebastien Roche, Jeremy Sheffield; Cameos: John Gielgud; D: Steven Barron; W: David Stevens, Edward Khmara; C: Sergei Kozlov; M: Trevor Jones; V: James Earl Jones. TV**

Merlin *♂♂½* 1992 (PG-13) In a remote California town reporter Christy Lake is stunned to discover her ancient heritage. Turns out she's the reincarnated daughter of legendary Merlin the magician and it is her duty to protect the Sword of Power from the evil sorcerer Pendragon. And aided by a handsome warrior and an ancient sage, that's just what she intends to do. **112m/C VHS, Nadia Cameron, Peter Phelps, Richard Lynch, James Hong, Ted Markland, Desmond Llewelyn; D: Paul Hunt; W: Nick McCarty.

Merlin and the Sword *♂* the King 1985 Poor use of a good cast in this treatment of the legend of Merlin, Arthur and Excalibur. **94m/C VHS, Malcolm McDowell, Edward Woodward, Candice Bergen, Dyan Cannon; D: Clive Donner.

Merlin's Apprentice *♂½* 2006 Disappointingly cheesy sort of sequel to the 1998 miniseries "Merlin." Merlin (Neill again) takes a 50-year nap and awakens to find Arthur dead, the Holy Grail missing, and Camelot under siege. When a young thief, Jack (Reardon), tries to steal his abilities and takes Jack on as his apprentice to help save Camelot. Richardson is back too, but this time she plays the Lady of the Lake. **185m/C DVD, US CA Sam Neill, John Reardon, Miranda Richardson, Duncan Fraser, Christopher Jacot, Andrew Jackson, Gavin Sanford, Meaghan Ory, Alexander Kalugin; D: David Wu; W: Christian Ford, Roger Soffer; C: John Spooner; M: Lawrence Shragge. CABLE

Merry-Go-Round *♂♂♂* 1923 A handsome Austrian count is engaged to a woman of his class when he meets the beautiful Agnes, who works as an organ grinder for the local merry-go-round. He disguises himself to woo her but finally decides to marry his fiance, although Agnes continues to love him. But the story doesn't end for the two lovers who are destined to be together. Producer Thalberg and director von Stroheim battled over the expense and length of the film until Thalberg had the director replaced. However, much of the film still shows the von Stroheim brilliance and attention to lavish detail. **110m/B VHS, DVD, Norman Kerry, Mary Philbin, Cesare Gravina, George Hackathorne; D: Rupert Julian, Erich von Stroheim.

A Merry War *♂♂♂* Keep the Aspidistra Flying 1997 Gordon Comstock (Grant) is a frustrated ad-man in London, circa 1935. He believes that his creativity (he is mistakenly lead to believe that he is a poet when he gets published). Convinced that slumming is the only way to tap into his supposed talent, he quits his advertising job and moves into a shabby little apartment to augment his misery, despite the doubts of girlfriend Rosemary (Bonham Carter). Based on George Orwell's only comedy, which fictionalizes his own experiences in London and Paris, in spite of being a comedy (and a funny one at that), story has that Orwellian feel of at its best. **

Merry Christmas, Mr. Lawrence *♂♂♂* 1983 (R) An often overlooked drama about a WWII Japanese POW camp. Taut psychological drama about clashing cultures and physical and emotional survival focusing on the tensions between English POW and camp commander Sakamoto, who also composed the outstanding score. A haunting and intense film about the horrors of war. Based on the novel by Laurens van der Post. **124m/C VHS, DVD. JP GB David Bowie, Tom Conti, Ryuichi Sakamoto, Takeshi "Beat" Kitano, Jack Thompson, Takashi Naito, Alistair Browning, Johnny Okura, Yuya Uchida, Ryunosuke Kaneda, Kan Mikami, Yuji Honma, Diasuke Iijima; D: Nagisa Oshima; W: Nagisa Oshima, Paul Mayersberg; C: Toichiro Narushima. Natl. Bd. of Review '83: Actor (Conti).

Merrill's Marauders *♂♂♂* 1962 The Aqua Sex 1962 A marine biologist and a criminal travel to a remote island off Mexico in search of elusive, expensive "fire pearls." There they encounter a kingdom of lovely mermaids who promptly liven things up. Filmed in "Aquascope" for your viewing pleasure. **77m/C VHS, Diane Webber, George Rowe, Timothy Carey, Jose Gonzalez-Gonzalez, John (Jack) Mylong, Gil Barreto, Vicki Kanternwine, Nani Morrissey, Judy Edwards, Jean Carroll, Diana Crook, Karen Goodman, Nancy Burns; D: John Lamb; M: John Lamb.

The Mermaids of Tiburon *♂* The Aqua Sex 1962 A marine biologist and a criminal travel to a remote island off Mexico in search of elusive, expensive "fire pearls." There they encounter a kingdom of lovely mermaids who promptly liven things up. Filmed in "Aquascope" for your viewing pleasure. **77m/C VHS, Diane Webber, George Rowe, Timothy Carey, Jose Gonzalez-Gonzalez, John (Jack) Mylong, Gil Barreto, Vicki Kanternwine, Nani Morrissey, Judy Edwards, Jean Carroll, Diana Crook, Karen Goodman, Nancy Burns; D: John Lamb; M: John Lamb.

Mermaid *♂♂♂* 2000 Young Desi is mourning her father's death. She writes a letter to him and lies it to a balloon, hoping that it will fly to heaven so he can read it. Instead, the winds blow the balloon to Canada's St. Edward's Island and the small town of Mermaid. When the letter is found, the islanders decide to respond to Desi's message. **94m/C VHS, DVD. Samantha Mathis, Ellen Burstyn, David Kaye, Jodelle Ferland, Blu Mankuma, Tom Heaton; D: Peter Masterson; W: Todd Robinson; C: Jon Joffin; M: Peter Melnick. CABLE

Mermaids *♂♂♂* 1990 (PG-13) Mrs. Flax (Cher) is the flamboyant mother of two who hightails out of town every time a relationship threatens to turn serious. Having moved some 18 times, her daughters, Charlotte (Ryder), 15, and Kate (Ricci), 8, are a little worse for the wear, psychologically speaking. One aspires to be a nun though not Catholic, and the other holds her breath under water. Now living in Massachusetts, Mrs. Flax starts having those "I got you, babe" feelings for Hoskins, a shoestore owner. Amusing, well-acted multi-generational coming of ager based on a novel by Patty Dann. **110m/C VHS, DVD, Cher, Winona Ryder, Bob Hoskins, Christina Ricci, Michael Schoeffling, Caroline McWilliams, Jan Miner; D: Richard Benjamin; W: June Roberts; C: Howard Atherton; M: Jack Nitzsche. Natl. Bd. of Review '90: Support. Actress (Ryder).

chops. Very British pic will appeal to fans of '30s era dialogue. 101m/C VHS, DVD. Richard E. Grant, Helena Bonham-Carter, Julian Wadham, Jim Carter, Harriet Walter, Liz Smith, Barbara Leigh-Hunt; **D:** Robert Bierman; **W:** Alan Plater; **C:** Giles Nuttgens; **M:** Mike Batt.

The Merry Widow ♂♂♂½ *The Lady Dances* 1934 The first sound version of the famous Franz Lehar operetta, dealing with a playboy from a bankrupt kingdom who must woo and marry the land's wealthy widow or be tried for treason. A delightful musical comedy, with a sterling cast and patented Lubitschian gaiety. Made as a silent in 1912 and 1925; remade in color in 1952. ♫Girls, Girls, Girls; Vilia; Tonight Will Teach Me to Forget; Melody of Laughter; Maxim's; The Girls at Maxim's; The Merry Widow Waltz; If Widows are Rich; Russian Dance. 99m/B VHS. Maurice Chevalier, Jeanette MacDonald, Edward Everett Horton, Una Merkel, George Barbier, Minna Gombell, Ruth Channing, Sterling Holloway, Henry Armetta, Barbara Leanard, Donald Meek, Akim Tamiroff, Herman Bing; **D:** Ernst Lubitsch; **M:** Franz Lehar, Lorenz Hart.

The Merry Widow ♂♂½ 1952 Rich widow Turner travels to her husband's homeland of Marshovia to dedicate a statue to his memory. The country is deeply in debt and the king would like the widow to marry a local count and remain (along with her fortune). Lamas is charming as the intended bridegroom but Turner, though lovely looking, is miscast; her singing was dubbed by Erwin. Uninspired remake of the 1934 film only benefits from being shot in color and the lavish production values. Based on the operetta by Lehar. ♫The Merry Widow Waltz; Can-Can; Girls, Girls, Girls; I'm Going to Maxim's. 105m/C VHS. Lana Turner, Fernando Lamas, Una Merkel, Richard Haydn, Thomas Gomez, John Abbott, Marcel Dalio, King Donovan, Robert Coote, Joi Lansing; **Cameos:** Gwen Verdon; **D:** Curtis Bernhardt; **W:** Sonya Levien, William Ludwig; **C:** Joseph Ruttenberg; **M:** Franz Lehar; **V:** Trudy Erwin.

The Merry Wives of Windsor ♂♂ *Die Lustigen Weiber von Windsor* 1950 Fat, ribald, and boastful Sir John Falstaff indulges in excess at his favorite Windsor tavern. He also likes the ladies and has taken to flattering both Mistress Reich and Fluth. The ladies and the townspeople eventually decide that Falstaff needs to be taught a lesson. German with subtitles. 96m/B VHS. Paul Esser, Sonja Ziemann, Camilla Spira; **D:** Georg Wildhagen; **W:** Georg Wildhagen, Wolff von Gordon; **C:** Karl Plintzner, Eugen Klagemann; **M:** Otto Nikolai.

Merton of the Movies ♂♂½ 1947 Skelton stars as star-struck, small town theater usher Merton Gill who wins a trip to Hollywood. He's befriended by stunt double Phyllis (O'Brien) who recognizes his comedic talents and works to get him that big break. Based on the play by George S. Kaufman and Marc Connelly and previously filmed in 1924 and 1932 (as "Make Me a Star"). 82m/B VHS. Red Skelton, Virginia O'Brien, Gloria Grahame, Leon Ames, Alan Mowbray, Charles D. Brown, Hugo Haas, Harry Hayden; **D:** Robert Alton; **W:** George Wells, Lou Breslow.

Mesa of Lost Women WOOF! *Lost Women; Lost Women of Zarpa* 1952 Mad scientist creates brave new race of vicious women with long fingernails. So bad it's a wanna-B. Addams Family buffs will spot the Fester in Coogan. 70m/B VHS, DVD. Jackie Coogan, Richard Travis, Allan Nixon, Mary Hill, Robert Knapp, Tandra Quinn, Lyle Talbot, Katherine Victor, Angelo Rossitto, Dolores Fuller, John Martin; **D:** Ron Ormond, Herbert Tevos; **W:** Herbert Tevos; **C:** Gilbert Warrenton, Karl Struss; **M:** Hoyt Curtin.

Mesmer ♂♂ 1994 Rickman gives a bravura performance in the title role of controversial 18th-century Austrian doctor Franz Anton Mesmer, who put the term "mesmerize" in the dictionary. This court (in Vienna and Paris) physician's unorthodox healing practices were concerned with filtering out negative magnetism through hypnotism and positive thinking. Was he a charlatan or merely a man ahead of his time? 107m/C VHS, DVD, GB. Alan Rickman, Donal Donnelly, Peter Dvorsky, David Hemblen, Simon McBurney, Gillian Barge, Jan

Rubes; **D:** Roger Spottiswoode; **W:** Dennis Potter; **C:** Elemer Ragalyi; **M:** Michael Nyman.

Mesmerized ♂♂ *Shocked* 1984 Based on the work by Jerzy Skolimowski, the film is a dramatization of the Victoria Thompson murder case in 1880s New Zealand. A teenaged orphaned girl marries an older man and decides after years of abuse to kill him through hypnosis. An unengaging drama, though the lovely New Zealand landscape serves as a fitting contrast to the film's ominous tone. 90m/C VHS, DVD, GB NZ AU John Lithgow, Jodie Foster, Michael Murphy, Dan Shor, Harry Andrews; **D:** Michael Laughlin; **W:** Michael Laughlin; **C:** Louis Horvath; **M:** Georges Delerue.

Mesquite Buckaroo ♂ 1939 Two cowboys bet over who is the better bronco buster, but one of them gets kidnapped. 59m/B VHS. Bob Steele, Carolyn Curtis, Frank LaRue, Juanita Fletcher, Charles "Blackie" King; **D:** Harry S. Webb.

The Message ♂♂ *Mohammad: Messenger of God; Al-Ris-Alah* 1977 (PG) Sprawling saga of the genesis of the religion of Islam, with Quinn portraying Mohammad's uncle, Hamza, an honored warrior. The story behind the movie might prove much more successful as a sequel than did the movie itself. The filming itself created a religious controversy. 220m/C VHS, DVD. GB Damien Thomas, Anthony Quinn, Irene Papas, Michael Ansara, Johnny Sekka, Michael Forest, Neville Jason; **D:** Moustapha Akkad; **W:** H.A.L. Craig; **C:** Jack Hildyard; **M:** Maurice Jarre.

Message in a Bottle ♂♂ 1998 (PG-13) Romantic drama that's paced slower than the method of mail delivery in the title. Wright Penn is a divorced mother who finds a love note written to a mystery man's lost love floating in the Atlantic. She tracks the note to strong silent guy Costner, still grieving for his dead wife. She tries to get him to open up and move on with his life (with her preferably), but this takes a mind-numbingly long time. The two are destined to be together, but half of those watching are destined to be asleep by the time it happens. The sole reason to watch this movie is to see old pro Paul Newman steal every scene he's in as Costner's father. 132m/C VHS, DVD. Kevin Costner, Robin Wright Penn, Paul Newman, John Savage, Illeana Douglas, Robbie Coltrane, Jesse James, Bethel Leslie, Tom Aldredge, Viveka Davis, Raphael Sbarge, Richard Hamilton, Rosemary Murphy, Stephen Eckholdt; **D:** Luis Mandoki; **W:** Gerald Di Pego; **C:** Caleb Deschanel; **M:** Gabriel Yared.

Messalina vs. the Son of Hercules ♂ 1964 A Roman slave leads a rebellion against the emperor Messalina. Italian; dubbed into English. 105m/C VHS. **D:** Umberto Lenzi.

The Messenger ♂ 1987 (R) A man right out of prison sets out to avenge his wife's murder by an Italian drug syndicate. 95m/C VHS. Fred Williamson, Sandy Cummings, Christopher Connelly, Cameron Mitchell; **D:** Fred Williamson; **W:** Brian Johnson, Anthony Wisdom; **C:** Giancarlo Ferrando, Craig Greene; **M:** William Stuckey.

Messenger of Death ♂♂½ 1988 (R) A tough detective investigates the slaughter of a Mormon family, and uncovers a conspiracy centering around oil-rich real estate. 90m/C VHS, DVD. Charles Bronson, Trish Van Devere, Laurence Luckinbill, Daniel Benzali, Marilyn Hassett, Jeff Corey, John Ireland, Penny Peyser, Gene Davis; **D:** J. Lee Thompson; **W:** Paul Jarrico; **M:** Robert O. Ragland.

The Messenger: The Story of Joan of Arc ♂♂½ 1999 (R) Besson's take on the legendary 15th-century French teen martyr Joan of Arc (Jovovich) leans heavily on gory battle scenes, stilted dialogue, and spectacle to tell her story. After seeing her sister murdered and raped (actually in that order) by English soldiers, Joan begins to hear "heavenly voices" that tell her that she must free her country and king from the invaders. After a visit with the Dauphin, several bloody battles ensue, and Joan is eventually captured and put on trial for sorcery and heresy. Awaiting her fate, she has conversations with a character that is actually billed

as her Conscience (Hoffman), which brings up questions in her mind whether she was really divinely inspired or merely a cake du fruit. Jovovich's pop-eyed, semi-intelligible performance helps this poor effort go up in flames. 148m/C VHS, DVD. Milla Jovovich, John Malkovich, Faye Dunaway, Dustin Hoffman, Pascal Greggory, Vincent Cassel, Tcheky Karyo, Richard Ridings, Desmond Harrington; **D:** Luc Besson; **W:** Luc Besson, Andrew Birkin; **C:** Thierry Arbogast; **M:** Eric Serra.

The Messengers ♂½ 2007 (PG-13) Hong Kong filmmakers, the Pang brothers, go Americana with a derivative haunted farmhouse tale. The Solomon family moves onto a dilapidated North Dakota farm (the previous owners were slaughtered) in a last-ditch effort to forestall personal and economic ruin. No one believes sullen teenager Jess (Stewart), who thinks the place has some bad juju, and only toddler Ben (the Turner twins) can see the ghosts skittering around. Dull rather than ominous. 84m/C DVD, Blu-ray Disc, HD DVD. US Kristen Stewart, Dylan McDermott, Penelope Ann Miller, John Corbett, Evan Turner, Theodore Turner, Dustin Milligan; **D:** Danny Pang, Oxide Pang; **W:** Mark Wheaton; **C:** David Geddes; **M:** Joseph LoDuca.

The Messiah ♂♂½ *Il Messia* 1975 Rossellini's final film, a rarely seen version of the life of Christ, completely passed over any notions of divinity to portray him as a morally perfect man. In Italian with subtitles. 145m/C VHS. IT Tina Aumont, Flora Carabella, Vernon Dobtcheff, Jean Martin; **D:** Roberto Rossellini; **W:** Roberto Rossellini; **C:** Mario Montuori; **M:** Mario Nascimbene.

Messiah of Evil ♂ *Dead People; Return of the Living Dead; Revenge of the Screaming Dead; The Second Coming* 1974 (R) California coastal town is invaded by zombies. Confusing low-rent production from the writers of "American Graffiti." 90m/C VHS, DVD. Marianna Hill, Joy Bang, Royal Dano, Elisha Cook Jr., Michael Greer; **D:** Gloria Katz, Willard Huyck; **W:** Gloria Katz, Willard Huyck.

Messidor ♂♂ 1977 Bored university student Jeanne (Amouroux) and shop assistant Marie (Retore) meet while hitchhiking and decide to travel together through Europe—committing robberies when they run out of money. French with subtitles. 118m/C VHS. S/Clementine Amouroux, Catherine Retore, Franziskus Abgottspon, Gérald Battiaz, Hansjörg Bedschart; **D:** Alain Tanner; **W:** Alain Tanner; **C:** Renato Berta; **M:** Arie Dzierlatka.

Metal Skin ♂½ 1994 Nihilistic nightmare, set in Melbourne, plays like an unintentional parody of '50s "B" juvenile delinquent movies. Aimless Joe (Young) has been taken under the wing of local Romeo Dazey (Mendelsohn), who's been romancing Roslyn (Garner) and Savina (Morice), two girls Joe is also interested in. Dazey also has Joe involved in illegal drag racing, leading, after much interim angst, Joe to a racing battle between the two. Director Wright has shown his way with violent characters living on the fringes of society (see "Romper Stomper") but this is too much of a bad thing. 115m/C DVD. AU Aden Young, Ben Mendelsohn, Tara Morice, Nadine Garner; **D:** Geoffrey Wright; **W:** Geoffrey Wright.

Metallica ♂ 1985 Alien warmongers endeavor to conquer Earth and scientists try to stop them. 90m/C VHS. Anthony Newcastle, Sharon Baker; **D:** Al (Alfonso Brescia) Bradley.

Metallica: Some Kind of Monster ♂♂♂ 2004 "Headbangers' 'Let It Be' is a story of celebrity confession and, possibly, redemption. No Metallica career overview, concert showcases, or archival clips included. What you'll see is the psychoanalytically-assisted recording misadventure of St. Anger, a warts and all portrait exposing artist insecurity. Originally Elektra Records commissioned Bruce Sinofsky and Joe Belinger to create a film promoting the making of an album, but when talk of turning the footage into a half-hour reality series ensued, Metallica quickly reimbursed the $2 million to the label and added another $2.3 to have it completed. 140m/C DVD. James Hetfield, Lars Ulrich, Kirk Hammett, Robert Trujillo, Jason Newsted, Dave Mustaine, Bob Rock, Phil Towle; **D:** Joe

Berlinger, Bruce Sinofsky; **C:** Robert Richman. Ind. Spirit '05: Feature Doc.

Metalstorm: The Destruction of Jared Syn ♂ 1983 (PG) It's the science fiction battle of the ages with giant cyclopes and intergalactic magicians on the desert planet of Lemuria. 84m/C VHS, DVD. Jeffrey Byron, Mike (Michael) Preston, Tim Thomerson, Kelly Preston, Richard Moll; **D:** Charles Band; **W:** Alan J. Adler; **C:** Mac Ahlberg; **M:** Richard Band.

Metamorphosis ♂ 1990 (R) Novice scientist foolishly uses himself as the guinea pig for his anti-aging experiments. He quickly loses control of the project. 90m/C VHS. Gene Le Brock, Catherine Baranov, Stephen Brown, Harry Cason, Jason Arnold; **D:** G.L. Eastman.

Metamorphosis: The Alien Factor ♂♂½ 1993 (R) Gerard is a genetic engineer who is bitten by a frog injected with a mutation sample from outer space. He turns into a slimy virus that infects everything he touches. 92m/C VHS, DVD. George Gerard, Tony Gigante, Katharine Romaine; **D:** Glen Takakjian.

Meteor WOOF! 1979 (PG) American and Soviet scientists attempt to save the Earth from a fast-approaching barrage of meteors from space in this disaster dud. Destruction ravages parts of Hong Kong and the Big Apple. 107m/C VHS, DVD. Sean Connery, Natalie Wood, Karl Malden, Brian Keith, Martin Landau, Trevor Howard, Henry Fonda, Joseph Campanella, Richard Dysart; **D:** Ronald Neame; **W:** Stanley Mann; **C:** Paul Lohmann; **M:** Laurence Rosenthal.

Meteor & Shadow ♂♂ *Meteoro Kai Skia* 1985 Based on the life of esteemed Greek poet Napoleon Lapathiotis (1888-1944), whose openly gay lifestyle shocked conservative Athenian society. A leftist charmer, Lapathiotis indulged in the bohemian life until it finally destroyed him. Greek with subtitles. 101m/C VHS, DVD. GR Takis Moschos; **D:** Takis Spetsiotis; **W:** Takis Spetsiotis.

The Meteor Man ♂♂♂ 1993 (PG) Townsend is a school teacher who reluctantly becomes a hero when he acquires semi-super powers after being hit by a meteor. Meteor Man flies only four feet off the ground (because he's afraid of heights) and wears costumes fashioned by his mother. Funny premise satires "superhero" movies, but is inconsistent with some hilarious gags and others that fall flat. Includes interesting cameos by Cosby, Sinbad, Vandross, and Page. 100m/C VHS, DVD. Robert Kevin Townsend, Robert Guillaume, Marla Gibbs, James Earl Jones, Frank Gorshin, Bill Cosby, Sinbad, Luther Vandross, LaWanda Page, Louis Freese; **D:** Robert Kevin Townsend; **W:** Robert Kevin Townsend; **C:** John A. Alonzo.

The Method ♂♂♂ *El Metodo* 2005 Seven job applicants for a high-end position at a corporation in Madrid participate in the Gronholm method of selection. Individuals play games using the monitor and keyboard provided them, setting out to destroy the competition while proving their own credibility. After each round the monitor shuts down on the candidate being eliminated and an electronic voice announces "It's over." Humorous, dark, and engaging view of business culture. English and Spanish with subtitles. 115m/C DVD. AR IT SP Eduardo Noriega, Najwa Nimri, Eduardo Fernandez, Pablo Echarri, Ernesto Alterio, Natalia Verbeke, Adriana Ozores, Carmelo Gomez; **D:** Marcelo Piñeyro; **C:** Alfredo Mayo; **M:** Frederic Begin.

Metro ♂♂½ 1996 (R) Murphy has now officially made this exact movie one kajillion times. He plays fast-talking, fast-shooting cop Axel Fo... er... Scott Roper, who's forced to accept a partner that he doesn't want... played by Nick... um... Judge... uh... Michael Rapaport! When a villain kills his best friend, he vows revenge. He and his sidekick are involved in car chases, shoot-outs and a tense situation where his girlfriend is taken hostage. Any of this ring a bell? Maybe it was in that "Another 48 Beverly Hills Cop Movies." 117m/C VHS, DVD. Eddie Murphy, Michael Rapaport, Michael Wincott, Carmen Ejogo, Denis Arndt,

Art Evans, Donal Logue, Paul Ben-Victor, Kim Miyori, David Michael Silverman; **D:** Thomas Carter; **W:** Randi Feldman; **C:** Fred Murphy; **M:** Steve Porcaro.

Mexican Blow 🐾 *Warner* **2002 (R)** Dangerous drug lords invade the deepest jungles of South America to build their drug manufacturing and distribution headquarters. Dreadmon (Klyn) watches the marauders kill his adopted father and then scares them away with his supernatural powers, but they're not happy to go. Dreadmon must fight inner battles and overcome both his own demons and the drug lords. Shot in the urban setting of Puerto Vallarta, and the urban setting of the jungles of Costa Azul. **M:** Alan Silvestri.

Metroland 🐾🐾 **1997 (R)** Marital ennui and male friendship is explored in this adaptation of Julian Barnes' 1980 novel. In 1977, advertising exec Chris Lloyd (Bale) is settled in a London suburb with his wife, Marion (Watson), and their baby. His predictable existence is blasted when his old chum, Toni (Rossi), arrives. The duo once shared a dream of living a bohemian life and Chris is reminded of his wild spent in Paris in the late-'60s and his wild French lover. Toni increasingly tries to undermine Chris' marriage as he struggles to decide what he expects from life. 105m/ C VHS, DVD, GB FR Christian Bale, Emily Watson, Lee Ross, Elsa Zylberstein, Ifan Meredith, Rufus, Amanda Ryan; **D:** Philip Saville; **W:** Adrian Hodges; **C:** Jean-Francois Robin; **M:** Mark Knopfler.

Metropolis 🐾🐾🐾 **1926** Now a classic meditation on futurist technology and mass mentality, this fantasy concerns mechanized society. Original set design and special effects made this an innovative and influential film in its day. Is now considered one of the hippest films of the sci-fi genre. Silent, with musical score. The 1984 re-release features some color tinting, reconstruction, and a digital score with songs by Pat Benatar, Bonnie Tyler, Giorgio Moroder, and Queen. 115m/B VHS, DVD, GEEnglitte Helm, Alfred Abel, Gustav Froehlich, Rudolf Klein-Rogge, Fritz Rasp, Heinrich George, Theodore Loos, Erwin Biswanger, Olaf Storm, Hans Leo Reich, Heinrich Gotho, Fritz Alberti, Max Dietze; **D:** Fritz Lang; **W:** Fritz Lang, Thea von Harbou; **C:** Karl Freund, Gunther Rittau, Eugen Shuftan; **M:** Gottfried Huppertz.

Metropolitan 🐾🐾🐾 **1990 (PG-13)** The Izod set comes of age on Park Avenue during Christmas break. Tom Townsend (Clements), a member of the middle class, finds himself drawn into a circle of self-proclaimed urban haute bourgeoisie types. They're embarrassingly short on male escorts for the holiday season's parties so he stands in and gets an inside look at life with the brat pack. Intelligently written and carefully made, it transcends the flirting-with-adulthood genre. 98m/C VHS, DVD, Carolyn Farina, Edward Clements, Taylor Nichols, Christopher Eigeman, Allison Rutledge-Parisi, Dylan Hundley, Isabel Gillies, Bryan Leder, Will Kempe, Elizabeth Thompson; **D:** Whit Stillman; **W:** Whit Stillman; **C:** John Thomas; **M:** Mark Suozzo, Ind. Spirit '91: First Feature; N.Y. Film Critics '90: Director (Stillman).

The Mexican 🐾🐾 **2001 (R)** South-of-the-border sniffer has Jerry (Pitt), an inept go-fer for mobster Margolese (Hackman), on a mission to retrieve a priceless antique gun with a name which gives the movie its title. Jerry's quirky girlfriend Samantha (Roberts) wants him to go straight and, when he refuses, heads to Vegas to pursue her dreams of becoming a croupier. Sam's dreams are temporarily sidetracked when she's kidnapped as leverage 'or the supposedly cursed gun by homosexual hitman Leroy (Gandolfini). Gandolfini is far-and-away the standout as the sensitive hood with whom Samantha bonds during her captivity. Screwball romantic comedy outshone by Pitt and Roberts are easily scenes with Pitt and Roberts are easily outshone 'with Pitt and Roberts' chemistry with Gandolfini. Pitt does his part, providing some comic moments in Mexico but can't save the cliched tale. 123m/C VHS, DVD, US Brad Pitt, Julia Roberts, James Gandolfini, Bob Balaban, Gene Hackman, J.K. Simmons, David Krumholtz, Michael Cavens; **D:** Gore Verbinski; **W:** J.H. Wyman; **C:** Darius Wolski; **M:** Alan Silvestri.

Mexican Bus Ride 🐾🐾 *Ascension to Heaven; Subida Al Cielo* **1951** A good-natured Bunuel effort about a newlywed peasant who travels to the big city to attend to his mother's will, who en route, he encounters a diversity of people on the bus and some temptation. In Spanish with English subtitles. 85m/B VHS, MX Lilia Prado, Esteban Marquez, Carmelita Gonzalez; **D:** Luis Bunuel.

Mexican Hayride 🐾🐾 **1948** Bud heads a gang of swindlers and Lou is the fall guy. When things up north get too hot, the boys head south of the border to cool off and start a mining scam. Watch for the hilarious bullfighting scene. Believe it or not, this is based on a Cole Porter musical—minus the music. 77m/B VHS, Bud Abbott, Lou Costello, Virginia Grey, Luba Malina, John Hubbard, Pedro de Cordoba, Fritz Feld, Tom Powers, Pat Costello, Frank Fenton; **D:** Charles T. Barton; **W:** Oscar Brodney.

Mexican Spitfire 🐾🐾 **1940** Velez is typecast as the title character—newlywed Carmelita who has some problems to deal with in her brand-new marriage to Dennis (Woods). There's her fiery temper, a meddling aunt, and an ex-fiancee who's determined to wreck the twosome. First in the series. 67m/B VHS, DVD, Lupe Velez, Leon Errol, Donald Woods, Linda Hayes, Elisabeth Risdon, Cecil Kellaway; **D:** Leslie Goodwins; **W:** Joseph Fields, Charles E. Roberts; **C:** Jack Mackenzie.

Mexican Spitfire at Sea 🐾½ **1942** The feisty wife from South of the Border heads for Hawaii to close a deal for her husband. He goes along to help her, impersonating nobility. The thin storyline keeps it from being quite as good as the action takes place aboard ship. 73m/B VHS, Lupe Velez, Leon Errol, Charles "Buddy" Rogers, Zasu Pitts, Elisabeth Risdon, Florence Bates, Marion Martin, Eddie Dunn, Harry Holman; **D:** Leslie Goodwins.

Mexico City 🐾🐾½ **2000 (R)** This one gets points for having a strong heroine in Edwards. She plays Mitch who takes a holiday in Mexico with photographer brother Sam (Zander). On y Sam disappears and Mitch enlists the help of a local taxi driver (Robles) to help her find him. Shows the seedy underworld side of Mexico City—not exactly a tourist mecca. 88m/C VHS, DVD, Stacy Edwards, Jorge Robles, Johnny Zander, Robert Patrick, Alexander Gould; **D:** Richard Shepard; **W:** Richard Shepard, Jonathan Stern. VIDEO

Mi Vida Loca 🐾🐾 *My Crazy Life* **1994 (R)** Looks at the lives of Latina gang members from L.A.'s Echo Park. The women talk about their romantic dreams, friendships, families, and raising children amidst the pervasive violence and despair of their tough neighborhood. Small budget and some unpolished performances don't lessen film's impact—about the stupidity of violence and how "average" the hopes and dreams of these women are. 92m/C VHS, DVD, Angel Aviles, Jacob Vargas, Jesse Borrego, Seidy Lopez, Mario Marror, Nelida Lopez, Benilia Damas, Art Esquer, Christina Solis, Salma Hayek, Magali Alvarado, Julian Reyes, Panchito Gomez; **D:** Allison Anders; **W:** Allison Anders; **M:** John Taylor.

Miami Beach Cops 🐾 **1993** Two vets return home expecting life to be routine when they become sheriff's deputies. But when bad guys murder a local merchant things heat up fast. 97m/C VHS, Frank Maldonatti, Salvatore Rendino, William Childers, Joyce Geier, Reff Baker, Dan Preston, Deborah Daniels; **D:** James R. Winburn.

Miami Blues 🐾🐾 **1990 (R)** Cold-blooded killer plays cat-and-mouse with blissfully easygoing, dangerously deep undercover cop while diddling with an unflappable prostitute. Violent and cynical, with appropriate performances from three leads. Based on the novel by Charles Willeford. 97m/C VHS, DVD, Fred Ward, Alec Baldwin, Jennifer Jason Leigh, Nora Dunn, Charles Napier, Jose Perez, Paul Gleason, Shirley Stoler; **D:** George Armitage; **M:** Gary Chang, N.Y. Film Critics '90: Support. Actress (Leigh).

Miami Vice 🐾🐾 **1984** Pilot for the popular TV series paired Crockett and Tubbs for the first time on the trail of a killer in Miami's sleazy underground. Music by Jan Hammer and other pop notables. 99m/C VHS, DVD, Don Johnson, Philip Michael Thomas, Saundra Santiago, Michael Talbott, John Diehl, Gregory Sierra; **D:** Thomas Carter TV

Miami Vice 🐾🐾½ **2006 (R)** Writer/director Michael Mann gives his Miami cop story the big-screen treatment in this update of his popular '80s TV series. Today's Crockett (Colin Farrell) and Tubbs (Jamie Foxx) find themselves dangerously deep undercover with the same curious access to super-fast, super-expensive cars and boats as their small-screen predecessors, essential, no-doubt, to catching the multicultural, drug-dealing bad guys and attracting their "average" girlfriends. The actors' pursuit of "cool" comes across as stiff and void of expression, while the story is overly complicated and ultimately secondary to film's style, which really is everything in this case. But then, did you really expect that to change? 132m/C DVD, HD DVD, US Colin Farrell, Jamie Foxx, Gong Li, Naomie Harris, Luis Tosar, John Ortiz, Barry (Shabaka) Henley, Ciaran Hinds, Justin Theroux, Elizabeth Rodriguez, John

Miami Vendetta 🐾 **1987** L.A. vice cop risks it all to avenge his friend's death at the hands of Cuban drug smugglers. 90m/C VHS, Sandy Brooke, Frank Gangari, Maarlen Gosins, Barbara Pilavin; **D:** Steven Seemayer

Miami Cops 🐾 **1989** When a cop's father is killed by a drug smuggler, his partner pursue the murderer over two continents. Italian-made adventure is a bit drawn-out. 103m/C VHS, IT Richard Roundtree, Harrison Muller, Dawn Baker, Michael J. Aronin; **D:** Al (Alfonso Brescia) Bradley.

Miami Horror 🐾 **1987** A Florida scientist is experimenting with bacteria from space, trying to recreate a human only to have his efforts stolen by a crook. His intentions for the use of the experiment are not exactly for the furtherance of science. De martino used the pseudonym Martin Herbert. 85m/C VHS, IT David Warbeck, Laura Trotter, Lawrence Lodd, John Ireland; **D:** Alberto De Martino.

Miami Hustle 🐾½ **1995 (R)** Con artist Marsha (Ireland) is forced by a sleazy lawyer to impersonate a bar waitress (England) who's about to inherit a fortune. But when things turn sour, she gets a computer mogul (Enos) to figure out who's setting her up. 81m/C VHS, DVD, Kathy Ireland, John Enos, Audie England, Richard Sarafian; **D:** Lawrence Lanoff. C ABLE

Miami Rhapsody 🐾🐾 **1995 (PG-13)** Woody Allen-ish romantic comedy about a young, neurotic copywriter who becomes disillusioned with the idea of marriage as she discovers every member of her family is having an affair. Parker plays the newly engaged Gwyn who is not entirely sure if she wants to marry her cute, zoologist boyfriend. Most of the acters come across as annoying, self-absorbed whiners, except for Banderas, who charms as a sexy Cuban nurse. Film movies along with its light-hearted narrative, but never reaches the comic or emotional depth of Allen's work. Director/writer Frankel shows promise, but should come out from behind the Woodman's shadow. Filmed on location in Miami. 95m/C VHS, DVD, Sarah Jessica Parker, Gil Bellows, Antonio Banderas, Mia Farrow, Paul Mazursky, Kevin Pollak, Barbara Garrick, Carla Gugino, Bo Eason, Naomi Campbell, Jeremy Piven, Kelly Bishop, Ben Stein; **D:** David Frankel; **W:** David Frankel; **C:** Jack Wallner; **M:** Mark Isham.

Miami Supercops 🐾 **1985** Two goofy policemen strike out against such threats as a gang that hassles buses, the attempted kidnapping of an Orange Bowl quarterback, and a multi-million-dollar robbery. 97m/C VHS, Terence Hill, Bud Spencer, Jackie Castellano, C.V. Wood Jr.; **D:** Bruno Corbucci.

Michael 🐾🐾½ **1996 (PG)** Following up "Phenomenon" with another celestial storyline, Travolta tries on the giant, molting wings of Michael, an atypical archangel with an amazing jole de vive and an appetite for alcohol, women, and sugar. Residing in Iowa with the elderly Pansy (Stapleton), Michael is being tracked by a cynical tabloid reporter (Hurt) and an angel expert (MacDowell), so he figures he might as well play cupid. The now standard dance sequence in Travolta movies takes place in a bar to the tune of "Chain of Fools" and is one of the movie's standout performance. Hurt and MacDowell have little to do but play out their tired romantic subplot in a script that could've used some inspiration from its lead character. 105m/C VHS, DVD, John Travolta, William Hurt, Andie MacDowell, Bob Hoskins, Robert Pastorelli, Jean Stapleton, Teri Garr; **D:** Nora Ephron; **W:** Nora Ephron, Delia Ephron, Pete Dexter; **C:** John Lindley; **M:** Randy Newman.

Michael Clayton 🐾🐾🐾½ **2007 (R)** The titular Clayton (Clooney) is a ruthless, conflicted "fixer" for a giant law firm—the guy you bring in to do whatever it takes, no matter how unethical, to secure a win for the firm. When Clayton's friend and top-notch litigator Arthur (Wilkinson) suffers a breakdown over a pollution case where their client is clearly in the wrong, Clayton's boss (Pollack) tells him to fix the problem, but Clayton can't help but see just how in the wrong his firm truly is. Unfortunately, he's too good, and in too deep, to give it all up. The ending is in doubt right up until the final, powerful scene. A heady, fascinating exploration of a world where people spend so much time inhabiting grey areas, they've forgotten what black and white look like. 119m/C DVD, US George Clooney, Tom Wilkinson, Tilda Swinton, Sydney Pollack, Michael O'Keefe, Jennifer Van Dyck, Ken Howard, Robert Prescott; **D:** Tony Gilroy; **W:** Tony Gilroy; **C:** Robert Elswit; **M:** James Newton Howard. Oscars '07: Support. Actress (Swinton); British Acad. '07: Support. Actress (Swinton).

Michael Collins 🐾🐾🐾 **1996 (R)** Collins (Neeson) was a revolutionary lead-er with the Irish Volunteers, a guerilla force (an early version of the IRA) dedicated to freeing Ireland from British rule by any means necessary. After a number of successful moves against British intelligence, Collins is unwillingly drawn into a statesman's role as negotiations for an Anglo-Irish Treaty begin in 1921, ultimately dividing the country in two and leading to Collins' own assassination. Controversy surrounded the film as historians, politicians, and the media took potshots at director Jordan's admittedly personal look at the complexities of Irish life and one of its equally controversial heroes. 117m/C VHS, DVD, Liam Neeson, Aidan Quinn, Alan Rickman, Stephen Rea, Julia Roberts, Ian Hart, Sean McGinley, Gerard McSorley, Stuart Graham, Brendan Gleeson, Charles Dance, Jonathan Rhys Meyers; **D:** Neil Jordan; **W:** Neil Jordan; **C:** Chris Menges; **M:** Elliot Goldenthal. L.A. Film Fest. '96: Golden Lion, Actor (Neeson).

Michael Shayne: Private Detective 🐾🐾½ **1940** Brett Halliday's shamus made it to the big screen in a seven-film series starring Nolan. Shayne is a wisecracking, usually broke PI whose ethics, which is why he first refuses the suspicious job: offer made by wealthy Hiram Brighton (Kolb). Hiram wants him to keep an eye on Phyllis (Weaver), his gambling-addicted daughter, who's been betting on the ponies. When a shady money lender is murdered, Shayne is set up to take the fall but he learns the suspect list is long. First in the series. 77m/B DVD, Lloyd Nolan, Clarence (C. William) Kolb, Marjorie Weaver, Douglass Dumbrille, George Meeker, Walter Abel, Joan Valerie, Donald MacBride, Elizabeth Patterson, Charles Coleman; **D:** Eugene Forde; **W:** Stanley Rauh, Manning O'Connor; **C:** Cyril Mockridge.

The Michigan Kid 1928 Two boys fight for the same girl in this silent love triangle set in Alaska. Film's most notable scene is of a raging forest fire, considered a classic even today. 62m/B VHS. C: Conrad Nagel, Renee Adoree, Fred Esmelton, Virginia Grey, Adolph Milar, Lloyd Whitlock; D: Irvin Willat.

Mickey 1917 A penniless young woman moves in with relatives and works as the family's maid. Silent film. 105m/B VHS. Mabel Normand, Lew Cody, Minta Durfee; D: Mack Sennett.

Mickey 1948 A tomboy becomes a woman even as she plays matchmaker for her own father and sings a few songs. Not too exciting; you may fall asleep if you're slipped this "Mickey." Based on the novel "Clementine," by Peggy Goodin. 87m/C VHS, DVD. Lois Butler, Bill Goodwin, Irene Hervey, John Sutton, Hattie McDaniel; D: Ralph Murphy.

Mickey Blue Eyes 1999 (PG-13) Grant reprises his role as the maddeningly polite, apologetic British guy for about the bazillionth time. This time he plays Michael Felgate, an art auctioneer who proposes to schoolteacher Gina (Tripplehorn). Her father Frank (Caan) turns out to be a mobster, whose boss wants to use his auction house as a front for money laundering. After Michael tells a string of lies to hide his involvement with Gina, a series of wild events and misunderstandings leads to Michael posing as mobster Little Big Mickey Blue Eyes from Kansas City. Listening to tea-and-crumpety Grant trying to pronounce "fuhgeddaboudit" briefly brings the movie to life, but the premise is quickly abandoned and he sinks back into his droopy British bit again. All is wrapped up in your standard issue romantic comedy ending. 103m/C VHS, DVD. Hugh Grant, Jeanne Tripplehorn, James Caan, Burt Young, Gerry Becker, James Fox, Joe (Johnny) Viterelli, Maddie Corman, Tony Darrow, Kathryn Witt, Vincent Pastore, Frank Pellegrino, Scott Thompson, John Ventimiglia; D: Kelly Makin; W: Robert Kuhn, Adam Scheinman; C: Donald E. Thorin; M: Wolfgang Hammerschmid.

Micki & Maude 1984 (PG-13) When a man longs for a baby, he finds that his wife, Micki, is too busy for motherhood. Out of frustration, he has an affair with Maude that leads to her pregnancy. Still shocked by the news of his upcoming fatherhood, the man learns that his wife is also expecting. 117m/C VHS, DVD. Dudley Moore, Amy Irving, Ann Reinking, Richard Mulligan, Wallace Shawn, George Gaynes, Andre the Giant; D: Blake Edwards; W: Jonathan Reynolds; C: Harry Stradling Jr. Golden Globes '85: Actor—Mus./Comedy (Moore).

Mickey One 1965 Nightclub comic Mickey (Beatty) gets into trouble when he can't pay his gambling debts. So he hides out in Chicago under an assumed name, working as a janitor, but can't live without the applause. His agent finds him a club job but Mickey panics, thinking the place is under mob control, trying to clear his debts. Finally, returning to the club, Mickey resigns himself to a bleak fate. Beatty's jumpy character is an acquired taste—as is the film. 93m/B VHS. Warren Beatty, Hurd Hatfield, Alexandra Stewart, Franchot Tone, Teddy Hart, Jeff Corey; D: Arthur Penn; W: Alan M. Surgal; C: Ghislan Cloquet; M: Jack Shaindlin, Eddie Sauter.

Mickey the Great 1939 Stitched together from several late '20s Mickey McGuire shorts, starring 10-year-old Rooney. 70m/B VHS. Billy Barty, Mickey Rooney.

Microcosmos 1996 (G) Warning: Do not attempt to smash the bugs on the screen with your shoe. They're supposed to be there. This French documentary uses delicate cameras and sound recording devices to explore the world of insects like never before. The editing and score also add a human dimension to the creepy-crawly world under the lawn, making amorous snails and workaholic beetles seem like people you know (well, if they had an extra set of legs and a shell-like carapace). Of course, if you don't like bugs, then this is just a 77-minute gross out. Cameo appearances by some birds and frogs. 77m/C VHS, DVD. FR D: Claude Nuridsany, Marie Perennou; C: Claude Nuridsany, Marie Perennou; Hughes Ryffel. Thierry Machado; M: Bruno Coulais. Cesar '97: Art Dir./Set Dec., Cinematog., Film Editing, Sound, Score.

Microwave Massacre 1983 (R) Killer kitchen appliances strike again in a late lounge comic Vernon murders nagging wife and 'waves her. Overcome by that Betty Crocker feeling, he goes on a microwave murdering/feeding spree of the local ladies. Lots of Roger Corman copying. 80m/C VHS, DVD. Jackie Vernon, Loren Schein, Al Troupe, Claire Ginsberg, Lou Ann Webber, Sarah Alt; D: Wayne Berwick; W: Thomas Singer; C: Karen Grossman; M: Leif Horvath.

Mid-Channel 1920 A married couple become bored with each other and the wife seeks diversion with other men. Surprise ending. 70m/B VHS. Clara Kimball Young, J. Frank Glendon, Edward M. Kimball, Bertram Grassby, Eileen Robinson, Helen Sullivan, Katherine Griffith, Jack Livingston; D: Harry Garson.

Mid Knight Rider *Hard Knocks; Hollywood Knight* 1979 Penniless actor becomes a male prostitute at the service of bored, rich women. At an all-night orgy, he suddenly goes on a rampage, nearly killing one of his customers. 76m/C VHS. Michael Christian, Keenan Wynn, Donna Wilkes, Henry (Kleinbach) Brandon; D: David Worth.

Midaq Alley *The Alley of Miracles; El Callejon de los Milagros* 1995 Amusing melodrama based on the 1947 novel by Egyptian Naguib Mahfouz and transported from Cairo's backstreets to this city neighborhood known as "The Alley of Miracles." Four segments all begin on the same Sunday afternoon and follow a variety of the Alley's inhabitants, including a married man who becomes attracted to a young male clerk, a beauty who falls prey to a suave pimp, and a homely woman looking for love and finding Mr. Wrong. Spanish with subtitles. 140m/C VHS, DVD. MX Ernesto Cruz, Maria Rojo, Salma Hayek, Bruno Bichir, Claudio Obregon, Delia Casanova, Margarita Sanz, Juan Manuel Bernal, Luis Felipe Tovar, Daniel Gimenez Cacho; D: Jorge Fons; W: Vicente Lenero; C: Carlos Marcovich; M: Lucia Alvarez.

The Midas Touch *Eldorado* 1989 A flea market merchant in 1956 Budapest has the ability to turn items into gold. In Hungarian with English subtitles. 100m/C VHS. HU Karoly Eperies, Judith Pogany, Eniko Eszenyi, Barnabas Toth; D: Geza Beremenyi; W: Geza Beremenyi; C: Sandor Kardos; M: Ferenc Darvas.

Middle Age Crazy 1980 (R) Story of a Texas building contractor who takes life pretty lightly until his own father dies. Then he becomes immersed in a mid-life crisis and has an affair with a Dallas Cowboys' cheerleader. Ann-Margret plays the victim wife of the middle aged swingin' guy. 95m/C VHS. CA Bruce Dern, Ann-Margret, Graham Jarvis, Eric Christmas, Deborah Wakeham; D: John Trent.

The Middleman *Jana Aranya* 1976 Recent college graduate Somnath has struggled to find a job and eventually enters the business world as a middleman, where he soons discovers that success will depend on his willingness to break the rules. Bengali with subtitles. 131m/B VHS. IN Pradip Mukherjee; D: Satyajit Ray; W: Satyajit Ray; C: Soumendu Roy.

Middlemarch 1993 Stylish British TV costume drama, adapted from George Eliot's 1872 novel, finds idealistic Dorothea Brooke (Aubrey) determined to be a helpmate to the older scholar, the Rev. Edward Casaubon (Malahide), whom she marries. Too bad that he takes so little interest in her ability (or in Dorothea herself). This leads Casaubon's distant cousin, young and handsome Will Ladislaw (Sewell), to discreetly make his interest clear. Naturally, Eliot has a number of other plots (some dealing with the impact of the Industrial Revolution on 19th-century life) and romances worked into the mix. Filmed in Stamford, England. On three cassettes. 360m/C VHS, DVD. GB Juliet Aubrey, Patrick Malahide, Rufus Sewell, Douglas Hodge, Trevyn McDowell, Michael Hordern, Robert Hardy; John Savident, Jonathan Firth, Peter Jeffrey, Simon Chandler, Julian Wadham; D: Anthony Page; W: Andrew Davies, Stanley Myers; C: Brian Tufano.

Midnight 1934 A jury foreman's daughter is romantically involved with a gangster who is interested in a particular case before it appears in court. The foreman, who sentenced a girl to death, faces a dilemma when his own daughter is arrested for the same crime. An early Bogart appearance in a supporting role led to a re-release of the film as "Call it Murder" after Bogart made it big. Weak melodrama. 74m/B VHS, DVD. Humphrey Bogart, Sidney (Sydney) Fox, O.P. Heggie, Henry Hull, Richard Whorf, Margaret Wycherly, Lynne Overman; D: Chester Erskine; W: Chester Erskine.

Midnight 1939 Struggling showgirl Colbert masquerades as Hungarian countess in sophisticated comedy of marital conflicts. Near-classic film scripted by Wilder and Brackett. Based on a story by Edwin Justus Mayer and Franz Schulz. Remade as "Masquerade in Mexico." 94m/B VHS, DVD. Claudette Colbert, Don Ameche, John Barrymore, Francis Lederer, Mary Astor, Hedda Hopper, Rex O'Malley; D: Mitchell Leisen; W: Billy Wilder, Charles Brackett; C: Charles B(ryant) Lang Jr.

Midnight *Backwoods Massacre* 1981 (R) Russo, who cowrote the original "Night of the Living Dead," wrote and directed this film about a runaway girl who is driven out of her home by a lecherous stepfather and meets two young thieves and then a family of cultists. Russo adapted his own novel. He also attains some of "Night of the Living Dead's" low-budget ambience. 88m/C VHS, DVD. Lawrence Tierney, Melanie Verlin, John Hall, John Amplas; D: John A. Russo.

Midnight 1989 Murder-thriller involving the vampirish hostess of a TV horror movie showcase and a fanatical fan. 90m/C VHS. Lynn Redgrave, Tony Curtis, Steve Parrish, Rita Gam, Gustav Vintas, Karen Witter, Frank Gorshin, Wolfman Jack; D: Norman Thaddeus Vane.

Midnight 2: Sex, Death, and Videotape 1993 Sequel to "Midnight" finds the sole surviving member of the crazed family stalking a beautiful unsuspecting teller with a video camera. Only she's teamed up with a detective to solve the murder of her best friend—even if it means she's bait for a psycho. 70m/C VHS. Matthew Jason Walsh, Jo Norcia; D: John A. Russo.

Midnight at the Wax Museum *Midnight at Madame Tussaud's* 1936 A man attempts to spend an evening in a wax museum's chamber of horrors, only to find that he is the target of a murder plot. 66m/B VHS. Lucille Lisle, James Carew, Charles Oliver, Kim Peacock; D: George Pearson.

Midnight Auto Supply *Love and the Midnight Auto Supply* 1978 Dealers in hot car parts, working out of the garage behind the local brothel, become persuaded to donate some of their profits to the cause of Mexican farm workers. 91m/C VHS. Michael Parks, Rory Calhoun, Scott Jacoby, Rod Cameron, Colleen Camp, Linda Cristal, John Ireland; D: James Polakof.

Midnight Blue 1996 (R) Martin Blake (Chapa) is a lonely banker on a trip to Atlanta where he meets prostitute Martine (Schofield). They have a one-nighter and Martin later decides he loves her and hires a detective (Stockwell) to find her—only Martine has disappeared. After Martin has moved to L.A., he discovers his new boss' wife, Georgine, just happens to be a double for Martine. Naturally, Martin becomes obsessed and this leads to big trouble. 95m/C VHS. Damian Chapa, Annabel Schofield, Steve Kanaly, Dean Stockwell, Harry Dean Stanton, Jennifer Jostyn; D: Skott Snider; W: Douglas Brode; C: Mark Vicente; M: Eric Allaman.

Midnight Cabaret 1990 Woof! A New York nightclub-based Satanic cult selects a child actress to bear Satan's child. 94m/C VHS. Michael Des Barres, Thom Mathews, Carolyn Seymour, Leonard Termo, Norbert Weisser, Lydie Denier, Wilhelm von Homburg; D: Pece Dingo; W: Pece Dingo; M: Michel Colombier.

A Midnight Clear 1992 (PG) Sensitive war drama that takes place in the Ardennes Forest, near the French-German border in December 1944. It's Christmastime and six of the remaining members of a 12-member squad are sent on a dangerous mission to an abandoned house to locate the enemy. Filmed in a dreamy surreal style, the setting is somewhat reminiscent of a fairytale, although a sense of anguish filtrates throughout the picture. A solid script, excellent direction, and a good cast make this a worthwhile film that pits the message of peace against the stupidity of war. Adapted from the novel by William Wharton. 107m/C VHS, DVD. Peter Berg, Kevin Dillon, Arye Gross, Ethan Hawke, Gary Sinise, Frank Whaley, John C. McGinley, Larry Joshua, Curt Lowens, David Jensen, Rachel Griffin, Tim Shoemaker; D: Keith Gordon; W: Keith Gordon; C: Tom Richmond; M: Mark Isham.

Midnight Clear 2006 (PG-13) Five strangers, battling misfortune and loneliness, cross paths on Christmas Eve and find their lives changed by acts of kindness. Keeps its Christian themes low-key. Jenkins directs from an adaptation of his father Jerry's short story. 102m/C DVD. Stephen Baldwin, K. Callan, Kirk B.R. Woller, Victoria Jackson, Richard Riehle, Richard Fancy, Mary Thornton, Mitchell Jarvis; D: Dallas Jenkins; W: Wes Halula; C: Randall Walker Gregg; M: Jeehun Hwang.

Midnight Confessions 1995 (R) Provocative night-time DJ Vannesse (Hoyt) lures her listeners into revealing their sexual fantasies. But when an obsessed fan begins killing women just how deeply is she involved? 98m/C VHS, DVD. Carol Hoyt, Julie Strain, Monique Parent, Richard Lynch; D: Allan Shustak; W: Jake Jacobs, Allan Shustak, Marc Cushman, Timothy O'Rawe; C: Tom Frazier; M: Scott Singer.

Midnight Cop 1988 (R) A young woman gets tangled up in a web of murder, intrigue, prostitution and drugs, and she enlists the aid of a cop to help get her out of it. 100m/C VHS, DVD. Michael York, Morgan Fairchild, Frank Stallone, Armin Mueller-Stahl; D: Peter Patzak.

Midnight Cowboy 1969 (R) Drama about the relationship between a naive Texan hustler and a seedy derelict, set in the underbelly of NYC. Graphic and emotional character study is brilliantly acted and engaging. Shocking and considered quite risque at the time of its release, this film now carries an "R" rating. It was the only "X"-rated film ever ever to win the Best Picture Oscar. From James Leo Herlihy's novel. 113m/C VHS, DVD. Dustin Hoffman, Jon Voight, Sylvia Miles, Brenda Vaccaro, John McGiver, Bob Balaban, Barnard Hughes; D: John Schlesinger; W: Waldo Salt; C: Adam Holender; M: John Barry. Oscars '69: Adapt. Screenplay, Director (Schlesinger), Picture; AFI '98: Top 100; British Acad. '69: Actor (Hoffman), Director (Schlesinger), Film, Screenplay; Directors Guild '69: Director (Schlesinger); Natl. Film Reg. '94; N.Y. Film Critics '69: Actor (Voight); Natl. Soc. Film Critics '69: Actor (Voight); Writers Guild '69: Adapt. Screenplay.

Midnight Crossing 1987 (R) Two married couples are subjected to jealousy, betrayal and uncloseted-skeletons as their pleasure cruise on a yacht turns into a ruthless search for sunken treasure. 96m/C VHS, DVD. Faye Dunaway, Daniel J. Travanti, Kim Cattrall, John Laughlin, Ned Beatty; D: Roger Holzberg.

Midnight Dancer 1987 A young ballerina is forced to work as an erotic dancer. 97m/C VHS. AU Deanne Jeffs, Mary Regan; D: Pamela Gibbons.

Midnight Dancers 1994 Seamy look at Manila's gay subculture and male prostitution. Sonny and his older brothers Dennis and Joel work as dancers at a sleazy club whose upstairs apartments are used for prostitution. The boys need the money to help their impoverished family survive in the slums but the emotional wear and tear (not to mention police raids and assorted brutalities) provide lots of melodrama. Filipino with subtitles. 115m/C VHS, DVD. PH Alex Del Rosario,

Gandong Cervantes, Laurence David, Pera Bautista, Sexy Topacio; **D:** George Tulanes; **M:** Nonong Buenaamino.

Midnight Edition 1993 (R) Investigative reporter Jack Travers (Patton) returns to his Georgia hometown's newspaper just in time to write the story of his life. Nineteen-year-old Darryl Weston (DeLuise) massacres a local family for no apparent reason, is tried, convicted, and sentenced to die. Jack's death row interviews with Darryl become hot news but his reporter's objectivity is lost and he becomes a pawn in an escape plan. Good interplay between the charming sociopath and the self-deluded reporter in a sometimes confusing thriller. Based on the autobiography "Escape of My Dead Men" by Charles Postell. 96m/C VHS, Wii DVD. **C:** Will Patton, Michael Stewart; **M:** Murray Attaway.

Midnight Express 1978 (R) Gripping and powerful film based on the true story of Billy Hayes (Davis), a young American busted in Turkey for trying to smuggle hashish. He is sentenced to a brutal and nightmarish prison for life as an example to other potential smugglers. After enduring tremendous mental and physical torture, Billy seeks the "Midnight Express" his chance at escape. Not always easy to watch, but the overall effect is riveting and unforgettable. Adapted from the book by Hayes and William Hoffer. 120m/C VHS, DVD. John Hurt, Randy Quaid, Brad Davis, Paul Smith, Bo Hopkins, Oliver Stone; **D:** Alan Parker; **W:** Oliver Stone; **C:** Michael Seresin; **M:** Giorgio Moroder. Oscars '78: Adapt. Screenplay, Orig Score; British Acad. '78: Director (Parker), Support. Actor (Hurt); Golden Globes '79: Film—Drama, Screenplay, Support. Actor (Hurt); Writers Guild '78: Adapt. Screenplay.

Midnight Faces 1926 Mysterious doings abound in a house in the Florida bayous, recently inherited by Bushman. Silent, with original organ music. 72m/B VHS, DVD. Francis X. Bushman, Jack Perrin, Kathryn McGuire; **D:** Bennett Cohen; **W:** Bennet Cohen; **C:** King Gray.

Midnight Fear 1990 When a sexually demented killer skins a woman alive, Sheriff Hanley sets out to find who-dunit. He suspects two weird brothers, who turn out to be holding a woman hostage, but the situation may not be so simple. Carradine plays the good-guy sheriff in this creeper. 90m/C VHS. Doris Day, David Carradine, Craig Wasson; **D:** William Crain.

Midnight Girl 1925 A fading opera impresario plots to steal a family's fortune. Lugosi before he became Dracula. Silent 84m/B VHS. Charlotte Walker Gareth Hughes, Dolores Cassinelli, Bela Lugosi, Lila Lee; **D:** Wilfred Noy; **W:** Jean Conover; **C:** Frank Zucker.

Midnight Heat 1996 *Black Out* 1995 (R) Football player is the prime suspect when his lover's husband (who happens to be the team owner) is murdered. 97m/C VHS, DVD. Tim Matheson, Stephen Mendel, Mimi (Meyer) Craven; **D:** Harvey Frost.

The Midnight Hour 1986 A group of high schoolers stumbles upon a vintage curse that wakes up the dead. More humor than horror. 97m/C VHS, DVD. Shari Belafonte, LeVar Burton, Lee Montgomery, Dick Van Patten, Kevin McCarthy, Jonelle Allen, Peter DeLuise, Dedee Pfeiffer, Mark Blankfield; **D:** Jack Bender; **C:** Rexford Metz; **M:** Brad Fiedel. TV

Midnight in Saint Petersburg 1997 (R) Caine once again returns to his role of super spy Harry Palmer, who's after terrorists buying stolen plutonium to use in nuclear weapons. He's aided by Nikolai (Connery), whose girlfriend Tatiana is kidnapped, leading the men to a link between the kidnapping, the terrorists, and recent art thefts from the Hermitage Museum. Adapted from stories by Len Deighton. 90m/C VHS. Michael Caine, Jason Connery, Michael Sarrazin, Michele Rene Thomas. CABLE.

Midnight in the Garden of Good and Evil 1997 (R) An all-star cast can't save Eastwood's grossly mishandled adaptation of John Berendt's best-selling novel on the eccentric citizens of Savannah. New York journalist John Kelso (Cusack) is sent on assignment to report on the glamourous Christmas parties of famed citizen and a dull romance between Kelso and local flower Mandy (Eastwood's daughter), the rich subject which made the book a top-seller for four years is all but lost and the answer to the above question moot. "Midnight" has the star power for greatness, but looks certainly are deceiving. 155m/C VHS, DVD. Kevin Spacey, John Cusack, Jack Thompson, Alison Eastwood, The Lady Chablis, Irma P. Hall, Paul Hipp, Jack Law, Dorothy Loudon, Anne Haney, Kim Hunter, Geoffrey Lewis; **D:** Clint Eastwood; **W:** John Lee Hancock; **C:** Jack N. Green; **M:** Lennie Niehaus.

Midnight Kiss 1993 (R) When a woman police detective investigates a mysterious series of deaths—women whose blood has been drained—she gets more than she bargains for. She's attacked by a vampire and is herself turned into a reluctant bloodsucker. Quick moving and some gross special effects. Also available in an unrated version. 85m/C VHS, DVD. Michelle Owens, Gregory A. Greer, Celeste Yarnall; **D:** Joel Bender; **W:** John Weidner, Ken Lamplugh.

Midnight Lace 1960 Acceptable thriller about a woman in London who is being harassed by a telephone creep. Day is at her frantic best, and Harrison is suitably charming. Handsome Gavin later became American ambassador to Mexico. Adapted from the play "Matilda Shouted Fire." 108m/C VHS. Doris Day, Rex Harrison, John Gavin, Myrna Loy, Roddy McDowall, Elspeth March; **D:** David Miller; **W:** Ivan Goff; **C:** Russell Metty.

Midnight Limited 1940 A detective sets out to thwart the criminals who would rob the "Midnight Limited" train on its route from New York to Montreal. 61m/B VHS, DVD. John "Dusty" King, Marcine Reynolds, George Cleveland, Edward Kean, Keene Keane, Pat Flaherty, Monte (Monty) Collins Jr., I. Stanford Jolley; **D:** Howard Bretherton.

Midnight Madness 1980 (PG) Five teams of college stereotypes search the city of Los Angeles for clues as part of a wacky scavenger hunt designed by a fellow student. Features the big-screen debut of Michael J. Fox as the little brother of David "I'm a Pepper" Naughton (look closely to see the former Pepper pitchman drinking a bottle of the stuff; it's the only near-vérity moment). Also casts Stephen "Flounder" Dort, making this flick somewhat of an "It's a Mad, Mad, Mad, Mad Animal House," but to say that is an insult to both of those films. Even the presence of arch-geek Eddie Deezen can't save the outing. 110m/C VHS, DVD. David Naughton, Stephen Furst, Debra Clinger, Eddie Deezen, Michael J. Fox, Maggie Roswell; **D:** David Wechter; **C:** Frank Phillips; **M:** Julius Wechter.

Midnight Murders *Manhunt in the Dakotas; In the Line of Duty: Manhunt in the Dakotas* 1991 (R) Steiger stars as a farmer and Posse Committatus member whose paramilitary pretensions lead to a bloody confrontation with federal marshals. Gross is the FBI agent sent to hunt him down. Made for TV. 95m/C VHS. Rod Steiger, Michael Gross, Gary Basaraba, Christopher Rich, Henderson Forsythe; **D:** Dick Lowry. TV

The Midnight Phantom 1935 Incredibly rare horror film featuring a bizarre murder at a midnight lecture. 63m/B VHS, DVD. Reginald Denny, Lloyd Hughes, Claudia Dell, Jim Farley, John Elliott, Barbara Bedford.

D: Bernard B. Ray; **W:** John Thomas "Jack" Neville; **C:** Pliny Goodfriend.

Midnight Ride 1992 Lots of silly action fails to save this slight tale of a cop (Cudikoff) chasing after his runaway wife (Gersak), who has made the mistake of picking up a psycho hitchiker (Hamill, gleefully overacting). 95m/C VHS. Michael Biddikoff, Mark Hamill, Savina Gersak; **D:** Robert Braiver.

Midnight Run 1988 (R) An ex-cop, bounty hunter must bring in an ex-mob accountant who has embezzled big bucks from his former boss. After he catches up with the thief, the hunter finds that bringing his prisoner from New York to Los Angeles will be very trying, especially because it is apparent that the Mafia and FBI are out to stop them. The friction between the two leads—De Niro and Grodin—is fun to watch, as the action and comic moments are enjoyable. 125m/C VHS, DVD, HD DVD. Robert De Niro, Charles Grodin, Yaphet Kotto, John Ashton, Dennis Farina, Joe Pantoliano, Richard Foronjy, Wendy Phillips; **D:** Martin Brest; **M:** Danny Elfman.

Midnight Tease 1994 Strip bar, the Club Fugazi, is having trouble with its help—the dancers keep getting murdered. Dancer Samantha (Leigh) actually dreams about the murders before they occur, so naturally she becomes the prime suspect. Leigh can actually do more than look fetching but plot is barely apparent. 87m/C VHS, DVD. Cassandra Leigh, Rachel Reed, Edmund Halley, Ashlie Rhey, Todd Joseph; **D:** Scot Levy; **M:** Christopher Lennertz.

Midnight Tease 2 1995 (R) Jen Brennan (Kelly) goes undercover at an L.A. strip club to find out who's been murdering the dancers, including her sister. 95m/C VHS, DVD. Kimberly Kelly, Tane McClure, Ross Hagen; **D:** Richard Styles; **W:** Richard Styles; **C:** Gary Graver.

Midnight Warning 1932 A woman thinks she's going off the deep end when her brother and all records of his existence disappear. Based on an urban legend that appeared somewhere around the time of the 1893 World's Fair. Remade in 1952 as "So Long at the Fair." 63m/B VHS, DVD. William Boyd, Claudia Dell, Henry Hull, John Harron, Hooper Atchley; **D:** Spencer Gordon Bennet.

Midnight Warrior 1989 A reporter strikes it big when he investigates the underside of L.A. nightlife, but things go terribly wrong, when he becomes wrapped up in the sleaze. 90m/C VHS, DVD. Bernie Angel, Michele Berger, Kevin Bernhardt, Lilly Melgar; **D:** Joseph Merhi.

Midnight Witness 1993 (R) Guy finds himself on the run when after he videotapes the beating of a young drug dealer by corrupt cops. Plot bears more than a little resemblance to the Rodney King incident, but according to writer Foldy it was written before it took place. Low-budget thriller went direct to video. 90m/C VHS, DVD. Maxwell Caulfield, Jan-Michael Vincent, Paul Johansson, Karen Moncrieff, Mark Pellegrino, Virginia Mayo; **D:** Peter Foldy; **W:** Peter Foldy; **M:** Grayden Hillock. VIDEO

Midnight's Child 1993 Another Nanny-from-Hell story, only this time it's literal. D'Abo is the Nanny in question, who belongs to a Satanic cult. Her mission is to select the young daughter in her care as a bride for the devil, even if the girl's parents don't approve of the match. 89m/C VHS, DVD. Olivia D'Abo, Marcy Walker, Cotter Smith, Elisabeth Elisapeth, Elizabeth, Liz Moss, Jim Norton, Judy Parfitt, Roxann Biggs-Dawson, Mary Larkin; **D:** Colin Bucksey; **W:** David Chaskin.

Midnite Spares 1985 A young man's search for the men who kidnapped his father leads him into the world of car thieves and chop-shops. 90m/C VHS. Bruce Spence, Gia Carides, James Laurie; **C:** Geof Burton; **M:** Cameron Allan.

A Midsummer Night's Dream 1935 Famed Reinhardt version of the Shakespeare classic, featuring nearly every star on the Warner Bros. lot. The plot revolves around the amorous battle between the king (Jory) and queen (Louise) of a fairy kingdom, and the humans who are drawn into their sport. Features de Havilland's first film role (as Hermia, although Rooney, as the fairy Puck, seems to be having the most fun). Classic credit line: Dialogue by William Shakespeare. 117m/B VHS. James Cagney, Dick Powell, Joe E. Brown, Hugh Herbert, Olivia de Havilland, Ian Hunter, Mickey Rooney, Victor Jory, Arthur Treacher, Billy Barty, Ross Alexander; **D:** Max Reinhardt, William Dieterle; **W:** Mary C. McCall, Charles Kenyon; **C:** Hal Mohr. Oscars '35: Cinematog., Film Editing.

A Midsummer Night's Dream 1966 Fine acting from the Royal Shakespeare Company cast in this filmed version of the play. Makes very little use of the Athens, Greece scenery. 124m/C VHS, DVD. GB David Warner, Diana Rigg, Ian Richardson, Judi Dench, Ian Holm, Barbara Jefford, Nicholas Selby, Helen Mirren, Sebastian Shaw, Bill Travers, Paul Rogers; **D:** Peter Hall.

A Midsummer Night's Dream 1996 (PG-13) The Royal Shakespeare Company offers their version of the play in which the spat between Oberon and Titania, the king and queen of the fairies, leads to a romantic and comedic woodland fantasy for a quartet of would-be lovers who get caught up in their spells, as well as a group of rustics rehearsing their own play. 103m/C VHS, DVD. GB Lindsay Duncan, Alex Jennings, Desmond Barrit, Barry Lynch, Monica Dolan, Emily Raymond; **D:** Adrian Noble; **C:** Ian Wilson; **M:** Howard Blake.

A Midsummer Night's Sex Comedy 1982 (PG) Allen's homage to Shakespeare, Renoir, Chekhov, Bergman, and who knows who else is an engaging ensemble piece about the jinks among friends and acquaintances gathered at a country house at the turn of the century. Standouts include Ferrer as pompous professor and Steenburgen as his sexually repressed wife, Mia's first gathered at a country house at the turn of the century. 88m/C VHS, DVD. Woody Allen, Mia Farrow, Mary Steenburgen, Tony Roberts, Julie Hagerty, Jose Ferrer, Kate McGregor-Stewart; **D:** Woody Allen; **W:** Woody Allen; **C:** Gordon Willis.

A Midwinter's Tale 1995 (R) *In the Bleak Midwinter* 1995 (R) Branagh assembles a largely unknown cast in this low-budget backstage saga about an out-of-work thesp, Joe Harper (Maloney), who assembles a shaggy crew of actors to stage an alternative "Hamlet" in a small English country church. The diverse cast squabble, stumble, and emote their way through rehearsals, finally pulling together for the big show. Funny and interesting performances manage to show through the dense and somewhat cliched script. Maloney's Joe, who exhibits the frustration of being forced to deal with amateurs and Sessions as a camp queen playing the Queen (Gertrude, that is) stand out, as does Briers as the aging player. 99m/B VHS, GB Michael Maloney, Richard Briers, Mark Hadfield, Nicholas Farrell, Gerard Horan, John Sessions, Celia Imrie, Hetta Charnley, Julia Sawalha, Joan Collins, Jennifer Saunders; **D:** Kenneth Branagh; **W:** Kenneth Branagh; **C:** Roger Lanser; **M:** Jimmy Yuill.

Midway 1976 (PG) The epic WWII battle of Midway, the turning point in the war, is retold through Allied and Japanese viewpoints by a big all-star cast saddled with dumsy dialogue and enough weaponry to seize Hollywood on any given Wednesday. 132m/C VHS, DVD. Sab Shimono, Robert Webber, Ed Nelson, James Shigeta, Monte Markham, Biff McGuire, Glenn Corbett, Gregory Walcott, Noriyuki "Pat" Morita, John Fujioka, Dabney Coleman, Erik Estrada, Clyde Kusatsu, Robert Ito, Steve Kanaly, Kip Niven, Michael Ryan, Susan Sullivan, Charlton Heston, Henry Fonda, James Coburn, Glenn Ford, Hal Holbrook, Robert Mitchum, Cliff Robertson, Robert Wagner, Kevin Dobson, Christopher George, Toshiro Mifune, Tom Selleck; **D:** Jack Smight; **W:** Donald S. Sanford; **C:** Harry Stradling Jr.; **M:** John Williams.

Mifune 1999 (R) Third release for the Danish film collective Dogma 95 (following "The Idiots" and "The Celebration") is a comedy/romance with a couple of twists. Yuppie Kresten (Berthelsen) travels to the family's run-down farm to check on his mentally handicapped brother, Rud (Asholt), after their father's death. Kresten needs a housekeeper and winds up with attractive Livia (Hjejle), who neglects to tell him she is a hooker on the lam from her threatening pimp and also shows up with her younger brother (Tarding). Kresten and Livia soon share a mutual attraction and lots of obstacles. Title refers to Rud's hero worship of actor Toshiro Mifune. Danish with subtitles. **102m/C VHS, DVD.** *DK* Iben Hjejle, Anders W. Berthelsen, Jesper Asholt, Emil Tarding, Anders (Totfing) Hove, Sofie Grabol, Paprika Steen, Mette Bratlann; **D:** Soeren Kragh-Jacobsen; **W:** Soeren Kragh-Jacobsen, Anders Thomas Jensen; **C:** Anthony Dod Mantle; **M:** Karl Bille, Christian Sievert.

The Mighty ♂♂♂ **1998 (PG-13)** Like "Simon Birch," this one also features a central character, Kevin (Culkin), who's smart and brave despite suffering from Morquio's syndrome. His new neighbor, Max (Henson), is just the opposite: large in size, not too bright, and afraid of everything. The two quickly find they're much stronger as a team than individually. When Kevin becomes Max's reading tutor, he brings along a book on the legend of King Arthur. Kevin rides Max's shoulders and, dubbing themselves "Freak the Mighty" (the title of Rodman Philbrick's novel, on which the film is based), the inspired boys embark on knightly neighborhood quests, even facing the evil Black Knight—in the form of Max's ex-con father. Henson is amazing as the at-first introverted Max, and Culkin does a good job as Kevin. Stone's understated performance as Kevin's mom shows she's more than a sexpot. **100m/C VHS, DVD.** Kieran Culkin, Elden (Ratliff) Henson, Sharon Stone, Gillian Anderson, Harry Dean Stanton, Gena Rowlands, James Gandolfini, Joe Perrino, Meat Loaf Aday, Jenifer Lewis; **D:** Peter Chelsom; **W:** Charles Leavitt; **C:** John de Borman; **M:** Trevor Jones.

Mighty Aphrodite ♂♂½ **1995 (R)** Neurotic (Surprise!) New York sportswriter Lenny Weinrib (Allen) is trapped in an unhappy marriage to art dealer Amanda (Bonham Carter), who talks him into adopting a child. Lenny comes alive when Lenny tracks down his son's biological mother, consummate dumb blond and hooker/porno actress Linda, played with over-the-top (in a good way) gusto by Sorvino. Lenny attempts to reform his son's real mother while a Greek chorus (including Abraham and Dukakis) provide a running commentary on the tragedy/comedy of Lenny's predicaments. Allen's 31st film treads into familiar Woodman waters but falls short of his past comic genius. **95m/C VHS, DVD.** Woody Allen, Helena Bonham-Carter, Mira Sorvino, F. Murray Abraham, Michael Rapaport, Jack Warden, Olympia Dukakis, Peter Weller, Claire Bloom, David Ogden Stiers; **D:** Woody Allen; **W:** Woody Allen; **C:** Carlo Di Palma; **M:** Dick Hyman. Oscars '95: Support. Actress (Sorvino); Golden Globes '96: Support. Actress (Sorvino); Nat'l Bd. of Review '95: Support. Actress (Sorvino); N.Y. Film Critics '95: Support. Actress (Sorvino).

The Mighty Ducks ♂♂½ **1992 (PG)** Bad News Bears on skates. Selfish yuppie lawyer is arrested for drunk driving and as part of his community service sentence, he is forced to coach an inner-city hockey team full of the usual misfits and underachievers. Although sarcastic and skeptical, Coach Gordon Bombay (Estevez) eventually bonds with the Ducks and learns to treat them with respect. Dual themes of teamwork and redemption are repeated constantly, and it gets a bit hokey at times, but the kids won't mind with this fun Disney film, while adults will appreciate the sarcasm. Followed by "D2: The Mighty Ducks." **114m/C VHS, DVD.** Emilio Estevez, Joss Ackland, Lane Smith, Heidi Kling, Josef Sommer, Matt Doherty, Steven Brill, Joshua Jackson, Elden (Ratliff) Henson, Shaun Weiss; **D:** Stephen Herek; **W:** Brian Hohlfeld, Steven Brill; **C:** Thomas Del Ruth; **M:** David Newman.

A Mighty Heart ♂♂♂ **2007 (R)** Based on Mariane Pearl's memoir about the kidnapping and execution of her husband, Wall Street Journal reporter Daniel, when he was on assignment in Karachi, Pakistan in 2002. His beheading by Islamic extremists was videotaped for broadcast on the Internet while the pregnant Mariane (a journalist herself) worked her way through bureaucrats and false leads to get answers. Brit director Winterbottom has done films on the complexities of the Mideast before, and he treats this harrowing story matter-of-factly. Jolie (a somewhat controversial choice for the role) does a fine, low-key job with Futterman, as Daniel, in flashbacks during happier times. **103m/C DVD, HD DVD.** *US* Angelina Jolie, Dan Futterman, Will Patton, Archie Panjabi, Irfan Khan, Denis O'Hare, Sajid Hasan, Gary Wilmes; **D:** Michael Winterbottom; **W:** Michael Winterbottom, Laurence Coriat, John Orloff; **C:** Marcel Zyskind; **M:** Molly Nyman, Harry Escott.

Mighty Joe Young ♂♂♂½ **1949** Tongue-in-cheek King Kong variation and features giant ape brought to civilization and exploited in a nightclub act, whereupon things get darned ugly. Bullied and given the key to the liquor cabinet, mild-mannered Joe goes on a drunken rampage, but eventually redeems himself by rescuing orphans from a fire. Special effects (courtesy of Willis O'Brien and the great Ray Harryhausen) are probably the film's greatest asset. Also available colorized. **94m/B VHS, DVD.** Terry Moore, Ben Johnson, Robert Armstrong, Frank McHugh; **D:** Ernest B. Schoedsack.

Mighty Joe Young ♂♂½ **1998 (PG)** Loose adaptation of the 1949 film has special effects wizard Rick Baker creating a very life-like model of the 15-foot, 2,000-lb. gorilla. With his elaborate features, including a pair of huge brown eyes, this Joe has more personality than his human allies Jill (Theron) and O'Hara (Paxton) who, in between saving Joe from evil South African poachers, spend most of the film giving each other the goo-goo eyes. Wholesome, harmless, lightweight (the movie, not the gorilla) family entertainment. **114m/C VHS, DVD.** Bill Paxton, Charlize Theron, David Paymer, Regina King, Rade Serbedzija, Peter Firth, Lawrence Pressman, Linda Purl, Ray Harryhausen; **D:** Ron Underwood; **W:** Mark Rosenthal, Larry Konner; **C:** Don Peterman; Oliver Wood; **M:** James Horner.

Mighty Jungle ♂♂ **1964** Lost in the Amazon jungle, a hunter must fight off killer iguanas, man-eating crocodiles and bloodthirsty natives who prefer human sacrifices. **90m/C VHS.** Marshall Thompson, David Dalie, Antonio Gutierrez, Rosenda Monteros; **D:** David Dalue, Arnold Belgard; **C:** J. Carlos Carbajal; **M:** Les Baxter.

Mighty Morphin Power Rangers: The Movie ♂½ **1995 (PG)** From the living room onto the big screen, these six suburban teenagers with super powers battle the evil Ivan Ooze to save Earth. Offers more special effects, new Zord animals, more ooze and more growth to the retail toy industry than the small screen could provide. A child's dream come true, but a parent's nightmare. **93m/C VHS, DVD.** Paul Freeman, Jason Harold Yost, Amy Jo Johnson, Jason David Frank, John Yong Bosch, Stephen Antonio Cardenas; **D:** Bryan Spicer; **W:** Arne Olsen, John Kamps; **C:** Paul Murphy; **M:** Graeme Revell.

The Mighty Pawns **1987** Inner-city kids turn to chess when their teacher inspires them to stay off the streets. Originally aired on PBS as part of the "Wonderworks" family movie series. **58m/C VHS.** Paul Winfield, Alfonso Ribeiro, Terence Knox, Rosalind Cash, Teddy Wilson; **D:** Eric Laneuville.

The Mighty Peking Man woof! *Goliathon* **1977 (PG-13)** A ten-story-tall gorilla resides in the jungle and is sought by a group of Hong Kong businessmen who want to display the creature. Johnny, the hunter hired to find the beast, discovers both the gorilla and a beautiful jungle goddess. Incredibly campy, with badly dubbed and hilariously awful dialogue. **91m/C VHS, DVD.** *HK* Evelyn Kraft, Danny Lee, Chen Cheng-Fen; **D:** Ho Meng-Hua; **W:** Yi Kuang; **C:** Tsao Hui-Chi, Wu Cho-Hua; **M:** Chuen Yung-Yu, Chuen Yung-Yu.

The Mighty Quinn ♂♂♂ **1989 (R)** While investigating the local murder of a rich white guy, the black Jamaican head of police becomes convinced that the prime suspect, a childhood friend, is innocent. As the police chief, Denzel is good in this off-beat comedy mystery. **98m/C VHS, DVD.** Denzel Washington, Robert Townsend, James Fox, Mimi Rogers, M. Emmet Walsh, Sheryl Lee Ralph, Esther Rolle, Art Evans, Norman Beaton, Keye Luke; **D:** Carl Schenkel; **W:** Hampton Fancher; **C:** Jacques Steyn; **M:** Anne Dudley.

A Mighty Wind ♂♂♂ **2003 (PG-13)** Folk music and its aging practitioners are the targets for Guest and company's observant eye and sharp wit. When legendary folk music producer/promoter Irving Sheinbloom dies, his neurotic son Jonathan organizes a tribute concert of his father's favorite acts. They include the earnest, WASPy trio The Folksmen; nine-member, terminally perky cult/troupe New Main Street Singers; and former marrieds Mitch and Mickey. While the dead-on satire is still present, it's muted and more subtle than in Guest's previous outings, maybe because the characters are more fully-realized and engaging, maybe because Guest knows this particular genre may be running out of air. Virtually all of the excellent ensemble from "Best in Show" returns, with co-writer Levy standing out as the depressed Mitch. Too Young to remember folk? Don't worry Good satire done right is worth a look, no matter the subject. **92m/C VHS, DVD.** *US* Bob Balaban, Christopher Guest, John Michael Higgins, Jane Lynch, Eugene Levy, Catherine O'Hara, Michael McKean, Parker Posey, Harry Shearer, Fred Willard, Ed Begley Jr., Larry Miller, Jennifer Coolidge, Michael Hitchcock; **C:** Christopher Guest; **W:** Christopher Guest, Eugene Levy; **C:** Arlene Donnelly Nelson; **M:** John Michael Higgins, Eugene Levy, Catherine O'Hara, Michael McKean, Harry Shearer, Annette O'Toole, C.J. Vanston. N.Y. Film Critics '03: Support. Actor (Levy).

The Migrants ♂♂♂ **1974** Adaptation of the Tennessee Williams play about the hard-scrabble world of a migrant family yearning for a better life. Made for TV. **83m/C VHS.** Cloris Leachman, Ron Howard, Sissy Spacek, Cindy Williams, Ed Lauter, Lisa Lucas, Mills Watson, Claudia McNeil, Dolph Sweet; **D:** Tom Gries; **W:** Lanford Wilson. **TV**

Mike's Murder ♂♂ **1984 (R)** Disjointed drama about a shy bank teller who falls for a slick tennis player. When he is murdered, she investigates the circumstances, placing herself in dangerously close contact with his seedy, drug-involved buddies. The twists and confused plot leave the viewer bewildered. **109m/C VHS.** Debra Winger, Mark Keyloun, Paul Winfield, Darrell Larson, Dan Shor, William Ostrander; **D:** James Bridges; **W:** James Bridges; **M:** John Barry.

Mikey ♂½ **1992 (R)** Mikey seems like such a sweet little boy—but these awful things keep happening all around him. At every foster home and every school people have such dreadful, and deadly, accidents. But innocent Mikey couldn't be to blame—or could he. **92m/C VHS, DVD.** Brian Bonsall, John Diehl, Lyman Ward, Josie Bissett, Ashley Laurence, Mimi (Meyer) Craven, Whitby Hertford; **D:** Dennis Dimster-Denk; **W:** Jonathan Glassner; **C:** Thomas Jewett; **M:** Tim Truman.

Mikey & Nicky ♂♂½ **1976 (R)** Quirky, uneven film about longtime friends dodging a hit man during one long night. Bears little evidence of time and money invested. Cassavetes and Falk, however, provide some salvation. **105m/C VHS, DVD.** John Cassavetes, Peter Falk, Ned Beatty, Oliver Clark, William Hickey; **D:** Elaine May; **W:** Elaine May.

The Milagro Beanfield War ♂♂♂½ **1988 (R)** Redford's endearing adaptation of John Nichols's novel about New Mexican townfolk opposing development. Seemingly simple tale provides plenty of insight into human spirit. Fine cast, with especially stellar turns from Blades, Braga, and Vennera. **118m/C VHS, DVD.** Chick Vennera, John Heard, Ruben Blades, Sonia Braga, Daniel Stern, Julie Carmen, Christopher Walken, Richard Bradford, Carlos Riquelme, James Gammon, Melanie Griffith, Freddy Fender, M. Emmet Walsh; **D:** Robert Redford; **W:** David S. Ward; **C:** Robbie Greenberg; **M:** Dave Grusin. Oscars '88: Orig. Score.

Mildred Pierce ♂♂♂ **1945** Gripping melodrama features Crawford as hard-working divorcee rivaling daughter for man's love. Things, one might say, eventually get ugly. Adaptation of James M. Cain novel is classic of its kind. **113m/B VHS, DVD.** Joan Crawford, Jack Carson, Zachary Scott, Eve Arden, Ann Blyth, Bruce Bennett; **D:** Michael Curtiz; **W:** Ranald MacDougall; **M:** Max Steiner. Oscars '45: Actress (Crawford), Nat'l. Film Reg. '96.

Miles from Home ♂♂ *Farm of the Year* **1988 (R)** Times are tough for farmers Frank and Terry Roberts. The brothers are about to have another bad harvest and the bank is threatening to foreclose. In a symbolic last ditch effort to save their pride, they decide to burn the farm and leave. On their journey, they meet strangers who recognize the pair and help them escape the police. A melodrama with many members of Chicago's Steppenwolf Theater. **113m/C VHS.** Richard Gere, Kevin Anderson, John Malkovich, Brian Dennehy, Judith Ivey, Penelope Ann Miller, Laurie Metcalf, Laura San Giacomo, Daniel Roebuck, Helen Hunt; **D:** Gary Sinise; **W:** Chris Gerolmo; **C:** Elliot Davis; **M:** Robert Folk.

Miles to Go ♂♂½ **1986** A successful businesswoman tries to enjoy her last days after learning she has terminal cancer. **88m/C VHS, DVD.** Mimi Kuzyk, Tom Skerritt, Jill Clayburgh; **D:** David Greene.

Miles to Go Before I Sleep ♂♂½ **1974** A retired, lonely man and a delinquent girl distrust each other but eventually reach out in mutual need. **78m/C VHS.** Martin Balsam, MacKenzie Phillips, Kitty Winn, Elizabeth Wilson; **D:** Fielder Cook. **TV**

Militia ♂ **1999 (R)** ATF agents Ethan Carter (Cain) and Julie Sanders (Beals) must enlist the help of William Fain (Forrest), an imprisoned member of a radical militia group, in order to stop the deployment of three stolen missiles and an assassination attempt on the President. **97m/C VHS, DVD.** Dean Cain, Jennifer Beals, Frederic Forrest, Stacy Keach, John Beck, Jeff Kober, Brett Butler; **D:** Jim Wynorski; **W:** Steve Latshaw, William Carson; **C:** Mario D'Ayala; **M:** Neal Acree. **VIDEO**

Milk and Honey ♂ **2003** Manhattan stockbroker Rick Johnson (Jordan) goes on a midlife freak-out touched off by his suspicion that his wife Joyce (Russell) is cheating on him. What ensues is a string of events that spirals downward, ensnaring people along the way in the most incredibly absurd ways. The digital video filming suits the frenzied nature of this off the wall romp, but the characters are utterly unsympathetic and the string of events falls just outside of the realm of believability. **91m/C DVD.** *US* Clint Jordan, Kirsten Russell, Eleanor Hutchins, Dudley Findlay Jr., Anthony Howard, Greg Amici; **D:** Joe Maggio; **W:** Joe Maggio; **C:** Gordon Chou; **M:** Hal Hartley, Yo La Tengo.

Milk Money ♂½ **1994 (PG-13)** Twelve year-old Frank (Carter) talks his pals into pooling their milk money and heading to the big city so they can get a look at a naked woman. They find a prostitute (Griffith) for the job, whom Frank decides would be perfect to bring home to his widower dad (Harris). Although Griffith is generally adorable and the movie is actually less salacious than the premise might suggest, overall, it's sappy and an affront in the long line of cute-hooker/Cinderella fairytales. **110m/C VHS, DVD.** Michael Patrick Carter, Melanie Griffith, Ed Harris, Malcolm McDowell, Casey Siemaszko, Anne Heche, Philip Bosco; **D:** Richard Benjamin; **W:** John Mattson; **M:** Michael Convertino.

Milky Way ♂♂½ **1936** Loopy comedy about milkman who finds unhappiness after accidentally knocking out champion boxer. Adequate, but not equal to Lloyd's fine silent productions. **89m/B VHS, DVD.** Harold Lloyd, Adolphe Menjou, Verree Teasdale, Helen Mack, William Gargan; **D:** Leo McCarey.

The Milky Way 🐾🐾🐾 1968 Wicked anti-clerical farce. Two bums team on religious pilgrimage and encounter seemingly all manner of strangeness and sacrilege in this typically peculiar Buñuel work. Perhaps the only film in which Jesus is encouraged to shave. In French with English subtitles. 102m/C VHS, FR Laurent Terzieff, Paul Frankeur, Delphine Seyrig, Alain Cuny, Bernard Verley, Michel Piccoli, Edith Scob; **D:** Luis Buñuel; **W:** Jean-Claude Carriere.

The Milky Way 🐾🐾 1997 *Shvil Hahalav* 1997 The Palestinian occupants of a small village in the Galilee try to balance their traditions against the Israeli military occupation in 1964. Many of the villagers were traumatized as children by the 1948 war and old fears and resentments linger as the village's mukhtar (Khoury) tries to placate the occupiers. Meanwhile, the Israelis are investigating forged work passes and a village murder leads to trouble for everyone. Arabic and Hebrew with subtitles. 104m/C VHS, IS Muhamad Bakri Suheil Haddad, Makram Khoury, Yussef Abu-Warda; **D:** Ali Nassar; **W:** Ali Nassar, Ghalib Shaath; **C:** Amnon Salomon; **M:** Nachum Heiman.

Mill of the Stone Women 🐾🐾½ 1960 *Il Mulino delle Donne di Pietra; Horror of the Stone Women; The Horrible Mill Women; Drops of Blood* 1960 Sculpture-studying art student encounters strange carousel with beautiful babes rather than horsies, and soon finds out that the statues contain shocking secrets. Filmed in Holland; it's offbeat and creepy. 94m/C VHS, DVD, FR IT Pierre Brice, Scilla Gabel, Dany Carrel, Wolfgang Preiss, Herbert Boenne, Liana Orfei, Marco Guglielmi, Olga Solbelli; **D:** Giorgio Ferroni, Giorgio Stegani, Remigio del Grosso, Ugo Liberatore; **C:** Pier Ludovico Pavoni; **M:** Carlo Innocenzi.

The Mill on the Floss 🐾🐾 1937 Based on George Eliot's classic novel, this film follows the course of an ill-fated romance at student encounters strange carousel with beautiful babes rather than horsies, and soon finds out that the statues contain shocking secrets. Filmed in Holland; it's offbeat and creepy. 94m/C VHS, DVD, FR IT Pierre Brice, Scilla Gabel, Dany Carrel, Wolfgang Preiss, Herbert Boenne, Liana Orfei, Marco Guglielmi, Olga Solbelli; **D:** Giorgio Ferroni, Giorgio Stegani, Remigio del Grosso, Ugo Liberatore; **C:** Pier Ludovico Pavoni; **M:** Carlo Innocenzi.

The Mill on the Floss 🐾🐾½ 1997 Maggie Tulliver (Watson) is a smart, emotional young woman painfully at odds with her conventional times. She adores her intolerant older brother Tom (Meredith) but when Maggie becomes involved with Philip Wakeum (Frain), the son of their father Edward's (Hill) greatest enemy, she reluctantly acquieses when Tom forbids the romance. When Stephen Guest (Weber-Brown), the fiance of Maggie's cousin Lucy (Whybrow), falls in love with her, his attentions bring scandal and tragedy to both Maggie and Tom. Watson is fine as the harried heroine but Meredith seems too young in his role, upsetting the sibling balance between the two. Based on the novel by George Eliot. 90m/C VHS, GB Emily Watson, Ifan Meredith, James Frain, Bernard Hill, James Weber-Brown, Lucy Whybrow, Nicholas Jecks, Cheryl Campbell; **D:** Graham Theakston; **W:** Hugh Stoddart; **C:** David Clark.

Mille Bolle Blu 🐾🐾 1993 Follows the lives of the inhabitants of a single block in 1961 Rome, on the eve of a solar eclipse. The neighborhood children take the opportunity to spy on their elders, including the engaged Elvira, whose old boyfriend Antonio wants her back, escaped convict Caligiuri who returns to his loving wife, and blind Guido, who's undergone an operation to restore his sight. Italian with subtitles. 83m/C VHS, IT Stefano Dionisi, Claudio Bigagli, Paolo Bonacelli, Nicoletta Boris; **D:** Leone Pompucci; **W:** Leone Pompucci; **M:** Franco Piersanti.

Millennium 🐾🐾½ 1989 (PG-13) The Earth of the future is running out of time. The people are sterile and the air is terrible. To keep the planet viable, Ladd and company must go back in time and yank people off planes that are doomed to crash. Great special effects and well-thought out script make this a ball of fun. 108m/C VHS, DVD Kris Kristofferson, Cheryl Ladd, Daniel J. Travanti, Lloyd Bochner, Robert Joy, Brent Carver, Maury Chaykin, David McIlwraith, Al Waxman; **D:** Michael Anderson Sr.; **W:** John Varley; **C:** Rene Ohashi; **M:** Eric N. Robertson.

Miller's Crossing 🐾🐾🐾½ 1990 (R) From the Coen brothers comes this extremely dark entry in the gangster movie sweepstakes of 1990. Jewish, Italian, and Irish mobsters spin webs of deceit, protection, and revenge over themselves and their families. Byrne is the protagonist, but no hero, being as deeply flawed as the men he battles. Hardan stuns as the woman who sleeps with Byrne and his boss, Finney, in hopes of a better life and protection for her small-time crook brother. Visually exhilarating, excellently acted and perfectly paced. 115m/C VHS, DVD, Albert Finney, Gabriel Byrne, Marcia Gay Harden, John Turturro, Jon Polito, J.E. Freeman, Albert Finney, Jon Polito, J.E. Freeman, **C:** Barry Sonnenfeld; **M:** Carter Burwell.

Millie 🐾🐾½ 1931 Creaky melodrama about a divorcee who wants every man but one. He pursues her teenage daughter instead, leading to tragedy and a courtroom hand-wringing. Twelve-tress still stands out in this hokum, based on a Donald Henderson novel considered daring in its day. 85m/B VHS, Helen Twelvetrees, Robert Ames, Lilyan Tashman, Joan Blondell, John Halliday, James Hall, Anita Louise, Frank McHugh; **D:** John Francis Dillon.

Million Dollar Baby 🐾🐾🐾½ 2004 (PG-13) Multi-Oscar winning flick, left conservative pundits frothing at the baseless allegations at the ever-gracious Eastwood (directing his 25th film). As always, you should make up your own mind's. Old school boxing trainer Frankie Dunn (Eastwood) manages a rundown LA gym, aided by his best friend, former boxer Scrap (Freeman, who also narrates). Abrasive Frankie, long estranged from his own daughter, is very reluctant to have anything to do with 30-ish, uneducated waitress Maggie (Swank), whom he deems too old to train. But Maggie fiercely wants to box and can change her life—and it does, although not in a way anyone could have expected. Downer ending doesn't negate the heart-tugging vulnerability of its characters or its emotional power. A knockout. Based upon "Rope Burns: Stories From the "Corner" by Jerry Boyd. 133m/C VHS, DVD, Blu-ray Disc, HD DVD, US Clint Eastwood, Hilary Swank, Morgan Freeman, Anthony Mackie, Jay Baruchel, Mike Colter, Lucia Rijker, Brian F. O'Byrne, Margo Martindale, Riki Lindhome; **D:** Clint Eastwood; **W:** Paul Haggis; **C:** Tom Stern; **M:** Clint Eastwood. *Oscars '04: Actress (Swank), Director (Eastwood), Film, Support. Actor (Freeman); Directors Guild '04: Director (Eastwood); Golden Globes '05: Actress—Drama (Swank), Director (Eastwood); Screen Actors Guild '04: Actress (Swank), Support. Actor (Freeman).*

Million Dollar Duck 🐾½ 1971 (G) A family duck is doused with radiation and begins to lay gold eggs. Okay Disney mogul's son in a sleazy, run-down hotel. FBI special agent Skinner (Gibson) is sent to investigate and discovers a group of oddballs and losers inhabit the hotel, including mildly retarded narrator Tom Tom (Davies), intellectual hooker Eloise (Jovovich), creepy artist Geronimo (Smits), and self-proclaimed "Fifth Beatle" Dixie (Stormare). Skinner carries on the investigation by spying on the tenants and making life even more miserable for them. The scattered storyline is countered somewhat by Wenders always brilliant visual style, but the performances are mixed, with Gibson, Bono, lead singer for the rock group U2, allegedly came up with the original idea for the film, as was the one on which U2 performed in the movie video for "Where the Streets Have No Name." 122m/C VHS, DVD, US Conrad Roberts, Mel Gibson, Jeremy Davies, Milla Jovovich, Jimmy Smits, Peter Stormare, Amanda Plummer, Gloria Stuart, Tom Bower, Donal Logue, Bud Cort, Julian Sands, Tim Roth, Richard Edson, Harris Yulin, Charlaine Woodard; **D:** Wim Wenders; **M:** Brian Eno, Bono, Daniel Lanois, John Hassell.

The Million Dollar Hotel 🐾🐾 1999 (R) Director Wenders displays his obsession with disposable Americana in this tale of the murder of an entertainment mogul's son in a sleazy, run-down hotel. FBI special agent Skinner (Gibson) is sent to investigate and discovers a group of oddballs and losers inhabit the hotel, including mildly retarded narrator Tom Tom (Davies), intellectual hooker Eloise (Jovovich), creepy artist Geronimo (Smits), and self-proclaimed "Fifth Beatle" Dixie (Stormare). Skinner carries on the investigation by spying on the tenants and making life even more miserable for them. The scattered storyline is countered somewhat by Wenders always brilliant visual style, but the performances are mixed, with Gibson, Bono, lead singer for the rock group U2, allegedly came up with the original idea for the film, as was the one on which U2 performed in the movie video for "Where the Streets Have No Name." 122m/C VHS, DVD, US Conrad Roberts, Mel Gibson, Jeremy Davies, Milla Jovovich, Jimmy Smits, Peter Stormare, Amanda Plummer, Gloria Stuart, Tom Bower, Donal Logue, Bud Cort, Julian Sands, Tim Roth, Richard Edson, Harris Yulin, Charlaine Woodard; **D:** Wim Wenders; **M:** Brian Eno, Bono, Daniel Lanois, John Hassell.

The Millionairess 🐾🐾½ 1960 Loren is an incredibly rich woman who has ended a bad marriage, and feels that the only thing she still needs to fulfill her life is a good husband. She meets a humble doctor from India, in the person of Sellers, and finds he evades her every effort to snare him. In the process she learns that money can't buy everything. From a play by George Bernard Shaw. 90m/C VHS, DVD, GB Sophia Loren, Peter Sellers, Alastair Sim, Vittorio De Sica, Dennis Price; **D:** Anthony Asquith; **C:** Jack Hildyard.

The Millionaire's Express 🐾🐾 *Shanghai Express; Fu Gui Lie Che* 1986 Hung returns to his village with a plan to derail the local train, which carries a number of wealthy passengers, in hopes of saving his poor hometown. Chinese with subtitles or dubbed. 107m/C VHS, DVD, HK Sammo Hung, Yuen Biao, Cynthia Rothrock, Richard Norton, Yukari Oshima; **D:** Sammo Hung; **W:** Sammo Hung.

A Million to One 🐾 1937 An athlete trains for the Olympic decathlon, and catches the eye of an upper-class woman in the process. The lead Bennett was actually a shot-putter in the 1932 Olympic Games. 60m/B VHS, Bruce Bennett, Joan Fontaine, Monte Blue, Kenneth Harlan, Reed Howes; **D:** Lynn Shores.

A Million to Juan 🐾🐾 1994 (PG) Familiar rags-to-riches tale, this time set in a L.A. barrio, centers on Juan Lopez (Rodriguez), an uneducated good guy struggling to raise his son. Juan gets his lucky break when a stranger hands him a check for $1 million, explains it's a loan, and if Juan can use the money properly for a month, he'll get a reward. Juan remains incredibly noble; the movie remains mushy. Loose adaptation of the Mark Twain story "The Million Pound Bank Note." Directorial debut for Rodriguez. 97m/C VHS, DVD, Paul Rodriguez, Polly Draper, Edward James Olmos, Paul Williams, Cheech Marin, David Rasche, Liz Torres; **C:** Tony Plana, Rubén Blades, Richard "Cheech" Marin, Edward James Olmos, Gerardo Mejia, Victor Rivers, Jonathan Hernandez, Pepe Serna, Bert Rosario, Jonathan Hernandez; **D:** Paul Rodriguez; **W:** Francisca Matos, Robert Grasmere.

Million Dollar Kid 🐾🐾 1944 From the notorious "Bowery Boys" series comes this entry. 65m/B VHS, DVD, Leo Gorcey, Huntz Hall, Gabriel Dell, Louise Currie, Noah Beery Jr., Iris Adrian, Mary Gordon; **D:** Wallace Fox.

The Million Dollar Kid 🐾🐾½ 1999 (PG) A $50 million lottery jackpot is up for grabs and the winning ticket goes missing. Now Shane and his family must find their lost prize before someone else does. 92m/C VHS, DVD, Richard Thomas, Maureen McCormick, John Ritter, C. Thomas Howell, Howard Freeman, Randy Travis, Andrew Sandler; **D:** Neil Mandt. VIDEO

Million Dollar Mermaid 🐾🐾 1952 The prototypical Williams aquashow, with the requisite awesome Berkeley dance numbers. As a biography of swimmer Annette Kellerman it isn't much, but as an MGM extravaganza, it fits the bill. 115m/C VHS, Esther Williams, Victor Mature, Walter Pidgeon, Jesse White, David Brian, Maria Tallchief, Howard Freeman, Jesse White, Maria Tallchief, Howard Freeman; **C:** George J. Folsey.

Million Dollar Mystery 🐾½ 1987 (PG) A dying man's last words indicate that several million dollars have been stashed near a diner. Chaos breaks out as nearly everyone in town tries to dig up the loot. 95m/C VHS, DVD, Eddie Deezen, Penny Baker, Tom Bosley, Rich Hall, Wendy Sherman, Rick Overton, Mona Lyden; **D:** Richard Fleischer; **W:** Rudy DeLuca, Tim Metcalfe; **C:** Jack Cardiff.

Milo 🐾🐾 1998 (R) Four young girls are lured to the home of creepy kid Milo where they witness the murder of one of their friends. Sixteen years later, the girls are reunited for a wedding and Milo returns as well. 94m/C VHS, DVD, Jennifer Joslyn, Maya Schavelli, Antonio Fargas, Rae'Ven Aelia Larry-Mamanakis; **D:** Pascal Franchot; **M:** Kevin Manthei. VIDEO

Milo & Otis 🐾🐾½ 1989 (G) Charming tale of a kitten named Milo and a puppy named Otis. The two live on a farm and, when exploring the countryside, Milo is swept down a rushing river. Otis goes after to rescue his friend, and the two begin a series of adventures as they try to return home. 76m/C VHS, DVD, Dudley Moore. **Nar:** Dudley Moore.

The Milpitas Monster 🐾 1975 Comedy about some very silly French people who propose to steal the Venus de Milo from the Louvre. 110m/C VHS, GR GE GR Mario Adorf, Andrea Ferreol, Andreas Katsulas, Christopher Penekis; **W:** Christopher Doherty, Nicos Penekis; **C:** Dietrich Lohmann; **M:** Nikos Mamangakis.

Milwaukee, Minnesota 🐾🐾 2003 (R) Chaotic comedy features a number of oddballs who inhabit a weird Midwestern world. Albert (Garity in a strong performance) is a champion ice fisherman looked after by his overprotective mother Ecma (Monks) since he's a bit slow and overly eager to please. When mom dies suddenly, Albert is left at the mercy of various con artists who want a piece of his inheritance and fishing prize money. Dern plays a kindly protector to Albert, who has more on the ball than people suspect. Mindel's feature debut. 96m/C VHS, US Troy Garity, Alison Folland, Randy Quaid, Bruce Dern, Hank Harris, Debra Monk, Josh Brolin, Holly Woodlawn; **D:** Allan Mindel; **W:** Richard R. (R.D.) Murphy; **C:** Bernd Heinl.

Millions 🐾🐾½ 1990 (R) To a family of millionaires, money is everything, and the heir to the family fortune is willing to do anything to get his hands on all that money. Even if it means sleeping with his sister-in-law and cousin. Lucky for him they happen to be beautiful models. 118m/C VHS, DVD, IT Billy Zane, Lauren Hutton, Carol Alt, Alexandra Paul, Catherine Hickland, Donald Pleasence; **D:** Carlo Vanzina.

Millions 🐾🐾 2005 (PG) Boyle shows he can do sweet family entertainment with the same ease he does violent and creepy (a la "Trainspotting" and '28 Days Later"). Set just before Christmas, practical 9-year-old Anthony (McGibbon) and his dreamer 7-year-old brother Damian (Etel) have just moved with their recently widowed father Ronnie (Nesbitt) into a new neighborhood outside Liverpool. Damian is hanging out near the rail line when a bag filled with (stolen) English pound notes literally comes flying through the air. Damian, who sees and talks to a variety of saints, wants to use the money to help the poor while Anthony would prefer to keep it for themselves. In any case, the boys have only a few days to use the loot since the currency will become scrap paper as Britain makes an (imagined) switch to the euro. Child-centered story may be whimsical but stays firmly away from the sappy. 97m/C VHS, DVD, James Nesbitt, Christopher Fulford, Alun Armstrong, Kathyn Pogson, Alexander Nathan) Etel, Lewis Owen McGibbon, Daisy Donovan, Pearce Quigley, Jane Hogarth, Enzo Cilenti, Nasser Memarzia, Harry Kirkham, Cornelius Macarthy, Kolade Agbooke; **Cameos:** Leslie Phillips; **D:** Danny Boyle; **W:** Frank Cottrell Boyce; **C:** Anthony Dod Mantle; **M:** John Murphy.

Mimi ♂♂ 1935 Melodrama with a down-on-his-luck playwright falling for a poor lass who provides him with the needed inspiration to be a winner. The question is, will she die before he hits the big time? Loosely based on "La Vie de Boheme" by Henri Murger. **98m/B VHS.** *GB* Douglas Fairbanks Jr., Gertrude Lawrence, Diana Napier, Harold Warrender, Carol Goodner, Richard Bird, Austin Trevor, Lawrence Hanray, Paul Graetz, Martin Walker; **D:** Paul Stein.

Mimic ♂♂½ 1997 (R) Married biotech scientists Sorvino and Northam upset the balance of nature when they cure a plague only to have their insectoid concoction unleashed in the New York subways. This causes giant cockroaches to mimic—and kill—humans. Far-fetched story is furthered with a unique script (both John Sayles and Steven Soderbergh made additions) and original kills and thrills. Plenty of gore also makes it a worthy addition to the horror genre. **105m/C VHS, DVD.** Jeremy Northam, Mira Sorvino, Josh Brolin, Charles S. Dutton, Giancarlo Giannini, F. Murray Abraham, Alexander Goodwin; **D:** Guillermo del Toro; **W:** John Sayles, Steven Soderbergh, Matthew Robbins; **C:** Dan Laustsen; **M:** Marco Beltrami.

Mimic 2 ♂♂½ 2001 (R) If you like squishy giant bug movies, this direct-to-video sequel is for you. New York detective Campos and entomologist Koromzay discover that a mutant six-foot cockroach is responsible for three murders where the victims' face has been ripped off. And now it wants to mate. **82m/C VHS, DVD.** Alix Koromzay, Bruno Campos, Will Estes, Edward Albert, Jon Polito, Gaven Eugene Lucas; **D:** Jean De Segonzac; **W:** Joel Soisson; **C:** Nathan Hope. **VIDEO**

Mimic 3: Sentinel ♂♂ 2003 (R) Patchy early talkie about two houseboat dwellers fighting to preserve their waterfront lifestyle and keep their daughter from being taken to a "proper" home. **66m/B VHS.** Marie Dressler, Wallace Beery, Marjorie Rambeau, Dorothy Jordan; **D:** George Hill. Oscars '31: Actress (Dressler).

Mina Tannenbaum ♂♂ 1993 Touching but unsentimental look at the 25-year friendship between two Jewish women in Paris. Mina (Bohringer) and Ethel (Zylberstein) meet as seven-year-olds and go through various childhood and teenage tramas together, including the desperate pangs of first love. Mina becomes an intense artist while flirty Ethel works as a freelance journalist. And, naturally, their friendship undergoes its own relentless changes. Pacing problems cause something of a letdown. Directorial debut for cinematographer Dugowson. French with subtitles. **128m/C VHS.** *FR* Romane Bohringer, Elsa Zylberstein, Nils (Niels) Tavernier, Florence Thomassin, Jean-Philippe Ecoffey, Stephane Slima; **D:** Martine Dugowson; **W:** Martine Dugowson; **C:** Dominique Chapuis; **M:** Peter Chase.

Minbo—Or the Gentle Art of Japanese Extortion ♂♂ 1993 *Minbo No Onna; The Gangster's Moll; The Anti-Extortion Woman* 1992 Satire on Japanese mobsters, known as the Yakuza, focusing on the blackmail and intimidation that gives these criminals a great deal of their power. The ill-mannered group like to congregate at a local hotel—much to the detriment of business—and hotel management finally hire a hardball-playing female lawyer to solve their problems with the thugs. Japanese with subtitles. **123m/C VHS.** *JP* Nobuko Miyamoto, Akira Takarada, Takehiro Murata, Yasuo Daichi, Hideji Otaki; **D:** Juzo Itami; **W:** Juzo Itami; **C:** Yonezo Maeda; **M:** Toshiyuki Honda.

Mind, Body & Soul ♂♂ 1992 (R) When a woman witnesses a human sacrifice performed by her boyfriend's satanic cult, she goes to the police. The cops, however, believe she is part of the cult, so she is forced to rely on the public defender to protect her from angry cult members. Pretty dull, but Hauser and Allen add some spice to this hokey thriller. **93m/C VHS, DVD.** Wings Hauser, Ginger Lynn Allen, Jay Richardson, Ken Hill, Jesse Kaye, Tami Bakke; **D:** Rick Sloane; **W:** Rick Sloane; **C:** Robert Hayes; **M:** Alan Der Marderosian.

Mind Games ♂♂½ 1989 (R) A young couple and their ten-year-old son pick up a hitcher in their mobile home, never suspecting that he's a deranged psychology student ready to pit the family against each other as an experiment. **93m/C VHS, DVD.** Edward Albert, Shawn Weatherly, Matt Norero, Maxwell Caulfield; **D:** Bob Yari.

Mind Lies ♂♂ *Mind Rage* 2000 Middle-aged detective Jack Stillman is investigating a series of stabbings, where the killer has left messages implicating Jack's estranged brother, Michael. So Jack decides he and Michael have to work together to find out who's setting Michael up. The problem is all the likely suspects keep turning up dead. **m/C VHS.** Charles Hallahan, Dennis Christopher, Tippi Hedren, Max Gail; **D:** Mark Allen Michaels. **VIDEO**

Mind Snatchers ♂♂½ 1972 (PG) An American G.I. becomes involved in U.S. Army experimental psychological brain operations when he is brought into a western European hospital for treatment. Also know as "The Happiness Cage." **94m/C VHS, DVD.** Christopher Walken, Ronny Cox, Ralph Meeker, Joss Ackland; **D:** Bernard Girard.

Mind the Gap ♂♂ 2004 (R) Fate brings five lonely people together in New York City to deal with past guilt and unhappiness in an effort to make a fresh start. Cranky senior citizen Herb (King in his last role) plans to fulfill a promise to his late wife; single dad Sam (Schaeffer) suspects he's terminally ill; introverted folkie busker Jody (singer-songwriter Sobule) has heart trouble; John's (Parnell) a suicidal yuppie; and Malissa's (Reaser) an eccentric country gal saddled with a nasty dying mom. Film is less indulgent than Schaeffer's usual oeuvre but it's also less than noteworthy. **130m/C DVD.** Eric Schaeffer, Alan King, John Heard, Mina (Badiyi) Badie, Elizabeth Reaser, Jill Sobule, Charles Parnell, Christopher Kovaleski, Kim Raver, Todd Weeks, Deirdre Kingsbury; **D:** Eric Schaeffer; **W:** Eric Schaeffer; **C:** Marc Blandori; **M:** Veigar Margeirsson.

A Mind to Kill ♂♂ 1995 When a murdered girl is found in a small English seaside town, the crime is linked to a previous death. Police call on a university professor for help but then a new victim, with ties to the professor, is discovered and the police detective in charge finds that his own loved ones are now in danger. **95m/C VHS.** *GB* Hywel Bennett, Philip Madoc, Sue Jones-Davies, Nicola Beddoe; **D:** Peter Edwards.

A Mind to Murder ♂♂½ *P.D. James: A Mind to Murder* 1996 Scotland Yard Commander Adam Dalgliesh (Marsden) is still depressed over the murder of a colleague some months earlier when he's discreetly called in to investigate the stabbing death of the administrator of the Steen Clinic, located in East Anglia. The exclusive psychiatric facility is home to some politically sensitive patients and Dalgliesh is under pressure to solve the crime quickly and quietly. His work would go a lot easier if people cooperated, but naturally the investigation doesn't go smoothly at all. Based on the 1963 novel by P.D. James and updated for the TV movie. **100m/C VHS, DVD.** *GB* Roy Marsden, Sean Scanlan, Robert Pugh, Mairead Carty, Frank Finlay, Cal Macaninch, Ann-Gisel Glass, Sian Thomas, Jerome Flynn, Suzanne Burden, Donald Douglas, Christopher Ravenscroft; **Cameos:** David Hemmings; **D:** Gareth Davies; **C:** Bill Broomfield. **TV**

Mind Trap ♂♂½ 1991 A beautiful movie star's family is killed due to her father's involvement with naval research. The government wants no part of her trou-

bles so she is forced to take the law into her own hands. **90m/C VHS.** Dan Haggerty, Lyle Waggoner, Martha Kincare, Thomas Elliot, Samuel Steven; **D:** Eames Demetrios.

Mind Twister ♂♂½ 1993 (R) Erotic thriller finds a tough police detective on the trail of a sadistic killer with a twist. An unrated version is available at 94 minutes. **87m/C VHS.** Telly Savalas, Gary Hudson, Richard Roundtree, Erica Nann, Suzanne Slater; **D:** Fred Olen Ray.

Mind Warp ♂½ 1989 *Grey Matter; The Brain Machine* 1972 ½ A future society exercises mental control and torture over its citizens. **92m/C VHS, DVD.** James Best, Barbara Burgess, Gil Peterson, Gerald McRaney, Marcus J. Grapes, Doug Collins, Anne Latham; **D:** Joy Houck Jr.

Mindfield ♂½ 1989 (R) An innocent man gets trapped by the CIA and is used by them in mind control experiments. **91m/C VHS.** *CA* Michael Ironside, Lisa Langlois, Christopher Plummer, Stefan Wodoslowsky, Sean McCann; **D:** Jean-Claude Lord.

Mindhunters woof! 2005 (R) A group of FBI profilers-in-training are sent to a deserted island for their final test but end up victims of a real serial killer through a gamut of enormously complicated, special-effect-laden murders. Disappointing execution of an interesting premise. **106m/C DVD.** *US GB NL FI* Val Kilmer, Christian Slater, LL Cool J, Eion Bailey, Clifton (Gonzalez) Collins Jr., Will(iam) Kemp, Jonny Lee Miller, Kathryn Morris, Patricia Velasquez; **D:** Renny Harlin; **W:** Wayne Kramer, Kevin Brodbin; **C:** Robert Gantz; **M:** Tuomas Kantelinen.

Mindkiller ♂½ 1987 A tongue-in-cheek gore-fest about a shy young guy who develops his brain in an effort to be socially accepted. Unfortunately, he overdoes it and his brain mutates, bursts from his head, and runs around on its own. **84m/C VHS.** Joe McDonald, Christopher Wade, Shirley Ross, Kevin Hart; **D:** Michael Krueger.

Mindstorm ♂♂½ 2001 (R) The plot has holes big enough to fly a helicopter through but the action keeps things from being boring. Psychic private eye Tracy Wellman (Vaugier) is hired to free Senator Armitage's (Ironside) daughter from the clutches of cult leader David Mendez (a prototypically evil Roberts) and is aided by FBI hunk Dan Oliver (Sabato). Turns out that Mendez and Wellman have a past together—they're both telepaths as the result of a government mind control experiment when they were children—a project headed by Armitage. **106m/C VHS, DVD.** *CA* Emmanuelle Vaugier, Antonio Sabato Jr., Eric Roberts, Michael Ironside, Clarence Williams III, Michael Moriarty, Ed O'Ross, William B. Davis; **D:** Richard Pepin; **W:** Paul A. Birkitt; **C:** Adam Sliwinski; **M:** John Sereda. **CABLE**

Mindwalk: A Film for Passionate Thinkers ♂♂♂ 1991 (PG) A feature-length intellectual workout; a physicist, poet and politician stroll the ancient grounds of Mont St. Michel monastery in France and discuss the need to change mankind's view of the universe. Uncinematic? Perhaps, but it entertainingly conveys the epochal ideas of scientist/author Fritjof Capra (whose book was adapted for the screen by younger brother Berni). **111m/C VHS.** Liv Ullmann, Sam Waterston, John Heard, Ione Skye; **D:** Bernt Capra; **W:** Fritjof Capra, Floyd Byars; **M:** Philip Glass.

Mindwarp ♂♂ 1991 (R) After an ecological disaster, residents of Earth move to a sterile haven known as "Inworld." When survivor Judy (Alicia) seeks answers about her missing father (accidentally killing her mother in the process), she is cast from "Inworld" into Earth's wasteland, where she and human compatriot Stover (Campbell) are left to fight the elements and learn the awful truth about Judy's father. **91m/C VHS.** Marta Alicia, Bruce Campbell, Angus Scrimm, Elizabeth Kent, Mary Becker; **D:** Steve Barnett; **W:** John Brancato, Michael Ferris.

Mine Own Executioner ♂♂♂ 1947 Determined but unstable psychologist struggles to treat schizophrenic who suffered torture by Japanese while wartime prisoner. Strong, visually engrossing fare. **102m/B VHS.** *GB* Burgess Meredith, Kieron Moore, Dulcie Gray,

Christine Norden, Barbara White, John Laurie, Michael Shepley; **D:** Anthony Kimmins.

Mines of Kilimanjaro ♂♂½ 1987 (PG-13) An archaeology student heads for Africa to investigate his professor's murder and comes up with a heap of trouble. **88m/C VHS.** Christopher Connelly, Tobias Hoesl, Gordon Mitchell, Elena Pompei; **D:** Mino Guerrini.

The Minion ♂♂ 1998 (R) *Fallen Knight* Lucas (Lundgren) is a modern-day Knights Templar, the emissary of an ancient religious order that guards a temple door, which is the gateway to the antichrist. When the key to the door is discovered, Lucas must battle an ancient demon who has risen from hell to claim possession. But since the demon can inhabit anyone, how's Lucas going to know who to fight? **97m/C VHS, DVD.** *CA* Dolph Lundgren, Francoise Robertson, Roc Lafortune, Michael Greyeyes, David Nerman, Karen Goodleaf; **D:** Jean-Marc Piche; **W:** Matt Roe, Ripley Highsmith; **C:** Barry Parrell.

Ministry of Fear ♂♂♂ 1944 Creepy noir based on the novel by Graham Greene. Stephen Neale (Milland) has just been released from two years in an insane asylum. As he waits for a train, he decides to visit a nearby carnival that turns out to be fronted by a Nazi organization, where Neale's mistaken for an agent. After finally reaching London, he's later accused of murder, being sought by the police, and is aided by the sympathetic Carla (Reynolds). No one and nothing is as it seems, however, and soon the unwitting Neale is deeply involved in espionage. Since the viewer sees only what Neale does, it's just as puzzling for the audience as it is for the character. **85m/B VHS.** Ray Milland, Marjorie Reynolds, Percy Waram, Dan Duryea, Carl Esmond, Hillary Brooke, Alan Napier, Erskine Sanford; **D:** Fritz Lang; **W:** Seton I. Miller; **C:** Henry Sharp; **M:** Victor Young.

Ministry of Vengeance ♂ 1989 (R) A psychotic murderer who hates grapes of any kind finds the woman of his dreams—she's a psychotic murderer who hates grapes! Together they find bliss—until the plumber discovers their secret! **90m/C VHS, DVD.** John Schneider, Ned Beatty, George Kennedy, Yaphet Kotto, James Tolkan, Apollonia; **D:** Peter Maris; **W:** Mervyn Emerys; **C:** Mark Harris; **M:** Scott Roewe.

The Miniver Story ♂♂ 1950 Weepy sequel to "Mrs. Miniver" reunites the family in post-WWII England, but clearly lacks the inspiration of the original. Garson is again Mrs. Miniver and she's secretly suffering from a never-named fatal disease. She decides to straighten out the family troubles before her time is up, including her daughter's love life and her husband's plan to move to Brazil. Depressing and glum. **104m/B VHS.** *GB* Greer Garson, Walter Pidgeon, John Hodiak, Leo Genn, Cathy O'Donnell, Reginald Owen, Anthony Bushell; **D:** H.C. Potter; **W:** Ronald Millar, George Froeschel; **C:** Joseph Ruttenberg; **M:** Miklos Rozsa.

Minna von Barnhelm or The Soldier's Fortune ♂♂ *Minna von Barnhelm oder das Soldatenglück* 1962 Prussian nobleman Major von Tellheim becomes engaged to noblewoman Minna von Barnhelm during the Seven Year's War. But after the war has ended, the King inexplicably deprives von Tellheim of his title, leaving him humiliated and impoverished. But Minna loves her man and refuses to let him go. Based on the drama by Gotthold Ephraim Lessing. German with subtitles. **103m/C VHS.** *GE* Martina Bohme, Otto Mellies, Manfred Krug; **D:** Martin Hellberg.

Minnesota Clay ♂½ 1965 *L'Homme du Minnesota* 1965 A blind gunman, who aims by sound and smell, is marked by two rival gangs and a tempestuous tramp. **89m/C VHS, DVD.** *FR IT* Cameron Mitchell, Diana Martin; **D:** Sergio Corbucci.

Minnie and Moskowitz ♂♂½ 1971 Minnie's (Rowlands) about to turn 40 and wants out of her affair with married man, Jim (Cassavetes). She accepts a blind date with Zelmo (Avery) and when he turns out to be a nut, Minnie's rescued by parking attendant Moskowitz (Cassel).

Through the opposites attract ploy, Minnie and Moskowitz start dating and soon decide to get married. It's basically a Cassavetes home movie, featuring a number of family and friends who probably had a better time making it than you'll have watching it. **114m/C** VHS, DVD. Gena Rowlands, Seymour Cassel, Val Avery, Timothy Carey, Holly Near, Katherine Cassavetes, Mary Allen "Lady" Rowlands, David Rowlands, Elizabeth Deering, Elsie Adams, John Cassavetes; **C:** Arthur Ortiz. **D:** Terell Tannen.

A Minor Miracle ⅋⅋ 1983 (G)
Tender family fare about a group of orphaned children, who band together under the loving guidance of their guardian (Huston) to save St. Francis School for boys from the town planners. Warms the cockles. **100m/C** VHS, John Huston, Pele, Peter Fox. **W:** John Cassavetes; **C:** Arthur Ortiz.

Minority Report ⅋⅋⅋½ 2002
(PG-13) In 2054 Washington, D.C., a law enforcement agency employs seers called Pre-Cogs to anticipate homicides. Cruise plays John Anderton, chief of the Pre-Crime unit, created to go after potential perps before they can commit the crime. When one of the Pre-Cogs names Anderton as a suspect, however, he's forced to go on the run. Realistic mix of '9th century tradition (classic architecture) and cool, new innovations (retinal scanning robotic spiders) blend into a detailed and believable future world. Engaging story and interesting character's help pic race along, figuratively and literally, with visual sophistication and technical wizardry that Spielberg does so well. Based on a 1956 short story by Philip K. Dick. **145m/C** VHS, DVD, US Tom Cruise, Samantha Morton, Colin Farrell, Max von Sydow, Neal McDonough, Lois Smith, Peter Stormare, Tim Blake Nelson, Steve Harris, Kathryn Morris, Mike Binder, Daniel London, Spencer (Treat) Clark, Jessica Capshaw, Patrick Kilpatrick, Jessica Harper, Ashley Crow, Arye Gross; **D:** Steven Spielberg; **W:** Scott Frank, Jon Cohen; **C:** Janusz Kaminski; **M:** John Williams.

The Minus Man ⅋⅋ 1999 (R)
Vann Siegart (Wilson) is the blandest, nicest serial killer you are ever likely to meet. A drifter, Vann has settled into a small California town where he boards with a troubled married couple, Doug (Cox) and Jane (Ruehl), who come to think of ever-smiling Vann as a surrogate son. Vann gets a job at the post office (!), and calmly proceeds to off some of the locals. Eerie thriller offers no explanations for Vann's behavior, which makes it all the creepier. Adapted from the 1990 novel by Lew McCreary, who has a cameo as a victim. **112m/C** VHS, DVD. Owen Wilson, Brian Cox, Mercedes Ruehl, Janeane Garofalo, Dwight Yoakam, Dennis Haysbert, Eric Mabius, Sheryl Crow, Larry Miller; **D:** Hampton Fancher; **W:** Hampton Fancher; **C:** Bobby Bukowski; **M:** James Grundmith.

The Miracle ⅋⅋⅋ 1991 (PG)
An innocent peasant woman is seduced by a shepherd and becomes convinced that her pregnancy will produce a second Christ. Controversial, compelling film derived from a story by Federico Fellini. In Italian with English subtitles. **43m/B** VHS. **D:** Federico Fellini. **C:** Aldo Tonti.

A Minute to Pray, a Second to Die ⅋⅋ Un Minuto Per Pregare, Un Istante Per Morire; Dead or Alive; Outlaw Gun 1967
A notorious, wanted-dead-or-alive gunman retreats to the amnesty of the New Mexico Territory, but finds he cannot shake his past. **100m/C** VHS. Alex Cord; **D:** Franco Giraldi.

The Miracle ⅋⅋½ 1991 (PG) Irish teens, whose strong friendship is based upon their equally unhappy home lives, find both tested when a secretive American woman turns up in town. Excellent debut from Byrne and Pilkington but tedious pacing in a dreamy script that tells too much too soon. Worth watching just for D'Angelo's smouldering rendition of "Stardust." **97m/C** VHS, GB Beverly D'Angelo, Donal McCann, Niall Byrne, Lorraine Pilkington, J.G. Devlin; **D:** Neil Jordan; **W:** Neil Jordan; **C:** Philippe Rousselot; **M:** Anne Dudley.

Miracle ⅋⅋⅋ 2004 (PG) Russell stars as coach Herb Brooks, who led the upstart 1980 U.S. Olympic hockey team to victory against the Russians and a gold medal. Brooks, driven by his own failure to capture a medal as an Olympic player, uses aggressive mind-games and innovative strategy to take a squad of college hotshots and turn them into a single unit capable of defeating the Russian powerhouse. Russell is excellent as Minnesotan Brooks, down to his clipped accent and bad pants. O'Connor, directing newcomer Guggenheim's script, manages to push all the right buttons while mostly avoiding heavy-handed cliches. The end result is a solid sports movie. Most of the actors had real on-ice scenes. Brooks served as an advisor but died during post-production. **135m/C** VHS, DVD, US Kurt Russell, Patricia Clarkson, Noah Emmerich, Sean McCann, Kenneth Welsh, Nathan West, Kenneth Mitchell, Eddie Cahill, Patrick O'Brien Demsey, Michael Mantamu to, Eric Peter-Kaiser, Bobby Hanson, Joseph Cure, Billy Schneider, Nate Miller; **D:** Gavin O'Connor; **W:** Eric Guggenheim; **C:** Dan Stoloff; **M:** Mark Isham.

Miracle at Midnight ⅋⅋½ 1998
Having occupied Denmark for several years, the Nazis decide to round up all Danish Jews on October 1, 1943. Word is leaked and a number of citizens risk their lives to warn and hide the Jews, spiriting more than 7,000 to safety in Sweden. This Disney version focuses on the non-Jewish Kloster family and how each of them become involved in the rescue. **89m/C** VHS. DVD. Sam Waterston, Mia Farrow, Justin Whalin, Nicola Mycroft, Barry McGovern, Patrick Malahide; **D:** Ken Cameron; **W:** Chris Bryant, Monte Merrick. TV

Miracle at Moreaux 1986 Three Jewish children fleeing from Nazis find sanctuary with a nun and her wards. Based on Clare Huchet Bishop's book "Twenty and Ten." Originally aired on PBS as part of the "Wonderworks" family movie series. **58m/C** VHS, DVD. Loretta Swit, Marsha Moreau, Robert Joy, Ken Pogue, Robert Kosoy, Talya Rubin; **D:** Paul Shapiro; **M:** Jonathan Goldsmith.

Miracle at Sage Creek ⅋⅋½ 2005 (PG) Uplifting drama begins in 1888 Wyoming. Crusty rancher Ike (Carradine) is still enraged by the murder of his wife by a Sioux war party 10 years earlier. This draws him against his neighbor John (Abell), whose white Sunny (Bedard) is Sioux, although she and Ike's married daughter Mary (Aldrich) are close friends. Ike tries to take their ranch until a tragedy and a Christmas miracle occur. **85m/C** DVD. David Carradine, Tim Abell, Irene Bedard, Wes Studi, Sarah Aldrich, Daniel Quinn, Fred Griffith; **D:** James Intveld; **W:** Thadd Turner; **C:** Virgil Harper; **M:** James Intveld. VIDEO

Miracle Beach ⅋½ 1992 (PG-13) Scotty McKay has lost his job, his apartment, and his girl. Then he gets rejected by Dana, the super model he's secretly adored. Can things get any worse? Scotty decides to take a walk along the beach and sort things out when he stumbles across a girl genie, named Jeanie, who has been sent to Earth on a good will mission. Scotty gets Jeanie in order to dazzle model material wish in order to dazzle model Dana. But when Jeanie falls in love with Scotty can she get him to recognize the difference between true love and fantasy? **88m/C** VHS. Dean Cameron, Felicity Waterman, Ami Dolenz, Alexis Arquette, Martin Mull, Noriyuki "Pat" Morita, Vincent Schiavelli; **D:** Skot Snider.

Miracle Dogs ⅋⅋½ 2003 After accidentally running over a stray springer spaniel, the Logans (Jackson, Shackelford) discover that the dog has cancer and must have a foreleg amputated. Son Charlie (Hutcherson) cares for the dog in the basement of the hospital where his folks work. When dog Annie recovers, she takes to visiting patients and miraculously starts making them feel better too. **105m/C** DVD. US Josh Hutcherson, Kate Jackson, Ted Shackelford, Rue McClanahan, Stacy Keach, Alana Austin, Wayne Rogers; **D:** Craig Clyde; **W:** Craig Clyde. **C:** Neal Brown; **M:** Joseph Conlan. CABLE.

Miracle Dogs Too ⅋⅋½ 2006 When 10-year-old Zack (Evans) discovers two stolen cocker spaniels caged and abandoned in the woods, he frees the dogs and takes them home. Turns out Sissy and Buddy have healing powers that change those around them. When the crooks discover that they want the dogs back. **90m/C** DVD. US Dustin Hunter Evans, Casey Spacek, Patrick Muldoon, Janine Turner, Lesley Ann Warren, Jaleel White, Alana Austin, Charles Durning, Stepin Fetchit, Hilda Offley, Lawrence Criner, Monte Hawley; **D:** Jack Kemp.

Miracle in Harlem ⅋⅋ 1948 A gang tries to take over a candy shop and when the gang leader is killed, the evidence points to the foster daughter of the shop owner. The script suffers from clichéd dialog and less-than-believable situations, but the all-black cast turns in good performances. **69m/B** VHS. Sheila Guyse, Stepin Fetchit, Hilda Offley, Lawrence Criner, Monte Hawley; **D:** Jack Kemp.

Miracle in Lane Two ⅋⅋ 2000 Based on the true story of 12-year-old Justin Yoder (Muniz) who's confined to a wheelchair but still wins a national soap box derby championship. **89m/C** VHS, DVD. Frankie Muniz, Roger Aaron Brown, Molly Hagan, Rick Rossovich, Tuc Watkins; **D:** Greg Beeman. CABLE

Miracle in Milan ⅋⅋⅋ Milano Miracolo a Milano 1951 An innocent, child-like fantasy tells out of a Milanese ghetto and helping the poor to fly to a new Utopia. Happy mixture of whimsy and neo-realism. In Italian with English subtitles. **95m/B** VHS, DVD. **IT** Francesco Golisano, Brunella Bovo, Emma Gramatica, Paolo Stoppa; **D:** Vittorio De Sica. **W:** Cesare Zavattini, Cannes '51: Film; N.Y. Film Critics '51: Foreign Film.

Miracle in Rome ⅋⅋ 1988 Margarito Duarte digs up his dead daughter and finds her body in perfect condition despite 12-year internment. Attempting to convince the local clergy that she's miracle material, he finds himself less than eager to elect her to sainthood. Based on a story by Gabriel García Márquez; made for Spanish TV. In Spanish with English subtitles. **76m/C** VHS. SP Frank Ramírez, Gerardo Arellano, Amalia Duque García, Lisandro Duque, Daniel Priolett; **D:** Lisandro Duque; **W:** Lisandro Duque Naranjo, Gabriel García Márquez. TV

Miracle in the Wilderness ⅋⅋½ 1991 A Christmas western based on Paul Gallico's novella, "The Snow Goose." Kristofferson stars as Jericho Adams, a former Indian fighter, who turns to farming to support his wife and child. When they are captured by a raiding party of Blackfeet, Adams discovers they have never heard the story of the Nativity. **88m/C** VHS. Kris Kristofferson, Kim Cattrall, John Dennis Johnston, Joanelle Romero, Dennis Olivers, Sheldon Peters Wolfchild, David Oliver; **D:** Kevin James Dobson; **W:** Jim Byrnes.

Miracle Kid ⅋⅋ 1942 Standard story of a young boxer who'd rather be something else. His romance is interrupted when he becomes successful in the ring. **66m/B** VHS. Tom Neal, Carol Hughes, Betty Blythe, Minta Durfee, Gertrude Messinger; **D:** William Beaudine.

The Miracle Maker: The Story of Jesus ⅋⅋½ 2000 Elaborate 3-D claymation is surprisingly effective in telling the story of Jesus, based on the Gospel of St. Luke. Christ's ministry is seen through the eyes of sickly child, Tamar, who is healed by one of his miracles. **87m/C** VHS. Art Garney, Casey Siemaszko, Jack Bannon; **D:** Georg Stanford Brown. TV

Miracle in Harlem (continued)

Miracle Mile ⅋⅋⅋ 1989 (R) A riveting, apocalyptic thriller about a mild-mannered misfit who, while inadvertently standing on a street corner at 2 a.m., answers a ringing pay phone. The caller is a panicked missile-silo worker who announces that the bombs have been launched for an all-out nuclear war. With about an hour left before the end, he races to head into the city and rendezvous with his new girlfriend. A surreal, wicked farce sadly overlooked in theatrical release. Music by Tangerine Dream. **87m/C** VHS, DVD. Anthony Edwards, Mare Winningham, John Agar, Denise Crosby, Lou Hancock, Mykelti Williamson, Kelly Jo Minter, Kurt Fuller, Robert DoQui, Danny De La Paz, O-lan Jones, Alan Rosenberg, Claude Earl Jones; **D:** Steve DeJarnatt; **W:** Steve DeJarnatt; **C:** Theo van de Sande; **M:** Tangerine Dream.

The Miracle of Marcelino ⅋⅋½ Marcelino, Pan y Vino; Marcelino 1955 Marcelino (Calvo) was left at birth on a monastery doorstep and raised by the Franciscan friars. The highspirited young boy finds a life-sized crucifix in the church attic and, believing the figure of Christ to be real, befriends the image, bringing it food and wine. Then, one day, the image of Jesus comes to life. Spanish with subtitles. **90m/B** VHS, DVD. SP Pablito Calvo, Fernando Rey, Rafael Riveles; **D:** Ladislao Vajda; **C:** Enrique Guerner; **M:** Pablo Sorosábal.

Miracle of Morgan's Creek ⅋⅋⅋½ 1944 Sturges's breakneck comedy details the misadventures of wartime floozy Trudy Kockenlocker (Hutton) who gets drunk at a party, thinks she married a soldier on leave, gets pregnant, forgets the whole thing, and sometimes boyfriend Norval (Bracken) to take responsibility. Oh yeah, and it turns out Trudy's expecting sextuplets. Hilarious, out-to-make-trouble farce that shouldn't have, by all rights, made it past the censors of the time. The director's most scathing assault on American values. Loosely remade as 1958's "Rock-A-Bye Baby" starring Jerry Lewis. **98m/B** VHS, DVD. Eddie Bracken, Betty Hutton, Diana Lynn, Brian Donlevy, Akim Tamiroff, Porter Hall, Emory Parnell, Alan Bridge, Julius Tannen, Victor Potel, Almira Sessions, Chester Conklin, William Demarest, Jimmy Conlin; **D:** Preston Sturges; **W:** Preston Sturges; **M:** Leo Shuken, Charles Bradshaw. Natl. Film. Reg. '01.

The Miracle of Our Lady of Fatima ⅋⅋ The Miracle of Fatima 1952 Slick cold-war version of the supposedly true events surrounding the sighting of a holy vision by three children in Portugal during WWI. **112m/C** VHS, DVD. Gilbert Roland, Susan Whitney, Sherry Jackson, Sammy Ogg, Angela (Carol) Clarke, Frank Silvera, Jay Novello; **D:** John Brahm; **M:** Max Steiner.

The Miracle of the Bells ⅋⅋ 1948 A miracle occurs after a dead movie star is buried in the cemetery of her modest hometown. Given the premise, the casting is all the more peculiar. Adapted by Ben Hecht from Russell Janney's novel. **120m/B** VHS. Fred MacMurray, Alida Valli, Frank Sinatra, Lee J. Cobb; **D:** Irving Pichel.

Miracle of the Heart: A Boys Town Story ⅋⅋ 1986 Based on the story of Boys Town, and an old priest who sticks up for Boys Town's principles in the face of a younger priest with rigid ideas. **100m/C** VHS. Art Garney, Casey Siemaszko, Jack Bannon; **D:** Georg Stanford Brown. TV

Miracle of the White Stallions ⅋½ The Flight of the White Stallions 1963 A disappointing Disney adventure about the director of a Viennese riding academy who guides his prized Lipizzan stallions to safety when the Nazis occupy Austria in WWII. **92m/C** VHS, DVD. Robert Taylor, Lilli Palmer, Eddie Albert, Curt Jurgens; **D:** Arthur -Hiler; **W:** A.J. Carothers.

Miracle Down Under ⅋⅋ 1987 A family endures arduous times in 1890s Australia before a Christmas miracle changes their fortunes. Inoffensive Disney-produced drama, Australia has more directors named George Miller—one directs this, the other directs family fare such as "The Man from Snowy River." This Miller is the latter. **101m/C** VHS. AU Dee Wallace Stone, John Waters, Charles "Bud" Tingwell, Bill Kerr, Andrew Ferguson; **D:** George Miller.

Miracle Mile (continued below)

CABLE.

Miracle ernes, Rebecca Callard, Michael Bryant, Julie Christie, James Frain, Richard E. Grant, Ian Holm, William Hurt, Daniel Massey, Alfred Molina, Bob Peck, Miranda Richardson, Anthony Sher, Ken Stott, David Thewis. TV

Miracle on Ice ✗✗½ 1981 Occasionally stirring TV film recounts the surprise triumph of the American hockey team over the touted Soviet squad during the 1980 Winter Olympics at Lake Placid. **150m/C VHS.** Karl Malden, Steve Guttenberg, Andrew Stevens, Lucinda Dooling, Jessica Walter; **D:** Steven Hilliard Stern. **TV**

Miracle on 34th Street ✗✗✗½ *The Big Heart* 1947 The actual Kris Kringle is hired as Santa Claus for the Macy's Thanksgiving parade but finds difficulty in proving himself to the cynical parade sponsor. When the boss's daughter also refuses to acknowledge Kringle, he goes to extraordinary lengths to convince her. Holiday classic equal to "It's a Wonderful Life," with Gwenn and Wood particularly engaging. Also available colorized. **97m/B VHS, DVD.** Maureen O'Hara, John Payne, Edmund Gwenn, Natalie Wood, William Frawley, Porter Hall, Gene Lockhart, Thelma Ritter, Jack Albertson; **D:** George Seaton; **W:** George Seaton; **C:** Lloyd Ahern, Charles Clarke; **M:** Cyril Mockridge. Oscars '47: Screenplay, Story, Support. Actor (Gwenn); Golden Globes '48: Screenplay, Support. Actor (Gwenn); Natl. Film Reg. '05.

Miracle on 34th Street ✗✗½ 1994 (PG) Updated remake of the 1947 Christmas classic in which a jolly, bearded gent (Attenborough) claiming to be Santa Claus brings happiness to a doubting girl (Wilson) and her jaded mother (Perkins). Before he can prove himself to the precocious child, he must prove himself in a court of law with the help of Perkins's impossibly perfect neighbor (McDermott), a lawyer with a heart of gold (talk about your Christmas miracles). This version can't compete with the original's "classic" status, but Attenborough and Wilson bring soul and substance to this otherwise average adaptation. **114m/C VHS, DVD.** Richard Attenborough, Elizabeth Perkins, Dylan McDermott, J.T. Walsh, Mara Wilson, Joss Ackland, James Remar, Jane Leeves, Simon Jones, Robert Prosky, William Windom; **D:** Les Mayfield; **W:** John Hughes, George Seaton; **M:** Bruce Broughton.

The Miracle Rider ✗✗ 1935 A 15-chapter serial finds the bad guys trying to run the Indians off their lands in this saga of the old west. **295m/B VHS.** Tom Mix, Joan Gale, Charles Middleton, Jason Robards Sr., Pat O'Malley, Robert Frazer, Wally Wales, Tom London, George Chesebro, Lafe (Lafayette) McKee; **D:** B. Reeves Eason, Armand Schaefer.

The Miracle Woman ✗✗✗½ 1931 Stanwyck's particularly fine as evangelist Florence "Faith" Fallon, who becomes very successful thanks to her way with words, some fake miracles, and the talents of shady promoter Hornsby (Hardy). After blind ex-pilot John Carson (Manners) hears her on the radio, he decides Faith might be able to cure him. Florence winds up falling in love with John but Hornsby starts to worry she's going soft and will end their scam. Even Capra apparently thought this film was corny but it still works. Based on the play "Bless You Sister" by John Meehan and Robert Riskin. **90m/B VHS.** Barbara Stanwyck, David Manners, Sam Hardy, Beryl Mercer, Russell Hopton, Charles Middleton, Eddie Boland; **D:** Frank Capra; **W:** Dorothy Howell, Jo Swerling; **C:** Joseph Walker.

The Miracle Worker ✗✗✗½ 1962 Depicts the unconventional methods that teacher Anne Sullivan used to help the deaf and blind Helen Keller adjust to the world around her and shows the relationship that built between the two courageous women. An intense, moving experience. William Gibson adapted his own play for the screen. **107m/B VHS, DVD.** Anne Bancroft, Patty Duke, Victor Jory, Inga Swenson, Andrew Prine, Beah Richards; **D:** Arthur Penn; **W:** William Gibson; **C:** Ernesto Caparros; **M:** Laurence Rosenthal. Oscars '62: Actress (Bancroft), Support. Actress (Duke); British Acad. '62: Actress (Bancroft); Natl. Bd. of Review '62: Actress (Bancroft).

The Miracle Worker ✗✗ 1979 Remade for TV story of blind, deaf and mute Helen Keller and her teacher, Annie Sullivan, whose patience and perseverance finally enable Helen to learn to communicate with the world. Duke was Keller in the 1962 original, but plays the teacher in this version. **98m/C VHS.** Patty Duke, Melissa Gilbert; **D:** Paul Aaron; **M:** Billy Goldenberg. **TV**

The Miracle Worker ✗✗✗½ 2000 Yet another remake of William Gibson's Tony award-winning play, following the 1962 movie and the 1979 TV version. This time around precocious Eisenberg is young Helen Keller and Elliott (particularly good) is her dedicated teacher Annie Sullivan. Rather a genteel retelling although Annie's breakthrough with Helen still carries a strong emotional power. **90m/C VHS, DVD.** Hallie Kate Eisenberg, Alison Elliott, David Strathairn, Lucas Black, Kate Greenhouse; **D:** Nadia Tass; **W:** Monte Merrick; **C:** David Parker; **M:** William Goldstein. **TV**

Miracles ✗✗½ 1986 (PG) Comedic misfire pairs a recently divorced couple as reluctant adventurers dodging jewel thieves and peculiar tribes in South America. In a desperate move to create a plot, Mexican jewel thieves, strange tribal rites, and some outrageously unlikely coincidences reunite the family. If this sounds good, see "Romancing the Stone" instead. **90m/C VHS.** Tom Conti, Teri Garr, Paul Rodriguez, Christopher Lloyd, Jorge Russek, Charles Rocket, Bob Nelson; **D:** Jim Kouf; **M:** Peter Bernstein.

Miracles ✗✗½ *Qiji; Black Dragon* 1989 (PG-13) Chan stars (and writes and directs) as a bumpkin who saves the life of a mob boss and is thrust into the world of crime in 1930s Hong Kong. He gets some social help from a mysterious woman that gives him the confidence to romance nightclub singer Mui. But when his mob patron is murdered, Chan decides he has to show his loyalty by seeking justice. Humor and action turn out to be a winning combo. **106m/C VHS, DVD.** HK Jackie Chan, Anita (Yim-Fong) Mui, Richard Ng, Yuen Biao; **D:** Jackie Chan; **W:** Jackie Chan.

Mirage ✗✗✗ 1966 An amnesiac finds himself the target of a dangerous manhunt in New York City in this offbeat thriller. Peck is particularly sympathetic in the lead, and McCarthy, Matthau, and Kennedy all shine in supporting roles. Worth it just to hear thug Kennedy grunt, "I owe him some some pain!" **108m/B VHS.** Gregory Peck, Diane Baker, Walter Matthau, Jack Weston, Kevin McCarthy, Walter Abel, George Kennedy; **D:** Edward Dmytryk; **M:** Quincy Jones.

Mirage ✗✗½ 1994 (R) Neo-noir with plot problems has former Palm Springs cop Matteo Juarez (Olmos) hired to protect Jennifer (Young), the wife of wealthy environmentalist Donald Gale (Williams). But Jennifer just happens to suffer from multiple personality disorder, leading a not-so-secret second life as a stripper and having trouble always on her heels. **106m/ C VHS.** Edward James Olmos, Sean Young, James Andronica, Paul W. Williams; **D:** Paul W. Williams; **W:** James Andronica.

Miranda ✗✗½ 2001 (R) A romantic fantasy that takes too many complicated turns for its own good. Naive librarian Frank (Simm) is instantly smitten by the oh-so-experienced Miranda (Ricci), who is working on a real estate scam. She heads to London after one night with Frank for a new target, twisted tycoon Nailor (MacLachlan), with her foolish lover trailing behind. Miranda tries to get Frank to leave and instead he gets overly involved in her business. Ricci gets to play dress-up as Miranda goes through a lot of disguises and she's intriguing—the movie's not. **92m/ C VHS, DVD.** *GB* Christina Ricci, John Simm, Kyle MacLachlan, John Hurt, Julian Rhind-Tutt, Matthew Marsh; **D:** Marc Munden; **W:** Rob Young; **C:** Benjamin Davis; **M:** Murray Gold.

Mirele Efros ✗✗✗ 1938 A widowed but successful businesswoman finds herself at odds with her daughter-in-law in this film set in the turn of the century. In Yiddish with English subtitles. **80m/B VHS.** Berta Gersten, Michael Rosenberg, Ruth Elbaum, Albert Lipton, Sarah Krohner, Moishe Feder; **D:** Joseph Berne.

The Mirror ✗✗✗ *Zerkalo; A White Mirror* White Boy1975 Wonderful child's view of life in Russia during WWII. Black and white flashbacks of important events in the country's history are interspersed with scenes of day-to-day family life. In Russian with English subtitles. **106m/C VHS, DVD.** *RU* Margarita Terekhova, Philip Yankovsky, Ignat Daniltsev, Oleg (Yankovsky) Jankovsky; **C:** Georgy Rerberg; **M:** Eduard Artemyev.

The Mirror Crack'd ✗✗ 1980 (PG) While filming a movie in the English countryside, an American actress is murdered and Miss Marple must discover who the killer is. Based on the substantially better Agatha Christie novel. **105m/C VHS, DVD.** *GB* Angela Lansbury, Wendy Morgan, Margaret Courtenay, Charles Gray, Maureen Bennett, Carolyn Pickles, Elizabeth Taylor, Rock Hudson, Kim Novak, Tony Curtis, Edward Fox, Geraldine Chaplin, Pierce Brosnan; **D:** Guy Hamilton; **W:** Barry Sandler; **C:** Christopher Challis; **M:** John Cameron.

The Mirror Has Two Faces ✗✗ 1996 (PG-13) Gregory (Bridges) is a hunky, but flustered, professor (hunky professor?) looking for romance without all that complicated sex, which shortly leads him to plain but soulful Rose (Streisand), the ugly duckling of her family. Rose's mother (Bacall) seems more happy with her much married sister (Rogers), who is headed down the aisle again with gorgeous Alex (Brosnan). Rose decides it's her turn, despite Gregory's protests, and she weds the bow-tied (and perhaps hog-tied?) educator anyway. When Gregory leaves her on a promotional book tour, frumpy Babs decides a big makeover is in order. Her newfound outer beauty, however, becomes the beast on the inside. Premise is marred by Streisand's unwillingness to look bad, and there's a too-subtle transformation between the "ugly" Rose and the updated version. Bacall gives a memorable, Oscar-nominated performance. Remake of 1959 French film. La Streisand added to her reputation for being a "difficult" perfectionist with her constant reshoots and personnel firings that extended the film's schedule. **127m/C VHS, DVD.** Barbra Streisand, Jeff Bridges, Pierce Brosnan, Mimi Rogers, Lauren Bacall, Brenda Vaccaro, Austin Pendleton, George Segal, Elle Macpherson; **D:** Barbra Streisand; **W:** Richard LaGravenese; **C:** Dante Spinotti, Andrzej Bartkowiak; **M:** Barbra Streisand, Marvin Hamlisch. Golden Globes '97: Support. Actress (Bacall); Screen Actors Guild '96: Support. Actress (Bacall).

Mirror Images ✗✗½ 1991 (R) Although sexy twins Kaitlin and Shauna may look alike, they couldn't have more diverse personalities. Yet the gorgeous twins find their lives thrown together in a mad tornado of passion and danger when they each encounter a handsome, mysterious stranger. Could it be that this guy has something more on his mind than love, something like... murder? Also available in an steamier unrated version. **94m/C VHS.** Delia Sheppard, Jeff Conaway, Richard Arbolino, John O'Hurley, Korey Mall, Julie Strain, Nels Van Patten; **D:** Alexander Gregory (Gregory Dark) Hippolyte.

Mirror Images 2 ✗✗ 1993 Direct-to-video erotic thriller features identical twins Carrie and Terrie (Whirry in a dual role). Carrie's Miss Goody Two-Shoes and Terrie's a murderous nympho who likes Carrie's guys. Terrie dies in a mysterious fire and Carrie sets out to investigate. Sex and nudity sells. **92m/C VHS.** Shannon Whirry, Luca Bercovici, Tom Reilly; **D:** Alexander Gregory (Gregory Dark) Hippolyte.

Mirror, Mirror ✗✗ 1990 (R) The prolific Ms. Black turns on the ol' black magic when her daughter's classmates decide it's open season for taunting shrinking violets. Thanks to a magical mirror on the wall, the cheerleading classmates are willing to the great pep rally in the sky. **105m/C VHS, DVD.** Karen Black, Rainbow Harvest, Kristin Dattilo-Hayward, Ricky Paull Goldin, Yvonne De Carlo, William Sanderson, Charlie Spradling, Ann Hearn, Stephen Tobolowsky; **D:** Marina Sargenti; **W:** Marina Sargenti; **C:** Robert Brinkmann; **M:** Jimmy Lifton.

Mirror, Mirror 2: Raven Dance ✗✗½ 1994 (R) Teenaged Marlee (Wells) and her brother are temporarily housed in a convent after the death of their parents. The mystery mirror is discovered and looking into it causes Marlee

to become partially blind. Meanwhile, her inheritance is threatened and a mysterious stranger, living in the convent's basement, may be Marlee's only hope. **91m/C VHS, DVD.** Tracy Wells, Roddy McDowall, Sally Kellerman, Veronica Cartwright, William Sanderson, Lois Nettleton; **D:** Jimmy Lifton; **W:** Jimmy Lifton, Virginia Perfili; **C:** Troy Cook; **M:** Jimmy Lifton.

Mirror, Mirror 3: The Voyeur ✗✗½ 1996 Artist discovers a mirror in an abandoned mansion and sees that it reflects the presence of his lost lover, who is now able to manipulate his dreams. **91m/C VHS, DVD.** Billy Drago, Monique Parent, David Naughton, Mark Ruffalo, Elizabeth Baldwin, Richard Cansino; **D:** Rachel Gordon, Virginia Perfili; **W:** Steve Tymon; **C:** Nils Erickson.

Mirror of Death ✗✗ *Dead of Night* 1987 A woman subject to physical abuse gets more than she bargains for when she seeks revenge by when she unleashing the gruesome Queen of Hell. Watch this if you dare! **85m/C VHS, DVD.** Julie Merrill, Kurt Browne, John Reno, Deryn Warren; **D:** Deryn Warren; **W:** Jerry Daly; **M:** David Michael Frank.

Mirror Wars: Reflection One woof! 2005 Something obviously got lost in translation with the Russian portion of this otherworldly escapade from the cast and crew since this minor actioner is a muddled mess. A terrorist wants to steal a new Russian stealth-fighter prototype and provoke a war between Russia and the USA, but the plane's young plot proves uncooperative. The "names" in the cast apparently were just picking up a paycheck. **109m/C VHS, DVD.** Malcolm McDowell, Armand Assante, Rutger Hauer, Alexander Efimov, Olga Yakovtseva; **D:** Vasili Chiginsky; **W:** Alex Kustanovich; **M:** David Robbins.

MirrorMask ✗✗ 2005 (PG) McKean teams with "Sandman" author Neil Gaiman in this otherworldly story. Helena (Leonidas) is the teenaged daughter of circus performers who longs for a "normal" life. But when her mom (McKee) lapses into a coma, Helena has to travel into a fantasy world to recover the MirrorMask from the Queen of Shadows. McKean's trippy CGI landscapes (rendered on a bare-bones budget) produce some of the most exciting film visuals in years, but you'll be so bored waiting for the story to kick in that the sugar rush from the eye candy wears off way too fast. **101m/C DVD, UMD.** Jason Barry, Stephanie Leonidas, Gina McKee, Rob Brydon, Dora Bryan, Stephen Fry; **D:** Dave McKean; **W:** Neil Gaiman, David McKean; **C:** Antony Shearn; **M:** Ian Ballamy.

Mirrors ✗✗ 1978 Woman finds that her dreams lead to death and destruction in New Orleans. **83m/C VHS.** Kitty Winn, Peter Donat, William Swetland, Mary-Robin Redd, William Burns; **D:** Noel Black.

Mirrors ✗✗½ 1985 A Detroit-born ballerina goes to the Big Apple in search of fame and glory, leaving behind her journalist boyfriend. This upbeat love story features some spectacular dance routines and a behind-the-scenes look at a Broadway dancer's lifestyle. **99m/C VHS.** Timothy Daly, Marguerite Hickey, Antony (Tony) Hamilton; **D:** Harry Winer. **TV**

The Misadventures of Merlin Jones ✗✗½ 1963 (G) A pair of college sweethearts become embroiled in a rollicking chimp-napping scandal. Disney pap done appropriately. A sequel, "The Monkey's Uncle," followed. **90m/C VHS, DVD.** Tommy Kirk, Annette Funicello, Leon Ames, Stuart Erwin, Connie Gilchrist, Kelly Thordsen; **D:** Robert Stevenson; **W:** Alfred Lewis Levitt, Helen Levitt; **C:** Edward Colman; **M:** Buddy (Norman Dale) Baker.

The Misadventures of Mr. Wilt ✗✗ *Wilt* 1990 (R) Bumbling college lecturer has to convince inept inspector that he murdered a blowup doll, which he had to have their bundle of joy thanks to artifical insemination. Only psycho donor daddy Billy Crapshoot (Dillon) finds out who they are and decides to come for his soon-to-be-born offspring. **97m/C VHS,** Kevin Dillon, Nick Mancuso, Lysette Anthony, Robert Lewis, Matthew (Matt) Walker, Stefan Arngrim; **D:** Mark L. Lester; **W:** Larry Cohen; **C:** Mark Irwin. CABLE

Misbehaving Husbands ♂½ **1941** Weak story finds store-owner Langton suspected of being untrue by wife Blythe—thanks to rumors spread by a shyster lawyer only too happy to console the lady after the divorce. **65m/C VHS, DVD,** Harry Langdon, Betty Blythe, Ralph Byrd, Esther Muir, Luana Walters; **D:** William Beaudine.

Mischief ♂♂ **1985 (R)** Alienated youths form a friendship during James Dean's heyday. Warning: this film offers a fairly convincing recreation of the 1950s. **97m/C VHS, DVD,** Doug Mckeon, Catherine Mary Stewart, Kelly Preston, Chris Nash, J.W. Brown, Jami Gertz, Margaret Blye, Graham Jarvis, Terry O'Quinn; **D:** Mel Damski; **W:** Noel Black.

Misery ♂♂♂ **1990 (R)** Author Caan decides to chuck his lucrative but unfulfilling pulp novels and write seriously by finally convincing his most popular character, Misery Chastain. However, fate intervenes when he crashes his car near the home of Bates, his "biggest fan ever," who saves his life, but then tortures him for resurrecting her "favorite character." Bates is chillingly glib and calmly brutal—watch your ankles. Based on the novel by Stephen King. **107m/C VHS, DVD,** James Caan, Kathy Bates, Lauren Bacall, Richard Farnsworth, Frances Sternhagen, Graham Jarvis; **D:** Rob Reiner; **W:** William Goldman; Oscars '90: Actress (Bates); Golden Globes '91: Actress—Drama (Bates).

The Misfit Brigade ♂♂♂ *Wheels of Terror* **1987 (R)** Variation on the "Dirty Dozen" finds German misfits recruited for warfare by desperate Nazis during WWII. **99m/C VHS,** Bruce Davison, Oliver Reed, David Carradine, David Patrick Kelly, D.W. Moffet, Keith Szarabajka; **D:** Gordon Hessler.

Misfits of Science ♂ **1985** Pilot for a failed TV series about a group of teens with special powers who fight to save the world. **96m/C VHS,** Dean Paul Martin Jr., Marin, Kevin Peter Hall, Mark Thomas Miller, Kenneth Mars, Courteney Cox; **D:** Philip DeGuere. TV

The Misfits ♂♂♂ **1961** A cynical floozy befriends grim cowboys in this downbeat drama. Compelling performances from leads Clift, Monroe (screenwriter Miller's wife), and Gable. Last film for the latter two performers, and nearly the end for Clift. **124m/B VHS, DVD,** Clark Gable, Marilyn Monroe, Montgomery Clift, Thelma Ritter, Eli Wallach, James Barton, Estelle Winwood; **D:** John Huston; **W:** Arthur Miller; **C:** Russell Metty.

Mishima: A Life in Four Chapters ♂♂♂ **1985 (R)** Somewhat detached account and indulgent portrayal of the narcissistic Japanese author (and actor, filmmaker, and militarist) alternates between stylized interpretations of his books and a straightforward account of his life. Culminates in a pseudo-military operation that, in turn, resulted in Mishima's ritualistic suicide. Innovative design by Eiko Ishioka. In Japanese with English subtitles. **121m/C VHS, DVD,** Ken Ogata, Kenji Sawada, Yasosuke Bando; **D:** Paul Schrader; **C:** John Bailey; **W:** Leonard Schrader, Paul Schrader, Chieko Schrader; *Nar:* Roy Scheider.

Misleading Lady ♂½ **1932** A dingy well-to-do socialite tries to bribe herself a part as a seductress in an upcoming film, proving her worthiness for an unsavory bachelor. **70m/B VHS,** Claudette Colbert, Edmund Lowe, Stuart Erwin, Robert Strange, Edmund Lowe, Stuart Erwin, Robert Strange; **D:** Stuart Walker; **W:** Paul Dickey, Adelaide Heilbron, Charles W. Goddard, Caroline Francke. VIDEO

Miss A & Miss M ♂½ **1966** A young girl is shocked when she realizes that two teachers she has befriended also live together. **60m/C VHS,** Kika Markham, Jennifer Hilary; **D:** Robert Knights.

Miss All-American Beauty ♂½ **1982** A behind-the-scenes look at a small-time Texas beauty pageant. Lane stars as a contestant who comes to realize her self-respect is more important than winning an award. Meanwhile the lady wearing the number one sash—Lane—has a mean pageant director adds an ironic edge that the movie as a whole lacks. **96m/C VHS, DVD,** Diane Lane, Cloris Leachman, David Dukes, Gus Meadows, Alice Hirson, Brian Kerwin; **D:** Gus Trikonis. TV

Miss Annie Rooney ♂♂ **1942** (G) Intended to bill the child star in a more mature role, Temple receives her first screen kiss in this story about a poor Irish girl who falls in love with a wealthy young man. The well-worn plot is weighed down by lifeless dialogue. **86m/B VHS,** Shirley Temple, Dickie Moore, William Gargan, Guy Kibbee, Peggy Ryan, Jana Lockhart; **D:** Edwin L. Marin.

Miss Austen Regrets ♂♂½ **2007** A "what-if" biography of the writer, Jane Austen (Williams) receives a proposal from a wealthy suitor but changes her mind when she realizes that a wife's duties will prevent her from writing. So she insists on asking Jane's opinion on her own potential suitors, though she doesn't like the advice she's given. This causes Jane to wonder as she gains success as an author about the choices even she made the right choices even as she gains success as an author about the choices even she made the right. **90m/C DVD,** GB Olivia Williams, Greta Scacchi, Phyllida Law, Pip Torrens, Adrian Edmondson, Hugh Bonneville, Imogen Poots, Jack Huston, Tom Hiddleston; **D:** Jeremy Lovering; **W:** Gwyneth Hughes; **C:** Michael Kotz; **M:** Luke Dunkley. TV

Ms. Bear ♂♂½ **1997 (G)** Logging operations in a Canadian forest have disturbed the local bear population and down-on-his-luck Barney decides to make some money by tranquilizing the animals and selling them to a zoo importer. A cub escapes and wanders into the yard of lonely, seven-year-old Emily, who befriends the cute critter. Then, with Emily's help, Barney learns the importer is actually killing the bears and are giving their paws to the overseas market. So a rescue is in order. **95m/C VHS,** Ed Begley Jr., Kaitlyn Burke, Shawn Johnston; **D:** Paul Ziller.

Miss Cast Away ♂ *Miss Castaway and the Island Girls* **2004** Absurd antics abound in this wide-ranging parody of big-budget flicks such as "The Perfect Storm" and "The Lord of the Rings." An airplane filled with beauty-pageant contestants crash-lands on a deserted island on its way to Japan and as its two pilots (Roberts and Schlatter) must protect the ladies by fending off all manner of strange inhabitants including ape people. Features cameo by the former King of Pop himself, Michael Jackson, as Special Agent M. Surely you can't be serious if you think this ranks anywhere near the Zucker/Abrahams/Zucker ouvre. **91m/C VHS, DVD,** Eric Roberts, Charlie Schlatter, Joyce Giraud, Stuart Pankin, Evan Marriott; **D:** Bryan Michael Stoler; **W:** Bryan Michael Stoler. VIDEO

Miss Congeniality ♂♂ **2000 (PG-13)** Tough FBI agent Gracia Hart (Bullock) must go undercover at the Miss USA Pageant after the event is threatened by terrorists. Eric (Bratt) is a helpful fellow agent (and potential beau) while down-on-his-luck consultant Victor Melling (Caine) is hired to girly-up Gracie and make her pageant material. Predictable comedy shows flashes of witty satire that lives up to its name by easing up on intended targets at the moment of truth, Bullock, as always, is game and both Bergen as a former beauty queen turned pageant manager and Shatner as unctuous pageant host add a spark to the proceedings. **111m/C VHS, DVD,** Sandra Bullock, Benjamin Bratt, Michael Caine, William Shatner, Ernie Hudson, Candice Bergen, Heather Burns, Melissa De Sousa, Steve Monroe, John DiResta, Jennifer Gareis, Wendy Raquel Robinson; **D:** Donald Petrie; **W:** Marc Lawrence; **C:** Laszlo Kovacs.

Miss Congeniality 2: Armed and Fabulous ♂½ **2005 (PG-13)** It took five years for Sandra Bullock to make this contrived sequel and you have to wonder why she bothered. Set a few weeks after the first flick, Gracie has become such a celebrity that she can no longer work undercover and has been reassigned as the public face of the FBI. Gracie, accompanied by her flamboyant personal stylist Joel (Bader), even has her own FBI bodyguard, Sam Fuller (King). When the current Miss United States (Burns), and pageant director Stan (Shatner) are kidnapped, Gracie and her entourage head for Vegas where the agent is expected to be the bureau spokesperson. Heather decides she's her only friend. Many slapstick shenanigans follow in this trifling female buddy comedy. **115m/C DVD,** Sandra Bullock, Regina King, Enrique Murciano, William Shatner, Ernie Hudson, Heather Burns, Diedrich Bader, Treat Williams, Abraham Benrubi, Nick Offerman, Elisabeth Rohm; **D:** John Pasquin; **W:** Marc Lawrence; **C:** Peter Menzies Jr.

Miss Evers' Boys ♂♂½ **1997 (PG)** Wrenching docudrama covers a 40-year U.S. Public Health Service study in which black men suffering from syphilis were monitored but not treated for the disease. Eunice Evers (Woodard) is a nurse assisting Dr. Brodus (Morton) in the care of the afflicted men. White Dr. Douglas (Sheffer) first has a funded government program for treatment but when the program is cut, he's offered funding only for the study of syphilitic black men and establishing whether the disease affects blacks and whites differently. Brodus and Evers both lie to their patients as each comes to realize that treatment will never be re-established and only the deaths of their patients will provide the final information for the study. Based on the play by David Feldshuh. **120m/C VHS, DVD,** Alfre Woodard, Laurence Fishburne, Joe Morton, Craig Sheffer, Obba Babatunde, Ossie Davis, E.G. Marshall; **D:** Joseph Sargent; **W:** Walter Bernstein; **C:** Donald M. Morgan; **M:** Charles Bernstein. CABLE

Miss Firecracker ♂♂♂ **1989 (PG)** Hunter, longing for love and self-respect, decides to change her promiscuous image by entering the local beauty pageant in her conservative southern hometown. The somewhat drippy premise is transformed by a super script and cast into an engaging and upbeat film. Henley's script was adapted from her own Off-Broadway play where Hunter created the role. Actress Lahti, wife of director Schlamme, makes a brief appearance. **102m/C VHS, DVD,** Holly Hunter, Scott Glenn, Mary Steenburgen, Tim Robbins, Alfre Woodard, Trey Wilson, Bert Remsen, Ann Wedgeworth, Christine Lahti, Amy Wright; **D:** Thomas Schlamme; **W:** Beth Henley; **C:** Arthur Albert; **M:** David Mansfield.

Ms. 45 ♂♂♂ **1981** *Angel of Vengeance* **(R)** Rough, bristling cult favorite about a mute girl who, in response to being raped and beaten twice in one night, goes on a man-killing murder spree. Wild ending. **84m/C VHS, DVD,** Abel Ferrara, Zoe Tamerlis, Steve Singer, Jack Thibeau, Peter Yellen, Darlene Stuto, Editta Sherman, Albert Sinkys; **D:** Abe Ferrara; **W:** Nicholas St. John; **C:** James (Momel) Lemmo; **M:** Joe Della.

Miss Grant Takes Richmond ♂♂ *Innocence Is Bliss* **1949** Zipperhead secretary finds herself in hot water a la Lucy when she finds out the company she's been working for is really the front for a gambling getup. Only Lucy fans need apply. **87m/B VHS,** Lucille Ball, William Holden, Janis Carter, James Gleason, Gloria Henry, Frank McHugh, George Cleveland, Arthur Space, Will Wright, Jimmy Lloyd; **D:** Lloyd Bacon.

Miss Julie ♂♂ *Froken Julie* **1950** Melodramatic stew adapted from the August Strindberg play about a confused noblewoman who disgraces herself when she allows a servant to seduce her. In Swedish with English subtitles. **90m/B VHS,** SW Anita Bjork, Ulf Palme, Anders Henriksson, Max von Sydow; **D:** Alf Sjoberg; **C:** Goran Strindberg; **W:** Alf Sjoberg; Cannes '51: Film.

Miss Mary ♂♂½ **1986 (R)** A compassionate English governess in Buenos Aires conflicts with the honor-obsessed family she works for and Argentina's tumultuous history. Christie gives a wonderful performance. **100m/C VHS, DVD,** Julie Christie, Nacha Guevara, Sofia Viruboff, Luisina Brando; **D:** Maria-Luisa Bemberg; **W:** Jorge Goldenberg, Maria-Luisa Bemberg.

Miss Melody Jones ♂ **1973** A beautiful young black woman's dreams of stardom unravel as she is forced to pander to prurient men by disrobing publicly for financial recompense. **86m/C VHS,** Philomena Nowlin, Ronald Warren, Jacqueline Dalya, Peter Jacob; **D:** Bill Brame; **W:** Bill Brame.

Miss Monday ♂♂ **1998 (R)** A commonplace but charming romance. **90m/C DVD,** Andrea Hart, James Hicks, Nick Moran, Michael Coles, Benson Lee, Richard Morel; **M:** Woody Pak.

Miss Pettigrew Lives for a Day ♂♂ **2008 (PG-13)** As a middle-aged governess, and a lousy one at that, Miss Guinevere Pettigrew (McDormand) was a genteel spinster from a nouveau riche family (the film covers 1902-06). Her talents were generally dismissed until the elder editors at the Warne family publishing firm decide the project will keep young-est brother Norman (McGregor) busy. He turns out to be enthusiastic for not only the book but for Beatrix herself, and she is soon friendly with both Norman and his unmarried sister, Millie (Watson). Noonan has Potter's drawings come to life when she talks to them, otherwise this is standard fare. Watson and McGregor make a lively, charming duo while Zellweger seems rather too restrained. **92m/C DVD, GB** US Renee Zellweger, Ewan McGregor, Emily Watson, Barbara Flynn, Bill Paterson, Matyclock Gibbs, Anton Lesser, David Bamber, Phyllida Law, Lloyd Owen; **D:** Chris Noonan; **W:** Richard Maltby Jr.; **C:** Andrew Dunn; **M:** Nigel Westlake.

Miss Potter ♂♂½ **2006 (PG)** Charming, though staid, bio of the creator of Peter Rabbit. Beatrix Potter (Zellweger) is a genteel spinster from a nouveau riche family (the film covers 1902-06). Her talents were generally dismissed until the elder editors at the Warne family publishing firm decide the project will keep youngest brother Norman (McGregor) busy. He turns out to be enthusiastic for not only the book but for Beatrix herself, and she is soon friendly with both Norman and his unmarried sister, Millie (Watson). **96m/C VHS, DVD,** William Tepper, Karen Black, Virna Lisi, Margot Kidder; Marie-France Pisier; **D:** Paul Williams.

Miss Right ♂ **1981 (R)** A young man determines to find the ideal woman for himself and casts aside his other romantic interests. Sputtering lightweight comedy. **96m/C VHS, DVD,** William Tepper, Karen Black, Virna Lisi, Margot Kidder; Marie-France Pisier; **D:** Paul Williams.

Miss Julie ♂♂ **1999 (R)** Dry adaptation of August Strindberg's 1889 banned-in-Sweden play about the turbulent relationship between an imperious young noblewoman and an ambitious servant. Neurotic Miss Julie (Burrows), restless and bored, strides into the servants' kitchen where mutual loathing, humiliation, and psycho/sexual clashes over an evening self-destruction are the only means of communication. **107m/C VHS, DVD,** GB Saffron Burrows, Peter Mullan, Maria Doyle Kennedy; **D:** Mike Figgis; **W:** Helen Cooper; **C:** Benoit Delhomme; **M:** Mike Figgis.

Miss Rose White 1992 (PG) Sedgwick is Rose, a modern young career woman in post-WWII New York, as American as apple pie, who lives two very separate lives. Born Rayzel Weiss, a Polish Jew, she immigrated to the U.S. with her father as a very young girl, before the holocaust devastated her remaining family in Poland. After the war her older sister, thought dead, comes to America. The haunted Luisa causes Rose to question whether she can ever leave her past behind. Above average Hallmark Hall of Fame presentation has a good cast, particularly Plummer as Luisa. Based on the play "A Shayna Maidel" by Barbara Lebow. 95m/C VHS. Kyra Sedgwick, Amanda Plummer, Maximilian Schell, D.B. Sweeney, Penny Fuller, Milton Selzer, Maureen Stapleton; D: Joseph Sargent; W: Anna Sandor. TV

Miss Sadie Thompson 1953 Based on the novel "Rain" by W. Somerset Maugham. Promiscuous tart Hayworth arrives on a Pacific island occupied by a unit of Marines and a sanctimonious preacher played by Ferrer While Hayworth parties with the Marines and becomes involved with Ray's Sgt. O'Hara, Ferrer moralizes and insists she return to the mainland to face moral charges. Quasi-musical with a scattering of dubbed songs by Hayworth includes a memorable erotic dance scene complete with tight dress and dripping sweat. Hayworth's strong performance carries the picture with Ferrer and Ray turning in cardboard versions of their Maugham characters. Originally filmed in 3-D. 91m/C VHS. Rita Hayworth, Jose Ferrer, Aldo Ray, Charles Bronson; D: Curtis Bernhardt.

Missile to the Moon 1959 First expedition to the moon encounters not acres of dead rock but a race of gorgeous women in lingerie and high heels. A bad but entertaining remake of "Cat Women of the Moon," featuring a bevy of beauty contest winners from New Hampshire to Yugoslavia. Who says truth is stranger than fiction. 78m/B VHS, DVD. Gary Clarke, Cathy Downs, K.T. Stevens, Laurie Mitchell, Michael Whalen, Nina Bara, Richard Travis, Tommy Cook, Marjorie Hellen; D: Richard Cunha; W: Vincent Fotre, H.E. Barrie; G: Meredith Nicholson; M: Nicholas Carras.

Missiles of October 1974 Cuban Missile of the October 1962 Cuban Missile crisis, this TV drama keeps you on the edge of your seat while unfolding the sequence of events within the U.S. government. Well written, with a strong cast including Devane, who turns in a convincing performance as—guess who—J.F.K. 155m/C VHS, DVD. James Hong, James Callahan, Keene Curtis, John Dehner, Peter Donat, Andrew Duggan, Charles Cyphers, Dana Elcar, Arthur Franz, Larry Gates, Richard Kartan, Michael Lerner, Stacy Keach Sr., Wright King, Will Kuluva, Paul Lambert, Doreen Lang, Byron Morrow, Stewart Moss, James Olson, Dennis Patrick, Albert Paulsen, Nehemiah Persoff, William Prince, John Randolph, Kenneth Tobey, Harris Yulin, George Wyner, William Devane, Ralph Bellamy, Martin Sheen, Howard da Silva; D: Anthony Page; M: Laurence Rosenthal. TV

Missing 1982 (PG) At the height of a military coup in Chile (never named in the movie), a young American writer (Shea) disappears. His right-wing father (Lemmon) tries to get to the bottom of his disappearance while bickering with Shea's wife, played by Spacek, a bohemian who is the political opposite of her father-in-law. Outstanding performances by Spacek and Lemmon along with excellent writing and direction result in a gripping and thought-provoking thriller. Based on the book by Thomas Hauser from the true story of Charles Horman. 122m/C VHS, DVD. Jack Lemmon, Sissy Spacek, John Shea, Melanie Mayron, David Clennon, Charles Cioffi, Joe Regalbuto, Richard Venture, Janice Rule; D: Constantin Costa-Gavras; W: Constantin Costa-Gavras, Donald Stewart; M: Vangelis. Oscars '82: Adapt. Screenplay; British Acad. '82: Screenplay; Cannes '82: Actor (Lemmon), Film; Writers Guild '82: Adapt. Screenplay.

The Missing 2003 (R) Director Ron Howard successfully tries his hand at a gritty western. Blanchett plays Maggie Gilkeson, a mother of two daughters, who supports her family by working the ranch and serving as a healer to the community. Maggie is estranged from her father Samuel Jones (the perfectly craggy-faced Jones) who left her and her mother years ago to live with the Apache tribe. But she soon seeks her father's help after her oldest daughter Lilly (Wood) is kidnapped by an evil Native American shaman (Schweig). Blanchett and Jones both have the acting chops to keep this story interesting and well worth watching. Based on the Thomas Eidson novel "The Last Ride." 135m/C VHS, DVD. US Tommy Lee Jones, Cate Blanchett, Eric Schweig, Jenna Boyd, Evan Rachel Wood, Steve Reevis, Ray McKinnon, Val Kilmer, Aaron Eckhart, Simon Baker, Jay Tavare, Sergio Calderon, Clint Howard, Elisabeth (Elisabeth, Liz) Moss, Max Perlich; D: Ron Howard; W: Ken Kaufman; C: Salvatore Totino; M: James Horner.

Missing Brendan 2003 After three painful decades, George Calden (Asner) goes to Vietnam with his two sons and grandson upon learning that his MIA son Brendan's crashed plane has been found. Desperate to fulfill his wife's dying wish to bring his remains home, the family grapples with many more challenges including lack of cooperation by the Vietnamese government, a father-son clash when his grandson dates a local girl, and George's hidden terminal illness. 100m/C VHS, DVD. Ed Asner, Robin Thomas, Illeana Douglas, Frank Cox, Adam Brody, Harold Sylvester, Kathleen Luong, Aki Aleong, Dale Dye, Brenda Strong; D: Eugene Brady; W: Christopher White; C: Jeffrey Smith. VIDEO

The Missing Corpse 1945 When a newspaper publisher's worst rival is murdered, he fears that he will be implicated. He decides the only thing to do is hide the body to prevent its being discovered. Enjoyable, light comedy/mystery. 62m/B VHS. J. Edward Bromberg, Eric Sinclair, Frank Jenks, Isabelle Randolph, Paul Guilfoyle, John Shay, Lorell Sheldon; D: Al(bert) Herman.

Missing in Action 1984 (R) An army colonel returns to the Vietnam jungle to settle old scores and rescue some POWs while on an MIA fact-finding mission. Box office smash. 101m/C VHS, DVD. Chuck Norris, M. Emmet Walsh; D: Joseph Zito; W: James Bruner; C: Joao Fernandes; M: Jay Chattaway.

Missing in Action 2: The Beginning 1985 (R) Set in Vietnam, this prequel to the original "Missing in Action" provides some interesting background on Norris's rocky relationship with communism. Packed with violence, bloodshed and torture. 96m/C VHS, DVD. Chuck Norris, Soon-Teck Oh, Cosie Costa, Steven Williams; D: Lance Hool; W: Steve Bing.

Missing Link 1988 (PG) A strange, meditative quasi-documentary depicting the singular adventures of a humanoid silently transversing the African wilderness and confronting various natural phenomena. Beautifully photographed. Make-up by Rick Baker. 92m/C VHS. Peter Elliott, Michael Gambon; D: David Hughes.

Missing Pieces 1983 A woman takes a job as a private investigator in order to find her journalist husband's killer. Effective mystery taken from the novel "A Private Investigation" by Karl Alexander. 96m/C VHS. Elizabeth Montgomery, Louanne, John C. Reilly, Ron Karabatsos, Robin Gammell, Julius W. Harris; D: Mike Hodges. TV

Missing Pieces 1991 (PG) Goof-ups Wuhl and Idle find out about a potential inheritance thanks to a fortune cookie. Now if they can just figure out what the riddle means. 93m/C VHS. Eric Idle, Robert Wuhl, Lauren Hutton; D: Leonard Stern; W: Leonard Stern.

Missing Pieces 2000 Rancher Atticus Cody (Coburn) leaves his home in Colorado to investigate his estranged artist son Scott's (Kersey) supposed suicide in a remote part of Mexico. And what he finds are more questions and lots of lies. Unfortunately lame script filled with cliches. Based on the Ron Hansen novel "Atticus." 90m/C VHS. James Coburn, Lisa Zane, Paul Kersey, Finn Carter, William R. Moses, Julio Oscar Mechoso, Maxwell Caulfield; D: Carl Schenkel; W: Philip Rosenberg, Richard Kletter, D.W. Owen, Peachy Markowitz; C: Karl Hermann; M: Lawrence Shragge. TV

The Mission 1986 (PG) Sweeping, cinematically beautiful historical drama about an 18th-century Jesuit mission in the Brazilian jungle. The missionaries struggle against the legalized slave trade of Portugal and political factions within the church. Written by Bolt (of "A Man for All Seasons" fame), its visual intensity is marred by length and so much overt symbolism that an emotional coolness surfaces when the action slows. Nonetheless, epic in ambition and nearly in quality. Magnificent musical score. 125m/C VHS, DVD. Robert De Niro, Jeremy Irons, Ray McAnally, Aidan Quinn, Liam Neeson, Cherie Lunghi, Rev. Daniel Berrigan, Ronald Pickup; D: Roland Joffe; W: Robert Bolt; C: Chris Menges; M: Ennio Morricone. Oscars '86: Cinematog.; British Acad. '86: Support. Actor (McAnally); Cannes '86: Film; Golden Globes '87: Screenplay, Score; L.A. Film Critics '86: Cinematog.

The Mission 1999 Cheung Fo A Hong Kong mobster hires five gunmen to be his bodyguards. Everything's cool until one of them has an affair with the boss's wife. Director To revisits Tarantino-Woo territory. Most of the guys have bad haircuts and all of them have big pistols. 84m/C DVD. HK Anthony Wong, Francis Ng, Roy Cheung, Simon Yam, Jackie Lui, Lam Suet; D: Johnny To; W: Nai-Hoi Yau.

Mission 2000 New York native Marvin (Coburn) moves to the Mission District of San Francisco to write a novel. He rooms with wannabe musician Jay (Leonard) and falls for beauty Ima (Holt), who tells him that he's too uptight to be a good writer. Well, if the Mission District can't loosen Marvin up, he's doomed. 87m/C VHS, DVD. Chris Coburn, Joshua Leonard, Sandrine Holt, Bellamy Young, Adam Arkin; D: Loren Marsh; W: Loren Marsh; C: Matthew Uhry.

Mission Batangas 1969 Unremarkable adventure-war-heist movie tells the story of a shallow American WWII pilot (Weaver) and a missionary nurse (Miles), who team up to steal the Philippine government's entire stock of gold bullion from the Japanese who captured it. Beautiful scenery, shot in the Philippines, adds something to an otherwise vacant effort. 100m/C VHS. Dennis Weaver, Vera Miles, Keith Larsen; D: Keith Larsen.

Mission Galactica: The Cylon Attack 1978 Spaceship Battlestar Galactica is stranded in space without fuel and open to attack from the chrome-plated Cylons. Adama (Greene) is forced to stop Commander Cain's (Bridges) efforts to launch an attack against the Cylons, while countering the attacks of the Cylon leader. Warmed over TV sci-fi. 108m/C VHS. Lorne Greene, Lloyd Bridges, Patrick Hatch, Dirk Benedict, Herbert Jefferson Jr., John Colicos, Maren Jensen, Laurette Spang, Anne Lockhart, Terry Carter, George Murdock; D: Vince Edwards, Christian Nyby; W: Jim Carlson, Glen Larson; C: H. John Penner, Frank Thackery. TV

Mission: Impossible 1996 (PG-13) Cruise and director DePalma did not completely succeed or fail in their mission to create a blockbuster hit based on the popular '60s TV series. Cruise (one of the film's producers) is Ethan Hunt, pointman extraordinaire of the IMF team headed by Jim Phelps (Jon Voight). Their team is sent to recover a computer disk with devastating information from a mercenary Russian spy. Smelling a double cross, Hunt confronts his conniving agency boss Kitteridge (the perfectly cast Czerny) and creates his own team of crack agents to get to the truth, mind-boggling plot twists and crazy train rides be damned. The plotline may have self-destructed two-thirds into the movie and the absence of a truly sinister villain causes some damage, but with solid acting talent, tight pacing, alluring European locales, and tension-inducing special effects, who has time to notice? $100 million gross in the first two weeks would seem to indicate a sequel is in order. 110m/C VHS, DVD, Blu-ray Disc, HD DVD. Tom Cruise, Jon Voight, Emmanuelle Beart, Ving Rhames, Henry Czerny, Emilio Estevez, Vanessa Redgrave, Jean Reno, Dale Dye; D: Brian De Palma; W: Robert Towne, David Koepp; C: Stephen Burum; M: Danny Elfman.

Mission: Impossible 2 2000 (PG-13) In this visually stunning sequel to the 1996 film, Ethan Hunt tracks a rogue IMF agent Ambrose (Scott), who threatens to release deadly virus on Sydney, Australia and corner the market on the cure. Ambrose's ex-girlfriend Nyah (Newton), a jewel thief, is recruited by Hunt to spy on Ambrose from inside. Of course Nyah and Hunt fall in love (the weakest element of the movie, by the way). Director Woo brings his trademark balletic style to the action, although it seems to take a while to actually get to it. The stunts and fights, while completely preposterous, are beautifully done. The plot is a lot less convoluted than the first "Mission," which is either good or bad, depending on how you feel about the original. 125m/C VHS, DVD, Blu-ray Disc, HD DVD. Tom Cruise, Anthony Hopkins, Dougray Scott, Thandie Newton, Ving Rhames, Brendan Gleeson, John Polson, Richard Roxburgh, Rade Serbedzija; D: John Woo; W: Robert Towne; C: Jeffrey L. Kimball; M: Hans Zimmer.

Mission: Impossible 3 2006 (PG-13) Tom Cruise may have transformed into Hollywood's most bizarre leading man (take that, Mel Gibson!), but you can't deny that this third MI chapter is a cracking good yarn. Abrams, in his feature debut, grounds the film by bringing back the cool gadgets and teamwork that everyone loved about the original TV show. Ethan Hunt (Cruise) is ready to retire from the IMF, when evil arms dealer Davian (a scene-stealing Hoffman) kills Hunt's protege and kidnaps his wife (Monaghan). Hunt goes into rescue/revenge mode and the non-stop action... well... never stops. Great example of a summer blockbuster that works. 126m/C DVD, Blu-ray Disc, UMD. Tom Cruise, Ving Rhames, Keri Russell, Philip Seymour Hoffman, Michelle Monaghan, Laurence Fishburne, Billy Crudup, Simon Pegg, Jonathan Rhys Meyers, Sasha Alexander, Greg Grunberg, Carla Gallo, Eddie Marsan, Jose Zuniga, Maggie Q; D: J.J. (Jeffrey) Abrams; W: J.J. (Jeffrey) Abrams, Alex Kurtzman, Roberto Orci; C: Dan Mindel; M: Michael Giacchino.

Mission in Morocco 1959 When an oilman scouting for oil fields in the Sahara is killed, his partner, Barker, hops a jet to Morocco to find the whereabouts of a microfilm that gives the location of a valuable oil deposit. The search for the secret microfilm is complicated by competing parties also interested in the black gold. Ho-hum action adventure. 79m/C VHS. Fernando Rey, Alfredo Mayo, Silvia Morgan, Lex Barker, Juli Reding; D: Anthony Squire, Carlos Arevalo; C: Cecilio Paniagua.

Mission Kashmir 2000 (R) Altaff (Roshan) is a young Kashmiri whose family is killed by state police hunting a rebel leader. He's adopted by Inayat Khan (Dutt), whom Altaff eventually learns was the man who lead the raid. Fleeing, Altaff seeks the tutelage of Hila Kohistani (Shroff), a militant whose only aim is the independence of Kashmir and Altaff is his weapon. But when Altaff returns to Kashmir, he unexpectedly meets his childhood girlfriend, Sufi (Zinta), and is torn between love and revenge. Hindi with subtitles or English dubbed. 157m/C VHS, DVD. IN Hrithik Roshan, Sanjay Dutt, Jackie Shroff, Preity Zinta, Sonali Kulkarni; D: Vidhu Vinod Chopra; W: Vidhu Vinod Chopra, Vikram Chandra; C: Vinod Pradhan.

Mission... Kill 1985 (R) An American demolitions expert (Ginty) joins a Latin American guerrilla force in battling tyrannical junta force. Fast-paced thriller is big on revenge and violence but not much else. 97m/C VHS, DVD. Robert Ginty, Olivia D'Abo, Cameron Mitchell; D: David Winters.

Mission Manila 1987 (R) An ex-CIA operative and Manila-based drug addict is called by his ex-lover to return to Manila to help his brother, who has gotten in much the same trouble he had. 98m/C

Mission Mars 🎬 1967 American astronauts McGavin and Adams, on a mission whatever it's out, are to accomplish. *112m/C VHS, DVD.* Tim Robbins, Gary Sinise, Don Cheadle, Connie Nielsen, Jerry O'Connell, Kim Delaney, Elise Neal, Peter Outerbridge, Jill Teed, Kavan Smith; *D:* Brian De Palma; *W:* Jim Thomas, John Thomas, Graham Yost; *C:* Stephen Burum; *M:* Ennio Morricone.

Mission of Death 🎬🎬 *Death* 1997 (R) Cop Jim Randall (Pare) has been accused of murder and suspended from the force. Something in his past of-fers the clue to proving his innocence but Randall doesn't want to remember. *96m/C VHS.* Michael Pare, Linda Hoffman, John Simon Jones, Anthony Fridjon, Justin Illuson; *D:* Yossi Wein; *M:* Dan Lerner, David Sparling; *C:* Peter Belcher; *M:* Serge Colbert. VIDEO

Mission of Justice 🎬🎬 1992 (R) *Merchant of Death* 1997 (R) Cop Jim Randall (Pare) has been accused of murder and suspended from the force. Something in his past of-fers the clue to proving his innocence but Randall doesn't want to remember. *95m/C VHS.* Brigitte Nielsen, Matthias Hues, Luca Bercovici, Cyndi Pass, Billy "Sly" Williams, Tony Burton; *D:* Steve Barnett.

Mission of the Shark 🎬🎬🎬 1991 A top secret naval mission leads to a scandal-ridden court martial in this true WWII saga, based on the worst sea disaster in naval history. The USS Indianapolis has just completed a secret mission when it is torpedoed by enemy subs. The survivors spend five days in shark-infested waters awaiting rescue and, when the Navy points fingers, the ship's highly decorated and well-respected Captain McVay accepts responsibility for the gooc of the service. Contains some harrowing scenes of sailors versus sharks. *92m/C VHS.* Stacy Keach, Richard Thomas, Steve Landesberg, Carrie Snodgress, Bob Gunton, Andrew Prine, Stacy Keach Sr., Don Harvey; *D:* Robert Iscove. TV

Mission Phantom 🎬 1979 A group of spies on a mission in Russia plans to steal some diamonds and help a woman get to the United States. Dubbed. *90m/C VHS.* Andrew Ray, Ingrid Sholder, Peter Martellan-za; *D:* James Reed.

Mission Stardust 🎬½ 1966 An internationally produced but thoroughly unambitious adaptation of the once-popular Perry Rhodan sci-fi serial in which Rhodan and his team bring ill aliens back to Earth and defend them against evil spies. *90m/C VHS.* 4...3...2...*More* 1968 An internationally produced. *GE T SP Easy Persson*, Gianni Rizzo, Lang Jeffries, Pinkas Braun; *D:* Primo Zeglio.

Mission to Death 🎬 1966 Small American patrol during WWII is beset by numerous attacks on their way to their final destination and each time more members of the unit are wounded or killed. *71m/C VHS, DVD.*

Mission to Glory 🎬🎬 1980 (PG) *The Father* ry of Father Francisco: "Kino" Kin, a tough, 17th-century priest in California who took on the Apaches and murderous Conquistadors in defense of his people. *100m/C VHS, DVD.* Richard Egan, John Ireland, Cesar Romero, Ricardo Montalban, Rory Calhoun, Michael Ansara, Keenan Wynn, Aldo Ray; *D:* Ken Kennedy.

Mission to Mars 🎬½ 2000 (PG) When the first manned flight tc Mars ends in disaster, leaving Commander Luke Graham (Cheadle) as the only survivor, NASA sends a rescue mission consisting of Gra-ham's best friend Jim (Sinise), married astronauts Woody (Robbins) and Terri (Niel-sen), and generic tech guy Phil (O'Connell). On the way to Mars they encounter problems you've seen in other...

---

they find the New Age-y, touchy-feely secrets of creation. DePalma is known for his visual wizardry, and on the element he doesn't display, but the horrible script and indifferent performances undermine whatever it's out. *112m/C VHS, DVD.*

Mission to Venice 🎬🎬 1963 Flynn plays a sleuth attempting to find a missing husband when he accidentally stumbles upon a ring of spies. *88m/C VHS.* Sean Flynn, Madeleine Robinson.

The Missionary 🎬🎬½ 1982 (R) A mild-mannered English missionary returns to London from his work in Africa and is recruited into saving the souls of a group of prostitutes. Aspiring to gentle comedy status, it's often formulaic and flat, with above script level. Still, good for some laughs, particularly during the near classic walking butler sequence. *86m/C VHS, DVD.* Michael Palin, Maggie Smith, Trevor Howard, Denholm Elliott, Michael Hordern; *D:* Richard Loncraine; *W:* Michael Palin. VIDEO

Missionary Man 🎬 2007 (R) Ryder comes into town on his hog and learns that a friend was murdered because he got in the way of John Reno's plans to build a casino on an Indian reservation. So Ryder decides to bring some of that old-time, eye-for-an-eye religion and an case of whup-ass on those evildoers. *92m/C DVD.* Dolph Lundgren, Matthew Tompkins, John Enos, August Schellenberg, James Chalke, Morgana Shaw; *D:* Dolph Lundgren; *W:* Dolph Lundgren, Frank Valdez; *C:* Xiaoling Rao; *M:* Ella Chiral. VIDEO

Mississippi 🎬🎬 1935 In this uneven musical comedy, Philadelphia Yankee Tom Grayson (Crosby) is engaged to southern belle Elvira Rumford (Patrick). But when he refuses to duel one of her other suitors, the engagement is off and he's branded a coward. Tom gets a job singing aboard a riverboat piloted by Commodore Orlando Jackson (Fields) and eventually realizes that his true love is actually Elvira's younger and more sympathetic sister Lucy (Bennett). Fields steals everything that's not nailed down, leaving ostensible star Bing in the dust. Based on the play "Magnolia" by Booth Tarkington. *80m/B DVD.* Bing Crosby, W.C. Fields, Joan Bennett, Gail Patrick, Fred Kohler Sr., Claude Gilling-water, Queenie Smith, John Miljan; *D:* Edward Sutherland; *W:* Francis Martin, Jack Cunningham, Herbert Fields, Claude Binyon; *C:* Charles Lang.

Mississippi Burning 🎬🎬🎬 1988 (R) Hard-edged social drama centers around the civil rights movement in Mississippi in 1964. When three activists turn up missing, FBI agents Anderson (Hackman) and Ward (Dafoe) are sent to head up the investigation. Unfortunately, this is another example of a "serious" film about racial conflict in which white characters predominate and blacks provide background. *127m/C VHS, DVD.* Gene Hackman, Willem Dafoe, Frances McDormand, Brad Dourif, R. Lee Ermey, Gailard Sartain, Stephen Tobolowsky, Michael Rooker, Pruitt Taylor Vince, Badja (Medu) Djola, Kevin Dunn, Frankie Faison, Tom Mason, Park Overall; *D:* Alan Parker; *W:* Chris Gerolimo; *C:* Peter Biziou; *M:* Trevor Jones. Oscars '88: Cinematog; Berlin Intl. Film Fest. '88: Actor (Hackman); Natl. Bd. of Review '88: Actor (Hackman), Director (Parker), Support. Actress (McDormand).

Mississippi Masala 🎬🎬🎬 1992 (R) "Masala" is an Indian seasoning blending different-colored spices, as this film is a blend of romance, comedy, and social conscience. An interracial romance sets off a cultural collision and escalates racial tensions in a small Southern town when Mina, a sheltered young Indian woman, falls in love with Demetrius, an ambitious black man with his own carpet-cleaning business. Washington and Choudhury are engaging as the lovers with Seth, as Mina's unhappy father, especially watchable. *118m/C VHS, DVD.* Denzel Washington, Sarita Choudhury, Roshan Seth...

---

better-done social drama. Once on Mars, they find the New Age-y, touchy-feely secrets of creation. *112m/C VHS, DVD.*

Mrs. 'Arris Goes to Paris 🎬🎬½ 1992 Ada Harris (Lansbury) is a widowed charwoman, living in '50s London, whose one dream is to visit Paris and buy a Christian Dior gown at the designer's own salon. Naturally, her dream comes true—and she even finds a little romance too. Adapted from the Paul Gallico novel; made for TV. *90m/C VHS.* Angela Lansbury, Omar Sharif, Diana Rigg, Lothaire Bluteau, Lila Kaye, John Savident. TV

Mrs. Brown 🎬🎬 1997 (PG) *Her Majesty Mrs. Brown* 1997 (PG) Unusual drama finds Queen Victoria (Dench), bereft by the death of Prince Albert, withdrawing from public life into her Scottish retreat at Balmoral. There she's looked after by coarse highlander John Brown (Connolly), who encourages her to have an interest in life. As he rises in the Queen's esteem, the brash commoner begins to become overly protective of her, leading to whispers of an affair. The powers-that-be, including the Prince of Wales (Westhead) and the oily Prime Minister Disraeli (Sher), then must persuade Brown to withdraw from her company in order to preserve her reputation. Merely hints at what may or may not have been a sexual relationship between the two, but isn't it that the Victorian way? *103m/C VHS, DVD.* Judi Dench, Billy Connolly, Geoffrey Palmer, Anthony Sher, Richard Pasco, Gerard Butler, David Westhead; *D:* John Madden; *W:* Jeremy Brock; *C:* Richard Greatrex; *M:* Stephen Warbeck. British Acad. '97: Actress (Dench), Costume Des.; Golden Globes '98: Actress—Drama (Dench).

Missourians 🎬🎬 1950 Small-town sheriff Hale helps a Polish rancher overcome ethnic prejudice among the townspeople. The situation worsens with the arrival in town of the rancher's outlaw brother. Strong direction and engaging story line. *60m/B VHS.* Roy Barcroft, Lyn Thomas, Lane Bradford, Scott Elliott, Monte Hale, Paul Hurst; *D:* George Blair; *W:* Arthur Orloff; *C:* John MacBurnie; *M:* Stanley Wilson.

Missouri Breaks 🎬🎬🎬 1976 (PG) Thomas McGuane wrote the screenplay for this offbeat tale of Montana ranchers and rustlers fighting over land and livestock in the 1880s. Promising combination of script, cast and director unfortunately yields rather disappointing results, though both Brando and Nicholson chew up scenery to their hearts' content. *126m/C VHS, DVD.* Jack Nicholson, Marlon Brando, Randy Quaid, Kathleen Lloyd, Frederic Forrest, Harry Dean Stanton; *D:* Arthur Penn; *W:* Thomas McGuane; *M:* John Williams.

Missouri Traveler 🎬🎬½ 1956 An orphan boy struggles to get his own farm in Missouri. Family fare based on John Bures' novel. *103m/C VHS, DVD.* Lee Marvin, Gary Merrill, Brandon de Wilde, Paul Ford; *D:* Jerry Hopper; *W:* Norman S. Hall; *C:* Winton C. Hoch; *M:* Jack Marshall.

Mrs. Harris 🎬🎬 2005 Jean Harris (Bening) is the head of a posh girls' school and the longtime mistress of Scarsdale diet doctor Herman Tarnower (Kingsley), a chronic womanizer. The depressed, pill-popping Jean gets fed up and kills her lover, and then endures a sensational trial, which Nagy revisits from both Jean's point of view as a suicide attempt gone wrong or that she committed cold-blooded murder. The cast is fine but the goings-on get tedious. True crime from the 1980s. *94m/C DVD.* Annette Bening, Ben Kingsley, Frances Fisher, Frank Whaley, Cloris Leachman, Chloe Sevigny, Bill Smitrovich, Michael Gross; *Cameos:* Ellen Burstyn; *D:* Phyllis Nagy; *W:* Phyllis Nagy; *C:* Steven Poster; *M:* John (Giann) Frizzell. CABLE

Mrs. Henderson Presents 🎬🎬🎬 2005 (R) The recently widowed Mrs. Henderson (Dench), in an attempt to relieve her own boredom, purchases the rundown 40s London Windmill Theatre in 1930s London. Working her way through the theatre's revitalization, she hires Vivian Van Damm (Hoskins) as the theatre's manager. The two come up with the idea of staging all-nude revues, which are suitably tasteful but still a bit racy for the time. Once World War II breaks out, the story becomes one of British determination to cling to fragile everyday life in the face of the difficulties of war. All told, an interesting look at homefront England. *102m/C DVD.* Judi Dench, Bob Hoskins, Christopher Guest, Kelly Reilly, Will Young, Thelma Barlow; *D:* Stephen Frears; *W:* Martin Sherman; *C:* Andrew Dunn; *M:* George Fenton. Natl. Bd. of Review '05: Cast.

Mrs. Mike 🎬🎬½ 1949 Boston-bred Kathy O'Fallon (Keyes) falls in love with Canadian Mountie Mike Flanigan (Powell) and then finds it hard to adjust to a...

Mississippi Mermaid 🎬🎬🎬 *La Sirene du Mississippi* 1969 (PG) Truffaut generally succeeds in merging his own directorial style with Hitchcockian suspense, but the U.S. release was cut by some 13 minutes and the restored version deserves a re-appraisal. Millionaire tobacco planter Louis (Belmondo) looks for a bride in the personals and finds Julie (Deneuve). Louis feels lucky landing this beauty until she leaves him and takes his money with her. After a breakdown, he finds his wife working in a dance-hall under another name. Louis agrees to a reconciliation, which proves to be a mistake. Look for numerous references to the movies, including Bogart, Balzac and Cocteau. Based on the Cornell Woolrich novel "Waltz into Darkness." French with subtitles. *110m/C VHS, DVD.* FR !T Jean-Paul Belmondo, Catherine Deneuve, Michel Bouquet, Nelly Borgeaud, Marcel Berbert, Martine Ferriere; *D:* Francois Truffaut; *W:* Francois Truffaut; *C:* Denys Clerval; *M:* Antoine Duhamel.

Mississippi Mermaid 🎬🎬🎬 *Le Sirene du Mississippi* 1969 (PG) Truffaut generally succeeds... Shamila Tagore, Charles S. Dutton, Joe Seneca, Ranjit (Chaudry) Chowdhry; *Cameos:* Mira Nair; *D:* Mira Nair; *W:* Sooni Taraporevala; *M:* L. Subramaniam.

Mrs. Brown, You've Got a Lovely Daughter 🎬½ 1968 (G) The Herman's Hermits gang inherits a greyhound and attempts to make a racer out of him while singing their songs. For the Brit group's diehard fans only. "It's Nice To Be Out in the Morning; Ooh, She's Done It Again; Lemon and Lime; The World is for the Young; Holiday Inn; The Most Beautiful Thing in My Life; Daisy Chain; Mrs. Brown, You've Got a Lovely Daughter; There's a King of Hush. *95m/C VHS.* Peter Noone, Stanley Holloway, Mona Washbourne; *D:* Saul Swimmer.

Mrs. Dalloway 🎬🎬🎬½ 1997 (PG-13) Mannered retelling of the Virginia Woolf novel has a radiant performance by Redgrave in the title role. Wealthy, middle-aged, and long-married to boring politician Richard (Standing), Clarissa Dalloway is making preparations for her latest soiree in 1923 London. But the past rudely intrudes when old flame Peter Walsh (Kitchen) suddenly re-enters, causing Clarissa to reflect on her youth and the choices she's made. She's also shaken out of her social ennui by the unexpected sight of a shell-shocked WWI veteran (Graves) whose tragic plight disturbs her placid life. Director Gorris' English-language debut. *97m/C VHS, DVD.* GB Vanessa Redgrave, Michael Kitchen, John Standing, Rupert Graves, Natascha (Natasha) McElhone, Alan Cox, Sarah Badel, Lena Headey, Robert Portal, Amelia Bullmore, Margaret Tyzack, Robert Hardy; *D:* Marleen Gorris; *W:* Eileen Atkins; *C:* Sue Gibson; *M:* Iona Sekacz.

Mrs. Doubtfire 🎬🎬🎬 1993 (PG-13) Williams is an unemployed voiceover actor going through a messy divorce. When his wife gets custody, the distraught father decides to dress up as a woman and become a nanny to his own children. He also trudges when old flame who re-enters his ex-wife's life. Williams schtick extraordinaire with more than a little sugary sentimentality. Based on the British children's book "Madame Doubtfire" by Anne Fine. *120m/C VHS, DVD.* Robin Williams, Sally Field, Pierce Brosnan, Harvey Fierstein, Robert Prosky, Mara Wilson, Paul Guilfoyle, Lisa Jakub, Joey Lawrence, Martin Mull, Polly Holliday; *D:* Chris Columbus; *W:* Randi Mayem Singer, Leslie Dixon; *C:* Donald McAlpine; *M:* Howard Shore. Oscars '93: Makeup; Golden Globes '94: Actor—Mus./Comedy (Williams), Film—Mus./Comedy; MTV Movie Awards '94: Comedic Perf. (Williams).

rural life in Northwest woods. Based on the novel by Benedict and Nancy Freedman. **98m/B VHS.** Evelyn Keyes, Dick Powell, J.M. Kerrigan, Angela (Clark) Clarke, John Miljan; *D:* Louis King; *W:* Alfred Lewis Levitt, DeWitt Bodeen; *C:* Joseph Biroc.

Mrs. Miniver ✓✓✓ **1942** A moving tale of a courageous, gentle middle-class British family and its struggle to survive during WWII. A classic that garnered six Academy Awards, it's recognized for contributions to the Allied effort. Contains one of the most powerful orations in the film history, delivered by Wilcoxon, who portrayed the vicar. Followed by "The Miniver Story." Adapted from Jan Struther's book. **134m/B VHS, DVD.** Greer Garson, Walter Pidgeon, Teresa Wright, May Whitty, Richard Ney, Henry Travers, Reginald Owen, Henry Wilcoxon, Helmut Dantine, Aubrey Mather, Rhys Williams, Tom Conway, Peter Lawford, Christopher Severn, Clare Sandars, Marie De Becker, Connie Leon, Brenda Forbes, John Abbott, Billy Bevan, John Burton, Mary Field, Forrester Harvey, Arthur Wimperis, Ian Wolfe; *D:* William Wyler; *W:* George Froeschel, James Hilton, Claudine West, Arthur Wimperis; *C:* Joseph Ruttenberg; *M:* Herbert Stothart. Oscars '42: Actress (Garson), B&W Cinematog., Director (Wyler), Picture, Screenplay, Support. Actress (Wright).

Mrs. Munck ✓✓ **1995** (R) Creepy cable thriller finds widowed Rose Munck (Ladd) agreeing to care for bitter father-in-law Patrick Leary (Dern, Ladd's real-life ex-hubby), who's suffered a debilitating stroke. But they share a nasty past—seems he seduced a teenaged Rose (played by Preston), she had a child, Patrick refused any responsibility, and the child died. So whacked-out Rose is really out for revenge. Based on a novel by Ella Leffland. Ladd's debut as writer/director. **99m/C VHS.** Diane Ladd, Bruce Dern, Kelly Preston, Shelley Winters; *D:* Diane Ladd; *W:* Diane Ladd; *C:* James Glennon; *M:* Leonard Rosenman. **CABLE**

Mrs. Palfrey at the Claremont ✓✓✓½ **2005** Charming, gentle and somewhat melancholy comedy about the unlikely friendship between a 70-something widow and a 20-something writer. Mrs. Palfrey (Plowright) lives as independently as possible at a London residential hotel for the elderly. She's hoping to become closer to her grandson Desmond (O'Toole), but he doesn't visit. Instead, she literally stumbles into young Ludovic Meyer (Friend), an equally lonely soul. A bond begins that extends to Ludovic passing himself off as the absent grandson to maintain Mrs. Palfrey's pride (which will cause later confusion). An adaptation of the Elizabeth Taylor novel, which was set in the 1950s. This film's budget couldn't stretch to such a re-creation so it was updated to the present, with some awkwardness. **108m/C DVD,** *GB* Joan Plowright, Rupert Friend, Zoe Tapper, Anna Massey, Robert Lang, Marcia Warren, Millicent Martin, Lorcan O'Toole, Anna Carteret; *D:* Dan Ireland; *W:* Ruth Sacks; *C:* Claudio Rocha; *M:* Stephen Barton.

Mrs. Parker and the Vicious Circle ✓✓✓½ *Mrs. Parker and the Round Table* **1994** (R) Bio of witty, suicidal writer Dorothy Parker and her equally witty friends, including theatre critics, playwrights, and novelists, who lunched together at New York's Algonquin Hotel for most of the 1920s. An irreverant band known as the Algonquin Round Table, their numerous bon mots were regularly reported in the papers. Their private lives were often less than happy with alcohol, drug addiction and depression prominent factors. Parker's downward spiral is depressing though compelling to watch, thanks to Leigh's performance (in spite of much criticism for her lockjawed accent) but many of the characters come and go so quickly they make little impression. **124m/C VHS, DVD.** Mina (Badiyi) Badie, Natalie Strong, Jennifer Jason Leigh, Matthew Broderick, Andrew McCarthy, Campbell Scott, Jennifer Beals, Rebecca Miller, Nick Cassavetes, Sam Robards, Gwyneth Paltrow, Wallace Shawn, Martha Plimpton, Tom McGowan, Lili Taylor; *D:* Alan Rudolph; *W:* Rudolph Coburn, Randy Sue Coburn; *C:* Jan Kiesser; *M:* Mark Isham. Natl. Soc. Film Critics '94: Actress (Leigh).

Mrs. Parkington ✓✓½ **1944** Overblown epic drama spanning six decades tells the story of the rise and fall of an American dynasty made on easy money. Garson plays the woman who goes from working as a maid in a boarding house to living a life of luxury when she marries a multimillionaire. This was the fifth pairing of Garson and Pidgeon and although it's not one of their best, it proved to be a big hit with audiences. Lavish costumes and good performances by Garson and Moorehead. Based on the novel by Louis Bromfield. **124m/B VHS.** Greer Garson, Walter Pidgeon, Edward Arnold, Frances Rafferty, Agnes Moorehead, Selena Royle, Gladys Cooper, Lee Patrick; *D:* Tay Garnett; *W:* Robert Thoeren, Polly James; *C:* Joseph Ruttenberg. Golden Globes '45: Support. Actress (Moorehead).

Mrs. R's Daughter ✓✓ **1979** An outraged mother fights the judicial systems in order to bring her daughter's rapist to trial. Based on a true story. **97m/C VHS.** Cloris Leachman, Season Hubley, Donald Moffat, John McIntire, Stephen Elliott, Ron Rifkin; *D:* Dan Curtis. **TV**

Mrs. Santa Claus ✓✓½ **1996** (G) Who better than Lansbury to star as the title character in this sweet TV musical set in 1910. Vivacious Mrs. C is tired of being left home during Santa's (Durning) annual trip and decides to borrow the sleigh for a test drive just before the big day. But bad weather and an injured reindeer force an emergency landing in New York City where she befriends the young sweatshop workers at villainous toy-maker A.P. Tavish's (Mann) factory and does a little matchmaking too. But Mrs. Claus still must make it back to the North Pole by Christmas Eve. ♫Avenue A; Almost Jolly; We Don't Go Together; Suffragette March; He Needs Me. **90m/C VHS, DVD.** Angela Lansbury, Charles Durning, Terrence Harris, Bryan Murray, Lynsey Bartilson, Michael Jeter; *D:* Terry Hughes; *W:* Mark Saltzman; *C:* Stephen M. Katz; *M:* Jerry Herman.

Ms. Scrooge ✓✓½ **1997** (G) Modern-day distaff version of the Dickens Christmas saga. Ebenita Scrooge (Tyson) is a miserly banker but you get the same familiar characters with the Cratchits and Tiny Tim as well as the various ghosts to show Ebenita the errors of her ways. **87m/C VHS.** Cicely Tyson, Katherine Helmond, Michael Beach, John Bourgeois, Arsinee Khanjian, William Greenblatt, Rae'ven (Alyia Larrymore) Kelly, Michael J. Reynolds; *D:* John Korty; *M:* David Shire. **CABLE**

Mrs. Silly ✓ **1985** Romance novel on tape, following the exploits of an aging woman who in losing material wealth, gains contentment. **60m/C** Maggie Smith, James Villiers, Cyril Luckham.

Mrs. Soffel ✓✓½ **1984** (PG-13) Falling in love with a convicted murderer and helping him flee confinement occupies the time of the prison warden's wife. Effectively captures the 1901 setting, yet a dark pall fairly strangles any emotion. Based on a true story. **110m/C VHS, DVD.** Diane Keaton, Mel Gibson, Matthew Modine, Edward Herrmann, Trini Alvarado, Terry O'Quinn, Jennifer (Jennie) Dundas Lowe, Danny Corkill, Maury Chaykin, Dana Wheeler-Nicholson; *D:* Gillian Armstrong; *W:* Ron Nyswaner; *C:* Russell Boyd; *M:* Mark Isham.

Mrs. Wiggs of the Cabbage Patch ✓✓½ **1934** A warm, funny, and altogether overdone story of a mother whose husband abandons her, leaving the woman to raise their four children alone. It's Thanksgiving, so the rich visit the poor household to deliver a turkey dinner, and in the end all live happily ever after. Not one of Fields' larger roles; he doesn't even make an appearance until midway through the schmaltz. **80m/B VHS.** Pauline Lord, Zasu Pitts, W.C. Fields, Evelyn Venable, Donald Meek, Kent Taylor, Charles Middleton; *D:* Norman Taurog; *M:* Val Burton.

Mrs. Winterbourne ✓✓ **1996** (PG-13) Pregnant loser Connie Doyle (Lake) is whisked into the lap of luxury when she's assumed to be the widowed Patricia Winterbourne after a train wreck. The grieving family (who had never met the bride) take her in and accept her and her baby as part of the household. Since her life is now going well, Connie decides to keep her true identity a secret while she falls for faux-brother-in-law Bill (Fraser). MacLaine is brilliant as the spirited matriarch of the family. Retooled as a comedy, the story is actually based on the noirish novel "I Married a Dead Man" by Cornell Woolrich and a remake of the equally dark "No Man of Her Own" from 1950. **106m/C VHS, DVD.** Ricki Lake, Brendan Fraser, Shirley MacLaine, Miguel (Michael) Sandoval, Loren Dean, Susan Haskell, Paula Prentiss; *D:* Richard Benjamin; *W:* Phoef Sutton, Lisa-Marie Radano; *C:* Alex Nepomniaschy; *M:* Patrick Doyle.

The Mist ✓✓✓ **2007** (R) Writer director Frank Derabant adapts Stephen King's short story into what on the surface appears to be a typical horror film, replete with fantastic creatures hell-bent on annihilating anyone or anything in their path. There's also tense drama, which unfolds in the grocery store of a typical Maine town, where locals and tourists are trapped by a thick, malevolent fog that follows after a freak storm. Local commercial artist David Drayton (Jane) and Mrs. Carmody (Harden), a bible-thumping kook, both try to lead the others through the crisis as people begin to crack under the pressure and turn on each other. Andre Braugher is a big-city lawyer, a thoroughly rational outsider who refuses to accept the small town mentality of the citizenry. Ultimately the inhumanity they direct at each other proves to be as great a threat as whatever is in the mist. The ending may be mildly disappointing but the movie is otherwise well done. **125m/C DVD.** *US* Thomas Jane, Marcia Gay Harden, Laurie Holden, Andre Braugher, Toby Jones, William Sadler, Jeffrey DeMunn, Alexa Davalos; *D:* Frank Darabont; *W:* Frank Darabont; *C:* Ronn Schmidt; *M:* Mark Isham.

Mistaken Identity ♪♫ **1936** A swank hotel is the setting for this so-so comedy about three con men who wind up conning each other as much as their supposed victims. A couple of light romances are also thrown in for good measure. **75m/B VHS.** Chick Chandler, Evelyn Knapp, Benton Churchill, Patricia Farr, Richard Carle, Bradley Page, Lew Kelly; *D:* Phil Rosen.

Mistaken Identity ♪♫½ **1999** *Music* **1941** All-black mystery set against the background of a nightclub, and featuring a production number, "I'm a Bangi from Ubangi." **60m/B VHS.** Nellie Hill, George Oliver, Noble Sissle; *D:* George P. Quigley; *W:* Victor Vicas; *C:* John Visconti, George Webster.

Mr. Accident ♪♫½ **1999** (PG-13) Australian director/writer/producer. Accident-prone Roger Crumpkin (Serious) finds out his egg-processing factory boss (Fiels) is planning to produce eggs that will become addicted. No, not to eggs!—to cigarettes! A lame attempt at comedy. **89m/C VHS, DVD.** *AU* Yahoo Serious, David Field, Helen Dallimore, Grant Piro, Jeanette Cronin; *D:* Yahoo Serious; *W:* Yahoo Serious; *C:* Steve Arnold; *M:* Nerida Tyson-Chew.

Mr. Ace ♪♫½ **1946** A congresswoman decides to run for governor without the approval of the loyal political kingpin, Mr. Ace. **85m/B VHS, DVD.** George Raft, Sylvia Sidney, Sara Haden, Stanley Ridges; *D:* Edwin L. Marin; *W:* Fred Finklehoffe; *C:* Karl Struss; *M:* Heinz Roemheld.

Mr. & Mrs. Bridge ✓✓✓✓ **1990** (PG-13) Set in the '30s and '40s in Kansas City, Ivory's adaptation of Evan S. Connell's novels painstakingly portrays an upper middle-class family struggling to survive within an emotional vacuum. Newman and Woodward, together for the first time in many years as Walter and India Bridge, bring a wealth of experience and insight to their characterizations. Many consider this to be Newman's best, most subtle and nuanced performance. **127m/C VHS, DVD.** Joanne Woodward, Paul Newman, Kyra Sedgwick, Blythe Danner, Simon Callow, Dianna McClain, Margaret Welsh, Austin Pendleton, Gale Garnett, Remak Ramsay; *D:* James Ivory; *W:* Ruth Prawer Jhabvala; *C:* Tony Pierce-Roberts; *M:* Richard Robbins. N.Y. Film Critics '90: Actress (Woodward), Screenplay.

Mr. & Mrs. Loving ✓✓✓ **1996** (PG-13) Fact-based movie, set in the 1960s, follows the romance, marriage, and struggle of Richard Loving (Hutton) and Mildred "Bean" Jeter (Rochon). Growing up in rural Virginia, their interracial relationship isn't considered uncommon. But when Bean gets pregnant, they aren't allowed to marry and live together because of Virginia's racial laws. Instead, the Lovings start a letter to the Attorney General's office. What results is young ACLU lawyer Bernie Cohen (Parker) taking on their case—which eventually leads to a landmark Supreme Court decision about miscegenation laws. **95m/C VHS, DVD.** Timothy Hutton, Lela Rochon, Corey Parker, Ruby Dee, Isaiah Washington IV, Bill Nunn, Charles Gray; *D:* Richard Friedenberg; *W:* Richard Friedenberg; *C:* Kenneth Macmillan; *M:* Branford Marsalis. **CABLE**

Mr. & Mrs. Smith ✓✓✓ **1941** Hitchcock's only screwball comedy, an underrated, endearing farce about a bickering but happy modern couple who discover their marriage isn't legitimate and go through courtship all over again. Vintage of its kind, with inspired performances and cracking dialogue. **95m/B VHS, DVD.** Carole Lombard, Robert Montgomery, Gene Raymond, Jack Carson, Lucile Watson, Charles Halton; *D:* Alfred Hitchcock; *W:* Norman Krasna.

Mr. & Mrs. Smith ✓✓✓ **2005** (PG-13) Who knew that pretty people shooting at each other could be so much fun? Director Liman fuses "The War of the Roses" with "The Killer" in this stylish tale of hitman love-gone-wrong. Suburban couple John (Pitt) and Jane (Jolie) are getting bored with their marriage, but they're both hiding a big secret—they're the world's top assassins who unwittingly fell in love and got hitched. When they're assigned to kill each other, every ounce of their simmering martial tensions finds expression through shotguns and dropkicks. The plot wanes and bad guys are ridiculously disposable, but the leads have such palpable on-screen chemistry that you'll find yourself wondering how to discreetly introduce a rocket launcher into your own bedroom. **119m/C DVD, Blu-ray Disc, UMD.** *US* Brad Pitt, Angelina Jolie, Adam Brody, Vince Vaughn, Kerry Washington, Chris Weitz, Keith David, Rachael Huntley; *D:* Doug Liman; *W:* Simon Kinberg; *C:* Bojan Bazelli; *M:* John Powell.

Mr. Arkadin ✓✓✓ *Confidential Report* **1955** Screenwriter, director, star Welles, adapting from his own novel, gave this plot a dry run on radio during early 1950s. Welles examines the life of yet another ruthless millionaire, but this one can't seem to remember the sordid source of all that cash. Investigator Arden follows the intriguing and descending trail to a surprise ending. As in "Citizen Kane," oblique camera angles and layered dialogue prevail, but this time only serve to confuse the story. Shot over two years around Europe, required seven years of post production before finding distribution in 1962. **99m/B VHS, DVD.** *GB* Orson Welles, Akim Tamiroff, Michael Redgrave, Patricia Medina, Robert Arden, Mischa Auer; *D:* Orson Welles; *W:* Orson Welles; *C:* Jean (Yves, Georges) Bourgoin.

Mr. Barrington ✓✓ **2003** Agoraphobic poet Lila (Porter) is at first charmed and then menaced by mysterious neighbor, Mr. Barrington (McArdle). Is this some reflection of her tragic past at St. Agatha's orphanage? Mr. Barrington certain wants to settle some old score and Samuel (Schweig), Lila's supportive husband, decides to investigate so they can overcome the danger. Filmed in Maine. **100m/C DVD.** Eric Schweig, Jonelle Allen, Jennifer Nicole Porter, Brian McArdle; *D:* Dana Packard; *C:* Eric Goldstein.

Mr. Baseball ✓✓ **1992** (PG-13) Washed-up American baseball player tries to revive his career by playing in Japan and experiences cultures clashing under

Mr. Bean's Holiday 🐶🐶 2007
(PG) Love him or hate him, Mr. Bean (Atkinson) has returned for yet another round of lowbrow slapstick. On his way to France for vacation, Mr. Bean manages to lose his wallet and gain a lost child (Baldry), and spends much of the rest of the movie in awkward situations trying to reunite the boy and his father. Plenty of Atkinson's physical gags and base jokes, Title is not much here for non-Bean fans. Title is an homage to Jacques Tati's 1953 comedy "M Hulot's Holiday." **90mC** VHS, **DVD**. **GB** *US* Rowan Atkinson, Emma de Caunes, Willem Dafoe, Jean Rochefort, Max Baldry, Karel Roden, Steve Pemberton; **D:** Steve Bendelack; **W:** Robin Driscoll, Hamish McColl; **C:** Baz Irvine; **M:** Howard Goodall.

Mr. Billion 🐶🐶 1977 (PG) Engaging chase adventure comedy about an Italian mechanic who stands to inherit a billion dollar fortune if he can travel from Italy to San Francisco in 20 days. Hill made his American debut in this film. **89mC/B** VHS, DVD. Jack-ie Gleason, Terence Hill, Valerie Perrine, Slim Pickens, Chill Wills; **D:** Jonathan Kaplan; **W:** Jonathan Kaplan, Ken Friedman; **M:** Dave Grusin.

Mr. Blandings Builds His Dream House 🐶🐶½ 1948 Jim Blandings (Grant), wife Muriel (Loy), and their two daughters must give up their Manhattan apartment for new digs. City boy Jim wants to become a suburbanite and the Blandings decide to build their dream house—with many complications. Timely at its release because of the post-WWII housing shortage and building boom, this classic comedy is still a humorous treat with Grant at his funniest. Loy and Douglas provide strong backup. A must for all homeowners. Based on the novel by Eric Hodgins. **93mB/B** VHS, DVD. Cary Grant, Myrna Loy, Melvyn Douglas, Lex Barker, Reginald Denny, Louise Beavers, Jason Robards Sr.; **D:** H.C. Potter; **W:** Norman Panama, Melvin Frank; **C:** James Wong Howe; **M:** Leigh Harline.

Mr. Brooks 🐶🐶 2007 (R) Costner invests in the bad guy route in this suspense thriller about a serial killer who's the family man next door (if more tightly wound). Earl Brooks is a loving father and husband, a successful businessman, and a philanthropist. If he just didn't have 'that pesky alter-ego, Marshall (Hurt), constantly telling him it's time to kill again. But Brooks makes an uncharacteristic mistake and is seen by Mr. Smith (Cook), who blackmails him into coming along on his next bloody excursion. Detective Tracy Atwood (Moore) is burdened by too many personal issues to be very effective. It's really the Brooks/Marshall show and if you're interested in either/both Costner and Hurt, you'll enjoy yourself. **120mC** DVD, Blu-ray Disc. *US* Kevin Costner, William Hurt, Marg Helgenberger, Demi Moore, Dane Cook, Danielle Panabaker, Reuben Santiago-Hudson, Lindsay Crouse, Jason Lewis, Reiko Aylesworth, Aisha Hinds, Matt Schulze, Michael Cole; **D:** Bruce A. Evans; **W:** Bruce A. Evans, Raynold Gideon; **C:** John Lindey; **M:** Ramin Djawadi.

Mr. Boggs Steps Out 🐶 1938 A pencil-pusher wins a bundle and invests it in a barrel factory. Trouble arises when a slickster tries to close it down. Even with the usual romantic entanglements, it's film has trouble staying interesting. **68mB** VHS, DVD. Stuart Erwin, Helen Chandler, Toby Wing, Tully Marshall, Spencer Charters, Otis Harlan, Walter Byron, Milburn Stone; **D:** Gordon Wiles.

Mr. Corbett's Ghost 🐶🐶 1990 A young man, displeased with his boss's managerial finesse, cuts a deal with a soul collector who pink slips the guy to the great unemployment line in the sky. Once

the ballpark lights. Semi-charmer swings and misses often enough to warrant return to minors. Film drew controversy during production when Universal was bought by the Japanese Matsushita organization and claims of both Japan- and America-bashing were thrown about. **109mC** VHS, DVD. Tom Selleck, Ken Takakura, Toshi Shioya, Dennis Haysbert, Aya Takanashi; **D:** Fred Schepisi; **W:** Gary Ross, Kevin Wade, Monte Merick; **C:** Ian Baker; **M:** Jerry Goldsmith.

Mr. Deeds 🐶½ 2002 (PG-13) With more chutzpah than money (and he's got $40 billion), Sandler plays the must miss Deeds of the joyless remake's title. Longfellow Deeds is an owner of a New Hampshire pizza joint and aspiring greeting card poet (gag) before learning of a multi-billion dollar inheritance that gives him control of the slimy CEO who secretly wants to bayseed Deeds to disappear back to the nonnies, while Ryder is tabloid reporter/love interest Babe Bennett, out to dupe manchild Deeds for a sensational story. Tuturro, as Deeds' sneaky butler is the sole reason to see this. Buscemi does his best Marty Feldman to no avail. Paired with the much-better-by-comparison "Little Nicky," Sandler's schtick is wearing thin. **97mC** VHS, DVD. *US* Adam Sandler, Winona Ryder, John Turturro, Peter Gallagher, Steve Buscemi, Jared Harris, Allen Covert, Erik Avari, Peter Dante, Conchata Ferrell, Harve Presnell, Blake Clark, JB Smoove, Rob Schneider; **Cameos:** John McEnroe; **D:** Steven Brill; **W:** Tim Herlihy; **C:** Peter Lyons Collister; **M:** Teddy Castellucci.

Mr. Deeds Goes to Town 🐶🐶🐶 1936 Typical Capra fare offers Cooper as small town Vermont-er and philanthropic fellow Longfellow Deeds, who inherits $20 million and promptly donates to a courtroom hearing on his sanity. He also manages to find time to fall in love with beautiful reporter and tough cookie, Babe Bennett (Arthur), who's determined to fathom the good guy's motivation. Superior entertainment. Based on the Clarence Budington Kelland's story "Opera Hat." **118mB** VHS, DVD, Gary Cooper, Jean Arthur, Raymond Walburn, Walter Catlett, Lionel Stander, George Bancroft, H.B. Warner, Ruth Donnelly, Douglass Dumbrille, Margaret Seddon, Margaret McWade; **D:** Frank Capra; **W:** Robert Riskin; **C:** Joseph Walker. Oscars '36: Director (Capra); N.Y. Film Critics '36: Film.

Mr. Destiny 🐶🐶 1990 (PG-13) Midlevel businessman Belushi has a mid-life crisis of sorts when his car dies. Wandering into an empty bar, he encounters bartender Caine who serves cocktails and acts omniscient before taking him on the ten-cent tour of life as it would've been if he hadn't struck out in a high school baseball game. Less than a wonderful rehash of "It's a Wonderful Life." **110mC** VHS, DVD. James Belushi, Michael Caine, Linda Hamilton, Jon Lovitz, Bill McCutcheon, Hart Bochner, Rene Russo, Jay O. Sanders, Maury Chaykin, Pat Corley, Douglas Seale, Courtney Cox, Kathy Ireland; **D:** James Orr; **W:** James Orr, Jim Cruickshank.

Mister Drake's Duck 🐶🐶½ 1950 American newlyweds Don (Fairbanks Jr.) and Penny (Donlan) Drake settle down on the English farm that Don has inherited. At a auction, Penny mistakenly buys five dozen ducks, one of which turns out to lay radioactive eggs. Soon the British Army has quarantined the farm and then other branches of the military turn up—all claiming the duck and turning the Drakes' life into chaos. Rather dated, but still amusing, satire on nuclear arms and the military. Based on a play by Ian Messiter. **80mB** VHS, DVD. *GB* Douglas Fairbanks Jr., Yolande Donlan, Reginald Beckwith, Howard Marion-Crawford, Wilfrid Hyde-White, Jon Pertwee, John Boxer, A.E. Matthews; **D:** Val Guest; **W:** Val Guest; **C:** Jack Cox, Harry Gillam; **M:** Bruce Campbell.

Mr. Emmanuel 🐶🐶½ 1944 An elderly Jewish widower leaves his English home in 1935 in quest of the mother of a German refugee boy, and is subjected to shocking treatment in Germany. **97mB** VHS. Felix Aylmer, Greta Gynt, Walter Rilla, Peter Mullins, Ursula Jeans, Elspeth March, Irene Handl; **D:** Harold French; **W:** Gordon Wellesley; **C:** Otto Heller; **M:** Mischa Spoliansky.

Mr. Fix It 🐶🐶½ 2006 (R) Charming romantic comedy. Lance Valentreen (Boreanaz) is a relationship fixer. Lovelorn guys who want to get back the gal who

dumped them come to Lance and he makes like Casanova with said ex. But he breaks their heart and, suddenly, that foreign boyfriend is the greatest guy in the world. Then Lance gets hired by Bob Meredith; **D:** Danny Huston; **C:** Robin Vidgeon; **M:** John Cameron. TV

Mr. Frost 🐶 1989 (R) Goldblum feigns fascination in this lackluster tale of the devil incarnate, who is imprisoned after owning out a series of grisly murders, and who hides his true identity until approached by a woman psychiatrist. **92mC** VHS. Jeff Goldblum, Kathy Baker, Alan Bates, Roland Giraud, Jean-Pierre Cassel; **D:** Philippe Setbon; **M:** Kevin Saunders Hayes.

Mr. Headmistress 🐶🐶½ 1998 Smalltime con man Tucker (Williams) is trying to avoid a couple of thugs out to collect a bad debt when he assumes the identity of the headmistress of the Rawlings Academy for Girls. Seems the school is about to receive a big donation if grades improve and Tucker wants the money. But of course, he learns more than how to walk like a lady along the way. **89mC** VHS. Harland Williams, Katey Sagal, Shawna Waldron; **D:** James Frawley. TV

Mr. Hobbs Takes a Vacation 🐶🐶🐶 1962 Good-natured comedy in which beleaguered parents try to resolve family squabbles while the entire brood is on a couple of thugs out to help resolve family squabbles while the entire brood is on vacation. Stewart and O'Hara are especially fine and their children, as the well-meaning parents. **116mC** VHS. James Stewart, Maureen O'Hara, Fabian, John Saxon, Marie Wilson, John McGiver, Reginald Gardiner; **D:** Henry Koster; **W:** Nunnally Johnson; **M:** Henry Mancini. Berlin Intl. Film Fest. '62.

Mr. Holland's Opus 🐶🐶🐶 1995 (PG) Well-done Disney tearjerker begins in 1965 as musician Glenn Holland (Dreyfuss) takes a teaching job to get himself off the wedding reception circuit and help support his wife, Iris (Headly), and their deadbeat son. Spanning three decades, with actual newsreel footage thrown in to highlight time passing, Holland sets aside his dream of composing a great symphony and finds his true calling—mentoring and inspiring young minds. Holland's son is born deaf might have proved corny, but their rocky relationship is deeply rooted to the storyline. Dreyfuss turns in his most vibrant performance in years and, while sentimental buttons are definitely pushed, director Herek avoids falling into sappiness. **142mC** VHS, DVD. Richard Dreyfuss, Glenne Headly, Jay Thomas, Olympia Dukakis, William H. Macy, Alicia Witt, Jean (Louisa) Kelly, Anthony Natale, Mark Daniels; **D:** Stephen Herek; **W:** Patrick Sheane Duncan; **C:** Oliver Wood; **M:** Michael Kamen.

Mr. Horn 🐶🐶 1979 Slow-paced film about "folk-hero Scott Tom Horn capturing the famous Apache warrior, Geronimo, is average at best. Light-hearted and dine, Richard Widmark, Karen Black, Jeremy Slate, Enrique Lucero, Jack Starrett; **D:** Jack Starrett; **W:** William Goldman.

Mr. Hulot's Holiday 🐶🐶🐶½ Les Vacances de Monsieur Hulot; Monsieur Hulot's Holiday 1953 Superior slapstick details the misadventures of an oblivious bachelor's seaside holiday, where disaster follows his every move. Inventive French comedian Tati at his best. Light-hearted and natural, with magical mime sequences. Followed by "Mon Oncle." French with subtitles. **86mB** VHS, DVD, FR Jacques Tati, Natalie Pascaud, Michelle Rolla; **D:** Jacques Tati; **W:** Jacques Tati, Henri Marquet, Jacques Lagrange, Pierre Aubert; **C:** Jacques Mercanton; **M:** Alain Romans.

Mr. Inside, Mr. Outside 🐶🐶 1974 Two N.Y.C. cops, one undercover, one not, try to infiltrate a tough diamond-smuggling ring. **74mC** VHS. Tony LoBianco, Hal Linden; **D:** Roy Battersby; **M:** Willy Russell.

Mr. Jealousy 🐶🐶½ 1998 (R) When Lester Grimm (Stoltz) was 15, he chickened out on a good night kiss with his girl, and later spied her necking with another boy. Ever since then, he's had this thing about infidelity and he trashes every relationship because of his suspicions. It's no different when he meets the vivacious Ramona (Sciorra), who has recently broken up with arrogant author Dashiell (Eigeman). Lester joins Dashiell's therapy group to spy on his possible competition. Writer-director Baumbach stretches this material by making the characters interesting and the dialogue funny. Fonda's role is a cameo as Dashiell's only witness. No wonder clowns have such bad reps, with flicks like these. **80mC** DVD. *US* Kalil Jensen, Jessica Hall, John Anton, Nathaniel Katcham, Heather Doba, Nicole Majdali; **D:** Tommy Brunswick; **W:** Todd Brunswick; **C:** Todd Erusnewick; **M:** James Scuva.

Mr. Jingles Woof! 2 S.I.C.K. (Serial Insane Clown Killer) 2006 (R) Angie has been in a psych ward for years, ever since the murder of her parents by Mr. Jingles (Gere) is a charmer who gets a rush from tightrope walking a high beam on a construction site, yet is prone to bad moods when he fails to remember his own name. Based on the novel by Joyce Cary. **105mC** VHS, DVD. *US* Michael (Mickey) Lonsdale, Juliet Berwin, Delroy Lindo, Bruce Altman, Lauren Tom; **D:** Joseph Losey; **W:** Franco Solinas; **C:** Gerry Fisher; **M:** Egisto Macchi. Cesar '77: Film.

Mr. Love 🐶🐶½ 1986 (PG-13) A meek gardener's perceived by neighbors as a fool until he dies and numerous women arrive for his funeral. Is it his cologne? The radishes? **91mC** VHS. *GB* Barry Jackson, Maurice Denham, Margaret Tyzack, Linda Marlowe; **D:** Roy Battersby; **M:** Willy Russell.

Mr. Jones 🐶½ 1993 (R) Psychiatrist (Olin) falls in love with her manic-depressive patient (Gere). Head case Mr. Jones (Gere) is a charmer who gets a rush from tightrope walking a high beam on a construction site, yet is prone to bad moods when he fails to remember his own name. He can't resist flirting with the seductive Dr. Bowen, who eagerly leaps past professional boundaries while trying to coax him out of his illness. Wastes the talents of its stars with Gere showy, Olin brittle, and the whole story as contrived as their prefunctory love affair. Psychiatrists are getting as bad a rep professionally as lawyers in their recent film appearances. **110mC** VHS, DVD. Richard Gere, Lena Olin, Anne Bancroft, Tom Irwin, Delroy Lindo, Bruce Altman, Lauren Tom; **D:** Mike Figgis; **W:** Michael Cristofer, Eric Roth; **C:** Juan Ruiz-Anchia; **M:** Maurice Jarre.

Mr. Klein 🐶🐶 1976 (PG) Cleverly plotted script and fine direction in this dark and intense story of French-Catholic art dealer Robert Klein (Delon) who buys valuables from Jews trying to escape Nazi occupied France in 1942, paying far less than what the treasures are worth. Ironically, he is mistaken for another Robert Klein, a Jew who's wanted for anti-Nazi activities. French with subtitles. **122mC** VHS, DVD, FR Alain Delon, Jeanne Moreau, Suzanne Flon, Michael (Mickey) Lonsdale, Juliet Berwin; **D:** Joseph Losey; **W:** Franco Solinas; **C:** Gerry Fisher; **M:** Egisto Macchi. Cesar '77: Film.

Mr. Kingstreet's War 🐶🐶½ 1971 An idealistic game warden and his wife defend the wildlife of Africa against the fighting Italian and British armies at the dawn of WWII. **92mC** VHS. John Saxon, Tippi Hedren, Rossano Brazzi, Brian O'Shaughnessy; **D:** Percival Rubens.

Mister Johnson 🐶🐶🐶 1991 (PG-13) In 1923 Africa, an educated black man working for the British magistrate constantly finds himself in trouble, thanks to backfiring schemes. This highly enjoyable film from the director of "Driving Miss Daisy" suffers only from the underdeveloped opment of the intriguing lead character, Based on the novel by Joyce Cary. **105mC** VHS, DVD. Pierce Brosnan, Edward Woodward, Maynard Eziashi, Beatie Edney, Denis Quilley, Nick Reding; **D:** Bruce Beresford; **W:** Bruce Beresford, William Boyd; **C:** Peter James; **M:** Georges Delerue.

Mister

Mr. Lucky
1943 Likeable wartime drama about a gambler who hopes to swindle a philanthropic organization, but then falls in love and determines to help the group in a fundraising effort. Grant is, no surprise, excellent as the seemingly cynical con artist who actually has a heart of gold. Cliched, but nonetheless worthwhile. 99m/B VHS, DVD. Cary Grant, Laraine Day, Charles Bickford, Gladys Cooper, Paul Stewart, Henry Stephenson, Florence Bates; D: H.C. Potter; C: George Barnes.

Mr. Magoo
1997 (PG) Ah Magoo, we wish you wouldn't have done it again! Live-action version of the cartoon character popular in the '50s and '60s. Elderly myopic millionaire Quincy Magoo (Nielsen) unwittingly comes into possession of a stolen gem that he gives to his bulldog Angus as a toy. Bumbling government agents and evil arch-criminals are after the gem and Magoo, but he avoids them through luck and bad plot devices. Meanwhile, Magoo is mistaking a mummy's sarcophagus for a phone booth, a riverboat paddle wheel for an escalator and...well, you get the idea. Nielsen puts a "Naked Gun" spin on Magoo, and that routine is getting a bit stale. Although criticized by some blind groups as an inaccurate portrayal of the visually challenged, after a very brief run in the theatres, no one was able to see it. Opening and closing sequences include animated Magoo bits. 87m/C VHS, DVD: Leslie Nielsen, Kelly Lynch, Matt Keeslar, Nicholas Chinlund, Ernie Hudson, Malcolm McDowell, Stephen Tobolowsky, Jennifer Garner, Miguel Ferrer; D: Stanley Tong; W: Pat Proft, Tom Sherohman; C: Jingle Ma; M: Michael Tavera.

Mr. Magorium's Wonder Emporium
2007 (G) Mr. Magorium (Hoffman) is the ageless owner of a magic toy store who's gearing up to retire and wants to turn the store over to his manager Mahoney (Portman), who dreams of being a classical pianist. In the meantime, he hires uptight accountant Henry (Bateman) to assess the value of the store (and perhaps find a little magic in himself). An unapologetically whimsical family movie, it has occasional charming moments but mostly leans on its far superior influences ("Pee-Wee's Big Adventure" and "Willie Wonka and the Chocolate Factory," to name a few) for inspiration, and much of the fairy-tale feel seems forced and unoriginal. 94m/C DVD. US Dustin Hoffman, Natalie Portman, Jason Bateman, Zach Mills; D: Zach Helm; W: Zach Helm; C: Roman Osin; M: Aaron Zigman, Alexandre Desplat.

Mister Mean
1977 A man who once worked for a mafia don is now given the task of rubbing him out. For Cosa Nostra diehards and gluttons for Roman scenery. 98m/C VHS. IT Fred Williamson; D: Fred Williamson.

Mr. Mike's Mondo Video
1979 (R) A bizarre, outrageous comedy special declared too wild for TV and conceived by the "Saturday Night Live" alumnus Mr. Mike. 75m/C VHS. Michael O'Donoghue, Dan Aykroyd, Jane Curtin, Carrie Fisher, Teri Garr, Joan Haskett, Deborah Harry, Margot Kidder, Bill Murray, Laraine Newman, Gilda Radner, Julius LaRosa, Paul Shaffer, Sid Vicious; W: Mitch Glazer.

Mr. Majestyk
1974 (PG) When a Vietnam veteran's attempt to start an honest business is thwarted by Mafia hitmen and the police, he goes after them with a vengeance. Based on Leonard's novel (he also did the screenplay). 103m/C VHS, DVD. Charles Bronson, Al Lettieri, Linda Cristal, Lee Purcell; D: Richard Fleischer; W: Elmore Leonard; M: Charles Bernstein.

Mr. Mom
1983 (PG) Tireless auto exec Jack (Keaton) loses his job and stays home with the kids while his wife Caroline (Garr) becomes the breadwinner. He's forced to cope with the rigors of housework and child care, resorting to drugs, alcohol and soap operas. Keaton's hilarious as the homebound dad chased by killer appliances and poker buddy to the ladies in the neighborhood. 92m/C VHS, DVD: Jeffrey Tambor, Michael Keaton, Teri Garr, Christopher Lloyd, Martin Mull, Ann Jillian, Edie McClurg, Valri Bromfield; D: Stan Dragoti; W: John Hughes; C: Victor Kemper; M: Lee Holdridge.

Mr. Moto in Danger Island
1939 Mr. Moto (Lorre) is after diamond smugglers (this sounds familiar) in Puerto Rico and is aided by wrestler Twister McGurk (Hymer). 7th in the series. 80m/B DVD. Peter Lorre, Warren Hymer, Jean Hersholt, Richard Lane, Amanda Duff, Leon Ames, Douglass Dumbrille, Charles D. Brown; D: Peter Milne; W: Herbert I. Leeds; C: Lucien N. Andriot; M: Samuel Kaylin.

Mr. Moto Takes a Chance
1938 Mr. Moto (Lorre), who also works for an international police agency, is told to destroy an armory hidden by a fanatical priest (Regas) in the jungles of Cambodia while also foiling anti-government plots against the French. He's helped by aviatrix (and fellow agent) Vicki Mason (Hudson) as well as a couple of fumbling newsreel photographers. 4th in the series. 63m/B DVD. Peter Lorre, Rochelle Hudson, Robert Kent, Chick Chandler, George Regas, J. Edward Bromberg, Frederick Vogeding; D: Norman Foster; W: Lou Breslow, John Patrick; C: Virgil Miller; M: Samuel Kaylin.

Mr. Moto's Gamble
1938 Mr. Moto (Lorre) is teaching a class for would-be sleuths and one of his students is Charlie Chan's son, Lee (Luke), who helps out when Moto investigates the murder of a boxer during a fight. Originally intended as a Charlie Chan film that was already in production, the script was rewritten because of Warner Oland's health problems and doesn't quite fit the other Moto adventures. 3rd in the series. 72m/B DVD. Peter Lorre, Keye Luke, Maxie "Slapsie" Rosenbloom, Lynn Bari, Dick Baldwin, Douglas Fowley, Jayne Regan, Harold Huber, Ward Bond, Lon Chaney Jr.; D: James Tinling; W: Charles Belden, Jerome Cady; C: Lucien N. Andriot; M: Samuel Kaylin.

Mr. Moto's Last Warning
1939 One of the better in the series of Mr. Moto, the wily detective! Lorre is convincing in the title role and gets good support from character villains Carradine and Sanders in this story of saboteurs converging on the Suez Canal plotting to blow up the French Fleet. 71m/B VHS, DVD. Peter Lorre, George Sanders, Ricardo Cortez, John Carradine, Virginia Field, Robert Coote; D: Norman Foster.

Mr. Muggs Rides Again
1945 The East Side Kids (think Dead End Kids, the Bowery Boys and the rest of their ilk) are featured in a horseracing adventure. Honest jockey Muggs (Gorcey) is framed by gamblers and barred from the track but must still find a way to save the horse farm of Ma Brown (Urecal) from foreclosure. 63m/B VHS. Leo Gorcey, Minerva Urecal, Huntz Hall, William Benedict, John Duncan, Buddy Gorman, Nancy Brinckman, Mende Koenig; D: Wallace Fox; W: Harvey Gates; C: Ira Morgan.

Mr. Music
1950 Crosby is a successful songwriter who would rather enjoy life on the golf course than pen any more tunes. He's persuaded by his secretary to help out an old-time producer who's fallen on hard times by writing a new Broadway show. Light-hearted fluff. Based on the play "Accent on Youth" by Samson Raphaelson which had been filmed in 1935. ♫Life is So Precious; Accidents Will Happen; High on the List; Wouldn't It Be Funny; Wasn't I There?; Mr. Music; Once More the Blue and White; Milady; Then You'll Be Home. 113m/B VHS. Bing Crosby, Nancy Olson, Charles Coburn, Robert Stack, Tom Ewell, Ruth Hussey, Charles Kemper, Donald Woods, Gower Champion, Marge Champion; Cameos: Groucho Marx, Peggy Lee; D: Richard Haydn.

Mr. Nanny
1993 (PG) For those who fear change, this predictable plot should serve as comforting assurance that Hollywood will still sacrifice substance for the quick buck. Basic storyline has the child-hating Hulkster playing nanny/bodyguard to a couple of bratty kids. Meanwhile, his arch rival (Johansen) hatches a scheme to gain world dominance by kidnapping the kids for the ransom of their father's top secret computer chip. Never fear—in this world, the good guys kick butt, naturally, and everyone learns a lesson. 85m/C VHS, DVD. Hulk Hogan, Sherman Hemsley, Austin Pendleton, Robert Gorman, Madeline Zima, Mother Love, David Johansen; D: Michael Gottlieb; W: Ed Rugoff, Michael Gottlieb; M: David Johansen, Brian Koonin.

Mr. Nice Guy
1986 (PG-13) In the near future, a hired gun strives for national recognition as the best of his now legitimate profession. Comedy with few laughs. 92m/C VHS. Jan Smithers, Joe Silver; D: Henry Wolford; W: Michael MacDonald, Henry Wolford; C: Leonard Smolsky; M: Paul Hoffert.

Mr. Nice Guy
1998 (PG-13) Jackie Chan brings another installment of his Bruce Lee-meets-Charlie Chaplin action adventure shenanigans to the screen. This time he plays a TV cooking show host who gets into boiling water when he saves a female reporter (Fitzpatrick) who has videotaped a drug deal. He ends up with the videotape, so reptilian bad guy Giancarlo (Norton) sends his lackeys out to chop-suey Jackie, though they turn out to be boneless chickens. The high action/low talk meter is cranked up in this outing, due to the fact that it's Chan's first movie filmed primarily in English (although it was still produced in Hong Kong). The plot seems to have been chopped up a bit while travelling over the Pacific, but Chan fans are well aware that the whirling dervish stunts are more important than a silly old story anyway. 90m/C VHS, DVD. HK Jackie Chan, Richard Norton, Gabrielle Fitzpatrick, Miki Lee, Karen McLymont, Vince Poletto, Barry Otto, Sammo Hung; D: Sammo Hung; W: Edward Tang, Fibe Ma; C: Raymond Lam; M: J. Peter Robinson.

Mr. North
1988 (PG) Capracorn fable about a charming, bright Yale graduate who encounters admiration and disdain from upper-crust Rhode Island residents when news of his miraculous "cures" spreads. Marks the directorial debut of Danny Huston, son of John Huston, who co-wrote the script and served as executive producer before dying several weeks into shooting. Set in the 1920s and adapted from Thornton Wilder's "Theophilus North." 90m/C VHS, DVD. Anthony Edwards, Robert Mitchum, Lauren Bacall, Harry Dean Stanton, Anjelica Huston, Tammy Grimes, David Warner, Virginia Madsen, Christopher Durang, Mark Metcalf, Katharine Houghton, Christopher Lawford; D: Danny Huston; W: John Huston, Janet Roach, James Costigan; C: Robin Vidgeon; M: David McHugh.

Mr. Peabody & the Mermaid
1948 Lightweight fish story about a middle-aged married man who hooks a beautiful mermaid while fishing in the Caribbean and eventually falls in love with her. Powell is smooth as always, though hampered by the unrealistic, strained absurdity of it all. Based on the novel by Guy and Constance Jones. Also available colorized. 89m/B VHS. William Powell, Ann Blyth, Irene Hervey, Andrea King, Clinton Sundberg, Art Smith; D: Irving Pichel; W: Nunnally Johnson.

Mr. Reeder in Room 13
1938 Based on the mystery stories created by Edgar Wallace, Mr. Reeder (Kellaway), a cultured English gentleman who fights crime) enlists the aid of a young man to find evidence on a gang of counterfeiters. 66m/B VHS. GB Gibb McLaughlin, Sally Gray, Malcolm Keen, Peter Murray-Hill, Leslie Perrins, D.J. Williams, Robert Cochran; D: Norman Lee; W: Victor Kendall, Doreen Montgomery; C: Eric Cross.

Mr. Reliable: A True Story
1995 (R) A "truth is stranger than fiction" comedy about Australia's first hostage situation. During the summer of 1968, recently released car thief Wally Mellish (Friels) rents a rundown cottage in a Sydney suburb. He finds a girlfriend in Beryl Muddle (McKenzie), who moves in with her two-year-old daughter. When Wally steals some trifles to brighten up the place, the cops come 'round and Wally, who's still on probation, pulls a gun. The authorities think Beryl and the baby are hostages and are afraid to storm the cottage while the standoff becomes hot media news. Wally and Beryl are thrilled with the attention but there's increasing political pressure to put an end to the farcical situation. 112m/C VHS. AU Colin Friels, Jacqueline McKenzie, Paul Sonkkila, Frank Gallacher, Barry Otto, Lisa Hensley, Ken Radley, Neil Fitzpatrick; D: Nadia Tass; W: Terry Hayes, Don Catchlove; C: David Parker; M: Phil Judd.

Mr. Rice's Secret
2000 (PG) Mysterious Englishman Mr. Rice (Bowie) lives next door to 13-year-old Owen (Switzer), who has cancer. He's struggling but Mr. Rice offers words of wisdom (that come from the fact he's lived hundreds of years). When Mr. Rice suddenly does die, it's not before letting Owen in on some posthumous life-saving secrets. 113m/C VHS, DVD. CA David Bowie, Garwin Sanford, Bill Switzer, Teryl Rothery; D: Nicholas (Nick) Kendall; W: J.H. Wyman; C: Gregory Middleton; M: Simon Kendall, Al Rodger.

Mister Roberts
1955 Crew of a Navy cargo freighter in the South Pacific during WWII relieves the boredom of duty with a series of elaborate practical jokes, mostly at the expense of their long-suffering and slightly crazy captain, who then determines that he will get even. The ship's cargo officer, Mr. Roberts, longs to be transferred to a fighting vessel and see some action. Originally a hit Broadway play (based on the novel by Thomas Heggen) which also featured Fonda in the title role. Great performance from Lemmon as Ensign Pulver. Powell's last film. Sequelled in 1964 by "Ensign Pulver," and later a short-lived TV series as well as a live TV special. Newly transferred in 1988 from a pristine stereo print. 120m/C VHS, DVD. Henry Fonda, James Cagney, Jack Lemmon, William Powell, Betsy Palmer, Ward Bond, Harry Carey Jr., Nick Adams, Phil Carey, Ken Curtis, Martin Milner, Jack Pennick, Perry Lopez, Patrick Wayne, Tige Andrews, William Henry; D: John Ford, Mervyn LeRoy; W: Frank Nugent, Joshua Logan, Thomas Heggen; C: Winton C. Hoch; M: Franz Waxman. Oscars '55: Support. Actor (Lemmon).

Mr. Rock 'n' Roll: The Alan Freed Story
1999 In the early 1950s, Cleveland disc jockey Alan Freed (Nelson) decides to play the newfangled rock 'n' roll on his station, where it becomes an immediate hit and an immediate controversy. Freed's success takes him to New York and further celebrity but career missteps lead to the payola scandal and his eventual disgrace. Original recordings are used and they turn out to be the most exciting thing about this TV movie. Based on the book by John A. Jackson. 91m/C VHS. Judd Nelson, Madchen Amick, Leon, Paula Abdul; Cameos: Bobby Rydell, Fabian; D: Andy Wolk; W: Matt Dorff; C: Derick Underschultz. TV

Mr. Robinson Crusoe
1932 Rollicking adventure in the South Seas as Fairbanks makes a bet that he can live on a desert island for a year without being left any refinements of civilization. Lucky for him, a woman arrives. Also written by Fairbanks. 76m/B VHS, DVD. Douglas Fairbanks Sr., William Farnum, Maria Alba, Earle Brown; D: Edward Sutherland; W: Douglas Fairbanks Sr.; M: Alfred Newman.

Mr. St. Nick
2002 Agreeable Christmas comedy with a little twist. It seems that being Santa is a family business—each St. Nick gets 100 years on the job. The current Santa (Durning) should be settling into retirement and leaving things to Santa Jr. (Grammer) soon, but Junior's been waiting so long that he's more bah-humbug than ho-ho-ho. So, it's

about time that he learned the true meaning of the holiday. 100m/C DVD. Kelsey Grammer, Charles Durning, Katherine Helmond, Brian Bedford, Elaine Hendrix, Lupe Ontiveros, Wallace Shawn, Ara Ortiz. **D:** Craig Zisk; **W:** Maryedith Burrell, Steve Hayes, Debra Frank; **C:** David Franklin. Cameos: Taylor Negron, Ron Perlman, Nia Peeples. **D:** John Amiel. **TV**

Mr. Sardonicus ✓✓ *Sardonicus* **1961** Tidy little horror film finds the title character's (Rolfe) face frozen in a hideous grin after being cursed for stealing a winning lottery ticket from his father's corpse. Sardonicus has been experimenting with solutions to his problem (each more disgusting than the last) and finally forces ne.rosurgeon, Sir Robert Cargrave (Lewis), to assist him with his dilemma. 89m/B VHS, DVD. Guy Rolfe, Ronald Lewis, Oscar Homolka, Audrey Dalton, Vladimir Sokoloff. **D:** William Castle; **W:** Ray Russell; **C:** Burnett Guffey.

Mr. Saturday Night ✓✓✓½ **1992** (R) Crystal, in his directorial debut, stars as Buddy Young Jr., a self-destructive comedian whose career spans five decades. His nasty one-liners and witty jokes combine with poignancy in this satisfying comedy/drama. Paymer is excellent as Young's long-suffering, faithful brother and manager. Watch for Lewis in a cameo role. Expectations were very high and the boxoffice results were disappointing, but fans of Crystal shouldn't miss this one. 118m/C VHS, DVD, Billy Crystal, David Paymer, Julie Warner, Helen Hunt, Mary Mara, Jerry Orbach, Ron Silver, Sage Allen, Jackie Gayle, Carl Ballantine, Slappy (Melvin) White, Conrad Janis, Jerry Lewis. **D:** Billy Crystal; **W:** Babaloo Mandel, Lowell Ganz, Billy Crystal; **C:** Burnett Guffey; **M:** Marc Shaiman.

Mr. Scarface ✓✓½ **1977** (R) A young man searches for the man who murdered his father years earlier in a dark alley. 85m/C VHS, DVD. Jack Palance, Edmund Purdom, 4. Oliver, Harry Baer, Gisela Hahn; **D:** Fernando Di Leo.

Mr. Skeffington ✓✓✓ **1944** A super-grade soap opera spanning 26 years in the life of a ravishing, spoiled New York socialite. The beauty with a fondness for bedrooms marries for convenience, abuses her husband, then enjoys a highly equitable divorce settlement. Years later when cynthenia leaves her totally deformed and no man will have her, she is saved by her former husband. Based on the novel by "Elizabeth" (Mary Annette Beauchamp Russell) and adapted by "Casablanca's" Julius and Philip Epstein. 147m/B VHS, DVD. Bette Davis, Claude Rains, Walter Abel, Richard Waring, George Coulouris, John Alexander. **D:** Vincent Sherman.

Mr. Skitch ✓✓ **1933** Weak Rogers offering. Couple loses their farm and begins cross country jaunt with mishaps at every tuTl. All ends well when their daughter meets an Army cadet, but few laughs and lots of loose ends. 70m/B VHS. Will Rogers, Zasu Pitts, Rochelle Hudson, Charles Starrett. **D:** James Cruze.

Mr. Smith Goes to Washington ✓✓✓✓ **1939.** Another classic from Hollywood's golden year of 1939. Jimmy Stewart is an idealistic and naive young man selected to fill in for an ailing Senator. Upon his arrival in the Capitol, he is inundated by a multitude of corrupt politicians. He takes a stand for his beliefs and tries to denounce many of those he feels are unfit for their positions, meeting with opposition from all sides. Great cast is highlighted by Stewart in one of his most endearing performances. Quintessential Capra tale sharply adapted from Lewis Foster's story. Outstanding in every regard. 130m/B VHS, DVD. James Stewart, Jean Arthur, Edward Arnold, Claude Rains, Thomas Mitchell, Beulah Bondi, Eugene Pallette, Guy Kibbee, Harry Carey Sr., H.B. Warner, Porter Hall, Jack Carson, Charles Lane. **D:** Frank Capra; **W:** Sidney Buchman; **M:** Dimitri Tiomkin. Oscars '39: Story. AFI '98: Top 100. Natl. Film Reg. '89; N.Y. Film Critics '39: Actor (Stewart).

Mr. Stitch ✓ **1995** (R) Demented scientist (!-Lauer) plays Frankenstein and makes a creature, named Lazarus (Wheaton), from the body parts of more than 80 men and women. Unfortunately, the sensitive Lazarus has retained the collective memories of all these people and becomes obsessed with finding the reason for his existence. He receives compassion from a shrink (Peeples) but his maker has enlisted a Japanese soldier to be held hostage to discover that his nemesis is now dating his mother Beverly (Sarandon). Vulgar jokes, slapstick, and cruel antics ensue. Thornton plays a character he's played a million times before, while Scott serves up a meltdown of epic proportions, all leading up to a contrived happy ending that makes any legitimate bite the movie had ring false. Everyone involved should overcome first, including her dim bulb boyfriend and obnoxious father. Adapted from the play by Howard J. Morris.

Mr. Superinvisible ✓✓ **1973** (G) Searching to cure the common cold, a bumbling scientist invents a bizarre virus, then strives to at otherwise banal flag-waving comedy that is based on a novel by Theodore Pratt. 80m/B VHS, Edward G. Robinson, Ruth Warrick, Richard Gaines, Robert Armstrong, Ted Donaldson. 90m/C VHS, IT GE SP Dean Jones, Ingeborg (Inge) Schoener, Gastone Moschin. **D:** Anthony M. Dawson.

Mr. Sycamore ✓✓½ **1974** A sappy mail carrier escapes his badgering wife by sprouting into a tree. A potentially whimsical piece that wilts. 85m/C VHS. Jason Robards Jr., Jean Simmons, Sandy Dennis; **D:** Pancho Kohner; **M:** Maurice Jarre.

Mr. 3000 ✓✓½ **2004** (PG-13) Lackluster sports comedy follows egotistical Milwaukee Brewers star Stan Ross (Mac), who abruptly quit the team as soon as he got his 3,000 hit. His comfy retirement of 10 years is interrupted when an old record-keeping error is corrected, revealing that Stan only has 2,997 career hits. So, the 47-year-old decides to come back long enough to get those missing hits. He must contend with resentful younger teammates, numerous strikeouts, the accompanying ridicule, and Mo, his beautiful former flame who's now a reporter for ESPN covering his comeback. Mac and Bassett have a lot of charm together but much of the film is predictable, and the on-field action lacks any urgency. 104m/C VHS, DVD. Bernie Mac, Angela Bassett, Michael Rispoli, Evan Jones, Dondre T. Whitfield, Paul Sorvino, Brian J. White, Ian Anthony Dale, Amaury Nolasco; Cameos: Tom Arnold, John Salley; **D:** Charles Stone III; **W:** Eric Champnella, Keith Mitchell; **C:** Shane Hurlbut; **M:** John Powell.

Mr. Toad's Wild Ride ✓✓ *The Wind in the Willows* **1996** (PG) Kenneth Grahame's 1908 children's book gets the Monty Python treatment. Set in Edwardian England, but with a definitely modern slant, Jones' adaptation removes much of the gentle whimsy and replaces it with Python skits. Mole (Coogan) wakes up one day to find his home being bulldozed by the industrialist weasels who have purchased the property from the motorcar-infatuated Mr. Toad (Jones). Toad keeps selling more land to buy more cars as his weasels take over the area and Toad is sent to jail for reckless driving. Mole, along with friends Rat (Idle) and Badger (Williamson) must help him escape and reclaim his land. Grahame's early 20th century fable railing against modern industrialism's encroachment on the countryside becomes a satire on '90s consumerism and corporate greed. Mighty heady stuff for a kid's movie. 88m/C VHS, DVD, GB Terry Jones, Steve Coogan, Eric Idle, Antony Sher, Nicol Williamson, John Cleese, Stephen Fry, Bernard Hill, Michael Palin, Nigel Planer, Julia Sawalha, Victoria Wood, Richard James; **D:** Terry Jones; **W:** Terry Jones.

Mr. Vampire ✓✓ **1986** Undertaker Uncle Kau (Ying) is also a master vampire hunter—necessary when your town is under siege from a vampire army who can make new converts with a single bite. Vampire movie with a Chinese twist combines elements of both comedy and horror, presenting a vampire who comes closer to resembling a corpse, who, when not levitating, hops like a bunny. Chinese with subtitles or dubbed. 99m/C VHS, DVD, CH Wong; **D:** Ricky Lau; **M:** Roy Szeto; **C:** Peter Ngor, Moon Lee, Ching-Ying Lam, Ricky Hui, Pauline Wong.

Mr. Walkie Talkie ✓✓ **1952** Tired of a sergeant's jabber-jaws, a soldier requests to be relocated to the front lines, only to find his catty comrade has followed. Set during the Korean War and

featuring some truly amusing escapades set between the lulls in the war. 65m/B VHS. William Tracy, Joseph (Joe) Sawyer, Margia Dean, Robert Shayne, Alan Hale Jr., Russell Hicks; **D:** Fred Guiol; **W:** George Carleton Brown, Edward E. Seabrook; **C:** Walter Strenge; **M:** Leo Klatzkin.

Mr. Winkle Goes to War ✓✓ *Arms and the Woman* **1944** A weak, nerdy former banker is drafted for service during WWII and proves himself a hero by bulldozing a Japanese foxhole. Bits of genuine war footage add a measure of realism to an otherwise banal flag-waving comedy that is based on a novel by Theodore Pratt. 80m/B VHS, Edward G. Robinson, Ruth Warrick, Richard Gaines, Robert Armstrong, Ted Donaldson. **D:** Alfred E. Green; **W:** Waldo Salt, Louis Solomon; **C:** Joseph Walker; **M:** Paul Sawtell, Carmen Dragon.

Mr. Wise Guy ✓✓ **1942** The East Side Kids break out of reform school to clear one of the kids' brother of a murder charge. Typical pre-Bowery Boys vehicle. 70m/B VHS, DVD. Billy Gilbert, Guinn "Big Boy" Williams, Benny Rubin, Douglas Fowley, Ann Doran, Jack Mulhall, Warren Hymer, David Gorcey; **D:** William Nigh.

Mr. Wonderful ✓✓ **1993** (PG-13) Bittersweet (rather than purely romantic) look at love and romance. Divorced Con Ed worker Gus (Dillon) is hard up for cash and tries to marry off ex-wife Lee (Sciorra) so he can use her for alimony to invest in a bowling alley with his buddies. Routine flick's saved by the cast, who manage to bring a small measure of believability to a transparent plot. This was director Minghella's sophomore effort, between "Truly, Madly, Deeply" and "The English Patient." 99m/C VHS, DVD. James Gandolfini, Bruce Kirby, Jessica Harper, Bruce Altman, Paul Bates, Matt Dillon, Annabella Sciorra, William Hurt, Mary-Louise Parker, Luis Guzman, Dan Hedaya, Vincent D'Onofrio; **D:** Anthony Minghella; **W:** Amy Schor, Vicki Folon; **C:** Geoffrey Simpson; **M:** Michael Gore.

Mr. Wong, Detective ✓✓ **1938** The first in the Mr. Wong series, the cunning detective traps a killer who feigns guilt to throw suspicion away from himself. The plot is loaded with the usual twists and villains. However, Karloff is a standout. 69m/B VHS, DVD. Boris Karloff, Grant Withers, William Royle, Maxine Reynolds, Evelyn Brent, Lucien Prival; **D:** William Nigh; **W:** Houston Branch; **C:** Harry Neumann.

Mr. Wong in Chinatown ✓✓½ **1939** Third of the Mr. Wong series finds James Lee Wong investigating the murder of a wealthy Chinese woman. She had been helping to fund the purchase of airplanes to equip China in its 1930s struggle with Japan. 70m/B VHS, DVD. Boris Karloff, Grant Withers, William Royle, Marjorie Reynolds, Peter George Lynn, Lotus Long, Richard Loo; **D:** William Nigh.

Mr. Woodcock ✓✓½ **2007** (PG-13) Thornton plays yet another misanthropic, nasty tormentor of kids, this time as the world's nastiest (and most unfortunately named) gym teacher, Mr. Woodcock. Former student John (Scott) has turned his childhood trauma at Woodcock's hands into a self-help book, and he returns home to discover that his nemesis is now dating his mother Beverly (Sarandon). Vulgar jokes, slapstick, and cruel antics ensue. Thornton plays a character he's played a million times before, while Scott serves up a meltdown of epic proportions, all leading up to a contrived happy ending that makes any legitimate bite the movie had ring false. Everyone involved should have been taught to use the spices turn on Tilo (and her clients), make some money by acting in commercials. He falls for ad exec Nicole (Tuck) but there are some complications to be overcome first, including her dim bulb boyfriend and obnoxious father. Adapted from the play by Howard J. Morris. 88m/C VHS.

Mr. Write ✓ **1992** (PG-13). Modest advertising satire mixed with romance. Aspiring writer Charlie (Reiser) decides to make some money by acting in commercials. He falls for ad exec Nicole (Tuck) but there are some complications to be overcome first, including her dim bulb boyfriend and obnoxious father. Adapted from the play by Howard J. Morris. 88m/C VHS. Paul Reiser, Jessica Tuck, Doug Davidson, Martin Mull, Wendie Jo Sperber, Eddie Barth, Darryl M. Bell, Thomas F. Wilson, Jane Leeves, Calvert DeForest, Ben Stein; **D:** Charles Loventhal; **W:** Howard J. Morris; **C:** Elliot Davis.

Mr. Wrong ✓✓ **1995** (PG-13) In her feature film debut, DeGeneres plays Martha, a 30-something single woman with wacky friends who's being pressured by parents toward marriage while having little luck in the dating scene. Hmm... sounds familiar. Pullman plays Whitman, her dreamboat who quickly turns into the Titanic. Along the relationship road to ruin she's forced to deal with bad poetry, charades and...gum in her hair! The usually entertaining DeGeneres is given little to do on around her. Those that have had an experience with "the ex that would not go away" might want to rent something more calming, such as "Psycho." 97m/C VHS. DVD. Ellen DeGeneres, Bill Pullman, Joan Cusack, Dean Stockwell, Joan Plowright, John Livingston, Robert Goulet, Ellen Cleghorne, Brad Henke, Polly Holliday, Briant Wells; **D:** Nick Castle; **W:** Chris Matheson, Kerry Ehrin, Craig Munson; **C:** John Schwartzman; **M:** Craig Safan.

Mistral's Daughter ✓✓½ **1984** Frothy miniseries, based on the Judith Krantz novel, about a French artist and his relationship with three beautiful women. Formulaic TV melodrama offers several scenes and revealing glimpses. Produced-like other Krantz miniseries, by author's husband, Steve. 390m/C VHS. Stefanie Powers, Lee Remick, Stacy Keach, Robert Urich, Timothy Dalton; **D:** Douglas Hickox; **M:** Vladimir Cosma. **TV**

Mistress *Wild Geese* **1953** A classic Japanese period piece about an innocent woman who believes she's married to a ruthless industrialist, only to find he is already married and she is but his mistress. Her love for a medical student unleashes tragedy. Subtly moving in a low-key way starkly beautiful in black and white. In Japanese, with English subtitles. 106m/B VHS. JP Hideko Takamine, Hiroshi Akutagawa; **D:** Shiro Toyoda.

Mistress ✓✓½ **1987** Weepy melodrama about a woman who makes a living as a mistress. When her lover dies, she must learn to stand on her own two feet. 96m/C VHS. Victoria Principal, Alan Rachins, Don Murray; **D:** Michael Tuchner; **M:** Michael Convertino. **TV**

Mistress ✓✓ **1991** (R) A weak script goes in a formidable cast in a behind-the-scenes look at movie making. Wuhl plays Marvin Landisman, a failed director/screenwriter, who's approached by has-been producer Jack Roth (Landau) who says he's found a backer to finance a movie from one of Marvin's old scripts. It turns out Roth has three men (De Niro, Aiello, and Walach) ready to finance the film as long as each of their mistresses, who all have acting ambitions, gets the starring role. Double-dealing at a bargain basement level sets up the rest of this little comedy. 100m/C VHS, DVD. Robert Wuhl, Martin Landau, Robert De Niro, Danny Aiello, Sheryl Lee Ralph, Jean Smart, Tuesday Weld, Jace Alexander, Laurie Metcalf, Christopher Walken, Ernest Borgnine; **D:** Barry Primus; **W:** J.F. Lawton, Barry Primus; **C:** Sven Kirsten; **M:** Galt MacDermot.

The Mistress of Spices ✓✓½ **2005** Beautiful but remarkably inert attempt at magical realism. Tilo (Rai) has second sight and has been taught to use the magic of various spices to help others. She emigrates from India and opens a spice shop in Oakland, but there are three severe restrictions she must follow: she can't use the spices for personal gain; she can't touch the skin of another human being; and she can't ever leave the shop. Tilo seems okay with all this until shortly outside. She helps him, he helps her, and the spices turn on Tilo (and her clients). Although it hardly seems fair that anyone as luscious as Rai should be held back by saffron (which attracts love by the way). 95m/C DVD. US GB Aishwarya Rai, Dylan McDermott, Ayesha Dharker, Nitin Ganatra, Anupam Kher; Adewale Akinnuoye-Agbaje, Sonny Gill Dulay, Padma Lakshmi; **D:** Paul Mayeda Berges; **W:**

Paul Mayeda Berges, Gurinder Chadha; **C:** Santosh Sivan; **M:** Craig Pruess.

Mistress of the Apes woof!

1979 (R) A woman searches for her missing husband in Africa with a group of scientists and discovers a tribe of near-men, who may be the missing link in evolution (or perhaps, a professional football team). Into their little group she is accepted, becoming their queen. Buchanan earned his reputation as a maker of horrible films honestly. Includes the songs "Mistress of the Apes" and "Ape Lady." **88m/C VHS.** Jenny Neumann, Barbara Leigh, Garth Pillsbury, Walt Robin, Stuart Lancaster, Suzy Mandel; **D:** Larry Buchanan; **W:** Larry Buchanan.

Mistress of the World 🐾🐾

1959 A scientist, aided by Swedish Intelligence agent Ventura, works to protect his gravity-altering invention from Chinese agents. Partly based on a German serial from the silent film era, but not up to director Dieterle's usual fare. A must-see for Ventura fans and Mabuse mavens. **107m/C VHS.** Martha Hyer, Micheline Presle, Gino Cervi, Lino Ventura, Sabu, Wolfgang Preiss; **D:** William Dieterle.

Mistress Pamela 🐾1/2

1974 (R) When young Pamela goes to work in the household of handsome Lord Devonish, he sets about in wild pursuit of her virginity. Loosely based on the 1740 work "Pamela" by Samuel Richardson, considered the first modern English novel. Read the book unless you only have 95 minutes to spend finding out who gets what. **95m/C VHS.** Anne Michelle, Julian Barnes, Anna Quayle, Rosemary Dunham; **D:** Jim O'Connor.

Mistrial 🐾🐾

1996 (R) NYC cop Steve Donohue (Pullman) is incensed when acquited cop killer Eddie Rios (Seda) is acquited and Donohue himself is about to be charged in the wrongful deaths of the suspect's wife and brother, which occurred during his pursuit. So he takes the entire courtroom hostage. **90m/C VHS, DVD.** Bill Pullman, Robert Loggia, Jon Seda, Blair Underwood, Casey Siemaszko, Josef Sommer, Roberta Maxwell, James Rebhorn, Leo Burmester, Roma Maffia, Kate Burton; **D:** Heywood Gould; **W:** Heywood Gould; **C:** Paul Sarossy; **M:** Brad Fiedel.

Mists of Avalon 🐾🐾

2001 A womancentric version of the story of Camelot based on Marion Zimmer Bradley's 1982 bestseller. Morgaine (Margulies) is the niece of the Lady of the Lake, Viviane (Huston), who raises her in the mother/ goddess religion even as Christianity takes hold of the land. Morgaine is reunited with her half-brother Arthur (Atterton), who is betrothed to the Christian Gwenhwyfer (Mathis), who falls for Arthur's best friend and knight, Lancelot (Vartan). But as the years pass, Viking invasions and familial circumstances threaten to tear Arthur's kingdom apart and Morgaine can only watch as the vision of Avalon disappears as well. **180m/C VHS, DVD.** Julianna Margulies, Anjelica Huston, Samantha Mathis, Edward Atterton, Joan Allen, Michael Vartan, Hans Matheson, Caroline Goodall, Michael Byrne, Clive Russell, Mark Lewis Jones; **D:** Uli Edel; **W:** Gavin Scott; **C:** Vilmos Zsigmond; **M:** Lee Holdridge. **CABLE**

Misty 🐾🐾1/2

1961 Ladd and Smith are two kids who capture a wild pony and teach it to run around in circles and step over things. Based on Marguerite Henry's bestselling "Misty of Chincoteague," and filmed on an island off the coast of Virginia. **92m/C VHS, DVD.** David Ladd, Arthur O'Connell, Pam Smith; **D:** James B. Clark; **W:** Ted Sherdeman; **C:** Leo Tover; **M:** Paul Sawtell, Bert Shefter.

Misunderstood 🐾🐾1/2

1984 (PG) A former black market merchant has to learn how to relate to his sons after his wife dies. The father, now a legitimate businessman, is more concerned with running his shipping business than growing closer to his boys. Fine acting can't overcome a transparent plot. **92m/C VHS.** Gene Hackman, Susan Anspach, Henry Thomas, Rip Torn, Huckleberry Fox; **D:** Jerry Schatzberg; **C:** Pasqualino De Santis.

Misunderstood

1987 A father learns his lonely son is full of love and sensitivity when a tragedy reveals that it is this son who takes the blame for all the wrongs his brother commits. **101m/C VHS.** Anthony Quayle, Stefano Colagrande, Simone Gianozzi, John Sharp; **D:** Luigi Comencini.

Mitchell 🐾

1975 (R) Tough cop battles drug traffic and insipid script. Big screen release with that certain TV look. **90m/C VHS, DVD.** Joe Don Baker, Linda Evans, Martin Balsam, John Saxon, Merlin Olsen, Harold J. Stone, Robert Phillips; **D:** Andrew V. McLaglen; **W:** Ian Kennedy Martin; **C:** Harry Stradling Jr.; **M:** Jerry Styner.

Mixed Blood 🐾🐾1/2

1984 (R) From the renowned underground film-maker, a dark comedy that examines the seedy drug subculture in New York. Violent, fast, and funny. **98m/C VHS, DVD.** Marília Pera, Richard Vlacia, Linda Kerridge, Geraldine Smith, Angel David; **D:** Paul Morrissey; **W:** Paul Morrissey.

Mixed Nuts 🐾

Lifesavers 1994 (PG-13) Misfits man a suicide hotline on Christmas Eve in this unfunny, pathetic comedy that's a real downer. Director/writer Ephron (along with her co-writer sister Delia) try way too hard to fashion a hip, racy, madcap farce reminiscent of the screwball comedies that Hollywood churned out in the 1930s and '40s. Film never finds its style and the storyline is very weak. Most of the performances are over the top, although Martin, Shandling, and Kahn are good for a few amusing scenes. Ephron and the cast are capable of doing so much better, it's a shame their talents are virtually wasted here. Adapted from the French film "Le Pere Noel Est une Ordure." **97m/C VHS, DVD.** Steve Martin, Madeline Kahn, Robert Klein, Anthony LaPaglia, Juliette Lewis, Rob Reiner, Adam Sandler, Rita Wilson, Garry Shandling, Liev Schreiber; **D:** Nora Ephron; **W:** Nora Ephron, Delia Ephron; **M:** George Fenton.

Mixing Nia 🐾1/2

1998 (R) Biracial ad exec Nia (Parsons) becomes upset when she is asked to head a new beer campaign aimed at black youth. She quits, and decides to write a novel about the black experience and then realizes that she's lost touch with that part of her heritage. So, Nia decides to regain her roots and finds a real culture clash. **93m/C VHS, DVD.** Karyn Parsons, Isaiah Washington IV, Eric Thal, Diego Serrano, Heidi Schanz, Rosalyn Coleman; **D:** Alison Swan.

M'Lady's Court 🐾

1973 A lawyer searching for an heiress in a convent of lusty maidens has loads of fun. None too captivating. **92m/C VHS. GE** Gabriele Tinti, Femi Benussi, Sonia Jeanine, Maja Hoppe; **D:** Franz Antel; **M:** Kurt Nachmann; **C:** Siegfried Holt; **M:** Stelvio Cipriani.

Mo' Better Blues 🐾🐾1/2

1990 (R) Not one of his more cohesive or compelling works, Lee's fourth feature is on the surface a backstage jazz biopic. But all Lee features are vitally concerned with complicated racial issues, and though subtle, this is no exception. Bleek Gilliam is a handsome, accomplished jazz trumpeter who divides his limited extra-curricular time between Clarke (newcomer Williams) and Indigo (junior Lee sibling Joie). What's interesting is not so much the story of self-interested musician and ladies' man Gilliam, but the subtle racial issues his life draws into focus. The Branford Marsalis Quartet provides the music for Bleek's group, scored by Lee's dad Bill Lee. **129m/C VHS, DVD.** Denzel Washington, Spike Lee, Joie Lee, Wesley Snipes, Cynda Williams, Giancarlo Esposito, Robin Harris, Bill Nunn, John Turturro, Dick Anthony Williams, Ruben Blades, Nicholas Turturro, Samuel L. Jackson, Abbey Lincoln, Tracy C. Johns, Joe Seneca; **D:** Spike Lee; **W:** Spike Lee; **C:** Ernest R. Dickerson; **M:** Bill Lee, Branford Marsalis.

Mo' Money 🐾🐾1/2

1992 (R) Damon Wayans is a small-time con-artist who is inspired to go straight by a beautiful woman (Dash). He lands a job at the credit card company she works for, but temptation overcomes him, he swipes some plastic, and the scamming begins anew. With the help of his younger brother (played by real-life younger brother Marlon), they get involved in an even bigger, more dangerous scam being operated by the credit card company's head of security. Crude formula comedy driven by energetic, inventive performances by the brothers Wayans. Needless to say, will be especially enjoyed by fans of TV's "In Living Color." **97m/C VHS, DVD.** Damon Wayans, Marlon Wayans, Stacey Dash, Joe Santos, John Diehl, Harry J. Lennix, Mark Beitzman, Quincy Wong, Larry Brandenburg, Almayvonne; **D:** Peter Macdonald; **W:** Damon Wayans; **C:** Don Burgess; **M:** Jay Gruska.

Moana, a Romance of the Golden Age 🐾🐾🐾1/2

1926 An early look through American eyes at the society of the people of Samoa, in the Pacific Islands. Picturesque successor to Flaherty's "Nanook of the North." **76m/B VHS. Ta'avale, Fa'amgase, Moana; D:** Robert Flaherty.

Mob Boss 🐾

1990 (R) Gangster films spoof starring Hickey as the head of a successful California crime ring. When his beautiful wife conspires to have him killed, he is left just breaths away from his demise. He calls his nerdy son to his bedside to ask him to take over the family business. But this kid thinks that money laundering requires detergent! Take this one down for a walk by the river in its new cement shoes. **93m/C VHS.** Eddie Deezen, Morgan Fairchild, William Hickey, Stuart Whitman; **D:** Fred Olen Ray.

Mob Queen 🐾🐾

1998 Dim low-level Brooklyn mobsters George (Proval) and Dip (Moran) want to impress their boss, Joey "The Heart" Aorta (Sirico), by giving him a memorable birthday present. So George sets up a "date" with sexy new prostitute on the docks, Glorice (Cayne). And it works—Joey's smitten by the tough babe and George and Dip figure they're in clover. Until they find out that Glorice is actually a he—and they decide the safest thing would be to end the budding romance before Joey finds out too. Set in 1957. **87m/C VHS, DVD.** David Proval, Dan Moran, G. Anthony "Tony" Sirico, Candis Cayne, Marlene Forte, Jerry Grayson, Gerry Cooney; **D:** Jon Carfano; **W:** Mike Horelick; **C:** Nils Kenaston; **M:** Jonathan Cossu.

Mob Story 🐾1/2

1990 (R) Vernon stars as a big-wig mob boss on the run from the government and a few of his "closest" friends. He plans to disappear into Canada, but if his girl (Kidder) and best friend (Waxman) find him first he'll be traveling in a body-bag. Very silly, but fun. **98m/C VHS, DVD.** John Vernon, Margot Kidder, Al Waxman, Kate Vernon; **D:** Gabriel Markiw, Jancarlo Markiw.

Mob War 🐾🐾

1988 (R) A war breaks out between the head of New York's underworld and a media genius. After deciding to become partners, the "family" tries to take over. For fun, count how many times the word "respect" pops up in the script. Tries hard but fails. **96m/C VHS, DVD.** John Christian, David Henry Keller, Jake LaMotta, Johnny Stumper; **D:** J. Christian Ingvordsen; **W:** J. Christian Ingvordsen, John Weiner; **C:** Steven Kaman.

Mobsters 🐾🐾1/2

1991 (R) It sounded like a great idea, casting the hottest young actors of the '90s as youthful racketeers "Lucky" Luciano, Meyer Lansky, Bugsy Siegel, and Frank Costello. But it would take an FBI probe to straighten out the blood-choked plot, as the pals' loyalties get tested the hard way in a dismembered narrative. Sicker than the violence is a seeming endorsement of the glamorous hoods. **104m/C VHS, DVD, HD DVD.** Joe (Johnny) Viterelli, Christian Slater, Patrick Dempsey, Richard Grieco, Costas Mandylor, Anthony Quinn, F. Murray Abraham, Lara Flynn Boyle, Michael Gambon, Christopher Penn; **D:** Michael Karbelnikoff; **W:** Nicholas Kazan; **C:** Lajos Koltai.

Moby Dick 🐾🐾1/2

1956 This adaptation of Herman Melville's high seas saga features Peck as Captain Ahab. His obsession with revenge upon the great white whale, Moby Dick, isn't always believable, but the moments that click make the film more than worthwhile. **116m/C VHS, DVD.** Gregory Peck, Richard Basehart, Orson Welles, Leo Genn, Harry Andrews, Friedrich Ledebur; **D:** John Huston; **W:** Ray Bradbury, John Huston; **C:** Oswald Morris. Natl. Bd. of Review '56: Director (Huston); N.Y. Film Critics '56: Director (Huston).

Moby Dick 🐾🐾1/2

1998 (PG) TV adaptation of Herman Melville's 1851 novel, starring a mesmerizing Stewart as the obsessive peg-legged Captain Ahab. Novice seaman Ishmael (Thomas) signs aboard the whaling ship Pequod, making friends with Polynesian native, harpooner Queequeg (Waretini). Soon enough Ishmael learns about the great white whale who claimed the captain's leg and Ahab's determination to seek revenge on the beast, no matter what the cost to himself, his crew, or the ship. Peck, who starred as Ahab in the 1956 movie version, takes on the role of Jonah-and-the-whale sermonizing Father Mapple. **145m/C VHS, DVD.** Patrick Stewart, Henry Thomas, Ted Levine, Piripi Waretini, Gregory Peck, Bill Hunter, Hugh Keays-Byrne, Norman D. Golden II, Bruce Spence; **D:** Franc Roddam; **W:** Franc Roddam, Anton Diether; **C:** David Connell; **M:** Christopher Gordon. **TV**

Mockery 🐾🐾1/2

1927 Chaney plays a peasant working for a Russian countess. He becomes involved in a peasant revolution against the rich and threatens the countess but eventually saves her from the mob. **75m/B VHS, DVD.** Lon Chaney Sr., Barbara Bedford, Ricardo Cortez, Emily Fitzroy; **D:** Benjamin Christiansen.

Mockingbird Don't Sing 🐾🐾

2001 Based on the true story of Katie, which came to light in 1970. She is rescued from some 12 years of abuse and isolation imposed by her mentally unbalanced parents. Unable to speak and with no social skills, Katie is little more than a lab rat to a variety of psychologists and doctors who see her more as a case study than a person. Even her caring social worker Sandra (Errico) is unable to beat a system that just offers a different type of abuse to the young girl. **98m/C VHS, DVD.** Tarra Steele, Melissa Errico, Sean Young, Joe Regalbuto, Michael Lerner; **D:** Harry Bromley-Davenport; **W:** Daryl Haney; **C:** Jeff Baustert; **M:** Mark Hart.

The Mod Squad 🐾🐾

1999 (R) Tangled rehash of the '60s series tries very hard to be cool, but ends up as hip as a $2 haircut. Attempts to update the premise, but teen criminals-turned-cops Pete (Ribisi), Linc (Epps), and Julie (Danes) merely look like they're guilty of shoplifting from The Gap and making unwise career decisions. They all glower sullenly as they try to crack a convoluted case involving drugs, prostitution and their dead boss Capt. Greer (Farina). Director Silver manages to crush what little dramatic tension was left in the stale script into a bland pulp. This shameless attempt to hijack youth culture in order to sell jeans will keep you down. **94m/C VHS, DVD.** Claire Danes, Giovanni Ribisi, Omar Epps, Dennis Farina, Josh Brolin, Richard Jenkins, Larry Brandenburg, Steve Harris, Sam McMurray, Michael Lerner, Bodhi (Pine) Elfman, Holmes Osborne, Dey Young, Eddie Griffin, Carmen (Lee) Llywelyn; **D:** Scott Silver; **W:** Scott Silver, Stephen Kay, Kate Lanier; **C:** Ellen Kuras; **M:** B.C. Smith.

Model Behavior 🐾🐾1/2

1982 Fresh from college, an aspiring photographer pines for a glamorous model. **86m/C VHS.** Richard Bekins, Bruce Lyons, Cindy Harrel, Anne Marie Howard; **D:** Bud Gardner.

Model Behavior 🐾🐾

2000 Shy, boyfriendless, 16-year-old Alex (Lawson) is your typically anguished teen. She wishes she had the life of teen supermodel Janine and gets her chance when the girls accidentally meet and realize they are lookalikes. So they decide to trade places for a week—Alex gets to do fashion shoots, go to parties, and hang-out with hottie model Jason (played by 'N Sync's Timberlake) and Janine gets to go to high school, eat stuff that's bad for her, and laze around. It's kind of a "The Prince and the Pauper" for girls with no one threatening their lives. Based on the book by Michael Levin. **90m/C VHS.** Maggie Lawson, Justin Timberlake, Kathie Lee Gifford, Cody Gifford, Jim Abele, Daniel Clark, Karen Hines, Jesse Nilsson; **Cameos:** Vendela Thommessen; **D:** Mark Rosman; **W:** David Kukoff, Matt Roshkow; **C:** Laszlo George; **M:** Eric Colvin. **TV**

Model by Day 🦴½ 1994 (R) When New York model Janssen is murdered, she takes up martial arts training and becomes the vengeful "Lady X." Then she becomes the prime suspect in a murder and finds herself falling for a plainclothes cop. Fair amount of action, somewhat less exploitive than usual for the genre. 88m/C VHS, DVD. Frankie Janssen, Stephen Shellen, Shannon Tweed, Sean Young; D: Christian Duguay.

The Modern Adventures of Tom Sawyer 🦴 1999 (PG) Title sums it up. Mark Twain's mischievous hero is still getting into trouble only this time in the present-day. Harmless, but involves a sperm bank. M: Jan Hammer.

A Modern Affair 🦴🦴 1994 (R) Single executive Grace Rhodes (Eichorn) biological clock is ringing and LA rock groupies and their various wild adventures during a single night on the LA. Right in sight, she decides to visit a sperm bank. Grace gets pregnant and also very curious about her anonymous donor—who of course doesn't stay anonymous. Grace even manages to fall for photographer Peter Kessler (Tucci) but how does she tell him she's carrying his baby when they haven't even had sex yet? 91m/C VHS. Lisa Eichhorn, Stanley Tucci, Caroline Aaron, Tammy Grimes, Robert Joy, Wesley Addy, Cynthia Martells, Mary Jo Salerno; D: Vern Oakley; W: Paul Zimmerman; C: Howard Wexler; M: Kristopher Carter. VIDEO

Modern Girls 🦴½ 1986 Mr. 247 Teen comedy about three bubble-headed LA rock groupies and their various wild adventures during a single night on the town. Surprising in that the three lead actresses waste their talents in this lesson in exploitation. Bruce Springsteen's younger sister portrays a drug user. 82m/C VHS. Cynthia Gibb, Daphne Zuniga, Virginia Madsen; D: Jerry Kramer; W: Laurie Craig; M: Eddie Arkin.

Modern Love 🦴 1990 (R) An average slob realizes that marriage, fatherhood and in-law-ship isn't quite what he expected. Benson stars, directs and produces as well as co-starring with real-life wife DeVito. A plotless hodgepodge of bits that were more successful in "Look Who's Talking" and "Parenthood." 107m/C VHS, DVD. Robby Benson, Karla DeVito, Rue McClanahan, Kaye Ballard, Frankie Valli, Cliff Bemis, Louise Lasser, Burt Reynolds, Lyric Benson; D: Robby Benson; W: Robby Benson.

Modern Problems 🦴🦴 1981 (PG) A man involved in a nuclear accident discovers he has acquired telekinetic powers, which he uses to turn the tables on his professional and romantic rivals. A fine cast but an unsuccessful fission trip. 93m/C VHS, DVD. Chevy Chase, Patti D'Arbanville, Mary Kay Place, Brian Doyle-Murray, Neil Carter, Dabney Coleman; D: Ken Shapiro.

Modern Romance 🦴🦴🦴 1981 (R) The romantic misadventures of a neurotic film editor who is hopelessly in love with his girlfriend but can't seem to maintain a normal relationship with her. Smart and hilarious at times and always simmering with anxiety. Offers an honest look at relationships as well as an accurate portrait of filmmaking. 102m/C VHS, DVD. Albert Brooks, Kathryn Harrold, Bruno Kirby, George Kennedy, James L. Brooks, Bob Einstein; D: Albert Brooks; W: Albert Brooks, Monica Johnson.

Modern Times 🦴🦴🦴 1936 This mostly silent film finds Chaplin playing a factory worker who goes crazy from his repetitious job on an assembly line and his boss's demands for greater speed and efficiency. Ultimately encompassing the tyranny of machine over man, it's cinematic masterpiece has more relevance today than ever. Chaplin wrote the musical score, which incorporates the tune "Smile." Look for a young Gloria De Haven as one of Goddard's sisters; she's the real-life daughter of Chaplin's assistant director. 87m/B VHS, DVD. Charlie Chaplin, Paulette Goddard, Henry Bergman, Stanley Sandford, Gloria De Haven, Chester Conklin; D: Charlie Chaplin; W: Charlie Chaplin; C: Ira Morgan, Roland H. Totheroh; M: Charlie Chaplin. AFI '98: Top 100, Natl. Film Reg. '89.

Modern Vampires 🦴½ 1998 (R) Think vampire-lite. A community of European vamps have moved to L.A., decide to make their own porn flick. Genial loser Andy (Bridges) comes up with the initial idea and gets local video store clerk Emmett (Frugé) to operate the camera while closeted Moose (Danson) offers to be the on-camera stud, and the appropriately nicknamed Some Idiot (Pantoliano) is writer-director. Other pals fill in as needed. One-note joke with equally one-note roles for the women involved. 100m/C DVD. 95m/C VHS, DVD. Casper Van Dien, Natasha Gregson Wagner, Rod Steiger, Robert Pastorelli, Kim Cattrall, Natasha Andreichenko, Gabriel Casseus, Udo Kier, Natasha Lyonne; D: Richard Elfman; W: Matthew Bright; C: Denis Maloney.

The Moderns 🦴🦴🦴 1988 (R) One of the quirkier directors around, this time Rudolph tries a comedic period piece (Ernest Hemingway, Gertrude Stein) and some strange art-world types. The tone is not consistently funny but, instead, romantic as the main characters clash over art and love. 126m/C VHS, DVD. Keith Carradine, Linda Fiorentino, John Lone, Genevieve Bujold, Geraldine Chaplin, Wallace Shawn, Kevin J. O'Connor, Elsa Raven, Kathleen Lloyd; D: Alan Rudolph; W: Alan Rudolph, Jon Bradshaw; C: Toyomichi Kurita; M: Mark Isham. L.A. Film Critics '88: Support. Actress (Bujold).

Modesty Blaise 🦴🦴½ 1966 Adaptation of Peter O'Donnell's comic strip about tough British babe spy embodied by Italian beauty Vitti, aided by her right-hand man Willie Garvin (Stamp). The secret agent is watching out for a diamond shipment, which is the target of her archrival Gabriel (Bogarde). Very campy and '60s pop-arty, with everyone having fun and not taking any situation seriously. 2001. 118m/C VHS, DVD. GB Monica Vitti, Terence Stamp, Dirk Bogarde, Harry Andrews, Michael Craig, Clive Revill, Alexander Knox, Rossella Falk; D: Joseph Losey; W: Evan Jones; C: Jack Hildyard; M: John Dankworth.

Modigliani 🦴🦴½ Montparnasse 19. The Lovers of Montparnasse, Montparnasse 19. 1958 Life of dissolute 19th-century painter Modigliani (Philipe), which tracks his affairs with British poet Beatrice Hastings (Palmer) and later mistress Jeanne (Aimee), who commits suicide shortly before his death. Tender performances from director Max Ophuls, who co-wrote the screenplay but who died before the start of production. In French with English subtitles. 110m/B VHS. FR Gerard Philipe, Lilli Palmer, Anouk Aimee, Gerard Blain; D: Jacques Becker; W: Max Ophuls, Henri Jeanson, Jacques Becker.

Modigliani 🦴 2004 (R) Garcia is miscast as debauched Italian Jewish artist Amedeo Modigliani, who's living it up in Paris, circa 1919, and having a tragic love affair with his beautiful Catholic mistress, Jeanne (Zylberstein), who leaves her family for him. Writer/director Davis invents a feud between Modigliani and a glowering Picasso (Dialii) to further liven up the action, which is almost a melodramatic parody of screen bios about the art world. It doesn't work and neither does the film, which is almost a melodramatic parody. 128m/C DVD. FR IT RO GE GB US Andy Garcia, Elsa Zylberstein, Omid Djalili, Hippolyte Girardot, Udo Kier, Peter Capaldi, Miriam Margolyes, Eva Herzigova, Susie Amy, Louis Hilyer, Stevan Rimkus, Frederico Ambrosino, Irina Dinescu, Theodor Danetti, Ion Simirie, Lance Henriksen, Beatrice Chiricai; D: Mick Davis; W: Mick Davis; C: Emmanuel Chiriac; M: Guy Farley.

Mogambo 🦴🦴🦴 1953 Remake of "Red Dust," this is the steamy story of a love triangle between an African game hunter, a proper British lady, and an American showgirl in the jungles of Kenya. 115m/C VHS, DVD. Clark Gable, Ava Gardner, Grace Kelly, Donald Sinden, Philip Stainton, Eric Pohlmann, Denis O'Dea; D: John Ford; W: John Lee Mahin; C: Robert L. Surtees. Golden Globes '54: Support. Actress (Kelly).

Moliere 🦴🦴 Meanwhile, Molière flirts with Jourdain's wife Elmire (Morante) and she returns his interest, although she thinks his name is Tartuffe. French with subtitles. 120m/C DVD. FR Romain Duris, Laura Morante, Fabrice Luchini, Ludivine Sagnier, Edouard Baer, Fanny Valette, Gillian Petrovsky, Gonzague Requillart; D: Lauren Tirard; W: Gregoire Vigneron; C: Gilles Henry; M: Frederic Talgorn.

Moliere 🦴🦴 2007 Bittersweet costume farce that explores the lost months in 1644 between the French satirist's release from prison and his return to Paris. In order to avoid his creditors, Molière (Duris) agrees to board at the home of wealthy bourgeois Jourdain (Luchini) who wants acting lessons so he can perform in a play he has written to impress the marquise Celimene (Sagnier). Meanwhile, Molière

Moll Flanders 🦴🦴½ 1996 (PG-13) Writer/director Densham takes only the title character and the 18th-century London setting from Daniel Defoe's 1722 novel in telling of spirited heroine Moll Flanders' (Wright) life. Orphaned Moll eventually finds herself working at the brothel of greasy, scheming Mrs. Allworthy (Channing). Her life as a prostitute leads her to drink and near suicide—despite the unwavering friendship of Hibble (Freeman) and Allworthy's dignified servant—until she falls for an impoverished artist (Lynch) and briefly finds happiness. Wright's heartfelt performance holds everything together but things get dreary. 120m/C VHS, DVD. Robin Wright Penn, Morgan Freeman, Stockard Channing, John Lynch, Brenda Fricker, Aisling Corcoran, Geraldine James, Jim Sheridan, Jeremy

The Moguls 🦴 The Amateurs 2005 (R) Good cast is wasted in a lame comedy about middle-aged small-town guys who ne.

Mojave Moon 🦴🦴½ 1996 (R) Middle-aged car dealer Al (Aiello) is asked by nymphet Ellie (Jolie) to drive her home—a trailer in the desert where Al meets her perky-yet-kinky mom Julie (Archer) and Julie's violent boyfriend Boyd (Biehn). A series of strange happenings finds Al tied to the trio and discovering both adventure and romance. 95m/C VHS, DVD. Danny Aiello, Anne Archer, Angelina Jolie, Michael Biehn, Alfred Molina; D: Kevin Dowling; W: Leonard Glasser; C: James Glennon.

Mohawk 🦴½ 1956 A cowboy and his Indian maiden try to stop a war between Indian tribes and fanatical landowners. 80m/C VHS, DVD. Rita Gam, Neville Brand, Scott Brady, Lori Nelson; D: Kurt Neumann; W: Maurice Geraghty, Milton Krims; C: Karl Struss; M: Edward L. Alperson Jr.

The Mole People 🦴 1956 A really bad '50s creature feature which finds two archeologists accidentally discovering an underground civilization of albinos who shun all forms of light. They've also enslaved the local populace of half-human, half-mole creatures who decide to help the good guys escape by rising up in a revolt against their evil masters. When the weapon of choice is a flashlight you know not to expect much. 78m/B VHS, DVD. John Agar, Cynthia Patrick, Hugh Beaumont, Alan Napier, Nestor Paiva, Phil Chambers; D: Virgil W. Vogel; W: Laszlo Gorog.

Mole Men Against the Son of Hercules 🦴 1961 Italian muscleman Maciste battles the pale-skinned denizens of an underground city. 99m/C VHS. IT Moira Orfei, Raffaella Carra, Paul Wynter, Enrico Glori, Roberto Miali, Mark Forest; D: Antonio Leonviola; W: Marcello Baldi, Giuseppe Mangione; C: Avaro Mancori; M: Armando Trovajoli.

Moll Flanders 🦴🦴½ 1996 The Fortunes and Misfortunes of Moll Flanders 1996 Rousing, bawdy retelling of Daniel Defoe's 1722 novel about the wickedly seductive Moll (Kingston). Born in London's Newgate prison, Moll becomes a house servant, embarks on her first marriage, is soon widowed, and decides to make her own way (and fortune). She becomes a thief, a whore, marries several more times, and eventually winds up back in prison and a likely candidate for the gallows. But the ever-enterprising Moll always finds her way. TV miniseries on two cassettes. 210m/C VHS, DVD. GB Alex Kingston, Daniel Craig, Diana Rigg, Colin Buchanan, Christopher Fulford, James Fleet, Ian Driver, Tom Ward; D: David Attwood; W: Andrew Davies; C: Ivan Strasburg; M: Jim Parker. TV.

Molly and Gina 🦴🦴 1994 (R) The very different lives of Molly and Gina intersect suddenly when their boyfriends die in a violent... 90m/C VHS, DVD. Frances Fisher, Natasha Gregson Wagner, Bruce Weitz, Stella Stevens, Peter Fonda; D: Paul Leder; W: Reuben Leder; M: Dane Walden.

Molly & Lawless John 🦴🦴 1972 Average western with Miles the wife of a sadistic sheriff who helps a prisoner escape the gallows so they can run away together. Enough clichés for the whole family to enjoy. 90m/C VHS, DVD. Sam Elliott, Vera Miles; D: Gary Nelson.

Molly Maguires 🦴🦴½ 1970 (PG) Dramatization based on a true story, concerns a group of miners called the Molly Maguires who resort to using terrorist tactics in their fight for better working conditions during the Pennsylvania Irish coal mining rebellion in the 1870s. During their reign of terror, the Mollies are infiltrated by a Pinkerton detective who they mistakenly believe is a new recruit. It has its moments but never fully succeeds. Returned less than 15% of its initial $11 million investment. 123m/C VHS, DVD. Sean Connery, Richard Harris, Samantha Eggar, Frank Finlay; D: Martin Ritt; W: Walter Bernstein; C: James Wong Howe; M: Henry Mancini.

The Mollycoddle 🦴🦴 1920 Fairbanks is a British-educated American... 115m/C VHS. Douglas Fairbanks Sr., Wallace Beery, Ruth Renick; D: Victor Fleming; W: Douglas Fairbanks Sr.

Molokai: The Story of Father Damien 🦴🦴½ 1999 In the 19th century, the government sent suspected lepers to the island of Molokai in an effort to stop the spread of infection. The inhabitants were dependant on the efforts of the church to ease their suffering. Father Damien (Wenham) volunteers to go to the island to provide spiritual and physical comfort and care, even at the risk of contracting the disease himself. Based on a true story. 112m/C VHS, DVD. *D:* David Wenham, Derek Jacobi, Alice Krige, Kris Kristofferson, Peter O'Toole, Sam Neill, Leo McKern, Tom Wilkinson; *C:* Paul Cox; *W:* John Briley; *M:* Wim Mertens. **VIDEO**

Mom WOOF! 1989 (R) When his mother is bitten by a flesh-eater, Clay Dwyer is at a loss as to what to do. How do you tell your own mother that she must be destroyed, lest she continue to devour human flesh? A campy horror/comedy. 95m/C VHS. Mark Thomas Miller, Art Evans, Mary (Elizabeth) McDonough, Jeanne Bates, Brion James, Stella Stevens, Claudia Christian; *D:* Patrick Rand.

Mom & Dad WOOF! 1947 An innocent young girl's one night of passion leads to an unwanted pregnancy. Stock footage of childbirth and a lecture on the evils of syphilis concludes this campy schlock that features the national anthem. Banned or denied release for years, this movie is now a cult favorite for its time-capsule glimpse at conventional 1940s sexual attitudes. 97m/B VHS. Hardie Albright, Sarah Blake, George Eldredge, June Carlson, Jimmy Clark, Bob Lowell; *D:* William Beaudine; *W:* Mildred Horn; *C:* Barney A. Sarecky.

Mom and Dad Save the World ♂♂½ 1992 (PG) A suburban housewife (Garr) is transported along with her husband in the family station wagon to the planet Spengo, ruled by King Tod Spengo (Lovitz), who has fallen in love with her and wants to save her from his plans to blow up Earth. While trying to prevent the king from marrying her and killing him, Garr and Jones wind up in many goofy situations and wind up saving the Earth from its imminent doom. Uninspired comedy just isn't funny, and the excellent cast is misused, especially the one with Shawn. Save this one for the kiddies. 87m/C VHS, DVD. Teri Garr, Jeffrey Jones, Jon Lovitz, Eric Idle, Wallace Shawn, Dwier Brown, Kathy Ireland, Thalmus Rasulala; *D:* Greg Beeman; *M:* Jerry Goldsmith.

Mom, Can I Keep Her? ♂½ 1998 (PG) Goofy family film features 12-year-old Timmy who's having problems at school and at home with a too-busy father and a new stepmom. But that's nothing compared to the new friend that follows Timmy home—a 500 lb. gorilla. 90m/C VHS, DVD. Gil Gerard, Kevin Dobson, Terry Funk, Justin Berfield, Alana Stewart, Henry Darrow, Don Mcleod; *D:* Fred Olen Ray; *W:* Sean O'Bannon; *C:* Jesse Weathington. **VIDEO**

Mom, the Wolfman and Me ♂♂½ 1980 An 11-year-old girl arranges and manages the love affair of her mother, an ultra-liberated photographer, and an unemployed teacher, who is also the owner of an Irish wolfhound. Charming adaptation of a novel by Norma Klein. 100m/C VHS. Patty Duke, David Birney, Danielle Brisebois, Keenan Wynn, Viveca Lindfors, John Lithgow; *D:* Edmond Levy. **TV**

Momentum ♂♂ 2003 Although reluctant to use his unwanted telekinetic powers, physics professor Zach Shefford (McCouch) agrees to help FBI agent Raymond Addison (Gossett Jr.) by going undercover in a gang of telekinetic troublemakers. But things get a little blurry when he learns that the group's leader Adrian Greer (Massee) was once part of a government project that went fatally awry at the hands of Addison. Meanwhile another agent (a wickedly fun Hatcher) tails both Shefford and Addison. Created for cable's Sci-Fi Channel. 97m/C VHS, DVD. Louis Gossett Jr., Teri Hatcher, Grayson McCouch, Michael Massee, Nicki Aycox, Daniel Dae Kim; *D:* James Seale; *W:* Deverin Karol; *C:* Maximo Munzi; *M:* Joseph Williams. **CABLE**

Mommie Dearest ♂♂ 1981 (PG) Film based on Christina Crawford's memoirs of her incredibly abusive and violent childhood at the hands of her adoptive mother, actress Joan Crawford. The story is controversial and sometimes trashy, but fairly well done nevertheless. However, it is also so campy and the immortal Crawford/Dunaway screech "No wire hangers—ever!" became so associated with Dunaway's over-the-top performance that it was thought by some to have damaged the actress's career. 129m/C VHS, DVD. Faye Dunaway, Diana Scarwid, Steve Forrest, Mara Hobel, Rutanya Alda, Harry Goz, Howard da Silva; *D:* Frank Perry; *W:* Frank Perry, Robert Getchell, Frank Yablans; *C:* Paul Lohmann; *M:* Henry Mancini. Golden Raspberries '81: Worst Picture, Worst Actress (Dunaway), Worst Support. Actor (Forrest), Worst Support. Actress (Scarwid), Worst Screenplay.

Mommy ♂♂½ 1995 Schoolteacher is stalked by murderous mom who'll do anything for her daughter. Mommy McCormack was the original "Bad Seed" child. Filmed in Muscatine, Iowa. 89m/C VHS, DVD. Patty McCormack, Majel Barrett, Jason Miller, Brinke Stevens, Rachel Lemieux, Mickey Spillane, Michael Cornelison, Sarah Jane Miller; *D:* Max Allan Collins; *W:* Max Allan Collins; *C:* Phillip W. Dingeldein; *M:* Richard Lowry.

Mommy's Day ♂♂½ 1996 Murderous Mommy (McCormack) returns as does her beloved daughter (now rebellious teenager), Jessica Ann (Lemieux). Mommy's on Death Row, awaiting execution after her murder spree but the Mommy-style killings continue. Shot on location in Iowa. 89m/C VHS, DVD. Patty McCormack, Rachel Lemieux, Brinke Stevens, Michael Cornelison, Sarah Jane Miller, Mickey Spillane, Gary Sandy, Paul Petersen, Arlen Dean Snyder, Todd Eastland, Del Close; *D:* Max Allan Collins; *W:* Max Allan Collins; *C:* Phillip W. Dingeldein; *M:* Richard Lowry.

Mom's Outta Sight ♂ 2001 (PG) Substandard kiddie SF comedy exudes cheapness. Special effects and props are bargain-basement material. The story has something to do with a matter transmission machine that turns a sexy woman into a mincing man and makes another (Williamson) invisible. The only redeeming feature is an all-too-brief cameo by Brinke Stevens. 89m/C VHS, DVD. Hannes Jaenicke, Melissa Williamson, Steve Sciorti, Arianna Albright, Brinke Stevens; *D:* Stewart Peter; *M:* Jay Bolton. **VIDEO**

Mon Amie Max ♂♂ 1994 Marie-le's (Bujold) longtime best friend Alexandrine (Max) Babant (Bujold) is a middle-aged former pianist who returns to her native Quebec City after 25 years of self-imposed exile. Pregnant at 15, Max was forced to give her son up for adoption and ran away from friends and family. Now, she's meet former best friend Catherine (Keller), who's had the concert career Max never did, who's also agreed to help Max find her son. Slow-going melodrama with little emotional impact. 107m/C VHS. *CA FR* Genevieve Bujold, Marthe Keller, Michel Rivard, Johanne McKay; *D:* Michel Brault; *W:* Jefferson Lewis.

Mon Homme ♂♂ *My Man* 1996 Marie-le's (Grinberg) a very happy hooker (think male fantasy) whose kindly impulses wind up getting her into difficulty. She picks up the homeless Jeannot (Lanvin), invites him in for a meal, offers him sex, and is enthralled by his unexpected prowess. Marie decides Jeannot should become her pimp but, unfortunately for her, he takes to his new job with great zeal, seducing manicurist Sanguine (Bruni-Tedeschi) as another lover/prostitute. But when Jeannot gets arrested, his two women decide to abandon him and turn respectable. Nothing exactly works out. French with subtitles. 95m/C VHS. *FR* Anouk Grinberg, Gerard Lanvin, Valeria Bruni-Tedeschi, Olivier Martinez; *Cameos:* Mathieu Kassovitz, Jean-Pierre Leaud; *D:* Bertrand Blier; *W:* Bertrand Blier; *C:* Pierre Lhomme.

Mon Oncle ♂♂♂½ *My Uncle; Mon Uncle; Mr. Hulot* 1958 Tati's celebrated comedy contrasts the simple life of Monsieur Hulot with the technologically complicated life of his family when he aids his nephew

---

in war against his parents' ultramodern, push-button home. An easygoing, delightful comedy that is also the director's first piece in color. Sequel to "Mr. Hulot's Holiday," followed by "Playtime." In French with English subtitles. 110m/C VHS, DVD. *FR* Jacques Tati, Jean-Pierre Zola, Adrienne Serrantie, Alain Bacourt; *D:* Jacques Tati; *C:* Jean (Yves, Georges) Bourgoin; *M:* Alain Romans, AMG. Oscars '58: Foreign Film; Cannes '58: Grand Jury Prize; N.Y. Film Critics '58: Foreign Film.

Mon Oncle Antoine ♂♂♂½ 1971 A splendid tale of young Benoit, who learns about life from a surprisingly compassionate uncle, who works as everything from undertaker to grocer in the depressed area where they live. 104m/C VHS, DVD. *CA* Jean Duceppe, Olivette Thibault; *D:* Claude Jutra.

Mon Oncle d'Amerique ♂♂♂½ *Les Sommanbules* 1980 (PG) Three French characters are followed as they try to find success of varying kinds in Paris, interspersed with ironic lectures by Prof. Henri Laborit about the biology that impels human behavior. Their disappointments lead them to dream of a legendary American uncle, who could make their desires come true. An acclaimed, witty comedy by former Nouvelle Vague filmmaker, dubbed into English. 123m/C VHS, DVD. *FR* Gerard Depardieu, Nicole Garcia, Roger-Pierre, Marie DuBois; *D:* Alain Resnais; *W:* Jean Gruault; *C:* Sacha Vierny; *M:* Arie Dzierlatka. Cannes '80: Grand Jury Prize; N.Y. Film Critics '80: Foreign Film.

Mona Lisa ♂♂♂½ 1986 (R) Jordan's wonderful, sad, sensitive story of a romantic, small-time hood who gets personally involved with the welfare and bad company of the high-priced whore he's been hired to chauffeur. Hoskins is especially touching and Caine is chilling as a suave gangster. Fine film debut for Tyson. Brilliantly filmed and critically lauded. 104m/C VHS, DVD. *GB* Bob Hoskins, Cathy Tyson, Michael Caine, Clarke Peters, Kate Hardie, Robbie Coltrane, Zoe Nathenson, Sammi Davis, Rod Bedall, Joe Brown, Pauline Melville; *D:* Neil Jordan; *W:* David Leland, Neil Jordan; *C:* Roger Pratt; *M:* Michael Kamen. British Acad. '86: Actor (Hoskins); Cannes '86: Actor (Hoskins); Golden Globes '87: Actor—Drama (Hoskins); L.A. Film Critics '86: Actor (Hoskins), Support. Actress (Tyson); N.Y. Film Critics '86: Actor (Hoskins); Natl. Soc. Film Critics '86: Actor (Hoskins).

Mona Lisa Smile ♂♂½ 2003 (PG-13) Julia Roberts is Katherine Watson, an art history professor from California who takes a position at Wellesley College, an all girl college of impeccable standing. Watson, of course, wants to enlighten her students to the possibilities that lay outside of their safe, WASPish upbringing and expectations. You've seen the "Maverick-teacher-tries-to-inspire-the-complacent" plot before (think "Dead Poet's Society" on estrogen), and really there's nothing new here but the gender. Strong ensemble cast doesn't have much to work with. 117m/C VHS, DVD. *US* Julia Roberts, Kirsten Dunst, Julia Stiles, Maggie Gyllenhaal, Ginnifer Goodwin, Juliet Slattery, Dominic West, Topher Grace, John Slattery, Marcia Gay Harden, Jordan Bridges, Marian Seldes, Donna Mitchell, Terence Rigby; *D:* Mike Newell; *W:* Larry Konner, Mark Rosenthal; *C:* Anastas Michos; *M:* Rachel Portman.

Monaco Forever ♂ 1983 An enigmatic American meets a mysterious Frenchwoman and they set off on a string of unusual romantic adventures. Set around the 1956 marriage of Grace Kelly to Prince Rainier of Monaco. Film debut of Van Damme. 79m/C VHS. Charles Pitt, Martha Farris, Sydney Lassick, Jean-Claude Van Damme; *D:* William A. Levey; *W:* C. William Pitt, William A. Levey.

Monday Night Mayhem ♂♂½ 2002 Behind-the-scenes look at "Monday Night Football," the unexpectedly sucessful televised game sanctioned by the NFL in 1969 and produced for ABC by Roone Arledge (Heard). TV broadcaster Howard Cosell (John Turturro) makes his mark but comes to resent players-turned-commentators Frank Gifford (Anderson) and Don Meredith (Beyer) who join him. 98m/C VHS, DVD. John Turturro, John Heard, Kevin Anderson,

---

Nicholas Turturro, Brad Beyer, Patti LuPone, Eli Wallach; *D:* Ernest R. Dickerson; *W:* Bill Carter; *C:* Jonathan Freeman; *M:* Van Dyke Parks. **CABLE**

Mondays in the Sun ♂♂ *Los Lunes al Sol* 2002 (R) Hard times and no easy answers in this biting drama—often filled with corrosive humor—about unemployment and its consequences. The shipyard where Santa (Bardem) and his friends work has been shut down after being sold to a Korean company. Rico (Climent), the only one to accept a management severance package, opens a waterfront bar where the others hang out: hot-headed activits Santa is deeply in debt and, dreams of emigrating, Jose (Tosar) drinks too much and is resentful his working wife is supporting the family, and Lino (Egido) finds himself unqualified and competing against much younger men in a tight job market. Spanish with subtitles. 113m/C VHS, DVD. *SP* Javier Bardem, Luis Tosar, Jose Angel Egido, Joaquin Climent, Nieve De Medina, Enrique Villen, Celso Bugallo; *D:* Fernando Leon de Aranoa; *W:* Fernando Leon de Aranoa, Ignacio del Moral; *C:* Alfredo Mayo; *M:* Lucio Godoy.

Mondo ♂♂ 1996 Orphaned gypsy boy Mondo (Balan) winds up living on the streets of Nice looking for a new family. He's befriended and sheltered by various street people as he hides from the police who want to place him in care. Based on the novel "Ed. Gallinard" by J.M.G. Le Clezio. French with subtitles. 80m/C VHS. *FR* Ovidiu Balan, Philippe Petit, Pierrette Fesch, Jerry Smith; *D:* Tony Gatlif; *W:* Tony Gatlif; *C:* Eric Guichard.

Mondo Balordo ♂ 1964 Translated as "Crazy World," this is crude sensationalism masked as a horror story. Karloff guides the viewer through a curious mixture of society's fringe elements. A loosely connected series of sketches includes portraits of a reincarnated Rudolph Valentino, practitioners of transvestism, Roman coke whores, and an Italian-Japanese rock 'n roll midget (Drago) in director Montero's unusual vision of an anti-paradise. Includes standard lesbian club scene. Volume 11 of Frank Henenlotter's Sexy Shockers. 86m/C VHS, DVD. Franz Drago; *D:* Robert Bianchi Montero; *W:* Albert T. Viola; *Nar:* Boris Karloff.

Mondo Cane ♂♂ *A Dog's Life* 1963 (R) A documentary showcasing the eccentricities of human behavior around the world, including cannibalism, pig killing and more. Dubbed in English. Inspired a rash of "shockumentaries" over the next several years. The song "More" made its debut in this film. 105m/C VHS, DVD. *IT D:* Gualtiero Jacopetti; *W:* Gualtiero Jacopetti; *C:* Antonio Climati, Benito Frattari; *M:* Riz Ortolani, Nino Oliviero; *Nar:* Stefano Sibaldi.

Mondo Cane 2 ♂♂ *Mondo Pazzo; Mondo Insanity; Crazy World; Insane World* 1964 (R) More documentary-like views of the oddities of mankind and ethnic rituals around the world. Enough, already. 94m/C VHS, DVD. *IT D:* Gualtiero Jacopetti, Franco Prosperi.

Mondo Trasho WOOF! 1969 A major trasho film of the last day in the life of a most unfortunate woman, complete with sex and violence. First full length effort from cult filmmaker Waters, who was also writer, producer, and editor. 95m/B VHS. Mary Vivian Pearce, Divine, John Leisening, Mink Stole, David Lochary, Chris Atkinson, Mark Isherwood; *D:* John Waters; *W:* John Waters; *C:* John Waters.

The Money ♂♂ 1975 (R) The quest for money drives a young man to kidnap the child that his girlfriend is baby-sitting. Average but Workman's direction is right

Mondovino ♂♂½ 2004 (PG-13) French/American documentary looks at the wine industry in the context of the rise of globalization, marketing, and corporate groupthink vs. craftsmanship, independent thought, and tradition. Thought-provoking, if somewhat meandering and bloated piece also explores issues such as relations between the U.S and France, and America's perceived economic imperialism. 131m/C DVD. *US D:* Jonathan Nossiter; *C:* Jonathan Nossiter, Stephanie Pommez.

on the money. 88m/C VHS, DVD, Laurence Luckinbill, Elizabeth Richards, Danny DeVito, Graham Beckel. D: Chuck Workman.

Money Buys Happiness 1999 Money (Weatherford) and Georgia (Murphy) are on the verge of divorce when a friend commits suicide and leaves them an upright piano. Their problems crystal-lize as they attempt to transport the instru-ment 50 books across town. That's a curi-ous premise for a comedy but this one manages to generate some genuine wit. 104m/C VHS, Cynthia Whalen, Caveh Zahedi; D: Gregg Lachow; W: Gregg Lachow; C: Jamie Hook; M: Jim Ragland.

Money Talks 1997 (R) Hustler Franklin Hatchet (Tucker) is falsely ac-cused of orchestrating a violent jail break. Ratings-hungry TV reporter James Rus-sell (Sheen) agrees to help Franklin clear his name in return for exclusive rights to his story. The mismatched pair search for stolen jewels, dodge bullets and endure explosive escapes, but this being an ac-tion-comedy, there needs to be some laughs. These are provided (intermittently)

Money for Nothing 1993 (R) $1.2 million falls off a truck in the ware-house district of Philadelphia where a sim-ple-minded unemployed longshoreman (Cusack) finds the chance of a lifetime. Indiscreetly leaving behind a trail of spending, he soon has a detective (Mad-sen) snooping around dangerously close. But he only digs himself deeper by enlist-ing the assistance of the mob to help him launder the money. At this point the film disintegrates into a limp diatribe on the injustice of capitalism on society's down-trodden. Mazar plays Joey's ex-girlfriend who double-times it back to the fold after his find. Based on a true story. 100m/C VHS, DVD, John Cusack, Michael Madsen, Beni-cio Del Toro, Michael Rapaport, Debi Mazar, Fion-nula Flanagan, Maury Chaykin, James Gandolfini, Elizabeth Bracco, Ashleigh Dejon, Lanny Venito; D: Ramon Menendez; W: Ramon Menendez, Car-ol Sobieski; M: Craig Safan.

Money Kings Vlg 1998 (R) Slow-starter is worth the time it takes to get the story moving. Soft-hearted Vinnie Glenn (Falk) runs a Boston bar and serves as a small-time bookie to some backroom gambling. Then the local mob decide Vin-nie needs an assistant to help him collect on the bad debts and send in a young hothead, Anthony (Prinze). Vinnie would like to restore the status quo before he heads to a Florida vacation with loyal wife Ellen (Daly), if only Anthony will listen. 96m/C VHS, DVD, Peter Falk, Freddie Prinze Jr., Lauren Holly, Timothy Hutton, Tyne Daly; D: Gra-ham Theakston.

Money Madness 1947 Beau-turned thief in this curiosity. 73m/C VHS, Hugh Beaumont, Frances Rafferty, Harlan Warde, Cecil Weston, Ida Moore, Danny Morton, Joel Friedkin, Lane Chandler; D: Sam Newfield; W: Al Martin; C: Jack Greenhalgh.

Money Movers 1978 Aussie thieves plan megabuck bank robbery but heist and plot go sour. An oft told tale based on a true story. Features early ap-pearance from burly boy Brown. 94m/C VHS, AU Terence Donovan, Ed Devereaux, Tony Bonner, Lucky Grills, Charles "Bud" Tingwell, Can-dy (Candice) Raymond, Bryan Brown, Alan Cas-sell; D: Bruce Beresford; W: Bruce Beresford.

The Money Pit 1986 (PG) A young yuppie couple encounter sundry problems when they attempt to renovate their newly purchased seemingly self-de-structive Long Island home. However, the collapse of their relationship is the collapse of their relationship as well. Somewhat modeled after "Mr. Blandings Builds His Dream House." Hanks and Long fail to jell as partners and the many sight gags are on the predictable side. A Spielberg production. 91m/C VHS, DVD, Tom Hanks, Shelley Long, Alexander Godunov, Mau-reen Stapleton, Philip Bosco, Joe Mantegna, Josh Mostel, Yakov Smirnoff, Carmine Caridi, Brian Backer, Wendell Pierce, Mike Starr, Frankie Fai-son, Nestor Serrano, Michael Jeter; D: Richard Benjamin; W: David Giler; C: Gordon Willis; M: Michel Colombier.

The Moneytree 1993 A care-free would-be actor decides to make some money by harvesting a huge marijuana crop in the California hills, all the while tending of his girlfriend, the cops, and some wild boars. 92m/C VHS, Christopher Dienstag; D: Alan Dienstag.

A Mongolian Tale Hei Ma 1994 Nai Nai has raised her granddaughter Somiya and the abandoned Bayingbalag among the Mongolian steppes. Eventual-ly, Bayingbulag leaves to get an education but promises to return and marry Somiya. Away three years, he comes back only to discover Somiya pregnant, so he takes off, finds success as a folk singer, and doesn't return for 12 years. Somiya now has a drunken husband, four sons, and an illegitimate 12-year-old daughter who is desperate for a father. Mongolian dia-logue. Adapted by Chengzhi from his story "A Song of the Grassland." 105m/C VHS, CH HK Narenhua, Tengger; D: Xie Fei; W: Zhang Chengzhi; C: Jing Sheng Fu; M: Tengger. Montre-al World Film Fest. '95: Director (Fei).

Mongrel woof! 1983 El-cheapo ken-nel horror about a man who dreams he's a wild murderous mutt. His relief upon wak-ing up is short-lived, however, when he discovers the people he jailed in his dreams are actually dead. Flick will make you want to gnaw on a bone. 90m/C VHS. Aldo Ray, Terry Evans; D: Robert Burns.

The Mongols Les Mongols 1960 Splashy Italian production has Gen-ghis Khan's son repelling invading hordes while courting buxom princess. Pairing of Palance and Ekberg makes this one wor-thy of consideration. 105m/C VHS, IT FR Jack Palance, Anita Ekberg, Antonella Lualdi, Franco Silva, Gianni 'John' Garko, Roldano Lupi, Gabriel-la Pallotta; D: Andre de Toth, Leopoldo Savona, Riccardo Freda.

by the frenzied comic style of Tucker, who easily eclipses Sheen's straight man de-meanor (which could be mistaken for act-ing if you've never seen any of Sheen's previous films). Tucker shows flashes of when the girl becomes pregnant and gives deserving better material than he has to work with here. 92m/C VHS, DVD Chris Tuck-er, Charlie Sheen, Heather Locklear, Paul Sorvino, Veronica Cartwright, Elise Neal, Paul Gleason, Larry Hankin, Daniel Roebuck, David Warner, Mi-chael Wright, Gerard Ismael; D: Brett Ratner; W: Joel Cohen, Alec Sokolow; C: Russell Carpenter, Robert Primes; M: Lalo Schifrin.

Money to Burn 1983 Aging high school counselor and two senior cit-izens develop a plan to steal $50 million from the Federal Reserve Bank. Harmless bit of fun. 90m/C VHS, Jack Kruschen, Meegan King, David Wallace, Phillip Pine; D: Virginia Lively Stone.

Money to Burn 1994 (R) Two buddies go off on a wild spending spree when $2 million in cash falls into their laps. Only one problem—a crazy cop who's de-termined to stop them squandering the money. 96m/C VHS, Chad McQueen, Don Swayze, Joe Estevez, Julia Strain, Sydney Las-sick; D: John Sjogren; W: John Sjogren, Scott Ziehl.

Money Train 1995 (R) Snipes and Harrelson team up again, this time as New York City transit cops (and foster brothers) who decide to rob the money train—a subway car that collects all the cash accrued from the transit system each day. To complicate matters, they're both in love with their new Latina partner (Lopez). Lame attempt to cash in on the Snipes and Harrelson chemistry leaves out one important ingredient—a competent script. The movie is almost over before the train actually becomes part of the plotline. Film came under criticism when it was blamed for a series of "copycat" arsons in which a New York City subway clerk was killed. 110m/C VHS, DVD, Skipp (Robert L.) Sudduth, Enrico Colantoni, Jose Zuniga, Bill Nunn, ...ary (Lawrence) Gilliard Jr., Michael Artura, Woody Harrelson, Wesley Snipes, Jennifer Lopez, Robert (Bobby) Blake, Chris Cooper, Joe Grifasi; D: Jo-seph Ruben; W: Doug Richardson, David Lough-ery; C: John Lindley; M: Mark Mancina.

Monika 1952 Two teenagers who run away togeth-er for the summer find the winter brings more responsibility than they can handle when the girl becomes pregnant and gives birth. Lesser, early Bergman, sensitively directed, but dull. Adapted by Bergman from a Per Anders Fogelstrom novel. In Swedish with English subtitles. 96m/B VHS, SW Harriet Andersson, Lars Ekborg, John Harry-son, Georg Skarstedt, Dagmar Ebbesen, Ake Gronberg; D: Ingmar Bergman; W: Ingmar Berg-man; M: Les Baxter.

Monique 1976 A sophisticated ca-reer woman is about to unleash a terrify-ing secret on her new husband. 96m/C VHS, Florence Giorgetti, John Ferris; D: Jacques Scandelari; W: Louisa Rose.

Monkey Boy 1990 Decent sci-fi horror from Britain, about a cunning humar-ape hybrid that escapes from a ge-netics lab after massacring the staff. Not excessively gruesome or vulgar, and some sympathy is aroused for the killer mutant. Based on the novel "Chimera." 104m/C VHS, John Lynch, Christine Kavanagh, Kenneth Cranham; D: Lawrence Gordon-Clark.

Monkey Business 1931 Marx Brothers run amok as stowaways on ocean liner. Fast-paced comedy provides seemingly endless amount of gags, quips, and pratfalls, including the fab four imitat-ing Maurice Chevalier at immigration. This film, incidentally, was the group's first to be written—by noted humorist Perel-man—directly for the screen. 77m/B VHS, DVD, Groucho Marx, Harpo Marx, Chico Marx, Zeppo Marx, Thelma Todd, Ruth Hall, Harry Woods, Tom Kennedy, Rockliffe Fellowes, Maxine Castle; D: Norman Z. McLeod; W: S.J. Perelman, Arthur Sheekman; C: Arthur L. Todd.

Monkey Business 1952 A scientist invents a fountain-of-youth po-tion, a lab chimpanzee mistakenly dumps it into a water cooler, and then grown-ups start turning into adolescents. Top-flight comedy, though comic moments shine. Monroe is the secretary sans skills, while absent-minded Grant and sexy wife Rog-ers race hormonally as teens. 97m/B VHS, DVD, Charlotte Austin, Cary Grant, Ginger Rogers, Charles Coburn, Marilyn Monroe, Hugh Marlowe, Larry Keating, George Winslow; D: Howard Hawks; W: Ben Hecht, Charles Lederer, I.A.L. Dia-mond; C: Milton Krasner; M: Leigh Harline.

Monkey Grip 1982 An un-married woman copes with parenthood and a drug-addicted boyfriend while work-ing on the fringe of Australia's music busi-ness. Grim but provocative, based on Hel-en Graham's novel. 101m/C VHS, AU Noni Hazlehurst, Colin Friels, Alice Garner, Harold Hop-kins, Candy (Candida) Raymond; D: Ken Camer-on; W: Ken Cameron, Australian Film Inst. '82: Ac-tress (Hazlehurst).

Monkey Hustle 1977 (PG) Vin-tage blaxploitation has trouble hustling laffs. The Man plans a super freeway through the ghetto, and law abiding do gooders join forces with territorial dudes to fight the project. Shot in the Windy City. 90m/C VHS, DVD, Yaphet Kotto, Rudy Ray Moore, Rosalind Cash, Debbi (Deborah) Morgan, Thomas Carter; D: Arthur Marks.

Monkey Shines 1988 (R) Monkey Shines: An Experiment in Fear, Ella 1988 (R) Based on the novel by Michael Stuart, this is a sick, scary yarn after a quadriplegic who is given a specially trained capuchin monkey as a helpmate. However, he soon finds that the beast is assuming and act-ing on his subconscious rages. 108m/C VHS, DVD, Jason Beghe, John Pankow, Kate McNeil, Christine Forrest, Stephen (Steve) Root, Joyce Van Patten, Stanley Tucci, Janine Turner; D: George A. Romero; W: George A. Romero; C: James A. Contner; M: David Shire.

Monkey Trouble 1994 (PG) Lonely schoolgirl Birch is feeling aban-doned when mom and stepdad shower at-tention on her new baby brother. Then a ...

ered monkey, who steals the show. Birch is amusing as the youngster caught in all sorts of uncomfortable situations. Formula abounds, but the milk and cookies set won't notice; fine family fare. 95m/C VHS, DVD, Thora Birch, Harvey Keitel, Mimi Rogers, Christopher McDonald; D: Franco Amurri; W: Franco Amurri, Stu Krieger; M: Mark Mancina.

Monkeybone 2001 (PG-13) Weird comedy about comatose cartoonist Stu Miley (Fraser), who must escape from his own consciousness in order to return to consciousness after an accident. Monkeybone, a chimp embodiment of the teenager's libido from his "Show Me the Monkey" animated pilot is the focus of the rest of the film as he escapes from the underworld and "steals" Stu's body to ro-mance his awaiting girlfriend (Fonda). Kat-tan is funny as the organ donor and Tur-turro, who puts his considerable talent to voicing a monkey, is successful, but one note libidinous simian humor makes flimsy material for a film. Based on the graphic novel "Dark Town" by Kaja Blackley. 92m/C VHS, DVD, US Brendan Fraser, Bridget Fonda, Whoopi Goldberg, Chris Kattan, Dave Foley, Gian-carlo Esposito, Rose McGowan, Megan Mullally, Lisa Zane; D: Henry Selick; W: Sam Hamm; C: Andrew Dunn; M: Anne Dudley; V: John Turturro.

Monkeys, Go Home! 1966 Dumb Disney yarn about young American who inherits a badly neglected French olive farm. When he brings in four chim-panzees to pick the olives, the local town-speople go on strike. People can be so sensitive. Based on "The Monkeys" by G. K. Wilkinson. Chevalier's last film appear-ance. 89m/C VHS, DVD, Dean Jones, Yvette Mimieux, Maurice Chevalier, Clement Harari, Yvonne Constant; D: Andrew V. McLaglen; M: Robert F. Brunner.

The Monkey's Mask 2000 Lesbian private detective Jill Fitzpatrick (Porter) is hired by the parents of missing student Mickey Norris (Cornish). Jill meets Mickey's married poetry professor Diana (McGillis) and the two soon embark on a torrid affair. Then Mickey is found stran-gled and Jill searches (rather ineptly) for the killer and nearly becomes a victim her-self. Who knew poetry could be so dan-gerous? Based on the 1994 nonrhyming verse thriller by Dorothy Porter. 94m/C VHS, DVD, AU Susie Porter, Kelly McGillis, Marton Cso-kas, Francoise Varley, Caroline Gillmer, Jean-Pierre Mignon, Jim Holt, John Noble, Linden Wil-kinson; D: Samantha Lang; W: Anne Kennedy; C: Garry Phillips.

Monkey's Uncle 1965 A se-quel to Disney's "The Misadventures of Merlin Jones" and featuring more bizarre antics and scientific hoopla, including chimps and a flying machine. 90m/C VHS, Tommy Kirk, Annette Funicello, Leon Ames, Arthur O'Connell; D: Robert Stevenson; W: Alfred Lewis Levitt, Helen Levitt; C: Edward Colman; M: Buddy Baker.

The Monocle 1964 Steele plays a seductive villainess in this rare spy/comedy thriller. 100m/C VHS, FR Paul Meurisse, Barbara Steele, Marcel Dalio; D: Georges Lautner; W: Jacques Robert; C: Maurice Fellous; M: Michel Magne.

Monolith 1993 (R) Tucker (Paxton) and Flynn (Frost) are unlikely partners on the LAPD. But they're teamed up on an unlikely case a Russian scientist commits a seemingly senseless murder and is taken away by a mystery man (Hurt) before she can be interrogated. What the curious duo discover is a lethal alien force capable of possessing any living creature and whose objective is the de-struction of the planet. 96m/C VHS, Bill Pax-ton, Lindsay Frost, John Hurt, Louis Gossett Jr.; D: John Eyres; W: Stephen Lister.

The Monolith Monsters 1957 A geologist investigates a meteor shower in Arizona and discovers strange crystals. The crystals attack humans and absorb their silicone, causing them to grow into monsters. Good "B" movie fun. 76m/B VHS, Grant Williams, Lola Albright, Les Tremayne, Trevor Bardette; D: John Sherwood; W: Jack Arnold, Norman Jolley, Robert M. Fresco; M: Joseph Gershenson.

Monsieur Beaucaire 1924 The Duke of Chartres ditches France posing as a barber, and once in Britain, becomes a lawman. At once a classic Valentino vehicle. 100m/B VHS. Rudolph Valentino, Bebe Daniels, Lois Wilson, Doris Kenyon, Lowell Sherman, John Davidson; **D:** Sidney Olcott.

Monsieur Beaucaire 1946 Entertaining Hope vehicle that casts him as a barber impersonating a French nobleman in the court of Louis XV. He's set to wed a Spanish princess in order to prevent a full-scale war from taking place. However, he really wants to marry social-climber chambermaid Caulfield. Director Marshall was at his best here. Based on the novel by Booth Tarkington. 93m/B VHS, DVD. Bob Hope, Joan Caulfield, Patric Knowles, Marjorie Reynolds, Cecil Kellaway, Joseph Schildkraut, Reginald Owen, Constance Collier; **D:** George Marshall; **W:** Melvin Frank, Norman Panama; **C:** Lionel Lindon.

Monsieur Hire 1989 (PG-13) The usual tale of sexual obsession and suspense. Mr. Hire spends much of his time trying to spy on his beautiful young neighbor woman, alternately alienated and engaged by her love affairs. The voyeur soon finds his secret desires have entangled him in a vicious intrigue. Political rally set-piece is brilliant. Excellent acting, intense pace, elegant photography. Based on "Les Fiancailles de M. Hire" by Georges Simenone and adapted by Leconte and Patrick Dewolf. In French with English subtitles. 81m/C VHS. *FR* Michel Blanc, Sandrine Bonnaire, Luc Thuillier, Eric Berenger, Andre Wilms; **D:** Patrice Leconte; **W:** Patrice Leconte. Cesar '90: Sound.

Monsieur Ibrahim *Ibrahim and the Flowers of the Koran; Monsieur Ibrahim et les Fleurs du Coran* 2003 (R) Coming-of-age story set in the low-rent district of 1960s Paris. Momo (Boulanger) is a Jewish street youth burdened with a chronically depressed father (Melki) and a mother who deserted him. Sharif excels as Ibrahim, a philosophy-spouting Turkish Muslim shopkeeper who befriends and adopts Momo after his father kills himself. Ibrahim tends to Momo's spiritual development while the local prostitutes and the girl next door teach him about sex and romance. Duperyon creates a lighthearted, sentimental fairytale about tolerance and spirituality. Adapted from writer Schmitt's semi-autobiographical book and play. 94m/C DVD. *FR* Omar Sharif, Pierre Boulanger, Gilbert Melki, Lola Naymark, Anne Suarez, Isabelle Renauld, Isabelle Adjani; **D:** Francois Dupeyron; **W:** Francois Dupeyron; **C:** Remy Chevrin.

Monsieur N. 2003 (R) A charming work of historical speculation that wonders if the body believed to belong to Napoleon Bonaparte truly is the corpse of the legendary French emperor. Opening in 1840, when Napoleon's remains were returned to Paris, the narrative shifts back in time to the emperor's exile on the island of St. Helena after 1815. The narrator, Basil Heathcote (Rodan), is the liaison between Napoleon's (Torreton) staff and Sir Hudson Lowe (Grant), the British governor of the island. Plots against Bonaparte abound as Lowe fumes at the expense of the exile and the emperor's retinue lusts after their promised inheritance. Caunes deftly keeps the mystery brisk and engaging, while Torreton delivers a hypnotic portrayal of the tactical genius. 127m/C DVD. Philippe Torreton, Richard E. Grant, Jay Rodan, Elsa Zylberstein, Bruno Putzulu, Stephane Freiss, Frederic Pierrot, Roschdy Zem, Siobhan Hewlett; **D:** Antoine de Caunes; **W:** Rene Manzor; **C:** Pierre Aim; **M:** Stephan Eicher.

Monsieur Verdoux 1947 A thorough Chaplin effort, as he produced, directed, wrote, scored and starred. A prim and proper bank cashier in Paris marries and murders rich women in order to support his real wife and family. A mild scandal in its day, though second-thought pacifism and stale humor date it. A bomb upon release (leading Chaplin to shelve it for 17 years) and a cult item today, admired for both its flaws and complexity. Raye fearlessly chews scenery and croissants. Initially based upon a suggestion from Orson Welles. 123m/B VHS, DVD. Charlie Chaplin, Martha Raye, Isobel Elsom, Mady Correll, Marilyn Nash, Irving Bacon, William Frawley, Allison Roddan, Robert Lewis; **D:** Charlie Chaplin; **W:** Charlie Chaplin; **C:** Curt Courant, Roland H. Totheroh; **M:** Charlie Chaplin.

Monsieur Vincent 1947 True story of 17th century French priest who became St. Vincent de Paul (Fresnay). He forsakes worldly possessions and convinces members of the aristocracy to finance his charities for the less fortunate. Inspirational. French with subtitles. 112m/B VHS. *FR* Pierre Fresnay, Lisa (Lise) Delamare, Aime Clariond, Jean Debucourt, Pierre Dux, Gabrielle Dorziat, Jean Carmel, Michel Bouquet; **D:** Maurice Cloche; **W:** Jean Anouilh, Jean-Bernard Luc; **C:** Claude Renoir. Oscars '48: Foreign Film.

Monsignor woof! 1982 (R) Callow, ambitious priest befriends worldly Vatican's business affairs. No sparks generated by Reeve and Bujold (who appears nude in one scene), and no real conviction related by most other performers. Absurd, ludicrous melodrama best enjoyed as unintentional comedy. Based on Jack Alain Leger's book. 121m/C VHS. Christopher Reeve, Fernando Rey, Genevieve Bujold, Jason Miller; **D:** Frank Perry; **W:** Abraham Polonsky, Wendell Mayes; **C:** Billy Williams; **M:** John Williams.

Monsignor Quixote 1991 A small town priest takes on the persona of his ancestor, Don Quixote, and prepares to battle the evil he sees around him. Based on the novel by Graham Greene. 118m/C VHS. Alec Guinness, Ian Richardson, Graham Crowden, Maurice Denham, Philip Stone, Rosalie Crutchley, Valentine Pelka, Don Fellows, Leo McKern; **D:** Rodney Bennett.

Monsoon 1997 Ambitious project from director Mundhra (known best for his erotic thrillers) is set in Goa, India. That's where Kenneth Blake (Tyson) and his fiancee Sally Stephens (McShane) go to visit his friend (McCoy). But in a previous incarnation Kenneth was a lover of Leela (Brodie), who's now married to the local drug lord Miranda (Grover). Their centuries-spanning affair causes the usual complications. Local color is actually much more interesting and the film looks very sharp. 96m/C DVD. Richard Tyson, Matt McCoy, Gulshan Grover, Jenny (Jennifer) McShane, Doug Jeffery, Helen Brodie; **D:** Jag Mundhra; **C:** Blain Brown; **M:** Alan Dermot Derosian.

Monsoon Wedding 2001 (R) Outlines the clash of India's traditional culture with the growing modern sensibilities of the new Delhi. Aditi Vermas (Das) is promised in marriage to Hemant (Dabas) an Indian computer programmer living in Houston, whom she has yet to meet. The problem is, Aditi has a life of her own, including a married TV host for a boyfriend. When the couple eventually meet, tensions and attraction arises as a bevy of romantic subplots swirl like the title's monsoon around them. Film's large, Altman-esque cast of characters include both sides of the intendeds' family. Nair's engaging storylines, fresh premise and lush cinematography succeed in depicting the turbulent modern life in Delhi. In English, and Hindi and Punjabi (with English subtitles). 113m/C VHS, DVD. *IN US* Naseeruddin Shah, Lillete Dubey, Shefali Shetty, Vasundhara Das, Parvin Dabas, Vijay Raaz, Tilotama Shome, Rajat Kapoor; **D:** Mira Nair; **W:** Sabrina Dhawan; **C:** Declan Quinn; **M:** Mychael Danna.

The Monster 1925 This silent horror film has all the elements that would become genre standards. Mad scientist Dr. Ziska (Chaney), working in an asylum filled with lunatics, abducts strangers to use in his fiendish experiments to bring the dead back to life. There's the obligatory dungeon and even a lovely heroine (Olmsted) that needs rescuing. Great atmosphere and Chaney's usual spine-tingling performance. Based on the play by Crane Wilbur. 86m/B VHS. Lon Chaney Sr., Gertrude (Olmstead) Olmsted, Johnny Arthur, Charles Sellon, Walter James, Hallam Cooley; **D:** Roland West; **W:** Albert Kenyon, Willard Mack; **C:** Hal Mohr.

Monster 1978 (R) Bloodthirsty alien indiscriminately preys on gaggle of teens in wilds of civilization. Performers struggle with dialogue and their own self-esteem. 98m/C VHS. Jim Mitchum, Diane McBain, Roger Clark, John Carradine, Phil Carey, Anthony Eisley, Keenan Wynn; **D:** Herbert L. Strock.

The Monster *Il Monstro; Le Monstre* 1996 (R) Italian impresario of comedy Benigni co-wrote, directed and starred in this film that has become the highest grossing film in Italian history to date. Jaded American audiences, however, may find the broad comedy of errors all too familiar territory with Loris (Benigni) as a criminal Clouseau, an incompetent petty thief whom police mistake for a serial murderer on the loose. Cops install an attractive female detective (Braschi), Benigni's wife) in the sexually strained shyster's apartment to tempt him into striking again. Sight gags aplenty populate Benigni's highly physical performance, including: being pulled wildly around a garage attached to an out-of-control chainsaw; contending with a lit cigarette down his pants; and scores of pratfalls, all of which garner comparisons to comedy phenom, Jim Carrey. French director and actor Blanc ("Dead Tired") is great as the loony police psychiatrist. 110m/C VHS, DVD. *IT* Roberto Benigni, Nicoletta Braschi, Michel Blanc, Dominique Lavanant, Jean-Claude Brialy, Ivano Marescotti, Laurent Spielvogel, Massimo Girotti, Franco Mescolini; **D:** Roberto Benigni; **W:** Roberto Benigni, Vincenzo Cerami; **C:** Carlo Di Palma; **M:** Evan Lurie.

Monster 2003 (R) Charlize Theron plays Aileen Wuornos, the first woman serial killer executed in the U.S., who murdered seven men on the highways of Florida in the 1980s. Focuses on the love affair between Selby Wall (Ricci) and Wuornos. While the film itself has some flaws, not the least of which is portraying Wournos as a victim whose motive was self-defense, Theron's complete transformation for and commitment to the role is fascinating to watch. Her performance alone is worth the rental. 111m/C DVD. *US* Charlize Theron, Christina Ricci, Bruce Dern, Scott Wilson, Pruitt Taylor Vince, Lee Tergesen, Annie Corley; **D:** Patty Jenkins; **W:** Patty Jenkins; **C:** Steven Bernstein; **M:** BT (Brian Transeau). Oscars '03: Actress (Theron); Golden Globes '04: Actress—Drama (Theron); Ind. Spirit '04: Actress (Theron); First Feature; Natl. Soc. Film Critics '03: Actress (Theron); Screen Actors Guild '03: Actress (Theron).

Monster a Go-Go! woof! 1965 Team of go-go dancers battle a ten-foot monster from outerspace whose mass is due to a radiation mishap. He can't dance, either. 70m/B VHS, DVD. Phil Morton, June Travis, Bill Rebane, Herschell Gordon Lewis, Lois Brooks, George Perry; **D:** Bill Rebane, Herschell Gordon Lewis; **W:** Herschell Gordon Lewis.

The Monster and the Girl 1941 It's the mob vs. the ape in this tale of revenge. Scott (Terry) discovers innocent sister Susan (Drew) is being lead down the path to prostitution by suave mobster Reed (Paige). But Reed manages to frame Scott for murder and he's executed, although not before donating his brain to science. Then scientist Parry (Zucco) decides to transplant the brain into the body of an ape who goes on a rampage aimed at the mobster. 65m/B VHS. Ellen Drew, Robert Paige, Phillip Terry, Paul Lukas, Joseph Calleia, Onslow Stevens, Rod Cameron, George Zucco, Marc Lawrence, Gerald Mohr; **D:** Stuart Heisler; **W:** Stuart Anthony; **C:** Victor Milner.

The Monster Club 1985 Price and Carradine star in this music-horror compilation, featuring songs by Night, B.A. Robertson, The Pretty Things and The Viewers. Soundtrack music by John Williams, UB 40 and The Expressos. 104m/C VHS, DVD. *GB* Vincent Price, Donald Pleasence, John Carradine, Stuart Whitman, Britt Ekland, Simon Ward, Patrick Magee; **D:** Roy Ward Baker.

The Monster Demolisher 1960 Nostradamus' descendent shares the family penchant for sanguine cocktails, and threatens a professor who protects himself with an electronic wonder of modern technology. Edited from a sombrero serial; if you make it through this one, look up its Mexican siblings, "Curse of Nostradamus" and "Genie of Darkness." 74m/B VHS. *MX* Domingo Soler, Julio Aleman, Aurora Alvarado, German Robles; **D:** Frederick Curiel; **W:** Alfredo Ruanova; **C:** Fernando Colin; **M:** Jorge Perez.

Monster Dog woof! 1982 A rock band is mauled, threatened, and drooled upon by an untrainable mutant canine. Rock star Cooper plays the leader of the band. No plot, but the German shepherd is worth watching. 88m/C VHS, DVD. Alice Cooper, Victoria Vera; **D:** Clyde (Claudio Fragasso) Anderson.

Monster from Green Hell 1958 An experimental rocket containing radiation-contaminated wasps crashes in Africa, making giant killer wasps that run amok. Stinging big bug horror. 71m/B VHS, DVD. Jim Davis, Robert E. (Bob) Griffin, Barbara Turner, Eduardo Ciannelli; **D:** Kenneth Crane; **W:** Endre Bohem, Louis Vittes; **C:** Ray Flin; **M:** Albert Glasser.

Monster from the Ocean Floor *It Stalked the Ocean Floor; Monster Maker* 1954 An oceanographer in a deep-sea diving bell is threatened by a multi-tentacled creature. Roger Corman's first production. 66m/C VHS, DVD. Anne Kimball, Stuart Wade, Jonathan Haze, Wyott Ordung, David Garcia, Dick Pinner; **D:** Wyott Ordung; **W:** William Danch; **C:** Floyd Crosby; **M:** Andre Brummer.

Monster High 1989 (R) Bloodthirsty alien indiscriminately preys on gaggle of teens in wilds of civilization. Even the people who made this one may not have seen it all the way through. 89m/C VHS, DVD. David Marriot, Dean Iandoli, Diana Frank, D.J. Kerzner; **D:** Rudiger Poe.

Monster House 2006 (PG) Artistically and effectively creepy outing from executive producers Zemeckis and Spielberg is just the second film to utilize stop-motion animation (their "Polar Express" was the first). Halloween-worthy story follows a trio of kids who investigate the neighborhood haunted house, which devours anything or anyone who gets too close. State-of-the-art technique allows animated characters, including the house, to show emotion and expression while excellent voice work from the likes of Buscemi and Gyllenhaal lend real human talent to the eye-popping visual technology. 91m/C DVD. Blu-ray Disc. *US D:* Gil Kenan; **V:** Steve Buscemi, Maggie Gyllenhaal, Jon Heder, Mitchel Musso, Spencer Locke, Nick Cannon, Kevin James, Jason Lee, Catherine O'Hara, Kathleen Turner, Fred Willard.

Monster in a Box 1992 (PG-13) Master storyteller Gray spins a wonderful tale about his life, revolving stories about his adventures at a Moscow film festival, a trip to Nicaragua, and his first experience with California earthquakes. Filled with wit, satire, and hilarity. Filmed before an audience, this is based on Gray's Broadway show of the same title. By the way, the monster in the box is a 1,900-page manuscript of his autobiography and the box in which he lugs it around. 88m/C VHS, DVD. Spalding Gray; **D:** Nick Broomfield; **W:** Spalding Gray; **C:** Michael Coulter; **M:** Laurie Anderson.

Monster-in-Law 2005 (PG-13) Awfully nice girl from Venice Beach (Lopez) has a whirlwind courtship and romance with an Adonis-like surgeon (Vartan) but meets with great resistance from his has-been television reporter mother (Fonda) upon the announcement of their engagement. A bevy of battles to put-down or one-up one another ensues. Lopez's character is nothing new, Vartan shows no personality, and although Fonda makes the atrocious behavior of her character palatable, one still wonders why she choose this one-dimensional and craven comedy for a comeback. 100m/C VHS, DVD. *US* Jane Fonda, Jennifer Lopez, Michael Vartan, Wanda Sykes, Will Arnett, Adam Scott, Annie Parisse, Monet Mazur, Elaine Stritch, Stephen Dunham; **D:** Robert Luketic; **W:** Anya Kochoff, Scott

Monster in the Closet 1986 (PG) A gory horror spoof about a rash of San Francisco murders that all take place inside closets. A news reporter and his scientist friend decide they will be the ones to protect California from the evil but shy creatures. From the producers of "The Toxic Avenger." 87m/C VHS. **C:** R. Russell Carpenter; **M:** David Newman, Dana Sano.

The Monster Maker 1944 Low-budget gland fest in which deranged scientist develops serum that inflates heads, feet, and hands. He recklessly inflicts others with this potion, then must contend with deformed victims while courting a comely gal. 65m/B VHS, DVD. J. Carrol Naish, Ralph Morgan, Wanda McKay, Terry Frost, Glenn Strange, Tala Birell; **D:** Sam Newfield; **C:** Robert E. Cline; **M:** Albert Glasser.

Monster Man 2003 (R) Horror flick rule number one: don't be the idiots who rile up the disfigured, ill-tempered guy with the big truck. College buddies Adam and Harley, road tripping to reach the girl they both love to prevent her impending nuptials, are just idiots. Could be enjoyable, genre fun if you're in the mood. 95m/C VHS, DVD. Eric Jungmann, Justin Urich, Aimee Brooks, Michael Bailey Smith, Robert (Bob) Wick; **D:** Michael Davis; **C:** Matthew Irving; **M:** John Coda. VIDEO

The Monster of London City 1964 *Das Ungeheuer von London City* During a stage play about Jack the Ripper, murders occur paralleling those in the production. The lead actor finds himself to be the prime suspect. Lightweight horror from Germany. 87m/B VHS, DVD. GE: Hansjorg Felmy, Marianne Koch, Dietmar Schonher, Hans Nielsen; **D:** Edwin Zbonak.

The Monster of Piedras Blancas WOOF! 1957 During a seaside festival, two fisherman are killed by a bloodthirsty oceanic critter with no respect for holidays. The fishing village is determined to find it and kill it. Low-budget, with amateurish effects and poor acting. 72m/B VHS. Les Tremayne, Jeanne Carmen, Forrest Lewis, John Harmon, Don Sullivan; **D:** Irvin Berwick; **W:** H. Haile Chace; **C:** Philip Lathrop.

The Monster Squad 1987 (PG-13) Youthful monster enthusiasts find their community inundated by Dracula, Frankenstein creature, Wolf Man, Mummy, and Gill Man(!?!), who are all searching for a life-sustaining amulet. Somewhat different, but still somewhat mediocre. 82m/C VHS, DVD. Andre Gower, Stephen Macht, Tom Noonan, Duncan Regehr, Mary Ellen Trainor; **D:** Fred Dekker; **W:** Fred Dekker, Shane Black; **M:** Bruce Broughton.

The Monster That Challenged the World 1957 Huge, ancient eggs are discovered in the Salton Sea and eventually hatch into killer, crustaceous caterpillars. Superior monster action. 83m/B VHS, DVD. Tim Holt, Audrey Dalton, Hans Conried, Harlan Ward, Max (Casey Adams) Showalter, Mimi Gibson, Gordon Jones; **D:** Arnold Laven; **W:** Pat Fielder, David Duncan.

The Monster Walks 1932 A whodunit thriller, complete with stormy nights, suspicious cripples, weird servants, a screaming gorilla, and a spooky house. Nor unique but entertaining. 60m/B VHS, DVD. Rex Lease, Vera Reynolds, Mischa Auer, Willie Best; **D:** Frank Strayer.

Monster on the Campus 1959 *Monster on the Campus; Stranger on the Night*. Science-fiction thriller about the blood of a prehistoric fish turning college professor into murderous beast. Will the halls of Dunsfield University ever be safe again? 76m/B VHS, DVD. Arthur Franz, Joanna Moore, Judson Pratt, Nancy Walters, Troy Donahue; **D:** Jack Arnold.

Monster's Ball 2001 (R) Georgia death-row prison guard Hank (Thornton) is following in his father Buck's (Boyle) footsteps as a guard, and as a bigot. His son (Ledger) also has joined the family business, but doesn't seem to have the heart or stomach for it. When his son throws up during the execution of Lawrence Musgrove (Combs), Hank flies into a rage that makes him reexamine his life. Soon after, he helps the waitress, Leticia (Berry) from the diner he frequents after an auto accident. Leticia is Musgrove's widow, unbeknownst to Hank, who begins what at first is a desperate, sexual relationship with Hank that changes both of them. Director Forster and scriptiers Addica and Rokos provide a well-done, raw, and unflinching story that the excellent cast, especially Berry (who won the Best Actress Oscar) and Thornton inhabit perfectly. Boyle is also powerful as the racist patriarch. Everything comes together before they can announce Forster's arrival as a director. 111m/C VHS. US Billy Bob Thornton, Halle Berry, Heath Ledger, Peter Boyle, Sean (Puffy, Puff Daddy, P. Diddy) Combs, Coronji Calhoun, Mos Def, Will Rokos, Milo Addica; **C:** Roberto Schaefer; Oscars '01: Actress (Berry); Natl. Bd. of Review '01: Actor (Thornton), Actress (Berry); Screen Actors Guild '01: Actress (Berry).

Monsters, Inc. 2001 (G) Sweet-natured animated film from Pixar that's geared more towards the younger end of the family spectrum than films like "Toy Story." Monstropolis is a town that is powered by the screams of human children, which are captured in tanks thanks to "scarers" who invade the kids' bedrooms via their closet doors. Sully (Goodman) is the best there is, with the help of buddy Mike (Crystal), but he has a problem when human toddler Boo (Gibbs) accidentally gets loose in monster town, which is a big no-no, and Sully has to get her safely home. There's also some sinister goings-on at a company level causing problems for our boys. Very colorful and more silly than scary (what's scary is the familiar toddler behavior). 92m/C VHS, DVD. US **C:** Pete Docter. **W:** Andrew Stanton, Daniel Gerson; **M:** Randy Newman; **V:** John Goodman, Billy Crystal, Steve Buscemi, Mary Gibbs, James Coburn, Jennifer Tilly, John Ratzenberger, Frank Oz, Bob Peterson, Bonnie Hunt. Oscars '01: Song ("If I Didn't Have You").

Monster's Crash the Pajama Party 1965 Mad scientist is discovered conducting weird experiments in a group of teens who enter a supposedly haunted house. This one was much better in the theatre, because "monsters" would run through the audience and select a victim. Then the monsters and the victim would magically appear on the screen. Weird. 31m/C VHS, DVD. Peter J. D'Noto, Vic McGee, James Reason, Pauline Hilcurt, Charles Egan, Joseph Ormond; **D:** David L. Hewitt; **W:** David L. Hewitt, Jay Lister; **C:** David L. Hewitt, Austin McKay.

Montana 1997 (R) Claire (Sedgwick) is a professional killer, who works with partner Nick (Tucci) for the eccentric Boss (Coltrane). When Boss' drug addict mistress Kitty (Tunney) runs away, Claire and Nick are given the thankless task of retrieving her and have to also endure the presence of the man's imbecile son, Jimmy (Embry). Then Kitty kills Jimmy and Claire and Nick are also accused of embezzling from the organization—so the trio are now being hunted by their own syndicate. Good cast is hampered by a not particularly memorable story. 96m/C VHS. Kyra Sedgwick, Stanley Tucci, Robbie Coltrane, Robin Tunney, Philip Seymour Hoffman, John Ritter, Ethan (Randall) Embry; **D:** Jennifer Leitzes; **W:** Erich Hoeber, Jon Hoeber; **C:** Ken Kelsch; **M:** Cliff Eidelman.

Montana 1990 (PG) Hoyce and Bess Guthrie are long-married and strong-willed ranchers who are at odds over the family ranch in Montana. He wants to sell the land to a power company and she wants to keep the land in the family. 91m/C VHS. Gena Rowlands, Richard Crenna, Lea Thompson, Justin Deas, Elizabeth Berridge, Scott Coffey, Darren Dalton; **D:** William A. Graham; **W:** Larry McMurtry. CABLE

Montana Belle 1952 A buxom bandit teams with the notorious Dalton Brothers before embarking on a life of reform. In the card game of life, Russell is always holding a pair. 81m/C VHS. Jane Russell, George Brent, Scott Brady, Forrest Tucker, Andy Devine, Jack Lambert, John Litel, Ray Teal; **D:** Allan Dwan.

Monte Carlo 1930 Poor Countess Vera (MacDonald) dumps her boring, rich fiance, Prince Otto (Allister) and heads to Monte Carlo to win big. Shy Count Rudolph (Buchanan) thinks Vera will bring him good luck and asks to stroke her blonde curls. When Vera wins instead, she decides to hire Rudolph, whom she mistakenly believes is a hairdresser. When her fortunes reverse, Vera contemplates marrying the boring prince again without realizing that Rudolph is in love with her (and that he has loads of cash). 90m/B DVD. Jeanette MacDonald, Jack Buchanan, Claud Allister, Lionel Belmore, Tyler Brooke, John Roche; **D:** Ernst Lubitsch; **W:** Ernest Vajda; **C:** Victor Milner; **M:** W. Franke Harling.

Monte Carlo 1986 A sexy Russian woman aids the Allies by relaying important messages during WWII. Fun TV production featuring Collins in her seductive best. 200m/C VHS. Joan Collins, George Hamilton, Lisa Eilbacher, Lauren Hutton, Robert Carradine, Malcolm McDowell; **D:** Anthony Page. TV

Monte Carlo Nights 1934 Wrongly convicted murderer determines to prove his innocence even as he is tracked by police. 60m/B VHS. Mary Brian, John Darrow, Kate Campbell, Robert Frazer, Astrid Allwyn, George "Gabby" Hayes, George Cleveland; **D:** William Nigh.

Monte Walsh 1970 (PG) Aging cowboy sees declining of Old West, embarks on mission to avenge best friend's death. Subdued, moving western worthy of genre greats Marvin and Palance. Cinematographer Fraker proves himself a proficient director in this, his first venture. Based on Jack Schaefer's novel. 100m/C VHS. Lee Marvin, Jack Palance, Jeanne Moreau, Jim Davis, Mitchell Ryan; **D:** William A. Fraker; **W:** David Zelag Goodman; **M:** John Barry.

Monte Walsh 2003 Tried-and-true horse opera adapted from the novel by Jack Schaefer and a remake of the 1970 film. Aging cowpoke Monte Walsh (Selleck) realizes that life in 1892 Wyoming's Antelope Junction is changing. An eastern company is taking over the western free-range society and fewer cowboys are making a living. Monte has his loyal love Martine (Rossellini) to sustain him, but pal Chet (Carradine) needs a way to support his family and hot-headed Shorty (Eads) has turned to crime. Selleck has become a comfortable old hand at these roles; the pleasures may be predictable but they're still present. 120m/C DVD. Tom Selleck, Isabella Rossellini, Keith Carradine, George Eads, William Devane, Barry Corbin, James Gammon, William Sanderson, Wallace Shawn, Joanna Miles; **D:** Simon Wincer; **W:** Robert B. Parker, Michael Brandman, David Zelag Goodman, Lukas Heller; **C:** David Eggby; **M:** Eric Colvin. CABLE

Montenegro 1981 *Or Pigs and Pearls.* Offbeat, bawdy comedy details experiences of bored, possibly mad housewife who lands in a coarse, uninhibited ethnic community. To its credit, this film remains unpredictable to the end. And Anspach, an intriguing, resourceful—and attractive—actress, delivers what is perhaps her greatest performance. 97m/C VHS, DVD. SW Susan Anspach, Erland Josephson; **D:** Dusan Makavejev; **W:** Dusan Makavejev; **C:** Tomislav Pinter; **M:** Kornell Kovac.

Monterey Pop 1968 This pre-Woodstock rock 'n' roll festival in Monterey, California features landmark performances by some of the most popular '60s rockers. Compelling for the performances and historically important as the first significant rock concert film. Appearances by Jefferson Airplane, Janis Joplin, Jimi Hendrix, Simon and Garfunkel, The Who, and Otis Redding. 72m/C VHS, DVD. **D:** James Desmond, Richard Leacock, D.A. Pennebaker, Nicola Piovani.

Montana Sky 2007 Jack Mercy's will is very clear—his three daughters must live on his Montana ranch for one year in order to claim their inheritance. But the women, who are half-sisters, are strangers to each other and they anticipate trouble with their forced family reunion. What they get is a saboteur who is determined to drive them from the ranch before they can claim dad's fortune. Lifetime original movie based on the novel by Nora Roberts. 96m/C DVD. Charlotte Ross, John Corbett, Diane Ladd, Nathaniel Arcand, Ashley Williams, Laura Mennell, Aaron Pearl; **D:** Mike Robe; **W:** April Smith; **C:** Eric Van Haren Noman; **M:** Steve Porcaro.

A Month by the Lake 1995 (PG) Redgrave takes the plunge into highly familiar "romantic comedy of the somewhat wooden, but gradually warming, English Major Wilshaw (Fox). Petulant American nanny Miss Beresford (Thurman) arrives to provide an arresting diversion for Wilshaw, while Gassman proves an unwilling pawn for Miss Bentley's game of "get the major." Touching and lighthearted performances, especially by heavyweight Redgrave, Edward Fox, Uma Thurman, Alida Valli, Alessandro Gassman, Carlo Cartier; **D:** John Irvin; **W:** Trevor Bentham; **C:** Pasqualino De Santis; **M:** Nicola Piovani.

A Month in the Country 1987 The reverently quiet story of two British WWI veterans, one an archaeologist and the other a church painting restorer, who are working to heal their emotional wounds. Based on the novel by J.L. Carr. 92m/C VHS, DVD. GB: Colin Firth, Kenneth Branagh, Natasha Richardson, Patrick Malahide, Tony Haygarth, Jim Carter; **D:** Pat O'Connor; **W:** Simon Gray; **C:** Kenneth Macmillan; **M:** Howard Blake.

Monty Python and the Holy Grail 1975 (PG) Britain's famed comedy band assaults the Arthurian legend in a cult classic replete with a Trojan rabbit and an utterly dismembered, but inevitably pugnacious, knight. Fans of manic comedy—and graphic violence—should get more than their fill here. 90m/C VHS, DVD, UMD. GB Graham Chapman, John Cleese, Terry Gilliam, Eric Idle, Terry Jones, Michael Palin, Carol Cleveland, Connie Booth, Neil Innes, Patsy Kensit; **D:** Terry Gilliam, Terry Jones; **W:** Graham Chapman, John Cleese, Terry Gilliam, Eric Idle, Terry Jones, Michael Palin; **C:** Terry Bedford; **M:** De Wolfe, Neil Innes.

Monty Python's Life of Brian 1979 (R) Often riotous spoof of Christianity tracks hapless peasant mistaken for the messiah in A.D. 32. Film reels from routine to routine, and only the most pious will remain unmoved by a chorus of crucifixion victims. Probably the group's most daring, controversial venture. 94m/C VHS, DVD. GB Graham Chapman, John Cleese, Terry Gilliam, Eric Idle, Michael Palin, George Harrison, Terry Jones, Kenneth Colley, Spike Milligan, Carol Cleveland, Neil Innes, Andrew MacLachlan; **D:** Terry Jones; **W:** Graham Chapman, John Cleese, Terry Gilliam, Eric Idle, Michael Palin, Terry Jones; **C:** Peter Biziou; **M:** Geoffrey Burgon.

Monty Python's The Meaning of Life 1983 (R) Funny, technically impressive film conducts various inquiries into the most profound questions confronting humanity. Notable among the sketches here are a live sex enactment performed before bored schoolboys, a student-faculty rugby game that turns quite violent, and an encounter between a physician and a reluctant, untimely organ donor. Another sketch provides a memorable portrait of a glutton prone to nausea. And at film's end, the meaning of life is actually revealed. 107m/C VHS, DVD, HD DVD. GB Graham Chapman, John Cleese, Terry Gilliam, Eric Idle, Terry Jones, Michael Palin, Carol Cleveland.

Cleveland, Matt Frewer, Simon Jones, Patricia Quinn, Andrew MacLachlan; **D:** Terry Gilliam, Terry Jones; **W:** Graham Chapman, John Cleese, Terry Gilliam, Eric Idle, Terry Jones, Michael Palin; **C:** Peter Hannan; **M:** John Du Prez, Graham Chapman, John Cleese, Eric Idle, Terry Jones, Michael Palin. Cannes '83: Grand Jury Prize.

Monument Ave. 🦴🦴½ *Snitch* 1998 Updated, Irish-American version of Martin Scorsese's "Mean Streets" focuses on a group of petty thieves from Boston's mostly Irish Charleston neighborhood. The hoods, lead by Bobby O'Grady (Leary), pass time stealing cars, snorting cocaine, and waxing poetic about their dead-end lives. But when a recently paroled member of their gang is murdered by the neighborhood kingpin Jackie O' (Meaney), Bobby must decide between upholding the gang's code of silence and avenging his pal's death. Excellent performances all around, especially from Leary, who grew up in this neighborhood. Originality, however, is not the film's strong suit. In addition to borrowing from Scorsese, script is full of Tarantinoesque banter. Worthy effort, just don't expect anything you haven't seen before. **90m/C VHS, DVD.** Denis Leary, Billy Crudup, Famke Janssen, Colm Meaney, Martin Sheen, Jeanne Tripplehorn, Ian Hart, Jason Barry, John Diehl, Noah Emmerich, Greg Dulli; **D:** Ted (Edward) Demme; **W:** Mike Armstrong; **C:** Adam Kimmel; **M:** Amanda Scheer-Demme.

Moolaade 🦴🦴 *Protection* 2004 Eighty-one-year-old Senegalese filmmaker/activist Sembene focuses on the practice of female genital mutilation that still occurs in a number of African countries. In a small village, Colle (Coulibaly), the fearless second wife of a village elder, refuses to allow her daughter Amasatou (Traore) to undergo the purification ceremony that has caused her own lifelong pain. She then becomes the protector of four young girls, also fleeing the ceremony, who seek sanctuary. To defend the girls, Colle invokes the traditional protective spirit of the title so the girls cannot be removed from her care and discovers her resistance is considered a threat to the social order of village life. Bambara and French with subtitles. **124m/C** Fatoumata Coulibaly, Malmouna Helene Diarra, Salimata Traore, Dominique T. Zeida, Mah Compaore, Aminata Dao; **D:** Ousmane Sembene; **W:** Ousmane Sembene; **C:** Dominique Gentil; **M:** Boncana Maiga.

The Moon and Sixpence 🦴🦴🦴 1943 Stockbroker turns ambitious painter in this adaptation of W. Somerset Maugham's novel that was, in turn, inspired by the life of artist Paul Gauguin. Fine cast, taut pacing. Filmed in black and white, but uses color sparingly to great advantage. Compare this one to "Wolf at the Door," in which Gauguin is played by Donald Sutherland. **89m/B VHS, DVD.** George Sanders, Herbert Marshall, Steven Geray, Doris Dudley, Eric Blore, Elena Verdugo, Florence Bates, Albert Bassermann, Heather Thatcher; **D:** Albert Lewin.

Moon 44 🦴🦴½ 1990 (R) A space prison is overrun by thugs who terrorize their fellow inmates. Fine cast, taut pacing. Filmed in Germany. **102m/C VHS, DVD. GE** Malcolm McDowell, Lisa Eichhorn, Michael Pare, Stephen Geoffreys, Roscoe Lee Browne, Brian Thompson, Dean Devlin, Mechmed Yilmaz, Leon Rippy; **D:** Roland Emmerich.

Moon in Scorpio 🦴½ 1986 Three Vietnam-vet buddies go sailing and are attacked by the back-from-the-dead victims of a bloody war crime. **90m/C VHS.** John Philip Law, Britt Ekland, William (Bill) Smith; **D:** Gary Graver.

Moon in the Gutter 🦴🦴 *Dans le Caniveau* 1983 (R) In a ramshackle harbor town, a man searches despondently for the person who killed his sister years before. Various sexual liaisons and stevedore fights intermittently spice up the action. Nasty story that doesn't make much sense on film; adapted from a book by American pulp writer David Goodis. In French with English subtitles. **109m/C VHS. FR** Gerard Depardieu, Nastassja Kinski, Victoria Abril, Vittorio Mezzogiorno, Dominique Pinon; **D:** Jean-Jacques Beineix; **W:** Jean-Jacques Beineix; **C:** Philippe Rousselot; **M:** Gabriel Yared. Cesar '84: Art Dir/Set Dec.

The Moon Is Blue 🦴🦴½ 1953 A young woman flaunts her virginity in this stilted adaptation of F. Hugh Herbert's play. Hard to believe that this film was once considered risque. Good performances, though, from Holden and Niven. **100m/B** William Holden, David Niven, Maggie McNamara, Tom Tully; **D:** Otto Preminger; **C:** Ernest Laszlo. Golden Globes '54: Actor—Mus./Comedy (Niven).

Moon of the Wolf 🦴🦴 1972 A small town in bayou country is terrorized by a modern-day werewolf that rips its victims to shreds. **74m/C VHS, DVD.** Barbara Rush, Bradford Dillman, John Beradino, Geoffrey Lewis, Royal Dano; **D:** Daniel Petrie; **W:** Alvin Sapinsley; **C:** Richard C. Glouner; **M:** Bernardo Segall. **TV**

Moon over Broadway 🦴🦴🦴 1998 Filmmakers (and spouses) Pennebaker and Hegedus follow the Broadway-bound comedy "Moon over Buffalo" in its evolution from pen to premiere—a lot like "Waiting for Guffman," but for real. Along the way we see how a bunch of professionals try to fine-tune a very average script into a funny comedy, and all the rewrites, conflicts, and jealousies that entails. As the celebrity of the cast, Burnett is at first resented (this isn't TV and she hasn't been on Broadway in 30 years), but winds up the life of the party, injecting most of the humor, and shows herself to be the real trouper among them. All in all an interestingly tense, and sometimes funny, behind-the-scenes look—with the biggest disappointment being the play itself, which did manage to run for nine months, probably thanks to Burnett. **92m/C VHS, DVD.** Carol Burnett, Philip Bosco; **D:** D.A. Pennebaker, Chris Hegedus; **C:** D.A. Pennebaker, James Desmond.

Moon over Harlem 🦴🦴 1939 A musical melodrama about a widow who unwittingly marries a fast-talking gangster involved in the numbers racket. The film features 20 chorus girls, a choir, and a 60-piece orchestra. **67m/B VHS, DVD.** Bud Harris, Cora Green, Alec Lovejoy, Sidney Bechet; **D:** Edgar G. Ulmer.

Moon over Miami 🦴🦴🦴 1941 Manhunting trio meet their match in this engaging musical. A remake of 1938's "Three Blind Mice," this was later remade in 1946 as "Three Little Girls in Blue." ♪Moon Over Miami; I've Got You All To Myself; What Can I Do For You?; Kindergarten Congo; You Started Something; Oh Me Oh Mi-Am-Mi; Solitary Seminole; Is That Good?; Loveliness and Love. **91m/C VHS, DVD.** Don Ameche, Betty Grable, Robert Cummings, Carole Landis, Charlotte Greenwood, Jack Haley; **D:** Walter Lang; **W:** Mitch Glazer; **C:** Leon Shamroy.

Moon over Parador 🦴🦴½ 1988 (PG-13) An uneven comedy about a reluctant American actor who gets the role of his life when he gets the chance to pass himself off as the recently deceased dictator of a Latin American country. A political strongman wants to continue the charade until he can take over, but the actor begins to enjoy the benefits of dictatorship. Look for a cameo by director/writer Mazursky in drag. **103m/C VHS, DVD.** Richard Dreyfuss, Sonia Braga, Raul Julia, Jonathan Winters, Fernando Rey, Ed Asner, Dick Cavett, Michael Greene, Sammy Davis Jr., Polly Holliday, Charo, Marianne Sagebrecht, Dana Delany, Ike Pappas, Paul Mazursky; **D:** Paul Mazursky; **W:** Leon Capetanos, Paul Mazursky; **M:** Maurice Jarre.

Moon over Tao 🦴🦴 1997 In 16th-century Japan, a Samurai (Abe) and a sorcerer (Nagashima) are dispatched to discover the origins of a strange sword which can cut through solid stone. Once on their quest, they learn that the sword was forged from a meteorite, which also housed a strange orb. This orb contains the power to destroy the world. Meanwhile, three mysterious alien females are dispatched to Earth to retrieve the orb. Unfortunately, it has fallen into the hands of an evil tyrant (Enoki) who wants to use its powers to rule the planet. Successfully mixes sword & sorcery action with a science fiction slant. Director Amemiya is best known for making films featuring futuristic creatures, but he tones that down here, evoking an interesting narrative and impressive fight scenes. American viewers familiar with similar films will find the pacing here a bit different, but the film is engrossing all the same. **96m/C DVD. JP** Toshiyuki Nagashima, Hiroshi Abe, Takaaki Enoki; **D:** Keito Amamiya.

Moon Pilot 🦴🦴 1962 An astronaut on his way to the moon encounters a mysterious alien woman who claims to know his future. **98m/C VHS,** Tom Tryon, Brian Keith, Edmond O'Brien, Dany Saval, Tommy Kirk; **D:** James Neilson.

The Moon-Spinners 🦴🦴½ 1964 (PG) Lightweight Disney drama featuring Mills as a young tourist traveling through Crete who meets up with a young man, accused of being a jewel thief, and the two work together to find the real jewel thieves. Watch for silent film star Pola Negri. **118m/C VHS, DVD.** Hayley Mills, Peter McEnery, Eli Wallach, Pola Negri, Joan Greenwood, Irene Papas, Sheila Hancock; **D:** James Neilson; **W:** Michael Dyne; **M:** Ron Grainer.

The Moon Stallion 🦴🦴½ 1985 A charming tale of mystery and fantasy for children and adults. Professor Purwell is researching King Arthur. His blind daughter soon becomes involved with supernatural events and a white horse that appears to lead her into adventures not of this age. **95m/C VHS. GB** Sarah Sutton, David Haig, James Greene, John Abineri, Caroline Goodall; **D:** Dorothea Brooking.

Moonbase 🦴🦴 1997 (R) In the year 2045, John Russell, manager of the Moonbase Waste Disposal Plant, has his hands full with more than garbage when a group of prison escapees take over the facility. **89m/C VHS, DVD.** Scott Plank, Jocelyn Seagrave, Kurt Fuller, Robert O'Reilly; **D:** Paolo Mazzucato; **W:** Brian DiMuccio, Dino Vindeni; **M:** Michael Sherwood. **VIDEO**

Mooncussers 🦴½ 1962 A children's film detailing the exploits of a precocious 12-year-old determined to exact revenge upon a band of ruthless pirates. **85m/C VHS.** Kevin Corcoran, Rian Garrick, Oscar Homolka; **D:** James Neilson.

Moondance 🦴🦴 1995 (R) When lovely young German tourist Anya (Brendler) comes to an Irish fishing village on a summer holiday, two young brothers, Patrick (Shaw) and Dominic (Conroy), vie for her affections causing a family rift. Adapted from the novel "The White Hare" by Francis Stuart. **96m/C VHS, DVD. GB** Ruaidhri Conroy, Ian Shaw, Julia Brendler, Marianne Faithfull, Gerard McSorley, Kate Flynn, Brendan Grace; **D:** Dagmar Hirtz; **W:** Burt Weinshanker, Matt Walters; **C:** Steven Bernstein; **M:** Van Morrison, Fiachra Trench.

Moondance Alexander 🦴🦴½ 2007 (G) Appealing family film. Awkward 15-year-old Moondance (Panabaker) lives with her eccentric mom Gelsey (Loughlin) and expects to have an uneventful summer. Then she finds pinto pony Checkers has jumped his paddock fence, so she returns him to ranch owner Dante Longpre (Johnson). Convinced that Checkers is a champion jumper just waiting for his chance, Moondance then convinces Dante to train her and Checkers for an upcoming competition. **94m/C DVD.** Kay Panabaker, Don Johnson, Lori Loughlin, James Best, Sasha Cohen, Whitney Sloan, Joe Norman Shaw; **D:** Michael Damian; **W:** Michael Damian, Janeen Damian; **C:** Julien Eudes; **M:** Mark Thomas. **VIDEO**

Moonfleet 🦴🦴½ 1955 Follows the adventures of an 18th century buccaneer who tries to swindle a young lad in his charge of a valuable diamond. From J. Meade Falkner's novel. **89m/C VHS.** Stewart Granger, Jon Whiteley, George Sanders, Viveca Lindfors, Joan Greenwood, Ian Wolfe; **D:** Fritz Lang; **M:** Miklos Rozsa.

Moonlight and Valentino 🦴🦴 1995 (R) To help her recover from the death of her husband, Rebecca turns to the comfort of flaky neighbor Sylvie (Paltrow), self-destructive sis Lucy (Paltrow) and overbearing ex-stepmother Alberta (Turner). Together they sit around and talk some of the more contrived and cliched "women talk" ("Chicken soup is the most womanly thing on the face of the planet") in recent film history. The finale, a hokey ritual in a cemetery, will have you pulling out hair rather than hankies. Rock star Bon Jovi makes his screen debut as the beefcake (discussion of his butt takes up about two-thirds of the dialogue) who puts the fire back into Rebecca's life. Not for the estrogen impaired. **104m/C VHS, DVD.** Elizabeth Perkins, Whoopi Goldberg, Gwyneth Paltrow, Kathleen Turner, Jon Bon Jovi, Jeremy Sisto, Josef Sommer, Peter Coyote; **D:** David Anspaugh; **W:** Ellen Simon; **C:** Julia Macat; **M:** Howard Shore.

Moonlight Mile 🦴🦴🦴 2002 (PG-13) Quirky look at dealing with grief in the aftermath of tragedy. Circa 1973, Joe Nast (Gyllenhaal) has attended the funeral of his fiancee Diana Floss at the home of her parents Ben (Hoffman) and JoJo (Sarandon). Literally at a loss, Joe moves in to the Floss home and forms an unusual bond with these virtual strangers. To fill his void, Ben tries to get Joe to go into the real estate development business with him. The strident JoJo guesses there's more to Joe's loss than meets the eye. Joe is aided in his grief when he meets attractive postal worker Bertie (Pompeo) who has experienced similar loss. Coleman gives an animated performance as the local rich guy who shatters Ben's dreams. Great performances all around, especially by newcomer Pompeo. Loosely based on director Silberling's experience as the boyfriend of murdered actress Rebecca Schaffer. **112m/C VHS, DVD. US** Jake Gyllenhaal, Dustin Hoffman, Susan Sarandon, Holly Hunter, Ellen Pompeo, Richard T. Jones, Allan Corduner, Dabney Coleman, Akelsia Landeau, Roxanne Hart; **D:** Brad Silberling; **W:** Brad Silberling; **C:** Phedon Papamichael; **M:** Mark Isham.

Moonlight Sonata 🦴🦴½ 1938 Professional concert pianist Paderewski performs his way through a confusing soap-opera of a film. Includes performances of Franz Liszt's "Second Hungarian Rhapsody" and Frederic Chopin's "Polonaise." **80m/B VHS, DVD. GB** Ignace Jan Paderewski, Charles Farrell, Marie Tempest, Barbara Greene, Eric Portman; **D:** Lothar Mendes.

Moonlighting 🦴🦴🦴½ (PG) Compelling drama about Polish laborers illegally hired to renovate London flat. When their country falls under martial law, the foreman conceals the event and pushes workers to complete project. Unlikely casting of Irons as foreman is utterly successful. **97m/C VHS, DVD. PL GB** Jeremy Irons, Eugene Lipinski, Jiri Stanislav, Eugeniusz Haczkiewicz; **D:** Jerzy Skolimowski; **C:** Tony Pierce-Roberts; **M:** Hans Zimmer.

Moonlighting 🦴🦴🦴½ 1982 (PG) Pilot for the popular detective show, where Maddie and David, the daffy pair of impetuous private eyes, meet for the first time and solve an irrationally complex case. **93m/C VHS, DVD.** Cybill Shepherd, Bruce Willis, Allyce Beasley; **D:** Robert Butler; **W:** Glenn Gordon Caron; **C:** Michael D. Margulies; **M:** Lee Holdridge. **TV**

The Moonraker 🦴🦴½ 1958 Compelling action scenes highlight this tale set at the end of the English Civil War, as the Royalists attempt to sneak the king out of England and into France. **82m/C VHS. GB** George Baker, Sylvia Syms, Peter Arne, Marius Goring, Clive Morton, Gary Raymond, Richard Leech, Patrick Troughton; **D:** David MacDonald.

Moonraker 🦴🦴 1979 (PG) Uninspired Bond fare has 007 unraveling intergalactic hijinks. Bond is aided by a female CIA agent, assaulted by a giant with jaws of steel, and captured by Amazons when he sets out to protect the human race. Moore, Chiles, and Lonsdale all seem to be going through the motions only. **136m/C VHS, DVD. GB** Roger Moore, Lois Chiles, Richard Kiel, Michael (Michel) Lonsdale, Corinne Clery, Geoffrey Keen, Emily Bolton, Walter Gotell, Bernard Lee, Lois Maxwell, Desmond Llewelyn; **D:** Lewis Gilbert; **W:** Christopher Wood; **C:** Jean Tournier; **M:** John Barry.

The Moon's Our Home 🦴🦴½ 1936 A fast-paced, breezy, screwball comedy about an actress and adventurer impulsively marrying and then bickering through the honeymoon. Silliness at its height, Fonda and Sullivan were both married and then divorced before filming this movie. **80m/B VHS.** Margaret Sullavan, Henry Fonda, Beulah Bondi, Charles Butterworth, Margaret Hamilton, Walter Brennan, Grace Hayle, Lucien Littlefield, Spencer Charters, Henrietta Crosman, Margaret Fielding, Dub Taylor, Dorothy Parker; **C:** Alan Campbell, Isabel Dawn, Dorothy Parker; **C:** Joseph Valentine.

Moonshine County Express 1977 (PG). Three sexy daughters of a hillbilly moonshiner set out to run the still and avenge their father's murder. **97m/C VHS.** John Saxon, Susan Howard, William Conrad, Morgan Woodward, Claudia Jennings, Jeff Corey, Dub Taylor, Maureen McCormick, Albert Salmi, Candice Rialson; **D:** Gus Trikonis.

Moonshine Highway 1996 (PG-13). Redneck alert '50s Tennessee moonshiner Jed Muldoon (MacLachlan) clashes with Sheriff Miller (Quaid), who's not only aggrieved about Jed's illegal liquor running but is not happy that his estranged wife Ethel (Del Mar) has taken up with the miscreant. Lots of backwoods car chases. **96m/C VHS.** Kyle MacLachlan, Randy Quaid, Maria Del Mar, Gary Farmer, Jeremy Ratchford; **D:** Andy Armstrong; **W:** Andy Armstrong; **C:** Dick Quinlan. **CABLE.**

Moonshine Mountain Woof! 1964 A country-western star travels with his girlfriend to the singer's home in backwoods Carolina. When the girl is killed by a lusting resident, all hell breaks loose. One of gore-meister Lewis' excursions into the dramatic. **90m/C VHS.** Chuck Scott, Adam Sorg, Bonnie Hinson, Carman Sotir, Ben Moore, Pat Patterson, Mark Douglas, Colin Baker; **D:** Herschell Gordon Lewis; **W:** Herschell Gordon Lewis; **C:** Herschell Gordon Lewis.

The Moonstone 1972 The moonstone is a fabulous jewel from India that lovely Rachel Verinder (Heilbron) receives on her birthday. However, the gem is stolen property and is now stolen from Rachel, which brings Sgt. Cuff (Welsh) of Scotland Yard in to solve the crime. Adaptation of the 1868 Wilkie Collins novel. **221m/C DVD.** GB Vivien Heilbron, John Welsh, Robin Ellis, Martin Jarvis, Basil Dignam, Colin Baker; **D:** Paddy Russell; **W:** Hugh Leonard. TV.

The Moonstone 1997 In the mid-19th century, the Moonstone, a sacred Hindu diamond, is stolen from a shrine in India. The jewel, which carries a curse, winds up in the hands of heiress Rachel Verinder (Hawes), thanks to her suitor Franklin Blake (Wise). But when the diamond is stolen from Rachel, police Sergeant Cuff (Sher) investigates and uncovers deception and a variety of villains. Based on the novel by Wilkie Collins and considered the first detective story, some 20 years before Conan Doyle's Sherlock Holmes. **120m/C VHS, DVD.** Greg Wise, Anthony Sher, Keeley Hawes, Patricia Hodge; **D:** Robert Bierman. TV.

Moonstruck 1987 (PG-13). Winning romantic comedy about widow engaged to one man but falling in love with his younger brother in Little Italy. Excellent performances all around, with Cher particularly fetching as attractive, hapless widow. Unlikely casting of usually domineering Aiello, as unassuming mama's boy also works well, and Cage is at his best as a tormented one-handed opera lover/baker. **103m/C VHS, DVD.** Cher, Nicolas Cage, Olympia Dukakis, Danny Aiello, Vincent Gardenia, Julie Bovasso, Louis Guss, Anita Gillette, Feodor Chaliapin Jr., John Mahoney; **D:** Norman Jewison; **W:** John Patrick Shanley; **C:** David Watkin; **M:** Dick Hyman. Oscars '87: Actress (Cher), Orig. Screenplay, Support. Actress (Dukakis); Berlin Intl. Film Fest. '87: Director (Jewison); Golden Globes '88: Actress—Mus./Comedy (Cher), Support. Actress (Dukakis); L.A. Film Critics '87: Support. Actress (Dukakis); Natl. Bd. of Review '87: Support. Actress (Dukakis); Writers Guild '87: Orig. Screenplay.

Moontrap 1989 An astronaut discovers an alien frozen in space and returns to Earth with it. Once thawed, the creature reveals its horrible secret. **92m/C** VHS. Walter Koenig, Bruce Campbell, Leigh Lombardi; **D:** Robert Dyke.

Morals for Women 1931 This soap-opera's so old it almost predates soap. A secretary becomes the Kept Woman of her boss in the Big Bad City. She escapes, but not for long. **65m/B VHS.** Bessie Love, Conway Tearle, John Holland, Natalie Moorhead, Emma Dunn, June Clyde; **D:** Mort Blumenstock.

Moran of the Lady Letty 1922 Seaweed saga of Ramon Laredo (Valentino), a high society guy who's kidnapped aboard a pirate barge. When the salty dogs rescue(cap-ture Moran (a theme ahead of its time?) from a ship turning with burning coal. Ramon is smitten in a big way with the boyish girl and battles contagiously to prevent the pirates from selling her as a slave. Excellent fight scenes with much hoistepping over gangplanks and swinging from masts, and a 60-foot death dive from above. Little known Dalton was a celluloid fave in the 'teens and twenties, and Valentino is atypically cast as a man's man. The one because it undermined his image as a ladies' man. **71m/B VHS.** Dorothy Dalton, Rudolph Valentino, Charles Brinley, Walter Long, Emil Jorgenson; **D:** George Melford.

More 1969 Smells like 'teen angst as an '60s when a German college grad falls for an American in Paris, to the tune of sex, drugs, and Pink Floyd, naturally. Schroeder's first effort as director, its definitely a '60s pic. In French with English subtitles. **110m/C VHS, DVD.** Mimsy Farmer, Klaus Grunberg, Heinz Engelmann, Michel Chanderli; **D:** Barbel Schroeder; **C:** Nestor Almendros.

More about the Children of Noisy Village 1987 *More About the Children of Bullerby Village/Mem on oss barn i Bullerby* 1987 The six adventurous children, who live in an idyllic Swedish village before WWII, return. This time they're ready to start a new school year, including playing pranks on the teacher, getting stranded during a blizzard, and enjoying a memorable New Year's Eve. Based on stories by Astrid Lindgren. Dubbed. **85m/C VHS.** SW Linea Bergstrom, Ellem Demerus, Crispin Wendenius, Henrik Larsson; **D:** Lasse Hallstrom; **C:** Jens Fischer; **M:** George Riedel.

More American Graffiti 1979 (PG) Sequel to 1973's acclaimed '50s homage "American Graffiti" charts various characters' experiences in the more radical '60s. George Lucas didn't direct, Richard Dreyfuss didn't reprise. Ron Howard doesn't direct, he acts. B.W.L. Norton doesn't direct either, though he's credited. Pass on this one and have that root canal done instead. **111m/C VHS, DVD.** Paul LeMat, MacKenzie Phillips, Charles Martin Smith, Anna Blom, Richard Bradford, Cindy Williams, Scott Glenn; **D:** Bill W.L. Norton; **W:** Gloria Katz, Willard Huyck; **C:** Caleb Deschanel.

More Dead Than Alive 1968 Gunslinger Cain (Walker) is released from an 18-year prison stint and is soon taking his sharpshooter credentials to a cheap wild west show run by Ruffalo (Price). But Cain's presence upsets former headliner, hot-headed young shooter Billy (Hampton). Surprise ending. **101m/C DVD.** Clint Walker, Vincent Price, Anne Francis, Paul Hampton, Mike Henry, Craig Littler; **D:** Robert Sparr; **W:** George Schenck; **C:** Jacques "Jack" Marquette; **M:** Philip Springer.

More Dogs Than Bones 2000 (R) Crook Victoria (Ruehl) is on the lam, so she decides to hide $1 million in the luggage of Indian tourist Raj (Giraff), who's on his way to L.A. When she sends her boys (Mantegna, Hipp) to retrieve the loot, they discover Raj is staying at his nephew Andy's (Naidu) apartment and no one knows where. Too bad the pooch couldn't have buried this movie as well. **92m/C VHS, DVD.** Mercedes Ruehl, Joe Mantegna, Paul Hipp, Peter Coyote, Chaim Giraff, Ajay Naidu, Debi Mazar, Louise Fletcher, DB Woodside, Whoopi Goldberg, Kevin Weisman, Eddie Kaye Thomas; **D:** Michael Browning; **W:** Michael Browning.

A Mormon Maid 1917 Young woman and her family, after being saved from an Indian attack by a Mormon group, come to live among them without converting to their beliefs. Considered a shocking expose of controversial Mormon practices, including polygamy. **78m/B VHS.** Mae Murray, Frank Borzage, Hobart Bosworth, Noah Beery Sr.; **D:** Robert Z. Leonard.

The Morning After 1986 (R) A predictable suspense-thriller about an alcoholic actress who wakes up one morning with a corpse in bed next to her, but cannot remember anything about the night before. She evades the police, accidentally meets up with an ex-cop, and works with him to unravel an increasingly complicated mystery. **103m/C VHS, DVD.** Jane Fonda, Jeff Bridges, Raul Julia, Diane Salinger, Richard Foronjy, Geoffrey Scott, Kathleen Wilhoite, Frances Bergen, Rick Rossovich, Kathy Bates; **D:** Sidney Lumet; **W:** James Cresson; **C:** Andrzej Bartkowiak.

Morituri *Morituri; Code Name: Morituri; The Saboteur;* 1965 Gripping wartime drama in which an Allied spy tries to persuade German gunboat captain to surrender the vessel. Brando is—no surprise—excellent. **123m/C VHS, DVD.** Marlon Brando, Yul Brynner, Trevor Howard, Janet Margolin, Wally Cox, William Redfield; **D:** Bernhard Wicki; **W:** Daniel Taradash; **C:** Conrad L. Hall; **M:** Jerry Goldsmith.

Morgan's Ferry 1999 (PG-13) Kinder, gentler "Desperate Hours" has three escaped cons, Sam (Zane), Monroe (Rollins), and Darcy (Galecki) happen upon the modest cottage of spinster Vonee (McGillis) and hold her hostage. Not only is she not afraid of the trio, but she falls in love with charming, sensitive Sam and hides him when his buddies decide to split. Interesting cast and nice twist on the escaped-cons-take-hostage story make this one better than it should be. **91m/C VHS, DVD.** Billy Zane, Kelly McGillis, Henry Rollins, Johnny Galecki, Roscoe Lee Browne, Muse Watson; **D:** Sam Pillsbury; **C:** Johnny E. Jensen; **M:** Reuben.

Morgan the Pirate *Capitaine Morgan; Morgan il Pirata* 1960 Steve Reeves at his finest as Morgan, an escaped slave who becomes a notorious pirate in the Caribbean and is wrongly condemned to death in this brisk, sea-going adventure. **95m/C VHS, FF.** IT Steve Reeves, Valerie Lagrange; **D:** Andre de Toth.

Morgan Stewart's Coming Home *Home Front* 1987 (PG-13) When Dad needs a good family image in his political race, he brings Morgan home from boarding school. Fortunately, Morgan can see how his parents are using him and he doesn't approve at all. He decides to turn his family's life upside down while pursuing his true love life. **96m/C VHS, DVD.** Jon Cryer, Lynn Redgrave, Nicholas Pryor, Viveka Davis, Paul Gleason, Savely Kramorov, Maureen Stapleton, Andrew Duncan; **D:** Alan Smithee; **W:** Peter Bernstein.

Morgan: A Suitable Case for Treatment *Morgan!; A Suitable Case for Treatment* 1966 Offbeat comedy in which deranged artist copes with divorce by donning ape suit. Some laughs ensue. Based on David Mercer's play. **93m/B VHS, DVD.** GB Vanessa Redgrave, David Warner, Robert Stephens, Irene Handl, Bernard Bresslaw, Arthur Mullard, Newton Blick, Nan Munro, Graham Crowden, John Rae, Peter Collingwood, Edward Fox; **D:** Karel Reisz; **W:** David Mercer; **C:** Larry Pizer; **M:** John Dankworth. British Acad. '66: Actress (Redgrave); Cannes '66: Actress (Redgrave).

More Wild, Wild West 1980 Another feature-length continuation of the satirical TV western series, with Winters taking on Conrad and Martin. **94m/C VHS.** Robert Conrad, Ross Martin, Jonathan Winters, Victor Buono; **D:** Burt Kennedy. TV.

The More the Merrier 1943 Likeable romantic comedy in which working girl must share apartment with two bachelors in Washington, D.C., during WWII. Arthur is especially endearing as a young woman in male company. **104m/B VHS, DVD.** Jean Arthur, Charles Coburn, Joel McCrea, Richard Gaines, Bruce Bennett, Ann Savage, Ann Doran, Frank Sully, Grady Sutton; **D:** George Stevens. Oscars '43: Support. Actor (Coburn); N.Y. Film Critics '43: Director (Stevens).

Morning Departure 1950 Suspenseful disaster story. During a post-war mission a British submarine hits a forgotten electric mine and sinks to the sea—only working snorkel equipment to get to safety while the sub's captain, Armstrong (Mills), tries to keep a stiff upper lip and keep the remaining three sailors calm while they await rescue. **102m/B DVD.** GB John Mills, Richard Attenborough, James Hayter, Nigel Patrick, Bernard Lee, Kenneth More; **D:** Roy Ward Baker; **W:** William Fairchild; **C:** Desmond Dickinson.

Morning Glory 1933 Small-town girl finds love and fame in the big city. Predictable fare nonetheless boasts fine performances from Hepburn and Fairbanks. Adapted from Zoe Atkins' stage play. **74m/B VHS, DVD.** Katharine Hepburn, Douglas Fairbanks Jr., Adolphe Menjou, Mary Duncan; **D:** Lowell Sherman; **M:** Max Steiner. Oscars '33: Actress (Hepburn).

Morning Glory 1993 (PG-13). Sappy romance, set during the Depression, about a pregnant widow (Raffin) trying to survive on her hardscrabble farm in Georgia. Elly Dinsmore advertises for a husband, and is answered by Will Parker (Reeve), an ex-con trying to live down his past. When a local floozy who's been eyeing Will is killed, the sheriff (Walsh) is only too happy to go after the stranger in town. Light-weight with some unbelievable plot twists. Based on the novel "Morning Glory" by LaVyrle Spencer. **90m/C VHS.** Deborah Raffin, Christopher Reeve, Lloyd Bochner, Nina Foch, Helen Shaver, J.T. Walsh; **D:** Steven Hilliard Stern; **W:** Charles Jarrott, Deborah Raffin.

Morocco 1930 A foreign legion soldier "falls for a world-weary chanteuse along the desert sands. Cooper has never been more earnest, and Dietrich has never been more blase and exotic. In her American film debut, Dietrich sings "What Am I Bid?" A must for anyone drawn to improbable, gloriously well-done kitsch. Based on the novel "Amy Jolly." **92m/B VHS, DVD.** Marlene Dietrich, Gary Cooper, Adolphe Menjou, Ullrich Haupt, Francis McDonald, Eve Southern, Paul Porcasi; **D:** Josef von Sternberg; **C:** Lee Garmes. Natl. Film Reg. '92.

Morons from Outer Space 1985 (PG) Slow-witted aliens from elsewhere in the universe crash onto Earth, but unlike other sci-fi's, these morons become internationally famous, despite them acting like intergalactic stooges. Plenty of sight gags. **87m/C VHS, DVD.** GB Griff Rhys Jones, Mel Smith, James B. Sikking, Dinsdale Landen, Jimmy Nail, Joanne Pearce, Paul Brown; **D:** Mike Hodges; **W:** Griff Rhys Jones, Mel Smith; **C:** Phil Meheux; **M:** Peter Brewis.

Mortal Challenge 1997 (R) A corrupt police force, known as the Centurions, guard a futuristic L.A., which is divided into rich and poor sectors. When wealthy Trci is captured visiting her wrong-side-of-the-sectors boyfriend, the Centurions decide to have some fun by matching her with a cyborg in a death game. **77m/C VHS, DVD.** Timothy Bottoms, David McCallum, Evan Lurie, Nick Hilt; **D:** Rancolph Cheveldave. **VIDEO**

Mortal Danger *Turn Your Pony Around* 1994 (PG-13) Kathy and Phil are suicidal teens finding different solutions to their difficulties over the same weekend. Comes across like a TV movie but does maintain an honest message with affecting performances. **86m/C VHS.** Ami Dolenz, Noah Hathaway, Paul Coufos, Larry Gatlin, Charles Napier; **D:** Brianne Murphy.

Mortal Kombat 1: The Movie 1995 (PG-13) Inevitable film version of the mega popular arcade game intended to cash in fast on the game's popularity. Shameless nirvana for youngin's with permanent joystick scars on their

Mortal (continued)

hands. Grown-ups forced to sit through it may get into some of the eye-popping special effects and nifty martial arts sequences if they can block out the contrived plot, lame acting, and Lambert's presence as Thunder God. **101m/C VHS, DVD.** Christopher Lambert, Talisa Soto, Cary-Hiroyuki Tagawa; Bridgette Wilson-Sampras; **D:** Paul W.S. Anderson; **W:** Kevin Droney; **C:** John R. Leonetti; **M:** George S. Clinton.

Mortal Kombat 2: Annihilation ♪½ **1997 (PG-13)** The treacherous Shao-Khan brings his evil horde of video-game villians through a portal ripped in the universe and threatens to destroy the Earth in this highly unnecesary sequel. Liu Kang and his buds are on the scene to once again do battle to save humanity. Moves from one badly staged fight scene to another with little story or acting (except for Remar in the role of Rayden, replacing Christopher Lambert in the first "Kombat"), and adults should quickly tire of the non-stop back flips and somersaulting that combine with computer graphics to give each character their own special abilities. Kids and gamers, however, should enjoy the new characters, the same-sounding pulse-pounding techno music, and the non-stop, but fairly bloodless, violence. **96m/C VHS, DVD.** James Remar, Robin Shou, Talisa Soto, Daron McBee, Sandra Hess, Brian Thompson, Reiner Schone, Musetta Vander, Marjean Holden, Litefoot, Lynn Red Williams, Irina Pantaeva; **D:** John R. Leonetti; **W:** Brent Friedman, Bruce Zabel; **C:** Matthew F. Leonetti; **M:** George S. Clinton.

Mortal Passions ♪♪½ **1990 (R)** Another "Double Indemnity" rip-off, with a scheming tramp manipulating everyone around her with betrayal, sex, and murder. Her dead husband's brother eventually ignites old flames to steer her away from his money. **93m/C VHS.** Roxann Biggs-Dawson, Francis Dunan, Weston McMillan, Phillip R. Allen, Lisa Vultaggio, Christopher Reeve; **D:** Bradford May; **W:** Dennis Paoli, Greg Martinelli; **C:** Peter Woeste; **M:** Joseph Conlan.

Mortal Sins ♪ **1990 (R)** A TV evangelist finds more than salvation at the altar, when bodies begin to turn up. The detective he hires is close-mouthed, but more than a little interested in the preacher's daughter. A tense psycho-sexual thriller. **85m/C VHS.** Brian Benben, Anthony LaPaglia, Debrah Farentino; **D:** Yuri Sivo.

Mortal Sins ♪♪ **1992 (PG-13)** Reeve stars as parish priest Thomas Cusack, who hears the confession of a serial killer. What's worse is that the killer is preying on the women of Cusack's parish. Since he can't break the seal of the confessional, the good Father tries to stop the killer himself before another murder takes place. **93m/C VHS.** Christopher Reeve; **D:** Bradford May; **W:** Peter Woeste; **M:** Joseph Conlan.

The Mortal Storm ♪♪♪½ **1940** Phyllis Bottome's famous novel comes to life in this extremely well acted film about the rise of the Nazi regime. Stewart and Sullavan are young lovers who risk everything to escape the country after their families are torn apart by the Nazi takeover. Although Germany is never identified as the country, it is obvious in this story about the early days of WWII. Hitler took one look at this and promptly banned all MGM movies in Nazi Germany. **100mB VHS.** Margaret Sullavan, James Stewart, Robert Young, Frank Morgan, Robert Stack, Bonita Granville, Irene Rich; **D:** Frank Borzage; **W:** Claudine West, George Froeschel, Anderson Ellis; **C:** William H. Daniels.

Mortal Thoughts ♪♪½ **1991 (R)** Best friends find their relationship tested when the brutal husband of one of them is murdered. Moore and Headly are exceptional, capturing the perfect inflections and attitudes of the hard-working New Jersey beauticians sure of their friendship. Excellent pacing, fine supporting cast, with Keitel and Willis stand-outs. **104m/C VHS, DVD.** Demi Moore, Bruce Willis, Glenne Headly, Harvey Keitel, John Pankow, Billie Neal; **D:** Alan Rudolph; **W:** William Reilly, Claude Kerven; **C:** Elliot Davis; **M:** Mark Isham. Natl. Soc. Film Critics '91: Support. Actor (Keitel).

Mortuary ♪ **1981 (R)** Young woman's nightmares come startlingly close to reality. **91m/C VHS.** Christopher George, Lynda Day George, Paul Smith; **D:** Howard (Hikmet) Avedis; **W:** Howard (Hikmet) Avedis.

Mortuary WOOF! **2005 (R)** The Doyle family (widowed mom and two kids) move to a small California town where mom (Crosby) thinks it's a great idea to reopen the long-abandoned funeral home that has a cemetery in the yard. According to townspeople, the mortuary is built on haunted property and soon some sort of toxic killer fungus that's oozing around is raising the corpses. lck in more ways than one. **94m/C DVD.** Denise Crosby, Dan Byrd, Courtney Peldon, Bug Hall, Stephanie Patton; **D:** Tobe Hooper; **W:** Jace Anderson, Adam Grerasch; **C:** Jaron Presant; **M:** Joseph Conlan. **VIDEO**

Mortuary Academy ♪ **1991 (R)** To win an inheritance two brothers must attend the family mortician school, a situation paving the way for aggressively tasteless jokes on necrophilia. An attempt to recapture the successful black humor of the earlier Bartel/Woronov teaming "Eating Raoul," this one's dead on arrival. **86m/ C VHS, DVD.** Christopher Atkins, Perry Lang, Paul Bartel, Mary Woronov, Tracey Walter, Lynn Danielson-Rosenthal, Cesar Romero, Wolfman Jack; **D:** Michael Schroeder; **W:** William Kelman; **C:** Roy Wagner, Ronald Víctor; **M:** David Spear.

Morvern Callar ♪♪½ **2002** A young woman (Morton) wakes on Christmas morning to find her boyfriend's body, wrists slashed, beside her bed. His legacy is a personalized compilation tape, his cash card, and a novel he's written for her, complete with publishers to send it to. After she dismembers and disposes of his body, replaces his name on the manuscript with her own and sends it off to a publisher (who buys it), she goes off on a holiday to Spain with her sex and drug crazed girlfriend (McDermott). Morvern's emotions are revealed through the lyrics of the compilation tape constantly pounding through her headphones. Morton, known for other speech-challenged roles in "Sweet and Low Down" (mute girlfriend) and "Minority Report" (precognitive psychic) has become adept at making passivity riveting. Ramsey's second film, based on a novel by Alan Warner, is a moody beauty that's not altogether gratifying. **97m/C VHS, DVD.** GB CA Samantha Morton, Kathleen McDermott; **D:** Lynne Ramsay; **W:** Lynne Ramsay, Liana Dognini; **C:** Alwin Kuchler.

The Mosaic Project ♪♪½ **1995 (R)** Action junkies should be happy with the chases, explosions, and other mayhem engendered by this story of two buddies who find themselves the victims of a mad scientist. Now they have experimental computer chips implanted in their brains that make them skilled in 25 martial arts forms (and some other stuff that doesn't matter much). **89m/C VHS.** Jon Tabler, Ben Marley, Joe Estevez, Julie Strain, Colleen T. Coffey, Robert Z'Dar; **D:** John Sjogren; **W:** John Sjogren.

Mosby's Marauders ♪♪ **1966** A young boy joins a Confederate raiding company during the Civil War and learns about bravery, war, and love. **79m/C VHS.** Kurt Russell, James MacArthur, Jack Ging, Peggy Lipton, Nick Adams; **D:** Michael O'Herlihy.

Moscow Does Not Believe in Tears ♪♪♪ *Moscow Distrusts Tears; Moskva Sljesam Nje Jerit* **1980** Three provincial girls—Lyuda (Muravyova), Tonya (Ryazanova), and Katya (Alentova)—realize very different fates when they pursue their dreams in 1958 Moscow. The film picks up 20 years later to see what became of the women. Bittersweet, moving fare that seems a somewhat surprising production from pre-Glasnost USSR. In Russian with English subtitles. A 150-minute version has also been released. **115m/ C VHS, DVD.** RU Vera Alentova, Irina Muravyova, Raisa Ryazanova, Natalie Vavilova, Alexei Batalov, Alexander Fatyushin, Yuri Vasilyev; **D:** Vladimir Menshov; **W:** Valentin Chernykh; **C:** Igor Slabnevich; **M:** Sergei Nikitin. Oscars '80: Foreign Film.

Moscow on the Hudson ♪♪♪ **1984 (R)** Good-natured comedy has Williams as Soviet defector trying to cope with new life of freedom in fast-paced, freewheeling melting pot of New York City. Williams is particularly winning as naive jazzman, though Alonso also scores as his Hispanic love interest. Be warned though, it's not just played for laughs. **115m/C VHS, DVD.** Robin Williams, Maria Conchita Alonso, Cleavant Derricks, Alejandro Rey, Elya Baskin; **D:** Paul Mazursky; **W:** Paul Mazursky, Leon Capetanos; **C:** Donald McAlpine; **M:** David McHugh.

Moscow Parade ♪♪ *Prova* **1992** Sexy cabaret singer gets caught up in the shifting alliances caused by war. Set in Russia before the Nazi invasion. Russian with subtitles. **103m/C VHS.** RU Ute Lemper, Vladimir Simonov; **D:** Ivan Dykhovichny.

Moses WOOF! **1976 (PG)** Lancaster gets biblical as Moses, the man with the tablets. Edited from the 360-minute British TV series, with no improvement obvious from the economy, except that the bad parts are shorter. Poor chatter and scattered bouts of acting are surpassed in inadequacy only by special effects. **141m/C VHS, DVD.** Burt Lancaster, Anthony Quayle, Ingrid Thulin, Irene Papas, William Lancaster; **D:** Gianfranco DeBosio; **W:** Anthony Burgess, Vittorio Bonicelli; **M:** Ennio Morricone.

Moses ♪♪½ **1996** Another entry in TNT's series of Bible stories finds a humble Moses (Kingsley), raised in the Egyptian court, finding his way to his own people, the Israelites. Chosen by God to be his messenger and lead his people out of bondage, Moses must unleash a series of plagues upon Egypt before pharaoh Mernefta (Langella) will let them go. If you want action, look to "The Ten Commandments," since this is a faithful but tedious retelling. Filmed on location in Morocco; on two cassettes. **185m/C VHS, DVD.** Ben Kingsley, Frank Langella, David Suchet, Christopher Lee, Anna Galiena, Enrico Lo Verso, Geraldine McEwan, Maurice Roeves, Anthony (Corlan) Higgins, Anton Lesser; **D:** Roger Young; **W:** Lionel Chetwynd; **C:** Raffaele Mertes; **M:** Marco Frisina.

Mosley ♪♪ **1998** Looks at the life and political career of Oswald "Tom" Mosley (Cake), the leader of the British Fascist Movement from the end of WWI to his rise to prominence and eventual imprisonment during WWII. **240m/C VHS.** GB Jonathan Cake, Hugh Bonneville, Jeremy Child, Eric Allan, Caroline Langrishe, Jemma Redgrave, Windsor Davies; **D:** Robert Knights. **TV**

Mosquito ♪ **1995 (R)** Alien forces transform the annoying insects into monstrous mutants. Schlocky special effects are good for laughs. **92m/C VHS, DVD.** Gunnar Hansen, Ron Asheton, Steve Dixon, Rachel Loiselle, Tim Lovelace; **D:** Gary Jones; **W:** Gary Jones, Steve Hodge, Tom Chaney; **C:** Tom Chaney; **M:** Allen Lynch, Randall Lynch.

The Mosquito Coast ♪♪½ **1986 (PG)** Ambitious adaptation of Paul Theroux's novel about an asocial inventor who transplants his family to a rainforest to realize his utopian dream. A nightmare ensues. Ford tries hard, but supporters Mirren and Phoenix are main appeal of only intermittently successful drama. **119m/ C VHS, DVD.** Harrison Ford, Helen Mirren, River Phoenix, Andre Gregory, Martha Plimpton, Conrad Roberts, Butterfly McQueen, Jadrien Steele, Hilary Gordon, Rebecca Gordon, Dick O'Neill, Jason Alexander; **D:** Peter Weir; **W:** Paul Schrader; **C:** John Seale; **M:** Maurice Jarre.

Mosquitoman ♪♪½ *Mansquito* **2005** Break out the giant can of mosquito repellent for this genre cheese of 50s big bug flicks. A death row convict (Jordan) is used for scientific experiments and exposed to a DNA-altering concoction that turns him into the blood-slurping creature of the title. Cop Tom Randall (Nemec) tracks the blood trail while scientist babe Jennifer Allen (Vander) tries to prevent the change from happening again—to her. Originally shown on the Sci-Fi Channel. **m/** C DVD. Corin "Corky" Nemec, Musetta Vander, Jay Benedict, Patrick Drekauss, Austin Jordan; **D:** Tibor Takas; **W:** Michael Hurst; **C:** Emil Topuzov; **M:** Joseph Conlan, Sophia Morizet. **CABLE**

The Most Dangerous Game ♪♪♪ *The Hounds of Zaroff* **1932 (R)** Shipwrecked McRae washed ashore on the island of Banks's Count Zaroff, a deranged sportsman with a flair for tracking humans. Guess who becomes the mad count's next target. Oft-told tale is compellingly related in this, the first of many using Richard Connell's famous short story. If deja vu sets in, don't worry. This production uses most of the scenery, staff, and cast from its studio cousin, "King Kong." Remade in 1945 as "A Game of Death" and in 1956 as "Run for the Sun." **78m/B VHS, DVD.** Joel McCrea, Fay Wray, Leslie Banks, Robert Armstrong, Noble Johnson; **D:** Ernest B. Schoedsack, Irving Pichel; **W:** James A. Creelman; **C:** Henry W. Gerrard; **M:** Max Steiner.

Most Wanted ♪½ **1976** A psychopath with a penchant for raping nuns and collecting crucifixes is tracked down by a special police unit in this successful TV pilot. **78m/C VHS.** Robert Stack, Shelly Novack, Leslie Charleson, Tom Selleck, Sheree North; **D:** Walter Grauman. **TV**

Most Wanted ♪♪½ **1997 (R)** Marine Sgt. James Dunn (Wayans), framed for the assassination of the first lady, is on the run from the CIA, FBI, LAPD, and the covert team he was working with, which is led by Voight, the gung-ho general who set up the whole scam. Wayans, who wrote and produced, seems convinced that an action hero must be of the strong-silent-superhero mold, and appears at a loss without a joke to crack. Voight, however, is right at home in the bad-guy role, employing an overdone but effective southern drawl. Plenty of elaborate stunts, oversized fireballs, shootings, and chases provide the expected wild ride, including the film's funniest sequence as thousands of L.A. natives spontaneously become wild-in-the-street bounty hunters. **99m/C VHS, DVD.** Keenen Ivory Wayans, Jon Voight, Jill(ian) Hennessey, Eric Roberts, Paul Sorvino, Robert Culp, Wolfgang Bodison, Simon Baker; **D:** David Hogan; **W:** Keenen Ivory Wayans; **C:** Marc Reshovsky; **M:** Paul Bruckmaster.

Mostly Martha ♪♪♪ *Drei Sterne; Bella Martha* **2001 (PG)** Martha, a top chef at a fancy French restaurant in Hamburg, is so obsessed with her job that she really only connects with life through food. Things get stirred up when two new ingredients are added. First, a new sous-chef (Castellitto); scruffy and care-free as opposed to Martha's icy professionalism, enters her kitchen. Then, she takes in her 8-year-old neice (Foerste) after the death of the child's mother (Martha's sister). Appealing romantic comedy benefits form excellent performances by the leads, as well director Nettlebeck's assured style. German with subtitles. **107m/C VHS, DVD. GE AT SI IT** Martina Gedeck, Sergio Castellitto, Ulrich Thomsen, Maxime Foerste, Sibylle Canonica, August Zirner; **D:** Sandra Nettlebeck; **W:** Sandra Nettlebeck; **C:** Michael Bertl.

Motel Blue ♪♪½ **1998 (R)** Kyle Rivers (Frye) is an agent with the Department of Defense, who's doing a security clearance check on scientist Lana Hawking (Young). Lana maintains an expensive lifestyle that suggests she may be selling government secrets. But when Lana finds out about Kyle's suspicions, she frames her and Kyle gets suspended. But she decides to continue the investigation on her own terms. No particular surprises but there are a number of sleazy sex scenes. **96m/C VHS, DVD.** Sean Young, Soleil Moon Frye, Seymour Cassel, Robert Vaughn, Robert Stewart, Lou Rawls, Spencer Rochfort; **D:** Sam Firstenberg; **W:** Marianne S. Wibberley, Cormac Wibberley; **C:** Moshe Levin. **VIDEO**

Motel Hell ♪½ **1980 (R)** A completely tongue-in-cheek gore-fest about a farmer who kidnaps tourists, buries them in his garden, and reaps a human harvest to grind into his distinctive brand of smoked, preservative-free sausage. **102m/ C VHS, DVD.** Rory Calhoun, Nancy Parsons, Paul (Link) Linke, Nina Axelrod, Wolfman Jack, Elaine Joyce, Dick Curtis, Rosanne Katon, Monique St. Pierre, John Ratzenberger; **D:** Kevin Connor; **W:** Robert Jaffe, Steven-Charles Jaffe; **C:** Thomas Del Ruth; **M:** Lance Rubin.

Mother 🐾🐾🐾 1926 Pudovkin's innovative classic about a Russian family shattered by the uprising in 1905. A masterpiece of Russian cinema that established Pudovkin, and rivaled only Eisenstein for supremacy in montage, poetic imagery, and propagandistic ideals. Based on Maxim Gorky's great novel, it's one of cinematic history's seminal works. Striking cinematography, stunning use of montage make this one important. Silent with English subtitles. **70m/B VHS, DVD, RU** ***V. Baranovskaya, Nikolai Batalov; D: Vsevolod Pudovkin.***

Mother 🐾🐾½ *Okasan* 1952 A Japanese family is undone after the devastation of WWII. An uncharacteristically dramatic, and thus more accessible, film from one of the Japanese cinema's greatest masters. In Japanese with English subtitles. **98m/B VHS, JP** ***Kinuyo Tanaka, Kyoko Kagawa, Eiji Okada, Akihiko Katayama; D: Mikio Naruse.***

Mother 🐾🐾 1994 (R) Olivia Hendrix (Ladd) is a very over-protective mom—even though son Tom (Weisser) is nineteen and anxious to untie the apron strings. But Mom thinks she knows best and she's willing to kill to make certain Tom stays home where he belongs. **90m/C VHS, DVD** ***Diane Ladd, Olympia Dukakis, Morgan Weisser, Eli Keats; D: Frank Laloggia.***

Mother 🐾🐾½ 1996 (PG-13) Yes, you will shake your head in recognition of that parent-child bond. Twice-divorced writer John Henderson (Brooks) decides it's all Mom's fault he has problems with women, so he decides to move back home and figure out what went wrong. Mom Beatrice (Reynolds) is exasperated and married younger brother Jeff (Morrow) winds up jealous of mom's attentions to his sibling. Reynolds' first feature film in 25 years. **104m/C VHS, DVD** ***Albert Brooks, Debbie Reynolds, Rob Morrow, Lisa Kudrow, John C. McGinley, Isabel Glasser, Peter White; D: Albert Brooks; W: Albert Brooks, Monica Johnson; C: Lajos Koltai; M: Marc Shaiman. N.Y. Film Critics '96: Screenplay; Natl. Soc. Film Critics '96: Screenplay.***

The Mother 🐾🐾🐾 2003 (R) Reid gives a ferociously honest performance as the 60-ish May, a lifelong suburban wife and mother left bereft of purpose when her husband (Vaughn) suddenly dies. She moves to London to live temporarily with her preoccupied son Bobby (Mackintosh) and his indifferent wife Helen (Wilson Jones) and tries to straighten out the life of her self-pitying divorce daughter, Paula (Bradshaw). Paula is involved in a messy relationship with rugged married builder, Darren (Craig). May finds herself attracted to the younger man's unexpected kindness and, unresigned to going quietly into old age, also begins an affair with the weak-willed Darren—the revelation of which causes no end of drama. The only false note comes in a late scene when May allows Paula to take her rage out on her mother by hitting her. The newly liberated May should have instead knocked her whiny child on her ass. **111m/C VHS, DVD, GB** ***Anne Reid, Daniel Craig, Steven Mackintosh, Cathryn Bradshaw, Oliver Ford Davies, Peter Vaughan, Anne Wilson Jones; D: Roger Michell; W: Hanif Kureishi; C: Alwin Kuchler; M: Jeremy Sams.***

Mother & Daughter: A Loving War 🐾🐾 1980 Three women experience matherhood. Special appearance by Harry Chapin as himself. **96m/C VHS. Tuesday Weld, Frances Sternhagen, Kathleen Beller, Jeanne Lang, Edward Winter; D: Burt Brinckerhoff. TV**

Mother and Son 🐾🐾 1931 Melodrama finds the wayward Young shielding her son from the fact that she runs a gambling hall. He grows up to be a society gal before discovering the devastating truth. **67m/B VHS. Clara Kimball Young, Bruce Warren, Millard Golden, John Elliott, Gordon Wood, Ernest Hilliard. D: John P. McCarthy.**

She eventually goes back to her bed where they discuss death and she falls asleep, never to waken, Russian with subtitles. **73m/C VHS, DVD, RU GE Gudrun Geyer, Alexei Ananishnov; D: Alexander Sokurov; W: Yuri Arabov; C: Aleksei Federov; M: Otmar Nussio.**

The Mother and the Whore 🐾🐾🐾 *La Maman et la Putain* 1973 Alexander (Leaud) lives with slightly older Marie (Lebrun) but still can't resist picking up sexy Veronika (Lebr.n). Their menage works for a while but then tensions between the sexual threesome force them to discuss their situation. Talky, witty, provocative example of French New Wave, which Eustache shot in his own apartment and local bistros. French with subtitles. **210m/B VHS, FR Jean-Pierre Leaud, Bernadette Lafont, Francoise Lebrun, Isabelle Weingarten, Jean-Noel Picq, Jessa Darrieux, Genevieve Mnich, Marinka Matuszewski; D: Jean Eustache; W: Jean Eustache; C: Pierre Lhomme.**

Mother Goose Rock 'n' Rhyme 🐾🐾🐾 1990 Duvall follows the success of her "Faerie Tale Theatre" series with a new comedic fable, starring some of Hollywood's top names. Great fun for the whole family. **96m/C VHS. Shelley Duvall, Teri Garr, Howie Mandel, Jean Stapleton, Ben Vereen, Bobby Brown, Art Garfunke., Dan Gilroy, Deborah Harry, Cyndi Lauper, Little Richard, Paul Simon, Harry Anderson, Elayne Boosler, Woody Harrelson, Anna Ciepielewska, Maria Chwalibog; D: Jerzy Kawalerowicz; W: Jerzy Kawalerowicz, Tadeusz Konwicki; M: Adam Walacinski. Cannes '61: Grand Jury Prize.**

Mother Joan of the Angels 🐾🐾🐾 *The Devil and the Nun; Matka Joanna Od Aniolow* 1960 A priest investigating demonic possession among nuns in a 17th-century Polish convent becomes involved in a mutual attraction with the Mother Superior. A powerful allegory complemented by the stylized narrative and performances. Polish with subtitles. Based on actual events at Loudon and also the subject of a play by Aldous Huxley, "The Devils of Loudon" novel by Krzysztof Penderecki, era by Krzysztof Penderecki, "The Devils" movie by Ken Russell's movie "The Devils." **108m/B VHS, DVD, PL Lucyna Winnicka, Mieczyslaw Voit, Anna Ciepielewska, Maria Chwalibog; D: Jerzy Kawalerowicz; W: Jerzy Kawalerowicz, Tadeusz Konwicki; M: Adam Walacinski.**

Mother, Jugs and Speed 🐾½ 1976 (PG) Black comedy about the day-to-day tragedies encountered by a group of ambulance drivers. Interesting mix of stars. **95m/C VHS, DVD, Bill Cosby, Raquel Welch, Harvey Keitel, Allen (Goorwitz) Garfield, Larry Hagman, Bruce Davison, Dick Butkus, L.Q. Jones, Toni Basil; D: Peter Yates; M: Tom Mankiewicz.**

Mother Teresa: In the Name of God's Poor 🐾🐾 1997 Bio of the missionary begins when she learned of the project **93m/C VHS, DVD, Geraldine Chaplin, Keene Curtis, William Katt, Alan Sheerman, Cornelia Hayes O'Herlihy; D: Kevin Connor; W: Dominique Lapierre, Carol Kaplan. CABLE**

Mother Wore Tights 🐾🐾🐾 1947 Colorful nostalgic musical stars Grable as Myrtle McKinley Burt, who leaves the small-town turn-of-the-century vaudevillian stage to raise her two daughters. Once they're grown, Myrtle decides to rejoin husband Frank (Dailey) in the theatre again, thus embarrassing daughter Iris (Freeman) who's at a snotty finishing school. Of course, Iris learns what's really important in life. **107m/C VHS. Betty Grable, Dan Dailey, Mona Freeman, Connie Marshall, Vanessa Brown, Robert Arthur, Sara Allgood, William Frawley; D: Walter Lang; M: Lamar Trotti; C: Harry Jackson; M: Josef Myrow, Alfred Newman, Mack Gordon. Oscars '47: Scoring/Musical.**

Mother's Boys 🐾🐾 1994 (R) Estranged mother Curtis attempts to reunite with the family she abandoned only to be snubbed, inspiring in her a ruthless effort to win back the children and oust father Gallagher's new live-in girlfriend Whalley-Kilmer. With an almost psychotic devotion, she terrorizes everyone in the family, including her 12-year-old son Ed-wards into a nude bathtub game of peek-a-too. Film lacks the tension necessary to carry suspense. Based on the novel by Bernard Taylor. **96m/C VHS, DVD, Jamie Lee Curtis, Peter Gallagher, Joanne Whalley, Luke Edwards, Vanessa Redgrave, Colin Ward, Joss Ackland, Paul Guilfoyle, John C. McGinley, J.E. Freeman.**

Mother Kusters Goes to Heaven 🐾🐾🐾 *Mutter Kusters Fahrt Zum Himmel* 1976 Mrs. Kusters's husband is a frustrated factory worker who goes over the edge and kills the factory owner's son and himself. Left alone, she learns that everyone is using her husband's death to further their own needs, including her daughter, who uses the publicity to enhance her singing career. A statement that you should trust no one, not even your family and friends. This film was banned from the Berlin Film Festival because of its political overtones. In German with English subtitles. **108m/C VHS, DVD, GE Brigitte Mira, Ingrid Caven, Armin Meier, Irm Hermann, Gottfried John, Margit Carstensen, Karl-Heinz Boehm; D: Rainer Werner Fassbinder; W: Rainer Werner Fassbinder; C: Michael Ballhaus.**

Mother Lode 🐾½ *Search for the Mother Lode; The Last Great Treasure* 1982 (PG) The violent conflict between twin brothers (played by Heston) is intensified by greed, near madness, and the all-consuming lust for gold in this action-adventure. Heston's novel. He poses as a Nazi sympathizer in this adaptation of Kurt Vonnegut's 1962 novel. He poses as a Nazi sympathizer in broadcasts to American troops, but his anti-semitic diatribes are actually coded information crucial to the Allies. After the war, Campbell's life unravels as he loses his young wife (Lee) and the U.S. government refuses to acknowledge his efforts. He is smuggled back to the U.S., where both Israeli Nazi-hunters and twisted neo-Nazis search for him. After being captured, imprisoned in Israel, and conversing with fellow prisoner Adolf Eichmann (Gibson), Campbell realizes the moral of this dark comedy: "We are what we pretend to be." Arkin is excellent as his Greenwich Village neighbor who also has some secrets. If you look closely, you can see author Vonnegut in a cameo. **111m/C VHS, DVD, Nick Nolte, Sheryl Lee, Alan Arkin, John Goodman, Kirsten Dunst, David Strathairn, Arye Gross, Frankie Faison, Bernard Behrens, Henry Gibson; D: Keith Gordon; W: Robert B. Weide; C: Tom Richmond; M: Michael Convertino.**

Mother of Mine 🐾🐾🐾 *Aidelsta Parhein* 2005 During World War II, when conflict breaks out between Finland and Russia, 9-year-old Eero (Majaniemi) is sent to live with a neutral family in Sweden by his Finnish mother (Maliala) after his soldier father is killed. She believes he will be safer there. The lad adapts well to the new language and although his immediate family (Nygvist) takes a shine to him, and finally returns home, all parties have much some time to warm up to him. When he finally returns home, all parties have much trauma to endure, the final repair coming when Eero attends his surrogate mother's funeral and then visits his elderly Finnish mother, finally understanding the motive behind her difficult choice long ago. Visually pleasing, emotionally engaging, with a fabulous score to boot. Finnish and Swedish with subtitles. **111m/C VHS, DVD, FI Michael Nyquist, Topi Majaniemi, Maria Lundqvist, Kari-Pekka Toivonen; D: Klaus Haro; W: Jimmy Karlsson, Kirsi Vikman; C: Jarkko T. Laine; M: Tuomas Kantelinen.**

Mother of Kings 🐾🐾🐾 1982 Livin' ain't easy for a widowed charwoman thanks to WWII and Stalinism. Innovative use of newsreel scenes, in Polish with English subtitles. **126m/C VHS, PL Zbigniew Zapasiewicz, Franciszek Pieckza, Boguslaw Linda, Adam Ferency, Magda Teresa Wojcik; D: Janusz Zaorski; W: Janusz Zaorski; C: Edward Klosinski; M: Przemyslaw Gintrowski.**

Motives 🐾½ 2003 (R) Handsome, successful, and married businessman Emery Simms (Moore) indulges in a dangerous fling with free-spirited Allanah (Brooks) and winds up involved in murder. **87m/C VHS, DVD, Shemar Moore, Vivica A. Fox, Keisha Knight Pulliam, Golden Brooks, Victoria Rowell, Mel Jackson, Joe Torry, Sean Blakemore; D: Craig Ross Jr.; W: Kelsey Scott; C: Ken Stipe. VIDEO**

Mothra 🐾🐾🐾 *Mosura; Daikaiju Mosura* 1962 Classic Japanese monster shenanigans about an enraged giant caterpillar that invades Tokyo while searching for the Ailenas, a set of very tiny, twin princesses who've been kidnapped by an evil nightclub owner - in the pursuit of big profits. After tiring of crushing buildings and wreaking incidental havoc, the enormous crawly thing zips up into a cocoon and emerges as Mothra, a moth distinguished by both its size and bad attitude. Mothra and the wee babes make appearances in later Godzilla epics. **101m/C VHS, JP Frankie Sakai, Hiroshi Koizumi, Kyoko Kagawa, Yumi Ito, Emi Ito, Lee Kresel, Ken Uehara, Akihiko Hirata, Kenji Sahara, Takashi Shimura; D: Inoshiro Honda; W: Shinichi Sekizawa; C: Hajime Koizumi; M: Yuji Koseki.**

Mr. Takes a Vacation 🐾½ 1939 Lorre was bored with his character and afraid of being typecast and it shows in this 8th and final entry in the series. Mr. Moto must act his holiday short to protect the priceless crown of the Queen of Sheba, which s on display at a New York museum. But he's up against international jewel thief Metaxa as well as gangsters

man, Ken Lerner, Lorraine Toussaint, Joey Zimmerman, Jill Freedman; D: Yves Simoneau; M: George S. Clinton.

Mother's Day 🐾½ 1980 Three women who were former college roommates plan a reunion together in the wilderness. All goes well until they are dragged into an isolated house by two insane boys who constantly watch TV, are dependently consume the products advertised, and then terrorize and torture people to please their mom. Sanitized gore with black satiric intentions. **98m/C VHS, DVD, Tiana Pierce, Nancy Hendrickson, Deborah Luce, Holden McGuire, Billy Ray McQuade, Rose Ross; D: Charles Kaufman; W: Charles Kaufman, War-Lee Rose; C: Eric Van Haren Nomani; M: Tom Scott. CABLE**

A Mother's Prayer 🐾🐾 1995 (PG-13) 1980 Fact-based story about young mom Rosemary Holmstrom (Hamilton), who has AIDS, and is determined to find a home for her eight-year-old son T.J. (Fleiss) before she dies. Guaranteed to make the tear ducts flow, with a deter-mired performance from Hamilton that lessens the sentimentality. Holmstrom died at the age of 36 in 1994. **94m/C VHS, Linda Hamilton, Noah Fleiss, Bruce Dern, Kate Nelligan, S. Epatha Merkerson, Corey Parker, Jennifer O'Hara, RuPaul Charles; D: Larry Elikann; W: Charles Kaufman; M: Phil Gallo. CABLE**

The Mothman Prophecies 🐾🐾 2002 (PG-13) Supernatural thriller based on true events occurring in Point Pleasant, WV, in the mid-1960s. John and Mary Klein (Gere and Messing) are happily married, until a car crash with a moth-like creature only seen by Mary, who later dies, but not before making some preliminary sketches of the insect-like beast. Two years later John, a "Washington Post" reporter, mysteriously ends up in the town of Point Pleasant, where things get weird. John boasts cop Connie (Linney) the sole voice of reason in the superstitious bunch of locals, some of whom have seen the same creature Mary did, and John and Connie team to solve the Mothman mystery. Gere and Linney are fine actors wasted in this ho-hum story. Movie does have an aptly creepy tone, however, and Bates is good as the hermitish psychic phenomena expert. **119m/C VHS, DVD, US Richard Gere, Laura Linney, Will Patton, Debra Messing, Lucinda Jenney, Alan Bates, David Eigenberg, Nesbitt Blaisdell; D: Mark Pellington; W: Richard Hatem; C: Fred Murphy; M: Tomandandy.**

who want the prize. **63m/B DVD.** Joseph Schildkraut, Lionel Atwill, Virginia Field, Peter Lorre, John "Dusty" King, G.P. (Tim) Huntley Jr.; **W:** Norman Foster, Philip MacDonald; **C:** Charles Clarke; **M:** Samuel Kaylin.

Motor Home Massacre *woof* **2005 (R)** Typical low-budget slasher that has the good sense not to take itself seriously. Seven friends set out for a woodland adventure in a vintage RV and come under attack from a power-tool wielding psycho. **91m/C DVD.** *US* Shan Holleman, Nelson Bonilla, Justin Geer, Tanya Fraser, Breanne Ashley, Greg Corbett; **D:** Allen Wilbanks; **W:** Allen Wilbanks; **C:** Allen Wilbanks. CABLE

Motor Patrol *woof 1/2* **1950** A cop poses as a racketeer to infiltrate a car-stealing ring. **66m/B VHS.** Don Castle, Jane Nigh, Charles Victor, Reed Hadley, William Henry, Sid Melton, Richard Travis, Frank Jenks, Onslow Stevens; **D:** Sam Newfield; **W:** Orville H. Hampton; **C:** Ernest Miller.

Motor Psycho WOOF! *Motor Rods and Rockers* **1965** When a motorcycle gang rapes a woman, she and her husband pursue them into the desert to seek their brutal revenge. **73m/B VHS, DVD.** Haji, Alex Rocco, Stephen Oliver, Holle K. Winters, Joseph Cellini, Thomas Scott, Coleman Francis, Sharon Lee, Russ Meyer; **D:** Russ Meyer; **W:** William E. Sprague, Russ Meyer; **C:** Russ Meyer.

Motorama *woof woof* **1991 (R)** A 10-year-old juvenile delinquent becomes obsessed with winning a gas station contest which involves collecting game cards. So he steals a car and hits the road where he gets his first tattoo and encounters a beautiful "older" woman (Barrymore) and lots of trouble. **89m/C VHS, DVD.** Jordan Christopher Michael, Martha Quinn, Flea, Michael J. Pollard, Meat Loaf Aday, Drew Barrymore, Garrett Morris, Robin Duke, Sandy Baron, Mary Woronov, Susan Tyrrell, John Laughlin, John Diehl, Robert Picardo, Jack Nance, Vince Edwards, Dick Miller, Allyce Beasley, Shelley Berman; **D:** Barry Shils; **W:** Joe Minion; **C:** Joseph Yacoe; **M:** Andy Summers.

The Motorcycle Diaries *woof woof woof* **Diarios de motocicleta 2004 (R)** Unadorned narrative about the life of a pre-revolutionary Che Guevara, based on his diaries and a memoir from his best friend. In 1952, naive, asthmatic 23-year-old middle-class medical student Ernesto Guevara (Garcia Bernal) and his rowdy, older compadre, Alberto Granado (de la Serna) decide to take what will be a life-changing adventure. They spend a few months on Ernesto's motorcycle traveling from Buenos Aires to Venezuela. By the time they reach Chile, and then Peru, Ernesto is dismayed by the poverty and injustice he sees around him; an extended stay caring for the sick in the San Pablo leper colony provides an emotional turning point. The film avoids being either a travelogue or a political polemic, thanks to the skill of both director Salles and his two leads. Spanish with subtitles. **128m/C DVD.** *CL US AR PY* Gael Garcia Bernal, Rodrigo de la Serna, Mia Maestro, Gustavo Bueno, Jorge Chiarella; **D:** Walter Salles; **W:** Jose Rivera; **C:** Eric Gautier; **M:** Gustavo Santaolalla. Oscars '04: Song ("Al Otro Lado Del Rio"); British Acad. '04: Foreign Film; British Acad. '05: Orig. Score; Ind. Spirit '05: Cinematog., Debut Perf. (de la Serna).

Motorcycle Gang *woof* **1957** It's the summer of '57, and Randy plans to bring home the title at the Pacific Motorcycle Championships for his club, the "Skyriders." But first his old rival Nick, who's just out of jail, turns up and challenges Randy to an illegal street race. Will Randy succumb to peer pressure and race? Lame plot = lame acting = lame movie. **78m/B VHS.** Paul Blaisdell, Steven Terrell, John Ashley, Anne Neyland, Carl "Alfalfa" Switzer, Raymond Hatton; **D:** Edward L. Cahn; **W:** Lou Rusoff.

Motorcycle Squad *woof 1/2* **Double Cross 1941** A policeman is dishonorably discharged so he can get the "inside" dope on a gang of crooks in this 'B' thriller. **61m/B VHS.** Kane Richmond, Wynne Gibson, Pauline Moore, John Miljan, Mary Gordon, Frank Moran; **D:** Albert Kelley; **W:** Milton Raison; **C:** Arthur Martinelli.

Mouchette *woof woof woof 1/2* **1967** A lonely 14-year-old French girl, daughter of a drunk father and dying mother, eventually finds spiritual release by committing suicide. Typically somber, spiritual fare from unique master filmmaker Bresson. Perhaps the most complete expression of Bresson's austere, Catholic vision. In French with English subtitles. **80m/B VHS, DVD.** *FR* Nadine Nortier, Maria Cardinal, Paul Hebert; **D:** Robert Bresson; **C:** Ghislain Cloquet.

Moulin Rouge *woof woof woof 1/2* **1952** Colorful, entertaining portrait of acclaimed Impressionist painter Toulouse-Lautrec, more famous for its production stories than on-screen drama. Ferrer delivers one of his most impressive performances as the physically stunted, cynical artist who basked in the seamy Montmartre nightlife. **119m/C VHS, DVD.** Jose Ferrer, Zsa Zsa Gabor, Christopher Lee, Peter Cushing, Colette Marchand, Katherine Kath, Michael Balfour, Eric Pohlmann, Suzanne Flon, Claude Nollier, Muriel Smith, Mary Clare, Walter Crisham, Harold Kasket, Jim Gerald, George Lannes, Lee Montague, Maureen Swanson, Tutte Lemkow, Jill Bennett, Theodore Bikel; **D:** John Huston; **W:** John Huston, Anthony Veiller; **C:** Oswald Morris. Oscars '52: Art Dir/Set Dec., Color, Costume Des. (C).

Moulin Rouge *woof woof woof* **2001 (PG-13)** Luhrmann resurrects the famed Parisian Montmartre nightclub decadence in his surreal quasi 1899-set movie musical that stars Kidman as the club's star singer/dancer/courtesan Satine, who entrances McGregor's naive poet, Christian. Naturally, their love is doomed—in part because she has this nasty cough. Leguizamo shows up as artist Toulouse Lautrec. Luhrmann likes to shake up staid genres (witness "Strictly Ballroom" and "Romeo + Juliet") and in this case he married pop music (uneasily) with extraordinary elaborate visuals. This doesn't always work but the director deserves points for sheer chutzpah and Kidman has never looked more stunning. **126m/C VHS, DVD.** *AU US* Nicole Kidman, Ewan McGregor, John Leguizamo, Jim Broadbent, Garry McDonald, Kylie Minogue, Richard Roxburgh, David Wenham, Natalie Mendoza; **D:** Baz Luhrmann; **W:** Baz Luhrmann, Craig Pearce; **C:** Donald McAlpine; **M:** Craig Armstrong. Oscars '01: Art Dir./Set Dec., Costume Des.; Australian Film Inst. '01: Cinematog., Costume Des., Film Editing, Sound; British Acad. '01: Sound, Support. Actor (Broadbent); Golden Globes '02: Actor (Broadbent), Score; L.A. Film Critics '01: Support. Actor (Kidman), Score; N.Y. Film Critics '01: Support. Actor (Broadbent); Natl. Bd. of Review '01: Film, Support. Actor (Broadbent).

The Mountain *woof woof* **1956** A man and his shady younger brother set out to inspect a Paris-routed plane that crashed in the French Alps. After some harrowing experiences in climbing the peak, it becomes evident that one brother has designs to save whatever he can, while the other intends to loot it. Many real, as well as staged, climbing scenes. Based on Henri Troyat's novel. **105m/C VHS.** Spencer Tracy, Robert Wagner, Claire Trevor, William Demarest, Richard Arlen, E.G. Marshall; **D:** Edward Dmytryk.

Mountain Charlie *woof woof 1/2* **1980** Mountain girl's life is destroyed by three drifters. **96m/C VHS.** Denise Neilson, Dick Robinson, Rick Guinn, Lynn Seus; **D:** George Stapleford.

Mountain Family Robinson *woof woof* **1979 (G)** An urban family, seeking escape from the hassles of city life, moves to the Rockies, determined to get back to nature. They soon find that nature may be more harsh than rush-hour traffic and nasty bosses when a bear comes calling. More "Wilderness Family"-type adventures. **102m/C VHS, DVD.** Robert F. Logan, Susan Damante-Shaw, Heather Rattray, Ham Larsen, William (Bill) Bryant, George "Buck" Flower; **D:** John Cotter.

Mountain Justice *woof woof 1/2* **1977 Kettle Creek 1930** Maynard's first all-talkie western finds our hero in search of his father's murderer. Good action sequences (with stunts performed by Maynard), including those aboard a moving train and a buckboard. **73m/B VHS.** Ken Maynard, Otis Harlan, Kathryn Crawford, Paul Hurst; **D:** Harry Joe Brown.

Mountain Man *woof woof 1/2* **1967** *Guardian of the Wilderness* **1977** Historically accurate drama about Galen Clark's successful fight in the 1860s to save the magnificent wilderness area that is now Yosemite National Park. Together with naturalist John Muir, he fought a battle against the lumber companies who wanted the timber and won President Lincoln's support for his cause. **96m/C VHS.** Denver Pyle, John Dehner, Ken Berry, Cheryl Miller, Don Shanks, Cliff Osmond, Jack Kruschen, Ford Rainey; **D:** David O'Malley; **W:** David O'Malley.

The Mountain Men *woof woof 1/2* **1980 (R)** Dull adventure drama set in the American West of the 1880s. Two trappers argue about life and have trouble with Indians. **102m/C VHS.** Charlton Heston, Brian Keith, John Glover, Seymour Cassel, Victor Jory; **D:** Richard Lang; **W:** Fraser Heston; **C:** Michael Hugo; **M:** Michel Legrand.

Mountain of the Cannibal God WOOF! *Il Montagna di Dio Cannibale; Slave of the Cannibal God* **1979** Beautiful Andress is captured by "native" cannibals; Keach must save her. **103m/C VHS, DVD.** *IT* Stacy Keach, Ursula Andress, Claudio Cassinelli, Franco Fantasia; **D:** Sergio Martino; **M:** Guido de Angelis, Maurizio de Angelis.

Mountain Patrol: Kekexili *woof woof* **Kekexili 2004** Kekexili is a brutally dangerous, remote, and beautiful part of Tibet that is home to the endangered chiru antelopes, which are prized by poachers for the price that their wool coats bring. The slaughter is so bad that the mountain people have formed their own patrol to hunt the poachers. In 1996, young Beijing journalist Ga Yu (Zhang) shows up to shadow the patrol and bring attention to the animals' plight. Based on a true story. Mandarin and Tibetan with subtitles. **92m/C DVD.** *CH HK* Duo Bujie, Zhang Lei, Qi Lang, Zhao Xueying; **D:** Lu Chuan; **W:** Lu Chuan; **C:** Cao Yu; **M:** Lao Zai.

The Mountain Road *woof woof 1/2* **1960** Listless drama of an American squadron stationed in China during the last days of WWII. Only Stewart makes this drab film worthwhile. **102m/B VHS.** James Stewart, Harry (Henry) Morgan, Glenn Corbett, Mike Kellin; **D:** Daniel Mann.

Mountains of the Moon *woof woof woof* **1990 (R)** Sprawling adventure detailing the obsessive search for the source of the Nile conducted by famed British rogue/explorer Sir Richard Burton and cohort John Hanning Speke in the late 1800s. Spectacular scenery and images. Director Rafelson, better known for overtly personal films such as "Five Easy Pieces" and "The King of Marvin Gardens," shows considerable skill with this epic. From William Harrison's novel "Burton and Speke." **140m/C VHS, DVD.** Patrick Bergin, Iain Glen, Fiona Shaw, Richard E. Grant, Peter Vaughan, Roger Rees, Bernard Hill, Anna Massey, Leslie Phillips, John Savident, James Villiers, Delroy Lindo, Roshan Seth; **D:** Bob Rafelson; **W:** Bob Rafelson; **C:** Roger Deakins; **M:** Michael Small.

Mountaintop Motel Massacre WOOF! **1986 (R)** A resort motel's hostess is a raving lunatic who regularly slaughters her guests. **95m/C VHS, DVD.** Bill (Billy) Thurman, Anna Chappell, Will Mitchell; **D:** Jim McCullough; **W:** Jim McCullough Jr.; **C:** Joseph M. Wilcots; **M:** Ron Di Lulio.

Mountbatten: The Last Viceroy *woof woof 1/2* **1986** Originally a British TV miniseries detailing English viceroy Lord Mountbatten's (Williamson) turning over ruling power from Great Britain to India in 1947 and the birth of Pakistan. **107m/C VHS, DVD.** *GB* Nicol Williamson, Janet Suzman, Sam Dastor, Nigel Davenport, Wendy Hiller, Ian Richardson, Julian Wadham; **D:** Tom Clegg; **W:** David Butler; **C:** Peter Jessop; **M:** John Scott.

Mouse and His Child *woof woof 1/2* **1977** A gentle animated fantasy adventure about a toy wind-up mouse and his child who fall into the clutches of a villainous rat when they venture into the outside world. **83m/C VHS.** **D:** Fred Wolf; **V:** Peter Ustinov, Cloris Leachman, Andy Devine.

Mouse Hunt *woof woof woof* **1997 (PG)** The Smuntz brothers (Lane and Evans) inherit a run-down mansion from their wealthy string magnate father (Hickey, in his last role). Since the boys are involved in a bitter long-standing argument over cord versus twine, they're happy to learn about an offer from a preservation society for a small fortune. The boys try to fix up the house, only to be foiled by the mouse who had been the sole occupant. There are plenty of new mouse traps and tricks thanks to the 65 trained mice (along with 3-D animation) who play the hero. The plucky rodent must also battle a psychotic cat and an obsessed exterminator (Walken, or Lord High King Psycho). If you've ever laughed at a cartoon character taking an anvil to the head, you'll like this. The cartoon-like action livens up the otherwise dismal setting of the mansion and its surroundings. Directorial debut by Verbinski, the man who brought us the Bud frogs. **97m/C VHS, DVD.** Nathan Lane, Lee Evans, Christopher Walken, William Hickey, Vicki Lewis, Maury Chaykin, Eric Christmas, Michael Jeter, Debra Christofferson, Camilla Soeberg; **D:** Gore Verbinski; **W:** Adam Rifkin; **C:** Phedon Papamichael; **M:** Alan Silvestri.

The Mouse on the Moon *woof woof woof* **1962** Sort-of sequel to "The Mouse That Roared" lacks the presence of Peter Sellers but maintains the whimsical tone of the original. The prime minister (Moody) of the Duchy of Grand Fenwick asks for American aid in setting up a space program. (Actually, he wants the money for indoor plumbing.) When it turns out that the local wine is actually rocket fuel, his amiable goof of a son (Cribbins) fulfills his lifelong dream of becoming an astronaut. The mild spoof of cold war politics lacks the anarchic spirit that director Lester has brought to "Help!" and his "Musketeer" films. **85m/C DVD.** *GB* Margaret Rutherford, Ron Moody, Bernard Cribbins, Terry-Thomas, June Ritchie, David Kossoff; **D:** Richard Lester; **W:** Michael Pertwee; **C:** Wilkie Cooper; **M:** Ron Grainer.

The Mouse That Roared *woof woof woof* **1959** With its wine export business going down the drain, a tiny, desperate country decides to declare war on the United States in hopes that in the U.S., after its inevitable triumph, will revive New York go 20 chain-mail clad warriors armed with bow and arrow. Featured in three roles, Sellers is great as the duchess, less effective (though still funny) as the prime minister, and a military leader. A must for Sellers' fans; maintains a sharp satiric edge throughout. Based on the novel by Leonard Wibberley. **83m/C VHS, DVD.** *GB* Peter Sellers, Jean Seberg, Leo McKern, David Kossoff, William Hartnell, Timothy Bateson, MacDonald Parke, Monte Landis; **D:** Jack Arnold; **W:** Roger MacDougall, Stanley Mann; **M:** Edwin Astley.

Mouth to Mouth *woof woof* **Boca a Boca 1995 (R)** Budding actor Victor (Bardem) is working in Madrid as a phone sex operator while waiting to hear about his big break on an American picture. Victor's regularly called by repressed gay surgeon Ricardo (Flotats) and Amanda (Sanchez-Gijon), who says she's Ricardo's wife. Naive Victor falls for Amanda—who of course isn't Ricardo's wife but seems to be involved in a plot to kill Ricardo masterminded by his real wife Angela (Barranco) and her lover David (Gutierrez Caba). The plot's a little tangled but there's lots of visual gags and bedroom farce and the virile Bardem turns out to be a gifted comedian. Spanish with subtitles. **97m/C VHS, DVD.** *SP* Javier Bardem, Aitana Sanchez-Gijon, Josep Maria Flotats, Maria Barranco, Emilio Gutierrez-Caba, Fernando Guillen, Myriam Meziere; **D:** Manuel Gomez Pereira; **W:** Manuel Gomez Pereira, Joaquin Oristrell, Naomi Wise, Juan Luis Iborra; **C:** Juan Amoros; **M:** Bernardo Bonezzi.

Movements du Desir *woof woof* **Desire in Motion 1994** Sex-on-a-train sequences add more than a little steam to this romantic drama. Catherine (Kaprisky) is travelling with her young daughter on the Montreal to Vancouver train in order to forget a failed relationship. She meets shy Vincent (Pichette), who is supposed to be on his way to meet his lover, but somewhere on the journey the sexual sparks start igniting. There are some eccentric fellow passengers to contend with (and director Pool drops in some surreal dream sequences as well) but the heat generated by the leads is genuine enough. Not apt to move you. **89m/C VHS, CA SL. D:** Lea Pool; **W:** Lea Pool; **C:** Pierre Mignot; **M:** Zbigniew Preisser.

Move Over, Darling ♂♂½ **1963** Remake of 1938's "My Favorite Wife" has widower Garner having his wife Ellen (Day) declared legally dead five years after a plane crash. He remarries, only to have Ellen turn up on his doorstep. Turns out she was stranded on a desert island for those years, and she wasn't alone. Fluffy but enjoyable Day vehicle is the second attempt to remake Day's ill-fated "Something's Gotta Give," the film Marilyn Monroe was working on when she died. Garner and Day are fine, but are often upstaged by the excellent supporting cast. **103m/C VHS, DVD.** Doris Day, James Garner, Polly Bergen, Thelma Ritter, Chuck Connors, Fred Clark, Don Knotts, Edgar Buchanan, Elliott Reid, John Astin, Pat Harrington, Eddie Quillan, Max (Casey Adams) Showalter, Alvy Moore; **D:** Michael Gordon; **W:** Hal Kanter, Leo McCarey, Jack Sher; **C:** Daniel F. Fapp; **M:** Lionel Newman. Golden Globes '63: Actress—Mus./Comedy (Day).

Movers and Shakers ♂½ **1985 (PG)** An irreverent spoof of Hollywood depicting a filmmaker's attempt to render a best-selling sex manual into a blockbuster film. Fails to live up to its potential and wastes a star-studded cast. **100m/C VHS.** Walter Matthau, Charles Grodin, Gilda Radner, Vincent Gardenia, Bill Macy, Tyne Daly, Steve Martin, Penny Marshall, Luana Anders; **D:** William Asher. **W:** Charles Grodin.

The Movie House Massacre ♂ **1978** A psychopath runs rampant in a theatre killing and maiming moviegoers. No refunds are given. **80m/C VHS.** Jenny Cunningham, Jonathan Blakely, Andrew Cofrin, Mary Woronov; **D:** Rick Sloane; **W:** Rick Sloane; **C:** Bill Fishman; **M:** Rick Sloane.

Movie, Movie ♂♂½ **1978 (PG)** Acceptable spoof of 1930s films features Scott in twin-bill of black and white "Dynamite Hands," which lampoons boxing dramas, and "Baxter's Beauties," a color send-up of Busby Berkeley musicals. There's even a parody of coming attractions. Wholesome, mildly entertaining. **107m/B VHS.** Stanley Donen, George C. Scott, Trish Van Devere, Eli Wallach, Red Buttons, Barbara Harris, Barry Bostwick, Harry Hamlin, Art Carney; **D:** Stanley Donen; **W:** Larry Gelbart. **M:** Ralph Burns. Writers Guild '78: Orig. Screenplay.

Movie Maker ♂ Smart Alec **1986** A young filmmaker ineptly raises money for his next film. **87m/C VHS.** Zsa Zsa Gabor, Antony Alda, Orson Bean, Bill Henderson; **D:** Jim Wilson.

Movie... In Your Face ♂ **1990** Japanese mobsters want to take over a movie studio. This supposed comedy comes with a "PU-13" rating—"Stinks to anyone with an I.Q. over 13," make of that what you will and be forewarned that it's also sophomoric and tasteless. **85m/C VHS.**

Movie Sturtmen ♂ Hollywood Stunt Man **1953** A retired Hollywood stunt man takes a job for a dead friend so that the friend's widow can receive the fee. Good stunt work taken mostly from old Richard Taldmadge movies almost makes up for poor production. **56m/B VHS.** James Gleason, William Henry; **D:** Bernard B. Ray.

Movies Money Murder ♂♂ **1996** Ruthless actress Lee McNight (Purcell) seduces Dr. Jim (Mull) into helping her produce a movie when invites her to his beach house. Too bad the writer (Black), to his beach house. Too bad the doc's wife (Kazan) shows up unexpectedly and the doc kills her. And when Dr. Jim hears the plot of the movie (about a murder in a doctor's house), he figures he's being blackmailed and decides to get rid of the

suspects. **?m/C VHS.** Martin Mull, Lee Purcell, Karen Black, Lainie Kazan; **D:** Arthur Webb.

Moving ♂ **1988 (R)** An engineer must relocate his family from New Jersey to Idaho in order to have a better job. Predictable calamities ensue. Not apt to move you. **89m/C VHS.** Richard Pryor, Randy Quaid, Dana Carvey, Dave Thomas, Rodney Dangerfield, Stacey Dash; **D:** Alan Metter; **W:** Andy Breckman; **M:** Howard Shore.

Moving McAllister ♂½ **2007 (PG-13)** Rick Robinson (Gourley) is a lowly intern at a Miami law firm. Desperate to score points with his boss, Maxwell McAllister (Hauer), he agrees to move McAllister's seductive niece Michelle (Kunis), her pet pig Dorothy, and various possessions cross-country. They pick up quirky hitchhiker Orrick Prescott Hope (Heder), and Rick finds his adventures just beginning. Unfortunately, they're boring and predictable and so's the movie. **90m/C DVD.** Mila Kunis, Jon Heder, Rutger Hauer, Ben Gourley; **D:** Andrew Black; **W:** Ben Gourley; **C:** Douglas Chamberlain; **M:** Didier Rachou.

Moving Out ♂♂ **1983** Adolescent migrant Italian boy finds it difficult to adjust to his new surroundings in Melbourne, Australia. **91m/C VHS.** Vince Colosimo, Sally Cooper, Maurice Devincentis, Tibor Gyapjas; **D:** Michael Pattinson.

Moving Target ♂½ **1989 (R)** A young woman witnesses the brutal murder of her boyfriend by mobsters and flees to Florida. Unbeknownst to her the thugs are still after her. Although top-billed, Blair's role is actually a supporting one. **85m/C VHS.** Linda Blair, Ernest Borgnine, Stuart Whitman, Charles Pitt, Jainine Linde, Kurt Woodruff; **D:** Marius Mattei.

Moving Target ♂½ **1996 (R)** Sonny McClean (Dudikoff) is a bounty hunter. But his latest job has him framed for murder and caught up in the middle of mob rivalries. So in order to clear his name, Sonny has to avoid getting killed by violent gangs and quick-draw cops. **106m/C VHS, DVD. CA** Michael Dudikoff, Billy Dee Williams; **D:** Don "The Dragon" Wilson, Bill Murphy, Hillary Kavanagh, Terry McMahon, Eileen McCloskey, Lisa Duane; **D:** Paul Ziller; **W:** Paul Ziller; **C:** Yoram Astrakhan; **M:** Cerek Gleeson.

Moving Target ♂♂ **2000 (R)** Martial arts expert Wilson is framed for murder and must battle the mob to clear his name. **86m/C VHS, DVD.** Don "The Dragon" Wilson, Billy Dee Williams; **D:** Damian Lee; **W:** Paul Whitworth, John Doe; **D:** Suri Krishnamme; **C:** David Pelletier; **M:** David Lawrence.

Moving Targets ♂♂ **1987** A young girl and her mother find themselves tracked by a homicidal maniac. **95m/C VHS, DVD. AU** Michael Aitkens, Carmen Duncan, Annie Jones, Shane Briant; **D:** Chris Langman.

Moving Violation ♂♂ **1976 (PG)** Crooked cops chase two young drifters who have witnessed the local sheriff commit a murder. Corman car chase epic. **91m/C VHS, DVD.** Eddie Albert, Kay Lenz, Stephen McHattie, Will Geer, Lonny (Lonnie) Chapman; **D:** Charles S. Dubin; **W:** William W. Norton Sr.

Moving Violations ♂ **1985 (PG-13)** This could be entitled "Adventures in Traffic Violations School." A wise-cracking tree planter is sent to traffic school after accumulating several moving violation's is-sued to him by a morose traffic cop. Bill Murray's little brother in feature role. **90m/C VHS, DVD.** John Murray, Jennifer Tilly, James Keach, Clara Peller, Wendie Jo Sperber, Fred Willard; **D:** Neal Israel; **W:** Pat Proft; **C:** Robert Elswit; **M:** Ralph Burns.

Mozart: A Childhood Chronicle ♂♂♂ **1976** An experimental, semi-narrative portrait of the immortal composer, from the ages of seven to twenty, filmed on authentic locations and with the original instruments of the era. Entire soundtrack is composed of Mozart's music. In German with English subtitles. **224m/B VHS.** GE Pavlos Bekiaris, Diego Crovetti, Santiago Ziesmer, Marianne Lowitz, Karl Maria Schley; **D:** Klaus Kirschner, Marianne Lowitz, Karl Maria Schley; **D:** Klaus Kirschner; **C:** Philip Koch.

Mozart and the Whale ♂♂½ **2005 (PG-13)** Based on a true story. Donald (Hartnett) and Isabelle (Mitchell) both have Asperger's Syndrome (a form of autism), which results in problems dealing with the outside world or other people. Donald has assembled a support group, which Isabelle decides to join. Since Donald is so shy, she makes the first romantic move at a Halloween party where she's dressed as Mozart and Donald hides inside a whale costume. The relationship grows stronger but has a lot of pitfalls as Donald gains self-confidence while Isabelle grows more uncertain. Filmed in Spokane, Washington. **93m/C DVD.** Josh Hartnett, Radha Mitchell, Gary Cole, Sheila Kelley, John Carroll Lynch, Rusty Schwimmer, Robert Wisdom; **D:** Petter Naess; **W:** Ronald Bass; **C:** Svein Krovel; **M:** Deborah Lurie.

The Mozart Brothers ♂♂♂ **1986** An angst-ridden Swedish opera director decides to break all the rules while doing an innovative production of Mozart's "Don Giovanni." At first he horrifies his conservative opera company but as his vision is gradually realized their resistance breaks down. A wonderful look at behind-the-scenes chaos and not just for opera aficionados. In Swedish with English subtitles. **111m/C VHS, SW** Etienne Glaser, Philip Zanden, Henry Bronett; **D:** Suzanne Osten.

The Mozart Story ♂♂ **1948** After Mozart's death, music minister to the Emperor, Antonio Salieri, reflects on how his jealousy and hatred of the musical genius held the great composer back and contributed to his death. Originally filmed in Austria in 1937, scenes were added for the U.S. release in 1948. **91m/B VHS.** Hans Holt, Winnie Marcus, Irene von Meyendorf, Rene Deltgen, Edward Vedder, Wilton Graff, Walther Janssen, Curt Jurgens, Paul Hoerniger; **D:** Karl Hartl.

MTV's Wuthering Heights ♂½ **2003 (PG-13)** MTV pop-rock version, set in California, of Emily Bronte's classic romantic tragedy. The star-crossed lovers are bionce beauty Cate (Christensen) and a motorcycle-riding, up-and-coming rocker named Heath (Vogel). Cate's brother Hendrix (Whitworth) is suspicious and jealous and Cate, who's scared of her feelings, impulsively decides to marry nice guy Edward (Masterton). Certainly not for purists—or anyone out of their teen years. **89m/C VHS, DVD.** Erika Christensen, Mike Vogel, Christopher K. Masterson, Katherine Heigl, Johnny Whitworth, John Doe; **D:** Suri Krishnamme; **W:** Max Enscoe, Annie de Young; **C:** Claudio Chea; **M:** Stephen Trask. C.A.B.L.E.

Much Ado about Nothing ♂♂♂½ **1993 (PG-13)** Shakespeare for the masses details romance between two sets of would-be lovers—the battling Beatrice and Benedick (Thompson and Branagh) and the ingenuous Hero and Claudio (Beckinsale and Leonard). Washington is the noble warrior leader, Reeves his evil half-dressed halfbrother, and Keaton serves comic relief as the officious, bumbling Dogberry. Sunlit, lusty, and revealing about all the vagaries of love, Branagh brings passion to the quest of making Shakespeare more approachable. His second attempt after "Henry V" at breaking the stuffy Shakespearean tradition. Filmed on location in Tuscany, Italy. **110m/C VHS, DVD.** GB Kenneth Branagh, Emma Thompson, Robert Sean Leonard, Kate Beckinsale, Denzel Washington, Keanu Reeves, Michael Keaton, Brian Blessed, Phyllida Law, Imelda Staunton, Gerard Horan, Jimmy Yuill, Richard Clifford, Ben Elton, Richard Briers; **D:** Kenneth Branagh; **W:** Kenneth Branagh; **C:** Roger Lanser; **M:** Patrick Doyle.

The Mudge Boy ♂♂½ **2003 (R)** Duncan Mudge (Hirsch) is not your average teenage boy. Wearing his dead mother's clothing, he bikes around town with his pet chicken in tow. Not surprisingly, he's picked on by the other boys and scorned by his own father (Jenkins). But investigating the murder of his ex-mistress, Nolte and cohorts belatedly relate to his loneliness, led by one boy is drawn to Duncan, a tough kid named Perry (Guiry). Perry's confused sexuality leads him to abuse and then resentment, with gruesome results. Explores the pain of loss and youth well. Cast is uniformly good, particularly Hirsch and Jenkins. And hey, who knew you could calm a chicken by sticking its head in your mouth? **94m/C DVD.** Emile Hirsch, Tom Guiry, Richard Jenkins, Pablo Schreiber, Zachary Knighton, Ryan Donowho, Meredith Handelman, Beckie King; **D:** Michael Burke; **W:** Michael Burke; **C:** Vanja Cernjul; **M:** Marcelo Zarvos.

Mugsy's Girls ♂ Delta Pi **1985 (R)** A messy comedy about six sorority women, educated in the refined skills of bar mud wrestling, who wallow in a Las Vegas championship tournament. Features pop singer Laura Branigan. **87m/C VHS.** Ruth Gordon, Laura Branigan, Eddie Deezen; **D:** Kevin Brodie.

Mulan ♂♂½ **1998 (G)** Disney's 36th animated tale is taken from a Chinese fable. The Emperor (Morita) sends out an order that one man from every family must become a soldier in order to repel the advances of Shan-Yu (Ferrer) and his army of Huns. But Mulan's (Wen) father (Oh) is old and she's afraid he won't return, so she decides to take his place and disguises herself as a warrior. While Murphy's Mushu does have the funniest lines, he doesn't quite fit the more serious tone. Impressive visuals, and careful characterization by the voice actors make up for any formulaic missteps so that adults as well as kids, should enjoy the show. **87m/C VHS, DVD. D:** Barry Cook, Tony Bancroft; **W:** Philip LaZebnik, Raymond Singer, Rita Hsiao, Christopher Sanders, Eugenia Bostwick-Singer; **M:** Eddie Murphy, B.D. Wong, Miguel Ferrer, Soon-Teck Oh, Noriyuki "Pat" Morita, Harvey Fierstein, Gedde Watanabe, James Hong, Freda Foh Shen, June Foray, Marni Nixon, George Takei, Miriam Margolyes, James Shigeta, Frank Welker, Lea Salonga, Donny Osmond, Jerry S Tondo.

Mulholland Drive ♂♂♂ **2001 (R)** David Lynch is back to his old trippy surrealistic tricks again, folks. Lush visuals and atmospheric Badalamenti music are once again the key ingredients in this hypnotic look at Hollywood through a kaleidoscope. Betty (Watts), an aspiring actress, comes home to find mystery girl Rita (Harring) taking a shower there. Rita, who has taken her name from a movie poster, has amnesia, and Betty tries to help her piece her life together. Meanwhile, successful young director Adam (Theroux) is threatened with death unless he casts a certain actress favored by a wheelchair-bound dwarf who issues orders over a cell phone. Then if you can believe it) things get even weirder. Originally conceived as a pilot for ABC television, but reshot as a feature. Execs must have guessed the public wasn't ready for "Laverne and Shirley Drop Acid." **146m/C VHS, DVD. US** Naomi Watts, Laura Elena Harring, Justin Theroux, Ann miller, Dan Hedaya, Lafayette Montgomery, Melissa George, James Karen, Katharine Towne, Billy Ray Cyrus, Angelo Badalamenti, Mark Pellegrino, Robert Forster, Missy Crider, Brent Briscoe, Marcus Graham, Vincent Castellanos, Michael Des Barres; **D:** David Lynch; **W:** David Lynch; **C:** Peter Deming; **M:** Angelo Badalamenti. Cesar '01: Foreign Film; Ind. Spirit '02: Cinematog.; L.A. Film Critics '01: Director (Lynch); Natl. Bd. of Review '01: Breakthrough Perf. (Watts); N.Y. Film Critics '01: Film, Director (Lynch); Natl. Soc. Film Critics '01: Actress (Watts), Film.

Mulholland Falls ♂♂½ **1995 (R)** Noir meets the nuclear age in this stylish period piece from New Zealand director Tamahori. Nolte plays the leader of the Hat Squad, a vicious group of fedora-sporting detectives assigned to bust organized crime in '50s L.A. at all costs. While investigating the murder of his ex-mistress (Connelly), who hung with General (Malkovich) in charge of the top secret nuclear program,

Although the cast is dripping with big name stars, the best performance is put in by the glossy set design of Richard Sylbert, who probably had a strong case of deja vu, having previously done "Chinatown." **107m/C VHS, DVD.** Nick Nolte, Melanie Griffith, Chazz Palminteri, Michael Madsen, Christopher Penn, Treat Williams, Jennifer Connelly, Andrew McCarthy, John Malkovich, Daniel Baldwin, Bruce Dern, Ed Lauter; *Cameos:* William L. Petersen, Rob Lowe; *D:* Lee Tamahori; *W:* Pete Dexter; *C:* Haskell Wexler; *M:* Dave Grusin. Golden Raspberries '96: Worst Support. Actress (Griffith).

Multiple Maniacs 1970 Waters at his most perverse. Divine's travelling freak show, acts, is the vehicle used for robbing and killing hapless spectators. One of the best scenes of a sordid lot is Divine being raped by Lobstora, a 15-foot broiled lobster. **90m/B VHS.** Divine, David Lochary, Mary Vivian Pearce, Edith Massey, Mink Stole, Susan Lowe, Cookie Mueller, Pat Moran, Paul Swift, Jack Walsh, Susan Walsh, Ed Peranio, George Figgs; *D:* John Waters; *W:* John Waters; *C:* John Waters.

Multiplicity 1996 (PG-13) With too many business and personal responsibilities, construction supervisor Doug Kinney (Keaton) is a prime candidate for the cloning experiments of Dr. Leeds (Yulin). Since the cloning process isn't exactly perfect, each clone (Doug winds up with three) has a different dominant personality trait—a hard-charger, a "Mister Mom," and a dopey slacker. Confusion reigns as wife Laura (MacDowell) deals with separation anxiety on a grand scale. Pleasant comedy shows Keaton can still be funny given the chance. Keaton had his choice of cloning comedies and chose this one over Chris Columbus's "More. **117m/C VHS, DVD.** Michael Keaton, Andie MacDowell, Harris Yulin, Richard Masur, Eugene Levy, Obba Babatunde, Ann Cusack, Brian Doyle-Murray, Julie Bowen; *D:* Harold Ramis; *W:* Harold Ramis, Chris Miller, Lowell Ganz, Babaloo Mandel, Mary Hale; *C:* Laszlo Kovacs; *M:* George Fenton.

Mumford 1999 (R) Writer/director Lawrence Kasdan creates another ensemble gem in this story of small town psychologist Mumford (Dean), who uses unusual methods to help the quirky townsfolk deal with their problems. His ability to actually listen to people helps out the young skateboarding millionaire (Lee) who employs most of the town, a shopaholic wife (McDonnell), her loutish husband (Danson), and nearly everyone else in town whose screws are put loose. Everyone except a slimy lawyer (Short) who the good doctor fires as a patient. He begins to dig up facts that may prove that Mumford isn't even a doctor. Since there's no big plot payoff or mind-boggling twists, some viewers may find it a bit boring. Those who enjoy deeper character development will love it, however. **112m/C VHS, DVD.** Loren Dean, Alfre Woodard, Hope Davis, Jason Lee, Mary McDonnell, Pruitt Taylor Vince, Zooey Deschanel, Martin Short, David Paymer, Jane Adams, Dana Ivey, Kevin Tighe, Ted Danson, Jason Ritter, Elissabeth (Elisabeth, Elizabeth, Liz) Moss, Robert Stack; *D:* Lawrence Kasdan; *W:* Lawrence Kasdan; *C:* Ericson Core; *M:* James Newton Howard.

The Mummy 1932 A group of scientists examine a sarcophagus taken from an unmarked grave at an archeological dig in 1921 Egypt. There is a warning on the box that it should not be opened. Does this stop anyone? Of course not! So Im-Ho-Tep (Karloff), a 4000-year-old priest who was disgraced and buried alive, is revived. Then, of course, ther's his objective—heroine Helen (Johann) whom the wrapped one believes is the reincarnation of his long-gone love Anck-es-en-Amon. Eerie chills mark this classic horror tale that found Karloff undergoing eight hours of extraordinary makeup (by Jack Pierce) to transform him into the macabre mummy. Marked the directing debut of famed German cinematographer Freund. The first in the Universal series. **72m/B VHS, DVD.** Boris Karloff, Zita Johann, David Manners, Edward Van Sloan, Arthur Byron, Bramwell Fletcher, Noble Johnson, Leonard Mudie, Henry Victor; *D:* Karl Freund; *W:* John Lloyd Balderston; *C:* Charles Stumar.

The Mummy 1959 A group of British archaeologists discover they have made a grave mistake when a mummy kills off those who have violated his princess' tomb. A summation of all the previous "mummy" films, this one has a more frightening mummy (6'4" Lee) who is on screen much of the time. Additionally, there is pathos in this monster, not merely murder and revenge. An effective remake of the 1932 classic. **88m/C VHS, DVD. GB** Peter Cushing, Christopher Lee, Felix Aylmer, Yvonne Furneaux, Eddie Byrne, Raymond Huntley, George Pastell, Michael Ripper, John Stuart; *D:* Terence Fisher; *W:* Jimmy Sangster; *C:* Jack Asher.

The Mummy 1999 (PG-13) Cheesy fun in the Saturday matinee tradition, this horror tale is a loose remake of the 1932 Boris Karloff-starrer. In the 1920s, American adventurer Rick O'Connell (Fraser) is hired by British librarian Evelyn (Weisz) and her Egyptologist brother Jonathan (Hannah) to escort them to the ancient Egyptian city of the dead. Unfortunately, their meddling results in the release of cursed mummified priest Imhotep (Vosloo), who manages to regenerate into living flesh and who wants to use Evelyn to resurrect his dead girlfriend. Lots of zombies, mummies, skeletons, and flesh-eating beetles ensue. **124m/C VHS, DVD, HD DVD.** Brendan Fraser, Rachel Weisz, Arnold Vosloo, John Hannah, Kevin J. O'Connor, Jonathan Hyde, Oded Fehr, Erik Avari, Tuc Watkins, Stephen Dunham, Corey Johnson, Bernard Fox, Aharon Ipale, Omid Djalili, Patricia Velasquez; *D:* Stephen Sommers; *W:* Stephen Sommers; *C:* Adrian Biddle; *M:* Jerry Goldsmith.

Mummy & Curse of the Jackal WOOF! 1967 Upon opening the tomb of female mummy, a man is cursed to roam the streets of Las Vegas as a werejackal. Impossibly inept. **86m/C VHS.** Anthony Eisley, Martina Pons, John Carradine, Saul Goldsmith; *D:* Oliver Drake.

The Mummy Lives 1993 (PG-13) Vengeance-minded mummy goes on a murderous rampage against the defilers of his tomb and becomes obsessed with a woman he believes is his reincarnated lost love. **97m/C VHS.** Tony Curtis, Greg Wrangler, Muhamad Bakri, Leslie Hardy; *D:* Gerry O'Hara; *W:* Nelson Gidding; *C:* Avi Koren; *M:* Dov Seltzer.

The Mummy Returns 2001 (PG-13) Bombastic sequel to the 1999 hit is set a decade later and finds married Rick (Fraser) and Evelyn (Weisz) living in London with their 8-year-old son, Alex (Boath). Unfortunately, a reincarnated Anck-Su-Namun (Velasquez) manages to bring crispy Imhotep (Vosloo) back again to rule the world. Fehr returns as desert warrior Ardeth Bay, as does Hannah as Evelyn's ne'er-do-well brother. Wrestler Dwayne "The Rock" Johnson briefly shows up as a new villain—The Scorpion King, who's already going to have his own film. As usual there's too much going on—it's loud and crowded, sacrificing the original's unexpected charm for visual overkill. **129m/C VHS, DVD, HD DVD. US** Brendan Fraser, Rachel Weisz, Oded Fehr, John Hannah, Patricia Velasquez, Dwayne "The Rock" Johnson, Arnold Vosloo, Flip Kobler, Adewale Akinnuoye-Agbaje, Shaun Parkes, Alun Armstrong; *D:* Stephen Sommers; *C:* Adrian Biddle; *M:* Alan Silvestri.

The Mummy: Tomb of the Dragon Emperor 2008 Fraser's back (after 2001's "The Mummy Returns") as explorer Rick O'Connell but Rachel Weisz took a pass so wife Evelyn is now played by Bello. In 1946, the duo are do one last job for the foreign office, returning a priceless artifact to Shanghai. China also happens to be the location of Evelyn's wastrel brother (Hannah) and the O'Connells' adventurous son Alex (Ford), who has uncovered an entombed terra cotta army. In the distant past, a ruthless sorceress (Yeoh) placed a spell on the Dragon Emperor (Li) and his warriors and Alex had the misfortune to break it. That long sleep has made the supernatural Emperor even more determined to rule—and not just China. Not yet reviewed. **?m/C** Brendan Fraser, Jet Li, Maria Bello, John Hannah, Luke Ford, Michelle Yeoh, Anthony Wong, Russell Wong, Isabella Leong; *D:* Rob Cohen; *W:* Alfred Gough, Miles Millar; *C:* Simon Duggan; *M:* Randy Edelman.

The Mummy's Curse 1944 Sequel to "The Mummy's Ghost" and Chaney's last outing as Kharis. Construction by a government order causes Kharis and Ananka (Christine) to be dug up in a Louisiana bayou (how they got there from a New England swamp is anyone's guess) and taken to Cajun country for study by archaeologists. The usual havoc ensues. Includes lots of stock footage from earlier mummy movies. Based on a story by Leon Abrams and Dwight V. Babcock. **61m/B VHS, DVD.** Lon Chaney Jr., Peter Coe, Virginia Christine, Kay Harding, Dennis Moore, Martin Kosleck, Kurt Katch; *D:* Leslie Goodwins; *W:* Bernard Schubert; *C:* Virgil Miller.

The Mummy's Ghost 1944 The fourth in the Universal series and the sequel to "The Mummy's Tomb" has Kharis (Chaney Jr.) searching for the reincarnation of his ancient love, Princess Ananka, who just happens to be New England college coed Amina (Ames). The high priest (Zucco) sends fellow priest Yousef Bey (Carradine) along to assist but he makes the mistake of declaring his own love for Amina and the mummy gets very, very mad. Oh, and both Kharis and Amina sink into a swamp, thus setting up the next (and last) film in the series. **61m/B VHS, DVD.** Lon Chaney Jr., John Carradine, Ramsay Ames, Robert Lowery, Barton MacLane, George Zucco; *D:* Reginald LeBorg; *W:* Griffin Jay, Henry Sucher, Brenda Weisberg; *C:* William Sickner; *M:* Hans J. Salter.

The Mummy's Hand 1940 Although this is the followup to 1932's "The Mummy," it actually has little to do with the original film. Archaeologists Steve Banning (Foran) and Babe Jensen (Ford) are searching for the tomb of ancient Egyptian Princess Ananka. Crazy high priest Andoheb (Zucco) sends mummy Kharis (Tyler), who is the tomb's guardian, to kill anyone who defiles her rest. So Kharis shuffles off but finds Marta (Moran) instead. And being a guy, albeit a long-dead guy, wants to make the beauty his bride. Low-budget but the mix of scares and comedy make this worth watching. **70m/B VHS, DVD.** Dick Foran, Wallace Ford, Peggy Moran, Cecil Kellaway, George Zucco, Tom Tyler, Eduardo Ciannelli, Charles Trowbridge; *D:* Christy Cabanne; *W:* Griffin Jay, Maxwell Shane; *C:* Elwood "Woody" Bredell; *M:* Hans J. Salter.

The Mummy's Revenge *La Venganza de la Momia* 1973 A fanatic revives a mummy with virgin blood. The first mummy movie to feature an intact gore. **91m/C VHS. SP** Paul Naschy, Jack Taylor, Maria Silva, Helga Line, Luis Davila, Eduardo Calvo; *D:* Carlos Aured; *W:* Paul Naschy.

The Mummy's Shroud 1967 Hammer's next-to-last Mummy horror is a handsomely produced but tepid affair. The plot trots out the familiar elements—British archeological dig led by Sir Basil Walden (Morell) discovers the remains of Pharaoh Kah-to-Bey; hieroglyphics from the shroud are read aloud...you know the drill. Lots of talk, comparatively little action. **90m/C DVD, GB** Andre Morell, John Phillips, David Buck, Elizabeth Sellars; *D:* John Gilling; *W:* John Gilling; *C:* Arthur Grant; *M:* Don Banks.

The Mummy's Tomb 1942 Chaney Jr. is in wraps for the first time in this sequel to "The Mummy's Hand." Kharis is transported to America by a crazed Egyptian high priest to kill off surviving members of the expedition. Weakened by a lame script and too much stock footage. Based on a story by Neil P. Varnick. **71m/B VHS, DVD.** Lon Chaney Jr., Dick Foran, John Hubbard, Elyse Knox, George Zucco, Wallace Ford, Turhan Bey; *D:* Harold Young; *W:* Griffin Jay, Henry Sucher; *C:* George Robinson.

Munchie 1992 (PG) A forgotten alien critter is discovered in a mine shaft by young Gage. Munchie turns out to be a good friend, protecting Gage from bullies and granting other wishes. Frequent sight gags help keep the film moving but it's still awfully slow. Sequel to "Munchies" (1987). **80m/C VHS, DVD.** Loni Anderson, Andrew Stevens, Arte Johnson, Jamie McEnnan; *D:* Jim Wynorski; *V:* Dom DeLuise.

Munchies 1987 (PG) "Gremlins" rip-off about tiny aliens who love beer and fast food, and invade a small town. Lewd and ribald. **83m/C VHS, DVD.** Harvey Korman, Charles Stratton, Nadine Van Der Velde, Alix Elias, Jon Stafford, Charlie Phillips, Hardy Rawls, Robert Picardo, Wendy Schaal, Paul Bartel; *D:* Bettina Hirsch; *W:* Lance Smith; *C:* Jonathan West.

Munich 2005 (R) Back in "Schindler's List" mode, Spielberg explores in horrifying magnification the politics and far-reaching aftermath of the real-life shocking murders of 11 Israeli athletes at the 1972 Munich Olympics. However, the film is primarily about a team of Israeli agents (Bana, Craig, Hinds, Kassovitz) hired to exact revenge on the Palestinian assassins. Gold standard screenwriters Kushner and Roth draw liberally from George Jonas's nonfiction tome "Vengeance," and, like his other fact-based dramas, Spielberg delivers a thought-provoking and intense experience, making us cringe at the transforming power of revenge. **164m/C DVD. US** Eric Bana, Daniel Craig, Ciaran Hinds, Mathieu Kassovitz, Hanns Zischler, Geoffrey Rush, Michael (Michel) Lonsdale, Mathieu Amalric, Lynn Cohen, Marie Josee Croze, Makram Khoury, Moritz Bleibtreu, Gila Almagor, Moshe Ivgi, Yvan Attal, Hiam Abbass, Valeria Bruni-Tedeschi, Meret Becker, Ayelet Zurer, Igal Naor, Omar Metwally, Mostefa Djadjam; *D:* Steven Spielberg; *W:* Tony Kushner, Eric Roth; *C:* Janusz Kaminski; *M:* John Williams.

Munster, Go Home! 1966 Herman learns he's inherited the stately manor Munster Hall so he and the family head for jolly old England to claim their family history. Will the Brits ever recover? **96m/C VHS, DVD.** Fred Gwynne, Yvonne De Carlo, Al Lewis, Butch Patrick, Debbie Watson, Terry-Thomas, Hermione Gingold, Robert Pine, John Carradine, Bernard Fox, Richard Dawson, Arthur Malet; *D:* Earl Bellamy; *W:* Joe Connelly, Bob Mosher, George Tibbles; *C:* Benjamin (Ben H.) Kline; *M:* Jack Marshall.

The Munsters' Revenge 1981 Based on the continuing adventures of the 1960s comedy series characters. Herman, Lily, and Grandpa have to contend with robot replicas of themselves that were created by a flaky scientist. **96m/C VHS, DVD.** Fred Gwynne, Yvonne De Carlo, Al Lewis, Jo McDonnell, Sid Caesar, Ezra Stone, Howard Morris, Bob Hastings, K.C. Martel; *D:* Don Weis; *M:* Vic Mizzy. TV

The Muppet Christmas Carol 1992 (G) Christmas classic features all the muppet favorites together and in Victorian garb. Storyline is more or less faithful to Dickens original, with pleasant special effects. Gonzo the Great as Dickens narrates the tale as Scrooge (Caine) takes his legendary Christmas Eve journey escorted by three (flannel) spirits. The Cratchits are led by Kermit and Miss Piggy. Directed by Brian Henson, Jim's son, the film is as heartwarming as the Cratchit's crackling fire, but doesn't quite achieve the former muppet magic. Also features some sappy songs by Williams, including "Love is Like a Heatwave" and "Island in the Sun." **120m/C VHS, DVD.** Michael Caine; *D:* Brian Henson; *C:* John Fenner; *M:* Paul Williams, Miles Goodman; *V:* Dave Goetz, Steve Whitmire, Jerry Nelson, Frank Oz.

The Muppet Movie 1979 (G) Seeking fame and footlights, Kermit the Frog and his pal Fozzie Bear travel to Hollywood, and along the way are joined by sundry human and muppet characters, including the lovely Miss Piggy. A delightful cult favorite filled with entertaining cameos, memorable (though somewhat pedestrian) songs and crafty special effects—Kermit rides a bike and rows a boat! A success for the late Jim Henson. ♫The Rainbow Connection; Frog's Legs

So Fine; Movin Right Along; Can You Picture That?; Never Before; Something Better; This Looks Familiar; I'm Going Back There Someday. **94m/C VHS, DVD, GB Cameos:** Edgar Bergen, Milton Berle, Mel Brooks, Madeline Kahn, Steve Martin, Carol Kane, Paul Williams, Charles Durning, Bob Hope, James Coburn, Dom DeLuise, Elliott Gould, Cloris Leachman, Telly Savalas, Orson Welles; **D:** James Frawley; **W:** Jack Burns, Jerry Juhl; **C:** Isicore Mankofsky; **M:** Paul Williams; **V:** Jim Henson, Frank Oz, Jerry Nelson, Richard Hunt, Dave Goelz.

Murda Muzik ♪½ 2003 Up-and-coming rapper Fresh can't keep the hard life on the mean Queens' streets behind him, risking more than just his big record-ing contract. Music from popular hip-hop and rap stars, including 50 Cent, Snoop Dogg, and Mobb Deep, are the main draw. **72m/C VHS, DVD,** Nas, Big Noyd, Havoc, Cormega, Chinky, Prodigy; **D:** Lawrence Page; **M:** Prodigy. VIDEO

Muppet Treasure Island ♪♪½ 1996 (G) Literary classic gets its first coat of felt as Kermit the Frog, Miss Piggy and the entire Muppet gang hit the high seas in an adaptation of Robert Lous Stevenson's 1883 well-worn adventure tale. De-lightful settings, from an old English tavern to an exotic south sea island, frame the journey of young Jim Hawkins (flesh and blood Bishop), who along with tavern own-ers Rizzo the Rat (Whitmire) and the Great Gonzo (Goelz) search for buried treasure. Long John Silver is played to the hilt by Curry, master of the over-the-top villain. Helmer Henson steers a steady ship, with over 400 Muppet critters making an appearance. **99m/C VHS, DVD,** Tim Curry, Kevin Bishop, Billy Connolly, Jennifer Saunders; **D:** Brian Henson; **C:** John Fenner; **M:** Hans Zimmer; **V:** Steve Whitmire, Frank Oz, Dave Goelz, Steve Whitmire.

The Muppets Take Manhattan ♪♪½ 1984 (G) Following a smashing success with a college musi-cal, the Muppets take their show and tal-ents to Broadway, only to face misfortune in the form of an unscrupulous producer. A less imaginative script than the first two Muppet movies, yet an enjoyable experi-ence with numerous major stars making cameo appearances. **94m/C VHS, DVD, Cam-eos:** Dabney Coleman, James Coco, Art Carney; Joan Rivers, Gregory Hines, Linda Lavin, Liza Min-nelli, Brooke Shields, John Landis; **D:** Frank Oz; **W:** Frank Oz, Tom Patchett, Jim Henson.

The Muppets' Wizard of Oz ♪♪ 2005 (PG) The sock-puppets that made the world fall in love with the "Rainbow Connection" find themselves somewhere over the rainbow in this made-for-TV feature. Granted, the Muppets have been much, much funnier in the past, but after stinkers like "Muppets Christmas Carol" and "Muppets Treasure Island," it's nice to see the return of their creations to their comedic roots. Sure, Ashanti is a pretty dull lead, but the sup-porting cast is strong and the humor is surprisingly adult. The Muppets might be owned by Disney now, but you can still enjoy Wizard's Quentin Tarantino cameos and jokes about Gonzo's n.pples. (Hon-estly.) **100m/C DVD,** Ashanti, Queen Latifah, David Alan Grier, Jeffrey Tambor; **Cameos:** Quentin Tarantino; **D:** Kirk R. Thatcher; **W:** Debra Frank, Steve Hayes, Adam F. Goldberg, Tom Martin; **C:** Tony Westman; **V:** Steve Whitmire, Dave Goelz, Bill Berretta, Eric Jacobson. VIDEO

Muppets from Space ♪♪½ 1999 (G) The sixth full-length movie featur-ing Jim Henson's uberpuppets centers on Gonzo and his search for his real family. He discovers that he is an alien from a distant planet and announces his findings on Miss Piggy's talk show. Soon, govern-ment bad guy K. Edgar Singer (Tambor) is after him. After escaping Singer (Tambor) and the foursome...

Murder ♪♪ 1930 Believing in a young woman's innocence, one jurist be-gins to organize the pieces of the crime in order to save her. Fine early effort by Hitchcock based on play "Enter Sir John," by Clemense Dane and Helen Simpson. **92m/B VHS, DVD, GB** Herbert Marshall, Nora Baring, Phyllis Konstam, Miles Mander; **D:** Alfred Hitchcock; **W:** Alfred Hitchcock; **C:** .ack Cox; **M:** John Reynders.

Murder Ahoy ♪♪ 1964 Miss Marple looks perplexed when dead bodies surface on a naval cadet training ship. Dame Marge is the dottie detective in the final, and least appealing, of her four Aga-tha Christie films of the '60s (although it was released in the States prior to "Murd-er Most Foul"). **74m/B VHS, DVD,** Margaret Rutherford, Lionel Jeffries, Charles "Bud" Tingwell, William Mervyn, Francis Matthews; **D:** George Pollock.

Murder at Devil's Glen ♪♪½ 1999 Henry (Schro-der) is a manipulative ex-con who returns to his hometown with a proposition for three of his former college buddies, who have all become successful. They all share a secret—during a frat party hazing incident a young woman accidentally died and the foursome buried her body in an isolated area in the woods. Now Henry wants to develop that particular piece of property, so they have to go back and dig up the evidence of their crime. Ah, if only it were that easy. The sweet-faced Schroder makes a remarkably capable and creepy bad guy. **90m/C VHS, DVD,** Rick Schroder, Jack Noseworthy, Michael Easton, Jayce Bartok, Jenni-fer Jostyn, Tara Reid; **D:** Paul Shapiro; **W:** Eric Haitacher; **C:** Brian Reynolds; **M:** Dana Kaproff. TV

Murder at 45 R.P.M. ♪♪ Meur-tre en 45 Tours 1965 A singer and her lover suspect each other of a gruesome murder. Things become sticky when she receives a recorded message from her dead husband. Average. **98m/C VHS, FR** Danielle Darrieux, Michel Auclair, Jean Servais, Henri Guisol; **D:** Etienne Perier.

Murder at Midnight ♪♪ 1931 The killings begin with a game of cha-rades in which the gun wasn't supposed to be loaded, and continue as members of English high society take one by one. "Blondie" director Strayer still working on his change of pace. **69m/B VHS, DVD,** Alice White, Leslie Fenton, Aileen Pringe, Hale Hamil-ton, Robert Elliot, Clara Blandick, Brandon Hurst; **D:** Frank Strayer.

Murder at 1600 ♪♪ 1997 (R) Jad-ed D.C. detective Harlan Regis (Snipes) is called to investigate the murder of Carla Town (Moore), a secretary found dead in a White House bathroom. He's reluctantly assisted by hard-boiled Secret Service agent Chance (Lane), with head of secu-rity Nick Spikings (Benzali) wants the quietly—justice not being his main con-cern. Cliche-fest script gives stereotypical characters a little more development than you may be used to seeing, but doesn't give them anything new or interesting to say or do. Snipes and Lane make a good team, however, and Miller fulfills his usual wise-cracking sidekick role effortlessly. **107m/C VHS, DVD,** Wesley Snipes, Diane Lane, Daniel Benzali, Dennis Miller, Alan Alda, Ronny Cox, Tate Donovan, Diane Baker, Mary Moore, Harris Yulin, Richard Blackburn; **D:** Dwight Little; **W:** Wayne Beach, David Hodgin; **C:** Steven Bern-stein; **M:** Christopher Young.

Murder at the Baskervilles ♪♪ Silver Blaze; Sher-lock Holmes: The Silver Blaze 1937 Sherlock Holmes is invited to visit Sir Henry Basker-ville at his estate, but then finds that Bas-kerville's daughter's fiance is accused of stealing a race horse and murdering its keeper. Based on Sir Arthur Conan Doyle's story "Silver Blaze." Remade in 1977. **67m/B VHS, DVD, GB** Arthur Wontner, Ian Fleming, Lyn Harding; **D:** Thomas Bentley.

Murder at the Vanities ♪♪½ 1934 Vintage murder mystery set against a musical revue format, in which a tough de-tective must find a killer before the Earl Carroll-based cabaret ends and he or she will escape with the exciting crowd. Also featured is a mind-boggling production number based on the song "Marijuana." ♫Marijuana; Lovely One; Where Do They Come From Now; Live and Love Tonight; Cocktails for Two; Ebony Rhapsody. **91m/B VHS,** Victor McLaglen, Kitty Carlisle Hart, Jack Oakie, Duke Ellington, Carl Brisson, Dorothy Stick-ney, Gertrude Michael, Jessie Ralph, Charles Mid-dleton, Gail Patrick, Donald Meek, Toby Wing, Lu-cille Ball, Ann Sheridan; **D:** Mitchell Leisen; **W:** Agnes Brackner; **C:** Leo Tover; **M:** Arthur Johnston.

Murder by Death ♪♪♪½ 1976 (PG) Capote is an eccentric millionaire who invites the world's greatest detectives to dinner, offering $1 million to the one who can solve the evening's murder. En-tertaining and hammy spoof of Agatha Christie's "And Then There Were None" and the earlier "Ten Little Indians." **95m/C VHS, DVD,** Peter Falk, Alec Guinness, David Ni-ven, Maggie Smith, Peter Sellers, Eileen Brennan, Elsa Lanchester, Nancy Walker, Estelle Winwood, James Coco; **D:** Robert Moore; **Support:** Actress (Bujold.) **M:** Dave Grusin.

Murder by Decree ♪♪♪ 1979 (PG) Realistic and convincing version of the Jack the Ripper story. Sherlock Holmes and Dr. Watson find a vast web of conspiracy which they investigate the murders of Whitechapel prostitutes. Based partially on facts, it's a highly de-tailed suspenser with interesting camera work and fine performances. **120m/C VHS, DVD, CA** Christopher Plummer, James Mason, Donald Sutherland, Genevieve Bujold, Susan Clark, David Hemmings, Frank Finlay, John Giel-gud, Anthony Quayle; **D:** Bob (Benjamin) Clark; **W:** John Hopkins. Genie '80: Actor (Plummer), Direc-tor (Clark), Support: Actress (Bujold).

Murder by Moonlight ♪♪ 1991 (PG-13) Rival agents investigate a mysteri-ous murder in a prosperous mining colony on the moon. Not only do they discover a dastardly trail that leads all the way back to Earth, but a strange romantic attraction for each other. Originally broadcast on British TV. **94m/C VHS, GB** Julian Sands, Bri-gitte Nielsen, Gerald McEnany, Jane Lapotaire, Brian Cox; **D:** Michael Lindsay-Hogg; **M:** Trevor Jones.

Murder by Natural Causes ♪♪ 1979 A made-for-TV brain teaser in which a woman and her lover plot to kill her mind-reader husband. Lots of twists make this fun for viewers who enjoy a challenge. **96m/C VHS,** Hal Hol-brook, Barry Bostwick, Katharine Ross, Richard Anderson; **D:** Robert Day.

Murder by Night ♪♪½ 1989 (PG-13) Amnesia victim Urich is found next to a dead body, the result of a gruesome murder. Urich is the only witness and thinks he may be the next victim. Others think he's the killer. Mystery, with enough twists to keep it worthwhile. **95m/C VHS,** Robert Urich, Kay Lenz, Jim Metzler, Richard Mon-sen; **D:** Paul Lynch. CABLE

Murder at the Gallop ♪♪½ 1963 Snooping Miss Marple doesn't be-lieve a filthy rich old-timer died of natural causes, despite the dissenting police point of view. Wheedling her way into the police investigation, she discovers the secret of the Gallop club, a place where people bounce up and down on top of horses. Much mugging between Dame Margaret and Morley, Marple's assistant, Mr. String-er, is the real life Mr. Dame Margaret. Based on Christie's Poirot mystery "After the Funeral." **81m/B VHS, DVD,** Margaret Ruth-erford, Robert Morley, Flora Robson, Charles "Bud" Tingwell, Duncan Lamont, Stringer Davis; **D:** George Pollock; **W:** James P. Cavanagh; **C:** Arthur Ibbetson; **M:** Ronald Goodwin.

Murder by Numbers ♪♪½ 2002 (R) Homicide detective Cassie May-weather (Bullock) is a crime-scene spe-cialist saddled with a by-the-book new partner, Sam Kennedy (Chaplin). This isn't good since she has to prove that two wealthy young men (Gosling, Pitt) have committed what they think is the perfect murder (shades of Leopold and Loeb with nods to Hitchcock). Naturally, Cassie has baggage and must come to terms with her past in order to solve the crime. Gos-ling's downright scary while Pitt well-plays his weaker partner; Bullock works against being likeable as a loner toughie. **120m/C VHS, DVD, US** Sandra Bullock, Ben Chaplin, Ryan Gosling, Michael Pitt, Christopher Penn, R.D. Call, Agnes Bruckner; **D:** Barbet Schroeder; **W:** Tony Gayton; **C:** Luciano Tovoli; **M:** Clint Mansell.

Murder by Phone ♪♪ 1982 (R) A deranged technician has turned his phone into an instrument of electronic death. Chamberlain is the visit-ing professor trying to discover who's per-petrating the numbers of his students. Good cast decides to test schlock meter. **79m/C VHS, CA** Richard Chamberlain, John Houseman, Sara Botsford; **D:** Michael Anderson Sr.; **W:** Michael Butler, John Kent Harrison; **M:** John Barry.

Murder by Television ♪½ 1935 Low-budget murder mystery with Lugosi in a dual role as twins—one good, one not so. When a professor and his evil twin are murdered, the instrument of death sometimes invoked fear and suspicion in the general public. Historically interesting and Lugosi fans will appreciate seeing him in a non-vampiric role. **55m/B VHS, DVD,** Bela Lugosi, George Meeker; **D:** Clifford Sanforth.

Murder by the Book ♪½ 1987 A-ter Ego 1987 A mystery writer finds that his fictional character, a hard-boiled private eye, has taken control of his life. With his new macho persona the writer solves a crime and saves the obligatory damsel. Based on the novel "Alter Ego" by Mel Arrighi. **100m/C VHS,** Robert Hays, Fred Gwynne, Chris-topher Murney; **D:** Mel Damski. TV

Murder Czech Style ♪♪ Vrazda po Cesky 1966 Chubby and boring office clerk Frantisek (Hrusinsky) is amazed when a colleague, the beautiful Alice (Fia-lova), agrees to marry him. He can't be-lieve his good fortune—and he's right—Frantisek soon discovers his wife has a married lover. So, he plots to murder her in several increasingly silly fantasies. Czech with subtitles. **87m/C VHS, CZ** Rudolf Hrusinsky, Kveta Fialova, Vacav Voska, Vladimir Mensik; **D:** Jiri Weiss; **W:** Jiri Weiss, Jan Otcena-sek; **C:** Jan Nemecek; **M:** Zdenek Liska.

Murder Elite ♪½ 1986 A murder in maniac terrorizes the rural English countryside, where MacGraw has re-turned after losing all her money in Ameri-ca. Poor acting and direction leave one a dust-gatherer. **98m/C VHS,** Ali MacGraw, Billie Whitelaw, Hywel Bennett; **D:** Claude Whatham.

Murder for Sale ♪ OSS 177 - Dou-ble Agent 1968 Secret Agent 117 stages an elaborate scam in order to infiltrate a ring of terrorists and criminals. Ask for Bond next time. **9?m/C VHS, FR** John Garvin, Margaret Lee, Curt Jurgens, Luciana Paluzzi, Robert Hos-sein, Rosalba Neri; **D:** Renzo Cerrato; **W:** Renzo Cerrato; **C:** Torino Delli Colli; **M:** Piero Piccioni.

Murder, He Says ♪♪♪½ 1945 Sinister comedy finds insurance salesman Peter Marshall (MacMurray) sent to gather statistics in the Ozarks and encountering the murderous hillbilly Fleagle family and various other looney characters. Naturally, the prettiest girl in the area, Claire (Walk-er), also happens to be the only sane per-son, which is lucky for Peter. **91m/B VHS,** Fred MacMurray, Helen Walker, Marjorie Main, Pe-ter Whitney, Barbara Pepper, Jean Heather, Mabel Paige, Porter Hall; **D:** George Marshall; **W:** Lou

Murder by Numbers ♪½ ... Behrens, Shari Belafonte, Ronee Blakley, Stanley Kamel, Jayne Meadows, Debra Sandlund, Dick Sargent, Cleavon Little; **D:** Paul Leder; **W:** Paul Leder.

Breslow; **C:** Theodor Sparkuhl; **M:** Robert Emmett Dolan.

Murder in a Small Town ♂♂1/2 1999
It's the 1930s and Broadway director Wilder has moved to Connecticut after his wife's murder and runs the community theatre. But soon he finds himself surrounded by dead bodies and, with the aid of an opera-loving cop (Starr), Wilder decides to do some detecting. **100m/C VHS.** Gene Wilder, Mike Starr, Cherry Jones, Frances Conroy, Deirdre O'Connell, Terry O'Quinn; **D:** Joyce Chopra; **W:** Gene Wilder; **C:** Bruce Surtees; **M:** John Morris. **CABLE**

Murder in Coweta County ♂♂1/2 1983
Griffith and Cash are strong in this true-crime drama based on the book by Margaret Anne Barnes. Griffith is a Georgia businessman who thinks he's gotten away with murder, Cash is the lawman who tenaciously pursues him. Based on an actual 1948 case. **100m/C VHS, DVD.** Johnny Cash, Andy Griffith, Earl Hindman, June Carter Cash, Cindi Knight, Ed Van Nuys; **D:** Gary Nelson; **W:** Dennis Nemec; **C:** Larry Pizer; **M:** Brad Fiedel. **TV**

Murder in Greenwich ♂♂ Dominick Dunne Presents Murder in Greenwich 2002
(R) Based on former LAPD detective Mark Fuhrman's book. Fuhrman (Meloni) investigates the unsolved 25-year-old murder of 15-year-old Martha Moxley (Grace), which happened in Greenwich, CT in the 1970's. This is the case that eventually led to the arrest and conviction of Kennedy nephew Michael Sakal for the crime. **88m/C VHS, DVD.** Christopher Meloni, Robert Forster, Maggie Grace, Toby Moore, Jon Foster, Andrew Mitchell; **D:** Tom McLoughlin; **W:** Dave Erickson; **C:** Mark Wareham; **M:** John Davis. **CABLE**

Murder in Greenwich Village ♂♂1/2 1937
Heiress Kay Cabot (Wray) is accused of a murder that she naturally didn't commit and it's up to her defense attorney, Steve Jackson (Arlen), to get her off so that they can live happily ever after. **68m/B VHS.** Fay Wray, Richard Arlen, Raymond Walburn, Scott Kolk, Thurston Hall, Marc Lawrence, Leon Ames, Marjorie Reynolds, Wyn Cahoon, Mary Russell; **D:** Albert Rogell; **W:** Michael L. Simmons; **C:** Henry Freulich.

Murder in Mind ♂♂1/2 1997 **(R)**
Caroline Walker's (Parker) accused of murdering her husband (Smits) but can't remember doing so. She tries to figure out the truth by undergoing regression therapy with a hypnotherapist (Hawthorne). But what she supposedly uncovers are a lot of ugly secrets that were better left hidden. Adapted by Cooney from his stage play. **89m/C VHS.** Nigel Hawthorne, Mary-Louise Parker, Jimmy Smits, Jason Scott Lee, Gailard Sartain; **D:** Andrew Morahan; **W:** Michael Cooney; **C:** John Aronson; **M:** Paul Buckmaster.

Murder in New Hampshire: The Pamela Smart Story ♂♂1/2 1991 **(PG-13)**
A sleazy true story about a young high school teacher who seduces an impressionable student into murdering her husband. Hunt's fine as the seductress but this TV fare is just average. **93m/C VHS, DVD.** Helen Hunt, Chad Allen, Larry Drake, Howard Hesseman, Ken Howard, Michael Learned; **D:** Joyce Chopra; **M:** Gary Chang. **TV**

Murder in Space ♂♂ 1985
Nine multinational astronauts are stranded aboard a space station when they discover one of them is a murderer. This creates anxiety, particularly since the killer's identity is unknown. Oatmeal salesman Brimley is the earth-bound mission control chief trying desperately to finger a space-chief while the bodies pile up. **95m/C VHS.** Wilford Brimley, Martin Balsam, Michael Ironside; **D:** Steven Hilliard Stern. **TV**

Murder in Texas ♂♂♂ 1981
Docudrama looks at the strange but true events surrounding the death of society woman Joan Robinson Hill, first wife of prominent plastic surgeon, Dr. John Hill,

---

and daughter of wealthy oilman Ash Robinson. Well-crafted script and effective performances keep your interest. Griffith was Emmy nominated. From the book "Prescription Murder," written by the doctor's second wife. **200m/C VHS.** Farrah Fawcett, Katharine Ross, Andy Griffith, Sam Elliott, Craig T. Nelson, Barbara Sammeth; **D:** William (Billy) Hale. **TV**

Murder in the First ♂♂1/2 1995
(R) Hours after leaving a three-year stint in solitary confinement at Alcatraz, petty thief Henri Young (Bacon) kills the inmate he thinks ratted him out. Young, eager-puppy lawyer James Stamphill (Slater) defends Young by claiming that inhumane and brutal prison treatment turned him into a murderer. Heavy-handed and uneven despite excellent performances by top-notch cast. Oldman does his usual fine job with yet another unsympathetic character, the sadistic warden. Major professional landmark for both Slater and Bacon. Loosely based on a true story that led to the closing of Alcatraz. **123m/C VHS, DVD.** Christian Slater, Kevin Bacon, Gary Oldman, Embeth Davidtz, William H. Macy, Stephen Tobolowsky, Brad Dourif, R. Lee Ermey, Mia Kirshner, Stefan Gierasch, Kyra Sedgwick; **D:** Marc Rocco; **W:** Dan Gordon; **C:** Fred Murphy; **M:** Christopher Young. Broadcast Film Critics '95: Actor (Bacon).

Murder in the Footlights ♂♂ 1946
The Trojan Brothers 1946 Murder drama involving a socialite and a vaudeville team. **85m/B VHS.** Lesley Brook, David Hutcheson, Patricia Burke, David Farrar, Bobby Howes, Barbara Mullen, Finlay Currie; **D:** Maclean Rogers; **W:** Maclean Rogers; **C:** Moray Grant, Ernest Palmer.

Murder in the Old Red Barn ♂ 1936
Maria Marten 1936 Based on the real murder of an unassuming girl by a randy squire. Stiff, melodramatic performances are bad enough, but the playstyle production, unfamiliar to modern viewers, is the last nail in this one's coffin. **67m/B VHS, DVD.** Tod Slaughter, Sophie Stewart, D.J. Williams, Eric Portman; **D:** Milton Rosmer.

A Murder Is Announced ♂♂
Agatha Christie's Miss Marple: A Murder Is Announced 1987 From the critically acclaimed BBC series. While on holiday, supersleuth Miss Marple encounters a murder that was advertised in the local newspaper one week prior to its occurrence. Based on the 1952 Agatha Christie novel, Hickson shines once again as Christie's detective extraordinaire. **155m/C VHS, DVD.** Joan Hickson; **D:** David Giles. **TV**

Murder Mansion ♂1/2 1970
Some decent scares ensue when a group of travelers is stranded in an old haunted mansion. **84m/C VHS, DVD.** Evelyn Stewart, Analia Gade; **D:** Francisco Lara Polop.

Murder Most Foul ♂♂♂ 1965
Erstwhile school marm Dame Margaret is excellent as the only jury member to believe in the accused's innocence. Posing as a wealthy actress to insinuate herself into the local acting troupe, she sniffs out the true culprit. Based on the Poirot mystery "Mrs. McGinty's Dead." **90m/B VHS, DVD.** Margaret Rutherford, Ron Moody, Charles "Bud" Tingwell, Megs Jenkins, Dennis Price, Ralph Michael; **D:** George Pollock.

Murder Motel ♂ 1974
Inept spine-tingler about a motel keeper who makes a practice of killing his customers. There's always a vacancy at the Murder Motel, at least until the fiancee of one of his victims decides to look into the matter. **80m/C VHS.** Robyn Millan, Derek Francis, Ralph Bates, Edward Judd; **D:** Malcolm Taylor; **W:** Brian Clemens. **TV**

Murder, My Sweet ♂♂♂ 1944
Farewell, My Love 1944 Down-on-his-luck private detective Philip Marlowe (Powell) searches for an ex-convict's missing girlfriend through a dark world of murder, mayhem, and ever-twisting directions. Classic film noir screen version of Raymond Chandler's tense novel "Farewell, My Lovely," which employs flashback fashion using that crisp Chandler narrative. A breakthrough dramatically for singer Powell; Chandler's favorite version. Remade using the novel's title in 1975. **95m/B VHS, DVD.** Dick Powell, Claire Trevor, Mike Ma-

---

zurki, Otto Kruger, Anne Shirley, Miles Mander, Douglas Walton, Esther Howard, Donald Douglas; **D:** Edward Dmytryk; **W:** John Paxton; **C:** Harry Wild; **M:** Roy Webb.

A Murder of Crows ♂♂1/2 1999 **(R)**
Alcoholic, disbarred New Orleans attorney Lawson Russell (Gooding Jr.) decides to write a book. He happens to meet an elderly man who lets him read his own murder mystery manuscript and when the man unexpectedly dies, Lawson gets the book published as his own. It's a success—only it seems the the story about five lawyers being murdered is real and a detective (Berenger) thinks that since Russell knows so much about the crimes, he must be the killer. **102m/C VHS, DVD.** Cuba Gooding Jr., Tom Berenger, Marianne Jean-Baptiste, Eric Stoltz; **D:** Rowdy Herrington; **W:** Rowdy Herrington.

The Murder of Mary Phagan ♂♂♂1/2 1987 **(PG)**
Lemmon stars as John Slaton, governor of Georgia during one of America's most notorious miscarriages of justice. In 1913, timid, Jewish factory manager Leo Frank is accused of the brutal murder of a female worker. Prejudice and a power hungry prosecuting attorney conspire to seal the man's fate at the end of the hangman's noose. Sensing the injustice, Slaton reopens the case, causing riots in Atlanta. Top-notch TV drama, featuring a superb re-creation of turn-of-the-century atmosphere and a compelling, true story which was not finally resolved until the 1970s. **251m/C VHS.** Jack Lemmon, Peter Gallagher, Richard Jordan, Robert Prosky, Paul Dooley, Rebecca Miller, Kathryn Walker, Charles S. Dutton, Kevin Spacey, Wendy J. Cooke; **D:** William (Billy) Hale; **M:** Maurice Jarre. **TV**

A Murder of Quality ♂♂1/2 1990
Spymaster George Smiley (Elliott) comes to aid of colleague Ailsa Brimley (Jackson) when he agrees to investigate the nefarious goings-on at the Carne School for boys. It seems a schoolmaster's wife predicted her murder and named her husband as the killer. Now she's dead but her husband has a very solid alibi. Based on the novel by John Le Carre. **103m/C VHS, DVD.** Denholm Elliott, Glenda Jackson, Joss Ackland, Billie Whitelaw, David Threlfall, Ronald Pickup, Christian Bale, Matthew Scurfield; **D:** Gavin Millar; **C:** Denis Crossan; **M:** Stanley Myers. **TV**

The Murder of Stephen Lawrence ♂♂♂ 1999
Institutional racism is explored in this fact-based drama about the 1993 murder of black teenager Stephen Lawrence (Black) in London. Lawrence is waiting at a bus stop when he's attacked by five teenaged neo-Nazis. His Jamaican-born parents (Baptiste and Quarshie) seek justice but are treated indifferently by the police. Then the charges against the suspects are thrown out for lack of evidence and the Lawrences insist on a private prosecution (civil suit) that studies the incompetent police investigation. **120m/C VHS.** Marianne Jean-Baptiste, Hugh Quarshie, Leon Black, Joseph Kpobie, Kenneth Cranham, David Calder; **D:** Paul Greengrass; **W:** Paul Greengrass; **C:** Ivan Strasburg. **TV**

Murder on Approval ♂ Barbados Quest 1956
Conway is a carbon-copy Sherlock Holmes, called in to verify the authenticity of a stamp and finds himself involved in murder. Slow-paced, weak and transparent. **70m/B VHS.** Tom Conway, Delphi Lawrence, Brian Worth, Michael Balfour, John Colicos; **D:** Bernard Knowles.

Murder on Flight 502 ♂♂ 1975
A crisis arises on a 747 flight from New York to London when a terrorist runs amuck. Big cast of TV stars and Stack as the pilot keep this stale flick from getting lost in the ozone. **97m/C VHS, DVD.** Farrah Fawcett, Sonny Bono, Ralph Bellamy, Theodore Bikel, Dane Clark, Polly Bergen, Laraine Day, Fernando Lamas, George Maharis, Hugh O'Brian, Molly Picon, Walter Pidgeon, Robert Stack; **D:** George McCowan. **TV**

Murder on Lenox Avenue ♂♂1/2 1941
When the lead-fork of the Harlem Better Business Bureau is overthrown, he swears revenge. **60m/C**

VHS, Mamie Smith, Norman Astwood, Augustus Smith, Alberta Perkins, Alec Lovejoy; **D:** Arthur Dreifuss; **W:** Vincent Valentini; **C:** George Webber; **M:** Donald Heywood.

Murder on Line One ♂♂ 1990
A London murderer films his crimes for his later viewing pleasure. The police arrest a suspect, but the killings continue. Both the police and viewer are soon aware that they've made a mistake. **103m/C VHS.** Emma Jacobs, Peter Blake, Simon Shepherd, Allan Surtees, Andrew Wilde, Dirkan Tulane, Neil Duncan, Brett Forrest; **D:** Anders Palm; **W:** Anders Palm.

Murder on the Bayou ♂♂♂ A Gathering of Old Men 1991 **(PG)**
Down on the L'siana bayou, a white guy who thinks civil rights are color coded is murdered, and an elderly black man is accused of the crime. Made for TV, well performed, engaging. From the novel by Ernest J. Gaines. **91m/C VHS, DVD.** Louis Gossett Jr., Richard Widmark, Holly Hunter, Woody Strode, Joe Seneca, Papa John Creach, Julius W. Harris, Will Patton; **D:** Volker Schlondorff. **TV**

Murder on the Campus ♂♂
Out of the Shadow 1952 A reporter investigates the apparent suicide of his brother at Cambridge University. He discovers that a number of other mysterious deaths have occurred as well. Interesting characterizations hampered by predictability. **61m/B VHS, DVD.** Terence Longdon, Donald Gray, Diane Clare, Robertson Hare, Dermot Walsh; **D:** Michael Winner; **W:** Michael Winner.

Murder on the High Seas ♂♂ 1932
Infidelity and murder aboard a cruise ship. **65m/B VHS.** Natalie Moorhead, Jack Mulhall, Edmund Breese, Montagu Love, Clara Kimball Young, Alice Day, Roy D'Arcy; **D:** Robert F. "Bob" Hill; **W:** Robert F. "Bob" Hill, George Plympton; **C:** E. Fox Walker.

Murder on the Midnight Express ♂1/2 *Night is the Time for Killing* 1974
Mystery about spies, thieves, honeymooners, and a corpse aboard an all-night train. All aboard. **70m/C VHS.** Judy Geeson, James Smilie, Charles Gray, Alister Williamson; **W:** Brian Clemens. **TV**

Murder on the Orient Express ♂♂♂ 1974 **(PG)**
An Agatha Christie mystery lavishly produced with an all-star cast. In 1934, a trainful of suspects and one murder victim make the trip from Istanbul to Calais especially interesting. Super-sleuth Hercule Poirot sets out to solve the mystery. An entertaining who-dunit, ably supported by the remarkable cast. Followed by "Death on the Nile." **128m/C VHS, DVD.** Albert Finney, Martin Balsam, Ingrid Bergman, Lauren Bacall, Sean Connery, Richard Widmark, Anthony Perkins, John Gielgud, Jacqueline Bisset, Jean-Pierre Cassel, Wendy Hiller, Rachel Roberts, Vanessa Redgrave, Michael York, Colin Blakely, George Coulouris, Denis Quilley, Vernon Dobtcheff, Jeremy Lloyd; **D:** Sidney Lumet; **W:** Paul Dehn; **C:** Geoffrey Unsworth; **M:** Richard Rodney Bennett. Oscars '74: Support. Actress (Bergman); British Acad. '74: Support. Actor (Gielgud), Support. Actress (Bergman).

Murder on the Yukon ♂1/2 1940
An installment in the "Renfrew of the Royal Mounted" series. Newill and O'Brien's vacation plans are ruined when they find a corpse in a canoe and must investigate. Lots of action, but a somewhat threadbare production. Based on "Renfrew Rides North" by Laurie York Erskine. **57m/B VHS, DVD.** James Newill, Dave O'Brien, Polly Ann Young; **D:** Louis Gasnier.

Murder Once Removed ♂♂1/2 1971
A private eye discovers that a respectable doctor has a bedside manner that women are dying for. **74m/C VHS, DVD.** John Forsythe, Richard Kiley, Barbara Bain, Joseph Campanella; **D:** Charles S. Dubin; **M:** Robert Jackson Drasnin.

Murder One ♂♂ 1988 **(R)**
Two half-brothers escape from a Maryland prison and go on a killing spree, dragging their younger brother with them. Low-budget and it shows. Based on a true story. **83m/C VHS, DVD.** Henry Thomas, James Wilder, Stephen Shellen, Errol Slue; **D:** Graeme Campbell.

Murder 101 ♂♂♂ 1991 **(PG-13)**
Brosnan plays Charles Lattimore, an author and English professor who specializes in murder mysteries. He gives his students a

Murder or Mercy ♂♂½ 1974
Still timey story of a famous doctor accused of killing his terminally ill wife. Forever picturing the demise of their spouses. Good acting for this sort of thing. In two-cassette package. **183**m/C VHS, Keith Carradine, JoBeth Williams, Terry Kinney, Guy Boyd, Terence Knox, Darrell Larson, M. Emmet Walsh, Kathy Baas; **D:** Mike Robe. **TV**

Murder Ordained ♂♂½ 1987
Yet another true-crime network miniseries, this time about a Kansas minister and her lover plotting the demise of their spouses. Good acting for this sort of thing. In two-cassette package. **183**m/C VHS, Keith Carradine, JoBeth Williams, Terry Kinney, Guy Boyd, Terence Knox, Darrell Larson, M. Emmet Walsh, Kathy Baas; **D:** Mike Robe. **TV**

Murder over New York ♂♂ 1940
Episode in the Charlie Chan mystery series. Chan visits New York City and becomes involved in an investigation at the airport. With the aid of his klutzy son, he sleuths his way through a slaw of suspects until the mystery is solved. Standard fare for the Chan fan. **65**m/B VHS Sidney Toler, Marjorie Weaver, Robert Lowery, Ricardo Cortez, Donald MacBride, Melville Cooper, Victor Sen Yung; **D:** Harry Lachman.

Murder Rap ♂ 1987 An aspiring musician/sound technologist becomes involved with a mysterious woman and her plot to kill her husband. Complications galore, especially for the viewer. **90**m/C VHS, **DVD.** John Hawkes, Sella Kathleen Feigny; **D:** Kliff Keuhl.

Murder She Said: A Mrs. Murphy Mystery ♂♂½ 1998
Mrs. Murphy is a cat, who along with her doggie housemate Tucker, a Welsh Corgi who complains about his short legs, assists their human owner, postmistress Mary "Harry" Haristeen (Lake), in investigating a murder in their small Virginia town. Based on the mystery series by Rita Mae Brown. **88**m/C VHS, Ricki Lake, Linden Ashby, Bruce McGill, Ed Begley Jr., Christina Pickles, Judith Scott, Wayne Robson, D: Simon Wincer. **W:** Jim Cox; **V:** Blythe Danner, Anthony Clark. **TV**

Murder So Sweet ♂♂½ 1993 Poisoned by Love. The Kern County, Murders Hamlin stars as a slick small-town loser, with an apparently limitless appeal to women. He marries five of them but two wives and his mother mysteriously die of poisoning. Then an ex gets suspicious and tries to make certain it'll never happen again. Based on a true story. **94**m/C VHS, Harry Hamlin, Helen Shaver, Faith Ford, Daphne Ashbrook, Eileen Brennan, K.T. Oslin, Terence Knox, Ed Lauter. **D:** Larry Peerce. **W:** Calliope Brattlesteet, Tony Imi, Stephen Glantz; **M:** Steve Dorff. **TV**

Murder Story ♂♂½ 1989 (PG) An aspiring mystery writer finds himself mixed up in a real murder and winds up involving his mentor as well. An overdone story, but a reasonably enjoyable film. **90**m/C VHS, DVD. Christopher Lee, Bruce Boa; **D:** Eddie Arno. Markus Innocent; **W:** Eddie Arno.

Murder: Ultimate Grounds for Divorce ♂ 1984 A quiet weekend of camping turns into a night of horror for two couples when one of them plans an elaborate murder scheme. **90**m/C VHS. GB Roger

---

Murder with Music ♂♂ 1945 A musical drama featuring an all-black cast. Markel's hamburger are discovered by a young, deaf girl. Beware of filler. **60**m/B VHS, Bob Howard, Noble Sissle, Nellie Hill; **D:** George P. Quigley.

Murder Without Conviction ♂♂½ 2004 When exnun Christine Bennett (Ward) visits her cousin in a mental facility, she meets servant James Talley (Proval). He and his twin, Edward, have been separated for 30 years, ever since they were accused, but not convicted, of their mother's murder on Good Friday, 1974, and a judge sent them to separate hospitals. Christine becomes suspicious and teams up with handsome detective Jack Brooks (Weisser) to have the case re-opened. But someone is deadly serious about wanting Christine to mind her own business. **90**m/C VHS, Megan Ward, Morgan Weisser, David Proval, Rutanya Alda, Matt Lutz, Patty Duke; **D:** Kevin Connor; **W:** Bruce Franklin Singer; **C:** Dane Peterson; **M:** Roger Belton. **CABLE**

Murder Without Motive ♂♂½ 1992 When two African American teenagers harrass and one teen ends up dead. Was the struggle racially motivated, or did the police act justifiably? **93**m/C VHS, DVD. Curtis McClaren, Anna Maria Horsford, Carla Gugino, Christopher Daniel Barnes, Cuba Gooding Jr., Georg Stanford Brown; **D:** Kevin Hooks.

Murderball ♂♂½ 2005 (R) Fast-paced yet fluid film catches the warriors of Quad Rugby on and off the court. Quadriplegics candidly answer the questions people are afraid to ask them and boast about sexual escapades. Joe Soares has been a fierce American team leader until being cut from the roster due to age. His revenge is to coach the Canadian team to their first victory over the U.S. in 12 years. Mark Zupan is the best U.S. player. We also witness breakthroughs for motocross champ Keith Cavill as he returns home after months of rehabilitation. Attending a quad rugby demonstration, the thought of learning a new sport recharges Cavill. Powerful, must see film. **85**m/C DVD. US US D: Henry Alex Rubin, Dana Adam Shapiro; **C:** Henry Alex Rubin; **M:** Jamie Saft.

Murdered Innocence ♂♂ 1994 (R) In 1972, a rookie New York cop is called to a crime scene where a woman has been stabbed to death. Her young son is hysterical and her husband panics and tries to flee. When the husband panics back. Now it's 1992, the convicted killer is out of prison and out for revenge (seems the son said his mother's lover committed the crime but there was a police coverup). Bruce believes his hands full. **93**m/C VHS. Bruce Boxleitner, aura Johnson, Robert Culp; **D:** Gary Sherman. **TV**

The Murderers Are Among Us ♂♂ 1946 Die Mörder Sind Unter Uns 1946 In post WWII Germany, Suzanne Wallner (Knel) returns from a concentration camp occupied by Dr. Hans Mertens (Borchert). Haunted by his wartime experiences, Mertens has turned to women and alcohol. Suzanne refuses to give up her claim and moves in with Hans, eventually finding love with him. In turn, Hans decides to face his demons by going after his former superior, Colonel Otto Bruckner (Paulsen), who's living an untroubled life despite the war crimes he committed. German with subtitles. **84**m/B VHS, DVD. GE Hildegarde Knel, Ernst Borchert, Arno Paulsen; **D:**

Daltrey, Toyah Wilcox, Leslie Ash, Terry Raven; **D:** Moris Barry. **W:** Tim Purcell; **C:** Charles Toobey; **M:** Harlan Cockburn, Robin Langridge.

Murderer's Keep WOOF! 1988 Secret ingredients used in the Central Meat Market's hamburger are discovered by a young, deaf girl. Beware of filler. **89**m/C VHS, DVD. Vic Tayback, Talia Shire, Robert Walden; **D:** Paulmichel Miekhe.

Murderers' Row ♂½ 1966 Daredevil bachelor and former counter-espionage agent Matt Helm is summoned from his life of leisure to ensure the safety of an important scientist. Martin's attempt as a super-spy doesn't wash, and Margret is molaisable as the kidnapped scientist's daughter. Unless you want to hear Martin sing "I'm Not the Marrying Kind," don't bother. Second in the "Matt Helm" series. **108**m/C VHS, DVD. Dean Martin, Ann-Margret, Karl Malden, Beverly Adams, James Gregory, Camilla Sparv; **D:** Henry Levin; **W:** Herbert Baker; **C:** Sam Leavitt; **M:** Lalo Schifrin, Lalo Schifrin.

Murderlust WOOF! 1986 Employers in search of a security guard make a poor choice in offering the position to a sexually frustrated man whose hobbies include strangling prostitutes. Poor hiring decisions come into play later when he senses come into play later when he senses a job at an adolescent crisis center. **90**m/C VHS, Eli Rich, Rochelle Taylor, Dennis Gannon, Bonnie Schneider, Lisa Nichols; **D:** Donald M. Jones.

Murderous Intent ♂♂♂½ Like Minds 2006 Psychotic thriller set in an all-boys prep school includes a great mix of twists, flashbacks, investigative details ened by what he observes, he's also oddly fascinated. Then Nigel ends up dead. As views Alex she drops together behavioral clues that lead her on an intuitive case-solving mission. From script to score, act creation is a fine piece of film art. **110**m/C DVD. GB AU Toni Collette, Eddie Redmayne, Thomas Stange, Richard Roxburgh, Patrick Malahide, Kate Maberly; **D:** Gregory J. Reed; **W:** Gregory J. Reec; **C:** Nigel Bluck; **M:** Carlo Giacco.

Murderous Vision ♂♂ 1991 (R) Television fixture Boxleitner is a bored detective in this outing. But one day, while tracking a young mother in the missing persons bureau, he stumbles upon the trail of a serial killer. Enter a beautiful psychic who wants to help, add a race to catch the murderer, and Bruce Boxleitner has his hands full. **93**m/C VHS. Bruce Boxleitner, aura Johnson, Robert Culp; **D:** Gary Sherman. **TV**

Murders at Lynch Cross 1985 Mystery about a weird, isolated hotel on the Yorkshire moors. **60**m/C VHS, GB Jill Bennett, Joanna David, Barbara Jefford, Sylvie Syms; **D:** Patrick Lau; **W:** Frances Galleymore; **M:** Paul Lewis. **TV**

Murders in the Doll House ♂½ 1979 Private detective must find out who is systematically killing off the family of a Japanese toy executive. With English subtitles. **92**m/C VHS. JP Yusaku Matsuda, Shin Kishida, Hiraho Shiro; **D:** Susumu Kodama. **W:** Shuichi Nagahara; **M:** Masaharu Ueda; **M:** Yuji Ono.

Murders in the Rue Morgue ♂½ 1932 Lugosi stars as a deranged scientist (what a stretc) who wants to find a female companion for his pet gorilla. He kidnaps a beautiful woman and prepares to make her the gorilla's bride. Very loosely based on the story by Edgar Allan Poe, which has been remade several times. **61**m/B VHS, DVD, Bela Lugosi, Sidney (Sydney) Fox, Leon Ames, Brandon Hurst, Arlene Francis, Noble Johnson; **D:** Robert Florey; **W:** John Huston, Tom Reed, Dale Van Every; **C:** Karl Freund.

Murmur of the Heart ♂♂♂½ 1971 (R) Le Souffle au Coeur 1971 (R) Honest treatment of a 14-year-old's coming-of-age. After his older brothers take him to a prostitute for his first sexual experience, he comes down with scarlet fever. He then travels to a health spa with his mom to recover. There they find that their mother-son bond is stronger than most. Music by Charlie Parker is featured in the score. In French with English subtitles. **118**m/C VHS, DVD. FR Benoît Ferreux, Daniel Gelin, Lea Massari, Corinne Karsten, Jacqueline Chauveau, Marc Wincourt, Michael (Michel) Lonsdale; **D:** Louis Malle; **W:** Louis Malle; **C:** Ricardo Aronovich; **M:** Charlie Parker.

Wolfgang Staudte, **W:** Wolfgang Staudte; **C:** Friedl Behn-Gaund, Eugen Klagemann; **M:** Ernst Roberts.

Murders in the Rue Morgue ♂♂½ 1971 (PG) A young woman has frightening dreams inspired by a play that her father is producing in Paris at the turn of the century. After many people associated with the production become murder victims, the girl becomes involved with one of her father's former associates, a man who killed her mother years ago and then faked his own suicide. The fourth film based on Edgar Allan Poe's classic horror story. **87**m/C VHS, DVD. Jason Robards Jr., Lilli Palmer, Herbert Lom, Michael Dunn, Christine Kaufmann, Adolfo Celi; **D:** Gordon Hessler.

The Murders in the Rue Morgue ♂♂½ 1986 (PG) The fifth filmed version of the Edgar Allan Poe mystery. Set in 19th-century Paris; actors in a mystery play find their roles coming to life. Scott is terrific, with good supporting help. **92**m/C VHS, DVD. George C. Scott, Rebecca De Mornay, Val Kilmer, Ian McShane, Neil Dickson; **D:** Jeannot Szwarc; **C:** Bruno de Keyzer. **TV**

Murders in the Zoo ♂♂½ 1933 Zoologist Atwill has a reason to be insanely jealous since his wife (Burke) has been having lots of extramarital affairs. But his way of dealing with these other men is certainly unique—he feeds them to various zoo animals (after first sewing the victims' lips shut). Censors were outraged at the film when underwent various edits for its theatrical release. **62**m/B VHS, Lionel Atwill, Kathleen Burke, Charlie Ruggles, Randolph Scott, Gail Patrick, John Lodge, Harry Beresford; **D:** Edward Sutherland; **W:** Philip Wylie, Seton I. Miller.

Muriel ♂♂½ Muriel, Ou le Temps d'Un Retour; The Time of Return; Muriel, Or the Time of Return 1963 A complex, mosaic drama about a middle-aged woman who meets an old lover at Boulogne, and her stepson who cannot forget the needless suffering he caused a young woman named Muriel while he was soldier at war. Throughout, director Alain Resnais plumbs the essential meanings of memory, age, and the anxieties created from the tension between personal and public actions. Acclaimed; in French with subtitles. **115**m/C VHS, DVD. FR Delphine Seyrig, Jean-Pierre Kerien, Nita Klein, Jean-Baptiste Thierree; **D:** Alain Resnais **W:** Jean Cayrol; **C:** Sacha Vierny. **M:** Georges Delerue. Venice Film Fest. '63: Actress (Seyrig).

Muriel's Wedding ♂♂♂ 1994 (R) Muriel (Collette) can catch a bridal bouquet, but can she catch a husband? Her blonde, bitch-goddess friends don't think so. But dowdy, pathetic, overweight Muriel dreams of a fairy tale wedding anyway. How she fulfills her obsessive 'fantasy is the basis for this quirky, hilarious, and often touchingly poignant ugly duckling tale with the occasional over-the-top satiric moment. Strong casts led by sympathetic and engaging performances from Collette (who gained 40-plus pounds for the role) and Griffiths as her best friend, Rhonda. '70s pop supergroup ABBA lends its kitschy but catchy tunes to the plot and soundtrack. Not released in the U.S. until 1995. **105**m/C VHS, DVD. AU Toni Collette, Bill Hunter, Rachel Griffiths, Jeanie Drynan, Gennie Nevinson Brice, Matthew Day, Daniel Lapaine, Sophie Lee, Rosalind Hammond, Belinda Jarrett; **D:** P.J. Hogan; **W:** P.J. Hogan; **C:** Martin McGrath; **M:** Peter Best. Australian Film Inst. '94: Film (Collette), Film, Sound, Support, Actress (Griffiths).

Murph the Surf 🐾🐾½ *Live a Little, Steal a Lot; You Can't Steal Love* 1975 (PG) Fact-based, engrossing story of two beach bums turned burglars who grow bored with small-time robbery and plan a trip to New York City to steal the Star of Africa sapphire. Notable among the many action scenes is a boat chase through the inland waterways of Miami, Florida. 102m/C VHS, DVD. Robert Conrad, Don Stroud, Donna Mills, Luther Adler, Robyn Millan, Paul Stewart; D: Marvin J. Chomsky.

Murphy's Fault 🐾🐾 1988 (PG-13) Dark comedy about a night watchman/writer plagued by a series of bad luck incidents. 94m/C VHS. Patrick Dollaghan, Anne Curry, Stack Pierce; D: Robert J. Smawley.

Murphy's Law 🐾 1986 (R) A hard-headed cop gets framed for his ex-wife's murder and embarks on a mission to find the actual killer. He is slowed down by a smart-mouthed prostitute who is handcuffed to him during his search. Casting a female in the role of a psycho-killer is unique to the genre. 101m/C VHS, DVD. Charles Bronson, Carrie Snodgress, Kathleen Wilhoite, Robert F. Lyons, Richard Romanus, Angel Tompkins, Bill Henderson, James Luisi, Janet MacLachlan, Lawrence Tierney; D: J. Lee Thompson; C: Alex Phillips Jr.; M: Marc Donahue.

Murphy's Romance 🐾🐾🐾 1985 (PG-13) A young divorced mother with an urge to train horses pulls up the stakes and heads for Arizona with her son. There she meets a pharmacist who may be just what the doctor ordered to help her build a new life. 107m/C VHS, DVD. James Garner, Sally Field, Brian Kerwin, Corey Haim, Dennis Burkley, Charles Lane, Georgann Johnson; D: Martin Ritt; W: Harriet Frank Jr., Irving Ravetch; M: Carole King.

Murphy's War 🐾🐾 1971 (PG) In WWII, the Germans sink an English ship and gun down most of its crew. An Irishman, however, survives and returns to health with the help of a nurse. He then seeks revenge on those who killed his crewmates, even after he learns the war has ended. O'Toole is interesting as the revenge-minded seaman though saddled with a mediocre script. 106m/C VHS, DVD. GB Peter O'Toole, Siân Phillips, Philippe Noiret; D: Peter Yates; M: John Barry.

Murrow 🐾🐾½ 1986 Biography of the renowned chain-smoking journalist who changed broadcasting history by fearlessly voicing his liberal ideas on the air waves. His life was more interesting though Travanti does his best to breathe some life into the script. 114m/C VHS. Daniel J. Travanti, Dabney Coleman, Edward Herrmann, David Suchet, John McMartin, Robert Vaughn, Kathryn Leigh Scott; D: Jack Gold; W: Ernest Kinoy; M: Carl Davis. CABLE

Muscle Beach Party 🐾🐾 1964 Sequel to "Beach Party" finds Frankie and Annette romping in the sand again. Trouble invades teen nirvana when a new gym opens and the hardbodies try to muscle in on surfer turf. Meanwhile, Paluzzi tries to muscle in on Funicello's turf. Good clean corny fun, with the usual lack of script and plot. Lorre appears in a cameo, his final screen appearance. Watch for "Little" Stevie Wonder in his debut. Rickles' first appearance in the "BP" series; Lupus was credited as Rock Stevens. Followed by "Bikini Beach." ♫Muscle Bustle; My First Love; Surfin' Woodie; Surfer's Holiday; Happy Street; A Girl Needs a Boy; A Boy Needs a Girl. 94m/C VHS, DVD. Frankie Avalon, Annette Funicello, Buddy Hackett, Luciana Paluzzi, Don Rickles, John Ashley, Jody McCrea, Morey Amsterdam, Peter Lupus, Candy Johnson, Dolores Wells, Peter Lorre, Stevie Wonder, Donna Loren, Amadee Chabot, Dick Dale; D: William Asher; W: William Asher, Robert Dillon; C: Harold E. Wellman; M: Les Baxter.

The Muse 🐾🐾½ 1999 (PG-13) Brooks plays Steven, a screenwriter who finds he's unable to get a job when his creative well runs dry. He is introduced by fellow scribe Jack (Bridges) to Sarah (Stone, showing off some surprising comedy chops), who may actually be one of the Greek goddesses of inspiration. Of course, she may be a total lunatic too. After he discovers that some of the biggest names in Hollywood swear by her mojo, Steven is thrilled when he's deemed worthy of her service. Unfortunately for him, Sarah's inspiration requires a fancy hotel room, expensive gifts, and boatloads of cash, which draws the suspicion of his wife Laura (MacDowell). As he begins writing, Steven discovers that Sarah has also inspired his wife to start a career of her own and kick him out of bed. Lots of movie in-jokes and cameos from big shots like Rob Reiner, James Cameron and Martin Scorsese. 97m/C VHS, DVD. Albert Brooks, Sharon Stone, Jeff Bridges, Andie MacDowell, Steven Wright, Mark Feuerstein, Bradley Whitford, Dakin Matthews, Concetta Tomei, Stacey Travis; Cameos: James Cameron, Rob Reiner, Martin Scorsese, Jennifer Tilly, Lorenzo Lamas; D: Albert Brooks; W: Albert Brooks, Monica Johnson; C: Thomas Ackerman; M: Elton John.

Music & Lyrics 🐾🐾½ 2007 (PG-13) The somewhat smarmy, frequently self-deprecating charm of Grant is on full display, opposite Barrymore as his sunny romantic foil. Alex (Grant) is the less-successful half of the music of a long-disbanded '80s pop duo. Making a decent living on the nostalgia circuit, Alex gets another chance at a hit when current teen queen Cora (newcomer Bennett) wants her one-time crush to write a duet for them. Alex then stumbles onto insecure, would-be lyricist Sophie (Barrymore) and puts her to work. Grant and Barrymore don't make the most convincing romantic couple (she's too young and ditsy) but it's light-hearted fluff, and the pseudo-80s music videos are hysterical. 106m/C DVD, Blu-ray Disc, HD DVD. US Hugh Grant, Drew Barrymore, Brad Garrett, Kristen Johnston, Aasif Mandvi, Campbell Scott, Haley Bennett; D: Marc Lawrence; W: Marc Lawrence; C: Xavier Perez Grobet; M: Adam Schlesinger.

Music Box 🐾🐾🐾 1989 (R) An attorney defends her father against accusations that he has committed inhumane Nazi war crimes. As the case progresses, she must struggle to remain objective in the courtroom and come to terms with the possibility that her father is guilty. Lange's portrayal of an ethnic character is highly convincing. 126m/C VHS, DVD. Jessica Lange, Frederic Forrest, Lukas Haas, Armin Mueller-Stahl, Michael Rooker, Donald Moffat, Cheryl Lynn Bruce; D: Constantin Costa-Gavras; W: Joe Eszterhas; C: Patrick Blossier; M: Philippe Sarde.

Music from Another Room 🐾🐾½ 1997 (PG-13) Danny (Law) is a hopeless romantic who decided, at five, to marry Anna, whose birth he assisted. But the icy adult Anna (Mol) doesn't seem to be Danny's ideal when he doesn't seem to meet her again—and she's got a fiance. 104m/C VHS, DVD. Jude Law, Gretchen Mol, Brenda Blethyn, Jennifer Tilly, Martha Plimpton, Jon Tenney, Jeremy Piven, Vincent Laresca, Jane Adams, Kevin Kilner, Jan Rubes, Judith Malina, Jon Polito; D: Charlie Peters; W: Charlie Peters; C: Richard Crudo; M: Richard Gibbs.

Music in My Heart 🐾🐾½ 1940 Two taxi cabs crash and spur the love of Martin and Hayworth. She proceeds to break off her engagement to save Martin from deportation. Hayworth's last low-budget role before becoming a Hollywood goddess. 69m/B VHS, DVD. Rita Hayworth, Tony Martin, Edith Fellows, Alan Mowbray, Eric Blore, George Tobias, Joseph Crehan, George Humbert, Phil Tead; D: Joseph Santley; M: Robert Wright, Chet Forrest.

The Music Lovers 🐾🐾🐾 1971 (R) Russell's version of Tchaikovsky's tormented life and glorious achievements is a shocker, a movie that infuriates professed music lovers but, nonetheless, has introduced many a neophyte to the world of classical music via its sensationalism. Homosexual Tchaikovsky marries an admirer to placate the Russian government and his financial benefactor. Stunned when he discovers his wife is a nymphomaniac, he banishes her to a netherworld of prostitution and eventual insanity which Russell mercilessly explores. Tchaikovsky's own squalid life is hardly better, though he does enjoy success before the bottom falls out. 122m/C VHS. GB Richard Chamberlain, Glenda Jackson, Max Adrian, Christopher Gable, Kenneth Colley, Izabella Telezynska, Maureen Pryor; D: Ken Russell; W: Melvyn Bragg; C: Douglas Slocombe; M: Andre Previn.

The Music Man 🐾🐾🐾🐾 1962 (G) Con man in the guise of a traveling salesman gets off the train in River City, Iowa. After hearing about plans to build a pool hall, he argues it would be the gateway to hell for the young, impressionable males of the town. He then convinces the River Cityzens to look toward the future of the children's marching band. Although the huckster plans to take their money and run before the instruments arrive, his feelings for the town librarian cause him to think twice about fleeing the Heartland. This isn't just a slice of Americana; it's a whole pie. Acting and singing are terrific "with a capital 'T' and that rhymes with 'P' and that stands for" Preston, who epitomizes the charismatic pitchman. ♫Seventy-six Trombones; Trouble; Till There Was You; The Wells Fargo Wagon; Being in Love; Goodnight, My Someone; Rock Island; Iowa Stubborn. 151m/C VHS, DVD. Robert Preston, Shirley Jones, Buddy Hackett, Hermione Gingold, Paul Ford, Pert Kelton, Ron Howard; D: Morton DaCosta; W: Marion Hargrove; C: Robert Burks; M: Meredith Willson, Ray Heindorf. Oscars '62: Adapt. Score; Golden Globes '63: Film—Mus./Comedy, Natl. Film Reg. '05.

The Music of Chance 🐾🐾½ 1993 (R) Convoluted story about a small-time gambler (Spader) and a drifter (Patinkin) who wind up involved in a bizarre high stakes poker game with a Laurel and Hardyish pair (Durning and Grey) who live in an isolated mansion. When Spader and Patinkin lose, their debt forces them into an indentured servitude where they must construct a brick wall around their new masters' estate. Bloated with symbolism, this adaptation from cult fave novelist Auster (who has a small part), loses its eclectic significance in the translation to the big screen. Nonetheless, valiant effort by rookie director Haas. 98m/C VHS, DVD. James Spader, Mandy Patinkin, Joel Grey, Charles Durning, M. Emmet Walsh, Samantha Mathis, Christopher Penn, Pearl Jones, Paul Auster; D: Philip Haas; W: Philip Haas, Belinda Haas; C: Bernard Zitzermann; M: Philip Johnston.

Music of the Heart 🐾🐾½ *50 violins* 1999 (PG) Based on the true story of violin teacher Roberta Guaspari, who was the subject of the 1996 documentary, "Small Wonders." A divorced Guaspari (Streep) leaves suburbia with her two young sons and a dream to teach music to children, using the 50 violins she had purchased. Roberta finds herself working with a group of Harlem students on what will become the landmark East Harlem Violin Program. Despite numerous obstacles, their determination eventually leads to a performance at Carnegie Hall. Streep gives her usual professionally winning performance in this sentimental heart-tugger. 124m/C VHS, DVD. Meryl Streep, Angela Bassett, Aidan Quinn, Gloria Estefan, Cloris Leachman, Kieran Culkin, Charlie Hofheimer, Jay O. Sanders, Josh Pais; D: Wes Craven; W: Pamela Gray; C: Peter Deming; M: Mason Daring.

The Music Teacher 🐾🐾½ 1988 (PG) *Le Maître de musique* A Belgian costume drama dealing with a famed singer who retires to devote himself to teaching two students exclusively. In time, he sees his prized pupils lured into an international competition by an old rival of his. Although the singing is sharp, the story is flat. In French with yellow English subtitles. 95m/C VHS, DVD. BE Patrick Bauchau, Sylvie Fennec, Philippe Volter, Jose Van Dam, Johan Leysen, Anne Roussel; D: Gerard Corbiau.

Music Within 🐾🐾½ 2007 (R) True story plays like an inspirational movie of the week but is not without its appeal. Richard Pimentel (Livingston) has always wanted to be a public speaker; instead he winds up fighting in Vietnam where he loses most of his hearing in a bomb blast. He returns home, goes to college, and makes an unlikely connection with acerbic Art Honeyman (Sheen), who's wheelchair-bound because of cerebral palsy. Both are discriminated against and ostracized because of their disabilities, which leads Richard to his work as a motivational speaker and one of the leading advocates for what will become the Americans With Disabilities Act. 94m/C DVD. Ron Livingston, Michael Sheen, Melissa George, Yul Vazquez, Rebecca De Mornay, Hector Elizondo; D: Steven Sawalich; W: Brett McKinney, Mar Andrew Olsen, Kelly Kenmener; C: Irek Hartowicz; M: James T. Sale.

Musica Proibita 🐾🐾½ 1943 A serious opera-spiced drama about a young romance crushed by adultery in the teenage couple's ancestry. In Italian with English subtitles. 93m/B VHS. Tito Gobbi, Maria Mercader; D: Carlo Campogalliani; W: Carlo Campogalliani; C: Carlo Duse; C: Enzo Serafin; M: Ettore Campogalliani.

The Musketeer 🐾🐾 2001 (PG-13) Very, very loose adaptation of Dumas's "The Three Musketeers" features fight choreography from Hong Kong stunt master Xin-Xin Xiong. Unfortunately, the direction is murky and the action sequences are too cramped to be effective. In this version of the musketeer-go-round, D'Artagnan (Chambers) is motivated to join the famed battalion to avenge the murder of his parents by the evil Febre (Roth). He is disappointed to find that the musketeers have been decommissioned by the scheming Cardinal Richelieu (Rea), so he forms an alliance with Athos (Gregor), Porthos (Speirs) and Aramis (Moran) to set things aright. Along the way he falls for Francesca (Suvari), a close confidant of the queen (Deneuve). Despite the shortcomings of the fight scenes, the scenic French countryside is filmed beautifully and the actors do their best with the garbled yet overly familiar material. 105m/C VHS, DVD. US Justin Chambers, Mena Suvari, Tim Roth, Catherine Deneuve, Stephen Rea, Daniel Mesguich, David Schofield, Nick Moran, Jeremy Clyde, Michael Byrne, Steve Speirs, Jan Gregor Kremp, Jean-Pierre Castaldi; D: Peter Hyams; W: Gene Quintano; C: Peter Hyams; M: David Arnold.

Mussolini & I 🐾🐾½ 1985 *Mussolini: The Decline and Fall of Il Duce* 1985 Docudramatization of the struggle for power between Italy's Benito Mussolini and his son-in-law, Galeazzo Ciano. Narrated by Sarandon in the role of Il Duce's daughter. 130m/C VHS, DVD. Bob Hoskins, Anthony Hopkins, Susan Sarandon, Annie Girardot, Barbara DeRossi, Fabio Testi, Kurt Raab; D: Alberto Negrin. CABLE

Must Be Santa 🐾🐾 1999 (G) Santa is about to retire (three days before Christmas!) and Tuttle (Coleman), the CEO of the North Pole, is in desperate need of a replacement. And who does he find? Why classic loser Floyd (Pinnock), who decides that having the job will certainly get him his daughter's attention. 92m/C VHS. CA Dabney Coleman, Arnold Pinnock; D: Brad Turner; W: Douglas Berne; C: Albert J. Dunk; M: Jonathan Goldsmith. VIDEO

Must Love Dogs 🐾🐾 2005 (PG-13) Recently-divorced Sarah (Lane), a 40ish preschool teacher, is thrown into the online dating world by her family, a large group of cackling Irish Americans. But first Sarah meets Bob (Mulroney), the separated father of one of her students, and later Jake (super-witty Cusack), a romantic who builds wooden boats by hand, and the triangle ensues. Former TV director Goldberg and a star-loaded cast don't quite make a love connection, but a passable date movie is in here somewhere. The title is a good motto to live by, though. 98m/C VHS, DVD. US Diane Lane, John Cusack, Dermot Mulroney, Christopher Plummer, Stockard Channing, Elizabeth Perkins, Ben Shenkman, Julie Gonzalo, Brad Hall, Brad William Henke, Ali Hillis, Steve Schirripa, Laura Kightlinger, Jordana Spiro; D: Gary David Goldberg; W: Gary David Goldberg; C: John Bailey; M: Craig Armstrong.

Mutant 🐾½ *Night Shadows* 1983 (R) Another argument for the proper disposal of toxic waste. Hazardous materials transform the people of a southern town into monsters. 100m/C VHS, DVD. Wings Hauser, Bo Hopkins, Jennifer Warren, Lee Montgomery; D: John Cardos; W: Michael Jones; C: Alfred Taylor; M: Richard Band.

Mutant Hunt WOOF! *Matt Riker* 1987 Story of a battle between robots gone haywire and an all-American hero. The detective cyborgs are set free while high on a sexual stimulant called Euphoron to wreak their technological havoc on a rampage in Manhattan. **90m/C VHS.** *W:* Rick Gianasi, Mary-Anne Fahey. *D:* Tim Kincaid. *W:* Tim Kincaid. **VIDEO**

Mutant on the Bounty ⚡½ 1989 A musician, lost in space as a beam of light for 23 years, is transported aboard a spaceship. Once he materializes, it becomes apparent that he has undergone some incredible physical changes. As if that's not enough, the crew then must flee from a couple of thugs who are trying to steal a vial of serum they have on board. A space spoof that never gets into orbit. **93m/C VHS.** John Roarke, Deborah Benson, John Furey, Victoria Catlin, John Fleck, Kyle T. Heffner. *D:* Robert Torrance. **VIDEO**

Mutant Species ⚡ *Bio-Force* 1995 (R) Soldier is accidentally exposed to altered DNA and begins to mutate into a remorseless and terrifying killer. **100m/C VHS.** Leo Rossi, Ted Prior, Grant Gelt, Denise Crosby, Powers Boothe, Wilford Brimley; *D:* David A. Prior; *W:* David A. Prior, William Vigil; *C:* Carlos Gonzalez.

Mutants in Paradise WOOF! 1984 Comedy about a human guinea-pig who always gets involved in some sort of mishap. **76m/C VHS.** Brad Greenquist, Robert Ingraham, Anna Nicholas; *D:* Scott Apostolou; *W:* Scott Apostolou.

Mutator ⚡ *Time of the Beast* 1990 (R) A corporation makes a tiny genetic mistake and winds up creating a new life form...a demonic pussycat who preys on humans. **91m/C VHS.** Brion James, Carolyn Ann Clark, Milton Raphiel Murrill; *D:* John R. Bowey; *W:* Lynn Rose Higgins.

Mute Witness ⚡⚡½ 1995 (R) Low-budget British thriller, lensed in Moscow film studio, about U.S. filmers making a cheap thriller in Moscow film studio. Billy (Sudina) is the mute make-up artist of the title who, returning to the studio for a forgotten 'em, witnesses some of the crew shooting a snuff film with a real-life stabbing. First-timer Waller mocks both thriller genre and film biz, sometimes relying on, rather than spoofing, clichéd elements. Highlight is 20-minute long chase scene with the killers pursuing Billy in the cavernous studio. Guinness makes a surprise appearance in a cameo. **100m/C VHS, DVD.** GB Marina Sudina, Fay Ripley, Evan Richards, Oleg Yankovskij Jankowsky, Igor Volkom, Sergei Karlenkov; *Cameos:* Alec Guinness; *D:* Anthony Waller; *W:* Anthony Waller; *C:* Egon Werdin; *M:* Wilbert Hirsch.

The Muthers ⚡⚡ 1976 (R) Women prisoners escape from their confinement in a South American jungle. **DVD.** Jeannie Bell, Rosanne Katon, Jayne Kennedy, Trina Parks; *D:* Cirio H. Santiago.

The Mutilator WOOF! *Fall Break* 1985 (R) After accidentally bumping off his mother, a young man stalks five high school students wanting to cut them up into tiny bits. An unedited version is also available. Bloody boredom. **85m/C VHS.** Matt Mitler, Ruth Martinez, Bill Hitchcock; *D:* Buddy Cooper.

Mutiny ⚡⚡ 1952 In the War of 1812, the crew of an American ship carrying $10 million in gold fight among themselves for a part of France's donation to the war effort. The beautiful photography doesn't make up for the predictability of the storyline. **76m/C VHS, DVD.** Mark Stevens, Gene Evans, Angela Lansbury, Patric Knowles; *D:* Edward Dmytryk; *W:* Philip Yordan.

Mutiny ⚡⚡½ 1999 (PG-13) On July 17, 1944, a Victory ship anchored near San Francisco exploded, killing 323 sailors and injuring 390 (most of them black) defended by a young Thurgood Marshall in the worst homefront disaster of WWII. Three weeks later, 50 of the primarily untrained munition loaders who refused to continue working without safely equipment and proper training were charged with mutiny by the Navy. The men were defended by a young Thurgood Marshall (Morton) in a controversial case. **90m/C VHS.** Michael Jai White, Duane Martin, Joe Morton, Matthew Glave, Adrian Pasdar, James B. Sikking, Troy Winbush, David Ramsey; *D:* Kevin Hooks; *W:* James Henerson; *C:* Ron Garcia; *M:* Lee Holdridge. **TV**

Mutiny in the Big House ⚡⚡½ 1939 A man is sent to prison for writing a bad $10 check and must choose between seeking salvation with the prison chaplain or toughing it out with a hardened convict. Suprisingly good low-budget programmer. **83m/B VHS.** Charles Bickford, Barton MacLane, Pat Moriarty, Dennis Moore, William Royle, Charles Foy; *D:* William Nigh.

The Mutiny of the Elsinore ⚡ 1939 A writer on board an old sailing ship fights mutineers and wins back both the helm and the captain's daughter. Tedious British flotsam that made hash of an often-filmed Jack London tale. **66m/B VHS.** Paul Lukas, Lyn Harding, Kathleen Kelly, Clifford Evans, Ben Soutten, Jim Roy Lockwood.

Mutiny on the Blackhawk ⚡½ 1939 A swashbuckling western that deals with slave-running between Hawaii and California in 1840, including a battle between the Mexican army and small town California settlers that has even in 1939 for its sale of modern-day slang and clothing in the period setting. **74m/B VHS.** Richard Arlen, Andy Devine, Constance Moore, Guinn "Big Boy" Williams, Thurston Hall, Paul Fix, Richard Lane, Sandra Kane; *D:* Christy Cabanne; *W:* Michael L. Simmons; *C:* John Boyle.

Mutiny on the Bounty ⚡⚡⚡ 1935 Compelling adaptation of the true story of sadistic Captain Bligh, Fletcher Christian and their turbulent journey aboard the HMS Bounty and the subsequent mutiny in 1788. No gray here: Laughton's Bligh is truly a despicable character and extremely memorable in this MGM extravaganza. Remade twice, in 1962 and again in 1984 as "The Bounty." Much, much better than the 1962 remake. **132m/B VHS, DVD.** Clark Gable, Franchot Tone, Charles Laughton, Donald Crisp, Dudley Digges, Spring Byington, Henry Stephenson, Eddie Quillan, Herbert Mundin, Movita, Ian Wolfe; *D:* Frank Lloyd; *W:* Talbot Jennings, Jules Furthman, Carey Wilson; *M:* Herbert Stothart; Oscars '35: Picture; AFI '98: Top 100; N.Y. Film Critics '35: Actor (Laughton).

Mutiny on the Bounty ⚡⚡⚡ 1962 Based on the novel by Charles Nordhoff and James Norman Hall, this account of the 1789 mutiny led by Fletcher Christian and their turbulent journey on lauigh's. Based on Tamar Burnstein's book. **93m/C VHS.** Dom DeLuise, Jimmie Walker; *D:* Sam Firstenberg.

Mutiny on the Bounty ⚡⚡½ 1962 Based on the novel by Charles Nordhoff and James Norman Hall, this account of the 1789 mutiny led by Fletcher Christian against Captain Bligh of the Bounty is highlighted by lavish photography and an eccentric, though interesting, portrayal of the mutiny leader by Brando. Though overshadowed by Laughton's compelling performance in the original 1935 masterpiece, Howard's Bligh is ship-shape as the cold-hearted, single-minded captain determined to reach Tahiti and return with a hold full of breadfruit trees. Brando is highlighted by lavish photography over the top spirit of things. **177m/C VHS, DVD, HD DVD.** Marlon Brando, Trevor Howard, Richard Harris, Hugh Griffith, Richard Haydn, Percy Herbert, Noel Purcell; *D:* Lewis Milestone; *W:* Charles Lederer; *C:* Robert L. Surtees.

Mutual Needs 1997 (R) Man hires an escort to pose as his wife at a high school reunion. **90m/C VHS.** Richard Grieco, Charlotte Lewis, Christopher Atkins, Robert Davi, Dee Wallace Stone, Rochelle Swanson; *D:* Robert Achs; *W:* Dale Levenson, George Ayvas; *C:* Carl Oakwood; *M:* Bill Rogers. **VIDEO**

Mutual Respect ⚡½ 2000 (PG) Predicable and lackluster tale about a hockey-playing chimp and the team of loveable loser's that he helps to the inevitable "big game." **88m/C VHS.** Lloyd Bridges, Beau Bridges, Foy.

MVP (Most Valuable Primate) ⚡½ 2000 (PG) *Shimmering Light* 1977 (PG) A dying wealthy man sets out to find the son he never knew. Jack is a chimp with very human characteristics thanks to training from animal behavior specialist Dr. Kendall (Study). After Dr. Kendall dies, Jack mistakenly ends up in Nelson, British Columbia. He then makes contact with Tara (Smith), a deaf girl who is picked on by her classmates, and her older brother Steven, a hockey player on the worst team in the league. They discover that Jack has natural hockey skills, and recruit him for Steven's team. Unfortunately, the slimy Dr. Peabody (Muirhead) is searching for Jack due to his value as a lab animal, setting up a showdown between the kids and the evil grown-up. Hockey footage of the chimp was actually shot using three honest-to-God skating chimps named Mac, Bernie, and Louie. **91m/C VHS, DVD.** Kevin Zegers, Oliver Muirhead, Jamie Renee Smith, Lomax Study; *D:* Robert Vince; *W:* Robert Vince, Anne Vince; *C:* Glen Winter; *M:* Brahm Wenger.

MVP2: Most Vertical Primate ⚡½ 2001 Takes up where those "Air Bud" movies left off. In this equally dumb sequel, Jack the chimp is thrown out of the ZHL hockey league and goes on the lam for authorities. He meets homeless boy Ben (Goodman), who introduces the hairy one to amateur skateboarding. Of course, the chimp is a natural and many monkeyshines ensue. **97m/C VHS, DVD.** Scott Goodman, Bob Burnquist; *D:* Robert Vince; *W:* Robert Vince, Anne Vince; *M:* Brahm Wenger. **VIDEO**

MXP: Most Xtreme Primate ⚡⚡ MVP 3 2003 (G) Jack the chimp is at it again. This time he finds himself in Colorado, befriending lonely kid Pete, who's having trouble adjusting to a new town. Of course, Pete is an avid snowboarder, and teaches Jack some moves (Why wouldn't you?). They team up for a 'tournament while trying to avoid kidnappers. Third in the series again proves the comedy axiom "Monkeys are funny." Plot isn't great, but Jack's monkeyshines will keep the whole family amused anyway. **71m/C VHS, DVD, CA Robby Benson, Davin Douglas Drewitz, Gwynyth Walsh, Trevor Wright, Nicole McKay, Ian Bagg; *D:* Robert Vince; *W:* Robert Vince, Anne Vince, Anna McRoberts; *C:* Mike Southon; *M:* Brahm Wenger.

My African Adventure WOOF! 1987 Silly tale of an ambassador's son discovering a talking monkey in Africa and meeting a slew of opportunistic misfits in his travels. A comedy unfortunately short on laughs. **93m/C VHS.** **VIDEO**

My American Cousin ⚡⚡⚡ 1985 (PG) Award-winning autobiographical Canadian coming-of-age comedy set in 1959 on a British Columbia farm. 12-year-old Sandy (Langrick) exasperates her parents and has just discovered the appeal of boys when her rebellious, fun-loving, rich (Wildman) shows up (in a red Cadillac convertible) over summer vacation. Followed by "American Boyfriends" (1989) **94m/C VHS.** CA Margaret Langrick, John Wildman, Richard Donat, Jane Mortifee; *D:* Sandy Wilson; *W:* Sandy Wilson. Genie '86: Actor (Wildman), Actress (Langrick), Director (Wilson), Film.

My Antonia ⚡⚡½ 1994 (PG) Orphaned teenaged farm boy Jim Burden (Harris) discovers first romance with poor immigrant girl Antonia (Lowensohn) in 1886 Nebraska. They fall in love, separate, but maintain a 30-year friendship. Based on the book by Willa Cather. **92m/C VHS.** Neil Patrick Harris, Jason Robards Jr., Eva Marie Saint, Elina Lowensohn, Norbert Weisser, Travis Fine, Jan Triska, Anne Tremko, Mira Furlen, Boris Krutonog; *D:* Joseph Sargent; *C:* Jean-Marie Drejou; *M:* Xavier Demerliac.

My Apprenticeship ⚡⚡⚡ 1939 eur Am 2006 (PG-13) The second film of Donskoi's trilogy on Maxim Gorky has the writer earning his living, at the age of eight, as an apprentice to a bourgeois family. Although they promise him an education, Gorky is forced to learn to read on his own and eventually sets off on a series of land and sea voyages. In Russian with English subtitles.

My Best Friend Is a Vampire ⚡⚡½ 1988 (PG) Another teenage vampire story, about trying to cope with certain changes that adolescence and bloodsucking bring. Good supporting cast. **90m/C VHS.** Robert Sean Leonard, Evan Mirand, Cheryl Pollak, Rene Auberjonois, Cecelia

My Architect: A Son's Journey ⚡⚡⚡½ 2003 Slow but moving documentary about the life of famed architect Louis Kahn, written and directed by his son, Nathaniel. The movie begins with Kahn's death in 1974, when Nathaniel discovers in the obituary that his father had children by two other women. From there, he tries to uncover the mystery of Kahn's secretive life while highlighting his public achievements. What results is a film as much about a son trying to find his place in his father's life as Kahn's life and loneliness in a world of consumerism. A depressing, poignant film only occasionally marred by Nathaniel's focus on his personal relationship, he still creates a complex father but empathetic portrait of his complex father. **116m/C VHS, DVD, US** Oscars '04: Feature Doc. Nom. *D:* Nathaniel Kahn; *W:* Nathaniel Kahn; *C:* Robert Richman; *M:* Joseph Vitarelli; *Narr:* Nathaniel Kahn.

My Baby's Daddy ⚡⚡ 2004 (PG-13) Three irresponsible doofuses end up fathers in the hip-hop rehash of an old formula. Lonnie (Griffin) and his buddies G (Anderson) and Dominic (Imperioli) struggle with how new fatherhood will affect their lives as South Philly small-time playboys. He 'reunites with Johnny (Day Lewis), a child-hood friend and a working class street punk, and they go into the business together. They find themselves battling the prejudice of each other's families and friends in order to succeed. An intelligent look at the sexuality, race relations and economic problems of Thatcher's London. Great performances by a relatively unknown cast (for contrast, note Day Lewis' performance in the same year.) View," released in the same year.) **86m/C VHS, DVD, Gordon Warnecke, Daniel Day-Lewis, Saeed Jaffrey, Roshan Seth, Shirley Anne Field, Derrick Branche, Rita Wolf, Souad Faress, Richard Graham, Dudley Thomas, Garry Cooper, Charu Bala Choksi, Neil Cunningham, Walter Donovan, Stephen Marcus, Badi Uzzaman; *D:* Stephen Frears; *W:* Hanif Kureishi; *C:* Oliver Stapleton; *M:* Ludus Tonalis, Stanley Myers, Neal. Bd. of Review '86: Support. Actor (Day-Lewis); N.Y. Film Critics '86: Screenplay, Support. Actor (Day-Lewis); Natl. Soc. Film Critics '86: Screenplay.

My Beautiful Laundrette ⚡⚡⚡ 1985 (R) Omar (Warnecke), the nephew of a Pakistani businessman, is given the opportunity to better himself by turning his uncle's run-down laundry into a profitable business. He 'reunites with Johnny (Day Lewis), a child-hood friend and a working class street punk, and they go into the business together. They find themselves battling the prejudice of each other's families and friends in order to succeed. An intelligent look at the sexuality, race relations and economic problems of Thatcher's London.

My Best Friend ⚡⚡⚡ *Mon Meilleur Ami* 2006 (PG-13) Arrogant loner art dealer Francois (Auteuil) bets his business partner (Gayet) that he has a friend, and he is willing to do anything to win. He recruits taxi driver Bruno (Boon) to help him find a friend, only to discover that friendship isn't as easy to pin down (or buy) as he thought. Director Leconte thoughtfully turns it into an examination of friendship and loneliness in a world of consumerism. **94m/C DVD.** FP Daniel Auteuil, Dany Boon, Julie Gayet, Julie Durand; *D:* Patrice Leconte; *W:* Patrice Leconte, Jerome Tonnerre; *C:* Jean-Marie

abuse he has suffered is typical of the lives of most Russians and he encounters the beginnings of revolution. In Russian with English subtitles. Preceded by "My Universal Childhood" and followed by "My Universities." **100m/C VHS.** RU Varvara O. Massalitinova, Aleksei Lyarskv, Irina Zarubina, Ivan Kudryavtsev; *D:* Mark Donskoi; *W:* Mark Donskoi; *C:* Pyotr Yermolov; *M:* Lev Shvarts.

Peck, Fannie Flagg, Kenneth Kimmins, David Warner, Paul Winfield, Kathy Bates; **D:** Jimmy Huston; **W:** Tab Murphy; **C:** James Bartle; **M:** Steve Dorff.

My Best Friend's Girl 1984 Coy, sardonic *La Femme De Mon Pote* French romance about a woman who slaloms between two buddies working at a ski resort. Despite fine performances from all, it never quite makes it to the top of the hill. In French with English subtitles. **99m/C VHS.** *FR* Isabelle Huppert, Thierry Lhermitte, Coluche, Francois Perrot; **D:** Bertrand Blier; **W:** Bertrand Blier, Gerard Brach.

My Best Friend's Wedding 1997 (PG-13) Yes, it's a romantic comedy, but like director Hogan's previous effort, "Muriel's Wedding," there's some snap among the smiles. Restaurant critic Julianne (Roberts) and sports writer Michael (Mulroney) are best friends who have a pact that they'll marry each other if neither has found someone else by the age of 28. Michael finds sweet, wealthy Kimmy (Diaz) and invites Julianne to his nuptials. Naturally, Julianne realizes she's in love with Michael and she'll stop at nothing to break up the wedding, even enlisting gay friend George (Everett) to pose as her new beau. Roberts appears as the critics prefer her (long hair and smiling) while she extends her range of physical comedy. Diaz gets to be nice, Everett gets to steal every scene he's in, and Mulroney gets to be the lucky object of two lovely women's affections. Shot on location in Chicago. **105m/C VHS, DVD.** Julia Roberts, Dermot Mulroney, Cameron Diaz, Rupert Everett, Philip Bosco, M. Emmet Walsh, Rachel Griffiths, Susan Sullivan; Paul Giamatti; **D:** P.J. Hogan; **W:** Ronald Bass; **C:** Laszlo Kovacs; **M:** James Newton Howard.

My Best Girl 1927 Plucky Maggie (Pickford) is a store clerk who is the main support for her eccentric family. She falls in love with the store owner's son (future hubby Rogers) but his father is skeptical of the match. A gentle satire on middle-American life in the 1920s. **88m/B VHS, DVD.** Mary Pickford, Charles "Buddy" Rogers, Lucien Littlefield, Carmelita Geraghty, Sunshine Hart, Hobart Bosworth; **D:** Sam Taylor; **W:** Hope Loring, Tim Whelan, Allen McNeil; **C:** Charles Rosher, David Keeson.

My Big Fat Greek Wedding 2002 (PG) This is a big fat wet smooch of a movie—the kind you get from an enthusiastic older relative at a spare-no-expense wedding. Toula (Vardalos) is a frumpy 30-year-old waitress at her Greek parents' Chicago restaurant. They expect her to marry a Greek boy, have babies, and feed everyone. Then she meets handsome Ian Miller (Corbett), a non-Greek vegetarian schoolteacher who really, really likes her. Enough to want to marry her—if Toula's family can ever recover from the shock of her marrying outside their heritage. Every cliche imaginable is trotted out and you won't care as you'll laugh and groan at the too-recognizable family behavior (no matter what your ethnicity). Based on Vardalos' stage monologue. **95m/C VHS, DVD.** *US* Nia Vardalos, John Corbett, Lainie Kazan, Michael Constantine, Gia Carides, Louis Mandylor, Andrea Martin, Joey Fatone, Bruce Gray, Fiona Reid, Bess Meisler, Ian Gomez; **D:** Joel Zwick; **W:** Nia Vardalos; **C:** Jeffrey Jur; **M:** Chris Wilson, Alexander Janko. Ind. Spirit '03: Debut Perf. (Vardalos).

My Bloody Valentine 1981 (R) Psychotic coal miner visits the peaceful little town of Valentine Bluffs on the night of the yearly Valentine Ball. Many of the townspeople have their hearts removed with a pick axe and sent to the sheriff in candy boxes. The bloodiest scenes were cut out to avoid an X-rating. **91m/C VHS, DVD.** *CA* Paul Kelman, Lori Hallier, Neil Affleck, Keith Knight, Alf Humphreys, Cynthia Dale, Terry Waterland, Peter Cowper, Don Francks, Jack Van Evera; **D:** George Mihalka; **W:** John Beaird; **C:** Rodney Gibbons.

My Blue Heaven 1950 Sentimental musical comedy-drama has successful husband and wife showbiz team Grable and Dailey try to start a family. When pregnant Molly (Grable) loses her baby in a car accident, she and husband/partner Jack (Dailey) decide to adopt, as they also try to make the transition from a popular radio show to TV. Some dialogue considered risque at the time of release wouldn't raise an eyebrow today. **96m/C DVD.** Betty Grable, Dan Dailey, David Wayne, Jane Wyatt, Mitzi Gaynor, Una Merkel, Dan Hicks, Louise Beavers, Mae Marsh, Elinor Donahue; **D:** Henry Koster; **W:** Claude Binyon, Lamar Trotti; **C:** Arthur E. Arling.

My Blue Heaven 1990 (PG-13) After agreeing to rat on the Mafia, Martin is dropped into suburbia as part of the witness protection program. Moranis plays the FBI agent assigned to help the former mobster become an upstanding citizen. Adjusting to life in the slow lane isn't easy for an ex con who has grown accustomed to the big time. Not the typical role for Martin, who plays a brunette with a New York accent and is handcuffed by bad writing. **96m/C VHS, DVD.** Steve Martin, Rick Moranis, Joan Cusack, Melanie Mayron, Carol Kane, Bill Irwin, William Hickey, Daniel Stern; **D:** Herbert Ross; **W:** Nora Ephron; **C:** John Bailey; **M:** Ira Newborn.

My Blueberry Nights 2007 (PG-13) Director Wong Kar Wai's first English-language feature sets up a bit of a road movie. New Yorker Elizabeth (crooner Jones), in the wake of an ugly breakup, happens into a Manhattan cafe where she orders a piece of blueberry pie and meets waiter/cook Jeremy (Law). Elizabeth is headed out of town to get over her painful split but promises to stay in touch with her new pal. While on the road, she works various jobs and encounters other wandering souls, including an alcoholic cop (Strathairn) and his gorgeous ex-wife (Weisz) in Memphis, and a hard-luck card shark (Portman) in Las Vegas who cons her out of her savings. Finally she heads back to New York, perhaps hungry for another slice of blueberry pie. Don't look for any real plot here—Wong has just artfully strung together a series of vignettes, which works if that's your thing. **90m/C DVD.** *FR HK* Jude Law, David Strathairn, Rachel Weisz, Natalie Portman, Norah Jones, Chan Marshall; **D:** Wong Kar-Wai; **W:** Larry Block, Wong Kar-Wai; **C:** Darius Khondji; **M:** Ry Cooder.

My Bodyguard 1980 (PG) An undersized high school student fends off attacking bullies by hiring a king-sized, withdrawn lad as his bodyguard. Their "business" relationship, however, develops into true friendship. An adolescent coming of age with intelligence and sensitivity than most of its ilk, and a pack of up and coming stars as well as old stand-bys Houseman and Gordon. **96m/C VHS, DVD.** Chris Makepeace, Adam Baldwin, Martin Mull, Ruth Gordon, Matt Dillon, John Houseman, Joan Cusack, Craig Richard Nelson, Tim Kazurinsky, George Wendt, Jennifer Beals; **D:** Tony Bill; **W:** Alan Ormsby; **C:** Michael D. Margulies; **M:** Dave Grusin.

My Boss's Daughter 2003 (PG-13) Spoof-meister Zucker should have let this one stay on the shelf where someone had wisely left it. Instead, Kutcher and Reid are at the center of a gaggle of tasteless and largely unfunny mishaps and gags. Tom (Kutcher) is a clueless schlub who works for Jack (Stamp), a tough-as-nails publishing exec. Wanting to further his career and get in good with Jack's party-hearty but pretty daughter Lisa (Reid), Tom takes a job house-sitting for his cantankerous, and very particular, boss. You can just smell the comic possibilities. Unfortunately, that's not the odor emanating here, despite a solid supporting cast, which includes a typically pneumatic appearance from Dimension Films Electra. The whirlwind of destructive disaster, and Kutcher's deer-in-the-headlights routine runs as thin as Electra's t-shirts. **84m/C VHS, DVD.** *US* Ashton Kutcher, Tara Reid, Terence Stamp, Jeffrey Tambor, Andy Richter, Michael Madsen, Jon Abrahams, David Koechner, Carmen Electra, Molly Shannon, Kenan Thompson; **D:** David Zucker; **W:** David Dorfman; **C:** Martin McGrath; **M:** Teddy Castellucci.

My Boy 1921 Coogan stars as a foreign orphan who faces deportation. Instead he escapes and follows an old man home. This rare film includes an organ score. **56m/B VHS.** Jackie Coogan, Claude Gillingwater, Mathilde Brundage; **D:** Albert Austin; **W:** Victor Heerman.

My Boy Jack 2007 British author Rudyard Kipling (Haig, who also wrote the 1997 play the TV movie is based on) pulls strings that allow his only son, teenager Jack (Radcliffe), to enlist in the army in WWI in spite of the boy's bad eyesight. This is done over the objections of his American wife Caroline (Cattrall). When Jack is reported missing in 1915 in his first battle, the patriotic Kipling is overwhelmed by guilt and grief and spends years searching for answers before Jack's death is confirmed. **120m/C DVD.** *GB* David Haig, Daniel Radcliffe, Kim Cattrall, Carey Mulligan, Julian Wadham, Martin McCann, Richard Dormer; **D:** Brian Kirk; **W:** David Haig; **C:** David Odd; **M:** Adrian Johnston. TV

My Boyfriend's Back 1989 *Johnny Zombie* 1993 (PG-13) Embarrassingly dumb flick about a teenage boy who wants to take the prettiest girl in the school to the prom. The only problem is that he's become a zombie. Bits of him keep falling off (his girl thoughtfully glues them back on) and if he wants to stay "alive" long enough to get to the dance he has to munch on human flesh. Yuck. **85m/C VHS, DVD.** Andrew Lowery, Traci Lind, Edward Herrmann, Mary Beth Hurt, Danny Zorn, Austin Pendleton, Jay O. Sanders, Paul Dooley, Bob (Robert) Dishy, Cloris Leachman, Matthew Fox, Paxton Whitehead; **D:** Bob Balaban; **W:** Dean Lorey; **C:** Mac Ahlberg.

My Boys Are Good Boys 1978 (PG) A young foursome steal from an armored car and have to face the consequences. Quirky with an implausible storyline. **90m/C VHS, DVD.** Ralph Meeker, Ida Lupino, Lloyd Nolan, David Doyle; **D:** Bethel Buckalew.

My Brilliant Career 1979 (G) Sybella (Davis) is a poor, headstrong young woman spurns the social expectations of turn-of-the-century Australia and pursues opportunities to broaden her intellect and preserve her independence. This despite the fact that she loves Harry (Neill), a handsome, wealthy farmer. Davis is wonderful as the energetic and charismatic community trendsetter, especially in the scenes transforming her from a tomboy to a "lady." Has an excellent supporting cast. Based on an autobiographical novel by Miles Franklin which has been marvelously transferred to the screen. Armstrong deserves credit for her fine direction. **101m/C VHS, DVD.** *AU* Judy Davis, Sam Neill, Wendy Hughes, Robert Grubb, Patricia Kennedy, Aileen Britton, Peter Whitford, Alan Hopgood, Julia Blake; **D:** Gillian Armstrong; **W:** Nathan Waks. Australian Film Inst. '79: Film; British Acad. '80: Actress (Davis). VIDEO

My Brother Has Bad Dreams *Scream Bloody Murder* 1972 Young man with sibling tosses and turns in bed. **97m/C VHS.** Nick Kleinholz, Marlena Lustic; **D:** Robert Emery; **C:** Jack L. Richards; **M:** James Guglielmo.

My Brother Tom 1986 The rural village of St. Helens is scarcely disturbed by WWII. But a burgeoning love affair between young Peggy MacGibbon and Tom Quayle, and the conflict between their two religions, does threaten to tear their country town apart. Based on the novel by James Aldridge. On three cassettes. **200m/C VHS.** Gordon Jackson, Keith Michell, Catherine McClements, Tom Jennings, Christopher Mayer, Christopher Cummings; **D:** Pino Amenta. TV

My Brother's Keeper 1995 Twin brothers, Bob and Tom Bradley, fight for an experimental procedure when Tom is declared HIV positive. **94m/C DVD.** John Lithgow, Annette O'Toole, Veronica Cartwright, Ellen Burstyn, Richard Masur, Zeljko Ivanek, Brian Doyle-Murray, Amy Aquino, Julie Fulnek, Mark Harelik; **D:** Glenn Jordan; **W:** Gregory Goodell.

My Brother's War 1997 (R) Brothers Gerry (Foy) and Liam (Xuereb) find themselves on opposite sides of the troubles in Ireland. Then, CIA operative Hall (Brolin) arrives to prevent Liam kidnapping three politicians who are trying to reach a peace accord. Some plot twists help out this standard actioner. **85m/C VHS. DVD.** Salvator Xuereb, Patrick Foy, James Brolin, Josh Brolin, Jennie Garth, Cristi Conaway; **D:** James Brolin; **W:** Alex Simon; **C:** Michael Bucher; **M:** John Graham.

My Brother's Wife 1989 (PG) Barney (Ritter), the black sheep of a wealthy family, spends two decades pursuing Eleanor (Harris), the woman of his dreams. Unfortunately, she's already married—to the brother he despises. Adapted from the play "The Middle Ages" by A.R. Gurney. **94m/C VHS, DVD.** John Ritter, Mel Harris, Polly Bergen, Dakin Matthews, David Byron, Lee Weaver; **D:** Jack Bender; **W:** Percy Granger. TV

My Champion *Aitou Champion* 1981 Chance meeting propels Mike Gorman and Miki Tsuwa into a relationship based on the strong bonds of love and athletic competition. **101m/C VHS.** *JP* Yoko Shimada, Chris Mitchum; **D:** Gwen Amer; **W:** Richard Martini.

My Chauffeur 1986 (R) When a wise-cracking female is hired on as a chauffeur at an all-male chauffeur service, sparks fly. And when the owner takes a definite liking to her work, things take a turn for the worse. As these sort of sexploitation flicks go, this is one of the better ones. **94m/C VHS, DVD.** Deborah Foreman, Sam Jones, Howard Hesseman, E.G. Marshall, Sean McClory; **D:** David Beaird; **W:** David Beaird.

My Childhood *Childhood of Maxim Gorky* 1938 The first of director Donskoi's trilogy on the life of Maxim Gorky, based on Gorky's autobiographical stories. In this first film, Donskoi depicts Gorky's childhood of abuse and poverty with his grandparents in the 1870s. Eventually, Gorky is forced into the streets and becomes a wandering beggar. In Russian with English subtitles. Followed by "My Apprenticeship" and "My Universities." **100m/B VHS.** *RU* Varvara O. Massalitinova, Aleksei Lyarsky, Mikhail Troyanovsky, Yelizaveta Alekseyeva; **D:** Mark Donskoi; **W:** Ilya Gruzdev; **C:** Pyotr Yermolov; **M:** Lev Shvarts.

My Cousin Vinny 1992 (R) Vinny Gambini (Pesci), a lawyer who took the bar exam six times before passing, goes to Wahzoo City, Alabama to get his cousin and a friend off the hook when they're accused of killing a store clerk. Leather jackets, gold chains, Brooklyn accents, and his fiancee Tomei's penchant for big hair and bold clothing don't go over well with conservative judge Gwynne, causing plenty of simplistic story reaches. Surprising hit with simplistic story reaches popular heights via entertaining performances by the entire cast. Tomei in particular steals every scene she's in and has an Oscar to prove it. **120m/C VHS, DVD.** Joe Pesci, Ralph Macchio, Marisa Tomei, Mitchell Whitfield, Fred Gwynne, Lane Smith, Austin Pendleton, Bruce McGill; **D:** Jonathan Lynn; **W:** Dale Launer; **C:** Peter Deming; **M:** Randy Edelman. Oscars '92: Support. Actress (Tomei); MTV Movie Awards '93: Breakthrough Perf. (Tomei).

My Darling Clementine 1946 One of the best Hollywood westerns ever made, this recounts the precise events leading up to and including the gunfight at the O.K. Corral. Fonda's the lawman, with Bond, Holt, and Garner as his brothers, and Mature co-stars as best friend, Doc Holliday. Schoolteacher Clementine (Downs) is Earp's gal, but the real revelation should be Brennan as old man Clan-

My Date With Drew 🐾🐾🐾 2005 (PG) That would-be actress Drew Barrymore, whom struggling filmmaker Herzlinger idolizes. He gives himself 30 days (since Herzinger must return his video camera to the electronics store in that time in order to get a refund—yes, it's really low-budget). He must also attract her attention and not have her think he's a crazed stalker (he's actually kind of funny in an insecure way). And in the case of this documentary, it's all about the quest and not the outcome, which will not be revealed. 90m/C DVD. *US* Brian Herzinger; *D:* Jon Gunn, Brian Herzinger, Brett Winn; *C:* Jon Gunn, Brian Herzinger, Brett Winn; *M:* Steven Stern, Stuart Hart.

My Daughter's Keeper 🐾🐾 1998 Hallie, the President's sheltered daughter, just wants to go out with a boy and have a little fun. But between her father's re-election campaign and those darn Secret Service agents, what's a teen to do? 94m/C VHS, DVD. Nicholas Guest, Jocelyn Broderick, Ana Padraic; *D:* Heinrich Damms.

My Dear Secretary 🐾🐾½ 1949 After she marries her boss, a woman grows jealous of the secretary that replaces her. Comedic dialogue and antics result. 94m/B VHS, DVD. Kirk Douglas, Laraine Day, Keenan Wynn, Rudy Vallee, Florence Bates, Alan Mowbray, Charles Halton; *D:* Charles Martin; *W:* Charles Martin.

My Demon Lover 🐾🐾 1987 (PG-13) This sex comedy is complicated by the hero's transformation into a demon whenever he is aroused. Saved from complete mediocrity by Family Ties's Valentine in a likable performance. 90m/C VHS, DVD. Scott Valentine, Michelle Little, Arnold Johnson, Gina Gallego; *D:* Charles Loventhal; *M:* David Newman, Ed Alton.

My Dinner with Andre 🐾🐾🐾½ 1981 Two friends talk for hours over dinner one night. A wonderful exploration in storytelling, the conversation juxtaposes the experiences and philosophies of nerdish, bumbling Shawn and the globe-trotting spiritual pilgrimage of Gregory, in this sometimes poignant, sometimes comic little movie that starts you thinking. 110m/C VHS, DVD. Andre Gregory, Wallace Shawn, Roy Butler, Jean Lenauer; *D:* Louis Malle; *W:* Andre Gregory, Wallace Shawn; *C:* Jeri Sopanen; *M:* Allen Shawn.

My Dog Skip 🐾🐾🐾 1999 (PG) This is just the kind of movie people are talking about when they complain that there's no family friendly movies being made anymore. In 1940s Mississippi, awkward only child Willie (Muniz) sees his life change when, over the protests of his overprotective father (Bacon), he gets a puppy. Skip, for his ninth birthday. Amid much nostalgia and sentiment, Willie learns to be more outgoing and has many coming-of-age moments. Even if some of the plot elements are weak, the look and feel of the period is captured well, and Muniz does a fine job, although no human is likely to compete with the pooch, anyway. Kids will love the antics of Skip, and adults will enjoy having their hearts, and memories, tugged. Based on the book by Willie Morris. 95m/C VHS, DVD. Frankie Muniz, Diane Lane, Kevin Bacon, Luke Wilson, Caitlin Wachs, Bradley Coyell, Daylan Honeycutt, Cody Linley; *D:* Jay Russell; *W:* Gail Gilchriest; *C:* James L. Carter; *M:* William Ross; *Nar:* Harry Connick Jr.

My Dog Shep 🐾½ 1946 An orphan and his dog run away and are pursued diligently when it is discovered that he is a wealthy heir. 71m/B VHS. Tom Neal, William Farnum, Lannie Rees, Russell Simpson, Sarah Padden, Al "Fuzzy" St. John, Helen Chapman, Douglas Evans, Reed Howes, Grady Sutton; *D:* Ford Beebe; *W:* Ford Beebe; *C:* Fred Mandl.

My Family 🐾🐾🐾½ *Mi Familia* 1994 (R) Patriarch Jose Sanchez (Rojas) comes to America in the early 1900s from Mexico and soon finds that the grass is not always greener on the other side. Thus begins the multigenerational saga of the Sanchez family in L.A., which chronicles their struggles and hopes over a time span of 60 years. Overlooked in the glut of Hispanic-themed movies released, featuring soulful performances from the ensemble cast, especially Smits and Morales as troubled men from separate generations. Their deep-seated need to assimilate matched by a disdain for authority provide most of the family's heartaches. English and Spanish dialogue. 126m/C VHS, DVD. Jimmy Smits, Esai Morales, Eduardo Lopez Rojas, Jenny Gago, Elpidia Carrillo, Lupe Ontiveros, Jacob Vargas, Jennifer Lopez, Scott Bakula, Edward James Olmos, Michael Delorenzo, Maria Canals, Leon Singer, Jonathan Hernandez, Constance Marie, Enrique Castillo, Mary Steenburgen; *D:* Gregory Nava; *W:* Gregory Nava, Anna Thomas; *C:* Edward Lachman; *M:* Pepe Avila, Mark McKenzie; *Nar:* Edward James Olmos.

My Family Treasure 🐾🐾½ 1993 Mother tells her children about her dangerous trip into Russia to recover a family legacy—a priceless Faberge egg. 95m/C VHS. Dee Wallace Stone, Theodore Bikel.

My Date With Drew — [see column above]

My Dog, the Thief 🐾 1969 A helicopter weatherman is unaware that the lovable St. Bernard he has accepted as a value—a—has just been... Vicky's complicated love life, unsuccessful career tryouts, and her father's increasing bewilderment. It's meant as a sort of reverse, and perverse, innocents abroad, with the two Germans adrift in zany New York but this only works fitfully. 82m/C VHS. GE Shelley Kastner, Alfred Edel, David Bronstein, Mary Lou Graulau, Michael Massee, Annie Sprinkle, Bruce Benderson; *D:* Monika Treut; *W:* Monika Treut.

My Dream Is Yours 🐾🐾½ 1949 Day plays an up-and-coming radio star in this Warner Bros. musical comedy with a cameo from Bugs Bunny in a dream sequence. This fresh, fun remake of "Twenty Million Sweethearts" is often underrated, but is well worth a look. *♪My Dream is Yours; Love Finds a Way; I'll String Along with You; Canadian Capers; Freddie Get Ready; You Must Have Been a Beautiful Baby; Jeepers, Creepers.* 101m/C VHS, DVD. Jack Carson, Doris Day, Lee Bowman, Adolphe Menjou, Eve Arden, S.Z. Sakall, Selena Royle, Edgar Kennedy; *D:* Michael Curtiz.

My Fair Lady 🐾🐾🐾½ 1964 (G) Colorful production of Lerner and Loewe's musical version of "Pygmalion," about ill-mannered cockney Eliza (Hepburn) who is plucked from her job as a flower girl by Professor Henry Higgins (Harrison). Higgins makes a bet with a colleague that he can turn this rough diamond into a "lady." Winner of eight Academy Awards. Hepburn's singing voice is dubbed by Marni Nixon, who was also responsible for the singing in "The King and I" and "West Side Story." The dubbing may have undermined Hepburn's chance at an Oscar nomination. Typecasting role for Harrison as the crusty, egocentric Higgins. A timeless classic. *♪Why Can't the English?; Wouldn't It Be Lovely?; I'm an Ordinary Man; With a Little Bit of Luck; Just You Wait; 'Enry 'Iggins; The Servant's Chorus; The Rain in Spain; I Could Have Danced all Night; Ascot Gavotte.* 170m/C VHS, DVD. Audrey Hepburn, Rex Harrison, Stanley Holloway, Wilfrid Hyde-White, Theodore Bikel, Mona Washbourne, Jeremy Brett, Robert Coote, Gladys Cooper; *D:* George Cukor; *W:* Alan Jay Lerner; *C:* Harry Stradling Sr.; *M:* Frederick Loewe, Alan Jay Lerner. Oscars '64: Actor (Harrison), Adapt. Score, Art Dir./Set Dec., Color, Color Cinematog., Costume Des. (C), Director (Cukor), Picture, Sound; AFI '98: Top 100; British Acad. '65: Film, Directors Guild '64: Director (Cukor); Golden Globes '65: Film, Director (Cukor), Actor (Harrison).

My Father, My Hero 🐾🐾 1993 (PG) Another adaptation of a French film ("Mon Pere, Ce Heroes") finds 14-year-old Heigl on an island paradise with divorced dad Depardieu, passing him off as her boyfriend (without his knowledge) to impress a cute boy, causing obvious misunderstandings. Depardieu shows a flair for physical comedy, but his talent is wasted in a role that's vaguely disturbing; one of the few funny moments finds him unwittingly singing "Thank Heaven For Little Girls" to a horrified audience. For the preteen set only, others will probably find it a waste of time. Top notch actress Thompson's surprising (uncredited) cameo's due to her friendship with Depardieu. 90m/C VHS, DVD. Gerard Depardieu, Katherine Heigl, Dalton James, Lauren Hutton, Faith Prince, Emma Thompson; *D:* Steve Miner; *W:* Francis Veber, Charlie Peters; *M:* David Newman.

My Father, My Rival 🐾 1985 A high school student's crush on his teacher leads to emotional complications when his widowed father becomes romantically involved with her. 60m/C VHS. Wendy Crewson, Thomas Hauff, Helen Hughes, Andrew Gunn, Marissa Griben.

My Father, My Mother, My Brothers and My Sisters 🐾🐾 *Mon Pere, Ma Mere, Mes Freres et Mes Soeurs* 1999 Free-spirit Anne (Abril) has three children by three different men and has never bothered to inform any of them about their offspring. She's surprised when her young son Victor expresses an interest in meeting his dad, which just happens to be possible since Anne and her brood are vacationing at the same Mexican resort where all three of her ex-lovers happen to also be staying with their significant others. French with subtitles. 95m/C VHS, DVD. FR Victoria Abril, Alain Bashung, Pierre-Jean Chert, Charlotte de Turckheim, Philippe Gianheim; *W:* Charlotte de Turckheim; *M:* Cyril de Turckheim; *greco:* *C:* Javier Salmones.

My Family is Coming 🐾🐾 1991 German immigrant, Vicky, is trying to get an acting career off the ground in New York. She shares her apartment with Ben, a gay man, and generally does more work as a waitress than actress. Vicky's alarmed when her father, Hans, arrives for a visit. She's told him she's married (Vicky's also gay), so Ben agrees to pose as her husband. The film details [...]

My Father is Coming 🐾🐾 1991 [continued] Alex Vincent, Bitty Schram; *D:* Rolfe Kanefsky; *Ed:* ward Staroselsky.

My Favorite Blonde 🐾🐾🐾 1942 Beautiful British spy Carroll convinces Hope to aid her in carrying out a secret mission. Lots of fun as Hope and his trained penguin, along with Carroll, embark on a cross-country chase to elude the Nazis. Hope's behavior is hilarious and the pacing of the film is excellent. Based on a story by Melvin Frank and Norman Panama. 78m/B VHS. Bob Hope, Madeleine Carroll, Gale Sondergaard, George Zucco, Lionel Royce, Walter Kingsford, Victor Varconi, Bing Crosby; *D:* Sidney Lanfield; *W:* Frank Butler, Don Hartman; *C:* William Mellor.

My Favorite Brunette 🐾🐾½ 1947 Detective parody starring Hope as a photographer turned grumbling private eye. He becomes involved with a murder, a spy caper, and a dangerous brunette (Lamour). 85m/B VHS, DVD. Bob Hope, Dorothy Lamour, Peter Lorre, Lon Chaney Jr., Alan Ladd, Reginald Denny, Bing Crosby; *D:* Elliott Nugent; *W:* Edmund Beloin, Jack Rose; *C:* Lionel Lindon; *M:* Robert Emmett Dolan.

My Favorite Martian 🐾🐾½ 1998 (PG) This retread of the semi-successful '60s TV sitcom adds to the growing pile of evidence that the words "original" and "thought" are not used in the same sentence in Hollywood anymore. Tim (Daniels) is a TV producer cajoled into hiding his "Uncle Martin." Martin (Lloyd) is actually an alien whose spaceship has crashed and he's on the run from a government agency and he's on the prying press. Tim must throw racy reporter Hurley off the trail as well, although he has a crush on her. Numerous animated and computer morphed sight gags, including a horny wisecracking spacesuit named Zoot (who brings new meaning to the term "skirt chasing"), take the place of a plot. Sets new standards for mediocrity, but the kid dies might enjoy it. 93m/C VHS, DVD. Jeff Daniels, Christopher Lloyd, Elizabeth Hurley, Daryl Hannah, Wallace Shawn, Christine Ebersole, Ray Walston, Michael Lerner; *C:* Thomas Ackerman; *M:* John Dabney.

My Favorite Wife 🐾🐾🐾 1940 Handsome widower Nick (Grant) has just married Bianca (Patrick) only to discover that first wife Ellen (Dunne), shipwrecked seven years earlier and presumed dead, has reappeared. Ellen wants Nick back and makes him jealous by revealing the style and wit of this presentation. 88m/B VHS, DVD. Ann Shoemaker, Granville Bates, Irene Dunne, Cary Grant, Randolph Scott, Gail Patrick, Scotty Beckett; *D:* Garson Kanin; *W:* Samuel Spewack, Balla Spewack, Leo McCarey; *C:* Rudolph Mate; *M:* Roy Webb.

My Favorite Year 🐾🐾🐾 1982 (PG) *My Favourite Year* 1982 (PG) A young writer on a popular live TV show in the 1950s is asked to keep a watchful eye on that week's guest star—his favorite swashbuckling movie hero. Through a series of misadventures, he discovers his matinee idol is actually a drunkard and womanizer who has trouble living up to his cinematic standards. Sterling performance from O'Toole, with memorable portrayal from Bologna as the show's host, King Kaiser (a take-off of Sid Caesar from "Your Show of Shows"). 92m/C VHS, DVD. Peter O'Toole, Mark Linn-Baker, Joseph Bologna, Jessica Harper, Lainie Kazan, Bill Macy, Anne DeSalvo, Lou Jacobi, Adolph Green, Cameron Mitchell, Gloria Stuart; *D:* Richard Benjamin; *W:* Norman Steinberg; *M:* Ralph Burns.

My Fellow Americans 🐾🐾 1996 (PG-13) Political "Odd Couple" pits cantankerous conservative Kramer (Lemmon) against womanizing liberal Douglas (Garner) when a current President Aykroyd frames his two predecessors for a White House scandal. The age-old adversaries must set aside their differences long enough to clear their names by reaching Kramer's presidential library, where the two encounter adventure, danger and "the people," the average Americans they used to work for. "Grumpy Old Men" veteran Lemmon is plenty cranky while Garner's charisma is a suitable foil. The ironic

VideoHound's Golden Movie Retriever | 657

My

My

'charm' of course banter from the mouths of two ex-Presidents is supposed to carry much of the humor, but instead wears thin. Supporting characters (Aykroyd, Bacall) aren't as well used as the two main characters. Mainly for Lemmon, Garner, and "Grumpy" fans. **96m/C VHS, DVD.** Dan Aykroyd, James Garner, Jack Lemmon, John Heard, Sela Ward, Wilford Brimley, Everett McGill, Bradley Whitford, Lauren Bacall, James Rebhorn, Esther Rolle, Conchata Ferrell, Jack Kehler, Tom Everett, Jeff Yagher; **D:** Peter Segal; **W:** E. Jack Kaplan, Richard Chapman, Peter Tolan; **C:** Julio Macat; **M:** William Ross.

My First Mister ♦♦♦ **2001 (R)** Explores the delicate friendship between two lost and lonely souls. Teenaged Jennifer (Sobieski) is a goth girl whose look and attitude alienates both school and family members. Looking for a job, she is unexpectedly hired as a stock clerk by men's clothing salesman, Randall (Brooks), a middle-aged conservative in both dress and manner. They discover they have a number of feelings in common, although Randall is careful never to let their relationship get out of control. Film does take an unfortunate turn towards the maudlin when we learn that Randall is dying but the leads keep sentimentality fairly well-checked. **109m/C VHS, DVD.** *US* Albert Brooks, Leelee Sobieski, Desmond Harrington, Carol Kane, Michael McKean, Mary Kay Place, John Goodman, Lisa Jane Persky; **D:** Christine Lahti; **W:** Jill Franklyn; **C:** Jeffrey Jur; **M:** Steve Porcaro.

My First Wedding WOOF! **2004 (PG-13)** Disastrous and raunchy would-be rom-com with unlikable characters and ridiculous situations. Bride-to-be Vanessa (Cook) is having sex fantasies about other men just days before her wedding and heads to confession. Horndog carpenter Nick (Doughty) happens to be fixing the confessional booth and is mistaken for the priest. Vanessa pleads with the faker to save her from sin. Of course Nick wants to sin big time and does his best to persuade Vanessa to call off the nuptials. **100m/C DVD.** Rachael Leigh Cook, Kenny Doughty, Paul Hopkins, Valerie Mahaffey; **D:** Laurent Firode; **W:** Joan Carr-Wiggin; **C:** Vernon Layton; **M:** Michel Cusson.

My 5 Wives ♦♦ **2000 (R)** Dangerfield is a thrice-divorced real estate tycoon who discovers the Utah land he's invested in comes complete with five wives. **100m/C VHS, DVD.** Rodney Dangerfield, Andrew (Dice Clay) Silverstein, John Byner, Molly Shannon, Jerry Stiller, John Pinette, Emmanuelle Vaugier, Fred Keating, Kate Luyben, Judy Tylor, Angelika Baran, Anita Brown; **D:** Sidney J. Furie; **W:** Rodney Dangerfield, Harry Basil; **C:** Curtis Petersen; **M:** Robert Carli. VIDEO

My Foolish Heart ♦♦½ **1949** Women's weepie starred Hayward as Eloise Winters, the tippling and unhappily married wife of Lew Wengler (Smith). Eloise stole Lew away from her college roommate, Mary Jane (Wheeler), when she got pregnant by another man. Lew has asked Eloise for a divorce so he and Mary Jane can finally get hitched. But an old evening dress has Eloise remembering her true love and the father of her daughter—Walt Dreiser (Andrews)—whom she fatefully met in 1941. Eloise finally owns up to the unhappiness her deception has caused and at least someone is happy by the closing credits. Based on the short story "Uncle Wiggily in Connecticut" by J.D. Salinger. **98m/B VHS.** Dana Andrews, Susan Hayward, Kent Smith, Lois Wheeler, Jessie Royce Landis, Robert Keith, Gigi Perreau, Karin (Karen, Katharine) Booth; **D:** Mark Robson; **M:** Julius J. Epstein, Philip G. Epstein; **C:** Lee Games; **M:** Victor Young.

dren would be able to deal with some unhappy occurrences in the film, but most seemed to classify it as a movie the whole family would enjoy. **102m/C VHS, DVD.** Dan Aykroyd, Jamie Lee Curtis, Macaulay Culkin, Anna Chlumsky, Griffin Dunne, Raymond Buktenica, Richard Masur, Ann Nelson, Peter Michael Goetz, Tom Villard; **D:** Howard Zieff; **W:** Laurice Elehwany; **C:** Paul Elliot; **M:** James Newton Howard. MTV Movie Awards '92: Kiss (Macaulay Culkin/Anna Chlumsky).

My Forbidden Past ♦♦½ **1951** Melodrama set in 1890 New Orleans centers on a young woman (Gardner) with an unsavory past who unexpectedly inherits a fortune and vows to break up the marriage of the man (Mitchum) she loves. His wife is murdered and he is charged with doing the deed until Gardner, exposing her past, wins his love and helps to extricate him. **81m/B VHS.** Ava Gardner, Melvyn Douglas, Robert Mitchum. **D:** Robert Stevenson.

My Friend Flicka ♦♦♦ **1943** Boy makes friends with four-legged beast. Dad thinks the horse is full of wild oats, but young Roddy trains it to be the best gosh darned horse in pre-Disney family faredom. Based on Mary O'Hara book, followed by "Thunderhead, Son of Flicka," and TV series. **89m/C VHS, DVD.** Roddy McDowall, Preston Foster, Rita Johnson, James Bell, Jeff Corey; **D:** Harold Schuster.

My Friend Irma ♦♦½ **1949** An adaptation of the radio series, featuring Wilson as the dumb blonde with boyfriend trouble and Lynn as her sensible pal. The film debut of Martin (singing) and Lewis (mugging) as juice-bar operators. Followed by a sequel, "My Friend Irma Goes West," and later by a TV series. **103m/B VHS.** Marie Wilson, Diana Lynn, John Lund, Don DeFore, Dean Martin, Jerry Lewis, Hans Conried; **D:** George Marshall; **W:** Cy Howard; **C:** Leo Tover; **M:** Roy Webb.

My Friend Walter ♦♦½ **1993** Bess Throckmorten attends a family reunion in London with her Aunt Ellie and discovers one of her ancestors is Sir Walter Raleigh. Visiting the Tower of London, Bess finds Sir Walter's ghost who wants to follow her home to Devon to see how the family is doing. He finds that the Throckmorten's are about to lose the family farm but Sir Walter comes up with a plan to restore their fortunes. Shot on location in England and based on the book by Michael Morpurgo. **87m/C VHS.** *GB* Polly Grant, Ronald Pickup, Prunella Scales, Louise Jameson, James Hazeldine, Lawrence Cooper, Constance Chapman; **D:** Gavin Millar.

My Geisha ♦♦½ **1962** MacLaine and husband experience bad karma because she wants to be in his new film. In pancake makeup and funny shoes, she poses as a geisha girl and is cast as Madame Butterfly. Her husband, however, is one sharp cookie. Filmed in Japan. **120m/C VHS, DVD.** Shirley MacLaine, Yves Montand, Edward G. Robinson, Robert Cummings; **D:** Jack Cardiff.

My Giant ♦♦ **1998 (PG)** Billy Crystal plays a short, annoying, Hollywood-type guy and Romanian-born NBA player Gheorghe Muresan plays a really tall Romanian guy, so you know there's not exactly an Olivier thing happening here. Billy Crystal is the brutish showbiz agent Sammy, who accidently stumbles onto Muresan's Max. The gentle Max is at peace in his monastery, but Sammy, being an agent, quickly finds a way to make money off of him. Max is talked into a movie career so he can be reunited with his childhood crush Lillianna (Pacula). The odd couple schtick is milked until bone dry, and then the sentimentality floodgates open when it's discovered Max has a serious medical condition. Warning: although presented as a family film, unless you want to recreate that whole "Why did Bambi's mom have to die?" scene (with you as the parent this time), you might want to reconsider renting this movie for small children. **103m/C VHS, DVD.** Michael (Mike) Papajohn, Billy Crystal, Gheorghe Muresan, Kathleen Quinlan, Joanna Pacula, Rider Strong, Harold Gould, Doris Roberts, Philip Sterling, Heather Thomas, Zane Carney; **Cameos:** Steven Seagal; **D:** Michael Lehmann; **W:** David Seltzer; **C:** Michael Coulter; **M:** Marc Shaiman.

My Girl ♦♦½ **1991 (PG)** Chlumsky is delightful in her film debut as an 11-year-old tomboy who must come to grips with the realities of life. Culkin plays her best friend Thomas, who understands her better than anyone else, including her father, a mortician, and his girlfriend, the makeup artist at their funeral parlor. Some reviewers questioned whether young chil-

My Girl 2 ♦♦½ **1994 (PG)** It's 1974 and Chlumsky is back as Vada (this time without Culkin, given the killer bee attack in MG1) in this innocent coming-of-ager. Portly Aykroyd and flaky Curtis return as parental window dressing who encourage Vada's search for information on her long-dead mother. She tracks down old friends of her mom's (Masur and Rose) who are having difficulties with their obnoxious adolescent son (O'Brien). Predictable, but enjoyable. Certain to fail the credibility test of nit-pickers who may wonder why the only thing Aykroyd can remember of his first wife is that she fell behind a paper bag with a date scribbled on it. **99m/C VHS, DVD.** Anna Chlumsky, Dan Aykroyd, Jamie Lee Curtis, Austin O'Brien, Richard Masur, Christine Ebersole, Ben Stein; **D:** Howard Zieff; **W:** Janet Kovalcik; **C:** Paul Elliott; **M:** Cliff Eidelman.

My Girl Tisa ♦♦½ **1948** Chronicles the experiences of a young immigrant woman who struggles to survive in the U.S. at the turn of the century and hopes to bring her father over from their home country. Based on a play by Lucille S. Prumbs and Sara B. Smith. **95m/B VHS.** Lilli Palmer, Sam Wanamaker, Akim Tamiroff, Alan Hale, Hugo Haas, Gale Robbins, Stella Adler; **D:** Elliott Nugent; **M:** Max Steiner.

My Grandpa Is a Vampire ♦♦½ **1992 (PG)** When 12 year-old Lonny and his pal visit Grandpa Cooger in New Zealand Lonny discovers a long-hidden family secret—Grandpa's a vampire! This doesn't stop either boy from joining with Grandpa in lots of scary adventures. **90m/C VHS.** AL Lewis, Justin Gocke, Milan Borich, Noel Appleby; **D:** David Blyth.

My Heroes Have Always Been Cowboys ♦♦½ **1991 (PG)** An aging rodeo rider returns to his hometown to recuperate and finds himself forced to confront his past. His ex-girlfriend, his dad and his sister all expect something from him. He learns how to give it, and gains the strength of purpose to get back on the bull that stomped him. Excellent rodeo footage, solid performances, but the story has been around the barn too many times to hold much interest. **106m/C VHS.** Scott Glenn, Kate Capshaw, Ben Johnson, Balthazar Getty, Mickey Rooney, Gary Busey, Tess Harper, Clarence Williams III, Dub Taylor, Clu Gulager, Dennis Fimple; **D:** Stuart Rosenberg; **W:** Joel Don Humphreys; **M:** James Horner.

My House in Umbria ♦♦♦ **2003** Quality HBO production adapted from the novella by William Trevor. Romance writer Emily Delahunty (Smith) is aboard a Milan-bound train when her peace is shattered by a bomb. Emily invites the other survivors from her train car to recuperate at her house in Umbria, including young American Aimee (Clarke), whose parents were killed in the explosion. Aimee begins to lean on Emily (who loves having a ready-made family) and opens the snake appears in the Garden of Eden; Aimee's frosty Uncle Thomas (Cooper) has come to pick up his unknown niece. Emily's voiceover ramblings are sometimes distracting but Smith finds the pathos in her character without going overboard. The versatile Cooper also offers excellent support in an unsympathetic role. And, naturally, the scenes at the villa, shot on the Tuscany-Umbria border, are entrancing. **103m/C VHS, DVD.** Maggie Smith, Chris Cooper, Timothy Spall, Emmy Clarke, Benno Furmann, Ronnie Barker, Giancarlo Giannini, Libero De Rienzo; **D:** Richard Loncraine; **W:** Hugh Whitemore; **C:** Marco Pontecorvo; **M:** Claudio Capponi. CABLE

My Husband's Double Life ♦♦½ *The Familiar Stranger* **2001** Men are scum. Cable drama based on a true story finds Elizabeth Welsh (Sanders) trying to cope with the apparent suicide of her embezzling husband Patrick (Sanders). She has to sell the house and get a job to support their kids. Then, 10 years later, the Social Security Department informs Elizabeth that the weasel is alive and living in Maine. Naturally, Elizabeth heads off to confront the two-timer. **96m/C VHS, DVD.** Margaret Colin, Jay O. Sanders, Will Estes, Aaron Ashmore, Gary Hudson, Victoria Snow; **D:** Alan Metzger; **W:** Alan Hines. CABLE

My Husband's Secret Life ♦♦ **1998 (PG-13)** Nonsensical thriller about cop's widow Archer who discovers her late hubby had a mistress (Alonso). Unlikely as it seems, the two pair up to investigate police corruption after it seems their mutual honey was also taking payoffs from the mob. The two actresses are much classier than their material. Based on the novel "Tin Wife" by Joe Flaherty. **93m/C VHS.** Anne Archer, Maria Conchita Alonso, Garry Chalk, James Russo, Gerard Plunkett; **D:** Graeme Clifford; **W:** Georgia Jeffries; **C:** David Geddes; **M:** Roger Bellon. CABLE

My Lady of Whims ♦♦ **1925** Clara Bow's dad disapproves of debutante daughter's desire to hang out with the girls who just want to have fun. **42m/B VHS.** Clara Bow, Betty Baker, Carmelita Geraghty, Donald Keith, Lee Moran; **D:** Dallas Fitzgerald; **W:** Doris Schroeder; **C:** Jack Young.

My Left Foot ♦♦♦♦ **1989 (R)** A gritty, unsentimental drama based on the life and autobiography of cerebral-palsy victim Christy Brown. Considered an imbecile by everyone but his mother (Fricker, in a stunning award-winning performance) until he teaches himself to write. He survives his impoverished Irish roots to become a painter and writer using his left foot, the only appendage over which he has control. He also falls in love and finds some heartaches along the way. Day-Lewis is astounding; the supporting cast, especially Shaw and Cusack, match him measure for measure. **103m/C VHS, DVD.** IR Daniel Day-Lewis, Brenda Fricker, Ray McAnally, Cyril Cusack, Fiona Shaw, Hugh O'Conor, Adrian Dunbar, Ruth McCabe, Alison Whelan; **D:** Jim Sheridan; **W:** Shane Connaughton, Jim Sheridan; **C:** Jack Conroy; **M:** Elmer Bernstein. Oscars '89: Actor (Day-Lewis), Support. Actress (Fricker); British Acad. '89: Actor (Day-Lewis), Support. Actor (McAnally); Ind. Spirit '90: Foreign Film; L.A. Film Critics '89: Actor (Day-Lewis), Support. Actress (Fricker); Montreal World Film Fest. '89: Actor (Day-Lewis); N.Y. Film Critics '89: Actor (Day-Lewis); Film; Natl. Soc. Film Critics '89: Actor (Day-Lewis).

My Life ♦♦½ **1993 (PG-13)** Maudlin, sometimes depressing production preaches the power of a well-examined life. Public relations exec Keaton is diagnosed with cancer and the doctors predict he will most likely die before the birth of his first child. Film follows his transition from uncommunicative and angry to acceptance, a role to which Keaton brings a sentimental strength. Kidman is window dressing as the ever-patient, nobly suffering wife, a cardboard character notable mainly for her beauty. **114m/C VHS, DVD.** Michael Keaton, Nicole Kidman, Haing S. Ngor, Bradley Whitford, Queen Latifah, Michael Constantine, Toni Sawyer, Rebecca Schull, Lee Garlington; **D:** Bruce Joel Rubin; **W:** Bruce Joel Rubin; **C:** Peter James; **M:** John Barry.

My Life and Times with Antonin Artaud ♦♦♦ *En Compagnie d'Antonin Artaud* **1993** Postwar Parisian bohemia is depicted in the obsessive friendship between ambitious young poet Jacques Prevel (Barbe) and famed intellectual/poet/impressario Antonin Artaud (Frey), who founded the Theatre of Cruelty. Artaud has returned to Paris after spending nine years in an asylum and is suffering from terminal cancer, the misery of which is partially alleviated by the opiates that Prevel can provide. Delusional and paranoid, Artaud makes his self-destruction into genius while Prevel documents Artaud's last two years in diaries,

My Life As a Dog 🐾🐾🐾 *Mitt Liv Som Hund* 1985 A troublesome boy is separated from his brother and is sent to live with relatives in the country when his mother is taken ill. Unhappy and confused, he struggles to understand sexuality and love and tries to find security and acceptance. Remarkable Swedish film available with English subtitles or dubbed. 101m/C VHS, DVD, SW Anton Glanzelius, Tomas von Bromssen, Ank Liden, Melinda Kinnaman, Kicki Rundgren, Ing-mari Carlsson; D: Lasse Hallström; W: Lasse Hallström, Per (Pelle) Berglund, Brasse Brannström, Reidar Jönsson; M: Björn Isfält. Golden Globes '88; Foreign Film; Ind. Spirit '88; Foreign Film; N.Y. Film Critics '87; Foreign Film.

My Life on Ice 🐾🐾 *The True Story of My Life in Rouen; Ma Vraie Vie a Rouen* 2002 Sixteen-year-old Etienne (Tavares) has two obsessions: figure skating and filming everything that happens around him with the video camera he got for his birthday. He films his mom, Caroline (Ascaride), and her new boyfriend Laurent (Zaccai), his grandmother (Surgère), and his best friend Ludovic (Bonnifait)—few of whom are happy to constantly be in the camera's eye. The viewer also becomes aware (although those around him seem oblivious) of a crush on Etch Laurent, who happens to be his history teacher, and pal Ludovic, who can't deal with any sexual revelations. French with subtitles. 100m/C VHS, DVD, FR Jimmy Tavares, Ariane Ascaride, Helene Surgère, Jonathan Zaccai, Lucas Bonnifait; D: Olivier Ducastel, Jacques Martineau; W: Olivier Ducastel, Jacques Martineau; M: Mathieu Poirot-Delpech, Pierre Milon; M: Philippe Miller.

My Life So Far 🐾🐾½ 1998 (PG-13) In the 1920s, the Pettigrews live on the family estate of Gamma Macintosh (Harris) in the Scottish Highlands. Eccentric would-be inventor Edward (Firth) ineffectually manages the property, with wife Moira (Mastrantonio) and his children, including mischievous 10-year-old Fraser (Norman). Fraser's safe world is rocked by the arrival of his businessman Uncle Morris (McDowell) and his uncle's seductive French fiancée, Heloise (Jacob), who draws the immediate and overly attentive gaze of Edward. Based on the autobiographical book "Son of Adam" by Sir Denis Forman. 93m/C VHS, DVD, GB Colin Firth, Mary Elizabeth Mastrantonio, Irene Jacob, Malcolm McDowell, Rosemary Harris, Tcheky Karyo, Robert Norman, Kelly Macdonald; D: Hugh Hudson; W: Simon Donald; M: Howard Blake.

My Life to Live 🐾🐾🐾 *Vivre Sa Vie; It's My Life* 1962 A woman turns to prostitution in this probing examination of sexual and social relations. Idiosyncratic Godard has never been more starstruck than in this vehicle for the endearing Karina, his wife at the time. A classic. In French with English subtitles. 85m/B VHS, DVD, FR Anna Karina, Sady Rebbot, Andre S. Labarthe, Guylaine Schlumberger; D: Jean-Luc Godard; W: Jean-Luc Godard; C: Raoul Coutard; M: Michel Legrand. Venice '62: Special Jury Prize.

My Life Without Me 🐾🐾🐾½ 2003 (R) Writer/director Coixet delivers a weepy drama about a young, married woman who keeps her impending death a secret from her family. Diagnosed with inoperable ovarian cancer, the happily married 23-year-old Ann (Polley) decides against telling husband Don (Speedman) and their two daughters about her condition. With only a few months to live, Ann draws up a list of things to do before dying, one of which is to really fall in love with another man. She soon finds a cooperative lover in Lee (Ruffalo), who falls for her too. She also tries to set her husband up with a replacement wife, also named Ann (Watling). Despite the far-fetched soap operatic script and less than sympa-

thetic main character, earnest performances (especially from the likeable Polley) ratchet up the believability factor. 106m/C VHS, DVD, CA SP Sarah Polley, Scott Speedman, Mark Ruffalo, Deborah Harry, Alfred Molina, Leonor Watling, Amanda Plummer, Julian Richings, Maria De Medeiros; D: Isabel Coixet; W: Isabel Coixet; C: Jean-Claude Larrieu; M: Alfonso de Villalonga.

My Life's in Turnaround 🐾🐾 1994 (R) Amusing low-budget comedy takes a behind-the-scenes, semi-autobiographical look at the lives of two would-be filmmakers. They try for cool but manage only goofy. 84m/C VHS, DVD, Eric Schaeffer, Donal Lardner Ward, Lisa Gerstein, Dana Wheeler-Nicholson, Debra Clein, Sheila Jaffe, Casey Siemaszko, John Sayles, Martha Plimpton, Phoebe Cates; D: Eric Schaeffer, Donal Lardner Ward; W: Eric Schaeffer, Donal Lardner Ward; M: Reed Hays.

My Little Assassin 🐾🐾 1999 In 1959, idealistic 19-year-old Marta Lorenz is in Cuba with her CIA operative mother (Clayburgh), when she falls for revolutionary leader Fidel Castro (Mantegna). She winds up pregnant and alone in New York, where the CIA tries to convince her that Fidel's a bad guy. So, she decides to return to Cuba and assassinate him. In 1993, Lorenz wrote a book detailing her affair, the birth of their daughter, and Lorenz's involvement in a failed plot to poison the dictator in 1960. If you can suspend your credulity, you'll discover a watchable potboiler with Mantegna as a charismatic Cuban leader. 90m/C VHS, DVD, Joe Mantegna, Gabrielle Anwar, Jill Clayburgh, Robert Davi, Scott Paulin, Tony Plana, Reiner Schone, Mike Moroff, Glenn Mershower, Dean Norris; D: Jack Bender; W: Howard Korder; M: David Schwartz. CABLE

My Little Chickadee 🐾🐾🐾 1940 Classic comedy about a gambler and a fallen woman who marry for convenience so they can respectably enter an unsuspecting town. Sparks fly in their adventures together. Fields and West are both at their best playing their larger-than-life selves. 91m/B VHS, DVD, W.C. Fields, Mae West, Joseph Calleia, Dick Foran, Margaret Hamilton, Donald Meek, Ruth Donnelly, Fuzzy Knight; D: Edward F. (Eddie) Cline; W: W.C. Fields, Mae West; C: Joseph Valentine; M: Frank Skinner.

My Little Girl 🐾🐾 1987 (R) A rich Philadelphia girl idealistically volunteers her time to help local institutionalized orphans, but meets with opposition. 118m/C VHS, Mary Stuart Masterson, James Earl Jones, Geraldine Page, Anne Meara, Peter Gallagher, George Newbern; D: Connie Kaiserman.

My Louisiana Sky 🐾🐾½ 2002 Twelve-year-old Tiger Ann (Keel) lives with her grandma Jewel (Knight) and her "slow" parents in Saitler, Louisiana. She's looking forward to the summer when her glamorous aunt, Dorie Kay (Lewis), will visit but Jewel's unexpected death has Tiger Ann re-thinking what matters to her after she goes to live with her aunt in the city. Based on the book by Kimberly Willis Holt. 99m/C VHS, DVD, Kelsey, Keel, Shirley Knight, Juliette Lewis, Karen Robinson, Amelia Campbell, Chris Owens, Michael Cera; D: Adam Arkin; W: Anna Sandor; C: Gavin Smith; M: Mader. CABLE

My Love For Yours 🐾🐾½ Ho-neymoon in Bali 1939 The romantic tale of a young man hoping to win the love of a beautiful but icy girl. A tad silly in parts, but the clever dialogue moves the story along. 99m/B VHS, DVD, Fred MacMurray, Madeleine Carroll; D: Edward H. Griffith.

My Lucky Star 🐾🐾½ 1938 Skating star Henie plays a department store clerk that gets sent off to college to model clothes from the store's sports line. She somehow manages to convince school officials to stage their winter ice show on department store, where she gets to show off her stuff. Don't miss the grand finale, a performance of "Alice in Wonderland Ice Ballet." Based on the story "They Met in Chicago," by Karl Tunberg and Don Ettlinger. "I've Got a Date With a Dream; Could You Pass in Love; This May Be the Night; The All-American Swing; Plymouth University Song. 81m/B VHS Sonja Henie, Richard Greene, Joan Davis, Cesar Romero, Bud-

dy Ebsen, Arthur Treacher, George Barbier, Gypsy Rose Lee; D: Roy Del Ruth; W: Harry Tugend, Jack Yellen.

My Magic Dog 🐾🐾½ 1997 Lucky is eight-year-old Toby's dog. Lucky happens to be invisible. Which turns out to be a good thing when evil Aunt Violet tries to steal Toby's inheritance. 98m/C VHS, DVD, Leo Millbrook, Russ Tamblyn, John Phillip Law; D: John Hough. VIDEO

My Man Adam 🐾🐾 1986 (R) A dreamy, Mitty-esque high schooler falls in love with a girl (Daryl's auburn-haired sister, Page Hannah), and becomes ensnared in a real life crime, leaving his friend to bail him out. Typical boy-meets-girl, boy-gets-in-trouble yarn. 84m/C VHS, Raphael Sbarge, Veronica Cartwright, Page Hannah, Larry B. Scott, Charlie Barnett, Arthur Penderson, Dave Thomas; D: Roger L. Simon.

My Man Godfrey 🐾🐾🐾 1936 Spoiled rich girl Irene Bullock (Lombard) picks up someone she assumes is a bum (Powell) as part of a scavenger hunt and decides to keep him on as her family's butler. In the process, Godfrey teaches her about life, money, and happiness—and that everything is not as it seems. Top-notch screwball comedy defines the genre. Lombard is a stunner alongside the equally charming Powell. Watch for Jane Wyman as an extra in the party scene. Remade in 1957 with June Allyson and David Niven. 95m/B VHS, DVD William Powell, Carole Lombard, Gail Patrick, Alice Brady, Mischa Auer, Eugene Pallette, Alan Mowbray, Franklin Pangborn, Jean Dixon; D: Gregory La Cava, Morrie Ryskind; C: Ted Tetzlaff; M: Charles Previn. Natl. Film Reg. '99.

My Man Godfrey 🐾🐾½ 1957 Inferior remake of the 1936 sophisticated screwball comedy about a butler who brings a touch of the common man to the filthy rich. Niven stars as the butler and Allyson plays the rich girl, but nothing compares to the original roles created by Powell and Lombard. 92m/C VHS, DVD, June Allyson, David Niven, Martha Hyer, Jessie Royce Landis, Robert Keith, Eva Gabor, Jay Robinson, Jeff Donnell; D: Henry Koster; W: Everett Freeman, Peter Berneis, William Bowers; C: William H. Daniels.

My Michael 🐾🐾🐾 1975 Sensitive adaptation of Amos Oz's novel set in Jerusalem in the late 1950s. A young woman is stifled by marriage and the conventions of her bourgeois life and her fantasies begin to take over. In Hebrew with English subtitles. 90m/C VHS, DVD, Susan Blakely, John Saxon, Oded Kotler; D: Dan Wolman.

My Mom's a Werewolf 🐾½ 1989 (PG) An average suburban mother gets involved with a dashing stranger and soon, to her terror, begins to turn into a werewolf. Her daughter and companion must come up with a plan to regain dear, sweet mom. 90m/C VHS, DVD, Susan Blakely, Marilyn McCoo, Marcia Wallace, Diana Barrows; D: Michael Fischa; W: Mark Pirro; C: Bryan England; M: Dana Walden, Barry Fasman.

My Mother Likes Women 🐾🐾 *A mi madre le gustan las mujeres* 2002 Screwy, somewhat strained, Spanish comedy has successful, middle-aged classical pianist Sofia (Sarda), introducing her younger, female lover Eliska (Sirova), a shy Czech immigrant, to her three shocked daughters. Conservative, married Jimena (Pujalte) is the eldest, would-be writer Elvira (Watling) is the neurotic middle child, and the youngest, Sol (Abascal), is a breezy pop singer willing to follow her sisters' opinion. Which is that Eliska is a gold-digger and has to be gotten rid of. Czech and Spanish with subtitles. 96m/C DVD, SP Leonor Watling, Rosa Maria Sarda, Silvia Abascal, Chisco Amado, Alex Angulo, Maria Pujalte, Eliška Sirova, Xabier Elorriaga, Aitor Mazo, Sergio Otegui; D: Ines Paris, Daniela Fejerman; C: Ines Paris, Daniela Fejerman; M: Juan Bardem.

My Mother's Castle 🐾🐾🐾½ *Le Chateau de Ma Mere* 1991 (PG) The second half of the two part film series based on the autobiography of Marcel Pagnol. Picking up where "My Father's Glory" left off,

the family begins a series of vacations in a beautiful country home. Dynamically acted and tenderly directed, charming and suitable for the entire family. In French with English subtitles. 98m/C VHS, DVD, FR Philippe Caubere, Nathalie Roussel, Didier Pain, Therese Liotard, Julien Ciamaca, Victorien Delmare; D: Yves Robert; M: Vladimir Cosma.

My Mother's Courage 🐾🐾 🐾 *Mutters Courage* 1995 Based on writer George Tabori's memoir of his Jewish mother, Elsa (Collins), who managed to escape deportation from Budapest in 1944. Her husband is in prison, her sons have left the country, but an unwavering Elsa remains to care for her asthmatic sister. Finally, she is detained and sent to the railyard to be deported—until she confronts a Nazi official and manages to obtain her release. German with subtitles. 88m/C VHS, DVD, GE Pauline Collins, Ulrich Tukur, Natalie Morse; D: Michael Verhoeven; W: Michael Epp, Theo Bierkes; M: Julian Nott, Simon Verhoeven.

My Mother's Secret Life 🐾½ 1984 Dull drama focusing on a long-forgotten hooker who suddenly appears on her mother's doorstep and discovers that she is really as a high-priced hooker. 100m/C VHS, Loni Anderson, Paul Sorvino, Amanda Wyss, James Sutorius, Sandy McPeak; D: Robert Markowitz; M: Brad Fiedel.

My Mother's Smile 🐾🐾🐾 *L'ora di religione; Il sorriso di mia madre* 2002 Controversial drama about religion and family. Artist—and atheist—Ernesto (Castellitto) is disdainful when he learns from a church emissary that his deceased mother (Conti) is a candidate for canonization. Ernesto loathed his pious, cold mother, who was murdered by his mentally unstable brother, and his attitude deepens the rift with his family, who are looking at monetary and social gains should the beatification take place. Both melodramatic and mystical, the narrative is also sometimes puzzling. Italian with subtitles. 103m/C DVD, IT Sergio Castellitto, Jacqueline Lustig, Chiara Conti, Alberto Mondini, Gianni Schicchi, Maurizio Donadoni, Gigio Alberti; D: Marco Bellocchio; W: Marco Bellocchio; C: Pasquale Mari; M: Riccardo Giagni.

My Name Is Bill W. 🐾🐾 🐾 1989 Woods gave an Emmy-winning performance as Bill Wilson, a successful stockbroker who loses everything in the 1929 crash. Bill turns to alcohol for solace and, after realizing his life is in a downward spiral, forms a support group with Dr. Bob (Garner), which will become Alcoholics Anonymous. 100m/C DVD, James Woods, James Garner, JoBeth Williams, Gary Sinise, Fritz Weaver; D: Daniel Petrie; W: William G. Borchert; C: Neil Roach; M: Laurence Rosenthal. TV

My Name Is Ivan 🐾🐾½ *Ivan's Childhood; The Youngest Spy* 1962 Tarkovsky's first feature film is a vivid, wrenching portrait of a young Soviet boy surviving as a spy behind enemy lines during WWII. Technically stunning, heralding the coming of modern cinema's greatest formalist. In Russian with English subtitles. 84m/B Anonymous. 100m/C DVD, RU Kolya Bunyayev, Valentin Zubkov, Ye Zharikov, S. Krylov; D: Andrei Tarkovsky. Venice Film Fest. '62: Film.

My Name Is Joe 🐾🐾 1998 (R) Set in Glasgow, where the Scots accents prove a distinct challenge in this story of working-class romance. Unemployed alcoholic Joe Kavanagh (Mullan) is 10 months sober and does odd jobs to get by, while coaching the local no-hoper football team. By chance he meets community health worker Sarah (Goodall) and the two are drawn together by their similar outlooks on life and begin a cautious romance. But Joe's loyalty to his mates and his efforts to get his friend Liam (McKay) out of trouble helps to put a strain on the relationship, as does odd jobs to get by, while coaching the local no-hoper football team. By man, Gary Lewis, Lorraine McIntosh; D: Ken Loach; W: Paul Laverty; C: Barry Askroyd; M: George Fenton. Cannes '98: Actor (Mullan).

My Name is Modesty: A Modesty Blaise Adventure 🐾 2004 (R) Based Modesty Blaise: The Beginning on the comic strip/novels by Peter O'Donnell, this cheap quickie filmed in

Romania) was turned out by Miramax so it could retain its rights to the potential franchise. So what we get is mighty Modesty's backstory as an orphan learning to survive in the war-torn Balkans, who winds up working at a small casino in Tangiers. Her criminal boss Louche is killed by bad guy Miklos, who wants what's in Louche's safe and doesn't care how he gets it. Modesty plays roulette with Miklos to save the day (and her fellow workers who are being held hostage). There's little action and Staden is a mannequin in a role that calls for beauty, brains, and butt-kicking. **77m/C DVD.**

My Name Is Nobody *Mio Nome e Nessuno* 1974 (PG) Fast-paced spaghetti-western wherein a cocky, soft-hearted gunfighter is sent to kill the famous, retired outlaw he reveres, but instead they band together. **115m/C VHS, DVD.** *IT* Henry Fonda, Terence Hill, R.G. Armstrong; **D:** Tonino Valerii; **M:** Ennio Morricone.

My Neighbor Totoro 1988 (G) Rather gooey Japanese animated movie about Satsuki and her younger sister Lucy, whose new house in the country is filled with magic, including a friendly creature named Totoro. Totoro is a cuddly, if weird, mix of bear, owl, and seal, with whiskers and a gentle roar. He can fly, has a magic bus, and can only be seen by children. Naturally, every time the two girls get into mischief Totoro is there to rescue them. Dubbed into English. **76m/C VHS, DVD.** *JP* **D:** Hayao Miyazaki; **W:** Hayao Miyazaki; **V:** Frank Welker, Lea Salonga, Timothy Daly, Paul Butcher, Pat Carroll.

My New Gun 1992 (R) Uneven, restless dark comedy about Debbie and Gerald Bender, yuppified suburban couple whose lives are disrupted by a gun. When their newly engaged friends get a gun, Gerry decides they need a gun as well. Debbie is very uncomfortable about having a weapon in the house and doesn't want anything to do with it. When mysterious neighbor LeGros steals the gun, it sets off a bizarre chain of events that culminate at the wedding of their friends. Impressive first effort for writer/director Cochran. **99m/C VHS, DVD.** Diane Lane, Stephen Collins, James LeGros, Tess Harper, Bill Raymond, Bruce Altman, Maddie Corman; **D:** Stacy Cochran; **W:** Stacy Cochran; **M:** Pat Irwin. Cannes '92: Film.

My New Partner *Les Ripoux* 1984 (R) Amiable French comedy in which cynical veteran cop is saddled with straight arrow rookie partner. French Cesars for best film and best director, but remember: They like Jerry Lewis too. In French with English subtitles. **106m/C VHS.** *FR* Philippe Noiret, Thierry Lhermitte, Regine, Grace de Capitani, Claude Brosset, Julien Guiomar; **D:** Claude Zidi; **W:** Claude Zidi; **C:** Jean-Jacques Tarbes; **M:** Francis Lai.

My Night at Maud's *My Night with Maud; Ma Nuit Chez Maud* 1969 Typically subtle Rohmer entry concerns quandary of upright fellow who finds himself drawn to comparatively carefree woman. Talky, somewhat anti-dramatic and film is one of director's Six Moral Tales. You'll either find it fascinating or wish you were watching "Rocky XXIV" instead. In French with English subtitles. **111m/B VHS, DVD.** *FR* Jean-Louis Trintignant, Francoise Fabian, Marie-Christine Barrault, Antoine Vitez; **D:** Eric Rohmer; **W:** Eric Rohmer; **C:** Nestor Almendros. N.Y. Film Critics '70: Screenplay; Natl. Soc. Film Critics '70: Cinematog., Screenplay.

My Old Man 1979 Plucky teen and her seedy horsetrainer father come together over important horse race. Oates makes this one worth watching on a slow evening. Based on a Hemingway story. **102m/C VHS, DVD.** Kristy McNichol, Warren Oates, Eileen Brennan; **D:** John Erman. **TV**

My Old Man's Place 1971 (R) A veteran, with two war buddies and a girl, returns to his father's run-down farm, hoping to fix it up. Sexual tensions arise and violence erupts. **93m/C VHS.** Arthur Kennedy, Michael Moriarty, Mitchell Ryan, William Devane, Topo Swope; **D:** Edwin Sherin.

My Other Husband *Attention! Une Femme Peut en Cacher une Autre* 1985 (PG-13) A woman has two husbands and families, one in Paris and one in Trouville, who eventually meet each other. Seems silly but grows into a sensitive and sad portrait of married life. In French with English subtitles. **110m/C VHS.** *FR* Miou-Miou, Rachid Ferrache, Roger Hanin; **D:** Georges Lautner.

My Outlaw Brother *My Brother, the Outlaw* 1951 A man travelling West to visit his brother in Mexico meets a Texas Ranger on the train. The man discovers that his brother is an outlaw, and teams up with the Ranger to capture him. Based on the novel "South of the Rio Grande" by Max Brand. **82m/B VHS, DVD.** Mickey Rooney, Wanda Hendrix, Robert Preston, Robert Stack, Jose Torvay; **D:** Elliott Nugent; **W:** Gene Fowler Jr.; **C:** Jose Ortiz Ramos.

My Own Country 1998 (R) Abraham Verghese (Andrews) is an Indian immigrant who becomes the head of infectious diseases at the rural Johnson City, Tennessee hospital, where he had interned, in 1985. Considered an outsider, the doctor also finds himself dealing with the area's first AIDS cases, and his patients who are discriminated against. In fact, Verghese becomes so obsessed with their care that he neglects his own wife and children. Based on Verghese's memoirs. **106m/C VHS, DVD.** Naveen Andrews, Glenne Headly, Marisa Tomei, Hal Holbrook, Swoosie Kurtz, Sean Hewitt, William Webster; **D:** Mira Nair; **W:** Sooni Taraporevala, Jim Leonard Jr. **CABLE**

My Own Private Idaho 1991 (R) Director Van Sant of "Drugstore Cowboy" returns to the underworld to examine another group of outsiders, this time young, homosexual hustlers. On the streets of Seattle, narcoleptic hustler Mike meets slumming rich boy Scott, and together they begin a search for Mike's lost mother, which leads them to Idaho and Italy. Stunning visuals, an elliptical plot, and a terrific performance by Phoenix highlight this search for love, the meaning of life, and power. Van Sant couples these activities with scenes from Shakespeare's "Henry IV" for a sometimes inscrutable, but always memorable film. Look for director Richert's Falstaff role as an aging chickenhawk. **105m/C VHS, DVD.** River Phoenix, Keanu Reeves, James Russo, William Richert, Rodney Harvey, Michael Parker, Flea, Chiara Caselli, Udo Kier, Grace Zabriskie, Tom Troupe; **D:** Gus Van Sant; **W:** Gus Van Sant; **C:** John Campbell, Eric Alan Edwards. Ind. Spirit '92: Actor (Phoenix), Screenplay; Natl. Soc. Film Critics '91: Actor (Phoenix).

My Pal, the King 1932 Amusing western with Rooney as the boy king of Ruritania, who's bored with his official duties. He meets Mix, the proprietor of a traveling wild west show which just happens to be performing in the country. Good thing too because Rooney has an evil prime minister who wants the throne for himself and kidnaps the kid. Naturally Mix and his friends arrive to save him in the nick of time. **62m/B VHS.** Tom Mix, Mickey Rooney, Stuart Holmes, Paul Hurst, Noel Francis, James Kirkwood, Jim Thorpe, Clarissa Selwynne; **D:** Kurt Neumann; **W:** Jack Natteford, Thomas J. Crizer; **C:** Daniel B. Clark.

My Pal Trigger 1946 Roy is unjustly imprisoned in this high adventure on the plains. Better than usual script and direction makes this is one of the more entertaining of the singing cowboy's films. **79m/B VHS, DVD.** Roy Rogers, George "Gabby" Hayes, Dale Evans, Jack Holt; **D:** Frank McDonald.

My Pleasure Is My Business 1974 (R) Cinematic autobiography of Xaveria Hollander, the world's most renowned prostitute of the '70s, and the zany occurrences which abound in her profession. **85m/C VHS.** *CA* Xaviera Hollander, Henry Ramer, Colin Fox, Ken Lynch, Jayne (Jane) Eastwood; **D:** Al Waxman.

My Reputation 1946 Dated melodrama. Jessica Drummond (Stanwyck) is an attractive young widow who's lonely and chafing under the restrictions of her overbearing long-widowed mother (Watson). While vacationing with friends, Jess meets Major Scott Landis (Brent) and sparks are struck, though Landis makes it clear he's not interested in marriage. Nevertheless, Jess sees him back in Chicago and gossip follows, thanks to some busybodies, though nothing has actually happened. Jess sets the record straight, Landis has a change of heart, and the ending is rather abrupt and sappy even for the times. Ah yes, the old "wave goodbye at the train station" scenario. Actually filmed in 1944. **94m/B DVD.** Barbara Stanwyck, George Brent, Warner Anderson, Lucile Watson, Eve Arden, John Ridgely, Jerome Cowan; **D:** Curtis Bernhardt; **W:** Catherine Turney; **C:** James Wong Howe; **M:** Max Steiner.

My Samurai 1992 (R) When young Peter McCrea witnesses a gang murder he turns to his martial-arts expert friend Young Park to help him. On the run from both the gang and the police Peter learns self-defense and the courage to face his fears. **87m/C VHS.** Julian Lee, Mako, Terry O'Quinn, Bubba Smith, Jim Turner, Carlos Palomino, John Kallo; **D:** Fred Dresch.

My Science Project 1985 (PG) Teenager Stockwell stumbles across a crystal sphere with a funky light. Unaware that it is an alien time-travel device, he takes it to school to use as a science project in a last-ditch effort to avoid failing his class. Chaos follows and Stockwell and his chums find themselves battling gladiators, mutants, and dinosaurs. Plenty of special effects and a likeable enough, dumb teenage flick. **94m/C VHS, DVD.** John Stockwell, Danielle von Zerneck, Fisher Stevens, Raphael Sbarge, Richard Masur, Barry Corbin, Ann Wedgeworth, Dennis Hopper, Candace Silvers, Beau Dremann, Pat Simmons, Pamela Springsteen; **D:** Jonathan Betuel; **M:** Peter Bernstein.

My Sex Life... Or How I Got into an Argument *Ma Vie Sexuelle...Comment Je Me Suis Dispute* 1996 Paul (Amalric) is unhappy personally and professionally. He's a bored grad student/assistant professor of philosophy and breaking up with lover of ten years, Esther (Devos). Soon Paul's romancing other women, one of whom, Sylvia (Denicourt), is already involved with Paul's best friend Nathan (Salinger). Very talky and Frenchly intellectual. French with subtitles. **178m/C VHS, DVD.** *FR* Mathieu Amalric, Marianne (Cuau) Denicourt, Emmanuelle Devos, Emmanuel Salinger, Jeanne Balibar, Michel Vuillermoz; **D:** Arnaud Desplechin; **W:** Arnaud Desplechin, Emmanuel Bourdieu; **C:** Eric Gautier; **M:** Krishna Levy.

My Side of the Mountain 1969 (G) A 13-year-old boy decides to emulate his idol, Henry David Thoreau, and gives up his home and his family to live in the Canadian mountains. **100m/C VHS, DVD,** *CA* Teddy Eccles, Theodore Bikel; **D:** James B. Clark.

My Sister Eileen 1955 Ruth and Eileen are two small-town Ohio sisters who move to Manhattan seeking excitement. They live in a basement apartment in Greenwich Village with an assortment of oddball tenants as they pursue success and romance. Everyone is daffy and charming, as is the film. Fun, but unmemorable songs, however the terrific choreography is by Fosse, who also appears as one sister's suitor. Remake of a 1942 film which was based on a Broadway play which was based on a series of autobiographical stories published in the New Yorker. The play was later turned into a Broadway musical known as "Wonderful Town," which has nothing to do with this version of the original stories. ♫Give Me a Band and My Baby; It's Bigger Than You and Me; There's Nothing Like Love; As Soon As They See Eileen; I'm Great; Conga; Atmosphere. **108m/C VHS, DVD.** Janet Leigh, Betty Garrett, Jack Lemmon, Bob Fosse, Kurt Kasznar, Dick York, Lucy Marlow, Tommy (Thomas) Rall, Barbara Brown, Horace McMahon; **D:** Richard Quine; **W:** Blake Edwards, Richard Quine; **M:** Jule Styne.

My Sister, My Love *The Mafu Cage* 1978 (R) Odd tale of two sisters' incestuous relationship and what happens when one of them takes another lover. The cage of the alternate titles refers to the place where their pet apes are kept and seems to symbolize the confining nature of their life together. **102m/C VHS, DVD.** Lee Grant, Carol Kane, Will Geer, James Olson; **D:** Karen Arthur.

My Sister's Keeper 2002 Christina (Bates) and her sister Judy (Perkins) couldn't have more different lives. Christina struggles to cope with her schizophrenia and her dependence on others while Judy is a work-obsessed art editor in New York. When their mother Helen (Redgrave) dies, Judy is suddenly responsible for Christina's care and they must struggle to accept and support one another. Based on the memoir by Margaret Moorman. **98m/C VHS, DVD.** Kathy Bates, Elizabeth Perkins, Lynn Redgrave, Bobby Harwell, Kimberly J. Brown, Hallee Hirsh, Kathleen Wilhoite, Jascha Washington; **D:** Ron Lagomarsino; **W:** Susan Tarr; **C:** Lloyd Ahern II; **M:** Lawrence Shragge. **TV**

My Son, My Son 1940 The spoiled son (Hayward) of a successful businessman (Aherne) doesn't think twice about making everyone miserable in his quest to get everything he wants. He even goes as far as trying to steal his dad's new bride. When world war comes, he has a chance to redeem himself. Melodrama is kept from sinking to overwrought soap opera by Hayward and Aherne. **115m/B VHS.** Louis Hayward, Brian Aherne, Scotty Beckett, Lionel Belmore, Laraine Day, Madeleine Carroll, Henry Hull, Howard Davies, Pat Flaherty, Leyland Hodgson, Josephine Hutchinson, Sophie Stewart, Stanley Logan; **D:** Charles Vidor; **W:** Lenore Coffee; **C:** Harry Strading Sr.

My Son the Fanatic 1997 (R) Pakistani immigrant Parvez (Puri) has been driving a cab in Bradford, England and trying to fit in his new country for 25 years. He ekes out a living driving prostitutes around town, which leads to a relationship with hooker Bettina (Griffiths). His working-class life is disrupted when Parvez realizes his son, Farid (Kurtha) is exploring his cultural roots by turning to Islamic fundamentalism. Moral and religious tensions lead to a climactic conflict between father and son. **86m/C VHS, DVD.** *GB* Om Puri, Rachel Griffiths, Stellan Skarsgard, Akbar Kurtha; **D:** Udayan Prasad; **W:** Hanif Kureishi; **C:** Alan Almond; **M:** Stephen Warbeck.

My Son, the Vampire *Mother Riley Meets the Vampire; The Vampire and the Robot; Vampire Over London; Mother Riley Meets the Vampire* 1952 Last of Britain's Old Mother Riley series in which Lucan plays the Irish housekeeper who thinks he's a vampire and wants to take over the world with his giant robot. Mother Riley interferes. Theme song by Alan Sherman. **72m/B VHS, DVD.** *GB* Bela Lugosi, Arthur Lucan, Dora Bryan, Richard Wattis; **D:** John Gilling; **W:** Val Valentine; **C:** Stanley Pavey.

My Song Goes Round the World 1934 Chronicles the romantic foibles of a singing trio and the one girl they decide they all love. **68m/B VHS.** Joseph Schmidt, John Loder, Charlotte Ander; **D:** Richard Oswald.

My Stepmother Is an Alien 1988 (PG-13) When eccentric physicist Aykroyd sends a message beam to another galaxy on a stormy night, the last thing he expects is a visit from beautiful alien Basinger. Unfortunately, he does not realize that this gorgeous blonde is an alien and he continues to court her despite her rather odd habits. Only the daughter seems to notice the strange goings on, and her dad ignores her warnings, enabling Basinger's evil sidekick to continue in its plot to take over the Earth. **108m/C VHS, DVD.** Dan Aykroyd, Kim Basinger, Jon Lovitz, Alyson Hannigan, Joseph Maher, Seth Green, Wesley Mann, Adrian Sparks, Juliette Lewis, Tanya Fenmore; **D:** Richard Benjamin; **W:** Jerico Stone, Herschel Weingrod, Timothy Harris, Jonathan Reynolds; **C:** Richard H. Kline; **M:** Alan Silvestri.

My Summer of Love 2005 (R) Teenaged Mona (Press) lives with her ex-con brother, Phil (Considine), over the closed family pub in a dull Yorkshire village. Phil has become a born-again

My Summer Story 🐾🐾½ *It Runs in the Family* 1994 (PG) Humorist Shepherd and director Clark re-team for another period family comedy in the tradition of their first collaboration, "A Christmas Story," now a video classic. This time the Parkers find themselves battling their crazy new neighbors, the Bumpus family, Ralphie (Kieran Culkin) has troubles with a neighborhood bully and tries to bond with his dad (Grodin) while fishing, and mom (Steenburgen) goes loopy over gravy boats. Charming family fun. Based on Shepherd's novels "In God We Trust, All Others Pay Cash" and "Wanda Hickey's Night of Golden Memories and Other Disasters." 85m/C VHS, DVD. Charles Grodin, Mary Steenburgen, Kieran Culkin, Chris Culkin, Al Mancini, Troy Evans, Glenn Shadix, Dick O'Neill, Wayne Grace; D: Bob (Benjamin) Clark; W: Jean Shepherd, Bob (Benjamin) Clark, Leigh Brown; C: Stephen M. Katz; M: Paul Zaza; Nar: Jean Shepherd.

My Super Ex-Girlfriend 🐾🐾 2006 (PG-13) "Fatal Attraction" meets "Wonder Woman" in this weak effort from veteran director Ivan Reitman. Uma Thurman plays the dual role of Jenny Johnson, Manhattan art curator by day, and G-Girl, crime-fighting superheroine at night, who, unfortunately for her unsuspecting new boyfriend, Matt (Luke Wilson), is super-insecure as well. When Matt makes the mistake of dumping the possessive Jenny, she unleashes the fury of her powers on him. Reitman doesn't know what he wants—comedy, girl-power statement, relationships/date movie—and fails on all fronts as a result. 96m/C DVD. US Uma Thurman, Luke Wilson, Anna Faris, Rainn Wilson, Eddie Izzard, Wanda Sykes, Mark Consuelos; D: Ivan Reitman; W: Don Payne; C: Don Burgess; M: Teddy Castellucci.

My Sweet Charlie 🐾🐾½ 1970 Unwed, pregnant white woman hides out with black lawyer in backwater Texas. Better than it sounds, with nice performances by Duke and Freeman. 97m/C VHS. Patty Duke, Al Freeman Jr., Ford Rainey, William Hardy, Chris Wilson, Archie Moore, Noble Willingham; D: Lamont Johnson. TV

My Sweet Little Village 🐾🐾½ 1986 Gentle comedy set in a rural village and dealing with everyday events, including a romantic teenager who develops a crush on a schoolteacher, an adulterous wife and her boyfriend, the accident-prone doctor, a Laurel and Hardy duo of truck drivers, and others. Czech with subtitles. 100m/C VHS, CZ Rudolf Hrusinsky, Janos Ban, Marian Labuda, Milena Dvorska, Ladislav Zupanic, Petr Cepek; D: Jiri Menzel; W: Zdenek Sverak; C: Jaromir Sofr; M: Jiri Sust.

My Sweet Suicide 🐾🐾 1998 Very low-budget comedy about staging the perfect suicide. Depressed Kevin (Aldrich) can't even manage to kill himself. He confides his dilemma to eccentric bookstore clerk Thompson, who agrees to help him out. 78m/C VHS. Matthew Aldrich, Michelle Leigh Thompson, Eric Wheeler; D: David Michael Flanagan.

My Sweet Victim 🐾 *Murder: By Reason of Insanity* 1985 A young couple who recently moved to the United States from Poland try to make a go of their own business. The business fails, and so does their marriage. Will it end in murder? 92m/ C VHS. Candice Bergen, Jurgen Prochnow, Michael Flanagan.

My Teacher Ate My Homework 🐾🐾 *Shadow Zone: My Teacher Ate My Homework* 1998 (PG) Jesse is convinced that his teacher Mrs. Fink has it in for him. When he finds a doll that looks just like her, Jesse can live out all his revenge fantasies but bad things start happening when the doll takes on an attitude of its own. Based on J.R. Black's "Shadowzone" books. 91m/C VHS, DVD, CA MacKenzie Gray, Gregory Edward Smith, Shelley Duvall, Dara Perlmutter, Tim Progosh, Shelley McCarthy, Edwin Hodge, Dan Warry-Smith, Dana Theodore, John Novak, Karen Robinson, Margot Kidder, Damon D'Oliveira; D: Stephen Williams; W: Garfield Reeves-Stevens, Judith Reeves-Stevens; C: Curtis Petersen; M: John McCarthy. VIDEO

My Teacher's Wife 🐾🐾½ 1995 (R) High-schooler London has big college plans, which won't get anywhere if he doesn't pass math. So he asks Carrere to tutor him, only the problems they study become more personal. 90m/C VHS, DVD, CA Tia Carrere, Jason London, Christopher McDonald, Leslie Lyles, Zak Orth, Jeffrey Tambor; D: Bruce Leddy; W: Bruce Leddy, Seth Greenland; C: Bruce Leddy; M: Kevin Gilbert. VIDEO

My Therapist woof! 1984 A sex therapist's boyfriend cannot bear the thought of her having intercourse with others as part of her work. Soft core. 81m/C VHS. Marilyn Chambers; D: Gary Legon.

My Tutor 🐾½ 1982 (R) When a high school student is in danger of flunking French, his parents hire a private tutor to teach him the lessons. It becomes clear that his studies will involve many more subjects, however. Standard teen sex comedy. 97m/C VHS, DVD. Caren Kaye, Matt Lattanzi, Kevin McCarthy, Clark Brandon, Bruce Bauer, Arlene Golonka, Crispin Glover, Shelley Taylor Morgan, Amber Denyse Austin, Francesca "Kitten" Natividad, Jewel Shepard, Marilyn Tokuda; D: George Bowers; M: Joe Roberts; C: Mac Ahlberg; W: Webster Lewis.

My Twentieth Century 🐾🐾🐾 *Az en XX. Szazadom* 1990 This quirky gem of a movie is a charming, sentimental journey through the early 1900s. Twins Dora and Lili are separated in early childhood. They reunite as grown, very different women on the Orient Express after they both (unknowingly) have sex with the same man. Dora is a sex kitten, while Lili is a radical equipped with explosives. When the two sisters come together, they both lose their destructive, dependent selves (Dora on men, Lili on politics) and become independent women. Lots of sidelights and subjects that are sure to amuse the viewer. In Hungarian with English subtitles. 104m/B VHS, HU CA Dorotha Segda, Oleg (Yankovsky) Jankovsky, Peter Andorai, Gabor Mate, Paulus Manker, Laszlo Vidovszky; D: Ildiko Enyedi; W: Ildiko Enyedi.

My Uncle 🐾🐾½ 1996 (PG) Kelly, President Sullivan's teenaged daughter, travels to L.A. to visit a children's shelter at Christmas. When she finds out the shelter needs money to stay open, she eludes the Secret Service and does have someone watching out for her—no, not a guardian angel, a guardian girl! As his obsession grows, his behavior becomes stranger. Interesting and well-acted. The early 1900s. Summer in the early 1900s. Charlotte Rampling, Joe Prosperor, Annabelle Apsion; D: Philip Saville. TV

My Uncle Silas 🐾🐾½ 2001 Finney certainly has fun in the title role as an aging reprobate (with an eye for the ladies) who teaches his 10-year-old grand-nephew Edward (Prospero) how to enjoy life. Based on the short stories by H.E. Bates and set during a rural English summer in the early 1900s. TV

The Mysterians 🐾🐾½ *Chikyu Boeigun* 1958 A race of gigantic scientific intellects from a doomed planet attempts to conquer Earth. They want to rebuild their race by reproducing with earth women. Earth fights back. From the director of "Godzilla." Dubbed in English from Japanese. 85m/C VHS, DVD, JP Kenji Sahara, Yumi Shirakawa, Takashi Shimura; D: Inoshiro Honda.

Mysteries 🐾½ 1984 A rich tourist becomes obsessed by a beautiful local girl. 100m/C VHS, DVD. Rutger Hauer, Sylvia Kristel, David Rappaport, Rita Tushingham; D: Paul de Lussanet.

Mysterious Desperado 🐾½ 1949 Young man, about to inherit a large estate, is framed on a murder charge by land grabbers. 61m/B VHS. Tim Holt, Richard Martin, Edward Norris, Movita, Frank Wilcox, William Tannen, Robert "Bob" Livingston, Robert B. Williams; D: Lesley Selander; W: Norman Houston; C: Nicholas Musuraca; M: Paul Sawtell.

The Mysterious Dr. Fu Manchu 🐾½ 1929 Early talkie with Oland starring as evil Fu Manchu. Fu vows vengeance on the English Petrie family, whom he holds responsible for the deaths of his loved ones during the Boxer Rebellion. He hypnotizes sweet Lia (Arthur) to do his fiendish bidding but the Petries are warned by Scotland Yard to be on the lookout. Based on the novel by Sax Rohmer. Followed by "The Return of Dr. Fu Manchu." 80m/B VHS. Warner Oland, Jean Arthur, O.P. Heggie, William Austin, Claude King, Noble Johnson; D: Rowland V. Lee; W: Lloyd Corrigan, Florence Ryerson; C: Harry Fischbeck.

Mysterious Doctor Satan 🐾🐾 1940 A mad satanic scientist builds an army of mechanical robots to rob and terrorize the nation. In 15 episodes. 250m/B VHS. William "Billy" Newell, C. Montagus Shaw, Dorothy Herbert, Charles Trowbridge, Eduardo Ciannelli, Robert Wilcox, Ella Neal; D: John English, William Witney; W: Frank (Franklyn) Adreon, Joseph Poland, Barney A. Sarecky; C: William Nobles.

Mysterious Island 🐾🐾½ 1961 Exhilarating sci-fi classic adapted from Jules Verne's novel about escaping Civil War soldiers who go up in Verne balloon and come down on a Pacific island populated by giant animals. They also encounter two shipwrecked English ladies, pirates, and Captain Nemo (and his sub). Top-rate special effects by master Ray Harryhausen. 101m/C VHS, DVD, GB Michael Craig, Joan Greenwood, Michael Callan, Gary Merrill, Herbert Lom, Beth Rogan, Percy Herbert, Dan Jackson, Nigel Green; D: Cy Endfield; M: John Prebble, Daniel Ullman, Crane Wilbur; C: Wilkie Cooper; M: Bernard Herrmann.

Mysterious Island of Beautiful Women 🐾 1979 Amid soft-focus nudity, a husband and his lover conspire to institutionalize his wife. 90m/C VHS. Amber Lee, Sandy Carey.

Mysterious Jane 🐾 1981 Amid soft-focus nudity, a male sextet is stranded on a South Sea island, where they must encure the films of an angry tribe of conveniently bikini-clad women. 100m/C VHS, DVD. Jamie Lyn Bauer, Jayne Kennedy, Kathryn Davis, Deborah Shelton, Susie Coelho, Peter Lawford, Steven Keats, Clint Walker; D: Joseph Pevney.

The Mysterious Lady 🐾🐾½ 1928 Pre-Ninotchka Garbo plays Russian spy who betrays her mother country because she does not want to be alone. 99m/ B VHS, DVD. Greta Garbo, Conrad Nagel, Gustav von Seyffertitz, Richard Alexander, Albert Pollet, Edward Connelly; C: William H. Daniels.

The Mysterious Magician 🐾🐾½ 1965 Entertaining suspense story of the mad murderer known as "The Wizard," who was thought by Scotland Yard to be dead, but the current murderwave in London suggests otherwise. Based on an Edgar Wallace story. 95m/C VHS, GE Joachim Fuchsberger, Eddi Arent, Sophie Hardy, Karl John, Heinz Drache; D: Alfred Vohrer.

Mysterious Mr. Moto 🐾🐾 1938 Mr. Moto (Lorre) poses as a criminal to escape with killer Paul Brissac (Ames) from Devil's Island. Brissac is part of a gang of assassins, operating out of London, and Moto is not only after their leader (Wilcoxon) who is being blackmailed by the gang. 5th in the series. 63m/B DVD. Peter Lorre, Leon Ames, Henry Wilcoxon, Mary Maguire, Erik Rhodes, Harold Huber, Frederick Vogeding; D: Norman Foster; W: Norman Foster, Philip MacDonald; C: Virgil Miller; M: Samuel Kaylin.

Mysterious Mr. Wong 🐾🐾 1935 The Thirteen Coins of Confucius put San Francisco's Chinatown in a state of terror until Mr. Wong arrives. 56m/B VHS. Bela Lugosi, Arline Judge, Wallace Ford, E. Alyn (Fred) Warren, Lotus Long; D: William Nigh; W: Nina Howatt; C: Harry Neumann.

Myra Breckinridge woof! 1970 Softcore gristle out of a beautiful tramp climbing the social ladder via the boudoir. A tasteless version of the Gore Vidal novel. An alleged satire of a film critic who undergoes a sex change operation and then plots the destruction of the American male movie star stereotype. Created an outcry from all sides, and hung out to dry by studio where it is reportedly still blowing in the wind. 94m/C VHS, DVD. Mae West, John Huston, Raquel Welch, Rex Reed, Farrah Fawcett, Jim Backus, John Carradine, Andy Devine, Tom Selleck; D: Michael Sarne; W: Michael Sarne, David Giler; C: Richard Moore; M: Lionel Newman.

Myrt and Marge 🐾½ 1933 Vail and daughter Damerel repeat their radio serial roles as sisters Myrt Minter and Marge Spear, two chorus girls in a popular Broadway show. The Three Stooges provide some laughs. 62m/B VHS, Myrtle Vail, Eddie Foy Jr., Trixie Friganza, Ted Healy, Bonita Damerel, Curly Howard, Moe Howard, Larry Fine; D: Al Boasberg; W: Al Boasberg, Beatrice Banyerd; C: Joseph Valentina.

My Very Best Friend 🐾🐾 1996 (PG) Former model Dana Griffin (Smith) has the good life and seems to have latched onto the prize when a multi-millionaire (Mason) proposes marriage. But Dana has a nasty habit of lying and when things fall, she turns to her oldest friend, Barbara (Eikenberry) to help rebuild her life. But instead of rebuilding her own life, Dana decides she'd just rather take over Barbara's. 92m/C VHS, Jaclyn Smith, Jill Eikenberry, Tom Mason, Torri Irwin, Mary Kay Place, Garwin Sanford, Robert Lewis, Beverley Elliott; D: Joyce Chopra; W: John Robert Bensink; C: James Glennor; M: Patrick Williams. TV

My Wicked, Wicked Ways 🐾🐾½ 1984 Cleverly cast, low-budget drama based on the autobiography of Errol Flynn. 95m/C VHS, Duncan Regehr, Barbara Hershey, Hal Linden, Darren McGavin; D: Don Taylor. TV

My Wife is an Actress 🐾🐾½ *Ma Femme est une Actrice* 2001 (R) Yvan (Attal) is a TV sports journalist married to famous actress Charlotte (Gainsbourg). He's irritated by the attention and jealous of her co-stars when she films sex scenes. Charlotte's off to London for her latest project, with a courtly and seductive older leading man, John (Stamp). Charlotte can't understand her husband's neuroses and Yvan's fretting increases. Self-mocking and frequently charming although the sub-plot concerning Yvan's pregnant sister is an unnecessary distraction. French with subtitles. 93m/C VHS, DVD. FR Yvan Attal, Charlotte Gainsbourg, Terence Stamp, Noemie Lvovsky, Ludivine Sagnier, Keith Allen, Lionel Abelanski, Laurent Bateau, Jo McInnes; D: Yvan Attal; W: Yvan Attal; C: Remy Chevrin.

My Wonderful Life 🐾 1990 (R) Softcore gristle about a beautiful tramp climbing the social ladder via the boudoir. 107m/C VHS. IT Pierre Cosso, Jean Rochefort, Massimo Venturiello, Carol Alt, Elliott Gould; D: Carlo Vanzina.

The Mysterious Rider ✍✍ ½ 1938 *The Fighting Phantom* 1933 A cowboy tries to prevent unscrupulous homesteaders from being cheated out of their land. 59m/B VHS, DVD. Kent Taylor, Lona Andre, Gail Patrick, Warren Hymer, Berton Churchill; *D:* Fred Allen.

The Mysterious Rider ✍½ *Mark of the Avenger* 1938 A man framed for murder must help innocent homesteaders from being cheated out of their land. 75m/B VHS. Douglass Dumbrille, Sidney Toler, Russell Hayden, Charlotte Field; *D:* Lesley Selander.

The Mysterious Rider ✍✍ 1942 Routine oater has Crabbe and St. John helping a couple of kids protect their inheritance. 56m/B VHS. Buster Crabbe, Al "Fuzzy" St. John, Caroline Burke, John Merton, Kermit Maynard, Jack Ingram, Charles "Slim" Whitaker; *D:* Sam Newfield.

Mysterious Skin ✍✍✍ 2004 (NC-17) As 8-year-olds in 1981, clumsy Brian and athletic Neil both play for the same Kansas Little League team. They have something else in common; both are sexually abused by their Coach (Sage). By 1991, Neil (Gordon-Levitt) has become a reckless hustler—first in his dull hometown and later in New York, where he's followed his best friend Wendy (Trachtenberg). Brian (Corbet) has grown into an awkward misfit who (having suppressed the abuse) believes he was abducted and experimented upon by aliens. He has a vague memory of Neil and decides to track the other teen down to find out what really happened—a confrontation that takes place in a challenging scene set on Christmas Eve. Araki displays a fearless candor in showing the damage that was wrought without exploiting his inflammatory subject matter Both leads give strong, gut-wrenching performances. Based on the 1995 novel by Scott Heims. 103m/C DVD. *US* Brady Corbet, Joseph Gordon-Levitt, Michelle Trachtenberg, Elisabeth Shue, Jeff(rey) Licon, Mary Lynn Rajskub, Chris Mulkey, Richard Riehle, Lisa Long, Billy Drago, William Sage, George Webster, Chase Ellison; *D:* Gregg Araki; *W:* Gregg Araki; *C:* Steve Gainer; *M:* Harold Budd, Robin Guthrie.

The Mysterious Stranger ✍✍ 1982 Printer's apprentice is given to bouts of daydreaming about a magic castle in Austria. Based on Twain tale. 89m/C VHS. Chris Makepeace, Lance Kerwin, Fred Gwynne; *D:* Peter H. Hunt.

Mysterious Two ✍✍½ 1982 Two aliens visit the Earth in an effort to enlist converts to travel the universe with them. 100m/C VHS, DVD. John Forsythe, Priscilla Pointer, Noah Beery Jr., Vic Tayback, James Stephens, Karen Werner, Robert Englund, Robert Pine; *D:* Gary Sherman.

Mystery, Alaska ✍✍½ 1999 (R) Amiable sports comedy that plays like a TV movie (with a little more sex and language). Journalist and ex-local Charles Danner (Azaria) does a Sports Illustrated feature on his hometown's weekly cutthroat hockey game. Danner's story draws NHL interest and, for a publicity stunt, the New York Rangers fly in for an exhibition game. This heads up hurt feelings since aging team captain (and local sheriff) John Biebe (Crowe) is asked to step aside for young phenom Stevie Weeks (Northcott). Expect cliches. 118m/C VHS, DVD. Russell Crowe, Hank Azaria, Mary McCormack, Burt Reynolds, Ron Eldard, Lolita (David) Davidovich, Colm Meaney, Maury Chaykin, Ryan Northcott, Scott Grimes, Judith Ivey, Rachel Wilson, Mike Myers; *Cameos:* Little Richard; *D:* Jay Roach; *W:* David E. Kelley, Sean O'Byrne; *C:* Peter Deming; *M:* Carter Burwell.

Mystery Date ✍✍ 1991 (PG-13) A sort of teen version of "After Hours," in which a shy college guy gets a date with the girl of his dreams, only to be mistaken for a master criminal and pursued by gangsters, police and a crazed florist. Not terrible, but if you're old enough to drive you're probably too old to watch with amusement. 98m/C VHS, DVD. Ethan Hawke, Teri Polo, Brian McNamara, Fisher Stevens, B.D. Wong; *D:* Jonathan Wacks; *W:* Terry Runte, Parker Bennett; *M:* John Du Prez.

Mystery in Swing ✍✍ 1940 An all-black mystery with music, about a trumpet player who has snake venom put on his mouthpiece. 66m/B VHS. F.E. (Flourney) Miller, Monte Hawley, Marguerite Whitten, Tommie Moore, Ceepee Johnson; *D:* Arthur Dreifuss.

Mystery Island ✍✍½ Beautifully filmed underwater scenes in this children's film about four youths who discover a deserted island which they name Mystery Island, and a retired pirate who lives there. When the children find counterfeit money and the bad guys return for it, the old pirate's clever plans keep the kids safe. 75m/C VHS. AU Jayson Duncan, Niklas Juhlin, Mozelle McGlinchey, Melissa Woodhams; *D:* Gene W. Scott; *W:* Clifford Green, Geoff Beak; *C:* Phil Pike.

Mystery Kids ✍✍½ 1999 (PG) Preteens Herford and Baltes spend their summer snooping into the disappearance of high school girl Lakin in order to claim a reward. They first think her boyfriend killed her but then discover Lakin has just run away and is working as a singer in a local bar. So the kids decide to try and reconcile the troubled teen with her family. Innocuous family fare but the two would-be sleuths are good. 88m/C VHS, DVD. Brighton Herford, Jameson Baltes, Christine Lakin; *D:* Lynn Hamrick. VIDEO

Mystery Liner ✍✍½ *The Ghost of John Holling* 1934 Dead bodies are found aboard ocean liner and passengers are concerned about it. Slow-moving sea cruise. 62m/B VHS, DVD. Noah Beery Sr., Astrid Allwyn, Cornelius Keefe, Gustav von Seyffertitz, Edwin Maxwell, Boothe Howard, George "Gabby" Hayes; *D:* William Nigh.

The Mystery Man ✍✍½ 1935 A Chicago reporter goes on a drinking binge and ends up in St. Louis. There he stumbles upon a mystery which may involve the paper for which he works. He teams up with a beautiful woman to try to crack the case. 65m/B VHS, DVD. Robert Armstrong, Maxine Doyle, Henry Kolker, Leroy Mason, James Burke; *D:* Ray McCarey.

Mystery Man ✍✍ 1944 Below-average episode has rancher Hoppy being bothered by rustlers. Boyd solves things in the usual way, while Clyde provides the laughs. 58m/B VHS, DVD. William Boyd, Andy Clyde, Jimmy Rogers, Don Costello, Francis McDonald, Forrest Taylor, Eleanor Stewart; *D:* George Archainbaud.

Mystery Mansion ✍✍ 1983 (PG) Fortune in gold and a hundred-year-old mystery lead three children into an exciting treasure hunt. Family fare. 95m/C VHS, DVD. Dallas McKennon, Greg Wynne, Jane Ferguson, Barry Hostetler; *D:* David S. Jackson; *W:* David S. Jackson; *C:* Milas C. Hinshaw; *M:* William Loose.

Mystery Men ✍✍½ 1999 (PG-13) A cast of quirky comedy all-stars, including Garofalo, Stiller and Macy, help deflate the superhero genre by playing a team of bush league crimefighters. The superhero washouts use their dubious powers to save Champion City from party monster villain Casanova Frankenstein (Rush), who has kidnapped real superhero Captain Amazing (Kinnear). Great concept and dialogue are stretched a bit thin over the long running time. Based on the Dark Horse comic book. 120m/C VHS, DVD, HD DVD. Ben Stiller, Hank Azaria, William H. Macy, Paul (Pee-wee Herman) Reubens, Claire Forlani, Wes Studi, Janeane Garofalo, Kel Mitchell, Geoffrey Rush, Lena Olin, Greg Kinnear, Tom Waits, Eddie Izzard, Ricky Jay, Louise Lasser, Stacey Travis, Artie Lange, Jenifer Lewis, Pras, Dane Cook; *D:* Kinka Usher; *W:* Neil Cuthbert; *C:* Stephen Burum; *M:* Stephen Warbeck.

Mystery Mountain ✍½ 1934 Twelve episodes depict the villain known as the "Rattler" attempting to stop the construction of a railroad over Mystery Mountain. 156m/B VHS, DVD. Ken Maynard, Gene Autry, Smiley Burnette; *D:* Otto Brower, B. Reeves Eason.

The Mystery of Alexina ✍½ *Mystere Alexina* 1986 True story of Herculine Adelaide Barbin, a 19th-century French hermaphrodite, who, after growing up a woman, fell in love with another woman and was actually revealed to be a man. Subtitled. 86m/C VHS. *FR* Vuillemin, Valeri Stroh; *D:* Rene Feret; *W:* Jean Gruault.

The Mystery of Edwin Drood ✍✍½ 1935 Nicely creepy gothic atmosphere highlights this version of Charles Dickens' final novel, which was unfinished at the time of his death. English choirmaster and opium addict John Jasper (Rains) is visited by his nephew Edwin Drood (Manners), who's soon to enter into an arranged marriage with Rosa (Angel). Unbeknownst to anyone, Jasper has long desired Rosa for himself and kills his nephew in a jealous rage. Now that Drood's disappeared, will Jasper have Rosa to himself? 85m/B VHS. Claude Rains, Heather Angel, Douglass Montgomery, Valerie Hobson, David Manners, Francis L. Sullivan, Ethel Griffies, E.E. Clive; *D:* Stuart Walker; *W:* John Lloyd Balderston, Gladys Unger; *C:* George Robinson; *M:* Edward Ward.

The Mystery of Edwin Drood ✍✍½ 1993 When Edwin Drood vanishes on Christmas Eve, his disappearance leads to a terrifying mystery that unfolds amidst the slums of Victorian England. Adapted from Charles Dickens' last novel, which was left unfinished at his death. 98m/C VHS. *GB* Robert Powell, Michelle Evans, Jonathan Phillips, Finty Williams, Rupert Rainsford, Nanette Newman, Freddie Jones, Rosemary Leach, Ronald Fraser; *D:* Timothy Forder; *W:* Timothy Forder.

Mystery of Mr. Wong ✍½ 1939 The largest star sapphire in the world, the "Eye of the Daughter of the Moon," is stolen from a museum in its home country of China. Mr. Wong becomes involved in trying to trace its trail and the perpetrator of the murders that follow in its wake. One in the series of detective films. 67m/B VHS, DVD. Boris Karloff, Grant Withers, Dorothy Tree, Lotus Long; *D:* William Nigh.

The Mystery of Rampo ✍✍✍ 1994 (R) Visually dazzling fantasy that propels mystery writer Edogawa Rampo (Takenaka) into his own stories. Set just before WWII, Rampo is despondent when his latest novel (about a woman suffocating her husband in a trunk) is censored by the government and then amazed when a newspaper story reveals a similar crime. So Rampo decides to meet the widow Shizuko (Hada) and discovers she's a double again finds reality and fiction blending into the bizarre. Rampo was the pseudonym for renowned writer Hirai Taro, regarded as the Japanese Edgar Allan Poe. The film had its own complications when the version filmed by original director Rentaro Mayusumi was rejected by producer Okuyama, who then reshot much of the film himself. Japanese with subtitles. 96m/C VHS, DVD. *JP* Naoto Takenaka, Michiko Hada, Masahiro Motoki, Teruyuki Kagawa, Mikijiro Hira; *D:* Kazuyoshi Okuyama; *W:* Kazuyoshi Okuyama, Yuhei Enoki; *C:* Yasushi Sasakibara; *M:* Akira Senju.

Mystery of the Hooded Horseman ✍✍ 1937 Tex finds himself pitted against a very strange adversary. 61m/B VHS, DVD. Tex Ritter, Iris Meredith, Charles "Blackie" King, Joseph Girard, Late (Lafayette) McKee; *D:* Ray Taylor.

The Mystery of the Mary Celeste ✍✍ *The Phantom Ship; The Mystery of the Marie Celeste* 1935 Tale of terror based on the bizarre case of the "Marie Celeste," an American ship found adrift off the coast of England with her sails set but minus any of her crew on December 5, 1872. 64m/B VHS, DVD. Bela Lugosi, Shirley Grey, Edmund Willard, Arthur Margetson, Dennis Hoey, George Mozart, Ben Welden, Clifford McLaglen; *D:* Denison Clift; *W:* Denison Clift; *C:* Eric Cross, Geoffrey Faithfull.

Mystery of the Million Dollar Hockey Puck ✍½ 1975 Sinister diamond smugglers learn a lesson on ice from a pair of orphan lads. Features the National Hockey League's Montreal Canadians in one of their few film appearances. 88m/C VHS. Michael MacDonald, Angele Knight; *D:* Jean LaFleur, Peter Svatek.

Mystery of the Riverboat ✍✍½ 1944 Louisiana and the Mississippi River are the background for these 13 episodes of mystery and murder. 90m/B VHS. Robert Lowery, Eddie Quillan, Lyle Talbot, Francis McDonald, Arthur Hohl; *D:* Ray Taylor, Lewis D. Collins.

Mystery of the Wax Museum ✍✍✍ 1933 Rarely seen, vintage horror classic about a wax-dummy maker who, after a disfiguring fire, resorts to murder and installs the wax-covered bodies of his victims in his museum. Famous for its pioneering use of two-strip Technicolor. Remade in 1953 in 3-D as "House of Wax." 77m/C VHS. Lionel Atwill, Fay Wray, Glenda Farrell, Frank McHugh, Allen Vincent, Holmes Herbert; *D:* Michael Curtiz; *W:* Carl Erickson, Don Mullaly; *C:* Ray Rennahan.

Mystery Plane ✍½ 1939 An inventor devises a new bomb-dropping mechanism, and must evade secret agents on his way to deliver it to the government. 60m/B VHS, DVD. John Trent, Marjorie Reynolds, Milburn Stone, Peter George Lynn, Polly Ann Young; *D:* George Waggner.

Mystery Ranch ✍½ 1934 A cowboy finds himself in strange predicaments out on the range. 52m/B VHS, DVD. George O'Brien, Charles Middleton, Cecilia Parker; *D:* David Howard.

Mystery Science Theater 3000: The Movie ✍✍✍ 1996 (PG-13) Mad scientist Dr. Clayton Forrester (Beaulieu) maroons Mike Nelson on the Satellite of Love, forces him to watch bad movies, and monitors his reactions. Mike and his robotic pals, Tom Servo and Crow T. Robot, save their sanity by wisecracking their way through the movies. Today's experiment is "This Island Earth," an uncharacteristically semi-respectable flick. As regular viewers know, the jokes come fast and in bunches. Not all of them work, but the ones that do will be remembered and repeated often. Audience participation is inevitable. Weekend theme-party status is virtually assured. 73m/C VHS, DVD. Trace Beaulieu, James Mallon, Michael J. Nelson, Kevin Murphy, John Brady; *D:* James Mallon; *W:* Trace Beaulieu, James Mallon, Michael J. Nelson, Kevin Murphy, Mary Jo Pehl, Paul Chaplin, Bridget Jones; *C:* Jeff Stonehouse; *M:* Billy Barber.

Mystery Squadron ✍✍ 1933 Twelve chapters, 13 minutes each. Daredevil air action in flight against the masked pilots of the Black Ace. 240m/B VHS, DVD. Bob Steele, Guinn "Big Boy" Williams, Lucille Browne, Jack Mulhall, J. Carrol Naish, Jack Mower; *D:* Colbert Clark.

Mystery Street ✍✍ 1950 Unusual for two reasons: an immigrant detective who ignores race baiting for a shot at his first big case and the use of forensics (then a new science) to solve it. Bar girl Vivian (Sterling) gets the brush-off from her married lover and decides to confront him. She persuades drunken Henry (Thompson) to loan her his car so she can meet the louse. Months later a skeleton turns up on a Cape Cod beach and Portuguese-American detective Peter Morales (Montalban) gets his chance to move up the cop ladder. He enlists the aid of Harvard forensic expert Dr. McAdoo (Bennett) to identity the bones. Then the car turns up, putting foolish Henry (who reported it stolen) in the hot seat. McAdoo insists forensics show Henry is the wrong guy but Morales is skeptical. 93m/B DVD. Ricardo Montalban, Bruce Bennett, Marshall Thompson, Jan Sterling, Elsa Lanchester, Edmon Ryan, Sally Forrest, Wally Maher; *D:* John Sturges; *W:* Richard Brooks, Sydney (Sidney) Boehm; *C:* John Alton; *M:* Rudolph Kopp.

Mystery Train ✍✍✍ 1989 (R) A run down hotel in Memphis is the scene for three vignettes concerning the mythic foreigners to the U.S. Themes of dying Americana, Elvis, and life on the fringe pervade this hip and quirky film. The three vignettes all tie together in clever and funny overlaps. Waits fans should listen for his performance as a DJ. 110m/C VHS, DVD. Masatoshi Nagase, Youki Kudoh, Screamin' Jay Hawkins, Cinque Lee, Joe Strummer, Nicoletta Braschi, Elizabeth Bracco, Steve Buscemi, Tom

Mystery Trooper ⅞ *Trail of the Royal Mounted* 1932 Adventures in the great wilderness full of prospecting, greed, and Indians all being observed by the Royal Mounties. Ten chapters of the serial at 20 minutes each. 200m/B VHS, Blanche Mehaffey, Al Ferguson, Charles King, William Bertram, Robert Frazer, Buzz Barton; *D:* Stuart Paton; *W:* Harry S. Webb, Carl Krusada; *C:* Edward Kull, William Nobles.

Mystery Woman: Mystery Weekend ⅞⅞½ 2005 Samantha Kinsey (Martin) inherits a struggling mystery bookstore and tries to boost business by inviting three successful authors to speak as part of a mystery weekend. Only the mystery really begins when one of the writers is murdered. Originally shown on the Hallmark Channel. 87m/C DVD, Kellie Martin, Clarence Williams III, Nina Siemaszko, Colleen Camp, Casey Sander, Deborah Van Valkenburgh, Paul Satterfield, Beth Broderick; *D:* Mark Griffiths; *W:* Joyce Burdett; *C:* Maximo Munzi; *M:* Joe Kraemer. CABLE.

Mystic Circle Murder ⅞ *Religious Racketeers* 1939 Reporter sets out to uncover phony mediums, particularly the Great La Gagge, whose fake apparitions are so convincing that it caused one of his clients to have a heart attack. Cheaply made, and it's obvious. Watch for a cameo by Harry Houdini's wife, who talks about life after death. Based on a story by director O'Connor. 69m/B VHS, DVD, Betty Compson, Robert (Fisk) Fiske, Helene Le Berthon, Arthur Gardner; *D:* Frank O'Connor.

The Mystic Masseur ⅞⅞½ 2001 (PG) Ganesh (Mandvi), a disgruntled schoolteacher, is part of the Indian community of Trinidad. He longs to become a writer and is inspired when he returns to his rural village for the funeral of his father, a famed masseur and healer. Ganesh discovers he also has a talent for healing, together they go on a wonderful journey, finds success as a writer, and even tries his hand at politics before finding a private contentment. Based on a novel by V.S. Naipaul. 117m/C VHS, DVD, GB IN Aasif Mandvi, Om Puri, Ayesha Dharker, Jimi Mistry, Zohra Sehgal, James Fox; *D:* Ismail Merchant; *W:* Caryl Phillips; *C:* Ernest Vincze; *M:* Richard Robbins, Zakir Hussain.

Mystic Pizza ⅞⅞⅞ 1988 (R) Intelligent coming of age drama centers on two sisters and their best friend as they struggle with their hopes, loves, and family rivalries in the small town of Mystic, Connecticut. At times predictable, there are enough unexpected moments to keep interest high; definite appeal to young women, but others may not relate. The relatively unknown Roberts got most of the attention, but is the weakest of the three leads, so watch this one for the strong performances from Gish and Taylor. 101m/C VHS, DVD, Annabeth Gish, Julia Roberts, Lili Taylor, Vincent D'Onofrio, William R. Moses, Adam Storke, Conchata Ferrell, Joanna Merlin, Matt Damon, Arthur Walsh; *D:* Donald Petrie; *W:* Amy Holden Jones, Perry Howze, Alfred Uhry; *C:* Tim Suhrstedt; *M:* David McHugh, Ind. Spirit '89: First Feature.

Mystic River ⅞⅞⅞½ 2003 (R) Complex drama is right up in the controlled Eastwood's directorial alley (it's his 24th film)—especially with his three leads giving their all. Jimmy (Penn), Dave (Robbins), and Sean (Bacon) have grown up together in a working-class Irish neighborhood in Boston. As a child, Dave was kidnapped as his buddies looked on helplessly and he's never completely recovered from his ordeal. Decades later, Sean is now a homicide detective; Dave, a subdued loser; and Jimmy, an ex-con who manages a local market. Tragedy brings the guys back in close contact when Jimmy's beloved 19-year-old daughter Katie (Rossum) is murdered and he wants to get the killer before the cops do. There are some strange circumstances surrounding Katie's death and suspicion soon falls on Dave, leading to a climax filled with irony, regret, oss, and the perils of vigilante justice. Based on the novel by Dennis Le-

hane. 137m/C VHS, DVD, US Sean Penn, Tim Robbins, Kevin Bacon, Laurence Fishburne, Marcia Gay Harden, Laura Linney, Tom Guiry, Kevin Chapman, Emmy Rossum, Spencer (Treat) Clark, Adam Nelson, Jenny O'Hara, Andrew Mackin, Robert Wahlberg; *D:* Clint Eastwood; *W:* Brian Helgeland *C:* Tom Stern; *M:* Clint Eastwood. Oscars '03: Actor (Penn), Support. Actor (Robbins); Golden Globes '04: Actor—Drama (Penn), Support. Actor (Robbins); Natl. Bd. of Review '03: Actor (Penn); Film; Natl. Soc. Film Critics '03: Director (Eastwood); Screen Actors Guild '03: Support Actor (Robbins).

The Myth of Fingerprints ⅞⅞½ 1997 (R) Four adult siblings and their various partners return to their New England home to spend Thanksgiving with their parents. As with most movie families of upper-middle class status, old resentments and issues abound. Dad (Scheider), a sullen, misanthropic near-recluse, isn't thrilled about the reunion. Younger son Warren (Wyle) hopes to reconcile with his high school sweetheart. Older sister Mia (Moore) can't think of anything nice to say about anyone, and tomboy sister Leigh (Holloman) does the sibling rivalry dance with her. Subdued and interesting, Freundlich's debut doesn't go for a grand conclusion or startling revelation. Depending on your taste for pat endings and easy answers, that could be it's greatest asset or a reason not to bother. Excellent performances by a great cast should have a bearing on the decision. 91m/C VHS, DVD, Blythe Danner, Roy Scheider, Julianne Moore, Noah Wyle, Michael Vartan, Laurel Holloman, Hope Davis, Brian Kerwin, James LeGros; *D:* Bart Freundlich; *W:* Bart Freundlich; *C:* Stephen Kazmierski; *M:* David Bridie, John Phillips.

Nabonga ⅞⅞ *Gorilla; Jungle Woman* 1944 The daughter of an embezzler, whose plane crashes in the jungle, befriends a gorilla who protects her. Soon a young man comes looking for the embezzler's cash, meets the woman and the ape, and together they go on a wonderful journey. 72m/B VHS, DVD, Buster Crabbe, Fifi d'Orsay, Barton MacLane, Julie London, Herbert Rawlinson; *D:* Sam Newfield.

Nacho Libre ⅞⅞ 2006 (PG) Surprising misfire offers a few chuckles and the chance to see Black in spandex and a cape but not much else. Ignacio is a cook at a Mexican orphanage who assumes the alter ego of masked wrestler Nacho Libre in order to help out the tykes. He even has a tag-team buddy, skinny Esqueleto (Jimenez), and they somewhat resemble a cheap version of Laurel and Hardy. It's also not nearly as outrageous as the actual Lucha Libre wrestling it features. 91m/C DVD, Blu-ray Disc, HD DVD, US Jack Black, Peter Stormare, Ana de la Reguera, Hector Jimenez, Richard Montoya, Darius A. Rose, Moises Arias, Diego Eduardo Gomez, Carlos Maycotte, Cesar Gonzalez; *D:* Jared Hess; *W:* Jared Hess, Jerusha Hess, Mike White; *C:* Xavier Perez Grobet; *M:* Danny Elfman.

Nadia ⅞⅞ 1984 Entertaining account of the life of Nadia Comaneci, the Romanian gymnast who earned six perfect 'ens with her stunning performance at the 1976 Olympic Games. 100m/C VHS, DVD, Talia Balsam, Jonathan Banks, Simone Blue, Johann Carlo, Carrie Snodgress; *D:* Alan Cooke. TV

Nadine ⅞⅞½ 1987 (PG) In Austin circa 1954, an almost divorced beautician witnesses a murder and goes undercover with her estranged husband to track down the murderer, before he finds her. Plenty of low-key humor. Well-paced fun; Basinger is terrific. 83m/C VHS, DVD, Jeff Bridges, Kim Basinger, Rip Torn, Gwen Verdon, Glenne Headly, Jerry Stiller, Jay Patterson; *D:* Robert Benton; *W:* Robert Benton; *C:* Nestor Almendros; *M:* Howard Shore.

Nadja ⅞⅞⅞ 1995 (R) Fresh, modern family take on the vampire tale is about the power and the lure of home, with the required AIDS analogy and lesbian sex scenes. Tired of nightly blood-letting, the daughter of the now-deceased Count, Nadja (Lowensohn), lives in New York's East Village, hoping to charge her life. She seduces and falls in love with Lucy (Craze), whose husband is the nephew of

old family nemesis Van Helsing (Fonda, in a surprisingly comedic role). Manic Fonda, Van Helsing sets out to save Lucy and steal the twin brother (Harris, son of Richard) and Lucy discovers sex with a "toy Pixelvision camera and blown up to 35mm for a moody, grainy look) and a great score keep "Nadja" very watchable despite some missteps in the plot. (Director Almereyda pioneered use of the Pixel-vision camera in an "Another Girl Another Planet.") Executive producer David Lynch contributes a cameo as a guard at the morgue where Nadja claims her father's body. 92m/B VHS, DVD, Elina Lowensohn, Suzy Amis, Galaxy Craze, Martin Donovan, Peter Fonda, Karl Geary, Jared Harris; *Cameos:* David Lynch; *D:* Michael Almereyda; *W:* Michael Amereyda; *C:* Jim Denault; *M:* Simon Fisher Turner.

Nail Gun Massacre Woof! 1986 A crazed killer with a penchant for nailing bodies to just about anything goes on a hammering spree. In horrific, vivid co-or. 90m/C VHS, DVD, Rocky Patterson, Ron Queen, Beau Leland, Michele Meyer; *D:* Bill Lesley.

Nails ⅞½ 1992 (R) Harry "Nails" Niles (Hopper) is a tough, experienced cop whose partner has been killed by drug dealers. Harry doesn't take this well and decides to go on a violent search for revenge. Archer is wasted as Harry's estranged wife and Nappo can sleepwalk through this type of clichéd wildman role. 96m/C VHS, Dennis Hopper, Anne Archer, Tomas Millan, Cliff DeYoung; *D:* John Flynn. CABLE.

Nairobi Affair ⅞⅞ 1988 (PG) Savage and Heston fight poachers and each other in Kenya, where the father has an affair with his son's ex-wife. Mediocre, derivative script, but beautiful scenery. 95m/C VHS, Charlton Heston, John Savage, Maud Adams, John Rhys-Davies, Connie Booth; *D:* Marvin J. Chomsky. TV

Nais ⅞⅞⅞ 1945 Vintage Pagnolian peasant drama. A hunchback sacrifices himself for the girl he loves. She escapes to another man's arms. Adapted from the Emile Zola novel "Nais Micoulin." In French with English subtitles. 105m/B vhs, FR Fernandel; *D:* Fernand Lauteier. *W:* Marcel Pagnol.

Naked ⅞⅞⅞ 1993 *Mike Leigh's Naked* 1993 (R) Existential angst in a '90s London filled with Leigh's usual eccentrics. The unemployed Johnny (Thewlis) comes to London and bunks with former girlfriend Louise (Sharp). After seducing her flatmate Sophie (Cartledge), Johnny leaves to wander the streets, exchanging philosophical, foul-mouthed dialogues with a variety of odd characters. Thewlis gives an explosive performance as the calculatingly brutal and desolate Johnny. Chaotic shifts in mood from comedy to violence to love prove a challenge and the pervasive abuse of all the women characters is very disturbing. Critically acclaimed; see it as a reflection on the mess of modern England. 131m/C VHS, DVD, GB David Thewlis, Lesley Sharp, Katrin Cartlidge, Greg Cruttwell, Claire Skinner, Peter Wight, Ewen Bremner, Susan Vidler, Deborah MacLaren, Gina McKee; *D:* Mike Leigh; *W:* Mike Leigh; *C:* Dick Pope. *M:* Andrew Dickson. Cannes '93: Actor (Thewlis), Director (Leigh); N.Y. Film Critics '93: Actor (Thewlis); Natl. Soc. Film Critics '93: Actor (Thewlis).

The Naked and the Dead ⅞⅞½ 1958 Sanitized adaptation of Norman Mailer's bestselling novel of army life in the Pacific during WWII. Resentment between officers and enlisted men proves to be almost as dangerous as the Japanese. Uneven acting and clichéd characterizations make this an average outing. Don't expect to hear the profane language that sensationalized the book, because most of it was edited out of the screenplay. 131m/C VHS, Aldo Ray, Cliff Robertson, Joey Bishop, Raymond Massey, Lili St. Cyr, James Best; *D:* Raoul Walsh; *C:* Joseph La Shelle.

The Naked Angels ⅞ 1969 (R) Rape, mayhem, beatings, and road-hogging streetbikes highlight this biker film, acted, in part, by actual bikers, and in part

by others who were actually (almost) actors. The gang war rages from Los Angeles to Las Vegas. Roger Corman was the executive producer. 83m/C VHS, Michael Greene, Richard Rust, Felicia Guy; *D:* Bruce (B.D.) Clark; *W:* Bruce (B.D.) Clark.

The Naked City ⅞⅞⅞½ 1948 Film noir classic makes spectacular use of its NYC locations. Beautiful playgirl is murdered and police detectives Fitzgerald and Taylor are left without clues. They spend most of their time running down weak leads and interviewing various suspects and witnesses. When they finally get a break, it leads to playboy Duff. Spectacular ending on the Brooklyn Bridge between cops and killer. Producer Hellinger provided the hard-boiled narration, patterned after an ambitious newscaster. The film seems. Based on the 1948 film "The Naked City." 107m/C VHS, Scott Glenn, Courtney B. Vance, Laura Leighton, Barbara Williams, Nigel Bennett, Lisa Vidal, Al Waxman, Jason Blicker, Richard McMillan; *D:* Jules Dassin; *M:* Albert (John B. Sherry) Maltz; *C:* William H. Daniels; *Narr:* Mark Hellinger; Oscars '48: B&W Cinematog., Film Editing; Natl. Film Reg. '07.

Naked City: A Killer Christmas ⅞⅞½ 1998 Cops Muldoon (Glenn) and Halloran (Vance) are on the case of a serial killer who's sent New York into a panic, thanks to the media circus Quentin Crisp, who came out of the closet in his native England, long before his lifestyle would be tolerated by Britain's. mature audiences. 80m/C VHS, DVD, John Hurt; *D:* Jack Gold; *M:* Carl Davis.

Naked City: Justice with a Bullet ⅞⅞½ 1998 Undercover NYC detectives Scott Muldoon (Glenn) and James Halloran (Vance) come to the rescue of naïve tourists Sarah (Erbe) and Merri (Tunney) who unwittingly become involved in a drug dealer's murder. And then Halloran has to deal with a boyfriend pal from the 'hood who isn't the friend he seems. Based on the 1948 film "The Naked City." 107m/C VHS, Scott Glenn, Courtney B. Vance, Giancarlo Esposito, Robin Tunney, Kathryn Erbe, El Wallach, Tony Bill, Sebastian Roché, Barbara Williams; *D:* Jeff Freilich; *W:* Jeff Freilich; *C:* Miroslaw Baszak; *M:* Ashley Irwin. CABLE.

The Naked Civil Servant ⅞⅞⅞½ 1975 Remarkable film, based on the life of flamboyant homosexual Quentin Crisp, who came out of the closet in his native England, long before his lifestyle would be tolerated by Britain's mature audiences. 80m/C VHS, DVD, John Hurt; *D:* Jack Gold; *M:* Carl Davis.

The Naked Country ⅞½ 1985 (R) In the untamed frontier of Australia rancher bigot Lance Dillion and his sensual wife Mary are determined to make their way. But when Lance finds out that the neglected Mary is fooling around with a local cop, he goes on a killing spree on land sacred to the Aborigines. Plodding plot. 90m/C VHS, AU John Stanton, Rebecca Gilling, Ivar Kants; *D:* Tim Burstall; *C:* David Eggby; *M:* Bruce Smeaton.

The Naked Edge ⅞⅞ 1961 Cooper stars as a middle-aged businessman whose wife suspects him of murder after she begins snooping into his business affairs. Cooper's last film and far from his best. Poor direction and holes in the screenplay divert from what could have been a tight thriller. 99m/C VHS, GB Gary Cooper, Deborah Kerr, Eric Portman, Diane Cilento, Hermione Gingold, Peter Cushing, Michael Wilding, Ronald Howard; *D:* Michael Anderson Sr.; *W:* Joseph Stefano.

Naked Cage Woof! 1986 (R) Brutal women's prison film that is borderline soft-core, about an innocent country woman, a horsending fanatic, who is framed for a robbery and sent to the slammer. There, she contends with lesbian wardens and inmates. Disgusting. 97m/C VHS, Shari Shattuck, Angel Torpines, Lucinda Crosby, Christina Whitaker; *D:* Paul Nicholas.

The Naked Face 🐾🐾 1984 (R) A psychiatrist tries to find out why his patients are being killed. He gets no help from police, who suspect he is the murderer. A dull affair featuring unusual casting of Moore, while Steiger's suspicious police captain character provides spark. Based on the novel by Sidney Sheldon. 105m/C VHS. Roger Moore, Rod Steiger, Elliott Gould, Art Carney, Anne Archer, David Hedison; **D:** Bryan Forbes.

The Naked Flame 1968 (R) O'Keefe plays an investigator in a strange town inhabited by weird, religious fanatics. After he arrives, the womenfolk shed their clothes in this pitiful, pathetic hilarity. 90m/C VHS. CA Dennis O'Keefe, Kasey Rogers, Al Ruscio, Linda Bennett, Tracey Roberts, Barton Heyman, Robert Howay; **D:** Larry Matanski; **W:** Al Everett Dennis; **C:** Paul Ivano.

The Naked Gun: From the Files of Police Squad 🐾🐾🐾 1988 (PG-13) More hysterical satire from the creators of "Airplane!" The short-lived TV cop spoof "Police Squad" moves to the big screen and has Lt. Drebin uncover a plot to assassinate Queen Elizabeth while she's visiting Los Angeles. Nearly nonstop gags and pratfalls provide lots of laughs. Nielsen is perfect as Drebin and the supporting cast is strong; cameos abound. 85m/C VHS, DVD. Leslie Nielsen, Ricardo Montalban, Priscilla Presley, George Kennedy, O.J. Simpson, Nancy Marchand, John Houseman; **Cameos:** Weird Al Yankovic, Reggie Jackson, Dr. Joyce Brothers; **D:** David Zucker; **W:** Jerry Zucker, Jim Abrahams, Pat Proft, David Zucker; **M:** Ira Newborn.

Naked Gun 33 1/3: The Final Insult 🐾🐾 1994 (PG-13) Ever dumb, crass, and crude, Lt. Drebin returns to the big screen and finds difficulty in adjusting. A notch down from the previous entry but still hilarious cop parody. Nielsen has this character down to a tee, and gets a laugh every minute. 85m/C VHS, DVD. Leslie Nielsen, Priscilla Presley, O.J. Simpson, Fred Ward, George Kennedy, Gary Cooper, Kathleen Freeman, Raquel Welch; **Cameos:** Pia Zadora, James Earl Jones, Weird Al Yankovic, Ann B. Davis; **D:** Peter Segal; **W:** Robert Locash, David Zucker, Pat Proft; **M:** Ira Newborn. Golden Raspberries '94: Worst Support. Actor (Simpson), Worst New Star (Smith).

Naked Gun 2 1/2: The Smell of Fear 🐾🐾 1991 (PG-13) Lt. Drebin returns to rescue the world from a faulty energy policy devised by the White House and oil-lords. A notch down from the previous entry but still hilarious cop parody. Nielsen has this character down to a tee, losing his wife and family. 72m/C VHS, DVD. David Wayne, Keenan Wynn, James Barton, Marcia Henderson, Jim Backus, Denver Pyle, Myrna Dell, Frank Fenton, Fuzzy Knight; **D:** Josef Shaftel; **W:** Josef Shaftel.

Naked Hills 🐾🐾1/2 1956 Meandering tale about a man (Wayne) who, suffering from gold fever, searches for 40 years in 19th Century California and ends up out of luck, losing his wife and family. 72m/C VHS, DVD. David Wayne, Keenan Wynn, James Barton, Marcia Henderson, Jim Backus, Denver Pyle, Myrna Dell, Frank Fenton, Fuzzy Knight; **D:** Josef Shaftel; **W:** Josef Shaftel.

Naked in New York 🐾🐾1/2 1993 (R) Aspiring New York playwright Jake Briggs (Stoltz) and his girlfriend Joanne (Parker), an aspiring photographer, find their relationship in jeopardy when their respective careers start to take off. Offspring from the "Annie Hall" school of neurotic romance examines a number of issues, including ambition, commitment, and the societal dynamics of theatre and art. Celebrity appearances abound, including Allen Ginsberg, and Jack Paul Bowles, Allen Ginsberg, and Jack Kerouac. 117m/C VHS, DVD, CA GB Peter Weller, Judy Davis, Ian Holm, Julian Sands, Roy

Dalton, Lynne Thigpen, Roscoe Lee Browne; **Cameos:** Whoopi Goldberg, William Styron, Eric Bogosian, Quentin Crisp; **D:** Dan Algrant; **W:** Dan Algrant, John Warren; **M:** Angelo Badalamenti; **V:** David Johansen.

Naked in the Night 🐾 *Madeleine Tel. 13 62 11* 1958 Cheap German exploitation film about the dangers of promiscuous women. Dubbed in English. 85m/B VHS. GE Eva Bartok, Alexander Kerst, Heinz Drache, Ilse Steppat, Sabine Sesselmann; **D:** Kurt Meisel; **W:** Will Berthold; **C:** Kurt Grigoleit; **M:** Willy Mattes.

Naked in the Sun 🐾🐾 1957 The true story of events leading to the war between the Osceola and Seminole Indians and a slave trader. Somewhat slow. 90m/C VHS. James Craig, Lita Milan, Barton MacLane, Tony Hunter; **D:** R. John Hugh.

Naked Is Better 🐾 1973 A couple of buffoons pose as hospital workers so they can play doctor with a hospitalized actress. 93m/C VHS. Alberto Olmedo, Jorge Porcel, Jorge Barreiro, Maria Casan.

Naked Jungle 🐾🐾🐾 1954 Suspenseful, well-done jungle adventure of a plantation owner (Heston) in South America and his North American mail-order bride (Parker), who do battle with a deadly, miles-long siege of red army ants. Realistic and worth watching. Produced by George Pal, shot by Ernest Laszlo and based on the story "Leiningen vs. the Ants" by Carl Stephenson. 95m/C VHS, DVD. Charlton Heston, Eleanor Parker, Abraham Sofaer, William Conrad; **D:** Byron Haskin; **W:** Philip Yordan; **C:** Ernest Laszlo.

Naked Killer 🐾 *Chiko Gouyeung* 1992 Kitty (Ching) turns to a female assassin to learn the art of killing so that she may avenge her father's death. When her teacher is herself unceremoniously murdered, Kitty and her policeman boyfriend (Yam) have two scores to settle. Sex and violence. Subtitled in English. 86m/C VHS, DVD. HK Chingmy Yau, Simon Yam, Carrie Ng, Kelly Yao, Svenvara Madoka; **D:** Clarence Fok Yiu Leung; **W:** Jing Wong; **C:** Peter Pau, William Yim; **M:** Lowell Lo.

Naked Kiss 🐾🐾1/2 *The Iron Kiss* 1964 Fuller's most savage, hysterical film noir. A brutalized prostitute escapes her pimp and tries to enter respectable small-town society. She finds even more perversion and sickness there. 92m/B VHS, DVD. Constance Towers, Anthony Eisley, Michael Dante, Virginia Grey, Patsy Kelly, Betty Bronson, Edy Williams, Marie Devereux, Karen Conrad, Linda Francis, Barbara Perry, Walter Matthews, Betty Robinson; **D:** Samuel Fuller; **W:** Samuel Fuller; **C:** Stanley Cortez; **M:** Paul Dunlap.

Naked Lie 🐾🐾 1989 A District Attorney and a judge engage in an altogether steamy affair and inevitably clash when she is assigned as a prosecutor on the politically explosive case over which he is presiding. 89m/C VHS, DVD. Victoria Principal, James Farentino, Glenn Withrow, William Lucking, Dakin Matthews; **D:** Richard A. Colla; **M:** Robert Alcivar.

Naked Lies 🐾🐾 1998 (R) FBI agent Cara Landry (Tweed) gets transferred to treasury after a drug bust goes bad and is assigned to work an undercover operation that reunites Cara with ex-lover Mitch Kendall (Baker). Kendall has been trying to bust international counterfeiter Damian Medina (Allende) and sends Cara in to bust one of Medina's casinos. But Cara finds herself drawn to the bad guy, putting both her career and her life in jeopardy. 93m/C VHS, DVD. Shannon Tweed, Jay Baker, Fernando Allende, Steven Bauer, Hugo Stiglitz; **D:** Ralph Portillo. VIDEO

Naked Lunch 🐾🐾🐾 1991 (R) Whacked-out movie based on William S. Burroughs's autobiographical account of drug abuse, homosexuality, violence, and weirdness set in the drug-inspired land called Interzone. Hallucinogenic images are carried to the extreme: typewriters metamorphose into beetles, bloblike creatures with sex organs scurry about, and characters mainline insecticide. Some of the characters are clearly based on writers of the Beat generation, including Jane and Paul Bowles, Allen Ginsberg, and Jack Kerouac. 117m/C VHS, DVD, CA GB Peter Weller, Judy Davis, Ian Holm, Julian Sands, Roy

Scheider, Monique Mercure, Nicholas (Nick) Campbell, Michael Zelniker, Robert A. Silverman, Joseph Scorsiani; **D:** David Cronenberg; **W:** David Cronenberg; **C:** Peter Suschitzky; **M:** Howard Shore. Genie '92: Adapt. Screenplay, Art Dir/Set Dec., Cinematog., Director (Cronenberg), Film, Sound, Support. Actress (Mercure); N.Y. Film Critics '91: Screenplay, Support. Actress (Davis); Natl. Soc. Film Critics '91: Director (Cronenberg), Screenplay.

The Naked Maja 🐾🐾 1959 Elaborate, yet dull drama about the tumultuous romance between a Spanish duchess and the legendary painter Francisco Goya. Even the gorgeous costumes and spectacular sets can't overcome the weak script and poor direction that plague the film. Based on a story by Oscar Saul and Talbot Jennings. 111m/C VHS. Ava Gardner, Anthony (Tony) Franciosa, Amedeo Nazzari, Gino Cervi, Lea Padovani, Massimo Serato, Carlo Rizzo, Renzo Cesana; **D:** Henry Koster, Mario Russo; **W:** Norman Corwin, Giorgio Prosperi.

The Naked Man 🐾🐾 1998 (R) When a pharmaceutical conglomerate muscles into his small town, chiropractor Rapaport decides to take action to save the livelihood of his family's drugstore—by becoming a professional wrestler. 96m/C VHS. Michael Rapaport, Michael Jeter, Rachael Leigh Cook, Joe Grifasi, John Slattery; **D:** J. Todd Anderson; **W:** J. Todd Anderson, Ethan Coen.

Naked Obsession 🐾1/2 1991 (R) A city councilman running for mayor is mugged in one of the seedier parts of the city. He's found by a homeless man who takes him to a kinky nightclub where the councilman is promptly seduced by a topless bar hostess with secrets of her own. Also available in an unrated version. 93m/C VHS. William Katt, Maria Ford, Rick Dean; **D:** Dan Golden.

Naked Paradise *Black Emmanuelle, White Emmanuelle; Black Velvet* 1978 (R) A young woman moves in with her mother and step-sister and finds difficulty in adjusting. 86m/C VHS. IT Al Cliver, Gabriele Tinti, Feodor Chaliapin Jr., Laura Gemser, Annie Belle; **D:** Brunello Rondi; **W:** Brunello Rondi; **C:** Gastone Di Giovanni; **M:** Alberto Baldan Bembo.

The Naked Prey 🐾🐾🐾 1966 Unnerving African adventure which contains some unforgettably brutal scenes. A safari guide (Wilde), leading a hunting party, must watch as an indigenous tribe murders all his companions, and according to their customs, allows him to be set free, sans clothes or weapons, to be hunted by the best of the tribe. 96m/C VHS. Cornel Wilde, Gertrude Van Der Berger, Ken Gampu; **D:** Cornel Wilde.

Naked Souls 🐾 1995 (R) Artist Brit Clark (Anderson) must save scientist fiance Edward (Krause) from the evil experiments of murderous scientist Longstreet (Warner). Like you'll care as long as the Anderson body is on display. 90m/C VHS. Michael (Mike) Papajohn, Pamela Anderson, Brian Krause, Clayton Rohner, Justina Vail, David Warner; **Cameos:** Dean Stockwell; **D:** Lyndon Chubbuck; **W:** Frank Dietz; **C:** Eric Goldstein; **M:** Nigel Holton.

The Naked Spur 🐾🐾🐾 1953 A compulsive bounty hunter tracks down a vicious outlaw and his beautiful girlfriend. An exciting film from the Mann-Stewart team and considered one of their best, infusing the traditional western with psychological confusion. Wonderful use of Rockies locations. 93m/C VHS, DVD. James Stewart, Robert Ryan, Janet Leigh, Millard Mitchell, Ralph Meeker; **D:** Anthony Mann; **W:** Sam Rolfe, Harold Jack Bloom; **C:** William Mellor; **M:** Bronislau Kaper. Natl. Film Reg. '97.

The Naked Sword of Zorro 🐾 1969 Deadly Don Luis taxes the town by day and violates the women by night, but Zorro takes a stand and saves the town. When he's not dressed as Zorro, he is Don Diego, an inept fool, but when he puts that suit on, look out. The ladies can't keep their hands off of him. There are more lusty females than villains, but there's still lots of swordplay and action. 94m/C VHS.

Naked Tango 🐾1/2 1991 (R) A lurid recreation of the Argentinian underworld in 1924. Stephanie is a bored wife with an older husband who, while traveling with her husband on a cruise ship, pretends to fall overboard in order to establish a new identity. The problem is she becomes the supposed mail-order bride of a young man who promptly sells her into white slavery. One of her customers is a charismatic killer named Cholo who isn't interested in Stephanie for sex, he just wants to dance the tango with her. This is meant to be taken seriously but is one of the many pretensions, erotic and otherwise, that hamper the film. 90m/C VHS. Mathilda May, Vincent D'Onofrio, Esai Morales, Fernando Rey; **D:** Leonard Schrader; **W:** Leonard Schrader; **M:** Thomas Newman.

The Naked Truth 🐾🐾1/2 *Your Past is Showing* 1958 A greedy publisher tries to get rich quick by publishing a scandal magazine about the "lurid" lives of prominent citizens. Well-drawn characters in an appealing offbeat comedy. 92m/C VHS, DVD. GB Peter Sellers, Terry-Thomas, Shirley Eaton, Dennis Price; **D:** Mario Zampi.

Naked Vengeance WOOF! *Satin Vengeance* 1985 (R) A woman's husband is murdered, she is beaten and raped, and she becomes a vengeful, vicious killing machine. Gratuitous violence, distasteful to the max. 97m/C VHS. Deborah Tranelli, Kaz Garas, Bill McLaughlin; **D:** Cirio H. Santiago.

Naked Venus 🐾1/2 1958 Ulmer's last film is a slow-paced tale about an American artist, married to a model who poses in the nude and belongs to a nudist camp, whose wealthy mother tries to tear the marriage apart. Discrimination and intolerance of nudist camps is explored. 80m/B VHS, DVD. Patricia Conelle; **D:** Edgar G. Ulmer.

Naked Wishes 🐾🐾 2000 Sex therapist Taj inherits a trunk from his uncle that contains only a dusty old bottle. When he cleans it up, very sexy genie Samathia is released and she lets Taj knows that they were lovers in a previous life and she's ready to resume their affair, besides granting his every wish. Taj, silly guy, wavers because he's engaged but then Samthia disturbs his therapy sessions by having his patients act out their deepest sexual fantasies. 99m/C VHS. Jennifer Marks, Jeff Kueppers, Chanda Marie, Lance Moseley; **D:** Mike Sedan. VIDEO

The Naked Witch 🐾 1964 College students researching witchcraft dig up the grave of a long-dead witch. She comes back to life to take revenge on the descendants of the villagers who killed her. Nude shots feature a finger over the camera lens to cover up the witch's, uh, vital organs. 60m/C VHS, DVD. Jack Herman, Libby Hall, Robert Short, Jo Maryman, Denis Adams, Charles West, Marilyn Pope; **D:** Larry Buchanan, Claude Alexander; **W:** Larry Buchanan, Claude Alexander.

Naked Youth WOOF! *Wild Youth* 1959 Seedy drive-in cheapie about two punks breaking out of juvenile prison and heading south of the border on a trail filled with crime, drugs, and loose women. 80m/B VHS, DVD. Robert Hutton, John Goddard, Carol Ohmart, Jan Brooks, Robert Arthur, Steve Rowland, Clancy Cooper; **D:** John F. Schreyer.

Nam Angels 🐾 1988 (R) Hell's Angels enter Southeast Asia and rescue POWs. 91m/C VHS, DVD. PH Brad Johnson, Vernon Wells, Kevin Duffis, Fred Bailey, Archie Adamos, Rick Dean, Jeff Griffith, Eric Hahn, Ken Metcalfe, Tonichi Fructuoso, Leah Navarro, Ruben Ramos; **D:** Cirio H. Santiago; **C:** Ricardo Remias, Chris Squires; **M:** Jaime Fabregas.

A Name for Evil 🐾 1970 (R) Having grown tired of city living, a couple moves to an old family estate out in the country near the Great Lakes. Strange sounds in the night are the first signs of the terror to come. 74m/C VHS, DVD. Robert Culp, Samantha Eggar, Sheila Sullivan, Mike Lane; **D:** Bernard Girard.

The Name of the Rose 🐾🐾1/2 1986 (R) An exhaustive, off-center adaptation of the bestselling Umberto Eco novel about violent murders in a 14th-century Italian abbey. An English monk struggles

The Namesake 🐾🐾🐾 2006 (PG-13) Nair's thoughtful and emotional adaptation of Jhumpa Lahiri's novel about two generations of a Bengali family living in the U.S. Ashoke (Khan) enters into an arranged marriage with Ashima (Tabu) and they move to New York, settling uneasily into their new lives. The couple's first child, Nikhil, is nicknamed Gogol after Ashoke's favorite writer. The name confusion continues as the boy accepts and then rejects his various monikers, growing into a young man (Penn) torn between tradition and pursuing his own life. Naturally, he's also torn (at least at first) between WASP princess Maxine (Barrett) and fellow Bengali Moushumi (Robinson). Penn has his dramatic presence to go along with his real familiar comic gifts. 122m/C DVD, US Kal Penn, Tabu, Irfan Khan, Jacinda Barrett, Zuleika Robinson; D: Mira Nair; W: Sooni Taraporevala. C: Frederick Elmes; M: Nitin Sawhney.

Nancy Drew and the Hidden Staircase 🐾🐾 1939 Nancy Drew (Granville) and trusty Ted Nickerson (Thomas) are charged with both solving a murder and saving a couple of elderly women from losing their family home, which, by coincidence, seems haunted by some mysteries of its own, like moving walls and hidden staircases. 60m/B VHS, Bonita Granville, Frankie Thomas Jr., John Litel.

Nancy Drew 🐾½ 2007 (PG) Poor sleuth is awkward and dull. Nancy (the appealing but rather stiff Roberts) accompanies her lawyer dad Carson (Donovan) to L.A. She discovers the scene of movie star Dehlia Draycott's (I-starring) murder, an unsolved case that Nancy can't resist. However, the story really falls apart with Nancy in high school, where her anachronisms make her an object of popular girl scorn (toc bad Nancy wasn't doing her sleuthing on vacation). But Nancy's sheer perky tenaciousness can overcome any obstacle (okay, except this script). Based on the Carolyn Keene character. 98m/C DVD, US Emma Roberts, Tate Donovan, Josh Flitter, Max Thieriot, Rachael Leigh Cook, Amy Bruckner, Kay Panabaker, Laura Elena Harring, Belly Vitz, Marshall Bell, Caroline Aaron, David Doty, Kay Panabaker, Daniela Monet, Barry Bostwick, Daniela Monet; D: Andrew Fleming; W: Andrew Fleming, Tiffany Paulsen; C: Alexander Gruszynski; M: Ralph Sall.

Nana 🐾🐾½ 1982 A lavishly photographed graphic adaptation of the Emile Zola novel about a Parisian whore who seduces the high society of Paris in the late 1880s, and suffers a heart-breaking downfall and death. Film has three remakes of the original 1926 version. 118m/C VHS, FR Charles Boyer, Martine Carol, Jacques Casteiot, Paul Frankeur, Noel Roquevert, Walter Chiari, Jean Debucourt, Elisa Cegani; L: Christian-Jaque; W: Christian-Jaque, Jean Ferry, Henri Jeanson; C: Christian Matras; M: Georges Van Parys.

Namu, the Killer Whale 🐾🐾 1966 Based on the true story of a marine biologist (Lansing) who gets the perfect opportunity to study killer whales when one is confined to a small cove. The local fisherman want to kill the creature because it feeds on the salmon they catch but they are persuaded against their baser instincts. Filmed on location in the San Juan Islands of Puget Sound. The real Namu lived at the Seattle Public Aquarium. 89m/C VHS, DVD, Robert Lansing, John Anderson, Robin Mattson, Richard Erdman, Lee Meriwether, Joe Higgins; D: Laszlo Benedek.

The Nanny 🐾🐾½ 1965 Creepfest stars Davis as a seemingly proper nameless nanny who's been accused by her young charge Joey (Dix) of drowning his sister in the bathtub. But is it Joey who's sent away to a home for disturbed children and when he returns two years later (and just why is the nanny still around a childless home?) it's a battle of wills between the duo over who's responsible for some evil goings-on. Based on a novel by Evelyn Piper. 93m/B VHS, GB Bette Davis, William Dix, Wendy Craig, Jill Bennett, James Villiers, Pamela Franklin, Jack Watling, Alfred Burke, Maurice Denham; D: Seth Holt; W: Jimmy Sangster; C: Henry Waxman; M: Richard Rooney Bennett.

The Nanny Diaries 🐾🐾 2007 (PG-13) Recent NYU graduate Annie (Johansson), unsure of herself after bombing a job interview, accepts a nanny job from Manhattan power-mommy extraordinaire Mrs. X (Linney), whose number one priority is herself, and her husband, uptight jerk Mr. X (Giamatti). Meanwhile, she's got the hots for a Harvard man (Adams), the neighbor upstairs. Johansson somehow manages not to give Annie any depth or humor, which is sorely missed amid the satire, but the result is weak social commentary about the class divide between insanely rich Manhattanites and white, college educated upwardly mobile wannabes. Based on a novel fictionalizing its authors' real life Manhattan nanny experiences. 105m/C DVD, US Scarlett Johansson, Laura Linney, Paul Giamatti, Chris Evans, Nicholas Reese Art, Alicia Keys, Donna Murphy, Judith Anne Roberts, Nathan Corddry; D: Shari Springer Berman; W: Shari Springer Berman; C: Terry Stacey; M: Mark Suozzo.

Nanny McPhee 🐾🐾½ 2006 (PG) Thompson wrote the screenplay and stars as the spectacularly ugly title character, who comes complete with magical abilities and a no-nonsense manner destined to overcome the horrors wrought by the seven motherless Brown children. Their clueless 'father, Cedric (Firth), counts on a stipend from Aunt Adelaide (Lansbury) to

Napoleon and Samantha 🐾🐾 1972 Disney adventure about Napoleon, an orphan (Whitaker), who is befriended by Danny, a college student (Douglas). After the death of his grandfather, Napoleon decides to take Major, his elderly pet lion, and follow Danny.

Nancy Drew—Detective 🐾🐾 1938 Nancy Drew (Granville) and Ted Nickerson (Thomas) are on the case of a kidnapping, or, well-to-do elderly lady napee and the nappers. 66m/B VHS, Bonita Granville, John Litel, James Stephenson, Frankie Thomas Jr., Frank Orth, Helena Phillips Evans, Renie Riano; D: William Clemens; W: Kenneth Gamet, Mildred Wirt Benson.

Nancy Drew, Reporter 🐾🐾 1939 The young sleuth gets to play reporter after winning a newspaper contest. In no time at all she's involved in a murder mystery. 68m/B VHS, DVD, Bonita Granville, Frankie Thomas Jr., Mary Lee, Sheila Bromley, Betty Amann, Dickie Jones, Olin Howlin, Charles Halton; D: William Clemens.

Nancy Drew—Trouble Shooter 🐾🐾 1939 Nancy Drew's uncle Matt gets slapped with a murder charge, only he's no murderer and it takes Nancy and Ted Nickerson (Thomas) to clear him. They have to find the real murderer, and they're stuck in some perilous situations in order to do just that. 66m/B VHS, Bonita Granville, Frankie Thomas, John Litel, Aldrich Bowker, Charlotte Wynters, Renie Riano, Edgar Edwards; D: William Clemens; W: Kenneth Gamet, Mildred Wirt Benson.

Nancy Goes to Rio 🐾🐾½ 1950 Actresses Powell and Sothern compete for the same part in a play and for the same man. Catch is, they're mother and daughter. Zany consequences ensue. Sothern's last film for MGM. 99m/C VHS, Ann Sothern, Jane Powell, Barry Sullivan, Carmen Miranda, Louis Calhern, Scotty Beckett, Hans Conried, Glenn Anders; D: Robert Z. Leonard; W: Sidney Sheldon.

Napoleon 🐾🐾½ 1996 (G) Cute p/c for young kiddies who like animals. A very curious golden retriever puppy named Muffin manages to slip into a balloon-covered basket and finds himself airborne across Australia. Deciding he likes the idea of adventuring, Muffin renames himself Napoleon because it sounds braver. He lands unexpectedly near Sydney Harbor and is befriended by Birdo, who before end is befriended by Birdo, who becomes his guide when Napoleon decides he wants to join along the way with kangaroos, koalas, snakes, and lizards to help or hinder along the way. 81m/C VHS, DVD, AU JP D: Mario Andreacchio; W: Mario Andreacchio, Mark Saltzman; C: Roger Dowling; M: Bill Conti V: Jamie Croft, Philip Quast, Carole Skinner, Anne Louise Lambert, David Argue, Joan Rivers, Steven Vidler, Susan Lyons.

Napoleon 🐾🐾½ 2003 Epic miniseries starts off with a bedraggled general Napoleon Bonaparte (Clavier) managing to make both personal and professional marks in 1794 Paris; he thwarts a royalist riot at the end of the French Revolution and he meets Josephine (Rossellini). Soon, Napoleon is rising through the military ranks, winning the loyalty of the people, and proclaiming himself Emperor. But since Josephine can't give him a child, he has to make some dynastic decisions and begins to lose control. A lavish spectacle and a charismatic titular performance by Clavier. Based on the biography by Max Gallo. 360m/C VHS, DVD, Christian Clavier, Isabella Rossellini, Gerard Depardieu, John Malkovich, Anouk Aimee, Heino Ferch, Ennio Fantastichini, Claude Brasseur, Sebastian Koch, Julian Sands, Toby Stephens, John Wood, Mavie Hörbiger, Yves Jacques; D: Yves Simoneau; W: Didier Decoin; C: Guy Dufaux; M: Richard Gregoire CABLE

The Narcotics Story woof! The Dreaded Persuasion 1958 Bad film on the same vein as "Reefer Madness." Originally intended as a police training film, this shows the evils and destruction of heroin addiction. Portrayals of drug addicts are become palpable. Carnahan's tale is cruelly intended as a police training film, this shows the evils and destruction of heroin addiction. Portrayals of drug addicts are hilarious. 75m/C VHS, Sharon Strand, Darlene W. Larsen; Nar: Art Gilmore.

Napoleon 🐾🐾🐾 1927 A vivid, near-complete restoration of Gance's epic silent masterpiece of the famed emperor's early years, from his youth through the Italian Campaign. An innovative, spectacular achievement in its use of multiple split screens, montage, color, and triptychs. Given a gala theatrical release in 1981. Remade in 1955. 235m/B VHS, FR Albert Dieudonne, Antonin Artaud, Pierre Batcheff, Gina Manes, Armand Bernard, Harry Krimer, Albert Bras, Abel Gance, Georges Cahuzac, Annabella, Georges Lampin, Max Maxudian, Maurice Schultz, Marguerite Gance, Conrad Veidt, Edmond Van Daele, Alexandre Koubitzky, W. Percy Day, Yvette Dieudonne, Nicolas Koline, Vladimir Roudenko, Suzy Vernon, Robert Vidalin, Paul Amiot, Suzanne Blanchetti, Louis Sance; D: Abel Gance; W: Abel Gance; C: Leonce-Henri Burel, Roger Hubert, Jules Kruger; M: Carmine Coppola, Arthur Honegger, Carl Davis.

Napoleon 🐾🐾 1955 Depicts life story of Napoleon from his days as a soldier in the French army to his exile on the island of Elba. Falls short of the fantastic 1927 silent classic as it attempts to delve into Napoleon the man, as opposed to his conquests. Some might find it too slow for their tastes. 123m/C VHS, DVD, FR Raymond Pellegrin, Orson Welles, Maria Schell, Yves Montand, Erich von Stroheim, Jean Gabin, Jean-Pierre Aumont; D: Sacha Guitry.

Napoleon Dynamite 🐾🐾🐾 2004 (PG) Filmed in Preston, Idaho, the debut of director Hess (co-written by his wife) is a small-budget, small-scale, overreaching effort about the unfortunately named title character (Heder), an awkward, frizzy-haired, high school uber-nerd whose life is even up by the jocks, can't score with the babes, and his only friend is a shy Mexican immigrant, Pedro (Ramirez), whom Napoleon assists in his campaign for class president against popular blonde goddess, Summer (Duff, Hilary's sister). His much-older brother Kip (Ruell) is even more of a misfit and has a creepily macho life since Grandma (Martin) had an ATV-riding accident. You should want to root for the underdog but you may become just as exasperated as everyone watching this flick. 86m/C VHS, DVD, UMD Jon Heder, Jon Gries, Efren Ramirez, Haylie Duff, Tina Majorino, Diedrich Bader, Aaron Ruell, Sandy Martin, Trevor Snarr, Shondrella Avery; D: Jared Hess; W: Jared Hess, Jerusha Hess; C: Munn Powell; M: John Swihart.

Narc 🐾🐾½ 2002 (R) Patric is Det. Nick Tellis, an undercover narcotics cop on suspension for a bust that went tragically wrong. He seeks a desk job, but the suits want him to investigate the murder of another undercover cop. He's teamed with the deceased's former partner, Henry Oak (Liotta), who's out to nail the killers, proceedures be damned, although his motives may be more than just revenge. As the investigation continues, and the dead and leads mount, the tension and suspense become palpable. Carnahan's tale is cruelly gripping, and he uses cop drama conventions to great effect. Both Patric and Liotta take well to their roles, with Patric embodying Nick's despair and Liotta swallowing scenes whole with Oak's barely (and sometimes unsuccessfully) suppressed rage. 105m/C VHS, DVD, US Ray Liotta, Jason Patric, Chi McBride, Busta Rhymes, Richard Chevolleau, John Ortiz, Alan Van Sprang, Krista Bridges, Anne Openshaw; D: Joe Carnahan; W: Joe Carnahan; C: Alex Nepomniaschy; M: Cliff Martinez.

The Narrow Margin 🐾🐾🐾 1990 (R) Archer reluctantly agrees to testify against the mob after witnessing a murder, and a cop who is in charge of transporting a gangster's widow to a trial where she is to testify. On the train through the Rockies back to L.A. Bad idea, she finds out. No match for its '52 predecessor. 99m/C VHS, DVD, Gene Hackman, Anne Archer, James B. Sikking, J.T. Walsh, M. Emmet Walsh; D: Peter Hyams; W: Peter Hyams; M: Bruce Broughton.

Narrow Trail 🐾🐾🐾½ 1917 A silent classic that still stands as one of the best Westerns ever made. A tough cowboy with a troubled past hopes a good woman can save him. But she's some trouble, too. They meet up again in San Francisco's Barbary Coast. A horse race might

---

support the unruly brood but she has now demanded that he marry in 30 days or lose the money. Cedric is in love with unsuitable scullery maid Evangeline (Macdonald) but decides on garish, greedy widow Mrs. Quickly (Imrie) instead. Naturally, Nanny will put everything right. Loosely based on "Christianna Brand's 1960s "Nurse Matilda" series. 97m/C DVD, US GB Emma Thompson, Colin Firth, Kelly Macdonald, Derek Jacobi, Pat Barlow, Celia Imrie, Imelda Staunton, Thomas Sangster, Angela Lansbury, Jenny Jaylin, Eliza Bennett, Raphael Coleman, Samue Honywood, Holly Gibbs, Hebe Barnes, Zinnia Barnes; D: Kirk Jones; W: Emma Thompson, Matt Robinson; C: Henry Braham; M: Patrick Doyle.

ny, who is herding goats for the summer, across the American northwest mountains and they are joined by Samantha (Foster in her film debut). Worth watching 91m/C VHS, DVD, Jocie Foster, Johnny Whitaker, Michael Douglas, Will Geer, Henry Jones; D: Bernard McEveety; W: Stewart Raffill; C: Monroe Askins; M: Buddy (Norman Dale) Baker.

hold the answer. **56m/B VHS.** William S. Hart, Sylvia Bremer, Milton Ross; **D:** William S. Hart.

Nashville 🐾🐾🐾🐾 1975 (R) Altman's stunning, brilliant film tapestry that follows the lives of 24 people during a political campaign/music festival in Nashville. Seemingly extemporaneous vignettes, actors playing themselves (Elliott Gould and Julie Christie), funny, touching, poignant character studies concerning affairs of the heart and despairs of the mind. Repeatedly blurs reality and fantasy. 🎵 **I'm Easy;** Two Hundred Years; Keep A'Goin'; One, I Love You; Let Me Be the One; The Day I Looked Jesus in the Eye; For the Sake of the Children; I Never Get Enough; It Don't Worry Me. **159m/C VHS, DVD.** Allan Nichols, Keith Carradine, Lily Tomlin, Henry Gibson, Ronee Blakley, Keenan Wynn, David Arkin, Geraldine Chaplin, Lauren Hutton, Shelley Duvall, Barbara Harris, Allen (Goorwitz) Garfield, Karen Black, Christina Raines, Michael Murphy, Ned Beatty, Barbara Baxley, Scott Glenn, Jeff Goldblum, Gwen Welles, Bert Remsen, Robert DoQui, Elliott Gould, Julie Christie; **C:** Paul Lohmann; **M:** Richard Baskin. Oscars '75: Song ("I'm Easy"); Golden Globes '76: Director (Altman); N.Y. Film Critics 75: Director (Altman). Film, Support. Actress (Blakley); Natl. Film Reg. '92; N.Y. Film Critics 75: Director (Altman), Film, Support. Actress (Tomlin); Natl. Soc. Film Critics '75: Director (Altman), Film, Support. Actor (Gibson), Support. Actress (Tomlin).

Nashville Beat 🐾🐾 1989 Gang targets the citizens of Nashville, Tennessee, until two tough cops stomp the country music scene, rises to the top the Nashville success ladder, by compromising everything and hanging out with stereotyped no-goods in the show biz world. It's as good as a yawn. **90m/C VHS.** Monica Gayle, Johnny Rodriguez; **D:** Gus Trikonis.

Nashville Girl 🐾 *Country Music Daughter; New Girl in Town* 1976 (R) Innocent country girl who wants to make good in the country music scene, rises to the top the Nashville success ladder, by compromising everything and hanging out with stereotyped no-goods in the show biz world.

The Nasty Girl 🐾🐾🐾½ *Das Schreckliche Madchen* 1990 (PG-13) A bright young German model plans to enter a national essay contest on the topic of her hometown's history during the Third Reich. While researching the paper, she's harassed and even brutalized, but refuses to cease her sleuthing. Excellent performances, tight direction, with comedic touches that charmingly imparts an important message. Based on a true story. In German with English subtitles. **93m/C VHS, DVD. GF** Lena Stolze, Monika Baumgartner, Michael Gahr; **D:** Michael Verhoeven; **W:** Michael Verhoeven; **C:** Axel de Roche. British Acad. '91: Foreign Film; N.Y. Film Critics '90: Foreign Film.

Nasty Habits 🐾🐾 1977 (PG) Broad farce depicting a corrupt Philadelphia convent as a satiric parallel to Watergate, with nuns modeled on Nixon, Dean and Mitchell. Includes cameo appearances by various media personalities. Based on the British novel "The Abbess of Crewe" by Muriel Spark. **92m/C VHS, DVD. GB** Glenda Jackson, Geraldine Page, Anne Jackson, Melina Mercouri, Sandy Dennis, Susan Penhaligon, Anne Meara, Edith Evans, Rip Torn, Eli Wallach, Jerry Stiller; **Cameos:** Mike Douglas, Bill Jorgensen, Jessica Savitch, Howard K. Smith; **D:** Michael Lindsay-Hogg.

Nasty Hero 🐾½ 1989 (PG-13) Hardboiled ex-con comes to Miami to get revenge on the car thieves who framed him and got him sent to the slammer. This is car-chase scene heaven—little plot or drama. **79m/C VHS.** Robert Sedgwick, Carlos Palomino, Scott Feraco, Mike Starr, Rosanna DaVon, Jon Tenney, Raymond Serra; **D:** Nick Barwood; **C:** Oliver Wood.

Nasty Rabbit 🐾 *Spies-A-Go-Go* 1964 Ridiculous spoof about Soviet spies intent on releasing what with a hideous Communist disease into the U.S. Everyone gets in on the chase: Nazi forces, cowboys and Indians, sideshow freaks, banditos—what is the point? **88m/C VHS, DVD.** Arch Hall Jr., Micha(el) Terr, Liz Renay, John Akana; **D:** James Landis.

Natas... The Reflection 🐾 1983 (PG) A reporter persists in validating an Indian demon myth. **90m/C VHS.** Randy Mulkey, Pat Bolt, Craig Hensley, Kelli Kuhn; **D:** Jack Dunlap; **W:** Jack Dunlap.

Nate and Hayes 🐾🐾½ 1983 (PG) Set during the mid-1800s in the South Pacific, the notorious real-life swashbuckler Captain "Bully" Hayes ("good pirate") helps young missionary Nate recapture his fiancee from a cutthroat gang of evil slave traders. Entertaining "jolly rogers" film. **100m/C VHS, DVD. NZ** Tommy Lee Jones, Michael O'Keefe, Max Phipps, Jenny Seagrove; **D:** Ferdinand Fairfax; **M:** Trevor Jones.

Nathalie 🐾½ 2003 Remarkably dull psycho-sexual tease finds Catherine (Ardant) distressed to learn that Bernard (Depardieu), her husband of 25 years, has been cheating. So Catherine hires a beautician/prostitute named Marlene (Beart) to become Bernard's sex partner and report back to her. In great detail. Oh, and Marlene should call herself Nathalie. French with subtitles. **105m/C DVD. FR** Fanny Ardant, Emmanuelle Beart, Gerard Depardieu; **D:** Anne Fontaine; **W:** Anne Fontaine, Jacques Fieschi; **C:** Jean-Marc Fabre; **M:** Michael Nyman.

A Nation Aflame 🐾½ 1937 Anti-Klan film is based on a story by Thomas L. Dixon, the author of "The Clansman," from which D.W. Griffith made "The Birth of a Nation." In this story, a con man gains control of the state's government through an ultra-nationalistic secret society, and eventually pays for his corruption. **70m/B VHS.** Lila Lee, Noel Madison, Snub Pollard, Norma Trelvar; **D:** Victor Halperin.

National Lampoon Goes to the Movies 🐾🐾 1981 Parodies of popular Hollywood genres, including cop thrillers, melodramas, and inspirational biographies, done in goofy "Lampoon" style. **89m/C VHS, DVD.** Robby Benson, Candy Clark, Diane Lane, Christopher Lloyd, Peter Riegert, Richard Widmark, Henny Youngman, Bobby DiCicco; **D:** Henry Jaglom.

National Lampoon's Adam & Eve 🐾🐾 *Adam & Eve* 2005 (R) Raunchy, gross, yet amusing and occasionally intelligent sex comedy. Adam (Douglas) falls for virginal sorority babe Eve (Chriqui), who doesn't believe in putting out to keep some horny frat dude around. She's after true love and Adam waits... and waits. But both are pressured by their so-called friends (not to mention hormonal urges) to either consummate the relationship or break up. **91m/C VHS.** Cameron Douglas, Emmanuelle Chriqui, Chad Lindberg, Courtney Peldon, Jake Hoffman, George Dzundza, Lisa Wilhoit; **D:** Jeff Kanew; **W:** Justin Kanew; **C:** John Darbonne.

National Lampoon's Animal House 🐾🐾🐾 *Animal House* 1978 (R) Classic Belushi vehicle running amuck. Set in 1962 and responsible for launching Otis Day and the Knights and defining cinematic food fights. Every college tradition from fraternity rush week to the homecoming pageant is irreverently and relentlessly mocked in this wild comedy edge. Clifmaxes with the homecoming parade from hell. Sophomoric, but very funny, with a host of young stars who went on to more serious work. Remember: "Knowledge is good." **109m/C VHS, DVD, UMD, HD DVD.** John Belushi, Tim Matheson, John Vernon, Donald Sutherland, Peter Riegert, Stephen Furst, Bruce McGill, Mark Metcalf, Verna Bloom, Karen Allen, Tom Hulce, Mary Louise Weller, James Widdoes, Kevin Bacon, Doug Kenney, Martha Smith, Cesare Danova, Stephen Bishop, Sarah Holcomb; **D:** John Landis; **W:** Harold Ramis, Chris Miller, Doug Kenney; **C:** Charles Correll; **M:** Elmer Bernstein. Natl. Film Reg. '01.

National Lampoon's Attack of the 5 Ft. 2 Women 🐾🐾 *the 5 Ft. 2 Women* 1994 (R) Brown parodies two of 1994's most notorious tabloid queens in "Tonya: The Battle of Wounded Knee" and "He Never Give Me Orgasm: The Lenora Babbitt Story." **82m/C VHS.** Julie Brown, Sam McMurray, Adam Storke, Priscilla Barnes, Lauren Tewes, Dick Miller, Rick Overton, Stanley DeSantis, Anne DeSalvo, Liz Torres, Vicki Lawrence, Stella Stevens, Peter DeLuise, Stacey

Travis; **D:** Richard Wenk, Julie Brown; **W:** Charlie Coffey, Julie Brown; **M:** Christopher Tyng. **CABLE**

National Lampoon's Christmas Vacation 🐾🐾🐾 *Christmas Vacation* 1989 (PG-13) The third vacation for the Griswold family finds them hosting repulsive relatives for Yuletide. The sight gags, although predictable, are sometimes on the mark. Quaid is a standout as the slovenly cousin. **93m/C VHS, DVD, Blu-ray Disc.** Chevy Chase, Beverly D'Angelo, Randy Quaid, Diane Ladd, John Randolph, E.G. Marshall, Doris Roberts, Julia Louis-Dreyfus, Mae Questel, William Hickey, Brian Doyle-Murray, Juliette Lewis, Johnny Galecki, Nicholas Guest, Miriam Flynn; **D:** Jeremiah S. Chechik; **W:** John Hughes; **C:** Thomas Ackerman; **M:** Angelo Badalamenti.

National Lampoon's Christmas Vacation 2: Cousin Eddie's Big Island Adventure 🐾🐾 *National Lampoon's Cousin Eddie's Christmas Vacation Lost: Christmas Vacation 2: Cousin Eddie; Christmas Vacation 2: Cousin Eddie's Island Adventure* 2003 Quaid is back as boorish Cousin Eddie. This time his nutty gaggle gets to spend the holidays on a South Pacific island as a payoff from his old boss for a monkey mishap. But their fateful trip instead ends up on an uncharted desert isle. Again, the lessons of "Caddyshack 2" and "Blues Brothers 2000" go tragically unheeded. **83m/C VHS, DVD.** Randy Quaid, Miriam Flynn, Dana Barron, Jake Thomas, Beverly Garland, Stephen Furst, Eric Idle, Fred Willard, Ed Asner, Sung Hi Lee, Julian Stone, Kate Bradley; **D:** Nick Marck; **W:** Matty Simmons; **M:** Nathan Furst. **TV**

National Lampoon's Class of '86 🐾🐾½ *Class of '86* 1986 This is a live stage comedy show written and sponsored by the infamous adult humor magazine, featuring a new cast of comics. **86m/C VHS.** Rodger Bumpass, Veanne Cox, Annie Golden, John Michael Higgins, Tommy Koenig.

National Lampoon's Class Reunion 🐾 *Class Reunion* 1982 (R) Class reunion with some very wacky guests and a decided bad of plot or purpose. Things go from bad to worse when a crazed killer decides to join in on the festivities. Disappointing with very few laughs. **85m/C VHS, DVD.** Shelley Smith, Gerrit Graham, Michael Lerner; **D:** Michael Miller; **W:** Marc Bonilla. **CABLE**

National Lampoon's Dad's Week Off 🐾 *Dad's Week Off* 1997 (R) Jack (Winkler) is a stressed-out salesman who decides he needs time away from both his job and his family. His wife agrees to take their kids camping while Jack spends a week peacefully at home. But before he knows it, Jack's bud (Jeni) has introduced him to kooky Cherice (d'Abo) and it's party-time at Jack's place. **92m/C VHS.** Henry Winkler, Olivia d'Abo, Richard Jeni, Justin Louis, Ken Pogue, Wendel Meldrum; **D:** Neal Israel; **W:** Neal Israel; **C:** Jan Kiesser; **M:** Marc Bonilla.

National Lampoon's European Vacation 🐾½ *European Vacation* 1985 (PG-13) Sappy sequel to "Vacation" that has witless Chase and his family bumbling around in the land "across the pond." The Griswolds never redefine the term "ugly American." Stonehenge will never be the same. **94m/C VHS, DVD.** Chevy Chase, Beverly D'Angelo, Dana Hill, Jason Lively, Victor Lanoux, John Astin, Cameos: Eric Idle; **D:** Amy Heckerling; **W:** John Hughes, Robert Klane, Eric Idle; **M:** Charles Fox.

National Lampoon's Favorite Deadly Sins 🐾🐾½ 1995 (R) Three sketches about greed, anger, and lust. In "Lust," Leary plays a security guard who spies on a neighbor; "Anger" finds Clay as an irate convenience store shopper; and "Greed," stars as a sleazoid producer who helps a young woman kill her wicked stepmother and stepsisters in order to make a movie about it. **95m/C VHS.** Joe Mantegna, Denis Leary, Annabella Sciorra, Andrew (Dice Clay) Silverstein, Cassidy Rae, Brian Keith, William Ragsdale, Farrah Forke, Tanya Pohlkotte; **D:** Denis Leary, David Jablin; **M:** Mi-

chael Barrie, Jim Mulholland, Lee Biondi, Ann Lembeck.

National Lampoon's Gold Diggers WOOF! *Lady Killers* 2004 (PG-13) Why does anyone bother releasing this tripe on the big screen when it barely qualifies for basic cable or direct-to-video? The gold diggers of the title are a couple of inept twenty-something con men (Friedle, Owen) who plot to marry two elderly sisters (Taylor, Lasser) who are supposed to be wealthy Beverly Hills heiresses. Only the gals (who are, of course, broke) have their own insurance scam in mind. Can't even be enjoyed as trash. **82m/C DVD.** Will Friedle, Chris Owen, Louise Lasser, Renee Taylor, Nikki Ziering; **D:** Gary Preisler; **W:** Gary Preisler; **C:** Thomas Callaway.

National Lampoon's Golf Punks 🐾½ 1999 (PG-13) Innocuous comedy finds luckless former golf pro Al Oliver (Arnold) in desperate need of cash to pay off his gambling debts. So, he becomes an instructor to a bunch of teen misfits and decides to enter the uncoordinated group in a prestigious tournament. **90m/C VHS, DVD.** Bryan Cranston, Judge Reinhold, Reece Thompson, Penelope Ann Miller, Hallie Todd, Brittney Irvin, Anthony Holland, Noel Fisher, Noel Fisher, David Paetkau; **D:** Neal Israel; **W:** Marc Warren; **M:** Robert Folk, Brad Segal. **TV**

National Lampoon's Holiday Reunion 🐾 *Thanksgiving Family Reunion* 2003 (PG-13) Think "Christmas Vacation" but without the Griswolds, or the funny. Thanksgiving stands in for Wally World, Europe, Christmas, and Vegas. Cousin Woodward—you, sir, are no Cousin Eddie! **90m/C VHS, DVD.** Bryan Cranston, Judge CA Tom Arnold, James Kirk, Rene Tardif; **D:** Harvey Frost; **W:** Jill Mazursky; **C:** Patrick Williams; **M:** Richard Bronskill. **VIDEO**

National Lampoon's Last Resort 🐾½ 1994 (PG-13) Retired film actor finds his long-time movie nemesis can't separate screen life from the real thing anymore and is planning an invasion of the actor's private island. So, he calls on his nephew (who brings along a friend) to help him out. **91m/C VHS, DVD.** Corey Feldman, Corey Haim, Geoffrey Lewis, Robert Mandan; **D:** Rafal Zielinski.

National Lampoon's Loaded Weapon 1 🐾🐾 *Loaded Weapon 1* 1993 (PG-13) Cop Jack Colt (Estevez) and partner Wes Luger (Jackson) attempt to recover a microfilm which contains a formula for turning cocaine into cookies. Essentially a sendup of the popular "Lethal Weapon" series, although other movies and themes make an appearance, well sort of. Short on plot and long on slapstick, but that's the whole point. Tired formula creates nostalgia for the granddaddy of them all, "Airplane." Lots of cameos, including one from sibling spoof star Sheen. The magazine folded while the movie was in production, an ominous sign. **83m/C VHS, DVD.** Emilio Estevez, Samuel L. Jackson, Jon Lovitz, Tim Curry, Kathy Ireland, William Shatner, Dr. Joyce Brothers, James Doohan, Richard Moll, F. Murray Abraham, Denis Leary, Corey Feldman, Phil Hartman, J.T. Walsh, Erik Estrada, Larry Wilcox, Allyce Beasley, Charlie Sheen; **D:** Gene Quintano; **C:** Peter Deming; **M:** Robert Folk.

National Lampoon's Senior Trip 🐾 *Senior Trip* 1995 (R) According to the promotion, "They came, they saw, they passed out." Good dumb fun is hard to come by, perfectly effortful in a long line of lesser "Lampoon" effort in a long line of lesser Lampoons is about midwestern high school seniors who take a bus trip to Washington to meet the President. Along the way they have hijinks, including manipulation by a stereotypically political opponent. Frewer is the inept principal who leads the dopey corridors of power. Somehow, even the Coreys avoided this one. **91m/C VHS, DVD.** Matt Frewer, Valerie Mahaffey, Lawrence Dane, Thomas Chong, Kevin McDonald; **D:** Kelly Makin; **W:** I. Marlene King, Roger Kumble.

National Lampoon's The Don's Analyst 🐾 Don's Analyst 1997 (R) Don Vito (Loggia) has lots of problems—his wife has left him, his sons are too stupid to take over the business, and his mob rival wants both his business and his wife. The Don's so upset he's thinking of going legit. Instead, his sons kidnap therapist Dr. Riceputo (Polak) to straighten the Don out. 103m/C VHS, Robert Loggia, Kevin Pollak, Joseph Bologna, Angie Dickinson, Sherilyn Fenn; **D:** David Jablin. **CABLE**

National Lampoon's Vacation 🐾🐾 Vacation 1983 (R) The Clark Griswold (Chase) family of suburban Chicago embarks on a westward cross-country vacation via car to the renowned "Wally World." Ridiculous and hysterical misadventures, including a falling asleep at the wheel sequence and the untimely death of Aunt Edna. 98m/C VHS, DVD, HD DVD, Chevy Chase, Beverly D'Angelo, Imogene Coca, Randy Quaid, Christie Brinkley, James Keach, Anthony Michael Hall, John Candy, Eddie Bracken, Brian Doyle-Murray, Eugene Levy, Dana Barron, Jane Krakowski, Miriam Flynn, Frank McRae, John Diehl, Mickey Jones; **D:** Harold Ramis; **W:** John Hughes, Harold Ramis; **C:** Victor Kemper; **M:** Ralph Burns.

National Lampoon's Van Wilder 🐾 Van Wilder 2002 (R) Cliched and crass college comedy of suave coed Van Wilder (Reynolds) who gets cut off by his dad. (Matheson, in a nice bit of ironic casting), who realizes his son's seven college years have not yielded a degree. The universally adored, high-profile, frat house toastmaster then uses his charm to help fund his education by helping the underprivileged undergrads have fun—for a price, of course. A circus of gross-out jokes and sight gags that would make the Farrelly brothers blush ensue. Reid is typically vapid as the lackluster Lois Lane college reporter and love interest. An unrated version is also available. 92m/C VHS, DVD, Blu-ray Disc, UMD, US Ryan Reynolds, Tara Reid, Tim Matheson, Kal Penn, Teck Holmes, Daniel Cosgrove, Deon Richmond, Alex Burns, Paul Gleason, Tom Everett Scott, Chris Owen, Curtis Armstrong, Kim Smith, Erik Estrada, Michelle Rene Thomas; **D:** Walt Becker; **W:** Brent Goldberg, David T. Wagner; **C:** James R. Bagdonas; **M:** David Lawrence.

National Lampoon's Van Wilder 2: The Rise of Taj WOOF! 🐾 Van Wilder 2: The Rise of Taj 2006 (R) Despite the title, Ryan Reynolds-MIA as its former underling Taj Mahal Badalandabad (Penn) is all grown up and ready to tackle the countless and pointless sexual innuendo. Taj goes off to Camford University in England as a student-teacher and gets his own crew of flunkies to whip into shape. They must prove themselves to the school's elite in order to win the coveted Camford Cup. Shamelessly—and poorly—rips off scenes from too many other movies to keep track of. So bad it makes the original look good. 95m/C DVD, US Lauren Cohan, Daniel Percival, Glen Barry, Kal Penn, Anthony Cozens, Steven Rathman, Holly Davidson; **D:** Mort Nathan; **W:** David Gallagher; **C:** Hubert Taczanowski; **M:** Robert Folk.

National Security 🐾🐾 (PG-13) Earl Montgomery (Lawrence, seeming surprisingly bored) is a police academy reject and Hank Rafferty (Zahn) is a disgraced cop. Working as security guards, they uncover a smuggling operation in standard buddy-cop fashion. What the problem is? Car chases and Lawrence's rapid-fire "comic" rantings replace any semblance of plot or direction to make a mess that wastes the time of all involved. But at least it has spiteful racial politics played for laughs. 90m/C VHS, DVD, US Martin Lawrence, Steve Zahn, Eric Roberts, Bill Duke, Colm Feore, Timothy Busfield, Robine Lee, Matt McCoy, Brett Cullen, Stephen Tobolowsky, Joe Flaherty; **D:** Dennis Dugan; **W:** Jay Scherick, David Ronn; **C:** Oliver Wood; **M:** Randy Edelman.

National Treasure 🐾🐾 2004 (PG) Old-fashioned and underwhelming adventure tale. Once upon a time, the Knights Templar unearthed the legendary treasure of King Solomon during a crusade. After

---

being hidden in Europe, the treasure supposedly made its way to colonial-era America where the Freemasons, who included many of our Founding Fathers, protected it. The treasure is a longtime obsession for the Gates family, including Benjamin Franklin Gates (Cage), who thinks his best clue is concealed on the reverse side of the Declaration of Independence. When his sinister benefactor Howe (Bean) plots to steal the document, patriotic Ben and his techie sidekick Riley (Bartha) try to alert the authorities, including hottie conservator Abigail (Kruger). Many uninvolving twists and less-than-exciting action sequences follow. 130m/C DVD, UMD, US Nicolas Cage, Diane Kruger, Justin Bartha, Sean Bean, Jon Voight, Harvey Keitel, Christopher Plummer; **D:** Jon Turteltaub; **W:** Jim Kouf, Marianne S. Wibberley, Cormac Wibberley; **C:** Caleb Deschanel; **M:** Trevor Rabin.

National Treasure: Book of Secrets 🐾🐾🐾 2007 (PG) Equally old-fashioned sequel to the 2004 treasure hunt. Ben Gates (Cage) and dad Patrick (Voight) defend the family honor from dastardly southerner Mitch Wilkinson (Harris), who insists a Gates ancestor was actually behind Lincoln's assassination. Interesting historical clues combine with a presidential book of secrets and a global hunt for missing gold to create an enjoyable adventure. Includes all the players from the original, along with new addition, Gates matriarch Emily (an admirably game Mirren). 124m/C DVD, US Nicolas Cage, Jon Voight, Diane Kruger, Justin Bartha, Helen Mirren, Harvey Keitel, Ed Harris, Bruce Greenwood, Alicia Coppola, Michael Maize, Timothy Murphy, Joel Gretsch; **D:** Jon Turteltaub; **W:** Cormac Wibberley, Marianne S. Wibberley; **C:** John Schwartzman, Amir M. Mokri; **M:** Trevor Rabin.

National Velvet 🐾🐾🐾 1944 (G) Velvet Brown (Taylor) wins a horse in a raffle and is determined to train it to compete in the famed Grand National race. With the help of her best friend, Mi (Rooney), Taylor, only 12 at the time is superb in her first starring role. Rooney also gives a fine performance. Filmed with a loving eye on lushly decorated sets, this is a masterpiece version of the story of affection between a girl and her pet. Based on the novel by Enid Bagnold and followed by the dismal "International Velvet" in 1978. 124m/C VHS, DVD, Elizabeth Taylor, Mickey Rooney, Anne Revere, Donald Crisp, Angela Lansbury, Reginald Owen, Norma Varden, Terry Kilburn; **D:** Clarence Brown; **W:** Theodore Reeves, Helen Deutsch; **C:** Leonard Smith; **M:** Herbert Stothart. Oscars '45: Film Editing, Support. Actress (Revere); Natl. Film Reg. '03.

Native Son 🐾🐾½ 1951 (R) A young black man from the ghettos of Chicago is hired as a chauffeur by an affluent white family. His job is to drive their head-strong daughter anywhere she wants to go. Unintentionally, he kills her, tries to hide, and is ultimately found guilty. Based on the classic novel by Richard Wright, who also stars. Remade in 1986. Unprofessional direction and low budget work against the strong story. 91m/B VHS, Richard Wright, Jean Wallace, Nicholas Joy, Gloria Madison, Charles Cane; **D:** Pierre Chenal.

Native Son 🐾🐾½ 1986 (R) This second film adaptation of the classic Richard Wright novel is chock full of stars and tells the story of a poor black man who accidentally kills a white woman and then hides the body. Changes in the script soft-soap some of the novel's disturbing truths and themes—so-so except for those who have not read the book. 111m/C VHS, Geraldine Page, Oprah Winfrey, Matt Dillon, John Karlen, Elizabeth McGovern, Akosua Busia, Carroll Baker, Victor Love, John McMartin, Art Evans, Willard Pugh, David Rasche; **D:** Jerrold Freedman; **W:** Richard Wesley; **C:** Thomas Burstyn; **M:** James Mtume.

Nativity 🐾🐾 1978 Unmemorable, made-for-TV portrayal of the romance between Mary and Joseph (of the Bible story), Joseph's response to Mary's pregnancy, and the birthing of Jesus. Not exactly a Bible epic, the direction and acting are uninspirec. 97m/C VHS, John Shea, Madeleine

---

Stowe, Jane Wyatt, John Rhys-Davies, Kate O'Mara **D:** Bernard L. Kowalski.

The Nativity Story 🐾🐾½ 2006 (PG) Faithful retelling of the events leading to the birth of Jesus, from the arrangement of Mary's (Castle-Hughes) marriage to Joseph (Isaac) to their journey to Bethlehem. A sort of kinder, gentler companion to Mel Gibson's "The Passion of the Christ," it conveys "the hope that Jesus' arrival brings amid the mayhem caused by King Herod (Hinds). Though it plays mostly as a Sunday school lesson, director Hardwicke uses her skills as a former teacher well, performance is solid and mature, 102m/C VHS, DVD, US Keisha Castle-Hughes, Shohreh Aghdashloo, Hiam Abbass, Shaun Toub, Oscar Isaac, Stanley Townsend, Ciaran Hinds, Alexander Siddig, Alessandro Giuggioli, Nadim Sawalha, Eriq Ebouaney; **D:** Catherine Hardwicke; **W:** Mike Rich; **C:** Elliot Davis; **M:** Mychael Danna.

The Natural 🐾🐾🐾 1984 (PG) A beautifully filmed movie about baseball as myth. A young man, whose gift for baseball sets him apart, finds that trouble dogs him, particularly with a woman. In time as an aging rookie, he must fight against his past to lead his team to the World Series, and win the woman who is meant for him. From the Bernard Malamud story. 134m/C VHS, DVD, Robert Redford, Glenn Close, Robert Duvall, Kim Basinger, Wilford Brimley, Barbara Hershey, Richard Farnsworth, Robert Prosky, Darren McGavin, Joe Don Baker, Michael Madsen; **D:** Barry Levinson; **W:** Roger Towne, Phil Dusenberry; **C:** Caleb Deschanel; **M:** Randy Newman.

Natural Born Killers 🐾🐾 1994 (R) An old script by Tarantino is resurrected by Stone and is invested with its own unique subtle nuance and style. Controversial (natch, considering the director and writer) look at the way the media portrays criminals. Harrelson and Lewis are the lovestruck, white-trash serial killers who become tabloid-TV darlings, thanks to a sensationalistic press led by Downey Jr. Stone's dark and manic comment on America's fascination and revulsion with violence is strictly of the love it or leave it variety. Bloodshed galore, dazzling photography, and a dynamite soundtrack (with over 75 selections) add up to sensory overload. 119m/C VHS, DVD, Woody Harrelson, Robert Downey Jr., Juliette Lewis, Tommy Lee Jones, Richard Lineback, Tom Sizemore, Rodney Dangerfield, Rachel Ticotin, Arliss Howard, Russell Means, Denis Leary, Steven Wright, Pruitt Taylor Vince, Dale Dye, Lanny Lombard, O-Lan Jones, Edie McClurg, Evan Handler, Kirk Baltz, Maria Pitillo, Jared Harris, Balthazar Getty, Joe Grifasi, James Gammon, Mark Harmon; **D:** Oliver Stone; **W:** Oliver Stone; **C:** Robert Richardson; **M:** Trent Reznor.

Natural Causes 🐾½ 1994 (PG-13) Muddled political thriller finds Dr. Jessie McCarthy (Purl) traveling to Thailand by McCarthy on a pleasant distraction. While there Rachel's increasing alienation and despair. 90m/C VHS, Linda Purl, Cary-Hiroyuki Tagawa, Will Patton, Tim Thomerson, Janis Paige, Ali MacGraw; **D:** James Becket; **W:** Jake Raymond Needham; **C:** Denis Maloney; **M:** Nathan Wang.

Natural Enemies 🐾🐾½ 1979 (R) A successful publisher begins to consider suicide and murder as the cure for his family's increasing alienation and despair. Dark and depressing drama. 100m/C VHS, Hal Holbrook, Louise Fletcher, Jose Ferrer, Viveca Lindfors; **D:** Jeff Kanew; **W:** Jeff Kanew.

Natural Enemy 🐾🐾 1996 (R) Unsuspecting married couple become the target of a disturbed man with a big secret. 88m/C VHS, DVD, Donald Sutherland, William McNamara, Lesley Ann Warren, Joe Pantoliano, Tia Carrere; **D:** Douglas Jackson; **W:** Kevin Bernhard; **C:** Rodney Gibbons; **M:** Alan Reeves. **CABLE**

The Natural History of Parking Lots 🐾🐾 1990 What's a rich L.A. father to do when his teenage son hot-wires antique cars for kicks? Why pay his gun-running older brother to keep an eye on him. And the whackiness is just beginning. 92m/C VHS, Charlie Bean, B. Wyatt, Eli Guralnick; **D:** Everet Lewis; **W:** Everet Lewis; **C:** Hisham Abed; **M:** Johannes Hammers.

Nature of the Beast 🐾🐾 1994 (R) A businessman and a drifter are both hiding deadly secrets as police search for both a serial killer and the $1 million missing. Is a Vegas casino robbery. Just which man is involved in what crime? 91m/C VHS, DVD, Eric Roberts, Lance Henriksen, Brion James; **D:** Victor Salva.

Nature's Playmates 🐾 1962 A distinctive tattoo on his posterior. One of H.G. Lewis' obscure "nudie" flicks, sexual any standards. 56m/B VHS, Vicki (Allison Louise Downe) Miss, Allison Louise Downe, Scott Osborne, Terry Stevens, Peter Lathrop, Fred Gordon; **D:** Herschell Gordon Lewis; **W:** Ben T. Williams; **C:** William R. Johnson.

Naughty Knights 🐾 Up the Chastity Belt 1971 (PG) Soft-core romp in a medieval setting. Toss it in the moat. Arranged marriage, and is captured by pirates. When she's saved by a dashing Indian scout, it's love at first sight. The first MacDonald-Eddy match-up and very popular in its day. 72m/C VHS, Frankie Howerd, Graham Crowden, Bill Fraser, Roy Hudd, Hugh Paddick, Anna Quayle, Eartha Kitt, Dave King, Fred Emney; **D:** Bob Kellett; **M:** Carl Davis.

Naughty Marietta 🐾🐾½ 1935 A French princess switches identities with a mail-order bride to escape from her arranged marriage, and is captured by pirates. When she's saved by a dashing Indian scout, it's love at first sight. The first MacDonald-Eddy match-up and very popular in its day. 7 Italian Street Song; Chansonette; Antoinette and Anatole; Prayer; Tramp, Tramp, Tramp; The Owl and the Bobcat; Neath the Southern Moon; Mon Ami Pierrot; Ship Ahoy. 106m/B VHS, Jeanette MacDonald, Nelson Eddy, Frank Morgan, Elsa Lanchester, Douglass Dumbrille, Cecilia Parker; **D:** W.S. Van Dyke; **C:** William H. Daniels. Oscars '35: Sound. Natl. Film Reg. '03.

The Naughty Nineties 🐾🐾 1945 Bud and Lou help a showboat owner fend off crooks in the 1890s. Usual slapstick shenanigans, but highlighted by verbal banter. Includes the first on-screen rendition of the classic "Who's on First?" routine. J Rolling Down the River; Uncle Tom's Cabin I Can't Get You Out of My Mind; On a Sunday Afternoon; I'd Leave My Happy Home for You; Nora Malone; Ma Blushin' Rosie; The Showboat's Comin' to Town; A Blarney from Killarney. 76m/B VHS, Bud Abbott, Lou Costello, Henry Travers, Alan Curtis, Joseph (Joe) Sawyer, Rita Johnson, Joe (Joseph) Kirk, Lois Collier; **D:** Jean Yarbrough.

Nautilus 🐾🐾 1999 (R) In the year 2100, the planet has been destroyed by a series of cataclysms caused by a scientific experiment. An scientist decides to go back in time aboard a futuristic submarine in order to change the past and save the future. 99m/C VHS, DVD, Richard Norton, Hannes Jaenicke, Miranda Wolfe; **D:** Rodney McDonald; **W:** C. Courtney Joyner; **M:** Eric Wurst. **VIDEO**

Navajo Blues 🐾🐾 1997 (R) Police detective Nicholas Epps is installed in the federal witness protection program after seeing a mob hit on his partner. He's sent to a Native American reservation to hide out until the trial but can't resist investigating a series of local murders. 99m/C VHS, DVD, Steven Bauer, Irene Bedard, Charlotte Lewis, Ed O'Ross, Michael Horse, Tom Fridley; **D:** Joey Travolta; **C:** Dan Heigh.

Navajo Joe 🐾🐾½ 1967 The sole survivor of a massacre single-handedly kills each person involved in the atrocity, which aids a terrorized, though unappreciative, town in the process. Low-budget Spanish-Italian western only worth watching because of Reynolds. Filmed in Spain. 89m/C VHS, IT SP Burt Reynolds, Aldo Sambrel, Tanya Lopez, Fernando Rey; **D:** Sergio Corbucci; **M:** Ennio Morricone.

The Navigator 🐾🐾🐾 1924 Ever the quick thinker, Keaton actually bought a steamer headed for the scrap heap and used it to film an almost endless string of sight gags. Rejected by a socialite, millionaire Keaton finds himself alone with her on the abandoned boat. As he saves her from various and sundry perils, the gags and thrills abound—including one stunt that was inspired by a near-accident on the set. Too bad they don't make 'em like this anymore. Silent. **60m/B VHS, DVD.** Buster Keaton, Kathryn McGuire, Frederick Vroom, Noble Johnson, Clarence Burton, H. M. Clugston; **D:** Donald Crisp, Buster Keaton; **W:** Clyde Bruckman, Jean C. Havez, Joseph A. Mitchell; **C:** Byron Houck, Elgin Lessley.

The Navigator 🐾🐾🐾 1988 (PG) A creative time-travel story of a 14th-century boy with visionary powers who leads the residents of his medieval English village away from a plague by burrowing through the earth's core and into late-20th-century New Zealand. Quite original and refreshing. **92m/C VHS, DVD. NZ** Hamish McFarlane, Bruce Lyons, Chris Haywood, Marshall Napier, Noel Appleby, Paul Livingston, Sarah Pierse; **D:** Vincent Ward; **W:** Vincent Ward. Australian Film Inst. '88: Cinematog., Director (Ward), Film.

The Navigators 🐾🐾 2001 (R) In 1995, British Rail is privatized and a portion of the South Yorkshire line is now serviced by two competing companies. The new owners break up the union system—some of the former workers decide to retire while others, including four friends, have to stick it out. Since fewer men are employed in maintaining the railway depot and lines, accidents increase and the increased stress just isn't professional but personal as well. **92m/C VHS, DVD. GB GE SP** Steve Huison, Dean Andrews, Tom Craig, Joe Duttine, Venn Tracey; **D:** Ken Loach; **W:** Rob Dawber; **C:** Barry Ackroyd, Mike Eley; **M:** George Fenton.

Navy Blue and Gold 🐾🐾½ 1937 Three football-playing midshipmen (Young, Stewart, and Brown) at Annapolis share a friendship. Stewart has registered under a false name since his dad was unfairly cashiered from the service. When he hears some slander about his old man he stands up and tells the truth and gets suspended, just before the big game with Army. Naturally, he's reinstated just in time to make the big play and carry the team to victory. Well-done, old-fashioned hokum. **94m/B VHS.** James Stewart, Florence Young, Tom Brown, Lionel Barrymore, Florence Rice, Billie Burke, Samuel S. Hinds, Paul Kelly, Frank Albertson, Minor Watson; **D:** Sam Wood; **W:** George Bruce.

The Navy Comes Through 🐾🐾 1942 Salty sailors aboard a mangy freighter beat the odds and sink Nazi warships and subs with the greatest of ease. Boy meets girl subplot is added for good measure. Morale booster includes newsreel footage. **81m/B VHS.** Pat O'Brien, George Murphy, Jane Wyatt, Jackie Cooper, Carl Esmond, Max Baer Sr., Desi Arnaz Sr., Ray Collins, Lee Bonnell, Frank Jenks, Helmut Dantine; **D:** Edward Sutherland.

Navy SEALS 🐾🐾 1990 (R) A group of macho Navy commandos, whose regular work is to rescue hostages from Middle Eastern underground organizations, finds a stash of deadly weapons. They spend the balance of the movie attempting to destroy the arsenal. Sheen chews the scenery as a crazy member of the commando team. Lots of action and violence, but simplistic good guys-bad guys philosophy and plot weaknesses keep this from being more than below average. **113m/C VHS, DVD.** Charlie Sheen, Michael Biehn, Joanne Whalley, Rick Rossovich, Cyril O'Reilly, Bill Paxton, Dennis Haysbert, Paul Sanchez, Ron Joseph, Nicholas Kadi; **D:** Lewis Teague; **W:** Gary Goldman; **C:** John A. Alonzo; **M:** Sylvester Levay.

Navy vs. the Night Monsters Woof! *Monsters of the Night* 1966 When horrifying, acid-secreting plant monsters try to take over the world, Van Doren and the Navy must come to the rescue, with the action taking place in a tropical South Pole setting. Amazing deployment of talents. **87m/C VHS.** Mamie Van Doren, Anthony Eisley, Pamela Mason, Bobby Van, Russ Bender; **D:** Michael Hoey; **W:** Michael Hoey.

Navy Way 🐾 1944 Hurriedly produced war propaganda film in which a boxer gets inducted into the Navy just before his title shot. **74m/B VHS, DVD.** Robert Lowery, Jean Parker, Roscoe Karns, William Henry, Robert Armstrong, Tom Keene; **D:** William Berke; **W:** Maxwell Shane; **C:** Fred H. Jackman Jr.; **M:** Willy Stahl.

Nazarin 🐾🐾🐾 1958 Buñuel's scathing indictment of Christianity finds its perfect vehicle in the adventures of a defrocked priest attempting to relive Christ's life. Gathering a group of disciples, he wanders into the Mexican desert as a cross between Christ and Don Quixote. Filmed in Mexico, this is Buñuel at his grimmest. Based on a novel by Benito Perez Galdos; Spanish with subtitles. **92m/B VHS.** MX Francesco Rabal, Rita Macedo, Margo Lopez, Rita McLedo, Ignacio Lopez Tarso, Jesus Fernandez; **D:** Luis Buñuel.

Nea 🐾🐾½ 1978 (R) Comic drama about a young girl from a privileged home who writes a best selling pornographic novel anonymously. When her book writing talents are made public through betrayal, she gets even in a most unique way. Subtitled "A Young Emmanuelle." Kaplan also performs. Appealing and sophisticated. **101m/C VHS, DVD.** Sami Frey, Ann Zacharias, Heinz Bennent; **D:** Nelly Kaplan.

Near Dark 🐾🐾🐾 1987 (R) Southwestern farm boy Caleb (Pasdar) is attracted to the pretty Mae (Wright) and falls in unwillingly with a family of thirsty, outlaw-fringe vampires who roam the West in a van. The first mainstream effort by Bigelow, and a rollicking, blood-saturated, slaughterhouse of a movie, with enough laughs and stunning imagery to move the place as the performers crank up the mixups to maximum frenzy, but with little effect since you really don't care much about these fools. **95m/C VHS, DVD, UMD.** Adrian Pasdar, Jenny Wright, Bill Paxton, Jenette Goldstein, Lance Henriksen, Tim Thomerson, Joshua John Miller; **D:** Kathryn Bigelow; **W:** Kathryn Bigelow, Eric Red; **C:** Adam Greenberg; **M:** Tangerine Dream.

Near Misses 🐾🐾½ 1991 Missable farce with Reinhold as a bigamist in the foreign service. To make time for a mistress he swaps identities with a young Marine in Paris, but then the KGB kidnaps the imposter. Doors slam in hallways all over the world. **57m/B VHS, DVD.** Bob Steele, Lafe (Lafayette) McKee, Louise Lorraine, Al Ferguson, Al Hewston; **D:** (John) (Paterson) McGowan.

Near the Rainbow's End 🐾½ 1930 Cattle rancher Steele (in his first talking western) finds out that rustlers are aggravating the trouble between the cattlemen and the sheep herders. So he goes after the bad guys and then settles the feud by marrying a sheep herder's daughter. **57m/B VHS, DVD.** Bob Steele, Lafe (Lafayette) McKee, Louise Lorraine, Al Ferguson, Al Hewston; **D:** (John) (Paterson) McGowan.

Nearing Grace 🐾🐾 2005 (R) In 1978, responsible high school senior Henry Nearing (Smith) is trying to cope with the death of his mother, while his dad (Morse) and older brother (Moscow) take to drink, drugs, and reckless behavior. Henry can't see that his gal pal Merna (Johnson) is perfect for him and instead he pants after sexy tease Grace (Brewster), until he learns better. Smith and Johnson are a cute twosome but the story's familiar. Based on Scott Sommers' 1979 novel. **105m/C DVD.** Gregory Edward Smith, Jordana Brewster, Ashley Johnson, David Moscow, David Morse, Chad Faust, Brian Murray, Logan Bartholomew; **D:** Rick Rosenthal; **W:** Jacob Aaron Estes; **C:** David Geddes; **M:** John E. Nordstrom.

'Neath Brooklyn Bridge 🐾🐾 1942 The Boys from the Bowery get tangled up in crime when they try to help a young girl whose guardian was murdered. **61m/B VHS, DVD.** Leo Gorcey, Huntz Hall, Bobby Jordan, Sammy (Earnest) Morrison, Ann Gillis, Noah Beery Jr., Marc Lawrence, Gabriel Dell; **D:** Wallace Fox.

'Neath Canadian Skies 🐾 1946 Mounted lawman who says "eh" a lot tracks murdering gang of mine looters. **41m/B VHS.** CA Russell Hayden, Inez Cooper, Cliff Nazarro, Kermit Maynard, Jack Mulhall; **D:** B. Reeves Eason; **W:** Arthur V. Jones; **C:** Marcel Le Picard; **M:** Carl Hoefle.

'Neath the Arizona Skies 🐾🐾 1934 Low budget oater epic about a cowhand who finds all the action he and his friends can handle as they try to rescue a young Indian girl (and oil heiress) who has been kidnapped. "Nuff said. **54m/B VHS, DVD.** John Wayne, George "Gabby" Hayes, Shelia Terry; **D:** Harry Fraser.

Necessary Parties 1988 Based on Barbara Dana's book that has a 15-year-old boy filing a lawsuit to stop his parents' divorce. Originally aired on PBS as part of the "Wonderworks" family movie series. **120m/C VHS, DVD.** Alan Arkin, Mark Paul Gosselaar, Barbara Dana, Adam Arkin, Donald Moffat, Julie Hagerty, Geoffrey Pierson, Taylor Fry; **D:** Gwen Amer.

Necessary Roughness 🐾🐾 1991 (PG-13) After losing their NCAA standing, the Texas Southern University (passing for the real Texas State) Armadillos football team looks like it's headed for disaster. The once proud football factory is now composed of assorted goofballs instead of stud players. But hope arrives in the form of a 34-year-old farmer with a golden arm, ready to recapture some lost dreams as quarterback. Can this unlikely team rise above itself and win a game, or will their hopes be squashed all over the field? **108m/C VHS, DVD.** Scott Bakula, Robert Loggia, Harley Jane Kozak, Sinbad, Hector Elizondo, Kathy Ireland, Jason Bateman; **D:** Stan Dragoti; **W:** Rick Natkin, David Fuller; **C:** Peter Stein; **M:** Bill Conti.

Necromancer: Satan's Servant 🐾🐾 1988 (R) After a woman is brutally raped, she contacts a sorceress and makes a pact with the devil to ensure her successful revenge. Plenty of graphic violence and nudity. **90m/C VHS, DVD.** Elizabeth Kaitan, Russ Tamolyn, Rhonda Dorton; **D:** Dusty Nelson; **W:** William T. Naud; **C:** Eric Cayla, Richard Clabaugh; **M:** Kevin Klinger, Bob Mamet, Gary Stockdale.

Necropolis 🐾 1987 (R) A witch burned at the stake 300 years ago is brought back to life as a motorcycle punkette in New York (or New York?). New waver should have been watchable. **77m/C VHS.** Leeanne Baker, Michael Conte, Jacquie Fritz, William Reed, Paul Ruber; **D:** Tim Kincaid.

Ned Kelly 🐾🐾½ 1970 (PG) Dramatizes the life of Australia's most notorious outlaw. Kelly (Jagger) and his family start off as horse thieves and proceed from there. A manhunt results in death.and the eventual capture and execution of Kelly. The very contemporary British Jagger was miscast as a period Australian and British director Richardson seems to have lacked an empathy for the material, given his lethargic direction. **100m/C VHS, DVD.** GB Mick Jagger, Allen Bickford, Geoff Gilmour, Mark McManus, Serge Lazareff, Peter Sumner, Ken Shorter, James Elliott, Diane Craig, Sue Lloyd, Clarissa Kaye; **D:** Tony Richardson; **W:** Ian Jones, Tony Richardson; **M:** Shel Silverstein.

Ned Kelly 🐾🐾½ 2003 (R) Another telling of the legend of Australian outlaw Ned Kelly (Ledger), based on the novel "Our Sunshine" by Robert Drewe. Kelly was falsely imprisoned for three years and faced such harassment from corrupt law officers that he took up bank robbery with a gang of four others and became a folk hero for the lower class. Ledger fits the role well but Orlando Bloom (as Kelly's Gang member Joe Byrne) is a scene-stealer. Very genuine, well-made effort with a brutal final showdown between the police and the gang, but the presentation doesn't always flow well. **109m/C DVD. AU** Heath Ledger, Orlando Bloom, Geoffrey Rush, Naomi Watts, Joel Edgerton, Laurence Kinlan, Kris McQuade, Emily Browning, Kiri Paramore, Rachel Griffiths, Charles "Bud" Tingwell, Peter Phelps, Russell Dykstra, Phil Barantini, Kerry Condon, Saskia Burmeister; **D:** Gregor Jordan; **W:** John M. McDonagh; **C:** Oliver Stapleton; **M:** Klaus Badelt.

Needful Things 🐾🐾½ 1993 (R) Stephen King film adaptations are becoming as prolific as his novels, though few seem to improve in the transition from page to screen. This time a scheming Maine shopkeeper (Von Sydow) sells unsuspecting small towners peculiar items that, not surprisingly, begin to cause horror and mayhem. Harris is the town sheriff who tries to warn everyone that he's the devil in disguise. Big screen directorial debut for Heston (yes, Charlton's son). **120m/ C VHS, DVD.** Ed Harris, Bonnie Bedelia, Max von Sydow, Amanda Plummer, J.T. Walsh, William Morgan Sheppard; **D:** Fraser Heston; **W:** W.D. Richter; **C:** Tony Westman; **M:** Patrick Doyle.

Nefertiti, Queen of the Nile 🐾🐾 1964 Woman, married against her will, turns into Nefertiti. For fans of Italo-Biblical epics only. **97m/C VHS.** IT Jeanne Crain, Vincent Price, Edmund Purdom, Amedeo Nazzari, Liana Orfei; **D:** Fernando Cerchio.

Negatives 🐾🐾 1968 A couple indulge in sexual fantasies to dangerous extremes, with the man first impersonating Dr. Crippen, the early 1900s murderer, and later a WWI flying ace. When a photographer friend joins the fun, the action careens off the deep end. **90m/C VHS. GB** Peter McEnery, Diane Cilento, Glenda Jackson, Maurice Denham, Norman Rossington; **D:** Peter Medak.

The Negotiator 🐾🐾½ 1998 (R) Police hostage negotiator Danny Roman (Jackson) has had his life destroyed by false accusations of theft and murder. So he decides to go after his accusers by taking the Chicago Internal Affairs Bureau staff (what else?) hostage. Chris Sabian (Spacey), a negotiator from another precinct, is Roman's only hope to save himself and find the real culprits. Jackson and Spacey are excellent in their scenes together, and the supporting cast does a fine job. Nice action sequences and suspenseful storyline make for a thrilling ride, as long as you don't contemplate the details for too long. **115m/C VHS, DVD.** Samuel L. Jackson, Kevin Spacey, David Morse, Ron Rifkin, John Spencer, Regina Taylor, J.T. Walsh, Siobhan Fallon, Paul Giamatti, Paul Guilfoyle, Carlos Gomez, Nestor Serrano; **D:** F. Gary Gray; **W:** James DeMonaco, Kevin Fox; **C:** Russell Carpenter; **M:** Graeme Revell.

The Neighbor 🐾🐾½ 1993 (R) See nice city couple John and Mary move to small town Vermont. See their nice retired obstetrician neighbor Myron welcome them. See Mary get pregnant and Myron take an obsessional interest. See John arrested for murder. See Mary left alone—except for Myron's tender care. **93m/C VHS, DVD.** Linda Kozlowski, Ron Lea, Rod Steiger, Frances Bay, Bruce Boa, Jane Wheeler; **D:** Rodney Gibbons; **W:** Kurt Wimmer.

The Neighbor No. Thirteen 🐾½ *Rinjin 13-go* 2005 (R) Excessively horrific violence abounds when a Japanese man, Juzo (Oguri), meets up with his childhood tormentor Akai (Arai). Seeing that Akai's brutish behavior hasn't changed and that he doesn't even recall Juzo or the suffering he endured causes Juzo's maniacal side to emerge and seek vengeance. **115m/C DVD.** Hirofumi Arai, Takashii Milke, Shido Nakamura, Shun Oguri, Yumi Yoshimura, Tomoya Ishii; **W:** Ha-jime Kado; **C:** Taro Kawazu; **M:** Riji Kitazato.

Neighbors 🐾🐾 1981 (R) The Keeses (Belushi and Walker) live in a quiet, middle-class suburban neighborhood where life is calm and sweet. But their new neighbors, Ramona and Vic (Aykroyd and Moriarty), prove to be loud, obnoxious, crazy, and freeloading. Will Earl and Enid Keese mind their manners as their neighborhood disintegrates? Some funny moments, but as the script fades, so do the laughs. Belushi's last waltz is based on Thomas Berger's novel. **90m/C VHS, DVD.** John Belushi, Dan Aykroyd, Kathryn Walker, Cathy Moriarty; **D:** John G. Avildsen; **W:** Larry Gelbart; **M:** Bill Conti.

Neil Gaiman's NeverWhere 🐾🐾½ 1996 Ordinary Londoner Richard Mayhew never before realized there's an extraordinary world beneath his feet. Until he helps an injured mystery woman named Door. The next morning, Richard's world is turned upside down—no one he knows remembers him and he's now jobless and homeless. When Richard finds his way into London Below, he sees Door again and discovers a feudal society and much strangeness as he tries to get back to his old reality. **180m/C DVD, GB** *Gary Bakewell, Laura Fraser, Hywel Bennet, Clive Russell, Peter Capaldi, Stratford Johns;* **D:** *Dewi Humphreys;* **W:** *Neil Gaiman; Lenny Henry;* **C:** *Steve Murray, Steve Saunderson;* **M:** *Brian Eno.* **TV**

Nelly et Monsieur Arnaud ♦♦♦
Nelly and Mr. Arnaud 1995 Chatty adult May/December would-be romance between 25-year-old secretary

Nell ♦♦½ 1994 (R) "Wild child" story—adult version. When illiterate, barely verbal backwoods Nell (Foster) is discovered after her stroke-afflicted mother's death, she's placed in the care of a doctor (Neeson) and psychologist (Richardson) who have different ideas about how to bring her into society. Unfairly dismissed by some as self-indulgent, Foster's raw physical performance is truly mesmerizing, dull script, unconvincingly tidy ending, and gross over-sentimentality are what disappoint. From the play "Idioglossia" by Mark Handley. **114m/C VHS, DVD,** *Jodie Foster, Liam Neeson, Natasha Richardson, Richard Libertini;* **D:** *Michael Apted '94; Actress (Foster). Screen Actors Guild '94.*

Nekromantik 2 ♦♦ 1991 Includes highlights from the first "Nekro", the sequel picks up with a new nekro-chick who obtains the head of Rob, the jilted necrophile of the previous movie. Sicker than its predecessor, with less non-stop shock and a little more plot. In German with English subtitles. **100m/C VHS, DVD, GE** *Monika M., Daktari Lorenz, Harald Lundt, Henri Boeck, Clemens Schwender, Holger Suhr, Jorg Buttgereit;* **D:** *Jorg Buttgereit;* **W:** *Franz Rodenkirchen;* **C:** *Uwe Bohrer;* **M:** *Herman Kopp, Daktari Lorenz*

Nekromantik ♦♦½ 1987 How much can we say—not to everyone's taste? How's this: a romantic story of necrophilia. Followed by "Nekromantik 2". In German with English subtitles. **74m/C VHS, DVD, GE** *Bernd Daktari Lorenz, Beatrice M., Harald Lundt, Colloseo Schulzendorff, Susa Kohlstedt;* **D:** *Jorg Buttgereit;* **W:** *Jorg Buttgereit;* **C:** *Uwe Bohrer;* **M:** *Herman Kopp, Daktari Lorenz*

Neil Young: Heart of Gold ♦♦♦ 2006 (R) Demme shot two acoustic concert performances by Young at Nashville's fabled Ryman Auditorium on August 18 and 19, 2005, where Young featured songs from his new album "Prairie Wind" as well as some old favorites. In April of that year, Young had been diagnosed with a life-threatening brain aneurysm and wrote and recorded the album before his surgery. The concerts were the first after his recovery. **103m/C DVD, US D:** *Jonathan Demme;* **C:** *Ellen Kuras;* **M:** *Nei Young.*

Neil Simon's The Odd Couple 2 ♦♦½ *The Odd Couple 2* 1998 (PG-13) In the not-too-grand tradition of "Caddyshack II," "Son of the Pink Panther," and "Blues Brothers 2000" they waited too long. And like the others, they shouldn't have even bothered. Oscar (Matthau) and Felix (Lemmon) reunite when their respective kids (Silverman as Oscar's son, Waltz as Felix's daughter) marry. Meeting at LAX, the duo immediately falls into the old routine of annoying each other and, this time out, the audience. Simon fills his script with leftover road movie clichés and vaudeville jokes, leaving Lemmon and Matthau nothing to do but mug and yell. Since almost everything these two have done together since the original has been a de facto sequel, it's a shame that the real thing falls so flat. **96m/C VHS, DVD,** *Jack Lemmon, Walter Matthau, Jonathan Silverman, Lisa Waltz, Christine Baranski, Jean Smart, Barnard Hughes, Doris Belack, Ellen Geer, Jay O. Sanders, Rex Linn, Mary Beth Peil, Alice Ghostley, Rebecca Schull, Florence Stanley, Lou (Cotel) Cutell;* **D:** *Howard Deutch;* **W:** *Neil Simon;* **C:** *Jamie Anderson;* **M:** *Alan Silvestri.*

Nelly (Bear) and Pierre Arnaud (Serrault), she's working. The arrogant divorced Arnaud is intrigued by the independent Nelly, by whom he finds he can't control, while she comes to appreciate their emotional ties (altogether different from the selfishness of the younger men she knows). Conclusion avoids a neat resolution to a situation beset by bad timing. French with subtitles. **105m/C VHS, DVD,** *FR GE FR Emmanuelle Beart, Michel Serrault, Jean-Hugues Anglade, Francoise Brion, Claire Nadeau, Michele (Michel) Lonsdale, Charles Bering, Michele Laroque;* **D:** *Claude Sautet;* **W:** *Jacques Fieschi, Claude Sautet;* **C:** *Jean-Francois Robin;* **M:** *Philippe Sarde, Cesar '96; Actor (Serrault), Director (Sautet).*

Nemesis ♦♦½ 1993 (R) Futuristic thriller that combines cybernetics and cyborgs in post-nuclear Los Angeles. Gruner plays a human (although he's mostly composed of mechanical replacement parts) boys, information terrorists, bio-enhanced in a world overwrought with system cowboys, gangsters, and cyborg outlaws. Film's biggest flaw is the extremely confusing script that makes no attempt at logic whatsoever. Special visual effects are good despite the obviously low f/x budget. **95m/C VHS, DVD,** *Olivier Gruner, Tim Thomerson, Cary-Hiroyuki Tagawa, Marie Kennedy, Yuji Okumoto, Merle Kennedy, Nicholas Guest, Vincent Klyn, Marjorie Monaghan;* **D:** *Albert Pyun;* **W:** *Rebecca Charles;* **C:** *George Mooradian;* **M:** *Michel Rubini.*

Nemesis 3: Time Lapse ♦½ 1994 (R) Superhuman mutant Alex is the last hope for mankind as the cyborgs once again prepare to destroy civilization. **90m/C VHS, DVD,** *Sue Price, Tim Thomerson, Norbert Weisser, Xavier DeClie, Sharon Bruneau, Debbie Muggli;* **D:** *Albert Pyun;* **W:** *Albert Pyun;* **C:** *George Mooradian;* **M:** *Tony Riparetti.*

Nemesis 2: Nebula ♦ 1994 (R) Cyborg goes on a rampage across time with a superhuman in pursuit. **83m/C VHS,** *Sue Price, Tina Cote, Earl White, Jahi JJ Zuri, Tracy Davis;* **D:** *Albert Pyun.*

Nemesis 3: Prey Harder 1996 (R) *Nemesis 4: Cry of Angels* ♦ 1997 (R) Alex (Price) is an assassin in the year 2082. When she mistakenly kills the son of crimelord Bernardo (Dvoff), a bounty is placed on her head. Cartoonish dreck. **80m/C VHS, DVD,** *Sue Price, Norbert Weisser, Andrew Divoff, Simon Poland, Nicholas Guest;* **D:** *Albert Pyun;* **W:** *Albert Pyun;* **C:** *George Mooradian.* **VIDEO**

Nemesis Game ♦♦½ 2003 (R) Vern (Paul) is a comic-book store owner who introduces introverted college student Sara (Pope) to a mysterious game that involves finding various riddles located in out-of-the-way places and answering them to move on to the next clue. But then Sara notices when she solves a riddle, people start to die. **91m/C VHS, DVD, CA** *Adrian Paul, Carly Pope, Brendan Fehr, Jay Banchel, Ian McShane, Rena Owen, Vanessa Guy, Brian Rhodes;* **D:** *Jesse Warn;* **W:** *Jesse Warn;* **C:** *Aaron Morton;* **M:** *Matthew Fletcher.* **VIDEO**

Nenette and Boni ♦♦ 1996 Boni (Colin) is a 19-year-old pizza chef in Marseilles who likes to have sexual fantasies about the local baker's sensuous wife (Bruni-Tedeschi). His life is basically carefree until his pregnant, rebellious 15-year-old sister Nenette (Houri) shows up at his door, having run away from school. Nenette really doesn't want to deal with the pregnancy until Boni forces her to do so and, just to make the teens lives more complicated, their estranged small-time gangster dad (No!ot) has learned about Nenette's condition and wants to help her out. Fine performances, French with subtitles. **103m/C VHS, FR** *Gregoire Colin, Alice Houri, Valeria Bruni-Tedeschi, Jacques Nolot, Vincent Gallo, Gerard Meylan, Alex Descas, Jamila Farah, Christine Gaya;* **D:** *Claire Denis;* **W:** *Claire Denis, Jean-Pol Fargeau;* **C:** *Agnes Godard.*

The Neon Bible ♦♦ 1995 Beautifully crafted, yet thin telling of the struggles of a rural family in 1940s Georgia. The stories unfold in a series of flashbacks, as a 15-year-old boy travels alone on a train, reflecting on his dysfunctional early adolescence. An abusive father (Leary) who dies in the war, suicidal mom

(Scarwid), and ex-showgirl visiting aunt (Rowlands) provide plenty of opportunities for familial angst. Starts out strong, with some stunning scenes sprinkled throughout, but director Davies never ventures far from the narrative territory he's covered thoroughly in his other films ("Distant Voices, Still Lives" and "The Long Day Closes"). Adapted from the novel by Pulitzer Prize winning author John Kennedy Toole. **92m/C VHS, DVD,** *Gena Rowlands, Jacob Tierney, Diana Scarwid, Drake Bell, Denis Leary, Leo Burmester, Frances Conroy, Peter McRobbie, Joan Glover, Dana Dick, Virgil Graham Hopkins;* **D:** *Terence Davies;* **W:** *Terence Davies;* **C:** *Michael Coulter.*

Neon City ♦♦ 1991 (R) Title refers to a rumored city of refuge in the year 2053, where eight misfit adventurers in an armored transport seek safety from the Earth's toxic environment and "Mad Max" clichés. **99m/C VHS,** *Michael Ironside, Vanity, Lyle Alzado, Valerie Wildman, Nick Klar, Juliet Landau, Arsenio "Sonny" Trinidad, Richard Sanders;* **D:** *Monte Markham.*

The Neon Empire ♦♦ 1989 (R) Tepid tale of two gangsters battling inner mob opposition and backstabbing to build Las Vegas. Ostensibly based on the story of Bugsy Siegel and Meyer Lansky. **120m/C VHS,** *Martin Landau, Ray Sharkey, Gary Busey, Harry Guardino, Julie Carmen, Linda Florentino, Dylan McDermott;* **D:** *Larry Peerce;* **M:** *Pete Hamill.* **CABLE.**

Neon Maniacs WOOF! 1986 (R) An even half-dozen fetish-ridden zombies stalk the streets at night, tearing their victims into teensy weensy bits. Brave teenagers try to stop the killing. Brave viewers will stop the tape. **90m/C VHS, DVD,** *Allan Hayes, Leilani Sarelle Ferrer, Bo Sabato, Donna Locke, Victor Elliot Brandt;* **D:** *Joseph Mangine.*

The Nephew ♦♦ 1997 Part culture clash, part melodrama. Teenager Chad (Harper) heads to his Dora, a small island off the Irish coast, in order to fulfill his mother Karen's last request—that her ashes be scattered in her homeland. Karen was long estranged from her family and they're shocked to discover that Chad's father is black. Everyone tries to make the best of the situation but Chad's would-be romance with Aislin (McGuckin), whose father Joe (Brosnan) once loved Karen, causes a lot of friction. **104m/C VHS, IR** *Hill Harper, Aislin McGuckin, Pierce Brosnan, Donal McCann, Sinead Cusack, Lorraine Pilkington;* **D:** *Eugene Brady;* **W:** *Jacqueline O'Neill, Sean P. Steele;* **C:** *Jack Conroy;* **M:** *Stephen McKeon.*

Neptune Factor ♦ *The Neptune Disaster; An Underwater Odyssey* 1973 (G) Scientists board a special new deep-sea sub to search for their colleagues lost in an undersea earthquake. Diving ever deeper into the abyss that swallowed their friend's Ocean Lab II, they and up trapped themselves. The plot's many holes sink it. **94m/C VHS,** *Ben Gazzara, Yvette Mimieux, Walter Pidgeon, Ernest Borgnine;* **D:** *Daniel Petrie;* **W:** *Jack DeWitt.*

Neptune's Daughter ♦♦ 1949 A swim-happy bathing suit designer finds romance and deep pools of studio water to dive into. Typically lavish and ridiculous Williams aqua-parade. ♪Baby It's Cold Outside; I Love Those Men; My Heart Beats Faster. **92m/C VHS, DVD,** *Esther Williams, Red Skelton, Ricardo Montalban, Betty Garrett, Keenan Wynn, Xavier Cugat, Ted de Corsia, Mike Mazurki, Mel Blanc, Juan Duval, George Mann, Joi Lansing;* **D:** *Edward Buzzell;* **C:** *Charles Rosher, Oscars '49: Song ("Baby It's Cold Outside").*

Nerolio ♦♦ 1996 Three imagined episodes depicting the final months of an unnamed poet/director (Cavicchioli), who is actually based on homosexual writer/filmmaker Pier Paolo Pasolini. The contradictory, hypocritical, aging Poet is shown buying sex, while extolling the virtues of male beauty in voiceover, and as the making of his own doom (Pasolini was murdered in 1975). "Nerolio" is a contraction of "nero" (black) and "Petrolio" (oil), which refers to Pasolini's posthumous novel "Petrolio." Italian with subtitles. **82m/B VHS, DVD,** *IT Marco Cavicchioli, Vincenzo Crivello, Salvatore Lazzaro;* **D:** *Aurelio Grimaldi;* **W:** *Aurelio Grimaldi;* **C:** *Maurizio Calvesi;* **M:** *Maria Soldatini.*

man investigating his mysterious, dead father travels to this ancestral plantation in the bayou. To its horror, he discovers that his father was involved in the black arts. Now two beautiful young witches are after him. Can he possibly survive this madness? **87m/C VHS, DVD,** *Michael C. Ben...*

Neptune's Daughter

Net Games ♦♦ 2003 (R) Married Adam (Howell) is just looking for a little fantasy fun when he logs on to a website called cyber-chat. He thinks it's all eye candy and no risk—especially when he meets seductive Angel (Sloatman). Too bad she's your basic psycho-babe, who soon has Adam involved in blackmail and murder. **97m/C VHS, DVD,** *C. Thomas Howell, Lala Sloatman, Ed Begley Jr., Marina Sirtis, Samuel Ball, Lochlyn Munro, Maeve Quinlan, Monique Demers, Joan Van Ark;* **D:** *Andrew Van Slee;* **M:** *William Richter.* **VIDEO**

The Net 2.0 ♦♦ 2006 (R) Computer systems analyst Hope (DeLoach) takes a job in Istanbul where her identity is stolen and she's framed for criminal activities that land her in prison. But no, it's not a lame go-on-the-run-and-prove-it's-a-innocent adventure. **95m/C DVD,** *Nikki Deloach, Keegan Connor Tracy, Demet Akbag, Neil Hopkins;* **D:** *Charles Winkler;* **W:** *Rob Cowan;* **C:** *S. Douglas Smith;* **M:** *Stephen Endelman.* **VIDEO**

The Net ♦♦½ 1995 (PG-13) The ever-spunky Bullock gets stuck behind a computer screen rather than the wheel of a bus as reclusive computer systems analyst Angela Bennett. She's puzzled by a mysterious Internet program, which Angela finds can easily access highly classified databases. It's soon apparent that somehow it knows because every record of her identity has been erased and the conspirators decide to take care of one last detail by eliminating her as well. Miller's the ex she turns to for help and Northam's a seductive British hacker. **114m/C VHS, DVD,** *Sandra Bullock, Jeremy Northam, Dennis Miller, Diane Baker, Ken Howard, Wendy Gazelle, Ray McKinnon;* **D:** *Irwin Winkler;* **W:** *John Brancato, Michael Ferris;* **C:** *Jack N. Green;* **M:** *Mark Isham.*

The Nesting ♦½ 1980 (R) Too long tale of a neurotic author who rents a haunted Victorian manor and finds herself a pawn in a ghostly plan for revenge. Features Grahame's last performance. **104m/C VHS,** *Robin Groves, John Carradine, Gloria Grahame, Christopher Loomis, Michael David Lally;* **D:** *Armand Weston;* **C:** *Joao Fernandes.*

The Nest ♦♦ 1988 (R) A small island is overcome by giant cockroaches created by you guessed it, a scientific experiment gone wrong. Special effects make it watchable. **89m/C VHS, DVD,** *Robert Lansing, Lisa Langlois, Franc Luz, Terri Treas, Stephen Davies, Diana Bellamy, Nancy Morgan;* **D:** *Terence H. Winkless;* **W:** *Robert King;* **C:** *Ricardo Jacques Gae;* **M:** *Rick Conrad.*

The Nest ♦♦½ *El Nido* 1980 Tragic romance of an elderly man and a 13-year-old girl in other shenanigans, and then he discovers he's going to live after all. Once there, he becomes romantically entangled with the sheriff's fiancee, uses a wrench to hold up a gas station, and gets involved in other shenanigans, and then **70m/B VHS,** *Harrison Ford, Phyllis Haver, Chester Conklin, Mack Swain, Hobart Bosworth, Charles Gerrard;* **D:** *Scott Sidney.*

The Nervous Wreck ♦♦♦ 1926 Harrison Ford (not the one from "Indiana Jones") heads West, seeking a cure for what he believes is a terminal illness. Once there, he becomes romantically entangled with the sheriff's fiancee, uses a wrench to hold up a gas station, and gets involved in other shenanigans, and then **70m/B VHS,** *Harrison Ford, Phyllis Haver, Chester Conklin, Mack Swain, Hobart Bosworth, Charles Gerrard;* **D:** *Scott Sidney.*

Nervous Ticks ♦♦½ 1993 (R) Ninety minutes in the life of airline employee York Daley. All he needs to do is get off work, go home, grab his luggage, pick up his married girlfriend, and get back to the airport for a flight to Rio De Janeiro. Simple, right? Not in this movie. **95m/C VHS, Bill Pullman, Julie Brown, Peter Boyle, James LeGros, Brent Jennings;** **D:** *Rocky Lang;* **W:** *David Frankel.*

detti, Denise Gentile, Anjanette Comer, Holly Floria, Robert Burr, Robert Sampson; *D:* David Schmoeller; *W:* Billy Chicago; *C:* Adolfo Bartoli; *M:* Edgar Winter.

Network 🦴🦴🦴½ **1976 (R)** As timely now as it was then: a scathing indictment of the TV industry and its propensity towards self-prostitution. A television newscaster's mental breakdown turns him into a celebrity when the network tries to profit from his illness. The individual characters are startlingly realistic and the acting is excellent. **121m/C VHS, DVD.** Faye Dunaway, Peter Finch, William Holden, Robert Duvall, Wesley Addy, Ned Beatty, Beatrice Straight, Lane Smith, Conchata Ferrell, William Prince, Ted (Theodore) Sorel, Lance Henriksen, Marlene Warfield; *D:* Sidney Lumet; *W:* Paddy Chayefsky; *C:* Owen Roizman. Oscars '76: Actor (Finch), Actress (Dunaway), Orig. Screenplay, Support. Actress (Straight); AFI '98: Top 100; British Acad. '77: Actor (Finch); Golden Globes '77: Actor—Drama (Finch), Actress—Drama (Dunaway), Director (Lumet), Screenplay; L.A. Film Critics '76: Director (Lumet). Film, Natl. Film Reg. '00; N.Y. Film Critics '76: Screenplay. Writers Guild '76: Orig. Screenplay.

Neurotic Cabaret 🦴½ **1990** Would-be actress dances exotically and finds more exotic ways to roll in dough. **90m/C VHS.** Edwin Neal, Tammy Stone; *D:* John Woodward; *C:* Daniel Anaya; *M:* John Mills.

Neutron and the Black Mask 🦴 **1961** Man wears mask with lightning bolts and gains comic book style powers to do deathly battle with a scientist with a neutron bomb up his sleeve. First Neutron feature. **80m/B VHS.** *MX* Wolf Ruvinskis, Julio Aleman, Armando Silvestre, Rosita (Rosa) Arenas, Claudio Brook; *D:* Frederick Curiel.

Neutron vs. the Amazing Dr. Caronte 🦴 **1961** Dr. Caronte from "Neutron and the Black Mask" just won't give up that neutron bomb and let the series die. **80m/B VHS.** *MX* Wolf Ruvinskis, Julio Aleman, Armando Silvestre, Rosita (Rosa) Arenas, Rodolfo Landa; *D:* Frederick Curiel.

Neutron vs. the Death Robots 🦴 **1962** Guy with a mask takes on army of killer robots and neutron bomb to protect the world from future sequels. **80m/B VHS.** *MX* Wolf Ruvinskis, Julio Aleman, Armando Silvestre, Rosita (Rosa) Arenas; *D:* Frederick Curiel.

Neutron vs. the Maniac 🦴 **1962** Man in mask hunts guys who kill people. **80m/B VHS.** *MX* Gina Romand, Rodolfo Landa, Wolf Ruvinskis; *D:* Alfredo B. Crevenna.

Nevada 🦴🦴 **1944** Cowpoke Mitchum is mistaken for the killer of a homesteader and narrowly escapes the rope by finding the real killer. First leading role for Mitchum as the tough but laconic hero. Based on a novel by Zane Grey. **62m/B VHS, DVD.** Robert Mitchum, Anne Jeffreys, Nancy Gates, Craig Reynolds, Guinn "Big Boy" Williams, Richard Martin, Harry Woods; *D:* Edward Killy.

Nevada 🦴🦴½ **1997 (R)** Women run a small Nevada town Monday through Friday while their men work at a dam several hours away, returning only on the weekends. When stranger Chrysty (Brenneman) shows up, the townswomen become curiously unsettled at their normally placid lives—accusing her of being a troublemaker or seeing her as a hopeful sign of change. **108m/C VHS.** Amy Brenneman, Kirstie Alley, Gabrielle Anwar, Saffron Burrows, Angus MacFadyen, Kathy Najimy, Dee Wallace Stone, James Wilder, Bridgette Wilson-Sampras; *D:* Gary Tieche; *W:* Gary Tieche; *C:* Nancy Schreiber; *M:* Robert Perry.

Nevada City 🦴½ **1941** Roy outwits a financier who is trying to monopolize transportation in California. **54m/B VHS, DVD.** Roy Rogers, George "Gabby" Hayes, Sally Payne, George Cleveland, Billy Lee, Joseph Crehan, Fred Kohler Jr., Pierre Watkin; *D:* Joseph Kane; *W:* James R. Webb; *C:* William Nobles; *M:* Cy Feuer.

Nevada Smith 🦴🦴 **1966** The halfbreed Nevada Smith (previously introduced in Harold Robbins' story "The Carpetbaggers" and film of same name) seeks the outlaws who killed his parents. Standard western plot, characters. Later remade as a TV movie. **135m/C VHS, DVD.** Steve McQueen, Karl Malden, Brian Keith, Arthur Kennedy, Raf Vallone, Suzanne Pleshette, Paul Fix, Pat Hingle, Janet Margolin, Howard da Silva, John Doucette, Gene Evans, Val Avery, Lyle Bettger; *D:* Henry Hathaway; *W:* John Michael Hayes; *C:* Lucien Ballard; *M:* Alfred Newman.

The Nevadan 🦴½ **1950** *The Man From Nevada* A marshal goes in search of an outlaw's gold cache, only to be opposed by a crooked rancher. Good scenery and action, but not one of Scott's best. **81m/C VHS.** Randolph Scott, Dorothy Malone, Forrest Tucker, Frank Faylen, George Macready, Charles Kemper, Jeff Corey, Tom Powers, Jock Mahoney, George Cleveland; *W:* Rowland Brown, George W. George; *D:* Gordon Douglas; *C:* Charles Lawton Jr.; *M:* Arthur Morton.

Never a Dull Moment 🦴🦴 **1950** New York songwriter falls for rodeo Romeo, moves out West, and finds welcome wagon deficient. Mediocre songs; many dull moments. ♪Once You Find Your Guy; Sagebrush Lullaby; The Man With the Big Felt Hat. **89m/B VHS.** Irene Dunne, Fred MacMurray, William Demarest, Andy Devine, Gigi Perreau, Natalie Wood, Philip Ober, Jack Kirkwood, Ann Doran, Meg Gibson; *D:* George Marshall.

Never a Dull Moment 🦴🦴 **1968 (G)** Mobsters mistake an actor for an assassin in this gag-filled adventure. They threaten the thespian into thievery, before the trouble really starts when Ace, the actual assassin, arrives. **90m/C VHS, DVD.** Dick Van Dyke, Edward G. Robinson, Dorothy Provine, Henry Silva, Joanna Moore, Tony Bill, Slim Pickens, Jack Elam; *D:* Jerry Paris; *W:* A.J. Carrothers; *M:* Robert F. Brunner.

Never Again 🦴🦴 **2001 (R)** The best thing is seeing a radiant fiftysomething Clayburgh back on the big screen. Divorcee Grace (Clayburgh) winds up meeting cute with exterminator/jazz musician Christopher (Tambor). Both vow to maintain a no-strings relationship, no matter how great the sex is, though they can't help becoming emotionally involved. Unfortunately, the film is often more contrived and crude than romantic. **97m/C VHS, DVD.** *US* Jill Clayburgh, Jeffrey Tambor, Michael McKean, Caroline Aaron, Sandy Duncan, Bill Duke; *D:* Eric Schaeffer; *W:* Eric Schaeffer; *C:* Tom Ostrowski; *M:* Amanda Kravat.

Never Back Down 🦴 **2008 (PG-13)** Mild-mannered teen Jake Tyler (Faris) is set off by the school bully's trash talk, exploding into an ugly fist fight. Soon after, boxing trainer Jean (Honsou) takes Jake under his wing, teaching him the ways of the sport and the meaning of self-respect, eventually leading to an inevitable rematch with the bully. And, yes, he wins the girl, rehashing "The Karate Kid" and countless other underdog sports dramas. Oddly preaches a message of non-violence while cheering on Jake's bloody bareknuckle beat-downs. **110m/C DVD.** *US* Sean Faris, Amber Heard, Djimon Hounsou, Leslie Hope, Cam Gigandet, Evan Peters, Wyatt Smith; *D:* Jeff Wadlow; *W:* Chris Hauty; *C:* Lukas Ettlin; *M:* Michael Wandmacher.

Never Been Kissed 🦴🦴 **1999 (PG-13)** Lightweight and logic-defying, Barrymore's producing debut hypothesizes that the people who were unpopular in high school want another chance at it. Not. Still-nerdy newspaper copy editor Josie is assigned to go undercover as a student and write about high school life. She see it as a chance to be a big-time journalist and one of the "cool kids." When it turns that not much has changed for her, she enlists the help of her brother (Arquette) and a coworker (Shannon), and Barrymore is sweet, but doesn't exactly stretch here, and the script sounds a lot like the John Hughes comedies of the '80s. Probably more enjoyable if you're actually high school age. **107m/C VHS, DVD.** Drew Barrymore, David Arquette, Leelee Sobieski, Michael Vartan, Molly Shannon, John C. Reilly, Garry Marshall, Sean M. Whalen, Jordan Ladd, Jessica Alba, Carmen (Lee) Llywelyn; *D:* Raja Gosnell; *W:* Abby Kohn, Marc Silverstein; *C:* Alex Nepomniaschy; *M:* David Newman.

Never Been Thawed 🦴 **2005** Mockumentary follows the obsessions of the members of the Mesa Frozen Entree Enthusiasts' Club (frozen food addicts). Besides his obsession with frozen entrees, Shawn has converted to Christianity and fronts a once hard-core punk band that has turned into a Christian rock group so they can increase their music sales. Easy targets, lame humor. **87m/C DVD.** *US* John Morris, Sean Anders; *W:* John Morris, Sean Anders, Le Vinus Chuck; *C:* Sean Anders; *M:* Sean Anders, Thomas Laufenberg.

Never Cry Wolf 🦴🦴🦴 **1983 (PG)** A young biologist is sent to the Arctic to study the behavior and habitation of wolves, then becomes deeply involved with their sub-society. Based on Farley Mowat's book. Beautifully photographed. **105m/C VHS, DVD.** Charles Martin Smith, Brian Dennehy, Samson Jorah; *D:* Carroll Ballard; *W:* Curtis Hanson, Sam Hamm; *C:* Hiro Narita; *M:* Mark Isham. Natl. Soc. Film Critics '83: Cinematog.

Never Die Alone 🦴🦴½ **2004 (R)** King David (DMX) is a drug dealer and a vicious dude to boot, and the opening scene shows him paying the price for his deeds as he is fatally stabbed. This is where Paul (Arquette), a struggling writer desperate for a story to tell, comes in. When King David passes on he gives Paul all of his possessions, including a stack of audiotapes he'd made detailing the events of his wretched life (which provide the means for the at-times tedious narrative), but Paul doesn't realize how dangerous a predicament this really is. Director Dickerson presents powerful images and purposefully avoids garnering sympathy for King David. DMX is engrossing as the suave seducer/violent hoodlum. Based on the 1974 novel by ex-convict Donald Goines. **88m/C DVD, UMD.** *US* DMX, Michael Ealy, Antwon Tanner, David Arquette, Clifton Powell, Tommy (Tiny) Lister, Aisha Tyler, Michele Shay, Reagan Gomez-Preston, Jennifer Sky, Drew Sidora; *D:* Ernest R. Dickerson; *W:* James Gibson; *C:* Matthew Libatique; *M:* DMX, George Duke.

Never Down 🦴🦴 **2006** Latino con Rico (LaSardo) is fresh out of the joint after a five-year stint. He's hoping his ex-wife will allow him access to their young daughter but new forces conspire to send him back down that criminal path. Vonnegut (in his last role) makes a brief appearance as a benefactor. **82m/C DVD.** Robert LaSardo, Mary Kelsey; *Cameos:* Kurt Vonnegut Jr., James Toback; *D:* Robert Oppel. **VIDEO**

Never Forget 🦴🦴 **1991** True story of California resident Mel Mermelstein (played by Nimoy), a survivor of Hitler's death camps who accepted a pro-Nazi group's challenge to prove in court that the Holocaust of six million Jews really happened. A sincere, well-meaning courtroom drama that just can't surmount the uncinematic nature of the source material. **94m/C VHS.** Leonard Nimoy, Blythe Danner, Dabney Coleman; *D:* Joseph Sargent; *M:* Henry Mancini. **CABLE**

Never Give a Sucker an Even Break 🦴🦴🦴 **1941** *What a Man* An almost plotless comedy, based on an idea reputedly written on a napkin by Fields (he took screenplay credit as Otis Criblecoblis), and features Fields at his most unleashed. It's something of a cult favorite, but not for all tastes. Classic chase scene ends it. Fields' last role in a feature-length film. **71m/B VHS, DVD.** W.C. Fields, Gloria Jean, Franklin Pangborn, Leon Errol, Margaret Dumont, Susan Miller; *D:* Edward F. (Eddie) Cline; *W:* John Thomas "Jack" Neville, Prescott Chaplin, W.C. Fields; *C:* Charles Van Enger; *M:* Frank Skinner.

Never Let Go 🦴🦴 **1960** A man unwittingly tracks down the mastermind of a gang of racketeers. Sellers sheds his comedic image to play the ruthless and brutal gang boss, something he shouldn't have done. **91m/C VHS, DVD.** *GB* Peter Sellers, Richard Todd, Elizabeth Sellars, Carol White; *D:* John Guillermin; *M:* John Barry.

Never Let Me Go 🦴🦴½ **1953** Implausible yet entertaining account of American newsman Gable trying to smuggle ballerina wife Tierney out of Russia. Hard to believe Gable as a one-man assault force infiltrating Russia, but enjoyable nonetheless. Based on the novel "Came the Dawn" by Roger Bax. **94m/B VHS.** Clark Gable, Gene Tierney, Richard Haydn, Bernard Miles, Kenneth More, Karel Stepanek, Theodore Bikel; *D:* Delmer Daves; *W:* Ronald Millar, George Froeschel.

Never Love a Stranger 🦴🦴 **1958** A young man becomes a numbers runner for a mobster and ultimately winds up heading his own racket. Later he finds himself in conflict with his old boss and the district attorney. No surprises here. Based on the Harold Robbins' novel. **93m/B VHS, DVD.** John Drew (Blythe) Barrymore Jr., Steve McQueen, Lita Milan, Robert Bray; *D:* Robert M. Stevens.

Never Met Picasso 🦴🦴½ **1996** Thirty-year-old artist Andrew (Arquette) lives with self-absorbed actress/mom Genna (Kidder) in Boston, struggling with both his lack of work and romantic prospects. Andrew's one consolation is gay Uncle Alfred (Epstein), who serves as a role model. Until, unexpectedly, Andrew meets confident Jerry (McKellar) at his mother's dreadful opening night bash. After Alfred dies suddenly, Andrew discovers some hidden photos of his uncle's lover and seeks to make connections between the past and the present. **97m/C VHS.** Alexis Arquette, Margot Kidder, Don McKellar, Alvin Epstein, Georgia Ringsdale; *D:* Stephen Kijak; *W:* Stephen Kijak; *C:* David Tames; *M:* Kristen Hersh.

Never on Sunday 🦴🦴🦴 **1960** An American intellectual tries to turn a Greek prostitute into a refined woman. Fine performances and exhilarating Greek photography. Fun all around. ♪Never on Sunday. **91m/B VHS, DVD.** *GR* Melina Mercouri, Titos Vandis, Jules Dassin, Mitsos Liguisos; *D:* Jules Dassin; *W:* Jules Dassin; *M:* Manos Hadjidakis. Oscars '60: Song ("Never on Sunday"); Cannes '60: Actress (Mercouri).

Never on Tuesday 🦴🦴 **1988 (R)** Two jerks from Ohio head to California and find themselves stuck midway in the desert with a beautiful girl, who has plans of her own. **90m/C VHS.** Claudia Christian, Andrew Lauer, Peter Berg; *Cameos:* Charlie Sheen, Emilio Estevez; *D:* Adam Rifkin; *W:* Adam Rifkin.

Never Pick Up a Stranger 🦴🦴 *Bloodrage* **1979** When a local hooker is murdered, her cop boyfriend, who never gives up on a case, hunts her killer with a vengeance. Extremely graphic. **82m/C VHS.** Ian Scott, Judith-Marie Bergan, James Johnston, Lawrence Tierney; *D:* Joseph Bigwood.

Never Say Die 🦴🦴½ **1939** Wealthy John Kidley (Hope) is at the Swiss spa of Bad Gasswasser, thinking he only has a few weeks to live. So he marries Mickey Hawkins (Raye) to save her from a crazy Russian, Prince Smirnov (Mowbray), and ends up fighting a duel! Oh, and Mickey thinks she's in love with bus driver Henry Munch (Devine), who accompanies the duo on their honeymoon. Much silliness. Based on the play by William H. Post. **82m/B VHS.** Bob Hope, Martha Raye, Alan Mowbray, Andy Devine, Gale Sondergaard, Monty Woolley, Sig Rumann; *D:* Elliott Nugent; *W:* Preston Sturges, Don Hartman, Frank Butler; *C:* Leo Tover.

Never Say Die 🦴🦴 **1990** Two innocents are thrown into a web of international intrigue and car crashes for a film shot in New Zealand. **98m/C VHS.** *NZ* George Wendt, Lisa Eilbacher; *D:* Geoff Murphy.

Never Say Die 🦴🦴 **1994 (R)** Ex-Special Forces soldier John Blake (Zagarino), ambushed and left to die, returns to seek vengeance on the renegade commander who betrayed him. And he has the perfect opportunity when his nemesis kidnaps a general's daughter. **99m/C VHS.**

Frank Zagarino, Billy Drago, Todd Jensen, Jenny (Jennifer) McShane, Robin Smith, Jennifer Wein; **W:** Jeff Albert. **M:** Wendy Oldfield, Adrian Levy.

Never Say Goodbye 🐾🐾 1946 Cliche-ridden story about a man trying to win back his divorce-bound wife. Flynn tries hard, but the material just isn't up to par. Based on the story "Don't Ever Leave Me" by Ben and Norma Barzman. Co-screenwriter Diamond later became famous when he teamed up with Billy Wilder to script "Some Like it Hot" and "The Apartment." 97m/B VHS. Errol Flynn, Eleanor Parker, Lucile Watson, S.Z. Sakall, Forrest Tucker, Donald Woods, Peggy Knudsen, Tom D'Andrea, Hattie McDaniel; **D:** James V. Kern; **W:** James V. Kern, I.A.L. Diamond, Lewis R. Foster.

Never So Few 🐾🐾 1959 A military commander and his outnumbered troops overcome incredible odds against the Japanese. There is a lot of focus on romance, but the script and acting make a strong impression nonetheless. Based on the novel by Tom T. Chamales. 124m/C VHS, DVD. Frank Sinatra, Gina Lollobrigida, Peter Lawford, Steve McQueen, Richard Johnson, Paul Henreid, Charles Bronson; **D:** John Sturges; **C:** William H. Daniels.

Never Steal Anything Small 🐾½ 1959 A tough union boss pushes everyone around in the battles the mob for control of the waterfront. A strange musical-drama combination that kind of interest only to the most ardent Cagney and Jones fans. Based on the Maxwell Anderson/Rouben Mamoulian play "The Devil's Hornpipe." Largely forgettable songs. 🎵"I'm Sorry, I Want a Ferrari; I Haven't Got a Thing to Wear; It Takes Love to Make a Home; Never Steal Anything Small; Helping Out Friends. 94m/C VHS. James Cagney, Shirley Jones, Cara Williams, Wendell Holmes, Nehemiah Persoff, Anthony Caruso, Jack Albertson, Roger Smith, Royal Dano, Horace McMahon, Virginia Vincent, Robert J. Wilke; **D:** Charles Lederer; **M:** Henry Mancini.

Never Talk to Strangers 🐾🐾 1995 (R) Sarah Taylor (DeMornay) is an uptight criminal psychologist who gets involved with handsome stranger Tony Ramirez (Banderas) while working on the case of a serial killer (Stanton). Then Sarah finds herself the target of an increasingly malevolent stalker—and she has lots of suspects to choose from. Typical woman-in-peril film with equally standard frights but the leads certainly look good (and Banderas is a fine sex object in a bit of role reversal). Filmed in Toronto. 86m/C VHS, DVD. Rebecca De Mornay, Antonio Banderas, Harry Dean Stanton, Dennis Miller, Len Cariou, Beau Starr; **D:** Peter Hall; **W:** Lewis Green, Jordan Rush; **C:** Elemer Ragalyi; **M:** Pino Donaggio.

Never Too Late to Mend 🐾🐾 1937 Victorian British play about the abuses of the penal system which had, upon its initial London West End run, caused Queen Victoria to institute a sweeping program of prison reform. The movie caused considerably less stir. 67m/B VHS, DVD. Tod Slaughter, Marjorie Taylor, Jack Livesey, Ian Colin; **D:** David MacDonald.

Never Too Young to Die 🐾 1986 (R) A young man is drawn into a provocative espionage adventure by his late father's spy associates. Together they try to discover who killed the young man's father.

Never Steal Anything Small ...

Never 2 Big 🐾🐾 1998 (R) A young record company exec wants to prove that someone at the company murdered his singer sister in order to protect her from leaving and signing with another label. Only he's been framed for the crime and has to stay out of jail and prove his own innocence. 100m/C VHS, DVD. Ernie Hudson, Nia Long, Tony Todd, Donnie Wahlberg, Terrence Howard, Donald Adeosun Faison, Tommy (Tiny) Lister, Salli Richardson, Shemar Moore; **D:** Terry Gatlings Bunche; **W:** Peter Gatlings Bunche; **C:** Nancy Schreiber.

Never Wave at a WAC 🐾🐾½ 1952 A Washington socialite joins the Women's Army Corps hoping for a commission that never comes. She has to tough it out as an ordinary private. A reasonably fun ancestor of "Private Benjamin," with a cameo by Gen. Omar Bradley as himself. 87m/B VHS, DVD. Rosalind Russell, Paul Douglas, Marie Wilson, William Ching, Arleen Whelan, Leif Erickson, Hillary Brooke, Regis Toomey; **Cameos:** Omar Bradley; **D:** Norman Z. McLeod; **M:** Elmer Bernstein.

The NeverEnding Story 🐾🐾½ 1984 (PG) A lonely young boy helps a warrior save the fantasy world in his book from destruction by the Nothing. A wonderful, intelligent family script. Petersen's first English-language film, based on the novel by Michael Ende. 94m/C VHS, DVD. Barret Oliver, Noah Hathaway, Gerald McRaney, Moses Gunn, Tami Stronach, Patricia Hayes, Sydney Bromley, Thomas Hill; **D:** Wolfgang Petersen; **W:** Wolfgang Petersen, Herman Weigel; **C:** Jost Vacano; **M:** Klaus Doldinger, Giorgio Moroder.

NeverEnding Story 2: The Next Chapter 🐾🐾 1991 (PG) Disappointing sequel to the first story that didn't end. Bastian (Brandis) must again save Fantasia, this time from the evil sorceress Xayride (Burt). So dull, the kids may wander away. But wait: contains the first Bugs Bunny theatrical cartoon in 26 years, "Box Office Bunny." 90m/C VHS, DVD. Jonathan Brandis, Kenny Morrison, Clarissa Burt, John Wesley Shipp, Martin Umbach; **D:** George Miller; **M:** Robert Folk.

The NeverEnding Story 3: Escape from Fantasia 🐾 1994 (G) The third time was not the charm in this case. Bastian, on the edge of puberty, is being bullied by a group at school called the Nasties. He seeks refuge in the library and enters the world of Fantasia through the "Neverending Story" tome. When the book is stolen by the Nasties, it is up to Bastian to return it. Unfortunately, the story does not have the charm of the original, trying to incorporate too much reality and not enough of dreamland. 95m/C VHS, DVD. Jason James Richter, Melody Kay, Freddie Jones, Jack Black, Ryan Bollman, Tracey Ellis, Kevin McNulty; **D:** Peter MacDonald; **C:** Robert Smith; **M:** Peter Wolf.

The New Adventures of Pippi Longstocking 🐾½ 1988 (G) Deexcent cast is trapped in another musical rehashing of the Astrid Lindgren children's books about a precocious red-headed girl and her fantastic adventures with horses, criminals, and pirates. 101m/C VHS, DVD. Tami Erin, Eileen Brennan, Dennis Dugan, Dianne Hull, George DiCenzo, John Schuck, Dick Van Patten; **D:** Ken Annakin; **C:** Roland Smith; **M:** Misha Segal.

Nevil Shute's The Far Country 🐾½ 1985 The Far Country (York), once a doctor in Hitler's army, escapes to Australia from postwar Europe to begin a new life with a new identity. Falling in love with the beautiful Jennifer Morton (Thornton), Carl hopes he's left his past behind. But nothing is ever that simple. Adaptation of the Shute novel. 200m/C VHS, AU Michael York, Sigrid Thornton, Fred Steele; **D:** George Miller. **TV**

The NeverEnding Story ...

High point may be Simmons as a crazed hermaphrodite plotting to poison Goddess 1935 Twelve episodes, each 22 minutes long, depict the adventures of Edgar Rice Burroughs's tree-swinging character—Tarzan. 260m/B VHS, DVD. Bruce Bennett, Ula Holt, Frank Baker, Dale Walsh, Lewis Sargent; **D:** Edward Kull.

The New Age 🐾🐾 1994 (R) Illusions in L.A. centering on talent agent Peter (Weller) and art designer Katherine (Davis) Witner, Katherine loses her job the same day Peter decides to quit his and suddenly the caustic duo are dependent upon each other. The trendy couple decide to open a boutique and quickly find themselves in a fiscal sinkhole and on a downhill slide. The acting is fine but the story is empty. 106m/C VHS, Peter Weller, Judy Davis, Adam West, Patrick Bauchau, Corbin Bernsen, Jonathan Hadary, Samuel L. Jackson, Patricia Heaton, Audra Lindley, Paula Marshall, Maureen Mueller, Bruce Ramsay, Sandra Seacat; **D:** Michael Tolkin; **W:** Michael Tolkin.

New Best Friend 🐾½ 2002 (R) Depraved Indifference; Mary Jane's Last Dance 2002 (R) Obvious and sleazy whodunit wastes its cast. Alicia (Krshner) is in a cocaine-induced coma after getting in with the wrong college crowd. Working-class mom Connie (O'Connor) raises a stink with new sheriff Bonner (Diggs) out to investigate. 91m/C VHS, DVD. Mia Kirshner, Dominique Swain, Rachel True, Meredith Monroe, Scott Bairstow, Taye Diggs, Glynnis O'Connor, Eric Michael Cole, Oliver Hudson; **D:** Zoe Clarke-Williams; **W:** Victoria Strouse; **C:** Tom Priestley; **M:** David A. Hughes, John Murphy.

New Blood 🐾🐾 1999 (R) Violent thriller that has a few nifty twists. After seven years, Danny White (Moran) turns up on the doorstep of his estranged father Alan (Hurt). Danny is bleeding from a gunshot wound and makes the devil's own deal with dad: Danny's twin sister needs a heart transplant and Danny offers his own organ if dad will participate in a mob ordered kidnapping that's gone wrong once already. Solid performances are an asset. 92m/C VHS, DVD. GB Nick Moran, John Hurt, Carrie-Anne Moss, Shawn Wayans, Joe Pantoliano, Eugene Robert Glazer, Richard Fitzpatrick, Rob Freeman; **D:** Michael Hurst; **W:** Michael Hurst; **C:** David Pelletier; **M:** Jeff Danna.

The New Centurions 🐾🐾½ 1972 (R) Rookies training for the Los Angeles Police Department get the inside info from retiring cops. Gritty and realistic drama based on the novel by former cop Joseph Wambaugh. Tends to be disjointed at times, but overall is a good adaptation of the bestseller. Scott, excellent as the retiring beat-walker, is supported well by the other performers. 103m/C VHS, DVD. George C. Scott, Stacy Keach, Jane Alexander, Scott Wilson, Erik Estrada, James B. Sikking; **D:** Richard Fleischer; **W:** Stirling Silliphant; **M:** Quincy Jones.

New Crime City: Los Angeles 2020 🐾½ 1994 (R) Prisoner Tony Ricks (Roscovich) is executed and then revived thanks to technology. But there's a price to pay for his life and freedom—he must retrieve a biowarfare weapon from a prison gang and he has only has 24 hours to do it. 95m/C VHS, Rick Rosovich, Stacy Keach, Sherrie Rose; **W:** Rick Rosovich.

New Eden 🐾🐾 1994 (R) In the year 2237 wartime prisoners are condemned to a desert planet where they are preyed upon by brutal Sand Pirates. An idealistic engineer falls in love and seeks to protect his new family from a deadly confrontation. 88m/C VHS, Stephen Baldwin, Lisa Bonet, Tobin Bell, Michael Bowen, Janet Hubert-Whitten, Kate McGregor-Stewart; **D:** Alan Metzger; **M:** Dan Gordon.

The New Eve 🐾🐾 1999 La Nouvelle Eve 1998 (R) Camille (Viard in an astonishing performance) is a hard-partying Parisienne whose hedonistic life is changed when she meets Alexis (Rajot). He's a political activist, married with a couple of kids—not at all the sort of drugged-up

New Jack City 🐾🐾½ 1991 (R) Just say no ghetto-melodrama. Powerful performance by Snipes as wealthy Harlem drug lord sought by rebel cops Ice-T and Nelson. Music by Johnny Gill. 🎵 2 Live Crew, Ice-T and others. 101m/C VHS, DVD. MX Wesley Snipes, Ice-T, Mario Van Peebles, Chris Rock, Judd Nelson, Tracy C. Jones, Allen Payne, Kim Park, Vanessa Williams, Nick Ashford, Thalmus Rasulala, Michael Michele, Bill Nunn, Russell Wong; **D:** Mario Van Peebles; **W:** Keith Critchlow, Barry Michael Cooper; **C:** Francis Kenny; **M:** Roger Colombier.

The New Adventures of Tarzan 🐾🐾 Tarzan and the Green

playboy she is used to. Their rocky relationship is both sexual and emotional. French with subtitles. 90m/C VHS, DVD. FR Karin Viard, Pierre-Loup Rajot, Catherine Frot, Sergi Lopez, Mireille Roussel, Nozha Khouadre; **D:** Catherine Corsini; **W:** Catherine Corsini, Marc Syrigas; **C:** Agnes Godard.

New Faces of 1952 🐾🐾½ 1954 Based on the hit Broadway revue. The plot revolves around a Broadway show that is about to be closed down, and the performers who fight to keep it open. Lots of hit songs. Mel Brooks is credited as one of the writers, under the name Melvin Brooks. 🎵C'est Si Bon; Santa Baby; Uskadara; Monotonous; Eal Petit Bal; Ronny Graham; Time for Tea. 98m/C VHS, DVD. Eartha Kitt, Robert Clary, Alice Ghostley, Paul Lynde; **D:** Harry Horner.

New Fist of Fury 🐾 1935 Xin Ching-wu Men 1976 During WWII, a former pickpocket becomes a martial arts whiz with the assistance of his fiancee, and fights the entire Imperial Army. 120m/C VHS, DVD. Jackie Chan; **D:** Lo Wei; **W:** Lo Wei.

The New Frontier 🐾½ 1935 Wayne is a small-town sheriff whose predecessor, his father, was murdered. The everything they can to prevent Wayne from bringing the culprit to justice. 59m/B VHS. John Wayne, Muriel Evans, Murdock MacQuarrie, Mary MacLaren, Warner Richmond; **D:** Carl Pierson.

The New Gladiators woof! 1983 In the future, criminals try to kill each other on TV for public entertainment. Two such gladiators discover that the network's computer is using the games in order to take over mankind, and they attempt to stop it. Even if the special effects were any good, they couldn't save this one. 90m/C VHS, DVD. Jared Martin, Fred Williamson, Eleanor Gold, Howard (Red) Ross, Claudio Cassinelli; **D:** Lucio Fulci; **W:** Elisa Briganti, Dardano Sacchetti; **C:** Giuseppe Pinori; **M:** Riz Ortolani.

The New Guy 🐾½ 2002 (PG-13) Dorky high school senior Dizzy (Qualls) wants to transform himself into a cool guy—by getting expelled and transferring to another school. Instead, he winds up in prison where he meets Luther (Griffin), who gives him an attitude makeover. Once he hits the new school, his newfound popularity has him winning a hottie cheerleader (Dushku) and uniting the various school cliques. Long (but not quite long enough) delayed high school flick shows a certain lack of effort on most everyone's part, most notably the director, writer, and cinematographer. Qualls is likable, Deschanel is better than flick deserves, and Dushku supplies the expected sexual spark. 88m/C VHS, DVD. US DJ Qualls, Eddie Griffin, Eliza Dushku, Zooey Deschanel, Lyle Lovett, Jerod Mixon, Parry Shen, Sunny Mabrey, Ross Patterson, Matt Gogin, Illeana Douglas, Kurt Fuller, M.C. Gainey, Julius J. Carry III, Horatio Sanz, Geoffrey Lewis; **Cameos:** Henry Rollins, Gene Simmons, Vanilla Ice, Tommy Lee, Dr. Joyce Brothers; **D:** Ed Decter; **W:** David Kendall; **C:** Michael D. O'Shea; **M:** Ralph Sall.

The New Invisible Man 🐾 H.G. Wells' New Invisible Man 1958 A SD-SO Mexican adaptation of the popular H.G. Wells novel has a prisoner receiving a vanishing drug from his brother, who created it—perhaps to aid an escape attempt. 95m/B VHS. MX Arturo de Cordova, Ana Luisa Peluffo, Jorge Mondragon; **D:** Alfredo B. Crevenna.

New Jersey Drive ⊘⊘½ 1995 (R) Jason (Corley) has dreams of life outside the mean streets of Newark, but he jeopardizes his future by stealing cars and joyriding around the neighborhood with his friends. Unblinking realism, provided by credible actors (especially Corley, a former gang member), dialogue, and filming in the projects of Brooklyn and Queens, is neutralized by stereotypical characters (especially the lily-white, sadistically brutal cops) and lack of a sympathetic point of view. Loosely based on a series of articles by Michel Marriott, a reporter for the "New York Times." 98m/C VHS, DVD. Sharron Corley, Gabriel Casseus, Saul Stein, Andre Moore, Donald Adeosun Faison, Conrad Meerin Jr., Devin Eggleston, Gwen McGee, Koran C. Thomas, Samantha Brown, Christine Baranski, Robert Jason Jackson, Roscoe Orman, Dwight Errington Myers, Gary DeWitt Marshall; D: Nick Gomez; W: Nick Gomez, Michel Marriott; C: Adam Kimmel; M: Wendy Blackstone.

The New Kids ⊘⊘ 1985 (R) An orphaned brother and sister find out the limitations of the good neighbor policy. A sadistic gang terrorizes them after their move to a relatives' home in Florida. They go after expected revenge. 90m/C VHS, DVD. Shannon Presby, Lori Loughlin, James Spader, Eric Stoltz; D: Sean S. Cunningham; W: Brian Taggert, Stephen Gyllenhaal.

A New Kind of Love ⊘⊘½ 1963 Romantic fluff starring real-life couple Newman and Woodward who meet en route to Paris and end up falling in love. Newman plays a reporter and Woodward is a fashion designer in this light comedy set amidst the sights of Paris. 110m/C VHS, DVD. Paul Newman, Joanne Woodward, Thelma Ritter, Eva Gabor, Maurice Chevalier, George Tobias; D: Melville Shavelson; W: Melville Shavelson; C: Daniel F. Fapp.

The New Land ⊘⊘⊘ Nybyggarna 1973 (PG) Sequel to "The Emigrants" follows Von Sydow and his family as they struggle to make their new home in the new world. Hardships include severe weather which devastates the farm, a Sioux Indian uprising, and a disastrous trek to the Southwest to search for gold. Sensitive performances and direction. Based on the novels by Vilhelm Moberg. Dubbed into English. 161m/C VHS. SW Max von Sydow, Liv Ullmann, Allan Edwall, Eddie Axberg, Hans Alfredson, Halvar Bjork, Peter Lindgren, Monica Zetterlund, Pierre Lindstedt, Per Oscarsson; D: Jan Troell; W: Jan Troell, Bengt Forslund; C: Jan Troell; M: Bengt Ernryd, George Oddner. Natl. Bd. of Review '73: Actress (Ullmann); Natl. Soc. Film Critics '73: Actress (Ullmann).

A New Leaf ⊘⊘½ 1971 (G) A playboy who has depleted his financial resources tries to win the hand of a clumsy heiress. May was the first woman to write, direct and star in a movie. She was unhappy with the cuts that were made by the studio, but that didn't seem to affect its impact with the public. Even with the cuts, the film is still funny and May's performance is worth watching. 102m/C VHS. Walter Matthau, Elaine May, Jack Weston, George Rose, William Redfield, James Coco; D: Elaine May; W: Elaine May.

A New Life ⊘⊘½ 1988 (PG-13) An uptight stockbroker is abandoned by his wife. The New York singles scene beckons both of them to a new chance at life. Appealing performances cannot completely mask the old story line, but it's definitely worth a look. 104m/C VHS. Alan Alda, Ann-Margret, Hal Linden, Veronica Hamel, John Shea, Mary Kay Place, Cynthia Belliveau, Beatrice Alda; D: Alan Alda; W: Alan Alda; M: Joseph Turrin.

New Mafia Boss ⊘½ Crime Boss 1972 (PG) Italian-made plodder has Savalas taking over a huge Mafia family and all hell breaking loose. 90m/C VHS, DVD. IT Telly Savalas, Lee Van Cleef, Antonio (Tony) Sabato, Paola Tedesco; D: Alberto De Martino.

New Moon ⊘⊘⊘ 1940 An adaptation of the operetta by Sigmund Romberg and Oscar Hammerstein II. A French heiress traveling on a boat that is captured by pirates falls in love with their leader. Remake of the 1930 film. Includes the 1935 Robert Benchley MGM short "How to Sleep." ♪Dance Your Cares Away; Stranger in Paris; The Way They Do It in Paris; Lover Come Back; Shoes; Softly as in a Morning Sunrise; One Kiss; Troubles of the World; No More Weeping. 106m/B VHS. Jeanette MacDonald, Nelson Eddy, Buster Keaton, Joe Yule, Jack Perrin, Mary Boland; D: Robert Z. Leonard.

New Orleans ⊘⊘ 1947 The great legends of jazz re-enact its birth in this song-filled tribute to the town where it all began. When the proprietor (de Cordova) of a Bourbon Street gambling joint (and haven for musicians) falls for an opera-singing socialite, he realizes that only through music will he gain responsibility. He begins a campaign to bring jazz to the highbrow American stage. 90m/B VHS, DVD. Arturo de Cordova, Dorothy Patrick, Louis Armstrong, Billie Holiday, Woody Herman, Richard Hageman; D: Arthur Lubin; W: Elliot Paul, Dick Irving Hyland; C: Lucien N. Andriot.

New Orleans After Dark ⊘⊘ 1958 A pair of New Orleans detectives tour the city, crime-buster style, and bag a dope ring. Average crime tale, shot on location in the Big Easy. 69m/B VHS. Stacy Harris, Louis Sirgo, Ellen Moore; D: John Sledge.

New Pastures ⊘⊘½ 1962 Three ex-convicts run into some humorous situations when they go back to their small hometown. A semi-acclaimed Czech comedy, with subtitles. 92m/B VHS. CZ D: Vladimir Cech.

New Police Story ⊘⊘⊘ Ging Chaat Goo Si 2004 (R) Of course it's the action that carries these pics and 19 years after the 1985 original, star Chan still made it work. Inspector Wing hits the bottle after his team is killed in a shootout with evil Joe (Wu) and his gang. But rookie Frank (Tse) dries Wing out so he can return to the force and finally settle the score. Chinese with subtitles. 123m/C DVD. HK Jackie Chan, Nicholas Tse, Daniel Wu, Charlene (Cheuk-Yin) Choi, Charlie Yeung; D: Benny Chan; W: Alan Yuen; C: Anthony Pun; M: Tommy Wai.

New Rose Hotel ⊘½ 1998 (R) Corporate raider Fox (Walken) and his assistant X (Dafoe) are hired to get scientific genius Hiroshi (Amano) into working for another company. Slinky Sandii (Argento) is the lure. She succeeds but double-crosses her employers who now expect to be killed for their contract. (Industrial espionage is apparently quite hazardous.) Frustrating as director Ferrara repeats scenes with minor variations, leaving viewers bewildered if nothing else. Based on a story by William Gibson. 92m/C VHS, DVD. Christopher Walken, Willem Dafoe, Asia Argento, Yoshitaka Amano, Annabella Sciorra, Gretchen Mol, John Lurie, Ryuichi Sakamoto; D: Abel Ferrara; W: Abel Ferrara, Chris Zois; C: Ken Kelsch.

New Waterford Girl ⊘⊘½ 1999 Mooney Pottie (Balaban) is a 15-year-old stuck in a small coal-mining community in Nova Scotia in the 1970s. Mooney has won a scholarship to a prestigious arts school and is desperate to attend but her parents refuse to let her. But careful observation has shown Mooney that girls who get themselves into "trouble" leave the community to have their babies in secret and she decides to transform herself into a slut (while keeping her virginity) and get out of town. Sweetly amusing with a compelling debut performance from Balaban. 97m/C VHS, DVD. CA Liane Balaban, Tara Spencer-Nairn, Andrew McCarthy, Nicholas (Nick) Campbell, Mary Walsh, Cathy Moriarty; D: Allan Moyle; W: Tricia Fish; C: Derek Rogers.

A New Wave ⊘⊘ 2007 (R) Bank teller Desmond (Keegan) hates his job and follows his movie-obsessed pal Rupert (Krasinski) to talk him into being the inside man in a heist he's lifted from the plots of his favorite flicks. Surprise! Things start to go wrong when Desmond begins having second thoughts and the heist is botched. 94m/C DVD. Andrew Keegan, Lacey Chabert, John Krasinski, William Sadler, Dean Edwards; D: Jason Carvey; W: Jason Carvey; C: Kambui Olujimi; M: Chris Blackburn. VIDEO

New World ⊘½ Le Nouveau Monde 1995 (R) Unflattering portrait of American soldiers in postwar France in the 1950s. Their presence is resented by most of the locals, who are still suffering the depredations caused by WWII unlike their American counterparts, who won't even learn a little French to get by. Young Patrick (Chatel), however, is smitten with American culture, thanks to his meeting with soldier Will (Gandolfini) and All-American girl Trudy (Silverstone). President DeGaul would eventually force the American bases to close. English and French dialogue with subtitles. 117m/C VHS, DVD. FR Nicolas Chatel, James Gandolfini, Alicia Silverstone, Sarah Grappin, Guy Marchand; D: Alain Corneau; C: William Lubtchansky.

The New World ⊘⊘⊘ 2005 (PG-13) Malick's vision offers the story of Pocahontas (Kilcher), stripped of its revisionist history and cartoon-fantasy world and elevated to a mythic retelling of the establishment of an American colony by the London based Virginia Co., which brought Captain John Smith (Farrell) in contact with the Powhatan Indians. As the story surrounding Fort James unfolds, Malick brings into question the motives and desires of Pocahontas, Smith, and later John Rolfe (Bale), the tobacco farmer who eventually marries Pocahontas and brings her back home to England. Ends up as a beautifully crafted metaphor for the effect Europe had on the new world and vice versa. 160m/C DVD. US Colin Farrell, Christopher Plummer, Christian Bale, August Schellenberg, Wes Studi, David Thewlis, Yorick Van Wageningen, Ben Mendelsohn, Raoul Trujillo, Brian F. O'Byrne, Irene Bedard, John Savage, Jamie Harris, Alex Rice, Michael Greyeyes, Noah Taylor, Jonathan Pryce, Q'orianka Kilcher, Kianai Queypo, Alexandra Malick; D: Terrence Malick; W: Terrence Malick; C: Emmanuel Lubezki; M: James Horner. Natl. Bd. of Review '05: Breakthrough Perf. (Kilcher).

New World Disorder ⊘⊘ 1999 Action thriller combines familiar elements of the formula with high-tech computer jargon. A gang of thieves led by the bestudded Bishop (McCarthy) blasts into a computer chip company and steals the Rosetta encryption program. Young computer-savvy FBI agent Paddock (Fitzgerald) winds up working with old-fashioned local cop Marx (Hauer) to catch the bad guys. The action scenes are fairly ambitious for a video premiere. 94m/C VHS, DVD. Rutger Hauer, Andrew McCarthy, Tara Fitzgerald; D: Richard Spence; W: Ehren Kruger, Jeffrey Smith; C: Ivan Strasburg; M: Gast Waltzing. VIDEO

New Year's Day ⊘⊘⊘ 1989 (R) Jaglom continues this look at modern relationships in this story of a man reclaiming his house from three female tenants. Introspective character study lightened by humor and insight. 90m/C VHS, DVD. Maggie Jakobson, Gwen Welles, Melanie Winter, Milos Forkobson, Michael Emil, David Duchovny, Tracy Reiner, Henry Jaglom; D: Henry Jaglom; W: Henry Jaglom.

New Year's Evil woof! 1978 (R) Every hour during a New Year's Eve concert, a madman kills an unsuspecting victim. After each killing, the murderer informs a local disc jockey of his deed. Little does he know that she will soon be next on his list. No suspense, bad music makes this slash and crash a holiday wrecker. 88m/C VHS. Roz Kelly, Kip Niven, Chris Wallace, Louisa Moritz, Grant Cramer, Jed Mills; D: Emmett Alston; W: Emmett Alston; M: W. Michael Lewis.

New York Cop ⊘⊘ 1994 (R) Japanese martial arts expert Toshi (Nakamura) joins the NYPD and is given an undercover assignment to infiltrate a gun-running gang that supplies both drug lords and Japanese mobsters. But internal rivalries force Toshi to bond with gang leader Hawk (McQueen) and the duo to do battle together. 88m/C VHS, DVD. Toru Nakamura, Chad McQueen, Mira Sorvino; D: Toru Murakawa.

New York Doll ⊘⊘⊘ 2005 (PG-13) Arthur "Killer" Kane was the bassist for the 1970s glam-rock band the New York Dolls, going from the excesses of rock 'n' roll (the Dolls broke up in 1975) to obscurity and battling a variety of demons (chemical and otherwise) until a belated recovery and his adoption of the Mormon faith. In 2004, diehard fan Morrissey persuaded Kane to reunite with his two remaining bandmates for a London music festival. Whiteley follows Kane from his settled life in LA to the Dolls' bittersweet reunion. Kane died of leukemia shortly after the concert. 73m/C DVD. US D: Greg Whiteley; C: Rod Santiano, Seth Gordon.

New York Minute ⊘½ 2004 (PG) Sporting different hair color, way too much make-up, and a sheen only multi-millions from straight-to-video hits can bring, the Olsen twins take New York City in this dumb semi-screwball, wanna-be action comedy. Blonde do-gooder Jane (Ashley) and dark-haired rebel Roxy (Mary-Kate) have recently lost their mom and live with their dad (Pinsky) in the Long Island suburbs. The couldn't-be-more-different twins share a ride into The City in search of their respective dreams (Jane's is an Oxford fellowship; Roxy's a career in rock) when things go awry and they end up running amok to marginal comic effect, while being tailed by truant officer Levy. The twins' TV dad Saget shows up in an amusing cameo. 91m/C VHS, DVD. US Ashley (Fuller) Olsen, Mary-Kate Olsen, Eugene Levy, Andy Richter, Riley Smith, Jared Padalecki, Darrell Hammond, Andrea Martin, Alannah Ong; Cameos: Bob Saget; D: Dennie Gordon; W: Emily Fox, Adam Cooper, Bill Collage; C: Greg Gardiner; M: George S. Clinton.

New York, New York ⊘⊘⊘ 1977 (PG) Tragic romance evolves between a saxophonist and an aspiring singer/actress in this salute to the big-band era. A love of music isn't enough to hold them together through career rivalries and life on the road. Fine performances by De Niro and Minnelli and the supporting cast. Re-released in 1981 with the "Happy Endings" number, which was cut from the original. Look for "Big Man" Clarence Clemons on sax. ♪New York, New York; There Goes the Ball Game; Happy Endings; But the World Goes 'Round; Night in Tunisia; Opus One; Avalon; You Brought a New Kind of Love to Me; I'm Getting Sentimental Over You. 163m/C VHS, DVD. Robert De Niro, Liza Minnelli, Lionel Stander, Barry Primus, Mary Kay Place, Dick Miller, Dianne Abbott; D: Martin Scorsese; W: Mardik Martin; M: Ralph Burns.

New York Nights ⊘ 1984 (R) The lives of nine New Yorkers intertwine in a treacherous game of passion and seduction. Liberal borrowing from plot of "La Ronde." 104m/C VHS. Corinne Alphen, George Auyer, Bobbi Burns, Peter Matthey, Cynthia Lee, Willem Dafoe; D: Simon Nuchtern.

New York Ripper woof! Lo Squartatore de New York; The Ripper 1982 A New York cop tracks down a rampaging murderer in this dull, mindless slasher flick. 88m/C VHS, DVD. IT Jack Hedley, Antonella Interlenghi, Howard (Red) Ross, Andrea Occhipinti, Alessandra Delli Colli, Paolo Malco; D: Lucio Fulci; W: Lucio Fulci, Gianfranco Clerici, Vincenzo Mannino, Dardano Sacchetti; C: Luigi Kuveiller; M: Francesco De Masi.

New York Stories ⊘⊘⊘ 1989 (PG) Entertaining anthology of three separate short films by three esteemed directors, all set in New York. In "Life Lessons" by Scorsese, an impulsive artist tries to prevent his live-in girlfriend from leaving him. "Life Without Zoe" by Coppola involves a youngster's fantasy about a wealthy 12-year-old who lives mostly without her parents. Allen's "Oedipus Wrecks," generally considered the best short, is about a 50-year-old man who is tormented by the specter of his mother. 124m/C VHS, DVD. Nick Nolte, Rosanna Arquette, Woody Allen, Mia Farrow, Mae Questel, Julie Kavner, Talia Shire, Giancarlo Giannini, Don Novello, Patrick O'Neal, Peter Gabriel, Paul Herman, Deborah Harry, Steve Buscemi, Heather McComb, Chris Elliot, Carole Bouquet, Edward I. Koch; D: Woody Allen, Martin Scorsese, Francis Ford Coppola; W: Woody Allen, Francis Ford Coppola, Richard Price, Sofia Coppola; C: Sven Nykvist, Nestor Almendros; M: Carmine Coppola.

New York's Finest 🎬 1987 (R) Three prostitutes are determined to leave their calling and marry very eligible millionaires. But becoming society ladies is more difficult than they thought. Would-be sophisticated comedy misfires. 80m/C VHS. C: Jennifer Delora, Scott Thompson Baker, Heidi Paine, Jane (Veronica Hart) Hamilton, Alan Naggar, John Altamura, Alan Fisler, Jesey Duval; D: Chuck Vincent.

The Newlydeads 🎬½ 1987 (R) An uptight, conservative, honeymoon resort owner murders one of his guests and finds out that "she" is really a he. Fifteen years later, on his wedding night, all of his guests are violently murdered by the transvestite's vengeful ghost. Oddball twist to the usual slasher nonsense. 84m/C VHS, DVD. Scor: Kaske, Jim Williams, Jean Levine, Jay Richardson; D: Joseph Merhi; W: Joseph Merhi, Louis Zorich; M: John Gonzalez.

Newman's Law 🎬🎬 1974 (PG) A city detective is implicated in a corruption investigation. While on suspension, he continues with his own investigation of a large drug ring and finds corruption is closer than he thought. Director Heffron's first feature film. 99m/C VHS. George Peppard, Roger Robinson, Eugene Roche, Gordon Pinsent, Abe Vigoda; D: Richard T. Heffron.

News at Eleven 🎬🎬 1986 A fading news anchorman is pressured by his ambitious young boss to expose a touchy local sex scandal, forcing him to consider the public's right to know versus the rights of the individual. About average for TV drama. 96m/C VHS, DVD. Martin Sheen, Peter Riegert, Barbara Babcock, Sheree J. Wilson, Sydney Penny, David S. Sheiner, Christpher Allport; D: Mike Robe. TV

News from Home 🎬🎬 1975 Scenes of life in New York are juxtaposed with voiceover from the letters of a mother to her young daughter. Plotless narrative deals with the small details of life. 85m/C VHS. D: Chantal Akerman; Nar: Chantal Akerman.

Newsbreak 🎬🎬 2000 (R) Reckless and arrogant reporter John McNamara (Rooker) has made a lot of enemies. When he decides to investigate the disappearance of a fellow journalist, John uncovers citywide corruption that involves the president of a construction company (Reinhol) and his own father (Culp), a judge with a sterling reputation. 95m/C VHS, DVD. Michael Rooker, Robert Culp, Kelly Miller, Kim Darby, Noele Parker; D: Serge Rodnunsky; W: Serge Rodnunsky; Paul Tarantino; C: Howard Wexler; M: Evan Evans. VIDEO

Newsfront 🎬🎬🎬 1978 A story about two brothers, both newsreel filmmakers, and their differing approaches to life and their craft in the 1940s and '50s. Tribute to the days of newsreel film combines real stories and fictionalized accounts with color and black and white photography. Noyce's feature film debut. 110m/C VHS, DVD. AJ Bill Hunter, Gerard Kennedy, Angela Punch McGregor, Wendy Hughes, Chris Haywood, John Ewart, Bryan Brown; D: Phillip Noyce. Australian Film Inst. '78: Actor (Hunter), Film.

Newsies 🎬½ 1992 (PG) An unfortunate attempt at an old-fashioned musical with a lot of cute kids and cardboard characters and settings. The plot, such as it is, concerns the 1899 New York newsboys strike against penny-pinching publisher Joseph Pulitzer. Bale plays the newsboy's leader and at least shows some charisma in a strictly cartoon setting. Tt e songs are never, none of it moves the story along. Add a bone for viewers under 12. Choreographer Ortega's feature-film directorial debut. 121m/C VHS, DVD. Christian Bale, Bill Pullman, Robert Duvall, Ann-Margret, Michael Lerner, Kevin Tighe, Charles Cioffi, Luke Edwards, Max Casella, David Moscow; D: Kenny Ortega; W: Bob Tzudiker; C: Noni White; M: Alan Menken; Song ("High Times, Hard Times").

The Newton Boys 🎬🎬½ 1997 (PG-13) Fact-based drama chronicling the careers and love lives of the bank robbing Newton brothers, who robbed their way from Texas to Toronto during the 20s and

'30s. They lived and worked by a romantic credo: no killing, stealing from women or children, and no rating each other out. McConaughey and Ulrich lead the group as Willis and Joe, respectively, and both prove likeable gangsters. Hawke and D'Onfrio do their best in less developed roles. Highlight is the great tran robbery, which garnered the outlaws $3 million and eventually landed the boys in court. Though well-acted with interesting material, Linklater's departure lacks precise and gle, which keeps the story from really humming. Stealing the show is the real-life footage of a 1980 "Tonight Show" where Johnny Carson interviews the genson able Joe. 122m/C VHS, DVD. Matthew McConaughey, Skeet Ulrich, Ethan Hawke, Vincent D'Onofrio, Julianna Margulies, Dwight Yoakam, Gail Cronauer, Chloe Webb, Charles Gunning, Becket Gremmels, Richard Jones; D: Richard Linklater; W: Claude Stanush, Clark Lee Walker; C: Peter James; M: Edward D. Barnes.

Next 🎬🎬 2007 (PG-13) Struggling Vegas magician Cris (Cage) has the ability to see two minutes into the future. Somehow, FBI agent Ferris (Moore) becomes aware of his ability and wants him to help them find a nuclear weapon that's been smuggled into L.A. Cris would rather focus on meeting his dream girl, Liz (Biel), but the two plot points soon collide and Cage stays low-key, Biel is beautiful and bewildered, and director Tamahori handles the action well, but it's ultimately a forgettable gimmick. Adapted from a story by Philip K. Dick. 96m/C VHS, DVD, Blu-ray Disc, HD DVD. US Nicolas Cage, Jessica Biel, Julianne Moore, Thomas Kretschmann, Tory Kittles, Peter Falk, Jose Zuniga, Jim Beaver, Michael Trucco, Jason Butler Harner; D: Lee Tamahori; W: Gary Goldman, Jonathan Hensleigh, Paul Bernbaum; C: David Tattersall; M: Mark Isham.

The Next Best Thing 🎬🎬 2000 (PG-13) L.A. yoga instructor Abbie (Madonna) manages to get preggers thanks to a drunken one-nighter with gay best friend, Robert (Everett). She has the kid, they decide to live together and share parental responsibilities (but nothing more), and for six years things just go along swimmingly. Then Abbie meets the perfect guy—investment banker Ben (Bratt). But Ben is planning to relocate to New York and suddenly sole custody is all that matters to Abbie—even it means a court case. Sappy, predictable story falls prey to Madonna's limited acting ability 'though both Everett and Bratt supply charm galore. 108m/C VHS, DVD, US Madonna, Rupert Everett, Benjamin Bratt, Michael Vartan, Josef Sommer, Lynn Redgrave, Malcolm Stumpf, Neil Patrick Harris, Illeana Douglas, Mark Valley, Stacy Edwards; D: John Schlesinger; W: Tom Ropelewski; C: Elliot Davis; M: Gabriel Yared. Golden Raspberries '00: Worst Actress (Madonna).

The Next Big Thing 🎬½ 2002 (R) Gus Bishop (Eigeman) is a struggling New York artist who meets con man Deech Scumble (Harris) when Deech steals his wallet and, later, a painting. Deech sells the painting, signed "GB" to art gallery owner Arthur (Granger) by inventing a tragic background for the artist he's renamed Geoff Buonardi. Deech manages to convince Gus to continue the scam since his new artistic persona is making them a lot of money. But soon more and more people become aware of the deception. 85m/C VHS, DVD. US Christopher Eigeman, Jamie Harris, Connie Britton, Janet Zarish, Farley Granger, Mike Starr, Marin Hinkle; D: P.J. Posner; W: P.J. Posner, Joel Posner; C: Oliver Bokelberg; M: Ferdinand Jay Smith.

Next Door 🎬½ 1994 (R) College professors Matt (Woods) and Karen (Capshaw) have the perfect suburban home—complete with the perfect blue-collar neighbor. Then their boorish blue-collar neighbor Lenny (Quaid) takes to enthusiastic lawn watering and ruins their flowers. One thing leads to a full-scale feud. 95m/C VHS. James Woods, Randy Quaid, Kate Capshaw, Lucinda Jenney; D: Tony Bill; W: Barney Cohen; C: Thomas Del Ruth. CABLE

Next Friday 🎬🎬 2000 (R) Amiable, meandering sequel to 1995's surprise hit "Friday" finds Craig (Ice Cube) fleeing to the suburbs to escape Debo (Lister),

who's out of prison and looking for payback. Uncle Elroy (Curry) has hit the lotto and moved to the 'burbs, giving Craig and a whole new bunch of central casting characters a new place to hang out and cause some mischief. The original's biggest success came on home video and cable, and this one's likely to duplicate that pattern. 93m/C VHS, DVD. Ice Cube, Tommy Lister, John Witherspoon, Justin Pierce, Jacob Vargas, Lopo Sebastian, Rolando Molina, Tamala Jones, Mike Epps, Don "DC" Curry, Lisa Rodriguez, Kym E. Whitley, Amy Hill, Robin Allen, Kirk "Sticky Fingaz" Jones; D: Steve Carr; W: Ice Cube; C: Christopher Baffa; M: Terence Blanchard.

The Next Karate Kid 🎬🎬½ 1994 (PG) Fourth installment in the "Kid" series finds martial arts expert Miyagi (Morita) training Julie Pierce (Swank), the orphaned tomboy daughter of an old war buddy who saved his life 50 years earlier. He even teaches her the waltz, just in time for the prom, but she's still tough enough to scrap with a guy. A must-see for "Karate K'd" fans, if there are any left. 107m/C VHS, DVD. Noriyuki "Pat" Morita, Hilary Swank; D: Christopher Cain; W: Mark Lee; M: Bill Conti.

Next of Kin 🎬🎬 1982 A daughter moves into her dead mother's retirement home and discovers an unspeakable evil that lurks there. Typical horror stuff has some very creepy moments; filmed in New Zealand. 72m/C VHS, DVD, CA Jackie Kerin, John Jarratt, Gerda Nicholson, Alex Scott; D: Tony Williams.

Next of Kin 🎬🎬 1984 A young man experiencing familial difficulties undergoes experimental video therapy where he views a videotape of an Armenian family who gave their son up for adoption. When he discovers the actual family he insinuates himself into their life, determined to be their long-lost son. 72m/C VHS, DVD, CA Patrick Tierney; D: Atom Egoyan; W: Atom Egoyan.

Next of Kin 🎬🎬 1989 (R) A Chicago cop returns to his Kentucky home to avenge his brother's brutal murder. Swayze's return to action films after his success in "Dirty Dancing" is unimpressive. 108m/C VHS, DVD. Patrick Swayze, Adam Baldwin, Bill Paxton, Helen Hunt, Andreas Katsulas, Ben Stiller, Michael J. Pollard, Liam Neeson; D: John Irvin; C: Steven Poster; M: Jack Nitzsche.

Next One 🎬½ 1984 A mysterious visitor from another time winds up on an isolated Greek island as the result of a magnetic storm. The local inhabitants are amazed when the visitor displays some Christ-like characteristics. 105m/C VHS. Keir Dullea, Adrienne Barceau, Jeremy Licht, Peter Hinton; D: Nico Mastorakis.

The Next Step 🎬🎬½ 1995 Nick Mendez (Negron) is a 35-year-old Broadway dancer who's feeling the wear and tear of his profession. A practiced seducer, Nick does have a devoted girlfriend in ex-dancer turned physical therapist, Amy (Moreu). Amy gets a job offer in Connecticut just as Nick's confidence is shaken when he's rejected for a dance role he originated in favor of a younger performer. Amy wants Nick to retire and move away with her but life away from Broadway leaves Nick wondering what he'd do. Negron is a former Broadway dancer and of course a compelling performance in a film that's ripe with showbiz clichés. 97m/C VHS, DVD. Rick Negron, Kristin Moreu, Denise Faye, Taylo: Nichols; D: Christian Faber; W: Aaron Reed; C: Zack Winestine; M: Mio Morales, Brian Otto, Roni Skies.

Next Stop, Greenwich Village 🎬🎬🎬 1976 (R) An affectionate, autobiographical look by Mazursky at a Brooklyn boy with acting aspirations, who moves to Greenwich Village in 1953. Good performances, especially by Winters as the overbearing mother. 109m/C VHS. Lenny Baker, Christopher Walken, Ellen Greene, Shelley Winters, Lou Jacobi, Mike Kellin; D: Paul Mazursky; W: Paul Mazursky; M: Bill Conti.

Next Stop, Wonderland 🎬🎬½ 1998 (R) Charming romance, set in Boston, about a couple of odd ducks who are totally right for each other. Waifish Eric (Davis)

is a nurse whose boyfriend Sear (Hoffman) has just left her. So her meddling mom Piper (Taylor) secretly places a personal ad to get her daughter some dates. They're a bunch of losers but plumber/marine-biology student Alan (Gelfant) whom Erin keeps seeing on the subway is Mr. Right. If only the duo could get together. Intelligent characters and a terrific bossa nova soundtrack. Title refers to the name of an actual subway stop. 96m/C VHS, DVD. Hope Davis, Alan Gelfant, Holland Taylor, Robert Klein, Cara Buono, Jose Zuniga, Phil Hoffman, Lyn Vaus, Larry (Lawrence) Gilliard Jr., Victor Argo, Roger Rees, Robert Stanton, Pamela Hart; D: Brad Anderson; W: Brad Anderson, Lyn Vaus; C: Uta Briesewitz; M: Claudio Ragazzi.

Next Summer 🎬🎬🎬 L'Eté Prochain 1984 A large, character-studded French family pursues power, love and beauty. Excellent performances. In French with English subtitles. 100m/C VHS, FR Jean-Louis Trintignant, Claudia Cardinale, Fanny Ardant, Philippe Noiret, Marie Trintignant; D: Nadine Trintignant.

Next Time I Marry 🎬½ 1938 Lucy fraternizes with ditch digger Ellison because she needs to hitch a Yankee in order to inherit $20 mill. Seems she really loves a foreigner, though. Not much to balloo about. Director Kanin's second effort. 65m/B VHS. Lucille Ball, James Ellison, Lee Bowman, Granville Bates, Mantan Moreland, Florence Lake; D: Garson Kanin.

Next Time We Love 🎬🎬½ 1935 Ambitious reporter Chris Tyler (Stewart) and actress Cicely (Sullivan) impulsively marry. With the help of their best friend Tommy (Milland), Cicely gets a shot on Broadway while Chris is assigned to his paper's Rome bureau. Cecily learns she's pregnant and Chris comes back to New York, losing his job. Tommy pulls some strings but Chris' new position is overseas again and Cecily basically raises their son alone while becoming a Broadway star. Eventually, Tommy admits he loves her and Cecily goes to Europe to settle things with Chris only to learn that he's dying. Romantic melodrama also suffers because Cecily isn't a particularly likeable character. An uncredited Preston Sturges worked on the first draft of the script. 87m/B DVD. James Stewart, Margaret Sullavan, Ray Milland, Grant Mitchell, Robert McWade, Anna Demetrio; D: Edward H. Griffith; W: Melville Baker; C: Joseph Valentine; M: Franz Waxman.

The Next Victim 🎬 Lo Strano Vizio Della Signora Wardh 1971 (PG) The unfaithful wife of an Austrian diplomat attempts to find out who has been slicing up beautiful jet-setters. Tepid mystery. 87m/C VHS. George Hilton, Edwige Fenech, Christina Airoldi, Ivan Rassimov; D: Sergio Martino.

The Next Voice You Hear 🎬🎬 1974 A beautiful woman confined to a wheelchair is stalked by a lunatic killer. You've seen it before and done better. 80m/C VHS, GB Carroll Baker, James Whitmore, Nancy Davis, Gary Gray, Lillian Bronson, Art Smith, Tom D'Andrea, Jeff Corey, George Chandler; D: William A. Wellman.

Next Year if All Goes Well 🎬🎬½ 1983 Two young lovers struggle to overcome insecurities while establishing a relationship. Dubbed. 95m/C VHS. FR Isabelle Adjani, Thierry Lhermitte, Marie-Anne) Chazel; D: Jean-Loup Hubert.

Next Year in Jerusalem 🎬🎬 1980 Lives are changed forever when a group of people hear the voice of God on the radio. Interesting premise presented seriously. 84m/B VHS.

Next Time 🎬🎬½ 1999 Offbeat romance tells the story of the relationship between Matt (Campbell), a young white guy, and Evelyn (Allen), a 39-year-old black woman, who meet at a laundrette. 97m/C DVD. Jonelle Allen, Christian Campbell, Ishtar, Robert Harper, Iona Morris; D: L. Alan Frazer; W: L. Alan Frazer; C: William Hooke; M: James S. Mulholian Jr.

up at the family Passover seder, where he meets Manny. Devout Manny is supposed to marry the Rabbi's daughter, only he's got a secret too. The duo soon begin a relationship they keep from their families but it becomes clear that Charlie and Manny need to be honest about who they truly are. 103m/C VHS, DVD. Peter J. Byrnes, Reed McGowan, Georgina Spelvin, Louis Edmonds; *D:* David Nahmod; *W:* David Nahmod; *C:* Kelvin Walker; *M:* Richard Barone.

Niagara ✗✗½ 1952 During their honeymoon in Niagara Falls, a scheming wife (Monroe) plans to kill her crazed warvet husband (Cotten). Little does she know that she is plotting to double-cross her. Steamy, quasi-Hitchcockian mystery ably directed, with interesting performances. Monroes sings "Kiss." 89m/B VHS, DVD. Joseph Cotten, Jean Peters, Marilyn Monroe, Max (Casey Adams) Showalter, Don Wilson, Denis O'Dea, Lurene Tuttle, Harry Carey Jr., Russell Collins, Minerva Urecal; *D:* Henry Hathaway; *W:* Charles Brackett, Walter Reisch; *C:* Joe MacDonald; *M:* Sol Kaplan.

Niagara, Niagara ✗✗ 1997 (R) Marcy (Tunney) is a victim of Tourette's Syndrome, which causes the sufferer to twitch and unleash strings of profanity that would make a longshoreman blush. She meets shy, introverted Seth (Thomas) while they're both shoplifting, and it's love at first sight. They hit the road, supposedly for a doll that Marcy believes can be found in Toronto, but in reality because they are already outcasts at home. When Seth is injured in a botched pharmacy robbery, they're taken in by fellow oddball Walter, a tow truck driver who dotes on a pet chicken named after his dead wife. All of these lost characters are on a road to nowhere, and are pulled apart by Marcy's bourbon-fueled tics and tantrums. Compelling performance by Tunney carries the rest of this dull, flat movie on its back. 96m/C VHS, DVD. Robin Tunney, Henry Thomas, Michael Parks, Stephen Lang, John MacKay; *D:* Bob Gosse; *W:* Matthew Weiss; *C:* Michael Spiller; *M:* Michael Timmins, Jeff Bird.

Nice Girl? ✗✗½ 1941 Jane (Durbin) develops a crush on visiting professor Richard Calvert (Tone), much to his embarrassment. But her steady beau Don (Stack) sticks around to provide support while Calvert seeks a way to let Jane down easy. The video includes a 3-minute alternate ending. 96m/B VHS. Deanna Durbin, Franchot Tone, Robert Stack, Robert Benchley, Walter Brennan, Ann Gillis, Helen Broderick, Anne Gwynne; *D:* William A. Seiter; *W:* Richard Connell, Gladys Lehman; *C:* Joseph Valentine.

Nice Girl Like Me ✗✗ 1969 (PG) An orphaned young girl roams Europe, getting pregnant twice by two different men. She eventually finds love in the form of a kind caretaker. Harmless fluff. Based on Anne Piper's novel "Marry At Leisure." 91m/C VHS. GB Barry Andrews, Barbara Ferris, Gladys Cooper, Bill Hinnant, James Villiers; *D:* Desmond Davis.

Nice Girls Don't Explode ✗✗ 1987 (PG) A girl telekinetically starts fires when sexually aroused. This puts a bit of a damper on her relationship with O'Leary, much to her mother's delight. Matchless entertainment. 92m/C VHS. Barbara Harris, Wallace Shawn, Michelle Meyrink, William O'Leary; *D:* Chuck Martinez; *M:* Brian Banks.

Nice Guys Sleep Alone ✗✗ 1999 (R) Overachieving independent romantic comedy finds nice guy Carter (O'Bryan) hearing those three dreaded words "let's be friends" at the end of each date. He has resolved to take a new approach when he meets Maggie (Temchen), who recently arrived in Louisville from New York. The complications keep the plot moving are familiar, and Carter's rival Robert (Murray) is such a swine that it's impossible any intelligent woman would pay attention to him, no matter how rich he is. But the characters are engaging, especially Carter's stepsister Erin (Marcil), and the film has its heart in the right place. 92m/C DVD. Sean O'Bryan, Sybil Temchen, Vanessa Marcil, Blake Steury, Christopher Murray, Morgan Fairchild, William Sanderson; *D:* Stu Pollard; *C:* Nathan Hope.

Nice Neighbor ✗✗ 1979 An acclaimed film about an outwardly self-sacrificing neighbor who cold-bloodedly manipulates his fellow rooming house tenants for his own ends. In Hungarian with English subtitles. 90m/C VHS. HU Laszlo Szabo, Margit Dayka, Agi Margittay; *D:* Zsolt Kedzi-Kovacs.

Nicholas and Alexandra ✗✗½ 1971 (PG) Epic chronicling the final years of Tsar Nicholas II, Empress Alexandra, and their children. Their lavish royal lifestyle gives way to imprisonment and eventual execution under the new Lenin government. Beautiful, but overlong costume epic that loses steam in the second half. Based on the biography by Robert Massie. 183m/C VHS, DVD. Michael Jayston, Janet Suzman, Tom Baker, Laurence Olivier, Michael Redgrave, Harry Andrews, Jack Hawkins, Alexander Knox, Curt Jurgens; *D:* Franklin J. Schaffner; *W:* James Goldman; *C:* Frederick A. (Freddie) Young; *M:* Richard Rodney Bennett. Oscars '71: Art Dir/Set Dec., Costume Des.

Nicholas Nickleby ✗✗✗ *The Life and Adventures of Nicholas Nickleby* 1946 An ensemble cast works hard to bring to life Charles Dickens' novel about an impoverished family dependent on their wealthy but villainous uncle. Young Nicholas is an apprentice at a school for boys, and he and a student run away to a series of exciting adventures. An enjoyable film, though it is hard to tell the entire story in such a small amount of time. 108m/B VHS. GB Cedric Hardwicke, Stanley Holloway, Derek Bond, Alfred Drayton, Sybil Thorndike, Sally Ann Howes, Bernard Miles, Mary Merrall, Cathleen Nesbitt; *D:* Alberto Cavalcanti; *C:* Georges Perinal.

Nicholas Nickleby ✗✗✗ 2002 (PG) Director McGrath reliably takes on another period piece with this sprawling Dickens classic, which he nicely condenses for mass consumption. Nicholas (Hunnam) is a 19 year-old in England forced to grow up quickly when his father dies and he takes over as head of the family. Well acted, with Hunnam able but not outstanding in an overall light-hearted and lively production. 130m/C VHS, DVD. US Charlie Hunnam, Christopher Plummer, Jamie Bell, Jim Broadbent, Juliet Stevenson, Tom Courtenay, Alan Cumming, Edward Fox, Romola Garai, Anne Hathaway, Timothy Spall, Nathan Lane, Barry Humphries, Gerard Horan, Stella Gonet; *D:* Douglas McGrath; *W:* Douglas McGrath; *C:* Dick Pope; *M:* Rachel Portman.

Nick and Jane ✗✗ 1996 (R) See John sleep with another woman. See Jane see John sleep with another woman. See Jane run out of the building to catch a cab. See Nick pick her up in the cab. This is just a glimpse of all the hilarious fun you'll see when New Yorker Jane (Wheeler-Nicholson) gets a fake boyfriend, Nick (McCaffrey), to upset two-timing John (Dossett). Predictable romantic comedy does have something to offer in sparks between the leads, but they're buried amid the bizarre subplots and off-beat supports. The opening scene where Jane catches her boyfriend cheating is the lone unique and funny segment. Cost-saving camera work, devoid of close-ups and reaction shots, shows. 94m/C VHS. Dana Wheeler-Nicholson, James McCaffrey, Lisa Gay Hamilton, John Dossett, David Johansen, Gedde Watanabe, Saundra Santiago, George Coe, Clinton Leupp; *D:*

Rich Mauro; *W:* Rich Mauro, Peter Quigley, Neil Alumkai; *C:* Christopher Norr; *M:* Mark Suozzo.

Nick Knight ✗✗ 1989 An L.A. cop on the night beat is really a good-guy vampire, who quaffs cattle blood as he tracks down another killer who's draining humans of their plasma. A gimmicky pilot for a would-be TV series that eventually morphed into "Forever Knight." 92m/C VHS, DVD. Rick Springfield, Michael Nader, Laura Johnson, John Kapelos; *D:* Farhad Mann; *W:* James D. Parriott; *C:* Frank Beascoechea; *M:* Joseph Conlan. TV

Nick of Time ✗✗½ 1995 (R) A malicious stranger (Walken) and his cohort coerce ordinary accountant Gene Watson (Depp) 90 minutes to assassinate the governor of California (Mason) or his little girl will be killed. Walken as an evil psycho...now there's a stretch. On the other hand, Depp as a button-down, conservative widower is a bit of a switch after his usually quirky roles of the recent past. This may be the first time Depp's picked up a gun since "21 Jump Street." Illogical scenarios (even for an action flick) and curiously uneven pacing do this one in. Shot almost entirely in L.A's Bonaventure Hotel in real time with a handheld camera. 98m/C VHS, DVD. Johnny Depp, Christopher Walken, Charles S. Dutton, Peter Strauss, Roma Maffia, Gloria Reuben, Marsha Mason, Courtney Chase, Bill Smitrovich, G.D. Spradlin; *D:* John Badham; *W:* Patrick Duncan; *C:* Roy Wagner; *M:* Arthur B. Rubinstein.

Nickel & Dime ✗✗ 1992 (PG) A con artist's luck turns bad when the IRS catches up with him, impounds all his worldly goods, and sticks him with an officious auditor. But if Jack can find the heiress to a fortune, within 48 hours, he can claim a hefty finder's fee and his money worries will be a thing of the past. 96m/C VHS. C. Thomas Howell, Wallace Shawn, Lise Cutter, Lynn Danielson-Rosenthal, Roy Brocksmith; *D:* Ben Moses; *W:* Seth Front, Eddy Polon, Ben Moses.

Nickel Mountain ✗✗½ 1985 Heartwarming story of a suicidal 40-year-old man who finds a new reason to live when he falls in love with a pregnant 16-year-old girl who works at his diner. Langenkamp is particularly appealing. Based on a John Gardner novel. 88m/C VHS. Michael Cole, Patrick Cassidy, Grace Zabriskie, Don Beddoe; *D:* Drew Denbaum.

Nico and Dani ✗✗½ 2002 *Krampack* 2000 Best buddies Nico (Vilches) and Dani (Ramallo) are 17-year-old virgins who hope to change that situation while on a Spanish beach vacation. Nico has the hots for pretty Elena (Orozco), who returns his interest, which leaves her cousin Berta (Nubiola) pining for Dani. Too bad Dani realizes that he not only loves Nico, he's IN love with him and that Nico doesn't share his sexual feelings. Dani finds a mentor in an older gay man (Amado) but the situation remains tangled in an all-too realistic (if somewhat overly sunny) way. Based on the play "Krampack" by Jordi Sanchez. Spanish with subtitles. 90m/C VHS, DVD. SP Fernando Ramallo, Jordi Vilches, Marieta Orozco, Esther Nubiola, Chisco Amado, Ana Gracia; *D:* Cesc Gay; *W:* Cesc Gay, Tomas Aragay; *C:* Andreu Rebes; *M:* Riqui Sabates, Joan Diaz, Jordi Prats.

Nico Icon ✗✗✗ 1995 (R) Documentary probes the life of Velvet Underground sensation and Warhol superstar Nico. A pastiche showing V.U. concert footage and movie clips from Nico's most famous film appearances: Fellini's "La Dolce Vita" and Warhol's "The Chelsea Girls." Also features interviews from Warhol's Factory inhabitants, band members, and Nico's grown son Ari. Visually as interesting as the subject herself, film manages to bring the viewer closer to the untouchable Teutonic figure without being sensational or overly flashy. Director Paul Morrissey and musician Jackson Browne make appearances. Some French and German language; subtitled. 75m/C VHS, DVD. GE *D:* Susanne Ofteringer; *W:* Susanne Ofteringer; *C:* Judith Kaufman.

Nicole ✗ 1972 (R) The downfall of a wealthy woman who is able to buy everything she wants except love. 91m/C VHS. Leslie Caron, Catherine Bach, Ramon Bieri; *D:* Istvan Ventilla.

The Night After Halloween ✗ *Snapshot* 1979 (R) A young woman gets the shock of her life when she discovers that her boyfriend is a crazed killer. 90m/C VHS. AU Chantal Contouri, Robert Bruning, Sigrid Thornton; *D:* Simon Wincer; *M:* Brian May.

Night After Night ✗✗½ 1932 West's screen debut finds her in an unaccustomed secondary role, although a prime scene-stealer. In Raft's first starring role, he's a monied low-life who opens a fancy nightclub and becomes infatuated with Park Avenue beauty Cummings. His problems are compounded by the arrival of raucous ex-flames West and Gleason. When a hatcheck girl cries "Goodness!" over West's diamonds, she replies, in suggestive West-style, "Goodness had nothing to do with it, dearie." Adapted from the novel "Single Night" by Louis Bromfield. 73m/B VHS, DVD. George Raft, Constance Cummings, Mae West, Wynne Gibson, Alison Skipworth, Roscoe Karns, Louis Calhern; *D:* Archie Mayo; *W:* Mae West, Kathryn Scola, Vincent Lawrence.

Night Ambush ✗✗½ *Ill Met By Moonlight* 1957 A Nazi general is kidnapped on Crete by British agents, who embark on a dangerous trip to the coast where a ship awaits to take them to Cairo. The general tries to thwart their plans, but they outwit him at every turn. Based on a novel by W. Stanley Moss that details a similar real-life event. 100m/B VHS. GB Dirk Bogarde, Marius Goring, David Oxley, Cyril Cusack, Christopher Lee; *D:* Michael Powell, Emeric Pressburger.

Night and Day ✗✗ 1946 Sentimental musical about the life of bon-vivant composer-extraordinaire Cole Porter. His intensity and the motivations for his music are dramatized, but this film succeeds best as a fabulous showcase for Porter's songs. ♪ Begin the Beguine; My Heart Belongs to Daddy; You're the Top; I've Got You Under My Skin; Just One of Those Things; I Get a Kick Out of You; Night and Day; What Is This Thing Called Love; Do I Love You. 128m/C VHS, DVD. Cary Grant, Alexis Smith, Jane Wyman, Eve Arden, Mary Martin, Alan Hale, Monty Woolley, Ginny Simms, Dorothy Malone; *D:* Michael Curtiz; *M:* Max Steiner.

Night and Day ✗✗✗ ½ *Nuit et Jour* 1991 Charming adult romance about Jack and Julie, young lovers newly arrived in Paris. When Jack gets a night job driving a cab, Julie finds her evenings lonely. But not for long. She meets Joseph, a cab driver on the day shift. Soon, Julie is juggling sexual affairs with both men and everything gets increasingly complicated. Her lovers find out about each other but Julie doesn't want to fully commit to either of them. In French with English subtitles. 90m/C VHS. FR BE SI Guilaine Londez, Thomas Langmann, Francois Negret; *D:* Chantal Akerman; *W:* Pascal Bonitzer, Chantal Akerman; *M:* Marc Herouet.

Night and the City ✗✗✗ ½ 1950 A film noir classic about a hustler's money-making schemes. Widmark is Harry Fabian, a small-time promoter working for slimy nightclub owner Sullivan, whose job is to hustle the marks into the club where his girlfriend Tierney is the singer. Widmark also happens to be romancing Sullivan's wife, Withers, and wants her to back his latest con. But his schemes go awry and Fabian's on the run for his life. Widmark gives a riveting performance of a lowlife whose brains don't match his ambitions. Filmed in London with appropriate brooding tawdriness. Adapted from the novel by Gerald Kersh; remade in 1992. 95m/B VHS, DVD. GB Richard Widmark, Gene Tierney, Googie Withers, Francis L. Sullivan, Hugh Marlowe, Herbert Lom, Mike Mazurki, Charles Farrell; *D:* Jules Dassin; *W:* Jo Eisinger; *M:* Franz Waxman.

Night and the City ✗✗✗ 1992 (R) Harry Fabian (De Niro), a con-artist/ ambulance-chaser, concocts a scheme to make it big, and approaches an old boxing

Niagara Motel ✗✗ 2006 A rundown motel in Niagara Falls houses the usual malcontents and oddballs, beginning with its drunken Scottish manager, Phillie (Ferguson). Lily (Crewson) is thinking about turning tricks since her husband can't find a job; waitress and wannabe actress Caroline (Dhavernas) is being pushed into filming porn by her sleazy agent Michael (Pollak); and drug addict Denise (Friel) wants to reclaim her daughter from foster care. 88m/C DVD. CA Craig Ferguson, Anna Friel, Wendy Crewson, Caroline Dhavernas, Kevin Pollak, Peter Keleghan, Kris Holden-Ried, Tom Barnett, Gary Yates, Dani Romain; *W:* George F. Walker; *C:* Ian Wilson; *M:* Guy Fletcher.

The Night and the Moment 🐾½ 1994 (R) Dull, mishmashy costume drama (set in the 17th century) about an imprisoned author (Da Tito) who became intrigued with the mystery woman who had occupied the next cell. They exchanged notes, and he vows to find her when he's released from prison. But first he spends a seductive night at the chateau of the Marquise (Olin), who, of course, turns out to be the mystery lady. Based on the novel "La Nuit et le Moment" by Claude-Prosper de Jolyot Crebillon. **89m/C** VHS, DVD. **GB FR IT** Willem Dafoe, Lena Olin, Miranda Richardson, Jean-Claude Carriere, Carole Richert; **D:** Anna Maria Tato; **W:** Anna Maria Tato, Jean-Claude Carriere; **C:** Giuseppe Rotunno; **M:** Ennio Morricone.

Night Angel 🐾 1990 (R) A beautiful seductress lures men into a deadly trap and Kattan) continue their fruitless quest... Mic has gone legit and wants them to move from L.A. to Vegas to work in a casino. Mic takes his pal back to the sleazy Golden Eagle hotel where he's been living. Unfortunately, their plans are soon derailed by a dead hooker (Lyonne) who works for vicious pimp Rodan (Jones). Paralleling the Tommy/Mic friendship is that of veteran whore Sally (Magnuson) to whom Rodan gives runaway teenager Lori Ann (Jacobs) for training. **87m/C** VHS, DVD. Donnie Montemarano, Vinny Argiro, Ann Magnuson, Vinnie Jones, Nicole Jacobs, Natasha Lyonne, Fayard Nicholas, Sam Moore, Francesca Feuer, Helen Martin, Karen Black, Doug Jones, Gary Hudson, Sam Hennings; **D:** Dominique Othenin-Girard; **W:** Joe Augustyn.

Night at the Golden Eagle 🐾🐾 2002 (R) As bleak as the Tom Waits song on the soundtrack, Tommy (Montemarano) is an aging small-time crook fresh out of a seven year prison stint. He meets up with old partner Mic (Agiro) and is dismayed to find out that seductress lures men into a deadly trap.

A Night at the Opera 🐾🐾🐾 1935 The Marx Brothers get mixed up with grand opera in their first MGM-produced epic and their first without Zeppo. Jones, great (Warden) to come out of retirement. Problem is, although Harry has energy and ambition, he also has a talent for making enemies out of the wrong people, like the mobster. Filled with details more interesting than the plot, more about fast-living, fast-talking New Yorkers, a fine showcase for De Niro's talent. Winkler's remake of the 1950 Jules Dassin film. **98m/C** VHS, DVD. Joseph (Joe) D'Onofrio, Michael Badalucco, Michael Rispoli, Robert De Niro, Jessica Lange, Cliff Gorman, Alan King, Jack Warden, Eli Wallach, Barry Primus, Gene Kirkwood, Fred Sanchez; **Cameos:** Regis Philbin, Joy Philbin, Richard Price; **D:** Irwin Winkler; **W:** Richard Price; **C:** Tak Fujimoto; **M:** James Newton Howard.

Night at the Museum 🐾🐾 2006 (PG) Wanting to impress his 10-year-old son (Cherry) when his ex-wife's (Raver) new fiance (Rudd)—a successful businessman—proves to be a better role model, Larry (Stiller) decides to change his flighty ways and takes a night guard job at NYC's Museum of Natural History. He gets more than he bargained for when the displays, from the giant T-Rex to a wax figure o' Teddy Roosevelt (Williams) to an Old West cowboy (an uncredited Owen Wilson) come alive at night, a minor detail left unrevealed by his predecessors (the comic-legend trio of Rooney, Van Dyke, and Cobbs). But it's not as fun as it sounds—the hyper CGI effects, combined with the weak tale of Larry's life woes, chase away the charm of Milan Trenc's original children's book. **108m/C DVD, Blu-ray Disc.** **US** Ben Stiller, Carla Gugino, Dick Van Dyke, Mickey Rooney, Bill Cobbs, Kim Raver, Ricky Gervais, Robin Williams, Jake Cherry, Owen Wilson, Steve Coogan, Patrick Gallagher, Mizuo Peck, Paul Rudd, Anne Meara, Rami Malek; **D:** Shawn Levy; **W:** Robert Ben Garant, Thomas Lennon; **C:** Guillermo Navarro; **M:** Alan Silvestri.

A Night at the Roxbury 🐾½ 1998 (PG-13) The Butabi brothers, like so many Saturday Night Live veterans before them, make the leap to the big screen with limited success. Steve and Doug (Ferrell and Kattan) continue their fruitless quest to gain entrance into the hallowed Roxbury night club. Their luck changes when they get into a fender bender with former "21 Jump Street" star Richard Greco (playing himself), who gets them in. Typical of the SNL skits-to-big-screen formula, the bit works as a three-minute sketch but isn't funny or interesting enough to sustain even its meager 82 minute running time. **83m/C** VHS, DVD, Will Ferrell, Chris Kattan, Molly Shannon, Dan Hedaya, Loni Anderson, Richard Grieco, Elisa Donovan, Lochlyn Munro, Dwayne Hickman, Mark McKinney; **D:** John Fortenberry; **W:** Steve Koren, Will Ferrell, Chris Kattan; **C:** Francis Kenny; **M:** David Kitay.

Night Beast 🐾 1983 Alien creature lands his spaceship near a small town and begins a bloody killing spree. Recycled plot. **90m/C** VHS, DVD. Tom Griffin, Richard Dyszel, Jamie Zemarel, George Stover; **D:** Donald M. Dohler.

The Night Before 🐾🐾½ 1988 (PG-13) Snobby high school beauty Lough-lin loses a bet and has to go to the prom with the school geek Reeves. On the way, they get lost on the wrong side of the tracks, and become involved with pimps, crime, and the police. A drunken Reeves loses Loughlin as well as his father's car. Typical teen farce. **90m/C** VHS. Keanu Reeves, Lori Loughlin, Trinidad Silva, Michael Greene, Theresa Saldana, Suzanne Snyder, Morgan Lofting, Gwil Richards; **D:** Thom Eberhardt; **W:** Gregory Scherick, Thom Eberhardt.

Night Beat 🐾½ 1948 A labored crime drama from postwar Britain. Two army pals pursue diverging careers. One becomes a cop, the other a crook. Want to bet that they meet again? **96m/B** VHS. **GB** Anne Crawford, Maxwell Reed, Ronald Howard, Christine Norden; **D:** Harold Huth.

Night Birds 🐾 1931 Early British thriller about a notorious crook named "Flash Jack," who heads a gang of that hatted criminals that rob the wealthy. Poor production quality and Raine's standoffish screen presence contribute to this below-average film. **76m/B** VHS. **GB** Jameson Thomas, Jack Raine, Muriel Angelus, Eve Gray; **D:** Richard Eichberg; **W:** Miles Malleson.

The Night Brings Charlie 🐾🐾 1990 A disfigured tree surgeon is the prime suspect in some grisly murders committed with a tree trimming saw. Obviously, everyone in the town fears him as a result. Not a sequel to "Roots." **90m/C** VHS. Kerry Knight, Joe Fishback, Aimee Tenaila, Monica Simmons; **D:** Tom Logan.

Night Call Nurses 🐾 Young L.A. Nurses 2 1972 (R) Three gorgeous nurses find danger and intrigue on the night shift at a psychiatric hospital. Third in the "nurse" quintet is back on target, shrugging off the previous film's attempts at "serious" social commentary. "Miller provides comic relief. Preceded by "The Student Nurses" and "Private Duty Nurses," and followed by "The Young Nurses" and "Candy Stripe Nurses." **85m/C** VHS, DVD. Patricia T. Byrne, Alana Collins, Mittie Lawrence, Clinton Kimbrough, Felton Perry, Stack Pierce, Richard Young, Dennis Dugan, Dick Miller; **D:** Jonathan Kaplan; **W:** George Armitage.

The Night Evelyn Came Out of the Grave 🐾½ La Notte Che Evelyn Usca Dalla Tomba 1971 (R) A wealthy Italian playboy, obsessed with his dead, flame-haired wife, lures living redheads into his castle, where he tortures and kills them. Standard '70s Euro/horror/sex stuff enlivened by the presence of the incredible Erika Blanc as a stripper who works out of a coffin. **99m/C** VHS, DVD. **IT** Anthony Steffen, Marina Malfatti, Rod Murdock, Erika Blanc, Giacomo "Jack" Rossi-Stuart, Umberto Raino; **D:** Emilio P. Miraglio; **W:** Tom Citrano.

Night Eyes 🐾 Hidden Vision 1990 (R) Surveillance can be a dangerous profession, especially when your boss happens to be the jealous husband of a very sexy woman. Watching turns to yearning for this professional peeper, but he may just get more than he bargained for. Roberts is worth watching. **95m/C** VHS, Andrew Stevens, Tanya Roberts, Cooper Huckabee; **D:** Emilio P. Miraglio.

Night Eyes 2 🐾 1991 (R) A security expert assigned to protect the sultry wife of a foreign diplomat finds himself spending a little too much time eyeing her as a budding opera singer warbles "Al, one" and "Cosi Cosa." One of their best films, blessed with a big budget—used to reach epic anarchic heights. Some scenes were based on live audiences before inclusion, including the Groucho/Chico paper-tearing contract negotiation and the celebrated stateroom scene, in which the boys are joined in a small closet by two maids, the ship's engineer, his assistant, a manicurist, a young woman, a cleaning lady, and four food-laden waiters. **92m/B** VHS, DVD. Groucho Marx, Chico Marx, Harpo Marx, Allan Jones, Kitty Carlisle Hart, Sig Rumann, Margaret Dumont, Walter Woolf King, Edward (Ed) Keane, Keane) Keane, Robert Emmett O'Connor; **D:** Sam Wood; **W:** George S. Kaufman, Morrie Ryskind, Bert Kalmar, Harry Ruby, Al Boasberg; **C:** Merritt B. Gerstad; **M:** Herbert Stothart, Nat'l Film Reg. '93.

Night Caller from Outer Space 🐾½ Blood Beast from Outer Space; The Night Caller 1966 When a woman-hunting alien arrives in London, women begin to disappear. At first, incredibly, no one makes the connection, but then the horrible truth comes to light. **84m/B** VHS, DVD. **GB** John Saxon, Maurice Denham, Patricia Haines, Alfred Burke, Jack Watson, Aubrey Morris, Warren Mitchell; **D:** John Gilling; **W:** James O'Connolly; **C:** Stephen Dade; **M:** Johnny Gregory.

The Night Caller 🐾🐾 1997 (R) Radio psychologist attracts the attentions of a deranged listener. **94m/C** VHS, DVD. Shanna Reed, Tracy Nelson, Mary Crosby, Cyndi Pass; **D:** Rob Malenfant; **W:** Frank Rehwaldt; **C:** M. David Mullen.

Night Children 🐾 1989 (R) Tough L.A. cop teams with a parole officer to battle a nasty gang leader. The battle is quite violent and senseless. **90m/C** VHS, David Carradine, Nancy Kwan, Griffin O'Neal, Tawny (Ellis) Fere; **D:** Norbert Meisel.

The Night Club 🐾 1925 Swinging single stands to gain fortune if he weds a certain girl, and, as luck would have it, he falls for her. When the usual hearts and roses don't convince her he's earnest, he tries to prove his love is true by attempting suicide and hiring a hit man. **62m/B** VHS, Raymond Griffith, Vera Reynolds, Wallace Beery, Louise Fazenda; **D:** Frank Urson.

Night Creature 🐾 Out of the Darkness; Fear 1979 (PG) A tough, Hemingway-type writer is determined to destroy the man-eating black leopard which nearly killed him once before. Filmed in Thailand. **83m/C** VHS, DVD. Donald Pleasence, Nancy Kwan, Ross Hagen; **D:** Lee Madden.

Night Cries 🐾🐾½ 1978 After a woman's baby dies at birth, she has persistent dreams that he is alive and in trouble. She insists she believes her when she tells them that something is wrong. **100m/C** VHS. Susan St. James, Michael Parks, William Conrad; **D:** Richard Lang. **TV**

Night Crossing 🐾🐾 1981 (PG) The fact-based story of two East German families who launch a daring escape to the West in a homemade hot air balloon. Exciting action for the whole family. **106m/C** VHS, DVD. John Hurt, Jane Alexander, Glynnis O'Connor, Doug McKeon, Beau Bridges; **D:** Delbert Mann; **W:** John McGreevey.

The Night Cry 🐾🐾 1926 Silent canine melodrama has sheep-murdering dog sentenced to death row until he saves little girl from unbelievably big bird. **65m/B** VHS. John Harron, June Marlowe, Mary Louise Miller; **D:** Herman C. Raymaker.

Night Divides the Day 🐾🐾 2001 A serial killer is stalking the students at Hollow Pointe University. The exceptionally low-budget film is more of a serious independent effort than exploitation. **125m/C** DVD. Tiffany Richards, John Stumr, David Stirwell, Jeff Burton, Michael McCallum, Lynn Cottormouth, Jeff Burton; **M:** Jeff Burton.

Night Eyes 3 🐾🐾 1993 (R) Night Eyes Security boss Stevens' latest assignment is to protect the superstar lead (Shannon Tweed) of a top TV cop show from a stalker. They wind up in very close contact but someone is videotaping their private moments which don't stay private for long. Maybe on-screen partner Tracy (Shannon's sister) has something to do with it. Also available in an unrated version. **97m/C** VHS, Andrew Stevens, Shannon Tweed, Tracy Tweed, Tristan Rogers; **D:** Andrew Stevens, Michel W. Potts, Stevens; **W:** Andrew Stevens, Michel W. Potts.

Night Eyes 4: Fatal Passion 🐾½ 1995 (R) Beverly Hills shrink Angela Cross (Barbieri) gets involved with bodyguard Steve Caldwell (Trachta), who's been hired to protect her from a stalker, who may also be the same person who stole some sexual explosive patient files. Also available unrated. **101m/C** VHS. Casper Van Dien, Chick Vennera, Paula Barbieri, Jeff Trachta, Andrew Stevens; **D:** Rodney McDonald; **W:** Jon Eubanks, Henry Krinkle; **C:** Gary Graver; **M:** Patrick Seymour.

Night Falls on Manhattan 🐾🐾 1996 (R) One man's search for truth runs into serious problems in this adaptation of "Tainted Evidence" by Robert Daley. Former cop turned junior D.A., Sean Casey (Garcia), is chosen to lead the prosecution in a sensational NY trial involving a drug dealer/cop killer, who also seriously wounded Sean's long-time cop father, Liam (Hom). His wins but allegations of police corruption rather unexpectedly becomes the new district attorney, the issue becomes a full-blown scandal, leading the naive Sean very close to home. Veteran director Lumet knows this scandal-ridden territory very well and is aided by fine performances from his leads. **114m/C** VHS, DVD. Dominic Chianese, Andy Garcia, Ian Holm, Richard Dreyfuss, Lena Olin, James Gandolfini, Ron Leibman, Colm Feore, Sheik Mahmud-Bey, Paul Guilfoyle; **D:** Sidney Lumet; **W:** Sidney Lumet; **C:** David Watkin; **M:** Mark Isham.

Night Fire 🐾½ 1994 (R) Barry wants wife Lydia to try to rekindle the passion in their marriage by getting away for the weekend at their remote ranch. But they're interrupted in their leisure by the stranded Cal and Gwen. Only it turns out Barry has hired the duo, who like Kinky games, to peak Lydia's interest. She's merely disgusted and Barry gets nasty. Also available unrated. **93m/C** VHS, DVD. Shannon Tweed, John Laughlin, Martin Hewitt, Rochelle Swanson; **D:** Mike Sedan; **W:** Zoran Hochstatter; **M:** Nan Cutler.

Night Flight 🐾🐾½ 1933 Riviere (John Barrymore) is obsessively devoted to his air delivery service, Trans Andean European Air Mail, putting prompt delivery over the safety of his own men. His best pilot, Jules (Gable), tries to satisfy Riviere's schedule, which includes dangerous night flights over the Andes Mountains. Based on the novel by Antoine de Saint-Exupery. Lionel Barrymore manages to steal scenes from his brother as an airline mechanic. **84m/B** VHS, John Barrymore, Clark Gable, Helen Hayes, Lionel Barrymore, Robert Montgomery, Myrna Loy, William Gargan; **D:** Clarence Brown; **W:** Oliver H.P. Garrett; **C:** Elmer Dyer, Oliver Marsh, Charles A. Marshall; **M:** Herbert Stothart.

Night Flight from Moscow 🐾🐾½ The Serpent 1973 (PG) A Soviet spy defects with a fistful of secret documents that implicate every free government. Then the CIA must decide if he's telling the truth. Complex espionage thriller. **113m/C DVD. FR IT GE** Yul Brynner, Henry Fonda, Dirk Bogarde, Virna Lisi, Philippe Noiret, Farley Granger, Robert Alda, Marie DuBois, Elga Andersen; **D:** Henri Verneuil; **M:** Ennio Morricone.

A Night for Crime 1942 A movie star disappears during the filming of a movie. When she turns up dead, a bumbling cop suspects everyone on the set. 75m/B VHS. Glenda Farrell, Lyle Talbot, Lena Basquette, Donald Kirke, Ralph Sanford; *D:* Alexis Thurn-Taxis.

Night Friend 1987 (R) A priest sets out to help a young woman caught up in a world of drug abuse and prostitution. Exploitation morality flick. 94m/C VHS. Art Carney, Chuck Shamata, Jayne (Jane) Eastwood, Heather Kjollesdal; *D:* Peter Gerretsen.

A Night Full of Rain *End of the World (in Our Usual Bed in a Night Full of Rain)* 1978 (R) Italian communist tries unsuccessfully to seduce vacationing American feminist. They meet again in San Francisco and argue more. They argue. They put all but rabid Wertmuller fans to sleep. The director's first English-language film. 104m/C VHS. *IT* Giancarlo Giannini, Candice Bergen, Anne Byrne, Flora Carabella; *D:* Lina Wertmuller; *W:* Lina Wertmuller.

Night Gallery 1969 Serling is the tour guide through an unusual art gallery consisting of portraits that reflect people's greed, desire, and guilt. Pilot for the 1969-1973 TV series. Three stories, including "Eyes," which saw novice Spielberg directing veteran Crawford. 95m/C VHS, DVD. Joan Crawford, Roddy McDowall, Tom Bosley, Barry Sullivan, Ossie Davis, Sam Jaffe, Kate Greenfield, Richard Kiley, George Macready, Norma Crane, Barry Atwater; *D:* Steven Spielberg, Boris Sagal, Boris Shear; *W:* Rod Serling; *C:* Richard Batcheller; *M:* Billy Goldenberg. **TV**

Night Game 1989 (R) A cop links a string of serial killings to the night games won by the Houston Astros. Brave cast tries hard, but is retired without a hit. 95m/C VHS. Roy Scheider, Karen Young, Paul Gleason, Lane Smith, Carlin Glynn; *D:* Peter Masterson; *M:* Pino Donaggio.

The Night God Screamed woof! 1980 (R) Raped as a child, California girl Pickett has trouble relating to her husband. To overcome her sexual anxieties, she engages in a number of bizarre fantasies. 85m/C VHS. Michael Sugich, Jeanne Crain, James B. Sikking; *D:* Lee Madden.

The Night Has Eyes *Terror House* 1942 Tense melodrama concerns a young teacher who disappears on the Yorkshire moors at the same spot where her girlfriend had vanished the previous year. Early film appearance for Mason. 79m/B VHS, DVD. *GB* James Mason, Joyce Howard, Wilfred Lawson, Mary Clare; *D:* Leslie Arliss.

The Night Heaven Fell *Les Bijoutiers du Clair de Lune* 1957 Ursula (Bardot) returns from the convent to the Spanish town where her Aunt Florentine (Vaili) lives unhappily with Count Ribera (Nieto), a macho brute and womanizer. A local malcontent, Lambert (Boyd) has returned from political exile to find his sister dead by suicide over the Count; and a deadly feud is reignited. Complicating matters is Aunt Florentine's unwillingness to admit her love for Lambert, and virgin Ursula's instantaneous attraction to him. It's serious, and typically overheated melodrama in a commercial package that reveals Vadim to be basically the sex merchant everyone accuses him of being. 95m/C DVD. *FR IT* Brigitte Bardot, Stephen Boyd, Alida Valli, Pepe Nieto; *D:* Roger Vadim; *W:* Roger Vadim, Peter Viertel, Jacques Remy; *C:* Armand Thirard; *M:* Georges Auric.

Night Hunter 1995 (R) Cutter's (Wilson) vampire-hunting parents were killed by a group of bloodsuckers so he teams up with a tabloid reporter (Smith) to eliminate the last nine vampires who have gathered together in Los Angeles and plan to multiply. 86m/C VHS, DVD. Don "The Dragon" Wilson, Melanie Smith, Maria Ford; *D:* Rick Jacobson.

A Night in Casablanca 1946 Groucho, Harpo and Chico find themselves in the luxurious Hotel Casablanca, going after some leftover Nazis searching for treasure. One of the later Marx Brothers' films, but still loaded with the familiar wisecracks and mayhem. 85m/B VHS, DVD. Groucho Marx, Harpo Marx, Chico Marx, Charles Drake, Dan Seymour, Sig Rumann, Lisette Verea, Lois Collier, Paul Harvey, Lewis L. Russell; *D:* Archie Mayo; *W:* Roland Kibbee, Frank Tashlin, Joseph Fields; *C:* James Van Trees; *M:* Werner Janssen.

A Night in Heaven woof! 1983 (R) A college teacher gets involved with one of her students, who moonlights as a male stripper. Will he earn that extra credit he needs to pass? Uninspired, overly explicit. Look for Denny Terrio of "Dance Fever" fame. 85m/C VHS, DVD. Christopher Atkins, Lesley Ann Warren, Carrie Snodgrass, Andy Garcia; *D:* John G. Avildsen; *W:* Joan Tewkesbury. Golden Raspberries '83: Worst Actor (Atkins).

Night in the Life of Jimmy Reardon 1988 (R) A high school Casanova watches his friends leave for expensive schools while he contemplates a trip to Hawaii with his rich girlfriend, a ruse to avoid the dull business school his father has picked out. Well photographed, but acting leaves something to be desired. Based on Richert's novel "Aren't You Even Going to Kiss Me Good-bye?" 95m/C VHS, DVD. River Phoenix, Meredith Salenger, Matthew Perry, Louanne, Ione Skye, Ann Magnuson, Paul Koslo, Jane Hallaren, Jason Court; *D:* William Richert; *W:* William Richert; *C:* John J. Connor; *M:* Elmer Bernstein, Bill Conti.

Night Is My Future *Music in Darkness* 1947 A young musician, blinded in an accident, meets a girl who tries to bring him happiness. Usual somber Bergman, but unimportant story. In Swedish with English subtitles. 89m/B VHS, DVD. *SW* Mai Zetterling, Birger Malmsten, Naima Wifstrand, Olof Winnerstrand, Hilda Borgstrom; *D:* Ingmar Bergman.

Night Junkies 2007 (R) Twist on the familiar vampire genre makes this one worth watching. Exotic dancer Ruby is turned by her philosophical vampire lover Vincent and the two hunt for victims along London's seedy waterfront while dealing with their blood addiction. 90m/C DVD. *GB* Katia Winter, Giles Anderson, Jonathan Coyne, Sasha Jackson; *D:* Lawrence Pearce; *W:* Lawrence Pearce; *C:* Sadik Ahmed; *M:* Michael England. **VIDEO**

Night Life 1990 (R) A teenager gets the all-out, high-stakes ride of his life when four cadavers are re-animated in his uncle's mortuary. 92m/C VHS. Scott Grimes, John Astin, Cheryl Pollak, Alan Blumenfeld; *D:* David Acomba; *W:* Keith Critchlow; *M:* Roger Bourland.

Night Life in Reno 1931 When a man leaves his wife, she sets out for Reno and falls in love with a married man. When her new love is killed by his jealous wife, the woman returns to her husband and they begin their marriage anew. Watchable melodrama. 58m/B VHS. Jameson Thomas, Dorothy Christy, Virginia Valli, Carmelita Geraghty, Dixie Lee, Pat O'Malley, Clarence Wilson; *D:* Raymond Cannon; *W:* Arthur Hoerl; *C:* M.A. Andersen.

The Night Listener 2006 Williams does drama in this adaptation of Maupin's novel. New York radio show host Gabriel Noone is distracted by his breakup with longtime lover, Jess (Cannavale), which is affecting his work. His outlook changes when a friend gives him a memoir purportedly written by dying teenaged fan, Pete. Gabriel begins a telephone relationship with Pete (Culkin) and his foster mother, Donna (Collette), but becomes suspicious about Pete's actual existence when Donna won't let them meet. 90m/C DVD. *US* Robin Williams, Toni Collette, Bobby Cannavale, Joe Morton, Rory Culkin, Sandra Oh, John Cullum; *D:* Patrick Stettner; *W:* Patrick Stettner, Armistead Maupin, Terry Anderson; *C:* Lisa Rinzler; *M:* Peter Nashel.

Night Master 1987 A handful of karate students practice their homework with much higher stakes away from the classroom. For them, deadly Ninja games are the only way to study. 87m/C VHS, DVD. Tom Jennings, Nicole Kidman, Vince Martin; *D:* Mark Joffe.

Night Monster *Mystery* 1942 A maniac wears artifical limbs to hunt down and murder the doctors responsible for amputating his legs. Picture was shot in 11 days. Fire scene was stock footage from "The Ghost of Frankenstein." 80m/B VHS. Bela Lugosi, Ralph Morgan, Lionel Atwill, Leif Erickson, Don Porter, Irene Hervey, Nils Asther; *D:* Ford Beebe; *W:* Clarence Upson Young; *C:* Charles Van Enger.

'night, Mother 1986 (PG-13) A depressed woman, living with her mother, announces one evening that she is going to kill herself. Her mother spends the evening reliving their lives and trying to talk her out of it, but the outcome seems inevitable. Well acted, though depressing. Based on Marsha Norman's Pulitzer Prize-winning novel. 97m/C VHS. Sissy Spacek, Anne Bancroft, Ed Berke, Carol Robbins, Jennifer Roosendahl; *D:* Tom (Thomas R.) Moore; *W:* Marsha Norman; *M:* David Shire.

Night Moves 1975 (R) Smalltime L.A. detective Harry Moseby (Hackman) is hired by fading actress Arlene Iverson (Ward) to find her wild teenaged daughter Delly (Griffith) who has taken off for the Florida Keys. Delly winds up dead and Harry uncovers a bizarre smuggling ring. Hackman is realistic as the detective whose own life is unraveling and Penn and screenwriter Sharp tweaked the detective convention with Harry being an ultimately ineffectual hero. Underrated when released and worth a view. 100m/C VHS, DVD. Gene Hackman, Susan Clark, Jennifer Warren, Melanie Griffith, Harris Yulin, Edward Binns, Kenneth Mars, James Woods, Dennis Dugan, Max Gail, Janet Ward; *D:* Arthur Penn; *W:* Alan Sharp; *C:* Bruce Surtees; *M:* Michael Small.

Night Must Fall 1937 Effective thriller based on the play by Emlyn Williams. Wheelchair-bound grand dame Mrs. Branson (Whitty) hires personable Danny (Montgomery) as a handyman for the cottage she lives in with niece, Olivia (Russell). Danny is, of course, too good to be true. He's a creepy killer after moolah, which Olivia discerns but does nothing about until he strikes again. Oh yeah, he also keeps a suspicious hatbox in his room. Remade in 1964 with Albert Finney. 72m/B VHS. Robert Montgomery, May Whitty, Rosalind Russell, Merle Tottenham, Alan Marshal, Kathleen Harrison, Matthew Boulton; *D:* Richard Thorpe; *W:* John Van Druten; *C:* Ray June; *M:* Edward Ward.

Night Nurse 1931 Stanwyck is a nurse who uncovers a sordid plot involving the murder of two young children for an inheritance. An entertaining, overlooked crime-drama, initially notorious for Stanwyck and roommate Blondell's continual onscreen dressings and undressings. Gable is compelling in an early, villainous role. 72m/B VHS. Barbara Stanwyck, Ben Lyon, Joan Blondell, Charles Winninger, Charlotte Merriam, Eddie Nugent, Blanche Frederici, Allan "Rocky" Lane, Walter McGrail, Ralf Harolde, Clark Gable; *D:* William A. Wellman.

Night of a Thousand Cats *La Noche de los Mil Gatos; Blood Feast; Cats* 1972 (R) A reclusive playboy cruises Mexico City in his helicopter, searching for beautiful women. It seems he needs their bodies for his cats who, for some reason, eat only human flesh. He keeps the heads, for some reason, for his private collection. A really odd '70s cannibal cat entry, but it moves along nicely and features some truly groovy fashions (floppy hats, translucent blouses, etc.). Not to be confused with the 1963 film of the same name. From the director of "Night of the Bloody Apes" and "Survive!" 83m/C VHS. *MX* Anjanette Comer, Zulma Faiad, Hugo Stiglitz, Christa Linder, Teresa Velazquez, Barbara Ange; *D:* Rene Cardona Jr.

Night of Bloody Horror 1969 (R) Tale of a former mental patient who is believed to be responsible for the brutal murders of his ex-girlfriends. A night of bloody horror indeed, as the gore is liberally spread. 89m/C VHS, DVD. Gaye Yellen, Evelyn Hendricks, Gerald McHaney, Michael Anthony; *D:* Joy Houck Jr.; *W:* Joy Houck Jr., Robert A. Weaver; *C:* Robert A. Weaver.

Night of Dark Shadows *Curse of Dark Shadows* 1971 (PG) Underrated, atmospheric follow-up to "House of Dark Shadows." When newlyweds Quentin (Selby) and Tracy Collins (Jackson) move into the family mansion, they find the place haunted by a ghostly woman named Angelique (Parker). As Quentin is disturbed by visissss of the past, he finds himself possessed by the spirit of Angelique's lover (also Selby) and Tracy's life in danger from the vengeful specter. Though occasionally muddled due to last-minute cuts ordered by the studio, the film still delivers a surplus of chills and is beautifully photographed. 94m/C VHS. David Selby, Kate Jackson, Lara Parker, Grayson Hall, John Karlen, Nancy Barrett, James Storm, Thayer David; *D:* Dan Curtis; *W:* Sam Hall; *C:* Richard Shore. **TV**

Night of Evil 1962 Girl is released from reform school and promptly wins a beauty contest. Her bid to win the Miss America title is blown to smithereens however, when it is discovered that she has been secretly married all along. From there she resorts to working in strip joints and attempts to pull off an armed robbery. As exploitation fare goes, a winner. 88m/B VHS. Lisa Gaye, William Campbell; *D:* Richard Galbreath; *Nar:* Earl Wilson.

Night of Horror 1978 (R) Zombies attack four young people stranded in the wilderness. 76m/C VHS. Steve Sandkuhler, Gae Schmitt, Rebecca Bach, Jeff Canfield; *D:* Tony Malanowski; *W:* Rebecca Bach; *C:* Jeff Canfield.

Night of January 16th 1941 Tycoon Bjorn Faulkner (Asther) is accused of embezzlement by his board of directors. When he's apparently murdered, his secretary Kit Lane (Drew) becomes the prime suspect. But good guy Steve Van Ruyle (Preston) sets out to prove that Kit is innocent. Adapted from a play by Ayn Rand. 80m/B VHS. Robert Preston, Ellen Drew, Clarence (C. William) Kolb, Willard Robertson, Cecil Kellaway, Donald Douglas, Paul Stanton, Nils Asther; *D:* William Clemens; *W:* Delmer Daves, Robert Pirosh; *C:* John Mescall.

A Night of Love *Manifesto* 1987 (R) Because of an assassination threat on the new king, Inspector Avanti (Molina) is charged with rounding up the town's troublemakers. Among them is a beguiling debutante (Soeberg) whose sexual appetites are matched only by her passion to kill the king. Based on a story by Emile Zola. 97m/C VHS. Alfred Molina, Camilla Soeberg, Eric Stoltz, Gabrielle Anwar; *D:* Dusan Makavejev.

The Night of the Nights *Heaven on a Shoestring* 1939 Drunk Broadway show producer Dan O'Farrell (O'Brien) makes his comeback after a long hiatus. 86m/B VHS. Pat O'Brien, Olympe Bradna, Roland Young; *D:* Lewis Milestone; *W:* Donald Ogden Stewart.

Night of Terror *He Lived to Kill* 1933 A swami, a couple of Hindu servants, a pretty heroine, a reporter, and all stalked by a killer who's after a formula that can put people in a state of suspended animation. Lame chiller. 64m/B VHS. Bela Lugosi, Sally Blane, Wallace Ford, Tully Marshall, George Meeker, Edwin Maxwell; *D:* Ben Stoloff; *C:* Joseph Valentine.

Night of Terror 1987 A bizarre family conducts brain experiments on themselves and then begins to kill each other. Bloodshed for the whole family. 105m/C VHS. Renee Harmon, Henry Lewis; *D:* Felix Girard.

Night of the Assassin 1977 Priest leaves his pulpit to become a terrorist. He plans a surprise for a U.N. secretary visiting Greece that would put the U.S. and Greek governments in the palm of his hand. Hard to believe. 98m/C VHS,

DVD, Klaus Kinski, Michael Craig, Eva Renzi; D: Robert McMahon.

Night of the Blood Beast ♪½ *Creature from Gaaxy 27* 1958 An astronaut comes back from space with an alien growing inside his body. The low-budget defeats a valiant attempt at a story. 65m/B VHS, DVD, Michael Emmet, Angela Greene, John Baer, Ed Nelson, Georgianna Carter, Tyler McVey; D: Bernard L. Kowalski; W: Martin Varno; C: John M. Nickolaus Jr.; M: Alexander Laszlo.

Night of the Bloody Apes *Woof!* *Gomar the Human Gorilla; La Horriplane Bestia Humana* 1968 (R) When a doctor transplants an ape's heart into his dying son's body, the son goes berserk. Gory Mexican-made horror at its finest. 84m/C VHS, DVD, MX Jose Elias Moreno, Armando Silvestre, Norma Lazareno, Augustin Martinez Solares, Gina Morel, Noelia Noel, Gerard Zepeda, Carlos Lopez Moctezuma; D: Rene Cardona Jr.; W: Rene Cardona Jr.; D: Raul Martinez Solares; M: Antonio Diaz Conde.

Night of the Bloody Transplant *Woof!* 1986 (R) Some scientist switches hearts from one person to another in this bloody gorefest. Footage of real surgery adds authenticity, but not believeability. 50m/C with W. Hanson.

Night of the Cobra Woman ♪ 1972 (R) A woman who can turn herself into a cobra needs constant sex and snake venom to keep her eternally young. Shot on location in the Philippines. One-time underground filmmaker Meyer co-wrote the script, for the Corman factory. 85m/C VHS, PH Joy Bang, Marlene Clark, Roger Garrett, Slash Marks, Vic Diaz; D: Andrew Meyer.

Night of the Comet ♪♪½ 1984 (PG-13) After surviving the explosion of a deadly comet, two California girls discover that they are the last people on Earth. When zombies begin to chase them, things begin to lose their charm. Cute and funny, but the script runs out before the movie does. 90m/C VHS, DVD, Catherine Mary Stewart, Kelli Maroney, Robert Beltran, Geoffrey Lewis, Mary Woronov, Sharon Farrell, Michael Bowen; D: Thom Eberhardt. W: Thom Eberhardt. C: Arthur Albert.

Night of the Creeps ♪♪½ *Creeps; Homecoming Night* 1986 (R) In 1958 an alien organism lands on earth and a person who is then frozen. Thirty years later he is accidentally unfrozen and starts spreading the infection throughout a college town. B-movie homage contains every horror cliché there is. Director Dekker's first film. 89m/C VHS, Jason Lively, Jill Whitlow, Tom Atkins, Steve Marshall, Wally Taylor, Bruce Solomon, Kenneth Tobey, Dick Miller, David Oliver; D: Fred Dekker; W: Fred Dekker; C: Robert New; M: Barry DeVorzon.

Night of the Cyclone ♪♪ 1990 (R) A complex, but not overly interesting thriller about a big city cop who goes to an island paradise in search of his missing daughter and finds murder. 89m/C VHS, Kris Kristofferson, Jeffrey Meek, Marisa Berenson, Winston Ntshona, Gerrit Graham; D: David Irving.

Night of the Death Cult ♪♪ *Night of the Seagulls* 1975 After moving to a quiet seaside community, a young couple is plagued by cult practising human sacrifice in order to appease the Templars, a zombie-like pack of ancient clergymen who rise from the dead and torture the living. Last in a four film series about the Templars. 90m/C VHS, DVD, SP Victor Petit, Julie James, Maria Kosti, Sandra Mozarowsky; D: Armando de Ossorio.

Night of the Demon *Woof!* 1980 Anthropology students are attacked by the legendary Bigfoot. Later they discover that he has raped and impregnated a young woman. Gore and sex prevail. 97m/C VHS, Jay Allan, Michael J. Cutt, Bob Collins, Jodi Lazarus. D: James C. Watson.

Night of the Demons ♪♪ 1988 (R) A gory, special-effects-laden horror farce about teenagers calling up demons in a haunted mortuary. On Halloween, of course. 92m/C VHS, DVD, Linnea Quigley, Cathy Podewell, Alvin Alexis, William Gallo, Mimi Kinkade, ance Fenton; D: Kevin S. Tenney; W: Joe Augustyn.

Night of the Demons 2 ♪♪ 1994 (R) Some horror and reasonable special effects help this rise above the usual teen-slasher horror sequels. The demonic Angela (complete with her skull-shaped lollipops) lives on in legend, handily haunting her creepy old house where a group of dumb teens end up on Halloween (and soon wind up dead). With each casualty, a new victim also joins the ranks of the Un-dead. Funniest parts come with heroic rescuer, yardstick-wielding Sister Gloria, who's not about to let any of Satan's helpers get the better of her. 96m/C VHS, Amelia Kinkade, Jennifer Rhodes, Merle Kennedy, Bobby Jacoby, Rod McCary, Zoe Trilling, Cristi Harris, Johnny Moran, Rick Peters, Christine Taylor, Ladd York, Darin Heames; D: Brian Trenchard-Smith; W: Joe Augustyn; M: Jim Manzie.

Night of the Demons 3 *Woof!* *Demon House* 1997 (R) Yet another bunch of moronic teenagers take refuge in Hull House funeral home on Halloween. Don't they know the mansion houses a blood-thirsty demon by now? May the demon win. 85m/C VHS, Amelia Kinkade, Kris Holden-Fried, Vlasta Vrana; D: Jim Kaufman.

The Night of the Following Day ♪♪ 1968 (R) Four professional criminals kidnap a young girl at France's Orly airport, demanding a large ransom from her wealthy father. Each kidnapper turns out to be beset by personal demons, hindering their plans and leading to a bloody climax. Then, there's a final twist to the entire story. Brando and Boone are properly chilling but the plot is muddled and melodramatic. From the novel "The Snatchers" by Lionel White. 93m/C VHS, DVD, Marlon Brando, Richard Boone, Rita Moreno, Pamela Franklin, Jess Hahn, Jacques Marin, Gerard Buhr, Hugues Wanner; D: Hubert Cornfield; W: Robert Phippeny, Hubert Cornfield.

Night of the Fox ♪♪ 1990 (R) An American officer with top secret knowledge is captured by Germans on the brink of D-Day. His home team plans to kill him if he cannot be rescued before spilling the beans. On-location filming adds much. 95m/C VHS, Michael York, Deborah Raffin, George Peppard; D: Charles Jarrott. CABLE.

Night of the Generals ♪♪♪ *La Nuit de Generaux* 1967 (R) A Nazi intelligence officer is pursuing three Nazi generals who may be involved in the brutal murder of a Warsaw prostitute. Dark and sinister, may be too slow for some tastes. Based on Hans Helmut Krist's novel. 148m/C VHS, Peter O'Toole, Omar Sharif, Tom Courtenay, Joanna Pettet, Donald Pleasence, Christopher Plummer, Philippe Noiret, John Gregson, Charles Gray; D: Anatole Litvak; M: Maurice Jarre.

Night of the Ghouls *Woof!* *Revenge of the Dead* 1959 Second to last in Wood's celebrated series of inept horror films that began with "Bride of the Monster" and "Plan 9 from Outer Space." This one tells of a phony spiritualist who swindles the grieving by pretending to raise the dead. To his great surprise he actually does enliven some cadavers, who then go after him. Unreleased for over 20 years because Wood couldn't pay the film lab. Not quite as classically bad as his other films, but still a laugh riot. 69m/B VHS, DVD, Paul Marco, Tor Johnson, Duke Moore, Kenne Duncan, John Carpenter, Criswell, Bud Osborne, Anthony Cardoza, Valda Hansen, Karl Johnson; D: Edward D. Wood Jr.; W: Edward D. Johnson; D: William C. Thompson.

Night of the Grizzly ♪♪ 1966 An ex-lawman's peaceful life as a rancher is threatened when a killer grizzly bear goes on a murderous rampage terrorizing the residents of the Wyoming countryside. 99m/C VHS, Clint Walker, Martha Hyer; D: Joseph Pevney.

Night of the Howling Beast ♪ *La Maldicion de la Bestia; The Werewolf and the Yeti* 1975 (R) The selling point of this one is an epic, first-time battle between a werewolf and a Yeti. Unfortunately it lasts about 15 seconds; the wolfman. 87m/C VHS, SP Paul Naschy, Grace Mills, Castillo Escalona, Silvia Solar, Gil Vidal, Luis Indurni; D: Miguel Iglesias Bonns; W: Paul Naschy; C: Tomas Pladeval.

The Night of the Iguana ♪♪♪ 1964 An alcoholic ex-minister acts as a tour guide in Mexico, becoming involved with a spinster and a hotel owner. Based on Tennessee Williams' play. Excellent performances from Burton and Gardner. 125m/B VHS, DVD, Richard Burton, Deborah Kerr, Ava Gardner, Grayson Hall, Sue Lyon, Emilio Fernandez, Cyril Delevanti; D: John Huston; W: John Huston, Anthony Veiller; C: Gabriel Figueroa; M: Benjamin Frankel. Oscars '64: Costume Des. (B&W).

Night of the Juggler ♪♪½ 1980 (R) An ex-cop encounters countless obstacles in trying to track down his daughter's kidnapper in NYC. Just a tad too complicated for some tastes. 101m/C VHS, James Brolin, Cliff Gorman, Richard S. Castellano, Mandy Patinkin, Julie Carmen; D: Robert Butler; W: William W. Norton Sr.

Night of the Kickfighters ♪ 1991 A mighty band of martial artists takes on a terrorist group that has in their possession a secret weapon that could destroy the world. 87m/C VHS, GB Andy Bauman, Adam West, Marcia Karr; D: Buddy Reyes.

The Night of the Laughing Dead ♪♪½ *Crazy House; House in Nightmare Park* 1975 Veteran British comedy cast perform unsuitable spoof. Man stands to inherit loasa money as his family members kick the bucket one by one. 90m/C VHS, GB Ray Milland, Frankie Howerd, Rosalie Crutchley, Kenneth Griffith; D: Peter Sykes.

Night of the Lepus ♪♪ 1972 (PG) Giant mutant bunny wabbits lay waste to the countryside after a failed hormone experiment goes horribly awry. Debate still rages about whether this is an incompetent B-movie horror flick or an intentionally campy spoof of giant critter flicks. Watch it as the latter to get maximum enjoyment out of it. 88m/C DVD, Stuart Whitman, Janet Leigh, Rory Calhoun, De-Forest Kelley, Paul Fix, William (Bill) Elliott; D: William F. Claxton; W: Don Holliday, Gene R. Kearney; C: Ted Voightlander; M: Jimmie Haskell.

Night of the Living Babes *Woof!* 1987 Two yuppie men go looking for fun at a brothel. They get their just deserts in the form of sex-seeking female zombies. 60m/C VHS, Michelle Bauer, Connie Woods, Andrew Nichols, Louie Bonanno; D: Jon Valentine.

Night of the Living Dead ♪♪½ *Night of the Flesh Eaters; Night of the Anubis* 1968 Cult favorite is low budget but powerfully frightening. Space experiments set off a high level of radiation that makes the newly dead return to life, with a taste for human flesh. Handful of holdouts find shelter in a farmhouse. Claustrophobic, terrifying, gruesome, extrema, and yes, humorous. Followed by "Dawn of the Dead" (1979) and "Day of the Dead" (1985). Romero's directorial debut. Available in a colorized version. 90m/B VHS, DVD, Judith O'Dea, Duane Jones, Karl Hardman, Marilyn Eastman, Keith Wayne, Judith Ridley, Russell Streiner, Bill "Chilly Billy" Cardille, John A. Russo, Kyra Schon, Bill (William Heinzman), Hinzman, John Simpson, Vincent Survinski, George A. Romero; D: George A. Romero; W: John A. Russo, George A. Romero; C: George A. Romero. Natl. Film Reg. '99.

Night of the Living Dead ♪♪ 1990 (R) A bunch of people are trapped in a farmhouse and attacked by ghouls with eating disorders. Remake of the '68 classic substitutes high tech blood 'n' guts for bona fide frights. 92m/C VHS, DVD, Tony Todd, Patricia Tallman, Tom Towles, William Butler, Bill Moseley, McKee Anderson, Kate Finneran, Bill "Chilly Billy" Cardille; D: Tom Savini; W: George A. Romero, John A. Russo; C: Frank Prinzi; M: Paul McCollough.

Night of the Living Dead, 25th Anniversary Documentary ♪♪½ 1993 Features behind the scenes look at low-budget 1968 classic film about legions of dead people who stalk the earth looking for live humans to feed on. 83m/C VHS.

The Night of the Hunter ♪♪♪♪ 1955 The nightmarish story of psychotic bogus preacher Harry Powell (Mitchum) who has the words H-A-T-E tattooed on the knuckles of his left hand and L-O-V-E on his right. He marries lonely widow Willa Harper (Winters), who has two children, in the hopes of finding the cache of money her thieving husband (Graves) had stashed. Gish plays Rachel, the shotgun-wielding, Bible-reading old lady who defends the kids with heroic threatens them. A dark, terrifying tale, completely unique in Hollywood's history. Mitchum is terrific. From novel by Davis Grubb and, sadly, Laughton's only directorial effort. 93m/B VHS, DVD, Robert Mitchum, Shelley Winters, Lillian Gish, Don Beddoe, Evelyn Varden, Peter Graves, James Gleason, Billy Chapin, Sally Jane Bruce, Gloria Castillo, Mary Ellen Clemons, Cheryl Callaway, Corey Allen, Paul Stanley, Co-rez; M: James Agee. C: Charles Laughton; W: James Agee; C: Stanley Cortez; M: Walter Schumann. Natl. Film Reg. '92.

The Night of the Running Man ♪½ 1994 (R) Las Vegas cab driver McCarthy finds $1 million stolen from a casino and goes on the run from hit man Glenn, who's been hired to recover the loot. 90m/C VHS, Scott Glenn, Andrew McCarthy, John Glover; D: Mark L. Lester.

Night of the Scarecrow ♪♪½ 1995 (R) Hundreds of years before a small town makes a pact with a warlock (Lazar) to ensure prosperity. After regretting the deal, the townspeople kill him and bury the body in a field where it's eventually uncovered. Now the warlock's ghost is off on a murderous rampage. Formula horror with some decent production values. Based on a comic book. 90m/C VHS, Elizabeth Barondes, John Mese, Stephen (Steve) Root, Bruce Glover, Dirk Blocker, Howard Swain, Gary Lockwood, John Lazar, John Hawkes, Martine Beswick; D: Jeff Burr; W: Reed Steiner, Dan Mazur; C: Thomas Callaway; M: Jim Manzie.

Night of the Sharks *Woof!* 1987 Mercenaries in a downed plane go after a jewel-ridden shipwreck despite a plethora of sharks. 87m/C VHS, DVD, Treat Williams, Christopher Connelly, Antonio Fargas, Janet Agren; D: Anthony Richmond.

The Night of the Shooting Stars ♪♪♪♪ *La Notte di San Lorenzo; The Night of San Lorenzo* 1982 (R) Set in an Italian village during the last days of WWII, this film highlights the schism in the village between those who support the retreating fascists and those who sympathize with the Allies. A poignant, deeply moving final scene. A powerful, deeply moving film. 106m/C VHS, DVD, IT Omero Antonutti, Margarita Lozano, Claudio Bigagli, Massimo Bonetti, Norma Martelli; D: Paolo Taviani, Vittorio Taviani; W: Tonino Guerra, Giuliani G. De Negri, Paolo Taviani, Vittorio Taviani; C: Franco Di Giacomo; M: Nicola Piovani. Cannes '82: Grand Jury Prize; Natl. Soc. Film Critics '83: Director (Taviani), Direc-

Night of the Sorcerers *Woof!* *La Noche de los Brujos* 1973 (R) ...

Night of the Strangler ♪ 1973 (R) A love affair between a white society girl and a young black man causes a chain of events that end with brutal murders in New Orleans. 88m/C VHS, Mickey Dolenz, James Ralston, Susan McCullough; D: Joy Houck Jr.

Night of the Twisters ♪♪½ 1995 Teenager Dan (Sawa) and his new stepfather Jack (Schneider) must work to protect the family when tornadoes rip through their small Nebraska town. Based on the book by Ivy Ruckman. 91m/C VHS, DVD, John Schneider, Devon Sawa, Lori Hallier, Helen Hughes; D: Timothy Bond; M: Lawrence Shragge. CABLE.

Night of the Warrior ♪ 1991 (R) ...

Lamas, Anthony Geary, Kathleen Kinmont, Arlene Dahl, Wilhelm von Homburg; *D:* Rafal Zielinski; *W:* Thomas Ian Griffith; *C:* Edward Pei; *M:* Ed Tomney.

Night of the Wilding 🎬 **1990** Very, very loosely based on the story of the female jogger who was gang-raped and left for dead in New York's Central Park. Made soon after the actual incident occurred. **90m/C VHS, DVD.** Erik Estrada, Kathrin Lautner; *D:* Joseph Merhi. **TV**

Night of the Zombies 🎬 **1981 (R)** *Gamma 693; Night of the Wehrmacht Zombies* 1981 (R) WWII soldiers with eating disorders shuffle through 88 minutes of gratuitous gore, while pursued by porn star cum intelligence agent. From the director of "Bloodsucking Freaks." **88m/C VHS, DVD.** James Gillis, Ryan Hilliard, Samantha Grey, Joel M. Reed; *D:* Joel M. Reed; *W:* Joel M. Reed.

Night on Earth 🎬🎬🎬 **1991 (R)** Jarmusch's "road" movie comprises five different stories taking place on the same night in five different cities—Los Angeles, New York, Paris, Rome, and Helsinki—between cabbies and their passengers. As with any anthology some stories work better than others but all have their moments in this ambitious film with its outstanding international cast. Subtitled in English for the three foreign segments. **125m/C VHS, DVD.** Winona Ryder, Gena Rowlands, Giancarlo Esposito, Armin Mueller-Stahl, Rosie Perez, Beatrice Dalle, Roberto Benigni, Paolo Bonacelli, Matti Pellonpaa, Kari Vaananen, Sakari Kuosmanen, Tomi Salmela, Lisanne Falk, Isaach de Bankole, Alan Randolph Scott, Anthony Portillo, Richard Boes, Pascal Nzonzi, Emile Abossolo-M'Bo; *D:* Jim Jarmusch; *W:* Jim Jarmusch; *C:* Frederick Elmes; *M:* Tom Waits, Kathleen Brennan. Ind. Spirit '93: Cinematog.

Night Orchid 🎬🎬🎬 **1997 (R)** Filmmaker Mark Atkins heads for Stephen King territory with the story of a young psychic (Paris) who arrives in a rural hamlet and has visions of murders. For a low-budget video premiere, this one looks very good. It's made with a degree of style and originality. Fans have seen worse. **93m/C VHS, DVD.** Dale Paris, Alyssa Simon, Mary Ellen O'Brien; *D:* Mark Atkins; *C:* Paul Atkins; *M:* C.C. Adcock.

Night Partners 🎬½ **1983** Bored housewives assist the police to patrol the streets after the kids have gone to bed. Originally a TV pilot, but the script doesn't hold water. **100m/C VHS.** Yvette Mimieux, Diana Canova, Arlen Dean Snyder, M. Emmet Walsh, Patricia (Patti) Davis, Larry Linville; *D:* Noel Nosseck. **TV**

Night Passage 🎬🎬½ **1957** Stewart is Grant McLaine, an ex-lawman hired to protect a railroad's payroll from a band of outlaws who've heisted previous attempts to get the payroll through. Unbeknownst to Grant, the gang is led by his brother (Murphy), who's known as the "Utica Kid." Eventually Grant and the Kid will have to have a showdown, unless Grant can convince him to go straight. Anthony Mann was set to direct, at Stewart's request, but declined, damaging his relationship with Stewart. Fans of the stars and the genre will enjoy this solid outing, but will also wonder how much better it could've been with Mann at the helm. Stewart plays accordian and sings two songs. **90m/C DVD.** James Stewart, Audie Murphy, Dan Duryea, Dianne Foster, Elaine Stewart, Brandon de Wilde, Jay C. Flippen, Herbert Anderson, Robert J. Wilke, Hugh Beaumont, Jack Elam, Tommy Cook, Paul Fix, Olive Carey, James Flavin, Donald Curtis, Ellen Corby; *D:* James Neilson; *W:* Borden Chase; *C:* William H. Daniels; *M:* Dimitri Tiomkin.

The Night Patrol 🎬🎬½ **1926** Talmadge is a cop who winds up arresting his girlfriend's brother for murder. Convinced the boy is innocent, Talmadge disguises himself in order to infiltrate the gang he thinks is actually responsible for the crime. Lots of derring-do and a last-minute rescue from the electric chair. **53m/B VHS.** Richard Talmadge, Mary Carr, Rose Blossom, Josef Swickard, Gardner James; *D:* Noel Mason Smith.

Night Patrol WOOF! **1985 (R)** The streets of Hollywood will never be the same after the night patrol runs amuck in the town. Crude imitation of "Police Academy." **87m/C VHS, DVD.** Linda Blair, Pat Paulsen, Jaye P. Morgan, Jack Riley, Murray Langston, Billy Barty, Noriyuki "Pat" Morita, Sydney Lassick, Andrew (Dice Clay) Silverstein; *D:* Jackie Kong; *C:* Hanania Baer. Golden Raspberries '85: Worst Actress (Blair).

The Night Porter 🎬🎬 **1974** *Il Portiere de Notte* 1974 (R) Max, an ex-SS concentration camp officer, unexpectedly meets his former lover-victim at the Viennese hotel where he works as the night porter. After they get reacquainted, the couple must hide from the porter's ex-Nazi friends who want the women dead because they fear she will disclose their past. A sado-masochistic voyage not for the faint-hearted. **115m/C VHS, DVD.** *IT* Dirk Bogarde, Charlotte Rampling, Philippe LeRoy, Gabriele Ferzetti, Isa Miranda; *D:* Liliana Cavani; *W:* Liliana Cavani; *C:* Alfio Contini; *M:* Daniele Paris.

Night Rhythms 🎬½ **1992 (R)** Nick West is a radio talk show host with a sexy voice that causes his women listeners to reveal their most intimate fantasies and problems to him on the air. When one listener goes too far, it's murder, and Nick must work to prove his innocence to save his career—and there's a hero (and a heroine) to take care of the evildoers. Also available in an unrated version. **99m/C VHS.** Martin Hewitt, Delia Sheppard, David Carradine, Terry Tweed, Sam Jones, Deborah Driggs, Julie Strain; *D:* Alexander Gregory (Gregory Dark) Hippolyte.

Night Ride Home 🎬🎬½ **1999** Nora Mahler (DeMornay) loves running the family ranch with her teenaged children (Clea (Birch) and Simon (Brower) and her somewhat indifferent husband, Neil (Carradine). Then Simon is killed in a riding accident and Nora falls apart. Neil thinks the family needs to make a fresh start but Nora's too shattered to make decisions until her mother, Maggie (Burstyn), comes to visit and help her daughter cope with the family's tragedy—and failing marriage. **94m/C VHS.** Rebecca De Mornay, Keith Carradine, Ellen Burstyn, Thora Birch, Lynne Thigpen, Jordan Brower; *D:* Glenn Jordan. **TV**

Night Rider 🎬 **1932** A cowboy possing as a gunman ends a trail of murder and violence in a small frontier town. **54m/B VHS.** Elinor Fair, Julian Rivero, Harry Carey Sr., George "Gabby" Hayes; *D:* William Nigh; *W:* Harry Fraser; *C:* James Diamond.

Night Riders of Montana 🎬 **1950** A state ranger helps a group of ranchers to fight off a band of rustlers. **60m/B VHS.** Roy Bacroft, Claudia Barrett, Arthur Space, Chubby Johnson, Allan "Rocky" Lane; *D:* Fred Brannon; *W:* M. Coates Webster; *C:* John MacBurnie; *M:* Stanley Wilson.

Night Ripper 🎬 **1986** A psychopathic killer stalks high fashion models and kills them by carving them up. Lots of violence. **88m/C VHS.** James Hansen, April Anne, Larry Thomas; *D:* Jeff Hathcock.

Night School 🎬 **1981 (R)** *Terror Eyes* 1981 (R) A police detective must find out who has been decapitating the women attending night school at Wendell College. Ward's first film. **89m/C VHS.** Leonard Mann, Rachel Ward, Drew Snyder, Joseph R. Sicari, Nicholas Cairis, Bill McCann, Margo Skinner; *D:* Ken Hughes; *W:* Ruth Avergon; *C:* Mark Irwin; *M:* Brad Fiedel.

Night Screams 🎬 **1987** Violent scare-monger about two escaped convicts who crash a high school house party. Kids and convicts start getting killed, one by one. **85m/C VHS, DVD.** Joe Manno, Ron Thomas, Randy Lundsford, Megan Wyss; *D:* Allen Plone.

Night Shade 🎬🎬½ **1997 (R)** Grief widower Scott Travers (Abell) is still grieving over the death of his wife, although his friends are persistent that he should get out and mingle. So he goes to a club and notices one of the dancers looks very familiar—yep, it's the missus, and she's only kinda dead: she's become a vampire. **90m/C VHS.** Tim Abell, Tane McClure, Teresa Langley; *D:* Fred Olen Ray; *W:* Sean O'Bannon; *C:* James Lawrence Spencer.

Night Shadow 🎬 **1990 (R)** A woman, returning home after being away for years, picks up a hitchhiker. Soon after her arrival, terrible serial killings begin, and only she has the nerve to track down the killer. **90m/C VHS, DVD.** Brenda Vance, Dana Chan, Tom Boylan; *D:* Randolph Cohlan; *W:* Randolph Cohlan.

Night Shift 🎬🎬 **1982 (R)** Two morgue attendants, dull Winkler and manic Keaton, decide to spice up their latenight shift by running a call-girl service on the side. Keaton turns in a fine performance in his film debut, and Howard's sure-handed direction almost overcomes the silly premise. Watch closely for Costner in the morgue frat party scene. **106m/C VHS, DVD.** Henry Winkler, Michael Keaton, Shelley Long, Kevin Costner, Pat Corley, Bobby DiCicco, Nita Talbot, Richard Belzer, Shannen Doherty, Clint Howard, Joe Spinell; *D:* Ron Howard; *W:* Babaloo Mandel, Lowell Ganz; *C:* James A. Crabe; *M:* Burt Bacharach; *V:* Vincent Schiavelli.

Night Siege Project: Shadowchaser 2 🎬🎬½ *Project Shadowchaser 2* 1994 (R) Smooth actioner finds a terrorist android taking over a nuclear arsenal and threatening to make Washington, D.C. a mushroom cloud. Naturally, there's a hero (and a heroine) to take care of the evildoers. **97m/C VHS, DVD.** Bryan Genesse, Frank Zagarino, Beth Toussaint; *D:* John Eyres; *W:* Nick Davis; *M:* Stephen (Steve) Edwards.

Night Slasher 🎬 *Night After Night After Night* 1969 A madman enjoys spilling the innards of London prostitutes with his dagger. **87m/C VHS.** Justine Lord, Gilbert Wynne, Jack May, Linda Marlowe; *D:* Lindsay Shonteff; *W:* Dail Ambler; *C:* Douglas Hill; *M:* Douglas Gamley.

Night Stage to Galveston 🎬½ **1952** Autry leads his Texas Rangers on a mission to uncover corruption in the Texas State Police during the turbulent post-Civil War era. **61m/B VHS.** Gene Autry, Pat Buttram, Virginia Huston, Thurston Hall; *D:* George Archainbaud.

The Night Stalker 🎬🎬½ **1971** Pilot movie for the TV series finds veteran reporter Carl Kolchak (McGavin) investigating a series of murders that lead him to believe a modern-day vampire is stalking the streets of Vegas. **73m/C VHS, DVD.** Darren McGavin, Carol Lynley, Simon Oakland, Ralph Meeker, Claude Akins, Kent Smith, Larry Linville, Barry Atwater; *D:* John Llewellyn Moxey; *W:* Richard Matheson; *M:* Robert Colbert. **TV**

Night Stalker 🎬🎬 **1987 (R)** A bloodthirsty serial killer is tracked by a detective through the streets in New York. The usual rigamarole of fisticuffs, gunplay, and car chases ensure. Impressive acting from Napier raises the film from the run-of-the-mill. **91m/C VHS, DVD.** Charles Napier, John Goff, Robert Viharo, Robert Z'Dar, Joseph Gian, Gary Crosby, Joan Chen, Michelle Reese; *D:* Max Cleven; *C:* Don Burgess.

The Night Strangler 🎬🎬½ **1972** Still creepy sequel to 1971's "The Night Stalker" finds reporter Carl Kolchak (McGavin) investigating a series of murders with female victims. He discovers that similar crimes have been committed in Seattle every 21 years for more than a century and the killer's description is always the same. **90m/C VHS, DVD.** Darren McGavin, Richard Anderson, Simon Oakland, Wally Cox, Margaret Hamilton, John Carradine, Al Lewis; *D:* Dan Curtis; *W:* Richard Matheson; *M:* Robert Colbert. **TV**

Night Sun 🎬🎬½ **1990** *Il Sole Anche di Notte, Sunshine Even by Night* 1990 Sergio (Sands) is an 18th-century nobleman who discovers his (past) wife was once the king's mistress. He abandons worldly pursuits to become a monk and find some peace but temptation follow him. Based on the Tolstoy story "Father Sergius." Sands' voice was dubbed by Italian actor Giancarlo Giannini. Italian with subtitles. **112m/C VHS, DVD.** *IT* Julian Sands, Charlotte Gainsbourg, Massimo Bonetti, Margarita Lozano, Ruediger Vogler; *D:* Paolo Taviani, Vittorio Taviani; *W:* Tonino Guerra, Paolo Taviani, Vittorio Taviani; *C:* Giuseppe Lanci; *M:* Nicola Piovani.

Night Terror 🎬 **1976** Everyone's after a hausfrau who saw a highway patrolman murdered on an expressway...including the psychotic murderer. Pretty standard fare. **73m/C VHS.** Valerie Harper, Richard Romanus, Michael (Lawrence) Tolan, Beatrice Manley, John Quade, Quinn Cummings, Nicholas Pryor; *D:* E.W. Swackhamer. **TV**

Night Terror 🎬🎬 **1989** A man wakes up from a nightmare only to find that his terrors are still present. **90m/C VHS.** Lloyd B. Mote, Jeff Keel, Guy Ecker, Jon Hoffman, Michael Cooper; *D:* Harry Falk; *W:* Paul Howard.

The Night the City Screamed 🎬🎬½ **1980 (PG)** It's the hottest day of the year, the city experiences a massive blackout, and nighttime brings out less-than-noble emotions amongst the citizenry. **96m/C VHS.** Raymond Burr, Georg Stanford Brown, Linda Purl, Robert Culp, Clifton Davis, David Cassidy, Shelley Smith, Vic Tayback, Dick Anthony Williams; *D:* Harry Falk. **TV**

The Night the Lights Went Out in Georgia 🎬🎬 **1981 (PG)** Loosely based on the popular hit song, the film follows a brother and sister as they try to cash in on the country music scene in Nashville. McNichol is engaging. **112m/C VHS, DVD.** Kristy McNichol, Dennis Quaid, Mark Hamill, Don Stroud; *D:* Ronald F. Maxwell; *W:* Bob Bonney; *C:* Bill Butler; *M:* David Shire.

The Night They Raided Minsky's 🎬🎬🎬 *The Night They Invented Striptease* 1969 (PG) Chaotic but interesting period comedy about a young Amish girl who leaves her tyrannical father to come to New York City in the 1920s. She winds up at Minsky's Burlesque and accidentally invents the striptease. Lahr's last performance—he died during filming. ♪The Night They Raided Minsky's; Take Ten Terrific Girls But Only 9 Costumes; How I Love Her; Perfect Gentleman; You Rat, You; Penny Arcade; Wait For Me. **97m/C VHS.** Jason Robards Jr., Britt Ekland, Elliott Gould, Bert Lahr, Norman Wisdom, Denholm Elliott; *D:* William Friedkin; *W:* Norman Lear, Arnold Schulman.

The Night They Robbed Big Bertha's 🎬 **1975 (R)** Bungling burglar attempts to knock off Big Bertha's massage parlor. **87m/C VHS.** Robert Nichols, Doug Hale, Gary Allen, Hetty Galen; *D:* Peter Kares; *W:* Albert T. Viola.

The Night They Saved Christmas 🎬🎬½ **1987** A Christmas special in which Santa's North Pole headquarters are endangered by the progress of an expanding oil company. Will the attempts of three children be enough to save the day? **94m/C VHS.** Art Carney, Jaclyn Smith, Paul Williams, Paul LeMat; *D:* Jackie Cooper.

Night Tide 🎬🎬 **1963** Hopper in another off the wall character study, this time as a lonely sailor. He falls for a mermaid (Lawson) who works at the dock. She may be a descendent of the man-killing Sirens. Interesting and different little love story, sometimes advertised as horror, which it is not. **84m/B VHS, DVD.** Dennis Hopper, Gavin Muir, Linda Lawson, Luana Anders, Marjorie Eaton, Tom Dillon, Bruno VeSota; *D:* Curtis Harrington; *W:* Curtis Harrington; *C:* Vilis Lapenieks; *M:* David Raksin.

Night Time in Nevada 🎬🎬 **1948** Young woman heads West to claim $50,000 trust left by dear old dad, but his crooked lawyer and associate figure they'd rather keep their hands in the pot. Cowboy Roy rides horse and flexes dimples while helping helpless girl. **67m/B VHS, DVD.** Roy Rogers, Adele Mara, Andy Devine, Grant Withers, Joseph Crehan; *D:* William Witney.

A Night to Remember 🎬🎬½ **1942** A murder-mystery writer's wife convinces him to move to a new apartment because she thinks the change might help him finish a novel he started long ago. When they find a dead body behind their new building, they try their hands at sleuthing. A clever and witty mystery, indeed, supported by likeable performances. **91m/B VHS.** Loretta Young, Brian Aherne, Sidney Toler, Gale Sondergaard, William Wright.

Wright, Donald MacBride, Blanche Yurka. *D:* Richard Wallace.

A Night to Remember 🎬🎬🎬 **1958** Gripping tale of the voyage of the Titanic with an interesting account of action in the face of danger and courage amid despair. Large cast is effectively used. Adapted by Eric Ambler from the book by Walter Lord. **119m/C VHS, DVD.** Kenneth More, David McCallum, Anthony Bushell, Honor Blackman, Michael Goodliffe, George Rose, Laurence Naismith, Frank Lawton, Alec McCowen, Jill Dixon, John Cairney, Joseph Tomelty, Jack Watling, Richard Clarke, Ralph Michael, Kenneth Griffith. *D:* Roy Ward Baker. *W:* Eric Ambler. *C:* Geoffrey Unsworth. *Golden Globes '59. Foreign Film.*

Night Vision 🎬 **1987** A young writer in the big city's given a video monitor by a street thief which is equipped with some remarkable features, including the ability to present scenes of future murders and demon worship. **102m/C VHS.** Ellie Martins, Stacy Carson, Shirley Ross, Tony Carpenter. *D:* Michael Krueger.

Night Vision 🎬🎬 **1997(R)** Burned-out detective Dak Smith (Williamson) has been demoted to motorcycle cop on the graveyard shift. But he unexpectedly becomes involved with the case of a serial killer who likes to stalk and videotape his victims. Now Dak and his new partner Kristen O'Conner (Rothrock) are working to capture this psychopath. **95m/C VHS, DVD.** Fred Williamson, Cynthia Rothrock, Robert Forster, Frank Pesce, Willie Gault, Amanda Welles, Nina Richardson. *D:* Gil Bettman. *W:* Michael Thomas Montgomery. *C:* Trey Smith. **VIDEO**

Night Train *Night Train; Gestapo 1940* **1934(R)** Strange things start happening on the train where a rock band makes its last appearance. Clips from other horror flicks were pieced together to make this film that's so bad it's almost good. **96m/C VHS, DVD.** John Phillip Law, Cameron Mitchell, Marc Lawrence, Charles Moll, Ferdinand "Ferdy" Mayne. *D:* Jay Schlossberg-Cohen. *W:* Philip Yordan.

Night Train Murders woof! *L'Ultimo Treno della Notte, The Last Train of the Night* **1975** If you're a fan of the Italian giallo genre then this is the horror for you—if you're not, then ick, ick, ick, ick, ick, Lisa (D'Angelo) and Margaret (Miracle) are taking the train from Germany to Italy to visit Lisa's family. On board, they encounter a sicko trio (DeGrassi, Bucci, Merli) who torture, rape, and eventually kill the girls. The only comic relief's the completely ridiculous English dubbing of the Italian dialogue. **94m/C DVD.** *IT* Flavio Bucci, Macha Meril, Irene Miracle, Enrico Maria Salerno, Marina Berti, Gianfranco de Grassi, Laura D'Angelo. *D:* Aldo Lado; *W:* Aldo Lado, Renato Izzo. *C:* Gábor Pogány. *M:* Ennio Morricone.

Night Train to Kathmandu 🎬🎬 **1988** A young girl accompanies her parents on a research expedition to Nepal, where her head is turned by an exotically handsome young Sherpa. Old story without much help from actors or director. **102m/C VHS.** Milla Jovovich, Pernell Roberts, Eddie Castrodac. *D:* Robert Wiemer. **CABLE**

Night Train to Munich 🎬🎬🎬 **1940** There's Nazi intrigue galore aboard a big train when a scientist's daughter joins allied intelligence agents in retrieving some secret documents. From the book "Report on a Fugitive" by Gordon Wellesley. **93m/B VHS, DVD.** *GB* Margaret Lockwood, Rex Harrison, Paul Henreid, Basil Radford, Naunton Wayne, James Harcourt, Felix Aylmer, Roland Culver, Raymond Huntley, Austin Trevor, Kenneth Kent, C.V. France, Frederick Valk, Morland Graham, Wally Patch, Irene Handl, Albert Lieven, David Horne; *D:* Carol Reed; *W:* Frank Launder, Sidney Gilliat; *C:* Otto Kanturek.

Night Train to Terror woof! *Shiver* **1984(R)** Strange things start happening on the train where a rock band makes its last appearance. Clips from other horror flicks were pieced together to make this film that's so bad it's almost good. **96m/C VHS, DVD.** John Phillip Law, Cameron Mitchell, Marc Lawrence, Charles Moll, Ferdinand "Ferdy" Mayne. *D:* Jay Schlossberg-Cohen; *W:* Philip Yordan.

Night Train to Venice 🎬½ **1993(R)** Martin (Grant) is aboard the Orient Express on his way to Venice to deliver his book about the rise of neo-Nazism. He meets a mystery man (McDowell) and an actress (Welch) with ties to a neo-Nazi group, who also happen to be aboard the train and anxious to stop Martin from delivering his expose. Extended dream sequences and flashbacks tend to stop the story cold but Grant is a draw (and probably the only reason this mishmash has been released to video). **98m/C VHS.** Hugh Grant, Malcolm McDowell, Tahnee Welch, Kristina Söderbaum; *D:* Carlo U. Quinterio; *W:* Toni Hirtreiter; *M:* Alexander Bubenheim.

Night Visitor 🎬 *Never Cry Devil* **1989 (R)** A retired police detective teams up with a teenage peeping tom to disclose the identity of a satanic serial killer. The killer, of course, is one of the youth's teachers. **95m/C VHS, DVD.** Derek Rydall, Shannon Tweed, Elliott Gould, Allen (Goorwitz) Garfield, Michael J. Pollard, Richard Roundtree, Henry Gibson. *D:* Rupert Hitzig; *W:* Randal Viscovich.

The Night Visitor 🎬🎬½ **1970** Stanwyck is always worth watching and she has the best moments in this psychothriller which suffers from a low-budget and confused script. The basic story has Stanwyck as a rich widow with a recurring nightmare featuring a faceless lover. There's also a too-helpful lawyer (Taylor), a suspicious private detective (Bochner), and maybe her husband isn't so dead after all. Taylor and Stanwyck, who had once been married, worked together for the first time in 27 years. **86m/B VHS.** Barbara Stanwyck, Robert Taylor, Lloyd Bochner, Hayden Rorke, Judith Meredith, Rochelle Hudson; *D:* William Castle; *W:* Robert Bloch.

The Night Walker 🎬🎬½ **1964** Stanwyck is always worth watching and she has the best moments in this psycho-thriller which suffers from a low-budget and confused script. The basic story has Stanwyck as a rich widow with a recurring nightmare featuring a faceless lover.

The Night Visitor 🎬🎬½ **1970**

Night Warning 🎬🎬 *Nightmare Maker; Butcher Baker (Nightmare Maker)* **1982 (R)** A slasher gorefest redeemed by Tyrrell's go-for-broke performance. She plays a sexually repressed aunt who has to deal with problems by going on murderous rampages. Hide the kitchen knives! **96m/C VHS.** Susan Tyrrell, Julia Duffy; *D:* William Asher; *W:* Stephen Breimer.

Night Wars 🎬🎬 **1988** Two ex-POWs who are plagued by their memories return to dream therapy to relive their escape. Eventually, they rescue a buddy they left behind. **90m/C VHS.** Dan Haggerty, Brian O'Connor, Cameron Smith; *D:* David A. Prior.

The Night We Called It a Day 🎬🎬½ *All the Way* **2003** Taken-from-reality tale finds Frank Sinatra (Hopper) in Australia doing a tour in 1974 with Ol' Blue Eyes barely gets off the airplane before mouthing off at reporter Hillary Hunter (de Rossi) when asked some too-personal questions. The resulting country-wide brouhaha keeps him captive in his hotel as unions protest outside and demand that he apologize. Hopper is a natural at doing Sinatra, though Tom Burlinson—often a Sinatra impersonator—performed the vocals. **97m/C VHS, DVD.** *AU US* Dennis Hopper, Melanie Griffith, Portia de Rossi, Joel Edgerton, Rose Byrne, David Hemmings, David Field, Nicholas Hope; *D:* Paul Goldman; *W:* Peter Clifton, Michael Thomas; *C:* Danny Ruhlmann; *M:* Rupert Gregson-Williams. **VIDEO**

The Night We Never Met 🎬🎬 **1993 (R)** Three yuppies bring different visions of romance and a case of mistaken identity to a time-share apartment in New York's Greenwich Village. Sam (Broderick) needs a quiet space to get over being dumped by a flaky performance artist (Tripplehorn). Ellen (Sciorra) is looking for space to paint away from the confines of her thick-headed spouse (Mantell). Brian, the organizer of the living arrangement, wants a space where he can be one of the boys and escape from his cloying fiancee (Bateman). Fairly predictable but enjoyable romantic comedy. **99m/C VHS.** Paul Guilfoyle, Matthew Broderick, Jeanne Tripplehorn, Kevin Anderson, Justine Bateman, Annabella Sciorra, Christine Baranski, Doris Roberts, Dominic Chianese, Michael Mantell, Tim Guinee, Greg Germann, Dana Wheeler-Nicholson, Louise Lasser, Billy Campbell, Ranjit Chowdry, Garry Shandling, Katharine Houghton, Brooke Smith; *D:* Warren Leight; *W:* Warren Leight; *M:* Evan Lurie.

Night Watch 🎬🎬 *Le Trou; Il Buco* **1972** A woman recovering from a nervous breakdown witnesses a murder, but no one will believe her. **100m/C VHS, GB** Elizabeth Taylor, Laurence Harvey, Billie Whitelaw; *D:* Brian G. Hutton; *C:* Billy Williams.

Night Watch 🎬🎬 *Nochnoi Dozor* **2004(R)** Russian take on the battle between the forces of good and evil, set in present-day Moscow. A prologue establishes that a diplomatic truce exists between the two: the Night Watch keeps a check on the dark side and the Day Watch on the light. But after centuries, a prophecy about the Great Other, who will tip the balance, seems about to come true. Somewhat chaotic and convoluted but still intense. The first in a trilogy, based on the novels of co-writer Lukyanenko. Russian with subtitles. **114m/C DVD, RU** Vladimir Menshov, Viktor Verzhbisky, Konstantin Khabensky, Maria Poroshina, Galina Tyunina, Gosha Kutsenko, Alexei Chadov, Zhanna Friske, Ilya Lanciten-ko, Anna Dubrovskaya, Aleksandr Samoilenko, Rimma Markova, Maria Mironova, Alexei Maklakov, Anna Slyusareva, Dmitry Martynov; *D:* Timur Bekmambetov; *W:* Timur Bekmambetov, Sergei Lukyanenko; *C:* Sergei Trofimov; *M:* Yuri Poyarenko, Valera Viktorov, Mukstar Mirzakeev.

The Night Watchman 🎬🎬 **2002** Decent yet flawed thriller that borrows a bit too much from its acknowledged influences ("Magnolia," "American Beauty,"

Nightbreed 🎬 **1990 (R)** A teenager flees a maniacal past to slowly become a member of a bizarre race of demons that live in a huge, abandoned Canadian graveyard; a place where every sin is forgiven. Based on Barker's novel "Caba," and appropriately gross, nonsensical and strange. Good special effects almost save this one. **102m/C VHS, DVD.** Craig Sheffer, Anne Bobby, David Cronenberg, Charles Haid; *D:* Clive Barker; *W:* Clive Barker; *C:* Robin Vidgeon; *M:* Danny Elfman.

The Nightcomers 🎬 **1972 (R)** A pretend "prequel" to Henry James's "The Turn of the Screw," wherein an Irish gardener trysts with the nanny of two watchful children who believe that lovers unite in death. Don't be fooled: stick to the original. **96m/C VHS, GB** Marlon Brando, Stephanie Beacham, Thora Hird, Harry Andrews, Christopher Ellis, Verna Harvey, Anna Palk; *D:* Michael Winner;

Nightbreaker 🎬🎬 **1989** Revelation of the U.S. government's deliberate exposure of servicemen to atomic bomb tests and the resulting radiation in 1950s and his son. Estevez, portray a U.S. doctor in the 1980s and the 1950s, respectively. **100m/C VHS.** Martin Sheen, Emilio Estevez, Joe Pantoliano; *D:* Peter Markle; *W:* T.S. Cook; *M:* Peter Bernstein.

Night Zoo 🎬🎬 *Un Zoo, La Nuit* **1987** A confusing story about a father/son reconciliation and the lurid underworld of drugs and sex in Montreal. The graphic sex and violence undermines the sensitive aspects of the film. **115m/C VHS, CA** Gilles Maheu, Roger Le Bel, Lynne Adams, Germain Houde; *D:* Jean-Claude Lauzon, Genie '88: Actor (Le Bel), Director (Lauzon). Film; Support. Actor (Houde).

Nightforce 🎬 **1986** Five buddies plunge into Central American jungles to rescue a young girl held by terrorists. **81m/C VHS, DVD.** Linda Blair, James Van Patten, Chad McQueen, Richard Lynch, Cameron Mitchell; *D:* Lawrence Foldes.

Nightfall 🎬🎬 **1956** Ray, accused of a crime he didn't commit, is forced to flee from both the law and the underworld. Classic example of film noir, brilliantly filmed by Tourneur. **78m/B VHS.** Aldo Ray, Brian Keith, Anne Bancroft, Jocelyn Brando, James Gregory, Frank Albertson; *D:* Jacques Tourneur; *W:* Stirling Silliphant.

Nightfall 🎬🎬 **1988 (PG-13)** Adaptation of the classic Isaac Asimov short story. A planet that has two suns (and therefore no night) experiences an eclipse and its inhabitants go mad. **87m/C VHS, DVD.** David Birney, Sarah Douglas, Alexis Kanner, Andra Millian; *D:* Paul Mayersberg; *C:* Darius Woski. **TV**

Nightflyers 🎬½ **1987 (R)** Aboard a weathered space freighter, the crew experience a series of deadly accidents caused by an unknown evil presence. From a novella by George R.R. Martin; *T.C.* Blake is better known as Robert Collector. **88m/C VHS.** Michael Praed, Michael Des Barres, Catherine Mary Stewart, John Standing, Lisa Blount; *D:* T.C. Blake.

Nighthawks 🎬🎬½ **1981 (R)** NYC cops scour Manhattan to hunt down an international terrorist on the loose. They look for ways to help her fellow slaves. **113m/C VHS, DVD.** *GB* Ken Robinson. *D:* Ron Peck; *W:* Ron Peck, Paul Hallam; *C:* Johanna Davis; *M:* David Graham Ellis.

Nighthawks 🎬🎬 **1981 (R)** NYC cops scour Manhattan to hunt down an international terrorist on the loose. Exciting and well paced. Hauer's American film debut. **100m/C VHS, DVD.** Rutger Hauer, Sylvester Stallone, Billy Dee Williams, Lindsay Wagner, Nigel Davenport, Persis Khambatta, Catherine Mary Stewart, Joe Spinell; *D:* Bruce Malmuth; *W:* David Shaber; *C:* James A. Contner; *M:* Keith Emerson.

The Nightingale 🎬🎬🎬 **1983** From "Faerie Tale Theatre" comes the story of an Emperor who discovers the value of true friendship and loyalty from his palace kitchen maid who gives him a tramway. **60m/C VHS, DVD.** Mick Jagger, Barbara Hershey, Bud Cort, Mako; *D:* Ivan Passer.

Nightjohn 🎬🎬½ **1996 (PG-13)** Nightjohn (Lumbly) is the new slave purchased by Southern plantation owner Clel Walker (Bridges). He moves into the cabin shared by 12-year-old Sarny (Jones) and Delie (Toussaint). When Sarny finds out that Nightjohn can read and write (illegal for slaves), she's determined to learn from him. And with her new knowledge, Sarny looks for ways to help her fellow slaves. Based on Gary Paulsen's 1993 novel; filmed on location at Flip Raps Plantation in Sumter, South Carolina. **96m/C VHS, DVD.** Carl Lumbly, Allison Jones, Beau Bridges, Lorraine Toussaint, Bill Cobbs, Kathleen York, Gabriel Casseus, Tom Nowicki, Monica Ford, Joel Thomas Traywick; *D:* Charles Burnett; *W:* Bill Cain; *C:* Elliot Davis; *M:* Stephen James Taylor. **CABLE**

Nightkill 🎬🎬½ **1980 (R)** Simple love affair turns into a deadly game of cat and mouse when a bored wife plots to do away with her wealthy, powerful husband with the aid of her attractive lover. Mitchum is the reluctant investigator pulled into the game. **104m/C VHS.** Jaclyn Smith, Mike Connors, James Franciscus, Robert Mitchum, Sybil Danning; *D:* Ted Post.

Nightlife 🎬🎬 **1990** An ancient vampiress who rises from the dead spends her time haunting a blood clinic, where she finds a hematologist starts to fall for her. **93m/C VHS.** Ben Cross, Maryam D'Abo, Keith Szarabajka, Jesse Conti, Oliver Clark, Glenn Shadix, Camille Saviola; *D:* Daniel Taplitz.

W: Michael Hastings; *C:* Robert Paynter; *M:* Jerry Fielding.

Nightlife

The Nightman ♂♂ 1993 (R) Ex-soldier Marcoux becomes the night manager of a failing southern resort, run by sexy, and lonely, Kerns. They begin an affair, which turns sour when Robertson, Kerns's teenaged daughter, also falls for the stud. Then mom is murdered and Marcoux goes to prison. But 18 years later Robertson's past comes back to haunt her. Just what did happen all those years ago? Made-for-TV thriller with additional footage. 96m/C VHS, DVD. Ted Marcoux, Jenny Robertson, Joanna Kerns; **D:** Charles Haid; **W:** James Poe; **M:** Gary Chang. **TV**

Nightmare WOOF! *Blood Splash; Nightmare in a Damaged Brain* 1982 (R) Boring splatterthon has a young boy hacking his father and his aggressive mistress to pieces when he discovers them in bed. He grows up to be a psycho who continues along the same lines. Humorless and dreadful, the original ads claimed Tom Savini did the special effects. He had nothing to do with it. 97m/C VHS. Baird Stafford, Sharon Smith, C.J. Cooke, Mik Cribben, Kathleen Ferguson, Danny Ronan; **D:** Romano Scavolini; **W:** Romano Scavolini; **C:** Gianni Fiore; **M:** Jack Eric Williams.

Nightmare ♂♂ 1991 (PG-13) Single mom Linda Hemmings (Principal) takes matters into her own hands when her daughter Dana (Harris) is kidnapped. Though Dana escapes and her assailant, Edward Ryter (Banks), is arrested, he's soon released and threatening Dana to prevent her from testifying. So mom teams up with police detective Jake Willman (Sorvino) to get the goods on the psycho before he can do further harm. 84m/C VHS, DVD. Victoria Principal, Jonathan Banks, Paul Sorvino, Danielle Harris; **D:** Edmund Goulding; **W:** Jules Furthman; **C:** Lee Garmes; **M:** Cyril Mockridge.

Nightmare Alley ♂♂♂1/2 1947 Dark and disturbing noir has Power, in one of his best roles, as con man/carny who learns the secrets of a mentalist act and turns it into fame and fortune. When a femme fatale shrink persuades him to join a scheme to bilk the rich, it leads to a fascinating and precipitous downfall. Power fought to get the film made, and for the chance to play against his matinee idol type. 111m/B DVD. Tyrone Power, Joan Blondell, Coleen Gray, Helen Walker, Taylor Holmes, Ian Keith, Mike Mazurki; **D:** Edmund Goulding; **W:** Jules Furthman; **C:** Lee Garmes; **M:** Cyril Mockridge.

Nightmare at Bittercreek ♂♂ 1991 (PG-13) Four babes and a tour guide are pursued by psycho gang in the Sierra mountains. Made for TV nightmare in your living room. 92m/C VHS, DVD. Tom Skerritt, Joanna Cassidy, Lindsay Wagner, Constance McCashin, Janne Mortil; **D:** Tim Burstall. **TV**

Nightmare at 43 Hillcrest 1974 A family's life becomes a living hell when the police mistakenly raid their house. Based on a true story. 72m/C VHS. Jim Hutton, Mariette Hartley; **D:** Dan Curtis; **W:** William Katz; **M:** Robert Cobert.

Nightmare at Noon ♂ 1987 (R) Watered-down thriller about a small desert town beset by violent terrorists (who are really locals gone mad from a chemical experiment dumped into the water system). Only the sheriff's small staff is there to stop them. 96m/C VHS, DVD. Wings Hauser, George Kennedy, Bo Hopkins, Brion James, Kimberly Beck, Kimberly Ross; **D:** Nico Mastorakis.

The Nightmare before Christmas ♂♂♂ *Tim Burton's The Nightmare before Christmas* 1993 (PG) Back when he was an animator trainee at Disney, Burton came up with this adventurous idea but couldn't get it made; subsequent directorial success brought more clout. Relies on a painstaking stop-motion technique that took more than two years to film and is justifiably amazing. The story

revolves around Jack Skellington, the Pumpkin King of the dangerously weird Halloweentown. Suffering from ennui, he accidentally discovers the wonders of Christmastown and decides to kidnap Santa and rule over this peaceable holiday. Fast pace is maintained by the equally breathless score. Not cuddly, best appreciated by those with a feel for the macabre. 75m/C VHS, DVD, UMD. **D:** Henry Selick; **W:** Caroline Thompson, Tim Burton, Michael McDowell; **C:** Pete Kozachik; **M:** Danny Elfman; **V:** Danny Elfman, Chris Sarandon, Catherine O'Hara, William Hickey, Ken Page, Ed Ivory, Paul Pee-wee Herman) Reubens, Glenn Shadix.

Nightmare Castle ♂♂ *Amanti d'Oltretomba; Night of the Doomed; The Faceless Monsters; Lovers from Beyond the Tomb* 1965 Jealous sadist murders his wife and her lover. Then he conducts a bizarre experiment, using the dead couple's blood to rejuvenate an old servant. Not satisfied with his revenge, he then seeks to marry his late wife's sister after realizing that she has been left the inheritance. In time, the perturbed ghosts of the late lovers appear and seek revenge. A real nightmare. 90m/B VHS, DVD. **IT:** Barbara Steele, Paul Muller, Helga Line; **D:** Allan Grunwald; **M:** Ennio Morricone.

Nightmare in Badham County ♂ *Nightmare* 1976 Two girls get arrested on trumped-up charges in a small backwoods town. They soon discover that the prison farm is a front for a slavery ring. 100m/C VHS. Deborah Raffin, Lynne Moody, Chuck Connors, Della Reese, Robert Reed, Ralph Bellamy, Tina Louise; **D:** John Llewellyn Moxey; **M:** Charles Bernstein. **TV**

Nightmare in Blood ♂ *Horror Convention* 1975 Vampires lurk in San Francisco and wreak havoc on the night life. 90m/C VHS, DVD. Kerwin Mathews, Jerry Walter, Barrie Youngfellow; **D:** John Stanley.

Nightmare in Wax ♂1/2 *Crimes in the Wax Museum* 1969 After suffering disfigurement in a fight with a studio boss, a former make-up man starts a wax museum. For fun, he injects movie stars with a formula that turns them into statues. 91m/C VHS, DVD. Cameron Mitchell, Anne Helm; **D:** Bud Townsend.

A Nightmare on Elm Street ♂♂1/2 1984 (R) Feverish, genuinely frightening horror film about Freddy Krueger (Englund), a scarred maniac in a fedora and razor-fingered gloves who kills neighborhood teens in their dreams and, subsequently, in reality. Of the children fight-back genre, in which the lead victim (Langenkamp) ingeniously goes to great lengths to destroy Freddy. In the tradition of "Friday the 13th"'s Jason and "Halloween"'s Michael Myers, "Elm Street" spawned a "Freddy" phenomenon: seven sequels (including the upcoming "Freddy Vs. Jason," linking "Elm Street, Part 8" with "Friday the 13th, Part 10"); a TV series ("Freddy's Nightmares," a horror anthology show hosted by Englund to capitalize on his character); and an army of razor-clawed trick or treaters at Halloween. 92m/C VHS, DVD. John Saxon, Heather Langenkamp, Ronee Blakley, Johnny Depp, Charles Fleischer; **D:** Wes Craven; **W:** Wes Craven; **C:** Jacques Haitkin; **M:** Charles Bernstein.

A Nightmare on Elm Street 2: Freddy's Revenge ♂1/2 1985 (R) Mediocre sequel to the popular horror film. Freddy, the dream-haunting psychopath with the ginsu knife hands, returns to possess a teenager's body in order to kill again. Nothing new here, however praise is due for the stunning high-tech climax sequence. 87m/C VHS, DVD. Mark Patton, Hope Lange, Clu Gulager, Robert Englund, Kim Myers, Robert Rusler, Marshall Bell, Sydney Walsh; **D:** Jack Sholder; **W:** David Chaskin; **C:** Jacques Haitkin.

A Nightmare on Elm Street 3: Dream Warriors ♂♂ 1987 (R) Chapter three in this slice and dice series. Freddy Krueger is at it again, haunting the dreams of unsuspecting suburban teens. Langenkamp, the nightmare-freaked heroine from the first film, returns to counsel the latest victims of Freddy-infested

dreams. Noted for the special effects wizardry but little else. Part Three was produced on over a $4.5 million shoe string and took in more than $40 million, making it one of the most successful independently produced films in Hollywood. Followed by "A Nightmare on Elm Street 4: Dream Master." 96m/C VHS, DVD. Patricia Arquette, Robert Englund, Heather Langenkamp, Craig Wasson, Laurence Fishburne, Priscilla Pointer, John Saxon, Brooke Bundy, Jennifer Rubin, Rodney Eastman, Nan Martin, Dick Cavett, Zsa Zsa Gabor; **D:** Chuck Russell; **W:** Chuck Russell, Bruce Wagner, Wes Craven, Frank Darabont; **C:** Roy Wagner; **M:** Angelo Badalamenti.

A Nightmare on Elm Street 4: Dream Master ♂♂1/2 1988 (R) Freddy Krueger is still preying on people in their dreams, but he may have met his match as he battles for supremacy with a telepathically talented girl. What Part 4 lacks in substance, it makes up for in visual verve, including scenes of a kid drowning in his waterbed, and a pizza covered with pepperoni-like faces of Freddy's previous victims. This boxoffice bonanza set a new record as the most successful opening weekend of any independently released film. Followed by "A Nightmare on Elm Street 5: Dream Child." 99m/C VHS, DVD. Robert Englund, Rodney Eastman, Danny Hassel, Andras Jones, Tuesday Knight, Lisa Wilcox, Ken Sagoes, Toy Newkirk, Brooke Theiss, Brooke Bundy; **D:** Renny Harlin; **W:** Brian Helgeland, Scott Pierce; **C:** Steven Fierberg; **M:** Craig Safan.

A Nightmare on Elm Street 5: Dream Child ♂♂ 1989 (R) The fifth installment of Freddy Krueger's never-ending adventures. Here, America's favorite knife-wielding burn victim, unable to best the Dream Master from the previous film, haunts the dreams of her unborn fetus. Gore fans may be disappointed to discover that much of the blood and guts ended up on the cutting room floor. 90m/C VHS, DVD. Robert Englund, Lisa Wilcox, Kelly Jo Minter, Danny Hassel, Erika Anderson, Nicholas Mele, Beatrice Boepple; **D:** Stephen Hopkins; **W:** Leslie Bohem; **C:** Peter Levy; **M:** Jay Ferguson. **C A B L E** Golden Raspberries '89: Worst Song ("Bring Your Daughter to the Slaughter").

Nightmare on the 13th Floor ♂ 1990 (PG-13) A travel writer at an old hotel glimpses murder on a supposedly non-existent floor. Nasty devil-worshippers are afoot, but the chills in this mild cable throwaway seldom dip below room temperature. 85m/C VHS. Michael Greene, John Karlen, Louise Fletcher, Alan Fudge, James Brolin; **D:** Walter Grauman. **C A B L E**

Nightmare Sisters WOOF! 1987 (R) Three sorority sisters become possessed by a demon and then sexually ravage a nearby fraternity. 83m/C VHS, DVD. Brinke Stevens, Michelle (McClellan) Bauer, Linnea Quigley; **D:** David DeCoteau.

Nightmare Weekend ♂ 1986 (R) A professor's evil assistant lures three young women into his lab and performs cruel and vicious experiments that transform the girls and their dates into crazed zombies. 86m/C VHS, DVD. Dale Midkiff, Debbie Laster, Debra Hunter, Lori Lewis; **D:** Henry Sala.

The Nightmare Years ♂♂1/2 1989 An American reporter in Nazi Germany dares to report the truth to an unbelieving world. Based on a true story. Two cassettes. 237m/C VHS. Sam Waterston, Marthe Keller, Kurtwood Smith; **D:** Anthony Page; **M:** Vladimir Cosma.

Nightmares ♂♂ 1983 (R) A less-than-thrilling horror anthology featuring four tales in which common, everyday occurrences take on the ingredients of a nightmare. In the same vein as "Twilight Zone" and "Creepshow." 99m/C VHS, DVD. Emilio Estevez, Moon Zappa, Lance Henriksen, Richard Masur, Veronica Cartwright; **D:** Joseph Sargent; **W:** Christopher Crowe, Jeffrey Bloom; **C:** Mario DiLeo, Gerald Perry Finnerman; **M:** Craig Safan.

Nights and Days ♂♂1/2 1976 Adaptation of writer Maria Dabrowska's tale about a Polish family chronicles the persecution, expulsions, and land grabbing that occurred after the unsuccessful Uprising of 1864. In Polish with English

subtitles. 255m/C VHS, DVD. **PL** Jadwiga Baranska, Jerzy Binczycki; **D:** Jerzy Antczak.

Nights in White Satin ♂1/2 1987 A made-for-video Cinderella story about the growing love between a fashion photographer and a young model whose boyfriend has just been murdered. 96m/C VHS. Kenneth Gilman, Priscilla Harris; **D:** Michael Bernard.

Nights of Cabiria ♂♂♂1/2 *Le Notti de Cabiria; Cabiria* 1957 Fellini classic which details the personal decline of a naive prostitute who thinks she's found true love. In Italian with English subtitles or dubbed. Basis for the musical "Sweet Charity." 117m/B VHS, DVD. **IT** Giulietta Masina, Amedeo Nazzari, Francois Perier, Franca Marzi, Dorian Gray, Aldo Silvani, Ennio Girolami; **D:** Federico Fellini; **W:** Federico Fellini, Tullio Pinelli, Ennio Flaiano; **C:** Aldo Tonti; **M:** Nino Rota. Oscars '57: Foreign Film; Cannes '57: Actress (Masina).

Nightscare ♂1/2 *Beyond Bedlam* 1993 (R) When Dr. Stephanie Lyell's (Hurley) drug behavior-modification experiment goes wrong it allows serial killer Marc Gilmour (Allen) to get to his victims through their dreams. The doc tries to prove to Detective Inspector Terry Hamilton (Fairbrass) that the drug is safe by injecting them both but things get out of hand. Adapted from the novel by Harry Adam Knight. 89m/C VHS. **GB** Craig Fairbrass, Elizabeth Hurley, Keith Allen, Jesse Birdsall, Craig Kelly; **D:** Vadim Jean; **W:** Vadim Jean.

NightScreams ♂1/2 1997 Cameron is having terrible nightmares and also sees the ghost of a young woman—the same woman involved in the unexplained murder/suicide that caused the death of Cameron's boyfriend. 90m/C VHS, DVD. Casper Van Dien, Teri Garr, Candace Cameron; **D:** Noel Nosseck; **W:** Raymond Singer, Eugenia Singer. **C:** Paul Maibaum; **M:** Garry Schyman. **VIDEO**

Nightstalker WOOF! *Don't Go Near the Park* 1981 A brother and sister who were condemned to eternal death 12,000 years ago must eat virgins to keep their bodies from rotting. Trouble is, while they search for dinner, the movie decomposes. For mature audiences with no fantasies of celluloid nirvana. 90m/C VHS, DVD. Meeno Peluce, Tamara Taylor, Linnea Quigley, Aldo Ray; **D:** Lawrence Foldes; **W:** Lawrence Foldes; **C:** William de Diego.

Nightstalker ♂♂ 2002 (R) Based on the '80s true crime saga of L.A. serial killer Robert Ramirez, aka the Nightstalker. Cop Gabriella Martinez (Sanchez), who discovered some of the victims, is offered a promotion to the task force investigating the murders. But she makes a judgement error when she leaks info to reporter Adrianne Deloia (Emma) and is suspended. However, Gabriella's old partner Frank Luis (Trejo) has some info of his own and Gabriela learns that she's become one of the Nightstalker's targets. 95m/C VHS, DVD. Roselyn Sanchez, Danny Trejo, Evan Dexter Parke, Bret Roberts, Derek Hamilton, Douglas Spain, Brandi Emma; **D:** Chris Fisher; **W:** Chris Fisher; **C:** Eliot Rockett; **M:** Ryan Beveridge.

Nightstick ♂1/2 *Calhoun* 1987 (R) New York vigilante cop fights nasties who threaten to blow the lid off the city. Worse, they kidnap super cop's girl forcing him to save her along with the city. Lots of violence, predictable plot, and mediocre acting leave this one without much bang. 90m/C VHS. Bruce Fairbairn, Kerrie Keane, John Vernon, Robert Vaughn, Isaac Hayes, Leslie Nielsen; **D:** Joseph L. Scanlan.

Nightwatch ♂♂ 1996 (R) Law student Martin (McGregor) takes a job as a night watchman in a morgue at the same time a serial killer is killing prostitutes and gouging out their eyes. As if that weren't enough, he has to deal with a cop (Nolte) who suspects him, a sadistic best friend (Brolin) who likes to scare him on the job, and a creepy boss (Dourif) who doesn't like him. Adapted by director Bornedal from his Danish film "Nattevagten," this one's effectively creepy, but disjointed. Excellent cast is misused, as hardly any of the characters are developed beyond simple types. If you enjoyed the murky, depressing atmosphere of "Seven," you'll

Nightwaves ✂✂ 2003 (PG-13) A car accident cripples widows Shelby, who battles pain and boredom by picking up neighbors' lives via their phone calls on her police scanner. But when a woman winds up in a body bag Shelby is shoved into a mess that is... seems and makes her a target. **99m/C VHS, DVD.** Sherilyn Fenn, Ivan Sergei, Frank Fontaine, Emma Campbell, Jennifer Moreho, Francis X. (Frank) McCarthy, Joanna Noyes, Kevin Jubinville; **D:** John Kaufman; **M:** Melissa Jo Peltier. **C:** Georges Archambault; **M:** Simon Carpenter. **TV**

Nightwish ✂✂½ 1989 (R) Students do more than homework when a professor leads them into their own horrifying dreams. Soon it becomes impossible to distinguish dreams from reality. **96m/C VHS.** Jack Starrett, Robert Tessier, Clayton Rohner, Elizabeth Kaitan, Alisha Das, Tom Dugan, Brian Thompson; **D:** Bruce Cook Jr.

Nijinsky ✂✂ 1980 (R) An opulent biography of the famous ballet dancer. His exciting and innovative choreography gets little attention. The film concentrates on his infamous homosexual lifestyle and his relationship with impresario Sergei Diaghilev (Bates), in a tour-de-force performance. Lovely to look at, but slow and unconvincing. **125m/C VHS.** Alan Bates, George de la Pena, Leslie Browne, Alan Badel, Carla Fracci, Colin Blakely, Ronald Pickup, Ronald Lacey, Vernon Dobtcheff, Jeremy Irons, Frederick Jaeger, Janet Suzman, Sian Phillips; **D:** Herbert Ross.

Nikki, the Wild Dog of the North ✂✂ 1961 (G) When a Malemute pup is separated from his Canadian trapper master, he teams up with a bear cub for a series of adventures. Later the pup is reunited with his former master for still more adventures. Adapted from a novel by James Oliver Curwood for Disney. **73m/C VHS, DVD.** CA Jean Coutu, Emile Genest, Uriel Luft, Robert Rivard; **D:** Jack Couffer, Don Haldane.

Nil by Mouth ✂✂ 1998 (R) Oldman draws on his own dysfunctional working-class London background for his impressive writer/director debut, which casually puts you into the middle of one Cockney family's life. There's brutal Ray (Winstone), husband to Val (Burke) and brother-in-law to young addict Billy (Creed-Miles), as well as his tough mother-in-law Janet (Morse) and her mother, Kath (Dore). Billy gets kicked out of the house by Ray and struggles to survive outside his family while a drunken Ray beats the pregnant Val, prompting a display of female solidarity. Formless yet... characters' lives at random, showcasing family loyalty and generosity amidst the violence. **128m/C VHS, DVD.** GE Ray Winstone, Kathy Burke, Charlie Creed-Miles, Lala Morse, Edna Dore, Steve Sweeney, Chrissie Cotterill, Jon Morrison, Jamie Foreman; **D:** Gary Oldman; **W:** Gary Oldman. **'97: Actress (Burke).**

Nim's Island ✂✂½ 2008 (PG) A sweet fantasy adventure for kids featuring some excellent special effects, although adult viewers may find the limited plausibility too distracting to buy into the story of... probably like this. **101m/C VHS, DVD.** Jodie Foster, Gerard Butler, Abigail Breslin, Michael Carman, Mark Brady, Maddison Joyce; **D:** Jennifer Flackett, Mark Levin; **W:** Jennifer Flackett, Mark Levin; **C:** Stuart Dryburgh; **M:** Patrick Doyle.

Nina Takes a Lover ✂✂ 1994 (R) Romantic comedy finds Nina (San Giacomo) deciding that the passion is gone from her three-year marriage so, while her husband is out of town, she picks up a nameless Welsh photographer (Rhys) and begins an affair. The affair is over as the movie begins but Nina tells her story to a tabloid journalist (O'Keefe) who's writing about adultery. Gimmicky, with shallow if attractive characters and an equally attractive San Francisco setting. **100m/C VHS.** Laura San Giacomo, Paul Rhys, Michael O'Keefe, Cristi Conaway, Fisher Stevens; **D:** Alan Jacobs; **W:** Alan Jacobs; **C:** Phil Parmet; **M:** Todd Boekelheide.

The Nine Lives of Elfego Baca ✂✂ 1958 Venerable Western hero Loggia faces a veritable army of gunfighters and bandits. Action-packed but not too violent; family fun. **78m/C VHS, DVD.** Robert F. Simon, Lisa Montell, Nestor Paiva; **D:** Norman Foster.

Nine Lives of Fritz the Cat ✂✂ 1974 Fritz feels that life's too square in the '70s, so he takes off into some of his other lives for more adventures. Cleaner but still naughty sequel to the X-rated "Fritz the Cat" featuring neither the original's writer/director Ralph Bakshi nor cartoonist Robert Crumb. Animated. **77m/C VHS.** **DVD.** **D:** Robert Taylor; **W:** Robert Taylor, Eric Monte; **V:** Skip Hinnant.

Nine Men ✂✂½ 1943 Nine British troops must fend for themselves in the African desert when their supply convoy truck is destroyed. Besieged by Axis forces, they find a decrepit fort and attempt to hold out by making it seem as if they have more men and ammo than they do. Well-done British production has suspense aplenty. Similarly set and themed for a double feature. **68m/B VHS, GB** Jack Lambert, Gordon Jackson, Frederick Piper, Grant Sutherland, Eric Micklewood, John Varley, Harry Watt, Bill Blewitt, Jack Horseman, Richard Wilkinson; **D:** Roy Kellino; **M:** John Greenwood.

Nine Months ✂✂½ 1995 (PG-13) Happily single Samuel (Grant) gets girlfriend Rebecca (Moore) pregnant and promptly wigs out. He makes amends to the lovely Rebecca, they marry, and true happily ever after. Bachelor pal Sean (Goldblum) and an expectant couple (Arnold and Cusack) with three kids round out the cast, with Williams offering his usual manic flair as a Russian obstetrician, improvising his scenes with glee. Grant's knack for clumsy befuddlement fits well with the warm, fuzzy style of Columbus. "Nine" doesn't go out on any limbs, but is a pleasant diversion anyway. Remake of the French film "Neuf Mois." **103m/C VHS, DVD.** Hugh Grant, Julianne Moore, Tom Arnold, Joan Cusack, Jeff Goldblum, Robin Williams, Alexa Vega, Ashley Johnson, Mia Cottet, Kristen Davis, Joey Simmrin; **D:** Chris Columbus; **W:** Chris Columbus; **C:** Donald McAlpine; **M:** Hans Zimmer.

Nine Queens ✂✂✂ Nueve Reinas 2000 (R) Juan (Pauls) is a rookie con man in Buenos Aires, who is taken under the wing of the more-experienced Marcos (Darin). Marcos stumbles across an opportunity to fence the Nine Queens, a famous set of detectively printed stamps from Weimar Germany. Actually, Marcos's ruse is peddle a counterfeit set to a stamp-collecting patsy named Gandolfo (Abacollecting patsy named Gandolfo (Abacanti). Things get complicated when Marcos needs his angry sister Valeria's (Bredice) help, the stamps are stolen, and even Argentina's economic woes come to play a significant role. Just who's scamming

976-EVIL ✂✂ 1988 (R) England (the infamous Freddy from the Nightmare on Elm Street epics) directs this horror movie about a lonely teenager dials direct to demons from hell. **102m/C VHS, DVD.** Stephen Geoffreys, Jim Metzler, Maria Rubell, Sandy Dennis, Robert Picardo, Lezlie (Dean) Deane, Pat O'Bryan, J.J. Cohen; **D:** Robert Englund; **M:** Brian Helgeland, Rhet Topham; **C:** Paul Elliott; **M:** Tom Chase, Steve Rucker.

976-EVIL 2: The Astral Factor ✂✂½ 1991 (R) Satan returns in this supernatural thriller that sequels the original film. **93m/C VHS.** Pat O'Bryan, Rene Assa, Debbie James; **D:** Jim Wynorski; **W:** Erik Anjou.

The Nines ✂✂✂ 2007 (R) Three stars play three roles in three different, interconnected stories in this ambitious puzzle of a movie whose twists and turns mostly succeed. Each story features Reynolds, McCarthy, and Davis dealing with conflicts internal and external that all seem to come back to "the nines," what-ever that may be. Each story connects to the other while you're guessing throughout the build-up but the resolution doesn't entirely pay off. **99m/C VHS, DVD.** Ryan Reynolds, Hope Davis, Melissa McCarthy; **D:** John August; **W:** John August; **C:** Nancy Schreiber; **M:** Alex Wurman.

1900 ✂✂ Novecento 1976 (R) Bertolucci's impassioned epic about two Italian families, one land-owning, the other peasant. Shows the sweeping changes of the 20th century begun by the trauma of WWI and the onslaught of Italian socialism. Edited down from its original 360-minute length and dubbed in English from three other languages, the film suffers a serious lack of commitment to any genre. Based on the novel by Roger MacDonald. **255m/C VHS, DVD.** FR IT GE Robert De Niro, Gerard Depardieu, Burt Lancaster, Donald Sutherland, Dominique Sanda, Sterling Hayden, Laura Betti, Francesca Bertini, Werner Bruhns, Stefania Sandrelli, Anna Henkel, Alida Valli; **D:** Bernardo Bertolucci; **W:** Giuseppe Bertolucci, Bernardo Bertolucci; **C:** Vittorio Storaro.

1915 ✂✂ 1982 Aussie mates Billy and Walter decide to leave their country homes and enlist in the army, dreaming of heroics in WWI, only to be shocked by the realities of war. Based on the novel by William Converse-Roberts, Rochelle Oliver, Michael Higgins, Horton Foote Jr., William McGhee, Jeanne McCarthy; **D:** Ken Harrison; **W:** Willie Nelson.

1918 ✂✂½ 1985 An adaptation of the Horton Foote play about the effects of WWI and an influenza epidemic on a small Texas town. Slow-moving but satisfying. Score by Willie Nelson. Originally produced for PBS's "American Playhouse." Prequelled by "On Valentine's Day." **89m/C VHS, DVD.** Matthew Broderick, Hallie Foote, William Converse-Roberts, Rochelle Oliver, Michael Higgins, Horton Foote Jr., William (Bill) McGhee, Jeanne McCarthy; **C:** Peter Hendry; **M:** Bruce Smeaton. **TV**

1931: Once Upon a Time in New York ✂✂ 1972 Prohibition-era gangsters war, beat each other up, make headlines, and drink bathtub gin. **90m/C**

who? Spanish with subtitles. **115m/C VHS, DVD.** AR Ricardo Darin, Gaston Pauls, Leticia Bredice, Ignasi Abadal, Tomas Fonzi, Felician Bielinsky; **W:** Fabian Bielinsky; **C:** Marcelo Camorino; **M:** Cesar Lerner.

9 to 5 ✂✂½ 1980 (PG) In this caricature of large corporations and women in the working world, Coleman plays the male chauvinist boss who calls the shots and keeps his employees, all female, under his thumb. Three of the office secretaries daydream of Coleman's disposal and rashly kidnap him after a silly set of occurrences threaten their jobs. While they have him under lock and key, the trio take office matters into their own hands and take a stab at running things their own way, with amusing results. Basis for a TV series. **111m/C VHS, DVD.** Jane Fonda, Lily Tomlin, Dolly Parton, Dabney Coleman, Sterling Hayden, Norma Donaldson; **D:** Colin Higgins; **W:** Patricia Resnick; **C:** Reynaldo Villalobos; **M:**

Nine Lives ✂✂ 2005 (R) Character study that captures brief but intense moments in the lives of nine women, ranging from a pregnant married woman (Wright Penn) running into a former lover (Isaacs) at a supermarket to a teenager's daughters. Writer/director Garcia (the son of famed actress Gabriel Garcia Marquez) showcases his leading ladies while not forgetting to support his equally talented supporting males. **115m/C VHS.** US Kathy Baker, Amy Brenneman, Elpidia Carrillo, Glenn Close, Stephen (Dillon) Dillane, Dakota Fanning, William Fichtner, Lisa Gay Hamilton, Holly Hunter, Jason Isaacs, Joe Mantegna, Ian McShane, Molly Parker, Mary Kay Place, Sydney Tamiia Poitier, Aidan Quinn, Miguel (Michael) Sandoval, Amanda Seyfried, Sissy Spacek, Robin Wright Penn; **W:** Rodrigo Garcia; **C:** Xavier Perez Grobet; **M:** Ed Shearmur.

The Nine Lives of Elfego Baca (see above entry)

Nina Takes a Lover ... (see above)

9 1/2 Weeks ✂✂½ 1986 (R) Chance meeting between a Wall Street exec and an art gallery employee evolves into an experimental sexual relationship bordering on sado-masochism. Video version is more explicit than the theatrical release, but not by much. Strong character, with strength of male and female personalities nicely balanced. Intriguing, but not for all tastes. **114m/C VHS, DVD.** Mickey Rourke, Kim Basinger, Margaret Whitton, Karen Young, David Margulies, Christine Baranski, Roderick Cook, Dwight Weist; **D:** Adrian Lyne; **W:** Patricia Louisiana Knop, Zalman Kirg; **C:** Peter Biziou; **M:** Jack Nitzsche.

9 1/2 Ninjas ✂½ 1990 (R) A cautious and disciplined martial artist trains a young and flirtatious woman in the ways of the ninja. His life becomes exciting in more ways than one, when the realizes she's being followed by ninjas with more on their minds than her training— they want to assassinate her Crazy mixture of sex, kung fu and humor make this film one surprise after another. **88m/C VHS.** Michael Phenicie, Andee Gray, Tommy (Tiny) Lister; **D:** Aaron Worth; **W:** Bill Crounse.

Nine Ages of Nakedness ✂ 1969 The story of a man whose ancestors have been plagued by a strange problem: beautiful, naked women who create carnal chaos. **88m/C VHS, DVD.** George Harrison Marks; **D:** George Harrison Marks; **Nar:** Charles Gray.

Nine Days a Queen ✂✂✂ Lady Jane Gray; Tudor Rose 1936 An historical drama based on the life of Lady Jane Grey, proclaimed Queen of England after the death of Henry VIII of England and summarily executed for treason by Mary Tudor after a nine-day reign. An obscure tragedy with good performances and absorbing story line. Remade as "Lady Jane" (1985). **80m/B VHS, GB** John Mills, Cedric Hardwicke, Nova Pilbeam, Sybil Thorndike, Leslie Perrins Felix Aylmer, Miles Mallesor, Frank Cellier, Desmond Tester, Gwen Francon-Davies, Martita Hunt, John Laurie, Roy Emerton, John Turnbull, J.H. Roberts; **D:** Robert Stevenson; **W:** Robert Stevenson; **C:** Mutz Greenbaum.

Nine Deaths of the Ninja WOOF! 1985 (R) Faceless ninja warrior Kosugi leads a team of commandos on a mission to rescue a group of political prisoners held captive in the Philippine jungles. Features Ozone-depleted plot, incongruous performances, and inane dialogue, not to mention two main villains—a neurotic Nazi in a wheelchair and a black lesbian amazon—who chew jungle air and bring bad art to a new level of appreciation. Amazing in its total badness.

VHS, DVD. *IT* Tony Anthony, Richard Conte, Adolfo Celi, Lionel Stander, Irene Papas; *D:* Luigi Vanzi; *W:* Tony Anthony; *C:* Riccardo (Pallton) Pallotti.

1941 ♂♂½ **1979 (PG)** Proved to be the most expensive comedy of all time with a budget exceeding $35 million. The depiction of Los Angeles in the chaotic days after the bombing of Pearl Harbor combines elements of fantasy and black humor. 120m/C VHS, DVD. John Belushi, Dan Aykroyd, Patti LuPone, Ned Beatty, Slim Pickens, Murray Hamilton, Christopher Lee, Tim Matheson, Toshiro Mifune, Warren Oates, Robert Stack, Nancy Allen, Elisha Cook Jr., Lorraine Gary, Treat Williams, Mickey Rourke, John Candy, Wendie Jo Sperber, Lucille Benson, Eddie Deezen, Bobby Di Cicco, Dianne Kay, Perry Lang, Frank McRae, Lionel Stander, Dub Taylor, Joe Flaherty, David Lander, Michael McKean, Samuel Fuller, Audrey Landers, John Landis, Walter Olkewicz, Donovan Scott, Penny Marshall; *D:* Steven Spielberg; *W:* Robert Zemeckis, Bob Gale, John Milius; *C:* William A. Fraker; *M:* John Williams.

1969 ♂♂♂ **1989 (R)** Three teenage friends during the 1960s become radicalized by the return of one of their friends from Vietnam in a coffin. Critically lambasted directorial debut for "On Golden Pond" author Ernest Thompson. 96m/C VHS, DVD. Kiefer Sutherland, Robert Downey Jr., Winona Ryder, Bruce Dern, Joanna Cassidy, Mariette Hartley, Christopher Wynne; *D:* Ernest Thompson; *W:* Ernest Thompson; *C:* Jules Brenner; *M:* Michael Small.

1984 ♂♂♂ **1956** Winston Smith and Julia struggle to find happiness within forbidden love in a dystopian totalitarian future ruled by omnipresent dictator Big Brother. Excellently dreary adaptation of the George Orwell novel was made only seven years after the novel's debut, and at the height of the noir age and Cold War, making it that much scarier to contemporary audiences. Seen today, it still captures the dread and paranoia of the novel. 90m/B VHS, DVD. *GB* Edmond O'Brien, Jan Sterling, Michael Redgrave, David Kossoff, Mervyn Johns, Donald Pleasence, Carol Wolveridge, Ernest Clark, Ronan O'Casey, Kenneth Griffith; *D:* Michael Anderson Sr.; *W:* William Templeton, Ralph Gilbert Bettinson; *C:* N. Peter Rathvon.

1984 ♂♂♂½ **1984 (R)** A very fine adaptation of George Orwell's infamous novel, this version differs from the overly simplistic and cautionary 1954 film because of fine casting and production design. The illegal love affair of a government official becomes his attempt to defy the crushing inhumanity and lack of simple pleasures of an omniscient government. Filmed in London, it skillfully visualizes our time's most central prophetic nightmare. 117m/C VHS, DVD. *GB* John Hurt, Richard Burton, Suzanna Hamilton, Cyril Cusack, Gregor Fisher, Andrew Wilde, Rupert Baderman; *D:* Michael Radford; *C:* Roger Deakins.

1990: The Bronx Warriors WOOF! *1990 I Guerrieri del Bronx; Bronx Warriors* **1983 (R)** Good street gang members combat evil corporate powers in a semi-futuristic South Bronx. Lame copy of "Escape from New York." 86m/C VHS, DVD. *IT* Vic Morrow, Christopher Connelly, Fred Williamson; *D:* Enzo G. Castellari.

1991: The Year Punk Broke ♂♂½ **1992** Documents a grunge rock tour of European festivals in 1991 when the alternative bands were largely unknown to all but hardcore fans. Follows Sonic Youth, Nirvana, Dinosaur Jr., Babes in Toyland, Gumball, and granddaddy punk idols, The Ramones, behind-the-scenes and through their performances. 95m/C VHS. *D:* David Markey.

1999 ♂♂♂½ **1998 (R)** On New Year's Eve, Rufus King (Futterman) is partying like it's 1999 (which it is), deciding it's the perfect opportunity to make some life-changing decisions. Like dumping his sweet girlfriend for the office sexpot (Peet). 93m/C VHS, DVD. Dan Futterman, Jennifer Garner, Matt McGrath, Amanda Peet, Steven Wright, Sandrine Holt, Buck Henry, Margaret Devine, Daniel Lapaine, David Gelb, Nick Davis; *D:* Nick Davis; *W:* Nick Davis; *C:* Howard Krupa; *M:* Sue Jacobs, Lynne Geller.

90 Days ♂♂♂ **1986** Charming independently made Canadian comedy about two young men handling their respective romantic dilemmas—one awaiting an oriental fiancee he's never met, the other who is being kicked out of his house by his wife. 99m/C VHS. *CA* Stefan Wodoslawsky, Sam Grana, Christine Pak; *D:* Giles Walker.

92 in the Shade ♂♂♂ **1975 (R)** Based upon McGuane's novel, the film deals with a bored, wealthy rogue who becomes a fishing guide in the Florida Keys, and battles against the competition of two crusty, half-mad codgers. Sloppy, irreverent comedy as only a first-time writer-turned-director can fashion. 91m/C VHS. Peter Fonda, Warren Oates, Margot Kidder, Burgess Meredith, Harry Dean Stanton; *D:* Thomas McGuane; *W:* Thomas McGuane.

99 & 44/100 Dead ♂ *Call Harry Crown* **1974 (PG)** Familiar patters with this silly gangster flick. Harris is hired to kill Dillman, by local godfather O'Brien. Originally written as a satirical look at gangster movies, but it doesn't stick to satire, and as a result is disappointing. 98m/C VHS. Richard Harris, Chuck Connors, Edmond O'Brien, Bradford Dillman, Ann Turkel; *D:* John Frankenheimer; *W:* Robert Dillon; *M:* Henry Mancini.

99 Women ♂½ *Isle of Lost Women* **1969 (R)** Sympathetic prison warden attempts to investigate conditions at a women's prison camp. Thin and exploitative view of lesbianism behind bars that sensationalizes the subject. 90m/C VHS, DVD. *GB SP GE IT* Maria Schell, Herbert Lom, Mercedes McCambridge, Luciana Paluzzi; *D:* Jess (Jesus) Franco.

Ninja 3: The Domination ♂♂ **1984 (R)** Ninja master must remove the spirit of a deadly ninja assassin from a young woman intent on wreaking havoc among the Phoenix police department. Extremely silly super ninja epic utterly uninhibited by the usual plot conventions. 92m/C VHS. Lucinda Dickey, Sho Kosugi; *D:* Sam Firstenberg; *W:* James R. Silke; *C:* Hanania Baer.

Ninja Academy ♂♂½ **1990 (R)** Seven wimps, losers, and spoiled brats come to the Ninja Academy to learn the art. Will they make it? 93m/C VHS, DVD. Will Egan, Kelly Randall, Gerald Okomura, Michael David, Robert Factor, Jeff Robinson; *D:* Nico Mastorakis.

Ninja: American Warrior ♂½ **1990** An evil ninja takes on the U.S. Drug Enforcement Agency when the authorities threaten to shut him down. 90m/C VHS. Joff Houston, John Wilford; *D:* Godfrey Ho.

Ninja Champion WOOF! **1980** White-clad and masked ninja heros come to the aid of some Interpol agents tracking down a sleazy diamond smuggler. Invisible storyline features very little actual ninja. Extremely unconvincing and poorly dubbed. 90m/C VHS, DVD. *HK* Bruce Baron, Richard Harrison; *D:* Godfrey Ho; *W:* Godfrey Ho.

Ninja Commandments ♂ **1987** Everything is at stake when an evil warrior takes on the greatest fighter in the land: the winner will rule the empire! 90m/C VHS. Richard Harrison, Dave Wheeler; *D:* Joseph Lai.

Ninja Condors ♂ **1987** A young man grows up to avenge the murder of his father. 85m/C VHS. Alexander Lou, Stuart Hugh; *D:* James Wu.

Ninja Connection ♂ **1990** Ninja terrorism is employed as a scare tactic to deter a group who wants to break up an international drug ring. 90m/C VHS, DVD. Patricia Greenford, Jane Kingsly, Joe Nelson, Louis Roth, Henry Steele, Stuart Steen; *D:* York Lam.

Ninja Death Squad ♂ **1987** A ninja team specializing in political assassinations is hunted down by a special agent. 88m/C VHS. Glen Carson, Patricia Goodman, Joff Houston, Billy "Red" Jones, Wallace Jones, John Wilford; *D:* Godfrey Ho.

Ninja Destroyer ♂ **1970 (R)** Ninja warriors battle over an emerald mine. 92m/C VHS. *HK* Bruce Baron, Stuart Smith; *D:* Godfrey Ho; *W:* Godfrey Ho.

Ninja Fantasy WOOF! **1986** Ninja drug smugglers and government officials battle over a large drug shipment. Everybody go chop socky. Not much in way of ninja fantasy. Dubbed. 95m/C VHS, DVD. *HK* Adam Nell, Ian Frank, Jordan Heller, Ken Ashley, Jenny Mills, Jack Rodman; *D:* Godfrey Ho; *W:* Anthony Green.

Ninja Hunt WOOF! **1987** This time, ninjas kick international terrorists in the head while searching for secret formula. Poorly dubbed pseudo ninja developed by Godfrey Ho. 92m/C VHS. *HK* Bruce Baron, Stuart Smith; *D:* Joseph Lai; *W:* Stephen Saul.

Ninja in the U.S.A. ♂½ **1988** Evil drug kingpin Tyger McFerson (Albergo) is acquitted of murder charges because all witnesses against him have been killed by his ninja army. Cops Rodney Kuen and Jerry Wong (Lou) give McFerson the benefit of the doubt because he saved their lives in Viet Nam. But when Jerry's reporter wife is kidnapped by Tyger's ninja suits up with all his ninja gear and storms McFerson's compound. Despite the video release title, there's no reason to believe any of this takes place anywhere in the United States. 93m/C VHS, DVD. *TW* Alexander Lou, George Nicholas Albergo, Eugene Thomas, Alex Yip; *D:* Dennis Wu; *W:* Ed Jones; *C:* Owen Casey; *M:* Sherman Chow.

Ninja Masters of Death ♂ **1985** Terrorists reign supreme until the white ninja saves the city. 90m/C VHS. Mick Jones, Chris Petersen, Daniel Wells, Richard Young; *D:* Godfrey Ho.

Ninja Mission ♂½ **1984 (R)** First Scandinavian ninja epic follows CIA agent and his group of ninja fighters as they embark on a hazardous mission to rescue two people from a Soviet prison. They use their fighting skills (Swedish ninjas favor guns more than ninjutsu) against Russian soldiers. Dubbed. 96m/C VHS. *SW* Christopher Kohlberg, Curt Brober, Hanna Pola; *D:* Mats Helge.

Ninja of the Magnificence ♂½ **1989** When the ninja master is killed, factions within his group battle for control. 90m/C VHS. UMD. Sam Baker, Patrick Frbezar, Clive Hadwen, Tim Michael, Renato Sala; *D:* Godfrey Ho.

Ninja Operation: Licensed to Terminate ♂ **1987** Two warriors risk broken noses and twisted limbs to take on the Black Ninja Empire. 89m/C VHS. Richard Harrison, Paul Marshall, Jack McPeat, Grant Temple; *D:* Joseph Lai.

Ninja Phantom Heroes ♂ **1987** Two Vietnam vets are imprisoned for war crimes. One escapes and forms his own secret ninja society. 90m/C VHS. Glen Carson, George Dickson, Allen Leung, Christine Wells; *D:* Godfrey Ho.

Ninja Powerforce ♂½ **1990** Two childhood friends end up as members of rival ninja gangs in the midst of a bloody war. Usual assortment of ninja-inflicted injuries result. 90m/C VHS. Jonathan Bould, Richard Harrison; *D:* Joseph Lai.

Ninja Showdown ♂ **1990** A warrior or must take on a number of vicious bandits in order to defend his small town. He vows revenge on anyone who threatens his people. 92m/C VHS. Richard Harrison; *D:* Joseph Lai.

Ninja Strike Force ♂½ **1988** The Black Ninjas steal the powerful "spirit sword," and go on a bloody rampage. 89m/C VHS. Richard Harrison, Gary Carter; *D:* Joseph Lai.

Ninja the Battalion ♂ **1990** Agents from America, the Soviet Union, and China try to recover germ warfare secrets stolen by the Japanese secret service. 90m/C VHS. Roger Crawford, Sam Huxley, Alexander Lou, Dickson Wam; *D:* Victor Sears.

Ninja, the Violent Sorcerer ♂½ **1986** Murderer, with the help of Chinese vampires, does battle with the ghost of a dead gambling lord's wife and the gambling lord's living brother. Often tedious even with above average production and incredible plot. 90m/C VHS. *D:* Godfrey Ho; *W:* Daniel Clough.

Ninja Vengeance ♂½ **1993 (R)** The corrupt sheriff of a small Texas town, who also leads the KKK, is terrorizing a young African-American local. Then our lone hero rides into town on his trusty motorcycle to save the day. Only this time instead of your average gunman, he's a ninja. 87m/C VHS. Stephen K. Hayes, Janet K. Pawiak, Craig Boyett, David Paul Lord; *D:* Karl Armstrong; *W:* Carrie Armstrong, Karl Armstrong.

Ninotchka ♂♂♂½ **1939** Delightful romantic comedy. Garbo is a cold Russian agent sent to Paris to check up on her comrades, who are being seduced by capitalism. She inadvertently falls in love with a playboy, who melts her communist heart. Garbo talks and laughs. Satirical, energetic, and witty. Later a Broadway musical called "Silk Stockings." 110m/B VHS, DVD. Greta Garbo, Melvyn Douglas, Ina Claire, Sig Rumann, Felix Bressart, Bela Lugosi; *D:* Ernst Lubitsch; *W:* Billy Wilder; *C:* William H. Daniels. Natl. Film Reg. 90.

The Ninth Configuration ♂♂♂ *Twinkle, Twinkle, Killer Kane* **1979 (R)** Based on Blatty's novel "Twinkle, Twinkle, Killer Kane" (also the film's alternate title), this is a weird and surreal tale of a mock rebellion of high-ranking military men held in a secret base hospital for the mentally ill. Keach is good as the commander who is just as insane as the patients. Available in many different lengths, this is generally considered to be the best. 115m/C VHS, DVD. Stacy Keach, Scott Wilson, Jason Miller, Ed Flanders, Neville Brand, Alejandro Rey, Robert Loggia, George DiCenzo; *D:* William Peter Blatty; *W:* William Peter Blatty. Golden Globes '81; Screenplay.

The Ninth Day ♂♂♂ *Der Neunte Tag* **2004** Examines Nazism from the side of its victims through the plight of Rev. Henri Kremer, a Roman Catholic priest from Luxembourg imprisoned at Dachau. The cruel logic behind totalitarian power is revealed in the plot to use Kremer in coercing his bishop to declare Nazism compatible with church doctrine, upon which they will 'grant' him a nine-day furlough. Failure will result in the execution of 18 Luxembourg priests in his Dachau block and will also bring harm to his family. All performances, in German with English subtitles, are stellar. Schlondorff lays out the theological and ethical debates of potent themes without over-dramatizing them. 90m/C DVD. *GE* Ulrich Matthes, August Diehl, Germain Wagner, Bibiana Beglau, Jean-Paul Raths, Ivan Jirik, Karel Hromadka, Miroslav Sichman, Adolf Filip, Vladimir Fiser, Petr Varga, Petr Janis, Zdenek Pechacek, Karel Dobry, Goetz Burger, Hilmar Thate; *D:* Volker Schlondorff; *W:* Eberhard Goemer, Andreas Pflueger; *C:* Tomas Erhart; *M:* Alfred Schnitke.

The Ninth Gate ♂♂ **1999 (R)** Less-than-scrupulous rare-book dealer Dean Corso (Depp) is hired by wealthy publishing mogul Balkan (Langella) to find and authenticate three copies of a 17th-century book that supposedly holds the secrets to conjuring up the devil. Naturally, he encounters many spooky and deadly people along the way. Depp is perfectly cast as the sleazy bookworm and every scene is appropriately atmospheric, but Polanski's glacial pace and lack of any dramatic tension keeps this flick from getting its due. 127m/C VHS, DVD. *FR SP* Johnny Depp, Frank Langella, Lena Olin, Emmanuelle Seigner, Barbara Jefford, Jack Taylor, James Russo, Jose Lopez Rodero; *D:* Roman Polanski; *W:* Roman Polanski, John Brownjohn, Enrique Urbizu; *C:* Darius Khondji; *M:* Wojciech Kilar.

Nirvana ♂♂ **1997 (R)** Jimi Dini (Lambert) is a computer game designer whose latest creation, Nirvana, has a lead character called Solo (Abatantuono). But when Jimi plays the game, he finds out that a computer virus has imparted self-awareness to Solo who pleads to be deleted from his virtual world. Jimi's agreeable but this doesn't turn out to be so easy. 108m/C VHS, DVD. *FR IT* Christopher Lambert, Diego Abatantuono, Emmanuelle Seigner, Sergio Rubini; *D:* Gabriele Salvatores; *W:* Gabriele Salvatores.

Nitti: The Enforcer 1988 (PG-13) Made-for-TV saga about Al Capone's brutal enforcer and right-hand man, Frank Nitti. Diversified cast (Moriarty in particular) do their best to keep things moving along, and the atmosphere is consistently and appropriately violent. Made to capitalize on the success of 1987's "The Untouchables." 94m/C VHS, DVD. Anthony LaPaglia, Vincent Guastaferro, Trini Alvarado, Michael Moriarty, Michael Russo, Louis Guss, Bruno Kirby; D: Michael Switzer.

Nixon 1995 (R) Stone again "interprets" historical events of the '60s and '70s with a sprawling, bold bio of Richard Nixon. Covering all the highlights of Nixon's public life, and speculating on his private one. Hopkins convincingly portrays "Tricky Dick" as an embattled lonely political genius. Gigantic all-star cast is lead by Oscar-caliber performance of Joan Allen as Pat Nixon. Even at over three hours, there isn't nearly enough time to explore the significance of all the events covered. As usual, Stone has taken some creative license which lead to the Nixon daughters publicly trashing the film, and Walt Disney's daughter expressing "shame" at being affiliated with it. 192m/C VHS, DVD. Anthony Hopkins, Joan Allen, Ed Harris, Bob Hoskins, David Paymer, Paul Sorvino, J.T. Walsh, James Woods, Madeline Kahn, Brian Bedford, Mary Steenburgen, Powers Boothe, E.G. Marshall, David Hyde Pierce, Kevin Dunn, Annabeth Gish, Tony Goldwyn, Larry Hagman, Edward Herrmann, Saul Rubinek, Tony LoBianco, Kamar De Los Reyes; D: Oliver Stone; W: Oliver Stone, Christopher Wilkinson, Stephen J. Rivele; C: Robert Richardson; M: John Williams. L.A. Film Critics '95. Support. Actress (Allen); Natl. Soc. Film Critics '95. Support. Actress (Allen).

No 1998 Based on a segment of writer-director Lepage's play "The Seven Branches of the River Ota," which juxtaposes events at the 1970 World's Fair in Osaka, Japan with an infamous event in Canadian history, as separatist terrorists in Quebec kidnap a British diplomat and a government cabinet minister. Sophie is performing in Osaka while her boyfriend Michel (Martin) is back home watching the political upheaval on TV. Sophie has a number of personal crises to contend with, while Michel gets so wrapped up in politics he contemplates taking radical actions of his own. The cultural and political differences won't necessarily travel well outside French-speaking Canada. 85m/C VHS, CA Anne-Marie Cadieux, Alexis Martin, Marie Brassard, Richard Frechette, Marie Gignac, Eric Bernier; D: Robert Lepage; W: Robert Lepage, Andre Morency; C: Pierre Mignot '98: Canadian Feature Film.

No Alibi 2000 (R) Upstanding businessman Bob Valenz (Cain) becomes involved with beautiful Camille (Doig), who also has something kinky going on with Bob's smalltime crook brother, Phil (Stebbings). Phil gets dead and it leads back not only to Camille but to the third man in her life, criminal slickster Vic (Roberts). But by then Bob and Camille are married and she's pregnant. But Bob won't stop investigating his brother's death and he's not going to like what he finds out. 94m/C VHS, DVD. CA Dean Cain, Eric Roberts, Lexa Doig, Peter Stebbings, Richard Chevolleau, Frank Schorpion, Melissa Di Marco; D: Bruce Pittman; W: Ivan Kane, John Scharer; C: Michael Storey; M: Marty Simon. VIDEO

No Big Deal 1983 (PG-13) Dillon is a streetwise teenager who makes friends at his new school. Blah promise: bad acting makes this no big deal. 86m/C VHS, DVD. Kevin Dillon, Sylvia Miles, Tammy Grimes, Jane Krakowski, Christopher Gartin, Mary Joan Negro; D: Robert Charlton.

No Code of Conduct 1998 (R) Veteran cop Bill Peterson (Sheen) is working with the DEA on a sting operation to recover millions in heron but when things go wrong, Bill suspects corruption within his own department. So he calls on hot-headed cop son Jake (Charlie Sheen) for help. 90m/C VHS, DVD. Mark Dacascos, Joe Estevez, Charlie Sheen, Martin Sheen, Courtney Gains, Paul Gleason, Joe Lando, Meredith Salenger, Bret Michaels; D: Bret Michaels; W: Charlie Sheen, Paul Sorvino.

No Contest 1994 (R) International terrorists, lead by Oz (Clay), hold the TV host (Tweed) and contestants of the Ms. Galaxy beauty pageant hostage, demanding a $10 million ransom demand. 98m/C VHS, DVD. Andrew (Dice Clay) Silverstein, Shannon Tweed, Robert Davi, Roddy Piper, Nicholas (Nick) Campbell; D: Paul Lynch; W: Robert Cooper.

No Country for Old Men 2007 (R) When cowboy Llewelyn Moss (Brolin) happens upon a drug deal gone bad in the West Texas wilderness and grabs a case holding more than $2 million, it's up to world-weary sheriff Ed Tom Bell (Jones) to track him down. However, both men find themselves tangled up with cold-blooded killer Anton Chigurh (Bardem), who's determined to track down the missing money and willing to kill anyone in his way. Expertly adapted from the Cormac McCarthy novel, writers/directors/producers Joel and Ethan Coen have crafted a masterpiece; a painstakingly intense, dark thriller that doubles as a meditation on the role of violence in American society. 122m/C DVD, US Tommy Lee Jones, Javier Bardem, Josh Brolin, Woody Harrelson, Kelly Macdonald, Tess Harper, Garret Dillahunt, Barry Corbin; D: Joel Coen, Ethan Coen; W: Joel Coen, Ethan Coen; C: Roger Deakins; M: Carter Burwell. Oscar's '07. Adapt. Screenplay, Director (Coen, Coen), Film, Support. Actor (Bardem); British Acad. '07. Cinematog., Director (Coen, Coen), Support. Actor (Bardem); Directors Guild '07. Director (Coen); Golden Globes '08. Screenplay, Support. Actor (Bardem); Screen Actors Guild '07. Support. Actor (Bardem); Cast; Writers Guild '07. Adapt. Screenplay.

No Dead Heroes 1987 Green Beret Vietnam war hero succumbs to Soviet scheming when they plant a computer chip in his brain. Unoriginal and unworthy. 86m/C VHS. Max (Michael) Thayer, John Dresden, Toni Nero; D: J.C. Miller.

No Deposit, No Return Double Trouble 1976 (G) Tedious, silly, pointless Disney action comedy. Rich brats persuade bumbling crooks to kidnap them, offer them for ransom to millionaire grandfather. 115m/C VHS, DVD. David Niven, Don Knotts, Darren McGavin, Barbara Feldon, Charles Martin Smith; D: Norman Tokar; W: Arthur Alsberg; M: Buddy (Norman Dale) Baker.

No Dessert Dad, 'Til You Mow the Lawn 1994 (PG) Suburban parents Ken and Carol Cochran (Robert Hays and Joanna Kerns) are harassed at home by their annoying offspring. Justin, Monica, and Tyler. When they try hypnosis tapes to quit smoking, the kids discover by doctoring the tapes they can plant suggestions resulting in parental capers. 80m/C VHS, DVD. Robert Hays, Joanna Kerns, Joshua Schaefer, Allison Meek, Jimmy Marsden, Richard Moll, Larry Linville; D: Clyde Ware.

No Drums, No Bugles 1971 (G) A West Virginia farmer and conscientious objector leaves his family to live alone in a cave for three years during the Civil War. Bad direction spoils Sheen's good performance. 85m/C VHS. Martin Sheen, Davey Davison, Denine Terry, Rod McCary; D: Clyde Ware.

No End Bez Konca 1984 The ghost of a dead lawyer watches as his wife and young son struggle to survive without him, including the woman getting involved in her husband's last case about a worker arrested for organizing a strike. Well-acted but overly solemn and slow. Set during Poland's martial law in 1982. In Polish with English subtitles 108m/C VHS, DVD. PL Grazyna Szapolowska, Jerzy Radziwilowicz, Maria Pakulnis, Aleksander Bardini, Artur Barcis, Michal Bajor; D: Krzysztof Kieslowski; W: Krzysztof Pieslewicz, Krzysztof Kieslowski.

No End in Sight 2007 Brookings Institute scholar and political science PhD Charles Ferguson's documentary of the war in Iraq is a powerful, compelling analysis and critique of U.S. policy. Rather than criticize the war as a whole, Ferguson focuses in on the period immediately following the overthrow of Saddam and the Bush Administration's lack of a plan to rebuild Iraq. Most compelling are the interviews with individuals such as Ambassador Barbara Bodine and Major General Paul Eaton, who were hands-on involved in that initial post-Saddam period and found their efforts hindered by disorganization and ideological agendas. By focusing on experts involved in the war rather than outside critics, Ferguson skips partisanship to create a sharp, hard to ignore film. 102m/C DVD, US Antonic Rossi; M: Peter Nashel.

No Escape 1994 (R) In 2022, Captain Robbins (Liotta) has been banished to a prison colony island inhabited by the most dangerous criminals. With no walls and no guards, the prisoners are left to kill each other. Then Robbins discovers a relatively peaceful community of prisoners who help each other. But this group is soon bedeviled by the evil nasties on the other side of the island. Attempts at escape define the plot, so the film is filled with superhuman feats of sheer courage, determination, and guts. Adapted from the book "The Penal Colony" by Richard Herley. 118m/C VHS, DVD. Ray Liotta, Lance Henriksen, Stuart Wilson, Kevin Dillon, Kevin J. O'Connor, Jack Shepherd; D: Martin Campbell; W: Michael Gallagher, Joel Gross; C: Phil Meheux; M: Graeme Revell.

No Escape, No Return 1993 (R) An FBI agent (Nouri) and a police captain (Saxon) force three renegade cops (Nguyen, Caulfield, and Loveday) to infiltrate a drug syndicate. But things go from bad to worse when a war breaks out between rival drug gangs, leaving a lot of bodies, and a large chunk of money gone missing. Now the trio is sought by both the cops and the crooks. 93m/C VHS, DVD. Max Caulfield, Dustin Nguyen, Denise Loveday, John Saxon, Michael Nouri, Kevin Brannan; D: Charles Kanganis; W: Charles Kanganis; M: Jim Halfpenny.

No Fear, No Die 1990 To make some quick cash two black immigrants in France train and sell birds for illegal cockfights at a roadside restaurant. Jocelyn, who trains the cocks, pays them lavish, obsessive attention. But cultural conflicts and repressed passions are just waiting to explode. In French with English subtitles. 97m/C VHS, FR Alex Descas, Isaach de Bankole, Jean-Claude Brialy, Solveig Dommartin, Christopher Buchholz, Jean-Pol Fargeau; D: Claire Denis; W: Claire Denis, Jean-Pol Fargeau; M: Abdullah Ibrahim.

No Good Deed The House on Turk Street 2002 (R) Fairly mild thriller adapted from the Dashiell Hammett story, "The House on Turk Street." Diabetic, cello-playing cop Jack Friar (Jackson) postpones his vacation to look for a neighbor's runaway daughter. While checking around Turk Street, he comes to the aid of elderly Mrs. Quarre (Zabriskie) and winds up the hostage of a gang planning a bank robbery, mastermind Tyrone (Skarsgard) and hot-head Hoop (Hutchinson), inside man David (Higgins), and Tyrone's sexy and duplicitous girlfriend Erin (Jovovich), who's given the job of guarding Jack. Naturally, Jack's diabetes and his cello-playing will both come into play. 97m/C VHS, DVD. Samuel L. Jackson, Milla Jovovich, Stellan Skarsgard, Doug Hutchison, Grace Zabriskie, Joss Ackland, Jonathan Higgins; D: Bob Rafelson; W: Christopher Canaan, Steve Barancik; C: Juan Ruiz-Anchia; M: Jeff Beal.

No Greater Love 1943 Capraesque Soviet war movie. A peasant woman mobilizes her village against the Nazis to avenge her family's death. Dubbed into English by the Soviets for Western circulation during WWII. 74m/B Vera Mareskaya; D: Frederic Ermler.

No Highway in the Sky 1951 Eccentric scientist Theodore Honey (Stewart) works for the Royal Aircraft Establishment, which has just produced a new plane, the Reindeer. But Honey tells his boss Dennis Scott (Hawkins) that he has a serious defect. While flying to examine a Reindeer crash site, Honey befriends Monica (Dietrich), a musical star, and stewardess Marjorie (Johns), who support him when his company accuses him of maliciously damaging the aircraft's reputation. Dietrich steals every scene with her Christian Dior wardrobe and star attitude. Based on the novel "No Highway," by Nevil Shute. 98m/B VHS, GB James Stewart, Marlene Dietrich, Glynis Johns, Jack Hawkins, Ronald Squire, Niall MacGinnis, Elizabeth Allan, Kenneth More, David Hutcheson; D: Henry Koster; W: R.C. Sherriff, Oscar Millard; M: Malcolm Arnold.

No Holds Barred 1989 (PG-13) Cheesy campy remake of cheesy, campy 1952 wrestling movie. Hulk Hogan on the big screen, at last. 98m/C VHS. Hulk Hogan, Kurt Fuller, Joan Severance, Tommy (Tiny) Lister; D: Thomas J. Wright.

No Laughing Matter 1997 (PG-13) The widow of a policeman, outgoing Emma (Somers) is especially close to her teenaged son Charlie (Christ), and Emma needs protection since she has a long-standing drinking problem and has become increasingly impaired just as Charlie needs her most—seems his girlfriend Lauren (Blair) is pregnant. Finally, together, Charlie turns hostile over his own volatile situation. 90m/C VHS. Suzanne Somers, Chad Christ, Selma Blair, Robert Desiderio; D: Michael Elias; W: Michael Elias, Ted Kristian.

No Looking Back Long Time, Nothing New 1998 (R) Small-town 30ish waitress Claudia (Holly) is about to settle for a boring life with decent-but-dull Michael (Bon Jovi) when her ne'er-do-well former boyfriend Charlie (Burns) comes home looking to relive the glory days. Burns stays with the working-class, northeastern setting, but goes for drama this time. With themes that cover economic hopelessness and a yearning to escape, Burns seems to be trying for a cinematic distillation of Bruce Springsteen's (very cinematic) music. In fact, many Springsteen songs are used to set scenes. Like Bruce, Burns knows the working class vernacular, and uses it well. But this time, all traces of subtlety are gone, and the story plays out pretentiously much, barely registering in the crucial role. She also looks too damn good to be a washed-up waitress with no options. 96m/C VHS, DVD. Lauren Holly, Edward Burns, Jon Bon Jovi, Blythe Danner, Connie Britton; D: Edward Burns; W: Edward Burns; C: Frank Prinzi; M: Joe Delia.

No Love for Johnnie 1960 Well acted if unoriginal political drama. Finch is a British M.P. who falls in both public and private life. Based on the novel by Wilfred Fienburgh. 105m/B VHS, GB Peter Finch, Stanley Holloway, Donald Pleasence, Mary Peach, Mervyn Johns, Dennis Price, Oliver Reed, Billie Whitelaw; D: Ralph Thomas; W: Mordecai Richter; M: Malcolm Arnold. British Acad. '61. Actor (Finch).

No Man is an Island 1962 Wartime adventure based on the exploits (Hollywoodized) of U.S. Naval radio operator George R. Tweed (Hunter), who is stationed on Guam when the Japanese invade. He hides out in the jungle to avoid capture and is aided by the natives for nearly three years until he's able to contact some American warships. Thanks to Tweed's info, the Americans are able to recapture the island. Slow-paced. 114m/C VHS, DVD. Jeffrey Hunter, Marshall Thompson, Ronald Remy, Rolf Bayer, Barbara Perez, Joseph de Cordova; D: John Monks Jr., Richard Goldstone; W: John Monks Jr., Richard Goldstone; C: Carl Kayser; M: Restie Umali.

No Man of Her Own 1932 Gable and Lombard in their only screen pairing. Gambler Babe Stewart (Gable) marries small town librarian (Lombard) on a bet and exposes small town life from her. Neither star's best film. 81m/B VHS. Carole Lombard, Clark Gable, Grant Mitchell, Elizabeth Patterson, Dorothy Mackaill, George Barbier, J. Farrell MacDonald, Walter Walker, Paul Ellis; D: Wesley Ruggles; W: Benamin Glazer, Edmund Goulding, Maurine Watkins; C: Leo Tover; M: W. Franke Harling.

No Man's Land 1987 (R) Undercover cop Sweeney tails playboy car thief Sheen but is seduced by wealth and glamour. Flashy surfaces, shiny cars, little substance. 107m/C VHS, DVD. Charlie Sheen, D.B. Sweeney, Lara Harris, Randy Quaid; *D:* Peter Werner; *W:* Dick Wolf; *M:* Basil Poledouris.

No Man's Land 2001 (R) Let's talk about the futility and stupidity of war. In Bosnia in 1993, Croatian soldier Ciki (Branko Djuric) and Serbian Nino (Rene Bitorajac) wind up sharing the same trench between enemy lines, which is booby-trapped by a land mine. Laying on the mine is the injured Croat Cera (Filip Sovagovic) and if he moves, they all die. Reluctantly brought into the already tense situation is ineffectual U.N. officer Col. Soft (Callow) and then journalist Jane (Cartlidge) also shows up. Bosnian with subtitles. 98m/C VHS, DVD. *BS FR IT BE GB* Branko Djuric, Rene Bitorajac, Filip Sovagovic, Georges Siatidis, Serge-Henri Valcke, Simon Callow, Katrin Cartlidge; *D:* Danis Tanovic; *W:* Danis Tanovic; *C:* Walther Vanden Ende; *M:* Danis Tanovic. Oscars '01: Foreign Film; Cannes '01: Screenplay; L.A. Film Critics '01: Foreign Film.

No Man's Law 1927 Hardy plays the depraved villian desperate to get the goldmine owned by an old prospector and his beautiful daughter. But the mine is protected by Rex the Wonder Horse! 7m/B VHS. Oliver Hardy, Barbara Kent, James Finlayson, Theodore von Eltz; *D:* Fred W. Jackman.

No Man's Range *No Man's Land* 1935 Unremarkable, typical, predictable Western: good guys, bad guys, guns, bullets, horses. 56m/B VHS, DVD. Buck Connors, Steve Clark, Charles French, Roberta Gale, Bob Steele; *D:* Robert North Bradbury; *W:* Forbes Parkhill; *C:* William Nobles.

No Marriage Ties 1933 Reporter Bruce Foster (Dix) loses his job because he's a boozer but finds his way with words appeals to ad man Perkins (Dinehart). The two partner up successfully but Perkins begins to disapprove of the way Bruce goes after a cosmetics account and its owner (Deane). 72m/B VHS. Richard Dix, Alan Dinehart, Doris Kenyon, Elizabeth Allan, David Landau; *D:* J. Walter Ruben; *W:* Sam Mintz; *C:* Henry Cronjager.

No Mercy 1986 (R) A Chicago cop (Gere) plunges into the Cajun bayou in order to avenge the murder of his partner. He falls for a beautiful girl enslaved by the killer, but that doesn't stop him from using her to flush out the powerful swamp-inhabiting crime lord. Absurd story without much plot. 108m/C VHS, DVD. Richard Gere, Kim Basinger, Jeroen Krabbe, George Dzundza, William Atherton, Ray Sharkey, Bruce McGill; *D:* Richard Pearce; *W:* James (Jim) Carabatsos; *C:* Michel Brault; *M:* Alan Silvestri.

No Money Down *The Definite Maybe* 1997 (R) When Eric (Lucas) needs a new place to live, his best pal Ziggy (Beuhl) takes him to the Hamptons for the weekend to look at houses and enjoy the cocktails parties and other amenities—such as fraud, adultery, and attempted murder. 90m/C DVD. Josh(ua) Lucas, Bob Balaban, Jeffrey Beuhl, Claudia Rocafort; *D:* Sam Bokolow, Rob Rollins Lobl; *W:* Sam Sokolow, Rob Rollins Lobl; *C:* Ella Lyssy; *M:* Tree Adams, Billy Jay Stein.

No More Women 1934 A beautiful young woman inherits a boat employing two divers. When she decides to keep only one in her employ, it leads to fights, attempted murder, jail time, and broken hearts. 76m/B VHS. Edmund Lowe, Victor McLaglen, Sally Blane, Minna Gombell; *D:* Albert Rogell; *W:* Lou Breslow, Delmer Daves, Grant Leenhouts, John Mikale Strong.

No Name on the Bullet 1959 Aloof gunman John Gant (Murphy) is seeking revenge from someone in the town of Lordsburg, only none of the inhabitants know who the intended victim is. And slowly the town's citizens begin to panic. Great final showdown. 77m/C VHS, DVD. Audie Murphy, Charles Drake, Joan Evans, Edgar Stehli, Warren Stevens, R.G. Armstrong, Whit Bissell, Karl Swenson; *D:* Jack Arnold; *W:* Gene L. Coon; *C:* Harold Lipstein.

No News from God *Sin Noticias de Dios; Don't Tempt Me!* 2001 (R) Angel Lola (Abril) is a nightclub singer in heaven who is sent by her boss Marina (Ardant) to Earth to save the soul of boxer Many (Bechir). But when Jack (Garcia Bernal), Marina's counterpart in hell, hears the news, he sends devil waitress Carmen (Cruz) to do the deed first. To Many, Lola appears to be his ex, while Carmen is a cousin. Naturally, Lola tries to get Many to be good and Carmen wants him to be bad-and Many is well on his way to the latter. Starts out offbeat but then goes conventional. Spanish, French, and English dialogue. 115m/C VHS, DVD. *SP FR IT MX* Victoria Abril, Penelope Cruz, Damian Bechir, Fanny Ardant, Gael Garcia Bernal, Juan Echanove, Bruno Bichir, Emilio Gutierrez-Caba; *D:* Agustin Diaz Yanes; *W:* Agustin Diaz Yanes; *C:* Paco Femenia; *M:* Bernardo Bonezzi.

No, No Nanette 1940 Lackluster filming of the Broadway production which fared better on the stage. Stock story of a young woman (Neagle) who rescues her uncle from financial ruin and finds romance in the process. 96m/B VHS. Anna Neagle, Richard Carlson, Victor Mature, Roland Young, Zasu Pitts, Eve Arden, Billy Gilbert, Keye Luke; *D:* Herbert Wilcox; *C:* Russell Metty.

No One Cries Forever woof! 1985 When a prostitute breaks away from a gangster-madam after finding love, she is tracked down and disfigured. Swedish; dubbed. 96m/C DVD. Elke Sommer, Howard Carpendale, Zoli Marks; *D:* Jans Rautenbach.

No One Man 1932 Palm Beach socialite Penelope (Lombard) is a bored divorcee who marries ne'er-do-well Bill (Cortez) who, fortunately, soon drops dead. (Must have been all that extramarital activity.) Thus leaving her free to pursue old flame and idealistic doctor, Karl Bernis (Lukas). Adapted from the novel "No One Man" by Rupert Hughes. 73m/B VHS. Carole Lombard, Ricardo Cortez, Paul Lukas, George Barbier, Juliette Compton, Virginia Hammon; *D:* Lloyd Corrigan; *W:* Sidney Buchman, Percy Heath, Alice Leahy; *C:* Charles B(ryant) Lang Jr.

No One Sleeps 2001 Berlin medical researcher Stefan Hein (Wlaschiha) is attending an AIDS conference in San Francisco just as a serial killer is targeting men who are HIV positive. Stefan also wants to investigate his late father's theory that U.S. researchers used prisoners to test a virus that created HIV by trying to find an alleged list of the injected prisoners. Along the way Stefan meets detective Louise Tolliver (Levi) and discovers the two investigations may be linked. 108m/C VHS, DVD. Tom Wlaschiha, Irit Levi, Jim Thalman, Kalene Parker; *D:* Jochen Hick; *W:* Jochen Hick; *C:* Thomas M. Harting, Michael Maley; *M:* James Hardway.

No Other Woman 1933 Stand by your man despite the fact that he's a cheating, lying louse. Pittsburgh steelworker Jim Stanley (Bickford) is persuaded by wife Anna (Dunne) to invest in a dyeworks that brings them big bucks. Instead of staying home, Jim takes up with a gold-digging blonde (Andre) and causes lots of heartache for his faithful spouse. Adapted from Eugene Walter's play "Just a Woman". 58m/B VHS. Irene Dunne, Charles Bickford, Christian Rub, J. Carrol Naish, Gwili Andre, Eric Linden, Leila Bennett; *D:* J. Walter Ruben; *W:* Bernard Schubert, Wanda Tuchock; *C:* Edward Cronjager.

No Place to Hide 1981 A girl's father drowns and she blames herself. Her mother and psychologist try to convince the girl that her father's spirit isn't stalking her, but she doesn't believe them. 120m/C VHS. Keir Dullea, Mariette Hartley, Kathleen Beller, Arlen Dean Snyder, Gary (Rand) Graham, John Llewellyn Moxey; *D:* John Llewellyn Moxey. TV

No Place to Hide 1993 (R) Barrymore is the target of a psycho who's already killed her sister. Kristofferson plays the hard-edged cop who's out to protect her and trap the killer. 90m/C VHS, DVD. Drew Barrymore, Kris Kristofferson, Martin Landau, O.J. Simpson, Dey Young, Bruce Weitz; *D:* Richard Danus; *W:* Richard Danus.

No Place to Run 1972 An elderly man fights for custody of his grandson, then kidnaps him and flees with him to Canada. Made for TV. 78m/C VHS. Herschel Bernardi, Larry Hagman, Stefanie Powers, Neville Brand; *D:* Delbert Mann. TV

No Prince for My Cinderella 1978 A schizophrenic girl who has turned to prostitution is sought desperately by her social worker. 100m/C VHS. Robert Reed.

No Problem *Pas de Probleme!* 1975 A man is pursued, shot, and drops dead in the apartment of an unsuspecting man who doesn't know what to do with the body. Dubbed in English. 94m/C VHS. *FR* Miou-Miou, Bernard Menez, Jean (Lefevre) Lefebvre, Henri Guybet, Anny (Annie Legras) Duperey, Renee (Raymonde-Renee Vittorel) Saint-Cyr; *D:* Georges Lautner; *W:* Jean-Marie Poire; *C:* Roger Fellous; *M:* Philippe Sarde.

No Regrets for Our Youth 1946 A feminist saga depicting the spiritual growth of a foolish Japanese girl during the tumultuous years of WWII. In Japanese with English subtitles. 110m/B VHS. *JP* Setsuko Hara, Susumu Fujita, Denjiro Okochi, Haruko Sugimura, Eiko Miyoshi; *D:* Akira Kurosawa; *W:* Akira Kurosawa; *C:* Asakazu Nakai; *M:* Tadashi Hattori.

No Reservations 2007 (PG) Uptight, temperamental chef Kate (Zeta-Jones) meets her match romantically and professionally in laid back sous chef Nick (Eckhart). He's perfect, but she's too neurotic to recognize it, and just for a touch of extra conflict she's saddled with an orphaned pre-teen niece (Breslin). Aspires to be the romantic comedy version of fine dining but the end result is a bland and uninspired dish. Remake of popular German film "Mostly Martha." 105m/C DVD, Blu-ray Disc, HD DVD. *US* Catherine Zeta-Jones, Aaron Eckhart, Abigail Breslin, Patricia Clarkson, Jenny Wade, Bob Balaban, Brian F. O'Byrne, Lily Rabe, Celia Weston, John McMartin, Stephanie Barry; *D:* Scott Hicks; *W:* Carol Fuchs; *C:* Stuart Dryburgh; *M:* Philip Glass.

No Retreat, No Surrender 1986 (R) A young American kick-boxer battles a formidable Russian opponent and wins, quite improbably, after having been tutored by the ghost of Bruce Lee in an abandoned house. Notable as Van Damme's debut, but little else recommends this silly "Rocky" rehash. Followed by "No Retreat, No Surrender II." 85m/C VHS. Kurt McKinney, J.W. Falls, Jean-Claude Van Damme; *D:* Corey Yuen.

No Retreat, No Surrender 2 1989 (R) With help from two karate experts, a man sets out to find his girlfriend who has been kidnapped by Soviets. Has little or nothing to do with the movie to which it is ostensibly a sequel. High level kick-boxing action sequences. 92m/C VHS, Loren Avedon, Max (Michael) Thayer, Cynthia Rothrock; *D:* Corey Yuen; *W:* Maria Elene Celllino.

No Retreat, No Surrender 3: Blood Brothers 1991 (R) Sibling martial arts rivals decide to bond in a manly way when CIA agent dad is most heinously slain by terrorists. Answers the burning question: "Whatever became of Joseph Campanella?" 97m/C. Keith Vitali, Loren Avedon, Joseph Campanella; *D:* Lucas Lowe; *W:* Keith W. Strandberg; *C:* John Huneck; *M:* Richard Huen.

No Room to Run 1978 Concert promoter's life turns into a nightmare of deadly espionage intrigue when he arrives in Australia. Luckily, he finds time to fall in love. 101m/C VHS, *AU* Richard Benjamin, Paula Prentiss, Barry Sullivan; *D:* Robert Lewis. TV

No Safe Haven 1987 (R) A government agent seeks revenge for his family's death. 92m/C VHS, DVD. Wings Hauser, Marina Rice, Robert Tessier; *D:* Ronnie Rondell; *W:* Nancy Locke, Wings Hauser; *C:* Steve McWilliams; *M:* Joel Goldsmith.

No Secrets 1991 (R) A young man on the run seeks refuge with three girls in an isolated house. His dread secret isn't so dread, leaving this mild teen-oriented thriller starved for lack of menace. 92m/C VHS. Adam Coleman Howard, Amy Lo-cane, Heather Fairfield, Traci Lind; *D:* Dezso Magyar.

No Sex Please—We're British 1973 Silly—and now dated—sex farce finds a postman accidentally delivering a parcel of pornography to a conservative bank. The contents inflame the bank's stuffy employees and suddenly it's a sexual free-for-all! Based on the play by Anthony Marriott and Alistair Foot. 90m/C VHS. *GB* Ronnie Corbett, Beryl Reid, Arthur Lowe, Ian Ogilvy, Susan Penhaligon, Michael Bates, Gerald Sim, David Swift; *D:* Cliff Owen; *W:* John Mortimer, Anthony Marriott, Brian Cooke; *C:* Ken Hodges; *M:* Eric Rogers.

No Sleep 'Til Madison 2002 Thirty-something Owen (Gaffigan) rounds up his old high school buddies for their yearly trek back to sweet home Wisconsin for their alma mater's hockey tournament. Along the way, he discovers that growing up is hard to do as his chums desert him when adulthood beckons. The message in this lighthearted flick is as subtle as a crosscheck to the face, but the likeable Gaffigan won't be sent to the penalty box for his efforts. 88m/C VHS, DVD. Jim Gaffigan, Rebekah Louise Smith, Ian Brennan, T.J. Jagodowski, Michael Gillo, Jed Resnik, Molly Glynn, Jason Wells, David Fleer, Erik Moe; *D:* David Fleer, Erik Moe, Peter Rudy; *W:* David Fleer, Erik Moe, Peter Rudy; *C:* Bradley W. Milsap; *M:* Stephen (Steve) Edwards.

No Small Affair 1984 (R) A 16-year-old aspiring photographer becomes romantically involved with a sultry 22-year-old rock star. 102m/C VHS, DVD. Jon Cryer, Demi Moore, George Wendt, Peter Frechette, Elizabeth (E.G. Dailey) Daily, Tim Robbins, Jennifer Tilly, Ric(k) Ducommun, Ann Wedgeworth; *D:* Jerry Schatzberg; *C:* John A. Alonzo; *M:* Rupert Holmes.

No Strings Attached 1998 (R) Mark Demetrius (Spano) is a reporter working on a story about women's sexual fantasies. To the distress of his fiancee, he enters a relationship with a mysterious woman he knows only through telephone conversations. To nobody's surprise, murder ensues. 97m/C VHS, DVD. Vincent Spano, Cheryl Pollak, Traci Lind, David Packer, Michael McKean; *D:* Josef Rusnak; *W:* Nicholas Bogner, Michael Holden; *C:* Wedigo von Schultzendorff; *M:* Eric Lundmark.

No Such Thing 2001 (R) This "Beauty and the Beast" fairytale for grownups doesn't always work but it's at least intriguing. Burke stars as an ill-tempered, drunken, ageless, nameless monster who has been terrorizing the remote areas of Iceland. When timid Beatrice (Polley) learns that her fiance, part of a news crew, has been slaughtered by the beast, she persuades her ratings-driven TV news show boss (Mirren) to send her to follow up on the story. Monster and Beatrice develop an unexpected rapport and she brings him back to New York where he's exploited, not unknowingly, as the lastest celeb. 103m/C VHS, DVD. *US* Sarah Polley, Robert Burke, Helen Mirren, Julie Christie, Baltasar Kormakur; *D:* Hal Hartley; *W:* Hal Hartley; *C:* Michael Spiller; *M:* Hal Hartley.

No Surrender 1986 (R) An unpredictable, darkly charming comedy about a Liverpool nightclub newly managed by Angelis. On New Year's Eve, a small drunken war is triggered when two groups of irate senior citizens are booked into the club and clash over their beliefs. The group is made up of Protestants and Catholics and the fight resembles the ongoing conflicts in modern-day Northern Ireland, although most of the action takes place in the loo. Watch for Costello as an inept magician. 100m/C VHS. *GB* Ray McAnally, Michael Angelis, Avis Bunnage, James Ellis, Tom Georgeson, Mark Mulholland, Joanne Whalley, Elvis Costello, Bernard Hill, Michael Ripper; *D:* Peter Smith; *W:* Alan Bleasdale; *C:* Michael Coulter; *M:* Daryl Runswick.

No Survivors, Please *Der Chef Wuenscht Keine Zeugen; The Chief Wants No Survivors* 1963 Aliens from Orion take over politicians in order to rule the Earth. Bizarre, obscure, dated-looking story. 92m/B VHS. *GE* Maria Perschy, Uwe Friedrichsen, Robert Cunningham, Karen Blanguernon, Gustavo Rojo; *D:* Hans Albin, Peter Bemeis.

No Time for Romance ✍ *1948* A sprightly musical with an all-black cast. First such film to be shot in color. *?m/* C VHS. **Joel** Fluellen, Eunice Wilson, Austin McCoy, Shirley Haven, Bill Walker.

No Time for Sergeants ✍✍✍ *1958* Hilarious film version of the Broadway play by Ira Levin, which was based on the novel by Mac Hyman. Griffith is excellent as Georgia farm boy Will Stockdale, who gets drafted into the service and creates mayhem among his superiors and colleagues. Of course, Griffith had already played the role both on stage and in a TV version. McCormick was also repeating his Broadway role of Sgt. King. Note Don Knotts in a small role along with Jameel Farah, who went on to star in TV's "M*A*S*H" after changing his name to Jamie Farr. *119m/B* VHS. Andy Griffith, Nick Adams, Murray Hamilton, Myron McCormick, Howard Smith, Will Hutchins, Sydney Smith, Don Knotts, Jamie Farr; *D:* Mervyn LeRoy; *W:* John Lee Mahin; *C:* Harold Rosson; *M:* Ray Heindorf.

No Tomorrow ✍✍ *1999 (R)* Criminal Busey works with shipping-company employee Daniels to broker a multimillion-dollar arms deal. As word of the deal spreads, both a gangster (Master P) and an FBI agent (Grier) get involved as well. Lots of shootouts and explosions cover the threadbare plot. *95m/C* VHS, DVD. Gary Busey, Gary Daniels, Pam Grier, Jeff Fahey, Master P; *D:* Master P. VIDEO

No Time to Die ✍ *1984* In Indonesia, two corporate pawns and a beautiful reporter battle for the possession of a new laser cannon. *87m/C* VHS. GE Chris Mitchum, John Phillip Law, Grazyne Dylong; *D:* Helmut Ashley; *W:* Wolfgang Grasshoff; *M:* Hans Hammerschmid.

No Turning Back ✍✍½ *2001 (R)* Intriguing, based-on-real-events story of Pablo Hernandez (Nebot), an illegal immigrant who came to southern California after losing everything except his six-year-old daughter, Cristina (Rendon), during 1998's Hurricane Mitch in Honduras. After Pablo unintentionally mows down a well-to-do young girl with a borrowed truck, the pair is on the run with Sofd (Pr'ce), a struggling journalist who agrees to aid the desperate man in exchange for filming the getaway. Along with playing the lead role, Nebot also co-wrote and makes his debut as co-director. *98m/C* VHS, DVD. Jesus Nebot, Lindsay Price, Vernee Watson-Johnson, Susan Haskell, Chelsea Rendon, Joe Estevez, Niki Botelho, Kenya Moore, Gage Hunter Bejarik; *D:* Jesus Nebot, Julia Montejo; *W:* Jesus Nebot, Julia Montejo; *C:* Ian Fox; *M:* Steven Chesne. VIDEO

No Trace ✍✍ *1950* A writer who broadcasts his crime stories as part of a radio show is the victim of blackmail. It seems a former associate is aware that the stories are all based in fect. A Scotland Yard detective investigates when murder rears its ugly head. *76m/B* VHS. GB Hugh Sinclair, Dinah Sheridan, John Laurie, Barry Morse, Michael Brennan, Cora Bryar; *D:* John Gilling.

No Way Back woof! *Ah'ti No Way Back* *1990 (R)* Two men find themselves in a trashy mess when they come to the aid of a damsel in distress while hunting the backwoods. One man dies and the other, Fletcher (Scott), must stop a family feud if he hopes to survive. Actually filmed in 1989, this terrible terror movie sat on the shelf for 16 years before our good friends at Troma decided to rescue it. *90m/C* DVD. Campbell Scott, Virginia Lantry, Berne (Bernard) White, John Durbin, Sean McGuirk, Dennis Ott; *D:* Frank Kerr.

No Way Back ✍✍ *1996 (R)* FBI agent Zack Grant (Crowe) has never dealt with the death of his wife in childbirth and his career has suffered. His last professional chance is a sting operation involving the Mafia and the Yakuza. But when the operation goes wrong, Giant has a vendetta on his hands. Mafia toss Serafino (Lerner) kidnaps Zack's young son so Zack will turn over his prisoner—Yuji (Toyokawa), a Yakuza whom Serfano believes is responsible for his own son's death, and he doesn't care who gets in his way, including his fellow feds and the gangsters. *92m/C* VHS, DVD. Russell Crowe, Helen Slater, Michael Lerner, Etsushi Toyokawa, Ian Ziering; *D:* Frank Cappello; *M:* Frank Cappello; *C:* Richard Clabaugh; *M:* David Williams.

No Way Home ✍✍ *1996 (R)* Joey (Roth), who's mentally a little slow, returns to his tough Staten Island neighborhood after being paroled from prison. He goes to live with his low-level drug dealer older brother Tommy (Russo) and Tommy's wife, Lorrain (Unger), who's rct too happy with the situation—at first. But Joey's basically a decent guy and Lorran begins to respond to his consideration. Meanwhile, shark and his behavior may once again find Joey taking the rap for his brother's misdeeds. (Potlier) works on in cast definitely rises above the material. *101m/C* VHS, DVD. Catherine Kellner, Joe Ragno, Tim Roth, James Russo, Deborah Kara Unger; *D:* Buddy Giovinazzo; *W:* Buddy Giovinazzo; *C:* Claudia Raschke; *M:* Ricky Giovinazzo.

No Way Out ✍✍ *1950* When bigoted bad guy Roy Biddle (Bellaver) and his brother George (Bellaver) are shot, they're taken to a small hospital run by Dr. Wharton (McNally), who believes in giving all his doctors a fair chance. So black doctor Luther Brooks (Potlier) works on George, who dies. Naturally, Roy blames the doctor and gets his hoodlum pals to cause some bloody confrontations. *105m/B* VHS. Sidney Poitier, Richard Widmark, Stephen McNally, Linda Darnell, Harry Bellaver, Stanley Ridges, Ruby Dee, Ossie Davis; *D:* Joseph L. Mankiewicz; *W:* Joseph L. Mankiewicz, Lesser Samuels; *C:* Milton Krasner; *M:* Alfred Newman.

No Way Out ✍✍✍ *1987 (R)* Career Navy man Tom Farrel (Costner) is involved with a beautiful, sexy party girl, Susan (Young), who gets killed. Turns out she was also the mistress of Secretary of Defense Brice (Hackman), Tom's boss. Assigned to investigate her suspicious death, Tom suddenly finds himself set up as the chief suspect. A tight thriller based on 1948's "The Big Clock," with a new surprise ending. Costner looks fine in his Navy whites and there's a backseat limousine sex scene that's quite steamy. *114m/C* VHS, DVD. Kevin Costner, Sean Young, Gene Hackman, Will Patton, Howard Duff, George Dzundza, Iman Chris D, Marshall Bell, Jason Bernard, Fred Dalton Thompson, David Paymer, Iman; *D:* Roger Donaldson; *W:* Robert Garland; *C:* John Alcott; *M:* Maurice Jarre.

No Way to Treat a Lady ✍✍✍ *1968* Steiger is a psychotic master of disguise who stalks and kills various women in this suspenseful cat-and-mouse game. Segal, as the detective assigned to the case, uncovers clues, falls in love, and discovers that his new girl may be the killer's next victim. *108m/C* VHS, DVD. Rod Steiger, Lee Remick, George Segal, Eileen Heckart, Murray Hamilton; *D:* Jack Smight; *W:* John Gay; *C:* Jack Priestley.

No Vacancy ✍✍½ *1999 (R)* LA's Pink Motel may be a dump but it feels like home to the kooky folks who are hanging out there, such as Lillian (Ricco), who's shook up to see that the man in her bed isn't her fiance. Also, there's two druggies who stiff their working girls andhave to deal with the gals' super-slick pimp (Wagner). *83m/C* VHS, DVD. Olek Krupa, Lolita (David) Davidovich, Timothy Olyphant, Christina Ricci, Ryan Bollman, Steven Schub, Tracy Tutor, Joaquim de Almeda, Patricia Velasquez, Graham Beckel, Gabriel Mann, Robert Wagner, Rhona Bennet, June Velar, Tracey Minner, Micaela Lookridge, 'rina Gasanova, Tom Todoroff; *D:* Marius Balchunas; *W:* Marius Balchunas; *C:* Denis Maloney; *M:* Jeff Marsh, Alex Wurman. VIDEO

No Way Back ✍✍ *1974* Way. Writer, director, and producer Williamson portrays Jess Crowder, a man-for-hire who is an expert with guns, fists, and martial arts. An angry look at the white establishment. *92m/C* VHS. Fred Williamson, Charles Woolf, Tracy Reed, Virginia Gregg, Don Cornelius; *D:* Fred Williamson.

No Witness ✍½ *2004 (R)* Shady Senator Gene Haskell (Fahey) is having some problems staying on the right side of the law and makes his gopher Leiter (Feldman) his pawn in covering up the misdeeds. The thorough hit man Paul (Barnes) hired by gives even the senator the willies. All-too-familiar thriller-wannabe includes some familiar faces who don't further the cause. *95m/C* DVD. Jeff Fahey, Corey Feldman, Michael Damian, Steve Barnes, Marisa Petroro; *D:* Michael Valverde, Steve Antczak. VIDEO

The Noah ✍✍ *1975* Bouria's only appearance on the festival circuit in 1951 is allegorically depicted by the school vs. murky B&W post-apocalyptic nightmare. Former soldier Noah (character actor Strauss) is the only survivor of a nuclear holocaust. He finds himself marooned on an island that once housed a Communist Chinese military facility, thus offering him shelter. Unable to cope with his solitude, Noah begins hearing voices that grow into problems, including a war, which Noah must battle. A definite cinematic oddity. *107m/B* DVD. Robert Strauss; *D:* Daniel Bourla; *C:* Jerry Kalogeratos; *V:* Geoffrey Holder, Sally Kirkland, Jim Blackmore.

Noah ✍✍ *1998* Contemporary update of the biblical story of Noah and his ark, retold for laughs (and morals). Busy widowed contractor Norman Waters (Danza) has three sons to provide for and can't spend as much time with them as he may like. Then a heavenly bureaucrat (Shawn) comes down and tells Norman to build an ark in the usual 40 days. At least it brings the family together. *90m/C* VHS. Tony Danza, Wallace Shawn, Jane Sibbett; *D:* Ken Kwapis. TV

Noah's Ark ✍✍ *1999* Made-for-TV biblical epic of the Old Testament story that doesn't exactly stay close to its biblical roots. It's eccentric, special effects-laden, and borders on the irreverent. Noah builds his ark, gathers the animals (and his family), watches as the world is destroyed, and survives the 40 days and nights of flooding. *178m/C* VHS, DVD. Jon Voight, Mary Steenburgen, F. Murray Abraham, Carol Kane, James Coburn, Jonathan Cake, Alexis Denisof, Emily Mortimer, Sydney Tamiia Poitier, Sonya Walger; *D:* John Irvin; *W:* Peter Barnes; *C:* Mike Molloy; *M:* Paul Grabowsky. TV

Noble House ✍✍½ *1988* Continuation of James Clavell's "Hong Kong series, following "Tai-Pan," and set in the present day. Ian Dunross (Brosnan) is the head of Struan and Company, Hong Kong's leading trading company, which is being undermined by the nefarious Quillan Gornt (Rhys-Davies) who plots to destroy his archrival. American businesswoman Casey Tcholok (the bland Raffin) serves as Dunross' love interest. Originally a four-part TV miniseries partially filmed on location. *350m/C* VHS. Pierce Brosnan, John Rhys-Davies, Deborah Raffin, Ben Masters, Julia Nickson-Soul, Khigh (Kaie Deei) Deigh, Tia Carrere, Gordon Jackson; *D:* Gary Nelson; *W:* Eric Bercovici; *C:* Cristiano Pogany; *M:* Paul Chihara.

Nobody ✍✍ *1999* Three business-men get involved in a bar fight that isn't your average brawl. In fact, the situation begins to take over their lives and there no longer certain even who they're fighting. Japanese with subtitles. *100m/C* VHS, DVD. JP Masaya Kato, Jinpachi Nezu, Riki Takeuchi, Hideo Nakano; *D:* Shundo Okuawa, Toshimichi Ohkawa; *W:* Shundo Ohkawa.

Nobody Knows ✍✍✍½ *Dare mo shiranai* *2004 (PG-13)* Inspired by a true story that happened in 1988, Koreeda's overly long drama follows the lives of four abandoned children. Irresponsible Keiko (You) smuggles her brood into a Tokyo apartment, refusing to let them attend school and giving them bizarre rules to follow so they won't be discovered. 12-year-old Akira (Yuya) is the ce facto head of the family, especially when mom leaves a little cash and takes off with her latest boyfriend. Akira soon realizes she isn't returning and struggles to keep the family together under increasingly dire circumstances. Japanese with subtitles. *141m/C* DVD. Yuya Yagira, Ayu Kitaura, Momoko Shimizu, Hanae Kan, Hiei Kimura; *D:* Hirokazu Kore-eda; *C:* Yutaka Yamazaki; *M:* Gontiti.

Nobody's Baby ✍✍ *2001 (R)* Proman's "Raising Arizona" with Ulrich and Oldman playing hick vs. hick in the battle for an orphaned baby. Orphaned themselves at a young age, hillbilly brothers Billy and Buford have turned to crime, facing hard prison time and a court-ordered separation from one another until they escape from the paddy wagon on the way to the young-un National. Splitting up, dim Billy triggers a car crash which kills everyone aboard except a baby. Absconding with the child, Billy gets and caring for the tot from truck stop waitress Shauna (Mitchell). Buford joins the party with the plan to ransom the kid off to still-living relatives, only to discover that Billy has grown attached to the two attempt to secure funds to raise the child as their own. Only Ulrich is able to bring any interest to the weak, patchy script and unmemorable performances. *113m/C* VHS, DVD. Skeet Ulrich, Gary Oldman, Radha Mitchell, Mary Steenburgen, Gordon Tootoosis, Anna Gunn, Peter Greene, Ed O'Neill, Matthew Modine; *D:* David Seltzer; *M:* Christopher Taylor; *M:* Brian Tyler; *C:* Joseph Vitarelli.

Nobody's Daughter ✍✍ *1976* The tragedy of an eight-year-old orphan shuttled from one family to another, all of whom are only interested in the money the government will pay for her care. In Hungarian with English subtitles. *90m/C* VHS. HU Zsuzsi Czinkoczi; *D:* Lazlo Ranody.

Nobody's Fool ✍✍ *1986 (PG-13)* Another entry in the genre of quirky Americana, this romantic comedy concerns a travelling stage-hand. *107m/C* VHS, DVD. Rosanna Arquette, Eric Roberts, Mare Winningham, Louise Fletcher, Jim Youngs, Gwen Welles, Stephen Tobolowsky, Charlie Barnett, Lewis Arquette; *D:* Evelyn Purcell; *W:* Beth Henley; *C:* Mikhail Suslov; *M:* James Newton Howard.

Nobody's Fool ✍✍✍½ *1994 (R)* Newman shines as 60-year-old Donald "Sully" Sullivan, a construction worker who, in spite of himself, begins mending his many broken relationships over the course of the holiday season. Seemingly plotless scenario is sprinkled with enough humor, hope, and understated celebration of a perfectly ordinary man. Characters-driven story is blessed with commendable performances by supporting players—obviously inspired by Newman's brilliant portrayal. Based on the novel by Richard Russo. *110m/C* VHS, DVD. Paul Newman, Jessica Tandy, Bruce Willis, Melanie Griffith, Dylan Walsh, Pruitt Taylor Vince, Gene Saks, Josef Sommer, Philip Seymour Hoffman, Philip Bosco, Margo Martindale, Jay Patterson; *D:* Robert Benton; *C:* John Bailey; *M:* Howard Shore, Benin Intl. Film Fest. '94: Actor (Newman); N.Y. Film Critics '94: Support. Actor (New-man); N.Y. Film Critics '94: Actor (Newman); Nat. Soc. Film Critics '94: Actor (Newman).

Nobody's Perfect woof! *1990* Where "Tootsie" and "Some Like it Hot" collide (or more likely crash and burn). A lovesick teenager masquerades as a girl and joins the tennis team to be near his dream girl. Takes its title from Joe E. Brown's famous last line in "Some Like It Hot." *90m/C* VHS. Chad Lowe, Gail O'Grady, Patrick Breen, Kim Flowers, Robert Vaughn; *D:* Robert Kaylor; *W:* Joel Block.

Nobody's Perfekt woof! *1979 (PG)* Supposed comedy about three psychiatric patients who decide to extort $650,000 from the city of Miami when their car is wrecked. Lacks laughs and generally considered a turkey. *95m/C* VHS. Gabe Kaplan, Robert Klein, Alex Karras, Susan Clark; *D:* Peter Bonerz.

Nocturna woof! *Nocturna, Granddaughter of Dracula* 1979 (R) Hard times have fallen upon the house of Dracula. To help pay the taxes on the castle, the owners have converted it to the Hotel Transylvania. In order to increase business and the blood supply at the hotel, Nocturna books a disco group to entertain the guests. Hard times fell on this script, too. It's no wonder that director Tampa hid behind the alias Harry Hurwitz. **82m/C VHS.** Yvonne De Carlo, John Carradine, Antony (Tony) Hamilton, Nai Bonet; **D:** Harry (Hurwitz) Tampa; **C:** Mac Ahlberg.

Nocturne 🐾🐾½ 1946 A police lieutenant investigates the supposed suicide of a famous composer and uncovers dark secrets that suggest murder is afoot. An overlooked RKO production shines thanks to Raft's inimitable tough guy performance and some offbeat direction. For film noir completists. **88m/B VHS.** George Raft, Lynn Bari, Virginia Huston, Joseph Pevney, Myrna Dell, Edward Ashley, Walter Sande, Mabel Paige; **D:** Edwin L. Marin; **W:** Rowland Brown, Jonathan Latimer; **C:** Harry Wild; **M:** Leigh Harline.

Noel 🐾½ 2004 (PG) Not designed for Christmas cheer, this coal-in-your-stocking drama (Palmintieri's directorial debut) follows the intertwined stories of several lonely New Yorkers searching for happiness on Christmas Eve. Rose (Sarandon) is a divorced, workaholic book editor desperately trying for a final reconciliation with a mother who's in the last stages of Alzheimer's. Nina (Cruz) and Mike (Walker) are engaged but Mike's pathological jealousy is about to destroy the relationship. Walter Artie (Arkin) thinks Mike is the reincarnation of his dead wife(!) and follows him around constantly. And homeless Jules's (Thomas) one happy holiday memory was a party in the hospital emergency room so he decides to have an "emergency." When Robin Williams shows up (unbilled) to give advice, you know you're in trouble. **96m/C DVD.** *US* Penelope Cruz, Susan Sarandon, Paul Walker, Alan, Arkin, Marcus Thomas, Chazz Palminteri, Robin Williams; **D:** Chazz Palminteri; **W:** David Hubbard; **C:** Russell Carpenter; **M:** Alan Menken.

Noi 🐾🐾 *Noi Albinoi; Noi the Albino* 2003 (PG-13) Feature debut of Kari is set in a remote Icelandic fjord village cut off from the world by winter weather. Noi (Lemarquis) is a misfit 17-year-old who lives with his eccentric grandma (Fridriksdottir) and gets expelled from school for being a smart-ass. He begins a diffident romance with newcomer Iris (Hansdottir) and wants to escape the constraints of his life, but just can't manage to get anywhere—much like the film. Icelandic with subtitles. **90m/C DVD. IC GE GB DK** Tomas Lemarquis, Throstur Leo Gunnarson, Elin Hansdottir; Anna Fridriksdottir, Hjalti Rognvaldsson; **D:** Dagur Kari; **W:** Dagur Kari; **C:** Rasmus Videbaek.

Noir et Blanc 🐾🐾 1986 Antoine (Frappat) is a shy accountant who takes a job in a health club and begins an increasingly sado-masochistic relationship with black masseur, Jacques (Martial). The violence is inferred not actually shown but still makes for some kinky adult fare. Based on a short story by Tennessee Williams; debut film for director Devers. French with subtitles. **82m/B VHS.** *FR* Francis Frappat, Jacques Martial, Josephine Fresson, Marc Berman, Claire Rigollier; **D:** Claire Devers; **W:** Claire Devers.

Noises Off 🐾🐾½ 1992 (PG-13) An Americanization of a British farce about a group of second-rate actors touring a group of second-rate actors touring a sex comedy and their convoluted private lives. Wretched rehearsals and equally disasterous preformances, backstage sniping, lovers' quarrels, and a beleaguered director all bumble along together. It worked better on the stage, where it was a Broadway hit, but the actors at least have some fun with the material. Based on the play by Michael Frayn. **101m/C VHS, DVD.** Michael Caine, Carol Burnett, Denholm Elliott, Julie Hagerty, Marilu Henner, Mark Linn-Baker, Christopher Reeve, John Ritter, Nicolette Sheridan; **D:** Peter Bogdanovich; **W:** Marty Kaplan; **M:** Phil Marshall.

Nomad Riders 🐾 1981 A la "Mad Max," (though with an even smaller budget and a decided lack of originality) one rugged man goes after the bikers who killed his wife and daughter. **82m/C VHS.** Wayne Chema, Richard Cluck, Ron Gregg; **D:** Frank Roach.

Nomads 🐾🐾½ 1986 (R) A supernatural thriller set in Los Angeles about a French anthropologist who is mysteriously killed, and the woman doctor who investigates and becomes the next target of a band of strange street people with nomadic spirits. Nomad notables include pop stars Adam Ant and Josie Cotton. **91m/C VHS, DVD.** Pierce Brosnan, Lesley-Anne Down, Adam Ant, Anna Maria Monticelli, Mary Woronov, Hector Mercado; **D:** John McTiernan; **W:** John McTiernan; **C:** Stephen Ramsey; **M:** Bill Contl.

Nomads of the North 🐾🐾½ 1920 Vintage silent melodrama set in the North Woods about a requisite young girl beset by evil villians, a climactic forest fire, and a dashing Mountie who allows a man wrongly sought by the law to be reunited with the woman he secretly loves. Also available at 75 minutes. **108m/B VHS, DVD.** Lon Chaney Sr., Lewis Stone, Betty Blythe; **D:** David M. Hartford.

Nomugi Pass 🐾🐾½ 1979 A young woman working in a Japanese silk mill in the early 1900s must endure hardship and abuse. English subtitles. **154m/C VHS.** *JP* Shinobu Otake, Meiko Harada, Rentaro Mikuni, Takeo Jii; **D:** Satsuo Yamamoto; **W:** Satsuo Yamamoto; **C:** Setsuo Kobayashi; **M:** Masaru Sato.

Non-Stop New York 🐾🐾½ 1937 Mystery tale with interesting twist. A wealthy woman can give an alibi for a murder suspect, but no one will listen, and she is subsequently framed. Pays homage to Hitchcock with its photography and humor. Quick and charming. **71m/B VHS.** Anna Lee, John Loder, Francis L. Sullivan, Frank Cellier, Desmond Tester, Athene Seyler, William Dewhurst, Drusilla Wills, Jerry Verno, James Pirrie, Ellen Pollock, Arthur Goullet, James Carew, Alf Goddard, Danny Green; **D:** Robert Stevenson; **W:** Curt Siodmak, Roland Perlwee, Derek Twist, J.O.C. Orton, E.V.H. Emmett; **C:** Mutz Greenbaum.

None But the Brave 🐾🐾 1965 During WWII, an American bomber plane crash-lands on an island already inhabited by stranded Japanese forces. After a skirmish, the two groups initiate a fragile truce, with the understanding that fighting will resume if one or the other sends for help. The Americans repair their radio unit and must decide on their next actions. Sinatra's directorial debut is a poor effort. **105m/C VHS.** Frank Sinatra, Clint Walker, Tommy Sands, Brad Dexter, Tony Bill, Tatsuya Mihashi, Takeshi Kato, Sammy Jackson; **D:** Frank Sinatra; **M:** John Williams.

None But the Lonely Heart 🐾🐾🐾 1944 In the days before WWII, a Cockney drifter (Grant) wanders the East End of London. When his get-rich-quick schemes fail, his dying shopkeeper-mother tries to help and lands in prison. Interesting characterization of life in the slums. Odets not only directed, but wrote the screenplay. **113m/B VHS, DVD.** Cary Grant, Ethel Barrymore, Barry Fitzgerald, Jane Wyatt, Dan Duryea, George Coulouris, June Duprez; **D:** Clifford Odets; **W:** Clifford Odets; **C:** George Barnes. Oscars '44: Support. Actress (Barrymore).

Noon Sunday 🐾 1975 (PG) A cold war situation in the Pacific explodes into an orgy of death. **104m/C VHS.** Mark Lenard, John Russell, Linda Avery, Keye Luke; **D:** Terry Bourke; **W:** Terry Bourke; **C:** Akira Mimura; **M:** Nick Demuth.

Noon Wine 🐾🐾🐾 1984 Dramatization of Katherine Anne Porter's classic story about a Swedish worker on a Texas farm who becomes the center of a family battle. Made for PBS' American Playhouse. **60m/C VHS.** Fred Ward, Lise Hilboldt, Stellan Skarsgard, Jon Cryer; **D:** Michael Fields. **TV**

The Noose Hangs High 🐾🐾 1948 This broad comedy has our heroes as window washers mistaken for gamblers and getting involved with a bunch of gang-

sters. Much physical and verbal shenanigans as only these two can do it. The bits may be a bit old, but they're done with a fresh twist. Some good word play with the phrase "You can't be here" runs in the same vein as their classic "Who's on first?" routine. Genuinely funny. **77m/B VHS, DVD.** Bud Abbott, Lou Costello, Cathy Downs, Joseph Calleia, Leon Errol, Mike Mazurki, Jack Overman, Fritz Feld, Vera Martin, Joe (Joseph) Kirk, Matt Willis, Benny Rubin; **D:** Charles T. Barton.

Nora 🐾🐾½ 2000 (R) In a film about the passionate relationship between two people, there's actually little heat to be found, although the leads are effective. Ambitious would-be writer James Joyce (McGregor) and hotel maid Nora Barnacle (Lynch) meet in Dublin in 1904. Nora soon becomes his muse, common-law wife, and the mother of his children but insecure Joyce is mistrustful of her faithfulness and the two are locked in a constant battle as they travel between Italy and Ireland and Joyce seeks to find a publisher for his work. Based on the book by Brenda Maddox. **106m/C VHS, DVD.** *IR GB GE* Ewan McGregor, Susan Lynch, Peter McDonald, Roberto Citran, Andrew Scott, Vincent McCabe, Veronica Duffy, Aedin Moloney, Darragh Kelly; **D:** Pat Murphy; **W:** Gerard Stembridge, Pat Murphy; **C:** Jean-Francois Robin; **M:** Stanislas Syrewicz. **VIDEO**

Nora's Hair Salon 🐾🐾 2004 (R) Girlfriends get together and dish the dirt at Nora's (Lewis) L.A. salon in this lively yet not quite as folksy female take on "Barbershop" where Nora plays mom to her staff and customers. Whitney Houston cameos. **84m/C VHS, DVD.** Jenifer Lewis, Tatyana Ali, Bobby Brown, Christine Carlo, Tamala Jones, Pras, Kimberly (Lil' Kim) Jones; **D:** Jerry LaMothe; **W:** Jean-Claude La Marre; **C:** Robert Humphreys. **VIDEO**

Nora's Hair Salon 2: A Cut Above 🐾🐾 2008 (PG-13) Nora willed her beauty salon to her two nieces, but the estranged cousins have very different ideas for the business: Lilliana (Ali) wants to keep the shop open and Simone (Dash) wants to sell. There's some sassiness, some romance, and some thoughts on what it means to be family. **80m/C DVD.** Stacey Dash, Tatyana Ali, Bobby Brown, Mekhi Phifer, Christine Carlo, Lucille Soong, Malik Barnhardt; **D:** Jill Maxcy; **W:** Jill Maxcy, Chanel Capra; **C:** Laura Beth Love; **M:** John "Flexx" Simeus. **VIDEO**

Norbit 🐾½ 2007 (PG-13) Eddie does triple duty as meek Norbit, raised in an orphanage by Mr. Wong (Murphy), the worst Asian stereotype since Mickey Rooney in "Breakfast at Tiffany's"), who is bullied into marriage with gargantuan Rasputia (yeah, it's Murphy inside the fat suit). But he's really in love with slender beauty Kate (Newton), whose fiance (Gooding Jr.), is in shady cahoots with Rasputia's intimidating brothers. Like you care, as long as Eddie delivers the predictable laughs. Rick Baker does the special effects makeup. **95m/C DVD, Blu-ray Disc, HD DVD.** *US* Eddie Murphy, Thandie Newton, Terry Crews, Clifton Powell, Cuba Gooding Jr., Eddie Griffin, Katt Micah Williams, Marlon Wayans, Lester "Rasta" Speight; **D:** Brian Robbins; **W:** Charles Murphy, Jay Scherick, David Ronn; **C:** Clark Mathis; **M:** David Newman. Golden Raspberries '07: Worst Actor (Murphy), Worst Support. Actor (Murphy), Worst Support. Actress (Murphy). **CABLE**

Noriega: God's Favorite 🐾🐾½ 2000 Hoskins is the reason to watch this cable drama about Panamanian strongman Gen. Manuel "Tony" Noriega who was deposed in 1989 after the U.S. invasion. He has a complicated political existence that includes Castro, the CIA, Colombian drug cartels, and various rivals for power. **115m/C VHS.** Bob Hoskins, Jeffrey DeMunn, Richard Masur, Nestor Carbonell, Tony Plana, Luis Avalos, Edward Edwards, David Marshall Grant, Rosa Blasi, Denise Blasor, John Verea, Michael Sonich; **D:** Roger Spottiswoode; **W:** Lawrence Wright; **C:** Pierre Mignot. **CABLE**

The Norliss Tapes 🐾🐾 1973 This failed NBC TV pilot is best viewed for its nostalgia value (especially those special effects). Troubled journalist David Norliss (Thinnes) disappears while investi-

gating an attack by an alleged dead man. When his publisher (Porter) investigates, he finds only the recordings that Norliss left behind, which point to some supernatural forces at work. Curtis and Nolan were also responsible for "Kolchak: The Night Stalker." **72m/C DVD.** Roy Thinnes, Don Porter, Angie Dickinson, Claude Akins, Vonetta McGee, Nick Dimitri; **D:** Dan Curtis; **W:** William F. Nolan; **C:** Ben Colman; **M:** Robert Cobert. **TV**

Norma Jean and Marilyn 🐾🐾½ 1995 (R) Blonde screen goddess Marilyn Monroe (Sorvino) is haunted by her past, literally, since she never escapes the legacy of ambitious Norma Jean Baker (Judd). As her relationships and career falter, Norma Jean is always there (thanks to drug-induced hallucinations) to remind Marilyn how worthless she is. Drama deals with Norma Jean's troubled past and how she was willing to do anything to be in the movies, although it (apparently) brought her little happiness. The dual stars work surprisingly well and director Fywell offers the proper camp flair. **133m/C DVD.** Mira Sorvino, Ashley Judd, Josh Charles, Peter Dobson, Ron Rifkin, David Dukes, Taylor Nichols, Lindsay Crouse, John Rubinstein, Steven Culp, Perry Stephens, Earl Boen; **D:** Tim Fywell; **W:** Jill Isaacs; **C:** John Thomas; **M:** Christopher Young. **CABLE**

Norma Rae 🐾🐾🐾 1979 (PG) A poor, uneducated textile worker joins forces with a New York labor organizer to unionize the reluctant workers at a Southern mill. Field was a surprise with her fully developed character's strength, beauty, and humor; her Oscar was well-deserved. Ritt's direction is top-notch. Jennifer Warnes sings the theme song, "It Goes Like It Goes," which also won an Oscar. ♪It Goes Like It Goes. **114m/C VHS, DVD.** Sally Field, Ron Leibman, Beau Bridges, Pat Hingle; **D:** Martin Ritt; **W:** Harriet Frank Jr., Irving Ravetch; **C:** John A. Alonzo; **M:** David Shire. Oscars '79: Actress (Field), Song ("It Goes Like It Goes"); Cannes '79: Actress (Field); Golden Globes '80: Actress—Drama (Field); L.A. Film Critics '79: Actress (Field); Natl. Bd. of Review '79: Actress (Field); N.Y. Film Critics '79: Actress (Field); Natl. Soc. Film Critics '79: Actress (Field).

Normal 🐾🐾 2003 No guts, no glory. And both Wilkinson and Lange had to have guts to make this story work. Roy and Irma Applewood (Wilkinson, Lange) have been married for 25 years and are respected church-going members of their small Illinois farming community. Chronic headaches and stress have Roy seeking counseling—and finally admitting that he has always felt like a woman trapped in a man's body. He's determined to undergo sex-change surgery and tells Irma that he still loves her and wants them to continue living together. Irma's not unreasonably confused, resentful, angry, and, ultimately, loving and supportive as the community turns its back on Roy and his family. Adapted from Anderson's play "Looking for Normal." **108m/C VHS, DVD.** Tom Wilkinson, Jessica Lange, Hayden Panettiere, Joe Sikora, Clancy Brown, Richard Bull, Randall Amey, Mary Seibel; **D:** Jane Anderson; **W:** Jane Anderson; **C:** Alar Kivilo; **M:** Alex Wurman.

Normal Life 🐾🐾 1996 (R) Straightarrow, smalltown Illinois rookie cop Chris Anderson (Perry) comes to the aid of sexy, impetuous biker chick Pam (Judd) and they impulsively marry. Fast forward two years and the willfully irresponsible Pam has turned their lives into a disaster but for some reason Chris (now a security guard) sticks it out, even pulling bank jobs to afford Pam's luxuries. When she finds out what Chris has been doing, Pam insists on joining in, leading to a bitter end. Based on the true story of Jeffrey and Jill Erickson, who went on a bank robbing spree and were killed in 1991. Great lead performances though character motivation is lacking. **108m/C VHS, DVD.** Luke Perry, Ashley Judd, Bruce A. Young, Jim True-Frost, Dawn Maxey, Penelope Milford, Tom Towles, Kate Walsh; **D:** John McNaughton; **W:** Bob Schneider, Peg Haller; **C:** Jean De Segonzac.

Norman Conquest 🐾🐾 *Park Plaza* 1953 Conway finds himself drugged and framed for murder in this bargain-basement thriller. Bartok is the leader of a dia-

The Norman Conquests, Part 1: Table Manners 🎬🎬🎬 1978 Part one of playwright Alan Ayckbourn's comic trilogy of love unfulfilled, as the charmingly unreliable Norman (Conti) works his amorous wiles on three women. 108m/C VHS. *GB* Tom Conti, Penelope Keith Richard Briers, Fiona Walker, David Troughton, Fiona Walker, Penelope Wilton; *D:* Herbert Wise; *W:* Alan Ayckbourn; *C:* Peter Coombs.

The Norman Conquests, Part 2: Living Together 🎬🎬🎬 1978 Part two concerns the happenings in the living room during Norman's disastrous weekend of unsuccessful seduction. 93m/C VHS. *GB* Tom Conti, Penelope Keith Richard Briers, Fiona Walker, David Troughton, Penelope Wilton; *D:* Herbert Wise; *W:* Alan Ayckbourn; *C:* Peter Coombs.

The Norman Conquests, Part 3: Round and Round the Garden 🎬🎬🎬 1978 Part three concerns Norman's furtive appearance in the garden, which suggests that the weekend is going to misfire. 108m/C VHS. *GB* Tom Conti, Penelope Keith Richard Briers, David Troughton, Fiona Walker, Penelope Wilton; *D:* Herbert Wise; *W:* Alan Ayckbourn; *C:* Mike Hobbs.

Norman, Is That You? 🎬1/2 1976 Ursuccessful film adaptation based on the unsuccessful Broadway play about one family's sexual revolution. Revamped by a host of black stars, it's basically a one-joke affair when Foxx discovers his son is gay and living with his white lover. Shot on videotape and transferred to film. 91m/C VHS. Redd Foxx, Pearl Bailey, Dennis Dugan, Michael Warren, Tamara Dobson, Vernee Watson-Johnson, Jayne Meadows, George Furth; *D:* George Schlatter; *W:* George Schlatter, Ron Clark, Sam Bobrick; *M:* William Goldstein.

Norman Loves Rose 🎬1/2 1982 (R) A precocious 13-year-old and his married sister-in-law join forces in this substandard comedy. When Rose tries to help Norman by teaching him about sex, she learns a little too—she's pregnant. 95m/C VHS. Au Carol Kane, Tony Owen, Warren Mitchell, Myra de Groot; *D:* Henri Safran.

Norman's Awesome Experience Woof! 1988 🎬1/2 Three adolescents are transported back in time to the Roman Empire. Bill and Ted, anyone? 90m/C VHS. Tom McCamus, Laurie Paton, Jaques Lussier; *D:* Paul Conovan.

Norseman 🎬1/2 1978 (PG) Leader of a band of Norsemen sets sail for the New World in search of his missing royal father. Low-budget Viking adventure. 90m/C VHS. Lee Majors, Cornel Wilde, Mel Ferrer, Christopher Connelly, Jack Elam; *D:* Charles B. Pierce; *W:* Charles B. Pierce.

North 🎬🎬 1994 (PG) Some laughs with a message in family fare from Reiner. Eleven-year-old ace kid actor Wood divorces his workaholic parents Alexander and Louis-Dreyfus and searches the world for a "functional family (good luck). Willis, who's a treat in a pink bunny suit, acts as guardian angel/narrator and shows the kid what's really important. Illustrious comedic cast inhabits story based on a book by original "Saturday Night Live" screenwriter (and "Gary Shandling Show" co-creator) Zweibel, who put things in motion ten years ago when he asked Reiner to write a book jacket quote for the novel. 87m/C VHS. Elijah Wood, Jason Alexander, Julia Louis-Dreyfus, Bruce Willis, Jon Lovitz, Alan Arkin, Dan Aykroyd, Kathy Bates, Faith Ford, Graham Greene, Reba McEntire, John Ritter, Abe Vigoda, Kelly McGillis, Alexander Godunov, Noriyuki "Pat" Morita, Ben Stein; *D:* Rob Reiner; *M:* Marc Shaiman.

North and South Book 1 🎬🎬🎬 1985 Lavish spectacle about a friendship tested by the turbulent times leading up to Civil War. Orry Main (Swayze) is a South Carolina plantation owner while his best friend George Hazard (Read) comes from a Pennsylvania industrial family. Orry is also involved in a doomed romance with the beautiful Made-line (Down), who's forced to marry the odious Justin LaMotte (Carradine). Lots of intrigue and excitement. Based on the novel by John Jakes. Filmed on location in Charleston, South Carolina. Originally broadcast as a six-part TV miniseries. Available on six cassettes. 561m/C VHS. Patrick Swayze, James Read, Lesley-Anne Down, David Carradine, Kirstie Alley, Jean Simmons, Inga Swenson, Jonathan Frakes, Genie Francis, Terri Garber, Georg Stanford Brown, Olivia Cole, David Ogden Stiers, Robert Guillaume, Hal Holbrook, Gene Kelly, Robert Mitchum, Johnny Cash, Penelope Wilton; *D:* Herbert Wise; *W:* Alan Ayckbourn; *C:* Peter Coombs.

North and South Book 2 🎬🎬 1986 Equally dramatic sequel follows the southern Main clan and the northern Hazard family into the Civil War as friendship and romance struggle to survive the fighting. Casnoff is a notable presence as the aptly named Bent, who will go to any length to settle old scores with both families. Based on the John Jakes novel "Love and War." Originally broadcast as a six-part TV miniseries; on six cassettes. The last of the Jakes trilogy, "Heaven and Hell," was finally filmed for TV in '94 but proved a major disappointment. 570m/C VHS. Patrick Swayze, James Read, Lesley-Anne Down, Terri Garber, Genie Francis, Jean Simmons, Kirstie Alley, Philip Casnoff, Hal Holbrook, Lloyd Bridges, James Stewart, Morgan Fairchild, Nancy Marchand, Parker Stevenson, Lewis Smith; *M:* Bill Conti.

The North Avenue Irregulars 🎬🎬1/2 1979 (G) Slapstick Disney comedy along the same lines as some of their earlier laugh-fests. A priest and three members of the 'ocal ladies' club try to bust a crime syndicate. Though the premise is silly, there are still lots of laughs in this family film. 99m/C VHS, DVD. Edward Herrmann, Barbara Harris, Susan Clark, Karen Valentine, Michael Constantine, Cloris Leachman, Melora Hardin, Alan Hale Jr., Ruth Buzzi, Patsy Kelly, Virginia Capers; *D:* Bruce Bilson; *W:* Don Tait; *C:* Leonard J. South; *M:* Robert F. Brunner.

North by Northwest 🎬🎬🎬🎬 1959 Self-assured Madison Avenue ad exec Roger Thornhill (Grant) inadvertently gets involved with international spies when they mistake him for someone else. His problems are compounded when he's framed for murder and winds up on a cross-country train trip with pretty Eve Kendall (Saint) who offers her help. The movie where Grant and Saint dangle from the faces of Mount Rushmore and a plane chases Grant through farm fields. Exceptional performances, particularly Grant's. Plenty of plot twists are mixed with tongue-in-cheek humor. 136m/C VHS, DVD. Cary Grant, Eva Marie Saint, James Mason, Leo G. Carroll, Martin Landau, Jessie Royce Landis, Philip Ober, Adam Williams, Josephine Hutchinson, Edward Platt; *D:* Alfred Hitchcock; *W:* Ernest Lehman; *C:* Robert Burks. *M:* Bernard Herrmann. AFI '98. 100. Natl. Film Reg. '95.

North Country 🎬🎬1/2 2005 (R) Theron de-glamorizes once again to play Josey Aimes, a hard luck single mom who returns to her Minnesota home town to make a new start. Since the best-paying jobs are working in the mines, Josey decides to become a miner. Eventually fed up with the blatant sexual harassment of her male co-workers and the indifference of her employer, Josey files the first class action lawsuit for sexual harassment in the country (the actual plaintiff, Lois Jenson, sued her employer in 1984). An old-fashioned exercise in social responsibility and the search for justice. 123m/C DVD. US Charlize Theron, Frances McDormand, Sean Bean, Richard Jenkins, Jeremy Renner Michelle Monaghan, Woody Harrelson, Sissy Spacek, Rusty Schwimmer, Jillian Armenante, Thomas Curtis, Elizabeth Peterson, Linda Emond, Amber Heard, Cole Williams; *D:* Niki Caro; *W:* Michael Seitzman; *C:* Chris Menges; *M:* Gustavo Santaolalla.

North Dallas Forty 🎬🎬🎬 1979 (R) Based on the novel by former Dallas Cowboy Peter Gent, the film focuses on the labor abuses in pro-football. One of the best football movies ever made it contains searing commentary and very good acting, although the plot is sometimes dropped behind the line.

Northanger Abbey 🎬🎬 2005 (R) Catherine is a young woman whose head is turned by her romance readings of dark secrets, sinister castles, dashing heroes, and helpless women. When the hardsome Henry Tilney invites her to visit his ancestral home, Northanger Abbey, it seems all her fancies have come to life. A somewhat tepid adaptation of Jane Austen's parody of the popular Gothic romances of her day. 90m/C VHS, DVD. *GB* Peter Firth, Katharine Schlesinger, Google Withers, Robert Hardy; *D:* Giles Foster; *W:* Maggie Wacey; *C:* Nat Crosby; *M:* Ilona Sekacz.

Northanger Abbey 🎬🎬1/2 2007 Spirited teenager Catherine Moreland (Jones) has an over-active imagination, fueled by the popular gothic romances she reads. Taken to fashionable Bath by family friends, Catherine falls in with two different families: the Thorpes and the Tineys. Catherine becomes romantically interested in gentle Henry Tilney (Field) and is invited to their rather sinister family estate.

North Shore 🎬1/2 1987 (PG) A young surfer from Arizona hits the beaches of Hawaii and discovers love, sex, and adventure. Only redeeming quality is surfing footage. 96m/C VHS, DVD. Matt Adler, Nia Peeples, John Philbin, Gregory Harrison, Christina Raines; *D:* Will Phelps.

North Shore Fish 🎬🎬 1997 (R) North Shore Fish is a failing Massachusetts fish-packing factory with various cyndivorcee Flo (Puehl); who's just found out she's pregnant by her married boss Sal (Danza); 60ish Arlyne (Baker), who regards her co-workers as family; and Josie (Schwimmer), whose husband has left her for a younger woman. It's on this one day that they realize how uncertain all their futures are. Based on the play by Israel Horovitz. 95m/C VHS. Mercedes Ruehl, Peter Riegert, Carroll Baker, Tony Danza, Rusty Schwimmer, Wendie Malick, Cordelia Richards; *D:* Steve Zuckerman; *W:* Israel Horovitz; *C:* Levie Isaacks. Copland.

North Star 🎬🎬 1996 (R) Formulaic actioner where no one seems very enthusiastic. Half-breed trapper Hudson (psehawk (Lambert) refuses to mine the gold on his Alaskan property because the land is considered sacred. This doesn't concern greedy miner Sean. McLennon (Caan) who wants the property for himself. Oh yeah, there's also a babe, Sarah (McCormack), that both men are interested in. Norway substitutes for Alaska. Based on the novel by Will Henry. 89m/C VHS. Christopher Lambert, James Caan, Catherine McCormack, Burt Young; *D:* Nils Gaup; *W:* Paul Ohl, Sergio Donati, Lorenzo Donati; *C:* Bruno de Keyzer; *M:* Bruce Rowland.

North to Alaska 🎬🎬 1960 A gold prospector encounters many problems when he agrees to pick up his partner's fiancee in Seattle to bring her home to Nome, Alaska, in the 1890s. Overly slapstick at times, but great fun nonetheless. Loosely based on Laszlo Fodor's play "The Birthday Gift." 120m/C VHS, DVD. John Wayne, Stewart Granger, Ernie Kovacs, Fabian, Capucine; *D:* Henry Hathaway; *C:* Leon Shamroy.

North of the Great Divide 🎬1/2 1950 Standard Rogers programmer, with Roy as a half-breed mediator between salmon fisherman and Indians. 67m/C VHS, DVD, Roy Rogers, Penny Edwards, Gordon Jones, Roy Barcroft, Jack Lambert, Douglas Evans, Noble Johnson; *D:* William Witney.

119m/C VHS, DVD, Nick Nolte, Mac Davis, Charles Durning, Bo Svenson, John Matuszak, Dayle Haddon, Steve Forrest, Dabney Coleman, G.D. Spradlin; *D:* Ted Kotcheff; *W:* Ted Kotcheff, Frank Yablans; *C:* Paul Lohmann; *M:* John Scott.

Northeast of Seoul 🎬 1972 (PG) Three people will stop at nothing to steal a legendary jewel-encrusted sword out of Korea. 84m/C VHS. Anita Ekberg, John Ireland, Victor Buono; *D:* David Lowell Rich.

Northern Extremes 🎬1/2 Buried on Sunday 1993 (PG) Silly comedy about an eccentric Canadian island village whose fishing livelihood is threatened. So the town mayor captures an errant nuclear submarine and uses it as a big bargaining chip. Filmed in Nova Scotia, Canada. 80m/C VHS, DVD. CA Paul Gross, Denise Vireux, Henry Czerny, Jeff Leder, Tommy Sexton, Louis de Grande, Wauny Chaykin; *D:* Paul Donovan; *W:* Rob Nilsson.

Northern Lights 🎬🎬🎬 1979 A small, black-and-white independent drama depicting the struggle of a lowly farmer combating governmental forces in the wilderness. 97m/C VHS. CA Jacques Weber, Lorne Brass, Jeff Faney, Neve Campbell; *D:* Arnaud Selignac; *M:* Jonathan Hales; *C:* Michel Mardero; *M:* Alan Chamfort.

Northern Passage 🎬🎬1/2 1995 (PG-13) Cowboy tries to protect a young Native American woman from harm in the wilderness. 94m/B VHS. Errol Flynn, Helmut Dantine, Julie Bishop, Gene Lockhart, Tom Tully; *D:* Raoul Walsh.

Northern Pursuit 🎬🎬1/2 1943 A Canadian Mountie disguises himself to infiltrate a Nazi spy ring in this exciting adventure film. Based on Leslie White's "Five Thousand Trojan Horses." 94m/B VHS. Errol Flynn, Helmut Dantine, Julie Bishop, Gene Lockhart, Tom Tully; *D:* Raoul Walsh.

Northfork 🎬🎬 2003 (PG-13) Surrealistic fairy tale, with pretensions of examining death and the afterlife, crossed with comical Americana circa 1955. The town of Northfolk is being evacuated to make way for an incoming hydroelectric plant, as a band of strange gypsy angels search for the "unknown angel," thought to be a sick orphan boy who has been left to the town preacher. Patchwork script is a jumble of pompous spiritual pronouncements, kitschy sitcom catch-phrasery, and Lynchian confusion. At least the beautifully-filmed landscape gives you something nice to look at while wondering what the heck is going on. 103m/C VHS, DVD. US James Woods, Nick Nolte, Claire Forlani, Daryl Hannah, Ben Foster, Anthony Edwards, Robin Sachs, Graham Beckel, Peter Coyote, Jon(athan) Gries, Marshall Bell, Kyle MacLachlan, Michele Hicks, Josh Barker; *C:* Michael Polish, Mark Polish, Michael Polish; *C:M.* David Mullen; *M:* Michael Nesmith.

Northville Cemetery Massacre 🎬 The Northfield Cemetery Massacre 1976 (R) Gang of bikers comes to town and all hell breaks loose. The result is a horribly bloody war between the townsfolk and the gang. Yup, it was a massacre. 81m/C VHS, DVD. David Hyry, Craig Collicott, Jan Sisk, Carson Jackson; *D:* William Dear, Thomas ﹘. Dyke; *C:* William Dear, Thomas L. Dyke; *M:* Michael Nesmith.

Northwest Outpost 🎬1/2 Era of the Rainbow 1947 Eddy is a California cavalry officer in this lightweight operetta. He helps a young woman who is trying to free her husband from jail, and after his death they are able to pursue their relationship. 91m/B VHS. Nelson Eddy, Ilona Massey, Hugo Haas, Esa Lanchester, Lenore Ulric; *D:* Allan Dwan.

Carried away by her surroundings, Catherine thoughtlessly upsets Henry and is then left to wonder about her future. Based on the novel by Jane Austen. 90m/C DVD. *GB* Felicity Jones, J.J. Feild, Carey Mulligan, Catherine Walker, Liam Cunningham, Hugh O'Connor, Sophie Yevaisseur, Sylvestra Le Touzel, William Beck, Mark Dymond, Shauna Taylor, Desmond Barrit, Julia Dearden; *D:* Jon Jones; *W:* Andrew Davies; *C:* Ciaran Tanham; *M:* Sue Wyatt; *Nar:* Geraline James. TV.

Northwest Passage ♂♂♂ 1940
The lavish first half of a projected two-film package based on Kenneth Roberts' popular novel, depicting the troop of Rogers' Rangers fighting the wilderness and hostile Indians. Beautifully produced; the second half was never made and the passage itself is never seen. **126m/C VHS.** Spencer Tracy, Robert Young, Ruth Hussey, Walter Brennan, Nat Pendleton, Robert Barrat, Lumsden Hare; **D:** King Vidor.

Northwest Trail ♂♂ 1946 Royal Canadian Mountie Steele's assignment is to escort Woodbury across the wilderness. She's carrying a large sum of money to save her uncle's business. Problem is, killers are on their trail. **75m/C VHS, DVD.** Bob Steele, Joan Woodbury, John Litel, Raymond Hatton, Madge Bellamy, Charles Middleton; **D:** Derwin Abrahams.

Nosferatu ♂♂♂♂ *Eine Symphonie des Grauens; Nosferatu, A Symphony of Terror; Nosferatu, the Vampire; Nosferatu, Die Zwölfte Stunde* 1922 The first film adaptation of Bram Stoker's "Dracula" remains one of the creepiest and most atmospheric versions. Murnau knew how to add just the right touches to make this one of the best vampire films ever made. All it lacks is the name of Dracula, which was changed due to copyright problems with Stoker's widow. Filmed in Bavaria. Silent with music and English titles. Remade by Werner Herzog in 1979. **63m/B VHS, DVD.** *GE* Max Schreck, Alexander Granach, Gustav von Wagenheim, Greta Schroder, John Gottowt, Ruth Landshoff, G.H. Schnell; **D:** F.W. Murnau; **W:** Henrik Galeen; **C:** Fritz Arno Wagner, Gunther Krampf.

Nosferatu the Vampyre ♂♂ *Nosferatu: Phantom der Nacht* 1979 Herzog's tribute to fellow countryman's F.W. Murnau's 1922 silent film interpretation of Bram Stoker's "Dracula" story. It features Kinski as the disgustingly rodent-like Count, with Ganz as Jonathan Harker, and Adjani as Harker's wife and the beautiful object of the Count's lust. Released in a German language version with subtitles and an English language version. **107m/C VHS, DVD.** *FR GE* Klaus Kinski, Isabelle Adjani, Bruno Ganz, Roland Topor, Walter Ladengast; **D:** Werner Herzog; **C:** Jorge Schmidt-Reitwein; **M:** Popul Vuh, Florian Fricke.

Nostalghia ♂♂ 1983 Russian academic Jankovsky comes to Tuscany to research the life of an 18th-century composer and meets the mysterious Josephson, who's convinced the end of the world is near. And soon the homesick Russian is in a search for himself. Filled with Christian iconography and some extraordinary images, Tarkovsky's first film outside his native Russia. Russian and Italian with subtitles; the Russian sequences are filmed in B&W. **126m/C VHS.** *IT* Oleg (Yankovsky) Jankowsky, Erland Josephson, Domiziana Giordano, Delia Boccardo; **D:** Andrei Tarkovsky; **W:** Andrei Tarkovsky, Tonino Guerra; **C:** Giuseppe Lanci.

Nostradamus ♂♂ 1993 (R) Historical soap opera about unconventional 16th-century French physician and astrologer Michel de Nostradame. Persecuted by the Inquisition, he comes under the protection of Queen Catherine de Medici of France, although his visions of destruction and death continue to haunt him. Nostradamus' prophecies, first published in 1555, have continued to fascinate, being used to predict everything from the death of historical leaders to WWI. The film, however, is slow going and fails to hold much interest. **118m/C VHS.** *FR* Tcheky Karyo, F. Murray Abraham, Julia Ormond, Rutger Hauer, Amanda Plummer, Assumpta Serna, Anthony (Corlan) Higgins, Diana Quick, Michael Gough; **D:** Roger Christian; **W:** Knut Boeser, Piers Ashworth.

The Nostradamus Kid ♂♂ 1992 (R) Young man, convinced the world is about to end, decides his last goal will be to make love (for the first time) with his girlfriend. **120m/C VHS.** Miranda Otto, Arthur Dignam; **D:** Bob Ellis.

Nostromo ♂♂ *Joseph Conrad's Nostromo* 1996 Tediously drawn-out TV adaptation of the 1904 novel by Joseph Conrad takes place in the 1890s in the fictional South American country of Costaguana. Englishman Charles Gould (Firth) is determined to reopen his family's silver mine—a plan supported by the local regime, which is, however, soon to be overthrown. Amidst the revolution is the title character Nostromo (Amendola), a contraction of "nostro uomo" or "our man," an enigmatic Italian immigrant who is thrust into the role of hero. Filmed on location in Cartagena, Colombia. On three cassettes. **360m/C VHS.** Colin Firth, Albert Finney, Claudio Amendola, Serena Scott Thomas, Claudia Cardinale, Brian Dennehy, Lothaire Bluteau, Ruth Gabriel, Joaquim de Almeida; **D:** Alastair Reid; **W:** John Hale; **M:** Ennio Morricone. **TV**

Not Another Teen Movie ♂♂½ 2001 (R) Unsuccessful parody of the recent proliferation of bad teen movies and the better John Hughes films of the '80s. Teen moviedom's stereotypes are hammered up to the extreme, from the bitchy teenager to the dumb jock, nerdy beauty-in-waiting and fat guy for comic relief. Which is okay if you like really obvious, unoriginal humor. Film's self-awareness is sometimes amusing but more often sinks to the level of what it's supposed to be satirizing, and of course, there's enough "bodily-function and base sexual jokes to fill three Tom Green flicks. If there was ever a genre begging to be parodied, it's teen movies, but this entry flunks. Entertaining cameos by Molly Ringwald and John Vernon, though. **90m/C VHS, DVD, UMD.** *US* Chyler Leigh, Chris Evans, Eric Jungmann, Eric Christian Olsen, Cody McMains, Sam Huntington, Ron Lester, Samm Levine, Deon Richmond, Jaime Pressly, Mia Kirshner, Riley Smith, Lacey Chabert, Cerina Vincent, Beverly Polcyn, Joanna Garcia, Randy Quaid, Ed Lauter, Mr. T, Paul Gleason, Molly Ringwald; **D:** Joel Gallen; **W:** Michael G. Bender, Adam Jay Epstein, Andrew Jacobson, Phil Beauman, Buddy Johnson; **C:** Reynaldo Villalobos; **M:** Theodore Shapiro.

Not as a Stranger ♂♂½ 1955 Glossy film about the medical profession and the varying degrees of dedication shown by doctors. Mitchum stars as an medical student who can't afford to pay his tuition, so he marries nurse de Havilland and continues going to school on her money, although their relationship is far from being a loving one. Producer Kramer's directorial debut. Based on the book by Morton Thompson. **135m/B VHS.** Olivia de Havilland, Robert Mitchum, Frank Sinatra, Gloria Grahame, Broderick Crawford, Charles Bickford, Myron McCormick, Lon Chaney Jr.; **D:** Stanley Kramer; **W:** Edward Anhalt.

Not for Publication ♂♂ 1984 (R) A woman working as both a tabloid reporter and a mayoral campaign worker uncovers governmental corruption with the help of a shy photographer and a midget. Meant to be on par with older screwball comedies but lacking the wit and subtlety. **87m/C VHS, DVD.** Nancy Allen, David Naughton, Richard Paul, Alice Ghostley, Laurence Luckinbill; **D:** Paul Bartel; **W:** Paul Bartel.

Not in This Town ♂♂½ 1997 (PG-13) Fact-based drama stars Baker as Billings, Montana, housewife Tammie Schnitzer, who is shocked when white supremacists, led by Henry Whitcomb (Begley Jr.), begin harassing religious and ethnic minorities in her town. She forms the Montana Coalition for Human Rights and begins a public appeal to rally the community but soon Tammie and her family need some protection of their own. **95m/C VHS.** Kathy Baker, Adam Arkin, Ed Begley Jr., Bradford Tatum, Max Gail; **D:** Donald Wrye; **W:** Adam Gilad; **M:** Don Davis. **CABLE**

Not Like Us ♂♂½ 1996 (R) Bored Anita's (Pacula) tired of life in her small town and glad to make a new friend in Janet (Grant). But she's shocked to discover Janet may be involved in several mysterious deaths (oh yeah, and she happens to be an alien). **87m/C VHS.** Joanna Pacula, Annabelle Gurwitch, Peter Onorati, Morgan Englund, Rainer Grant; **D:** Dave Payne; **W:** Daniela Purcell.

Not My Kid ♂♂½ 1985 The 15-year-old daughter of a surgeon brings turmoil to her family when she becomes heavily involved in drugs. Producer Polson, along with Dr. Miller Newton, wrote the original book for this emotional story that is one of the better treatments of this important subject. **120m/C VHS.** George Segal, Stockard Channing, Viveka Davis, Andrew (Andy) Robinson, Gary Bayer, Nancy Cartwright, Tate Donovan; **D:** Michael Tuchner; **W:** Christopher Knopf. **TV**

Not of This Earth ♂½ 1988 (R) In a remake of the 1957 Roger Corman quickie, an alien wearing sunglasses makes an unfriendly trip to Earth. In order to save his dying planet he needs major blood donations from unsuspecting Earthlings. Not a match for the original version, some may nevertheless want to see exporn star Lords in her role as the nurse. **92m/C VHS, DVD.** Traci Lords, Arthur Roberts, Lenny Juliano, Rebecca Perle, Ace Mask, Roger Lodge, Michael Delano, Monique Gabrielle, Becky LeBeau; **D:** Jim Wynorski; **W:** Jim Wynorski, R.J. Robertson, Charles B. Griffith, Mark Hanna; **C:** Zoran Hochstatter; **M:** Chuck Cirino.

Not of This Earth ♂♂ 1996 (R) Corman remake of his own 1957 cheapie is both camp and sexy. Sunglass-wearing mystery millionaire Paul Johnson (York) apparently suffers from a rare condition and must have constant blood transfusions, so he hires a sexy live-in nurse (Barondes) to be at his beck-and-call. Yes, he does turn out to be a vampire but of the space alien-with-telepathic-powers variety who has a particular purpose for coming to earth. **92m/C VHS, DVD.** Michael York, Elizabeth Barondes, Richard Belzer, Parker Stevenson; **D:** Terence H. Winkless; **W:** Charles Philip Moore. **CABLE**

Not of This World ♂♂½ *Fuori dal Mondo* 1999 Sister Caterina (Buy) is a novice, about to take her final vows, when she discovers a baby abandoned in a park. Although she takes the baby to a hospital and learns the child will be put up for adoption, Caterina can't ignore her surge of maternal feelings and decides to search for the baby's parents. When she traces a cleaning tag from the sweater the baby was wrapped in, Caterina meets Ernesto (Orlando), the middle-aged owner of a local laundry who suspects he may be the baby's father. The duo both take long looks at their lives and wonder if they should may some changes. Italian with subtitles. **100m/C VHS, DVD.** *IT* Margherita Buy, Silvio Orlando, Carolina Freschi, Maria Cristina Minerva; **D:** Giuseppe Piccioni; **W:** Gualtiero Rosella, Giuseppe Piccioni, Lucia Maria Zei; **C:** Luca Bigazzi; **M:** Ludovico Einaudi.

Not One Less ♂♂½ *Yi Ge Dou Bu Neng Shao* 1999 (G) Gao is teaching in a rundown rural Chinese school when he is called away to visit his dying mother. The only substitute he can find is 13-year-old Wei Minzhi, who's scarcely older than her would-be students. Because so many children are forced to leave school because of their poverty-stricken families, Gao promises the girl extra money if she will keep all the pupils in class until he returns. When Zhang Huike must go to work in the city, Wei Minzhi is stubbornly determined to find and bring him back. Mandarin with subtitles. **106m/C VHS, DVD.** *CH* Wei Minzhi, Zhang Huike, Gao Enman; **D:** Yimou Zhang; **W:** Shi Xiangsheng; **C:** Hou Yong; **M:** San Bao.

Not Quite Human ♂♂ 1987 When Jonas Carson builds himself an android teenage son, he must keep the technology from falling into the hands of an evil toy manufacturer with plans of his own. Humorous hijinks abound. Based on the book series "Not Quite Human" by Seth McEvoy. Followed by two sequels. **91m/C VHS.** Alan Thicke, Robyn (Robyn) Lively, Robert Harper, Joseph Bologna, Jay Underwood; **D:** Steven Hilliard Stern. **CABLE**

Not Quite Human 2 ♂♂½ 1989 In this sequel, Dr. Jonas Carson sends his cyber-son off to college where Chip meets the not-quite-human girl of his dreams. Followed by "Still Not Quite Human." **91m/C VHS.** Alan Thicke, Jay Underwood, Robin (Ro-byn) Lively, Greg Mullavey, Katie Barberi, Mark Arnott; **D:** Eric Luke. **CABLE**

Not Quite Paradise ♂ *Not Quite Jerusalem* 1986 (R) A young American medical student falls in love with a young Israeli girl living on a kibbutz. **106m/C VHS.** Sam Robards, Joanna Pacula; **D:** Lewis Gilbert.

Not Tonight Darling ♂ 1972 (R) A bored suburban housewife becomes involved with a fast-talking businessman who leads her into a web of deceit and blackmail. **90m/C VHS.** *GB* Luan Peters, Vincent Ball, Jason Twelvetrees, James Hayter; **D:** Anthony Slocombe; **W:** Christopher Gregory, James Pillock; **C:** Harry Waxman.

Not Without My Daughter ♂♂½ 1990 (PG-13) Overwrought drama shot in Israel about American Field, who travels with her Arab husband and their daughter to his native Iran, where (he must have forgotten to tell her) she has no rights. He decides the family will stay, using beatings and confinement to persuade his uncooperative wife, but she risks all to escape with daughter. Based on the true story of Betty Mahmoody. **116m/C VHS, DVD.** Sally Field, Alfred Molina, Sheila Rosenthal, Roshan Seth, Sarah Badel, Mony Rey, Georges Corraface; **D:** Brian Gilbert; **W:** David W. Rintels; **C:** Peter Hannan; **M:** Jerry Goldsmith.

The Notebook ♂♂ 2004 (PG-13) An elderly man (Garner) tries patiently to reawaken beloved wife's (Rowlands) failing memory of their life together by reading the story to her. Couple is seen in flashback of youth and follows them through the struggles of romance. There are two stories here: one very interesting, the other rehashed saccharine. Story of the young lovers is harlequin romance cliche in which noble blue collar overreaches his station, but pretty rich girl just can't help herself. They love, they lose one another, they're reunited again. Sure to make many tender hearts quiver. When Garner and Rowlands share the screen there's true magic. Their chemistry is genuine and finally heartbreaking, and too little time is spent exploring it. A frustrating schizophrenic letdown. **120m/C DVD.** *US* Rachel McAdams, Ryan Gosling, Gena Rowlands, James Garner, Joan Allen, James Marsden, Kevin Connolly, Sam Shepard; **D:** Nick Cassavetes; **W:** Jan Sardi, Jeremy Leven; **C:** Robert Fraisse; **M:** Aaron Zigman.

Notes from Underground ♂♂ 1995 Modern adaptation of the Dostoevsky novella has Czerny starring as a nameless, alienated civil servant who can only find pleasure in the petty torments his job allows him to inflict on others. Everything he does to broaden his world backfires in humiliating ways. Most of the film consists of monologues that Czerny records on a homevideo camera as he recalls the worst moments in his life. Fortunately, Czerny is up to the nearly one-man task of carrying this odd film. **90m/C VHS, DVD.** Henry Czerny, Sheryl Lee, Jon Favreau, Charles Stratton; **D:** Gary Walkow; **W:** Gary Walkow; **C:** Dan Gillham; **M:** Mark Governor.

Notes on a Scandal ♂♂ 2006 (R) Compelling look at obsession based on Zoe Heller's 2003 novel. Attractive Sheba Hart (Blanchett) is a novice art teacher who's given guidance by acerbic veteran Barbara Covett (Dench). Sheba has a much older husband (Nighy), two children, and a vague dissatisfaction with her comfortable life, which soon leads her into a relationship with her very willing 15-year-old pupil Steven (Simpson). When the bitter, lonely Barbara discovers Sheba's indiscretion, she ruthlessly uses emotional blackmail to tether the younger woman to her. But as Barbara's neediness grows, even the self-destructive Sheba finally has enough until the inevitable showdown. Disturbing and dazzling, thanks to the no-holds-barred performances of both Dench and Blanchett. **91m/C DVD.** *GB US* Judi Dench, Cate Blanchett, Bill Nighy, Andrew Simpson, Juno Temple, Max Lewis; **D:** Richard Eyre; **W:** Patrick Marber; **C:** Chris Menges; **M:** Philip Glass.

Nothin' 2 Lose ♂♡ 2000 Kwame (Hooks) can't bring him himself to commit to marriage with his girlfriend, Yasmine (Bayete). He prefers to spend his time hanging with his friends, gambling on playground basketball games, and chattering with his racist, misogynist buddies. Racist language serves for humor and women serve as objects in what proves to be a bad excuse for an urban comedy. 100m/C DVD. Brian Hooks, Shani Bayete, Cedric Pendleton, Crystal Sessions, Michael A. LaMelle, Martin C. Jones, Michael Sekina Williams, Malik Jones; D: Barry Bowles. W: Barry Bowles.

Nothing but a Man ♂♂½ 1964 Duff Anderson (Dixon) is a black laborer trying to make a life in a small Alabama town. He falls for the daughter of a minister, they marry, and he gets a job at a local sawmill. When he won't bend to his racist white employers, he's fired and labeled a troublemaker. Unsentimental portrait of the times. 95m/B VHS, DVD. Ivan Dixon, Abbey Lincoln, Gloria Foster, Julius W. Harris, Martin Priest, Yaphet Kotto, Leonard Parker, Stanley Greene, Helen Lounck, Helene Arndldt; D: Michael Roemer. W: Michael Roemer, Robert M. Young; C: Robert M. Young, Nat'l Film Reg. '93.

Nothing But Trouble ♂♂½ 1944 Laurel & Hardy's last film for MGM is a complicated tale of two servants who wind up protecting an exiled boy king from the machinations of his power-mad uncle. 70m/B VHS, DVD. Stan Laurel, Oliver Hardy, Henry O'Neil, Mary Boland, David Leland, John Warburton, Connie Gilchrist, Philip Merivale; D: Sam Taylor.

Nothing But Trouble ♂ 1991 (PG-13) Yuppie couple out for weekend drive find themselves smoldering in small town hell thanks to a traffic ticker. Horror and humor mix like oil and water in Aykroyd's debut as director. 93m/C VHS, DVD. Dan Aykroyd, Demi Moore, Chevy Chase, John Candy, Taylor Negron, Bertila Darnas, Valri Bromfield; D: Dan Aykroyd; W: Dan Aykroyd, Peter Aykroyd; C: Dean Cundey. Golden Raspberries '91: Worst Support. Actor (Aykroyd).

Nothing in Common ♂♂½ 1986 (PG) In his last film, Gleason plays the abrasive, diabetic father of immature advertising agency worker Hanks. After his parents separate, Hanks learns to be more responsible and loving in caring for his father. Comedy and drama are blended well here with the help of satirical pokes at the ad business and Hanks turns in a fine performance, but the unorganized, lengthy plot may lose some viewers. 119m/C VHS, DVD. Tom Hanks, Jackie Gleason, Eva Marie Saint, Bess Armstrong, Hector Elizondo, Barry Corbin, Sela Ward, John Kapelos, Jane Morris, Dan Castellaneta, Tracy Reiner; D: Garry Marshall; W: Rick Podell; C: John A. Alonzo; M: Patrick Leonard.

Nothing Personal ♂♂ 1980 (PG) Confused mix of romantic comedy and environmental themes. Lawyer (?) Somers attempts to help college professor Sutherland prevent the slaughter of seals. Enter romance (hey, but what about the baby seals?). Enlivened by appearances of Canadian SCTV vets and Somers's first starring theatrical role. 96m/C VHS. Donald Sutherland, Suzanne Somers, Dabney Coleman, John Dehner, Roscoe Lee Browne, Catherine O'Hara; D: George Bloomfield.

Nothing Personal ♂♂♂ 1995 (R) Uncompromising drama about the sectarian violence in northern Ireland that engulfs even the innocent. The IRA bombing of a Protestant pub sets a Loyalist unit, led by dedicated Kenny (Fraa) and psychotic Ginger (a terrifying Harty), on an increasingly deadly, 24-hour rampage through Belfast (in 1975). Catholic single father Liam Kelly (Lynch) finds himself in the wrong part of town and only wants to return to his two children but is inexorably drawn into the violence, which leads to tragedy for all. Adapted from the novel "All Our Fault" by Mornin, who wrote the screenplay. 86m/C VHS. GB IR Ian Hart, John Lynch, James Frain, Michael Gambon, Ruaidhri Conroy, Jeni Courtney, Gary Lydon, Maria Doyle Kennedy, Gerard McSorley, Gareth O'Hare, Thaddeus O'Sullivan; W: Daniel Mornin; C: Dick Pope; M: Philip Appleby.

Nothing Sacred ♂♂♂ 1937 Slick, overzealous reporter takes advantage of a small-town girl's situation. As a publicity stunt, his newspaper brings her to the Big Apple to distract her from her supposedly imminent death in order to manipulate the public's sentiment as a means to sell more copy. Innocent young Lombard, however, is far from death's door, and deftly exploits her exploitation. Scathing indictment of the mass media and bovine mentality of the masses. Both hysterically funny and bitterly cynical, boasts Lombard's finest performance as the small-town rube who orchestrates the ruse. Remade in 1954 as "Living It Up." DVD version includes home movie footage of a Lombard-Gable hunting trip and two Mack Sennett shorts—"Campus Vamp" (1928) and "Matchmaking Maria." 75m/C VHS, DVD. Fredric March, Carole Lombard, Walter Connolly, Sig Rumann, Charles Winninger, Margaret Hamilton; D: William A. Wellman; W: Ben Hecht; C: William Howard Greene; M: Oscar Levant.

Nothing to Lose ♂♂½ 1996 (R) Ad exec Nick Beam (Robbins) is having a very bad day. He loses his job, finds his wife is having an affair, then gets carjacked by street-wise but dim-witted thief T-Paul (Lawrence). T-Paul picked the wrong day to rob Nick, who ironically takes T-Paul hostage. The unlikely pair find they have more in common than realized. Screwball buddy comedy shows its originality in casting, and not much else. Robbins and Lawrence are an inspired pair with great comedic potential but are trapped in a mundane story. Filming was delayed due, in part, to Lawrence's consort run-ins with the law. 97m/C VHS, DVD. Tim Robbins, Martin Lawrence, John C. McGinley, Giancarlo Esposito, Kelly Preston, Michael McKeanIma P. Hall, Susan Barnes, Rebecca Gayheart, Patrick Cranshaw; D: Steve Oedekerk. W: Steve Oedekerk; C: Donald E. Thorin; M: Robert Folk.

Nothing Underneath ♂½ 1985 An American guy goes to Rome to search for his model twin sister, who may be one of the victims of a series of scissor killings. 95m/C VHS. Tom Schanley, Renee Simonsen, Nicola Perring Donald Pleasence; C: Carlo Varzina.

Notorious ♂♂♂♂ 1946 Post-WWII story of beautiful playgirl Alicia (Bergman) who's sent by the U.S. government to marry a suspected spy (Rains) living in Brazil. Cynical agent Devlin (Grant) is assigned to watch her. Duplicity and guilt are important factors in this brooding, romantic spy thriller. Suspenseful throughout, with a surprise ending. The acting is excellent all around and Hitchcock makes certain that suspense is maintained throughout this classy and complex thriller. 101m/B VHS, DVD. Cary Grant, Ingrid Bergman, Claude Rains, Louis Calhern, Leopoldine Konstantin, Reinhold Schunzel, Moroni Olsen; D: Alfred Hitchcock; W: Ben Hecht; C: Ted Tetzlaff; M: Roy Webb. Nat'l Film Reg. '06.

The Notorious Bettie Page ♂♂½ 2006 (R) The ultimate 50s fetish pinup, Bettie (M(?)) is a sweet, religious Southern gal with a rocky past (bad childhood, bad men), who comes to the Big Apple and looks great—dark hair curvy body, come-hither smile, and an open sexuality that soon has her doing nude photo shoots. After Bettie meets the Klaws, Irving (Bauer) and his sister Paula (Taylor), she becomes a sensation in the specialty market of leather and bondage. This being the 50s, morality soon wags a disapproving finger when Senator Estes Kefauver (Strathairn) convenes his indecency hearings and Bettie gets caught in the crossfire. Mol is charming but Bettie remains a cipher. 91m/C DVD, US Gretchen Mol, Chris Bauer, Jared Harris, Sarah Paulson, Cara Seymour, Lili Taylor, David Strathairn, John Cullum, Matt McGrath, Austin Pendleton, Norman Reedus, Dallas Roberts, Victor Slezak, Tara Subkoff, Kevin Carroll, Ann Dowd, Michael Gaston, Jefferson Mays, Peter McRobbie, Jonathan M. Woodward; D: Mary Harron; W: Mary Harron, Guinevere Turner; C: W. Mott Hupfel III; M: Mark Suozzo.

The Notorious Lady ♂♂½ 1927 Englishman Stone kills the man he finds in Bedford's room, believing him to be his wife's lover. He's mistaken but she lies to save him and Stone ends up in prison, sentenced to death for the murder. Answers are at the point in this psy. 79m/B VHS, Lewis Stone, Barbara Bedford, Earl Metcalfe, Francis McDonald; D: King Baggot; C: Gaetaro Antonio "Tony" Gaudio.

Notre Histoire ♂♂ Our Story: Separate Rooms 1984 Confusing and frequently surreal drama. Middle-aged alcoholic Robert (Delon) is in despair about his life as he sits alone in a train compartment. Suddenly, beautiful Donatienne (Baye) enters and just as suddenly leaves (after they have sex, of course) and the unexpected twosome are soon spending a lot of time together. Trouble immediately begins when the paparazzi find out about their affair and William finds his face splashed all over the tabloids and reporters camped out in his garden. (fans is a scene stealer as William's grubby and crazy housemate. 123m/C VHS, DVD. HD DVD. Julia Roberts, Hugh Grant, Hugh Bonneville, Rhys Ifans, Tim McInerny) McHenry, Gina McKee, James Dreyfus, Richard McCabe, Emma Chambers; D: Roger Michell; W: Richard Curtis; C: Michael Couter; M: Trevor Jones.

Nous N'Irons Plus au Bois ♂♂ 1968 On the outskirts of a forest held by the Germans, a small group of French resistance fighters capture a German soldier during WWII. He actually wants to join forces with them, however, after falling in love with a lovely young French girl. In French; subtitled in English. 98m/C VHS. FR Marie-France Pisier, Siegfried Rauch, Richard Leduc; D: Georges Dumoulin.

Nouvelle Vague ♂♂ 1990 New Wave 1990 Delon is a philosopher king and Giordaro a wealthy countess involved in Godard's usual sexual and political themes. which has society geared toward support of the rich. Dialogue is composed entirely of quotations, in French with English subtitles. 89m/C VHS. SI FR Alain Delon, Domiziana Giordano, Roland Amstutz, Laurence Cote, Christophe Odent; D: Jean-Luc Godard; W: Jean-Luc Godard.

Novel Desires ♂½ 1992 (R) Brian Freedman is a best-selling author who teams up with his writing rival, Vicky Chance. But it isn't just their imaginations they give free reign to, it's all their desires as well. 80m/C VHS, DVD. Tyler Gains, Caroline Monteith, Mitchell Clark, Lisa Hayland; D: Lawrence Unger.

Novel Romance ♂♂ 2006 (R) Hearing her biological clock ticking very loudly, magazine editor Max (Lord) decides to have a baby and looks for a suitable cherished sperm donor. She picks a suitably matic unpublished writer (Johansson) and offers to make him a literary success if he will do his part (baby-making wise) and then get lost. He does, she does, and Max raises their daughter while he moves to France. But they just can't quite let go completely. 92m/C DVD. Traci Lords, Paul Johansson, Sherilyn Fenn, Mariette Hartley, Jacqueline Pinol; D: Emily Skopov; C: David Klein; M: Raney Shockne. VIDEO

Now and Forever ♂♂ 1934 Penny (Temple) is the young daughter of charming widower and con man Jerry Day (Cooper). Penny's been in the care of her uncle but Jerry's decided to settle down in Paris with his lady love Toni (Lombard) and figures he can give the tyke a home. But the hard-up Jerry can't resist stealing a valuable necklace and there's much trouble ahead (and not your average happy ending). Temple steals the te film from her elders. Adapted from the story "Honor Bright" by Jack Kirkland and Melville Baker. Colorized. 82m/C VHS, DVD. Gary Cooper.

Notting Hill ♂♂♂ 1999 (PG-13) Romantic comedy that can coast by on charm alone. Roberts is not playing herself (okay, so there are, possibly, some similarities). She is playing a famous and neurotic movie star, Anna Scott, who's filming on location in London. She meets cute with shy travel bookstore owner William Thacker (Grant) and the unexpected twosome are soon spending a lot of time together... 123m/C VHS. Alain Delon, Nathalie Baye; D: Bernard Blier; W: Bernard Blier; C: Jean Penzer; M: Laurent Rossi.

November ♂♂♂ 2005 (R) A young woman (Le Gros) enters an L.A. convenience store to buy ice cream for his girlfriend Sophie (Cox) who is waiting in the car, but unwittingly walks into a holdup anc is shot dead. The fatalist date is replayed in three sections, "Denial," "Despair," and "Acceptance," each offering clues to what's behind the actual event, as Sophie begins to question her grip on her life and reality. 73m/C DVD. US Courteney Cox, James LeGros, Nora Dunn, Anne Archer, Michael Ealy, Nick Offerman Brand; C: Nancy Schreiber; M: Lew Baldwin.

November Conspiracy ♂♂½ 1996 (R) Journalist Jenny Baron (Turco) is covering the presidential campaign of a senator (Segal) when she uncovers a conspiracy linking a number of assassinations and murder attempts. A computer disk reveals more information but when her lover (Benedict) is murdered during an attempt ed political assassination, Baron goes on the run to save her own life. 103m/C VHS. Paige Turco, George Segal, Elliott Gould, Bo Hopkins, Dirk Benedict, Conrad Janis; D: Conrad Janis; W: Maria Grimm; M: Tony Hurecke.

November Moon ♂♂ November-mond 1985 On the eve of WWII, Jewish November Messing (Osurg) flees Germany for what she hopes will be safety in Paris. She meets Ferial (Millei) and the two become lovers, but Ferial must hide however. After the Nazis occupy the city, Ferial also decides to take a position on a Nazirun newspaper in order to gather information and protect them both. German with subtitles. 106m/C VHS, DVD. GE Gabriele Osburg, Christiane Millet, Gerhard Olschewski, Daniele Delorme, Bruno Pradal, Werner Stocker; C: Alexandra von Grote; W: Alexandra von Grote; C: Bernard Zitzerman.

Novocaine ♂♂ 2001 (R) Ambitious, occasionally successful blend of black comedy and film noir framed in toothy imagery. Frank (Martin) is a humdrum dentist with a thriving practice and perfect if nutty, hygienist/fiancee (Dern). The normalcy is crushing and dread is palpable. Enter Susan (Carter), a seductive, if grungy, first-time patient with a need for painkillers. She appeals to Frank's latent desire for danger by allowing a cavity search of another kind right in the dentist's chair. From there, playing the classic noir role of the stooge, Frank makes a lot of really bad decisions. Story is pretty unbelievable, but the screwball quality keeps it afloat to a point. Ultimately the plot stumbles and during tones bump into each other. Martin has some funny moments but Carter is still in "Fight Club" mode and falls into caricature. Laughing gas would've been preferable to the numbness of the film's ending. 95m/C US Steve Martin, Helena Bonham-Carter, Laura Dern, Elias Koteas, Scott Caan, Keith David, Lynne Thigper, Kevin Bacon; D: David Atkins; W: David Atkins; C: Vilko Filac; M: Steve Bartek.

The November Men ♂½ 1993 In 1992, liberal Hollywood director Arthur Gwenlyn (Williams) begins filming a thriller about an assassin after a presidential candidate. But cinematographer Elizabeth (Bevis) begins to suspect that Gwenlyn's actually serious about killing off some real-life politicos and is using the production as a cover. Doesn't make a lot of sense. 98m/C VHS. Paul W. Williams, James Andronica, Leslie Bevis, Robert Davi; D: Paul W. Williams; W: James Andronica.

Carole Lombard, Shirley Temple, Guy Standing, Charlotte Granville, Gilbert Emery; **D:** Henry Hathaway; **W:** Vincent Lawrence, Sylvia Thalberg; **C:** Harry Fischbeck.

Now and Forever ♂♂ 1982 (R)
Young wife's life is shattered when her unfaithful husband is wrongly accused and convicted of rape. After he is sent to prison, she begins drinking and taking drugs. From the novel by Danielle Steel, it will appeal most to those who like their romances a la Harlequin. 93m/C VHS, DVD. **AU** Cheryl Ladd, Robert Coleby, Carmen Duncan, Christine Amor, Aileen Britton; **D:** Adrian Carr.

Now & Forever ♂♂ 2002 (R)
Childhood friends Angela Wilson and John Myron live in small-town Saskatchewan and come from different backgrounds (he's Cree, she's white). Angela's plagued by major family woes and longs to be an actress; John is mystical and grounded by his culture, and has loved Angela from the moment he met her. She takes up with a jerk who does the unthinkable (we're not spoiling it) and she leaves town. But the connection between Angela and John proves strong enough to bring them back together. Too many elements make the film too convoluted, but it is earnest. 101m/C DVD. **CA** Mia Kirshner, Adam Beach, Theresa Russell, Gordon Tootoosis, Gabriel Olds, Callum Keith Rennie, Alexandra Purvis, Simon Baker; **D:** Bob (Benjamin) Clark, Billy Boyle; **C:** Jan Kiesser; **M:** Paul Zaza.

Now and Then ♂♂ 1995 (PG-13)
Four women hold a reunion 25 years after their most eventful childhood summer to relive the good ol' days of prepubescent triumphs and tragedies. Flashback, which thankfully comprises about 85% of the movie, explores about 85% of the movie, explores first kisses, budding breasts, death and divorce. Despite good intentions, this nostalgic coming-of-ager for the girls is a jumbled mass of borrowed formulas that just can't shake that feeling of forced sentimentality. The young actresses are talented and charming, but their less convincing adult counterparts serve mostly as big names to draw crowds and studio support. 97m/C VHS, DVD. Rosie O'Donnell, Melanie Griffith, Demi Moore, Rita Wilson, Christina Ricci, Thora Birch, Gaby Hoffman, Ashleigh Aston Moore, Cloris Leachman, Lolita (David) Davidovich, Bonnie Hunt, Brendan Fraser; **W:** I. Marlene King; **C:** Ueli Steiger; **M:** Cliff Eidelman.

Now, Voyager ♂♂♂♂½ 1942
Davis plays a lonely spinster who is transformed into a vibrant young woman by therapy. She comes out of her shell to have a romantic affair with a suave European (who turns out to be married) but still drowns his sorrows with buds Gil (Anderson) and Biscuit (Fehrman) while Jerry (Jones) and gal pal Marti (Kent). Finally, Jeremy just decides to ask Keri what went wrong. Lame comedy about the "Clerks" sidekick Anderson, making his directorial debut. 102m/C DVD. Jeremy Sisto, Rashida Jones, Trevor Fehrman, Paget Brewster, Heather Paige Kent, Anthony John (Tony) Denison, Jeff Anderson; **D:** Jeff Anderson; **W:** Jeff Anderson; **C:** Marco Cappetta; **M:** Lanny Cordola, Matt Sorum. VIDEO

Now You See Him, Now You Don't ♂♂ 1972 (G)
Light Disney comedy involving a gang of crooks who want to use a college student's invisibility formula to rob a local bank. Sequel to Disney's "The Computer Wore Tennis Shoes." 85m/C VHS, DVD. Kurt Russell, Joe Flynn, Cesar Romero, Jim Backus, Kelly Thordsen; **D:** Robert Butler; **W:** Robert F. Brunner.

Nowhere ♂♂ 1996 (R)
Third in Araki's teen trilogy, following "Totally F***ed Up" and "The Doom Generation" is a basic day-in-the-life look at alienated L.A. 18-year-old Dark Smith (Duval), adrift in a world of consumerism and looking for love. He loves Mel (True) but she's torn between Dark and girlfriend Lucifer (Robertson), so Dark turns to Montgomery (Bexton). His friends have their own trials with drugs and sex (in various combos), and violence. Angst to the Nth degree, with Araki's imagination in wild disarray. 82m/C VHS, James Duval, Rachel True, Kathleen Robertson, Nathan Bexton, Guillermo Diaz, Alan Boyce, Christina Applegate, Jeremy Jordan, Chiara Mastroianni, Debi Mazar, Jordan Ladd, Thyme Lewis, Sarah Lassez, Ryan Phillippe, Heather Graham, Scott Caan, Jaason Simmons, Mena Suvari, Christopher Knight, Eve Plumb, Beverly D'Angelo, David Leisure, Traci Lords, Shannen Doherty, John Ritter, Rose McGowan, Charlotte Rae, Denise Richards, Teresa Hill, Lauren Tewes, Staci Keanan, Joshua Gibran Mayweather; **D:** Gregg Araki; **W:** Gregg Araki; **C:** Arturo Smith.

Nowhere in Africa 2002 (R)
Nirgendwo in Afrika 2002 (R) Walter Redlich (Ninidze), a German Jew, has fled Breslau for a job as a farm manager in British-colonized Kenya. In 1938, his wife Jettel (Koehler) and their 5-year-old daughter Regina (Kurka) join him. Jettel is unhappy with their harsh new life and isolation but Regina quickly adapts. When war is declared, Walter is briefly interned and eventually joins the British Army, leaving Jettel behind to manage things. As Regina (Eckertz) grows up, she becomes ever-more adapted to life in Kenya and is dismayed when, in 1947, her father is offered a prestigious job and wants to return "home" to Germany. German with subtitles. From the novel by Stefanie Zweig. 141m/C VHS, DVD. **GE** Juliane Kohler, Merab Redlich, Karoline Eckertz, Lea Kurka, Matthias Habich, Sidede Onyulo; **D:** Caroline Link; **W:** Caroline Link; **C:** Gernot Roll; **M:** Niki Reiser. Oscars '02: Foreign Film.

Nowhere in Sight ♂♂½ 2001
Rehash of "Wait until Dark" has little to add that masterpiece of suspense/horror. This time, Carly Bauer (Slater) is the blind woman who's tormented in her apartment by a couple of nasty thugs. The cast does credible work with familiar material. 94m/C DVD, Helen Slater, Mark Camacho, Richard Jutras, Max Perlius, Andrew McCarthy; **D:** Douglas Jackson; **W:** James (Momel) Lemmo; **C:** Bruno Philip; **M:** Helen Slater, David Findlay.

Nowhere to Hide ♂♂ 1998 (R)
A widow whose Marine officer husband has been assassinated is chased by some bad guys who are after a helicopter part (say what?) and she must fight for survival for herself and her six-year-old son. 91m/C VHS, DVD. Beau Cox, Ray Meagher, Amy Madigan, Daniel Hugh-Kelly, Michael Ironside; **D:** Mende Brown, Mario Azzopardi; **W:** Michael Fisher; **C:** Paul Onorato; **M:** Laurie Lewis, Brad Fiedel.

Nowhere to Land ♂♂½ 2000
Familiar plotline still manages to be suspenseful. A bomb filmed with nerve gas is stashed aboard a Boeing 747 flying from Australia to California. It's up to pilot John Prescott (Wagner) and the feds to get the situation under control. 90m/C VHS. Jack Wagner, Christine Elise, James B. Sikking, Ernie Hudson, Mark Lee, Helen Thomson; **D:** Armand Mastroianni. CABLE

Nowhere to Run ♂♂ 1988 (R)
Slipshod version of a true story about a series of murders in Caddo, Texas in 1960. Carradine, paroled from prison, murders for revenge while six high school seniors get involved in the chase and in the seedy side of politics, police, and their own puberty. 87m/C VHS. David Carradine, Jason Priestley, Kieran Mulroney, Henry Jones; **D:** Carl Franklin.

Nowhere to Run ♂♂½ 1993 (R)
Kickboxer with heart seeks cross-over movie to establish real acting career. Unfortunately, even if such a movie existed, Van Damme wouldn't know what to do with it. Arquette plays the damsel in distress, facing eviction from the family farm with her two small children. Fortunately for Van Damme's escaped convict character, she is also a very lonely widow (nudge, nudge). He saves the day by abusing the daylights out of the big bad bankers, yet also finds time to play surrogate dad. Whatta guy. 95m/C VHS, DVD. Jean-Claude Van Damme, Rosanna Arquette, Kieran Culkin, Tiffany Taubman, Joss Ackland, Ted Levine; **D:** Robert Harmon; **W:** Joe Eszterhas, Leslie Bohem, Randy Feldman; **C:** David Gribble, Doug Milsome; **M:** Mark Isham.

Nuclear Conspiracy ♂♂½ 1985
A reporter disappears while investigating a huge nuclear waste shipment, and his wife searches for him. 115m/C VHS. GE Birgit Doll, Albert Fortell; **D:** Rainer Erler; **W:** Rainer Erler; **C:** Wolfgang Grasshoff; **M:** Eugen Thomass.

The Nude Bomb ♂♂½ 1980 (PG)
The Return of Maxwell Smart 1980 (PG) Proof that old TV shows never die—they just get made into big screen movies. Maxwell Smart from "Get Smart" (would you believe?) tries to save the world from a bomb intended to destroy clothing and leave everyone in the buff. Old hat lines. Followed by the TV movie "Get Smart, Again!" 94m/C VHS. Don Adams, Dana Elcar, Pamela Hensley, Sylvia Kristel, Norman Lloyd, Rhonda Fleming, Joey Forman; **D:** Clive Donner; **W:** Bill Dana; **M:** Lalo Schifrin.

Nude on the Moon WOOf! 1961
Lunar expedition discovers moon inhabited by people who bare skin as hobby. Groovy theme song, "I'm Mooning Over You, My Little Moon Doll." Part of Joe Bob Brigg's "Sleaziest Movies in the History of the World" series. 83m/C VHS, DVD. Shelby Livingston, Pat Reilly; **D:** Doris Wishman; **W:** Doris Wishman; **C:** Raymond Phelan; **M:** Daniel Hart.

Nudity Required ♂ 1990
Two pals go to the casting couch, pretending to be Hollywood producers, to seduce young women. Silly comedy with gratuitous nudity (Ms. Newmar included). Hardly a laugh to be found. 90m/C VHS. Julie Newmar, Troy Donahue, Brad Zutaut, Billy Frank, Mindi Miller, Alvin Silver, Eli Rich, Phil Hock; **D:** John Bown.

Nudo di Donna ♂ 1983
Portrait of a Woman, Nude 1983 A witty comedy about a Venetian bookseller who is becoming tired of marital struggles with his sexy wife of 16 years. He wanders into a fashion photography shop, sees a backside nude photo of a model who looks like his wife, and he takes off in fiery pursuit to find the subject of the photo. Venetian location photography is quite nice. In Italian with English subtitles. 112m/C VHS. IT Nino Manfredi, Jean-Pierre Cassel, Georges Wilson, Eleonora Giorgi; **D:** Nino Manfredi.

Nueba Yol ♂♂ 1995
Balbuena (Marti) is a recent widower with nothing much to look forward to in his native Dominican Republic, so he's easily persuaded by fast-talking friend Felito (Carbonell) into immigrating to New York (illegally). He has trouble finding any kind of work, is confused and intimidated by the city, and finds himself at odds with more acclimated immigrants from his homeland. Spanish with subtitles. 105m/C VHS. Luisito Marti, Caridad Ravelo, Raul Carbonell, Joel Garcia; **D:** Angel Muniz; **W:** Angel Muniz; **C:** Christopher Norr.

The Nugget ♂♂ 2002 (R)
Aussie-made comedy jokes may be better understood by the locals. Three working-class blokes spend their weekends out in the bush allegedly gold prospecting but mostly sitting around drinking beer. But on one trip, they finally find a huge nugget, and their greed leads to a disruption in their friendship, until their windfall gets stolen. 90m/C DVD. **AU** Eric Bana, Alan Brough, Max Cullen, Dave O'Neil, Stephen Currie, Peter Moon, Belinda Emmett, Sallyanne Ryan, Karen Pang; **D:** Bill Bennett; **W:** Bill Bennett; **C:** Danny Ruhlmann; **M:** Nigel Westlake.

Nukie ♂♂½ 1993 (G)
Brothers from another planet crash land on Earth. The first one is subjected to a dizzying array of scientific experiments in Florida involving electric cattle prods. The other one, Nukie, lands in Africa and is befriended by twins from a remote tribal village. They join him in his quest to free his brother from the sadistic clutches of suntanned professionals who have lost all compassion. Important message for our youth about the dangers of a runaway technocracy. 99m/C VHS. Glynis Johns, Steve Railsback; **D:** Sias Odendal.

Numb ♂♂½ 2007 (R)
Screenwriter Hudson Milbank (Perry) suffers from depersonalization disorder (DPD), a mental illness where the person cannot feel normal human emotion. Hudson feels neither love nor fear, just a depressed blank nothingness that permeates his life. He's tried many different drugs and therapies with no success until Sarah (Collins) enters his life. Hudson knows there's an attraction but cannot demonstrate it despite his desire to get better and Sarah's supportiveness. Funny rather than mawkish, and personal as director/writer Goldberg suffers from DPD himself. 94m/C DVD. Matthew Perry, Lynn Collins, Kevin Pollak, Mary Steenburgen, Bob Gunton, Helen Shaver, William B. Davis; **D:** Harris Goldberg; **W:** Harris Goldberg; **C:** Eric Steilberg; **M:** Ryan Shore.

Number One Fan ♂♂½ 1994 (R)
Hollywood action star Zane Barry (McQueen) is stalked by Blair (Ammann), a fan with whom he had a brief romance. Zane manages to patch things up when fiancee Holly (Stewart) finds out but Blair's determined to be the only woman in his life. 93m/C VHS, Chad McQueen, Catherine Mary Stewart, Renee Griffin, Hoyt Axton, Paul Bartel, Eric (DaRe) Da Re, Charles Matthau; **D:** Jane Simpson; **W:** Anthony Laurence Greene.

Number 1 of the Secret Service ♂♂½ 1977 (PG)
A handsome secret agent must foil the plans of a millionaire industrialist to destroy the economy. Spy spoof that's marginally interesting. 87m/C VHS. GB Nicky Henson, Geoffrey Keen, Sue Lloyd, Aimi MacDonald, Richard Todd; **D:** Lindsay Shonteff.

Number One with a Bullet ♂♂ 1987 (R)
Two unorthodox "odd couple" detectives are demoted after losing a key witness, but still set out on their own to unearth a drug czar. Carradine and Williams are better than this standard action material. 103m/C VHS. Bobby DiCicco, Doris Roberts, Mykelti Williamson, Jon(athan) Gries, Vanessa Bell Calloway, Shari Shattuck, Barry Corbin, Billy Dee Williams, Peter Graves, Valerie Bertinelli; **D:** Jack Smight; **C:** Alex Belushi, Andrew Kurtzman, Rob Riley; **C:** Alex Phillips Jr.; **M:** Alf Clausen.

No. 17 ♂♂♂ 1932
A humorous early thriller by the Master Hitchcock, filmed before the likes of "The 39 Steps." An unsuspecting hobo accidentally discovers a jewel thief's cache. The chase is on—superb final chase sequence involving a bus and a train. Based on the play by J. Jefferson Farjeon. 64m/B VHS, DVD. GB Leon M. Lion, Anne Grey, John Stuart, Donald Calthrop; **D:** Alfred Hitchcock; **W:** Alfred Hitchcock; **C:** Jack Cox, Bryan Langley.

The Number 23 ♂♂½ 2007 (R)
Disappointing, gimmicky, and generally incoherent effort stars Carrey as dog catcher Walter Sparrow, who's given a mystery novel by wife Agatha (Madsen in another supportive wife role). It's about a noirish detective (also played by Carrey), and all the significant events in the book are oddly connected to the number 23. Walter also becomes obsessive about the number and begins to fear that he will follow the book's plot, which includes murder. Walter eventually gets a grip but the film never recovers. 95m/C DVD. US Jim Carrey, Virginia Madsen, Logan Lerman, Danny Huston, Rhona Mitra, Lynn Collins, Mark Pellegrino, Ed Lauter; **D:** Joel Schumacher; **W:** Fernley Phillips; **C:** Matthew Libatique; **M:** Harry Gregson-Williams.

Numero Deux ♂♂ Number Two 1975
Godard explores politics, sex, and the trials of the modern family. A dissatisfied wife suffers from chronic constipation, her exhausted husband is impotent, they, their

The Nun ✍✍ 1966 A young woman, unable to meet financial obligations, is forced into a convent. Victimized by the mother superior and betrayed by a clergyman who befriends her, she escapes from the convent and eventually ends up in a bordello, despairing and suicidal. Not a creepy story. Banned in France for two years. In French with English subtitles. 95m/C VHS, FR Anna Karina, Lilo (Lisolete) Pulver, Micheline Presle, Christine Lenier, Francine Berge, Francesco Rabal, Wolfgang Reichmann, Catherine Diamant, Yori Bertin; D: Jacques Rivette.

children, and grandparents all try to cope with daily life. For nine-tenths of the film Godard only used small portions of the screen (the upper left and lower right corners); it's only at the end that the full-screen is used to offer some sort of relief. In French with English subtitles. 90m/C VHS, FR Sandrine Battistella, Pierre Oudry, Alexandre Rignault, Rachel Stefanopoli; D: Jean-Luc Godard; W: Anne-Marie Mieville, Jean-Luc Godard.

Nuns on the Run ✍✍½ 1990
Two nonviolent members of a robbery gang who double-cross their boss during a hold-up run from both the Mob and the police. Catholic humor, slapstick, and much fun with habits dominate. Idle and Coltrane do with its one-joke premise. 95m/C VHS, DVD. Eric Idle, Robbie Coltrane, Janet Suzman, Camille Coduri, Robert Patterson, Tom Hickey, Doris Hare, Lila Kaye; D: Jonathan Lynn; W: Jonathan Lynn; C: Mike Garfath.

The Nun's Story ✍✍½ 1959
The melancholy tale of a young nun working in the Congo and Belgium during WWII, and struggling to reconcile her free spirit with the rigor's of the order. Gabrielle (Hepburn) is the daughter of a Belgian doctor (Jagger), who leaves the convent as Sister Luke. Her assignment in the Congo is at a European hospital where's she influenced by dedicated surgeon, Dr. Fortunai (Finch). But Sister Luke comes to question her vocation and her homeland. Highly acclaimed; from the Kathryn Hulme novel. 152m/C VHS, DVD. Audrey Hepburn, Peter Finch, Edith Evans, Peggy Ashcroft, Mildred Dunnock, Dean Jagger, Beatrice Straight, Colleen Dewhurst; D: Fred Zinnemann; W: Franz Waxman, British Acad. '59; Actress (Hepburn); Natl. Bd. of Review '59; Director (Zinnemann); Support. Actress (Evans); N.Y. Film Critics '59; Actress (Hepburn), Director (Zinnemann).

Nuremberg ✍✍½ 2000 A decent
but not overly compelling intro to the allied prosecution of Nazi war criminals at Nuremberg, Germany in 1945/46. Supreme Court Justice Robert H. Jackson (Baldwin) is asked to take a leave from the bench to head up the prosecution and he decides to try a representative sample of Third Reich leaders, including Hitler's No. 2 man, Hermann Goering (the always chilling Cox). The trial secenes generally work but there's also the needless byplay of a romance between Jackson and his secretary Elsie (Hennessy). Based on the book "Nuremberg: Infamy on Trial" by Joseph E. Persico. 240m/C VHS, DVD Alec Baldwin, Jill(ian) Hennessey, Brian Cox, Michael Ironside, Christopher Plummer, Matt Craven, Max von Sydow, Len Cariou, Len Doncheff, Herbert Knaup, Yves Simoneau; W: David W. Rintels; C: Alan Dostie; M: Richard Gregoire. CABLE

Nurse ✍✍½ 1980 A recently widowed woman resumes her career as a nurse in a large urban hospital, after her son leaves for college. Based on Peggy Anderson's book. Pilot for a TV series. 94m/C VHS, DVD. Lisa Zane, John Stockwell, Jennie Rose, Jay Underwood, Michael Fairman; D: David Lowell Rich. TV

The Nurse ✍✍ 1997 (R) Nurse Laura Harriman (Zane) seeks revenge from the man she holds responsible for her father's suicide by destroying his family. 105m/C VHS, Michael Learned, Robert Reed, Antonio Fargas; D: Bret Lowell Rich.

Nurse Betty ✍✍✍ 2000 (R) Small-time waitress Betty (Zellweger) "antisizes her favorite soap opera doc David Ravell (Kinnear). But she confuses fantasy and reality after witnessing the murder of her sleazoid husband (Eckhart) over a drug deal and thinks she's a character in the soap herself. So she travels to Hollywood to be reunited with her true love, trailed by her husband's two killers (Rock and Freeman). LaBute's unpredictable black comedy represents a departure from his previous claustrophobic, misanthropic work, but retains a cynical edge. Zellweger and Freeman stand out in a stellar cast that includes Kinnear at his smarmy best. 110m/C VHS, DVD, Renee Zellweger, Morgan Freeman, Chris Rock, Greg Kinnear, Aaron Eckhart, Crispin Glover, Allison Janney, Pruitt Taylor Vince, Kathleen Wilhoite, Harriet Samson Harris, Susan Barnes, Sheila Kelley, Tia Texada; D: Neil LaBute; W: John C. Richards; C: Jean-Yves Escoffier; M: Rolfe Kent. Golden Globes '01; Actress—Mus./Comedy (Zellweger).

Nurse Edith Cavell ✍✍✍ 1939
Fine performances in this true story of Britain's famous nurse who aided the Belgian underground during WWI, transporting wounded soldiers out of the German-occupied country. Decidedly opposes war and, ironically, was released just as WWII began in 1939. 95m/3 VHS, DVD. George Sanders, Edna May Oliver, Zasu Pitts, Robert Coote, May Robson, Anna Neagle; D: Herbert Wilcox.

Nurse Marjorie ✍✍ 1920 Aristocratic nurse Marjorie (Minter) 'falls in love and marries the leader of the Labor Party, much to her family's dismay. Based on the play by Israel Zangwill. Minter made four films with director Taylor, whose made four 1922 has never been solved. 88m/B VHS. Mary Miles Minter, Clyde Fillmore, George Periolat, Mollie McConnell, Frank Leigh, Vera Lewis; D: William Desmond Taylor; W: Julia Crawford Ivers.

Nurse on Call ✍ 1988 A bevy of trampy nurses cavort throughout a big city hospital. Softcore. 80m/C VHS, D: Herman Martinez, Christopher Floye.

The Nut ✍✍½ 1921 Charlie Jackson (Fairbanks) is a wacky, wealthy inventor who falls for Estrell Wynn (De La Motte), a society gal dedicated to improving the lives of underprivileged children. He tries to aid her in a variety of ways— none of which work out as he expects. The usually swashbuckling Fairbanks does get to rescue the heroine. 61m/B VHS. Douglas Fairbanks Sr., Marguerite de la Motte, William E. (W.E., William A., W.A.) Lowery; D: Theodore Reed; W: William Parker.

Nutcase ✍ 1983 A trio of young children in New Zealand attempt to thwart a group of terrorists who threaten to reactivate a large city's volcanoes unless they are given a large sum of money. Novel twist there. 49m/C VHS, NZ Nevan Rowe, Ian Watkin, Michael Wilson; D: Roger Donaldson.

The Nutcracker Prince ✍ 1991 The classic children's Christmas tale comes alive in this feature-length animated special. 75m/C VHS, DVD, CA D: Paul Schibli; V: Kiefer Sutherland, Megan Follows, Michael McDonald, Phyllis Diller, Peter O'Toole.

Nutcracker Sweet ✍ 1984 Ridiculous drama about a beautiful and powerful socialite (Collins) who runs a renowned ballet company with an iron fist. A Russian ballerina defects and infiltrates Collins's company to try out her own treacherous motives. 105m/C VHS, Joan Collins, Finola Hughes, Paul Nicholas; D: Anwar Kawadri.

Nutcracker: The Motion Picture ✍✍½ 1986 A lavish stage-bound filmization of the Tchaikovsky ballet, designed by Maurice Sendak. 82m/C VHS, D: Carroll Ballard.

Nuts ✍✍½ 1987 (R) A high-priced prostitute attempts to prove her sanity when she's accused of manslaughter. Ashamed of her lifestyle, and afraid of her reasons for it, her parents attempt to institutionalize her. A filmed version of Tom Topor's play that manages to retain its mesmerizing qualities. Fine performances, although the funnygirl goes over the top on several occasions. 116m/C VHS, DVD, Barbra Streisand, Richard Dreyfuss, Maureen Stapleton, Karl Malden, James Whitmore, Robert Webber, Eli Wallach, Leslie Nielsen, Robert Prince, Dakin Matthews, Hayley Taylor Block; D: Martin Ritt; W: Tom Topor, Darryl Ponicsan, Alvin Sargent; C: Andrzej Bartkowiak; M: Barbra Streisand.

Nuts in May ✍½ 1976 Two smug, middle-aged, middle-class vegetarians go on a camping trip and clash with their cynical, working-class fellow campers. 84m/C VHS, DVD, GB Alison Steadman, Anthony O'Donnell, Roger Sloman; D: Mike Leigh; W: Mike Leigh; C: Michael Williams. TV

The Nutt House ✍½ 1995 (PG-13) Identical twins—separated at birth—grow up to be a slimy politician and a nutcase (living up to the family name) with multiple personalities. Naturally, when the two are reunited it makes for lots of outrageous complications. 89m/C VHS, DVD, Stephen Keamey, Traci Lords, Amy Yasbeck; Cameos: Stella Stevens, Robert Mandan, Catherine Bach; D: Adam Rifkin; W: Ron Zwang, Scott Spiegel, Sam Raimi; C: Bernd Heinl; M: Cameron Allan.

The Nutty Professor ✍✍✍ 1963 A mild-mannered chemistry professor creates a potion that turns him into a suave debonair, playboy type with an irresistible attraction to women. Lewis has repeatedly denied the slick character s a Dean Martin parody, but the evidence is quite strong. Easily Lewis's best film. 107m/C VHS, DVD. Jerry Lewis, Stella Stevens, Del Moore, Kathleen Freeman, Howard Morris, Les Brown, Med Flory, Norman Alden, Milton Frome, Buddy Lester, Henry Gibson; D: Jerry Lewis; W: Bill Richmond, Jerry Lewis; C: Wallace Kelley; M: Walter Scharf. Natl. Film Reg. '04.

The Nutty Professor ✍✍✍ 1996 (PG-13) Remake of the 1963 Jerry Lewis comedy stars Murphy as Professor Sherman Klump, a severely overweight but bright man whose heft gets in the way of his love life. He takes a swig of his own secret potion and is transformed into the slim and suave Buddy Love. Only the formula isn't perfect and seems to wear off at the worst possible times. After a string of bad movies, Murphy may have stumbled upon his own formula for a comeback by relincuishing creative control and concentrating on the comedy. Reminiscent of "Coming to America," Murphy plays eight different roles. The fat and fart jokes are plentiful and so are the laughs. 96m/C VHS, DVD, HD DVD. Eddie Murphy, Jada Pinkett Smith, James Coburn, Dave Chappelle; D: Tom Shadyac; W: David Sheffield, Barry W. Blaustein, Steve Oedekerk, Tom Shadyac; C: Julio Macat; M: David Newman. Oscars '96; Makeup; Natl. Soc. Film Critics '96; Actor (Murphy).

Nutty Professor 2: The Klumps ✍✍½ 2000 (PG-13) Sequel to the 1996 hit finds Sherman Klump working over-time as Sherman Klump attempts to re-move the DNA of his alter ego Buddy Love from his system. Once Buddy escapes, he steals Sherman's latest experiment, a youth serum. Buddy also complicates Sherman's relationship with a beautiful colleague (Jackson) and the entire Klump clan. Expanding a one-joke scene from the original is risky, but Murphy and the writers manage to pull it off rather impressively. Yes, the humor is crude, (the more uptight may even say offensive) but the story is funny and interesting while the characters, if not always appealing, are sympathetic and genuine. 105m/C VHS, DVD, HD DVD. Eddie Murphy, Janet Jackson, Anna Maria Horsford, Melinda McGraw, Richard Gant, John Ales, Larry Miller, Chris Elliot, Earl Boen, Kathleen Freeman, Charles Napier, Jamal Mixon, Nikki Cox; D: Peter Segal; W: Barry W. Blaustein, David Sheffield, Paul Weitz, Steve Oedekerk; C: Dean Semler; M: David Newman.

O Fantasma ✍✍ Phantom 2000 The darker side of sexuality is explored as lonely, twentysomething trash collector Sergio (Menses) drifts through his life in a dreamlike haze, indulging in anonymous sexual encounters. He discovers a taste for the sexual extreme and becomes obsessed with the unobtainable Joao (Barbosa)—stalking him until Sergio can act on his desires. Explicit sex—fuzzy narrative. Portuguese with subtitles. 90m/C VHS, DVD. PT Ricardo Menses, Andre Barbosa, Beatriz Torcato, Eurico Vieira; D: Joao Pedro Rodrigues; W: Joao Pedro Rodrigues, Jose Neves, Paulo Rebelo, Alexandre Melo; C: Rui Pocas.

O Lucky Man! ✍✍✍ 1973 (R) Surreal, black comedy following the rise and fall and eventual rebirth of a modern British coffee salesman. Several actors play multiple roles with outstanding performances throughout. Price's excellent score combines with the hilarity for an extraordinary experience. 178m/C VHS, GB Malcolm McDowell, Ralph Richardson, Rachel Roberts, Arthur Lowe, Alan Price, Helen Mirren, Mona Washbourne, Warren Clarke; D: Lindsay Anderson; M: Alan Price, British Acad. '73; Support. Actor (Lowe).

O Pioneers! ✍✍½ 1991 (PG) Lange plays Alexandra Bergson, an unmarried woman at the turn of the century, who inherits her family's Nebraska homestead because she loves the land and is alive, a voluptuous nymphoid barbarian—much she loves the land. Although the family has prospered through Alexandra's smart investments, her brothers come to

O Brother, Where Art Thou? ✍✍½ 2000 (PG-13) Clooney stars as chain gang escapee Ulysses Everett McGill, who, along with fellow escapees Pete and Delmar (Turturro and Nelson), sets out on an "Odyssey"-like journey through Depression-era Mississippi bound for home, where waits McGill's wife, Penny (Hunter). What the trio encounter along the way are a number of Coenesque situations and characters that when all is said and done, seem like just that—individual situations that never really add up to a cohesive whole. They fit well enough to comprise a pretty enjoyable film, though. Fine performances by Clooney, Nelson, and Coen regulars Goodman and Turturro. 103m/C VHS, DVD, George Clooney, Tim Blake Nelson, John Turturro, Holly Hunter, John Goodman, Charles Durning, Del Pentecost, Michael Badalucco, Brian "Roddy", Wayne Duvall, Ed Gale, Ray McKinnon, Daniel von Barger, Royce D. Applegate, Frank Collison, Lee Weaver, Stephen (Steve) Root, Musetta Vander, Chris Thomas King, Mia Tyler, Christy Taylor; D: Joel Coen; W: Ethan Coen, Joel Coen; C: Roger Deakins; M: T-Bone Burnett, Chris Thomas King, Carter Burwell. Golden Globes '01; Actor—Mus./Comedy (Clooney).

Nyoka and the Tigermen ✍✍ Nyoka and the Lost Secrets of Hippocrates; Perils of Nyoka 1942 The adventures of the jungle queen Nyoka and her rival Vultura in their search for the lost tablets of Hippocrates. In 15 episodes. 250m/B VHS. Kay Aldridge, Clayton Moore; D: William Witney.

O ✍✍ 2001 (R) Apparently Hollywood has discovered that this Shakespeare fella can do some writin'. An exclusive South Carolina high school serves as background for this updated teen "Othello," which substitutes basketball court hoops prowess. He has an intimate relationship with Desi (Stiles, in her third Bard adaptation in as many years), the daughter of the schoo's dean, Hugo (Hartnett). plots Odin's disgrace and destruction by poisoning his mind against Desi. Although blasted by some critics as full of skimpy plot devices, there's not much that's not taken straight from the source material. Filmed in 1999, it was pulled by skittish studio bigwigs following the Columbine shootings and not released until 2001. 94m/C VHS, Mekhi Phifer, Josh Hartnett, Julia Stiles, Elden (Ratliff) Henson, Andrew Keegan, Rain Phoenix, John Heard, A.J. (Anthony) Johnson, Martin Sheen; D: Tim Blake Nelson; W: Brad Kaaya; C: Russell Fine; M: Jeff Danna.

O

resent her influence. When her first love returns after 15 years and the romance is rekindled, family resentments surface once again. Based on the novel by Willa Cather. A Hallmark Hall of Fame presentation. **99m/C VHS, DVD.** Jessica Lange, David Strathairn, Tom Aldredge, Reed Edward Diamond, Anne Heche, Heather Graham, Josh Hamilton, Leigh Lawson, Graham Beckel; **D:** Glenn Jordan; **W:** Glenn Jordan. **TV**

O Quatrilho 1995 Two young couples from Italy immigrate to southern Brazil in the 1910s, hoping to find their fortunes. Thrifty peasant Angelo (Paternost) marries romantic Teresa (Pillar) and goes into business with the equally romantic Massimo (Campos), who's married to the thrifty Pierina (Pires). The grain mill thrives but the romantic half of each couple delve into some illicit amore and decide to flee while their left-behind spouses discover their own attractions. A happy ending is had by all (this must be a fairytale). Lots of high-gloss gush. Based on the novel by Jose Clemente Pozenat. Portuguese and Italian with subtitles. **120m/C VHS.** *BR* Gloria Pires, Patricia Pillar, Bruno Campos, Alexandre Paternost; **D:** Fabio Barreto; **W:** Leopoldo Serran; **C:** Felix Monti; **M:** Caetano Veloso.

The Oak 1993 Morgenstern grieves over the loss of her father until she realizes she can't get rid of the body. Her difficulties in locating adequate medical facilities reflect the nightmarish realities of pre-1990 communist Romania. Potentially farcical aspects of storyline are successfully removed by violence in following scene involving Morgenstern and a band of roaming soldiers. A tragicomic look at obstinate communist bureaucrats and the wily, willful bureaucrats who overcome them. Based on a novel by Ion Baiesu. In Romanian with English subtitles. **105m/C VHS.** *RO* Maia Morgenstern, Razvan Vasilescu, Victor Rebengiuc, Dorel Visan, Mariana Mihut, Dan Condurache, Virgil Andriescu, Leopoldina Balanuta, Matei Alexandru, Gheorghe Visu, Magda Catone, Lucian Pintilie; **D:** Lucian Pintilie; **W:** Lucian Pintilie.

Oasis of the Zombies *Bloodsucking Nazi Zombies; Treasure of the Living Dead* 1982 European students set out to find lost buried treasure in Saharan oasis but instead find bevy of hungry Nazis with eating disorders. Franco directed under the name "A.M. Frank." **75m/C VHS, DVD.** *SP FR* Manuel Gelin, France Jordan, Jeff Montgomery, Miriam Landson, Eric Saint-Just, Caroline Audret, Henry Lambert; **D:** Jess (Jesus) Franco; **W:** Jess (Jesus) Franco.

The Object of Beauty 1991 **(R)** Two Americans, trapped in Europe by their love of pleasure and their lack of money, bicker over whether to sell their one object of value—a tiny Henry Moore sculpture. When it disappears, their relationship is challenged. Excellent acting and telling direction. Forces an examination of one's own value placement. **105m/C VHS, DVD.** Andie MacDowell, John Malkovich, Joss Ackland, Lolita (David) Davidovich, Peter Riegert, Bill Paterson, Rudi Davies, Ricci Harnett; **D:** Michael Lindsay-Hogg; **W:** Michael Lindsay-Hogg; **C:** David Watkin; **M:** Tom Bahler.

The Object of My Affection 1998 **(R)** Nina (Aniston) is a Brooklyn social worker with an overbearing boyfriend, Vince (Pankow), she doesn't really love. Unfortunately, the man she does fall for is handsome gay teacher George (Rudd), who's just broken up with his pretentious boyfriend Joley (Daly), and who winds up renting Nina's spare room. When Nina discovers she's pregnant, she decides George would make a terrific father and asks him to raise the baby with her. But both turn out to have very unrealistic expectations about friendship and romance. Mix of humor and tears, with good performances, particularly by the appealing leads. Adapted from the novel by Stephen McCauley. **112m/C VHS, DVD.** Jennifer Aniston, Paul Rudd, John Pankow, Timothy Daly, Alan Alda, Nigel Hawthorne, Allison Janney, Amo Guinello, Steve Zahn, Daniel Cosgrove; **D:** Nicholas Hytner; **W:** Wendy Wasserstein; **C:** Oliver Stapleton; **M:** George Fenton.

Object of Obsession 1995 **(R)** One wrong phone call propels divorcee Margaret into an affair with a stranger that leads to kinky psycho/sexual games and revenge. **91m/C VHS, DVD.** Erika Anderson, Scott Valentine; **D:** Alexander Gregory (Gregory Dark) Hippolyte; **W:** Brad (Sean) Marlowe; **C:** Wally Pfister.

Objective, Burma! 1945 Deemed by many to be the greatest and most moving WWII production released during the war. American paratroopers are dropped over Burma where their mission is to destroy a Japanese radar station. The Americans led by Flynn are successful in wiping out the station, but they are spotted and descended upon by Japanese forces. Impeded from returning to Allied lines, the American soldiers must try to survive enemy encounters, exhaustion, starvation, and the elements until they are rescued. Splendid performance by Flynn and exceptional direction from Walsh; excellent performances enhanced by energetic score. **142m/B VHS, DVD.** Errol Flynn, James Brown, William Prince, George Tobias, Henry Hull, Warner Anderson, Richard Erdman, Mark Stevens, Anthony Caruso, Hugh Beaumont, John Alvin, William (Bill) Hudson, Lester Matthews, George Tyne, Erville Alderson; **D:** Raoul Walsh; **W:** Ranald MacDougall, Lester Cole; **C:** James Wong Howe; **M:** Franz Waxman.

Oblivion 1994 **(PG-13)** In this sci-fi western, set in the year 3031, its cowboys versus the aliens. A sheriff's son (Paul) returns to the town of Oblivion to avenge his father's murder and finds a reptilian extraterrestrial (Divoff) terrorizing the community. **94m/C VHS, DVD.** Richard Joseph Paul, Andrew Divoff, Jackie Swanson, Meg Foster, Isaac Hayes, Julie Newmar, Carel Struycken, George Takei; **D:** Sam Irvin; **W:** Peter David; **M:** Pino Donaggio.

Oblomov *A Few Days in the Life of I.I. Oblomov; Neskolko Dnei iz Zhizni I.I. Oblomov* 1981 A production of the classic Goncharov novel about a symbolically inert Russian aristocrat whose childhood friend helps him find a reason for action. Well made, with fine performances. In Russian with English subtitles. **145m/C VHS, DVD.** *RU* Oleg Tabakov, Elena Solovei; **D:** Nikita Mikhalkov.

The Oblong Box *Edgar Allen Poe's The Oblong Box* 1969 **(PG)** Coffins, blood, and live corpses fill drawn-out and lifeless adaptation of Edgar Allan Poe story. English aristocrat Price attempts to hide his disfigured brother in an old tower. Brother predictably escapes and rampages through town before being killed. **91m/C VHS, DVD.** *GB* Vincent Price, Christopher Lee, Alister Williamson, Hilary Dwyer, Peter Arne, Harry Baird, Carl Rigg, Sally Geeson, Maxwell Shaw; **D:** Gordon Hessler; **C:** John Coquillon.

The Obsessed *The Late Edwina Black* 1951 Uninspiring story with Farrar suspected of murdering his wife. Competent performances, but this mystery isn't developed with any sense of style and the killer's real identity will make any differences don't add anything. **77m/B VHS, DVD.** David Farrar, Geraldine Fitzgerald, Roland Culver, Jean Cadell, Mary Merrall, Harcourt Williams, Charles Heslop, Ronald Adam, Sydney Monkton; **D:** Maurice Elvey; **W:** Charles Frank, David Evans; **C:** Stephen Dade.

Obsessed 1988 **(PG-13)** Semi-realistic tale of a woman's exhausting desire for revenge against hit-and-run driver who killed her son. Cast acceptable but lack of psychological foundation weakens plot. **100m/C VHS.** Allan Nicholls, Kerrie Keane, Alan Thicke, Colleen Dewhurst, Saul Rubinek, Daniel Pilon, Lynne Griffin; **D:** Robin Spry. **Genie '89:** Support. Actress (Dewhurst).

Obsession 1976 **(PG)** A rich, lonely businessman meets a mysterious young girl in Italy, the mirror image of his late wife who was killed by kidnappers. Intriguing suspense film that's not quite up to comparisons with Hitchcock thrillers. Music by Hitchcock-collaborator Herrmann. **98m/C VHS, DVD.** Cliff Robertson, Genevieve Bujold, John Lithgow; **D:** Brian De Palma; **W:** Paul Schrader; **C:** Vilmos Zsigmond; **M:** Bernard Herrmann.

Obsession 1997 Pierre (Berling) is Miriam's (Makatsch) longtime lover. They seem happy until Miriam has a chance encounter at the Berlin train station with Jack McHale (Craig), who's investigating a family secret. The romantic triangle is inexplicable (Pierre's accepting, Jack's suddenly obsessed, and Miriam waffles) and John's family quest is confusing and ends in an unsatisfying manner. **105m/C DVD.** *FR GE* Heike Makatsch, Charles Berling, Daniel Craig, Seymour Cassel, Allen (Gorowitz) Garfield, Marie-Christine Barrault, Daniel Gelin; **D:** Peter Sehr; **W:** Peter Sehr, Marie Noelle; **C:** David Watkin; **M:** Micki Meuser.

Obsession: A Taste for Fear 1989 **(R)** Diane's high fashion models are being killed and although there are plenty of suspects, she can't find the killer. **90m/C VHS.** Virginia Hey, Gerard Darmon, Carlo Mucari; **D:** Piccio Raffanini.

Obsessive Love 1984 A lonely, mentally unstable typist (Mimieux) becomes obsessed with her soap opera hero and decides to go to Hollywood to seduce him. She transforms herself into a sleek and stunning Hollywood temptress to woo him, and at first he goes along with her—until he realizes that she is insane. An average made-for-TV movie of the older woman/younger man genre. **97m/C VHS.** Yvette Mimieux, Simon MacCorkindale, Kin Shriner, Constance McCashin, Allan Miller, Lainie Kazan; **D:** Steven Hilliard Stern.

O.C. and Stiggs 1987 **(R)** Two teens spend a summer harassing a neighbor and his family. Flimsy attempts at comedy fall flat. A failed adaptation of a National Lampoon short story, it was held for three years before release. **109m/C VHS, DVD.** Daniel H. Jenkins, Neill Barry, Jane Curtin, Tina Louise, Jon Cryer, Dennis Hopper, Paul Dooley, Ray Walston, Louis Nye, Martin Mull, Melvin Van Peebles; **D:** Robert Altman; **W:** Donald Cantrell.

An Occasional Hell 1996 **(R)** Ernest DeWalt (Berenger) is an ex-cop turned writer and college professor. He investigates the death of a fellow professor (Lang) at the behest of the beautiful widow (Golino) and then learns the lady is the prime suspect. Filmed in South Carolina and based on the novel by Silvis, who wrote the screenplay. **93m/C VHS, DVD.** Tom Berenger, Valeria Golino, Kari Wuhrer, Robert Davi, Stephen Lang, Richard Edson, Geoffrey Lewis; **D:** Salome Breziner; **W:** Randall Silvis; **C:** Mauro Fiore; **M:** Anton Sanko.

The Occultist WOOF! 1989 Satan worshippers do the dance of death as they skin men alive for their evil purposes. **82m/C VHS, DVD.** Rick Gianasi; **D:** Tim Kincaid; **W:** Tim Kincaid.

Occupation: Dreamland 2005 Documentary directors Scott and Olds spent six weeks in 2004 in the very dangerous city of Fallujah, following an eight-man squad of the Army's 82nd Airborne as they deal with hostile fire, isolation, bewildering customs, and whether their presence really will make any difference to the Iraqis. **78m/C DVD.** *US* Garrett Scott, Ian Olds.

An Occurrence at Owl Creek Bridge/Coup de Grace 1962 "Occurrence at Owl Creek Bridge" (1962), from a story by Ambrose Bierce documents the last moments of a man about to be hanged for sabotage. "Coup de Grace" (1978) tells the story of a group of friends who are caught up amongst the turmoil of the Bolshevik revolution. **123m/B VHS, DVD.** Margarethe von Trotta, Matthias Habich, Rudiger Kirschstein, Matthieu Carriere, Valeska Gert; **D:** Volker Schlondorff, Robert Enrico.

Ocean Drive Weekend WOOF! 1985 **(PG-13)** Several college students congregate at "Ocean Drive" for a weekend of beer, sex, and dancing. Stereotypical characters, lack of plot, and poor versions of 1960 classics combine for boring and inane comedy. **96m/C VHS.** Robert Peacock, Charles Redmond, Tony Freeman; **D:** Brian Thomas Jones.

Ocean's 11 1960 A Rat Pack romp. Spyros Acebos (Tamiroff) comes up with a plan to simultaneously rob five Las Vegas casinos on New Year's Eve. Danny Ocean (Sinatra) will lead his buddies—all of whom are veterans of the 82nd Airborne Division—in the action by shutting off all the electricity. The planning's elaborate but the plan itself goes wrong (so what else is new) and the gang can't get their stolen loot out of the city. **148m/C VHS, DVD.** Frank Sinatra, Dean Martin, Sammy Davis Jr., Angie Dickinson, Peter Lawford, Richard Conte, Cesar Romero, Joey Bishop, Akim Tamiroff, Henry Silva, Buddy Lester, Norman Fell, Red Skelton, Shirley MacLaine, George Raft; **D:** Lewis Milestone; **W:** Harry Brown, Charles Lederer; **C:** William H. Daniels; **M:** Nelson Riddle.

Ocean's Eleven 2001 **(PG-13)** Stylish, fun remake of the 1960 Rat Pack caper flick measures up to the original in Cool Factor and surpasses it in plot and action. In this version, Danny Ocean (Clooney) is an ex-con with a taste for the grift and a grudge against powerful casino owner Benedict (Garcia). Backed by an eclectic, amusingly quirky crew, he encounters complications when his ex (Roberts) turns out to be involved with Benedict. Great cast looks like they're having a blast (especially Gould and Reiner, who make the most of small but showy roles) as Soderbergh's "Midas touch" streak continues. **116m/C VHS, DVD, UMD.** *US* George Clooney, Brad Pitt, Andy Garcia, Matt Damon, Julia Roberts, Don Cheadle, Casey Affleck, Scott Caan, Elliott Gould, Bernie Mac, Carl Reiner, Edward Jemison, Shaobo Qin; **Cameos:** Henry Silva, Angie Dickinson, Holly Marie Combs, Joshua Jackson, Topher Grace, Steve Lawrence, Eydie Gorme, Wayne Newton; **D:** Steven Soderbergh; **W:** Ted Griffin; **C:** Steven Soderbergh; **M:** David Holmes.

Oceans of Fire 1986 **(PG)** Average rehash of the tension-filled world of oil riggers. Lives of two ex-cons are threatened when they hire on as divers for world's deepest undersea oil rig. **100m/C VHS, DVD.** Gregory Harrison, Billy Dee Williams, Cynthia Sikes, Lyle Alzado, Tony Burton, Ray "Boom Boom" Mancini, David Carradine, Ken Norton; **D:** Steve Carver.

Ocean's Thirteen 2007 **(PG-13)** The neo-Rat Pack returns to Vegas, baby, where they belong. Reuben (Gould) has been screwed out of his share of the strip's newest luxury hotel/casino by double-dealing egomaniac Willie Banks (Pacino). So Danny (Clooney) and Rusty (Pitt) assemble their usual team and concoct an elaborate plan (including simulating an earthquake) to sabotage the opening, bankrupt the casino, and ruin Banks. Old nemesis Garcia gets to join in on the fun this time out. Barkin comes in to cherchez la femme. So should you. **122m/C DVD, Blu-ray Disc, HD DVD.** *US* George Clooney, Brad Pitt, Matt Damon, Andy Garcia, Al Pacino, Bernie Mac, Ellen Barkin, Casey Affleck, Scott Caan, Elliott Gould, Shaobo Qin, Don Cheadle, Edward Jemison, Carl Reiner, Eddie Izzard, Michael Mantell, David Paymer, Vincent Cassel, Julian Sands, Bob Einstein, Noureen DeWulf; **D:** Steven Soderbergh; **W:** Brian Koppelman, David Levien; **C:** Steven Soderbergh; **M:** David Holmes.

Ocean's Twelve 2004 **(PG-13)** The gang's all back, enjoying themselves mightily in this undemanding but fun sequel. It's taken three years but casino boss Terry Benedict (Garcia) has tracked down Danny Ocean (Clooney), who's now remarried to Tess (Roberts), and demands repayment of his $160 mil or else. Having spent his share of the dough, Danny gets the boys together and he and partner Rusty (Pitt) come up with a plan that takes them all a-thieving in various picturesque European cities. New to the adventure are Interpol agent Isabel Lahiri (Zeta-Jones), who has an amorous past with Rusty, and top Euro thief Francois Toulour (Cassel) out to prove just who's the best criminal. A frivolous, good-looking romp all the way. **125m/C VHS, DVD.** *US* George Clooney, Brad Pitt, Matt Damon, Cathenne Zeta-Jones, Andy Garcia, Don Cheadle, Bernie Mac, Casey Affleck, Scott Caan, Vincent Cassel, Edward Jemison, Shaobo Qin, Carl Reiner, Elliot Gould, Robbie Coltrane, Eddie Izzard, Cherry Jones, Jeroen Krabbé, Julia Roberts, Jared Harris; **D:** Steven Soderbergh; **W:** George Nolfi; **C:** Steven Soderbergh; **M:** David Holmes.

Octagon 🐶🐶 1980 (R) Norris protects a woman from threatening Ninja warriors in average kung-fu adventure. Enough action and violence for fans of the genre. 103m/C VHS, DVD, UMD. Chuck Norris, Karen Carlson, Lee Van Cleef, Kim Lankford, Art Hindle, Jack Carter; **D:** Eric Karson; **W:** Paul Aaron, Leigh Chapman.

Octaman 🐶🐶 1971 Comical thriller featuring non-threatening octopus-man discovered by scientists in Mexico. Rip-off of director Essex's own "Creature from the Black Lagoon." Not without its curiosity factor: young Rick Baker designed the octopus man, while actress Angeli died of a drug overdose during filming. 79m/C VHS, DVD. Kerwin Mathews, Pier Angeli, Harry Guardino, David Essex, Jeff Morrow, Norman Fields; **D:** Harry Essex; **W:** Harry Essex; **C:** Robert Caramico.

Octavia 🐶 1982 (P) A contemporary fable about a blind girl who befriends a stranger with mental problems must prove his innocence to others and himself. Strong characters make good suspense. 95m/C VHS. GB John Mills, Joan Greenwood, Edward Chapman, Joyce Carey, Kay Walsh, Felix Aylmer, Juliet Mills; **D:** Roy Ward Baker; **W:** Eric Ambler.

The October Man 🐶🐶🐶 1948 Relates the true story of young Homer Hickam Jr. (Gyllenhaal), who rose from a gloomy West Virginia mining town to become a NASA engineer. Spurred by the launch of Sputnik and a supportive teacher (Dern), Homer and three of his friends experiment with rockets with the hope of winning college scholarships. Adapted from Hickam's memoir "Rocket Boys." The boys battle the skepticism of their peers and families as well as the looming possibility of a future in the mines. Entertaining and uplifting without resorting to melodrama and sentimentality. Adapted from Hickam's memoir "Rocket Boys." 108m/C VHS, DVD. Jake Gyllenhaal, Chris Cooper, Laura Dern, Chris Owen, William Lee Scott, Chad Lindberg, Natalie Canerday, Scott Miles, Randy Stripling, Chris Ellis; **D:** Joe Johnston; **W:** Lewis Colick; **C:** Paul M. rphy; **M:** Mark Isham.

October Sky 🐶🐶🐶 1999 (PG) Relates the true story of young Homer Hickam Jr.

Octopus 🐶🐶 2000 (PG-13) Giant mutant octopus lurking in the ocean depths is disturbed by a U.S. Navy submarine and decides to make it lunch. This, however, is not the only bad news. Seems the sub was transporting a terrorist who escapes in the confusion, and winds up on a cruise ship. He thinks he's safe but our eight-legged horror is just getting started. Special effects are pretty lame but the humor doesn't take itself seriously a d the horror covers a lot of holes. 99m/C VHS, DVD. Jay Harrington, Ravil Isyanov; **D:** John Eyres; **W:** Michael D. Weiss; **C:** Adolfo Bartoli; **M:** Marco Marinangeli. VIDEO

Octopus 2: River of Fear 🐶🐶 2002 (R) After two Russian tourists are killed on the waterfront of the Hudson River, scuba diver cop Nick (Burke) discovers a giant man-eating octopus. Not wanting to spoil the city's 4th of July celebrations, the mayor refuses to do anything. So Nick and his partner Walter (Lane) must stop the rampaging creature—who attacks the Statue of Liberty. That's just wrong. 95m/C VHS, DVD. Michael Reilly Burke, Frederic Lenne, Duncan Fraser, Meredith Morton, John Thaddeus; **D:** Yossi Wein; **W:** Michael D. Weiss; **C:** Peter Belcher; **M:** Bill Wandel. VIDEO

Octopussy 🐶🐶 1983 (PG) The Bond saga continues as Agent 007 is on a mission to prevent a crazed Russian general from launching a nuclear attack against the NATO forces in Europe. Lots of special effects and gadgets keep weak plot moving. 140m/C VHS, DVD. GB Roger Moore, Maud Adams, Louis Jourdan, Kristina Wayborn,

---

The Odd Angry Shot 🐶🐶½ 1979 Australian soldiers fighting in Vietnam discover the conflict is not what they expected. Ironic perspective of men struggling with their feelings about the war. More of an unremarkable drama with comic overtones than a combat film, it will appeal to those who prefer good direction to bloodshed. 90m/C VHS. AU Graham Kennedy, John Hargreaves, John Jarratt, Bryan Brown, Graeme Blundell, Richard Moir, Ian Gilmour, John Allen, Brandon Burke, Graham Rouse, Tony Barry, Max Cullen, John Fitzgerald, Ray Meagher; **D:** Tom Jeffrey; **W:** Tom Jeffrey; **C:** Donald McAlpine; **M:** Walter (Wendy) Carlos.

Odd Birds 🐶🐶½ 1985 Coming of age drama set in 1965 California. Shy 15-year-old Joy Chan is a Chinese-American dreaming of becoming an actress. Her widowed immigrant mother wants Joy to have a practical profession—like nursing. Longing for someone to understand Joy, meets Brother Murphy, a math teacher at the loca boys school. Murphy's been trying to reconcile his religious commitment with his unorthodox views. It isn't long before these two individuals recognize a fellow kindred spirit. 87m/C VHS. Michael Moriarty, Donna Lai Ming Lew, Nancy Lee, Bruce Gray, Karen Maruyama, Scott Crawford; **D:** Jeanne Collachia; **W:** Jeanne Collachia.

The Odd Couple 🐶🐶🐶½ 1968 Two divorced men with completely opposite personalities move in together. Lemmon's obsession with neatness drives slob Matthau up the wall, and their inability to see eye-to-eye results in many hysterical escapades. A Hollywood rarity, it is actually better in some ways than Neil Simon's original Broadway version. Simon based the characters on brother Danny and his roommates. Basis for the hit TV series. 106m/C VHS, DVD. Jack Lemmon, Walter Matthau, Herb Edelman, John Fiedler, Monica Evans, Carole Shelley; **D:** Gene Saks; **W:** Neil Simon; **C:** Robert B. Hauser.

The Odd Job 🐶🐶 1978 Insurance salesman Chapman, depressed after his wife leaves him, hires a hit man to kill him. Chapman then has a hard time shaking his stalker after deciding he wants to live. Monty Python fans will enjoy seeing extroupe member Chapman again, but the comic's heart isn't in this unoriginal story. 100m/C VHS. GB Graham Chapman; **D:** Peter Medak; **M:** Howard Blake.

Odd Jobs 🐶🐶 1985 (PG-13) When five college friends look for jobs during summer break, they wind up running their own moving business with the help of the mob. Good comic talent, but a silly slapstick script results in only a passable diversion. 89m/C VHS, DVD. Paul Reiser, Scott McGinnis, Rick Overton, Robert Kevin Townsend; **D:** Mark Story; **W:** Robert Conte; **C:** Arthur Albert; **M:** Robert Folk.

Odd Man Out 🐶🐶🐶½ 1947 An Irish revolutionary is injured during a robbery attempt. Suffering from gunshot wounds and closely pursued by the police, he must rely on the help of others who could betray him at any moment. A gripping tale of suspense and intrigue that will keep the proverbial seat's edge warm until the final credits. Adapted from "F.L. Greer's novel, previously filmed as 'The Last Man.' 111m/B VHS, DVD. GB James Mason, Robert Newton, Dan O'Herlihy, Kathleen Ryan, Cyril Cusack, Dan O'Herlihy, F.J. McCormick, W.G. Fay; **D:** Carol Reed; **W:** F.L. Green, R.C. Sherriff; **C:** Robert Krasker; **M:** William Alwyn. British Acad. '47: Film.

Odd Obsession 🐶🐶🐶½ 1960 One of Ichikawa's first films, about an elderly Japanese gentleman with a young wife whose feelings of jealousy and impotence eventually wreak havoc on the marriage. In Japanese with English subtitles. 96m/C VHS. JP Machiko Kyo, Ganjiro Nakamura; **D:** Kon Ichikawa. Golden Globes '60: Foreign Film.

The Odd Squad 🐶🐶½ 1986 (R) The Key Gls in WWII defend a bridge from the enemy, and manage in doing so to have loads of laughs. 82m/C VHS. Johnny Dorelli, Vincent Gardenia; **D:** E.B. (Enzo Barboni) Clucher.

Oddballs WOOF! 1984 (PG-13) In another attempt to capitalize on the success of Bill Murray's "Meatballs," this summer camp story features three campers and their pathetic attempts to lose their virginity. Brooks has his moments, but there is little else to recommend here. 92m/C VHS. DVD. Foster Brooks, Jason Sorokin, Wally Wodchis, Konnie Krome; **D:** Miklos Lente.

Odds Against Tomorrow 🐶🐶🐶 1959 Compulsive gambler/nightclub singer Johnny Ingram (Belafonte) owes big money to gangster Bacco (Kuluva). He hooks up with racist ex-con Earl Slater (Ryan) and former policeman Dave Burke (Begley) to rob a bank but everything goes wrong. Ingram and Slater manage to escape to a nearby oil storage area but the racial tensions between the two are proving deadlier than the cops on their trail. Based on the novel by William P. McGivern; because of the blacklist screenwriter Polonsky was "fronted" by John O. Killens. Polonsky officially received credit for this work in 1996. 120m/B VHS, DVD. Harry Belafonte, Robert Ryan, Shelley Winters, Ed Begley Sr., Gloria Grahame, Will Kuluva, Richard Bright; **C:** Robert Burks; **D:** Robert Wise; **W:** Abraham Polonsky, Nelson Gidding; **C:** Joseph Brun.

Odds and Evens 🐶½ 1978 (PG) Italian supercops pretend they don't have badges in order to clean up illegal betting and gambling rings in sunny Miami. Odds are this spaghetti cop-o-rama won't keep work well together. 106m/C VHS. Robby Benson, Glynnis O'Connor, Joan Hotchkis, Sandy McPeak, James Best; **D:** Max Baer Jr.

Ode to Billy Joe 🐶🐶½ 1976 (PG) The 1967 Bobby Gentry hit song of the same title is expanded to tell why a young man jumped to his death off the Tallahatchie Bridge. The problems of growing up in the rural South and teenage romance do not match the appeal of the theme song. Benson and O'Connor, however, work well together. 106m/C VHS, DVD. Robby Benson, Glynnis O'Connor, Joan Hotchkis, Sandy McPeak, James Best; **D:** Max Baer Jr.

The Odessa File 🐶🐶½ 1974 (PG) During 1963, a German journalist attempts to track down some SS war criminals who have formed a secret organization called ODESSA. The story, from Frederick Forsyth's novel, drags in some places, but the scene where bad guy Schell and reporter Voight finally confront each other is a high point. 128m/C VHS. DVD. GB Jon Voight, Mary Tamm, Maximilian Schell, Maria Schell, Derek Jacobi, Peter Jeffrey, Klaus Lowitsch, Kurt Meisel, Hannes Messemer, Garfield Morgan, Shmuel Rodensky, Ernst Schroder, Noel Willman, Hans Caninenberg, Towje Kleiner, Gunnar Moller; **D:** Ronald Neame; **W:** Kenneth Ross, George Markstein; **C:** Oswald Morris; **M:** Andrew Lloyd Webber.

The Odyssey 🐶🐶½ 1997 (PG-13) Lavish TV miniseries based on Homer's 2,700-year-old epic poem, relating the adventures of King Odysseus of Ithaca. On the day his son is born to faithful wife Penelope (Scacchi), Odysseus (Assante) is commanded by the goddess Athena (Rossellini) to leave his home and travel to battle the Trojans. Little does he realize that this is the beginning of a 20-year sojourn, where additional trials include sea monsters, the Cyclops, the Kingdom of the Dead, enchantress Circe (Peters), and getting shipwrecked on the isle of Calypso (Williams), who wants to keep the hunk around. But even Odysseus realizes there's no place like home. 203m/C VHS. 96m/C VHS. JP Machiko Kyo, Ganjiro Nakamura, Bernadette Peters, Irene Papas, Vanessa Williams, Christopher Lee, Isabella Rossellini, Jeroen Krabbé, Nicholas Clay, Ron Cook, Michael J. Pollard, Paloma Baeza, Armand Assante, Greta Scacchi, Geraldine Chaplin, Eric Roberts, Bernadette Peters, Irene Papas; **D:** Andrei Konchalovsky; **W:** Andrei Konchalovsky, Chris Solimine; **C:** Sergei Kozov; **M:** Eduard Artemyev. TV

Oddball Hall 🐶🐶 1991 (PG) Two aging jewel thieves hide out in the African wilds, masquerading as powerful "wizards." When they head back to civilization, an African tribe beseeches the phony sorcerers to cure their long drought. 87m/C VHS. Don Ameche, Burgess Meredith; **D:** Jackson Hunsicker.

Oedipus Rex 🐶🐶🐶 1967 Edipo Re A new twist on the famous tragedy as Pasolini gives the story a modern prologue and epilogue. The classic plot has Oedipus spiraling downward into moral horror as he tries to avoid fulfilling the prophecy that he will murder his father and sleep with his mother. Cross-cultural curiosities include Japanese music and Lenin-inspired songs, some written by Pasolini who also stars as the high priest. In Italian with English subtitles. 110m/C VHS, DVD. IT Franco Citti, Silvana Mangano, Alida Valli, Julian Beck, Pier Paolo Pasolini; **D:** Pier Paolo Pasolini; **W:** Pier Paolo Pasolini; **C:** Pasqualino De Santis; **M:** Pier Paolo Pasolini.

The Odyssey of the Pacific 🐶🐶½ 1982 L'Empereur de Peru Three young Cambodian refugees encounter retired train engineer Rooney living in the woods where a railway station once thrived. Together they work to restore an old locomotive. The ordinary, inoffensive script will not endanger any family time. 82m/C VHS. CA Mickey Rooney, Monique Mercure; **D:** Fernando Arrabal.

Of Freaks and Men 🐶🐶 1998 Pro Urodov I Lyudei 1998 Kinky Russian melodrama set in pre-revolutionary St. Petersburg. Pornographer Johann and his assistant Viktor specialize in selling photos and films featuring half-naked women getting flogged. They manage to insinuate themselves into two upper class Russian households and involve the families in some secret sadomasochistic games. Russian with subtitles. 93m/C VHS, DVD. RU Tatiana Polonskaya, Sergei Makovetsky, Dinara Drukarova, Anzhelika Nevolina, Viktor Sukhorukov, Aleksei De, Chingiz Tsydendambayev, Vadim Prokhorov, Ale-sandr Mezentsev, Igor Shibanov, Darya Lesnikova; **D:** Aleksei Balabanov; **W:** Aleksei Balabanov; **C:** Sergei Astakhov; **M:** Eric Neveux.

Of Human Bondage 🐶🐶🐶 1934 The first movie version of W. Somerset Maugham's classic novel in which a young, handicapped medical student falls in love with a crude cockney waitress, in a mutually destructive affair. Established Davis's role as the tough, domineering woman. Remade in 1946 and 1964. 84m/B VHS, DVD. Bette Davis, Leslie Howard, Frances Dee, Reginald Owen, Reginald Denny, Alan Hale, Kay Johnson; **D:** John Cromwell; **W:** Lester Cohen; **C:** Henry W. Gerrard; **M:** Max Steiner.

Of Human Bondage 🐶🐶 1964 An essentially decent man falls fatally in love with an alluring but heartless waitress, who subtly destroys him. Based on the W. Somerset Maugham novel. Miscast and least interesting of the three film versions, although Novak gives a good performance. 100m/B VHS, DVD. GB Kim Novak, Laurence Harvey, Robert Morley, Roger Livesey, Siobhan McKenna; **D:** Henry Hathaway, Ken Hughes; **W:** Bryan Forbes; **C:** Oswald Morris.

Of Human Hearts 🐶🐶½ 1938 Rural life just before the Civil War sets up this compone tale of family strife. Huston is a stern preacher who has his family living in near poverty as an example of sacrifice to his flock. Son Stewart wants to study medicine and fund his dream. Only Stewart becomes so engrossed by his ambitions that he ignores the family, even after his father dies and his mother is left poor and alone. Then Stewart joins the Civil War as a doctor where he meets President Lincoln (Carradine), who tells him he should never neglect his mother. Oy. Well, the cast is good. Adapted from the story "Benefits Forgot" by Honore Morrow. 100m/B VHS. James Stewart, Beulah Bondi, Walter Huston, John Carradine, Guy Kibbee, Charles Coburn, Ann Rutherford, Charley Grapewin, Gene Lockhart; **D:** Clarence Brown; **W:** Bradbury Foote; **C:** Clyde De Vinna.

Of Love and Shadows 🐶🐶 1994 (R) Political photojournalist Francisco (Banderas) begins investigating the disappearance of a self-proclaimed saint after the bloody 1973 coup in Chile. He's aided by aristocratic Chilean Irene (Connelly), who's engaged to her Army captain cousin Gustavo (Gallardo) but can't resist Francisco's ever-smoldering charms. The intrepid duo naturally find lots of corruption. Based on the novel by Isabel Allende;

Of

shot on location in Argentina. **103m/C VHS, DVD.** Antonio Banderas, Jennifer Connelly, Stefania Sandrelli, Camillo Gallardo, Patricio Contreras; **D:** Betty Kaplan; **W:** Donald Freed; **C:** Felix Monti; **M:** Jose Nieto.

Of Mice and Men 🦴🦴🦴 **1939** A powerful adaptation of the classic Steinbeck tragedy about the friendship between two itinerant Southern ranch hands during the Great Depression. Chaney is wonderful as the gentle giant and mentally retarded Lenny, cared for by migrant worker Meredith. They both get into an irreversible situation when a woman is accidentally killed. **107m/C VHS, DVD.** Lon Chaney Jr., Burgess Meredith, Betty Field, Bob Steele, Noah Beery Jr., Charles Bickford; **D:** Lewis Milestone; **W:** Eugene Solow; **C:** Norbert Brodine; **M:** Aaron Copland.

Of Mice and Men 🦴🦴🦴 **1981** TV remake of the classic Steinbeck tale, casting TV's Baretta (Blake) as George and Quaid as Lenny. Worth watching. **150m/C VHS, DVD.** Robert (Bobby) Blake, Randy Quaid, Lew Ayres, Mitchell Ryan, Ted Neeley, Cassie Yates, Pat Hingle, Whitman Mayo, Dennis Fimple, Pat Corley; **D:** Reza Badiyi. **TV**

Of Mice and Men 🦴🦴🦴 **1992** (PG-13) Set on the migratory farms of California, John Steinbeck's novel covers the friendship of the simple-minded Lenny, his protector George, and a flirtatious farm wife who doesn't know Lenny's strength. Director Sinise got permission from Steinbeck's widow to film the novel (actually the third adaptation). **110m/C VHS, DVD.** John Malkovich, Sherilyn Fenn, Casey Siemaszko, Joe Morton, Ray Walston, Gary Sinise, John Terry, Richard Riehle, Joe Garre; **W:** Horton Foote; **C:** Kenneth Macmillan; **M:** Mark Isham.

Off and Running 🦴1/2 **1990** (PG-13) Struggling actress Cyd (Lauper) is working as a mermaid at a Miami hotel lounge when her horse trainer boyfriend Woody is suddenly murdered by a psycho thug (Belzer). Turns out he's after a key hidden in a necklace now in Cyd's possession. Cyd goes on the run and gets some help from failed golf pro Jack (Keith) as they try to stay one step ahead of the killer and discover what the key unlocks. **91m/C VHS.** Cyndi Lauper, David Keith, Richard Belzer, David Thornton, Anita Morris; **D:** Edward Bianchi; **C:** Eugene Robert Glazer; **C:** Andrzej Bartkowiak; **M:** Mason Daring.

Off Beat 🦴1/2 **1986** (PG) A shy librarian unluckily wins a spot in a police benefit dance troupe, and then falls in love with a tough police woman. With a screenplay by playwright Medoff, and a good supporting cast, it still manages to miss the mark. **92m/C VHS.** Judge Reinhold, Meg Tilly, Cleavant Derricks, Fred Gwynne, John Turturro, Jacques D'Amboise, James Tolkan, Joe Mantegna, Harvey Keitel, Amy Wright, Christopher Noth; **D:** Michael Dinner; **W:** Mark Medoff; **C:** Carlo Di Palma; **M:** James Horner.

Off Limits 🦴🦴1/2 **1953** When a boxing manager is drafted into the Army, he freely breaks regulations in order to train a fighter as he sees fit. Hope and Rooney, while not in peak form, make a snappy duo in this amusing romp. **89m/B VHS.** Bob Hope, Mickey Rooney, Marilyn Maxwell, Marvin Miller; **D:** George Marshall.

Off Limits 🦴🦴1/2 **1987** (R) A spree of murders involving Vietnamese hookers draws two cops from the Army's Criminal Investigation Department into the sleazy backstreets of 1968 Saigon. There is little mystery as to who the killer is in this tale that seems written more for the sake of foul language and gratuitous gunfights than actual plot. **102m/C VHS, DVD.** Willem Dafoe, Gregory Hines, Fred Ward, Scott Glenn, Amanda Pays, Keith David, David Alan Grier; **D:** Christopher Crowe; **W:** Christopher Crowe, Jack Thibeau; **M:** James Newton Howard.

Off Season 🦴🦴1/2 **2001** A Christmas movie set in July or, rather, a spirit of Christmas movie set in July. Recently orphaned Jackson (Culkin) is now living with his Aunt Patty in Florida. She tends bar in a tacky hotel where they also live and Jackson likes to make up stories about the guests. He decides that cranky Sam Clausner (Cronyn) is actually Santa Claus on vacation, although the elderly man is more Scrooge-like than jolly. Then hotel manager Mel Breskin (McBeath) gets the idea to use Jackson's tall tale in a tasteless promotion scheme and things just snowball from there. **95m/C VHS, DVD.** Rory Culkin, Hume Cronyn, Sherilyn Fenn, Tom McBeath, Adam Arkin, Bruce Davison; **D:** Bruce Davison; **W:** Glen Gers; **C:** Tony Westman; **M:** Daniel Licht. **CABLE**

Off the Lip 🦴1/2 **2004** (R) Rookie reporter Kat gets to rove the wilds of Hawaii when her first beat puts her in pursuit of slippery surfing legend The Monk. While the search might have stalled, what she learns about herself means so golly gosh more. **88m/C VHS, DVD.** Marguerite Moreau, MacKenzie Astin, Adam Scott, Mark Fite, David Rasche, Jim Turner, Rick Overton, Matty Liu; **D:** Robert Mickelson; **W:** Shem Bitterman; **C:** Joey Forsyte; **M:** Andrew Gross. **VIDEO**

Off the Map 🦴🦴🦴 **2003** (PG-13) Folksy, quirky melodrama gets an extra bone for the strength of its performances. In 1974, eccentric IRS agent William Gibbs (True-Frost) is assigned to audit the Groden family and manages to stumble across their isolated New Mexico desert house. The Grodens, who live off the grid, are in the midst of a crisis: Grizzled Charley (Elliott) has slipped into clinical depression and hasn't spoken in months while free-spirited, unsentimental wife Arlene (Allen) gardens in the nude, and their pre-teen daughter Bo (de Angelis) longs for friends and a "normal" life. Gibbs becomes so involved with the Grodens that he throws his job aside to stay with them and his presence alters the family's precarious balance. Film is narrated by the grown-up Bo (Brenneman); Ackermann adapted from her play. **111m/C DVD. US** Joan Allen, Sam Elliott, J.K. Simmons, Amy Brenneman, Valentina de Angelis, Jim True-Frost; **D:** Campbell Scott; **W:** Joan Ackermann; **C:** Juan Ruiz-Anchia; **M:** Gary DeMichele.

Off the Mark 🦴1/2 **1987** (R) Neely is a young athlete suffering from a childhood affliction that causes spasms in his legs. Facing the ultimate challenge, he must overcome his handicap and defeat a talented woman athlete and a Russian student in a triathalon competition. An unremarkable effort, it had a limited one-week run in theatres. **89m/C VHS.** Mark Neely, Terry Farrell, Jon Cypher, Clarence Gilyard Jr.; **D:** Bill Berry; **C:** Aledge Armenaki.

Off the Wall 🦴 **1982** (R) Two hitchhikers wind up in a southern maximum security prison after being accused of a crime they did not commit. What follows is a series of shenanigans as they try to escape. This supposed comedy falls flat in every way with the possible exception of Arquette's portrayal of the governor's daughter. **86m/C VHS.** Paul Sorvino, Rosanna Arquette, Patrick Cassidy, Billy Hufsey, Monte Markham, Mickey Gilley; **D:** Rick Friedberg.

Off Your Rocker 🦴1/2 **1980** Representatives of a corporate conglomerate find that the residents of Flo Adler's Mapleview Nursing Home can still muster stiff resistance to a threatened takeover. **99m/C VHS.** Milton Berle, Red Buttons, Lou Jacobi, Dorothy Malone, Sharon Acker, Helen Hughes; **D:** Morley Markson, Larry Pall.

The Offence 🦴🦴🦴 Something Like the Truth **1973** (R) Connery plays a London detective who beats a suspected child molester to death during a police interrogation. Turns out he's reacting to a long-buried molestation incident from his own childhood. A chilling psycho-drama highlighted by a strong lead performance by Connery. **108m/C VHS. GB** Sean Connery, Trevor Howard, Vivien Merchant, Ian Bannen, Derek Newark, John Hallam, Peter Bowles; **D:** Sidney Lumet; **W:** John Hopkins.

Offerings 🦴 **1989** (R) After a boy is tormented by a gang of children who cause him to fall down a well, his resulting brain injuries turn him into a psychopathic killer. Seeking revenge ten years later, he systematically murders his oppressors, offering bits of their anatomy to the one girl who treated him kindly. A typical slasher movie, the plot is only slightly better than the worst examples of the genre. **96m/C VHS, DVD.** G. Michael Smith, Loretta L. Bowman; **D:** Christopher Reynolds.

Office Killer 🦴 **1997** (R) Just when you thought it was safe to run with scissors! Dorine (Kane) is a meek copy editor who is in danger of losing her job. After securing her position by accidentally electrocuting a fellow employee, Dorine begins some downsizing of her own. Pent up frustrations cause her sanity to take a personal leave of absence, and she begins to streamline her department by folding, spindling and mutilating her co-workers. Office tramp Kim (Ringwald) suspects the truth, but no one believes her. Stab at horror-black comedy isn't very scary or very funny. First directorial effort by still photographer Cindy Sherman, who didn't adapt very well to people moving around. **83m/C VHS, DVD.** Carol Kane, Molly Ringwald, Jeanne Tripplehorn, Barbara Sukowa, Michael Imperioli, David Thornton, Alice Drummond, Mike Hodge; **Cameos:** Eric Bogosian; **D:** Cindy Sherman; **W:** Tom Kalin, Todd Haynes, Elise MacAdam; **C:** Russell Fine; **M:** Evan Lurie.

Office Romances 🦴🦴 **1986** A woman who has moved to London from the country is seduced by her employer. Because of her plain appearance, she is flattered by his attention even though he is married and has no real feelings for her. Competently made, nonetheless hard to watch because of the slow pace. **60m/C VHS. GB** Judy Parfitt, Ray Brooks, Suzanne Burden; **D:** Mary McMurray; **W:** Hugh Whitemore.

Office Space 🦴🦴1/2 **1998** (R) Cartoon bigwig Mike Judge tries his hand at live action in this satire of white collar corporate drudgery. Peter (Livingston) is a drone for a software company well on his way to a nervous breakdown when a hypnosis mishap opens his eyes. He becomes so apathetic toward his job that he can't even muster up the energy to quit. His new no-work ethic is mistaken by a pair of corporate headhunters as "middle-management potential," and he is promoted as his pals Michael (Herman) and Samir (Naidu) are laid off. Frustrated in his attempts to be down-sized, Peter hatches a plot to embezzle the company. Stephen Root, as disgruntled nerd Milton, steals scenes like they were office supplies in an unlocked cabinet. Adapted from animated shorts begun by Judge before the Beavis and Butthead gravy train rolled into the station. **89m/C VHS, DVD, UMD.** Mike Judge, Jennifer Aniston, Ron Livingston, Gary Cole, Diedrich Bader, Stephen (Steve) Root, Richard Riehle; **D:** Mike Judge; **W:** Mike Judge; **C:** Tim Sunstedt; **M:** John (Gianni) Frizzell.

An Officer and a Gentleman 🦴🦴🦴 **1982** (R) Young drifter Gere, who enters Navy Officer Candidate School because he doesn't know what else to do with his life, becomes a better person almost despite himself. Winger is the love interest who sets her sights on marrying Gere, and Gossett is the sergeant who whips him into shape. Strong performances by the whole cast made this a must-see in 1982 that is still appealing, despite the standard Hollywood premise. ♪Up Where We Belong; Hungry for Your Love; An Officer and a Gentleman; Treat Me Right; Tunnel of Love. **126m/C VHS, DVD.** Richard Gere, Louis Gossett Jr., David Keith, Lisa Eilbacher, Debra Winger, David Caruso, Robert Loggia, Lisa Blount; **D:** Taylor Hackford; **W:** Douglas Day Stewart; **C:** Donald E. Thorin; **M:** Jack Nitzsche. Oscars '82: Song ("Up Where We Belong"); Support. Actor (Gossett); Golden Globes '83: Song ("Up Where We Belong"), Support. Actor (Gossett).

Official Denial 🦴🦴1/2 **1993** A victim of an alien abduction becomes the only hope for a captured space being. Can Paul help the alien escape from a special Air Force UFO group and what secrets will he uncover if he does? **86m/C VHS.** Parker Stevenson, Erin Gray, Dirk Benedict, Chad Everett; **D:** Brian Trenchard-Smith; **W:** Bruce Zabel; **M:** Garry McDonald, Laurie Stone. **TV**

The Official Story 🦴🦴🦴1/2 **1993** La Historia Oficial; The Official History; The Official Version **1985** (R) A devastating drama about an Argentinian woman who realizes her young adopted daughter may be a child stolen from one of the thousands of citizens victimized by the country's repressive government. A powerful, important film. In Spanish with English subtitles or dubbed. **112m/C VHS, DVD. AR** Norma Aleandro, Hector Alterio, Chunchuna Villafane, Patricio Contreras; **D:** Luis Puenzo; **W:** Luis Puenzo, Aida Bortnik. Oscars '85: Foreign Film; Cannes '85: Actress (Aleandro); Golden Globes '86: Foreign Film; L.A. Film Critics '85: Foreign Film; N.Y. Film Critics '85: Actress (Aleandro).

The Offspring 🦴🦴 From a Whisper to a Scream **1987** (R) In four stories of past evils Price reveals his hometown can force folks to kill. Not the usual Price character: dismemberment, cannibalism, and necrophilia clash with his presence. Strong yuk factor. **99m/C VHS, DVD, UMD.** Vincent Price, Cameron Mitchell, Clu Gulager, Terry Kiser, Susan Tyrrell, Harry Caesar, Rosalind Cash, Martine Beswick, Angelo Rossitto, Lawrence Tierney; **D:** Jeff Burr; **W:** Jeff Burr, C. Courtney Joyner; **M:** Jim Manzie.

The Ogre 🦴🦴 Der Unhold **1996** Misfit Abel (Malkovich) desperately believes in his own personal power to change the world around him. He winds up captured by the Germans in 1939 and is held in a POW camp until chance lands him in the service of a group of high-ranking Nazis, including Hermann Goring (Spengler). Goring sends Abel out to recruit young boys into becoming military conscripts and he gains the nickname of the Ogre, the mythic devourer of children. Adapted from Michael Tournier's novel "The Erl King." **117m/C VHS, DVD. GE FR GB** John Malkovich, Volker Spengler, Armin Mueller-Stahl, Gottfried John; **D:** Volker Schlondorff; **W:** Volker Schlondorff, Jean-Claude Carriere; **C:** Bruno de Keyzer; **M:** Michael Nyman.

Oh, Alfie 🦴 Alfie Darling **1975** (R) In every man's life, there comes a time to settle down... but never when you're having as much fun as Alfie! Inadequate sequel to "Alfie." **99m/C VHS, DVD. GB** Joan Collins, Alan Price, Jill Townsend; **D:** Ken Hughes; **W:** Ken Hughes.

Oh, Bloody Life! 🦴🦴1/2 **1988** Young actress faces deportation during the Stalin era in Hungary because of her aristocratic family. In Hungarian with English subtitles. **115m/C VHS. HU** Udvaros Dorottya, Szacsvay Laszlo, Kern Andras, Bezeredi Zoltan, Oze Lajos, Lukacs Margit; **D:** Peter Bacso; **W:** Peter Bacso; **C:** Bruno de Keyzer; Montreal World Film Fest. '88: Actress (Dorottya).

Oh! Calcutta! 🦴1/2 **1972** Film version of the first nude musical to play on Broadway, which caused a sensation in the late 1960s. It's really a collection of skits, some of which were written by such notables as John Lennon, Sam Shepard, and Jules Feiffer. And it's really not that funny or erotic. **105m/C VHS, DVD.** Bill Macy, Mark Dempsey, Raina Barrett, Samantha Harper, Patricia Hawkins, Mitchell McGuire; **D:** Guillaume Martin Aucion; **W:** Robert Benton, Jules Feiffer, Dan Greenberg, John Lennon, Jacques Levy, Sam Shepard, Leonard Melfi, David Newman, Clovis Trouille, Sherman Yellen; **C:** Frank Biondo, Arnold Giordano, Jerry Sarcone; **M:** Prof. Peter Schickele, Robert Dennis.

Oh Dad, Poor Dad (Momma's Hung You in the Closet & I'm Feeling So Sad) 🦴🦴 **1967** Cult fave black comedy about a bizarre family on a vacation in Jamaica. The domineering mother travels with a coffin containing the stuffed body of her late husband. Based on the play by Arthur L. Kopit. **86m/C VHS.** Rosalind Russell, Robert Morse, Barbara Harris, Hugh Griffith, Lionel Jeffries, Jonathan Winters, Cyril Delevanti, Hiram Sherman, George Kirby,

Janis Hansen; **D:** Richard Quine; **W:** Herbert Baker, Pat McCormick, Ian Bernard; **C:** Geoffrey Unsworth.

Oh, God! 🐾🐾½ 1977 (PG) God, in the person of Burns, recruits Denver as his herald in his plan to save the world. Despite initial skepticism, Denver, in his film debut, keeps faith and is rewarded. Sincere performances and optimistic and make for satisfying story. Followed by "Oh, God! Book 2" and "Oh God! You Devil." 104m/C VHS, DVD. George Burns, John Denver, Paul Sorvino, Ralph Bellamy, Teri Garr, William Daniels, Donald Pleasence, Barnard Hughes, Barry Sullivan, Dinah Shore, Jeff Corey, David Ogden Stiers; **D:** Carl Reiner; **W:** Larry Gelbart. Writers Guild '77. Adapt. Screenplay.

Oh, God! Book 2 🐾 1980 (PG) Burns returns as the "Almighty One" in strained sequel to "Oh God!" This time he enlists the help of a young girl to remind others of his existence. The slogan she concocts saves God's image, but not the movie. Followed by "Oh, God! You Devil." 94m/C VHS. George Burns, Suzanne Pleshette, David Birney, Louanne, Conrad Janis, Wilfrid Hyde-White, Hans Conried, Howard Duff, Anthony Holland; **D:** Gilbert Cates; **M:** Charles Fox.

Oh, God! You Devil 🐾🐾 1984 (PG) During his third trip to earth Burns plays both the Devil and God as the first takes a struggling musician's soul, then gives it back. A few zingers and light atmosphere save unoriginal pict. The second sequel to "Oh, God!" 96m/C VHS, DVD. George Burns, Ted Wass, Roxanne Hart, Ron Silver, Eugene Roche, Robert Desiderio; **D:** Paul Bogart; **M:** Andrew Bergman; **M:** David Shire.

Oh, Heavenly Dog! 🐾🐾 1980 (PG) A private eye returns from the dead as a dog to solve his own murder. Man's best friend and intelligent to toot. The famous dog Benji's third film, and his acting improves with each one. Adults may find this movie slow, but kids will probably love it. 104m/C VHS, DVD. Chevy Chase, Jane Seymour, Omar Sharif, Robert Morley, Susan Kellerman; **D:** Joe Camp; **M:** Euel Box.

Oh, Mr. Porter 🐾🐾 1937 Billeted at an obscure railway post, the station-master hero renovates the place and hires a special train to transport the areas soccer team. Trouble arises when the train is hijacked by gun smugglers. 85m/B VHS, GB. Will Hay, Moore Marriott, Graham Moffatt, Frederick Piper; **D:** Marcel Varnel.

Oh Susannah 🐾🐾½ 1938 Robbed and thrown from a train, Autry and the two drifters who rescue him follow the thieves to Mineral Springs. Their journey is plagued by too many songs and the bad guys are predictably punished in the end. 59m/B VHS, DVD. Gene Autry, Boothe Howard, Smiley Burnette, Frances Grant, Donald Kirke, Clara Kimball Young; **D:** Joseph Kane.

Oh! What a Lovely War 🐾🐾½ 1969 Scathing musical re-creation of British soldiers in WWI using the era's popular songs and presenting the story as a music hall review as seen through the eyes of the working-class Smith family. All their sons are seduced into enlisting and get killed, while the generals and the politicians are safely behind the lines or complaining at home. Attenborough's directorial debut features an all-star cast but comes off as somewhat disjointed and obvious due to its adaptation in and around Brighton. Filmed on location from a stage production. 144m/C VHS. GB Colin Farrell, John Rae, Corin Redgrave, Maurice Roeves, Kim Smith, Angela Thorne, Mary Wimbush, Paul Daneman, Vanessa Redgrave, Olivier, Michael Redgrave, Vanessa Redgrave, John Gielgud, Ralph Richardson, Maggie Smith, Susannah York, John Mills, Isabel Dean, Vincent Ball, Christian Doermer, Robert Flemyng, Ian Holm, David Lodge, Guy Middleton, Juliet Mills, Nanette Newman, Cecil Parker, Natasha Perry, Gerald Sim, Thorley Walters, Penelope Allen, Michael Bates, Edward Fox, Peter Gilmore, Ben Howard, Dirk Bogarde, Phyllis Calvert, Jean-Pierre Cassel, John Clements, Jack Hawkins, Kenneth More, Jane Seymour, Pippa Steele, Wendy Allnutt, Malcolm McFee, Paul Shelley; **D:** Richard Attenborough; **W:** Len Deighton; **C:** Gerry Turpin; **M:** Alfred Ralston. British: Acad. '69. Art Dir/Set Dec. (Olivier); Costume Des., Support. Actor (Olivier); Golden Globes '70: Foreign Film.

Oh, What a Night 🐾🐾 1992 Bittersweet coming o' age tale about a lonely 17-year-old (Haim) who has moved with his father and stepmother to a chicken farm in 1955 Ontario. After struggling with the untimely death of his mother, Haim falls in love with an older woman who has a husband and two kids. Features a great '50s soundtrack and beautiful scenes of the Canadian countryside. 93m/C VHS. CA Corey Haim, Barbara Williams, Keir Dullea, Genevieve Bujold, Richie Coltrane; **D:** Eric Till.

O'Hara's Wife 🐾🐾 1982 Loving wife Harey continues to care for her family even after her untimely death. Only her husband Asner, however, can see her ghost. Lightweight drama traps a good cast. 87m/C VHS, DVD. Ed Asner, Mariette Hartley, Jodie Foster, Tom Bosley, Perry Lang, Ray Walston; **D:** William S. Bartman; **W:** William S. Bartman; **M:** Artie Butler. TV

O.H.M.S. 🐾🐾½ 1937 Convoluted story about a New York hood (Ford) who flees to England where he joins the British Army by posing as a Canadian. He buddies up with Mills and they both fall for Lee. His regiment is sent to China, via ship, and Lee just happens to be a stowaway. In China, Ford manages to prove his worth by saving Lee from bandits. Maybe it's not supposed to make sense. 71m/B VHS, GB. Wallace Ford, John Mills, Anna Lee, Frank Cellier, Frederick Leister, Peter Croft; **D:** Raoul Walsh.

Oil 🐾 1978 (PG) Seven men fight a raging oil fire that threatens to destroy an entire country. Unfortunately, the movie is unable to ignite any interest at all. 95m/C VHS, DVD. Ray Milland, Woody Strode, Stuart Whitman, Tony Kendall, William Berger; **D:** Mircea Dragan.

The O.J. Simpson Story 🐾 1994 Tacky tabloid TV movie follows, incredibly exploited story about former gridiron star Simpson (Hosea) who's accused of murdering blonde babe ex-wife Nicole (Tuck). Mainly stolid performances though Weitz 's slick as Simpson lawyer Robert Shapiro. Told in flashbacks, the actual murder is never depicted. Director Jerry Friedman took his name off of the credits, leaving the standard Smithee pseudonym as a replacement. 90m/C VHS. Bobby Hosea, Jessica Tuck, James Handy, Kimberly Russell, David Roberson, Bruce Weitz; **D:** Alan Smithee; **W:** Stephen Harrigan; **M:** Harald Kloser.

Okoge 🐾🐾🐾 *Fag Hag* 1993 Rueful sexual comedy about a triangular friendship. Sayoko is a single young working woman living in a tiny Tokyo apartment. She meets the gay Noh and his older married love. Tochi and when they become friendly, Sayoko lets them use her apartment as their love nest—to the complications of all concerned. Title is a slang term used to refer to women who prefer the company of gay men. In Japanese with English subtitles. 120m/C VHS. JP Misa Shimizu, Takehiro Murata, Takeo Nakahara, Masayuki Shionoya, Noriko Sengoku, Kyozo Nagatsuka, Toshie Negishi; **D:** Takehiro Nakajima; **W:** Hiroshi Ariyoshi; **M:** Yoshimasa Hakata.

Oktober 🐾🐾 1998 A multinational pharmaceutical company is behind a sinister plot for global domination as a young teacher becomes both a walking experiment and a marked target in this medical thriller. 90m/C VHS, DVD. GB Stephen Tompkinson, Mara Lennon, James McCarthy, Lydzia Englert; **D:** Stephen Gallagher; **W:** Stephen Gallagher; **C:** Bruce McGowan; **M:** Alan Parker. TV

Oklahoma! 🐾🐾🐾 1955 (G) Jones's film debut, a must-see for musical fans. A cowboy and country girl fall in love, but she is tormented by another unwelcomed suitor. At over two hours, cuteness wears thin for some. Actually filmed in Arizona. Adapted from Rodgers and Hammerstein's broadway hit with original score; choreography by Agnes de Mille. 🎵Oh, What a Beautiful Morning; Surrey with the Fringe on Top; I Cain't Say No; Many a New Day; People Will Say We're in Love; Poor Jud Is Dead; All 'Er Nuthin'; Everything's Up to Date in Kansas City; The Farmer and the Cowman. 145m/C VHS, DVD. Gordon MacRae, Shirley Jones, Rod Steiger, Gloria Grahame, Eddie Albert, Charlotte Greenwood, James Whitmore, Gene Nelson, Barbara Lawrence, Jay C. Flippen; **D:** Fred Zinnemann; **W:** Sonya Levien, William Ludwig; **C:** Robert L. Surtees; **M:** Richard Rodgers, Oscar Hammerstein. Oscars '55: Sound, Scoring/Musical; Natl. Film Reg. '07.

Oklahoma Annie 🐾 1951 Storekeeper Canova joins the new sheriff in booting undesirables out of town, and tries to sing her way into his heart. Amazingly, it works—not for delicate ears. 90m/C VHS. Judy Canova, Fuzzy Knight, Grant Withers, John Russell, Denver Pyle, Allen Jenkins, Almira Sessions; **D:** R.G. Springsteen.

Oklahoma Badlands 🐾🐾 1948 Lane and his horse outsmart a corrupt newspaper publisher trying to steal land from a female rancher. An early directorial work for veteran stuntman Canutt. 59m/B VHS. Allan "Rocky" Lane, Mildred Coles; **D:** Yakima Canutt.

Oklahoma Bound 🐾 1981 A feisty farmer tries to save his failing farm through a series of ostensibly comedic, unsuccessful schemes. 92m/C VHS. F.E. Bowling, Dan (Daniel) Jones; **D:** Patrick C. Poole, Thomas Bentley.

Oklahoma Crude 🐾🐾½ 1973 (PG) Sadistic oil trust rep Palance battles man-hating Dunaway for her well. Drifter Scott helps her resist on the promise of shared profits. In this 1913 setting, Dunaway tells Scott she wishes she could avoid men altogether, but later settles for him. 108m/C VHS. George C. Scott, Faye Dunaway, John Mills, Jack Palance, Harvey Jason, Woodrow Parfrey; **D:** Stanley Kramer; **W:** Marc Norman; **C:** Robert L. Surtees; **M:** Henry Mancini.

Oklahoma Cyclone 🐾🐾 1930 A group of bronco busters find action and adventure on the prairie. Second of eight talkies in Steele series, includes his first of few singing roles. 64m/B VHS, DVD. Bob Steele, Al "Fuzzy" St. John, Nita Ray, Charles "Blackie" King; **D:** John P. McCarthy.

Oklahoma Kid 🐾🐾🐾 1939 Offbeat, hilarious western with Bogie as the villain and gunfighter Cagney seeking revenge for his father's wrongful death. Continuity buffs will note Hale wears the same outfit in most scenes. 80m/C VHS, DVD. James Cagney, Humphrey Bogart, Rosemary Lane, Ward Bond, Donald Crisp, Charles Middleton, Harvey Stephens; **D:** Lloyd Bacon; **C:** James Wong Howe; **M:** Max Steiner.

The Oklahoman 🐾🐾 1956 A routine western with some trivia value. Town doc McCrea helps Indian Pate keep his land. Talbot plays Indian maiden in lame year as her title role in Daughter of Jekyll. McCrea, Barbara Hale, Brad Dexter, Gloria Talbott, Verna Felton, Douglas Dick, Michael Pate, Scott Beckett; **D:** Francis D. Lyon.

Old Barn Dance 🐾🐾 1936 Autry and his singing cowboys are selling horses until a crooked tractor company puts them out of business. They join a radio program, discovers that it is owned by the same company that put them out of the horse-selling business, and runs the crooks out of town. 54m/B VHS, DVD. Gene Autry, Smiley Burnette, Roy Rogers; **D:** Joseph Kane.

Old Boyfriends 🐾🐾 1979 (R) Shire is weak as a psychologist searching for old boyfriends in order to analyze her past. Strange combination of Carradine and Belushi may draw curious fans. 103m/C VHS, DVD. Talia Shire, Richard Jordan, John Belushi, Keith Carradine, John Houseman, Buck Henry; **D:** Joan Tewkesbury; **W:** Leonard Schrader; **M:** David Shire.

Old Corral 🐾🐾 *Texas Serenade* 1936 Sheriff Autry protects the love interest, a girl fleeing the Mob. 54m/B VHS, DVD. Gene Autry, Roy Rogers, Smiley Burnette; **D:** Joseph Kane.

Old Enough 🐾🐾 1984 (PG) Slow-moving coming-of-age comedy on the rich kid-poor kid friendship theme. Silver's directing debut. 91m/C VHS. Sarah Boyd, Rainbow Harvest, Neill Barry, Danny Aiello, Susan Kingsley, Roxanne Hart, Alyssa Milano, Fran Brill, Anne Pitoniac; **D:** Marisa Silver; **W:** Marisa Silver. Sundance '84: Grand Jury Prize.

Old Explorers 🐾🐾½ 1990 (PG) Two old friends refuse to let old age lessen their want for excitement, so they get together on a regular basis to set out on dangerous, imaginary adventures. They search for Atlantis, explore the Himalayan Mountains, and visit the Bermuda Triangle. After one of the men survives a stroke, the two set out on a real-life adventure. Although the leads put in strong performances, they can't hide the slow-moving plot or the thin action sequences. Based on the play by James Cada and Mark Keller. 91m/C VHS. Jose Ferrer, James Whitmore, Jeffrey Gadbois, Caroline Kaiser, William Warfield, Christopher Pollard, Storm Richardson, William M. Pohlad; **D:** William M. Pohlad; **W:** William M. Pohlad; **C:** William F. Carlson.

Old Gringo 🐾🐾½ 1989 (R) Adapted from Carlos Fuentes' novelization of the revolution in Mexico during the revolution of 1913. Features Fonda in the unlikely role of a virgin schoolteacher, Smits as her hero, and Peck as her bro. Soggy acting by all but Peck, whose prestigious presence is wasted in a sketchy character.

ruin their lives by evicting them and forcing them into a life of poverty. Remade as "Mr. Quip" in 1957. 90m/B VHS, Ben Webster, Elaine Benson, Hay Petrie, Beatrix Thompson, Gibb McLaughlin, Reginald Purcell; **D:** Thomas Bentley.

The Old Curiosity Shop 🐾🐾 *Mr. Quilp* 1975 (G) Flat musical version of the Charles Dickens story about an evil man who wants to take over a small antique shop run by an elderly man and his granddaughter. 🎵When a Felon Needs a Friend; Somewhere; Love Has the Longest Memory; Happiness Pie; The Sport of Kings; What Shouldn't Happen to a Dog; Quilp. 118m/C VHS, GB Anthony Newley, David Hemmings, David Warner, Jill Bennett, Peter Duncan, Michael Hordern; **D:** Michael Tuchner; **M:** Herbert Bernstein.

The Old Curiosity Shop 🐾🐾 1994 (PG) Another adaptation of Charles Dickens's 1840 tale of Grandfather Trent (Ustinov), an antiques dealer who has lost his fortune through gambling and makes matters worse by borrowing money from the miserable Mr. Quip (Courtenay). Unable to repay the debt, Trent and young granddaughter Sally (Walsh) try to escape London, which turns Quip's wrath upon them. Fine performances and a colorful production. 280m/C VHS, DVD. Peter Ustinov, Tom Courtenay, James Fox, Sally Walsh, Anna Fielding, Christopher Ettridge, Julia McKenzie, Anna White, Jean Marlow, Cornelia Hayes O'Herlihy, Michael Meam; **D:** Kevin Connor; **W:** John Goldsmith; **C:** Doug Milsome; **M:** Mason Daring. CABLE.

The Old Curiosity Shop 🐾🐾½ 1935 Webster and Ben-scn are an old gambler and his daughter in this well-made film adaptation of the Dickens's tale. Their miserly landlord tries to

The Old Dark House 🐾🐾🐾 1932 An atmospheric horror film, with more than a touch of comedy, well-directed by Whale. In an old haunted house five scarred, and psychotic butler (Karloff's first starring role). Into this strange group wander five unsuspecting stranded travelers who set all sorts of dastardly plots in motion. Based on the novel "Benighted" by J.B. Priestley. John Dudgeon is actually actress Elspeth Dudgeon who's playing in drag. Remade in 1963 by William Castle. 71m/B VHS, DVD. Boris Karloff, Melvyn Douglas, Charles Laughton, Gloria Stuart, Ernest Thesiger, Raymond Massey, Lilian Bond, Eva Moore, Brember Wills, Elspeth (John) Dudgeon; **D:** James Whale; **W:** Benn W. Levy, R.C. Sherriff; **C:** Arthur Edeson.

Technical problems and cheesy sets and costumes—look for the dusk backdrop in the dance scene and Smits' silly moustache. Better to read the book. **119m/C VHS, DVD.** Jane Fonda, Gregory Peck, Jimmy Smits, Patricio Contreras, Jenny Gago, Gabriela Roel, Sergio Calderon, Guillermo Rios, Anne Pitoniak, Pedro Armendariz Jr., Jim Metzler; *D:* Luis Puenzo; *W:* Aida Bortnik, Luis Puenzo; *M:* Lee Holdridge.

Old Gun 1976 A grief-plagued doctor finds he must seek out and kill each Nazi involved in the slaughter of his wife and child to ease his pain. Excellent directing and a fully formed main character. **141m/C VHS.** Philippe Noiret, Romy Schneider, Jean Bouise; *D:* Robert Enrico.

Old Ironsides 1926 Silent, black-and-white version of the big budget/important director and stars action-adventure. Merchant marines aboard the famous Old Ironsides battle 19th century Barbary pirates in rousing action scenes. Home video version features an engaging organ score by Gaylord Carter. Based on the poem "Constitution" by Oliver Wendell Holmes. **111m/B VHS.** Esther Ralston, Wallace Beery, Boris Karloff, Charles Farrell, George Bancroft; *D:* James Cruze; *M:* Gaylord Carter.

Old Joy 2006 Two 30-something buddies who spent their younger days smoking pot and fighting the system embark on a reunion road trip to an Oregon natural hot springs. While their time together is pleasant enough, the pair doesn't quite reconnect—Kurt (Oldham) is still living in the past, while Mark (London) has a career, wife, and child on the way. Not much in the way of action but their talks—or, even, what isn't talked about—show how the glory days of friendship can't always be recaptured. Drawn from Jonathan Raymond's short story. **76m/C DVD.** US William Oldham, Daniel London, Tanya Smith; *D:* Kelly Reichardt; *W:* Kelly Reichardt, Jonathan Raymond; *C:* Peter Sillen.

The Old Lady Who Walked in the Sea 1991 *La Vieille qui Marchait dans la Mer* Eccentric Lady M (Moreau) and her equally aging ex-lover Pompilius (Serrault) have spend their lives conning the rich. Summering on the French Riviera, Lady M spots handsome beach boy/thief Lambert (Thuiller) and decides to groom him for their latest caper, a jewel heist. Meanwhile, Pompilius pursues the young Noemie (Danon) and brings her into their menage, where Lambert is instantly smitten. Their lust leads to some unexpected complications but the real drama in the film is watching old pros Moreau and Serrault at work. Based on the novel by San Antonio; French with subtitles. **95m/C VHS.** FR Jeanne Moreau, Michel Serrault, Luc Thuillier, Geraldine Danon; *D:* Laurent Heynemann; *W:* Dominique Roulet; *C:* Robert Alazraki; *M:* Philippe Sarde.

The Old Maid 1939 After her beau is killed in the Civil War, a woman allows her cousin to raise her illegitimate daughter, and therein begins a years-long struggle over the girl's affections. High grade soaper based on Zoe Akdin's stage adaptation of Edith Wharton's novel. **96m/B VHS.** Bette Davis, Miriam Hopkins, George Brent, Donald Crisp, Jane Bryan, Louise Fazenda, Henry Stephenson; *D:* Edmund Goulding; *C:* Gaetano Antonio "Tony" Gaudio; *M:* Max Steiner.

The Old Man and the Sea 1958 Cuban fisherman Santiago hooks a giant marlin and battles sharks and the sea to bring his trophy home. Tracy's performance as the tough, aging fisherman garnered him his sixth Academy Award nomination and Tiomkin's beautiful score was an Oscar winner. **86m/C DVD.** Spencer Tracy, Felipe Pazos, Harry Bellaver, Don Diamond, Don Blackman, Joey Ray; *D:* John Sturges; *W:* Peter Viertel; *C:* James Wong Howe, Floyd Crosby; *M:* Dimitri Tiomkin. Oscars '58: Orig. Dramatic Score.

The Old Man and the Sea 1990 Quinn is wonderful as Hemingway's aging Cuban fisherman Santiago, who battles a band of marauding sharks in the Gulf Stream. Unfortunately, this made-for-TV adaptation is ordinary. **97m/C VHS, DVD.** Anthony Quinn, Gary Cole, Alexis Cruz, Patricia Clarkson, Francesco Quinn; *D:* Jud Taylor; *W:* Roger O. Hirson; *C:* James Wong Howe; *M:* Bruce Broughton. TV

Old Mother Riley Headmistress 1950 Irish washerwoman Mrs. Riley (Lucan) winds up the headmistress of a girls' school that is threatened when a railroad line is planned to go through the property. **76m/B VHS.** GB Arthur Lucan, Kitty McShane, Enid Hewitt, Jenny Mathot, Cyril Smith; *D:* John Harlow; *W:* Jack Marks, Con West; *C:* Ken Talbot.

Old Mother Riley's Ghosts 1941 A group of spies "haunt" Mother Riley's castle home in a futile attempt to scare her out; she turns the tables. Some good scares and laughs. Part of the Old Mother Riley series. Look for similarities to later Monty Python films. **82m/B VHS, DVD.** GB Arthur Lucan, Kitty McShane, John Stuart; *D:* John Baxter.

Old Mother Riley's Jungle Treasure 1951 Mother Riley (Lucan) and daughter Kitty (McShane) are working in an antiques shop where they discover a treasure map. So they head for the South Seas and a pirate's ghost as well. **75m/B VHS.** GB Arthur Lucan, Kitty McShane, Sebastian Cabot, Garry Marsh, Roddy Hughes; *D:* Maclean Rogers; *W:* Val Valentine; *C:* James Wilson.

Old Mother Riley's New Venture 1949 Old Mother Riley (Lucan) is hired as the manager of a hotel that's been victimized by a series of robberies. But she's soon framed for a real jewel heist by the real thief. **80m/B VHS.** GB Arthur Lucan, Kitty McShane, Chili Boucher, Willer Neal, Sebastian Cabot; *D:* James Wilson.

Old School 2003 (R) Thirty-something pals Mitch (Wilson), Frank (Ferrell), and Beanie (Vaughn) start a frat at the nearby college so they can have a place to escape their everyday troubles. Mitch's girlfriend hosts orgies during his business trips, the recently-married Frank longs for beery bachelor freedom, and Beanie has never grown up despite having a nice family and owning an electronics store chain. Nonsensical plot threads lead only to frat-boy fun and confrontation with the dean, a stereotypical villain who used to be the butt of their jokes. Despite the plot breakdowns and generally one-dimensional characters, everyone, including the audience, manages to have a pretty good time, thanks largely to the likeability of the cast. Vaughn plays Beanie as if Trent from "Swingers" had ended up with a wife and two kids. **90m/C VHS, DVD, HD DVD.** US Luke Wilson, Will Ferrell, Vince Vaughn, Ellen Pompeo, Juliette Lewis, Leah Remini, Perrey Reeves, Elisha Cuthbert, Jeremy Piven, Rick Gonzalez, Terry O'Quinn, Artie Lange, Matthew Carey, Harve Presnell, Seann William Scott, Craig Kilborn; *Cameos:* Andy Dick, Snoop Dogg; *D:* Todd Phillips; *W:* Todd Phillips, Scot Armstrong; *C:* Mark Irwin; *M:* Theodore Shapiro.

The Old Settler 2001 Elizabeth Barney (Rashad) is middleaged and has never been married, thus making her an old settler according to sister Quilly (Allen), much to the bitter Quilly's astonishment. Based on the play by John Henry Redwood. **90m/C VHS, DVD.** Phylicia Rashad, Debbie Allen, Bumper Robinson, Eartha D. Robinson, Crystal Fox, Randy J. Goodwin; *D:* Debbie Allen; *W:* Shaunelle Perry. TV

Old Spanish Custom 1936 Only a Keaton fan could love this comedy, set in Spain and filmed in England. One of his rarest—and poorest—sound films. He plays a bumbling rich yachtsman smitten with Tovar, a Spanish maiden who uses him to make her lover jealous. **58m/B VHS.** GB Buster Keaton, Lupita Tovar, Lyn Harding, Esme Percy; *D:* Adrian Brunel.

Old Swimmin' Hole 1940 Small-town friends Moran and Jones try to bring their single parents together; his mother can't afford to finance his dream to be a doctor. Dull, melodramatic look at heartland America, reminiscent of "Our Town." **78m/B VHS, DVD.** Marcia Mae Jones, Jackie Moran, Leatrice Joy, Charles D. Brown; *D:* Robert McGowan.

Old Yeller 1957 (G) Disney Studios' first and best boy-and-his-dog film, set in Texas in 1869. 15-year-old Travis Coates (Kirk) is left in charge of the family farm while dad Jim (Parker) is away on a cattle drive. When his younger brother Arliss (Corcoran) brings home a stray dog, Travis is displeased but lets him stay. Yeller saves Travis's life, but contracts rabies in the process. Keep tissue handy, especially for the kids. Strong acting, effective scenery—all good stuff. Based on the novel by Fred Gipson. Sequel "Savage Sam" released in 1963. **84m/C VHS, DVD.** Dorothy McGuire, Fess Parker, Tommy Kirk, Kevin Corcoran, Jeff York, Beverly Washburn, Chuck Connors; *D:* Robert Stevenson; *W:* Fred Gipson, William Tunberg; *C:* Charles P. Boyle; *M:* Oliver Wallace.

Oldboy 2003 (R) Winner of the 2004 Cannes Grand Jury Award, this Korean thriller takes the emotionally charged terror of a David Fincher film and multiples it by a factor of ten. After a drunken evening, Oh Dae-su (Choi, in a brilliant performance) awakens to find himself trapped inside a small room, barred from escape by a thick steel door. Oh spends the next fifteen years in captivity, with no explanation ever offered from his jailers. With no warning, Oh—now half crazy from isolation and his thirst for vengeance—is suddenly freed and a mysterious figure gives him five days to figure out why he's been imprisoned. Park should be applauded for his vicious, unflinching insight into human sexuality and violence in this sad, surrealistic mystery. **120m/C DVD, Blu-ray Disc, UMD.** KN Min-Sik Choi, Yu Ji-tae, Hye-jeong Kang, Dae-su; *W:* Park Chan-wook, Hwang Jo-yun, Lim Jun-hyeong; *C:* Jeong-hun Jeong; *M:* Yeong-wook Jo, Shim Hyeon-jeong; Lee Ji-su, Choi Sung-hyeon.

Oldest Confederate Widow Tells All 1995 TV drama starts with the recollections of 99-year-old Lucy Marsden (Bancroft), the widow of the title, as she revisits her marriage to troubled Civil War veteran Capt. William Marsden (Sutherland), sporting an impressive set of whiskers). In 1899, the teenaged Lucy (played by Lane) marries the eccentric 50-year-old, who constantly relives battlefield horrors and the loss of his boyhood friend, while she deals with family and various domestic crises. Somewhat meandering story with fine performances based on Allan Gurganus' novel. **180m/C VHS, DVD.** Diane Lane, Donald Sutherland, Anne Bancroft, Cicely Tyson, Blythe Danner, E.G. Marshall, Gwen Verdon, Maureen Mueller, Wil Horneff; *D:* Ken Cameron; *W:* Joyce Eliason; *M:* Mark Snow.

Oldest Living Graduate 1980 Fonda is memorable in his last single role as the oldest graduate of a Texas military academy. He and his son clash when Fonda refuses to give up his land. Teleplay features strong performances from Leachman and other big-name cast members. **75m/C VHS.** Cloris Leachman, Henry Fonda, John Lithgow, Timothy Hutton, Harry Dean Stanton, David Ogden Stiers, George Grizzard, Penelope Milford; *D:* Jack Hofsiss. TV

Oldest Profession 1967 *Le Plus Vieux Metier du Monde* A study of prostitution from prehistoric times to the future. Generally unexciting and unfunny. In six segments meant as vehicles for their directors. **97m/C VHS.** FR GE IT Raquel Welch, Jeanne Moreau, Elsa Martinelli, Michele Mercier, Jean-Luc Godard, Philippe De Broca, Claude Autant-Lara, Franco Indovina, Mauro Bolognini, Michael Pfleghar; *W:* Jean-Luc Godard.

Oleanna 1994 Mamet directs the big-screen version of his controversial play about political correctness, sexual harrassment, and the gender gap. Pompous, burned-out college professor (Macy) is accused of sexual harassment by dense, shrill, academically weak student (Eisenstadt) after she misconstrues a self-important speech as a come-on. Unbalanced perspective, obvious stereotyping of unsympathetic characters, and weak performances remove any hint of the intended drama. **90m/C VHS, DVD.** William H. Macy, Debra Eisenstadt; *D:* David Mamet; *W:* David Mamet; *C:* Andrzej Sekula; *M:* Rebecca Pidgeon.

Olga's Girls *Mme. Olga's Massage Parlor; Olga's Massage Parlor; Olga's Parlor* 1964 Sadistic Olga deals in narcotics and white slavery in New York's Chinatown. Her drug addicted girls turn to each other for comfort but Olga suspects there's a snitch in her outfit. She'll stop at nothing to get the informant but the girls think it's about time for revenge. Campy sexploitation. **72m/B VHS, DVD.** Audrey Campbell, Alice Linville; *D:* Joseph P. Mawra; *M:* Claude Otis.

Oliver! 1968 (G) Splendid big-budget musical adaptation of Dickens' "Oliver Twist." An innocent orphan is dragged into a life of crime when he is befriended by a gang of pickpockets. ♪Food, Glorious Food; Oliver; Boy For Sale; Where Is Love?; Consider Yourself; Pick a Pocket or Two; I'd Do Anything; Be Back Soon; As Long As He Needs Me. **145m/C VHS, DVD.** GB Mark Lester, Jack Wild, Ron Moody, Shani Wallis, Oliver Reed, Hugh Griffith; *D:* Carol Reed; *W:* Vernon Harris; *C:* Oswald Morris; *M:* Lionel Bart. Oscars '68: Adapt. Score, Art Dir./Set Dec., Director (Reed), Picture, Sound; Golden Globes '69: Actor—Mus./Comedy (Moody), Film—Mus./Comedy.

Oliver & Company 1988 Animated animal retelling of Dickens' "Oliver Twist"—Disney style. Kitten Oliver (Lawrence) is left to fend for himself on the mean streets of New York until he's taken under the paw of Dodger (Joel) the dog. Dodger heads up a gang of doggy thieves, who help down-and-out human Fagin (DeeLuise), who owes money to ruthless loan shark Sykes (Loggia). Out on his first job, Oliver's found by rich little Jenny (Gregory) and happily adopted. But his pals think he's been kidnapped and are off to rescue him. ♪Once Upon a Time in New York City; Why Should I Worry?. **72m/C VHS, DVD.** *D:* George Scribner; *V:* Jim Cox, James Mangold; *V:* Joey Lawrence, Billy Joel, Richard "Cheech" Marin, Bette Midler, Dom DeLuise, Roscoe Lee Browne, Richard Mulligan, Sheryl Lee Ralph, Robert Loggia, Taurean Blacque, Carl Weintraub, Natalie Gregory, William Glover.

Oliver Twist 1922 Silent version of the Dickens classic as a vehicle for young Jackie Coogan. As orphan Oliver Twist, he is subjected to many frightening incidents before finding love and someone to care for him. Remade numerous times, most notably in 1933 and 1948 and as the musical "Oliver!" in 1968. **77m/B VHS, DVD.** Jackie Coogan, Lon Chaney Sr., Gladys Brockwell, George Siegmann, Esther Ralston, James A. Marcus, Aggie Herring, Nelson McDowell, Lewis Sargent, Joan Standing, Carl Stockdale, Edouard Trebaol, Lionel Belmore; *D:* Frank Lloyd; *W:* Frank Lloyd, Harry Weil; *C:* Glen MacWilliams, Robert Martin.

Oliver Twist 1933 The first talking version of Dickens's classic about an ill-treated London orphan involved with youthful gang of pickpockets. Moore was too young—at seven—to be very credible in the lead role. The 1948 version is much more believable. **70m/B VHS, DVD.** Dickie Moore, Irving Pichel, William "Stage" Boyd, Barbara Kent; *D:* William J. Cowen.

Oliver Twist 1948 Charles Dickens' immortal story of a workhouse orphan who is forced into a life of crime with a gang of pickpockets. The best of many film adaptations, with excellent portrayals by the cast. **116m/C VHS, DVD.** GB Robert Newton, John (Howard) Davies, Alec Guinness, Francis L. Sullivan, Anthony Newley, Kay Walsh, Diana Dors, Henry Stephenson; *D:* David Lean; *C:* Guy Green; *M:* Arnold Bax.

Oliver Twist 🐾🐾 1982 Good version of the classic Dickens's tale of a boy's rescue from a life of crime. Scott's Fagin is a treat, and period details are on the mark. 100m/C VHS. George C. Scott, Tim Curry, Michael Hordern, Timothy West, Lysette Anthony, Eileen Atkins, Cherie Lunghi, Clive Donner **W:** James Goldman; **M:** Nick Bicat. **TV**

Oliver Twist 1985 Miniseries adaptation of the Charles Dickens classic about an orphan boy plunging into the underworld of 19th-century London. Scott's Fagin spins another tale of frantic family life with his alter ego, Ralphie. This time the family is off on a summer vacation—with all its inherent problems. 96m/C VHS, James B. Stikking, Dorothy Lyman, Jonny O'Connell, Richard Bartlett. **TV**

Oliver Twist 🐾🐾½ 1997 Lavish TV version of the Dickens tale finds orphaned Oliver (Trench) escaping to 1837's London and being befriended by the wicked Fagin (Dreyfuss) and his gang of pickpocketing youngsters, including the Artful Dodger (Wood). 92m/C VHS, DVD. Alex Trench, Richard Dreyfuss, Elijah Wood, David O'Hara, Antoine Byrne, Olivia Caffrey; **D:** Tony Bill; **W:** Monte Merrick. **C:** Keith Wilson; **M:** Van Dyke Parks. **TV**

Oliver Twist 🐾🐾🐾 2000 The umpteenth version of the Dickens saga is a well-done British miniseries that includes the backstory of Oliver's parents, an inheritance, scheming relatives, and finally young Oliver (Smith) himself and his adventures with Fagin (Lindsay) and his criminal elements of London. 360m/C VHS, DVD. Sam Smith, Robert Lindsay, Andy Serkis, Emily Wood, Julie Walters, Michael Kitchen, Annette Crosbie, Alex Crowley, David Ross, Tim Dutton, Lindsay Duncan, Sophia Myles, Keira Knightley; **D:** Renny Rye; **W:** Alan Bleasdale; **C:** Walter McGill; **M:** Elvis Costello, Paul Pritchard. **TV**

Oliver's Story 🐾 1978(PG) A "not so equal" sequel to "Love Story," where widower O'Neal wallows in grief until rich heiress Bergen comes along. He falls in love again, this time with money. 90m/C VHS, DVD. Ryan O'Neal, Candice Bergen, Ray Milland, Edward Binns, Nicola Paget Charles Haid; **D:** John Korty; **C:** Pawel Edelman; **M:** Rachel Portman.

Olivia 🐾½ 1983 Abused housewife moonlights as a prostitute and begins killing her customers. She falls in love with an American businessman and flees to America when her husband finds out about the result. 90m/C VHS, DVD. Suzanna Love, Robert Walker Jr., Jeff Winchester; **D:** Ulli Lommel.

Olivier, Olivier 🐾🐾🐾 1992 (R) Holland's directorial follow-up to "Europa, Europa" is based on a 1984 French newspaper story and evokes "The Return of Martin Guerre" and its update, "Sommersby." Beloved nine-year-old boy disappears from his home in a small French town and his dysfunctional family falls apart. Mom obsesses and falls into trances, dad escapes to North Africa, and sister Nadine develops telekinetic powers in order to cope. Six years later a detective brings an amnesiac teenager, who has been working as a hustler in Paris, to the boy's family. Is it the missing Olivier? Spooky, provocative, and emotionally resonate. In French with English subtitles. 110m/C VHS. FH Francois Cluze, Brigitte Rouan, Gregoire Colin, Marina Golovine, Faye Gatteau, Frederic Quiring; **D:** Agnieszka Holland; **W:** Agnieszka Holland. LA. Film Critics '93. Score.

Ollie Hopnoodle's Haven of Bliss 🐾🐾½ 1988 Humorist Jean Shepherd (of "A Christmas Story" fame) spins another tale of frantic family life with his alter ego, Ralphie. This time the family is off on a summer vacation—with all its inherent problems. 96m/C VHS, James B. Stikking, Dorothy Lyman, Jonny O'Connell, Richard Bartlett. **TV**

Olly Olly Oxen Free 🐾🐾 The Great Balloon Adventure 1978 Junkyard owner Hepburn helps two boys fix up and fly a hot-air balloon, once piloted by McKenzie's grandfather, as a surprise for the film's birthday. Beautiful airborne scenes over California and a dramatic landing to the tune of the "1812 Overture," but not enough to make the film interesting. 83m/C VHS, DVD. Katharine Hepburn, Kevin McKenzie, Dennis Dimster-Denk, Peter Kilman, Richard A. Colla; **M:** Robert Alcivar.

Omaha (the movie) 🐾🐾 1995 Gen-Xer Simon (Walkinshaw) flees his native Nebraska and eccentric, dysfunctional family for enlightenment in Tibet. He's instructed in Buddhism and returns home but doesn't find the peace he's seeking and decides to hit the road with former girlfriend Gina (Anderson). 85m/C VHS, Hughston Walkinshaw, Jill Anderson; **D:** Dan Mirvish; **W:** Dan Mirvish; **C:** Oslo Anderson.

Omar Khayyam 🐾🐾 1957 In medieval Persia, Omar (Wilde) becomes involved in a romance with the Shah of Persia's fiancee, while trying to fight off a faction of assassins trying to overthrow the Shah. Although this film has a great cast, the script is silly and juvenile, defeating the cast's fine efforts. 101m/C VHS. Cornel Wilde, Michael Rennie, Debra Paget, Raymond Massey, John Derek, Yma Sumac, Margaret (Maggie) Hayes, Joan Taylor, Sebastian Cabot; **D:** William Dieterle.

The Omega Code 🐾½ 1999 (PG-13) This entry in the God vs. Devil steel cage apocalypse smackdown genre was actually financed by the Christian cable network TBN. Therefore, you can be sure that it's not evil, although it's plenty bad. In this corner, representing good, is motivational speaker Gillen Lane (Van Dien), who believes that hidden truths may be discovered by applying mathematical equations to sections of the Bible or by overacting. In that corner, representing evil, is Stone Alexander (York), AKA The Antichrist, who uses the hidden codes for nefarious purposes such as taking over the world government and overacting. In the stunning climax stolen from "Raiders of the Lost Ark," evil is overthrown and we find that the whole thing was a fix from the beginning. Caused a minor stir with semi-big boxoffice numbers, but much of the business was a case of preaching to the choir of fervent TBN viewers in its opening weeks. 99m/C VHS, DVD. Casper Van Dien, Michael York, Catherine Oxenberg, Michael Ironside, Jan Triska, William Hootkins, Devon Odessa, George Coe, Robert F. Lyons; **D:** Robert Marcarelli; **W:** Stephan Bliss, Hollis Barton; **C:** Carlos Gonzalez; **M:** Harry Manfredini.

Omega Cop 🐾 1990 In a post-apocalyptic future, there's only one cop left. He uses his martial arts skills and tons of guns attempting to rescue three women, but the violence doesn't cover the poor acting and shoddy production. Fans of TV's Batman might enjoy this for West's presence. 89m/C VHS, DVD. Adam West, Stuart Whitman, Troy Donahue, Meg Thayer, Jennifer Joslyn, Chryst Jimenez; **D:** Wil Landingham, Chuck Katzakian; **C:** Paul Kyriazi.

Omega Doom 🐾🐾 1996 (PG-13) Four hundred years after an apocalyptic war the most organic thing around are the cyborgs, who exist along with androids and robots in a ruined amusement park, the Roms and Droids, two rival cyborg groups, maintain an uneasy truce and when Doom wanders in they unite to destroy the intruder. But they don't know what they're up against. 84m/C VHS, DVD.

Omen 4: The Awakening 🐾🐾 1991 It turns out Damien of Omens past had a daughter, Delia, who takes up where dear old devilish Dad left off. Delia is adopted by your basic clueless couple and proceeds to wreak havoc wherever she goes, including getting rid of several interfering adults. She also plans to make her adoptive father, a U.S. senator, President, so that his delightful child anti-Christ can have him carry out all her evil plans. 97m/C VHS, DVD. Faye Grant, Michael Woods, Michael Lerner, Asia Vieira; **D:** Jorge Montesi, Dominique Othenin-Girard. **TV**

Omoo Omoo, the Shark God 🐾 1949 A sea captain is cursed when he removes the black pearls from a store shark god in this extremely cheap adventure. 58m/B VHS, DVD. Ron Randall, Devera Burton, Trevor Bardette, Pedro de Cordoba, Richard Benedict, Rudy Robles, Michael Whalen, George Meeker; **D:** Leo Leonard.

On a Clear Day 🐾🐾½ 2005 (PG-13) Frank (Mullan) is a 55-year-old Glasgow shipbuilder who has been laid off after 35 years. At odds with himself and his family, Frank regularly meets his mates at the local swimming pool, where he begins training in secret, thus causing his anxious wife Joan (Blethyn) to suspect he's having an affair. Frank also grapples with some painful past sorrows that have caused

---

The Omen 🐾🐾½ Birthmark 1976 (R) American diplomat's family adopts a young boy who always seems to be around when bizarre and inexplicable deaths occur. Of course, what else would you expect of Satan's son? The shock and subsequent bloodletting ("The Exorcist" is replaced with more suspense and believable effects. Well-done horror film doesn't insult the viewer's intelligence. Followed by three sequels: "Damien: Omen 2," "The Final Conflict," and "Omen 4." 111m/C VHS, DVD, Gregory Peck, Lee Remick, Harvey Stephens, Billie Whitelaw, David Warner, Holly Palance, Robert Rietty, Patrick Troughton, Martin Benson, Leo McKern, Richard Donner; **D:** Richard Donner; **W:** David Seltzer; **C:** Gilbert Taylor. **M:** Jerry Goldsmith. Oscars '76: Orig. Score.

The Omen 🐾🐾½ 2006 (R) Robert Thorn (Schreiber), American ambassador to England, adopts an orphaned newborn after his own son dies, without telling his fragile wife Katherine (Stiles). Damien (newcomer Davey-Fitzpatrick) grows into a spooky little boy looked after by overprotective nanny Mrs. Baylock (Farrow). Sinister happenings lead Thorn to believe he's raising the antichrist. The remake uses the same screenwriter—David Seltzer—as the 1976 original with some modest updates so nothing's very surprising. But it's still pretty scary (and bloody). 110m/C VHS, Blu-ray DVD. Liev Schreiber, Julia Stiles, Mia Farrow, David Thewlis, Pete Postlethwaite, Seamus Davey-Fitzpatrick; **D:** John Moore; **W:** David Seltzer; **C:** Jonathan Sela; **M:** Marco Beltrami.

Omega Man 🐾🐾½ 1971 (PG) In post-holocaust Los Angeles, Heston is immune to the effects of a biologically engineered plague and battles those who aren't—an army of albino victims bent on destroying what's left of the world. Strong suspense with considerable violence, despite the PG rating. Based on the science fiction thriller "I Am Legend" by Richard Matheson, which is also the basis for the film "The Last Man on Earth." 98m/C VHS, DVD. Blu-ray Disc. Charlton Heston, Anthony Zerbe, Rosalind Cash, Paul Koslo, Eric Laneuville, Lincoln Kilpatrick, Anna Aries, John Dierkes, Moniika Joyce H. Corrington; **C:** Russell Metty; **M:** Ron Grainer.

Omega Syndrome 🐾½ 1987 (R) Neo-Nazis kidnap Wahl's daughter. He and Vietnam buddy DiCenzo get her back. Ho hum. DiCenzo's is the best performance. Tolerable for vigilante film fans. 90m/C VHS, Ken Wahl, Ron Kuhlman, George DiCenzo, Doug McClure, Di-Anne Thorne, Nicholas Grabowski.

On a Clear Day You Can See Forever 🐾🐾 1970 (G) A psychiatric hypnotist helps a girl stop smoking and finds that in trances she remembers previous incarnations. He falls in love with one of the women she used to be. Alan Jay Lerner of "My Fair Lady" and "Camelot" wrote the lyrics and the book. Based on a stage musical by Lerner and Burton Lane. J'On a Clear Day, You Can See Forever; Come Back to Me; What Did I Have That I Don't Have?; He Isn't You; Hurry, It's Lovely Up Here; Go To Sleep; Love with All the Trimmings; Melinda. 129m/C VHS, DVD. Barbra Streisand, Yves Montand, Bob Newhart, Jack Nicholson, Simon Oakland; **D:** Vincente Minnelli.

On an Island with You 🐾🐾½ 1948 Williams plays a movie star who finds romance on location in Hawaii in this musical extravaganza. Contains many of Williams' famous water ballet scenes and plenty of bathing beauties. 80m/B VHS, DVD. GB Clive Brook. Beatrice Lillie, Googie Withers, Roland Culver, O.B. Clarence, Lawrence Hanray, Elliot Mason, Hay Petrie, Marjorie Munks, Molly Munks; **D:** Clive Brook; **W:** Terence Young, Clive Brook; **C:** Claude Friese-Greene; **M:** William Alwyn.

On Borrowed Time 🐾🐾🐾 1939 Engrossing tale of Death (Hardwicke) coming for an old man (Barrymore) who isn't ready to die so he traps him in his backyard apple tree. Performances are first rate in this good adaptation of the stage success (originally by Eugene O'Neill). Hardwicke is especially a standout; he gave up theatre for Hollywood after making this film. 99m/B VHS, Lionel Barrymore, Cedric Hardwicke, Beulah Bondi, Una Merkel, Bobs Watson, Henry Travers; **D:** Harold Bucquet; **C:** Joseph Ruttenberg.

On Approval 🐾🐾🐾 1944 Hilarious British farce in which two women trade boyfriends. Lillie's performance provides plenty of laughs. Brook runs the show as leading man, co-author, director, and co-producer. Based on the play by Frederick Lonsdale. 80m/B VHS, DVD. GB Clive Brook, Beatrice Lillie, Googie Withers, Roland Culver.

On Dangerous Ground 🐾🐾🐾 1951 A world-weary detective is sent to the countryside to investigate a murder. He encounters the victim's revenge-hungry father and the blind sister of the murderer. Directorial debut for Seagal keep from laughing when stoneyfaced Steven intones "What does it take to change the essence of man?" A better script, for one. 82m/B VHS, Robert Ryan, Ida Lupino, Ward Bond, Ed Begley Sr., Cleo Moore, Charles Kemper; **D:** Nicholas Ray; **M:** Bernard Herrmann.

On Deadly Ground Woof! 1994 (R) Seagal nearly destroys Alaska in an effort to save it in this inane, preachy story of an oil-rig roughneck out to protect the landscape from an evil oil company's drilling habits. Directorial debut for Seagal lumbers from scene to scene. Violence is expected, as is silly dialogue—just try to keep from laughing when stoneyfaced Steven intones "What does it take to change the essence of man?" A better script, for one. Michael Caine, Joan Chen, John C. McGinley; **C:** Ric Waite; **M:** Basil Poledouris. Golden Raspberries '94: Worst Director (Seagal).

a rift between himself and son Rob (Sives). Mullan portrays Frank as such a gruff bloke that the mawkishness is kept at bay. 99m/C VHS, DVD. GB Peter Mullan, Brenda Blethyn, Sean McGinley, Jamie Sives, Billy Boyd, Ron Cook, Jodhi May, Benedict Wong, Shaun Dingwall, Anne-Marie Timoney, Tony Roper, Paul Ritter; **D:** Gaby Dellal; **W:** Alex Rose; **C:** David Johnson; **M:** Stephen Warbeck.

On Edge ⚫⚫ 2003 (R). Figure skaters Wendy (Winokur), Veda (Swatek), and J.C. (Langer) are three Olympic hopefuls vying for the Southern California regional figure skating championship amidst the usual jealousies and craziness. Alexander is the Zamboni driver who observes it all and a number of professional skaters play skating judges. **93m/C VHS, DVD. A-J, A-J** (Allison Joy) Langer, Jason Alexander, Barret Swatek, Marissa Jaret Winokur, John Glover, Kathy Griffin, Chris Hogan, Wallace (Wally) Langham, Sabrina Lloyd, Wendie Malick; **D:** Karl Slovin; **W:** Karl Slovin, Laura Wolf; **C:** Chris Squires; **M:** Jim Latham. **VIDEO**

On Golden Pond ⚫⚫⚫ 1981 (PG) Henry Fonda won his first—and long overdue—Oscar for his role as the curmudgeonly patriarch of the Thayer family. He and his wife have grudgingly agreed to look after a young boy while at their summer home in Maine. Through his gradually affectionate relationship with the boy, Fonda learns to allay his fears of mortality. He also gains an understanding of his semi-estranged daughter. Jane Fonda plays his daughter and Hepburn is his loving wife in this often funny adaptation of Ernest Thompson's 1978 play. Predictable but deeply moving. Henry Fonda's final screen appearance. **109m/C VHS, DVD.** Henry Fonda, Jane Fonda, Katharine Hepburn, Dabney Coleman, Doug McKeon, William Lanteau; **D:** Mark Rydell; **W:** Ernest Thompson; **C:** Billy Williams; **M:** Dave Grusin. Oscars '81: Actor (H. Fonda), Actress (Hepburn), Adapt. Screenplay; British Acad. '82: Actress (Hepburn); Golden Globes '82: Actor—Drama (H. Fonda), Film—Drama, Screenplay; Natl. Bd. of Review '81: Actor (H. Fonda). Writers Guild '81: Adapt. Screenplay.

On Guard! ⚫⚫⚫½ Le Bossu; En Garde 2003 Thrilling story of revenge and long swordplay set in 18th century France. Lagardere (Auteuil) attempts to kill the Duke of Nevers (Perez) for money and ends up being taken in and trained by him. Nevers' cousin, the evil Gonzague (Luchini), murders him to grab the family fortune and Lagardere is forced to go into hiding and raise Nevers' daughter Aurore. 16 years later, Lagardere and grown Aurore (Gillain) find themselves in the court of Gonzague, where they put their plot for vengeance into effect. Fantastic swordfighting scenes, complex intrigue, and excellent acting make this a world-class swashbuckler. Based on the frequently adapted 1857 French serial "Le Bossu" by Paul Feval. In French with subtitles. **128m/C VHS, DVD. FR IT GE** Daniel Auteuil, Fabrice Luchini, Vincent Perez, Marie Gillain, Jean-Francois Stevenin, Didier Pain, Claire Nebout, Philippe Noiret, Yann Collette; **D:** Philippe de Broca; **W:** Philippe de Broca, Jean Cosmos, Jerome Tonnerre; **C:** Jean-Francois Robin; **M:** Philippe Sarde.

On Her Majesty's Secret Service ⚫⚫½ 1969 (PG) In the sixth 007 adventure, Bond again confronts the infamous Blofeld, who is planning a germwarfare assault on the entire world. Australian Lazenby took a crack at playing the super spy, with mixed results. Many feel this is the best-written of the Bond films and might have been the most famous, had Sean Connery continued with the series. Includes the song "We Have All the Time in the World," sung by Louis Armstrong. **144m/C VHS, DVD. GB** George Lazenby, Diana Rigg, Telly Savalas, Gabriele Ferzetti, Ilse Steppat, Bernard Lee, Lois Maxwell, Desmond Llewelyn, Catherine Schell, Julie Ege, Joanna Lumley, Mona Chong, Anouska (Anoushka) Hempel, Jenny Hanley; **D:** Peter Hunt; **W:** Richard Maibaum; **M:** John Barry.

On Moonlight Bay ⚫⚫½ 1951 Set in small-town Indiana in 1917 with Day as the tomboyish Marjorie who falls for college man MacRae. Her father (Ames) doesn't approve but the trouble really begins when Marjorie's younger brother gets into trouble at school. The incorrigible Wesley (Gray) blames everything on dear old dad and MacRae feels he must come to Marjorie's rescue! Gray steals the movie as the bratty brother—otherwise its business as usual. Based on Booth Tarkington's "Penrod" stories and followed by "By the Light of the Silvery Moon." "Love Ya; On Moonlight Bay; Till We Meet

Again; Pack Up Your Troubles In Your Old Kit Bag; I'm Forever Blowing Bubbles; Christmas Story; Tell Me Why Nights Are Lonely; Cuddle Up a Little Closer; Every Little Movement Has a Meaning All Its Own. **95m/C VHS, DVD.** Doris Day, Gordon MacRae, Leon Ames, Billy Gray, Rosemary DeCamp, Mary Wickes, Ellen Corby, Esther Dale; **D:** Roy Del Ruth; **M:** Melville Shavelson, Jack Rose; **M:** Max Steiner.

On My Own ⚫⚫ 1992 Fifteen-year-old Simon Henderson (Ferguson) struggles to cope with his life when he's sent away to school after his mother (Davis) suffers a nervous breakdown. Just as he begins to adjust and make friends, his mother pays a disturbing visit and reveals the source of her troubles. **96m/C VHS. CA** Judy Davis, Matthew Ferguson, David McIlwraith; **D:** Antonio Tibaldi.

On Our Merry Way ⚫⚫½ A Miracle Can Happen 1948 Episodic comedy with Meredith starring as Oliver Pease, a would-be newspaper reporter (he actually works on the classifieds), asking the question "How has a child changed your life?" Among those queried are a couple of jazz musicians (Fonda, Stewart), Hollywood bit players (Lamour, Moore), and con men (Demerest, MacMurray). Goddard, who was married to Meredith at the time, plays his wife in the film. **107m/B VHS, DVD.** Burgess Meredith, Paulette Goddard, Dorothy Lamour, Victor Moore, James Stewart, Henry Fonda, Fred MacMurray, William Demarest, Hugh Herbert, Eilene Janssen, Dorothy Ford, David Whorf; **D:** King Vidor, Leslie Fenton; **W:** Laurence Stallings, Lou Breslow; **C:** John Seitz, Ernest Laszlo, Gordon Avil, Joseph Biroc, Edward Cronjager; **M:** Heinz Roemheld.

On the Air ⚫⚫ En el Aire 1995 DJ Alberto (Gimenez Cacho) is facing job loss with the shutdown of the radio station where he does his psychedelic music show. This isn't his only loss as Alberto's marriage to Laura (Heredia) is also failing. He explores his problems on air as he flashes back to his life growing up in the '60s and '70s. Spanish with subtitles. **90m/C VHS, DVD. MX** Daniel Gimenez Cacho, Dolores Heredia, Angelica Aragon, Alberto Estrella; **D:** Juan Carlos de Llaca; **W:** Juan Carlos de Llaca; **C:** Claudio Rocha; **M:** Alejandro Giacoman.

On the Air Live with Captain Midnight ⚫½ Captain Midnight 1979 Socially challenged teen finds hipness as a rebel DJ operating an illegal radio station from his van. Leading actor is the son of the director/writer/producer but nepotism does not a good film make. **90m/C VHS.** Tracy Sebastian; **D:** Ferd Sebastian.

On the Avenue ⚫⚫½ 1937 Broadway showman Powell opens up a new musical, starring Faye as the richest girl in the world, in this musical-comedy satirizing upper-crust society. Debutante Carroll is outraged because she realizes it's mocking her actual life. Carroll tries to get Powell to change the show, they fall in love, Faye gets her nose out of joint, and after lots of fuss everything ends happily. Fine Berlin score. "He Ain't Got Rhythm; You're Laughing at Me; This Year's Kisses; Slumming on Park Avenue; The Girl on the Police Gazette; I've Got My Love to Keep Me Warm. **90m/B VHS, DVD.** Dick Powell, Madeleine Carroll, Alice Faye, George Barbier, Al Ritz, Harry Ritz, Jimmy Ritz, Alan Mowbray, Cora Witherspoon, Walter Catlett, Stepin Fetchit, Sig Rumann, Douglas Fowley, Joan Davis; **D:** Roy Del Ruth; **W:** Gene Markey; **M:** Irving Berlin.

On the Beach ⚫⚫⚫½ 1959 A group of survivors attempt to live normal lives in post-apocalyptic Australia, waiting for the inevitable arrival of killer radiation. Astaire is strong in his first dramatic role. Though scientifically implausible, still a good anti-war vehicle. Based on the best-selling novel by Nevil Shute. **135m/B VHS, DVD.** Gregory Peck, Anthony Perkins, Donna Anderson, Ava Gardner, Fred Astaire; **D:** Stanley Kramer; **W:** John Paxton; **C:** Daniel F. Fapp; **M:** Ernest Gold. Golden Globes '60: Score.

On the Beach ⚫⚫½ 2000 Remake of the 1959 anti-nuke film (based on the 1957 novel by Nevil Shute) is well-acted but so low-key that it never generates real tension. In 2006, the bomb has been

dropped and Australia is the current refuge and the destination of sub commander Dwight Towers (Assante). A radio transmission from Alaska offers some hope but Towers needs the help of Melbourne scientist Julian Osborne (Brown), who happens to be the ex- of Towers' sultry love, Moira (Ward). **180m/C VHS, DVD.** Armand Assante, Rachel Ward, Bryan Brown, Jacqueline McKenzie, Grant Bowler; **D:** Russell Mulcahy; **W:** David Williamson, Bill Kerby; **C:** Martin McGrath; **M:** Anna Borghesi. **CABLE**

On the Border ⚫⚫½ 1998 (R) Familiar neo-noir revolves around a bank heist. Ex-bank robber Jake (Van Dien) is now a security guard. Kristin (Roos) entices him into a plot involving Brown, Baldwin, and Mitchum. The humor is intentional, and the Texas locations are well utilized. Overall, this is an overachieving video premiere. **103m/C DVD.** Casper Van Dien, Bryan Brown, Bentley Mitchum, Camilla Overbye Roos, Rochelle Swanson, Daniel Baldwin; **D:** Bob Misiorowski; **W:** Josh Olson; **C:** Lawrence Sher; **M:** Serge Colbert. **VIDEO**

On the Borderline ⚫⚫½ 2001 (R) On their way to California with their new baby, Luke (Mabius) and Nicole (Shelton) find themselves short of funds in a border town. She takes work as a waitress while he becomes involved with transporting Mexican aliens. Curious little road thriller actually works pretty well. The leads and a solid supporting cast handle the material well. Some scenes are curiously tinted to disguise the less-than-lavish production values. **93m/C DVD.** Eric Mabius, Marley Shelton, Elizabeth Pena, R. Lee Ermey; **D:** Michael Oblowitz; **W:** Kevin R. Frech; **C:** Michael Barrow; **M:** Michael Wandmacher.

On the Comet ⚫⚫⚫ Na Komete 1968 Hector Servadac's Ark 1968 Zeman's fourth fantasy based on Jules Verne stories. A chunk of the Earth's crust suddenly becoming a comet and giving its passengers a ride through the galaxy. Complete with Zeman's signature animation fantasias. In English. **76m/C VHS, CZ** Emil Horvath Jr., Magda Vasaryova, Frantisek Filipovsky; **D:** Karel Zeman.

On the Edge ⚫⚫½ 1986 (PG-13) A drama about the inevitable Rocky-esque triumph of Dern as an aging marathon runner. Simultaneous to his running endeavor, Dern is trying to make up for lost time with his father. Available in two versions, one rated, the other unrated with a racy appearance by Pam Grier as the runner's interracial lover. **86m/C VHS, DVD.** Bruce Dern, John Marley, Bill Bailey, Jim Haynie, Pam Grier; **D:** Rob Nilsson; **W:** Rob Nilsson.

On the Edge ⚫⚫½ 2000 (R) Troubled 19-year-old Jonathan Breech (Murphy) deals with his depression over his father's death by stealing a car and driving it over a cliff. Surviving with very minor injuries, Jonathan is faced with prison or spending time in a mental institution. He chooses the latter, where he meets his caring therapist, Dr. Figure (Rea), and some fellow patients to bond with—Rachel (Vessey) and Toby (Jackson). Much teen angst is explored before the resolution and the material may not be fresh but it is heartfelt. **86m/C VHS, DVD. IR** Cillian Murphy, Tricia Vessey, Jonathan Jackson, Stephen Rea; **D:** John Carney, Jonathan James, John Carney; **C:** Eric Alan Edwards.

On the Edge: The Survival of Dana ⚫⚫ 1979 Another entry from the world of low-quality made-for-TV films. A young girl moves with her family to a new town. When she falls in with the "bad" crowd, her ethical standards are challenged. A stinker that may appeal to those with campy tastes. Not for the discriminating palate. **92m/C VHS.** Melissa Sue Anderson, Robert Carradine, Marion Ross, Talia Balsam, Michael Pataki, Kevin Breslin, Judge Reinhold, Barbara Babcock; **D:** Jack Starrett. **TV**

On the Fiddle ⚫⚫½ Operation Snafu; Operation Warhead 1961 Conniving Horace Pope (Lynch) gets his mate Pedlar Pascoe (Connery) to join the Royal Air Force with him during WWII. Horace sets up a number of rackets but, despite their larceny, they become unintentional heroes. Based on the novel "Stop at a Win-

ner" by R.F. Delderfield. **93m/B VHS. GB** Alfred Lynch, Sean Connery, Cecil Parker, Stanley Holloway, Wilfrid Hyde-White; **D:** Cyril Frankel; **W:** Harold Buchman; **C:** Edward Scaife; **M:** Malcolm Arnold.

On the Line ⚫⚫½ 1983 Two Mexico–US border guards, one hard-bitten, the other sympathetic to the illegal immigrants' plight, battle it out over a beautiful Mexican whore. Disjointed and confusing. **95m/C VHS, DVD. SP** David Carradine, Victoria Abril, Scott Wilson, Sam Jaffe, Jesse Vint; **D:** Jose Luis Borau; **W:** Jose, Luis Borau.

On the Line ⚫½ 2001 (PG) Insipid romance featuring Bass and Fatone from the teenybopper group 'N Sync. Kevin (Bass) meets Abbey (Chriqui), the girl of his dreams, on a train in Chicago. How does he know she's the one for him? Well, they can both name all the presidents in order and they both like the Cubs. Gee! Ain't that sweet? Unfortunately, Kevin is too shy to ask for her number, and he lets her slip away. He laments to his friends Rod (Fatone), Eric (GQ) and Randy (Bulliard) and they decide to help him find her by posting flyers all over town. A local reporter (Montgomery) picks up the story and a gaggle of girls claiming to be "The L Girl" respond. Further plot contrivances keep the two apart. Love wins out in the end, however, much to the delight of squealing 12-year-old girls everywhere. **90m/C VHS, DVD. US** Lance Bass, Joey Fatone, Emmanuelle Chriqui, GQ, Al Green, Tamala Jones, Dave Foley, Dan Montgomery Jr., Jerry Stiller; **D:** Eric Bross; **W:** Paul Stanton, Eric Aronson; **C:** Michael Bernard; **M:** Stewart Copeland.

On the Nickel ⚫⚫ 1980 (R) An ex-alcoholic returns to Fifth Street in Los Angeles to save his friend from a life of despair. Waits' musical score enhances this sentimental skid row drama. Scripted, directed, and produced by "The Waltons" Waite. **96m/C VHS.** Ralph Waite, Donald Moffat, Hal Williams, Jack Kehoe; **D:** Ralph Waite; **W:** Ralph Waite; **M:** Tom Waits.

On the Night Stage ⚫⚫ 1915 Gruff bandit (legendary Hart) loses his girl-of-questionable-values to town preacher. One of the first feature length westerns. **83m/B VHS.** William S. Hart, Robert Edeson, Rhea Mitchell, Shorty Hamilton; **D:** Reginald Barker.

On the Old Spanish Trail ⚫⚫½ 1947 Rogers becomes a singing cowboy with a traveling tent show in order to pay off a note signed by the Sons of the Pioneers. **56m/B VHS, DVD.** Roy Rogers, Jane Frazee, Andy Devine, Tito Guizar; **D:** William Witney.

On the Outs ⚫⚫ 2005 (R) Three teen girls find the mean streets more than they can handle. Suzette (Mariano) is pregnant by a crack dealer who leaves her literally holding the gun that killed a rival. Crack addict Marisol (Mendoza) is a single mom who loses her daughter to child welfare and learns that even if she stays clean it could take years to regain parental custody. Oz (Marte) is herself a crack dealer, trying to raise her mentally retarded younger brother. Based on case studies of young women who were held in a Jersey City juvenile detention center. **86m/C DVD.** Judy Marte, Anny Mariano, Paola Mendoza, Dominic Colon; **D:** Lori Silverbush, Michael Skolnik; **W:** Lori Silverbush; **C:** Mariana Sanchez du Antunano; **M:** Richard Leigh, Brian Satz.

On the Right Track ⚫⚫½ 1981 (PG) Young orphan living in Chicago's Union Station has the gift of being able to pick winning race horses. May be appealing to fans of Coleman and "Different Strokes" TV show, but lacks the momentum to keep most viewers from switching tracks. **98m/C VHS.** Gary Coleman, Lisa Eilbacher, Michael Lembeck, Norman Fell, Maureen Stapleton, Herb Edelman; **D:** Lee Philips.

On the Run ⚫ Country Blue; One for the Money, Two for the Show 1973 (R) An ex-con and his gal cut a law-defying swath through the Bayou. **110m/C VHS.** Jack Conrad, Rita George, Dub Taylor, David Huddleston; **D:** Jack Conrad; **W:** Jack Conrad; **C:** Emmett Alston.

On the Run 🎬🎬 1983 A hitman is hired to kill a young boy who witnesses a brutal murder. The hitman, however, decides he's already killed too many people and wants to get out of the business. Will he become the next murder target? 101m/C VHS. Paul Winfield, Rod Taylor, Shirley Cameron. Beau Cox; C: Mende Brown; M: Leonie Lewis.

On the Sunny Side 🎬🎬 1942 English boy Hugh Ayelsworth (McDowall) is sent to live with Hugh Aylesworth (McDowall) family in order to escape the American Andrew politeness endears him to many people but causes friction with son Tom (Clements) until the two boys unite against the neighborhood bully. 69m/B VHS. Roddy McDowall, Katherine Alexander, Stanley Clements, Jane Darwell, Donald Douglas, William Benedict, Jill Esmond, Freddie Mercer; D: Harold Schuster; W: Lillie Hayward; George Templeton; C: Lucien N. Andriot.

On the Third Day 🎬 1983 A headmaster finds a mysterious stranger in his house who turns out to be his long-lost illegitimate son. 101m/C VHS. Richard Marant, Catherine Schell, Paul Williamson. D: Stanley O'Toole; W: Stanley O'Toole; C: Alec Mills; M: Michael Lewis.

On the Town 🎬🎬🎬½ 1949 Kelly's directorial debut features three sailors on a one day leave search for romance in the Big Apple. Filmed on location in NYC, with uncompromising authentic flavor. Based on the successful Broadway musical. 🎵New York, New York; I Feel Like I'm Not Out of Bed Yet; Come Up to My Place; Miss Turnstiles Ballet; Main Street; You're Awful; On the Town; You Can Count on Me; Pearl of the Persian Sea. 98m/C VHS, DVD, Gene Kelly, Frank Sinatra, Vera-Ellen, Ann Miller, Betty Garrett Jules Munshin. D: Stanley Donen, Gene Kelly; W: Betty Comden, Adolph Green; M: Leonard Bernstein. Oscars '49: Scoring/Musical.

On the Waterfront 🎬🎬🎬 1954 A trend-setting, gritty portrait of New York dock workers embroiled in union violence. Cobb is the gangster union boss, Steiger his crooked lawyer, and Brando, Steiger's ex-fighter brother who "could've been a contender!" Intense performances and excellent direction on stand up well today. The picture was a a huge financial success. 108m/B VHS, DVD. Marlon Brando, Rod Steiger, Eva Marie Saint, Lee J. Cobb, Karl Malden, Pat Henning, Leif Erickson, Tony Galento, John Hamilton, Nehemiah Persoff; D: Elia Kazan; W: Budd Schulberg; C: Boris Kaufman; M: Leonard Bernstein. Oscars '54: Actor (Brando), Art Dir/Set Dec., B&W. B&W Cinematog., Director (Kazan), Film Editing, Picture, Story & Screenplay, Support. Actress (Saint); AFI '98: Top 100; British Acad. '54: Actor (Brando); Directors Guild '54: Director (Kazan); Golden Globes '55: Actor—Drama (Brando), Director (Kazan); Film—Drama, Natl. Film Reg. '89; N.Y. Film Critics '54: Actor (Brando), Director (Kazan), Film.

On the Yard 🎬🎬 1979 (R) An attempt to realistically portray prison life. Focuses on a murderer who runs afoul of the leader of prisoners and the system. A fairly typical prison drama with above average performances from Heard and Kellerman.

lin. 102m/C VHS. Dominic Chianese, John Heard, Thomas G. Waites, Mike Kellin, Joe Grifasi; D: Raphael D. Silver; W: Malcolm Braly.

On Top of Old Smoky 🎬½ 1953 Autry and the Cass County Boys are mistaken for Texas Rangers by a gang of land poachers. 59m/B VHS. Gene Autry, Smiley Burnette, Gail Davis, Sheila Ryer; D: George Archainbaud.

On Top of the Whale 🎬🎬 1982 Two scholars move onto the estate of strange but wealthy benefactor to conduct research on the few survivors of a disappearing clan of Indians. Two tribesmen speak bizarre dialect which utilizes only one word while others confound the researchers with stories of ghosts and graveyards. Dutch comedy subtitled in English. 93m/C VHS. NL Willeke Van Ammelroy, Fernando Bordeu, Jean Badin, Herbert Curiel; D: Raul Ruiz; W: Raul Ruiz; C: Henri Alekan; M: Jorge Arriagada.

On Valentine's Day 🎬🎬½ 1986 *Story of a Marriage* 1986 (PG) Author Horton Foote based this story loosely on his parents' lives. A wealthy young Southern girl marries a poor but decent young man and finds herself ostracized from her family. A prequel to the same author's "1918." Produced with PBS for "American Playhouse." 106m/C VHS, DVD. Hallie Foote, Matthew Broderick, Michael Higgins, Steven Hill, William Converse-Roberts, Rochelle Oliver, Richard Jenkins, Horton Foote Jr., Carol Goodheart; D: Ken Harrison; W: Horton Foote; M: Jonathan Shifter.

On Wings of Eagles 🎬🎬½ 1986 During the 1979 Iranian revolution two American executives are imprisoned by Islamic radicals. Help arrives in the form of covert agents of their boss—Texas tycoon H. Ross Perot (played by Crenna). Don't expect strict historical veracity or insight from this network miniseries (based on the "nonfiction novel" by Ken Follett), an okay but lengthy "mission impossible." It came out in a two-cassette set, just in time for Perot's 1992 presidential campaign. 221m/C VHS. Burt Lancaster, Richard Crenna, Paul LeMat, Esai Morales, Constance Towers, Jim Metzler, James Sutorius, Lawrence Pressman, Karen Carlson, Cyril O'Reilly; D: Andrew V. McLaglen.

Onassis 🎬½ *World: The Richest Man in the World: The Story of Aristotle Onassis* 1988 Romanticized biography of Greek shipping magnate Aristotle Onassis, from the poverty of his youth to his later wealth and family and romantic liaisons and tragedies. Julia is adequate as the character but English actress Annis is badly miscast as Jackie Kennedy Onassis. However, Seymour is terrific as Onassis's. How played Onassis in "The Greek Tycoon," plays Onassis's father in this one. Miniseries based on the novel by Peter Evans. 120m/C VHS, DVD. Raul Julia, Jane Seymour, Francesca Annis, Anthony Quinn, Anthony Zerbe, Lorenz Quinn; D: Waris Hussein. TV

Once 🎬🎬½ 2006 (R) Simple story, cool soundtrack. A homeless guy (singer-songwriter Hansard) works at his dad's vacuum repair shop and busks on the Dublin streets, still hoping to make his musical dreams come true. He meets a young Czech immigrant (Irglova), also a musician-songwriter, who wants them to team up. There's a hint of romance but it's the music that really drives the film, as it gains fame for TV's "In Living Color" and "Ace Ventura, Pet Detective". 86m/C DVD. /R Glen Hansard, Markéta Irglová; D: John Carney; W: John Carney; C: Tim Fleming; M: Glen Hansard, Markéta Irglová. Oscars '07: Song ("Falling Slowly"); Ind. Spirit '08: Foreign Film.

Once a Hero 🎬🎬 1988 The dregs of society, the Cicero Gang, have taken Captain Justice's number one fan and his mother hostage. Is it really curtains for rosy cheeks, bubble gum, and apple pie? But wait, it's Captain Justice to the rescue! 74m/C VHS. Jeff Lester, Robert Forster, Milo O'Shea; D: Claudia Weill.

Once a Thief 🎬🎬 1990 (R) Minor kids children are raised to be thieves by crime boss/surrogate father Chow (Tsang). As adults, Joe (Chow), Jim (Cheung), and Cherie (Chung) have just completed an[...]

other successful art heist and Cherie thinks it's time they retire. Instead, they agree to one last job—stealing a painting from a heavily guarded French villa. But it turns out to be a set-up and Joe is apparently killed. He returns, in a wheelchair, two years later—seeking revenge against Chow, who betrayed them. Chinese with subtitles. Woo went on to use a variation of this premise for his TV movie/series of the same name. 108m/C VHS; HK Chow Yun-Fat, Leslie Cheung, Cherie Chung, Kenneth Tsang; D: John Woo; W: John Woo.

Once a Thief 🎬🎬 1996 (R) A fun action-packed TV movie finds adopted children Li Ann (Holt) and Mac (Sergei) being raised along with natural son Michael (Wong) by Hong Kong crime head Tang (Ito) and trained as daring professional thieves. A falling out finds Li Ann in Vancouver, involved with ex-cop Victor (Lea), and both of them working for a co... ever crime-fighting agency headed by a very tough director (Dale). Then Mac is forced to join the duo in an elaborate heist to bring down Michael and his family's criminal empire. Woo's director's cut contains additional footage. 101m/C VHS, DVD. Ivan Sergei, Sandrine Holt, Nicholas Lea, Michael Wong, Robert Ito, Jennifer Dale, Alan Scarfe; D: John Woo; W: Glenn Davis, William Laurin; C: Bill Wong; M: Amin Bhatia.

Once Around 🎬🎬½ 1991 (R) 30ish, lonely Renata Bella (Hunter) meets boisterous, self-assured (read utterly obnoxious) Lithuanian salesman Sam Sharpe (Dreyfuss). He sweeps her off her feet, showers her with affection and gifts, and then tries hard—too hard—to please her close-knit Italian family. Casting doesn't get much better than the group assembled here and Hallstrom steers everyone to wonderful performances in his American directorial debut. The major flaw is the script, a light romantic comedy that sometimes swerves into heavy drama, so much so that you may need Kleenex. 115m/C VHS, DVD. Richard Dreyfuss, Holly Hunter, Danny Aiello, Gena Rowlands, Laura San Giacomo, Roxanne Hart, Danton Stone, Tim Guinee, Greg Germann, Griffin Dunne; D: Lasse Hallstrom; W: Malia Scotch Marmo; M: James Horner.

Once Before I Die 🎬🎬½ 1965 Army soldiers caught in in the Philippines during WWII struggle to survive and elude the Japanese. A single woman traveling with them becomes the object of their spare time considerations. A brutal, odd, and gritty war drama. Director/actor Derek was Andress' husband at the time. 97m/C VHS. PH Ursula Andress, John Derek, Richard Jaeckel, Rod Lauren, Ron Ely; D: John Derek.

Once Bitten 🎬½ 1985 (PG-13) Centuries-old though still remarkably youthful vampiress comes to LA to stalk male virgins. That may be the wrong city, but she needs their blood to retain her young countenance. Vampire comedy theme was more effectively explored in 1979's "Love at First Bite," notable however for the screen debut of comic Carrey who would later gain fame for TV's "In Living Color" and "Ace Ventura, Pet Detective". 94m/C VHS, DVD. Lauren Hutton, Jim Carrey, Cleavon Little, Karen Kopins, Thomas Ballatore, Skip Lackey; D: Howard Storm; W: Jonathan Roberts, David Hines, Jeffrey Hause; C: Adam Greenberg; M: John Du Prez.

Once in Paris... 🎬🎬½ 1979 (PG) A bittersweet romance about a screenwriter working in Paris, the chauffeur who befriends him, and the aristocratic British woman with whom the writer falls in love. Beautiful French scenery and the engaging performance of Lenoir as the chauffeur make this into a diverting piece of entertainment. 100m/C VHS. Wayne Rogers, Gayle Hunnicutt, Jack Lenoir; D: Frank D. Gilroy; W: Frank D. Gilroy.

Once in the Life 🎬🎬½ 2000 (R) Fishburne transfers his 1995 Off Broadway play "Riff Raff" to the big screen but its stage antecedents are apparent. 20/20 Mike (Fishburne) has hooked up with his heroin-addicted white half-brother Torch (Wolliver) and they have trouble finding a drug score gone wrong that has enraged

local boss Manny (Calderon). Manny has

sent henchman Tony the Tiger (Wake) to take care of things, even though Tony and Mike are old prison buddies. The film basically turns into a talky, one-set triangle leading to inevitable tragedy. 107m/C VHS, DVD. Laurence Fishburne, Titus Welliver, Eamonn Walker, Paul Calderon, Dominic Chianese, Gregory Hines, Annabella Sciorra, Michael Paul Chan, Nicholas Chinlund, Jim Breuer; D: Laurence Fishburne; W: Laurence Fishburne; C: Richard Turner; M: Branford Marsalis.

Once Is Not Enough 🎬½ *Jacqueline Susann's Once is Not Enough* 1975 (R) Limp trash-drama concerning the young daughter of a has-been movie producer who has a tempestuous affair with a writer who reminds her of her father. Based on the novel by Jacqueline Susann. 121m/C VHS. Kirk Douglas, Deborah Raffin, David Janssen, George Hamilton, Brenda Vaccaro, Alexis Smith, Melina Mercouri; D: Guy Green; W: Julius J. Epstein; C: John A. Alonzo; M: Henry Mancini. Golden Globes '76: Support. Actress (Vaccaro).

Once Upon a Brothers Grimm 🎬🎬 1977 An original musical fantasy in which the Brothers Grimm meet a succession of their most famous storybook characters, including Hansel and Gretel, the Gingerbread Lady, Little Red Riding Hood, and Rumpelstiltskin. 102m/C VHS. Kirk Douglas, Paul Sand, Cleavon Little, Ruth Buzzi, Chita Rivera, Teri Garr; D: Norman Campbell; M: Mitch Leigh. TV

Once Upon a Crime 🎬½ 1992 (PG) Extremely disappointing comedy featuring a high profile cast set in Europe. The plot centers around Young and Lewis finding a dachshund and travelling from Rome to Monte Carlo to return the stray and collect a $5,000 reward. Upon arrival in Monte Carlo, they find the dog's owner dead and they end up getting implicated for the murder. Other prime suspects include Belushi, Candy, and Shepherd. Weak script is made bearable only by the comic genius of Candy. 94m/C VHS. John Candy, James Belushi, Cybill Shepherd, Sean Young, Richard Lewis, Ornella Muti, Giancarlo Giannini, George Hamilton, Joss Ackland, Elsa Martinelli; D: Eugene Levy; M: Richard and Gibbs.

Once Upon a Forest 🎬🎬 1993 (G) Animated tale of three woodland creatures in a daring race against time when their young friend's life is at stake. Ecologically correct story by "American Tail" creator David Kirschner is light on humor and heavy on gloom, as little animals encounter oppressive human society and their big, bad machines. Servicable animation, though not up to Don Bluth standards (and a long, long way from Disney). Crawford, the voice of the wise old uncle, has a song, while Vereen breaks into a fervent gospel number as a marsh bird with a yen for preaching. For an evening of anti-pollution, see it with "Ferngully." 80m/C VHS, DVD. D: Charles Grosvenor; W: Mark Young, Kelly Ward; V: Michael Crawford, Ben Vereen.

Once Upon a Honeymoon 🎬🎬½ 1942 Set in 1938, Grant is an American radio broadcaster reporting on the oncoming war. Rogers is the ex-showgirl who unknowingly marries a Nazi. In this strange, uneven comedy, Grant tries to get the goods on him and also rescue Rogers. The plot is basic and uneven with Grant attempting to expose the Nazi and save Rogers. However, the slower moments are offset by some fairly surreal pieces of comedy. 116m/B VHS. Ginger Rogers, Cary Grant, Walter Slezak, Albert Dekker, Harry Shannon; D: Leo McCarey; C: George Barnes.

Once Upon a Midnight Scary 🎬🎬 1990 Price narrates a collection of three tales of terror. "The Ghost Belonged to Me," "The Legend of Sleepy Hollow," and "The House with a Clock in its Walls." Aimed at the kiddies. 50m/C VHS. Rene Auberjonois, Severn Darden; C: Cox; Nar: Vincent Price.

Once Upon a Scoundrel 🎬🎬 1973 (G) A ruthless Mexican land baron arranges to have a young woman's fiance thrown in jail so he can have her all to himself. 90m/C

VHS. Zero Mostel, Katy Jurado, Titos Vandis, Priscilla Garcia, A. Martinez; **D:** George Schaefer; **M:** Alex North.

Once Upon a Time in America 🦴🦴🦴½ **1984 (R)** The uncut, original version of Leone's epic saga of five friends from a rough Jewish neighborhood in Brooklyn who grow up to be powerful Mob figures during Prohibition and try to keep their friendships and loyalties intact. Told, mostly in flashback, from the perspective of "Noodles" Aaronson (De Niro) as an old man looking back on a lifetime of crime, love, and death; with a sweeping and violent elegance. **229m/C VHS, DVD.** Robert De Niro, James Woods, Elizabeth McGovern, Tuesday Weld, Treat Williams, James Hayden, Joe Pesci, Danny Aiello, William Forsythe, Burt Young, Darlanne Fluegel, Robert Harper, Richard Bright, Mario Brega, Frank Gio, Jennifer Connelly, Brian Bloom, James Russo, Tandy Cronyn, Marcia Jean Kurtz, Estelle Harris; **D:** Sergio Leone; **W:** Sergio Leone, Leonardo Benvenuti, Piero De Bernardi, Enrico Medioli, Franco Arcalli, Franco Ferrini; **C:** Tonino Delli Colli; **M:** Ennio Morricone. British Acad. '84: Costume Des., Orig. Score.

Once Upon a Time in China 🦴🦴🦴 *Wong Fei-hung* **1991** Martial arts expert Wong Fei-hung (Li) is dismayed as his country is overrun with western influences and the slave trade that provides labor to the California gold fields. When his aunt is kidnapped by slavers, Wong is determined to get revenge. The DVD edition clocks in at 134 minutes. **100m/C VHS, DVD.** HK Jet Li, Yuen Biao, Jacky Cheung, Rosamund Kwan, Kent Cheng; **D:** Tsui Hark; **W:** Tsui Hark; **C:** Arthur Wong Ngok Tai; David Chung; **M:** James Wong.

Once Upon a Time in China II 🦴🦴🦴 *Wong Fei-hung Ji Yi: Naam Yi Dong Ji Keung* **1992** Wong (Li), his assistant Foon, and his aunt arrive in the city of Canton for a medical conference at which Wong is to demonstrate the Chinese art of acupuncture. But the city is on the brink of anarchy as a crumbling dynasty threatens its stability. So Wong joins the revolutionary Sun Yat Sen when a terrorist group initiates a campaign of violence. Dubbed into English. **112m/C VHS, DVD.** HK Jet Li, Rosamund Kwan, Mok Siu Chung, Xin-Xin Xiong, Zhang Tie Lin, Yen Chi Tan; **D:** Tsui Hark; **W:** Tsui Hark; **C:** Wong Ngok Tai; **M:** Richard Yuen.

Once Upon a Time in China III 🦴🦴🦴 *Wong Fei-hung Tsi Sam: Siwong Tsangba* **1993 (R)** Wong Fei-Hung, his young aunt-by-adoption Yee (to whom he is secretly engaged), and his friend Chung arrive in Peking just as the Empress announces an important martial arts contest. Wong faces rivals on two fronts: a brutal martial arts foe and a Russian diplomat who has a history with Yee. **105m/C VHS, DVD.** HK Jet Li, Rosamund Kwan, Mok Siu Chung, Xin-Xin Xiong, Shun Lau; **D:** Tsui Hark; **W:** Tsui Hark; **C:** Wai Keung (Andrew) Lau; **M:** Wai Lap Wu.

Once Upon a Time in Mexico 🦴🦴🦴 **2003 (R)** The last in Rodriguez's "El Mariachi" trilogy. El Mariachi (Banderas) is enlisted by corrupt CIA agent Sands to take part in a coup against the President of Mexico. The coup is being planned by vicious cartel leader Barillo (Dafoe) and crooked Gen. Marquez, both of whom want to see El Mariachi dead (and the feeling is mutual). Confusing plot twists and twirls around flashbacks, doublecrosses, triplecrosses, and at least three different subplots to keep you guessing about what's going on and who's on whose side. The top-notch cast keeps it all together (especially Depp, who walks away with every scene he's in), under the playful guidance of Rodriguez, who doesn't disappoint with several spectacular action scenes. **101m/C VHS, DVD, UMD.** US Antonio Banderas, Johnny Depp, Willem Dafoe, Salma Hayek, Mickey Rourke, Eva Mendes, Danny Trejo, Enrique Iglesias, Marco Leonardi, Richard "Cheech" Marin, Ruben Blades, Pedro Armendariz Jr., Gerardo Vigil; **D:** Robert Rodriguez; **W:** Robert Rodriguez; **C:** Robert Rodriguez; **M:** Robert Rodriguez.

Once Upon a Time in the Midlands 🦴🦴 **2002 (R)** Small-time criminal Jimmy (Carlyle) decides to take a second chance on romance in this fitfully engaging comedy. Jimmy sees ex-girlfriend Shirley (Henderson) on a TV chat show where she's just turned down the marriage proposal of her current beau Dek (Ifans). He decides to try to win Shirley back—and he needs to get out of town after literally being left holding the bag after a bungled robbery. Jimmy tries to insinuate himself into Shirley's good graces by making like a dad to their daughter Marlene (Atkins) and having several ineffectual showdowns with Dek. Then Jimmy's pissed-off cohorts come to town looking for their share of the loot and more trouble ensues. **104m/C VHS, DVD.** GB Robert Carlyle, Rhys Ifans, Shirley Henderson, Kathy Burke, Ricky Tomlinson, Finn Atkins; **D:** Shane Meadows; **W:** Shane Meadows, Paul Fraser; **C:** Brian Tufano; **M:** John Lunn.

Once Upon a Time in the West 🦴🦴🦴½ **1968 (PG)** The uncut version of Leone's sprawling epic about a band of ruthless gunmen who set out to murder a mysterious woman waiting for the railroad to come through. Filmed in John Ford's Monument Valley, it's a revisionist western with some of the longest opening credits in the history of the cinema. Fonda is cast against type as an extremely cold-blooded villain. Brilliant musical score. **165m/C VHS, DVD.** IT Henry Fonda, Jason Robards Jr., Charles Bronson, Claudia Cardinale, Keenan Wynn, Lionel Stander, Woody Strode, Jack Elam; **D:** Sergio Leone; **W:** Sergio Leone, Bernardo Bertolucci, Dario Argento; **C:** Tonino Delli Colli; **M:** Ennio Morricone.

Once Upon a Time ... When We Were Colored 🦴🦴🦴 **1995 (PG)** Actor Reid makes a fine directorial debut with the story of a black youngster growing up parentless in '50s Mississippi. His family faces the usual troubles of the time, including poor wages and white bigotry, but manages to provide a positive and loving home life for him. Nostalgic, sensitive, and heartwarming adaptation of Clifton Taulbert's autobiographical book. **112m/C VHS, DVD.** Al Freeman Jr., Paula Kelly, Phylicia Rashad, Polly Bergen, Richard Roundtree, Charles Taylor, Willie Norwood, Jr., Damon Hines, Leon; **D:** Tim Reid; **W:** Paul Cooper; **C:** Johnny (John W.) Simmons; **Nar:** Phill Lewis.

Once Upon a Wedding 🦴🦴 **2005 (PG)** Margarita (Ayanna), the daughter of an eccentric Caribbean dictator (Martinez), is just a week away from an arranged marriage to wealthy Manolo (de la Fuente). She accidentally runs over poor-but-handsome Rogelio (Becker) and takes him to the palace to recover. Of course when Margarita realizes she's fallen in love Dad isn't happy. **92m/C DVD.** Charlotte Ayanna, A. Martinez, Kuno Becker, Christian de la Fuente, Esai Morales; **D:** Matia Karrell; **W:** Reuben Gonzalez; **C:** Steven Finestone; **M:** Douglas G. Cuomo. **VIDEO**

Once Were Warriors 🦴🦴🦴 **1994 (R)** Violent story of the struggling Maori Heke family, who have left their rural New Zealand roots to live in the city. Feisty mom Beth (Owen) is struggling with five kids and volatile hubby Jake (Heke), who's continuously out of work, boozing, and fighting. Eldest son Nig (Arahanga) has left home and joined a street gang and the rest of the kids hate Jake for beating up on their mother. They also fall victim to his temper and his habit of bringing his brawling, drunk buddies home-leading to further tragedy. Intense drama showcases great performances, with Owen honored as best actress at the Montreal World Film Festival. Based on the novel by Alan Duff. Feature-film directorial debut of Tamahori. **102m/C VHS, DVD.** NZ Rena Owen, Temuera Morrison, Mamaengaroa Kerr-Bell, Julian (Sonny) Arahanga, Taungaroa Emile, Rachael Morris, Joseph Kairau, Pete Smith; **D:** Lee Tamahori; **W:** Riwia Brown; **C:** Stuart Dryburgh; **M:** Murray Grindlay, Murray McNabb. Australian Film Inst. '95: Foreign Film; Montreal World Film Fest. '94: Actress (Owen), Film.

The One 🦴🦴 **2001 (PG-13)** The premise of this action-intensive martial arts flick is that there are 125 parallel universes, and that each person has a counterpart in all of them. Gabriel Yulaw (Li) is a renegade Multiverse Bureau of Investigation agent who is killing his fellow selves in order to absorb their energy. He has fellow MBI agents Roedecker (Lindo) and Funsch (Statham) after him, but he only has one Gabe left to kill, this one a hard-working L.A. deputy sheriff. Bad Gabe kills good Gabe's wife, and the stage is set for a showdown in a grungy factory. Did you follow all of that? Well, it doesn't matter, because it's all just an excuse to have Jet Li kick Jet Li's butt on a catwalk to the sounds of grating techno/metal. Should have added a touch of humor to a completely ludicrous plot instead of concentrating on stealing special effects from "The Matrix." **80m/C VHS, DVD.** US Jet Li, Delroy Lindo, Carla Gugino, Jason Statham, Dylan Bruno, Richard Steinmetz, James Morrison; **C:** James Wong; **W:** Glen Morgan, James Wong; **C:** Robert McLachlan; **M:** Trevor Rabin.

One Against the Wind 🦴🦴🦴 **1991 (PG)** A true story of one woman's courage against great odds. British Mary Liddell and her children are living in Paris during the WWII Nazi occupation. Mary's secret agenda is to smuggle downed Allied pilots out of the country to safety without arousing Nazi suspicions. Great performances by Davis as the resourceful Mary and Neill as one of the pilots she rescues. A Hallmark Hall of Fame presentation. **96m/C VHS.** Judy Davis, Sam Neill, Denholm Elliott, Anthony (Colin) Higgins, Christien Anholt, Kate Beckinsale, Frank Middlemass, Benedick Blythe, Peter Cellier, Stefan Gryff, Mark Wing-Davey, John Savident; **D:** Larry Elikann; **W:** Chris Bryant; **C:** Denis Lewiston; **M:** Lee Holdridge. **TV**

One A.M. 🦴🦴½ **1916** Charlie is a drunk who must first battle a flight of stairs in order to get to bed. Silent with music track. **34m/B VHS, DVD.** Charlie Chaplin, Albert Austin; **D:** Charlie Chaplin; **W:** Charlie Chaplin; **C:** Roland H. Totheroh, William C. Foster.

The One and Only 🦴🦴½ **1978 (PG)** An egotistical young man is determined to make it in show business. Instead, he finds himself in the world of professional wrestling. Most of the humor comes from the wrestling scenes, with Winkler and Darby's love story only serving to dilute the film. **98m/C VHS.** Henry Winkler, Kim Darby, Gene Saks, William Daniels, Harold Gould, Herve Villechaize; **D:** Carl Reiner.

The One and Only, Genuine, Original Family Band 🦴🦴🦴 **1968 (G)** A harmonious musical family comes divided when various members take sides in the presidential battle between Benjamin Harrison and Grover Cleveland, a political era that has been since overlooked. **110m/C VHS, DVD.** Walter Brennan, Buddy Ebsen, Lesley Ann Warren, Kurt Russell, Goldie Hawn, Wally Cox, Richard Deacon, Janet Blair; **D:** Michael O'Herlihy.

One Arabian Night 🦴🦴🦴 *Sumurun* **1921** When an exotic dancer in a traveling carnival troupe is kidnapped into a harem, a dwarf acts on his unrequited love and avenges her death by murdering the sheik who killed her. Secured a place in American filmmaking for director Lubitsch. **85m/B VHS, DVD.** GE Pola Negri, Ernst Lubitsch, Paul Wegener; **D:** Ernst Lubitsch.

One Armed Executioner 🦴🦴 **1980 (R)** An Interpol agent seeks revenge on his wife's murderers. **90m/C VHS.** Franco Guerrero, Jody Kay; **D:** Bobby A. Auarez.

One Away 🦴 **1976** Gypsy escapes from a South African prison and the police are in hot pursuit. **83m/C VHS.** Elke Sommer, Bradford Dillman, Dean Stockwell; **D:** Sidney Hayers.

One Body Too Many 🦴🦴 **1944** A mystery spoof about a wacky insurance salesman who's mistaken for a detective. The usual comedy of errors ensues. A contrived mish-mash—but it does have Lugosi going for it. **75m/B VHS, DVD.** Jack Haley, Jean Parker, Bela Lugosi, Lyle Talbot,

Blanche Yurka, Douglas Fowley, Fay Helm, Lucien Littlefield, Dorothy Granger; **W:** Maxwell Shane, Winston Miller; **C:** Fred H. Jackman Jr; **M:** Alexander Laszlo.

One Brief Summer WOOF! **1970 (R)** Love triangles and intrigues abound on a spectacular country manor. An aging woman is mortified by her father's interest in a young seductress, who finds herself attracted to the old man, but not only him. **86m/C VHS.** Clifford Evans, Felicity Gibson, Jennifer Hilary, Jan Holden, Peter Egan; **D:** John MacKenzie.

One Christmas 🦴🦴½ *Truman Capote's One Christmas* **1995** Conman father uses his estranged son as a pawn to gain access to New Orleans high society. Based on the story "One Christmas" by Truman Capote. **91m/C VHS, DVD.** Katharine Hepburn, Henry Winkler, Swoosie Kurtz, T.J. Lowther, Pat Hingle, Julie Harris; **D:** Tony Bill; **W:** Duane Poole; **M:** Van Dyke Parks. **TV**

One Cooks, the Other Doesn't 🦴🦴 **1983** A most unlikely story of a man's ex-wife and his son moving back into his house, where he's now living with his new wife. **96m/C VHS.** Suzanne Pleshette, Joseph Bologna, Rosanna Arquette, Oliver Clark; **D:** Richard Michaels. **TV**

One Crazy Night 🦴🦴½ **1993 (PG-13)** In 1964, three Australian teenagers try to get into the Melbourne hotel where the Beatles are staying on tour. They wind up trapped in the basement, swapping secrets, and finding out how much they have in common. **92m/C VHS, DVD.** AU Noah Taylor, Beth Champion, Malcolm Kennard, Danni Minogue, Malcolm Braly; **D:** Michael Pattinson.

One Crazy Summer 🦴🦴½ **1986 (PG)** A group of wacky teens spends a fun-filled summer on Nantucket Island in New England. Follow-up to "Better Off Dead." It's offbeat and fairly charming, led by Cusack's perplexed cartoonist and with comic moments delivered by Goldthwait. **94m/C VHS, DVD.** John Cusack, Demi Moore, William Hickey, Curtis Armstrong, Bob(cat) Goldthwait, Mark Metcalf, Joel Murray, Tom Villard, Joe Flaherty; **D:** Savage Steve Holland; **W:** Savage Steve Holland; **M:** Cory Lerios.

One Dark Night 🦴🦴½ *Entity Force; Mausoleum* **1982 (R)** Two high school girls plan an initiation rite for one of their friends who is determined to shed her "goody-goody" image. West is the caped crusader of TV series "Batman" fame. **94m/C VHS, DVD.** Meg Tilly, Adam West, David Mason Daniels, Robin Evans, Elizabeth (E.G. Dailey) Daily; **D:** Tom McLoughlin.

One Day in the Life of Ivan Denisovich 🦴 **1971** The film version of Nobel Prize-winner Alexander Solzhenitsyn's novel about a prisoner's experiences in a Soviet labor camp. A testament to human endurance. Photography be Sven Nykvist. **105m/C VHS. NO GB** Tom Courtenay, Alfred Burke, Espen Skjonberg, James Maxwell, Eric Thompson; **D:** Casper Wrede; **W:** Ronald Harwood; **C:** Sven Nykvist.

One Deadly Owner 🦴 **1974** A possessed Rolls-Royce tortures its new owner. Quite a vehicle for the usually respectable set of wheels. **80m/C VHS.** GB Donna Mills, Jeremy Brett, Robert Morris, Laurence Payne; **D:** Ian Fordyce; **W:** Brian Clemens; **M:** Laurie Johnson. **TV**

One Deadly Summer 🦴🦴🦴 *L'Ete Meurtrier* **1983 (R)** Revenge drama about a young girl who returns to her mother's home village to ruin three men who had assaulted her mother years before. Very well acted. From the novel by Sebastien Japrisot. In French with English subtitles. **134m/C VHS.** FR Isabelle Adjani, Alain Souchon, Suzanne Flon; **D:** Jean Becker; **M:** Georges Delerue. Cesar '84: Actress (Adjani), Support. Actress (Flon), Writing.

One Down, Two to Go! WOOF! **1982 (R)** When the mob is discovered to be rigging a championship karate bout, two dynamic expert fighters join in a climactic battle against the hoods. Example of really bad "blaxploitation" that wastes talent, film, and the audience's time. **84m/C VHS, DVD.** Jim Brown, Fred Williamson, Jim Kelly, Richard Roundtree, Tom Signorelli, Joe Spinell, Paula Sills, Laura Loftus; **D:** Fred Williamson; **M:** Jeff

187 &&½ 1997 (R) Jackson's a Brooklyn high school teacher who is brutally attacked by one of his students. His physical scars are healed, but his emotional state is troubled as he takes some pretty unorthodox teaching methods in a troubled L.A. school. Very dark, psychological drama with a powerful performance by Jackson. Tough film whose title refers to the California penal code number for murder. First film from director Reynolds after his "Waterworld" fiasco. **119mC VHS, DVD.** Samuel L. Jackson, John Heard, Katy Rowan, Clifton (Gonzalez) Collins Jr., Tony Plana, Lobo Sebastian, Jack Kehler, Demetrius Navarro, Karina Arroyave; **D:** Kevin Reynolds; **W:** Scott Yagemann; **C:** Ericson Core.

One-Eyed Jacks &&&½ 1961 An often engaging, but lengthy, psychological western about an outlaw who seeks to settle the score with a former partner who became a sheriff. Great acting by all, particularly Brando, who triumphed both as star and director. Stanley Kubrick was the original director, but Brando took over mid-way through the filming. The photography is wonderful and reflects the effort that went into it. **141mC VHS, DVD.** Marlon Brando, Karl Malden, Katy Jurado, Elisha Cook Jr., Slim Pickens, Ben Johnson, Pina Pellicer, Timothy Carey; **D:** Marlon Brando; **W:** Calder Willingham; **C:** Charles Bryant] Lang Jr.

One-Eyed Soldiers & 1967 Young woman, criminal, and dwarf follow trail to mysterious key to unlock $15 million treasure. Much cheesy intrigue. **83mC VHS, DVD.** *J.P.* Tetsuro Tamba, Haruko Wanibuchi; **D:** Seiichiro Uchikawa.

One-Eyed Swordsman & 1963 A handicapped samurai battles shogun warriors. With English subtitles. **95mC VHS.** *JP* Tetsuro Tamba, Hanuko Wanibuchi; **D:** Seichiro Uchikawa.

One False Move &&& 1991 (R) Black psycho Pluto, his white-trash partner Ray, and Ray's biracial lover Fantasia are three low-level drug dealers on the streets of Los Angeles who get involved in murder. Fleeing the city for Fantasia's small hometown in Arkansas they come up against the local sheriff and two L.A. cops sent to bring them back. Not a typical crime thriller, first-time feature director Franklin is more interested in a psychological character study of racism and small town mores than in your average shoot 'em up action picture. Good performances, especially by Williams as the deceptive bad girl. **105mC VHS, DVD.** Bill Paxton, Cynda Williams, Michael Beach, Jim Metzler, Earl Billings, Billy Bob Thornton, Natalie Canerday, Robert Ginnaven, Robert Anthony Bell, Kevin Hunter; **D:** Carl Franklin; **W:** Billy Bob Thornton, Tom Epperson; **C:** James L. Carter; **M:** Peter Haycock, Derek Holt. Ind. Spirit '93: Director (Franklin); MTV Movie Awards '93: New Filmmaker (Franklin).

One Fine Day &&½ 1996 (PG) Marshmallows. That's what this movie is like—light, fluffy, not much substance, but enjoyable when you're in the mood. Nod to the classic screwball comedies of the '40s and '50s throws harried single mom/ architect Pfeiffer and political columnist/ devilish grin thing working overtime weekend dad Clooney together when their kids, who attend the same school, miss a class field trip. Naturally, they take an instant dislike to each other, but are forced to cooperate to solve the daycare situations. An accidental switching of cell phones provides the chance for repeated encounters, and growing mutual interest. Predictable, but pleasantly so. No matter how hard she tries, Pfeiffer always looks good, and Clooney has that cocked head, devilish grin thing. **108mC VHS, DVD.** Michelle Pfeiffer, George Clooney, Alex D. Linz, Mae Whitman, Charles Durning, Jon Robin Baitz, Ellen Greene, Joe Grifasi, Pete Hamil, Anna Maria Horsford, Sheila Kelley, Barry Kivel, Robert Klein, George Martin, Holland Taylor, Rachel York; **D:** Michael Hoffman; **W:** Terrel Seltzer, Ellen Simon; **C:** Oliver Stapleton; **M:** James Newton Howard.

Williamson; **C:** James (Mome) Lemmo; **M:** Herb Hetzer, Joe Trunzo.

One Flew Over the Cuckoo's Nest &&&& 1975 (R) Touching, hilarious, dramatic, and completely effective adaptation of Ken Kesey's novel. Nicholson is two-bit crook Randle Patrick McMurphy, who, facing a jail sentence, feigns insanity to be sentenced to a cushy mental institution. The hospital is anything but cushy, with tyrannical head nurse Ratched (Fletcher) out to squash any vestige of the patients' independence. Nicholson proves to be a crazed messiah and catalyst for these mentally troubled patients. Classic performs superbly on nu-merous levels. **129mC VHS, DVD.** Jack Nicholson, Louise Fletcher, Will Sampson, William Redfield, Danny DeVito, Christopher Lloyd, Scatman Crothers, Vincent Schiavelli, Michael Berryman, Peter Brocco, Louisa Moritz; **D:** Milos Forman; **W:** Ken Kesey, Bo Goldman; **C:** Haskell Wexler, Bill Butler; **M:** Jack Nitzsche. Oscars '75: Actor (Nicholson), Actress (Fletcher), Director (Forman), Picture; AFI '98: Top 100; British Acad. '76: Actor (Nicholson), Actress (Fletcher), Director (Forman), Film, Support. Actor (Dourif); Directors Guild '75: Director (Forman); Golden Globes '76: Actor—Drama (Nicholson), Actress—Drama (Fletcher), Director (Forman), Film—Drama, Screenplay; Natl. Bd. of Review '75: Actor (Nicholson); N.Y. Film Critics '75: Actor (Nicholson); Natl. Film Reg. '93; N.Y. Film Critics '75: Actor (Nicholson); Natl. Film Reg. '93; N.Y. Film Critics '75: Actor, Film Reg. Soc. Film Critics '75: Actor. (Nicholson) Writers Guild '75: Adapt. Screenplay.

One for the Road & *Against All Odds* 1982 An eccentric millionaire informs his family members that he is leaving each of them $1 million...as long as 'his long-lost granddaughter doesn't reappear. Guess who comes to dinner. **69m/B VHS, DVD.** Mary Carlisle, Wallace Ford, Hedda Hopper, Charley Grapewin; **D:** Christy Cabanne.

One Frightened Night &&½ 1935 An eccentric millionaire informs his family members that he is leaving each of them $1 million...as long as 'his long-lost granddaughter doesn't reappear. Guess who comes to dinner. **69m/B VHS, DVD.** Mary Carlisle, Wallace Ford, Hedda Hopper, Charley Grapewin; **D:** Christy Cabanne.

One from the Heart && 1982 (R) The film more notable for sinking Coppola's Zoetrope Studios than for its cinematic context. Garr and Forrest are a jaded couple who seek romantic excitement with other people. An extravagant (thus a much-needed plus. **100mC VHS, DVD.** Teri Garr, Frederic Forrest, Nastassja Kinski, Raul Julia, Laina Kazan, Rebecca De Mornay, Harry Dean Stanton; **D:** Francis Ford Coppola; **W:** Armyan Bernstein, Francis Ford Coppola; **M:** Tom Waits, Robert Acivar.

One Good Cop &&½ 1991 (R) A noble, inconsistent attempt to do a police thriller with a human face, as a young officer and his wife adopt the three little daughters of his slain partner from the force. But it reverts to a routine action wrapup, with 'Batman' Keaton even donning a masked-avenger get-up to get revenge. **105mC VHS, DVD.** Michael Keaton, Rene Russo, Anthony LaPaglia, Kevin Conway, Rhea Silver-Smith, Grace Johnston, Blair Swenson, Charlaine Woodard, Lisa Anthony, Benjamin Bratt, Heywood Gould; **W:** Heywood Gould; **C:** Ralf Bode; **M:** William Ross.

One Good Turn && 1995 (R) Matt Forrest (Von Dohlen) and his wife Laura (Annis) seemingly have it all only to have their fortunes take a radical turn for the worse. Matt "accidentally" runs into Simon Jury (Remar), the man who saved his life 12 years before. But the seemingly friendly Jury is actually intent on destroying everything they have. **90mC VHS, DVD.** Lenny Von Dohlen, James Remar, Suzy Amis, John Savage; **D:** Tony Randel; **W:** Jim Piddock; **C:** Jacques Haitkin; **M:** Joel Goldsmith.

One Hour Photo &&& 2002 (R) Creepy thriller with Williams treading new ground as Seymour Parrish, Sy the Photo Guy, a disturbed and disturbing one-hour photo clerk. While seeming the mild Milquetoast, Sy becomes a tad obsessed with the suburban Yorkin family, idealizing

---

One Hour with You &&½ 1932 Lubitsch remade this 1924 silent, "The Marriage," in this musical comedy. Parisian doctor Andre Bertier (Chevalier) may be wed to Colette (MacDonald) but that doesn't stop his roving eye. Married Mitzi (Tobin) has designs on Andre and when her suspicious husband (Young) threatens to name him in a divorce suit, Andre is forced to reveal all to the miffed Colette, who decides to cheat right back. Andre is out as director but quit because of production differences and he finished the picture himself. **80m/B VHS, DVD.** US Robin Williams, Connie Nielsen, Michael Vartan, Gary Cole, Eriq La Salle, Dylan Smith, Erin Daniels, Andy Comeau; **D:** Mark Romanek; **W:** Mark Romanek; **C:** Jeff Cronenweth; **M:** Reinhold Heil, Johnny Klimek.

One Hundred and One Nights && *Les Cent et Une Nuits; Les Cent et Une Nuits de Simon Cinéma* 1995 Simon Cinéma (Piccoli) is a 100-year-old producer/director whose memory is fading. So he hires young film student Camille (Gayel) to prompt his memory. Numerous cameo appearances to talk about film and numerous film clips are shown. **101mC VHS, DVD, FR GB** Michel Piccoli, Marcello Mastroianni, Henri Garcin, Julie Gayel, Mathieu Demy, Emmanuel Salinger; **D:** Agnes Varda; **W:** Agnes Varda; **C:** Eric Gautier.

100 Days Before the Command && *Sto Dnej Do Pri Kaza* 1990 "Five young Red Army recruits struggle for survival and to preserve their humanity against the violence of their daily lives by learning on each other. Russian with subtitles. **71mC VHS, DVD, RU** Vladimir Zamansky, Armen Dzhigarkhanyan, Oleg Vasilkov, Roman Grekov, Valeri Troshin; **D:** Hussein Erkenov; **W:** Vladimir Kholodov, Yuri Polyakov; **C:** Vladislav Menshikov.

100 Girls && 2000 (R) College freshman Tucker (Tucker) scores an unexpected sexual encounter with a co-ed in the girls' dorm elevator during a black-out. He can't see her face and doesn't know her name, so he spends the semester investigating the 100 possibilities in search of his mystery girl. Actually funny and not as sleazy as it may sound. **95mC VHS, DVD.** Jonathan Tucker, James DeBello, Emmanuelle Chriqui, Larisa Oleynik, Jaime Pressly, Katherine Heigl; **D:** Michael Davis; **W:** Michael Davis; **C:** James Lawrence Spencer; **M:** Kevin Bassinson.

100 Men and a Girl &&& 1937 Charming musical features Durbin as the daughter of an unemployed musician, who decides she will try to persuade Leopold Stokowski to help her launch an orchestra that will employ her father and his musician friends. Beautiful mix of classical and pop music. Based on a story by Hans Kraly. ♫Hungarian Rhapsody No. 2; Symphony No. 5; Alleluja; It's Raining Sunteams; A Heart That's Free. **85m/B VHS, DVD.** Deanna Durbin, Leopold Stokowski, Adolphe Menjou, Alice Brady, Eugene Pallette, Mischa Auer, Billy Gilbert, Alma Kruger, Christian Rub, Jed Prouty, Jack Mulhall; **D:** Henry Koster; **W:** Charles Kenyon, Bruce Manning; **C:** Joseph Valentine. Oscars '37: Score.

100 Mile Rule &&½ 2002 (R) Dark comedy has a trio of salesmen from Detroit discussing the "100 Mile Rule" en route to a business meeting in L.A. The rule states that a man is free to cheat on his girlfriend/spouse if he's over 100 miles away. Jerry is all for it, while family man Bobby wants no part of it. Bobby changes his tune when he meets Monica (Bello). After she seduces him, she blackmails him with a tape of the encounter, leading

---

them in the process. After years of viewing their happiest moments frozen in time, he decides to get involved in their lives when he sees trouble brewing. A breakthrough performance by Williams, he creates an off-kilter character that is surprisingly sympathetic. Romanek's direction is clever and extremely stylish, avoiding cliche, to craft a gripping psychodrama. **96mC VHS, DVD.** US Robin Williams, Connie Nielsen, Michael Vartan, Gary Cole, Eriq La Salle, Dylan Smith, Erin Daniels, Andy Comeau; **D:** Mark Romanek; **W:** Mark Romanek; **C:** Jeff Cronenweth; **M:** Reinhold Heil, Johnny Klimek.

101 Ways (The Things a Girl Will Do to Keep Her Volvo) &&½ 2000 Actually, struggling writer Watson (Hoopes) doesn't seem to be trying too hard to keep that car which her mother insisted she purchase because of its safety record. Watson has moved from the bright lights of the Big Apple to the suburbs of Connecticut in order to concentrate on her career but since she has to pay the bills, she works intellectually at a couple of nothing jobs. The flick itself is ineffectual and Watson isn't terribly likeable so who wonders what happens to her (Varney), who routinely abused her. Rae's anger grows, fueled by cocaine and alcohol, until she snaps and begins shooting people. **94mC VHS, DVD.** Jim Brown, Raquel Welch, Burt Reynolds, Fernando Lamas; **D:** Tom Gries; **M:** Jerry Goldsmith.

101 Dalmatians &&&½ 1961 (G) Disney classic is one of the highest-grossing animated films in the history of Hollywood. Dogowners Roger and Anita, and their respective pets Pongo and Perdita are shocked when their puppies are kidnapped by Cruella de Vil, villainess extraordinaire, to make a simply fabulous spotted coat. The aid of various animals including a dog named Colonel, a horse, a cat, and a goose is enlisted to rescue the doomed pups. Imagine their surprise when they find not only their own puppies, but 84 more as well. You can expect a happy ending and lots of spots—6,469,952 to be exact. Based on the children's book by Dodie Smith. Technically notable for the first time use of the Xerox process to transfer the animator's drawings onto cel celluloid, which made the film's opening sequence of dots evolving into 131 barking dogs possible. ♫Remember When; Cruella de Vil; Dalmatian Plantation; Kanine Krunchies Kommercial. **79mC VHS, DVD.** *D:* Clyde Geronimi, Wolfgang Reitherman, Hamilton Luske; **W:** Bill Peet; **M:** George Bruns; **V:** Rod Taylor, Betty Lou Gerson, Lisa Davis, Ben Wright, Frederick Worlock, J. Pat O'Malley.

100 Rifles && 1969 (R) Native American bank robber and Black American lawman join up with a female Mexican revolutionary to help save the Mexican Indians from annihilation by a despotic military governor. What it lacks in political correctness it makes up for in fits of action. Although quite racy in its day for its interracial sex sizzle of Brown and Welch, it's tame and overblown by today's standards. **110mC VHS, DVD.** Jim Brown, Raquel Welch, Burt Reynolds, Fernando Lamas; **D:** Tom Gries; **M:** Jerry Goldsmith.

100 Proof && 1996 Based on a 1966 murder rampage in Lexington, Kentucky. Rae (Stewart) and her compliant sidekick Cara (Bellando) are a couple of smalltime, small-town hustlers, with drug, booze habits, who turn tricks to get by. The day begins in its usual bleak fashion until Rae encounters her degenerate father. **100mC VHS, DVD.** US Wendy Hoopes, Fitzgerald, Jamie Harrold, Jack Gilpin, Patricia Elliott, Gabriel Macht; **D:** Jennifer B. Katz; **W:** Jennifer B. Katz; **C:** Jeffrey A. Splett; **M:** John Hodian.

to murder and corporate backstabbing. Think "Very Bad Things" on business. Standard fare is helped along by McKean and Bello. **98mC VHS, DVD.** Jake Weber, Maria Bello, David Dorfman, Shawn Huff; **C:** Chinland, David Dorfman, Shawn Huff; **D:** Brent Huff; **W:** Drew Pillsbury; **C:** Giovani Lampassi; **M:** Tor Hyams.

---

may be too scary for the little ones. The Hound is always happy to see another dog movie but still feels some classics should be left alone. **103m/C VHS, DVD.** Glenn Close, Jeff Daniels, Joely Richardson, Joan Plowright, Hugh Laurie, Mark Williams; *D:* Stephen Herek; *W:* John Hughes; *C:* Adrian Biddle; *M:* Michael Kamen.

102 Dalmatians 🦴🦴½ **2000 (G)** Lackluster sequel to the 1996 live-action Disney film finds Cruella De Vil (Close) being released from prison and teaming up with fur designer Jean Pierre Le Pelt (Depardieu). She still wants that dalmatian fur coat (and this time a hood as well). The puppies are as cute as ever, with the addition of digitally de-spotted Oddball, but this one just seems like another excuse for Disney to print money and Close to chew scenery. Stick with the original (that is). **100m/C VHS, DVD.** Glenn Close, Gerard Depardieu, Ioan Gruffudd, Tim (McInnerny) McInnery, Ian Richardson, Ben Crompton, Jim Carter, Ron Cook, David Horovitch, Timothy West, Alice Evans, Carol MacReady; *D:* Kevin Lima; *W:* Brian Regan; *C:* Adrian Biddle; *M:* David Newman; *V:* Eric Idle.

125 Rooms of Comfort 🦴🦴 **1983** A mental patient has bizarre fantasies that create havoc among those who stand in his way. **82m/C VHS.** Tim Henry, Jackie Burroughs, Bob Warner, Bob Silverman, Les Barker; *D:* Patrick Loubert; *W:* Patrick Loubert, Bill Freut.

One in a Million 🦴🦴🦴 **1936** Debut film of Norwegian skating star Henie centers around a Swiss girl whose father is training her for the Olympics. Features good comedy by the Ritz Brothers and Sparks, as well as the beautiful skating of Henie. ♫One in a Million; We're Back in Circulation Again; Who's Afraid of Love; Lovely Lady in White; The Moonlight Waltz. **95m/B VHS.** Sonja Henie, Adolphe Menjou, Jean Hersholt, Al Ritz, Harry Ritz, Jimmy Ritz, Arline Judge, Don Ameche, Ned Sparks, Montagu Love, Leah Ray; *D:* Sidney Lanfield; *W:* Leonard Praskins, Mark Kelly.

One in a Million: The Ron LeFlore Story 🦴🦴½ **1978** The true story of Detroit Tigers' star Ron LeFlore, who rose from the Detroit ghetto to the major leagues. Adaptation of LeFlore's autobiography, "Breakout." A well-acted and compelling drama with Burton in a standout performance. **90m/C VHS.** LeVar Burton, Madge Sinclair, Billy Martin, James Luisi; *D:* William A. Graham; *C:* Jordan Cronenweth.

One Kill 🦴🦴🦴 **2000 (PG-13)** Fact-based drama focuses on a murder and a trial. Mary Jane O'Malley (Heche) is a decorated Marine captain and divorced mom who is having an affair with her troubled senior officer, Maj. Nelson Gray (Shepard). Mary Jane breaks things off when she finds out Nelson is married but he's obsessed and when he breaks into her home, she shoots him in self-defense. At least, the D.A. says justifiable homicide but the military will be harmed. **93m/C VHS.** Anne Heche, Sam Shepard, Eric Stoltz, Bill MacDonald, Kate McNeil, Carl Marotte; *D:* Christopher Menaul; *W:* Shelley Evans; *C:* Michael Storey; *M:* Eric Allaman. **CABLE**

One Last Ride 🦴🦴 **2003 (R)** Hard slice-of-life look at L.A. gambling addict Michael (Cupo), who's in deep to loan shark Tweat (Palminteri). Tweat tells the fabric salesman to do what he says or he can be harmed. Despite the threats, Michael is still sure he is just one win from everything going his way. Low-budget with a familiar story; Cupo adapted from his play. **90m/C DVD.** *US* Chazz Palminteri, Anita Barone, Mario Roccuzzo, Robert Davi, Charles Durning, Jack Carter, Pat Cupo, Joe Marinelli; *D:* Tony Vitale; *W:* Pat Cupo; *C:* Mark Doering-Powell; *M:* Judy G. Abrahams.

One Last Run 🦴½ **1989** It's drama on the slopes as a variety of individuals confront their pasts/fears/personal demons via extreme skiing. Features the performances of champion skiers Franz Weber and Scot Schmidt. **82m/C VHS.** Russell Todd, Ashley Laurence, Craig Branham, Jimmy Aleck, Tracy Scoggins, Nels Van Patten, Chuck Connors; *D:* Peter Winograd, Glenn Gebhard; *W:* Peter Winograd, Glenn Gebhard.

One Last Thing 🦴🦴½ **2005 (R)** Dylan (Angarano) is 16 and dying from brain cancer. When a charity chooses to grant his final wish, he decides that rather than spending time with his football hero Jason O'Malley (Messner), he wants to meet supermodel Nikki Sinclair (Mabrey). Well, duh. Self-destructive Nikki needs the good publicity but bails as quickly as possible. Still, Jason offers Dylan and his buddies Ricky (Bush) and Slap (Glick) a luxury weekend in New York during which Nikki is given a chance to redeem herself. Ping-pongs between sentiment and reality. Ethan Hawke appears uncredited in flashbacks as Dylan's dead father. **93m/C DVD.** *US* Cynthia Nixon, Michael Angarano, Sunny Mabrey, Michael Rispoli, Brian Stokes Mitchell, Gina Gershon, Nelust Wyclef Jean, Matthew Bush, Gideon Glick; *D:* Alex Steyermark; *W:* Barry Stringfellow; *C:* Christopher Norr; *M:* Anton Sanko.

One Little Indian 🦴🦴 **1973** AWOL cavalry man Garner and his Indian ward team up with a widow (Miles) and her daughter (Foster) in an attempt to cross the New Mexican desert. A tepid presentation from the usually high quality Disney studio. **90m/C VHS, DVD.** James Garner, Vera Miles, Jodie Foster, Clay O'Brien, Andrew Prine, Bernard McEveety; *D:* Bernard McEveety; *M:* Jerry Goldsmith.

One Magic Christmas 🦴🦴½ **1985 (G)** Disney feel-good film about a disillusioned working woman whose faith in Christmas is restored when her guardian angel descends to Earth and performs various miracles. Somewhat cliched and tiresome, but partially redeemed by Stanton and Steenburgen's presence. **88m/C VHS, DVD.** Mary Steenburgen, Harry Dean Stanton, Gary Basaraba, Michelle Meyrink, Arthur Hill, Elisabeth Harnois, Robbie Magwood; *D:* Phillip Borsos; *W:* Thomas Meehan; *C:* Frank Tidy; *M:* Michael Conway Baker.

One Man Army 🦴½ **1993 (R)** Kickboxer decides to visit gramps in small town, only to discover the old guy has been murdered and corruption and cover-ups abound. So he decides to kick some butt and set things right. **95m/C VHS, DVD.** Jerry Trimble; *D:* Cirio H. Santiago.

One Man Force 🦴🦴 **1989 (R)** L.A. narcotics cop Jake Swan goes on a vigilante spree. Huge in body and vengeful in spirit, he makes short work of his partner's murderers—pay! **92m/C VHS, DVD.** John Matuszak, Ronny Cox, Charles Napier, Sharon Farrell, Sam Jones, Chance Boyer, Richard Lynch, Stacey Q; *D:* Dale Trevillion; *W:* Dale Trevillion; *M:* Charles Fox.

One Man Jury 🦴½ **1978 (R)** LAPD lieutenant, wearied by an ineffective justice system, becomes a one-man vigilante avenger. Pale Dirty Harry rip-off with over acting and an excess of violence. **95m/C VHS.** Jack Palance, Chris Mitchum, Joe Spinell, Pamela Shoop; *D:* Charles Martin.

One Man Out 🦴🦴 **1989 (R)** An ex-CIA agent diverts his psychological problems into his new job: assassin for a South American despot. His jaded view of life changes when he meets and falls in love with an American journalist. Trouble in paradise when he is ordered to kill her. One man out was not enough, they should have done away with the entire crew of this stinker. **90m/C VHS.** Stephen McHattie, Deborah Van Valkenburgh, Aharon Ipale, Ismael Carlo, Michael Champion, Dennis A. Pratt; *D:* Michael Kennedy.

One Man's Hero 🦴½ **1998 (R)** Heavy-handed retelling of the U.S.-Mexican war of the 1840s. Irish Catholic Army Sgt. John Riley (Berenger) is tired of the constant harassment he and his fellow Irishmen are subjected to. After disobeying an officer, Riley leads his men into Mexico where they eventually join the Mexican army as the St. Patrick's Battalion just in time to battle the U.S. troops of Gen. Zachary Taylor (Gammon). The history's confusing and isn't helped when the action stops for romantic interludes between Riley and rebel girl, Marta (Romo). **122m/C VHS, DVD.** Tom Berenger, Joaquim de Almeida, Daniela Romo, James Gammon, Mark Moses, Stuart Graham, Stephen Tobolowsky, Carlos Carrasco, Patrick Bergin; *D:* Lance Hool; *W:* Milton S. Gelman; *C:* Joao Fernandes; *M:* Ernest Troost.

One Man's Justice 🦴🦴½ **1995 (R)** Army drill sergeant John North (Bosworth) heads for the streets of Venice, California to get the drug-dealing, gun-running scum who killed his wife and daughter. And a streetwise 10-year-old may be his best chance for finding them. **100m/C VHS, DVD.** Brian Bosworth, Bruce Payne, Jeff Kober, DeJuan Guy, Hammer; *D:* Kurt Wimmer; *W:* Steven Selling; *C:* Jurgen Baum, John Huneck; *M:* Anthony Marinelli.

One Man's War 🦴🦴½ **1990 (PG-13)** A human-rights crusader in repressive Paraguay won't be silenced, even after government thugs torture and murder his son. He fights obsessively to bring the killers to justice. The true story of the Joel Filartiga family is heartfelt but ultimately a dramatic letdown; an epilogue proves that full story hasn't been told. **91m/C VHS, DVD.** Anthony Hopkins, Norma Aleandro, Fernanda Torres, Ruben Blades; *D:* Sergio Toledo.

One Man's Way 🦴🦴 **1963** Murray is appropriately devout as charasmatic religious leader Norman Vincent Peale. With the support of his wife (Hyland), he survives the adulations and accusations of blasphemy for his rather unorthodox theological ideas and his book, "The Power of Positive Thinking." Based on the book "Norman Vincent Peale: Minister to Millions" by Arthur Gordon. **105m/B VHS.** Don Murray, Diana Hyland, William Windom, Virginia Christine, Carol Ohmart, Veronica Cartwright, Liam Sullivan, June Dayton, Ian Wolfe; *D:* Denis Sanders; *W:* Eleanore Griffin, John W. Bloch.

One Million B.C. 🦴🦴🦴½ *The Cave Dwellers; Cave Man; Man and His Mate* **1940** The strange saga of the struggle of primitive cavemen and their battle against dinosaurs and other monsters. Curiously told in flashbacks, this film provided stock footage for countless dinosaur movies that followed. Portions of film rumored to be directed by cinematic pioneer D. W. Griffith. **80m/B VHS, DVD.** Victor Mature, Carole Landis, Lon Chaney Jr.; *D:* Hal Roach, Hal Roach Jr.

One Million Years B.C. 🦴🦴½ **1966 (R)** It's Welch in a fur bikini and special FX expert Ray Harryhausen doing dinosaurs so who cares about a plot (which involves Welch and her boyfriend, who's from a rival clan). Remake of the 1940 film "One Million B.C." **100m/C VHS, DVD.** *GB* Raquel Welch, John Richardson, Percy Herbert, Robert Brown, Martine Beswick; *D:* Don Chaffey.

One Minute to Zero 🦴🦴 **1952** Korean War action film divides its time between an army romance and war action. The lukewarm melodrama features Mitchum as a colonel in charge of evacuating American civilians but who ends up bombing deaths. **105m/B VHS.** Robert Mitchum, Ann Blyth, William Talman, Charles McGraw, Margaret Sheridan, Richard Egan, Eduard Franz, Robert Osterloh, Robert Gist; *D:* Tay Garnett.

One Missed Call woof! **2008 (PG-13)** Yet another technophobic Japanese horror remake, this one looking for scares from college students who receive cell phone calls from their future selves that capture the sounds of their own looming deaths. Burns and Cho are cringe-worthy as the good cop/bad cop tandem investigating at the behest of the dewy and earnest co-ed (Sossamon), who also brings a child-abuse subplot into play. Meanwhile, director Valette fails to conjure much oogidy-boogidy, and even the gore is boring. **87m/C DVD.** *GE JP US GB* Shannyn Sossamon, Edward Burns, Ana Claudia Talancon, Ray Wise, Azura Skye, Jason Beghe, Margaret Cho, Meagan Good; *D:* Eric Valette; *W:* Andrew Klavan; *C:* Glen MacPherson; *M:* Reinhold Heil, Johnny Klimek.

One More Chance 🦴🦴½ **1990** While he's in jail, an ex-con's family moves away without leaving a forwarding address. When he's released he strikes up a friendship with a woman from the neighborhood who knows where they've gone. **102m/C VHS.** Kirstie Alley, John Lamotta, Logan Clarke, Michael Pataki, Hector Maisonette; *D:* Sam Firstenberg.

One More Kiss 🦴🦴 **1999** Scottish immigrant Sarah (Edmond) leaves New York to return to her hometown when she learns she's dying from cancer. On her to-do list is getting closer to her former flame Sam (Butler), which doesn't please his wife Charlotte (Gogan). Tear-jerker, although Sarah comes across as selfish rather than your standard noble character. **98m/C DVD.** *GB* Valerie Edmond, Gerard Butler, James Cosmo, Valerie Gogan, Carl Proctor; *D:* Vadim Jean; *W:* Suzie Halewood; *C:* Mike J. Fox; *M:* David A. Hughes, John Murphy.

One More Saturday Night 🦴🦴 **1986 (R)** Franken and Davis, "Saturday Night Live" alumni, wrote this film about a small town going wild on the weekend. Dry, taxing, and unfunny. Averages about one laugh per half hour—at one-and-a-half hours, that's way too long. **96m/C VHS.** Al Franken, Tom Davis, Nan Woods, Dave Reynolds; *D:* Dennis Klein; *W:* Al Franken, Tom Davis.

One Night at McCool's 🦴🦴 **2001 (R)** Quirky and inventive, this poor man's "Rashomon" gets points for effort, but the execution doesn't always live up to the ambition. Easygoing bartender Randy (Dillon) is involved in a murder by aggressively materialistic con artist Jewel (Tyler) and before he knows it, he's in love. Somehow his sleazy lawyer cousin (Reiser) becomes involved, as well as Det. Dehling (Goodman) who is investigating the murder of Jewel's former partner (Clay). Of course, all three fall in love, and we see the preceding night's events through each set of love-struck eyes as they spill their guts to a hitman (Douglas), a shrink (McIntire), and a priest (Jenkins), respectively. Douglas's outlandish toupee and understated portrayal of the hitman, as well as some fine comic touches by Dillon, are highlights. **93m/C VHS, DVD.** *US* Liv Tyler, Matt Dillon, Paul Reiser, John Goodman, Michael Douglas, Reba McEntire, Richard Jenkins, Andrew (Dice Clay) Silverstein, Leo Rossi, Eric Schaeffer; *D:* Harald Zwart; *W:* Stan Seidel; *C:* Karl Walter Lindenlaub; *M:* Marc Shaiman.

One Night in the Tropics 🦴🦴½ **1940** The film debut of radio stars Abbott & Costello who play secondary roles to a love triangle (set to music). Jones is an insurance salesman who falls in love with Kelly, the fiance of Cummings. Based on the novel "Love Insurance" by Earl Derr Biggers. ♫Back in My Shell; Remind Me; You and Your Dream; Your Dream is the Same as My Dream. **83m/B VHS, DVD.** Allan Jones, Robert Cummings, Nancy Kelly, Bud Abbott, Lou Costello, Mary Boland, Peggy Moran, William Frawley, Leo Carrillo; *D:* Edward Sutherland; *W:* Kathryn Scola, Gertrude Purcell, Charles Grayson, Francis Martin.

One Night of Love 🦴🦴🦴½ **1934** Moore's best quasi-operetta, about a young American diva rebelling in response to her demanding Italian teacher. "Pygmallion"-like story has her falling in love with her maestro. Despite being nearly 60 years old, this film is still enchanting and fresh. ♫One Night of Love; Ciri-Biri-Bin; Sempre Libera; Sextet; Indian Love Call; 'Tis the Last Rose of Summer; Habanera; Un bel di; None But the Lonely Heart. **95m/B VHS.** Grace Moore, Tullio Carminati, Lyle Talbot, Jane Darwell, Nydia Westman, Mona Barrie, Jessie Ralph, Luis Alberni; *D:* Victor Schertzinger. Oscars '34: Sound, Score.

One Night Only 🦴🦴 **1984** A gorgeous law student decides to make big money by hiring herself and her friends out as hookers to the school football team. **87m/C VHS.** Lenore Zann, Jeff Braunstein, Grant Ailanak; *D:* Timothy Bond.

One Night Stand 🦴🦴 **1978** Woman's chance encounter with a man in a singles bar leads to an evening of unexpected terror. Billed as a horror flick, it is really more of a drama. **90m/C VHS.** *CA* Chapelle Jaffe, Brent Carver, Susan Hogan, Len Doncheff; *D:* Allan King; *W:* Carol Bolt; *C:* Kenneth Gregg. **TV**

One Night Stand 🎬🎬 1984
Four young people attempt to amuse themselves at the empty Sydney Opera House on the night WWIII begins. An odd commentary on nuclear war that sees the bomb as the ultimate bad joke. Features an appearance by alternative rock group Midnight Oil. **94m/C VHS.** Tyler Coppin, Cassandra Delaney, Jay Hackett, Saskia Post. **D:** John Duigan.

One Night Stand 🎬🎬1/2 1995 (R)
Lonely Michelle (Sheedy) visits a nightclub and allows herself to be picked up by your basic handsome stranger, Jack (Marinez) in this case. She wakes up alone and learns from a jealous rock group owner Josslyn (Fornest) that the apartment is up for lease. Obsessed with finding her mystery man, Michelle discovers Jack's wife was murdered—possibly by him or maybe by Josslyn, who turns out to be the dead woman's father. Debut feature for director Shire covers familiar territory, with Sheedy giving a strong performance. **82m/C VHS, DVD.** Ally Sheedy, A. Martinez, Frederic Forrest, Don Novello, Diane Salinger, Millie Slavin; **D:** Talia Shire; **W:** Mary Casella; **C:** Arthur Albert; **M:** David Shire.

1-900 🎬🎬 1994
Based on the play "06" by Doesburg, which refers to the Dutch exchange for phone-sex numbers. Sarah (Schuler) and Thomas (van Kempen) are both lonely professionals who "meet" when Thomas answers Sarah's personal ad. Their weekly phone chats lead to descriptions of sexual fantasies but relationship issues begin to intrude as time passes. Dutch with subtitles. **80m/C VHS, DVD.** NL Ariane Schuiter, Ad van Kempen, Johan Doesburg, Marcel Theron; **D:** Theo van Gogh; **W:** Ariane Schuiter, Ad van Kempen; **C:** Ruud Bos.

One of Her Own 🎬🎬1/2 1997
Based on the true story of a police officer (Laughlin) who decides to press charges against the fellow cop (Evigan) who raped her, despite the consequences to her career. **91m/C VHS.** Lori Loughlin, Greg Evigan, Martin Sheen, Val Johnson; **D:** Armand Mastroianni; **W:** Pablo F. Fenjves, Valerie West. **TV**

One of My Wives Is Missing 🎬🎬 1976
An ex-New York cop tries to solve the mysterious disappearance of a newlywed socialite. Things become strange when she reappears but is discovered as an imposter. Above-average acting in a film adapted from the play "The Trap" or a Lonely Man." **97m/C VHS.** Jack Klugman, Elizabeth Ashley, James Franciscus; **D:** Glenn Jordan. **TV**

One of Our Aircraft Is Missing 🎬🎬1/2 1941
The crew of an R.A.F. bomber downed in the Netherlands, struggle to escape Nazi capture. A thoughtful study of wars and the men who fight them, with an entertaining melodramatic plot. Look for the British version, which runs 106 minutes. Some of the American prints only run 82 minutes. **103m/B VHS.** GB Godfrey Tearle, Eric Portman,

Hugh Williams, Pamela Brown, Googie Withers, Peter Ustinov; **D:** Emeric Pressburger, Michael Powell.

One of Our Dinosaurs Is Missing 🎬🎬 1975 (G)
An English nanny and her cohorts help British Intelligence retrieve a microfilm—concealing dinosaur fossil from the bad guys that have stolen it. Disney film was shot on location in England. **101m/C VHS.** Peter Ustinov, Helen Hayes, Derek Nimmo, Clive Revill, Robert Stevenson, Joan Sims; **D:** Robert Stevenson.

One of Them WOOF! 200¢ (R) Really bad dead teen flick. Elizabeth (Carmichael) and her friends are trapped in a school of horrors (Satanism is involved). Uncle Don (Crenna) tries to come to the rescue. **93m/C VHS.** Richard Anthony Crenna, Kelly Carmichael, Brian Sheridan, Erin Byron, Paul Jeffre; **D:** Ralph Portillo; **W:** Geoff Levin. **VIDEO**

One on One 🎬🎬 1977 (PG) A Rocky-esque story about a high school basketball star from the country who accepts an athletic scholarship to a big city university. He encounters a demanding coach and intense competition. Light weight drama that is economically entertaining. **100m/C VHS.** Robby Benson, Annette O'Toole; **D:** G.D. Spradlin, Gail Strickland, Melanie Griffith; **D:**amont Johnson; **W:** Robby Benson; **M:** Charles Fox.

One Plus One 🎬 Exploring the Kinsey Report 1961 A dramatization, believe it or not, of the Kinsey sex survey of the 1950s. Participants in a sex lecture talk about and demonstrate various "risque" practices, such as premarital sex and extramarital affairs. Despite this film, the sexual revolution went on as planned. **114m/B VHS.** CA Leo G. Carroll, Hilda Brawner, William D: Arch Oboler.

One-Punch O'Day 🎬 1926 Boxing boy tries to buy back hometown's oil livelihood by winning prizefight. Much patient waiting by his honey. **60m/B VHS.** Billy Sullivan, Charlotte Merriam; **D:** Harry Joe Brown.

One Rainy Afternoon 🎬🎬 1936 A bit-player kisses the wrong girl in a Paris theatre causing a massive uproar that brands him as a notorious romantic "mon-ster." Patterned after a German film the story lacks depth and zest. **80m/B VHS, DVD.** Francis Lederer, Ida Lupino, Hugh Herbert, Roland Young, Donald Meek; **D:** Rowland V. Lee.

One Russian Summer WOOF! 1973 (R) During the Russian Revolution, a cripple seeks revenge on the corrupt land-baron who murdered his parents. An unfortunate attempt to dramatize a novel by M. Lermontov. **112m/C VHS.** Oliver Reed, Claudia Cardinale, John McEnery, Carole Andre, Ray Lovlock; **D:** Antonio Calenda.

One Shoe Makes It Murder 🎬🎬 1982
A shady casino owner hires ex-cop Mitchum to investigate the disappearance of his unfaithful wife. Adapted from Eric Bercovici's novel, the story does little to enhance Mitchum's TV debut. **100m/C VHS.** Robert Mitchum, Angie Dickinson, Mel Ferrer, Howard Hesseman, Jose Perez; **D:** William (Billy) Hale; **M:** Bruce Broughton.

One Sings, the Other Doesn't 🎬🎬1/2 L'Une Chante, l'Autre Pas 1977 Seeking contentment, a conservative widow and a liberal extrovert help each other cope in a man's world. Endearing characters, but a superficial treatment of dated feminist issues. In French with English subtitles. **105m/C VHS.** FR BE Valerie Mairesse, Therese Liotard, Robert Dadles, Ali Affi, Jean-Pierre Pellegrin; **D:** Agnes Varda; **W:** Agnes Varda. **C:** Charlie Van Damme; **M:** Francois Wertheimer.

One Small Hero 🎬1/2 1999 (PG) Dopey family entertainment might not be a complete waste of time for easygoing viewers. Joey Cooper (Killey) can't pass the tests to become a member of the Wilderness Club and go on their camping trip. He fails once again (he's physically too small) but can't tell his mom after she surprises Joey with camping gear. So, he trails behind the campers and is the only one who can save them from kidnappers. **90m/C VHS, DVD.** Nathan Kiley, Matthew Peters,

Lindsay Lewis, Bonnie Burroughs; **D:** Jennifer Malcheise; **C:** Denis Maloney; **M:** Herman Beethin. **CABLE**

One Special Night 🎬🎬1/2 1999 (PG) Robert (Garner) is visiting his Alzheimer's-stricken wife in the hospital and is unable to get a taxi home because of a snowstorm. Doctor Catharine (Andrews) offers him a ride but her car gets stuck on a deserted road and they find shelter in a small cabin. The twosome are drawn to each other during that snowy refuge but will a romance be possible when they return home? **90m/C VHS, DVD.** Julie Andrews, James Garner, Patricia Charbonneau, Stacy Grant, Stewart Bick; **D:** Robert M. Young; **W:** Nancy Silvers; **C:** Guy Dufaux; **M:** Richard Bellis. **TV**

One Step to Hell 🎬🎬 Caccia Ai Violenti; King of Africa 1967 Good cop rescues gold-miner's widow from three escaped convicts. Beautiful African scenery helps save an otherwise mediocre film. **90m/C VHS.** Ty Hardin, Rossano Brazzi, Pier Angeli, George Sanders, Helga Line, Jorge (George) Rigaud; **D:** Sandy Howard **C:** Julio Ortas; **M:** Gianni Marchetti.

One Summer Love 🎬1/2 1976 Man checks out from loony bin, searches for family ties and befriends beautiful woman who works in a movie-house. **95m/C VHS.** Beau Bridges, Susan Sarandon, Mildred Dunnock, Ann Wedgeworth, Michael B. Miller, Linda Miller, James Noble, Frederick Coffin; **D:** Gilbert Cates; **W:** N. Richard Nash.

The One That Got Away 🎬🎬 1957 A loyal German Luftwaffe pilot captured by the British becomes obsessed with escape. Fast paced and exciting. Based on a true story. **111m/B VHS.** Hardy Kruger, Colin Gordon, Alec Gordon; **D:** Roy Ward Baker.

The One That Got Away 🎬🎬1/2 1996 A badly prepared SAS patrol is dropped 300 miles behind enemy lines during the British obsession with the Gulf War to destroy Scud missile launchers that are aimed at Israel. Only when they are under fire, the soldiers discover that they cannot call for reinforcements and things get very bad indeed. Based on a true story. **104m/C VHS, DVD.** GB Paul McCann, David Morrissey, Nick Brimble, Simon Burke, Steven Waddington; **D:** Paul Greengrass; **M:** Barrington Phelong. **TV**

One Third of a Nation 🎬🎬 1939 Depression era film contrasts the conditions of slum life with those in high society. A young entrepreneur inherits a city block in ruins, unwilling to fall in love with a young woman who lives there and help her crippled brother. Timely social criticism. **79m/B VHS.** Sylvia Sidney, Leif Erickson, Myron McCormick, Sidney Lumet; **D:** Dudley Murphy.

1001 Arabian Nights 🎬🎬1/2 1959 In this Arabian nightmare, the nearsighted Mr. Magoo is known as "Azziz" Magoo, lamp dealer and uncle of Aladdin. **76m/C VHS.** Jim Backus, Kathryn Grant, Hans Conried, Herschel Bernardi.

One to Another 🎬 Chacun sa Nuit 2006 Lucie investigates the beating death of her troubled bisexual brother Pierre, a member of a rock band made up of equally beautiful and bored teenagers. More of an excuse for bed-hopping and showing off good-looking bodies than a true murder mystery. French with subtitles. **95m/C VHS.** FR Pierre Perrier, Valerie Mairesse Lizzie Brochere, Arthur Dupont, Guillaume Bache, Nicolas Nollet; **D:** Jean-Marc Barr, Pascal Arnold; **C:** Pascal Arnold; **D:** Jean-Marc Barr, **M:**

One Too Many 🎬 The Important Story of Alcoholism; Killer With a Label 1951 Exploitation film depicting the evils of alcoholism. Campy, but slick. **110m/B VHS.** Ruth Warrick, Richard Travis, Victor Killian, Onslow Stevens, Lyle Talbot; **D:** Erie C. Kenton; **W:** Malcolm Stuart Boylan; **C:** Carl Berger; **M:** Bert Shefter.

One Touch of Venus 🎬🎬1/2 1948 Love fills a department store when a window dresser kisses a statue of the goddess Venus—and she comes to life. Appealing adaptation of the Broadway musical. Speak Low; The Trouble with Women; That's Him; Don't Look Now But My Heart Is Showing; My Week. **82m/B**

One, Two, Three 🎬🎬1/2 1961 Cagney, an American Coca-Cola exec in Germany, zealously pursues an opportunity to run Coke's European operations. He does this by promising to keep an eye on the boss's wild daughter, who promptly falls for an East German Communist. Fast-paced laughs, wonderful cinematography, and a fine score. **110m/B VHS, DVD.** James Cagney, Horst Buchholz, Arlene Francis, Pamela Tiffin; **D:** Billy Wilder; **W:** Billy Wilder, I.A.L. Diamond; **C:** Daniel F. Fapp; **M:** Andre Previn.

One Way Out 🎬🎬 1955 Frank (Gwaltney) gets out of jail, teams up with Bobby (Monahan) and his stripper girlfriend Eve (Golden), and the trio go to visit Frank's brother, Snooky (Turano). When Frank learns that Snooky's lowlife boss (Ironside) has been tipping him off, they plan to steal the score. Naturally, the heist goes wrong and they wind up with a hostage (Gillies) and on the lam. **106m/C VHS.** Jack Gwaltney, Jeff Monahan, Annie Golden, Robert Turano, Michael Ironside, Isabel Gillies; **D:** Keven Lynn.

One Way Passage 🎬🎬1/2 1932 Joan Ames (Francis) is dying and decides to spend her last days having fun aboard a cruise ship. She meets cute Dan Hardesty

VHS, Ava Gardner, Robert Walker, Eve Arden, Dick Haymes, Olga San Juan, Tom Conway; **D:** William A. Seiter; **W:** Frank Tashlin, Harry Kurnitz; **C:** Franz Planer; **M:** Kurt Weill.

One Tough Cop 🎬🎬 1998 (R) Baldwin proves he's more than just a goofy face in a potential breakthrough role as headstrong NYPD detective Bo Dietl. Together with partner Finnerty (Penn), Dietl investigates a brutal rape and mutilation of a nun in East Harlem. Despite Brazilian director Barreto's good eye for the mean streets of New York and Baldwin's stellar performance, this is just or a more derivative police drama without distinction. Based on the autobiography by real-life retired cop Bo Dietl. **94m/C VHS, DVD.** Stephen Baldwin, Gina Gershon, Christopher Penn, Mike Mcglone, Paul Guilfoyle, Amy Irving, Victor Slezak, Luis Guzman; **D:** Bruno Barreto; **W:** Jeremy Iacone; **C:** Ron Fortunato; **M:** Bruce Broughton.

One Trick Pony 🎬🎬1/2 1980 (R) Once-popular rock singer/songwriter struggles to keep his head above water in a turbulent marriage and in the changing currents of popular taste. Simon wrote the autobiographical screenplay and score, but let's hope he is more sincere in real life. A good story. **100m/C VHS.** Paul Simon, Blair Brown, Rip Torn, Joan Hackett, Mare Winningham, Lou Reed, Harry Shearer, Allen (Goorwitz) Garfield, Daniel Stern; **D:** Robert M. Young;

One True Thing 🎬🎬🎬 1998 (PG-13) Better check for the family-sized box of tissues before you take home this tearjerker about cancer-stricken mother Kate (Streep) and her relationship with ar-rogant, career-oriented daughter Ellen (Zellweger). After being guilted by her stuffy college professor dad (Hurt), Ellen agrees to care for Kate as the disease progresses, and the two bridge their emotional distance. Lifted above the disease-of-the-week formula by the fine performance of the stellar trio of Streep and Hurt and by the presence of star power. Based on the novel by Anna Quindlen. **128m/C VHS, DVD.** Meryl Streep, Renee Zellweger, William Hurt, Tom Everett Scott, Nicky Katt, Lauren Graham, James Eckhouse, Patrick Breen, Gerrit Graham; **D:** Carl Franklin; **W:** Karen Croner; **C:** Declan Quinn; **M:** Cliff Eidelman.

One

(Powell) but keeps her illness a secret from him. Dan's got a big secret of his own: he's an escaped killer being returned to San Francisco for execution by Steve (Hymer), who begins his own flirtation with con woman Betty (MacMahon). Betty and fellow con man Skippy (McHugh) hope to help Dan escape but when he learns of Joan's condition, he refuses to abandon her. **68m/B VHS.** Kay Francis, William Powell, Aline MacMahon, Frank McHugh, Warren Hymer, Frederick Burton; *D:* Tay Garnett; *W:* Robert Lord, Wilson Mizner, Joe Jackson; *C:* Robert B. Kurle.

One Wild Moment 1978 (R) Comic complications arise when a divorced man is seduced by his best friend's daughter while vacationing. Warm and charming. Later re-made as "Blame It on Rio." In French with English subtitles. **88m/C VHS.** *FR* Jean-Pierre Marielle, Victor Lanoux, Agnes Soral, Christine Dejoux, Martine Sarcey; *D:* Claude Berri.

One Wish Too Many 1955 A young boy finds a marble that grants wishes. He has the time of his life with his teachers and the school bullies, but runs into trouble when he creates a giant steam roller which overruns London. Winner of Best Children's Film, 1956 Venice Film Festival, but it is hard to say why. **55m/B VHS.** *GB* Anthony Richmond, Rosalind Gourgey, John Pike; *D:* John Durst.

One Woman or Two *Une Femme ou Deux* 1985 (PG-13) Paleontologist Depardieu is duped by beautiful exec who plans to use his findings to push perfume. Remake of "Bringing Up Baby," this screwball comedy has a few screws loose. Dubbed. **100m/C VHS.** *FR* Gerard Depardieu, Sigourney Weaver, Dr. Ruth Westheimer, Michel Aumont, Zabou; *D:* Daniel Vigne; *W:* Elisabeth Rappeneau, Daniel Vigne.

One Wonderful Sunday *Subarashiki Nichiyobi* 1947 It's postwar Tokyo, so just how wonderful can things be? Well, perky Masako (Nakakita) is determined to make the day as bright as possible for her depressed fiance, Yuzo (Numasaki), despite the fact they have no money and can't afford to do much more than walk around together. More of a curiosity in Kurosawa's oeuvre than a substantial work. Japanese with subtitles. **108m/B VHS.** *JP* Chieko Nakakita, Isao Numasaki; *D:* Akira Kurosawa; *W:* Akira Kurosawa, Keinosuke Uegusa; *C:* Asakazu Nakai; *M:* Tadashi Hattori.

Onegin 1999 Fiennes family affair, with Martha assuming directorial duties, brother Magnus providing the score, and Ralph starring as the titular 18th-century Russian aristocrat. The cynical sophisticate inherits a vast country estate in the 1820s, where Onegin befriends his young neighbor Lensky (Stephens) and his featherbrained fiancee, Olga (Headey). But Onegin is intrigued by Olga's older sister, lovely innocent Tatyana (Tyler), though he rejects her impulsive romantic gestures. This isn't the only mistake that Onegin makes—all of which cost him dearly. Film looks beautiful but doesn't have much soul. Based on the Aleksandr Pushkin novel "Eugene Onegin." **106m/C VHS, DVD.** *GB* Ralph Fiennes, Liv Tyler, Toby Stephens, Lena Headey, Martin Donovan, Alun Armstrong, Harriet Walter, Irene Worth, Francesca Annis; *D:* Martha Fiennes; *W:* Peter Ettedgui, Michael Ignatieff; *C:* Remi Adefarasin; *M:* Magnus Fiennes.

101 Reykjavik 2000 Icelandic comedy about a slacker and his mom. The slacker is the pushing 30 Hlynur (Gudnason) who lives with indulgent mom Berglind (Karlsdottir), he's cynical, jobless and unambitious (though not unintelligent). Then Berglind invites her Spanish friend Lola (Abril), who's teaching flamenco at the local dance school, to stay. Hylnur falls for the hottie bigtime and they have a drunken New Year's Eve fling while Berglind is away—and before she manages to tell her son that Lola is her own lover. And then Lola finds out she's pregnant. Oh, the complications! Icelandic and English dialogue. **90m/C VHS, DVD. IC DK FR NO** Hilmir Snaer Guonason, Victoria Abril, Baltasar Kormakur, Hanna Maria Karlsdottir, Olafur Darri Olafsson, Pruour Vilhjalmsdottir; *D:* Baltasar Kormakur; *W:* Baltasar Kormakur; *C:* Peter Stueger; *M:* Damon Albarn, Einar Orn Benediktsson.

Ong-Bak 2003 (R) Over-the-top action is the centerpiece of this breakthrough Thai martial arts film. Loose-cannon Thai kickboxer Ting (Jaa) travels to Bangkok in search of the stolen head to his tiny village's Buddha. Mayhem ensues. What little plot exists is just a vehicle for superb action sequences that are exceptionally violent yet highly inventive, especially when one considers that all the action was filmed without digital effects, wires, or other modern-day trickery. The result is a 70's-style martial-arts movie for the modern era, refreshingly real and a heck of a lot of fun. Thai with English subtitles. **107m/C DVD.** *TH* Tony Jaa, Wannakit Siriput, Sukhaow Phongwilai, Petchthai Wongkamlao, Pumwaree Yodkamol, Rungrawee Borriindakul; *D:* Prachya Pinkaew; *W:* Suphachai Sithiamphian; *C:* Nattawut Kitthun; *M:* Atomix Clubbing.

Onibaba *The Demon; The Devil Woman* 1964 A brutal parable about a mother and her daughter-in-law in war-ravaged medieval Japan who subsist by murdering stray soldiers and selling their armor. One soldier beds the daughter, setting the mother-in-law on a vengeful tirade. Review of the film varied widely, hailed by some as a masterpiece and by others as below average, in Japanese with subtitles. **103m/B VHS, DVD.** *JP* Nobuko Otowa, Jitsuko Yoshimura, Kei Sato; *D:* Kaneto Shindo.

The Onion Field 1979 (R) True story about the mental breakdown of an ex-cop who witnessed his partner's murder. Haunted by the slow process of justice and his own feelings of insecurity, he is unable to get his life together. Based on the novel by Joseph Wambaugh, who also wrote the screenplay. Compelling script and excellent acting. **126m/C VHS, DVD.** John Savage, James Woods, Ronny Cox, Franklyn Seales, Ted Danson, David Huffman, Christopher Lloyd, Dianne Hull, Priscilla Pointer, Richard Venture, William Sanderson, Michael Pataki; *D:* Harold Becker; *W:* Eric Roth; *C:* Charles Rosher Jr.; *M:* Eumir Deodato.

OnLine 2001 (R) Neurotic John Roth (Hamilton) and his partner Moe Curley (Perrineau) run an online sex site called IntercomX. John is obsessive about documenting his life via a daily Webcam and becomes mesmerized by watching the beautiful Jordan (Ferlito), who does her own erotic fantasy thing on the website. He tries a real-live date with her but finds reality too much to handle. Other characters wander into the online world and Weintrob shows them (usually in split screen) interacting in various ways via computer and in person, but the characters aren't particularly appealing and it all seems dated. **87m/C VHS, DVD.** Josh Hamilton, Harold Perrineau Jr., Isabel Gillies, Vanessa Ferlito, John Fleck, Eric Millegan, Liz Owens; *D:* Jed Weintrob; *W:* Andrew Osborne, Jed Weintrob; *C:* Toshiaki Ozawa; *M:* Roger Neill.

Only Angels Have Wings 1939 Melodramatic adventure about a broken-down Peruvian air mail service. Large cast adds to the love tension between Grant, a pilot, and Arthur, a showgirl at the saloon. Nominated for special effects, a category recognized by the Academy that year for the first time. William Rankin and Eleanor Griffin are uncredited writers. **121m/B VHS, DVD.** Cary Grant, Thomas Mitchell, Richard Barthelmess, Jean Arthur, Noah Beery Jr., Rita Hayworth, Sig Rumann, Allyn Joslyn; *D:* Howard Hawks; *W:* Jules Furthman; *C:* Joseph Walker; *M:* Dimitri Tomkin.

Only Love *Erich Segal's Only Love* 1998 Sappy made for TV romance adapted from the Segal novel. Neurosurgeon Matthew Heller (Morrow) is shocked by the reappearance of former fiancee Silvia Rinaldi (May) some 15 years after they broke up. She's dying of a brain tumor and needs his medical help. His longtime (platonic) female friend Evie (Tomei) can't understand his obsession and you won't either. (The scenery's nice though). **130m/C VHS.** Rob Morrow, Marisa Tomei, Mathilda May, Jeroen Krabbe, Paul Freeman, Georges Corraface; *D:* John Erman; *W:* Gerald Christopher; *M:* John Morris. **TV**

Only Once in a Lifetime 1979 A love story about an Hispanic immigrant painter looking for success in America. **90m/C VHS.** Miguel Robelo, Estrellita Lopez, Sheree North; *D:* Alejandro Grattan; *C:* Turner Browne; *M:* Robert O. Ragland.

Only One Night *En Enda Natt* 1942 Upon finding out that he's the illegitimate son of an aristocrat, a happy-go-lucky carousel operator in a circus joins high society and is promptly matched with a beautiful but repressed woman. In Swedish with English subtitles. **87m/B VHS.** *SW* Ingrid Bergman, Edvin Adolphson, Aino Taube, Olof Sandborg, Erik "Bullen" Berglund, Marianne Lofgren, Magnus Kesster; *D:* Gustaf Molander.

Only the Brave 1994 Gay coming-of-age story about two teenaged, working-class girls living on the seedy fringes of Melbourne. Alex (Manadalis), her wild best friend Vicki (Kaskanis), and their equally tough girlfriends seem to spend most of their time hanging out, smoking dope, and getting into trouble. But Alex slowly recognizes her feelings for Vicki are also sexual, and their friendship drastically changes. **62m/C VHS.** *AU* Elena Mandalis, Dora Kaskanis, Moudo Davey, Bob Bright; *D:* Ana Kokkinos; *W:* Ana Kokkinos, Mira Robertson.

Only the Lonely 1991 (PG) Middle-aged cop, Candy, falls in love with a shy undertaker's assistant, Sheedy, and is torn between love and dear old Mom, O'Hara, in her first role in years. Candy is an unlikely leading man and even the jokes are forced. But the restaurant scene makes the whole thing well worth seeing. **104m/C VHS, DVD.** John Candy, Ally Sheedy, Maureen O'Hara, Anthony Quinn, Kevin Dunn, James Belushi, Milo O'Shea, Bert Remsen, Macaulay Culkin, Joe V. Greco; *D:* Chris Columbus; *W:* Chris Columbus; *M:* Maurice Jarre.

Only the Strong 1993 (PG-13) Louis (Dacascos) is a special forces officer who has mastered capoeira, a Brazilian form of kung fu. In Miami, he works with his old teacher (Lewis) to instill discipline in the 12 toughest punks in school by teaching them his martial arts skills. A neighborhood drug lord, related to two of the students, decides to cause trouble for Louis. Dascascos displays some charm along with his physical abilities but the story's ridiculous and the movie hastily put together. **96m/C VHS, DVD.** Mark Dacascos, Stacey Travis, Todd Susman, Geoffrey Lewis, Paco Christian Prieto; *D:* Sheldon Lettich; *W:* Sheldon Lettich, Luis Esteban; *M:* Harvey W. Mason.

Only the Strong Survive 2003 (PG-13) Documentary filmmakers Hegedus and Pennebaker showcase R&B and soul legends of the late fifties to the early seventies in where-are-they-now features and in concert performances, including a number of performers from Memphis and Stax-Volt Records. Featured are Carla and Rufus Thomas, Issac Hayes, William Bell, Chi-Lites, Jerry Butler, Sam Moore, Ann Peebles, Wilson Pickett, and Mary Wilson. **95m/C DVD. US** *D:* Chris Hegedus, D.A. Pennebaker; *C:* Chris Hegedus, D.A. Pennebaker; James Desmond, Nick Doob, Jehane Noujaim.

Only the Valiant 1950 Action-packed story of a cavalry officer who struggles to win his troops respect while warding off angry Apaches. Fast-paced Western fun requires little thought. **105m/B VHS.** Gregory Peck, Ward Bond, Gig Young, Lon Chaney Jr., Barbara Payton, Neville Brand; *D:* Gordon Douglas; *C:* Lionel Lindon.

The Only Thrill *Tennessee Valley* 1997 Old-fashioned small town romance based on Ketron's play "The Trading Post." In 1966, Reece McHenry (Sheppard) decides to open a used clothing store in his Tennessee hometown and hires widowed seamstress Carol Fitzsimmons (Keaton) to help him out. Reece is married but his wife is in an irreversible coma and soon the aw-shucks storekeeper is interested in romancing his new employee. Meanwhile, Reece's son Tom (Patrick) and Carol's daughter Katherine (Lane) have also discovered a reciprocated love. However, neither romance runs smoothly. **108m/C VHS.** Sam Shepard, Diane Keaton, Robert Patrick, Diane Lane, Tate Donovan, Sharon Lawrence, Stacey Travis; *D:* Peter Masterson; *W:* Larry Ketron; *C:* Don E. Fauntleroy; *M:* Peter Melnick.

Only Two Can Play 1962 Sellers is a hilarious Casanova librarian who puts the moves on a society lady to get a promotion. Funny, of course, and based on Kingsley Amis' novel "That Uncertain Feeling." **106m/C VHS.** *GB* Peter Sellers, Virginia Maskell, Mai Zetterling, Richard Attenborough; *D:* Sidney Gilliat; *M:* Richard Rodney Bennett.

The Only Way 1970 (G) A semi-documentary account of the plight of the Jews in Denmark during the Nazi occupation. Despite German insistence, the Danes succeeded in saving most of their Jewish population from the concentration camps. **86m/C VHS.** Jane Seymour, Martin Potter, Benjamin Christiansen; *M:* Carl Davis.

The Only Way Home 1972 (PG) Two bikers end up in big trouble when one of them kills a wealthy man, and they kidnap his wife. Filmed entirely in Oklahoma. **86m/C VHS.** Bo Hopkins, Beth Brickel, Steve Sandor, G.D. Spradlin; *D:* G.D. Spradlin.

Only When I Laugh *It Hurts Only When I Laugh* 1981 (R) Neil Simon reworked his Broadway flop "The Gingerbread Lady" to produce this poignant comedy about the relationship between an aging alcoholic actress and her teenage daughters. **120m/C VHS.** Marsha Mason, Kristy McNichol, James Coco, Joan Hackett, David Dukes, Kevin Bacon, John Bennett Perry; *D:* Glenn Jordan; *W:* Neil Simon; *M:* David Shire. Golden Globes '82: Actress (Hackett).

Only with Married Men 1974 Carne's hassle-free dating routine is disrupted when a sly bachelor pretends that he's married to get a date. A middle-aged persons answer to a teenage sex comedy. Pretty bad. **74m/C VHS, DVD.** David Birney, Judy Carne, Gavin MacLeod, John Astin; *D:* Jerry Paris.

Only You 1992 (PG-13) A shy guy has always searched for true romance. But his cup runneth over when he meets, and must choose between, two beautiful women—your basic beach babe and a sensible beauty. What's a guy to do? **85m/C VHS.** Andrew McCarthy, Kelly Preston, Helen Hunt; *M:* Wendy Blackstone.

Only You *Just in Time* 1994 (PG) According to her ouija board, young Faith's (Tomei) soul mate is named Damon Bradley. But as the years pass, Faith is about to settle for a podiatrist—until an old school friend of her fiance's calls from Venice, Italy, with best wishes. Guess what his name is. So Faith and best friend Kate (Hunt) hop on a plane in search of Mr. Right. Then Faith meets charming shoe salesman Peter Wright (Downey) and wonders if ouija got things wrong. Slight romantic comedy with Jewison creating satisfactory chemistry with charming Downey and the somewhat miscast Tomei (and the Venetian scenery is gorgeous). **108m/C VHS, DVD.** Marisa Tomei, Robert Downey Jr., Bonnie Hunt, Fisher Stevens, Billy Zane, Joaquim de Almeida; *D:* Norman Jewison; *W:* Diane Drake; *C:* Sven Nykvist; *M:* Rachel Portman.

Open Cam *OpenCam* 2005 Lots of skin, but not too much mystery or plot logic in this gay crime thriller. A D.C. serial killer finds his victims through an adult webcam site, all of whom are somehow connected to aspiring artist Manny. Police detective Hamilton is investigating while behaving in a decidedly unprofessional manner with his protagonist. **100m/C DVD.** Andreau Thomas, Amir Darvish, Ben Green, J. Matthew Miller, Christian Jones; *D:* Robert Gaston; *W:* Robert Gaston; *C:* Doug Gritzmacher; *M:* Jerry Walterick.

Open City *Roma, Citta Aperta; Roma, Open City* 1945 A leader in the Italian underground resists Nazi control of the city. A stunning film, making Rossellini's realistic style famous. In Italian with English subtitles. **103m/B VHS, DVD.** *IT* Anna Magnani, Aldo Fabrizi, Marcel Pagliero, Maria Michi, Vito Annicchiarico, Nando (Fernando) Bruno,

Harry Feist. *D:* Roberto Rossellini; *W:* Federico Fellini, Sergio Amidei; *C:* Ubaldo Arata; *M:* Renzo Rossellini. N.Y. Film Critics '46. Foreign Film.

Open Doors 1989 (R) *Porte Aperte* Bitter review of Fascist rule and justice. The Fascist regime promises security, safety, and tranquility. So, on the morning that a white collar criminal murderers his former boss, murders the man who got his job, and then rapes and murders his wife, tensions rise and the "societal" structures are tested. The people rally for his death. A judge and a juror struggle to uphold justice rather than serve popular passions. Winner of four Donatello Awards, Italian Golden Globes for Best Film, Best Actor, and Best Screenplay. 93m/C VHS. *IT* Gian Marie Volonte, Ennio Fantastichini, Lidia Alfonsi; *D:* Gianni Amelio; *W:* Gianni Amelio.

Open Fire 1994 (R) Alex McNeil (Wincott) is an ex-FBI agent, haunted by the death of his partner. But when a group of terrorists threaten to release a cloud of nerve gas over L.A. and hold McNeil's family hostage, he comes back full force. 93m/C VHS. Jeff Wincott, Patrick Kipatrick, Lee DeRoux, Mimi (Meyer) Craven, Amanda Kurt Anderson; *W:* Thomas Ritz; *C:* Jurgen Baum.

Open House 1986 Radio psychologist and beautiful real estate agents search for the killer of real estate agents and their clients. A mystery-thriller for the very patient. 95m/C VHS. Joseph Bottoms, Adrienne Barbeau, Mary Slavin, Rudy Ramos; *D:* Jag Mundhra.

Open Range 2003 (R) Proving definitively that he should stick to sports and cowboys, Costner revives the glory of the classic Western with overwhelming success. Cowpokes Boss (Duvall) and Charley (Costner) peacefully graze their cattle on the open range during the late 1800s. That is, until they run up against cranky, land-grabbing 'rancher Baxter (Gambon) who dislikes the free-spirited, free-grazers and Boss's posse in particular. Bening is excellent as Costner's love interest. Their chemistry is only slightly less palpable than the reverence for lone rangers Costner and a superb Duvall. Actor Costner handles familiar role with aplomb, while director Costner displays an eye for detail and a reverence for the genre. Alberta, Canada subs for the Wild West. Based on the novel by Lauran Paine. 135m/C VHS, DVD. *US* Robert Duvall, Kevin Costner; Annette Bening, Michael Gambon, Michael Jeter, Diego Luna, James Russo, Abraham Benrubi, Dean McDermott, Kim Coates; *D:* Kevin Costner; *W:* Craig Storper; *C:* J. (James) Michael Muro; *M:* Michael Kamen.

Open Season 1995 (R) Stuart Sain (Wuhl) is an ambitious executive at Fielding, a TV ratings company (think Nielsen) whose boxes turn out to be defective. The ratings error causes public television programming to be number one, forcing the networks to counter-program culturally in order to regain their market share. Meanwhile, the public TV executives get overconfident and everything's just up for grabs. Flawed satire. 97m/C VHS. Robert Wuhl, Rod Taylor Gailard Sartain, Maggie Han, Joe Piscopo, Helen Shaver, Dina Merril, Saul Rubinek, Steven C. White, Timothy Arrington, Barry Ratman, Tom Selleck, Alan Thicke, Jimmie Walker; *D:* Robert Wuhl; *W:* Robert Wuhl; *C:* Stephen Lighthill; *M:* Marvin Hamlisch.

Open Season 2006 (PG) Harmless animated flick about the plight of animals vs. man. Boog (Lawrence) is a grizzly bear, raised in captivity, who's released into the woods a few days before the opening of hunting season. He relies on the help of his friend Elliot (Kutcher), a spastic mule deer, to find his way to safety, which means returning to human civilization since Boog really doesn't like this life-in-the-wild stuff. Abounds with standard bathroom humor, with sprinkles of wit for the grown-ups. 99m/C DVD, Blu-ray Disc. *US D:* Roger Allers, Jill Culton; *V:* Martin Lawrence, Ashton Kutcher, Gary Sinise, Debra Messing, Billy Connolly.

Open Secret 1948 Jewish residents are plagued by a gang of anti-semitic thugs. Violence and destruction escalate until a fed up police lieutenant, tenaciously played by Ireland, and a victimized shop owner (Tyne) join forces to just say no more. When the gang learns the shop keeper has caught their dastardly deeds on camera, the battle begins in earnest. Fast-paced and intriguing suspense. 70m/B VHS, DVD. John Ireland, Jane Randolph, Roman Bohnen, Sheldon Leonard, George Tyne, Morgan Farley, Ellen Lowe, Anne O'Neal, Arthur O'Connell; *D:* John Reinhardt.

Open Water 2003 (R) Daniel (Travis) and Susan (Ryan) are an overworked couple who badly need a vacation. Fighting cold, hunger, dehydration, sharks (which were real) and worst of all, their own fear and insecurities, the couple stay afloat for more than 24 hours hoping the boat will discover they are missing. Kentis and his wife Laura Lua shot or location in the Bahamas using a digital camera. The resulting visceral images add to the realism, and, subsequently, the fear and tension. Based on actual events. 79m/C DVD. Blanchard Ryan, Daniel Travis, Estelle Lau, Michael E. Williamson, John Charles, Christina Zenaro; *D:* Chris Kentis; *W:* Chris Kentis, Laura Lau; *M:* Graeme Revell.

Open Your Eyes *Abra Los Ojos* 1997 (R) Reality gets taken for a mind-bending spin in this Spanish thriller. Gorgeous womanizer, Cesar (Noriega), meets equally gorgeous Sofia (Cruz) and thinks he's finally found the one. Only his crazy ex-girlfriend Nuria (Nimri) causes a car crash that kills her and disfigures Cesar. He awakens in a prison hospital wearing a mask, accused of murder, and with confused memories. But maybe he's had an operation to restore his looks and is actually back together with Sofia but then Cesar keeps seeing Nuria's ghost. So just what is going on? Spanish with subtitles. 117m/C VHS, DVD. *SP* Eduardo Noriega, Penelope Cruz, Najwa Nimri, Chete Lera, Fele Martinez; Gerard Barray; *D:* Alejandro Amenabar; *W:* Alejandro Amenabar, Mateo Gil; *C:* Hans Burman; *M:* Alejandro Amenabar, Mariano Ma'in.

Opening Night 1977 (PG-13) Very long study about an actress (Rowlands) and the play she's about to open in on Broadway. Backstage turmoil increases her own insecurities and the bad luck persists when an adoring fan is struck by a car while the play is in try-outs in New Haven. Performances carry this neurotic epic along, including Cassavetes as Rowland's co-star and Blondell as the playwright. 144m/C VHS, DVD. Gena Rowlands, John Cassavetes, Joan Blondell, Ben Gazzara, Paul Stewart, Zohra Lampert, Laura Johnson; *D:* John Cassavetes; *W:* John Cassavetes; *C:* Frederick Elmes; *M:* Bo Harwood.

Opera *Terror at the Opera* 1988 (R) A bizarre staging of Verdi's "Macbeth" is plagued by depraved gore murders. But the show must go on, as one character chirps in badly dubbed English, Italian horrormeister Argento's ever-fluid camera achieves spectacular shots, but the lurid, ludicrous script make this one for connoisseurs only. The operatic scenes employ the voice of Maria Callas. Available in an edited "R" rated version. 107m/C VHS, DVD. *IT* Christina Marsillach, Ian Charleson, Urbano Barberini, William McNamara, Antonella Vitale, Barbara Cupisti, Coralina Cataldi-Tassoni, Daria Nicolodi; *D:* Dario Argento; *W:* Dario Argento, Franco Ferrini; *C:* Ronnie Taylor; *M:* Claudio Simonetti.

Opera do Malandro 1987 A lavish Brazilian take off of "The Threepenny Opera." Married hustler falls for a beautiful entrepreneur longing to get rich off of American goods. Based on Chico Buarque's musical play. In Portuguese, with subtitles. 106m/C VHS, DVD. *BR* Edson Celulari, Claudia Ohana, Elba Ramalho, Ney Latorraca; *D:* Ray Guerra.

Operation Amsterdam 1960 Four agents have 14 hours to snare $10 million in diamonds from under the noses of local Nazis. Based on a true story. Full of 1940s wartime action and suspense. 103m/B VHS, DVD. Peter Finch, Eva Bartok, Tony Britton, Alexander Knox; *D:* Michael McCarthy.

Operation Bikini 1963 Although set in WWII, this AIP flick was aimed at the teen market with Avalon pop-singing his way through the unlikely action. Old salt Brady and his submarine crew must deliver Frankie and his pals to Bikini Island for a super-secret mission. 53m/C VHS. Frankie Avalon, Tab Hunter, Scott Brady, Jim Backus, Gary Crosby, Jody McCrea, Michael Dante, Eva Six; *D:* Anthony Carras; *W:* John Tomerlin; *C:* Gilbert Warrenton; *M:* Les Baxter.

Operation C.I.A. *Last Message From Saigon* 1965 A plot to assassinate the U.S. ambassador in Saigon inspires brave CIA agent Reynolds to wipe out the bad guys. Action-packed and somewhat exciting. 90m/C VHS. Burt Reynolds, John Hayt, Kieu Chinh, Danielle Aubry; *D:* Christian Nyby.

Operation Condor 1991 (PG-13) Secret agent Jackie (Chan) is sent by the United Nations to retrieve 240 tons of gold buried by the Nazis in a Moroccan desert during WWII. Naturally, he's not the only one after the treasure. Lots of typical guys. 92m/C VHS, DVD. *HK* Jackie Chan, Carol Cheng, Eva Cabo De Garcia, Ikeda Shoko; *D:* Jackie Chan; *W:* Edward Tang, Jackie Chan; *C:* Wong Ngok Tai; *M:* Stephen Endelman.

Operation Condor 2: The Armour of the Gods *Armour of the Gods; Longxiong Hudi* 1986 (PG) Prequel to "Operation Condor" was re-released in 1997. Chan plays an adventurous treasure-hunter who is asked by his ex-girlfriend's new fiancee Alan (Tam), who used to be Jackie's best friend, to rescue her from an evil cult. The kidnappers want Jackie and Alan to deliver a priceless medieval set of armour, thought to contain mysterious powers, to them. Naturally, Char must come up with some spectacular saves of both the armour and the girl. In Cantonese with English subtitles. 88m/C VHS, DVD. *HK* Jackie Chan, Alan Tam, Rosamund Kwan, Lola Forner; *D:* Jackie Chan; *W:* Jackie Chan, Edward Tang, John Sheppard; *C:* Peter Ngor; *M:* Michael Lai.

Operation Cross Eagles 1969 Routine WWII military thriller with Conte and Calhoun on a mission to rescue an American general in exchange for their German prisoner. Their mission is complicated by a traitor in the group. Conte's only directorship. 90m/C VHS, DVD. *YU* Richard Conte, Rory Calhoun, Aili King, Phil Brown; *D:* Richard Conte.

Operation Crossbow *The Great Spy Mission; Code Name: Operation Crossbow* 1965 Action-packed espionage tale in which a trio of agents are assigned to destroy a Nazi munitions installation. Exciting ending and sensational pyrotechnics. 116m/C VHS. Sophia Loren, George Peppard, Trevor Howard, John Mills, Richard Johnson, Tom Courtenay, Jeremy Kemp, Anthony Quayle, Helmut Dantine; *D:* Michael Anderson Sr.; *W:* Ray Rigby, Duilo Coletti.

Operation Dames 1959 A squadron of soldiers must go behind Korean enemy lines to locate a missing U.S.O. troupe and bring them to safety. Low budget and not very funny for a supposed comedy. 73m/B VHS. Eve Meyer, Chux Henderson, Don Devlin, Ed Craig, Cindy Girard; *D:* Louis Clyde Stouman.

Operation: Delta Force 1997 (R) Nash (Lara) and his South African terrorist band have stolen two vials of Ebola virus in order to provide some cleansing of the population. So the Delta Force, lead by Lang (Fahey), are flown into Mozambique to stop 'em. Macho guys and lots of firepower. 93m/C VHS. Jeff Fahey, Ernie Hudson, Frank Zagarino, Joe Lara, Todd Jensen, Hal Holbrook; *D:* Sam Firstenberg; *W:* David Sparling; *C:* Yossi Wein; *M:* Serge Colbert.

'Nam 1965 A group of bored Vietnam vets return to 'Nam to rescue their leader from a POW camp. Nothing special, but features John Wayne's son. De Angelis used the pseudonym Larry Ludman. 85m/C VHS. Oliver Tobias, Christopher Connelly, Manfred Lehman, John Steiner, Ethan Wayne, Donald Pleasence; *D:* Fabrizio de Angelis.

Operation Intercept 1995 (R) Francesca (Andrichenko) suspects that the government is behind her father's murder after he develops technology that causes enemy planes to crash. So she threatens to destroy civilian aircraft until the killer is brought to justice. 94m/C VHS. Natasha Andrichenko, Bruce Payne, John Stockwell, Lance Henriksen, Dennis Christopher, Michael Champion, Curt Lowens, Corbin Bernsen; *D:* Paul Levine; *W:* Paul Levine; *C:* John Newby.

Operation Julie 1985 A detective searches out a huge drug ring that manufactures LSD. 100m/C VHS. Colin Blakehoney.

Operation Orient 1978 A statue laden with drugs is stolen when an international drug smuggler tries to bring to the U.S. 94m/C VHS. GR Gianni Gori, Gordon Mitchell; *D:* Ilias Milonakos.

Operation Delta Force 2: Mayday 1997 (R) Russian terrorist Lukash (Campbell) is threatening atomic mayhem unless he's paid $25 billion dollars. It's up to the elite combat action Delta Force, tc stop him. Standard action-er is less than memorable. 98m/C VHS, DVD. Michael McGrady; J. Kenneth Campbell, Dale Dye, Simon Jones; *D:* Yossi Wein; *W:* David Sparling; *C:* Peter Belcher; *M:* Russell Stirling.

Operation Delta Force 3: Clear Target 1998 (R) When the Delta Force destroys a billion-dollar cocaine operation, the drug cartel is out for revenge. Drug lord Umberto Salvatore steals a submarine and programs its warheads to fire on New York City. Of course, Delta Force has to get to the sub first. 96m/C VHS. Bryan Genesse, Danny Keogh, Jim (James) Fitzpatrick, Greg Collins, Darcy La Pier, Wessel Van Rensurg. VIDEO

Operation Dumbo Drop 1995 (PG) It's 1968 and tough Green Beret captain (Glover), rescued by Vietnamese villagers, promises to replace their prized elephant, which was killed during his mission. He and a group of commandos use land, sea, and air to transport the reluctant beast, learning way more about elephant hygiene and eating habits than they ever wanted to know in the process. Wincer, who also directed "Free Willy," seems to be going for the title of "greatest large mammal director of all time." Anything with good-guy U.S. troops, a paratrooper elephant, and a family-friendly plot should be a Bob Dole favorite. 107m/C VHS, DVD. Danny Glover, Ray Liotta, Doug E. Doug, Denis Leary, Corin "Corky" Nemec, Thein Le Dihn; *D:* Simon Wincer; *C:* Russell Boyd; *M:* David Newman.

Operation Golden Phoenix 1994 (R) A security specialist (Mehri) is betrayed with a valuable medallion. Seems the medal reveals the location of an ancient mountain of gold—desired by a ruthless warlord (Hong). Martial arts fights are well done in this routine action-er. 94m/C VHS. Jalal Mehri, James Hong, Al Waxman, Loren Avedon; *D:* Jalal Mehri.

Operation Haylift 1950 The true story of the U.S. Air Force's efforts to rescue starving cattle and sheep herds during Nevada's blizzards of 1949. The Air Force provided realism for the film with planes, equipment, and servicemen. 73m/C B VHS. Bill Williams, Tom Brown, Ann Rutherford, Jane Nigh, Joseph (Joe) Sawyer, Dean Riesner, Richard Travis, Raymond Hatton, Jimmy Conlin, Tommy "TV." Ivo; *D:* William Berke; *W:* Joseph (Joe) Sawyer, Dean Riesner; *C:* Benjamin (Ben H.) Kline.

Operation Petticoat ✓✓✓½ 1959 Submarine captain Grant teams with wheeler-dealer Curtis to make his sub seaworthy. They're joined by a group of Navy women, and the gags begin. Great teamwork from Grant and Curtis keeps things rolling. Jokes may be considered sexist these days. Later remake and TV series couldn't hold a candle to the original. 120m/C VHS, DVD: Cary Grant, Tony Curtis, Joan O'Brien, Dina Merrill, Gene Evans, Arthur O'Connell, Virginia Gregg; D: Blake Edwards; W: Stanley Shapiro, Maurice Richlin; C: Russell Harlan; M: David Rose.

Operation Sandman: Warriors in Hell ✓✓ 2000 (R) Scientist Perlman develops a serum for the military that allows soldiers to remain awake for weeks with heightened senses. Only there turns out to be a disturbing side effect—the soldiers eventually begin hallucinating and turn violent. Very disturbing. 89m/C VHS, DVD: Ron Perlman, Richard Tyson, Mary B. Ward, John Haymes Newton; D: Nelson McCormick; W: Nelson McCormick; D: Larry Blanford. TV

Operation Thunderbolt ✓✓½ Entebbe: Operation Thunderbolt 1977 Israeli-produced depiction of Israel's July 14, 1976 commando raid on Entebbe, Uganda to rescue the passengers of a hijacked plane. Better than the American versions "Raid on Entebbe" and "Victory at Entebbe" in its performances as well as the information provided, much of it unavailable to the American filmmakers. 120m/C VHS, DVD: Yehoram Gaon, Assaf Dayan, Ori Levy, Klaus Kinski; D: Menahem Golan.

Operation Warzone ✓ 1989 A platoon of soldiers uncovers a plot by corrupt officers to continue the Vietnam war and sell weapons. 86m/C VHS: Joe Spinell, John Cianetti, Sean Holton, William Zipp, David Marriott; D: David A. Prior; W: David A. Prior, Ted Prior; C: Andy Parke.

The Operator ✓ 2001 Scumdog lawyer Gary Whelan (Laurence) gets his comeuppance when he insults the wrong telephone operator (Kim). Calling herself Shiva (the Hindu goddess of destruction), she decides to even the karmic balance by stripping Gary of all his worldly possessions, breaking up his marriage, and framing him for murder. Set in Dallas, Texas. 102m/C VHS, DVD: Jacqueline Kim, Michael Laurence, Christa Miller, Stephen Tobolowsky, Brion James, Frances Bay; D: Jon Dichter; W: Jon Dichter. TV

The Opponent ✓½ 1989 (R) After years of domestic violence, Patty (Eleniak) finds an outlet for her anger in the boxing ring of the community center. With the encouragement of her trainer (Colby), she decides to take it to the next level and go for a pro career. But when Patty embarks on a romance with the guy, she also gets distracted from her goals. 90m/C VHS, DVD: Erika Eleniak, Aunjanue Ellis, James Colby, John Doman; C: Joe Di Gennaro. VIDEO

The Oppermann Family ✓✓½ Die Geschwister Oppermann 1982 Long epic (made for German TV) about a family trying to survive in Berlin during the rise of Hitler. In German with subtitles. 238m/C VHS. GE Peter Fitz, Wolfgang Kieling, Rosel Zech, Andrea Dahmen, Michael Degen, Til Topf; D: Egon Monk; C: Wolfgang Treu; M: Alexander Goehr. TV

Opportunity Knocks ✓✓½ 1990 (PG-13) Carvey's first feature film has him impersonating a friend of a rich suburbanite's family while hiding from a vengeful gangster. They buy it, and give him a job and the daughter. Not hilarious, but not a dud either. 105m/C VHS, DVD: Dana Carvey, Robert Loggia, Todd Graff, Milo O'Shea, Julia Campbell, James Tolkan, Doris Belack, Sally Gracie, Del Close; D: Donald Petrie; W: Mitchel Katlin, Nat Bernstein; M: Miles Goodman.

Opposing Force ✓✓½ Hellcamp 1987 (R) The commander of an Air Force camp simulates prisoner-of-war conditions for realistic training, but he goes too far, creating all too real torture situations. He preys on the only female in the experiment, raping her as part of the training. A decent thriller. 97m/C VHS: Tom Skerritt, Lisa Eichhorn, Anthony Zerbe, Richard Roundtree, Robert Wightman, John Considine, George Kee Cheung, Paul Joynt, Jay Louden, Ken Wright, Dan Hamilton; D: Eric Karson; W: Gil Cowan; M: Marc Donahue.

Opposite Corners ✓✓ 1996 (R) Bryant Donatello (Warlock) is looking for a shot at the Golden Gloves boxing championship, something his father (Dennison) has been obsessed about ever since his own chance was taken away. Then Bryant realizes just what kind of "connections" his dad has. 106m/C VHS: Billy Warlock, Cathy Moriarty, Anthony John (Tony) Dennison, Jay Acovone, Robert Miano; D: Louis D'Esposito.

The Opposite of Sex ✓✓✓½ 1998 (R) Teenaged terror Dedee (Ricci) wreaks havoc with the life of gay halfbrother Bill (Donovan). She seduces his boyfriend Matt (Sergei), gets pregnant, steals his savings, and nearly costs him his high school teacher's job. Then she takes off for L.A., with Bill, his best friend Lucia (Kudrow), and sheriff Carl (Lovett) in pursuit. Quirky black comedy isn't shy, especially when Ricci's vamping across the screen, and features fine work by Kudrow (in a welcome departure from the dumb blonde roles) and Ricci (who can definitely remove the words "child actress" from her resume). Dedee's acerbic narration is another highlight. 105m/C VHS, DVD. Christina Ricci, Martin Donovan, Lisa Kudrow, Ivan Sergei, Lyle Lovett, Johnny Galecki, William Lee Scott, Colin Ferguson; D: Don Roos; W: Don Roos; C: Hubert Taczanowski; M: Mason Daring. Ind. Spirit '98: First Feature, Screenplay; Natl. Bd. of Review '98: Support. Actress (Ricci); N.Y. Film Critics '98: Support. Actress (Kudrow).

The Opposite Sex ✓✓ 1956 Bevy of women battle mediocre script in adaptation of 1939's "The Women." "The Opposite sex's surf. Yellow Gold on de Trees (De Banana): A Perfect Love; Rock and Roll Tumbleweed; Now! Baby, Now; Jungle Red; Young Man with a Horn. 115m/C VHS: June Allyson, Joan Collins, Dolores Gray, Ann Sheridan, Ann Miller, Leslie Nielsen, Agnes Moorehead, Joan Blondell; D: David Miller; W: Fay Kanin, Michael Kanin.

The Opposite Sex and How to Live With Them ✓✓½ 1993 (R) Yuppies (Gross and Cox) from different backgrounds (he's Jewish, she's a WASP) meet, fall in love, fight, break up, and reunite, inspiring yawning disinterest. All this while their two best buddies (Pollak and Brown) offer what are meant to be "candid insights" delivered directly to the camera. Flat and formulaic romantic comedy wants to sparkle, but script lacks both purpose and point, and worse, takes way too much time not getting there. Winner of the annual Grammar Police award for the worst example of a semantically incorrect title in recent years. 86m/C VHS: Arye Gross, Courteney Cox, Kevin Pollak, Julie Brown, Mitchell Ryan, Philip Bruns, Mitzi McCall, B.J. Ward; D: Matthew Meshekoff; W: Noah Stern; M: Ira Newborn.

Optic Fiber ✓✓ Fibra Optica 1997 Marco (Sosa) is an unemployed journalist in Mexico who is hired by an anonymous telephone caller to investigate the murder of a labor union leader. The man's mistress, a Brazilian, has been framed for the crime. Marco enlists the help of his photographer girlfriend Maria (Cavazos) and they both plunge into a world of corruption and cover-ups. Spanish with subtitles. 105m/C VHS, DVD. MX Roberto Sosa, Lumi Cavazos, Angelica Aragon, Alberto Estrella; D: Francisco Athie; W: Francisco Athie; C: Rodrigo Prieto.

Options ✓ 1988 (PG) Nerdy Hollywood agent Salinger treks to Africa to "option" a princess's life story—hence the title. He gets mixed up with her kidnapping and with her. Misplaced cameos by Roberts and Anton drag down the overall comedy content, which isn't to high to begin with. 105m/C VHS, Matt Salinger, Joanna Pacula, John Kani, James Keach; Cameos: Susan Anton, Eric Roberts; D: Camilo Vila; W: Edward Decter.

Or (My Treasure) ✓✓ Mon tresor 2004 Feature debut of Israeli director Yedaya is naive, irritating, and compelling. Set in a modern-day, working-class neighborhood of Tel Aviv, it follows the struggles of prostitute Ruthie (Elkabetz) and her teenage daughter Or (Ivgy). Or is responsible one—going to school, working, and looking after her self-destructive mother. Ruthie makes promises to go straight but inevitably goes back to the streets, thus breaking the heart of the daughter she refers to as "my treasure." Hebrew with subtitles. 100m/C DVD. IS Ronit Elkabetz, Dana Ivgy, Meshar Cohen; D: Keren Yedaya; W: Sari Ezouz, Keren Yedaya; C: Laurent Brunet.

The Oracle ✓ 1985 A woman takes a new apartment only to find that the previous occupant's spirit is still a resident. The spirit tries to force her to take revenge on his murders. Not bad for a low-budget thriller, but bad editing offers a distraction. 94m/C VHS, DVD. Caroline Capers Powers, Roger Neil; D: Roberta Findlay.

Orange County ✓✓½ 2002 (PG-13) Pedigreed star Hanks (son of Tom) enters the world of leading men alongside character-meister Black in this pleasant buddy comedy. Equally credible Tinseltown offspring continue aplenty with love-interest Fisk (daughter of Sissy Spacek and Jake Fisk) and director Jake Kasdan (son of Lawrence). Typical Orange County, California teen Shaun Brumder trades his surf board for a pen when he accidentally discovers the joys of literature via a Marcus Skinner (an uncredited Kline) novel on the beach. Determined to study under Skinner at Stanford, Brumder is bummed when the wrong test scores are submitted to the college who summarily rejects him. Enter stoner brother Lance, to help him straighten everything out. Dynamic comedy with character development of a surprisingly sophisticated nature with this type of film. 81m/C VHS, DVD. US Colin Hanks, Jack Black, Schuyler Fisk, Catherine O'Hara, John Lithgow, Harold Ramis, Jane Adams, Garry Marshall, Dana Ivey, Chevy Chase, Lily Tomlin, George Murdock, Leslie Mann, Kyle Howard, Kevin Kline; D: Jake Kasdan; W: Mike White; C: Greg Gardiner; M: Michael Andrews.

Oranges Are Not the Only Fruit ✓✓½ 1989 Lesbian coming of age story about young Jess (Coleman), who must escape her evangelical religious upbringing and mother (McEwan) in order to be true to herself. When the teenaged Jess gets a schoolgirl crush on her friend Melanie, the congregation finds out and condemns the girls until Jess finds the strength to break away. Based on the novel by Winsterson, who also wrote the screenplay. Made for TV. 165m/C VHS, DVD. GB Charlotte Coleman, Geraldine McEwan, Cathryn Bradshaw, Kenneth Cranham, Freda Dowie, Richard Henders, Elizabeth Spriggs, Sophie Thursfield; D: Beeban Kidron; W: Jeanette Winterson; M: Rachel Portman. TV

Orca WOOF! Orca—Killer Whale; The Killer Whale 1977 (PG) Ridiculous premise has a killer whale chasing bounty hunter Harris to avenge the murder of its pregnant mate. Great for gore lovers, especially when the whale chomps Derek's leg off. 92m/C VHS, DVD. Richard Harris, Charlotte Rampling, Bo Derek, Keenan Wynn, Will Sampson, Robert Carradine; D: Michael Anderson Sr.; W: Sergio Donati, Luciano Vincenzoni; C: Ted Moore; M: Ennio Morricone.

Orchestra Rehearsal ✓✓ Prova d'Orchestra 1978 Italian orchestra musicians gather in a 13th-century chapel to film a TV documentary, protest the increasing authoritarianism of their German conductor, but are eventually persuaded to play amidst the chaos. Rota's last score. Italian with subtitles. 72m/C VHS, DVD. IT Balduin Baas, Clara Colosimo, Elisabeth Labi, Ronaldo Bonacchi, Ferdinando Villella, Giovanni Javarone, David Mauhsell, Francesco Aluigi; D: Federico Fellini; W: Federico Fellini, Brunello Rondi; C: Giuseppe Rotunno; M: Nino Rota.

Orchestra Wives ✓✓ 1942 A drama bursting with wonderful Glenn Miller music. A woman marries a musician and goes on the road with the band and the other wives. Trouble springs up with the sultry singer who desperately wants the woman's new husband. The commotion spreads throughout the group. ♫People Like You and Me; At Last; Serenade in Blue; I've Got a Gal in Kalamazoo. 98m/B VHS, DVD. George Montgomery, Glenn Miller, Lynn Bari, Carole Landis, Jackie Gleason, Cesar Romero, Ann Rutherford, Virginia Gilmore, Mary Beth Hughes, Harry (Henry) Morgan; D: Archie Mayo.

Orde Wingate ✓✓ 1976 Capable biography of Orde Wingate (Foster), who was one of Britain's most celebrated and unorthodox commanders during WWII. While serving in Palestine, Wingate becomes a passionate Zionist and develops guerrilla tactics he teaches to the future leaders of the Israeli Defense Force. 174m/ C DVD. GB Barry Foster, James Cosmo, Denholm Elliott, Bernard Hepton, Sheila Ruskin, Arnold Diamond; D: Bill Hays; W: Don Shaw. TV

Ordeal by Innocence ✓✓½ 1984 (PG-13) Sutherland is an amateur sleuth in 1950s England convinced he has proof that a convicted murderer is innocent, but no one wishes to reopen the case. Big-name cast is essentially wasted. Based on an Agatha Christie story. 91m/C VHS. Donald Sutherland, Christopher Plummer, Faye Dunaway, Sarah Miles, Ian McShane, Diana Quick, Annette Crosbie, Michael Elphick; D: Desmond Davis; C: Billy Williams; M: Pino Donaggio.

Ordeal in the Arctic ✓✓½ 1993 (PG) Military transport plane, piloted by Capt. John Couch (Chamberlain), crashes into the remote glaciers of the Arctic. The survivors face a blizzard and freezing to death unless a rescue team can get to them quickly. Based on the book "Death and Deliverance" by Robert Mason Lee. 93m/C VHS, DVD. CA Richard Chamberlain, Melanie Mayron, Catherine Mary Stewart, Scott Hylands, Page Fletcher, Christopher Bolton, Richard McMillan; D: Mark Sobel; W: Paul F. Edwards; C: Miklos Lente; M: Amin Bhatia. CABLE

The Ordeal of Dr. Mudd ✓ 1980 His name was Mudd—a fitting moniker after he unwittingly aided President Lincoln's assassin. Dr. Mudd set John Wilkes Boothe's leg, broken during the assassination, and was jailed for conspiracy. He became a hero in prison for his aid during yellow fever epidemics and was eventually released. A strong and intricate performance by Weaver keeps this TV drama interesting. Mudd's descendants are still trying to completely clear his name of any wrongdoing in the Lincoln assassination. 143m/C VHS, DVD. Dennis Weaver, Susan Sullivan, Richard Dysart, Michael McGuire, Nigel Davenport, Arthur Hill; D: Paul Wendkos. TV

The Order ✓ Sin Eater 2003 (R) Dark and logy religious thriller stars a dour and underwhelming Ledger as Alex, a Catholic priest investigating the death of his mentor (Carmelutti). His sleuthing eventually leads to a character known as a "Sin Eater" (Furmann), who literally ingests a wide range of normally unforgivable sins. These sins are represented by creatures similar to those in "Alien," as they also come bursting out of the chests of the unfortunate, but soon to be forgiven, souls. Upbeat subplot involves Alex's roll in the hay with a mentally deranged girl (Sossamon) who once attempted to kill him. What this poor man's "Exorcist" lacks in action, sufficient pacing, and a believable story line, it more than makes up for in gloomy lethargy, heavy-handed dialogue, and humorless characters. 102m/ C VHS, DVD. US Heath Ledger, Shannyn Sossamon, Benno Furmann, Mark Addy, Peter Weller, Francesco Carnelutti; D: Brian Helgeland; W: Brian Helgeland; C: Nicola Pecorini; M: David Tom.

Order of the Black Eagle ✓½ 1987 (R) A Bond-ish spy and his sidekick, Typhoon the Baboon, battle neo-Nazis planning to bring Hitler back to life in this silly tongue-in-cheek thriller. 93m/C VHS. GB

Ian Hunter, Charles K. Bibby, William T. Hicks, Jill Donnellan; **D:** Worth Keeter.

Order of the Eagle ♂½ 1989 An innocent scouting trip turns into a non-stop nightmare when an Eagle Scout uncovers some dangerous information. 88m/C VHS. Frank Stallone; **D:** William Zipp; **W:** William Zipp.

Order to Kill ♂♂ 1973 A gambling boss puts out a contract on a hit man. 110m/C VHS, DVD. Jose Ferrer, Helmut Berger, Sydne Rome, Kevin McCarthy; **D:** Jose Maesso.

Ordet ♂♂♂ *The Word* 1955 A man who believes he is Jesus Christ is ridiculed until he begins performing miracles, which serve to reaffirm the crumbling religious faith vs. fanaticism by the profoundly religious Dreyer, and based on the play by Kaj Munk. In Danish with English subtitles. 126m/B VHS, DVD, DK Henrik Malberg, Birgitte Federspiel, Cay Kristiansen Emil Hass Christiansen; **D:** Carl Theodor Dreyer; **W:** Carl Theodor Dreyer, Kaj Munk. **C:** Henning Bendtsen. Golden Globes '56: Foreign Film; Venice Film Fest. '55: Film.

Ordinary Decent Criminal ♂♂ 1999 (R) Lightweight caper flick loosely based on the life of Irish thief Martin Cahill was shot in 1998 but only recently received limited runs abroad. Kevin plays Michael Lynch, a self-styled blue collar criminal who enjoys high-profile heists and making the local cops look bad. When he steals a Caravaggio painting worth $45 million, he gets caught up with the IRA and an obsessive cop (Dillane) bent on catching him. Passes the time pleasantly enough, with a jovial performance by Spacey, but John Boorman's "The General" tells this story better. 90m/C VHS, DVD, IR GB Kevin Spacey, Linda Fiorentino, Helen Baxendale, Stephen (Dillon) Dillane, Peter Mullan, Patrick Malahide, Gerard McSorley, Colin Farrall; **D:** Thaddeus O'Sullivan; **W:** Gerard Stembridge; **C:** Andrew Dunn; **M:** Damon Albarn.

Ordinary Heroes ♂♂½ 1985 The story is familiar but the leads make it worthwhile. Anderson is strong as a blinded Vietnam vet readjusting to life at home. Bertinelli's portrayal of his former girlfriend is eloquent. Nice work on an overdone story. 105m/C VHS. Richard Dean Anderson, Valerie Bertinelli; **D:** Peter H. Cooper.

Ordinary Magic ♂♂½ 1993 Teenaged Jeffrey was raised in India, picking up more than a little eastern wisdom along the way. After the death of his parents Jeffrey comes to the U.S. to live with his aunt where he sticks out not only as the new kid but as a decided oddball. But he manages to make some new friends and teach a few lessons about individuality along the way. Adapted from the novel by Malcolm Bosse. 96m/C VHS. David Fox, Glenna Headly, Heath Lamberts, Ryan Reynolds; **Cameos:** Paul Anka; **D:** Giles Walker; **W:** Jefferson Lewis.

Ordinary People ♂♂♂♂ 1980 (R) Powerful, well-acted story of a family's struggle to deal with one son's accidental death and the other's subsequent guilt-ridden suicide attempt. Features strong performances by all, but Moore is especially believable as the cold and rigid mother. McGovern's film debut as well as Redford's directorial debut. Based on the novel by Judith Guest. 124m/C VHS, DVD. Mary Tyler Moore, Donald Sutherland, Timothy Hutton, Judd Hirsch, M. Emmet Walsh, Elizabeth McGovern, Adam Baldwin, Dinah Manoff, James B. Sikking, Frederic Lehne; **D:** Robert Redford; **W:** Alvin Sargent; **C:** John Bailey; **M:** Marvin Hamlisch. Oscars '80: Adapt. Screenplay, Director, Picture, Support. Actor (Hutton); Director Guild '80: Director (Redford); Golden Globes '81: Adapt. Screenplay, Director (Redford), Film—Drama, Support. Actor (Hutton); L.A. Film Critics '80: Support. Actor (Hutton); Natl. Bd. of Review '80: Director (Redford), N.Y. Film Critics '80: Film; Writers Guild '80: Adapt. Screenplay.

Ordinary Sinner ♂♂½ 2002 Peter (Hines) has dropped out of an Episcopal seminary, having had his faith shaken while working as a teen counselor. He's come to a small Vermont college town where his shy childhood friend Alex (Park) is going to school. Alex has a crush on sexy student Rachel (Banks), who's more interested in the depressed Peter. Meanwhile, Peter's one-time mentor Father Ed (Martinez) publicly reveals he's gay when a series of gay-bashing incidents strike the campus. A death causes more emotional upheaval and adds some unnecessary whodunit elements to an already overstuffed plot. Well-meaning plea for tolerance does border on the preachy. 92m/C VHS, DVD. Brendan P. Hines, Kris Park, Elizabeth Banks, A. Martinez, Peter Onorati, Nathaniel Marston; **D:** John Henry Davis; **W:** Brian Adler.

Orfeu ♂♂♂ 1999 Diegues's musical drama is adapted from the Vinicius de Moraes play that also inspired Marcel Camus's 1959 film "Black Orpheus." The retelling of the Greek Orpheus and Eurydice features pop singer Garrido as egotistical Orfeu who becomes smitten with country girl Eurydice (Franca). Portuguese with subtitles. 112m/C VHS, DVD, BR Toni Garrido, Patricia Franca, Murilo Benicio, Zeze Motta, Milton Goncalves, Isabel Fillardis; **D:** Carlos Diegues; **W:** Carlos Diegues; **C:** Affonso Beato; **M:** Caetano Veloso.

The Organization ♂♂♂ 1971 (PG) Poitier's third and final portrayal of Detective Virgil Tibbs, first seen in "In the Heat of the Night." This time around he battles a drug smuggling ring with a vigilante group. Good action scenes and a realistic ending. 108m/C VHS, DVD. Sidney Poitier, Barbara McNair, Sheree North, Raul Julia; **D:** Don Medford; **W:** James R. Webb; **C:** Joseph Biroc; **M:** Gil Melle.

The Organizer ♂♂ / *Compagni. Comrades* 1964 In 19th-century Turin, impoverished and oversized aristocratic professor Mastroianni unites a group of textile workers striking against unsafe working conditions. Italian with subtitles. 127m/B VHS, IT Marcello Mastroianni, Annie Girardot, Renato Salvatori, Bernard Blier, Francois Perier, Folco Lulli; **D:** Mario Monicelli; **M:** Mario Monicelli; **C:** Giuseppe Rotunno.

Organized Crime & Triad Bureau ♂♂ *Chungon Sattuk Linggei* 1993 Determined Lee and his cop team seal a crowded Hong Kong island Cheung Chai to trap mob boss Tung and his tootsie. And the bystanders better just get out of the way. Lots of action; Chinese with subtitles. 91m/C VHS, DVD, HK Danny Lee, Anthony Wong, Cecilia Yip, Roy Cheung, Elizabeth Lee; **D:** Kirk Wong; **W:** Winky Wong; **C:** Wing-Hung Wong, Kwong-Hung Chan; **M:** Danny Chung, Ding-Yat Tsung.

Orgazmo ♂½ 1998 (NC-17) "South Park" co-creator Trey Parker plays Mormon porn star Joe Young in this tale of sinners and Latter Day Saints in the dirty movie biz. When his sidekick (Bachar) invents an orgasm ray gun, they become superheroes and ride the one-joke premise like a rented Ferrari. Although hung with an NC-17 rating, it's guilty of bad humor more than bad taste. Parker is likeable, however, and provides intermittent laughs. 95m/C VHS. Trey Parker, Dian Bachar, Ron Jeremy, Matt Stone, Robyn Lynne, Michael Dean Jacobs, Andrew W. Kemler, David Dunn; **D:** Trey Parker; **W:** Trey Parker; **C:** Kenny Gioseffi; **M:** Paul Robb.

Orgy of the Dead Woof! 1965 Classic anti-canon film scripted by Ed Wood Jr., from his own novel. Two innocent travelers are forced to watch an even dozen nude spirits dance in a cardboard graveyard. Hilariously bad. 90m/C VHS, DVD. Criswell, Fawn Silver, William Bates, Pat Barringer; **D:** A.C. (Stephen Apostolof) Stephen; **W:** Edward D. Wood Jr.; **C:** Robert Caramico.

Orgy of the Vampires ♂ *Vampire's Night Orgy* 1973 (R) Tourists wander into village during cocktail hour. 86m/C VHS, DVD. SP IT Jack Taylor, Charo Soriano, Dianik Zurakowska, John Richard; **D:** Leon Klimovsky.

Oriana ♂♂ 1985 Marie (Silverio) learns that her Aunt Oriana (Wells) has willed her the family estate, a remote Venezuelan hacienda she visited as a girl. While preparing the house for sale and going through her aunt's things, Marie remembers her long-ago stay and tries to discover why Oriana never left the property, what happened to her first love, and what other secrets she kept. Spanish and French with subtitles. 88m/C DVD, FR VZ Daniela Silverio, Doris Wells, Rafael Briceno, Luis Armando Castillo, Maya Oloe, Mirtha Borges; **D:** Fina Torres; **W:** Tina Torres, Antoine Lacomblez; **C:** Jean-Claude Larrieu; **M:** Eduardo Marturet.

The Original Fabulous Adventures of Baron Munchausen ♂♂½ *The Fabulous Baron Munchausen* 1961 An adventure fantasy that takes the hero all over, from the belly of a whale, eventually landing him on the moon. 84m/C VHS, CZ Milos Kopecky, Hana Brejchova, Rudolf Jelinek, Jan Werich; **D:** Karel Zeman.

Original Gangstas ♂♂ 1996 (R) Everything old eventually becomes new again. John Bookman (Williamson) returns to his old neighborhood in Gary, Indiana, after his father is brutally shot by a gang leader. Things have changed from Bookman's day, with the streets swarming with young machine gun-toting lowlifes. Bent on revenge, cigar-chewing Bookman, aided by childhood friends Jake (Brown), Slick (Roundtree), and Bubba (O'Neal), decide to take back their streets with a little help from Foxy Brown herself (Grier), as a grieving mother. The nostalgia quotient is high watching these '70s blaxploitation stars together in one movie, older, more gray and a little wider, but still able to kick butt. Serious topic (gang violence) is lost in a conventional vigilante vehicle, which sacrifices a message for an all-too-familiar and bloody showdown. 99m/C VHS, DVD. Jim Brown, Fred Williamson, Pam Grier, Ron O'Neal, Richard Roundtree, Paul Winfield; **D:** Larry Cohen; **W:** Aubrey Rattan; **C:** Carlos Gonzalez; **M:** Vladimir Horunzhy.

Original Intent ♂♂ 1991 (PG) A successful lawyer, facing a mid-life crisis, jeopardizes both his family and career when he decides to defend a homeless shelter from eviction proceedings. What might have been a powerful drama about one man's crusade to help the homeless instead merely melodramatic. Actor/activist Sheen appears briefly as a homeless man. 37m/C VHS. Jay Richardson, Candy Clark, Kris Kristofferson, Vince Edwards, Cindy Pickett, Robert DoQui, Joseph Campanella; **Cameos:** Martin Sheen; **D:** Robert Marcarelli; **W:** Robert Macarelli.

Original Sin ♂♂ 2001 (R) 1880s Cuban coffee-plantation owner Luis (Banderas) sends to America for a mail-order bride, seeking only someone loyal and of child-bearing years. To discourage gold diggers, he describes himself as a clerk. When his bride-to-be Julia (Jolie) shows up, Luis discovers that she's much more attractive than her picture. She claims that she wanted to be desired for something other than her beauty. With a start like that, what could go wrong? Well, American private detective arrives on the scene, hired by Julia's family to report on her well-being. This fuels doubts in Luis, but a little too late. Soon he's cleaned out, shamed and on the trail of his former "wife." Banderas and Jolie torch the scenes as the couple in lust, but the ham-handed dialogue and direction derail this period potboiler. Loosely based on the Cornell Woolrich novel "Waltz Into Darkness," which was also the source for Truffaut's "Mississippi Mermaid." 112m/C VHS, DVD, US Antonio Banderas, Angelina Jolie, Thomas Jane, Jack Thompson, Gregory Itzin, Joan Pringle, Allison Mackie, Cordelia Richards, Pedro Armendariz Jr.; **D:** Michael Cristofer; **W:** Michael Cristofer; **C:** Rodrigo Prieto; **M:** Terence Blanchard.

Orlando ♂♂♂ 1992 (PG-13) Potter's sumptuous film adaptation of Virginia Woolf's 1928 novel, which covers 400 years in the life of an English nobleman, who not only defies death but evolves from a man to a woman in the intervening years. Orlando (Swinton) is first seen as a young man in the court of Queen Elizabeth I (Crisp) but after a deep sleep it's suddenly 40 years later. Things like this just keep happening and by 1750 he (now a she and remains so), finding and losing love, and eventually gaining fulfillment in the 20th century. Elaborate productions move overwhelm Swinton's serene, self-assured performance. 93m/C VHS, DVD, GB Tilda Swinton, Billy Zane, Lothaire Bluteau, John Wood, Quentin Crisp, Heathcote Williams, Dudley, Sutton, Thom Hoffman, Peter Eyre, Jimmy Somerville; **D:** Sally Potter; **W:** Sally Potter; **C:** Alexei Rodionov; **M:** Bob Last.

Orloff and the Invisible Man ♂ *Orloff Against the Invisible Man; The Invisible Dead; Dr. Orloff's Invisible Monster* 1970 So many invisible man movies, so little time. A scientist creates an invisible man, imprisons and tortures him. A bit miffed with this host, he who can't be seen escapes and vents his invisible spleen. 76m/C VHS. Howard Vernon, Brigitte Carpio, Fernando (Fernand) Sancho, Isabel Del Rio, Paco Valladares; **D:** Pierre Chevalier; **W:** France Villon; **M:** Camille Sauvage.

An Orphan Boy of Vienna ♂♂ 1937 A homeless street urchin with a beautiful singing voice is accepted into the wonderful world of the Choir, but is later unjustly accused of stealing. Performances by the Vienna Boys' Choir redeem the melodramatic plot. In German with English subtitles. 87m/B VHS. GE **D:** Max Neufeld.

The Orphan ♂½ 1979 A young orphaned boy seeks revenge against his cruel aunt who is harassing him with sadistic discipline. 80m/C VHS. Mark Evans, Joanna Miles, Peggy (Margaret) Feury; **D:** John Ballard.

Orphan Train ♂♂♂ 1979 A woman realizes her New York soup kitchen can't do enough to help the neighborhood orphans, so she takes a group of children out West in hopes of finding families to adopt them. Their journey is chronicled by a newspaper photographer and a social worker. Based on the actual "orphan trains" of the mid- to late 1800s. From the novel by Dorothea G. Petrie. 100m/C VHS. Jill Eikenberry, Kevin Dobson, Glenn Close, Linda Manz; **D:** William A. Graham. TV

The Orphanage ♂♂♂ 2007 (R) Laura (Rueda) returns to the orphanage of her youth with husband Carlos (Cayo) and adopted son Simon (Princep), three decades after leaving with her adoptive parents. Laura and Carlos have purchased the abandoned building with plans to establish a home for sick and disabled children. Their plans are preempted by the arrival of an imaginary playmate for Simon, which forces long-repressed frightening memories to the surface for Laura and leads to Simon's disappearance. What follows is Laura's nightmarish attempt to sort reality from haunting fantasy as she desperately tries to simultaneously find her son and cling to sanity. Well acted and well crafted, this terrifying ghost story is gripping, anxious, and truly scary, and an antidote to the torture porn that passes for horror of late. 100m/C VHS, DVD, SP Belen Rueda, Geraldine Chaplin, Mabel Rivera, Fernando Cayo, Roger Princep, Montserrat Carulla; **D:** Juan Antonio Bayona; **W:** Sergio G. Sanchez; **C:** Oscar Faura; **M:** Fernando Velazquez.

The Orphans ♂♂♂ *Podranki* 1977 A sensitive edge-of-glasnost portrait of a young boy's discovery of love, friendship, and literature. In Russian with English subtitles. 97m/C VHS. RU Nikolai Gubenko, Y. Boudraitis, A. Toberstvov, A. Kailagune, E. Bouratis, A. Bikov, E. Evstigneyev; **D:** Nikolai Gubenko; **W:** Nikolai Gubenko; **C:** Alexander Kniajinsky.

The Orphans ♂♂♂ 1987 (R) A gangster on the run is kidnapped by a tough New York orphan but soon takes control of his benefactor, befriending this abductor's maladjusted brother. Eventually each brother realizes his need for the older man, who has befriended them. This very quirky film is salvaged by good performances. Based on the play by Lyle Kessler. 116m/C VHS. Albert Finney, Matthew Mod-...

ine, Kevin Anderson; **D:** Alan J. Pakula; **W:** Lyle Kessler; **M:** Michael Small.

Orphans 🐾🐾 1997 Three brothers and their handicapped sister come unraveled in the 24-hour period following their mother's death. The four Flynn siblings head for the pub the night before the funeral where eldest brother Thomas (Lewis) takes to singing, drawing amusement from the onlookers. This upsets Michael (Henshall), who then gets stabbed in the subsequent bar fight, leading youngest brother John (McCole) to vow to get revenge. Meanwhile, angry, wheelchair-bound Sheila (Stevenson) is bored and decides to take a little roll around Glasgow on her own. Frustrated characters all lash out at one another. Feature directorial debut of actor Mullan. **102m/C VHS, DVD, GB** Douglas Henshall, Gary Lewis, Stephen McCole, Rosemarie Stevenson, Alex Norton, Frank Gallagher, Malcolm Shields; **D:** Peter Mullan; **W:** Peter Mullan; **C:** Grant Scott Cameron; **M:** Craig Armstrong.

Orphans of the North 🐾 1940 The story of Bedrock Brown's search for gold and his lost partner. Filmed on location in Alaska with non-professional actors. Impressive footage of America's "last frontier," including the flora and fauna. **56m/C VHS. D:** Norman Dawn; **W:** Susan Denis; **Nar:** Norman Dawn.

Orphans of the Storm 🐾🐾🐾½ 1921 Two sisters are separated and raised in opposite worlds—one by thieves, the other by aristocrats. Gish's poignant search for her sister is hampered by the turbulent maelstrom preceding the French Revolution. Silent. Based on the French play "The Two Orphans." **190m/B VHS, DVD.** Lillian Gish, Dorothy Gish, Monte Blue, Joseph Schildkraut; **D:** D.W. Griffith; **W:** D.W. Griffith; **C:** Billy (G.W.) Bitzer, Hendrik Sartov; **M:** Louis F. Gottschalk, William F. Peters.

Orpheus 🐾🐾🐾½ *Orphee* 1949 Cocteau's fascinating, innovative retelling of the Orpheus legend in a modern, though slightly askew, Parisian setting. Classic visual effects and poetic imagery. In French with English subtitles. **95m/B VHS, DVD.** Jean Marais, Francois Perier, Maria Casares, Marie Dea, Edouard Dermithe, Juliette Greco; **D:** Jean Cocteau; **W:** Jean Cocteau; **C:** Nicolas Hayer; **M:** Georges Auric.

Orpheus Descending 🐾🐾½ 1991 Lust and hatred in small Southern town. Confusing, poorly paced, but interesting for Anderson as Elvis-style drifter and Redgrave as woman addicted to him. Cable version of the 1989 Broadway revival of Tennessee Williams play. **117m/C VHS.** Vanessa Redgrave, Kevin Anderson, Anne Twomey, Miriam Margolyes, Brad Sullivan, Sloane Shelton, Patti Allison; **D:** Peter Hall; **W:** Peter Hall, Tennessee Williams. **CABLE**

Orwell Rolls in His Grave 🐾 2003 Wordy talking-head dominated movie parallels George Orwell's Big Brother totalitarianism in "1984" with the current relationship of U.S. media and government. Interviews conducted in dull settings and comically ominous soundtrack music detract from the main objective. Basically a poor rehashing of like "Fahrenheit 9/11," "The Corporation," and "Outfoxed." **95m/C DVD. D:** Robert Kane Pappas; **W:** Robert Kane Pappas, Tom Blackburn; **C:** Robert Kane Pappas, Alan Hostetter; **M:** Eric Wood.

Osa 🐾½ 1985 Yet another post-nuke flick with the usual devastated landscape, leather-clad survivors, and hokey dialog. It's sometimes funny, despite everyone's effort to make it dramatic. The supposed plot centers on one woman's efforts to break up a man's monopoly on clean water. **94m/C VHS.** Kelly Lynch, Daniel Grimm, Phillip Vincent, Etienne Chicot, John Forristal, Pete Walker, David Hausman, Bill Moseley; **D:** Oleg Egorov; **M:** Mason Daring.

Osaka Elegy 🐾🐾½ *Woman of Osaka* 1936 A study of Japanese cultural rules when society condemns a woman for behavior that is acceptable for a man. In Japanese with English subtitles. **71m/B VHS. JP** Isuzu Yamada; **D:** Kenji Mizoguchi.

Osama 🐾🐾🐾🐾 2003 First post-Taliban movie produced in Afghanistan shows the oppression suffered by women under that regime in the story of a young girl forced to pose as a boy. Osama (Golbahari) breaks the law, disguising herself to work in a grocery to support her family after her father and brother are killed. This ends quickly as she's rounded up with all the boys of her village and forced into the local religious/military training camp run by the Taliban, where she does everything she can to keep her disguise from being discovered. Director Barmak has an exceptional eye for detail and uses handheld cameras and nonprofessional actors on the streets of Kabul to create a brutally realistic portrait of Afghanistan under the Taliban. A brilliant, intense portrait of one girl's quest to survive hopelessness, horrible cruelty, and overbearing oppression. In Dari with English subtitles. **82m/C DVD, B VHS.** Alan Ladd, Geraldine Fitzgerald, Patric Knowles, John Hoyt, Richard Benedict, Gloria Saunders, Bobby Driscoll, Don Beddoe, Richard Webb, Gavin Muir, Onslow Stevens, Joseph Crehan, Leslie Denison; **D:** Irving Pichel; **W:** Richard Malbaum; **C:** Lionel Lindon; **M:** Daniele Amitheatrof.

The Oscar 🐾½ 1966 (R) Unless you enjoy razzing bad acting, this is not for you. Meant as a comeuppance for Hollywood, by Hollywood, this story of movie star Frank Fane (Boyd), climbing the ladder of success and squashing fingers on every rung is too schlocky to succeed. The climax, when the scumbag star thinks he's won an Oscar and stands up, only to find it's for someone else, was based on Frank Capra's embarrassing experience in 1932 with the same situation. Adapted from the novel by Richard Sale. **119m/C VHS.** Stephen Boyd, Elke Sommer, Jill St. John, Tony Bennett, Milton Berle, Eleanor Parker, Joseph Cotten, Eddie Adams, Ernest Borgnine, Ed Begley Sr., Walter Brennan, Broderick Crawford, James Dunn, Peter Lawford, Merle Oberon, Bob Hope, Frank Sinatra; **D:** Russell Rouse; **W:** Russell Rouse, Harlan Ellison, Clarence Greene; **C:** Joseph Ruttenberg.

Oscar 🐾🐾 1991 (PG) The improbable casting of Stallone in a 1930s style crime farce (an attempt to change his image) is hard to imagine, and harder to believe. Stallone has little to do as he plays the straight man in this often ridiculous story of a crime boss who swears he'll go straight. Cameos aplenty, with Curry's the most notable. Based on a French play by Claude Magnier. **109m/C VHS, DVD.** Sylvester Stallone, Ornella Muti, Peter Riegert, Vincent Spano, Marisa Tomei, Kirk Douglas, Art LaFleur, Ken Howard, Chazz Palminteri, Tim Curry, Don Ameche, Richard Romanus; **D:** John Landis; **W:** Michael Barrie, Jim Mulholland; **C:** Mac Ahlberg; **M:** Elmer Bernstein.

Oscar and Lucinda 🐾🐾½ 1997 (R) A priest and a glassworks heiress are united by a shared passion for gambling; together they attempt to transport a glass church through 1860s Australian wilderness. Fiennes' performance as the vulnerable and flailing Oscar is particularly good. Narrated by Geoffrey Rush. Based on the Booker Prize-winning novel by Peter Carey. **131m/C VHS, DVD.** Ralph Fiennes, Cate Blanchett, Ciaran Hinds, Tom Wilkinson, Richard Roxburgh, Clive Russell, Bille Brown, Josephine Byrnes, Barnaby Kay, Barry Otto, Linda Bassett; **D:** Gillian Armstrong; **W:** Laura Jones; **C:** Geoffrey Simpson; **M:** Thomas Newman; **Nar:** Geoffrey Rush. Australian Film Inst. '98: Cinematog., Score.

Osmosis Jones 🐾🐾 2001 (PG-13) Combo of animation and live-action concerns a slob named Frank (Murray) who's suffering from an evil virus (Fishburne) that's taking over his body. To the rescue are white blood cell Osmosis Jones (Rock) and cold tablet Drix (Pierce). The Farrellys once again push the envelope of gross-out humor, but this time it's a PG envelope, and the live-action sequences suffer for it, especially when compared to the funny, clever, and high-energy animated sequences. Luckily, the animation comprises about two-thirds of the movie. Kids will enjoy the lively animation and the gross stuff, while the adults should have a good enough time picking out the puns and references to other movies. Murray goes to heroic lengths to portray Frank's devotion to self-degradation.

95m/C VHS, DVD. US Bill Murray, Molly Shannon, Chris Elliott, Elena Franklin; **D:** Bobby Farrelly, Peter Farrelly, Piet Kroon, Tom Sito; **W:** Marc Hyman; **C:** Mark Irwin; **M:** Randy Edelman; **V:** Chris Rock, Laurence Fishburne, David Hyde Pierce, Brandy Norwood, William Shatner, Ron Howard.

O.S.S. 🐾🐾🐾 1946 John Martin (Ladd) has been recruited by Commander Brady (Knowles) as a would-be spy for the new Office of Strategic Services. Martin's teamed with Ellen Rogers (Fitzgerald) and they parachute into France with orders to obtain information on German troop movements and destroy an important railroad tunnel. A turncoat Gestapo agent sells them information but German colonel Meister (Hoyt) is after them and it's a race to see if their mission can be completed before they're caught. The O.S.S. allowed Paramount studio a look at their WWII files for story purposes and numerous agents served as technical advisors. **108m/B VHS.**

Ossessione 🐾🐾🐾 1942 An adaptation of "The Postman Always Rings Twice," transferred to Fascist Italy, where a drifter and an innkeeper's wife murder her husband. Visconti's first feature, which initiated Italian neo-realism, was not released in the U.S. until 1975 due to a copyright dispute. In Italian with English subtitles. **135m/B VHS, DVD. IT** Massimo Girotti, Clara Calamai, Juan deLanda, Elio Marcuzzo; **D:** Luchino Visconti; **W:** Giuseppe de Santis, Mario Alicata; **C:** Aldo Tonti, Domenico Scala.

The Osterman Weekend 🐾🐾 1983 (R) Peckinpah was said to have disliked the story and the script in this, his last film, which could account for the convoluted and confusing end result. Adding to the problem is the traditional difficulty of adapting Ludlum's complex psychological thrillers for the screen. The result: cast members seem to not quite "get it" as they portray a group of friends, one of whom has been convinced by the CIA that the others are all Soviet spies. **120m/C VHS, DVD.** Burt Lancaster, Rutger Hauer, Craig T. Nelson, Dennis Hopper, John Hurt, Chris Sarandon, Meg Foster, Helen Shaver; **D:** Sam Peckinpah; **M:** Lalo Schifrin.

Otaku No Video 🐾🐾🐾 *Fan's Video* 1991 The title of this satirized bio of Gainax animation studio and its founders can be read as "Fan's Video." The tape contains two installments, one made in 1982 and one in 1985. In 1982, college freshman Kubo is reunited with his old friend Tanaka and slowly gets sucked into the world of hopelessly obsessed anime and science fiction fans or "otaku." Both the fun and social costs of his new hobby are examined in Japan, like the U.S., the coolest guys aren't sitting inside watching TV all day). The second installment finds Kubo and Tanaka starting two different businesses that are directly related to their beloved hobby. As if the animated stories weren't hilarious enough (and, perhaps, all-too familiar to some anime fans), there are live-action, fake documentary segments. These examine different aspects of "otakudom." People less familiar with the world of anime should be able to understand the basic story which is very funny (keeping in mind that practically nothing about this video is to be taken seriously). More experienced anime fans will have the added fun of trying to spot all the anime references and in-jokes liberally woven into the script. **100m/C VHS, DVD. JP** Takeshi Mori; **W:** Toshio Okada; **C:** Tadashi Sano; **M:** Kohei Tanaka; **V:** Kohi Tsujitani, Toshiharu Sakurai.

Otello 🐾🐾½ 1986 (PG) An uncommon film treat for opera fans, with a stellar performance by Domingo as the troubled Moor who murders his wife in a fit of jealousy. Walker is convincingly impassioned but Eccleston's slimy manipulation is rather too obvious. **96m/C VHS, DVD. GB** Eamonn Walker, Christopher Eccleston, Keeley Hawes, Richard Coyle, Del Synnot, Christopher Fox, Allan Cutts, Patrick Myers; **C:** Geoffrey Sax; **W:** Andrew Davies; **C:** Daf Hobson; **M:** Debbie Wiseman. **TV**

Italian with English subtitles. **123m/C VHS, DVD. IT** Placido Domingo, Katia Ricciarelli, Justino Diaz; **D:** Franco Zeffirelli.

Othello 🐾🐾🐾 1922 A silent version of Shakespeare's tragedy, featuring Jannings as the Moor. Titles are in English; with musical score. **81m/B VHS, DVD. GE** Emil Jannings, Lya de Putti, Werner Krauss; **D:** Dimitri Buchowetzki.

Othello 🐾🐾🐾 *Orson Welles's Othello; The Tragedy of Othello: The Moor of Venice* 1952 Welles's striking adaptation of the Shakespeare tragedy casts him as the self-deluding Moor, with MacLiammoir as the despicable Iago and Cloutier as innocent victim, Desdemona. Welles filmed his epic over a four-year period due to budget difficulties, which also resulted in his filming in a number of different countries and settings. The film underwent a $1 million restoration, supervised by Welles's daughter, prior to its limited theatrical re-release in 1992. **90m/B VHS, DVD.** Orson Welles, Michael MacLiammoir, Suzanne Cloutier, Robert Coote, Hilton Edwards, Michael Lawrence, Nicholas Bruce, Fay Compton, Doris Dowling, Jean Davis, Joseph Cotten, Joan Fontaine; **D:** Orson Welles; **W:** Orson Welles; **C:** Anchise Brizzi, George Fanto, Alberto Fusi, Aldo (G.R. Aldo) Graziatti, Oberdan Troiani; **M:** Alberto Barberis, Angelo Francesco Lavagnino. Cannes '52: Film.

Othello 🐾🐾🐾½ 1965 Olivier (in blackface) gives another towering performance as Shakespeare's tragic Moor, led to disaster by his own jealousy. He's ably supported by Finlay's insinuating performance as Iago, Smith as a sweetly vulnerable Desdemona, and Jacobi as unwitting rival Cassio. The production, however, doesn't stray far from its stage-bound roots. **150m/C VHS.** Laurence Olivier, Frank Finlay, Maggie Smith, Derek Jacobi, Joyce Redman, Anthony Nicholls, Sheila Reid, Roy Holder; **D:** Stuart Burge; **W:** Margaret Unsworth; **C:** Geoffrey Unsworth; **M:** Richard Hampton.

Othello 🐾🐾🐾 1995 (R) Fishburne stars as Shakespeare's tragic Moor, with Branagh as silken agitator Iago, and Jacob as the tragic Desdemona. First time director Oliver Parker (brother Nathaniel is also in the film) drastically cut the play, rearranging scenes (and even adding material)—purists will no doubt scream, but performances carry the production. Through the clever use of asides directed at the camera, Branagh's Iago makes the viewer feel like an accomplice in the plot. French-speaking Jacob, however, seems to have a hard time pronouncing the Shakespearean dialogue. **125m/C VHS, DVD.** Laurence Fishburne, Irene Jacob, Kenneth Branagh, Nathaniel Parker, Michael Maloney, Anna Patrick, Nicholas Farrell, Indra Ove, Michael Sheen, Andre Oumansky, Philip Locke, John Savident, Gabriele Ferzetti, Pierre Vaneck; **D:** Oliver Parker; **W:** Oliver Parker; **C:** David C(lark) Johnson; **M:** Charlie Mole.

Othello 🐾🐾🐾 2001 Updated version (with modern dialogue) of Shakespeare's "Othello" set in contemporary London. John Othello (Walker) is a respected police officer who has just been installed as the first black commissioner of the Metropolitan force. His promotion comes at the expense of his mentor/friend Ben Jago (Eccleston) who does not handle the slight well as he is now second-in-command. So Ben plays the race card and works on John's jealousy of his heiress white wife, Dessie (Hawley), by suggesting that she is unfaithful. Walker is convincingly impassioned but Eccleston's slimy manipulation...

The Other 🐾🐾🐾 1972 (PG) Eerie, effective thriller adapted by Tyron from his supernatural novel. Twin brothers represent good and evil in a 1930s Connecticut farm town beset with gruesome murders and accidents. A good scare. **100m/C VHS, DVD.** Martin Udvarnoky, Chris Udvarnoky, Uta Hagen, Diana Muldaur, Norma Connolly, Victor French, John Ritter, Loretta Leversee, Lou Frizzell, Portia Nelson, Jenny Sullivan; **D:** Robert Mulligan;

The Other Boleyn Girl 🎬🎬 2003 Truncated, low-budget TV version of Philippa Gregory's novel about Mary Boleyn (McElhone), who first won the favor of King Henry VIII (Harris) while a young married woman at court. When Mary becomes pregnant, the restless Henry turns his attentions to Mary's older and much-more ambitious sister, Anne (May), who refuses to give in until Henry is free to marry her. **90m/C DVD, GB** Natasha McElhone, Jodhi May, Jared Harris, Jack Shepherd, Philip Glenister, John Woodvine, Ron Cook, Anthony Howell, Yolanda Vazquez, Steven Macintosh, Jane Gurnett. **C:** Graham Smith; **M:** TV.

The Other Boleyn Girl 🎬🎬½ 2008 (PG-13) Big-budget Elizabethan period piece that comes off more like a Hollywood soap opera, starring three non-British leads that seem too hip and contemporary for it's kind of melodramatic material. Divided into two sections: the first depicting two sisters, Anne (Portman) and Mary Boleyn (Johansson), competing for the love of King Henry VIII (Bana), and the second being a fast-forward through history showing Anne's ascent to the throne. The costumes and scenery are expectedly great, and script is surprisingly tight (even if it's occasionally anachronistic), but the execution is often confusing and awkward, reducing what could have been excellent by just plain old good. Based on the novel by Phillipa Gregory. **115m/C DVD, GB US** Eric Bana, Natalie Portman, Scarlett Johansson, David Morrissey, Mark Rylance, Jim Sturgess, Eddie Redmayne, Benedict Cumberbatch, Ana Torrent, Juno Temple, Oliver Coleman, Kristin Scott Thomas; **D:** Justin Chadwick; **W:** Peter Morgan; **C:** Kieran McGuigan; **M:** Paul Cantelon.

The Other Brother 🎬🎬½ 2002 (R) Nice guy Martin (Phifer) is shocked to discover his girlfriend in bed with another woman. Uncertain about his judgement of the fair sex, he reluctantly agrees to listen to his player brother Junnie's (Blake) advice, which results in some awkward pick-up moments. Of course, Martin has already meet the perfect new girlfriend, his new upstairs neighbor Paula (Miller), if only he would listen to what his own heart says. **94m/C VHS, DVD** Mekhi Phifer, André B. Blake, Michele Morgan, Targi Miller, Ebony Jo-Ann, Regina Hall, Collette Wilson; **D:** Matthew Clark.

Other Hell 🎬 1985 (R) Schlocky Italian-made chiller has the devil inhabiting a convent where he does his darnest to upset the nuns. Gross, but not scary—lots of cliche dark-hallway scenes and fright music. **88m/C VHS, DVD, IT** Carlo De Mejo, Francesca Carmeno; **D:** Stefan Oblowsky.

Other People's Money 🎬🎬½ 1991 (R) DeVito is "Larry the Liquidator," a corporate raider with a heart of stone and a penchant for coughnuts. When he sets his sights on a post-smokestack era, family-owned cable company, he gets a taste of love for the first time in his life. He and Miller, the daughter of the company president and also its legal advisor, court one another while sparring over the fate of the company. Unbelievably clipped ending otherwise enterprising comedy. Based on the off-Broadway play by Jerry Sterner. **101m/C VHS, DVD** Danny DeVito, Penélope Ann Miller, Jean Jones, Gregory Peck, Piper Laurie, Tom Aldredge, R.D. Call; **D:** Norman Jewison; **W:** Alvin Sargent; **C:** Haskell Wexler; **M:** David Newman.

The Other Side of Heaven 🎬🎬 2002 (PG) Well-meaning if heavy-handed bio-drama based on Groberg's memoir "In the Eye of the Storm." John Groberg (Gorham) is a Mormon college student at Brigham Young University in 1953, who's pining for Jean (Hathaway), the girl of his dreams. Then he receives his missionary assignment—to Tonga in the South Seas. Groberg has to struggle with native culture, the language barrier, and various hardships and natural disasters before he can accomplish his goals. Film's sincere although you never get much of an idea of how Groberg feels about all that befalls him except for his enduring faith. Picture was filmed in the Cook Islands. **113m/C VHS, DVD** Christopher Gorham, Anne Hathaway, Joe Folau, Miriama Smith, Nathaniel Lees, Whetu Fala; **D:** Mitch Davis; **W:** Mitch Davis; **C:** Brian J. Breheny; **M:** Kevin Kiner.

The Other Side of Midnight woof! 1977 (R) The dreary, depressingly shallow life story of a poor French girl, dumped by an American GI, who sleeps her way to acting stardom and a profitable marriage, then seeks revenge for the jilt. Based on Sidney Sheldon's novel, it's not even titillating—just a real downer. **160m/C VHS, DVD** Susan Sarandon, Marie-France Pisier, John Beck, Raf Vallone, Clu Gulager, Sorrell Booke; **D:** Charles Jarrott; **W:** Daniel Taradash; **C:** Fred W. Koenekamp.

The Other Side of Sunday 🎬🎬 *Søndagsengler* 1996 A small town in 1959 Norway is the setting for th's coming of age comedy. Maria doesn't seem to be part of her religion, but puberty is hitting Maria hard and she longs to join in with the livelier crowd of her school friend Brigit (Salvesen), who listens to rock 'n' roll, wears makeup, and makes out with boys. Maria does find a compassionate listener in Mrs. Tunheim (Riise), who urges the teenager to learn how to think for herself. Based on the novel "Sunday" by Reidun Nortvedt. Norwegian with subtitles. **103m/C VHS, DVD, NO** Marie Theisen, Bjorn Sundquist, Hildegunn Riise, Sylvia Salvesen, Jan Berit Nesheim; **W:** Berit Nesheim, Lasse Glomm; **C:** Anne Borsheim; **M:** Geir Bohren, Bent Aserud.

The Other Side of the Bed 🎬🎬 *El Otro Lado de la Cama* 2003 (R) Two sexy and self-absorbed Madrid couples slyly swap partners—yet still find time to break out in song and dance when the mood strikes—in this lively, sex-packed, high-camp Spanish import. In Spanish with subtitles. **114m/C VHS, DVD, SP** Ernesto Alterio, Guillermo Toledo, María Esteve; **W:** David Serrano; **C:** Juan Molina; **M:** Roque Baños.

VIDEO

The Other Side of the Law 🎬🎬 1995 (R) Man makes a wilderness hideout with his son after killing his wife's murderer. But when the cold gives up, dad decides to send him back into civilization for education, leading to nothing but trouble. **96m/C VHS, CA** Johnny Morina, Maggie Castle, Yves Renier, Xavier Deluc, Jurgen Prochnow; **D:** Gilles Carle; **W:** Gilles Carle; **M:** Jean Delorme.

The Other Side of the Mountain 🎬🎬 *A Window to the Sky* 1975 (PG) Tear-jerking true story of Olympic hopeful skier Jill Kinmont, paralyzed in a fall. Bridges helps her pull her life together. A sequel followed two years later. Based on the book "A Long Way Up" by E. G. Valens. **102m/C VHS** Marilyn Hassett, Beau Bridges, Dabney Coleman, John David Garfield, Griffin Dunne; **D:** Larry Peerce; **W:** David Seltzer; **M:** Charles Fox.

The Other Side of the Mountain, Part 2 🎬🎬 1978 (PG) Quadriplegic Jill Kinmont, paralyzed in a skiing accident that killed her hopes for the Olympics, overcomes depression and the death of the man who helped her to recover. In this chapter, she falls in love again and finds happiness. More tears are jerked. **99m/C VHS** Marilyn Hassett, Timothy Bottoms; **D:** Larry Peerce.

The Other Sister 🎬🎬 1998 (PG-13) Carla (Lewis) is the mentally challenged but exuberant member of the re-pressed Tate family. After leaving a "special school," she convinces her uptight parents Elizabeth (Keaton) and Radley (Skerritt) to let her enroll in a vocational program. She meets and falls for fellow retarded student Danny (Ribisi), much to her parents' dismay. Love wins out, but jerked. **99m/C VHS.** Marilyn Hassett, Timothy Bottoms; **D:** Larry Peerce.

(continued) the script is so sappy that a maple syrup factory could be built on it. Lewis and Ribisi give an admirable job of rising above the material, which was co-written by schmaltz-meister director Garry Marshall.

Other Voices, Other Rooms 🎬🎬½ 1995 Adaptation of Truman Capote's 1948 novel (his first) is the semi-autobiographical story of a young boy's search for his father set against the backdrop of a decaying Bayou mansion, Southern saga, narrated by Capote sound-alike Kingdom, starts when 12-year-old Joel's mother dies and he's sent by his aunts to live with his father. Instead of being greeted by his father, Joel (Speck) instead meets an odd collection of guests, including Amy (Thomson), a fragile and pretty Southern belle and her cousin Randolph (Bluteau), a sensitive, effete, and charming alcoholic. Pic deals with the secrets of the father's illness and what lies behind the unhappiness of the two cousins, who try to keep the child from fleeing the wacky "family." Lacks the danger and suspense of Capote's novel, but sets proper mood and shows off actors talents. Best known as a documentary director/producer, this is Rocksavage's feature debut. **98m/C VHS, DVD** Lothaire Bluteau, Anna Thomson, David Speck, April Turner, Audrey Dollar; **D:** David Rocksavage; **C:** Paul Ryan; **M:** Chris Tajima; **Nar:** Bob Kingdom.

The Other Woman 🎬½ 1992 (R) Investigative reporter Jessica is working on a murder case when she finds incriminating sex photos showing her husband with another woman. She becomes obsessed with finding the woman in the pictures but it would be dangerous for Jessica to forget there's still a murderer on the loose. **90m/C VHS** Adrian Zmed, Lee Ann Beaman, Daniel Moriarty, Jenna Persaud, Sam Jones; **D:** Jag Mundhra.

The Others 🎬🎬🎬 2001 (PG-13) Twisting Gothic haunt-fest centers on Grace (Kidman) and her two children Anne (Mann) and Nicholas (Bentley), living in a mansion on Britain's remote Isle of Jersey. She waits for her husband's return from WWII, although she fears he may be dead. After her servants disappear in the middle of the night, she's surprised when Grace is demanding and high-strung to the point of mania. Because of rare allergies, the kids must be kept out of the sunlight. Maybe the solitude is preying on Grace's mind, maybe she's crazy, or maybe their house is haunted. Kidman is at her chilly best as the audience is kept guessing. **101m/C VHS, DVD, US** Nicole Kidman, Fionnula Flanagan, Alakina Mann, James Bentley, Christopher Eccleston, Elaine Cassidy, Eric Sykes, Renee Asherson; **D:** Alejandro Amenábar; **W:** Alejandro Amenábar; **C:** Javier Aguirresarobe; **M:** Alejandro Amenábar.

Oubliette 🎬🎬 1914 A peripheral version of François Villon, in what is a recently discovered and restorec film, the earliest extant Chaney film. **35m/B VHS.** Lon Chaney Sr., Murdock MacQuarrie, Pauline Bush, Doc (Harry F.) Crane, Chester Withey; **D:** Charles Giblyn; **W:** H.G. Stafford; **C:** Lee Bartholomew.

Our Brand Is Crisis 🎬🎬 2005 Unsettling documentary follows the American political consultancy firm of Greenberg Carville and Shrum as they work on the 2002 Bolivian presidential campaign. Their candidate is unpopular former president Gonzalo Sanchez de Lozada, and the consultants work to spin him as the new and improved version, with the focus ("brand") being that Bolivia is in crisis and needs an experienced politco at the helm. English and Spanish with subtitles. **87m/C DVD, US** **D:** Rachel Boynton; **C:** Michael Ancerson, Tom Hurwitz, Christine Burrill, Jerr Risius; **M:** Marcelo Zavros.

Our Daily Bread 🎬🎬🎬 *Miracle of Life* 1934 Vidor's sequel to the 1928 "The Crowd." A young couple inherit a farm during the Depression and succeed in managing the land. A near-classic, with several sequences highly influenced by directors Alexander Dovshenko and Sergei Eisenstein. Director Vidor also co-scripted this film, risking bankruptcy to finance it. **80m/B VHS, DVD** Karen Morley, Tom Keene, John Qualen, Barbara Pepper, Addison Richards; **D:** King Vidor; **W:** King Vidor, Elizabeth Hill; **C:** Robert Planck.

Our Dancing Daughters 🎬🎬½ 1928 Flapper (Crawford on the brink of stardom) falls hard for millionaire who's forced into arranged marriage, but obliging little missus kicks bucket so Crawford can step in. **98m/B VHS** Joan Crawford, Johnny Mack Brown, Nils Asther, Dorothy Sebastian, Anita Page; **D:** Harry Beaumont; **C:** George Barnes.

Our Family Business 🎬🎬 1981 TV pilot; this generally plodding "Godfather"-type story is saved by good performances by Wanamaker and Milland. **74m/C VHS, DVD.** Sam Wanamaker, Vera Miles, Ray Milland, Ted Danson, Chip (Christopher) Mayer; **D:** Robert E. Collins; **M:** TV.

Our Hospitality 🎬🎬🎬 1923 One of Keaton's finest silent films, with all the elements in place. William McKay (Keaton) travels to the American South on a quaint train (a near-exact replica of the Stephenson Rocket), to claim an inheritance as the last survivor of his family. En route, a young woman traveler informs him that her family has had a long, deadly feud with his, and that they intent to kill him. McKay resolves to get the inheritance, depending on the Southern rule of hospitality to guests to save his life until he can make his escape. Watch for the river scene somewhere, during filming, Keaton's own discovers when his two kids, 7m/C DVD, IT Buster Keaton, Joe Keaton, Joe Roberts, Monte (Monty) Collins; **D:** John Blystone, Buster Keaton; **W:** Jean C., Havez, Joseph A. Mitchell, Clyde Bruckman; **C:** Elgin Lessley, Gordon Jennings.

Our Italian Husband 🎬½ 2004 (PG-13) Lame comedy. Vincenzo is a struggling artist, living with his pregnant American wife Charlene in New York. Ex-writer, who has returned to his hometown of Medellín, Colombia to die. After 30 years away, Fernando discovers a crime-ridden city with drug trafficking, gangs, and violence to be the norm. At a party, Fernando is introduced to 16-year-old street tough Alexis (Ballesteros), who soon moves in with him. But when Alexis's past catches up with him, Fernando seeks the truth in a city of lies. Not for the faint-hearted; Spanish with subtitles. **98m/C VHS, DVD. CL FR** German Jaramillo, Anderson Ballesteros, Juan David Restrepo, Manuel Busquets; **D:** Barbet Schroeder; **W:** Fernando Vallejo; **C:** Fodrigo Lalinde; **M:** Jorge Arriagada.

Our Little Girl 🎬🎬 1935 (PG) A precocious little tyke tries to reunite her estranged parents by running away to their favorite vacation spot. Sure to please Shirley Temple fans, despite a lackluster script. **65m/B VHS.** Shirley Temple, Joel McCrea, Rosemary Ames, Lyle Talbot, Erin O'Brien-Moore; **D:** John S. Robertson.

Our Man Flint 🎬🎬 1966 James Bond clone Derek Flint uses gadgets and his ingenuity to save the world from an evil organization, GALAXY, that seeks world domination through control of the weather. The plot moves quickly around many bikini-clad women, but still strains for effect. Spawned one sequel: "In Like Flint." **107m/C VHS, DVD** James Coburn, Lee J. Cobb, Gila Golan, Edward Mulhare, Benson Fong, Shelby Grant, Sigrid Valdis, Gianna Serra, James Brolin, Helen Funai, Michael St. Clair; **D:** Daniel Mann; **W:**

Our Lady of the Assassins 🎬🎬 *La Virgen de los Sicarios* 2001 (R) Based on Vallejo's 1994 autobiographical novel, the film follows Fernando (Jaramillo), an older gay man and a writer.

129m/C VHS, DVD. Juliette Lewis, Giovanni Ribisi, Diane Keaton, Tom Skerritt, Poppy Montgomery, Linda Thorson, Juliet Mills, Héctor Elizondo, Sarah Paulson, Joe Flanigan, Dina Merrill; **D:** Garry Marshall; **W:** Garry Marshall, Bob Brunner; **C:** Dante Spinotti; **M:** Rachel Portman.

Hal Fimberg, Ben Starr; **C:** Daniel F. Fapp; **M:** Jerry Goldsmith.

Our Man in Havana 🐾🐾🐾 1959 Excellent noir—with plenty of veddy British black comedy—has ordinary, but not very successful, Havana-based vacuum salesman Guinness joining the British spy service to make some extra money. He begins spinning elaborate tales of intrigue to justify himself, and his lies eventually spiral out of control and into some very real, very dangerous situations. Kovacs, Richardson, and Coward stand out among a great cast. See "The Tailor of Panama" for a post-Cold War re-telling of the tale, but see this one first. 111m/B VHS, DVD, GB Alec Guinness, Burl Ives, Maureen O'Hara, Noel Coward, Ernie Kovacs, Ralph Richardson, Jo Morrow, Paul Rogers, Gregoire Aslan, Joseph Prieto, Timothy Bateson, Duncan MacRae, Maurice Denham, Raymond Huntley, Ferdinand "Ferdy" Mayne, Rachel Roberts; **D:** Carol Reed; **W:** Graham Greene; **C:** Oswald Morris.

Our Miss Brooks 🐾🐾 1956 Quietly pleasing version of the TV series. Miss Brooks pursues the "mother's boy" biology professor. The father of the child she begins tutoring appears taken with her. The professor sees notice. 85m/B VHS, Eve Arden, Gale Gordon, Nick Adams, Richard Crenna, Don Porter; **D:** Al Lewis.

Our Modern Maidens 🐾🐾½ 1929 Scandalous jazz-age drama in which Crawford and Fairbanks both fall in love with other people before their wedding is to take place. This sequel to "Our Dancing Daughters" features beautiful gowns and lush, opulent Art Deco interiors. Based on a story by Josephine Lovett. 75m/B VHS, Joan Crawford, Rod La Rocque, Douglas Fairbanks Jr., Anita Page, Josephine Dunn; **D:** Jack Conway; **W:** Josephine Lovett.

Our Mother's Murder 🐾🐾½ 1997 (PG-13) Title says it all in this drama based on the true story of publishing heiress Anne Scripps Douglas (Hart) who, in 1989, marries volatile young carpenter, Scott (Wilder), and begins an abusive four-year marriage that will end with her beating death in 1993. Scripps Douglas's two daughters by her first marriage, Alexandra and Annie (portrayed on screen by Clarke and Combs), cooperated with the production. 92m/C VHS. Roxanne Hart, Holly Marie Combs, Sarah Chalke, James Wilder, Jonathan Scarfe; **D:** Bill W.L. Norton; **W:** Richard De Long Adams. **CABLE**

Our Music 🐾🐾 *Our Musique* 2004 Godard divides his film into three kingdoms, using Dante's "The Divine Comedy" as his structure. First there's Hell, with a montage showing war and genocide throughout history. Next is the longest section, Purgatory, set in Sarajevo at a literary conference where we meet Israeli journalist Judith (Adler), and Olga (Dieu), a Russian Jew now living in Israel, and the theme is reconciliation and sacrifice. Then we get to Heaven, which again features Olga under very different circumstances. If you're a Godard fan, you'll know what strangeness you're getting into; others beware. French with subtitles. 80m/C DVD. **FR** S/ Nade Dieu, Sarah Adler; **D:** Jean-Luc Godard; **W:** Jean-Luc Godard; **C:** Julien Hirsch, Jean-Christophe Beauvallet.

Our Mutual Friend 🐾🐾½ 1998 Charles Dickens's last completed novel follows the complicated saga of John Harmon (Mackintosh), who must consent to a prearranged marriage if he's to inherit a fortune. But when fate allows Harmon to assume a new identity, he decides to see what anonymity will bring him. Meanwhile, Harmon's life and death also brings together low-born Lizzie Hexum and wastrel lawyer Eugene Wrayburn, who develops an unexpected affection for the lovely young woman. On 3 cassettes. 339m/C VHS. **GB** Steven Mackintosh, Anna Friel, Paul McGann, Keeley Hawes, David Morrissey, Dominic Mafham, Peter Vaughan, Pam Ferris, Kenneth Cranham, Timothy Spall, David Bradley, Margaret Tyzack; **D:** Julian Farino; **W:** Sandy Welch; **C:** David Odd; **M:** Adrian Johnston. **TV**

Our Relations 🐾🐾½ 1936 Confusion reigns when Stan and Ollie meet the twin brothers they never knew they had, a pair of happy-go-lucky sailors. Laurel directs the pair through madcap encounters with their twins' wives and the local underworld. One of the pair's best efforts, though not well-remembered. Based on a story by W.W. Jacobs. 94m/B VHS, Stan Laurel, Oliver Hardy, Alan Hale, Sidney Toler, James Finlayson, Daphne Pollard; **D:** Harry Lachman.

Our Song 🐾🐾 2001 (R) Not your average teen drama. McKay's second dramatic feature concerning the troubled lives of adolescent girls faced with tough choices is a quietly affecting, poetic and solid effort. First-time actors Washington, Simpson and Martinez bring poignancy and realism to their roles as high school friends living in the Brooklyn projects and rehearsing for a marching band competition. The expected issues are present, but the film's treatment of them is what makes it unique. Bold in its way of forgoing major plot drama in favor of finding powerful moments in small places and offering food for thought. Real-life marching band the Jackie Robinson Steppers, who were the inspiration for the film, provide a focal point for the story and punch to the mostly languid pacing. 96m/C VHS, DVD. US Kerry Washington, Anna Simpson, Melissa Martinez, Marlene Forte, Rosalyn Coleman, Ray Anthony Thomas, D'Monroe, Kim Howard, Carmen Lopez; **D:** Jim McKay; **W:** Jim McKay; **C:** Jim Denault.

Our Sons 🐾🐾½ 1991 Two middle-aged moms strike up an unlikely friendship over their gay sons in this TV weeper. Arkansas waitress Luanna (Ann Margret) hasn't talked to son Donald (Ivanek) in years—now he's dying of AIDS. Successful career woman Audrey (Andrews in her TV-movie debut) has seemingly accepted son James' (Grant) life with Donald and it's James who urges his mother to make contact with Luanna and persuade her to see Donald one last time. 100m/C VHS, DVD. Julie Andrews, Ann-Margret, Hugh Grant, Zeljko Ivanek, Tony Roberts; **D:** John Erman; **W:** John Erman, William Hanley.

Our Time 🐾🐾 1974 *Death of Her Innocence* An exclusive girls finishing school in the '50s is the setting for the friendship of Abby (Martin) and Muffy (Slade) and their first stirrings of romance. But when Muffy gets pregnant, tragedy awaits. Sappy. 91m/C VHS. Pamela Sue Martin, Betsy Slade, Parker Stevenson, George O'Hanlon Jr., Roderick Cook, Edith Atwater, Meg Wyllie, Debralee Scott, Nora Heflin, Kathryn Holcomb, Robert Walden, Helene Winston; **D:** Peter Hyams; **W:** Jane C. Stanton.

Our Town 🐾🐾🐾 1940 Small-town New England life in Grover's Corners in the early 1900s is celebrated in this well-performed and directed adaptation of the Pulitzer Prize-winning play by Thornton Wilder. Film debut of Scott. 90m/B VHS, DVD. Martha Scott, William Holden, Thomas Mitchell, Fay Bainter, Guy Kibbee, Beulah Bondi, Frank Craven; **D:** Sam Wood; **W:** Harry Chandlee, Frank Craven; **C:** Bert Glennon; **M:** Aaron Copland.

Our Town 🐾🐾 1977 TV version of Thornton Wilder's classic play about everyday life in Grovers Corners, a small New England town at the turn of the century. It hews more closely to the style of the stage version than the earlier film version. 120m/C VHS, DVD. Ned Beatty, Sada Thompson, Ronny Cox, Glynnis O'Connor, Robby Benson, Hal Holbrook, John Houseman; **D:** Franklin J. Schaffner. **TV**

Our Town 🐾🐾½ 1989 Filmed TV version of the Tony Award-winning Lincoln Center production of the Thornton Wilder play focusing on small-town life in Grover's Corners, New Hampshire. Gray is the omniscient Stage Manager, with Stolz and Miller as the young couple brought together by the everyday cycle of happiness and hardship. 104m/C VHS, DVD. Eric Stoltz, Penelope Ann Miller, Spalding Gray; **D:** Gregory Mosher.

Our Town 🐾🐾½ 2003 Filmed version of the 1938 Thornton Wilder play as staged by the Westport County Playhouse. Newman makes his first stage appearance in nearly 40 years as the Stage Manager, who narrates the story of the townspeople of Grover's Corners, New Hampshire at the turn of the 20th century. At the play's heart are Emily Webb and George Gibbs, who will grow up, marry, and start a family with tragic results as the ghosts of the town watch the lives of those they've left behind. 120m/C DVD. Paul Newman, Margaret Lacey, Frank Converse, Jayne Atkinson, Jeffrey DeMunn, Jane Curtin, Stephen Spinella, Mia Dillon; **D:** James Naughton; **W:** Thornton Wilder. **CABLE**

Our Very Own 🐾🐾 1950 At 18, and about to graduate from high school, Gail (Blyth) discovers she was adopted. So she decides to find her birth mother and then comes to realize what her foster parents really mean to her. Pretty sappy all the way 'round. 93m/B VHS. Ann Blyth, Jane Wyatt, Donald Cook, Farley Granger, Ann Dvorak, Joan Evans, Natalie Wood, Martin Milner, Phyllis Kirk; **D:** David Miller; **W:** F. Hugh Herbert; **C:** Lee Garmes; **M:** Victor Young.

Our Vines Have Tender Grapes 🐾🐾🐾½ 1945 A change of pace role for the volatile Robinson who plays a kind Norwegian farmer, living in Wisconsin with his daughter, the spunky O'Brien. The film is made-up of small-town moments as O'Brien learns a few of life's lessons, eased by the thoughtful compassion of Robinson. Based on the novel "For Our Vines Have Tender Grapes" by George Victor Martin. 105m/B VHS. Edward G. Robinson, Margaret O'Brien, James Craig, Agnes Moorehead, Jackie "Butch" Jenkins, Morris Carnovsky, Frances Gifford, Sara Haden, Louis Jean Heydt; **D:** Roy Rowland; **W:** Dalton Trumbo; **C:** Robert L. Surtees.

Out 🐾🐾½ 1988 A drifter's travels throughout the U.S. from the '60s to the '80s. Successfully manages to satirize just about every conceivable situation but keeps from posturing by not taking itself too seriously. Adapted from an experimental novel by Ronald Sukenick. 88m/C VHS, DVD. Peter Coyote, Danny Glover, O-Lan Shepard, Jim Haynie, Scott Beach, Semu Haute; **D:** Eli Hollander; **M:** David Cope.

Out Cold 🐾🐾 1989 (R) Black comedy follows the misadventures of a butcher who believes he has accidentally frozen his business partner; the iced man's girlfriend, who really killed him; and the detective who tries to solve the crime. Too many poor frozen body jokes may have the viewer cold. 91m/C VHS, DVD. John Lithgow, Teri Garr, Randy Quaid, Bruce McGill; **D:** Malcolm Mowbray; **M:** Michel Colombier.

Out Cold 🐾🐾 2001 (PG-13) Dumb snowboarding comedy (the snowboarding scenes are the only cool things about the movie) focuses on a ragged ski resort in Bull Mountain, Alaska that developer Jack Majors (Majors) wants to turn into a family-oriented resort. That means getting rid of the resort's raucous loser employees, including Rick (London) and his buddies. 90m/C VHS, DVD. Jason London, Willie Garson, Lee Majors, A.J. Cook, Derek Hamilton, Zach Galifianakis, Flex Alexander, Caroline Dhavernas, Victoria Silvestedt; **D:** Brendan Malloy, Emmett Malloy; **W:** Jon Zack; **C:** Richard Crudo; **M:** Michael Andrews.

Out for Blood 🐾🐾 1993 (R) Attorney John Decker is living a happy life until his family is murdered by drug dealers. He turns vigilante, dubbed "Karateman" by the press, and finds himself hunted by the cops and the criminals. 90m/C VHS, DVD. Don "The Dragon" Wilson, Shari Shattuck, Michael Delano, Kenneth McLeod, Todd Curtis, Timothy Baker, Howard Jackson, Bob Schott, Eric Lee; **D:** Richard W. Munchkin; **W:** David S. Green.

Out for Justice 🐾🐾½ 1991 (R) A psycho Brooklyn hood goes on a murder spree, and homeboy turned lone-wolf cop Seagal races other police and the mob to get at him. Bloodthirsty and profane, it does try to depict N.Y.C.'s Italian-American community—but 90 percent of them are dead by the end so what's the point? Better yet, why does it open with a quote from Arthur Miller? Better still, what's Daffy Duck doing on this tape peddling Warner Bros. T-shirts to kid viewers?! 91m/C VHS, DVD, Blu-ray Disc, HD DVD. Dominic Chianese, Steven Seagal, William Forsythe, Jerry Orbach, Julianna Margulies, Gina Gershon, John Leguizamo, Julie Strain; **D:** John Flynn; **W:** David Lee Henry; **C:** Ric Waite; **M:** David Michael Frank.

Out in Fifty 🐾🐾½ 1999 (R) Con is released from prison only to be pursued by a psycho detective who wants him back in the slammer and a mystery babe who has her own plans for the guy. 95m/C VHS, DVD. Mickey Rourke, Bojesse Christopher, Christina Applegate, Scott Leet, Balthazar Getty, Peter Greene; **D:** Bojesse Christopher, Scott Leet.

VIDEO

Out of Africa 🐾🐾🐾 1985 (PG) An epic film of the years spent by Danish authoress Isak Dinesen (her true name is Karen Blixen) on a Kenya coffee plantation. She moved to Africa to marry, and later fell in love with Denys Finch-Hatten, a British adventurer. Based on several books, including biographies of the two lovers. Some critics loved the scenery and music; others despised the acting and the script. A definite "no" for those who love action. 161m/C VHS, DVD. Meryl Streep, Robert Redford, Klaus Maria Brandauer, Michael Kitchen, Malick Bowens, Michael Gough, Suzanna Hamilton, Rachel Kempson, Graham Crowden, Shane Rimmer, Donal McCann, Iman, Joseph Thiaka, Stephen Kinyanjui; **D:** Sydney Pollack; **W:** Kurt Luedtke; **C:** David Watkin; **M:** John Barry. Oscars '85: Adapt. Screenplay, Art Dir./Set Dec., Cinematog., Director (Pollack), Picture, Sound, Orig. Score; British Acad. '86: Adapt. Screenplay; Golden Globes '86: Film—Drama, Support. Actor (Brandauer), Score; L.A. Film Critics '85: Actress (Streep), Cinematog.; Natl. Bd. of Review '85: Support. Actor (Brandauer); N.Y. Film Critics '85: Cinematog., Support. Actor (Brandauer).

Out of Annie's Past 🐾🐾½ 1994 (R) Successful career woman Annie Carver (Stewart) has managed to hide a dreadful secret from family and co-workers for some 10 years. But now the past is back to haunt her—seems Annie was once the prime suspect in a murder. 91m/C VHS. Catherine Mary Stewart, Dennis Farina, Scott Valentine, Carsten Norgaard, Michael Flynn; **D:** Stuart Cooper; **W:** Pablo F. Fenjves. **CABLE**

Out of Bounds 🐾🐾½ 1986 (R) An Iowa farmboy picks up the wrong bag at the Los Angeles airport, and is plunged into a world of crime, drugs, and murder. Plenty of action, but the fast pace can't hide huge holes in the script or the silliness of Hall playing a tough kid on the run from the law. 93m/C VHS. Anthony Michael Hall, Jenny Wright, Jeff Kober; **D:** Richard Tuggle; **C:** Bruce Surtees; **M:** Stewart Copeland.

Out of Control 🐾🐾 1985 (R) A plane full of rich teenagers crash on a secluded island and must battle a gang of vicious smugglers to survive. A teen sex theme keeps working its way in, leaving the viewer as confused as the actors and actresses appear to be. 78m/C VHS. Betsy Russell, Martin Hewitt, Claudia Udy, Andrew J. Lederer; **D:** Allan Holzman; **W:** Vicangelo Bulluck; **C:** John A. Alonzo.

Out of Order 🐾🐾 1984 A German-made film about people stuck in an office building's malevolent, free-thinking elevator. Dubbed. 87m/C VHS. GE Renee Soutendijk, Goetz George, Wolfgang Kieling, Hannes Jaenicke; **D:** Carl Schenkel.

Out of Order 🐾🐾 2003 (R) The pilot episode of the Showtime series finds Stoltz and Huffman starring as a long-married, successful Hollywood screenwriting couple Mark and Lorna Colm. Lorna is going through a deep depression, which leaves Mark caring for their son and vulnerable to the unhappily married Danni (Dickens). Meanwhile, Lorna finds some solace with bitter best pal Steven (Macy), a not very successful producer. 97m/C VHS, DVD. Eric Stoltz, Felicity Huffman, Kim Dickens, William H. Macy, Justine Bateman, Peter Bogdanovich; **D:** Wayne Powers; **W:** Wayne Powers, Donna Powers. **CABLE**

Out of Season 🐾🐾 *Winter Rates* 1975 (R) Mother and teenage daughter compete for the attentions of the mother's mysterious ex-lover. We never know who wins the man in this enigmatic drama set

Out of Sight ✗✗✗ 1998 (R) Cerebral director Soderbergh turns up the heat in this fine adaptation (with fine performances) of the Elmore Leonard crime caper. Jack Foley (Clooney) is a charming bank robber who's current one being served in a Florida pen from which he escapes with the aid of partner Buddy (Rhames). Even the escape doesn't go as planned since federal marshal Karen Sisco (Lopez) becomes an unexpected (temporary) hostage. Sparks fly between the duo but Karen's still determined to bring Jack to justice, even as he plans his next heist. A heist involving shady financier Richard Ripley (Brooks) that will take Jack and Buddy to Detroit and more complications. **122m/C** VHS, DVD, HD DVD, GB *C:* George Clooney, Jennifer Lopez, Ving Rhames, Don Cheadle, Albert Brooks, Steve Zahn, Dennis Farina, Catherine Keener, Luis Guzman, Isaiah Washington IV, Keith Loneker, Nancy Allen; *Cameos:* Michael Keaton, Samuel L. Jackson; *D:* Steven Soderbergh; *W:* Scott Frank; *C:* Elliot Davis; *M:* Cliff Martinez. Natl. Soc. Film Critics '98: Director (Soderbergh), Film, Screenplay; Writers Guild '98: Adapt. Screenplay.

Out of Sight, Out of Her Mind ✗✗ *Cut of Sight, Out of Mind* 1989 (R) After witnessing her daughter burned alive, Alice is released from a mental institution. She tries to start a new life, but her daughter won't stay dead. She keeps appearing, crying out for help. Hip-hop soundtrack may provide the only interest. **105m/C** VHS, DVD, LL Cool J, Victoria Dillard, Howard Hessman Ramy Zada, Don Yesso, Yaphet Kotto; *D:* Debbie Allen; *W:* Robert E. Dorn; *C:* Nicholas Mankowski; *M:* Steve Tyrell.

Out of the Black ✗✗1/2 2001 In 1976, 10-year-old Cole Walby is told to forgive everything he thinks he saw regarding the death of his Pennsylvania coal miner father and the shooting that paralyzed his mother (Kirkland). Thirteen years later, Cole (Christopher) and his younger brother Patrick (Widener) struggle on the family farm and decide it's past time to find out the truth. Naturally, there are a lot of people determined to make the brothers sorry for their interference. **105m/C** VHS, DVD, TV *C:* Sally Kirkland, Dee Wallace Stone, Jason J. Pollard, Miles O'Keeffe, Sally Struthers, Allison Lange, John Capodice, Tom Atkins; *D:* Karl Kozak; *W:* Karl Kozak, Joel Eisenberg; *C:* Maximo Munzi; *M:* Lawrence Nash Groupe.

Out of the Blue ✗✗✗ 1947

Out of the Blue ✗✗1/2 1980 (R) A harsh, violent portrait of a shattered family. When an imprisoned father's return fails to reunite this Woodstock-generation family, the troubled teenage daughter takes matters into her own hands. "Easy Rider" star Hopper seems to have reconsidered the effects of the 1960s. **94m/C** VHS, DVD, Dennis Hopper, Linda Manz, Raymond Burr, Don Gordon; *D:* Dennis Hopper *C:* Marc Champion; *M:* Tom Lavin.

Out of the Body ✗ 1988 (R) A man is possessed by a spirit that likes to kill young, beautiful women. This makes him (and the viewer) uncomfortable. **91m/C** VHS. AU: Mark Hembrow, Tessa Humphries, John Clayton, John Ley, Carrie Zivetz, Linda Newton; *D:*

in an English village, and hints of incest make the story even murkier. Had only a short run in the U.S. **90m/C** VHS, DVD, GB George; *D:* Alan Bridges.

Cliff Robertson, Vanessa Redgrave, Susan

Out of Sync ✗1/2 1995 (R) Deejay Jason St. Julian gets in trouble with his bookies and L.A. detectives, one of whom forces him into an undercover job with a drug-dealing club owner. Then Jason falls for the dealer's girlfriend. Hip-hop sound-track may provide the only interest. **105m/C** VHS, DVD, LL Cool J, Victoria Dillard, Howard Hessman Ramy Zada, Don Yesso, Yaphet Kotto; *D:* Debbie Allen; *W:* Robert E. Dorn; *C:* Nicholas Mankowski; *M:* Steve Tyrell.

Out of the Cold ✗1/2 1999 (R) Jewish tap dancer Dan Scott (Carradine) decides to take his fading cabaret act to his family's homeland of Estonia on the eve of WWII. Bad idea. Trapped between the Nazis and the Soviets, Dan still finds time to romance local beauty Deborah (Kirshner), although their love affair is cut short by tragedy. Blah film whose plot goes nowhere quickly. **111m/C** VHS, DVD. AU: Keith Carradine, Mia Kirshner, Judd Hirsch, Brian Dennehy, Mercedes Ruehl, Bronson Pinchot, Kim Hunter, Mark Sheppard; *D:* Aleksandr (Sasha) Baranavsky; *W:* Aleksandr (Sasha) Baranavsky; *C:* Vladimir Klimov; *M:* Maksim Dunayevsky.

Brian Trenchard-Smith; *W:* Kenneth Ross; *C:* Kevan Lind; *M:* Peter Westheimer.

Out of the Dark ✗1/2 1988 (R) The female employees of a telephone-sex service are stalked by a killer wearing a clown mask in this tongue-in-cheek thriller. A few laughs amid the slaughter. Look for Divine. **96m/C** VHS, Cameron Dye, Divine, Karen Black, Bud Cort, Lynn Danielson, Geoffrey Lewis, Paul Bartel, Tracey Walter, Silvana Gallardo, Starr Andreeff, Lainie Kazan, Tab Hunter, John DeBello; *D:* Michael Schroeder; *W:* James DeFelice, Zane W. Levitt; *C:* Julio Macat; *M:* Paul Antonelli, David Wheatley.

Out of the Darkness ✗✗✗ 1985 (R) TV movie about the personal life of the New York detective who hunted and arrested sexual killer Son of Sam. Sheen shines in a tight suspenser. **96m/C** VHS. Martin Sheen, Hector Elizondo, Matt Clark, Jennifer Salt, Eddie Egan, Robert Trebor; *D:* Jud Taylor; *W:* T.S. Cook. TV

Out of the Past ✗✗✗1/2 *Build My Gallows High* 1947 A private detective gets caught in a complex web of love, murder, and money in this film noir classic. The plot is torturous but clear thanks to fine directing. Mitchum became an overnight star after this film, which was overlooked but now considered one of the best in its genre. Based on Daniel Homes's novel as "Against All Odds." "Build My Gallows High." Remade in 1984 as "Against All Odds." **97m/B** VHS, DVD. Robert Mitchum, Kirk Douglas, Jane Greer, Rhonda Fleming, Steve Brodie, Dickie Moore, Richard Webb, Virginia Huston, Ken Niles, Paul Valentine; *D:* Jacques Tourneur; *W:* Daniel Mainwaring, Geoffrey Homes; *C:* Nicholas Musuraca; *M:* Roy Webb. Natl. Film Reg. '91.

Out of the Rain ✗✗ 1990 (R) A small town becomes a hotbed of deceit and lies due to the influence of drugs. A man and and a woman engage in a passionate struggle to free themselves from the town's grip. **91m/C** VHS. Bridget Fonda, John E. O'Keefe, John Seitz, Michael O'Keefe, Al Shannon; *C:* Gary Winick; *M:* Shem Bitterman.

Out of the Shadows ✗✗✗ 1988. Scotland Yard Chief Inspector Michael Hayden (Dance) investigates a series of international art thefts that lead him to believe the goods are being smuggled out of the country through diplomatic channels. **95m/C** VHS, GB Charles Dance, Alexandra Paul, Wanda Ventham; *D:* Will Patterson. TV

Out of Time ✗1/2 2000 Dull update of the Rip Van Winkle legend. While waking in the woods outside his small Oregon town, Jack Epson (McDaniels) takes a drink from a spring and falls asleep for 20 years. He wakes up to find his natural surroundings are under siege from developers and his now-grown daughter has a child of her own. **94m/C** VHS, DVD, James McDaniel, Mel Harris, August Schellenberg, Ken Pogue; *D:* Ernest Thompson; *W:* Ernest Thompson, Rob Gilmer; *C:* Stephen McNift; *M:* Terry Frewer. CABLE

Out of Time ✗✗1/2 2003 (PG-13) Far-fetched thriller gets by on the charms of its lead. Matt Lee Whitlock (Washington) is an easy-going police chief in a sleepy Florida town who is having an affair with Ann (Lathan), who's married to jealous Chris (Cain). Ann reveals she has cancer and Matt decides to "borrow" money he recovered in a drug bust and give it to Ann to help with her treatment. Then, there's a mysterious fire, a couple of charred bodies, and soon Matt is trying to

Out on a Limb ✗✗ 1992 (PG) Lame comedy follows the misadventures o f financial whiz Bill Campbell (Broderick). His young sister is convinced their stepfather is a criminal and persuades her brother to return home. On his way, Bill is robbed and abandoned by a woman hitchhiker, then found by two moronic brothers. It also turns out his stepfather has a twin brother who wants revenge for past crimes. Frantic chase scenes and lots of noise do not a comedy make. Broderick and Jones also appeared together in "Ferris Bueller's Day Off." **82m/C** VHS. Matthew Broderick, Jeffrey Jones, Heidi Kling, John C. Reilly, Marian Mercer, Larry Hankin, David Margulies; *D:* Francis Veber.

Out on Bail ✗✗ 1989 (R) A law-abiding citizen witnesses a murder, only to discover the crooked town council is behind the slaying. **102m/C** VHS. Robert Ginty, Kathy Shower, Tom Badal, Sydney Lassick; *D:* Gordon Hessler; *W:* Tom Badal, Jason Booth.

Out There ✗✗1/2 1995 (PG-13) Cable sci-fi comedy finds photographer Delbert Mosley (Campbell) buying a Brownie camera at a garage sale and discovering the 25-year-old film shows pictures of a UFO encounter. Mosley then tries to verify the photos with a supermarket tabloid, the military, and UFO fanatics all on his trail. Fast-paced amusement with appealing performances. **98m/C** VHS. Richard Spright Jr., Billy Campbell, Wendy Schaal, Julie Brown, David Rasche, Paul Dooley, Bill Cobbs, Bobcat Goldthwait, Rod Steiger, June Lockhart, Jill St. John, Carel Struycken, Billy Bob Thornton, P.J. Soles; *D:* Sam Irvin; *W:* Thomas Strelich, Alison Nigh; *C:* Gary Tieche; *M:* Deborah Holland, Frank e Blue.

Out on a Limb ✗✗ 1987 Laine plays herself in this miniseries based on her best-selling book by the same name. In the midst of love affairs with an unnamed British politician and a mysterious teacher, she learns about her past, present and future through reincarnation. Features footage of psychics performing spiritual channeling. Beautiful scenery filmed on location in California, Hong Kong, London, Hawaii, Sweden, and Peru, but the acting is just average, and the movie is slow in some parts. **150m/C** VHS, Shirley MacLaine, Charles Dance, Anne Jackson, Jerry Orbach; *D:* Robert Butler. TV

The Out-of-Towners ✗✗✗ 1970 (G) A pair of Ohio rubes travels to New York City and along the way every-thing that could go wrong does. Lemmon's performance is excellent and Simon's script is, as usual, both wholesome and funny. **98m/C** VHS, DVD, Jack Lemmon, Sandy Dennis, Anne Meara, Sandy Baron, Billy Dee Williams; *D:* Arthur Hiller; *W:* Neil Simon. Writers Guild '70: Orig. Screenplay.

The Out-of-Towners ✗✗ 1999 Henry Clark, middle-aged Ohio empty-nesters headed for Henry's job interview in New York. Along the way, they're thwarted by every tourist nightmare obstacle imaginable: rerouting to Boston, missed trains, rental car mishaps, muggings, maxed credit cards, snooty hotel personnel, etc. Martin's seen all this before (in "Planes, Trains and Automobiles") and so have we, in any number of movies, including the original 1970 Neil Simon script. Mostly uninspired and inconsistent with flashes of fine physical comedy from Hawn and Martin. Cleese plays a needlessly pompous hotel manager. **92m/C** VHS, DVD, Mark McKinney, Goldie Hawn, Steve Martin, John Cleese, Oliver Hudson; *D:* Sam Weisman; *W:* Marc Lawrence; *C:* John Bailey; *M:* Marc Shaiman.

The Outcast ✗1/2 1984 Story of three brothers who live by the ax, love from the heart, hate with passion, and die violently. Trouble is they have to recite their screenplay's "The Coming Plague." **128m/C** VHS, DVD. Dustin Hoffman, Rene Russo, Morgan Freeman, Donald Sutherland, Cuba Gooding Jr., Kevin Spacey, J.T. Walsh, Dale Dye; *D:* Wolfgang Petersen; *W:* Laurence Dworet, Robert Roy Pool; *C:* Michael Ballhaus; *M:* James Newton Howard, N.Y. Film Critics '95. Support.

The Outcast ✗✗ 1954 A young tough heads west to seize the family ranch wrongfully held by a conniving uncle. Of course he finds love as well, and enjoys gun and fistfights in this exciting cle. **90m/C** VHS. John Derek, Jim Davis, Joan Davis; *D:* William Witney.

Outcasts of the City ✗✗✗ 1958

The Outcasts ✗✗✗ 1986 A Taiwanese film about young gay boys in an urban jungle who are given shelter and protection by an aging photographer. In Chinese with English subtitles. **102m/C** VHS, TW *D:* Yu-Kan-Ping.

Outcasts of the Trail ✗✗1/2 1949

Outbreak ✗✗✗ 1994 (R) Smuggled African monkey spits on someone who kisses someone else who sneezes on a bunch of people, thus initiating the spread of a highly infectious mystery disease in a northern California town. Crusading two-man team of scientists is in a search for the anti-serum, but it's a secret government plot to exterminate the victims that literally sends Hoffman and crew into action movie cliché overdrive (add "helicopter" to the list of chase scene vehicles). Based on Richard Preston's "The Hot Zone" and Laurie Garratt's "The Coming Plague." **128m/C** VHS, DVD. Dustin Hoffman, Rene Russo, Morgan Freeman, Donald Sutherland, Cuba Gooding Jr., Kevin Spacey, J.T. Walsh, Dale Dye; *D:* Wolfgang Petersen.

Out to Sea ✗✗1/2 1997 (PG-13) Charlie (Matthau) persuades brother-in-law Herb (Lemmon) to become a dance instructor aboard a cruise ship so they can meet women and con them out of money. Charlie sets his sights on feisty socialite Liz (Cannon), while Herb romances Vivian (DeHaven), who's tagging along on her daughter's honeymoon. Both of these "salty old dogs" have to avoid the wrath of militaristic cruise director Gil (Spiner). The duo still has great comic timing, as they continue to defy the odds that this is the one that's gonna flop. Great supporting cast which includes O'Connor in a couple of nifty dance scenes, seems to be having a great time. **106m/C** VHS, DVD, Joe (Johnny) Viterelli, Walter Matthau, Jack Lemmon, Dyan Cannon, Gloria De Haven, Brent Spiner, Elaine Stritch, Hal Linden, Donald O'Connor, Edward Mulhare, Rue McClanahan; *D:* Martha Coolidge; *W:* Robert Nelson Jacobs, Danny Jacobson; *C:* Lajos Koltai; *M:* David Newman.

The Outer Limits: Sandkings ✗✗✗ *Sandkings* 1995 Cable revival of the '60s sci-fi series is creepier than ever with this tale of loony scientist Simon Kress (Bridges). He discovers tiny alien eggs while doing an analysis of

Martian soil samples and decides to take his research home with him when the government cuts off funding. Big mistake—the critters he successfully hatches in his barn are mean and hungry. Features both dad Lloyd and Beau's 10-year-old son, Dylan, in roles. **93m/C VHS.** Beau Bridges, Lloyd Bridges, Helen Shaver, Dylan Bridges, Kim Coates; **D:** Stuart Gillard; **W:** Melinda M. Snodgrass. **CABLE**

The Outfit ♪♪½ **1993 (R)** It's the 1930s and a mob war is brewing between Lucky Luciano, Legs Diamond and Dutch Schultz. A maverick FBI agent gets in good with Diamond and works to end their reign of crime—only he winds up being the spark to light a war between the rival bosses. **92m/C VHS.** John Christian, Billy Drago, Lance Henriksen, Martin Kove, Josh Moby, Rick Washburne; **D:** J. Christian Ingvordsen; **W:** J. Christian Ingvordsen, Steven Kaman, Whitney Ransick.

Outfoxed: Rupert Murdoch's War on Journalism ♪♪♪ **2004** Greenwald's doc rails against what he views as unscrupulous, political bias, and smear-campaign tactics used to further the conservative agenda of Fox News Channel. Uses internal Fox News Department memos to illustrate and ask hard questions about the line between news coverage and commentary. **77m/C DVD. D:** Robert Greenwald; **C:** Bob Sullivan, James Curry, Will Miller, Glen Pearcy, Richard Perez, Luke Rifle, Eugene Thompson; **M:** Nicholas O'Toole.

The Outing ♪♪ *The Lamp* **1987 (R)** A group of high school kids sneaks into a museum at night to party, and get hunted down by a 3,000-year-old genie-in-a-lamp. The genie idea is original enough to make things interesting. Mediocre special effects and run-of-the-mill acting. **87m/C VHS, DVD.** Deborah Winters, James Huston, Andra St. Ivanyi, Scott Bankston, Mark Mitchell, Andre Chimene, Damon Merrill, Barry Coffing; **D:** Tom Daley; **W:** Warren Chaney; **C:** Herbert Raditschnig.

Outing Riley ♪♪ **2004** Chicago architect Bobby Riley (Jones) is a regular guy in his thirties from an Irish-Catholic family. At the urging of his sister (Pearl) and his boyfriend (McDonald), Bobby finally decides to come out to his three brothers. Only they don't believe him. **86m/C DVD.** Pete Jones, Nathan Fillion, Michael McDonald, Stoney Westmoreland, Dev Kennedy, Julie R. Pearl, Dana Gilhooley; **D:** Pete Jones; **W:** Pete Jones; **C:** Pete Biagi.

Outland ♪♪ **1981 (R)** On a volcanic moon of Jupiter, miners begin suffering from spells of insanity. A single federal marshal begins an investigation that threatens the colony's survival. No more or less than a western in space, and the science is rather poor. Might make an interesting double feature with "High Noon," though. **109m/C VHS, DVD.** Kika Markham, Clarke Peters, Steven Berkoff, John Ratzenberger, Manning Redwood, Angus MacInnes, Sean Connery, Peter Boyle, Frances Sternhagen, James B. Sikking; **D:** Peter Hyams; **W:** Peter Hyams; **C:** Stephen Goldblatt; **M:** Jerry Goldsmith.

Outlaw ♪♪½ **2007 (R)** Good Brit cast in a revenge flick with lots and lots (and lots) of violence. Embittered ex-soldier Danny Bryant (Bean) forms a vigilante group after becoming disgusted by the brazenness of the city's criminals and the weakness of the PC judicial system. His recruits have all been victimized by violence and Danny has an inside man with longtime copper Lewis (Hoskins), who passes along information on the whereabouts of various scum that need dealing with. **105m/C DVD. GB** Sean Bean, Bob Hoskins, Danny Dyer, Rupert Friend, Sean Harris, Lennie James; **D:** Nick Love; **W:** Nick Love; **C:** Sam McCurdy; **M:** David Julyan.

The Outlaw and His Wife ♪♪♪½ **1917** An early silent film about a farmer, accused of a petty crime, who flees with his wife into the mountains to escape the police. This powerful drama was a breakthrough film for the early Swedish movie industry. **73m/B VHS. SW** Victor Sjostrom, Edith Erastoff; **D:** Victor Sjostrom.

The Outlaw Bikers—Gang Wars ♪ **1970** The original road warriors take it to the streets as rival biker gangs square off. **90m/C VHS.** Clancy Syrko, Des Roberts, John King III, Linda Jackson; **D:** Laurence Merrick.

Outlaw Blues ♪♪ **1977 (PG)** An ex-convict becomes a national folk hero when he sets out to reclaim his stolen hit song about prison life. St. James is charming in her first major movie role. A grab bag of action, drama, and tongue-in-cheek humor. **101m/C VHS.** Peter Fonda, Susan St. James, Johnny Crawford, Michael Lerner, James Callahan; **D:** Richard T. Heffron; **M:** Charles Bernstein.

Outlaw Country ♪♪½ **1949** LaRue has a dual role as the marshal who is after a band of counterfeiters and an outlaw who's part of the gang. **72m/B VHS.** Lash LaRue, Al "Fuzzy" St. John, House Peters Jr., Ted Adams, Dan(iel) White, Steve Dunhill; **D:** Ray Taylor.

Outlaw Express ♪♪½ **1938** After the annexing of California, a U.S. marshall is sent to stop a gang of outlaws who have been raiding Spanish landowners. **57m/B VHS.** Bob Baker, Cecilia Callejo, Leroy Mason, Don Barclay, Carleton Young; **D:** George Waggner.

The Outlaw Deputy ♪♪ **1935** The law-abiding McCoy as an outlaw! It's really a mistake and Lane helps him clear his name. Based on the story "King of Cactusville" by Johnston McCulley. **55m/B VHS, DVD.** Tim McCoy, Nora Lane, Bud Osborne, Si Jenks, George Offerman Jr.; **D:** Otto Brower.

Outlaw Force ♪ **1987 (R)** A Vietnam country singer tracks down the vicious rednecks that kidnapped his daughter and raped and killed his wife. Heavener did all the work in this low-budget, low-quality take-off on "Death Wish." **95m/C VHS.** David Heavener, Frank Stallone, Paul Smith, Robert Bjorklund, Devin Dunsworth; **D:** David Heavener.

Outlaw Fury ♪ *Hostile Country* **1950** Another Shamrock Ellison epic, this time dealing with a coward proving himself by killing the bad guys. **55m/B VHS.** James Ellison, Russell Hayden, Julie Adams, Raymond Hatton, Tom Tyler, George Lewis, John Cason, Stanley Price, I. Stanford Jolley; **D:** Thomas Carr; **W:** Ron Ormond, Maurice Tombragel; **C:** Ernest Miller.

Outlaw Gang ♪ *The Dalton Gang* **1949** A marshal investigates a rash of rancher killings, leading to a conflict between Indians and local land and water companies. **59m/B VHS.** Donald (Don "Red") Barry, Robert Lowery, Betty Adams, James Millican, Byron Foulger, J. Farrell MacDonald, Greg McClure, George Lewis, Stanley Price, Tom Tyler; **D:** Ford Beebe; **W:** Ford Beebe; **C:** Ernest Miller.

The Outlaw Josey Wales ♪♪♪ **1976 (PG)** Eastwood plays a farmer with a motive for revenge—his family was killed by Union guerillas, and he was betrayed and hunted. His desire to play the lone killer is, however, tempered by his need for family and friends. He kills plenty, but in the end finds peace. Considered one of the last great Western performances, with many superb performances. Eastwood took over directorial chores during filming from Kaufman, who co-scripted. Adapted from "Gone To Texas" by Forest Carter. **135m/C VHS, DVD.** Clint Eastwood, Chief Dan George, Sondra Locke, Matt Clark, John Vernon, Bill McKinney, Sam Bottoms, Will Sampson, Woodrow Parfrey, Royal Dano, John Quade, John Russell, John Mitchum, Kyle Eastwood; **D:** Clint Eastwood; **W:** Philip Kaufman; **C:** Bruce Surtees; **M:** Jerry Fielding. Natl. Film Reg. '96.

Outlaw Justice ♪♪ **1932** Worn oater plot has our hero infiltrating a gang of outlaws to bring them to justice and save the heroine. **56m/C VHS.** Jack Hoxie, Dorothy Gulliver, Donald Keith, Kermit Maynard, Charles "Blackie" King, Tom London; **D:** Armand Schaefer.

Outlaw Justice ♪♪½ **1998 (R)** Aging gunslingers Nelson and Kristofferson meet up with buddy Tritt in order to avenge the death of their old partner. Nothing new storywise but the cast is certainly comfortable with the material. **94m/C VHS, DVD.** Kris Kristofferson, Willie Nelson, Sancho Garcia, Travis Tritt, Chad Willet, Waylon Jennings; **D:** Bill Corcoran; **W:** Gene Quintano; **C:** Federico Ribes; **M:** Jay Gruska. TV

Outlaw of Gor ♪♪½ **1987 (PG)** Once again, the mild professor is transported to Gor, where he has new, improved, bloody adventures. Lots of swordplay, but no magic. Sequel to "Gor." From the novel by John Norman. **89m/C VHS.** Rebecca Ferratti, Urbano Barberini, Jack Palance, Donna Denton; **D:** John Cardos; **W:** R.J. Marx.

Outlaw of the Plains ♪ **1946** Another of Crabbe's cowboy pictures in which he played hero Billy Carson, now bailing his trouble-prone sidekick out of a land swindle. Very plain indeed. **56m/B VHS.** Buster Crabbe, Al "Fuzzy" St. John, Patti McCarty, Charles "Blackie" King, Karl Hackett, John Cason, Bud Osborne, Budd Buster, Charles "Slim" Whitaker; **D:** Sam Newfield.

Outlaw Riders ♪ **1972 (PG)** Three outlaw bikers take it on the lam after committing a series of disastrous bank robberies. **84m/C VHS.** Bryan (Sonny) West, Darlene Duralia, Bambi Allen, Bill Bonner; **D:** Tony Houston.

Outlaw Roundup ♪ **1944** The Texas Rangers battle an outlaw gang. Guess who wins. **51m/B VHS.** Tex O'Brien, James Newill, Guy Wilkerson, Helen Chapman, Jack Ingram, I. Stanford Jolley; **D:** Harry Fraser.

Outlaw Rule ♪♪½ **1936** Standard action-packed western adventure pitting outlaws against the law of the West. **61m/B VHS.** Reb Russell, Betty Mack, Yakima Canutt, Jack Rockwell, John McGuire, Alan Bridge; **D:** S. Roy Luby.

The Outlaw Tamer ♪ **1933** Even though Chandler is on the run he still helps capture some horse thieves. **56m/B VHS, DVD.** Lane Chandler, J(ohn) P(aterson) McGowan, Janet Morgan, George "Gabby" Hayes; **D:** J(ohn) P(aterson) McGowan.

Outlaw Trail ♪♪½ **1944** The Trail Blazers put an end to a counterfeiter's evil ways. **53m/B VHS.** Hoot Gibson, Bob Steele, Chief Thundercloud, Jennifer Holt, Cy Kendall; **D:** Robert Emmett Tansey.

Outlaw Trail ♪♪♪ **2006 (PG)** In 1951, teenager Roy Parker (Kelley) sets out to prove that his late great-uncle was actually Butch Cassidy, who survived a Bolivian ambush to return to the States with a fortune in gold. Roy wants to clear the family name and, thanks to a handy map, find Butch's missing treasure, but he's not the only one looking. Lively family fare. **90m/C DVD.** Ryan Kelley, Arielle Kebbel, Dan Byrd, Bruce McGill, Brian Wimmer, James Gammon, James Karen, Ryan Kelley, Ryan Little; **W:** David Piller; **C:** Geno Salvatori; **M:** J Bateman.

Outlaw Women ♪ **1952** A western town is run by a woman who won't let male outlaws in—one wins her heart. **76m/C VHS.** Marie Windsor, Jackie Coogan, Carla Balenda; **D:** Sam Newfield.

The Outlaws Is Coming! ♪♪♪ **1965** Three magazine staffers (Larry, Moe, and Curly Joe) and their editor (West) encounter Wyatt Earp, Wild Bill Hickock, Jesse James, and Annie Oakley when they journey out West to save the buffalo. Last, and one of the best, of the Three Stooges feature films. **90m/B VHS, DVD.** Moe Howard, Larry Fine, Joe DeRita, Adam West, Nancy Kovack, Emil Sitka, Henry Gibson; **D:** Norman Maurer.

Outlaws of Sonora ♪♪½ **1938** A man transports money to a neighboring town while his outlaw double tries to steal it from him. **58m/B VHS, DVD.** Robert "Bo" Livingston, Ray Corrigan, Max Terhune, Jack Mulhall, Otis Harlan; **D:** George Sherman.

Outlaws of the Desert ♪♪½ **1941** Having run out of bad guys in the Old West, Hoppy and his pals head to Arabia to buy some horses. Once there, they get involved in a kidnapping. Russell Hayden is replaced as Hoppy's sidekick by Brad King. Duncan ("The Cisco Kid") Renaldo plays the sheik. **66m/B VHS, DVD.** William Boyd, Brad King, Andy Clyde, Forrest Stanley, Jean Phillips, Duncan Renaldo, George Lewis; **D:** Howard Bretherton.

Outlaws of the Range ♪♪½ **1936** Action western featuring outlaws who terrorize the countryside. **60m/B VHS, DVD.** Bill Cody, Marie Burton, William (Bill, Billy) McCall, Gordon Griffith; **D:** Al(bert) Herman.

Outlaw's Paradise ♪♪ **1939** Cowboy hero McCoy plays not only a lawman out to catch mail thieves, but also the chief outlaw he's hunting! That's one way to keep the budget low. **62m/B VHS.** Tim McCoy, Ben (Benny) Corbett, Joan Barclay, Ted Adams, Forrest Taylor, Bob Terry; **D:** Sam Newfield.

Outpost in Morocco ♪♪ **1949** A desert soldier is sent to quiet the restless natives and falls for the rebel leader's daughter. The good guys win, but the love interest is sacrificed. Glory before love boys, and damn the story. **92m/B VHS, DVD.** George Raft, Marie Windsor, Akim Tamiroff, John Litel, Eduard Franz; **D:** Robert Florey; **W:** Charles Grayson, Paul de Sainte-Colombe; **C:** Lucien N. Andriot; **M:** Michel Michelet.

Outrage! ♪♪½ **1986** An upstanding citizen guns down his daughter's killer and turns himself in to police. His ambitious lawyer fights an open-and-shut homicide case with both fair and foul means. Not a shootout like the cassette box suggests, but an okay courtroom drama attacking excesses of the legal system. From a novel by Henry Denker, made for TV by producer Irwin Allen. **96m/C VHS.** Robert Preston, Beau Bridges, Anthony Newley, Mel Ferrer, Burgess Meredith, Linda Purl, William Allen Young; **D:** Walter Grauman. TV

Outrage ♪♪ *Dispara* **1993 (R)** Journalist Marco Vallez's (Banderas) latest assignment is a story about a traveling circus. Bored with the usual acts, he's intrigued by equestrian/sharpshooter Anna (Neri) and asks her for an interview, which leads to passion. While Marco is on assignment in Barcelona, Anna is attacked and raped in her trailer. Rather than calling the police, Anna decides to take her own revenge. Spanish with subtitles or dubbed. **108m/C VHS, DVD. SP** Antonio Banderas, Francesca Neri, Eulalia Ramon, Walter Vidarte, Coque Malla; **D:** Carlos Saura; **W:** Carlos Saura; **C:** Javier Aguirresarobe; **M:** Alberto Iglesias.

Outrageous! ♪♪ **1977 (R)** An offbeat, low-budget comedy about the strange relationship between a gay female impersonator and his pregnant schizophrenic friend. The pair end up in New York, where they feel right at home. Russell's impersonations of female film stars earned him the best actor prize at the Berlin Film Festival. **100m/C VHS, DVD. CA** Craig Russell, Hollis McLaren, Richard Easley, Allan Moyle, Helen Shaver, Martha Gibson, Helen Hughes, David McIlwraith, Andree Pelletier; **D:** Richard Benner; **W:** Richard Benner; **C:** James Kelly; **M:** Paul Hoffert.

Outrage ♪♪ **1998** Average guy Tom Casey (Lowe) thinks he's being a good citizen when he reports some teens stealing from cars to the cops. Instead, he and wife Sally (Grey) are terrorized by the punks and Tom decides the best solution is to take care of the miscreants himself. **90m/C VHS, DVD.** Rob Lowe, Jennifer Grey, Eric Michael Cole, Shane Meier, Nathaniel DeVeaux, Kathryn Harrold, Robert Wisden; **D:** Robert Allan Ackerman; **W:** Ellen Weston; **C:** Tobias Schliessler. TV

Outrageous Fortune ♪♪ **1987 (R)** An off-beat, low-budget comedy about the strange relationship between a gay female impersonator and his pregnant schizophrenic friend. The pair end up in New York, where they feel right at home. Russell's impersonations of female film stars earned him the best actor prize at the Berlin Film Festival. 100m/C VHS, DVD. CA Craig Russell, Hollis McLaren, Richard Easley, Allan Moyle, Helen Shaver, Martha Gibson, Helen Hughes, David McIlwraith, Andree Pelletier; D: Richard Benner; W: Richard Benner; C: James Kelly; M: Paul Hoffert.

Outrageous Fortune ♪♪ **1987 (R)** Two would-be actresses—one prim and innocent and one wildly trampy—chase after the same two-timing boyfriend and get involved in a dangerous CIA plot surrounding a deadly bacteria. Tired plot. Mediocre acting and formula jokes, but somehow still funny. Disney's first foray into comedy for grown-ups. **112m/C VHS,**

Outside Chance of Maximilian Glick 🐾🐾 1988 (G) A sentimental Canadian comedy about a boy's dreams and his tradition-bound Jewish family. **94m/C VHS.** CA Noam Zylberman, Fairuza Balk, Saul Rubinek; *D:* Allan Goldstein; *C:* an Elkin. Toronto-City '88: Canadian Feature Film.

Outside Ozona 🐾🐾 1998 (R)

Outside the Man 🐾 1978 A soapy, sanitized remake of Mimieux's film. "Jack-son County Jail," wherein an innocent woman is persecuted in a small Southern jail. **92m/C VHS.** Yvette Mimieux, Royce D. Applegate; *D:* Michael Miller. **TV**

The Outside Man 🐾🐾 *Est Mort* 1973 (PG) A French hit mar is called -C Los Angeles to knock off a crime boss, which he does. But then an American hit man is hired to do in the Frenchman. The climatic showdown is set around the crime boss' body, which happens to be en-tained in a sitting position. Decidely off-beat. **104m/C VHS.** FR Jean-Louis Trintignant, Roy Scheider, Ann-Margret, Angie Dickinson, Georgia Engel, Carlo De Mejo, Umberto Orsini, Ted de Corsia, Felice Orlandi, John Hillerman; *D:* Jacques Deray.

Outside Providence 🐾🐾½ 1999 (R) Although heavily promoted as created "by the makers of 'There's Some-thing About Mary'" upon its release to craw fans of lowbrow humor, this coming-of-age comedy is actually a bit more sen-sitive. Based on Peter Farrelly's semi-au-tcbiographical novel, it tells the story of Dunph (Hatosy), a stoner teen from Paw-tucket who's sent to a snooty prep school by his father (Baldwin) after he and his high-on friends crash into a police car. He has immediate trouble fitting in, although he manages to hook up with coed Jane (Smart), whose book smarts help his rele-mic GPA. Unfortunately, his pranks put her Ivy League hopes in danger. Baldwin gives a good performance as the gruff-but-loving dad, but too many of the char-acters are merely skinned over before they have a chance to develop. **103m/C VHS, DVD.** Shawn Hatosy, Alec Baldwin, George Wendt, Jonathan Brandis, Amy Smart, Gabriel Mann, Jon Abrahams, Adam LaVorgna, Mike Cer-rone, Richard Jenkins; *D:* Michael Corrente; *W:* Peter Farrelly, Michael Corrente, Bobby Farrelly; *C:* Richard Crudo; *M:* Sheldon Mirowitz.

Outside the Law 🐾🐾½ 1995 (R) Maverick cop Brad Kingsbury (Bradley) crosses the line when he falls for Luscious "Tanya Borgman (Thomson)," who's the prime suspect in a murder investigation. Also available unrated. **94m/C VHS.** David Bradley, Anna Thomson, Ashley Laurence; *D:* Boaz Davidson; *W:* Dennis Dimster-Denk; *C:* (Avraham) Karpik; *W:* Blake Leyh.

Outside the Law 🐾 1921 Lon Chaney plays dual roles of the underworld hood in "Black Mike Sylva," and a Chi-nese servant in "Ah Wing." Silent. 77m/B V/HS, DVD. Lon Chaney Sr., Priscilla Dean, Wheeler Oakman; *D:* Tod Browning; *W:* Lu-cien Hubbard; *C:* William Fildew.

The Outsider 🐾🐾½ 2002 R) Re-becca Yoder (Watts) is part of a religious community that has settled in Montana in 1886, hoping to escape the prejudice that plagued them in Ohio. But the local cattle ranchers are angry over a land dispute

DVD. Shelley Long, Bette Midler, George Carlin, Peter Coyote; *D:* Arthur Hiller; *W:* Leslie Dixon; *C:* David M. Walsh; *M:* Alan Silvestri.

Outside Chance 🐾 1978 A soapy, sanitized remake of Mimieux's film, "Jack-son County Jail," wherein an innocent woman is persecuted in a small Southern jail. **92m/C VHS.** Yvette Mimieux, Royce D. Applegate; *D:* Michael Miller. **TV**

---

and kill Rebecca's husband, hoping to force her to sell her farm. Then, a wound-ed stanger staggers onto her property, whom Rebecca nurses back to health. Of course, Johnny Gault (Daly) is not only worldly but dangerous and Rebecca may be forced to choose between her new man and the religious community that dis-approves. Adapted from the book by Pe-nelope Williamson. **111m/C VHS, DVD.** Timothy Daly, Naomi Watts, Keith Carradine, David Carradine, Jason Clarke, Grant Prio; *D:* Randa Haines; *W:* Jenny Wingfield; *C:* Ben Nott; *M:* Todd Boekelheide. **CABLE.**

The Outsiders 🐾🐾½ 1983 (PG) Based on the popular S.E. Hinton book, the story of a teen gang from the wrong side of the tracks and their conflicts with society and each other. Melodramatic and over-done, but teenagers still seem to relate to it. Good soundtrack and cast ripples with up and coming stars. Followed by a TV series. Coppola adapted another Hinton novel the same year, "Rumble Fish," and C VHS, DVD. C: Thomas Howell, Matt Dillon, Ralph Macchio, Patrick Swayze, Diane Lane, Tom Cruise, Emilio Estevez, Rob Lowe, Tom Waits, Leif Garrett; *D:* Francis Ford Coppola; *W:* Kathleen Rowell; *C:* Stephen Burum **M:** Carmine Coppola.

Outta Time 🐾🐾 *The Courier* 2001 (R) Tijuana native David Morales (Lopez) has gotten an athletic scholarship to the Uni-versity of San Diego but loses it because of a knee injury. Needing cash to pay his tuition, David doesn't ask a lot of ques-tions when ex-professor Darabont (Saxon) asks David to transport some sealed packages of serum for testing across the border. Naturally, this job isn't as easy as David has been told. **90m/C VHS, DVD.** Mario Lopez, John Saxon, Ali Landry, Nancy O'Dell, Taya Smiley, Tim Siharz; *C:* Lorena David; *M:* Scott Duncan, Ned Kerwin; *C:* Lisa Wiegand; *M:* Scott Gilman.

The Oval Portrait 🐾½ 1988 An adaptation of the Edgar Allan Poe sus-pense tale about a Civil War-era maiden, her illicit love for a Confederate soldier and her eventual death. **88m/C VHS.** Giselle MacKenzie, Barry Coe; *D:* Fegelio A. Gonzalez Jr.

Over Her Dead Body 🐾½ 2008 (PG-13) Henry (Rudd) and Kate (Lon-goria Parker) are about to tie the knot at their perfectly orchestrated wedding when a freak ice sculpture accident leads to the bride-to-be's *untimely* demise. A year later, the still-mourning Henry is en-couraged by his sister Chloe (Sloane) to see her psychic friend Ashley (Bell) to help him get over his grief. Of course sparks fly, but ghostly Kate shows up to put the kibosh on Henry's new romance. Bell's charming and Rudd's likable in a premise that's been done to death, but the inexpli-cably top-billed Longoria Parker grates in every scene she stomps through. **95m/C DVD.** *US* Eva Longoria, Paul Rudd, Lake Bell, Ja-son Biggs, Lindsay Sloane, Stephen Root, William Morgan Sheppard; *D:* Jeff Lowell; *W:* Jeff Lowell; *C:* John Bailey; *M:* David Kitay.

Over the Brooklyn Bridge 🐾🐾 *My Darling Shiksa* 1983 (R) A young Jewish man (Gould) must give up his Catholic girlfriend (Hemingway) in or-der to get his uncle (Caesar) to lend him the money he needs to buy a restaurant in Manhattan. Nowhere near as funny as it should be, and potentially offensive to boot. **100m/C VHS.** Elliott Gould, Sid Caesar, Shelley Winters, Margaux Hemingway, Carol Kane, Burt Young; *D:* Menaham Go'an; *M:* Pino Donaggio.

Over the Edge 🐾🐾🐾½ 1979 (PG) The music of Cheap Trick, The Cars, and The Ramones highlights this realistic tale of alienated suburban youth on the ram-page. Dillon makes his screen debut in the's updated, well-done "Rebel Without a Cause." Shelved for several years, the movie was finally released after Dillon made it big. Sleeper with excellent direc-tion and dialogue. **91m/C VHS, DVD,** Michael Kramer, Matt Dillon, Pamela Ludwig, Vincent Spa-

---

no, Tom Fergus, Harry Northrup, Andy Romano, Ellen Geer, Richard Jamison, Julia Pomeroy, Tiger Thompson; *D:* Jonathan Kaplan; *W:* Charles Haas, Tim Hunter; *C:* Andrew Davis; *M:* Sol Ka-plan.

Over the Hedge 🐾🐾🐾 2006 (PG) Hilarious, somewhat shallow comedy 'has a group of woodland creatures awakening from their winter hibernation, surprised to see a subdivision has sprouted up just be-side a hedge. Opportunistic raccoon RJ (Willis) tells his pals, including cautious turtle Verne (Shandling), that humans venture into this strange new world. Of course, the humans, in the form of harpie Gladys (Janney) and "Verminator" (Church) view these new neigh-bors as pests. Plenty of laughs and excel-lent voice performances, especially from Carell and Shatner, but trades some of the satire of Michael Fry and T. Lew's's source comic strip for fuzzy se-itimentality. **84m/C DVD.** *D:* Tim Johnson, Karey Kirkpa-trick; *W:* Karey Kirkpatrick, Len Blum, Lorne Cam-eron, David Hoselton; *M:* Rupert Gregson-Wi-liams; *V:* Bruce Willis, Garry Shandling, Steven Carell, William Shatner, Catherine O'Hara, Eugene Levy, Wanda Sykes, Nick Nolte, Thomas Haden Church, Allison Janney, Avn Lavigne, Omid Djalil, Sami Kirkpatrick, Shane Baumel, Madison Daven-port.

Over the Hill 🐾🐾 1993 (PG) Du-kakis stars as Alma, an eccentric widow who decides to leave her well-meaning but restrictive home in the form of her-estranged daughter Elizabeth in Sydney, Australia. Embarassed by her peculiarities Elizabeth arranges a 'noliday away but Mom has her own plans. She wants to "loop the loop," and make a complete cir-cuit around the Australian continent. Soon Alma is on the road, meeting fellow eccen-trics and experiencing a variety of adven-tures. **102m/C VHS.** Olympia Dukakis, Sigrid Thornton, Derek Fowlds, Pippa Grandison; *D:* George Miller; *W:* Robert Caswell; *C:* David Con-nell.

Over the Hill Gang 🐾🐾 1969 A quirky cast is the only real reason to watch this made-for-TV western about a retired Texas Ranger and his pals who clean up a corrupt town. **75m/C DVD** Walter Brennan, Ed-gar Buchanan, Andy Devine, Jack Elam, Gypsy Rose Lee, Kristin Harmon, Ricky Nelson, Chill Wills, Edward Andrews; *D:* Jean Yarbrough; *W:* Jameson Brewer; *C:* Henry Croniger Jr. **TV**

Over the Summer 🐾🐾½ 1985 Strong drama about a troubled teen who escapes the city for a summer with her grandparents. No cliches here—the grandmother hires a hitman after his grandfather lusts after the granddaughter and eventually kills himself, and problems remain at the end. Intelligent and enter-taining, though marred by nee-tless nude scenes. **97m/C VHS.** Laura Hunt, Johnson West, Catherine Williams, David Romero; *D:* Teresa Sparks.

Over the Top 🐾½ 1986 (PG) The film that started a nationwide arm-wres-tling craze. A slow-witted trucker decides the only way he can retain custody of his estranged son, as well as win the boy's respect, is by winning a big arm-wrestling competition. Stallone is an expert at grind-ing these movies out by now, and the kid (General Hospital's Mikey) is all right, but the end result is boredom, as it should be with an arm-wrestling epic. **94m/C VHS.** Sylvester Stallone, Susan Blakely, Robert Loggia, David Mendenhall; *D:* Menahem Golen; *W:* Sylvester Stallone, Gary Conway, Stirling Sili-phant; Golden Raspberries '87: Worst Support, Ac-tor (Mendenhall), Worst New Star (Mendenhall).

Over the Wire 🐾½ 1995 Tele-phone lineman Bruce (Christensen) acci-dentally overhears a conversation where a woman hires a hitman to kill her sister. He finds out that the sisters live together and tries to figure out just who the target is before it's too late (of course, he has to seduce both of them to accomplish this). Ray used the pseudonym Nicholas Medi-na. **90m/C VHS, DVD.** Fred Olen Ray; *W:* Pete Slate; *C:* Howard Wexler.

Overboard 🐾🐾 1987 (PG) A wealthy, spoiled woman falls off of her yacht and into the arms of a low-class carpenter she picks her up and convinces her she is in fact his wife, and mother to his four brats. Just when she learns to like her life, the tables are turned again. Even though it's all been done before, there's still enough to laugh at the screwy gags. **112m/C VHS.** **DVD.** Goldie Hawn, Kurt Russell, Katherine Hel-mond, Roddy McDowall, Edward Herrmann; *D:* Garry Marshall; *W:* Leslie Dixon; *C:* John A. Alon-zo; *M:* Alan Silvestri.

The Overcoat 🐾🐾🐾½ *The Cloak* *Shinel* 1959 An adaptation of Nikolai Gogol's classic story about the dehumanizing life endured in 20th-century bureaucracy. All a menial civil servant wants is a new over-coat. When he finally gets one, this trea-sured article not only keeps him warm but makes him feel self-satisfied as well. In Russian with English subtitles. **93m/B VHS.** *RU* Rolan Bykov, Yuri Tolubeyev; *D:* Alexei Bata-lov; *W:* L. Solovyov; *C:* Heinrich Mararidzhian; *M:* N. Sidelnikov.

Overdrawn at the Memory Bank 🐾🐾 1983 In a futuristic tyranny, a romantic rebel becomes somehow fused with the spirit of Humphrey Bogart in a cliched version of the film character's ad-ventures. **84m/C VHS.** Raul Julia, Linda Griffiths, Wanda Cannon, Louis Negin, Chapelle Jaffe, Jackie Burroughs, Maury Chaykin, Sheila Moore, Bill Smtrovich; *D:* Douglas Williams; *W:* John Var-ley.

Overexposed 🐾🐾 1990 (R) All the wackics love the sultry soap star Oxen-burg; one is a killer. Eighty minutes and a bunch of bodies later the killer is un-masked. Plenty of suspense and some original gore. Based on the true stories of fans who stalk celebrities. **83m/C VHS.** Cath-erine Oxenberg, David Naughton, Jennifer Ed-wards, Karen Black; *D:* Larry Brand; *M:* Larry Brand.

Overkill 🐾 1986 (R) A detective and the vengeance-minded brother of a dead Japanese-American fight back against the controlling Yakuza in Little Tokyo. **81m/C** Steve Fahy, John Nishio, Laura Burkett, Roy Sum-merset; *D:* Uli Lommel.

Overkill 🐾🐾 1996 (R) Burnt-out cop Jack Hazard (Norris) heads for vacation in Costa Rica and winds up being the prey for demented hunter Lloyd Wheeler (Nouri). **92m/C VHS.** Aaron Norris, Michael Nouri; *D:* Dean Ferrandini; *W:* Dear Ferrandini.

Overland Mail 🐾🐾 1942 Fifteen episodes of the vintage serial filled with western action. **225m/B VHS, DVD.** Lon Cha-ney Jr., Helen Parrish, Don Terry, Bob Baker, Noah Beery Sr., Noah Beery Jr., Tom Chatterton, Charles Stevens; *D:* Ford Beebe, John Rawlins; *W:* Paul Huston; *C:* George Robinson, William Sickner.

Overland Stage Raiders 🐾🐾🐾 1938 The "Three Mesquiteers" ride again, this time to guard a Greyhound bus! The trio must protect a shipment of gold from hijackers. This is the last film for Brooks, who had starred in the German master-piece "Pandora's Box" in 1929. **55m/B VHS.** John Wayne, Ray Corrigan, Max Terhune, Louise Brooks, John Archer, Frank LaRue, Yakima Ca-nutt; *D:* George Sherman.

Overlanders 🐾🐾🐾 1946 The japa-nese may invade, but rather than kill 1,000 head of cattle, these Aussies drive the huge herd across the continent, facing danger along the way. Beautifully photo-graphed, featuring the "Australian Gary Cooper" and a stampede scene to chal-lenge "Dances with Wolves." **9m/3 VHS.** *AU* Chips Rafferty, Daphne Campbell, Jean Blue, John Nugent Hayward; *D:* Harry Watt.

Overnight 🐾🐾 2003 (R) Troy Duf-fy's "The Boondock Saints" has garnered a cult following on video, but this docu-mentary about the story behind the film will make viewers recoil in disbelief at how one man's hubris and self-delusion can sink a promising career. During the indie film boom of the 1990s, Miramax offered Duffy $1 million for his "Boondock" script and signed his band to a record deal. Con-vinced of his own greatness, Duffy alien-ates and bullies everyone around him in he loses every opportunity he's been handed. It's hard to sympathize with Duffy, particularly because he originally hired Montana and Smith to direct the doc as a chronicle of his rise to the top. Weak in spots, but it's still schadenfreude at its best. **81m/C DVD.** *US* **D:** Mark Smith; **C:** Mark Smith; **M:** Troy Duffy.

Overnight Delivery 🦴🦴 **1996 (PG-13)** Convinced his girlfriend (Taylor) has been cheating on him, Wyatt (Rudd) sends her a nasty breakup letter via overnight mail. But when he realizes the letter's wrong, Wyatt enlists the aid of friendly stripper Ivy (Witherspoon) to help him retrieve the letter. **87m/C VHS, DVD.** Larry Drake, Tobin Bell, Reese Witherspoon, Paul Rudd, Christine Taylor; **D:** Jason Bloom; **W:** Steven L. Bloom; **C:** Edward Pei; **M:** Andrew Gross.

Overseas: Three Women with Man Trouble 🦴🦴🦴 **1990** Three beautiful sisters in French colonial Algeria surround themselves in a life of luxury to avoid the incredible social changes going on around them. Each sister has a different perspective on her life, and the perspectives are graphically revealed. Lush photography set in the Mediterranean. In French with English subtitles. **96m/C VHS.** *FR* Nicole Garcia, Marianne Basler, Philippe Galland, Pierre Doris, Brigitte Rouan; **D:** Brigitte Rouan; **W:** Brigitte Rouan. Cannes '90: Film.

Overthrow 🦴½ **1982 (R)** American sportswriter finds himself caught up in violence and intrigue in Buenos Aires. De Angelis used the pseudonym Larry Ludman. **90m/C VHS.** John Phillip Law, Lewis Van Bergen, Roger Wilson; **D:** Fabrizio de Angelis.

Overture to Glory 🦴🦴½ *Der Vilner Shtot Khazn* **1940** A Jewish cantor longs for the world of opera. He leaves his wife and son to fulfill his passion, but eventually he loses his voice and humbly returns home on Yom Kippur, the Jewish Day of Atonement. He learns that his son has passed away. Grief-stricken, he goes to the synagogue. There, the cantor regains his voice as he performs Kol Nidre in a passionate and melodious rendering. In Yiddish with English subtitles. **85m/B VHS.** Helen Beverly, Florence Weiss.

The Owl and the Pussycat 🦴🦴🦴 **1970 (PG)** Nerdy author gets the neighborhood hooker evicted from her apartment. She returns the favor, and the pair hit the street—and the sack—in Buck Henry's hilarious adaptation of the Broadway play. Streisand's first non-singing role. **96m/C VHS, DVD.** Barbra Streisand, George Segal, Robert Klein, Allen (Goorwitz) Garfield; **D:** Herbert Ross; **W:** Buck Henry; **C:** Harry Stradling Sr., Andrew Laszlo; **M:** Dick Halligan.

Owning Mahowny 🦴🦴🦴½ **2003 (R)** Dan Mahowny (Hoffman) is a vice president at a Toronto bank. He is also a compulsive gambler and in order to clear his gambling debts, he embezzles (millions of dollars as it turns out). Even Dan's fiancee Belinda (Driver) can't pull him away from the casino tables when they are supposed to on a romantic getaway (why she's so loyal is something of a mystery). Hoffman excels as an everyday schlub who's completely absorbed in his addiction and Hurt is fascinatingly reptilian as the Atlantic City casino boss who is happy to enable Mahowny's addiction. Based on a true story; adapted from the book "Stung: The Incredible Obsession of Brian Molony" by Gary Ross. **107m/C VHS, DVD.** *CA GB* Philip Seymour Hoffman, Minnie Driver, Maury Chaykin, John Hurt, Sonja Smits, Ian Tracey, Roger Dunn, Jason Blicker, Chris Collins; **D:** Richard Kwietniowski; **W:** Richard Kwietniowski, Maurice Chauvet; **C:** Oliver Curtis; **M:** Richard Grassby-Lewis.

The Ox 🦴🦴½ **1991** Slow-moving, simple tale, set in rural Sweden in the 1860s during a famine. Desperate to feed his family a tenant farmer kills his employer's ox. Consumed by guilt, the man is quickly found out and sentenced to life imprisonment. Pardoned after six years, the farmer returns to his family, to find out his wife has survived by doing things he finds difficult to forgive. Based on a true story. Directorial debut of Nykvist, the longtime cinematographer for Ingmar Bergman, well displays his familiarity with composition and lighting to heighten mood. In Swedish with English subtitles. **93m/C VHS.** *SW* Stellan Skarsgard, Ewa Froling, Lennan Hjulstrom, Max von Sydow, Liv Ullmann, Bjorn Granath, Erland Josephson; **D:** Sven Nykvist; **W:** Lasse Summanen, Sven Nykvist.

The Ox-Bow Incident 🦴🦴🦴 **1996** *Strange Incident* **1943** A popular rancher is murdered, and a mob of angry townspeople can't wait for the sheriff to find the killers. They hang the young man, despite the protests of Fonda, a cowboy with a conscience. Excellent study of mob mentality with strong individual characterizations. A brilliant western based on a true story by Walter Van Tilburg Clark. Also see "Twelve Angry Men"—less tragic but just as moving. **75m/B VHS, DVD.** Henry Fonda, Harry (Henry) Morgan, Dana Andrews, Anthony Quinn, Frank Conroy, Harry Davenport, Jane Darwell, William Eythe, Mary Beth Hughes; **D:** William A. Wellman; **W:** Lamar Trotti; **C:** Arthur C. Miller; **M:** Cyril Mockridge. Natl. Bd. of Review '43: Director (Wellman). Natl. Film Reg. '98.

Oxford Blues 🦴🦴 **1984 (PG-13)** An American finagles his way into England's Oxford University and onto the rowing team in pursuit of the girl of his dreams. Beautiful scenery, but the plot is waferthin. Remake of "Yank at Oxford." **98m/C VHS.** Rob Lowe, Ally Sheedy, Amanda Pays, Julian Sands, Michael Gough, Gail Strickland, Cary Elwes, Jeffrey S. (Jeff) Perry; **D:** Robert Boris; **W:** Robert Boris; **M:** John Du Prez.

Oxygen 🦴🦴 **1999 (R)** Madeline (Tierney) is a troubled police detective who's married to another cop (Kinney) and involved in a kinky extramarital affair. Harry (Brody) is an escape artist who fancies himself the new Houdini—he kidnaps the wife (Robbins) of wealthy Clarke Hannon (Naughton) and buries her alive. Madeline's assigned to the case and Harry takes to taunting her and their dangerous game could have more than one victim. **92m/C VHS, DVD.** Madeline Stowe, Adrien Brody, Maura Tierney, Terry Kinney, James Naughton, Laila Robins, Dylan Baker; **D:** Richard Shepard; **W:** Richard Shepard; **C:** Sarah Cawley; **M:** Rolfe Kent.

P2 🦴 **2007 (R)** Late on Christmas Eve, Angela (Nichols) decends to level PS of her office's parking garage, only to find that her car won't start and the parking lot attendant Thomas (Bentley) is a homicidal maniac obsessed with her. After she initially escapes, she again finds herself trapped, with Thomas menacingly creeping her out. Standard gory "woman in danger" thriller fare with the occasional imaginative twist. **98m/C DVD.** *US* Wes Bentley, Rachel Nichols; **D:** Franck Khalfoun; **W:** Franck Khalfoun, Alexandre Aja, Gregory Levasseur; **C:** Maxime Alexandre; **M:** Tomandandy.

Pace That Kills 🦴 **1928** An anti-drug cautionary drama from the Roaring '20s, one of many now marketed on cassette as campy fun. Beware, though, a little bit of this stuff goes a long way. A young man goes to the big city to find his missing sister and winds up hooked on heroin. **87m/B VHS.** Owen Gorin, Virginia Roye, Florence Turner; **D:** William A. O'Connor, Norton S. Parker; **W:** Ruth Todd; **C:** Ernest Laszlo.

Pacific Heights 🦴🦴🦴 **1990 (R)** Young San Francisco couple takes on mammoth mortgage assuming tenants will write their ticket to the American dream, but psychopathic tenant Keaton moves in downstairs and redecorates. He won't pay the rent and he won't leave. Creepy psycho-thriller has lapses but builds to effective climax. It's a treat to watch mother/daughter actresses Hedren and Griffith work together. Watch for D'Angelo as Keaton's lover. **103m/C VHS, DVD.** Melanie Griffith, Matthew Modine, Michael Keaton, Mako, Nobu McCarthy, Laurie Metcalf, Carl Lumbly, Dorian Harewood, Luca Bercovici, Tippi Hedren, Sheila McCarthy, Dan Hedaya, Beverly D'Angelo, Nicholas Pryor, Miriam Margolyes, D.W. Moffett, Tracey Walter, Dabbs Greer, O-lan Jones; **D:** John Schlesinger; **W:** Daniel Pyne; **C:** Amir M. Mokri; **M:** Hans Zimmer.

Pacific Inferno 🦴🦴 **1985** During WWII, American POWs endeavor to break out of a Japanese prison camp in the Philippines. Their goal is to prevent their captors from retrieving millions of dollars worth of sunken U.S. gold. **90m/C VHS, DVD.** Jim Brown, Richard Jaeckel, Timothy Brown; **D:** Rolf Bayer. **CABLE**

The Pacifier 🦴🦴½ **2005 (PG)** Schwarzenegger had "Kindergarten Cop," Hulk Hogan had "Mr. Nanny," and wooden Diesel has this. Shane Wolfe is a Navy SEAL who fails to prevent the death of a scientist at the hands of terrorists and is then assigned to protect the scientist's five kids and find some top-secret disk hidden in their home. Mom Ford is conveniently absent for much of the time. He retrofits his gadgets to hold baby formula and other child-friendly necessities and tries to promote military discipline on the bratty, unwilling clan. There's also a pet duck who doesn't like the new babysitter. It's all obvious and silly. **95m/C VHS, DVD.** *US* Vin Diesel, Lauren Graham, Faith Ford, Brittany Snow, Max Thieriot, Chris Potter, Morgan York, Scott Thompson, Carol Kane, Brad Garrett, Tate Donovan, Denis Akiyama, Mung-Ling Tsui; **D:** Adam Shankman; **W:** Robert Ben Garant; **C:** Peter James; **M:** John Debney.

The Pack 🦴🦴½ **1977 (R)** A group of dogs become wild when left on a resort island. A marine biologist leads the humans who fight to keep the dogs from using vacationers as chew toys. Fine production valves keep it from going to the dogs. Made with the approval of the American Humane Society who helped with the treatment of stage hands. **99m/C VHS.** Joe Don Baker, Hope Alexander-Willis, R.G. Armstrong, Richard B. Shull; **D:** Robert Clouse; **W:** Robert Clouse.

The P.A.C.K. 🦴🦴 **1996** The P.A.C.K. are alien warriors who mistakenly land on earth, which doesn't prevent them from killing all but one of a team of government agents sent to investigate. Now lone agent Rachel (Bergman) reluctantly teams up with a second alien who's been sent to destroy the P.A.C.K. **90m/C VHS.** Sandahl Bergman, Ted Prior, Red West.

Pack of Lies 🦴🦴½ **1987** In the early 1960s, MI5 agents manipulate a British family, quietly living in the suburbs, into allowing them to use their home for a surveillance mission. Only it turns out they're watching the Jackson's neighbors who are actually Soviet spies. Based on a true story. **100m/C DVD.** Ellen Burstyn, Teri Garr, Alan Bates, Ronald Hines, Daniel Benzali, Sammi Davis, Clive Swift; **D:** Anthony Page; **W:** Hugh Whitemore; **C:** Kenneth Macmillan; **M:** Stanley Myers. **TV**

Pack Up Your Troubles 🦴🦴½ **1932** Laurel and Hardy make good on a promise to help find the grandfather of a girl whose father was killed in WWI. All they know is the grandfather's last name though—Smith. Wholesome R and R. **68m/B VHS, DVD.** Stan Laurel, Oliver Hardy, James Finlayson, Jacquie Lyn; **D:** George Marshall.

The Package 🦴🦴🦴 **1989 (R)** An espionage thriller about an army sergeant who loses the prisoner he escorts into the U.S. When he tries to track him down, he uncovers a military plot to start WWIII. Hackman is believable in his role as the sergeant. **108m/C VHS, DVD.** Gene Hackman, Joanna Cassidy, Dennis Franz, Pam Grier, John Heard, Reni Santoni, Thalmus Rasulala, Ike Pappas, Kevin Crowley, Wilhelm von Homburg; **D:** Andrew Davis; **W:** John Bishop; **M:** James Newton Howard.

Packin' It In 🦴🦴 **1983** A Los Angeles family is in for a rude awakening when they leave the city for a quieter life in the Oregon woods. There they encounter a band of survivalists with semi-comedic results. **100m/C VHS.** Richard Benjamin, Paula Prentiss, Molly Ringwald, Tony Roberts, Andrea Marcovicci; **D:** Jud Taylor.

Paco 🦴½ **1975 (G)** A young, South American boy heads for the city, where he meets his uncle. He discovers his uncle is the leader of a gang of youthful thieves. Predictable and sluggish. **89m/C VHS, DVD.** Jose Ferrer, Panchito Gomez, Allen (Goorwitz) Garfield, Pernell Roberts, Andre Marquis; **D:** Robert Vincent O'Neil,

The Pact 🦴🦴 *The Secret Pact* **1999 (R)** When teenager Greg (Frost) witnesses his parents' murder by the mob, he's sent to a private school in Montreal as part of the witness protection program. He makes a new best friend with a fellow student (Strong) but discovers his fellow teen is actually a hit man sent to kill him. Only they come to a strange sort of deal instead. **94m/C VHS, DVD.** *CA* Rider Strong, Adam Frost, John Heard, Nick Mancuso, Jack Langedijk, Lisa Zane; **D:** Rodney Gibbons; **W:** William Lee, Brian Cameron Fuld; **C:** Bert Tougas; **M:** Antonio Battista. **VIDEO**

Paddy 🦴🦴 *Goodbye to the Hill* **1970 (PG)** A young Irish lad realizes his sexual potential by seducing every woman he can find. Freudians will have a field day. **97m/C VHS.** *IR* Des Cave, Milo O'Shea, Dearbhla Molloy, Peggy Cass; **D:** Daniel Haller.

Padre Nuestro 🦴🦴½ **1985** Religious satire about a dying priest who wishes to reunite his family, who include an atheist brother, a mistress from his youth, and his illegitimate daughter who's a notorious prostitute. In Spanish with English subtitles. **91m/C VHS.** *SP* Fernando Rey, Francisco Rabal, Victoria Abril; **D:** Francisco Regueiro.

Padre Padrone 🦴🦴🦴½ *Father Master; My Father, My Master* **1977** The much acclaimed adaptation of the Gavino Ledda autobiography about his youth in agrarian Sardinia with a brutal, tyrannical father. Eventually he overcomes his handicaps, breaks the destructive emotional ties to his father and successfully attends college. Highly regarded although low budget; in an Italian dialect (Sardinian) with English subtitles. **113m/C VHS, DVD.** *IT* Omero Antonutti, Saverio Marconi, Marcella Michelangeli, Fabrizio Forte; **D:** Paolo Taviani, Vittorio Taviani; **W:** Paolo Taviani, Vittorio Taviani; **C:** Mario Masini; **M:** Egisto Macchi. Cannes '77: Film.

Pagan Island 🦴 **1960** A man is stranded on a desert island with 30 beautiful girls who tie him up and abandon him. Maki, to be sacrificed by the rest, saves Dew and they fall in love. They go off in search of a reputed treasure, which they find, but at a deadly cost. **67m/B VHS, DVD.** Eddie Dew, Nani Maka, Yanka (Doris Keating) Mann; **D:** Barry Mahon; **W:** Clelie Mahon; **C:** Mark Dennis.

Pagan Love Song 🦴🦴 **1950** A dull musical which finds Keel in Tahiti taking over his uncle's coconut plantation and falling in love with Williams. Surprise! Williams performs one of her famous water ballets, which is the only saving grace in this lifeless movie. ♫The House of Singing Bamboo; Singing in the Sun; Etiquette; Why is Love So Crazy; Tahiti; The Sea of the Moon; Pagan Love Song; Coconut Milk. **76m/C DVD.** *FR* Debora Kerr, Esther Williams, Howard Keel, Minna Gombell, Rita Moreno; **D:** Robert Alton.

The Page Turner 🦴🦴🦴 *La Tourneuse de Pages* **2006** As a child, aspiring pianist Melanie has her dreams carelessly ruined by concert pianist Ariane (Frot). She nurses a grudge and when Melanie (Francois) grows up, she puts her plan for revenge into action by insinuating herself into Ariane's family life. Okay thriller, but nothing that hasn't been seen before. French with subtitles. **85m/C DVD.** *FR* Deborah Francois, Catherine Frot, Pascal Gregory, Clothilde Mollet; **D:** Denis Dercourt; **W:** Denis Dercourt; **C:** Jerome Peyrebrune; **M:** Jacques Lemonnier.

The Pagemaster 🦴🦴½ **1994 (G)** Timid Richard (Macauley) is basically scared of his own shadow but, during a storm, he's forced to take refuge in a mysterious library with an even odder librarian, Mr. Dewey (Lloyd). Richard's intrigued by the library's mural, which turns out to be the doorway to an animated universe where the wizardlike Pagemaster (voiced by Lloyd) and other literary characters help Richard discover his strengths and overcome his fears. Mildly amusing but kids may not know who the characters refer to unless they're readers (a good intro, perhaps?) **76m/C VHS, DVD.** Macaulay Culkin, Christopher Lloyd, Ed Begley Jr., Mel Harris; **D:** Joe Johnston, Maurice Hunt; **W:** David Casci, David Kirschner, Ernie Contreras; **M:** James Horner,

Paid in Full ⚐⚐½ 2002 (R) Based on the true story of the rise and fall of three Harlem drug dealers in the mid '80s during the height of the crack cocaine trade and the beginnings of "Gangsta" culture. The trio rises to the top of their dubious profession dealing with the issues of staying friends while also becoming rivals and making obscene amounts of money. Story hinges on Ace (Harris, who also narrates), a good kid who quickly goes bad after seeing the money to be made on the streets. Phifer is excellent as his best friend whose business he takes over after he's been busted. Cam'ron is the third friend, who may end up as Ace's replacement. Highlights the unsavory side of a business that makes Ace a fortune, but steals his soul. Acting all around is too-familiar territory about the price of greed and the politics of poverty. 93m/C VHS, DVD. Wood Harris, Mekhi Phifer, Kevin Carroll, Esai Morales, Chi McBride, Cynthia Martells, Elise Neal, Cam'ron, Regina Hall, Remo Greene, Anthony Clark; D: Charles Stone III; W: Azie Faison Jr., Austin Phillips, Matthew Cirulnick, Thulani Davis; C: Paul Sarossy; M: Vernon Reid, Frank Fitzpatrick.

The Paint Job ⚐⚐ 1993 (R) GB Dane Clark, Paul Carpenter, Thea Gregory, Howard Marion-Crawford, Peter Gawthorne; D: Montgomery Tully; W: Paul Tabori; C: Walter J. (Jimmy W.) Harvey.

Pain in the A— ⚐⚐ 1977 (PG) A hit man helps a suicidal shirt salesman solve his marital problems in this black comedy that was later Americanized as "Buddy, Buddy." Not for all tastes, but has acquired a reputation for its dark wit. In French with English subtitles. 90m/C VHS. Lino Ventura, Jacques Brel, Caroline Cellier; D: Edouard Molinaro; W: Edouard Molinaro, Francis Veber.

Paint It Black ⚐⚐½ 1989 (R) A violent/steamy mystery and action flick from the director of "River's Edge." In which a young man from the silver-spoon set develops a fascination for an artist. Margaret is drawn to Wesley and bored with Wily. But one of the men turns out to be a serial killer. What's a gal in love to do? 99m/C VHS. Sally Kirkland, Rick Rossovich, Martin Landau, Doug Savant, Peter Frechette, Jason Bernard, Julie Carmen, Monique Van De Ven; D: Tim Hunter.

The Paint Job ⚐⚐ 1993 (R) A seedy, tiny, lonely house painter, falls in love with his neighbor, Margaret. Unfortunately, Margaret is married—to Wesley and Willy, his boss. 101m/C VHS, DVD. Will Patton, Bebe Neuwirth, Robert Pastorelli; D: Micheal Taav. W: Micheal Taav; M: John Wesley Harding.

Paint Your Wagon ⚐⚐½ 1969 (PG) Big-budget western musical-comedy about a gold mining boom town, and two prospectors sharing the same Mormon wife complete with a classic Lerner and Lowe score. Marvin chews up the sagebrush and Eastwood attempts to sing, although Seberg was mercifully dubbed. Overlong, with patches of interest, pretty songs, and plenty of panoramic scenery. Adapted from the L & L play. ♫I Talk to the Trees; I Still See Elisa; I'm on My Way; Wand'rin Star; There's a Coach Comin' In; Hand Me Down That Can o' Beans; Whoop-Ti-Ay; They Call the Wind Maria; Best Things. 164m/C VHS, DVD. Lee Marvin, Clint Eastwood, Jean Seberg, Harve Presnell; D: Joshua Logan; W: Paddy Chayefsky; M: Frederick Loewe, Andre Previn, Alan Jay Lerner.

Painted Desert ⚐⚐ 1931 Gable's first film role of any consequence came in this early sound western. Gable plays a villain opposite "good guy" William Boyd. 80m/B VHS, DVD. William Boyd, Helen Twelvetrees, George O'Brien, Clark Gable, William Farnum; D: Howard Higgin.

Painted Hero ⚐⚐½ 1995 (R) Rodeo clown Virgil Kidder (Yoakum) has to watch out for more than rampaging bulls when he returns to Waco, where he's accused of murder and reunites with his actor mother of his now-dead son. 105m/C VHS, DVD. Dwight Yoakam, Bo Hopkins, Cindy Pickett, Michelle Joyner; D: Terry Benedict; M: Rick Marotta.

The Painted Hills ⚐⚐½ 1951 (G) Lassie outsmarts crooked miners and rescues her friends. Surprise, Surprise! Overly sentimental, but action packed and beautifully shot. Lassie's last outing with MGM. 70m/C VHS, DVD. Paul Kelly, Bruce Cowling, Gary Gray, Art Smith, Ann Doran; D: Harold F. Kress.

A Painted House ⚐⚐ 2003 Loose adaptation of the John Grisham novel finds 10-year-old Luke Chandler (Lerman) living on a struggling Arkansas farm in 1952 with his parents and grandparents. The family needs to hire local "hill" people and Mexican migrant workers to pick their cotton crop and there's the trouble between the groups as well as with Luke and his family. Title refers to the fact that the Chandlers' bare clapboard farmhouse gets mysteriously painted (they can't afford to do it themselves). 110m/C VHS, DVD. Scott Glenn, Melinda Dillon, Robert Sean Leonard, Logan Lerman, Geoffrey Lewis, Arija Bareikis, Pablo Schreiber, Luis Esteban Garcia, Luke Ebert, Diane Delano, Maria Anderson; D: Alfonso Arau; W: Patrick Sheane Duncan; M: Ray Folquera. TV

The Painted Lady ⚐⚐ 1997 Maggie Sheridan (Mirren) is a hard-living ex-blues singer (with some destructive habits. After bottoming out some years before, she was taken in by Sir Charles Stafford (Cuthbertson), the father of childhood friend Sebastian (Glen). Sir Charles is murdered during a botched robbery, a 16th-century painting stolen, and Sebastian becomes the victim of a brutal attack, so Maggie decides to get involved. And finds herself deeply enmeshed in the illegal art trade, posing at a very dangerous man (Nero). 204m/C VHS. GB Helen Mirren, Franco Nero, Iain Glen, Michael Maloney, Leslie Manville, Roland Gift, Iain Cuthbertson, Michael Liebman, Indro Montanelli; D: Julian Jarrold. TV

Painted Skin ⚐⚐ Hua Pi Zhi Yinyang Faweng 1993 Historical supernatural tale concerns a ghost (Joey Wang) who's trapped on Earth and must paint her skin to pass among humans. The evil Demon King is responsible. 93m/C DVD. HK Adam Cheng, Joey Wang, Sammo Hung; D: King Hu; W: King Hu, Chiang A. Cheng; C: Stephen Yip; M: Ng Tai Kong.

The Painted Stallion ⚐⚐ 1937 This 12-chapter serial features a mysterious figure on a painted stallion who attempts to maintain peace between Mexicans and Indians. Sammo Hung costars as a monk. 212m/B VHS, DVD. Ray Corrigan, Hoot Gibson, Duncan Renaldo, LeRoy Mason, Yakima Canutt; D: William Witney, Ray Taylor.

The Painted Veil ⚐⚐½ 1934 Adaptation of a W. Somerset Maugham story. Garbo, once again the disillusioned wife turning to the affections of another man, is responsible for the deaths of another. Lost money at the box office, but for Garbo fans, an absolute must. 83m/B VHS. Greta Garbo, Herbert Marshall, George Brent, Warner Oland, Jean Hersholt; D: Richard Boleslawski; C: William H. Daniels.

The Painted Veil ⚐⚐ 2006 (PG-13) The third film version of Maugham's 1925 novel takes some liberties with his story. Garbo, once again the disillusioned wife turning to the affections of another man, is responsible for the deaths of another. Lost money at the box office, but for Garbo fans, an absolute must. Did I Go Wrong?; Pajama Party; Beach Ball; Among the Young; Stuffed Animal. 82m/C VHS, DVD. Tommy Kirk, Annette Funicello, Elsa Lanchester, Harvey Lembeck, Jesse White, Jody McCrea, Donna Loren, Susan Hart, Bobbi Shaw, Cheryl Sweeten, Luree Holmes, Candy Johnson, Dorothy Lamour, Toni Basil, Frankie Avalon, Don Rickles, Teri Garr, Ben Lessy; Cameos: Buster Keaton; D: Don Weis; W: Louis M. Heyward; C: Floyd Crosby; M: Les Baxter.

Pajama Tops ⚐⚐½ 1983 A stage production of the classic French bedroom farce, taped live at the Music Hall Theatre in Toronto, Canada. Includes all the trials and tribulations of marriage including adultery and deceit. 105m/C VHS. Robert Klein, Susan George, Pia Zadora.

Pal Joey ⚐⚐⚐ 1957 Musical comedy about an opportunistic singer who courts a wealthy socialite in hopes that she will finance his nightclub. His play remains in comedic complications. Stellar choreography, fine direction, and beautiful costumes complement performances headed by Hayworth and Sinatra. Oscar-overlooked his pal Joey when awards were handed out. Songs include some of Rodgers and Hart's best. Based on John O'Hara's book and play. ♫Zip; Bewitched, Bothered and Bewildered; I Could Write a

---

Painted Hero ⚐⚐½ 1995 (R) Ro-their orphanage amidst the rise of Chinese nationalism (as if an epidemic and problematic marriage aren't trouble enough). 125m/C CH US Naomi Watts, Edward Norton, Liev Schreiber, Toby Jones, Diana Rigg, Anthony Wong; D: John Curran; W: Ron Nyswaner, Nichols, Hank Henry, Elizabeth Patterson; D: George Sidney; W: Dorothy Kingsley; C: Harold Lipstein; M: Richard Rodgers, Golden Globes '58; Nelson, Kris Kristofferson; Rip Torn, Helen Shaver, Emily Warfeld, Michael Maright; D: Aaron Lipstadt. TV

Pair of Aces ⚐⚐½ 1990 Kristofferson is a Texas Ranger who's on the trail of a serial killer. His only other problem is being saddled with Nelson, a philosophical safecracker who's awaiting trial and in the reluctant cop's custody. Low-key western with good buddy pairing of Nelson and Kristofferson. 94m/C VHS. Willie Nelson, Kris Kristofferson, Rip Torn, Helen Shaver, Emily Warfeld, Michael Maright; D: Aaron Lipstadt. TV

Paisan ⚐⚐⚐ 1946 Six episodic tales of life in Italy, several featuring Allied soldiers and nurses during WWII. One of the stories tells of a man who tries to develop a relationship without being able to speak Italian. Another focuses on a young street robber who is confronted by one of his victims. Strong stories that covers a wide range of emotions. In Italian with English subtitles. 115m/B VHS, DVD. IT Maria Michi, Carmela Sazio, Gar Moore, William Tubbs, Harriet White, Robert Van Loon, Dale Edmonds, Carlo Pisacane, Dots Johnson; D: Roberto Rossellini; W: Federico Fellini, Roberto Rossellini. Natl. Bd. of Review '48: Director (Fellini); N.Y. Film Critics '48: Foreign Film.

The Pajama Game ⚐⚐⚐½ 1957 A spritely musical about the striking workers of the Sleepite Pajama Flactory and their plucky negotiator, Katie (Day). (Raitt). Based on the hit Broadway musical, which was based on Richard Bissell's book "Seven and a half Cents" and adapted for the screen by Bissell and Abbott. Bob Fosse choreographed the dance numbers. ♫I'm Not at All in Love; Small Talk; There Once Was a Man; Steam Heat; Hernando's Highway; Hey There; Once-a-Year Day; Seven and a Half Cents; I'll Never Be Jealous Again. 101m/C VHS, DVD. Doris Day, John Raitt, Eddie Foy Jr., Reta Shaw, Carol Haney; D: Stanley Donen, George Abbott; W: George Abbott, Richard Bissell; C: Harry Stradling Sr.

Pajama Party ⚐⚐ 1964 Follow-up to "Bikini Beach" takes the party inside in this fourth entry in the popular "Beach Party" series. Plot is up to beach party realism. Funicello is Avalon-ess (although he does have a cameo) so she falls for Martian Kirk instead. He's spouting for an alien invasion, but after he falls into Annette's lap decides to save the planet instead. Typical fluff with the usual beach movie faces present. look for a young Garr as a dancer. Followed by the classic "Beach Blanket Bingo." ♫It's That Kind of Day; There Has to Be a Reason; Where Did I Go Wrong?; Pajama Party; Beach Ball; Among the Young; Stuffed Animal. 82m/C VHS, DVD. Tommy Kirk, Annette Funicello, Elsa Lanchester, Harvey Lembeck, Jesse White, Jody McCrea, Donna Loren, Susan Hart, Bobbi Shaw, Cheryl Sweeten, Luree Holmes, Candy Johnson, Dorothy Lamour, Toni Basil, Frankie Avalon, Don Rickles, Teri Garr, Ben Lessy; Cameos: Buster Keaton; D: Don Weis; W: Louis M. Heyward; C: Floyd Crosby; M: Les Baxter.

Pale Saints ⚐⚐½ 1997 (R) Small-time hoods Louis (Flanery) and Dody (Zahn) decide that they will do one last job for crime broker Quick Vic and use their share of the money to head off to California. They travel to Montreal and wind up with a botched heist, a case of mistaken identity, and a lot of double-dealing. The plot gets too convoluted, although it's so last-paced you may not notice the holes. 98m/C VHS, DVD. CA Sean Patrick Flanery, Michael Riley, Saul Rubinek, Maury Chaykin, Rachael Crawford, Gordon Pinsent; D: Joel Wyner; M: Lennie Niehaus.

The Paleface ⚐⚐⚐ 1948 A cowardly dentist becomes a gunslinging hero when Calamity Jane starts aiming for him. A rip-roarin' good time as the comic inventions of the Old West are turned upside down. Includes the Oscar-winning song "Buttons and Bows." The 1952 sequel is "Son of Paleface." Remade in 1968 as "The Shakiest Gun in the West." ♫Buttons and Bows; Get a Man!; Meetcha 'Round the Corner. 91m/C VHS, DVD. Bob Hope, Robert Armstrong, Iris Adrian, Russell, Bob Hope, Robert Armstrong, Iris Adrian, Jane Russell; D: Norman Z. McLeod; C: Ray Rennahan. Oscars '48: Song ("Buttons and Bows").

The Palermo Connection ⚐⚐ 1991 (R) Not the action-thriller the cassette box claims, but a cynical study of a crusading N.Y.C. mayoral candidate who journeys to Sicily and learns that the war on crime has already been lost. Remote adaptation of "To Forget Palermo" by Edmonde Charles-Roux. 100m/C VHS, DVD. James Belushi, Mimi Rogers, Joss Ackland, Philippe Noiret, Vittorio Gassman, Carolina Rosi; D: Francesco Rosi; W: Francesco Rosi, Gore Vidal, Tonino Guerra; C: Pasqualino De Santis; M: Ennio Morricone.

Palindromes ⚐⚐⚐ 2004 As if having abortion as his central topic wasn't challenging enough, Solondz raises the art-house ante exponentially by having his protagonist, Aviva, played by eight different actors, including Jennifer Jason Leigh, an African-American woman, and a boy. Thirteen-year-old Aviva dreams of motherhood, but after she's impregnated, her over-caring parents insist she get an abortion. To keep the baby, Aviva runs away, meeting an eccentric cast of characters on the road. Solondz masterfully conducts the pitfalls of both sides of the abortion issue until the audience's moral compass is helplessly askew. May be too

---

Palais Royale ⚐⚐ 1988 (R) Craven plays an exec who gets involved in the world of gangsters in the late 50s. 100m/C VHS. CA Matt Craven, Kim Cattrall, Dean Stockwell; D: Martin Lavut; M: Jonathan Goldsmith.

Pale Blood ⚐½ 1991 (R) A serial killer in Los Angeles is leaving his victims drained of blood. Could it be that a vampire is stalking the modern American empire, or is this merely the workings of a bloodthirsty psychopath? 93m/C VHS. George Chakiris, Wings Hauser, Pamela Ludwig, Diana Frank, Darcy Demoss, Earl Garnes; D: V.V. Dachin Hsu; W: V.V. Dachin Hsu, Takeshi Matsuo.

Pale Rider ⚐⚐⚐ 1985 (R) A mysterious nameless stranger rides into a small California gold rush town to find himself in the middle of a feud between a mining syndicate and a group of independent prospectors. Christ-like Eastwood evokes comparisons to "Shane." A classical western with clear references to that genre. Its theme treated well complemented by excellent photography and a rock-solid cast. 116m/C VHS, DVD. Clint Eastwood, Michael Moriarty, Carrie Snodgress, Sydney Penny, Richard Dysart, Richard Kiel, Christopher Penn, John Russell, Charles Hallahan, Doug McGrath, Fran Ryan; D: Clint Eastwood; W: Michael Butler, Dennis Shryack; C: Bruce Surtees; M: Lennie Niehaus.

Book; That Terrific Rainbow; What Do I Care for a Dame?; Happy Hunting Horn; Plant You Now, Dig You Later; Do It the Hard Way; Take Him. 111m/C VHS, DVD. Frank Sinatra, Rita Hayworth, Kim Novak, Barbara Nichols, Hank Henry, Elizabeth Patterson; D: George Sidney; W: Dorothy Kingsley; C: Harold Lipstein; M: Richard Rodgers. Golden Globes '58:

esoteric for most, but that's half the fun anyway. 100m/C DVD. US Jennifer Jason Leigh, Ellen Barkin, Richard Masur, Debra Monk, Emani Sledge, Valerie Shusterov, Hannah Freiman, Rachel Corr, Will Denton, Shayna Levine, Sharon Wilkins, Stephen Adly Guirgis, Matthew Faber, Steve Singer, Richard Riehle, Robert Agri, John Gemberling, Alexander Brickel, Walter Bobbie; **D:** Todd Solondz; **W:** Todd Solondz; **C:** Tom Richmond; **M:** Nathan Larson.

The Pallbearer 🦴🦴½ **1995 (PG-13)** You probably liked this one better when it was called "The Graduate," as this one shares some key plot points with, but lacks the edge and cultural impact of the 1967 classic. Basset-faced Schwimmer plays Tom, who is asked to be a pallbearer for an old high school classmate whom he can't quite remember. He is then seduced by the mother (Hershey) of the deceased, while trying to kindle a romance with the fabulous Julie DeMarco (Paltrow), an old classmate who can't quite remember him. The spurned older woman then begins to exact her revenge, while Tom tries to figure out how to court Julie while living at home with his mom. Good performances make it watchable. 98m/C VHS, DVD. Joseph (Joe) D'Onofrio, David Schwimmer, Gwyneth Paltrow, Barbara Hershey, Michael Rapaport, Carol Kane, Toni Collette, Michael Vartan; **D:** Matt Reeves; **W:** Matt Reeves, Jason Katims; **C:** Robert Elswit; **M:** Stewart Copeland.

Palm Beach 🦴🦴 **1979** The lives of two petty thieves, a runaway, and a private detective intertwine at Palm Beach Down Under. Best appreciated by fans of things Aussie. 90m/C VHS. AU Bryan Brown, Nat Young, Ken Brown, Amanda Berry; **D:** Albie Thomas.

The Palm Beach Story 🦴🦴 **1942** Young architect Tom Jeffers (McCrea) dreams of building an airport and his adoring wife Gerry (Colbert) decides to help him out—by divorcing him. That way she can head to Palm Beach, marry rich, and finance Tom's ambitions. So Gerry sets her considerable charms on catching eccentric J.D. Hackensacker (Vallee). When Tom follows, he becomes prey for J.D.'s tart-tongued sister (Astor). Takes amusing aim at the idle rich with sophisticated, witty dialogue. 88m/B VHS, DVD. Claudette Colbert, Joel McCrea, Mary Astor, Rudy Vallee, William Demarest, Franklin Pangborn; **D:** Preston Sturges; **C:** Victor Milner.

Palm Springs Weekend 🦴🦴½ **1963** A busload of love-hungry kids head south and get involved in routine hijinks. Actually shot on Palm Springs with above average performances by a handful of teen stars. 100m/C VHS, DVD. Troy Donahue, Ty Hardin, Connie Stevens, Stefanie Powers, Robert Conrad, Jack Weston, Andrew Duggar; **D:** Norman Taurog.

Palmetto 🦴½ **1998 (R)** Contempo-noir film that misses the mark has bitter ex-con Harry (Harrelson) partnered with seductress Rhea (Shue) in a phony kidnapping of her step-daughter Odette (Sevigny). Newly released from the joint after a rotten frame-up job, Harry is lured back by ex Nina (Gershon), to the backwater town that sent him up, where he winds up in trouble as all three women go to work on him. Originality and character development go AWOL, as the normally adept Harrelson flounders for an identity alongside Shue's broad characterization of a vamp who teeters on high heels and the brink of satire. Feels like Tennessee Williams as written by Joe Esterhas. From Rene Raymond's (a.k.a. James Hadley Chase) novel, "Just Another Sucker." 114m/C VHS, DVD. Angela Featherstone, Woody Harrelson, Elisabeth Shue, Michael Rapaport, Gina Gershon, Chloe Sevigny, Rolf Hoppe, Tom Wright; **D:** Volker Schlondorff; **W:** E. Max Frye; **C:** Thomas Kloss; **M:** Klaus Doldinger.

Palmy Days 🦴🦴½ **1931** Shy Eddie (Cantor) is involved with a phony medium, a scam involving a bakery, theft, romance, singing, and a disguise as a woman (in the other bakery workers and the Goldwyn Girls, including Betty Grable). Silly fun, with choreography by Busby Berkeley. ♪Bend Down, Sister; Goose Pimples; Dunk Dunk Dunk; My Honey Said Yes, Yes, Yes; There's Nothing Too Good for My Baby. 77m/B VHS. Eddie Cantor, Charlotte Greenwood, Charles Middleton, George Raft, Harry Woods, Spencer Charters, Barbara Weeks, Paul Page; **D:** Edward Sutherland; **W:** Morrie Ryskind, Keene Thompson, Eddie Cantor; **C:** Gregg Toland.

Palombella Rossa 🦴🦴 **1989** Political comedy about the fate of Italian communism. When communist politician Michele loses his memory in a car crash, he finds himself trying to reconstruct his life during a game of water polo as well as trying to answer political questions and keep track of the people from his life who randomly appear and disappear. In Italian with English subtitles. 87m/C VHS. IT Nanni Moretti, Silvio Orlando, Asia Argento; **D:** Nanni Moretti; **W:** Nanni Moretti; **C:** Giuseppe Lanci; **M:** Nicola Piovani.

Palooka 🦴🦴½ **1934 (G)** Based on the comic strip, "Joe Palooka; The Great Schnozzle" this film portrays a fast-talking boxing manager and his goofy, lovable protege. The young scrapper fights James Cagney's little brother. Durante sings his classic tune, "Inka-Dinka-Doo," and packs a punch in the lead. A two-fisted comedy with a witty dialogue and fine direction. Not a part of the Palooka series of the 1940s. 86m/B VHS, DVD. Jimmy Durante, Stuart Erwin, Lupe Velez, Robert Armstrong, Thelma Todd, William Cagney; **D:** Ben Stoloff.

Palookaville 🦴🦴🦴 **1995 (R)** Nostalgic comedy of three under-employed friends who take up crime, temporarily, just until they can secure legit work. Using a little-known 1950s crime movie as their tutor, the trio of criminal cretins encounter a variety of setbacks on their way to financial security. Planning an elaborate scheme to rob an armored car, they decide to use toy guns, so Jerry (Trese) rounds up a most intimidating assortment of the neon orange plastic variety. Later, while chiseling through a wall to a jewelry store, they find themselves in the bakery next door, with Jerry delighted to score some pastries instead. The other two aren't much brighter—Russ (Gallo) is the leader of the three and a small-time ladies man while Sid (Forsythe) is a devout dog lover whose dreams of a taxi service for the aged are shattered when customers are driven away by his kennel on wheels. Adapted from short stories written in the 1940s by the Italian Italo Calvino, modern adaptation manages to retain a '40s feel and charm. 92m/C VHS, DVD. William Forsythe, Vincent Gallo, Adam Trese, Lisa Gay Hamilton, Frances McDormand, Davis Boulton, James David Hilton, Gareth Williams, Bridget Ryan, Kim Dickens, Suzanne Shepherd, Robert LuPone; **D:** Alan Taylor; **W:** David Epstein; **C:** John Thomas; **M:** Rachel Portman.

Pals 🦴½ **1987** Old friends stumble across $3 million in cash and learn the predictable lesson that money can't buy happiness. A terribly trite TV-movie with an exceptional cast. 90m/C VHS, DVD. Don Ameche, George C. Scott, Sylvia Sidney, Susan Rinell, James Greene; **D:** Lou Antonio.

Pals of the Range 🦴 **1935** A framed ranch owner breaks out of jail in order to catch the real cattle thieves. Ho hum in the Old West. 55m/B VHS. Frances Morris, Yakima Canutt, George Chesebro, Robert "Blackie" Whiteford, Rex Lease; **D:** Elmer Clifton; **W:** Elmer Clifton; **C:** Edward Linden.

Pals of the Saddle 🦴🦴½ **1938** The intrepid trio go after enemy agents who are trying to smuggle chemicals for poisonous gas into Mexico. This is the first of the series in which the Duke played the part of Stony Brooke. Somewhat convoluted plot, but nevertheless enjoyable. 55m/B VHS. John Wayne, Ray Corrigan, Max Terhune, Doreen McKay, Josef Forte, Ted Adams, Curley Dresden; **D:** George Sherman.

The Pamela Principle 🦴🦴 **1991 (R)** A bored, middle-aged man thinks his prayers are answered when he meets a sexy 20-year-old model and begins a sordid affair with her. Soon, however, he finds himself in a tense situation when he must choose between his family or his fantasy. Also available in an unrated version. 94m/C VHS. J.K. Dumont, Veronica Cash, Shelby Lane, Troy Donahue, Frank Pesce; **D:** Paul Thomas.

Panama Flo 🦴½ **1932** While stranded in Panama, honky-tonk chanteuse Flo (Twelvetrees) steals the wallet of mining engineer Don McTeague (Bickford), but gets caught. Instead of calling the cops, the mark insists Flo go with him to his mining camp and work off the debt as his housekeeper. Eventually, Flo's louse of a boyfriend (Armstrong) shows up to cause more trouble and ruin a budding romance. 72m/B VHS. Helen Twelvetrees, Charles Bickford, Robert Armstrong, Maude Eburne, Paul Hurst, Marjorie Peterson; **D:** Ralph Murphy; **W:** Garrett Fort; **C:** Arthur C. Miller.

Panama Hattie 🦴🦴 **1942** Screen adaptation of Cole Porter's delightful Broadway musical. Unfortunately, something (like a plot) was lost in transition. Southern runs a saloon for our boys down in Panama. Among the musical numbers and vaudevillian acts some spies show up. Several screenwriters and directors, including Vincente Minnelli, worked uncredited on this picture, to no avail. Home's second screen appearance. ♪It Was Just One of Those Things; Fresh as a Daisy; I've Still Got My Health; Let's Be Buddies; Make It Another Old Fashioned; Hattie from Panama; Good Neighbors; I'll Do Anything for You; The Son of a Gun Who Pick on Uncle Sam. 79m/B VHS. Ann Sothern, Dan Dailey, Red Skelton, Virginia O'Brien, Rags Ragland, Alan Mowbray, Ben Blue, Carl Esmond, Lena Home; **D:** Norman Z. McLeod; **C:** George J. Folsey; **M:** George Bassman, Cole Porter.

Panama Lady 🦴½ **1939** Ball stars as the sexy, sultry "Panama Lady" in this old-fashioned romance. She gets involved in some shady business south of the border. A lackluster remake of "Panama Flo." 65m/B VHS. Lucille Ball, Evelyn Brent, Allan "Rocky" Lane, Steffi Duna, Don Briggs, Bernadene Hayes; **D:** Jack B. Hively; **W:** Michael Kanin; **C:** J. Roy Hunt.

Panama Menace 🦴 *South of Panama* **1941** An agent heads to Panama to thwart spies who are after a special paint that makes things invisible. Poor effort all around, in spite of Beaumont's presence. 68m/B VHS. Roger Pryor, Virginia Vale, Lionel Royce, Lucien Prival, Duncan Renaldo, Lester Dorr, Hugh Beaumont; **D:** Jean Yarbrough.

Panama Patrol 🦴🦴½ **1939** Just as they are about to be married, two Army officers are called to duty in Panama. It seems that the Chinese have infiltrated the area with spies and something's got to be done. Too much attention to minor parts of the plot slows the story occasionally, but performances for some of the sluggishness compensate for some of the story. 67m/B VHS, DVD. Leon Ames, Charlotte Wynters, Weldon Heyburn, Adrienne Ames, Abner Biberman, Hugh McArthur, Donald (Don "Red") Barry; **D:** Charles Lamont.

Panamint's Bad Man 🦴🦴 **1938** Ballaw is a poor man's Gary Cooper fighting for justice against stagecoach robbers. Almost as much flavor as tumbleweed. 59m/B VHS, DVD. Smith Ballew, Evelyn Daw, Noah Beery Sr.; **D:** Ray Taylor.

Pancho Barnes 🦴🦴½ **1988 (PG)** Routine biography of one of the first female pilots of the 1920s. Barnes is a bored debutante who finds her challenge in life when she learns to fly, becoming a barnstormer and movie stunt pilot. Her ambitions naturally get in the way of her romantic life. Good flying scenes. 150m/C VHS. Valerie Bertinelli, Ted Wass, Sam Robards, James Stephens, Cynthia Harris, Geoffrey Lewis; **D:** Richard T. Heffron; **W:** John Michael Hayes. TV

Pancho Villa 🦴½ **1972 (PG)** Savalas has the lead in this fictional account of the famous Mexican, he leads his men in a raid on an American fort after being hoodwinked in an arms deal. Connors tries to hold the fort against him. The finale, in which two trains crash head on, is the most exciting event in the whole darn movie. 92m/C VHS, DVD. SP Telly Savalas, Clint Walker, Anne Francis, Chuck Connors, Angel Del Pozo, Luis Davila; **D:** Eugenio (Gene) Martin; **W:** Julian Zimet; **C:** Alejandro Ulloa; **M:** Anton Abril.

Pancho Villa Returns 🦴🦴 **1950** It's 1913, and noble Mexican General Pancho Villa leads his merry men against the assassins of President Madera. This Mexican production (filmed in English) paints a partisan portrait of title character as a good-hearted revolutionary folk hero, not the roving bandit later notorious north of the border. 95m/B VHS. MX Leo Carrillo, Esther Fernandez, Jeanette Comber, Rodolfo Acosta; **D:** Miguel Contreras Torres; **W:** Miguel Contreras Torres.

Pandaemonium 🦴🦴🦴 **2000 (PG-13)** Friendship, rivalry, and jealousy between 19th century English romanticists William Wordsworth (Hannah) and Samuel Taylor Coleridge (Roache), in 1813, debilitated by opium abuse, Coleridge attends a reception for the now-distant Wordsworth and flashes back to their first meeting some 20 years before. Coleridge and his wife Sara (Morton) move to a country cottage with Wordsworth and his sister Dorothy (Woof) living nearby as the two men collaborate on a poetry collection. Coleridge becomes (mutually) attracted to Dorothy and finds inspiration in drugs. A rift between the two men deepens when Wordsworth marries and Coleridge dependency on drugs worsens—even as his poetry soars. 125m/C VHS, DVD. GB Linus Roache, John Hannah, Samantha Morton, Emily Woof, Emma Fielding, Andy Serkis, Samuel West, Guy Lankester; **D:** Julien Temple; **C:** John Lynch; **M:** Dario Marianelli.

Pandemic 🦴½ **2007** Dr. Kayla Martin (Thiessen) and her partner Carl (Stewart) face the frightening effects of a biological attack when a young man dies on a plane following a fever and violent convulsions. Other passengers on board are now filtering into the city and infecting areas of Los Angeles. The virus and panic continue to spread. Fairly entertaining but overly saturated with unsupported improbability (starting with Thiessen as a doctor). 170m/C DVD. Tiffani-Amber Thiessen, Vincent Spano, Eric Roberts, Faye Dunaway, French Stewart, Bruce Boxleitner, Bob Gunton, Renee Taylor, Tamlyn Tomita, Clyde Kusatsu; **D:** Armand Mastroianni; **W:** Bruce Zabel, Jackie Zabel; **C:** Amit Bhattacharya. CABLE

Pandemonium 🦴🦴½ **1982 (PG)** A spoof of teen slasher films involving murder at Bambi's Cheerleading School. Seems that nationwide, cheerleaders have been brutally eliminated from their squads, leaving Bambi's as the last resort for the terminally perky. Smothers is interesting and more intelligent than his TV persona (although not by much) as the Mountie hero, assisted by Paul Reubens in a pre-Pee-Wee role. Kane steals the show as Candy, a pleasant lass with hyperkinetic powers. 82m/C VHS. CA Tom Smothers, Carol Kane, Miles Chapin, Paul (Pee-wee Herman) Reubens, Judge Reinhold, Tab Hunter, Marc McClure, Donald O'Connor, Eve Arden, Eileen Brennan, Edie McClurg; **D:** Alfred Sole.

Pandora and the Flying Dutchman 🦴🦴 **1951** Feverish romantic fantasy has playgirl/nightclub singer Pandora Reynolds (Gardner) living in '30s Spain and being romanced by every man in sight. Naturally, she cares for none of them until she meets enigmatic Dutch captain Hendrick van der Zee (Mason) who is, in fact, the legendary Flying Dutchman—condemned to wander the seas forever unless a woman is willing to give up her life for him. Gardner is, as usual, exotically lovely. 123m/C VHS, DVD. Ava Gardner, James Mason, Nigel Patrick, Sheila Sim, Harold Warrender, Mario Cabre; **D:** Albert Lewin; **W:** Albert Lewin; **C:** Jack Cardiff; **M:** Alan Rawsthorne.

Pandora's Box 🦴🦴🦴 *Die Buechse der Pandora; Lulu* **1928** This silent classic marked the end of the German Expressionist era and established Brooks as a major screen presence. She plays the tempestuous Lulu, who destroys everyone she comes in contact with, eventually sinking to prostitution and a fateful meeting with Jack the Ripper. Silent with orchestral score. 110m/B VHS, DVD. GE Louise Brooks, Fritz Kortner, Francis Lederer, Carl Goetz, Alice Roberts, Gustav Diesl; **D:** G.W. Pabst; **W:** G.W. Pabst; **C:** Gunther Krampf.

Panic ✓✓½ *Bakterion* 1976 A scientist terrorizes a small town when he becomes hideously deformed by one of his bacteria experiments. He should have known better. **90m/C VHS.** *IT/SP* David Warbeck, Janet Agren; *D:* Tonino Ricco; *W:* Victor Andres Catena, Jaime Comas Gil; *C:* Giovanni Bergamini; *M:* Marcello Giombini.

Panic ✓✓½ 2000 (R) Hangdog Macy is perfect as middle-aged Alex, who is not having your usual midlife crisis since he's a hit man. As a matter of fact, he learned his trade from his ruthless dad Michael (Sutherland), who still calls the shots. But Alex has been keeping the truth from his wife Martha (Ullman) and his beloved son Sammy (Dorfman) and he needs to talk. So he goes to shrink Josh Parks (Ritter) and, in the waiting room, Alex meets neurotic Sarah (Campbell), with whom he contemplates an affair. Alex wants to make some changes but when you're a professional killer, it's not that easy. **93m/C VHS, DVD.** William H. Macy, John Ritter, Neve Campbell, Donald Sutherland, Tracey Ullman, Barbara Bain, David Dorfman; *D:* Henry Bromell; *W:* Henry Bromell; *C:* Jeffrey Jur; *M:* Brian Tyler.

Panic Button ✓½ 1962 Mel Brooks took the plot from this film and made "The Producers," which was much better. Italian gangsters produce a TV show and stack the deck so it will fail. Unbeknownst to them, the star has figured out what they are doing when you're a doctor races against time to find the cause of an epidemic that is threatening the health of a city. Good performances compensate for a predictable plot. **76m/C VHS, DVD.** Dorian Harewood, Robin Gammell, Catlin Adams, Ramon Bieri, Movita; *D:* John Llewellyn Moxey. **TV**

Panic in Echo Park ✓✓ 1977 A doctor races against time to find the cause of an epidemic that is threatening the health of a city. Good performances compensate for a predictable plot.

Panic in Needle Park ✓✓✓ 1971 (R) Drugs become an obsession for a young girl who goes to New York for an abortion. Her new boyfriend is imprisoned for robbery in order to support both their habits. She resorts to prostitution to continue her drug habit, and trouble occurs when her boyfriend realizes she was instrumental in his being sent to jail. Strikes a vein in presenting an uncompromising look at drug use. May be too much of a depressant for some. Pacino's first starring role. **90m/C VHS, DVD.** Al Pacino, Kitty Winn, Alan Vint, Richard Bright, Kiel Martin, Warren Finnerty, Raul Julia, Paul Sorvino; *D:* Jerry Schatzberg; *W:* Joan Didion, John Gregory Dunne; *C:* Adam Holender. Cannes '71: Actress (Winn).

Panic in the Skies ✓✓ 1996 The cockpit of a Boeing 747 is struck by lightning in mid-flight, killing the pilot and co-pilot. Flight attendant Jackson and passenger Marinaro try to figure out a way to safely land the passenger-filled jet. **90m/C VHS, DVD.** Kate Jackson, Ed Marinaro, Erik Estrada, Maureen McCormick, Billy Warlock, Robert Guillaume; *D:* Paul Ziller; *W:* Robert Hamilton; *C:* Rod Parkhurst. **M:** Todd Hayen. **TV**

Panic in the Streets ✓✓✓ 1950 The Black Death threatens New Orleans in this intense tale. When a body is found on the waterfront, a doctor (Widmark) is called upon for a diagnosis. The carrier proves to be deadly in more ways than one. Fine performances, taut direction (this was one of Kazan's favorite movies). Filmed on location in New Orleans. **96m/B VHS, DVD.** Richard Widmark, Jack Palance, Barbara Bel Geddes, Paul Douglas, Zero Mostel; *D:* Elia Kazan; *W:* Edward Anhalt. Oscars '50: Story.

Panic in the Year Zero! ✓✓½ *End of the World* 1962 Milland and family leave Los Angeles for a fishing trip just as the city is hit by a nuclear bomb. Continuing out into the wilderness for safety, the family now must try to survive as their world crumbles around them. Generally considered the best of Milland's five directorial efforts. **92m/B VHS, DVD.** Ray Milland, Jean Hagen, Frankie Avalon, Mary Mitchell, Joan Freeman, Willis Bouchey, Rex Holman, Richard Bakalyan.

Neil Nephew; *D:* Ray Milland; *W:* Jay Simms, John Morton; *C:* Gilbert Warrenton; *M:* Les Baxter.

Panic on the 5:22 ✓✓ 1974 Wealthy commuters are kidnapped and held hostage by terrorist hoodlums in a suburban train club car. **78m/C VHS** Lynda Day George, Laurence Luckinbill, Ina Balin, Bernie Casey; *D:* Harvey Hart. **TV**

Panic Room ✓✓½ 2002 (R) Recently divorced mom Meg (Foster) moves with daughter Sarah (Stewart) into a huge, ominous four-story brownstone in New York. The house comes equipped with a "panic room" a fortress-like room on the par. Before the night is over, the room comes into play as three intruders came looking for something. The three happen to be looking for something that's in the room, where the women have holed themselves up. And thus the cat-and-mouse game begins. Fincher's talents for visual style, creative camera work, and squirmy set pieces are well-used here as the tension mounts with each scene. The plot isn't especially original, but the twists are well-done the performers acquit themselves nicely. **112m/C VHS, DVD.** Jodie Foster, Forest Whitaker, Dwight Yoakam, Jared Leto, Kristen Stewart, Ann Magnuson, Patrick Bauchau, Ian Buchanan, Paul Schulze; *C:* David Fincher; *W:* David Koepp; *C:* Conrad W. Hall. Darius Khondji; *M:* Howard Shore.

Panic Station ✓✓ *The Pains of Heaven* 1982 Two guys get lonely at remote satellite relay station. **90m/C VHS.** AV Richard Moir, Reg Evans, Gerard Kennedy; *D:* Ian Pringle.

Panique ✓✓✓ *Panic* 1947 A study of mob psychology in slums of post-WWII Paris. Two lovers frame a stranger for murder. Dark and tautly paced thriller taken from the novel by Georges Simenon in French with English subtitles. **87m/B VHS.** FR Michel Simon, Viviane Romance; *D:* Julien Duvivier.

Pan's Labyrinth ✓✓✓ *El Laberinto del Fauno* 2006 (R) When her loving soldier father dies in combat during Spain's civil war, young Ofelia (Baquero) is stuck with Captain Vidal (Lopez), a brute of a stepfather, when her mother, Carmen (Gil), remarries. Ofelia sees an escape from her miserable situation when she stumbles upon a garden labyrinth that leads to a freakish-yet-bewitching underground fantasy world inhabited by strange creatures led by Pan (Jones), who is part goat, part man. He tells Ofelia that she might be their lost princess but must perform three tasks in order to prove herself worthy of the crown. Despite feeling guilty about abandoning her mother, whose difficult pregnancy leaves her bedridden, Ofelia takes on the risky, off-the-wall missions. Eventually the line between the two worlds blurs, causing dire consequences. Complex and entertaining fairy tale mixes vivid scenery with computer-generated effects that is violence and adult themes are too intense for the kiddies. In Spanish with subtitles. **112m/C DVD, Blu-ray Disc, HD DVD, MX SP** Sergi Lopez, Maribel Verdu, Doug Jones, Alex Angulo, Ivana Baquero, Ariadna Gil, Roger Casamajor; *D:* Guillermo del Toro; *W:* Guillermo del Toro; *M:* Javier Navarrete. Oscars '06: Art Dir./Set Dec., Cinematog., Makeup; British Acad; Ind. Spirit '07: Cinematog., Foreign Film, Makeup; Ind. Spirit '07: Cinematog., Foreign Film.

Pantaloons ✓✓ 1957 A man who fancies himself to be irresistible chases women for sport. A quaint and lively period film. **93m/C VHS.** FR Fernandel, Carmen Sevilla, Fernando Rey; *D:* John Berry.

Panther ✓✓✓ 1995 (R) The Van Peebles family teaches Oliver Stone History 101 with a fictionalized account of the Black Panthers' emergence as a voice for African Americans and as a fixture on the FBI's most wanted list in the '60s. Judge (Hardison), a Vietnam vet forced by the FBI to become an informant, chronicles the activities of leaders Bobby Seale (Vance) and Huey P. Newton (Chong) and serves as witness to the Panthers' rise and subsequent fall into corruption and disintegration. Scatter-shot editing is meant to signify the chaos of the times, but instead adds to the action-flick feel.

---

and further detracts from the professed intent of being a message movie. **124m/C VHS, DVD.** Kadeem Hardison, Marcus Chong, Courtney B. Vance, Bokeem Woodbine, Joe Don Baker, Anthony Griffith, Nefertiti, James Russo, Richard Dysart, M. Emmet Walsh, Mario Van Peebles, Sybil Danning; *D:* Pierre Chevalier; *W:* Georges Friedland; *C:* Max Montellier; *M:* Douglas Cooper.

The Panther's Claw ✓ 1942 Litter of sex kittens led by Danning get into major scraps to save world. **77m/C VHS.** FR Jack Taylor, Analia Ivars, Jean-Pierre Gossart, Karin Schubert, Sybil Danning; *D:* Pierre Chevalier; *W:* Georges Friedland; *C:* Max Montellier.

Panther Squad ✓ 1984 Litter of sex kittens led by Danning get into major scraps to save world.

Paparazzi ✓✓½ 2004 (PG-13) An actor's revenge? Produced by Mel Gibson (who has a cameo) and his icon production company, this overheated melodrama follows newly-crowned action star Bo Laramie (Hauser), whose celebrity has led to his being stalked by those degenerate paparazzi. When Bo's family is critically injured in a car crash caused by the relentless shutterbug pursuit, Bo turns vigilante to get revenge. Sleazy as it is slimy nastiest as the lead sleazy photog. **85m/C VHS, DVD.** US Cole Hauser, Robin Tunney, Dennis Farina, Daniel Baldwin, Tom Hollander, Kevin Gage, Tom Sizemore, Duane Davis, Blake Bryan, Chris Rock, Matthew McConaughey, Vince Vaughn; *D:* Paul Abascal; *W:* Forrest Smith; *C:* Daryn Okada; *M:* Brian Tyler.

Papa's Angels ✓✓ 2000 (PG) Sappy Christmas drama set in the 1930s. The Jenkins family, headed by gruff furniture maker Grins (Bakula), live a hard-but-happy life in the Appalachia mountains, with mom Sharon (Nixon) raising their four kids. Then Sharon is diagnosed with tuberculosis and is sent to a sanatorium. But Grins bulics a glass room on to the house so she can see the children without infecting them, and brings her home to die. After her death, Grins takes to the moonshine and the kids aren't even want to celebrate Christmas! Based on the book by Collin Wilcox Paxton and Gary Carden. **95m/C VHS.** Scott Bakula, Cynthia Nixon, Eva Marie Saint, Kimberly Warnat, Branston James Olson, Jenny Lynn Hutcheson, Lachlan Murdoch, Kirsten Bishopric; *D:* Dwight Little; *W:* Bill Cain. **TV**

Papa's Delicate Condition ✓✓ 1963 Based on the autobiographical writings of silent screen star Corinne Griffith. Gleason is Papa whose "delicate condition" is a result of his drinking. His antics provide a cornucopia of humor and warmth at the turn-of-the-century family life. No I.D.s required whole family. Features the Academy Award-winning song "Call Me Irresponsible." *D:* "Call Me Irresponsible; Bill Bailey, Won't You Please Come Home?. **98m/C VHS.** Jackie Gleason, Glynis Johns, Charlie Ruggles, Laurel Goodwin, Elisha Cook Jr., Murray Hamilton; *D:* George Marshall; *W:* Jack Rose; *C:* Loyal Griggs. Oscars '63: Song ("Call Me Irresponsible").

The Paper ✓✓✓ 1994 (R) Another crowd pleaser from director Howard follows a red letter day in the life of an editor at the tabloid New York Sun (modeled on the trashy Post). Fresh, fast-moving script by the Koepp brothers (who appear as reporters) offers a fairly accurate portrayal of the business of journalism (including the "brisk" language), with a few Hollywood exceptions. Pace suffers from cutaways to life outside, while script and direction sometimes coast past targets. Propelled by a fine cast, with cola-swigging editor Keaton the focus as he juggles his personal and professional lives. As a managing editor married to her work and ready to run over anyone in her way, Close is both funny and scary. Duvall contributes salt as

the old newsroom warhorse. Tons of cameos, though those outside of the business may not notice them. **112m/C VHS, DVD.** Michael Keaton, Robert Duvall, Marisa Tomei, Glenn Close, Randy Quaid, Jason Robards Jr., Jason Alexander, Spalding Gray, Catherine O'Hara, Lynne Thigpen; *C:* John Seale; *M:* Randy Newman.

The Paper Brigade ✓✓½ 1996 (PG) Fifteen-year-old Gunther (Howard) gets a paper-route-to pay for the concert tickets he bought to impress a girl. Now he has to contend with his crazy neighbor (England) and a gang of bullies, as well as other obstacles. **89m/C VHS.** Kyle Howard, Robert England, Travis Wester; *D:* Blair Treu.

Paper Bullets ✓ 1999 (R) Cop John Rourke's son is kidnapped by a Chinese drug lord and, naturally, he'll do anything to get his boy back, including aligning himself with a beautiful woman who has an equal obsession for revenge. **55m/C VHS, DVD.** James Russo, Kyle McNamara, Ernie Hudson, Nicole Billderback, Jeff Wincott, Francois Chau; *D:* Serge Rodnunsky; *C:* Greg Patterson; *M:* Serge Rodnunsky. **VIDEO**

The Paper Chase ✓✓✓ 1973 (PG) Students at Harvard Law School suffer and struggle through their first year. A realistic, sometimes acidly humorous look at Ivy League ambitions, with -housman at his best as the tough professor. Wonderful adaptation of the John Jay Osborn novel which later became the basis for the acclaimed TV series. **111m/C VHS, DVD.** Timothy Bottoms, Lindsay Wagner, John Houseman, Graham Beckel, Edward Herrmann, James Naughton, Craig Richard Nelson, Bob Lydiard; *D:* James Bridges; *W:* James Bridges; *C:* Gordon Willis; *M:* John Williams. Oscars '73: Support. Actor (Houseman); Golden Globes '74: Support. Actor (Houseman); Natl. Bd. of Review '73: Support. Actor (Houseman).

Paper Clips ✓✓✓ 2004 (G) A middle school class in Whitwell, Tennessee, a small rural town with virtually no Jews, few minorities, and within 100 miles of the KKK's headquarters inspires the world through a class project in this powerful Holocaust, the students discovered that in Norway, where the paper clip was invented, citizens wore paper clips on their lapels in protest of the Nazis. They begin writing letters to public figures asking for one paper clip each, in hopes of collecting 6 million to match the number of Jews that lost their lives. They receive an overwhelming response from around the world, eventually collecting 29 million. At times a little too tedious and self-congratulatory for its own good, but makes a great tool for discussing diversity education. **87m/C DVD.** US *D:* Jeffrey Ventimilia, Elliot Berlin; *W:* Jeffrey Ventimilia; *C:* Michael Marton; *M:* Charlie Bernett.

Paper Lion ✓✓½ 1968 A comedy "documentary" about bestselling writer George Plimpton's tryout game as quarterback with the Detroit Lions. Film debut of Alan Alda. Helped Karras make the transition from the gridiron to the silver screen. Moves into field goal range but doesn't quite score. **107m/C VHS.** Alan Alda, Lauren Hutton, Alex Karras, Ann Turkel, John Gordy, Roger Brown, "Sugar Ray" Robinson, Roy Scheider, David Doyle; *D:* Alex Marchi.

Paper Man ✓✓ 1971 A group of college students create a fictitious person in a computer for a credit card scam. The scheme snowballs, resulting in murder and hints of possible artificial intelligence. But it's just standard network TV fare, with a creepy performance by Stockwell as a computer whiz. **90m/C VHS.** Dean Stockwell, Stefanie Powers, James Stacy, Elliot Street, Tina Chen, James Olson, Ross Elliott; *D:* Walter Grauman.

Paper Marriage ✓✓½ 1988 In Canada, a less-than-successful Chinese boxer agrees to marry a Hong Kong girl for a promise of payment in order that she may become a citizen. The money never comes, but the nearly betrothed pair discover that they love each other, after all in Cantonese with English subtitles. **102m/C VHS.** C/-Sammo Hung, Maggie Cheung; *D:* Alfred Cheung.

Paper Marriage 1993 Yet another variation on the marriage in order to gain citizenship but yes we're going to fall in love films. A young Polish woman has fallen for an upper-crust English doctor she's met in Warsaw. When Alicia arrives in England, she's promptly dumped by the cad. She's ambitious and wants to stay in England so Alicja arranges a marriage of convenience with small-time crook Aiden, who finds his new bride is more than he bargained for. 88m/C VHS. GB PL Gary Kemp, Joanna Trepechinska, Rita Tushingham, Richard Hawley, David Horovitch, William Ilkley, Mark McKellen, Ann Mitchell, Sadie Frost; D: Krzysztof Lang; W: Marek Kreutz, Krzysztof Lang.

Paper Mask 1991 (R) When a promising young doctor is killed in an auto accident, an unscrupulous, psychotic porter assumes his identity. He uses said identity to, among other things, initiate an affair with a sultry co-worker. How long will this madman play his unholy game, and at what cost? 105m/C VHS. GB Paul McGann, Amanda Donohoe, Frederick Treves, Barbara Leigh-Hunt, Jimmy Yuill, Tom Wilkinson; D: Christopher Morahan; W: John Collee; C: Nat Crosby; M: Richard Harvey.

Paper Moon 1973 (PG) Award-winning story set in depression-era Kansas with Ryan O'Neal as a Bible-wielding con who meets up with a nine-year-old orphan. During their travels together, he discovers that the orphan (his daughter, Tatum) is better at "his" game than he is. Irresistible chemistry between the O'Neals, leading to Tatum's Oscar win (she is the youngest actor ever to take home a statue). Cinematically picturesque and cynical enough to keep overt sentimentalism at bay. Based on Joe David Brown's novel, "Addie Pray." The director's version contains a prologue that... 102m/B VHS, DVD. Ryan O'Neal, Tatum O'Neal, Madeline Kahn, John Hillerman, Randy Quaid; D: Peter Bogdanovich; W: Alvin Sargent. Oscars '73: Support. Actress (O'Neal); Writers Guild '73: Adapt. Screenplay.

Paper Tiger 1974 Niven plays an imaginative English tutor who fabricates fantastic yarns fictionalizing his past in order to impress his student, the son of the Japanese ambassador to a Southeast Asian country. Poorly executed karate, misdirection, and a simplistic story line work against it. 104m/C VHS. GB David Niven, Toshiro Mifune, Eiko Ando, Hardy Kruger; D: Ken Annakin; W: Jack Davies.

A Paper Wedding Les Noces de Papier 1989 A middle-aged literature professor with a dead-end career and equally dead-end romance with a married man is persuaded by her lawyer sister to marry a Chilean political refugee to avoid his deportation. Of course, they must fool an immigration official and their fake marriage does turn into romance, but this is no light-hearted "Green Card." Bujold shines. In French and Spanish with English subtitles. 90m/C VHS. CA Genevieve Bujold, Manuel Aranguiz, Dorothee Berryman; D: Michel Brault; C: Sylvain Brault.

Paperback Hero 1973 A hotshot hockey player turns to crime when his team loses its financial backing. Choppy storyline could use a Zamboni, while Dullea should be penalized for occasionally losing his rustic accent. Still the supporting actors skate through their roles and, for periods, it works. A slapshot that ultimately clangs off the goal post. 94m/C VHS. CA Keir Dullea, Elizabeth Ashley, John Beck, Dayle Haddon; D: Peter Pearson.

Paperback Hero 1999 Engaging leads help carry a weak story in this fluffy romantic comedy. Studly Jack (Jackman) is a long-distance trucker who makes his home in a remote part of the Australian outback and is the secret author of a bodice-ripper that has become a bestseller. What Jack has neglected to tell his best friend, Ruby (karvan), is that he used her name as his nom de plume. Now the book's publisher wants Ruby to come to Sydney for a face-to-face meeting and Jack has a tough time getting her to go along with the deception. 96m/C VHS. AU Hugh Jackman, Claudia Karvan, Andrew S. Gilbert, Angie Milliken, Jeanie Drynan, Tony Barry, Ritchie Singer, Bruce Venables, Charlie Little; D: Antony J. Bowman; W: Antony J. Bowman; C: David Burr; M: Burkhard Dallwitz.

Paperback Romance Lucky Break 1996 (R) Sophie (Carides) is a writer of erotica who doesn't act on her own impulses because she's embarrassed by her polio-crippled leg. But when she breaks her leg, the cast allows her to pass the injury off as a skiing accident and Sophie decides to go after the man of her dreams, a charmingly shady jewelry dealer named Eddie (LaPaglia)—who just happens to be engaged. 99m/C VHS, DVD. AU Gia Carides, Anthony LaPaglia, Rebecca Gibney; D: Ben Lewin; W: Ben Lewin; C: Vincent Monton; M: Paul Grabowsky.

The Paperboy 1994 (R) Melissa Thorpe (Paul) returns to her small hometown to settle her mother's estate, only to become the obsession of Johnny (Marut), the 12-year-old paperboy she mistakenly jealous when Melissa takes up with an old flame (Katt) and dead bodies become all too common as old newspapers. 93m/C VHS. Alexandra Paul, Marc Marut, William Katt, Brigid Tierney; D: Douglas Jackson; W: David Peckinpah; M: Milan Kymlicka.

Paperhouse 1989 An odd fantasy about a young girl plagued by recurring dreams that begin to influence real life. Very obtuse, British-minded film with "Twilight Zone" feel that manages to capture genuine dream-ness. Not for all audiences, but intriguing nonetheless. Based on the novel "Marianne Dreams" by Catherine Storr. 92m/C VHS. GB Glenne Headly, Ben Cross, Charlotte Burke, Elliott Spiers, Gemma Jones, Sarah Newbold; D: Bernard Rose; W: Matthew Jacobs; M: Hans Zimmer, Stanley Myers.

Papillon 1973 (PG) McQueen is a criminal sent to Devil's Island in the 1930s determined to escape from the Lemote prison. Hoffman is the swindler he befriends. A series of escapes and recaptures follow. Boxoffice winner based on the autobiographical writings of French thief Henri Charriere. Excellent portrayal of prison life and fine performances from the prisoners. Certain segments would have been better left on the cutting room floor. The film's title refers to the lead's butterfly tattoo. 150m/C VHS, DVD. Steve McQueen, Dustin Hoffman, Victor Jory, George Coulouris, Anthony Zerbe; D: Franklin J. Schaffner; W: Dalton Trumbo, Lorenzo Semple Jr.; C: Fred W. Koenekamp; M: Jerry Goldsmith.

Paprika 2006 (R) "Tokyo Godfathers" creator Satoshi Kon is back with the warped tale of a company that has created a machine that allows therapists to enter their patient's dreams. Head researcher Dr Chiba—known to her patients as Paprika—enlists the help of a police detective because a madman has stolen a prototype and is mucking about with the minds of her colleagues. The animation is mind-blowing, but the surreal and disturbing nature of the dream sequences will make it too spicy for some. 90m/C DVD. JP D: Seishi Minakimi; W: Seishi Minakimi, Seishi Minakimi; C: Michiya Kato; M: Susumu Hirasawa; V: Akio Ohtsuka, Toru Furuya, Satoshi Kon.

Parade 1974 A series of vignettes in a circus, "Parade" is actually a play within a play, meshing the action with events offstage. 85m/C VHS. FR Jacques Tati; D: Jacques Tati; W: Jacques Tati.

The Paradine Case 1947 A passable Hitchcock romancer about a young lawyer who falls in love with the woman he's defending for murder, not knowing whether she is innocent or guilty. Script could be tighter and more cohesive. $70,000 of the $3 million budget were spent recreating the original Bailey courtroom. Based on the novel by Robert Hichens. 125m/B VHS, DVD. Gregory Peck, Alida Valli, Ann Todd, Louis Jourdan, Charles Laughton, Charles Coburn, Ethel Barrymore, Leo G. Carroll; D: Alfred Hitchcock; W: David O. Selznick; C: Lee Garmes; M: Franz Waxman.

Paradise 1982 (R) Young American boy and beautiful English girl on a 19th-century jaunt through the Middle East are the sole survivors when their caravan is massacred. Left to their own devices, they discover a magnificent oasis and the joys of frolicking naked and experience (surprise) their sexual awakening. Do a double-take: it's the "Blue Lagoon" all over, with a bit more nudity and a lot more sand. 96m/C VHS. Phoebe Cates, Willie Aames, Richard Curnock, Tuvia Tavi; D: Stuart Gillard.

Paradise 1991 (PG-13) Young boy is sent to the country to live with his pregnant mother's married friends (real life husband and wife Johnson and Griffith). From the outset it is clear that the couple are experiencing marital troubles, making the boy's assimilation all the more difficult. Help arrives in the form of a sprightly tentening relationship. Largely predictable, this remake of the French film "Le Grand Chemin" works thanks to the surprisingly good work of its ensemble cast, and the gorgeous scenery of South Carolina, where the movie was filmed. 112m/C VHS, DVD. Melanie Griffith, Don Johnson, Elijah Wood, Thora Birch, Sheila McCarthy, Eve Gordon, Louise Latham, Greg Travis, Sarah Trigger; D: Mary Agnes Donoghue; W: Mary Agnes Donoghue; M: David Newman.

Paradise Alley 1978 (PG) Rocky tires of boxing, decides to join the WWF. Three brothers brave the world of professional wrestling in an effort to strike it rich and move out of the seedy Hell's Kitchen neighborhood of New York, circa 1946. Stallone wrote, stars in, and makes his directorial debut in addition to singing the title song. He makes a few good moves as director, but is ultimately pinned to the canvas. 109m/C VHS, DVD. Sylvester Stallone, Anne Archer, Armand Assante, Lee Canalito, Kevin Conway; D: Sylvester Stallone; W: Sylvester Stallone; M: Bill Conti.

Paradise Canyon 1935 Early Wayne "B" thriller, in which he plays an undercover government agent sent to track down a group of counterfeiters. 59m/B VHS, DVD. John Wayne, Yakima Canutt, Marion Burns; D: Carl Pierson; W: Lindsley Parsons, Robert Emmett Tansey; C: Archie Stout.

Paradise, Hawaiian Style 1966 (G) Out-of-work pilot returns to Hawaii, where he and a buddy start a charter service with two helicopters. Plenty of gals are wooed by "the Pelvis." Filmed four years after Elvis's first Pacific piece, "Blue Hawaii." Presley, showing the first signs of slow-down, displays no surprises here. ♫Paradise, Hawaiian Style; Scratch My Back (Then I'll Scratch Yours); Stop Where You Are; This Is My Heaven; House of Sand; Queenie Wahine's Papaya; Datin'; Drums of the Islands; A Dog's Life. 91m/C VHS, DVD. Elvis Presley, Suzanna Leigh, James Shigeta, Donna Butterworth, Irene Tsu, Julie Parrish, Philip Ahn, Mary Treen, Marianna Hill, John Doucette, Grady Sutton; D: Michael D. Moore; W: Anthony Lawrence, Allan Weiss; C: Wallace Kelley; M: Joseph J. Lilley.

Paradise in Harlem 1940 All-black musical in which a cabaret performer witnesses a gangland murder, sees his sick wife die, and is pressured into leaving town by the mob. Have a nice day. 83m/B VHS, DVD. Frank Wilson, Mamie Smith, Edna Mae Harris, Juanita Hall; D: Joseph Seiden.

Paradise Island 1930 Downscale musical romance about an ingenue on her way to join her fiance in the South Seas, only to find that he has gambled away his money. The opportunistic saloon owner tries to put the moves on her. Will the two lovers be reunited? ♫I've Got a Girl In Every Port; Drinking Song; Lazy Breezes; Just Another Dream. 68m/B VHS, DVD. Kenneth Harlan, Marceline Day, Thomas Santschi, Paul Hurst, Victor Potel, Gladden James, Will Stanton; D: Bert Glennon.

Paradise Motel 1984 (R) Teen exploitation film centered around a local motel predominantly used for one-night rendezvous. High school heroes and jocks battle for the affections of a beautiful classmate. 87m/C VHS. Bob Basso, Gary Hershberger, Jonna Leigh Stack, Robert Krantz; D: Cary Medoway; C: James L. Carter.

Paradise Now 2005 (PG-13) Al-Jenna-An Recounts how two young Palestinians go from garage mechanics to suicide bombers preparing for a mission to Tel Aviv. Best friends Said (Nashef) and Khaled (Suliman) live in Nablus on the West Bank and apparently have guerrilla ties. They are informed that that they have been chosen and have 24 hours to prepare; the men seem more resigned than fanatical. Director Abu-Assad pays close attention to the details. 90m/C DVD. Lubna Azabal, Hiam Abbass, Kais Nashef, Ali Suliman, Amer Hlehel, Ashraf Barhoum; D: Hany Abu-Assad; W: Hany Abu-Assad, Bero Beyer; C: Antoine Heberle. Golden Globes '06: Foreign Film; Ind. Spirit '06: Foreign Film; Natl. Bd. of Review '05: Foreign Film.

Paradise Road 1997 (R) Fleeing Singapore during WWII, a group of British, American, and Australian women straggle to the shore of Sumatra after their ship is bombed, where they're taken prisoner by the Japanese. Headed by Close, the prisoners form a vocal ensemble that crosses their collective national differences and attempts to lift the spirits of the brutalized women. Familiar ground is trod in this prisoner-of-war saga, but the music is genuinely moving, and excellent performances from the cast help sustain interest. The symphonic choral pieces were taken from actual sheet music used by a similar group of real-life WWII prisoners. 115m/C VHS, DVD. Glenn Close, Frances McDormand, Julianna Margulies, Pauline Collins, Jennifer Ehle, Elizabeth Spriggs, Tessa Humphries, Sab Shimono, Cate Blanchett, Wendy Hughes, Johanna Ter Steege, Pamela Rabe, Clyde Kusatsu, Stan(ford) Egi, Susie Porter, Lisa Hensley, Penne Hackforth-Jones, Pauline Chan; D: Bruce Beresford; W: Bruce Beresford, David Giles, Martin Meader; C: Peter James; M: Margareth Dryburgh, Ross Edwards.

Paradise, Texas 2005 (PG) Mack Cameron (Bottoms) is an action actor whose career has faded, which is why he agrees to star in an indie drama being made in his Texas hometown. Mack also hopes that bringing his family along will help him re-establish the bonds with his wife (Baxter) and sons. He even mentors his star-struck young co-star (Estus), until a professional setback turns Mack into a morose drunk who needs some tough love (personal and professional). 90m/C DVD. Timothy Bottoms, Meredith Baxter, Sheryl Lee, Polly Bergen, Ben Estus, Rider Strong, Brandon Smith; D: Lorraine Senna; W: Joe Conway; C: Shane F. Kelley; M: Jay Ferguson.

A Paradise Under the Stars Un Paraiso Bajo las Estrellas 1999 Sissy wants to perform at Cuba's Tropicana nightclub, just as her mother did, but her strict father Candido forbids it. But Sissy has more problems when she discover her new lover Sergio may also be her brother! Spanish with subtitles. 90m/C VHS, DVD. CU SP Vladimir Cruz, Thais Valdes, Enrique Molina, Amparo Munoz, Daisy Granados, Litico Rodriguez, Saitiago Alfonso, Jacqueline Arenal; D: Gerardo Chijona; W: Gerardo Chijona, Senel Paz; C: Raul Perez Ureta; M: Carlos Faruolo.

Paradisio 1961 (R) Dying inventor wills Oxford professor an authentic pair of X-ray specs. Spies come gunning for the professor, chasing him through Europe. Doc keeps forgetting he's being chased while using the special specs to see (sometimes in 3-D) nudie exploitation. 82m/C VHS. Arthur Howard, Eva Waegner; D: Jacques Henrici; M: John Bath.

The Parallax View 1974 (R) Lee (Prentiss) was a witness to the assassination of a senator and is worried for her own safety, so she goes to newspaper reporter Joe Frady (Beatty) with her fears. He becomes suspicious after her alleged suicide and starts to investigate, discovering a mysterious corporation that hires assassins. As Joe digs deeper and deeper, he uncovers more than he bargained for and becomes a pawn in the conspirators' further plans. Beatty is excellent and the conspiracy is never less than believable. A lesser-

Parallel Corpse ♂ 1983 A mortuary attendant finds a murder victim hidden in a coffin and blackmails the remorseless killer. 88m/C VHS. Buster Larsen, Jørgen Kiil, Agneta Ekmanner, Masja Dessau; D: Hans-Erik Philip; W: Hans-Erik Philip, Søren Melson; M: Hans-Erik Philip.

Parallel Lives ♂♂½ 1994 (R) Sorority sisters and frat brothers (and their various spouses and lovers), from the classes of both 1948 and 1973, gather for an on-campus weekend reunion and discover old and new jealousies, rivalries, and lots of lust (requited and not). There's also an unexpected death and a police investigation as well. Director Yellen had her cast improvise much of their dialogue—the same method she used in "Chantilly Lace." 105m/C VHS. James Belushi, James Brolin, LeVar Burton, Lindsay Crouse, Jill Eikenberry, Ben Gazzara, Jack Klugman, David Lansbury, Liza Minnelli, Dudley Moore, Gena Rowlands, Ally Sheedy, Helen Slater, Mira Sorvino, Paul Sorvino, Robert Wagner, Patricia Wettig, JoBeth Williams, Treat Williams; D: Linda Yellen; W: Gisella Bernice; M: Patrick Seymour. CABLE

Parallel Sons ♂♂ 1995 No-budget first feature from Young has an awkward construction but a couple of fine performances. Teen Seth (Mick) lives in a conservative upstate New York farming community—exactly the wrong place for a young white man with a penchant for black culture and both artistic and homosexual desires. He's working at the local diner, which just happens to get held up by Knowledge (Mason), a black con shot during an escape from the local prison. Seth shelters Knowledge, whose hostility is gradually overcome by both Seth's concern and a mutual sexual attraction. However, more plot complications lead to melodrama. 93m/C VHS, DVD. Heather Gottlieb, Gabriel Mick, Laurence Mason, Murphy Guyer, Graham Alex Johnson; D: John G. Young; W: John G. Young; M: E.D. Menasche.

Paramedics ♂♂½ 1988 (PG-13) A motley crew of cavorting paramedics ply their evil captain. Another parody of people in uniform. A comedy with little pulse. 91m/C VHS. George Newbern, Christopher McDonald, John P. Ryan, Ray Walston, Lawrence-Hilton Jacobs; D: Stuart Margolin.

Paranoia ♂ Orgasmo; A Beautiful Place to Kill; A Quiet Place to Kill 1969 Beautiful jetset widow is trapped in her own Italian villa by a young couple who drug her to get her to perform in various sex orgies, which are probably the most interesting part of this muddled affair. 94m/C VHS. /T Carroll Baker, Lou Castel, Colette Descombes; D: Umberto Lenzi.

Paranoia ♂♂ 1998 (R) An imprisoned killer uses a computer to harass the surviving member of the family he murdered. 86m/C VHS, DVD. Larry Drake, Sally Kirkland, Scott Valentine, Brigitte Bako; D: Larry Brand; W: Larry Brand; M: Martin Trum. VIDEO

Paranoia 1.0 ♂♂ 1998 (R) Computer programmer Simon J (Sisto) keeps finding mysterious empty packages left in his rundown apartment. Are the boxes really empty? (Maybe they contain an airborne contaminant.) Is one of his freaky neighbors leaving them? Is Simon J (Reed) wants the family inheritance to himself even if it means driving sister Eleanor (Scott) insane. This may not be so... One Point O 2004 Jeremy Sisto, Deborah Kara Unger, Udo Kier, Eugene Byrd, Bruce Payne, Richard Rees; D: Jeff Renfroe, Marteinn Thorsson; C: Christopher Soos; M: Terry Huud.

Paranoiac ♂♂½ 1962 Greed and terror set in a country mansion. Simon just nuts? Well, he's paranoid and having hallucinations, so he's got a reason. Note the tagline. "Are you infected?" (Maybe they contain... RO IC US Jeremy Sisto...)

Parasite WOOF 1982 (R) A small town is beset by giant parasites. An "Alien" rip-off originally filmed in 3-D, during that technique's brief return in the early '80s. Bad films like this killed it both the first and second times. An unpardonable mess that comes off as a stinky sixth-grade film project. 90m/C DVD. US Taylor Momsen, Scott Green, Gabe Nevins, Lauren MacKenzie, Daniel Lu; D: Gus Van Sant; W: Gus Van Sant; C: Christopher Doyle, Rain Kathy Li.

Parasite ♂½ 2003 (R) Ah, the far reaches of the North Sea...what a perfect spot to gather a team of engineers on an old oil rig to test out some cleaning fluid. But those pesky environmental do-gooders have to come and ruin the fun by hijacking the rig and holding them captive. Then to really top things off there's the parasite that's absolutely famished and happy to see so many items on the menu. 93m/C VHS, DVD, GB Saskia Gould, Conrad Whitaker, G.W. Stevens, Gary Condes, Margaret Thompson, Oliver Price, Michell Azuma; D: Andrew Prendergast; W: Andrew Prendergast; C: Tom Wright; M: Tom Bible. VIDEO

Parasite Eve ♂♂♂ 1997 Hiroshi Mikami stars as Dr. Nagashima, a scientist who has discovered that mitochondria, the organisms which provide energy for cells, appear to have their own DNA and life-cycle. Nagashima has put this theory to work in his research, as he attempts to cure diseases in lab animals, using the mitochondrial energy. When Nagashima's young wife Kiyomi (Riona Hakuzi) is killed in an auto accident, Nagashima takes her liver in order to try and clone her, once again, using the energy of the mitochondria. He doesn't realize is that her death may be the first step in an evolutionary leap, in which the mitochondria will rise up and dominate the world. 120m/C DVD. JP Hiroshi Mikami, Riona Hakuzi, Tomoko Nakajima; D: Masayuki Ochiai.

Pardners ♂♂½ 1956 Spoiled New York millionaire (Lewis) becomes the sheriff of small western town, with Martin as a ranch foreman. The two team up to rid the town of bad guys and romance two local cuties. Western spoof (with music) is a remake of 1936's "Rhythm on the Range." ♫"Buckskin Beauty"; "Pardners; The Wind!; The Wind!; Me 'N You 'N the Moon. 88m/C VHS, DVD. Jerry Lewis, Dean Martin, Lori Nelson, Jackie Loughery, Jeff Morrow, John Baragrey, Agnes Moorehead, Lon Chaney Jr., Milton Frome, Lee Van Cleef, Jack Elam, Bob Steele, Emory Parnell; D: Norman Taurog; W: Sidney Sheldon, Jerry Davis.

Paranoid Park ♂♂½ 2007 (R) A security guard is murdered at Portland, Oregon's famous skater hangout, Paranoid Park, and police home in on high-school student Alex (Nevins) as a suspect. But that's just one of Alex's problems; he has schoolwork, his girlfriend (Momsen) and the fallout of his parents' divorce to deal with as well. As the investigation continues, the pieces fall into place both for viewers and for Alex, who finds his own outlets to cope with the consequences of his actions. Clean 35-millimeter is interspersed with grainy Super-8 footage of Alex and his friends at the skate park, and a mostly newcomer cast is a plus, giving the teen characters a natural, easy credibility. But with this dark, ambivalent tone, it's hardly the usual teen skating flick. 90m/C DVD. US Taylor Momsen, Scott Green, Gabe Nevins, Lauren MacKenzie, Daniel Lu; D: Gus Van Sant; W: Gus Van Sant; C: Christopher Doyle, Rain Kathy Li.

The Parent Trap ♂♂♂½ 1961 Mills plays a dual role in this heartwarming comedy as twin sisters Susan and Sharon, who were separated at birth by their divorcing parents Mitch (Keith) and Maggie (O'Hara), discover each other during a stay a summer camp. They decide to switch lives and when they realize that dear old dad is about to get married to just the wrong woman (Barnes), the twins conspire to bring their divorced parents back together. Well-known Disney fluff. Followed by several made-for-TV sequels featuring the now grown-up twins (Mills reprised her role). 127m/C VHS, DVD. Hayley Mills, Maureen O'Hara, Brian Keith, Charlie Ruggles, Una Merkel, Leo G. Carroll, Joanna Barnes, Cathleen Nesbitt, Ruth McDevitt; D: David Swift; W: David Swift; C: Lucien Ballard; M: Paul J. Smith.

The Parent Trap ♂♂♂½ 1998 (PG) Updated remake of Disney's 1961 family film about long-separated identical twins, Hallie and Annie (both played by Lohan), who meet accidentally at camp and decide to reunite their divorced parents. Quaid is Napa vineyard-owning dad while Richardson is London fashion designer mom. The twins switch places and foil gold digging publicist Meredith (Hendrix) in order to get their parents back together. Since it's both Disney and a remake, you can assume that it works. However, it's doubtful that parents that don't even tell their kid that they have a twin are going to be winning any PTA awards. ♫"Let's Get Together." The song that the guitar strummin' Hayley Mills made popular with the original makes a cameo in an elevator. 128m/C VHS, DVD. Dennis Quaid, Natasha Richardson, Lindsay Lohan, Polly Holliday, Elaine Hendrix, Joanna Barnes, Ronnie Stevens, Lisa Ann Walter.

Pardon Us ♂♂½ Jail Birds 1931 Laurel and Hardy are thrown into prison for bootlegging. Plot meanders along aimlessly, but the duo have some inspired moments. The first Laurel and Hardy feature. 78m/B VHS, DVD. Stan Laurel, Oliver Hardy, June Marlowe, James Finlayson; D: James Parrott.

Pardon My Trunk ♂♂ Hello Elephant; Buongiorno, Elefante 1952 Struggling against poverty on his teacher's salary, a man and his family receive a gift from a Hindu prince—an elephant. De Sica carries this silly premise beyond mere slapstick. Dubbed. 85m/B VHS, DVD. /T Sabu, Vittorio De Sica; D: Gianni Franciolini.

Pardon My Gun ♂♂½ 1930 Cowpoke falls for the boss' daughter but has a rival in a wealthy rancher, who stages sabotage to get the girl. 64m/B VHS, DVD. Tom Keene, Harry Woods, Sally Starr, Lee Moran, Mona Ray; D: Robert De Lacy; W: Hugh Cummings.

Pardon My Sarong ♂♂½ 1942 Bud and Lou star as Chicago bus drivers who end up shipwrecked on a South Pacific island when they get involved with notorious jewel thieves. The island natives think Lou is a god! Standard Abbott & Costello fare. 83m/B VHS, DVD, Bud Abbott, Lou Costello, Virginia Bruce, Robert Paige, Lionel Atwill, Leif Erickson, William Demarest, Samuel S. Hinds; D: Erle C. Kenton; C: Milton Krasner.

Pardon Mon Affaire ♂♂♂ Un Elephant a Trompe Enormement 1976 (PG) When a middle-aged civil servant gets a look at a model in a parking garage, he decides it's time to cheat on his wife. Enjoyable French farce. Re-made as in the United States by "Pardon Mon Affair" and followed by "Pardon Mon Affair, Too!" Subtitled. 107m/C VHS. FR Jean Rochefort, Claude Brasseur, Guy Bedos, Victor Lanoux, Daniele Delorme, Martine Sarcey, Anny (Anne Legras) Duperey; D: Yves Robert; M: Vladimir Cosma. Ce

Pardon Mon Affaire, Too! ♂♂½ We Will All Meet in Paradise 1977 Pale sequel to the first popular French comedy, "Pardon Mon Affair." This time the four fantasy-minded buddies withstand the trials of marriage and middle-class life. With English subtitles or dubbed. 105m/C VHS, FR Jean Rochefort, Claude Brasseur, Guy Bedos; D: Yves Robert.

Paris Belongs to Us ♂♂½ Paris Nous Appartient; Paris is Ours 1960 An early entry in the French "new wave" of naturalistic cinema, this psychological mystery drama has a woman investigating a suicide linked to a possible worldwide conspiracy. Interesting, if somewhat dated by Cold War elements. 120m/B VHS, FR Jean-Claude Brialy, Betty Schneider, Gianni Esposito, Francoise Prevost; D: Jacques Rivette; W: Jacques Rivette, Jean Gruault.

Paris Blues ♂♂½ 1961 Two jazz musicians, one white, one black, strive for success in Paris and become involved with American tourists who want to take them back to the States. Score by Duke Ellington and an appearance by Armstrong make it a must-see for jazz fans. 100m/B VHS, Paul Newman, Sidney Poitier, Joanne Woodward, Diahann Carroll, Louis Armstrong, Barbara Laage; D: Martin Ritt; W: Jack Sher, Walter Bernstein; M: Duke Ellington.

Paris Express ♂♂½ 1953 When a man boards the Paris Express to escape from the police. A bit convoluted, but well acted. Based on the George Simenon novel. 82m/C VHS, Claude Rains, Herbert Lom, Felix Aylmer, Marius Goring, Anouk Aimée, Maria Toren; D: Harold French; W: Paul Jarrico.

Paris, France ♂♂ 1994 (NC-17) Watched Trains Go By 1953 When a man steals money from his employer, he boards the Paris Express to escape from the police. Lucy (Hope) is a frustrated writer, living in Toronto, who decides to pursue the pursuit of sexual passion will unleash her blocked creative urges. Her main partner is poet Sloan (Outerbridge), the young man Lucy is trying to fashion in the image of a deceased Parisian lover, and also the one whose poetry her husband (and publisher) Michael (Ertmanis) is promoting. Lots of self-delusion and literary pretensions as well as erotic grappling. Adapted from the novel by Tom Walmsley. 111m/C VHS, DVD, CA Leslie Hope, Peter Outerbridge, Victor Ertmanis, Raoul Trujillo, Dan Lett; D: Gerard Ciccoritti; W: Tom Walmsley; M: John McCarthy.

Pardon Mon Affaire... / Parental Guidance / Parenthood / Parents

Parental Guidance ♂♂ 1989 (PG-13) Kinfolks 1998 (R) Sean (Lee) is part of a crazy extended family in South Central L.A. who is reluctant to bring his upscale girlfriend Lisa (Johnson) home for the family's Christmas dinner. 87m/C VHS, DVD. Maia Campbell, Shadi Jae Johnson, Casey Lee; C: A.M. Cali; W: A.M. Cali; C: Scott Edelstein; M: Horace Washington.

Parenthood ♂♂♂ 1989 (PG-13) Dark satire of middle class suburban life in the '50s, centering on a young boy who discovers that his parents aren't getting their meat from the local butcher. Gives new meaning to leftovers and boasts a very disturbing barbecue scene. Balaban's debut is a strikingly visual and creative gorefest with definite cult potential. The eerie score is by Badalamenti, who also composed the music for "Blue Velvet," "Wild at Heart," and "Twin Peaks." 81m/C VHS, DVD. Randy Quaid, Mary Beth Hurt, Bryan Madorsky, Sandy Dennis, Kathryn Grody, Deborah Rush, Graham Jarvis, Juno Mills-Cockell; D: Bob Balaban; W: Christopher Hawthorne; C: Robin Vidgeon, Ernest Day; M: Angelo Badalamenti, Jonathan Elias, Sherman Foote.

Parents ♂♂♂ 1989 (R) Dark satire of middle class suburban life in the '50s, centering on a young boy who discovers that his parents aren't getting their meat from the local butcher. Four grown siblings and their parents struggle with various levels of parenthood. From the college drop-out to the nervous single mother, to the yuppie couple raising an overachiever, every possibility is explored, including the perspective from the cider generation, portrayed by Roards. Genuinely funny with cinematic moments that work most of the time, with an affecting performance from Martin and Wiest. Director Howard has four kids and was inspired to make this film when on a European jaunt with them. 124m/C VHS, DVD. Steve Martin, Mary Steenburgen, Dianne Wiest, Martha Plimpton, Keanu Reeves, Tom Hulce, Jason Robards Jr., Rick Moranis, Harley Jane Kozak, Joaquin Rafael (Leaf) Phoenix, Paul (Link) Linke, Dennis Dugan; D: Ron Howard; W: Ron Howard, Lowell Ganz, Babaloo Mandel; C: Donald McAlpine; M: Randy Newman.

Parental Guidance ♂♂ Kinfolks 1998 (R) Simon Kunz, Meggie Wheeler; D: Nancy Meyers; W: Nancy Meyers, Charles Shyer, David Swift; C: Dean Cundey; M: Alan Silvestri.

Paris Holiday ✶✶½ 1957 An actor heading for Paris to buy a noted author's latest screenplay finds mystery and romance. Entertaining chase scenes as the characters try to find the elusive script. 100m/C VHS, DVD. Bob Hope, Fernandel, Anita Ekberg, Martha Hyer, Preston Sturges; D: Gerd Oswald; W: Edmund Beloin, Dean Reisner; C: Roger Hubert.

Paris in Spring ✶✶✶½ 1935 Romance, Paris, springtime... ahhhh. But love in the air leads to heartbreak when Simone (Ellis) breaks it off with Paul de Lille (Carminati) because she's not into the whole marriage thing. Meanwhile Mignon (Lupino) and Albert (Blakely) call it splits for exactly the same reason. 82m/B VHS. Mary Ellis, Tullio Carminati, Ida Lupino, Lynne Overman, James Blakely, Jessie Ralph; D: Lewis Milestone; W: Franz Schulze, Samuel Hoffenstein.

Paris Is Burning ✶✶✶ 1991 (R) Livingston's documentary portrayal of New York City's transvestite balls where men dress up, dance, and compete in various categories. Filmed between 1985 and 1989, this is a compelling look at a subculture of primarily black and Hispanic men and the one place they can truly be themselves. Madonna noted this look and attitude (much watered down) in her song "Vogue." 71m/C VHS. Dorian Corey, Pepper Labeija, Venus Xtravaganza, Octavia St. Laurant, Willi Ninja, Anji Xtravaganza, Freddie Pendavis, Junior Labeija; D: Jennie Livingston; C: Paul Gibson. Natl. Soc. Film Critics '91: Feature Doc.; Sundance '91: Grand Jury Prize.

Paris, je t'aime ✶✶ *Paris, I Love You* 2006 (R) Eighteen—count 'em—eighteen uneven vignettes by 20 international directors all set in various Parisian neighborhoods. Some are little slice of life tales while others are fantasies (vampires?). Some are about love and some about friendship and some are serious while some are light-hearted. All are so brief that if one doesn't strike your fancy, the next one may, especially given the variety of the cast. English and French with subtitles. 120m/C DVD. FR SI Leila Bekhti, Marianne Faithfull, Elias McConnell, Gaspard Ulliel, Steve Buscemi, Catalina Sandino Moreno, Barbet Schroeder, Sergio Castellitto, Miranda Richardson, Leonor Watling, Juliette Binoche, Willem Dafoe, Hippolyte Girardot, Yolande Moreau, Nick Nolte, Ludivine Sagnier, Bob Hoskins, Fanny Ardant, Maggie Gyllenhaal, Aissa Maiga, Elijah Wood, Emily Mortimer, Rufus Sewell, Natalie Portman, Melchior Beslon, Gerard Depardieu, Ben Gazzara, Gena Rowlands, Margo Martindale, Bruno Podalydes, Florence Muller, Cyril Descours, Julie Bataille, Axel Kiener, Li Xin, Paul Putner, Lionel Dray, Seydou Boro, Olga Kurylenko; D: Gerard Depardieu, Gurinder Chadha, Gus Van Sant, Joel Coen, Ethan Coen, Walter Salles, Daniela Thomas, Christopher Doyle, Isabel Coixet, Sylvain Chomet, Alfonso Cuaron, Richard LaGravenese, Olivier Assayas, Oliver Schmitz, Vincenzo Natali, Wes Craven, Alexander Payne, Tom Tykwer, Nobuhiro Suwa; W: Gurinder Chadha, Gus Van Sant, Joel Coen, Ethan Coen, Walter Salles, Daniela Thomas, Christopher Doyle, Isabel Coixet, Sylvain Chomet, Alfonso Cuaron, Richard LaGravenese, Olivier Assayas, Oliver Schmitz, Vincenzo Natali, Wes Craven, Alexander Payne, Tom Tykwer, Nobuhiro Suwa; C: Christopher Doyle, Matthieu Poirot-Delpech, Pascal Rabaud, Bruno Delbonnel, Eric Gautier, Jean-Claude Larrieu, Pascal Marti, Eric Guichard, Gerard Sterin, Michel Amathieu, Michael Seresin, Pierre Aim, J. Eddie Peck, Tetsuo Nagata, David Quesemand, Frank Greibe; M: Tom Tykwer, Michael Andrews, Reinhold Heil, Johnny Klimek.

Paris, Texas ✶✶✶½ 1983 (PG) After four years a drifter returns to find his son is being raised by his brother because the boy's mother has also disappeared. He tries to reconnect with the boy. Introspective script acclaimed by many film critics, but others found it to be too slow. 145m/C VHS, DVD. FR GE Harry Dean Stanton, Nastassja Kinski, Dean Stockwell, Hunter Carson, Aurore Clement; D: Wim Wenders; W: Sam Shepard, L.M. Kit Carson; M: Ry Cooder. British Acad. '84: Director (Wenders). Cannes '84: Film.

Paris Trout ✶✶✶½ 1991 (R) Believing himself above the law, southern Trout (Hopper) shoots the mother and sister of a young black man who reneged on his IOU. Lawyer Harris is forced to defend a man he knows deserves to be punished. ...and wife Hershey suffers long. Adapted by Pete Dexter from his National Book Award-winning novel. 98m/C VHS. Dennis Hopper, Barbara Hershey, Ed Harris, Tina Lifford, Darnita Henry, Eric Ware, Ray McKinnon; D: Stephen Gyllenhaal; W: Pete Dexter; C: Robert Elswit. CABLE

Paris When It Sizzles ✶✶ 1964 A screenwriter and his secretary fall in love while working on a film in Paris, confusing themselves with the script's characters. Star-studded cast deserves better than this lame script. Shot on location in Paris. Holden's drinking—he ran into a brick wall while under the influence—and some unresolved romantic tension between him and Hepburn affected shooting. 110m/C VHS, DVD. William Holden, Audrey Hepburn, Gregoire Aslan, Raymond Bussieres, Tony Curtis, Fred Astaire, Frank Sinatra, Noel Coward, Marlene Dietrich, Mel Ferrer; D: Richard Quine; W: George Axelrod; C: Charles B(ryant) Lang Jr.; M: Nelson Riddle.

Parisian Love ✶✶ 1925 Marie (Bow) is a streetwise Paris urchin who makes her living by fleecing the tourists. When her lover Armand (Keith) is shot, wealthy Pierre Marcel (Tellegen). With the help of some underworld friends, Marie transforms herself into a beauty in order to seduce Pierre. 62m/B VHS, DVD. Clara Bow, Donald Keith, Lou Tellegen, Lillian (Lillianne, Lyllian) Leighton; D: Louis Gasnier; W: Lois Hutchinson; C: Allen Siegler.

Park Avenue Logger ✶✶½ 1937 Silly story has blue-blood Ingraham believing son O'Brien is a panty-waist, so he sends him to a lumber camp to prove his manhood. But junior is actually a wrestling champ (known as The Masked Marvel) and manages just fine, even winning the gal. 65m/B VHS. George O'Brien, Beatrice Roberts, Lloyd Ingraham, Ward Bond, Willard Robertson; D: David Howard.

The Park Is Mine ✶✶ 1985 A deranged and desperate Vietnam vet takes hostages in Central Park. Semi-infamous film, notable for being the first movie made for HBO, and for being filmed in Toronto, before the inexpensive practice of filming in Canada became widespread. 102m/C VHS. Tommy Lee Jones, Yaphet Kotto, Helen Shaver; D: Steven Hilliard Stern; M: Tangerine Dream. CABLE

Parker ✶✶ 1984 An executive is kidnapped, then released, but does not know why. Unable to live with the mystery, he tracks his kidnappers down into a world of blackmail, drugs, and intrigue. 100m/C VHS. GB Cherie Lunghi, Elizabeth Spriggs, Bob Peck, Bryan Brown, Kurt Raab; D: Jim Goddard; W: Trevor Preston; C: Peter Jessop; M: Richard Hartley.

Parlor, Bedroom and Bath ✶✶ *Romeo in Pyjamas* 1931 A family tries to keep a young woman from seeing that her love interest is flirting with others. Doesn't live up to the standard Keaton set in his silent films. Keaton spoke French and German for foreign versions. 75m/B VHS, DVD. Buster Keaton, Charlotte Greenwood, Cliff Edwards, Reginald Denny; D: Edward Sedgwick.

Parole, Inc. ✶✶ 1949 FBI takes on the underground in this early crime film. Criminals on parole have not served their sentences, and the mob is responsible. A meagerly financed yawner. 71m/B VHS, DVD. Michael O'Shea, Evelyn Ankers, Turhan Bey, Lyle Talbot; D: Alfred Zeisler.

Paroled to Die ✶✶ 1937 A man frames a young rancher for a bank robbery and a murder he committed in this wild west saga. Predictable and bland. 66m/B VHS, DVD. Karl Hackett, Horace Murphy, Steve Clark, Bud Steele, Kathleen Elliott; D: Sam Newfield; W: George Plympton; C: Robert E. Cline.

Parrish ✶✶½ 1961 Parrish McLean (Donohue) is a very ambitious young man, determined to work in the rich world of the tobacco growers of the Connecticut River Valley. But his ruthless stepfather (Malden) would like to thwart his plans. As befits Donohue's teen idol status, he also gets to romance three beautiful girls. Very silly and much too long. Based on the novel by Mildred Savage. 138m/C VHS. Troy Donahue, Claudette Colbert, Karl Malden, Dean Jagger, Diane McBain, Connie Stevens, Sharon Hugueny, Dub Taylor, Hampton Fancher, Bibi Osterwald, Madeline Sherwood, Sylvia Miles, Carroll O'Connor, Vincent Gardenia; D: Delmer Daves; W: Delmer Daves; C: Harry Stradling Sr.; M: Max Steiner.

Parting Glances ✶✶ 1986 (R) Low-budget but acclaimed film shows the relationship between two gay men and how they deal with a close friend's discovery of his exposure to the AIDS virus. Touching and realistic portrayals make this a must see. In 1990 Sherwood died of AIDS without completing any other films. 90m/C VHS, DVD. John Bolger, Richard Ganoung, Steve Buscemi, Adam Nathan, Patrick Tull, Kathy Kinney; D: Bill Sherwood; W: Bill Sherwood; C: Jacek Laskus.

Parting Shots ✶✶½ 1998 Harry's feeling like a bunch of folks have done him wrong—from his ex-wife to his thieving best buddy to the local chef—so once he learns he's only got six weeks to live, he aims to settle the score...with a gun. "Death Wish" director Winner shoots for edgy humor but misses. 98m/C VHS, DVD. Chris Rea, Felicity Kendal, Bob Hoskins, Ben Kingsley, Joanna Lumley, Oliver Reed, Diana Rigg, John Cleese, Gareth Hunt, Peter Davison, Patrick Ryecart, Edward Hardwicke, Nicholas Gecks, Ruby Snape, Nicola Bryant, Brian Poyser, Nicky Henson, Caroline Langrishe, Taryn Kay, Alison Reynolds, Roland Curram, Craig Jelley, Jenny Logan, Sarah Reeves, Anthony Smee, Donald Standen, Warren Weaver; D: Michael Winner; W: Michael Winner, Nick Mead; C: Ousama Rawi; M: Chris Rea, Chris Rea, Les Reed. VIDEO

Partition ✶✶ 2007 Predictable historical romance/drama. Gian Singh (Mistry) is an ex-soldier from a Sikh regiment who fought for the Brits in WWII. In 1947, when India and Pakistan have become separate countries, Gian watches the violent upheavals from his Punjab village and then rescues Muslim refugee Naseem (Kruek) from an angry mob. The two fall in love and marry despite the religious complications but Naseem eventually hears word of her family in Pakistan and goes to see them. Her brothers are horrified that she's married an enemy and hold her prisoner, which causes more trouble when Gian travels to bring his wife home. 115m/C DVD. CA Jimi Mistry, Kristen Kreuk, Neve Campbell, John Light, Madhur Jaffrey, Irfan Khan, Jesse Moss; D: Vic Sarin; W: Vic Sarin, Patricia Finn; C: Vic Sarin; M: Brian Tyler.

Partner ✶✶ 1968 An extremely shy young man invents a strong alter ego to cope with the world but this second personality comes to dominate—with tragic results. In Italian with English subtitles. 110m/C VHS, DVD. IT Pierre Clementi, Stefania Sandrelli, Tina Aumont; D: Bernardo Bertolucci; M: Ennio Morricone.

Partners ✶✶ 1982 (R) A straight, macho cop must pose as the lover of a gay cop to investigate the murder of a gay man in Los Angeles' homosexual community. Sets out to parody "Cruising", unfortunately, the only source of humor is the makers could find was in ridiculous homosexual stereotypes that are somewhat offensive and often unfunny. 93m/C VHS. Ryan O'Neal, John Hurt, Kenneth McMillan, Robyn Douglass, Jay Robinson, Rick Jason; D: James Burrows; W: Francis Veber; M: Georges Delerue.

Partners ✶✶✶ 1999 (R) All of the usual suspects are rounded up for this action comedy. Mild-mannered Bob (Paymer) steals a super-secret computer program from his company. Then it's stolen from him by hunky thief Axel (Van Dien). A series of double-crosses and chases—involving the obligatory Caddy convertible—ensue. Toss in the sexy girlfriend (Angel) and a cheap L.A. motel with a heart-shaped bed. 90m/C VHS, DVD. Casper Van Dien, Vanessa Angel, David Paymer, Jenifer Lewis, Yuji Okumoto, Donna Pescow; D: Joey Travolta; W: Jeff Ferrell; C: Kristian Bernier; M: Jeff Lass.

Partners in Crime ✶✶✶ 1999 (R) Local detective Gene Reardon (Hauer) is assigned to investigate the kidnapping of a wealthy man from a small town. But soon the FBI is called in, including Reardon's ex-wife Wallis Longworth (Porizkova). Then the victim turns up dead on Reardon's property and he's suddenly suspect numero uno. Since Wallis doesn't think Gene's guilty, she decides to secretly help him prove who really done it. 90m/C VHS, DVD. Rutger Hauer, Paulina Porizkova, Michael Flynn, Raymond Hatton, Lloyd Ingraham, Christine McIntyre, Robert Frazer; D: Lambert Hillyer.

Partners of the Trail ✶✶✶ 1944 U.S. marshals Brown and Hatton try to find out who's murdering ranchers which leads them to gunplay with Ingraham's band of outlaws. 57m/B VHS. Johnny Mack Brown, Raymond Hatton, Lloyd Ingraham, Christine Larner; D: Lambert Hillyer.

The Party ✶✶✶ 1968 Disaster-prone Indian actor wreaks considerable havoc at a posh Hollywood gathering. Laughs come quickly in this quirky Sellers vehicle. 99m/C VHS, DVD. Peter Sellers, Claudine Longet, Marge Champion, Sharron Kimberly, Denny Miller, Gavin MacLeod, Carol Wayne; D: Blake Edwards; W: Blake Edwards; C: Lucien Ballard; M: Henry Mancini.

Party Animal ✶✶ 1983 (R) A college stud teaches a shy farm boy a thing or two about the carnal aspects of campus life. 78m/C VHS, DVD. Timothy Carhart, Matthew Causey, Robin Harlan; D: David Beaird; W: David Beaird; C: Bryan England.

Party ✶✶ 1996 Leonor (Silveira) and Rogerio (Samora) are having a 10th anniversary party at their seaside villa. As the celebration continues, Leonor is pursued by aging playboy Michel (Piccoli) while her husband stands idly by. Maybe that has something to do with the secret Rogerio's about to reveal. French and Portuguese with subtitles. 91m/C VHS, DVD. FR PT Leonor Silveira, Michel Piccoli, Rogerio Samora, Irene Papas; D: Manoel de Oliveira; W: Manoel de Oliveira, Augustina Bessa-Luis; C: Renato Berta.

Party Camp ✶ 1987 (R) A rowdy summer camp counselor endeavors to turn a tame backwoods camp into a non-stop party. Late entry in the "Meatballs"-spawned genre fails to do anything of even minor interest. 96m/C VHS. Andrew Ross, Billy Jacoby, April Wayne, Kirk Cribb; D: Gary Graver.

Party Favors WOOF! 1989 (R) Erotic dancing, strip tease acts, and general hilarity are featured in this party tape. 83m/C VHS. Jeannie Winters, Marjorie Miller, Gail Thackray; D: Ed Hansen.

Party Girl ✶✶½ 1958 A crime drama involving an attorney representing a 1920s crime boss and his henchmen when they run afoul of the law. The lawyer falls in love with a nightclub dancer who successfully encourages him to leave the mob, but not before he is wounded in a gang war attack, arrested, and forced to testify against the mob as a material witness. The mob then takes his girlfriend hostage to prevent his testifying, leading to an exciting climax. Must-see viewing for Charisse's steamy dance numbers. 99m/C VHS. Robert Taylor, Cyd Charisse, Lee J. Cobb, John Ireland, Kent Smith, Claire Kelly, Corey Allen; D: Nicholas Ray.

Party Girl ✶✶✶ 1994 (R) In the "girls just wanna have fun" category comes this spritely saga of 20-something Manhattan club gal Mary (Posey), who needs some steady income after the cops bust her for throwing an illegal rent party. So, since Mary's godmother is a librarian, she gets a job as a library clerk and discovers the wonders of the Dewey Decimal system (no, I'm not joking but presumably director Mayer is). Parker's Mary is a properly flaunting poseur but a little nightlife tends to go a long way. 94m/C VHS, DVD. Parker Posey, Omar Townsend, Anthony De Sando, Guillermo Diaz, Sasha von Scheler, Liev Schreiber; D: Daisy von Scherler Mayer; W: Harry Birckmayer, Daisy von Scherler Mayer; C: Michael Slovis; M: Anton Sanko.

Party Girls ✶✶½ 1929 Escort service girls run afoul of the law in this hokey melodrama. 67m/B VHS, DVD. Douglas Fairbanks Jr., Jeanette Loff, Judith Barrie, Marie Prevost, John St. Polis, Lucien Prival; D: Victor Halperin.

Party Girls for Sale ♂ Violate (PG) An ambitious adaptation of E.M. For- which a young girl's body is found on the ster's complex novel about relations be- beach in Rio de Janeiro. **80m/B VHS, US GE** tween Brits and Indians in the 1920s. Dra- to pay it off. Also known as "Party Girls." ma centers on an Indian doctor razed **80m/C VHS, Marilyn Chambers, Kurt Woodruff,** accusations that an attack on a young British woman's Christine Veronica, Kimberly Taylor **D:** Chuck Vin- her while serving as a guide in some rath- cent. er ominous caves. Film occasionally flags, but is usually compelling. Features partic-

Party Incorporated ♂♂ ulary strong performances from Banner- **1989 (R) Marilyn Chambers (of "Behind the** jee, Fox, and Davis. **163m/C VHS, DVD, GB** Green Door" fame) stars as a young wid- Peggy Ashcroft, Alec Guinness, James Fox, Judy ow with a huge tax load who gives parties Davis, Victor Banerjee, Nigel Havers; **D:** David **80m/C VHS, Marilyn Chambers, Kurt Woodruff,** Lean. **W:** David Lean; **C:** Ernest Day; **M:** Maurice Richard -latch, Shawn Weatherly, Richard Round- Orig. Score; British Acad. '85; Foreign Film, Actress tree, Lief Garrett, Gina Blackburn; **D:** William Golden Globes '85; Foreign Film, Support. Actress Webb; **W:** Richard Brandes. (Banerjee), Actress (Ashcroft); L.A. Film Critics '84; Support. Actress (Ashcroft); Nat. Bd. of Review '84; Actor **Party Line** ♂ **1988 (R)** A veteran po- (Ashcroft), Director (Lean); N.Y. Film Critics '84; Actress (Ashcroft), lice captain and a district attorney team up N.Y. Film Critics '84; Actress (Ashcroft), Director to track down a pair of killers who find their (Lean), Film. victims through party lines. **90m/C VHS, Bob** Davis, Victor Banerjee, Nigel Havers; **D:** Judy **Passage to Marseilles** ♂♂♂ Leon, **W:** David Lean; **C:** Ernest Day; **M:** Maurice **1944** Hollywood propaganda in which con-

Party Monster ♂♂½ **2003 (R)** victs escape from Devil's Island and help Culkin impressively crosses over into on- French freedom fighters combat Nazis. screen adulthood, starring as Michael Routine but entertaining. What else could Alig, the real-life club kid turned murderer. it be with Bogart, Raines, Greenstreet, Alig, a misunderstood kid from Indiana, and Lorre, who later made a pretty good travels to the Big Apple where he quickly film set in Casablanca? **110m/B VHS, DVD,** finds his niche in the decadent and flam- Humphrey Bogart, Claude Rains, Sydney Green- boyant club scene of NYC circa 1990s. street, Peter Lorre, Helmut Dantine, George To- There, he hooks up with mentor James St. bias, John Loder, Eduardo Ciannelli, Michele Mor- James (Green) also a former Midwester- gan; **D:** Michael Curtiz; **C:** James Wong Howe; **M:** kin, wro teaches him the ropes. Alig Max Steiner. quickly surpasses his master, becoming a celebrated party promoter at the famed **Passed Away** ♂½ **1992 (PG-13)** disco Limelight. As Michael spirals out of Family patriarch Jack Scanlan dies and control both in his addictions and emotion- his entire family gets together for the fu- ally, St. James, as his best friend, at- neral and a big Irish wake. The family, of tempts to intervene to curb Alig's lead. course, is made up of a weird group of Based on the book "Disco Bloodbath" by characters, good steadfast son Petersen, St. James. **98m/C VHS, DVD, US Macaulay Cul-** dim-witted but good-looking son Petersen, kin, Seth Green, Chloe Sevigny, Natasha Lyonne, rebellious daughter Reed, and a left-wing Wilson Cruz, Wilmer Valderrama, Dylan McDer- nun who works in Central America and is mott; **D:** Fenton Bailey, Randy Barbato; **W:** Fenton accompanied by an illegal alien (McDor- Bailey, Randy Barbato; **C:** Teodoro Maniaci; **M:** mand). Throw in a mysterious female Jimmy Harry. mourner and a pregnant granddaughter who goes into labor at the graveside and **Party! Party!** **1983** A bunch of kids you come up with a movie that manages go nuts and have a party when their par- to use every comic death cliche ever im- ents leave. **100m/C VHS, GB Daniel Peacock,** agined. Talented cast is wasted in a movie Karl Howman, Perry Fenwick, Sean Chapman, that should have passed away. **96m/C VHS,** Phoebe Nicholls **D:** Terry Winsor; **W:** Daniel Pea- Bob Hoskins, Jack Warden, William L. Petersen, cock, Terry Winsor; **C:** Syd Macartney; **M:** Sting, Helen Lloyd Breed, Maureen Stapleton, Pamela David Bowie, Joe Jackson, Elvis Costello. Reed, Tim Curry, Peter Riegert, Blair Brown, Par- rick Breen, Nancy Travis, Teri Polo, Frances

Party Plane ♂ **1990** Softcore fun- McDormand; **D:** Charlie Peters; **W:** Charlie Peters; fest about a plane full of oversexed ste- **C:** Arthur Albert. **M:** Richard Gibbs. wardesses. French with subtitles. **100m/B VHS, FR Anemone, Christine Boisson, Michel Di-** **Passenger** ♂♂♂ dym, Grégoire Colin, Denis Podalydès, Roland **1963** Pasazerka 1961 Bertin, Bernard Verley, Michel Roux; **Cameos:** While on a cruise ship Lisa (Slaska), a Micheline Presle; **D:** Tonie Marshall; **W:** Tonie former camp guard at Auschwitz, realizes Marshall; **C:** Dominique Chapuis. that fellow passenger Martha (Ciepliews- ka) was once one of her prisoners. Their **Pas Tres Catholique** ♂♂ Some- meeting triggers a series of flashbacks to thing Fishy **1993** Pleasant comedy finds the Holocaust and to domination, suffer- 40ish, chain-smoking, unconventional P.I. ing, and resistance. Director Munk was Maxine (Anemone) investigating her ex- killed in a car crash during filming, which husband or an insurance scam, drawing was completed by his colleague Witold closer to her estranged son, and trying to Lesiewicz. Based on the novel by Zofia decide romantically between long-time Posmysz-Piasecka; Polish with subtitles. friend Florence and handsome economist **53m/B VHS, PL Aleksandra Slaska, Anna Ciepie-** Jacques. French with subtitles. **100m/B** lewska, Marek Walczewski, Jan Kreczewski, Irena **VHS, FR Anemone, Christine Boisson, Michel Di-** Malkiewicz; **D:** Andrzej Munk; **W:** Andrzej Munk, dym, Grégoire Colin, Denis Podalydès, Roland Zofia Posmysz-Piasecka; **C:** Krzysztof Winiewicz; Bertin, Bernard Verley, Michel Roux; **Cameos:** **M:** Tadeusz Baird. Micheline Presle; **D:** Tonie Marshall; **W:** Tonie Marshall; **C:** Dominique Chapuis. **The Passenger** ♂♂♂½ **1975 (PG-13)** Profes- sion: Reporter **1975 (PG)** A dissatisfied TV re-

Pascali's Island ♂♂½ **1988** porter changes identities with a dead man **(PG-13)** A Turkish spy becomes involved while on assignment in Africa, then learns with an adventurer's plot to steal rare arti- that he is posing as a gunrunner. Mysteri- facts, then finds himself ensnared in politi- ous, elliptical production from Italian mas- cal and personal intrigue. Superior trage- ter Antonioni, who co-wrote. Nicholson is dy features excellent performances from fine in the low-key role, and Schneider is Kingsley, Dance, and Mirren. **106m/C VHS,** surprisingly winning as the woman drawn eB Ben Kingsley, Helen Mirren, Charles Dance, to him. The oddest of much debate, hailed Sheila Allen, Vernon Dobtcheff; **D:** James Dear- by some as quintessential cinema and by den, **W:** James Dearden; **C:** Roger Deakins; **M:** others as slow and unrewarding. **119m/C** Loek Dikker. **VHS, Jack Nicholson, Maria Schneider,** Ian Hendry, Jenny Runacre, Steven Berkoff; **D:**

Pass the Ammo ♂♂½ **1988 (R)** Michelangelo Antonioni; **W:** Mark Peploe, Miche- Entertaining comedy about a young cou- langelo Antonioni; **C:** Luciano Tovoli. ple who attempt to steal back $50,000 of inheritance money that a televangelist **Passenger 57** ♂♂ **1992 (R)** Classic swindled from the family. One of the more movie-of-the-week fare. Anti-terrorist spe- creative satires on this religious TV phe- cialist John Cutter (Snipes) leaves his pro- nomenon. **93m/C VHS, Bill Paxton, Tim Curry,** fession because of his wife's murder, and Linda Kozlowski, Annie Potts, Anthony Geary, coincidentally boards the same plane as Dennis Burkley, Glenn Withrow, Richard Paul; **D:** Charles Rane (Payne) an apprehended David Beaird; **W:** Neil Cohen, Joel Cohen; **M:** Pet- evil terrorist headed to trial in L.A. Some- er Burwell. how, Rane's thugs have also sneaked

aboard with plans to hijack the plane, and it's up to Cutter to use his skills and save the day. Athletic Snipes is convincing in his role but can't make up for the plot's lack of premise. **84m/C VHS, DVD, Wesley Snipes, Bruce Payne, Tom Sizemore, Alex Datch-** Hurley, Michael Horse; **D:** Kevin Hooks; **W:** Dan Gordon, David Loughery; **C:** Mark Irwin; **M:** Stan- ley Clarke.

The Passing ♂♂½ **1988** Two men find themselves trapped in the darker vicissitudes of life. The two lead almost parallel lives until an extraordinary event unites them. **96m/C VHS, DVD, James Plaster,** Welton Benjamin Johnson, Lynn Dunn, Albert B. Smith; **D:** John Huckert.

Passing Glory ♂♂♂ **1999** The script may not be a three-pointer but the acting is a slam-dunk in this fact-based drama. Joseph Verrett (Braugher) is a black priest in segregationist New Orleans in the early '60s, teaching at St. Augustine High and coaching the school's unbeaten varsity basketball squad. Verrett is a go- getter who wants to integrate the league now, and his boss, Father Robert Grant (Tom) preaches patience. Despite numer- ous obstacles, Verrett manages to chal- lenge white Jesuit High to an unofficial city championship game. **94m/C VHS, Andre Braugher, Rip Torn, Bill Nunn, Sean Squire, Ruby Dee, Diane Hugh-Kelly, Anderson Bowell, Khali Kain; D: Steve James; W: Harold Sylvester; C: Bill Butler; M: Stephen James.** CABLE

The Passing of Evil ♂♂ **The Grasshopper, Passions 1970 (R)** Bisset is a starstruck Canadian woman drawn by the bright lights and big cities of America. By age 22, she's a burnt-out prostitute in Las Vegas. Cheerless but compelling. **96m/C VHS, Jac- queline Bisset, Jim Brown, Joseph Cotten, Corbett Monica, Ramon Bieri, Christopher Stone, Roger Garrett, Stanley Adams, Dick Richards, Tim O'Kelly, Ed Flanders; D: Jerry Paris; C: Sam Leav- itt. M: Billy Goldenberg.**

The Passing of the Third Floor Back ♂♂♂ **1936** Boarding house tenants improve their lives after be- ing inspired by a mysterious stranger. They revert, though, when he leaves. Now you know. Based on a Victorian morality play. **80m/B VHS, DVD, GB Conrad Veidt, Rene Ray, Frank Cellier, Anna Lee, John Turnbull, Cath- leen Nesbitt; D: Berthold Viertel.**

Passion ♂♂ **1919** Paris, and the decadent Louis XV falls for the lovely Jeanne, making her his mistress, much to the scandal of the nation. Respectable si- lent version of "Madame DuBarry" is a rel- atively realistic costume drama, but it doesn't rate with the best German films of this period. **135m/B VHS, GE Pola Negri, Emil Jannings, Harry Liedtke; D: Ernst Lubitsch.**

Passion ♂♂ **1954** When a rancher's young family falls victim to rampaging des- perados, he enlists an outlaw's aid to avenge the murders of his loved ones. **84m/C VHS, DVD, Cornel Wilde, Yvonne De Carlo, Lon Chaney Jr., John Qualen; C: Allan Dwan.**

Passion ♂♂ **1982 (R)** A Polish film director (Radziwilowicz) is making a movie called "Passion" and practicing what he's filming by having an affair with the film owner (Schygulla) where the film crew are staying. Then the money for the film be- gins to run out. Meanwhile, Schygulla's husband, Piccoli, is having problems at his factory because of a labor dispute called by worker Huppert. French with subtitles. **88m/C VHS, FR Jerzy Radziwilowicz, Hanna Schygulla, Michel Piccoli, Isabelle Huppert, Laszlo Szabo; D: Jean-Luc Godard; W: Jean-Luc Godard; C: Raoul Coutard.**

Passion in the Desert ♂♂ ½ **Si- moom, A Passion in the Desert 1997 (PG-13)** Definitely one of the stranger plots going. Augustin Roberts (Daniels) is a French of- ficer in Napoleon's Egyptian campaign. He's escorting artist Venture de Paradis (Piccoli), who's been commissioned to record the country's monuments. The duo are lost and separated in a desert sand- storm, with Roberts eventually finding shelter in the ruins of an ancient city. But he's not alone—his dangerous companion is a female leopard, who decides to help out the two-legged interloper. Based on a novella by Honoré de Balzac. **93m/C VHS, DVD, Ben Daniels, Michel Piccoli; D: Lavinia Curri- er; W: Lavinia Currier, Martin Edmunds; C: Alexei Rodionov; M: Jose Nieto.**

The Passion of Anna ♂♂♂ **1970 (R)** A complicated psychological dra- ma about four people on an isolated island. Von Sydow is an ex-con living a hermit's existence when he becomes in- volved with a crippled widow (Ullmann) and her two friends—all of whom have se- crets in their pasts. Brutal and disturbing. Wonderful cinematography by Sven

Passion Fish ♂♂♂ **1992 (R)** McDonnell plays May-Alice, a soap opera actress who is paralyzed after a taxi acci- dent in New York. Confined to a wheel- chair, the bitter woman moves back to her Louisiana home and alienates a number of live-in nurses until Chantelle (Woo- dard), who has her own problems, comes along. Blunt writing and directing by Sayles overcome the story's inherent sen- timentality as do the spirited performances of the leads, including Curtis-Hall as the rogue romancing Chantelle and Strathairn as the Cajun bad boy McDonnell once loved. **136m/C VHS, DVD, Mary McDonnell, Alfre Woodard, David Strathairn, Vondie Curtis-Hall, Nora Dunn, Sheila Kelley, Angela Bassett, Mary Portser, Maggie Renzi, Leo Burmester, Shaunitsa Willis, John Henry, Michael Laskin; D: John Sayles; W: John Sayles; C: Roger Deakins; M: Mason Daring, Ind. Spirit '93: Support. Actress (Woodard).**

Passion Flower ♂♂♂ **1986 (PG-13)** L'Ecole Buissonnière; I Have a New Master **1985** A new teacher uses revolutionary methods to en- gage students, but draws ire from the staid parents in rural France. Worthwhile dra- ma. In French with English subtitles. **89m/B VHS, Bernard Blier, Juliette Faber, Edouard Del- mont; D: Jean-Paul LeChanois.**

Passion for Life ♂♂ **1985** Two men involved in a drug-smuggling syndicate at- tempt to take over the business. Compli- cations arise when they both fall for a beautiful, deceitful woman who turns them against one another. **94m/C VHS, SP Hector Suarez, Sasha Montenegro, Manuel Capetillo, Ale- jandra Peniche.**

Passion for Power ♂♂½ A tropical romantic melodrama made for network TV and set in Singapore, where a spoiled rich girl who marries a handsome gigolo (As- sante), much to daddy big bucks' (Steiger) displeasure. Then daddy is murdered and the son-in-law becomes the key suspect. Trashy, but Assante's fine. **100m/C VHS, Ar- mand Assante, Catherine Mary Stewart, Rod Steiger, Marlette Hartley, Wayne Rogers; D: Har- vey Hart.** TV

Passion in Paradise ♂♂♂ **1988** Fact-based mystery set in the Baha- mas in 1943. Stewart is a spoiled rich girl who marries a handsome gigolo (As- sante) is a French con of Augustin Roberts (Daniels) is a French of-

folk songs. But his home life is a twisted psychosexual drama as his devoted moth- er (Hershey), Rose (Hershey), suffers from syphilitic rela- tionship and Grainger's own masochistic impulses, which are catered to by his pi- ano and student, Karen (Woof). **98m/C VHS, DVD, AU Richard Roxburgh, Barbara Hershey, Emily Woof, Claudia Karvan, Simon Burke, Linda Cropper, Julia Blake; D: Peter Duncan; W: Don Watson; C: Martin McGrath; Australian Film Inst. '99: Art Dir./Set Dec. Cinematog., Costume Des.**

Nykvist. Filmed on the island of Faro. In Swedish with English subtitles. **101m/C VHS, DVD.** *SW* Max von Sydow, Liv Ullmann, Bibi Andersson, Erland Josephson, Erik Hell; *D:* Ingmar Bergman; *W:* Ingmar Bergman; *C:* Sven Nykvist. Nat. Soc. Film Critics '70: Director (Bergman).

The Passion of Ayn Rand 🐾🐾½ 1999
Warts-and-all bio of the Russian-born novelist/philosopher that focuses on the 20-year friendship between Rand (Mirren) and psychoanalyst Nathaniel Branden (Stoltz). When the pic opens in 1951, self-important Rand is already famous for "The Fountainhead" and has a longtime marriage to the overshadowed Frank (Fonda). Nathaniel and Barbara (Delpy) are college students pushed to marry by mentor Rand, who soon becomes Nathaniel's lover and encourages his ambitions—to the dismay of both spouses. Based on the 1986 memoir by Barbara Branden, so there's an axe to grind. **104m/C VHS, DVD.** Helen Mirren, Eric Stoltz, Julie Delpy, Peter Fonda, Tom McCamus, Sybil Temchen, Don McKellar, David Ferry; *D:* Christopher Menaul; *W:* Howard Korder, Mary Gallagher; *C:* Ronald Orieux; *M:* Jeff Beal. **CABLE**

The Passion of Darkly Noon 🐾½ 1995
Strange religious/sexual allegory. Running through the woods, Darkly Noon (Fraser) stumbles across the rural home of Callie (Judd) and Clay (Mortensen). Callie sees that the young man is ill and allows him to stay, discovering his parents have recently died and he's escaped from the ultra-religious community where he was raised. The sexy Callie is an uncomfortable attraction for the naive lad and when he meets a crazy old woman, Roxy (Zabriskie), in the woods, he's inclined to listen to her ravings against Callie, leading Darkly to believe he's been sent to punish the transgressors. **106m/C VHS.** *GB GE BE* Brendan Fraser, Ashley Judd, Viggo Mortensen, Grace Zabriskie, Loren Dean; *D:* Philip Ridley; *W:* Philip Ridley; *C:* John de Borman; *M:* Nick Bicat.

Passion of Joan of Arc 🐾🐾🐾🐾 1928
Dreyer's version of the life of France's Joan of Arc ignores all the battlefield dramatics and confines itself to showing Joan in her cell and at her trial, with only one exterior shot—that of Joan (stage actress Falconetti in her only film role) on her way to the stake. The script is drawn from the Latin text of the heresy trial itself and Dreyer uses numerous close-ups (the actors wore no make-up) to show the bewilderment, fear, and anger of the participants. Dreyer refused to have his film shown with musical accompaniment but the tape includes Richard Einhron's oratorio, "Voices of Light." **114m/B VHS, DVD.** *FR* Renee (Marie) Falconetti, Eugene Sylwan, Maurice Schutz, Antonin Artaud, Michel Simon; *D:* Carl Theodor Dreyer; *W:* Carl Theodor Dreyer, Joseph Delteil; *C:* Rudolph Mate.

Passion of Love 🐾🐾🐾 1982
Passione d'Amore Military captain becomes the obsession of his commander's mysterious cousin when he reports to an outpost far from home. Daring and historical romance guaranteed to heat up the VCR. Available dubbed or with subtitles. **117m/C VHS.** *IT FR* Laura Antonelli, Bernard Giraudeau, Valeria (Valerie Dobson) D'Obici, Jean-Louis Trintignant; *D:* Ettore Scola; *W:* Ettore Scola.

Passion of Mind 🐾½ 2000
(PG-13) Moore plays two roles: Marie is an American widow and mother living in France while Marty is a hard-charging single New York literary agent. Marie falls asleep and wakes up as Marty and vice versa. Marie/Marty can't tell anymore which of her two worlds is real and things get even more complicated when each (Marie's persona falls for an appealing man (Skarsgard in France, Fichtner in New York). It's not really confusing since the script is so simplistic and both her lives turn out to be remarkably dull (as is Moore's performance). English-language debut for Berliner and Moore's first film since 1997's "G.I. Jane." **105m/C VHS, DVD.** Demi Moore, Stellan Skarsgard, William Fichtner, Peter Riegert, Joss Ackland, Sinead Cusack; *D:* Alain Berliner;

W: Ronald Bass, David Field; *C:* Eduardo Serra; *M:* Randy Edelman.

The Passion of the Christ 🐾🐾🐾 2004
(R) Calling Gibson's record-breaking, graphic version of the last 12 hours in the life of Jesus Christ "controversial" s an understatement on par with calling the Sahara Desert "warm." Film begins as Jesus (Caviezel) is arrested and taken before Hebrew and Roman authorities for crimes of heresy. Although some backstory is told in flashback, the movie assumes the viewer's knowledge of Jesus's life and focuses on giving as graph c a portrayal of his torture and crucifixion as possible (including a 45-minute flogging scene) in a movie as painful and intense to watch as any put on film. Very bold and well-crafted, but the obsessive focus on gore and violence will leave many asking where the spirituality is supposed to be. Endorsed by many church leaders but drew complaints for its negative depiction of the Hebrew leaders, as well as some violent scenes that Gibson invented. Gibson funded the film with $30 million of his own money. In Aramaic, Latin, and Hebrew with English subtitles. **126m/C DVD.** *US* James (Jim) Caviezel, Monica Bellucci, Maia Morgenstern, Claudia Gerini, Sergio Rubini, Toni Bertorelli, Mattia Sbragia, Luca Lionello, Hristo Naumov Shopov, Giancinto Ferro, Rosalinda Celentano, Francesco De Vito, Hristo Jivkov, Roberto Bestazzrni, Adel Ben Ayed, Fabio Sartor, Luca De Dominics, Pietro (Pedro) Sarubbi, Chokri Ben Zagden, Janeth Merz, Matt Patresi, Francesco Cabras, Giovanni Capaldo, Olek Mincer; *D:* Mel Gibson; *W:* Mel Gibson, Benedict Fitzgerald; *C:* Caleb Deschanel; *M:* John Debney.

A Passion to Kill 🐾½ 1994
Rules of Obsession Formulaic thriller finds psychologist David (Bakula) getting sexually involved with his best friend Jerry's (Getz) wife, who has a lurid past. Seems Diana (Field) stuck a kitchen knife into her abusive first husband and now Jerry's prospects don't look too good. **93m/C VHS.** Scott Bakula, Chelsea Field, Sheila Kelley, John Getz, Rex Smith, France Nuyen, Michael Warren; *D:* Rick King; *W:* William F. Deligan.

Passionate Thief 🐾🐾½
Risate de Gioia; Joyous Laughter 1960 Two pickpockets and a bumbling actress plan to rip off the guests at a posh New Year's Eve party with slightly comic results. Not much to recommend in this slow moving flick. **100m/C VHS.** *IT* Anna Magnani, Ben Gazzara, Fred Clark, Toto, Edy Vessel; *D:* Mario Monicelli; *C:* Leonida Ba'boni.

The Passover Plot 🐾🐾 1975
(PG) A controversial look at the crucifixion of Christ which depicts him as a Zealot leader who, aided by his followers, faked his death and then "rose" to win new converts. **105m/C VHS.** Harry Andrews, Hugh Griffith, Zalman King, Donald Pleasence, Scott Wilson; *D:* Michael Campus; *M:* Alex North.

Passport to Pimlico 🐾🐾½ 1949
Farce about a London neighborhood's residents who discover an ancient charter proclaiming their right to form their own country within city limits. Passable comedy. **81m/B VHS, DVD.** *GB* Stanley Holloway, Margaret Rutherford, Hermione Baddeley, Naunton Wayne, Basil Radford; *D:* Henry Cornelius.

Past Midnight 🐾🐾½ 1992
(R) Richardson plays a social worker who believes recently paroled killer Hauer was wrongly convicted. She attempts to prove his innocence while also falling in love—a dangerous combination. Richardson's beautiful and Hauer's making a successful career out of playing handsome psychos. **100m/C VHS, DVD.** Natasha Richardson, Rutger Hauer, Clancy Brown, Guy Boyd; *D:* Jan Eliasberg; *W:* Frank Norwood; *M:* Steve Bartek.

Past Perfect 🐾🐾½ 1998
(R) Gun battles, car chases, and fights move this actioner right along. Cop Dylan Cooper's (Roberts) job is made harder because his city is overrun with juvenile crime. But even he's shocked when the young criminals start turning up dead. Then Cooper discovers a group of futuristic bounty hunters have teen sent back in time to eliminate these violent delinquents before they become adult killers. **92m/C VHS.** Eric Rob-

erts, Nick Mancuso, Saul Rubinek, Laurie Holden; *D:* Jonathan Heap; *W:* John Penney; *C:* John Houtman; *M:* Christophe Beck.

Past Tense 🐾🐾🐾½ 1994
(R) Complicated thriller about a cop with a gorgeous but mysterious neighbor, a murder to solve, and problems separating reality from his nightmares. **91m/C VHS.** Scott Glenn, Lara Flynn Boyle, Anthony LaPaglia, David Ogden Stiers, Sheree J. Wilson, Marita Geraghty, Stephen Graziano; *D:* Graeme Clifford. **CABLE**

Past the Bleachers 🐾🐾½ 1995
(PG) Sentimental TV movie finds Anderson starring as Bill Parish—a man still lost by the death of his 11-year-old son. Reluctantly, he agrees to coach the Little League team his son had played on, with the help of an opinionated senior citizen (scene-stealer Hughes), and is drawn to the boy who turns out to be the team's star player. The appropriately named Lucky Diamond (Fricke) is both mute and of a mysterious family background, and bonding proves therapeutic for both Bill and the youngster. Based on a novel by Christopher A. Bohjalian. **120m/C VHS.** Richard Dean Anderson, Barnard Hughes, Grayson Fricke, Glynis O'Connor, Ken Jenkins; *D:* Michael Switzer; *W:* Don Rhymer; *M:* Stewart Levin.

Pastime 🐾🐾🐾 1991
(PG) A bittersweet baseball elegy set in the minor leagues in 1957. A 41-year-old pitcher can't face his impending retirement and pals around with the team pariah, a 17-year-old black rookie. Splendidly written and acted, it's a melancholy treat whether you're a fan of the game or not, and safe for family attendance. The only drawback is a grungy, low-budget look. **94m/C VHS, DVD.** William Russ, Scott Plank, Glenn Plummer, Noble Willingham, Jeffrey Tambor, Deirdre O'Connell, Ricky Paull Goldin; *Cameos:* Ernie Banks, Harmon Killebrew, Duke Snider, Bob Feller, Bill Mazeroski, Don Newcombe; *D:* Robin B. Armstrong; *W:* David Eyre; *C:* Tom Richmond. Sundance '91: Aud. Award.

Pat and Mike 🐾🐾🐾 1952
War of the sexes rages in this comedy about a leathery sports promoter who futilely attempts to train a woman for athletic competition. Tracy and Hepburn have fine chemistry, but supporting players contribute too. Watch for the first on-screen appearance of Charles Bronson (then Charles Buchinski) as a crook. **95m/B VHS, DVD.** Spencer Tracy, Katharine Hepburn, Aldo Ray, Jim Backus, William Ching, Sammy White, Phyllis Povah, Charles Bronson, Chuck Connors, Mae Clarke, Carl "Alfalfa" Switzer; *D:* George Cukor; *W:* Garson Kanin, Ruth Gordon; *C:* William H. Daniels; *M:* David Raksin.

Pat Garrett & Billy the Kid 🐾🐾🐾 1973
Coburn is Garrett, one-time partner of Billy the Kid (Kristofferson), turned sheriff. He tracks down and eventually kills the outlaw. The uncut director's version released on video is a vast improvement over the theatrical and TV versions. Dylan's soundtrack includes the now famous "Knockin' on Heaven's Door." **106m/C VHS, DVD.** Kris Kristofferson, James Coburn, Bob Dylan, Richard Jaeckel, Katy Jurado, Chill Wills, Charles Martin Smith, Slim Pickens, Harry Dean Stanton; *D:* Sam Peckinpah; *W:* Rudy Wurlitzer; *M:* George Duning.

Patch Adams 🐾🐾 1998
(PG-13) Maverick medical student Hunter "Patch" Adams (Williams) takes the expression "laughter is the best medicine" literally and treats terminally ill patients with slapstick routines. Naturally, his stodgy old boss, won't to mention the rest of the medical establishment, frown on his antics and prefer more conventional treatments (like medicine). But Patch thumbs his nose at The Man and tries to defend his unorthodox ways to fellow students, including the requisite love interest (Potter). Director Shadyac and screenwriter Oedekerk seem to let Williams unleash his rapid-fire wackiness without much direction. Ultimately, flick is brought down by sappy melodrama and sincere emotion. **115m/ C VHS, DVD, HD DVD.** Robin Williams, Philip Seymour Hoffman, Monica Potter, Bob Gunton, Josef Sommer, Irma P. Hall, Daniel London, Frances Lee McCain, Harve Presnell, Peter Coyote, Michael Jeter, Harold Gould, Frank Gould; *D:*

dyk, Barry (Shabaka) Henley; *D:* Tom Shadyac; *W:* Steve Oedekerk; *C:* Phedon Papamichael; *M:* Marc Shaiman.

A Patch of Blue 🐾🐾🐾½ 1965
A kind-hearted blind girl falls in love with a black man without acknowledging racial differences. Good performances from Hartman and Poitier are film's strongest assets. **108m/C DVD.** Sidney Poitier, Elizabeth Hartman, Shelley Winters, Wallace Ford, Ivan Dixon, John Qualen, Elisabeth Fraser, Kelly Flynn; *D:* Guy Green; *C:* Robert Burks; *M:* Jerry Goldsmith. Oscars '65: Support. Actress (Winters).

Patchwork Girl of Oz 🐾🐾 1914
You wonder what Baum might have been imbibing when he wrote each of his Oz books. In this story a mysterious Emerald City doctor is working on a powder of life that his wife accidentally tests on a patchwork servant doll that suddenly comes alive. **80m/B VHS, DVD.** Frank Moore, Violet MacMillan, Raymond Russell, Leontine Dranet, Pierre Couderc, Richard Rosson, Bobbie Gould, Marie Wayne; *D:* J. Farrell MacDonald; *W:* L. Frank Baum; *C:* James A. Crosby.

Paternity 🐾🐾 1981
(PG) Routine comedy about middle-aged manager of Madison Square Gardens (Reynolds) who sets out to find a woman to bear his child, no strings attached. The predictability of the happy ending makes this a yawner. **94m/C VHS.** Burt Reynolds, Beverly D'Angelo, Lauren Hutton, Norman Fell, Paul Dooley, Elizabeth Ashley; *D:* David Steinberg; *W:* Charlie Peters; *M:* David Shire. Golden Raspberries '81: Worst Song ("Baby Talk").

Path to Paradise 🐾🐾 1997
(R) Based on the true story of the 1993 World Trade Center bombing, which focuses on both the terrorists and the FBI investigators. FBI agent John Anticev (Gallagher) is investigating a rabbi's murder, which leads him to Islamic extremists. An informant warns Anticev that the group are planning terrorist activities in Manhattan but the conspirators are closer to their target than the FBI imagine. **95m/C VHS.** Peter Gallagher, Art Malik, Ned Eisenberg, Marcia Gay Harden, Paul Guilfoyle, Andreas Katsulas, Shiek Mahmud-Bey, Mike Starr; *D:* Larry Williams, Leslie Libman; *W:* Ned Curren; *C:* Jean De Segonzac. **CABLE**

Path to War 🐾🐾½ 2002
Covers the period from the night of President Lyndon B. Johnson's (Gambon) inauguration in 1965 to his 1968 decision not to seek re-election because of the escalating war in Vietnam. While the British Gambon has Johnson's mannerisms down, he can't manage the Texas drawl, which is a real handicap. Baldwin plays Defense Secretary Robert McNamara and Sutherland is Johnson adviser Clark Clifford. **160m/C VHS, DVD.** Michael Gambon, Alec Baldwin, Donald Sutherland, John Aylward, Cliff DeYoung, Christopher Eigeman, Frederic Forrest, James Frain, Philip Baker Hall, Felicity Huffman, Patricia Kalember, Bruce McGill, Tom Skerritt, Diana Scarwid, Gary Sinise; *D:* John Frankenheimer; *W:* Daniel Giat; *C:* Stephen Goldblatt, Nancy Schreiber; *M:* Gary Chang. **CABLE**

Pather Panchali 🐾🐾🐾🐾 *The Song of the Road; The Saga of the Road; The Lament of the Path* 1954
Somber, moving story of a young Bengali boy growing up in impoverished India. Stunning debut from India's master filmmaker Ray, who continued the story in "Aparajito" and "World of Apu." A truly great work. In Bengali with English subtitles. **112m/B VHS, DVD.** *IN* Kanu Bannerjee, Karuna Bannerjee, Uma Das Gupta, Subir Banerji, Runki Banerji, Chunibala Devi; *D:* Satyajit Ray; *W:* Satyajit Ray; *M:* Ravi Shankar.

Pathfinder 🐾🐾🐾½ 1987
A young boy in Lapland of 1,000 years ago comes of age prematurely after he falls in with cutthroat nomads who already slaughtered his family and now want to wipe out the rest of the village. Gripping adventure in the ice and snow features stunning scenery. In Lappish with English subtitles and based on an old fable. **88m/C VHS.** *NO* Mikkel Gaup, Nils Utsi, Svein Scharffenberg, Helgi Skulason, Sara Marit Gaup, Sverre Porsanger; *D:* Nils Gaup; *W:* Nils Gaup.

The Pathfinder 🐾🐾½ 1994
(PG-13) TV adaptation of the 1840 James Fenimore Cooper novel that finds legendary woodsman Natty Bumppo, his adop-

tive Indian father Chingachgook and lovely Mabel Dunham trying to aid a besieged British fort during the French and Indian wars. If it sounds familiar, it's because also the basis for "Leatherstocking Tales" were Cooper's. **104m/C VHS, DVD.** Kevin Dillon, Russell Means, Jaïrz Woolvett, Laurie Holden, Russell Greene; *D:* Donald Shebib; *W:* James Means, Stacy Keach; *M:* Reg Powell.

Pathfinder ☆ 2007 (R) Shelved for a year and then released after blockbuster "300." Coincidence? We think not. Violent and gory (although with fewer ripped abs), this epic wannabe doesn't even have the camp factor to save it. Abandoned by his father during a North American raid, a Viking lad is raised by a peaceful Native American tribe. When the Vikings return for more pillaging and slaughter, now-grown Ghost (Urban) takes on the intruders. Soon all the action cliches commence. Loosely inspired by the 1988 Norwegian pic "Ofelas. **99m/C DVD, Blu-ray Disc.** US Karl Urban, Russell Means, Moon Bloodgood, Clancy Brown, Ralph (Ralf) Moeller, Jay Tavare, Clancy Brown; *D:* Marcus Nispe; *W:* Laeta Kalogridis; *C:* Daniel Pearl; *M:* Jonathan Elias.

Pathology ☆☆ 2008 (R) Grisly, perverse horror thriller finds amoral young doctor Ted Grey (Ventimiglia) beginning his residency in pathology. His fellow docs are a sex-and-drugs crazed bunch led by bony Jack (Weston). Jack has devised a game in which one of the team commits a murder and then the others perform an autopsy to decide how it was done (so much for the Hippocratic Oath). Ted's soon involved up to his scalpel but discovers French officer who knows... the French officer who knows. **86m/B VHS, DVD.** Kirk Douglas, Adolphe Menjou, George Macready, Ralph Meeker, Richard Anderson, Wayne Morris, Timothy Carey, Susana Christian, Bert Freed, Joe Turkel, Peter Capell; *D:* Stanley Kubrick; *W:* Stanley Kubrick, Calder Willingham, Jim Thompson; *C:* Georg Krause; *M:* Gerald Fred. Natl. Film Reg. '92.

Paths of Glory ☆☆☆ 1957 Classic anti-war drama set in WWI France. A vain, ambitious officer imposes unlikely battle strategy on his hapless troops, and when it fails, he demands that three soldiers be selected for execution as cowards. Menjou is excellent as the bloodless French officer with Douglas properly heroic as the French officer who knows about the whole disgraceful enterprise. Fabulous, wrenching fare from filmmaking great Kubrick, who co-wrote. Based on a true story from Humphrey Cobb's novel of the same name. **86m/B VHS, DVD.** Kirk Douglas, Adolphe Menjou, George Macready, Ralph Meeker, Richard Anderson, Wayne Morris, Timothy Carey, Susana Christian, Bert Freed, Joe Turkel, Peter Capell; *D:* Stanley Kubrick; *W:* Stanley Kubrick, Calder Willingham, Jim Thompson; *C:* Georg Krause; *M:* Gerald Fred. Natl. Film Reg. '92.

Paths to Paradise ☆☆☆ 1925 Compson and Griffith share criminal past, reunite at gala event to snatch priceless necklace, and head south of the border. Word-class chase scene. **78m/B VHS.** Raymond Griffith, Betty Compson, Thomas Santschi, Bert Woodruff, Fred Kelsey; *D:* Clarence Badger.

Patrick ☆☆½ 1978 (PG) Coma patient suddenly develops strange powers and has a weird effect on the people he comes in contact with. **115m/C VHS, DVD.** AU Robert Helpmann, Susan Penhaligon, Rod Mullinar; *D:* Richard Franklin; *M:* Brian May.

The Patriot ☆☆ 1986 (R) An action film about an ex-Navy commando who battles a band of nuclear-arms smuggling terrorists. Edited via George Lucas' electronic editor, Edit Droid. **83m/C VHS, DVD.** Gregg Henry, Simone Griffith; *D:* Frank Harris; *W:* Andy Ruben, Katt Shea; *M:* Jay Ferguson.

The Patriot ☆☆ 1999 (R) Wesley McClaren (Seagal) is a former government immunologist who's now the local doctor for a small ranching community. The peaceful community becomes a plague town when an extremist militia group take over and turn out to be carriers of a mysterious disease. McClaren might be a healer but he also can kick some extremist butt when necessary. **90m/C VHS,** DVD. Steven Seagal, Gaïlard Sartain, L.Q. Jones; *D:* Dean Semler; *C:* Stephen Windon; *M:* Stephen (Steve) Edwards.

The Patriot ☆☆½ 2000 (R) Bloody, long, and melodramatic. Revolutionary War revenge pic with a strong lead by Gibson as a notably hissable villain in Isaacs. Benjamin Martin (Gibson) is a former guerilla soldier in the French and Indian wars who just wants to raise his family in peace. Unfortunately, local redcoat leader, Col. Tavington (Isaacs), has other ideas and when Martin's idealistic soldier son Gabriel (Ledger) is captured, dad gets caught up in the action. Producing partners Roland Emmerich and Dean Devlin did "Independence Day" and "Godzilla," so spectacle is their middle name. Film inaccuracies. But who won, anyway? **164m/C VHS, DVD, Blu-ray Disc.** Mel Gibson, Heath Ledger, Jason Isaacs, Chris Cooper, Tcheky Karyo, Joely Richardson, Tom Wilkinson, Donal Logue, Rene Auberjonois, Adam Baldwin, Leon Rippy, Jay Arlen Jones, Gregory Edward Smith, Logan Lerman, Mika Boorem, Skye McCole Bartusiak, Trevor Morgan, Mary Jo Deschanel, Joey D. Viera, Bryan Chafin; *D:* Roland Emmerich; *W:* Robert Rodat; *C:* Caleb Deschanel; *M:* John Williamson.

Patriot Games ☆☆☆ 1992 (R) Jack Ryan, retired CIA analyst, takes his wife and daughter to England on a holiday and ends up saving a member of the Royal Family from assassination by IRA extremists. Ryan, who has killed one of the terrorists, then becomes the target of revenge by the dead man's brother. Good action sequences but otherwise predictable adaptation of the novel by Tom Clancy. Companion to "The Hunt for Red October," with Ford taking over the role of Ryan from Alec Baldwin. Since this movie did well, we can probably expect two more from Ford, who's becoming the king of trilogies. Followed by "Clear and Present Danger." **117m/C VHS, DVD.** Harrison Ford, Anne Archer, Patrick Bergin, Thora Birch, Sean Bean, Richard Harris, James Earl Jones, James Fox, Samuel L. Jackson, Polly Walker, Theodore (Ted) Raimi; *D:* Phillip Noyce; *W:* Donald Stewart, W. Peter Iliff; *C:* Donald McAlpine; *M:* James Horner.

The Patriots ☆☆☆ 1933 A German prisoner works as a shoemaker in a small village during WWI. A lyrical drama in German and Russian with English titles. **82m/B VHS, DVD.** RU Sergei Komarov, Nikolai Kryuchkov, Aleksandr Chistyakov, Yelena Kuzmina; *D:* Boris Barnet; *W:* Eciris Barnet; *C:* Mikhail Krillov; *M:* Sergei Vasilenko.

The Patsy ☆☆ 1964 Shady producers attempt to transform a lowly bellboy into a comedy superstar. Not one of Lewis's better efforts; Lorre's last film. **101m/C VHS, DVD.** Jerry Lewis, Ina Balin, Everett Sloane, Phil Harris, Keenan Wynn, Peter Lorre, John Carradine, Hans Conreid, Richard Deacon, Scatman Crothers, Del Moore, Neil Hamilton, Buddy Lester, Nancy Kulp, Norman Alden, Jack Albertson, Jack Albertson; *D:* Jerry Lewis; *W:* Jerry Lewis.

Pattern for Plunder ☆☆½ 1962 Ex-commando leader rounds up his former comrades to head back to Normandy in search of buried Nazi plunder. **73m/B VHS.** GB Keenan Wynn, Maï Zetterling, Ronald Howard, Edward Underdown; *D:* John Ainsworth; *W:* Christopher Davis.

Patterns ☆☆☆ 1956 Realistic depiction of big business. Heflin starts work at a huge New York office that is under the ruthless supervision of Sloane. Serling's astute screenplay (adapted from his TV play) is adept at portraying ruthless, power-struggling executives and the sundry workings of a large corporation. Film has aged slightly, but it still has some edge to it. Originally intended for television. **83m/B VHS, DVD.** Van Heflin, Everett Sloane, Ed Begley Sr., Beatrice Straight, Elizabeth Wilson; *D:* Fielder Cook; *W:* Rod Serling. *C:* Boris Kaufman.

Pattes Blanches ☆☆½ — *Paws of Power 1956*

Pattes Blanches ☆☆½ *White Paws* 1949 A reclusive aristocrat always wears white spats, causing ridicule in the small fishing village where he lives. Trouble comes when a local saloon-keeper becomes resentful of the rich man's advances on his girlfriend. Moody, sensual.

Paul and Michelle ☆ 1974 (R) The equally dull sequel to "Friends" finds the two lovers a little older but no wiser. Paul has graduated from his British school and returns to France to seek out Michelle and their child. They try to rekindle their romance but the stresses of everyday life cause them problems. **102m/C VHS, DVD.** GB FR Sean Bury, Anicee Alvina, Keir Dullea, Ronald Lewis, Catherine Allegret, Georges Beller; *D:* Lewis Gilbert; *M:* Michel Colombier.

Paul Bartel's The Secret Cinema ☆☆½ *The Secret Cinema 1969*

Paul Robeson ☆☆ 1977 Major events in the life of the popular actor are recounted in this one-man performance. Originally staged by Charles Nelson Reilly. **118m/C VHS, DVD.** James Earl Jones; *D:* Lloyd Richards.

Paulie ☆☆½ 1998 (PG) Dreamworks follows up "Mouse Hunt" with this tale of a conversant parrot (voiced by Mohr) whose mouth keeps getting him in trouble. Trapped in a dingy basement, Paulie tells a lonely Russian janitor (Shalhoub) the story of his cross-country quest to return to his original owner, the little girl (Eisen-

French melodrama exploring class, money and sex. Adaptation of a play by Jean Anouilh. In French with English subtitles. **92m/B VHS.** FR Suzy Delair, Fernand Ledoux, Paul Bernard, Michel Bouquet; *D:* Jean Grémillon.

Patti Rocks ☆☆☆ 1988 (R) Offbeat, realistic independent effort concerns a foul chauvinist who enlists a friend to accompany him on a visit to a pregnant girlfriend who turns out to be less than the bimbo she's portrayed as en route. Mulkey shines as the sexist. Same characters featured earlier in "Loose Ends." **86m/C VHS.** Chris Mulkey, John Jenkins, Karen Landry; David L. Turk, Stephen Yoakam; *D:* David Burton Morris; *W:* Chris Mulkey, John Jenkins, Karen Landry, David Burton Morris; *M:* Doug Maynard.

Patton ☆☆☆½ — *Patton—Lust for Glory*

Patton ☆☆☆½ 1970 (PG) Lengthy but stellar bio of the vain, temperamental American general who masterminded significant combat triumphs during WWII. "Old Blood and Guts" who was considered himself an 18th-century commander living in the wrong era, produced victory after victory in North Africa and Europe, but not without a decided impact upon his troops. Scott is truly magnificent in the title role, and Malden shines in the supporting role of General Omar Bradley. Not a subtle film, but neither is its subject. Interesting match-up with the 1986 TV movie "The Last Days of Patton," also starring Scott. **171m/C VHS, DVD.** George C. Scott, Karl Malden, Stephen Young, Michael Strong, Frank Latimore, James Edwards, Lawrence (Larry) Dobkin, Michael Bates, Tim Considine, Edward Binns, John Doucette, Morgan Paull, Siegfried Rauch, Paul Stevens, Richard Muench; *D:* Franklin J. Schaffner; *W:* Francis Ford Coppola, Edmund H. North; *C:* Fred W. Koenekamp; *M:* Jerry Goldsmith. Oscars '70: Actor (Scott), Art Dir./Set Dec., Director (Schaffner), Film Editing, Picture, Sound, Story & Screenplay; AFI '98: Top 100; Directors Guild '70: Director (Schaffner); Golden Globes '71: Actor—Drama (Scott); Natl. Bd. of Review '70: Actor (Scott); Natl. Film Reg. '03: N.Y. Film Critics '70: Actor (Scott); Natl. Soc. Film Critics '70: Actor (Scott); Writers Guild '70: Orig. Screenplay.

Patty Hearst ☆☆½ 1988 (R) Less than fascinating, expressionistic portrait of Hearst from her kidnapping through her brainwashing and eventual criminal participation with the SLA. An enigmatic film that seems to only make Hearst's transformation into a Marxist terrorist all the more mysterious. Based on Hearst's book, "Every Secret Thing." **108m/C VHS.** Natasha Richardson, William Forsythe, Ving Rhames, Frances Fisher, Jodi Long, Dana Delany; *D:* Paul Schrader; *W:* Nicholas Kazan; *C:* Bojan Bazelli.

Pauline and Paulette ☆☆ 2001 French melodrama exploring class, money and sex... (see adjacent column)

Pavilion of Women ☆☆ 2001 (R) Dull adaptation of the 1946 Pearl S. Buck novel. As the Japanese prepare to invade Manchuria in 1938, Madame Wu (Luo), tired of her husband's brutality, decides to give him a peasant girl concubine, Chiuming (Cing), whom he promptly rejects. However, the pretty girl attracts the interest of the Wu's youngest son, Fengmo (Cho), just as Madame becomes interested in American missionary doctor, Father Andre (Dafoe), who runs the local orphanage. The film is in English and the Chinese actors do struggle with their dialogue which doesn't help the emotional balance of the production. **120m/C VHS, DVD.** Luo Yan, Willem Dafoe, John Cho, Yi Ding, Shek Sau, Amy Hill, Anita Loo, Kate McGregor-Stewart; *W:* Luo Yan, Paul R. Collins; *C:* Hang-Seng Poon; *M:* Conrad Pope.

Pauline at the Beach ☆☆☆½ 1983 (R) Fifteen-year-old Pauline (Langlet) accompanies her more experienced divorced cousin Marion (Dombasle) to the French coast for a summer of sexual hijinks. Contemplative, not coarse, though the leads look great indeed, her will states that her beachfront dies, her will states that her beachfront divided in thirds on condition that one of the two remaining sisters, Breezy, typically talky fare from small-film master Rohmer. Third film in the director's Comedies & Proverbs series. French with subtitles. **95m/C VHS, DVD.** FR Amanda Langlet, Arielle Dombasle, Pascal Greggory, Rosette, Feodor Atkine, Simon de la Brosse; *D:* Eric Rohmer; *C:* Nestor Almendros.

Pauline and Paulette ☆☆ 2001 (PG) Pauline (van der Groen) is a 66-year-old mentally retarded woman living happily with her sister Martha (De Bruyn) is a Flemish town near Brussels. When Martha dies, her will states that her beachfront will be divided in thirds on condition that one of the two remaining sisters, Pauline (Peter-sen) or Cecile (Bergmans), must take in Pauline. Otherwise the money will go to set Pauline up in a special care facility. Pauline agrees to care for Pauline, at least temporarily, and finds there are some obligations that aren't easy to get rid of. French and Flemish with subtitles. **78m/C VHS, DVD.** BE FR NL Dora van de Groen, Ann Petersen, Rosemarie Bergmans, Julienne De Bruyn, Idwig Stephane; *D:* Lieven Debrauwer; *W:* Lieven Debrauwer, Jacques Boon; *C:* Michael Van Laer; *M:* Frederic Devreese.

berg), who raised him from a fledgling. Alternately funny and saccharine, Pauline goes through a procession of owners: a smart-aleck pawn shop owner (Hackett); a kindly old woman (Rowlands) who drives him to L.A. in her RV; a petty criminal (Mohr again); a taco stand owner (Marin) who manages a parrot dancing act; and a scientist (Davison) looking to cash in on the bird's talent. Not a whole lot of action for a kiddie movie, and some of the jokes may go over their heads, but fine performances all around and a charming story keep pic aloft. **91m/C VHS, DVD.** Jay Mohr, Gena Rowlands, Tony Shalhoub, Richard Davison, Trini Alvarado, Buddy Hackett, Matt Craven, Bill Cobbs, Laura Harrington, Tia Texada; *D:* John Roberts; *W:* Laurie Craig; *C:* Tony Pierce-Roberts; *M:* John Debney; *V:* Jay Mohr.

The Pawnbroker ☆☆☆½ 1965 A Jewish pawnbroker in Harlem is haunted by his grueling experiences in a Nazi camp during the Holocaust. Powerful and well done. Probably Steiger's best performance. Adapted from a novel by Edward Lewis Wallant. **120m/B VHS, DVD.** Rod Steiger, Brock Peters, Geraldine Fitzgerald, Jaime Sanchez, Thelma Oliver; *D:* Sidney Lumet; *C:* Boris Kaufman; *M:* Quincy Jones. Berlin Intl. Film Fest. '65: Actor (Steiger); British Acad. '66: Actor (Steiger).

Pawnshop ☆☆½ 1916 Charlie is employed as a pawnbroker's assistant. Silent with music track. **32m/B VHS, DVD.** Charlie Chaplin, Henry Bergman, Edna Purviance, John Rand; *D:* Charlie Chaplin; *W:* Charlie Chaplin; *C:* Roland H. Totheroh.

Pay It Forward ☆☆ 2000 (PG-13) Seventh-grade student Trevor (Osment) takes his social studies assignment very seriously. His teacher Eugene (Spacey) has his students think of an idea to change the world and tells them to put it into action. Trevor comes up with the idea of doing a good deed for someone who is then supposed to do a favor for someone else as a way to "pay the favor forward." Trevor's cocktail waitress/recovering alcoholic mom Arlene (Hunt) finds herself wary of both the project and the teacher. Trevor, however, has decided to use the two of them as his first "pay it forward" subjects. Cloyingly emotional and more than a little manipulative. Based on the novel by Catherine Ryan Hyde. **122m/C VHS, DVD.** Haley, Joel Osment, Kevin Spacey, Helen Hunt, Jay Mohr, James (Jim) Caviezel, Jon Bon Jovi, Angie Dickinson, David Ramsey, Gary Werntz; **D:** Mimi Leder; **W:** Leslie Dixon; **C:** Oliver Stapleton; **M:** Thomas Newman.

Pay Off 1989 A lunatic psychiatrist seeks murderous revenge on his ex-patient/girlfriend and her family. **87m/C VHS.** Michael Fitzpatrick, Veronika Mattson, Margareta Krook; **D:** Jiri (George) Trif.

Pay or Die 1983 (M) A crime boss' men turn on him and kidnap his daughter, prompting the intervention of an unusual martial arts team. **92m/C VHS.** Dick Adair, Johnny Wilson; **D:** Bobby Suarez.

Payback 1989 A brawny young man uses firepower to avenge those who have wronged him. **90m/C VHS.** Jean Carol, Alex Meneses; **D:** Addison Randall.

Payback 1990 (R) A convict sets out to avenge his brother's death, and creates all sorts of mayhem in the process. Produced by Bob "Newlywed Game" Eubanks and scored by Daryl "Captain and Tenille" Dragon. **94m/C VHS.** Corey Michael Eubanks, Michael Ironside, Teresa Blake, Bert Remsen, Vincent Van Patten, Don Swayze; **D:** Russell Solberg; **M:** Daryl Dragon.

Payback 1994 (R) An old, dying con (Armstrong) tells fellow inmate Oscar Bonsetter (Howell) the whereabouts of a fortune if he'll promise to kill cruel jail guard Gully (Bell) who made the geezer's life a misery. Years later, the now ex-con finds the ex-guard running a diner near the spot where the money is buried and decides to carry out his plan for revenge. If Oscar doesn't get too distracted by Gully's hot-to-trot wife, Rose (Severance), first. Also available in an unrated version. **92m/C VHS.** C. Thomas Howell, Joan Severance, Marshall Bell, R.G. Armstrong; **D:** Anthony Hickox; **W:** Sam Bernard; **C:** David Bridges.

Paycheck 2003 (PG-13) Michael Jennings (Affleck) is a brilliant engineer hired by his old friend Jimmy Rethrick (Eckhart) to work on a top-secret project. The one condition is that he gets his mind erased after his job is completed. Three years later, Jennings awakes, sans memories, finds that he had forfeited his fee of $90 million in exchange for a manila envelope full of seemingly random objects. It turns out that he was framed for murder and his former employers want him dead. The objects become clues to figuring out what the heck is going on. Surprisingly lackluster adaption of a Phillip K. Dick short story, considering that John Woo is the director. **110m/C DVD. US** Ben Affleck, Aaron Eckhart, Uma Thurman, Paul Giamatti, Colm Feore, Joe Morton, Michael C. Hall; **D:** John Woo; **W:** Dean Georgaris; **C:** Jeffrey L. Kimball; **M:** John Powell. Golden Raspberries '03: Worst Actor (Affleck).

Payday 1973 Tom stars as a declining country music star on tour in this portrayal of the seamy side of show business, from groupies to grimy motels. Well-written script and fine performances make this an engaging, if rather draining, drama not easily found on the big screen. **98m/C VHS, DVD.** Sonny Shroyer, Rip Torn, Anna Capri, Michael C. Gwynne, Jeff Morris; **D:** Daryl Duke; **W:** Don Carpenter; **C:** Richard C. Glouner; **M:** Ed Bogas, Shel Silverstein, Ian Tyson.

The Payoff 1943 The old-fashioned newspaper-reporter-as-crime-fighter routine. When the city's special prosecutor is murdered a daring newshawk investigates and tracks the bad guys. But will he spell their names right? **74m/B VHS, DVD.** Lee Tracy, Tom Brown, Tina Thayer, Evelyn Brent, Jack La Rue, Ian Keith, John Maxwell; **D:** Arthur Dreifuss.

Payoff 1991 (R) An ex-cop discovers the identity of gangsters who killed his parents. He traces them to a Lake Tahoe resort and plots revenge. Familiar crime story with a good cast. **111m/C VHS.** Keith Carradine, Kim Greist, Harry Dean Stanton, John Saxon, Jeff Corey; **D:** Stuart Cooper; **W:** Douglas S. Cook; **M:** Charles Bernstein.

P.C.U. 1994 (PG-13) Satire on campus political correctness follows freshman Tom Lawrence's (Young) adventures as he navigates the treacherous waters of Port Chester University (PCU). He falls in with the gang from the Pit, the militantly non-PC dorm, who encourage bizarre and offensive behavior. Essentially a modern update of "National Lampoon's Animal House," but without the brilliance; add half a bone for tackling the thorny sensitivity issue in a humorous way that parodies, but shouldn't offend. Actor Bochner's directorial debut. **81m/C VHS, DVD.** Jeremy Piven, Chris Young, David Spade, Sarah Trigger, Jessica Walter, Jon Favreau, Megan Ward, Jake Busey, Alex Desert; **Cameos:** George Clinton; **D:** Hart Bochner; **W:** Adam Left, Zak Penn; **M:** Steve Vai.

P.D. James: Death in Holy Orders 2003 *Death in Holy Orders* 2003 When murder and suicide shockwave St. Anselm's, a remote theological college, one victim's wealthy father pressures Scotland Yard to investigate. Adam Dalgleish (Shaw), who spent childhood summers at the school, is sent and discovers that the Church of England wishes to close the school, and Archdeacon Matthew Crampton (Wood) is particularly interested in seeing that its valuable art works have more suitable settings. What the widowed Dalgleish doesn't expect to encounter is potential romance with visiting professor Emma Lavenham (Dee). **180m/C DVD. GB** Martin Shaw, Jesse Spencer, Alan Howard, Clive Wood, Hugh Fraser, Robert Hardy, Janie Dee; **D:** John Campbell; **W:** Robert C. Jones; **C:** Martin Fuhrer; **M:** Julian Nott. TV

P.D. James: The Murder Room 2004 *The Murder Room* 2004 A macabre family legacy leads to murder and other crimes. London's Dupayne Museum houses exhibits from some of Britain's most gruesome real-life homicides. When Neville (Maloney), one of the Dupayne heirs, dies in a terrible fire, Adam Dalgleish (Shaw) investigates and discovers that the killing is similar to a notorious case on display. But there are also family secrets the remaining Dupaynes don't want exposed. **180m/C DVD. GB** Martin Shaw, Samantha Bond, Michael Maloney, Nicholas Le Prevost, Sam Phillips, Kerry Fox, Janie Dee; **D:** Diarmuid Lawrence; **W:** Robert C. Jones; **C:** Simon Richards; **M:** John Lunn. TV

Peace, Propaganda & the Promised Land 2004 Expose lashing out at the American media's coverage of the Israeli-Palestinian conflict. Another long-winded attempt at a Michael Moore-style "documentary." Cites twists on terms, such as "retaliate" when Israel makes a move, but using the word "attack" when describing Palestinian operations. On-camera interviews come from unabashedly biased academics and advocates. Makes some stirring observations, but its lack of humor and tunnel-visioned hoopla will turn off most audiences. Ironically, it falls into the category it sets out to derail: juicy propaganda. **80m/C DVD. US D:** Sut Jhally, Bathsheba Ratzkoff; **C:** Kelli Garner; **M:** Thom Monahan.

Peaceful Warrior 2006 (PG-13) It's not quite the new "Karate Kid" despite that whole Zen mentor aspect that Nolte brings to the role of Socrates. Dan (Mechlowicz) is a hotshot college gymnast on his way to realize his dreams are over after a bad motorcycle crash. Socrates offers his own spiritual take on Dan's dilemma and Dan goes on to—well, the actual Dan Millman goes on to write a 1980 New Age memoir called "Way of the Peaceful Warrior," which this film is based on. **121m/C DVD. US** Nick Nolte, Scott Mechlowicz, Amy Smart, Tim DeKay, Paul Wesley, Ashton Holmes, Agnes Bruckner, Ray Wise, B. J. Britt; **D:** Victor Salva; **W:** Victor Salva, Kevin Bernhardt; **C:** Sharon Meir; **M:** Bennett Salvay.

The Peacekeeper 1998 (R) Frank Cross (Lundgren) is one unlucky man. While guarding the president (Scheider), he manages to lose the briefcase containing nuclear launch codes to a terrorist group. Now, they're blackmailing the government and Cross needs to breach the terrorist's stronghold to save the day. **98m/C VHS, DVD. CA** Dolph Lundgren, Roy Scheider, Michael Sarrazin, Montel Williams, Monica Schnarre; **D:** Frederic Forestier; **W:** James H. Stewart, Robert Geoffrion; **C:** John Berrie; **M:** Francois Forestier.

Peacekillers 1971 A mean bunch of bikers visit a commune to kidnap a young woman. The gang has a big surprise in store for them when the girl escapes. **86m/C VHS.** Michael Ontkean, Clint Ritchie, Paul Krokop; **D:** Douglas Schwartz.

Peacemaker 1990 (R) Two aliens masquerading as human cops stalk each other through a major city. **90m/C VHS, DVD.** Robert Forster, Lance Edwards, Hilary Shepard, Bert Remsen, Robert Davi; **D:** Kevin S. Tenney; **W:** Kevin S. Tenney.

The Peacemaker 1997 (R) First-time feature director Leder teams up with fellow "ER" vet Clooney on the first theatrical release for Dreamworks SKG. Clooney's Army Intel officer Lt. Col. Thomas Devoe works with White House nuke expert Dr. Julia Kelly (Kidman) when a renegade Russian colonel diverts some nuclear warheads, scheduled for dismantling, into the hands of a Bosnian diplomat (lures) with a grudge against the West. Plenty of well-constructed action set pieces and a reasonably plausible plot overcome a lack of snappy dialogue. Extra credit for making the terrorist human instead of the usual evil caricature, and for letting the two leads work together without having to sleep together. **123m/C VHS, DVD.** George Clooney, Nicole Kidman, Armin Mueller-Stahl, Marcel lures, Alexander Baluyev, Randall Batinkoff, Jim Haynie, Michael Boatman, Gary Werntz, Holt McCallany, Joan Copeland, Carlos Gomez, Rene Medvesek, Alexander Strobele; **D:** Mimi Leder; **W:** Michael Schiffer; **C:** Dietrich Lohmann; **M:** Hans Zimmer.

The Peacock Fan 1929 The Peacock Fan is protected by a deadly curse, with certain death to anyone who possesses it. **50m/B VHS.** Lucian Preval, Dorothy Dwan, Rosemary Theby, Gladden James; **D:** Phil Rosen; **W:** Arthur Hoerl; **C:** M.A. Anderson.

The Peanut Butter Solution 1985 (PG) An imaginative 11-year-old boy investigates a strange old house which is haunted by friendly ghosts who are in possession of a magic potion. **96m/C VHS.** Matthew Mackay, Siluck Saysanasy, Alison Podbrey, Michael Maillot, Griffith Brewer, Michael Hogan, Helen Hughes; **D:** Michael Rubbo; **W:** Michael Rubbo; **M:** Lewis Furey.

The Pearl 1948 Based on a John Steinbeck story, a Mexican fisherman, living in poverty, finds a magnificent pearl and he thinks it will improve the lives of his family. He is bewildered by what this pearl really brings—liars and thieves. Simple, yet larger-than-life film, beautifully photographed; a timeless picture capturing human nature. **77m/B VHS. MX** Pedro Armendariz Sr., Maria Elena Marques, Fernando Wagner, Charles Rooner; **D:** Emilio Fernandez. Natl. Film. Reg. '02.

Pearl 1978 Sweeping miniseries covers the careers and private lives of those who live and work at the naval base at Pearl Harbor, Hawaii, from right before the Japanese attack to its aftermath. **233m/C VHS.** Robert Wagner, Dennis Weaver, Lesley Ann Warren, Brian Dennehy, Max Gail, Mary Crosby, Gregg Henry, Katherine Helmond, Angie Dickinson, Tiana Alexandra, Richard Anderson, Adam Arkin, Marion Ross, Allan Miller, David Elliott; **D:** Hy Averback, Alexander Singer; **W:** Stirling Silliphant; **C:** Gayne Rescher, **M:** John Addison; **Nar:** Joseph Campanella. TV

Pearl Harbor 2001 (PG-13) Director Bay has also done "The Rock" and "Armageddon" so he knows his way around big-budget, action-packed event movies. The problem, besides his usual difficulties with characterization and subtlety, is that we have to wade through the trite romantic triangle between U.S. Army Air aviator Hartnett, flyboy Affleck, and Navy nurse Beckinsale before we get to the well-done spectacle of the bombing on December 7, 1941, as well as the subsequent U.S. raid on Tokyo led by James Doolittle (Baldwin). It's probably quicker, and more enjoyable, to skip to the attack sequence between a rented double feature of "From Here to Eternity" and "Thirty Seconds Over Tokyo." **183m/C VHS, DVD. US** Ben Affleck, Josh Hartnett, Kate Beckinsale, Alec Baldwin, Cuba Gooding Jr., Dan Aykroyd, Mako, Tom Sizemore, Jon Voight, William Lee Scott, Colm Feore, Michael Shannon, Peter Firth, Jennifer Garner, Catherine Kellner, Jaime (James) King, Scott Wilson, William Fichtner, Ewen Bremner, Leland Orser, Graham Beckel, Tomas Arana, Guy Torry, Brian Haley, Tony Curran, Kim Coates, Glenn Morshower, John Fujioka, Tim Choate, John Diehl, Ted McGinley, Raphael Sbarge; **D:** Michael Bay; **W:** Randall Wallace; **C:** John Schwartzman; **M:** Hans Zimmer.

The Pearl of Death 1944 Holmes and Watson investigate the theft of a precious pearl. **69m/B VHS, DVD.** Basil Rathbone, Nigel Bruce, Dennis Hoey, Miles Mander, Rondo Hatton, Evelyn Ankers; **D:** Roy William Neill.

Pearl of the South Pacific *South Sea Woman* 1955 A trio of adventurers destroy a quiet and peaceful island when they ransack it for pearl treasures. **85m/C VHS, DVD.** Dennis Morgan, Virginia Mayo, David Farrar; **D:** Allan Dwan; **W:** Edwin Blum; **C:** John Alton; **M:** Louis Forbes.

Peau D'Ane 1971 Charming fairy tale about a widowed king in search of a beautiful wife. Gorgeous color production. In French with English subtitles. **90m/C VHS, DVD. FR** Catherine Deneuve, Jacques Perrin, Jean Marais, Delphine Seyrig; **D:** Jacques Demy.

The Pebble and the Penguin 1994 (G) Animated musical about a shy, romantic penguin named Hubie (Short), who must present his lady love Marina (Golden) with a beautiful pebble to win her hand forever before the villainous Drake (Curry) can claim her. Hubie is helped along the way by a cantankerous new friend (Belushi) he meets when stranded on a boat to Tahiti. Together the two race back to Antarctica fighting enemies and the elements along the way. Based on a true mating custom of the Adeli penguins, the story is satisfying for younger viewers, but does not have the animation magic of other recents films to keep adults interested. Beware of the sugary Manilow tunes. **74m/C VHS, DVD. D:** Don Bluth; **W:** Rachel Koretsky, Steve Whitestone; **M:** Barry Manilow, Bruce Sussman, Mark Watters; **V:** Martin Short, Annie Golden, Tim Curry, James Belushi; **Nar:** Shani Wallis.

Pecker 1998 (R) A kinder, gentler Waters? To be sure, he doesn't laugh at, but with, his working-class Baltimoreans. Still, you've got strippers (of both sexes), a "talking" statue of the Virgin Mary, and rats having sex, so this isn't a Disney film. Pecker (Furlong), who gets his name from pecking at his food, who takes pictures of what's around him. His work catches the eye of New York art

Peck's Bad Boy 🐾🐾 1921 Impudent, precocious brat causes his parents considerable grief. Someone should lock this kid in a room with W.C. Fields or the other assorted pals. Warning: Not to be confused with Peck's Bad Boy with the Circus. Warning: Not to be confused with Peck-wee's Big Adventure. 60m/B VHS, DVD. Paul (Pee-wee Herman) Reubens, John Moody, John Paragon, Tito Lorna, Nicole Panter. D: Marty Callner. W: Bill Steinkellner. M: Danny Elfman.

Peck's Bad Boy 🐾🐾 1934 A wedge is driven between a young boy and his adoptive father when the man's sister son to be number one in, causing much discord. Cooper is excellent in his role as the adopted son. 70m/B VHS, DVD. Tommy Kelly, Ann Gillis, George "Spanky" McFarland, Edgar Kennedy, Billy Gilbert; D: Edward F. (Eddie) Cline.

Peck's Bad Boy with the Circus 🐾🐾 1938 The circus will never be the same after the mischievous youngster and his buddies get done with it. Gilbert and Kennedy provide the high points. 67m/B VHS, DVD. Tommy Kelly, Ann Gillis, George "Spanky" McFarland, Edgar Kennedy, Billy Gilbert; D: Edward F. (Eddie) Cline.

Pecos Kid 1966 Meet the man who used the Grand Canyon for a swimmin' hole, dug the Rio Grande, and used the Texas panhandle for a fryin' pan. From Shelly Duvall's "Tall Tales and Legends" cable series. 50m/C VHS, DVD. Steve Guttenberg, Martin Mull, Claude Akins, Rebecca De Mornay. CABLE

Pecos Bill 1935 A child has his parents killed, and grows up embittered, vengeful and thirsty for blood. 56m/B VHS. Roger Williams, Edward Cassidy, Wally Wales, Ruth Findlay, Earl Dwire, Fred Kohler Jr.; D: Harry Fraser; W: Henry Hess.

Pedale Douce 🐾🐾½ What a Drag 1996 Irreverent comedy features a romantic triangle involving content gay businessman Adrien (Timsit), whose confidante is the liberal Eva (Ardant), owner of a trendy Paris eatery, with an all-gay staff and predominantly gay clientele. Adrien persuades Eva to pose as his wife in order to close a deal with conservative, married banker Alexandre (Berry). Alexandre becomes enchanted with Eva and begins to pursue her, causing a comedy of errors and unexpected jealousy for Adrien, who tries to derail their affair. French with subtitles. 102m/C VHS. FR Patrick Timsit, Fanny Ardant; D: Gabriel Aghion. W: Patrick Timsit, Gabriel Aghion, Pierre Palmade; C: Fabio Conversi; M: Herve Masini, Philippe Chopin. Cesar '97: Actress (Ardant).

Peddlin' in Society 🐾🐾 Da Barcarola a Bancarella 1947 A fruit vendor makes it big on the black market and lives the good life, until poor investments force her back to her old means. Strong performances by Magnani and De Sica. In Italian with English subtitles. 97m/C VHS. GE IT Anna Magnani, Vittorio De Sica, Virgilio Riento, Laura Gore; D: Gennaro Righelli.

The Pedestrian 🐾🐾🐾½ Der Fussgaenger 1973 (PG) A prominent German industrialist is exposed as a Nazi officer who supervised the wholesale devastation of a Greek village during WWII. Impressive debut for director Schell, who also appears in a supporting role. 97m/C VHS. GE Maximilian Schell, Peggy Ashcroft, Lil Dagover, Francoise Rosay, Elisabeth Bergner; D: Maximilian Schell. Golden Globes '74: Foreign Film.

Peeping Tom 🐾🐾🐾½ Face of Fear; The Photographer of Panic 1960 Controversial, unsettling thriller in which psychopath Mark Lewis (Boehm) lures women before his film camera, then records their deaths at his hand. Unnerving subject matter is rendered impressively by British master Powell, who plays the part of Mark's abusive father who's s own in home movies tormenting the boy. A classic of its kind, but definitely not for everyone. Critical brickbats effectively derailed Powell's career and the original uncut version was not released until 1979. 88m/C VHS, DVD, GB Karl-Heinz Boehm, Moira Shearer, Anna Massey, Maxine Audley, Esmond Knight, Shirley Anne Field, Brenda Bruce, Pamela Green, Jack Watson, Nigel Davenport, Susan Travers, Veronica Hurst, Martin Miller, Miles McRoberts, Michael Powell; D: Michael Powell; W: Leo Marks; C: Otto Heller; M: Brian Easdale.

Peephole 🐾 1993 Prison psychiatrist is asked by the DA to keep Rick, who committed a sex crime against a little girl, in jail any way he can. So he visits Rick's prostitute girlfriend Sheena for info but instead winds up or e of her clients. Meanwhile, Rick has been released and a little girl has been found dead, but nothing's that clear cut. Based on director/writer Bitterman's play. 90m/C VHS. Patrick Husted, Rick Dean, William Dennis Hunt, Kristen Trucksess, Peter Crook; D: Shem Bitterman; W: Shem Bitterman.

The Pee-wee Herman Show 🐾🐾🐾 1982 The original HBO special which introduced Pee-wee to the world. Hilarious stuff, with help from Captain Carl (Harman), Miss Yvonne, and other assorted pals. Warning: Not to be confused with Pee-wee's children's show. 60m/C VHS, DVD. Paul (Pee-wee Herman) Reubens, John Moody, John Paragon, Tito Lorna, Nicole Panter; D: Marty Callner; W: Bill Steinkellner. Edie McClurg; D: Marty Callner; W: Bill Steinkellner. CABLE

Pee-wee's Big Adventure 🐾🐾🐾 1985 (PG) Zany, endearing comedy about an adult nerd's many adventures while attempting to recover his stolen bicycle. Chock full of classic sequences, including a barroom encounter between Pee-wee and several ornery bikers, and a tour through the Alamo. A colorful, exhilarating experience. 92m/C VHS, DVD. Paul (Pee-wee Herman) Reubens, Elizabeth (E.G. Daley) Daily, Mark Holton, Diane Salinger, Judd Omen, Cassandra Peterson, James Brolin, Morgan Fairchild, Tony Bill, Jan Hooks, Phil Hartman, Jason Hervey, John Paragon; D: Tim Burton; W: Michael Varhol, Paul (Pee-wee Herman) Reubens, Phil Hartman; C: Victor Kemper; M: Danny Elfman.

Pelle the Conqueror 🐾🐾🐾 1988 Overpowering tale of a Swedish boy and his widower father who serve land-owners in late 19th-century Denmark. Compassionate saga of human spirit contains numerous memorable sequences. Hvenegaard is wonderful as young Pelle, but von Sydow delivers what is probably his finest performance as a sympathetic weakling. American distributors foolishly trimmed the film by some 20 minutes (140 minute version). From the novel by Martin Anderson Nexo. In Swedish with English subtitles. 160m/C VHS, DVD, SW DK Max von Sydow, Pelle Hvenegaard, Erik Paaske, Bjorn Granath, Axel Strobye, Troels Asmussen, John Wittig, Anne Lise Hirsch Bjerrum, Kristina Tornqvist, Morten Jorgensen; D: Billie August; W: Billie August. Oscars '88: Foreign Film; Cannes '88. Film; Golden Globes '89: Foreign Film.

The Penalty 🐾🐾½ 1920 Legless madman Blizzard (Chaney) is after revenge on his family doctor, and society. Chaney's properly creepy. 93m/B VHS, DVD. Lon Chaney Sr., Claire Adams, Kenneth Harlan, Charles Clary; D: Wallace Worsley II; W: Charles Kenyon, Philip Lonergan; C: Don Short.

Pendulum 🐾🐾 1969 (PG) A police captain struggles to prove himself innocent of his wife's—and his wife's lover's—murders. 106m/C VHS. George Peppard, Jean Seberg, Richard Kiley, Madeleine Sherwood, Charles McGraw, Marj Dusay; D: George Schaefer; C: Lionel Lindon.

Penalty Phase 🐾🐾 1986 An up-for-election judge must decide a murder case in which his future, as well as the defendant's, is in question 94m/C VHS. Peter Strauss, Melissa Gilbert, Jonelle Allen; D: Tony Richardson; M: Ralph Burns. TV

The Pelican Brief 🐾🐾½ 1993 (PG-13) Tulane law student Darby Shaw (Roberts) writes a speculative brief on the murders of two Supreme Court justices that results in more murder and sends her running for her life. Fairly faithful to the Grisham bestseller, but the multitude of characters is confusing. Pakula adds style and star-power, but much will depend on your tolerance for paranoid political thrillers and ability to accept Roberts as the smart cookie who hits on the right answer and then manages to keep herself alive while bodies are dropping all around her. Washington, as sharp as reporter Gray Grantham, the guy Roberts looks like she falls hard for (but the book's romance is nowhere to be seen). 141m/C VHS, DVD. Julia Roberts, Denzel Washington, John Heard, Julia Roberts, Stanley Tucci, James B. Sikking, William Atherton, Robert Culp, John Lithgow, Sam Shepard, Hume Cronyn; D: Alan J. Pakula; W: Alan J. Pakula; C: Stephen Goldblatt; M: James Horner.

Penitentiary 🐾🐾½ 1979 (R) A realistic story of a black fighter who survives his prison incarceration by winning bouts against the other prisoners. Well-made and executed, followed by two progressively worse sequels. 99m/C VHS, DVD. Leon Isaac Kennedy, Jamaa Fanaka, Badja (Medu) Djola, Chuck "Porky" Mitchell; D: Jamaa Fanaka. C: Marty Ollstein.

Penitentiary 2 🐾 1982 (R) A welterweight fighter is after the man who murdered his girlfriend, who, luckily, is incarcerated in the same prison as Our Hero. Sometimes things just work out right. 108m/C VHS, DVD. Leon Isaac Kennedy, Mr. T, Leon Erickson, Ernie Hudson, Glynn Turman; D: Jamaa Fanaka; W: Jamaa Fanaka; C: Stephen Posey; M: Jack Wheaton.

Penitentiary 3 🐾½ 1987 (R) Once again, Kennedy, as the inmate boxer extraordinaire punches his way out of various prison battles. Another punch-drunk sequel. 91m/C VHS, DVD. Leon Isaac Kennedy, Anthony Geary, Steve Antin, Ric Mancini, Kessler Raymond, Jim Bailey, Mindi Miller; D: Jamaa Fanaka; W: Jamaa Fanaka.

Penn and Teller Get Killed 🐾 1990 (R) The comedy team with a cut following are pursued by an assassin through dozens of pratfalls in this dark comedy. 91m/C VHS. Penn Jillette, Teller, Caitlin Clarke, Leonardo Cimino, David Patrick Kelly; D: Arthur Penn.

Pennies from Heaven 🐾🐾🐾½ 1936 Bing plays Larry, a singer wrongly imprisoned, who promises to help the family imprisoned of a man killed by a death row inmate Larry has befriended. Once in the out-side world, he finds the family, sassy little girl Patsy (Fellows) and her grandfather (Meek), enduring hard times. A social worker (Evans) is trying to keep Patsy out of the orphanage, and the gift of a home that Larry brings may help accomplish that. Complications arrive, however, when they try to turn the place into a cafe and find it may even be haunted. Typical of Crosby's 1930s work, it's pleasant enough and relies on Bing's charm and singing. He sings the Oscar-nominated title song no less than three times. Louis Armstrong appears to great effect, for the film and his subsequent career. 80m/C DVD, Bing Crosby, Madge Evans, Edith Fellows, Donald Meek, Louis Armstrong, John Gallaudet, Tom Dugan, Nana Bryant, Charles C. Wilson, Harry Tyler, William Stack; D: Norman Z. McLeod; W: Jo Swerling; C: Robert Pittack; M: Johnny Burke, Arthur Johnston. Oscars '36: Song ("Pennies from Heaven").

Pennies from Heaven 🐾🐾🐾½ 1981 (R) Underrated, one-of-a-kind musical about a horny sheet-music salesman in Chicago and his escapades during the Depression. Extraordinary musical sequences have stars lip-synching to great effect. Martin is only somewhat acceptable as the hapless salesman, but Peters and Harper deliver powerful performances as the women whose lives he ruins. Walken brings down the house in a stunning song-and-dance sequence. Adapted by Dennis Potter from his British TV series. ("The Clouds Will Soon Roll By"; Let's Face the Music and Dance; Let's Misbehave; Life Is Just a Bowl of Cherries; Let's Face the Music and Dance. 107m/C VHS, DVD. Steve Martin, Bernadette Peters, Christopher Walken, Jessica Harper, Vernel Bagneris; D: Herbert Ross; W: Dennis Potter; C: Gordon Willis; M: Ralph Burns, Marvin Hamlisch. Golden Globes '82: Actress—Mus./Comedy (Peters); Natl. Soc. Film Critics '81: Cinematog. (Willis), Screenplay.

Penny Serenade 🐾🐾🐾 1941 Newlyweds adopt a child, but tragedy awaits. Simplistic story nonetheless proves to be a moving experience. They don't make 'em like this anymore, and no one plays Grant better than Grant. Dunne is adequate. Also available colorized. 120m/B VHS, DVD. Cary Grant, Irene Dunne, Beulah Bondi, Edgar Buchanan, Ann Doran, Wallis Clark; D: George Stevens; M: W. Franke Harling.

Peg o' My Heart 🐾🐾 1922 Taylor portrays the motherless Irish charmer sent to live with her mother's English relatives during the Irish rebellion. Of course, she must overcome her upper-class English snobbery to become a part of the family. 85m/B VHS. Laurette Taylor, Mahon Hamilton, Russell Simpson, Ethel Grey, D. Mahon Hamilton; D: King Vidor; C: George Barnes.

Peggy Sue Got Married 🐾🐾🐾½ 1986 (PG-13) Uneven but entertaining comedy about an unhappily married woman seemingly unable to relive her life when she falls unconscious at a high school reunion and awakens to find herself back in school. Turner shines, but the film flags often, and Cage isn't around enough to elevate entire work. O'Connor scores, though, as a sensitive biker. Look for musician Marshall Crenshaw as part of the reunion band. 103m/C VHS, DVD. Kathleen Turner, Nicolas Cage, Catherine Hicks, Maureen O'Sullivan, John Carradine, Helen Hunt, Lisa Jane Persky, Barbara Harris, Joan Allen, Kevin J. O'Connor, Barry Miller, Don Murray, Leon James, Sofia Coppola, Sachi (VacLaine) Parker, Jim Carrey; D: Francis Ford Coppola; W: Jerry Leichtling, Arlene Sarner; C: Jordan Cronenweth; M: John Barry. Natl. Bd. of Review '86: Actress (Turner).

The Peking Blond 🐾½ The Blonde From Peking; La Blonde de Pekin 1968 The French-fried spy film boasts lousy acting unencumbered by plot. Amnesiac may or may not hold secrets coveted by Americans, Russians and Chinese. 80m/C VHS. FR Mireille Darc, Claudio Brook, Edward G. Robinson, Pascale Roberts, Marc Behm. D: Nicolas Gessner; W: Nicolas Gessner, Marc Behm.

Penelope 🐾🐾½ 2005 (PG) Modern-day retelling of an old fairy tale casts Ricci as Penelope, the lonely girl cursed with a pig's snout. Raised by overbearing and bizarre upper-crust parents (O'Hara and Grant), Penelope is presented with a long line of suitors, all of whom hope to marry into the family's wealth but immediately ball at the sight of their daughter's schnoz. Penelope soon flees to the Big Apple in search of a companion equally cursed and reviled, but instead meets Max (McAvoy), a sweet and charming rocker who sees her inner beauty instead. First-time director Mark Palansky successfully blends a sense of fantasy with the modern world, even throwing a few political jabs along the way. Still, as hard as he may try, he's no Tim Burton. 101m/C DVD, GB Christina Ricci, James McAvoy, Catherine O'Hara, Peter Dinklage, Richard E. Grant, Reese Witherspoon, Simon Woods, Michael Feast, Nigel Havers, Lenny Henry, Ronni Ancona; D: Mark Palansky; W: Leslie Caveny; C: Michel Amarthieu; M: Joby Talbot.

The Penitent 🐾🐾 1988 (PG-13) A remote village's annual reenactment of the crucifixion of Christ serves as the backdrop for Assante's affair with his friend's (Julia) wife. Quirky little tale that focuses on a small town whose lives and problems of the trio rather than the intriguing religious practices going on around them. 94m/C VHS. Raul Julia, Armand Assante, Rona Freed, Julie Carmen; D: Cliff Osmond; M: Alex North.

The Pentagon Wars ⊘⊘½
1998 (R) Based on the true story of Air Force Col. James G. Burton (Elwes) whose mandate in the 1980s was to monitor weapons testing. What he discovers is the ultimate in white elephants—the Bradley Fighting Vehicle, an armored troop transport project that cost the taxpayers $14 billion over 17 years. Grammer is the scheming and pompous Army General Patridge (a composite character) who'll brook no "The Pentagon Wars" by James Burton. 104m/C VHS, DVD. Cary Elwes, Kelsey Grammer, Olympia Dukakis, Richard Benjamin, John C. McGinley, Tom Wright, Clifton Powell, Richard Schiff; D: Richard Benjamin; W: Martyn Burke, Jamie Malanowski; C: Robert Yeoman; M: Joseph Vitarelli. CABLE

Pentathlon ⊘⊘½ 1994 (R) East German Olympic athlete Eric Brogar (Lundgren) defects to the U.S. a year before the crash of the Berlin Wall, causing embarrassed German authorities to seek revenge on him and his family. 101m/C VHS. Dolph Lundgren, David Soul, Roger E. Mosley, Renee Coleman; D: Bruce Malmuth.

Penthouse ⊘⊘ Crooks in Clover 1933 Baxter is a corporation lawyer who, for a change of pace, defends a gangland boss (Pendleton). His success loses him his high-society clientele but wins him Pendleton's respect and protection. But Baxter then gets involved in a further series of gang-related crimes, which nearly cost him his life. Also aiding Baxter is Loy, playing a smart-cookie gun moll, who would take her wisecracks to "The Thin Man" the following year. Good combo of melodrama, suspense, and humor. 90m/B VHS. Warner Baxter, Myrna Loy, Nat Pendleton, C. Henry Gordon, Mae Clarke, Charles Butterworth, Phillips Holmes; D: Woodbridge S. Van Dyke.

The Penthouse ⊘⊘ 1992 Givens stars as a wealthy young woman stalked by an old boyfriend who just happens to have escaped from a mental institution. When he traps her in her home, she has two choices—love him or die. Based on the novel by Elleston Trevor. 93m/C VHS, DVD. Robin Givens, David Hewlett, Cedric Smith, Donnelly Rhodes, Robert Guillaume; D: David Greene.

The People ⊘⊘ 1971 A young teacher takes a job in a small town and finds out that her students have telepathic powers and other strange qualities. Adapted from a novel by Zenna Henderson. Good atmosphere, especially for a TV movie. 74m/C VHS, DVD. Kim Darby, Dan O'Herlihy, Diane Varsi, William Shatner; D: John Korty; M: Carmine Coppola.

People Are Funny ⊘⊘ 1946 Battling radio producers vie to land the big sponsor with an original radio idea. Comedy ensues when one of them comes up with a great idea—stolen from a local station. 94m/B VHS, DVD. Jack Haley, Rudy Vallee, Ozzie Nelson, Art Linkletter, Helen Walker; D: Sam White.

People I Know ⊘⊘½ 2002 (R) Pacino forgoes the over-the-top style that's been his forte lately for a more restrained, meticulous portrayal of burned-out publicist Eli Wurman, and his performance saves the intriguing but muddled character study/political caper. Wurman's down to his last bigtime client, movie star Cary Launer (O'Neal), a shallow, womanizing, preening actor trying to break into politics. His bid for office is endangered when an actress with whom Launer had a drug-fueled fling is arrested. Eli is sent to bail her out, but becomes entangled in her murder and mysterious political hijinks, all while trying to stage a benefit for African refugees. Fine supporting cast delivers but plot gets a little busy for its own good when not focused on Eli's inner struggle. 95m/C VHS, DVD. US Al Pacino, Kim Basinger, Ryan O'Neal, Tea Leoni, Richard Schiff, Bill Nunn, Robert Klein, Mark Webber, Polly Adams; D: Dan Algrant; W: Jon Robin Baitz; C: Peter Deming; M: Terence Blanchard.

The People Next Door ⊘⊘ 1970 Seventies attempt at exposing the drug problems of suburban youth. Typical middle-class parents Wallach and Harris

are horrified to discover that daughter Winters is strung out on LSD. They fight to expose the neighborhood pusher while daughter descends into addiction. Based on J.P. Miller's television play. 93m/C VHS. Deborah Winters, Eli Wallach, Julie Harris, Stephen McHattie, Hal Holbrook, Cloris Leachman, Nehemiah Persoff; D: David Greene; W: (James) P(inckney) Miller.

The People That Time Forgot ⊘⊘½ 1977 (PG) Sequel to "The Land That Time Forgot," based on the Edgar Rice Burroughs novel. A rescue team returns to a world of prehistoric monsters to locate a man left there after the first film. 90m/C VHS, DVD. GB Doug McClure, Patrick Wayne, Sarah Douglas, Dana Gillespie, Thorley Walters, Shane Rimmer; D: Kevin Connor; W: Patrick Tilley; C: Alan Hume; M: John Scott.

The People under the Stairs ⊘⊘½ 1991 (R) Adams is part of a scheme to rob a house in the slums owned by a mysterious couple (Robie and McGill), both of "Twin Peaks" fame). After his friends are killed off in a gruesome fashion, he discovers that the couple aren't the house's only strange inhabitants—homicidal creatures also lurk within. 102m/C VHS, DVD. Everett McGill, Wendy Robie, Brandon Adams, Ving Rhames, A.J. (Allison Joy) Langer, Sean M. Whalen, Kelly Jo Minter; D: Wes Craven; W: Wes Craven; C: Sandi Sissel; M: Don Peake.

The People vs. Jean Harris ⊘⊘ 1981 Follows the trial of Jean Harris. Shortly before the trial was released, she had been convicted of murder in the death of Dr. Herman Tarnower, the author of "The Scarsdale Diet." Harris was headmistress in a private school and all the while. Burstyn was nominated for an Emmy Award for best actress. 147m/C VHS, DVD. Ellen Burstyn, Martin Balsam, Richard Dysart, Peter Coyote, Priscilla Morrill, Sarah Marshall, Millie Slavin; D: George Schaefer; M: Brad Fiedel. TV

The People vs. Larry Flynt ⊘⊘½ 1996 (R) Controversy surrounded director Forman's look at unrepentant pornographer and Hustler Magazine publisher, Larry Flynt (Harrelson). While feminists decried what they saw as a whitewash of Flynt's career, Forman insisted his movie was about Flynt's legal battles concerning the First Amendment and freedom of speech. If you can set aside your prejudices, you'll find a master storyteller at work and some great performances from Harrelson as Flynt, Love as his drug-addicted and ultimately tragic wife Althea, and Norton as Flynt's sometimes impatient attorney, Alan Isaacman, who does get his big moment before the U.S. Supreme Court (his speeches are taken from actual court transcripts). 130m/C VHS, DVD. Woody Harrelson, Courtney Love, Edward Norton, James Cromwell, Crispin Glover, Brett Harrelson, James Carville, Vincent Schiavelli, Richard Paul, Donna Hanover, Norm MacDonald, Miles Chapin, Jan Triska; Cameos: Larry Flynt; D: Milos Forman; W: Larry Karaszewski, Scott M. Alexander; C: Philippe Rousselot; M: Thomas Newman. Golden Globes '97: Director (Forman); L.A. Film Critics '96: Director (Forman); Natl. Bd. of Review '96: Support. Actor (Norton); N.Y. Film Critics '96: Support. Actress (Love).

People Who Own the Dark WOOF! 1975 (R) A group of wealthy men and a coterie of call girls are having an orgy in the basement of an old home when a nuclear war breaks out. Everyone outside is blinded by the blast but some survivors manage to make their way to the house where they try to attack the inhabitants. Don't bother. 87m/C VHS. Paul Naschy, Tony Kendall, Maria Perschy, Terry Kemper, Tom Weyland, Anita Brock, Paul Mackey; D: Armando de Ossorio; W: Armando de Ossorio.

People Will Talk ⊘⊘½ 1951 Grant plays Dr. Noah Praetorius, a doctor and educator who believes that the mind is a better healer than medicine. Archenemy Cronyn is the fellow instructor with a vengeance. Sickened by Grant's goodwill and the undying attention he receives, Cronyn reports Grant's unconventional medical practices to the higher-ups in hopes of ruining his reputation as doctor/

educator. Witty and satirical, this well-crafted comedy-drama is chock-full of interesting characters and finely tuned dialogue. Adapted from the play "Dr. Praetorius" by Curt Goetz. 110m/B VHS, DVD. Cary Grant, Jeanne Crain, Finlay Currie, Hume Cronyn, Walter Slezak, Sidney Blackmer, Basil Ruysdael, Katherine Locke, Margaret Hamilton, Carleton Young, Billy House, Stuart Holmes; D: Joseph L. Mankiewicz; W: Joseph L. Mankiewicz; C: Milton Krasner.

People's Choice ⊘⊘½ 1946 A small town boy suffers laryngitis, becomes a radio personality via his new huskiness, and claims he's a notorious criminal. 68m/B VHS. Drew Kennedy, Louise Arthur, George Meeker, Rex Lease, Fred Kelsey, Bill Kennedy; D: Harry Fraser.

Pep Squad ⊘⊘½ 1998 (R) Director Steve Balderson does a John Waters riff with the story of evil Cherry (Brooke Balderson) who reacts inappropriately when she's not chosen for the high school pep squad. The Kansas production is driven by broad, nasty slapstick humor. 97m/C DVD. Brooke Balderson, Jennifer Dreiling, Adrian Pujol, Summer Makowkin; D: Steve Balderson; W: Steve Balderson; C: Rhet W. Bear; M: Johnette Napolitano.

Pepe Le Moko ⊘⊘⊘ 1937 An influential French film about a notorious gangster holed up in the Casbah, emerging at his own peril out of love for a beautiful woman. Stirring film established Gabin as a matinee idol. Cinematography is particularly fine too. Based upon the D'Ashelbe novel. The basis for both "Algiers," the popular Boyer-Lamarr melodrama, and the musical "The Casbah." In French with English subtitles. 87m/B VHS, DVD. FR Jean Gabin, Mireille Balin, Gabriel Gabrio, Lucas Gridoux; D: Julien Duvivier; W: Julien Duvivier, Henri Jeanson; C: Jules Kruger; M: Vincent Scotto.

Pepi, Luci, Bom and Other Girls on the Heap ⊘⊘½ Pepi, Luci, Bom y Otras Chicas del Monton 1980 Almodovar's low-budget directorial debut will be of interest primarily to the director's aficionadoes. Pepi (Maura's debut role) is a Madrid heiress who gets in trouble when her neighbor, a policeman, notices her marijuana plants. She offers sexual favors in return for silence but is raped instead. Pepi later decides on revenge by seducing Luci, the policeman's wife, aided by her girlfriend, Bom. There's lots of partying, drugs, promiscuity, and violence, none of it very involving. In Spanish with English subtitles. 80m/C VHS. SP Carmen Maura, Eva Siva, Olivido Gara, Felix Rotaeta; D: Pedro Almodovar; W: Pedro Almodovar.

Pepper and His Wacky Taxi ⊘½ 1972 (G) Father of four buys a '59 Cadillac and starts a cab company. Time-capsule fun. 79m/C VHS. John Astin, Frank Sinatra Jr., Jackie Gayle, Alan Sherman; D: Alex Grasshof.

Peppermint Soda ⊘⊘⊘ 1977 Kurys' affecting directorial debut is a semi-autobiographical tale of two teenaged sisters set in 1963 Paris. Seen through the eyes of the 13-year-old Anne, who lives with 15-year-old sister Frederique and their divorced mother, this is the year of first loves, strict teachers, dreaded family vacations, and a general awareness of growing up. Sweet look at adolescence and all its embarrassing tribulations. In French with English subtitles. 97m/C VHS. FR Eleonore Klarwein, Odile Michel, Anouk Ferjac, Tsilia Chelton, Coralie Clement, Marie-Veronique Maurin, Puterflam; D: Diane Kurys; W: Diane Kurys; C: Philippe Rousselot.

Perceval ⊘⊘ Perceval Le Gallois 1978 Rohmer's extremely stylized version of Chretien de Troyes unfinished 12th century poem. Young Welsh knight Perceval (Luchini) comes to a mysterious castle although he doesn't recognize it. In the morning, the castle is deserted and Perceval resumes his wanderings. When he finally realizes what he has seen, the castle has disappeared and Perceval continues with his search for the Grail. French with subtitles. 140m/C VHS, DVD. FR Fabrice Luchini, Andre Dussollier, Arielle Dombasle, Marie-

Christine Barrault; D: Eric Rohmer; W: Eric Rohmer; C: Nestor Almendros.

Percy & Thunder ⊘⊘½ 1993 Percy Banks (Jones) is an old-school boxing trainer who believes in hard work and he sees a likely prospect in Wayne "Thunder" Carter (Vance), a middleweight on a chance to be a champ. That is, if big time boxing promotion doesn't get in the way. 90m/C VHS. James Earl Jones, Billy Dee Williams, Courtney B. Vance, Robert Wuhl, Gloria Foster, Zakes Mokae, Gloria Reuben; D: Ivan Dixon; W: Art Washington; M: Tom Scott.

The Perez Family ⊘⊘½ 1994 (R) Juan Paul Perez (Molina) has spent 20 years in Cuban jails, dreaming of being reunited with wife Carmela (Huston) and daughter Teresa (Alvarado) who successfully escaped to Miami. Part of the 1980 Mariel exodus, Juan meets exuberant Dottie (Tomei), who learns families get sponsored first at the refugee camps. She convinces Juan to pose as her husband, while Carmela, who's being wooed by cop Pirelli (Palminteri), mistakenly believes Juan has literally missed the boat. Tomei's spunky (but with a garish accent), Huston's regal, Palminteri courtly, and Molina morose. The film's inconsistently whimsical, wistful, and clunky. From the novel by Christine Bell. 135m/C VHS, DVD. Marisa Tomei, Alfred Molina, Anjelica Huston, Chazz Palminteri, Trini Alvarado, Celia Cruz; D: Mira Nair; W: Robin Swicord; C: Stuart Dryburgh; M: Alan Silvestri.

Perfect ⊘⊘½ 1985 (R) A "Rolling Stone" reporter goes after the shallowness of the Los Angeles health club scene, and falls in love with the aerobics instructor he is going to write about. "Rolling Stone" publisher Wenner plays himself. As bad as it sounds. 120m/C VHS, DVD. John Travolta, Jamie Lee Curtis, Carly Simon, Marilu Henner, Laraine Newman, Jann Wenner, Anne DeSalvo; D: James Bridges; W: James Bridges, Aaron Latham; C: Gordon Willis; M: Ralph Burns.

Perfect Alibi ⊘⊘½ 1994 Woman's suspicions of her husband's affair leads to murder. 90m/C VHS. Teri Garr, Hector Elizondo, Kathleen Quinlan, Anne Ramsey, Rigg Kennedy; D: Kevin Meyer.

Perfect Assassins 1998 FBI profiler pursues a killer on a murder spree. 100m/C VHS. Andrew McCarthy, Robert Patrick, Nick Mancuso, Portia de Rossi, Matthew Laurance, Lisa Jane Persky, Aki Aleong; D: H. Gordon Boos; W: John Pennsey; C: Bruce Douglas Johnson; M: Geoff Levin. VIDEO

The Perfect Bride ⊘½ 1991 (R) A pretty young nurse prepares to marry her fiance, but his sister thinks she is hiding a secret. Could the bride-to-be have murder on her mind? 95m/C VHS. John Agar, Sammi Davis, Kelly Preston, Linden Ashby, Marie-Terrence O'Hara; M: Richard Bronsill. CABLE

Perfect Crime ⊘⊘ 1997 (PG-13) Indagine su un Delitto Perfetto 1979 A Scotland Yard inspector must find out who has been killing off executives of a powerful world trust. 90m/C VHS. IT Joseph Cotten, Anthony Steel, Janet Agren, Leonard Mann, Alida Valli, Adolfo Celi; D: Giuseppe Rosati; W: Giuseppe Rosati; M: Carlo Savina.

The Perfect Daughter ⊘⊘ 1996 (PG-13) A near-fatal hit-and-run accident reintroduces Alexandra Michelson (Gold) to her family—mother, Jill (Armstrong), father, Tom (Joy), and younger brother, Josh (Shulman). They'd cut the ties to the troubled drug abuser and runaway but the accident has erased Alexandra's memory of her recent life. Unfortunately for them all, Alex's sordid and dan-

A Perfect Day _gerous past will leave neither her nor her family alone._ 90m/C VHS. Tracey Gold, Bess Armstrong, Mark Joy, Michael Shulman, Harold P. Pruett, Jay Edward Anthony, Brian Gamble; **D:** Harry S. Longstreet; **W:** Sean Silas; **C:** Stephen Lighthill; **M:** Don Davis. CABLE

A Perfect Day ✶✶ 2006 Rather maudlin story based on the novel by Richard Paul Evans. Author Rob Harlan (Lowe) writes an unexpected bestseller and his fame has him ignoring his wife and daughter. Then his supposed guardian angel (Lloyd) appears to show Mr. Selfish the error of his ways, especially when he tells Rob that if he doesn't change his attitude, he dies on Christmas. Fear--what an incentive to become a better person. 90m/C DVD. Rob Lowe, Christopher Lloyd, Paget Brewster, Frances Conroy, Jude Ciccolella, Rowena King, Kevin Dunn; **D:** Peter Levin; **W:** Joyce Eliason; **C:** Kees Van Oostrum; **M:** Jeff Beal. CABLE

The Perfect Family ✶✶ 1992 (R) Standard woman-and-kids-in-peril-from-psycho tale. Maggie is a recent widow with two young daughters who's looking for a nanny and a handyman. She hires both--a stranger combo Janice and Alan, who, of course, are too good to be true. One is a sociopath who has murdered a family once before. Guess along with Maggie and the nut might get. 92m/C VHS. Jennifer O'Neill, Bruce Boxleitner, Joanna Cassidy, Juliana Hansen, Shiri Appleby; **D:** E.W. Swackhamer. **W:** Christian Stolainovich, Phoebe Dorin; **M:** Nicholas Pike.

Perfect Furlough ✶✶½ _Strictly for Pleasure_ 1959 Paul Hodges (Curtis) is an Army corporal who wins three weeks in Paris with a movie star (Cristal) as a publicity gimmick. It's the idea of a female Army psychologist (Leigh), who thinks the guys need a morale booster, and she accompanies Hodges on his trip. One is a bit bizarre, but it works. 93m/C VHS. Tony Curtis, Janet Leigh, Keenan Wynn, Linda Cristal, Elaine Stritch, Marcel Dalio, King Donovan; **D:** Blake Edwards; **W:** Stanley Shapiro.

The Perfect Game ✶✶½ 2000 Kanin Crosby (Finley) and his equally uncoordinated friends are determined to make it into the winning park league baseball team, the Bulldogs, but they're all surprised when they're chosen by the team's arrogant coach, Bobby Geiser (Duffy). Eventually the kids learn that Geiser is only playing and coaching his best players, leaving the others to warm the bench. A confrontation leads to Kanin's mom Diane (Nelson) taking over along with grumbling retired coach Billy Hicks (Asner) and the kids are on their way once again. 99m/C VHS, DVD. Cameron Finley, Tracy Nelson, Patrick Duffy, Ed Asner; **D:** Dan Guntzelman; **M:** David Benoit. VIDEO

The Perfect Gift ✶✶ 1995 (R) Suzanne decides to fulfill her boyfriend's menage-a-trois fantasy and discovers that the partner they involve just may be the woman of her dreams. 90m/C VHS. John McCafferty, Kim (Kimberly Dawn) Lawson, Monique Parent; **D:** Michael Paul Girard; **W:** Paul Girard; **M:** Michael Paul Girard.

Perfect Harmony ✶✶½ 1991 Facial conflict at an exclusive Southern boys school in 1950s South Carolina is overcome through friendship and the love of music in this sentimental tale. 90m/C VHS, DVD. Peter Scolari, Darren McGavin, Catherine Mary Stewart, Moses Gunn, Cleavon Little, Justin Whalin, David Faustino, Richie Havens, Eugene Boyd; **D:** Will Mackenzie. CABLE

The Perfect Holiday ✶✶½ 2007 (PG) Nancy (Union), a struggling single mother of three who is desperately searching for a good man, finds love in Benjamin (Chestnut), a mall Santa and aspiring songwriter. The only problem is that Nancy's ex-husband and famous rapper, J-Jizzy (Murphy), is recording one of Benjamin's songs and doesn't know Nancy and Benjamin have fallen in love. Benjamin doesn't know J-Jizzy is Nancy's ex, and Nancy is just plain clueless. A predictable and lukewarm romantic comedy saved in part by Queen Latifah's cameo appearance. Despite the marketing ploy, this is not a sequel to "The Last Holiday." 90m/C DVD. US Gabrielle Union, Morris Chestnut, Queen Latifah, Terrence Howard, Charlie (Charles Q.) Murphy, Faizon Love, Katt Micah Williams, Jill Jones, Malik Hammond, Khail Bryant, Jeremy Gumbs, Rachel True; **D:** Lance Rivera; **W:** Lance Rivera, Nat Mauldin, Jeff Stein, Marc Calixte; **C:** Teodoro Maniaci; **M:** Christopher Lennertz.

The Perfect Husband ✶✶

Perfect Killer ✶✶½ _Satanic Mechanic_ 1977 (R) Van Cleef stars as a world weary Mafia hit-man who is double-crossed by his girl, set up by his best friend, and hunted by another hired assassin. 85m/C VHS, DVD. Lee Van Cleef, Tina Barker, John Ireland, Robert Widmark; **D:** Marlon Sirko.

Perfect Lies ✶✶ 1997 Trying to pull her life back together, private eye Toby Merck (Friess) winds up being blackmailed by her former lover, an FBI agent, who wants her to infiltrate a drug kingpin's operation. 94m/C VHS. Brittanya Friess, Charis Michelsen, Eric Leffler, William Laney, Geoff Thompson, Carolyn Smith; **D:** Bret Stern; **W:** Steve Arthur. VIDEO

Perfect Love ✶✶ _Parfait Amour_ 1996 Divorced Frederique (Renauld) has an affair with volatile younger man, Christophe (Renaud). When she realizes he's also seeing another woman, she's angry and the tension builds as each seeks to psychologically wound the other. The only thing they still agree upon is sex. But then Christophe loses control. French with subtitles. 110m/C VHS, DVD, FR Isabelle Renauld, Francis Renaud, Laura Saglio; **D:** Catherine Breillat; **W:** Catherine Breillat; **C:** Laurent Dailland.

A Perfect Little Murder ✶✶½ _A Quiet Little Neighborhood, A Perfect Little Murder_ 1990 Marsha is expecting an uneventful life of barbecues and Little League when her family settles down in the suburbs. But then she overhears a murder plot and someone finds out she knows. 94m/C VHS. Teri Garr, Robert Urich, Susan Ruttan, Jeffrey Tambor, Tom Poston, Florence Stanley, Gail Edwards, Alex Rocco; **D:** Anson Williams; **W:** Mark Stein. TV

Perfect Match ✶✶ 1988 (PG) A timid young woman and an unambitious young man meet each other through the personal ads and then lie to each other about who they are and what they do for a living. 93m/C VHS. Marc McClure, Jennifer Edwards, Diane Stilwell, Rob Paulsen, Karen Witter; **D:** Mark Deimel.

The Perfect Marriage ✶✶ 1946 Tired comedy about a perfect couple who decide they can't stand each other anymore after ten years of marriage. Good cast makes the most of weak script. Based on the play by Samuel Raphaelson. 88m/B VHS. Loretta Young, David Niven, Eddie Albert, Charlie Ruggles, Zasu Pitts, Jerome Cowan, Rita Johnson; **D:** Lewis Allen; **W:** Leonard Spigelgass.

A Perfect Murder ✶✶ 1998 (R) ...who's having a torrid affair with hippie artist David (Mortensen). The love triangle gets shaken when Steven devises a solution to his wife's infidelities and his financial woes by paying David to kill Emily. Things go a little bit astray, and the psychological cat and mouse game begins. Glossy production is only eye candy while the unsympathetic characters (led by a weak protagonist in Paltrow) march to the beat of many plot points that all come together in a rushed and dull climax. Hitchcock's 1954 film "Dial M for Murder" is the better, more taut, and far superior original. 105m/C VHS, DVD. Michael Douglas, Gwyneth Paltrow, Viggo Mortensen, David Suchet, Sarita Choudhury, Constance Towers, Novella Nelson; **D:** Andrew Davis; **W:** Patrick Smith Kelly; **C:** Darius Wolski; **M:** James Newton Howard.

The Perfect Man ✶✶ 2005 (PG) Whenever 16-year-old Holly's (Duff) single mom, the gloomy Jean (Locklear), loses at love she packs up Holly and younger sister Zoe for a brand new city in a desperate search for a fresh start. Fed up with the chaos, Holly concocts a secret admirer based on her best friend Amy's suave Uncle Ben (Noth)--when she sees another potentially lame suitor on the horizon. Naturally the ruse gets dicey, and Holly feels the humor, plus it's hard to believe the knockout Locklear would have trouble finding a decent man. 100m/C DVD. US Hilary Duff, Heather Locklear, Christopher Noth, Vanessa Lengies, Aria Wallace, Ben Feldman, Michael O'Malley, Caroline Rhea, Kym E. Whitley; **D:** Mark Rosman; **W:** Gina Wendkos; **C:** John R. Leonetti; **M:** Christophe Beck.

Perfect Murder, Perfect Town ✶✶ 2000 Re-telling of the (still unsolved) murder of six-year-old JonBenet Ramsey in Boulder, Colorado, the subsequent investigation and the media frenzy that descended on the community. Miniseries is based on the book by director Schiller. 178m/C VHS, DVD. Marg Helgenberger, Ronny Cox, Kris Kristofferson, Ken Howard, John Heard, Ann-Margret, Sean Cohen, John Rubinstein, Dennis Boutsikaris, Scott M. Whalen; **D:** Lawrence Schiller; **W:** Tom Topor; **C:** Peter Sova; **M:** John Cacavas. TV

The Perfect Nanny ✶✶ 2000 Andrea McBride (Nelson) gets released from a mental institution and manages to get a job as a nanny to the children of a wealthy widower (Boxleitner). But Andrea expects a fairy-tale life and will do anything to make her romantic happy ending come true. 90m/C VHS, DVD. Tracy Nelson, Bruce Boxleitner, Dana Barron, Susan Blakely, Katherine Helmond; **D:** Rob Malenfant; **W:** Victor Schiller, Christine Conrad, Richard Gilbert Hill; **C:** Don E. Fauntleroy; **M:** Richard Bowers. VIDEO

The Perfect Score ✶✶½ 2004 (PG-13) Anxious high school seniors stressing about the SATs decide to steal the answers in this slightly above-average teen movie of the "Breakfast Club" variety. Kyle (Chris Evans), worried that his lousy test scores will prevent him from becoming an architect, assembles a crew of high school stereotypes to do the crime, including Chris's slacker buddy Matty (Greenberg), angry rich girl Francesca (Johansson), star athlete Desmond (Christiansen), overachiever Anna (hipster Miles) and stoner Roy (Nam), who happens to be the smartest of the bunch. The plot takes a backseat to the interaction between the misfits, but none of it adds up to much more than average fare, with the exception of scene-stealers Johansson and Nam. 93m/C DVD. US Erika Christensen, Chris Evans, Scarlett Johansson, Tyra Ferrell, Bryan Greenberg, Darius Miles, Leonardo Nam, Matthew Lillard, Vanessa Angel, Fulvio Cecere; **D:** Brian Robbins; **W:** Mark Schwahn, Marc Hyman, Jon Zack; **C:** Clark Mathis; **M:** John Murphy.

The Perfect Son ✶✶ 2000 When their father dies, estranged brothers Theo (Cubitt) and Ryan (Feore) are reluctantly reunited. Theo is out of rehab and hoping to make a fresh start with ex-lover Sarah (West) but it's his "perfect brother" Ryan who has some revelations. The overly responsible, successful lawyer reveals to his younger bro that he is gay and dying of AIDS. They try to set aside old rivalries as one struggles to start over and the other struggles with facing his mortality. Strong drama with two exceptional lead performances, although the story is simple and somewhat old-fashioned. 93m/C VHS, DVD. CA David Cubitt, Colm Feore, Chandra West; **D:** Leonard Farlinger; **W:** Leonard Farlinger; **C:** Barry Stone; **M:** Ron Sures.

A Perfect Spy ✶✶ _John Le Carre's A Perfect Spy_ 1988 In this BBC miniseries, John Le Carre takes a break from the world of George Smiley to take a look at spying from a personal view. Magnus Pym (Evan) would seem to be the perfect English gentleman, having gone to the right schools he proceeds to join the covert world of espionage. But Magnus hides the secret that his estranged father is a con man par excellence and it leads him to his own betrayals. Adapted from the novel, which Le Carre is said to have drawn from his own past. On three cassettes. 360m/C VHS, DVD. GB Peter Egan, Ray McNally, Frances Tomelty, Benedict Taylor, Tim Healy; **W:** Arthur Hopcraft.

Perfect Strangers ✶✶½ 2003 It's too bad when a girl (Blake) can't go out on the town, get plastered, and pick up an honorable, upstanding guy. No, he (Neill) has to turn out to be a charming kidnapper (aren't those the worst kind?) who holds her hostage at his shack on a desolate island (off of New Zealand's west coast). But, this captivating yet contrived tale might just reveal that there's just no escaping the true bliss that demented love brings. 96m/C VHS, DVD. Sam Neill, Rachael Blake, Joel Tobeck, Robyn Malcolm, Madeleine Sami; **D:** Gaylene Preston; **W:** Gaylene Preston; **C:** Alun Bollinger; **M:** Neil Finn. VIDEO

Perfect Strangers ✶✶ _Blind Alley_ 1984 (R) Thriller develops around a murder and the child who witnesses it. The killer attempts to kidnap the young boy, but he falls in love with the boy's mother (which is how Grace met him). Rowena is unethical, Hill is smug, and it turns into a stereotypical disaster flick. 90m/C VHS, DVD. US Halle Berry, Bruce Willis, Giovanni Ribisi, Anne Carlisle, Brad Rijn, John Woehrle, Matthew Stockley, Ann Magnuson, Stephen Lack; **D:** Larry Cohen.

Perfect Stranger ✶✶½ 2007 (R) Efficient, if routine, thriller. Rowena (Berry) is an investigative reporter whose childhood friend Grace (Ayvox) is murdered shortly after admitting to an affair with married corporate hotshot Harrison Hill (Willis). She goes undercover at Hill's ad firm, with the help of sorta creepy/geeky tech whiz Miles (Ribisi), to get to the truth and double-plays Hill by also posing as an online tart. 109m/C VHS, DVD, Blu-ray Disc. US Halle Berry, Bruce Willis, Giovanni Ribisi, Richard Portnow, Nicki Aycox, Gary Dourdan, Kathleen Chalfant, Florencia Lozano; **D:** James Foley; **W:** Todd Komarnicki; **C:** Anastas Michos; **M:** Antonio Pinto.

The Perfect Storm ✶✶½ 2000 (PG-13) Based on the true story of the Andrea Gail, a swordfishing boat lost at sea in 1991 during a freak storm--one of the biggest of the century--off the coast of Newfoundland. Film briefly sets up the backgrounds of the six men who will be the captain and crew on the tragic voyage, but not even Clooney and Wahlberg can compete with the watery special effects and it turns into a stereotypical disaster flick. Adapted from Sebastian Junger's bestselling nonfiction account of the tragedy. 129m/C VHS, DVD, HD DVD. George Clooney, Mark Wahlberg, Mary Elizabeth Mastrantonio, John C. Reilly, Diane Lane, William Fichtner, Allen Payne, John Hawkes, Karen Allen, Bob Gunton, Cherry Jones, Christopher McDonald, Dash Mihok, Josh Hopkins, Michael Ironside, Janet Wright, Rusty Schwimmer; **D:** Wolfgang Petersen; **W:** William D. Wittliff; **C:** John Seale; **M:** James Horner.

Perfect Target ✶✶ 1998 (R) An ex-CIA agent is forced to work as a mercenary, protecting the president of Santa Brava. Naturally, this assignment doesn't go well and he becomes the fall guy for the politico's murder. Only he doesn't intend to stay that way. VIDEO

Perfect Tenant ✶✶ 1999 (R) Overly familiar thriller. Because of financial problems Jessica (Purl) is forced to rent out her guesthouse. She thinks she's found the perfect tenant in Bryan (Caulfield) since he's oh so handsome but polite and tidy. But it's all a facade since Bryan actually wants revenge on the woman he blames for his father's suicide. 97m/C VHS, DVD. Linda Purl, Maxwell Caulfield, Tracy Nelson, Earl Holliman, Melissa Behr, Stacy Hogue; **D:** Doug Campbell; **W:** Jim Vines. **M:** Todd Boric; **C:** M. David Mullen. VIDEO

Perfect Timing WOOF! 1984 Softcore film about a fledgling photographer who can't turn his orgy-like photo sessions into anything profitable. 87m/C VHS. **D:** Rene Bonniere.

Perfect Victims 🦴 *Hidden Rage* 1987 (R) Beautiful models are being hunted by a killer, and a police officer wants to catch the psychopath before he strikes again. 100m/C VHS. John Agar, Deborah Shelton, Clarence Williams III, Lyman Ward; **D:** Shuki Levy.

The Perfect Weapon 🦴🦴 1991 (R) Kenpo karate master Speakman severs family ties and wears funny belt in order to avenge underworld murder of his teacher. 85m/C VHS. Jeff Sanders, Jeff Speakman; **D:** Mark DiSalle; **W:** David Wilson; **C:** Russell Carpenter; **M:** Gary Chang.

The Perfect Wife 🦴 2000 Liza (Sturges) is another of those vengeful blondes who, in the wake of "Hand that Rocks the Cradle," thrive on video premieres. She goes after everyone she blames for her beloved brother's death, including the doctor (King) who did not save his life after an auto accident. How does she get close to the good doctor? She marries him, of course, and sets about to ruin everyone he cares for. The pace moves along briskly while production values are strictly of the made-for-TV level. 92m/C DVD. Shannon Sturges, Perry King, Lesley-Anne Down, William R. Moses; **D:** Don E. FauntleRoy; **M:** Frank Rehwaldt, George Saunders.

Perfect Witness 🦴🦴½ 1989 A restaurant owner witnesses a mob slaying and resists testifying against the culprit in New York City. 104m/C VHS, DVD. Brian Dennehy, Aidan Quinn, Stockard Channing, Laura Harrington, Joe Grifasi; **D:** Robert Mandel; **M:** Brad Fiedel. CABLE

A Perfect World 🦴🦴½ 1993 (PG-13) Butch Haynes (Costner) is an escaped con who takes eight-year-old fatherless Phillip (Lowther) as a hostage in 1963 Texas and is pursued by Texas Ranger Red Garnett (Eastwood). Butch is a bad guy and the film never tries to make him heroic but it also allows him to grow attached to Phillip and acknowledge him as a surrogate son. Costner gives a quiet and strong performance and the remarkable Lowther never goes wrong in his role as the needy little boy. Eastwood's role is strictly secondary as the well tested lawman who understands justice without seeking vengeance. Somewhat draggy—especially the protracted final scene. 138m/C VHS, DVD. Kevin Costner, T.J. Lowther, Clint Eastwood, Laura Dern, Keith Szarabajka, Leo Burmester, Paul Hewitt, Bradley Whitford, Ray McKinnon, Wayne Dehart, Jennifer Griffin, Linda Hart; **D:** Clint Eastwood; **W:** Eugene Lipinski; Paul Quarrington.

Perfectly Normal 🦴🦴 1991 (R) Two friends end up in hilarious situations when one opens an eccentric restaurant with a mysterious, newly found fortune. 106m/C VHS. Michael Riley, Robbie Coltrane, Kenneth Welsh, Eugene Lipinski; **D:** Yves Simoneau; **W:** Eugene Lipinski, Paul Quarrington.

Performance 🦴🦴🦴 1970 (R) Grim and unsettling psychological account of a criminal who hides out in the bizarre house occupied by a peculiar rock star Scott (James) and his two female companions. Entire cast scores high marks, with Pallenberg especially compelling as a somewhat mysterious and attractive housemate to mincing Jagger. A cult favorite, with music by Nitzsche under the direction of Randy Newman. 104m/C VHS, DVD. *GB* James Fox, Mick Jagger, Anita Pallenberg, Michele Breton, Ann Sidney, John Bindon, Stanley Meadows, Allan Cuthbertson, Antony Morton; **D:** Donald Cammell, Nicolas Roeg; **W:** Donald Cammell; **C:** Nicolas Roeg; **M:** Jack Nitzsche.

Perfume 🦴½ 1991 Five beautiful, black childhood friends join together to conquer the cosmetics industry with their new perfume, Sassy. But can they resist all the temptations success brings and keep both their company and their friendship? 98m/C VHS. Cheryl Francis Harrington, Kathleen Bradley Overton, Shy Jefferson, Lynn Martin, Eugina Wright, Ted Lange; **D:** Roland S. Jefferson.

Perfume 🦴🦴 2001 (R) Rymer worked from an outline rather than a complete script and had his actors improvise this satire on the fashion world but the film fumbles on fuzzy plots and characters. English photog Anthony (Harris) deals with professional and personal crises; gay fashion mogul Lorenzo (Sorvino) learns he has family and 'lover; magazine editor Janice (Baron) is suddenly confronted by the daughter (Williams) she hasn't seen in years; and various designers (Epps, Wilson, Mann) have various problems. 106m/C VHS, DVD. Rita Wilson, Leslie Mann, Jared Harris, Michelle Forbes, Paul Sorvino, Peter Gallagher, Sonia Braga, Omar Epps, Jeff Goldblum, Harris Yulin, Michelle Williams, Joanne Baron, Mariel Hemingway, Carmen Electra, Coolio, Harry Hamlin, Mariska Hargitay, Gaby Hoffman, Robert Joy, Chris Sarandon, Angela Bettis, Kyle MacLachlan; **D:** Michael Rymer; **W:** Michael Rymer, L.M. Kit Carson; **C:** Rex Nicholson; **M:** Adam Plack.

Perfume: The Story of a Murderer 🦴🦴 2006 (R) Patrick Suskind's "unfilmable" 1985 novel offered a unique challenge to director Tykwer: how do you visualize the sense of smell? Jean-Baptiste Grenouille (Whishaw), orphaned in filthy, smelly 18th-century Paris, has two unique characteristics: he has no natural body odor and he possesses an unparalleled sense of smell that leads to an apprenticeship with perfumer Baldini (Hoffman). Grenouille soon becomes obsessed with the natural scent of young women and turns to serial killing in order to preserve that smell and turn it into the perfect perfume. Ironically, the flick may be too faithful to the book and could have used some judicious editing; it also appeals more to the intellect than to the heart or any of the other senses. 145m/C DVD. *SP FR GE* Ben Whishaw, Dustin Hoffman, Alan Rickman, Rachel Hurd-Wood, Corinna Harfouch; **D:** Tom Tykwer; **W:** Tom Tykwer, Andrew Birkin, Bernd Eichinger; **C:** Frank Griebe; **M:** Tom Tykwer, Johnny Klimek, Reinhold Heil; **Nar:** John Hurt.

Perfumed Nightmare 🦴🦴🦴 1989 Unique, appealing fable about a Filipino youth who discovers the drawbacks of social and cultural progress when he moves to Paris. Director Tahimik also plays the lead role. Imaginative, yet remarkably economical, this film was produced for $10,000 and received the International Critics Award at the Berlin Film Festival. Its Tagalog with English dialogue and subtitles. 93m/C VHS. *PH* Kidlat Tahimik, Dolores Santamaria, Georgette Baudry, Katrin Muller, Hartmut Lerch; **D:** Kidlat Tahimik.

Peril 🦴🦴½ *Peril en la Demeure* 1985 (R) From the novel "Sur La Terre Comme Au Ciel" by Rene Belletto. Deals with a music teacher's infiltration into a wealthy family and the sexually motivated, back-stabbing murder plots that ensue. DeVille does poorly with avant-garde technique. In French with English subtitles. 100m/C VHS. *FR* Michel Piccoli, Christophe MaLavoy, Richard Bohringer, Nicole Garcia, Anaïs Jeanneret; **D:** Michel DeVille; **W:** Michel DeVille. Cesar '86: Director (DeVille)

Peril 🦴 2000 (R) Out-of-control plot dooms this women-in-peril saga. Terry (Fairchild) and her semi-disabled hubby Scott (James) are facing financial ruin but have one chance to save themselves. Unfortunately, Scott falls and gets trapped in a storm drain and when Terry goes for help, she gets captured by an escaped mental patient (Pare) who uses her as a hostage against the cops. Oh, and the water is rising in the storm drain, so Scott's gonna drown unless Terry can get free. Very dumb. 90m/C VHS, DVD. Morgan Fairchild, Michael Pare, John James, Steve Eastin, Thom Christopher; **D:** David Giancola. VIDEO

The Perils of Gwendoline 🦴🦴½ *Gwendoline; The Perils of Gwendoline in the Land of the Yik-Yak* 1984 (R) A young woman leaves a convent to search for her long-lost father, in this adaptation of a much funnier French comic strip of the same name. What ends up on the screen is merely a very silly rip-off of the successful "Raiders of the Lost Ark," and of primary interest for its numerous scenes of amply endowed Kitaen in the buff. 88m/C VHS, DVD. *FR* Tawny Kitaen, Brent Huff, Zabou, Bernadette LaFont, Jean Rougerie; **D:** Just Jaeckin; **M:** Pierre Bachelet.

The Perils of Pauline 🦴🦴 1934 All 12 episodes of this classic melodrama/adventure serial in one package, featuring dastardly villains, cliff-hanging predicaments, and worldwide chases. 238m/B VHS, DVD. Evelyn Knapp, Robert "Tex" Allen, James Durkin, Sonny Ray, Pat O'Malley; **D:** Ray Taylor.

The Perils of Pauline 🦴🦴 1947 A musical biography of Pearl White, the reigning belle of silent movie serials. Look for lots of silent film stars. 96m/C VHS, DVD. Betty Hutton, John Lund, Constance Collier, William Demarest, Billy DeWolfe; **D:** George Marshall; **C:** Ray Rennahan; **M:** Frank Loesser.

Perils of the Darkest Jungle 🦴🦴½ *The Tiger Woman; Jungle Gold* 1944 Tiger Woman battles moneymad oil profiteers to protect her tribe. This 12-episode serial comes on two tapes. 180m/B VHS. Linda Stirling, Allan "Rocky" Lane, Duncan Renaldo, George Lewis; **D:** Spencer Gordon Bennet.

Period of Adjustment 🦴🦴🦴 1962 Heartwarming comedy about young newlyweds adjusting to the pressures of domestic life and trying to help the troubled marriage of an older couple. Based on the play by Tennessee Williams. 112m/B VHS. Anthony (Tony) Franciosa, Jane Fonda, Jim Hutton, Lois Nettleton, John McGiver, Jack Albertson; **D:** George Roy Hill; **W:** Isobel Lennart.

Permanent Midnight 🦴🦴½ 1998 (R) Stiller stars as TV writer Jerry Stahl in this film version of his 1995 autobiography, which follows his plunge from a guy who has it all to a loser junkie who's as unlikable as this movie itself. At its real-life peak, Stahl's heroine habit reached $6,000 a week. There are some great flashes of dark humor—Jerry is obsessed with exercising and eating right even while pumping himself full of drugs—and some truly horrific sequences (at one low point, Stahl both scores and shoots up with his baby daughter by his side). The problem is that we don't care. Stiller's comic timing makes most of the bleak jokes work, and it's the only thing that makes the movie bearable; however, his brooding performance (possibly due to writer/director Veloz) lacks any charisma. Watch for Stahl himself as a pessimistic doctor at a methadone clinic. 85m/C VHS, DVD. Ben Stiller, Elizabeth Hurley, Maria Bello, Owen Wilson, Lourdes Benedicto, Peter Greene, Cheryl Ladd, Fred Willard, Charles Fleischer, Janeane Garofalo, Jerry Stahl; **D:** David Veloz; **W:** David Veloz; **C:** Robert Yeoman; **M:** Daniel Licht.

Permanent Record 🦴🦴½ 1988 (PG-13) Hyper-sincere drama about a popular high schooler's suicide and the emotional reactions of those he left behind. Great performance from Reeves. 92m/C VHS, DVD. Alan Boyce, Keanu Reeves, Michelle Meyrink, Jennifer Rubin, Pamela Gidley, Michael Elgart, Richard Bradford, Barry Corbin, Kathy Baker, Dakin Matthews; **D:** Marisa Silver; **W:** Jarre Fees, Alice Liddle, Larry Ketron; **C:** Frederick Elmes; **M:** Joe Strummer.

Permanent Vacation 🦴🦴 1984 A young man disenchanted with New York City decides to escape to Europe to forget about his problems. 80m/C VHS. John Lurie, Chris Parker; **D:** Jim Jarmusch; **W:** Jim Jarmusch; **M:** John Lurie.

Permission To Kill 🦴🦴½ 1975 (PG) Grim spy drama features Bogard as an agent determined to prevent the return of a third-world radical to a totalitarian state. 96m/C VHS. *GB* Dirk Bogarde, Ava Gardner, Timothy Dalton, Frederic Forrest; **D:** Cyril Frankel; **C:** Frederick A. (Freddie) Young; **M:** Richard Rodney Bennett.

Perpetrators of the Crime 🦴🦴 1998 (R) Dumb criminals—dumb crime. Jones (Burgess) comes up with a kidnapping scheme but his sidekicks, Phil (Strong) and Ed (Devine), kidnap the wrong girl (Spelling) and take her to the wrong hideout. That makes things difficult when Jones tries to shake down their mark (Davis) for the ransom. 85m/C VHS, DVD. *CA* Danny Strong, Tori Spelling, Mark Burgess, Sean Devine, William B. Davis; **D:** John Hamilton; **W:** Max Sartor.

Perry Mason Returns 🦴🦴 1985 Perry Mason returns to solve another baffling mystery. This time he must help his longtime assistant, Della Street, when she is accused of killing her new employer. 95m/C VHS. Raymond Burr, Barbara Hale, William Katt, Patrick O'Neal, Richard Anderson, Cassie Yates, Al Freeman Jr.; **D:** Ron Satlof.

Perry Mason: The Case of the Lost Love 🦴🦴½ 1987 Superlawyer Mason defends the husband of a former lover he hasn't seen in 30 years. The solution to the mystery may catch viewer off guard. 96m/C VHS. Raymond Burr, Barbara Hale, William Katt, Jean Simmons, Gene Barry, Robert Walden, Stephen Elliot, Robert Mandan, David Ogden Stiers; **D:** Ron Satlof. TV

Persepolis 🦴🦴🦴 2007 (PG-13) Animated universal coming-of-age tale spans the life of a young Iranian girl beginning at the tumultuous period from the end of the rule of the Shah through the abrupt transition to the fundamentalist Muslim regime that followed. The profound impact of the many changes Marjane (Satrapi) endures is heartrending. Although she is part of a modern and progressive Iranian family, she is forced to don a face-covering veil; she then finds that she is an outsider in her native land, and she is forced yet again to flee. Adapted from the semi-autobiographical graphic novel by Marjane Satrapi, the characters are expressed as rather low-tech line drawings when compared to other contemporary animation, but the resulting images and storyline are relatable. 95m/B DVD. *FR* **D:** Marjane Satrapi, Vincent Paronnaud; **M:** Olivier Bernet; **V:** Chiara Mastroianni, Danielle Darrieux, Simon Abkarian, Gabrielle Lopes, Catherine Deneuve, Francois Jerome.

Persona 🦴🦴🦴 1966 A famous actress turns mute and is treated by a talkative nurse at a secluded cottage. As their relationship turns increasingly tense, the women's personalities begin to merge. Memorable, unnerving—and atypically avant garde—from cinema giant Bergman. First of several collaborations between the director and leading lady Ullmann. In Swedish with English subtitles. 100m/C VHS, DVD. *SW* Bibi Andersson, Liv Ullmann, Gunnar Bjornstrand, Margareta Krook, Jorgen Lindstrom; **D:** Ingmar Bergman; **W:** Ingmar Bergman; **C:** Sven Nykvist; **M:** Lars Johan Werle. Natl. Soc. Film Critics '67: Actress (Andersson), Director (Bergman), Film.

Personal Best 🦴🦴🦴 1982 (R) Lesbian lovers compete while training for the 1990 Olympics. Provocative fare often goes where few films have gone before, but overly stylized direction occasionally overwhelms characterizations. It gleefully exploits locker-room nudity, with Hemingway in her pre-implant days. Still, an ambitious, often accomplished production. 126m/C VHS, DVD. Mariel Hemingway, Scott Glenn, Patrice Donnelly; **D:** Robert Towne; **W:** Robert Towne; **C:** Michael Chapman; **M:** Jack Nitzsche.

Personal Exemptions 🦴½ 1988 (PG) In this stock comedy a frenzied IRS auditor learns that her daughter is smuggling aliens into the country, her son is brokering with some businessmen she's

Personal Maid ✗ 1931 Poor Irish lassie, Nora Ryan (Carroll), dreams of bettering herself and decides to start by becoming a maid for New York's wealthy Gary family and seeing how the other half lives. Wayward son Dick Gary (Raymond) immediately starts flirting with Nora but true love has some bumps in the road. 74m/B VHS, Nancy Carroll, Gene Raymond, Pat O'Brien, Mary Boland, Donald Meek, George Fawcett, Lewis Drayton, Jessie Busley, Hugh O'Connell; *D:* Monta Bell, Lothar Mendes; *W:* Adelaide Heilbron; *C:* Karl Freund.

Personal Property ✗✗½ 1937 The Man in Possession 1937 Taylor tries every trick in the book to win Harlow over in this MGM romantic fluff. Not that big on laughs, but plenty of good shots of Harlow and a beefcake scene of Taylor in the tub who was the darling of the MGM lot and worked with every leading lady. This and would with Harlow and Taylor made together. Remake of the 1931 film "The Man in Possession." 84m/B VHS, Robert Taylor, Jean Harlow, Reginald Owen, Una O'Connor, E.E. Clive, Henrietta Crosman, Cora Witherspoon; *D:* Woodbridge S. Van Dyke; *W:* Hugh Mills.

Personal Services ✗✗½ 1987 (R) A bawdy satire loosely based on the life and times of Britain's modern-day madam, Cynthia Payne, and her rise to fame in the world of prostitution. Payne's earlier years were featured in the film "Wish You Were Here." 104m/C VHS, DVD, GB Julie Walters, Alec McCowen, Shirley Stelfox, Tim Woodward, Dave Atkins, Danny Schiller, Victoria Hardcastle; *D:* Terry Jones; *W:* David Leland; *C:* Roger Deakins; *M:* John Du Prez.

Personal Velocity: Three Portraits ✗✗✗ 2002 (R) Fictional triptych of three New York women undergoing moments of epiphany. Delia (Sedgwick) summons the courage to take her children and leave her broke, abusive spouse and Catskill trailer life. Greta (Posey), a Manhattan cookbook editor realizes that her work does have merit but in order to really move forward in life she needs to leave her slouch of a husband. And finally Paula (Balk), a pregnant, misdirected young woman driving nowhere in particular, connects with her maternal instincts through an encounter with a hitchhiker. Ellen Kuras's cinematography is notable in its attention to detail and Miller (playwright Arthur's daughter) mixes great storytelling with flashbacks, montages, and narrator commentary to provides a well-rounded understanding of each situation, leaving final judgment to the audience. 86m/C VHS, DVD, US Kyra Sedgwick Davenance, Ben Shenkman, Fairuza Balk, Seth Gilliam, David Patrick Kelly, Lou Taylor Pucci, Patti D'Arbanville; *D:* Rebecca Miller; *W:* Rebecca Miller; *C:* Ellen Kuras; *M:* Michael Rohatyn; *Nar:* John Ventimiglia.

The Personals ✗✗½ 1983 (PG) A recently divorced young man takes out a personal ad in a newspaper to find the woman of his dreams. But it isn't quite that simple in this independent comedy shot entirely in Minneapolis. 90m/C VHS, DVD, Bill Schoppert, Karen Landry, Paul Eiding, Michael Laskin, Vickie Dakil; *D:* Peter Markle.

Personals ✗✗ 1990 Chilling drama that casts O'Neill as an unnoticed librarian until she begins to meet (and kill) the men who answer her ads. Zimbalist is a widow who is determined to learn the truth. 93m/C VHS, Stephanie Zimbalist, Jennifer O'Neill, Robin Thomas, Clark Johnson, Gina Gallego, Rosemary Dunsmore, Colm Feore; *D:* Steven Hilliard Stern. TV

Personals ✗✗ 2000 New Yorker Keith (Yoba) is juggling two girlfriends and a writing job and sucking at all three endeavors. So it's no big surprise when he loses it all. Entertaining debut for filmmaker Sargent. 91m/C VHS, DVD, Malik Yoba, Stacey Dash, Sheryl Lee Ralph, Rhonda Foss, Kendrick, Monteria Ivey; *D:* Mike Sargent; *W:* Mike Sargent. VIDEO

Persons Unknown ✗✗ 1996 Melodramatic noir with a decent cast. Disgraced ex-cop Jim Holland (Mantegna) now runs a security firm in Long Beach, CA. He has a one-nighter with foxy Amanda (Lynch) and wakes up to discover she's stolen confidential files. So, with colleague Cake (Walsh), he tracks Amanda down and discovers that she and her wheelchair-bound sister, Molly (Watts), are planning a robbery that involves ripping off Columbian drug lords. But, as usual, nothing works out as intended. 99m/C VHS, Joe Mantegna, Kelly Lynch, J.T. Walsh, Naomi Watts, Xander Berkeley, Jon Favreau, Channon Roe, Michael Nicolosi; *D:* George Hickenlooper; *W:* Craig Smith.

The Pest ✗ 1996 (PG-13) Movie certainly lives up to its title. A hyperkinetic Leguizamo stars as Pesterio (Pest) Vargas, a small-time Miami con man, who owes 50 large to the mob. Eccentric German businessman Gustav Shank (Jones) offers this money to Pest—the catch being that Pest will become the human prey for Gustav's private island hunting party. You'll be rooting for the hunter. 86m/C VHS, DVD, FrI Lina Romay, Robert Woods, Howard Vernon, Alice Arno, Caroline Riviere; *D:* Jess (Jesus) Franco.

Pet Sematary ✗✗ 1989 (R) A quirky adaptation of Stephen King's best-seller about a certain patch of woods in the Maine wilderness that "rejuvenates the dead, and how a newly located college MD eventually uses it to restore his dead son. Mildly creepy. 103m/C VHS, DVD, Dale Midkiff, Fred Gwynne, Denise Crosby, Blaze Berdahl, Brad Greenquist, Miko Hughes, Stephen King; *D:* Mary Lambert; *W:* Stephen King; *C:* Peter Stein; *M:* Elliot Goldenthal.

Pet Sematary 2 ✗½ 1992 (R) Lame sequel to the original Stephen King flick. After seeing his mother electrocuted, a teen and his veterinarian father move to the Maine town where the legendary Pet Sematary is located. Horror begins when the boy's friend's dog is shot by his stepfather, and the boys bury the dog in the "sematary." King wasn't involved with this film, so the story isn't very coherent, but shock value and special effects are great. Not recommended for those with a weak stomach. 102m/C VHS, DVD, Anthony Edwards, Edward Furlong, Clancy Brown, Jared Rushton, Darlanne Fluegel, Lisa Waltz, Jason McGuire, Sarah Trigger; *D:* Mary Lambert; *W:* Richard Outten; *C:* Russell Carpenter.

Pet Shop ✗✗½ 1994 (PG) Pair of evil galaxy-travelling aliens take over the local pet store in a remote desert town and is forced to stand up against a brutal racketeer. The melodramatic plot is brightened by a nonstop flow of jazz tunes sung by Lee and Fitzgerald and played by an all-star lineup that includes Dick Cathcart, Matty Matlock, Eddie Miller and George Van Eps. 72m/C VHS. *C:* Russell Carpenter.

Pete Kelly's Blues ✗✗ 1955 A jazz musician in a Kansas City speakeasy is forced to stand up against a brutal racketeer. The melodramatic plot is brightened by a nonstop flow of jazz tunes sung by Lee and Fitzgerald and played by an all-star lineup that includes Dick Cathcart, Matty Matlock, Eddie Miller and George Van Eps. 95m/C VHS, Jack Webb, Janet Leigh, Edmond O'Brien, Lee Marvin, Martin Milner, Peggy Lee, Ella Fitzgerald, Andy Devine; *D:* Jack Webb.

Pete 'n' Tillie ✗✗½ 1972 (PG) Amiable comedy turns to less appealing melodrama as couple meets, marries, and endures tragedy. Film contributes little to director Ritt's fresh-and-miss reputation, but shine in leads. Adapted by Julius J. Epstein from a Peter de Vries' story. 100m/C VHS, Walter Matthau, Carol Burnett, Geraldine Page, Barry Nelson, Rene Auberjonois, Lee Montgomery, Henry Jones, Kent Smith; *D:* Martin Ritt; *W:* Julius J. Epstein; *C:* John A. Alonzo; *M:* John Williams. British Acad. '73: Actor (Matthau).

Peter and Paul ✗✗½ 1981 TV miniseries follows the lives of the two apostles, Peter (Foxworth) and Paul (Hopkins), from the Crucifixion through the next three decades as they travel spreading the word of Christ, until both are executed in Rome. Tries valiantly, but falls a bit short. 194m/C VHS, Anthony Hopkins, Robert Foxworth, Eddie Albert, Raymond Burr, Jose Ferrer, Jon Finch, David Gwillim, Herbert Lom, Jean Peters; *D:* Robert Day; *W:* Christopher Knopf.

The Pest ✗ 1996 (PG-13) Movie certainly lives up to its title. A hyperkinetic Leguizamo stars as Pesterio (Pest) Vargas, a small-time Miami con man, who owes 50 large to the mob. Eccentric German businessman Gustav Shank (Jones) offers this money to Pest—the catch being that Pest will become the human prey for Gustav's private island hunting party. You'll be rooting for the hunter. 86m/C VHS, FrI Lina Romay, Robert Woods, Howard Vernon, Alice Arno, Caroline Riviere; *D:* Jess (Jesus) Franco.

Peter Gunn ✗✗ 1989 Detective Peter Gunn returns, only to find himself being hunted by both the mob and the Feds. A TV movie reprise of the vintage series that has none of the original cast members. 97m/C VHS, DVD, Peter Strauss, Barbara Williams, Jennifer Edwards, Charles Cioffi, Pearl Bailey, Peter Jurasik, David Rappaport; *D:* Blake Edwards; *M:* Henry Mancini. TV

Peter Lundy and the Medicine Hat Stallion ✗✗½ The Medicine Hat Stallion; Pony Express 1977 A teenaged Pony Express rider must outrun the Indians and battle the elements in order to carry mail from the Nebraska Territory to the West Coast. Good family entertainment. 85m/C VHS, Leif Garrett, Mitchell Ryan, Bibi Besch, John Quade, Milo O'Shea; *D:* Michael O'Herlihy. TV

Peter Pan ✗✗✗ 1953 (G) Disney classic about a boy who never wants to grow up. Based on J.M. Barrie's book and play. Still stars his head and shoulders above any recent competition in providing fun family entertainment. Terrific animation and lovely hummable music. 76m/C VHS, DVD, Hamilton Luske; *W:* Milt Banta, William Cottrell, Winston Hibler, Bill Peet, Erdman Penner, Joe Rinaldi, Ted Sears, Ralph Wright; *M:* Edward Plumb, Oliver Wallace; *V:* Bobby Driscoll, Kathryn Beaumont, Hans Conried, Heather Angel, Candy Candido, Bill Thompson; *Nar:* Tom Conway.

Peter Pan ✗✗✗ 1960 A TV classic, this videotape of a performance is the 1954 Broadway musical adaptec from the play. Mary Martin returns once again, this time around, teaches the Darling children how to fly and leads them to Never-never-land. Newcomer Rachel Hurd-Wood shines as Wendy Darling. Goes deeper into the relationships and emotions between the characters, including Peter and Hook, than in previous versions. 113m/C VHS, DVD, US Jason Isaacs, Jeremy Sumpter, Rachel Hurd-Wood, Olivia Williams, Ludivine Sagnier, Richard Briers, Lynn Redgrave, Geoffrey Palmer, Harry Newell, Freddie Popplewell; *D:* P.J. Hogan; *W:* P.J. Hogan, Michael Goldenberg; *C:* Donald McAlpine; *M:* James Newton Howard; *Nar:* Saffron Burrows.

Peter Pan ✗✗✗ 2003 (PG) Much more literal adaptation of the J.M. Barrie novel is surprisingly serious in its tone. Peter Pan (Sumpter), played by an actual boy this time around, teaches the Darling children how to fly and leads them to Never-never-land. Newcomer Rachel Hurd-Wood shines as Wendy Darling. Goes deeper into the relationships and emotions between the characters, including Peter and Hook, than in previous versions. 113m/C VHS, DVD, US Jason Isaacs, Jeremy Sumpter, Rachel Hurd-Wood, Olivia Williams, Ludivine Sagnier, Richard Briers, Lynn Redgrave, Geoffrey Palmer, Harry Newell, Freddie Popplewell; *D:* P.J. Hogan; *W:* P.J. Hogan, Michael Goldenberg; *C:* Donald McAlpine; *M:* James Newton Howard; *Nar:* Saffron Burrows.

Peter the First: Part 1 ✗✗ 1937 The first half of Petrov's Soviet epic about the early years of Tsar Peter I's reign. Lavish, in Russian with English subtitles. 95m/B VHS, RU Nikolai Simonov, Nikolai Cherkasov, Mikhail Zharov, Mikhail Tarkanov, Vladimir Petrov; *W:* Vladimir Petrov; *C:* Vyacheslav Gordanov; *M:* Vladimir Scherbachov.

Peter the First: Part 2 ✗✗ 1938 The second half of Petrov's epic, covering the triumphs and final years of the famous Tsar. In Russian with English subtitles. 104m/B VHS, RU Nikolai Simonov, Mikhail Zharov, Nikolai Cherkasov, Alla Tarasova, Irina Zarubina, Vladimir Gardin; *D:* Vladimir Petrov; *C:* Vyacheslav Gordanov; *M:* Vladimir Scherbachov.

Peter the Great ✗✗ 1936 Dry but eye-pleasing TV miniseries follows the life of Russia's colorful, very tall ruler, from childhood on. Much of the interesting cast is wasted in tiny roles. 371m/C VHS, Maximili-

The Personals ✗✗ 1998 Fed up with her boring love life, Dr. Du Jazhen (Liu) takes out a personal ad and begins to meet (and kill) the responses. The body of the film is made up of the interviews she conducts with these men—well, most of them are men. Other filmmakers have made more of the same premise, but director Kuo-fu targeted for tax fraud, and her husband having an affair with a high-school girl. 100m/C VHS, Nanette Fabray, John Cotton; *D:* Peter Rowe.

Persuasion ✗✗✗ 1995 (PG) Charming British costume romance, based on Jane Austen's final novel, deals with the constricted life of practical, plain, put-upon Anne Elliot (Root). Thanks to the marriage proposal of the manly Frederick Wentworth (Hinds) and instead stuck by her snobbish (and demanding) family. Eight years later, Anne is given a second chance at love when the now-wealthy Wentworth happens back into her life—but she still has her obnoxious relations to contend with. It's wonderful to see Anne blossom from mouse to lioness although the swirl of supporting players (and settings) provide some confusion. 104m/C VHS, DVD, GB Amanda Root, Ciaran Hinds, Susan Fleetwood, Corin Redgrave, Fiona Shaw, John Woodvine, Phoebe Nicholls, Samuel West, Sophie Thompson, Judy Cornwell, Felicity Dean, Simon Russell Beale, Victoria Hamilton, Emma Roberts; *D:* Roger Michell; *W:* Nick Dear, Jeremy Sams.

Persuasion ✗✗ 2007 Poor, put-upon spinster Anne Elliot (Hawkins)! Some years before, having respected the wishes of family and friends, she turned down the marriage proposal of Captain Wentworth (Penny-Jones) to care for her selfish and self-centered family. But Wentworth unexpectedly re-enters the scene—now a wealthy, rather dashing, and very eligible bachelor. Can Anne still catch his eye? And will she allow her own feelings to rule what's still expected of her? Based on the novel by Jane Austen. 90m/C DVD, GB Sally Hawkins, Rupert Penny-Jones, Anthony Head, Julia Davis, Amanda Hale, Sam Hazeldine, Alice Krige, Michael Fenton-Stevens, Mary Stockley, Maisie Dimbleby; *D:* Adrian Shergold; *W:* Simon Burke; *C:* David Odd; *M:* Martin Phipps. TV

The Perverse Countess ✗ La Comtesse Perverse 1973 Romay is a bored tourist who spends a fee weekend on a fling with Woods, who procures 'human flesh for the cannibalistic Count and Countess Zaroff (Vernon and Arno). Romay accompanies her lover to the haunted castle on a delivery, not realizing she is the Countess sees what a succulent bon-bon Romay is, she faces difficult choices. Subtitled in English. 86m/C VHS, FrI Lina Romay, Robert Woods, Howard Vernon, Alice Arno, Caroline Riviere; *D:* Jess (Jesus) Franco.

Chen keeps his camera squarely on his characters. The Taiwan setting is a bit exotic. Liu's performance is a model of restraint. Mandarin with subtitles. 104m/C VHS, TWRene Liu, Wu Bai; *D:* Kuo-fu Chen; *C:* Nan-hong Li; *M:* Kuo-fu Chen, Shih-chich Chen; *W:* Kuo-fu Chen, Shih-chich an Schell, Laurence Olivier, Omar Sharif, Vanessa Redgrave, Ursula Andress; **D:** Marvin J. Chomsky; **W:** Edward Anhalt; **C:** Vittorio Storaro; **M:** Laurence Rosenthal. **TV**

Peter's Friends ♥♥1/2 **1992 (R)** Peter has recently inherited a grand manor house located outside London and invites some chums to celebrate a New Year's Eve weekend, ten years after they've been at university together. So begins another nostalgic trip down memory lane ala "The Big Chill," but unlike other clones, this one can stand on its own, with a lightweight and sly script by talented comedienne Rudner (in her film debut) and her husband Bergman. If the script sometimes falls a little flat, the fine cast will make up for it. Thompson's mother, actress Law, plays the housekeeper. **102m/C VHS, DVD.** *GB* Kenneth Branagh, Rita Rudner, Emma Thompson, Stephen Fry, Hugh Laurie, Imelda Staunton, Alphonsia Emmanuel, Tony Slattery, Alex Lowe, Alex Scott, Phyllida Law, Richard Briers; **D:** Kenneth Branagh; **W:** Rita Rudner, Martin Bregman.

Pete's Dragon ♥♥1/2 **1977 (G)** Elliot, an enormous, bumbling dragon with a penchant for clumsy heroics, becomes friends with poor orphan Pete. Combines brilliant animation with the talents of live actors for an interesting effect. **128m/C VHS, DVD.** Helen Reddy, Shelley Winters, Mickey Rooney, Jim Dale, Red Buttons, Sean Marshall, Jim Backus, Jeff Conaway; **D:** Don Chaffey; **W:** Malcolm Marmorstein; **C:** Frank Phillips; **M:** Irwin Kostal; **V:** Charlie Callas.

Pete's Meteor ♥♥1/2 **1998 (R)** A meteor lands in the Dublin backyard where Mickey and his two siblings are living with their grandmother (Fricker) after the death of their parents. They think the rock is a gift from mom and dad (who now live up in the stars). But when the government takes the meteor and sends it to a university scientist (Molina) for study, the kids decide to get it back. And if this wasn't plot enough, the trio's junkie Uncle Pete (Myers), who promised to look after them, is in trouble with the mob. Don't be fooled—this is a gritty and thoughtful drama, not a kid flick or a comedy despite Myers presence. **103m/C VHS, DVD.** Mike Myers, Brenda Fricker, Alfred Molina, Ian Costello; **D:** Joe O'Byrne; **W:** Joe O'Byrne; **C:** Paul Sarossy.

Petit Con ♥♥1/2 **1984 (R)** A live-action version of the popular French comic strip wherein a young rebel drops out of society to live with aging hippies. With English subtitles. **90m/C VHS.** *FR* Guy Marchand, Michel Choupon, Caroline Cellier, Bernard Brieux, Souad Amidou; **D:** Gerard Lauzier.

Petits Freres ♥♥1/2 *Little Fellas* **2000** Troubled 13-year-old Talia (Touly) takes her pitbull Kim and runs away from her brutal stepfather. She hangs out in the projects with a group of boys her own age whom she warily befriends, only to be victimized when they steal and sell Kim to a dogfighting ring. Despite their denials, Talia knows what they did, even when they promise to help her rescue the dog. Kids, who are non-professionals, do fine but the story meanders it's way to a predictable ending. French with subtitles. **92m/C VHS, DVD.** *FR* Stephanie Touly, Illes Sefraoui, Mapha Goumane, Nassim Izem, Rachid Mansouri, Gerald Dantoff; **D:** Jacques Doillon; **W:** Jacques Doillon; **C:** Manuel Teran.

Petrified Forest ♥♥♥♥1/2 **1936** Writer Alan Squier (Howard) is hitchhiking through the Arizona desert when he stops at a run-down gas station/diner run by Maple (Hall) and his daughter Gabrielle (Davis). Once an idealist, Alan now feels he has little to live for, which may explain his attitude when the diner patrons and employees are held hostage by on the lam gangster Duke Mantee (Bogart) and his boys. Often gripping, with memorable performances from Davis, Howard, and Bogart. Based on the play by Robert Sherwood with Howard and Bogart re-creating their stage roles. **83m/B VHS, DVD.** Bette Davis, Leslie Howard, Humphrey Bogart, Dick Foran, Charley Grapewin, Porter Hall, Genevieve Tobin, Joseph (Joe) Sawyer; **D:** Archie Mayo; **W:** Delmer Daves; **C:** Sol Polito; **M:** Bernhard Kaun.

expert Rocky to try to defeat the creep. That's if they can get past his zombie cohorts and flesh-eating ghouls. **91m/C VHS, DVD.** Reggie Bannister, A. Michael Baldwin, Bill Thornbury, Gloria Lynne Henry, Kevin Connor, Angus Scrimm; **D:** Don A. Coscarelli; **W:** Don A. Coscarelli.

Petty Crimes ♥♥ *Aller-Simple Pour Manhattan* **2002** Evading jail time in France, two-bit thief Michel immigrates to the Big Apple and falls for the zesty Zoe who works on his deportation battle when his visa expires. But he needs to scrounge up some major coinage pronto. Enter the persistent old partner tempting him back into his rotten ways of yore. All goes pleasantly enough until the Frenchman faces a puzzling, perturbing twist at the end—mais non! **78m/C VHS, DVD.** *FR* Andrew Pang, Ann Hu, Jeremie Covillault, Sarah Zoe Canner; **D:** Michel Ferry; **W:** Sarah Zoe Canner, Michel Ferry; **C:** Jean Coudsi; **M:** Jean-Claude Ghrenessia. **VIDEO**

Petulia ♥♥♥♥ **1968 (R)** Overlooked, offbeat drama about a flighty woman who spites her husband by dallying with a sensitive, recently divorced surgeon. Classic '60s document and cult favorite offers great performance from the appealing Christie, with Scott fine as the vulnerable surgeon. On-screen performances by the Grateful Dead and Big Brother. Among idiosyncratic director Lester's best. From the novel "Me and the Arch Kook Petulia" by John Haase. **105m/C VHS, DVD.** George C. Scott, Richard Chamberlain, Julie Christie, Shirley Knight, Arthur Hill, Joseph Cotten, Pippa Scott, Richard Dysart, Kathleen Widdoes, Austin Pendleton, Rene Auberjonois, Roger Bowen, Ellen Geer; **D:** Richard Lester; **W:** Lawrence B. Marcus; **C:** Nicolas Roeg; **M:** John Barry.

Peyton Place ♥♥♥ **1957** Passion, scandal, and deception in a small New England town set the standard for passion, scandal, and deception in soap operadom. Shot on location in Camden, Maine. Performances and themes now seem dated, but produced a blockbuster in its time. Adapted from Grace Metalious' popular novel and followed by "Return to Peyton Place." **157m/C VHS, DVD.** Lana Turner, Hope Lange, Lee Philips, Lloyd Nolan, Diane Varsi, Lorne Greene, Russ Tamblyn, Arthur Kennedy, Terry Moore, Barry Coe, David Nelson, Betty Field, Mildred Dunnock, Leon Ames, Alan Reed Jr.; **D:** Mark Robson; **W:** John Michael Hayes; **C:** William Mellor; **M:** Franz Waxman.

Phaedra ♥♥ **1961** Loose and updated adaptation of Euripides' "Hippolytus." Mercouri, the second wife of a rich Greek shipping magnate, is dispatched to London to convince her husband's adult son (Perkins) to come home to Greece. Merkouri and Perkins immediately begin a steamy affair but their return home brings problems for all. Dubbed. **116m/B VHS.** *GR FR* Melina Mercouri, Anthony Perkins, Raf Vallone, Elizabeth Ercy; *Cameos:* Jules Dassin; **D:** Jules Dassin; **W:** Jules Dassin, Margarita Liberaki; **M:** Mikis Theodorakis.

Phantasm ♥♥♥1/2 *The Never Dead* **1979 (R)** A small-budgeted, hallucinatory horror fantasy about two parentless brothers who discover weird goings-on at the local funeral parlor, including the infamous airborne, brain-chewing chrome ball. Creepy, unpredictable nightmare fashioned on a shoestring by young independent producer Coscarelli. Scenes were cut out of the original film to avoid "X" rating. Followed by "Phantasm II". **90m/C VHS, DVD.** Michael Baldwin, Bill Thornbury, Reggie Bannister, Kathy Lester, Terrie Kalbus, Kenneth V. Jones, Susan Harper, Lynn Eastman, David Arntzen, Angus Scrimm, Bill Cone; **D:** Don A. Coscarelli; **W:** Don A. Coscarelli; **C:** Don A. Coscarelli; **M:** Fredric Myrow, Malcolm Seagrave.

Phantasm 2 ♥♥ **1988 (R)** Teen psychic keeps flashing on villainous Tall Man. A rehash sequel to the original, cultishly idiosyncratic fantasy, wherein more victims are fed into the inter-dimensional abyss and Mike discovers that the horror is not all in his head. Occasional inspired gore, bloodier than its predecessor. More yuck for the buck. **97m/C VHS.** James LeGros, Reggie Bannister, Angus Scrimm, Paula Irvine, Samantha (Sam) Phillips, Ken Tigar; **D:** Don A. Coscarelli; **W:** Don A. Coscarelli; **C:** Daryn Okada.

Phantasm 3: Lord of the Dead ♥♥1/2 **1994 (R)** Murderous mortician The Tall Man and his killer silver spheres return once again in this continuing gore fest. Mike, whose brother Jody was one of The Tall Man's victims, teams up with the cynical Reggie and martial arts

Phantasm 4: Oblivion ♥1/2 **1998 (R)** At least this sequel can boast the original's lead actors, which allows for footage from the first movie to be used in telling a familiar story. The Tall Man (Scrimm) is still transporting corpses and Mike (Baldwin) is now becoming one of the evil guy's minions. But some time travel takes Mike back to the Tall Man's origins and he tries to take care of the problem at the source. **90m/C VHS, DVD.** Angus Scrimm, A. Michael Baldwin, Reggie Bannister, Bill Thornbury, Bob Ivy; **D:** Don A. Coscarelli; **W:** Don A. Coscarelli; **C:** Chris Chomyn; **M:** Christopher Stone. **VIDEO**

Phantom ♥♥ **1922** A mild-mannered clerk, dreaming of bettering himself by becoming a famous poet, becomes obsessed with a wealthy beauty. Restored and hand-tinted silent from legendary German director Murnau with a 2003 orchestral score by Israel. **120m/B DVD.** *GE* Alfred Abel, Lya de Putti, Lil Dagover; **D:** F.W. Murnau; **W:** Thea von Harbou; **C:** Axel Graatkjaer, Theophan Ouchakoff; **M:** Robert Israel.

The Phantom ♥♥ **1931** Rare cheapie of a hooded killer terrorizing a group of people in a haunted house. **62m/C VHS, DVD.** Guinn "Big Boy" Williams, Wilfrid Lucas, Sheldon Lewis, William (Bill) Gould; **D:** Alan James.

The Phantom ♥♥1/2 **1996 (PG)** Based on the Lee Falk comic created in 1936. Deep in the Bengala jungle, a mysterious costumed figure honors a 400-year-old legacy by fighting piracy, greed, and cruelty. With the help of a beautiful newspaper heiress (Swanson), the latest guardian (Zane) must keep an American industrialist (Williams) and a secret brotherhood of pirates from finding three sacred skulls that contain the power to dominate the world. Old-fashioned swashbuckling story is helped along by Zane's enthusiastic portrayal of the stalwart hero. Action set pieces, while done more dynamically elsewhere, are fun and exciting. Older kids (read: teenagers) may find the proceedings a bit hokey, but everyone seems to be having a good time. **100m/C VHS, DVD.** Billy Zane, Kristy Swanson, Treat Williams, Catherine Zeta-Jones, James Remar, Jon Tenney, Patrick McGoohan, Samantha Eggar, Cary-Hiroyuki Tagawa, Robert Coleby, David Proval; **D:** Simon Wincer; **W:** Jeffrey Boam; **C:** David Burr; **M:** David Newman.

The Phantom Broadcast ♥♥1/2 *Phantom of the Air* **1933** A popular radio crooner is murdered. The main suspect is his hunchbacked accompanist and manager. A tightly plotted minor thriller that holds up surprisingly well. **63m/B VHS, DVD.** Ralph Forbes, Gail Patrick, Vivienne Osborne, Guinn "Big Boy" Williams, George "Gabby" Hayes; **D:** Phil Rosen.

The Phantom Brother ♥♥ **1988** A semi-spoof about a teenager left orphaned by a car crash that wiped out his entire family, and who is subsequently haunted by his dead brother. Even thinner than it sounds. **92m/C VHS.** Jon Hammer, Patrick Molloy, John Gigante, Mary Beth Pelshaw; **D:** William Szarka.

The Phantom Bullet ♥♥1/2 **1926** Hoot wants to holler at his father's murderers. **60m/B VHS.** Eileen (Elaine Persey) Percy, Alan Forrest, Nelson McDowell, Pat Harmon, Hoot Gibson; **D:** Cliff(ord) Smith; **W:** Curtis Benton; **C:** Harry Neumann.

The Phantom Chariot ♥♥1/2 **1920** A fantasy depicting the Swedish myth about how Death's coach must be driven by the last man to die each year. Silent. **89m/B VHS.** *SW* Hilda Borgstrom, Tore Svenberg, Astrid Holm; **D:** Victor Sjostrom; **W:** Victor Sjostrom; **C:** Julius Jaenzon.

The Phantom Creeps ♥♥ **1939** Evil Dr. Zorka, armed with a meteorite chunk which can bring an army to a standstill, provides the impetus for this enjoyable serial in 12 episodes. **235m/B VHS,** DVD. Bela Lugosi, Dorothy Arnold, Robert Kent, Regis Toomey; **D:** Ford Beebe, Saul Goodkind.

The Phantom Empire ♥♥ *Radio Ranch* **1935** Autry faces the futuristic "Thunder Riders" from the subterranean city of Murania, located 20,000 feet beneath his ranch. A complete serial in 12 episodes. If you only see one science-fiction western in your life, this is the one. Also available in an edited theatrical version at 80 minutes. **245m/B VHS, DVD.** Gene Autry, Frankie Darro, Betsy King Ross, Smiley Burnette; **D:** B. Reeves Eason, Otto Brower.

Phantom Empire ♥♥ **1987 (R)** A woman who rules over a lost city takes a bunch of scientists prisoner and forces them to be slaves. **85m/C VHS, DVD.** Ross Hagen, Jeffrey Combs, Dawn Wildsmith, Robert Quarry, Susan Stokey, Michelle (McClellan) Bauer, Russ Tamblyn, Sybil Danning; **D:** Fred Olen Ray; **W:** Fred Olen Ray, T.L. Lankford.

Phantom Express ♥♥ **1932** Experienced old engineer is dismissed from his job because no one believes his explanation that a mysterious train caused the wreck of his own train. He aims to find justice. **65m/B VHS, DVD.** J. Farrell MacDonald, Sally Blane, William "Buster" Collier Jr., Hobart Bosworth; **D:** Emory Johnson.

Phantom Fiend ♥♥1/2 **1935** A gentle musician becomes a suspect when a series of Jack-the-Ripper type murders terrorize London. Is he the nice guy known by his girlfriend and the people in his lodging house, or is the musician really JTR? Based on the novel "The Lodger" by Marie Belloc-Lowndes. **70m/B VHS, DVD.** *GB* Ivor Novello, Elizabeth Allan, A.W. Baskcomb, Jack Hawkins, Barbara Everest, Peter Gawthorne, Kynaston Reeves; **D:** Maurice Elvey.

The Phantom Flyer ♥♥1/2 **1928** Stunt pilot helps out a cattle-owning frontier family bedeviled by rustlers. Silent. **54m/B VHS.** Al Wilson, Buck Connors, Billy "Red" Jones, Lillian Gilmore, Myrtis Crinley, Larry Steers; **D:** Bruce Mitchell; **C:** William S. Adams.

Phantom from Space ♥♥1/2 **1953** An invisible alien lands on Earth, begins killing people, and is pursued by a pair of scientists. **72m/B VHS, DVD.** Ted Cooper, Rudolph Anders, Noreen Nash, James Seay, Harry Landers; **D:** W. Lee Wilder; **C:** William Clothier.

The Phantom from 10,000 Leagues ♥ **1956** Slimy sea monster attacks swimmers and fishermen; investigating oceanographer pretends not to notice monster is hand puppet. Early AIP release, when still named American Releasing Company. **80m/B VHS, DVD.** Kent Taylor, Cathy Downs, Michael Whalen, Helene Stanton, Phillip Pine; **D:** Dan Milner; **W:** Lou Rusoff; **C:** Brydon Baker; **M:** Ronald Stein.

Phantom Gold ♥♥1/2 **1938** The wicked Whitaker claims to have struck it rich but it's really a scam to lure unsuspecting miners to the claim and then rob and murder them. Luden's suspicious and proves Whitaker's a bad guy. **56m/B VHS.** Jack Luden, Charles "Slim" Whitaker, Beth Marion, Hal Taliaferro, Art Davis; **D:** Joseph Levering.

The Phantom in the House ♥♥ **1929** A woman commits a murder and has her inventor husband take the rap. While he's in prison, she gets rich off of his work. Things get hairy when he is released 15 years later and is introduced to his daughter as a friend of the family. Melodramatic film was originally made with and without sound. **64m/B VHS, DVD.** Ricardo Cortez, Nancy Welford, Henry B. Walthall, Grace Valentine; **D:** Phil Rosen.

Phantom Killer ♥♥ **1942** A district attorney tries to hang a murder rap on a most improbable suspect. When the man is acquitted, the DA quits his job to find the truth, which takes a disturbing twist. The plot is a thinly veiled rehash of "The Sphinx" (1933). **61m/B VHS, DVD.** Dick Purcell, Joan Woodbury, John Hamilton, Warren Hymer, Kenneth Harlan, J. Farrell MacDonald, Mantan Moreland; **D:** William Beaudine.

Phantom Lady ♥♥♥ **1944** After an argument with his wife Scott Henderson (Curtis) walks into a bar and chats up a mystery woman (Helm). When he returns home, the police are there and his wife has been strangled with his necktie.

Since he doesn't know his bar mate's name and no one professes to remember her, Scott is quickly convicted of the crime. Only his loyal secretary Carol (Raines) believes him and she sets out to solve the crime. Based on the novel by Cornell Woolrich. **37m/B VHS, DVD**. Alan Curtis, Franchot Tone, Thomas Gomez, Elisha Cook Jr., Fay Helm, Aurora Miranda, Andrew Tombes, Regis Toomey, Joseph Crehan, Virginia Brissac, Milburn Stone; **D:** Robert Siodmak; **W:** Bernard C. Schoenfeld; **C:** Elwood "Woody" Bredell.

The Phantom Light ✓½ 1935 A lighthouse keeper is murdered under strange circumstances and a mysterious light keeps appearing at the scene. Detective Hale joins up with a navy man and another lighthouse keeper to solve the crime. A low-budget mystery with good atmosphere and some humor. 75m/B VHS. **GB** Binnie Hale, Gordon Harker, Ian Hunter, Donald Calthrop; **D:** Michael Powell.

Phantom of Chinatown ✓ 1940 Mr. Wong is called in to solve another murder in the final entry in the series. The first to have an Asian actor portray the lead, as Luke replaced Boris Karloff. 61m/B VHS, DVD. Keye Luke, Lotus Long, Grant Withers, Paul McVey, Charles F. Miller; **D:** Phil Rosen; **W:** George Waggner; **C:** Fred H. Jackman Jr.; **M:** Edward Kay.

Phantom of Death ✓ 1987 (R) A brilliant pianist, stricken by a fatal disease that causes rapid aging, goes on a murderous rampage. 95m/C VHS. **IT** Michael York, Donald Pleasence, Edwige Fenech; **D:** Ruggero Deodato; **M:** Pino Donaggio.

Phantom of 42nd Street ✓½ 1945 An actor and a cop team up to find the killer of a wealthy uncle. 58m/B VHS, DVD. Dave O'Brien, Kay Aldridge, Alan McWray, Frank Jenks; **D:** Albert Herman.

Phantom of Liberty ✓✓✓ Le Fantome de la Liberte; The Specter of Freedom 1974 Master surrealist Bunuel's episodic film wanders from character to character and from event to event. Animals wander through a man's bedroom, soldiers conduct military exercises in an inhabited area, a missing girl stands before her parents even as they futilely attempt to determine her whereabouts, and an assassin is found guilty, then applauded and led to freedom. They don't get much more surreal than this. If you think you may like it, you'll probably love it. Bunuel, by the way, is among the filming squad victims in the film's opening enactment of Goya's May 3, 1808. In French with English subtitles. 104m/C VHS, DVD. **FR** Adriana Asti, Jean-Claude Brialy, Michel Piccoli, Adolfo Celi, Monica Vitti, Milena Vukotic, Michael Lonsdale, Claude Pieplu, Julien Bertheau, Paul Le Person, Bernard Verley; **D:** Luis Bunuel, Jean-Claude Carrier; **C:** Edmond Richard.

The Phantom of Soho ✓✓ Das Phantom von Soho 1964 A Scotland Yard detective investigates the murders of several prominent businessmen and is assisted by a beautiful mystery writer. 92m/B VHS, DVD. **GE** Dieter Borsche, Barbara Rutting, Hans Sohnker, Peter Vogel, Helga Sommerfeld, Werner Peters; **D:** Franz Gottlieb.

Phantom of the Air 1933 Twelve chapters of high-flying adventure with Tom Tyler. 230m/B VHS, DVD. Tom Tyler, Gloria Shea, William Desmond, Leroy Mason, Walter Brennan; **D:** Ray Taylor.

Phantom Lover ✓✓ 1995 Bang Ge Sheng It's "The Phantom of the Opera" Hong Kong style, although it's a adult fairytale rather than a horror story. In 1936 a theatrical troupe hopes to restore a burned-out opera house for their performances. Legendary singer Sung Dan-Ping (Cheung) was thought to have died in the fire, instead, horribly disfigured, he hides out in the ruins and dreams of his lost love (Chien-Lien). Chinese with subtitles or dubbed (ewwww). 102m/C VHS, DVD, **HK** Leslie Cheung, Chie-Lien Wu, Philip Kwok, Roy Szeto, Peter Pau; **M:** Chris Babida.

The Phantom of the Opera ✓✓ 1925 Deranged, disfigured music lover haunts the sewers of a Parisian opera house and kills to further the career of an unsuspecting young soprano. First of many film versions still packs a wallop, with fine playing from Chaney Sr. Silent with two-color Technicolor "Bal Masque" sequence. Versions with different running times are also available, including 79 and 88 minutes. 101m/B VHS, DVD. Lon Chaney Sr., Norman Kerry, Mary Philbin, Gibson Gowland, Arthur Edmund Carewe, John St. Polis, Snitz Edwards, Virginia Pearson; **D:** Rupert Julian, Edward Sedgwick, Lon Chaney Sr.; **W:** Elliot J. Clawson, Raymond L. Schrock, Frank M. McCormack; **C:** Virgil Miller, Charles Van Enger, Milton Bridenbecker; **Natl. Film Reg. '98.**

The Phantom of the Opera ✓✓✓ 1943 Second Hollywood version (following the 1925 silent) of Gaston Leroux's novel, remade by the same studio (Universal), suffers by dispersing the chills with too many opera scenes (no doubt to give Eddy, something to do) and weak comedy. Enrique (a sympathetic Rains) is a disfigured musician in the Paris Opera who sacrifices himself for the love of young singer Christine (DuBois), who doesn't even know he exists. Rains is only briefly seen in his horror visage. 92m/C VHS, DVD. Nelson Eddy, Susanna Foster, Claude Rains, Edgar Barrier, Leo Carrillo, Hume Cronyn, J. Edward Bromberg; **D:** Arthur Lubin; **W:** Samuel Hoffenstein, Eric Taylor; **C:** Hal Mohr, William Howard Greene; **M:** Edward Ward. Oscars '43: Color Cinematog.

The Phantom of the Opera ✓✓½ 1962 Hammer version of the Gaston Leroux novel transfers the action from Paris to London but keeps the basic story of a young singer (Sears) and her masked benefactor (Lom), who lives in the sewers beneath the opera house. There's also the wimpy fiance (De Souza), a come between them. Good gothic melodrama. Sears' singing was dubbed by opera performer Pat Clark; producer Hinds used the pseudonym John Elder for his screenplay. 85m/C VHS, DVD. Herbert Lom, Heather Sears, Edward De Souza, Thorley Walters, Michael Gough, Martin Miller, Ian Wilson; **D:** Terence Fisher; **W:** John (Hinds) Elder; **C:** Arthur Grant; **M:** Edwin Astley.

The Phantom of the Opera ✓½ 1989 (R) A gory, "Elm Street"-ish version of the Gaston Leroux classic, attempting to cash in on the success of the Broadway musical. 93m/C VHS, DVD. Robert Englund, Jill Schoelen, Alex Hyde-White, Bill Nighy, Terence Harvey, Stephanie Lawrence, Nathan Lewis, Peter Clapham, Molly Shannon; **D:** Dwight Little; **W:** Duke Sandefur; **C:** Elemer Ragalyi; **M:** Misha Segal.

The Phantom of the Opera ✓½ 1990 Yet another version of the tragic tale of a disfigured maskwearing opera lover who lurks in the depths of the Paris Opera House, and his desire for lovely young singer, Christine. Dance plays the Phantom as doomed romantic, with Lancaster his protective "father. Kopit adapted from his 1983 play. Made for TV drama, originally shown in two parts. 200m/C V-S, DVD. **GB** Charles Dance, Burt Lancaster, Teri Polo, Ian Richardson, Andrea Ferreol, Adam Storke, Jean-Pierre Cassel; **D:** Tony Richardson; **W:** Arthur Kopit; **C:** Steve Yaconelli; **M:** John Addison. **TV**

The Phantom Planet ✓✓½ 1961 An astronaut crash-lands on an asteroid and discovers a race of tiny people living there. Having breathed the atmosphere, he shrinks to their diminutive size and aids them in their war against brutal invaders. Infamously peculiar. 82m/B VHS, DVD. Dean Fredericks, Coleen Gray, Tony Dexter, Dolores Faith, Francis X. Bushman, Richard Kiel; **D:** William Marshall.

Phantom of the Mall: Eric's Revenge ✓ 1989 A murderous spirit haunts the local mall. Gore flows like water. 91m/C VHS, DVD. Morgan Fairchild, Kari Whitman, Jonathan Goldsmith, Derek Rydall, Pauly Shore, Robert Estes, Brinke Stevens; **D:** Richard Friedman; **W:** Robert King; **C:** Harry Mathias; **M:** Stacy Widelitz.

The Phantom of the Opera ✓✓ 2004 (PG-13) Andrew Lloyd Webber's London musical finally hit the big-screen in this extravagant version from director Schumacher. This umpteenth adaptation ramps up the romance over the hideousness of the title character. As played here by brawny Scottish actor Butler, the Phantom is positively swoon-worthy. Story is simple: Paris Opera engenue Christine (Rossum) gets her big chance when diva Carlotta (Driver) huffs off the stage. Christine is then torn between two would-be loves: well-mannered opera patron Vicompte Raoul de Chagny (Wilson) and that mystery man. Some changes are made from stage to screen but fans won't be unduly alarmed although the film's cheesy romanticism is unlikely to find new converts. Sets and costumes are eye-catching. 143m/C VHS, DVD. Blu-ray Disc, HD DVD. Gerard Butler, Emmy Rossum, Patrick Wilson, Miranda Richardson, Minnie Driver, Simon Callow, Ciaran Hinds, James Fleet, Kevin McNally, Murray Melvin, Victor McGuire, Jennifer Ellison; **D:** Joel Schumacher; **W:** Joel Schumacher, Andrew Lloyd Webber; **C:** John Mathieson; **M:** Andrew Lloyd Webber.

Phantom of the Paradise ✓✓ 1974 (PG) A rock 'n' roll parody of "Phantom of the Opera." Splashy, only occasionally horrific spoof in which cruel music executive Williams, much to his everlasting regret, swindles a songwriter. Violence ensues. Not for most, or even many, tastes. Graham steals the film as rocker Beef. A failure at the boxoffice, and now a cult item (small enthusiastic cult with few outside interests) for its oddball humor and outrageous rock star parodies. Williams also wrote the turgid score. ♪ Goodbye, Eddie, Goodbye; Faust; Upholstery; Special to Me; Old Souls; Somebody Super Like You; Life At Last; The Hell of It; Beef. 92m/C VHS, DVD, Paul Williams, William Finley, Jessica Harper, Gerrit Graham, George Memmoli, Archie Hahn; **D:** Brian De Palma; **W:** Brian De Palma; **M:** George Alison Tipton, Paul Williams.

The Phantom of the Range ✓½ 1938 Marion is trying to sell her grandfather's ranch only, his "ghost" is scaring everyone away. She and cowpoke Tyler find out a group of evil treasure hunters are searching the property for hidden gold. 59m/B VHS, DVD. Tom Tyler, Beth Marion, Charles "Blackie" King, Forrest Taylor, John Elliott, Soledad Jimenez, Sammy Cohen; **D:** Robert F. "Bob" Hill.

Phantom of the Ritz ✓✓ 1988 (R) Bizarre accidents begin to take place when Ed Blake and his girlfriend start renovating the old Ritz Theatre which re-theatre is inhabited by a rather angry ghost and someone's got to deal with it before the Ritz can rock and roll. Features the fabulous sounds of the '50s. 88m/C VHS. Peter Bergman, Deborah Van Valkenburgh; **D:** Allen Plone.

Phantom of the West ✓✓ 1931 Ten-episode serial about a "rancher who becomes "The Phantom of the West" in order to smoke out his father's killer. 166m/C VHS, DVD. William Desmond, Thomas Santschi, Tom Tyler; **D:** David Ross Lederman.

Phantom Patrol ✓½ 1936 A mystery writer is kidnapped and someone impersonates him. Mountie Maynard must come to the rescue. 60m/B VHS. Kermit Maynard, Joan Barclay, Paul Fix, Julian Rivero, Eddie Phillips, Roger Williams; **D:** Charles (Hutchison) Hutchison.

---

alone. 100m/C VHS, DVD. **IT** Julian Sands, Asia Argento, Andrea Di Stefano, Nadia Rinaldi, Coralina Cataldi-Tassoni, Istvan Bubik, Zoltan Barabas; **D:** Dario Argento; **W:** Dario Argento, Gerard Brach; **C:** Ronnie Taylor; **M:** Ennio Morricone.

The Phantom of the Opera ✓✓½ See p. (see main entry above).

Phantom Ranger ✓ 1938 A federal agent masquerades as a crook to catch a band of counterfeiters. 54m/B VHS. DVD. Tim McCoy, Suzanne Kaaren, Karl Hackett, John St. Polis, John Merton, Harry Strang; **D:** Sam Newfield.

The Phantom Rider ✓✓✓ 1936 Mystery fills the old West in this serial composed of 15 chapters. 152m/B VHS. Buck Jones, Maria Shelton, Joey Ray, Diane Gibson, Harry Woods, Frank LaRue, George Cooper, Eddie Gribbon; **D:** Ray Taylor; **W:** Basil Dickey, George Plympton, Ella O'Neill; **C:** John Hickson, Allen Q. Thompson.

Phantom Stallion ✓½ 1954 Four-time oater has a ranch owner believing a wild stallion is enticing away horses from his herd. But Rex thinks the answer is human and lies close to home. 54m/B VHS, DVD. Rex Allen, Slim Pickens, Carla Balenda, Harry Shannon; **D:** Harry Keller; **W:** Gerald Geraghty; **C:** Bud Thackery; **M:** R. Dale Butts.

Phantom Thunderbolt ✓½ 1933 A man who has falsely spread the rumor that he's a gunfighter is hired to bring a town some good-for-nothings. 62m/B VHS, DVD. Ken Maynard, Frances Lee, Frank Rice, William (Bill) Gould, Robert F. (Bob) Kortman; **D:** Alan James.

Phantom Tollbooth ✓½ 1969 (G) A young boy drives his car into an animated world, where the numbers are at war with the letters and he has been chosen to save Rhyme and Reason, to bring stability back to the Land of Wisdom. Completely unique and typically Jonesian in its intellectual level and interests. Bright and funny on its own level, but this is really for adults who will understand the allegorical novel. 89m/C VHS, DVD. **C:** Chuck Jones; **V:** Mel Blanc, Hans Conried.

Phantom 2040 Movie: The Ghost Who Walks ✓✓½ 1995 Teenager Kit Walker discovers his destiny when a mysterious stranger tells him about his late father and how Kit must carry on his father's legacy as a superhero called the Phantom. A purple suit renders his dad's old nemesis, Rebecca Madison, who's out to destroy the Earth's re-sources. Based on the TV and comic book series. 97m/C VHS, DVD. **V:** Scott Valentine, Margot Kidder, Ron Perlman, Carrie Snodgress, Mark Hamill.

Phantoms ✓ 1997 (R) Dr. Jennifer Palley (Going) and her sister Lisa (McGowan) arrive in a Colorado resort town and discover that the entire population has been wiped out by a mysterious force. They team up with local sheriff Hammond (Affleck) and his odd deputy (Schnieber) to battle the evil force thingie, which a' so seems to have an adverse affect on acting ability. Peter O'Toole appears as an expert on ancient plagues, and to show the rest of the cast what a real actor looks like. Schnieber plays the part of the squirmy deputy very well, but the rest of the characters are cheap plywood. Will they stop the amorphous monster who is taking over the corpses of its victims? Will they remember their lines if someone drops the cue card? Based on the novel by Dean Koontz, w'ro also adapted it for the screen and produced. 91m/C VHS, DVD. Peter O'Toole, Joanna Going, Rose McGowan, Ben Affleck, Liev Schreiber,

William Telaak; **C:** Elwood J. Nicholson; **M:** Hayes Pagel.

Phantom Rancher ✓½ 1939 Roaring melodrama finds Maynard donning a mask to find the real Phantom, who is causing havoc. 61m/B VHS, DVD. Ken Maynard, Dorothy Short, Harry Harvey, Ted Adams, Dave O'Brien, Tom London, John Elliott, Reed Howes; **D:** Harry Fraser; **W:** William Lively; **C:** William (Bill) Hyer; **M:** Lew Porter.

Nicky Katt, Clifton Powell, Adam Nelson, John Hammil, John Scott Clough; **W:** Joe Chappelle; **M:** David Williams.

Phar Lap ✶✶½ 1984 (PG) *Phar Lap: Heart of a Nation* 1984 (PG) Saga of a legendary Australian racehorse who rose from obscurity to win nearly 40 races in just three years before mysteriously dying in 1932. American version runs 10 minutes shorter than the Aussie one. **107m/C** VHS. *AU* Ron Leibman, Tom Burlinson, Judy Morris, Celia de Burgh; **D:** Simon Wincer; **W:** David Williamson; **C:** Russell Boyd.

Pharaoh ✶✶ 1966 An expensive Polish epic about the power plays of royalty in ancient Egypt. Dubbed. **125m/B** VHS. *PL* Wieslawa Mazurkiewicz, Barbara Brylska, Krystyna Mikolajewska, Jerzy Zelnick; **D:** Jerzy Kawalerowicz; **C:** Jerzy Wojcik; **M:** Adam Walacinski.

Pharmacist ✶✶½ 1932 A day in the life of a hapless druggist undone by disgruntled customers and robbers. Typical Fields effort. **19m/B** VHS, DVD. Elise Cavanna, Marjorie "Babe" Kane, W.C. Fields; Grady Sutton; **D:** Arthur Ripley.

Pharoah's Army ✶✶½ 1995 (PG-13) Five Union soldiers are foraging for food at a small Kentucky farm when one young soldier (John Abston (Cooper), is forced to stay put while he treats the wounds. The farm is home to Sarah Anders (Clarkson) and her young son (Lucas) while her husband is off fighting for the Confederates. Sarah isn't happy about the arrangement but the decent Abston, a farmer himself in peacetime, begins slowly to win her over. Their friendship, however, doesn't sit well with either his men nor Sarah's son. Fine performances in a restrained drama. **90m/C** VHS, DVD. Chris Cooper, Patricia Clarkson, Kris Kristofferson, Richard Tyson, Huckleberry Fox, Will Lucas; **D:** Robby Henson; **W:** Robby Henson; **C:** Doron Schlair.

Phase 4 ✶✶ 1974 (PG) A tale of killer ants retaliating against the humans attempting to exterminate them. **84m/C** VHS. Nigel Davenport, Michael Murphy, Lynne Frederick; **D:** Saul Bass; **C:** Dick Bush.

Phat Beach ✶✶ 1996 (R) Generic but basically harmless buddies-at-the-beach comedy with a hip-hop beat. Fast-talking, slickster Durrell (Hooks) manipulates sensitive, overweight pal Benny (Hopkins), who's real life nickname is "Huggy") into emptying his savings, "borrowing" his dad's Mercedes convertible, and taking off for some Southern California fun. Scores of scantily clad beach bunnies aren't the only ones threadbare—so's the whole premise of this flick—but that's not the point of this lighthearted romp. The likable Hopkins/Hooks comedy team is a hit with precise, lowbrow humor. Coolio, prominent in the ads, is barely window dressing with minimal screen time. Kickin' SugaT featuring The Click. **99m/C** VHS, DVD. Jermaine "Huggy" Hopkins, Brian Hooks, Jennifer Lucienne, Claudia Kaleem, Gregg D. Vance, Tommy (Tiny) Lister, Erick Fleeks, Alma Collins, Candice Merideth, Sabrina De Pina, Coolio; **D:** Doug Ellin; **W:** Doug Ellin, Brian E. O'Neal, Ben Morris; **C:** Jurgen Baum; **M:** Paul Stewart.

Phat Girlz ✶✶ 2006 (PG-13) Sassy, plus-sized comedienne Mo'Nique stars as Jazmin, a salesclerk at a store catering to the snooty skinny with designs on creating her own plus-sized fashion line. Her self-esteem a little battered, Jazmin and her equally-fleshy best friend Stacey (Johnson) are happy to indulge themselves on a Palm Springs resort, especially when they meet a couple of buff Nigerian doctors (Jean-Louis and Godfrey) who happen to like their ladies with some extra curves. Thus inspired, Jazmin decides to pursue her fashion dream. **99m/C** DVD, *US* Mo'Nique, Jimmy Jean-Louis, Godfrey, Jack Noseworthy, Kendra C. Johnson, Joyful Drake, Eric Roberts; **D:** Nnegest Likke; **W:** Nnegest Likke; **C:** Dean Lent; **M:** Gerald John L. (Ndiaga) Demps Jr.; **M:** Stephen Endelman.

Phedre ✶✶½ 1968 Jean Racine's adaptation of the Greek legend involving Phedre, Theseus, and Hippolyte. Bell is the only one worth watching in this weak and stagy picture. In French with English subtitles. **93m/C** VHS. Claude Giraud, Jacques Dacqmine, Jean Chevrier, Marie Bell; **D:** Pierre Jourdan; **C:** Michel Kelber.

Phenomenon ✶✶½ 1996 (PG) Average small town schmoe George Malley (Travolta) is turned into a genius when he's struck by a bright light on his 37th birthday. This development brings him to the attention of the scientific community and, of course, the military. The locals scorn him, thus fulfilling the Hollywood stereotype of rural folks fearing anything they don't understand. Good-natured weeper plays the Gump card (but turns too paranoid) and wins as Travolta gets to be the nice guy, while attractive Sedgwick is fine as romantic interest Lace. **123m/C** VHS, DVD. John Travolta, Robert Duvall, Kyra Sedgwick, Forest Whitaker, Richard Kiley, Brent Spiner; **D:** Jon Turteltaub; **W:** Gerald Di Pego; **C:** Phedon Papamichael; **M:** Thomas Newman.

Phffft! ✶✶½ 1954 Holliday and Lemmon are a bored couple who decide to divorce, date others, and take mambo lessons. By no stretch of plausibility, they constantly run into each other and compete in the same mambo contest. **91m/B** VHS. Judy Holliday, Jack Lemmon, Jack Carson, Kim Novak, Luella Gear, Merry Anders; **D:** Mark Robson; **W:** George Axelrod; **C:** Charles B(ryant) Lang Jr.

Philadelphia ✶✶✶½ 1993 (PG-13) AIDS goes Hollywood as hot-shot corporate attorney Andrew Beckett (Hanks) is fired because he has the disease, hires brilliant but homophobic personal injury attorney Washington as his counsel when he sues for discrimination. Boxoffice winner was criticized by some gay activists as too mainstream, which is the point. It doesn't probe deeply into the gay lifestyle, focusing instead on justice and compassion. Boasts a good script, make-up that transforms Hanks, sure direction, great soundtrack, and a strong supporting cast, but all would mean little without Hanks' superb performance. Hanks's best to date. ♫*Streets of Philadelphia.* **125m/C** VHS, DVD. Tom Hanks, Denzel Washington, Antonio Banderas, Jason Robards Jr., Joanne Woodward, Mary Steenburgen, Ron Vawter, Robert Ridgely, Obba Babatunde, Robert Castle, Daniel Chapman, Roger Corman, John Bedford Lloyd, Roberta Maxwell, Warren Miller, Anna Deavere Smith, Kathryn Witt, Andre B. Blake, Ann Dowd, Bradley Whitford, Chandra Wilson, Charles Glenn, Peter Jacobs, Kathryn Witt, Dan Olmstead, Joey Perillo, Lauren Roselli, Bill Rowe, Lisa Talerico, Daniel Drake, Tracey Walter; **Cameos:** Karen Finley, David Drake, Quentin Crisp; **D:** Jonathan Demme; **W:** Ron Nyswaner; **C:** Tak Fujimoto; **M:** Howard Shore. Oscars '93: Actor (Hanks), Song ("Streets of Philadelphia"); Berlin Intl. Film Fest. '94: Actor (Hanks); Golden Globes '94: Actor—Drama (Hanks), Song ("Streets of Philadelphia"); MTV Movie Awards '94: Male Perf. (Hanks); Blockbuster '95: Drama Actor, V. (Hanks).

The Philadelphia Experiment ✶✶½ 1984 (PG) A WWII sailor falls through a hole in time and lands in the mid-1980s, whereupon he woos a gorgeous woman. Sufficient chemistry between Pare and Allen, but PG rating is an indication of the film's less-than-graphic love scenes. **101m/C** VHS, DVD. Michael Pare, Nancy Allen, Eric Christmas, Bobby DiCicco; **D:** Stewart Raffill; **W:** Don Jakoby; **C:** Dick Bush; **M:** Kenneth Wannberg.

Philadelphia Experiment 2 ✶✶ 1993 (PG-13) Melodramatic sci-fi what-ifer has Germany winning WWII by dropping a bomb on Washington. So southern California is now one big labor camp with an evil mad scientist (Graham) and a beleaguered hero (Johnson) who must time-travel back to 1943 to prevent the Germans from dropping that bomb. **98m/C** VHS, DVD. Brad Johnson, Gerrit Graham, Marjean Holden, James Greene, Geoffrey Blake, John Christian Grass, Cyril O'Reilly; **D:** Stephen Cornwell; **W:** Kevin Rock, Nick Paine; **M:** Gerald Gouriet.

The Philadelphia Story ✶✶✶✶ 1940 A woman's plans to marry again go awry when her dashing ex-husband arrives on the scene. Matters are further complicated when a loopy reporter—assigned to spy on the nuptials—falls in love with the blushing bride. Classic comedy, with trio of Hepburn, Grant, and Stewart all serving aces. Based on the hit Broadway play by Philip Barry, and remade as the musical "High Society" in 1956 (stick to the original). Also available colorized. **112m/B** VHS, DVD. Katharine Hepburn, Cary Grant, James Stewart, Ruth Hussey, Roland Young, John Howard, John Halliday, Virginia Weidler, Henry Daniell, Hillary Brooke, Mary Nash; **D:** George Cukor; **W:** Donald Ogden Stewart; **C:** Joseph Ruttenberg; **M:** Franz Waxman. Oscars '40: Actor (Stewart), Screenplay; AFI '98: Top 100, Natl. Film Reg. '95;; N.Y. Film Critics '40: Actress (Hepburn).

Philby, Burgess and MacLean: Spy Scandal of the Century ✶✶✶ 1984 The true story of the three infamous British officials who defected to the Soviet Union in 1951, after stealing some vital British secrets for the KGB. **83m/C** VHS. *GB* Derek Jacobi, Anthony Bate, Michael Culver; **D:** Gordon Flemyng; **W:** Ian Curteis.

Phobia Woof! 1980 (R) Patients at a hospital are mysteriously being murdered. Stupid and unpleasant story that lasts too long and probably should never have started. **91m/C** VHS. *CA* Paul Michael Glaser, Susan Hogan; **D:** John Huston; **W:** Peter Bellwood, Lew Lehman, Gary Sherman, Ronald Shusett, Jimmy Sangster.

Phoenix ✶½ *Hi No Tori; The Firebird* 1978 Aging queen summons her marksman to find the Phoenix, a mythical bird that she believes will bring her eternal life. With English subtitles. **137m/C** VHS, DVD. *JP* Tomisaburo Wakayama, Ken Tanaka, Reiko Ohara, Micko Takamine, Tatsuya Nakadai; **D:** Kon Ichikawa; **W:** Shuntaro Kangawa; **C:** Kiyoshi Hasegawa; **M:** Jun Fukamachi.

Phoenix ✶✶ 1995 The Titus 4 deep-space outpost has problems when the creators of a killing machine are targeted for death by their creation, which has begun to think for itself. **94m/C** VHS, DVD. Stephen Nichols, Billy Drago, William Sanderson, Brad Dourif; **D:** Troy Cook; **W:** Troy Cook, Jimmy Lifton.

Phoenix ✶✶ 1998 (R) With a cast like this, you hope for a bit more than the usual cliched crime drama. Gambling addict/Phoenix cop Harry Collins (Liotta) is in big debt to loansharks. He decides the best way to get the money is to rob the nightclub of a local sleaze where fellow corruptible officer Mike Henshaw (LaPaglia) moonlights. But beyond the inherent stupidity of such a plan is the lurking presence of internal affairs officer Clyde Webb (Berkley). **104m/C** VHS, DVD. Ray Liotta, Anthony LaPaglia, Daniel Baldwin, Jeremy Piven, Xander Berkley, Giancarlo Esposito, Anjelica Huston, Tom Noonan, Kari Wuhrer, Brittany Murphy; **D:** Danny Cannon; **W:** Eddie Richey; **C:** James L. Carter; **M:** Graeme Revell.

The Phoenix and the Magic Carpet ✶✶½ 1995 (PG) Visiting England to settle her father's estate, Mrs. Wilson and her three children discover an egg from which a phoenix emerges. This mythical firebird proceeds to take the children on a magic adventure. Adapted from the book by Edith Nesbit. **80m/C** VHS. Dee Wallace Stone, Timothy Hegeman, Nick Klein, Laura Kamrath, Peter Ustinov; **D:** Zoran Perisic; **W:** Florence Fox; **M:** Alan Parker.

Phoenix the Warrior ✶ 1988 Sometime in the future, female savages battle each other for control of the now ravaged earth. A newcomer seeks the tribe most worthy of receiving the last man on the planet, thereby continuing the human race. **90m/C** VHS. Persis Khambatta, James H. Emery, Peggy Sands, Kathleen Kinmont; **D:** Robert Hayes; **W:** Robert Hayes.

Phone Booth ✶✶ 2002 (R) Stu (Farrell), a slimy Broadway publicist, uses a phone booth to call a would-be actress he's been stringing along. After he hangs up, the phone rings and he answers it, only to be informed that if he hangs up or runs, he'll be shot. To prove his point, the unseen sniper (voiced by Sutherland), kills a pimp who's been wanting the booth for himself. After the interesting premise and set-up, what follows is a disappointing mix of suspense thriller cliches and Schumacher's trademark visual stunts. It all adds up to nothing more than a showcase for Farrell, who does a great job as the weasel who must face and confess the fact that he hasn't been a very nice guy. Whitaker, Holmes and Mitchell are wasted in one-dimensional roles. Cohen has been trying to get the script, filmed in real time, made for about 30 years. **81m/C** VHS, DVD, Blu-ray Disc. *US* Colin Farrell, Forest Whitaker, Katie Holmes, Radha Mitchell, Kiefer Sutherland, Richard T. Jones, Keith Nobbs, John Enos, James MacDonald, Josh Pais, Paula Jai Parker, Tia Texada; **D:** Joel Schumacher; **W:** Larry Cohen; **C:** Matthew Libatique; **M:** Harry Gregson-Williams.

The Phone Call ✶✶ 1989 (R) 900-number morality tale about high-powered executive who calls phone sex line and is connected with escaped homicidal maniac who takes a toll on him and his family. **95m/C** VHS. Michael Sarrazin, Linda Smith, Ron Lea, Lisa Jakub; **D:** Allan Goldstein.

Phone Call from a Stranger ✶✶½ 1952 After a plane crash, a survivor visits the families of three of the victims whom he met during the flight. **96m/B** VHS. Bette Davis, Gary Merrill, Michael Rennie, Shelley Winters, Hugh Beaumont, Keenan Wynn, Eve Arden, Craig Stevens; **D:** Jean Negulesco; **W:** Nunnally Johnson; **C:** Milton Krasner.

Photographer ✶ 1975 (PG) A photographer turns into a murderer, showing the negative side of his personality. **94m/C** VHS. Michael Callan; **D:** William B. Hillman.

Photographing Fairies ✶✶ 1997 (R) Haunting story that's not quite as compelling as it could be. After Anne-Marie (Shelley), the bride of photographer Charles Castle (Stephens), is killed on their honeymoon, Charles shuts down emotionally, and the horrors he photographs in WWI only numb him further. After the war, Charles sets up a studio in London and becomes an expert in unmasking doctored photos. When Beatrice (Barber) shows him photos of fairies taken by her young daughters, Charles travels to her country home to expose them as fakes. Instead, Charles comes to believe that the fairies represent the "Other Side" and if he can photograph their spirit world, he can enter it and be reunited with his lost love. Based on the novel by Steve Szilagyi. The premise involving the young girls and the faked fairy photos is also the basis of the film "Fairytale: A True Story." **107m/C** VHS. *GB* Toby Stephens, Frances Barber, Ben Kingsley, Emily Woof, Philip Davis, Rachel Shelley, Edward Hardwicke, Hannah Bould, Miriam Grant, Clive Merrison; **D:** Nick Willing; **W:** Nick Willing, Chris Harrald; **C:** John de Borman; **M:** Simon Boswell.

Physical Evidence ✶✶ 1989 (R) A lawyer finds herself falling for an ex-cop turned murder suspect while she tries to defend him for a crime he doesn't remember committing. **99m/C** VHS, DVD. Burt Reynolds, Theresa Russell, Ned Beatty, Kay Lenz, Ted McGinley; **D:** Michael Crichton; **W:** Bill Phillips; **C:** John A. Alonzo; **M:** Henry Mancini.

Pi ✶✶✶ 1998 (R) Definitely a first—a religious/mathematical thriller about a man obsessed with decoding the real name of God. Max (Gullette) is a genius mathematician who believes everything can be understood in terms of numbers, so he works on his homebuilt supercomputer to unravel the stock market. Max begins to suffer hallucinations and blackouts just as his work draws the interest of both a high-powered Wall Street firm and a Hasidic cabalistic sect. **85m/B** VHS, DVD. Sean Gullette, Mark Margolis, Ben Shenkman, Pamela Hart, Stephen Perlman, Samia Shoaib, Ajay Naidu; **D:** Darren Aronofsky; **W:** Darren Aronofsky, Eric Watson, Sean Gullette; **C:** Matthew Libatique; **M:** Clint Mansell. Ind. Spirit '99: First Screenplay; Sundance '98: Director (Aronofsky).

P.I. Private Investigations ✶ 1987 (R) Corrupt, drug-dealing cops stalk another cop who can finger them. **91m/C** VHS. Clayton Rohner, Ray Sharkey, Paul LeMat,

Piaf 🐾 1981 (PG) Musical drama chronicles the life of Edith Piaf, France's legendary singer of the Roaring '20s. Her rise from the streets, bout with temporary blindness, and many self-destructive attempts at experiencing life are retold in flashbacks. 114m/C VHS. Jane Lapotaire; **Nar:** Patti LuPone.

The Pianist 🐾🐾 1991 As teenagers in Toronto, sisters Jean (Travers) and Colette (Grenon) become infatuated with Yoshi Takahashi (Okuda), a Japanese concert pianist who lived across the street. Ten years later, they have a family reunion in Vancouver and learn Yoshi is giving a concert in the city. Jean is excited to renew their ties but Colette is reluctant—buy some land that their grandfather had worked as a slave. But the past, carved into the piano's panels, has a strong hold—one that Berniece refuses to give up. Set in 1936. Adaptation by Wilson of his 1990 Pulitzer Prize-winning play. 99m/C VHS, DVD. Alfre Woodard, Charles S. Dutton, Courtney B. Vance, Carl Gordon, Tommy Hollis, Zelda Harris, Lou Myers, Rosalyn Coleman, Tommy La Fitte; **D:** Lloyd Richards; **W:** August Wilson; **M:** Stephen James Taylor, Dwight Andrews. TV

The Pianist 🐾🐾🐾½ 2002 (R) Polanski effectively turns his personal knowledge of the Holocaust into a spellbinding portrait of fellow Holocaust survivor Wladyslaw Szpilman, the renowned Polish-Jewish pianist of the title. Brody's dead-on portrayal of Szpilman, who as a gifted artist scarcely believes he will be affected by the war, effectively registers the horrifying transition from life of luxury to ending up in the Warsaw ghetto. An interesting feeling of hopefulness that lies beneath the barbarism shows Polanski's attention to the humanity and kindness that still may be found in the most savage conditions, and winningly captures the feel of one of recent history's darkest times. Based on the autobiography of Wladyslaw Szpilman. 148m/C VHS, DVD, HD DVD, FR PL GE GB Adrien Brody, Thomas Kretschmann, Frank Finlay, Maureen Lipman, Emilia Fox, Ed Stoppard, Julia Rayner, Jessica Kate Meyer, Ruth Platt; **D:** Roman Polanski; **W:** Ronald Harwood; **C:** Pawel Edelman; **M:** Wojciech Kilar. Oscars '02: Actor (Brody), Adapt. Screenplay, Director (Polanski); British Acad. '02: Director (Polanski), Film; Cannes '02: Film; Natl. Soc. Film Critics '02: Actor (Brody), Director (Polanski), Film, Screenplay.

The Piano 🐾🐾🐾½ 1993 (R) In the 1850s, Ada (Hunter), a mute Scottish widow with a young daughter, agrees to an arranged marriage with Stewart (Neill), a colonial landowner in New Zealand. The way she expresses her feelings is by playing her cherished piano, left behind on the beach by her new husband. Another settier, George (Keitel), buys it, arranges for lessons with Ada, and soon the duo begin a grand passion leading to a cruelly calculated revenge. Fiercely poetic and well acted (with Keitel in a notably romantic role), though the film may be too dark and intense for some. Fine original score with Hunter doing her own piano playing. 120m/C VHS, DVD, AU Holly Hunter, Harvey Keitel, Sam Neill, Anna Paquin, Kerry Walker, Genevieve Lemon; **D:** Jane Campion; **W:** Jane Campion; **C:** Stuart Dryburgh; **M:** Michael Nyman. Oscars '93: Actress (Hunter), Orig. Screenplay, Support. Actress (Paquin); Australian Film Inst. '93: Actor, Actress (Hunter), Cinematog., Costume Des., Director (Campion), Film, Film Editing, Screenplay, Sound, Score; British Acad. '93: Actress (Hunter); Cannes '93: Actress (Hunter), Film; Golden Globes '94: Actress—Drama (Hunter), Ind. Spirit '94: Foreign Film; L.A. Film Critics '93: Actress (Hunter), Director (Campion), Screenplay; Natl. Bd. of Review '93: Actress (Hunter); N.Y. Film Critics '93: Actress (Hunter), Cinematog., Director (Campion), Screenplay; Natl. Soc. Film Critics '93: Actress (Hunter), Screenplay; Writers Guild '93: Orig. Screenplay.

A Piano for Mrs. Cimino 🐾🐾½ 1982 Declared senile and incompetent, a widowed woman fights for control of her own life. Good script helps this made for TV soaper. 100m/C VHS. Bette Davis, Keenan Wynn, Alexa Kenn, Penny Fuller, Christopher Guest, George Hearn; **D:** George Schaefer. TV

The Pick-Up Artist 🐾½ 1987 The adventures of a compulsive Don Juan who finds he genuinely loves the daughter of an alcoholic who's in debt

to the mob. Standard story with no surprises. **Pinball Pick-Up** 1979 (R) Two suburban boys cruise their town after school lets out, chasing a pair of voluptuous sisters. 90m/C VHS, DVD. C: Michael Zelniker, Carl Marotte; **D:** George Mihalka.

Pick a Card 🐾🐾 Alula Express 1997 (PG-13) David (Hadar) is an unemployed mechanic who dreams of becoming a magician while his girlfriend Batia (Zakheim) just wants to get married. So how can they reconcile their reality with their reality? 94m/C VHS, DVD. IS Zvika Hadar, Esti Zakheim, Ayeth Moskona, Orli Perl, Ze Julie Shites; **W:** Amit Leor, **C:** Itzik Portal; **M:** Yuval Shafrir.

Pick a Star 🐾🐾 Movie Struck 1937 Lawrence is a small-town girl who wins a contest and is sent to Hollywood. Only no one pays any attention to her except for publicity man Haley, who arranges her screen test. Naturally, she knocks the studio bosses for a loop and becomes a star. Laurel & Hardy are featured in a couple of comedy segments showing the newcomer some backstage silliness and movie business on the set of a Western with a film-ing (with Finlayson, better known as a director, cast as the duo's director). Pick Novak provides a couple pointers too. Lavish Hollywood adaptation of the William Inge play, including the popular tune "Moonglow/Theme from Picnic." Remade for TV in 2000 with Josh Brolin in the Holden role. 113m/C VHS, DVD. Willem Holden, Kim Novak, Rosalind Russell, Susan Strasberg, Arthur O'Connell, Cliff Robertson, Betty Field, Verna Felton, Reta Shaw, Nick Adams, Phyllis New-

Picasso Trigger 🐾🐾 1989 (R) An American spy tries to catch an elusive murderer. The sequel to "Hard Ticket to Hawaii" and "Malibu Express." 99m/C VHS, DVD. Steve Bond, Dona Speir, John Aprea, Hope Marie Carlton, Guich Koock, Roberta Vasquez, Bruce Penhall, Harold Diamond, Rodrigo Obregon; **D:** Andy Sidaris; **W:** Andy Sidaris; **C:** Howard Wexler. **M:** Gary Stockdale.

Piano Tuner of Earthquakes 🐾🐾 L'Accordeur de tremblements de terre 2005 Appropriately bizarre but unfortunately stale experimental film from the Quay brothers has beautiful operatic star Malvina (Casar) killed before her wedding by the evil Cr. Droz (John), who then steals her corpse to revive it. He then hires piano tuner Felisberto (Sasachu) to write and choreograph an opera depicting the events. Since he resembles her former love, Malvina falls in love with him and he plots their escape. Interesting staging and visuals can't make up for the many weaknesses. 99m/C DVD, FR GB GE Amira Casar, Gottfried John, Assumpta Serna, Cesar Saracuf; **D:** Stephen Quay, Timothy Quay; **C:** Nicholas D. Knowland; **M:** Christopher Slask.

Pickpocket 🐾🐾🐾½ 1959 Slow moving, documentary-like account of a petty thief's existence as a moral tragedy inspired by 'Crime and Punishment.' Ending is particularly moving. Classic filmmaking from Bresson, France's master of austerity. In French with English subtitles. 75m/B VHS, DVD. FR Martin LaSalle, Marika Green, Pierre Leymarie, Pierre Etaix, Jean Pelegri, Dolly Scal; **D:** Robert Bresson; **W:** Robert Bresson; **C:** Leonce-Henri Burel.

Pickup on South Street 🐾🐾🐾 1953 Petty thief Widmark lifts woman's wallet only to find it contains top secret Communist micro-film for which pinko agents will stop at nothing to get back. Intriguing look at the politics of the day. The creme of "B" movies. 80m/B VHS. Richard Widmark, Jean Peters, Thelma Ritter, Murvyn Vye, Richard Kiley, Milburn Stone; **D:** Samuel Fuller; **W:** Samuel Fuller; **C:** Joe MacDonald; **M:** Leigh Harline.

The Pickwick Papers 🐾🐾½ 1954 Comedy based on the Dickens classic wherein Mrs. Bardell sues the Pickwick Club for breach of promise. 109m/B VHS. GB James Hayter, James Donald, Nigel Patrick, Hermione Gingold, Hermione Baddeley, Kathleen Harrison; **D:** Noel Langley.

Picnic 🐾🐾🐾½ 1955 Drifter Hal Carter (Holden) arrives in a small town and immediately wins the love of his friend's girl, Madge (Novak). The other women in town seem interested too. Strong, romantic work, with Holden excelling in the lead.

The Piano Lesson 🐾🐾🐾 1994 (PG) The prized heirloom of the Charles family is an 80-year-old, ornately carved upright piano, jealously guarded by widowed Berniece Woodard, and housed in the Pittsburgh home of Uncle Doaker (Gordon). When Berniece's brother Willie Boy (Dutton) visits from Mississippi, the persuade her to sell the piano in order to

The Piano Teacher 🐾🐾 La Pianiste 2001 Middle-aged Erika (Huppert) teaches piano at the Vienna Conservatory where she is demanding—if not cruel—to her students. Erika lives with her controlling mother (Girardot) and spends her off hours, mutilating herself, watching porn, and engaging in other bizarre behavior. Which doesn't improve when she agrees to a questionable sexual relationship (on her masochistic terms) with hot new student Walter (Magimel). Not for the faint-hearted; adapted from the 1983 novel by Elfriede Jelinek. French with subtitles. 130m/C VHS, DVD, FR FR Isabelle Huppert, Benoit Magimel, Annie Girardot, Udo Samel, Susanne Lothar, Anna Sigalevitch; **D:** Michael Haneke; **W:** Michael Haneke; **C:** Christian Berger. Cannes '01: Actor (Magimel), Grand Jury Prize.

The Pickle 🐾 1993 (R) Self-indulgent comedy about a middle class, Aiello stars as a middle-aged manic-depressive film director certain that his new film is going to be an abysmal flop (as have all his recent pictures). He seeks comfort and reassurance from various ex-wives, children, lovers, and others, though he abuses them all. This dispirited tale also shows clips of the director's dreadful film about children who launch a giant pickle into space. It couldn't possibly be worse than what Mazursky actually put up on the screen. 103m/C VHS, DVD. Danny Aiello, Dyan Cannon, Woody Allen, David Schwimmer, Maria Grazia Cucinotta, Kiefer Sutherland, Sharon Stone, Alfonso Arau, Richard "Cheech" Marin, Lou Diamond Phillips, Danny De La Paz, Andy Dick, Fran Drescher, Joseph Gordon-Levitt, Elliott Gould, Eddie Griffin, Lupe Ontiveros, Di Alfonso Arau; **W:** Bill Wilson; **C:** Vittorio Storaro; **M:** Ruy Folguera.

Pick-Up Summer 🐾 Pinball Summer; Pinball Pick-Up 1979 (R) Two suburban boys cruise their town after school lets out, chasing a pair of voluptuous sisters. 81m/C VHS, DVD. Robert Downey Jr., Molly Ringwald, Dennis Hopper, Harvey Keitel, Danny Aiello, Vanessa Lisymer, Williams, Robert Towne, Mildred Dunnock, Lorraine Bracco, Joe Spinell, Victoria Jackson, Polly Draper, Brian Hattie; **D:** James Toback; **W:** James Toback; **C:** Gordon Willis; **M:** Georges Delerue.

Picking Up the Pieces 🐾🐾 1999 (R) Tex (Allen) is a kosher cowboy in a New Mexico town, who's also a butcher. When he cuts off the hand of his adulterous wife (Ullman)—to the local church where it becomes a shrine for pilgrims seeking miracle cures. Meanwhile, Tex just wants to rebury the evidence. If you can buy Allen as any kind of cowboy, you can buy the rest of this would-be comedy. 95m/C VHS, DVD. Woody Allen, David Schwimmer, Maria Grazia Cucinotta, Kiefer Sutherland, Sharon Stone, Alfonso Arau, Richard "Cheech" Marin, Lou Diamond Phillips, Danny De La Paz, Andy Dick, Fran Drescher, Joseph Gordon-Levitt, Elliott Gould, Eddie Griffin, Lupe Ontiveros; **D:** Alfonso Arau; **W:** Bill Wilson; **C:** Vittorio Storaro; **M:** Ruy Folguera.

Picture Bride 🐾🐾 1994 (PG-13) Le De-jeuner sur l'herbe; Lunch on the Grass strange, whimsical flop here's through scenes at Berniece refuses to give up. Japanese immigrant saga finds 17-year-old Japanese Riyo (Kudoh) setting off for Hawaii in 1918 as a "picture bride" to a husband she's never met but with whom she's exchanged photos (hence the title). Riyo's shocked to discover her intended, sugarcane worker Matsuji (Takayama), has deceived her with an out-of-date picture and is at least 25 years older than she. She refuses to consummate the marriage and goes to work in the fields, intending to earn money for her passage home but of course things don't work out quite as she intends. Japanese with subtitles. 95m/C VHS, DVD. JP Yoko Sugi, Youki Kudoh, Akira Takayama, Tamlyn Tomita, Cary-Hiroyuki Tagawa; **D:** Kayo Hatta; **W:** Kayo Hatta, Mari Hatta, Diane Mark; **C:** Claudio Rocha; **M:** Cliff Eidelman. Sundance '95: Aud. Award.

Picture Claire 🐾 2001 (R) Lewis is miscast as the independent French-speaking Claire, who leaves Montreal for Toronto to find a one-time boyfriend. Instead, Claire gets in the middle of a diamond heist between shady lady Lily (Germann), sleazy Eddie (Rourke) and sadistic thug Laramie (Rennie)—all because she can't speak English. Bleech, English and Juliette Lewis, Callum Keith Rennie, Gina Gershon, Mickey Rourke; **D:** Bruce McDonald; **W:** Semi Chellas; **C:** Miroslaw Baszak; **M:** Paul Haslinger.

Picture Mommy Dead 🐾🐾 1966 Well acted melodrama involving a scheming shrew who struggles to drive her mentally disturbed stepdaughter insane for the sake of cold, hard cash. 88m/C VHS. Don Ameche, Zsa Zsa Gabor, Martha Hyer, Susan Gordon; **D:** Bert I. Gordon; **C:** Ellsworth Fredericks.

Picture of Dorian Gray 🐾🐾🐾 1974 Another version of Wilde's renowned novel about a man who retains his youthful visage while his portrait shows the physical ravages of aging. Davenport is particularly appealing in the lead. 130m/C VHS, DVD. Shane Briant, Nigel Davenport, Charles Aidman, Fionnula Flanagan, Linda Kelsey, Vanessa Howard; **D:** Glenn Jordan. TV

Picture Perfect 🐾🐾½ 1996 (PG-13) While trying to impress her new boss, ad exec Kate (Aniston) claims Nick (Mohr), the man standing with her in a photo, is her fiance. Unfortunately, the boss now wants to meet the guy (a strange picture at Hanging Rock 🐾🐾🐾 who was at the same party) anc she must find him and get him to play along. The story's cliched, but Aniston's appeal-man, Raymond Bailey; **D:** Joshua Logan; **W:** Daniel Taradash; **C:** James Wong Howe; **M:** George Duning. Oscars '55: Art Dir./Set Decor., Color, Film Editing; Golden Globes '56: Director (Logan).

Picnic at Hanging Rock 🐾🐾🐾 1975 (PG) School outing in 1900 into a mountainous region ends tragically when three girls disappear. Eerie film is strong on atmosphere, as befits mood master Weir. Lambert is extremely photogenic—gorgeously beautiful when photographed on location. From the novel by Joan Lindsey. 110m/C VHS, DVD, AU Margaret Nelson, Rachel Roberts, Dominic Guard, Helen Morse, Jacki Weaver, Vivean Gray, Anne Louise Lambert; **D:** Peter Weir; **W:** Cliff Green; **C:** Russell Boyd; **M:** Bruce Smeaton.

Picnic on the Grass 🐾🐾 Le De-jeuner sur l'herbe; Lunch on the Grass 1959 A strange, whimsical fantasy heavily evocative of the director's Impressionist roots; a science-minded candidate for the president of Europe throws a picnic as public example of his earthiness, and falls in love with a peasant girl. In French with English subtitles. 92m/C VHS, FR Paul Meurisse, Catherine Rouvel, Fernand Sardou, Jacqueline Morane, Jean-Pierre Granval; **D:** Jean Renoir.

ing screen presence perks things up a bit. **100m/C VHS, DVD.** Jennifer Aniston, Jay Mohr, Kevin Bacon, Illeana Douglas, Olympia Dukakis, Kevin Dunn, Faith Prince, Anne Twomey; **D:** Glenn Gordon Caron; **W:** Glenn Gordon Caron; **C:** Paul Sarossy; **M:** Carter Burwell.

Picture Snatcher ♪♪ 1933 Former gangster Danny Kean (Cagney) tries to make himself over as a photographer for a tabloid, using his criminal know-how to get scoops. But his sometimes underhanded ways cause problems when Danny romances Patricia (Ellis), who happens to be the daughter of the cop (O'Connor) who once put Danny behind bars. **76m/B DVD.** James Cagney, Patricia Ellis, Ralph Bellamy, Alice White, Ralf Harolde, Robert Emmett O'Connor, Ralf Harolde; **D:** Lloyd Bacon; **W:** P.J. Wolfson, Allen Rivkin; **C:** Sol Polito.

Picture Windows ♪♪ 1995 (R) Three short cable movies inspired by works of art. "Lightning," based on Frederic Remington sketches and a Zane Grey short story, finds western codger Keith striking gold with the help of his trusty mule. A David Hockney painting suggested "Armed Response," which features a confrontation between a wealthy lawyer (Loggia) and a burglar (Zahn). And an anonymous 16th-century canvas "Two Nudes Bathing" is given an imaginative history. **95m/C VHS, DVD.** Brian Keith, Robert Loggia, Steve Zahn, Charley Boorman; **D:** Joe Dante, Bob Rafelson, John Boorman. **CABLE**

Pictures ♪♪½ 198? The silent-film era in England is spoofed in this look at ambitious waitress Ruby Sears, who's determined to be a film star, and writer Bill Trench, who winds up a novice screenwriter. Bill's first movie script is based on Ruby's life and she desperately wants to star in the production, if only she can convince the producer and the drunken male lead that she has the talent. **208m/C VHS. GB** Wendy Morgan, Peter McEnery, Harry Towb, Anton Rodgers, Annette Badland, Malcom Jamieson, Marc Smith; **W:** Roy Clarke. **TV**

Pictures of Hollis Woods ♪♪½ 2007 Twelve-year-old Hollis Woods (Ferland) was found abandoned as a baby and has spent her life in various foster homes. Her dedicated social worker Edna (Woodard) had hoped that Hollis' last family, the Reagans, would be permanent but an incident put Hollis on the move again and into the care of retired schoolteacher Josie (Spacek). Only Josie's forgetfulness turns out to be the early stages of Alzheimer's—a fact Hollis tries to cover up so she won't be moved again. Adapted from Patricia Reilly Giff's novel. **110m/C DVD.** Jodelle Ferland, Sissy Spacek, Alfre Woodard, Judith Ivey, James Tupper, Julie Ann Emery, Ridge Canipe; **D:** Tony Bill; **W:** Ann Peacock, Daniel Petrie Jr.; **C:** Camille Thomasson; **M:** Paul Sarossy, Van Dyke Parks. **TV**

Pie in the Sky ♪♪½ 1995 (R) Charles Dunlap (Charles) is a traffic geek, fascinated by the flow of cars on the nearby freeway, which hero in this stunning, occasionally confusing classic from iconoclast Godard. A hallmark in 1960s improvisational porter Alan Davenport (Goodman), with whom he eventually gets a job in L.A. Charles' other interest is dancer/waitress Amy (Heche)—their first attempt at romance goes awry but persistence pays off. Optimistic and corny. **94m/C VHS, DVD.** Josh Charles, Anne Heche, John Goodman, Christine Lahti, Peter Riegert, Christine Ebersole, Wil Wheaton, Bob Balaban, Dey Young; **C:** Bernd Heinl; **M:** Michael Covertino.

Piece of Cake ♪♪½ 1988 Adaptation of the Derek Robinson novel follows the flyboys of the RAF Hornet Squadron during the early years of WWII. They have trouble taking the war seriously but tangles with the Luftwaffe and increasing casualties put a strain on everyone. Great aerial photography and the British planes are vintage Spitfires not repros. Made for British TV miniseries on six cassettes. **312m/C VHS, DVD. GB** Tom Burlinson, Tim Woodward, Boyd Gaines, Nathaniel Parker, Neil Dudgeon, David Horovitch, Richard Hope, Jeremy Northam, Michael Elwyn, Corinne Dacla, Helena Michell; **D:** Ian Toynton; **W:** Leon Griffiths; **C:** Peter Jessop; **M:** Peter Martin. **TV**

in everyone around. Violent and sordid melodrama. French with subtitles. **93m/C VHS, DVD. FR** Francis Renaud, Vera Briole, Bianca Li, Raymond Gil, Younesse Boudache, Philippe Ambrosini, Jean-Claude Grenier; **D:** Karim Dridi; **W:** Karim Dridi; **C:** John Mathieson.

A Piece of Pleasure ♪♪♪ Un *Partie de Plaisir* 1974 Marriage declines due to a domineering husband in this familiar domestic study from French master Chabrol. Good, but not among the director's best efforts. In French with English subtitles. **100m/C VHS, DVD. FR** Paul Gegauff, Danielle Gegauff, Clemence Gegauff, Paula Moore, Michel Valette, Cecile Vassort; **D:** Claude Chabrol; **W:** Paul Gegauff; **C:** Jean Rabier; **M:** Pierre Jansen.

Piece of the Action ♪♪ 1977 (PG) An ex-cop beats two con men at their own game when he convinces them to work for a Chicago community center. **135m/C VHS, DVD.** Sidney Poitier, Bill Cosby, James Earl Jones, Denise Nicholas, Hope Clarke, Tracy Reed, Titos Vandis, Janet DuBois; **D:** Sidney Poitier; **M:** Curtis Mayfield.

Pieces woof! 1983 (R) Chain-saw wielding madman roams a college campus in search of human parts for a ghastly jigsaw puzzle. Gory and loathsome. **90m/C VHS, DVD. IT SP** Christopher George, Lynda Day George, Paul Smith; **D:** J(uan) Piquer Simon.

Pieces of April ♪♪♪½ 2003 (PG-13) Delightfully dysfunctional family meets for a chaotic Thanksgiving when tattooed New Yorker April (Holmes) has her suburban family join her for holiday dinner. The family trip to NYC is rife with humorous dramas and sidetracks involving roadkill and Mom bogarting little bro's stash. Meanwhile in the city, domestically-challenged April's oven breaks down while seemingly nice new boyfriend Bobby's behavior hints that something dark is afoot. Despite a misleading and slightly disturbing subplot involving Bobby (Luke) and a somewhat hasty ending, film is entertaining and original. Completed in three weeks on a limited budget ($200,000) with surprisingly slick digital camerawork. **81m/ C VHS, DVD. US** Katie Holmes, Patricia Clarkson, Oliver Platt, Derek Luke, Alison Pill, Alice Drummond, Sean P. Hayes, John Gallagher Jr., Sisqo, Isiah Whitlock Jr., Lillias White; **D:** Peter Hedges; **W:** Peter Hedges; **C:** Tami Reiker; **M:** Stephin Merritt. Nat'l. Bd. of Review '03: Support. Actress (Clarkson); Nat'l. Soc. Film Critics '03: Support. Actress (Clarkson).

The Pied Piper of Hamelin ♪♪ 1957
The evergreen classic of the magical piper who rids a village of rats and then disappears with the village children into a mountain when the townspeople fail to keep a promise. **90m/C VHS, DVD.** Van Johnson, Claude Rains, Jim Backus, Kay Starr, Lori Nelson; **D:** Bretaigne Windust. **CABLE**

The Pied Piper of Hamelin ♪♪ 1984
From Shelley Duvall's "Faerie Tale Theatre" comes the story of how a man with a magic flute charmed the rats out of Hamelin. **60m/C VHS, DVD.** Eric Idle; **D:** Nicholas Meyer.

Pier 23 ♪♪ 1951 A private eye is hired to bring a lawless ex-convict to a priest's custody, but gets an imposter instead. A web of intrigue follows. **57m/B VHS.** Hugh Beaumont, Ann Savage, David Bruce, Raymond Greenleaf, Joi Lansing, Edward Brophy, Richard Travis, Peter Mamakos, Mike Mazurki, Margia Dean, Harry Hayden, Richard Monahan; **D:** William Berke; **W:** Julian Harmon, Herbert Margolis, Louis Morheim; **C:** Jack Greenhalgh; **M:** Bert Shefter.

Pierrot le Fou ♪♪♪½ 1965 A woman fleeing a gangster joins a man leaving his wife in this stunning, occasionally confusing classic from iconoclast Godard. A hallmark in 1960s improvisational filmmaking, with rugged Belmondo and always-photogenic Karina effortlessly excelling in leads. In French with English subtitles. **110m/C VHS, DVD. FR IT** Samuel Fuller, Jean-Pierre Leaud, Jean-Paul Belmondo, Anna Karina, Dirk Sanders; **D:** Jean-Luc Godard; **W:** Jean-Luc Godard; **C:** Raoul Coutard; **M:** Antoine Duhamel.

Pigalle ♪♪ 1995 Dridi's feature debut focuses on the red light district of Paris and the company of various lowlifes, including pickpocket Fifi (Renaud), who's involved with both stripper Vera (Brile) and transvestite hooker Divine (Li). There's also an increasingly violent turf war between a couple of drug dealers that takes

Piglet's Big Movie ♪♪½ 2003 (G) An adaptation of three stories by A.A. Milne. Piglet (voiced by Fielder) is a very small animal and something of a fraidy pig. He's feeling too small to be of help to his friends and decides to take a little hike into the Hundred Acre Woods when he's ignored once again. However, when best bud Pooh (Cummings) thinks Piglet is missing, he organizes a search party and everyone realizes how important Piglet is to them. Best for the wee ones with its gentle lessons on friendship, even if it can't live up to the original shorts of the '60s and early '70s. **75m/C VHS, DVD. US D:** Francis Glebas; **W:** Brian Hohlfeld; **M:** Carly Simon, Carl Johnson, Carly Simon; **V:** John Fiedler, Jim (Jonah) Cummings, Kath Soucie, Nikita Hopkins, Andre Stojka, Thomas Wheatley, Peter Cullen, Ken Sansom.

Pigs ♪½ *Daddy's Deadly Darling; The Killers* 1973 Young woman who has escaped from a mental hospital teams up with an evil old man to go on a murdering spree. They complement each other beautifully. She kills them and he disposes of the bodies by making pig slop out of them. **90m/C VHS, DVD.** Toni Lawrence, Marc Lawrence, Jesse Vint, Katharine Ross; **D:** Marc Lawrence; **M:** Charles Bernstein.

Pigs ♪♪ 2007 In this lame oink-fest about young men behaving, well, like pigs, Miles (Brown) takes a bet from his best buddy Cleaver (Lucio) that he can have sex with 26 girls, alphabetically A-Z. Only he doesn't intend to fall for Miss X—Gaby Xeropolus (Marden). Tries to go from wacky sex romp to heartfelt romance but can't really pull it off. **85m/C DVD.** Chris Elliott, Jefferson Brown, Melanie Marden, Darryn Lucio; **D:** Karl DiPelino; **W:** Karl DiPelino, Chris Ragaonet; **C:** Gurjeet Mann; **M:** John Jamieson. **VIDEO**

A Pig's Tale ♪♪½ *Summer Camp* 1994 (PG) Rich kids rule at Kamp Kipperman but one 13-year-old forms the Pig Pen club and a college goes to great lengths to give his team a chance by recruiting a famboy (Erwin) who's a natural phenom. (Garland's co-boy's singing sister.) ♪Balboa; The Texas Tornado; It's Love I'm After; You're Simply Terrific; You Do the Darndest Things, Baby; T.S.U. Alma Mater; Hold That Bulldog; Down with Everything; We'd Rather Be In College. **95m/B VHS, DVD.** Jack Haley, Patsy Kelly, Stuart Erwin, Judy Garland, Johnny Downs, Betty Grable, Arline Judge, Tony Martin, Fred Kohler Jr., Elisha Cook Jr.; **D:** David Butler; **W:** Harry Tugend, Jack Yellen; **C:** Arthur C. Miller.

Pilgrim, Farewell ♪♪ 1982 Dramatic story about a dying woman who needs to tie up loose ends before her death and goes looking for her estranged teenage daughter. Made for PBS's "American Playhouse." **110m/C VHS.** Elizabeth Huddle, Christopher Lloyd, Laurie Pranage, Lesley Paxton, Shelley Wyant, Robert Brown; **D:** Michael Roemer. **TV**

Pilgrimage ♪♪ 1933 Overbearing Hannah Jessop (Crosman) is horrified when her son Jim (Foster) takes up with the unsuitable Mary (Nixon), so she sends him off to fight in WWI. Jim doesn't know Mary is pregnant and after he is killed, Hannah refuses to have anything to do with her grandson. It's not until she takes a trip to France to visit her son's grave that she realizes her heartlessness and makes amends. Crosman was a grand dame of the theater and well-suited to her part. **96m/B DVD.** Henrietta Crosman, Marion (Marian) Nixon, Norman Foster, Heather Angel, Charley Grapewin, Lucille La Verne, Maurice Murphy, Hed-

da Hopper; **D:** John Ford; **W:** Philip Klein, Barry Connors, Dudley Nichols; **C:** George Schneiderman; **M:** R. H. Bassett.

The Pillow Book ♪♪ 1995 (NC-17) Greenaway's usual chilliness gives way to some true erotic heat that still keeps to arcane subjects, violence, and dazzling visuals. Japanese model Nagiko (Wu) longs for the childhood rituals enacted by her calligrapher father (Ogata) as he literally painted birthday greetings on her face with brush and ink. As an adult, Nagiko searches out calligrapher/lovers willing to use her body as their paper but she's still unsatisfied until she meets bisexual Englishman Jerome (McGregor) and he insists Nagiko write on him. When Nagiko learns Jerome's male lover is the publisher (Oida) who was once involved with her father, her jealousy triggers tragic consequences. Title refers to the 10th century diary "The Pillow Book of Sei Shonagon." Some subtitled Japanese dialogue. **126m/ C VHS, DVD. NL FR GB** Vivian Wu, Ewan McGregor, Yoshi Oida, Ken Ogata, Hideko Yoshida, Judy Ongg, Ken Mitsuishi, Yutaka Honda, Ronald Guttman; **D:** Peter Greenaway; **W:** Peter Greenaway; **C:** Sacha Vierny.

Pillow Talk ♪♪♪½ 1959 Sex comedy in which a man woos a woman who loathes him. By the way, they share the same telephone party line. Narrative provides minimal indication of the film's strengths, which are many. Classic '50s comedy with masters Day and Hudson exhibiting considerable rapport, even when fighting. Lighthearted, constantly funny. **102m/C VHS, DVD.** Rock Hudson, Doris Day, Tony Randall, Thelma Ritter, Nick Adams, Lee Patrick; **D:** Michael Gordon; **W:** Maurice Richlin, Stanley Shapiro; **C:** Arthur E. Arling; **M:** Frank DeVol. Oscars '59: Story & Screenplay.

The Pilot's Wife ♪♪ 2001 (PG-13) *Mister V* Kathryn Lyons (Lahti) learns that her husband Jack (Heard), a commercial airline pilot, has died in a crash over Ireland. She's angry when she discovers investigators think he caused the crash and bewildered when she finds out Jack led a double life. Accompanied by union rep Robert Hart (Scott), Kathryn heads to England and Ireland to get some answers. Shreve co-scripted the teleplay from her own novel. **89m/C VHS, DVD.** Christine Lahti, Campbell Scott, John Heard, Alison Pill, Nigel Bennett; **D:** Robert Markowitz; **W:** Anita Shreve, Christine Berardo; **C:** Rudolf Blahacek; **M:** Lee Holdridge. **TV**

Pimpernel Smith ♪♪½ 1942 Seemingly scatterbrained archaeology professor is actually a dashing agent rescuing refugees from evil Nazis in WWII France. Howard is well cast, but the film is somewhat predictable, and it's too long. Wonderful scene, though, in which a Nazi officer champions Shakespeare as Aryan. **121m/B VHS. GB** Leslie Howard, Mary Morris, Francis L. Sullivan, David Tomlinson; **D:** Leslie Howard.

Pin... ♪♪½ 1988 (R) A boy's imaginary friend assists in the slaying of various enemies. Horror effort could be worse. **103m/C VHS, DVD.** Cynthia (Cyndy, Cindy) Preston, David Hewlett, Terry O'Quinn, Bronwen Mantel, Helene Udy, Patricia Collins, Steven Bednarski, Katie Shingler, Jacob Tierney, Michelle Anderson; **D:** Sandor Stern; **W:** Sandor Stern; **C:** Guy Defaux.

Pin Down Girls ♪♪ 1951 *Racket Girls; Pin Down Girl* 1951 Great schlock about girl wrestlers. **81m/B VHS, DVD.** Clara Mortensen, Rita Martinez, Peaches Page, Timothy Farrell; **D:** Robert Derteno; **W:** Robert Derteno; **C:** William C. Thompson.

Pin-Up Girl ♪♪ 1944 Grable plays a secretary who becomes an overnight sensation during WWII. Loosely based on her famous pinup poster that was so popular at the time, the movie doesn't even come close to being as successful. The songs aren't particularly memorable, although Charlie Spivak and his Orchestra perform. ♪Once Too Often; Yankee Doodle Dandy; I'll Be Marching to a Love Song; You're Very Merry Widow; Time Alone Will Tell; Don't Carry Tales Out of School; Red Robins, Bob Whites and Blue Birds. **83m/C VHS, DVD.** Betty Grable, Martha Raye, Jon Har-

Pineapple Express 🎬 2008 (R) Stoner Dale Denton (Rogen) visits his dealer Saul Silver (Franco) to purchase a rare new strain of weed called Pineapple Express. While Dale is toking in his car, he happens to witness a murder committed by a drug lord (Cole) and a crooked cop (Perez), is seen by the baddies, and then drops his doobie. Dale goes to Saul and learns that the rare weed can be traced back to them so the incoherent duo go on the lam. Not yet reviewed. 7min/C VHS, DVD. Gary Cole, Rosie Perez, Amber Heard, James Remar, Bill Hader, Danny McBride, Nora Dunn; D: David Gordon Green; W: Evan Goldberg; C: Tim Orr.

Ping! 🎬🎬 1999 (PG) Silly family comedy that gets an extra half-bone from the Hound for being about a dog—in this case, smart little chihuahua Ping who's been rescued from the pound by Ethel. And the little guard dog is not about to let a couple of inept burglars (Reinhold, Howard) cause problems on his new turf. 100m/C VHS, DVD. Robert Lee, Lam Fung, Victor Kan, Ric Young; D: Po-Chih Leung.

Pink Cadillac 🎬🎬 1/2 1989 (PG-13) A grizzled, middle-aged bondsman is on the road, tracking down bail-jumping crooks. He helps the wife and baby of his latest target escape from her husband's more evil associates. Eastwood's performance is good and fun to watch, in this otherwise lightweight film. 121m/C VHS, DVD. Clint Eastwood, Bernadette Peters, Timothy Carhart, Michael Des Barres, William Hickey, John Dennis Johnston, Geoffrey Lewis, Jim Carrey, Tiffany Gail Robinson, Angela Louise Robinson; D: Buddy Van Horn; M: Steve Dorff.

The Pink Chiquitas 🎬 1986 (PG-13) Sci-fi spoof about a detective battling a mob of meteorite-traveling Amazons. 85m/C VHS, DVD. Frank Stallone, Elizabeth Edwards, Claudia Udy; D: Anthony Currie.

Pink Flamingos 🎬🎬 1972 (NC-17) Divine, the dainty 300-pound transvestite, faces the biggest challenge of his/her career when he/she competes for the title of World's Filthiest Person. Tasteless, crude, and hysterical film; this one earned Waters its title as "Prince of Puke." If there are any doubts about this honor—or Divine's rep—watch through to the end to catch Divine chewing real dog excrement. It all the time wearing a you-know-what-eating grin. 95m/C VHS, DVD. Divine, David Lochary, Mary Vivian Pearce, Cookie Mueller, Mink Stole, Edith Massey, Danny Mills; D: John Waters; W: John Waters.

Pink Floyd: The Wall 🎬🎬 1/2 1982 (R) Film version of Pink Floyd's 1979 LP "The Wall." A surreal, impressionistic tour-de-force about a boy who grows up

---

Pinero 🎬🎬 2001 (R) Charge of pace role for Bratt, best known for clean-cut characters on the right side of the law. Not so here as he plays a dynamic actor/Miguel Pinero, Bratt gives a dynamic portrayal as the street smart hustler/heroin addict who died at age 40 in 1988. An ex-con who did time at Sing-Sing, Pinero put his experience to use with the "Short Eyes," and was one of the founders of the Nuyorican Cafe. Film is non-chronological, which can get confusing, and few of the secondary characters have enough screen time to make strong impressions. 103m/C VHS, DVD. Benjamin Bratt, Talisa Soto, Giancarlo Esposito, Rita Moreno, Mandy Patinkin, Michael Irby, Michael Wright, Nelson Vasquez, Jaime Sanchez, Rome Neal; D: Leon Ichaso; W: Leon Ichaso; C: Claudio Chea.

Ping Pong 🎬🎬 1/2 1987 (PG) A Chinese patriarch drops dead in London's Chinatown, leaving a young law student to disentangle his will, and get mixed up with his cross-cultured family. 100m/C VHS. David Yip, Lucy Sheen, Robert Lee, Lam Fung.

Pink Motel WOOF! Motel 1982 (R) Several people spend a night meant to be romantic at a pink stucco motel which caters to couples. Comic stiff with Diller and Pickens as the owners of said pink motel. 90m/C VHS. Phyllis Diller, Slim Pickens, Terri Berland, Squire Fridell; D: Mike MacFarlane.

Pink Nights 🎬 1987 (PG) A high school nebbish is suddenly pursued by three beautiful girls, and his life gets turned upside-down. 87m/C VHS, Shaun Aitcovic Michaels; D: Philip Koch.

The Pink Panther 🎬🎬🎬 1964 Bumbling, disaster-prone inspector invades a Swiss ski resort and becomes obsessed with capturing a jewel thief hoping to lift the legendary "Pink Panther" diamond. Said thief is also the inspector's wife's lover, though the inspector doesn't know it. Slick slapstick succeeds on strength of Sellers' classic portrayal of Clouseau, who accidentally destroys everything in his path while speaking in a funny French accent. Followed by "A Shot in the Dark," "Inspector Clouseau" (without Sellers), "The Return of the Pink Panther," "The Pink Panther Strikes Again," "Revenge of the Pink Panther," "Trail of the Pink Panther," "Curse of the Pink Panther." Memorable theme supplied by Mancini. 113m/C VHS, DVD, GB Peter Sellers, David Niven, Robert Wagner, Claudia Cardinale, Capucine, Brenda de Banzie; D: Blake Edwards; W: Blake Edwards; C: Philip Lathrop; M: Henry Mancini.

The Pink Panther 🎬🎬 2006 (PG) Martin returns to his slapstick roots as he takes over the character of bumbling Inspector Jacques Clouseau. When soccer coach Gluant (Statham) is murdered, the Pink Panther diamond he was about to give his girlfriend, hottie pop diva Xania (Knowles), disappears. Ambitious Inspector Dreyfus (Kline) assigns the clueless Clouseau and his partner Ponton (Reno) knowing they will botch it and he can take over and save the day. Martin maintains a ridiculous accent and leaves destruction in his wake, but the effort is wasted in a tired retread. Clive Owen has a cameo as Agent 006, spoofing superspy James Bond. 92m/C DVD, UMD. US Steve Martin, Kevin Kline, Jean Reno, Emily Mortimer, Henry Czerny, Kristin Chenoweth, Roger Rees, Beyonce Knowles, Clive Owen; D: Shawn Levy; W: Steve Martin, Len Blum; C: Jonathan Brown, George Folsey Jr.; M: Christophe Beck, Randall Poster.

The Pink Panther Strikes Again 🎬🎬🎬 1976 (PG) Fifth in the series has the incompetent inspector tracking his former boss, who has gone insane and has become preoccupied with destroying the entire world. A must for Sellers buffs and anyone who appreciates slapstick. 103m/C VHS, DVD, GB Peter Sellers, Herbert Lom, Lesley-Anne Down, Colin Blakely, Leonard Rossiter, Burt Kwouk; D: Blake Edwards; W: Edwards Waldman, Frank Waldman; C: Harry Waxman; M: Henry Mancini.

---

numb from society's pressures. The concept is bombastic and overwrought, but Geldof manages to remain somewhat like-able as the cynical rock star and the Gerald Scarfe animation perfectly complements the film. 95m/C VHS, DVD. GB Bob Geldof, Christine Hargreaves, Bob Hoskins, James Laurenson, Eleanor David, Kevin McKeon, David Bingham, Jenny Wright, Alex McAvoy, Neil Campbell, Joanne Whalley; D: Alan Parker; W: Roger Waters; C: Peter Biziou; M: Michael Kamen, David Gilmour, Roger Waters.

The Pink Jungle 🎬🎬 1968 Ben Morris (Garner) is a fashion photographer on assignment with model Allison (Renzi) in South America where they become entangled with eccentric Sammy Ryderbeit (Kennedy) who's searching for a lost diamond mine. Caught up in the adventure, the duo accompany Sammy and find the mine, only to discover Raul Ortega (Ansara) and his band of revolutionaries have gotten there first. Based on the novel "Snake Water" by Alan Williams. 104m/C VHS. James Garner, Eva Renzi, George Kennedy, Michael Ansara, Nigel Green, George Rose; D: Delbert Mann; W: Charles Williams; C: Russell Metty; M: Ernie Freeman.

Pinky 🎬🎬🎬 1949 Early Hollywood treatment of the tragic choice made by some black Americans to pass as white in order to attain a better life for themselves and their families. The story is still relevant today. Waters and Barrymore are also stars, but the lead black character is portrayed by a white actress. Based on the novel "Quality" by Cyd Ricketts Sumner. 102m/B VHS. Jeanne Crain, Ethel Barrymore, Ethel Waters, Nina Mae McKinney, William Lundigan; D: Elia Kazan; W: Philip Dunne, Dudley Nichols; M: Alfred Newman.

Pinocchio 🎬🎬🎬 1940 (G) Second Disney animated film featuring Pinocchio, a little wooden puppet, made with love by the old woodcarver Geppetto, and brought to life by a good fairy. Except Pinocchio isn't content to be just a puppet—he wants to become a real boy. Lured off by a sly fox, Pinocchio undergoes a number of adventures as he tries to return safely home. Has some scary scenes, including Geppetto, Pinocchio, and their friend Jiminy Cricket getting swallowed by a whale, and Pleasure Island, where naughty boys are turned into donkeys. An example of animation at its best and a Disney classic that has held up over time. ♪When You Wish Upon a Star; Give a Little Whistle; Turn on the Old Music Box; Hi-Diddle-Dee-Dee (An Actor's Life For Me); I've Got No Strings. 87m/C VHS, DVD. D: Hamilton Luske, Ben Sharpsteen; W: Aurelius Battaglia, William Cottrell, Otto Englander, Erdman Penner, Joseph Sabo, Ted Sears, Webb Smith; V: Dickie Jones, Cliff Edwards, Evelyn Venable, Walter Catlett, Frankie Darro, Charles Judels; M: Leigh Harline, Paul J. Smith; Oscars '40: Song ("When You Wish Upon a Star"), Orig. Score, Mat.

Pinocchio 🎬🎬 1983 Pee-wee Herman is the puppet who wants to be a real little boy in this "Faerie Tale Theatre" adaptation of this children's classic. 60m/C VHS, DVD. James Belushi, Paul (Pee-wee Herman) Reubens, Lanie Kazan; D: Peter Medak. C.A.B.L.E.

Pinocchio 🎬🎬 1/2 2002 (G) Benigni's faithful version of Carlo Collodi's Italian fairy tale suffers from a disastrous decision to dub the dialogue for an American audience and forced portrayal of the wooden boy. Set against this wall-to-wall performance, the rest of the proceedings seem lifeless and dull, with the exception of the opening sequence (before Benigni shows up). By the time you read this, a subtitled version could be around, which may help with the humor, but will still leave the other problems. One thing that is not a problem is Spinotti's wonderful cinematography. Production is the most expensive in Italian history, at $45 million. 108m/C VHS, DVD. IT Roberto Benigni, Nicoletta Braschi, Mino Bellei, Carlo Giuffre, Peppe Barra, Max Cavallari, Bruno Arena, Kim Rossi-Stuart; D: Roberto Benigni; W: Roberto Benigni, Vincenzo Cerami; C: Dante Spinotti; M: Nicola Piovani; V: Breckin Meyer, Glenn Close, Eric Idle, David Suchet, John Cleese, Richard "Cheech" Marin, Eddie Griffin, Topher Grace, Golden Raspberries '02: Worst Actor (Benigni).

Pinocchio's Revenge 🎬 1996 (R) Man murders his child and buries the body with a wooden Pinocchio puppet. Somehow before his execution, his lawyer, Jennifer Garrick (Allen), and her cute daughter Zoe (Smith) wind up with the grisly toy. Naturally, this is not a good thing. 96m/C VHS, DVD. Rosalind Allen, Brittany Alyse Smith, Todd Allen, Lewis Van Bergen, Aaron Lustig, Ron Canada; D: Kevin S. Tenney; W: Kevin S. Tenney; M: Dennis Michael Tenney.

Pink String and Sealing Wax 🎬🎬 1945 A British pub owner in Victorian England is poisoned by his abused wife. She tries to involve the son of a chemist with the idea of blackmailing the father. Fine period flavor. 89m/B VHS. GB Mervyn Johns, Mary Merrall, Gordon Jackson, Googie Withers, Sally Ann Howes, Catherine Lacey, Garry Marsh, Frederick Piper, Don Stannard, Valentine Dyall; D: Robert Hamer; C: Richard S. Pavey.

Pinochet's Last Stand 🎬🎬 Pinochet in Suburbia 2006 (R) Pinochet took control of Chile in violent coup and ruled as a dictator for 17 years. But in 1998, in a surprise move, the elderly ex-leader (Jacobi) was arrested in Britain (where he was seeking medical treatment) and charged with crimes against humanity. Confined to a house in a London suburb, Pinochet waited in exile while government ministers vacillated and the judicial system took over. 77m/C DVD. GB Derek Jacobi, Peter Capaldi, Phyllida Law, Micheel Maloney, Jessica Stevenson, Pip Torrens, Yolanda Vasquez, Anna Massey, Susan Wooldridge; D: Richard Smith; W: Richard Smith; C: Jeff Baynes; M: Jeff Beal.

Pinto Canyon 🎬🎬 1944 An hongusto sheriff does away with a band of cattle rustlers. 55m/B VHS. Bob Steele, Louise Stanley, Kenne Duncan, Ted Adams, Steve Clark, Budd Buster; D: Bernard B. Ray.

Pinto Rustlers 🎬🎬 1/2 1936 A cowboy left orphaned by a gang of rustlers seeks revenge. 52m/C VHS. Tom Tyler, George Walsh, Marie Burton, Earl Dwire, Al "Fuzzy" St. John, George Chesebro, William (Bill) Gould, Roger Williams, Charles "Slim" Whitaker, Murcock MacQuarrie; D: Harry S. Webb; W: Robert Emmett Tansey; C: William (Bill) Hyer.

The Pioneers 🎬🎬 1/2 1941 Lawman out to protect a wagon train. 59m/B VHS. Tex Ritter, Red Foley, Wanda McKay, George Chesebro, Slim Andrews; D: Al (bert) Herman; W: Charles E. Anderson; C: Marcel Le Picard; M: Frank Sanucc.

Pioneer Marshal 🎬 1949 Lawman Hale disguises himself as a criminal to track down an embezzler. 60m/B VHS. Nan Leslie, Roy Barcroft, Monte Hale, Paul Hurst; D: Philip Ford; W: Robert Creighton Williams; C: John MacEntee; M: Stanley Wilson.

Pioneer Woman 🎬🎬 1973 Pioneers 1973 A family encounters hostility when they set up a frontier homestead in Nebraska in 1867. Told from the feminine perspective, the tale is strewn with hurdles, both personal and natural. 74m/C VHS, DVD. Joanna Pettet, William Shatner, David Janssen, Helen Hunt; D: Buzz Kulik. TV

Pipe Dream 🎬🎬 1/2 2002 (R) David (Donovan) is a New York City plumber who is tired of being taken for granted by clueless David appropriate showbiz lines. So he steals a screenplay of writer/neighbor Toni (Parker), and pretends to be a casting director with the help of industry pal R.J. (Carroll). He holds auditions for his nonexistent movie and suddenly the buzz is that the film is hot and everyone wants a piece of the action, including Toni, who feeds the clueless Toni's father broken marriage. The cast is good but the film turns out to be mildly amusing rather than satiric. 94m/C VHS, DVD. US Martin Donovan, Mary-Louise Parker, Kevin Carroll, Rebecca Gayheart, Peter Jacobson, Cynthia Kaplan, Tim Hopper, Guinevere Turner, Maria Suciarezza; D: John C. Walsh; C: Peter Nelson; M: Alexander Lasarenko.

Pippi Goes on Board 🎬🎬 1/2 1976 (PG) A couple tries to repair their broken marriage against the backdrop of the Alaskan pipeline's construction. 89m/C VHS. Gladys Knight, Barry Henderson, Bruce French, Sally Kirkland, Sherry Bain; D: Stephen Verona.

Pippi Goes on Board 🎬🎬 1969 (G) The fourth and last film in the Swedish series finds Pippi's father arriving one day to take her sailing to Taka-Tuka, his island kingdom. She can't bear to leave her friends and jumps off the ship to return home. The series is poorly dubbed and technically flawed, which the kids probably won't notice. Based on the books by Astrid Lindgren. Preceded by "Pippi Longstocking," "Pippi in the South Seas," and "Pippi on the Run." 83m/C VHS, DVD. SW Maria Persson, Par Sundberg, Margot Trooger, Hans Clarin, Inger Nilsson; D: Olle Hellbom; W: Astrid Lindgren; C: Kalle Bergholm; M: Christian Bruhn.

Pippi in the South Seas 🎬🎬 1/2 Pippi Langstrump Pa de Sju Haven 1970 (G) Pippi, a fun-loving, independent, red-haired little girl, and her two friends decide to rescue her father who is being held captive by a band of pirates on

---

a South Sea island. Naturally, clever Pippi saves the day. Poorly dubbed and edited. Based on the children's book by Astrid Lindgren. Follows "Pippi Longstocking" and precedes "Pippi on the Run" and "Pippi Goes on Board." 99m/C VHS, DVD. *SW* Maria Persson, Par Sundberg, Beppe Wolgens, Inger Nilsson; *D:* Olle Hellbom; *W:* Olle Hellbom; *C:* Kalle Bergholm; *M:* Jan Johansson.

Pippi Longstocking 🦴🦴½ 1969 (G) This little red-headed, pigtailed terror is left alone by her sailor father as he heads out to sea. Not that Pippi minds, since it gives her the chance to create havoc in her town through the antics of her pets, a monkey and a horse. Pippi's antics may amuse the kiddies but adults will find her obnoxious. Poorly dubbed and technically somewhat shaky. Based on the children's book by Astrid Lindgren. Followed by "Pippi Goes on Board," "Pippi in the South Seas," "Pippi on the Run," and "Pippi Goes on Board." 99m/C VHS, DVD. *SW* Inger Nilsson, Hans Alfredson, Maria Persson, Par Sundberg; *D:* Olle Hellbom; *M:* Konrad Elfers.

Pippi on the Run 🦴🦴½ 1970 (G) The third time finds Pippi on the trail of two friends who have run away from home. The three have many adventures before deciding home is best. Preceded by "Pippi Longstocking" and "Pippi Goes on Board," followed by "Pippi in the South Seas." Films lacks technical and dubbing skills. Based on the children's book by Astrid Lindgren. 99m/C VHS, DVD. *SW* Inger Nilsson, Hans Alfredson; *W:* Astrid Lindgren; *C:* Kalle Bergholm; *M:* Christian Bruhn.

Pippin 🦴🦴🦴 1981 Video version of the stage musical about the adolescent son of Charlemagne finding true love. Adequate version of Bob Fosse's Broadway smash. Features Vereen re-creating his original Tony Award-winning role. 120m/C VHS, DVD. Ben Vereen, William Katt, Martha Raye, Chita Rivera, Leslie Denniston, Benjamin Rayson; *D:* David Sheehan; *W:* Roger O. Hirson; *M:* Stephen Schwartz. TV

Piranha 🦴🦴½ 1995 (R) *Piranha 2: Flying Killers; The Spawning* 1982 (R) Diving instructor and a biochemist seek to destroy piranha mutations that are murdering tourists at a club. Early Cameron exercise in gore tech that's a step down from original "Piranha." 88m/C VHS, DVD. Tricia O'Neil, Steve Marachuk, Lance Henriksen, Ricky Paul; *D:* James Cameron; *W:* H.A. Milton; *C:* Roberto D'Ettorre Piazzoli.

Piranha 2: The Spawning 🦴½ 1978 (R) A rural Texas resort area is plagued by attacks from ferocious man-eating fish which a scientist created to be used as a secret weapon in the Vietnam War. Spoofy horror film features the now-obligatory Dante film in-jokes in the background. 90m/C VHS, DVD. Bradford Dillman, Heather Menzies, Kevin McCarthy, Keenan Wynn, Barbara Steele, Dick Miller, Paul Bartel, John Sayles, Richard Deacon; *D:* Joe Dante; *W:* John Sayles; *C:* Jamie Anderson; *M:* Pino Donaggio.

The Pirate 🦴🦴½ 1948 A traveling actor poses as a legendary pilot to woo a lonely woman on a remote Caribbean island. Minnelli always scores with this type of fare, and both Garland and Kelly make the most of the Cole Porter score. ♪Be a Clown; Nina; Mack the Black; You Can Do No Wrong; Sweet Ices, Papayas, Berry War; Sea Wall; Serafin; The King; Judy Awakens. 102m/C VHS, ♪ Judy Garland, Gene Kelly, Walter Slezak, Gladys Cooper, George Zucco, Reginald Owen; *D:* Vincente Minnelli; *C:* Harry Stradling Sr.

Pirate Movie 🦴½ 1982 (PG) Gilbert and Sullivan's "The Pirates of Penzance" is combined with new pop songs in this tale of fantasy and romance. Feeble attempt to update a musical that was fine the way it was. 98m/C VHS, DVD. Kristy McNichol, Christopher Atkins, Ted Hamilton, Bill Kerr, Garry McDonald; *D:* Ken Annakin; *M:* Tony Britten. Golden Raspberries '82: Worst Director (Annakin), Worst Song ("Pumpin' and Blowin'").

Pirate Ship 🦴½ 1949 *The Mutineers* 1949 Slow-moving story has sailor Hall discovering new captain Reeves is involved with a gang of gun-runners and counterfeiters. 60m/C VHS. Jon Hall, George Reeves, Adele Jergens, Noel Cravat, Tom Kennedy, Lyle Talbot; *D:* Jean Yarbrough.

Pirate Warrior 🦴🦴 1964 Grade-B pirate flick about slavery and the evil Tortuga. 86m/C VHS. Ricardo Montalban, Vincent Price, Liana Orfei; *D:* Mary Costa.

Pirates 🦴🦴 1986 (PG-13) Blustery, confused effort at a big-budgeted retro-adventure, about a highly regarded pirate and his gains and losses on the high seas. Broad comedy, no story to speak of. 124m/C VHS. Walter Matthau, Cris Campion, Damien Thomas, Richard Pearson, Charlotte Lewis, Olu Jacobs, David Patrick Kelly, Roy Kinnear, Bill Fraser, Jose Santamaria; *D:* Roman Polanski; *W:* Gerard Brach, Roman Polanski; Cesar '87: Art Dir./Set Dec., Costume Des.

The Pirates of Penzance 🦴🦴 1983 (G) Gilbert and Sullivan's comic operetta is the story of a band of fun-loving pirates, their reluctant young apprentice, the "very model of a modern major general," and his lovely daughters. An adaptation of Joseph Papp's award-winning Broadway play. 112m/C VHS, DVD. Kevin Kline, Angela Lansbury, Linda Ronstadt, Rex Smith, George Rose; *D:* Wilford Leach.

The Pirates of Silicon Valley 🦴🦴½ 1999 Fact-based docudrama covering the early days of Apple and Microsoft. The partners in both companies tend to get the short end of the story as the telepic focuses on charismatic manipulator Steve Jobs (Wyle) and shrewd geek kingpin Bill Gates (Hall), who not only kept an eye on each other but outmaneuvered industry giants such as IBM and Xerox to virtually begin the personal computer market. 95m/C VHS, DVD. Noah Wyle, Anthony Michael Hall, Joey Slotnick, John DiMaggio, Josh Hopkins, Gema Zamprogna, Allan Royal, Bodhi (Pine) Elfman, Gailard Sartain; *D:* Martyn Burke; *W:* Martyn Burke; *C:* Ousama Rawi; *M:* Frank Fitzpatrick. CABLE

Pirates of the Caribbean: At World's End 🦴🦴 2007 (PG-13) Like a good captain, this latest (and last?) entry in the "Pirates" franchise goes down with the ship. Familiar heroes and villains must band together to fight even worse villains, perform rescues, and go head-to-head with Chow-Yun Fat, and much is lost to the hectic pace and CGI effects that jump off the screen. Still, the swashbuckling and action are excellent, and it all adds up to a fun, if over-stuffed, mess of a movie. Enjoy it, just don't expect it to make sense. 168m/C DVD, Blu-ray Disc. *US* Johnny Depp, Keira Knightley, Orlando Bloom, Geoffrey Rush, Bill Nighy, Chow-Yun-Fat, Jack Davenport, Stellan Skarsgard, Jonathan Pryce, Naomie Harris, Tom Hollander, Kevin McNally, Marshall Manesh; *D:* Gore Verbinski; *W:* Terry Rossio, Ted Elliott; *C:* Darius Wolski; *M:* Hans Zimmer.

Pirates of the Caribbean: Dead Man's Chest 🦴🦴½ 2006 (PG-13) The second installment of Disney's amusement-park-ride-turned-flick finds Capt. Jack Sparrow (Depp) swishing and swashbuckling in and out of one perilous predicament after another. This time he must contend with a ghost ship full of half-men/half-sea creatures in an attempt to repay a debt. This absurdly long chapter serves up plenty of Depp hamming up one scene more than the next, with little substance nor a meaningful story, and seems to aspire merely to showing off the tens of millions likely spent on CGI and special effects. Somewhat effective follow-up doesn't have the charm of the first. This and the third installment were shot back-to-back. 150m/C DVD, Blu-ray Disc. *US* Johnny Depp, Orlando Bloom, Keira Knightley, Stellan Skarsgard, Bill Nighy, Naomie Harris, Jack Davenport, Jonathan Pryce, Kevin McNally, Tom Hollander, Mackenzie Crook, Lee Arenberg, Alex Norton, David Bailie, Martin Klebba, David Schofield; *D:* Gore Verbinski; *W:* Ted Elliott, Terry Rossio; *C:* Darius Wolski; *M:* Hans Zimmer. Oscars '06: Visual FX; British Acad. '06: Visual FX.

Pirates of the Caribbean: The Curse of the Black Pearl 🦴🦴🦴 2003 (PG-13) Yes, the film was inspired by the Disney theme park ride but unlike "The Country Bears," this one is a lot of fun, thanks primarily to star Depp. He swashes his buckle with added glee as pirate captain Jack Sparrow—a cross, Depp said, between Keith Richards and Pepe Le Pew—whose ship, the Black Pearl, has been commandeered by Capt. Barbossa (Rush, having an equally good teeth-gnashing time). Barbossa and his crew are cursed and need a gold medallion, unwittingly held by feisty Governor's daughter Elizabeth (Knightley), to break the spell. This involves kidnapping the girl and a rescue mission led by her true love, blacksmith Will (Bloom), and Sparrow, who has a score to settle. There's a few too many plot twists and extended sword fights but the action and humor keep things moving along with relative ease. 134m/C VHS, DVD, Blu-ray Disc, UMD. *US* Johnny Depp, Geoffrey Rush, Orlando Bloom, Keira Knightley, Jonathan Pryce, Jack Davenport, Kevin McNally, Zoe Saldana, Treva Etienne, Lee Arenberg, Trevor Goddard, David Bailie, Mackenzie Crook, Isaac C. Singleton Jr., Brye Cooper; *D:* Gore Verbinski; *W:* Ted Elliott, Terry Rossio; *C:* Darius Wolski; *M:* Klaus Badelt. British Acad. '03: Makeup; Screen Actors Guild '03: Actor (Depp).

Pirates of the Coast 🦴½ 1961 A Spanish naval commander teams up with a group of pirates to even the score with an evil governor during the 1500s. 102m/C VHS. Lex Barker, Estella Blain, Livio Lorenzon, Liana Orfei; *D:* Domenico Paolella.

Pirates of the High Seas 🦴½ 1950 Crabbe helps a friend save his shipping line from sabotage. A serial in 15 chapters. 7m/C VHS. Buster Crabbe, Lois Hall, Tommy Farrell, Gene Roth, Tristram Coffin; *D:* Spencer Gordon Bennet, Thomas Carr.

Pirates of the Seven Seas 🦴½ 1962 In the further tales of "Sandokan the Great," the pirate hero helps save the heroine's father from an evil English Imperialist. 90m/C VHS. Steve Reeves, Jacqueline Sassard, Andrea Bosic; *D:* Umberto Lenzi.

The Pirates Who Don't Do Anything: A Veggie Tales Movie 🦴🦴 2008 (G) Three produce-aisle pals—a cucumber, a gourd, and a giant grape—find themselves transformed from dinner theater waiters into 17th-century pirates charged with the task of saving a princess and thwarting the bad guy. The faith-based, kid-friendly franchise backs off on its usual religiosity in favor of a more Oz-like tone to convey the virtues of moral fortitude, but the young'uns will be too into the bright colors, silly voices, and funny faces to care about the message, let alone the fact that the characters are fresh from the middle strata of the food pyramid. 85m/C DVD. *US M:* Kurt Heinecke; *V:* Cam(eron) Clarke, Mike Nawrocki, Phil Vischer, Laura Gerow, Yuri Lowenthal.

Pistol: The Birth of a Legend 🦴🦴½ 1990 (G) Biography of "Pistol" Pete Maravich, the basketball star who defied age limitations in the 1960s to play on his varsity team. 104m/C VHS, DVD. Adam Guier, Nick Benedict, Boots Garland, Millie Perkins; *D:* Frank C. Schroeder; *W:* Darrel A. Campbell.

Pistol Whipped 🦴 2008 (R) Seagal lumbers through with his usual inexpressiveness. Alcoholic ex-cop Matt has a gambling problem and big debts. So when a stranger (Henriksen) offers to take care of Matt's money issues in exchange for his assassinating some mobsters, he's not as unwilling as you might imagine. Of course, it's just not that simple. The real problem is that there's not enough Henriksen on-screen. 96m/C DVD. Steven Seagal, Lance Henriksen, Paul Calderon, Blanchard Ryan, Renee Goldsberry, Lydia Grace Jordan; *D:* Roel Reine; *W:* J.D. Zeik; *C:* Richard Crudo; *M:* Jerry Brunskill.

Pistoleros Asesinos 🦴🦴 1987 Plenty of action, plus a little romance, when a man falls in love with a crooked landowner's daughter and must battle her father's henchmen for her hand. 83m/C VHS. *SP* Maria de Lourdes, Federico Villa, Victor Alcocer, Arturo Benavides, Polo Ortin, Rosa Gloria; *D:* Angel Rodriguez Vazquez.

The Pit 🦴½ 1981 (R) Autistic boy gets his chance for revenge. The townspeople who humiliate him are in for a surprise after he stumbles across a huge hole in the forest, at the bottom of which are strange and deadly creatures. 96m/C VHS, DVD. Sammy Snyders, Sonja Smits, Jeannie Elias, Laura Hollingsworth; *D:* Lew Lehman.

The Pit and the Pendulum 🦴🦴🦴 1961 A woman and her lover plan to drive her brother mad, and he responds by locking them in his torture chamber, which was built by his loony dad, whom he now thinks he is. Standard Corman production only remotely derived from the classic Poe tale, with the cast chewing on a loopy script. A landmark in Gothic horror. 80m/C VHS, DVD. Vincent Price, John Kerr, Barbara Steele, Luana Anders, Antony Carbone, Charles Victor, Lynn Bernay, Patrick Westwood; *D:* Roger Corman; *W:* Richard Matheson; *C:* Floyd Crosby; *M:* Les Baxter.

The Pit & the Pendulum 🦴🦴½ 1991 (R) Retelling of the classic Poe short story, mixed with his "A Cask of Amantillado" and set during the Spanish Inquisition. Great special effects and professional scary guy, Lance Henriksen. 97m/C VHS, DVD. Lance Henriksen, Rona De Ricci, Jonathan Fuller, Jeffrey Combs, Tom Towles, Stephen Lee, Frances Bay, Oliver Reed; *D:* Stuart Gordon; *W:* Dennis Paoli; *M:* Richard Band.

Pit Fighter 🦴 2005 (R) A pit fighter suffering from amnesia, now living in Mexico, comes under the gun once old enemies find out he's not dead. Over-the-top low budget fight flick guarantees many crashes. Brian Donlevy is the promoter who involves young racers Sid Haig and Dick Davalos in his plans. 91m/B DVD. Brian Donlevy, Richard (Dick) Davalos, Ellen Burstyn, Sid Haig, Beverly Washburn; *D:* Jack Hill; *W:* Jack Hill; *C:* Austin McKinney.

Pit Stop 🦴🦴🦴 1967 On the DVD commentary track, director Jack Hill admits that he made this for the short-lived phenomenon of figure-8 racing, where the shape of the track guarantees many crashes. Brian Donlevy is the promoter who involves young racers Sid Haig and Dick Davalos in his plans. 91m/B DVD. Brian Donlevy, Richard (Dick) Davalos, Ellen Burstyn, Sid Haig, Beverly Washburn; *D:* Jack Hill; *W:* Jack Hill; *C:* Austin McKinney.

Pitch Black 🦴🦴🦴 2000 (R) Scary sci-fier with some familiar elements. Freak meteor storm causes a spaceship to make a crash landing on an unknown planet with three suns and apparently no life. Hah! In this version of "they only come out at night," the survivors discover that very nasty hunting creatures attack after dark—and the planet is in for a total eclipse. Diesel gives a hard-ass performance as a convicted murderer who has nothing to lose. Shot in Queensland, Australia. 108m/C VHS, DVD, UMD, HD DVD. Vin Diesel, Radha Mitchell, Cole Hauser, Keith David, Lewis Fitz-Gerald, John Moore, Simon Burke, Claudia Black, Rhiana Griffith; *D:* David N. Twohy.

Pitfall 🐾🐾🐾 1948 Gritty tale in which an insurance salesman, bo'ed with his routine suburban life and family, follows his less noble instincts—and finds himself up to his ears in stolen goo,ds, adultery and murder. 85m/B VHS, DVD. C: Dick Powell, Jane Wyatt, Lizabeth Scott, Raymond Burr, John Litel, Byron Barr, Ann Doran, Jimmy Hunt, Selmer Jackson, Margaret Wells, Dick Wessell; D: Andre de Toth; W: Karl Kamb; C: Harry Wild; M: Louis Forbes.

Pittsburgh 🐾🐾 1942 Slow-moving drama about a love triangle combined with class differences. Dietrich loves Wayne, but he's more interested in a factory worker on his way to a arm wrestling competition and they become friends, so rival Scott steps in. Although limited by standard plot, picture works because of excellent performances by leads. Based on a screen story by George Owen and Tom Reed. 88m/B VHS, DVD. C: Marlene Dietrich, Randolph Scott, John Wayne, Frank Craven, Louise Allbritton, Shemp Howard, Thomas Gomez, Ludwig Stossel; D: Lewis Seiler; W: Kenneth Gamet, Tom Reed, John Twist.

Pixote 🐾🐾🐾 1981 Wrenching, documentary-like account of an orphan-boy's life on the streets in a Brazil metropolis. Graphic and depressing, it's not for all tastes but nonetheless masterfully done. In Portuguese with English subtitles. 127m/C VHS, DVD, BR Pixote: A Le do Mais Fraco. C: Fernando Ramos Da Silva, Marilia Pera, Jorge Juliao, Gilberto Moura, Jose Nilson dos Santos, Edilson Lino; D: Hector Babenco; W: Hector Babenco, Jose Louzeiro.

Pizza 🐾🐾½ 2005 This pizza has a lot of extra cheese. An overweight misfit, Cara-Ethyl (Sparks) throws herself on an 18th birthday party, but none of the guests show up. Finally, pizza delivery guy Matt (Embry) arrives. Maybe he feels sorry for her, 'cause Matt invites C–E to come along on his pizza runs. Misadventure and strangeness ensue while two band together. 82m/C DVD. US: Kylie Sparks, Ethan (Randall) Embry, Julie Hagerty, Joey Kern, Alexis Dziena, Mary Birdsong, Maryjouise Burke, Judah Friedlander; D: Mark Christopher; W: Mark Christopher; C: Ken Ferris; M: John Kimbrough.

Pizza Man 🐾🐾 1991 (PG-13) Pizza deliveryman Elmo Bunn is minding his own business, delivering an extra large with anchovies and sausage, when he finds himself mixed up in a political scandal. Lawton directed under alias "J.D. Athers." 90m/C VHS. C: Bill Maher, Annabelle Gurwitch; D: J.F. Lawton; W: J.F. Lawton.

Pizzicata 🐾🐾 1996 When an American fighter plane is shot down over southern Italy in 1943, the pilot, Italian-American Tony Marciano (Frascaro), is rescued by peasant family, the Panaleos, who nurse the wounded man despite the danger. When Tony is discovered by a neighbor, he pretends to be a family cousin and tries to fit into the community—all while falling for young Cosima Panaleo (Torelli); even though she's engaged to Pasquale (Massafra). During a community dance, everyone's feelings become dramatically clear. Italian with subtitles. 95m/C VHS. If Fabio Frascaro, Chiara Torelli, Cosimo Cinieri, Paolo Massafra; D: Edoardo Winspeare; W: Edoardo Winspeare; C: Paolo Carrera.

Place of Weeping 🐾🐾½ 1986 (PG) Early entry in the anti-apartheid sweepstakes (made in South Africa, no less). A South African woman opposes her nation's racist policies. A reporter supports her. 88m/C VHS. SA: James Whyle, Geina Mhlophe; D: Darrell Roodt.

P.K. and the Kid 🐾🐾 1985 A runaway kid meets up with a factory worker on his way to a arm wrestling competition and they become friends. 90m/C VHS. C: Molly Ringwald, Paul LeMat, Alex Rocco, John Madden, Esther Rolle; D: Lou Lombardo; W: Neal Barbera; M: James Horner.

A Place Called Glory 🐾🐾 Die Holle von Manitoba 1966 Barker comes to the aid of local townsfolk in Dodge city who have their hands full with a gang of blood-thirsty outlaws. 92m/C VHS. GE SP/Lex Barker, Pierre Brice, Marianne Koch; C: Federico G. Larraya; M: Angel Arteaga.

A Place Called Today 🐾 City in minutes. 105m/C VHS.

A Place Called Truth 🐾½ A jeweler with a shop on the fashionable Place Vendome, he was unable to confess that the business is bankrupt and his connections shady. Instead he leaves Marianne with seven priceless diamonds that turn out to be stolen, which rekindles her business instincts (she's a former gem broker) and places her in danger. French with subtitles; originally released at 117 minutes. 105m/C VHS. C: Sheldon Reynolds; W: Edward Di Lorenzo; C: Federico G. Larraya.

A Place for Annie 🐾🐾½ 1994 (PG) Lots of tears in this drama of devoted pediatrics nurse Susan Lansing (Spacek) who decides to become the foster mother of abandoned baby girl Annie, who's been diagnosed as HIV-positive. Then Annie's destitute birth mother (Parker), a former junkie dying of AIDS, resurfaces and decides she wants her daughter back. Sputters into melodrama but good performances by strong women, including Plowright as the nanny and Merkerson as a concerned hospital social worker. Based on a true story. 98m/C VHS. C: Sissy Spacek, Mary-Louise Parker, Joan Plowright, S. Epatha Merkerson, Jack Noseworthy; D: John Gray; W: Cathleen Young, Lee Guthrie. TV

Place in Hell 🐾½ 1969 The Japanese armed forces camouflage a Pacific island beach which they are holding and invite the American forces to invade it during WWII. 106m/C VHS. IT Guy Madison, Helene Chanel, Monty Greenwood; D: Giuseppe Vari; W: Adriano Bolzoni; C: Stelvio Massi; M: Roberto Pregadio.

A Place in the Sun 🐾🐾🐾 1951 Melodramatic adaptation of "An American Tragedy." Theodore Dreiser's realist classic about an ambitious laborer whose aspirations to the high life with a gorgeous debutante are threatened by his lower-class lover's pregnancy. Clift is magnificent in the lead, and Taylor and Winters also shine in support. Burr, however, grossly overdoes his role of the vehement prosecutor. Still, not a bad effort from somewhat undisciplined director Stevens. 120m/B VHS, DVD. Montgomery Clift, Elizabeth Taylor, Shelley Winters, Raymond Burr, Anne Revere, Keefe Brasselle, Shepperd Strudwick, Herbert (Hayes) Heyes, Frieda Inescort; D: George Stevens; W: Harry Brown, Michael Wilson; C: William Mellor; M: Franz Waxman. Oscars '51: B&W Cinematog., Costume Des. (B&W), Director (Stevens), Film Editing, Screenplay, Orig. Dramatic Score; AFI '98: Top 100; Directors Guild '51: Director (Stevens); Golden Giobes '52: Film—Drama. Natl. Film Reg. '91.

A Place in the World 🐾🐾🐾 1992 Returning from exile to their native Argentina during a military dictatorship, Mario and Ana (Luppi and Roth) work to help the less advantaged in their society, determined to make a difference. Story is seen as a flashback from point-of-view of the couple's son Ernesto (Eatyi). Well-crafted, finely acted piece exploring political, social, and interpersonal themes. 1993 Oscar bid retracted due to controversy over country of film's origin. 120m/C VHS, AR/Jose Sacristan, Federico Luppi, Cecilia (Celia) Roth, Leonor Benedetto, Gaston Batyi, Lorena Del Rio; D: Adolfo Aristarain; W: Alberto ,echhi, Adolfo Aristarain; C: Ricardo De Angelis; M: Emilio Kauderer.

Plain Clothes 🐾🐾½ 1988 (PG) An undercover cop masquerades as a high school student to solve the murder of a teacher. He endures all the trials that made him hate high school the first time around. 98m/C VHS. Arliss Howard, George Wendt, Suzy Amis, Diane Ladd, Abe Vigoda, Robert Stack, Seymour Cassel, Larry Pine, Jackie Gayle, Alexandra Powers, Peter Dobson, Harry Shearer, Loren Dean, Reginald VelJohnson, Max Perlich; D: Martha Coolidge; W: Scott Frank; M: Scott Wilk.

Plain Dirty 🐾🐾 Briar Patch; Killing Edgar 2004 Abused wife Inez (Swain) has smitten local hermit Flowers (Svenson) help kill her husband (Thomas) then runs off with a rich lawyer (Urbaniak). Well, Flowers is none too pleased with that development, and sets out to vent his displeasure. 98m/C VHS. C: Brian Patch: Killing Edgar 2004 C: Dominique Swain, Henry Thomas, Arie Verveen, James Urbaniak, Karen Allen, Debra Monk, Blake Lindsley; D: Zev Berman; W: Christian Carion; C: Scott Kevan; M: Nathan Barr. VIDEO

Place Vendome 🐾🐾🐾 1998 Deneuve stars as elegant alcoholic Marianne Malivert, who finds a new interest after her husband's (Fresson) suicide. A prominent jeweler with a shop on the fashionable Place Vendome, he was unable to confess that the business is bankrupt and his connections shady. Instead he leaves Marianne with seven priceless diamonds that turn out to be stolen, which rekindles her business instincts (she's a former gem broker) and places her in danger. French with subtitles; originally released at 117 minutes. 105m/C VHS. FR Catherine Deneuve, Jean-Pierre Bacri, Emmanuelle Seigner, Jacques Dutronc, Bernard Fresson, Francois Berleand, Philippe Clevenot; D: Nicole Garcia; W: Nicole Garcia, Jacques Fieschi; C: Laurent Dailland; M: Richard Robbins.

Places in the Heart 🐾🐾🐾 1984 (PG) A young widow determines to make the best of a bad situation on a small farm in Depression-era Texas, fighting poverty, racism, and sexism while enduring back-breaking labor. Support group includes a blind veteran and a black drifter. Hokey but nonetheless moving film is improved significantly by strong performances by virtually everyone in the cast. Malkovich shines through this stellar group. Effective dust-bowl photography by Nestor Almendros. 113m/C VHS, DVD. Sally Field, John Malkovich, Danny Glover, Ed Harris, Lindsay Crouse, Amy Madigan, Terry O'Quinn, Ned Dowd, Ray Baker; D: Robert Benton; W: Robert Benton. Oscars '84: Actress (Field), Orig. Screenplay; Golden Globes '85: Actress (Field); N.Y. Film Critics '84: Screenplay; Natl. Soc. Film Critics '84: Support., Actor (Malkovich).

The Plague 🐾🐾 1992 (R) An outbreak of bubonic plague has turned the South American city of Oran into a prison, with no one permitted to leave until the disease has run its course. Hurt is the doctor trying to balance his duties with his own fears. Necessarily bleak adaptation of the Albert Camus novel is also slow-moving and long-winded—an equally deadly combination for the viewer. 105m/C VHS. FR/SP William Hurt, Robert Duvall, Raul Julia, Sandrine Bonaire, Jean-Marc Barr; D: Luis Puenzo.

The Plague Dogs 🐾🐾½ 1982 Two dogs carrying a plague escape from a research center and are tracked down in this unlikely animated film. A bit ponderous. And yes, that is Hurt's voice. From the novel by Richard Adams, author of "Watership Down." 99m/C VHS, DVD. D: Martin Rosen; W: Martin Rosen; M: Patrick Gleeson; V: John Hurt, Christopher Benjamin, Judy Geeson, Barbara Leigh-Hunt, Patrick Stewart.

Plague of the Zombies 🐾🐾½ 1966 The local doctor in a Cornish village gets suspicious when its inhabitants begin suddenly dying off and the local squire refuses to allow any autopsies. That's because he's learned voodoo rites while staying in Haiti and is turning the dead locals into zombies. 90m/C VHS, DVD. GB Andre Morell, John Carson, Diane Clare, Alex Davion, Jacqueline Pearce, Brook Williams, Michael Ripper, Marcus Hammond, Roy Royston; D: John Gilling; W: Peter Bryan, John (Anthony Hinds) Elder; C: Arthur Grant; M: James Bernard.

Plain Jane 🐾🐾½ 2001 In 1911, David Bruce (Whately) has just moved to London with his wife (Manville) and baby daughter. Newly prosperous, the family can afford to hire live-in maid, Jane (Cunniffe). But David begins to take too much of an interest in Jane (and doesn't realize that his grown son is also involved with her) and sexual obsession leads to murder. 150m/C VHS, DVD. GB Kevin Whately, Emma Cunniffe, Leslie Manville, Jason Hughes; D: John Woods; W: Lucy Gannon; M: Ray Russell. TV

The Plainsman 🐾🐾½ 1937 Western legends Wild Bill Hickock, Buffalo Bill, and Calamity Jane team up for adventure in this big, empty venture. Just about what you'd expect from splashy director DeMille. 113m/B VHS, DVD. Gary Cooper, Jean Arthur, Charles Bickford, Anthony Quinn, George "Gabby" Hayes, Porter Hall, James Mason; D: Cecil B. DeMille; C: Victor Milner.

Plan B 🐾🐾½ 1997 Comedy, set between Halloween and New Year's Eve, about a group of 30-ish friends who realize their lives aren't going the way they'd planned. Walter Stuart (Cryer) despairs of being a serious writer and has instead penned a lurid serial killer novel; aspiring actor Ricky (Matheison) freaks about growing older; Gina (Monnell) is successful in business but unlucky in love; while Gina's older sister Clare (Darr) is happily married to Jack (Guest) but fretting over not being a mother yet. It's pretty familiar but not a complete waste of time, thanks to the appealing cast. 102m/C VHS. Jon Cryer, Mark Matheison, Sara Monnell, Lisa Darr, Lance Guest; D: Gary Leva; W: Gary Leva; C: Yoram Astrakhan; M: Andrew Rose.

Plan 9 from Outer Space woof! Grave Robbers from Outer Space 1956 Two or three aliens in silk pajamas conspire to resurrect several slow-moving zombies from a cardboard graveyard in order to conquer the Earth. Space ships that look suspiciously like paper plates blaze across the sky. Pitifully, inadvertently hilarious fright worth a look if you're desperate to kill time since it's in the running for the "dumbest movie ever made" award. Lugosi's actual screen time is under two minutes, since he had the good sense to die before the film was complete. Enjoy the taller and younger replacement (the chiropractor of Wood's wife) they found for Lugosi, who remains hooded to protect his identity. 78m/B VHS, DVD. Bela Lugosi, Tor Johnson, Lyle Talbot, Vampira, Gregory Walcott, Tom Keene, Dudley Marlove, Mona McKinnon, Duke Moore, Joanna Lee, Bunny Breckinridge, Criswell, Carl Anthony, Paul Marco, Norma McCarty, David DeMering, Bill Asf, Conrad Brooks, Karl Johnson, Edward D. Wood Jr.; D: Edward D. Wood Jr.; W: Edward D. Wood Jr.; C: William C. Thompson; M: Trevor Duncan, Van Phillips, James Stevens, Bruce Campbell.

Plan 10 from Outer Space 🐾🐾½ 1995 The play on the infamous Ed Wood title is the only connection between the two fringe features as director Harris takes aim at his hometown of Salt Lake City, Utah. Heroine Lucinda (Russell) discovers a mysterious bronze plaque buried near the Great Salt Lake and uncovers a UFO conspiracy loosely conforming to Mormon mythology. There's a basic mass hysteria/alien invasion scene, cheesy special effects, dumb sexual humor, and not much else. 82m/C VHS. Stefene Russell, Pat Collins, Curtis James, Karen Black; D: Trent Harris; W: Trent Harris; C: Bryan Duggan; M: Fredric Myrow.

Planes, Trains & Automobiles 🐾🐾½ 1987 (R) One-joke Hughes comedy, saved by Martin and Candy. Strait-laced businessman Neal Page (played straight by Martin) on the way home for Thanksgiving meets up with a oafish, bad-luck-ridden boor Del Griffith (Candy) who turns his efforts to get home upside down. Martin and Candy both turn in fine performances, and effectively straddle a thin line between true pathos and hilarious buffoonery. Bacon and McClurg, both Hughes alumni, have small but funny roles. **93m/C VHS, DVD:** Steve Martin, John Candy, Edie McClurg, Kevin Bacon, Michael McKean, William Windom, Laila Robins, Martin Ferrero, Charles Tyner, Dylan Baker, Ben Stein, Lyman Ward; **D:** John Hughes; **W:** John Hughes; **C:** Don Peterman; **M:** Ira Newborn.

Planet Burg 🎬🎬½ 1962 A classic Soviet sci-fi flick about a space exploration team landing on Venus. Their job becomes a rescue mission when one of the crew is stranded. Although there are some silly moments, some good plot twists and acting make up for them. In Russian with English subtitles. **90m/C VHS.** *RU* Vladimir Temelianov, Gennadi Vernov, Kyunna Ignatova; **D:** Pavel Klushantsev.

Planet Earth 🎬🎬½ 1974 In the year 2133, a man who has been in suspended animation for 154 years is revived to lead the troops against a violent group of women (and mutants, too). **78m/C VHS.** John Saxon, Janet Margolin, Ted Cassidy, Diana Muldaur, Johanna DeWinter, Christopher Gary; **D:** Marc Daniels.

Planet of Blood 🎬🎬 *Queen of Blood* 1966 Space opera about an alien vampire discovered on Mars by a rescue team. If you've ever seen the Soviet film "Niebo Zowiet," don't be surprised if some scenes look familiar; the script was written around segments cut from that film. **81m/C VHS, DVD.** John Saxon, Basil Rathbone, Judi Meredith, Dennis Hopper, Florence Marly, Forrest J Ackerman; **D:** Curtis Harrington; **W:** Curtis Harrington; **C:** Vilis Lapenieks; **M:** Leonard Morand.

Planet of the Apes 🎬🎬🎬½ 1968 (G) Astronauts crash land on a planet where apes are masters and humans are merely brute animals. Superior science fiction with sociological implications married only by unnecessary humor. Heston delivers one of his more plausible performances. Superb ape makeup creates realistic pseudo-simians of McDowall, Hunter, Evans, Whitmore, and Daly. Adapted from Pierre Boulle's novel "Monkey Planet." Followed by four sequels and two TV series. **112m/C VHS, DVD.** Charlton Heston, Roddy McDowall, Kim Hunter, Maurice Evans, Linda Harrison, James Whitmore, James Daly; **D:** Franklin J. Schaffner; **W:** Rod Serling, Michael Wilson; **C:** Leon Shamroy; **M:** Jerry Goldsmith. **Natl. Film Reg. '01.**

Planet of the Apes 🎬🎬🎬 2001 (PG-13) Burton's "re-imagining" of the story looks more of the original novel by Pierre Boulle than it does to the 1968 classic. Wahlberg, as generic action hero Leo Davidson, takes over the Heston role, but with nowhere near the bravado or screen presence. Roth excels as Gen. Thade, an angry militarist with a loathing for all humans and a contempt for polite ape society. Needless to say, Leo becomes the focus for his rage. Come to think of it, all of the actors in the ape makeup do a fine job. The makeup effects, courtesy of Rick Baker, are astounding, (and light-years ahead of where they were in '68), and the action moves along at a satisfyingly brisk pace. The screenplay provides plenty of sly and clever references to the original, but doesn't have its sense of social commentary (this is, after all, a summer blockbuster). What it does have is a twist ending that seems tacked on for the purpose of setting up a sequel. **125m/C VHS, DVD, Blu-Ray Disc, UMD.** *US* Mark Wahlberg, Tim Roth, Helena Bonham-Carter, Michael Clarke Duncan, Paul Giamatti, Estella Warren, Cary-Hiroyuki Tagawa, David Warner, Kris Kristofferson, Erik Avari, Luke Eberl, Charlton Heston, Evan Dexter Parke, Michael Jace; **D:** Tim Burton; **W:** William Broyles Jr., Larry Konner, Mark Rosenthal; **C:** Philippe Rousselot; **M:** Danny Elfman. **Golden Raspberries '01: Worst Remake/Sequel; Worst Support. Actor (Heston), Worst Support. Actress (Warren).**

Planet of the Dinosaurs 🎬🎬 1980 (PG) Survivors from a ruined spaceship combat huge savage dinosaurs on a swampy uncharted planet. **85m/C VHS, DVD.** James Whitworth, Max (Michael) Thayer, Louie Lawless, Pamela Bottaro, Charlotte Speer; **D:** James K. Shea; **W:** Ralph Lucas.

Planet of the Vampires 🎬🎬½ *The Demon Planet; The Haunted Planet; The Outlawed Planet; Planet of Terror; Planet of the Damned; Space Mutants; Terror in Space; Terrore nello Spazio; Terreur dans l'Espace* 1965 Astronauts search for missing comrades on a planet dominated by mind-bending forces. Acceptable atmospheric filmmaking from genre master Bava, but it's not among his more compelling ventures. **86m/C VHS, DVD.** *IT SP* Barry Sullivan, Norma Bengell, Angel Aranda, Evi Marandi, Stelio Candelli, Ivan Rassimov, Fernando Villena; **D:** Mario Bava; **W:** Mario Bava, Alberto Bevilacqua, Callisto Cosulich, Louis M. Heyward, Ib Melchior, Antonio Roman, Rafael J. Salvia; **C:** Antonio Rinaldi; **M:** Gino Marinuzzi Jr.

Planet on the Prowl 🎬🎬 *War Between the Planets* 1965 A fiery planet causes earthly disasters, so a troop of wily astronauts try to destroy it with the latest technology. They fail, leading one sacrificial soul to do it himself. **80m/C VHS, DVD.** *IT* Giacomo "Jack" Rossi-Stuart, Amber Collins, Peter Martellanza, John Bartha, Halina Zalewska, James Weaver; **D:** Anthony M. Dawson.

Planet Terror 🎬🎬½ *Robert Rodriguez's Planet Terror; Grindhouse: Planet Terror* 2007 For the first time in his career, Rodriguez trumps his pal Quentin Tarantino by directing the better half of the Weinstein Bros. B-movie double-feature "Grindhouse." Almost every schlock-film cliche makes an appearance, which is the point, really. After a rogue military team sets loose a nerve gas that turns people into surprisingly gross zombies, it's up to El Wray (Rodriguez), his gal Cherry Darling (McGowan), and a gaggle of terrified Texans to try to stop the gas from spreading. McGowan steals the show with her M16-prosthetic leg, but the flurry of cheap thrills starts to feel... well... "cheap" after an hour or so. **105m/C DVD.** Rose McGowan, Freddy Rodriguez, Josh Brolin, Marley Shelton, Jeff Fahey, Michael Biehn, Bruce Willis, Naveen Andrews, Julio Oscar Mechoso, Stacy "Fergie" Ferguson, Nicky Katt, Tom Savini, Carlos Gallardo, Michael Parks, Quentin Tarantino, Rebel Rodriguez; **D:** Robert Rodriguez; **W:** Robert Rodriguez; **C:** Robert Rodriguez; **M:** Graeme Revell.

Planets Against Us 🎬½ *I Pianeti Contro di Noi; The Man with the Yellow Eyes; Hands of a Killer; The Monster with Green Eyes* 1961 Science fiction tale of escaped alien humanoid robots who take refuge on Earth, but whose touch is fatal. Good special effects. **85m/B VHS.** *IT FR* Michel Lemoine, Maria Pia Luzi, Jany Clair; **D:** Romano Ferrara.

The Plastic Age 🎬🎬½ 1925 Cynthia (Bow) is a flapper college babe who likes boys and parties. She easily manages to charm naive newcomer Hugh (Keith), who pays more attention to her than his athletic career. But Cynthia's not heartless—when she sees that Hugh is ruining his chances, she decides to give him up. **73m/B VHS, DVD.** Clara Bow, Donald Keith, Gilbert Roland, Henry B. Walthall, Mary Alden; **D:** Wesley Ruggles; **W:** Eve Unsell, Frederica Sagor; **C:** Gilbert Warrenton, Allen Siegler.

Platinum Blonde 🎬🎬🎬 1931 *Trouble at 16; Rich, Young, and Deadly* 1960 Divorced father Rooney is appalled when his son is "accidentally" killed while off at an exclusive military academy. His suspicions are aroused by the prevaricating school commander and he discovers some horrible truths about his son's death and life at the school. **91m/B VHS.** Mickey Rooney, Terry Moore, Dan Duryea, Conway Twitty, Warren Berlinger, Yvette Mimieux, Jimmy Boyd, Richard Jaeckel, Harold Lloyd Jr., Elisha Cook Jr.,

Jimmy Murphy; **D:** Charles F. Haas; **W:** Robert Smith; **M:** Van Alexander.

Platoon 🎬🎬🎬½ 1986 (R) A grunt's view of the Vietnam War is provided in all its horrific, inexplicable detail. Sheen is wooden in the lead, but both Dafoe and Berenger are resplendent as, respectively, good and bad soldiers. Strong, visceral filmmaking from fearless director Stone, who based the film on his own GI experiences. Highly acclaimed; considered by many to be the most realistic portrayal of the war on film. **113m/C VHS, DVD.** Charlie Sheen, Willem Dafoe, Tom Berenger, Francesco Quinn, Forest Whitaker, John C. McGinley, Kevin Dillon, Richard Edson, Reggie Johnson, Keith David, Johnny Depp, Dale Dye, Mark Moses, Chris Pederson, David Neidorf, Tony Todd, Ivan Kane, Paul Sanchez, Corey Glover, Oliver Stone; **D:** Oliver Stone; **W:** Oliver Stone; **C:** Robert Richardson; **M:** Georges Delerue. **Oscars '86:** Director (Stone), Film Editing, Picture, Sound; **AFI '98:** Top 100; **Brit. Acad. '87:** Director (Stone); Directors Guild '86: Director (Stone); **Golden Globes '87:** Director (Stone), Film—Drama, Support. Actor (Berenger); Ind. Spirit '87: Cinematog., Director (Stone), Film, Screenplay.

Platoon Leader 🎬🎬 1987 (R) A battle-drenched portrait of a West Point lieutenant in Vietnam. When he first arrives, he must win the trust of his men, who have been on their tours for a much longer time. As time goes on, he slowly becomes hardened to the realities of the brutal life in the widely acclaimed "Platoon," but it doesn't have the same power. Norris is martial arts king Chuck Norris' brother. **97m/C VHS.** Michael Dudikoff, Brian Libby, Rupert F. Lyons, Rick Fitts, Jesse Dabson, William (Bill) Smith, Michael DeLorenzo; **D:** Aaron Norris; **W:** R.J. Marx; **M:** George S. Clinton.

Platoon the Warriors 🎬 1988 The underworld rages with violence when two kingpins, Rex and Bill, become bitter and declare war over a botched drug deal. **90m/C VHS.** David Coley, Dick Crown, James Miller, Don Richard, Alex Sylvian; **D:** Philip Ko.

Plato's Run 🎬🎬 1996 (R) Ex-CIA agent agrees to free a Cuban who's been falsely imprisoned. But once the job is done, the agent learns he's been double-crossed and the prisoner turns out to be a professional assassin. **96m/C VHS, DVD.** Gary Busey, Roy Scheider, Steven Bauer, Jeff Speakman; **D:** James Becket; **W:** James Becket; **C:** Richard Clabaugh; **M:** Robert O. Ragland.

Platypus Cove 🎬 1986 An adopted boy tracks down the culprits responsible for the sabotage of his family's boat, a crime for which he was suspected. Australian. **72m/C VHS.** Paul Smith; **D:** Peter Maxwell.

Play Dead 🎬 1981 *Satan's Dog* Poor Yvonne De Carlo plays a psychotic woman who trains a dog to rip people to shreds. **89m/C VHS.** Yvonne De Carlo, Stephanie Dunham, David Cullinane, Glenn Kezer, Ron Jackson, Carolyn Greenwood; **D:** Peter Wittman.

Play for Me 🎬 *Toca Para Mí* 2001 Punk rock drummer Carlos goes on a search for identity after his adoptive father dies. He travels to the town of his birth in the Argentine pampas and meets hooker Fabiana who helps him on his journey. Spanish with subtitles. **101m/C VHS, DVD.** *AR* Hermes Gaido, Maria Laura Frigerio, Alejandro Fiore, Emilio Urdapilleta; **D:** Rodrigo Furth; **W:** Rodrigo Furth, Eduardo Ruderman; **C:** Paula Grandio; **M:** Fernando Manuel Dieguez.

Play It Again, Sam 🎬🎬🎬½ 1972 (PG) Allen is—no surprise—a nerd, and this time he's in love with his best friend's wife. Modest story line provides a framework of endless gags, with Allen borrowing heavily from "Casablanca." Bogey even appears periodically to counsel Allen on the ways of wooing women. Superior comedy isn't hurt by Ross directing instead of Allen, who adapted the script from his own play. **86m/C VHS, DVD.** Woody Allen, Diane Keaton, Tony Roberts, Susan Anspach, Jerry Lacy, Jennifer Salt, Joy Bang, Viva; **D:** Herbert Ross; **W:** Woody Allen, Herbert Ross; **C:** Owen Roizman; **M:** Billy Goldenberg.

Play It to the Bone 🎬🎬 1999 (R) Harrelson and Banderas are fading boxers and best friends Vince and Cesar, who unexpectedly wind up in an under-

card bout against each other. Since they need to get to Vegas, and didn't think to get travel money from the promoter, Cesar's girlfriend (and Vince's ex) Grace (Davidovich) agrees to drive them. Along the way, she uses her wiles to whip up their competitive juices to use in the fight. It works, as the excessively brutal fight sequence shows. Shelton's fifth attempt at sports movie success doesn't quite connect, as it's more realistic portrayal of boxing-movie cliches tacked onto both ends. **124m/C VHS, DVD.** Woody Harrelson, Antonio Banderas, Lolita (David) Davidovich, Lucy Liu, Tom Sizemore, Robert Wagner, Richard Masur, Willie Garson, Cylk Cozart, Jack Carter; **D:** Ron Shelton; **W:** Ron Shelton; **C:** Mark Vargo; **M:** Alex Wurman.

Play Misty for Me 🎬🎬🎬 1971 (R) A radio deejay obliges a psychotic woman's song request and suddenly finds himself the target of her obsessive behavior, which rapidly turns from seductive to murderous. Auspicious directorial debut for Eastwood, borrowing from the Siegel playbook (look for the director's cameo as a barkeep). Based on a story by Heims. **102m/C VHS, DVD.** Jessica Walter, Donna Mills, John Larch, Irene Hervey, Jack Ging, Clint Eastwood; **Cameos:** Donald Siegel; **D:** Clint Eastwood; **W:** Jo Heims, Dean Riesner; **C:** Bruce Surtees; **M:** Dee Barton.

Play Murder for Me 🎬🎬 1991 (R) Saxophonist performing in a seedy Buenos Aires nightclub has his world turned upside down when a former lover suddenly re-enters his life. She still has her eye on him, but she's now the woman of a notorious mobster. Soon the musician finds himself drawn into the usual deadly world of crime, deceit, and unharnessed passion. **80m/C VHS.** Jack Wagner, Tracy Scoggins; **D:** Hector Olivera.

Play Nice 🎬½ 1992 (R) A detective hunts down a murderous psychopath but is shocked when he discovers his suspect is a woman—and someone he knows. Also available in an unrated version. **90m/C VHS, DVD.** Ed O'Ross, Michael Zand, Bruce McGill, Ron Canada, Louise Robey; **D:** Terri Treas; **W:** Michael Zand, Chuck McCollum; **M:** Gary Stevan Scott.

Play Time 🎬🎬 1994 Jeannie, Lindsay, and their husbands are on vacation in Palm Springs where they get up to some naughty sexual games that test the limits of friendship. Available in an unedited version at 95 minutes. **90m/C VHS.** Monique Parent, Craig Stepp, Jennifer Burton, Elliot David, Julie Strain, Tammy Parks, Ashlie Rhey; **D:** Dale Trevillion; **W:** Mary Ellen Hanover; **C:** Sven Kirsten; **M:** Joel Derouin.

Playback 🎬½ 1995 (R) Young couple think they've finally captured the gold ring when hubby David (Grant) gets a chance at a million dollar merger deal. But David's set-up by sexy co-worker Karen (Whirry) and his slimy boss Gil (Hamilton) tries to seduce his wife Sara (Kitaen). **91m/C VHS.** Charles Grant, Shannon Whirry, George Hamilton, Tawny Kitaen, Harry Dean Stanton; **D:** Oley Sassone; **W:** Oley Sassone, David DuBos; **C:** Russ Brandt.

Playboy of the Western World 🎬🎬½ 1962 An innkeeper's daughter is infatuated with a young man who says he murdered his father. Adapted from the classic play by John Millington Synge. **96m/C VHS.** *IR* Siobhan McKenna, Gary Raymond; **D:** Brian Desmond Hurst.

The Playboys 🎬🎬🎬 1992 (PG-13) In 1957 in a tiny Irish village, unmarried Tara Maguire (Wright Penn), causes a scandal by having a baby. Her beauty attracts lots of men—there's a former beau who kills himself, the obsessive, middle-aged Sergeant Hegarty (Finney), and the newest arrival, Tom Castle (Quinn), an actor with a rag-tag theatrical troupe called the Playboys. Slow-moving and simple story with particularly good performances by Wright as the strong-willed Tara and Finney as Hegarty, clinging to a last chance at love and family. The Playboys' hysterically hammy version of "Gone With the Wind" is a gem. Directorial debut of co-writer Mackinnon. Filmed in the village of Redhills, Ireland, the hometown of co-writer

Played 🎬 **2006** VHS, DVD, Albert Finney, Aidan Quinn, Robin Wright Penn, Milo O'Shea, Alan Devlin, Niamh Cusack, Ian McElhinney, Niall Buggy, Adrian Dunbar; **D:** Gilles Mackinnon; **W:** Shane Connaughton, Kerry Crabbe; **C:** Jack Conroy; **M:** Jean-Claude Petit. Connaughton, 114m/C VHS, DVD, low-budget crime drama that the name actors seem to have done as a favor to Rossi. Ray (Rossi), the fall guy for a botched heist, gets out of prison and is hired by London crime boss Rawlings (Dotrice) to take out rival gangster Riley (Bergin) who was behind the bungled job. 87m/C DVD, GB Patrick Bergin, Roy Dotrice, Val Kilmer, Gabriel Byrne, Mick Rossi, Vinnie Jones, Anthony LaPaglia, Bruno Kirby, Joanne Whalley, Patsy Kensit; **D:** Sean Stanek; **C:** Michael Pavelism; **M:** Danny Saber.

The Player 🎬🎬½ **1992** (R) Clever, entertaining, and biting satire of the movie industry and the greed that controls it. Robbins is dead-on as Griffin Mill, a young studio exec who becomes the chief suspect in a murder investigation. He personifies Hollywood's ethics (or lack thereof) in a performance both cold and vulnerable, and as he looks for the right buttons to push and the proper back to stab. Strong leading performances are supplemented by 65 star cameos. Some viewers may be put off by the inside-Hollywood jokes, but Altman fans will love it. 123m/C VHS, DVD, Tim Robbins, Greta Scacchi, Fred Ward, Whoopi Goldberg, Peter Gallagher, Brion James, Cynthia Stevenson, Vincent D'Onofrio, Dean Stockwell, Richard E. Grant, Dina Merrill, Sydney Pollack, Lyle Lovett, Randall Batinkoff, Gina Gershon, Nick Nolte, Jack Lemmon, Lily Tomlin, Marlee Matlin, Julia Roberts, Bruce Willis, Angelica Huston, Elliott Gould, Sally Kellerman, Steve Allen, Richard Anderson, Harry Belafonte, Shari Belafonte, Karen Black, Gary Busey, Robert Carradine, James Coburn, Cathy Lee Crosby, John Cusack, Brad Davis, Peter Falk, Teri Garr, Leeza Gibbons, Scott Glenn, Jeff Goldblum, Joel Grey, Buck Henry, Kathy Ireland, Sally Kirkland, Andie MacDowell, Martin Mull, Mimi Rogers, Jill St. John, Susan Sarandon, Rod Steiger, Joan Tewkesbury, Robert Wagner. Cameos: Burt Reynolds, Cher; **D:** Robert Altman; **W:** Michael Tolkin; **C:** Jean Lepine; **M:** Thomas Newman. British Acad. '92; Actor (Robbins), Director. '92. Actor (Robbins), Director (Altman). Cannes '92. Actor (Robbins), Director (Altman); Golden Globes '93. Actor—Mus./Comedy (Robbins). Film—Mus./Comedy; Ind. Spirit '93: Film; N.Y. Film Critics '92: Director (Altman); Film; Writers Guild '92: Adapt. Screenplay.

Players 🎬 **1979** (PG) Young tennis hustler touring Mexico hooks up with beautiful and mysterious older woman. They seem to be from different worlds yet their love grows. She inspires him enough to enter Wimbledon. Several tennis pros appear, including Guillermo Vilas, John McEnroe, and Ilie Nastase. Almost as boring as watching a real tennis game. 120m/C VHS, Ali MacGraw, Dean Paul (Dino Martin Jr.) Martin, Maximilian Schell, Pancho Gonzales; **D:** Anthony Harvey; **W:** Arnold Schulman; **M:** Jerry Goldsmith.

Players 🎬🎬½ **1998** (R) Pledge of Allegiance 2003 (R) Star high school football player Sean (Rodriguez) dates Sophia (Marsala), the daughter of local Nevada wiseguy Salvi (Dobson). Then Sean discovers that having dad's friendship means throwing some championship games to help the sports betting line. Trouble follows. 90m/C DVD, Freddy Rodriguez, Peter Dobson, Rena Owen, Carmine D. Giovinazzo, Melissa Marsala, Joseph Bologna, John Doe, Theodore (Ted) Raimi, James DeBello, James Duval; **D:** Lee Madser; **W:** Lee Madsen; **C:** Ben Kufrin; **M:** Ben Sanborne.

The Players Club 🎬🎬½ **1998** (R) Rapper-turned-auteur Ice Cube directs this look at the seamy and steamy world of strip clubs from his own screenplay. Diana (LisaRaye) is a single mom and college student by day, and a dancer at a strip club owned by the bombastic Dollar Bill (Mac) by night. When her naive cousin Ebony (Calhoun) is lured into turning tricks by fellow stripper Ronnie (Wilson), trouble starts. Blue (Foxx) is the deejay who falls for Diana, and is persuaded to act honorably by Diana's disapproving (and target for Diana's disapproving...) father (Williams); Ice Cube appears as a customer who inadvertently lights the fuse for the movie's climax. While not in Woody Allen territory yet, Mr. Cube brings both humor and reality to the seedy world of strip joints. 103m/C VHS, DVD, LisaRaye, Bernie Mac, Monica Calhoun, A.J. Johnson, Tommy (Tiny) Lister, John Amos, Faizon Love, Alex Thomas, Chrystale Wilson, Adele Givens, Larry McCoy, Dick Anthony Williams; **D:** Ice Cube; **W:** Ice Cube; **C:** Malik Hassan Sayeed; **M:** Hidden Faces.

Playgirl Killer 🎬 Decoy for Terror **1966** After impulsively murdering a restless model, an artist continues to kill indiscriminately, keeping his spoils on ice. Sedaka croons between kills and luxuriates poolside—seemingly oblivious to the plot of the film—while a female decoy is sent to bait the killer for the police. For adult viewers. 86m/C VHS, DVT, CA Allan Nicholls, William Kerwin, Jean Christopher, Andree Champagne, Neil Sedaka; **D:** Erick Santamaria.

Playing Around 🎬½ **1930** Flapper Sheba Miller (White) is bored with poor good guy boyfriend Jack (Bakewell) and all-too eager to spend time with flashy playboy Nickey Solomon (Morris). Only Nickey can't afford his lavish spending without resorting to armed robbery and Sheba learns the error of her ways. 66m/B VHS, Alice White, Chester Morris, William 'Billy' Bakewell, Richard Carlye; **D:** Mervyn LeRoy; **W:** Harvey Thew; **C:** Sol Polito.

Playing Away 🎬 **1987** A team of Caribbean cricket players meet a team of stuffy Brits on the field in a clash of the cultures. 100m/C VHS, GB Norman Beaton, Robert Urquhart; **D:** Horace Ove.

Playing by Heart 🎬🎬 Dancing about Architecture **1998** (R) Excellent ensemble cast doesn't save this episodic film about several L.A. couples falling in and out of love. Theatre director Anderson tries to avoid becoming involved with architect Stewart; loud-mouthed night-club ber Jolie won't give up on Phillipe; Quaid uses bad lines and lies on Stowe, tools around with Edwards; Connery and Rowlands (in the best-acted segments) find their 40-year marriage threatened by emotional and health problems; and Burstyn tries to comfort her son Mohr, in the last stages of AIDS. Writer/director Carroll claims he was inspired by the saying "talking about love is like dancing about architecture," and appropriately the working title was "Dancing about Architecture." 121m/C VHS, DVD, Sean Connery, Gena Rowlands, Ryan Phillippe, Angelina Jolie, Ellen Burstyn, Gillian Anderson, Dennis Quaid, Jay Mohr, Anthony Edwards, Madeleine Stowe, Jon Stewart, Patricia Clarkson, Nastassja Kinski, Jeremy Sisto; **D:** Willard Carroll; **W:** Willard Carroll; **C:** Vilmos Zsigmond; **M:** John Barry.

Playing Dangerous 🎬½ **1995** (PG-13) Eleven-year-old computer whiz must outsmart computer thieves with the aid of a water gun and a remote-controlled car. 86m/C VHS, David Keith Miller; **D:** Lawrence Lanoff.

Playing Dead 🎬🎬½ **1915** Drew and his wife portray a married couple in this silent farce. The insecure husband decides to fake his death so his wife can be with the man he thinks she loves. 58m/B VHS, Sidney Drew, Lucille Drew, Alice Lake, Donald Hall, Harry English, Isadore Marcil; **D:** Sidney Drew.

Playing for Keeps 🎬 **1986** (PG-13) Three high school grads inherit a dilapidated hotel into a rock 'n' roll resort. Music by Pete Townshend, Peter Frampton, Phil Collins, and others. 103m/C VHS, DVD, Daniel Jordano, Matthew Penn, Leon Grant, Harold Gould, Jimmy Baio; **D:** Bob Weinstein.

Playing for Time 🎬🎬 **1980** Compelling, award-winning TV drama based on actual experiences of a Holocaust prisoner who survives by leading an inmate orchestra. Strong playing from Redgrave and Mayron. Pro-Palestinian Redgrave's political beliefs made her a controversial candidate for the role of Jewish Fania Fenelon, but her stunning performance is on the mark. 148m/C VHS, Vanessa Redgrave, Jane Alexander, Maud Adams, Verna Bloom, Melanie Mayron; **D:** Daniel Mann; **M:** Brad Fiedel. TV

Playmaker 🎬½ **1994** (R) Jaime (Rubin) is a struggling actress whose coach Talbert (Firth) guarantees success as long as she follows his bizarre training methods, which include seduction, abuse, and betrayal. Good chemistry between the leads but a mishmash of a script. Claire decides to adopt a Mona Lisa smile and see what life has to offer. 91m/C VHS, DVD, Alicia Witt, Ivan Sergei, Brooke Langton, Johnny Galecki, Jeff(rey) Perry; **D:** Yuri Zeltser; **W:** Yuri Zeltser; **C:** James Glennon.

Playing God 🎬½ **1996** (R) Eugene (Duchovny), a disgraced junkie doctor who has lost his license, saves the life of a hood in a bar while trying to score more drugs. This brings him to the attention of Raymond (Hutton), the head of a counterfeiting and smuggling ring, who saves the life of an undercover cop. While sufficiently bloody and nasty, flick tries too hard to be offbeat and hip. 94m/C VHS, DVD, David Duchovny, Timothy Hutton, Angelina Jolie, Michael Massee, Peter Stormare, Andrew Tiernan, Gary Dourdan; **D:** Andy Wilson; **W:** Mark Haskell Smith; **C:** B. Richmond; **M:** Richard Harvey.

Playing Mona Lisa 🎬🎬½ **2000** Piano prodigy Claire (Witt) gets dumped by her boyfriend on the night of her college graduation and then is humiliated at a piano competition. So, while trying to cope with her problems, Claire decides to adopt a Mona Lisa smile and see what life has to offer. While patching up crooks so they don't get arrested at the hospital, Eugene develops more than a doctor-patient relationship with Raymond's pillow-lipped girlfriend Claire (Jolie). Things begin to get a little slicey and nasty, flick tries too hard to cope with her problems... While patching up crooks so they don't get arrested at the hospital, Eugene develops more than a doctor-patient relationship... a little slicey and nasty. 97m/C VHS, DVD, Alicia Witt, Ivan Sergei, Brooke Langton, Elliot Gould, Mario Thomas, Harvey Fierstein, Molly Hagan, Estelle Harris, Sandra Bernhard, Shannon Finn; **D:** Matthew Huffman; **W:** Mani Freedman, Carlos De Los Rios; **C:** James Glennon.

Playmates 🎬 **1941** Barrymore is practically wasted in his last film as a down-on-his-luck actor who agrees to turn bandleader Kyser into a Shakespearean actor. Bizarre comedy is funny at times, but leaves the audience wondering what Barrymore thought he was doing. 96m/B VHS, Kay Kyser, John Barrymore, Ginny Simms, Lupe Velez, May Robson, Patsy Kelly, Peter Lind Hayes, George Cleve and; **D:** David Butler.

Playmates 🎬🎬½ **1972** Two divorced buddies fall in love with each other's ex-wives. Typical Alda vehicle isn't bad. 78m/C VHS, Doug McClure, Alan Alda, Connie Stevens, Barbara Feldon, Eileen Brennan, Tiger Williams, Severn Darden; **D:** Theodore J. Flicker. TV

Playroom 🎬🎬 **1990** (R) Archaeologist McDonald is completing his father's search for the tomb of a medieval boy-prince. But someone, or something, has been waiting for him for a long, long time. When he finally reaches the long-sought after tomb, he discovers that it is a torture chamber where the demonic prince who was buried in the tomb has picked Chris as his playmate, and the rest of the staff as his personal toys. 87m/C VHS, Lisa Aliff, Aron Eisenberg, Christopher McDonald, James Purcell, Jamie Rose, Vincent Schiavelli; **D:** Manny Coto; **C:** James L. Carter.

Playtime 🎬🎬🎬 **1967** Occasionally enterprising comedy, in which the bemused Frenchman Hulot tries in vain to maintain an appointment in an urban landscape of glass and steel. The theme of cold, unfeeling civilization is harshly unique, but the film is nonetheless enjoyable. The third in the Hulot trilogy, preceded by "Mr. Hulot's Holiday" and "Mon Oncle." In French with English subtitles. 108m/C VHS, DVD, FR Jacques Tati, Barbara Dennek, Jacqueline Lecomte, Jack Gautier; **D:** Jacques Tati.

Please Don't Eat the Daisies 🎬🎬½ **1960** City couple and kids leave the Big Apple for the suburbs when dad gets a job as a drama critic. The fun starts when they buy a broken-down mansion that needs fixing up and everybody gets into the act. Based on the book by Jean Kerr. From the TV series. 111m/C VHS, DVD, Doris Day, David Niven, Janis Paige, Spring Byington, Richard Haydn, Patsy Kelly, Jack Weston, Margaret Lindsay; **D:** Charles Walters; **W:** Isobel Lennart; **C:** Robert Bronner; **M:** David Rose.

Please Not Now! 🎬🎬 Only for Love: La Bride sur le Cou **1961** Parisian model Bardot discovers her boyfriend R.berolies is cheating on her and she decides to shoot him. He's warned by Subor, who wants Bardot for himself, and takes off with new gal pal James, but Bardot and Subor are in pursuit. Then Bardot and James commiserate over the fact that their lovers, French with subtitles. 53m/B VHS, Conway, Teerle, Roscoe Karns, Carmel Myers, Lena Basquette, Frances Dade, Paul Page, Harold Goodwin, George "Gabby" Hayes; **D:** Otto Brower; **W:** Jo Van Ronkel, Thomas Thibley, John Varley.

Pleasantville 🎬🎬🎬½ **1998** (PG-13) Nerdy David (Maguire) and his slut wannabe sister Jennifer (Witherspoon) are sucked into the sterile and innocent world of Pleasantville, a 1950s B/W TV show in the roles of Bud and Mary Sue, the blandly adorable children of George and Betty Parker (Macy and Allen). After Jennifer shows a classmate what lovers lare is really for, the townspeople begin to lose their innocence; the black-and-white world becomes more colorful as each new human passion is realized. The performances are dead-on, particularly Allen as the sexually awakening mom. The transition from straight comedy to social commentary is adeptly handled. The great character actor J.T. Walsh gives this usual excellent (and sadly, last) performance as the stubborn head of the chamber of commerce bitterly fighting change. 124m/C VHS, DVD, Tobey Maguire, Reese Witherspoon, William H. Macy, Joan Allen, Jeff Daniels, J.T. Walsh, Don Knotts; **D:** Gary Ross; **W:** Gary Ross; **C:** John Lindley; **M:** Randy Newman. L.A. Film Critics '98: Support. Actress (Allen); Broadcast Film Critics '98: Support. Actress (Allen).

A Pleasure Doing Business 🎬 **1979** (R) Three high school buddies, now in their 40s, are reunited at a stag party, where they decide to go into business as managers of the...

Pleasure 🎬🎬½ **1931** A saga of love, treachery, and melodrama in English society in which a married author begins an affair with a model, unaware that she also has someone on the side, and it turns out to be his brother. 53m/B VHS, Conway, Teerle, Roscoe Karns, Carmel Myers, Lena Basquette, Frances Dade, Paul Page, Harold Goodwin, George "Gabby" Hayes; **D:** Otto Brower.

Plaza Suite 🎬🎬🎬 **1971** (PG) Three alternating skits from Neil Simon's play about different couples staying at the New York hotel. Matthau shines in all three vignettes. Some of Simon's funnier stuff. Matthau and Stapleton are a couple celebrating their first sketch being the best. Matthau and Stapleton are a couple celebrating their 24th anniversary. She's sentimental, while he's yearning for his mistress. Number two has producer Matthau p.tting the make on old flame Harris, while it'e finale has father Matthau coaxing his anxious daughter out of the bathroom on her wedding day. 114m/C VHS, DVD, Walter Matthau, Maureen Stapleton, Barbara Harris, Lee Grant, Louise Sorel; **D:** Arthur Hiller; **W:** Neil Simon; **C:** Jack Marta.

est profession." 86m/C VHS. Conrad Bain, John Byner, Alan Oppenheimer, Misty Rowe, Phyllis Diller. D: Steve Vagnino.

The Pleasure Drivers ♂♂½ **2005** Disjointed plot follows the efforts of caregiver Daphne (Holly) to get what's due from cult leader Marvin (Zane), who refuses to pay for his son's care. Daphne decides to kidnap her patient's mentally unstable sister to get dad's attention. Meanwhile, psychology professor Bill (Macfadyen) takes a road trip with sex-obsessed student Faruza (Chabert) after his wife leaves him for another woman. Somehow a lesbian hitwoman (Bennett) becomes involved. All ultimately meet in the desert where justice is meted out. 99m/ C DVD. Lauren Holly, Lacey Chabert, Billy Zane, Jill Bennett, Angus MacFadyen, Steffany Huckaby, Angelo Spizzirri, Meat Loaf Aday, Jason Mewes, Rachel Dratch, Haynes; C: Andrzej Sekula; M: Steve Gutheinz. VIDEO

Pleasure Palace ♂♂ **1980** A gambling ladies' man (Sharif) meets his match when he helps a woman casino owner (Lange). 96m/C VHS. Omar Sharif, Victoria Principal, J.D. Cannon, Gerald S. O'Loughlin, Jose Ferrer, Hope Lange, Alan King; D: Walter Grauman. TV

The Pledge ♂♂♂ **2000 (R)** Retired Reno homicide detective Nicholson is obsessed with the unsolved murder of a little girl, which bares a resemblance to past unsolved child murders. Unconventional thriller's dark subject matter will no doubt dissuade some potential viewers, but Penn's third (and best) directorial outing is impressive, thanks in large part to Nicholson's subtle, intense work. 124m/C VHS, DVD. US Jack Nicholson, Robin Wright Penn, Aaron Eckhart, Vanessa Redgrave, Patricia Clarkson, Benicio Del Toro, Costas Mandylor, Helen Mirren, Tom Noonan, Michael O'Keefe, Mickey Rourke, Sam Shepard, Lois Smith, Harry Dean Stanton, Dale Dickey, Pauline Roberts; D: Sean Penn; W: Jerzy Kromolowski, Mary Olson-Kromolowski; C: Chris Menges; M: Hans Zimmer.

Pledge Night ♂♂ **1990 (R)** Tale of horror and revenge. Killed years before in a fraternity hazing, Sid returns for the brothers who did him in. Gory and violent. 90m/C VHS. Will Kempe, Shannon McMahon, Todd Eastland; D: Paul Ziller.

The Plot Against Harry ♂♂♂ **1969** Jewish racketeer Harry Plotnik checks out of prison, and finds the outside world ain't what it used to be. Attempting to lead an honest life only makes matters worse. Completely overlooked when first released in 1969 (and quickly shelved) because it was considered to have no commercial potential, Roemer's crime comedy found an enthusiastic audience when it was rediscovered 20 years later. 81m/B VHS, DVD. Martin Priest, Ben Lang, Maxine Woods, Henry Nemo, Jacques Taylor, Ellen Herbert, Sandra Kazan; D: Michael Roemer; W: Michael Emil; C: Robert M. Young; M: Frank Lewin.

The Ploughman's Lunch ♂♂♂ **1983** A BBC news reporter claws and lies his way to the top. He then discovers that he is the victim of a far more devious plan. Engrossing and well made, although some of the political views are simplistic. 107m/C VHS, DVD. Jonathan Pryce, Charlie Dore, Tim Curry, Rosemary Harris, Frank Finlay, Bill Paterson; D: Richard Eyre.

Plucking the Daisy ♂♂½
Please! Mr. Balzac; While Plucking the Daisy; En Effeuillant la Marguerite; Mademoiselle Striptease **1956** Agnes Dumont (Bardot) anonymously writes a scandalous romantic novel that becomes a best-seller and causes her straitlaced father to send Agnes to a convent school. Only she escapes to her brother's in Paris instead, where she decides to earn some money by entering a titicing Bardot's ample charms on display). French with subtitles. 100m/B VHS, DVD. FR Brigitte Bardot, Robert Hirsch, Daniel Gelin, Jacques Dumesnil; D: Marc Allegret; W: Marc Allegret, Roger Vadim; C: Louis Page; M: Paul Misraki.

Plughead Rewired: Circuitry Man 2 ♂♂ *Circuitry Man 2* **1994 (R)** Earth's atmosphere has been destroyed and survivors are forced underground, where they're terrorized by the humanoid Plughead, who likes to literally plug into the minds of his victims. Plughead wants to rule what's left of life on Earth and all that stands in his way is the android Circuitry Man and FBI agent Kyle. Special effects are strictly bargain basement reel. 97m/C VHS, DVD. Vernon Wells, Deborah Shelton, Jim Metzler, Dennis Christopher, Nicholas Worth, Traci Lords; D: Steven Lovy, Robert Lovy; W: Steven Lovy, Robert Lovy; C: Stephen Timberlake; M: Tim Kelly.

Plumber ♂♂½ **1979** A plumber who makes a house call extends his stay to psychologically torture the woman of the house. Originally made for Australian TV. 76m/C VHS. AU Judy Morris, Ivar Kants, Robert Coleby; D: Peter Weir; W: Peter Weir. TV

Plump Fiction ♂ **1997 (R)** The movie that proves beyond a doubt that when you make fun of Quentin Tarantino, you should stick to his truly horrible acting. Instead, this spoof attacks his already over-the-top characters from "Pulp Fiction" and "Natural Born Killers." Julius (Davidson) and Jimmy (Dinello) are the loser hit men, and Mimi (Brown) is the gangster's wife. You see, Mimi has a substance abuse problem, but it's not cocaine. It's food! She's fat, get it? Hal Haha. Ha? Hmm. Intersecting storylines feature Nicky (Glave) and Vallory (Segall), doing a dead-on Juliette Lewis) as "Natural Blonde Killers." The only redeeming scene is that of Kane Picoy (doing an uncanny impersonation of the king of the psychos. 82m/C VHS, DVD. Tommy Davidson, Julie Brown, Sandra Bernhard, Paul Dinello, Dan Castellaneta, Colleen Camp, Pamela Segall, Kevin Meaney, Matthew Glave, Jennifer Rubin, Robert Costanzo, Philippe Bergerone; D: Bob Koherr; W: Bob Koherr; C: Rex Nicholson; M: Michael Muhlfriedel.

Plunder Road ♂♂½ **1957** Eddie (Raymond) masterminds plan to rob a train bound for the San Francisco Mint that's carrying a fortune in gold bullion. The heist's a success but actually getting away with the loot becomes a problem. Top notch B-film noir. 76m/B VHS. Gene Raymond, Jeanne Cooper, Wayne Morris, Elisha Cook Jr., Stafford Repp, Steven Ritch; D: Hubert Cornfield; W: Steven Ritch; C: Ernest Haller; M: Irving Gertz.

Plunge Into Darkness ♂½ **1977** Quiet weekend in the mountains turns into a nightmare for an ex-Olympic runner and his family. 77m/C VHS. Bruce Barry, Olivia Hamnett, Ashley Greenville, Wallace (Wallas) Eaton, Tom Richards; D: Peter Maxwell.

Plunkett & Macleane ♂♂½ **1998 (R)** Will Plunkett (Carlyle) is a lower-class thief who teams up with wastrel aristocrat Macleane (Miller) to make a living as highwaymen in 18th-century London. The rogues are aided by hedonistic Lord Rochester (Cumming) and opposed by Lord Chief Justice Gibson (Gambon), whose vixenish niece, Lady Rebecca (Tyler), becomes Macleane's inamorata. Carlyle and Miller make a fine criminal duo but the film has lots of flaws to distract the viewer. (Son of Ridley) Scott's directorial debut. 102m/C VHS, DVD. GB Robert Carlyle, Jonny Lee Miller, Liv Tyler, Michael Gambon, Alan Cumming, Ken Stott, Terence Rigby, Claire Rushbrook, Iain Robertson, Jake Scott; D: Jake Scott; W: Robert Wade, Neal Purvis, Charles McKeown; C: John Mathieson; M: Craig Armstrong.

Plutonium Baby ♂♂ **1987** A mutated kid, whose mother was killed by the same radiation exposure that infected him, tracks down the guilty party in New York in this comic-book style film. 85m/C VHS. Patrick Molloy, Danny Guerra; D: Ray Hirschman.

Plutonium Incident ♂♂ **1982** A female technician at a nuclear power plant suspects the facility to be less safe than it appears, and faces a diabolical plan of harassment when she attempts to bring attention to the hazards. 90m/C VHS. Janet Margolin, Powers Boothe, Bo Hopkins, Joseph Campanella; D: Richard Michaels.

Pocahontas ♂♂♂ **1995 (G)** It's 1607 and spirited Powhatan maiden Pocahontas and British settler Captain John Smith strike an unlikely but doomed romance in Disney's 33rd animated feature, its first based on the life of a historical figure. Lovely Poca, a virtual post-adolescent Native American superbabe, introduces the roguish captain (spoken and sung by Gibson) to the wonders of unspoiled nature and serves as peacemaker in the clash of European and Native American cultures. Disney puts its spin on history but maintains cultural sensitivity: several characters are voiced by Native American performers, including Chief Powhatan, spoken by American Indian activist Means, who led the 1973 siege at Wounded Knee, and Bedard as Pocahontas. Just don't tell the kids the real Pocahontas married someone else, moved to England, and died of smallpox at 21. Stunningly animated, but its mediocre soundtrack and decidedly somber tone leave it lacking in typical Disney majesty and charm. Premiered at New York's Central Park, for the usual theatre crowd of 100,000 or so. 90m/ C VHS, DVD. D: Mike Gabriel, Eric Goldberg; W: Carl Binder, Susannah Grant, Philip LaZebnik; M: Alan Menken, Stephen Schwartz; V: Irene Bedard, Billy Connolly, James Apaumut Fall, Linda Hunt, John Kassir, Danny Mann, Bill Cobbs, David Ogden Stiers, Michelle St. John, Gordon Tootoosis, Frank Welker. Oscars '95: Song ("Colors of the Wind"), Orig. Score; Golden Globes '96: Song ("Colors of the Wind").

Pocahontas: The Legend ♂♂½ **1995** Live-action version of the increasingly familiar story of the psychos. Native American girl who aids Virginia settler, John Smith. 101m/C VHS, DVD. CA Sandrine Holt, Miles O'Keeffe, Tony Goldwyn, Gordon Tootoosis; D: Daniele Suissa; W: Daniele Suissa.

The Pocatello Kid ♂♂½ **1931** Maynard stretches in a dual role as the wrongly convicted Kid and the Kid's no-good sheriff brother. 60m/B VHS, DVD. Ken Maynard, Marceline Day, Charles "Blackie" King, Lafe (Lafayette) McKee; D: Phil Rosen.

Pocket Money ♂♂ **1972 (PG)** Down-on-their-luck cowpokes foolishly do business with crooked rancher in attempt to make comeback in faltering acting careers. Star-powered, moderately entertaining modern western-comedy based on the novel "Jim Kane" by J.K.S. Brown. 100m/C VHS, DVD. Paul Newman, Lee Marvin, Strother Martin, Christine Belford, Wayne Rogers, Hector Elizondo, Gregory Sierra; D: Stuart Rosenberg; W: Terrence Malick; M: Alex North.

Pocketful of Miracles ♂♂♂ **1961** Capra's final film, a remake of his 1933 "Lady for a Day," is just as corny and sentimental but doesn't work quite as well. Davis is delightful as Apple Annie, a down-on-her-luck street vendor who will go to any extreme to hide her poverty from the well-married daughter she adores. Ford is terrific as the man who financed Annie into a lady in time for her daughter's visit. Touching. Maybe too touching. Also marks Ann-Margret's film debut. 136m/C VHS, DVD. Bette Davis, Glenn Ford, Peter Falk, Hope Lange, Arthur O'Connell, Ann-Margret, Thomas Mitchell, Jack Elam, Edward Everett Horton, David Brian, Mickey Shaughnessy; D: Frank Capra; W: Hal Kanter, Harry Tugend; C: Robert J. Bronner; M: Walter Scharf. Golden Globes '62: Actor—Mus./Comedy (Ford).

A Pocketful of Rye ♂♂ *Agatha Christie's Miss Marple: A Pocketful of Rye* **1987** Based on Agatha Christie's novel featuring the sleuthing Miss Marple. She faces another murderous puzzle, this one based on an old nursery rhyme. 101m/C VHS, DVD. GB Joan Hickson; D: Guy Slater. TV

Poco ♂ **1977** The story of Poco, a shaggy little dog who travels across the country to search for the young girl who owns him. 88m/C VHS. Chill Wills, Michelle Ashburn, John Steadman; D: Dwight Brooks; W: William Carville; C: Dwight Brooks.

Poetic Justice ♂♂½ **1993 (R)** Justice (Jackson) in her movie debut, for better or worse) gives up college plans to follow a career in cosmetology after her boyfriend's brutal murder. She copes with her loss by dedicating herself to poetry writing (provided by no less than poet Maya Angelou) and meets postal worker Shakur. Singleton's second directorial effort is about the girlz n the hood and boasts a lighter script (well, it is about a hairdresser) focusing less on the Boyz-style morality and more on the trials and tribulations of justice. Production stopped on the South Central L.A. set during the '92 riots, but the aftermath provided poignant pictures for later scenes. 109m/C VHS, DVD. Janet Jackson, Tupac Shakur, Tyra Ferrell, Regina King, Joe Torry, Norma Donaldson; D: John Singleton; W: John Singleton; C: Peter Lyons Collister; M: Stanley Clarke. MTV Movie Awards '94: Female Perf. (Jackson), Most Desirable Female (Jackson); Golden Raspberries '93: Worst New Star (Jackson).

Poil de Carotte ♂♂♂ *The Red Head* **1931** A semi-famous French melodrama about a young boy harassed by his overbearing mother to the point of disaster, redeemed finally by the love of his father. In French with English subtitles. 90m/ B VHS. FR Harry Baur, Robert Lynen, Catherine Fontenoy; D: Julien Duvivier.

The Point ♂♂½ **1971** Charming and sincere animated feature about the rejection and isolation of a round-headed child in a world of pointy-headed people. Excellent score. 74m/C VHS, DVD. D: Fred Wolf; M: Harry Nilsson; V: Paul Frees; Nar: Ringo Starr. TV

Point Blank ♂♂♂ **1967** Adapted from Stark's "The Hunter." The film's techniques are sometimes compared to those of Resnais and Godard. Double-crossed and believed dead, gangster Marvin returns to claim his share of the loot from the Organization. Hard-nosed examination of the depersonalization of a mechanized urban world. 92m/C VHS, DVD. Lee Marvin, Angie Dickinson, Keenan Wynn, Carroll O'Connor, Lloyd Bochner, Michael Strong, James B. Sikking; D: John Boorman.

Point Blank ♂♂ **1998 (R)** A bus carrying death-row convicts is ambushed but the cons don't go their separate ways. Instead, they take over a shopping mall and begin fighting among themselves. 90m/C VHS, DVD. Mickey Rourke, Danny Trejo, Kevin Gage, Michael Wright, Frederic Forrest, James Gammon; D: Matt Earl Beesley. VIDEO

Point Break ♂♂½ **1991 (R)** If you can suspend your disbelief—and you'd need a crane—then this crime adventure is just dandy. Reeves is a young undercover FBI kid sent to infiltrate a gang of bank-robbing surfer dudes. Swayze is the leader of the beach subculture, a thrill-seeker who plays cat-and-mouse with the feds in a series of excellent action scenes. Silly brain candy. 117m/C VHS, DVD. Jack Kehler, Lee Tergesen, Christopher Pettiet, Elizabeth Berkley, Tom Sizemore, Anthony Mangano, Patrick Swayze, Keanu Reeves, Gary Busey, Lori Petty, John C. McGinley, Chris Pederson, Bojesse Christopher, Julian Reyes, Daniel Beer, Sydney Walsh, Vincent Klyn, James LeGros, John Philbin; D: Kathryn Bigelow; W: W. Peter Iliff; C: Don Peterman; M: Mark Isham. MTV Movie Awards '92: Most Desirable Male (Reeves).

Point of Impact ♂♂ *Spanish Rose* **1993 (R)** A Miami customs officer is killed in an explosion and his partner is blamed. He knows a Cuban crime boss was actually behind it and goes undercover to bring the criminal organization down. But there's also the temptation of the the criminal's sexy ladyfriend. Also available in an unrated version. **96m/C VHS, Michael Pare, Barbara Carrera, Michael Ironside. D:** Yassi Wein. **M:** Vladimir Horunzhy.

Point of No Return 🐾🐾 1993
(R) Fonda is Maggie, a drugged-out loser condemned to death for her part in a murder spree, but if she agrees to work as a government assassin, she'll be given a reprieve. Fonda displays a certain perkiness; Keitel is creepy as an other assassin. Flashy, exacting, but ultimately innocuous remake of the 1990 French thriller "La Femme Nikita." **108m/C VHS, DVD, Bridget Fonda, Gabriel Byrne, Dermot Mulroney, Michael Ferrer, Anne Bancroft, Olivia D'Abo, Harvey Keitel, Richard Romanus, Lorraine Toussaint, Geoffrey Lewis, Calvin Levels; D:** John Badham; **W:** Robert Getchell, Alexandra Seros; **C:** Michael Watkins; **M:** Hans Zimmer.

The Pointsman 🐾🐾🐾 De Wisselwachter 1986 (R) A quirky, small film based on the novel by Jean-Paul Franssens. A beautiful Scandinavian woman accidentally gets off a train in Northern Scotland, where the only shelter is a small railway outpost, and the only company is a mysterious pointsman who lives by the comings and goings of the trains. The couple's increasing isolation as winter falls and their lack of a common language persists is portrayed with both humor and poignancy. **95m/C VHS, NL Jim Van Jer Woude, Stephane Excoffier; D:** Jos Stelling.

Point of Origin 🐾🐾½ 2002 Captain John Orr (Liotta) is an arson investigator with the Glendale fire department. He's investigating a six-year string of fires in southern California (in the 1980s) along with protege/inspector Keith Lang (Leguizamo). Everyone's a suspect, including the firefighters themselves. Based on a true story. **86m/C VHS, DVD, Ray Liotta, John Leguizamo, Colm Feore, Clifford Curtis, Bai Ling, Illeana Douglas, Ronny Cox; D:** Newton Thomas Sigel; **W:** Matthew Tabak; **C:** Anthony B. Richmond. CABLE

Point of Terror 🐾 1971 (R) A handsome rock singer seduces a record company executive's wife in order to further his career. **88m/C VHS, DVD, Peter Carpenter, Dyanne Thorne, Lory Hansen, Leslie Simms; D:** Alex Nicol.

Poison 🐾🐾🐾 1991 (R) A controversial, compelling drama weaving the story of a seven year-old boy's murder of his father with two other tales of obsessive, fringe behavior. From the director of the underground hit "Superstar: The Karen Carpenter Story," which was shot using only a cast of "Barbie" dolls. **85m/C VHS, DVD, Edith Meeks, Larry Maxwell, Susan Norman, Scott Renderer, James Lyons, Millie White, Buck Smith, Anne Giotta, Al Quagliata, Michelle Sullivan, John R. Lombardi, Tony Pemberton, Andrew Harpending; D:** Todd Haynes; **W:** Todd Haynes. Excoffier, Jim Van Dort. **D:** Jos Stelling. **Maryse Alberti; M:** James Bennett. Sundance '91: Grand Jury Prize.

Poison Thy Neighbor's Wife 2001 (R) Ann believes that an ordinary housewife is responsible for the death of her husband. So Ann disguises herself, gets a job with the family, and decides to extract the proper revenge. Of course, Ann's crazy. **92m/C VHS, DVD, Karl Wuhrer, Jeff Trachta, Barbara Crampton, Michael Cavanaugh, Larry Poindexter; D:** Jim Wynorski; **W:** Sean O'Bannon; **C:** Andrea V. Rossotto. VIDEO

Poison Ivy 🐾🐾 1985 A routine comedy about a chaotic and lusty summer camp. **97m/C VHS, Michael J. Fox, Nancy McKeon, Robert Klein, Carer Kaye; D:** Larry Elikann; **M:** Miles Goodman. TV

Poison Ivy 🐾🐾 1992 (R) Barrymore is right on target as a junior femme fatale in this trashy tale of a wayward teenager and her takeover of her best friend's family. Ivy has no discernable family life and cuckily attaches herself to the lonely, neglected Cooper (Gilbert) who ends up watching as she systematically seduces both her mother (emotionally) and her father (physically). But when Ivy's homewrecking turns lethal, Cooper must fight her "friend" to save herself. Glossy, over-done

pulp. An unrated version is also available. **91m/C VHS, DVD, Drew Barrymore, Sara Gilbert, Tom Skerritt, Cheryl Ladd; D:** Katt Shea; **W:** Katt Shea, Andy Ruben; **C:** Phedon Papamichael; **M:** David Michael Frank.

Poison Ivy 2: Lily 🐾½ 1995 (R) Art student Lily (Milano) finds the provocative Ivy's diary and becomes intrigued enough to decide to take a walk on the wild side herself, which gets her into all sorts of trouble. Also available unrated. **110m/C VHS, DVD, Alyssa Milano, Xander Berkeley, Johnathon Schaech, Belinda Bauer; D:** Anne Goursaud; **W:** Chloe King; **C:** Suki Medencevic; **M:** Joseph Williams.

Poison Ivy 3: The New Seduction 🐾½ 1997 (R) Now Ivy has a long-lost sister, appropriately named Violet (Pressly), who heads to their childhood home to get revenge on those she believes betrayed them. Naturally, it's all sex and men being led around by their...zippers. Also available unrated. **93m/C VHS, DVD, Jaime Pressly, Megan Edwards, Michael Des Barres, Greg Vaughan; D:** Kurt Voss; **W:** Karen Kelly; **C:** Feliks Parnell; **M:** Reg Powell.

Pokemon 3: The Movie 🐾🐾 2001 (G) As opposed to what: "Pokemon 3: The Dinner Theater?" This installment of the interminable franchise has a young girl, who's father has disappeared, turning her surroundings into a land of icy crystal. Ash, Pikachu and the other Pokemon (Pokemen?) show up to save the day with various pocket monster battles. Lessons are learned, battles are fought and won or lost, and days are saved, except for the days wasted by parents who have to sit through it all. **88m/C VHS, DVD, D:** Kunihiko Yuyama, Michael Haigney; **W:** Michael Haigney, Norman Grossfeld, Takeshi Shudo, Hideki Sonoda; **V:** Veronica Taylor, Eric Stuart, Rachael Lillis, Maddie (Maddelene) B. Lisstein, Ikue Otani.

Pokemon: The First Movie 🐾 1999 (G) If your kid is saying things like "Pikachu," "Squirtle," and "Charizard" then you've already been introduced to the multimedia (and mucho dollar) world of Pokemon. In that case you'll be forced to rent or buy this movie regardless of any criticism (unless by the time you read this the craze has gone the way of the Teenage Mutant Ninja Turtle). This full-length version of the popular cartoon series (video game, trading card game, toy line, etc...) hero Ash and his pals Misty and Brock go to New Island to do battle with a wicked genetically engineered Pokemon called Mewtwo. Mewtwo defeats all the Pokemon trainers in battle, and is ready to clone hideous monsters from the defeated critters when he is challenged by the mysterious and rare Mew. Several new characters are introduced along with clever marketing ties, because regardless of any criticism the craze has gone. This short "Pikachu's Vacation." **75m/C VHS, DVD, D:** Kunihiko Yuyama, Michael Haigney; **W:** Michael Haigney, Takeshi Shudo; **C:** Hisao Shirai; **V:** Veronica Taylor, Mayumi Iizuka, Tomokazu Seki.

Poker Alice 🐾🐾 1987 A lively Western starring Elizabeth Taylor as a sometime gambler who wins a brothel in a poker game. **100m/C VHS, DVD, Elizabeth Taylor...**

lor, George Hamilton, Tom Skerritt, Richard Mulligan, David Wayne, Susan Tyrrell, Pat Corley; **D:** Arthur Allan Seidelman; **W:** James Lee Barrett.

Pola X 🐾🐾 1999 French film continues to push the sexual envelope even when it's inspired by Herman Melville's 1852 novel, "Pierre, or, the Ambiguities." Pierre (Depardieu) lives with his beautiful widowed mother, Marie (Deneuve), in a country chateau. He's about to marry his faithful girlfriend, Lucie (Chuillet), when a strange woman named Isabelle (Golubeva) shows up claiming to be Pierre's half-sister. Soon Pierre is living the grunge life with Isabelle in Paris and the two are involved in an incestuous relationship (some of which is explicitly displayed.) Another bizarre film from auteur Carax. French with subtitles. **134m/C VHS, DVD, FR Guillaume Depardieu, Catherine Deneuve, Delphine Chuillet, Laurent Lucas; D:** Leos Carax; **W:** Leos Carax, Jean-Pol Fargeau, Lauren Sedofsky; **C:** Eric Gautier; **M:** Scott Walker.

The Polar Bear King 🐾🐾½ 1994 (PG) When a handsome prince refuses to marry the evil witch of Summerland, the wicked woman uses her power to turn him into a polar bear. The polar bear prince embarks on a journey to Winterland where he meets and falls in love with a beautiful princess. Together they return to Summerland and try to break the witch's spell. Filmed on location in Norway and Sweden. **87m/C VHS, DVD, Maria Bonnevie, Jack Fjeldstad, Tobias Hoesl, Anna-Lotta Larsson; D:** Ola Solum.

The Polar Express 🐾🐾½ 2004 (G) Your capacity to enjoy this Christmas story will depend on whether or not you find the so-called performance or motion capture animation technique (think Gollum from "Lord of the Rings") enthralling or creepy. An extended version of Chris Van Allsburg's popular children's book, the story opens on Christmas Eve when nameless skeptic Hero Boy is suddenly awakened by the steam train of the title, which appears outside his window. The train is leaving for the North Pole and Hero Boy, encouraged by a kindly conductor (one of Hanks' many roles), joins the passengers on their journey to meet Santa. There are various adventures intended to rather melancholy tale with which to entertain the tykes. **100m/C DVD, Blu-ray Disc, HD DVD, US Tom Hanks, Michael Jeter, Nona Gaye, Peter Scolari, Eddie Deezen, Charles Fleischer, Steven Tyler, Daryl Sabara, Leslie Zemeckis, Andre Sogliuzzo, Jimmy Bennett, Isabella Peregrina; D:** Robert Zemeckis; **C:** Don Burgess. Robert Presley; **M:** Alan Silvestri; **V:** Daryl Sabara.

Poldark 🐾🐾 1975 Tempestuous love, political intrigue, and family struggles all set in 18th-century Cornwall, then the copper-producing center of England. Heroic Ross Poldark has just returned from fighting upstart Americans in the Revolutionary War only to discover that his father has died and the family mines are about to be sold to the scheming Warleggan family. Ross struggles to pay off family debts, reclaim his heritage, resolve his feelings for an old love, and fight his attraction to the beguiling, but completely unsuitable, Demelza. Adapted from the novels by Winston Graham. **720m/C VHS, GB Robin Ellis, Angharad Rees, Jill Townsend, Judy Geeson, John Baker, Jill Townsend, Clive Francis, John Baskcomb, Paul Curran, Tilly Tremayne, Mary Wimbush, Nicholas Selby; D:** Paul Annett, Christopher Barry, Kenneth Ives; **W:** Paul Wheeler, Peter Draper, Jack Pulman. TV

Poldark 🐾🐾 1996 Picks up the story of Ross and Demelza Poldark and their family from where the 1970s BBC series ended. It's 1310 and Ross is spending most of his time in London as a Member of Parliament while at their Cornwall home, Demelza deals with the continuing Warleggan feud. Poldark son, Jeremy, struggles to keep the mine going and daughter Clowance is in the throes of her first romance. Based on the novel "The Stranger from the Sea" by Winston Graham. **105m/C VHS, DVD, GB John Bowe, Mel Martin, Ioan Gruffudd, Michael Attwell, Kelly Reilly, Hans Matheson, Amanda Ryan, Nicholas Gleaves, Gabrielle Lloyd.**

Police 🐾🐾 1985 French police drama with the intense Depardieu as a cop hunting an Algerian drug boss. Matters grow complicated when he falls for the elusive crook's girlfriend. Sometimes gripping, but uneven; the actors were encouraged to improvise. Inspired by the novel "Bodies Are Dust" by P.J. Wolfson. In French with English subtitles. **120m/C VHS, FR Gerard Depardieu, Sophie Marceau, Sandrine Bonnaire, Pascale Rocard, Richard Anconina; D:** Maurice Pialat; **W:** Catherine Breillat. Venice Film Fest. '85: Actor (Depardieu).

Police Academy 🐾🐾½ 1984 (R) In an attempt to recruit more cops, a big-city police department does away with all its job standards. The producers probably didn't know that they were introducing bad comedy's answer to the "Friday the 13th" series, but it's hard to avoid heaping the sins of its successors on this film. Besides, it's just plain dumb. **96m/C VHS, DVD, Steve Guttenberg, Kim Cattrall, Bubba Smith, George Gaynes, Michael Winslow, Leslie Easterbrook, Georgina Spelvin, Debralee Scott; D:** Hugh Wilson; **W:** Hugh Wilson, Pat Proft, Neal Israel; **C:** Michael D. Margulies. **M:** Robert Folk.

Police Academy 2: Their First Assignment 🐾 1985 (PG-13) More predictable idiocy from the cop shop. This sequel, the bumbling cops find their arena mater is threatened by a budget crunch and they must compete with a rival precinct to see which school survives. The "return to school" plot allowed the filmmakers to add new characters to replace those who had some scruples about picking up yet another "Police Lobotomy" check. Followed by three more sequels. **87m/C VHS, DVD, Steve Guttenberg, Bubba Smith, David Graf, Michael Winslow, Marion Ramsey, Art Metrano, Colleen Camp, Howard Hessemann, David Graf, George Gaynes; D:** Jerry Paris; **W:** Barry W. Blaustein.

Police Academy 3: Back in Training 🐾 1986 (PG) In yet another sequel, the cop cutups from the first three films aid a citizen's patrol group in their unnamed, but still wacky, hometown. Moronic high jinks ensue. Fourth in the series of five (or is it six?) that began with "Police Academy." **88m/C VHS, DVD, James Carroll, Steve Guttenberg, Bubba Smith, Michael Winslow, David Graf, Tim Kazurinsky, George Gaynes, Colleen Camp, Bobcat Goldthwait, Sharon Stone; D:** Jim Drake; **W:** Gene Quintano; **M:** Robert Folk.

Police Academy 4: Citizens on Patrol 🐾 1987 (PG) The comic cop cutups from the first three films aid a citizen's patrol group in their unnamed, but still wacky, hometown. Moronic high jinks ensue. **88m/C VHS, DVD, Michael Winslow, Leslie Easterbrook, Rene Auberjonois, Marion Ramsey, Janet Jones, George Gaynes, Matt McCoy; D:** Alan Myerson; **W:** Stephen J. Curwick; **M:** Robert Folk.

Police Academy 5: Assignment Miami Beach Woof! 1988 (PG) The fourth sequel, wherein the misfits-with-badges go to Miami and bumble along in the usual manner. It's about time these cops were retired from the force. **89m/C VHS, DVD, Bubba Smith, David Graf, Michael Winslow, Leslie Easterbrook, Rene Auberjonois, Marion Ramsey, George Gaynes, Sarah Carpenter; D:** Richard Laxton; **W:** Robin Mukherjee; **M:** Ian Hughes. TV

Poldark 2 🐾🐾🐾 1975 The further adventures of Ross Poldark, wife Demelza, and assorted family, friends, and enemies, all set in 18th-century Cornwall, Demelza's two meddlesome younger brothers come to live at Nampera, enemy George Warleggan and Ross' old love Elizabeth move too close for comfort, and the uncertainties of the copper mining economy all bring their share of trouble. Adapted from the novels by Winston Graham. Made for British TV; six cassettes. **720m/C VHS, GB Robin Ellis, Angharad Rees, Jill Townsend, Judy Geeson, Ralph Bates, Kevin McNally, Brian Stirner, Michael Cadman, Jane Wymark, David Delve, Christopher Biggins, Trudie Styler; D:** Philip Dudley, Roger Jenkins; **W:** Alexander Baron, John Wiles, Mark Worth. TV

Police Academy 6: City under Siege ☆ 1989 (PG) In what is hoped to be the last in a series of bad comedies, the distinguished graduates pursue three goofballs responsible for a crime wave. 85m/C VHS, DVD. Bubba Smith, David Graf, Michael Winslow, Leslie Easterbrook, Marion Ramsey, Matt McCoy, Bruce Mahler, G.W. Bailey, George Gaynes; D: Peter Bonerz; W: Stephen J. Curwick; M: Robert Folk.

Police Academy 7: Mission to Moscow ☆ 1994 (PG) The seventh in the series is another inept comedy, which finds the chaotic crew tackling a Russian mobster on his Moscow turf—all because of a popular computer game with some sinister software. Like you'll care about the plot anyway. 83m/C VHS, DVD. George Gaynes, Michael Winslow, David Graf, Leslie Easterbrook, G.W. Bailey, Charlie Schlatter, Ron Perlman, Christopher Lee; D: Alan Metter; W: Michele S. Chodos, Randolph Davis; M: Robert Folk.

Police Court ☆☆ 1932 The son of a faded, alcoholic screen star tries to bring the old fellow back to prominence. 62m/B VHS. Henry B. Walthall, Leon Janney, Al "Fuzzy" St. John, Aileen Pringle, King Baggot, Lionel Belmore, Edmund Breese, Walter James; D: Louis King; C: Stuart Anthony; C: Archie Stout.

Police Story ☆☆½ *Jackie Chan's Police Force: Jackie Chan's Police Story; Ging Chaat Goo Si* 1985 (PG-13) Chopsocker Chan's assigned to protect a witness in a drug case. Faced by unsavory thugs, he flies through the air with the greatest of ease. Very cool stunts. 92m/C VHS, DVD. HK Jackie Chan, Brigitte Lin, Maggie Cheung, Cho Yuen, Bill Tung, Kenneth Tong; D: Jackie Chan; C: Yiu-tsou Cheung.

Policewoman Centerfold ☆ 1983 Exploitative rendering based on the true story of a cop who posed for a pornographic magazine. Anderson is appealing in the lead. 100m/C VHS. Melody Anderson, Ed Marinaro, Donna Pescow, Bert Remsen, David Spielberg; D: Reza Badiyi. TV

Policewomen ☆☆½ 1973 (R) Female undercover agent must stop a ring of gold smugglers. 99m/C VHS, DVD. Sondra Currie, Tony Young, Phil Hoover, Elizabeth Stuart, Jeannie Bell; D: Lee Frost.

A Polish Vampire in Burbank ☆ 1980 A shy vampire in Burbank tries again and again to find blood and love. Wacky. 84m/C VHS, DVD. Mark Pirro, Lori Sutton, Eddie Deezen; D: Mark Pirro.

Polish Wedding ☆☆½ 1997 (PG-13) Strong-willed teenager Hala (Danes) throws her working-class Polish/American family into a tizzy when she becomes pregnant and the family decides she must get married. But Hala's not the only one whose life is romntically complicated—her mom Jadzia's (Olin) had a longtime affair with Roman (Serbedzija), which husband Bolek (Byrne) tolerates because he's afraid of losing her. Too slapsticky but the cast is game and it does have heart. 107m/C VHS, DVD. Claire Danes, Lena Olin, Gabriel Byrne, Adam Trese, Rade Serbedzija, Mili Avital, Daniel Lapaine, Kristen Bell; D: Theresa Connelly; W: Theresa Connelly; C: Guy Dufaux; M: Luis Bacalov.

Pollock ☆☆☆ 2000 (R) First-time director Harris (who also stars) scores a personal triumph with his bio of abstract expressionist artist Jackson Pollock (whom the actor resembles quite astonishingly). Pollock is a troubled soul, beset by alcoholism and insecurity, who leads himself down a self-destructive path. The film covers 1941-1956 as Pollock struggles to find his celebrated breakthrough and marries fellow artist Lee Krasner (Harden), a tough New Yorker who takes his career in hand, but his success only exacerbates Pollock's problems. Solid production with a couple of great leading performances; based on the book by Steven Naifeh and Gregory White Smith. 122m/C VHS, DVD. Ed Harris, Marcia Gay Harden, Amy Madigan, Jennifer Connelly, Jeffrey Tambor, Bud Cort, John Heard, Val Kilmer; D: Ed Harris; W: Barbara Turner, Susan J. Emshwiller; C: Lisa Rinzler; M: Jeff Beal. Oscars '00: Support. Actress (Harden); N.Y. Film Critics '00: Support. Actress (Harden).

Pollyanna ☆☆½ 1920 A young orphan girl is adopted by her cold, embittered aunt and does her best to bring joy and gladness to all the new people she meets. Silent with music score. 60m/B VHS. Katherine Griffith, Helen Jerome Eddy, Wharton James, George Berrell, Howard Ralston, Mary Pickford; D: Paul Powell; W: Frances Marion; C: Charles Hosmer.

Pollyanna ☆☆☆½ 1960 Based on the Eleanor Porter story about an enchanting young girl whose contagious enthusiasm and zest for life touches the hearts of all she meets. Mills is perfect in the title role and was awarded a special Oscar for outstanding juvenile performance. A distinguished supporting cast is the icing on the cake in this delightful Disney confection. Original version was filmed in 1920 with Mary Pickford. 134m/C VHS, DVD. Hayley Mills, Jane Wyman, Richard Egan, Karl Malden, Nancy Olson, Adolphe Menjou, Donald Crisp, Agnes Moorehead, Kevin Corcoran; D: David Swift; W: David Swift; C: Russell Harlan; M: Paul J. Smith.

Poltergeist ☆☆☆ 1982 (PG) This production has Stephen Spielberg written all over it. A young family's home becomes a house of horrors when they are terrorized by menacing spirits who abduct their five-year-old daughter...through the TV screen! Roller-coaster thrills and chills, dazzling special effects, and perfectly timed humor highlight this stupendously scary ghost story. 114m/C VHS, DVD. JoBeth Williams, Craig T. Nelson, Beatrice Straight, Heather O'Rourke, Zelda Rubinstein, Dominique Dunne, Oliver Robins, Richard Lawson, James Karen, Michael McManus; D: Tobe Hooper; W: Steven Spielberg; C: Matthew F. Leonetti; M: Jerry Goldsmith.

Poltergeist 2: The Other Side ☆☆½ 1986 (PG-13) Adequate sequel to the Spielburg-produced venture into the supernatural, where demons follow the Freeling family in their efforts to recapture the clairvoyant young daughter Carol Anne. The film includes sojourns into Indian lore and a four-foot high agave worm designed by H.R. Giger. 92m/C VHS, DVD. Craig T. Nelson, JoBeth Williams, Heather O'Rourke, Will Sampson, Julian Beck, Geraldine Fitzgerald, Oliver Robins, Zelda Rubinstein; D: Brian Gibson; W: Mark Victor, Michael Grais; C: Andrew Laszlo; M: Jerry Goldsmith.

Poltergeist 3 ☆½ 1988 (PG-13) Wrestling with the supernatural has finally unnerved Carol Ann and she's sent to stay with her aunt and uncle in Chicago where she attends a school for gifted children with emotional disorders. Guess who follows her? Uninspired acting, threadbare premise, and one ghastly encounter too many. Oddly, O'Rourke died suddenly four months before the film's release. 97m/C VHS, DVD. Tom Skerritt, Nancy Allen, Heather O'Rourke, Lara Flynn Boyle, Zelda Rubinstein; D: Gary Sherman; W: Gary Sherman, Brian Taggert; C: Alex Nepomniaschy.

Poltergeist: The Legacy ☆☆½ 1996 Pilot for the cable series about a secret international society, the Legacy, which is devoted to the paranormal and to protecting mankind from supernatural evil. Derek Rayne (De Lint), the head of the San Francisco Legacy house, must find the last of five sepulchers containing the evil spirits of five fallen angels. This takes him and his cohorts to Ireland where Rachel Corrigan (Shaver) and her young psychic daughter Kat (Purvis) come into unwitting possession of the fifth box and untold danger. 86m/C VHS, DVD. Derek de Lint, Helen Shaver, Alexandra Purvis, Martin Cummins, Robbi Chong, Patrick Fitzgerald, Jordan Bayne, William Sadler, Daniel Pilon, Chad Krowchuk; D: Stuart Gillard; W: Brad Wright; C: Manfred Guthe. CABLE

Polyester ☆☆½ 1981 (R) Amusing satire on middle-class life, described by producer, director and writer Waters as "Father Knows Best' gone berserk." Forlorn housewife Divine pines for the man of her dreams while the rest of her life is falling apart at the seams. Filmed in "Odorama," a hilarious gimmick in which theatre goers were provided with scratch-n-sniff cards, containing specific scents corresponding to key scenes. Video watchers will have to use their imagination to experiencing a wide range of smells. The first of Waters' more mainstream films. Features songs by Murray and Harry. 86m/C VHS, DVD. Divine, Tab Hunter, Edith Massey, Mink Stole, Stiv Bators, David Samson, Mary Garlington, Kenneth King, Joni-Ruth White, Jean Hill, Hans Kramm, Mary Vivian Pearce, Cookie Mueller, Susan Lowe, George Stover, George Figgs, Steve Yeager; D: John Waters; W: John Waters; C: David Insley; M: Deborah Harry, Michael Kamen.

Pom Pom Girls ☆½ 1976 (R) High school seniors, intent on having one last fling before graduating, get involved in crazy antics, clumsy romances, and football rivalries. 90m/C VHS, DVD. Robert Carradine, Jennifer Ashley, Michael Mullins, Cheryl "Rainbeaux" Smith, Dianne Lee Hart, Lisa Reeves, Bill Adler; D: Joseph Ruben; W: Joseph Ruben; C: Stephen M. Katz; M: Michael Lloyd. VIDEO

The Pompatus of Love ☆☆½ 1995 (R) Remember Steve Miller's song "The Joker"?—well, that's where the title comes from—and we still don't know what it means. But the film's about four New York guys, and the mystery of women. They may be (reasonably) bright and literate but they still don't have a clue about love or how to grow-up. Naturally, the women they know—or meet—are all too smart for them. 99m/C VHS, DVD. Jon Cryer, Tim Guinee, Adrian Pasdar, Adam Oliensis, Kristen Wilson, Dana Wheeler-Nicholson, Paige Turco, Mia Sara, Kristin Scott Thomas, Arabella Field, Jennifer Tilly, Roscoe Lee Browne; D: Richard Schenkman; W: Jon Cryer, Adam Oliensis, Richard Schenkman; C: Russell Fine; M: John Hill. VIDEO

The Ponder Heart ☆☆½ 2001 Eccentric Daniel Ponder (MacNicol) wants to give all his inherited fortune away. So folks in his Mississippi community considered him a mite peculiar, especially after he suddenly marries the teenaged Bonnie Dee (Bettis). Then Bonnie disappears and Ponder is put on trial for the alleged murder of his bride. Easy-going southern charm and smalltown craziness. Based on the novel by Eudora Welty. 120m/C VHS. Peter MacNichol, JoBeth Williams, Angela Bettis; D: Martha Coolidge. TV

Ponette ☆☆ 1995 Four-year-old Ponette (Thivisol) is hard-pressed to understand what's happening to her family after her mother is killed in a car accident. Her father can't seem to explain it properly, so Ponette comes to her own acceptance with the help of some school friends. Film drew some controversy when the very young Thivisol was awarded the best actress award at the Venice Film Festival—since Thivisol was thought by some critics to be too young to "act," director Doillon was accused of manipulating the youngster in order to get a performance. French with subtitles. 92m/C VHS, DVD. FR Victoire Thivisol, Matiaz Trintignant, Claire Nebout, Xavier Beauvois; D: Jacques Doillon; W: Jacques Doillon; C: Caroline Champetier; M: Philippe Sarde. N.Y. Film Critics '97: Foreign Film; Venice Film Fest. '96: Actress (Thivisol).

Pontiac Moon ☆½ 1994 (PG-13) Danson plays a high school teacher who takes his son on a road trip to Spires of the Moon National Park hoping to arrive simultaneously with the astronauts' first lunar landing. His wife (Steenburgen) decides to follow them, although she's phobic about leaving the house and hasn't set foot outside in seven years. Sincere yet tedious film about father-son bonding has a few heartfelt moments, but not enough to sustain interest for entire viewing period. Best (and only) reason for watching: Monument Valley scenery. 108m/C VHS, DVD. Ted Danson, Mary Steenburgen, Ryan Todd, Eric Schweig, Cathy Moriarty, Max Gail, Lisa Jane Persky; D: Peter Medak; W: Finn Taylor, Jeffrey Brown; M: Randy Edelman.

The Pony Express ☆☆½ 1925 Melodramatic western about an evil senator (Hart) who's out to establish his own empire. His scheme is thwarted by pony express rider Cortez. Based on the novel by Henry James Forman and Walter Woods. 67m/B VHS. Ricardo Cortez, Al Hart, Betty Compson, Ernest Torrence, Wallace Beery, George Bancroft, Frank Lackteen; D: James Cruze; W: Walter Woods.

Pony Express ☆☆☆ 1953 Buffalo Bill Cody and Wild Bill Hickok join forces to extend the Pony Express mail route west to California through rain and sleet, snow and hail. Far from a factual account but good for extending the myth of the Old West. 101m/C VHS. Charlton Heston, Rhonda Fleming, Jan Sterling, Forrest Tucker; D: Jerry Hopper; C: Ray Rennahan.

Pony Express Rider ☆☆☆ 1976 (G) Young man with a mission joins up with the Pony Express hoping to bag the male responsible for killing his pa. The well-produced script boasts a bevy of veteran western character actors, all lending, solid, rugged performances. 100m/C VHS. Stewart Petersen, Henry Wilcoxon, Buck Taylor, Maureen McCormick, Joan Caulfield, Ken Curtis, Slim Pickens, Dub Taylor, Jack Elam; D: Robert Totten.

Pony Post ☆½ 1940 Standard horse opera has Brown running a pony express station where he battles Indians and typical villains. 59m/B VHS. Johnny Mack Brown, Fuzzy Knight, Nell O'Day, Dorothy Short, Kermit Maynard, Lane Chandler; D: Ray Taylor; W: Sherman Lowe.

The Pooch and the Pauper ☆☆ 1999 (G) This may be the first film where dogs switch identities. So the Presidential pooch has been replaced by a lookalike and the confused interloper can only be considered a, well, bad dog. Meanwhile, the First Pup is being pursued by a dogcatcher on those mean D.C. streets. Hey, it's Disney, so every dog has its day. 88m/C VHS. Fred Willard, George Wendt, Richard Kam, Vincent Schiavelli; D: Alex Zamm; W: Mark Steilen, Bennett Yellin; C: Albert J. Dunk; M: Chris Hajian; V: Peter MacNichol, Daryl (Chill) Mitchell. VIDEO

Poodle Springs ☆☆ 1998 In 1963, Philip Marlowe (Caan) has a wealthy young wife (Meyer) and is living in Palm Springs. Bored, he decides to get back into the PI biz and is soon dealing with land swindlers and dead bodies (and a confusing plot) that lead to a political conspiracy. Raymond Chandler died before finishing his novel and his estate eventually hired Robert B. Parker to complete it from Chandler's outline. 96m/C DVD. James Caan, Dina Meyer, David Keith, Brian Cox, Julia Campbell, Nia Peeples, Joe Don Baker; D: Bob Rafelson; W: Tom Stoppard; C: Stuart Dryburgh; M: Michael Small. CABLE

Pooh's Heffalump Movie ☆☆½ 2005 (G) Another addition to Disney's Winnie-the-Pooh collection. The Hundred Acre gang suspects that a heffalump has been wandering the forest. Pooh, Piglet, Eeyore, Tigger, Rabbit and Kanga all decided to go capture what they think is a fearsome creature. Roo wants to join, too, but is told he is too young. He decides to go on his own adventure, where in the course of events, he meets and befriends Lumpy, the not-so-fearsome heffalump. Mild story has a nice moral about accepting differences in people, which should please the parents. Not Disney glory days great, but kids will like it. 63m/C VHS, DVD. US D: Frank Nissen; W: Brian Hohlfeld, Evan Spiliotopolos; M: Joel McNeely; V: Jim (Jonah) Cummings, John Fiedler, Nikita Hopkins, Kath Soucie, Ken Sansom, Peter Cullen, Brenda Blethyn, Kyle Stanger.

Pool Hustlers ☆½ 1983 A romantic comedy about an amateur billiards whiz who finds love and successfully defeats the national champ. In Italian with English subtitles. 101m/C VHS. IT Francesco Nuti, Guiliana de Sio, Marcello Loti; D: Maurizio Ponzi.

Pool Sharks ☆☆½ 1915 W.C. Fields' first film features the comedian's antics while playing a pool game to win the love of a woman. Silent. 10m/B VHS, DVD. W.C. Fields; W: W.C. Fields.

Poolhall Junkies ☆☆½ 2002 (R) Johnny Doyle (writer-director Callahan) is a pool hustler who always aspired to greatness, and could've had it. His mentor/backer Joe (Palminteri) sabotaged his chance at the pro tour a while back. When Johnny left him, Joe broke his wrist and found himself a new boy, Brad (Schroder). Johnny impresses his girlfriend's uncle Mike (Walken) who agrees to bankroll his road to the final showdown with Brad and Joe. Gritty but enthusiastic debut for Callahan doesn't wallow in cliches; it revels in 'em. Fortunately, it all works because of Callahan's obvious joy at getting to make the movie, the work of the elder actors (including Steiger in his last role), and the good sense of the younger ones to stay out of their way. Walken's performance alone is worth the price of a rental. Excellent pool hall action makes up for the thin one-note comedy. **90m/C DVD.** Leslie Uggams, Shelley Winters performing a strip act. Mars Callahan, Michael Rosenbaum, Chazz Palminteri, Rod Steiger, Christopher Walken, Rick Schroder, Alison Eastwood, Glenn Plummer, Ernie Reyes Jr., Peter Mark Richman, Arson Mount; **C:** Robert Morris. **W:** Mars Callahan, Chris Corso; **D:** Michael Apted.

Poor Pretty Eddie ⚔️⚔️ *1973 (R) A young black singer gets waylaid and taken in by a twisted white Southern clan. An incredibly sleazy movie which boasts Shelly Winters performing a strip act.* **90m/C DVD.** Leslie Uggams, Shelley Winters, Michael Christian, Ted Cassidy, Slim Pickens, Dub Taylor; **D:** Richard Robinson.

The Poor Little Rich Girl ⚔️⚔️½ *1936 A motherless rich girl wanders away from home and is "adopted" by a pair of struggling vaudevillians. With her help, they rise to the big time. ♪Oh My Goodness, Buy a Bar of Barry's; Wash Your Neck With a Cake of Peck's; Military Man; When I'm with You; But Definitely; You've Gotta Eat Your Spinach, Baby.* **79m/B VHS.** Shirley Temple, Jack Haley, Alice Faye, Gloria Stuart, Michael Whalen, Sara Haden, Jane Darwell; **D:** Irving Cummings.

A Poor Girl, a Ghost Story ⚔️⚔️ *1974 A young girl takes a job as a governess at an English mansion and is besieged by a el manner of strange goings on.* **52m/C VHS.** Au Lynn Miller, Angela Thorne; **D:** Michael Glasse.

A Poor Little Rich Girl ⚔️⚔️⚔️ *1917 Mary Pickford received raves in this film, in which she portrayed Gwendolyn, with everything money could buy, except the attention of her family. Gwendolyn has a bizarre dream in which she sees a number of horrors and is tempted by death. Elaborate sets and special effects, as well as Pickford's delicate performance, make this one special. Organ score, **64m/B VHS.** Mary Pickford, Madeline Traverse, Charles Wellesley, Gladys Fairbanks; **D:** Maurice Tourneur. Natl. Film Reg. '91.*

The Poor Little Rich Girl: The Barbara Hutton Story ⚔️⚔️½ *1987 Bio-drama of the one-time richest woman in America, Woolworth heiress Barbara Hutton (Fawcett), and her extravagant lifestyle. She married seven times (including actor Cary Grant) until falling into self-destructive alcohol and drug addictions. Lavishly presented but superficial. Based on the book by C. David Heyman. **98m/C VHS.** Farrah Fawcett, Bruce Davison, Kevin McCarthy, Burl Ives, James Read, Stephane Audran, Anne Francis, David Ackroyd, Tony Peck, Zoe Wanamaker, Amadeus August; **D:** Charles Jarrott. **M:** Dennis Turner. **TV**.*

Poor Man's Game ⚔️⚔️⚔️ *Boy's Game 2006 (R) Provocative look at racism and redemption. White wo king-class Donnie Rose 'Sutherland, son of Donald) is released from prison after serving 10 years for the brutal beating of a black man named Keith Carvery, who was left brain damaged. The racially-motivated incident has continued to divide the black and white communities of Halifax. Having boxed in the joint, Donnie agrees to a grudge match with local fisticuffs star Ossie (Alexander, a violent friend of the Carvery family). After much soul-searching, George Carvery (a strong Glover) decides that an eye-for-an-eye has to stop, and he offers to become Donnie's trainer so he'll have a chance to survive. **104m/C DVD, CA** Danny Glover, Russell Sutherland, Flex Alexander, Stephen McHattie, Tonya Lee Williams, Greg Bryk, K.C. Collins, Laura Reagan; **D:** Clement Virgo; **C:** Luc Montpellier, Chaz Thorne, Clement Virgo; **M:** Bryon Kent Wong.

Popcorn ⚔️⚔️ *1989 (R) A killer stalks a movie audience who is unaware that his crimes are paralleling those in the very film they are watching. **93m/C VHS, DVD, JII** Schoelen, Tom Villard, Dee Wallace Stone, Derek Rydall, Elliott Hurst, Kelly Jo Minter, Malcolm Denare, Ray Walston, Tony Roberts, Karen Witter; **C:** Mark Herrier, Alan Ormsby; **D:** Leslie Goldwins.

Pop Always Pays ⚔️⚔️ *1940 A father gets in a jam when he has to make good on a bet with his daughter's boyfriend. **67m/B VHS.** Leon Errol, Pamela Blake; **D:** Willy Kurant.*

Pootie Tang ⚔️½ *2001 (PG-13) The gibberish-babbling Pootie Tang (Crouther) was mildly amusing as a three-minute one-joke sketch on "The Chris Rock Show." Stretched to 80 minutes, it turns into "It's Pat 2: Electric Boogaloo." The premise here is that Pootie talks so cool, no one wants to admit they don't have a clue what he's saying. He's also a role model to all the kids and fights crime with his whip-crackin' belt, which he wields like a kung-fu master. Evil captain of industry Lecter (Vaughn) tricks Pootie into encore-ing his empire of cigarettes, booze and junk food by using the feminine wiles of slinky treenie (Coolidge). Pootie retires in disgrace to his hometown before he can come back and make everything wambly again. Or something like that it really is hard to figure out what that cude is saying. **81m/C VHS, DVD.** US Lance Crouther, Jennifer Coolidge, Robert Vaughn, Chris Rock, Reg E. Cathey, Wanda Sykes, Dave Attell, Mario Joyner, JB Smoove, Cathy Trien, Andy Richter, Kristen Bell; **Cameos:** Bob Costas; **D:** Louis CK; **W:** Louis CK. **C:** Willy Kurant.

Poor White Trash ⚔️½ *1957 An architect arrives in bayou country with plans to design a new building. He meets with resistance from the locals but falls for the sensual daughter of one of his staunchest detractors. **83m/B VHS.** Peter Graves, Lita Milan, Douglas Fowley, Timothy Carey, Jonathan Haze; **D:** Harold Daniels.*

Poor White Trash 2 ⚔️ *Scum of the Earth 1975 (R) A young couple, vacationing in Louisiana's bayou country, are introduced by an unusual brand of hospitality by the eponymous group of roma Moore, Camilla Carr; **D:** S.F. Brownrigg.*

Poor White Trash ⚔️½ *2000 (R) One-note comedy. Buddies Mike (Danson) and Lennie (Tierney) prank on a local store owner backfires and the boys are in bigtime trouble that could be eased if they had money for defense attorney Ron (Devane). So Mike's trailer-trash mom, Linda (Young), and her boy toy Brian (London) agree to help him out. They raise the money through some burglaries that, of course, get botched. The gags are repeated so often that they lose whet humor they minimally possessed. **85m/C VHS, DVD.** Jacob Tierney, Sean Young, Jason London, Tony Denman, William Devane, Jaime Pressly, M. Emmet Walsh, Tim Kazurinsky; **D:** Michael Addis; **W:** Michael Addis; **C:** Peter Kowalski; **M:** Tree Adams.*

Popeye ⚔️⚔️ *1980 (PG) The cartoon sailor brought to life is on a search to find his long-lost father. Along the way, he meets Olive Oyl and adopts little Sweet Pea. Williams accomplishes the near-impossible feat of physically resembling the character, and the whole movie does accomplish the maker's stated goal of "looking like a comic strip," but it isn't any-where near as funny as it should be. **114m/ C VHS, DVD.** Ned Dowd, Allan Nicholls, Robin Williams, Shelley Duvall, Ray Walston, Paul Dooley, Bill Irwin, Paul Smith, Linda Hunt, Richard Libertini; **D:** Robert Altman; **W:** Jules Feiffer; **M:** Harry Nilsson.

Popeye's Voyage: The Quest for Pappy ⚔️⚔️½ *2004 Popeye's searching the seas for his Pappy with Olive Oyl and Sweet Pea n tow so they don't miss any happy, holiday family time. Hag all pop up in this animated romp. **44m/ C VHS, DVD.** Kathy Bates, Manoel Jonker, Garry Chalk, Billy West, Tabitha St. Germain, Sanders Whiting; **D:** Ezekiel Norton. **W:** Paul Reiser, Jim Hardison. **VIDEO***

Popi ⚔️⚔️⚔️ *1969 (G) Arkin is the heart and soul of this poignant charmer in his role as a Puerto Rican immigrant hell-bent on securing a better life outside the ghetto for his two sons. His zany efforts culminate in one outrageous scheme to set them adrift off the Florida coast in hopes they will be rescued and raised by a wealthy family. Far fetched, but ultimately heartwarming. **115m/C VHS, DVD.** Alan Arkin, Rita Moreno, Miguel Alejandro, Reuben Figueroa; **D:** Arthur Hiller.*

The Poppy Is Also a Flower ⚔️⚔️ *Poppies Are Also Flowers; Opium Connection 1966 (PG) A star-laden, anti-drug drama produced by the United Nations. Filmed on location in Iran, Monaco, and Italy. Based on a drug trade thriller by Ian Fleming that explains how poppies, converted into heroin, are brought into the United States. **100m/C VHS, DVD.** E.G. Marshall, Trevor Howard, Stephen Boyd, Eli Wallach, Marcello Mastroianni, Angie Dickinson, Rita Hayworth, Yul Brynner, Trini Lopez, Bessie Love; **D:** Terence Young. **TV***

Population 436 ⚔️⚔️ *2006 (R) Census investigator Steve Kady (Sisto) is sent to the reclusive town of Rockwell Falls, where the population has remained unchanged at 436 people for more than 100 years. The town seems idyllic although excess residents have a tendency to succumb to a strange fever. Can Steve stay alive long enough to figure out what's really going on? Sisto plays the horror straight and Limp Bizkit frontman Durst is amiable as the town law. **92m/C DVD, CA** Jeremy Sisto, Fred Durst, R.H. Thomson, Peter Outerbridge, Charlotte Sullivan, David Ames, David Fox; **D:** Michelle Maxwell MacLaren; **W:** Michael Crompton, Nigel Hawthorne, John McEntye; Brian Cox; **D:** Herbert Wise. **TV**

Porcelet ⚔️⚔️ *Pigsty; Porcherie 1969 Pasolini interviews the story of a soldier cannibal living in a medieval past and that of an ex-Nazi industrialist in present day German. Both the soldier and the young German (who prefers pigs to his fiance) become sacrificial victims of their differing societies. A grotesque fable on Pasolini's hatred of m ddle class mores and the 20th century. In Italian with English subtitles. **90m/C VHS, DVD. JT FR** Pierre Clementi, Franco Citti, Jean-Pierre Leaud, Anne Wiazemsky, Ugo Tognazzi; Alberto Lionello; **D:** Pier Paolo Pasolini.*

The Pope of Greenwich Village ⚔️⚔️½ *1984 (R) Two Italian-American cousins (Rourke and Roberts) struggle to escape the trap of poverty in New York's Greenwich Village. When a small crime goes wrong in a big way, the two must learn about deception and loyalty. Mostly character study; Page is exceptional. Interior re-run of the "Mean Streets" idea does have its moments. **122m/C VHS, DVD.** Eric Roberts, Mickey Rourke, Daryl Hannah, Geraldine Page, Tony Musante, M. Emmet Walsh, Kenneth McMillan, Burt Young, Jack Kehoe, Philip Bosco, Val Avery, Joe Grifasi, Tony DiBenedetto; **D:** Stuart Rosenberg; **W:** Vincent Patrick; **C:** John Bailey; **M:** Dave Grusin.

The Pope Must Diet ⚔️½ *The Pope Must Die 1991 (R) Coltrane stars as a misfit who accidentally becomes Pope Dave I. Living up to the benevolence suggested by his title, Pope Dave proposes to use Vatican money to create a children's fund. But there are those in the organization who have different, less noble plans for the cash, and soon Dave finds himself the target of a mob hit. Frantic comedy caused a stir with its original title "The Pope Must Die," with many newspapers refusing to run ads for the film. This couped with lukewarm critical reviews, led to a very brief stint at the boxoffice. **87m/C VHS, GB** Robbie Coltrane, Alex Rocco, Beverly D'Angelo, Herbert Lom, Paul Bartel, Salvatore*

Pope John Paul II ⚔️⚔️⚔️ *1984 Biography of the Pontiff, from childhood to world eminence. **150m/C VHS.** Albert Finney, Michael Crompton; **D:** Herbert Wise. **TV**

Porridge ⚔️⚔️ *Doing Time 1991 A British comedy inspired by the popular BBC situation comedy of the title, about a habitual criminal and convict who makes the*

The Pope of Greenwich Village — **M:** Cascio, Balthazar Getty; **D:** Peter Richardson; **M:** Anne Dudley.

Pork Chop Hill ⚔️⚔️½ *1959 A powerful, hard-hitting account of the last hours of the Korean War. Peck is totally believable as the man ordered to hold his ground against the hopeless onslaught of Chinese Communist hordes. A chilling, stark look in the face of a no-win situation. Top notch cast and masterful directing. **97m/B VHS, DVD.** Gregory Peck, Harry Guardino, Rip Torn, George Peppard, James Edwards, Bob Steele, Woody Strode, Robert (Bobby) Blake, Martin Landau, Norman Fell, Ben Rensen, Boyd Gaines, Douglas McGrath, Susan Clark, Art Hindle, Wayne Maunder, Chuck "Porky" Mitchell, Eric may induce laughter. **100m/C VHS, DVD, CA** Bill Wiley, Dan Monahan, Wyatt Knight, Cyril O'Reilly, Roger Wilson, Tony Ganios, Mark Herrier, Scott Colomby, Kaki Hunter, Nancy Parsons, Eric Christmas, Art Hindle; **D:** Bob (Benjamin) Clark; **W:** Alan Ormsby, Bob (Benjamin) Clark, Roger E. Swaybill; **C:** Reginald Morris; **M:** Paul Zaza, Carl Zittrer.*

Porky's ⚔️⚔️½ *1962 (R) Investigation of teen horniness set in South Florida during the fab '50s. Irreverent comedy follows the misadventures of six youths imprisoned in Angel Beach High School who share a common interest: girls. Their main barrier to sexual success: the no-touch stupid adults who run the world. Fairly dumb and tasteless with occasional big laughs that earned mega bucks at the drive-in and created perceived popular outcry for more porky. **94m/C VHS, DVD.** Dan Monahan, Wyatt Knight, Scott Colomby, Tony Ganios, Mark Herrier, Cyril O'Reilly, Roger Wilson, Alex Karras, Kim Cattrall, Kaki Hunter, Nancy Parsons, Boyd Gaines, Douglas McGrath, Susan Clark, Art Hindle, Wayne Maunder, Chuck "Porky" Mitchell, Eric Christmas, Bob (Benjamin) Clark; **C:** Reginald Morris; **M:** Paul Zaza, Carl Zittrer.*

Porky's Revenge ⚔️ *1985 (R) The Angel Beach High School students are cut to get revenge against Porky who orders the school basketball coach to throw the championship game. The second of the "Porky's" sequels. **95m/C VHS, CA** Dan Mona-han, Wyatt Knight, Tony Ganios, Nancy Parsons, Chuck "Porky" Mitchell, Kaki Hunter, Kimberly Evenson, Scott Colomby, Mark Herrier, Eric Christmas, Rose McVeigh; **D:** James Komacc; **M:** Ziggy Steinberg; **C:** Robert C. Jesup; **M:** Dave Edmunds.*

Porky's 2: The Next Day ⚔️⚔️ *1983 (R) More tame tomfoolery about teenage sex drives. Shakespeare fat high school teachers, the Ku Klux Klan, and streaking in the Florida high school where it all began. Outright caricature shares the stage with juvenile humor, some of which may induce laughter.*

The Pornographer ⚔️⚔️ *2000 (R) In his introduction, director Atchison says that the inspiration for this story of lonely guy Paul Ryan (Degood) who becomes a porno filmmaker almost by accident came from his own situation. While trying to raise money for his own legitimate movies, he skin flicks to raise money. Instead, he came up with an intriguing little video premiere. **88m/C VHS, DVD.** Michael Degood, Craig Wasson, Monique Parent, Katryan Cain; **D:** Doug Atchison; **W:** Doug Atchison; **C:** Christopher Mo-sic; **M:** Warner David Jansen.*

The Pornographers ⚔️⚔️⚔️ *1966 Bizarre, black comedy focuses on a part-time porno filmmaker lusting after the daughter of the widow he lives with and trying to cope with his family, the world, and himself. A perversely fascinating exploration of contemporary Japanese society and the many facets of sexual emotion. In Japanese with English subtitles. **128m/B VHS, DVD. JP** Shoichi Ozawa, Masaomi Konda, Sumiko Sakamoto, Haruo Tanaka, Keiko Sagowa; **D:** Shohei Imamura.*

Porridge

most of his time in prison. **105m/C VHS, DVD. *GB* Ronnie Barker, Fulton Mackay, Peter Vaughan, Julian Holloway, Geoffrey Bayldon; *D:* Dick Clement.

Port of Call 🐶🐶🐶 1948 Early Bergman drama about a seaman on the docks who falls for a troubled woman whose wild, unhappy past has earned her an unsavory reputation. The hopeful, upbeat tone seems incongruous with the grim harbor/slum setting. It's minor Bergman but the seeds of his trademark themes can be seen taking shape, making it a must-see for avid fans. In Swedish with English subtitles. **100m/B VHS, DVD. *SW*** Nine-Christine Jonsson, Bengt Eklund, Erik Hell, Berta Hall, Mimi Nelson; *D:* Ingmar Bergman.

The Port of Missing Girls 🐶 1938 A young woman implicated in a murder stows away on a freighter. There she becomes caught up in a waterfront world of pirates, smugglers and other assorted undesirables. **56m/B VHS. Harry Carey Sr., Judith Allen, Milburn Stone, Betty Compson; *D:* Karl Brown.

Portfolio 1988 (R) Real-life models star in this gritty drama about rising to the top of the fashion heap. Music by Eurythmics, Fun Boy Three and others. **83m/C VHS. DVD. Scott Brady, Yul Brynner, K.T. Stevens; *D:* Laszlo Benedek.

Portnoy's Complaint 🐶1/2 1972 (R) Limp screen adaptation of Philip Roth's novel follows the frustrating experiences of a sexually obsessed young man as he relates them to his psychiatrist. **101m/C VHS. Richard Benjamin, Karen Black, Lee Grant, Jeannie Berlin, Jill Clayburgh; *D:* Ernest Lehman; *W:* Ernest Lehman.

The Portrait 🐶🐶🐶 1993 Longtime real-life friends Bacall and Peck on-screen together for the first time in 37 years prove they are still shining stars as they play aging parents to Peck's real-life daughter, Cecilia Peck. The younger Peck is an artist preparing to sit for a portrait. This is the pole around which their relationships and reconciliations swing in this emotional drama based loosely on Tina Howe's 1983 off-Broadway play, "Painting Churches." **89m/ C VHS. Lauren Bacall, Gregory Peck, Cecilia Peck, Paul McCrane, Joyce O'Connor, Donna Mitchell, Mitchell Laurance, William Prince, Augusta Dabney; *M:* Michael Conway Baker. CABLE

Portrait in Black 🐶🐶1/2 1960 Invalid shipping magnate Matthew Cabot (Nolan) is contemptuous of second wife Sheila (Turner), who can't leave the marriage because of young son Peter (Kohler). She finds comfort in the arms of her husband's doctor, David Rivera (Quinn), and the duo decide the only way to find happiness is to kill off Cabot, which they do. Then Sheila begins to get anonymous letters accusing her of murder. Turner's glamor can't hide the gaping holes in the contrived plot. Adapted from the Goff/Roberts play. **113m/C VHS. Lana Turner, Lloyd Nolan, Anthony Quinn, Richard Basehart, Sandra Dee, John Saxon, Ray Walston, Anna May Wong, Virginia Grey, Dennis Kohler; *D:* Michael Gordon; *W:* Ivan Goff, Ben Roberts; *C:* Russell Metty; *M:* Frank Skinner.

Portrait in Terror 🐶🐶🐶 1966 A master thief and a deranged artist plan a heist of a Titian painting in an oddball suspense piece. Not a great success, but atmospheric and weird. **81m/B VHS, DVD. Patrick Magee, William Campbell, Anna Pavane; *D:* Jack Hill.

Portrait of a Hitman 🐶 *Jim Buck* 1977 Aspiring painter leads a double life as a professional hitman. Ragged feature feels more abandoned than finished, as if most of the movie had been shot and then the money ran out. All leads turn in paycheck performances, no more. **85m/C VHS, DVD. Jack Palance, Rod Steiger, Bo Svenson, Ann Turkel; *D:* Allan A. Buckhantz.

Portrait of a Lady 🐶🐶1/2 1967 A spirited young American woman is taken to England and insists on complete freedom to choose her own future and make her own choices. Based on the 1881 novel by Henry James. On two cassettes. **240m/C VHS, DVD. *GB* Richard Chamberlain, Suzanne Neve, Edward Fox; *D:* James Cellan Jones; *W:* Jack Pulman.

Portrait of a Lady 🐶🐶🐶 1996 (PG-13) Adapted from the century-old Henry James novel, "Portrait" paints the story of independent and newly wealthy American, Isabel Archer (Kidman). Abroad in Europe, she falls under the influence of the bitter, opportunistic Madame Merle (Hershey, in a strong portrayal), who manages to steer the innocent Isabel into a disastrous marriage with Gilbert Osmond (Malkovich). From there, film deals with Isabel's efforts to flee the domineering Osmond and find herself again. Kidman plays her role with never-before-seen efficiency. Malkovich is suitably evil but plays his villain card a bit too early. Director Campion's modern voice carries the film through, but is sometimes out of place, as in the opening segment. Filmed in England and Italy. **142m/C VHS, DVD. *GB* Nicole Kidman, John Malkovich, Barbara Hershey, Martin Donovan, Christian Bale, Shelley Winters, Shelley Duvall, Mary-Louise Parker, Richard E. Grant, John Gielgud, Viggo Mortensen; *D:* Jane Campion; *W:* Laura Jones; *C:* Stuart Dryburgh; *M:* Wojciech Kilar. L.A. Film Critics '96: Support. Actress (Hershey); Natl. Soc. Film Critics '96: Support. Actress (Donovan). VIDEO

Portrait of a Rebel: Margaret Sanger 🐶🐶1/2 1982 TV docudrama about the struggle of Margaret Sanger to repeal the Comstock Act of 1912, which prohibited the distribution of birth control information. **96m/C VHS. Bonnie Franklin, David Dukes, Milo O'Shea; *D:* Virgil W. Vogel.

Portrait of a Showgirl 🐶 1982 Inexperienced showgirl learns the ropes of Las Vegas life from a veteran of the Vegas stages. **100m/C VHS, DVD. Lesley Ann Warren, Rita Moreno, Tony Curtis, Dianne Kay, Howard Morris; *D:* Steven Hilliard Stern. TV

Portrait of a Stripper 🐶 1979 A widowed mother works part-time as a stripper to support her son. Trouble arises when her father-in-law attempts to prove that she is an unfit mother. **100m/C VHS. Lesley Ann Warren, Edward Herrmann, Vic Tayback, Sheree North; *D:* John A. Alonzo.

Portrait of a White Marriage 🐶🐶1/2 1988 An extended cable comedy special revamping certain old "Mary Hartman, Mary Hartman" and "Fernwood 2-Night" conventions; a moronic talk show host moves his cheap show to his hometown of Hawkins Falls in an unsuccessful bid to boost the ratings. **81m/C VHS. Martin Mull, Mary Kay Place, Fred Willard, Michael McKean, Harry Shearer, Jack Riley, Conchata Ferrell; *D:* Harry Shearer. CABLE

Portrait of an Assassin 🐶🐶 1949 Unhappy with his marriage to a nagging wife (Arletty), carnival daredevil Fabius (Brasseur) goes so far as to tell her that he killed a woman by mistake, thinking it was her. Can this marriage be saved? Before it's over, more infidelity and the paralyzed Eric (the inimitable Von Stroheim) have come into play. French with subtitles. **86m/B VHS, DVD. *FR* Pierre Brasseur, Arletty, Maria Montez, Erich von Stroheim; *D:* Bernard Roland; *W:* Marcel Rivet; *C:* Roger Hubert; *M:* Maurice Hinel.

Portrait of Jennie 🐶🐶🐶1/2 *Jennie; Tidal Wave* 1948 In this haunting, romantic fable, a struggling artist is inspired by and smitten with a strange and beautiful girl who he also suspects may be the spirit of a dead woman. A fine cast works wonders with what could have been a forgettable story. The last reel was tinted green in the original release with the last scene shot in technicolor. Oscar-winning special effects. Based on a novella by Robert Nathan. **86m/B VHS, DVD. Joseph Cotten, Jennifer Jones, Cecil Kellaway, Ethel Barrymore, David Wayne, Lillian Gish, Henry Hull, Florence Bates, Felix Bressart, Anne Francis; *D:* William Dieterle; *W:* Leonardo Bercovici, Peter Berneis, Paul Osborn; *C:* Joseph August; *M:* Dimitri Tiomkin. Venice Film Fest. '49: Actor (Cotten).

Portrait of Teresa 🐶🐶🐶 1979 Havana housewife has to balance motherhood, textile job, and cultural group activities without the cooperation of her husband. Vega skillfully portrays the lingering archaic attitudes and insulting assumptions that still confront post-revolution women. A fine eye for the revealing moments and movements of everyday life. In Spanish with English subtitles. **115m/C VHS. Daisy Granados, Aldofo Llaurado, Alina Sanchez, Alberto Molina; *D:* Pastor Vega.

Portraits Chinois 🐶🐶1/2 *Shadow Play* 1996 Uneven romantic drama finds English fashion designer Ada (Bonham Carter) living in Paris with her screenwriter boyfriend Paul (Ecoffey). They have just moved into an apartment together though dissatisfaction looms. Paul's writing partner, Guido (Castellito), has broken up with his girlfriend thus complicating their latest assignment, and Ada's fellow designer Lise (Bohringer) has not only impressed their boss Rene (Brialy) but has fallen for Paul. Various other friends interact and everything breaks apart and re-forms over the course of several months. French with subtitles. **105m/C VHS, DVD. *FR* Helena Bonham-Carter, Jean-Philippe Ecoffey, Romane Bohringer, Sergio Castellitto, Marie Trintignant, Elsa Zylberstein, Yvan Attal, Miki (Predrag) Manojlovic, Jean-Claude Brialy; *D:* Martine Dugowson; *W:* Martine Dugowson, Peter Chase; *C:* Vincenzo Marano; *M:* Peter Chase.

Portraits of a Killer 🐶🐶 *Portraits of Innocence* 1995 Attorney Elaine Taylor (Grey) is getting all hot and bothered by her client—photographer George Kendell (Mandylor), who's suspected (on the murders of five hookers. But the detective (Ironside) on the case thinks she's just asking for trouble. **93m/C VHS. Jennifer Grey, Costas Mandylor, Michael Ironside, Patricia Charbonneau, Kenneth Welsh, M. Emmet Walsh; *D:* Bill Corcoran.

Posed for Murder 🐶🐶 1989 (R) A young centerfold is stalked by a psycho who wants her all for himself. **90m/C VHS. Charlotte J. Helmkamp, Carl Fury, Rick Gianasi, Michael Merrins; *D:* Brian Thomas Jones.

Poseidon 🐶1/2 2006 (PG-13) Uninspired remake of 1972's "The Poseidon Adventure" sunk faster at the box office than the flick's luxury cruise ship. A rogue wave capsizes the liner on New Year's Eve but a few of the passengers defy the captain's orders to remain in the ballroom and await rescue and decide to make their own way to the surface through the treacherous wreckage. The cast is stuck with recognizable genre types (hero, coward, protective parent) but no one stands out amidst the watery water. **99m/C DVD, HD DVD. *US* Joshua) Lucas, Kurt Russell, Emmy Rossum, Jacinda Barrett, Jimmy Bennett, Mia Maestro, Andre Braugher, Richard Dreyfuss, Mike Vogel, Kevin Dillon, Freddy Rodriguez, Gabe Jarret, Stacy "Fergie" Ferguson; *D:* Wolfgang Petersen; *W:* Mark Protosevich; *C:* John Seale; *M:* Klaus Badelt.

The Poseidon Adventure 🐶🐶🐶1/2 1972 (PG) The cruise ship Poseidon is on its last voyage from New York to Athens on New Year's Eve when it is capsized by a tidal wave. The ten survivors struggle to escape the water-logged tomb. Oscar-winning special effects, such as Shelley Winters floating in a boiler room. Created an entirely new genre of film making—the big cast disas-

ter flick. ♫The Morning After. **117m/C VHS, DVD. Gene Hackman, Ernest Borgnine, Shelley Winters, Red Buttons, Jack Albertson, Carol Lynley, Roddy McDowall; *D:* Ronald Neame; *W:* Wendell Mayes, Stirling Silliphant; *C:* Harold E. Stine; *M:* John Williams. Oscars '72: Song ("The Morning After"), Visual FX; Golden Globes '73: Support. Actress (Winters).

Posers 🐶1/2 *Viperes 2002* (R) An unwary woman is fatally pummeled in a nightclub bathroom by four jealous party chicks. When the leader of the pack is suspiciously AWOL the terrible trio just totally freaks out thinking that—gasp!—someone is after them to avenge the killing. Cue the customary finger-pointing as the girls disintegrate along with this tale of woe. **86m/C VHS, DVD. *CA* Jessica Pare, Stefanie von Pfetten, Emily Hampshire, Adam Beach, Sarain Boylan, Chad Connell, Danielle Kind, Adrian Langley, Alexandra Sinclair; *D:* Katie Tallo; *W:* Katie Tallo; *C:* Claudine Sauve; *M:* Serge Cote. VIDEO

Positive I.D. 🐶🐶 1987 (R) A troubled housewife learns that the man who raped her years before is getting released on parole. She devises a second persona for herself with which to entrap him and get her revenge. **96m/C VHS, DVD. Stephanie Rascoe, John Davies, Steve Fromholz; *D:* Andy Anderson; *W:* Andy Anderson; *C:* Paul Barton.

The Positively True Adventures of the Alleged Texas Cheerleader-Murdering Mom 🐶🐶🐶 1993 (R) Satirical melodrama about Texas housewife Wanda Holloway (Hunter), accused of hiring a hitman to murder the mother of her daughter's chief cheerleading rival. She figures the girl will be so distraught that her own daughter can easily replace her. Ruthless and hilarious, this fact-based cable movie goes way over the top in satirizing suburban life-style excess and media overkill. Hunter, complete with whiney Texas twang, is perfect in her role as self-absorbed Wanda and Bridges is great as her loopy ex-brother-in-law and partner in planned homicide. A riot compared to the usual dramatic movies served up by the networks. **99m/C VHS, DVD. Andy Richter, Jack Kehler, Holly Hunter, Beau Bridges, Swoosie Kurtz, Gregg Henry, Matt Frewer, Frankie Ingrassia, Elizabeth Ruscio, Megan Berwick; *D:* Michael Ritchie; *W:* Jane Anderson; *M:* Lucy Simon. CABLE

Posse 🐶🐶🐶 1975 Big, brawny western shot with MTV in mind that tells the tale in part of how more than 8,000 black cowboys helped tame the American frontier. Or, as the advertising put it, "The untold story of the wild West." Or, spaghetti western meets blaxploitation meets the magnificent seven meets the L.A. riots, with characters actually saying, "No justice, no peace" and "Can't we all get along." However categorized, the intent is to show a side of Americana seldom seen, a goal realized. Strode, perhaps the greatest black Western star, appears at both the beginning and ending, while several other veteran black performers, including Hunky Van Peebles, appear in cameos. Hunky Van Peebles is the leader of the usual misfits in the "Dirty Dozen" tradition, infantry deserters holding a load of gold. Between them and freedom is a gang of goons led by Zane. Lots of flash and dash, but lacking soul. **113m/C VHS, DVD. Mario Van Peebles, Stephen Baldwin, Charles Lane, Tommy (Tiny) Lister, Big Daddy Kane, Billy Zane, Blair Underwood, Tone Loc, Salli Richardson, Reginald (Reggie) Hudlin, Richard Edson, Reginald VelJohnson, Warrington Hudlin; *Cameos:* Melvin Van Peebles, Pam Grier, Isaac Hayes, Robert Hooks, Richard Jordan, Paul Bartel, Nipsey Russell, Woody Strode, Aaron Neville, Stephen J. Cannell; *D:* Mar-

Possessed 🐾🐾½ **1931** A poor factory girl becomes a wealthy Park Avenue sophisticate when she falls in love with a rich lawyer who wants to be governor. Not to be confused with Crawford's 1947 movie of the same name, but worth a look. Gable and Crawford make a great couple! 77m/B VHS. Joan Crawford, Clark Gable, Wallace Ford, Richard "Skeets" Gallagher, John Miljan; **D:** Clarence Brown.

The Possessed 🐾🐾 **1947** Crawford is at her melodramatic best as a crazed gal who can't find happiness with either hunk Heflin or bland Massey... *C:* Peter Menzies Jr.; *M:* Michel Colombier. io Van Peebles; **W:** Sy Richardson, Dario Scardapane.

The Possessed 🐾½ **1977 (PG-13)** Farentino is a priest who loses his faith, but regains it after an apparently fatal auto accident. Hackett is the headmistress of a private girls' school which is in need of an exorcist, since one of her student's appears to be possessed, and Farentino seems just the man for the job. Fairly tame, since originally made for TV. 75m/C VHS. James Farentino, Joan Hackett, Diana Scarwid, Claudette Nevins, Eugene Roche, Ann Dusenberry, Dinah Manoff, P.J. Soles; **D:** Jerry Thorpe. **TV**

The Possessed 🐾🐾 ...as Possesses **1988** Based on the Dostoevsky novel which follows a young aristocrat who's torn between love and politics during the failed Russian revolution of the 1870s. French with subtitles. 124m/C VHS. FR Lambert Wilson, Jean-Philippe Ecoffey, Isabelle Huppert, Jutta Lampe, Laurent Malet, Remi Martin, Omar Sharif, Bernard Blier; **D:** Andrzej Wajda; **W:** Jean-Claude Carriere, Agnieszka Holland; **C:** Witold Adamek. 🐾 Zygmunt Konieczny.

Possessed 🐾🐾 **2000** William Bowden (Dalton) is a troubled priest in 1949 St. Louis, who has taken to drink because of his WWII nightmares. He's called on to help 11-year-old Robbie (Malen) who is apparently possessed by a damon. Will reluctant Archbishop Hume (Plummer) allow Bowdern to perform an arcane exorcism and does Robbie's strange Aunt Hanna (Laurie) have anything to do with his condition? Based on the true story of the only documented exorcism performed by the Catholic Church in the U.S. 111m/C VHS, DVD. Timothy Dalton, Christopher Plummer, Henry Czerny, Jonathan Malen, Shannon Lawson, Piper Laurie, Michael Rhoades; **D:** Steven E. de Souza; **W:** Steven E. de Souza, Michae Lazarou; **C:** Edward Pe; **M:** John (Gian) Frizzell. **CABLE**

Possessed by the Night 🐾🐾 **1993 (R)** Kinky sex games ensue between a married writer and a sexy other woman thanks to a mysterious fetish object. Un-rated version also available. Unrated Prior, Shannon Tweed, Sandahl Bergman, Chad McQueen, Henry Silva; **D:** Fred Olen Ray.

Possession 🐾🐾 **1981 (R)** Returned from a long mission, a secret agent notices that his wife is acting very strangely. She's about to give birth to a manifestation of the evil within her! Gory, hysterical, over-intellectual, and often unintelligible. 123m/C VHS, DVD. FR GE Johanna Hoier, Isabelle Adjani, Sam Neill, Heinz Bennent, Margit Carstensen, Shaun Lawtor; **D:** Andrzej Zulawski; **W:** Andrzej Zulawski, Frederic Tuten; **C:** Bruno Nuytten; **M:** Andrzej Korzynski. A.t Phillips. Cesar '82. Actress (Adjani).

Possession 🐾🐾 **2002 (PG-3)** English lilt life in this uninvolving romance from LaBute, based on the 1990 novel by A.S. Byatt. Brash and scruffy (doesn't the...

Possible Loves 🐾🐾🐾 Amores Possiveis **2000** Romantic comedy with a Brazilian beat and three possible outcomes. College student Carlos (Benicio) is waiting for his girlfriend Julia (Ferraz) outside a Rio cinema. Fifteen years later, the viewer learns what happens if she does—or doesn't—show up. In the first, Julia and Carlos has a dull marriage to Maria (Goulart) until he leaves his wife and son for Pedro (de Mello) as he tries to decide whom he loves. In the third plot, Julia doesn't show again and Carlos is a swinging bachelor looking for the perfect woman. Guess who. Portuguese with subtitles. 98m/C VHS, DVD. BR Murilo Benicio, Carolina Ferraz, Beth Goulart, Emilio de Mello, Irene Ravache; **D:** Sandra Werneck; **W:** Paulo Halm. **C:** Walter Carvalho; **M:** Chico Buarque, Joao Nabuco.

Possums 🐾½ **1999 (PG)** Beat-up small town can't endure the local high school football team's quarter-century of losing seasons and pulls the plug on the pathetic Possums. But their announcer, Will (Davis), breathes new life into the downtrodden fans by calling fictional wins. It's all high-fives until the real champs want to square off and. Will has to assemble a first-rate squad. 97m/C VHS, DVD. Mac Davis, Cynthia Sikes, Greg Coolidge, Andrew Prine, Dennis Burkley, Monica Creel, Jay Underwood, Clive Revill; **D:** J. Max Burnett; **W:** J. Max Burnett; **C:** Christopher Duskin; **M:** Justin Caine Burnett. **VIDEO**

Post Concussion 🐾🐾 **1999 (PG-13)** Matthew (Yoon) is a ruthless corporate "consultant" who specializes in downsizing and layoffs until he's hit by a car and suffers a severe head injury. Unable to work because of lingering symptoms, he re-evaluates his life, starts a romance with a neighbor, and explores New Age remedies. Writer-director Yoon based his refreshing, inventive, and gently humorous debut on his own experience with a brain-injuring accident and its subsequent effect on his own life and career. 82m/C VHS, DVD. Daniel Yoon, Jennifer Welch; **D:** Daniel Yoon; **W:** Daniel Yoon; **C:** Daniel Yoon.

The Possession of Joel Delaney 🐾🐾½ **1972 (R)** Blend of occult horror and commentary on social mores works for the most part, but some viewers may be put off by the low production values and spottiness of the script. MacLaine is a wealthy divorcee who must deal with the mysterious transformations affecting her brother. Skeptical at first, she begins to suspect he is the victim of Caribbean voodoo. 105m/C VHS, Shirley MacLaine, Perry King, Michael Hordern, David Elliott, Robert Burr; **D:** Waris Hussein.

Possession: Until Death Do You Part 🐾 **1990** When one man's attraction for a beautiful young woman becomes an obsession, a bizarre series of inexplicable events unravels a terrifying account of passion and revenge. 93m/C VHS. Monica Marko, John R. Johnston, Sharlene Martin, Cat Williamson; **D:** Michael Mazo, Lloyd A. Simandl.

Postal Inspector 🐾🐾 **1936** An extraordinary tale of a postal inspector's life. Crime, romance, and natural disaster all overtake this civil servant. Catch the song "Let's Have Bluebirds On All Our Wallpaper". 58m/B VHS, DVD, Carlos Cortez, Patricia Ellis, Michael Loring, Bela Lugosi, David Oliver, Wallis (Shaw) Clark; **D:** Otto Brower; **W:** Robert Presnell Sr., Horace McCoy; **C:** George Robinson.

Postcards from America 🐾🐾 **1995 (R)** Traces the non-artistic aspects of the life of writer/artist David Wojnarowicz, who died of AIDS. Nosphyre McLean contentrates on troubled childhood with an abusive father and teen years spent as a street hustler years. Choppy narrative uses little of Wojnarowicz's dialogue, save the voice-over narration by the lead character. Based on two semi-autobiographical novels by the artist. 93m/C VHS, DVD. James Lyons, Michael Tighe, Maggie Low; **D:** Steve McLean; **W:** Steve McLean; **C:** Ellen Kuras; **M:** Stephen Endelman.

Postcards from the Edge 🐾🐾½ **1990 (R)** Fisher adapted her best-selling novel, tamed and tempered, for the big screen with a tour-de-force of talent. Streep very fine as a delightfully harried actress struggling with her career, her drug dependence, and her career. competitive, overwhelming, show-biz mother. Autobiographical script is bitingly clever and filled with refreshingly witty dialogue. Lots of cameos by Hollywood's hippest. 101m/C VHS, DVD. Mery Streep, Shirley MacLaine, Dennis Quaid, Gene Hackman, Richard Dreyfuss, Rob Reiner, Mary Wickes, Conrad Bain, Annette Bening, Michael Ontkean, Dana Ivey, Robin Bartlett, Anthony Heald, Oliver Platt, CCH Pounder; **D:** Mike Nichols; **W:** Carrie Fisher; **C:** Michael Ballhaus; **M:** Shel Silverstein, Carly Simon, Stephen Sondheir, Howard Shore, Paul Shaffer, Gilda Radner.

Poster Boy 🐾🐾 **2004 (R)** Right-wing senator Jack Kray (Lerner) decides to use his college-student son Henry (Newton) in his reelection campaign in order to attract the youth vote. Except Henry's gay, and while he's living it up within his college confines, he's not out to his family, including his parents. Over-the-top soapiness and preachiness ensue as secrets and truth affect the dynamics of family, friendship, and public image. Alien is excellent as the smile-and-wave political wife who likes a cocktail, but the good performances are crushed by a heavy-handed script. 98m/C DVD. US Matt Newton, Karen Allen, Michael Lerner, Jack Noseworthy, Valerie Geffner, Len Reed Kesler, Sheff Stevens; **D:** Zak Tucker; **W:** Ryan Shiraki, Leca Rosenthal; **C:** Wolfgang Held; **M:** Mark Garcia.

The Postman 🐾🐾🐾½ **1994 (PG)** Il Postino Bittersweet, charming film about Mario (Troisi), a shy villager who winds up the personal postman of poet Pablo Neruda (Noiret), who is exiled from his beloved Chile in 1952, granted asylum by the Italian government, and who finds himself living in the tiny Italian community of Isla Negra. The tongue-tied Mario has fallen in love with barmaid Beatrice (Cucinotta) and asks the poet's help in wooing the dark-eyed beauty, striking up an unlikely friendship with the worldly Neruda. Based on the novel "Burning Patience" by Antonio Skarmeta. Italian with subtitles. Troisi, a beloved comic actor in his native Italy, was gravely ill, needing a heart transplant, during the making of the film (all-too apparent, day, after filming was completed. 115m/C VHS, DVD. IT Massimo Troisi, Philippe Noiret, Maria Grazia Cucinotta, Linda Moretti, Renato Scarpa, Anna Buonaiuto, Mariana Rigillo; **D:** Michael Radford; **W:** Massimo Troisi, Michael Radford, Furio Scarpelli, Anna Pavignano, Giacomo Scarpelli; **C:** Franco Di Giacomo; **M:** Luis Bacalov. Oscars '95. Orig. Dramatic Score; British Acad. '95; Director (Radford), Foreign Film, Score; Broadcast Film Critics '95; Foreign Film.

The Postman 🐾 **1997 (R)** It's postapocalypse time (the year's 2013), with a nameless drifter (Costner) assuming the role of a postal carrier in order to bring hope to a devasted town terrorized by marauding hooligans, led by General Bethlehem (Patton). If you fancy deadpan dialogue and can swallow the image of a mail carrier as the symbol for patriotism, then this one's for you. Overall, Costner offers lust-laden lovers in his lurid tale of fatal attraction. Garfield steals the show as the streetwise drifter who blows into town and lights a fire in Turner. As their affair steams up the two conspire to do away with her husband and circumstances begin to spin out of control. Tense and compelling. A classic. 113m/B VHS, DVD, Lana Turner, John Garfield, Cecil Kellaway, Hume Cronyn, Leon Ames, Audrey Totter, Alan Reed; **D:** Tay Garnett; **W:** Harry Ruskin, Niven Busch; **C:** Sidney Wagner; **M:** George Bassman.

The Postman Always Rings Twice 🐾🐾 **1946** Even without the brutal sexuality of the James M. Cain novel, Garfield and Turner sizzle as the lust-laden lovers in his lurid tale of fatal attraction. Garfield steals the show as the streetwise drifter who blows into town and lights a fire in Turner. As their affair steams up the two conspire to do away with her husband and circumstances begin to spin out of control. Tense and compelling. A classic. 113m/B VHS, DVD, Lana Turner, John Garfield, Cecil Kellaway, Hume Cronyn, Leon Ames, Audrey Totter, Alan Reed; **D:** Tay Garnett; **W:** Harry Ruskin, Niven Busch; **C:** Sidney Wagner; **M:** George Bassman.

The Postman Always Rings Twice 🐾🐾½ **1981 (R)** It must be true because he's ringing again in Mamet's version of James M. Cain's depression-era novel. This time Nicholson plays the drifter and Lange the amoral wife with an aged husband. Truer to the original story then the 1946 movie in its use of brutal sex scenes. It nevertheless lacks the power of the original. Nicholson works well in this time era and Lange adds depth and realism to the character of Cora. But in the end it remains dreary and easily forgettable. 123m/C VHS, DVD. Jack Nicholson, Jessica Lange, John Colicos, Anjelica Huston, Michael Lerner, John P. Ryan, Christopher Lloyd; **D:** Bob Rafelson; **W:** David Mamet; **C:** Sven Nykvist; **M:** Michael Small.

Post Mortem 🐾🐾 **1999** Single mom Linda (Moreau) will do anything to safeguard her daughter Charlotte, which in reality means Linda robs every man she dates after whacking him with some heavy object. Then there's lonely Ghislain (Arcand), who is abruptly arrested by the cops and accused of a crime. Naturally, his life and Linda's intersect. French with subtitles. 92m/C VHS. CA Gabriel Arcand, Sylvie Moreau, Helene Loiselle; **D:** Louis Belanger; **W:** Louis Belanger; **C:** Jean-Pierre St.-Louis; **M:** Guy Belanger. Genie '99. Actress (Moreau), Screenplay.

Postmark for Danger 🐾🐾 **1956** Detectives do their best to smash a diamond smuggling ring that operates between Britain and the U.S. Along the way a number of people are killed. 84m/B VHS. GB Terry Moore, Robert Beatty, William Sylvester, Josephine Griffin, Geoffrey Keen, Henry Oscar; **D:** Guy Green.

Postmortem 🐾🐾 **1998 (R)** Sheen is an FBI serial killer profiler who leaves the job to become a novelist and find peace in a small town. But his quiet life is shattered by a murderer who writes the obituaries of his victims before he kills. 105m/C VHS, DVD. Charlie Sheen, Michael Halsey, Stephen McCole, Gary Lewis, Hazel Ann Crawford; **D:** Albert Pyun; **W:** John Lamb; **C:** George Mooradian; **M:** Tory Ripairati.

Pot o' Gold 🐾🐾 **1941** The Golden Hour Stewart plays a wealthy young man who signs on with a struggling band. He convinces his uncle, who has a radio program, to let the band perform during a radio giveaway show; he has concocted. Slight comedy. Stewart notwithstanding. 87m/B VHS, DVD. Paulette Goddard, James Stewart, Charles Winninger, Horace Heidt, Art Carney; **D:** George Marshall; **W:** Walter DeLeon; **C:** Hal Mohr.

Pot, Parents, and Police *The Cat Ate the Parakeet* 1971 A 13-year-old boy goes crazy when his dog dies and soon gets in with a hippie crowd, drops acid, and gets in trouble with the cops. 86m/C VHS. Phillip Pine, Robert Mantell, Madelyn Keen, Arthur Battanides, Martin Margulies; **D:** Phillip Pine; **W:** Phillip Pine.

Pound Puppies and the Legend of Big Paw 1988 The Pound Puppies, known for breaking dogs out of pounds and delivering them to safe and secure homes, are featured in their first full-length musical (and merchandising effort). Fifties music. 76m/C VHS, DVD. **D:** Pierre de Celles; **W:** Jim Carlson; **V:** Nancy Cartwright, George Rose, B.J. Ward, Ruth Buzzi, Brennan Howard.

Pouvoir Intime 1987 (PG-13) What happens when robbers of an armored car lock the guard in the vehicle, and he decides to fight back? This film offers one possible scenario. Available in dubbed or subtitled versions. 86m/C VHS. *FR* Marie Tifo, Pierre Curzi, Yvan Ponton, Jaques Lussier; **D:** Yves Simoneau.

P.O.W. Deathcamp 1989 A combat unit is captured and tortured by the Vietcong in this typical Vietnam story. 92m/C VHS. Charles Black, Bill Balbridge, Rey Malonzo; **D:** Jett C. Espiritu.

The P.O.W. Escape *Behind Enemy Lines* 1986 (R) The adventures of a surly American commander captured as a POW during the final days of the Vietnam War. 90m/C VHS. David Carradine, Mako, Charles R. Floyd, Steve James; **D:** Gideon Amir; **W:** Malcolm Barbour, James Bruner, Jeremy Lipp, John Langway.

Powaqqatsi: Life in Transformation 1988 (G) Director Reggio's follow-up to "Koyaanisqatsi" doesn't pack the wallop of its predecessor. Still, the cinematography is magnificent and the music of Philip Glass is exquisitely hypnotic as we are taken on a spellbinding video collage of various third world countries and see the price they've paid in the name of progress. Part 2 of a planned trilogy. 95m/C VHS, DVD. **D:** Godfrey Reggio; **M:** Philip Glass.

Powder 1995 (PG-13) An electromagnetic albino with an I.Q. off the charts is discovered living in his grandparents' cellar and brought to live in a school for troubled teens. Revelations of Salva's criminal conviction for child molestation cast some scenes in a disturbing light and caused major headaches for Disney's publicity department. 111m/C VHS, DVD. Sean Patrick Flanery, Mary Steenburgen, Lance Henriksen, Jeff Goldblum, Brandon Smith, Bradford Tatum, Susan Tyrrell, Missy (Melissa) Crider, Ray Wise, Esteban Louis Powell; **D:** Victor Salva; **W:** Victor Salva; **C:** Jerzy Zielinski; **M:** Jerry Goldsmith.

Powder Burn 1996 Detective Jack Becker seeks to protect a Beverly Hills client's young daughter when he uncovers unsavory goings-on at her home. And then discovers he's being set up to be the patsy for a murder. 92m/C VHS. Jay Irwin, Elizabeth Barry; **D:** Serge Rodnunsky; **W:** Serge Rodnunsky; **C:** Pierre Chemaly; **M:** Jimmy Lifton.

Powder Keg 1970 Railroad company hires a rowdy team of investigators to retrieve a hijacked train. Action never quits. Inspired the TV pilot "The Bearcats." 93m/C VHS. Rod Taylor, Dennis Cole, Michael Ansara, Fernando Lamas, Tisha Sterling; **D:** Douglas Heyes.

Powdersmoke Range 1935 Crooked frontier politician plots to steal valuable ranch property. The new owners, however, have other ideas. First in "The Three Mesquiteers" series. 71m/B VHS. Harry Carey Sr., Hoot Gibson, Tom Tyler, Guinn "Big Boy" Williams, Bob Steele, Sam Hardy, Patricia "Boots" Mallory, Franklyn Farnum, William Desmond, William Farnum, Buzz Barton, Wally Wales, Art Mix, Buffalo Bill Jr., Buddy Roosevelt; **D:** Wallace Fox.

Power 1928 Two dam-building construction workers vie with each other for the local girls. Silent. 60m/B VHS. William Boyd, Alan Hale, Carole Lombard, Joan Bennett; **D:** Howard Higgin.

Power *Jew Suss* 1934 A Jewish ghetto inhabitant in 18th-century Wurtemburg works his way out of the gutter and into some authority by pleasing the whims of an evil duke. Based on the novel by Leon Fuechtwangler. 105m/B VHS. *GB* Conrad Veidt, Benita Hume, Frank Vosper, Cedric Hardwicke, Gerald du Maurier, Pamela Ostrer, Joan Maude, Paul Graetz, Mary Clare, Percy Parsons, Dennis Hoey, Gibb McLaughlin, Francis L. Sullivan; **D:** Lothar Mendes.

The Power 1980 (R) An ancient clay idol that was created by the Aztecs and possesses incredible destructive power is unleashed on modern man. 87m/C VHS. Warren Lincoln, Susan Stokey, Lisa Erickson, Jeffrey Obrow, Chad Christian, Ben Gilbert, Chris Morrill, Rod Mays; **D:** Stephen Carpenter, Jeffrey Obrow; **W:** Stephen Carpenter, John Penney, Jeffrey Obrow; **C:** Stephen Carpenter; **M:** Christopher Young.

Power 1986 (R) A study of corporate manipulations. Gere plays a ruthless media consultant working for politicians. Fine cast can't find the energy needed to make this great, but it's still interesting. Lumet did better with same material in "Network." 111m/C VHS, DVD. Richard Gere, Julie Christie, E.G. Marshall, Gene Hackman, Beatrice Straight, Kate Capshaw, Denzel Washington, Fritz Weaver, Michael Learned, J.T. Walsh; **D:** Sidney Lumet; **W:** David Himmelstein; **C:** Andrzej Bartkowiak; **M:** Cy Coleman.

Power and Beauty 2002 A titillating topic turns into a dull telepic. Judith Campbell Exner (Henstridge) is a beauty who, after a fling with Frank Sinatra (Ralston), becomes the mistress of JFK (Anderson). Sinatra is also the one who introduced Judith to wiseguy Sam Giancana (Friedman) and FBI honcho Herbert Hoover is convinced that the babe is some kind of messenger service between the White House and the Chicago crime boss. (In 1975, the real Exner is subpoenaed by a Senate committee who wants details and is briefly in the public eye.) 94m/C VHS, DVD. Natasha Henstridge, Kevin Anderson, Peter Friedman, Grant Nickalls, John Ralston; **D:** Susan Seidelman; **W:** William Bast, Dave Erickson, Paul Huson; **C:** Derick Underschultz; **M:** Patrick Williams. CABLE

Power 98 1996 (R) L.A. shock-jock Kaitlin Pickett (Roberts) takes inexperienced Jon Price (Gedrick) as his protege, much to the dismay of girlfriend Sharon (Garth). Since Pickett will do anything to get higher ratings, she's right to worry, especially after a caller confesses to murder during Pickett's show. Roberts refrains from scenery-chewing but co-stars Gedrick and Garth give new meaning to bland. 88m/C VHS. Eric Roberts, Jason Gedrick, Jennie Garth, Larry Drake, Stephen Tobolowsky; **D:** Jaime Hellman; **W:** Jaime Hellman; **C:** Kent Wakeford; **M:** Jeff Beal.

Power of Attorney 1994 (R) Ambitious up-from-the-streets lawyer Paul Diehl (Koteas) decides to defend Mafia don Joseph Scassi (Aiello) against federal charges of murder and extortion, convincing himself that the mobster is telling the truth. But Scassi decides to make certain his lawyer will do his best by threatening Diehl's drug-dealing brother Frankie (Wilson). 97m/C VHS, DVD. Danny Aiello, Elias Koteas, Nina Siemaszko, Rae Dawn Chong, Roger Wilson; **D:** Howard Himmelstein; **W:** George Erschbamer, Jeff Barmash; **M:** Hal Beckett.

The Power of One 1992 (PG-13) Good cast is generally wasted in liberal white look at apartheid. Set in South Africa during the 1940s, P.K. is a white orphan of British descent who is sent to a boarding school run by Afrikaaners (South Africans of German descent). Humiliated and bullied, particularly when England and Germany go to war, P.K. is befriended by a German pianist and a black boxing coach who teach him to box and stand up for his rights. Preachy and filled with stereotypes. Based on the novel by Bryce Courtenay. 126m/C VHS, DVD. Stephen Dorff, Armin Mueller-Stahl, Morgan Freeman, John Gielgud, Fay Masterson, Marius Weyers, Tracy Brooks Swope, John Osborne, Daniel Craig, Dominic Walker, Alois Mayo, Ian Roberts, Maria Marais; **D:** John G. Avildsen; **W:** Robert Mark Kamen; **C:** Dean Semler; **M:** Hans Zimmer.

The Power of the Ninjitsu 1988 A young man inherits the leadership of a martial arts crime gang, the Scorpions, but the elder members muscle him out of his place. He returns for revenge and has the old ones running scared. Power to the Ninjitsu! 90m/C VHS. Britton Lee, Adam Frank, Peter Ujaer; **D:** Joseph Lai.

Power, Passion & Murder 1983 A young, glamorous movie star has an affair with a married man which begins the end of her career in 1930s Hollywood. 104m/C VHS, DVD. Michelle Pfeiffer, Darren McGavin, Stella Stevens; **D:** Paul Bogart, Leon Ichaso.

Power Play *Operation Overthrow* 1981 Young army colonel from a small European country joins forces with rebels to overthrow the government. After the coup, the group discovers that in their midst is a traitor. So who is it? Suspense never builds adequately. 95m/C VHS. *CA GB* Peter O'Toole, David Hemmings, Donald Pleasence, Barry Morse; **D:** Martyn Burke; **W:** Martyn Burke.

Power Play 2002 (R) Connecting an energy company's greed to massive earthquakes in southern California is no small feat but reporter Matt Nash puts his life on the line to do just that. B-movie disaster flick is decidedly low-energy. 90m/C VHS, DVD. Dylan Walsh, Alison Eastwood, Tobin Bell, Julia Davis, Jaimz Woolvett; **D:** Joseph Zito; **W:** B.J. Davis, Brent Huff, Adrian Fulle; **C:** Gideon Porath. VIDEO

The Power Within 1979 An electrified stuntman finds he can send electrical shocks from his hands and becomes the victim of a kidnapping plot. 90m/C VHS. Eric (Hans Gudegast) Braeden, David Hedison, Susan Howard, Art Hindle; **D:** John Llewellyn Moxey.

The Power Within 1995 (PG-13) Evil Raymond Vonn has stolen an ancient ring of power but to acquire its complete strength he needs to find a second, matching ring. This is in the possession of teenaged Stan Dryer (Roberts), who must discover the ring's power if he expects to defeat Vonn. 97m/C VHS, DVD. Ted Jan Roberts, Karen Valentine, Keith Coogan, Liam O'Hurley, Gary Morgan, Sean Fitzgerald, William Zabka; **D:** Art Camacho; **W:** Jacobsen Hart, Susan Bowen; **M:** Jim Halfpenny.

The Powerpuff Girls Movie 2002 (G) Blossom, Buttercup, and Bubbles hit the big screen. The big-eyed trio of superpowered kindergartners came into existence after a botched science experiment by Professor Utonium, who mixed his sugar, spice, and everything nice recipe with a little Chemical X (thanks to Jojo the lab chimp). The "X" factor has left the seemingly normal tots with super powers. After a mishap leaves their father/creator in jail, the girls join up with Jojo (voice of Jackson), who since has been genetically altered by Chemical X himself and acquired a taste for world domination, unbeknownst to the Power Pack. Runs a bit long, but creator/ director McCracken's cool retro animation, fast-paced editing, and satiric fun makes a winner with kids and adults alike. 74m/C VHS, DVD. *US* **D:** Craig McCrackin; **W:** Craig McCrackin, Charlie Bean, Lauren Faust, Paul Rudish, John Roarke; **V:** Catherine Cavadini, Tara Strong, Elizabeth (E.G. Dailey) Daily, Roger L. Jackson, Tom Kane, Tom Kenny, Jennifer Hale, Jennifer Martin; **Nar:** Tom Kenny.

Powwow Highway 1989 (R) Remarkably fine performances in this unusual, thought-provoking, poorly titled foray into the plight of Native Americans. Farmer shines as the unassuming, amiable Cheyenne traveling to New Mexico in a beat-up Chevy with his Indian activist buddy, passionately portrayed by Martinez. On the journey they are constantly confronted with the tragedy of life on a reservation. A sobering look at government injustice and the lingering spirit of a people lost inside their homeland. 105m/C VHS, DVD. Gary Farmer, A. Martinez, Amanda Wyss, Sam Vlahos, Joanelle Romero, Graham Greene; **D:** Jonathan Wacks; **W:** Janet Heaney, Jean Stawarz; **C:** Toyomichi Kurita; **M:** Barry Goldberg. Sundance '89: Filmmakers Trophy.

Practical Magic 1998 (PG-13) Gillian (Kidman) and Sally (Bullock) are modern-day witch sisters whose family suffers from an unfortunate 100-year-old curse. Any man they fall in love with is doomed to an early death. One more dead body, Gillian's abusive boyfriend Jimmy (Visnjic), brings out detective Gary Hallet (Quinn) and spoils charms prove mighty attractive to the frantic Sally. Good cast, weak story. Based on the 1995 novel by Alice Hoffman. 105m/C VHS, DVD. Sandra Bullock, Nicole Kidman, Aidan Quinn, Stockard Channing, Dianne Wiest, Goran Visnjic; **D:** Griffin Dunne; **W:** Robin Swicord, Akiva Goldsman, Adam Brooks; **C:** Andrew Dunn; **M:** Alan Silvestri.

The Practice of Love 1984 A woman journalist's investigation of a murder casts suspicion on her two male lovers. The film raises the question of whether love is even possible in a world dominated by men's struggles for power. In German with English subtitles. 90m/C VHS. *GE* **D:** Valie Export.

A Prairie Home Companion 2006 (PG-13) Leisurely-paced adaptation of Keillor's radio show begins at the Fitzgerald Theater in St. Paul on a Saturday night. Only this night is the program's last broadcast because the radio station has been sold. Emcee Keillor (more or less playing himself) doesn't want to spoil things by making a fuss so the show goes on with the singing Johnson sisters—ditsy Yolanda (Streep) and caustic Rhonda (Tomlin)—and risque cowboy duo Lefty (Reilly) and Dusty (Harrelson), while backstage P.I. Guy Noir (Kline) wonders about the mysterious blonde in white (Madsen). Ensemble master Altman just lets his 39th feature meander gently along. 105m/C DVD. *US* Meryl Streep, Lily Tomlin, Lindsay Lohan, Woody Harrelson, John C. Reilly, Kevin Kline, Tommy Lee Jones, L.Q. Jones, Virginia Madsen, Maya Rudolph, Garrison Keillor, Marylouise Burke; **D:** Robert Altman; **W:** Garrison Keillor; **C:** Edward Lachman.

The Prairie King 1927 Will grants three people the same gold mine but stipulates only one may own it. Silent quandary. 58m/B VHS. Hoot Gibson, Barbara Worth, Charles Sellon, Albert Priscoe; **D:** B. Reeves Eason; **W:** Frank Howard Clark; **C:** Harry Neumann.

Prairie Moon 1938 Autry becomes the guardian of three tough kids from Chicago after they inherit a ranch. The kids help Autry round up a gang of rustlers. 58m/B VHS. Gene Autry, Smiley Burnette, Shirley Deane, Tommy Ryan, David Gorcey, Jack Rockwell, Tom London; **D:** Ralph Staub; **W:** Betty Burbridge, Stanley Roberts; **C:** William Nobles.

Prairie Pals 1942 Deputies go undercover to rescue a kidnapped scientist. 60m/B VHS. William Boyd, Lee Powell, Art Davis, Charles "Blackie" King, John Merton, Kermit Maynard, Al "Fuzzy" St. John; **D:** Sam Newfield.

The Prairie Pirate 1925 Carey is the western hero tracking down the dirty dogs who murdered his sister. Fast-paced. 59m/B VHS. Harry Carey Sr., Lloyd Whitlock, Jean Dumas, Trilby Clark; **D:** Edmund Mortimer.

Praise 1998 First-time director Curran scores big with this downbeat sex-and-drugs saga. Gordan (Fenton) has quit his convenience store job to spend his time drinking with his mates in his grubby Brisbane apartment. Former co-worker Cynthia (Holder) invites Gordon to her parents' empty house where the duo spend their time with various chemical substances, alcohol, and sex. They wind up sticking together out of mutual need and never rise above their marginal existence. Still, both director and actors deliv-

Prancer 🐾🐾 **1989 (G)** An eight-year-old girl whose mother has recently died thinks an injured reindeer she has found belongs to Santa. She lovingly nurses him back to health. Harmless family entertainment. **102m/C VHS, DVD.** Sam Elliot, Rebecca Harrell, Cloris Leachman, Rutanya Alda, John Joseph Duda, Ariana Richards, Michael Constantine, Abe Vigoda, Mark Rolston; **D:** John Hancock; **W:** Greg Taylor; **C:** Misha (Mikail) Suslov; **M:** Maurice Jarre.

Prancer Returns 🐾🐾½ **2001 (G).** When dad cuts out, 8-year-old Charlie, his mom and his brother move to a small Michigan town where Charlie hears about a local legend. Seems a young girl nursed a wounded deer back to health and set it free on Christmas Eve. The deer turned out to be Prancer and he rejoined Santa just in time to help pull the sleigh. So when Charlie finds a baby reindeer in the woods, he decides it must be a new Prancer and he has to make sure that the deer gets to Santa in time for Christmas. **90m/C VHS, DVD.** Jack Palance, John Corbett, Stacy Edwards, Gavin Fink, Michael O'Keefe, Joshua Butler; **W:** Greg Taylor. **CABLE**

Pray for the Wildcats 🐾½ **1974** Three advertising executives' promotional trip from (or to?) Hell. Anything to please a client. **90m/C VHS.** Andy Griffith, William Shatner, Angie Dickinson, Janet Margolin, Marjoe Gortner, Lorraine Gary; **D:** Robert Lewis.

Pray TV 🐾🐾 **1980 (PG)** A sly con man turns a failing TV station into a profitable one when the station starts to broadcast around-the-clock religious programming. **92m/C VHS.** Dabney Coleman, Archie Hahn, Joyce Jameson, Nancy Morgan, Roger E. Mosley, Marcia Wallace; **D:** Rick Friedberg; **W:** Nick Castle. **TV**

Pray TV 🐾🐾 **1982** Expose of broadcast religion in which a young preacher crosses between orthodox religion and lots of money. Not as cutting an indictment as it could have been. **100m/C VHS.** John Ritter, Ned Beatty, Madolyn Smith, Richard Kiley, Louise Latham, Jonathan Prince, Michael Currie. **TV**

A Prayer for Katarina Horovitzova 🐾🐾½ **1969** Stunning tale of a Polish singer who struggles to find the meaning and beauty of life while working to trade Nazi prisoners in U.S. jails for Jews hoping to emigrate. Based on the Arnost Lustig novel. Confiscated by the Czech Communist government and kept from the screen "for 21 years. In Czechoslovakian with English subtitles. **60m/C VHS. CZ** Jiri Adamira, Lenka Fiserova, Cestmir Randa; **D:** Arnost Lustig. **W:** Arnost Lustig; **C:** Jiri Kadanka; **M:** Bill Conti.

A Prayer in the Dark 🐾🐾½ **1997 (PG-13)** Pious Quaker wife and mother Emily Hayworth (Carter) is taken hostage in her own home by a former Quaker friend, Jimmy (Ferguson). He's escaped from prison with two armed cons, demanding that Emily steal $4 million from the bank where she works. Since they're

er a powerful production. Adapted from the novel by McGahan, who wrote the screenplay. **97m/C VHS, DVD.** A.J. Peter Fenton, Sacha Horler; **C:** Dion Beebe; Australian "Film Inst. '99. Actress (Horler). Adapt. Laskos.

also holding her family, she agrees. But when Emily's out of the house, she and others in the Quaker community try to find a peaceful solution to the volatile situation. **91m/C VHS.** Lynda Carter, Colin Ferguson, Teri Polo; **D:** Jerry Ciccoritti; **W:** Andrew Laskos; **C:** Peter E. Lengyel; **C:** Robert Barcoli; **M:** Nona Hendryx.

Prayer of the Rollerboys 🐾🐾½ **1991 (R)** Violent, futuristic, funky action as Halim infiltrates a criminal gang of syncopated roller-blading neo-nazi youth with plans for nationwide domination. Though routinely plotted and predictable, it's got great skating stunts and a wry vision of tomorrow's shattered USA—broke, drug-soaked, homeless, foreign-owned; even sharper when you realize this is a Japanese-American co-production. **94m/C VHS, DVD.** Corey Haim, Patricia Arquette, Christopher Collet, Julius W. Harris, J.C. Quinn, Jake Dengel, Devin Clark, Mark Pellegrino, Morgan Weisser; **D:** Rick King; **W:** Peter Iliff; **C:** Phedon Papamichael; **M:** Stacy Widelitz.

Praying Mantis 🐾🐾 **1983 (PG-13)** The professor's scheming nurse murdered his family and plans to marry him for his money. She enlists the aid of the professor's assistant in her evil plot. **119m/C VHS.** Jonathan Pryce, Cherie Lunghi, Anna Cropper, Carmen (De Sautoy) Du Sautoy, Pinkas Braun; **D:** Jack Gold; **M:** Carl Davis.

Praying Mantis 🐾🐾½ **1993 (PG-13)** Seymour stars as a femme fatale who likes to get married and then, in a rage against her own abusive childhood, kill her new husband's off. So far her total is five dead hubbies with number six (Bostwick) in her sights. Only this time, her almost-sister-in-law (Fisher) is very suspicious of the bride-to-be. **90m/C VHS.** Jane Seymour, Barry Bostwick, Frances Fisher, Chad Allen; **D:** James Keach; **W:** Duane Poole, William F. Delligan; **M:** Roy.

Pre-Madonnas: Rebels Without a Clue 🐾🐾½ **1995 (R)** **Social Surcide 1995 (PG-13)** Kim Sterling (Sturges) decides to rig the Beverly Hills Las Madonnas to the debutante ball to teach the snobs a lesson. **98m/C VHS.** Shannon Sturges, Bobbie Bressee, Peter Anthony Elliott, Kenn Cooper; **D:** Lawrence Foldes.

Preacherman 🐾½ **1983 (R)** Phony preacher travels through the south, fleecing gullible congregations (and providing for their sexual desires) wherever he goes. **90m/C VHS, DVD.** Amos Huxley, Marian Brown, Adam Hesse, Ilene Kristen, W. Henry Smith; **D:** Albert T. Viola; **W:** Albert T. Viola, Harvey Flaxman; **M:** W. Henry Smith, Roland Pope.

The Preacher's Wife 🐾🐾 **1996 (PG)** Remake of 1947's "The Bishop's Wife" finds troubled Newark minister Henry Biggs (Vance) praying for heavenly intervention. His prayers are answered with angel Dudley (Washington)—who isn't so holy that he can't appreciate the minister's choir-leading wife Julia (Houston). While trying to save his cash-strapped church from a greedy developer (Hines), Rev. Biggs is so mired in material problems that he is unable to believe that Dudley is actually an angel. Washington is the dictionary definition of debonair as the angel with a touch of the devil in his eye. All problems are, of course, wrapped up neatly with a bow on top in the end. The real stars of this Christmas tale, however, are Houston's vocal cords. Fans of her singing will love this movie, while others may want to rent the original. **124m/C VHS, DVD.** Denzel Washington, Whitney Houston, Courtney B. Vance, Gregory Hines, Jenifer Lewis, Loretta Devine, Lionel Richie, Paul Bates, Justin Pierre Edmund, Darvel Davis Jr., William James Stiggers Jr.; **D:** Penny Marshall; **W:** Nat Mauldin, Allan Scott; **C:** Miroslav Ondricek; **M:** Hans Zimmer.

Preaching to the Choir 🐾🐾 **2005 (PG-13)** Twin brothers Teshawn (Greene) and Wesley (Sills-Evans) Tucker have been estranged since the death of their parents. Te is the gangsta hip hop star Zulu while Wes is a minister at a Harlem church. When Te gets into big trouble with his LA record producer Bull Sharkey (Akinnaoye-Agbaje), he flees to Harlem to hide out and and he and Wes try to reconcile their differences, especially when Te of-

fers to whip the church's raggedy gospel choir into shape in time for a competition. But it's not all in the competition, as Te falls for the girl he married 2,000 and 10,000 meters but falters, thanks in part to the tragedy sur-

Precious Find 🐾🐾 **1996 (R)** In 2049 there's a new gold rush—this time into outer space. The moon's enclosed city is a staging area for mining operations throughout the solar system and draws the attention of three prospectors: Ben, who can "smell" gold, Crille (Hauer), who has a high-tech treasure map, and Sam (James), who owns a space hauler. They're all anxious to cash in when a newly discovered asteroid turns out to be literal gold mine as is claim jumper Camilla (Chen). **90m/C VHS.** Rutger Hauer, Brion James, Harold F. Pruett, Joan Chen; **D:** Philippe Mora; **W:** Jane Ubell, John Remark; **C:** Walter Bai; **M:** Roy Hay.

Predator 🐾🐾½ **1987 (R)** Schwarzenegger leads a team of CIA-hired mercenaries into the Central American jungles to rescue hostages. They encounter an alien force that begins to attack them one by one. Soon it's just Arnold and the Beast in this attention-grabbing, but sometimes silly, suspense film. **107m/C VHS, DVD, UMD.** Arnold Schwarzenegger, Jesse Ventura, Sonny Landham, Bill Duke, Elpidia Carrillo, Carl Weathers, R.G. Armstrong, Richard Chaves, Shane Black, Kevin Peter Hall; **D:** John McTiernan; **W:** Jim Thomas, John Thomas; **C:** Donald McAlpine; **M:** Alan Silvestri.

Predator 2 🐾🐾 **1990 (R)** Tough cop takes time away from battling drug dealers to deal with malicious extraterrestrial who exterminated Arnold's band of commandos in "Predator." Miss-billed as sequel, its only resemblance to the original is that the predator has inexplicably returned (this time to the thick of LA). Gory action aplenty, little logic. Fine cast dominated by minority performers can't save this one. **105m/C VHS, DVD.** Danny Glover, Gary Busey, Ruben Blades, Maria Conchita Alonso, Bill Paxton, Robert Davi, Adam Baldwin, Kent McCord, Morton Downey Jr., Calvin Lockhart, Teri Weigel, Kevin Peter Hall, Steve Kahan, Michael (Mike) Papajohn, Jsu Garcie; **D:** Stephen Hopkins; **W:** John Thomas, Jim Thomas; **C:** Peter Levy; **M:** Alan Silvestri.

Predator Island 🐾 **Hell's Beacon 2005 (R)** Teens and aliens—what could be more fun? A group of teens head off for a lovely weekend boat trip off the New England Coast. A meteor crash spurs bad weather and throws the crew off-course, stranding them on an island inhabited only by a creepy lighthouse keeper and his wife. The aliens, presumably having hitched a ride on the meteor, terrorize all. **75m/C DVD.** Daniel Gordon, Hank Torrance, Libby Kral, Tom Dahl, Ilana Becker, Michael Winans; **D:** Steven Charles Gordon; **C:** Peter Levy; **M:** Tony Bitten. **VIDEO**

Prefontaine 🐾🐾½ **1996 (PG-13)** Sports bio has appeal, thanks to lead actor Leto, in covering the brief career of early '70s runner Steve Prefontaine. Cocky and outspoken, the charismatic University of Oregon star soon owns every American record for distances between 2,000 and 10,000 meters but falters, thanks in part to the tragedy sur-

Preaching to the Perverted 🐾 **1997 (R)** Silly sex comedy finds politician Henry Harding (Bell) crusading against smut with his intention to close down London's S&M clubs. First up is the House of Thwax, run by New York fetish queen Tanya (Turner). To get evidence of naughtiness, Henry sends in his virginal volunteer Peter (Anholt), who becomes obsessed with Tanya. Tanya's intrigued by his innocence and teaches Peter a few sexual tricks which soon nears he has to choose between his job and his newly acquired interest in kink. **99m/C DVD, GB** Guinevere Turner, Christien Anholt, Tom Bell, Julie Graham, Julian Wadham, Georgina Hale, Ricky Tomlinson, Don Henderson; **D:** Stuart Urban; **W:** Stuart Urban; **C:** Sam McCurdy; **M:** Magnus Fiennes.

Prehistoric Bimbos in Armageddon City woof! **1993** Tirana and her tribe of Prehistoric Bimbos must prevent post-nuclear domination in Old Chicago City, the last remaining civ. **70m/C VHS, DVD.** Jared Leto, R. Lee Ermey, Ed O'Neill, Amy Locane, Lindsay Crouse, Laurel Holloman, Breckin Meyer, Kurwood Smith, Brian McGovern, Peter Anthony Jacobs; **D:** Steve James; **W:** Steve James, Eugene Corr; **C:** Peter Gilbert; **M:** Mason Daring.

Prehistoric Women woof! **1950** A tribe of prehistoric women look for husbands the old-fashioned way—they drag them back to their caves from the jungle. So bad it's almost good. **74m/C VHS, DVD.** Laurette Luez, Allan Nixon, Mara Lynn, Joan Shawlee, Judy Landon; **D:** Gregg Tallas.

Prehistoric Women 🐾 **See Slave Girls 1967** Essentially, an equally tacky remake of the 1950 wooler. Great white hunter David Marchant (Latimer) gets lost in a jungle where the local tribe worship the white rhino. He escapes from one group, only to recapture by some Amazons, who take the hunter to their queen, Kari (Berswick—the only reason to waste your time), who gives him two options—satisfy her or die. **90m/C VHS, DVD, GB** Michael Latimer, Martine Beswick, Edina Ronay, Carol White; **D:** Michael Carreras; **W:** Henry Younger; **C:** Michael Reed; **M:** Carlo Martelli.

Prehysteria 🐾🐾½ **1993 (PG)** Fantasy/adventure about a widower, his 11-year-old son and teenage daughter, and what happens when some mysterious eggs from South America accidentally wind up at their farm. Imagine their surprise when the eggs hatch and out pop a brood of pygmy dinosaurs. The dinosaurs are cute (as is the family), the villain is dumb, and the violence minimal. **84m/C VHS.** Brett Cullen, Austin O'Brien, Samantha Mills, Colleen Morris, Tony Longo, Stuart Fratkin, Steven Lee; **D:** Albert Band, Charles Band; **M:** Richard Band.

Prehysteria 2 🐾🐾½ **1994 (PG)** While their adoptive family is on vacation the pygmy dinosaurs get loose and aid a lonely rich boy whose governess is plotting to send him to military boarding school. **81m/C VHS.** Kevin R. Connors, Jennifer Harte, Dean Scofield, Betye Ackerman, Larry Hankin, Greg Lewis, Alan Palo, Michael Hagiwara, Owen Bush; **D:** Albert Band; **W:** Brent Friedman, Michae Davis; **M:** Richard Band.

Prehysteria 3 🐾🐾½ **1995 (PG)** The mini-dinos take up miniature golf. Seems Thomas MacGregor's (Willard) putt-putt business is about to sink when his daughter Ella (Anderson) finds the pygmy dinosaurs and a promotional bonanza is born. But Thomas' evil brother Hal (Weitz) hatches a plot to take over the now-successful enterprize. DeCoteau used the pseudonym Julian Breen. **85m/C VHS.** Fred Willard, Bruce Weitz, Whitney Anderson, Pam Matteson; **D:** David DeCoteau; **W:** Michael Davis, Neil Ruttenberg.

Prelude to a Kiss 🐾🐾 **1992 (PG-13)** Disappointing screen adaptation of Craig Lucas' hit play features Baldwin and Ryan as young lovers in this romantic fantasy. Ryan is Rita, a free-spirited bartender, and Baldwin is Peter, a conservative writer, who decide to marry after a whirlwind courtship. At their wedding reception, Rita obligingly kisses one of her guests, an old man (Walker). Then, on their honeymoon, Peter begins to notice a number of changes to Rita's character and comes to realize this is truly not the girl he married. The delicate fantasy which worked on stage struggles to survive this film up" of the screen adaptation though Baldwin (who reprises his stage role) and

Ryan are appealing. **106m/C VHS, DVD.** Alec Baldwin, Meg Ryan, Sydney Walker, Ned Beatty, Patty Duke, Kathy Bates, Stanley Tucci; *D:* Norman Rene; *W:* Craig Lucas; *C:* Stefan Czapsky; *M:* Howard Shore.

Premature Burial 🦴🦴½ **1962** A cataleptic Englishman's worst fears come true when he is buried alive. He escapes and seeks revenge on his doctor and his greedy wife. Based upon the story by Edgar Allan Poe. **81m/C VHS, DVD.** Ray Milland, Richard Ney, Hazel Court, Heather Angel, Alan Napier, John Dierkes, Dick Miller, Brendan Dillon Jr., Clive Halliday; *D:* Roger Corman; *W:* Charles Beaumont, Ray Russell; *C:* Floyd Crosby; *M:* Ronald Stein.

Premonition 🦴½ **1971 (PG)** Three drug-riddled '60s college students experience similar premonitions of death, and subsequently either die or become tormented. **83m/C VHS.** Carl Crow, Tim Ray, Winfrey Hester Hill, Victor Izay; *D:* Alan Rudolph; *W:* Alan Rudolph; *C:* John Bailey.

The Premonition **(PG)** Parapsychologist searching for a missing child is drawn into a frightening maze of dream therapy and communication with the dead. Well-done paranormal tale filmed in Mississippi. **94m/C VHS, DVD.** Richard Lynch, Sharon Farrell, Jeff Corey, Ellen Barber, Edward Bell, Danielle Brisebois; *D:* Robert Allen Schnitzer; *W:* Anthony Mahon.

Premonition 🦴🦴 **1998 (R)** Lloyd and Preston are tabloid reporters who investigate supernatural phenomena. Their latest find is a mental patient who predicts events that wind up leading back to a past they both share. Unfortunately, the film is more a series of horror cliches and makes little sense. **93m/C VHS, DVD.** Christopher Lloyd, Adrian Paul, Cynthia (Cyndy, Cindy) Preston, Blu Mankuma; *D:* Gavin Wilding; *W:* Gavin Wilding, Raul Inglis, John Fairley; *C:* Glen Winter. **VIDEO**

Premonition 🦴🦴½ **2007 (PG-13)** He's dead! No, he's not! He's in the shower! He's being buried! Whew—no wonder Linda (Bullock) thinks she's going nuts. Seems every time she wakes up the fate of her husband Jim (McMahon) has changed. Linda finally realizes her days are mysteriously out of order and if she can figure out the pattern (or have a little faith), maybe she can save her man. It's confusing however you look at it, though Bullock tries her best. **97m/C DVD, Blu-ray Disc.** *US* Sandra Bullock, Julian McMahon, Nia Long, Kate Nelligan, Amber Valletta, Peter Stormare, Courtney Taylor Burness, Shyann McClure; *D:* Mennan Yapo; *W:* Bill Kelly; *C:* Torsten Lippstock; *M:* Klaus Badelt.

Prep School 🦴 **1981 (PG-13)** A very proper New England prep school is turned topsy-turvy by two rambunctious co-eds. They're determined to break every one of the school's cardinal rules. **97m/C VHS.** Leslie Hope, Andrew Sabiston; *D:* Paul Almond.

The Preppie Murder 🦴🦴½ **1989** Made for TV crime drama based on the killing of Jennifer Levin in New York City's Central Park in 1987, with Baldwin cast as prep school grad Robert Chambers. Amid sensational headlines, the story told of drugs, sexual games, and idle and disaffected youth. **100m/C VHS.** William Baldwin, Lara Flynn Boyle, Danny Aiello, Joanna Kerns, Dorothy Fielding, James Handy, William Devane; *D:* John Herzfeld. **TV**

Preppies 🦴½ **1982 (R)** Yet another teen sex comedy, but this time Ivy Leaguer Drake must pass his exams to receive his $50 million inheritance. Lots of skirt chasing as his conniving cousin plans him astray. **83m/C VHS, DVD.** Dennis Drake, Peter Brady Reardon, Steven Holt, Nitchie Barrett, Cindy Manion, Katt Shea, Lynda Wiesmeier; *D:* Chuck Vincent.

Prescott Kid 🦴🦴 **1936** Legendary western star McCoy plays a law-abiding cowboy mistaken for the new Marshall in the outlaw town of San Lorenzo, which has been targeted by a gang of cattle rustling killers. **58m/B VHS.** Tim McCoy, Sheila (Manors) Mannors, Alden Chase, Hooper Atchley, Walter Brennan; *D:* David Selman; *W:* Ford Beebe.

Presenting Lily Mars 🦴🦴 **1943** A small-town girl comes to New York to make it on Broadway. Based on the Booth Tarkington novel. ♪When I Look at You; Three O'Clock in the Morning; Kulebiaka; Is It Love? (Or The Gypsy in Me); Broadway Rhythm; Sweethearts of America; Where There's Music; Every Little Movement Has a Meaning All Its Own; Tom, Tom the Piper's Son. **105m/B VHS, DVD.** Judy Garland, Van Heflin, Fay Bainter, Richard Carlson, Tommy Dorsey; *D:* Norman Taurog; *C:* Joseph Ruttenberg.

The President's Analyst 🦴🦴🦴½ **1967** A superbly written, brilliantly executed satire from the mind of Theodore J. Flicker, who wrote as well as directed. Coburn steals the show as a psychiatrist who has the dubious honor of being appointed "secret shrink" to the President of the U.S. Pressures of the job steadily increase his paranoia until he suspects he is being pursued by agents and counter agents alike. Is he losing his sanity or...? Vastly entertaining. **104m/C VHS, DVD.** James Coburn, Godfrey Cambridge, Severn Darden, Joan Delaney, Pat Harrington, Will Geer, William Daniels, Barry McGuire, Jill Banner, Arte Johnson; *D:* Theodore J. Flicker; *W:* Theodore J. Flicker; *C:* William A. Fraker; *M:* Lalo Schifrin.

President's Mistress 🦴½ **1978** A security agent searches for his sister's murderer, while trying to obscure the fact that she was having an affair with the President. **97m/C VHS.** Beau Bridges, Susan Blanchard, Larry Hagman, Joel Fabiani, Karen Grassle; *D:* John Llewellyn Moxey.

The President's Mystery 🦴½ *One For All* **1936** A lawyer decides to turn his back on society by giving up his practice and his marriage. Eventually he meets and falls in love with another woman. The most interesting aspect of the film is that it is based on a story by Franklin D. Roosevelt, which was published in "Liberty" magazine. The story was supposedly better than its screen adaptation. **80m/B VHS, DVD.** Henry Wilcoxon, Betty Furness, Sidney Blackmer, Evelyn Brent; *D:* Phil Rosen.

The President's Plane Is Missing 🦴🦴 **1971** When Air Force One disappears, the less than trustworthy Vice President takes control. Could there be a dire plot in the making? Based on a novel by Rod Serling's brother Robert J. Serling. **100m/C VHS.** Buddy Ebsen, Peter Graves, Arthur Kennedy, Rip Torn, Louise Sorel, Raymond Massey, James Wainwright, Mercedes McCambridge, Dabney Coleman, Joseph Campanella; *D:* Daryl Duke.

President's Target 🦴🦴 **1993** An anti-drug mission in South America is ambushed and CIA operative Peter Caine is the only survivor. Now he's out to see who planned the double-cross and how best to get his revenge. **82m/C VHS.** John Coleman, Martin Kove, Bo Hopkins, Brigitte Audrey; *D:* Yvan Chiffre.

The Presidio 🦴🦴 **1988 (R)** An easy going police detective must investigate a murder on a military base where he and the base commander have sparred before. The commander becomes downright nasty when his daughter shows an interest in the detective. Good action scenes in San Francisco almost covers up script weaknesses, but not quite. **97m/C VHS, DVD.** Sean Connery, Mark Harmon, Meg Ryan, Jack Warden, Mark Blum, Jenette Goldstein; *D:* Peter Hyams; *W:* Larry Ferguson; *M:* Bruce Broughton.

Pressure 🦴🦴 **2002 (R)** Med students Steve (Smith) and Patrick (Munro) find themselves on a road trip to hell when they make a stop in a smalltown bar. Patrick spends his time dancing with the cheerleaders inhabiting the premises while Steve is lured outside by vampy Amber (Featherstone). He's then knocked unconscious and set-up by her beau, Bo (Dorval), who accidentally shoots himself. This puts our boys in big trouble since Bo is the local corrupt sheriff's (Rhodes) kid. Then the chase is on! **90m/C VHS, DVD.** Kerr Smith, Lochlyn Munro, Angela Featherstone, Adrien Dorval, Donnelly Rhodes, Michelle Harrison; *D:* Richard Gale; *W:* Richard Gale, Craig Brewer; *M:* Christopher Brady. **VIDEO**

Pressure Point 🦴🦴🦴 **1962** Poitier stars as a prison psychiatrist treating an inmate who is a racist and a member of the Nazi party. Darin gives an excellent performance as the Nazi patient in this intelligent drama based on a true case. **87m/B VHS, DVD.** Sidney Poitier, Bobby Darin, Peter Falk, Carl Benton Reid, Barry J. Gordon, Howard Caine, Mary Munday; *D:* Hubert Cornfield; *M:* Ernest Gold.

The Prestige 🦴🦴🦴 **2006 (PG-13)** Nolan reunites with his "Batman Begins" stars Bale and Caine in this perplexing, complicated, and lavish period mystery that focuses on the increasingly violent rivalry between two London magicians. Posh Robert Angier (Jackman) is the more natural showman while Cockney Alfred Borden (Bale) is the risk taker; both are mentored by the conciliatory Cutter (Caine). One of Borden's risks causes the death of Robert's wife Julia (Perabo) and their feud is on. Eventually it will involve Alfred's unhappy missus, Sarah (Hall), lush magician's assistant Olivia (Johansson), reclusive inventor Nikola Tesla (Bowie), and murder. Situations turn fantastical but clues are aplenty if you pay attention. Definitely worth a second look. **128m/C DVD, Blu-ray Disc.** *GB US* Christian Bale, Hugh Jackman, Michael Caine, Scarlett Johansson, Piper Perabo, Rebecca Hall, David Bowie, Andy Serkis, Roger Rees, Ricky Jay, Samantha Mahurin, William Morgan Sheppard; *D:* Christopher Nolan; *W:* Christopher Nolan, Jonathan Nolan; *C:* Wally Pfister; *M:* David Julyan.

Presumed Guilty 🦴🦴 **1991** An innocent man is released from prison only to find he is once again a wanted man! So he gets his gal, who happens to be the sheriff's daughter, is beaten up and in the end winds up living happily ever after. **91m/C VHS, DVD.** Jack Vogel, Holly Floria, Sean Holton, Wayne Zanelotti, Bradley Rockwell, Sharon Young, Al Schuerman; *D:* Lawrence L. Simeone; *W:* Lawrence L. Simeone.

Presumed Innocent 🦴🦴🦴 **1990 (R)** Assistant district attorney is the prime suspect when a former lover turns up brutally murdered. Cover-ups surround him, and enemies switch sides. Slow-paced courtroom drama with excellent performances from Ford, Julia, and Bedelia. Skillfully adapted from the best-seller by Chicago attorney Scott Turow. **127m/C VHS, DVD.** Harrison Ford, Brian Dennehy, Bonnie Bedelia, Greta Scacchi, Raul Julia, Paul Winfield, John Spencer, Joe Grifasi, Anna Maria Horsford, Sab Shimono, Christine Estabrook, Michael (Lawrence) Tolan, Tom Mardirosian; *D:* Alan J. Pakula; *W:* Frank Pierson, Alan J. Pakula; *C:* Gordon Willis; *M:* John Williams.

Pretty Baby 🦴🦴🦴 **1978 (R)** Shield's launching pad and Malle's first American film is a masterpiece of cinematography and style, nearly upstaged by the plodding story line. Carradine manages to be effective but never succeeds at looking comfortable as the New Orleans photographer besotted with a, an 11-year-old prostitute (Shields). Low key, disturbingly intriguing story, beautifully photographed by Sven Nykvist. **109m/C VHS, DVD.** Brooke Shields, Keith Carradine, Susan Sarandon, Barbara Steele, Diana Scarwid, Antonio Fargas, Frances Faye, Gerrit Graham, Mae Mercer; *D:* Louis Malle; *W:* Polly Platt; *C:* Sven Nykvist; *M:* Jerry Wexler.

Pretty in Pink 🦴🦴🦴 **1986 (PG-13)** More teen angst from the pen of Hughes. Poor girl falls for a rich guy. Their families fret, their friends are distressed, and fate conspires against them. If you can suspend your disbelief that a teenager with her own car and answering machine is financially inferior, then you may very well be able to accept the entire premise. Slickly done and adequately, if not enthusiastically, acted. In 1987, Hughes essentially rewrote this film with "Some Kind of Wonderful," the same story with the rich/pauper characters reversed by gender. **96m/C VHS, DVD.** Molly Ringwald, Andrew McCarthy, Jon Cryer, Harry Dean Stanton, James Spader, Annie Potts, Andrew (Dice Clay) Silverstein, Margaret Colin, Alexa Kenin, Gina Gershon, Dweezil Zappa, Kristy Swanson; *D:* Howard Deutch; *W:* John Hughes; *C:* Tak Fujimoto; *M:* Michael Gore.

Pretty Persuasion 🦴 **2005** Nasty girls. Toxic Kimberly (Wood) rules her private high school roost, dragging along airhead best pal Brittany (Harnois) and new student Randa (Schnall) in her wake. The vicious teen targets her English teacher, Mr. Anderson (Livingston), who harbors fantasies about his female students, accusing him of sexual abuse and persuading her friends to back her up. The ensuing scandal and trial are played up by preening tabloid reporter Emily Klein (Krakowski). Woods is around as Kimberly's wealthy, aggressively nasty dad. Smug and offensive. **104m/C DVD.** *US* Evan Rachel Wood, Ron Livingston, James Woods, Jane Krakowski, Elisabeth Harnois, Selma Blair, Danny Comden, Stark Sands, Michael Hitchcock, Robert Joy, Jaime (James) King, Adi Schnall, Alex Desert; *D:* Marcos Siega; *W:* Skander Halim; *C:* Ramsay Nickell; *M:* Gilad Benamram.

Pretty Poison 🦴🦴🦴½ **1968** You won't need an antidote for this one. Original, absorbing screenplay, top-notch acting, and on target direction combine to raise this low-budget, black comedy above the crowd. Perkins at his eerie best as a burned-out arsonist who cooks up a crazy scheme and enlists the aid of a hot-to-trot high schooler, only to discover too late she has some burning desires of her own. Weld is riveting as the turbulent teen. **89m/C VHS, DVD.** Anthony Perkins, Tuesday Weld, Beverly Garland, John Randolph, Dick O'Neill, Joe (Joseph) Bova, Ken Kercheval; *D:* Noel Black; *W:* Lorenzo Semple Jr.; *C:* David Quaid; *M:* Johnny Mandel. N.Y. Film Critics '68: Screenplay.

Pretty Smart woof! **1987 (R)** Two diametrically opposed sisters at a European finishing school team up against a drug-dealing, voyeuristic teacher. Pretty lame. **84m/C VHS.** Tricia Leigh Fisher, Patricia Arquette, Dennis Cole, Lisa Lorient; *D:* Dimitri Logothetis; *M:* Eddie Arkin.

Pretty Village, Pretty Flame 🦴🦴🦴 *Lepa Sela, Lepo Gore* **1996** Powerful story of the Bosnian conflict that is loosely based on a true incident. Story flashes from the days of Yugoslavian unity under Marshal Tito to 1992 when members of a Serbian patrol are trapped (along with an American journalist) by Muslim militiamen in a tunnel connecting Zagreb and Belgrade with no hope for escape. Serbo-Croatian with subtitles. **125m/C VHS, DVD.** Dragan Bjelogrlic, Nikola Kojo, Bata Zivojinovic, Dragan Maksimovic, Zoran Cvijanovic, Nikola Pejakovic, Lisa Moncure; *D:* Srdjan Dragojevic; *W:* Srdjan Dragojevic, Vanja Bulic, Nikola Pejakovic; *C:* Dusan Joksimovic; *M:* Lazar Ristovski.

Pretty Woman 🦴🦴🦴 **1990 (R)** An old story takes a fresh approach as a successful but stuffy business man hires a fun-loving, energetic young hooker to be his companion for a week. The film caused some controversy over its upbeat portrayal of prostitution, but its popularity at the boxoffice catapulted Roberts to stardom. **117m/C VHS, DVD.** Richard Gere, Julia Roberts, Ralph Bellamy, Jason Alexander, Laura San Giacomo, Hector Elizondo, Alex Hyde-White, Elinor Donahue, Larry Miller, Jane Morris; *D:* Garry Marshall; *W:* J.F. Lawton; *C:* Charles Minsky; *M:* James Newton Howard. Golden Globes '91: Actress—Mus./Comedy (Roberts).

Prettykill woof! **1987 (R)** A confusing storyline with numerous subplots involves detective with a paramour/prostitute (Hubley) attempting to stalk a mad killer while contending with her split personality. **95m/C VHS.** David Birney, Susannah York, Season Hubley, Yaphet Kotto, Suzanne Snyder, Germane Houde; *D:* George Kaczender; *W:* Sandra K. Bailey; *C:* Joao Fernandes.

The Prey 🦴 **1980 (R)** Poorly done horror show about a predator who is looking for a mate in the Colorado Rockies and kills five campers in the process. **80m/C VHS.** Debbie Thuerson, Steve Bond, Lori Lethin, Jackie Coogan; *D:* Edwin Scott Brown; *W:* Edwin Scott Brown, Summer Brown.

Prey for Rock and Roll *♂♂♂*
2003 (R) Jacki (Gershon) is a punk rocker who heads the all-girl band Clam Dandy in the L.A. club scene. She's been trying to make it big for the past twenty years, and, fast approaching 40, wonders if it's time to call it quits. While the movie has heart and an authentic rock and roll attitude, it fails on some conventional tactics. That doesn't undermine the raw performance of Gershon, who co-produced the film, and sang her own songs, but it does have a buzz-killing effect on the rest of the proceedings. Adapted from the autobiographical play by Cheri Lovedog. **91m/C** VHS, DVD, **US** Gina Gershon, Drea De Matteo, Lori Petty, Shelly Cole, Marc Blucas, Ivan Martin; **D:** Alex Steyemark; **W:** Cheri Lovedog, Robin Whitehouse; **C:** Antonio Calvache.

Prey of the Chameleon *♂*
1991 (R) A female serial killer escapes from her asylum, ready to rip more men to shreds. However a tough lacy cop has other ideas and goes all out to put an end to the madwoman's doings. Can she stop this fiend before the man she loves becomes the next victim? **91m/C** VHS, Daphne Zuniga, James Wilder, Alexandra Paul, Don Harvey; **D:** Fleming J. Fuller.

Prey of the Jaguar *♂♂½*
1996 (R) Derek Leigh (Caulfield) is an ex-Special Ops agent who's the target of revenge-minded drug lord Damien Bandera (Goddard). When Bandera slaughters his family, Leigh transforms himself into costumed avenger, the Jaguar (after his son's drawing), and first goes after Bandera's drug network before hunting the man himself. Dopey costume but this vigilante prefers putting people to sleep (via a dart) rather than killing them so there's reduced gore and the violence is more martial-arts than slice-and-dice. **96m/C** VHS, Maxwell Caulfield, Trevor Goddard, Linda Blair, Stacy Keach, Paul Regina; **D:** David DeCoteau; **W:** Rory Johnston, Bud Robertson, Nick Spagnoli; **C:** Howard Wexler. **M:** Jeff Walton.

A Price above Rubies *♂♂½*
1997 (R) Evils of patriarchal society are exposed in this tale of an Orthodox Jewish wife who seeks fulfillment outside the lonely and oppressive world in which she lives. Zellweger shines as Sonia, who defies her frigid Hasidic husband Mendel (Fitzgerald) to take a job as a jeweler, then falls in love with a Puerto Rican artist ('Payne). Eccleston is Mendel's brother, who has a strange relationship with Sonia, and Margulies is his more traditional wife, who tries to help Sonia fit in with their way of life. Interesting, though not earth-shatteringly deep, characterization beyond film's female lead is scanty, with one-dimensional male models on display here. Second feature from writer/director Yakin. **117m/C** VHS, DVD, Renee Zellweger, Christopher Eccleston, Glenn Fitzgerald, Allen Payne, Julianna Margulies, Kim Hunter, John Randolph, Kathleen Chalfant, Edie Falco, Tim Jerome, Phyllis Newman; **D:** Boaz Yakin; **W:** Boaz Yakin; **C:** Adam Hoender; **M:** Lesiy Barber.

Price of Glory *♂♂*
2000 (PG-13) After seeing his promising boxing career destroyed by an unscrupulous manager, Arturo Ortega (Smits) tries to live his dreams through his three sons, Sonny (Seda) is the best boxer but can't please his father, Jimmy (Collins) is the rebel, and Johnny (Hernandez) shares his dad's passion and has talent. Complicating matters e're a powerful promoter (Perlman) and Arturo's self-destructive tendencies. You've seen this story before, even if the setting is changed to the Southwest, and except for excellent performances by Smits and Seda, there's nothing here to cover for the lack of originality and less-than-stellar execution. **118m/C** VHS, DVD, Jimmy Smits, Jon Seda, Clifton (Gonzalez) Collins Jr., Maria Del Mar, Sal Lopez, Louis Mandylor, Paul Rodriguez, Ron Perlman, Danielle Camastra, Ernesto Hernandez; **D:** Carlos Avila; **W:** Fil Berger; **C:** Alfonso Beato; **M:** Joseph Julian Gonzalez.

The Price of Milk *♂♂*
2000 (PG-13) Quirky modern fairy tale has Rob and Lucinda living a happy idyllic life on a New Zealand dairy farm when Lucinda becomes worried that they've become too happy. She decides, on the advice of her best friend Drosophilia, to test Rob's love. She does this by first jumping into a vat of fresh cow's milk worth $1,500. Rob koranges her, but things are about to get strange. Lucinda accidentally runs over a local Maori woman named "Auntie." The woman is unharmed but upset. Later, Auntie has her golf-playing nephews steal Lucinda's prized patchwork quilt, demanding the entire dairy herd in exchange for its return. Sinclair worked from a 30-page "outline" instead of a script, and it shows. Robust performances and the beautiful scenery do help make up for it, though. **87m/C** VHS, DVD, **NZ** Danielle Cormack, Karl Urban, Willa O'Neill, Michael Lawrence, Rangi Motu; **D:** Harry Sinclair; **W:** Harry Sinclair; **C:** Leon Narbey.

Pride and Prejudice *♂♂*
1940 Classic adaptation of Austen's classic novel of manners as a young marriageable woman spurns the suitor her parents choose for her. Excellent cast vividly recreates 19th-century England, aided by an Oscar. **114m/B** VHS, DVD, Greer Garson, Laurence Olivier, Edmund Gwenn, Edna May Oliver, Mary Boland, Maureen O'Sullivan, Ann Rutherford, Frieda Inescort; **D:** Robert Z Leonard; **C:** Karl Freund.

Pride and Prejudice *♂♂♂*
1985 BBC miniseries adaptation of the Jane Austen's novel about about 19th-century British mores and the attempts of five sisters to get married. **226m/C** VHS, DVD, **GB** Elizabeth Garvie, David Rintoul; **D:** Cyril Coke. TV

Pride and Prejudice *♂♂♂*
1995 Lavish TV adaptation of the Jane Austen novel finds bright Elizabeth Bennet (Ehle) forced to the right men, but headstrong daughter Elizabeth (Knightley) proves difficult. More manageable in scope than the BBC miniseries, this version is gorgeous and classic nonetheless, losing none of the essence of the story. Knightley brings a welcomed force and passion to her portrayal of Lizzie that, for some reason, brought mixed reviews. Sutherland is excellent as the brood's bemused patriarch. **127m/C** DVD, **HD** DVD, Keira Knightley, Matthew MacFadyen, Brenda Blethyn, Donald Sutherland, Tom Hollander, Judi Dench, Rosamund Pike, Jena Malone, Kelly Reilly, Claudie Blakley, Peter Wight, Penelope Wilton, Simon Woods, Rupert Friend, Carey Mulligan, Talulah Riley, Tamzin Merchant; **D:** Joe Wright; **W:** Deborah Moggach; **C:** Roman Osin. **M:** Dario Marianelli.

Pride and Prejudice *♂♂♂½*
2005 (PG) In 19th century England, Mrs. Bennet (Blethyn) must marry her daughters off to the right men, but headstrong daughter Elizabeth (Knightley) proves difficult...

Priceless *♂♂♂* Hors de Prix
2006 (PG-13) French fluff. Slinky/sweet gold digger Irene (Tautou) mistakes soulful hotel employee Jean (Elmaleh) for a wealthy mark and they spend a night together before she realizes her mistake. But Jean is smitten and circumstances eventually led to another comedy of errors in Monte Carlo where a rich widow (Adam) wants to make Jean her boy toy. So Jean asks for gigolo lessons from Irene, who's surprised to find herself miffed that someone else wants him. French with subtitles. **106m/C** DVD, **FR** Audrey Tautou, Gad Elmaleh, Vernon Dobtcheff, Annelise Hesme, Marie-Christine Adam, Jacques Spiesser; **D:** Pierre Salvadori; **W:** Pierre Salvadori, Benoit Graffin; **C:** Gilles Henry; **M:** Camille Bazbaz.

Priceless Beauty *♂♂½*
1990 (R) Musician Lambert was only looking when he spotted the bottle which changed his life. Beautiful genie (Lane) lives inside, and is waiting just for him! Fun premise, good score, nice chemistry between the two leads' outstanding performances. **94m/C** VHS, Christopher Lambert, Diane Lane, Francesco Quinn, J.C. Quinn, Claudia Cherna, Monica Scatini, Joaquim de Almeida; **D:** Charles Finch.

Prick Up Your Ears *♂♂♂*
1987 (R) Film biography of popular subversive playwright Joe Orton depicts his rise to fame and his eventual murder at the hands of his homosexual lover in 1967. Acclaimed for its realistic and sometimes humorous portrayal of the relationship between two men in a society that regarded homosexuality as a crime, the film unfortunately pays scant attention to Orton's theatrical success. The occasional sluggishness of the script detracts a bit from the three leads' outstanding performances. **110m/C** VHS, DVD, **GB** Gary Oldman, Alfred Molina, Vanessa Redgrave, Julie Walters, Lindsay Duncan, Wallace Shawn, James Grant, Frances Barber, Janet Dale, Dave Atkins; **D:** Stephen Frears; **W:** Alan Bennett; **C:** Oliver Stapleton. Film Critics '87: Supp. Actress (Redgrave).

Pride *♂♂½*
2007 (PG) Yet another inspirational true sports flick. Jim Ellis (Howard) experiences racism as a black collegiate swimmer in the 1960s and the same problem when he tries to get a job coaching in the early '70s. He finally accepts work at a dismal Philly rec center that does have an unused pool (the kids prefer basketball). Jim decides to pull a team together, instilling discipline and a winning attitude in his kids. It's predictable and is fault the performances. **108m/C** DVD, **US** Terrence Howard, Bernie Mac, Kimberly Elise, Tom Arnold, Alphonso McAuley, Nathaniel Parker, Kevin Phillips, Scott Reeves, Brandon Fobbs, Regine Nehy, Evan Ross, Gary Sturgis; **D:** Sunu Gonera; **W:** J Mills Goodloe, Norman Vance Jr., Kevin Michael Smith, Michael Gozzard; **C:** Matthew F. Leonetti.

Pride of the Clan *♂♂½*
1918 Silent drama with Pickford and Moore as Scottish sweethearts battling a bit of adversity. When Pickford's father is lost at sea, she moves onto his fishing boat. She meets Moore, a fishing boy, and falls in love. But, he inherits a fortune and his parents forbid him to see Pickford. He goes off to live the good life but comes back to dramatically rescue Pickford. **30m/B** VHS, Mary Pickford, Matt Moore; **D:** Maurice Tourneur.

Pride of the Bowery *♂* Here We Go Again
1941 The Dead End Kids versus a boxing, hopeful in training camp. **60m/B** VHS, DVD, Leo Gorcey, David Gorcey, Huntz Hall, Gabriel Dell, Billy Halop, Bobby Jordan; **D:** Joseph H. Lewis.

Pride of St. Louis *♂♂½*
1952 A romanticized and humorous portrait of famed baseball player-turned-commentator Dizzy Dean. **93m/B** VHS, Dan Dailey, Joanne Dru, Richard Crenna, Richard Haydn, Hugh Sanders; **D:** Harmon Jones; **W:** Herman J. Mankiewicz; **C:** Leo Tover; **M:** Arthur Lange.

Pride of Jesse Hallum *♂♂½*
1981 An illiterate man (played by country singer Cash) learns, after much trial and tribulation, to read. **105m/C** VHS, DVD, Johnny Cash, Brenda Vaccaro, Eli Wallach; **D:** Gary Nelson. TV

The Pride and the Passion *♂♂*
1957 (R) A small group of resistance fighters battling for Spanish independence in 1810 must smuggle a 6-ton cannon across the rugged terrain of Spain. Miscasting, especially of Sinatra as a Spanish peasant, hurts the film. **132m/C** VHS, DVD, Cary Grant, Frank Sinatra, Sophia Loren, Theodore Bikel, John Wengraf, Jay Novello, Philip Van Zandt; **D:** Stanley Kramer; **W:** Edward Anhalt; **C:** Franz Planer; **M:** George Antheil.

The Pride of the Yankees *♂♂♂½*
1942 Excellent portrait of baseball great Lou Gehrig. Beginning as the story of this great American through to his moving farewell speech as his career was tragically cut short by the disease that bears his name. Cooper is inspiring in the title role. **128m/B** VHS, DVD, **GB** Gary Cooper, Teresa Wright, Babe Ruth, Walter Brennan, Dan Duryea; **D:** Sam Wood; **W:** Herman J. Mankiewicz, Jo Swerling; **C:** Rudolph Mate; **M:** Leigh Harline. Oscars '42: Film Editing.

Priest *♂♂*
1994 (R) Father Greg (an intense performance by Roache) is a young, idealistic priest who gets a rude awakening when he's assigned to a tough inner-city Liverpool parish. His superior, Father Matthew (Wilkinson), is a middle-aged rabble rouser who's openly having an affair with their black housekeeper Maria (Tyson). But Father Greg has a secret of his own—despite struggles with his sexuality he gets involved with Graham (Carlyle), a man he meets in the local gay bar. Greg's inner turmoil is heightened when a young parishioner confesses that her father is sexually abusing her but, because he cannot report the problem. Director Bird walks a fine line between criticism and condemnation of Catholic doctrine. British feature provoked a storm of controversy in the U.S.; originally released at 105 minutes. **98m/C** VHS, DVD, **GB** Linus Roache, Tom Wilkinson, Cathy Tyson, Robert Carlyle, James Ellis, John Bennett, Rio Fanning, Jimmy Coleman, Lesley Sharp, Robert Pugh, Christine Tremarco; **D:** Antonia Bird; **W:** Jimmy McGovern; **C:** Fred Tammes; **M:** Andy Roberts.

Priest of Love *♂♂½*
1981 (R) Airy account of the final years of the life of then-controversial author D.H. Lawrence, during which time he published "Lady Chatterly's Lover." A slow-moving but interesting portrayal of this complex man and his wife as they grapple with his immanent death from tuberculosis. **125m/C** VHS, Helen Mirren, Jorge (George) Rivero, **D:** Christopher Miles; **W:** Alan Plater; **C:** Ted Moore.

Primal Fear *♂♂♂*
1996 (R) Chicago defense attorney Martin Vail (Gere) is torn between the fight for justice and the lure of fame. He seems to have found the spotlight when a gentle altar boy (newcomer Norton) is a standout) is accused of savagely murdering an archbishop. This leads to some courtroom fireworks due, in part, to the fact that the prosecutor (Linney) is Vail's former lover. Gere turns in a satisfying performance but, except when he's with his client, can't keep the script afloat. Lame plot revelations and an obvious "shocker" ending don't help matters. Feature directorial debut of Hoblit. Emmy winner for TV's "Hill Street Blues," "L.A. Law," and "NYPD Blue." Adapted from the book by William Diehl. **130m/C** VHS, DVD, Richard Gere, Laura Linney, Edward Norton, John Mahoney, Alfre Woodard, Frances McDormand, Terry O'Quinn, Andre Braugher, Steven Bauer, Joe Spano, Tony Plana, Stanley Anderson, Maura Tierney, Jon Seda; **D:** Gregory Hoblit; **W:** Steve Shagan, Ann Biderman; **C:** Michael Chapman; **M:** James Newton Howard, back on earth. **90m/C** VHS, //T Florinda Bolkan, Peter McEnery, Llia Kedrova, Nicoletta Elmi, Klaus Kinski; **D:** Luigi Bazzoni; **W:** Mario Fanelli; **C:** Vittorio Storaro **M:** Nicola Piovani.

Primal Impulse *♂½* Footprints 1974
1974 (R) A student is bitten by an experimental monkey, and begins to manifest his primal urges physically. Special effects by Carlo Rimbaldi. **92m/C** VHS, Bo Svensson, Patrick Lowe, Mitch Watson, Cheryl Arutt, Sarah Buxton; **D:** Vittoria Rambaldi.

Primal Rage *♂*
1990 (R) A student is bitten by an experimental monkey, and begins to manifest his primal urges physically...

An astronaut, stranded on the moon begins to have night terrors of a sinister experimental "double-cross, unleashes a mental scream which possesses a young woman's mind back

Priest *♂♂*
1994 (R) Father Greg...

Primal Scream ⚗️1/2 *Hellfire* 1987 (R) The Year is 1993. Earth's fuel sources are rapidly decaying and the top secret project to mine a revolutionary new energy source is underway—independently managed by a corrupt corporation. **95m/C VHS, DVD.** Kenneth Jon McGregor, Sharon Mason, Julie Miller, Jon Maurice, Mickey Shaughnessy; *D:* William Murray.

Primal Secrets ⚗️⚗️ *Trick of the Eye* 1994 Artist Tilly, who specializes in illusionary trompe l'oeil paintings, is commissioned to paint a mural in an attempt to end their demonic sacrifices. The question is, will this sister slide beneath Satan's cleaver? **87m/C VHS, DVD.** William Beckwith, Christine Moore; *D:* Roberta Findlay.

Primary Colors ⚗️⚗️1/2 1998 (R) Joe Klein's anonymously published political satire is adapted for the big screen, starting off humorously and shifting into somber. Southern good ole boy, Gov. Jack Stanton (Travolta), and his savvy wife (Thompson) are after the presidential nomination and encounter a lot of crazy associates, including skeptical first-time campaign manager Henry Burton (Lester). More about Henry's political baptism by fire than anything else, as he tries to accommodate his conscience to the continuous scandals and double-dealing. It really doesn't matter whether Travolta's channeling Clinton or if Thompson acts like Hillary, since the film has bigger problems. The change in tone is jarring, characters and situations disappear without warning. And given that the press act like salivating wolverines at the merest hint of scandal, the situation surrounding opponent Fred Picker (Hagman) seems far-fetched at best. Still the goings-on will hold your attention until they're over—and you realize it's all smoke-and-mirrors. **138m/C VHS, DVD.** John Travolta, Emma Thompson, Adrian Lester, Kathy Bates, Billy Bob Thornton, Larry Hagman, Maura Tierney, Stacy Edwards, Diane Ladd, Gia Carides, Paul Guilfoyle, Tommy Hollis, Robert Klein, J.C. Quinn, Rob Reiner, Caroline Aaron, Allison Janney, Mykelti Williamson, Tony Shalhoub, John Vargas, Ben Jones, Bonnie Bartlett; *D:* Mike Nichols; *W:* Elaine May; *C:* Michael Ballhaus; *M:* Ry Cooder. British Acad. '98: Adapt. Screenplay; Screen Actors Guild '98: Support. Actress (Bates); Broadcast Film Critics '98: Support. Actress (Bates).

Primary Motive ⚗️⚗️ 1992 (R) Taut political thriller with Nelson as Andy Blumenthal, a press secretary who finds that an opposing candidate's campaign is covered by a web of lies. Blumenthal exposes the lies, but the candidate denies them and pulls further ahead in the polls. When the candidate's wife gives Blumenthal an extremely damaging piece of information, will the polls finally turn against him? **93m/C VHS, DVD.** John Travolta, Richard Jordan, Sally Kirkland, Justine Bateman, John Savage; *D:* Daniel Adams; *W:* William Snowden III, Daniel Adams; *M:* John Cale.

Primary Target ⚗️⚗️ 1989 (R) A mercenary reunites his 'Nam guerilla unit to rescue a diplomat's wife kidnapped by a Laotian jungle lord. **85m/C VHS.** John Calvin, Miki Kim, Joey Aresco, Charles (Chip) Lucia, John Ericson, Colleen Casey; *D:* Clark Henderson.

Prime ⚗️⚗️1/2 2005 (PG-13) Streep plays Lisa, an interfering Jewish mama, fretting over her handsome 23-year-old son, David (Greenberg). Lisa's a shrink, one of her needier patients is newly divorced Rafi (Thurman) who's beautiful but insecure. Rafi is happy but fretful over a new romance with a much-younger guy, who, of course, turns out to be Lisa's son David. Lisa is the first to realize this and suffers agonies of embarrassment as Rafi enthusiastically describes her rejuvenated sex life. Lots more embarrassment to come for all concerned. Harmless comedic fluff. **105m/C DVD.** *US* Meryl Streep, Uma Thurman, Bryan Greenberg, Jon Abrahams, Zak Orth, Annie Parisse; *D:* Ben Younger; *W:* Ben Younger; *C:* William Rexer; *M:* Ryan Shore.

Prime Cut ⚗️⚗️1/2 1972 (R) Veritable orgy of drug trafficking, prostitution, extortion, loan sharking, fistcuffs and gangsters getting ground into mincemeat. Sleazy but well-made crime melodrama has its followers, but is best known as Spacek's film debut. **86m/C VHS, DVD.** Lee Marvin, Gene Hackman, Sissy Spacek, Angel Tompkins, Gregory Walcott; *D:* Michael Ritchie; *W:* Robert Dillon; *M:* Lalo Schifrin.

Prime Evil ⚗️⚗️ 1988 (R) A brave and determined nun infiltrates a sect of devil worshipping monks in an attempt to end their demonic sacrifices. The question is, will this sister slide beneath Satan's cleaver? **87m/C VHS, DVD.** William Beckwith, Christine Moore; *D:* Roberta Findlay.

The Prime Gig ⚗️⚗️ 2000 Wise (Vaughn) wants a telephone scam for a run-down company manafed by Mick (Tobolowsky) that soon goes under. He's then recruited by Caitlin (Ormond) for a telemarketing scheme involving selling stocks in a gold mine for guru Kelly Grant (Harris), whose previous schemes cost him jail time. Wise is a success but despite the money (and the girl) you know there's trouble ahead. Predictable plot with Harris giving the strong performance. **96m/C VHS, DVD.** Vince Vaughn, Julia Ormond, Ed Harris, Rory Cochrane, Wallace Shawn, George Wendt, Stephen Tobolowsky; *D:* Gregory Mosher; *W:* William Wheeler; *C:* John A. Alonzo; *M:* David Robbins.

The Prime of Miss Jean Brodie ⚗️⚗️⚗️ 1969 (PG) Oscar-winning performance by Smith as a forward-thinking teacher in an Edinburgh girls' school in 1932. She captivates with her impressionable young students with her fascist ideals and free-thinking attitudes in this adaptation of the play taken from Muriel Spark's novel. **116m/C VHS, DVD.** *GB* Maggie Smith, Pamela Franklin, Robert Stephens, Celia Johnson, Gordon Jackson, Jane Carr; *D:* Ronald Neame; *W:* Jay Presson Allen; *C:* Ted Moore. Oscars '69: Actress (Smith); British Acad. '69: Actress (Smith), Support. Actress (Johnson); Golden Globes '70: Song ("Jean"); Natl. Bd. of Review '69: Support. Actress (Franklin).

Prime Risk ⚗️⚗️ 1984 (PG-13) A young engineer who discovers an electronic method to break into automated teller machines finds that it leads to more trouble when she discovers that foreign agents are not on her trail. **98m/C VHS.** Toni Hudson, Lee Montgomery, Sam Bottoms; *D:* W. Farkas; *C:* Mac Ahlberg.

Prime Suspect ⚗️⚗️ 1982 An honest citizen becomes the prime suspect after the coverage of a murder by an over-ambitious television reporter. **100m/C VHS, DVD.** Mike Farrell, Teri Garr, Veronica Cartwright, Lane Smith, Barry Corbin, James Sloyan, Charles Aidman; *D:* Noel Black; *C:* Reynaldo Villalobos; *M:* Charles Gross. **TV**

Prime Suspect ⚗️⚗️ 1988 A young man escapes from a mental institution to clear his name after being wrongfully accused of murdering his girlfriend. **89m/C VHS, DVD.** Susan Strasberg, Frank Stallone, Billy Drago, Doug McClure; *D:* Mark Rutland.

Prime Suspect ⚗️⚗️ 1992 Mirren stars as Detective Chief Inspector Jane Tennison in this British TV police procedural. When a male inspector dies of a heart attack while investigating a rape-murder, Tennison, the only women of senior police status, wants the case. But she runs into multiple obstructions, not the least being the smug male police system. Then the case really takes a turn when it appears Tennison is searching for a serial killer. But Jane is no quitter and she has both the brains and the guts to back up her orders. Adapted from the book by Lynda La Plante, who also wrote the teleplay. Several other TV movies followed. **240m/C VHS, DVD.** *GB* Helen Mirren, Tom Bell, Zoe Wanamaker, John Bowe, Tom Wilkinson, Ralph Fiennes; *D:* Christopher Menaul; *W:* Lynda La Plante. **TV**

Prime Target ⚗️⚗️ 1991 (R) Small-town cop John Bloodstone (Heavener) is recruited by the FBI to transfer a mafia boss (Curtis) from a safehouse to the courthouse. He has to keep the former mobster alive long enough to testify against the "family." Their cross-country adventure is heightened by a murderous confrontation with evil forces that want them both dead. **87m/C VHS.** David Heavener, Tony Curtis, Isaac Hayes, Jenilee Harrison, Robert Reed, Andrew (Andy) Robinson, Don Stroud; *D:* David Heavener; *W:* David Heavener; *M:* Chris Boardman.

The Prime Time WOOF! 1960 Horrid film about a teen girl who leaves home and gets involved with a teen gang and a slimy detective. She's also kidnapped by a weird beatnik artist who forces her to pose nude. Black's film debut. Also known as "Hellkitten." **76m/B VHS.** JoAnn LeCompte, Frank Roche, James Brooks, Ray Gronwold, Maria Pavelle, Robert Major, Karen Black; *D:* Herschell Gordon Lewis.

Prime Time ⚗️1/2 *American Raspberry* 1977 (R) Forgotten satirical comedy about what would happen if the censors took a day off from American TV. **73m/C VHS.** Warren Oates, David Spielberg, Robert Ridgely, Joanna Cassidy, Harry Shearer, Hans Yulin, Dick O'Neill, George Furth, Stephen Furst, Larry Gelman, Fred (John F.) Dryer; *D:* Bradley R. Swinnoff; *W:* Steve Feinberg, Bradley R. Swinnoff; *C:* Matthew F. Leonetti; *M:* Ken Lauber.

Prime Time Murder ⚗️1/2 1992 (R) Freelance TV journalist hooks up with eccentric ex-cop to trail a psycho stalking street people. **95m/C VHS, DVD.** Tim Thomerson, Sally Kirkland, Anthony Finetti, Laura Reed; *D:* Gary Skeen Hall.

Primer ⚗️⚗️⚗️1/2 2004 (PG-13) Writer/director Carruth's debut film might be the the world's first thinking-man's time travel movie, beautifully shot for an absurdly low $7,500. Winner of the 2004 Sundance Grand Jury Prize, the plot revolves around two engineers, Aaron (Carruth) and Abe (Sullivan), who, while trying to develop a patentable invention, accidentally construct a box that allows them to move backwards through time. Carruth piles on the technical jargon, which will either hopelessly confuse viewers or make them love the director for respecting their intelligence. (No character ever whines, "Tell it to me in English, Doc!") At its core, Carruth's film is a meditation on trust, obsession, power, and the chaos surrounding innovation, combined with a nonlinear storyline that should inspire more repeated viewings than "Donnie Darko." **80m/C DVD.** Shane Carruth, David Sullivan, Casey Gooden, Anand Upadhyaya, Carrie Crawford, Samantha Thomson, Brandon Blagg; *D:* Shane Carruth; *W:* Shane Carruth, Anand Upadhyaya; *M:* Shane Carruth.

Primeval ⚗️⚗️ 2007 (R) What a croc—literally. Weird fact-based combo of horror and politics set in pre-2005, war-torn Burundi. Cynical reporter Tim (Purcell) is pressured into a tabloid story—capture a 25-foot croc, nicknamed Gustave, that has been eating the locals for years. The area is also the province of a vicious warlord who has nicknamed himself after the beastie. Brooding guide Jacob (Prochnow) takes Tim and his crew to the croc's favorite dining spot, but things don't go as planned. Neither as campy nor as gruesome as most of its ilk. **94m/C DVD, Blu-ray Disc.** *US* Dominic Purcell, Orlando Jones, Brooke Langton, Jurgen Prochnow, Gideon Emery, Dumisani Mbebe, Gabriel Malema; *D:* Michael Katleman; *W:* John Brancato, Michael Ferris; *C:* Edward Pei; *M:* John (Gianni) Frizzell.

The Primitive Lover ⚗️⚗️ 1916 Early silent comedy about young wife who decides she deserves more than her marriage is giving her. **67m/B VHS.** Constance Talmadge, Kenneth Harlan, Harrison Ford; *D:* Sidney Franklin.

Primrose Path ⚗️⚗️1/2 1940 Melodramatic soaper with comedic touches about a wrong-side-of-the-tracks girl falling for and then losing an ambitious young go-getter running a hamburger stand. **93m/B VHS.** Ginger Rogers, Joel McCrea, Marjorie Rambeau, Henry Travers, Miles Mander, Queenie Vasser, Joan Carroll, Vivienne Osborne; *D:* Gregory La Cava.

The Prince ⚗️⚗️1/2 1995 Young toy company executive Roy (Riley) is given cutthroat corporate advice by a sinister bartender (Williams) who uses the treatise on power by Machiavelli as his bible. Soon Roy is manipulating with the best of them and will do anything to get ahead. **89m/C VHS.** *CA* Billy Dee Williams, Michael Riley, Henry Silva, Lou Rawls, Timothy Bottoms, Liat Goodson, Edie McClurg; *D:* Pinchas Perry; *W:* Pinchas Perry; *C:* Hanania Baer; *M:* David Michael Frank.

The Prince & Me ⚗️⚗️ 2004 (PG) Dairy farmer's daughter Paige (Stiles) is a driven pre-med student who dreams of a future with Doctors Without Borders until Prince Charming shows up disguised as an average Joe. In this case his name is Eddie—actually Prince Edvard of Denmark (Mably)—and they fall in love, but as these young romance stories go the truth inevitably surfaces and the inner conflict begins. Should she give up on her life's passion? Or live the supposed fairy tale life of a princess? Of course in this modern day the larger question should be why does she have to choose? Only Stiles' engaging performance makes this sweet-yet-typical story at all worth watching. **110m/C VHS, DVD.** Julia Stiles, Luke Mably, Ben Miller, James Fox, Miranda Richardson, Eliza Bennett, Alberta Watson, John Bourgeois, Joanne Baron; *D:* Martha Coolidge; *W:* Mark Amin, Jack Amiel, Katherine Fugate, Michael Begler; *C:* Alex Nepomniaschy; *M:* Jennie Muskett.

The Prince & Me 2: Royal Wedding ⚗️ 2006 (PG) In this dull fluff sequel, Danish Prince Edvard (Mably) runs into a problem with his wedding plans to American commoner Paige (Heskin). Conniving cousin Albert (Holt) uses an ancient obscure law to proclaim that Edvard must marry someone of royal blood or he can't become king—and Albert offers his daughter, the equally sly Princess Kirsten (Burton-Hill), as a substitute. Apparently, Edvard is just too stupid to ask the Danish parliament to change the law, so Paige must find a loophole. **97m/C DVD.** Luke Mably, Kam Heskin, Jim Holt, Maryam D'Abo, Clemency Burton-Hill, Jonathan Firth; *D:* Catherine Cyran; *W:* Allison Robinson; *C:* Blake T. Evans; *M:* Andrew Gross. **VIDEO**

Prince and the Great Race ⚗️⚗️ *Bush Christmas* 1983 Three Australian children search the outback to find their kidnapped horse who is scheduled to run in the big New Year's Day Race. **91m/C VHS.** *AU* John Ewart, John Howard, Nicole Kidman; *D:* Henri Safran; *W:* Ted Roberts; *C:* Ross Berryman; *M:* Mike Perjanik.

The Prince and the Pauper ⚗️⚗️⚗️ 1937 Satisfying adaptation of the classic Mark Twain story of a young street urchin who trades places with the young king of England. Wonderful musical score by noted composer Korngold who provided the music for many of Flynn's adventure films. Also available in a computer-colorized version. **118m/B VHS, DVD.** Errol Flynn, Claude Rains, Alan Hale, Billy Mauch, Montagu Love, Henry Stephenson, Barton MacLane, Anne Howard; *D:* William Keighley; *M:* Erich Wolfgang Korngold.

The Prince and the Pauper ⚗️⚗️1/2 1962 A prince and a poor young boy swap their clothes and identities, thus causing a lot of confusion for their families. Based on the story by Mark Twain. **93m/C VHS.** Guy Williams, Laurence Naismith, Donald Houston, Jane Asher, Sean Scully; *D:* Don Chaffey; *W:* Jack Whittingham; *C:* Paul Beeson; *M:* Tristram Cary. **TV**

The Prince and the Pauper ⚗️⚗️1/2 *Crossed Swords* 1978 (PG) Remake of the 1937 Errol Flynn film employing lavish sets and a tongue-in-cheek attitude among the all-star cast, who occasionally wander adrift when the director stops for tea. When an English prince and a pauper discover that they have identical appearances, they decide to trade places with each other. From Mark Twain's classic. **113m/C VHS, DVD.** *GB* Oliver Reed, Raquel Welch, Mark Lester, Ernest Borgnine, George C. Scott, Rex Harrison, Charlton Heston, Sybil Danning; *D:* Richard Fleischer; *W:* Berta Dominguez, George MacDonald Fraser, Pierre Spengler; *C:* Jack Cardiff; *M:* Maurice Jarre.

The Prince and the Pauper ⚗️⚗️1/2 2001 Yet another version of the Mark Twain classic covers all the familiar bases but is briskly paced and has a good cast, including Prince Edward (Jonathan Timmins) exchanges identities with peasant Tom Canty (Robert Timmins) and both will always be a challenge. **D:** 90m/C VHS, DVD, Jonathan Timmins, Robert Timmins, Aidan Quinn, Alan Bates, Jonathan Hyde; **D:** Giles Foster. **W:** Duke Fenady, Dominic Minghella. **CABLE.**

The Prince and the Pauper ✗✗¹/₂ 2007 (PG) A modern-day retelling of the Mark Twain classic, starring the Sprouse twins. Tom Canty wants to be an actor so he sneaks onto the set of his favorite show to meet its lead, Eddie Tutor. A spoiled child star, Ed-die is about to get fired for his antics until the boys decide to trade places and see how the other half lives. But neither of the boys expects the TV production to suddenly go on location to Miami, leaving the duo in their assumed identities. 92m/C DVD, Dylan Sprouse, Cole Sprouse, Vincent Spano, Kay Panabaker, Decee Pfeiffer, Ed Lauter, Sally Kellerman, Nick Vallelonga; **D:** James Quattochi. **W:** Amanda Moresco; **C:** Jeff Bauslert; **M:** Dennis McCarthy. **VIDEO**

The Prince and the Showgirl ✗✗¹/₂ 1957 An American showgirl in 1910 London is wooed by the Prince of Carpathia. Part of the "A Night at the Movies" series, this tape simulates a 1957 movie evening, with a Sylvester the Cat cartoon, "Greedy for Tweety," a newsreel and coming attractions for "Spirit of St. Louis." 127m/C VHS, DVD, Laurence Olivier, Marilyn Monroe, Sybil Thorndike, Jeremy Spenser, Richard Wattis; **D:** Laurence Olivier; **W:** Terence Rattigan; **C:** Jack Cardiff. **VIDEO**

The Prince and the Surfer ✗✗¹/₂ 1999 (PG) A modern young prince, Edward, wants a chance to be a regular guy and changes places with young surfer teen double, Cash. Updated version of the Mark Twain story. 96m/C VHS, DVD, Vincent Schiavelli, Arye Gross, Robert Englund, Timothy Bottoms, C. Thomas Howell, Linda Cardellini; **D:** Gregory Gieras. **VIDEO**

Prince Brat and the Whipping Boy ✗✗✗ *The Whipping Boy* 1995 (G) Orphaned Jemmy (Munro) is living on the streets of the 18th-century German town of Brattenburg with his younger sister Annyrose (Salt). Neglected, spoiled Prince Horace (Knight) has been causing mischief in the castle but instead of being punished himself, the king's men catch Jemmy and use him as a punishment stand-in. Jemmy escapes the castle to get back to his sister and the Prince decides to go along for the adventure. Filmed on location in North Rhine-Westphalia and Burgundy, Germany. Adventurous TV movie with spunky leads; adapted from Sid Fleischman's novella. 96m/C VHS, Truan Munro, Nic Knight, Karen Salt, George C. Scott, Kevin Conway, Vincent Schiavelli, Andrew Bicknell, Jean Anderson, Mathilda Mayr; **D:** Syd Macartney; **W:** Max Brindle; **M:** Lee Holdridge.

Prince Jack ✗✗ 1983 Profiles the turbulent political career of President John F. Kennedy. 100m/C VHS, Lloyd Nolan, Dana Andrews, Robert Guillaume, Cameron Mitchell; **D:** Bert Lovitt; **M:** Elmer Bernstein.

Prince of Bel Air ✗¹/₂ 1987 (R) A pool-cleaning playboy who makes a habit of one night stands meets a woman and starts falling in love with her. 95m/C VHS, Mark Harmon, Kirstie Alley, Robert Vaughn, Patrick Laborteaux, Deborah Harmon; **D:** Charles Braverman; **M:** Robert Folk. **TV**

The Prince of Central Park ✗¹/₂ 1977 Two young orphans are forced by circumstance to live in a tree in New York's Central Park until they are befriended by a lonely old woman. An above-average adaptation of the novel by Evan H. Rhodes, the story was later used for a Broadway play. 76m/C VHS, Ruth Gordon, Timothy (John) Hargrave, Lisa Richards, Brooke Shields, Marc Vahanian, Dan Hecaya; **D:** Harvey Hart. **TV**

Prince of Central Park ✗¹/₂ 2000 (PG-13) JJ Somerfed (Nasso) is a 12-year-old stuck in the abusive foster home of Mrs. Ardis (Moriarty). Fed up, he takes off for the carousel at Central Park, where he had his last happy memory of his long-gone mother. In the park, JJ is befriended by all sorts of do-gooders and eccentrics. Bland non-musical reworking of a musical play. 105m/C VHS, DVD, Frank Nasso, Kathleen Turner, Danny Aiello, Harvey Keitel, Cathy Moriarty; **D:** Lauren Velez, Jerry Orbach, Tina Holmes; **D:** Jon Leekley; **W:** Jon Leekley; **C:** Jonatan Herron; **M:** Theodore Shapiro.

Prince of Darkness ✗¹/₂ 1987 (R) University students release Satan, in the form of a mysterious chemical, unwittingly on the world. Written by Martin Quatermass (a pseudonym of Carpenter). Strong personnel does not save this dreary and slow-moving cliche plot. 102m/C VHS, DVD, Alice Cooper, Donald Pleasence, Lisa Blount, Victor Wong, Jameson Parker, Dennis Dun, Susan Blanchard, Anne Marie Howard, Ken Wright, Dirk Blocker; **D:** John Carpenter; **W:** John Carpenter; **C:** Gary B. Kibbe; **M:** John Carpenter.

Prince of Egypt ✗✗✗ 1998 (PG) First animated musical from Dreamworks manages to tell the story of the Exodus without turning it into Mickey Moses, Killer voices the young Moses, who is adopted by the royal family; imperious pharaoh Seti (Stewart), his stately Queen (Mirren) and jockish son Rameses (Fiennes). Happily wed to Tzipporah (Pfeiffer), he's living it up at the dawn of civilization until a chance meeting with his real sister Miriam (Bullock) twists his conscience and destiny. Steve Martin and Martin Short provide a short comic break, but overall the joking is kept to a minimum. Successful in combining epic feeling with stylized animation. 99m/C VHS, DVD, **D:** Simon Wells, Brenda Chapman, Steve Hickner, Helen Mirren, Sandra Bullock, Jeff Goldblum, Danny Glover, Patrick Stewart, Ofra Haza, James Avery, Eden Riegel. Oscars '99: Song ("When You Believe"); Broadcast Film Critics '98: Song ("When You Believe").

Prince of Foxes ✗¹/₂ 1949 In 16th-century Italy, rascally Orsini (Power) is sent by his boss, the power-hungry Cesare Borgia (Welles), to seduce Camilla (Hendrix), the insipid young wife of an old duke (Aylmer), and turn the town over to the Borgias. But Orsini likes Count Varano and decide to switch sides, which doesn't please his now ex-boss. The story is plodding, the dialogue is deadly, and although it's lavishly picturesque (and filmed on location), it's a shame that the Fox didn't shoot the film in Technicolor. Based on the novel by Samuel Shellabarger. 107m/B DVD, Tyrone Power, Orson Welles, Wanda Hendrix, Felix Aylmer, Everett Sloane, Marina Berti, Katina Paxinou; **D:** Henry King; **W:** Milton Krims; **C:** Leon Shamroy; **M:** Alfred Newman.

Prince of Pennsylvania ✗¹/₂ 1988 (R) A mild comedy about a spaced-out youth who kidnaps his own father in hopes of nabbing a devoted wife, Annie (Ashbourne), and happy family. But the doctor has a secret passion for reckless adventure and gambling and his good life is about to crumble because of his debts. So what's his solution? Why, murder of course, so Palmer can collect on various insurance policies and dispose of his gambling rivals. 100m/C VHS, Fred Ward, Amy Madigan, Bonnie Bedelia, Jeff Hayenga; **D:** Ron Nyswaner; **W:** Ron Nyswaner; **M:** Thomas Newman.

Prince of Poisoners: The Life and Crimes of William Palmer ✗¹/₂ 1998 A true crime story set in mid-19th century England. Dr. William Palmer (Allen) appears to be a successful surgeon with a devoted wife, Annie (Ashbourne), and happy family. But the doctor has a secret passion for reckless adventure and gambling and his good life is about to crumble because of his debts. So... Excellent cast of newcomers. Based on a novel of the same name by Mark Schreiber. 103m/C VHS, CA Zachary Ansley, Nicholas Shields, Stacy Mistysyn, Alexander Chapman, Chuck Shamata; **D:** Giles Walker.

Princes in Exile ✗✗ 1990 (PG-13) Young people struggle with their life-threatening illnesses at a special summer camp. They find that love and friendship hold the key to dreams about the future. Excellent cast of newcomers. Based on a novel of the same name by Mark Schreiber. 103m/C VHS, CA Zachary Ansley, Nicholas Shields, Stacy Mistysyn, Alexander Chapman, Chuck Shamata; **D:** Giles Walker.

The Princess & the Call Girl ✗ 1984 Call girl Lucy Darling asks her look-alike college girlfriend Audrey Swallow (Levy in a dual role) to take her place in Monaco for a lavishly erotic weekend. Then when Audrey gets delayed, Lucy winds up taking her place in New York—at Audrey's engagement party. Weaker than Metzger's usual sexual romps. 90m/C VHS, DVD, Carol Levy, Shanrah Hall, Victor Bevine; **D:** Radley Metzger.

Princess Academy ✗ 1987 (R) A self-respecting young debutante battles the ways of her elitist finishing school. 91m/C VHS, FR Eva Gabor, Lu Leonard, Richard Paul, Lar Park-Lincoln, Carole (Raphaele) Davis; **D:** Bruce Block; **M:** Paul Antonelli, Roger Belon.

Princess Caraboo ✗✗¹/₂ 1994 (PG) Fluffy quasi-fairy tale (but based on a true story) finds an exotic beauty (Cates), appearing in an English village in 1817. She speaks a language no one understands and is taken under the wing of the local gentry; the Worralls, who believe she is an Asian princess washed ashore during a shipwreck. Meanwhile, the local journalist (Rea) is suspicious but protective, an Oxford linguist (Lithgow) is determined to prove her a fraud, and she must put up with the Worrall family's pompous Greek butler (Cate's husband Kline at his showy best). 97m/C VHS, DVD, Phoebe Cates, Stephen Rea, John Lithgow, Kevin Kline, Jim Broadbent, Wendy Hughes, Peter Eyre, Jacqueline Pearce, John Lynch, John Sessons, Arkie Whiteley, John Wells; **D:** Michael Austin; **W:** Michael Austin, John Wells; **C:** Freddie Francis; **M:** Richard Hartley.

Prince Valiant ✗✗ 1997 (PG-13) We're back at Camelot with a lot of colorful pageantry and clad-fashioned action. Young orphaned Valiant (Moyer) is the squire to Sir Gawain (Hickox), one of King Arthur's (Fox) knights. He is given the task of escorting Princess Ilene (Heigl) to her home in Wales and naturally the young twosome fall in love. Naturally, the sword Excalibur has been stolen by Viking leader Thagnar (Kretschmann) and somehow become embedded in this castle's stone floor. Then Ilene gets kidnapped and it's up to Valiant to rescue both Ilene and Excalibur. Based on the comic strip created by Harold R. Foster. 91m/C VHS, GB GE IR Stephen Moyer, Katherine Heigl, Thomas Kretschmann, Edward Fox, Benjamin Pullen, Anthony Hickox, Udo Kier, Warwick Davis, Zach Galligan, Ron Perlman, Joanna Lumley, Gavan O'Herlihy, Walter Gotell; **D:** Anthony Hickox; **W:** Michael Frost Beckner, Anthony Hickox; **C:** Roger Lanser; **M:** David Bergeaud.

Prince Valiant ✗✗ 1954 (FG-13) When his royal dad is exiled by an evil tyrant, brave young Wagner brushes aside bangs and journeys to Camelot to seek the help of King Arthur. Based on Harold Foster's classic comic strip. 100m/C VHS, DVD, James Mason, Janet Leigh, Robert Wagner, Debra Paget, Sterling Hayden, Victor McLaglen, Donald Crisp, Brian Aherne, Barry Jones, Mary (Phillips) Philips; **D:** Henry Hathaway; **W:** Dudley Nichols.

The Prince of Tides ✗✗✗¹/₂ 1991 (R) Conroy's sprawling southern-fried saga is neatly pared down to essentials in this tale of the dysfunctional Wingo family, whose dark tragedies are gradually revealed as twins Tom and Savannah come to grips with personal demons under the ministering aid of psychiatrist Streisand. Bravura performance by Nolte in what may be his best role to date; Streisand is restrained in both her performance and direction although a subplot dealing with her bad marriage and rebellious son is a predictable distraction. The South Carolina low country, and even New York City, never looked better. Conroy adapted the screenplay from his novel. 132m/C VHS, DVD, Nick Nolte, Barbra Streisand, Blythe Danner, Kate Nelligan, Jeroen Krabbe, Melinda Dillon, George Carlin, Jason Gould, Brad Sullivan; **D:** Barbra Streisand; **W:** Pat Conroy, Becky Johnston; **C:** Stephen Goldblatt; **M:** James Newton Howard. Golden Globes '92: Actor—Drama (Nolte); Film Critics '91: Actor (Nolte); L.A.

The Prince of Tides ✗✗✗¹/₂ 1991 (R) Treat Williams, Jerry Orbach, Richard Foronjy, Don Billett, Ken Marino, Lindsay Crouse, Lance Henriksen; **D:** Sidney Lumet; **W:** Jay Presson Allen, Sidney Lumet; **C:** Andrzej Bartkowiak, N.Y. Film Critics '81: Director (Lumet).

The Prince of Thieves ✗✗ 1948 Robin Hood helps Lady Marian extricate herself from a forced marriage in this adventure made with younger audiences in mind. 72m/C VHS, Jon Hall, Patricia Morison, Adele Jergens, Alan Mowbray, Michael Duane; **D:** Howard Bretherton; **W:** Charles Schnee, Maurice Tombragel; **C:** Fred H. Jackman Jr.

The Princess and the Goblin ✗✗ 1994 (G) Little kiddies may enjoy this animated adventure but it's a bland story with mediocre animation. Groups of ugly, underground-dwelling goblins like nothing better than to scare humans, especially castle-dwelling Princess Irene. Brave working-class Curdie helps to save the day. Based on a book by George MacDonald. 82m/C VHS, DVD, HU GB Jozsef Gemes; **W:** Robin Lyons; **M:** Istvan Laroh; **V:** Sally Ann Marsh, Peter Murray, Claire Bloom.

The Princess and the Pea ✗✗✗ 1983 From "Faerie Tale Theatre" comes the story of a princess who tries to prove that she's a blueblood by feeling the jump of a tiny pea under the thickness of 20 mattresses. 60m/C VHS, DVD, Liza Minnelli, Tom Conti, Tim Kazurinsky, Pat McCormick, Beatrice Straight; **D:** Tony Bill. **CABLE.**

The Princess and the Pirate ✗✗✗ 1944 Hope at his craziest as a vaudevillian who falls for a beautiful princess while on the run from buccaneers on the Spanish Main. Look for Crosby in a closing cameo performance. Available in digitally remastered stereo with original movie trailer. 94m/C VHS, DVD, Bob Hope, Walter Slezak, Walter Brennan, Virginia Mayo, Victor McLaglen, Bing Crosby; **D:** David Butler; **W:** Everett Freeman, Don Hartman, Melville Shavelson; **C:** Victor Milner; **M:** David Rose.

The Princess Bride ✗✗✗ 1987 (PG) A modern update of the basic fairy tale crammed with all the cliches, this adventurously irreverent love story centers around beautiful maiden Buttercup (Wright Penn) and her young swain Westley (Elwes) as they battle the evils of the mythical kingdom of Florin to be reunited with one another. Great dueling scenes and offbeat satire of the genre make this fun for adults as well as children. Based on William Goldman's cult novel. 98m/C VHS, DVD, Blu-ray Disc, UMD, Cary Elwes, Mandy Patinkin, Robin Wright Penn, Wallace Shawn, Peter Falk, Andre the Giant, Chris Sarandon, Christopher Guest, Billy Crystal, Carol Kane, Fred Savage, Peter Cook, Mel Smith; **D:** Rob Reiner; **W:** William Goldman; **C:** Adrian Biddle; **M:** Mark Knopfler.

The Princess and the Warrior ✗✗✗ *Der Krieger und die Kaiserin* 2000 (R) Writer/director Twyker reunites with Potente, the star of his breakthrough feature "Run Lola Run." Potente plays Sissi, a mental institution nurse whose life is saved by small-time crook Bodo (Furmann). On the way to the bank (which he was about to rob), she is run over by a truck (in an accident that he helped cause). He crawls under the truck to avoid the police, but ends up saving her as she's about to choke to death on her own blood. After she recovers, she sets out to find Bodo, still grieving the loss of his wife, realizes impossible to pigeonhole in one genre, as Twyker is clearly more concerned with his characters than with showing them into a conveniently labeled plot. 130m/C VHS, DVD, GE Franka Potente, Benno Furmann, Joachim Krol, Marita Breuer, Lars Rudolph, Jurgen Tarrach, Melchior Beslon, Ludger Pistor; **D:** Tom Tywker; **W:** Tom Tywker; **C:** Frank Griebe; **M:** Tom Tywker, Johnny Kimer, Reinhold Heil.

The Princess Comes Across 1936 Deft comedy-mystery finds Brooklyn actress Lombard deciding to take an ocean voyage and pass herself off as a Swedish princess in the hopes of furthering her career. Bandleader MacMurray is smitten but an old beau recognizes the ruse and demands hush money. Then he turns up dead and the duo fall under the suspicious eye of a German passenger (Rumann) who happens to be a detective. From the novel by Louis Lucien Rogger. 77m/B VHS, DVD. Carole Lombard, Fred MacMurray, Alison Skipworth, Sig Rumann, Douglass Dumbrille, William Frawley, Porter Hall, George Barbier, Lumsden Hare, Mischa Auer, Tetsu Komai; **D:** William K. Howard; **W:** Walter DeLeon, Francis Martin, Frank Butler, Don Hartman; **C:** Ted Tetzlaff.

Princess Daisy 1983 A beautiful model claws her way to the top of her profession while trying to find true love and avoid the clutches of her rotten half-brother. Adapted from Judith Krantz's glitzy best-selling novel. 200m/C VHS, DVD. Merete Van Kamp, Lindsay Wagner, Claudia Cardinale, Stacy Keach, Ringo Starr, Barbara Bach; **D:** Waris Hussein. **TV**

The Princess Diaries 2001 (G) Gently amusing comedy perfect for tweenies who worry about being misfits. Modern-day Cinderella story finds brainy-but-clumsy San Francisco teen Mia (newcomer Hathaway, who's a real find) learning that she's the heir to the European kingdom of Genovia after the death of her long-absent dad. And to teach her the ways of royalty is her very regal grandma (Andrews). Think Henry Higgins and Eliza Doolittle. Of course, Mia has her doubts about being a princess, especially when the kids at school learn her secret. There's even a little first romance thrown in for good measure. Based on the novel by Meg Cabot. 114m/C VHS, DVD. US Anne Hathaway, Julie Andrews, Hector Elizondo, Heather Matarazzo, Erik von Detten, Mandy Moore, Robert Schwartzman, Caroline Goodall, Larry Miller, Sandra Oh, Sean O'Bryan; **D:** Garry Marshall; **W:** Gina Wendkos; **C:** Karl Walter Lindenlaub; **M:** John Debney.

The Princess Diaries 2: Royal Engagement 2004 (G) Princess Mia (Hathaway), still sweet and klutzy, is now a college grad and on her way to Genovia to live with grandma, Queen Clarisse (Andrews), and assume her royal duties. But Clarisse is being forced to abdicate, and ancient law dictates that Mia must marry before she can become queen and she only has 30 days to find a suitable royal consort. If she can't, sneaky Viscount Mabrey's (Rhys-Davies) plastic-handsome nephew, Nicholas (Pine), is the next rightful heir. Nicholas tries to charm Mia while she dutifully agrees to marry affable British nobleman Andrew (Elizondo). 120m/C VHS, DVD. US Anne Hathaway, Julie Andrews, Hector Elizondo, John Rhys-Davies, Heather Matarazzo, Chris Pine, Callum Blue, Kathleen Marshall, Tom Poston, Joel McCrary, Kim Thomson, Larry Miller, Raven, Caroline Goodall, Sean O'Bryan, Matthew (Matt) Walker, Elinor Donahue, Paul Williams; **D:** Garry Marshall; **W:** Shonda Rhimes; **C:** Charles Minsky; **M:** John Debney.

Princess Mononoke 1998 (PG-13) Stunning animated feature by Japanese master Hayao Miyazaki is a bit too long and graphic for small children, but its a must-see for fans of anime. Dubbed into English by an all-star cast, the tale follows the plight of Ashitaka (Crudup), who tries to find some way to lift a curse inflicted upon him after he accidentally kills a rampaging forest spirit. He discovers the cause is the encroaching civilization of Iron Town, led by the cold Lady Eboshi (Driver) and its conflict with the forest spirits and their champion San (Danes)—the princess of the title. Also lending their voices are Billy Bob Thornton as a mischievous monk and Gillian Anderson as San's wolf protector. Became the first feature of any kind to gross over $150 million in its native Japan. 133m/C VHS, DVD. **D:** Hayao Miyazaki; **W:** Neil Gaiman; **M:** Joe Hisaishi; **V:** Claire Danes, Billy Crudup, Minnie Driver, Gillian Anderson, Jada Pinkett Smith, Billy Bob Thornton.

Princess of Thieves 2001 An aging Robin Hood and Will Scarlett return to England with a mortally wounded King Richard. Robin knows that Prince John will stop at nothing to assume the throne, including killing Richard's son Phillip. Unfortunately, the duo are captured by the Sheriff of Nottingham and it's up to Robin's feisty daughter Gwyn, who disguises herself as a boy, to rescue her father and Will and stop the bad guys from taking over the kingdom. 88m/C VHS, DVD. Malcolm McDowell, Keira Knightley, Roger Ashton-Griffiths, Jonathan Hyde, Del Synnott, Stephen Moyer, Stuart Wilson; **D:** Peter Hewitt; **W:** Sally Robinson, Robin Lerner. **TV**

Princess Tam Tam 1935 Pleasing French adaptation of Shaw's "Pygmalion," as a beautiful native African woman is "westernized" by a handsome writer and then introduced to high society as an exotic princess. A musical notable for its spectacular choreography and on-location Tunisian scenery. Story by Pepito Abatino, who was then Baker's husband. In French with English subtitles. 77m/B VHS, DVD. FR Josephine Baker, Albert Prejean, Germaine Aussey, Viviane Romance; **D:** Edmond T. Greville.

The Princess Who Never Laughed 1984 A stern king holds a laugh-off contest to make his morose daughter happy in this adaptation of the Brothers Grimm story from the "Faerie Tale Theatre" series. 60m/C VHS, DVD. Ellen Barkin, Howard Hesseman, Howie Mandel, Mary Woronov.

Princess Yang Kwei Fei 1955 Set in 8th-century China and based on the life of the last T'ang emperor and the beautiful servant girl he loves and makes his bride. She falls victim to court jealousies and he to his greedy family, though even death cannot end their love. Beautifully filmed and acted romantic tragedy. In Japanese with English subtitles. 91m/C VHS. JP Machiko Kyo, Masayuki Mori, Eitaro (Sakae, Saka Ozawa) Ozawa, So Yamamura; **D:** Kenji Mizoguchi. *Yokihi; The Empress Yang Kwei Fei*

The Principal 1987 (R) A tough, down-on-his-luck high school teacher is hired as the principal of a relentlessly violent, uncontrollable high school. Naturally he whips it into shape. 109m/C VHS, DVD. James Belushi, Louis Gossett Jr., Rae Dawn Chong, Michael Wright, Esai Morales, J.J. (Jeffrey Jay) Cohen, Troy Winbush, Jacob Vargas; **D:** Christopher Cain; **W:** Frank Deese; **C:** Arthur Albert; **M:** Jay Gruska.

The Principal Takes a Holiday 1998 John's (Bryan) parents threaten to deprive him of his grandmother's inheritance if he doesn't keep out of trouble during his senior year. But his latest prank is already underway and when the principal is mistakenly hospitalized because of it, John decides to manipulate the situation and sets up anti-establishment drifter Franklin (Nealon) as the school's temporary replacement. 89m/C VHS. Kevin Nealon, Zachery Ty Bryan, Jessica Steen; **D:** Robert King; **W:** Mark Amin. **VIDEO**

Prison 1988 (R) The zombified body of an unjustly executed inmate haunts Creedmore Prison, stalking the guard that killed him. His search is aided by the terrified inmates. 102m/C VHS. Lane Smith, Chelsea Field, Viggo Mortensen, Lincoln Kilpatrick, Tom Everett, Tommy (Tiny) Lister; **D:** Renny Harlin; **W:** C. Courtney Joyner; **C:** Mac Ahlberg; **M:** Richard Band.

Prison Break 1938 A convict plans a daring prison escape in order to clear his name for a murder he did not commit. 72m/B VHS, DVD. Barton MacLane, Glenda Farrell, Paul Hurst, Constance Moore, Edmund MacDonald, Ward Bond, Guy Usher, Victor Kilian; **D:** Arthur Lubin; **W:** Dorothy Davenport Reid; **C:** Harry Neumann; **M:** Frank Sanucci; Hayes Pagel.

Prison for Children 1993 Sixteen-year-old Chris is orphaned and put into a boys home where a supervisor sees his potential and helps him achieve it. 96m/C VHS. Raphael Sbarge, Kenny Ransom, Jonathan Chapin, Josh Brolin, James Callahan, Betty Thomas, John Ritter; **D:** Larry Peerce.

Prison of Secrets 1997 Mom Zimbalist gets convicted of racketeering and sent to the big house where she learns that some of the prison guards are pimping the inmates. After suffering degradation herself, Zimbalist finally decides to expose the abuse but she needs the other women to testify as well. 91m/C VHS, DVD. Stephanie Zimbalist, Dan Lauria, Finola Hughes, Rusty Schwimmer, Gary Frank, Kimberly Russell; **D:** Fred Gerber; **W:** Layce Gardner; **C:** John Fleckenstein; **M:** Nan Miskin. **CABLE**

Prison on Fire 1987 A mobster sent to prison for murdering his wife becomes friends with an innocent prisoner who has been framed. Violent portrayal of prison life. In Cantonese with English subtitles. 98m/C VHS, DVD. HK Chow Yun-Fat, Tony Leung Ka-Fai; **D:** Ringo Lam; **W:** Yin Nam; **M:** Lowell Lo.

Prison on Fire 2 1991 Ching is a hardtimer in a Hong Kong prison troubled by an ongoing battle between local inmates and those from Mainland China. He manages to escape to see his young son but is soon returned to prison where evil security chief Zau sets him up against the Mainland gang, a riot, revenge, and lots of action. Subtitled. 107m/C DVD. HK Chow Yun-Fat, Elvis Tsui, Kam-Kong Tsui, Yu Li; **D:** Ringo Lam; **M:** Lowell Lo. *Jian Yu Feng Yun Xu Ji*

Prison Planet 1992 (R) In the year 2200 Earth is under the dictatorship of an evil king, with only a band of intrepid rebels to oppose him. Blaine, one of the rebels, gets himself arrested and sent to prison in search of the true ruler, the king's brother. But the prison is protected by a brutal warlord and his equally sadistic warriors, whom Blaine must battle if he ever hopes to find truth and justice. 90m/C VHS. James Phillips, Jack Willcox, Michael Foley, Deborah Thompson-Carlin; **D:** Armand Gazarian; **W:** Armand Gazarian.

Prison Shadows 1936 Contrived programmer about a fighter (Nugent) who attempts to make a comeback after having served three years of a five-year sentence for killing an opponent in the boxing ring. He makes his comeback. Turns out that a gambling ring is behind the bizarre murders of the fighters and Nugent is their next victim. 67m/B VHS. Eddie Nugent, Lucille Lund, Joan Barclay, Forrest Taylor, Syd Saylor, Monte Blue; **D:** Robert F. "Bob" Hill; **W:** Al Martin.

Prison Stories: Women on the Inside 1991 Three short dramatic stories depict the life of women inside prison walls. "New Chicks," directed by Spheeris, tells the story of two life-long friends and partners in crime. "Esperanza," directed by Deitch, tells the story of a woman on the inside trying to prevent her family from following the same destructive path. Silver's "Parole Board" features Davidovich as a murderess up for parole but reluctant to leave the security of the prison. Blunt and gritty portrayal of prison gangs, the lifestyle of female inmates, and their fears of returning to life on the outside. 94m/C VHS. Rae Dawn Chong, Annabella Sciorra, Lolita (David) Davidovich, Talisa Soto, Rachel Ticotin, Grace Zabriskie, Silvania Gallardo, Francesca Roberts; **D:** Donna Deitch, Penelope Spheeris, Joan Micklin Silver; **W:** Dick Beebe. **CABLE**

Prison Train 1938 Travelogue of a convicted murderer's cross-country journey to begin his prison sentence at Alcatraz. 84m/B VHS, DVD. Fred Keating, Dorothy Comingore, Clarence Muse, Faith Bacon, Alexander Leftwich, Nestor Paiva, Franklyn Farnum; **D:** Gordon Wiles. *People's Enemy*

The Prisoner 1955 Gritty drama about a Cardinal imprisoned in a Soviet bloc country as his captors attempt to break his determination not to be used as a propaganda tool. Interactions between the prisoner and his interrogator are riveting. Based on the real-life experiences of Cardinal Mindszenty, a Hungarian activist during and after WWII. 91m/B VHS, DVD. GB Alec Guinness, Jack Hawkins, Raymond Huntley, Wilfred Lawson; **D:** Peter Glenville.

The Prisoner 1990 (R) Even though the cover of this bizarre import says "Jackie Chan is The Prisoner," he doesn't even show up for the first 20 minutes or so. Actually, the film is something of an ensemble piece that cheerfully borrows from American prison movies (most blatantly "Cool Hand Luke") between action scenes. The free-wheeling plot has Jackie, Sammo Hung, and Tony Leung battling fellow prisoners and corrupt officials. 94m/C DVD. HK Jackie Chan, Sammo Hung, Tony Leung Ka-Fai; **D:** Yen Ping Chu; **W:** Fu Lai, Yeh Yuen Chiao; **C:** Chan Wing Su; **M:** Eckart Seeber. *Jackie Chan Is the Prisoner; Huo Shao Dao*

Prisoner in the Middle 1974 (PG) Janssen is the only man who can stop a nuclear warhead from falling into the hands of rival Middle East factions. Originally released as "Warhead." 87m/C VHS, DVD. David Janssen, Karin Dor, Christopher Stone, Turia Tan, David Semadar, Art Metrano; **D:** John O'Connor.

Prisoner of Honor 1991 (PG) A cable retelling of notorious Dreyfus Affair, in which a Jewish officer in the 19th-century French military was accused of treason based on little evidence and lots of bigotry. George Piquart (Dreyfuss), the anti-Semitic counterintelligence head, grows to realize Dreyfuss's innocence and fights zealously for the truth. Russell's flamboyant direction takes the heroic tale into the realm of the surreal; this may not be a thoroughly accurate account, but it's one of the more eye-filling. 90m/C VHS, DVD. Richard Dreyfuss, Oliver Reed, Peter Firth, Jeremy Kemp, Brian Blessed, Peter Vaughan, Kenneth Colley, Lindsay Anderson; **D:** Ken Russell. **CABLE**

Prisoner of Love 1999 (R) After bartender Tracy (Campbell) witnesses a shakedown gone wrong, low-level stooge Jonny (Thal) is told to get rid of her. But since he's fallen in lust with Tracy after flirting with her in a nightclub, Jonny kidnaps her and holds her prisoner in a warehouse until he can figure out how to keep them both alive. Not nearly as kinky as it sounds—in fact the sheer blandness makes this a miss. 100m/C VHS, DVD. Eric Thal, Naomi Campbell, Beau Starr, Carl Marotte; **D:** Steve DiMarco; **M:** Norman Orenstein.

Prisoner of Paradise 2002 Stark PBS documentary profiling German singer/actor/director Kurt Gerron who gained fame during the 1920s and 1930s in "The Blue Angel," but, as a Jew, was not allowed to keep the Nazis in power and oddly declined a chance to escape. After being captured while touring with gypsies and sent to a camp, the Nazis forced him to create a pro-Nazi film, "The Fuhrer Gives a City to the Jews." His 23-minute work is curiously omitted. 96m/C DVD. **D:** Malcolm Clarke, Stuart Sender; **W:** Malcolm Clarke, Ian Holm. **TV**

Prisoner of Rio 1989 Satire of scruple-less TV evangelists and their nefarious schemes at acquiring their audience's money. 90m/C VHS. Steven Berkoff, Paul Freeman; **D:** Leoh Majewski; **M:** Hans Zimmer. **CABLE**

Prisoner of Second Avenue 1974 (PG) A New Yorker in his late 40s faces the future, without a job or even confidence in his ability, with the help of his understanding wife. Based on the Broadway play by Neil Simon. 98m/C VHS. Jack Lemmon, Anne Bancroft, Gene Saks, Elizabeth Wilson, Sylvester Stallone, F. Murray Abraham; **D:** Melvin Frank; **W:** Neil Simon; **M:** Marvin Hamlisch.

The Prisoner of Shark Island 1936 Dr. Samuel Mudd (Baxter) is wrongly convicted of conspiring to assassinate President Lincoln after he unwittingly sets the broken leg of assassin John Wilkes Booth (McDonald). He's sent to the titular island as his captors attempt to be used the inmates and guards, saving many during a yellow fever epidemic. Thanks to his heroism, Mudd's case is then re-opened. Baxter elicits audience sympathy without overplaying his role. **86m/B&W/D.** Warner Baxter, Gloria Stuart, Claude Gillingwater, Frank McGlynn, Francis McDonald, Harry Carey Sr., John Carradine, Fred Kohler Jr., Douglas Wood, Paul Fix; **D:** John Ford; **W:** Nunnally Johnson; **C:** Bert Glennon.

Prisoner of the Mountains *Kavkazsky Plennik; Prisoner of the Caucasus* 1996 (R) A modern-day, freely adapted version of Leo Tolstoy's novella "Prisoner of the Caucasus." Two Russian soldiers find themselves taken hostage in a remote Muslim village high in the Caucasus Mountains. Their captor, Abdul-Mourat (Skharulidze), wishes to exchange them for his own captive son. Seasoned veteran Sacha (Menshikov) and young recruit Vanya (Bodrov Jr.) slowly form a bond, not only with each other but gradually with their captors. But there's a tragic inevitability to the entire untenable situation. Russian with subtitles. **98m/C VHS, DVD, RU** Sergei Bodrov Jr., Oleg Menshikov, Djemal Skharulidze, Susanna Mekhalieva, Alexander Bureyev, Alexei Zharkov, Valentina Fedotova; **D:** Sergei Bodrov; **W:** Sergei Bodrov, Arif Aliev, Boris Giller; **C:** Pavel Lebeshev; **M:** Leonid Desyatnikov.

Prisoner of Zenda 1937 An excellent cast and splendid photography make this the definitive film adaptation of Anthony Hope's swashbuckling novel. A British commoner is forced to pose as King during the coronation of a small European country, to save the throne. Complications of the romantic sort ensue when he falls in love with the queen, and finds himself embroiled in a murder plot. Worth watching for the luxurious costumes and lavish sets. Cast as a Cardinal here, Stone starred in the 1922 version. **101m/B** **VHS, DVD.** Ronald Colman, Douglas Fairbanks Jr., Madeleine Carroll, David Niven, Raymond Massey, Mary Astor, Sir C. Aubrey Smith, Montagu Love, Byron Foulger, Alexander D'Arcy, Charles Halton; **D:** John Cromwell; **W:** Conald Coyce, Stewart, John Lloyd Balderston, Wells Root; **C:** James Wong Howe; **M:** Film Feg. '91.

Prisoner of Zenda 1952 Less-inspired remake of the 1937 version of Anthony Hope's novel, of a man's resemblance... is forced to pose as King during the coronation. Complications of the romantic sort ensue. **101m/C VHS, DVD.** Stewart Granger, Deborah Kerr, James Mason, Louis Calhern, Jane Greer, Lewis Stone, Robert Douglas; **D:** Richard Thorpe.

Prisoner of Zenda 1979 (PG) Flat comedic interpretation of Anthony Hope's swashbuckling tale of two identical men who switch places, only to find things complicated by a murder. Sellers stars in the double role of Prince Rudolph of Ruritania and Syd, the cockney cab driver who doubles for Rudolph when the Prince is imprisoned by his jealous brother Michael. **108m/C VHS, DVD.** Peter Sellers, Lynne Frederick, Lionel Jeffries, Elke Sommer, Gregory Sierra, Jane Greer, Lewis Stone; **D:** Richard Quine; **W:** Dick Clement, Ian La Frenais; **M:** Henry Mancini.

Prisoners of Inertia 1989 (R) Two newlyweds travel to New York city and find themselves caught up in a whirlwind adventure in this well-acted but lazily scripted comedy drama. **92m/C VHS.** Amanda Plummer, Christopher Rich, John C. McGinley; **D:** Jay Noyles Seeles.

Prisoners of the Lost Universe 1984 Talk-show hostess and her buddy are transported to a hostile universe by a renegade scientist. The two terrified humans search desperately for the dimensional door that is their only hope of escape. **94m/C VHS.** Richard Hatch, Kay Lenz, John Saxon; **D:** Terry Marcel. TV.

Prisoners of the Sun *Blood Oath* 1991 (R) Right after WWII an Australian captain fights to convict Japanese officers for atrocities against Allied

Private Affairs 1989 (R) The mistress of a well-known surgeon becomes jealous when the doctor decides to have a fling with a gorgeous young swim instructor. Italian-made creampie. **83m/C VHS, IT.** Giuliana de Sio, Kate Capshaw, David Naughton, Luca Barbareschi, Michele Placido; **D:** Francesco Massaro.

The Private Affairs of Bel Ami 1947 "This is the story of a scoundrel," proclaims the opening. Sanders is ideally cast as a suave cad who rises in 1880s Parisian society, largely through the strategic seduction of prominent women. Moralistically minded Old Hollywood toned down the talky adaptation of the Guy de Maupassant novel, but it's still drama of a high order. **112m/B VHS.** George Sanders, Angela Lansbury, Ann Dvorak, Frances Dee, John Carradine, Susan Douglas, Hugo Haas, Katherine Emery, Richard Fraser, Warren William, Marie Wilson, Albert Bassermann, Albert Dekker; **D:** Albert Lewin; **W:** Albert Lewin.

Private Benjamin 1980 (R) Lighthearted fare about a pampered New York Jewish princess who impulsively enlists in the U.S. Army after her husband dies on their wedding night. Hawn, who also produced, creates a character loveable even at her worst moments and brings a surprising amount of depth to this otherwise frivolous look at high society attitudes. Basis for a TV series. **110m/C VHS, DVD.** Goldie Hawn, Eileen Brennan, Albert Brooks, Robert Webber, Armand Assante, Barbara Barrie, Mary Kay Place, Sally K. Kland, Craig T. Nelson, Harry Dean Stanton, Sam Wanamaker; **D:** Howard Zieff; **W:** Nancy Meyers, Charles Shyer, Harvey Miller; **C:** David M. Walsh; **M:** Bill Conti. Writers Guild '80: Orig. Screenplay.

Private Buckaroo 1942 War time entertainment in which Harry James and his orchestra get drafted. They decide to put on a show for the soldiers and get help from the Andrews Sisters. "Don't Sit Under the Apple Tree with Anyone Else But Me; Three Little Sisters; Private Buckaroo; Johnny Get Your Gun Again; We've Got a Job to Do; You Made Me Love You; Six Jerks in a Jeep; That's the Moon My Son; I Love the South. **70m/B VHS, DVD.** The Andrews Sisters, Harry James, Joe E. Lewis, Dick Foran, Shemp Howard, Mary Wickes, Donald O'Connor; **D:** Edward F. (Eddie) Cline.

Private Confessions 1998 Continues Bergman's exploration of his parents' unhappy marriage (following "The Best Intentions"), set mostly in 1925. Restless Anna (August) is constantly at odds with her clergyman husband, Henrik (Froler), and she has an affair with divinity student Tomas (Hanzon). Anna confesses the affair to Pastor Jacob (von Sydow), who she regards as a surrogate uncle, and he advises her to tell Henrik. Anna's confrontation with Henrik will leave lasting scars—as Anna once again reveals to Jacob some ten years later. Swedish with subtitles. **127m/C VHS, SW.** Pernilla August, Samuel Froler, Max von Sydow, Thomas Hanzon; **D:** Liv Ullmann; **W:** Ingmar Bergman; **C:** Sven Nykvist.

Private Contentment 1983 This is a drama about a young soldier's experiences before he goes off to war in 1945. **90m/C VHS.** Trini Alvarado, Peter Gallagher, John McMartin, Kathryn Walker; **D:** Vivian Matalon.

Private Duty Nurses 1971 (R) Three nurses take on racism, war wounds, and a menage-a-trois (between one nurse, a doctor, and a drug addict). Second in Roger Corman's "nurse" quintet takes itself too seriously to be entertaining, but the gals make good use of those exciting new inventions, waterbeds. Preceded by "The Student Nurses" and followed by "Night Call Nurses," "The Young Nurses," and "Candy Stripe Nurses." **80m/C VHS.** Kathy Cannon, Joyce Williams, Pegi Boucher, Dennis Redfield, Herbert Jefferson Jr., Paul Hampton, Paul Gleeson; **D:** George Armitage; **W:** George Armitage; **C:** John McNichol; **M:** Sky.

The Private Eyes 1980 (PG) Light and uneven comedic romp with Knotts and Conway as bungling sleuths engaged to investigate two deaths. They're led on a merry chase through secret passages to a meeting with a ghostly adversary. **91m/C VHS, DVD.** Don Knotts, Tim Conway, Trisha Noble, Bernard Fox; **D:** Lang Elliott; **W:** John Myhers, Tim Conway; **C:** Jacques Haitkin; **M:** Peter Matz.

Private Fears in Public Places *Coeurs* 2006 Many short scenes make for a fitful stop-and-start story about six seemingly lonely people in Paris. Nicole (Morante) is looking for a new apartment for herself and fiance Dan (Wilson) with the help of broker Thierry (Dussollier). Thierry works with Charlotte (Azema), who knows bartender Lionel (Ardit) at the hotel where Dan likes to drink. Dan's drinking causes him to split with Nicole and he meets Gaelle (Carre), who happens to be Thierry's unhappy younger sister. The actors are pros but the production feels flat and constricted. French with subtitles. **120m/C DVD. FR, IT.** Laura Morante, Lambert Wilson, Pierre Arditi, Isabelle Carre, André Dussollier, Azema; **D:** Alain Resnais; **W:** Alain Resnais, Alan Ayckbourn, Jean-Michel Ribes; **C:** Eric Gautier; **M:** Mark Snow.

The Private Files of J. Edgar Hoover 1977 (PG) Scandal-mongering "biography" of J. Edgar Hoover's private, sex-filled life. **112m/C VHS.** Broderick Crawford, Dan Dailey, Jose Ferrer, Rip Torn, Michael Parks, Raymond St. Jacques, Ronee Blakley; **D:** Larry Cohen; **W:** Larry Cohen.

A Private Function 1984 (PG) A ribald gag-fest dealing with Pain in a Yorkshireman who steals and fattens a wily contraband pig against the backdrop of post-WWII rationing. The satire ranges from biting to downright nasty, but Pain is always likeable in the center of it all. **96m/C VHS, DVD, GB** Michael Palin, Maggie Smith, Denholm Elliott, Bill Paterson, Liz Smith, Richard Griffiths, Tony Haygarth, John Normington, Alison Steadman, Pete Postlethwaite; **D:** Malcolm Mowbray; **W:** Alan Bennett; **C:** Tony Pierce-Roberts; **M:** John Du Prez. British Acad. '84: Actress (Smith), Support. Actress (Smith), Support. Actor (Elliott).

Private Hell 36 1954 Two detectives become guilt-ridden after keeping part of some stolen money recovered after a robbery. Co-produced by Lupino. **81m/B VHS.** Ida Lupino, Howard Duff, Steve Cochran, Dean Jagger, Dorothy Malone, Bridget Duff, Jerry Hausner, Dabbs Greer, Chris O'Brien, Kenneth Patterson, George Dockstader, Jimmy Hawkins; **C:** Burnett Guffey; **D:** Donald Siegel; **W:** Ida Lupino.

The Private History of a Campaign That Failed 1981 Adaptation of the Mark Twain story about a cowardly troop of Confederate soldiers. **89m/C VHS.** Pat Hingle, Edward Herrmann; **D:** Peter Hunt; **W:** Philip Reisman Jr.; **C:** Walter Lassally; **M:** William Perry.

Private Investigations 1987 (R) A made-for-video thriller about a nosey reporter who gets himself and his son in trouble while investigating drug-pushing cops. **91m/C VHS.** Ray Sharkey, Clayton Rohner, Talia Balsam, Anthony Zerbe, Paul LeMat; **D:** Nigel Dick; **W:** John Dahl, David Warfield.

Private Lessons 1975 (R) Teenage boy is left alone for the summer in the care of an alluring maid and a nosey chauffeur. **83m/C VHS, DVD.** Eric Brown, Sylvia Kristel, Howard Hesseman, Ed Begley Jr.; **D:** Alan Myerson, Vittorio De Sisti; **W:** Vittorio Bonicelli; **D:** Jan De Bort, Mario Masini; **M:** Franco Micalizzi.

Private Lessons: Another Story 1994 (R) A New York photographer (Morgan) is sick of her philandering husband and decides to experience some sexual excitement of her own by, heading off to Miami. All that tropical heat inspires passion with her Cuban chauffeur (Garza). **86m/C/VHS.** Ray Garza, Theresa Merritt; **D:** Dominique Othenin-Girard; **W:** William Vernil.

Private Life *Chastnaya Zhizn* 1982 Suddenly with time on his hands, a Soviet official scrutinizes his relationships. After a number of revelations, he is forced to make new choices based on what he has learned. Oscar nominee in 1983. In Russian with English subtitles. **103m/C VHS. RU** Mikhail Ulyanov, Ita Saivina, Irina Gubanova; **D:** Edgar Ryazanov; **W:** Andrew Davies.

The Private Life of Don Juan *Don Juan* 1934 Appropriately slow-moving British costume drama set in 17th-century Spain finds an aging Don Juan struggling to maintain his usual antics in the pursuit of beautiful women. Far from the young matinee idol performer, he is forced to make new choices based on what he has learned. **86m/C VHS.** Douglas Fairbanks Sr., Merle Oberon, Binnie Barnes, Melville Cooper, Joan Gardner, Benita Hume, Athene Seyler; **D:** Alexander Korda; **C:** Georges Perinal.

The Private Life of Henry VIII 1933 Lavish historical spectacle lustily portraying the life and loves of notorious British Monarch, King Henry VIII. A tour de force for Laughton as the robust 16th-century king, with outstanding performances by the entire cast. **97m/B VHS, DVD. GB** Charles Laughton, Binnie Barnes, Elsa Lanchester, Robert Jonai, Merle Oberon, Miles Mander, Wendy Barrie, John Loder, Lady Tree, Franklin Dyall, Claud Allister, William Austin, Gibb McLaughlin, Sam Livesey, Lawrence Hanray, Everley Gregg, Judy Kelly, John Turnbull, Frederick Culley, Hay Petrie, Miles Malleson; **D:** Alexander Korda; **W:** Arthur Wimperis, Lajos Biro; **C:** Georges Perinal.

The Private Life of Sherlock Holmes 1970 (PG-13) Stylish unique perspective on the life of the famous detective reveals a complex character. Beautifully photographed, with fine performances by the supporting cast, the film boasts a haunting musical score but received surprisingly little recognition despite Wilder's high caliber direction. **125m/C VHS.** Robert Stephens, Colin Blakely, Genevieve Page, Irene Handl, Stanley Holloway, Christopher Lee, Clive Revill, Catherine Lacey, Tamara Toumanova, Mollie Maureen, Michael Balfour; **D:** Billy Wilder; **W:** Billy Wilder, I.A.L. Diamond; **C:** Christopher Challis; **M:** Miklos Rozsa.

Private Lives 1931 Stylish adaptation of Noel Coward play starring Shearer and Montgomery as a couple with a tempestuous relationship. Divorced and married other mates. While honeymooning at the same French hotel (Quelle coincidence!), they have trouble showing affection to their new spouses and realize they still feel passionately about one another. Excellent acting combined with Coward's witty dialogue makes this film a treat. **92m/B VHS.** Norma Shearer, Robert Montgomery, Reginald Denny, Una Merkel, Jean Hersholt; **D:** Sidney Franklin; **W:** Hans Kraly, Richard Schayer; **C:** Ray Binger.

The Private Lives of Elizabeth & Essex 1939 Cast reads like a Who's Who in Hollywood in this lavishly costumed dramatization of the love affair between Queen Elizabeth I (Davis) and Robert Devereaux (Flynn), the second Earl of Essex. Forced to choose between her Kingdom and her lover, Elizabeth's monarch is the epitome of a regal women. Fabray mace her first film appearance as an adult in this adaptation of Maxwell Anderson's 1930 play "Elizabeth the Queen." **106m/C VHS, DVD.** Bette Davis, Errol Flynn, Vincent Price, Nanette Fabray, Olivia de Havilland, Alan Hale, Donald Crisp, Leo G. Carroll; **D:** Michael Curtiz.

Private Manoeuvres Woof! *Sababa* 1983 A comely Swiss military adviser gives her all to uplift the morale of the men at Camp Samantha. **79m/C VHS GE S** Zachi Noy, Joseph Shiloah, Dvora Bekon; **D:** Tzvi Shissel; **W:** Boaz Davidson; **C:** Adam Greenberg; **M:** Jose Padilla.

A Private Matter 🦴🦴🦴 1992 (PG-13) Based on the true story of Sherri Finkbine (hostess of TV's "Romper Room") and the controversy surrounding her decision to terminate her pregnancy in 1962. Pregnant with her fifth child, she discovered her sleeping medication contained thalidomide, known to cause severe birth defects. Although technically illegal, her doctor agreed to quietly perform an abortion. Sherri warned as a local newspaper reporter about the drug's dangers and her identity was mistakenly revealed. A storm of adverse publicity forced her to Sweden for the abortion. Great performances highlight this complex and traumatic issue. 89m/C VHS, DVD. Sissy Spacek, Aidan Quinn, Estelle Parsons, Sheila McCarthy, Leon Russom, William H. Macy; D: Joan Micklin Silver; W: William Nicholson. CABLE

Private Navy of Sgt. O'Farrell 🦴🦴 1968 Serviceable World War II service comedy casts Hope as the titular NCO who must salvage a cargo ship full of beer that was sunk by the Japanese. He also tries to get some nurses assigned to the remote Pacific island where he's stationed. But Phyllis Diller proves to be a poor morale booster. The film doesn't come close to the "Road" comedies, but it's still worth a mild recommendation to the star's fans. 92m/C VHS, DVD. Bob Hope, Phyllis Diller, Jeffrey Hunter, Dick Sargent, Mako, Gina Lollobrigida; D: Frank Tashlin; W: Frank Tashlin; C: Alan Stensvold.

Private Obsession 🦴1/2 1994 (R) Model Emanuelle Griffith (Whirry) is missing—kidnapped by obsessed admirer Richard (Christian) who wants the beauty for himself alone. Emanuelle may be blonde but she's not dumb and she decides to turn the tables on her captor. 93m/C VHS, DVD. Shannon Whirry, Michael Christian, Bo Swenson, Rip Taylor; D: Lee Frost; W: Lee Frost; C: William Boatman; M: Dean Andre.

Private Parts 🦴🦴 1972 (R) A bizarre first attempt at feature length for Bartel. Black comedy featuring a runaway, a voyeuristic photographer and a hotel full of strange people who participate in murder and a variety of freakish sexual acts. 87m/C VHS, DVD. Ayn Ruymen, Lucille Benson, John Ventantonio, Laurie Main, Stanley Livingston, Charles Woolf, John Lupton, Dorothy Neumann, Gene Simms; D: Paul Bartel; W: Philip Kearney, Les Rendelstein; C: Andrew Davis; M: Hugo Friedhofer.

Private Parts 🦴🦴1/2 1996 (R) Howard Stern's movie debut as...himself. Self-effacing yet self-aggrandizing bio traces Stern's rise from gawky kid to gawky college student to awkward small-market DJ to New York madman to inauguration as self-proclaimed King of All Media. Funny, and at times, touching flick features good performances by the rookie actors in Stern's inner circle, as well as by the pros. Giamatti is exceptional as the young WNBC exec assigned to tame Howard. Script manages to show Stern's outrageousness and still make him likeable. While this is clearly a whitewash job, and under other circumstances Stern himself might make fun of its sentimentality, pic should please everyone but the most rabid Stern-hater. 109m/C VHS, DVD. Howard Stern, Robin Quivers, Mary McCormack, Paul Giamatti, Fred Norris, Gary Dell'Abate, Bobby Borriello, Michael Maccarone, Matthew Friedman, Jackie Martling, Carol Alt, Richard Portnow, Kelly Bishop, Henry Goodman, Jonathan Hadary, Paul Hecht, Allison Janney, Michael Murphy, James Murtaugh, Reni Santoni, Lee Wilkof, Theresa Lynn, Amber Smith; D: Betty Thomas; W: Len Blum, Michael Kalesniko; C: Walt Lloyd; M: Van Dyke Parks.

Private Passions 🦴🦴 1985 A sultry woman gives her teenaged cousin a lesson in love during his European vacation. 86m/C VHS, DVD. Sybil Danning, David J. Siegel, Susanne Ashley, Gavin Brennan; D: Kikuo Kawasaki; W: Kikuo Kawasaki; C: Ramon Suarez.

Private Property 🦴1/2 Nue Propriete 2006 Unpleasant dysfunctional family drama. Pascale lives with her lay-about twin sons Francois and Thierry in a run-down farmhouse that was part of her acrimonious divorce settlement. She and her sons have never cut those apron strings and the boys are appalled when Pascale hints at selling the dump, in part because she's found a boyfriend. Lots of bickering (and more) follows. French with subtitles. 95m/C DVD, BE FR LU Isabelle Huppert, Jeremie Renier, Patrick Descamps, Yannick Renier, Kris Cuppens; D: Joachim Lafosse; W: Joachim Lafosse, Francois Pirot; C: Hichame Alaouie.

Private Resort 🦴🦴 1984 (R) Curious house detective and a bumbling thief interrupt the highjinks of two girl-crazy teens on a quest for fun at an expensive Miami hotel. Occasionally funny plodder. 82m/C VHS, DVD. Johnny Depp, Rob Morrow, Karyn O'Bryan, Emily Longstreth, Tony Azito, Hector Elizondo, Dody Goodman, Leslie Easterbrook, Andrew (Dice Clay) Silverstein; D: George Bowers.

Private Road: No Trespassing 1987 (R) A stock car racer and a top engineer compete over a military project, cars and a rich heiress. 90m/C VHS. George Kennedy, Greg Evigan, Mitzi Kapture; D: Raphael Nussbaum.

Private School 🦴1/2 1983 (R) Two high school girls from the exclusive Cherryvale Academy for Women compete for the affections of a young man from nearby Freemount Academy for Men, while Cherryvale's headmistress is trying to raise funds to build a new wing. Banal teen sexploitation comedy with better-than-average cast. 89m/C VHS, DVD. Phoebe Cates, Betsy Russell, Kathleen Wilhoite, Sylvia Kristel, Ray Walston, Matthew Modine, Michael Zorek, Fran Ryan, Jonathan Prince, Kari Lizer, Richard Stahl; D: Noel Black; C: Walter Lassally.

The Private Secretary 🦴1/2 1935 Horton is a mild-mannered clergyman who finds out his identity has been usurped by a young man with a great many angry creditors. Horton has some amusing comic bits but the film, based on a popular Victorian farce "Der Bibliotheker" by Van Moser, did not translate well to the screen. 70m/B VHS. GB Edward Everett Horton, Barry Mackay, Oscar Asche, Judy Gunn, Michael Shepley, Alastair Sim; D: Henry Edwards.

Private War 🦴1/2 1990 (R) Training for an elite force turns deadly when the commanding officer makes the rules. Now it's a private war between two brutal fighting machines. Adapted from a Jan Guillou story. 95m/C VHS. Martin Hewitt, Joe Dallesandro, Kimberly Beck; D: Frank De Palma; W: Frank De Palma, Joe Borst.

The Private War of Major Benson 🦴🦴1/2 1955 Tough Army officer Major Bernard Benson (Heston) has his work cut out for him when he's ordered to take over an ROTC program at a military academy. First he finds out the school's run by nuns and then he treats his young cadets as he would adult troops, which naturally makes him very unpopular. But he manages to unbend enough to try for a romance with the school's doctor (Adams). And of course the kids teach him how to become a human being. Remade in 1995 as "Major Payne." 104m/C VHS. Charlton Heston, Julie Adams, Milburn Stone, Nana Bryant, William Demarest, Tim Considine, Sal Mineo; D: Jerry Hopper; W: William Roberts, Richard Alan Simmons; C: Harold Lipstein.

Private Wars 🦴🦴 1993 (R) A law-abiding community falls victim to gangland violence until the inhabitants hire a down-and-out private eye (Railsback) to show them how to fight back. He finds out that a greedy land developer (Champion) to let his goons do anything to get the people out so he can redevelop the land. 94m/C VHS, DVD. Steve Railsback, Michael Champion, Stuart Whitman, Holly Floria, Dan Tullis Jr., Michael Delano, James Lew, Brian Patrick Clarke; D: John Weidner; W: Ken Lamplugh, John Weidner.

Privates on Parade 🦴🦴1/2 1984 (R) Film centering around the comic antics of an Army song-and-dance unit entertaining the troops in the Malayan jungle during the late '40s. Occasionally inspired horseplay based on Peter Nichols play. 107m/C VHS, DVD. GB John Cleese, Denis Quilley, Simon Jones, Joe Melia, Nicola Paget, Julian Sands; D: Michael Blakemore.

Prix de Beaute 🦴1/2 Miss Europe 1930 A woman's boyfriend does not know that she has won a beauty contest. Brooks' last starring role and the only film she did in France. In French with English subtitles. 93m/B VHS, DVD. FR Louise Brooks, Jean Bradin, George Charlia, Gaston Jacquet; D: Augusto Genina.

The Prize 🦴🦴🦴 1963 Gripping spy story laced with laughs based on a novel by Irving Wallace (adapted by Lehman). In Stockholm, writer accepts the Nobel prize for dubious reasons and then finds himself in the midst of political intrigue. Newman and Sommer turn in great performances in this action drama. 136m/C VHS. Paul Newman, Edward G. Robinson, Elke Sommer, Leo G. Carroll, Diane Baker, Micheline Presle, Gerard Oury, Sergio Fantoni; D: Mark Robson; W: Ernest Lehman; C: William H. Daniels; M: Jerry Goldsmith.

Prize Fighter 🦴🦴 1979 (PG) Comedy team of Knotts and Conway take on Depression-era boxing. Fight manager Knotts and his pugilistic protege Conway unknowingly get involved with a powerful gangster, who convinces them to fight in a fixed championship match. Most enjoyable if intelligence is suspended at onset. 99m/C VHS, DVD. Tim Conway, Don Knotts; D: Michael Preece; W: Tim Conway.

Prize of Peril 🦴🦴 1984 A French TV game show rewards it winners with wealth and its losers with execution. Not always the best policy to learn what's behind Door #1. 95m/C VHS. FR Michel Piccoli, Marie-France Pisier; D: Yves Boisset.

The Prize Pulitzer 🦴🦴 1989 Watered-down account of the scandalous divorce between publishing heir Herbert "Pete" Pulitzer and his young wife Roxanne. Based on the book "The Prize Pulitzer" by Roxanne Pulitzer. 95m/C VHS, DVD. Perry King, Chynna Phillips, Courteney Cox, Betsy Russell, Sondra Blake, Caitlin Brown; D: Richard A. Colla. TV

The Prize Winner of Defiance, Ohio 🦴🦴🦴 2005 (PG-13) Based on a memoir by Terry Adams. The "prize winner" is Terry's mother Evelyn (Moore, who filmmakers seem to love casting as a 1950s housewife). The mother of ten children and the wife of a drunk (Harrelson), ever-cheerful Evelyn figures out how to (barely) hold it all together by becoming a successful jingle writer, winning money and prizes for her catchy advertising tunes. Maybe a little heavy and nostalgic at moments, but charming nonetheless. 99m/C DVD. Julianne Moore, Woody Harrelson, Laura Dern, Trevor Morgan, Simon Reynolds; D: Jane Anderson; W: Jane Anderson; C: Jonathan Freeman; M: John (Gianni) Frizzell.

The Prizefighter and the Lady 🦴🦴🦴 Every Woman's Man 1933 In his first film role boxer Baer (who won the heavyweight boxing crown in 1934) is a natural as a fighter who falls for a beautiful nightclub singer (Loy). Baer and Loy get, but don't stay, together but she does turn out to be his lucky charm in the big fight finale. Fellow professional boxer Carnera, Baer's opponent in the climatic fight scene, refused to lose as the script indicated and the film ending was eventually rewritten. The likeable Baer later earned his living as an actor. 102m/B Max Baer Sr., Myrna Loy, Otto Kruger, Primo Carnera, Walter Huston, Vince Barnett, Muriel Evans; D: Woodbridge S. Van Dyke.

Prizzi's Honor 🦴🦴🦴 1985 (R) Highly stylized, sometimes leaden black comedy about Vharley Partana (Nicholson), an aging and none-to-bright hit man from a New York mob family who breaks with family loyalties when he falls for Irene Walker (Turner), an upwardly mobile tax consultant who's also a hired killer. Skirting caricature in every frame, Nicholson is excellent in his portrayal of the thick-skulled mobster, as are Angelica Huston as the hot-to-trot Mafia daughter Maerose and Hickey as the Don Prizzi. Adapted by Condon and Roach from Condon's novel. 130m/C VHS, DVD. Jack Nicholson, Kathleen Turner, Robert Loggia, John Randolph, Anjelica Huston, Lawrence Tierney, William Hickey, Lee Richardson, Michael Lombard, Joseph Ruskin, CCH Pounder; D: John Huston; W: Richard Condon; C: Andrzej Bartkowiak; M: Alex North. Oscars '85: Support. Actress (Huston); British Acad. '85: Adapt. Screenplay; Golden Globes '86: Actor—Mus./Comedy (Nicholson), Actress—Mus./Comedy (Turner), Director (Huston), Film—Mus./Comedy; L.A. Film Critics '85: Support. Actress (Huston); N.Y. Film Critics '85: Actor (Nicholson), Director (Huston), Film, Support. Actress (Huston); Natl. Soc. Film Critics '85: Actor (Nicholson), Director (Huston), Support. Actress (Huston); Writers Guild '85: Adapt. Screenplay.

Probable Cause 🦴🦴 1995 (R) A knife-wielding serial killer specializes in murdering cops and the clues seem to point to a troubled veteran cop (Ironside), newly paired with a beautiful detective (Vernon). Some unexpected twists and a surprise ending. 90m/C VHS. Michael Ironside, Kate Vernon, Kirk Baltz, Craig T. Nelson, M. Emmet Walsh; D: Paul Ziller; W: Hal Salwen; C: Danny Nowak.

Probation 🦴🦴 Second Chances 1932 A dashing young man in trouble with the law receives an unusual sentence; he must become a chauffeur for a spoiled society girl. Grable's first film role is a small one. 60m/B VHS. Sally Blane, J. Farrell MacDonald, Eddie (Edward) Phillips, Clara Kimball Young, Betty Grable; D: Richard Thorpe.

Probe 🦴🦴1/2 1972 A detective uses computer-age technology to apprehend criminals. Pilot for the TV series "Search." 95m/C VHS. Hugh O'Brian, Elke Sommer, John Gielgud, Burgess Meredith, Angel Tompkins, Lilia Skala, Kent Smith, Alfred Ryder, Jaclyn Smith; D: Russ Mayberry; W: Leslie Stevens. TV

Problem Child 🦴🦴 1990 (PG) Ritter decides to adopt Oliver out of the goodness of his heart, but it seems young Oliver's already got a father figure named Beelzebub. Potential for laughs is unmet. 81m/C VHS, DVD. John Ritter, Michael Oliver, Jack Warden, Amy Yasbeck, Gilbert Gottfried, Michael Richards, Peter Jurasik; D: Dennis Dugan; W: Scott M. Alexander, Larry Karaszewski; C: Peter Lyons Collister; M: Miles Goodman.

Problem Child 2 🦴 1991 (PG-13) Ritter and his nasty adopted son are back, but this time there's an equally malevolent little girl. They team up to prevent Ritter's upcoming marriage to a socialite. Low slapstick junk. 91m/C VHS, DVD. John Ritter, Michael Oliver, Laraine Newman, Amy Yasbeck, Jack Warden, Ivyann Schwan, Gilbert Gottfried, James Tolkan, Charlene Tilton, Alan Blumenfeld, Paul Sutera; D: Brian Levant; W: Scott M. Alexander, Larry Karaszewski.

The Prodigal 🦴🦴1/2 1955 Luke's New Testament Bible story of the son seduced by greed slickly transferred to the silver screen by MGM. A colorful cast is the main attraction. 113m/C DVD. Lana Turner, Edmund Purdom, Louis Calhern, Audrey Dalton, Neville Brand, Walter Hampden, Taina Elg, Francis L. Sullivan, Joseph Wiseman, Sandy Descher, John Dehner, Cecil Kellaway, Henry Daniell, Paul Cavanagh, Tracey Roberts, Jay Novello, Dorothy Adams, Richard Devon; D: Richard Thorpe; C: Joseph Ruttenberg.

The Prodigal Planet 🦴🦴 1988 Small group of believers continue their struggle against the world government UNTIE by disrupting their communication network. Sequel to "Thief in the Night," "A Distant Thunder," and "Image of the Beast." 67m/C VHS, DVD. William Wellman Jr., Linda Beatie, Cathy Wellman, Thom Rachford; D: Donald W. Thompson.

The Prodigal Son 🦴🦴1/2 1982 Small-town martial arts champ Biao learns all his fights were fixed by his wealthy father. Determined to prove himself fairly, Biao learns the true wisdom and skills of kung fu from a traveling entertainer Ying. Typically over-the-top fight scenes. Chinese with subtitles or dubbed. 100m/C VHS, DVD. HK Yuen Biao, Ching-Ying Lam, Sammo Hung; D: Sammo Hung; W: Jing Wong.

The Prodigy 🦴🦴 1998 Well-intentioned but far-fetched drama posits that Nathan Jones (Earl), an illiterate 12-year-old black boy, is "adopted" by a fraternity and enrolled as a student as a child prodigy. Sounds like an after-school special gone tragically awry. 104m/C DVD. Robert Foreman, Jeremy Isiah Earl, Jennifer Rochester; D: Edward T. McDougal; W: Edward T. McDougal; Dale Chapman, Christopher Parneck; C: Ben Kufrin.

The Producers 🦴🦴½ 1968 A hilarious farce follows an attempted swindle by theater producer/con artist Max Bialystock (Mostel), who convinces his meek accountant Leo Bloom (Wilder) to go along with a scheme to deliberately stage a Broadway flop and abscond with the investors' money. They pick what they believe will be a surefire disaster, a musical entitled "Springtime for Hitler," only to see their plan backfire. Film achieved cult status and is considered one of Brooks' best. The phony play was later actually produced by Alan Johnson. 90m/C VHS. DVD. Zero Mostel, Gene Wilder, Dick Shawn, Kenneth Mars, Estelle Winwood, Lee Meredith, Frank Campanella, Mel Brooks; D: Mel Brooks; W: Mel Brooks; C: Joseph Coffey; M: John Morris. Oscars '68: Story & Screenplay; Natl. Film Reg. '96; Writers Guild '68: Orig. Screenplay.

The Producers 🦴🦴½ 2005 (PG-13) The wildly funny Mel Brooks 1968 film showed up in 2001 as a hit Broadway musical—this is the film version of that. Leo (Broderick) hatch a scheme to get rich by producing a flop and pocketing the leftover investor money after the show surely closes. Hideous Nazi musical "Springtime for Hitler" not only doesn't flop, it's a major success, which means trouble. Yes, it's all rehashed and old-schoolers will go back to the original film with a renewed fondness. Fun cast and hilarious musical numbers, help to somewhat mask the weaknesses. 129m/C DVD. US Nathan Lane, Matthew Broderick, Uma Thurman, Will Ferrell, Roger Bart, Eileen Essell, David Huddleston, Michael McKean, Debra Monk, Andrea Martin, Jon Lovitz, Jack Beach; D: Susan Stroman; W: Mel Brooks, Thomas Meehan; C: John Bailey, Charles Minsky; M: Mel Brooks.

The Professional 🦴🦴 Leon; The Cleaner 1994 (R) Leon (Reno) is an eccentric French hit man, working New York's mean streets, when his 12-year-old neighbor Mathilda (Portman) comes knocking. Seems her family has been murdered by minions of crooked drug enforcement agent Stansfield (Oldman) and she'd like Leon to teach her how to be a "cleaner" so she can get revenge. And Leon obliges. The lovely young Portman (in her film debut) is a little too Lolita-ish for comfort as she manipulates the stolid Reno, with Oldman suitably extravagant in the role of sadistic psycho. 109m/C VHS, DVD. FR Jean Reno, Natalie Portman, Gary Oldman, Danny Aiello, Michael Badalucco, Ellen Greene; D: Luc Besson; W: Luc Besson; C: Thierry Arbogast; M: Eric Serra.

The Professionals 🦴🦴🦴½ 1966 (PG-13) Action and adventure count for more than a story line in this exciting western about four mercenaries hired by a wealthy cattle baron to rescue his young wife from Mexican kidnappers. Breathtaking photography re-creates turn-of-the-century Mexico in this adaptation of the Frank O'Rourke novel. 117m/C VHS, DVD. Burt Lancaster, Lee Marvin, Claudia Cardinale, Jack Palance, Robert Ryan, Woody Strode, Ralph Bellamy; D: Richard Brooks; W: Richard Brooks; C: Conrad L. Hall; M: Maurice Jarre.

The Professor 🦴🦴½ 1958 Rare sci-fi thriller featuring a werewolf, an eccentric scientist and a communist plot. Also includes several newsreel oriented movie trailers. 30m/C VHS. Doug Hobart, John Copeland, Irene Barr; D: Tom McCan.

Profile 🦴🦴½ 1954 A newsman gets an editorial job for a magazine called "Profile," and promptly falls in love with the boss's daughter. Complications arise when the boss's wife puts the moves on him. As if that isn't trouble enough, he finds himself accused of embezzlement. Average entertainment with some notable performances and an interesting chase scene. 65m/B VHS. John Bentley, Kathleen Byron, Thea Gregory, Stuart Lindsell; D: Francis Searle.

Profile for Murder 🦴🦴 The Fifth Season 1996 (R) Criminal profiler Hanna Carras (Severance) and Detective Andy Sachs (Michael) are assigned by DA Michael Weinberg (Vincont) to investigate in a series of grisly murders of young women. Cross likes to play mind games and soon Carras is very personally involved with the suspect but does that also make him the killer? 95m/C VHS, DVD. Joan Severance, Lance Henriksen, Jeff Wincott, Ryan Michael; D: David Winning; W: Steve(n) Fisher; C: Bruce Worrall; M: Baron Abramovitch.

Progeny 🦴🦴 1998 Familiar horror ground with some scary creatures. Craig (Vosloo) and Sherry (McWhirter) are zapped by a bright light while in bed and don't remember what happened until a shrink (Crouse) and UFO investigator Clavell (Dourif) hypnotize them. Then Sherry remembers she was abducted and apparently impregnated by some slimy, tentacled aliens and it's all just kind of predictable. 100m/C VHS, DVD. Arnold Vosloo, Jillian McWhirter, Brad Dourif, Lindsay Crouse, Wilford Brimley; D: Briar Y-izna; W: Aubrey Solomon; C: James Hawkinson; M: Steven Morrell. VIDEO

The Program 🦴🦴½ 1993 (R) Sensitive tearjerker about college football players getting caught up in the drive for a championship. As the season takes its toll on both mind and body, players prepare for the big game. Caan is the team's gruff coach, who's willing to look the other way as long as his boys are winning. Film sparked controversy when the Disney studio pulled and recut it after release because one scene, where Shefter's character lies down in traffic, sparked copy-cat actions and several deaths. The scene was not recut for the video version. 110m/C VHS, DVD. James Caan, Craig Sheffer, Kristy Swanson, Halle Berry, Omar Epps, Duane Davis, Abraham Benrubi, Jon Maynard Pennell, Andrew Bryniarski, Joey Lauren Adams; D: David S. Ward; W: David S. Ward, Aaron Latham; M: Michel Colombier.

Programmed to Kill 🦴🦴 Retaliator 1986 (R) A beautiful terrorist is captured by the CIA and transformed into a buxom bionic assassin. 91m/C VHS. Robert Ginty, Sandahl Bergman, James Booth, Louise Caire Clark; D: Allan Holzman.

Project A 🦴🦴 Jackie Chan's Project A; A Gai Waak 1983 (PG-13) This period piece has several excellent physical routines. As Dragon Ma, a coast guard officer in 19th-century Hong Kong, Jackie Chan (who also directed) performs some of his most ingenious stunts, and pays overt homage to one of his greatest influences, Harold Lloyd. 105m/C VHS, DVD. HK Jackie Chan, Sammo Hung, Yuen Biao; D: Jackie Chan; W: Edward Tang, Jackie Chan.

Project A: Part 2 🦴🦴 Jackie Chan's Project A2 1987 Dragon Ma, the cop in Hong Kong on the high seas at the turn of the century, is back with a new set of adventures. In Cantonese with English subtitles. 101m/C VHS, DVD. HK Jackie Chan, Maggie Cheung, Carina Lau, David Lam; D: Jackie Chan; W: Edward Tang, Jackie Chan.

Project: Alien 🦴🦴 1989 (R) Science fiction fans in search of a good extraterrestrial flick should avoid this teaser, for it has nothing to do with aliens. As the title begins. Earth is allegedly being attacked by beings from space, and a vast array of scientists, militia and journalists track the aliens. What's actually happening revolves around the testing of deadly biological weapons. Shot in Yugoslavia. 92m/C VHS. Michael Nouri, Darianne Fluegel, Maxwell Caulfield, Charles Durning; D: Frank Shields; W: Anthony Able.

Project: Eliminator 🦴½ 1991 (R) A group of terrorists kidnap a designer of "smart" weapons, and it's up to a hard-hitting special forces unit to get him back. Filmed in New Mexico. 89m/C VHS, DVD. David Carradine, Frank Zagarino, Drew Snyder, Hilary English, Vivian Schilling; D: H. Kaye Dyal; W: Jon McCallum.

Project: Genesis 🦴🦴½ 1993 Pascal and a beautiful Alien Woman are shipwrecked on a desolate planet in the 23rd century. As they watch the worlds around them clash in war, they know it is up to them to create a new beginning at the end of the Universe. 75m/C VHS, DVD. Philip Jackson; M: Andy McNeil.

Project: Kill! 🦴🦴 1977 Head of a murder-for-hire squad suddenly disappears and his former assistant is hired 'to track him down dead or alive. 94m/C VHS. Leslie Nielsen, Gary Lockwood, Nancy Kwan, Vic Silayan, Vic Diaz, Donald G. Thompson; D: William Girdler; W: David Kidd.

Project Metalbeast: DNA Overload 🦴🦴½ 1994 (R) A CIA agent, cryogenically frozen for 10 years, becomes the guinea pig when a group of scientists decide to unthaw him for a DNA experiment involving living metallic skin. Too bad he turns into a metal beast by the light of the full moon. Sci-fi take on the werewolf saga. 92m/C VHS, DVD. Barry Boswick; D: Alessandro DeCeatano; W: Timothy E. Sabo; M: Conrad Pope.

Project Moon Base 🦴🦴 1953 Espionage runs rampant on a spaceship headed by a female officer. Eventually the ship's stranded or the moon. Actually filmed for the TV series "Ring Around the Moon." A cold-war sexist relic. 64m/B VHS. Donna (Dona Martel) Martell, Hayden Rorke, Ross Ford, Larry Johns, Herb Jacobs; D: Richard Talmadge; W: Robert Heinlein, Jack Seaman; C: William C. Thompson; M: Herschel Burke Gilbert.

Project: Nightmare 🦴½ 1995 Seems not all dreams are wish fulfillment, when these nightmares start coming true. 75m/C VHS, Elly Koslo, Lance Dickson; D: Donald M. Jones.

Project: Shadowchaser 🦴½ 1992 (R) Action-packed would-be thriller about a billion dollar android who escapes from a top secret government laboratory. Programmed with superhuman strength and human emotions the android and five terrorists take over a hospital (located in a skyscraper no less). Their hostages include the President's daughter and the terrorists demand a $150 million ransom. With a four-hour deadline the FBI calls in the hospital architect to advise them—only they've got the wrong man—and the android's creator, who wants his creation back—no matter what the cost. A low-budget Terminator clone. 97m/C VHS. Martin Kove, Meg Foster, Frank Zagarino, Paul Koslo, Joss Ackland; D: John Eyres.

Project Shadowchaser 3000 🦴½ 1995 (R) Deep space satellite station collides with a mining vessel carrying a killer android. The seven survivors of the station are then hunted by the android as the ship's nuclear core is also threatening to explode. 99m/C VHS, DVD. Brian Knudson, Sam Bottoms, Christopher Atkins, Musetta Vander, Nick Davis; D: John Eyres.

Project Vampire 🦴½ 1993 Vampire concocts a serum that will change humans into vampires within three days. His first guinea pig fights to stop the evil from succeeding. 90m/C VHS, DVD. Mary-Louise Gemmill, Christopher Cho, Myron Natwick; D: Peter Flynn.

Project X 🦴🦴½ 1987 (PG) A bemused Air Force pilot is assigned to a special project involving chimpanzees. He must decide where his duty lies when he realizes the semi-intelligent chimps are slated to die. 107m/C VHS, DVD. Matthew Broderick, Helen Hunt, William Sadler, Johnny Ray McGhee, Jonathan Stark, Robin Gammell, Stephen Lang, Jean Smart, Dick Miller; D: Jonathan Kaplan; W: Stanley Weiser, Lawrence Lasker; C: Dean Cundey; M: James Horner.

The Projectionist 🦴🦴🦴 1971 (PG) A must-see for movie buffs, Dangerfield made his screen debut in this story about a projectionist in a seedy movie house whose real-life existence begins to blur into the films he continuously watches. Made on a limited budget, this creative effort by Hurwitz was the first film to utilize the technique of superimposition. 84m/C VHS. Rodney Dangerfield, Chuck McCann, Ina Balin, Jara Kohout, Harry Hurwitz, Stephen Phillips, Clara Rosenthal, Jacquelyn Glenn, Robert Staats; D: Harry Hurwitz; W: Harry Hurwitz; C: Victor Petrashevich; M: Igo Kantor, Erna E. Levin.

Prom Night 🦴🦴 1980 (R) A masked killer stalks four high school girls during their senior prom as revenge for a murder which occurred six years prior. Sequelled by "Hello Mary Lou: Prom Night 2," "Prom Night 3: The Last Kiss," and "Prom Night 4: Deliver Us from Evil." 91m/C VHS, DVD. CA Jamie Lee Curtis, Leslie Nielsen, Casey Stevens, Eddie Benton, Antoinette Bower, Michael Tough, Pita Oliver, David Mucci, Joy Thompson, Mary Beth Rubens; D: Paul Lynch; W: William Gray; C: Robert New; M: Paul Zaza.

Prom Night 🦴 2008 (PG-13) Scream, run, die. Director McCormick's feature remake of the R-rated 1980 slasher with a merely adequate adequate story role. Donna (Snow) family was slain by obsessed teacher Richard Fenton (Schaech) and three years later, he's escaped from prison to finish his work while Donna and her friends party in their hotel suite on prom night. 88m/C DVD. US Brittany Snow, Johnathon Schaech, Idris Elba, Dana Davis, Jessica Stroup, Scott Porter, Johnathon Schaech, Collins Pennie, Kelly Blatz; D: Nelson McCormick; W: J.S. Cardone; C: Checco Varese; M: Paul Haslinger.

Prom Night 3: The Last Kiss 🦴 1989 (R) The second sequel in which the reappearing high school ghoul beguiles a lucky teenager. 97m/C VHS, DVD. Tim Conlon, Cynthia (Cyndy, Cindy) Preston, Courtney Taylor, David Stratton, Dylan Neal, Jeremy Ratchford; D: Ron Oliver, Peter Simpson; M: Ror Oliver; C: Rhett Morita.

Prom Night 4: Deliver Us from Evil 🦴 1991 (R) Yet another gory entry in the Prom series (one would hope it will be the last). Another group of naive teens decide that they can have more fun at a private party than at the prom. They host the party in a summer home that was once a monastery, but the festive affair soon turns into a night of terror when an uninvited guest crashes the party. For true fans of slasher flicks. 89m/C VHS, DVD. CA Nikki de Boer, Alden Kane, Joy Tanner, Alle Ghadban, James Carver; D: Clay Borris; W: Richard Beattie.

The Promise 🦴½ 1979 (PG) Weepie outdated story about star-crossed lovers Michael (Collins) and Nancy (Quinlan). A car accident leaves Michael comatose and Nancy badly disfigured. Michael's mother (Straight), who loathes Nancy, sees her chance to finally break them up. She offers to pay for Nancy's plastic surgery if she'll leave Michael forever, then Mom tells her son his girlfriend's dead. A year later Nancy, with her new face and new identity, and Michael meet. From the novel by Danielle Steele. 97m/C VHS. Stephen Collins, Kathleen Quinlan, Beatrice Straight, Laurence Luckinbill, William Prince, Michael O'Hare; D: Gilbert Cates; W: Gary Michael White; M: David Shire.

The Promise 🦴🦴½ Face of a Stranger; Das Versprechen 1994 (R) Young lovers Konrad (Zöller and Zirner) and Sophie (Harfouch and Becker) find themselves separated by the Berlin Wall after a botched escape attempt in 1961. The estranged lover's meet only four times during the next three decades as they adjust to the systems under which they're forced to live. Somewhat contrived and cliched, this bittersweet romance uses Konrad and Sophie as symbols of the social and political turmoil and triumphs of the divided Germany. Received some criticism from East Germans who found the film's severe portrayal of Communist rule too harsh. Gets points for...

ing the first post-fall film to explore the Wall's legacy. **115m/C VHS. GE** Corinna Harfouch, Meret Becker, August Zirner, Anian Zollner, Jean-Yves Gautier, Eva Mattes, Suzanne Uge, Hans Kremer, Pierre Besson, Tina Engel, Otto Sander, Hark Bohm; **D:** Margarethe von Trotta; **W:** Peter Schneider, Margarethe von Trotta; **C:** Franz Rath; **M:** Jurgen Knieper.

The Promise ♂♂½ *Wu Ji: Master of the Crimson Armor* 2005 (PG-13) Complicated and stylized martial arts fantasy in which a young orphan is offered a life of riches by a goddess (Hong) with the caveat that she will lose every man she loves. Qingcheng (Cheung) lives with her bargain until she falls for General Guangming (Sanada), of the crimson armor. Except it was his slave, Kunlun (Dong-Gun), who was wearing the armor and actually rescued the princess. Never really makes any sense (at least to Westerners). Mandarin with subtitles; also released at 121 minutes. **103m/C DVD. CH US** Hiroyuki (Henry) Sanada, Dong-Kun Jang, Cecilia Cheung, Nicholas Tse, Liu Yeh, Chen Hong, Qian Bo, Yu Xiaowei, Cheng Qian; **D:** Chen Kaige, Zhang Tan; **W:** Chen Kaige; **C:** Peter Pau; **M:** Klaus Badelt.

Promise Her Anything ♂♂ 1966 A widow (Caron) with a baby decides to make her boss (Cummings), a child psychologist who hates kids, her new husband. So she stashes the kid with her upstairs neighbor (Beatty), a would-be filmmaker who earns his living making blue movies. But the filmmaker has romantic designs on the widow and decides the baby may be his way to make a good impression. Beatty isn't very believable in this type of light-romantic comedy and the farcical situations are forced. **98m/C VHS. GB** Warren Beatty, Leslie Caron, Robert Cummings, Hermione Gingold, Lionel Stander, Keenan Wynn, Cathleen Nesbitt; **D:** Arthur Hiller; **W:** William Peter Blatty.

Promise to Murder ♂½ 1956 An early murder-drama episode from the "Climax" TV series. **60m/B VHS.** Peter Lorre, Louis Hayward, Ann Harding.

Promised Land ♂♂½ *Young Hearts* 1988 (R) Two high school friends from the rural northwestern U.S. come together several years after graduation under tragic circumstances. Writer Hoffman's semi-autobiographical, disillusioned look at the American Dream was re-discovered by movie goers due to its excellent dramatic performances, notable also as the first film produced by Robert Redford's Sundance Institute. **110m/C VHS, DVD.** Kiefer Sutherland, Meg Ryan, Tracy Pollan, Jason Gedrick, Googy Gress, Deborah Richter, Sandra Seacat, Jay Underwood, Oscar Rowland; **D:** Michael Hoffman; **W:** Michael Hoffman; **M:** James Newton-Howard.

Promises in the Dark ♂♂½ 1979 (PG) Drama focusing on the complex relationship between a woman doctor and her 17-year-old female patient who is terminally ill from cancer. Hellman's directorial debut. **118m/C VHS.** Marsha Mason, Ned Beatty, Kathleen Beller, Susan Clark, Paul Clemens, Donald Moffat, Michael Brandon; **D:** Jerome Hellman.

Promises! Promises! ♂½ 1963 Having difficulty getting pregnant, a woman goes on a cruise with her husband. While on board, they meet another couple, all get drunk, and change partners. Of course, both women find themselves pregnant, leaving the paternity in doubt. Famous primarily as the movie Mansfield told "Playboy" magazine she appeared "completely nude" in. **90m/B VHS, DVD.** Jayne Mansfield, Marie McDonald, Tommy Noonan, Fritz Feld, Claude Stroud, Mickey Hargitay, Marjorie Bennett, Vic Lundin; **D:** King Do-

novan; **W:** William Welch, Tommy Noonan; **C:** Joseph Biroc.

The Promoter ♂♂♂ *The Card* 1952 Horatio Alger comedy stars Guinness as an impoverished student who gives himself a surreptitious leg up in life by altering his school entrance exam scores. Outstanding performances enliven this subtle British comedy of morals. **87m/B VHS. GB** Alec Guinness, Glynis Johns, Petula Clark, Valerie Hobson, Michael Hordern; **D:** Ronald Neame; **W:** Eric Ambler.

Pronto ♂♂½ 1997 (R) Semi-retired bookie Harry Arno (Falk) is forced to head out of Miami when his mobster boss realizes Harry's been skimming. So he takes off for the Italian Riviera with ex-stripper girlfriend Joyce (Headly), while being trailed by doofus U.S. Marshal Raylan Givens (LeGros), who's trying to keep Harry alive so the feds can get his testimony against his gangster cohorts. Falk's gruff, Headly's smart, LeGros is a laugh, and the movie's vivid since it's taken from Elmore Leonard's 1993 novel. **100m/C VHS.** Peter Falk, Glenne Headly, James LeGros, Sergio Castellitto, Bradford Tatum, Walter Olkewicz, Glenn Plummer, Luis Guzman; **D:** Jim McBride; **W:** Michael Butler; **C:** Alfonso Beato; **M:** John Altman. **CABLE**

Proof ♂♂♂ 1991 (R) Directorial debut of Moorhouse tells a tale of manipulation, friendship, and obsessive love between a blind photographer, Martin, his housekeeper, and the young man he befriends. Martin, mistrustful of the world around him, takes photographs as "proof" of the reality of his life. A chance meeting with Andy provides Martin with his "eyes" and the opportunity to expand his world and emotions—something his housekeeper, Celia, would be only too happy to help him with. Unhealthy triangle leads all three to a re-evaluation of their lives. Propelled by terrific performances and enough humor to balance its emotional content. **90m/C VHS, DVD. AU** Hugo Weaving, Genevieve Picot, Russell Crowe, Heather Mitchell, Jeffrey Walker, Frank Gallacher; **D:** Jocelyn Moorhouse; **W:** Jocelyn Moorhouse. Australian Film Inst. '91: Actor (Weaving), Director (Moorhouse), Film, Film Editing, Screenplay, Support. Actor (Crowe).

Proof ♂♂♂½ 2005 (PG-13) Film adaptation of David Auburn's award-winning Broadway play makes the most of its four-character construct. Catherine (Paltrow) is the gifted daughter of a once-brilliant mathematician (Hopkins), who in the final years of his life suffered with dementia, sits at the center of the film. A brainy introvert by nature, Catherine is forced in the wake of her father's death to seek redeeming personal value as both an academic and a daughter, while contemplating her own fragile grip on sanity, **99m/C DVD. US** Gwyneth Paltrow, Anthony Hopkins, Jake Gyllenhaal, Hope Davis, Roshan Seth, Gary Houston; **D:** John Madden; **W:** Stephen Warbeck.

Proof of Life ♂♂½ 2000 (R) When Alicia's (Ryan) engineer husband (Morse) is kidnapped by anti-government guerrillas in South America, she hires professional negotiator Terry Thorne (Crowe) to get him back. Complications arise when Terry falls for the wife. Complications also arose when Ryan fell for Crowe and her marriage to Dennis Quaid fell apart. Crowe and Ryan subsequently broke up just in time for the marketing push, leaving director Hackford without his two biggest stars to promote the film. Despite the offscreen heat, the movie's a lot better when dealing with the husband's predicament and the rescue operations than when exploring Ryan's angst and the budding romance. **135m/C VHS, DVD.** Russell Crowe, Meg Ryan, David Morse, David Caruso, Pamela Reed, Anthony Heald, Stanley Anderson, Gottfried John, Alun Armstrong, Michael Kitchen, Margo Martindale, Mario Ernesto Sanchez, Pietro Sibille, Vicky Hernandez, Norma Martinez, Diego Trujillo; **D:** Taylor Hackford; **W:** Tony Gilroy; **C:** Slawomir Idziak; **M:** Danny Elfman.

Proof of the Man ♂ 1977 A Japanese co-production about a murder in Tokyo that takes on international importance. **100m/C VHS.** JP George Kennedy, Broderick Crawford, Toshiro Mifune; **D:** Junya Sato;

W: Zenzo Matsuyama; **C:** Sinsaku Himeda; **M:** Yuji Ono.

Prophecy ♂½ 1979 (PG) A doctor and his wife travel to Maine to research the effects of pollution caused by the lumber industry. They encounter several terrifying freaks of nature and a series of bizarre human deaths. Laughable horror film. **102m/C VHS, DVD.** Talia Shire, Robert Foxworth, Armand Assante, Victoria Racimo, Richard Dysart, George Clutesi; **D:** John Frankenheimer; **W:** David Seltzer; **C:** Harry Stradling Jr.

The Prophecy ♂♂½ 1995 (R) Modern variation of "Paradise Lost' carries a heavy load including possession. Native American mythology, and Walken as the archangel Gabriel. Not surprisingly, it stumbles under the weight. Gabriel is at odds with good angel Simon (Stolz) over the souls of humans, a battle that has its final showdown in a small Arizona community and crosses the paths of homicide detective Thomas Dagget (Koteas) and school teacher Katherine (Madsen). Successfully mixes humor and horror, but biblical jargon can lose horror fans just looking for a cheap thrill. Directorial debut of screenwriter Widen. **97m/C VHS, DVD.** Christopher Walken, Eric Stoltz, Elias Koteas, Virginia Madsen, Amanda Plummer, Viggo Mortensen; **D:** Gregory Widen; **W:** Gregory Widen; **C:** Bruce Douglas Johnson, Richard Clabaugh; **M:** David Williams.

The Prophecy 2: Ashtown ♂♂½ 1997 (R) It's post-apocalyptic L.A. and power-hungry fallen angel Gabriel (Walken) returns from hell to stop the creation of a half-human/half-angelic child who's prophesized as the new savior of mankind. Angel Danyael (Wong) is intended as the dad while nurse Valerie (Beals) is the woman chosen as the mother. The good guys get some help from angel Michael (Roberts). Lots of action and good special effects, though viewers who haven't seen the first film may be confused. **83m/C VHS, DVD.** Christopher Walken, Russell Wong, Eric Roberts, Jennifer Beals, Bruce Abbott, Brittany Murphy, Steve Hytner, Glenn Danzig; **D:** Greg Spence; **W:** Greg Spence, Matt Greenberg; **C:** Richard Clabaugh; **M:** David Williams. **VIDEO**

The Prophecy 3: The Ascent ♂♂ 1999 (R) Half-human/half-angel Danyael (Buzzotta) has grown up to be an anti-religious street preacher and is out to destroy new angel, Pyriel (Cleverdon). This doesn't sit well with angel Zophael (Spano) who decides to stop him. Walken seems to be having the most fun as he once again appears as Gabriel, who's become content in his mortal guise and with human pleasure. **83m/C VHS, DVD.** Christopher Walken, Vincent Spano, Brad Dourif, Dave Buzzotta, Steve Hytner, Scott Cleverdon, Kayren Ann Butler; **D:** Patrick Lussier; **W:** Joel Soisson, Carl DuPre; **C:** Nathan Hope. **VIDEO**

The Prophet's Game ♂♂ 1999 (R) Retired Seattle detective Vincent Swan (Hopper) gets a message from the Prophet, a serial killer that Swan supposedly killed years before. Then new victims turn up in L.A., killed in the Prophet's distinctive manner. So Swan heads south to help with the investigation and figure out is he dealing with a copycat—or did he just kill the wrong man? **107m/C VHS, DVD.** Dennis Hopper, Geoffrey Lewis, Stephanie Zimbalist, Joe Penny, Greg Lauren, Shannon Whirry, Michael Dorn, Don Swayze, Robert Ginty, Sondra Locke; **D:** David Worth; **W:** Carol Chrest; **C:** David Worth. **VIDEO**

The Proposal ♂♂½ 2000 (R) Morgan is an undercover cop who's forced to take on partner Esposito, who has no such experience, because he needs someone to pose as his wife in order to trap crime boss Lang. Only Esposito and Lang are starting to get a little too friendly, so Moran wonders how much she can be trusted. **90m/C VHS, DVD.** Nick Moran, Jennifer Esposito, Stephen Lang, William B. Davis; **D:** Richard Gale; **W:** Maurice Hurley; **C:** Curtis Petersen; **M:** Joseph Conlan.

The Proposition ♂♂½ 1996 (R) Unless widow Catherine Morgan (Russell) can find the money to pay her late husband's gambling debts, she and her two

daughters will be evicted from their Welsh farm. She refuses to take the easy way and marry local sheriff Huw (Lynch), instead making a bargain with his rakish, drunken bastard brother Rhys (Bergin) to drive her cattle to Gloucester market. Huw takes exception to this plan and tries every dirty trick he can to thwart them and naturally, Catherine and Rhys become more than antagonistic allies along the rough journey. **99m/C VHS, DVD.** Theresa Russell, Patrick Bergin, Richard Lynch, Nick Harrington, Jennifer Vaughan, Ian Huw Dafydd, Nick McGaughey, Owen Garmon; **D:** Strathford Hamilton; **W:** Paul Matthews; **C:** David Lewis; **M:** Ben Heneghan, Ian Lawson.

The Proposition ♂♂ *Tempting Fate: Shakespeare's Sister* 1997 (R) Convoluted and clunky story centering on wealthy-but-sterile Boston industrialist Hurt and his feminist writer wife Stowe, who decide to hire a surrogate (Harris) to get Stowe pregnant. But faltering priest Branagh, whom the couple consult, has some concerns. After the surrogate is murdered, the melodrama starts to fly and the movie plays out like a daytime soap opera, complete with dirty little secrets and earth-shaking revelations dropped with the subtlety usually reserved for an anvil on Wile E. Coyote. Hurt and Stowe give their characters a little fire, but everybody else seems to be wandering around on their own little acting planet. **115m/C VHS, DVD.** Pamela Hart, Kenneth Branagh, William Hurt, Madeleine Stowe, Blythe Danner, Neil Patrick Harris, Robert Loggia, Josef Sommer, David Byrd; **D:** Leslie Linka Glatter; **W:** Rick Ramage; **C:** Peter Sova; **M:** Stephen Endelman.

The Proposition ♂♂ 2005 (R) Brutal Aussie western set in the outback in the 1880s. Capt. Stanley (Winstone) is obsessed with bringing law to his patch of dirt, which means getting rid of the Burns brothers and their gang. He gets a break when he captures Charlie Burns (Pearce) and his younger brother, Mikey (Wilson). Stanley offers Charlie a devil's bargain—he will spare both brothers if Charlie will track and kill vicious older brother Arthur (a poetically psychotic Huston). Charlie has no choice but to agree but all that can be expected is more violence, blood, and death. **104m/C DVD. AU GB** Guy Pearce, Ray Winstone, Emily Watson, Danny Huston, John Hurt, David Wenham, Noah Taylor, David Gulpill, Leah Purcell, Tommy (Tom E.) Lewis, Richard Wilson; **D:** John Hillcoat; **W:** Nick Cave; **C:** Benoit Delhomme; **M:** Warren Ellis.

The Proprietor ♂♂ 1996 (R) Thinly disguised as a returning-to-your-roots and facing-your-ghosts drama, film is actually a celluloid French film and a current American remake, Mark's primary struggle to come to grips with her mother's death is overshadowed by a bevy of subplots that compete with one another. Young as a sassy and somewhat stereotypical Hollywood producer; Carter as Milly the loyal housekeeper; Waterston, an antique dealer; and Billy, NYC video artist and adoring Mark fan, all add to the confusion. Moreau tries her best to give life to the saintly lead figure, but the coma-inducing sugar level of her character's goodness is overwhelming. Director Merchant's sophomore effort, though well-acted, is a good idea, poorly told. **105m/C VHS,** Jeanne Moreau, Sean Young, Sam Waterston, Nell Carter, Austin Pendleton, Pierre Vaneck, Josh Hamilton, Marc Tissot; **D:** Ismail Merchant; **W:** Jean-Marie Besset, George Trow; **C:** Larry Pizer; **M:** Richard Robbins.

Pros & Cons ♂♂ 1999 (R) Opposites help each other out as new cellmates Davidson and Miller (both doing time for crimes they didn't commit) bumble their way into the good graces of convict kingpin Lindo. **103m/C VHS, DVD.** Larry Miller, Tommy Davidson, Delroy Lindo; **D:** Boris Damast; **W:**

Larry Miller. **C:** Jonathan Brown; **M:** Michel Colombier.

Prospero's Books 1991 (R) Greenaway's free-ranging adaptation of Shakespeare's "The Tempest" has all his usual hallmarks of the bizarre. Gielgud is the aged Prospero, exiled to a magical island with his innocent daughter Miranda and 24 beloved books containing the magician's recipe for life, each of which becomes a separate chapter in the film. Greenaway mixes film and high-definition video to create, with cinematographer Sacha Vierny, dazzling visuals that threaten to overwhelm but don't quite, thanks to both Greenaway's skill and the astonishing performance of the then 87-year-old Gielgud. 129m/C VHS, DVD. John Gielgud, Isabelle Pasco, Tom Bell, Kenneth Cranham, Michael Clark, Mark Rylance; **D:** Peter Greenaway; **W:** Peter Greenaway; **C:** Sacha Vierny; **M:** Michael Nyman.

Protecting the King 2007 When he was four, David Stanley's mother married widower Vernon Presley and the boy became Elvis's (Dobson) stepbrother. In 1972, David (Barr) began working as the singer's bodyguard until Presley's death five years later. In this biographical take, David witnesses the King's ever-increasing drug use and watches hopelessly as the singer's life spirals downward. 90m/C DVD. Peter Dobson, John Barr, Max Perlich, Mark Rolston, Jey Young; **D:** David Edward Stanley; **W:** David Edward Stanley; **M:** Joe Cruz.

Protection 2001 (R) Mobster Sal (Baldwin) and his family are relocated into the witness protection program and Sal gets a job with real estate broker Ted (Gallagher), who's putting together a low-income housing project. But Sal can't resist using his past and brings in local crime boss Lujack (Tager) to finance the deal. 97m/C VHS, DVD. Stephen Baldwin, Peter Gallagher, Kate Griffin, Deborah Odell, Vlasta Vrana, Aron Tager; **D:** John Flynn; **M:** Marc Charlebois. VIDEO

Protector 1985 (R) A semi-martial arts cops 'n' robbers epic about the cracking of a Hong Kong-New York heroin route. 94m/C VHS, DVD. Jackie Chan, Danny Aiello; **D:** James Glickenhaus.

Protector 1999 (R) Undercover cop Jack Valentine (Van Peebles) is supposed to be protecting a witness, but winds up being murdered. The cop is given 10 days to solve the crime or lose his badge. 97m/C VHS, DVD. Mario Van Peebles, Randy Quaid, Rae Dawn Chong, Ben Gazzara; **D:** Duane Clark. VIDEO

Proteus 1995 (R) Survivors of a boat wreck wash up on an off-shore oil rig that's actually a secret lab financed by looney millionaire Brinkstone (Bradley), who's seeking immortality. His DNA experiments have led to the creation of a disgusting parasite that travels from body to body. Naturally, the boat survivors also seek to survive this latest health threat. Based on the novel "Slimer" by Harry Adam Knight. 97m/C VHS. GB Doug Bradley, Craig Fairbrass, Toni Barry; **D:** Bob Keen.

Protocol 1984 (PG) A series of comic accidents lead a Washington cocktail waitress into the U.S. State Department's employ as a protocol official. Once there she is used as a pawn to make an arms deal with a Middle Eastern country. Typical Hawn comedy, with an enjoyable ending. 100m/C VHS, DVD. Goldie Hawn, Chris Sarandon, Andre Gregory, Cliff DeYoung, Ed Begley Jr., Gail Strickland, Richard Romanus, Keith Szarabajka, James Staley, Kenneth Mars, Kenneth McMillan, Archie Hahn, Amanda Bearse; **D:** Herbert Ross; **W:** Nancy Meyers, Harvey Miller, Charles Shyer, Buck Henry; **C:** William A. Fraker; **M:** Basil Poledouris.

Protocols of Zion 2005 Filmmaker Levin structures his documentary around "The Protocols of the Elders of Zion", a 19th-century screed that purports to reveal a Jewish plan to rule the world. Although exposed as a forgery (written by aides to the Russian czar to foment anti-Semitism), extremists of all own agendas, Levin examines recent examples of anti-Semitic propaganda, including the ridiculous belief that Jews were behind 9/11, and quizzes a wide variety of interviewees from skinheads to Holocaust survivors. 92m/C DVD, US **D:** Marc Levin; **C:** Mark Benjamin; **M:** John Zorn.

Prototype 1983 TV revision of the Frankenstein legend has award-winning scientist Plummer as the creator of the first android. Fearful of the use the military branch of government has in mind for his creation, he attempts to steal back his discovery, in this suspenseful adventure. 100m/C VHS, DVD. Christopher Plummer, David Morse, Frances Sternhagen, James Sutorius; **D:** David Greene; **M:** Billy Goldenberg. TV

Prototype X29A 1992 (R) The year is 2057 in a desolate, lawless Los Angeles. A research scientist is conducting experiments on a crippled ex-soldier named Hawkins when they suddenly go awry, turning him into a half-man, half-machine robot. Known as Prototype, the creature goes on a hunting and killing spree. Lame "Terminator" & "Robocop" takeoff. 98m/C VHS. Brenda Swanson, Robert Tossberg, Lane Lenhart; **D:** Phillip J. Roth; **W:** Phillip J. Roth.

The Proud and the Damned *Proud, Damned, and Dead* 1972 (PG) Five Civil-War-veteran mercenaries wander into a Latin American war.

The Proud Family Movie 2005 (G) The Disney Channel's original television series featuring an animated African American family gets a feature-length storyline. Teenager Penny Proud's parents treat her like a kid, banning her from dancing in a hip-hop half time show and dragging her off to a tropical island for a family vacation. The family finds themselves in trouble when their "vacation" turns out to be an excuse for the evil Dr. Carver to get his hands on dad's hot sauce recipe. Hijinx abound as Penny saves the recipe-and the day. Short enough to sit through with most pre-teens. 95m/C VHS, DVD. **D:** Bruce Smith; **W:** Calvin Brown Jr.; **M:** Elik Alvarez; **V:** Kyla Pratt, Tommy Davidson, Paula Jai Parker, Soleil Moon Frye, Omari (Omarion) Grandberry, Arsenio Hall, Orlando Brown, Jo Maria Payton. CABLE

Proud Men 1987 A cattle rancher and his excariate son are separated by bitterness toward each other. Good acting from Heston and Strauss, and good action sequences, but ordinary script. 95m/C VHS. Charlton Heston, Peter Strauss, Nan Martin, Alan Autry, Belinda Balaski, Red West; **D:** William A. Graham.

The Proud Ones *Les Orgueilleux* 1953 An aristocratic French woman and her husband are traveling through Mexico when he suddenly dies of a mysterious illness. Left penniless in a decaying seaside town, she falls for the local doctor who is mourning the death of his wife. Adaptation of the Satre novel "L'Amour Redempteur." In French with English subtitles. 105m/B VHS. FR Gerard Philipe, Michele Morgan, Victor Manuel Mendoza; **D:** Yves Allegret.

The Proud Ones 1958 A character study of a stubborn widower who searches for a doctor to aid him in dealing with the problems of his mute son, and of the woman who helps to tame the boy. Ladd's real-life son makes his acting debut. 99m/C VHS, DVD. Alan Ladd, Olivia de Havilland, Dean Jagger, Harry Dean Stanton; **D:** Michael Curtiz; **W:** Lillie Hayward, Joseph Petracca; **C:** Ted D. McCord; **M:** Jerome Moross.

Proud Rebel 1958 A character study of a stubborn widower...

Providence 1977 (R) An interesting drama of a dying writer envisioning his final novel as a fusion of the people from his past on a daily basis. The first English-language effort by French director Resnais. 104m/C VHS. GB John Gielgud, Dirk Bogarde, Ellen Burstyn, David Warner, Elaine Stritch; **D:** Alain Resnais; **W:** David Mercer; **C:** Ricardo Aronovich; Dir/Set Dec., Director (Resnais), Film, Sound.

Prozac Nation 2001 (R) Drama based on Elizabeth Wurtzel's (c) memoir of her depression, drug, and booze fueled college breakdown, which led her to seek the help of therapist Dr. Sterling (Heche). Unfocused script detracts from fine performance by Ricci, Williams and Biggs. 99m/C DVD. Christina Ricci, Jason Biggs, Anne Heche, Jonathan Rhys Meyers, Jessica Lange, Nicholas (Nick) Campbell, Emily Perkins; **D:** Erik Skjoldbjaerg; **W:** Frank Deasy; **C:** Erling Thurmann-Andersen; **M:** Nathan Larson.

Proximity 2000 (R) William Conroy (Lowe) gets prison time for vehicular manslaughter and learns that the big house is hazardous to his health. Seems the inmates have a bad habit of getting killed and Conroy is next when he learns too much about what's going on. Conroy manages to escape and seeks help to expose the whole sleazy situation. Unfortunately, the movie is really dopey and dull. 96m/C VHS, DVD. Rob Lowe, James Coburn, Kelly Rowan, Seana A. Avakian; **D:** Scott Ziehl; **W:** Ben Queen, Seamus Ruane; **M:** Stephen Cullo.

P.S. 2004 (R) Linney is a treasure but the same can't be said about this film, which is based on co-screenwriter Schulman's novel, "P.S. I Love You." Louise (Linney) is a quiet divorcee who works as a Columbia University admissions officer. She's intrigued by a young grad school applicant who bears the same name, F. Scott Feinstadt, as her lost first love. The young man (a game Grace) is bewildered but flattered by this attractive, lonely woman's attentions. F. Scott is basically a cipher, since it's Louise's emotional baggage we're supposed to be interested in, and she's got a lot of it (dysfunctional family, sex addict ex, back-biting best friend). Unfortunately, neither the movie nor the viewer can really handle all that weight without buckling. 97m/C DVD. US Laura Linney, Topher Grace, Paul Rudd, Lois Smith, Gabriel Byrne, Marcia Gay Harden; **D:** Dylan Kidd; **W:** Dylan Kidd, Helen Schulman; **C:** Joaquin Baca-Asay; **M:** Craig (Shudder to Think) Wedren.

P.S. I Love You 2007 (PG-13) In this painfully sappy romantic drama, happily marrieds Holly (Swank) and Gerry (Butler) soon aren't so happy when Gerry had enough time to plot out his widow's life for the next year—sending her a series of letters with various instructions to, you know, get out there and live! Kudrow and Gershon are gal pals while Connick and Morgan are potential new romances. Swank is game but Butler locked a lot more comfortable in leather and muscles in "300." 126m/C DVD. US Hilary Swank, Gerard Butler, Lisa Kudrow, Gina Gershon, Harry Connick Jr., Jeffrey Dean Morgan, Kathy Bates, James Marsters; **D:** Richard LaGravenese; **W:** Richard LaGravenese, Steven Rogers; **C:** Terry Stacey; **M:** John Powell.

P.S. Your Cat is Dead! 2002 (R) A moldy oldie. James Kirkwood's 1975 off-Broadway play was based on his 1972 novel and its attitudes towards gays appear quaint at best if not outright insulting. Jimmy Zoole (Guttenberg) is a failed actor/writer with a dead cat and a girlfriend, Kate (Watros), who's just dumped him. This leaves Jimmy alone in his L.A. apartment on New Year's Eve. Except for gay burglar Eddie (Boyar), who has the misfortune to be caught by a distraught Jimmy, who takes his gun and ties the men face down on a kitchen counter. Eddie proceeds to taunt Jimmy about his manhood, various humiliating things happen, and somehow male bonding occurs. 92m/C VHS, DVD. Steve Guttenberg, Lombardo Boyar, Cynthia Watros, Shirley Knight, Tom Wright, A.J. Benza; **D:** Steve Guttenberg; **W:** Steve Guttenberg, Jeff Korn; **C:** David Armstrong; **M:** Dean Grimsfelder.

Provincial Actors 1979 Ambitious Christopher is the leading actor of a rural theatre troupe, who dreams of moving to the city and becoming a star. But his wife Anna is fed up with his dreams and leaves him and Christopher must make a choice between his career and his marriage. Polish with subtitles. 104m/C VHS. PL Tadeysz Huk, Halina Labonaska, Ewa Dalkowska, Jerzy Stuhr; **D:** Agnieszka Holland.

Provocateur 1996 (R) Story revolves around the 1994 power struggle in North Korea. Spy Sook Hee (March) with close ties to dictator Kim Il Sung, takes a job as a nanny in South Korea in order to get access to sensitive info from her boss, a U.S. colonel. But her loyalties are torn when she befriends the colonel's teenaged son Chris (Brancato). When her true identity is revealed, there's trouble for all. 104m/C VHS. Jane March, Nick Mancuso, Lilo Brancato, Gary Hiroyuki Tagawa; **D:** Jim Donovan.

Provoked 1989 What would you do if your husband were being held hostage by a gang of ruthless, but stupid, escaped cons? Well, Maranne actually wants her husband back (maybe 'cause they're newlyweds) and no by-the-book police chief (Jones) is gonna stop her. 90m/C VHS. Cindy Maranne, McKeiver Jones III, Harold W. Jones, Sharon Blair, Bob Fail, Joe Sprosty, Phyllis Durant, Tera Unitedi; **D:** Rick Pamplin; **W:** Tara Steve Pake.

Prowler 1951 Heflin is a cop who responds to a prowler scare and finds the beautiful married Keyes worried about an intruder. He learns she will inherit a lot of money if anything happens to her husband so he seduces her and then "accidentally" kills her husband, supposedly mistaking him for a prowler. Keyes then marries Heflin but when she learns the truth her own life is in danger. Tidy thriller with Heflin doing a good job as the unpredictable villain. 92m/B VHS. Van Heflin, Evelyn Keyes, Katherine Warren, John Maxwell, Emerson Treacy, Madge Blake, Wheaton Chambers, Sherry Hall, Robert Osterloh, Matt Dorff; **D:** Joseph Losey; **W:** Hugo Butler, Dalton Trumbo; **C:** Arthur C. Miller; **M:** Lyn Murray.

The Prowler 1981 A soldier returns from duty curing WWII, only to find his girl in bed with another guy. He kills them, and for unclear reasons, returns to the same town 35 years later to kill more people. An effects-fest for Tom Savini. 87m/C VHS, DVD. Vicky Dawson, Christopher Goutman, Cindy Weintraub, Farley Granger, John Seitz, Lawrence Tierney; **D:** Joseph Zito; **W:** Neal Barbera; **M:** Richard Einhorn.

PSI Factor 1980 A civilian researcher working at the NASA space track station observes and records signals coming from planet Sirius B. 91m/C VHS. Peter Mark Richman, Gretchen Corbett, Tommy Martin; **D:** Bryan Trizers; **W:** Quentin Masters.

Psych-Out 1968 A deaf girl searches Haight-Ashbury for her runaway brother. She meets hippies and flower children during the Summer of Love. Psychedelic score with Strawberry Alarm Clock and The Seeds. Somewhere in this picture, Nicholson whangs on lead guitar. 95m/C VHS, DVD. Jack Nicholson, Bruce Dern, Susan Strasberg, Dean Stockwell, Henry Jaglom; **D:** Richard Rush; **W:** Richard Rush.

The Psychic 1978 (R) A psychic envisions her own death and attempts to alter the prediction. 90m/C VHS. Jennifer O'Neill, Marc Porel, Evelyn Stewart, Gabriele Ferzetti, Gianni "John" Garko; **D:** Lucio Fulci.

Psychic 1991 (R) A college student with psychic powers believes he knows who the next victim is; no one will believe him. And the victim is the woman he loves. 92m/C VHS. Michael Nouri, Catherine Mary Stewart, Zach Galligan; **D:** George

The Psychic woof! *Copenhagen's Psychic Loves* 1968 An ad executive gains psychic powers after he falls off a ladder and tries to conquer the world. A later effort by gore-king Lewis, notable only for sex scenes inserted by Lewis to make the movie salable. 90m/C VHS. Dick Genola, Robin Guest, Bobbi Spencer, Carol Saenz, Sandra Wolsfeld; **D:** Herschell Gordon Lewis, James F. Hurley; **C:** Herschell Gordon Lewis; **M:** Vincent Oddo.

persuasions still use the material to their Writing; Score; N.Y. Film Critics '77; Actor (Gielgud).

Mihalka; **W:** Paul Koval; **C:** Ludek Bogner; **M:** Milan Kymlicka.

Psychic ⚐⚐⚐ 1975 (PG) A wrongfully committed asylum inmate acquires psychic powers and decides to use them in a deadly revenge. Good cast in cheapie horror flick. **89m/C VHS, DVD.** Jim Hutton, Paul Burke, Julie Adams, Neville Brand, Aldo Ray, Rod Cameron, Della Reese; **D:** Ray Danton; **W:** Ray Danton, Mikel Angel, Greydon Clark; **C:** Herb Pearl; **M:** William Craft.

Psycho ⚐⚐⚐⚐ 1960 Hitchcock counted on his directorial stature and broke all the rules in this story of violent murder, transvestism, and insanity. Based on Robert Bloch's novelization of an actual murder, Leigh plays a fleeing thief who stops at the secluded Bates Motel where she meets her death in Hitchcock's classic "shower scene." Shot on a limited budget in little more than a month, "Psycho" changed the Hollywood horror film forever. Followed by "Psycho 2" (1983), "Psycho 3" (1986), "Psycho 4: The Beginning" (1990), and a TV movie. **109m/B VHS, DVD.** Anthony Perkins, Janet Leigh, Vera Miles, John Gavin, John McIntire, Martin Balsam, Simon Oakland, Ted (Edward) Knight, John Anderson, Frank Albertson, Patricia Hitchcock, Alfred Hitchcock; **D:** Alfred Hitchcock; **W:** Joseph Stefano; **C:** John L. "Jack" Russell; **M:** Bernard Herrmann; **V:** Virginia Gregg, Jeanette Nolan. AFI '98: Top 100; Golden Globes '61: Support. Actress (Leigh). Natl. Film Reg. '92.

Psycho 2 ⚐⚐½ 1983 (R) Since Hitchcock's "Psycho" is one of the most famous movies of all time, it would seem redundant to summarize the plot here. Although, redundant is a fitting description of Gus Van Sant's shot-for-shot recreation. Wisely, Van Sant doesn't meddle with a good thing. On the other hand, ya pretty much have to ask, "what's the point?" Significant to the success of the original was it that it pushed the envelope in 1960. (A shot of a toilet flushing! A woman taking a shower! Blasphemy!) But by today's standards, "Psycho" is utterly tame. Performances are excellent all around. As talented as Vaughn is, however, the inevitable comparison between him and Anthony Perkins reveals that Vaughn is just too cool for this role. Perkins' Norman Bates was geeky and frail, Vaughn just isn't. As the saying goes, "if it ain't broke, don't fix it." **106m/C VHS, DVD.** Vince Vaughn, Anne Heche, Julianne Moore, William H. Macy, Viggo Mortensen, Robert Forster, Philip Baker Hall, Anne Haney, James Remar, James LeGros; **D:** Gus Van Sant; **W:** Joseph Stefano; **C:** Christopher Doyle. Golden Raspberries '98: Worst Remake/Sequel, Worst Director (Van Sant).

Psycho 2 ⚐⚐ 1983 (R) This sequel to the Hitchcock classic finds Norman Bates returning home after 22 years in an asylum to find himself haunted by "mother" and caught up in a series of murders. In a surprisingly good horror film, Perkins and Miles reprise their roles from the original "Psycho." Perkins went on to direct yet another sequel, "Psycho 3." **113m/C VHS, DVD.** Claudia Bryar, Oz (Osgood) Perkins II, Anthony Perkins, Vera Miles, Meg Tilly, Robert Loggia, Dennis Franz; **D:** Richard Franklin; **W:** Tom Holland; **C:** Dean Cundey; **M:** Jerry Goldsmith.

Psycho 3 ⚐⚐ 1986 (R) The second sequel to Hitchcock's "Psycho" finds Norman Bates drawn into his past by "mother" and the appearance of a woman who reminds him of his original victim. Perkins made his directorial debut in this film that stretches the plausibility of the storyline to its limits, but the element of parody throughout makes this an entertaining film for "Psycho" fans. **93m/C VHS, DVD.** Anthony Perkins, Diana Scarwid, Jeff Fahey, Roberta Maxwell, Robert Alan Browne, Hugh Gillin, Lee Garlington; **D:** Anthony Perkins; **W:** Charles Edward Pogue; **C:** Bruce Surtees; **M:** Carter Burwell.

Psycho 4: The Beginning ⚐⚐ 1990 (R) Prequels "Psycho" when, at the behest of a radio talk show host, Norman Bates recounts his childhood and reveals the circumstances that aided in the development of his peculiar neuroses. Stefano wrote the original screenplay and the original score is used, but this doesn't even come close to the original. **96m/C VHS.** An-

thony Perkins, Henry Thomas, Olivia Hussey, CCH Pounder, Warren Frost, Donna Mitchell; **D:** Mick Garris; **W:** Joseph Stefano; **C:** Rodney Charters; **M:** Graeme Revell.

Psycho Beach Party ⚐⚐½ 2000 Busch adapted his own play—a spoof of 60s teen beach movies and psycho/thrillers. Perky teen tomboy Florence (Ambrose) desperately wants to fit into her SoCal ocean lifestyle by becoming the first female accepted into the local surfers who are led by hipster Kanaka (Gibson). The newly christened "Chicklet" has a dark side, however, a separate sultry personality named Anne that she fears is responsible for a series of murders that are thinning out the teen population. Busch plays the investigating officer, and former Kanaka girlfriend, Capt. Monica Stark. **95m/C VHS, DVD.** Lauren Ambrose, Thomas Gibson, Nicholas Brendon, Charles Busch, Kimberly Davies, Matt Keeslar, Nathan Bexton, Buddy Quaid, Beth Broderick, Amy Adams, Danni Wheeler, Kathleen Robertson; **D:** Robert Lee King; **W:** Charles Busch; **C:** Arturo Smith; **M:** Ben Vaughn.

Psycho Cop ⚐½ 1988 Six college undergrads on a weekend retreat are menaced and picked off one at a time by a crazed local cop. **89m/C VHS.** Robert (Bobby Ray) Shafer, Barbara Niven, Rod Sweitzer, Julie Strain; **D:** Wallace Potts.

Psycho Cop 2 ⚐½ 1994 (R) Four buddies plan a raunchy bachelor party, commandeering the company conference room for an after-hours orgy. Only Psycho Cop is on their case. Gore. Rifkin used the pseudonym Rif Coogan. **80m/C VHS, DVD.** Robert (Bobby Ray) Shafer, Barbara Lee (Niven) Alexander, Julie Strain; **D:** Adam Rifkin.

Psycho from Texas ⚐ *The Butcher* 1981 (R) Quiet Southern town is disrupted by the kidnapping of a wealthy oil man, followed by a string of meaningless murders. **85m/C VHS.** John King III, Candy Dee, Janel King, Herschel Mays; **D:** Jim Feazell, Jack Collins; **C:** Paul Hipp; **M:** Jaime Mendoza-Nava.

Psycho Girls ⚐ 1986 (R) Very low budget horror flick redeemed by spurts of weird black humor. Crazed woman is released from institution to seek out sister who should have been put away in the first place. She crashes anniversary celebration and, well, let's just say she's not the life of the party. Never released theatrically. **87m/C VHS.** CA John Haslett Cuff, Darlene Mignacco, Agi Gallus, Rose Graham, Silvio Oliviero, Michael Hoole, Pier Giorgia DiCicco, Femme Kane; **D:** Gerard Ciccoritti; **W:** Gerard Ciccoritti; Michael Boekner.

Psycho Sisters ⚐⚐½ 1998 As children, Jackie (North) and Jane (Lynn) witness shocking events that traumatize them into the titular killers. Actually, after seeing so many young women pursued by homicidal maniacs, it's nice that a couple of them get to turn the tables. This low-budget horror has developed a strong cult following. **90m/C DVD.** J.J. North, Theresa Lynn; **D:** Pete Jacelone; **W:** Pete Jacelone, James L. Edwards; **C:** Timothy Healy.

Psychomania ⚐½ *Violent Midnight* 1963 Semi-limpid mystery thriller about a former war hero and painter who is suspected of being the demented killer stalking girls on campus. To prove his innocence, he tracks the killer himself. **95m/C VHS, DVD.** Lee Philips, Shepperd Strudwick, Jean Hale, Dick Van Patten, Sylvia Miles, James Farentino; **D:** Richard Hilliard.

Psychomania ⚐⚐ *The Death Wheelers* 1973 (R) A drama of the supernatural, the occult, and the violence which lies just beyond the conventions of society for a group of dead motorcyclists, the Living Dead, who all came back to life after committing suicide with the help of the devil. **89m/C VHS, DVD.** GB George Sanders, Beryl Reid, Nicky Henson, Mary Laroche, Patrick Holt; **D:** Don Sharp; **W:** Arnaud d'Usseau; **C:** Ted Moore.

Psychopath ⚐½ 1968 A film about a modern-day, slightly unhinged, Robin Hood and his escapades, stealing from other thieves and giving to the victimized. **90m/C VHS.** GB Klaus Kinski, George Martin, Ingrid Schoeller; **D:** Guido Zurli.

Psychopath ⚐ *An Eye for an Eye* 1973 (PG) A nutso children's TV personality begins to murder abusive parents. Fairly gory, and definitely not for family viewing. **85m/C VHS.** Tom Basham, Gene Carlson, Gretchen Kanne; **D:** Larry G. Brown; **W:** John Williams.

Psychopath ⚐⚐½ 1997 (R) D.A. Rachel Dwyer (Amick) needs the help of serial killer Lennox (Mulkey), who targets female law students, in solving another crime. Low on the histrionics and high on the courtroom drama as well as being well-acted. **95m/C VHS, DVD.** Madchen Amick, Chris Mulkey, Bruce Dinsmore, Don Jordan, Lynne Adams, Cas Anvar, Tara Slone, James Bradford; **D:** Max Fischer; **W:** Cameron Kent, William Lee; **C:** Guy Kinkead; **M:** Normand Corbeil. **CABLE**

Psychos in Love WOOF! 1987 A psychotic murderer who hates grapes of any kind finds the woman of his dreams—she's a psychotic murderer who hates grapes! Together they find bliss—until the plumber discovers their secret **90m/C VHS.** Carmine Capobianco, Debi Thibeault, Frank Stewart; **D:** Gorman Bechard.

The Psychotronic Man ⚐½ 1991 An innocent man suddenly finds he possesses amazing and dangerous powers, enabling him to control outside events with a thought. **88m/C VHS.** Peter Spelson, Christopher Carbis, Curt Colbert, Robin Newton, Paul Marvel; **D:** Jack M. Sell.

PT 109 ⚐⚐ 1963 The WWII exploits of Lieutenant (j.g.) John F. Kennedy in the South Pacific. Part of the "A Night at the Movies" series, this tape simulates a 1963 movie evening, with a Foghorn Leghorn cartoon ("Banty Raids"), a newsreel on the JFK assassination, and coming attractions for "Critic's Choice" and "Four for Texas." **159m/C VHS.** Cliff Robertson, Ty Hardin, Ty Hardin, Robert (Bobby) Blake, Robert Culp, James Gregory; **D:** Leslie Martinson.

P.T. Barnum ⚐⚐½ 1999 Bio of Phineas Taylor Barnum (Beau Bridges) and his development of "The Greatest Show on Earth." A shopkeeper from Connecticut, P.T. was determined to make his fortune in New York, eventually purchasing Scudder's American Museum and its exhibits, which he turned into a traveling big top event, thanks to his promotional skills. Barnum's zest for work, however, made for a less than happy home life. Beau's son Jordan plays the young Barnum. Filmed in Montreal and Vancouver, Canada. **138m/C VHS, DVD.** Beau Bridges, George Hamilton, Henry Czerny, Charles Martin Smith, Josh Ryan Evans, R.H. Thomson, Stephanie Morgenstern, Isabelle Cyr, Michelle-Barbara Pelletier, Victoria Sanchez; **D:** Simon Wincer; **W:** Lionel Chetwynd; **C:** Pierre Mignot. **CABLE**

Pterodactyl Woman from Beverly Hills ⚐½ 1997 (R) California housewife Pixie Chandler (D'Angelo) is the victim of an eccentric witch doctor (James) when her paleontologist husband Dick (Wilson) disturbs an ancient burial site and the doc curses Pixie by turning her into a dinosaur. This is the first so-called family release from those madcap Troma people who brought you the Toxic Avenger. **97m/C VHS, DVD.** Beverly D'Angelo, Brion James, Brad Wilson, Moon Zappa, Aron Eisenberg; **D:** Philippe Mora; **W:** Philippe Mora; **C:** Walter Bal; **M:** Roy Hay.

PU-239 ⚐⚐½ *The Half Life of Timofey Berezin* 2006 Nuclear plant worker Timofey Berezin (Considine) is dosed with a lethal amount of radiation and becomes the victim of an administrative cover-up. To provide for his family, Timofey steals a tube of plutonium and turns to unstable Moscow gangster Shiv (Isaac) to help him sell it on the black market. But Shiv's general ineptitude just gets them into trouble with mob boss Starkov (Berkoff). Set in 1995. **107m/C DVD.** GB Paddy Considine, Radha Mitchell, Oscar Isaac, Jason Flemyng, Steven Berkhoff, Nikolaj Lie Kaas, Michael Fisher; **D:** Scott Burns; **W:** Scott Burns; **C:** Eigil Bryld; **M:** Abel Korzeniowski.

Puberty Blues ⚐½ 1981 (R) Two Australian girls become part of the local surfing scene in order to be accepted by the "in crowd" at their high school. **86m/**

C VHS. AU Neil Schofield, Jad Capelja; **D:** Bruce Beresford.

Public Access ⚐⚐ 1993 (R) Newcomer Whiley Pritcher (Marquette) manages to cause trouble in the small town of Brewster when he begins broadcasting a call-in program over a public-access cable station that encourages complaining about the town's problems. Skeletons start falling out of closets, leading to unexpected tragedy. Feature-film directorial debut of Singer. **90m/C VHS, DVD.** Ron Marquette, Dina Brooks, Burt Williams, Charles Kavanaugh, Larry Maxwell, Brandon Boyce; **D:** Bryan Singer; **W:** Bryan Singer, Christopher McQuarrie, Michael Feit Dougan; **C:** Bruce Douglas Johnson; **M:** John Ottman. Sundance '93: Grand Jury Prize.

A Public Affair ⚐⚐½ 1962 Exposes the evils and abuses of collection agencies without even a shred of humor. Certainly gets its point across, but will bore any audience to tears or spontaneous naps. **71m/B VHS.** Myron McCormick, Edward Binns, Harry Carey Jr.; **D:** Bernard Girard; **W:** Bernard Girard; **C:** Howard Schwartz; **M:** Joe "Mean Joe" Greene.

Public Cowboy No. 1 ⚐½ 1937 Cattle thieves use a radio, airplanes, and refrigerator trucks in their updated rustling schemes. **54m/B VHS, DVD.** Gene Autry, William Farnum, Smiley Burnette, Ann Rutherford, Arthur Loft, House Peters Jr.; **D:** Joseph Kane; **W:** Oliver Drake; **C:** Jack Marta.

Public Enemies ⚐⚐½ 1996 (R) It's nefarious Ma Barker (Russell) and her boys on a '30s crime spree that gets even bigger when they hook up with criminal Alvin Karpis (Stallone). But when Ma's lover Arthur (Roberts) dreams up a kidnapping plot, it's a fast road to ruin. **95m/C VHS.** Theresa Russell, Eric Roberts, Frank Stallone, Alyssa Milano, Joseph Lindsey, Richard Eden, James Marsden, Dan Cortese; **D:** Mark L. Lester; **W:** C. Courtney Joyner; **M:** Christopher Franke.

Public Enemy ⚐⚐⚐ ½ 1931 *Enemies of the Public* Cagney's acting career was launched by this story of two Irish boys growing up in a Chicago shantytown to become hoodlums during the prohibition era. Tom (Cagney) and Matt (Woods) work their way up the criminal ladder, hooking up with molls Kitty (Clarke) and Mamie (Blondell) on their rise to the top. Harlow's a tough blonde who knows how to handle Cagney when he gets tired of Clarke. Considered the most realistic "gangster" film, Wellman's movie is also the most grimly brutal due to its release prior to Hollywood censorship. The scene where Cagney smashes a grapefruit in Clarke's face was credited with starting a trend in abusing film heroines. **85m/B VHS, DVD.** James Cagney, Edward (Eddie) Woods, Leslie Fenton, Joan Blondell, Mae Clarke, Jean Harlow, Donald Cook, Beryl Mercer; **D:** William A. Wellman; **W:** Harvey Thew, John Bright, Kubec Glasmon; **C:** Devereaux Jennings. Natl. Film Reg. '98.

The Public Eye ⚐⚐½ 1992 (R) Underappreciated film noir homage casts Pesci as a crime photographer with an unsuspected romantic streak. It's 1942 in NYC and cynical freelancer Leon "Bernzy" Bernstein's always looking for the perfect shot. Hershey's the recent widow whose nightclub-owner husband had mob ties and perhaps Pesci would be a likely patsy for helping her out. Hershey seems quite develops, but Pesci delivers a rich, low-key performance as the visionary, hard-boiled artist. Climatic mob shootout is cinematic bullet ballet. Based loosely on the career of '40s photog Weegee, who defined New York and its times in his work. **98m/C VHS.** Joe Pesci, Barbara Hershey, Stanley Tucci, Richard Foronjy, Richard Riehle, Jared Harris, Jerry Adler, Dominic Chianese, Gerry Becker; **D:** Howard Franklin; **W:** Howard Franklin; **M:** John Barry.

Puccini for Beginners ⚐⚐ 2006 Snappy, droll, if occasionally labored comedy. Opera-loving Allegra (Reaser) breaks up with girlfriend Samantha (Nicholson) and drunkenly decides to have an affair after meeting appealing Philip (Kirk), who's dumped girlfriend Grace (Mol), who soon has her own rebound romance—with

Pucker Up and Bark Like a Dog 🐾 1989 (R) A young artist and his inspirationally lovely actress girlfriend find themselves in strange and crazy situations. Good cast gives this potential. 82m/C DVD. US Elizabeth Peaser, Justin Kirk, Gretchen Mol, Jennifer (Jenny) Dundas Lowe. D: Julianne Nicholson, Tina Benko, Brian Letscher; D: Maria Maggenti; W: Mara Maggenti; C: Mauricio Rubinstein; M: Terry Dane.

Pudd'nhead Wilson 🐾½ 1984 An adaptation of a Mark Twain story about a small-town lawyer who discovers the illicit exchange of a white infant for a light-skinned negro infant by a slave woman. Made as an "American Playhouse" presentation on PBS. 87m/C VHS. Lise Hilbolt, Dick Latessa, James Fritchet, Tom Aldredge, Steven Weber; Ken Howard; D: Alan Bridges; W: Philip Reisman Jr.; C: Walter Lassally. TV

Pueblo Affair 🐾🐾🐾 1973 A dramatization of the capture of the American spy ship "Pueblo" by the North Koreans, during which time the crew was tortured, imprisoned, and all intelligence documents were confiscated. 95m/C VHS. Hal Holbrook, Andrew Duggan, Richard Mulligan, George Grizzard, Gary Merrill, Mary Fickett. D: Anthony Page. TV

Puerto Vallarta Squeeze 🐾½ 2004 (R) Failed American writer Danny Paster (Wasson) is living in Mexico with his girlfriend Maria (Zacarias). Needing money, Danny agrees to drive Clayton Price (Glenn) to the border though he knows something is off and that officials are on high alert following two assassinations. Seems Price is a government hitman gone rogue and CIA operative Walter McGrane (Keitel) has been sent in to clean up the mess, which includes getting rid of Price. Based on the novel by Robert James Waller. 120m/C DVD. Scott Glenn, Harvey Keitel, Craig Wasson, Jonathan Brandis, Giovanna Zacarias; D: Arthur Allan Seidelman; W: Richard Alfieri; C: Chuy Chavez; M: Lee Holdridge.

Puff, Puff, Pass woof! 2006 (R) Excreta comedy about a couple of tokers who get locked out of their apartment for non-payment of rent and then get into various unpleasant situations as they seek a place to hang out. Not even worth watching stoned. 95m/C DVD US Danny Masterson, Mekhi Phifer, Ronnie Warner; D: Mekhi Phifer; W: Ronnie Warner, Kent George; C: Arthur Albert.

Putnstuf 🐾🐾½ 1970 (G). Surreal theatrical feature based on the "H.R. Pufnstuf" children's series by Sid and Marty Kroft. Jimmy (Wild) takes his talking flute to Living Island, where objects, plants, and animals can speak and where he meets mayor Pufnstuf, a dragon. But Jack's magic flute is stolen by Witchiepoo (Hayes) who wants to be named "Witch of the Year" at the annual witches convention. 98m/C VHS. Jack Wild, Billie Hayes, Martha Raye, "Mama" Cass Elliott, Billy Barry; D: Hollingsworth Morse; W: John Ferton Murray; C: Kenneth Pack Si.; M: Charles Fox.

Pulp 🐾🐾🐾 1972 (PG). Caine, playing a mystery writer, becomes a target for murder when he ghostwrites the memoirs of a movie gangster from the 1930s. played deftly by Rooney. 95m/C VHS, GB Michael Caine, Mickey Rooney, Lionel Stander, Lizabeth Scott, Nadia Cassini, Dennis Price, Al Lettieri. D: Mike Hodges. W: Mike Hodges.

Pulp Fiction 🐾🐾🐾🐾 1994 (R) Tarantino moves into the cinematic mainstream with his trademark violence and murder when he brings his style-ish crime trilogy. A day in the life of a criminal community unexpectedly shifts from outrageous, esoteric dialogue to violent mayhem with solid scripting that takes familiar stories to unexplored territory. Offbeat cast offers superb performances, led by Travolta in his best role to date as a hit man whose adventures with partner Jackson tie the seemingly unrelated stories together. Clever, almost gleeful look at everyday life on the fringes of mainstream society. Inspired by "Black Mask" magazine. 154m/C VHS, DVD, UMD Paul Calderon,

Allegra. Obviously, New York is a very small town. 82m/C DVD. US Elizabeth Reaser, Justin Kirk, Gretchen Mol, Jennifer (Jenny) Dundas Lowe. ...

The Puma Man woof! 1980 Puma Man is a super hero who must stop the evil Dr. Kobras from using an ancient mask in his attempt to become ruler of the world. Unreleased theatrically in the U.S. world. Unreleased theatrically in the U.S., this low budget sci-fi/horror mix is so bad one wonders why an actor like Pleasence would sign on. Special effects these days are so extraordinary that the ones employed here are laughable. 80m/C VHS. Donald Pleasence, Walter George Alton, Sydne Rome, Miguel Angel Fuentes; D: Alberto De Martino.

Pulse 🐾 1988 (PG-13) Electricity goes awry in this science-fiction thriller about appliances and other household devices that become super-charged and destroy property and their owners. 90m/C VHS. Film, Screenplay; MTV Movie Awards '95: Film, Dance Seq. (John Travolta/Uma Thurman); Natl. Bd. of Review '94: Director (Tarantino), Film; N.Y. Film Critics '94: Director (Tarantino), Screenplay; Natl. Soc. Film Critics '94: Actor (Jackson); Cannes '94: Film. Golden Globes '95: Screenplay; Ind. Spirit '95: Actor (Jackson), Director (Tarantino), Film, Screenplay; Film Critics '94: Actor (Travolta), Director (Tarant no), Film. Screenplay; M: Jay Ferguson.

Pulse 🐾🐾 Kairo 2001 Set in dirty and industrial Tokyo, a great example of Japanese horror. Don't look for logic because its not here. Instead there's tension and dread surrounding disquieting images hosted by a malevolent website. A group of friends are shocked by the suicide of another friend and are then haunted by ghostly computer images. Other people continue to die or disappear in strange ways, as Tokyo becomes an increasingly desolate place. 118m/C DVD. JP Kumiko Aso, Koyuki, Shun Sugata, Masayuki Shionoya, Shinji Takeda, Koji Yakusho, Haruhiko Kato, Kurume Arisaka, Masatoshi Matsuo, Kenji Mizuhashi, Jun Fukaki; D: Kiyoshi Kurosawa; W: Kiyoshi Kurosawa; C: Junichiro Hayashi; M: Takefumi Haketa.

Pulse 🐾🐾 Octane 2003 (R) Weirdo traveling vampire cult kidnaps teenage girl causing her anguished mom to descend into their world to attempt her rescue. 9cm/C VHS, DVD. Madeleine Stowe, Norman Reedus, Bijou Phillips, Mischa Barton, Jonathan Rhys Meyers, Samuel Froler, Tom Hunsinger, Leo Gregory; Amber Batty, Jenny Julen, Patrick O'Kane, Martin McDougall, Shauna Shim, Dean Gregory, Sarah Whitney, Stephen Lord, Dean Gregory, Sarah Hudgins, Emma Drews, Marcus Adams; D: Marcus Volk; W: Stephen Volk; C: Robin Shaw; M: Paul Hartnoll, Phil Hartnoll. Orbital. VIDEO

Pulse 🐾🐾½ 2006 (R) Remake of the 2001 Japanese horror flick "Kairo" that features an evil website. When the unsuspecting click on the creepy images of the dead, the supernatural force behind it re site invades the lives of those who log on and makes them commit suicide. Techniclogy is bad, but not as bad as this watered-down version, which forgoes creepy atmospherics and conceptualized fear for the occasional scare. 90m/C DVD, HD DVD, UMD Kristen Bell, Ian Somerhalder, Christina Milian, Rick Gonzalez, Zach Grenier, Ron Rifkin, Jonathan Tucker, Brad Dourif, Samm Levine; D: Jim Sonzero; W: Wes Craven, Ray Wright; C: Mark Plummer; M: Elia Cmira.

Pulsebeat woof! 1985 Flick about warring health club owners. As boring as it sounds unless you're in the mood for lots of on-screen aerobics. If so, rent Jane Fonda instead. Dubbed. 92m/C VHS, SP Daniel Greene, Lee Taylor Allen, Eoo Small Nica Moore, Helga Line, Alex Intriago, Peter Lupus; D: Marice Tobias.

Pumpkinhead 3: Ashes to Ashes 🐾 2006 (R) Cheapie forgetable franchise entry starts 20 years after the original although dead Ed Harley (Henriksen) still manages to return. Local mortician Doc Frasier (Bradley) has been stealing body parts from the dead and throwing the remains in the swamp rather than giving them a proper burial. After his desecration is discovered, outraged townsfolk turn to Haggis the witch to summon the cerimonic Pumpkinhead to give them revenge. 95m/C DVD, Doug Bradley, Lance Henriksen, Douglas Roberts, Lisa McAllister, Tess Panzer; D: Jake West; W: Lee West; C: Erik Wilson; M: Robert Lord. VIDEO

Pumpkinhead 4: Blood Feud 🐾½ 2007 (R) Jody Hatfield and Ricky McCoy fall in love despite their families' ongoing feud. But when Ricky's youngster sister dies, he decides to get the local witch to call up Pumpkinhead to kill all the Hatfields except for lover Jody. A ghostly Ed Harley tries to convince 'em that this is

Pumpkinhead 🐾🐾 1988 Vengeance: The Demon 1988 (R) A farmer evokes a demon from the earth to avenge his son's death. When it continues on its murdering rampage, the farmer finds he no longer has any control over the vicious killer. 89m/C VHS, DVD. Lance Henriksen, John DiAquino, Kerry Remsen, Matthew Hurley, Jeff East, Kimberly Ross, Cynthia Bain, Joel Hoffman, Florence Schauffler, George "Buck" Flower, Tom Woodruff Jr.; D: Stan Winston; W: Mark Patrick Carducci, Gary Gerani; C: Bojan Bazelli; M: Richard Stone.

Pumpkinhead 2: Blood Wings 🐾🐾½ 1994 (R) Five typically stupid teenagers resurrect a demon and the creature goes on a bloodthirsty rampage. His leaves his signature, a calling card in the shape of wings ahead its murder scene. 88m/C VHS, DVD. Ami Dolenz, Andrew (Andy) Robinson, Kane Hodder, R.A. Mihailoff, Linnea Quigley, Steve Kanaly, Caren Kaye, Gloria Hendry, Soleil Moon Frye, Mark McCracken, Roger Clinton; D: Jeff Burr; W: Ivan Chachornia, Constantin Chachornia.

Pump Up the Volume 🐾🐾½ 1990 (R) High school newcomer leads double life as Hard Harry, sarcastic host of an illegal radio broadcast and Jack Nicholson soundalike. Anonymously popular with his peers, he invites the wrath of the school principal due to his less than flattering comments about the school administration. Slater seems to enjoy himself as defiant deejay while youthful cast effectively supports. 105m/C VHS, DVD, Christian Slater, Scott Paulin, Ellen Greene, Samantha Mathis, Cheryl Pollak, Annie Ross, Andy Romano, Mimi Kennedy; D: Alan McVie; W: Allan Moyle; C: Walt Lloyd; M: Cliff Martinez.

Pumpkin 🐾🐾 2002 (R) Ambitious but over-reaching satire. California blonde sorority sister Carolyn McDuffy (Ricci) is a beauty—thus alienating her boyfriend, sorority sisters, and Pumpkin's mother. Too bad all the characters are little more than stereotypes. 118m/C VHS, DVD. US Christina Ricci, Brenda Blethyn, Dominique Swain, Hank Harris, Marisa Coughlan, Samuel Ball, Harry J. Lennix, Nina Foch, Caroline Aaron, Lisa Banes, Julio Oscar Mechoso, Amy Adams; D: Adam Larson Broder; C: Tim Suhrstedt; M: John Ottman.

The Pumpkin Eater 🐾🐾🐾 1964 British housewife Jo (Bancroft) has seemingly found contentment with her third husband, famous and wealthy writer Jake (Finch), and her eight children. But as Jo struggles to face middle age she discovers Jake is chronically unfaithful and goes into an emotional tailspin. Last film for Hardwicke. Slow-paced film with fine performances; based on the novel by Penelope Mortimer. 110m/C VHS, GB Anne Bancroft, Peter Finch, James Mason, Richard Johnson, Cedric Hardwicke, Maggie Smith, Alan Webb, Eric Porter; D: Jack Clayton; W: Harold Pinter; C: Oswald Morris; M: Georges Delerue. British Acad. '64: Screenplay.

Pump Up the Volume 🐾🐾½ a bad idea since Pumpkinhead isn't going to check IDs before he starts his slaughter. The usual biker stuff. 90m/C VHS, Stephen Falchi, Roxanne Rogers; Don Martin, Sandra Bogan; D: Stanley Lewis.

Punch-Drunk Love 🐾🐾🐾 2002 (R) Enjoy Adam Sandler's doofus americanus roles? Then don't put this on your shopping list. Looking for a new twist on the romantic comedy featuring Adam Sandler's best performance to date? Here's your flick. Barry Egan (Sandler), owner of a novelty toilet-plunger company, prone to sudden outbreaks of physical violence (mostly to glass doors and public bathrooms) serendipitously finds a woman (Watson) attracted to him. Amid the budding love stuff, Egan battles with a phone sex company's extortion attempts, and his discovery of a marketing mistake allowing him to obtain millions of frequent flyers miles for the price of some pudding cups (based on a true incident). Anderson arranges scenes like musical numbers, escalating sound and spectacle to a dizzying point, to good effect. 97m/C VHS, DVD. US Adam Sandler, Emily Watson, Philip Seymour Hoffman, Luis Guzman, Mary Lynn Rajskub, Ashley Clark; D: Paul Thomas Anderson; W: Paul Thomas Anderson; C: Robert Elswit. M: Jon Brion.

Punch the Clock 🐾🐾 1990 (R) Attractive female thief finds her self. Better than the previous entry but still standard monster fare. 95m/C DVD. Rob Freeman, Richard Durden, Louis Gossett Jr., Jeroen Krabbe, Kim Myori; D: Mark Goldblatt; W: Boaz Yakin; C: Ian Baker; M: Dennis Dreith.

Punchline 🐾🐾 1988 (R) A look at the lives of stand-up comics, following the career ups-and-downs of an embittered professional funny-man and a frustrated housewife hitting the stage for the first time. Some very funny and touching moments and some not-so-funny and touching moments as the movie descends into melodrama without a cause. 100m/C VHS, DVD. Tom Hanks, Sally Field, John Goodman, Mark Rydell, Kim Greist, Barry Sobel, Paul Mazursky, Pam Matteson, George Michael McGrath, Taylor Negron, Damon Wayans; D: David Seltzer; W: David Seltzer; C: Reynaldo Villalobos. L.A. Film Critics '88: Actor (Hanks).

The Punisher 🐾🐾 2004 (R) What this brutal revenger lacks in humor and cheeriness, it more than makes up for in gloomy, dour punishment, drunken brooding, and grisly deaths. The Punisher a.k.a. Frank Castle (Jane) is an FBI agent turned vigilante after an FBI sting which kills a wealthy mobster's son triggers the systematic murder of his entire family. Said mobster is the ironically named Mr. Saint (an uninspired Travolta). Despite a severe battering, Castle survives the slaughter. Rest of pic is his revenge plot against Saint, his right hand man (Patton) and assorted evil cohorts. Adding a touch of humanity are Castle's fellow rooming-house residents, including Romijn-Stamos, Pinette and Foster, who futilely attempt to socialize Castle. Based on the Marvel comic books. 124m/C VHS, DVD, Blu-ray Disc, UMD. US Thomas Jane, John Travolta, Will Patton, Roy Scheider, Rebecca Romijn, Geoff Wallace, Mark Collie, John Pinette, Russell Andrews, Marcus Johns, Ben Foster, Eduardo Yanez, Marcus Johns, Bonnie Johnson, Omar Avila; D: Jonathan Hensleigh; W: Jonathan Hensleigh, Michael France; C: Conrad W. Hall; M: Carlo Siliotto.

The Punisher 🐾 1990 (R) Lundgren portrays Frank Castle, the Marvel Comics anti-hero known as the Punisher. When his family is killed by the mob Castle set out on revenge. Filmed in Australia. 92m/C VHS, DVD. Dolph Lundgren, Louis Gossett Jr., Jeroen Krabbe, Kim Miyori; D: Mark Goldblatt; W: Boaz Yakin; C: Ian Baker; M: Dennis Dreith.

Punk Vacation 🐾 1990 A gang of motorcycle mamas terrorize a small town.

P.U.N.K.S. 1998 (PG) Preteen Drew (Redwine) and his friends are regularly beaten up by school bullies. Then they realize that evil industrialist Edward Crow (Winkler) has stolen an invention that turns weaklings into hulks and they decide to steal it back. 99m/C VHS, Randy Quaid, Cathy Moriarty, Henry Winkler, Ted Redwine, Patrick Renna; *D:* Sean McNamara. VIDEO

Puppet Master 1989 (R) Four psychics are sent to investigate a puppet maker who they think may have discovered the secret of life. Before they know it, they are stalked by evil puppets. Great special effects, not-so-great script. 90m/C VHS, DVD, Paul LeMat, Jimmie F. Skaggs, Irene Miracle, Robyn Frates, Barbara Crampton, William Hickey, Matt Roe, Kathryn O'Reilly; *D:* David Schmoeller; *W:* Joseph G. Collodi; *C:* Sergio Salvati; *M:* Richard Band.

Puppet Master 2 1990 (R) Puppets on a rampage turn hotel into den of special effects. Less effective string pulling than in original. Long live Pinocchio. 90m/C VHS, Elizabeth MacLellan, Collin Bernsen, Greg Webb, Charlie Spradling, Nita Talbot, Steve Welles, Jeff Weston; *D:* Dave Allen; *W:* David Pabian; *C:* Thomas Denove; *M:* Richard Band.

Puppet Master 3: Toulon's Revenge 1990 (R) Prequel about the origin of the whole gory Puppet Master shebang, set in Nazi Germany. The weapon-hungry Third Reich tries to wrest secrets of artificial life from sorceror Andre Toulon, who sics his deadly puppets on them. Toulon's a good guy here, one of many contradictions in the series. Fine cast, but strictly for the followers. 86m/C VHS, DVD, Guy Rolfe, Ian Abercrombie, Sarah Douglas, Richard Lynch, Walter Gotell; *D:* David DeCoteau; *W:* C. Courtney Joyner; *C:* Adolfo Bartoli; *M:* Richard Band.

Puppet Master 4 1993 (R) It's the puppets versus the totems, equally loathsome midget creatures who derive their power from the same eternal force as the puppets. No one wants to share and there's lots of gore while they battle for supremacy. 80m/C VHS, DVD, Gordon Currie, Chandra West, Jason Adams, Teresa Hill, Guy Rolfe; *D:* Jeff Burr; *W:* Todd Henschell, Steven E. Carr, Jo Duffy, Douglas Aarnikoski; *M:* Richard Band.

Puppet Master 5: The Final Chapter 1994 Greedy Dr. Jennings has come to Bodega Bay Inn to capture the puppets and discover the secret formula for their animation so he can sell it to the highest bidder. But he's not the only threat, it seems the demonic Eyad, a being from another dimension, also wants the secret and has sent his own evil puppet to fully the puppet master and steal their magic. 81m/C VHS, DVD, Gordon Currie, Chandra West, Ian Ogilvy, Teresa Hill, Nicholas Guest, Willard Pugh, Diane McBain, Kaz Garas, Guy Rolfe; *D:* Jeff Burr; *W:* Douglas Aarnikoski, Jo Duffy, Todd Henschell, Keith Payson, Steven E. Karr; *C:* Adolfo Bartoli; *M:* Richard Band.

The Puppet Masters 1994 (R) *A Heinlein's The Puppet Masters* Government official (Sutherland) discovers aliens are taking over the bodies of humans and if he doesn't find a way to stop the parasites they'll soon rule the Earth. Yes, it does sound like "Invasion of the Body Snatchers" but the film is based on Robert A. Heinlein's 1951 novel, written five years before. The parasites are sufficiently yucky but, unfortunately, this adaptation is mediocre and generally wastes a talented cast. 109m/C VHS, DVD, Donald Sutherland, Eric Thal, Julie Warner, Keith David, Will Patton, Richard Belzer, Yaphet Kotto, Dale Dye; *D:* Stuart Orme; *W:* Terry Rossio, David S. Goyer, Ted Elliott; *M:* Colin Towns.

Puppet on a Chain 1972 (PG) American narcotics officer busts an Amsterdam drug ring and the leader's identity surprises him. Slow-moving thriller based on the Alistair MacLean novel. 97m/C VHS. *GB* Sven-Bertil Taube, Barbara Parkins, Alexander Knox, Patrick Allen, Geoffrey Reeve; *D:* Geoffrey Reeve; *C:* Jack Hildyard.

The Puppetoon Movie 1987 (G) A compilation of George Pal's famous Puppetoon cartoons from the 1940s, marking his stature as an animation pioneer and innovator. Hosted by Gumby, Pokey, Speedy Alka Seltzer and Arnie the Dinosaur in newly directed scenes. 80m/C VHS, DVD. *D:* Arnold Leibowit; *M:* Buddy (Norman Dale) Baker.

Pups 1999 Surburban 13-year-old Stevie (Van Hoy) finds his mom's gun, which he shows to equally young girlfriend, Rocky (Barton). Instead of going to school, Stevie impulsively decides to rob a nearby bank, and nearly gets away with it until the cops and the FBI show up. Now the kids have hostages and no clue as to what they're doing, while hostage negotiator Daniel Bender (Reynolds) tries to get a volatile Stevie to listen to reason. 103m/C VHS, DVD. Cameron Van Hoy, Mischa Barton, Burt Reynolds, Darling Narita; *D:* Ash; *W:* Ash; *C:* Carolos Arguello.

The Purchase Price 1932 After a less than amorous beginning, farmer Brent and mail order bride Stanwyck fall into love and financial despair in this drama bordering on comedy. Good neighbor Landau is willing to help the poor agriculturalist out in exchange for the security of Stanwyck. Tragedy strikes again when Stanwyck's bootlegger ex-boyfriend shows up and further disasters continue to test the couple's commitment. Based on the story 'The Mud Lark' by Arthur Stringer. 70m/B VHS, Barbara Stanwyck, George Brent, Lyle Talbot, Hardie Albright, David Landau; *D:* William A. Wellman; *W:* Robert Lord.

Pure 2002 (R) Sentimental and brutal tale about Paul (Eden), a 10-year-old boy trying to stay in control of his life and save his mother from her addiction to heroin. Everyone around him is either an addict, a prostitute, or a pusher, yet he remains in confident denial of his true situation. The bad choices and ludicrous behavior of the adults in his life are perpetual by Eden; well shot but story on the whole is emotionally unsatisfying. 94m/C DVD, *GB* Molly Parker, David Wenham, Geraldine McEwan, Keira Knightley, Kate Ashfield, Gary Lewis, Marsha Thomason, Karl Johnson, Harry Eden, Vinni Ganatra, Levi Hayes, Vinni Hunter; *D:* Gilles Mackinnon; *W:* Alison Hume; *C:* John de Borman; *M:* Nitin Sawhney.

Pure Country 1992 (PG) An easygoing movie about a familiar subject is held together by the charm of Strait (in his movie debut) and the rest of the cast. Strait plays a country music superstar, tired of the career glitz, who decides to get out and go back to his home in Texas. He falls in love with the spunky Glasser and decides to run his career his own way. Warren is effective as his tough manager weathered as Glasser's gruff dad. 113m/C VHS, DVD. George Strait, Isabel Glasser, Lesley Ann Warren, Rory Calhoun, Kyle Chandler, John Doe, Molly McClure; *D:* Christopher Cain; *W:* Rex McGee; *C:* Rick Bota; *M:* Steve Dorff.

Pure Danger 1996 (R) Short order cook Johnny (Howell) and his waitress girlfriend Becky (Linn) stumble upon a bag of diamonds and think all their troubles are over. Wrong—they're just beginning, since some very nasty men want the jewels and don't care who they kill to get them. Howell keeps his directorial debut fast-paced and surprisingly entertaining. 99m/C VHS, DVD. C. Thomas Howell, Linn, Leon, Michael Russo; *D:* C. Thomas Howell; *W:* William Applegate Jr., Joseph John Barmettler Jr.; *C:* Ken Blakey; *M:* K. Alexander (Alex) Wilkinson.

A Pure Formality 1994 *Una Pura Formalita; Une Pure Formalite* (PG-13) Murky psycho-drama finds a disheveled man (Depardieu) winding up at an isolated police station in a nameless country (in the middle of a rainstorm, no less). The Inspector (Polanski) suspects him of a local murder, especially after he claims to be a famous writer named Onoff, yet, can remember nothing. The Inspector wants a confession and spends the night trying to exact one from his guileful suspect. French with subtitles. Film is rated at a much younger level than will possibly underdstand or enjoy it. 111m/C VHS. *FR IT* Gerard Depardieu, Roman Polanski, Sergio Rubini; *D:* Giuseppe Tornatore; *W:* Giuseppe Tornatore, Pascal Quignard; *C:* Blasco Giurato; *M:* Ennio Morricone.

The Pure Hell of St. Trinian's 1961 In this sequel to "Blue Murder at St. Trinian's," a sheik who desires to fill out his harem tries recruiting at a rowdy girls' school. Although it isn't as funny as the first, due to the lack of Alistair Sim, it is still humorous. Followed by "The Great St. Trinian's Train Robbery." Based on the cartoon by Ronald Searle. 94m/B VHS. *GB* Cecil Parker, Joyce Grenfell, George Cole, Thorley Walters; *D:* Frank Launder; *M:* Malcolm Arnold.

Pure Luck 1991 (PG) A who-asked-for-it remake of a 1981 Franco-Italian film called "La Chevre." The premise is the same: an accident-prone heiress disappears in Mexico, and her father tries to locate her using an equally clumsy accountant. The nebbish and an attendant tough private eye stumble and bumble south of the border until the plot arbitrarily ends. Pure awful. 96m/C VHS. Martin Short, Danny Glover, Sheila Kelley, Scott Wilson, Sam Wanamaker, Harry Shearer; *D:* Nadia Tass; *W:* Herschel Weingrod, Timothy Harris.

Purgatory 1989 While travelling abroad, two innocent women find themselves unjustly jailed. During their confinement they are tortured and raped. 90m/C VHS. Tanya Roberts, Julie Pop; *D:* Ami Artzi; *W:* Paul Aratow.

Purgatory 1999 A group of desperadoes head for what they think is the defenseless town of Refuge, where the sheriff (Shepard) doesn't carry a gun or allow cussing. But the town and its inhabitants are not what they seem and these cowpoke bad guys are in for quite a surprise. 94m/C VHS. Sam Shepard, Eric Roberts, Randy Quaid, Peter Stormare, Donnie Wahlberg; *D:* Uli Edel; *W:* Gordon Dawson. CABLE

Purgatory House 2004 (R) In a near-future Glasgow, rival gangs like to show off by holding martial arts battles. Crime boss Moses (McKidd) wants to organize the gangs but the Purifiers, led by John (Alexander), are eager to keep crime out of their 'hood and don't want to go along. Chop-socky with a Scottish brogue. 85m/C DVD. Kevin McKidd, Dominic Monaghan, Gordon Alexander, Rachel Grant; *D:* Richard Jobson; *W:* Richard Jobson; *C:* John Rhodes; *M:* Steven Severin.

Purlie Victorious *Gone are the Days; The Man from C.O.T.T.O.N* 1963 Preacher Purlie (Davis) returns to Georgia and tries to get an inheritance from the plantation owner, "Ol' Cap'n" Cotchipee (Booke), he used to serve. Cotchipee's progressive son (Alda) unexpectedly helps him in his cause. Presentation of Davis's award-winning Broadway hit. 93m/C VHS, DVD. Sorrell Booke, Beah Richards, Ossie Davis, Ruby Dee, Godfrey Cambridge, Alan Alda; *D:* Nicholas Webster; *W:* Ossie Davis; *C:* Boris Kaufman.

Purple Butterfly *Zi Hudie* 2003 (R) Stunning political thriller/noir set in 1930s Shanghai. Zhang stars as Cynthia/Ding Hui, an operative in the anti-Japanese underground Purple Butterfly. She's a fearless and dedicated patriot driven by the assassination of her brother years before. Her past comes to haunt her in the form of former lover Itami (Nakamura), who is now a Japanese agent assigned to bring down Purple Butterfly. Soon enough, the two are caught in a delicate balancing act, struggling between their duty and the love that may still exist between them, while all around them the conflict between Japanese and Chinese threatens not only them but innocent people as well. Director Lou mixes Western noir style with a distinct, dreamlike moodiness that ensnares while shocking with interesting twists 'in the complex plot. Chinese with English subtitles. 127m/C DVD. Ziyi Zhang, Toru Nakamura, Ye Liu, Yuanzheng Feng; *D:* Ye Lou; *W:* Ye Lou; *C:* Yu Wang; *M:* Jorg Lemberg.

The Purple Heart 1944 In this war drama, an American Air Force crew is shot down over Tokyo and taken into brutal POW camps. Intense wartime melodramatics. 99m/B VHS, DVD. Dana Andrews, Richard Conte, Farley Granger, Donald (Don "Red") Barry, Sam Levene, Kevin O'Shea, Tala Birell, Nestor Paiva, Benson Fong, Marshall Thompson, Richard Loo; *D:* Lewis Milestone; *C:* Arthur C. Miller.

Purple Hearts 1984 (R) Wahl stars as a Navy doctor who falls in love with nurse Ladd under the backdrop of the Vietnam war. Overlong and redundant. 115m/C VHS. Cheryl Ladd, Ken Wahl, Stephen Lee, Annie McEnroe, Paul McCrane, Cyril O'Reilly; *D:* Sidney J. Furie; *W:* Sidney J. Furie, Ron Nyswaner; *M:* Robert Folk.

The Purple Monster Strikes *D-Day on Mars; The Purple Shadow Strikes* 1945 A martian plots to conquer Earth to save his dying planet. Serial in 15 episodes. 188m/B VHS. Dennis Moore, Linda Stirling, Roy Barcroft; *D:* Spencer Gordon Bennet, Fred Brannon; *W:* Barney A. Saredy, Basil Dickey, Lynn Perkins, Joseph Poland, Albert DeMond; *C:* Bud Thackery.

Purple Noon *Plein Soleil; Lust for Evil* 1960 (PG-13) Don't let the ratings fool you, this isn't teen fodder. The gorgeous Delon stars as opportunistic Tom Ripley, who's hired by the father of his rich, arrogant playboy friend Philippe (Ronet) to persuade him to return home to San Francisco. Instead, Ripley covets the man's yacht, beautiful girlfriend Marge (Laforet), and money, so when Philippe pushes Tom too far he disposes of him and tries to divert police suspicions. Film noir set in the hedonistic Mediterranean sun. Based on the novel "The Talented Mr. Ripley" by Patricia Highsmith, although the ending of novel and film differ greatly. French with subtitles. 118m/C VHS, DVD. *FR* Alain Delon, Maurice Ronet, Marie Laforet, Erno Crisa, Billy Kearns; *D:* Rene Clement; *W:* Rene Clement, Paul Gegauff; *C:* Henri Decae; *M:* Nino Rota.

Purple People Eater 1988 (PG) The alien of the title descends to earth to mix with young girls and rock 'n' roll. Based on the song of the same name whose performer, Sheb Wooley, appears in the film. Harmless, stupid fun for the whole family. 91m/C VHS, Ned Beatty, Shelley Winters, Neil Patrick Harris, Kareem Abdul-Jabbar, Little Richard, Chubby Checker, Peggy Lipton; *D:* Linda Shayne.

Purple Rain 1984 (R) A quasi-autobiographical video showcase for the pop-star Prince. Film tells the tale of a lackluster life, escapes into a film playing at the local movie house where a blond film hero, tiring of the monotony of his role, makes a break from the celluloid to join her in the real world. The ensuing love story allows director-writer Allen to show his knowledge of old movies and provide his fans with a change of pace. Farrow's film sister is also her real-life sister Stephanie, who went on to appear in Allen's "Zelig." 82m/C VHS, DVD. Mia Farrow, Jeff Dan-

The Purple Rose of Cairo 1985 (PG) A diner waitress, disillusioned by the Depression and a lackluster life, escapes into a film playing at the local movie house. Song Score and/or Adapt.

The Purple Taxi 🐾🐾½ 1977 (R) Romantic drama revolving around several wealthy foreigners who have taken refuge in beautiful southern Ireland. From Michel Deon's bestselling novel. 93m/C VHS. FR Fred Astaire, Charlotte Rampling, Peter Ustinov, Philippe Noiret; Edward Albert; **D:** Yves Boisset; Oliver Drake; **C:** Ernest Miller.

Purpose 🐾🐾½ 2002 (R) College dropout turned Internet entrepreneur John Elias (Light) finds fame and fortune during the dot.com boom but things turn rough when his girlfriend (Dodds) and dad (Coyote) question his business ethics and John must prevent a hostil takeover of his company. 96m/C VHS, DVD. John Light, Megan Dodds, Peter Coyote, Jeffrey Donovan, Hal Holbrook, Mia Farow; Paul Reiser; **D:** Alan Ari Lazar; **W:** Alan Ari Lazar, **M:** Alan Ari Lazar, Steiner.

Pursued 🐾🐾🐾 1947 Excellent performances by Mitchum and Wright mark this suspenseful Western drama of a Spanish-American war veteran in search of his father's killer. 105m/B VHS. Teresa Wright, Robert Mitchum, Judith Anderson, Dean Jagger, Alan Hale, Harry Carey Jr., John Rodney; **D:** Raoul Walsh; **C:** James Wong Howe; **M:** Max Steiner.

Pursuit 🐾🐾 1972 A terrorist threatens to release a toxic nerve gas throughout a city hosting a political convention. Tension mounts as federal agents must beat the extremists' countdown to zero. Based on the novel by Crichton. 73m/C VHS. Ben Gazzara, E.G. Marshall, Martin Sheen, Joseph Wiseman, William Windom; **D:** Michael Crichton; **M:** Jerry Goldsmith.

Pursuit 🐾🐾 1990 (R) A mercenary comes out of retirement to join a renegade team recovering stolen gold. But they turn on him, stealing the treasure and taking a hostage. Now he must track them down, or there's no movie. 94m/C VHS. Robert Duvall, Treat Williams, Kathryn Harrold, Ed Flaenders; **D:** Roger Spottiswoode; **C:** Harry Stradling Jr.; **M:** James Horner.

The Pursuit of D.B. Cooper 🐾🐾 1981 (PG) Based on an actual hijacking that occurred on Thanksgiving Eve in 1971 in which a man (alias D.B. Cooper) parachuted out of an airliner with $200,000 of stolen money. Although his fate and whereabouts have remained a mystery, this story speculates about what may have happened. 100m/C VHS. Robert Duvall, Treat Williams, Kathryn Harrold, Ed Flanders; **D:** Roger Spottiswoode; **C:** John H. Parr.

Pursuit of Happiness 🐾🐾½ 1970 (PG) An idealistic man is convicted of manslaughter after accidentally running down a woman. Once in prison, he's faced with the decision to try to escape. 85m/C VHS. Michael Sarrazin, Arthur Hill, E.G. Marshall, Barbara Hershey, Robert Klein; **D:** Robert Mulligan.

Pursuit of Happiness 🐾🐾½ 2001 L.A. ad exec Alan Oliver (Whaley) always has his longtime best platonic friend Marissa (Gish) to turn to when his life spins out of control. And it's about to—his boss (Stapleton) takes him off his biggest account, his girlfriend moves out, and he's suddenly in a rebound romance with Tracy (Johnson). What Alan fails to realize is that Marissa is also having trouble since her marriage is falling apart. Oh, and as Alan pursues happiness, he should also realize that it's closer than he thinks. 93m/C VHS, DVD. Frank Whaley, Annabeth Gish, Amy Jo Johnson, Patrick Van Horn, Jean Stapleton, Alex Hyde-White, Cress Williams, Liz Vassey, Kieran Mulroney, Anne-Marie Johnson; **D:** John Robert Zaring; **W:** John Robert Zaring.

Purple Vigilantes 🐾🐾½ 1938 *The Three Mesquiteers* uncover a gang of vigilantes. Part of the series. 54m/B VHS. DVD. Robert "Bob" Livingston, Ray Corrigan, Max Terhune, Joan Barclay, Earle Dwire, Earle Hodgins, George Chaseburg, Robert (Fisk) Fiske; **D:** George Sherman; **W:** Betty Burbridge.

Pursuit of the Graf Spee 🐾🐾½ *The Battle of the River Plate* 1957 Three small British ships destroy the mighty Graf Spee a WWII German battleship. 106m/C VHS. GB Anthony Quayle, Peter Finch, Ian Hunter; **D:** Michael Powell.

Pursuit to Algiers 🐾🐾🐾 1945 The modernized Holmes and Watson guard a young heir of fictional Rovenia during a sea voyage, during which assassins close in. 65m/B VHS, DVD. Basil Rathbone, Nigel Bruce, Martin Kosleck, Marjorie (Reardon) Riordan, Rosalind Ivan, John Abbott; **D:** Roy William Neill.

Push 🐾 2006 (R) Unoriginal drug story set in Miami. Bartender Joe (Lindberg) gets his greedy pals Micky (DePaolo) and Kevin (Forsythe) involved in a scheme to push Ecstasy for drug lord Paul (Sanchez). Naturally, they get in too deep and bad things happen. 105m/C DVD. Chad Lindberg, Otto Sanchez, Chazz Palminteri, Charlotte Ayama, William DePaolo, Pierce Forsythe, Michael Rappaport; **D:** Dave Rodriguez; **C:** Steve Goodman; **M:** Tommy Finno.

Pushed to the Limit 🐾½ 1992 (R) Harry Lee, the most feared gangster in Chinatown, is about to meet his match in martial-arts queen Lesseos. She's out for revenge when she learns that Lee is responsible for her brother's murder but first she must get by Lee's lethal bodyguard, the equally skilled ninja. 88m/C VHS, DVD. Mimi Lesseos, Henry Hayashi, Verel Reed, Barbara Braverman, Greg Ostrin; **D:** Michael Mileham; **W:** Mimi Lesseos; **C:** Bado Holst; **M:** Miriam Cutler.

Pusher 🐾🐾 1996 Violent thriller was the directorial debut of 24-year-old Refn. Frank (Bodnia) and his buddy Tonny (Mikkelsen) sell heroin in Copenhagen. Their supplier is a Serbian gangster named Milo (Buric), to whom Frank owes money. Things get worse when Frank dumps his latest supply before being arrested—Milo warns him if he doesn't pay his debts in the next couple of days, he's a dead man. The more Frank tries to get the money, the worse things get for him. Danish with subtitles. 105m/C VHS, DVD, DK Kim Bodnia, Zlatko Buric, Mads Mikkelsen, Laura Drasbaek, Slavko Labovic, Lisbeth Rasmussen, **D:** Nicolas Winding Refn; **W:** Nicolas Winding Refn, Jens Dahl; **C:** Morten Soborg; **M:** Povl Kristian Mortensen.

Pushing Hands 🐾🐾½ 1992 Aging tai chi master Mr. Chu (Lung) leaves Beijing to live with his son Alex (Wang) and daughter-in-law Martha (Snyder) in suburban New York. High-strung Martha doesn't understand her tranquilly stubborn father-in-law, nor does Chu find disposable American society much to his liking. Naturally, and slowly, some accommodations are made. The title is a tai chi reference to keeping your opponent off-balance while maintaining your own equilibrium. Director Lee's debut feature is also the first in his trilogy of family films—followed by the more acclaimed "The Wedding Banquet" and "Eat Drink Man Woman." English and Mandarin Chinese with subtitles. 100m/C VHS, DVD. Sihung Lung, Deb Snyder, Bo Z Wang, Lai Wang; **D:** Ang Lee; **C:** Jong Lin; **M:** Xiao-Song Ou.

Pygmalion 🐾🐾🐾½ 1938 Oscar-winning film adaptation of Shaw's play about a cockney flower-girl who is transformed into a "lady" under the guidance of a stuffy phonetics professor. Shaw himself aided in writing the script in this superbly acted comedy that would be adapted into the musical "My Fair Lady," first on Broadway in 1956 and for the screen in 1964. 96m/B VHS, DVD. GB Leslie Howard, Wendy Hiller, Wilfred Lawson, Marie Lohr, Scott Sunderland, David Tree, Everley Gregg, Leueen McGrath, Jean Cadell, Eileen Beldon, Frank Atkinson, O.B. Clarence, Esme Percy, Violet Vanbrugh, Iris Hoey, Viola Tree, Irene Browne, Kate Cutler, Cathleen Nesbitt, Cecil Trouncer, Stephen Murray, Wally Patch, +.F. Marsh; **D:** Anthony Asquith, Leslie Howard; **W:** W.P. Lipscomb, Anatole de Grunwald, Cecil Lewis, Ian Dalrymple, George Bernard Shaw; **C:** Harry Stradling Sr. Oscars '38: Screenplay; Venice Film Fest. '38: Actor (Howard).

Pyrates 🐾 1991 (R) Real life husband-wife team of Bacon and Sedgwick try to provide fireworks as hot, hot lovers in the forgettable one. For the price of this one you can buy a newspaper and chewing gum instead. Use both at the same time and you'll be ahead of everyone involved in this senseless hoot. 98m/C VHS. Kevin Bacon, Kyra Sedgwick, Bruce Payne, Kristin Datillo-Hayward; **D:** Noah Stern.

A Pyromaniac's Love Story 🐾🐾 1995 (PG) Offbeat tale of romance has a neighborhood bakery burning down and every major character confessing to the crime. Earnest working stiffs, snotty rich kids, and kindly old shop owners all have really confusing reasons for wanting to do the heat most of which have to do with unrequited love. At times snake, the unfortunate viewer who picks up this woofer. American cargo plane carrying a secret weapon is shot down over war-torn Chechnya and Russian scientists go to investigate. The "weapon" turns out to be a biogenetically enhanced python that has a taste for human flesh. 85m/C VHS, DVD. William Zabka, Dana Ashbrook, Simone Mackinnon, Alex Jolig; **D:** Jeff Tanki; **W:** Lee McConnell. CABLE.

The Pursuit of Happyness 🐾🐾🐾 2006 (PG-13) Smith and too-cute son Jaden (in his film debut) easily fill the shoes of real-life father and son as Chris Gardner and 5-year-old Christopher. When Chris' bad decisions leave the family broke and soon homeless, until Chris pins his hopes on a six-month unpaid competitive internship at a brokerage firm that could lead to a full-time job and a stable life. The usual feel-good, never-give-up path ensues, and the Smiths make it a worthwhile journey. A story based on a New York Times article) of the tower scenes get things started in surprisingly exciting fashion, and the four leads keep the intensity going with excellent performances despite some script lapses and questionable plot devices. 124m/C VHS, DVD. John Cusack, Billy Bob Thornton, Cate Blanchett, Angelina Jolie, Vicki Lewis, Jake Weber, Kurt Fuller, Mary Grayson, Michael Willis; **D:** Mike Newell; **W:** Glen Charles, Les Charles; **C:** Gale Tattersal; **M:** Anne Dudley.

Puss 'n Boots 🐾🐾 1984 From "Faerie Tale Theatre" comes the story of a cat who makes his poor master a rich land-owning nobleman. 60m/C VHS, DVD. Ben Vereen, Gregory Hines; **D:** Robert Iscove. CABLE.

Putney Swope 🐾🐾🐾 1969 (R) Comedy about a token black ad man mistakenly elected Chairman of the board of a Madison Avenue ad agency who turns the company upside-down. A series of riotous spoofs on commercials and the hippocrit in this funny, though somewhat dated look at big business. 84m/B VHS, DVD, Arnold Johnson, Laura Greene, Stanley Gottlieb, Mel Brooks; **D:** Robert Downey; **W:** Robert Downey; **C:** Gerald Cotts; **M:** Charles Cura.

Puzzle 🐾🐾½ 1978 Franciscus searches for the urn that contains the remains of Buddha but instead finds danger and intrigue. 90m/C VHS, AU James Franciscus, Wendy Hughes, Robert Helpmann, Peter Gwynne, David Kennedy, Kerry McGuire; **D:** Gordon Hessler. TV

Puzzlehead 🐾🐾½ 2005 Hitchcock and Frankenstein collide in this ill-fated fable. Walter creates an android that not only looks like him but also has his psyche downloaded into its hard drive. As Puzzlehead starts to experience more of Walter's emotions, things get complicated and the two find themselves in love with the same Russian woman from the shop down the street. Conceptually and visually stunning with a regrettably flat-lined plot. 81m/C DVD. Stephen Galaida, Robbie Shapiro; **D:** James Bai; **W:** James Bai; **C:** Jeffrey Scott Lando; **M:** Max Lichtenstein.

The Pyx 🐾🐾 *The Hooker Cult Murders* 1973 (R) Canadian suspense thriller about the murder of a prostitute with satanic overtones. Police sergeant investigates the crime and enters a world of devil worship and decadence. Based on the novel by John Buell, Christopher Plummer, Donald Pilon; **D:** Harvey Hart.

Python 🐾🐾½ 2000 (R) Intelligence organization develops a perfect weapon in a gigantic python. Of course, the government screws up, the snake gets loose, and there's hell to pay. 90m/C VHS, DVD. Robert Englund, Casper Van Dien, Jenny McCarthy, Wil Wheaton, Frayne Rosenof; **D:** Richard Clabaugh; **W:** Chris Neal, Gary Hershberger, Paul J.M. Bogh; **C:** Patrick Rousseau, **M:** David J. Nelson. VIDEO

Python 2 *woof!* 2002 (R) HISSSSSSSSSS!!!!! No, not the titular snake, the unfortunate viewer who picks up this woofer. American cargo plane carrying a secret weapon is shot down over war-torn Chechnya and Russian scientists go to investigate. The "weapon" turns out to be a biogenetically enhanced python that has a taste for human flesh. 85m/C VHS, DVD. William Zabka, Dana Ashbrook, Simone Mackinnon, Alex Jolig; **D:** Jeff Tanki; **W:** Lee McConnell. CABLE.

Pushing Tin 🐾🐾🐾 1999 (R) Nick (Cusack) and Russell (Thornton) are rival air traffic controllers at the Long Island tower that oversees New York's three main airports (JFK, La Guardia, and Newark). Nick is a cool professional and a goofy plot twists sabotage any attempt to ignite much interest. 99m/C VHS, DVD. John Leguizamo, Sadie Frost, William Baldwin, Erika Eleniak, Michael Lerner, Joan Plowright, Armin Mueller-Stahl, Richard Crenna; **D:** Joshua Brand; **W:** Rachel Morgan Ward; **C:** John Schwartzman; **M:** Rachel Portman.

Python Wolf 🐾🐾 *C.A.T. Squad: Python Wolf* 1988 (R) It's non-stop action in South Africa as a counter-terrorist group sets out to thwart a drug smuggler's plans to export plutonium. As usual, intense pacing from director Friedkin. Sequel to "C.A.T. Squad" (1986). 100m/C VHS. Joe Cortese, Jack Youngblood, Steve James, Deborah Van Valkenburgh, Miguel Ferrer, Alan Scarfe; **D:** William Friedkin; **M:** Ennio Morricone. TV

Q & A 🐾🐾 1990 (R) Semi-taut thriller about a totally corrupt, hair-trigger cop trying to make his murder of a drug dealer look like self-defense. Assigned to the case is an ex-cop turned assistant DA (Hutton) who's supposed to sweep the case under the rug. Then he finds out another dealer (Assante) is a witness and he happens to be romancing Hutton's former girlfriend (film debut of director Lumet's daughter). Lots of violence and raw language. 132m/C VHS, DVD. CA Dominic Chianese, Nick Nolte, Timothy Hutton, Armand Assante, Patrick O'Neal, Lee Richardson, Luis Guzman, Charles S. Dutton, Jenny Lumet, Paul Calderon, Fyvush Finkel; **D:** Sidney Lumet; **W:** Sidney Lumet; **C:** Andrzej Bartkowiak; **M:** Ruben Blades.

Q Ships 🐾🐾½ 1928 Silent German drama about a submarine commander who has inner conflicts with his country's war effort. Uses actual WWI footage. 78m/B VHS. GF J.P. Kennedy, Roy Travers, Johnny Butt, Philip Hewland; **D:** Geoffrey Barkas, Michael Barringer.

Q (The Winged Serpent) 🐾🐾🐾 1982 (R) A cult of admirers surrounds this goony monster flick about dragonlike Aztec god Quetzlcoatl, summoned to modern Manhattan by gory human sacrifices and hungry for rooftop sunbathers and construction teams. Direction and special effects are pretty ragged, but witty script helps the cast shine, especially Moriarty as a lowlife crook who's been the beast's hidden nest. 92m/C VHS, DVD. Michael Moriarty, Candy Clark, David Carradine, Richard Roundtree, Malachy McCourt, James Dixon, Eddie Jones, Bruce Carradine, Tony Page, Fred J. Scollay, Mary Louise Weller; **D:** Larry Cohen; **W:** Larry Cohen; **C:** Fred Murphy; **M:** Robert O. Ragland.

Q

QB VII 🎬🎬½ **1974** A knighted physician brings a suit for libel against a novelist for implicating him in war crimes. Hopkins as the purportedly wronged doctor and Gazzara as the writer are both superb. Ending is stunning. Adapted from the novel by Leon Uris. **313m/C VHS, DVD.** Anthony Hopkins, Ben Gazzara, Lee Remick, Leslie Caron, Juliet Mills, John Gielgud, Anthony Quayle; **D:** Tom Gries; **W:** Edward Anhalt; **M:** Jerry Goldsmith. **TV**

Quackser Fortune Has a Cousin in the Bronx 🎬🎬½ **1970 (R)** An Irish fertilizer salesman *Fun* meets an exchange student from the U.S., who finds herself attracted to this unusual, earned, but not unknowing, man. An original love story with drama and appeal. **88m/C VHS, DVD.** *IR* Gene Wilder, Margot Kidder, Eileen Colgan, May Ollis, Seamus Ford, Danny Cummins, Liz Davis; **D:** Waris Hussein; **W:** Gabriel Walsh; **M:** Gilbert Taylor.

Quadrophenia 🎬🎬🎬 **1979 (R)** Pete Townshend's excellent rock opera about an alienated youth looking for life's meaning in Britain's music scene circa 1963. Jimmy (Daniels) and his pals are Mods who brawl with their rivals, the Rockers. Music by The Who is powerful and apt. Fine performance by Sting in his acting debut as The Ace Face. **115m/C VHS, DVD.** *GB* Phil Daniels, Mark Wingett, Philip Davis, Leslie Ash, Sting, Garry Cooper, Gary Shail, Toyah Willcox, Trevor Laird, Ray Winstone; **D:** Franc Roddam; **W:** Franc Roddam, Martin Stellman, Dave Humphries, Pete Townshend; **C:** Brian Tufano; **M:** John Entwistle, Pete Townshend.

Quake 🎬🎬½ **1992 (R)** Railsback stars as a stalker who takes advantage of the 1990 San Francisco earthquake to obtain the woman of his dreams. A surveillance expert, he's after a beautiful lawyer (Anderson) and when the earthquake leaves her trapped he rushes to rescue her—only to hold her captive himself. **83m/C VHS.** Steve Railsback, Erika Anderson, Eb Lottimer, Dick Miller; **D:** Louis Morneau; **W:** Mark Evan Schwartz.

Quality Street 🎬🎬 **1937** English lovers Tone and Hepburn are separated when he leaves to fight in the Napoleonic Wars. When Tone returns years later, he's forgotten his erstwhile heartthrob. He also fails to recognize that the 16-year old coquette who's caught his eye is his old beloved in disguise. Cast works hard to overcome the absurd premise, based on the play by Sir James Barrie. **84m/B VHS.** Katharine Hepburn, Franchot Tone, Fay Bainter, Eric Blore, Cora Witherspoon, Estelle Winwood, Florence Lake, Bonita Granville; **D:** George Stevens; **W:** J.M. Barrie.

The Quarrel 🎬🎬½ **1993** Chaim Kovler is a New York poet visiting Montreal in 1948. In a park he notices a group of Orthodox Jews and discovers one is his childhood friend Hersh. Fifteen years earlier their friendship broke over Chaim's decision to give up the religious life for his writing. Having lost their families to the Holocaust in Poland, both men have immigrated to new lives in North America. They immediately pick up their quarrel over religious faith and its value, particularly in light of the Holocaust. The two characters serve too much as careful ideologues to be compelling and the story turns cloyingly sentimental. Based on a short story by Yiddish writer Chaim Grade. **88m/C VHS, DVD.** *CA* Saul Rubinek, R.H. Thomson, Arthur Grosser; **D:** Eli Cohen; **W:** David Brandes; **M:** William Goldstein.

The Quarry 🎬🎬 **1998** A nameless fugitive (Lynch) accepts a ride from a minister, whom he accidentally kills. He takes over the man's identity and possessions and journeys to the minister's new posting in a nearby isolated South African town. When his goods are in turn stolen by a poor young black man, Valentine, the town's racist white police chief not only arrests Valentine for the theft but links him to the murder when the minister's body is discovered. The original fugitive is consumed by guilt but will justice prevail? English and Afrikaans with subtitles. **112m/C VHS, DVD.** *SA* John Lynch, Serge-Henri Valcke, Jonny Phillips, Oscar Petersen, Jody Abrahams, Sylvia Esau; **D:** Marion Hansel; **W:** Marion Hansel; **C:** Bernard Lutic; **M:** Takashi Kako.

Quarterback Princess 🎬🎬 **1985** Workaday telling of the real-life girl who goes out for football and becomes homecoming queen. Heartwarming, if you like that kinda stuff, but not exciting, except for the early appearances of such '90s stars as Helen Hunt (as said quarterback), Daphne Zuniga as her sister, and Tim Robbins as a teammate. **96m/C VHS.** Helen Hunt, Don Murray, John Stockwell, Barbara Babcock, Daphne Zuniga, Kathleen Wilhoite, Tim Robbins; **D:** Noel Black. **TV**

Quartet 🎬🎬🎬 **1981 (R)** A young French woman is taken in by an English couple after her husband goes to prison. The husband seduces her, and she becomes trapped emotionally and socially. Superbly acted, claustrophobic drama based on a Jean Rhys novel. **101m/C VHS, DVD.** *GB FR* Isabelle Adjani, Alan Bates, Maggie Smith, Anthony (Corlan) Higgins; **D:** James Ivory; **W:** Ruth Prawer Jhabvala. Cannes '81: Actress (Adjani).

Quartier Mozart 🎬🎬 **1992** Sexual farce presenting the assimilation of African American pop-culture into African traditions. A local sorceress uses witchcraft to give Queen of the "Hood" a first-hand look at sexual politics. The young girl enters the body of a boy struggling to find his place in the male hierarchy established by neighborhood Casanovas. In French with English subtitles. **80m/C VHS.** Pauline Andela, Jimmy Niyora, Essindi Mindja, Sandrine Ola'a; **D:** Jean-Pierre Bekolo; **W:** Jean-Pierre Bekolo; **C:** Regis Blondeau.

Quatermass 2 🎬🎬🎬 *Enemy from Space* **1957** In the well made sequel to "Quatermass Experiment," (also known as "The Creeping Unknown") Professor Quatermass battles blobs and brainwashed zombies to rescue government officials whose bodies have been invaded by aliens. "Five Million Years to Earth" concluded the trilogy. **84m/B VHS, DVD.** *GB* Brian Donlevy, John Longden, Sidney James, Bryan Forbes, William Franklyn, Vera Day, John Van Eyssen, Michael Ripper, Michael Balfour; **D:** Val Guest; **W:** Val Guest, Nigel Kneale; **C:** Gerald Gibbs; **M:** James Bernard.

Quatermass and the Pit 🎬🎬🎬½ *Five Million Years to Earth* **1958** From the original BBC production. Professor Quatermass is up to his ears in trouble as a Martian spacecraft is found by subway workers. Not long after a monster stalks the streets of London. Remade cinematically in 1968 as "Five Million Years to Earth." **105m/C VHS, DVD.** *GB* John Mills, Simon MacCorindale, Cec Linder; **D:** Rudloph Carrier; **W:** Nigel Kneale.

Quatermass Conclusion 🎬🎬 **1979** An elderly British scientist comes out of retirement to stop an immobilizing death ray from outer space from destroying Earth. Edited version of a TV miniseries continues earlier adventures of Quatermass on film and television. **105m/C VHS, DVD.** *GB* John Mills, Simon MacCorkindale, Barbara Kellerman, Margaret Tyzack; **D:** Piers Haggard. **TV**

The Quatermass Experiment 🎬🎬🎬 *The Creeping Unknown* **1956** Excellent British production about an astronaut who returns to Earth carrying an alien infestation that causes him to turn into a horrible monster. Competent acting and tense direction. Followed by "Enemy From Space." **78m/B VHS.** *GB* Brian Donlevy, Margia Dean, Jack Warner, Richard Wordsworth, Frank Phillips; **D:** Val Guest; **M:** James Bernard.

Quatorze Juillet 🎬🎬½ **1932** A taxi driver and a flower girl meet on Bastille Day and fall in love. When he becomes involved with gangsters, she steers him back to virtue in this minor French relic from director Clair. **85m/B VHS.** *FR* Anabella Rigaud, Jorge (George) Rigaud; **D:** Rene Clair.

Que Viva Mexico 🎬🎬🎬 *Da Zdravstvujet Meksika* **1932** Eisenstein's grand unfinished folly on the history of Mexico, reconstructed and released in 1979 by his protege, Grigori Alexandrov. Divided into five sections: "Sandunga" covers the Tehuantepec jungles and its inhabitants; "Manguel" is about a peasant and his bride; "Fiesta" devotes itself to bullfighting and romance; and "Soldadera" depicts the 1910 Mexican revolution through frescoes. Along with "Greed" and "Napoleon," it remains one of cinema's greatest irrecoverable casualties. Russian narration with English subtitles. **85m/B VHS, DVD.** *RU* **D:** Sergei Eisenstein; **W:** Sergei Eisenstein, Grigori Alexandrov; **C:** Eduard Tisse.

Queen 🎬🎬🎬 **1993** Epic miniseries from Pulitzer Prize-winner Alex Haley chronicles the life of his paternal greatgrandmother, who bore a baby girl, Queen, to her white slave master. At the heart is Queen's quest for identity as she experiences unique problems due to her mixed race. She finally finds love with a ferry operator (Glover) whose role is powerful but unfortunately brief. It is this union that produces Alex's father, Simon. Although Haley died during production, he had spent considerable time sharing his vision with the staff, who also worked with and a nice interpretation of Haley's tale to above average. Worth a watch. **360m/C VHS.** Halle Berry, Ann-Margret, Jasmine Guy, Timothy Daly, Danny Glover, Madge Sinclair, Martin Sheen, Paul Winfield, Ossie Davis, Raven, Victor Garber, Lonette McKee, Sada Thompson, Elizabeth Wilson; **D:** John Erman; **W:** David Stevens. **TV**

The Queen 🎬🎬🎬 **2006 (PG-13)** Mirren is royalty personified as Britain's Queen Elizabeth II, who maintains her regal authority while dealing with more annoying politicians. The timeline begins in 1997 with the election of Tony Blair (Sheen) as Labor prime minister and moves onto what happens when Princess Diana is killed in that car crash a few months later. Frankly, the Queen can't understand the fuss but, thanks to her professionalism, when she realizes the effect the tragedy has on the country, its politics, and, ultimately, her family, she rallies to put the best royal face on the public grief. **101m/C DVD, Blu-ray Disc.** *GB FR IT* Helen Mirren, Michael Sheen, James Cromwell, Helen McCrory, Alex Jennings, Sylvia Sims; **D:** Stephen Frears; **W:** Peter Morgan; Oscars '06: Actress (Mirren); British Acad. '06: Actress (Mirren), Film; Golden Globes '07: Actress—Drama (Mirren); Screenplay; Screen Actors Guild '06: Actress (Mirren).

Queen Bee 🎬🎬½ **1955** Crawford is at her manipulative best as Southern belle Eva Phillips, married to wealthy Georgia mill owner Avery (Sullivan). The ruthless Eva is despised by her bitter, tippling husband who finds a chance at romance when cousin Jennifer (Marlow) comes to visit. Naturally, Eva can't stand any competition, though she doesn't care about Avery, and tries to break up the duo even as she seeks to renew her own affair with a former lover (Ireland). Based on the novel by Edna Lee. **94m/B VHS.** Joan Crawford, Barry Sullivan, John Ireland, Lucy Marlow, Betsy Palmer, Fay Wray; **D:** Ranald MacDougall; **W:** Ranald MacDougall; **C:** Charles B(ryant) Lang Jr.; **M:** George Duning.

Queen Christina 🎬🎬🎬½ **1933** A stylish, resonant star vehicle for Garbo, portraying the 17th-century Swedish queen from ascension to the throne to her romance with a Spanish ambassador. Alternately hilarious and moving, it holds some of Garbo's greatest and most memorable moments. Gilbert's second to last film and his only successful outing after the coming of sound. **101m/B VHS, DVD.** Greta Garbo, John Gilbert, Lewis Stone, Sir C. Aubrey Smith, Ian Keith, Reginald Owen, Elizabeth Young; **D:** Rouben Mamoulian; **C:** William H. Daniels.

Horsie **1951** Three differing vignettes, based on a rather notorious radio and TV game show of the time, in which "deserving" (or sufficiently pathetic) working-class women were rewarded for their selflessness. Part one concerns a perfect suburban family whose son contracts polio. Part two has a teen spooking his immigrant parents by working as a carnival high diver to earn college cash. The finale is a Dorothy Parker farce about a homely but kindhearted nurse caring for the child of an unappreciative couple. So popular was this segment that the film was retitled after the main character. Overall, not bad considering the source. **107m/B VHS.** Phyllis Avery, Darren McGavin, Tristam Coffin, Adam Williams, Tracey Roberts, Jack Bailey, Jim Morgan, Fort Pearson; **D:** Arthur Lubin.

Queen Kelly 🎬🎬🎬 **1929** The popularly known, slapdash version of von Stroheim's famous final film, in which an orphan goes from royal marriage to white slavery to astounding wealth. Never really finished, the film is the edited first half of the intended project, prepared for European release after von Stroheim had been fired. Even so, a campy, extravagant and lusty melodrama. Silent. **113m/B VHS, DVD.** Gloria Swanson, Walter Byron, Seena Owen, Tully Marshall, Madame Sul Te Wan; **D:** Erich von Stroheim; **W:** Erich von Stroheim; **C:** Paul Ivano, Gordon Pollock.

Queen Margot 🎬🎬½ *La Reine Margot* **1994 (R)** Blood-soaked period of French history is duly rendered on screen in big-budget costume epic. Beautiful Catholic Princess Marguerite de Valois (Adjani), is the pawn of her devious mother, the widowed queen Catherine de Medicis (Lisi). Mom skillfully manipulates unstable son Charles IX (Anglade), the nominal ruler of 1570s France, while she plots to marry Margot off to Protestant Henri de Navarre (Auteuil). Margot is contemptuous of her new husband, preferring to find her amatory amusements in the Paris streets, where she takes a handsome lover de la Mole (Perez). But both Margot and Henri are united against the Queen when Catherine's minions order the murder of the rival Huguenots—a notably violent affair known as the St. Bartholomew's Day Massacre. The history's confusing, the violence graphic, the acting flamboyant, and the visuals top-notch. Based on the novel by Alexandre Dumas. French with subtitles; originally released at 161 minutes. **135m/C VHS, DVD.** *FR* Isabelle Adjani, Daniel Auteuil, Virna Lisi, Jean-Hugues Anglade, Vincent Perez, Pascal Greggory, Miguel Bose, Dominique Blanc, Claudio Amendola, Asia Argento, Julien Rassam, Jean-Claude Brialy; **D:** Patrice Chereau; **W:** Patrice Chereau, Daniele Thompson; **C:** Philippe Rousselot; **M:** Goran Bregovic. Cannes '94: Special Jury Prize, Actress (Lisi); Cesar '95: Actress (Adjani), Cinematog., Costume Des., Support. Actor (Anglade), Support. Actress (Lisi).

Queen of Diamonds 🎬🎬 *Popsy Pop; The Butterfly Affair* **1970 (PG)** A woman pulls off the biggest diamond heist of all time. **90m/C VHS.** *FR IT* Claudia Cardinale, Stanley Baker, Henri Charriere; **D:** Jean Herman; **W:** Jean Herman, Henri Charriere; **C:** Jean-Jacques Tarbes; **M:** Frederic Botton.

Queen of Diamonds 🎬🎬 **1991** The "Queen of Diamonds" is an alienated blackjack dealer in Vegas who, in between dealing cards, casually searches for her missing husband and looks after an old man in a motel. **77m/C VHS.** Tinka Menkes; **D:** Nina Menkes; **W:** Nina Menkes.

Queen of Hearts 🎬🎬🎬½ **1989 (PG)** Excellent, original romantic comedy and a directorial triumph for Amiel in his first feature. An Italian couple defy both their families and marry for love. Four children later, we find them running a diner in England. Humorous, dramatic, sad—everything a movie can and should be. Fine performances. **112m/C VHS.** *GB* Anita Zagaria, Joseph Long, Eileen Way, Vittorio Duse, Vittorio Amandola, Ian Hawkes; **D:** Jon Amiel; **M:** Michael Convertino.

The Queen of Mean 🦴🦴½ *Leona Helmsley: The Queen of Mean* 1990 Tabloid TV-movie based on Ransdell Pierson's scandal-sheet bio of the hotel magnate and convicted tax cheat. See Leona connive. See Leona bitch. What's the point? If you ask that you're too bright to watch. **94m/C** VHS, Suzanne Pleshette, Lloyd Bridges, Bruce Weitz, Joe Regalbuto; **D:** Richard Michaels; **C:** Hanania Baer. **TV**

Queen of Outer Space *woof!* 1958 Notorious male-chauvinist sci-fi cheapie starts out slow, but then the laughs keep coming as the cast plays the hyperdumb material straight. Space cadets crash on Venus, find it ruled by women—and the dolls have wicked plans in store for mankind. Don't be surprised if you've seen the sets before since they were borrowed from "World Without End," and "Flight to Mars." **80m/C** VHS, DVD, Zsa Zsa Gabor, Eric Fleming, Laurie Mitchell, Paul Birch, Barbara Darrow, Dave Willock, Lisa Davis, Patrick Waltz, Marilyn Buferd, Marjorie Durant, Lynn Cartwright, Gerry Gaylor; **D:** Edward L. Bernds; **W:** Charles Beaumont; **C:** William F. Whitley; **M:** Marlin Skiles.

The Queen of Spades 🦴🦴🦴 1949 Mystical drama about a Russian soldier who ruins his life searching for winning methods of card playing. Well-made version of the Pushkin story. **95m/B** VHS, DVD, GB Anton Walbrook, Edith Evans, Ronald Howard, Mary Jerrold, Yvonne Mitchell, Anthony Dawson; **D:** Thorold Dickinson.

Queen of the Amazons 🦴🦴½ 1947 A girl searches for her fiance and finds him reluctantly held captive by a tribe of women who rule the jungle. **60m/B** VHS, DVD, Robert Lowery, Patricia Morison, J. Edward Bromberg, Jo›n Miljan, Keith Richards, Bruce Edwards, Wilson Benge, Amira Moustafa; **D:** Edward Finney; **W:** Roger Merton; **C:** Robert Pittack.

Queen of the Damned 🦴🦴 2002 (R) Based on the third book in Anne Rice's "Vampire Chronicles" resurrects vampire Lestat (Townsend) to rock the new millennium after a 200-year nap. He's awakened to become the singing sensation of a goth band (what's more goth than a vampire?). He soon meets up with Jesse (Moreau) a reckless vampire researcher and fellow vampires Marius (Perez), and Maharet (Olin). Lestat's new lady love, however, is Akasha (late pop star Aaliyah) the mother of all the vampires who has big plans for her and her bloodsucking beau, to, (what else?) rule the world. Her followers feel differently, however. Camp, but not camp enough to excuse it's lameness and host of lifeless performances. One dimensional characters and lackluster plot leave this drag of a Queen to Rice and vampire fans only. **101m/C** VHS, DVD, US AU Aaliyah, Stuart Townsend, Marguerite Moreau, Vincent Perez, Lena Olin, Paul McGann, Claudia Black, Bruce Spence, Christian Manon; **D:** Michael Rymer; **W:** Scott Abbott; **C:** Ian Baker; **M:** Richard Gibbs, Jonathan Davis.

Queen of the Jungle 🦴 1935 Re-edited adventure serial featuring a white woman cast off in a hot-air balloon and landing in Africa, where she is hailed as a Queen. High camp, starring ex-Our Gang-er Kornman. **85m/B** VHS, Mary Kornman, Feed Howes; **D:** Robert F. "Bob" Hill.

Queen of the Road 🦴🦴 1984 A feisty Aussie schoolteacher starts a new life as a tractor-trailer driver. **96m/C** VHS, AU Joanne Samuel, Amanda Muggleton; **D:** Bruce Best.

Queen of the Stardust Ballroom 🦴🦴½ 1975 Well-made drama about a lonely widow who goes to a local dance hall, where she meets a man and begins an unconventional late love. **96m/C** DVD, Maureen Stapleton, Charles Durning, Michael Strong, Charlotte Rae, Sam O'Steen; **D:** Sam O'Steen; **M:** Billy Goldenberg. **TV**

Queenie 🦴🦴½ 1987 Miniseries loosely based on the life of actress Merle Oberon, exploring her rise to stardom. Based on the best-selling novel by marriage. Mary long, dry passages fit for leaving the room for snacks. **223m/C** VHS, Mia Sara, Kirk Douglas, Martin Balsam, Claire Bloom, Chaim Topol, Joel Grey, Sarah Miles, Joss Ackland; **D:** Larry Peerce; **M:** Georges Delerue. **TV**

Queens Logic 🦴🦴½ 1991 (R) Ensemble comedy in the tradition of "The Big Chill" featuring the trials and tribulations of the "old-neighborhood" gang, who gather again on hometurf and reminisce. Most of the film centers around Olin and girlfriend Webb and whether or not he will chicken out of their wedding. Not bad comedy, with Mantegna delivering most of the good lines. **116m/C** VHS, DVD, John Malkovich, Kevin Bacon, Jamie Lee Curtis, Linda Fiorentino, Joe Mantegna, Ken Olin, Tom Waits, Chloe Webb, Ed Marinaro, Kelly Bishop, Tony Spiridakis; **D:** Steve Rash; **W:** Tony Spiridakis; **C:** Amir M. Mokri; **M:** Joe Jackson.

Queen's Messenger II 🦴🦴 *Witness to a Kill* 2001 (R) Super-suave-James-Bond-wannabe Captain Strong's mission is to free two gorgeous women from their captors while cracking an international smuggling ring and preventing an African country's government from being overthrown. **90m/C** VHS, DVD, Gary Daniels, Nick Boraine, Anstey, Vusi Kunene, Ron Smerczak, Lindelani Buthelezi, Isaac Chokwe, Gideon Emery, Moagi Modise, Robert Whitehead, John Whiteley; **D:** Darrell Roodt, Mark Roper; **W:** Peter John, Harry Alan Towers, Michael Swan; **C:** Adolfo Bartoli, Giulio Biccari; **M:** Rene Veksman. **VIDEO**

Queens of Comedy 🦴🦴½ 2001 (R) This "sort of" companion piece to Spike Lee's "Original Kings of Comedy" is a concert recorded at the Orpheum Theatre in Memphis starring four black stand-up comediennes—Miss Laura Hayes, Adel Givens, Sommore, and Mo'Nique. **79m/C** DVD, Adele Givens, Mo'Nique, Miss Laura Hayes, Sommore; **D:** Steve Purcell.

The Queen's Sister 🦴🦴 2005 The queen would be the never-seen Elizabeth and the sister would be perennial tabloid fodder, Princess Margaret (Cohu), a fun-loving sort who never let royal restrictions impinge on her having a good time. Unable to marry her true love (a divorced man), Margaret settles for photographer Anthony Armstrong-Jones (Stephens), eventually leading to her own divorce (the first in the royal family) and a series of controversial liaisons. Cohu is properly flamboyant but, ultimately, Margaret's life is a sad decline. **155m/C** DVD, Toby Stephens, David Threlfall, Simon Woods, Meredith MacNeill, Lucy Cohu, Aiden Gillet; **D:** Simon Cellan Jones; **W:** Craig Warner; **C:** David Katzenson; **M:** John Altman. **TV**

Queer Duck: The Movie 🦴🦴 2006 An extension of the Showtime cartoons featuring a gay duck. Queer Duck breaks up with his partner Openly Gator for an unlikely love interest—aging diva Lola Buzzard. But this turn towards heterosexuality proves to be a mistake. Raucous humor and musical numbers further liven the rude proceedings. **72m/C** DVD, Kevin M. Richardson, Maurice LaMarche, Billy West, Jackie Hoffman, Tim Curry, Conan O'Brien, David Duchovny, Jim J. Bullock. **VIDEO**

Querelle 🦴🦴½ 1983 (R) Querelle, a handsome sailor, fincs himself involved in a bewildering environment of murder, drug smuggling, and homosexuality in the port of Brest. Highly stylized and erotic sets, along with a dark look, give the film an interesting feel. Nice performances by Davis, Nero, and Moreau. Fassbinder's controversial last film, based on the story by Jean Genet. Strange, difficult narrative (such as it is), alternately boring and engrossing. **106m/C** VHS, DVD, GE Brad Davis, Jeanne Moreau, Franco Nero, Laurent Malet; **D:** Rainer Werner Fassbinder; **W:** Rainer Werner Fassbinder, Burkhard Driest; **C:** Xaver Schwarzenberger; **M:** Peer Raben.

The Quest 🦴🦴 1986 (PG) Australian film never released theatrically in the United States. A young boy (Thomas, of "E.T." fame) raised in the outback investigates a local Aboriginal superstition about a monster living in an ancient cemetery. Not bad, just dull. **94m/C** VHS, AU Henry Thomas, Tony Barry, Dennis Miller, Rachel Friend; **D:** Brian Trenchard-Smith.

Quest of the Delta Knights 🦴🦴½ 1993 (PG) Swashbuckling fantasy about a kingdom suffering under an evil ruler and his equally sinister queen. They are opposed by the heroic Delta Knights whose only chance to defeat the fiendish powers of darkness is by unearthing a legendary storehouse containing technology from the age of Atlantis and all the powers of the Ancients. Not too much sex and lots of violence to go along with the fast pacing. **97m/C** VHS, David Warner, Olivia Hussey, Corbin Allred, Brigit Brannah, David Kriegel; **D:** James Dodson; **W:** Redge Mahaffey.

Quest for Fire 🦴🦴🦴 1982 (R) An interesting story sans the usual dialogue thing. A group of men (McGill, Perlman, El-Kadi) during the Ice Age must wander the land searching for fire after they lose theirs, fending off an attack. During their quest, they encounter and battle various animals and tribesmen in order to survive. The special language they speak was developed by Anthony Burgess, while the primitive movements were Desmond "The Naked Ape" Morris. Perlman went on to become the Beast in TV's "Beauty and the Beast"; Chong, as a primitive babe, is the daughter of Tommy Chong of the comic duo Cheech and Chong. **75m/C** VHS, DVD, FR Everett McGill, Ron Perlman, Nameer El-Kadi, Rae Dawn Chong; **D:** Jean-Jacques Annaud; **W:** Gerard Brach. Oscars '82: Makeup; Genie '63: Actress (Chong).

Quest for Love 🦴🦴½ 1971 Quirky sci-fi story of a man who passes through a time warp and finds himself able to maintain two parallel lives. Based on John Wyndham's short story. **90m/C** VHS, Tom Bell, Denholm Elliott, Laurence Naismith; **D:** Ralph Thomas.

Quest for the Mighty Sword 🦴 1990 (PG-13) A warrior battles dragons, demons and evil wizards. D'Amato used the pseudonym David Hills. **94m/C** VHS, Eric Allen Kramer, Margaret Lenzey, Donald O'Brien, Dina Marrone, Chris Murphy; **D:** Joe D'Amato.

The Quest 🦴🦴 1996 (PG-13) In his directorial debut, Van Damme plays pocket Christopher Dubois, who finds his adventures just beginning when he hops a freighter heading for the Far East in order to escape police trouble. He learns about a prestigious martial arts competition, where the prize could set him up for life, if he can manage to get into the invitation-only event. After many films set in the future, Van Damme chose to set this one in the '20s, with fairly good results. He piles on the beautiful location shots until the inevitable martial arts melee toward the end. Pacing is sketchy but Van Damme does display directorial talent. **95m/C** VHS, DVD, Jean-Claude Van Damme, Roger Moore, Aki Aleong, James Remar, Jack McGee, Janet Gunn, Abdel Qissi, Louis Mandylor; **D:** Jean-Claude Van Damme; **W:** Stuart Kain, Paul Mones; **C:** David Gribble; **M:** Randy Edelman.

Quest for Camelot 🦴🦴½ 1998 (G) Camelot's future lies in the hands of heroine Kayley, who sees an opportunity to win a spot at King Arthur's roundtable when Excalibur is stolen by evil knight Ruber (Oldman). On her quest to recover the sword, she meets blind hermit Garrett and two-headed dragon Devon and Cornwall (Idle and Rickles). With an all-star cast, this first full-length animated feature from Warner Bros. wants to be a contender for the Disney animation crown, but can't quite overcome its familiar story, one-dimensional villain, and forgettable songs. However, Kayley and Garrett are strong, non-stereotypical characters that children and adults will welcome. Based on the children's novel "The King's Damosel" by Vera Chapman. **85m/C** VHS, DVD, Voices of Jessalyn Gilsig, Cary Elwes, Gary Oldman, Eric Idle, Don Rickles, Jane Seymour, Pierce Brosnan, Gabriel Byrne, Bronson Pinchot, Jaleel White, John Gielgud. Golden Globes '99: Song ("The Prayer").

A Question of Love 🦴🦴½ 1978 Fine performances in this well-done TV movie about two lesbians—one of whom is fighting her ex-husband for custody of their child. **100m/C** VHS, Gena Rowlands, Jane Alexander, Ned Beatty, Clu Gulager, Bonnie Bedelia, James Sutorius, Jocelyn Brando; **D:** Jerry Thorpe; **M:** Billy Goldenberg. **TV**

Question of Silence 🦴🦴🦴 *De Stilte Rond Christine M* 1983 (R) Three women, strangers to each other, stand trial for a murdering a man. Intricately analyzed courtroom drama with much to say about male domination. In Dutch with English subtitles or dubbed. **92m/C** VHS, NL Cox Habema, Nelly Frijda, Henriette Tol, Edda Barends; **D:** Marleen Gorris.

Question of Faith 🦴🦴½ 1993 A happily married woman is diagnosed with a rare form of cancer. Much to her family's dismay, she turns to some unconventional medical therapies in order to heal herself. Based on real aspects. Basically noble, **90m/C** VHS, Anne Archer, Sam Neill, Frances Lee McCain, James Tolkan, James Hong, C2H ›under, Louis Giambalvo, Norman Parker, Michael Constantine; **D:** Stephen Gyllenhaal; **W:** Bruce Hart.

A Question of Guilt 🦴🦴½ 1980 When her child turns up dead, a free-wheeling divorcee is the prime suspect. **100m/C** VHS, Tuesday Weld, Ron Leibman, Peter Masterson, Alex Rocco, Viveca Lindfors, Lana Wood; **D:** Robert Butler. **TV**

A Question of Honor 🦴🦴 1980 Under governmental pressures, an honest narcotics cop decides to inform on his department's corruption. Co-written and produced by ex-cop Sonny Grosso, on whom "The French Connection" was based. **100m/C** VHS, Ben Gazzara, Paul Sorvino, Robert Vaughn, Tony Roberts, Danny Aiello, Anthony Zerbe; **D:** Jud Taylor; **W:** Budd Schulberg. **TV**

A Question of Attribution 🦴🦴½ 1991 Sir Anthony Blunt (Fox) is an internationally respected art expert who also serves as an art advisor to Queen Elizabeth II. His life unravels when an on-going British Intelligence investigation reveals him to be the fourth man in the Burgess-Maclean-Philby scandal involving Englishmen who spied for, and eventually defected to, the USSR. The investigation of Blunt's covert past is paralleled with his own art investigation of a painting attributed to Titian. Three men are depicted in the art work—with a fourth male figure discovered in the painted over. Alan Bennett adapted his play for this TV drama. **90m/C** VHS, GB James Fox, David Calder, Geoffrey Palmer, Prunella Scales, Mark Payton, Jason Flemyng, Edward De Souza, Ann Beach; **D:** John Schlesinger; **W:** Alan Bennett. **TV**

Quick 🦴🦴½ 1993 (R) Polo stars as Quick, a professional assassin whose latest job is Herschel (Donovan), a mob accountant turned federal witness. When Quick is double-crossed, she "takes off" with Herschel as her insurance and a couple of bad guys (Fahey and Davi) on her trail. **99m/C** VHS, DVD, Teri Polo, Martin Donovan, Jeff Fahey, Robert Davi, Tia Carrere; **D:** Rick King; **W:** Frederick Bailey; **M:** Robert Sprayberry.

The Quick and the Dead 🦴🦴 1987 Based on a Louis L'Amour story, this cable western features a lone gunslinger who protects a defenseless settler's family from the lawless West, only to become the source of sexual tension for the wife. **91m/C** VHS, DVD, Sam Elliott, Tom Conti, Kate Capshaw, Kenny Morrison, Matt Clark; **D:** Robert Day; **C:** Dick Bush; **M:** Steve Dorff. **CABLE**

The Quick and the Dead 🦴🦴½ 1995 (R) Stone is a tough gal gunslinger out to avenge the murder of her father. Ellen arrives in the frontier town of Redemption where arch-villain Herod

Quick *(continued)* (Hackman) rules by means of violence and intimidation. Director Raimi packs in so many cliches that you're amazed that it's not a parody of the spaghetti westerns it tries to emulate. Maybe if Stone and Raimi didn't take this film so seriously, it would have been a better movie, but it's still an entertaining one. Just sit back and enjoy the wildly staged gunfights, interesting camera angles, and excellent work by Hackman and Crowe. 105m/C VHS, DVD. Sharon Stone, Gene Hackman, Leonardo DiCaprio, Russell Crowe, Kevin Conway, Lance Henriksen, Roberts Blossom, Pat Hingle, Keith David, Michael Stone, Stacey Linn Ramsower, Gary Sinise; **D:** Sam Raimi; **W:** Simon Moore; **C:** Dante Spinotti; **M:** Alan Silvestri.

Quick Change 1990 (R) Murray, Davis, and Quaid form bumbling trio of New York bank robbers who can't seem to exit the Big Apple with loot. Based on Jay Cronley's book, it's Murray's directing debut (with help from screenwriter Franklin). Engaging minor caper comedy displaying plenty of NYC dirty boulevards. 89m/C VHS, DVD. Tony Shalhoub, Stanley Tucci, Jack Gilpin, Reg E. Cathey, Bill Murray, Geena Davis, Randy Quaid, Jason Robards Jr., Bob Elliott, Victor Argo, Kathryn Grody, Philip Bosco, Phil Hartman, Kurtwood Smith, Jamey Sheridan; **D:** Bill Murray, Howard Franklin; **W:** Howard Franklin; **C:** Michael Chapman; **M:** Randy Edelman, Howard Shore.

Quick, Let's Get Married Woof! *Seven Different Ways; The Confession* 1971 Quick, let's not watch this movie. Even the people who made it must have hated it; they waited seven years to release it. Rogers runs a whorehouse; Eden is a gullible, pregnant prostitute; Gould in his big-screen debut(!) is a deaf-mute. A must-not see. 96m/C VHS. Ginger Rogers, Ray Milland, Barbara Eden, Carl Schell, Michael Ansara, Walter Abel, Scott Meyer, Cecil Kellaway, Elliott Gould; **D:** William Dieterle.

Quicker Than the Eye 1988 When a magician gets mixed up in an assassination plot, he must use his wit, cunning, and magic to get out of it. 94m/C VHS. Ben Gazzara, Mary Crosby, Catherine Jarrett, Ivan Desny, Eb Lottimer, Sophie Carle, Wolfram Berger, Dinah Hinz, Jean Yanne; **D:** Nicolas Gessner.

The Quickie 2001 (R) Get your minds out of the gutter! Actually, this mob soap opera would have been a lot more fun if it had wallowed in the gutter itself. Conflicted Russian mobster Oleg (Mashkov) is celebrating his retirement with his family on New Year's Eve at their Malibu beach house. But Oleg has been targeted for extermination and maybe exterminator Lisa (Leigh), who is supposedly at the house to get rid of the vermin, is there to do the job. Bodrov's first English-language venture. 95m/C VHS, DVD. Vladimir Mashkov, Jennifer Jason Leigh, Dean Stockwell, Lesley Ann Warren, Henry Thomas, Sergei Bodrov Jr., Brenda Bakke, Jsu Garcia; **D:** Sergei Bodrov; **C:** Sergei Kozlov; **M:** Gia Kancheli.

Quicksand 1950 Mechanic Rooney borrows $20 from his boss's cash register, intending to return it. One thing leads to another, the plot thickens, and it's downhill (for Rooney) from there. Good, tense suspense drama. 79m/B VHS, DVD. Mickey Rooney, Peter Lorre, Jeanne Cagney, Irving Pichel; **D:** Irving Pichel; **W:** Peter Smith; **C:** Lionel Lindon; **M:** Louis Gruenberg.

Quicksand 2001 (R) Bill Turner (Dudikoff) is the new shrink on a marine base and one of his patients is Randi Stewart (Theiss), who's not only a sergeant (Theiss), who's the commanding officer's (Heyday) daughter. When General Stewart is murdered, Randi becomes the prime suspect. Turner, who has taken more than a professional interest in his patient, begins investigating and learns that the base has had an unusually high number of suicides as well. 92m/C VHS, DVD. Michael Dudikoff, Brooke Theiss, Dan Hedaya, Michael O'Hagan, Douglas Weston, Richard Kind, Pamela Salem; **D:** Sam Firstenberg; **W:** Steve Schoenberg, Ruben Gordon; **C:** Sameer Reddy; **M:** Curt Harpel. VIDEO

Quicksand 2001 (R) Bank exec Martin (Keaton) is sent to Monaco to investigate some questionable offshore accounts. Apparently the money is being laundered through financing various film productions—one of which is the currently filming "Quicksand" that stars washed-up actor Jake (Caine). Soon both are in over their heads in some real-life drama. 93m/C VHS, DVD. GB FR Michael Caine, Michael Keaton, Rade Serbedzija, Judith Godreche, Xander Berkeley, Elina Lowensohn, Kathleen Wilhoite; **D:** John MacKenzie; **W:** Tim Prager; **C:** Walter McGill; **M:** Hal Lindes, Anthony Marinelli. VIDEO

Quicksand: No Escape 1991 (PG-13) Scott Reinhardt (Matheson) is a successful architect whose partner decides to secure a building contract by bribing a city official. When his partner is murdered Reinhardt is approached by a former cop (Sutherland) asking a lot of money for some incriminating evidence. Reinhardt is then drawn ever deeper into the illicit dealings, endangering his life. 93m/C VHS. Tim Matheson, Donald Sutherland, Jay Acovone, Timothy Carhart, John Finn, Marc Alaimo, Felicity Huffman, Al Pugliese; **D:** Michael Pressman; **W:** Peter Baloff, Dave Wollert.

Quicksilver 1986 (PG) A young stockbroker loses all, then quits his job to become a city bicycle messenger. Pointless, self-indulgent yuppie fantasy. 106m/C VHS, DVD. Kevin Bacon, Jami Gertz, Paul Rodriguez, Rudy Ramos, Andrew Smith, Gerald S. O'Loughlin, Laurence Fishburne, Louie Anderson; **D:** Thomas Michael Donnelly; **W:** Thomas Michael Donnelly; **M:** Tony Banks.

Quicksilver Highway 1998 (R) Storyteller Aaron Quickselver (Lloyd) entertains with two horror tales, based on the stories "The Body Politic" by Clive Barker and "Chattery Teeth" by Stephen King. The Barker story has been re-set in America and now features a plastic surgeon whose hands decide to become independent from the rest of his body, while the King story is about a traveling salesman who purchases a pair of steel teeth at a Arizona gas station, which turn out to be lifesavers when he makes the mistake of picking up a nightmarish hitchhiker. 90m/C VHS. Christopher Lloyd, Matt Frewer, Raphael Sbarge, Missy (Melissa) Crider, Veronica Cartwright, Bill Nunn, Amelia Heinle; **Cameos:** Clive Barker; **D:** Mick Garris; **W:** Mick Garris; **C:** Shelly Johnson; **M:** Mark Mothersbaugh. TV

The Quiet 2005 (R) Dot (Belle), an orphaned deaf-mute teen, goes to live with her godparents (Donovan and Falco), much to the disdain of their catty cheerleader daughter Nina (Cuthbert). Dad twitches and Mom self-medicates, Nina snarks, and Dot sulks, but the otherwise socially rejected Dot becomes a convenient confessor for Nina and others, and the secrets they reveal are doozies. Too heavy to be a teen sex farce, too outlandish and gross to be poignant, the movie melts into cheesy ick despite good turns by the main players. 96m/C DVD. US Camilla Belle, Elisha Cuthbert, Martin Donovan, Edie Falco, Shawn Ashmore, Katy Mixon; **D:** Jamie Babbit; **W:** Abdi Nazemian, Micah Schraft; **C:** M. David Mullen; **M:** Jeff Rona.

The Quiet American 2002 (R) Caine well-deserves accolades in this role of a lifetime, portraying the aging and cynical journalist Thomas Fowler, a long-time correspondent based in 1950s Saigon. He's obsessed with his beautiful young Vietnamese mistress Phuong (Yen) who also becomes a romantic object for brash American Alden Pyle (Fraser). There's something about this do-gooder, who's supposedly on a medical mission, that makes Fowler both suspicious and jealous. Set amidst the communist insurgence of Ho Chi Minh into French-held Indo-China, which will then lead to American involvement. Based on the novel by Graham Greene. 118m/C VHS, DVD. US Michael Caine, Brendan Fraser, Do Thi Hai Yen, Rade Serbedzija, Tzi Ma, Robert Stanton, Holmes Osborne, Pham Thai Mai Hoa, Quang Hai, Ferdinand Hoang; **D:** Phillip Noyce; **W:** Christopher Hampton, Robert Schenkkan; **C:** Christopher Doyle; **M:** Craig Armstrong. Natl. Bd. of Review '02: Director (Noyce).

Quiet Cool 1986 (R) When his former girlfriend's family is killed, a New York cop travels to a sleepy California town run by a pot-growing tycoon. He subsequently kills the bad guys in a Rambo-like fit of vengeance. Dopey exercise in sleepy-eyed bloodshed. 80m/C VHS, DVD. James Remar, Daphne Ashbrook, Adam Coleman Howard, Jared Martin, Fran Ryan; **D:** Clay Borris; **W:** Clay Borris; **M:** Jay Ferguson.

Quiet Day in Belfast 1974 Tragedy occurs when northern Irish patriots and British soldiers clash in an Irish betting parlor. Kidder plays a duel role: an Irish woman in love with a British soldier (Foster) and the woman's twin sister, newly arrived from Canada, who becomes the victim of a case of mistaken identity. Convincingly adapted from a Canadian stage play by Andrew Dalrymple. 92m/C VHS. CA Barry Foster, Margot Kidder, Leo Leyden, Emmet Bergin, Joyce Campion, Sean McCann; **D:** Milad Bessada; **W:** Jack Gray.

Quiet Days in Hollywood 1997 (R) *The Way We Are* Sexual nondelay in Hollywood involves a prostitute, an actor, a crook, a waitress, a rape, a gay triangle, various affairs, and related sexual experimentation. Less titillating than it sounds; German director Rusnak was something got lost in the translation. 95m/C VHS, DVD. Peter Dobson, Chad Lowe, Steven Mailer, Daryl (Chill) Mitchell, Bill Cusack, Meta Golding, Hilary Swank, Natasha Gregson Wagner; **D:** Josef Rusnak; **W:** Josef Rusnak; **C:** Dietrich Lohmann; **M:** Harald Kloser.

A Quiet Duel *Akira Kurosawa's The Quiet Duel; Shizuka Naru Ketto* 1949 Kyoji (Mifune), a young, idealistic doctor working as an army surgeon, contracts syphilis from the blood of a patient during an operation. Because the disease was virtually incurable at the time, the tormented Kyoji abandons his fiance and decides to dedicate himself to his work. Based on a play by Kazuo Kikuta. Japanese with subtitles. 95m/B VHS, DVD. JP Toshiro Mifune, Takashi Shimura, Kenjiro Uemura; **D:** Akira Kurosawa; **W:** Senkichi Taniguchi, Akira Kurosawa; **M:** Akira Ifukube.

The Quiet Earth 1985 (R) Serious science fiction film about a scientist who awakens to find himself seemingly the only human left on earth as the result of a misfired time/space government experiment. He later finds two other people, a girl and a Maori tribesman, and must try to repair the damage in order to save what's left of mankind. 91m/C VHS, DVD. NZ Bruno Lawrence, Alison Routledge, Peter Smith, Norman Fletcher, Tom Hyde; **D:** Geoff Murphy; **W:** Sam Pillsbury, Bill Baer, Bruno Lawrence; **C:** James Bartle; **M:** John Charles.

Quiet Fire 1991 (R) A health-club owner tries to get the goods on the arms-dealing congressman who killed his best friend. Hilton-Jacobs looks properly pumped up since his sweathog days on TV's "Welcome Back Kotter." 100m/C VHS, DVD. Lawrence-Hilton Jacobs, Robert ZDar, Nadia Marie, Karen Black, Lance Lindsay; **D:** Lawrence-Hilton Jacobs.

The Quiet Man 1952 The classic incarnation of Hollywood Irishness, and one of Ford's best, and funniest films. Wayne is Sean Thornton, a weary American ex-boxer who returns to the Irish hamlet of his childhood and tries to take spirited lass Mary Kate (O'Hara) as his wife, despite the strenuous objections of her brawling brother Red Will (McLaglen). Thornton's aided by the leprechaun-like Michaleen Flynn (Fitzgerald) and the local parish priest (Bond). A high-spirited and memorable film filled with Irish stew, wonderful banter, and shots of the lush countryside. Listen for the Scottish bagpipes at the start of the horse race, a slight geographic inaccuracy. 129m/C VHS, DVD. John Wayne, Maureen O'Hara, Barry Fitzgerald, Victor McLaglen, Arthur Shields, Jack MacGowran, Ward Bond, Mildred Natwick, Ken Curtis, Mae Marsh, Sean McClory, Francis Ford, D.R.O. Hatswell; **D:** John Ford; **W:** Frank Nugent; **C:** Archie Stout; **M:** Victor Young. Oscars '52: Color Cinematog., Director (Ford); Directors Guild '52: Director (Ford); Venice Film Fest. '52: Director (Ford).

The Quiet Room 1996 (PG) A nameless seven-year-old girl (Chloe Ferguson) refuses to speak when she learns her constantly quarreling parents are separating. Film is shown from only the child's perspective and her fantasies of a different life as she goes about her daily routine. Although the girl remains silent, she answers her parents in her thoughts (the voiceover lets the viewer into the girl's world) and she has flashbacks to her younger self (played by Ferguson's sister Phoebe) and when her parents loved each other. 91m/C VHS. AU Chloe Ferguson, Celine O'Leary, Paul Blackwell, Phoebe Ferguson; **D:** Rolf de Heer; **W:** Rolf de Heer; **C:** Tony Clark; **M:** Graham Tardif.

Quiet Thunder 1987 (PG-13) A hard-drinking bush pilot in Africa and a beautiful senator's wife are thrown together on the run after both witness an assassination. Mindless, thoroughly derivative "adventure." 94m/C VHS. Wayne Crawford, June Chadwick; **D:** David Rice.

Quigley 2003 (G) When a ruthless, stinking-rich businessman suddenly dies, the powers-that-be won't let him into heaven unless he goes back and fixes his wrongdoings—as a cutesy pup named Quigley. 88m/C VHS, DVD. Gary Busey, Oz (Osgood) Perkins II, Curtis Armstrong, Christopher Atkins, P.J. Ochlan, Kieran Mulroney, Bill Fagerbakke, Jessica Ferrarone, Caryn Greenhut; **D:** William B. Hillman; **W:** William B. Hillman; **M:** Eric Lundmark. VIDEO

Quigley Down Under 1990 (PG-13) A Western sharpshooter moves to Australia in search of employment. To his horror, he discovers that he has been hired to kill aborigines. Predictable action is somewhat redeemed by the terrific chemistry between Selleck and San Giacomo and the usual enjoyable dramatics from Rickman as the landowner heavy. 121m/C VHS, DVD. AU Tom Selleck, Laura San Giacomo, Alan Rickman, Chris Haywood, Ron Haddrick, Tony Bonner, Roger Ward, Ben Mendelsohn, Jerome Ehlers, Conor McDermottroe; **D:** Simon Wincer; **W:** John Hill; **C:** David Eggby; **M:** Basil Poledouris.

The Quiller Memorandum 1966 An American secret agent travels to Berlin to uncover a deadly neo-Nazi gang. Refreshingly different from other spy tales of its era. Good screenplay adapted from Adam Hall's novel, "The Berlin Memorandum." 103m/C VHS, DVD. George Segal, Senta Berger, Alec Guinness, Max von Sydow, George Sanders; **D:** Michael Anderson Sr.; **W:** Harold Pinter; **M:** John Barry.

Quills 2000 (R) Follows the last years of the life of the Marquis de Sade (played by Rush), which he spent in an insane asylum as punishment for his erotic writings. Sade continues to write while imprisoned, and with the help of his secret courier, Madeleine (played by Winslet), is able to distribute his stories to the public. Unfortunately, the movie uses Sade's imprisonment to put forth lessons about the importance of freedom of expression and perils of censorship, thereby sacrificing a closer investigation of the real story—the man's boiling imagination. Worth viewing for the performances and for the glimpse into the life of one of histories most fascinating authors. Based on the off-Broadway play by David Wright. 123m/C VHS, DVD. Geoffrey Rush, Kate Winslet, Joaquin Rafael (Leaf) Phoenix, Michael Caine; **D:** Philip Kaufman; **W:** Doug Wright; **C:** Rogier Stoffers; **M:** Stephen Warbeck. Natl. Bd. of Review '00: Film, Support. Actor (Phoenix).

Quilombo 1984 The title refers to a legendary settlement of runaway slaves in 17th-century Brazil; an epic chronicles its fortunes as leadership passes from a wise ruler to a more militant one who goes to war against the government. Stunning scenery, tribal images, and folk songs, but the numerous characters seldom come to life as personalities. One of Brazil's most expensive films, in Portuguese with English subtitles. 114m/C VHS, DVD. BR Vera Fischer, Antonio Pompeo, Zeze Motta, Toni Tornado; **D:** Carlos Diegues; **W:** Carlos Diegues.

Quinceanera 🐾🐾🐾 2006 (R) Quinceanera is a traditional celebration that marks a coming-of-age at 15 for Mexican American girls. Magdalena (newcomer Rios) reaches this milestone with the revelation that she's pregnant (even though she swears she's a virgin). Banished from her home by her devout father, she takes refuge with her Uncle Tomas (Gonzalez), a wise octogenarian who is also sheltering her gay nephew Carlos (Garcia). Meanwhile, Tomas's modest but longstanding home is threatened by his new landlords, thus unfolding a complex story of tradition versus change, the definition of family, and gentrification. Effective coca-stylings illuminate life in L.A.'s Echo Park community and make the flick's ending utterly satisfying. 90m/C DVD. *C:* Emily Rios, Jesse Garcia, Chalo Gonzalez, Jesus Castanos-Chima; *D:* Richard Glatzer, Wash Westmoreland; *W:* Richard Glatzer, Wash Westmoreland. *C:* Eric Steelberg; *M:* Victor Bock.

Quintet 🐾🐾 1979 Atypical Altman sci-fi effort. The stakes in "Quintet," a form of backgammon, are high—you bet your life. Set during the planet's final ice age, Newman and wife Fossey wander into a dying city and are invited to play the game, with Fossey losing quickly. Bizarre and pretentious, with heavy symbolic going. 118m/C VHS, DVD. Paul Newman, Bibi Andersson, Fernando Rey, Vittorio Gassman, David Langton, Nina Van Pallandt, Brigitte Fossey; *D:* Robert Altman; *W:* Lionel Chetwynd, Patricia Resnick, Robert Altman, Frank Barhydt.

Quiz Show 🐾🐾🐾🐾 1994 (PG-13) Redford's intelligent, entertaining, and morally complex film about the TV game show scandals of the late '50s is his most accomplished work to date. At the center of the film is Charles Van Doren (Fiennes), an intellectual, golden boy who dethrones champion of the rigged "Twenty-One." The program's sponsor felt Stempel, a nerdy Jewish grad's everyman qualities were wearing thin and wanted a more polished image, which they found in hand-some, sophisticated Van Doren. Federal investigator Goodwin (Morrow) suspects 1970. Neophyte leads are appealing, natural. Based on a book by Doris Pilkington, ther. With strong script and gorgeous lens-ing, this modern Faust story is a brilliant reflection on corporate greed, class rivalry, and the powers of television. Based on the book "Remembering America: A Voice From the Sixties" by Richard N. Goodwin. 133m/C VHS, DVD. John Turturro, Rob Morrow, Ralph Fiennes, Paul Scofield, David Paymer, Hank Azaria, Christopher McDonald, Johann Carlo, Elizabeth Wilson, Mira Sorvino, Griffin Dunne, Martin Scorsese, Barry Levinson; *D:* Robert Redford; *W:* Paul Attanasio; *C:* Michael Ballhaus; *M:* Mark Isham, British Acad. '94. Adapt. Screenplay; N.Y. Film Critics '94.

Quo Vadis 🐾🐾🐾 1951 Larger-than-life production about Nero and the Christian persecution. Done on a giant scale; features exciting fighting scenes, romance, and fabulous costumes. Definitive version of the classic novel by Henryk Sienkiewicz. Remade for Italian TV in 1985. 171m/C VHS. Robert Taylor, Deborah Kerr, Peter Ustinov, Patricia Laffan, Finlay Currie, Abraham Sofaer, Marina Berti, Buddy Baer, Felix Aylmer, Nora Swinburne, Elspeth March; *Cameos:* Sophia Loren, Elizabeth Taylor; *D:* Mervyn LeRoy; *C:* Robert L. Surtees; *M:* Miklos Rozsa; Golden Globes '52: Support. Actor (Ustinov).

Quo Vadis 🐾🐾🐾½ 1912 One of the first truly huge Italian silent epics. The initial adaptation of the Henryk Sienkiewicz novel about Nero and ancient Rome. Probably the cinema's first great financial success. 45m/B VHS. Amleto Novelli, Gustavo Serena, Amelia Cattaneo, Carlo Cattaneo, Lea Giunchi; *D:* Enrico Guazzoni; *W:* Enrico Guazzoni; *C:* Eugenio Bava.

Quo Vadis 🐾🐾½ 1985 (R) Third screen version of Henryk Sienkiewicz's book. See the other two first. This one is slow and perfunctory. Brandauer is memorable as Nero; Quinn (in the lead) is the son of Anthony. 122m/C VHS. *C:* Klaus Maria Brandauer, Frederic Forrest, Christina Raines, Marina Therese Rein, Francesco Quinn, Barbara DeRossi, Phillippe LeRoy, Max von Sydow, Gabriele Ferzetti, Massimo Girotti, Leopoldo Trieste; *D:* Franco Rossi.

'R Xmas 🐾🐾 2001 Brancato and de Matteo star as the unnamed husband and wife whose idyllic Manhattan days disguise their shady heroin dealings by night in the Bronx. It's Christmas time and everything is just swell for the mom and pop drug dealers until they attempt to illegally obtain a hard-to-find toy for their daughter (Valens), which ends in dad getting kidnapped by a thug (Ice-T) who wants a huge ransom and asks that they refrain from dealing drugs in the future. They're then left to decide between their tarnished American Dream and going straight and being poor. Some racial issues are explored (she's Puerto Rican, he's Dominican) as well as the obvious moral and financial issues. De Matteo makes her character complex and eminently watchable through somewhat predictable and tired material. 83m/C VHS, DVD. Drea De Matteo, Ice-T, Victor Argo, Lisa Valens; *D:* Abel Ferrara; *W:* Abel Ferrara, Scott Pardo; *C:* Ken Kelsch.

Rabbit-Proof Fence 🐾🐾🐾½ 2002 (PG) Fascinating, true story of three mixed-race Aboriginal girls in 1930s Australia, who escape their forced incarceration at an institution designed to train such children, snatched from their parents by the government, as domestic workers. Embarking on an incredible 1,500 mile journey to return home, Molly (Sampi), Daisy (Sansbury) and Gracie (Monaghan) follow the line of a fence—the longest unbroken piece of fence ever created—built by the government to keep out the rabbits that had overrun the farmlands. Hunted by the authorities, the girls struggle to survive in a heartbreaking and riveting adventure. Mailman is a sympathetic white woman who helps the girls along the way while Branagh plays Neville, a first-class bigot who oversaw the racist policies that the Australian government enforced until 1970. Neophyte leads are appealing, natural. Based on a book by Doris Pilkington, daughter of one of the girls. 95m/C VHS, DVD. AU GB Everlyn Sampi, Tianna Sansbury, Laura Monaghan, Kenneth Branagh, David Gulpilil, Deborah Mailman, Jason Clarke, Garry McDonald, Ningali Lawford, Myarn_awford; *D:* Phillip Noyce; *W:* Christine Olsen; *C:* Christopher Doyle; *M:* Peter Gabriel; Natl. Bd. of Review '02: Director (Noyce).

Rabbit Test 🐾½ 1978 (PG) In Rivers' first directorial effort, a clumsy virginal guy becomes the world's first pregnant man. So irreverent it's almost never in good taste, and so poorly written it's almost never funny. 86m/C VHS. Sab Shimono, Billy Crystal, Roddy McDowall, Imogene Coca, Paul Lynde, Alex Rocco; George Gobel; *D:* Joan Rivers.

Rabid 🐾🐾 1977 (R) A young girl undergoes a radical plastic surgery technique and develops a strange and unexplained lesion in her armpit. She also finds she has an unusual craving for human blood. 90m/C VHS, DVD. *CA* Marilyn Ryshpan, Frank Moore, Joe Silver, Howard Ryshpan, Patricia Gage, Susan (Suzan) Roman, Roger Periard, Victor Desy; *D:* David Cronenberg; *W:* David Cronenberg; *C:* Rene Verzier.

Rabid Grannies WOOF! 1989 (R) Wicked satire about two aging sisters who receive a surprise birthday gift from their devil-worshipping nephew. The gift turns their party into a gorefest as they rip into various family members—literally. Any humor will be lost on any but the most die-hard Troma fans. Dubbed. 89m/C VHS, DVD. BE Catherine Aymerie, Caroline Brackman, Danielle Daven, Raymond Lescot, Anne Marie Fox, Richard Cotica, Patricia Davie; *D:* Emmanuel Kervyn; *W:* Emmanuel Kervyn; *C:* Hugh Labye; *M:* Jean-Bruno Castelain, Pierre-Damien Castelain.

Race to Freedom: The Story of the Underground Railroad 🐾🐾½ 1994 Story of four fugitive slaves, in 1850, who struggle to get from North Carolina to the safety of Canada through a network of safe-houses and people willing to risk smuggling them to asylum. 90m/C VHS, DVD. *CA* Courtney B. Vance, Janet Bailey, Glynn Turman, Tim Reid, Michael Riley, Dawnn Lewis, Ron White, Alfre Woodard; *D:* Don McBrearty; *W:* Nancy Trite Botkin, Diana Braithwaite; *M:* Christopher Dedrick. CABLE.

Race to Space 🐾🐾 2001 (PG) German rocket scientist Wilhelm Von Huber (Woods) and his young son Billy (Linz) move to Cocoa Beach, Florida, in 1960 so dad can work for NASA on the Mercury program. Billy, who's been lonely since his mother's death, is taken under the wing of vet Donni McGuinness (Gish), and bonds with Mac, one of the chimps being trained to go into space, which in turn helps him get closer to his father. The chimp steals the movie, which is heavy on the sentimentality. 104m/C VHS, DVD. Alex D. Linz, James Woods, William Devane, William Atherton, Chad Riley, Dawnn Lewis, Ron White, Alfre Woodard; *D:* Sean McNamara; *W:* Eric Gardner, Steven Kaplan; *D:* Sean McNamara; *C:* Christian Sebaldt; *M:* John Newfield.

Rachida 🐾🐾🐾 2005 Rachida is a young school teacher in terror-stricken 1990s Algeria. When stopped by street kids who demand she place a bomb in her classroom, she refuses. Shot point-blank and left for dead, Rachida miraculously survives. Under the care of her mother, far from the dangers of the city life, she begins to recover. Still, the struggle to find hope in such a violent world proves difficult for everyone. An unflinching portrait of fear with a brave performance from Djouadi; promising debut from writer/director Bachir. Arabic and French with English subtitles. 100m/C DVD, FR AL Ibtissem Djouad, Bahia Rachedi, Rachida Messaoui En, Zaki Boulenafed, Hamid Remas; *D:* Yamina Bachir; *W:* Yamina Bachir.

Rachel, Rachel 🐾🐾🐾½ 1968 (R) Such Men are Dangerous 1955 Douglas brings power to the role of a man determined to advance to the winners' circle. Exciting European location cinematography, but not much plot. 112m/C VHS, Gilbert Roland, Kirk Douglas. Car scenes are great. Standard, but less and salvage his career. Standard, but less. Rachel teaches by day, wearing simple, practical dresses and her hair up. By night she caters to her domineering mother by preparing refreshments for her parties. This sexually repressed, spinster school-teacher, however, gets one last chance at romance in her small Connecticut town. Woodward mixes just the right amounts of loneliness and sweetness in the leading role. A surprising award-winner that was an independent production of Newman's. Based on Margaret Laurence's "A Jest of God." 102m/C VHS, Joanne Woodward, James Olson, Estelle Parsons, Geraldine Fitzgerald, Donald Moffat; *D:* Paul Newman; *W:* Stewart Stern; Golden Globes '69: Actress—Drama (Woodward), Director (Newman); N.Y. Film Critics '68: Actress (Woodward), Director (Newman).

Rachel River 🐾🐾🐾 1987 (PG-13) A divorced radio personality struggles to make something of her life in her small Minnesota town. 88m/C VHS. Pamela Reed, Craig T. Nelson, Viveca Lindfors, James Olson, Zeljko Ivanek, Jo Henderson, Alan North, Jon Guest; *D:* Sandy Smolan; *W:* Judith Guest; *M:* Arvo Par.

Rachel's Man 🐾 1975 A big-screen version of the Biblical love story of Jacob and Rachel. 115m/C VHS, DVD. Mickey Rooney, Rita Tushingham, Leonard Whiting, Michal Bat-Adam; *D:* Moshe Mizrahi.

Race Against Time 🐾🐾 2000 Another bleak futuristic thriller but with fast-paced and suspenseful action. When Gabriel's (Roberts) son is diagnosed with a deadly virus, Gabriel learns that the vaccine will cost him mucho dinero—and he has only 12 hours to come up with the cash. So he agrees to sell his organs to the Lifecorps for harvesting in a year's time, then it's bye-bye for Gabe. But when his son dies anyway, Gabriel tries to get out of the agreement, especially when it seems this bargain wasn't so straightforward. 90m/C VHS, DVD. Eric Roberts, Cary Elwes, Sarah Wynter, Chris Sarandon; *D:* Geoff Murphy. CABLE.

Race for Glory 🐾🐾½ 1989 (R) A young motorcyclist builds a super-bike he hopes will help him win a world championship race. Will he win? Can you stand the suspense? Let's just say there's a happy ending. 102m/C VHS, Alex McArthur, Peter Berg, Pamela Ludwig; *D:* Rocky Lang; *M:* Jay Ferguson.

Race for Life 🐾½ 1955 Mask of Dust A race car driver attempts to make a comeback despite objections from his wife. He races around Europe (great scenery); she leaves him; he tries to win her back and salvage his career. Standard. 69m/B VHS. GB Richard Conte, Mari Aldon, George Coulouris, Alec Mango, Meredith Edwards, Richard Marner, Jeremy Hawk; *D:* Terence Fisher; *W:* Richard H. Landau; *C:* Walter J. (Jimmy W.) Harvey; *M:* Leonard Salzedo.

Race for Your Life, Charlie Brown 🐾🐾½ 1977 (G) Another in the popular series of "Peanuts" character films. This one features Charlie Brown, Snoopy, and all the gang spending an exciting summer in the American wilderness. 76m/C VHS. *D:* Bill Melendez, Phil Roman; *W:* Charles M. Schulz; *M:* Ed Bogas; *V:* Gail Davis, Melanie Kohn, Duncan Watson, Gregory Felton, Stuart Brotman, Liam Martin, Ed Bogas.

Race the Sun 🐾🐾 1996 (PG) There's nothin' new under this sun. Tired story of a group of young losers who band together to beat the odds and compete in an unusual contest. This time it's a Hawaiian high school solar car team traveling to Australia to go for the prize against the big shots and snobs. Based on true events, it features some nice scenery from Eerry and the main locations, but not much else. Uninspired but basically harmless, this one's fine for the kids. 100m/C VHS, DVD. Halle Berry, James Belushi, Casey Affleck, Eliza Dushku, Kevin Tighe, Anthony Michael Ruiwai, J. Moki Cho, Dion Basco, Sara Tanaka, Nadja Pionilla, Steve Zahn, Bill Hunter; *D:* Charles Kangan's; *W:* Barry Morrow; *C:* David Burr, *M:* Graeme Revell.

Race with the Devil 🐾🐾½ 1975 Vacationers are terrorized by devil worshippers after they witness a sacrificial killing. Heavy on car chases; light on plot and redeeming qualities. Don't waste your time. 88m/C VHS, DVD. Peter Fonda, Warren Oates, Loretta Swit, Lara Parker, R.G. Armstrong; *D:* Jack Starrett; *W:* Wes Bishop, Lee Frost; *C:* Robert C. Jessup.

The Racers 🐾🐾½ 1955 Such Men are Dangerous 1955 Douglas brings power to the role of a man determined to advance to the winners' circle. Exciting European location cinematography, but not much plot. 112m/C VHS, Gilbert Roland, Kirk Douglas...ee J. Cobb, Cesar Romero, Bella Darvi; *D:* Henry Hathaway. VIDEO

The Rachel Papers 🐾🐾🐾 1989 (R) Based on the Martin Amis novel, this is the funny/sad tale of an Oxford youth who plots via his computer the seduction of a beautiful American girl. For anyone who has ever loved someone just out of their reach. 92m/C VHS, DVD. Dexter Fletcher, Ione Skye, James Spacer, Jonathan Pryce Bill Paterson, Michael Gambon, Lesley Sharp; *D:* Damian Harris; *W:* Damian Harris; *M:* Chaz Jankel.

Rachel and the Stranger 🐾🐾½ 1948 A God-fearing farmer declares his love for his wife when a handsome stranger (Mitchum) nearly woos her away. Well-cast, well-paced, charming Western comedy-drama. 93m/B VHS, Loretta Young, Robert Mitchum, William Holden, Gary Gray; *D:* Norman Foster.

Racing Luck 🐾🐾 Red Hot Tires 1935 While working at a race track, a man is framed and forced to work for another stable. 56m/B VHS. William Boyd, Barbara Worth, George Ernest, Esther Muir, Dick Curtis; *D:* Sam Newfield.

Racing

Racing Stripes 🦴🦴 **2005 (PG)** Farmer Nolan Walsh (Greenwood), finds a baby zebra (voiced by Muniz) left by a traveling circus in rural Kentucky and raises him on his farm. Stripes grows up yearning to be a racing horse, just as Channing (Panettiere), the farmer's daughter, yearns to be a jockey. The plot thickens as Walsh is a former horse trainer whose wife died in a riding accident and has since forbidden Channing from racing. Strange combination of "Babe," "National Velvet" and "Charlotte's Web" uses live animals with creepy computer-enhanced mouths for the speaking parts. Kids will enjoy it, but mom and dad might get bored with its routine plotlines. 102m/C DVD. *US* Bruce Greenwood, Hayden Panettiere, M. Emmet Walsh, Wendie Malick; *D:* Frederick Du Chau; *W:* Frederick Du Chau, David F. Schmidt; *C:* David Eggby; *M:* Mark Isham; *V:* Frankie Muniz, Mandy Moore, Michael Clarke Duncan, Joshua Jackson, Jeff Foxworthy, Joe Pantoliano, Michael Rosenbaum, Steve Harvey, David Spade, Snoop Dogg, Fred Dalton Thompson, Dustin Hoffman, Whoopi Goldberg.

Racing with the Moon 🦴🦴🦴 **1984 (PG)** Sweet, nostalgic film about two buddies awaiting induction into the Marines in 1942. They have their last chance at summer romance. Benjamin makes the most of skillful young actors and conventional story. Great period detail. Keep your eyes peeled for glimpses of many rising young stars including Hannah and Carvey. 108m/C VHS, DVD. Sean Penn, Elizabeth McGovern, Nicolas Cage, John Karlen, Rutanya Alda, Max (Casey Adams) Showalter, Crispin Glover, Suzanne Adkinson, Page Hannah, Michael Madsen, Dana Carvey, Carol Kane, Michael Talbott, Michael Schoeffling; *D:* Richard Benjamin; *W:* Steven Kloves; *C:* John Bailey; *M:* Dave Grusin.

The Racket 🦴🦴🦴 **1951** Police captain Mitchum tries to break up mob racket of gangster Ryan. Internecine strife on both sides adds complexity. Mitchum and especially Ryan are super; fine, tense melodrama. 88m/B VHS, DVD. Robert Ryan, Robert Mitchum, Lizabeth Scott, Ray Collins, William Conrad, Don Porter; *D:* John Cromwell.

The Racketeer 🦴🦴½ **1929** A racketeer falls in love with a pretty girl and attempts to win her over. As part of his plan, the gangster arranges to help the girl's boyfriend begin his musical career in exchange for the girl's promise to marry him. 68m/B VHS, DVD. Robert Armstrong, Hedda Hopper; *D:* Howard Higgin.

Racketeers of the Range 🦴🦴½ **1939** Cattleman fights a crooked attorney who wants to sell his client's stock to a large meat packing company. 62m/B VHS. George O'Brien, Marjorie Reynolds, Chill Wills, Ray Whitley; *D:* David Ross Lederman.

Racquet 🦴 **1979** Tennis pro Convy searches for true love and a tennis court of to call his own in Beverly Hills. Lame, sophomoric, and unfunny. 87m/C VHS. Bert Convy, Edie Adams, Lynda Day George, Phil Silvers, Bobby Riggs, Bjorn Borg, Tanya Roberts; *D:* David Winters.

Rad 🦴½ **1986 (PG)** Teenage drama revolving around BMX racing and such dilemmas as: can the good guys beat the bad guys, who's got the fastest bike, must you cheat to win, and should our hero miss his SAT tests to compete in "the big race..." Directed by stunt-coordinator Needham. 94m/C VHS. Bill Allen, Bart Conner, Talia Shire, Lori Loughlin; *D:* Hal Needham; *W:* Sam Bernard.

Radar Men from the Moon

🦴🦴 **1986 (PG)** *Retik, the Moon Menace* 1952 Commando Cody, with his jet-pack, fights to defend the earth from invaders from the moon. Twelve-episode serial on two tapes. Silly sci-fi. 152m/B VHS, DVD. George D. Wallace, Aline Towne, Roy Barcroft, William Bakewell, Clayton Moore; *D:* Fred Brannon.

Radar Patrol vs. Spy King 🦴🦴½ **1949** Special agent Alyn and his buxom Vargas girl Jean Dean battle the deadly Baroda and his ring of saboteurs, hell-bent on destroying America. 12 episodes of the serial edited onto two cassettes. 167m/B VHS, Anthony Warde, George Lewis, John Merton, Eve Whitney, Kirk Alyn, Jeanne Dean; *D:* Fred Brannon; *W:* Ellis W. Carter; *M:* Stanley Wilson, Sol Shor.

Radar Secret Service 🦴½ **1950** Two servicemen witness the hijacking of a truck loaded with nuclear material. 59m/B VHS. John Howard, Adele Jergens, Tom Neal, Ralph Byrd; *D:* Sam Newfield; *C:* Ernest Miller; *M:* Russell Garcia, Richard Hazard.

Radiance 🦴🦴 **1998** Three half-sisters reunite in their rundown family home, located in the sugar cane country of Australia's tropical north, to bury their mother. Resentful Mae (Morton-Thomas) feels she was trapped into caring alone for their prematurely senile mother while sophisticated Cressy (Maza) became a successful opera singer and youngest sister Nona (Mailman) indulged her party girl ways. Old grievances are aired and the trio set off more than one kind of fireworks before... Adapted by Nowra from his play. 83m/C VHS. *AU* Trisha Morton-Thomas, Rachel Maza, Deborah Mailman; *D:* Rachel Perkins; *W:* Louis Nowra; *C:* Warwick Thornton; *M:* Alistair Jones.

Radio 🦴🦴½ **2003 (PG)** Feelgooder inspired by the true story of the mentally disabled James "Radio" Kennedy (Gooding Jr.), who befriends the kindly local football coach (Harris) and becomes a beloved mascot of sorts in Anderson, South Carolina circa 1976. Coach Jones finds Radio (so named for his ample, much-loved collection of discarded radios) locked in a storage shed after being taunted by a few players and is determined to help him. Radio, in turn, ends up teaching the town a lesson or two about the Golden Rule. Top notch cast and script can't completely save the somewhat saccharine but nonetheless inspirational story. Based on a *Sports Illustrated* story by Gary Smith. 109m/C VHS, DVD. *US* Cuba Gooding Jr., Ed Harris, Alfre Woodard, S. Epatha Merkerson, Chris Mulkey, Sarah Drew, Riley Smith, Patrick Breen, Brent Sexton, Debra Winger; *D:* Mike Tollin; *W:* Mike Rich; *C:* Don Burgess; *M:* James Horner.

Radio Days 🦴🦴🦴 **1987 (PG)** A lovely, unpretentious remembrance of the pre-TV radio culture. Allen tells his story in a series of vignettes centering around his youth in Brooklyn, his eccentric extended family, and the legends of radio they all followed. The ubiquitous Farrow is a young singer hoping to make it big. 89m/C VHS, DVD. Mia Farrow, Dianne Wiest, Julie Kavner, Michael Tucker, Wallace Shawn, Josh Mostel, Tony Roberts, Jeff Daniels, Kenneth Mars, Seth Green, William Magerman, Diane Keaton, Renee Lippin, Danny Aiello, Gina DeAngelis, Kitty Carlisle Hart, Mercedes Ruehl, Tito Puente; *D:* Woody Allen; *W:* Woody Allen; *C:* Carlo Di Palma; *Narr:* Woody Allen.

Radio Flyer 🦴🦴 **1992 (PG-13)** It's 1969 and Mike and Bobby have just moved to northern California with their divorced mom. Everything would be idyllic if only their mother hadn't decided to marry a drunken child abuser who beats Bobby whenever the mood strikes him. Mike decides to help Bobby escape by turning their Radio Flyer wagon into a magic rocketship that will carry Bobby to safety, but ultimately proves tragic. Appealing version of childhood dreams sans the child abuse angle (toned down though it was), which is abruptly and unsatisfactorily handled. 114m/C VHS, DVD. Elijah Wood, Joseph Mazzello, Lorraine Bracco, Adam Baldwin, John Heard, Ben Johnson; *D:* Richard Donner; *Nar:* Tom Hanks.

Radio Inside 🦴🦴½ **1994** Aimless Matthew (McNamara) comes to live with older brother Michael (Walsh) after their dad's death. Matthew needs someone to listen to him but, unfortunately, his picks his brother's neglected girlfriend Natalie (Shue). Aimless story, as well. 91m/C VHS. William McNamara, Dylan Walsh, Elisabeth Shue, Gil Goldstein; *D:* Jeffrey Bell; *W:* Jeffrey Bell. **CABLE**

Radio Patrol 🦴🦴 **1937** Plenty of action and thrills abound in this 12-chapter serial. Pinky Adams, radio cop, is assisted by his trusty canine partner, Irish (Silver-wolf). A cop's best friend is his dog. 235m/B VHS. Mickey Rentschler, Adrian Morris, Monte Montague, Jack Mulhall, Grant Withers, Catherine Hughes; *D:* Ford Beebe, Cliff(ord) Smith.

Radioactive Dreams 🦴🦴 **1986 (R)** Surreal, practically senseless fantasy wherein two men, trapped in a bomb shelter for 15 years with nothing to read but mystery novels, emerge as detectives into a post-holocaust world looking for adventure. 94m/C VHS. John Stockwell, Michael Dudikoff, Lisa Blount, George Kennedy, Don Murray, Michelle Little; *D:* Albert Pyun; *W:* Albert Pyun.

Radioland Murders 🦴🦴½ **1994 (PG)** Looks overwhelm weak plot in this mystery-comedy about 1939 Chicago radio station WBN. Lots of stock types (befuddled director, preening announcer, lusty vamp) with Masterson as Penny, the secretary holding everything together except for her marriage to head writer Roger (Benben). Then bodies start piling up during the live broadcast and everyone runs around frantically trying to solve the crimes and keep the broadcast going. Tiring and cliched. 112m/C VHS, DVD. Brian Benben, Mary Stuart Masterson, Ned Beatty, George Burns, Brion James, Michael Lerner, Scott Michael Campbell, Anita Morris, Jeffrey Tambor, Scott Michael Campbell, Christopher Lloyd, Larry Miller, Corbin Bernsen; *Cameos:* Robert Klein, Harvey Korman, Peter MacNichol, Joey Lawrence, Bob(cat) Goldthwait; *D:* Mel Smith; *W:* Willard Huyck, Gloria Katz, Jeff Reno, Ron Osborn; *C:* David Tattersall; *M:* Joel McNeely.

Rafferty & the Gold Dust Twins 🦴½ *Rafferty and the Highway Hustlers* **1975 (R)** Two women kidnap a motor vehicle inspector at gunpoint in Los Angeles and order him to drive to New Orleans. En route, they become pals. Wandering, pointless female buddy flick. 91m/C VHS. Alan Arkin, Sally Kellerman, MacKenzie Phillips, Charles Martin Smith, Harry Dean Stanton; *D:* Dick Richards; *M:* Arie Butler.

The Raffle 🦴🦴½ **1994 (R)** Frank and David travel the globe to find the world's most beautiful woman, who'll be the prize date of the lucky guy with the winning raffle ticket. 100m/C VHS. Nicholas Lea, Bobby Dawson, Jennifer Clement, Teri-Lynn Rutherford, Jay Underwood, Mark Hamill; *D:* Gavin Wilding; *W:* John Fairley; *M:* Robert O. Ragland.

Raffles 🦴🦴🦴 **1930** Debonair and dashing gentleman thief A.J. Raffles (Coleman) is a famed cricket player by day and a cat burglar by night, who's always been successful at eluding Scotland Yard. Then he falls for beautiful socialite Lady Gwen Manders (Francis) and gets invited to a weekend house party where Lady Kitty Melrose (Skipworth) just happens to own a very valuable necklace and one of the other guests is suspicious Scotland Yard inspector McKenzie (Torrance). Naturally Raffles goes after the jewels. Based on the novel "The Amateur Cracksman" by Ernest William Hornung. Director D'Arrast was fired by producer Goldwyn and Fitzmaurice finished the film. 72m/B VHS. Ronald Colman, Kay Francis, Alison Skipworth, David Torrence, Bramwell Fletcher, Frances Dade; *D:* Harry D'Abbadie D'Arrast, George Fitzmaurice; *W:* Sidney Howard; *C:* George Barnes; Gregg Toland.

Rage 🦴🦴 **1972 (PG)** Scott's directorial debut. A military helicopter sprays peaceloving rancher Scott and his son with nerve gas. The son's death is covered up; the rancher embarks on a vengeful rampage. Scott's sudden transformation to avenging killer is implausible and overwrought. 100m/C VHS, DVD. James Whitmore, Yaphet Kotto, Caroline McWilliams, Vic Tayback, Sharon Farrell, Craig T. Nelson, Garry Walberg; *D:* George C. Scott; *C:* Fred W. Koenekamp.

Rage 🦴🦴 **1980** Well-acted, well-written, nerve-wracking drama about a convicted rapist who finds help through difficult therapy. Focuses on how the sex offender discovers the "whys" behind his assaults. 100m/C VHS, David Soul, James Whitmore, Yaphet Kotto, Caroline McWilliams, Kenneth Tobey, Ed Lauter, Nicolas Beauvy, Dabbs Greer; *D:* George C. Scott; *C:* Allen Daviau. **TV**

Rage 🦴🦴½ **1995 (R)** When Alex Gainer (Daniels) is kidnapped in a high-tech lab experiment. Injected with chemicals that induce blind and killing rages, Alex escapes and unwillingly goes on a murderous rampage. Now he must find the antidote and clear his name before it happens again. 94m/C VHS, DVD. Gary Daniels, Ken Tigar, Jillian McWhirter, Fiona Hutchinson, Peter Jason, Mark Metcalf; *D:* Joseph Merhi; *W:* Jacobsen Hart, Joseph John Barmettler Jr.; *C:* Ken Blakey; *M:* Louis Febre.

The Rage 🦴🦴 **1996 (R)** Nick Travis (Lamas) is a burned-out FBI agent with a brand new partner Kelly McCord (Cloke), who has no real experience. He's after a gang of anti-government killers led by psycho Dacy (Busey). Good action sequences substitute for the lack of plot sense. 95m/C VHS, DVD. Lorenzo Lamas, Gary Busey, Kristen Cloke, Roy Scheider, David Carradine, Jenny (Jennifer) McShane; *D:* Sidney J. Furie; *W:* Greg Mellott; *C:* Donald M. Morgan; *M:* Paul Zaza.

The Rage 🦴🦴 **2007** Old-fashioned gorefest about a mad scientist and a deadly mutating virus. Russian scientist Viktor (Divoff) get the pharmaceutical shaft after discovering a cancer cure. To get even he develops the rage virus, which turns the infected into flesh-eating mutants. One of his test subjects escapes, dies in the woods, and becomes dinner for vultures. The infected birds then attack anyone/anything they find, some of whom eventually turn up at Viktor's cabin. There's lots of limb-ripping, blood-gushing, and flesh-noshing with some decent special effects. 99m/C DVD. Andrew Divoff, Misty Mundae, Reggie Bannister, Robert Kurtzman, Ryan Hooks; *W:* John Bisson; *M:* Edward Douglas. **VIDEO**

Rage and Honor 🦴🦴 **1992 (R)** Rothrock stars as Kris Fairfield, a high-school teacher who spends her spare time tutoring students in the martial-arts. Her present students are a group of cops, including Aussie visitor Preston Michaels. When Michaels witnesses a drug deal, he gets set-up by the dealers for a murder he didn't commit and only Kris can help him prove his innocence. 93m/C VHS, DVD. Cynthia Rothrock, Richard Norton, Brian Thompson, Terri Treas, Catherine Bach, Alex Datcher; *D:* Terence H. Winkless; *W:* Terence H. Winkless.

Rage and Honor 2: Hostile Takeover 🦴🦴½ **1993 (R)** Rothrock returns as black-belt CIA operative Kris Fairfield, whose latest assignment takes her to Jakarta where a banker is involved in a large-scale drug money laundering operation. She teams up with Preston Michaels (Norton), a renegade Australian cop, and winds up following a trail that leads to a fortune in diamonds and lots of trouble. 98m/C VHS, Cynthia Rothrock, Richard Norton, Patrick Muldoon, Frans Tumbuan, Ron Vreeken, Alex Tumundo; *D:* Guy Norris; *W:* Louis Sun, Steven Reich.

Rage at Dawn 🦴🦴 *Seven Bad Men* **1955** An outlaw gang is tracked by a special agent who must "bend" the rules a little in order to get the bad guys. Not surprisingly, he gets his girl as well. A solid standard of the genre, with some clever plot twists. 87m/C VHS, DVD. Randolph Scott, Forrest Tucker, Mala Powers, J. Carrol Naish, Edgar Buchanan; *D:* Tim Whelan; *W:* Horace McCoy; *C:* Ray Rennahan; *M:* Paul Sawtel.

The Rage: Carrie 2 🦴🦴 *Carrie 2* **1999 (R)** You don't need psychic powers to know that things probably aren't going to end well for the tormenting teens in this slightly altered sequel. The heroine this time is Rachel (Bergl), a semi-Goth outcast who has a crush on good guy jock Jesse (London). She also has the ability to rattle and explode things when she's upset. Sue (Irving), the sole survivor from Carrie White's little tantrum years earlier, discovers that Rachel is related to the late telekinetic prom queen and tries to warn her. Too late. Jesse's bitchy girlfriend sets out to humiliate Rachel at a big party held at an all too flammable mansion. Lacks the character development and shock value of the first installment. 97m/C VHS, DVD. Emily Bergl, Amy Irving, Jason London, J. Smith-Cameron, Zachery Ty Bryan, John Doe, Gordon Clapp, Rachel Blanchard, Mena Suvari, Eddie Kaye Thomas, Dylan Bruno, Charlotte Ayanna, Justin Urich, Elijah Craig; *D:* Katt Shea; *W:* Rafael Moreu; *C:* Donald M. Morgan; *M:* Danny P. Harvey.

A Rage in Harlem 🐾🐾🐾 1991 (R) The crime novels of Chester A. Himes were translated into the best movies of the early '70s blaxploitation era. Now, a woman with a band of gypsies. Gcod first directing effort by English actor Bob Hoskins. Unpretentious and engaging. **102m/C VHS, DVD.** Bob Hoskins, Dexter Fletcher, Zoe Nathenson, David Hill, Ian Dury, Zoe Wanamaker; **D:** Earl Ratt; **M:** Hal Mooney.

Ragin' Cajun 🐾 1990 Retired kickboxer is forced into a death match to save his girlfriend. **91m/C VHS, DVD.** David Heavener, Charlene Tilton, Sam Bottoms, Samantha Eggar; **D:** William B. Hillman.

Raging Angels 🐾 1995 (R) L.A. couple Chris (Flanery) and Lila (Mazur) are struggling to rock 'n' rollers when Lila gets a job as a backup singer to star Colin (Pare), who's part of a cult called the Coalition for World Unity. Turns out they're a recruiting org for Satan and are looking for new souls. Our young duo are aided by (Joe) Stewart, Virginia Christine (D: Lewis D. Collins. Fay Taylor; **W:** Morgan Cox; **D:** Harry Neumann, William Sickner.

Raiders of Leyte Gulf 🐾🐾 1963 A cattle company tries running homesteaders off their land to get control of it. The Lone Rider saves the day. **56m/B VHS.** Robert "Bob" Livingston, Al "Fuzzy" St. John, Mary na Dall, Edward Cassidy, Charles "Blackie" King, Charles "Slim" Whitaker; Kermit Maynard, George O'Brien; **D:** Sam Newfield; **W:** Joseph O'Donnell; **C:** Robert E. Cline.

Raiders of Sunset Pass 🐾🐾 1943 Wartime western quickie makes an interesting novelty today. With most cowboys off fighting the Axis, the ladies form the Women's Army of the Plains to watch out for 4-F rustlers. **57m/B VHS.** Eddie Dew, Smiley Burnette, Jennifer Holt, Roy Barcroft, Mozelle Cravens, Beverly Aadland, Nancy Worth, Kenne Duncan, Jack Rockwell, Bud Buster, Jack Ingram; **D:** John English.

Raiders of the Border 🐾🐾 1944 A white-hatted cowboy must prevent the takeover of a trading post. **55m/B VHS.** Johnny Mack Brown, Raymond Hatton, Ellen Hall; **D:** John P. McCarthy; **W:** Adele Buffington; **C:** Henry Neumann.

Raiders of the Lost Ark 🐾🐾🐾🐾 1981 (PG) Classic '30s-style adventure reminiscent of early serials spawned two sequels and numerous rip-offs and made Ford a household name as dashing hero and intrepid archeologist Indiana Jones. Set in 1936, Indy battles mean Nazis, decodes hieroglyphics, fights his fear of snakes, and even has time for a little romance in his quest for the biblical Ark of the Covenant. Allen is perfectly cast as his feisty ex-flame Marion, more than a little irritated with the smooth talker who dumped her years earlier. Asks viewers to suspend belief as every chase and stunt tops the last. Unrelated opening sequence does a great job of introducing the character. **115m/C VHS, DVD.** Harrison Ford, Karen Allen, Wolf Kahler, Paul Freeman, John Rhys-Davies, Denholm Elliott, Ronald Lacey, Anthony (Corrian) Higgins, Alfred Molina; **D:** Steven Spielberg; **W:** George Lucas, Philip Kaufman; **C:** Douglas Slocombe; **M:** John Williams. Oscars '81: Art Dir./Set Dec., Film Editing, Sound, Visual FX; AFI '98: Top 100. Natl. Film Reg. '99.

Raiders of the Sun 🐾 1992 (R) After the Earth has been turned in a biological disaster, a futuristic warrior arrives to help restore world peace and order. C-neap "Mad Max" ripoff. **80m/C VHS, DVD.** Richard Norton, Rick Dean, William (Bill) Steis, Blake Boyd, Brigitta Stenberg, Ned Hourani, Nick Nicholson, Nigel Hogge, Paul Holmes, Ernie Satana; **D:** Cirio H. Santiago; **W:** Frederick Bailey.

The Railway Children 🐾🐾🐾 2000 Heart-tugger about the three Waterbury children, who must move to a small village and live in reduced circumstances with their mother (Agutter) when their father is wrongly imprisoned. The threesome spend much of their time by the railroad with its stationmaster (Russell) and a kindly railroad tycoon (Attenborough), who takes an interest in their situation. Based on the novel by Edith Nesbitt. Agutter played the role of the eldest daughter in the 1970 film version. **90m/C VHS, DVD. GB** Jenny Agutter, William Mervyn, Bernard Cribbins, Dinah Sheridan, Iain Cuthbertson, Sally Thomsett, Peter Bromilow, Ann Lancaster, Gary Warren, Gordon Whiting, David Lodge; **D:** Lionel Jeffries; **C:** Arthur Ibbetson.

The Railway Station Man 🐾🐾🐾 1992 Set in present-day Ireland, Christie plays a widowed artist struggling to put her life back together after her husband's death in a terrorist bombing. She meets a mysterious American (Sutherland) who's working on restoring the local railway station and finds herself falling in love. When she stumbles upon an IRA bombing plot she also finds out some unpleasant truths about her new lover. Wonderful performances, tragic story. Shot on location in County Donegal, Northern Ireland. Based on the novel by Jennifer Johnston. **93m/C VHS.** Julie Christie, Donald Sutherland, John Lynch, Mark Tandy, Frank McCusker, Niall Cusack; **D:** Michael Whyte; **W:** Shelagh Delaney. CABLE

Rain 🐾🐾1/2 1932 W. Somerset Maugham's tale of a puritanical minister's attempt to reclaim a "lost woman" on the island of Pago Pago. Crawford and Huston work up some static. Remake of the

---

Rage of Angels 🐾🐾 1983 Lengthy miniseries adaptation of the Sidney Sheldon novel about an ambitious female attorney, her trials, and her men. Followed by "Rage of Angels: The Story Continues" (1986). **192m/C VHS.** Jaclyn Smith, Ken Howard, Armand Assante, Ronald Hunter, George D. Wallace; **D:** Bill Duke; **W:** John Toles-Bey, Bobby Crawford; **M:** Elmer Bernstein.

Rage of Angels: The Story Continues 🐾🐾 1986 In this sequel to the Sidney Sheldon trash-with-flash miniseries, Smith reprises her role as the beautiful lady lawyer who always gets involved with the wrong men. This time she tries to hide the fact that her illegitimate son is about to become a mobster. **VHS, DVD.** Jaclyn Smith, Ken Howard, Michael Nouri, Susan Sullivan, Brad Dourif, Angela Lansbury, Mason Adams; **D:** Paul Wendkos; **C:** Gordon Hessler; **W:** Wallace C. Bennett.

Rage of Honor 🐾🐾 1987 (R) A high-kicking undercover cop seeks vengeance on bad guys for his partner's murder. Standard of its type; why bother? **92m/C VHS, DVD.** Sho Kosugi, Lewis Van Bergen, Robin Evans, Gerry Gibson; **D:** Gordon Hessler.

The Rage of Paris 🐾🐾🐾 1938 Scheming ex-actress and head waiter hope to gain by helping a beautiful French girl (Darrieux) snag a rich hubby. She comes to her senses, realizing that love, true love, matters more than wealth. Well-acted, quaint comedy. **78m/B VHS, DVD.** Danielle Darrieux, Douglas Fairbanks Jr., Mischa Auer, Helen Broderick; **D:** Henry Koster; **C:** Joseph Valentine.

Rage of the Werewolf 🐾1/2 1999 Okay, try to follow this. It's 2010 in New York City after an asteroid has collided with the moon, which somehow causes thousands of people to become werewolves. Now Jake was already a werewolf, so he has more flexibility than these newbies, including the evil brother Lazio who wants to unite all the wolves and destroy humanity. But Jake doesn't want anything to do with this evil plot and goes on the run. And then there's some mystery babe Jake out. **90m/C VHS.** Santo Marotta, Tom Nonham, Hollis Granville, Debbie Rochon, Sasha Graham, Michael (Mick) McCleery, Jon Santome; **D:** Kevin J. Lindenmuth; **W:** Kevin J. Lindenmuth. VIDEO

Rage to Kill 🐾🐾 1988 (R) Jingoistic retelling of the 1982 Grenada invasion, complete with helpless American med students. Good-guy race car driver whips them into shape to fight the Soviet-supplied general (he's the bad guy). Guess who wins. **94m/C VHS.** Oliver Reed, James Ryan, Henry Cele, Cameron Mitchell; **D:** David Winters.

Raggedy Man 🐾🐾🐾 1981 (PG) Spacek in her signature role as a lonely small-town woman. Here she's raising two sons alone in a small Texas town during WWII. Spacek's strong acting carries a well-scripted story, unfortunately marred by an overwrought ending. **94m/C VHS, DVD.** Sissy Spacek, Eric Roberts, Sam Shepard, Tracey Walter, William Sanderson, Henry Thomas; **D:** Jack Fisk; **W:** William D. Wittliff; **C:** Ralf Bode; **M:** Jerry Goldsmith.

The Raggedy Rawney 🐾🐾1/2 1990 (R) A young Army deserter dresses in women's clothing and hides out as a mad woman with a band of gypsies. Good work by English actor Bob Hoskins in his directorial debut. Contains action footage from the 1967 film "Tobruk". **99m/C VHS, DVD.** Bob Hoskins, Dexter Fletcher, Zoe Nathenson, Ian Dury, Perry Fenwick; **D:** Bob Hoskins; **W:** J.G. Devlin, Perry Fenwick; **D:** Bob Hoskins; **W:** Nicole De Wilde; **M:** Michael Kamen.

Ragtime 🐾🐾🐾 1981 (PG) The lives and passions of a middle class family weave into the scandals and events of 1906 America. A small, unthinking act represents all the racist attacks on one man, who refuses to back down this time. Wonderful period detail. From the E.L. Doctorow novel, but not nearly as complex. Features Cagney's last film performance. **156m/C VHS.** James Cagney, Brad Dourif, Mary Steenburgen, James Olson, Elizabeth McGovern, Pat O'Brien, Debbie Allen, Jeff Daniels, Moses Gunn, Donald O'Connor, Mandy Patinkin, Norman Mailer, Jeffrey DeMunn, Robert Joy, Fran Drescher, Frankie Faison, Samuel L. Jackson, Michael Jeter, John Ratzenberger; **D:** Milos Forman; **W:** Michael Weller; **C:** Miroslav Ondricek; **M:** Randy Newman.

Rags to Riches 🐾 1987 A wealthy Beverly Hills entrepreneur decides to improve his public image by adopting six orphan girls. TV pilot. **96m/C VHS.** Joseph Bologna, Tisha Campbell; **D:** Bruce Seth Green; **W:** David Garber. TV

Raid on Entebbe 🐾🐾🐾 1977 (R) Dramatization of the Israeli rescue of passengers held hostage by terrorists at Uganda's Entebbe Airport in 1976. A gripping actioner all the more compelling because true. Finch received an Emmy nomination in this, his last film. **113m/C VHS, DVD.** Charles Bronson, Peter Finch, Horst Buchholz, John Saxon, Martin Balsam, Jack Warden, Yaphet Kotto, Sylvia Sidney; **D:** Irvin Kershner; **C:** Bill Butler; **M:** David Shire. TV

Raid on Rommel 🐾1/2 1971 (PG) A British soldier (Burton) poses as a Nazi and tries to infiltrate Rommel's team with his rag-tag brigade of misfits. Predictable drivel. **98m/C VHS, DVD.** Richard Burton, John Colicos, Clinton Greyn, Wolfgang Preiss; **D:** Henry Hathaway; **W:** Richard M. Bluel.

Raiders of Atlantis 🐾 The Atlantis Interceptors 1983 Battles break out when the lost continent surfaces in the Caribbean. The warriors in these apocalyptic frays defend atomic arsenals. **100m/C VHS.** Christopher Connelly; **D:** Roger Franklin.

Raiders of Ghost City 🐾🐾 1944 Serial in 13 chapters involves a Union Secret Service Agent after a ring of gold robbers who are posing as Confederate soldiers during the end of the Civil War. **225m/B VHS, DVD.** Dennis Moore, Lionel Atwill, Regis Toomey, Wanda McKay, Joe Sawyer, Virginia Christine; **D:** Ray Taylor; **W:** Morgan Cox; **D:** Harry Neumann, William Sickner.

Raiders of Red Gap 🐾🐾 1943 guerrillas who are setting the stage for MacArthur's return. Director Romero would go on to a busy career in horror and other genres. **80m/B VHS, DVD.** P.H. Leopold Salcedo, Michael Parsons, Jennings Sturgeon, Liza Mcreno; **D:** Eddie Romero; **W:** Ciari Kunize, E.F. Romero; **C:** Felipe Sacdalan; **M:** Tito Arayalo.

Rails & Ties 🐾🐾1/2 2007 (PG-13) Despite some good performances, this drama goes off track with some unbelievable plot machinations in (daughter of Clint) Eastwood's directorial debut. Emotionally distant train engineer Tom Stark (Bacon) can't cope with his wife Megan's (Harden) terminal cancer diagnosis and is glac to escape through work. At a rail crossing, a disturbed young woman (Ricci) deliberately parks her car on the tracks; the train/car crash kills her but her now-orphaned son Danny (Heizer) survives. Tom gets suspended and is brooding at home when Danny shows up on the Stark's doorstep, having run away from foster care. Childless Megan is happy to take the boy in over Tom and Danny are soon bonding. They eventually meet a new friend who helps them prove their father's innocence. Wonderfully directed by Jeffries. **104m/C VHS, DVD. GB** Kevin Bacon, Marcia Gay Harden, Marin Hinkle, Eugene Byrd, Miles Heizer, Margo Martindale, Bonnie Root, Micky Levy; **D:** Alison Eastwood; **W:** Kyle Eastwood; **M:** Michael Stevens.

Railroaded 🐾🐾 1947 The police seek a demented criminal who kills his victims with perfumed-soaked bullets. Tense, excellent noir. Anothony Mann crime drama. **72m/B VHS, DVD.** Sheila Ryan, Hugh Beaumont, Ed Kelly, Jane Randolph; **D:** Anthony Mann; **W:** John C. Higgins; **C:** Guy Roe; **M:** Alvin Levin.

Railroader 🐾🐾🐾 1965 Buster Keaton as the railroader in this slapstick short fumbles his way across Canada. As in the days of the silents, he speaks not a word. **25m/C VHS.** Buster Keaton; **D:** Gerald Potterton; **C:** Robert Humble; **M:** Eldon Rathburn.

Raging Bull 🐾🐾🐾🐾 1980 (R) Scorsese's depressing but magnificent vision of the dying American Dream and suicidal macho codes in the form of the rise and fall of middleweight boxing champ Jake LaMotta, a brutish, dull-witted animal who can express himself only in the ring and through violence. A photographically expressive, brilliant drama, with easily the most intense and brutal boxing scenes ever filmed. De Niro provides a vintage performance, going from the young LaMotta to the aging has-been, and is ably accompanied by Moriarty as his girl and Pesci as his loyal, much beat-upon brother. **128m/B VHS, DVD.** Robert De Niro, Cathy Moriarty, Joe Pesci, Frank Vincent, Nicholas Colasanto, Theresa Saldana; **D:** Martin Scorsese; **W:** Paul Schrader, Mardik Martin; **C:** Michael Chapman; **M:** Robbie Robertson. Oscars '80: Actor (De Niro), Film Editing; AFI '98: Top 100; Golden Globes '81: Actor—Drama (De Niro); L.A. Film Critics '80: Actor (De Niro), Film; Natl. B.d. of Review '80: Actor (De Niro), Support, Actor (Pesci), Natl. Film Reg. '90; N.Y. Film Critics '80: Actor (De Niro), Actor (Pesci), Support, Actor (Pesci); Natl. Soc. Film Critics '80: Cinematog., Director (Scorsese).

1928 silent film "Sadie Thompson." Remade again in 1953 as "Miss Sadie Thompson." Relies on her early years in vaudeville to her starring years at MGM. Based on the book by Christopher Finch. Directed by sometime-Garland flame Jackie Cooper. 100m/C VHS. Andrea McArdle, Jack Carter, Don Murray; *D:* Jackie Cooper; *M:* Charles Fox. **TV**

The Rainbow ♂♂♂ **1989 (R)** Mature, literate rendering of the classic D.H. Lawrence novel about a young woman's sexual awakening. Beautiful cinematography. Companion/prequel to director Russell's earlier Lawrence adaptation, "Women in Love" (1969). 104m/C VHS. *GB* Sammi Davis, Amanda Donohoe, Paul McGann, Glenda Jackson, Christopher Gable, David Hemmings, Glenda Jackson, Kenneth Colley; *D:* Ken Russell; *W:* Vivian Russell, Ken Russell; *C:* Billy Williams; *M:* Carl Davis.

Rainbow Bridge ♂ **1971 (R)** The adventures of a group of hippies searching for their consciousness in Hawaii. Features concert footage from Jimi Hendrix's final performance. 74m/C VHS, DVD. Chuck Wein, Herbie Fletcher, Pat Hartley; *D:* Chuck Wein; *C:* Vilis Lapenieks.

Rainbow Drive ♂♂½ **1990 (R)** Cop thriller promises great things but fails to deliver. Angie's a good cop trapped in the political intrigues of Hollywood. He discovers five dead bodies; when the official count is four, he detects funny business. From the novel by Roderick Thorp. 93m/C VHS. Peter Weller, Sela Ward, Bruce Weitz, David Caruso, James Laurenson, Chris Mulkey, Kathryn Harrold, Tony Jay, Jon(athan) Gries, Henry Sanders, David Neidorf, Chelcie Ross, Rutanya Alda, Megan Mullally, Rob Nilsson; *D:* Bobby Roth; *W:* Roderick Thorp, Bill Phillips, Bennett Cohen; *C:* Tim Suhrstedt; *M:* Tangerine Dream. **C A B L E**

The Rainbow Gang ♂ *Rainbow Boys* **1973** A trio of unlikely prospectors heads into a legendary mine in search of riches and fame. 90m/C VHS. *CA* Donald Pleasence, Don Calfa, Kate Reid; *D:* Gerald Potterton; *W:* Gerald Potterton; *C:* Robert Saad; *M:* Howard Blake.

Rainbow over Broadway ♂♂ **1933** A former Broadway star mother set is set against having her son and daughter try their luck on Broadway. 52m/C VHS. Joan Marsh, Frank Albertson, Lucien Littlefield, Grace Hayes, Dell Henderson, Harry C. (Henry) Myers, Gladys Blake, Glen Boles, Nat Carr; *D:* Richard Thorpe.

Rainbow Ranch ♂♂½ **1933** A Navy boxer returns home to his ranch to find murder and corruption. Needless to say, he rides off to seek revenge. 54m/B VHS. Rex Bell, Cecilia Parker, Robert F. (Bob) Kortman, Henry Hall, Gordon DeMain; *D:* Harry Fraser.

Rainbow Warrior ♂♂½ **1994 (PG)** True story of the bombing of the Greenpeace vessel and humiliation of the two men who set out to solve the crime. 90m/C VHS. Sam Neill, Jon Voight, Kerry Fox, Bruno Lawrence; *D:* Michael Tuchner.

Raining Stones ♂♂ **1993** A hard-up plumber becomes obsessed with buying an expensive first communion dress for his daughter and gets involved in numerous misadventures trying to get the money. Another of Loach's comedy-dramas about the British working class and their struggle to survive with dignity. 90m/C VHS, DVD. *GB* Bruce Jones, Julie Brown, Ricky Tomlinson, Tom Hickey, Gemma Phoenix, Jonathan James; *D:* Ken Loach; *W:* Jim Allen; *C:* Barry

Rain ♂♂ **1978** Broadway's "Annie" is badly miscast as Judy Garland from her early years in vaudeville to her starring years at MGM. Based on the book by Christopher Finch. Directed by sometime-Garland flame Jackie Cooper.

Rain ♂♂ **2001** Coming-of-age drama based on the 1994 novel by Kirsty Gunn. In 1972, 13-year-old Janey (Fulford-Wierzbicki) is spending the summer at a New Zealand beach cottage with her depressed mom Kate (Peirse), ineffectual father Ed (Browning), and her younger brother, Jim (Murphy). Trouble comes in the form of too much booze and the attentions of photographer Cady (Csokas), who not only catches Kate's eye but blossoming Janey's as well. Tensions build as the betrayals multiply. 90m/C VHS, DVD. *AU* Alicia Fulford-Wierzbicki, Sarah Peirse, Marton Csokas, Alistair Browning, Aaron Murphy; *D:* Christine Jeffs; *W:* Christine Jeffs; *C:* John Toon; *M:* Neil Finn, Edmund McWilliams.

The Rain Killer ♂♂ **1990 (R)** Big city cop and fed don goloshes to track serial killer who slays rich ladies during heavy precipitation. Soggy story. 94m/C VHS. Ray Sharkey, David Beecroft, Maria Ford, Woody Brown, Tania Coleridge; *D:* Ken Stein; *W:* Ray Cunneff.

Rain Man ♂♂♂½ **1988 (R)** When his father dies, ambitious and self-centered Charlie Babbit finds he has an older autistic brother who's been institutionalized for years. Needing him to claim an inheritance, he liberates him from the institution and takes to the road, where both brothers undergo subtle changes. The Vegas montage is wonderful. Critically acclaimed drama and a labor of love for the entire cast. Cruise's best performance to date as he goes from cad to recognizing something wonderfully human in his brother and himself. Hoffman is exceptional. 126m/C VHS, DVD. Dustin Hoffman, Tom Cruise, Valeria Golino, Jerry Molen, Jack Murdock, Michael D. Roberts, Ralph Seymour, Lucinda Jenney, Bonnie Hunt, Kim Robillard, Beth Grant; *D:* Barry Levinson; *W:* Ronald Bass, Barry Morrow; *C:* John Seale; *M:* Hans Zimmer. Oscars '88: Actor (Hoffman), Director (Levinson), Orig. Screenplay, Picture; Berlin Intl. Film Fest. '88: Golden Bear; Directors Guild '88: Director (Levinson); Golden Globes '89: Actor—Drama (Hoffman), Film—Drama.

The Rain People ♂♂♂ **1969 (R)** Pregnant housewife Knight takes to the road in desperation and boredom; along the way she meets retarded ex-football player Caan. Well directed by Coppola from his original script. Pensive drama. 102m/C VHS. Shirley Knight, James Caan, Robert Duvall, Tom Aldredge, Marya Zimmet, Andrew Duncan, Sally Gracie, Alan Manson, Laura Hope Crews; *D:* Francis Ford Coppola; *W:* Francis Ford Coppola; *C:* Bill Butler; *M:* Ronald Stein.

Rain Without Thunder ♂♂♂½ **1993 (PG-13)** Imagine the year 2042, a time when abortion is illegal and a fertilized egg has full Constitutional rights. Now imagine sitting through an 87 minute fake documentary that follows the story of a mother and daughter team who have been jailed for trying to go to Sweden so that the daughter can get an abortion. A one-sided, militant pro-choice effort that is neither entertaining nor informational. 87m/C VHS. Betty Buckley, Jeff Daniels, Ali Thomas, Frederic Forrest, Carolyn McCormick, Linda Hunt, Frank Earl Jones, Graham Greene, Iona Morris, Austin Pendleton; *D:* Gary Bennett; *W:* Gary Bennett; *M:* Randall Lynch, Alan Lynch.

Ackroyd; *M:* Stewart Copeland. Cannes '93: Special Jury Prize.

The Rainmaker ♂♂♂ **1956** Reminiscent of "Elmer Gantry" in his masterful performance, Lancaster makes it all believable as a con man who comes to a small midwestern town and works miracles not only on the weather but on spinster Hepburn, although both were a little long in the tooth for their roles. Written by Nash from his own play. 121m/C VHS, DVD. Burt Lancaster, Katharine Hepburn, Wendell Corey, Lloyd Bridges, Earl Holliman, Cameron Prudhomme, Wallace Ford; *D:* Joseph Anthony; *W:* N. Richard Nash; *C:* Charles B(ryant) Lang Jr.; *M:* Alex North. Golden Globes '57: Support. Actor (Holliman)

The Rains Came ♂♂½ **1939** Living within a loveless marriage in the mythical Indian city of Ranchipur, English socialite Loy pursues extramarital love interests, including the compassionate doctor Power, potential heir to the maharajah's throne, when an earthquake hits and brings major destruction to the city. Loy aids the doctor in helping the injured. Hankies should be kept handy. Adapted from the Louis Bromfield novel. 104m/B VHS, DVD. Myrna Loy, Tyrone Power, George Brent, Brenda Joyce, Nigel Bruce, Maria Ouspenskaya, Joseph Schildkraut, Laura Hope Crews, Marilyn Travers, Jane Darwell, Marjorie Rambeau, Henry Travers, H.B. Warner, William Royle, C. Montague Shaw, Harry Hayden, Abner Biberman, George Regas; *D:* Clarence Brown; *W:* Philip Dunne, Julien Josephson; *C:* Arthur C. Miller; *M:* Alfred Newman.

Raintree County ♂♂♂ **1957** A lavish, somewhat overdone epic about two lovers caught up in the national turmoil of the Civil War. An Indiana teacher (Clift) marries a southern belle (Taylor) just after the outbreak of war. The new wife battles mental illness. Producers had hoped this would be another "Gone with the Wind." Adapted from the novel by Ross Lockridge Jr. Film was delayed in mid-production by Clift's near-fatal and disfiguring car crash. 175m/C VHS, DVD. Elizabeth Taylor, Montgomery Clift, Eva Marie Saint, Lee Marvin, Nigel Patrick, Rod Taylor, Agnes Moorehead, Walter Abel; *D:* Edward Dmytryk; *C:* Robert L. Surtees.

Raise the Red Lantern ♂♂♂½ **1991 (PG)** Set in 1920s China, Zhang explores its claustrophobic world of privilege and humiliation. Songlian, an educated 19-year-old beauty, is forced into marriage as the fourth wife of a wealthy and powerful old man. She discovers that the wives have their own separate quarters and servants, and spend most of their time battling to attract their husband's attention. Over the course of a year, Songlian's fury and resentment grow until self-defeating rebellion is all she has. Gong Li is exquisite as the young woman struggling for dignity in a portrayal which is both haunting and tragic. 125m/C VHS, DVD. *CH* Gong Li, Ma Jingwu, He Caifei, Cao Cuifeng, Jin Shuyuan, Kong Lin, Ding Weimin; *D:* Yimou Zhang. British Acad. '92: Foreign Film; L.A. Film Critics '92: Cinematog.; N.Y. Film Critics '92: Foreign Film; Natl. Soc. Film Critics '92: Cinematog., Foreign Film.

Raise the Titanic woof! **1980 (PG)** A disaster about a disaster. Horrible script cannot be redeemed by purported thrill of the ship's emergence from the deep after 70 years. It's a shame, because the free world's security hangs in the balance. Based on Clive Cussler's best seller. 112m/C VHS. Jason Robards Jr., Richard Jordan, Anne Archer, Alec Guinness, J.D. Cannon; *D:* Jerry Jameson; *M:* John Barry.

Raise Your Voice ♂♂½ **2004 (PG)** Contrived tweenie fluff has eager 16-year-old Terri (Duff, blonde and bubbly as usual) longing to expand her singing talents by attending a performing arts summer school in L.A. Terri is encouraged by everyone but her overprotective dad (Keith) but finds the highly competitive atmosphere an eye-opener. Can sweet Terri realize her dreams and find mild romance with nice guy Jay (James)? Since this flick hits every teen cliche the answer should be obvious but it will still appeal to Duff's fans. 103m/C VHS, DVD. *US* Hilary Duff, Oliver

James, David Keith, Rita Wilson, Rebecca De Mornay, John Corbett, Jason Ritter, Robert Trebor, Dana Davis, Johnny Lewis, Kat Dennings, Lauren C. Mayhew; *D:* Sean McNamara; *W:* Sam Schreiber; *C:* John R. Leonetti; *M:* Machine Head, Aaron Zigman.

A Raisin in the Sun ♂♂♂ **1961** Outstanding story of a black family trying to make a better life for themselves in an all-white neighborhood in Chicago. The characters are played realistically and make for a moving story. Each person struggles with doing what he must while still maintaining his dignity and sense of self. Based on the 1959 Broadway play by Hansberry, who also wrote the screenplay. Remade for TV in 1989 with Danny Glover. 128m/B VHS, DVD. Diana Sands, John Fiedler, Ivan Dixon, Louis Gossett Jr., Sidney Poitier, Claudia McNeil, Ruby Dee; *D:* Daniel Petrie; *W:* Lorraine Hansberry; *C:* Charles Lawton Jr.; *M:* Laurence Rosenthal. Natl. Bd. of Review '61: Support. Actress (Dee), Natl. Film Reg. '05.

A Raisin in the Sun ♂♂♂ **1989** An "American Playhouse" presentation of the Lorraine Hansberry play about a black family threatened with dissolution by the outside forces of racism and greed when they move into an all-white neighborhood in the 1950s. 171m/C VHS, DVD. Danny Glover, Esther Rolle, Starletta DuPois; *D:* Bill Duke. **TV**

A Raisin in the Sun ♂♂♂½ **2008** The leads reprise their roles from the 2004 Broadway revival of Lorraine Hansberry's 1959 play. The Youngers live in a crowded Chicago tenement: mother Lena (Rashad) is a maid, daughter Beneatha (Lathan) is attending college, and son Walter (Combs) is a chauffeur with a long-suffering wife, Ruth (McDonald), and young son, Travis (Martin). When Lena receives a substantial insurance check, she decides to use the money to buy a house in a nice middle-class—and white—neighborhood. Walter wants to spend the money to open a family business, a liquor store, but Lena disapproves. 87m/C DVD. Phylicia Rashad, Sean (Puffy, Puff Daddy, P. Diddy) Combs, Audra McDonald, Sanaa Lathan, Justin Martin, Sean Patrick Thomas, David Oyelowo, John Stamos, Bill Nunn; *D:* Kenny Leon; *W:* Paris Qualles; *C:* Ivan Strasburg; *M:* Mervyn Warren; *Nar:* Morgan Freeman. **T V**

Raising Arizona ♂♂♂½ **1987 (PG-13)** Hi's an ex-con and the world's worst hold-up man. Ed's a policewoman. They meet, fall in love, marry, and kidnap a baby (one of a family of quints). Why not? Ed's infertile and the family they took the baby from has "more than enough," so who will notice? But unfinished furniture tycoon Nathan Arizona wants his baby back, even if he has to hire an axe murderer on a motorcycle to do it. A brilliant, original comedy narrated in notoriously loopy deadpan style by Cage. Innovative camera work by Barry Sonnenfeld. Wild, surreal, and hilarious. 94m/C VHS, DVD. Nicolas Cage, Holly Hunter, John Goodman, William Forsythe, Randall "Tex" Cobb, Trey Wilson, M. Emmet Walsh, Frances McDormand, Sam McMurray, T.J. Kuhn, Peter Benedek, M. Emmet Walsh; *D:* Joel Coen; *W:* Ethan Coen, Joel Coen; *C:* Barry Sonnenfeld; *M:* Carter Burwell.

Raising Cain ♂♂ **1992 (R)** Thriller evoking poor man's Hitchcock about a child psychiatrist who just happens to be nuts features Lithgow in five roles. Seems his supposedly dead Norwegian father has come to the United States and needs his son's help to steal babies for a child development experiment, so the son's alter ego, Cain, shows up to commit the nasty deed. Unfortunately Lithgow also catches his wife with another man, and that's when the bodies start piling up. 95m/C VHS, DVD. John Lithgow, Lolita Davidovich, Steven Bauer, Frances Sternhagen, Tom Bower, Mel Harris, Gabrielle Carteris, Barton Heyman; *D:* Brian De Palma; *W:* Brian De Palma; *C:* Stephen Burum; *M:* Pino Donaggio.

Raising Flagg ♂♂ **2006 (PG-13)** Flagg Purdy (Arkin) is a small-town handyman with a stubborn streak and a continuing feud with his neighbor Gus (Pendleton). Their latest fracas causes a public humiliation and a crisis for Flagg and he takes to his bed, sure he's about to meet his maker. So his family reluctantly gathers to figure out what to do about dad now. **102m/C DVD.** Alan Arkin, Austin Pendleton, Barbara Dana, Lauren Holly, Glenne Headly, Matthew Arkin, Daniel Quinn, Stephanie Lemelin, Dawn Maxey, Richard Kind, Clifton James, Vana O'Brien; **D:** Neal Miller; **W:** Nancy Miller, Dorothy Velasco; **C:** Erich Roland; **M:** Alan Barcus, Les Hooper.

Raising Genius ♂½ 2004 (R)
Weird teenaged math genius Hal (Long) locks himself in the bathroom to work on an equation that involves watching his cheerleader neighbor Lacy (McKellar) bounce on a trampoline. And it also sets his overbearing mother Nancy (Malick). But things get out of hand when a burglary brings out the cops who think Hal is being kept prisoner. **83m/C DVD.** Danica McKellar, Tippi Hedren, Shirley Jones, Justin Long, Wendie Malick, Stephen (Steve) Root, Danielle Voorhees, Bess Wiley; **W:** Linda Voorhees; **C:** Chris W. Johnson. VIDEO

Raising Helen ♂♂½ 2004 (PG-13)
Helen (Hudson) has a successful, carefree life as a modeling agency exec and is the favorite "cool" aunt of her sis Lindsay's (Huffman) three kids. However, Helen's shocked when Lindsay and her husband are killed in a car accident and she is given custody of the kids over perfect homemaker sis Jenny (Cusack). Helen soon gets fired, moves from Manhattan to Queens, finds a new job (working for Elizondo), and enrolls when Lindsay and her family. Good run by the single and hunky Pastor Dan (Corbett). Hudson is as winsome as ever, but this is just another mooch in her romantic comedy belt and it's all-too-familiar attire. **115m/C DVD.** US Kate Hudson, Joan Cusack, John Corbett, Helen Mirren, Hayden Panettiere, Spencer Breslin, Felicity Huffman, Sean O'Bryan, Hector Elizondo, Sakina Jaffrey, Abigail Breslin, Kevin Kilner; **D:** Garry Marshall; **W:** Jack Amiel, Michael Begler; **C:** Charles Minsky; **M:** John Debney.

Raising Heroes ♂♂ 1997 Josh (Sistillo) and Paul (White) are about to finalize their adoption of a child when Josh witnesses a mob hit. Now he's a target, trying to stay alive and protect his family, as well. **85m/C VHS, DVD.** Troy Sostillo, Henry White; **D:** Douglas Langway; **W:** Douglas Langway.

Raising the Heights ♂½ 1997 (R) Tensions escalate in the Brooklyn neighbor of Crown Heights when a drug deal, involving a high school teacher, results in the death of a young girl. So the neighborhood as he spends his summer vacation chasing the local hotties. His fisity, old-world Grandma (Guzman), who's raising Victor and his two younger siblings, begs to differ but the kids try to keep Grandma in the dark. Then Victor meets Judy (Marte), who's too smart to fall for his lines, and Victor really ge's some lessons in love. **87m/C VHS, DVD.** JE Victor Rasuk, Judy Marte, Melonie Diaz, Altagracia Guzman, Silvestre Rasuk, Krystal Rodriguez, Kevin Rivera; **D:** Peter Sollet; **W:** Peter Sollet; **C:** Tim O"-; **M:** Roy Nathanson.

Raising Victor Vargas ♂♂½ ...Long Way Home 2003 (R) Fifteen-year-old Latino Victor (Rasuk) thinks he's pretty not stuff in his Lower East Side New York neighborhood as he spends his summer vacation chasing the local hotties.

Rally 'Round the Flag, Boys! ♂½ 1958 Badly dated satire (from the novel by Max Shulman) turned slapstick comedy. Harry (Newman) and all-American guy Grace (Woodward) Bannerman live n the qu.et commuter community of P.tnam's Landing, CT. When the Air Force chooses t'e town as the site of a new missile base, the town joins a committee to embarrassment of his liaison. Local vamp Angela (Collins) regards their marital mis-understandings as her chance to console

Rambling Rose ♂♂ 1991 (R) Dern is Rose, a free-spirited, sexually liberated before her time young woman taken in by a Southern family in 1935. Rose immediately has an impact on the male members of the clan, father Duvall and son Haas, thanks to her inappressible sexuality. This causes consternation with the strait-laced patriarch, who attempts to control his desire for the girl. Eventually Rose decides she must try to stick to one man, but this only causes further problems. Dern gives her best performance yet in this excellent period piece, and solid support is offered from the rest of the cast, in particular Duvall and Dern's real-life mother Ladd. **115m/C VHS, DVD.** Laura Dern, Diane Ladd, Robert Duvall, Lukas Haas, John Heard, Kevin Conway, Robert John Burke, Lisa Jakub; **D:** Martha Coolidge; **W:** Elmer Calder Willingham; **C:** Johnny E. Jensen; **M:** Bernstein. Ind. Spirit '92: Director (Coolidge), Film, Support. Actress (Ladd).

Rambo ♂♂ 2008 (R) World-weary killing machine John Rambo (Stallone) is back, and this time the body count is higher than ever. Seemingly forgotten by the American military that used him in Vietnam and Afghanistan, Rambo's retired to isolation in the swamps of Thailand, but he's soon sucked back into the life of a mercenary when a group of missionaries recruit him to take them to Myanmar (Burma). Before the group has much time to help the innocents affected by the ongoing civil war, they're kidnapped by Burmese soldiers, and Rambo must swing into action, wiping out anyone in his path in the process. Passable if over-the-top action sequences highlight Stallone's freakishly buff 60-year-old bod. **93m/C DVD.** US Sylvester Stallone, Julie Benz, Paul Schulze, Ken Howard; **D:** Sylvester Stallone; **W:** Art Montersatelli; **C:** Glen MacPherson; **M:** Brian Tyler, Ashley Miller.

Rambo: First Blood, Part 2 ♂♂ 1985 (R) If anyone can save Our Rambo. Along the way he's tortured, flexes biceps, grunts, and then disposes of the bad guys by the dozen in one of filmdom's bigger dead body parades. Mindless action best enjoyed by testosterone-driven fans of the genre. Sequel to "First Blood" (1982); followed by "Rambo 3" (1988). **93m/C VHS, DVD, Blu-Ray Disc.** Sylvester Stallone, Richard Crenna, Charles Napier, Steven Berkoff, Julia Nickson-Soul, Martin Kove; **D:** George P. Cosmatos; **W:** Sylvester Stallone, James Cameron; **C:** Jack Cardiff; **M:** Jerry Goldsmith. Golden Raspberries '85: Worst Picture, Worst Actor (Stallone), Worst Screenplay, Worst Song ("Peace in Our Life").

Rambo 3 ♂½ 1988 (R) John Rambo, the famous Vietnam vet turned Buddhist monk, this time invades Afghanistan to rescue his mentor. Meets up with orphan and fights his way around the country. Typically exploitative, kill now, ask questions later Rambo attack, lacking the sheer volume of no-brainer action of the first two Rambos. At the time, the most expensive film ever made, costing $58 million. Filmed in Israel. **102m/C VHS, DVD.** Sylvester Stallone, Richard Crenna, Marc De Jonge, Kurnwood Smith, Soros Focas; **D:** Peter MacDonald; **W:** Sylvester Stallone; **C:** John Stanier Worst Actor (Stallone).

Rampage ♂♂ 1987 (R) Seemingly all-American guy Charles Reece (McArthur) goes on a murder spree, killing and then mutilating his victims. Fraser (Biehn) is a liberal district attorney who questions his own views as he argues during the trial that Reece was sane when he committed the murders and deserves the death penalty. Director Friedkin makes no bones about his concerns that if a criminal insan-

Rancho Deluxe ♂♂♂ 1975 Offbeat western spoof starring Bridges and Waterston as two carefree cowpokes. Cult favorite featuring music by Buffett, who also appears in the film. **93m/C VHS, DVD.** Jeff Bridges, Sam Waterston, Elizabeth Ashley, Charlene Dallas, Clifton James, Slim Pickens, Harry Dean Stanton, Richard Bright, Jimmy Buffett; **D:** Frank Perry; **W:** Thomas McGuane; **C:** William A. Fraser; **M:** Jimmy Buffett.

Rampage: The Hillside Strangler Murders ♂ 2004 (R) Has only the most tenuous connection with the true serial killer story involving the infamous Angelo Buono, and wasn't released until 1992 due to the production company's financial difficulties. Filmed in 1987, the movie wasn't released **87m/C VHS, DVD.** Nicholas (Nick) Campbell, Deborah Van Valkenburgh, John Harkins, Art LaFleur, Ennio Morricone.

Ramparts of Clay ♂♂♂ 1968 (PG) A young woman in a tiny village's traditional way of life and the modern world just after her country's independence from France. Brilliantly shot on location; exquisitely poignant. In Arabic with English subtitles. **87m/C VHS.** FR Leila Srenna, Jean-Louis Trintignant; **D:** Jean-Louis Bertucelli; **W:** Jean-Louis Bertucelli; **C:** Andreas Winding.

Ramrod ♂♂ 1947 Lake is a tough ranch owner at odds with her father, who is being manipulated by a big-time cattleman into trying to put them out of business. She fights back, and McCrea is the one caught in the middle as the only good guy. Nothing special. **94m/B VHS** Veronica Lake, Joel McCrea, Arleen Whelan, Don DeFore, Preston Foster, Charlie Ruggles, Donald Crisp, Lloyd Bridges; **D:** Andre de Toth.

Ran ♂♂♂ 1985 (R) The culmination of Kurosawa's career stands as his masterpiece. Loosely adapting Shakespeare's "King Lear," with plot elements from "Macbeth," he's fashioned an epic, heart-breaking statement about honor, ambition, and the futility of war. Aging medieval warlord Hidetora gives control of his empire to his oldest son, creating conflict with two other sons. Soon he's an outcast, as ambition and greed seize the two sons. Stunning battle scenes illuminate the full-blown tragedy of Kurosawa's vision. Superb acting with a scene-stealing Harada as the revenge-minded Lady Kaede, period costumes took three years to create. Japanese with English subtitles. **160m/C VHS, DVD.** JP FR Tatsuya Nakadai, Akira Terao, Jinpachi Nezu, Daisuke Ryu, Meiko Harada, Hisashi Igawa, Peter, Kazuo Kato, Takeshi Kato, Jun Tazeki, Toshiya Ito, Yoshiko Miyazaki, Masayuki Yui, Norio Matsui, Takashi Nomura; **D:** Akira Kurosawa; **W:** Akira Kurosawa, Hideo Oguni, Masato Ide; **C:** Asakazu Nakai, Takao Saito, Masaharu Ueda; **M:** Toru Takemitsu. Oscars '85: Costume Design; British Acad. '86: Foreign Film; L.A. Film Critics '85: Foreign Film; Nat. Bd. of Review '85: Director (Kurosawa); N.Y. Film Critics '85: Foreign Film; Natl. Soc. Film Critics '85: Cinematog., Film.

Rana: The Legend of Shadow Lake ♂♂ 1975 Gold at the bottom of a lake is guarded by a frog-monster, but treasure hunters try to retrieve it anyway. **96m/C VHS, DVD.** Alan Ross, Karen McDiarmid, Jerry Gregoris; **D:** Bill Rebane; **W:** Lyonna Denetz; **C:** Bill Rebane; **M:** Bruce Malm.

The Ranch ♂½ 1988 (PG-13) An executive who loses everything inherits a dilapidated ranch and renovates it into a health spa. **97m/C VHS.** Andrew Stevens, Gary Fjeligaard, Lou Ann Schmidt, Elizabeth Keefe; **D:** Stella Stevens.

Rancho Notorious ♂♂♂ ½ 1952 Kennedy, on the trail of his girlfriend's murderer, falls for dance hall girl Dietrich. Fine acting. A "period" sample of '50s westerns, but different. A must for Dietrich fans. **89m/C VHS.** Marlene Dietrich, Arthur Kennedy, Mel Ferrer, William Frawley, Jack Elam, George Reeves; **D:** Fritz Lang; **W:** Daniel Taradash; **C:** Hal Mohr.

Rancid Aluminium ♂♂½ 2000 Druggie Pete Thompson (Ifans) inherits his family's failing publishing business, which ticks off his friend (and the company's accountant) Sean Deery (Fiennes). So Sean decides to take over the business by borrowing money from Russian mobster, Mr. Kant (Berkoff). Pete thinks Sean is just getting an additional source of capital. Pete sleeps around and eventually learns what Sean is really up to. The Russian wants a return on his investment. But the viewer will wonder why he's wasting his time since this movie is dumb. Based on the novel by Hawes, who did the screenplay. **91m/C VHS, DVD, GB Rhys Ifans, Joseph Fiennes, Steven Berkoff, Tara Fitzgerald, Sadie Frost, Dani Behr, Keith Allen, Nick Moran; **D:** Edward Thomas; **W:** James Hawes; **C:** Tony Imi; **M:** John E.R. Hardy.

Random Encounter ♂½ 1998 Executive Berkley becomes involved in extortion and a murder cover-up all because she takes a shine to a mystery man. **100m/C VHS, DVD. CA** Elizabeth Berkley, Joel Wyner, Frank Schorpion, Barry Flatman, Mark Walker, Ellen David, Susan Glover, Frank Fontaine; **D:** Douglas Jackson; **W:** Matt Dorff; **C:** Georges Archambault; **M:** Daniel Scott. VIDEO

Random Harvest ♂♂♂ 1942 A classic romantic weepie. But the addition of some police corruption malarkey and a slow pace undermine the emotional payoff. Congresswoman Kay Chandler (Scott Thomas) and internal affairs cop Dutch Van Den Broeck (Ford) discover that their respective spouses, who were killed in the same airliner crash, had been having an affair. Dutch needs to know all the sordid details while Kay, who's up for re-election, wants to remain quiet. Based on the novel by Warren Adler. **133m/C VHS, DVD.** Harrison Ford, Kristin Scott Thomas, Sydney Pollack, Charles S. Dutton, Bonnie Hunt, Dennis Haysbert, Richard Jenkins, Paul Guilfoyle, Susanna Thompson, Peter Coyote, Dylan Baker, Lynne Thigpen, Bill Cobbs, Susan Floyd, Edie Falco, Kate Mara; **D:** Sydney Pollack; **W:** Kurt Luedtke; **C:** Philippe Rousselot; **M:** Dave Grusin.

Random Hearts ♂♂ 1999 (R) If this film had stuck to overcoming tragedy and finding new love, it could have been a beautiful match dancer and is made happy by a amnesiac meets and is made happy by a beautiful music hall dancer. He regains his memory and forgets about the dancer and their child. This is Garson's finest hour, and a shamelessly potent sobfest. **126m/B** VHS, DVD. Greer Garson, Ronald Colman, Reginald Owen, Philip Dorn, Susan Peters, Henry Travers, Margaret Wycherly, Bramwell Fletcher; **D:** Mervyn LeRoy; **W:** Claudine Wes:, George Froeschel, Arthur Wimperis; **C:** Joseph Ruttenberg; **M:** Herbert Stothart.

Range Busters ♂ 1940 Range Busters are called in to find the identity of the phantom killer, John 'Dusty' King, Luana Walters, ..leroy Mason, Eanie Hodgins, Kermit Maynard Frank LaRue; **D:** S. Roy Luby; **W:** John Rathmell; **C:** Edward Linden; **M:** Lew Porer.

Range Feud ♂♂ 1931 Wayne is a ranch owner's son falsely accused of murder. Just as he's about to 'nang,' Jones, as the heroic sheriff, saves the day and reveals the real killer's identity. **64m/C** VHS, DVD. John Wayne, Alberta Vaughn, George 'Gabby' Hayes; **D:** Ross Lederman.

Randy Rides Alone ♂♂ 1934 Very young Wayne is good in this slappapble but pleasant B effort. Wayne single-handedly cleans up the territory and rids the land of a passel o'bad guys. **53m/B** VHS, DVD. John Wayne, Alberta Vaughn, George 'Gabby' Hayes; **D:** Harry Fraser; **W:** Lindsey Parsons.

Range Law 🦴 1931 Another entry in the infamous Maynard series of horseplay, cliche, and repetitive plot elements. 60m/B VHS. **W:** Ken Maynard, Charles "Blackie" King, Late (Lafayette) McKee. **D:** Phil Rosen; **W:** Earle Snell; **C:** Arthur Reed.

Range Law 🦴½ 1944 Ranchers are being terrorized for their silver mine and its up to Brown and Hatton to catch the villains. 59m/B VHS. Johnny Mack Brown, Raymond Hatton, Lloyd Ingraham, Sarah Padden, Ellen Hall, Steve Clark, Jack Ingram, Bud Osborne; **D:** Lambert Hillyer.

Range of Motion 🦴½ 2000 After an accident, Lainie Berman's (De Mornay) husband slips into a coma but she's positive he can recover if she has enough faith. Based on the book by Elizabeth Berg. 120m/C VHS, DVD. Rebecca De Mornay, Henry Czerny, Melanie Mayron, Barclay Hope, Kimberly Roberts; **D:** Donald Wrye; **W:** Grace McKeaney; **C:** Malcolm Cross; **M:** Gary Chang. CABLE.

Range Renegades 🦴½ 1948 Sheriff Wakely and his pals have their hands full when his deputy gets involved with the leader of a gang of outlaw women. Predictable B oater reflects the then developing trend of using wicked female characters in westerns. Paved the way for films like "Johnny Guitar" and "Rancho Notorious." 54m/B VHS. Jimmy Wakely, Dub Taylor, Dennis Moore, Jennifer Holt, John James, Steve Clark, Frank LaRue; **D:** Lambert Hillyer; **W:** Ronald Davidson, William Lively.

Range Riders 1935 A gunman poses as a wimp and cleans out an outlaw gang. 46m/B VHS. Lew Meehan, Merrill McCormick, Horace Carpenter, Barbara Starr, Buddy Roosevelt; **D:** Sam Newfield; **W:** George Plympton; **C:** William (Bill) Hyer; **M:** Lew Porter.

Rangeland Empire 🦴 *West of the Brazos* 1950 Shamrock and Lucky are at it again, implicated as being members of an outlaw gang until that gang attacks them. 59m/B VHS. James Ellison, Russell Hayden, Stanley Price, John Cason, Raymond Hatton, Fuzzy Knight, Tom Tyler, George Lewis; **D:** Thomas Carr; **W:** Ron Ormond, Maurice Tombragel, Robert North Bradbury; **C:** Ernest Miller; **M:** Walter Greene.

Ranger and the Lady 🦴½ 1940 Texas Ranger Rogers romances the woman who is the leader of a wagon train. 54m/B VHS, DVD. Roy Rogers, George "Gabby" Hayes; **D:** Joseph Kane.

Rangers 🦴 2000 (R) McCoy leads an Army Rangers team in capturing a terrorist bomber and while they accomplish their mission, the unit is forced to leave behind Plummer, which turns out to be part of a government setup. Not happy about this, Plummer joins the terrorists to get revenge and goes after his ex-buddies while McCoy realizes there's a conspiracy going on. 100m/C VHS, DVD. Matt McCoy, Glenn Plummer, Corbin Bernsen, Dartanyan Edmonds, Rene Rivera; **D:** Jim Wynorski; **W:** Steve Latshaw; **C:** Ken Blakey; **M:** David Wurst, Eric Wurst. VIDEO

Ranger's Roundup 🦴 1938 The Rangers prove their courage by rounding up an outlaw gang. 57m/B VHS. Fred Scott, Al "Fuzzy" St. John.

The Rangers Step In 🦴½ 1937 Allen leaves the Texas Rangers when a feud between his family and that of the girl he loves heats up again. Turns out rustlers are stirring things up in order to get some of the disputed land. 56m/B VHS. Robert "Tex" Allen, Eleanor Stewart, John Merton, Hal Taliaferro, Jack Ingram, Jack Rockwell, Late (Lafayette) McKee, Robert F. (Bob) Kortman; **D:** Spencer Gordon Bennet.

Rangers Take Over 🦴½ 1942 Gunlords are driven out by the Texas Rangers. 62m/B VHS. Dave O'Brien, James Newill, Iris Meredith, Guy Wilkerson, Charles "Blackie" King, Forrest Taylor, I. Stanford Jolley; **D:** Albert Herman; **W:** Elmer Clifton; **C:** Robert E. Cline.

Ransom 🦴🦴🦴 1996 (R) Tight and crafty thriller proves millionaire airline magnate Tom Mullen (Gibson) is a force to be reckoned with when son Sean (Nolte, son of actor Nick) is kidnapped. A vigilante Donald Trump (only gorgeous and brave), Mullen treats this like a high-stakes business deal and decides to get his kid back by announcing on TV that the $2 million ransom demand will instead become a bounty on the kidnappers. Wife Kate (Russo), predictably flips out but Mullen, after a few encounters with the heinous abductors, has sized them up and is convinced he's done the right thing. Lindo is a by-the-book fed with bad dialogue and Sinise is a bad cop playing for the other team. Gibson's emergency appendectomy delayed filming but he was soon leaping over cars for director Howard's well-staged action scenes. Based on the 1956 flick starring Glenn Ford. 121m/C VHS, DVD. Mel Gibson, Rene Russo, Gary Sinise, Delroy Lindo, Brawley Nolte, Lili Taylor, Liev Schreiber, Evan Handler, Dan Hedaya, Paul Guilfoyle, Jose Zuniga, Donnie Wahlberg, Michael Gaston, Nancy Ticotin; *Cameos:* Richard Price; **D:** Ron Howard; **W:** Richard Price, Alexander Ignon; **C:** Piotr Sobocinski; **M:** James Horner.

Ransom Money 🦴½ 1988 A kidnapping scheme involving millions of dollars, in and around the Grand Canyon, backfires. 87m/C VHS, DVD. Broderick Crawford, Rachel Romen, Gordon Jump, Randy Whipple; **D:** DeWitt Lee.

Ranson's Folly 🦴½ 1926 Barthelmess makes a wager that he can impersonate a famous outlaw well enough to rob a stage with only a pair of scissors. When the army paymaster is killed, guess who gets caught with his swash unbuckled? 80m/B VHS. Richard Barthelmess, Dorothy Mackaill, Anders Randolf, Pat Hartigan, Brooks Benedict; **D:** Sidney Olcott.

Rapa Nui 🦴🦴½ 1993 (R) The title refers to the Polynesian name for Easter Island, with the film set in the 17th century (before Dutch explorers discovered the island). It depicts the annual rituals of the mysterious people who built the Island's moai—the famous giant stone statues. Lee plays the heroic Noroinia, with Morales as his rival Make, and Holt as Ramana, the object of their desires. Faux primitive but with some great on-location filming. 107m/C VHS. Jason Scott Lee, Esai Morales, Sandrine Holt; **D:** Kevin Reynolds; **W:** Kevin Reynolds, Tim Rose Price; **M:** Stewart Copeland.

Rape 🦴 1976 Two guys investigate a third pal's mysterious death. They discover that his supernatural-power-imbued girlfriend is at the root of the matter. 90m/C VHS. *SP* Gaspar Gonzalez, Alfred Lucchetti, Gil Vidal, Naduska; **D:** Miguel Iglesias; **W:** Miguel Iglesias; **C:** Tomas Pladevall.

Rape and Marriage: The Rideout Case 🦴🦴½ 1980 The true story of an Oregon wife who accused her husband of rape. Thoughtfully explores the legal and moral questions raised by the case. Interpreted well enough, though not superbly, by a decent cast (although Rourke is a little too intense). 96m/C VHS. Mickey Rourke, Linda Hamilton, Rip Torn, Eugene Roche, Conchata Ferrell, Gail Strickland, Bonnie Bartlett, Alley Mills; **D:** Peter Levin. TV

The Rape of the Sabines WOOF! *El Rapto de las Sabinas; The Mating of the Sabine Women; Shame of the Sabine Women* 1961 The story of Romulus, king of Rome, and how he led the Romans to capture the women of Sabina. The battles rage, the women plot, and Romulus fights and lusts. Dubbed in English. 101m/C VHS. *IT* FR Roger Moore, Mylene Demongeot, Jean Marais; **D:** Richard Pottier.

Rapid Assault 🦴 1999 (R) Terrorist Lars Rynaark (Scribner) is set to detonate a biochemical agent in the Atlantic Ocean that will decimate the population—unless he gets paid a lot of cash. Three government ops are sent to get to the terrorist first. Typical action fodder—the plot making any sense is besides the point. 90m/C VHS, DVD. Tim Abell, Don Scribner, Jeff Rector, Lisa Mazzetti; **D:** Fred Olen Ray. VIDEO

Rapid Fire 🦴 1989 Cheap, made-for-video quickie about a good guy U.S. agent who battles terrorists. Easy to skip. 90m/C VHS, DVD. Joe Spinell, Michael Wayne, Ron Waldron; **D:** David A. Prior.

Rapid Fire 🦴🦴½ 1992 (R) Lee (son of martial arts cult film star Bruce Lee) is a Chinese-American art student who also happens to be a martial arts expert. He's tapped by the police to help stem the violence between the Asian and Italian gangs fighting for control over Chicago's drug trade. Typical martial arts movie is made better by uniquely choreographed action sequences and Lee's attractive presence. 96m/C VHS, DVD. Brandon Lee, Powers Boothe, Nick Mancuso, Raymond J. Barry, Kate Hodge, Tzi Ma, Tony Longo, Michael Paul Chan, Dustin Nguyen, John Vickery; **D:** Dwight Little; **W:** Alan B. McElroy, Cindy Cirile, Paul Attanasio; **M:** Christopher Young.

Rappin' 🦴 1985 (PG) Ex-con Van Peebles gets into it with the landlord and a street gang leader. Forgettable action/music drivel. 🎵Rappin'; Two of a Kind; Call Me; Born to Love; Killer; Itching for a Scratch; Snack Attack; Dodge; Golly Gee. 92m/C VHS, DVD. Mario Van Peebles, Tasia Valenza, Harry Goz, Charles Flohe; **D:** Joel Silberg.

The Rapture 🦴🦴 1991 (R) A beautiful telephone operator engages in indiscriminate sexual adventures to relieve the boredom of her job and life. She becomes curious by, and eventually converted to, evangelical Christianity, which leads her to a contented happiness and the birth of a daughter. When her husband is tragically killed she becomes convinced that she and her child will be taken by God into heaven if she only waits for the proper sign. 100m/C VHS, DVD. Mimi Rogers, David Duchovny, Patrick Bauchau, Will Patton; **D:** Michael Tolkin; **W:** Michael Tolkin; **C:** Bojan Bazelli.

Rapturious 🦴🦴 2007 Surprisingly entertaining supernatural thriller. White rapper Rapturious (Oppel) takes a new street drug that causes murderous hallucinations, only it turns out, the rapper is the reincarnation of a 19th-century western serial killer hanged for his crimes and sent to Hell. And Hell wants him back. 95m/C DVD. Robert Oppel, Debbie Rochon, Cinque Lee, Joe Bob Briggs, Amin Joseph, Hoya Guerra; **D:** Kamal Ahmed; **W:** Kamal Ahmed; **C:** Tom Agnello; **M:** Kamal Ahmed.

Rapunzel 🦴🦴 1982 A beautiful young woman locked in a tall tower is saved by the handsome prince who climbs her golden tresses. Part of Shelly Duvall's "Faerie Tale Theatre" series. 60m/C VHS, DVD. Shelley Duvall, Gena Rowlands, Jeff Bridges; **D:** Gilbert Cates.

Rare Birds 🦴🦴 2001 Quirky Canadian comedy finds Dave Purcell (Hurt) depressed. His restaurant, located in the small town of Cape Spear, Newfoundland, is failing as is his long-distance marriage. But his eccentric neighbor Alphonse (Jones) comes up with a plan—he spreads the word among birders that a rare duck has been sighted and soon the area is flooded with amateur ornithologists, which is certainly good for Dave's business and his love life as he gets together with waitress Alice (Parker). Oh yeah, there's also Alphonse's plans for a cocaine shipment he's salvaged from a sunken boat, if he can keep away from the product himself. Based on the novel by Riche. 101m/C VHS, DVD. CA William Hurt, Molly Parker, Andy Jones, Cathy Jones, Sheila McCarthy, Vicky Hynes, Greg Malone; **D:** Sturla Gunnarsson; **W:** Edward Riche; **C:** Jan Kiesser; **M:** Jonathan Goldsmith.

The Rare Breed 🦴🦴½ 1966 Plodding but pleasant Western. A no-strings ranch hand (Stewart) agrees to escort a Hereford Bull to Texas, where the widow of an English breeder plans to crossbreed the bull with longhorn cattle. The widow (O'Hara) insists that she and her daughter accompany Stewart on the trip, which features every kind of western calamity imaginable. When all others believe the attempt to crossbreed has failed, Stewart sets out to prove them wrong. 97m/C VHS, DVD. James Stewart, Maureen O'Hara, Brian Keith, Juliet Mills, Jack Elam, Ben Johnson; **M:** Andrew V. McLaglen; **C:** William Clothier; **M:** John Williams.

A Rare Breed 🦴½ 1981 (PG) Real-life story of a kidnapped horse in Italy and a young girl's quest to retrieve it. Directed by David Nelson of TV's "Ozzie and Harriet" fame, this movie is cute and old-fashioned. 94m/C VHS. George Kennedy, Forrest Tucker, Tracy Vaccaro, Tom Hallick, Don DeFore; **D:** David Nelson.

The Rascals 🦴🦴½ 1981 (R) An irrepressible youth at a rural Catholic boys' school comes of age. 93m/C VHS. FR Bernard Brieux, Pascale Rocard, Etienne Draber, Pierre Vial, Thomas Chabrol; **D:** Bernard Revon; **W:** Bernard Revon; **C:** Gerard de Battista; **M:** Roland Romanelli.

Rashomon 🦴🦴🦴🦴 *In the Woods* 1951 In 12th century Japan, two travelers attempt to discover the truth about an ambush/rape/murder. They get four completely different versions of the incident from the three people involved in the crime and the single witness. An insightful masterpiece that established Kurosawa and Japanese cinema as major artistic forces. Fine performances, particularly Mifune as the bandit. Visually beautiful and rhythmic. Remade as a western, "The Outrage," in 1964. In Japanese with English subtitles. 83m/B VHS, DVD. JP Machiko Kyo, Toshiro Mifune, Masayuki Mori, Takashi Shimura, Minoru Chiaki, Kichijiro Ueda, Daisuke Kato; **D:** Akira Kurosawa; **W:** Akira Kurosawa, Shinobu Hashimoto; **C:** Kazuo Miyagawa; **M:** Fumio Hayasaka. Oscars '51: Foreign Film; Natl. Bd. of Review '51: Director (Kurosawa); Venice Film Fest. '51: Film.

Rasputin and the Empress 🦴🦴🦴 *Rasputin: The Mad Monk* 1933 Lavish historical epic teamed the three Barrymore sibs for the first and only time, as they vied for scene-stealing honors. Ethel is Empress Alexandra of Russia, tied to the weak-willed Nicholas II (Morgan) and under the spell of Rasputin, played by Lionel. John is a nobleman who seeks to warn the Russian rulers of their perilous perch on the throne, made only worse by Rasputin's spreading power and corruption. Ethel's first talkie role. Uncredited director Charles Brabin was replaced by Boleslawski due to his incompatability with the imperious Ethel. 123m/B VHS, DVD. Ethel Barrymore, John Barrymore, Lionel Barrymore, Ralph Morgan, Diana Wynyard, Tad Alexander, C. Henry Gordon, Edward Arnold, Gustav von Seyffertitz, Anne Shirley, Jean Parker, Henry Kolker; **D:** Richard Boleslawski; **W:** Charles MacArthur; **C:** William H. Daniels.

Rasputin: Dark Servant of Destiny 🦴🦴 1996 (R) Charismatic Russian peasant/mystic Grigori Rasputin (a mesmerizing Rickman), having received a vision of the Virgin Mary, comes to St. Petersburg in order to relieve the suffering of young hemophiliac, Prince Alexei (Findlay). Tsarina Alexandra (Scacchi) approves of anyone who can help her stricken son while Tsar Nicholas II (McKellen) tentatively agrees to accept the self-proclaimed holy man into the Russian court. Fine performances and beautiful photography. Filmed in St. Petersburg. 120m/C VHS. Alan Rickman, Ian McKellen, Greta Scacchi, Freddie Findlay, David Warner, John Wood, James Frain, Diana Quick, Ian Hogg, Peter Jeffrey, Ian McDiarmid, Julian Curry; **D:** Uli Edel; **W:** Peter Bruce; **C:** Elemer Ragalyi; **M:** Brad Fiedel. CABLE.

Rasputin the Mad Monk 🦴🦴 1966 Hammer's version of Russian history of course emphasizes the evil powers of the mad Russian monk (Lee) who gains entry into the court of the czar. Poor script but Lee's good. 90m/B VHS, DVD. GB Christopher Lee, Barbara Shelley, Richard Pasco, Francis

The Rat Pack ✓✓1/2 1998 Warts-and-all bio of ole blue eyes, Frank Sinatra (Liotta) and his pals, including Dean Martin (Mantegna), Sammy Davis Jr. (Don Cheadle), Joey Bishop (Slayton), and Peter Lawford (McFadyen). Story focuses on the time when Sinatra decides to support John F. Kennedy's (Petersen) bid for the presidency but his mobster ties eventually end their would-be association. TV effort is unauthorized and scorned by the late Sinatra's family. 120m/C VHS, DVD. Ray Liotta, Don Cheadle, Angus MacFadyen, Joe Mantegna, Bobby Slayton, William L. Petersen, Deborah Kara Unger, Phyllis Lyons, Megan Dodds; D: Rob Cohen; W: Kario Salem; C: Shane Hurlbut; M: Mark Adler. CABLE

Rat Pfink a Boo-Boo Woof! 1965 Parody on "Batman." Rat Pfink and Boo-Boo make it big, and end up sharing an apartment. Their relationship starts pleasantly and becomes romantic. Enjoyable farce. Well photographed and scripted, with the supporting characters stealing the show. Title story is legendary—it was misspelled accidentally and Steckler didn't have the cash to fix it. 72m/B VHS, DVD. Vin Saxon, Carolyn Brandt, Titus Moede, Mike Kannon, James Bowe, George Caldwell, Keith Wester; D: Ray Dennis Steckler; W: Ron Haydock; C: Fay Dennis Steckler; M: Andre Brummer.

The Rat Race ✓✓✓ 1960 A dancer and a musician venture to Manhattan to in which a bumbling superhero and his sidekick race around saving people. Notoriously inept. C: Alvin Kushler; M: Rachel Portman.

Rat Race ✓✓1/2 2001 (PG-13) Eccentric Las Vegas casino tycoon Cleese sends six ordinary gamblers on a treasure hunt for two million bucks while rich gamblers wager on the outcome. It's all in the tradition of "It's a Mad, Mad, Mad, Mad World" and the "Cannonball Run" movies, which means "s also old-fashioned. But in that good, solidly funny, anything-for-a-laugh way. But it doesn't go for the cheap, bodily-function humor that so many recent comedies have done to death. The mostly B-list cast has a lot of fun with the material, which is well-paced and expertly carried out by writer Breckman and director Zucker, who thankfully returns to the zany wall-to-wall comedy that put him on the map. 92m/C VHS, DVD. US John Cleese, Whoopi Goldberg, Cuba Gooding Jr., Jon Lovitz, Breckin Meyer, Amy Smart, Seth Green, Kathy Najimy, Rowan Atkinson, Wayne Knight, Dean Cain, Vince Vieluf, Lanei Chapman, Paul Rodriguez; D: Jerry Zucker; W: Andy Breckman; C: Thomas Ackerman; M: John Powell.

Ratas, Ratones, Rateros ✓✓ 1999 In poverty-stricken Ecuador, young Salvador (Bustos) tries to make his way as a petty thief. His life manages to mess up the TV industry. Early director-at effort by DeVito is uneven but funny. who stays with him and leads the boy down a self-destructive path. Spanish with subtitles. 107m/C VHS, DVD. Marco Bustos, Carlos Valencia, Simon Brauer, Cristina Dávila; D: Sebastian Cordero; W: Sergio Sacoto-Arias.

Ratatouille ✓✓✓ 2007 (G) Remy the rat (Oswalt) has a very refined palate, too refined for the garbage his colony hoards to survive. So he sneaks into the best restaurant in Paris to forage while the dreams of becoming a chef himself. This makes him odd-at-out with his dad and the rodent-averse community, not to mention the restaurant's human employees, named Linguini (Romano), a kitchen helper who helps the klutzy new guy, a renowned chef. Provides plenty to entertain all ages, with beautiful animation, excellent voice work, well-developed characters, and some surprising plot twists. 110m/C DVD, Blu-ray Disc. US D: Brad Bird; W: Brad Bird, Jan Pinkava, Jim Capobianco; C: Sharon Ca-

---

Ratboy ✓✓1/2 1986 (PG-13) An unscrupulous woman attempts to transform a boy with a rat's face into a celebrity, with tragic results. First directorial effort by Locke that gradually loses steam. 105m/C VHS. Sondra Locke, Sharon Baird, Robert Kevin Townsend; D: Sondra Locke; W: Rob Thompson; C: Bruce Surtees; M: Lennie Niehaus.

Ratcatcher ✓✓1/2 1999 Twelve-year-old James (Eadie) gets into a fight with another boy on the banks of the canal that runs through their 1970s working-class Glasgow neighborhood. Ryan 'falls' in and drowns and James keeps quiet while being endlessly drawn back to the scene. Meanwhile there's trouble at home and the family's hopes for a better life (by moving to new council housing) is also in jeopardy. 93m/C VHS, DVD. GB William Eadie, Tommy Flanagan, Mandy Matthews, Leanne Mullen, John Miller; D: Lynne Ramsay; W: Lynne Ramsay; C: Alwin Kushler; M: Rachel Portman.

Rated X ✓✓ 2000 (R) True story of smut kings, the Mitchell Brothers, as portrayed by brothers Sheen and Estevez. Porno pioneer Jim (Estevez) sees dollar signs and joins with younger brother Artie (Sheen) to film skin flicks in San Francisco, including their hard-core classic "Behind the Green Door." They get busted a lot on obscenity charges and fall victim to booze and drugs but while Jim finally cleans up his act, Artie just sinks deeper, leading to a deadly confrontation between the two. The brothers do a surprisingly impressive job but it's grim going. Based on the book by David McCumber. 114m/C VHS, DVD. Emilio Estevez, Charlie Sheen, Megan Ward, Danielle Brett, Rafer Weigel, Terry O'Quinn, Nikki de Boer, Peter Bogdanovich, Tracy Hutson; D: Emilio Estevez; W: Norman Snider, Anne Meredith, David Hollander; C: Paul Sarossy; M: Tyler Bates. CABLE

A Rather English Marriage ✓✓1/2 1998 Aging Reggie (Finney) and Roy (Courtenay) meet in a hospital waiting room after their wives have just died. The odd couple (Reggie is blustery ex-military while Roy was a milkman) are further thrown together when a social worker suggests that both should be ready to attack anyone in their path. their new situations with flashbacks to their younger selves. Based on the novel by Angela Carter. Finney and Courtenay starred together in 1983's "The Dresser." 104m/C VHS, DVD. GB Albert Finney, Tom Courtenay, Joanna Lumley, Sean Murray; D: Paul Seed; W: Andrew Davies; C: Gavin Finney; M: Jim Parker. TV

Ratings Game ✓✓ The Mogul 1984 A bitter, out-of-work actor and a woman who works at the ratings service manage an effort by DeVito is uneven but funny. 102m/C VHS, DVD. Danny DeVito, Rhea Perlman, Gerrit Graham, Kevin McCarthy, Jayne Meadows, Steve Allen, Ronny Graham, George Wendt, Barry Corbin, Huntz Hall, Louis Giambalvo, Basil Hoffman, Michael Richards, Ron Rifkin, Joe Santos, Vincent Schiavelli, Frank Sivero, Daniel Stern, Randi Brooks, Robert Costanzo, Allyce Beasley, Selma Diamond, Jason Hervey, James LeGros, Jerry Seinfeld, Damon Hines; D: Danny DeVito; M: Bruce Kimmel, David Spear. CABLE

Rats ✓✓ Rats: Night of Terror 1983 In 2225, the beleagured survivors of a nuclear holocaust struggle with a mutant rodent problem. Mattei used the pseudonym Vincent Dawn. 97m/C VHS, DVD. Ottaviano Del'Acqua, Richard Cross, Alex McBride; D: Bruno Mattei; W: Claudio Fragasso.

The Rats ✓✓ 2001 (R) Manhattan department store manager Susan Costello (Amick) calls in exterminator Jack Carver (Spano) to get rid of some rats but they discover these aren't the usual critters. Turns out these pesky rodents are geneti-

---

Rattle of a Simple Man ✓✓1/2 1964 A naive, chaste, middle-aged bachelor (Corbett) who lives in London must spend the night with a waitress (Cilento) to win a bet. She knows of the bet and kindly obliges. Enjoyable sex comedy. 91m/B VHS. GB Harry H. Corbett, Diane Cilento, Michael Medwin, Thora Hird; D: Muriel Box.

Rattled ✓✓1/2 1996 (PG-13) Indiana Jones won't be the only snake-hater after seeing what hundreds of rattlesnakes can do. When their den is disturbed by construction on a new water project, hundreds of rattlers slither down the mountainside ready to attack anyone in their path. Based on the book "Rattlers" by Joseph Gilmore. 90m/C VHS. William Katt, Shanna Reed, Michael Galeota, Monica Creel, Clint Howard, Ian Abercrombie; E: Lauter, Bibi Besch, Zack Eginton; D: Tony Randel; W: Jim Wheat, Ken Wheat.

Rattler Kid ✓ Un Hombre viene a matar 1968 Cavalry sergeant wrongly accused of murdering his commanding officer escapes from prison and finds the real killer. 86m/C VHS, DVD. IT SP Richard Wyler, Brad Harris, Jesus Puente, Femi Benussi; D: Len Kimovsky; W: Odoardo Fiory; C: Julio Ortas; M: Francisco De Masi.

Rattlers ✓ 1976 (PG) TV movie featuring poisonous rattlesnakes who attack at random. 82m/C VHS, DVD. Sam Chew, Elizabeth Chauvet, Dan Priest; D: John McCauley; TV

Ratz ✓✓ 1999 Dumb teen film about best friends Marci and Summer who get involved with a magic ring, an eccentric shopkeeper, and two rats (yes, the kind) who are transformed into a couple of datable young hunks so the girls will have escorts to the big spring dance. 95m/C VHS, DVD. Caroline Elliott, Vanessa Lengies, Jake Seeley, Lev James, Kathy Baker, Ron Silver, Barbara Tyson; D: Thom Eberhardt; W: Thom Eberhardt.

Ravager ✓1/2 1997 (R) When a space transport ship crashlands in the desert, former lovers Cooper Wayne (Payne) and Avedon Hammond (Butler), along with their crew, search for help. They discover an underground storage facility and some leaking hazardous material labeled "Ravenger" that infects one of their technicians. When they return the infected crewman to the ship, they also bring back a

---

A Rat's Tale ✓✓ 1998 (G) "Romeo & Juliet" for rats. A regular Joe, Manhattanite Monty Mad-Rat meets Isabella Nobel-Rat, the daughter of the rat President, and soon Monty is a goner for the girl. Bad romance sends the couple down into the common sewer creature. Adding to the intrigue, a land developer (Ostendorf) appears with a scheme to obliterate the rat population and build a parking garage. The rats band together to raise money to buy their land and prevent ratricide. Admirably lo-tech, kid pic nonetheless suffers from the cute but excessicisless and the much wired marionettes playing the rats—they're no muppets—and the broadly characterized roles of the human actors (Hutton, Stiller and D'Angelo). Marionettes complements of Germany's Augsburger Puppet Theatre. Based on the book by Tor Seidler. 90m/C VHS. GE Lauren Hutton, Jerry Stiller, Beverly D'Angelo, Josef Ostendorf; D: Michael F. Huse; W: Werner Morganroth, Peter Scheerbaum; C: Piotr Le'ar; M: Frederic Talgorn; V: Dee Bradley Baker, Lynsey Bartilson, Donald Arthur, Ray Guth, Scott MacDonald.

The Rats Are Coming! The Werewolves Are Here! Woof! 1972 (R) Low-budget schlock revolves around a family of werewolves and the daughter who decides to put an end to the curse. Imaginative title promises much more than movie delivers. The killer rats were thrown in as an afterthought to increase the run time. 92m/C VHS. Hope Stansbury, Jackie Skarvellis, Noel Collins, Joan Ogden, Douglas Phair, Bernard Kaler; D: Andy Milligan; C: Andy Milligan.

Rattle of a Simple Man ✓✓1/2 ...

Rave Review ✓✓ 1995 Desperate L.A. theatrical director wants to score a powerful critic into giving his latest production a glowing review so that his small theatre company can remain in business. Too bad he scares the critic to death. 91m/C VHS. Jeff Seymour, Ed Begley Jr., Lao Rossi, Joe Spano, Bruce Kirby, James Handy; D: Jeff Seymour.

The Raven ✓✓1/2 1915 An early, eccentric pseudo-biography of author Edgar Allen Poe. The film opens with a look at Poe's ancestors and follows the author to maturity when he turns to alcohol for solace. His drunken stupor produces hallucinations that lead to his tale of "The Raven." Silent with added music track. 80m/B VHS. Henry B. Walthall, Wanda Howard; D: Charles Brabin.

The Raven ✓✓✓ 1935 A lunatic surgeon (Lugosi), who has a dungeon full of torture gadgets inspired by Edgar Allan Poe's stories, is begged by a man to save his daughter's life. The surgeon does, and then falls in love with the girl. But when she rejects his love (she's already engaged), he plans revenge in his chamber of horrors. Karloff plays the criminal who winds up ruining the mad doctor's plans. Lugosi is at his prime in this role and any inconsistencies in the somewhat shaky script can be overlooked because of his chilling performance. 62m/B VHS, DVD. Boris Karloff, Bela Lugosi, Irene Ware, Lester Matthews, Samuel S. Hinds; D: Lew Landers; W: David Boehm, Jim Tully; C: Charles Stumar.

The Raven ✓✓ 1963 This could-have-been monumental teaming of horror greats Karloff, Lorre, and Price is more of a satire than a true horror film. One of the more enjoyable of the Corman/Poe adaptations, the movie takes only the title of the poem. As for the story line: Price and Karloff play two rival sorcerers who battle for supremacy, with Lorre as the unfortunate associate turned into the bird of the title. 86m/C VHS, DVD. Vincent Price, Boris Karloff, Peter Lorre, Jack Nicholson, Hazel Court, Olive Sturgess; D: Roger Corman; W: Richard Matheson; C: Floyd Crosby; M: Les Baxter.

Raven ✓1/2 1997 (R) Covert mercenary team codenamed Raven is after a Soviet satellite decoder. They're double-crossed by renegade CIA agents and their leader Reynolds decides to get his own brand of justice. 93m/C VHS, DVD. Burt Reynolds, Krista Allen, Matt Battaglia, David Ackroyd, Richard Gant; D: Russell Solberg; W: Jacobsen Hart; C: John Dirlam; M: Harry Manfredini.

Ravenhawk ✓✓ 1995 (R) Native American Ravenhawk (McLish) is falsely accused of murdering her parents and sent to a maximum security asylum. Twelve years later she returns to her home and learns that corporate slimeball Philip Thorne (Atherton) framed her. Now, she's built a nuclear waste plant on Shoshone land over the objections of the tribe and Ravenhawk is determined to even the score. 86m/C VHS. Rachel McLish, John Enos, William Atherton, Ed Lauter, Mitch Pileggi; D: Albert Pyun; W: Kevin Elders; C: George Mooradian; M: Johnny Harris.

Ravenous ✓✓1/2 1999 (R) Off-kilter tale of cannibalism in the American West in 1847 (loosely based on the Donner Party). Covert soldiers are off-killer; when it begins to use man-eating as a metaphor for settlers carving up the land. When stringy, twitch-

---

The Ravagers ✓✓ 1965 Capt. Kermit Dowling (Saxon) and ex-con Gaudial (Poe) led Filipino guerrillas against remnants of the Japanese forces on the Philippines. The Japanese have taken over a convent in their search for a ship of gold bullion and Gaudial manages to sneak inside where he encounters American can Sheila (Fitzsimmons), who's been sheltered by the nuns. In between the action, they take a liking to each other. 80m/B VHS, DVD. John Saxon, Fernando Poe Jr., Bronwyn Fitzsimmons, Robert Arevalo, Mike Parsons; D: Eddie Romero; W: Eddie Romero, Cesar Amigo; M: Tito Arevalo.

contagion that threatens the survival of everyone aboard. 92m/C VHS. Bruce Payne, Yancy Butler, Juliet Landau, Salvator Xuereck; D: James D. Deck; W: James D. Deck.

ing Colqhoun (Carlyle) shows up starving and nearly frozen at an army fort in the Sierra Nevadas, he tells Captain John Boyd (Pearce) that he was with a party that resorted to eating their dead when stranded. When a team is sent to investigate, more than the facts are digested. Soon Colqhoun is extolling the virtues of pan-frying your pals to Boyd. The unusual subject and offbeat attempts at humor make this a recipe not for all tastes. **100m/C VHS, DVD.** John Spencer, Stephen Spinella, Neal McDonough, Guy Pearce, Robert Carlyle, Jeremy Davies, Jeffrey Jones; **D:** Antonia Bird; **W:** Ted Griffin; **C:** Anthony B. Richmond; **M:** Michael Nyman, Damon Albarn.

Raven's Ridge 🦴🦴½ **1997 (R)** Imagine an exceptionally low-budget combination of Stanley Kubrick's heist movie "The Killing" and "Deliverance." That's essentially what this story boils down to. A group of friends knock over an armored car at a racetrack then stash the loot out in the woods. When they go to retrieve it, they're attacked by a grizzled local. **77m/C DVD.** William Kendall, Dawn Howard, John Rizzi; **D:** Mike Upton.

Ravishing Idiot 🦴🦴 *Adorable Idiot; The Warm-Blooded Spy; Bewitching Scatterbrain* **1964** An unemployed bank clerk becomes mixed up with Soviet spies. **99m/B VHS, DVD.** *FR* Brigitte Bardot, Anthony Perkins; **D:** Edouard Molinaro.

Raw Courage 🦴🦴 *Courage* **1984** Three long-distance runners relax in New Mexico, but are kidnapped by vigilantes. Loosely based on a James Dickey novel. **90m/C VHS.** Ronny Cox, Lois Chiles, Art Hindle, Tim Maier, M. Emmet Walsh; **D:** Robert L. Rosen.

Raw Deal 🦴🦴🦴 **1948** Sadistic Rick Coyle (Burr) framed one-time associate Joe Sullivan (O'Keefe), who wound up in prison. Joe's then pal Pat (Trevor) helps him to escape and they take prison social worker Ann (Hunt), who's befriended Joe, as a hostage. They go after Coyle and Joe begins to fall for the demure dame, who finds the underworld life exciting and even saves Joe from one of Coyle's henchmen. No good guys here but it is fine film noir. **79m/B VHS, DVD.** Dennis O'Keefe, Claire Trevor, Raymond Burr, Marsha Hunt, John Ireland, Curt Conway, Whit Bissell; **D:** Anthony Mann; **W:** John C. Higgins, Leopold Atlas; **C:** John Alton; **M:** Paul Sawtell.

Raw Deal 🦴½ **1986 (R)** Don't ever give Schwarzenegger a raw deal! FBI agent Schwarzie infiltrates the mob and shoots lots of people. **106m/C VHS, DVD.** Arnold Schwarzenegger, Kathryn Harrold, Darren McGavin, Sam Wanamaker, Paul Shenar, Steven Hill; **D:** John Irvin; **W:** Patrick Edgeworth, Gary De Vore; **C:** Alex Thomson.

Raw Force 🦴 *Shogun Island* **1981 (R)** Three karate buffs visit an island inhabited by a sect of cannibalistic monks who have the power to raise the dead (it could happen). They fix the villains by kicking them all in the head. **90m/C VHS.** *PH* Cameron Mitchell, Geoffrey Binney, John Dresden, John Locke, Ralph Lombardi; **D:** Edward Murphy.

Raw Justice 🦴 **1993 (R)** When the daughter of a powerful Southern mayor is murdered, tough ex-cop Mace (Keith) is hired to get the killer. Mace enlists the reluctant help of call girl Sarah (Anderson) to help him trap Mitch (Hayes), his prime suspect. Only things don't work out as Mace planned and the wary threesome must work together to save themselves from certain death. **92m/C VHS, DVD.** David Keith, Pamela Anderson, Robert Hays, Leo Rossi, Charles Napier, Stacy Keach; **D:** David A. Prior.

Raw Nerve 🦴 **1991 (R)** A cast with possibilities can't overcome this poorly reasoned suspenser. A young man has visions of the local serial killer, but when he reports them to police he becomes the suspect. There are a few twists beyond that, none too thrilling. **91m/C VHS.** Glenn Ford, Traci Lords, Sandahl Bergman, Randall "Tex" Cobb, Ted Prior, Jan-Michael Vincent; **W:** David A. Prior.

Raw Nerve 🦴🦴½ **1999 (R)** Rogue cop Blair (Van Peebles) has crossed the line one too many times and is being investigated for money laundering. He's in trouble with IAD and the mob, which also puts girlfriend Izabel (Sheridan) in danger. Blair turns for help to ex-cop buddy Ethan (Galligan) but won't change his violent ways and keeps sinking down. **102m/C VHS, DVD.** Mario Van Peebles, Nicolette Sheridan, Zach Galligan; **D:** Avi Nesher. **VIDEO**

Raw Target 🦴½ **1995 (R)** Ex-kickboxer Johnny Rider (Cook) finds himself a police decoy in a drug bust and then learns that the drug gang's leader Sparks (Hill) was also involved in his brother's death. **92m/C VHS, DVD.** Dale "Apollo" Cook, Ron Hall, Nick (Nicholas, Niko) Hill, Mychelle Charters; **D:** Tim Spring; **W:** Larry Maddox; **C:** Bruce Dorfman; **M:** Jun Lupito.

Rawhead Rex 🦴½ **1987 (R)** An ancient demon is released from his underground prison in Ireland by a plowing farmer, and begins to decapitate and maim at will. Adapted by Clive Barker from his own short story. But Barker later disowned the film, so make your own judgment. **89m/C VHS, DVD.** David Dukes, Kelly Piper, Niall Toibin, Niall O'Brien, Donal McCann, Gladys Sheehan, Cora Lunny, Heinrich von Schellendorf; **D:** George Pavlou; **W:** Clive Barker; **C:** John Metcalfe; **M:** Colin Towns.

Rawhide 🦴🦴 **1938** Rancher's Protection Association forces landowners to knuckle under resulting in friction. Lou Gehrig plays a rancher in a western released the year before he died. Bandleader Ballew could be more gripping in the lead. **60m/B VHS, DVD.** Lou Gehrig, Smith Ballew, Evalyn Knapp; **D:** Ray Taylor.

Rawhide 🦴🦴🦴 *Desperate Siege* **1950** Four escaped convicts hijack a stagecoach way station and hold hostages while waiting for a shipment of gold. A suspenseful B-grade western with a bang-up ending. Well paced and cast with an abundance of good talent. A remake of "Show Them No Mercy" (1938). **86m/B VHS.** Tyrone Power, Susan Hayward, Hugh Marlowe, Jack Elam, Dean Jagger, George Tobias, Edgar Buchanan, Jeff Corey; **D:** Henry Hathaway; **C:** Milton Krasner.

Rawhide Romance 🦴 **1934** Bill finds justice and love in this chap-slappin' opus, which finds him neglecting the thieves operating on the ranch as he romances his girl. Naturally he comes to his senses and gets after the crooks. **47m/B VHS.** Buffalo Bill Jr., Genee Boutell, Lafe (Lafayette) McKee, Si Jenks, William Barrymore, Marin Sais, Clyde McClary; **D:** Victor Adamson; **W:** L.V. Jefferson.

Ray 🦴🦴🦴 **2004 (PG-13)** If imitation is the sincerest form of flattery than Foxx (who did win an Oscar) has it all covered for his depiction of the legendary Ray Charles in an extended biography that covers 1930 to 1966. This detailed, colorful, and straightforward retelling starts with young Ray Charles Robinson being sent away to bolster himself at a school for the blind. Ray finds musical success in the Seattle jazz scene but also gets firsthand knowledge of the dark side of the biz. While touring, he picks up a 20-year heroin habit and an equally destructive addiction to women, although it's supportive wife Della Bea (Washington) who encourages Ray to develop his own style, a heady fusion of gospel and R&B. Hackford doesn't skimp on Ray's charms or faults and finds a workable balance between showcasing the musician's professional and personal lives. Foxx auditioned for Charles, who gave his approval for what became Foxx's breakout performance. **152m/C VHS, DVD, HD DVD.** *US* Jamie Foxx, Kerry Washington, Regina King, Clifton Powell, Aunjanue Ellis, Harry J. Lennix, Terrence Howard, Larenz Tate, Bokeem Woodbine, Curtis Armstrong, Richard Schiff, Wendell Pierce, Chris Thomas King, David Krumholtz, Warwick Davis, Robert Wisdom, Denise Dowse, Thomas Jefferson Byrd, Rick Gomez, Kurt Fuller, Sharon Warren, C.J. Sanders, Patrick Bauchau; **D:** Taylor Hackford; **W:** James L. White; **C:** Pawel Edelman; **M:** Craig Armstrong. Oscars '04: Actor (Foxx), Sound; Oscars '04: Actor (Foxx); British Acad. '04: Actor (Foxx), Sound; Golden Globes '05: Actor—Mus./Comedy (Foxx); Screen Actors Guild '04: Actor (Foxx).

Razor Blade Smile 🦴🦴 **1998 (R)** Kinky vampire tale with a really killer babe fond of leather fetish wear. She's Lilith Silver (Daley), a vampire hitwoman working in London. Lilith has been hired to murder members of the Illuminati—a secret society that has made inroads into the highest levels of business and government. Turns out the head of the Illuminati is Sethane Blake (Adamson), the vampire who originally made Lilith one of the undead. Low-budget, bloody camp with some watchable twists and turns. Also available in an unrated version. **101m/C VHS, DVD.** *GB* Eileen Daly, Christopher Adamson, Kevin Howarth, Jonathan Coote, Heidi James, David Warbeck; **D:** Jake West; **W:** Jake West; **C:** James Solan; **M:** Richard Wells.

The Razor; Sword of Justice 🦴🦴 *Hanzo the Razor: Sword of Justice* **1972** Reasonably honest cop Hanzo Itami knows he won't get a promotion under his corrupt boss Inspector Onishi unless he can blackmail him into it. And he finds a way when he discovers condemned prisoner Kanbei is actually living with his mistress Omino, who it turns out is busy with Onishi as well. A little knowledge could get Hanzo killed but he's willing to take the risk. Japanese with subtitles. **90m/C VHS, DVD.** *JP* Shintaro Katsu, Asaoka Yukiji, Atsumi Mari, Nishimura Akira; **D:** Kenji Misumi.

Razorback 🦴 **1984 (R)** Young American travels to the Australian outback in search of his missing journalist wife. During his quest, he encounters a giant killer pig that has been terrorizing the area. Firmly establishes that pigs, with little sense of natural timing, make lousy movie villains. **95m/C VHS.** *AU* Gregory Harrison, Bill Kerr, Arkie Whiteley, Judy Morris, Chris Haywood, David Argue; **D:** Russell Mulcahy; **W:** Everett DeRoche; **C:** Dean Semler.

The Razor's Edge 🦴🦴🦴 **1946** Adaptation of the W. Somerset Maugham novel. A rich young man spends his time between WWI & WWII searching for essential truth, eventually landing in India. A satisfying cinematic version of a difficult novel, supported by an excellent cast. Remade in 1984 with Bill Murray in the lead role. **146m/B VHS, DVD.** Tyrone Power, Gene Tierney, Anne Baxter, Clifton Webb, Herbert Marshall, John Payne, Elsa Lanchester, Lucile Watson, Frank Latimore, Cecil Humphreys, Harry Pilcer, Cobina Wright Sr., Noel Cravat, John Wengraf; **D:** Edmund Goulding; **W:** Lamar Trotti; **C:** Arthur C. Miller; **M:** Alfred Newman. Oscars '46: Support. Actress (Baxter); Golden Globes '47: Support. Actor (Webb), Support. Actress (Baxter).

The Razor's Edge 🦴🦴½ **1984 (PG-13)** A beautifully filmed but idiosyncratic version of the W. Somerset Maugham novel. WWI-ravaged Larry Darrell combs the world in search of the meaning of life. Murray is a little too old and sardonic to seem really tortured. Russell is great as the loser he rescues. Subtly unique, with real shortcomings. **129m/C VHS, DVD.** Bill Murray, Theresa Russell, Denholm Elliott, James Keach, Peter Vaughan, Saeed Jaffrey, Brian Doyle-Murray; **D:** John Byrum; **W:** John Byrum; **M:** Jack Nitzsche.

Razorteeth woof! **2005** No budget digital film rip-off of the 1978 cult classic "Piranha." **75m/C DVD.** Todd Carpent, Stevan Anselmi, Brian Berry, Brice Kennedy; **D:** John Polonia; **W:** John Polonia; **C:** Paul Alan Steele; **M:** Jon McBride. **VIDEO**

Re-Animator 🦴🦴🦴 **1984** Black humor cult classic, based on the H.P. Lovecraft story "Herbert West, The Re-Animator." Med student Herbert West (Combs) is determined to make a medical breakthrough by bringing the dead back to life. His experimental green goo is finally successful on a corpse but there's an unforgettable sex scene involving a lustful severed head and heroine Megan (Crampton). Followed by "Bride of Re-Animator." **86m/C VHS, DVD.** Jeffrey Combs, Bruce Abbott, Barbara Crampton, David Gale, Robert Sampson, Gerry Black, Carolyn Purdy-Gordon; **D:** Stuart Gordon; **W:** Stuart Gordon, Dennis Paoli, William J. Norris; **C:** Mac Ahlberg; **M:** Richard Band.

Reach for the Sky 🦴🦴½ **1956** WWII flying ace loses both legs in an accident and learns to fly again. He becomes a hero during the Battle of Britain, then is shot down over France and held prisoner by the Germans. At war's end he returns to England to lead 3,000 planes over London in a victory flight. Inspirationally told true story. **123m/B VHS, DVD.** *GB* Kenneth More, Alexander Knox, Nigel Green; **D:** Lewis Gilbert; **M:** John Addison. British Acad. '56: Film.

Reach the Rock 🦴 **1998 (R)** Robin (Nivola) is a minor troublemaker who gets tossed into his small hometown jail one hot summer night by Sgt. Quinn (Sadler), who blames Robin for his nephew's accidental drowning. Robin keeps escaping from lockup to cause more minor vandalism but always returns to his cell, since he's hoping his ex-girlfriend Lise (Langton), who's taking off for New York, will come and bail him out so they can have one last heart-to-heart. When she does so, Robin finally seems to reach some mature understanding (but the character's so weakly developed, it's hard to tell). **100m/C VHS.** Alessandro Nivola, William Sadler, Brooke Langton, Bruce Norris, Karen Sillas, Norman Reedus, Richard Hamilton; **D:** William Ryan; **W:** John Hughes; **C:** John Campbell; **M:** John McEntire.

Reaching for the Moon 🦴🦴 **1917** A day-dreaming department store employee finds himself in the unlikely position of ruling a kingdom. Vintage Fairbanks fun, based on a story by Anita Loos. Silent. **62m/B VHS.** Douglas Fairbanks Sr., Eileen Percy, Millard Webb; **D:** John Emerson.

Reaching for the Moon 🦴🦴½ **1931** Fairbanks is a businessman who falls for liquor and Daniels on a transatlantic cruise. Dull and cruel; not as light-hearted as it intends. One Irving Berlin song sung by Crosby. **62m/B VHS, DVD.** Douglas Fairbanks Sr., Bebe Daniels, Bing Crosby, Edward Everett Horton; **D:** Edmund Goulding.

Reactor 🦴 *War of the Robots* **1985** A low-budget sci-fi film about kidnapped scientists, alien ships and an activated nuclear reactor. **90m/C VHS.** *IT* Yanti Somer, Melissa Long, Giacomo "Jack" Rossi-Stuart, Robert Barnes, Aldo Canti; **D:** Alfonso Brescia; **W:** Alfonso Brescia; **C:** Silvio Fraschetti; **M:** Marcello Giombini.

Read My Lips 🦴🦴🦴 *Sur Mes Levres* **2001** Hearing-impaired Carla (Devos) is an office worker for a real-estate firm who is tired of being either ignored or unseen. When her boss has her hire an assistant, Carla chooses ex-con Paul (Cassel), who has no discernable office skills but does retain his shady criminal associations. He wants to heist some loot from an old associate, she wants revenge on a weaselly co-worker and it seems Carla's lip-reading skills are the key to both plans. French with subtitles. **115m/C VHS, DVD.** *FR* Emmanuelle Devos, Vincent Cassel, Olivier Gourmet, Olivier Perrier, Olivia Bonamy, Pierre Diot; **D:** Jacques Audiard; **W:** Jacques Audiard, Tonino Berancaquista; **C:** Mathieu Vadepied; **M:** Alexandre Desplat. Cesar '01: Actress (Devos), Screenplay.

The Reading Room 🦴🦴½ **2005 (PG)** Businessman William Campbell (Jones) fulfills his deceased wife's last wish by opening a free reading room in the gang-ridden inner-city neighborhood where he grew up. But his generosity is resented, and his dream threatened, by some in the neighborhood. **87m/C VHS.** James Earl Jones, Douglas Spain, Joanna Cassidy, Lynne Moody, Spencir Bridges, Tim Reid, Georg Stanford Brown; **D:** Georg Stanford Brown; **W:** Randy Feldman; **C:** James W. Wrenn; **M:** Elia Cmiral. **CABLE**

Ready to Rumble 🦴½ **2000 (PG-13)** Sanitation workers and best buds Gordie (Arquette) and Sean (Caan) decide to mastermind the comeback of their favorite wrestler, Jimmy "the King" (Platt). The reason he needs a comeback is that promoter Titus Sinclair (Pantaliano) has decided that he's outlasted his usefulness. Sort of like this movie. Arquette and wres-

Real Bullets ✗ 1990 Stunt team performs the real thing when two members get imprisoned in a bad guy's desert castle. *86m/C VHS.* *D:* Lance Lindsay.

A Real American Hero ✗✗½ 1978 Story of Tennessee sheriff Buford Pusser, the subject of three "Walking Tall" films. Here, he battles moonshiners, with the usual violence. *94m/C VHS, DVD.* Brian Dennehy, Brian Kerwin, Forrest Tucker. *D:* Lou Antonio. **TV**

The Real Blonde ✗✗½ 1997 (R) Entertaining ensemble pic that daringly exposes the business of show features a disillusioned actor, his beleaguered girlfriend, and a successful soap star (Caulfield) searching for a peroxide-free blonde in New York. On-the-outs couple Joe and Mary (Modine and Keener) is main focus but is undercut by the industry mania that surrounds them. Intelligent writing and caustic wit provide a few memorable scenes, such as the "Il Piano" debate in a crowded restaurant over a thinly veiled "acclaimed independent film" and Bob's resolution to his blonde quest. Modine also revs things up in an emotional improv. Thomas stands out from the crowd as a pretentious "fashion photog. DiCillo's lates: feature tackles the movie biz from the other side of the camera than his '995 acclaimed satire, "Living in Oblivion." *105m/C VHS, DVD.* Matthew Modine, Catherine Keener, Daryl Hannah, Maxwell Caulfield, Elizabeth Berkley, Marlo Thomas, Buck Henry, Bridgette Wilson-Sampras, Christopher Lloyd, Kathleen Turner, Denis Leary, Steve Buscemi; *D:* Tom DiCillo. *W:* Tom DiCillo; *C:* Frank Prinzi; *M:* Jim Farmer.

The Real Howard Spitz ✗✗½ 1998 (PG) Cranky has-been detective turned writer Spitz (Grammer) finds unlikely success with a children's book about a crime-solving cow, despite the fact that Howard hates kids. But even he can't resist 8-year-old Samantha's (Tessier) pleas to help her find her missing father. Amusing and Grammer even dresses in a cow costume. *93m/C VHS.* Kelsey Grammer, Amanda Donohoe, Genevieve Tessier, Cathy Lee Crosby; *D:* Vadim Jean; *W:* Glen MacPherson; *M:* John Murphy. **VIDEO**

Real Life ✗✗½ 1979 (R) Writer/comedian Brooks's first feature sags in places, but holds its own as a vehicle for his peculiar talent. Brooks plays a pompous director whose ambition is to make a documentary of a "typical" American family. *By:* Good, intelligent comedy. *99m/C VHS, DVD.* Charles Grodin, Frances Lee McCain, Albert Brooks; *D:* Albert Brooks; *W:* Monica Johnson, Harry Shearer, Albert Brooks; *C:* Eric Saarinen; *M:* Mort Lindsey.

The Real Macaw ✗✗½ 1998 (G) Mac (voiced by Goodman) is a 150-year-old parrot who lives with Benjamin Girdis (Robards), who is forced into a retirement home because of serious debt. Mac just happens to know where a pirate treasure is hidden and he's willing to share the info with Ben's grandson, Sarr (Croft) and the two set off for the South Pacific. *92m/C VHS.* AU Jason Robards Jr., Jamie Croft Deborah Lee Furness; *C:* David Foreman; *V:* John Goodman. **VIDEO**

Ready to Wear ✗✗ 1994 (R) *Pret-a-Porter* Altman travels to Paris to take on the fashion industry with a trademark satire, ensemble cast, and cameo players in tow. The untimely death of a random fashion player begins a swir of industry stereotypes. Loren and Mastroianni recreate their "Yesterday, Today, and Tomorrow" boudoir striptease scene. Coterie of one-dimensional characters is set adrift with no discernable plot, which might make for interesting people watching, but results in a tedious movie. Altman did it better with "The Player" and "Short Cuts." *132m/C VHS, DVD.* Sophia Loren, Marcello Mastroianni, Julia Roberts, Tim Robbins, Kim Basinger, Stephen Rea, Anouk Aimee, Lauren Bacall, Lili Taylor, Sally Kellerman, Tracey Ullman, Linda Hunt, Forest Whitaker, Richard E. Grant, Danny Aiello, Teri Garr, Lyle Lovett, Jean Rochefort, Michel Blanc, Anne Canovas, Jean-Pierre Cassel, Francois Cluzet, Rossy de Palma, Kasia (Katarzyna) Figura, Sam Robards, Cher, Harry Belafonte, Issey Miyata, Sonia Rykiel, Jean-Paul Gaultier, Thierry Mugler; *D:* Robert Altman; *W:* Barbara Shulgasser, Robert Altman; *C:* Jean Lepine, Pierre Mignot; *M:* Michel Legrand.

The Reagans ✗✗ 2004 Despite it being pulled from network broadcast due to allegations of character assassination, the production presents a compassionate and charitable portrayal of Ronald and Nancy Reagan's assent from Hollywood couple to First Family. Starting with their first date in 1949 and follows them through two White House terms. *180m/C VHS.* James Brolin, Judy Davis, Zeljko Ivanek, Mary Beth Peil, Bill Smitrovich, Shad Hart, Tom Barnett, Stewart Bick, Sean McCann, John Stamos, Lisa Bronwyn Moore, Zoie Palmer, Claudia Besso; *D:* Robert Allan Ackerman; *W:* Thomas (Tom) Rickman; *C:* James Chressanthis; *M:* John Altman. **TV**

The Real Glory ✗✗✗ 1939 After the U.S. capture of the Philippine Islands during the Spanish-American war, an uprising of Moro tribesmen spreads terror. After most of the islands are evacuated only a small group of Army officers is left to lead the Filipino soldiers against the rebels. Cooper plays the heroic doctor, who is not afraid to fight, especially when he comes to the rescue of the beseiged Army fort. Great action sequences and particularly good performances by Cooper and Niven. *95m/B VHS.* Gary Cooper, David Niven, Andrea Leeds, Reginald Owen, Broderick Crawford, Kay Johnson, Russell Hicks, Roy Gordon, Henry Kolker, Rudy Robles, Tetsu Komai, Roy Gordon, Vladimir Sokoloff; *D:* Henry Hathaway; *W:* Robert Presnell Sr., Jo Swerling; *C:* Rudolph Mate; *M:* Alfred Newman.

Real Genius ✗✗✗ 1985 (PG) Brainy kids in California work with lasers on a class project that is actually intended for use as an offensive military weapon. When they learn of the scheme, they use their brilliant minds to mount an amusingly elaborate strategic defense initiative of their own. Eccentric characters and an intelligent script provides a bevy of laughs for the family. *108m/C VHS, DVD.* Val Kilmer, Gabe Jarret, Jonjathan) Gries, Michelle Meyrink, William Atherton, Patt D'Arbanville, Steven Darden, Robert Prescott, Deborah Foreman, Ed Lauter, Tommy Swerdlow, Dean Devlin; *D:* Martha Coolidge. *W:* Peter Torokvei, Neal Israel, Pat Proft; *M:* Thomas Newman.

A Real Young Girl ✗✗ 1975 Breillat's explicit film was never commercially released—being too weird even for French cinema (at least at the time). It deals with the budding sexuality of the teenaged Alice (Alexandra) during her summer vacation as she becomes infatuated with Jim (Keller), a hunky laborer at her father's saw mill. Based on the director's novel "Le Soupirail" ("The Air Duct"). In French with subtitles. *93m/C VHS, DVD.* Charlotte Alexandra, Hiram Keller, Rita Maiden, Bruno Balp, Shirley Stoler; *D:* Catherine Breillat; *W:* Catherine Breillat; *M:* Mort Shuman.

Reality Bites ✗✗½ 1994 (PG-13) Humorous look at four recent college grads living, working, and slacking in Houston. Script by newcomer Childress is at its best when highlighting the trends: 7-Eleven Big Gulps, tacky '70s memorabilia, and games revolving around episodes of old TV shows like "Good Times," to name a few. Definite appeal for those in their early 20s, but anyone over 25 may encounter a "Generation X-er" gap, a notice-eble problem since "Reality" claims to speak for the entire twentysomething generation. Decent directorial debut for Stiller, good cast, particularly Garofalo, in the film debut. *99m/C VHS, DVD.* Winona Ryder, Ethan Hawke, Ben Stiller, Janeane Garofalo, Steve Zahn, Swoosie Kurtz, Joe Don Baker, John Mahoney; *Cameos:* David Pirner, Anne Meara, Jeanne Tripplehorn, Karen Duffy, Evan Dando; *D:* Ben Stiller; *W:* Helen Childress; *C:* Emmanuel Lubezki; *M:* Karl Wallinger.

Really Weird Tales ✗✗ 1986 Several SCTV alumni highlight this three-story movie, which is science fiction with a satirical edge. *85m/C VHS.* John Candy, Martin Short, Joe Flaherty, Catherine O'Hara, Clivia D'Albo, Sheila McCarthy, David Mcilwraith; *D:* John Blanchard, Paul Lynch, Don McBrearty.

The Reaper ✗✗ 1997 ✗✗½ A crime writer's most famous novel seems to be the basis for a copycat serial killer. Since the author is nearby the scene of every crime as well, he becomes the prime suspect. The investigating detective asks for his help but if the killer stays true to the plot, she's likely to become the next victim. *97m/C VHS, DVD.* CA Chris Sarandon, Catherine Mary Stewart, Vlasta Vrana, Joanna Noyes; *D:* John Bradshaw; *W:* Matt Dorff; *C:* Bruce Chun. **TV**

The Reaping ✗✗½ 2007 (R) Southern gothic revisits the 10 plagues from the bible in a small bayou town in Louisiana. Louisiana bayou town of Haven. Having lost her own faith, professor Katherine Winter (Swank), now a professional debunker of alleged miracles and religious phenomena, is called in to offer scientific explanations. Of course, she can't. CGI's decent. Swank's stoic, but the story is so much familiar hooey (and not very scary). *98m/C DVD, Blu-ray Disc, HD DVD, US* Hilary Swank, David Morrissey, Idris Elba, AnnaSophia Robb, William Ragsdale, Hilary Swank, David Morrissey, Idris Elba, AnnaSophia Robb, William Ragsdale, Hilary Swank, David Morrissey; *D:* Stephen Hopkins, Stephen Hopkins; *W:* Carey Hayes, Chad Hayes, Carey Hayes, Chad Hayes; *C:* Peter Levy, Peter Levy; *M:* John (Gianni) Frizzell, John Frizzell.

Rear Window ✗✗✗✗ 1954 A newspaper photographer with a broken leg (Stewart) passes the time recuperating by observing his neighbors through the window. When he sees what he believes to be a murder, he decides to solve the crime himself. With help from his beautiful girlfriend and his nurse, he tries to catch the murderer without getting killed himself. Top-drawer Hitchcock blends exquisite suspense with occasional on-target laughs. Based on the story by Cornell Woolrich. *112m/C VHS, DVD.* James Stewart, Grace Kelly, Thelma Ritter, Wendell Corey, Raymond Burr, Judith Evelyn; *D:* Alfred Hitchcock. *W:* John Michael Hayes; *C:* Robert Burks; *M:* Franz Waxman. AFI '98: Top 100. Natl. Film Reg. '97.

Rear Window 1998 Reeve stars as paralyzed architect Jason Kemp, whose wheelchair-bound existence has brought out the voyeur in the man. Kemp becomes convinced one of his neighbors is a murderer and has gotten rid of his drunken wife. Now all he needs to do is convince his friend and fellow architect, Claudia (Hannah), to help him prove his theory to skeptical police detective Moore (Forster), OR, and keep the murderer from discovering just what Kemp knows.

The Real Dirt on Farmer John ✗✗½ 2006 Eccentric John Peterson is the titular Illinois farmer whose life has been documented since the 1950s through home movies. John, who embraced the counterculture of the 1960s, later took over filming—and then—after his father died. Director Siegel befriended and started filming in the 1980s after a number of financial crises led him to sell most of the acreage, though the farm eventually rebounded as an organic co-op. *83m/C US D:* Taggart Siegel; *M:* Mark Orton.

The Real Charlotte ✗✗½ 1991 When young, lovely, and flirtatious Francie Fitzpatrick (Foth) is romantically betrayed by a young English officer, she wants to do its gc straight and raise her young son but her plans are thwarted by former associates who kidnap the child to force her into one last heist. Kilmer's a small-time thief, with a crush on Karen, who tries to help her out. Dumb, slow-moving story with a vapid performance by Basinger. *104m/C VHS, DVD.* Kim Basinger, Val Kilmer, Terence Stamp, Zach English, Gailard Sartain; *D:* Russell Mulcahy; *W:* William Davies, William Osborne; *C:* Denis Crossan; *M:* Brad Fiedel.

Real Men ✗✗½ 1987 (PG-13) The junior Belushi brother is a spy forced to recruit ordinary guy Ritter to help him negotiate with aliens to save the world. Bizarre premise shows promise, but spy spoof doesn't fire on all comedic pistons. Nice shoot-out. *86m/C VHS, DVD.* James Belushi, John Ritter, Barbara Barrie; *D:* Dennis Feldman; *C:* John A. Alonzo; *M:* Miles Goodman.

The Real Thing ✗✗ *Lives Ain't* *Cheap* 1997 (R) Ex-con Rupert (Russo) is trying the straight and narrow while his kid brother James (Buzzotta) continues to be a bad guy. But when James is shot, Rupert gets together with some criminal buddies to pull off a New Year's Eve heist to raise the money needed for James' care. This one's kind of dull until the ending shoot-out. *89m/C VHS.* James Russo, Jeremy Piven, Rod Steiger, Esai Morales, Gary Busey, Emily Lloyd, Dave Buzzotta, Ashley Laurence, Fabrizio Bentivoglio, Robert LaSardo; *D:* James Merendino; *W:* James Merendino; *C:* Greg Littlewood; *M:* Peter Leinheiser. **VIDEO**

Real Time: Siege at Lucas Street Market ✗✗ 2000 Deals with an armed robbery at a convenience store, which escalates into a hostage situation. What makes "Real Time" unique is that the story is played out through in-store security video, police-car cameras, and TV news footage. While this approach is interesting, it also depersonalizes the action, deflating the drama. At times, it feels like an extended episode of "Cops." On DVD, every scene can be viewed from a second angle, giving the movie the extra kick that it needs. Unfortunately, the inventiveness behind the camera never matches the on-screen action. *72m/C DVD.* Michael Cornelison, Chadrick Hoch, Tom Keane, Carol German, Sandy Gillies; *D:* Max Allan Collins; *W:* Max Allan Collins; *C:* Phillip W. Dingeldein.

The Real McCoy ✗✗½ 1993 Generally awful crime-caper film about female bank robber Karen McCoy (Basinger). Just out of prison, all Karen wants to do is gc straight and raise her small-time thief, with a crush on Karen, who tries to help her out. Dumb, slow-moving story with a vapid performance by Basinger. *104m/C VHS, DVD.* Kim Basinger, Val Kilmer, Terence Stamp, Zach English, Gailard Sartain; *D:* Russell Mulcahy; *W:* William Davies, William Osborne; *C:* Denis Crossan; *M:* Brad Fiedel.

Real Women Have Curves ✗✗✗ 2002 (PG-13) Coming-of-age comedy marks the debut of Ferrara as the young, headstrong and slightly plump Mexican-American Ana, who has decided to attend college cespite her overbearing mother Carmen (Ontiveros), who's decided that Ana would be better off married with children. Ana's plans are put on hold when she has 15 to help her sister Esela (Cruz) meet deadlines in a dress factory. While featuring such themes as the body image of larger women, work in a sweatshop and the rigid roles assigned to ethnic youngsters by their elders, the film manages to avoid cliches and preachiness. *93m/C VHS, DVD, US* America Ferrera, Lupe Ontiveros, Ingrid Oliu, George Lopez, Soledad St. Hilaire, Brian Sites, George Cerera Jr.; *D:* Patricia Cardoso; *W:* George ..aVoo, Josefina Lopez; *C:* Jim Denault; *M:* Heitor Pereira.

Reap the Wild Wind ✗✗✗ 1942 DeMille epic about salvagers off the Georgia coast in the 1840s featuring Wayne as the captain and Massey and his hep but if the killer stays true to the plot, she's likely to become the next victim. *123m/C VHS, DVD.* Ray Milland, John Wayne, Paulette Goddard, Raymond Massey, Robert Preston, Lynne Overman, Susan Hayward, Charles Bickford, Walter Hampden, Louise Beavers, Martha O'Driscoll, Elisabeth Risdon, Hedda Hopper, Raymond Hatton, Barbara Britton; *D:* Cecil B. DeMille; *W:* Charles Bennett, Jesse Lasky Jr., Alan LeMay; *C:* Victor Milner; *M:* Victor Young.

Reeve's first acting role since his own 1995 accident. **89m/C VHS.** Christopher Reeve, Daryl Hannah, Robert Forster, Ruben Santiago-Hudson, Anne Twomey, Allison Mackie, Rita Coster; **D:** Jeff Bleckner; **W:** Larry Gross, Eric Overmyer; **C:** Ken Kelsch; **M:** David Shire. **TV**

A Reason to Believe ♫♫ **1995 (R)** Campus date rape drama filmed at writer/director Tirola's alma mater, Miami University. Charlotte (Smith) goes to her boyfriend Wesley's (Quinn) big frat party, even though he's away and asked her not to. She drinks and flirts (a lot) with his best friend Jim (Underwood) and eventually leaves to collapse in a stupor on Wesley's bed. Jim follows and rapes her, though he'll tell his buddies Charlotte was a willing participant, which Wesley angrily believes. Meanwhile, the traumatized Charlotte is taken up by Linda (Emelin), the leader of the student feminist organization who wants the fraternities disbanded. Somewhat preachy and predicatable. **109m/C VHS, DVD.** Allison Smith, Jay Underwood, Daniel Quinn, Georgia Emelin, Obba Babatunde; **D:** Douglas Tirola; **C:** Sarah Cawley.

Reason to Die ♫ **1990 (R)** Bounty hunter uses his own girlfriend as a decoy to trap a psychotic prostitute killer. **86m/C VHS.** Liam Cundill, Wings Hauser, Anneline Kriel, Arnold Vosloo; **D:** Tim Spring.

A Reason to Live, a Reason to Die ♫♫ *Massacre al Fort Holman; Una Ragione Per Vivere e Una Per Morire* **1973** A bland Italian-French-German-Spanish western in which a group of condemned men attempt to take a Confederate fort. **90m/C VHS.** James Coburn, Telly Savalas, Bud Spencer, Guy Mairesse; **D:** Tonino Valerii.

Rebecca ♫♫♫♫ **1940** Based on Daphne Du Maurier's best-selling novel about a young unsophisticated girl who marries a moody and prominent country gentleman haunted by the memory of his first wife. Fontaine and Olivier turn in fine performances as the unlikely couple. Suspenseful and surprising, Hitchcock's first American film and only Best Picture Oscar. **130m/B VHS, DVD.** Joan Fontaine, Laurence Olivier, Judith Anderson, George Sanders, Nigel Bruce, Florence Bates, Gladys Cooper, Reginald Denny, Leo G. Carroll, Sir C. Aubrey Smith, Melville Cooper; **D:** Alfred Hitchcock; **W:** Joan Harrison, Robert Sherwood; **C:** George Barnes; **M:** Franz Waxman. Oscars '40: B&W Cinematog., Picture. **TV**

Rebecca of Sunnybrook Farm ♫♫ **1917** The original film version of the tale about an orphan who spreads sunshine and good cheer to all those around her. Silent with organ score. Based on the popular novel by Kate Douglas Wiggin; remade with Shirley Temple in 1938. **77m/B VHS.** Mary Pickford, Eugene O'Brien, Marjorie Daw, Helen Jerome Eddy; **D:** Marshall Neilan. **TV**

Rebecca of Sunnybrook Farm ♫♫½ **1938** Temple becomes a radio star over her aunt's objections in this bouncy musical that has nothing to do with the famous Kate Douglas Wiggin novel. Temple sings a medley of her hits, and dances the finale with Bill "Bojangles" Robinson. ♪On the Good Ship Lollipop/ When I'm With You/Animal Crackers medley; Crackly Corn Flakes; Alone With You; Happy Ending; Au Revoir; An Old Straw Hat; Come and Get Your Happiness; Parade of the Wooden Soldiers. **80m/B VHS, DVD.** Shirley Temple, Randolph Scott, Jack Haley, Phyllis Brooks, Gloria Stuart, Slim Summerville, Bill Robinson, Helen Westley, William Demarest; **D:** Allan Dwan; **C:** Arthur C. Miller.

Rebel ♫♫½ *No Place to Hide* **1970 (PG)** Mumbling student radical must decide between his love for a country girl and his loyalty to an underground terrorist organization. Notable (or not) for display of early Stallone. **80m/C VHS.** Sylvester Stallone, Anthony Page, Vickie Lancaster, Rebecca Grimes; **D:** Robert Allen Schnitzer; **W:** Robert Allen Schnitzer, Larry Beinhart.

Rebel ♫♫½ **1985 (R)** A U.S. Marine falls in love with a Sydney nightclub singer and goes AWOL during WWII. Stylish but empty and badly cast. **93m/C VHS.** *AU* Matt Dillon, Debbie Byrne, Bryan Brown, Bill Hunter, Ray Barrett; **D:** Michael Jenkins.

Rebel High ♫½ **1988 (R)** Hijinks occur at a high school where youngsters study guerilla warfare and teachers wear bullet-proof vests. **92m/C VHS.** Harvey Berger, Stu Trivax, Larry Gimple, Shawn Goldwater; **D:** Harry Jacobs.

Rebel Love ♫ **1985** Love grows between a northern widow and a Confederate spy. In better hands it might have been a good story. Here, it's overwrought and embarrassing historical melodrama. **84m/C VHS.** Terence Knox, Jamie Rose, Fred Ryan; **D:** Milton Bagby Jr.; **W:** Milton Bagby Jr.

Rebel Rousers ♫♫ **1969** A motorcycle gang wreaks havoc in a small town where a drag-race is being held to see who will get the pregnant girlfriend of Dern's high-school buddy as the prize. Young Nicholson in striped pants steals the show. **81m/C VHS, DVD.** Jack Nicholson, Cameron Mitchell, Diane Ladd, Bruce Dern, Harry Dean Stanton; **D:** Martin B. Cohen; **W:** Martin B. Cohen, Abe Polsky, Michael Kars; **C:** Laszlo Kovacs, Glen R. Smith; **M:** William Loose.

Rebel Run ♫ *Bolt* **1994 (R)** Biker Grieco moves west in order to escape his violent past but is then drawn into a rumble with arch-rival Ironside. **93m/C VHS, DVD.** Richard Grieco, Sean Young, Michael Ironside; **D:** Henri Colline; **W:** Henri Colline; **C:** Gerald Wolfe; **M:** Chris Squire. **VIDEO**

The Rebel Set ♫½ *Beatsville* **1959** The owner of a beat generation coffeehouse plans an armed robbery with the help of some buddies. Genuinely suspenseful, competently directed. **72m/B VHS, DVD.** Gregg (Hunter) Palmer, Kathleen Crowley, Edward Platt, John Lupton, Ned Glass, Don Sullivan, Vicki Dougan, I. Stanford Jolley; **D:** Gene Fowler Jr.; **W:** Bernard Girard, Louis Vittes; **C:** Karl Struss; **M:** Paul Dunlap.

Rebel Storm ♫ **1990 (R)** A group of freedom fighters team up to rescue America from the totalitarian rulers that are in charge in A.D. 2099. **99m/C VHS.** Zach Galligan, Wayne Crawford, June Chadwick, Rod McCary, John Rhys-Davies, Elizabeth Kiefer; **D:** Francis Schaeffer.

Rebel Vixens WOOF! *The Scavengers* **1969** Even though the war is over, ex-confederate soldiers continue looting and raping, until a brothel-full of prostitutes concoct a plan that has a lot to do with softcore sex. **94m/C VHS.** Maria Lease, Roda Spain, Jonathan Bliss, Michael Divoka, Wes Bishop, Bruce (Kemp) Kimball; **D:** Lee Frost; **W:** Robert W. Cresse; **C:** Robert Maxwell; **M:** Lee Frost, Robert W. Cresse.

Rebel without a Cause ♫♫♫♫ **1955** James Dean's most memorable screen appearance. In the second of his three films (following "East of Eden"), he plays troubled teen Jim Stark, who's alienated from both his parents and peers. He befriends outcasts Judy (Wood) and Plato (Mineo) in a police station and together they find a common ground. Many memorable scenes, including the "chickie run" between Jim and black leather-jacketed Buzz (Allen). Superb young stars carry this in-the-gut story of adolescence. All three leads met with real-life tragic ends. **111m/C VHS, DVD.** James Dean, Natalie Wood, Sal Mineo, Jim Backus, Nick Adams, Dennis Hopper, Ann Doran, William Hopper, Rochelle Hudson, Corey Allen, Edward Platt; **D:** Nicholas Ray; **W:** Irving Shulman, Stewart Stern; **C:** Ernest Haller; **M:** Leonard Rosenman. AFI '98: Top 100, Natl. Film Reg. '90.

The Rebels ♫♫ **1979** In the sequel to the TV miniseries "The Bastard," Philip Kent (Stevens) continues his Revolutionary War battle on the side of American independence. He is assisted by Southerner Judson Fletcher (Johnson) in thwarting an assassination attempt on George Washington. In addition to Bosley's Ben Franklin, "The Rebels" offers Backus as John Hancock. Followed by "The Seekers"; based on the novel by John Jakes. **190m/C VHS.** Andrew Stevens, Don Johnson, Doug McClure, Jim Backus, Richard Basehart, Joan Blondell, Tom Bosley, Rory Calhoun, MacDonald Carey, Kim Cattrall, William Daniels, Anne Francis, Peter Graves, Pamela Hensley, Wilfrid Hyde-White, Nehemiah Persoff, William (Bill) Smith, Forest Tucker, Tanya Tucker, Robert Vaughn, Desmond Richter; **D:** Russ Mayberry; **Nar:** William Conrad. **TV**

Rebirth of Mothra ♫♫ *Mosura; Mothra* **1996** A lumber company working in the Hokkaido rain forest accidently unearths the secret lair of Desghidorah, a three-headed monster, who teams up with the evil Belvera. It's up to twins More and Mona to call on Mothra to rescue the earth from their demonic powers. **106m/C VHS, DVD.** *JP* Megumi Kobayashi, Sayaka Yamaguchi, Hano Aki; **D:** Okihiro Yoneda.

Rebirth of Mothra 2 ♫½ *Mosura 2; Mothra 2* **1997** Garbage-eating monster Degehra and mutant marine lifeforms threaten Earth's oceans and it's up to Mothra and a magical treasure hidden in the underwater city of Nelikani to save the day. **103m/C VHS, DVD.** *JP* Megumi Kobayashi, Sayaka Yamaguchi, Hano Aki; **D:** Kunio Miyoshi; **W:** Masumi Suetani.

Reborn ♫♫ *Renacer* **1981** A faith healer and a talent scout hire actors to be cured of fake ailments. **105m/C VHS.** *SP* Dennis Hopper, Michael Moriarty, Francesco Rabal, Antonella Murgia; **D:** Bigas Luna; **W:** Bigas Luna; **C:** Juan Ruiz-Anchia; **M:** Scott Harper.

Rebound ♫♫ **2005 (PG)** Dumped as a college basketball coach after his usual sideline histrionics lead to the demise of an opposing team's avian mascot, Roy McCormick (Lawrence) decides to accept his old middle school's offer to take over their woeful team. From there, the tired, warm and fuzzy sports tale plays out as hard-nosed Roy becomes a softy while fashioning the losing squad into winners and finding love, too. Lawrence curbs his customary foul language for this family flick. **103m/C DVD.** *US* Martin Lawrence, Steven Anthony Lawrence, Horatio Sanz, Megan Mullally, Patrick Warburton, Wendy Raquel Robinson, Breckin Meyer, Fred Stoller, Oren Williams, Eddy Martin, Alia Shawkat, Steven Christopher Parker, Logan McElroy, Gus Hoffman, Tara Correa, Amy Bruckner; **D:** Steve Carr; **W:** Jon Lucas, Scott Moore; **C:** Glen MacPherson; **M:** Teddy Castellucci, Spring Aspers.

Rebound: The Legend of Earl "The Goat" Manigault ♫♫½ **1996 (R)** Earl "The Goat" Manigault (Cheadle) was a '60s Harlem playground basketball phenom who was taken under the wing of parks director Holcomb Rucker (Whitaker), who tries to steer the young man towards college and a career in the NBA. Unfortunately, the easily influenced Manigault also attracts the attention of local drug dealer Legrand (Beach) and when Manigault's life starts to fall apart, he drops out of college and turns to heroin, an inspirational true story. Manigault does turn his life around to found his own basketball tournament in Harlem. **111m/C VHS, DVD.** *US* Martin Lawrence, Don Cheadle, Michael Beach, James Earl Jones, Loretta Devine, Glynn Turman, Clarence Williams III, Ronny Cox, Eriq La Salle, Monica Calhoun, Tamara Tunie, Forest Whitaker; **Cameos:** Kareem Abdul-Jabbar; **D:** Eriq La Salle; **W:** Larry Golin, Alan Swyer; **C:** Alar Kivilo; **M:** Kevin in Eubanks. **CABLE**

The Reception ♫♫½ **2005** Jeannette, a wealthy, alcoholic Frenchwoman, lives with African American gay painter, Martin, under sadly codependent circumstances. Sierra, her estranged daughter, shows up one winter day with her new husband, coincidentally also African American, to collect on a promised inheritance. What unfolds is a scenario of shifting alliances that shadow the entanglement of racial prejudice, sexual orientation and addiction. Shooting in eight days on a $5,000 budget, Young presents an admirable effort. **75m/C DVD.** *US* Pamela Stewart, Darien Sills-Evans, Wayne Lamont Sims, Margaret Burkwit; **D:** John G. Young; **W:** John G. Young; **C:** Derek Wiesehahn.

Recipe for Disaster ♫♫½ **2003 (G)** The kids have to save the day when Mom (Warren) and Dad (Larroquette) get lost on their way home on the eve of their new restaurant's grand opening. Snooty owners of a neigboring restaurant complicate matters by trying to sabotage the kids' efforts at keeping the opening night crowd happy. Fun, well-paced family flick should go over well with the young'uns, especially with the "kids-save-the-day" theme and pop culture references. Younger children may be scared by the villains, who are a little more mean than they have to be for this type of movie. **92m/C VHS, DVD.** Lesley Ann Warren, John Larroquette, Michelle Brookhurst, Margo Harshman, Devon Werkheiser, Bill Dawes, Andrew James Allen, Melissa Peterman; **D:** Harvey Frost; **W:** William Propp; **C:** Christopher Pearson; **M:** William Goodrum. **TV**

Reckless ♫♫ **1935** Harlow, in a role originally intended for Joan Crawford, plays a showgirl coveted by a millionaire and secretly loved by her manager. Unfortunately, Harlow couldn't pull off the acting (much less the singing and dancing), although the plot strangely paralleled her own life. Songs include "Reckless," "Ev'rything's Been Done Before," "Trocadero," "Hear What My Heart Is Saying" and "Cyclone." **96m/B VHS.** Jean Harlow, William Powell, Franchot Tone, May Robson, Ted Healy, Nat Pendleton, Rosalind Russell; **D:** Victor Fleming; **C:** George J. Folsey.

Reckless ♫♫ **1984 (R)** A sincere movie about a "good" girl who finds herself obsessed with a rebel from the wrong side of her small town. Differs from 1950s' wrong-side-of-the-track flicks only in updated sex and music. **93m/C VHS.** Aidan Quinn, Daryl Hannah, Kenneth McMillan, Cliff DeYoung, Lois Smith, Adam Baldwin, Dan Hedaya, Jennifer Grey, Pamela Springsteen; **D:** James Foley; **W:** Chris Columbus; **C:** Michael Ballhaus; **M:** Thomas Newman.

Reckless ♫♫ **1995 (PG-13)** Rachel (Farrow) thinks she has a happy marriage and family but her husband (Goldwyn) informs her that he's hired a hit man to kill her. This startling revelation sends her on a 15-year journey in which she meets many other people who are not what they seem. Rene and Lucas go for an ultra-stylized fable theme, exploring Rachel's (and America's) aversion to dealing with the world as it really is. Quirky characters and situations are at turns amusing and annoying. Adapted by Lucas from his own play. **91m/C VHS.** Mia Farrow, Scott Glenn, Mary-Louise Parker, Tony Goldwyn, Stephen Dorff, Eileen Brennan, Giancarlo Esposito, Deborah Rush; **D:** Norman Rene; **W:** Craig Lucas; **C:** Frederick Elmes; **M:** Stephen Endelman.

Reckless ♫♫♫ **1997** British TV production's a combo of farce, romance, and drama that finds young doctor Owen Springer (Green) returning to Manchester to look after his feisty-but-ailing father (Bradley). He has a chance meeting with a beautiful middle-aged woman on the train, and then Anna Fairley (Annis) turns out to be his job interviewer. Reckless Owen falls impulsively in love—before learning Anna is also the wife of his new boss, Dr. Richard Crane (Kitchen). This doesn't deter Owen, and when he learns Crane is having an affair, Owen arranges for Anna to discover her husband's infidelity. Naturally, this leads to Owen and Anna hitting the sheets and things get very complicated. **312m/C VHS, DVD.** *GB* Robson Green, Francesca Annis, Michael Kitchen, David Bradley, Julian Rhind-Tutt, Daniela Nardini, Margery Mason, Conor Mullen; **D:** David Richards, Sarah Harding; **W:** Paul Abbott. **TV**

Reckless Disregard ♫♫½ **1984** A doctor whose career is ruined by a news report accusing him of involvement in a drug scam sues the newscaster. Based on Dan Rather's "60 Minutes" story and en-

Reckless Kelly 🐾🐾½ 1993 (PG) Australian bank robber, pop culture hero, and local video store owner Kelly is upset when his gang's Japanese conglomerate is about to be sold for a last-ditch defense of his home. So he prepares for a higher offer, unless he can come up with a higher offer. Slapstick homage to legendary Australian outlaw Ned Kelly. 81m/C VHS, AU Alexei Sayle, Hugo Weaving, Melora Hardin, Yahoo Serious, Bob Maza, Kathleen Freeman; **D:** Yahoo Serious; **W:** Yahoo Serious.

Reckless Moment 🐾🐾🐾 1949 A mother commits murder to save her daughter from an unsavory older man, and finds herself blackmailed. Gripping, intense thriller. 82m/B VHS, DVD; James Mason, Joan Bennett, Geraldine Brooks; **D:** Max Ophuls; **C:** Burnett Guffey.

Reckless: The Sequel 🐾🐾🐾 1998 A year later, Anna (Annis) has divorced philandering Richard (Kitchen) and is living with Owen (Green). The duo decide, somewhat impulsively, to marry, which drives the chronically jealous Richard into a frenzy and he vows to use any dirty trick necessary to break them up. But family interference and Anna and Owen's own doubts may do the job for him. 120m/C VHS. **GB** Robson Green, Francesca Annis, Michael Kitchen, David Bradley; **D:** David Richards; **W:** Paul Abbott; **C:** Lawrence Jones; **M:** Hal Lindes. TV

The Reckoning 🐾🐾🐾 2003 (R) Nicholas (Bettany) is a 14th century priest on the run from charges of adultery who joins a band of actors led by the bored Martin (Dafoe). They come upon a town where deaf-mute woman healer Martha is on trial for a boy's murder. Nicholas decides to perform a play based on the murder, which is a wild departure from performing only Bible-based stories, and find out that other boys have been killed recently in a similar manner. Nicholas becomes obsessed with proving Maria's innocence and uncovering the secrets of the village's "protector" Lord De Guise (Cassel). McGuigan makes excellent use of a deft story and exciting but not intrusive visuals to build suspense for the plot, and development for the interesting character development. Bettany and Dafoe shine. 110m/C VHS, DVD; Paul Bettany, Sarah Henderson, Thomas (Tom) Hardy, Willem Dafoe, Gina McKee, Stuart Wells, Vincent Cassel, Elvira Minguez, Ewen Bremner; **D:** Paul McGuigan; **W:** Mark Mills; **C:** Peter Sova; **M:** Adrian Lee, Mark Mancina.

Recoil 🐾🐾 1997 (R) L.A. detective Ray Morgan (Daniels) gets in trouble with a crime family and they target his wife and family. So, for Ray, it's a kill or be killed situation. 96m/C VHS, DVD; Gary Daniels Gregory McKinney; **D:** Art Camacho; **W:** Richard Preston Jr.; **C:** Ken Blakey; **M:** Tim Wynn. VIDEO

Reconstruction 🐾🐾 2003 One evening, photographer Alex (Kaas) dumps girlfriend Simone (Bonnevie) to follow blonde Swedish beauty Aimee (also Bonnevie) through the streets of Copenhagen. Sha's married to an older author, August (Henriksson), who also serves as narrator. Or is August actually narrating the plot? After a one-night stand, Alex's world is completely changed—no one recognizes him anc all he can think to do is find Aimee again. Danish and Swedish with subtitles. 91m/C VHS Lie Kaas, Maria Bonnevie, Krister Henriksson; **D:** Christofer Boe. **W:** Mogens Rukov, Christofer Boe. **C:** Manuel Alberto Claro; **M:** Thomas Knak.

Record of a Tenement Gentleman 🐾🐾🐾 1947 An abandoned chic picks a grumpy, middle-aged widow as a surrogate mother and she and her crazy neighbors come to love the little boy. Surprise ending. Japanese with subtitles. 72m/B VHS; JP Choko Iida, Hohi Aoki, Chishu Ryu, Eitaro (Sekae, Saka Ozawai Ozawa; **D:** Yasujiro Ozu.

The Recruit 🐾🐾½ 2003 (PG-13) In a role that should mean leading-man superstardom, Farrell is James Clayton, an MIT graduate on his way to the good life when he's approached by CIA "talent scout" Walter Burke (Pacino). Walter says James has the goods to be a top agent and entices him with the promise of info on his dad, who died in a plane crash in 1990. Once on the Farm, James learns the ropes and meets beautiful fellow spook-wannabe Layla (Moynahan), who may not be what she appears. Pacino is in full-on scenery-chewing mode, which helps when the plot heads into spy cliche territory near the end. Farrell and Moynihan provide good chemistry, which helps pick up the slack when Pacino's not around. 105m/C VHS, DVD. US Al Pacino, Colin Farrell, Bridget Moynahan, Gabriel Macht, Karl Pruner, Eugene Lipinski; **D:** Roger Donaldson; **W:** Roger Towne, Mitch Glazer, Kurt Wimmer; **C:** Stuart Dryburgh; **M:** Klaus Badelt.

Recruits 🐾 1986 (R) Sophomoric gagfest about an inept Californian police force. Typical '80s-style mindless "comedy": dumb gags ensue from perfunctory premise. 81m/C VHS; Alan Deveau, Annie McAuley, Lolita (David) Davidovich; **D:** Rafal Zielinski.

The Rector's Wife 🐾🐾 1994 Anna Bouverie (Duncan), has spent 20 years as a clergyman's wife, scrimping and slaving to raise a family, serve God, and work for the parish on limited means. Tired of the financial strain she takes a job at a local supermarket causing additional disturbances in her already shaky marriage, disapproval of the parish, and the sudden interest of three different men. Based on the novel by Joanna Trollope. 200m/C VHS, DVD, GB Lindsay Duncan, Jonathan Coy, Simon Fenton, Lucy Dawson, Joyce Redman, Stephen (Dillon) Dillane, Ronald Pickup, Miles Anderson, Prunella Scales, Jonathan Cecil; **C:** Giles Foster; **W:** Hugh Whitemore; **M:** Richard Hartley.

Red 🐾🐾🐾 1991 Lawrence Tierney stars in this dramatization of the "Red Tapes," a series of taped phone pranks in which a witty young man phones a tar and asks to speak to "Mike Hunt," "Al Koholic," "Stu, last name Pid," "Ben Dover," "Pepe, last name, Roney," etc., the prank made most commercially famous by Bart Simpson. Tierney plays Red, the bartender who receives these calls; he responds to the prankster with mounting incoherent expletives and unfavorable references to the caller's mother. Written and directed by "Film Threat" magazine founder Chris Gore. 35m/B VHS, DVD; Lawrence Tierney, Scott Spiegel, Carmen Von Daacke, Ron Zwang, J. J. Hommel; **D:** Christian Gore; **W:** Christian Gore; **C:** David E. Williams.

Red Alert 🐾🐾½ 1977 Good, suspenseful, topical made for television thriller about nuclear meltdown. Will Minneapolis be saved? Usually Barbeau's name in the credits is a red alert, but this one is better than most. 95m/C VHS; William Devane, Raph Waite, Michael Brandon, Adrienne Barbeau; **D:** William (Billy) Hale. TV

Red 🐾🐾 1977 L.A. detective Ray Morgan (Daniels) gets in trouble with a crime family and they target his wife and family. So, for Ray, it's a kill or be killed situation.

The Red and the Black 🐾🐾🐾 French adaptation of the classic Stendhal novel. A young man from the country seeks success, first in the Church and latter in the employment and seduction of the gentry. In French with English subtitles. 134m/B VHS. FR Danielle Darrieux, Gerard Philipe; **D:** Claude Autant-Lara.

The Red and the White 🐾🐾🐾 Csillgosok, Katonak 1968 Epic war drama about the civil war between the Red Army and the non-communist Whites in Russia in 1918. Told from the perspective of Hungarians who fought alongside the Reds. Little dialogue, in Hungarian with English subtitles. 92m/B VHS, DVD. HU Tibor Molnar, Andras Kozak, Josef Madaras, Gyula Hernadi, Giorgi Mdivani; **W:** Miklos Jancso; **D:** Miklos Jancso; **C:** Tamas Somlo.

Red Blooded American Girl 🐾 1990 (R) A scientist develops a virus that turns people into vampires. Those infected hit the streets in search of blood. 89m/C VHS, DVD, CA Christopher Plummer, Andrew Stevens, Heather Thomas, Kim Coates; **D:** David Blyth.

Red Cherry 🐾🐾🐾 Hong Ying Tao 1995 (PG-13) Based on a true story that focuses on the aftermath of the Chinese revolution in 1940 and the horrors of war. The orphaned Chuchu (Ke-Yu) and Luo (Xiaoi) are sent to a Russian school outside of Moscow and begin to settle into their new lives. But their precarious happiness is shattered when German troops invade Russia during WWII. Chinese and Russian with subtitles. 120m/C VHS, DVD, CH Guo Ke-Yu, Xu Xiaoli; **D:** Ye Ying.

Red Corner 🐾🐾½ 1997 (R) Wrong-man scenario features Gere as an American entertainment lawyer on business in China who is framed for murdering a Chinese model he spent the night with. A colossal bummer, Jack's beautiful, court-appointed attorney, Jia-ling] explains the Chinese legal process: "If you plead not guilty, you will be shot within a week and the cost of the bullet will be charged to your family." Gruesome jail scenes involving excrement and a hell-on-wheels

Red Blooded 2 🐾🐾 1996 Sequel to "Red Blooded American Girl" finds all-American college boy Trent Colbert (Winter) peacefully driving home when he's forced to rescue tough babe Miya (Salin) from rape and murder at a truck stop. Miya informs him that her violent trucker father is behind the attack and the duo are chased by 18-wheelers and the cops. However, ths doesn't prevent Miya from firting Trent to cheap motels, hot sex, and black leather. 86m/C VHS, CA Kari Salin, Kristofer Ryan Winters, Burt Young, David Keith, Nicholas Pasco; **D:** David Blyth; **W:** Nicolas Stiliadis. **C:** Edgar Egger; **M:** Paul Zaza.

Red Beard 🐾🐾🐾 Akahige 1965 An uncharacteristic drama by Kurosawa, about a young doctor in Japan awakening to life and love under the tutelage of a compassionate old physician. Highly acclaimed; in Japanese with English subtitles. 185m/B VHS, DVD. JP Toshiro Mifune, Yuzo Kayama, Yoshio Tsuchiya, Reiko Dan; **D:** Akira Kurosawa.

Red Barry 🐾🐾 1938 A comic strip detective tries to track down criminals who threaten the world. Thirteen episodes on one videotape. 7m/B VHS, Buster Crabbe Frances Robinson, Edna Sedgwick, Cyril Delevanti, Frank Lackteen; **D:** Ford Beebe, Alan Jarres.

The Red Balloon 🐾🐾🐾½ 1956 The story of Pascal, a lonely French boy which follows him everywhere. Lovely, finely done parable of childhood. imagine. 34m/C VHS, DVD. FR Pascal Lamorisse; **D:** Albert Lamorisse. Oscars '56: Orig. Screenplay.

Red Ball Express 🐾🐾½ 1952 Fast-paced action highlights this WWII story about the transportation corp that must supply the gas, food, and ammunition necessary for General Patton's tank assault on Nazi-held Paris. Tough compassion. 84m/B VHS, Jeff Chandler, Alex Nicol, Sidney Poitier, Judith Braun, Jacqueline Duval; **D:** Budd Boetticher; **W:** John Michael Hayes, Jeff Drake, Hugh O'Brian, Jack Kelly; **D:** Budd Boetticher; **W:** Maury Gertsman.

Red Dirt 🐾½ 1999 Teenaged cousins Griffith (Montgomery) and Emily (Palla-dino) spent their days lazying around their Mississippi town, sometimes in the company of their crazy Aunt Summer (Black). That is until the older Lee (Goggins) rents a cottage from the family and Griffith has some confused reactions to the newcomer, much to Emily's dismay. Unfortunately, this coming of age story is tritely told with laborious performances. 111m/C VHS, DVD. Dan Montgomery Jr., Walton Goggins, Aleksa Palladino, Karen Black, Glenn Sfradk, John Mese, Peg O'Keef; **D:** Tag Purvis; **W:** Tag Purvis; **C:** Ted Cohen; **M:** Nathan Barr.

Red Doors 🐾🐾½ 2005 (R) A cultural-clash family comedy. A red door is supposed to mean good luck in Chinese culture but it doesn't seem to be working for Ed (Ma) is in a suicidal funk since his retirement, wondering what happened to the three little girls he and his wife (Shen) raised, since they are so absorbed in their own lives and seem oblivious to his pain. Ed suddenly decides to immure himself in a monastery and then the family really gets crazy. 90m/C DVD. Tzi Ma, Jacqueline Kim, Freda Foh Shen, Sebastian Stan, Kathy Shao-Lin Lee, Elaine Kao, Jayce Barok, Rossif Sutherland, Mia Riverton; **D:** Georgia Lee; **W:** Georgia Lee; **C:** Zeus Morand; **M:** Robert Miller.

Red Dragon 🐾🐾½ 2002 (R) Prequel to "Silence of the Lambs" with film-quel to "Silence of the Lambs" with film-former FBI agent Will Graham (Norton). Graham needs the charismatic cannibal to crack the case of a serial killer (Fiennes) with good character development and a rare look at Lecter before incarceration. the franchise may have reached its expiration date. Second movie telling of Harris's first Lecter novel, following 1986's "Man-

The Red Desert 🐾🐾🐾 Il Deserto Rosso 1964 Antonioni's first color film, depicting an alienated Italian wife who searches for meaning in the industrial lunar landscape of northern Italy, to no avail. Highly acclaimed, but a master of visual form. In Italian with English subtitles. 120m/C VHS, DVD. IT Monica Vitti, Richard Harris, Carlo Chionetti; **D:** Michelangelo Antonioni; **W:** Michelangelo Antonioni, Tonino Guerra; **C:** Carlo Di Palma; **M:** Giovanni Fusco.

Red Desert 🐾 1950 The Pecos Kid is sent to track down the thief of a shipment of gold. 60m/B VHS, DVD. Jock Holt Don-ale (Don "Red") Barry, Tom Neal, Joseph Crenan, Tom London, Margia Dean, Byron Fouiger, John Cason; **D:** Charles Marquis Warren, Ford Beebe; **W:** Ford Beebe, Daniel Ullman, Ron Ormond **C:** George Slutzer.

Red Dawn 🐾🐾 1984 (PG-13) During WWIII, Russian invaders overrun America's heartland and take over the country. Eight small-town teenagers, calling themselves the Wolverines, hide out in the rugged countryside and fight the Russians. Swayze and Grey met again in "Dirty Dancing." 114m/C VHS, DVD, Patrick Swayze, C. Thomas Howell, Harry Dean Stanton, Powers Boothe, Lea Thompson, Charlie Sheen, Ben Johnson, Jennifer Grey, Ron C'Neal, William (Bill) Smith; **D:** John Milius; **W:** John Milius, Kevin Reynolds; **C:** Ric Waite; **M:** Basil Poledouris.

Red Desert Penitentiary 🐾 1983 A spoof of movie-making, featuring caricatures of industry-types. 104m/C VHS, James Michael Tayor, Cathryn Bissell, Will Rose; **D:** George Sluizer.

The Red Desert Antonioni's first color film...

female judge don't help his case much either. Pic suffers from some of the usua clichés but is aided by Ling an acclaimed performance by Ling and one of the better performances by Gere turns. Beijing was recreated on the DreamWorks studio lot in California. 118m/C VHS, DVD, Richard Gere, Bai Ling, Byron Mann, Bradley Whitford, Peter Donat, Robert Stanton, Tsai Chin, James Hong, Tzi Ma, Richard Venture; **D:** Jon Avnet; **W:** Robert King; **C:** Karl Walter Lindenlaub; **M:** Thomas Newman.

hunter." 124m/C VHS, DVD, HD DVD. *US* Anthony Hopkins, Edward Norton, Ralph Fiennes, Harvey Keitel, Emily Watson, Mary-Louise Parker, Philip Seymour Hoffman, Anthony Heald, Bill Duke, Stanley Anderson, Ken Leung, Azura Skye, Frankie Faison, Tyler Patrick Jones, Tom Verica, Dwier Brown, Conrad Palminisano, Mary Beth Hurt, Frank Whaley; *D:* Brett Ratner; *W:* Ted Tally; *C:* Dante Spinotti; *M:* Danny Elfman; *V:* Ellen Burstyn, Alex D. Linz.

Red Dust 🦴🦴🦴 1932 Dennis Carson (Gable) is the overseer of a rubber plantation in Indochina who causes all kinds of trouble when he falls in love with an engineer's (Raymond) new wife. Barbara (Astor). Harlow's the tart Vantine also interested in the big lug. Filled with free-spirited humor and skillfully directed; remarkably blend of... Remade in 1940 as "Congo Maisie" and Gable did his own remake with 1954's "Mogambo," co-starring Ava Gardner and Grace Kelly. 83m/B VHS. Tully Marshall, Clark Gable, Jean Harlow, Mary Astor, Gene Raymond, Donald Crisp; *D:* Victor Fleming; *W:* John Lee Mahin. Natl. Film Reg. '06.

The Red Dwarf 🦴🦴 1999 (R) Somewhat mawkish melodramatic fantasy about love-starved dwarf Lucien Lhotte (Thual) who works as a law clerk. He's summoned by aging opera singer Countess Paola Bendoni (Ekberg), who wants a divorce. The duo become improbable lovers, although he's humiliated (and avenged) when the Countess returns to her husband. Lucien is also innocently loved by young circus acrobat, Isis (Gauzy), and their profession leads Lucien to an unexpected escape from his restricted world. French with subtitles. 101m/B VHS, DVD. *FR* Anita Ekberg, Jean-Yves Thual, Dyna Gauzy, Arno Chevrier; *D:* Yvan Le Moine; *W:* Yvan Le Moine; *C:* Danny Elsen; *M:* Alexei Shelegin, Daniel Brandt.

Red Earth 🦴🦴 1982 A satire about life under Hungarian socialism. Szanto is a bauxite mixer whose pigs have rooted out high quality bauxite from his backyard. Only the local bauxite prospectors don't want to believe in luck (and pigs) and credit, instead, careful planning. When Szanto's village is turned into a vast open mine, he's blamed. In Hungarian with English subtitles. 105m/C VHS. *HU* Imre Nemeth, Sandor Kocsis, Kalman Toronyi, Ferenc Togh, Vilmos Gadori; *D:* Laszlo Vitezy; *W:* Istvan Darday.

Red Eye 🦴🦴🦴 2005 (PG-13) Lisa (McAdams) deftly handles calls, questions, and customers at the front desk of the high-end Miami hotel where she works. Jackson Rippner (Murphy) appears to be like any other guest—until he shows up next to her on her red-eye flight. Turns out she's his target, and Lisa's dad Joe (Cox) and an official of the Department of Homeland Security are at stake if Lisa doesn't figure out how to deal with the high-flying madman. Psychological thrills and chills at high-altitude don't disappoint, with McAdams scoring as a feisty and crafty heroine. 85m/C DVD, UMD. *US* Rachel McAdams, Cillian Murphy, Brian Cox, Kyle Gallner, Brittany Oaks, Jack Scalia; *Cameos:* Wes Craven, Carl Ellsworth; *D:* Wes Craven; *W:* Carl Ellsworth, Dan Foos; *C:* Robert Yeoman; *M:* Marco Beltrami.

Red Firecracker, Green Firecracker 🦴🦴½ *Paoda Shuang Deng* 1993 (R) Set in northern China before the 1911 revolution, this gorgeous saga focuses on the fortunes of the Cai family. The family, whose wealth depends on their fireworks business, has no male heirs and is headed by daughter Chun Zhi (Jing). To assume this lofty position, Chun Zhi must dress like a man and is forbidden to marry but that doesn't stop her from falling in love with bold young travelling artist Nie Bao (Gang). The household is thrown into a frenzy by their affair and it's decided that all Chun Zhi's potential suitors must undergo a firecracker ritual in order to win her hand. Mandarin Chinese with subtitles. 111m/C VHS, DVD. *HK CH* Ning Jing, Wu Gang, Zhao Xiaorui, Gai Yang; *D:* He Ping; *W:* Da Ying; *C:* Yang Lun.

Red Flag: The Ultimate Game 🦴🦴½ 1981 Pilots rival for success in battle simulation training with terrible consequences. Fine performances cover plot weaknesses. Well-written dialogue. 100m/C VHS. Barry Bostwick, William Devane, Joan Van Ark, Fred McCarren, Debra Feuer, George Coe, Linden Chiles, Arlen Dean Snyder; *D:* Don Taylor. TV

The Red Fury 🦴🦴 1984 Young Indian boy struggles to overcome prejudice and caring for his horse shows him his way. Good family viewing. 105m/C VHS, DVD. William Jordan, Katherine (Kathy) Cannon; *D:* Lyman Dayton; *W:* Joe Elliott; *C:* Arch Bryant; *M:* Merrill Jenson.

Red Garters 🦴🦴½ 1954 A musical parody of old-time westerns which doesn't quite come off. Mitchell plays the cowpoke who comes to town to avenge the death of his brother with Clooney as the saloon singer who uses him to make boyfriend Carson jealous. The adequate songs include "Red Garters," "Man and Woman," "A Dime and a Dollar," and "Vaquero." 91m/C VHS, DVD. Guy Mitchell, Rosemary Clooney, Jack Carson, Gene Barry, Pat(ricia) Crowley, Joanne Gilbert, Frank Faylen, Reginald Owen, Buddy Ebsen; *D:* George Marshall; *W:* Michael Fessier; *M:* Jay Livingston, Ray Evans.

The Red Half-Breed 🦴🦴 1970 A lonely half-breed Indian, wrongly accused of murder, discovers the real killer while running from the law. 103m/C VHS. Daniel Pilon, Genevieve Deloir; *D:* Gilles Carle.

Red Headed Stranger 🦴🦴½ 1987 Willie Nelson vehicle based on his 1975 album. Nelson is a gun-totin' preacher who kills his wife and is led to salvation by a good farm woman. But honestly, Morgan Fairchild as Willie Nelson's wife? Please. 108m/C VHS. Willie Nelson, Katharine Ross, Morgan Fairchild; *D:* William D. Wittliff; *W:* William D. Wittliff.

Red Headed Woman 🦴🦴½ 1932 Unscrupulous Lil (sultry Harlow in a red wig) vamps her boss Bill Legendre (Morris) into divorcing his wife (Hyams) and marrying her. But then she gets bored and takes up with the wealthier Gaerste (Stephenson), while keeping his chauffeur Albert (Boyer) on the side. Bill finally divorces her and Lil heads for Europe (with Albert) to play among the nobility. Audiences loved the scandalous material, but the Hays Office objected to the fact that the immoral woman goes unpunished. Boyer took the small but notable role in his third American film because of studio MGM's prestige and it made his career. 79m/B VHS, DVD. Jean Harlow, Chester Morris, Lewis Stone, Leila Hyams, Una Merkel, Henry Stephenson, May Robson, Charles Boyer, Harvey Clark; *D:* Jack Conway; *W:* Anita Loos; *C:* Harold Rosson.

Red Heat 🦴🦴½ 1985 Blair is a tourist in East Germany mistakenly arrested and sent to a rough women's prison. Her fiance tries to free her. Meanwhile, she has to deal with tough-lady fellow jail bird Kristel. Familiar and marginal. 104m/C VHS. Linda Blair, Sylvia Kristel, Sue Kiel, William Ostrander; *D:* Robert Collector.

Red Heat 🦴🦴 1988 (R) Two cops—one from the Soviet Union, one from Chicago—team up to catch the Eastern Bloc's biggest drug czar. Lots of action, but at times it seems too similar to Hill's earlier hit "48 Hours." Film claims to be the first major U.S. production shot in Red Square, Moscow. 106m/C VHS, DVD. Arnold Schwarzenegger, James Belushi, Peter Boyle, Ed O'Ross, Laurence Fishburne, Gina Gershon, Richard Bright; *D:* Walter Hill; *W:* Walter Hill; *C:* Matthew F. Leonetti; *M:* James Horner.

Red Hot 🦴🦴 1995 (PG) Alexi (Getty), a young Russian classical musician, is secretly smuggled American rock 'n' roll music (it's 1959) by his uncle. He immediately decides to form a band and plots the first underground Soviet rock concert. Too bad girlfriend Valentina's (Gugino) dad is a disapproving highly ranked Communist Party official and the KGB are giving Alexi the evil eye. 95m/C VHS. Balthazar Getty, Carla Gugino, Donald Sutherland, Armin Mueller-Stahl, Carol Bouquet, Jean-Pierre Gros; *D:* Cedric Kahm; *W:* Paul Haggis, Michael Maurer.

The Red House 🦴🦴🦴 1947 Robinson plays a crippled farmer who, after his daughter brings home a suitor, attempts to keep everyone from a mysterious red house located on his property. Strange film. Madness and murder prevail. Strange film noir about tangled relationships and unsuccessful attempts to bury the horrid past. Based on the novel by George Agnew Chamberlain. 100m/B VHS, DVD. Edward G. Robinson, Lon (Bud) McCallister, Judith Anderson, Allene Roberts, Rory Calhoun, Ona Munson, Julie London, Harry Shannon, Arthur Space, Walter Sande, Pat Flaherty; *D:* Delmer Daves; *W:* Delmer Daves; *C:* Bert Glennon; *M:* Miklos Rozsa.

The Red Inn 🦴🦴 1951 *L'Auberge Rouge* Yes, it is a comedy. An innkeeper and his wife have a second career involving the robbery and murder of stagecoach travellers staying at their isolated inn. And it's up to a monk (Fernandel) to stop the mayhem. French with subtitles. Yves Montand sings on the soundtrack. 95m/B VHS. *FR* Fernandel, Francoise Rosay, Julien Carette, Gregoire Aslan, Marie-Claire Olivia, Lud Germain; *D:* Claude Autant-Lara; *W:* Jean Aurenche, Pierre Bost; *C:* Andre Bac; *M:* Rene Cloerec.

Red Kimono 🦴🦴 1925 Exploitative silent melodrama about a young woman ditched by her husband. She becomes a prostitute, but is redeemed by true love. Interesting slice of its period. 95m/B VHS. Tyrone Power Sr., Priscilla Boner, Nellie Bly Baker, Mary Carr; *D:* Walter Lang.

Red King, White Knight 🦴🦴½ 1989 (R) An assassin tries to kill Mikhail Gorbachev during superpower peace talks. Ex-spook Skerritt returns to duty to thwart him. Better than most "topical" thrillers. 106m/C VHS. Tom Skerritt, Max von Sydow, Helen Mirren; *D:* Geoff Murphy. CABLE

Red Kiss 🦴🦴 1985 *Rouge Baiser* In 1952 Paris, Nadia, a 15-year-old French-Jewish Stalinist of Polish descent falls in love with Stephane, an older, apolitical photographer. She's torn between love and politics; he's worried (rightly) about her being under-age; and to make matters more complicated, her Polish mother has been reunited with her first love and Nadia's family may be split apart. The sensual Valandrey is a real find in her difficult coming-of-age role. In French with English subtitles. 110m/C VHS. *FR* Charlotte Valandrey, Lambert Wilson, Marthe Keller, Gunter Lamprecht, Laurent Terzieff; *D:* Vera Belmont; *W:* Vera Belmont, David Milnaud, Guy Konopnicki; *C:* Ramon Suarez; *M:* Jean-Marie Senia. Berlin Intl. Film Fest. '86: Actress (Valandrey).

Red Letters 🦴🦴 2000 (R) The plot veers wildly but the performances are worth a watch. Widowed college prof Dennis Burke (Coyote) has an eye for the ladies. He flirts with the dean's sexy young daughter, Gretchen (Balk), and is so taken with the imprisoned Lydia (Kinski) that he helps her escape so she can prove her innocence in a murder conviction. Not a good idea. 102m/C VHS, DVD. Peter Coyote, Nastassja Kinski, Fairuza Balk, Jeremy Piven, Ernie Hudson, Udo Kier; *D:* Bradley Battersby; *W:* Bradley Battersby, Tom Hughes; *C:* Steven Fierberg. VIDEO

Red Light Sting 🦴🦴 1984 A Justice Department rookie (Bridges) and a call girl (Fawcett) reluctantly team up to convict a San Francisco rackets czar. Goes down easy, but also easily forgotten or skipped. 96m/C VHS. Farrah Fawcett, Beau Bridges, Harold Gould, Paul Burke, Sunny Johnson; *D:* Rod Holcomb.

Red Lights 🦴🦴🦴 *Feux rouges* 2004 Troubled couple embarks on a trip to pick up their children from camp. They argue viciously as hubby repeatedly stops to drink along the way. When the missus finally ditches him and takes the train, the volatile and smashed husband continues by car but picks up an ominous stranger. Story of a man who regains his dignity through surprisingly violent twist of fate. Terrific French thriller in the vein of Hitchcock, with solid acting and direction. 106m/C VHS, DVD. *FR* Jean-Pierre Darroussin, Carole Bouquet, Jean-Pierre Gros; *D:* Cedric Kahn; *W:* Cedric Kahn; *C:* Patrick Blossier; *M:* Arvo Part.

Red Lights Ahead 🦴🦴 1936 Grandpa tries to save the day as he fights against spiritualism and crystal balls to help a friend prove that he is not running a scam. 63m/C VHS, DVD. Andy Clyde, Paula Stone, Roger Imhof, Frank "Junior" Coghlan, Ben Alexander, Matty Kemp, Sam Flint, Addison "Jack" Randall, Lucile Gleason, Dann Doran; *D:* Roland D. Reed.

Red Line 🦴½ 1996 (R) Stock-car racer Jim (McQueen) loses his sponsorship, turns to petty crime to settle his debts, and winds up in trouble with the mob when he hooks up with a couple of hoods to steal some diamonds. 102m/C VHS, DVD. Chad McQueen, Michael Madsen, Corey Feldman, Jan-Michael Vincent, Roxana Zal, Dom DeLuise, Julie Strain, Robert Z'Dar; *D:* John Sjogren; *W:* John Sjogren, Scott Ziehl, Rolfe Kanelsky; *C:* Kevin McKay; *M:* Craig Carothers, Junior Walker.

Red Line 7000 🦴🦴 1965 High stakes auto racers ride fast cars and date interchangeable women. Excellent racing footage in otherwise routine four-wheel fest. 110m/C VHS, DVD. James Caan, Laura Devon, Gail Hire, Charlene Holt, Marianna Hill, George Takei; *D:* Howard Hawks; *C:* Milton Krasner.

Red Lion 🦴🦴½ *Akage* 1969 A bumbling horse-tender in feudal Japan impersonates a military officer to impress his family, only to be swept into leading a liberating revolution. In Japanese with English subtitles. 115m/C VHS, DVD. *JP* Toshiro Mifune, Shima Iwashita; *D:* Kihachi Okamoto.

Red Meat 🦴🦴½ 1998 Stefan (Slattery) and Chris (Mailer) are the last (remaining members of the Red Meat Club, buddies who get together for macho posturing over steak dinners. They run into Victor (Frain) who's been out of touch. Stefan and Chris boast of their dating games (which are grown in flashback) and then it's Victor's turn to regale them with a lurid sexual saga. Only Victor's story involves his tender relationship with a dying woman, Ruth (Boyle). 94m/C VHS, DVD. James Frain, John Slattery, Steven Mailer, Lara Flynn Boyle, Jennifer Grey, Traci Lind; *D:* Allison Burnett; *W:* Allison Burnett; *C:* Charlie Lieberson.

The Red Menace woof! 1949 Anti-Communist propaganda, made with unknown actors in documentary style has little to offer today's viewers other than unintentional laughs. Picture the Commies offering naive Americans money and sex to join the party, and you'll have an idea of the intellectual talent that went into this movie. Rather too talky and obvious. 87m/B VHS. Robert Rockwell, Hannelore Axman, Shepard Menken, Betty Lou Gerson, Barbara Fuller; *D:* R.G. Springsteen.

Red Mercury 🦴½ 2005 (R) Three Islamic terrorists, planning a London bombing, have their cover blown and flee into a Greek restaurant, taking hostages. They're still carrying materials for their dirty bomb but the tension heightens as time passes and the bombers are forced to interact with their hostages as the police and government officials await the outcome. 106m/C VHS, DVD. *GB* Stockard Channing, Ron Silver, Pete Postlethwaite, Juliet Stevenson, David Bradley, Nigel Terry, Navin Chowdhry, Honeysuckle Weeks, Alex Caan; *D:* Roy Battersby; *W:* Farrukh Dhondy; *C:* Colin Towns, Uday Tiwari. VIDEO

Red Nights 🦴 1987 A country boy goes to Hollywood seeking success and finds instead corruption, decadence, and dishonesty. Excellent soundtrack by Tangerine Dream. 90m/C VHS. Chris Parker, Jack Carter, Brian Matthews; *D:* Izhak Hanooka.

Red Planet 🦴🦴½ 2000 (PG-13) It's 2050. Earth is dying, and the crew of the Mars-1 has been sent to the red planet to find out what went wrong with a previous colonization mission. Alas, something goes wrong with this mission, too (those pesky gamma rays), and some of the crew are forced to shuttle to the surface of Mars, where yet another mishap leaves them stranded without means of communication or escape. To make matters worse, the crew's AMEE (Autonomous Mapping Evaluation and Evasion) robot has turned nasty and intends to further

Red Planet Mars ✂✂ 1952 Anti-communist, pro-Christianity story about scientists discovering that the Voice of Radio Free Mars belongs to God. Incoherent film overburdened with messages about politics, religion, and science was ahead of its time. Based on the play "Red Planet" by John L. Balderson and John Hoare. **87m/B VHS, DVD.** Peter Graves, Andrea King, Marvin Miller, Herbert Berghof, House Peters Jr., Vince Barnett; **D:** Harry Horner; **W:** Anthony Veiller, John Lloyd Balderston.

The Red Pony ✂✂✂ 1976 Excellent TV remake of a classic 1949 adaptation of John Steinbeck. Fonda is superb as a troubled young boy's difficult father. **101m/C VHS.** Henry Fonda, Maureen O'Hara, Clint Howard, Jack Elam, Ben Johnson; **D:** Robert Totten. **TV**

The Red Pony ✂✂✂ 1949 A young boy escapes from his family's fighting through his love for a pet pony. Based on the novel by John Steinbeck. Timeless classic that the whole family can enjoy. **89m/C VHS, DVD.** Myrna Loy, Robert Mitchum, Peter Miles, Louis Calhern, Shepperd Strudwick, Margaret Hamilton, Beau Bridges; **D:** Lewis Milestone; **C:** Gaetano Antonio "Tony" Gaudio; **M:** Aaron Copland.

Red Riding Hood ✂ 2003 (R) Freakshow fairytale. Jenny (Satta) is a 12-year-old American who has been abandoned in a Rome apartment by her mother. She watched her politician father get assassinated, which obviously twisted her little psyche since Jenny roams the streets handing out her own brand of vigilante justice. She's accompanied by a big bad wolf named George (Dipascasio), who could be a figment of her crazy imagination. Then Granny (Archebald) shows up to take the little darling home, but Jenny's got other plans. English and Italian with subtitles. **90m/C DVD.** /T Susan Satta, Kathleen Archebald, Simone K. Dipascasio, Iaon Quinn, Roberto Purvis, Marco Firini, Justine Powell; **D:** Giacomo Cimini; **W:** Ovidio G. Assonitis, Andrew Benker; **C:** Sergio Salvati, Roberto Benvenuti; **M:** Alessandro Molinari.

Red Riding Hood ✂✂ 1988 Musical version of story of wolf who has little girl fetish. **81m/C VHS, DVD.** Isabella Rossellini, Craig T. Nelson, Rocco Sisto; **D:** Adam Brooks; **W:** Carole Lucia Satrina; **C:** Yuri Neyman; **M:** Stephen Lawrence. **VIDEO**

The Red Raven Kiss-Off ✂ 1990 (R) A seedy Hollywood detective becomes the key suspect in a movie-making murder. Based on the 1930s Dan Turner mystery stories. **93m/C VHS.** Marc Singer, Tracy Scoggins, Nicholas Worth, Arte Johnson; **D:** Christopher Lewis. **VIDEO**

Red River ✂✂✂ 1948 The classic Hawks epic about a grueling cattle drive and the battle of wills between father and son. Tom Dunston (Wayne), who owns a sprawling cattle empire, decides to make a difficult trek north, refusing to listen to any advice from his adopted son, Matthew Garth (Clift, in his first film). Matt is eventually forced to take over the drive from the obsessed Dunston, who swears revenge. Generally regarded as one of the best westerns ever made, with a great supporting cast headed by Brennan and Ireland, although Dru is a very nominal love interest. Restored version has eight minutes of previously edited material. Remade for TV in 1988 with James Arness and Bruce Boxleitner. **133m/B VHS, DVD.** John Wayne, Montgomery Clift, Walter Brennan, Joanna Dru, John Ireland, Noah Beery Jr., Paul Fix, Coleen Gray, Harry Carey Jr., Harry Carey Sr., Chief Yowlachie, Hank Worden; **D:** Howard Hawks; **W:** Borden Chase, Charles Schnee; **C:** Russell Harlan; **M:** Dimitri Tiomkin Natl. Film Reg. '90.

Red River Valley ✂✂ *Man of the Frontier* 1936 Autry and partner Burnette go undercover to find out who's plaguing a dam construction site with explosions. Not to be confused with a 1941 Roy Roger's epic bearing the same title. **60m/B VHS.** Gene Autry, Smiley Burnette, Frances Grant, Boothe Howard, Sam Flint, George Chesebro, Earle "Blackie" King, Eugene Jackson, Frank LaRue, Lloyd Ingraham; **D:** B. Reeves Eason.

Red River Valley ✂✂ 1941 Rogers helps the local ranchers get enough money together to build a much-needed water reservoir. Only gambler Bardette cons them out of the money, until Roy comes to the rescue. **62m/B VHS, DVD.** Roy Rogers, George "Gabby" Hayes, Trevor Bardette, Sally Payne; **D:** Joseph Kane; **W:** Malcolm Stuart Boylan; **C:** Jack Marta.

Red Road ✂✂ 2006 Debut feature for Brit helmer Arnold heightens suspense but fumbles the ending. Widowed Jackie (Dickie) works for a private security firm monitoring cameras that maintain surveillance on a rough North Glasgow neighborhood. She becomes obsessed watching ex-con Clyde (Curran) and his friends, who live in the decrepit Red Road housing estate. She contrives to meet him but it turns out Jackie has specific reasons for her interest in Clyde and they aren't going to make him happy. **113m/C DVD, GS '22** Tony Curran, Martin Compston, Kate Dickie, Andrew Armour; **D:** Andrea Arnold; **C:** Robbie Ryan.

Red Rock West ✂✂½ 1993 (R) Nothing is what it seems in this stylish and entertaining film noir set in a desolate Wyoming town. Perennial loser and nice guy Michael (Cage) is headed to a job at an oil rig, but blows his chance by admitting he has a bad leg. Landing in the tiny burg of Red Rock, he's mistaken for the hit man hired by local barkeep Walsh to kill his pretty wife (Boyle). Then Boyle decides Walsh's offer—what's a little cash to do? And Hopper, the real killer, strides into town. Full of twists, turns, and shades of "El Mariachi," this enjoyable, well-acted thriller is a real gem that escaped directly to cable before being rescued by a San Francisco exhibitor. **98m/C VHS, DVD.** Nicolas Cage, Dennis Hopper, Lara Flynn Boyle, J.T. Walsh, Timothy Carhart, Dan Shor, Dwight Yoakam, Bobby Joe McFadDen, Craig Reay, Vance Johnson, Robert Apel, Dale Gibson, Ted Parks, Babs Bram, Robert Guajardo, Sarah Sullivan; **D:** John Dahl; **W:** John Dahl, Rick Dahl; **C:** Marc Reshovsky; **M:** William Olvis.

The Red Rope ✂½ 1937 A Western hero cuts his honeymoon short to track down some villains. **56m/B VHS.** Bob Steele, Lois January, Forrest Taylor, Charles "Blackie" King, Karl Hackett, Bobby Nelson; **D:** S. Roy Luby; **W:** George Plympton; **C:** Bert Longenecker.

Red Salute ✂✂ 1935 Screwball comedy in the "It Happened One Night" tradition (only not as good) with an anti-Communist message. General's daughter Drue (Stanwyck) falls in love with a young communist. Patriotic dad tries to divert her attention by sending her on a Mexican vacation, where she meets an AWOL soldier. When the pair tries to sneak back into the U.S., he's arrested and she heads back to her leftist lover, whereupon dad releases her. AWOL beau and causes more confusion. Film caused much consternation among the left-leaning intelligensia at the time of its release. **88m/B VHS.** Barbara Stanwyck, Robert Young, Hardie Albright, Ruth Donnelly, Cliff Edwards, Gordon Jones, Lester Dorr; **D:** Sidney Lanfield; **W:** Manuel Seff, Elmer Harris, Humphrey Pearson; **C:** Robert Planck.

Red Scorpion ✂ 1989 (R) A Soviet soldier journeys to Africa where he is to assassinate the leader of a rebel group. Will he succeed or switch allegiances? Poor acting and directing abound. **102m/C VHS, DVD, UMD.** Dolph Lundgren, M. Emmet Walsh, Al White, T.P. McKenna, Carmen Argenziano, Brion James, Regopstaan; **D:** Joseph Zito; **W:** Arne Olsen, Jack A'zramoff, Robert Abramoff; **C:** Joao Fernandes; **M:** Jay Chattaway.

Red Scorpion 2 ✂½ 1994 (R) Another "Dirty Dozen" rip-off finds your average ethnically mixed good guys brought together by a government agency to be heroic. In this case the enemy is a neo-fascist businessman who uses skinheads to cause mayhem in minority communities. **90m/C VHS, Matt McColm, John Savage, Jennifer Rubin, Michael Irons'de, Michael Kennedy; **W:** Troy Bolotnick, Barry Victor; **M:** George Blondheim.

Red Shoe Diaries ✂✂ 1992 (R) After a woman's suicide her grieving lover discovers her diaries and finds out she's led a secret erotic life, revolving around her shoe-salesman lover and a pair of sexy red shoes. Also available in an unrated version. **105m/C VHS, DVD.** David Duchovny, Billy Wirth, Brigitte Bako; **D:** Zalman King. **CABLE**

Red Shoe Diaries 2: Double Dare ✂✂ 1992 (R) The erotic sequel to "Red Shoe Diaries" follows the libidinous fancies of three women. Severance begins a sexual affair with a stranger only to liaison—only to become intrigued with his lust. Johnson gets naked to tease an office worker in the building next door. Crosby is a cop who is rejected by the man she desires—so she arrests and handcuffs him in order to play some kinky games. Also available in an unrated version. **92m/C VHS.** Joan Severance, Laura Johnson, Denise Crosby, Steven Bauer, Arnold Vosloo, David Duchovny; **D:** Zalman King; **C:** Takas. **CABLE**

Red Shoe Diaries 3: Another Woman's Lipstick ✂✂ 1993 (R) Another sensual anthology focusing on three stories of desire. In "Another Woman's Lipstick," Zoey finds out her husband is having an affair and follows him to his lover. In "Just Like That" finds the up-tight Trudie falling for two way opposite men. "Talk to Me Baby" finds Ida and her lover Bud caught up in a very obsessional relationship. Also available in an unrated version. **90m/C VHS.** Nina Siemaszko, Matt LeBlanc, Tcheky Karyo, Maryam D'Abo, Richard Tyson, Lydie Denier, Christina Kristina) Fulton, Kevin Haley, David Duchovny; **D:** Ted Kotcheff, Rafael Eisenman, Zalman King; **W:** Zalman King, Chloe King. **CABLE**

Red Shoe Diaries 4: Auto Erotica ✂✂ 1993 (R) Yet another compilation of erotic tales courtesy of the Zalman King series. The first story finds the maid finding her employer's secret chamber and uncovering a very private fantasy. The second has an architect lured by a mystery woman into a game of seduction and the third finds a couple engaged in competitive obsessions. Also available in an unrated version. **83m/C VHS.** Ally Sheedy, Paula Barbieri, Claire Stansfield, Ely Pouget, Francesco Quinn, Ron Marchini; **D:** Zalman King, Patricia Louisianna Chirlund; **D:** Zalman King. **CABLE**

Red Shoe Diaries 5: Weekend Pass ✂ 1995 (R) Yet another erotic saga from the cable series that features a model (Barbieri) hustling a pool hustler, a bounty hunter (Stansfield) becoming captivated by her prey, and an army recruit (Pouget) whose furlough involves a sexy crifter. **85m/C VHS.** Paula Barbieri, Claire Stansfield, Ely Pouget, Francesco Quinn, Ron Marchini; **D:** Zalman King. **CABLE**

Red Shoe Diaries 6: How I Met My Husband ✂✂ 1995 (R) The mother of all series. "How I Met My Husband" finds Alice enrolling in a course on becoming a dominatrix and falling for Giuseppe, who's one of the training objects. Camille has inherited her father's vast fortune in "Na-ked in the Moonlight" on the condition that she take special care of his '57 Cadillac convertible—and the one mechanic allowed to work on the car. In "Midnight Bells," Claire reminisces about the mystery/lover she meets on only one night of the year—New Year's Eve. **85m/C VHS.** Luigi Amodeo, Keith Hunter, Raven Snow, Carsten Norgaard, John Enos, Charlotte Lewis, David Du-chovny; **D:** Arne Goursaud, Philippe Angers, Bernard Auroux. **CABLE**

Red Shoe Diaries 7: Burning Up ✂✂ 1996 (R) Yet another trilogy of TV eroticism. "Burning Up" finds Lynn becoming obsessed with a handsome fireman. "Kidnap" features the workaholic Sara taken hostage during a bank robbery and finding out that her captor has decided to marry her, Alia is a top model in "Runway," who falls in love with a cabby. **90m/C VHS,** Ub Kier, Ron Marquette, Jennifer Eliaso, Alexandra Vandernoot, Daniel Faitael Eisenmar. **CABLE**

Red Shoe Diaries 8: Night of Abandon ✂✂ 1997 (R) Three more adventures from the cable series. "Night of Abandon" finds Isabelle visiting her grandma in Rio de Janeiro and indulging in Carnival. "Liar's Table" has photojournalist Corey assigned to record LA's sex scene and becoming intrigued by a very expensive call girl. Married Kathryn's life changes "In the Blink of an Eye" when she meets a young boxer who's in training with her husband. **86m/C VHS,** Erika Andersen, Audie England, Daniel Lezz, Ann Cockburn; **D:** Rafael Eisenmen, Zalman King, David Womerek; **M:** Richard Baskin, Nellie Allard, Joelle Bentolila; **C:** Etienne Faudet, Manuel Tera, Marco Mazzei; **M:** George S. Clinton. **CABLE**

Red Shoe Diaries: Four on the Floor ✂✂ 1996 The late-night cable series continues with three more stories concerning a psychiatrist and her patient, two couples stranded on a rainy night, and the meeting of a rap star and a dancer. Contents: "The Psychiatrist," "Four on the Floor," "Emily's Dance." **85m/C DVD.** Denise Crosby, Georges Corraface, Christopher Atkins, Jsu Garcia, David Duchovny; **D:** Rafael Eli-sson, Zalman King, David Womerek; **M:** Brian Edwards, David Duchovny; **D:** Rafael Eisenman, Rene Manzor, James Gavin Bedford. **CABLE**

Red Shoe Diaries: Luscious Lola ✂✂½ 2000 In these three stories, shy Mimi (Phillips) fantasizes about winning her dream guy; a sailor on shore leave winds up with more women than he can handle; and a young woman toys with men. **87m/C DVD.** Bobbie Phillips, Michael C. Bender, Christina (Kristina) Fulton, Perrey Reeves, Ernie Banks, John Enos, Jesepn Whipp, David Duchovny, Andrew Bilgore, Heidi Mark, Michael Feally Burke; **D:** Zalman King, Pascal Franchot, Eliza D'Haene; **C:** Eagle Eglisson, David Stockton; **M:** George S. Clinton. **CABLE**

Red Shoe Diaries: Strip Poker ✂✂ 1996 Contains the episodes "Strip Poker," "Slow Train," "Hard Labor." **87m/C DVD.** Athena Massey, Jennifer Cesar, Carolyn Seymour, David Duchovny, Anissa Nezniakova, Larisa Tipikina, Andrew Calder, Mark Sueike, Maximo Morrone; **D:** Zalman King, Rafael Knop, Julie Marie Myatt, Elize D'Haene; **C:** Eagle Eglisson, Alexei Rodionov; **M:** George S. Clinton. **CABLE**

Red Shoe Diaries: Swimming Naked ✂✂½ 2000 The mother of all late-night cable series is still the artsiest. As such these stories are about a lifeguard, a skydiver and a dancer are told with lots of smoke and gauzy focus. Contents: "Swimming Naked," "Jump," "Tears," **85m/C DVD.** Michael Woods, Oyla Batten, Carolyn Seymour, Arabella Holzbog, David Duchovny, Kristi Frank, Omry Reznik, Sonya Ryzy-Ryski, Todd Gordon, Daniel Ezralow; **D:** Zalman King, Rafael Eisenman; **W:** Zalman King, Melanie Finn, Chloe King, Katarina Wittich, Kathryn MacQuarrie; **C:** Eagle Eglisson, David Knaus; **M:** George S. Clinton. **CABLE**

The Red Shoes ✂✂✂ 1948 British classic about a young ballerina torn between love and success. Boris Larr on (Walbrook) is the impresario of a ballet company who hires dancer Victoria Page (Shearer) and composer Julian Craster (Goring), giving them the chance at a break inspired by the Hans Christian Andersen fairy tale. But when the endea/or becomes a major success, Boris becomes jealous over the closeness that develops

Red Rock Outlaw ✂ 1947 A sleazy character tries to kill his twin brother and takes his place as an honest rancher. **56m/B VHS.** Billy Dix, Bob Gilbert, Ione Nixon, Forrest Clifton; **C:** Darian Cunha.

between his proteges. Noted for the 20-minute ballet at the heart of the film and for the lavish use of Technicolor. **136m/C VHS, DVD.** *GB* Anton Walbrook, Moira Shearer, Marius Goring, Leonide Massine, Robert Helpmann, Albert Basermann, Ludmilla Tcherina, Esmond Knight; **D:** Emeric Pressburger, Michael Powell; **W:** Emeric Pressburger, Michael Powell; **C:** Jack Cardiff; **M:** Brian Easdale. Oscars '48: Art Dir./Set Dec., Color, Orig. Dramatic Score; Golden Globes '49: Score.

Red Signals 1927 Mystery criminal makes trains collide. **70m/B VHS.** Wallace MacDonald, Earl Williams, Eva Novak, J(ohn) P(aterson) McGowan, Frank Rice; **D:** J(ohn) P(aterson) McGowan.

The Red Sneakers 2001 Reggie Reynolds (Pappion) is a high-school math whiz who figures he'll get more respect as a basketball star. He meets junkman Zeke (Hines), who gives Reggie a pair of worn red high-tops that he insists were worn by a legendary Harlem hoopster. When Reggie puts the shoes on, he suddenly seems to have inherited all the skill of their former owner and is suddenly drawing lots of attention as a star player. But there's a price to be paid. **109m/C VHS, DVD.** Gregory Hines, Vincent D'Onofrio, Vanessa Bell Calloway, Dempsey Pappion, Ruben Santiago-Hudson, Philip Akin; **D:** Gregory Hines; **W:** Mark Saltzman; **C:** John Bernie; **M:** Stanley Clarke. **CABLE.**

Red Snow 1991 High in the Cascade Mountains, Kyle Lewis is the new snowboard instructor for the Hurricane Ridge Ski Resort. The job is fine in the beginning, until Kyle learns of the tragic fate of the last instructor. Before he knows it, Kyle is the next target and is framed for two murders. He secures the help of his fellow snowboard buddies in hopes of solving the mystery and getting the girl, too. High speed ski scenes and danger-filled stunts are the film's only redeeming qualities. **86m/C VHS.** Carlo Scandiuzzi, Scott Galloway, Darla Haun, Mitchell Cox, Tamar Tibbs, Brian Mahoney; **D:** Phillip J. Roth.

Red Sonja 1985 (PG-13) Two warriors join forces against an evil queen in this sword and sorcery saga. Big, beautiful bodies everywhere, with Bergman returning from her Conan adventures. Little humor, few special effects, and weak acting make this a poor outing. **89m/C VHS, DVD.** Arnold Schwarzenegger, Brigitte Nielsen, Sandahl Bergman, Paul Smith; **D:** Richard Fleischer; **M:** Ennio Morricone. Golden Raspberries '85: Worst New Star (Nielsen).

Red Sorghum 1987 A stunning visual achievement, this new wave Chinese film (and Yimou's directorial debut) succeeds on many levels—as an ode to the color red, as dark comedy, and as a sweeping epic with fairy tale overtones. Set in rural China in the 1920s, during the period of the Japanese invasion. The sorghum plot nearby is a symbolic playing field in the movie's most stunning scenes. Here, people make love, murder, betray, and commit acts of bravery, all under the watchful eye of nature. In Mandarin with English subtitles. **91m/C VHS. CH** Gong Li, Jiang Wen, Ji Cun Hua; **D:** Yimou Zhang; **C:** Gu Changwei.

The Red Squirrel 1993 *La Ardilla Roja* Former pop star Jota (Novo) is distraught over breaking up with his girlfriend and contemplating throwing himself off a bridge when he witnesses a motorcycle accident and rushes to help the young woman (Suarez) involved. After learning she's suffering from amnesia, Jota tells both the woman and the hospital that her name is Lisa and she's his lover. Then Jota invents a fictitious life for her, according to his own desires. Spanish with subtitles. **104m/C VHS, DVD.** *SP* Nancho Novo, Emma Suarez, Maria Barranco, Carmelo Gomez, Ana Garcia; **D:** Julio Medem; **W:** Julio Medem; **C:** Gonzalo F. Berridi; **M:** Alberto Iglesias.

The Red Stallion 1947 Good film for animal lovers, but it loses something when it comes to human relationships. A young boy raises his pony into an award-winning racehorse that saves the farm when it wins the big race. Good outdoor photography. **82m/B VHS.** Robert Paige, Noreen Nash, Ted Donaldson, Jane Darwell; **D:** Lesley Selander.

Red Sun 1971 A gunfighter, a samurai, and a French bandit fight each other in various combinations in the 1860s. Ludicrous and boring. **115m/C VHS, DVD.** *FR IT SP* Charles Bronson, Toshiro Mifune, Alain Delon, Ursula Andress; **D:** Terence Young; **M:** Maurice Jarre.

Red Sun Rising 1994 (R) Kyoto cop Thomas Hoshino (Wilson) heads to L.A. in order to extradite a Japanese gangster, Yamata (Oh), and teams up with local detective Karen Ryder (Ferrell). Seems Yamata wants to start a turf war between two L.A. street gangs so he can sell guns to both sides. **95m/C VHS.** Don "The Dragon" Wilson, Terry Farrell, Soon-Teck Oh, Mako, James Lew, Edward Albert, Michael Ironside; **D:** Francis Megahy; **C:** John Newby.

Red Surf 1990 (R) Action abounds in this surfer film. A couple of hard-nosed wave-riders get involved with big money drug gangs and face danger far greater than the tide. **104m/C VHS, DVD.** George Clooney, Doug Savant, Dedee Pfeiffer, Gene Simmons, Rick Najera, Philip McKeon; **D:** H. Gordon Boos; **W:** Vincent Robert; **C:** John Schwartzman; **M:** Sasha Matson.

Red Tent 1969 (G) *Krasnaya Palatka* A robust, sweeping man-versus-nature epic based on the true story of Umberto to Nobile's expedition in 1928. A Russian-Italian co-production. **121m/C DVD.** Sean Connery, Claudia Cardinale, Peter Finch, Hardy Kruger, Massimo Girotti, Luigi Vannucchi; **D:** Mikhail Kalatozov; **M:** Ennio Morricone.

The Red Violin 1998 (R) *Le Violon Rouge* Spans 300 years in the life of one famed musical instrument that winds up in present-day Montreal on the auction block. Crafted by the Italian master Bussotti (Cecchi) in 1681, the red violin derives its unusual color from the human blood mixed into the finish. With this legacy, the violin travels to Austria, England, China, and Canada, leaving both beauty and tragedy in its wake. Most of the vignettes are dull, with the Montreal-set framing story holding the most interest. **131m/C VHS, DVD.** *CA* Samuel L. Jackson, Don McKellar, Carlo Cecchi, Irene Grazioli, Jean-Luc Bideau, Jason Flemyng, Greta Scacchi, Christoph Koncz, Sylvia Chang, Colm Feore, Monique Mercure, Liu Zi Feng; **D:** Francois Girard; **W:** Don McKellar, Francois Girard; **C:** Alan Dostie; **M:** John Corigliano. Oscars '99: Orig. Score; Genie '98: Art Dir./Set Dec., Cinematog., Costume Des., Director (Girard), Film, Screenplay, Score.

Red Water 2001 (R) Sanders is a Louisiana fisherman and ex-oil company worker who hooks up with his scientist wife to find natural gas in a Louisiana river. At the same time, gangsters and ex-con are heading to the same place looking for buried loot, and a freshwater shark picks the spot as well, looking for a buffet. The too-complicated plot only serves as a reason for everyone to show up and become shark bait for the ridiculously fake-looking maneater. If you're gonna spend time watching a shark movie, make it "Jaws" instead of this made-for-TV waste. **92m/C VHS, DVD.** Lou Diamond Phillips, Kristy Swanson, Coolio, Jaimz Woolvett; **D:** Charles Robert Carner; **W:** J.D. Feigelson, Chris Mack; **C:** Michael Goi. **TV**

Red, White & Busted 1975 *Outside the Law* Three friends are affected in different ways by the Vietnam War, whether or not they went. One who fled to Canada tries to return home for his father's funeral. **85m/C VHS.** Darrell Larson, Heather Menzies, Dennis Oliveri, John Bill, Peggy (Margaret) Feury, Logan Ramsey; **D:** Allen Baron, G.D. Spradlin; **W:** Allen Baron; **C:** Mario Tosi; **M:** Randy Edelman.

Red Wind 1991 (R) Kris Morrow is a psychotherapist whose latest patient, Lila, has a number of disturbing sadomasochistic fantasies. When Kris feels she's getting too close to the situation, she refers Lila to another therapist. But Lila calls and tells Kris she's already acted out one of her fantasies by killing her husband. In order to stop Lila from killing again, Kris goes on a dangerous search for her deadly patient. **93m/C VHS.** Lisa Hartman Black, Deanna Lund, Philip Casnoff, Christopher McDonald; **D:** Alan Metzger.

Redacted 2007 (R) A group of soldiers, compromised by the experience of war, find themselves in increasingly brutal and amoral situations, culminating in the group rape and murder of a 15-year-old girl. Izzy Diaz (Salazar), who's filming his experiences in Iraq in hopes of getting into film school, is disgusted by the actions of his comrades but fears retribution if he reports them. DePalma, who addressed similar issues in "Casualties of War," uses true stories from the Iraq War as inspiration and a "fictional documentary" technique, in which the entire film appears to be composed of assembled footage shot by Diaz, documentary makers, or other "real" sources. Story is powerful but ultimately heavy-handed, and the performances are inconsistent. Intense, depressing, and highly divisive, the pic received accusations of anti-American bias and bombed at the box office. **90m/C DVD.** *US CA* Kel O'Neill, Pat Carroll, Izzy Diaz, Rob Devaney, Daniel Stewart Sherman, Ty Jones; **D:** Brian De Palma; **W:** Brian De Palma; **C:** Jonathan Cliff.

Redbelt 2008 (R) Martial arts master Mike Terry (Ejiofor) lives by a strict code, staying away from the lucrative prize fighting circuit. He's struggling to hold onto the self-defense center he runs in west L.A. because he and his wife Sondra (Braga) are having money problems. An accident leads Terry down an unexpected path and unwillingly into some martial art bouts where he learns the fights are rigged. But Terry is not going to play that game. If you're a fan of writer/director Mamet, you'll notice some familiar faces from his other productions. Not yet reviewed. **99m/C** Chiwetel Ejiofor, Alice Braga, Tim Allen, Emily Mortimer, Rodrigo Santoro, Joe Mantegna, Rebecca Pidgeon, David Paymer, Ricky Jay; **D:** David Mamet; **W:** David Mamet; **C:** Robert Elswit; **M:** Stephen Endelman.

Redeemer 2002 Paul Freeman is a writing teacher in a prison program who decides to help inmate Charles Henderson (Babatunde), an articulate ex-Black Panther serving life for murder. After 20 years, Charles wants to write a letter to his victim's sister, Sharon Davidson (Greene), asking her forgiveness. The reaction to the letter turns out to be a catalyst for a second chance for each of them. **90m/C VHS, DVD.** Matthew Modine, Obba Babatunde, Michele Greene; **D:** Graeme Clifford; **W:** James Ricci; **C:** Norayr Kasper; **M:** Frankie Blue. **CABLE**

Redemption: Kickboxer 5 1995 (R) Retired kickboxer Matt Reeves (Dacascos) goes after the scum who murdered a friend. No surprises here. **87m/C VHS, DVD.** Mark Dacascos, James Ryan; **D:** Kristine Peterson; **M:** John Massari.

The Redhead from Wyoming 1953 Spirited sagebrush adventure with fiery-tempered O'Hara as a saloon proprietress with feelings for both a local cattle rustler and the town's sheriff. Based on a story by James. **81m/C VHS, DVD.** Maureen O'Hara, Alex Nicol, William Bishop, Robert Strauss, Alexander Scourby, Jack Kelly, Jeanne Cooper, Dennis Weaver; **D:** Lee Sholem; **W:** Polly James, Herb Meadow.

Redline 1997 (R) *Deathline* John Wade (Hauer) is double-crossed and murdered by his partner Merrick (Dacascos) who's involved with a Russian crime syndicate. But Wade is resurrected as a bionically enhanced creation and hunts for revenge. **96m/C VHS, DVD.** Rutger Hauer, Mark Dacascos, Yvonne Solo, John Thompson; **D:** Tibor Takacs, Brian Irving; **W:** Tibor Takacs, Brian Irving; **C:** Zoltan David; **M:** Guy Zerafa. **VIDEO**

Redline 2007 (PG-13) Self-financed and distributed by real estate tycoon Sadek, this action pic is most notable for its conspicuous consumption. Dissolute Michael (Macfadyen) instigates an illegal $100 million winner-take-all race with high-rollers Infamous (Griffin), a rapper, and movie producer Jerry (Matheson), and such drivers as the vengeful Natasha (Bjorlin) and daredevil Jason (Johnson). Plot—such as it is—is an excuse to watch some of the world's most expensive cars become scrap metal. **95m/C DVD.** *US* Nathan Phillips, Angus MacFadyen, Tim Matheson, Eddie Griffin, Nadia Bjorlin, Jesse Johnson, Barbara Niven, Louis Mandylor, Denyce Lawton, Neill Skylar; **D:** Andy Cheng; **W:** Richard Foreman; **C:** Bill Butler; **M:** Ian Honeyman, Andrew Raiher.

Redneck 1973 Implausible, distasteful purported "thriller" about criminals on the run. **92m/C VHS.** *IT GB* Telly Savalas, Franco Nero, Mark Lester, Ely Galleani, Duilio Del Prete, Maria Michi; **D:** Silvio Narizzano.

Redneck Zombies 1988 (R) A bunch of backwoods rednecks become zombies after chug-a-lugging some radioactive beer. Eating local tourists becomes a hard habit to break. Betcha can't have just one! **83m/C VHS, DVD.** Lisa DeHaven, W.E. Benson, Floyd Piranha, William-Livingston Dekker, Zoofeet, James Housely, Anthony Burlington-Smith, Martin J. Wolfman, Boo Teasdale, Darla Deans, Tyrone Taylor, Frank Lantz, Pericles Lewnes; **D:** Pericles Lewnes; **W:** Fester Smellman; **C:** Ken Davis; **M:** Adrian Bond.

Reds 1981 (PG) The re-creation of the life of author John Reed ("Ten Days that Shook the World"), his romance with Louise Bryant, his efforts to start an American Communist party, and his reporting of the Russian Revolution. A sweeping, melancholy epic about what they saw. See director Sergei Eisenstein's silent masterpiece "Ten Days that Shook the World," based on Reed's book, for the Russian view of some of the events depicted in Beatty's film. **195m/C VHS, DVD, Blu-ray Disc, HD DVD.** Warren Beatty, Diane Keaton, Jack Nicholson, Edward Herrman, Maureen Stapleton, Gene Hackman, Jerzy Kosinski, George Plimpton, Paul Sorvino, William Daniels, M. Emmet Walsh, Dolph Sweet, Josef Sommer; **D:** Warren Beatty; **W:** Warren Beatty; **C:** Vittorio Storaro; **M:** Dave Grusin, Stephen Sondheim. Oscars '81: Cinematog., Director (Beatty), Support. Actress (Stapleton); British Acad. '82: Support. Actor (Nicholson), Support. Actress (Stapleton); Directors Guild '81: Director (Beatty); Golden Globes '82: Director (Beatty); L.A. Film Critics '81: Cinematog., Director (Beatty), Support. Actress (Stapleton); Natl. Bd. of Review '81: Director (Beatty), Support. Actor (Nicholson); N.Y. Film Critics '81: Film; Natl. Soc. Film Critics '81: Support. Actress (Stapleton); Writers Guild '81: Orig. Screenplay.

Redwood Curtain 1995 (PG) Geri Riordan (Salonga) is an American teenager, with a brilliant future as a concert pianist before her, until she becomes obsessed with learning about her past. Her wealthy adoptive father, Laird Riordan (Lithgow), provides understanding but no answers so she turns to her sympathetic Aunt. Geneva (Monk), who lives in the redwood forest area of northern California. There Geri encounters homeless Vietnam vet Lyman Fellers (Daniels) and becomes convinced the troubled man is her birth father. Adapted from the play by Lanford Wilson; made for TV. **99m/C VHS.** Lea Salonga, John Lithgow, Jeff Daniels, Debra Monk, Catherine Hicks; **D:** John Korty; **W:** Ed Nanzug; **M:** Lawrence Shragge. **TV**

Redwood Forest Trail 1950 Environmental-themed oater about a camp for underprivileged city boys. The boys of the camp are blamed for the death of a landowner whose daughter then refuses to renew the camp's mortgage. Allen and Switzer set out to prove that the real culprits are sawmill workers out to control the area timber. Smokey the Bear also makes an appearance to lecture about careless forest fires and the need to preserve the woods. **67m/B VHS.** Rex Allen, Jeff Donnell, Carl "Alfalfa" Switzer, Jane Darwell, Marten Lamont, Pierre Watkin; **D:** Philip Ford; **W:** Bradford Ropes.

Reed: Insurgent Mexico 1950 *Reed, Mexico Insurgente* 1973 Dramatization of John Reed's newspaper reporting on the Mexican Revolution. Spanish with subtitles. **104m/B VHS.** *MX* Claudio Obregon, Eduardo Lopez Rojas, Eracio Zepeda; **D:** Paul Leduc.

Reefer Madness WOOF! *Tell Your Children; Dope Addict; Doped Youth; Love Madness; The Burning Question* 1938 (PG) Considered serious at the time of its release, this low-budget depiction of the horrors of marijuana has become an underground comedy favorite. Overwrought acting and lurid script contribute to the fun. **67m/B VHS, DVD.** Dave O'Brien, Dorothy Short, Warren McCollum, Lillian Miles, Thelma White, Carleton Young, Josef Forte, Harry Harvey Jr., Pat Royale; **C:** Jack Greenhalgh; **M:** Abe Meyer.

Reel Paradise 🐾🐾🐾 2005 (R) Follows film industry insider, John Pierson and his family during the final month of a one-year sabbatical in Taveuni, Fiji, from their suburban New York home. In Taveuni, the Piersons established the self-proclaimed "most remote theatre in the world" in the 180 Meridian Cinema, Taveuni's 52-year-old 288-seat theatre. Taps into the unbridled enthusiasm as the local Fijians pack the seats to view such films as "Jackass: The Movie" (later banned in Fiji), "Apocalypse Now Redux," "Bend it Like Beckham" and the Hindi film "Kaante." With free admission, the Piersons received little support from the Local Catholic mission—apparently the films were in competition with attendance at religious services. **110m/C DVD.** **D:** Steve James; **C:** P.H. O'Brien; **M:** Norman Arnold.

Reet, Petite and Gone 🐾🐾🐾 1947 All-Black musical featuring the music of neglected jive singer Louis Jordan, and his band, The Tympany Five. A girl's mother dies; sneaky lawyer tries to cheat her. Slick and enjoyable. **75m/B VHS, DVD.** Louis Jordan, June Richmond; **D:** William Forest Crouch.

The Ref 🐾🐾🐾 1993 (R) The couple from hell turn the tables on Gus (Leary), a hard-nosed fugitive who takes Caroline (Davis) and her husband Lloyd (Spacey) hostage. Gus then finds himself trapped in the traditional Christmas ordeal of a family suffering from industrial-strength dysfunction. He plots its getaway while masquerading as the couple's marriage counselor, hence the film's title. This sometimes brutal, frequently hysterical satire of male-female relationships, family ties, and compulsory holiday rituals uses consistently sharp dialogue and superb acting to tell an absurd but convincing tale. **97m/C VHS, DVD.** J.K. Simmons, Raymond J. Barry, Richard Bright, Adam LeFevre, Ellie Raab, Bill Raymond, Jim Turner, Robert Ridgely, Vincent Pastore, B.D. Wong, Rutanya Alda, Denis Leary, Judy Davis, Kevin Spacey, Glynis Johns, Robert J. Steinmiller Jr., Christine Baranski; **D:** Ted (Edward) Demme; **W:** Richard LaGravenese, Marie Weiss; **M:** David A. Stewart.

The Reflecting Skin 🐾🐾 1991 In a 1950s prairie town a small boy sees insanity, child-murder, and radiation sickness, leading him to fantasize that his tormented young widow next door is a vampire. The pretentious drama/freak show rationalizes its ghastly events as symbolizing the hero's loss of youthful innocence. But the Hound knows the score; this is "Faces of Death" for the arts crowd, a grotesque menagerie that dares you to watch. The exploiting-frog opener is already notorious. Beautiful photography, with vistas inspired by the painting of Andrew Wyeth. **116m/C VHS.** Viggo Mortensen, Lindsay Duncan, Jeremy Cooper, Duncan Fraser, Sheila Moore, David Longworth, Robert Koo's, David Bloom, Evan Hall; **D:** Philip Ridley; **W:** Philip Ridley; **C:** Dick Pope; **M:** Nick Bicat.

Reflections in a Golden Eye 🐾🐾½ 1967 Huston's film adaptation of Carson McCullers's novel about repressed homosexuality, madness, and murder at a Southern Army base in 1948, with family members dying of suspernatural causes. **90m/C VHS.** Robert Shaw, Sally Kellerman, Sondra Locke, Mary Ure; **D:** William A. Fraker; **W:** Lewis John Carlino.

A Reflection of Fear 🐾🐾 1972 (PG) Lane psycho-thriller about a young girl's jealousy of her father's girlfriend, with family members dying of supernatural causes. **90m/C VHS.** Robert Shaw, Sally Kellerman, Sondra Locke, Mary Ure; **D:** William A. Fraker; **W:** Lewis John Carlino.

Reflections in the Dark 🐾🐾 Beautiful Regina (Rogers) is on death row for murdering her overbearing husband James (Terry). On execution-eve she relates her tale to young guard Colin (Zane), dispatching hubby by a different method each time she varies her story. Takes itself too seriously though Rogers gives a star performance. **83m/C VHS.** Mimi Rogers, Billy Zane, John Terry, Kurt Fuller, Lee Garlington, Nancy Fish; **D:** Jon Purdy; **C:** Teresa Medina.

Reflections of Murder 🐾🐾 1974 Evil schoolteacher's wife and mistress decide to kill him off and then are plagued by his phantom. Well-done TV remake of the French film "Diabolique." Suspenseful, with a great ending. **97m/C VHS.** Tuesday Weld, Joan Hackett, Sam Waterston, Lucille Benson, F.G. Armstrong, Michael Lerner, Ed Bernard, Lance Kerwin; **D:** John Badham; **M:** Billy Goldenberg. **TV**

Reform School Girl 🐾 1957 A young girl ends up behind bars when her boyfriend steals a car, she joy-riding and is involved in a hit-and-run murder. Extremely cheap production and incredious story. Look for Kellerman in a bit part in her first screen appearance. **71m/B VHS.** Gloria Castillo, Ross Ford, Edward Byrnes, Ralph Reed, Jack Kruschen, Sally Kellerman, Luana Anders, Yvette Vickers, Diane Darrin, Edmund Burns, Ross Hunter; **C:** Floyd Crosby; **M:** Edward L. Bernds; **D:** Edward L. Bernds; **W:** Edward L. Bernds.

Reform School Girls 🐾 1986 (R) Satiric raucous women's prison film, complete with tough lesbian warders, brutal lesbian guards, sadistic lesbian inmates, and a single, newly convicted heterosexual heroine. Wendy O. Williams as a teenager? Come on. Overdone, over-campy, exploitative. **94m/C VHS, DVD.** Linda Carol, Wendy O. Williams, Pat Ast, Sybil Danning, Charlotte McGinnis, Sherri Stoner; **D:** Tom De Simone; **W:** Tom De Simone; **C:** Howard Wexler.

The Refrigerator 🐾½ 1991 Filmed on a miniscule budget, this comic/horror flick tells the story of the innocent Batemans of Ohio who move into a grubby New York apartment where they discover their battered Norge refrigerator is actually a doorway to hell. The fridge has a taste for flesh and tends to eat the unwary visitor as well as defrosting blood (very messy). All the previous tenants disappeared without a trace—will the Batemans be next? Cartoon satire is too amateurish to be successful. **86m/C VHS.** David Simonds, Julia McNeal, Angel Caban, Nena Segal, Jaime Rojo, Michelle DeCosta, Phyllis Sanz; **D:** Nicholas A.E. Jacobs; **W:** Nicholas A.E. Jacobs; **C:** Paul Gibson.

Regarding Henry 🐾🐾 1991 (PG-13) A cold-hearted lawyer gets shot in the head during a hold-up and survives with memory and personality erased. During recovery the new Henry displays compassion and conscience the old one never had. Though too calculated in its yuppie-bashing ironies, the picture works thanks to splendid acting and low-key, on-target direction. **107m/C VHS, DVD.** Harrison Ford, Annette Bening, Bill Nunn, Mikki Allen, Elizabeth Wilson, Robin Bartlett, John Leguizamo, Donald Moffat, Nancy Marchand; **D:** Mike Nichols; **W:** J.J. (Jeffrey) Abrams; **C:** Giuseppe Rotunno; **M:** Hans Zimmer.

Regeneration 🐾🐾 1915 Irish hoodlum Owen (Fellowes) is saved from this life of crime by social worker Mamie Rose (Nilsson). Walsh filmed on location in New York's Bowery district and used actual gangsters in roles. Also features the 10-minute 1910 short "The Police Force of New York City," produced by Thomas Edison. **72m/B VHS, DVD.** Rockliffe Fellowes, Anna Q. Nilsson; **D:** Raoul Walsh; **W:** Raoul Walsh, Carl Harbaugh; **C:** Georges Benoit. Natl. Film Reg. '00.

Reggie Mixes In 🐾🐾🐾 1916 Wealthy man brawls in bar room and falls for barmaid. Taking a job to be near his beloved, he wipes out local thugs while tending to her welfare. Exhilarating fight scenes in which Fairbanks lists it out with...

Reign of Fire 🐾½ 2002 (PG-13) Your average year 2020 post-apocalyptic world scenario: Fire-breathing dragons rule the earth. Yes, the film has dragons as the bad guys. These long dormant, London tunnel-dwelling beasties are out to incinerate what's left of humankind, which ain't much. Enter mismatched, macho American Van Zan (McConaughey), British fireman (Bale), and a foxy blond helicopter pilot (Scorupco), who took up to give the nasty critters a taste of their own medicine. By the looks of this rag tag reptile posse, apparently personal grooming has gone by the wayside in the near futuristic world and the filmmakers saw to it that character development and survive lievable plot went along with it, too. Throwaway humor scores points for the humans but after the dust settles, the coo FX drags ons definitely come out on top. **101m/C VHS, DVD, Blu-ray Disc, UMD. US** Matthew McConaughey, Christian Bale, Izabela Scorupco, Gerard Butler, Scott James Moutter, Alexander Siddig, David Kennedy, Alice Krige, Ned Dennehy, Rory Kennan, Terence Maynard, Ben Thornton; **D:** Rob Bowman; **W:** Matt Greenberg, Gregg Chabot, Kevin Peterka; **C:** Adrian Biddle; **M:** Ed Shearmur.

Reign of Terror 🐾🐾 *The Black Book* 1949 British-made adventure set during the French Revolution, with everyone after the black book that holds the names of those arch-fiend Robespierre plans to guillotine in his ambitious bid for power. Well-mounted, but historical personages and events are reduced to cartoon form. **89m/B VHS, DVD.** Robert Cummings, Arlene Dahl, Richard Hart, Arnold Moss, Richard Basehart; **D:** Anthony Mann; **W:** Philip Yordan; **C:** John Alton.

Reign Over Me 🐾🐾½ 2007 (R) Why is Adam Sandler wearing Bob Dylan's hair? Anyway, it's subtle pro Cheedle; you should be watching. Alan (Cheadle), a NYC dentist, is mildly bored with his successful life and perfect family. Then he runs into his old college roommate, Charlie (Sandler), who's acting weird. Turns out he had a family and life into a rage whenever the past is brought up. Low-ever, Alan's a compassionate guy and ties to do some male bonding that will result in bringing Charlie back to reality. Sandler restrains from doing shtick, although he's done the angry boy-man thing before, and Binder rushes this predictable ending. **128m/C DVD, Blu-ray Disc. US** Adam Sandler, Don Cheadle, Jada Pinkett Smith, Liv Tyler, Saffron Burrows, Donald Sutherland, Robert Klein, Melinda Dillon, Jonathan Banks, Mike Binder; **D:** Mike Binder; **W:** Mike Binder; **C:** Russ T. Alsobrook; **M:** Rolfe Kent.

Reg'lar Fellers 🐾🐾 1941 A gang of kids save the town and soften the heart of their grandmother, too. Production is sloppy. Based on a comic strip by Gene Byrnes. **66m/B VHS, DVD.** Billy Lee, Carl Alfalfa' Switzer, Buddy Boles, Janet Dempsey, Sarah Padden, Roscoe Ates; **D:** Arthur Dreifuss.

Regina 🐾🐾½ *Regina Roma* 1983 A woman controls all the activities of her husband and son. At age 36, her son is ready to leave home and she refuses to let him. Fine performances in this strange and disturbing film. **86m/C VHS, DVD.** Anthony Quinn, Ava Gardner, Fay Sharkey, Anna Karina; **D:** Jean-Yves Prate.

Regular Guys 🐾🐾½ *Echte Kerle; Real Men* 1996 Macho Frankfurt cop Christoph (Ohrt) gets blindingly drunk after discovering his girlfriend with another guy. She kicks him out—sans belongings—and after a very long night, Christoph wakes up in the bed of stud car mechanic, Edgar (Bergmann). Neither can't remember anything and Edgar won't say if something happened between them, although he agrees to let Christoph stay awhile while he sorts things out. Meanwhile, the cop's new colleague Helen (Tietze) is making eyes at him and rumors are flying at the police station about his living arrangements and sexual orientation. German with subtitles. **102m/C VHS, DVD. GE** Christoph M. Ohrt, Tim Bergmann, Carin C. Tietze, Oliver Stokowski; **D:** Rolf Silber; **W:** Rolf Silber, Rudolf Bergmann; **C:** Jürgen Hermann; **M:** Peter W. Schmitt.

Rehearsal for Murder 🐾🐾½ 1982 Movie star Redgrave is murdered on the night of her Broadway debut. Seems it might have been someone in the cast. Brought to you by the creative team behind "Columbo." Challenging whodunit as a team of good guys. **96m/C VHS, DVD.** Robert Preston, Lynn Redgrave, Patrick Macnee, Lawrence Pressman, Madolyn Smith, Jeff Goldblum, William Daniels; **D:** David Greene; **W:** Richard Levinson, William Link; **C:** Steven Larner; **M:** Billy Goldenberg. **TV**

The Reincarnate 🐾🐾 1971 (PG) Cult guarantees lawyer will live "forever" if he can find a new body. Enter gullible sculptor, who uncovers Russian secrets in 1901, allowing the Japanese to sink the Russian fleet and invade China. After a lively spy career for the British, Reilly eventually plots against the Bolsheviks and corresreincarnation of Golden Lotus, a counterpart of ancient China. In Mandarin Chinese with English subtitles. **99m/C VHS. HK** Joi Wong, Eric Tsang, Lam Chen Yen; **D:** Clara Law.

The Reincarnation of Golden Lotus 🐾🐾🐾 *Pan Jin Lian Zhi Qian Shi* 1987 Covers the exploits of the real-life swordspy and womanizer Sydney Reilly who uncovers Russian secrets in 1901, allowing the Japanese to sink the Russian fleet and invade China. After a lively spy career for the British, Reilly eventually plots against the Bolsheviks and corresreincarnation of Golden Lotus, a counterpart of ancient China. **572m/C VHS, DVD, GB** Sam Neill, Sebastian Shaw, Jeananne Crowley; **D:** Jim Goddard.

The Reincarnation of Peter Proud 🐾🐾 1975 (R) A college professor has nightmares which lead him to believe the spirit of a murdered man is now possessing him. Kinda scary, but predictable. Screenplay by Ehrlich from his novel. **105m/C VHS.** Michael Sarrazin, Jennifer O'Neill, Margot Kidder, Cornelia Sharpe, Paul Hecht; **D:** J. Lee Thompson; **W:** Max Ehrlich; **C:** Victor Kemper; **M:** Jerry Goldsmith.

Reindeer Games 🐾 2000 (R) Too much talking and not nearly enough gun-toting action bog down this already inane crime thriller that tries way too hard to impress with loopy plot twists that come at a dizzying pace. A miscast Affleck is Rudy Duncan, a just released convict who takes on the identity of his recently deceased cellmate in order to get cozy with Ashley (Theron), who had established a correspondence with the dead inmate. The couple spends blissful days together via aerobic sex until Ashley's sadistic "brother" Gabriel (Sinise) forces Rudy to help him and his skanky gang rob an Indian casino on Christmas Eve. Pic is surprisingly flat, deadening the impact of the surprise endings that come in rapid succession, which unintentionally transform the film into a parody of itself. **98m/C VHS, DVD.** Ben Affleck, Charlize Theron, Gary Sinise, Clarence Williams III, Dennis Farina, Donal Logue, James Frain, Isaac Hayes, Danny Trejo; **D:** John Frankenheimer; **W:** Ehren Kruger; **C:** Alan Caso; **M:** Alan Silvestri.

Reilly: Ace of Spies 🐾🐾🐾 1987 *Jim Saeng* 1989 In this highly erotic story of love and revenge, Wong escapes China for decadent Hong Kong by marrying a wealthy but foolish man. She has numerous sadomasochistic affairs and begins having flashbacks, revealing her to be the reincarnation of Golden Lotus. **89m/C VHS. CA** Jack Crieley, Jay Reynolds, Trudy Young, Terry Tweed; **D:** Don Haldane.

The Reivers 🐾🐾½ 1969 (PG) Young boy and two adult pals journey from small town Mississippi (circa 1905) to the big city of Memphis in a stolen car. Picaresque tale is delightful onscreen, as with all things Faulkner's enjoyable last novel. **107m/C VHS.** Steve McQueen, Sharon Farrell, Will Geer, Michael Constantine, Rupert Crosse; **D:** Mark Rydell; **W:** Harriet Frank Jr., Irving Ravetch; **M:** John Williams.

The Rejuvenator 🎬🎬½ *Rejuvenatrix* 1988 (R) An oft-told film story: an aging actress discovers a "youth" serum but finds out that the serum affects things other than her aging. Well-done. **90m/C VHS.** Marcus Powell, John MacKay, James Hogue, Vivian Lanko, Jessica Dublin; **D:** Brian Thomas Jones; **W:** Simon Nuchtern; **M:** Larry Juris.

Relative Fear 🎬½ 1995 (R) Little Adam has bad luck with his friends and relatives—they keep getting murdered all around him. His mother begins to suspect something unnatural is going on, and discovers Adam is not her natural child, but the son of a homicidal madwoman. Has Adam inherited some deadly traits? **94m/C VHS, DVD.** Darlanne Fluegel, M. Emmet Walsh, James Brolin, Denise Crosby, Martin Neufeld, Linda Sorensen, Matthew Dupuis; **D:** George Mihalka; **W:** Kurt Wimmer.

Relative Strangers 🎬½ 2006 (PG-13) Ticky-tacky and too familiar. Uptight self-help guru Richard Clayton (Livingston) learns from his oh-so-proper parents (Baranski, Herrman) that he was adopted. But when Richard finds his birth parents, the Menures (Bates, DeVito) turn out to be less-than-couth trailer park denizens. His fiancee Ellen (Campbell) thinks Richard should just roll with it but he's horrified. **86m/C DVD.** Ron Livingston, Neve Campbell, Kathy Bates, Danny DeVito, Christine Baranski, Edward Herrmann, Ed Begley Jr., Beverly D'Angelo; **C:** Greg Gilenna; **W:** Greg Gilenna, Jeff Baynes; **C:** Jeffrey Greeley, Tim Suhrstedt; **M:** David Kitay, Arnold Diamond.

Relax... It's Just Sex! 🎬🎬½ 1999 (R) Love and sex in the '90s surround gay looking-for-love writer Vincey (Anderson). His self-made extended family include best gal pal Tara (Tilly) and her boyfriend Gus (Perez), whose HIV-positive brother Javi (Garcia) has just attracted the attention of Buzz (Carson), the man Vincey had his eye on. Then there's troubled lesbian couple Megan (Scott Thomas), who has a fling with a guy (Wirth), and girlfriend Sarina (Williams), who's drawn into the arms of Robin (Petty). But romantic complications take a back seat when Javi and Vincey are subjected to a fag bashing in which Vincey violently turns the tables on one of his attackers. **110m/C VHS, DVD.** Mitchell Anderson, Jennifer Tilly, Cynda Williams, Serena Scott Thomas, Lori Petty, Eddie Garcia, Terrence "T.C." Carson, Timothy Paul Perez, Billy Wirth, Susan Tyrrell, Chris Cleveland, Gibbs Toldsdorf, Seymour Cassel, Paul Winfield; **D:** P.J. Castellaneta; **W:** P.J. Castellaneta; **C:** Lon Magdich; **M:** Lori Eschler Frystak.

Relentless 🎬🎬 1989 (R) Twisted psycho Nelson, once rejected by the LAPD Academy on psychological grounds, takes his revenge by murdering people and using his police training to cover his tracks. Good acting keeps spasmodically powerful but cliched thriller afloat. **92m/C VHS, DVD.** Edward (Eddie) Bunker, Judd Nelson, Robert Loggia, Meg Foster, Leo Rossi, Pat O'Bryan, Mindy Seeger, Angel Tompkins, Ken Lerner, George "Buck" Flower; **D:** William Lustig.

Relentless 2: Dead On 🎬🎬 1991 (R) Rossi, the detective from the first film, tracks yet another murderer whose occult-style mutilations mask an international political conspiracy. So-so slaughter with artsy camera work. Honestly, how many "Relentless" fans can you name who've been waiting with anticipation? **93m/C VHS, DVD.** Leo Rossi, Ray Sharkey, Meg

Foster, Miles O'Keefe, Dale Dye; **D:** Michael Schroeder.

Relentless 3 🎬🎬 1993 (R) A serial killer (Forsythe) likes to carve up his women victims and send various body parts to taunt the police. Then this sicko decides to really drive the cops crazy by stalking the beautiful girlfriend of the detective (Rossi) investigating the crimes. **84m/C VHS.** William Forsythe, Leo Rossi, Tom Bower, Robert Costanzo, Signy Coleman; **D:** James (Momel) Lemmo; **W:** James (Momel) Lemmo.

Relentless 4 🎬½ 1994 (R) A psychiatrist with a secret (Janssen) is the only clue Detective Sam Dietz (Rossi) has to a serial killer. Seems all the victims knew the shrink but what does she know? **91m/C VHS.** Leo Rossi, Famke Janssen, Ken Lerner, Colleen T. Coffey; **D:** Oley Sassone; **W:** Mark Sevi, Terry Plumeri.

The Relic 🎬🎬 1996 (R) Quiz time! Which is more implausible: a huge reptilian creature from South American mythology who is crazy for decapitations running amok in a Chicago museum, or Miller as an evolutionary biologist? That's right! Both are equally implausible. But we're forced to accept both after a ship from Brazil arrives with crates for the museum and a completely headless crew (extra credit if you said it's implausible for people with no heads to pilot a ship). Superstitious police detective Vincent D'Agosto (Sizemore) decides to close down the museum's exhibit of...Superstition. That does not sit well with museum director Ann Cuthbert (Hunt), who decides she needs grant money (and the movie needs victims). The monster proceeds to suck brains until the sassy scientist decides she's had enough and takes off her high heels, which everyone knows means the end is near for the creature. Sound interesting? Only if you like Lifestyles of the Rich and Headless. **110m/C VHS, DVD.** Penelope Ann Miller, Tom Sizemore, Linda Hunt, James Whitmore, Clayton Rohner, Thomas Ryan, Lewis Van Bergen, Chi Muoi Lo, Robert Lesser; **D:** Peter Hyams; **W:** Amy Holden Jones, John Raffo, Rick Jaffa, Amanda Silver; **C:** Peter Hyams; **M:** John Debney.

The Reluctant Agent 🎬🎬 1995 Waitress Linda (Jackee) is persuaded to take the place of injured twin sister Charlene, an FBI agent hot on the trail of shady-but-attractive businessman C. Gabriel Dash (Lawson). So, she goes undercover with the questionable assistance of agent John Fraser (Hedaya) to bring their criminal to justice. **94m/C VHS.** Jackee, Richard Lawson, Dan Hedaya, Bill Fagerbakke, Harold Sylvester, Cynthia Stevenson, Sharon Barr, Eda Reiss Merin; **D:** Paul Lynch; **W:** Jeff Cohn, Kristi Kane; **M:** Tim Truman.

The Reluctant Astronaut 🎬½ 1967 Roy Fleming (Knotts) is a carnival worker who operates the spaceship ride. Dad's upset the kid has no ambition and sends an application for Roy to NASA. Everyone's surprised when Roy gets accepted and the heads off to Florida but it turns out the job is janitorial. Still Roy does make friends with astronaut Red (Nielsen), who persuades Roy that Roy would be the perfect civilian to send up in an experimental capsule. Too bad Roy's terrified to fly in anything. **103m/C VHS, DVD.** Don Knotts, Leslie Nielsen, Joan Freeman, Arthur O'Connell, Jesse White, Jeanette Nolan, Joan Shawlee; **D:** Edward Montagne; **W:** James Fritzell, Everett Greenbaum; **C:** Rexford Wimpy; **M:** Vic Mizzy.

The Reluctant Debutante 🎬🎬🎬 1958 Harrison and Kendall are the urbane parents of Dee who are trying to find a suitable British husband for their girl. It seems their choices just won't do however, and Dee falls for American bad boy musician Saxon. A very lightweight yet extremely enjoyable romantic comedy thanks to Harrison and in particular his real-life wife Kendall, who unfortunately died the following year. **96m/C VHS.** Rex Harrison, Kay Kendall, John Saxon, Sandra Dee, Angela Lansbury, Diane Clare; **D:** Vincente Minnelli; **C:** Joseph Ruttenberg.

Washington, Will Patton, Donald Adeosun Faison, Wood Harris, Ethan Suplee, Nicole Ari Parker, Hayden Panettiere, Kate (Catherine) Bosworth, Ryan Hurst, Kip Pardue, Craig Kirkwood, Burgess Jenkins, Earl C. Poitier, Ryan Gosling; **D:** Boaz Yakin; **W:** Gregory Allen Howard; **C:** Philippe Rousselot; **M:** Trevor Rabin.

Remembering the Cosmos Flower 🎬🎬 1999 Teenager Akiko and her mother return to their small town home in Japan after seven years in South America. Akiko has contracted AIDS—a fact the entire community is aware of. While Akiko tries to cope with her illness, her childhood playmate Natsumi confronts the ignorance and fear of the village. Japanese with subtitles. **103m/C VHS, DVD.** *JP* Mari Natsuki, Megumi Matsushita, Akane Oda, Kai Shishido; **D:** Junichi Suzuki; **W:** Junichi Suzuki, Tetsuotomo Kosugi; **C:** Kaz Tanaka; **M:** Mamoru Samurakouchi.

Remo Williams: The Adventure Begins 🎬🎬 *Remo: Unarmed and Dangerous* 1985 (PG-13) Adaptation of "The Destroyer" adventure novel series with a Bond-like hero who can walk on water and dodge bullets after being instructed by a Korean martial arts master. Funny and diverting, and Grey is excellent (if a bit over the top) as the wizened oriental. The title's assumption is that the adventure will continue. **121m/C VHS, DVD.** Fred Ward, Joel Grey, Wilford Brimley, Kate Mulgrew, J.A. Preston, George Coe, Charles Cioffi, Patrick Kilpatrick, Michael Pataki, Marv Albert, Reginald Veljohnson, William Hickey; **D:** Guy Hamilton; **W:** Warren B. Murphy, Christopher Wood; **C:** Andrew Laszlo; **M:** Craig Safan.

Remolino de Pasiones 🎬🎬 1968 A young woman is driven to suicide after succumbing to her mother's persistent lover. **89m/C VHS.** *MX* Amparo Rivelles, Carlos Pinar, Susana Dosamantes; **D:** Alejandro Galindo; **C:** Alejandro Galindo; **C:** Alex Phillips Jr.; **M:** Gustavo Cesar Carrion.

Remote 🎬½ 1993 (PG) Thirteen-year-old Randy is a whiz designing high-tech remote-control gadgets. When one of his toys wipes out a friend's science project, Randy's parents try to put a halt to his tinkering but the kids, other than his innocuous rip-off of "Honey, I Shrunk the Kids" with some "Home Alone" thrown in as well. **80m/C VHS.** Chris Carrara, Jessica Bowman, John Diehl, Derya Ruggles, Tony Longo, Stuart Fratkin; **D:** Ted Nicolaou; **W:** Mike Farrow; **M:** Richard Band.

Remedy 🎬½ 2005 Will's life is perfect until his friend is fatally shot while the two are out partying. Too doped up to remember anything, he appears guilty thus forcing him to find the real killers amid New York City's sleaziest players. **82m/C VHS, DVD.** Christian Maelen, Arthur J. Nascarelli, Vincent Pastore, Nicholas Reiner; **D:** Christian Maelen; **W:** Jonathan Hanser; **C:** Brendan Flynt; **M:** Jon Doscher. **VIDEO**

Remedy for Riches 🎬🎬 1940 Another Sturges-scripted winner in which assistant D.A. MacMurray falls for sophisticated shoplifter Stanwyck, who has stolen a diamond bracelet amidst the Christmas holiday bustle. On a promise that she will return for the trial MacMurray postpones the trial and offers her a ride home for the holidays. Stanwyck is turned away by her mother and MacMurray brings her home for a real family Christmas, where love blooms. A sentimental, funny romance that boisters holiday cheer any time of year. **94m/B VHS.** Barbara Stanwyck, Fred MacMurray, Beulah Bondi, Elizabeth Patterson, Willard Robertson, Sterling Holloway; **D:** Mitchell Leisen; **W:** Preston Sturges; **C:** Ted Tetzlaff; **M:** Frederick "Friedrich" Hollander.

Remember Me 🎬 1985 Just as a woman is starting to gain control of her life, her husband returns home from the mental hospital. **95m/C VHS.** Robert Grubb, Wendy Hughes, Richard Moir; **D:** Lex Marinos.

Remember the Night 🎬🎬🎬 1940 Another Sturges-scripted winner in which assistant D.A. MacMurray falls for sophisticated shoplifter Stanwyck, who has stolen a diamond bracelet amidst the Christmas holiday bustle. On a promise that she will return for the trial MacMurray postpones the trial and offers her a ride home for the holidays. Stanwyck is turned away by her mother and MacMurray brings her home for a real family Christmas, where love blooms. A sentimental, funny romance that boisters holiday cheer any time of year. **94m/B VHS.** Barbara Stanwyck, Fred MacMurray, Beulah Bondi, Elizabeth Patterson, Willard Robertson, Sterling Holloway; **D:** Mitchell Leisen; **W:** Preston Sturges; **C:** Ted Tetzlaff; **M:** Frederick "Friedrich" Hollander.

Remember the Titans 🎬🎬 2000 (PG) Black coach Herman Boone (Washington) is hired to lead the football team at racially tense T. C. Williams High School in Alexandria, Virginia, a school that has been forced to integrate in 1971. This forces white coach Bill Yoast (Patton), who was close to reaching an important milestone, into the role of assistant. He and his former players almost sit out the season, but decide warily to show up for the team's first practices. The team works through initial stages of mistrust and ignorance, but finally learn to work together. As the school year begins, racial tensions are eased by the success of the team and the unified team goes to the state championship. A bit predictable and cliche-ridden, but heartfelt. Based on a true story. **114m/C VHS, DVD, Blu-ray Disc, UMD.** Denzel

Remote Control 🎬🎬½ 1988 (R) A circulating videotape of a 1950s sci-fi flick is turning people into murderous zombies, thanks to some entrepreneurial aliens. Silly, but performed by young actors with gusto. **88m/C VHS.** Kevin Dillon, Deborah Goodrich, Christopher Wynne, Jennifer Tilly; **D:** Jeff Lieberman; **M:** Peter Bernstein.

Remote Control 🎬🎬½ 1994 Quiet Axel lives with his mom, whose life revolves around the TV set, and his sister Maeja, who spends most of her time partying in a seedy club called Sodoma. Sodoma is run by three amateur gangsters who are anxious to get rid of a rival, Molli. Meanwhile, Axel falls in love with Molli's sister Unnur (who also happens to be Maeja's best friend). Then the gangsters kidnap Unnur and Axel sets out to rescue her. Icelandic with English subtitles. **85m/C VHS.** *IC* Bjorn Fridbjornsson, Margret H. Gustavsdottir, Helgi Bjornsson, Soley Eliasdottir; **D:** Oskar Jonasson; **W:** Oskar Jonasson.

Renaissance 🎬🎬½ 2006 (R) Stark noir/sci-fi animation set in 2054 Paris, a city that has become a gigantic labyrinth run by Avalon, a company and entity more like Big Brother, Inc. A female scientist who works for the company goes missing, setting off a classic noir adventure with the brooding cop hero, femme fatale, and enemies around every corner. The B&W design is striking but the story drags after awhile. The film was originally voiced by French actors and re-done for the English-language market. **103m/B DVD.** *GB FR LU* Romola Garai, Ian Holm, Jonathan Pryce, Christian Volckman; **W:** Alexandre de la Patellière, Matthieu Delaporte; **M:** Nicholas Dodd; **V:** Daniel Craig, Catherine McCormack.

Renaissance Man ♂♂½ 1994 (PG-13) Skeptical new teacher inspires a classroom of underachievers and finds his true calling. Based loosely on the experiences of screenwriter Burnstein at a base in Michigan. Civilian Bill Rago (DeVito) is an unemployed ad exec assigned to teach Shakespeare to a group of borderline Army recruits led by Hardison. Add half a bone for the recruits and in their Hamlet rap, a breath of fresh air in an otherwise state plot. Some funny moments, reminiscent of "Stripes," but not quite as wacky. On the other hand, Marshall does endearing well. Look for rapper Marky Mark with his shirt on (hard to recognize). Shot with his congressional aide, the co-operation of the Army. 128m/C VHS, DVD. Danny DeVito, Gregory Hines, James Remar, Stacey Dash, Ed Begley Jr., Mark Wahlberg, Lillo Brancato, Kadeem Hardison, Richard T. Jones, Khalil Kain, Peter Simmons, Jenifer Lewis; Cameos: Cliff Robertson; D: Penny Marshall; W: Jim Burnstein, Ned Mauldin. M: Hans Zimmer.

The Rendering ♂♂ 2002 Art student Sarah (Doherty) is attacked by a man who's obsessed with her. Recovering in the hospital, she renders a sketch that has Theodore Grey (Outerbridge) arrested and sent to prison. Ten years later, Sarah is married to Boston businessman Michael (Brennan) but has never told him what happened to her and her continued paranoia has caused a rift. Sarah has also continued to help the police as a sketch artist and her latest drawing of a suspect looks suspiciously like Michael. Has he committed a crime or is this a set-up by Grey, who happens to be out on parole. 92m/C VHS, DVD, CA Shannen Doherty, Peter Outerbridge, John Brennan, Tammy Isabell, Conrad Pla, Sean Devine; D: Peter Svatek; W: David Amann; C: Francois Dagenais; M: James Gelfand. CABLE

Rendez-vous ♂♂♂ 1985 (R) A racy, dark film about the sensitive balance between sex and exploitation, the real world and the stage world. Some may be disturbed by chillingly explicit scenes. Impressive tour de force of imagination, direction, and cinematography. In French with English subtitles. 82m/C VHS, DVD. FR Juliette Binoche, Lambert Wilson, Wadeck Stanczak, Jean-Louis Trintignant; D: Andre Techine; W: Olivier Assayas; C: Philippe Angers. Cannes '85.

Rendez-vous de Juillet ♂♂½ 1949 In postwar Paris Lucien dreams of becoming a documentary filmmaker, with his friends accompanying him to Africa to serve as his production team. His parents want him to get a regular job and Lucien's buddies are more concerned with love affairs, jazz, theatre, and other pleasures to take him too seriously. Includes a performance by American trumpeter Rex Stewart. French with subtitles; follows Becker's "Antoine et Antoinette." 110m/B VHS, FR Daniel Gelin, Brigitte Auber, Nicole Courcel, Maurice Fronet, Bernard Lajarrige; D: Jacques Becker; W: Jacques Becker, Maurice Griffe; C: Claude Renoir; M: Jean Wiener.

Rendezvous in Paris ♂♂♂ 1995 Les Rendez-vous de Paris 1995 includes three stories by Rohmer about the complications and disappointments of love. "Le Rendezvous de 7 heures" finds Esther (Bellar) upset when boyfriend Horace (Basler) is spotted with another girl at a cafe. She decides to make him jealous by showing up at the same cafe with another man. A bewitching "Les Bancs de Paris" and tries to decide on a possible new romance with a provincial professor (Renko). In "Mere et Enfant 1907," a painter (Kraft) goes to an art gallery where he spots a woman (Loyen) admiring Picasso's painting "Mother and Child" and he decides to pursue her. French with subtitles. 100m/C

Rendez-Moi Ma Peau ♂♂½ My Skin 1981 A modern-day witch gets in a traffic accident with a married couple and, as revenge, she transposes their personalities into the others' body. In French with subtitles. 82m/C VHS. FR Jean-Luc Biceau, Erik Colin, Bee Michelin, Chantal Neuwirth; D: Patrick Schulmann; C: Jacques Assueras, Andre Zarra; M: Patrick Schulmann.

Renegade Trail ♂♂ 1939 Hopalong Cassidy helps a marshall and a pretty widow round up ex-cons and rustlers. In King's Men, radio singers of the era, perform a fistful of songs. 61m/B VHS, William Boyd, George "Gabby" Hayes, Russell Hayden, Charlotte Wynters, Russell Hopton, Sonny Bupp, Jack Rockwell, Roy Barcroft, Eddie Dean; D: Lesley Selander; W: Harrison Jacobs, John Rathmell; C: Russell Harlan; M: Phil Ohman.

Renegades ♂♂ 1989 (R) A young cop from Philadelphia and a Lakota Indian begrudgingly unite to track down a gang of ruthless crooks. Good action, and just a bit not much story. 105m/C VHS, DVD. Kiefer Sutherland, Lou Diamond Phillips, Jami Gertz, Rob Knepper; D: Jack Sholder; C: Phil Meheux; M: Michael Kamen.

Renfrew of the Royal Mounted ♂♂ 1937 A Canadian Mountie goes after counterfeiters and sings a few songs in this mild adaptation of a popular kids' radio serial. Newill was a ruthless crooks. Good action, and just a bit not much story. 57m/B VHS, DVD. Carol Hughes, James Newill, Kenneth Harlan; D: Al(bert) Herman.

Renfrew on the Great White Trail ♂♂½ On the Great White Trail; Renfrew of the Royal Mounted on the Great White Trail 1938 A frustrated fur trader takes off after a pack of thieves. 58m/B VHS, DVD. James Newill, Terry Walker, Robert Frazer, Richard Alexander; D: Al(bert) Herman.

Reno 911!: Miami ♂♂ 2007 (R) If you're a fan of the Comedy Central TV show, you'll enjoy this expanded version in all its raunchy, silly glory. The Reno sheriffs go to a police convention in Miami and are left to patrol the city's streets (with their usual complete incompetence) when all the other cops are quarantined at the hotel. Improv is hit-or-miss and involves alligators, topless beaches, crazy mobsters, sexual frustration—and Lt. Dangle (Lennon) in this short-shorts. 84m/C DVD. US Thomas Lennon, Robert Ben Garant, Niecy Nash, Nick Swardson, Kerri Kenney-Silver, Carlos Alazraqui, Mary Birdsong, Wendi McLendon-Covey, Cedric Yarbrough, Paul Rudd; Cameos: Danny DeVito, Dwayne "The Rock" Johnson; D: Robert Ben Garant; W: Thomas Lennon, Robert Ben Garant, Kerri Kenney-Silver; C: Joe Kessler; M: Craig (Shudder to Think) Wedren.

Rendition ♂♂ 2007 (R) Egyptianborn, assimilated American citizen Anwar El-Ibrahimi (Metwally) is ripped from his suburban Chicago existence to the confusion of his pregnant wife Isabella (Witherspoon), who wonders when he doesn't return from a business trip. She turns to old boyfriend Alan Smith (Sarsgaard), a congressional aide, for access to Senator Hawkins (Arkin), although her pleas fall on deaf ears. Turns out Anwar's in North Africa being tortured by the local authorities (with Washington's secret blessing), for what they believe is his involvement in a terrorist bombing. Meanwhile, newly-promoted CIA analyst Douglas Freeman (Gyllenhaal) is privy to Anwar's interrogation and begins to have second thoughts. Corinne Whitman (Streep) runs the whole rendition program (an actual government policy that allows suspected terrorists to be extradited for interrogation with a steely resolve. Unfortunately it all fails to convince, and even an otherwise brilliant cast can't pull this topical nugget out of the trash bin. 120m/C DVD. US Meryl Streep, Reese Witherspoon, Jake Gyllenhaal, Peter Sarsgaard, Alan Arkin, Omar Metwally, Igal Naor, Moa Khouas, Zineb Oukach; D: Gavin Hood; W: Kelley Sane; C: D on Beebe; M: Paul Hepker, Mark Killian.

Renegade Girl ♂ 1946 A special agent is sent west to capture the female head of a band of outlaws. 65m/B VHS, DVD. Alan Curtis, Ann Savage, Edward Brophy, Ray Corrigan, Jack Holt, Russell Wade, Claudia Dreke, John "Dusty" King, Chief Thundercloud, Edmund Cobb; D: William Berke; W: Edwin Westrate; C: James S. Brown Jr.; M: Darrell Calker.

Rented Lips ♂♂ 1988 (R) Two documentary filmmakers sell out, taking over the production of a porno film at the request of a public television producer who promises to help their careers. Mull and Shawn are well supported by a impressive cast, but everyone's effort is wasted in unfunny script aimed at comedy. 82m/C VHS. Martin Mull, Dick Shawn, Jennifer Tilly, Kenneth Mars, Edy Williams, Robert Downey Jr., June Lockhart, Shelley Berman, Mel Welles, Pat McCormick, Eileen Brennan; D: Robert Downey.

Repentance ♂♂♂ 1998 (R) Hong Kong action star Chow Yun-Fat makes his American debut in this somewhat disappointing first feature from director Antoine Fuqua. Chow stars as John Lee, an assassin working for crime boss Mr. Wei ("sang). When Lee decides not to carry out a hit on a cop's (Rooker) son, he becomes the target of the men sent to replace him. Needing a passport to get back to China, Lee goes to forger Meg Coburn (Sorvino). Before she can finish the papers, Wei's men begin the first of many high body count gun battles. Fuqua, who was heavily influenced by John Woo (one of the film's exec producers), does a passable job of conveying the style of Chow and Woo's Hong Kong work, but doesn't leave much room for the substance. Chow's subtlety and charisma are crammed into a mechanical action plot, and only his talent saves the whole thing from imploding. 86m/C VHS, DVD, Blu-ray Disc, UMD. Chow Yun-Fat, Mira Sorvino, Michael Rooker, Kenneth Tsang, Jürgen Prochnow, Danny Trejo, Til Schweiger, Clifton (Gonzalez) Collins Jr., Carlos Gomez, Frank Medrano; D: Antoine Fuqua; W: Ken Sanzel; C: Peter Lyons Collister; M: Harry Gregson-Williams.

The Replacement Killers ♂♂½ 1998 (R) Pokayanie: Confession 1987 A popular, surreal satire of Soviet and Communist societies. A woman is arrested for repeatedly digging up a dead local despot, and put on trial. Wickedly funny and controversial; released under the auspices of glasnost. In Russian with English subtitles. 151m/C VHS, DVD. RU Avtandil Makharadze, Zeinab Botsvadze, Ketevan Abuladze, Ka-kh Kavsadze; D: Tengiz Abuladze. Grand Jury Prize.

Renoir Shorts ♂♂♂ 1927 Two early silent Renoir fantasies: "The Little Matchgirl," a lyrical adaptation of the Hans Christian Anderson fairy tale, and "Charleston," in which a space-traveling African and Parisian girl dance comically. 50m/B VHS. Catherine Hessling; D: Jean Renoir.

Rent ♂♂ 2005 (PG-13) Hit Broadway show makes its screen debut, though it all feels just a bit too late. For the uninitiated, the story follows a group of New York squatters and struggling artists in an update of La Boheme. The passion isn't an act—the film cast is the same group that developed the characters on stage, if you lost, young, and broke in a big city, the timing and uber-sentimentality won't matter. Themes of AIDS, homosexuality and drugs may be too much for stuffier viewers. 128m/C DVD, Blu-ray Disc, UMD. US Anthony Rapp, Adam Pascal, Rosario Dawson, Taye Diggs, Jesse L. Martin, Wilson Jermaine Heredia, Idina Menzel, Tracie Thoms; D: Chris Columbus; C: Stephen Goldblatt; M: Rob Cavallo.

Rent-A-Cop ♂♂ 1988 (R) A cop (Reynolds) is bounced from the force after he survives a drug-bust massacre under suspicious circumstances. He becomes a security guard and continues to track down the still-at-large killer with help from call girl Minnelli, who helps to keep an eye out on the Midnight. Themes of AIDS, homosexuality and mat-90m/C VHS, DVD. Burt Reynolds, Liza Minnelli, James Remar, Richard Masur, Dionne Warwick, Robby Benson, John P. Ryan, Bernie Casey, John Stanton, John P. Ryan, Dionne Warwick, Robby Benson; W: Michael Blodgett; C: Giuseppe Rotunno; M: Jerry Goldsmith. Golden Raspberries '38: Worst Actress (Minnelli).

Rent-A-Kid ♂♂½ 1955 (G) Businessman Harry Haber (Nielsen) is asked by his son to keep an eye out on the Midnight. Valley Orphanage for a week. Then Harry meets a young couple who are unsure about having a family so, since Harry's business is renting all sorts of things, he decides to rent the couple three orphans so they can get a taste of parenting. 89m/C VHS. Leslie Nielsen, Amos Crawley Cody Jones, Tabitha Lucien, Tony Rosato; D: Fred Gerber; W: Paul Bernbaum; C: Rene Ohashi; M: Ron Ramin.

Rentadick ♂♂ 1972 A precursor to the Monty Python masterpieces, written by future members Chapman and Cleese. Private eye spoof isn't as funny as later Python efforts; but it is an indication of what was yet to come and fans should enjoy it. 94m/C VHS. GB James Booth, Julie Ege, Ronald Fraser, Donald Sinden, Spike Milligan, Tsai Chin, Kenneth Cope, John Wells; D: Jim Clark; W: Graham Chapman, John Cleese; C: John Coquillon; M: Carl Davis.

Replicant ♂♂ 2001 (R) It takes a killer to catch a killer. In this case Van Damme is cloned by the government so he can go after himself (the original is a vicious serial killer). Cop Rooker, who's been unsuccessfully hunting the psycho for several years, teams up with the duplicate to get results. Lots of chases, fights, and high-tech thrills. 100m/C VHS, DVD. Jean-Claude Van Damme, Michael Rooker, Catherine Dent; D: Ringo Lam; W: Lawrence Riggin's, Les Weldon; C: Mike Sounion; M: Guy Zerafa. VIDEO

Repli-Kate ♂♂½ 2001 (R) Reporter Kate "Landry) is accidentally cloned by grad student Max (Roday) with a she's doing a story on his professor's (Levy) genetic experiments. Since Kate is a hot babe, Max's pal Henry (Askew) thinks this is a wonderful thing and promptly teaches Repli-Kate about the important things in every guy's life—sports, beer, and sex. 90m/C VHS, DVD. Ali Landry, James Roday, Desmond Askew, Eugene Levy; D: Frank Longo; W: Stuart Gibbs; C: Alan Caso; M: Teddy Castellucci. VIDEO

Repo Jake ♂♂½ 1990 Jake Bexter learns the myth of the carefree life of a repo man in this action thriller. His illusion is destroyed by angry clients, and a sinister crime boss. 90m/C VHS. Dan Haggerty, Robert Axelrod; D: Joseph Merhi; W: Joe Hart; C: Richard Pepin; M: John Gonzalez.

Reno and the Doc ♂♂½ 1984 Enjoyable comedy about two endearingly cranky middle-aged men battling mid-life crises join together and test their mettle in the world of professional skiing. 88m/C VHS. CA Kenneth Welsh, Henry Ramer, Linda Griffiths; D: Charles Dennis.

The Replacements ♂♂½ 2000 (PG-13) An NFL players' strike finds coach Hackman stuck with a bunch of replacement players, including washed-up quarterback Shane Falco (Reeves) and never-was receiver Clifford Franklin (Jones). If you can get past the fact that the heroes are scabs, this silly cliche-fest still isn't very good. It's better than it oughta be, but only because of Hackman's presence and Jones's comic talents. The odd assortment of misfits and goofballs is occasional men of comedy, but nothing you haven't seen in all the other "rag-tag-team-fights-the-odds" sports comedies. Based on the 1987 strike when players filling in for the Washington Redskins won three straight games. 105m/C VHS, DVD. Keanu Reeves, Gene Hackman, Jon Favreau, Orlando Jones, Jack Warden, Brooke Langton, Rhys Ifans, Brett Cullen, Gailard Sartain, Art LaFleur, Faizon Love, Michael "Bear" Taliferro, Troy Winbush, Michael Jace, Ace Yonamine, David Denman, Keith David, Pat Summerall, John Madden, Evan Dexter Parke; D: Howard Deutch; W: Vince McEwin; C: Tak Fujimoto; M: Alan Silvestri.

Replikator: Cloned to Kill ♂♂½ 1994 (R) In the 21st century, a ruthless criminal gets hold of replication technology that can duplicate anything, including people. So it's up to a cop and two cyberpunks to stop the destruction. 95m/C VHS. Michael St. Gerard, Brigitte Bako, Ned Beatty; D: G. Philip Jackson; W: Tony Johnston, Michelle Bellerose, John Dawson.

Repo Man ♪♪♪½ **1983 (R)** An inventive, perversely witty portrait of sick modern urbanity, following the adventures of punk stock boy Otto (Estevez), who takes a job as a car repossessor under the jaundiced eye of veteran Bud (Stanton). Then there's the lobotomized physicist Parnell (Harris), who carries around a strang glowing object in the trunk of his car that's wanted by the government. The L.A. landscape is filled with pointless violence, no-frills packaging, media hypnosis, and aliens. Executive producer: none other than ex-Monkee Michael Nesmith. **93m/C VHS, DVD.** Emilio Estevez, Harry Dean Stanton, Sy Richardson, Tracey Walter, Olivia Barash, Fox Harris, Jennifer Balgobin, Vonetta McGee, Angelique Pettyjohn, Biff Yeager; **D:** Alex Cox; **W:** Alex Cox; **C:** Robby Muller; **M:** Tito Larriva, Iggy Pop.

Report on the Party and the Guests ♪♪♪♪ **1966** A controversial, widely banned political allegory, considered a masterpiece from the Czech new wave, a picnic/lawn party deteriorates into brutality, fascist intolerance and persecution. Many Czech film makers, some banned at the time, appear. Based on a story by Ester Krumbachova, who also co-wrote the screenplay. In Czech with English subtitles. **71m/B VHS.** *CZ* Jiri Nemec, Evald Schorm, Ivan Vyskocil, Jan Klusak, Zdena Skvorecka, Pavel Bosek; **D:** Jan Nemec; **W:** Jan Nemec.

Report to the Commissioner ♪♪♪ *Operation Undercover* **1974 (R)** A rough, energetic crime-in-the-streets cop thriller. A young detective accidentally kills an attractive woman who turns out to have been an undercover cop, then is dragged into the bureaucratic cover-up. **112m/C VHS.** Michael Moriarty, Yaphet Kotto, Susan Blakely, Hector Elizondo, Richard Gere, Tony King, Michael McGuire, Stephen Elliott; **D:** Milton Katselas; **W:** Abby Mann; **M:** Elmer Bernstein.

Repossessed ♪♪ **1990 (PG-13)** A corny, occasionally funny takeoff on the human-possessed-by-the-devil films with Blair, as usual, as the afflicted victim. Nielsen, in another typecast role, plays the goofy man of the cloth who must save the day. Numerous actors appear in brief comedy sequences which lampoon current celebrities and constitute the film's highlights. For fans of "Airplane" and "The Naked Gun", not necessarily for others. **89m/C VHS, DVD.** Linda Blair, Ned Beatty, Leslie Nielsen, Anthony Starke, Jesse Ventura; **D:** Bob Logan; **W:** Bob Logan; **M:** Charles Fox. Golden Raspberries '90: Worst Song ("He's Comin' Back (The Devil)").

The Reptile ♪♪♪ **1966** The inhabitants of yet another Cornish village are turning up dead—mysteriously from snakebite. When Harry (Barrett) investigates his brother's death, he finds out Anna (Pearce) is the victim of a curse, which causes her to turn into a snake. Rather sympathetic characters for the horror genre. **90m/C VHS, DVD.** *GB* Jacqueline Pearce, Ray Barrett, Noel Willman, Jennifer Daniel, Michael Ripper, John Laurie, Marne Maitland, Charles Lloyd-Pack, George Woodbridge, David Baron; **D:** John Gilling; **W:** John (Anthony Hinds) Elder; **C:** Arthur Grant; **M:** Don Banks.

Reptilian ♪ **1999 (PG-13)** Archeologists Campbell (Livingston) and Hughes (Young) are searching for remains of a gigantic dinosaur. But guess who gets to them first? Evil aliens! Who want to take over the earth! So they ray-zap the dino remains back to life and the creature goes on a rampage until the military puts him down. But it doesn't end there—although you'll certainly wish it had. **99m/C VHS, DVD.** *KN* Harrison Young, Donna Philipson, Richard B. Livingston; **D:** Hyung Rae Shim; **W:** Marty Poole; **C:** Hong Kim An; **M:** Chris Desmong, Seung Woo Cho.

Reptilicus ♪♪ **1962** Oil drillers in Lapland bring up a sample of prehistoric flesh from a frozen bog deep deep below the earth, which is transported to Copenhagen. It proves to be alive and growing; eventually a lightning storm frees it from its holding tank. Soon thereafter the army has a real problem on its hands when it reappears as a completely regenerated monster, crawling across the landscape,

crushing buildings and eating farmers. The authorities have no luck ridding themselves of the scaly, snake-like dragon, until they corner it in the main square in downtown Copenhagen. This alternative epic comes in dead last in the list of movies where giant monsters attack cities. The several hundred extras who run politely through the streets in "panic" look bored or amused. Most of Reptilicus's scenes are artlessly shot in broad daylight, making its general artificiality even more obvious. **90m/C DVD.** *DK* Carl Ottosen, Ann Smyrner, Mimi Heinrich, Asbjorn Andersen, Bodil Miller, Bent Mejding, Dirch Passer, Ole Wisborg; **D:** Sidney W. Pink; **W:** Sidney W. Pink, Ib Melchior; **C:** Aage Wiltrup; **M:** Sven Gyldmark.

Repulsion ♪♪♪½ **1965** Character study of a young French girl who is repulsed when her sister goes on vacation, her cascade of stability begins to crack, with violent and bizarre results. Polanski's first film in English and his first publicly accepted full-length feature. Suspenseful, disturbing and potent. **105m/B VHS, DVD.** *GB* Catherine Deneuve, Yvonne Furneaux, Ian Hendry, John Fraser, Patrick Wymark, James Villiers, Renee Houston, Helen Fraser, Mike Pratt, Valerie Taylor; **D:** Roman Polanski; **W:** Roman Polanski, Gerard Brach, David Stone; **C:** Gilbert Taylor.

Requiem for a Dream ♪♪♪½ **2000** Amazing performances from the entire cast, particularly Burstyn, propel this harrowing story of drug addiction and crumbled dreams. Harry (Leto) and his friend Tyrone (Wayans) decide to become small-time drug dealers in order to raise the cash needed to help his designer girlfriend Marion (Connelly) open a clothing store. Unfortunately, they begin to sample the merchandise, and their plans slip away until all they can plan is how to get the next fix. In a parallel storyline, Harry's mother Sara (Burstyn) receives a call that she may be a contestant on her favorite game show. She begins gobbling diet pills to improve her appearance and soon can't live without them. Director Aronofsky has stated that addiction is the hero of this movie. Based on the novel by Hubert Selby, Jr. **102m/C VHS, DVD.** Jared Leto, Ellen Burstyn, Jennifer Connelly, Marlon Wayans, Christopher McDonald, Louise Lasser, Keith David, Sean Gullette; **D:** Darren Aronofsky; **W:** Darren Aronofsky, Hubert Selby Jr.; **C:** Matthew Libatique; **M:** Clint Mansell. Ind. Spirit '01: Actress (Burstyn), Cinematog.

Requiem for a Heavyweight ♪♪♪ **1956** Original TV version of the story about an American Indian heavyweight boxer played by Palance who risks blindness in order to help his manager pay off bookies. Highly acclaimed teleplay written for "Playhouse 90." **90m/B VHS.** Jack Palance, Keenan Wynn, Ed Wynn, Kim Hunter, Ned Glass; **D:** Ralph Nelson; **W:** Rod Serling. **TV**

Requiem for a Heavyweight ♪♪♪ *Blood Money Mountain Rivera* **1962** After 17 years, Mountain Rivera (Quinn) is a washed-up heavyweight risking his life if he continues boxing. He tries to find another job but his manager, Maish Rennick (Gleason), owes the mob big, and persuades the fighter to help him pay off his debts by joining the wrestling circuit, so Mountain humiliates himself to help out his old friend. The 1956 TV version is still more compelling but the film's performances are all first-rate. **100m/B VHS, DVD.** Anthony Quinn, Jackie Gleason, Mickey Rooney, Julie Harris, Stanley Adams, Spivy Levoe, Muhammad Ali, Jack Dempsey; **D:** Ralph Nelson; **W:** Rod Serling; **C:** Arthur Ornitz; **M:** Laurence Rosenthal.

Requiem for Dominic ♪♪♪½ *Requiem fur Dominic* **1991 (R)** A Communistbloc country in the midst of revolution accuses a man of terrorist activities. Can his friend, exiled for years, help him discover the truth? Interesting and timely premise matched with outstanding ensemble acting make for a superior thriller. Amnesty International receives partial proceeds from all sales of this video. In German with English subtitles. **88m/C VHS.** *GE* Felix Mitterer, Viktoria Schubert, August Schmolzer, Angelica Schutz; **D:** Robert Domhelm.

Requiem for Murder ♪♪½ **1999 (PG-13)** Psychotic fan of a classical radio DJ decides to murder her competition. **95m/C VHS, DVD.** Molly Ringwald, Chris Heyerdahl, Lynne Adams, Chris Mulkey, Jayne Heitmeyer; **D:** Douglas Jackson; **W:** Matt Dorff; **C:** Barry Gravelle; **M:** Milan Kymlicka. **VIDEO**

The Rescue ♪♪½ **1988 (PG)** An elite team of U.S. Navy Seals is captured after destroying a disabled submarine. When the U.S. government writes off the men, their children decide to mount a rescue. Puerile, empty-headed trash for teens. **97m/C VHS.** Marc Price, Charles Haid, Kevin Dillon, Christina Harnos, Edward Albert; **D:** Ferdinand Fairfax; **W:** Jim Thomas, John Thomas; **C:** Russell Boyd; **M:** Bruce Broughton.

Rescue Dawn ♪♪♪ **2006 (PG-13)** Brutal true survival story of Dieter Dengler, the only American POW to ever escape from a prison camp in the Laotian jungle and return alive to his own side. Director Herzog—who also helmed a documentary version of Dengler's epic experience a decade earlier with "Little Dieter Needs to Fly"—forgoes the flashy effects and plot complications of most modern war films in favor of raw storytelling. Funny guy Zahn is notable in a rare non-comic screen role. **125m/C DVD, Blu-ray Disc.** Christian Bale, Steve Zahn, Jeremy Davies, Evan Jones, Marshall Bell, Zach Grenier, Toby Huss, Abhijati Jusakul, Pat Healy, Galen Yuen, Chayan Chunsuttiwat; **D:** Werner Herzog; **W:** Werner Herzog; **C:** Peter Zeitlinger; **M:** Klaus Bartle.

Rescue from Gilligan's Island ♪♪½ **1978** Fifteen years after the cancellation of "Gilligan's Island" came this TV movie that reunited the principal cast (minus Tina Louise's original Ginger) and finally depicted the rescue of the castaways. When a tsunami sweeps the group's huts into the sea, they're discovered by the Coast Guard and return to civilization. Somewhat changed by their experiences on the island, the castaways face difficulties assimilating with modern life, while at the same time Gilligan is pursued by Russian spies sent to retrieve an information disc that landed on the island. This awkward return to the lame jokes and Keaton-inspired slapstick of the TV series seemed out of date even during the original broadcast, but the cast's chemistry is still evident. **92m/C VHS, DVD.** Bob Denver, Alan Hale Jr., Russell Johnson, Jim Backus, Natalie Schafer, Dawn Wells, Judith Baldwin; **D:** Leslie Martinson; **W:** David Harmon, Sherwood Schwartz, Elroy Schwartz, Al Schwartz; **C:** Robert Primes; **M:** Gerald Fried. **TV**

Rescue Me ♪♪½ **1993 (PG-13)** Geek photographer Fraser carries a torch for high school honey Ginny and just happens to be on the scene (with camera) when she's kidnapped. So he persuades a scruffy Vietnam vet to help him rescue his damsel in distress. Likeable adventure with lots of chases. **99m/C VHS.** Michael Dudikoff, Stephen Dorff, Peter DeLuise, Ami Dolenz, William Lucking, Dee Wallace Stone; **D:** Arthur Allan Seidelman; **W:** Michael Snyder; **C:** Hanania Baer; **M:** Al Kasha, Joel Hirschhorn, David Waters.

The Rescuers ♪♪♪ **1977 (G)** Bernard and Miss Bianca, two mice who are members of the Rescue Aid Society, attempt to rescue an orphan named Penny from the evil Madame Medusa, who's after the world's biggest diamond. They are aided by comic sidekick, Orville the albatross, and a group of lovable swamp creatures. Very charming in the best Disney tradition. Based on the stories of Margery Sharp. Followed by "The Rescuers Down Under." **76m/C VHS, DVD.** *D:* Wolfgang Reitherman, John Lounsbery; **M:** Artie Butler; **V:** Bob Newhart, Eva Gabor, Geraldine Page, Jim Jordan, Joe Flynn, Jeanette Nolan, Pat Buttram.

The Rescuers Down Under ♪♪♪½ **1990 (G)** "Crocodile" Dundee goes Disney; the followup to "The Rescuers" places its characters in Australia with only mild results for a Magic Kingdom product. Heroic mice Bernard and Bianca protect a young boy and a rare golden eagle from a poacher. The great bird closely resembles the logo of Republic Pictures. **77m/C VHS, DVD.** **D:** Hendel Butoy, Mike Gabriel; **W:** Jim Cox, Karey Kirkpatrick, Joe Ranft, Byron Simpson; **M:** Bruce Broughton; **V:**

Bob Newhart, Eva Gabor, John Candy, Tristan Rogers, George C. Scott, Frank Welker, Adam Ryen.

Rescuers: Stories of Courage—Two Couples ♪♪♪ **1998 (PG)** In "Aart and Joht Je Vos," Delaney and Donovan are Dutch newlyweds who turn their home into a refuge for Jews hiding from the Nazis. The second story, "Marie Taquel," features Hamilton in the title role as a Belgian who, along with her husband (Molina), hides Jewish students at their Catholic boarding school. These true stories are based on the book "Rescuers: Portraits of Moral Courage in the Holocaust." **109m/C VHS.** Dana Delany, Martin Donovan, Linda Hamilton, Alfred Molina, Jan Rubes, Nigel Bennett, James Kidnie, Nicholas Kilbertus, Scott Speedman; **D:** Tim Hunter, Lynne Chermack; **C:** Miroslaw Baszak; **M:** Pino Donaggio, Hummie Mann. **C A B L E**

Rescuers: Stories of Courage "Two Women" ♪♪♪ **1997 (PG-13)** Fact-based drama about Gentiles who sheltered Jews from Nazi persecution during WWII. In "Mamusha" Perkins plays Gertruda, a Catholic nanny in Poland, who poses as the mother of her orphaned Jewish charge. "The Woman on the Bicycle" is Frenchwoman Marie-Rose (Ward), who works for the Resistance and hides a Jewish family in the attic of her home. **107m/C VHS.** Elizabeth Perkins, Sela Ward, Fritz Weaver, Anne Jackson, Al Waxman, Gerard Parkes, Mireille Landes; **D:** Peter Bogdanovich; **W:** Ernest Kinoy, Terry Norris; **C:** Miroslaw Baszak; **M:** Hummie Mann. **C A B L E**

Reservation Road ♪♪ **2007 (R)** Dwight Arno (Ruffalo) is a small town Connecticut lawyer. Already running late returning his son to his ex-wife's home at the end of a visitation day spent at a Red Sox game, Dwight accidentally strikes and kills a young boy with his car, then in a panic flees the scene. The dead boy's father, Ethan Learner (Phoenix), is a local professor who, expectedly grief stricken and filled with anger, becomes dissatisfied with local law enforcement's inability to find his son's killer and seeks the assistance of an attorney—who ends up being Dwight. Dwight, meanwhile, is obviously conflicted. An unfortunate series of coincidences stretch believability and derail this overly melodramatic story. Fans of Joaquin Phoenix will still enjoy his raw, emotional performance. **102m/C DVD.** *US* Joaquin Rafael Phoenix, Mark Ruffalo, Jennifer Connelly, Mira Sorvino, Sean Curley, Eddie Alderson; **D:** John Lindley; **M:** Mark Isham.

Reservoir Dogs ♪♪♪½ **1992 (R)** Ultraviolent tale of honor among thieves. Six professional criminals known by code names to protect their identities (Misters Pink, White, Orange, Blonde, Blue, and Brown) are assembled by Joe Cabot (Tierney) to pull off a diamond heist. But two of the gang are killed in a police ambush. The survivors regroup in an empty warehouse and try to discover the informer in their midst. In probably the most stomachchurning scene (there is some competition here), a policeman is tortured (by Madsen) to the tune of the Stealers Wheel "Stuck in the Middle with You." Unrelenting; auspicious debut for Tarantino with strong ensemble cast anchored by Keitel as the very professional Mr. White. **100m/C VHS, DVD, Blu-ray Disc.** Harvey Keitel, Tim Roth, Michael Madsen, Steve Buscemi, Christopher Penn, Lawrence Tierney, Kirk Baltz, Randy Brooks; **D:** Quentin Tarantino; **W:** Quentin Tarantino; **C:** Andrzej Sekula; **M:** Karyn Rachtman; **V:** Steven Wright. Ind. Spirit '93: Support. Actor (Buscemi).

Resident Evil ♪♪ **2002 (R)** Yet another noisy movie adapted from a videogame, which never gets as creepy as a zombie movie should. Umbrella Corp. (AKA the Hive) is the front for a secret military tech and genetics operations. Its security operations are controlled by a A.I. computer known as the Red Queen, which instigates a series of defensive measures to contain a virus (that can reanimate the

Resident Evil: Apocalypse 🐾
2004 (R) While its predecessor was a moderately successful return to pulp science-fiction films, this outing is nothing of the kind. It's less of a sequel than a regurgitating of the earlier installment but with fewer thrills, less action, and an inconsequential story. Alice and a new batch of survivors are trying to escape the city above The Hive, which has been re-infected with the T-virus. By simply rehashing the first film, any fresh conflict is forgone. Lack of suspense and characterization make for an uninspired, unoriginal, and thoroughly unenjoyable genre pic. **93m/C VHS, DVD, Blu-ray Disc, UMD.** *GB CA* Milla Jovovich, Sienna Guillory, Oded Fehr, Thomas Kretschmann, Sophie Vavasseur, Jared Harris, Mike Epps, Sandrine Holt, Raz Adoti, Zack (Zach) Ward, Iain Glen; *D:* Alexander Witt. *W:* Paul W.S. Anderson; *C:* Christian Sebaldt, Derek Rogers; *M:* Jeff Danna.

Resident Evil: Extinction 🐾½
2007 (R) Video game franchise trades claustrophobic underground sets for "Road Warrior" style wasteland, but star Jovovich is stuck battling the same old zombies. This time super-powered Alice meets up with a convoy of refugees led by Larter and Fehr, trying to stay one step ahead of the zombie virus. Between the zombies and the evil corporation that created them, there's not much hope that they'll make a stand in a mostly sand-buried Las Vegas (created by Os-car-winning production designer Caballero). Short on originality, the movie depends on its mostly dull action scenes and its franchise status to keep viewers interested. **94m/C DVD, Blu-ray Disc.** *C:* GB Milla Jovovich, Oded Fehr, Ali Larter, Iain Glen, Ashanti, Christopher Egan, Spencer Locke, Matthew Marsden, Linden Ashby, Mike Epps, Jason O'Mara; *D:* Russell Mulcahy. *W:* Paul W.S. Anderson; *C:* Russell Carpenter; *M:* Charlie Clouser.

Resistance 🐾🐾
1992 Apocalyptic tale of rebels and soldiers. The poor have been driven from abandoned cities into working as farm hands for a large corporation. When the workers rebel, anti-terrorist squads manage to make the situation worse and a full-scale rebellion begins. **112m/C VHS, DVD.** Jack Thompson, Stephen Leeder, Robyn Nevin, Harold Hopkins, Helen Jones, Kris McQuade, Hugh Keays-Byrne; *D:* Paul Elliot.

A Respectable Trade 🐾🐾½
1998 Frances Scott (Fielding) has lost her position as a governess in 1788 Bristol, England. A job-search letter gathers Frances a marriage proposal from Josiah Cole (Clarke), an older, earnest, social climbing businessman whose trade happens to be slaves. Josiah wishes Frances to teach English to some of his property so they may be sold as house servants and Frances begins to feel something special for one of the group—Moses (Bakare)—who turns out to be much more of an educated gentleman than her own husband. Based on Gregory's 1995 novel. **240m/C VHS, DVD.** *GB* Emma Fielding, Warren Clarke, Ariyon Bakare, Anna Massey; *D:* Suri Krishnamma; *W:* Philippa Gregory. *TV*

The Respectful Prostitute 🐾🐾½
1952 Sartre's tale of a hooker who is cajoled into providing false testimony as a witness in the trial of a member of a prominent family. English language version of French drama. **75m/B VHS.** *FR* Ivan Desny, Barbara Laage, Walter Bryan; *D:* Marcel Pagero, Charles Brabant; *W:* Jean-Paul Sartre.

Respiro 🐾🐾🐾 / *Breathe; Respiro; Grazia's Island* **2002** (PG-13) Grazia (Golino—the only professional in the cast) does not fit into the usual life of the small Sicilian fishing village of Lempedusa. Although devoted to her husband Pietro (Amato) and their children, Grazia's emotions are volatile (even by Italian standards)—maybe she needs professional help? When Pietro tries to send his wife to Milan for treatment, she runs away to hide out in a local cave, depending on her 13-year-old son Pasquale (Casisa) to protect her. The film replaces reality (the part that Grazia has a mental illness) with poetics (she's really just a free-spirit) but you'll be lulled by its charms. *94m/C* **DVD.** *IT FR* Valeria Golino, Vincenzo Amato, Francesco Casisa, Veronica D'Agostino, Filippo Pucillo, Muzzi Loffredo, Elio Germano; *D:* Emanuele Crialese; *W:* Emanuele Crialese; *C:* Fabio Zamarion; *M:* John Surman.

Rest in Pieces 🐾
1987 (R) A young woman inherits a Spanish mansion, and weird things begin to happen. It seems a cult of Satan worshippers is already living on the estate. As one might infer from the title, quite a bit of hacking and slashing ensues. **90m/C VHS, DVD.** Scott Thompson Baker, Lorin Jean, Dorothy Malone; *D:* Joseph (Jose Ramon Larraz) Braunstein.

Restaurant 🐾🐾½
1998 (R) Would-be showbiz types all work at the same swanky New Jersey restaurant while experiencing alcoholic and aspiring play-wright Chris (Brody) is still carrying a torch for ex-girlfriend/co-worker Kenny (Baker), who's been cast in Chris' new play, much to his dismay. Meanwhile, Chris is trying a new romance with singer/waitress Jeanine (Neal). Although race doesn't seem to be a problem in personal relations (Chris is white, both his girlfriends are black), it starts to raise ugly problems at work (and his feature story is published) he realizes change the tenor of the movie). **107m/C DVD.** Adrien Brody, Elise Neal, David Moscow, Simon Baker, Catherine Kellner, Malcolm Jamal-Warner, Lauryn Hill, John Carroll Lynch, Sybil Temchen, Vonte Sweet, Michael Stoyanov; *D:* Eric Bross. *W:* Tom Cudworth; *C:* Horacio Marquinez; *M:* Theodore Shapiro.

Restless 🐾 / *The Beloved* **1972** A restless homemaker begins an affair with a childhood friend. Director Cosmatos later oversaw "Rambo." **75m/C VHS.** *GR* Raquel Welch, Richard Johnson, Jack Hawkins, Fiora Robson; *D:* George P. Cosmatos.

The Restless Breed 🐾🐾
1958 Son is restless after dad, a secret service agent, is slain by gunrunners. Routine career-revenge epic done in by listless script. **81m/C VHS.** Scott Brady, Anne Bancroft, Jay C. Flippen, Rhys Williams, Jim Davis; *D:* Allan Dwan.

Restless Spirits 🐾🐾½ / *Dead Aviators* **1999** Sullen Katie (Wimbles) and her young brother Simon (Swan) arrive to stay with their grandmother Lydia (Mason) in Porter's Point, Newfoundland. Both children are still grieving over the death of their aviator father in a crash four years before. While exploring a remote pond, Katie encounters the ghosts of French airmen Nungesser (Bluteau) and Coli (Monty). In 1927, they left Paris in a biplane on a nonstop trans-Atlantic flight to New York and disappeared. It seems their plane crashed into Porter's Pond and until the two can be recovered they are doomed to wander its banks. Katie's determined to help, though no one believes her story. **99m/C VHS, DVD.** *CA* Juliana Wimbles, Lothaire Bluteau, Michel Monty, Marsha Mason, Leslie Hope, Ben Cook, Eugene Lipinski, Nicholas Swan; *D:* David Wellington; *W:* Semi Chellas; *C:* Andra Fearnwort; *M:* Ron Sures. **C.A.B.L.E.**

Restoration 🐾🐾🐾
1994 (R) Set in the 17th century after Charles II is restored to the British throne, the title may instead refer to the restoration of one man's values. After curing one of the king's dogs, physician Downey is elevated to courtier and falls into drunken debauchery. He is soon forced to marry (but not touch) the king's favorite mistress. Unfortunately, he is caught trespassing on his majesty's main squeeze and banished from the court. Cast among the common rabble, he encounters the plague and the Great Fire of London while trying to redeem himself. Strong cast and sumptuous set design help to propel Downey's performance. Adapted from Rose Tremain's 1989 novel. Release was delayed a year because no one could seem to come up with a marketing strategy. **118m/C VHS, DVD.** Robert Downey, Jr., Meg Ryan, Sam Neill, Hugh Grant, David Thewlis, Polly Walker, Ian McKellen; *D:* Michael Hoffman; *W:* Rupert Walters; *C:* Oliver Stapleton; *M:* James Newton Howard. Oscars '95: Art Dir./Set Dec., Costume Des.

Restraining Order 🐾🐾
1999 (R) Lawyer Robert Woodfield (Roberts) witnesses a murder that's committed by a former client. He contacts a friend in the D.A.'s office but when that friend is also murdered and Woodfield's efforts to bring the killer to justice are futile, he decides to personally avenge the crimes. **95m/C VHS, DVD.** Eric Roberts, Hannes Jaenicke, Tatjana Patitz, Dean Stockwell; *D:* Lee H. Katzin; *W:* John Jarrell; *M:* David Wurst, Eric Wurst. **VIDEO**

The Resurrected 🐾🐾
One of the best recent H.P. Lovecraft horror adaptations, a fairly faithful try at "The Case of Charles Dexter Ward." Ward learns he has a satanic ancestor who possessed the secret of resurrection and eternal life—but as the warlock says, it is very messy. Surprisingly tasteful even with occasional gore and truly ghastly monsters; in fact this pic could have used a bit more intensity. **108m/C VHS, DVD.** Scott Chris Sarandon, Robert Romanus; *D:* Dan O'Bannon; *M:* Richard Band.

Resurrecting the Champ 🐾🐾
2007 (PG-13) Erik Kernan (Hartnett) is a sports reporter looking for a big story. He thinks he's found it in Bob "Champ" Satterfield (Jackson), a former contender now homeless in Denver. Moving from back page to the top of the heap, Erik pursues his big chance to make a name for himself without much concern for Champ. After his feature story is published he realizes a lesson to be learned. Hartnett tries but ultimately can't give his flawed character depth, and is forced to carry far more weight than he's capable of. Any energy Jackson gives to the movie disappears the second he's not on the screen. Loosely based on a true story about writer J.R. Moehringer and real-life boxer Satterfield. **111m/C VHS, DVD.** Samuel L. Jackson, Josh Hartnett, Teri Hatcher, Kathryn Morris, Alan Alda, David Paymer, Rachel Nichols, Dakota Goyo, Harry J. Lennix, Peter Coyote, Ryan McDonald; *D:* Rod Lurie. *W:* Michael Bortman, Allison Burnett; *C:* Adam Kane; *M:* Lawrence Nash Groupe.

Resurrection 🐾🐾½
1980 (PG) After a near-fatal car accident, a woman finds she has the power to heal others by touch. She denies that God is responsible, much to her Bible Belt community's dismay. Acclaimed and well-acted. **103m/C VHS.** Ellen Burstyn, Sam Shepard, Roberts Blossom, Eva LeGallienne, Clifford David, Richard Farnsworth, Pamela Payton-Wright; *D:* Daniel Petrie; *W:* Lewis John Carino; *M:* Maurice Jarre. Natl. Bd. of Review '80: Support. Actress (LeGallienne).

Resurrection 🐾🐾½
1999 (R) Chicago detectives John Prudhomme (Lambert) and Andrew Hollinsworth (Oser) are tracking a serial killer (C) who is killing men named after Christ's 12 apostles. He intends to use parts of his victims to reassemble the body of Christ in time for Easter Sunday resurrection. **108m/C VHS, DVD.** Christopher Lambert, Leland Orser, Robert Joy, Rick Fox, Barbara Tyson, James Kidnie, David Cronenberg; *D:* Russell Mulcahy; *W:* Brad Mirman; *C:* Jonathan Freeman; *M:* Jim McGrath.

Resurrection Man 🐾🐾
1997 (R) Sociopath Victor Kelly (Townsend) is in his element in 1975's Belfast when he's recruited to lead a group of Loyalist killers known as the "Resurrection Men." The gang's violence draws the attention of journalist Ryan (Nesbitt), who makes them media stars, and local cop Ferguson (Thompson), who wants to bring them down. Soon, though, Victor's capacity for bloodshed begins to worry older, hood, McLure (McGinley), who thinks they'll all be better off without Victor. Very creepy atmosphere sustained by some appalling violence. Based on the novel by McNamee, who also wrote the screenplay.

Retreat, Hell! 🐾🐾
1952 Korean War drama about the retreat from the Changjin Reservoir. Standard gun-ho military orientation with dismal results. **95m/B VHS.** Frank Lovejoy, Richard Carlson, Russ Tamblyn, Anita Louise; *D:* Joseph H. Lewis.

Retribution 🐾½
1988 (R) Struggling artist survives suicide attempt only to find himself possessed by the spirit of a criminal who was tortured to death. Seeing the he's working out a series of grisly murders that possibly lead back to the youthful protests of a group of activists. Tends to be confusing more than compelling. Based on the novel by Iain Banks. **106m/C VHS.** Dennis Lipscomb, Hoyt Axton, Leslie Wing, Suzanne Snyder; *D:* Guy Magar.

Retribution *Compactly* **1999** (R) Cameron Colley (Miller) is an investigative journalist who constantly runs into trouble with his editors. He's also addicted to cigarettes, cocaine, computer games, and sex with the married Yvonne (Hawes). Now he's working in pre-World War I Paris where he falls in love with the daughter of the Swiss ambassador. Of course, the puppets and other mini-critters are involved too. **90m/C VHS, DVD.** Guy Rolfe, Greg Sestero, Brigita Dau, Jack Donner, Stephen Blackehart; *D:* Joseph Tennent; *W:* Benjamin Carr; *C:* Viorel Sergovici Jr.; *M:* John Massari.

Retro Puppet Master 🐾🐾
1999 (PG-13) Most recent entry in the "Puppet Master" series is officially the first, finding a young Toulon in pre-World War I Paris where he falls in love with the daughter of the Swiss ambassador.

Retroactive 🐾🐾
1997 (R) Scientist Brian (Whaley) has been experimenting with reversing time and finally manages to make his project work. Meanwhile, police psychologist Karen (Travis) has her car trouble and been given a ride by Frank (Belushi) and his wife Rayanne (Whirry). Karen soon realizes Frank is a psycho and escapes, stumbling into Brian's lab. But Brian's just reversed time and Karen winds up back in Frank's car, trying to change the sequence of events. **91m/C VHS, DVD.** James Belushi, Kylie Travis, Shannon Whirry, Frank Whaley, Jesse Borrego, M. Emmet Walsh, Guy Boyd; *D:* Louis Morneau; *W:* Robert Strauss, Philip Badger; *C:* George Mooradian; *M:* Tim Truman.

The Return WOOF! *The Alien's Return* **1980** (PG) Vincent and Shepherd meet as adults and discover that they had both, as children, been visited by aliens who had given technology to a cattle-mutilating prospector. A mess with no idea of what sort of film it wants to be. **91m/C VHS.** Cybill Shepherd, Raymond Burr, Jan-Michael Vincent, Martin Landau, Vincent Schiavelli, Zachary Vincent, Farrah Bunch, Neville Brand, Susan Kiger; *D:* Greydon Clark.

Return 🐾🐾
1988 (R) A woman believes that the man she loves is the reincarnation of her dead grandfather. Interesting concept, but overall, a disappointing mystery. **78m/C VHS.** Frederic Forrest,

Resurrection of Zachary Wheeler 🐾🐾½
1971 (G) A president-elect, Sean McGinley, Derek Thompson, John Hannah, Geraldine O'Hare, Brenda Fricker, James Ellis, B.J. Hogg, Zara Turner; *D:* Marc Evans; *W:* Eoin McNamee; *D:* Pierre Aim; *M:* David Holmes, Gary Burns, Keith Tenniswood.

100m/C VHS. *GB* Stuart Townsend, James Nesbitt, who narrowly escaped death in an auto crash, is brought to a mysterious clinic in New Mexico. A reporter sneaks into the clinic and discovers the horrors of cloning. **100m/C VHS.** Angie Dickinson, Bradford Dillman, Leslie Nielsen, Jack Carter, James Daly; *D:* Bob Wynn.

Retrievers 🐾
1982 Young man and a former CIA agent team up to expose the unsavory practices of the organization. **90m/C VHS, DVD.** Max (Michael) Thayer, Roselyn Royce, Richard Anderson, Shawn Hoskins, Mary McCormick, Lenard Miller; *D:* Elliot Hong; *W:* Elliot Hong; *C:* Stephen Kim; *M:* Ted Asthoric.

Anne Francis, Karlene Crockett, John Walcutt, Lisa Richards; *D:* Andrew Silver.

The Return 🐾½ **2006 (PG-13)** Supernatural thriller that substitutes atmospheric moodiness for actual plot and dialogue. Joanna (Gellar) is a sales rep who uses the constant movement of her job to escape the visions and blackouts that have plagued her since her childhood. When business brings her back to her hometown, her hallucinations intensify. She begins seeing visions of a woman and the mysterious dirtbag who may have murdered her. Soon Joanna is being stalked by the killer, as well as by a jilted ex and a sexy stranger who also seems wrapped up in the mystery. **85m/C DVD.** *US* Sarah Michelle Gellar, Peter O'Brien, Adam Scott, Kate Beahan, Sam Shepard, J.C. MacKenzie, Erinn Allison; *D:* Asif Kapadia; *W:* Adam Sussman; *C:* Roman Osin; *M:* Dario Marianelli.

Return Engagement 🐾½ **1978** A lonely middle-aged ancient history professor falls in love with one of her students. **76m/C VHS.** Elizabeth Taylor, Joseph Bottoms, Peter Donat, James Ray; *D:* Joseph Hardy.

Return Fire 🐾½ *Jungle Wolf 2* **1991 (R)** A former employee of the government finds that he must now fight the system if he wants to save his son. Trivial action fare. **97m/C VHS.** Adam West, Ron Marchini, Mindi Miller; *D:* Neil Callaghan; *W:* Neil Callaghan; *D:* Dan Goodman.

Return from Witch Mountain 🐾🐾½ **1978 (G)** A pair of evil masterminds use a boy's supernatural powers to place Los Angeles in nuclear jeopardy. Sequel to Disney's ever-popular "Escape to Witch Mountain." **93m/C VHS, DVD.** Christopher Lee, Bette Davis, Ike Eisenmann, Kim Richards, Jack Soo, Helene Winston; *D:* John Hough; *W:* Malcolm Marmorstein.

The Return of a Man Called Horse 🐾🐾½ **1976 (PG)** Sequel to "A Man Called Horse" tells the story of an English aristocrat who was captured and raised by Sioux Indians, and then returned to his native homeland. Contains more of the torture scenes for which this series is famous, but not much of Harris. **125m/C VHS, DVD.** Richard Harris, Gale Sondergaard, Geoffrey Lewis; *D:* Irvin Kershner; *W:* Jack DeWitt; *C:* Owen Roizman.

The Return of Captain Invincible 🐾🐾½ *Legend in Leotards* **1983 (PG)** Arkin is a derelict superhero persuaded to fight crime again in this unique spoof. One liners fly faster than a speeding bullet. Lee gives one of his best performances as the mad scientist. Musical numbers by Rocky Horror's O'Brien and Hartley sporadically interrupt. Made on a shoe-string budget, offbeat film is entertaining but uneven. **102m/C VHS, DVD.** *AU* Alan Arkin, Christopher Lee, Kate Fitzpatrick, Bill Hunter, Graham Kennedy, Michael Pate, Hayes Gordon, Max Phipps, Noel Ferrier; *D:* Philippe Mora; *W:* Steven E. de Souza, Andrew Gaty; *C:* Louis Irving, Mike Molloy; *M:* William Motzing, Richard O'Brien.

The Return of Casey Jones 🐾🐾½ *Train 2419* **1934** Early adventure film featuring lots of great railroad action. **64m/B VHS, DVD.** Charles Starrett, Ruth Hall, George "Gabby" Hayes, Robert Elliot, Margaret Seddon, Jackie Searl; *D:* John P. McCarthy.

Return of Chandu 🐾🐾½ **1934** This serial in 12 chapters features Bela Lugosi as Chandu, who exercises his magical powers to conquer a religious sect of cat worshippers inhabiting the island of Lemuria. In the process, he fights to save the Princess Nadji from being sacrificed by them. **156m/B VHS, DVD.** Bela Lugosi, Maria Alba, Clara Kimball Young; *D:* Ray Taylor.

The Return of Count Yorga 🐾🐾 **1971 (R)** The vampire Count returns, taking up residence in a decrepit mansion nearby an orphanage. There he spies the toothsome Cynthia and Yorga decides to make her a vampiric bride. But the Count reckons without Cynthia's noble boyfriend who wants to keep his honey on this side of the grave. Preceded by "Count Yorga, Vampire." **97m/C VHS, DVD.** Robert Quarry, Mariette Hartley, Roger Perry, Yvonne Wilder, Rudy DeLuca, George Macready, Walter Brooke, Tom Toner, Karen Huston, Paul Hansen, Craig T. Nelson; *D:* Bob Kelljan; *W:* Bob Kelljan, Yvonne Wilder; *C:* Bill Butler.

The Return of Dr. Fu Manchu 🐾½ **1930** Fu Manchu (Oland) fakes his death and once again goes after Jack Petrie (Hamilton) and Scotland Yard Inspector Smith (Heggie), still determined to find revenge. Based on the novel by Sax Rohmer. Sequel to "The Mysterious Dr Fu Manchu." **73m/B VHS.** Warner Oland, O.P. Heggie, Neil Hamilton, Jean Arthur, Evelyn Hall, William Austin, Margaret Fealy; *D:* Rowland V. Lee; *W:* Lloyd Corrigan, Florence Ryerson; *C:* Archie Stout.

The Return of Dr. Mabuse 🐾🐾½ *Im Stahlnetz Des Dr. Mabuse; Phantom Fiend* **1961** The evil doctor is back, this time sending his entranced slaves to attack a nuclear power plant. Frobe, the inspector, and Barker, the FBI man, team up to thwart him. Fun for fans of serial detective stories. **88m/B VHS.** *GE FR IT* Gert Frobe, Lex Barker, Daliah Lavi, Wolfgang Preiss, Fausto Tozzi, Rudolph Forster; *D:* Harald Reinl.

Return of Dracula 🐾🐾 *The Curse of Dracula; The Fantastic Disappearing Man* **1958** Low-budget film about the Count killing a Czech artist and assuming his identity as he makes his way to the States. Once there, he moves in with the dead man's family and begins acting rather strangely. Retitled "The Curse of Dracula" for TV. **77m/C VHS.** Francis Lederer, Norma Eberhardt, Ray Stricklyn, Jimmy Baird, John Wengraf, Virginia Vincent, Greta Granstedt; *D:* Paul Landres; *W:* Pat Fielder; *C:* Jack MacKenzie.

Return of Draw Egan 🐾½ **1916** Vintage silent western wherein Hart is an outlaw-turned-greenhorn sheriff of a lawless town. Music Score. **64m/B VHS.** William S. Hart, Louise Glaum; *D:* William S. Hart.

The Return of Eliot Ness 🐾🐾 **1991 (R)** Ness comes out of retirement in 1947 Chicago to track down a friend's killer. And with Al Capone dead, Chicago mob bosses are fighting for their piece of illegal turf. Stack reprises his "The Untouchables" TV role from the early '60s in this made-for-TV movie. **94m/C VHS, DVD.** Robert Stack, Charles Durning, Philip Bosco, Jack Coleman, Lisa Hartman Black, Anthony De Sando; *D:* James A. Contner. TV

Return of Frank Cannon 🐾🐾 **1980** Portly private eye Frank Cannon comes out of retirement to investigate the alleged suicide of an old friend. **96m/C VHS.** William Conrad, Diana Muldaur, Joanna Pettet, Allison Argo, Arthur Hill, Ed Nelson; *D:* Corey Allen; *M:* Bruce Broughton. TV

Return of Frank James 🐾🐾🐾 **1940** One of Lang's lesser Hollywood works, this is nonetheless an entertaining sequel to 1939's "Jesse James." Brother Frank tries to go straight, but eventually has to hunt down the culprits who murdered his infamous outlaw sibling. Tierney's first film. **92m/C VHS, DVD.** Henry Fonda, Gene Tierney, Jackie Cooper, Henry Hull, John Carradine, Donald Meek, J. Edward Bromberg; *D:* Fritz Lang.

The Return of Grey Wolf 🐾🐾 **1922** A wild dog must fight for survival in Northern Quebec and is befriended by a fur trapper. An intelligent hound, he repays the trapper's generosity by helping him put the moves on some fur thieves. Silent. **62m/B VHS.** Walter Shumway, Helen Lynch, James Pierce; *D:* Jack Rollens.

The Return of Jafar 🐾🐾½ **1994 (G)** Clumsy thief Abis Mal inadvertently releases evil sorcerer Jafar from his lamp prison and now the powerful "genie Jafar" plots his revenge. So it's up to Aladdin and friends to save the Sultan's kingdom once again. Contains five new songs. ♫Just Forget About Love; Nothing in the World (Quite Like a Friend); I'm Looking Out for Me; You're Only Second Rate; Arabian Nights. **66m/C VHS, DVD.** *W:* Kevin Campbell, Mirith J.S. Colao; *V:* Scott Weinger, Linda Larkin, Gilbert Gottfried, Val Bettin, Dan Castellaneta, Jason Alexander.

Return of Jesse James 🐾🐾 **1950** Look-alike of dead outlaw Jesse James joins in with some former members of the James Gang, leading townsfolk to believe the notorious bank robber never died. It's up to brother Frank James, now an upstanding citizen, to set the record straight. A little slow moving at times, but still worth viewing. **77m/B VHS, DVD.** John Ireland, Ann Dvorak, Reed Hadley, Henry Hull, Hugh O'Brian, Tommy Noonan, Peter Marshall; *D:* Arthur Hilton.

The Return of Josey Wales 🐾 **1986 (R)** No match for the original featuring Clint Eastwood, the title character is played woodenly by Parks. This installment finds Wales pitted against a bumbling lawman. Sequel to 1976's "The Outlaw Josey Wales." **90m/C VHS.** Michael Parks, Rafael Campos, Bob Magruder, Paco Vela, Everett Sifuentes, Charlie McCoy; *D:* Michael Parks.

The Return of Martin Guerre 🐾🐾🐾½ *Le Retour de Martin Guerre* **1983** In this medieval tale, a dissolute village husband disappears soon after his marriage. Years later, someone who appears to be Martin Guerre returns, allegedly from war, and appears much kinder and more educated. Starring in a love story of second chances, Depardieu does not disappoint, nor does the rest of the cast. In French with English subtitles. Based on an actual court case. Remade in 1993 as "Sommersby." **111m/C VHS, DVD.** *FR* Gerard Depardieu, Roger Planchon, Maurice Jacquemont, Bernard Pierre Donnadieu, Nathalie Baye; *D:* Daniel Vigne; *W:* Daniel Vigne, Jean-Claude Carriere; *C:* Andre Neau; *M:* Michel Portal. Cesar '83: Writing, Score; Natl. Soc. Film Critics '83: Actor (Depardieu).

The Return of Peter Grimm 🐾🐾½ **1935** Man returns from death to try to tidy up the mess he left behind. Enjoyable if trite fantasy based on a play by David Belasco. **82m/B VHS.** Lionel Barrymore, Helen Mack, Edward Ellis, Donald Meek, George Breakston, James Bush; *D:* George Nicholls Jr.

Return of Sabata 🐾🐾½ **1971 (PG)** Van Cleef is back in this thoroughly confusing shoot-'em-up. Sabata is working as a trick-shot performer in a circus that arrives in the town of Hobsonville. Robber baron Joe McIntock heavily taxes the communists, who McIntock is turning his ill-gotten gains into gold so he can skip town with a fortune. Sabata discovers his plan. **100m/C DVD.** *IT* Lee Van Cleef, Giampiero Albertini, Reiner Schone, Ignazio Spalla, Annabella Incontrera; *D:* Gianfranco Parolini; *W:* Gianfranco Parolini, Renato Izzo; *C:* Sandro Mancori; *M:* Marcello Gombini.

The Return of Spinal Tap 🐾🐾½ **1992** Cult-fave mock rock group Spinal Tap is back with a feature-length video of performance and backstage footage from its recent reunion concert tour promoting their album "Break Like the Wind." Sequel to "This Is Spinal Tap" features lots of heavy metal songs including the title track, "Majesty of Rock," "Bitch School," "Diva Fever," "Clam Caravan," and "Stinkin' Up the Great Outdoors." Not as great as the original satire, but will appeal to Spinal Tap fans. **110m/C VHS, DVD.** Christopher Guest, Michael McKean, Harry Shearer, Rick Parnell, C.J. Vanston, June Chadwick; *Cameos:* Paul Anka, Jeff Beck, Jamie Lee Curtis, Richard Lewis, Martha Quinn, Kenny Rogers, Martin Short, Mel Torme, Rob Reiner, Paul Shaffer, Fred Willard, Bob Geldof; *W:* Christopher Guest, Michael McKean, Harry Shearer.

Return of Superfly 🐾 **1990 (R)** Man with insect moniker pesters drug dealers and cops in Harlem. Long-awaited sequel to urban epic "Superfly," scored again by Mayfield. **94m/C VHS.** Margaret Avery, Nathan Purdee, Samuel L. Jackson; *M:* Ice-T, Curtis Mayfield.

The Return of Swamp Thing 🐾½ **1989 (PG-13)** The DC Comics creature rises again out of the muck to fight mutants and evil scientists. Tongue-in-cheek, and nothing at all like the literate, ecologically oriented comic from which it was derived. **95m/C VHS, DVD.** Louis Jourdan, Heather Locklear, Sarah Douglas, Dick Durock; *D:* Jim Wynorski.

Return of the Aliens: The Deadly Spawn 🐾 *The Deadly Spawn* **1983 (R)** Aliens infect the earth and violently destroy humans. Extremely violent and gory. Watch out for those officious offspring. **90m/C VHS, DVD.** Charles George Hildebrandt; *D:* Douglas McKeown.

Return of the Ape Man 🐾🐾 **1944** Campy fun with Carradine and Lugosi. A mad scientist transplants Carradine's brain into the body of the "missing link." Hams galore. **51m/B VHS.** Bela Lugosi, John Carradine, George Zucco, Judith Gibson, Michael Ames, Frank Moran, Mary Currier; *D:* Phil Rosen.

Return of the Bad Men 🐾🐾 **1948** Scott is a retired marshall who must fight against a gang of outlaws lead by the Sundance Kid. Sequel to "Badman's Territory." **90m/C VHS.** Randolph Scott, Robert Ryan, Anne Jeffreys, George "Gabby" Hayes, Jason Robards Sr., Jacqueline White; *D:* Ray Enright; *W:* Charles "Blackie" O'Neal.

The Return of the Beverly Hillbillies 🐾🐾 **1981** The Clampett clan, along with now-government official Miss Jane help to solve the energy crisis using Granny's 'white lightening.' Adding to the whoops and hollers is Miss Jane's down-home Ozark wedding to her boss Mr. Medford. Entertaining enough but not quite the same with the loss of key players in the parts of Granny, Mr. Drysdale and Jethro. **100m/C VHS.** Buddy Ebsen, Donna Douglas, Nancy Kulp, Ray Young, Imogene Coca; *D:* Robert M. Leeds; *W:* Paul Henning. VIDEO

The Return of the Borrowers 🐾🐾🐾 **1996** Sweet sequel to 1993's "The Borrowers" finds the six-inch Clock family—father Pod (Holm), mother Homily (Wilton), and teenaged daughter Arrietty (Callard)—having to find a new home. Lots of misadventures ensue as they must avoid nasty humans, a giant bee, a storm, and other dangers on their way to safety. Based on the novels by Mary Norton. **165m/C VHS.** *GB* Ian Holm, Penelope Wilton, Rebecca Callard, Sian Phillips, Tony Haygarth, Judy Parfitt, Ben Chaplin, Paul Cross, Pamela Cundell, Ross McCall, Richard Vernon, Daniel Newman; *D:* John Henderson; *W:* Richard Carpenter; *C:* Clive Tucker; *M:* Howard Goodall.

Return of the Dragon 🐾🐾½ *Return of the Blind Dead; El Ataque de los Muertos Sin Ojos* **1973 (R)** In Lee's last picture, a Chinese restaurant in Rome is menaced by gangsters who want to buy the property. On behalf of the owners, Lee duels an American karate champ in the Roman forum. The battle scenes between Lee and Norris are great and make this a must-see for martial arts fans. **91m/C VHS, DVD.** *CH* Bruce Lee, Nora Miao, Chuck Norris; *D:* Bruce Lee; *W:* Bruce Lee; *C:* Ho Lang Shang; *M:* Joseph Koo.

Return of the Evil Dead 🐾🐾 *Return of the Blind Dead; El Ataque de los Muertos Sin Ojos* **1975** The sightless dead priests return to attack still more 1970s' Europeans in this second installment of the "blind dead" trilogy. Preceded by "Tombs of the Blind Dead" and followed by "Horror of the Zombies." Not to be confused with Raimi's "Evil Dead" slasher flicks. **85m/C VHS, DVD.** *SP PT* Tony Kendall, Esther Roy, Frank Blake, Fernando (Fernand) Sancho, Lone Fleming, Loretta Tovar, Jose Canalejas; *D:* Armando de Ossorio; *C:* Miguel Mlla; *M:* Anton Abril.

Return of the Family Man 🐾½ **1989** A mass murderer seems unstoppable as he continues to slash whole families at a time...the family man is redefined in this bloody gore-fest. **90m/C VHS.** Ron Smerczak, Liam Cundill, Terence Reis, Michelle Constant; *D:* John Murlowski.

Return of the Fly 🐾🐾 **1959** The son of the scientist who discovered how to move matter through space decides to continue his father's work, but does so against his uncle's wishes. He soon duplicates his dad's experiments with similar results. This sequel to "The Fly" doesn't buzz like the original. Followed by "Curse of the Fly." **80m/B VHS, DVD.** Vincent Price, Brett Halsey, John Sutton, Dan Seymour, David Frankham, Danielle De Metz, Ed Wolff; *D:* Edward L. Bernds; *W:* Edward L. Bernds, Brydon Baker.

Return of the Jedi 🐾🐾🐾½ 1983
(PG) Third film in George Lucas' popular space saga. Against seemingly fearsome odds, Luke Skywalker battles such worthies as Jabba the -tut and heavy-breathing Darth Vader to save his comrades and triumph over the evil Galactic Empire. Han and Leia reaffirm their love and team with C3PO, R2-D2, Ch'ewbacca, Calrissian, and a bunch of furry Ewoks to aid in the annihilation of the Dark Side. The special effects are still spectacular, even the third time around. Sequel to "Star Wars" (1977) and "The Empire Strikes Back" (1980). 132m/C VHS, DVD. Mark Hamill, Carrie Fisher, Harrison Ford, Billy Dee Williams, David Prowse, James Earl Jones, Kenny Baker, Denis Lawson, Anthony Daniels, Peter Mayhew, Sebastian Shaw, Jeremy Bulloch, Toby Philpot; **D:** Richard Marquand; **W:** George Lucas, Lawrence Kasdan; **C:** Alan Hume; **M:** John Williams; **V:** Alec Guinness, Frank Oz. Oscars '83: Visual FX.

Return of the Killer Tomatoes! 🐾 1988 (PG) The man-eating plant-life from 1977's "Attack of the Killer Tomatoes" is back, able to turn into people due to the slightly larger budget. Astin is mad as the scientist. Not as bad as "Attack," representing a small hurdle in the history of filmdom. Followed by "Killer Tomatoes Strike Back." 98m/C VHS, DVD. Anthony Starke, George Clooney, Karen Mistal, Steve Lundquist, John Astin, Charlie Jones, Rock Peace, Frank Davis, C.J. Dillon, Teri Weigel; **D:** John DeBello; **W:** John DeBello, Constantine Dillon, Steve Peace; **C:** Stephen Kent Welch; **M:** Neal Fox, Rick Patterson.

The Return of the King 1980
The third and final animated episode of J.R.R Tolkien's Middle Earth Trilogy. This one features Frodo, relative to Hobbit Bilbo Baggins, and his faithful servant, making middle Earth safe from Orcs, Gollums, and other ooky creatures. 120m/C VHS, DVD. **D:** Arthur Rankin Jr., Jules Bass; **M:** Maury Laws; **V:** Orson Bean, Roddy McDowall, John Huston, Theodore B rei, William Conrad, Glen Yarborough, Paul Frees, Casey Kasem, Sonny Meendrez.

Return of the Lash 🐾½ 1947
Lash LaRue once again defends settlers' rights from ruthless outlaws. 53mB VHS. Lash LaRue, Al "Fuzzy" St. John, Mary Maynard, George Chesebro; **D:** Ray Taylor.

Return of the Living Dead 🐾🐾½ 1985 (R) Poisonous gas revives a cemetery and a morgue rendering an outrageous spoof on the living-dead sub-genre with fast-moving zombies. p.nk humor, and exaggerated gore. Its humor does not diminish the fear factor, however. Sequel follows. Directed by "Alien" writer O'Bannon. 90m/C VHS, DVD, Clu Gulager, James Karan, Linnea Quigley, Don Calfa, Jewel Shepard, Beverly Randolph, Miguel A. Nunez Jr., Brian Peck; **D:** Dan O'Bannon; **W:** Dan O'Bannon, John A. Russo, Russell Streiner; **C:** Jules Brenner.

Return of the Living Dead 2 🐾½ 1988 (R) An inevitable sequel to the original Dan O'Barron satire about zombies attacking suburbia with zest and vigor. 89m/C VHS, DVD. Dane Ashbrook, Marsha Diette n, Philip Bruns, James Karen, Thom Mathews, Suzanne Snyder, Micheal Kenworthy, Thor Van Lingen; **D:** Ken Wiederhorn; **W:** Ken Wiederhorn; **C:** Robert Elswit.

Return of the Living Dead 3 🐾½ 1993 (R) When Curt's girlfriend Julie dies in a motorcycle accident you'd think that would be the end of romance. But not when your dad heads a secret project that involves reviving corpses. Only problem is now Julie's a zombie with a long metal claws and glass spikes sticking out of various body parts. Hey, if it's true love Curt will get over it. Macabre special effects. Also available unrated. 97m/C VHS, DVD. Melinda (Mindy) Clarke, J. Trevor Edmond, Kent McCord, Basil Wallace, Fabio Urena; **D:** Brian Yuzna; **W:** John Penney; **C:** Gerry Lively; **M:** Barry Goldberg.

Return of the Living Dead: Rave to the Grave 🐾 2005 (R)
Don't expect much from the franchise and you won't be disappointed. In this fifth installment, university chemist Garrison

(Coyote) creates a toxin that is discovered by a group of buds who made their own designer drug. One pill gets you high but use too many and you become a brain-eating zombie. Just in time to party at the campus Halloween rave. 86m/C DVD. Peter Coyote, Aimee-Lynn Chadwick, Cory Hardrict, Jenny Mollen; **D:** Ellory Elkayem; **W:** William Butler, Aaron Strongoni; **C:** Gabriel Kosuth.

VIDEO

Return of the Magnificent Seven 🐾🐾 1966 The first sequel to "The Magnificent Seven" features the original seven who is held hostage. Yawn. 96m/C VHS, Robert Vaughn, Yul Brynner, Warren Oates, Robert Fuller, John Saxon; **W:** Larry Cohen; **C:** Paul Vogel; **M:** Elmer Bernstein.

Return of the Man from U.N.C.L.E. 🐾 1983 Those dashing super agents Napoleon Solo and Illya Kuryakin come out of retirement to settle an old score with their nemesis THRUSH. 96m/C VHS. Robert Vaughn, David McCallum, Patrick Macnee, Gayle Hunnicutt, Geoffrey Lewis; **D:** Ray Austin. **TV**

The Return of the Musketeers 🐾🐾 1989 (PG) Lester's third Musketeers film (after his successful double-act in the '70s) is a good-natured but average costume/comedy film. Twenty years after D'Artagnan, Athos, Porthos, and Aramis saved the French queen from scandal its time to do it all over again. Milady DeWinter, who hatched the first plot, is dead but her equally devious daughter Justine is more than able to take mama's scheming place. Just to add a little more excitement, Athos' adopted son Raoul meets Justine and passions fly amidst the swordplay. Based on the Alexandre Dumas novel "Twenty Years After." 103m/C VHS, GB FR SP Michael York, Oliver Reed, Frank Finlay, Richard Chamberlain, Kim Cattrall, C. Thomas Howell, Geraldine Chaplin, Roy Kinnear, Christopher Lee, Philippe Noiret, Jean-Pierre Cassel, Billy Connolly, Eusebio Lazaro; **D:** Richard Lester; **W:** George MacDonald Fraser.

The Return of the Native 🐾🐾½ 1994 (PG) Wind-swept moors, a tempestuous heroine, two loves, and requisite tragedy all courtesy of Thomas Hardy's 1878 novel. Beautiful Eustacia Vye (Jones) longs to leave the boredom of Egdon Heath—even though she's involved with the roguish Damon Wildeve (Owen). Then businessman Clym Yeobright (Stevenson) returns from Paris and captures Eustacia's fancy. She marries him in the hope they'll return to the continent but she's bitterly disappointed when Clym wants to remain in Egdon. Meanwhile, Damon has married Clym's gentle cousin Thomasin (Skinner) but he and Eustacia can't seem to stay away from each other, leading to tragedy for all. 99m/C VHS, DVD. Catherine Zeta-Jones, Clive Owen, Ray Stevenson, Claire Skinner, Joan Pioneer, Steven Mackintosh, Celia Imrie, Paul Rogers; **D:** Jack Gold; **W:** Robert W. Lenski; **M:** Carl Davis. **TV**

Return of the Pink Panther 🐾🐾½ 1974 (G) Bumbling Inspector Clouseau is called upon to rescue the Pink Panther diamond stolen from a museum. Sellers manages to produce mayhem with a vacuum cleaner and other devices that, in his hands, become instruments of terror. Clever opening credits. Fourth installment in the Pink Panther series but the first with Sellers since 1964's "A Shot in the Dark." 113m/C VHS, DVD. Peter Sellers, Christopher Plummer, Catherine Schell, Herbert Lom, Victor Spinetti; **D:** Blake Edwards; **W:** Frank Waldman, Blake Edwards; **C:** Geoffrey Unsworth; **M:** Henry Mancini.

Return of the Rebels 🐾🐾 1981 TV fluff with Eden as a motorcycle matron whose campground is rid of riff-raff by the crow-lined participants in a 25-year reunion of a biker gang. 100m/C VHS. Barbara Eden, Robert Mandan, Jamie Farr, Patrick Swayze, Don Murray, Christopher Connelly; **D:** Noel Nosseck. **TV**

Return to Africa 🐾🐾 1989 Rebels threaten the familial paradise of the tightknit Mallory clan. 95m/C VHS, Stan Brock, Anne Collings, David Tors, Ivan Tors, Peter Tors, Steven Tors; **D:** Leslie Martinson.

Return to Boggy Creek 🐾🐾 1977 (PG) Townspeople in a small fishing village learn from a photographer that "killer" beast, whom they thought had disappeared, has returned and is living in Boggy Creek. Some curious children follow the shutterbug into the marsh, despite hurricane warnings, and the swamp monster reacts with unusual compassion. OK for the kiddies. Fictitious story unlike other "Boggy Creek" films, which are billed as semi-documentaries. Sequel to "Legend of Boggy Creek" and features Mary Ann from "Gilligan's Island." 87m/C VHS. Dawn

Return of the Secaucus 7 🐾🐾🐾½ 1980 Centers around a weekend reunion of seven friends who were activists during the Vietnam War in the turbulent '60s. Now turning 30, they evaluate their present lives and progress. Writer and director Sayles plays Howie in this excellent example of a low-budget film can and should be. A less trendy predecessor of "The Big Chill" (1983) which, perhaps, was a few years ahead of its time. 110m/C VHS, DVD. Mark Arnott, Gordon Clapp, Maggie Cousineau-Arndt, David Stratmann, Adam LeFevre, Bruce MacDonald, Maggie Renzi, Jean Passanante, Karen Trott; **D:** John Sayles; **W:** John Sayles; **C:** Austin De Besche; **M:** Mason Daring, L.A. Film. Reg. '97.

Return of the Soldier 🐾🐾🐾 1982 A shell-shocked WWI veteran has no memory of his marriage, leaving his wife, his childhood flame, and an unrequited love to vie for his affections. Adapted from the novel by Rebecca West. 101m/C VHS, DVD. GB Glenda Jackson, Julie Christie, Ann-Margret, Alan Bates, Ian Holm, Frank Finlay; **D:** Alan Bridges; **M:** Richard Rodney Bennett.

Return of the Street Fighter 🐾🐾½ 1974 Sequel to "The Street Fighter" finds Terry Tsuguri (Chiba) hired by a gang to silence a jailed informer. So, Terry gets arrested, practices his karate and does the guy in. Big mistake! Notice a pattern yet? Followed by "The Street Fighter's Last Revenge" and "Sister Street Fighter." 88m/C VHS. JP Sonny Chiba, Claude Gannon; **D:** Shigehiro (Sakae) Ozawa; **W:** Hajime Kowa, Koji Takada; **C:** Taiji Yoshida.

Return of the Tall Blond Man with One Black Shoe 🐾🐾 Le Retour du Grand Blond 1974 Sequel to "The Tall Blond Man with One Black Shoe." Again a "klutz" is mistaken for a master spy and becomes unknowingly involved in the world of international intrigue. In French with English subtitles. Not quite as good as the original. 84m/C VHS. FR Pierre Richard, Mireille Darc, Michel Duchaussoy, Jean Rochefort, Jean Carmet; **D:** Yves Robert; **W:** Francis Veber; **M:** Vladimir Cosma.

Return of the Tiger 🐾½ 1978 The Hoover Night Club in Bangkok fronts the operations of an international narcotics group headed by an American. When a rival Chinese gang tries to dominate the drug market, conflict and lots of kicking ensue. 95m/C VHS, DVD. Bruce Li, Paul Smith, Chiang I, Angela (Mao Ying) Mao; **D:** Jimmy Shaw.

Return of the Vampire 🐾🐾 1943 A Hungarian vampire and his werewolf servant seek revenge on the family who drove a spike through his heart two decades earlier. 69m/B VHS, DVD. Bela Lugosi, Nina Foch, Miles Mander, Matt Willis, Frieda Inescort, Roland Varno, Gilbert Emery, Ottola Nesmith; **D:** Lew Landers; **W:** Griffin Jay; **C:** L.W. O'Connell, John Stumar.

Return of Wildfire 🐾½ 1948 Two sisters are left to run the family horse ranch when their brother is killed. A drifter aids the sisters in bringing the murderer to justice. 83m/B VHS, Richard Arlen, Patricia Morison, Mary Beth Hughes, James Millican, Reed Hadley, Chris-Pin (Esther Criscin Martin) Martin, Stanley Andrews, Holly (Mike Ragan) Bane; **D:** Ray Taylor; **W:** Betty Burbridge; **C:** Ernest Miller.

Return to Cabin by the Lake 🐾½ 2001 Psychos never die—they always return to do evil. Presumed dead writer/serial killer Stanley Caldwell (Nelson) isn't dead at all. In fact, he infiltrates a movie crew making a film adaptation of the circumstances of his killing spree. But Stanley doesn't like the way events are being portrayed, so he bumps off the director (Krause) and takes control. Campy rather than scary. 89m/C VHS, DVD. Judd Nelson, Brian Krause, Dahlia Salem, P. Nortney, Emmanuelle Vaugier; **D:** Po-Chih Leung; **W:** Jeffrey Reddick; **C:** Stephen M. Katz; **M:** Frankie Blue. **CABLE**

Return to Earth 🐾🐾 1976 Drama deals with the self-doubts faced by Apollo 11 astronaut Buzz Aldrin after his thirty-third return to Earth. Based on Aldrin's own novel. 74m/C VHS, Cliff Robertson, Shirley Knight, Ralph Bellamy, Stefanie Powers, Charles Cioffi; **D:** Jud Taylor. **TV**

Return to Eden 🐾🐾 1989 A young woman falls in love with her philosophy tutor, but he can't return her affections. An interesting comparison between the passion of the primitive and the tangle of modern-day romance. 90m/C VHS, Sam Bottoms, Edward Bins, Renée Coleman; **D:** William Olsen.

Return to Fantasy Island 🐾🐾 1977 Boss, boss, it's da plane! The second full-length TV treatment of the once-popular series wherein three couples get their most cherished fantasy fulfilled by Mr. Roarke and company. 90m/C VHS, DVD. Ricardo Montalban, Herve Villechaize, Adrienne Barbeau, Patrick Duffy, Joseph Campanella, Karen Valentine, Laraine Day, George Maharis, Horst Buchholz, France Nuyen, Joseph Cotten, Cameron Mitchell, George Chakiris; **D:** George McCowan. **TV**

Return to Frogtown WOOF! 1992
(PG-13) Sequel to "Hell Comes to Frogtown" finds Texas Rocket Ranger Ferrigno captured by mutant frogs. As unbelievably bad as it sounds. 90m/C VHS, DVD. Lou Ferrigno, Charles Napier, Robert ZDar, Denice Duff, Don Stroud; **D:** Donald G. Jackson.

Return to Horror High 🐾 1987
(R) A horror movie producer makes a film in an abandoned and haunted high school, where a series of murders occurred years earlier. As in most "return" flicks, history repeats itself. 95m/C VHS, DVD. Alex Rocco, Vince Edwards, Philip McKeon, Brendan Hughes, Lori Lethin, Scott Jacoby, George Clooney, Maureen McCormick; **D:** Bill Froelich; **W:** Bill Froelich, Mark Lisson, Dana Escalante, Greg H. Sims, Nancy Forner; **C:** Roy Wagner; **M:** Stacy Widelitz.

Return to House on Haunted Hill 🐾½ 2007 (R) Typical haunted house fflick. Sarah survived the massacre at Vannacutt Mansion only to later commit suicide. Now her sister Ariel is investigating, aided by the diary of Dr. Vanacutt which speaks of a diabolical evil inhabiting the house. But the mansion also contains a relic worth millions, and several treasure-seekers come to claim it, although the house has other ideas. 81m/C DVD, Blu-ray Disc, HD DVD. Erik Palladino, Cerina Vincent, Tom Riley, Jeffrey Combs, Amanda Righetti, Andrew Lee Potts, Steven Pacey; **D:** Victor Garcia; **M:** Frederik Wiedmann. **VIDEO**

Return to Lonesome Dove 🐾🐾½ 1993 Routine sequel to successful western saga "Lonesome Dove" picks up after the burial of Gus McCrae by his friend, ex-Texas Ranger Woodrow F. Call (now played by Voight). The original dealt with a cattle drive, this one with horses. Along the way you'll run into the usual sidewinders as well as McCrae's lost love Clara (now Hershey) and Schroder, returning as Call's unacknowledged son Newt. Filmed on location in Montana. TV production was already in the works when author Larry McMurtry gave the producers his then unpublished sequel "Streets of Laredo" which differed from the book and changes were made but the book and miniseries don't match. 330m/C VHS. Dawn

Return of the Soldier Wells, Dana Plato, Louise Belaire, John Hoteus; **D:** Tom (Thomas R.) Moore.

Jon Voight, William L. Petersen, Rick Schroder, Barbara Hershey, Louis Gossett Jr., Oliver Reed, Reese Witherspoon, Nia Peeples, Dennis Haysbert, Timothy Scott, Barry Tubb, Chris Cooper, CCH Pounder, William Sanderson; **D:** Mike Robe; **W:** John Wilder. **TV**

Return to Macon County 🐾🐾
1975 Tale of three young, reckless youths who become involved with drag racing and a sadistic law enforcement officer. Nolte turns in a good performance in his first film, as does Johnson, despite a mediocre script and dialogue. Sequel to 1974's "Macon County Line." **90m/C VHS.** Nick Nolte, Don Johnson, Robin Mattson; **D:** Richard Compton; **W:** Richard Compton.

Return to Mayberry 🐾🐾 1985
Andy Taylor returns to Mayberry after 20 years to obtain his old job as sheriff. Sixteen of the original actors reappeared for this nostalgia-fest. **95m/C VHS.** Andy Griffith, Ron Howard, Don Knotts, Jim Nabors, Aneta Corsaut, Jada Dodson, George Lindsey, Betty Lynn; **D:** Bob Sweeney. **TV**

Return to Me 🐾🐾1/2 2000 (PG)
Widowed building contractor Bob (Duchovny) is uneasy about getting involved in a new romance (particularly after some pathetic blind dates) but meets waitress Grace (Driver) and suddenly love is in the air. However, Grace is reluctant to reveal that she's had a heart transplant. But what's she going to do when she discovers that the donor heart came from Bob's beloved late wife. The best romance, however, might be between the testily loving marrieds, the Daytons (Hunt, Belushi), who are Grace's best friends. Directorial debut of Hunt is soapy without being sappy. **113m/C VHS, DVD.** David Duchovny, Minnie Driver, James Belushi, Bonnie Hunt, Carroll O'Connor, Robert Loggia, David Alan Grier, Joely Richardson, Eddie Jones, Marianne Muellerleile, William Bronder; **D:** Bonnie Hunt; **W:** Bonnie Hunt, Don Lake; **C:** Laszlo Kovacs; **M:** Nicholas Pike.

Return to Never Land 🐾🐾1/2
2002 (G) Losing much of the charm and magic of the 1953 Disney animated classic "Peter Pan," this sequel picks up years after the other left off and finds Peter (Weaver), Tinker Bell, and the rest of the gang in Never Land. Wendy (Soucie), however, is now grown and married with a daughter of her own, the spunky Jane (Owen), whose skepticism about her mother's wild tales fades after she is kidnaped by Captain Hook (Burton), still on a quest for the treasure he believes Pan stole. She then finds her way to Peter and more adventure with her mom's old pals. Innocuous and generic but refined Disney entry works for the youngest viewers but older children and parents won't find anything deeper for them. Nice blend of digital and traditional animation. **72m/C VHS, DVD. US D:** Robin Budd; **V:** Temple Mathews; **M:** Joel McNeely; **V:** Blayne Weaver, Harriet Owen, Corey Burton, Jeff Glenn Bennett, Kath Soucie, Roger Rees, Spencer Breslin, Andrew McDonough.

Return to Oz 🐾🐾1/2 1985 (PG)
Picking up where "The Wizard of Oz" left off, Auntie Em and Uncle Ed place Dorothy in the care of a therapist to cure her "delusions" of Oz. A natural disaster again lands her in the land of the yellow brick road, where the evil Nome King and Princess Mombi are spreading terror and squalor. Based on a later L. Frank Baum book. Enjoyable for the whole family although some scenes may frighten very small children. **109m/C VHS, DVD.** Fairuza Balk, Piper Laurie, Matt Clark, Nicol Williamson, Jean Marsh; **D:** Walter Murch; **W:** Walter Murch, Gill Dennis; **C:** David Watkin; **M:** David Shire.

Return to Paradise 🐾🐾 1953
Cooper is a soldier of fortune wandering through the Polynesian islands in the late 1920s. On a remote atoll he comes across a crazy missionary intent upon subduing the native population. Cooper falls in love with a native beauty (Haynes in her screen debut) and leads the natives in a revolt against authority. Cliched but with nice scenery from the location shoot in Samoa. Loose adaptation of the short story "Mr. Morgan" by James Michener. **100m/C VHS.** Gary Cooper, Roberta Haynes, Barry Jones, John Hudson, Moira MacDonald; **D:** Mark Robson; **W:** Charles A. Kaufman.

Return to Paradise 🐾🐾 All for
One 1998 (R) Sheriff (Vaughn) and Tony (Conrad), along with their new friend Lewis (Phoenix), take a vice-filled vacation in Malaysia. Done with the partying, the two New Yorkers return home while Lewis stays in Asia to work with orangutans. Two years later, Lewis is in a Malaysian prison, facing execution for a brick of hashish, which Sheriff haphazardly tossed into the garbage. Enter Heche as lawyer Beth, who finds Sheriff and tells him that in order to save Lewis, he and Tony must return and take their share of the responsibility (and serve time in a squalid third-world prison). Despite contributing an important twist to the extremely powerful climax, Pinkett Smith's role feels too contrived and is the biggest flaw in the film. Loose retelling of the 1989 French film "Force Majeure." **112m/C VHS, DVD.** Vince Vaughn, Joaquin Rafaol (Leaf) Phoenix, Anne Heche, David Conrad, Jada Pinkett Smith, Vera Farmiga, Nick Sandow; **D:** Joseph Ruben; **W:** Wesley Strick, Bruce Robinson; **C:** Reynaldo Villalobos; **M:** Mark Mancina.

Return to Peyton Place 🐾🐾1/2
1961 A young writer publishes novel exposing town as virtual Peyton Place, and the townsfolk turn against her and her family. Sequel to the scandalously popular '50s original and inspiration for the just-as-popular soap opera. Astor is excellent as the evil matriarch. **122m/C VHS, DVD.** Carol Lynley, Jeff Chandler, Eleanor Parker, Mary Astor, Robert Sterling, Luciana Paluzzi, Tuesday Weld, Brett Halsey, Bob Crane; **D:** Jose Ferrer.

Return to Salem's Lot 🐾🐾
1987 (R) Enjoyable camp sequel to the Stephen King tale, this time involving a cynical scientist and his son returning to the town only to find it completely run by vampires. **101m/C VHS.** Michael Moriarty, Ricky Addison Reed, Samuel Fuller, June Havoc, Evelyn Keyes, Jill Gatsby, Jack Gatsby, Ronee Blakley, James Dixon, David Holbrook; **D:** Larry Cohen; **W:** Larry Cohen, James Dixon; **C:** Daniel Pearl. **VIDEO**

Return to Snowy River 🐾🐾🐾
1988 (PG) Continues the love story of the former ranch hand and the rancher's daughter in Australia's Victoria Alps that began in "The Man From Snowy River." Dennehy takes over from Kirk Douglas as the father who aims to keep the lovers apart. The photography of horses and the scenery is spectacular, making the whole film worthwhile. **99m/C VHS, DVD. AU** Tom Burlinson, Sigrid Thornton, Brian Dennehy, Nicholas Eadie, Mark Hembrow, Bryan Marshall; **D:** Geoff Burrowes; **W:** Geoff Burrowes.

Return to the Blue Lagoon 🐾
1991 (PG-13) Neither the acting nor the premise has improved with age. Another photogenic adolescent couple experiences puberty on that island; for continuity, the young man is the son of the lovers in the first "Blue Lagoon." Breathtaking scenery—just turn down the sound. **102m/C VHS, DVD.** Milla Jovovich, Brian Krause, Lisa Pelikan; **D:** William A. Graham; **C:** Robert Steadman.

Return to the Lost World 🐾🐾1/2 1993 (PG)
Rival scientists Challenger and Summerlee set out for the Lost World and find it threatened by oil prospectors. With a volcano about to explode the scientists set out to save their prehistoric paradise and its dinosaur inhabitants. Based on a story by Sir Arthur Conan Doyle. Sequel to "The Lost World." **99m/C VHS, DVD.** John Rhys-Davies, David Warner, Darren Peter Mercer, Geza Kovacs; **D:** Timothy Bond.

Return to Two Moon Junction 🐾1/2 1993 (R)
New York supermodel Savannah (Clarke) returns to her family's riverfront home in Georgia and promptly sheds her clothing for local sculptor Jake (Schafer). Must be something about the southern heat. This sequel should have the same video success as its predecessor since it keeps to the minimal plot/maximum teasing sex scenes outline. **96m/C VHS.** Melinda (Mindy) Clarke, John Clayton Schafer, Louise Fletcher; **D:** Farhad Mann.

Return to Waterloo 🐾🐾 1985 (PG-13)
Experimental musical concept from the Kinks' Ray Davies about an everyman commuter (Colley) who is either having a nervous breakdown or living in a fantasy world or both. As he rides the train tions, his fellow passengers burst into song and things get increasingly violent. Also includes "Come Dancing with the Kinks," with videos of eight songs, including "Lola" and "Come Dancing." **95m/C VHS, DVD. GB** Ray Davies, Gretchen Franklin, Tim Roth; **D:** Ray Davies; **W:** Ray Davies; **C:** Roger Deakins; **M:** Ray Davies.

Reuben, Reuben 🐾🐾🐾 1983 (R)
Brilliant, but drunken poet Conti turns himself around when he falls in love with early college girl McGillis in his film debut. The student's dog Reuben unwittingly alters Conti's progress, however, in the film's startling conclusion. Based on the writings of Peter DeVries. **100m/C VHS.** Tom Conti, Kelly McGillis, Roberts Blossom, E. Katherine Kerr, Cynthia Harris, Joel Fabiani, Kara Wilson, Lois Smith; **D:** Robert Ellis Miller; **W:** Julius J. Epstein; **M:** Billy Goldenberg. Natl. Bd. of Review '83: Actor (Conti); Writers Guild '83: Adapt. Screenplay.

Reunion 🐾🐾 1936
The Chamber of Commerce holds a testimonial dinner for the humble Dr. John Luke at which the Dionne quintuplets and many other townies join in sharing how he's helped them all. **80m/B VHS.** Jean Hersholt, Rochelle Hudson, Helen Vinson; **D:** Norman Tourog; **W:** Bruce Gould. **VIDEO**

Reunion 🐾🐾🐾 1988 (PG-13)
Robards stars as a Jewish businessman, living in the U.S., who returns to his boyhood home of Stuttgart, Germany some 50 years after his leaving in 1933. He hopes to find out what happened to a boyhood school chum—the son of an aristocractic (and Aryan) German family. Film uses extensive flashbacks to show the rise of anti-Semitism and how it affects the friendship of both youths. Thoughtful and well-acted though occasionally plodding drama based on Fred Uhlman's novel. **120m/C VHS. FR GE GB** Jason Robards Jr., Christien Anholt, Samuel West, Francoise Fabian, Maureen Kerwin, Barbara Jefford, Alexander Trauner; **D:** Jerry Schatzberg; **W:** Harold Pinter; **C:** Bruno De Keyzer.

Revelation 🐾 2000
In the continuing adventures based on the "Left Behind" novels (a conservative Christian interpretation of the Book of Revelation), a counter-terrorism expert (Fahey) goes up against a Messiah (Mancuso) out to rule the world, etc., etc. **97m/C DVD.** Jeff Fahey, Nick Mancuso, Carol Alt, Leigh Lewis; **D:** Andre Van Heerden; **W:** Peter LaLonde, Paul LaLonde; **C:** Jiri (George) Tirf.

Revenge 🐾🐾1/2 Terror under the House,
After Jenny Died; Inn of the Frightened People 1971 The parents of a girl who was brutally killed take the law into their own hands in this bloody, vengeful thriller. **89m/C VHS. GB** Joan Collins, James Booth, Ray Barrett, Sinead Cusack, Kenneth Griffith; **D:** Sidney Hayers.

Revenge woof! 1986 (R)
Sequel to "Blood Cult" about a cult led by horror king Carradine. Seems these dog worshippers want McGowan's land and Senator Carradine will stop at nothing to get it. Woofer filled with gratuitous violence. **104m/C VHS, DVD.** Patrick Wayne, John Carradine, Bennie Lee McGowan, Josef Hanet, Stephanie Kropke; **D:** Christopher Lewis; **W:** Christopher Lewis; **C:** Steve McWilliams; **M:** Rod Slane.

Revenge 🐾🐾 1990 (R)
Retired pilot Costner makes the mistake of falling in love with another man's wife. Quinn gives a first-rate performance as the Mexican crime lord who punishes his spouse and her lover, beginning a cycle of vengeance. Sometimes contrived, but artfully photographed with tantalizing love scenes. Based on the Jim Harrison novel. **123m/C VHS, DVD, Blu-ray Disc.** Kevin Costner, Anthony Quinn, Madeleine Stowe, Sally Kirkland, Joe Santos, Miguel Ferrer, James Gammon, Tomas Milian; **D:** Tony Scott; **W:** Jim Harrison; **M:** Jack Nitzsche.

Revenge in the House of Usher 🐾🐾 1985
Mad Eric Usher, the last of his equally insane family, lives in a creepy cliffside house with vampire-ghost Helen. Then he invites Alan Harker for a visit, and Alan's accepting is a big mistake on his part. **90m/C VHS, DVD. FR** Howard Vernon, Anthony (Jose J. Antonio, J.A.) Mayans, Dan Villers, Lina Romay; **D:** Jess (Jesus) Franco; **C:** Alain Hardy; **M:** Daniel White.

The Revenge of Frankenstein 🐾🐾1/2 1958
Frankenstein (Cushing) is rescued from the guillotine by his dwarf servant and decides to relocate to Carlsbruck where he becomes the popular society physician, Dr. Stein. But the misunderstood doc just can't stop his ghoulish experiments and plans to transfer his servant's brain into another sewn together creature. Nicely macabre sequel to "The Curse of Frankenstein"; followed by "The Evil of Frankenstein." **89m/C VHS, DVD. GB** Peter Cushing, Michael Gwynn, Francis Matthews, Oscar Quitak, Lionel Jeffries, Eunice Gayson, John Welsh; **D:** Terence Fisher; **W:** Jimmy Sangster.

Revenge of the Barbarians 🐾
La Vendetta dei Barbari 1960 As the barbarians descend on Rome, Olympus must decide whether to save the empire or the beautiful Gallo, the woman he loves. Decisions, decisions. **104m/C VHS. IT** Robert Alda, Anthony Steel, Tom Felleghi, Daniela Rocca; **D:** Giuseppe Vari; **C:** Gastone Ranazzotti; **C:** Sergio Pesce; **M:** Roberto Nicolosi.

Revenge of the Barbarians 🐾
Hrafnin Flygur; When the Raven Files 1985 A Scandinavian adventure about a young Celt seeking revenge against the Viking hordes that killed his family. **95m/C VHS, DVD. IC** Helgi Skulason, Jakob Thor Einarsson, Edda Bjorgvinsdottir, Egill Olafsson, Flosi Olafsson; **D:** Hrafn Gunnlaugsson; **W:** Hrafn Gunnlaugsson; **C:** Tony Forsberg.

Revenge of the Cheerleaders 🐾 1976 (R)
The cheerleaders pull out all the stops to save their school from a ruthless land developer. What spirit. **86m/C VHS, DVD.** Jerii Woods, Cheryl "Rainbeaux" Smith, Helen Lang, Patrice Rohmer, Susie Elene, Eddra Gale, William Bramley, Carl Ballantine, David Hasselhoff; **D:** Richard Lerner.

Revenge of the Creature 🐾 1955
In this follow up to "The Creature from the Black Lagoon," the Gill-man is captured in the Amazon and taken to a Florida marine park. There he is put on display for visitors and subjected to heartless experiments. Growing restless in his captive surroundings, the creature breaks free and makes for the ocean. Includes screen debut of Clint Eastwood as a lab technician. Originally shot in 3-D. Based on a story by William Alland. **82m/B VHS, DVD.** John Agar, Lori Nelson, John Bromfield, Nestor Paiva, Clint Eastwood, Grandon Rhodes, Charles Cane; **D:** Jack Arnold; **W:** Martin Berkeley; **C:** Charles S. Welbourne; **M:** Joseph Gershenson.

Revenge of the Dead 🐾 1984 (R)
European archeological team discovers the existence of a powerful force that allows the dead to return to life. **100m/C VHS, DVD. IT** Gabriele Lavia, Anne Canoras; **D:** Pupi Avati.

Revenge of the Living Zombies 🐾 1988 (R)
Teens on a Halloween hayride run headlong into flesh-craving zombies. Available in a slightly edited version. **85m/C VHS, DVD. Bill** (William

Heinzman) Hinzman, John Mowod, Leslie Ann Wick, Kevin Kindlin; **D:** Bill (William Heinzman) Hinzman.

Revenge of the Musketeers ♂♂½
Daughter, La Fille de D'Artagnan 1994 (R) Excitng swashbuckler that finds the beautiful Eloise (Marceau) uncovering a dastardly plot by the Duc de Crassac (Rich) to kill King Louis XIV (Legros). She goes to her father, aging Musketeer D'Artagnan (Noiret), and he seeks the aid of old compatriots Athos (Eideau), Porthos (Billeray), and Aramis (Frey). Since Eloise can handle a sword as well as any of the Musketeers, she gets her own share of derring-do. French with subtitles. **130m/C VHS, DVD** Sophie Marceau, Philippe Noiret, Sami Frey, Claude Rich, Nils Tavernier; **C:** Patrick Blossier; **M:** Philippe Sarde.

Revenge of the Nerds ♂♂½
1984 (R) When nerdy college freshmen are victimized by jocks, frat boys and the school's beauties, they start their own fraternity and seek revenge. Carradine and Edwards team as well as the geeks in this better than average teenage sex comedy. Guess who gets the girls? Sequel was much worse. **89m/C VHS, DVD, Robert Carradine, Anthony Edwards, Timothy Busfield, Andrew Cassese, Curtis Armstrong, Ted McGinley, Brian Tochi, Julia Montgomery, Michelle Meyrink, John Goodman, Bernie Casey; D: Jeff Kanew; W: Tim Metcalfe, Jeff Buhai; C: King Baggot; M: Thomas Newman.

Revenge of the Nerds 2: Nerds in Paradise ♂
1987 (PG-13) The nerd clan from the first film (minus Edwards who only makes a brief appearance) travels to Fort Lauderdale for a fraternity conference. They fend off loads of bullies and jocks with raunchy humor. Boy can Booger belch. Not as good as the first Nerds movie, a few laughs nonetheless. **89m/C VHS, DVD, Robert Carradine, Curtis Armstrong, Timothy Busfield, Andrew Cassese, Ed Lauter, Larry B. Scott, Courtney Thorne-Smith, Anthony Edwards, James Hong; D: Joe Roth; W: Dan Guntzelman, Steve Marshall; C: Charles Correll; M: Mark Mothersbaugh.

Revenge of the Nerds 3: The Next Generation ♂½
1992 Yes, even nerds deserve a little love. This time the gang get together for Booger's (Armstrong) wedding—complete with nerd bachelor party and wedding shower. Too reluctant to have a nerd in the family that he hires a sleazy detective to dig up some dirt. Made for TV. **90m/C VHS, Curtis Armstrong, Robert Carradine, Ted McGinley, Larry B. Scott, Donald Gibb, Joseph Bologna, Julia Montgomery, Corinne Bohrer, Christina Pickles, Jessica Tuck, Robert Picardo; D: Steve Zacharias; W: Steve Zacharias, Steve Buhai. TV

Revenge of the Ninja ♂♂½
1983 (R) Ninja Kosugi hopes to escape his past in Los Angeles. A drug trafficker, also with amusing surreal touches like a battling grandma ninja. Sequel to "Enter the Ninja," followed by "Ninja III." **90m/C VHS, DVD, Sho Kosugi, Arthur Roberts, Keith Vitali, Virgil Frye, Ashley Ferrare, Kane (Takeshi) Kosugi, John Lamotta, Grace Oshita, Melvin C. Hampton, Mario Gallo; D: Sam Firstenberg; W: Michael Lewis, Sites; M: Rob Walsh. W. Michael Lewis.

Revenge of the Pink Panther ♂♂½
1978 (PG) Inspector Clouseau survives his own assassination attempt, but allows the world to think he is

dead in order to pursue an investigation of the culprits in his own unique, bumbling way. The last "Pink Panther" film before Sellers died, and perhaps the least funny. **99m/C VHS, DVD, Peter Sellers, Herbert Lom, Dyan Cannon, Robert Webber, Burt Kwouk, Robert Loggia; D: Blake Edwards; W: Frank Waldman, Blake Edwards, Ron Clark; C: Ernest Day; M: Henry Mancini.

Revenge of the Radioactive Reporter ♂½
1991 Nuclear plant honchos don't like journalist who's about to hang their dirty laundry, so they toss him into vat of nuclear waste. He returns as a reporter with a cosmetic peel. **90m/C VHS, David Scammell, Kathryn Boese, Randy Pearlstein, Derrick Strange; D: Craig Pryce.

Revenge of the Red Baron ♂♂½
1993 (PG-13) Jim Spencer (Rooney) is the WWI pilot who shot down Germany's fearsome Red Baron. Now aged and infirm he's tormented by what he thinks is his enemy's ghost. A vengeful ghost who takes after Spencer's family. **90m/C VHS, DVD, Mickey Rooney, Tobey Maguire, Laraine Newman, Cliff DeYoung; D: Robert Gordon; W: Michael James McDonald; C: Christian Sebaldt.

Revenge of the Stepford Wives ♂½
1980 TV sequel to the Ira Levin fantasy about suburban husbands who create obedient robot replicas of their wives. In this installment, the wives are not robots, but are simply made docile by drugs. Strange casting pairs Johnson and Kavner as husband and stepford wife. Begat "The Stepford Children." **95m/C VHS, Sharon Gless, Julie Kavner, Don Johnson, Audra Lindley, Mason Adams, Arthur Hill; D: Robert Fuest. TV

Revenge of the Teenage Vixens from Outer Space ♂♂
1986 A low-budget film about three sex starved females from another planet who come to earth to find men. When the ones they meet do not live up to their expectations, the frustrated females turn the disappointing studies are turned into vegetables. **84m/C VHS, Lisa Schwedop, Howard Scott, Jeff Ferrell.

Revenge of the Virgins ♂
1962 A tribe of topless 'Indian' women protect their sacred land from the white men. Exhumed exploitation for bad-film junkies, narrated by Kenne Duncan, an Ed Wood cohort. **53m/B VHS, DVD, Jewell Morgan, Charles Veltman, Jodean Russo, Stanton Pritchard; D: Paul Perri; Nar: Kenne Duncan.

Revenge of the Zombies ♂½
1943 In this sequel of sorts to "King of the Zombies," Carradine is creating an army of the undead for use by an evil foreign entity. **61m/B VHS, John Carradine, Robert Lowery, Gale Storm, Veda Ann Borg, Mantan Moreland; D: Steve Sekely.

Revenge Quest ♂
1986 In the year 2031, Trent McCormic, L.A.'s most violent serial killer, escapes from a maximum security prison on Mars. He's determined to kill Julie Myers, the woman who testified against him. LAPD detective Rick Castle is equally determined to protect her. **90m/C VHS, DVD, Brian Glushak, Christopher Michael Egger, Jennifer Aguilar; D: Alan De Herrera; W: Alan De Herrera; C: Alan De Herrera; M: Joseph Andalino. VIDEO

The Revenge Rider ♂
1935 Orphan McCoy goes after the villains who killed his parents. Good performance from McCoy in an otherwise average film. **60m/ B VHS, Tim McCoy, Robert "Tex" Allen, Billie Seward, Edward Earle, Jack Clifford, Lafe (Lafayette) McKee; D: David Selman.

The Revenger ♂♂
1990 A framed man returns from prison and finds that a mobster has kidnapped his wife and wants $50,000 to give her back. **91m/C VHS, DVD, Oliver Reed, Frank Zagarino; D: Cedric Sundstrom.

Reversal of Fortune ♂♂½
1990 (R) True tale of wealthy socialite Claus von Bulow (Irons), accused of deliberately giving his wife Sunny [Close] a near-lethal overdose of insulin. Comatose Close narrates history of the couple's courtship and married life, a saga of unhappiness and substance abuse, while

Silver (as lawyer Dershowitz) et al prepare von Bulow's defense. An unflattering picture of the idle rich that never spells out what really happened. Irons is excellent as the eccentric and creepy defendant and richly deserved his Best Actor Oscar. From the novel by Dershowitz. **112m/C VHS, DVD, Jeremy Irons, Glenn Close, Ron Silver, Annabella Sciorra, Uta Hagen, Fisher Stevens, Julie Hagerty, Jack Gilpin, Christine Baranski, John David (J.D.) Cullum; D: Barbet Schroeder; W: Nicholas Kazan; GE HU Ferenc Zenthe, Mario Feliciani; D: Guido Malatesta.

The Revolt of Job ♂♂ *Job La-
zadása* 1984 An elderly Jewish couple adopts an eight-year-old Gentile boy although it is illegal in WWII-torn Hungary and against the beliefs of the orthodox community. Moving story with fine performances. **98m/C VHS, GE HU Hedi Temessy; D: Imre Gyongyossy, Barna Kabay.

Revolt of the Barbarians ♂ *La Rivolta dei Barbari* 1964 Ancient Rome is plagued by barbarian invasion and piracy. A consul travels to Gaul to try to put an end to their misdeeds. **99m/C VHS, IT Roland Carey, Maria Grazia Spina, Mario Feliciani.

Revolt of the Zombies ♂
1936 A mad scientist learns the secret of bringing the dead to life and musters the zombies into an unique, gruesome military unit during WWI. Strange early zombie flick looks silly by today's standards. **65m/B VHS, DVD, Dorothy Stone, Dean Jagger, Roy D'Arcy, Robert Noland, George Cleveland; D: Victor Halperin; W: Howard Higgin; C: Jockey A. Feindel, Arthur Martinelli.

Revolution ♂
1985 (R) The American Revolution is the setting for this failed epic centering on an illiterate trapper and his son who find themselves caught up in the fighting. Long and dull, which is unfortunate, because the story had some potential. The cast is barely believable in their individual roles. Where did you get that accent, Al? **125m/C VHS, DVD, GB Al Pacino, Donald Sutherland, Nastassia Kinski, Annie Lennox, Joan Plowright, Steven Berkoff, Dave King; D: Hugh Hudson; W: Robert Dillon.

Revolution! A Red Comedy ♂♂
1991 A group of students are lured away from their revolutionary tendencies by materialistic indulgences. This satirical comedy is in color and black and white. **84m/B VHS, Kimberly Flynn, Christopher Renstrom, Georg Osterman; D: Jeff Kahn; W: Jeff Kahn.

Revolution #9 ♂♂½
2001 James Jackson (Risley) is a late twenties worker drone in NYC who's just become engaged to Kim (Shelly) when his behavior undergoes a radical transformation. He's getting subliminal messages via commercials for a perfume called Revolution #9—the kind of messages that lead to worldwide conspiracy theories. His mental breakdown is diagnosed as schizophrenia with Kim bearing the brunt of James's paranoia and self-destructive behavior while she also tries to deal with the bureaucracy and inadequacies of the mental health system. Risley forgoes the histrionics often associated with playing a mentally ill character while Shelly displays the toughness of an ordinary woman confronted by a difficult situation. **91m/C VHS, DVD, US Michael Risley, Adrienne Shelly, Spalding Gray, Callie (Calliope) Thorne, Saxon Ryan, Marina Black; D: Tim McCann; W: Tim McCann; C: Tim McCann; M: Douglas J. Cuomo.

Revolver ♂♂
1992 (R) FBI agent Nick Sastro is paralyzed by an assassin's bullet when he tries to stop Aldo Testi, an arms and drug smuggler. But Nick decides to come out of retirement: when a chance to nail Testi comes his way. **95m/C VHS, Robert Urich, Dakin Matthews, Steven Williams, Assumpta Serna, Craig Hill; D: Gary Nelson.

Revolver ♂
2005 Director Ritchie sticks to lowlife criminals with little return. Ex-con Jake Green (Statham) decides to get even with casino-owning baddie Macha (Liotta), who set him up for a prison

stint. Jake wins big at the casino and Macha orders a hit to soothe his humiliation. Then Jake is picked up by con shark Zack (Pastore) and his partner Avi (Benjamin), who dispense a lot of silly psychobabble to no known purpose, which is par for the flick's general incoherence. **115m/C VHS, DVD, GB FR Jason Statham, Ray Liotta, Vincent Pastore, Andre Benjamin, Francesca Annis, Terence Maynard, Mark Strong, Andrew Howard; D: Guy Ritchie; W: Guy Ritchie; C: Tim Jones; M: Nathaniel Mechaly.

RFK ♂♂½
2002 Focuses on the years following the assassination of President John F. Kennedy (Donovan) as his brother Robert (Roache) pursued his own political career until his own assassination. **90m/C VHS, DVD, Linus Roache, James Cromwell, David Paymer, Martin Donovan, Ving Rhames, Mamie McPhail, Jacob Vargas, Sean Gregory Sullivan, Kevin Hare; D: Robert Dornhelm; W: Hank Steinberg; C: Derek Underschultz; M: Harald Kloser; Thomas Wanker CABLE

Rhapsody ♂♂½
1954 Taylor plays a wealthy woman torn between a famous young violinist and an equally talented pianist: in this long and overdrawn soap opera. Although Taylor gives a superb performance, it's not enough to save this surgarcoated musical romance. Includes lush European scenery and sequences of classical music dubbed in by Claudio Arrau and Michael Rabin. Based on the adaptation of the Henry Handel Richardson novel "Maurice Guest." **115m/C VHS, Elizabeth Taylor, Vittorio Gassman, John Ericson, Louis Calhern, Michael Chekhov, Barbara Bates, Celia Lovsky; D: Charles Vidor; W: Michael Karin, Fay Kanin.

Rhapsody ♂♂
2001 (R) In 1986, young hoods Jelly and Roughneck are caught out by an undercover cop in a drug deal. Jelly escapes arrest while Roughneck does time. Released from prison, Roughneck (Plummer) thinks his ex-partner (Phillips), who is now a successful music producer, owes him. **95m/C VHS, DVD, Glenn Plummer, Fred Williamson, Ice-T, Tee Phillips, Tone Loc, Freda Payne; D: Don Abernathy; W: Don Abernathy. VIDEO

Rhapsody in August ♂♂½
Hachigatsu no Kyohshikyoku 1991 (PG) Talky family drama has four children spending the summer with their grandmother Kane in Nagasaki. They become obsessed with the memorials and bomb sites commemorating the dropping of the atomic bomb in 1945 and their grandmother's experiences. Then Kane's Eurasian nephew (Gere) comes for a visit, inciting more family discussions. Adapted from the novel "Nabe-no-Naka" by Kiyoko Murata. Minor Kurosawa; in Japanese with English subtitles. **98m/C VHS, DVD, JP Sachiko Murase, Narumi Kayashima, Hisashi Igawa, Richard Gere; D: Akira Kurosawa; W: Akira Kurosawa; C: Takao Saito, Masaharu Ueda; M: Shinichiro Ikebe.

Rhapsody in Blue ♂♂
1945 Standard Hollywood biography of the great composer features whitewashed and non-existent characters to deal with the spottier aspects of George Gershwin's life. Still, the music is the main attraction and it doesn't disappoint. J.R.Rhapsody in Blue; Concerto in F; The Cuban Overture; Fascinatin' Rhythm; The Man I Love; Yankee Doodle Blues; Somebody Loves Me; Swanee; Mine. **139m/B VHS, Robert Alda, Joan Leslie, Alexis Smith, Charles Coburn, Julie Bishop, Albert Bassermann, Morris Carnovsky, Rosemary DeCamp, Herbert Rudley, Charles Halton, Robert Shayne, Johnny Downs, Al Joson; D: Irving Rapper; W: Howard Koch; M: Max Steiner, Ira Gershwin.

Rhapsody of Spring ♂♂
1998 Inspired by the life of one of China's most-respected composers. Zhao (Shao) comes of age during the Cultural Revolution and is torn between preserving the past and living in the present. He studies China's indigenous musical forms and becomes determined to compose a new type of opera that will combine traditional songs within a westernized orchestral arrangement, despite any disapproval. Mandarin with subtitles. **120m/C DVD, CH Bing Shao, Ying Qu, Quan Yuan; D: Wenji Teng; W: Wenji Teng, Ping He, Wu Hanqing; C: Lei Zhi; M: Yuhong Chang.

Rhinestone ♪ 1984 (PG) A country singer claims she can turn anyone, even a cabbie, into a singing sensation. Stuck with Stallone, Parton prepares her protege to sing at New York City's roughest country-western club, The Rhinestone. Only die-hard Dolly and Rocky fans need bother with this bunk. Some may enjoy watching the thick, New York accented Stallone learn how to properly pronounce dog ("dawg") in country lingo. Yee-haw. 111m/ C VHS, DVD. Sylvester Stallone, Dolly Parton, Ron Leibman, Richard Farnsworth, Tim Thomerson; D: Bob (Benjamin) Clark; W: Sylvester Stallone, Phil Alden Robinson. Golden Raspberries '84: Worst Actor (Stallone), Worst Song ("Drinkenstein").

Rhodes ♪♪♪½ Rhodes of Africa 1936 The story of Cecil Rhodes, a man who was instrumental in the Boer War in Africa and established the Rhodes Scholarships with $10 million, is told in this biography. Fine performance by Huston and Homolka. 91m/B VHS. GB Walter Huston, Oscar Homolka, Basil Sydney, Frank Cellier, Peggy Ashcroft, Renne De Vaux, Percy Parsons, Bernard Lee, Ndanisa Kumalo; D: Berthold Viertel.

Rhodes ♪♪½ 1997 British miniseries details the life of 19th-century colonialist, British-born Cecil Rhodes (Shaw), who makes his money in the South African diamond trade and decides to place as much African territory under Britain's flag as possible. Rhodes succeeded in begetting the nation of Rhodesia (now Zimbabwe), became involved in the bloody Boer War, and established the prestigious Rhodes scholarship at Oxford University. On three cassettes. 336m/C VHS. GB Martin Shaw, Frances Barber, Tim Dutton, David Butler, Ken Stott, Raymond Coulthard, Neil Pearson; D: David Drury; W: Antony Thomas; C: Alec Curtis; M: Alan Parker. TV

Rhythm on the Range ♪♪♪½ 1936 Crosby stars as a singing cowboy who befriends freight car stowaway Farmer while transporting his prize steer back to his ranch in California. He invites her to his domicile and she falls in love with life on the range and with the rancher himself. When the two fall in love they decide to strike off on their own but can't get their music heard since everyone assumes they've been copying Rathbone terrific as an insecure egomaniac. ♪Rhythm on the River; When the Moon Comes Over Madison Square; Ain't It a Shame About Mame?; What Would Shakespeare Have Said?; Only Forever; That's for Me; I Don't Want to Cry Anymore. 94m/B VHS, DVD. Bing Crosby, Mary Martin, Basil Rathbone, Oscar Levant, Oscar Shaw, Charley Grapewin, William Frawley, Charles Lane; D: Victor Schertzinger; W: Dwight Taylor; M: Victor Young.

Rhythm Parade ♪♪ 1943 A woman takes off for Hawaii, leaving her infant in the care of an L.A. nightclub singer. A jealous rival of the singer takes the opportunity to cause problems. The thin plot serves as a vehicle for lots of singing. ♪Tootin' My Own Horn; Petticoat Army; Mimi From Tahiti; You're Drafted; Wait Till the Sun Shines Nellie; Sweet Sue; 'Neath the Yellow Moon in Old Tahiti. 68m/B VHS. Nils T. Granlund, Gale Storm, Robert Lowery, Margaret Dumont, Chick Chandler, Cliff Nazarro, Jan

Wiley, Candy Candido, Yvonne De Carlo; D: Howard Bretherton.

Rhythm Romance ♪♪½ Some Like It Hot 1939 Gene Krupa and his Orchestra are the reason to see this lesser Hope comedy. Nicky Nelson (Hope) is a Coney Island carnival barker, who's latest scheme is to make a buck off the swing craze with Krupa. Meanwhile, Nelson's girl, Lily Racquel (Ross), is miffed at him and decides to take a job as Krupa's girl singer. Based on the play "The Great Magoo" by Ben Hecht and Gene Fowler. ♪The Lady's in Love with You; Some Like it Hot; Heat and Soul. 65m/B VHS. Bob Hope, Shirley Ross, Gene Krupa, Una Merkel; D: George Archainbaud; W: Lewis R. Foster, Gene Fowler Sr.; C: Karl Struss.

Rhythm Thief ♪♪ 1994 No-budget independent film finds alienated New York hustler Simon (Andrews) eking out a living selling tapes of local underground bands he has illegally recorded. He wants to be left alone but circumstances won't allow it. He's got one of the enraged bands after him, he's pestered by local "admirers," (Daniels) suddenly turns up—severely shaking Simon's emotionally barren existence. Quirky character study gets lots of impact from tiny bucks. 88m/B VHS. Jason Andrews, Eddie Daniels, Kimberly Flynn, Kevin Corrigan, Sean Haggerty, Mark Alfred, Christopher Cooke; D: Matthew Harrison; W: Matthew Harrison, Christopher Grimm; C: Howard Krupa; M: Danny Brenner. Sundance '95: Special Jury Prize.

Ricco ♪♪ Summertime Killer 1974 (PG) A young man swears vengeance against the mobsters who killed his father. He kidnaps the daughter of a mafia kingpin and the battle begins. 90m/C VHS, DVD. FR IT SP Chris Mitchum, Karl Malden, Olivia Hussey, Raf Vallone, Claudine Auger, Gerard Tichy; D: Antonio (Isasi-Isasmendi) Isasi.

R.I.C.C.O. ♪♪ 2002 (R) When a defense attorney saves a beautiful young woman from the clutches of sinister hitmen, they both become pawns in a deadly game of hide and seek, running from R.I.C.C.O. Detroit's mysterious ganglord. No budget action piece acts more like a decent tour video of Detroit. Other than that, there's not much to look at. Dismal acting and a silly score. 108m/C VHS, DVD. Walter Harris, Sophia Taylor; D: Shawn Woodard; W: Shawn Woodard. VIDEO

Rich and Famous ♪ 1981 (R) The story of the 25-year friendship of two women, through college, marriage, and success. George Cukor's last film. 117m/C VHS, DVD. Jacqueline Bisset, Candice Bergen, David Selby, Hart Bochner, Meg Ryan, Steven Hill, Michael Brandon, Matt Lattanzi; D: George Cukor; W: Gerald Ayres; M: Alfred Hitchcock; C: Jack Cox, Charles Martin.

Rich and Strange ♪♪½ East of Shanghai 1932 Early Hitchcock movie is not in the same class as his later thrillers. A couple inherits a fortune and journeys around the world. Eventually the pair gets shipwrecked. 92m/B VHS, DVD. GB Henry Kendall, Joan Barry, Betty Amann, Percy Marmont, Elsie Randolph; D: Alfred Hitchcock; W: Alfred Hitchcock, Alma Reville; C: Jack Cox, Charles Martin.

Rich Girl ♪ 1991 (R) A winsome, wealthy wench hides her millions by going to work in a rock 'n' roll bar and falls in love with the local Bruce Springsteen wanna-be. Despite the thick coating of music, sex, drugs, and profanity, this consists of cliches that were old before talkies. Too earnestly acted to be campy fun. Poor movie. 96m/C VHS. Jill Schoelen, Don Michael Paul, Ron Karabatsos, Sean Kanan, Willie Dixon, Paul Gleason; D: Joel Bender.

Rich in Love ♪♪½ 1993 (PG-13) Light-hearted look at the changes in a Southern family after matriarch Helen Odom leaves to pursue her own life, shattering the peaceful existence of those around her. Seen through the eyes of 17-year-old daughter Lucille who assumes the role of "mother" for her sister and father while trying to come to terms with her own confused feelings. Nice performances by newcomer Erbe and Finney can't overcome a mediocre script. Based

on the novel by Josephine Humphreys. 105m/C VHS. Albert Finney, Jill Clayburgh, Kathryn Erbe, Kyle MacLachlan, Piper Laurie, Ethan Hawke, Suzy Amis, Alfre Woodard; D: Bruce Beresford; W: Alfred Uhry; M: Georges Delerue.

Rich Kids ♪♪ 1979 (PG) A young girl trying to cope with the divorce of her parents is aided by a boyfriend whose parents have already split. 97m/C VHS. John Lithgow, Kathryn Walker, Trini Alvarado, Paul Dooley, David Selby, Jill Eikenberry, Olympia Dukakis; D: Robert M. Young; C: Ralf Bode.

Rich Man, Poor Man ♪♪♪ 1976 Classic TV miniseries covers 20 (sometimes bitter) years in the lives of the two Jordache brothers. It's 1945 in quiet Port Phillip, New York with embittered German baker Axel (Asner), his unfulfilled wife Mary (McGuire), and sons Tom (Nolte) and Rudy (Strauss). Tom is wild and irresponsible, Rudy is ambitious and college-bound, and Julie Prescott (Blakely), Rudy's girl, overshadows both their lives. Based on the novel by Irwin Shaw. The first series contained 12 episodes. A second series of 21 episodes primarily followed the tribulations of the next generation, although Strauss returned as Rudy. 720m/C VHS. Peter Strauss, Nick Nolte, Susan Blakely, Ed Asner, Dorothy McGuire, Bill Bixby, Robert Reed, Ray Milland, Kim Darby, Talia Shire, Lawrence Pressman, Kay Lenz; M: Alex North. TV

The Rich Man's Wife ♪½ 1996 (R) Modern noir strands unhappy wife Josie (Berry) on Martha's Vineyard without her loathsome spouse (McDonald), where she makes the mistake of confiding her marital woes to sympathetic, yet obviously deranged stranger Cole (Greene). She tells Cole sometimes she wishes her husband was dead. Poof! Before you can say "foreshadowing," hubby's murdered and she's the prime suspect. Increasingly nutso Cole stalks our heroine, seemingly innocent, but possibly not as blameless as it appears. Failed mystery/thriller delivers little of either and the attempt at a "Strangers on a Train" premise and a "Usual Suspects" type ending fail miserably. 95m/C VHS, DVD. Halle Berry, Christopher McDonald, Clive Owen, Peter Greene, Charles Hallahan, Frankie Faison, Clea Lewis; D: Amy Holden Jones; W: Amy Holden Jones; C: Haskell Wexler; M: John (Gianni) Frizzell.

Rich, Young and Pretty ♪ 1972 (G) Light-hearted, innocuous musical starring Powell as a Texas gal visiting Paris with her rancher father (Corey). Powell finds romance with Damone (in his screen debut) and a secret—the mother she has never known (Darrieux). Lamas (in his American screen debut) plays Darrieux's new heartthrob. ♪Dark is the Night; L'Amour Toujours, Tonight For Sure; Wonder Why; I Can See You; Paris; We Never Talk Much; How Do You Like Your Eggs in the Morning?; There's Dancing in Your Eyes, Cherie; The Old Piano Roll Blues. 95m/C VHS. Jane Powell, Danielle Darrieux, Wendell Corey, Vic Damone, Fernando Lamas, Marcel Dallo, Una Merkel, Richard Anderson, Jean Murat, Hans Conried; D: Norman Taurog; W: Sidney Sheldon, Dorothy Cooper; M: Sammy Cahn, Nicholas Brodszky.

Richard Petty Story ♪ 1972 (G) The biography of race car driver Petty, played by himself, and his various achievements on the track. 83m/C VHS. Richard Petty, Darren McGavin, Kathie Browne, Lynn(e) Marta, Noah Beery Jr., L.Q. Jones; D: Ed Lasko.

Richard III ♪♪ The Life and Death of King Richard III 1912 According to the American Film Institute, this is the oldest surviving American feature film and, in 1912, the most ambitious adaptation of Shakespeare ever attempted. Despite changes in conventions, it's still a lively work that's brightened considerably by a new Ennio Morricone score. 56m/B DVD. Frederick Warde, Robert Gomp, Albert Gardner, Violet Stuart; D: James Keane.

Richard III ♪♪♪½ 1955 This landmark film version of the Shakespearean play features an acclaimed performance by Laurence Olivier, who also directs. The plot follows the life of the men-

tally and physically twisted Richard of Gloucester and his schemes for the throne of England. 138m/C VHS, DVD. GB Laurence Olivier, Cedric Hardwicke, Ralph Richardson, John Gielgud, Stanley Baker, Michael Gough, Claire Bloom; D: Laurence Olivier; British Acad. '55: Actor (Olivier), Director (Olivier); Film; Golden Globes '57. Foreign Film.

Richard III ♪♪♪½ 1995 (R) The Brits once again bring the Bard's most notorious monarch to the screen, this time in a new setting. McKellen stars in the title role of the deformed and ruthless English king, now in an imagined 1930s London of swanky Art Deco, Black Shirt thugs and modern media. Purists may resent major dialogue cuts, but famous speeches (such as the "winter of our discontent" opener) are amusingly staged in this modern take. Gorgeously polished visuals are perfect foil for the slimy, evil goings-on. Based on both Shakespeare's play and Richard Eyre's stage adaptation (in which McKellen also starred). 105m/C VHS, DVD. GB Ian McKellen, Annette Bening, Jim Broadbent, Robert Downey, Jr., Nigel Hawthorne, Kristin Scott Thomas, Maggie Smith, John Wood; D: Richard Loncraine; W: Ian McKellen, Richard Loncraine; C: Peter Biziou; M: Trevor Jones.

Richard's Things ♪♪ 1980 (R) A man's wife and his girlfriend find love and comfort in each other after his death. Screenplay by Frederic Raphael, from his novel. Very slow and dreary, with a weak performance from Ullman. 104m/C VHS. GB Liv Ullmann, Amanda Redman; D: Anthony Harvey; W: Frederic Raphael; C: Frederick A. (Freddie) Young; M: Georges Delerue.

Richie Rich ♪♪½ 1994 (PG) Yet another adaptation from the comics. Richie (Culkin), the world's richest boy, takes over the family business when his madcap parents Richard (Herrmann) and Regina (Ebersole) disappear thanks to conniving Laurence Van Dough (Larroquette). But there's kindly valet Cadbury (McShane) to help Richie save the day. Some silliness but Culkin has clearly outgrown this type of kid role. Biltmore, the 8,000 acre Vanderbilt estate in Asheville, North Carolina, serves as the Rich family home. 94m/C VHS, DVD. Macaulay Culkin, John Larroquette, Edward Herrmann, Christine Ebersole, Jonathan Hyde, Michael McShane, Stephi Lineburg; Cameos: Reggie Jackson, Claudia Schiffer; D: Donald Petrie; W: Tom S. Parker, Jim Jennewein; C: Don Burgess; M: Alan Silvestri.

Rick ♪♪½ 2003 (R) Drawing from Verdi's "Rigoletto," the widower Rick is a detestable corporate exec who despises his annoying and much younger boss Duke yet degrades himself to score points when he learns that the punk has been sex-chatting online with his teenage daughter and figures putting a hit out on him is the only answer. 90m/C VHS, DVD. Bill Pullman, Aaron Stanford, Agnes Bruckner, Sandra Oh, Dylan Baker, Emmanuelle Chriqui, Marianne Hagan, Jamie Harris, Paz de la Huerta, P.J. Brown, Haviland (Hayle) Morris, Dan Moran, Jennifer Preston Bates, Marin Rathje, William Ryall, Daniel Handler, Dennis Parlato, Todd A. Kovner, Kimberly Anne Thompson, Vita Haas, Ben Hauck; D: Daniel Handler; C: Lisa Rinzler; M: Ted Reichman. VIDEO

Ricky 1 ♪½ 1988 Mumbling pugilist spoof. Da Mob wants to make Ricky da fall guy, but uh, he's not as dumb as he looks. 90m/C VHS, DVD. Michael Michaud, Maggie Hughes, James Herbert, Lane Montano; D: Bill Naud; M: Joel Goldsmith.

Ricochet ♪♪♪ 1991 (R) Rookie cop Washington causes a sensation when he singlehandedly captures notorious psychopath Lithgow. But this particular criminal is a twisted genius, and from his prison cell he comes up with a plan to destroy the young cop. Teaming up with old friend Ice-T, the rookie tries to outwit his evil archnemesis. Genuinely scary, tense and violent thriller. 104m/C VHS, DVD. Denzel Washington, John Lithgow, Ice-T, Jesse Ventura, Kevin Pollak, Lindsay Wagner, Mary Ellen Trainor, Josh Evans, Victoria Dillard, John Amos, John Cothran Jr.; D: Russell Mulcahy; W: Steven E. de Souza; C: Peter Levy; M: Alan Silvestri.

Ricochet River 🐾🐾 1998 (R) High school senior Lorna (Hudson) has big dreams that don't include staying around her tiny Oregon town. She is dating hotshot school quarterback Wade. The duo are also the only two to accept newcomer Jesse, a Native American who falls victim to the town's prejudice. A video. 87m/C VHS, DVD. Kate Hudson, Douglas Spain, Jason James Richter, Matthew Glave, Dan Lauria, John Cullum. **D:** Deborah Del Prete. **VIDEO**

Ride 'Em Cowboy 🐾🐾½ 1942 Two peanut and hotdog vendors travel west to try their hand as cowpokes. Usual Abbott and Costello fare with a twist—there are lots of great musical numbers. ♫A Tisket, A Tasket; I'll Remember April; Wake Up Jacob; Give Me My Saddle; Cow Boogie. 86m/B VHS, DVD. Bud Abbott, Lou Costello, Anne Gwynne, Samuel S. Hinds, Dick Foran, Richard Lane, Johnny Mack Brown, Ella Fitzgerald, Douglas Dumbrille. **D:** Arthur Lubin.

Ride 'Em Cowgirl 🐾 1941 Singing cowgirl, Page, enters a horse race to expose the crook who cheated her father. 51m/B VHS, DVD. Dorothy Page, Vince Barret, Milton Frome. **D:** Samuel Diege.

Ride to Glory 🐾🐾 *Spina Dorsale del Diavolo* 1971 In 1886, a cavalry officer deserts his troops to seek revenge on the Apaches that brutally killed his family. Hearing this, a general offers to pardon him if he will lead a dangerous group of men on a mission against the Apaches. Fast-paced and very bloody. 90m/C VHS. Bekim Fehmiu, Richard Crenna, Chuck Connors, Ricardo Montalban, Ian Bannen, Slim Pickens, Woody Strode, Patrick Wayne, John Huston. **D:** Burt Kennedy.

Ride with the Devil 🐾🐾½ 1999 (R) Clunky Civil War saga adapted from Daniel Woodrell's novel "Woe to Live On." Lee concentrates on the 1862 Border Wars between the Southern-sympathizers known as the Bushwackers. Best pals Jack Bull Chiles (Ulrich) and Jake Roedel (Maguire) join a group of Bushwhackers and both become involved with a young farm widow, Sue Lee (singer Jewel in her acting debut). After some losses, Jake and the remaining band join in Quantrill's (Ales) infamous raid on the abolitionist stronghold of Lawrence, Kansas. Film serves as a coming-of-age story for the teenaged Jake and Maguire, at least, is up to the challenge. 138m/C VHS, DVD. Tobey Maguire, Skeet Ulrich, Jeffrey Wright, Jewel, Simon Baker, Jonathan Rhys Meyers, James "Jim" Caviezel, Tom Guiry, Tom Wilkinson, Jonathan Brandis, John Ales, Matthew Faber, Steven Mailer, Zach Grenier, Margo Martindale, Mark Ruffalo, Celia Weston. **D:** Ang Lee. **W:** James Schamus. **C:** Frederick Elmes. **M:** Mychael Danna.

Riders of the Desert 🐾🐾½ 1932 Steele tracks down the loot from a stage-coach robbery. 57m/B VHS, DVD. Bob Steele, Gertrude Messinger, Al "Fuzzy" St. John, "Gabby" Hayes, John Elliott. **D:** Robert North Bradbury. **W:** Wellyn Totman. **C:** Archie Stout.

Riders of Pasco Basin 🐾½ 1940 Outlaws are tricking ranchers out of their money by falsely promising to build a dam. So Brown and his cohorts come to set things right. 56m/B VHS. Johnny Mack Brown, Fuzzy Knight, Bob Baker, Frances Robinson, Arthur Loft, Frank LaRue. (Lafayette) McKee, Kermit Maynard. **D:** Ray Taylor. **W:** Ford Beebe.

Riders of the Purple Sage 🐾🐾½ 1925 When Texas Ranger Jim Lassiter's (Mix) sister and niece are kidnapped by the evil Walters (Oland), he devotes his life to finding them. While working on a ranch (and falling in love with the beautiful ranch owner), he learns Walters has changed his name and is passing himself off as a judge. Promptly shooting the skunk dead, Lassiter and his sweetie must run from a posse. Based on the Zane Grey novel. 63m/B VHS. Tom Mix, Warner Oland, Mabel Ballin, Beatrice Burnham, Arthur Morrison, Fred Kohler Sr. **D:** Lynn F. Reynolds. **W:** Edfrid Bingham.

Riders of the Purple Sage 🐾🐾½ 1996 Legendary gunman er Jim Lassiter's (Mix) sister and niece are (are there any other kind?) Lassiter (Harris) helps save Bern (Thomas, from a beating in a town run by a conservative religious sect, led by Deacon Tull (Weisser). Seems Bern's befriended ranch owner (and nonmember) Jane (Madigan) and the Deacon is not only after Jane but her considerable land and cattle holdings. Lassiter rides to the rescue. Properly brooding TV adaptation of the 1912 Zane Grey novel (the Grey novel specifies that the sect are Mormons but this caused considerable fuss). Filmed in Utah. 90m/C VHS. Ed Harris, Amy Madigan, Henry Thomas, Norbert Weisser, Robin Tunney, G.D. Spradlin. **D:** Charles Haid. **W:** Gill Dennis. **C:** William Wages. **M:** Arthur Kempel. **TV**

Ride a Wild Pony 🐾🐾½ 1975 (G) A poor Australian farmer's son is allowed to pick a horse of his own from a neighboring rancher's herd. After he trains and grows to love the pony, the rancher's daughter, who is crippled and depends on the pony for her mobility, decides to claim it for herself. Enjoyable Disney story is based on the tale "Sporting Proposition," by James Aldridge. 86m/C VHS, AU. John Meillon, Michael Craig, Robert Bettles, Eva Griffith, Graham Rouse. **D:** Don Chaffey. **C:** Jack Cardiff. **M:** John Addison.

The Ride Back 🐾🐾½ 1957 Well-done western about lawman Hamish (Conrad) who decides to take outlaw Kallen (Quinn) across the Mexican border back to Texas—a four days' journey through hostile territory. At the site of a massacre they discover a lone survivor, a little girl whom they take with them. Then they are attacked by Apaches and when Hamish is wounded, Kallen sees his chance for escape. Good performances by the leads; feature debut for director Miner. 79m/B VHS. Anthony Quinn, Lita Milan, Ellen Hope Monroe, William Conrad, Anthony DeVol.

Ride Clear of Diablo 🐾🐾½ 1954 Crooked Sheriff Kenyon (Birch) and equally crooked lawyer Meredith (Pullen) murder Clay O'Mara's (Murphy) father and brother. He vows to get revenge, aided by gunslinger Whitey Kincade (Duryea). Then Laurie (Cabot), Kenyon's niece and Meredith's fiance, comes to Clay's attention. Macho Technicolor western with a likeable cast. 80m/C VHS. Audie Murphy, Dan Duryea, Susan Cabot, Paul Birch, William Pullen, Abbe Lane, Russell Johnson, Jack Elam, Lane Bradford, Holly (Mike Ragan) Bane, Denver Pyle. **D:** Jesse Hibbs. **W:** George Zuckerman. **M:** George Duning.

Ride Him, Cowboy 🐾🐾🐾 1932 Entertaining oater has Wayne saving horse Duke from being sentenced to death. The horse made for Warner's, all of which costarred his white wonder horse, Duke. This was the first of six series films. Wayne made for Warner's, all of which costarred his white wonder horse, Duke. Remake of the 1926 Ken Maynard silent "The Unknown Cavalier." Based on the story by Kenneth Perkins. 55m/B VHS, DVD. John Wayne, Ruth Hall, Henry B. Walthall, Harry Gribbon, Otis Harlan, Charles Sellon. **D:** Fred Allen. **W:** Scott Mason.

Ride in a Pink Car 🐾 1974 (R) When a Vietnam vet returns home, he discovers that his welcoming committee is really a lynch mob. 83m/C VHS. Glenn Corbet, Morgan Woodward, Ivy Jones. **D:** Robert Emery.

Ride in the Whirlwind 🐾🐾½ 1966 Three cowboys are mistaken for members of a gang by a posse. Screenplay for the offbeat western by Nicholson. 83m/C DVD. Jack Nicholson, Cameron Mitchell, Millie Perkins, Katherine Squire, Harry Dean Stanton, Rupert Crosse. **D:** Monte Hellman. **W:** Jack Nicholson. **C:** Gregory Sandor. **M:** Robert Drasin.

Ride Lonesome 🐾🐾½ 1959 The heroic Scott is a bounty hunter looking for a killer (Best). It's not just the money, Scott hopes Best will lead him to the man who murdered Scott's wife. Along the trail he meets a pretty widow and two outlaws who hope if they capture Best, they'll get a pardon. A well-done example of a "B" western with good performances. Co-burn's film debut. 73m/C VHS, Randolph Scott, James Best, Karen Steele, Pernell Roberts, Lee Van Cleef, James Coburn. **D:** Budd Boetticher. **W:** Burt Kennedy.

Ride, Ranger, Ride 🐾½ 1936 Texas Ranger Autry is out to stop a group of Comanches from raiding a wagon train. 56m/B VHS. Gene Autry, Smiley Burnette, Kay Hughes, Max Terhune, Monte Blue, Chief Thundercloud. **D:** Joseph Kane.

Ride the High Country 🐾🐾🐾 *Guns in the Afternoon* 1962 The cult classic western about two old friends who have had careers on both sides of the law. One, Joel McCrea, is entrusted with a shipment of gold, and the other, Randolph Scott, rides along with him to steal the precious cargo. Although barely promoted by MGM, the film became a critics' favorite. Grinacing and acting as a fitting tribute and farewell to the western. One of Bronson's best performances. 115m/C VHS, DVD. FR Marlene Jobert, Si Jenks, Lloyd Ingraham, John Elliott, Earl Drewe, Bob Steele. **D:** Foster North Bradbury. **W:** Jack Natteford. **C:** Gus Peterson.

Ride the Man Down 🐾🐾½ 1953 Story of a murderous land war between neighboring landowners tells the same old story: Greed knows no boundaries. 90m/C VHS. Brian Donlevy, Chill Wills, Jack La Rue, Rod Cameron, Ella Raines, Barbara Britton. **D:** Joseph Kane.

Ride the Wild Surf 🐾🐾½ 1964 It's fun in the sun when surfers Fabian, Hunter, and Brown head to Hawaii in search of the ultimate waves. Throw in a little romance and a cool title song by Jan and Dean and you've got your better than average beach movie. The surfing footage is excellent. Cowabunga! 101m/C VHS, DVD. Fabian, Tab Hunter, Barbara Eden, Peter Brown, Susan Hart, Shelley Fabares, Jim Mitchum. **D:** Don Taylor.

Ride the Wild Fields 🐾🐾½ 2000 Tender adaptation of Vacarro's play "And the Home of the Brave" finds 11-year-old Opal (Vega) and her mother Ruby (Whalley) struggling to manage their small North Carolina farm while their dad serves overseas during WWII. Ruby is grateful for the help of drifter Tom (Flanery), though others are suspicious of the young man, but complications arise when the adults develop stronger feelings for one another. 101m/C VHS. Joanne Whalley, Sean Patrick Flanery, Alexa Vega, Cotter Smith. **D:** Paul A. Kaufman. **W:** Rodney Vacarro. **C:** Thom Best. **M:** Laura Kaufman.

Riders 🐾 *Jilly Cooper's Riders* 1988 English aristocratic Rupert Campbell-Black (Gilbert) and half-gypsy Jake Lovell (Praed) have carried their rivalry into the competitive equestrian field. Of course, there's the added complication of Rupert's wife, whom Jake is also interested in. Based on Jilly Cooper's steamy novel. 210m/C VHS. GB Marcus Gilbert, Michael Praed, Stephanie Beacham, Gabrielle Beaumont, Serena Gordon, John Standing, Anthony Valentine, Cecile Paoli. **D:** Gabrielle Beaumont. **W:** Charlotte Bingham. **C:** Michae J. Davis. **M:** Roger Webb.

Riders of Death Valley 🐾🐾½ 1941 Splendid western action serial in 15 episodes. Foran, Jones, and Carrillo head a passel o'men watching for thieves and claim jumpers in a mining area. 320m/B VHS, DVD. Dick Foran, Buck Jones, Leo Carrillo, Lon Chaney Jr. **D:** Ford Beebe, Ray Taylor.

Riders of Destiny 🐾🐾½ 1933 Wayne plays a government agent sent to find out who is stealing water from the local farmers. Very early Wayne has the Duke looking awfully young as an agent securing water rights for ranchers. 59m/B VHS, DVD. John Wayne, George "Gabby" Hayes, Forest Taylor, A "Fuzzy" St. John.

Rider on the Rain 🐾🐾🐾 *Lepassager de la Pluie* 1970 A young housewife is viciously raped by an escaped sex maniac. She kills him and disposes of his body, not knowing that she is being relentlessly pursued by mysterious American Bronson. Suspenseful, French-made thriller featuring one of Bronson's best performances. 115m/C VHS, DVD. FR Marlene Jobert, Charles Bronson, Jill Ireland. **D:** Rene Clement.

Rider of the Law 🐾 1935 A government agent poses as a greenhorn easterner to nab a gang of outlaws. 56m/B VHS. Gertrude Messinger, Si Jenks, Lloyd Ingraham, John Elliott, Earl Drewe, Bob Steele. **D:** Robert North Bradbury. **W:** Jack Natteford. **C:** Gus Peterson.

Rider from Tucson 🐾🐾 1950 Two rodeo riders head out to Colorado for a friend's wedding. They find out the bride has been kidnapped by a bunch of claim jumpers after control of a gold mine. 60m/B VHS. Tim Holt, Richard Martin, Elaine Riley, Douglas Fowley, Veda Ann Borg. **D:** Lesley Selander.

Riders of the Range 🐾🐾 1924 Sheep invade the cattle range and a range war flares up between those who would herd and the ranchers. Silent flick of interest because of the stars. 62m/B VHS. Edmund Cobb, Dolly Dale. **D:** Otis Thayer.

Riders of the Range 🐾🐾 1950 Cowboy rides into town just in time to save a girl's brother from gamblers. 60m/B VHS. Tim Holt, Richard Martin, Jacqueline Wells, Reed Hadley, Robert Barrat, Robert Clarke, Tom Tyler, William Tannen. **D:** Lesley Selander. **W:** Norman Houston. **C:** J. Roy Hunt. **M:** Paul Sawtell.

Riders of the Rockies 🐾🐾½ 1937 An honest cowboy turns rustler in order to trap a border gang. One of Ritter's very best cowboy outings; good fun and a very toe-tap, fistfight with Kirg. 56m/B VHS, DVD. Tex Ritter, Yakima Canutt, Louise Stanley, Charles "Blackie" King, Snub Pollard. **D:** Robert North Bradbury.

Riders of the Storm 🐾½ 1988 (R) A motley crew of Vietnam vets runs a covert TV broadcasting station from an in-flight B-29, jamming America's legitimate airwaves. Interesting premise with boring end result. 92m/C VHS, DVD. Dennis Hopper, Michael J. Pollard, Eugene Lipinski, James Aubrey, Nigel Pegram. **D:** Maurice Phillips. **W:** Scott Roberts.

Riders of the Timberline 🐾🐾 1941 Unusual for a Hopalong Cassidy programmer in that it puts him in timber country. Yes, he's a lumberjack and he's okay, as he fights against land-grabbing crooks all day. 59m/B VHS. William Boyd, Brad King, Andy Clyde, J. Farrell MacDonald, Elaine Stewart, Anna Q. Nilsson, Hal Taliaferro. **D:** Lesley Selander.

Riders of the West 🐾 1942 An honest cowboy fights off a band of rustlers. 58m/B VHS, DVD. Buck Jones, Tim McCoy, Raymond Hatton, Sarah Padden, Harry Woods. **D:** Howard Bretherton.

Riders of the Whistling Pines 1949 Our ever-so-bland hero solves a murder perpetrated by a passel of lumber thieves and saves the day for yet another damsel in distress. 70m/B VHS, DVD. Gene Autry, Patricia Barry, Jimmy Lloyd; **D:** John English.

Riders of the Whistling Skull 1937 The Three Mesquiteers are guiding an expedition to an ancient Indian city. A gang of rustlers looting the city are holding an archeology professor hostage, and the Mesquiteers must rescue him. Swell cast; nifty, creepy plot; solid-as-usual leads. 58m/B VHS, DVD, Robert "Bob" Livingston, Ray Corrigan, Max Terhune, Yakima Canutt, Roland Winters; **D:** Mack V. Wright.

Riders to the Sea 1988 A mother envisions the death of her last son in the same manner her other sons died—by drowning. Based on the play by Irish dramatist John Millington Synge. 90m/C VHS. Geraldine Page, Amanda Plummer, Sachi Parker, Barry McGovern; **D:** Ronan O'Leary.

Ridicule 1996 (R) Fish-out-of-water drama has minor country aristocrat Pondeludon (Berling) enter the depraved world of the 18th-century court at Versailles. There, he hopes, the king will aid him in his quest to drain the disease-ridden swamps at his estate. The naive provincial finds he must master the weapons of choice for success within the court—wit, deadly ridicule, and impeccable lineage. After initial missteps due to lack of finesse, he quickly adapts, and finds some influential allies: the beautiful Madame de Blayac (Ardant) and sympathetic Marquis de Bellegarde (Rochefort). When the Marquis's spirited and attractive daughter, Mathilde (Godreche), shows up, the smitten Pondeludon must stop her loveless marriage of convenience. Perfectly cast, director Leconte's highly lauded period piece has all the emotional and technical elements of an engaging film. In French with subtitles. 102m/C VHS, DVD. FR Charles Berling, Jean Rochefort, Fanny Ardant, Bernard Giraudeau, Judith Godreche, Bernard Dheran, Carlo Brandt, Jacques Mathou; **D:** Patrice Leconte; **W:** Remi Waterhouse, Michel Fessler, Eric Vicaut; **C:** Thierry Arbogast; **M:** Antoine Duhamel. Oscars '96: Foreign Film; Cesar '97: Director (Leconte); Film; Broadcast Film Critics '96: Foreign Film.

Ridin' Down the Canyon 1942 Standard but entertaining entry in Rogers' popular series. It's Rogers to the rescue when a gang of outlaws are rustling cattle and selling to the government for wartime profits. Roy, along with the Sons of the Pioneers, also manages to croon a few tunes. Based on a story by Robert Williams and Norman Houston. 54m/B VHS, DVD. Roy Rogers, George "Gabby" Hayes, Linda Hayes, Addison Richards, Adrian Booth, James Seay; **D:** Joseph Kane; **W:** Albert DeMond.

Ridin' on a Rainbow 1941 Has-been performer on a steamboat decides to rob a bank in the hopes of starting a new life for himself and his daughter. The money he robs had just been deposited by some cattlemen, one of whom joins the steamboat's crew, wins the daughter's heart, and gets to the father. Slow and dull, with too much singing, and too little plot and scenery. Keep your ears open for the sound of airplanes—apparently Newfield forgot they hadn't been invented in the time of the wild west. From a story by E.B. Mann. 56m/B VHS, Bob Steele, Claire Rochelle, Charles "Blackie" King, Ernie Adams, Lew Meehan, Julian Rivero; **D:** Sam Newfield; **W:** Charles Francis Royal.

Ridin' the Lone Trail woof! 1937 Steele attempts to stop some criminals who've been harassing a stagecoach line. Republic was better than this weak western would lead us to believe. Steele, who went on to better things, is a bright spot in a film that sounds and looks bad. 56m/B

Ridin' the Trail 1940 Scott stars as a cowboy out to rid the countryside of bad guys in this western. 60m/B VHS. Fred Scott, Iris Lancaster, Harry Harvey, Jack Ingram, John Ward; **D:** Bernard B. Ray.

Ridin' Thru 1935 Another Tom Tyler western, in which the hero does battle with unscrupulous villains. 60m/B VHS, DVD, Tom Tyler, Ruth Hiatt, Lafe (Lafayette) McKee, Philo (Philip, P.H., P.M.) McCullough, Lew Meehan, Bud Osborne; **D:** Harry S. Webb.

Riding Alone for Thousands of Miles Qian Li Zou Dan Ji 2005 (PG) Small-scale, compelling human drama from Zhang. Japanese fisherman Gou-ichi Takata (Takakura) is called to Tokyo by his daughter-in-law, where his estranged son Ken-ichi (Nakai) is hospitalized with terminal cancer. Grief-stricken, Gou-ichi vows to fulfill his son's dying dream—to film celebrated Chinese opera star Li Jiamin (appearing as himself) in performance. This involves the elderly man traveling to a remote Chinese province and ultimately reuniting Li with his own illegitimate son. Hope triumphs amidst the hardships. Japanese and Chinese with subtitles. 108m/C CH HK JP Ken Takakura, Kiichi Nakai, Shinobu Terajima, Li Jiamin; **D:** Yimou Zhang; **W:** Zou Jingzhi; **C:** Xiaoding Zhao; **M:** Guo Wenjing.

The Riding Avenger 1936 To gain the love of a beautiful lady, a cowboy vows never to fight again, but is forced to break his promise when the town is terrorized. Aw, shucks. 56m/B VHS, DVD. Hoot Gibson, Ruth Mix, Buzz Barton; **D:** Harry Fraser.

Riding Giants 2004 (PG-13) Director Stacy Peralta does for surfing what she did for skateboarding in "Dogtown and Z-Boys" by capturing the consummate skill and infectious enthusiasm of those who dominate the sport. Includes an animated mini-history that sardonically traces surfing from its Polynesian roots through the 20th century. 105m/C DVD. US Jeff Clark, Darrick Doerner, Mickey Munoz, Brian L. Keaulana, Dick Brewer, Buzzy Kerbox, Ricky Grigg, Pat Curren, Laird Hamilton, Lyon Hamilton, Dave Kalama, Randy Rarick, Buffalo Keaulana, Evan Slater, Kelly Slater; **Cameos:** Sam George, Gabrielle Reece, Dr. Mark Renneker, Mike Stange; **D:** Stacy Peralta; **W:** Sam George, Stacy Peralta; **C:** Peter Pilafian; **M:** Alan Barker.

Riding High 1950 Capra remade his 1934 film "Broadway Bill" as this light-hearted musical. Horse trainer Crosby falls for the wealthy Gray who demands he choose between her and his horse. Bing chooses the horse who proves his loyalty by winning the big race and making Crosby a rich man. ♪Someplace on Anywhere Road; Sunshine Cake; We've Got a Sure Thing; The Horse Told Me; The Whiffenpoof Song; De Camptown Races. 112m/B VHS, DVD. Bing Crosby, Coleen Gray, Charles Bickford, William Demarest, Frances Gifford, Raymond Walburn, James Gleason, Ward Bond, Percy Kilbride, Harry Davenport, Margaret Hamilton, Douglass Dumbrille, Gene Lockhart, Charles Lane, Frankie Darro, Paul Harvey, Marjorie Lord, Dub Taylor, Max Baer Sr., Oliver Hardy; **D:** Frank Capra; **W:** Robert Riskin, Melville Shavelson, Jack Rose; **C:** George Barnes.

Riding High 1978 It's a battle for supremacy between the kings of the motorcycle stunt world. TV movie's soundtrack includes songs from The Police, Dire Straits, Jerry Lee Lewis, and more. 92m/C VHS. Murray Salem, Marella Oppenheim, Eddie Kidd, Irene Handl; **D:** Ross Cramer. TV

Riding in Cars with Boys 2001 (PG-13) Based on the memoir of Beverly Donofrio, the plot follows Beverly (Barrymore) from 1965, when she becomes pregnant at age 15, to 1986, when her son has grown up and she has completed her book. The story is more concerned with the way parents treat their children, however, and Beverly doesn't emerge as the spunky super-mom who prevailed despite the odds. Instead she comes off as a whiner who blames her loser husband Ray (Zahn) for getting her pregnant, her own parents (Woods and Bracco) for not talking to her, and even her son Jason (Garcia) for merely being around, but Barrymore gives a good performance, but Zahn outdoes her by breaking his "goofy guy" typecast and adding texture to the woeful Ray. 132m/C VHS, DVD. US Drew Barrymore, Steve Zahn, Brittany Murphy, Adam Garcia, Lorraine Bracco, James Woods, Sara Gilbert, Desmond Harrington, David Moscow, Maggie Gyllenhaal, Peter Facinelli, Marisa Ryan, Mika Boorem, Skye McCole Bartusiak, Logan Lerman; **D:** Penny Marshall; **W:** Morgan Ward; **C:** Miroslav Ondricek; **M:** Hans Zimmer.

Riding On 1937 Hayseed falls for the daughter of his father's arch rival. While his father battles it out over cattle, he pines for his enemy's daughter. Lots of action which is typical fare in mediocre western production. 59m/B VHS. Tom Tyler, Germaine Greer, Rex Lease, John Elliott, Earl Dwire; **D:** Harry S. Webb.

Riding on Air 1937 Small-town newspaper editor Brown discovers that his bumbling methods get him the right results. Smugglers and crazy inventions in a ho-hum Brown entry. 58m/B VHS. Joe E. Brown; **D:** Edward Sedgwick.

Riding Speed 1935 Our hero breaks up a gang of smugglers along the Mexican border. 50m/B VHS. Buffalo Bill Jr., Bud Osborne, Lafe (Lafayette) McKee, Clyde McClary; **D:** Buffalo Bill Jr.; **C:** Brydon Baker.

Riding the Bullet 2004 (R) A death-obsessed young man (Jackson) keeps running from and into the Grim Reaper and his agents. Lame Garris/King collaboration relying on obvious shocks instead of suspense for its thrills. Tired horror movie cliches abound, so it never gets under your skin the way it should. 98m/C DVD. US Jonathan Jackson, David Arquette, Cliff Robertson, Barbara Hershey, Erika Christensen; **D:** Mick Garris; **W:** Mick Garris; **C:** Robert New; **M:** Nicholas Pike.

Riding the California Trail 1947 The Cisco Kid is wanted dead or alive in several states. 40m/B VHS. Gilbert Roland, Martin Garralaga, Frank Yaconelli, Teala Loring, Ted Hecht; **D:** William Nigh; **W:** Clarence Upson Young; **C:** Harry Neumann.

Riding the Sunset Trail 1941 Top-notch tale of Keene trying to stop a con from cashing in on his dead half-brother's fortune. Solid production values and an enthusiastic performance by Keene make this one of his best films after a string of flops. 56m/B VHS. Tom Keene, Betty Miles, Frank Yaconelli, Sugar Dawn, Slim Andrews, Kenne Duncan; **D:** Robert Emmett Tansey; **W:** Robert Emmett, Frances Kavanaugh.

The Riding Tornado 1932 Bronc rider McCoy takes a job on Grey's ranch, promptly falling for Grey. Ranch foreman Oakman, who's really the leader of a gang of rustlers, kidnaps Grey and McCoy goes after them. 63m/B VHS. Tim McCoy, Shirley Grey, Wheeler Oakman, Wallace MacDonald, Russell Simpson, Montagu Love, Lafe (Lafayette) McKee, Bud Osborne; **D:** David Ross Lederman.

Riding with Death 1976 A man who can become invisible, thanks to a military experiment, uses his power to uncover a complex plot by a mad scientist. So-so TV pilot. 97m/C VHS. Ben Murphy, Andrew Prine, Katherine Crawford, Richard Dysart; **D:** Alan J. Levi. TV

Riel 1979 The story of Louis Riel, a half-French, half-Indian visionary who challenged the Canadian army in his fight for equality and self-rule. 150m/C VHS. Raymond Cloutier, Arthur Hill, William Shatner, Christopher Plummer, Leslie Nielsen; **D:** George Bloomfield.

Riff Raff Riffraff 1935. Melodramatic story about the relationship of two waterfront workers in the tuna fishing business. Confusing script saddled with too many characters, but there is some good sharp dialogue between the leads. Also features the scenic California waterfront. 80m/B VHS. Jean Harlow, Spencer Tracy, Joseph Calleia, Una Merkel, Mickey Rooney, Victor Kilian, J. Farrell MacDonald, Roger Imhof; **D:** J. Walter Ruben.

Riff-Raff 1947 Various dramatic and comic complications arise when a dying man gives Panama City con man O'Brien a map to oil deposits. Interesting and quick-moving melodrama. 80m/B VHS. Pat O'Brien, Walter Slezak, Anne Jeffreys, Jason Robards Sr., Percy Kilbride, Jerome Cowan; **D:** Ted Tetzlaff.

Riff Raff 1992 Unsparing black comedy about the British working class by director Loach. Ex-con Stevie comes to London from Scotland to look for work and escape his thieving past. He finds a nonunion job on a construction site, takes up squatter's rights in an abandoned apartment, and finds a girlfriend in equally struggling singer Susie, who turns out to be a junkie. Loach's characters deal with their unenviable lot in life through rough humor and honest sentiment. Regional accents are so thick that the film is subtitled. 96m/C VHS. GB Robert Carlyle, Emer McCourt, Jimmy Coleman, George Moss, Ricky Tomlinson, David Finch, Bill Jesse; **D:** Ken Loach; **W:** Bill Jesse; **M:** Stewart Copeland.

Rififi Du Rififi Chez les Hommes 1954 Perhaps the greatest of all "heist" movies. Four jewel thieves pull off a daring caper, only to fall prey to mutual distrust. The long scene of the actual theft, completely in silence, will have your heart in your throat. In French with English subtitles. 115m/B VHS, DVD. FR Jean Servais, Carl Mohner, Robert Manuel, Jules Dassin; **D:** Jules Dassin; **W:** Jules Dassin; **C:** Philippe Agostini; **M:** Georges Auric. Cannes '55: Director (Dassin).

Rift 1996 Bland romantic triangle set among Manhattan twentysomethings. Shy Tom (Sage) pines for Lisa (Bransford), the wife of his best friend, Bill (Cavanaugh). In fact, Tom begins having overwhelming nightmares, involving murder, about the situation. Not that you'll care since Tom is a mope, Lisa's a whiner, and Bill's a nasty-tempered bore. 87m/C VHS. William Sage, Timothy Cavanaugh, Jennifer Bransford, Alan Davidson; **D:** Edward S. Barkin; **C:** Lee Daniel.

Right at Your Door 2006 (R) Brad (Cochrane) is forced to seal up his house and lock his wife Lexi (McCormack) outside after she is exposed to deadly toxins caused by dirty bombs hitting Los Angeles. Basically a disaster flick with only two major characters, and that gets dull real fast (especially since Brad is obnoxious). 96m/C DVD. Rory Cochrane, Mary McCormack, Tony Perez; **D:** Chris Gorak; **W:** Chris Gorak; **C:** Tom Richmond; **M:** Tomandandy.

The Right Hand Man 1987 (R) A brother and sister must deal with their crusty patriarch's demise in the Victorian-era Australian outback. Disappointing and overwrought. 101m/C VHS, DVD. AU Rupert Everett, Hugo Weaving, Arthur Dignam; **D:** Di Drew.

Right of Way 1984 Stewart plays an elderly man who makes a suicide pact with his wife (Davis) when he learns of her terminal illness. Davis and Stewart's first film together is disappointing and stodgy, with an abrupt ending that looks like bad editing by a frightened studio. Made for TV. 102m/C VHS, James Stewart, Bette Davis, Priscilla Morrill, Melinda Dillon; **D:** George Schaefer. **M:** Brad Fiedel. TV

The Right Stuff 1983 (PG) A rambunctious adaptation of Tom Wolfe's nonfiction book about the beginnings of the U.S. space program, from Chuck Yeager's breaking of the sound barrier to the last of the Mercury missions. Featuring an all-star cast and an ambitious script. Rowdy, imaginative, and thrilling, though broadly painted and oddly uninvolving. Former astronaut John Glenn was running for president when this was out. 193m/C VHS, DVD. Ed Harris, Dennis Quaid, Sam Shepard, Scott Glenn, Fred Ward, Charles Frank, William Russ, Kathy Baker, Barbara Hershey, Levon Helm, David Clennon, Kim Stanley, Mary Jo Deschanel, Veronica Cartwright, Pamela Reed, Jeff Goldblum, Harry Shearer, Donald Moffat, Scott Paulin, Lance Henriksen, Scott Wilson, John P. Ryan, Royal Dano; **D:** Philip Kaufman; **W:** Philip Kaufman; **C:** Caleb Deschanel; **M:** Bill Conti. Oscars '83: Film Editing, Sound, Orig. Score.

The Right Temptation 2000 (R) Female PI Derian (De Mornay) is hired by a jealous wife (Delaney) to get the dirt on her adulterous rich husband (Sutherland). Too bad the PI then falls for her target, who may also be in bed with

The Right to Remain Silent 🐾🐾 1995 (R) Rookie cop Christine Paley (Thompson) learns all about human foibles in her job processing incoming suspects. Based on a play by Brent Briscoe and Mark Fauser. 96m/C VHS, DVD. Kiefer Sutherland, Rebecca De Mornay, Dana Delany, Adam Baldwin; D: Lyndon Chubbuck.

Rikisha-Man 🐾🐾🐾½ Man: Muhomatsu no issho 1958 A tragic melodrama about a rickshaw puller who helps raise a young boy after his father has died, and loves the boy's mother from afar. In Japanese with English subtitles. 105m/B In Japanese with English subtitles. 105m/B gaki's remake of his original 1943 version. JP Toshiro Mifune; D: Hiroshi Inagaki.

Rikky and Pete 🐾🐾½ 1988 (R) An engaging Australian comedy about a bizarre, precociously eccentric brother and sister. He's a Rube Goldberg-style mentor, she's a scientist-cum-country singer. They move together to the outback and meet a score of weird characters. A worthy follow-up to director Tass's "Malcolm." 103m/C VHS, DVD. AU Nina Landis, Stephen Kearney, Tetchie Agbayani, Bruce Spence, Bruno Lawrence, Bill Hunter, Dorothy Alison, Don Reid, Lewis Fitz-Gerald; D: Nadia Tass; W: David Parker; M: Phil Judd.

Rikyu 🐾🐾🐾 1990 Set in 16th century Japan, Rikyu is a Buddhist priest who elevated the tea ceremony to an art form. To him it is a spiritual experience, to his master, Lord Hideyoshi Toiyotomi, the ruler of Japan, mastery of the ceremony is a matter of prestige. Conflict arises between Rikyu's ideal of profound simplicity, symbolized by the ceremony, and Toiyotomi's planned conquest of China, which Rikyu opposes. In Japanese with English subtitles. 116m/C VHS, DVD. JP Rentaro Mikuni, Tsutomu Yamazaki; D: Hiroshi Teshigahara; W: Hiroshi Teshigahara, Genpei Akasegawa; C: Fujio Morita; M: Toru Takemitsu.

Rim of the Canyon 🐾½ 1949 Autry has a dual role as a lawman tracking villains who were jailed by his father years before. 70m/B VHS, DVD. Gene Autry, Nan Leslie, Thurston Hall, Clem Bevans, Water Sande, Jock Mahoney, Alan Hale Jr., Denver Pyle; D: John English.

Rimfire 🐾🐾½ 1949 An undercover agent tracks down some stolen U.S. Army gold, aided by the ghost of a wrongly hanged gambler. Fun B western. 65m/B VHS, DVD. Mary Beth Hughes, Henry Hull, Fuzzy Knight, James Millican, Victor Kilian, Marga Dean, Jason Robards Sr., Reed Hadley, Chris-Pin Martin, Crispin Martin, Martin, John Cason, George Cleveland, I. Stanford Jolley, Stanley Price; D: B. Reeves Eason; W: Ron Ormond, Arthur St. Claire, Frank Wisbar; C: Ernest Miller, Greene.

Rin Tin Tin, Hero of the West 🐾🐾½ 1955 In one of his last adventures, the famous German Shepherd proves his courage and hyper-canine intelligence. Colorized. 75m/C VHS. James Brown, Lee Aaker.

The Ring 🐾🐾½ 1927 Very early Hitchcock about boxer who marries carnival girl, loses carnival girl, and wins carnival girl back again. Standard romantic punch and roses yarn interesting as measure of young director's developing authority. 82m/B VHS, DVD. GB Carl Brisson, Lillian Hall-Davis, Ian Hunter, Gordon Harker; D: Alfred Hitchcock; W: Alfred Hitchcock.

The Ring 🐾🐾½ 1952 Poignant early fight movie that gives a lesson in prejudice against Chicanos. The main character feels that the only way to get respect from the world is to fight for it. Well-directed and perceptive. 79m/B VHS, DVD. Gerald Mohr, Rita Moreno, Kiri Te Kanawa, Robert Arthur, Art Aragon, Jack Elam; D: Kurt Neumann.

The Ring 🐾🐾½ 2002 (R) American adaptation of the novel and film that took Japan by storm in 1998. Upon hearing of an allegedly lethal videotape in urban legend fashion, teen Katie (Tamblyn) gets her hands on a copy and watches it with three of her friends. Immediately after viewing the tape, she gets a call telling her that she will die in exactly one week. A week later all four teens are dead. Katie's supposedly to be on vacation with his son and a beautiful forest ranger when they find themselves in the way of a violent group known as the Global Mafia. Seems Johnny has a computer disk that the gangsters want. 90m/C VHS, DVD. Don "The Dragon" Wilson, Bobbie Phillips, Robert Costanzo; D: Rick Jacobson.

that she will die in exactly one week. A week later all four teens are dead. Katie's reporter aunt Rachel (Watts) tries to get to the bottom of the mystery, but has only one week to do so after also viewing the tape. She is also trying to save her son (Dorfman) and ex-husband Noah (Henderson), who are not rather stupidly exposed to this Memorex of Mayhem. While the look is suitably atmospheric and creepy, the plot stretches plausibility to the breaking point. 115m/C VHS, DVD. US Naomi Watts, Martin Henderson, David Dorfman, Brian Cox, Jane Alexander, Lindsey Frost, Amber Tamblyn, Rachael Bella, Daveigh Chase, Pauley Perrette, Sara Rue, Shannon Cochran; C: Gale Tattersall; W: Ehren Kruger; M: Hans Zimmer.

The Ring 2 🐾½ 2005 (PG-13) Creepy demon-child Samara (Chase) continues to pursue reporter Rachel (Watts) and her son (Dorfman). This time around the killer videotape is dispensed with early on in favor of a more traditional possession theme. Samara wants all the comforts of Mommy and home, and seems to find them in the son's body. Excruciatingly slow, confused, and almost totally unfrightening wreck, this time helmed by the director of the original Japanese film, who should have known better. 111m/C VHS, DVD. US Naomi Watts, Simon Baker, David Dorfman, Elizabeth Perkins, Gary Cole, Sissy Spacek, Ryan Merriman, Emily Van Camp, Daveigh Chase, Kelly Overton, Kelly Stables, James Lesure; D: Hideo Nakata; W: Ehren Kruger, Hideo Nakata; C: Gabriel Beristain; M: Henning Lohner, Martin Tillman.

Ring of Bright Water 🐾🐾🐾 1969 (G) Well done story of a pet otter from Gavin Maxwell's autobiography. The film stars the couple that made the delightful "Born Free." Beautiful Scottish Highlands photography adds to this captivating and endearing tale of a civil servant who purchases an otter from a pet store and moves to the country. 107m/C VHS, DVD. GB Bill Travers, Virginia McKenna, Peter Jeffrey, Archie Duncan; D: Jack Couffer, Bill Travers; C: Wolfgang Suschitzky; M: Frank Cordell.

Ring of Darkness WOOF! 2004 (R) Eoy band zombies. Pop singer Shawn (Martinez) reluctantly agrees to girlfriend Stacy's (Starr) demands that he try out to be the replacement lead singer of boy band Take Ten. Shawn and two other finalists are whisked away to a secluded island and discover that the band members are zombies who use black magic to stay young and on the charts. An unfortunate Barbeau plays their evil manager. Grating music and no frights—except for that plotline. 85m/C DVD. Jeremy Jackson, Acrienne Barbeau, Mink Stole, Stephen Martines, Ryan Starr, Eric Dearborn, Greg Cipes; D: David DeCoteau; W: Matthew Jason Walsh, Ryan Carrara; Michael Gingold; C: Mateo Londono.

Ring of Death 🐾½ The Detective 1969 (R) A tough cop investigating a routine case becomes a hunted man after someone kills the man he is following. 103m/C VHS. IT Franco Nero, Florinda Bolkan, Adolfo Celi, Delia Boccardo, Susanna Martinkova; D: Romolo Guerrieri; W: Massimo D'Avak; C: Roberto Gerardi; M: Fred Bongusto.

Ring of Fire 🐾½ 1991 (R) Wilson is one of very few modern American kung-fu heroes of Asian descent, and he works messages against prejudice in this interracial Romeo-and-Juliet chopsocky tale. What foot through yonder window breaks? 100m/C VHS, DVD. Don "The Dragon" Wilson, Maria Ford, Vince Murdocco, Jale Jacoby; D: Richard W. Munchkin.

Ring of Fire 2: Blood and Steel 🐾½ 1992 (R) Wilson returns as Dr. Johnny Wu in this martial-arts actioner which finds the good doctor the witness to a robbery. When one of the robbers is killed, the gang's leader kidnaps Johnny's fiance and holds her for ransom. He decides to bypass the police and use his own expertise to rescue her. 94m/C VHS, DVD. Don "The Dragon" Wilson, Maria Ford, Vince Murdocco, Jale Jacoby, Vince Delano, Eric Lee; D: Richard W. Munchkin.

Ring of Fire 3: Lion Strike 🐾½ 1994 (R) Johnny Wu is supposed to be on vacation with his son and a beautiful forest ranger when they find themselves in the way of a violent group known as the Global Mafia. Seems Johnny has a computer disk that the gangsters want. 90m/C VHS, DVD. Don "The Dragon" Wilson, Bobbie Phillips, Robert Costanzo; D: Rick Jacobson.

Ring of Steel 🐾🐾 1994 (R) Alex, a one-time Olympic hopeful in fencing, is enticed into combat by the mysterious owner of a decadent nightclub where gladiator-type matches are staged for the thrill seekers; he no longer wants to fight, but when Alex discovers the club's dark secret, he must fight from a corpse. Unfortunately, this seemingly invincible guy has a deadly terror of the dead. Cheaply made flop allegedly based on an actual hazing incident. 94m/C VHS, DVD. Gary Kasper, Darlene Vogel; D: David Frost; W: Robert Chapin; M: Jeff Beal.

Ring of Terror 🐾 1962 College boy who wants to join a fraternity must survive the initiation rights, which include stealing a ring from a corpse. Unfortunately, this seemingly invincible guy has a deadly terror of the dead. Cheaply made flop allegedly based on an actual hazing incident. 72m/B VHS, DVD. George Mather, Esther Furst, Austin Green, Joseph Conway; D: Clark Paylow.

The Ringer 🐾🐾½ 2005 (PG-13) Contemporary spoof of the Musketeers saga finds three descendants of the swashbuckling heroes carrying on the family tradition of protecting the weak and innocent. They even get stuck with a Musketeer-wanna-be when they come to the rescue of a young boy who is kidnapped to prevent his dad from testifying against mobsters. 86m/C VHS, DVD. Johnny Knoxville, Brian Cox, Katherine Heigl, Geoffrey Arend, Leonard Earl Howze, Jed Rees, Bill Chott, Leonard Flowers; D: Barry W. Blaustein; W: Ricky Blitt; C: Mark Irwin; M: Mark Mothersbaugh.

Ringmaster WOOF! 1998 (R) Okay, this is it. Hug the kids, empty the bank accounts. It's the apocalypse. Jerry Springer's made a movie. And the first question would be: why? Sexual escapades and the thrill of being on "the TEE-vee" ensue. 85m/C VHS, DVD. Jerry Springer, John Capporice, Jaime Pressly, Molly Hagan, Michael Dudikoff, Michael Jai White, William McNamara, Dawn Maxey, Wendal Jon Benstein; C: Russell Lyster; M: Kennard Ramsey; Golden Raspberries '98: Worst New Star (Springer).

Ringmaster 1998 (R) Okay, this is it. Hug the kids, empty the bank accounts. It's the apocalypse. Jerry Springer's made a movie. And the first question would be: why? To cash in, of course, and to try to justify the show's existence. The second question is: Why should you bother? The answer is a resounding "You shouldn't." In case you couldn't (Dudikoff) who's devolved—welcomes a stepdad (Pressly) with her best friend. Sexual escapades and the thrill of being on "the TEE-vee" ensue. 85m/C DVD. Jerry Springer, John Capporice, Jaime Pressly, Molly Hagan, Michael Dudikoff, Michael Jai White, William McNamara, Dawn Maxey, Nicki Micheaux, Ashley Holbrook, Tangie Ambrose, Raquel Robinson, Jon Benstein; C: Russell Lyster; M: Kennard Ramsey; Golden Raspberries '98: Worst New Star (Springer).

Rio 🐾🐾½ 1993 Country singers abound in—what else—a made-for-TV Western movie. A bounty hunter (Rogers) and newlywed groom (Tritt) set off after a gang of thieving kidnappers who have snatched the young bride (Harring). Judd shows up at the owner of a desert hostelry, who happens to cross paths with the hunters. Watch out—this could be more than a Partridge Family reunion. 120m/C VHS. Kenny Rogers, Travis Tritt, Naomi Judd, Stacy Keach, Brion James, Bruce Greenwood, Laura Elena Harring; M: Larry Brown.

Rio Grande 🐾🐾🐾 1950 The last entry in Ford's cavalry trilogy; following "Fort Apache" and "She Wore a Yellow Ribbon," A U.S. cavalry unit on the Mexican border conducts an unsuccessful campaign against marauding Indians. The commander of the lonely outpost, Lt. Col. Claude Jarman Jr., Harry Carey Jr. Victor McLaglen, Chill Wills, J. Carrol Naish; D: John Ford; M: Victor Young.

Rio Grande Raiders 🐾 1946 A Stagecoach driver discovers that his kid brother is working for a crooked rival stage company. 54m/B VHS. Sunset Carson, Linda Stirling, Bob Steele; D: Thomas Carr.

Rio Lobo 🐾🐾½ 1970 (G) Hawks's final film takes place after the Civil War, when Union Colonel Wayne goes to Rio Lobo to take revenge on two traitors. Disappointing. The Duke has to carry weak supporting performances on his brawny shoulders—and nearly does. 114m/C VHS, DVD. John Wayne, Maureen O'Hara, Ben Johnson, John Wayne, Jack Elam, Chris Mitchum, David Huddleston, George Plimpton; D: Howard Hawks; M: Jerry Goldsmith.

Rio Rattler 🐾½ 1935 Tyler takes the place of a murdered lawman in order to find his killer. 60m/B VHS, DVD. Tom Tyler, Marion Shilling, Eddie Gribbon, William (Bill) Gould; D: Franklin Shamray.

Ringside 🐾½ 1949 A concert pianist turns boxer to avenge his brother who was blinded in a fight. 64m/B VHS. Donald O'Brien, Sheila Ryan, Tom Brown, Margia Dean, John Cason, Joseph Crehan, Lyle Talbot; D: Frank McDonald; W: Ron Ormond, Daniel Ullman.

The Rink 🐾🐾🐾 1916 Chaplin plays a waiter who spends his lunch hour on roller skates. Silent with musical soundtrack added. 20m/B VHS, DVD. Charlie Chaplin, Edna Purviance; D: Charlie Chaplin.

Rio 🐾🐾🐾 1939 John T. Principally set in a French penal colony. 64m/B VHS. Basil Rathbone, Victor McLaglen, Sigrid Gurie, Leo Carrillo, Robert Cummings; D: John Brahm.

Rio Bravo 🐾🐾½ 1959 John T. Chance (Wayne) is the sheriff of a Texas border town who takes murderer Joe (Akins) into custody. Since Joe is the brother of powerful local cattle baron Nathan Burdette (Russell), the sheriff faces a blockade of gunmen hired to keep his prisoner from being brought to justice. Chance has to make do with the help of a cripple (Brennan), a drunk (Martin), and a hot-headed kid (Nelson). Long, but continually entertaining film that didn't impress critics at the time but its reputation has improved over the years. Hawks and Wayne basically remade this or were with "El Dorado." 140m/C VHS, DVD, Blu-ray Disc, HD DVD. John Wayne, Dean Martin, Angie Dickinson, Ricky Nelson, Walter Brennan, Ward Bond, Claude Akins, Bob Steele, John Russell, Harry Carey Jr., Pedro Gonzalez-Gonzalez; D: Howard Hawks; W: Leigh Brackett, Jules Furthman; C: Russell Harlan; M: Dimitri Tiomkin.

Rio Conchos 🐾🐾🐾 1964 Nifty nonstop action in this western set in Texas after the Civil War. Three Army buddies search for 2,000 stolen rifles. Boone is undertstated, O'Brien is good, and Brown memorable in his debut. 107m/C VHS, DVD. Richard Boone, Stuart Whitman, Edmond O'Brien, Anthony (Tony) Franciosa, Jim Brown; D: Gordon Douglas; M: Jerry Goldsmith.

Rio Diablo 🐾🐾½ 1993 Country singers abound in—what else—a made-for-TV Western movie. A bounty hunter (Rogers) and newlywed groom (Tritt) set off after a gang of thieving kidnappers who have snatched the young bride (Harring). Judd shows up at the owner of a desert hostelry, who happens to cross paths with the hunters. Watch out—this could be more than a Partridge Family reunion. 120m/C VHS. Kenny Rogers, Travis Tritt, Naomi Judd, Stacy Keach, Brion James, Bruce Greenwood, Laura Elena Harring; M: Larry Brown.

Rio Rita 1942 Abbott & Costello are working on a ranch and somehow become involved with Nazi spies. Provides a few original comic bits for the duo but is otherwise mediocre. An updated remake of the 1929 Wheeler & Woolsey comedy. 91m/B VHS. Bud Abbott, Lou Costello, Kathryn Grayson, John Carroll, Patricia Dane, Tom Conway, Peter Whitney; D: S. Sylvan Simon; C: George J. Folsey.

Riot 1969 (R) Men in cages throw tantrums until warden returns from vacation. Filmed in Arizona State Prison with real convicts as extras. Strong performances by fullback Brown and durable Hackman. Based on story by ex-con Frank Elli. Too off-played theme song sung by Bill Medley of the Righteous Brothers. 97m/C VHS. Gene Hackman, Jim Brown, Mike Kellin, Ben Carruthers, Frank Eyman; D: Buzz Kulik; W: James Poe.

Riot 1996 (R) Dumb actioner set on Christmas Eve, 1999, amidst some L.A. riots. British Special Air Service officer Shane Alcott (Daniels) must rescue his kidnapped ex-girlfriend Anna-Lisa (Rowland), who just happens to be the British ambassador's daughter. She's being held by ghetto gangster Leon (Sanders), whose gang turn out to be pawns for IRA leader O'Flaherty (Kilpatrick), who has a score to settle. Predictable fights, lots of explosions. 95m/C VHS, DVD. Gary Daniels, Ray "Sugar Ray" Leonard, Patrick Kilpatrick, Paige Rowland, Dex Elliot Sanders, Charles Napier; D: Joseph Merhi; W: Joseph John Barmettler Jr., William Applegate Jr.; C: Ken Blakey; M: Jim Halfpenny.

Riot in Cell Block 11 1954 A convict leads four thousand prisoners in an uprising to improve prison conditions. Based on producer/ex-con Walter Wanger's own experience. Powerful and still timely. Filmed at Folsom Prison. 80m/B VHS. Neville Brand, Leo Gordon, Emile Meyer, Frank Faylen; D: Donald Siegel.

Riot in the Streets 1996 Four interwined stories revolving around the 1992 Los Angeles riots, on the day the Rodney King verdict was announced. Concerned are an African-American family, a white police officer, a Latino family, and Asian-American shopowners. Documentary footage of the actual riots is also included. 95m/C VHS, DVD. Mario Van Peebles, Melvin Van Peebles, Cicely Tyson, Luke Perry, Peter Dobson, Dante Basco, Mako, Kieu Chinh, Alexis Cruz, Douglas Spain, Yelba Osorio, John Ortiz; D: C. David Johnson, Richard Dilello, Galen Yuen, Alex Munoz; W: C. David Johnson, Richard Dilello, Galen Yuen, Joe Vasquez; C: Paul Elliott. CABLE

Riot Squad 1941 An intern poses as a doctor in order to find out who was responsible for putting a mob hit on a police captain. 55m/B VHS. Richard Cromwell, Rita Quigley, John Miljan, Mary Ruth, Herbert Rawlinson, Mary Gordon, Arthur Space; D: Edward Finney.

Rip It Off *Beyond the City Limits* 2002 (R) Lexi (Hannigan) and Misha (Kinski) have a couple of loser thug boyfriends (Denisof, McCardie) who are planning a casino heist with a couple of dirty cops. When the gals get fed up by the way they're treated, they hook up with pal Helena (Esposito) and decide to pull off the heist first and leave the guys out in the cold. Told from the POV of Helena's own dirty cop, Toretti (Field). 91m/C VHS, DVD. Nastassja Kinski, Alyson Hannigan, Jennifer Esposito, Brian McCardie, Alexis Denisof, Todd Field, Steve Harris, Freddy Rodriguez, Sophie B. Hawkins; D: Gigi Gaston; W: John McMahon; C: David Bridges.

Rip-Off 1977 Two Greek wanderers enter the American way of life via sex, drugs, syndicated crime, and terrorism. 78m/C VHS. Michael Benet, Michele Simone, James Masters, Johnny Dark; D: Manolis Tsatos.

The Rip Off 1978 (R) A colorful gang of hoodlums goes for the biggest heist of their lives—six million bucks in diamonds! 99m/C VHS. Lee Van Cleef, Karen Black, Robert Alda, Edward Albert; D: Anthony M. Dawson.

Rip Roarin' Buckaroo 1936 A fighter sets out to avenge himself when he is framed in a dishonest fight. 51m/B VHS, DVD. Tom Tyler, B.J. Quinn Jr., Beth Marion, Charles "Blackie" King; D: Robert F. "Bob" Hill.

Rip van Winkle 1985 Sleepy Coppola adaptation of the Washington Irving story about a man who falls asleep for 20 years after a group of ghosts get him drunk. From the "Faerie Tale Theatre" series. 60m/C VHS, DVD. Harry Dean Stanton, Talia Shire; D: Francis Ford Coppola.

Ripe 1997 (R) Fourteen-year-old fraternal twins Violet (Keena) and Rosie (Eagan) decide to make it on their own after their abusive parents are killed in a car crash. They wind up on a derelict southern army base where they're befriended by caretaker Pete (Currie) and M.P. Ken (Brice), who may not have the most innocent of intentions. 93m/C VHS, DVD. Monica Keena, Daisy Eagan, Gordon Currie, Ron Brice, Karen (Lynn) Gomey, Vincent Laresca; D: Mo Ogrodnik; W: Mo Ogrodnik; C: Wolfgang Held; M: Anton Sanko.

Ripley's Game 2002 (R) Tom Ripley (Malkovich) is still a sociopath, but now he's older, more refined, icier, married, and (not surprisingly) successful. When he overhears an insult by the host, Trevanny (Scott), of a dinner party, he decides to make him pay. His opportunity comes when British gangster Reeves (Winstone) asks him for an anonymous assassin to take out a Russian mobster. Ripley, knowing Trevanny is terminally ill and broke, suggests him as the hit man. Trevanny accepts, but is betrayed by Reeves, which conflicts with Ripley's sense of honor, who then intervenes. Malkovich is perfect as the steely Ripley, and has good support from the rest of the cast, as well as an enjoyably intricate plot. 100m/C VHS, DVD. John Malkovich, Dougray Scott, Ray Winstone, Lena Headey, Chiara Caselli; D: Liliana Cavani; W: Liliana Cavani, Charles McKeown; C: Alfio Contini; M: Ennio Morricone. VIDEO

The Ripper WOOF! 1986 The spirit of Jack the Ripper possesses a university professor's body. Ultra-violent. Shot on videotape for the video market. 90m/C VHS. Wade Tower, Tom Schreir, Mona Van Pernis, Andrea Adams; D: Christopher Lewis.

The Ripper 1997 (R) Yet another version of the Jack the Ripper saga. In 1888 London, ambitious Scotland Yard inspector Jim Hansen (Bergin) is investigating the murders of several East End prostitutes. Clues direct him to a member of the nobility, in fact, Queen Victoria's grandson, Prince Edward (West), but pursuing his inquiries could lead to the end of Hansen's career. 100m/C VHS. Patrick Bergin, Gabrielle Anwar, Michael York, Samuel West, Essie Davis, Olivia Hamnett; D: Janet Meyers; W: Robert Rodat; C: Martin McGrath; M: Mason Daring. CABLE

Ripper: Letter from Hell 2001 (R) Thankfully, there's more terror than gore in this slasher, which could be a bummer if you prefer the bloodier the better. Molly Keller (Cook) enrolls in a forensic science program taught by criminologist Marshall Kane (Payne). There's a spate of recent campus murders that Molly and her study group are investigating and the modus operandi resembles that of Jack the Ripper. Then they start becoming the killer's next victims. 113m/C VHS, DVD. A.J. Cook, Bruce Payne, Ryan Northcott, Jurgen Prochnow, Claire Keim, Derek Hamilton, Emmanuelle Vaugier; D: John Eyres; W: Patrick Bermel; C: Thomas M. Harting; M: Peter Allen. VIDEO

Ripper Man 1996 (R) Ex-cop is accused of murder when he finds a body at a nightclub and then becomes the killer's next target. 93m/C VHS. Timothy Bottoms, Robert F. Lyons, Charles Napier, Bruce Locke, Mike Norris; D: Phil Sears; W: Phil Sears; C: Blake T. Evans; M: Jim Ervin. VIDEO

Riptide 1934 Shearer is a carefree American married to stuffy English lord Marshall. He goes off to America on a business trip, she's bored and goes to a costume party (everyone dresses as insects!) where she meets old flame Montgomery. He gets drunk, follows her home in an effort to rekindle their passion, and winds up in the hospital after a drunken fall. The returning Marshall is appalled by the scandalous press and instigates divorce proceedings. Eventually, they come to their senses and decide they do love each other. Quality production with an entertaining cast. 90m/B VHS. Norma Shearer, Herbert Marshall, Robert Montgomery, Richard "Skeets" Gallagher, Ralph Forbes, Lilyan Tashman; D: Edmund Goulding; W: Edmund Goulding.

The Rise and Fall of Legs Diamond 1960 Not quite historically accurate but fast-paced and entertaining gangster bio of legendary booze trafficker Legs Diamond. Danton's debut. 101m/B VHS. Ray Danton, Karen Steele, Jesse White, Simon Oakland, Robert Lowery, Elaine Stewart; D: Budd Boetticher.

The Rise & Rise of Daniel Rocket 1986 A exceptional young boy believes he can fly without the aid of a flying machine. From the "American Playhouse" series. 90m/C VHS. Tom Hulce, Timothy Daly, Valerie Mahaffey; D: Emile Ardolino.

Rise: Blood Hunter 2007 Reporter Sadie (Liu) becomes a victim of the underground vampire cult she was investigating. She's not happy and, armed with a cross-bow, she decides to get revenge on the vamp leader (D'Arcy) and anyone else who brutalized her. Lots of violence, gore, and nakedness. 94m/C DVD. Lucy Liu, Michael Chiklis, Carla Gugino, James D'Arcy, Nick Lachey, Robert Forster, Mako; D: Sebastian Gutierrez; W: Sebastian Gutierrez; C: John Toll; M: Nathan Barr.

The Rise of Louis XIV *La Prise de Pouvoir Par Louis XIV* 1966 A masterful docudrama detailing the life and court intrigues of Louis XIV of France. Successfully captures the attitudes and mores of the royalty at the time. One of a series of historical films directed by Rossellini. Made for French TV; subtitled. 100m/C FR Jean-Marie Patte, Raymond Jourdan, Dominique Vincent, Giorgio Silvagni, Pierre Barrat; D: Roberto Rossellini. TV

The Rising Place 2002 (PG-13) Nostalgia and tears. Dying Emily Hodge (Drummond) recalls her sometimes unconventional life to her niece Virginia (Fisher) in a series of flashbacks. The young Emily (Holloman) is a small-town Southern belle who gets pregnant by her boyfriend who goes off to WWII, never to return. Having scandalized her conventional parents (Harper, Cole), Emily agrees to give her baby up for adoption but refuses to go into hiding. Instead, she becomes a schoolteacher along with her black best friend, Wilma (Neal), who encourages Emily to get involved in the civil rights movement. Based on the novel by David Armstrong. 93m/C VHS, DVD. Laurel Holloman, Elise Neal, Mark Webber, Billy Campbell, Gary Cole, Tess Harper, Alice Drummond, Frances Fisher; D: Tom Rice; W: Tom Rice; C: Jim Dollarhide; M: Conrad Pope.

Rising Son 1990 A family man who loses his job faces trauma when his factory closes at the same time his son informs him he's quitting medical school. Solid family drama and parable of economic hard times of the early '80s, sustained by top-drawer performances by Dennehy, Damon, and Laurie. Well directed by Coles. 92m/C VHS. Brian Dennehy, Matt Damon, Piper Laurie, Graham Beckel, Ving Rhames, Jane Adams, Richard Jenkins, Emily Longstreth; D: John David Coles; W: Bill Phillips. CABLE

Rising Sun 1993 (R) When a prostitute is found murdered in the boardroom of a powerful Japanese-owned corporation, seasoned cop (and partner Snipes expert) Connery and new partner Snipes are sent to investigate. Complicated yarn about business, prejudice, cops, and the differences between east and west. Filmed with stylized camera techniques, quick action, and good rapport between the two leads. Based on the book by Crichton, which offered ominous business and international politics and business. These aspects had the film labeled as Japan-bashing, one of the reasons the script was rewritten to focus more on the murder mystery. 129m/C VHS, DVD. Sean Shaw, Steve Buscemi, Peter Crombie, Alexandra Powers, Daniel von Bargen, Amy Hill, Clyde Kusatsu, Sean Connery, Wesley Snipes, Tia Carrere, Harvey Keitel, Kevin Anderson, Stan(ford) Egi, Mako, Cary-Hiroyuki Tagawa, Ray Wise, Tatjana Patitz, Michael Chapman; W: Philip Kaufman; W: Michael Backes, Michael Crichton, Philip Kaufman; C: Michael Chapman; M: Toru Takemitsu.

Risk 1994 Maya (Sillas) is a struggling, emotionally distant, New York artist when she meets overly friendly Joe (Ilku) on a bus. He follows her home and manages to entice Maya into letting him spend the night but Joe has some psychological problems, including criminal behavior, which manifests itself when he steals a car. Maya, nevertheless, agrees to drive with him to his older sister's home in rural Connecticut and finds bad blood and more mental anguish that she knows how to deal with. Terrifically honest performance by Sillas and an equally touching one by Ilku are highlights of this adult attempt at romance. 85m/C VHS. Karen Sillas, David Ilku, Molly Price, Jack Gwaltney; D: Deirdre Fishel; W: Deirdre Fishel; C: Peter Pearce; M: John Paul Jones.

Risk 2000 (R) Shady insurance guy John Kriesky (Brown) is tutoring young Ben (Long) in money, sex, and shifty deals, including involving him in insurance fraud. Then Kriesky's lawyer/girlfriend Louise (Karvan) decides to give Ben a few personal lessons as well. Fast-paced thriller with a cast that's well worth watching. 89m/C VHS, DVD. AU Bryan Brown, Tom Long, Claudia Karvan, Jason Clarke; D: Alan White; W: John Armstrong; C: Simon Duggan; M: Don Miller-Robinson. CABLE

Risky Business 1928 Fortune-seeking mother disapproves of daughter's doctor fiance, and educates girl in marital woes. Video includes early Pollard short "Sold at Auction." 104m/B VHS. Vera Reynolds, Zasu Pitts, Ethey Clayton; D: Alan Hale.

Risky Business 1983 With his parents out of town and awaiting word from the college boards, a teenager becomes involved in unexpected ways with a quick-thinking prostitute, her pimp, and assorted others. Cruise is likeable, especially when dancing in his underwear. Funny, well-paced, stylish prototypical '80s teen flick reintroduced Ray-Bans as the sunglasses for the wanna-be hip. What a party! 99m/C VHS, DVD. Tom Cruise, Rebecca De Mornay, Curtis Armstrong, Bronson Pinchot, Joe Pantoliano, Kevin Anderson, Richard Masur, Raphael Sbarge, Nicholas Pryor, Janet Carroll; D: Paul Brickman; W: Paul Brickman; C: Reynaldo Villalobos, Bruce Surtees; M: Tangerine Dream.

Rita Hayworth: The Love Goddess 1983 Drama details the tragic life of the beautiful film star. Carter, lovely though she is, plays Rita weakly and without depth. 100m/C VHS. Lynda Carter, Michael Lerner, Alejandro Rey, John Considine; D: James Goldstone. TV

Rita, Sue & Bob Too 1987 (R) A middle-aged Englishman gets involved in a menage a trois when two promiscuous teenagers, until the whole town gets wind of it. A raunchy, amoral British comedy. 94m/C VHS, DVD. GB Michelle Holmes, George Costigan, Siobhan Finneran, Lesley Sharp, Willie Ross, Patti Nicholls, Kulvinder Ghir; D: Alan Clarke; W: Andrea Dunbar; C: Ivan Strasburg; M: Michael Kamen.

The Rite *The Ritual; Riten* 1969 Members of a famous theatrical troupe are called before a judge to answer charges that a production is obscene. The judge's interrogation exposes their private and painful neuroses until the performers decide to turn on their accuser. Pessimistic even by Bergman standards and the first film the director made specifically for TV. Swedish with subtitles. 75m/B VHS, DVD. SW Ingrid Thulin, Gunnar Bjornstrand, Erik Hell, Anders Ek; D: Ingmar Bergman; W: Ingmar Bergman; C: Sven Nykvist.

Rites of Frankenstein *Erotic Rites of Frankenstein* 1972 (R) Ultra-low budget remake with plenty of blood, sex and perversions required of surreal horrors. Frankenstein (Price) is murdered and his

River Beat ✗✗ 1954. A woman aboard an American freighter is unwittingly used as a diamond smuggler, and is arrested when the ship docks in London. An inspector does his best to clear the hapless woman. **70m/B VHS.** Phyllis Kirk, John Bentley, Robert Ayres, Lenny White, Glyn Houston, Charles Lloyd-Pack. *D:* Guy Green.

The River ✗✗✗ 1984 (PG) Farmers battle a river whose flood threatens their farm. Spacek, as always, is strong and believable as the wife and mother, but Gibson falters. Beautiful photography. The third in an onslaught of films in the early '80s that dramatized the plight of the small American farmer. "The River" isn't as strong as "Country" and "Places in the Heart" which managed to convey important messages less cloyingly. **124m/C VHS, DVD, HD DVD.** Mel Gibson, Sissy Spacek, Scott Glenn, Billy Green Bush; *D:* Mark Rydell; *W:* Julian Barton, Robert Dillon; *C:* Vilmos Zsigmond; *M:* John Williams.

The River ✗✗✗ 1951 A massive-ly lauded late film by Renoir about three British girls growing up in Bengal, India, all developing crushes on a one-legged American vet. Lyrical and heartwarming, with hailed cinematography by Claude Renoir. Rumer Godden wrote the novel, and co-scripted the screenplay with director Renoir. Satyajit Ray, one of Indie's greatest filmmakers, assisted Renoir. **99m/C VHS, DVD, FR** Patricia Waters, Adrienne Corri, Nora Swinburne, Radha, Arthur Shields, Thomas E. Breen, Esmond Knight; *D:* Jean Renoir; *W:* Jean Renoir; *C:* Claude Renoir; *Nar:* June Hillman.

Rivals ✗✗✗ *Deadly Rivals* 1972 (R) Shallow, unconvincing drama about a stepmother challenged by his stepson, who wants to kill this new contender for his mother's love. Nice handling of cast credits, but otherwise details—nice acting, directing and photography—leave much to be desired. **103m/C VHS.** Robert Klein, Joan Hackett, Scott Jacoby; *D:* Krishna Shah.

Rituals ✗✗ *The Creeper* 1979 Group of five calm, rational men suddenly turn desperate after a chain of nightmarish events on a camping trip. Yet another low-budget "Deliverance" rip off. **100m/C VHS, CA** Hal Holbrook, Lawrence Dane; *D:* Peter Carter.

The Ritz ✗✗✗ 1976 (R) Weston tries to get away from his gangster brother-in-law by hiding out in a gay bathhouse in New York. Moreno plays a talentless singer Googie Gomez, who performs in the bathhouse while waiting for her big break. Moreno is great reprising her Tony-winning stage role, and Lester's direction is spiffy. Written by Terence McNally from his play. **91m/C VHS, DVD.** Rita Moreno, Jack Weston, Jerry Stiller, Kaye Ballard, Treat Williams, F. Murray Abraham; *D:* Richard Lester.

Rites of Passage ✗✗ 1999 (R) Suspense about fathers, son's, and masculinity has both awkwardness and intensity. Del Farraday (Stockwell) and his son D.J. (Keith) travel to their secluded mountain cabin for a heart-to-heart that only to discover the place is being used by Farraday's estranged gay son, Campbell (Behr). As if there weren't enough family angst, the trio are joined by violent escaped cons Frank (Remar) and Red (Wodiwelt). Tempers flare between Del and Frank and the entire situation is worsened by a secret that Campbell is keeping. Good performances. **94m/C VHS, DVD.** Dean Stockwell, Robert Keith, Jason Behr, Robert Faunleroy; *M:* Bennett Salvay.

VIDEO monster creation is stolen by his archenemy Dr. Cagliostro, a mad genius taken to kidnapping girls for their body parts, which he uses in dastardly experiments. Frankenstein's daughter (Savon) seeks to avenge her father's death through unconventional methods, of course. Just wacky enough to become a euro-trash classic. In Spanish with English subtitles. **94m/C DVD.** Jess (Jesus) Franco, Dennis Price, Howard Vernon, Anne Libert, Britt Nichols, Alberto Dalbes, Luis Barboo, Lina Romay, Daniel White, Beatriz Savon; *D:* Jess (Jesus) Franco; *W:* Jess (Jesus) Franco; *C:* Raul Artigot; *M:* Daniel White.

The River Niger ✗✗ 1976 (R) Jones is riveting, and Tyson is good in an otherwise muddling adaptation of the Tony-award winning play about black ghetto life. Realistic emotions and believable characters. **105m/C VHS, DVD.** James Earl Jones, Cicely Tyson, Glynn Turman, Louis Gossett Jr., Roger E. Mosley, Jonelle Allen; *D:* Krishna Shah.

River of Death ✗✗ 1990 (R) Absurd adventure, based on an Alistair McLean novel, about a white man entering the Amazon jungle world of a forgotten tribe in search of wealth, tripping over Neo-Nazi scientists and war criminals. Too complex for the harmlessly enjoyable, but too mindless for the complexity to be worth unraveling. **103m/C VHS.** Michael Dudikoff, Robert Vaughn, Donald Pleasence, Herbert Lom, L.Q. Jones, Cynthia Erland, Sarah Maur-Thorp; *D:* Steve Carver.

River of Diamonds ✗ 1990 A daring adventurer, with the standard beautiful woman at his side, battles evil curses and Nazis buried alive to find a fortune in diamonds. Yeah, sure. Another miserable "Indiana Jones" rip off. **88m/C VHS.** Dack Rambo, Angela O'Neill Ferdinand "Ferdy" Mayne, Graham Clark, David Sherwood, Tony Caprari, Dominique Tyawa; *D:* Robert J. Smawley.

River of Evil ✗1/2 1964 Action/adventure in which a young girl travels through the Amazon jungle searching for clues to her father's death. **83m/C VHS.** Barbara Rütting, Harald Leipritz, Oswaldo Louriero, Cyl Farney, Tereza Raquo; *D:* Franz Eichhorn; *C:* Edgar Eichhorn; *M:* Catulo Cearense.

A River Made to Drown In ✗✗ 1997 When wealthy lawyer Thaddeus MacKenzie (Chamberlain) learns he is dying from AIDS, he decides to get in touch with the two people he once loved, Allen and Jaime. Allen (Imperioli) is a struggling artist who once worked the streets and is now involved with gallery owner Eva (Lemper), who knows nothing about his former life. But he agrees to look for the still-hustling Jaime (Duval), even if this means confronting a past he'd rather forget. **98m/C VHS, DVD.** Michael Imperioli, Richard Chamberlain, James Duval, Ute Lemper, Austin Pendleton, Talia Shire, Mike Starr, Michael Saucedo, James Karen, Lewis Arquette; *D:* James Merendino; *W:* Paul Marius; *C:* Thomas Callaway.

The River King ✗ 2005 (R) Muddled and dull crime drama based on the novel by Alice Hoffman. Small town police detective Abel Grey (Burns) doesn't believe that the drowning death of a private school student leads him to the boy's photography teacher, Betsy Chase (Ehle), who aids in Abel's sleuthing. **104m/C VHS, DVD.** Tom Everett Scott, David Moscow, Cara Buono, Denis O'Hare, Leo Burmester, Thor Feldman, James Murtaugh, David Lowery, Michael Kelly; *D:* Eric Drilling; *W:* Eric Drilling; *C:* Steven Schueler; *M:* Johnny Hickman.

River of No Return ✗✗ 1954 During the gold rush, an itinerant farmer and his young son help a heart-of-gold saloon singer search for her estranged husband. Rather crummy script is helped by the mere presence of Mitchum and Monroe. Monroe sings the title song, as well as "Down in the Meadow," and "I'm Going to File My Claim." **91m/C VHS, DVD.** Robert Mitchum, Marilyn Monroe, Tommy Rettig, Roy Calhoun, Murvyn Vye, Douglas Spencer; *D:* Otto Preminger; *W:* Frank Fenton; *C:* Joseph LaShelle; *M:* Cyril Mockridge.

River of Unrest ✗✗ *Ourselves Alone* 1936. Remarkable visual expressiveness and emotional power mark this depiction of terrorism and open warfare during the Irish Rebellion. Based on a play, hence slow; but good acting pulls it up half a bone. **69m/B VHS.** John Lodge, John Loder, Antoinette Cellier, Clifford Evans; *D:* Brian Desmond Hurst; *W:* Philip MacDorald; *C:* Walter J. Harvey.

The River Pirates ✗✗1/2 *Good Ole Boy: A Delta Boyhood* 1988 (PG) Mississippi boy discovers a lot about life over the summer of his 12th birthday in 1942. He finds the secret hiding place of a band of river thieves, endures a tornado, has some adventures with his friends, and finds out that his crush on the prettiest girl in town is reciprocated. Based on a novel by Willie Morris. **108m/C VHS.** Ryan Francis, Richard Farnsworth, Gennie James, Doug Emerson, Anne Ramsey, Maureen O'Sullivan; *D:* Tom G. Robertson.

The River Rat ✗✗1/2 1984 (PG) Ex-con Jones is reunited with his daughter after spending 13 years in prison. There's something in there about stashed loot that should have been jettisoned in favor of more getting-to-know-you father-daughter drama, which is good. **93m/C VHS.** Tommy Lee Jones, Brian Dennehy, Martha Plimpton, Shawn Smith, Melissa Davis; *D:* Thomas (Tom) Rickman.

A River Runs Through It ✗✗1/2 1992 (PG) Contemplative exploration of family ties and coming of age with impact falling just short of the novel's is another well-crafted American tale directed by Redford. Set in Montana during the early part of the century, a Presbyterian minister teaches his two sons, one troubled and one on his way to rally, the story is both streamlined and naturally well served. **123m/C VHS, DVD.** Craig Sheffer, Brad Pitt, Tom Skerritt, Brenda Blethyn, Emily Lloyd, Edie McClurg, Stephen Shellen, Susan Traylor; *D:* Robert Redford; *W:* Richard Friedenberg; *C:* Philippe Rousselot; *M:* Mark Isham. Oscars '92: Cinematog.

The River is Red ✗✗ 1948 (R) Trying to save his younger brother Tom (Moscow) from the beatings Dad regularly gives him, Dave Holden (Scott), stabs their father to death. As a minor (and frankly dumb housewife/mom Cozy (Bowman) hooks up with the boozing Lee Ray (Fessenden) and the gal in the duo take an illegal gun and thinks she hit a man who suddenly appeared. Not bothering to find out if this is true, they decide to hold up in a motel until they car figure out what Reichardt does have a way with visuals so things aren't a total loss. **80m/C VHS, DVD.** Lisa Bowman, Larry Fessenden, Dick Russell; *D:* Kelly Reichardt; *M:* Jesse Harman, Kelly Reichardt; *C:* Jim Denault.

River of Grass ✗✗1/2 1994 No-budget noirish crime/romance set in the swampy, low-rent Florida area between Miami and the Everglades. Uncaring and workaholic husband Tom (Strathairn), a former guide (and white-river novices Gail comes to the aid of river novices Wade (boyishly menacing Bacon) and Terry (Reilly), who quickly turn out to be violent criminals needing Gail's help with their escape. Slow start leads to nonstop thrills with Streep an adept action heroine, though undercut by the flic's need to do something with Strathairn's thankless role. **111m/C VHS, DVD.** Lisa Bowman, Larry Fessenden, Dick Russell; *D:* Kelly Reichardt; *M:* Jesse Harman, Kelly Reichardt; *C:* Jim Denault.

River Street ✗✗ 1995 Ambitious real estate agent Ben Egan (Young) is engaged to marry Sharon (MacIntosh), has shady boss Vincent Pierce's (Hunter) daughter. But when he blows a big deal and winds up striking a cop, Ben's pampered center for street kids. He takes an interest in good-hearted center director Wendy (Davis) but can't change his ways so easily. The center stands on valuable 'river' front property and if Ben can get the land, he'll get back both his job and Sharon. The relationships don't convince and Ben's change of heart seems forced. **88m/C VHS.** AU Aden Young, Bill Hunter, Essie Davis, Tammy MacIntosh, Sullivan Stapleton, Lois Ramsay; *D:* Tony Mahood; *W:* Philip Ryall; *C:* Martin McGrath; *M:* David Bridie, John Phillips.

The River Wild ✗✗1/2 1994 (PG-13) Dissatisfied wife Gail (Streep) plans a family white-water rafting vacation with 10-year-old son Roerke (Mazzello) and workaholic husband Tom (Strathairn), a former guide (and white-river expert). Gail comes to the aid of river novices Wade (boyishly menacing Bacon) and Terry (Reilly), who quickly turn out to be violent criminals needing Gail's help with their escape. Slow start leads to nonstop thrills with Streep an adept action heroine, though undercut by the flic's need to do something with Strathairn's thankless role. Beautiful Montana and Oregon settings. **111m/C VHS, DVD.** Meryl Streep, David Strathairn, Joseph Mazzello, Kevin Bacon, John C. Reilly, Benjamin Bratt; *D:* Curtis Hanson; *W:* Raymond Gideon; *C:* Robert Elswit; *M:* Jerry Goldsmith.

Riverbend ✗✗ 1989 (R) A renegade black Army major escapes a rigged court martial only to be persecuted by racist whites in a small Southern town. **106m/C VHS.** Steve James, Tony Frank, Julius Tennon, Margaret Avery; *D:* Sam Firstenberg; *W:* Neal Jimenez; *C:* Frederick Elmes; *M:* Jurgen Knieper. Ind. Spirit '88: Film, Screenplay; Sundance '87: Special Jury Prize.

River's Edge ✗✗✗ 1987 (R) Drug-addled high school student strangles his girlfriend and casually displays the corpse to his apathetic group of friends, who leave the murder unreported for days. Harrowing and gripping; based on a true story. Aging biker Hopper is splendid. 99m/C VHS, DVD. Keanu Reeves, Crispin Glover, Daniel Roebuck, Joshua John Miller, Dennis Hopper, Ione Skye, Roxana Zal, Tom Bower, Constance Forslund, Leo Rossi, Jim Metzler; *D:* Tim Hunter; *W:* Neal Jimenez; *C:* Frederick Elmes; *M:* Jürgen Knieper.

Rize ✗✗✗ 2005 (PG-13) Intensely uptempo, hyped-up L.A. dancing form called "clowning" or "krumping" is vividly chronicled in this David LaChapelle documentary. Born from the 1992 riots as a peaceful means of expression by poverty-stricken inner-city dwellers, krumping was the invention of Tom Johnson, or Tommy the Clown, a reformed drug dealer who started the movement by dressing as a clown and, later, reenacting the Rodney King footage. Payoff comes in the form of a grand krumping contest held annually at the Great Western Forum. **85m/C DVD, US** Ronin Prods., Amy Marie Beauchamp, Jose Carcella.

RKO 281 ✗✗✗ 1999 (R) This retelling of Orson Welles (Schrieber) battles to make 1941's "Citizen Kane" is all about egos. Welles had the arrogance of youth, and Hearst the arrogance of power. The film, written with Herman J. Mankiewicz (Malkovich), was a thinly disguised look at newspaper magnate William Randolph Hearst (Cromwell) and his life with long-time mistress, blond actress Marion Davies (Griffith). Hearst was so outraged by Welles' movie that he tried to use his considerable influence with the Hollywood studios to have the film destroyed. Naturally, the story is both streamlined and altered but the leading roles are dramatically well served. **87m/C VHS, DVD.** Liev Schreiber, John Malkovich, James Cromwell, Melanie Griffith, Brenda Blethyn, Roy Scheider, David Suchet, Fiona Shaw, Liam Cunningham, Tim Woodward; *D:* Ridley Scott; *W:* John Logan; *C:* Mike Southon; *M:* John Altman. **CABLE.**

The Road ✗✗1/2 *El Camino* 2000 Manuel is on his way to a family funeral (by motorcycle) when he meets photographer Caroline on the road. Their romance is tested when Manuel is suddenly arrested and thrown in jail—only to escape after seeing a cop beat an inmate to death. The lovers are on the run but the end of the road is not the end of the journey. Spanish with subtitles. **107m/C VHS, DVD, AR** Ezequiel Rodriguez, Antonella Costa, Daniel Valenzuela, Hector Anglada, Alejandro Awada, Ruben Patagonia; *D:* Javier Olivera; *W:* Hector Olivera, Javier Olivera; *C:* Cristian Cottet; *M:* Axel Krygier.

Road Agent ✗1/2 *Texas Road Agent* 1926 Hoxie is the Kansas Kid, a fugitive hired by a crooked lawyer to pose as the long-lost' heir to a ranching fortune. Only the Kid develops a soft spot for his "family" and may not be able to go through with the evil plot. **70m/B VHS.** Al Hoxie, Lew Meehan, Florence Lee, Leon de la Mothe; **D:** J(ohn) P(aterson) McGowan; **W:** Charles Sexton; **C:** Robert Cline.

Road Ends 🦴🦴½ **1998 (R)** Small town sheriff Hopper and local innkeeper Hemingway unwittingly offer refuge to runaway FBI informant, Maceda (Sarandon), who's supposed to testify against his drug trafficking boss. FBI agent Gere (Coyote) is after Maceda as well as his ex-employers—and it's just a matter of who catches up to him first. **96m/C VHS, DVD.** Chris Sarandon, Peter Coyote, Dennis Hopper, Mariel Hemingway, Joanna Gleason; **D:** Rick King; **W:** Bill Mesce Jr.; **C:** Bruce Douglas Johnson; **M:** David Mansfield.

The Road from Coorain 🦴🦴½ **2002** Based on the 1989 memoir by historian Jill Ker Conway who was born and raised on a vast and isolated Australian sheep ranch called Coorain. The story, which opens in the early 1940s, deals with Jill's difficult relationship with her stoical mother Eve (Stevenson), who keeps Coorain even after being widowed and moving her family to Sydney. Jill proves to be an exceptional student and excels at university but family tragedies continue to haunt the Kers. **120m/C VHS.** *AU* Juliet Stevenson, Richard Roxburgh, Katherine Slattery, Alex Tomasetti, Tim Guinee, John Howard, Bernard Curry, Sean Hall; **D:** Brendan Maher; **W:** Sue Smith; **C:** Tristan Milani; **M:** Stephen Rae. **TV**

Road Games 🦴🦴 **1981 (PG)** Trucker Keach is drawn into a web of intrigue surrounding a series of highway "Jack the Ripper"-style murders. Curtis is a hitchhiker. Nothing special. Director Franklin later helmed "Psycho II." **100m/C VHS, DVD.** *AU* Stacy Keach, Jamie Lee Curtis, Marion Edwards, Grant Page, Bill Stacey, Thaddeus Smith, Alan Hopgood; **D:** Richard Franklin; **W:** Everett DeRoche; **C:** Vincent Monton; **M:** Brian May.

The Road Home 🦴🦴½ **1995 (PG)** Depression-era heart-tugger features two orphaned brothers who ride the rails from New York to Nebraska in search of a new home at Father Flanagan's Boys Town. **90m/C VHS.** Keegan Macintosh, Will Estes, Kris Kristofferson, Charles Martin Smith, Danny Aiello, Dee Wallace Stone, Mickey Rooney; **D:** Dean Hamilton.

The Road Home 🦴🦴🦴 *Wo De Fu Qin Mu Qin* **2001 (G)** Sweet story about enduring love. Luo Yuseng (Hongle) returns to his Chinese village to bury his father. He learns his mother wants to have a funeral ritual performed as a mark of respect, which involves carrying the coffin to the cemetery. Flashbacks show how young illiterate beauty Zhao Di (Ziyi) caught the eye of Luo Changyu (Hao), the new schoolteacher, who comes from the city and is of a higher class. But Changyu falls victim to the political climate of the '50s and must leave her behind, promising to return. And she promises to wait. The flashbacks are filmed in color while the present is filmed in B&W. Chinese with subtitles. **89m/C VHS, DVD.** *CH* Zhang Ziyi, Honglei Sun, Zheng Hao, Zhao Yuelin, Bin Li; **D:** Yimou Zhang; **W:** Bao Shi; **C:** Hou Yong; **M:** San Bao.

Road House 🦴🦴½ **1989 (R)** Bouncer Swayze is hired to do the impossible: clean up the toughest bar in Kansas City. When he lays down his rules he makes a lot of enemies, including ex-bar employees and local organized crime. Ample violence; an example of formula filmmaking at its most brain-numbing, with a rock soundtrack. **115m/C VHS, DVD, UMD.** Patrick Swayze, Sam Elliott, Kelly Lynch, Ben Gazzara, Kevin Tighe, Marshall Teague, Julie Michaels, Jeff Healey; **D:** Rowdy Herrington; **C:** Dean Cundey; **M:** Michael Kamen.

Road House 2: Last Call 🦴🦴½ **2006 (R)** Dopey sequel to the 1989 cheese-fest. Nate Tanner (Patton) is the owner of a rowdy Louisiana road house called the Black Pelican. When local drug runner Wild Bill (wildly overacted by Bussey) and his minions want to take over the place, Nate's DEA nephew Shane (Schaech) decides to forcibly discourage them. Many brawls follow. **86m/C DVD.** *US* Johnathon Schaech, Jake Busey, Will Patton, William Ragsdale, Ellen Hollman; **D:** Scott Ziehl; **W:** Johnathon Schaech, Richard Chizmar; **M:** Amotz Plessner. **VIDEO**

Road Kill USA 🦴🦴½ **1993** Two sleazy drifters on a cross-country murder spree pick up a hitchhiking college student and expect him to join in the fun. When he refuses, he has two choices: kill or be killed. **98m/C VHS.** Andrew Porter, Sean Bridges, Deanna Perry; **D:** Tony Elwood.

The Road Killers 🦴🦴 **1995 (R)** Sickening psycho Cliff (well-played by Sheffer) is head of a brutal quartet that terrorizes a family driving along a remote desert highway. Cliff kidnaps the family daughter and her mild-mannered dad (Lambert) must rescue her. **88m/C VHS.** Christopher Lambert, Craig Sheffer, Adrienne Shelly; **D:** Deran Sarafian; **W:** Ted Sarafian.

Road Movie 🦴🦴½ **1972** Cult favorite about a pair of brutish truck drivers (Bostwick and Drivas) who pick up a prostitute (Baff) on a trip across America. Baff delivers an emotional performance as the beaten and furious hooker who, after being abused and rejected, seeks her revenge. **82m/C DVD.** Barry Bostwick, Robert Drivas, Regina Baff; **D:** Joseph Strick; **W:** Judith Rascoe; **C:** Don Lenzer.

Road Racers 🦴🦴 **1959** The roar of the engine, fast cars, and family ties combine in this movie about the thrill of speed. **73m/B VHS, DVD.** Joel Lawrence, Marian Collier, Skip Ward; **D:** Arthur Swerdloff; **W:** Stanley Kallis, Ed Lasko.

Road Rage woof! *A Friday Night Date* **2001** The familiar plot wouldn't be so bad if there was some suspense or twists to this flick but there's not. Jim offers Sonia a ride home after breaking up a fight between Sonia and her possessive ex-boyfriend Bo. While driving, Jim cuts off a big rig, whose driver decides to get even. It won't be any surprise to discover the truck's driver is Bo. Blah. **96m/C VHS, DVD.** Casper Van Dien, Danielle Brett, Catherine Oxenberg, Joseph Griffin; **D:** Sidney J. Furie; **W:** Greg Mellott; **C:** Curtis Petersen; **M:** Robert Carli. **VIDEO**

Road Show 🦴🦴🦴 **1941** Hubbard stars as a young man wrongfully committed to an insane asylum. He escapes and joins a bankrupt carnival owned by Landis. Some really zany stuff keeps this from being just standard fare. Co-written by silent film comic Langdon. **87m/B VHS, DVD.** Adolphe Menjou, Carole Landis, John Hubbard, Charles Butterworth, Patsy Kelly, George E. Stone, Polly Ann Young, Edward Norris, Marjorie Woodworth, Florence Bates; **D:** Hal Roach; **W:** Harry Langdon.

The Road to Bali 🦴🦴🦴 **1953** Sixth Bob-n-Bing road show, the only one in color, is a keeper. The boys are competing for the love of—that's right—Lamour. She must be some gal, cuz they chase her all the way to Bali, where they meet cannibals and other perils, including the actual Humphrey Bogart. Jone's debut, in a bit role. ♪♪Moonflowers; To See You; The Merry-Go-Runaround; Chorale for Brass, Piano, and Bongo (instrumental). **90m/C VHS, DVD.** Bob Hope, Bing Crosby, Dorothy Lamour, Murvyn Vye, Ralph Moody, Jane Russell, Jerry Lewis, Dean Martin, Carolyn Jones; **D:** Hal Walker; **W:** Frank Butler, Hal Kanter, William Morrow; **C:** George Barnes.

The Road to El Dorado 🦴🦴½ **2000 (PG)** Spanish con men Tulio (Kline) and Miguel (Branagh) search for the legendary Lost City of Gold in this animated mix of the Crosby-Hope "Road" pictures and Kipling's "Man Who Would Be King." The duo hitch a ride with Cortes's expedition to South America, land among the natives, and are mistaken for gods. They also run into a beautiful local (Perez) who's onto their game and agrees to help them, and run afoul of the nasty priest who's fond of human sacrifice and wants to overthrow the kindly chief (Olmos). As usual, the animation is superb, and there are enjoyable moments throughout, but a weak plot and nondescript characters add up to a somewhat disappointing outing. **90m/C VHS, DVD.** **D:** Eric Bergeron, Don Paul; **W:** Ted Elliott, Terry Rossio; **M:** Elton John, Hans Zimmer, John Powell, Tim Rice; **V:** Kevin Kline, Kenneth Branagh, Rosie Perez, Armand Assante, Edward James Olmos; **Nar:** Elton John.

The Road to Galveston 🦴🦴🦴 **1996 (PG-13)** Texas widow Jordan Roosevelt (Tyson) needs to pay her mortgage so she turns her home into a residence for three Alzheimer patients. When her financial problems only worsen, Jordan decides to fulfill her lifetime goal and takes every one on a trip to Galveston to see the ocean. Sentimental, fact-based TV movie cuts the saccharine through compelling performances. **93m/C VHS.** Cicely Tyson, Piper Laurie, Tess Harper, Salle Ellis, Stafetta DuPois, James McDaniel, Penny Johnson, Clarence Williams III, Stephen (Steve) Root; **D:** Michael Toshiyuki Uno; **W:** Tony Lee; **M:** Stanley Clarke.

The Road to Guantanamo 🦴🦴 **2006 (R)** Political docudrama from Winterbottom and Whitecross focuses on the misfortunes of the "Tipton Three." These young British Muslims are in Pakistan for a wedding immediately after 9/11 and then travel to Afghanistan (apparently for humanitarian reasons). Big mistake—they get rounded up by Northern Alliance troops and are guilty until proven innocent, which takes years of military imprisonment and interrogation at Gitmo (film covers 2001-2004). **95m/C DVD.** *GB* Rizwan Ahmed, Farhad Harun, Waqar Siddiqui, Afran Usman; **D:** Michael Winterbottom, Matt Whitecross; **C:** Marcel Zyskind; **M:** Molly Nyman, Harry Escott. Ind. Spirit '07: Feature Doc.

The Road to Hong Kong 🦴🦴½ **1962** Last of the Crosby-Hope team-ups shows some wear, but still manages charm and humor. Lamour appears only briefly in this twisted comedy of hustlers caught in international espionage and cosmic goings-on. ♪♪Teamwork; Let's Not Be Sensible; It's The Only Way to Travel; We're On the Road to Hong Kong; Warmer Than a Whisper. **91m/B VHS, DVD.** Bing Crosby, Bob Hope, Joan Collins, Dorothy Lamour, Peter Sellers; **D:** Norman Panama; **C:** Jack Hildyard.

Road to Life 🦴🦴 *Putyovka V Zhizn* **1931** In the turmoil caused by Russia's Revolutionary and Civil wars, thousands of orphans roam the countryside resorting to petty crime to survive. One group is sent to a collective as part of an experimental program where they can be reformed and learn a trade but their criminal pasts seem inescapable. Russian with subtitles. **100m/B VHS.** *RU* Nikolai Batalov, Maria Gonta, Tsifan Kyria; **D:** Nicolai Ekk; **W:** Nicolai Ekk; **M:** Yakov Stolyar.

The Road to Morocco 🦴🦴🦴½ **1942** The third in the road movie series finds Hope and Crosby in Morocco. Crosby sells Hope into slavery to be the princess's (Lamour) personal plaything. Feeling guilty, Crosby returns to the palace to rescue Hope, only to find that he and the princess are getting married because the royal astrologer said it was in the stars. Crosby then tries to woo Lamour and, when the astrologer discovers the stars were mistaken, those two decide to marry. Quinn, however, also wants her and hilarious scenes ensue when the boys rescue Lamour from him. One of the funniest in the series. Watch for the camel at the end. ♪♪Constantly; Moonlight Becomes You; Ain't Got a Dime to My Name; Road to Morocco. **83m/C VHS, DVD.** Bing Crosby, Bob Hope, Dorothy Lamour, Anthony Quinn, Dona Drake, Vladimir Sokoloff, Yvonne De Carlo; **D:** David Butler; **W:** Frank Butler, Don Hartman; **C:** William Mellor. Natl. Film Reg. '96.

Road to Nashville 🦴🦴 **1967 (G)** An agent travels to Nashville to enlist talent for a new musical. Why do so many of these semi-musicals insist on having a plot? Good music. **110m/C VHS, DVD.** Marty Robbins, Johnny Cash, Doodles Weaver, Connie Smith, Richard Arlen; **D:** Robert Patrick.

Road to Nhill 🦴🦴 **1997** Very Aussie comedy filled with eccentric characters. An isolated, rural community is thrown into a tizzy when four female members of the local bowling team are in an accident that traps them in their overturned car. Volunteer emergency services rush into action but head off in the wrong direction and the women finally manage to free themselves, with various local yokels inept laid at the scene. Ensemble cast is fine. **95m/C VHS.** *AU* Lynette Curran, Patricia Kennedy, Lois Ramsey, Monica Maughan, Paul Chubb, Bill Hunter, Kerry Walker, Matthew Dyktynski, Terry Norris, Bill Young, Tony Barry, Alwyn Kurts; **D:** Sue Brooks; **W:** Alison Tilson; **C:** Nicolette Freeman; **M:** Elizabeth Drake.

Road to Perdition 🦴🦴🦴🦴 **2002 (R)** Michael Sullivan (Hanks) is a Depression-era hitman who must take his teenage son Michael Jr. (Hoechlin) on the run as he seeks revenge on the people who betrayed him and killed his wife and youngest son. Dark, atmospheric tale excels on the strength of the brilliantly understated screenplay and outstanding performances, highlighted by Hanks's tormented hitman/father and Newman's conflicted mob boss. Based on the 1998 graphic novel by Max Allan Collins and Richard Piers Rayner. **116m/C VHS, DVD.** *US* Tom Hanks, Paul Newman, Jude Law, Tyler Hoechlin, Jennifer Jason Leigh, Stanley Tucci, Daniel Craig, Liam Aiken, Ciaran Hinds, Dylan Baker, David Darlow, Mina (Badiyi) Badie; **D:** Sam Mendes; **W:** David Self; **C:** Conrad L. Hall; **M:** Thomas Newman. Oscars '02: Cinematog.; British Acad. '02: Cinematog.

Road to Riches 🦴🦴🦴 *Strange Hearts* **2001 (R)** This independent feature by first-timer Gallagher is a happy surprise, thanks especially to McGowan and Forster. Middleaged Jack (Forster) is very protective of the emotionally disturbed Moira (McGowan). Then cocky, handsome, and exceptionally lucky young Henry (Pardue) comes along and takes Moira away without realizing the extent of her problems. Jack is not about to let her go so easily, but he needs some good luck of his own to get her back. **90m/C VHS, DVD.** Robert Forster, Rose McGowan, Kip Pardue, Harry Hamlin; **D:** Michelle Gallagher; **W:** Michelle Gallagher; **C:** Adam Holender; **M:** Fletcher Beasley.

The Road to Ruin 🦴🦴🦴½ **1947** The wisecracking duo travel to Rio De Janeiro to prevent Spanish beauty Lamour (there she is again) from going through with an arranged marriage. Top-notch entry; fifth in the "Road" series. ♪♪But Beautiful; You Don't Have To Know The Language; For What?; Experience; Apalachicola, Florida; Cavaquinho; Brazil. **100m/B VHS, DVD.** Bing Crosby, Bob Hope, Dorothy Lamour, Gale Sondergaard, Frank Faylen, The Andrews Sisters; **D:** Norman Z. McLeod; **W:** Jack Rose; **C:** Ernest Laszlo.

The Road to Ruin 🦴🦴 **1928** The evils of smoking and drinking plummet a girl into a life of prostitution in this melodramatic, moralistic tale. An unintentional laugh-riot right up there with "Reefer Madness." Silent. **45m/B VHS, DVD.** Helen Foster, Grant Withers, Virginia Roye; **D:** Norton S. Parker; **W:** Erik Anjou; **C:** James Diamond.

Road to Ruin 🦴🦴 **1991 (R)** A rich playboy pretends to lose all his money to see if his girlfriend loves him for himself or for his wealth. But when his business partner embezzles his fortune, he must regain both his money and his girlfriend's trust. **94m/C VHS.** Peter Weller, Carey Lowell, Michel Duchaussoy; **D:** Charlotte Brandstrom.

Road to Salina 🦴🦴 **1968 (R)** A drifter is mistaken for (and might actually be) a desert-restaurant owner's long-lost son. He plays along, eventually seducing the family's daughter, who might be his sister. **97m/C VHS.** *FR* Robert Walker Jr., Rita Hayworth, Mimsy Farmer, Ed Begley Sr.; **D:** Georges Lautner.

The Road to Singapore *♂♂½* 1940 This is the movie that started it all. Crosby and Hope decide to swear off women and escape to Singapore to enjoy the free life. There they meet Lamour, a showgirl who is abused by Quinn. The boys rescue Lamour, but soon find they are both falling for her. She's in love with one of them, but won't reveal her feelings. Who will get the girl? Not as funny as some of the other 'road movies, but it's great for a first try. ♪Captain Custard; The Moon and the Willow Tree; Sweet Potato Piper; Too Romantic; Kaigoon. 84m/C VHS, DVD. Bing Crosby, Bob Hope, Dorothy Lamour, Charles Coburn, Judith Barrett, Anthony Quinn, Jerry Colonna, Johnny Arthur, Pierre Watkin; **D:** Victor Schertzinger; **W:** Frank Butler, Don Hartman; **C:** William Mellor.

The Road to Utopia *♂♂♂* 1946 Fourth of the "Road" films, wherein the boys wind up in Alaska posing as two famous escaped killers in order to locate a secret gold mine. One of the series' 'funniest and most spontaneous entries, abetted by Benchley's dry, upper-crust comments. ♪Put It There, Pal; Welcome to My Dreams; Would You?; Personality; Sunday, Monday, or Always?; Goodtime Charlie; It's Anybody's Spring. 90m/B VHS, DVD. Bing Crosby, Bob Hope, Dorothy Lamour, Jack La Rue, Robert Barrat, Douglass Dumbrille, Hillary Brooke, Robert Benchley, Nestor Paiva; **D:** Hal Walker; **W:** Norman Panama, Melvin Frank; **C:** Lionel Lindon; **M:** Johnny Burke, Leigh Harline, James Van Heusen.

The Road to Wellville *♂♂* 1994 (R) Corn flake magnate John Harvey Kellogg takes good health to an intestine-invading extreme in this spa satire featuring Hopkins as the buck-toothed Kellogg. Broderick and Fonda portray a wealthy couple who visit the turn-of-the-century sanitarium in search of Kellogg's cure, but receive only sexual frustration and anal humiliations. Bowel jokes and an essentially plotless scenario overshadow a gifted, but helpless cast. Adapted from T. Coraghessan Boyle's not-so-easily-adaptable novel. 120m/C VHS, DVD. Anthony Hopkins, Bridget Fonda, Matthew Broderick, John Cusack, Dana Carvey, Michael Lerner, Corn Meaney, John Neville, Lara Flynn Boyle, Corn Brooksmith, Norbert Weisser; **D:** Alan Parker; **W:** Alan Parker; **C:** Peter Biziou; **M:** Rachel Portman.

The Road to Yesterday *♂♂½* 1925 Two couples together on a crashing train are somehow thrown into the 18th century in roles parallel to their own lives. DeMille's first independent film, intriguing action/melodrama. Silent with musical soundtrack. 136m/B VHS, Joseph Schildkraut, William Boyd, Jetta Goudal, Vera Reynolds, Iron Eyes Cody; **D:** Cecil B. DeMille.

The Road to Zanzibar *♂♂♂* 1941 After selling a fake diamond mine to a criminal, Crosby and Hope flee to Zanzibar, where they meet up with Lamour and Merkel. The guys put up the money for a safari, supposedly to look for Lamour's brother, but they soon discover that they're on the road to Zanzibar; Crosby and Hope find themselves surrounded by hungry cannibals. Will they survive, or will they be someone's dinner? Not as funny as the other 'road movies, but amusing nonetheless. ♪It's Always You; You're Dangerous; On the Road to Zanzibar; Yo Lucky People You; Birds of a Feather; African Etude. 92m/C VHS, DVD. Bing Crosby, Bob Hope, Dorothy Lamour, Una Merkel, Eric Blore, Iris Adrian, Lionel Royce; **D:** Victor Schertzinger; **W:** Frank Butler, Don Hartman; **C:** Ted Tetzlaff.

Road Trip *♂♂* 2000 (R) Extremely low-brow comedy about four college buddies who set out on an 1,800-mile road trip (from New York to Texas) in order to intercept an incriminating videotape Josh (Meyer) has mistakenly mailed to his long-distance girlfriend. Green does disgusting things to a defenseless white mouse, and there's the usual frat-house sexual humor, but like most teen comedies these days, it's quotable, laugh-even-though-you-know-better funny, and basically harmless. 91m/C VHS, DVD. Breckin Meyer, Seann William Scott, Rachel Blanchard, DJ Qualls, Fred Ward, Andy Dick, Paulo Costanzo,

Tom Green, Amy Smart, Anthony Rapp, Ethan Suplee; **D:** Todd Phillips; **W:** Todd Phillips, Scot Armstrong; **C:** Mark Irwin; **M:** Mike Simpson.

The Road Warrior *♂♂♂½* 1982 (R) Mad Max 2 1982 (R) The first sequel to "Mad Max" takes place after nuclear war has destroyed Australia. Max helps a colony of oil-drilling survivors defend themselves from the roving murderous outback gangs and escape to the coast. The climactic chase scene is among the most exciting ever filmed; this film virtually created the "action-adventure" picture of the 1980s. 95m/C VHS, DVD, Blu-ray Disc, HD DVD, UMD. Mel Gibson, Bruce Spence, Emil Minty, Vernon Wells, Virginia Hey, Max Phipps, Mike (Michael) Preston, William Zappa; **C:** Dean Semler; **M:** Brian May, L.A.

Roadhouse Girl *♂* Marilyn 1953 A sexy woman kindles a romance with one of her husband's employees and the result is murder. Reminiscent of "The Postman Always Rings Twice," but with poor production values and performances. 70m/B VHS. GB Maxwell Reed, Sandra Dorne, Leslie Dwyer, Vida Hope, Ferdinand "Ferdy" Mayne; **D:** Wolf Rilla; **W:** Wolf Rilla.

Roadhouse 66 *♂½* 1984 (R) Utterly unoriginal broke-down-in-a-hick-town nonsense. Snooty Reinhold and scruffy Dafoe go through the motions, and of course find a pair of female companions. 90m/C VHS, DVD. Willem Dafoe, Judge Reinhold, Karen Lee, Kate Vernon, Stephen Elliott; **D:** John Mark Robinson; **C:** Thomas Ackerman.

Roadie *♂½* 1980 (PG) Supposedly a look at the back-stage world of rock 'n' roll. Meatloaf is a roadie who desperately wants to move. Features Art Carney, and musical names like Blondie, Roy Orbison, Hank Williams Jr., and Don Cornelius (of "Soul Train" fame). 105m/C VHS, DVD. Meat Loaf Aday, Kaki Hunter, Art Carney, Gailard Sartain, Alice Cooper, Roy Orbison, Hank Williams Jr., Ramblin' Jack Elliott; **D:** Alan Rudolph; **W:** Alan Rudolph, Michael Ventura.

Roadkill *♂* 1989 Cheap thriller about Ramona (Buhagiar), a concert promoter who tries to find a lost band, "The Children of Paradise," in the Canadian north woods. Along the way, she meets a would-be serial killer and other assorted weirdos. 85m/B VHS, DVD. CA Valerie Buhagiar, Don McKellar, Bruce McDonald; **D:** Bruce McDonald; **W:** Don McKellar. Toronto-City '89. Canadian Feature Film.

Roadracers *♂♂* 1994 (R) Made as part of Showtime's "Rebel Highway" series, Rodriguez basically takes the title from the 1959 AIP low-budgeter and goes his own way. Leather-clad rebel Dude Delaney (Arquette) has a voluptuous Latino dreamgirl named Donna (Hayek) and a gang which faces off against the clique led by rival Teddy Leather (Wiles) in drag races and roller rinks all around town. Great rockabilly soundtrack. 95m/C VHS, DVD. David Arquette, Jason Wiles, Salma Hayek, Jchn Hawkes, William Sadler, O'Neal Compton, Lerce LeGault, Karen Landry, Tommy Nix; **D:** Robert Rodriguez; **W:** Robert Rodriguez, Tommy Nik; **C:** Roberto Schaefer; **M:** Paul Bolt, Johnny Reno. C.A.B.L.E.

Roads to the South *♂♂½* Les Routes du Sud 1978 One-time Spanish revolutionary turned screenwriter returns to his homeland to fight fascism, but finds himself attracted to his son's beautiful girlfriend. Much soul searching. In French with English subtitles. 100m/C VHS. FR Yves Montand, Miou-Miou, Laurent Malet, Mario Gonzalez, Jose Luis Gomez, Jean'rine Mestre, Roger Planchon, Didier Sauvegrain; **D:** Joseph Losey; **W:** Jorge Sempron; **C:** Gerry Fisher; **M:** Michel Legrand.

Roadside Prophets *♂♂* 1992 (R) Counter-culture road trip, striking to be the '90s version of "Easy Rider," follows factory worker/biker Joe (Doe) on his mission to transport the ashes of a fellow biker to Nevada. He is accompanied by the pesky younger Sam (Horovitz), and together they meet up with lots of eccentrics and

stay at lots of cheap motels. Interesting cast meanders through sentimental and slow-moving buddy flick from debut director Wool, who wrote "Sid and Nancy." Quatsack completes the cameo hat trick, with appearances here and in 1992's "The Player" and "Shadows and Fog." 96m/C VHS, DVD. John Doe, Adam Horovitz, David Carradine, Timothy Leary, Arlo Guthrie, Barton Heyman, Jennifer Balgobin, John Cusack; **D:** Abbe Wool; **W:** Abbe Wool. Cameos: John Cusack; **D:** Abbe Wool; **W:** Abbe Wool.

The Roamin' Cowboy *♂♂* 1937 being threatened, a drifter comes to their rescue and wins both a girl and a job. 56m/C VHS. Fred Scott, Al "Fuzzy" St. John, Lois Januay, Forrest Taylor, Roger Williams; **D:** Robert F. "Bob" Hill.

Roamin' Wild *♂♂½* 1936 Exciting, action-packed early western with marshal Tyler saving a lady's stagecoach line from unsavory varmints. 60m/B VHS. Tom Tyler, Carol Wyndham, Al Ferguson, George Chesebro, Max Davidson, Fred Parker; **D:** Bernard B. Ray.

Roanoak *♂♂♂½* 1986 A dramatization in three parts of the mysterious fate of the early English settlement of Roancak in North Carolina, which disappeared without a trace. Long, but intriguing. Made for PBS' "American Playhouse." 180m/C VHS. **C:** William Nobles; **M:** Hugo Riesenfeld.

Roaring City *♂½* 1951 A hard-boiled detective searches for the person behind the murders of gangsters and prize fighters. 58m/B VHS. Hugh Beaumont, Edward Brophy, Richard Travis, Joan Valerie, Wanda McKay, Rebel Randall, Greg McClure, Stanley Price, William Tannen, Abner Biberman, Anthony Warde; **D:** William Berke; **W:** Julian Harmon, Herbert Margolis, Louis Morheim; **C:** Jack Greenhalgh.

Roaring Guns *♂♂* 1936 An unflappable McCoy rides in to thwart a despicable ranchowner trying to drive all the small ranchers out of business. Low-budget fun. 66m/B VHS. Tim McCoy, Rex Lease, Wheeler Oakman; **D:** Sam Newfield.

Roarin' Lead *♂½* 1937 Three Mesquiteers fight with a gang of rustlers while helping the orphans' and cattlemen's associations. 54m/B VHS, DVD. Robert Livingston, Ray Corrigan, Max Terhune, Christine Maple, Hooper Atchley, Yakima Canutt, George Chesebro, Tommy Bupp; **D:** Sam Newfield, Mack V. Wright; **W:** Oliver Drake, Jack Natteford, Oliver Drake; **C:** William Nobles; **M:** Samson; Victoria Racimo, Porky White, Adrian Sparks, Patrick Kilpatrick; **D:** Jan Egleson. TV

Roaring Ranch *♂½* 1930 Gibson is trying to protect his ranch from the evil Oakman while attempting to care for a baby as well. 66m/B VHS. Hoot Gibson, Wheeler Oakman, Sally Eilers, Bobby Nelson, Frank Clark; **D:** B. Reeves Eason; **W:** B. Reeves Eason.

The Roaring Road *♂♂* 1919 Romantic comedy about a car salesman named Toodles, who drives for his company in a big race. Vintage racing footage. 57m/B VHS. Wallace Reid, Ann Little, Theodore Roberts; **D:** James Cruze.

Roaring Roads *♂* 1935 An heir to a fortune acquires a lust for race car driving, and his family thinks, a reckless death wish. 60m/B VHS. Gertruce Messinger, David Sharpe, Mickey Daniels, Mary Kornman, Jack Mulhall; **D:** Charles E. Roberts, Mary Kornman, Jack Mulhall; **D:** Charles E. Roberts; **C:** Robert E. Cline.

Roaring Six Guns *♂* 1937 Maynard protects his property against his crooked partner and his fiancee's father. 60m/B VHS, DVD. Kermit Maynard, Mary Hayes, John Merton, Edward Cassidy, Sam Flint, Budd Buster, Robert (Fisk) Fiske, Charles "Slim" Whitaker; **D:** (John) Paterson) McGowan; **W:** Arthur Everett; **C:** Jack Greenhalgh.

Roaring Speedboats *♂* Mile a Minute Love 1937 Bakewell is a speedboat racer up against crooks who want to con him out of his money by tinkering with his invention. 62m/B VHS. William "Billy" Bakewell, Arletta Duncan, Duncan Renaldo, Vivien Oakland, Wilfrid Lucas; **D:** Elmer Clifton.

The Roaring Twenties *♂♂♂½* 1939 Eddie (Cagney), George (Bogart), and Lloyd (Lynn) are three WWI buddies who find their lives intersecting unexpectedly in Prohibition-era New York. Eddie

becomes a bootlegger and vies with George for status as crime boss. Lloyd is the attorney working to prosecute them. Great gangster flick was the last time Bogart and Cagney worked together after "The Oklahoma Kid" (1938). Cheesy script delivered with zest by top pros. ♪ "Angels with Dirty Faces" (1938) and "The Oklahoma Kid" (1939). 106m/B VHS, DVD. James Cagney, Humphrey Bogart, Jeffrey Lynn, Priscilla Lane, Gladys George, Frank McHugh, Paul Kelly, Joseph (Joe) Sawyer; **D:** Raoul Walsh; **W:** Robert Rossen, Frank Niblo and Macaulay; **C:** Ernest Haller; **M:** Heinz Roemheld, Ray Heindorf.

Rob Roy *♂♂♂* 1995 (R) Kilt-raising though overlong tale of legendary Scot Robert Roy MacGregor mixes love and honor with bloodlust and revenge. Neeson, with bloodlust and revenge. Neeson with an evil brother (Roth), a foppish twit with an evil brawl. Misty, highland scenery and intense romantic interplay between Neeson and Large as the spirited Mary MacGregor lend a passionate twist to an otherwise delightfully harmy performance as MacGregor's loathsome, bewigged nemesis delivers zip amid the high-minded speeches, plot lulls, and separated body parts. Visually stunning, with on-location shooting in the Scottish Highlands. More ambience is provided by Bruswell's evocative score. 144m/C VHS, DVD. Liam Neeson, Jessica Lange, Tim Roth, John Hurt, Eric Stoltz, Andrew Keir, Brian Cox, Brian McCardie, Gilbert Martin, Vicki Masson, David Hayman, Jason Fleming, Shirley Henderson, Gilly Gilchrist, John Murtagh, Ewan Stewart; **D:** Michael Caton-Jones; **W:** Alan Sharp; **C:** Karl Walter Lindenlaub, Roger Deakins; **M:** Carter Burwell. British Acad. '95: Suppor. Actor (Roth).

Rob Roy—The Highland Rogue *♂♂½* Rob Roy 1953 In the early 18th century, Scottish Highlancer Rob Roy must battle against the King of England's secretary, who would undermine the MacGregor clan. Elilled as the first made-for-cable movie. 95m/C VHS. John Marley, Simon MacCorkindale, Louise Val-lance, George Toulitatos; **D:** Harold French.

Robbers of the Sacred Mountain *♂♂* Falcon's Gold *♂♂* 1983 TV rip-off of "Raiders of the Lost Ark," loosely based on Arthur Conan Doyle's story "Challenger's Gold." Adventurers seek meteorites in the Mexican jungle. 95m/C VHS. John Marley, Simon MacCorkindale, Louise Val-lance, George Toulitatos; **D:** Harold French.

Robbery *♂♂½* 1967 Uncriginal but competent rendition of the hackneyed British Royal Mail robbery. Thieves plan and execute a heist of a late-night mail train carrying $10 million. 113m/C VHS, GB Stanley Baker, James Booth, Joanna Pettet, Frank Finlay, Barry Foster; **D:** Peter Yates.

Robbery *♂♂* 1985 A six-man platoon of Vietnam war veterans endeavors to assault and rob a mob of shiftless bookies. 91m/C VHS. John Sheerin, Tony Rickards, Tim Hughes; **D:** Michael Thornhill.

Robbery under Arms *♂♂½* 1957 From Australia in the 1800s, similar to the American wild west, comes a tale of love and robbery. Finch is the leader of a band of outlaws. Rather dull story redeemed by excellent photography of beautiful landscape. 83m/C VHS, GB Peter Finch, Ronald Lewis, Laurence Naismith, Maureen Swanson, David McCallum, Jill Ireland; **D:** Jack Lee.

Robby *♂♂* 1968 A young white boy and a young black boy shipwrecked on an island form a strong friendship that sees them through a series of adventures. Loosely based on "Robinson Crusoe." 65m/C VHS. Warren Raum, Ryp Siani, John Garces; **D:** Ralph Bluemke.

The Robe 🦴🦴🦴½ 1953 This moving, religious portrait follows the career and religious awakening of drunken and dissolute Roman tribune Marcellus (Burton), after he wins the robe of the just-crucified Christ in a dice game. Mature plays Burton's slave surprisingly well, and reprised the role in the sequel, "Demetrius and the Gladiators": Burton is wooden. "The Robe" was the first movie to be filmed in CinemaScope. Based on the novel by Lloyd C. Douglas. 133m/C VHS, DVD. Richard Burton, Jean Simmons, Victor Mature, Michael Rennie, Richard Boone, Dean Jagger, Jeff Morrow, Jay Robinson, Dawn Addams, Ernest Thesiger, Torin Thatcher; D: Henry Koster; W: Albert (John B. Sherry) Maltz, Philip Dunne; C: Leon Shamroy. Oscars '53: Art Dir/Set Dec., Color, Costume Des. (C); Golden Globes '54: Film—Drama; Natl. Bd. of Review '53: Actress (Simmons).

Robert et Robert 🦴🦴🦴 1978 Two 'ineligible' bachelors resort to using a computerized matrimonial agency to find the girls of their dreams. They become friends while they wait for their dates. Sensitive tale of loneliness and friendship. Warm and witty with fine performances throughout. French with English subtitles. 105m/C VHS. FR Charles Denner, Jacques Villeret, Jean-Claude Brialy, Macha Meril, Germaine Montero, Regine; D: Claude Lelouch; W: Claude Lelouch; C: Jacques Lefrancois. Cesar '79: Support. Actor (Villeret).

Robert Kennedy and His Times 🦴🦴½ 1990 Another look at the Kennedy clan, this time from the Bobby angle. Good acting. Based on the book by Arthur Schlesinger. 300m/C VHS. Brad Davis, Veronica Cartwright, Cliff DeYoung, Ned Beatty, Beatrice Straight, Jack Warden; D: Marvin J. Chomsky.

Robert Louis Stevenson's The Game of Death 🦴🦴½ The Suicide Club; The Game of Death; Robert Louis Stevenson's The Suicide Club 1999 (R) This version sticks to the spirit of Stevenson's story (which was filmed in 1936 as "Trouble for Two") but adds plotlines and characters. It's 1899 and Henry Joyce (Morrissey) has decided to kill himself because of his lover's betrayal. He and pal, Captain May (Shuke), meet the equally suicidal Shaw (Bettany), who takes them along to the Suicide Club. Run by the mysterious Bourne (Pryce), its members willingly want to die—and the next victim and their murderer are selected by a drawing of the cards. And you aren't allowed to change your mind. 89m/C VHS, DVD. David Morrissey, Jonathan Pryce, Paul Bettany, Neil Stuke, Catherine Siggins; C: Chris Manley; M: Adrian Johnston.

Roberta 🦴🦴🦴 1935 A football player inherits his aunt's Parisian dress shop and finds himself at odds with an incognito Russian princess. Dumb plot aside, this is one of the best Astaire-Rogers efforts. A later remake was titled "Lovely to Look At." ♪Lovely to Look At; I'll Be Hard to Handle; I Won't Dance; Yesterdays; Smoke Gets in Your Eyes; I'll Be Hard to Handle; Back Home Again in Indiana; The Touch of Your Hand; You're Devasting. 85m/B VHS, DVD. Fred Astaire, Ginger Rogers, Irene Dunne, Lucille Ball, Randolph Scott; D: William A. Seiter; M: Max Steiner.

Robin and Marian 🦴🦴🦴 1976 (PG) After a separation of 20 years, Robin Hood is reunited with Maid Marian, who is now a nun. Their dormant feelings for each other are reawakened as Robin spirits her to Sherwood Forest. In case you wanted to see Robin Hood robbed of all magic, spontaneity, and fun. Connery is dull, dull, working with an uninspired script. 106m/C VHS, DVD. GB Sean Connery, Audrey Hepburn, Robert Shaw, Richard Harris, Denholm Elliott, Ian Holm, Nicol Williamson, Ronnie Barker; D: Richard Lester; C: David Watkin; M: John Barry.

Robin and the 7 Hoods 🦴🦴½ 1964 Runyon-esque Rat Pack version of 1920s Chicago, with Frank and the boys as do-good gangsters in their last go-round. Fun if not unforgettable. ♪Bang! Bang!; Style; Mister Booze; Don't Be a Do-Badder; My Kind of Town, Chicago. 124m/C VHS, DVD. Frank Sinatra, Bing Crosby, Dean Martin, Sammy Davis Jr., Peter Falk, Barbara Rush, Victor Buono, Hank Henry, Robert Foulk, Allen Jenkins, Jack La Rue, Edward G. Robinson, Hans Conried, Tony Randall; D: Gordon Douglas; W: John Fenton Murray, David R. Schwartz; C: William H. Daniels; M: Nelson Riddle, James Van Heusen.

Robin-B-Hood 🦴🦴 2006 Rob-B-Hood Goofy two-men-and-a-baby crime comedy. Compulsive gamblers Thongs (Chan) and Octopus (Koo) steal to support their addiction. Their boss wants them to kidnap an infant for big bucks but they have to babysit the tyke until arrangements for transfer can be made. Despite many mishaps, the duo bond with baby and are reluctant to turn him over to a Triad leader, who thinks the boy is his grandson. Cantonese with subtitles. 134m/C DVD. CH HK Jackie Chan, Michael Hui, Yuen Biao, Chen Baoguo, Louis Koo, Yuanyuan Gao; D: Benny Chan; W: Jackie Chan, Benny Chan; C: Anthony Pun; M: Fai-young Chan.

Robin Cook's Invasion 🦴🦴½ Invasion 1997 College student Beau Stark (Perry) is one of many sickened by some kind of strange viral infection after being exposed to rocks of interstellar origin. The virus induces mutations and Beau works with scientists to find an antidote to the alien threat. A familiar story slickly done. 180m/C VHS, DVD. Luke Perry, Kim Cattrall, Rebecca Gayheart, Christopher Orr, Jon Polito, Neal McDonough, Jason Schomburg; D: Armand Mastroianni; W: Rockne S. O'Bannon; C: Bryan England; M: Don Davis. TV

Robin Cook's Terminal 🦴🦴 Terminal 1996 Mediocre medical thriller. Cancer researcher Sean O'Grady (Savant) has just gotten an internship at a medical clinic that has a phenomenal cure rate for a particular type of brain cancer. Sean gets suspicious about the treatment and works with ex-girlfriend (and nurse) Janet (Peeples) to find out the truth. Which is always a bad idea in these sorts of movies because then lots of unsavory, suspicious types come after you. 90m/C VHS, DVD. Doug Savant, Nia Peeples, Michael Ironside, James Brolin, Roy Thinnes, Jenny O'Hara, Khandi Alexander, Gregg Henry; D: Larry Elikann; W: Nancy Isaak; C: Eric Van Haren Noman; M: Garry Schyman. TV

Robin Hood 🦴🦴🦴 1922 Extravagant production casts Fairbanks as eponymous gymnastic swashbuckler who departs for Crusades as Earl of Huntington and returns as the hooded one to save King Richard's throne from the sinister Sheriff of Nottingham. Best ever silent swashbuckling. 110m/B VHS, DVD. Douglas Fairbanks Sr., Wallace Beery, Sam De Grasse, Enid Bennett, Paul Dickey, William E. (W.E. William A., W.A.) Lowery, Roy Coulson, Bill Bennett, Merrill McCormick, Wilson Benge, Willard Louis, Alan Hale, Maine Geary, Lloyd Talman; D: Allan Dwan; W: Douglas Fairbanks Sr.; C: Arthur Edeson.

Robin Hood 🦴🦴🦴 1973 This time the Sherwood Forest crew are portrayed by appropriate cartoon animals, hence, Robin is a fox, Little John a bear, etc. Good family fare, but not as memorable as other Disney features. 83m/C VHS, DVD. D: Wolfgang Reitherman; M: George Bruns; V: Roger Miller, Brian Bedford, Monica Evans, Phil Harris, Andy Devine, Carol(e) Shelley, Peter Ustinov, Terry-Thomas, Pat Buttram, George Lindsey, Ken Curtis.

The Robin Hood Gang 🦴🦴½ Angels in the Attic 1998 (PG) Brad (Taylor) and Frankie (Losack) are enterprising youngsters who collect empty soda cans to raise money to buy new bikes. But when they discover a suitcase full of cash in the attic of their apartment, they decide to share the wealth with their equally hard-up neighbors. When they learn that it's stolen bank loot, they must figure out how to catch the criminal and return the money. Nobody's going to mistake this modest kidvid for "Home Alone" but it's an acceptable time-waster for the short set. 86m/C DVD. Clayton Taylor, Steven Losak, Dalin Christiansen, Brenda Price, Scott Christopher; D: Eric Hendershot; W: Eric Hendershot; C: T.C. Christensen; M: Allen Williams. VIDEO

Robin Hood: Men in Tights 🦴🦴½ Men in Tights 1993 (PG-13) Brooksian rendition of the classic legend inspires guffaws, but doesn't hit the bullseye on all it promises. Hood aficionados will appreciate the painstaking effort taken to spoof the 1938 Errol Flynn classic while leaving plenty of room to poke fun at the more recent Costner non-classic "Robin Hood: Prince of Thieves." Elwes, last seen swinging swords in "The Princess Bride," is well cast as the Flynn look-alike. Expect the usual off-color humor that's so prevalent in all Brooks outings. 105m/C VHS, DVD. Cary Elwes, Richard Lewis, Roger Rees, Amy Yasbeck, Dave Chappelle, Isaac Hayes, Tracey Ullman, Mark Blankfield, Megan Cavanagh, Eric Allen Kramer, Tony Griffin, Dick Van Patten, Mel Brooks; D: Mel Brooks; W: Mel Brooks, J. David Shapiro, Evan Chandler; M: Hummie Mann.

Robin Hood of Texas 🦴🦴½ 1947 Autry finds his calm life disturbed when he is falsely accused of robbing a bank. Pretty good plot for once, in Autry's last Republic western, and plenty of action. 71m/B VHS, DVD. Gene Autry, Lynne Roberts, Sterling Holloway, Adele Mara; D: Lesley Selander.

Robin Hood of the Pecos 🦴🦴½ 1941 Ex-Confederate soldier takes on northern post-war politicians and carpetbaggers. Decent Rogers/Hayes outing. 56m/B VHS, DVD. Roy Rogers, George "Gabby" Hayes, Marjorie Reynolds, Jay Novello, Roscoe Ates; D: Joseph Kane.

Robin Hood: Prince of Thieves 🦴🦴½ 1991 (PG-13) Costner is the politically correct Rebel with a Cause, but a thinker, not a doer—and therein lies the problem. His quiet thoughtfulness doesn't add up to leadership and Costner's performance, though their comments about his lack of an English accent seem nitpicky in light of some basic plot problems. Still has lots of fun for lovers of action, romance and fairy tales. 144m/C VHS, DVD. Kevin Costner, Morgan Freeman, Mary Elizabeth Mastrantonio, Christian Slater, Alan Rickman, Geraldine McEwan, Michael McShane, Brian Blessed, Michael Wincott, Nick Brimble, Harold Innocent, Jack Wild; Cameos: Sean Connery; D: Kevin Reynolds; W: Pen Densham, John Watson; C: Billy Milton; M: Michael Kamen. British Acad. '91: Support. Actor (Rickman); MTV Movie Awards '92: Song ("Everything I Do) I Do for You"); Golden Raspberries '91: Worst Actor (Costner).

Robin Hood... The Legend: Herne's Son 🦴🦴½ 1985 When Robin Hood is killed by the Sheriff of Nottingham, he begs Robert of Huntington (Connery) to continue his work. Connery refuses, the band dissolves, Maid Marion is kidnapped, and they reunite to save her. Good entry in the BBC series. 101m/C VHS. GB Jason Connery, Oliver Cotton, Michael Craig, Nickolas Grace, George Baker; D: Robert M. Young. TV

Robin Hood... The Legend: Robin Hood and the Sorcerer 🦴🦴½ 1983 Robin Hood is chosen by the mystical Herne the Hunter to thwart the evil Sheriff of Nottingham and protect the English peasantry. He must defeat the supernatural powers of a sorcerer and gather together his men in this pilot for British TV. 115m/C VHS. GB Michael Praed, Anthony Valentine, Nickolas Grace, Clive Mantle, Peter Williams; D: Ian Sharp. TV

Robin Hood... The Legend: The Swords of Wayland 🦴🦴½ 1983 A wicked sorceress provides a supernatural threat to Robin and his merry men. Second entry in the BBC series. Convoluted, breathless plot makes for swashbuckling fun and much derring-do. 115m/C VHS. GB Michael Praed, Rula Lenska, Nickolas Grace; D: Robert M. Young. TV

Robin Hood... The Legend: The Time of the Wolf 🦴🦴½ 1985 Robin Hood finds out that an old enemy is about to release his evil doings on the world and only he can stop him, while Maid Marian comes to a momentous decision. 105m/C VHS. GB Jason Connery, Nickolas Grace, Richard O'Brien; D: Syd Roberson. TV

Robin Hood: The Movie 1955 A colorized and re-mixed version of several episodes of the British TV series adds up to a fine version of the classic tale. Excellent cast, clever editing, and stunning colorization. 90m/C VHS. GB Richard Greene, Bernadette O'Farrell, Alan Wheatley; D: Ralph Smart, Daniel Birt, Terence Fisher. TV

Robin of Locksley 🦴🦴½ 1995 (PG) A modern-day, teenaged Robin Hood (Sawa) battles the bullies at his private boys school (thanks to his archery prowess), meets a girl named Marian, and takes on sinister FBI agent Nottingham. 97m/C VHS, DVD. Devon Sawa, Sarah Chalke, Joshua Jackson; D: Michael Kennedy.

Robin's Hood 🦴🦴 2003 Robin (Turner) is a black social worker in Oakland who is about to lose her job for caring too much about her clients. She meets thief Brooklyn (Cates) and together they start robbing banks and distributing the money to the neighborhood needy. But their crime spree can't last for long. 81m/C DVD. US Khahtee V. Turner, Clody Cates; D: Sara Millman; W: Khahtee V. Turner, Sara Millman; C: Howard Shack.

Robinson Crusoe 🦴🦴 1936 A British silent film originally made in 1927, re-edited ten years later. Music and sound effects were added, along with a narration by children's radio personality Carney. Follows the plot of the famous adventure story by Daniel Defoe. 34m/B VHS. M.A. Wetherell, Fay Compton, Herbert Waithe; D: M.A. Wetherell; W: M.A. Wetherell; C: J. Rosenthal; Nar: Uncle Don Carney.

Robinson Crusoe & the Tiger 🦴½ 1972 (G) A tiger tells the famous story of how Robinson Crusoe became stranded on a desert island. 109m/C VHS, DVD. Hugo Stiglitz, Ahui; D: Rene Cardona Jr.

Robinson Crusoe of Clipper Island 🦴🦴 1936 Fourteen-episode serial featuring the investigative expertise of Mala, a Polynesian in the employ of the U.S. Intelligence Service. Each episode runs 16 minutes. Shortened version titled "Robinson Crusoe of Mystery Island." 256m/B VHS, DVD. Mala, Rex, Buck, Kate Greenfield, John Ward, Tracy Lane, Robert F. (Bob) Kortman, Herbert Rawlinson; D: Mack V. Wright.

Robinson Crusoe of Mystery Island 🦴🦴 1936 A Polynesian investigates saboteurs on a mysterious island. Would-be cliffhanger is a yawner, where are the chills and thrills? Edited from the serial "Robinson Crusoe of Clipper Island." 100m/B VHS. Mala, Rex, Buck, Herbert Rawlinson, Ray Taylor; D: Mack V. Wright.

Robinson Crusoe on Mars 🦴 1964 Sci-fi interpretation of Defoe classic. West is one of two daring scientists who take a monkey with them on a mission to outer space. When a meteor strikes their ship, it hurtles out of control towards the Earth. Now part cop, part machine, becomes defender of justice. They meet Lundin, an escaped slave and teach him English until evil slave traders spoil the fun. **109m/C VHS.** Adam West, Vic Lundin, Paul Mantee; **D:** Byron Haskin. **W:** Ib Melchior, John C. Higgins; **C:** Winton C. Hoch. **M:** Nathan Van Cleave.

Robo-Chic *Cyber-Chic* **1989** A woman who is part cop, part machine, becomes defender of justice. **90m/C VHS.** Kathy Shower, Jack Carter, Burt Ward, Lyle Waggoner; **D:** Ed Hansen, Jeffrey Mandel.

Robo Warriors *♂♂* **1996 (PG-13)** In the year 2036, Earth has been conquered by the Terridaxs, a half-human, half-reptile race. But 12-year-old Zac finds the last hi-tech fighting machine, the Robo Warrior (Remar), and convinces him to help destroy the invaders. **94m/C VHS.** James Remar, James Lew, Kyle Howard, Bernard Kates. **D:** Ian Barry. **W:** Michael Berlin. **M:** Richard Band.

Robot Holocaust *♂♂* **1987** Screwwhere in the doomed future, after viet Union. When he returns to the States as a cyborg, his friends seem tc notice a change. **91m/C VHS. GB** Elliot Gould, Tre-vor Howard, Joe (Joseph) Bova, Ed Grover, James Yoble, John Lerner. **D:** Jack Gold.

Robot in the Family *♂♂* **1994** wacky but endearing robot who embark on a race against time through the streets of New York to track down a priceless antique that could save Alex's family from financial ruin. **92m/C VHS.** Joe Pantolaro, John Cuff, Nadine Hart, Joel von Ornsteiner, Jennifer Debora, Andrew Howarth, Angelika Jager, Rick Gianasi. **D:** Tim Kincaid. **W:** Tim Kincaid.

Roboman *♂♂* Who? **1975 (PG)** American scientist gets in car crash in Soviet Union. When he returns to the States as a cyborg, his friends seem tc notice a change.

RoboCop 2 *♂♂* **1990 (R)** A nearly dead Detroit cop, Alex Murphy (Weller), is used as the brain for a crime-fighting robot in this bleak vision of the future. Humor, satire, action and violence keep this moving in spite of its underlying sadness. Slick animation techniques from Phil Tippet. Verhoeven's first American film. **103m/C VHS. DVD. UMD.** Peter Weller, Nancy Allen, Ronny Cox, Kurtwood Smith, Ray Wise, Miguel Ferrer, Dan O'Herlihy, Robert DoGui, Felton Perry, Paul McCrane, Del Zamora. **D:** Irvin Kershner. **C:** Mark Irwin. **M:** Leonard Rosenman.

RoboCop 3 *♂♂½* **1991 (PG-13)** Ro-bocop's new Japanese owners plan to build a huge, new, ultra-modern city (in place of the decrepit 21st-century Detroit) but first must evict thousands of people in this third installment of the "Robocop" films (which set on the studio shelf before finally being released in 1993). There's an android Ninja warrior to do battle with Robo, who's gone over to the rebel underground. Plot and action sequences are re-hashed from better films. Watch the original. **104m/C VHS. DVD.** Robert John Burke, Nancy Allen, John Castle, CCH Pounder, Bruce Locke, Rip Torn, Remi Ryan, Felton Perry, Stephen (Steve) Root; **D:** Fred Dekker; **W:** Fred Dekker, Frank Miller; **C:** Gary B. Kibbe; **M:** Basil Poledouris.

RoboCop *♂♂♂* **1987 (R)** Grimer, more violent sequel to the initial fascinating look at the future, where police departments are run by corporations hungry for profit at any cost. A new and highly addictive drug has made Detroit more dangerous than ever. Robocop is replaced by a stronger cyborg with the brain of a brutal criminal. When the cyborg goes berserk, Robocop battles it and the drug lords for control of the city. Dark humor and graphic savagery, with little of the tenderness and emotion of the original. **117m/C VHS. DVD.** Peter Weller, Nancy Allen, Belinda Bauer, Dan O'Herlihy, Tom Noonan, Gabriel Damon, Galyn Gorg, Felton Perry, Patricia Charbonneau; **D:** Irvin Kershner; **W:** Walon Green; **C:** Mark Irwin; **M:** Leonard Rosenman.

Robots *♂♂½* **2005 (PG)** Standing in the shadows of Pixar, the makers of "Ice Age" return with this tale of a small-town robot in the big city. Idealistic Rodney Copperbottom (McGregor) travels to Robot City to present his inventions to Bigweld Industries. However, Ratchet (Kinnear) and Madame Gasket (Broadbent) have taken over the company and are forcing old robots to upgrade or perish. Rodney organizes a motley band of schticky Fender, to topple the heartless cuo and the outcome is as predictable as it sounds. The CGI work is dazzling (tre kitschy character design is the highlight), but the generic character story ard characters fail to inspire. **91m/C VHS. DVD. UMD. US D:** Chris Wedge. **W:** Lowell Ganz, Babaloo Mandel, David Lindsay-Abaire. **M:** John Powell; **V:** Ewan McGregor, Halle Berry, Robin Williams, Greg Kinnear, Mel Brooks, Drew Carey, Jim Broadbent, Amanda Bynes, Jennifer Coolidge, Stanley Tucci, Dianne Wiest, Paul Giamatti, Natasha Lyonne, Lowell Ganz, Dan Hedaya, Jackie Hoffman, James Earl Jones, Harland Williams, Stephen Tobolowsky, Alan Rosenberg, Jay Leno, Terry Bradshaw, Paula Abdul.

Robot Jox *♂♂½* **1990 (PG)** Two futuristic warriors battle to the finish in giant mechanical robots. Preteen fare. **84m/C VHS. DVD.** Gary (Rand) Graham, Anne-Marie Johnson, Paul Koslo, Robert Sampson, Danny Kamekona, Hilary Mason, Michael Alldredge; **D:** Stuart Gordon; **W:** Joe Haldeman; **C:** Mac Ahlberg; **M:** Papo Gely, Ted Mason; **V:** Don Peoros.

Robot Monster *♂♂½* *Monster from Mars; Monsters from the Moon* **1953** Ludicrous cheapie is widely considered one of the worst films of all time, as a single alien dressed in a moth-eaten gorilla suit and diving helmet conspires to take over the Earth from his station in a small, bubble-filled California cava. Available in original 3-D format. **84m/B VHS. DVD.** George Nader, Claudia Barrett, Gregory Moffett, Selena Royle; **D:** Phil Tucker; **W:** Wyott Ordung; **C:** Jack Greenhalgh; **M:** Elmer Bernstein; **V:** John Brown.

Robot Pilot *♂* *Emergency Landing* **1941** Tucker stars as a WWII test pilot trying to promote a friend's invention. Along the way, he's involved in a subplot with enemy agents who steal a bomber. He also finds time to become romantically entangled with the boss' spoiled daughter. **66m/B VHS.** Forrest Tucker, Carol Hughes, Evelyn Brent, Emmett Vogan, William (Bill) Halligan; **D:** William Beaudine.

Robot Stories *♂♂½* **2003** Writer-director Pak's first theatrical venture gazes into the future and imagines the impact that robots and artificial intelligence will have on society via four short stories. Though the central theme is sci-fi, at its core each piece is really an intriguing exploration of timeless human emotions of grief, death, family, and love. **85m/C DVD. US** Tamlyn Tomita, James Saito, Joshua Spafford, Rist Tajiri, Vin Knight, Gina Quintos, Karen Tse Lee, Glen Kubota, Norma Fire, Tarista Eanes, Catherine Carcha, Wai Ching Ho, Cindy Cheung, Louis Ozawa Changchien, Angel Desai, Olivia Oguma, Sab Shimono, Antonio Roman, John Cariani, Greg Pak, Bill Coelius, Tim Kang, Julienne Hanzelka Kim, Vivian Bang, Julie Atlas Muz, Brian Nishii; **D:** Greg Pak; **W:** Greg Pak; **C:** Peter Olsen; **M:** Rick Knutsen; **V:** Ari Garin.

Robot Wars *♂♂* **1993 (PG)** When what seems to be the last mega-robot on earth falls into enemy hands, a renegade pilot unearths another with the help of an engineer and archeologist to fight for the future of mankind. **106m/C VHS.** Don Michael Paul, Barbara Crampton, James Staley, Lisa Fi-na, Danny Kamekona, Yuji Okumoto, J. Downing. **D:** Albert Band.

The Robot vs. the Aztec Mummy Woof! *El Robot Humano; La Momia Azteca Contra el Robot Humano* **1959** Grade-Z Mexican horror film pits a jealous mummy who guards a tomb against tomb robbers and the robot they invent. Special effects are laughable today—the robot's ears are lightbulbs—but true mummy movie fans might want to watch this one. Everyone else will probably be better off skipping it. **65m/B VHS. DVD. MX** Ramon Gay, Rosita (Rosa) Arenas, Crcx Alvarado, Luis Aceves Cantaneda, Emma Rolden; **D:** Rafael Portillo; **W:** Alfredo Salazar; **C:** Enrique Wallace; **M:** Antonio Diaz Conde.

Rock-a-Doodle *♂♂½* **1992 (G)** Little Edmond is knocked out during a storm and has an Elvis-influenced vision. He sees Chanticleer, the sun-raising rooster, tricked into neglecting his duties by an evil barnyard owl. Humiliated and scorned, the earnest young fowl leaves the farm and winds up in a Las Vegas-like city as an Elvis-impersonating singer (complete with pompadour) where he meets with success bland by today's standards of animation, with music which is certainly nothing to crow about. **77m/C VHS. DVD.** Don Bluth; **W:** Christopher Plummer, Phil Harris, Sandy Duncan, Ellen Greene, Charles Nelson Reilly, Eddie Deezen, Toby Scott Granger, Sorrell Booke.

Rock-A-Bye Baby *♂♂½* **1957** Clayton Poole (Lewis) is a big fan of glamorous movie star Carla Naples (Maxwell), a recent widow who gives birth to triplets—a fact she wants kept hush-hush in a religious epic. So Clayton comes to the rescue by agreeing to be the little bundles' babysitter. And as a job bonus he gets to fall in love with Carla's sweet sister, Sandy (Stevens). A very loose adaptation of the Preston Sturges comedy "The Miracle of Morgan's Creek." **103m/C VHS.** Jerry Lewis, Marilyn Maxwell, Connie Stevens, Salvatore Bac-caloni, Reginald Gardiner, Hans Conried, Ida Moore, George Sanders, James Gleason; **D:** Frank Tashlin; **C:** Haskell Boggs; **M:** Walter Scharf.

Rock, Baby, Rock It *♂* **1957** Weak and silly rock-and-roll crime drama about teens trying to fight the Mafia in Dallas in 1957. Features performances by many regional bands including Kay Wheeler, the Cel Block Seven, Johnny Carroll, Preacher Smith and the Deacons, and the Five Stars. If you grew up in Dallas in the '50s, the musical groups may bring back some fond memories; otherwise, this obscure film probably isn't worth your time. **84m/B VHS.** Kay Wheeler, John Carroll; **D:** Murray Douglas Sporup.

Rock Haven *♂♂* **2007** A devout Christian, 18-year-old Bradley has just moved with his overprotective mother to the titular coastal town in northern California. Settling in, he's surprised to find himself attracted to athletic neighbor Clifford. But will Bradley's beliefs cause him to turn away from his first romance? Sentimental story that doesn't negate the importance of Bradley's spirituality. **78m/C DVD.** Sean Hoagland, Owen Alabado, Laura Jane Coles, Katheryn Hecht, Erin Daly; **D:** David Lewis; **W:** Christian Bruno; **M:** Jack Curtis Du-bowsky.

Rock House *♂♂* **1988 (R)** When an L.A. narcotics officer's wife is murdered by drug runners he goes on an obsessive revenge mission to destroy the city's cocaine operations. **90m/C VHS.** Joseph Jennings, Michael Robbin, Alan Shearer; **D:** Jack Vacek; **M:** Mark Rappaport.

Rock My World *♂* *Global Heresy* **2002 (R)** Amazingly bad would-be comedy finds one-hit American band Global Heresy forced to hire newcomer Nat (Silverstone), when their original player suddenly disappears. The group is headed to an English country mansion to relax and rehearse and it turns out the cash-poor aristocratic owners (O'Toole, Plowright) are secretly posing as the butler and cook. Every culture clash cliche is trotted out. **106m/**

Rock All Night *♂♂* **1957** Typically trashy Corman quickie (filmed in five days on one set) about some wild '50s teens and, in this case, a couple of murderers. Saems Cloud Nine, the local teen hangout, is invaded by a couple of murderers who hold the kids hostage. Its up to the hipster bartender, known as Shorty because he's five-foot-one, to save the day. Unrelated concert footage of the Platters and the Blockbusters opens the film. **62m/B VHS.** Dick Miller, Abby Dalton, Russell Johnson, Jonathan Haze, Robin Morse, Chris Alcaide, Beach Dickerson, Bruno VeSota, Mel Welles; **D:** Roger Corman; **W:** Charles B. Griffin; **C:** Floyd Crosby.

Rock & Roll Cowboys *♂* **1992** Set in the near-future. Mickey LaGrange is a 'roadie who has dreams of playing his own songs and becoming a rock and roll star himself. When he meets the mysterious Damien Shard he just may get the opportunity and a lot more besides. Shard is the inventor of an instrument that taps directly into the brain to transform thought into music. When Mickey uses the instrument he becomes an instant success—until he notices some horrifying side effects. **83m/C VHS.** Peter Phelps, David Franklin, John (Roy Slaven) Doyle; **D:** Robert Stewart.

Rock & Rule *♂* **1983** Animated sword & sorcery epic with a rock soundtrack. Voices are provided by, Deborah Harry, Cheap Trick, Lou Reed and Iggy Pop. **85m/C VHS. DVD.** Clive A. Smith; **M:** Deborah Harry, Lou Reed, Iggy Pop; **V:** Paul Le-Mat, Susan (Suzan) Roman, Don Francks, Dan Hennessey, Chris Wiggins, Catherine Gallant, Catherine O'Hara.

Rock & the Money-Hungry Party Girls *♂* **1989** A struggling musician battles against Gabor-sister-worshipping bimbos in a bid to find unpublished songs by a '50s music legend. **90m/C VHS.** Paul Serou, Adam Small, Judi Durand, Mary Baldwin, Debra Lamb; **D:** Kurt MacCarley.

Rock Hudson's Home Movies *♂♂* **1992** Farr re-creates the character of the late actor over numerous film clips used to suggest homoerotic themes in Hudson's movies. Low-budget and high camp. **63m/C VHS. DVD.** Eric Farr; **D:** Mark Rappaport.

Rocco and His Brothers *♂♂♂½* *Rocco et Ses Freres; Rocco E I Suoi Fratelli* **1960** A modern classic from top director Visconti, about four brothers who move with their mother from the Italian countryside to Milan. Very long, complex drama. Available in original subtitles, but the unedited version is much more rewarding. In Italian with English subtitles. **168m/B VHS. DVD. F** Alain Delon, Renato Salvatori, Annie Girardot, Katina Paxinou, Claudia Cardinale, Roger Hanin, Alessandra Panaro, Spiros Focas, Max Cartier; **D:** Luchino Visconti; **W:** Luchino Visconti, Suso Cecci D'Amico, Pasquale Festa Campanile, Enrico Medioli, Massimo Franciosa; **C:** Giuseppe Rotunno; **M:** Nino Rota.

The Rock *♂♂♂* **1995 (R)** Cage follows up his Oscar win with a big-budget action hero turn, and with great results. In an attempt to get benefits for the families of soldiers killed in various covert operations, a decorated general (Harris) and his commando squad occupy Alcatraz Island, taking hostages and threatening to unleash a deadly gas bomb on San Francisco. Biochemical weapons expert Stanley Goodspeed (Cage) is called in to disarm the rockets, aided by John Patrick Mason (Connery), only man to successfully escape from the island prison. Like most Simpson/Bruckheimer productions, credibility is stretched to the limit, but the action scenes and crisp pacing don't leave much time for pondering details, anyway. Connery, cool as ever, hasn't lost a step. Cage, effectively plays up his character's inexperience at being the hero. Co-producer Don Simpson died of drug overdose during production. **136m/C VHS. DVD. Blu-ray Disc.** Nicolas Cage, Sean Connery, Ed Harris, Michael Biehn, William Forsythe, David Morse, John Spencer, John C. McGinley, Tony Todd, Bokeem Woodbine, Danny Nucci, Claire Forlani, Vanessa Marcil, Brendan Kelly, Todd Louiso, Willie Garson, Xander Berkeley, Sam Whipple, Raymond Cruz, David Marshall Grant, Philip Baker Hall; **D:** Michael Bay; **W:** Jonathan Hensleigh; **C:** John Schwartzman; **M:** Nick Glennie-Smith, MTV Movie Awards '97: On-Screen Duo (Sean Connery/Nicolas Cage).

C VHS, DVD. *GB CA* Peter O'Toole, Joan Plowright, Alicia Silverstone, Jaimz Woolvett, Lochlyn Munro, Martin Clunes; **D:** Sidney J. Furie; **W:** Mark Mills; **C:** Curtis Petersen.

Rock 'n' Roll High School ✶✶✶ 1979 (PG) The music of the Ramones highlights this non-stop high-energy cult classic about a high school out to thwart the principal at every turn. If it had been made in 1957, it would have been the ultimate rock 'n' roll teen movie. As it is, its 1970s' milieu works against it, but the performances are perfect for the material and the Ramones are great. Songs include "Teenage Lobotomy," "Blitzkrieg Bop," "I Wanna Be Sedated" and the title track, among others. Followed less successfully by "Rock 'n' Roll High School Forever." ♪"Teenage 'o' botomy; Blitzkrieg Bop; I Wanna Be Sedated; Rock and Roll High School. **94m/C** VHS, DVD, UMD. P.J. Soles, Vincent Van Patten, Clint Howard, Dey Young, Mary Woronov, Alix Elias, Dick Miller, Paul Bartel, Don Steele, Dee Dee Ramone, Joey Ramone, Johnny Ramone, Marky Ramone; **W:** Joe Dante, Russ Dvonch, Joseph McBride, Richard Whitley; **C:** Dean Cundey; **M:** The Ramones.

Rock 'n' Roll High School Forever ✶ 1991 (PG-13) Jesse Davis and his band just want to rock 'n' roll, but the new principal doesn't share their enthusiasm. Way late, way lame sequel to "Rock 'n' Roll High School" doesn't come close to the originality that made it a cult classic. Soundtrack includes music from The Divinyls, Dee Dee Ramone, Mojo Nixon, Will and the Bushmen, The Pursuit of Happiness, and more. **94m/C** VHS, DVD. Corey Feldman, Mary Woronov, Mojo Nixon, Evan Richards, Michael Ceveris, Patrick Malone, Larry Linville, Sarah Buxton, Liane (Alexandra) Curtis, Lewis Arquette, Jason Lively; **D:** Deborah Brock; **W:** Deborah Brock; **C:** James Mathers.

Rock 'n' Roll Nightmare ✶✶½ *The Edge of Hell* 1985 (R) A rock band is pursued by demons from another dimension. The usual lame garbage. **89m/C** VHS, DVD. *CA* Jon Mikl Thor, Paula Francescatto, Rusty Hamilton, Jillian Peri, Frank Dietz, David Lane, Teresa Simpson, Liane Abel, Nancy Bush; **D:** John Fasano; **W:** Jon Mikl Thor; **C:** Mark MacKay.

Rock, Pretty Baby ✶ 1956 Early rock-n-roll movie about a teenage band and high school riots. **89m/B** VHS. Sal Mineo, John Saxon, Rod McKuen, Luana Patten, Fay Wray, Edward Platt, Alan Reed Jr.; **D:** Richard Bartlett; **M:** Henry Mancini.

Rock River Renegades ✶ 1942 The Range Busters capture a band of renegades and restore peace to the territory once more. **59m/B** VHS, DVD. Ray Corrigan, John "Dusty" King, Max Terhune, Christine McIntyre, John Elliott, Weldon Heyburn, Kermit Maynard, Frank Ellis; **D:** S. Roy Luby; **W:** Earle Snell, John Vlahos; **C:** Robert E. Cline.

Rock, Rock, Rock ✶✶½ 1956 A young girl tries to earn enough money for a prom gown after her father closes her charge account. Screen debut of Tuesday Weld. Ultra-low-budget, but a classic after a fashion. Includes classic musical numbers performed by Chuck Berry and other rock 'n' roll pioneers. **78m/B** VHS, DVD. Alan Freed, Chuck Berry, Fats Domino, Tuesday Weld; **D:** Will Price.

Rock School ✶✶✶ 2005 (R) Director Argott's dynamic documentary lays bare the life of offbeat and intense music teacher Paul Green and his School of Rock Music, an after-school program in Philadelphia for highly-skilled nine to 17-year-olds. Flipping between cursing and berating his pupils to chumming around with them, Green prepares his most gifted group for an inspired appearance at the annual Zappanale festival in Germany (a tribute to the late rocker Frank Zappa). Green is often thought to be the basis for Jack Black's comedy "School of Rock," though its creators have refuted the claim. **93m/C** DVD. **D:** Don Argott; **C:** Don Argott.

Rock Star ✶✶ 2001 (R) Not a number one hit, but thanks to Mark Wahlberg, at least you won't choke on your own vomit. Working class (Wahlberg) spends his off-hours as the lead singer in Blood Pollution, a "tribute band" (don't call them a cover band!) to heavy metal demigods Steel Dragon. He gets a little too obsessive in the worship of his heroes, alienates the rest of the band, and is finally replaced for telling guitarist Rob (Olyphant) how to play. In a fantastical twist (and a none-too-subtle reference to real-life rockers Judas Priest), the musicians in Steel Dragon fire their secretly gay lead singer Bobby Beers (Flemyng) and recruit the amazed Chris to replace him. Real rock musicians and former rock star wives are scattered throughout the cast, but they don't add any glam to a rather bland depiction of a raunchy time period. **106m/C** VHS, DVD. *US* Mark Wahlberg, Jennifer Aniston, Timothy Olyphant, Timothy Spall, Jason Flemyng, Dominic West, Matthew Glave, Beth Grant, Stephan Jenkins, Jason Bonham, Heidi Mark, Michael Shamus Wiles, Dagmara Dominczyk, Rachel Hunter, Colleen (Ann) Fitzpatrick; **D:** Stephen Herek; **W:** John Stockwell; **C:** Ueli Steiger; **M:** Trevor Rabin.

Rockabye ✶✶½ 1986 Single mother Bertinelli is visiting New York with her two-year-old son when she's attacked and her child stolen. In her search for the boy, she discovers a black market in baby selling. **100m/C** VHS. Valerie Bertinelli, Rachel Ticotin, Jason Alexander, Ray Baker, Dick Latessa, James Rebhorn, Lynne Thigpen; **D:** Richard Michaels. **TV**

The Rocket ✶✶✶ *Maurice Richard* 2005 (PG) Inspiring biopic of hockey legend Maurice "The Rocket" Richard (perfectly portrayed by Dupuis), who, in the 1940s and 50s, rises from the Quebec working-class to stardom with the Montreal Canadiens and winner of multiple Stanley Cups. Although his speed and skill make him popular with the fans, Richard has to battle prejudice against French-speaking players from the controlling, Anglo hockey establishment. Injuries lead to constant trade talk and Richard also isn't afraid to push for much-needed NHL reforms, which doesn't endear him to the suits. English and French with subtitles. **124m/C** DVD. *CA* Roy Dupuis, Stephen McHattie, Charles Biname, Ken Scott, Patrice Robitaille, Julie Le Breton, Francois Langlois Vallieres, Ian Lapremere, Vincent Lecavalier, Serge Roude, Ted Dillon; **C:** Pierre Gill; **M:** Michel Cusson.

Rocket Attack U.S.A. WOOF! 1958 Antiquated and ridiculous tale of nuclear warfare about the time of Sputnik, with Russia's first strike blowing up New York City and environs. Mercifully short, with time for a little romance. Everything about this movie is so bad it's good for a laugh. **70m/B** VHS. Monica Davis, John MacKay, Dan Kern, Edward Czerniuk, Art Metrano; **D:** Barry Mahon.

Rocket Gibraltar ✶✶✶ 1988 (PG) On the occasion of a crusty patriarch's birthday, a large family unites in his remote estate to carry out his special birthday wish. Fine performance by Lancaster. Supported by a solid cast, overcomes a slim story, Culkin, later of "Home Alone," is loveable as the precocious five-year-old. Picturesque Long Island scenery. **92m/C** VHS, DVD. Burt Lancaster, Bill Pullman, John Glover, Suzy Amis, Macaulay Culkin, Patricia Clarkson, Frances Conroy, Sinead Cusack, Bill Martin, Kevin Spacey; **D:** Daniel Petrie; **W:** Amos Poe; **M:** Andrew Powell.

Rocket Science ✶✶✶ 2007 (R) Hal (Thompson) is having a tough time: his dad (O'Hare) has just walked out on his family, his brother Earl (Piazza) is a domineering bully, and his stutter is so intense that it gets him mocked at school. Along comes ambitious Ginny (Kendrick), who recruits him for the debate club. Hal slowly falls for Ginny, all the time unsure if she likes him or if she's just using him. Sweet and quirky meditation on first love and teenage awkwardness provides plenty of laughs, but director Blitz has a genuine sense of feeling for the characters as well in his first feature film; he previously directed the spelling bee documentary "Spellbound." **98m/C** DVD. *US* Reece Thompson, Anna Kendrick, Margo Martindale, Nicholas D'Agosto, Vincent Piazza; **D:** Jeffrey Blitz; **W:** Jeffrey Blitz; **C:** Jo Willems; **M:** Eef Barzelay.

Rocket to the Moon ✶✶ 1986 An adaptation of the Clifford Odets story about the mundane life of a 30-year-old Manhattan dentist and how he comes to terms with his life. From the PBS "American Playhouse" series. **118m/C** VHS. Judy Davis, John Malkovich, Eli Wallach; **D:** John Jacobs.

The Rocketeer ✶✶✶ 1991 (PG) Lightheaded fun. A stunt flyer in the 1930s finds a prototype jet backpack sought by Nazi spies. Donning a mask, he becomes a flying superhero. Breezy family entertainment with stupendous effects; even better if you know movie trivia, as it brims with Hollywood references, like a great villain (Dalton) clearly based on Errol Flynn. **109m/C** VHS, DVD. Billy Campbell, Jennifer Connelly, Alan Arkin, Timothy Dalton, Paul Sorvino, Melora Hardin, Tiny Ron, Terry O'Quinn, Ed Lauter, James Handy; **D:** Joe Johnston; **W:** Paul De Meo, Danny Bilson; **C:** Hiro Narita; **M:** James Horner.

RocketMan ✶✶½ *Rocket Man* 1997 (PG) Houston, we have a gastrointestinal problem. Well, dumb astronaut Fred Z. Randall (Williams) does, anyway. The bumbling computer geek is picked to go on the first manned mission to Mars, much to the dismay of crew commander "Wild Bill" Overbeck (Sadler) and specialist Julie Ford (Lundy). Beau Bridges plays Bud Nesbitt, the veteran astronaut back at NASA headquarters who is Randall's only supporter. While too much of the humor revolves around flatulence, Williams shows some talent while raiding the Disney archive for impressions. Remember, in space no one can hear you...pull my finger. **93m/C** VHS, DVD. Harland Williams, Jessica Lundy, Beau Bridges, William Sadler, Jeffrey DeMunn, James Pickens Jr., Peter Onorati; **D:** Stuart Gillard; **W:** Craig Mazin, Greg Erb; **C:** Steven Poster; **M:** Michael Tavera.

Rocketship ✶ *Flash Gordon: Rocketship* 1936 Flash Gordon battles sea monsters, ray guns, and robots in this sci-fi adventure, which is an edited version of a Flash serial. **97m/B** VHS, DVD. Buster Crabbe, Jean Rogers, Charles Middleton; **D:** Frederick Stephani; **C:** Jerome Ash; **M:** Clifford Vaughan.

Rocketship X-M ✶✶½ *Expedition Moon* 1950 A lunar mission goes awry and the crew lands on Mars, where they discover ancient ruins. Well acted and nicely photographed. Contains footage, a tinted sequence and previews of coming attractions from classic science fiction films. **77m/B** VHS. Lloyd Bridges, Osa Massen, John Emery, Hugh O'Brian, Noah Beery Jr.; **D:** Kurt Neumann; **W:** Kurt Neumann, Dalton Trumbo; **C:** Karl Struss; **M:** Ferde Grofe Jr.

Rockin' Road Trip ✶ 1985 (PG-13) A guy meets a girl in a Boston bar, and finds himself on a drunken, slapstick road trip down the Eastern seaboard with a rock band. **101m/C** VHS. Garth McLean, Katherine Harrison, Margaret Currie, Steve Boles; **D:** William Olsen; **W:** William Olsen; **C:** Austin McKinney; **M:** Ricky Keller.

The Rocking Horse Winner ✶✶✶½ 1949 Poignant tale of a young boy who discovers he can predict racehorse winners by riding his rocking horse. His spendthrift mother's greed leads to tragedy. Based on the short story by D.H. Lawrence. **91m/B** VHS, DVD. *GB* John (Howard) Davies, Valerie Hobson, Hugh Sinclair; **D:** Anthony Pelissier.

Rocktober Blood ✶✶ 1985 (R) A convicted and executed rock star comes back from the grave and starts killing people all over again. Yet another gorefest. **88m/C** VHS. Donna Scoggins, Tray Loren, Nigel Benjamin, Beverly Sebastian; **D:** Ferd Sebastian.

Rockula ✶✶ 1990 (PG-13) Teen rock comedy about a young-yet-300-year-old vampire looking to lose his virginity. Recommended only for hard-core Diddley fans. **90m/C** VHS, DVD. Dean Cameron, Bo Diddley, Tawny (Ellis) Fere, Susan Tyrrell, Thomas Dolby, Toni Basil; **D:** Luca Bercovici; **W:** Luca Bercovici.

Rockwell: A Legend of the Wild West ✶✶½ 1993 Black heroics in the wild west. U.S. Marshall Porter Rockwell and his posse of sharp shooters are after a vicious gang murdering supposed claim jumpers who just happen to be Rockwell's friends. **105m/C** VHS, DVD. Randy Gleave, Karl Malone, Michael Rudd, George Sullivan; **D:** Richard Lloyd Dewey; **W:** Richard Lloyd Dewey.

Rocky ✶✶✶✶ 1976 (PG) Boxoffice smash about a young man from the slums of Philadelphia who dreams of becoming a boxing champion. Stallone plays Rocky, the underdog hoping to win fame and self-respect. Rags-to-riches story seems to parallel Stallone's life; he had been previously virtually unknown before this movie. Intense portrayal of the American Dream; loses strength in the subsequent (and numerous) sequels. **125m/C** VHS, DVD, Blu-ray Disc. Sylvester Stallone, Talia Shire, Burgess Meredith, Burt Young, Carl Weathers, Pedro Lovell, Joe Spinell, Thayer David, Tony Burton, Michael Dorn; **D:** John G. Avildsen; **W:** Sylvester Stallone; **C:** James A. Crabe; **M:** Bill Conti. Oscars '76: Director (Avildsen), Film Editing, Picture; AFI '98: Top 100; Directors Guild '76: Director (Avildsen); Golden Globes '77: Film; Natl. Bd. of Review '76: Support. Actress (Shire), L.A. Film Critics '76: Film; Natl. Film Reg. '06:; N.Y. Film Critics '76: Support. Actress (Shire).

Rocky 2 ✶✶✶ 1979 (PG) Time-marking sequel to the boxoffice smash finds Rocky frustrated by the commercialism that followed his match to Apollo, but considering a return bout. Meanwhile, his wife fights for her life. The overall effect is to prepare you for the next sequel. **119m/C** VHS, DVD. Sylvester Stallone, Talia Shire, Burt Young, Burgess Meredith, Carl Weathers; **D:** Sylvester Stallone; **W:** Sylvester Stallone; **C:** Bill Conti.

Rocky 3 ✶✶✶ 1982 (PG) Rocky is beaten by big, mean Clubber Lang (played to a tee by Mr. T). He realizes success has made him soft, and has to dig deep to find the motivation to stay on top. Amazingly, Stallone regains his underdog persona here, looking puny next to Mr. T, who is the best thing about the second-best "Rocky" flick. **103m/C** VHS, DVD. Sylvester Stallone, Talia Shire, Burgess Meredith, Carl Weathers, Mr. T, Leif Erickson, Burt Young; **D:** Sylvester Stallone; **W:** Sylvester Stallone; **C:** Bill Conti.

Rocky 4 ✶✶ 1985 (PG) Rocky travels to Russia to fight the Soviet champ who killed his friend during a bout. Will Rocky knock the Russkie out? Will Rocky get hammered on the head a great many times and sag around the ring? Will Rocky ever learn? Lundgren isn't nearly as much fun as some of Rocky's former opponents and Stallone overdoes the hyper-patriotism and relies too heavily on uplifting footage from earlier "Rocky" movies. **91m/C** VHS, DVD. Sylvester Stallone, Talia Shire, Dolph Lundgren, Brigitte Nielsen, Michael Pataki, Burt Young, Carl Weathers; **D:** Sylvester Stallone; **W:** Sylvester Stallone; **C:** Bill Butler; **M:** Bill Conti. Golden Raspberries '85: Worst Actor (Stallone), Worst Support. Actress (Nielsen), Worst Director (Stallone), Worst Screenplay, Worst New Star (Nielsen).

Rocky 5 ✶✶ 1990 (PG) Brain damaged and broke, Rocky finds himself back where he started on the streets of Philadelphia. Boxing still very much in his blood, Rocky takes in a protege, training him in the style that made him a champ (take a lickin' and keep on tickin'). However an unscrupulous promoter has designs on the young fighter and seeks to wrest the lad from under the former champ's wing. This eventually leads to a showdown between Rocky and the young boxer in a brutal streetfight. Supposedly the last "Rocky" film, it's clear the formula has run dry. **105m/C** VHS, DVD. Sylvester Stallone, Talia Shire, Burt Young, Sage Stallone, Tom Morrison, Burgess Meredith; **D:** John G. Avildsen; **W:** Sylvester Stallone; **C:** Steven Poster; **M:** Bill Conti.

Rocky Balboa ✶✶½ 2006 (PG) The Italian Stallion finds himself put out to pasture after the demise of his boxing glory days and the death of his wife (whose name graces the restaurant he now runs)—until a computer simulation predicts that the 50-something former champ would beat the current heavyweight title holder, Mason "The Line" Dixon (Tarver). The new bout stirs up all that was good about the olden days—the music, the punching bag, and those infamous museum steps. But what about Rocky's previous brain damage? Why is Rocky Jr. (Ventimiglia) so whiny? Are those muscles or implants? None of it embarrass the franchise as much as the previous outing did. **101m/C DVD, Blu-ray Disc.** *US* Sylvester Stallone, Burt Young, Milo Ventimiglia, Tony Burton, Antonio Tarver, Geraldine Hughes, A.J. Benza, Francis Kelly III, Henry Sanders, Lahmard Tate, Pedro Lovell, Ana Gerena; *D:* Sylvester Stallone; *W:* Sylvester Stallone; *C:* Clark Mathis; *M:* Bill Conti.

The Rocky Horror Picture Show 🐾🐾🐾 1975 (R) When a young couple take refuge in a haunted castle, they find themselves the unwilling pawns in a warped scientist's experiment. Cult camp classic has been a midnight movie favorite for years and has developed an entire subculture built around audience participation. Includes a seven-minute short detailing the story behind the movie's popularity. May not be as much fun watching it on the little screen unless you bring the rice and squirt guns. 🎵 The Time Warp; Science Fiction Double Feature; Wedding Song; Sweet Transvestite; The Sword of Damocles; Charles Atlas Song; Whatever Happened to Saturday Night; Touch-a Touch-a Touch-a Touch Me; Ed die's Teddy. **105m/C VHS, DVD.** *GB* Tim Curry, Susan Sarandon, Barry Bostwick, Nell Campbell, Richard O'Brien, Patricia Quinn, Jonathan Adams, Peter Hinwood, Meat Loaf Aday, Charles Gray, Koo Stark; *D:* Jim Sharman; *W:* Jim Sharman, Richard O'Brien; *C:* Peter Suschitzky; *M:* Richard Hartley, Richard O'Brien. Natl. Film Reg. '05.

Rocky Jones, Space Ranger: Renegade Satellite 🐾🐾½ 1954 Nostalgia freaks may embrace this revived edition of the infamous early live-TV space cadet show. Rocky squares off against enemies of the United Solar System like Dr. Reno and Rudy DeMarco. Really cheap. **69m/B VHS.** Richard Crane, Sally Mansfield, Maurice Cass; *D:* Ernest Miller; *M:* Warren Wilson; *C:* Alexander Laszlo.

Rocky Marciano 🐾🐾½ 1999 (R) Boxing biopic about the up-from-poverty Rocky (Favreau) who, as heavyweight champ, had 43 knockouts and never retired undefeated. [He was killed in a 1969 plane crash]. Marciano has the usual tribulations—greedy managers and overly interested mobsters—and a climatic bout with his childhood hero, an aging Joe Louis (Davis). LoBianco, who plays a mobster, starred as Marciano in the 1979 TV movie, "Marciano." **90m/C VHS.** Jon Favreau, Judd Hirsch, Penelope Ann Miller, George C. Scott, Tony LoBianco, Duane Davis, Rhoda Gemignani, Rino Romano; *D:* Charles Winkler; *M:* Charles Winkler, Larry Golin; *D:* Paul Sarossy; *M:* Stanley Clarke. **CABLE.**

Rocky Mountain Rangers 🐾🐾 1940 The Three Mesquiteers do what they do best: save a town from bad guys. **58m/B VHS.** Robert "Bob" Livingston, Raymond Hatton, Duncan Renaldo, Leroy Mason, Dennis Moore, John St. Polis; *D:* George Sherman.

Rodan 🐾🐾 1956 A gigantic prehistoric bird is disturbed from his slumber by H-bomb tests. He awakens to wreak havoc on civilization. Big bugs also run amok. From the director of "Godzilla" and a host of other nuclear monster movies. **74m/C VHS, DVD.** *JP* Kenji Sahara, Yumi Shirakawa; *D:* Inoshiro Honda.

Rodeo Girl 🐾🐾 1980 Ross is a restless housewife who joins the rodeo in this drama based on the life of cowgirl Sue Pirtle. Particularly strong supporting cast c/ Hopkins, Clark, and Brimley. **100m/C VHS, DVD.** Katharine Ross, Bo Hopkins, Candy Clark, Jacqueline Brookes, Wilford Brimley, Parley Baer; *D:* Jackie Cooper. **TV**

Rodeo King and the Senorita 🐾🐾 1951 Rex and his horse Koko are hired on to a Wild West show, which DiSimone is struggling to run after the death of her dad. Her situation is more difficult because of a series of accidents that Rex doesn't think are so accidental. Remake of the 1946 Roy Rogers/Trigger

---

movie "My Pal Trigger." **67m/B VHS.** Rex Allen, Buddy Ebsen, Roy Barcroft, Bonnie DeSimone, Mary Ellen Kay, Tristram Coffin; *D:* Philip Ford; *W:* John K. Butler; *C:* Walter Strenge.

Rodgers & Hammerstein's South Pacific 🐾🐾½ 2001 Close may be a little mature tc be cockeyed optimist and smalltown nurse Nellie Forbush but she gives it her all [and served as one of the exective producers] in this TV remake of the Rodgers and Hammerstein musical. Filmed in Australia and Tahiti, the scenery, music, and capable cast [who can sing just fine], all contribute. Of course, Connick Jr. [as roman- tic Lt. Cable] has an advantage in the vocal area but Serbedzija's plantation owner, Emile de Becque has charisma to spare. **135m/C VHS, DVD.** Glenn Close, Rade Serbedzija, Harry Connick Jr., Robert Pastorelli, Jack Thompson, Ilene Graff, Lori Tan Chinn, Natalie Mendoza, Simon Burke, Steve Le Marquand, Steve Bastoni, Damon Herriman; *D:* Richard Pearce; *W:* Lawrence D. Cohen; *C:* Stephen Windon; *M:* Richard Rodgers. **TV**

Roe vs. Wade 🐾🐾🐾 1989 Hunter is excellent as the single woman from Texas who successfully challenged the nation's prohibitive abortion laws in a landmark Supreme Court case. Based on the actual 1973 case of Norma McCorvey. **92m/C VHS.** Holly Hunter, Amy Madigan, Terry O'Quinn, Stephen Tobolowsky, Dion Anderson, Kathy Bates, James Gammon, Chris Mulkey; *D:* Gregory Hoblit. **TV**

Roger & Me 🐾🐾½ 1989 (R) Hilarious, controversial and atypical semi-documentary detailing Moore's protracted efforts to meet General Motors president Roger Smith and confront him with the poverty and despair afflicting Flint, Michigan, after GM closed its plants there. Includes some emotionally grabbing scenes: a Flint family is evicted just before Christmas; a woman makes a living by selling rabbits for food or pets; and a then soon-to-be Miss America addresses the socioeconomic impact of GM's decision. One of the highest-grossing non-fiction films ever released, and Moore's first. **91m/ C VHS, DVD.** Michael Moore, Anita Bryant, Bob Eubanks, Pat Boone; *D:* Michael Moore; *W:* Michael Moore; *C:* Kevin Rafferty, Chris Beaver, John Prusak, Bruce Schiermer.

Roger Dodger 🐾🐾 2002 (R) Roger [Scott] is a slightly sleazy ad copywriter who believes he can talk his way into or out of anything, especially when I comes to women. After he's dumped by boss/girlfriend Joyce [Rosselini], however, he realizes that in his attempt to convince everyone else, he has cheated himself. While his relationship with Joyce is turning unsavory, his nephew Nick [Eisenberg] arrives unannounced and eager to learn the art of picking up women. Roger tutors Nick in his cynical methods, but the hotties respond more positively to Nick's innocence and honesty than to Roger's bag of tricks. Scott's performance adds a touch of warmth and compassion to a character who could have been totally odious. **104m/ C VHS, DVD.** *US* Campbell Scott, Jesse Eisenberg, Isabella Rossellini, Elizabeth Berkley, Jennifer Beals, Ben Shenkman, Mina [Badiy] Bad'e, Chris Stack, Colin Fickes; *D:* Dylan Kidd; *W:* Dylan Kidd; *C:* Joaquin Baca-Asay; *M:* Craig [Shudder to Think] Wedren. Natl. Bd. of Review '02: First Feature.

RoGoPaG 🐾🐾 1962 Four episodic films by four European masters (the title refers to their last names), satirizing the human condition. Rosselini's "Virginity" finds an airline stewardess (Schiaffino) fending off an amorous passenger (Balsibin). Godard's "The New World" features a post-nuclear Paris and its effect on romance. "La Ricotta" is Pasolini's controversial take on religion with Welles as the director of a religious epic. Gregoretti's "The Range Grown Chicken" finds Tognazzi the frazzled head of a family beset by consumerism. A mixed bag with Pasolini and Godard offering the most disturbing essays. **122m/B VHS.** *IT* Orson Welles, Ugo Tognazzi, Rosanna Schiaffino, Alexandra Stewart, Jean-Marc Bory, Renato Salvatori, Lisa Gastoni, Bruce Balaban; *D:* Roberto Rosselini, Jean-Luc Godard, Pier Paolo Pasolini, Ugo Gregoretti; *W:* Roberto Rosselini, Jean-Luc Godard, Pier Paolo Pasolini, Ugo Gregoretti; *M:* Carlo Rustichelli.

Rogue 🐾 1976 (R) The Rogue is a ruthless man who can make beautiful women do anything that he desires; so, of course, he does. **87m/C VHS.** Milan Galvoric, Barbara Bouchet, Margaret Lee; *D:* Gregory Simpson. **VIDEO**

Rogue Force 🐾½ 1999 (R) A renegade SWAT commander [Patrick] leads a vigilante group of ex-police officers in assignment is leading them. Predictable but delivers the action required of the genre. **90m/C VHS, DVD.** Robert Patrick, Michael Rooker, Louis Mandylor, Diane DiLascio; *D:* Martin Kitrosser; *W:* Earle Snell; *C:* Jack Greenhalgh.

Rogue Male 🐾🐾🐾 1976 TV movie finds '30s British aristocrat O'Toole plotting to assassinate Hitler. When his plan fails, he's on the run from both the Gestapo and the British police. Based on the novel by Geoffrey Household. **100m/C VHS.** *GB* Peter O'Toole, Alastair Sim, John Standing, Cyd Hayman; *D:* Clive Donner; *W:* Frederic Raphael.

Rogue of the Range 🐾 1936 A lawman pretends that he is a bandit in order to track down an outlaw gang. **60m/B VHS, DVD.** Lois January, Alden Chase, Phyllis Hume, George Ball, Johnny Mack Brown; *D:* S. Roy Luby; *W:* Earle Snell; *C:* Jack Greenhalgh.

Rogue of the Rio Grande 🐾½ 1930 Musical western in the peace-loving town of Sierra Blanca. One of Loy's earlier films. **60m/B VHS.** Myrna Loy, Jose Bohr, Raymond Hatton, Carmelita Geraghty, Walter Miller, Florence Dudley, Gene Morgan, William P. Burt; *D:* Spencer Gordon Bennet; *W:* Oliver Drake.

Rogue Trader 🐾🐾 1998 (R) Unremarkable recreation of the true story of futures trader Nick Leeson [McGregor] who singlehandedly brought down the Barings Merchant Bank in 1995. Working the floor of the Singapore International Money Exchange, Leeson quickly realizes he's completely out of his depth but can't admit it, so he hides his losses and continues to gamble until the deficit adds up to a $1 billion. Based on the book by Nicholas Leeson and Edward Whitley. The real Leeson was paroled from a Singapore jail in 1999. **101m/C VHS, DVD.** *GB* Ewan McGregor, John Standing, Anna Friel, Yves Beneyton, Tim [McInnerny] McInnery Betsy Brantley, Caroline Langrishe; *D:* James Dearden; *W:* James Dearden; *C:* Jean-Francois Robin; *M:* Richard Hartley.

Rogue's Gallery 🐾🐾 1944 A reporter and photographer covering the story of an inventor and his latest device are caught up in intrigue when he is found murdered. **60m/B VHS, DVD.** Frank Jenks, Robin Raymond, H.B. Warner, Ray Walker, Davison Clark, Robert E. Homans, Frank McGlynn, Pat Gleason, Edward [Ed Kea', Keene] Keane; *D:* Albert[?] Herman.

Rogue's Tavern 🐾🐾 1936 In this grade B curio, a blood-thirsty killer stalks the occupants of a country inn bodies are found with their throats crushed, and a psycho psychic is on the loose. Surprise ending. **70m/B VHS, DVD.** Wallace Ford, Joan Woodbury, Clara Kimball Young, Barbara Pepper, Jack Mulhall, John Elliott; *D:* Robert F. "Bob" Hill.

Rogue's Yarn 🐾🐾 1956 An investigator probes the death of a woman ostensibly the result of a boating accident. Gradually he uncovers a plot involving the woman's husband and his mistress in this semi-entertaining British mystery. **80m/B**

Roland the Mighty 🐾🐾½ 1956 Muscular, Herculeanesque hero takes on all comers in this sword and sandal epic set in the Asian steppes. **98m/C VHS.** *IT* Rick [Riki] Battaglia, Rosanna Schiaffino, Ivo Garrani, Fabrizio Mioni; *D:* Pietro Francisci; *W:* Ennio de Concini; *C:* Mario Bava; *M:* Angelo Francesco Lavagnino.

Roll Along Cowboy 🐾🐾 1937 A vintage sagebrush saga about a cowboy caught by love. Based on Zane Grey's "The Dude Ranger." **55m/B VHS.** Smith Ballew, Cecilia Parker; *D:* Gus Meins.

Roll Bounce 🐾🐾 2005 (PG-13) Even if you don't remember the roller-disco craze of the 70s, you'll relive it here. South-side Chicago kid Xavier [Bow Wow] and his buddies find their turf rink closes, so they're forced to go North to the swankier Sweetwater rink where the super-cool Sweetness [Jonathan] holds court. The summer rolls by with skating, flirting, and a growing rivalry until the kids square off in an end-of-summer skate-off. Based on rooted in true heart and offering a sweetness that sets it apart. **107m/C DVD.** *US* Bow Wow, Chi McBride, Mike Epps, Wesley Jonathan, Kellita Smith, Meagan Good, Khleo Thomas, Nick Cannon, Rick Gonzalez, Jurnee Smollett, Charlie [Charles G.] Murphy, Wayne Brady, Marcus T. Paulk, Brandon T. Jackson, Paul Wesley, Darryl "DMC" McDaniels; *D:* Malcolm Lee; *W:* Norman Vance Jr.; *C:* J.[James] Michael Muro; *M:* Stanley Clarke.

Roll of Thunder, Hear My Cry 🐾🐾½ 1978 A black family struggles to survive in Depression-era Mississippi in this inspiring, if somewhat predictable, production. Look for the always impressive Freeman in a supporting role. **110m/C VHS.** Claudia McNeil, Janet MacLachlan, Morgan Freeman; *D:* Jack Smight. **TV**

Roll on Texas Moon 🐾🐾 1946 A cowpoke is hired to prevent a feud between the sheep men and the cattle ranchers. **68m/B VHS, DVD.** Roy Rogers, George "Gabby" Hayes, Dale Evans, Dennis Hoey; *D:* William Witney.

Roll, Wagons, Roll 🐾🐾 1939 Tex Ritter leads a wagon train tc Oregon, who worship a "have a nice day" happy face, battle the forces of evil with martial arts and mysticism. Has to be seen to be believed. Extremely low-budget outing. **88m/C VHS.** Suzanne Solari, Jeff Hutchinson, Shaun Mitchelle, Michelle [McClellan] Bauer, Lisa Marie Barbara Pedziprauht; *D:* Donald G. Jackson; *M:* Robert Garrett.

Roller Blade 🐾 1985 In a post-holocaust world a gang of Amazon-style nuns, Kaitian; *D:* Donald G. Jackson; *W:* Randall Frakes; *C:* Dorald G. Jackson; *W:* Randall

Roller Blade Warriors: Taken By Force 🐾🐾½ 1990 Roller babes battle evil mutant while balancing on big boots with small wheels. **90m/C VHS.** Kathleen Kinmont, Roy Calhoun, Abby Dalton, Elizabeth Kaitian; *D:* Donald G. Jackson; *W:* Randall

Roller Boogie WOOF! 1979 (PG) A truly awful film made at the time of the mercifully brief roller-disco craze. Blair runs away from home and winds up helping some friends thwart a businessman looking to close the local roller rink. Everything about this one reeks amateur. Important for its historical importance to a sterile society. Flashy, violent, sometimes exhilirating. **123m/C VHS, DVD.** James Caan, John Houseman, Maud Adams, Moses Gunn, John Beck; *D:* Norman Jewison; *W:* William Harrison; *C:* Douglas Slocombe; *M:* Andre Previn.

Rollerball 🐾🐾½ 1975 (R) Caan is utterly convincing in this futuristic tale in which a brutal sport assumes alarming importance to a sterile society. Flashy, violent, sometimes exhilirating. **123m/C VHS, DVD.** James Caan, John Houseman, Maud Adams, Moses Gunn, John Beck; *D:* Norman Jewison; *W:* William Harrison; *C:* Douglas Slocombe; *M:* Andre Previn.

Rollerball 🦴 2002 (PG-13) Re-imagination of the 1975 cult classic. The sport of the near-future attracts extreme sports enthusiast Jonathan Cross (Klein), drawn by the big bucks and buddy (LL Cool J), who convinces him to try out. The sport itself, is sort of like pro wrestling on skates and motorcycles. Fleeing the law in the U.S., Jonathan heads to a former Soviet republic where the league is run by ex-KGB agent Petrovich (Reno) who wants to increase the sport's blood and gore factor to gain a stateside cable TV deal. Jonathan than finds love with fellow baller Aurora (Romijn-Stamos) whose nearly unnoticeable "deformity" doesn't dissuade the suicidal suitor. Laughable scenarios, seriously ailing editing, corny script, lackluster performances and grave miscasting (the sensitive Klein as a macho macho man) make this one a prime candidate for contraction. 98m/C VHS, DVD. US Chris Klein, LL Cool J, Rebecca Romijn, Jean Reno, Naveen Andrews, Oleg Taktarov; David Hemblen; D: John McTiernan; W: Larry Ferguson, John Pogue; C: Steve Mason; M: Eric Serra.

Rollercoaster 🦴🦴 1977 (PG) A deranged extortionist threatens to sabotage an amusement park ride. Plucky Segal must stop him. Video renters will be spared the nauseating effects of film's original "Sensurround." 119m/C VHS, DVD. Helen Hunt, Craig Wasson, Steve Guttenberg, George Segal, Richard Widmark, Timothy Bottoms, Henry Fonda, Susan Strasberg, Harry Guardino; D: James Goldstone; W: William Link; C: David M. Walsh; M: Lalo Schifrin.

Rollin' Plains 🦴 1938 A Texas Ranger tries to settle a feud between cattlemen and sheepmen over water rights. 60m/B VHS, DVD. Horace Murphy, Snub Pollard, Hobart Bosworth, Karl Hackett, Jennifer Tisdale, Tex Ritter; D: Al(bert) Herman; W: Lindsley Parsons; C: Edmond Kelso, Gus Peterson.

Rolling Family 🦴🦴 Familia Rodante 2004 Aged matriarch Emilia is invited to be the guest of honor at her grandniece's wedding. So she gathers four squabbling generations of her family and packs them into a worn-out motor home so they can travel cross-country from Buenos Aires to the ceremony. It's hot, there's no air-conditioning, they have repeated motor trouble, and all those smelly people packed into tight quarters leads to some temperamental behavior. Spanish with subtitles. 103m/C DVD. AR Graciana Chironi, Liliana Capuro, Ruth Dobel, Bernardo Forteza, Carlos Resta, Raul Vinoles, Leila Gomez, Laura Glave, Federico Esquirro; D: Pablo Trapero; W: Pablo Trapero; C: Guillermo Nieto; M: Leon Gieco.

Rolling Home 🦴🦴 1948 Tame tale about aging cowpoke, his grandson, and a really swell horse. Saddle up and snooze. 71m/B VHS, DVD. Jean Parker, Russell Hayden, Pamela Blake, Buss Henry, Raymond Hatton; D: William Berke; W: Edwin Westrate; C: Benjamin (Ben H.) Kline; M: Kierstin Koppell.

Rolling Thunder 🦴🦴½ 1977 (R) Vietnam vet turns vigilante when he arrives home from POW camp and sees his family slaughtered. Graphically violent, potentially cathartic. Typical of screenwriter Paul Schrader. 99m/C VHS. William Devane, Tommy Lee Jones, Linda Haynes; D: John Flynn; W: Paul Schrader, Heywood Gould; C: Jordan Cronenweth.

Rollover 🦴½ 1981 (R) Turgid big-budget drama about Arab undermining of American economy. Kristofferson is lifeless, Fonda is humorless. Supporting players Sommer and Cronyn fare better. 117m/C VHS, DVD. Jane Fonda, Kris Kristofferson, Hume Cronyn, Bob Gunton, Josef Sommer, Martha Plimpton; D: Alan J. Pakula.

Roman 🦴 2006 Alienated Roman (McKee) exists in his own lonely world until he becomes interested in his blonde neighbor (Bell). Too bad he accidentally kills her. Not knowing what to do, Roman starts dismembering the corpse and disposing of it piece by piece. Then death-obsessed Eva (Rose) becomes his new neighbor but maybe Roman should be careful about inviting her to visit. 92m/C DVD. Lucky McKee, Nectar Rose, Kristen Bell, James Duval, Jesse Hlubik, Ben Boyer; D: Angela Bettis; W: Lucky McKee; C: Kevin Ford; M: Jaye Barnes Luckett.

Roman Holiday 🦴🦴🦴½ 1953 Hepburn's first starring role is a charmer as a princess bored with her official visit to Rome who slips away and plays at being an "average Jane." A reporter discovers her little charade and decides to cash in with an exclusive story. Before they know it, love calls. Blacklisted screenwriter Trumbo was "fronted" by Ian McLellan Hunter, who accepted screen credit and the Best Story Oscar in Trumbo's stead. The Academy voted to posthumously award Trumbo his own Oscar in 1993. 118m/B VHS, DVD. Audrey Hepburn, Gregory Peck, Eddie Albert, Tullio Carminati; D: William Wyler; C: Henri Alekan; Story: British Acad. '53: Actress (Hepburn), Costume Des. (B&W); N.Y. Film Critics '53: Actress (Hepburn).

Roman Scandals 🦴🦴½ 1933 A penniless young man daydreams himself back to ancient Rome with uproarious results. Lucille Ball appears as one of the Goldwyn Girls. Dance sequences were choreographed by Busby Berkeley. ♫No More Love; Build A Little Home; Keep Young and Beautiful; Rome Wasn't Built in a Day; Put a Tax on Love. 91m/B VHS. Eddie Cantor, Ruth Etting, Gloria Stuart, Edward Arnold, Lucille Ball, Busby Berkeley; D: Frank Tuttle; C: Gregg Toland.

Roman Spring of Mrs. Stone 🦴🦴🦴 The Widow and the Gigolo 1961 An aging actress determines to revive her career in Rome but finds romance with a gigolo instead in this adaptation of Tennessee Williams's novella. Leigh and Beatty are compelling, but Lenya nearly steals the show as Leigh's distinctly unappealing confidant. 104m/C VHS, DVD. Warren Beatty, Vivien Leigh, Lotte Lenya, Bessie Love, Jill St. John, Elspeth March; D: Jose Quintero; W: Gavin Lambert.

The Roman Spring of Mrs. Stone 🦴🦴 Tennessee Williams: The Roman Spring of Mrs. Stone 2003 (R) In this slightly revised remake of the 1961 original, older actress Karen Stone (Mirren) becomes infatuated with conniving gigolo Paolo (Martinez) as she tries to rebound from the death of her rich husband while in Italy. 108m/C VHS, DVD. Helen Mirren, Olivier Martinez, Anne Bancroft, Rodrigo Santoro, Brian Dennehy, Suzanne Bertish, Jane Bertish, Roger Allam, Victor Alfieri, Dona Granata, Aldo Signoretti; D: Robert Allan Ackerman; W: Martin Sherman, Tennessee Williams; C: Ashley Rowe; M: John Altman. TV

Romance 🦴🦴 1930 In what her second talkie, Garbo stars an Italian opera star who seduces a young priest. Poor story and weak acting from everyone with the exception of Garbo. Even she can't save this one. Adapted from the play "Signora Cacllini." 77m/B VHS. Greta Garbo, Lewis Stone, Gavin Gordon, Elliott Nugent, Florence Lake, Clara Blandick; D: Clarence Brown; C: William H. Daniels.

Romance 🦴🦴 1999 This journey of erotic self-discovery caused raised eyebrows even among the blasé French. Schoolteacher Marie (Ducey) is sexually rejected by her bored male model boyfriend Paul (Stevenin). This so distresses her that Marie flings herself into sexual escapades, including bar-pickup Paolo (Italian porn star Siffredi) and bondage sessions with school principal Robert (Berleand). Very talky, very self-serious, and very explicit. French with subtitles. 93m/C VHS, DVD. FR Caroline Ducey, Sagamore Stevenin, Francois Berleand, Rocco Siffredi; D: Catherine Breillat; W: Catherine Breillat; C: Yorgos Arvanitis; M: D.J. Valentin, Raphael Tidas.

Romance & Cigarettes 🦴🦴 2005 Although made in 2005, Turturro's musical comedy didn't get much of a release until 2007 although it's not really bad—just, well, odd. Queens ironworker Nick (Gandolfini) is cheating on wife Kitty (Sarandon) with a slinky redhead—lingerie shop owner Tula (a foul-mouthed Winslet). When Kitty finds out, she decides to get even, aided by Cousin Bo (Walken) and the couple's three daughters (Aida Turturro, Parker, Moore). The score is mainly recognizable pop tunes, which the actors either sing or lip-synch to. 106m/C DVD. James Gandolfini, Susan Sarandon, Kate Winslet, Christopher Walken, Mary-Louise Parker, Aida Turturro, Mandy Moore, Bobby Cannavale, Steve Buscemi, Eddie Izzard, Elaine Stritch; D: John Turturro; W: John Turturro; C: Tom Stern; M: Paul Chihara.

Romance and Rejection 🦴🦴 So This Is Romance? 1996 Sad-sack Mike (Dinsdale) is looking for love in London. His father tells him to settle for good sex but Mike wants more. Then he meets a woman (Bellar) who may fulfill both parts of the equation. 98m/C VHS, DVD. GB Reece Dinsdale, Clara Bellar, John Hannah, Victoria Smurfit, Frank Finlay, Susannah York, Mayam D'Abo, Rowena King; D: Kevin W. Smith; W: Kevin W. Smith; C: Ian Savage; M: Howard J. Davidson.

Romance in Manhattan 🦴🦴 1934 Recent immigrant to New York struggles to build new life, in spite of unemployment, language barriers, and loneliness. He meets Broadway chorine Rogers and song and dance ensues. America, ain't it a great place? 78m/B VHS. Ginger Rogers, Francis Lederer, J. Farrell MacDonald; D: Stephen Roberts; M: Max Steiner.

Romance of a Horsethief 🦴🦴½ 1971 (PG) Brynner leads this entertaining but slow-paced "Fiddler on the Roof" comedic romp without the music. In 1904 Poland, a Cossack captain takes horses for the Russo-Japanese war. The residents of the town rise up, goaded on by Birkin. 100m/C VHS, DVD. YU Yul Brynner, Eli Wallach, Jane Birkin, Oliver Tobias, Lainie Kazan, David Opatoshu; D: Abraham Polonsky.

Romance on the High Seas 🦴🦴🦴 1948 A woman is scheduled to take a cruise vacation but skips the boat when she believes her husband is cheating on her. Her husband believes she is taking the cruise to cheat on him and hires a private detective to follow her. Pleasant comedy features the film debut of Doris Day. ♫It's Magic; It's You or No One; The Tourist Trade; Put 'Em in a Box; Tie 'Em with a Ribbon, and Throw 'Em in the Deep Blue Sea; Two Lovers Met in the Night; Run, Run, Run; I'm in Love; Cuban Rhapsody. 99m/C VHS, DVD. Jack Carson, Janis Paige, Don DeFore, Doris Day, Oscar Levant, S.Z. Sakall, Eric Blore, Franklin Pangborn, Leslie Brooks; William "Billy" Bakewell; D: Michael Curtiz; W: Julius J. Epstein.

Romance on the Orient Express 🦴½ 1989 Sparks fly when former lovers meet again on the Orient Express. Don't expect any flesh, though, as this was made for TV. 96m/C VHS. Cheryl Ladd, Stuart Wilson, John Gielgud; D: Lawrence Gordon-Clark. TV

Romance on the Range 🦴½ 1942 Rogers sets out to trap a gang of fur thieves and finds romance. 60m/B VHS. Roy Rogers, George "Gabby" Hayes, Sally Payne, Linda Hayes, Harry Woods, Glenn Strange; D: Joseph Kane; M: Tim Spencer, Glenn Spencer.

Romance with a Double Bass 🦴🦴🦴 1974 When a musician and a princess take a skinny dip in the royal lake and get their clothes stolen, comic complications arise. Reminiscent of Cleese's sojourn as a Monty Python member, with surreal, frequently raunchy humor. 40m/C VHS, DVD. GB John Cleese, Connie Booth, Graham Crowden, Desmond Jones, Freddie Jones, Andrew Sachs; D: Robert M. Young.

Romancing the Stone 🦴🦴🦴 1984 (PG) Uptight romance novelist Joan (Turner) lives out her fantasies after she receives a mysterious map from her murdered brother-in-law and her sister is kidnapped in South America—the ransom being the map. Out to rescue her sister, she's helped and hindered by American soldier of fortune Jack (Douglas) whose main concern is himself and the hidden treasure described in the map. Great

Romantic Comedy 🦴🦴 1983 (PG) Writing duo never seem to synchronize their desires for each other in this dull comedy. Engaging stars don't inspire each other much, and supporting cast can't make up the difference. Adapted from the Bernard Slade play. 102m/C VHS, DVD. Dudley Moore, Mary Steenburgen, Frances Sternhagen, Ron Leibman; D: Arthur Hiller; W: Bernard Slade; C: David M. Walsh; M: Marvin Hamlisch.

Romantic Englishwoman 🦴🦴🦴 1975 (R) Literate comedy-drama about the intertwined lives of several sophisticated and restrained Brits. Caine is a successful novelist with writer's block whose wife falls for another man while on a trip alone. He then invites his wife's lover to stay with them in order to generate ideas for his writing until his jealousy begins to surface. 117m/C VHS. GB Glenda Jackson, Michael Caine, Helmut Berger, Kate Nelligan; D: Joseph Losey; W: Tom Stoppard, Thomas Wiseman.

Rome Adventure 🦴🦴 Lovers Must Learn 1962 Spinster librarian Pleshette takes Roman vacation hoping to meet handsome prince. Donahue takes shine to her while girlfriend Dickinson is away, as does suave Roman Brazzi. Soapy, ill-paced romance. 119m/C VHS, DVD. Pam(ela) Austin, Troy Donahue, Angie Dickinson, Suzanne Pleshette, Rossano Brazzi, Constance Ford, Al Hirt, Chad Everett; D: Delmer Daves; W: Delmer Daves; M: Max Steiner.

Rome '78 🦴🦴½ 1978 Acclaimed underground film centered around Caligula and the Queen of Sheba in ancient Rome. 60m/C VHS. Arya Phillips, David McDermott, Eric Mitchell; D: James Nares.

Romeo and Juliet 🦴🦴🦴½ 1936 One of MGM producer Irving Thalberg's pet projects (and starring Thalberg's wife, Norma Shearer), this Shakespeare classic was given the spare-no-expense MGM treatment. Physically too old to portray teenage lovers, both Howard and Shearer let their acting ability supply all necessary illusions. Also notable is Barrymore's over-the-top portrayal of Mercutio. 126m/B VHS. Leslie Howard, Norma Shearer, John Barrymore, Basil Rathbone, Edna May Oliver; D: George Cukor; C: William H. Daniels.

Romeo and Juliet 🦴🦴🦴½ 1954 Unfulfilling adaptation of Shakespeare's timeless drama of young love cast against family antagonisms. Peculiar supporting cast features both Cabot and ubiquitous master Gielgud. 138m/C VHS. IT Laurence Harvey, Susan Shantall, Aldo Zollo, Sebastian Cabot, Flora Robson, Mervyn Johns, Bill Travers, John Gielgud; D: Renato Castellani; C: Robert Krasker. Natl. Bd. of Review '54: Director (Castellani).

Romeo and Juliet 🦴🦴🦴½ 1968 (PG) Young couple share love despite prohibitive conflict between their families in this adaptation of Shakespeare's classic play. Director Zeffirelli succeeds in casting relative novices Whiting and Hussey in the leads, but is somewhat less proficient in lending air of free-wheeling '60s appeal to entire enterprise. Kudos, however, to cinematographer Pasquale De Santis and costume designer Nina Rota. Also available in a 45-minute edited version. 138m/C VHS, DVD. GB IT Olivia Hussey, Leonard Whiting, Michael York, Milo O'Shea; D: Franco Zeffirelli; W: Franco Zeffirelli, Franco Brusati, Maestro D'Amico; C: Pasqualino De Santis; M: Nino Rota; Nar: Laurence Olivier. Oscars '68: Cinematog., Costume Des.; Golden Globes '69: Foreign Film; Natl. Bd. of Review '68: Director (Zeffirelli).

Romeo Is Bleeding 🦴🦴½ 1993 (R) Jack (Oldman) is a police detective accepting mobster payoffs from boss Falcone (Scheider) for fingering federally protected witnesses. But the next target

Romeo Must Die ✓✓½ **2000 (R)**
Romance is decidedly secondary to action in this kung fu/hip hop hybrid. After an over-extended (but flashy) credits sequence, the story kicks in. Black crime lord Isaak O'Day (a magnetic Lindo) and Asian crime boss Ch'u Sing (O) are maintaining an uneasy truce in order to do a mega-business deal. Then Sing's useless younger son is killed and soon O'Day's son father at his side. As melodramatic and often predictable as this coming-of-age tale may be, it's still got guts and an emotional punch. Based on the memoir by German-born, Australian-based philosopher Raimond Gaita. **109m/C DVD. AU** Eric Bana, Franka Potente, Russell Dykstra, Martin Csokas, Kodi Smit-McPhee, Jacek Koman; **D:** Geoffrey Roxburgh; **W:** Nick Drake; **C:** Geoffrey Simpson; **M:** Basil Hogios.

Romeo ✓✓ **1989 (R)**
Julia is riveting as the Salvadoran archbishop who championed his destitute congregation despite considerable political opposition. A stirring biography financed by the United States Roman Catholic Church. **102m/C VHS, DVD.** Raul Julia, Richard Jordan, Ana Alicia, Eddie Velez, Alejandro Bracho, Tony, Plana, Lucy Reina, Harold Gould, Al Ruscio, Robert Viharo; **D:** John Duigan; **W:** John Sacret Young; **C:** Geoff Burton; **M:** Gabriel Yared.

Romola ✓✓½ **1925**
Silent adventure. After Powell and his father are attacked by pirates, Powell escapes. But instead of rescuing his father, he opts for a life of corruption. Dad eventually escapes and returns to exact vengeance. A rather expensive film in its day, troubled by modern-day sights in what was supposed to be old Florence. Gish's drowning scene had to be re-shot because she wouldn't sink. Colman arranged for his then-wife Faye to have a bit part, but they were directed soon after the film was finished. **112m/B VHS.** Lillian Gish, Dorothy Gish, William Powell, Ronald Colman, Charles Lane, Herbert Grimwood, Bonaventure Ibarez, Frank Puglia; **D:** Henry King.

Romper Stomper ✓✓ **1992 (R)**
Violent confrontations between Australian skinheads and the Vietnamese community mixed in with a disturbed love story. Suburban rich girl Gabe (McKenzie) is drawn to the charismatic Hando (Crowe), the certifiably loony leader of a group of Melbourne's skinheads. Any romance takes a backseat to the carnage brought by the skinheads' attacks on the local Asian community, who fight back with equal force. Disturbing look at a brutal world which can't be ignored. Film caused a furor upon its Australian release with debates about whether the extreme violence was intended version and explicate the plot. An unrated version at 89 minutes is also available. **85m/C VHS, DVD.** AU Alex Scott, Leigh Russell, Daniel Wyllie, James McKenna, Samantha Bladon, Russell Crowe, Jacqueline McKenzie, Daniel Pollock; **D:** Geoffrey Wright; **W:** Geoffrey Wright; **C:** Ron Hagen; **M:** John Clifford White; Australian Film Inst. '92: Actor (Crowe), Sound, Score.

Romulus, My Father ✓✓ **2007 (R)**
Set in Australia's hard economic struggles of 1961 ten-year old Raimond Hispanic girl and white youth who has mastered martial arts dancing. "West Side Story." See this one and be the only person you know who has. **108m/C VHS, DVD.** Jason Gedrick, Troy Beyer, Eddie Velez, Tisha Campbell; **D:** Robert Wise; **W:** Allan Goldstein, Terrence (Terry) Brennan; **M:** Michael Kamen.

Ronin ✓✓½ **1998 (R)**
What a cast! What a director! What a disappointment! Okay, so it's not that bad—the scenery's spectacular (the action takes place between Paris and Nice) and there are some amazing car chases. But, they go on much too long and the story's less than involving. Sam (De Niro) is a world-weary, possibly ex-spy who gets involved with several international players (including Reno, Skarsgard, and Bean) to do a job for tough Irish lass Deirdre (McElhone). She's fronting (for the violent Pryce) a project to retrieve a mysterious suitcase from some Russian bad guys. One of the best things the film's got going for it is the wary buddy relationship that builds between De Niro and Reno. Title refers to a Japanese legend concerning 47 masterless samurai. Richard Weisz is the pseudonym for a rewriting David Mamet. **116m/C VHS, DVD, UMD.** Robert De Niro, Jean Reno, Stellan Skarsgard, Natascha (Natasha) McElhone, Jonathan Pryce, Skipp (Robert L.) Sudduth, Michael (Michel) Lonsdale, Sean Bean, Jan Triska, Feodor Atkine, Bernard Bloch, Katarina Witt; **D:** John Frankenheimer; **W:** David Weisz, J.D. Zeik; **C:** Robert Fraisse; **M:** Ella Cmiral.

Ronnie and Julie ✓✓½ **1997**
(PG) Yet another contemporary variation of "Romeo & Juliet" with high-school sweethearts Ronnie (Jackson) and Julie's (Finley) relationship threatened by their respective parents political rivalry in a mayoral campaign. At least this one has a happy ending. **99m/C VHS.** Joshua Jackson, Margot Finley, Alexandra Purvis, Tom Butler, Garwin Sanford; **D:** Philip Spink; **C:** Bruce Worrall.

The Roof ✓✓ **1956**
Uninteresting outing about a young couple who married against their families' wishes and find that setting up a home of their own is more difficult than they thought. In Italian with English subtitles. **98m/B VHS.** IT Gabriella Pallotta, Giorgio Listuzzi; **D:** Vittorio De Sica.

Rookie of the Year ✓✓½ **1993**
(PG) Kid's fluff fantasy come true. Twelve-year-old baseball fanatic Henry has dreams of baseball stardom in the big league. He falls, breaks his arm, and when it heals strangely is blessed with a pitching arm so spectacular he finds himself not only playing for the Chicago Cubs, but leading them to the World Series. Enjoyable family outing for first-time director Stern, who also plays a seasoned and very incredulous ballplayer.) Keep your eyes peeled for appearances by real-live sluggers Pedro Guerrero, Barry Bonds, and others. **'03m/C VHS, DVD.** Thomas Ian Nicholas, Gary Busey, Dan Hedaya, Daniel Stern; Stern, Gary Busey, Dan Hedaya, Daniel Stern; **W:** Sam Harper; **C:** John G. Green; **M:** Bill Conti. Blockbuster '95: Family Movie, V.

The Room ✓✓ **1987**
Altman takes on Pinter in this brooding mini-play about two young strangers who try to rent the room already occupied by a disconnected woman and her semi-catatonic husband. **49m/C VHS.** Julian Sands, Linda Hunt, Annie Lennox, David Hemblen, Donald Pleasence; **D:** Robert Altman. **W:** Harold Pinter. **TV.**

Room at the Top ✓✓½ **1959**
Ambitious factory man forsakes true love and marries boss's daughter instead in this grim drama set in industrial northern England. Cast excels, with Harvey and Sears as the worker and his wife. Signoret is also quite compelling as the abandoned woman. Adapted from John Braine's novel and followed by "Life at the Top" and "Man at the Top." **118m/B VHS, DVD.** GB Laurence Harvey, Simone Signoret, Heather Sears, Hermione Baddeley, Avril Ungar, Donald Wolfit,

Wendy Craig, Allan Cuthbertson, Ian Hendry, Donald Houston, Raymond Huntley, Miriam Karlin, Wilfred Lawson, Richard Pasco, Mary Peach, Prunella Scales, Beatrice Varley, John Westbrook, Delena Kidd; **D:** Jack Clayton. **W:** Neil Paterson; **C:** Freddie Francis; **M:** Mario Nascimbene. Oscars '59: Actress (Signoret), Adapt. Screenplay; British Acad. '58: Actress (Signoret), Film Cannes '59: Actress (Signoret).

Romy and Michele's High School Reunion ✓✓½ **1997 (R)**
Two vacuous ditz queens, Romy (Sorvino) and Michele (Kudrow), best friends and roommates since high school, decide they must impress at their 10-year Tucson high school reunion by passing themselves off as wealthy and successful. Since they're barely bright enough to walk and chew gum at the same time, this proves to be a challenge, especially when the arrival of cynical Heather (Garofalo), who knows the truth, threatens their deception. Music's good, and there are a (very) few funny moments, but you'll concentrate most on trying to ignore those annoying accents. You don't laugh with these would-be babes, you laugh at them. And even then, not all that much. Based on Schiff's play "The Ladies' Room." **91m/C VHS, DVD.** Mira Sorvino, Lisa Kudrow, Janeane Garofalo, Alan Cumming, Julia Campbell, Elaine Hendrix, Jacob Vargas, Camryn Manheim; **D:** David Mirkin; **W:** Robin Schiff; **C:** Reynaldo Villalobos; **M:** Steve Bartek.

The Rookie ✓✓ **1990 (R)**
Routine cop drama has worldly veteran and wide-eyed newcomer team to crack stolen-car ring managed by Germans, Eastwood and Sheen are reliable, but Hispanics Julia and Braga, though miscast, nonetheless steal this one as the German villains. **121m/C VHS, DVD.** Clint Eastwood, Charlie Sheen, Raul Julia, Sonia Braga, Lara Flynn Boyle, Pepe Serna, Marco Rodriguez, Tom Skerritt, Roberta Vasquez; **D:** Clint Eastwood. **VIDEO**

The Rookie ✓✓✓½ **2002 (G)**
Texas high school teacher and baseball coach Jim Morris (Quaid) challenges his high school team by promising his he also-ran team by promising to go on a major league tryout if they win the regional championship. The team wins, and the former minor-leaguer keeps his promise and attends a Devil Rays tryout and finds his now-rejuvenated arm can throw a baseball 98 mph. During his journey to the majors, he deals with his relationship with his old man, and life on the other side of 30. If this weren't a true story, it'd be one of the hokiest movies ever, but because you know it's real, it's, well, inspiring. It helps that Quaid nails the role, and Jones, as son Hunter, walks off with every scene he's in. One of the producers, Mark Ciardi, is a former teammate of Morris, and his original go-round in the minors. Based on Morris's book "The Oldest Rookie." **127m/C VHS, DVD.** JS Dennis Quaid, Rachel Griffiths, Angus T. Jones, Brian Cox, Beth Grant, Chad Lindberg, Royce D. Applegate, Jay Hernandez, Russell Richardson, Raynor Scheine, David Blackwell, Edward "Blue" Deckert, Dan Kamin, Trevor Morgan, Rick Gonzalez, Angelo Spizzirri; **D:** John Lee Hancock; **W:** Mike Rich; **C:** John Schwartzman; **M:** Carter Burwell.

Rooftops ✓✓ **1989 (R)**
Peculiar but predictable, centering on love between Hispanic girl and white youth who has mastered martial arts dancing. "West Side Story." See this one and be the only person you know who has. **85m/C VHS, DVD.** Jason Gedrick, Troy Beyer, Eddie Velez, Tisha Campbell; **D:** Robert Wise; **W:** Allan Goldstein, Terrence (Terry) Brennan; **M:** Michael Kamen.

A Room with a View ✓✓✓ **1986**
Engaging adaptation of E.M. Forster's novel of requited love. Lucy Honeychurch (Bonham Carter) is the feisty British iconoclast who rejects dashing George (Sands) for supericilious Cecil (Day-Lewis), then repents and finds (presumably) eternal passion. A multi-Oscar nominee, with great music (courtesy of Puccini), great scenery (courtesy of Florence), and great performances (courtesy of practically everybody), but supporters Smith, Dench, Callow, and Elliott must be particularly distinguished.) Truly romantic, and there's much humor too. **117m/C VHS, DVD, Blu-Ray Disc, HD DVD, GB** Helena Bonham-Carter, Julian Sands, Denholm Elliott, Maggie Smith, Judi Dench, Simon Callow, Daniel Day-Lewis, Rupert Graves, Rosemary Leach; **D:** James Ivory; **W:** Ruth Prawer Jhabvala; **C:** Tony Pierce-Roberts; **M:** Richard Robbins. Oscars '86: Adapt. Screenplay, Art Dir/Set Dec., Costume Des.; British Acad. '86: Actress (Smith), Film, Support. Actress (Dench); Golden Globes '87: Support. Actress (Smith); Ind. Spirit '87: Foreign Film; Natl. Bd. of Review '86: Support. Actor (Day-Lewis); N.Y. Film Critics '86: Cinematogr., Support. Actor (Day-Lewis); Writers Guild '86: Adapt. Screenplay.

Roommate **1984**
A valedictorian church-goer and a rebellious iconoclast room together at Northwestern University in 1952 with the expected humorous results. Public TV presentation based on a John Updike story. **96m/C VHS.** Lance Guest, Barry Miller, Elaine Wilkes, Melissa Ford, David Bachman. **D:** Neil Cox. **TV.**

Room 43 ✓✓½ **1958**
The Marx Brothers provide less than the usual mayhem here with Groucho as a penniless theatrical producer determined to remain in his hotel room until he can secure funds for his next play. Ball doesn't help matters much either. The story does certainly not up to the zany Marx clan's usual stuff. **78m/B VHS, DVD.** Groucho Marx, Chico Marx, Lucille Ball, Ann Miller, Harpo Marx, Zeppo Marx; **D:** William A. Seiter; **W:** Roy Webb.

Room Service ✓✓½ **1938**
The Marx Brothers provide less than the usual mayhem here with Groucho as a penniless theatrical producer determined to remain in his hotel room until he can secure funds for his next play. Features a young Ceine and future novelist Collins in bit parts. **93m/B VHS.** Diana Dors, Herbert Lom, Eddie Constantine, Michael Caine, Jackie Collins; **D:** Peter Graham Scott.

Room to Let ✓✓ **1949**
An elderly woman and her daughter take in boarders in Victorian England. They rent a room to a man who claims to be a doctor, but the two women eventually become prisoners of fear, believing the man is actually Jack the Ripper. Will there be a vacancy soon? Somewhat disturbing and suspenseful. **68m/B VHS.** GB Jimmy Hanley, Valentine Dyall, Christine Silver, Merle Tottenham, Charles Hawtrey, Constance Smith, Laurence Naismith; **D:** Godfrey Grayson.

Roommates ✓✓ **1995 (PG)**
Rocky Holeczek (Falk) is a cantankerous coot who, at age 75, decides to care for orphaned seven-year-old grandson Michael. Over the 30 years they are together, they fight over Rocky's old school ways and a grown-up Michael's (Sweeney), attempt to have a family of his own. But despite their bickering, Michael soon realizes that his 107-years-old grandfather's words are truly pearls of wisdom when faced with tragedy. Film hits the right sentimental buttons without going overboard with the tissues and Falk's performance, underneath the layers of latex make-up, is charmingly irascible. Based on co-writer Apple's own grandfather. **108m/C VHS, DVD.** Peter Falk, D.B. Sweeney, Julianne Moore, Ellen Burstyn; **D:** Peter Yates; **W:** Max Apple, Stephen Metcalfe; **C:** Mike Southon; **M:** Elmer Bernstein.

Rooms for Tourists 🐾🐾 *Habitaciones para Turistas* 2004 Creepy, gory feature (made more so by being filmed in B&W) set in a backwater section of Buenos Aires. Five girls miss their train and find room in a hostel owned by two brothers. Soon they're hunted by a masked killer throughout the dark, decrepit house. Spanish with subtitles. **90m/B DVD, AR** Jimena Krouco, Elena Siritto, Mariela Mujica, Brenda Vera, Victoria Witemburg, Rolf Garcia, Alejandro Lise; **D:** Adrian Garcia-Bogliano; **W:** Adrian Garcia-Bogliano, Ramiro Garcia-Bogliano; **C:** Dario Bermeo, Veronica Padron; **M:** Rodrigo Franco.

Rooster Cogburn 🐾🐾½ 1975 (PG) A Bible-thumping schoolmarm joins up with a hard-drinking, hard-fighting marshal in order to capture a gang of outlaws who killed her father. Tired sequel to "True Grit" but the chemistry between Wayne and Hepburn is right on target. **107m/C VHS, DVD.** John Wayne, Katharine Hepburn, Richard Jordan, Anthony Zerbe, John McIntire, Strother Martin, Paul Koslo, Tommy Lee; **D:** Stuart Millar; **W:** Martin Julien; **C:** Harry Stradling Jr.; **M:** Laurence Rosenthal.

Rooster: Spurs of Death! *woof!* 1983 (PG) An expose on cock fighting, in which a young idealist tries to stop the thriving sport in a small southern town. Dog of a movie that (not surprisingly) went straight to video. **90m/C VHS.** Vincent Van Patten, Ty Hardin, Kristine DeBell, Ruta Lee; **D:** Brice Mack; **W:** John Eastman; **C:** Eric Saarinen; **M:** Robert O. Ragland. **VIDEO**

Roosters 🐾🐾½ 1995 (R) Gallo Morales (Olmos) is returning home, after serving seven years in prison for manslaughter, anxiously awaited by wife Juana (Braga), 20-year-old rebellious son Hector (Nucci), neglected adolescent daughter Angela (Lassez), and sexy sister Chata (Alonso). Gallo is a noted breeder of fighting cocks, which for him represent machismo and power but, to his resentment, it's Hector who owns a potential prize-winning bird, precipitating some explosive family conflicts. Adapted by Sanchez-Scott from her 1987 play. **93m/C VHS, DVD.** Edward James Olmos, Sonia Braga, Maria Conchita Alonso, Danny Nucci, Sarah Lassez; **C:** Reynaldo Villalobos; **M:** David Kitay.

Rootin' Tootin' Rhythm 🐾 *Rhythm on the Ranch* 1938 All's not quiet on the range, but Autry comes along to sing things back to normal. Goofy, clumsy, ubiquitous sidekick Burnette is a symbol for this whole effort. **55m/B VHS.** Gene Autry, Smiley Burnette, Monte Blue; **D:** Mack V. Wright.

Roots 🐾🐾🐾🐾 1977 The complete version of Alex Haley's saga following a black man's search for his heritage, revealing an epic panorama of America's past. Dramatizing the shared heritage of millions of African Americans in an ennobling fashion, this milestone miniseries brought together dozens of black actors to create an accurate, if simplified, picture of several generations in one black family. The story begins with Kunta Kinte (Burton) going through his manhood trials in his Gambian village in Africa, only to be captured by slavers and shipped away to America. **573m/C VHS, DVD.** John Amos, Maya Angelou, Ed Asner, Lloyd Bridges, LeVar Burton, Chuck Connors, Cicely Tyson, Ben Vereen, Sandy Duncan, Tanya Boyd, Lynda Day George, Lorne Greene, Burl Ives, O.J. Simpson, Todd Bridges, Georg Stanford Brown, MacDonald Carey, Olivia Cole, Leslie Uggams, Ossie Davis; **D:** David Greene, Marvin J. Chomsky, John Erman, Gilbert Moses; **W:** William Blinn, Ernest Kinoy, M. Charles Cohen, James H. Lee; **C:** Stevan Larner, Joseph M. Wilcots; **M:** Quincy Jones, Gerald Fried. **TV**

Roots of Evil 🐾½ 1991 (R) This erotic thriller follows a cop on the trail of a murderer who specializes in killing Hollywood's most beautiful prostitutes. Also available in unrated and Spanish-language versions. **95m/C VHS.** Alex Cord, Delia Sheppard, Charles Dierkop, Jillian Kesner; **D:** Gary Graver.

Roots: The Gift 🐾🐾 1988 It's Christmas 1770, and Kunte Kinte (Burton) and Fiddler (Gossett) try to escape slavery via the Underground Railroad. In their attempt, they wind up giving the gift of freedom to several of their fellow slaves. **94m/C VHS.** Louis Gossett Jr., LeVar Burton, Michael Learned, Avery Brooks, Kate Mulgrew, Shaun Cassidy, John McMartin; **D:** Kevin Hooks; **C:** John A. Alonzo. **TV**

Roots: The Next Generation 🐾🐾🐾 1979 Sequel to the landmark TV miniseries continuing the story of author Alex Haley's ancestors from the Reconstruction era of the 1880s to 1967, culminating with Haley's visit to West Africa where he is told the story of Kunta Kinte. **685m/C VHS.** Georg Stanford Brown, Lynne Moody, Henry Fonda, Richard Thomas, Marc Singer, Olivia de Havilland, Paul Koslo, Beah Richards, Stan Shaw, Harry (Henry) Morgan, Irene Cara, Dorian Harewood, Ruby Dee, Paul Winfield, James Earl Jones, Debbie Allen; **Cameos:** Al Freeman Jr., Marlon Brando; **D:** John Erman; **W:** Sydney Glass; **C:** Joseph M. Wilcots; **M:** Gerald Fried. **TV**

Rope 🐾🐾🐾½ 1948 (PG) In New York City, two gay college students murder a friend for kicks and hide the body in a living room trunk. They further insult the dead by using the trunk as the buffet table and inviting his parents to the dinner party in his honor. Very dark humor is the theme in Hitchcock's first color film, which he innovatively shot in uncut ten-minute takes, with the illusion of a continuous scene maintained with tricky camera work. Based on the Patrick Hamilton play and on the Leopold-Loeb murder case. **81m/C VHS, DVD.** James Stewart, John Dall, Farley Granger, Cedric Hardwicke, Constance Collier; **D:** Alfred Hitchcock; **W:** Arthur Laurents; **C:** William V. Skall, Joseph Valentine; **M:** David Buttolph.

Rorret 🐾🐾 1987 "Rorret" is "terror" spelled backwards—a good indication of the psychological and physical terror Mr. Rorret, the owner of the Peeping Tom Cinema, inflicts upon his female patrons. The Cinema is devoted to the horror film and Rorret himself dresses like Peter Lorre in "M"; lives behind the movie screen, watching the films in mirror image; and enjoys the frightened reactions of his female patrons. He enjoys their reactions so much that he later stalks the women for real. Highlighted by recreated sequences from such psycho-terror classics as "Psycho," "Dial M for Murder," "Strangers on a Train," and "Peeping Tom." In Italian with English subtitles. **105m/C VHS. IT** Lou Castel, Anna Galiena, Massimo Venturiello; **D:** Fulvio Wetzl; **W:** Fulvio Wetzl.

Rory O'Shea Was Here 🐾🐾½ *Inside I'm Dancing* 2004 (R) Rory is the independence-seeking, fun-loving, skirt-chasing new arrival at Carrighmore nursing home. A muscular dystrophy patient, he befriends cerebral palsy sufferer Michael because he seems to be the only one who can understand him. When Rory is denied an independent-living grant because of his recklessness, he persuades Michael to apply, tagging along as his interpreter. They hire Siobhan, a cute supermarket clerk as their helper. Inevitably, they both fall for her. Excellent performances and some genuinely funning and touching scenes help elevate this Irish import above the usual disease-of-the-week fare. **104m/C DVD. JR GB FR** Steven Robertson, James McAvoy, Romola Garai, Brenda Fricker, Gerard McSorley, Tom Hickey, Ruth McCabe; **D:** Damien O'Donnell; **W:** Jeffrey Caine; **M:** David Julyan.

Rosa Luxemburg 🐾🐾 1986 Based on the life of the Jewish political radical, murdered in 1919. Involving herself with the German Social Democratic Party, Luxemburg undergoes numerous imprisonments and maintains a tempestuous personal life. Based primarily on Luxemburg's letters and speeches; charismatic performance by Sukowa. In German with English subtitles. **122m/C VHS. GE** Barbara Sukowa, Daniel Olbrychski, Otto Sander, Adelheid Arndt; **D:** Margarethe von Trotta; **W:** Margarethe von Trotta. Cannes '86: Actress (Sukowa).

The Rosa Parks Story 🐾🐾½ 2002 Rather prosaic bio on Rosa Parks (Bassett) goes into detail on her life (beginning when she was the new girl at a Montgomery school) to her involvement in the N.A.A.C.P. and the Montgomery, Alabama bus boycott sparked by her arrest. **90m/C VHS, DVD.** Angela Bassett, Peter Francis

James, Tonea Stewart, Cicely Tyson, Sonny Shroyer; **D:** Julie Dash; **W:** Paris Qualles. **TV**

Rosalie 🐾🐾½ 1938 A gridiron great from West Point falls for a mysterious beauty from Vassar. He soon learns that her father reigns over a tiny Balkan nation. Expensive, massive, imperfect musical; exotic romantic pairing fails to conceal plot's blah-ness. Oh well, at least Porter's music is good. 🎵I've a Strange New Rhythm in My Heart; Why Should I Care?; Spring Love Is in the Air; Rosalie; It's All Over But the Shouting; Who Knows?; In the Still of the Night; To Love or Not to Love; Close (instrumental). **118m/B VHS.** Nelson Eddy, Eleanor Powell, Frank Morgan, Ray Bolger, Ilona Massey, Reginald Owen, Edna May Oliver, Jerry Colonna; **D:** Woodbridge S. Van Dyke; **M:** Cole Porter.

Rosalie Goes Shopping 🐾🐾🐾 1989 (PG-13) Satire about American consumerism hiding behind slapstick comedy, and it works, most of the time. Misplaced Bavarian (Sagebrecht) moves to Arkansas and begins spending wildly and acquiring "things." Twisty plot carried confidently by confident wackiness from Sagebrecht and supporters. **94m/C VHS. GE** Marianne Saegebrecht, Brad Davis, Judge Reinhold, Willie Harlander, Alex Winter, Erika Blumberger, Patricia Zehnenmayr; **D:** Percy Adlon; **W:** Eleonore Adlon, Percy Adlon; **M:** Bob Telson.

The Rosary Murders 🐾🐾 1987 (R) Based on the William X. Kienzle mystery about a serial killer preying on nuns and priests. Father Koesler (Sutherland) must betray the confessional to stop him. Interesting, though sometimes muddled and too rarely tense. Filmed on location in Detroit. **105m/C VHS.** Donald Sutherland, Charles Durning, Belinda Bauer, Josef Sommer, James Murtaugh, John Danelle, Addison Powell, Kathleen Tolan, Janet Smith; **D:** Fred Walton; **W:** Fred Walton, Elmore Leonard; **C:** David Golia.

The Rose 🐾🐾🐾 1979 (R) Modeled after the life of Janis Joplin, Midler plays a young, talented and self-destructive blues/rock singer. Professional triumphs don't stop her lonely restlessness and confused love affairs. The best exhibition of the rock and roll world outside of documentaries. Electrifying film debut for Midler features an incredible collection of songs. 🎵Fire Down Below; I've Written A Letter to Daddy; Let Me Call You Sweetheart; The Rose; Stay With Me; Camellia; Sold My Soul To Rock 'n' Roll; Keep On Rockin'; When A Man Loves a Woman. **134m/C VHS, DVD.** Bette Midler, Alan Bates, Frederic Forrest, Harry Dean Stanton, David Keith; **D:** Mark Rydell; **C:** Vilmos Zsigmond. Golden Globes '80: Actress—Mus./Comedy (Midler). Song ("The Rose"); Natl. Soc. Film Critics '79: Support. Actor (Forrest).

The Rose and the Jackal 🐾🐾 1990 Fun, intriguing fictionalization about the founder of the Pinkerton detective agency. During the Civil War, bearded, Scottish Reeve tries to persuade a wealthy Southern lady to help save the Union. **94m/C VHS.** Christopher Reeve, Madolyn Smith, Granville Van Dusen, Carrie Snodgress, Kevin McCarthy; **D:** Jack Gold. **C A B L E**

The Rose Garden 🐾🐾½ 1989 (PG-13) In modern Germany, a Holocaust survivor is put on trial for assaulting an elderly man. The victim, it turns out, was a Nazi guilty of heinous war crimes. Ullmann and Schell lend substance, though treatment of a powerful theme is inadequate. **112m/C VHS.** Liv Ullmann, Maximilian Schell, Peter Fonda, Jan Niklas, Kurt Hubner; **D:** Fons Rademakers; **W:** Paul Hengge; **M:** Egisto Macchi.

Rose Hill 🐾🐾½ 1997 (PG) Adam, Travis, Douglas, and Cole are (unrelated) orphans, living on the streets of 1860s New York City, when they find an abandoned baby girl. They adopt the baby, whom they name Mary Rose, and decide to head west to start a new life as a family. As the years pass the boys build a cattle ranch in Montana they name Rose Hill and over-protect their headstrong teenaged sister, who would like the chance to flirt with some beaus without her brothers hovering around. TV movie based on the Julie Garwood novel "For the Roses." **90m/C VHS, DVD.** Jennifer Garner, Jeffrey D.

Sams, Tristan Tait, Zak Orth, Justin Chambers, Casey Siemaszko, David Newcom; **D:** Christopher Cain; **W:** Earl W. Wallace. **TV**

Rose Marie 🐾🐾🐾 *Indian Love Call* 1936 An opera star falls in love with the mountie who captured her escaped convict brother. Hollywood legend has it that when a British singer was presented with the first line in "Indian Love Song," which is "When I'm calling you-oo-oo-oo-oo-oo," "the confused performer sang, "When oo, I'm calling you, double oh, double oh, double oh..." Maybe true, maybe not, but funny anyway. Classic MacDonald-Eddy operetta. Remade in 1954. 🎵Indian Love Call; Pardon Me, Madame; The Mounties; Rose Marie; Totem Tom Tom; Just for You; Tex Yeux; St. Louis Blues; Dinah. **112m/B VHS.** Jeanette MacDonald, Nelson Eddy, James Stewart, Allan Jones, David Niven, Reginald Owen; **D:** Woodbridge S. Van Dyke; **C:** William H. Daniels; **M:** Rudolf Friml.

Rose Marie 🐾🐾🐾 1954 (G) Blyth is a lonely Canadian woman wooed by a mean spirited fur trapper and a gallant mountie. Unremarkable remake of the EddyMacDonald musical is saved by spectacular technicolor and CinemaScope photography. Choreography by Busby Berkeley. 🎵Rose Marie; Indian Love Call; Totem Tom Tom; The Mounties; I Have the Love; The Right Place For A Girl; Free to be Free; The Mountie Who Never Got His Man. **115m/C VHS.** Ann Blyth, Howard Keel, Fernando Lamas, Bert Lahr, Marjorie Main, Joan Taylor, Chief Yowlachie, Abel Fernandez, Al Ferguson, Dabbs Greer, Lumsden Hare; **D:** Mervyn LeRoy; **C:** Paul Vogel.

Rose of Rio Grande 🐾 1938 A western musical about a Mexican gang that avenges the deaths of members of the upper strata. **60m/B VHS.** John Carroll, Movita, Antonio Moreno, Lena Basquette, Duncan Renaldo; **D:** William Nigh.

Rose of Washington Square 🐾🐾 1939 Singer Faye gets involved with the no-account Power, much to the dismay of her friend Jolson. They marry, and she becomes a singing sensation in the Ziegfeld Follies while he becomes an embarrassment, eventually winding up on the wrong side of the law. Jolson stole the movie, singing some of his best numbers. This thinly disguised portrait of Fanny Brice caused the performer to sue for defamation of character; she eventually settled out of court. 🎵California, Here I Come; My Mammy; Pretty Baby; Toot Toot Tootsie Goodbye; Rock-A-Bye Your Baby with a Dixie Melody; My Man; I'm Just Wild About Harry; I Never Knew Heaven Could Speak; Rose of Washington Square. **86m/B VHS.** Alice Faye, Tyrone Power, Al Jolson, William Frawley, Joyce Compton, Hobart Cavanaugh, Moroni Olsen; **D:** Gregory Ratoff; **W:** Nunnally Johnson; **C:** Karl Freund.

The Rose Tattoo 🐾🐾½ 1955 Magnani, in her U.S. screen debut, is just right as a Southern widow who cherishes her husband's memory, but falls for virile trucker Lancaster. Williams wrote this play and screenplay specifically for Magnani, who was never as successful again. Interesting character studies, although Lancaster doesn't seem right as an Italian longshoreman. **117m/B VHS, DVD.** Anna Magnani, Burt Lancaster, Marisa Pavan, Ben Cooper, Virginia Grey, Jo Van Fleet; **D:** Daniel Mann; **W:** Tennessee Williams, Hal Kanter; **C:** James Wong Howe; **M:** Alex North. Oscars '55: Actress (Magnani), Art Dir./Set Dec., B&W, Cinematog.; British Acad. '56: Actress (Magnani); Golden Globes '56: Actress—Drama (Magnani), Support. Actress (Pavan); N.Y. Film Critics '55: Actress (Magnani).

Roseanne: An Unauthorized Biography 🐾 1994 Boring TV movie about the boorish (ex-)duo of Tom Arnold and Roseanne Barr Pentiand Arnold. Recounts her troubled upbringing in Salt Lake City, her later stormy marriage, and her long slog toward fame as a "domestic goddess" stand-up comedienne and TV series star. Miscasting of both leads hurts any chance this poor substitute had. **90m/C VHS.** Denny Dillon, David Graf, John Walcutt, John Karlen, Judith Scarpone, Danielle Harris; **D:** Paul Schneider; **W:** Kam-yuen Szeto; **C:** Yuri Neyman; **M:** Scott Harper.

Rosebud 🎬 1975 (PG) Embarrassingly dull film finds a group of PLO terrorists kidnapping five young women who were vacationing aboard O'Toole's yacht. He's supposedly a journalist but actually works for the CIA. Action ping-pongs between the plight of the victims and what's being done to rescue them but it's so boring you won't care. "Rosebud" is the name of the yacht. Based on a novel by Joan Hemingway and Paul Bonnecarrere. 126m/C VHS. D: Otto Preminger. W: Eric Lee Preminger; Marjorie Kellogg.

Roseland 🎬🎬🎬 1977 (PG) Three interlocking stories, set at New York's famous old Roseland Ballroom, about lonely people who live to dance. Not fully successful, but strong characters, especially in the second and third stories, make it worth watching, although it lacks energy. 103m/C VHS, DVD. C: Christopher Walken, Geraldine Chaplin, Joan Copeland, Teresa Wright, Lou Jacobi. D: James Ivory. W: Ruth Prawer Jhabvala.

Rosemary's Baby 🎬🎬🎬 1968 (R) A young woman, innocent and religious, and her husband, ambitious and agnostic, move into a new apartment. Soon the woman is pregnant, but she begins to realize that she has fallen into a coven of witches and warlocks, and that they claim the child as the antichrist. Gripping and powerful, subtle yet utterly horrifying, with luminous performances by all. Polanski's first American film; from Levin's best-seller. 136m/C VHS, DVD. Mia Farrow, John Cassavetes, Ruth Gordon, Sidney Blackmer, Maurice Evans, Patsy Kelly, Elisha Cook Jr., Ralph Bellamy, Charles Grodin, Hanna Landy, Emmaline Henry, William Castle; D: Roman Polanski; W: Roman Polanski. V: Tony Curtis. Oscars '68: Support. Actress (Gordon); Golden Globes '69. Support. Actress (Gordon).

Rosencrantz & Guildenstern Are Dead 🎬🎬🎬 1990 (PG) Playwright Stoppard adapted his own absurdist 1967 play to film—which at first look makes as much sense as a "Swan Lake" ballet on radio. Patience is rewarded for those who stick with it. Two tragicomic minor characters in "Hamlet" squabble theatrically and misperceive Shakespeare's plot "tightening" fatally around them. Uprooted from the stage environment, it's arcane but hilarious if you're paying attention. Roth and Oldman are splendid as the doomed duo. 118m/C VHS, DVD. GB Gary Oldman, Tim Roth, Richard Dreyfuss, Iain Glen, Joanna Miles, Ian Richardson, John Burgess, Vili Matula, Ljubo Zecevic; D: Tom Stoppard; W: Tom Stoppard. C: Peter Biziou; M: Stanley Myers. Venice Film Fest. '91. Picture.

Rosenstrasse 🎬🎬🎬 2003 (PG-13) Fact-based account of a forgotten incident of heroism in WWII Germany. When retraining Jews of Berlin are rounded up for deportation to death camps in 1943, those married to non-Jewish women, or children of such couples are diverted to temporary prison on Rosenstrasse ("Street of Roses"). Many of the detainees' wives gather outside prison to show support to families inside and demand their release. After several days of quiet courageous protest, prisoners were released and saved from gas chambers. Film tells this story through families directly involved in event. Moving and well-acted retelling of lost piece of history. 136m/C DVD, GE NL. Katja Riemann, Maria Schrader, Martin Feifel, Jutta Lampe, Doris Schade, Fedja Van Huet, Carola Regnier, Jan Decleir, Thekla Reuten, Lena Stolze, Iso de Barth, Martin Wuttke, Jürgen Vogel, Svea Lohde, Jutta Wachowiak, Nina Kunzendorf. D: Margarethe von Trotta; W: Margarethe von Trotta, Pamela Katz; C: Jan Betke; M: Loek Dikker.

Rosebud Beach Hotel 🎬 1985 (R) The Big Lobby; The No-Tell Hotel. Wimpy loser tries his hand at managing a rundown hotel in order to please his demanding girlfriend. Camp is okay, but his only excuse is horrible in every other way. 82m/C VHS, DVD. Colleen Camp, Peter Scolari, Christopher Lee, Fran Drescher, Eddie Deezen, Chuck McCann, Hank Garrett, Hamilton Camp, Cherie Currie; D: Harry Hurwitz; C: Joao Fernandes.

Roses Bloom Twice 🎬 1977 When a middle-aged widow decides to make up for some of the wild living that she missed during her marriage, she shocks her children. 87m/C VHS. Glynis McNicoll, Michael Craig, Diane Craig, John Allen, Jennifer West. D: David Stevens.

Rosetta 🎬🎬 1999 (R) Rosetta (Dequenne) is a desperate 17-year-old Belgian who lives in a trailer with her alcoholic mother. Her joyless routine includes caring for her passed-out mom and frantically searching for some kind of employment, even if it means betraying her one friend, Riquet (Rongione), who works at a waffle stand and whose job Rosetta comes to covet. Claustrophobic and depressing. French with subtitles. 95m/C VHS, DVD, FR BE Emilie Dequenne, Fabrizio Rongione, Anne Yernaux, Olivier Gourmet; D: Jean-Pierre Dardenne, Luc Dardenne; W: Jean-Pierre Dardenne, Luc Dardenne. C: Alain Marcoen. Cannes '99: Actress (Dequenne), Film.

Rosewood 🎬🎬🎬 1996 (R) Based on the true story of the well-off African American community of Rosewood, Florida, which was destroyed by white mob in 1923. Rhames is Mr. Mann, a war vet and drifter. Voight is a white shopkeeper who, together with Mann, blend of real-life characters and Hollywood machismo. Both performances are strong and Rhames succeeds as a detailed visual reminder of country's tragic history. Real-life survivors of the tragedy finally won reparation from the Florida legislature in 1993. Singleton's location shoots in the Florida swamps caused problems for the crew, one of whom was sent to the hospital after a snake bite. 142m/C VHS, DVD. Ving Rhames, Jon Voight, Don Cheadle, Michael Rooker, Bruce McGill, Loren Dean, Esther Rolle, Elise Neal, Catherine Kellner, Akosua Busia, Paul Benjamin, Mark Boone Jr., Muse Watson, Badja Djola, Kathryn Masle, Jaimz Woovett; D: John Singleton; W: Gregory Poirier. C: Johnny E. Jensen. M: John Williams.

Rosie 🎬🎬 1999 Rosie (Coppens) is 13 and is first seen living in an institution for delinquents. Her desperate story is told in flashbacks as the girl grows up in industrial Antwerp in a cramped apartment with her mother, Irene (de Roo), who insists Rosie say they are sisters when men come to visit, which they do frequently. When her moocher Uncle Michel (Vercruyssen) arrives, Rosie is even kicked out of her bedroom. It's no wonder she escapes into a romantic dreamworld she shares with a would-be boyfriend, Jimi (Wijnant), and the dangerous turn her real life takes. Flemish with subtitles. 97m/C VHS, BE Aranka Coppers, Sara de Roo, Joost Wijnant, Frank Vercruyssen; D: Patrice Toye; W: Patrice Toye. C: Richard Van Oosterhout; M: John Farish.

Rosie: The Rosemary Clooney Story 🎬🎬1/2 1982 Above-average biography of Clooney's up-and-down career. Locke lip-synches Clooney's voice in songs. Orlando doesn't help matters portraying Jose Ferrer. 100m/C VHS. Sondra Locke, Tony Orlando, Penelope Milford, Katherine Helmond, Kevin McCarthy, John Karlen, Cheryl Anderson, Robert Ridgely, Joey Travolta; D: Jackie Cooper. TV

Roswell: The U.F.O. Cover-Up 🎬🎬 1994 (PG-13) Fact-based drama finds intelligence officer Major Jesse Marcel (McLachlan) investigating the wreckage of a craft near his New Mexico air base in the summer of 1947. Marcel believes the craft is extraterrestrial—as are the strange bodies recovered from the wreckage. An Air Force press release announces a UFO but is quickly retracted and Marcel's suspicions ridiculed. A 30-year reunion still finds him obsessed and seeking to clear his name but this time Marcel's investigations may finally lead to the truth. Made 'for TV,' based on the book "UFO Crash at Roswell" by Kevin D. Randle and Donald R. Schmitt. 91m/C VHS, DVD. Kyle MacLachlan, Dwight Yoakam, Kim G'nist, Martin Sheen, Xander Berkeley, J.D. Daniels, Doug Wert, John M. Jackson, Peter MacNichol, Bob Gunton, Charles Martin Smith; D: Jeremy Paul Kagan, Arthur Kopit, Paul Davies; W: Jeremy Paul Kagan, Arthur Kopit. TV

R.O.T.O.R. 🎬 1988 R.O.T.O.R. (Robotic Officer of Tactical Operations Research). Officer of Tactical Operations (Research) is a law enforcement robot that is supposed to stop criminals. But watch out! It might go beserk and wreck your town. 90m/C VHS. Richard Gesswein, Margaret Trigg, Jane Smith. D: Cullen Blaine.

Rough Cut 🎬🎬 1980 (PG) American diamond thief Reynolds lives in London, pursued by an aging Scotland Yard detective who wants to end his career in a blaze of glory. A beautiful lady is the decoy. Good chemistry; lousy script. 112m/C VHS. Burt Reynolds, Lesley-Anne Down, David Niven, Timothy West, Joss Ackland, Patrick Magee; D: Donald Siegel; W: Larry Gelbart. C: Frederick A. (Freddie) Young.

Rough Justice 🎬1/2 1987 Spaghetti western about a lone gunfighter tracking down three killers. Kinski is a sexual assistant, with latent powers of her own. C: Mario Costa.

Rough Magic 🎬🎬 Miss Shumway Jette un Sort 1995 (PG-13) Fantasy-noir-romance-comedy-on-the-road-movie-nostalgia-fest can't decide what it wants to be when it grows up. Fonda is a magician's assistant, with latent powers of her own, who flees to Mexico after witnessing a murder. Her fiance (Moffett) turns out to be the culprit and he hires drifter Crowe to track her down. Along the way, they meet a quack doctor (Broadbent) trying to find a magic Mayan potion, a garage owner who becomes a sausage, and a shaman. Sure, it's confusing, but the performances are good, and you could always play "Name That Genre" afterwards. Adapted from the novel "Miss Shumway Waves a Wand" by James Hadley Chase. 104m/C VHS, DVD, GB FR Bridget Fonda, Russell Crowe, Jim Broadbent, Clare Peploe, Eva Anderson; D: Clare Peploe, Clare Peploe, Robert Mundy; W: William Brookfield; C: John Campbell; M: Richard Hartley.

Rough Night in Jericho 🎬🎬1/2 1967 Martin plays unredeemable scum in this cliched western. He's an ex-lawman trying to take over the town of Jericho and all that's left to own is the stagecoach line run by Simmons and McIntire. Coming to Simmons aid is Peppard, a former deputy marshall turned gambler. Predicatably violent. 104m/C VHS, DVD. Dean Martin, Jean Simmons, George Peppard, John McIntire, Slim Pickens, Don Galloway; D: Arnold Laven; W: Sydney (Sidney) Boehm, Marvin H. Albert; C: Russell Metty. M: Don Costa.

Rough Riders 🎬🎬1/2 1997 Miniseries covering the adventures of the Volunteer Cavalry, led by a pre-presidential Teddy Roosevelt (Berenger), and their travails during the Spanish-American War in 1898. Fighting in Cuba, the Calvary were a mixture of western outlaws and cowboys and eastern bluebloods—all of whom would have to learn to fight together. Filmed on locations in Texas. 240m/C VHS, DVD. Tom Berenger, Sam Elliott, Gary Busey, Brad Johnson, Christopher Noth, Brian Keith, George Hamilton, R. Lee Ermey, Nicholas Chinlund, Dale Dye, Holt McCallany, Illeana Douglas, Geoffrey Lewis, William Katt, Adam Storke, Dakin Matthews, Francesco Quinn, Titus Welliver; Mark Moses; D: John Milius; W: John Milius, Hugh Wilson; C: Anthony B. Richmond; M: Peter Bernstein. CABLE

Rough Riders of Cheyenne 🎬1/2 1945 Sunset Carson ends the feud between the Carsons and the Sterlings. 54m/B VHS. Sunset Carson, Peggy Stewart, Mira McKinney, Monte Hale, Wade Crosby, Kenne Duncan, Tom London, Eddy (Edward) Waller, Jack Rockwell; D: Thomas Carr; W: Elizabeth Beecher.

Rough Ridin' Rhythm 🎬1/2 1937 Wallace is kidnapped to care for the orphaned child of a bandit's sister with Maynard being accused of leaving nursing duty. But he's innocent and fights the gang to clear his name. Based on the story "Getting a Start in Life" by James Oliver Curwood. 59m/B VHS. Kermit Maynard, Beryl Wallace, Ralph Peters, Betty Mack, Curley Dresden; D: John Paterson.

Rough Riders' Roundup 🎬🎬 1939 Roy and the boys ric a mining 'own o' its crooked manager. Less yodeling than later Roger's outings; also better all around. 54m/B VHS, DVD. Roy Rogers, Raymond Hatton, Lynne Roberts, Dorothy Sebastian, Duncan Renaldo, George Montgomery; D: Joseph Kane.

Rough Riding Ranger 🎬1/2 1935 Threatening letters plague a western ranch family. 57m/B VHS. Rex Lease, Janet Chandler, Bobby Nelson, Yakima Canutt, George Chesebro, Mabel Strickland, Robert Walker; D: Elmer Clifton; M: Edward Linden.

Roughnecks 🎬🎬 1980 A team of Texas oil drillers attempt to dig the deepest oil well in history and chase women on the side. Too long, and not particularly action-packed or gripping. 240m/C VHS. Sam Melville, Cathy Lee Crosby, Vera Miles, Harry (Henry) Morgan, Steve Forrest, Stephen McHattie, Wilford Brimley; D: Bernard McEveety. TV

Round Midnight 🎬🎬🎬 1986 (R) An aging, alcoholic black American jazz saxophonist comes to Paris in the late 1950s seeking an escape from his self-destructive existence. A devoted young French fan spurs him to one last burst of creative brilliance. A moody, heartfelt homage to such expatriate bebop musicians as Bud Powell and Lester Young, in English and French with English subtitles. Available in a Spanish-subtitled version. 132m/C VHS, DVD. FR Dexter Gordon, Lonette McKee, Francois Cluzet, Martin Scorsese, Herbie Hancock, Sandra Reaves-Phillips; D: Bertrand Tavernier; W: Bertrand Tavernier, David Rayfiel; C: Bruno de Keyzer. Oscars '86: Orig. Score.

Round Numbers 🎬🎬 1991 (R) Judith Schweitzer believes her husband 'Big Al the Muffler King' is having an affair with the gorgeous Muffler Honey (Playboy Playmate Hope Marie Carlton). Determined to get revenge. 98m/C VHS. Kate Mulgrew, Samantha Eggar, Mary Ingels, Hope Marie Carlton, Shani Wallis, Natalie Barish, Debic Christohol, Nemo Zaia; W: Nancy Zaia.

Round Trip to Heaven 🎬🎬1/2 1992 (R) Party guy Larry (Feldman) and his innocent cousin' (Galligan) take off in a borrowed Rolls Royce to go meet Larry's dream centerfold in a super model contest. Unfortunately, the Rolls' trunk is loaded with stolen money and Stoneface (Sharkey), the felon who stashed the cash, wants the money back. With Stoneface in pursuit these guys are in for the ride of their lives. For the teen set only. Also available with Spanish subtitles. 97m/C VHS. Corey Feldman, Zach Galligan, Julie McCullough, Roxanne Brewer, Ray Sharkey; D: Alan Roberts.

The Round Up 🎬🎬🎬 Szegenylegenyek Nehezeletcek; The Hopeless Ones; The Poor Outlaws 1966 Brutal tale spins a realistic political web of fear. Set in 1868 in a prison camp, suspected Hungarian subversives, largely peasants and herdsmen, are thrown into jail and tortured. A direct and shocking exploration of life under dehumanizing, totalitarian rule, in Hungarian with English subtitles. 90m/B VHS. HU Janos Gorbe, Tibor Molnar, Andras Kozak. D: Miklos Jancso; W: Gyula Hernadi.

Round-Up Time in Texas 🎬🎬 1937 Autry delivers a herd of horses to his diamond-prospector brother in South Africa and has to deal with bandits after the jewels. Typical early Autry entry with singin' girl' on the side. 54m/B VHS, DVD. Gene Autry, Smiley Burnette. D: Joseph Kane.

The Rounders ✓✓½ 1965 Two aging, no-account cowboys (Ford and Fonda) dream of giving up their bronco-busting ways to open a bar in Tahiti where they can watch the world go by. But they have a habit of blowing all their money on women, whiskey, and bad bets. An ornery unbreakable horse may be the key to changing their luck. Mild-mannered comedy with beautiful Arizona scenery. **85m/C VHS, UMD.** Glenn Ford, Henry Fonda, Sue Ane Langdon, Kathleen Freeman, Joan Freeman, Denver Pyle; **D:** Burt Kennedy; **W:** Burt Kennedy; **C:** Paul Vogel.

Rounders ✓✓½ 1998 (R) Damon plays Mike, a law student who used to be a poker hustler, but is now ready to leave the game and settle down with girlfriend Jo (Mol). His good intentions are undermined by his "friend" Worm (Norton), whose gambling debts are mounting. Mike's return to the table doesn't reduce the debt; instead, he loses money and his reputation. Knowing he must get the money himself, Mike sets up a final showdown with Teddy KGB (Malkovich)—a tense game of Texas Hold 'Em in which Malkovich's drawn-out accent provides the most fun of the movie. Damon holds his own, using some elaborate monologues reminiscent of "Good Will Hunting," while Norton and Malkovich add a lot of spark. It's all style over substance, but that's what makes it (mostly) work. **120m/C VHS, DVD.** Matt Damon, Edward Norton, John Turturro, Gretchen Mol, Famke Janssen, John Malkovich, Martin Landau, Michael Rispoli, Melina Kanakaredes, Josh Mostel, Lenny Clarke, Tom Aldredge, Lenny Venito, Goran Visnjic; **D:** John Dahl; **W:** David Levien, Brian Koppelman; **C:** Jean-Yves Escoffier; **M:** Christopher Young.

Rounding Up the Law ✓✓ 1922 Good guy dupes bad guy while organ plays. **62m/B VHS.** Russell Gordon, Chet Ryan, Patricia Palmer, William (Bill, Billy) McCall, Guinn "Big Boy" Williams; **D:** Charles Seeling.

The Roundup ✓✓ 1941 Janet (Morison) is set to marry rancher Steve (Dix) on the rebound after her beloved fiance Greg (Foster) is killed (or so she thinks). But Greg shows up on the wedding day and he's none too happy that Janet's getting hitched to another guy. **90m/B VHS.** Richard Dix, Patricia Morison, Preston Foster, Don Wilson, Betty Brewer; **D:** Lesley Selander; **W:** Harold Shumate, Edmund Day.

Roustabout ✓✓ 1964 (PG) A roving, reckless drifter joins a carnival and romances the owner's daughter. Elvis rides on good support from Stanwyck et al. Welch has a bit part in her film debut; look for Terri Garr as a dancer. ♪Roustabout; Poison Ivy League; One Track Heart; Little Egypt; Wheels on My Heels; It's a Wonderful World; It's Carnival Time; Hard Knocks; There's a Brand New Day on the Horizon. **101m/C VHS, DVD.** Elvis Presley, Barbara Stanwyck, Joan Freeman, Leif Erickson, Sue Ane Langdon, Pat Buttram, Joan Staley, Dabbs Greer, Steve Brodie, Jack Albertson, Marianna Hill, Beverly Adams, Billy Barty, Raquel Welch; **D:** John Rich.

The Rousters ✓✓½ 1990 (PG) Cliched story has some decent performances. Two smalltown sheriff's deputies (MacLachlan and Williams) discover a couple of dead bodies, drugs, and a stash of cash, which they decide to keep. But their boss (Coyote) gets suspicious and then the feds come investigating. **102m/C VHS, DVD.** Kyle MacLachlan, Wade Andrew Williams, Peter Coyote, Roma Maffia, Amy Locane, Miguel (Michael) Sandoval, Scott Coffey; **D:** David Mackay; **W:** Brendan Broderick, Rob Kerchner; **C:** Brian Sullivan; **M:** Don Davis. **CABLE**

Route 666 ✓✓½ 2001 (R) Some very slick stylistic touches are brought to this action/horror that aspires to be another "From Dusk Til Dawn." Marshals Jack (Phillips) and Stephanie (Petty) are escorting a witness to a grand jury in Los Angeles when they become lost on a remote highway. Years ago, a chain gang was murdered there, and they return as inmates of the living dead for revenge. The ultra-violence is silly but some of the visual tricks are pretty cool. **90m/C DVD.** Lou Diamond Phillips, Lori Petty, Steven Williams, Dale Midkiff, Alex McArthur, Mercedes Colon, L.Q. Jones; **D:** William Wesley; **W:** William Wesley, Thomas N. Weber, Scott Fivelson; **C:** Philip Lee; **M:** Terry Plumeri.

The Rover ✓½ *The Adventurer* 1967 Peyrol (Quinn) is involved in counterrevolutionary forces during the Napoleonic War and takes refuge in the home of Caterina (Hayworth), where he falls in love with her shy and mentally slow niece, Arlette (Schiaffino). Very dull adaptation of the Joseph Conrad novel. **103m/C VHS.** *IT* Anthony Quinn, Rosanna Schiaffino, Rita Hayworth, Richard Johnson; **D:** Terence Young; **W:** Luciano Vincenzoni, Jo Eisinger; **C:** Leonida Barboni; **M:** Ennio Morricone.

Rover Dangerfield ✓✓ 1991 (G) Lovable Las Vegas hound Rover Dangerfield searches for respect but finds none. The results are hilarious. Quality animation from a project developed by Rodney Dangerfield and Harold Ramis. **78m/C VHS.** **D:** Jim George; **W:** Harold Ramis; **M:** David Newman; **V:** Rodney Dangerfield.

Row Your Boat ✓✓ 1998 Ex-con Jamey (Bon Jovi), who took a burglary rap for his brother (Forsythe), is determined to go straight after his release from prison. He gets a job as a census taker, which is how he meets Asian immigrant single mom Chun Hua (Ling) who will become a part of a scheme by Jamey's no-good brother. **106m/C VHS, DVD.** Jon Bon Jovi, William Forsythe, Bai Ling, Jill(ian) Hennessey, John Ventimiglia; **D:** Sollace Mitchell; **W:** Sollace Mitchell; **C:** Michael Barrow, Zoltan David; **M:** Phil Ramone.

The Rowdy Girls ✓✓ 2000 Sharp-shooting Tweed disguises herself as a nun and meets up with bullwhip-wielding wild woman Strain and runaway bride Brooks in order to cross the western frontier. And no amount of scurvy outlaws are going to stop them. Ogle to your heart's content. **88m/C VHS, DVD.** Shannon Tweed, Julie Strain, Deanna Brooks, Laszlo Vargo; **D:** Steve Nevius; **W:** India Allen.

Rowing Through ✓✓ 1996 Tiff Wood (Ferguson) is a top sculler at Harvard who is sacrificing everything in his obsession to win gold at the 1980 Moscow Olympics. And he has the best chance—until the U.S. decides to boycott the games. But Tiff refuses to give up his dream and struggles four more years towards proving himself against a younger group of competitors. **115m/C VHS, DVD.** *CA* JP Colin Ferguson, Leslie Hope, Peter Mumik, Kenneth Welsh, Michiko Hada, Helen Shaver, James Hyndman, Christopher Jacobs; **D:** Masato Harada; **W:** Masato Harada, Will Aitken; **C:** Sylvain Brault; **M:** Masahiko Kawasaki.

Rowing with the Wind ✓✓ *Remando al Viento* 1988 (R) The story behind Mary Shelley's (McInnerny) writing of "Frankenstein," amidst the decadence of Mary and Percy B.'s (Pelka) 1816 Swiss sojourn with Lord Byron (Grant). Hurley has the relatively small role of Claire, Mary's half-sister and Byron's former lover. **95m/C VHS.** *SP* Lizzy McInnerny, Hugh Grant, Valentine Pelka, Elizabeth Hurley, Jose Luis Gomez, Aitana Sanchez-Gijon; **D:** Gonzalo Suarez; **W:** Gonzalo Suarez; **C:** Carlos Suarez.

Roxanne ✓✓✓ 1987 (PG) A modern comic retelling of "Cyrano de Bergerac." The romantic triangle between a big nosed, small town fire chief, a shy fireman Martin gives his most sensitive and believable performance. Don't miss the bar scene where he gets back at a heckler. A wonderful adaptation for the modern age. **107m/C VHS, DVD.** Steve Martin, Daryl Hannah, Rick Rossovich, Shelley Duvall, Michael J. Pollard, Fred Willard, John Kapelos, Max Alexander, Damon Wayans, Matt Lattanzi, Kevin Nealon; **D:** Fred Schepisi; **W:** Steve Martin; **C:** Ian Baker; **M:** Bruce Smeaton. L.A. Film Critics '87: Actor (Martin); Natl. Soc. Film Critics '87: Actor (Martin); Writers Guild '87: Adapt. Screenplay.

Roxie Hart ✓✓½ 1942 Sassy '20s Chicago dance hall girl Roxie (Rogers) decides to take the fall when hubby (Chandler) murders a man. (She sees it as a publicity boost to her career). Slick lawyer Billy Flynn (Menjou) knows he can get the tootsie off if she justs flashes the jury her considerable sex appeal. Montgomery's a smitten reporter who catches Roxie's eye. Based on the play "Chicago" by Maurine Watkins and previously filmed in 1927. Bob Fosse later adapted the play for a Broadway musical. **75m/B VHS, DVD.** Ginger Rogers, Adolphe Menjou, George Montgomery, Lynne Overman, Nigel Bruce, Phil Silvers, Sara Allgood, William Frawley, Spring Byington, George Chandler; **D:** William A. Wellman; **W:** Nunnally Johnson; **C:** Leon Shamroy; **M:** Alfred Newman.

The Royal Bed ✓✓½ *The Queen's Husband* 1931 King Eric's queen really wears the pants in the family, and when she leaves on a trip, he's left helpless and hapless. A revolution erupts, and his daughter announces she plans to marry a commoner. What's a king to do? **74m/B VHS, DVD.** Lowell Sherman, Nance O'Neil, Mary Astor, Anthony Bushell, Gilbert Emery, Robert Warwick, J. Carrol Naish; **D:** Lowell Sherman; **W:** J. Walter Ruben; **C:** Leo Tover.

Royal Deceit ✓✓½ *Prince of Jutland* 1994 (R) Young Amled (Bale) is heir to the 6th century kingdom of Jutland. But when his father is murdered by Amled's jealous uncle Fenge (Byrne), the youth feigns insanity to save himself and then begins to plot his revenge. Very familiar story doesn't arouse more than mild interest despite the cast. **85m/C VHS, DVD.** *GB* Gabriel Byrne, Helen Mirren, Christian Bale, Brian Cox, Kate Beckinsale, Steven Waddington, Tom Wilkinson, Tony Haygarth, Saskia Wickham, Brian Glover; **D:** Gabriel Axel; **C:** Henning Kristiansen; **M:** Per Norgard.

Royal Flash ✓✓½ 1975 (PG) Satirical adventure picture, witty and fast paced, with a few real life period characters thrown in for good measure. Cowardly swashbuckler Flashman, wanting to enter high society, is used to advance a political cause when he is forced to impersonate a Prussian nobleman and marry a duchess. Script by Fraser and based on his series of novels featuring the Flashman character. **98m/C VHS, DVD.** *GB* Malcolm McDowell, Alan Bates, Florinda Bolkan, Oliver Reed, Britt Ekland, Lionel Jeffries, Tom Bell, Alastair Sim, Michael Hordern, Joss Ackland, Christopher Cazenove, Bob Hoskins; **D:** Richard Lester; **W:** George MacDonald Fraser; **C:** Geoffrey Unsworth.

A Royal Scandal ✓✓½ 1996 And you thought Chuck and Di made a hash of their marriage. The British should be used to marital scandal as this saga on the disasters befalling Princess Caroline of Brunswick (Lynch) and Prince George (Grant), aptly demonstrates. The extravagant George is forced to marry through political and financial pressure but loathes the unrefined Caroline practically on sight. As soon as a royal heir is on the way, they cease to live together and George goes back to his mistresses. But although Caroline will agree to a settlement, she refuses a divorce and when George becomes King George IV, Caroline fully intends to be Queen. **60m/C VHS, DVD.** Richard E. Grant, Susan Lynch, Frances Barber, Michael Kitchen, Denis Lawson, Oliver Ford Davies, Irene Richards; **D:** Sheree Folkson; **W:** Stanley Price; **C:** John Daly; **M:** John Altman; **Nar:** Ian Richardson.

The Royal Tenenbaums ✓✓✓½ 2001 (R) Anderson and Wilson's third and most ambitious film concerns a wildly eccentric family of kid geniuses who converge upon their childhood home as unhappy adults, just as their long-estranged father shows up looking for handouts and understanding, and mother is considering remarriage to the family accountant. Book lovers will appreciate the literary allusions—the Tenenbaum house seems lifted from the pages of J.D. Salinger or John Irving—and storybook and gruff narration. Inventive script and quirky dialogue carry a story that sometimes becomes cartoonish, as most of the characters are one-dimensional. Some may find the film's overt weirdness a bit much, but there's a heart underneath it all. Hackman's performance as the dastardly, tactless, and yet wholly lovable Royal is a supreme comic feat. Depression has never been so fun. **108m/C VHS, DVD.** *US* Gene Hackman, Anjelica Huston, Gwyneth Paltrow, Ben Stiller, Luke Wilson, Owen Wilson, Bill Murray, Danny Glover, Seymour Cassel, Kumar Pallana, Grant Rosenmeyer, Jonah Meyerson, Stephen Lea Sheppard; **D:** Wes Anderson; **W:** Owen Wilson, Wes Anderson; **C:** Robert Yeoman; **M:** Mark Mothersbaugh; **Nar:** Alec Baldwin. Golden Globes '02: Actor--Mus./Comedy (Hackman); Natl. Soc. Film Critics '01: Actor (Hackman).

Royal Warriors ✓✓ *In the Line of Duty: Police Assassins; Ultra Force; Huang Jia Zhan Shi* 1986 Watch Michelle kick major butt! Policewoman Yeoh teams up with a retired Japanese cop and an airport security officer to outsmart a terrorist highjacking. When the terrorist's associates decide to get even, the three must continue to fight together to save themselves. Chinese with subtitles or dubbed. **85m/C VHS, DVD.** *HK* Michelle Yeoh, Hiroyuki (Henry) Sanada, Michael Wong; **D:** David Chung.

Royal Wedding ✓✓✓ *Wedding Bells* 1951 Astaire and Powell play a brother-and-sister dance team who go to London during the royal wedding of Princess Elizabeth, and find their own romances. Notable for the inspired songs and Astaire's incredible dancing on the ceiling and walls; Lerner's first screenplay. The idea came from Adele Astaire's recent marriage to a British Lord. ♪Too Late Now; Sunday Jumps; How Can You Believe Me When I Said I Love You When You Know I've Been A Liar All My Life?; You're All the World to Me; The Happiest Day of My Life; Open Your Eyes; Ev'ry Night at Seven; I Left My Hat in Haiti; What A Lovely Day For A Wedding. **93m/C VHS, DVD.** Fred Astaire, Jane Powell, Peter Lawford, Keenan Wynn, Sarah Churchill; **D:** Stanley Donen; **W:** Alan Jay Lerner; **C:** Robert Planck; **M:** Johnny Green, Burton Lane, Albert Sendrey. **VIDEO**

Royce ✓✓ 1993 (R) After a successful mission, Royce's CIA team is disbanded. But some former agents aren't happy with early retirement and decide to go into business for themselves. **98m/C VHS.** James Belushi, Chelsea Field, Miguel Ferrer, Peter Boyle; **D:** Rod Holcomb; **M:** Paul Bernbaum.

R.P.M. ✓✓ 1997 (R) Professional car thief Luke (Arquette) takes up an offer to steal a prototype fuel-less supercar for a very large sum of money. However, he's not the only one after the goods. **91m/C VHS, DVD.** David Arquette, Famke Janssen, Emmanuelle Seigner, Jerry Hall; **D:** Ian Sharp; **C:** Harvey Harrison; **M:** Alan Lisk. **VIDEO**

R.P.M.* (*Revolutions Per Minute) ✓½ 1970 (R) Another chance to relive the 60s. Student activists force the university hierarchy to appoint their favorite radical professor president. Hip prof-turned-prez Quinn is between a rock and a hard place, and allows police to crack down. Could have been intriguing, but loses steam; in any case, the script and direction both stink. **90m/C VHS, DVD.** Anthony Quinn, Paul Winfield, Gary Lockwood, Ann-Margret, Rigg Kennedy; **D:** Stanley Kramer; **W:** Erich Segal; **M:** Perry Botkin.

R.S.V.P. ✓✓½ 1984 (R) Hollywood party honoring a writer turns tragic when a body is found in the guest of honor's pool. Most interesting part is watching the porn stars who make up most of the cast fail at acting while dressed. **87m/C VHS.** Harry (Herbert Streicher) Reems, Lynda Wiesmeier; **D:** Lem Amero.

R.S.V.P. ✓½ 2002 (R) Slacker college student Nick (Otto), who has an unhealthy interest in criminology, decides to invite ten friends to a Vegas penthouse for a

Rubberface 🐾 *1981 (PG)* Tony Maroni (Carrey) is a very bad but very determined comedian. And he may just catch a break when he teams up with joke writer Janet (Glassbourg). Made for Canadian TV. **48m/C VHS, DVD.** *CA* Jim Carrey, Adah Glassbourg; *D:* Glen Salzman, Rebecca Yates. **TV**

Rubdown 🐾 *1993* An ex-baseball player, turned Beverly Hills masseur, finds himself the victim of a frame-up when one of his clients is murdered. **88m/C VHS.** Jack Coleman, Michelle Phillips, Kent Williams, Alan Thicke, Catherine Oxenberg, William Devane; *D:* Stuart Cooper; *W:* Clyde Allen Hayes; *M:* Gerald Gouriet.

Rubin & Ed 🐾🐾 *1992 (PG-13)* Ed is a real estate groupie who bribes the eccentric Rubin to attend a get-rich-quick seminar. Rubin decides to cash in on the favor by taking Ed on the road in search of the perfect gravesite for Rubin's long-dead feline. If that sounds wacky, just wait—the fun really begins when the duo is stranded in Death Valley and begins to suffer from sunstroke and hallucinations. Those who dream of weirdos bonding in the desert may be enthused but other viewers may thirst for something more. **82m/C VHS.** Crispin Glover, Howard Hesseman, Karen Black, Michael Greene, Brittney Lewis; *D:* Trent Harris; *W:* Trent Harris; *C:* Bryan Duggan.

Ruby 🐾🐾 *1977 (R)* A young woman, christened in blood and raised in sin, has a love affair with the supernatural and murders up a storm at a drive-in. Confused, uneven horror a step up from most similar flicks. **85m/C VHS, DVD.** Roger Davis, Janit Baldwin, Piper Laurie, Stuart Whitman, Curtis Harrington; *M:* Barry Schneider; *C:* William Mendenhall; *M:* Don Ellis.

Ruby 🐾🐾½ *1992 (R)* Another in the increasing number of Kennedy assassination and conspiracy dramas—this one told from the viewpoint of Jack Ruby, Lee Harvey Oswald's killer. Confusing plot, somewhat redeemed by the performances of Aiello and Fenn. Combines actual footage of Ruby shooting Oswald with black-and-white filmed scenes. Based on the play "Love Field" by Stephen Davis. **111m/C VHS, DVD.** Danny Aiello, Sherilyn Fenn, Arliss Howard, Tobin Bell, David Duchovny, Richard Sarafian, Joe Cortese, Marc Lawrence; *D:* John Mackenzie; *W:* Stephen Davis; *C:* Phil Meheux; *M:* John Scott.

Ruby Bridges 🐾🐾½ *1998* On November 14, 1960, six-year-old Ruby Bridges (Monet) became the first black student to integrate the New Orleans public-school system. She started her first day of first grade classes at William Frantz Elementary School escorted by four federal marshals, enduring hostile crowds and death threats because of her mother Lucielle's (Rochon) desire for her daughter to get an education despite what the Bridges family would endure. **90m/C VHS, DVD.** Michael Beach, Penelope Ann Miller, Lela Rochon, Chaz Monet, Kevin Pollak, Diana Scarwid. *D:* Euzhan Palcy; *W:* Toni Johnson. **TV**

Ruby Gentry 🐾🐾½ *1952* White-trash girl Jones, cast aside by man-she-loves Heston, marries wealthy Malden to spite him, then seeks revenge. Classic Southern theme of comeuppance, good direction and acting lift it a notch. **82m/B VHS, DVD.** Charlton Heston, Jennifer Jones, Karl Malden; *D:* King Vidor.

Ruby in Paradise 🐾🐾🐾 *1993 (R)* Leaving her dead-end life in Tennessee, Gissing (Judd) moves to Panama City, Florida and lands a job selling souvenirs for no-nonsense Mildred Chambers (Lymen). Although pursued by two very different men, Ruby concentrates more on self-exploration, recording her thoughts in a journal. A seemingly effortless portrayal of friends in a gay bashing, and ex-con Luke (Wint) returns to his wife (now a police officer), and young son. He tries to resist returning to his drug dealing past and cope with a jealous younger brother (Johnson). Debut for director Virgo. **90m/C VHS, DVD.** *CA* Sharon M. Lewis, Richard Chevolleau, Rachael Crawford, Maurice Dean Wint, Stephen Ellen, Clark Johnson, Melanie Nicholls-King, Stephen Shellen; *D:* Clement Virgo; *W:* Clement Virgo; *C:* Barry Stone; *M:* Aaron David.

Ruby in the Smoke 🐾🐾½ *2005 (R)* Sally Lockhart Mysteries: Ruby in the Smoke 1872 in London and Sally Lockhart has just learned that her father has died while investigating suspicious activity in his shipping business. Spunky Sally is told about the Ruby of Agrapur and her father's part in the gem's disappearance decades before. It seems the cursed stone is leading Sally straight into danger. Based on the mystery by Philip Pullman. **90m/C DVD.** *GB* Julie Walters, J.J. Feild, David Harewood, Hayley Atwell, Billie Piper, Matt Smith, Ramon Tikaram; *D:* Brian Percival; *W:* Adrian Hodges; *C:* Peter Greenhalgh; *M:* Martin Phipps; *V:* Martin Jarvis. **TV**

Ruby Jean and Joe 🐾🐾 *1996* Aging rodeo star Joe Wade (Selleck) doesn't want to leave the circuit even though it's obvious that his body can't take the punishment anymore. Joe gets more depressed until he picks up hitchhiker Ruby Jean (Johnson), a sarcastic teenager in search of a future. The unlikely duo form a friendship that may end up being vulnerable. Which may be wry she allows Johnny come—that's right—yuppies. Rip Van Winkle-ian farce draws a few yuks, but could have been much funnier. Points for trying. **100m/C VHS.** Tom Selleck, JoBeth Williams, Rebekah Johnson, Ben Johnson; *D:* Geoffrey Sax; *W:* James Lee Barrett; *C:* James L. Carter; *M:* Stephen Graziano. **CABLE**

Ruby's Bucket of Blood 🐾🐾 *2001 (PG-13)* Life's not easy for Ruby Delacroix (Bassett), the sultry owner of a bayou roadhouse, colorfully called the "Bucket of Blood," especially since she's a black woman in the segregated south of 1960. Neglected by her husband Earl (Mitchell) and constantly battling with her teenaged daughter, Emerald (Smollet), Ruby is feeling vulnerable. Which may be why she allows Johnny (Plummer), the leader of the house band as a replacement singer. Billy's white—and married. But Ruby and Billy have an undeniable attraction—and when Earl leaves Ruby, it becomes harder and harder to resist. **96m/C VHS, DVD** Angela Bassett, Kevin Anderson, Brian Stokes Mitchell, Glenn Plummer, Jurnee Smollett, Angelica Torn; *D:* Peter Werner; *W:* Julie Hebert. **CABLE**

Ruby's Dream 🐾🐾 *The Loner 1981 (PG)* A Vietnam vet uses his training to defend himself when he runs into trouble in a small Alabama town. Less obnoxious than "First Blood," (which came later), but basically the same movie. **91m/C VHS, DVD.** Dirk Benedict, Linda Blair, Ben Johnson, Richard Farnsworth, Matt Clark; *D:* Max Kleven; *W:* Max Kleven; *C:* Don Burgess; *M:* Willie Nelson. **TV**

Rude 🐾🐾 *1996 (R)* Rude (Lewis) is a Jamaican-Canadian pirate-radio DJ in Toronto, who narrates three stories about urban life: window dresser Maxine (Crawford) struggles to recover from an abortion after her lover leaves her, frightened boxer Jordan (Chevolleau) tries to deal with his own homosexuality after participating with *derful 1982* A bowling alley and nightclub owner dreams of making it big in Las Vegas. After his dreams crash to the ground, however, he realizes just how important it all is in life. **100m/C VHS, DVD.** Joe Pesci, Ed O'Ross, Evan Handler, Ivy Ray Browning; *D:* Peter Lilienthal; *W:* Sam Koperwas; *C:* Michael Ballhaus; *M:* Claus Bantzer.

Rude Awakening 🐾🐾 *1989 (R)* Hippies Cheech and Roberts (where's Chong?) settled in a South American commune 20 years ago. Now they're back, and don't know what to make of old pals Carradine and Hagerty who have become yuppies. Rip Van Winkle-ian farce draws a few yuks, but could have been much funnier. Points for trying. **100m/C VHS.** Eric Roberts, Richard "Cheech" Marin, Julie Hagerty, Robert Carradine, Buck Henry, Louise Lasser, Cindy Williams, Andrea Martin, Cliff DeYoung; *D:* Aaron Russo, David Greenwalt; *W:* Richard LaGravenese; *M:* Jonathan Elias.

Rude Boy: The Jamaican Don 🐾 *2003 (R)* Wanting to escape his life of crime in Jamaica, DJ Julius instead becomes ensnared with even bigger drug lord/music producer who promises to make all his rap-reggae dreams come true if Julius serves as his personal hitman. Not much hop when the bullets aren't flying. **92m/C VHS, DVD.** Jimmy Cliff, Mark Danvers, Michael "Bear" Taifero, Robert Carradine, Marcia Griffith, Beenie Man, Ninja Man; *D:* Desmond Gumbs. **VIDEO**

Rudy 🐾🐾🐾 *1993 (PG)* Likeable, true story about a little guy who triumphs over big odds. Daniel "Rudy" Ruettiger (Astin) dreams of playing football for Notre Dame, no matter how farfetched the dream. He's a mediocre student, physically unsuitable for big time college ball, but sheer determination helps him attain his dream. Astin delivers an engaging performance and is backed up by a good supporting cast. Sentimental story stretches the truth with typical shameless Hollywood manipulation, but is still entertaining. From the director and writer of another David beats Goliath sports film, "Hoosiers." **112m/C VHS, DVD.** Robert J. Steinmiller Jr., Vince Vaughn, Sean Astin, Ned Beatty, Charles S. Dutton, Lili Taylor, Robert Prosky, Jason Miller, Ron Dean, Chelcie Ross, Jon Favreau, Greta Lind, Scott Benjaminson, Christopher Reed; *D:* David Anspaugh; *W:* Angelo Pizzo; *C:* Oliver Wood; *M:* Jerry Goldsmith.

Rudy: The Rudy Giuliani Story 🐾🐾½ *2003* Warts and all bio of former New York mayor Rudy Giuliani (Woods), in an Emmy-nominated performance). The bio begins on September 10, 2001 as the mayor is on his second and last term and what happens during the World Trade Center disaster. Flashbacks highlight Giuliani's political rise as well as his abrasive personality and his controversial private life. **120m/C VHS, DVD.** James Woods, Penelope Ann Miller, Michelle Nolden, John Bourgeois, Kirsten Bishop, Maxim Roy, Michael Woods; *D:* Robert Dornhelm; *W:* Stanley Weiser; *C:* Serge Ladouceur *M:* Harald Kloser. **CABLE**

Rudyard Kipling's The Jungle Book 🐾🐾🐾 *1994 (PG) The Jungle Book* Respectable live-action version from Disney of the Rudyard Kipling tale of Mowgli (Lee), the boy who's raised by a wolf pack after getting lost in an Indian jungle. This time around Mowgli gets to grow up—enough to have a romantic interest in the lovely Kitty (Headey), the daughter of British superciliousness Captain Boone (Elwes), who learns Mowgli knows the location of a hidden jungle treasure. Now Mowgli must count on his friends, Grey Brother the wolf, Baloo the bear, and Bagheera the black panther, to defeat the greedy Boone and win Kitty. Filmed in India. **111m/C VHS, DVD.** Jason Scott Lee, Cary Elwes, Sam Neill, Lena Headey, John Cleese; *D:* Stephen Sommers; *W:* Stephen Sommers.

Rudyard Kipling's the Second Jungle Book: Mowgli and Baloo 🐾🐾 *Mowgli and Baloo: Jungle Book 2: The Second Jungle Book: Mowgli and Baloo 1997 (PG)* Actually a prequel to "Rudyard Kipling's The Jungle Book," the story centers on the ten-year-old Mowgli (Williams) and his efforts to stay among his animal friends in the jungle. After he is spotted by scout for P.T. Barnum's circus (Campbell), who wants to capture and exploit him. He must also dodge the Bandars, a group of funky monkeys who want to make Mowgli their unwilling leader. The special effects are nowhere near as good as its predecessor, with matte shots that make some of the animals look like they were added with magic markers. The story is a classic, however, and the performances (especially Williams') are good. **88m/C VHS, DVD.** Jamie Williams, Billy Campbell, Roddy McDowall, Cornelia Hayes O'Herlihy, David Paul Francis, Gulshan Grover, Dyrk Ashton, B.J. Hogg, Amy Robbins, Hal Fowler; *D:* Duncan McLachlan; *W:* Bayard Johnson, Matthew Horton; *C:* Adolfo Bartoli; *M:* John Scott.

The Rue Morgue Massacres 🐾½ *1973 (R)* A modern reprise of the Poe story with touches of Frankensteinia thrown in; plenty of gore. **80m/C VHS, DVD.** *SP* Paul Naschy, Rossana Yanni, Maria Perschy, Vic Winner, Mary Ellen Arpon; *D:* Javier Aguirre.

Ruggles of Red Gap 🐾🐾🐾🐾 *1935* Classic comedy about an uptight British butler who is "won" by a barbarous American rancher in a poker game. Laughton as the nonplussed manservant is hilarious; supporting cast excellent. Third and far superior filming of Harry Leon Wilson story. One of the all-time great comedies, the film was remade musically with Bob Hope and Lucille Ball as "Fancy Pants" (1950). **90m/B VHS, DVD.** Charlie Ruggles, Zasu Pitts, Roland Young, Leila Hyams, James Burke, Maude Eburne; *D:* Leo McCarey; *W:* Walter De Leon; *M:* Ralph Rainger. **N.Y. Film Critics '35, Actor (Laughton).**

Rugrats Go Wild! 🐾🐾 *2003 (PG)* Two Nickelodeon animated series combine in this adventure when the Rugrats, who are vacationing with their parents, get stranded on an island to find a rare leopard berries, on the island to find a rare leopard for their TV show, come to the rescue. It must've seemed like a good idea to combine these two lucrative franchises into one movie, but the sum proved to be less than its parts. Less charming than previous outings for both series, there's just too many characters competing for too little screen time, and the wandering plotlines don't help the situation. Less-discriminating kids may enjoy it on video, but there's nothing for adults or older kids to enjoy. This entertaining viewing for the entire family. Tommy, Chuckie and the rest of the gang from the animated Nickelodeon series return for their second full-length feature, this time trekking out to the de mechanical dinosaur at a very EuroDisney-style theme park. Also, Chuckie's dad Chas is wooed by the kid-hating park operator Coco La Bouche (voice of Susan Sarandon), who only wants to marry him because she thinks that there's a promo. **81m/C VHS, DVD.** *US D:* Norton Virgien, John Eng; *W:* Kate Boutilier; *M:* Mark Mothersbaugh; *V:* Elizabeth (E.G. Dailey) Daily, Michael Bell, Jodi Carlisle, Nancy Cartwright, Lacey Chabert, Melanie Chartoff, Tim Curry, Cheryl Chase, Flea, Dannielle Harris, Tom Kane, Bruce Willis, Chrissie Hynde, Tara Strong, Jack Riley, Kath Soucie, Tress MacNeille, Cree Summer, Dionne Quan, LL Cool J.

Rugrats in Paris: The Movie 🐾🐾🐾 *2000 (G)* There are enough pop culture references and sly humor for the parents and enough diaper, booger and barf jokes for the kids to make tion in it for her. This all leads to a bizarre chase through Paris involving the giant dinosaur and a huge escargot. **80m/C VHS, DVD.** *D:* Stig Bergvist, Paul Demeyer; *W:* David N. Weiss, Jill Gorey, Barbara Herndon, Kate Boutilier; *V:* Mark Mothersbaugh; *V:* Elizabeth (E.G. Daily) Daily, Christine Cavanaugh, Susan Sarandon, Jack Riley, Michael Bell, Melanie Chartoff, Tara Strong, Kath Soucie, John Lithgow, Debbie Reynolds, Mako, James D. Stern, Cheryl Chase, Julia Kato, Lisa McClowry.

The Rugrats Movie 🦴🦴🦴 **1998** (G) Precocious one-year-old Tommy is afraid he'll be forgotten by his parents with the arrival of baby brother Dil, so he and his pals decide to return the infant to the hospital. Boarding a talking wagon named Reptar (invented by Tommy's father), they embark on an adventure that takes them to a scary forest where they run into wolves, a "wizard," and a band of escaped circus monkeys that kidnap Dil in the film's most frightening sequence. While dishing out lessons about responsibility, bravery, friendship, and jealousy, film also contains parodies of and homages to several films, including "Raiders of the Lost Ark." The humor works on many levels, so this one is enjoyable for all ages. **79m/C VHS, DVD.** *D:* Norton Virgien, Igor Kovalyov; *W:* David N. Weiss, J. David Stem; *M:* Mark Mothersbaugh; *V:* Elizabeth (E.G. Daily) Daily, Christine Cavanaugh, Tara Strong, Melanie Chartoff, Jack Riley, Joe Alaskey, Phil(ip) Proctor, Whoopi Goldberg, David Spade, Kath Soucie, Cheryl Chase, Cree Summer, Michael Bell, Tress MacNeille, Busta Rhymes.

The Ruins 🦴½ **2008** (R) Rather than being content hanging by the pool at their Mexican seaside resort, Jeff (Tucker), Amy (Malone), Eric (Ashmore), and Stacy (Ramsay) accept the questionable invite of Mathias (Anderson) to visit an archeological dig at a Mayan ruin. The armed locals are very unhappy by these turistas and chase them up the vine-covered pyramid, but it's definitely not to safety. There's a gruesomely creepy twist to what attacks them but otherwise it's horror business as usual. Scott B. Smith adapted his novel. **90m/C DVD.** *D:* Carter Smith; *W:* Scott B. Smith; *C:* Darius Khondji; *M:* Graeme Revell.

Rule #3 🦴🦴 **1993** "Never believe everything you see." That's the rule con artist Travis West lives by. This time he's got two scams planned—a Las Vegas real estate swindle and a cash ripoff of a former nemesis. Double- and triple-crosses abound. Based on the true story of West, who swindled more than $9 million in 15 years. **93m/C VHS.** Mitchell Cox, Marcia Swayze; *D:* Mitchell Cox.

Rulers of the City 🦴½ *(I Padroni della Citta; The Big Boss; Blood and Bullets; Mister Scarface)* **1976** Young gangster avenges his father's death. **91m/C VHS.** *IT* Gisela Hahn, Vittorio Caprioli, Jack Palance, Edmund Purdom, Al Cliver, Harry Baer; *D:* Fernando Di Leo; *W:* Fernando Di Leo, Peter Berling; *C:* Erico Menczer; *M:* Luis Bacalov.

The Rules of Attraction 🦴🦴 **2002** (R) Follows a group of shallow, overprivileged, drug-addled college students apparently attending Hedonism University. Drug dealer Sean (Van Der Beek) is in lust with campus goddess Lauren (Sossamon). Lauren's bisexual ex-boyfriend Paul (Somerhalder) has a crush on the straight Sean. Lauren yearns for Victor (Pardue), a coked up vacationing druggie who once slept with Paul. As a result of this turmoil, everyone does drugs and sleeps with everyone else. Avary uses many production tricks and a fluctuating timeline in order to convey the feeling of the Bret Easton Ellis novel on which the movie is based. The technique works, especially the fast-forward view of Victor's trip, but the characters are so unlikable that none of them deserves to get what they want. **104m/C VHS, DVD.** *US* James Van Der Beek, Ian Somerhalder, Shannyn Sossamon, Jessica Biel, Kip Pardue, Thomas Ian Nicholas, Kate (Catherine) Bosworth, Fred Savage, Eric Stoltz, Clifton (Gonzalez) Collins Jr., Faye Dunaway, Swoosie Kurtz, Russell

Sams, Matthew Lang; *D:* Roger Avary; *W:* Roger Avary; *C:* Robert Brinkmann; *M:* Tomandandy.

Rules of Engagement 🦴🦴½ **2000** (R) Marine Childers (Jackson) is assigned the task of rescuing an ambassador and his family from a hostile area in Yemen. The mission goes terribly wrong when, by orders given by Childers, resulting in the death of 83 Yemeni women and children. To keep the US from suffering any terrorist backlash, Childers is charged with mass murder. Effective courtroom drama (which spares us the cliched surprise witness), although it merely grazes the complex issues of military decision-making due to its skeletal script. Intensity and momentum is sustained by the towering performances of leads Jackson and Jones as Childers's buddy and lawyer. After two weeks as box-office leader, film received some protest over its negative portrayal of Arab-Americans. Based on a story by ex-Secretary of the Navy James Webb. **128m/C VHS, DVD.** Elayne J. Taylor, Samuel L. Jackson, Tommy Lee Jones, Guy Pearce, Bruce Greenwood, Blair Underwood, Philip Baker Hall, Anne Archer, Ben Kingsley, Mark Feuerstein, Dale Dye; *D:* William Friedkin; *W:* Stephen Gaghan; *C:* Nicola Pecorini, William A. Fraker; *M:* Mark Isham.

The Rules of the Game 🦴🦴🦴 *(Le Regle du Jeu)* **1939** Renoir's masterpiece, in which a group of French aristocrats, gathering for a weekend of decadence and self-indulgence just before WWII, becomes a metaphor for human folly under siege. The film was banned by the French government, pulled from distribution by the Nazis, and not restored to its original form until 1959, when it premiered at the Venice Film Festival. In French with English subtitles. Heavily copied and poorly remade in 1989 as "Scenes from the Class Struggle in Beverly Hills." **110m/B VHS, DVD.** Marcel Dalio, Nora Gregor, Jean Renoir, Mila Parely, Julien Carette, Gaston Modot, Roland Toutain, Paulette Dubost, Odette Talazac; *D:* Jean Renoir; *W:* Jean Renoir.

The Ruling Class 🦴🦴½ **1972** (PG) The classic cult satire features O'Toole as the unbalanced 14th Earl of Gurney, who believes that he is either Jesus Christ or Jack the Ripper. Tongue-in-cheek look, complete with dance and music, at eccentric upper-class Brits and their institutions. Uneven, chaotic, surreal and noteworthy. **154m/C VHS, DVD.** *GB* Peter O'Toole, Alastair Sim, Arthur Lowe, Harry Andrews, Coral Browne, Nigel Green, Michael Bryant, William Mervyn, Carolyn Seymour, James Villiers; *D:* Peter Medak; *W:* Peter Barnes; *C:* Ken Hodges; *M:* John Cameron. Natl. Bd. of Review '72: Actor (O'Toole).

Rumble Fish 🦴🦴🦴 **1983** (R) A young street punk worships his gang-leading older brother, the only role model he's known. Crafted by Coppola into an important story of growing up on the wrong side of town, from the novel by S.E. Hinton. Ambitious and experimental, with an atmospheric music score; in black and white. **94m/B VHS, DVD.** Matt Dillon, Mickey Rourke, Dennis Hopper, Diane Lane, Vincent Spano, Nicolas Cage, Diana Scarwid, Christopher Penn, Tom Waits; *D:* Francis Ford Coppola; *W:* Francis Ford Coppola; *C:* Stephen Burum; *M:* Stewart Copeland.

Rumble in the Bronx 🦴🦴½ **1996** (R) Singapore action star Chan plays a Hong Kong cop who comes to the South Bronx to attend his uncle's wedding and winds up caught in a crime war between the mob and a vicious motorcycle gang. Living special effect Chan choreographed and performed all of his own stunts, and they are remarkable (pay special attention to the hovercraft scene). Over-the-top cheesy dubbing and streets that are obviously not New York (filmed in Vancouver) add to the cartoonish fun. After several attempts to break into the American market, this is Chan's first release in the United States. **91m/C VHS, DVD.** *HK* Jackie Chan, Anita (Yim-Fong) Mui, Francoise Yip, Bill Tung, Morgan Lam, Marc Akerstream; *D:* Stanley Tong; *W:* Edward Tang, Fibe Ma; *C:* Jingle Ma; *M:* J. Peter Robinson.

Rumble in the Streets 🦴½ **1996** (R) Street-smart young Rowe discovers that a psycho cop has decided to clean up the streets of Dallas by hunting down and killing kids like her and she must use her own toughness to survive. **74m/C VHS.** Kimberly Rowe, David Courtemarche, Patrick DeFazio; *D:* Bret McCormick.

Rumor Has It... 🦴 **2005** (PG-13) Rumor has it... this movie blows. And, unfortunately, the rumor ain't gossip. Rob Reiner continues to explore the latter, significantly crappier stage of his directorial career in this monumental waste of time and talent. It's a nifty concept—at her sister's wedding, the engaged Sarah (Aniston) discovers that her family was the basis for "The Graduate" and finds herself falling for the man (Costner) who seduced both her mother and grandmother (MacLaine)—but everyone involved in the production looks uncomfortable and there are no laughs to be found. Nice job, Meathead. **96m/C DVD, Blu-ray Disc, HD DVD.** *US* Jennifer Aniston, Kevin Costner, Shirley MacLaine, Mark Ruffalo, Richard Jenkins, Christopher McDonald, Mena Suvari, Steve Sandvoss; *D:* Rob Reiner; *W:* T.M. Griffin; *C:* Peter Deming; *M:* Marc Shaiman.

The Rumor Mill 🦴🦴½ *(Malice in Wonderland)* **1986** The careers and titanic rivalry of influential Hollywood gossip writer Hedda Hopper and Louella Parsons, played with verve by Taylor and Alexander. Fictionalized script based on the book "Hedda and Louella" by George Eels. **94m/C VHS, DVD.** Elizabeth Taylor, Jane Alexander, Richard Dysart, Joyce Van Patten; *D:* Gus Trikonis; *W:* Jacqueline Feather, David Seidler; *M:* Charles Bernstein. **TV**

A Rumor of Angels 🦴🦴 **2000** (PG-13) Cloying coming-of-age tale somewhat complicated by the real-life experience of author Philip Caputo (based on his bestseller), from naive youth to seasoned soldier to bitter murder suspect at court martial. Succeeds where Stone's later, much-ballyhooed "Born on the Fourth of July" fails. Adapted by John Sacret Young. **195m/C VHS.** Brad Davis, Keith Carradine, Michael O'Keefe, Stacy Keach, Steve Forrest, Richard Bradford, Brian Dennehy, John Friedrich, Perry Lang, Chris Mitchum, Dan Shor, Jeff Daniels, Laurence Fishburne, Lane Smith, Gail Youngs, Bobby Ellerbee; *D:* Richard T. Heffron; *W:* John Sacret Young; *C:* Stevan Larner, Jorge Stahl Jr.; *M:* Charles Gross.

Rumpelstiltskin 🦴🦴 **1982** From "Faerie Tale Theatre" comes the story of a woman who can spin straw into gold (Duvall) and the strange man who saves her life (Villechaize). Enjoyable for the whole family. **60m/C VHS, DVD.** Bud Cort, Ned Beatty, Shelley Duvall, Herve Villechaize, Paul Dooley; *D:* Emile Ardolino. **CABLE**

Rumpelstiltskin 🦴🦴 **1986** (G) Musical retelling of the classic Brother Grimm fairy tale. Irving plays a young girl who says she can spin straw into gold. Barty is a dwarf who helps her. The catch: she must give up her first born to pay him. Lackluster direction and uninspired acting make this version a yawner. Irving's real-life mother (Pointer) and brother have roles too. **84m/C VHS, DVD.** Amy Irving, Billy Barty, Robert Symonds, Priscilla Pointer, Clive Revill, John Moulder-Brown; *D:* David Irving.

Rumpelstiltskin WOOF! **1996** (R) First director Jones inflicts "Leprechaun" upon us and now there's another warped dwarf on the loose. Single L.A. mom Shelly (Johnston-Ulrich) finds a wishing stone in a thrift shop and unwittingly summons up the little demon, who immediately tries to steal her young son. **91m/C VHS, DVD.** Kim Johnston-Ulrich, Tommy Blaze, Max Grodenchik, Allyce Beasley; *D:* Mark Jones; *W:* Mark Jones; *C:* Doug Milsome; *M:* Charles Bernstein.

Run 🦴½ **1991** (R) A high energy action cartoon, with little plot but lots of stunts. Dempsey is a super-smart law student hired to drive a car to Atlantic City. A stop on the way starts trouble. Instant romance with a local girl balances mayhem from crime boss. Expect to be happy with this lightweight fare. **91m/C VHS.** Patrick Dempsey, Kelly Preston, Ken Pogue, Alan C. Peterson, Sean McCann; *D:* Geoff Burrowes; *W:* Michael Blodgett; *C:* Bruce Surtees.

Run, Angel, Run! 🦴½ **1969** (R) Ex-biker Angel is on the run from his former gang after he helps expose them in a magazine article. He settles on a sheep ranch with his girl and then the gang shows up with revenge in mind. Prime drive-in fare with title song sung by none other than Ms. Tammy Wynette. **90m/C VHS, DVD.** William (Bill) Smith, Margaret Markov, Valerie Starrett; *D:* Jack Starrett.

Run, Fat Boy, Run 🦴🦴½ **2007** (PG-13) David Schwimmer makes his directorial debut, oddly enough, in British territory, but very much in the vein of a "Friends" episode. Like the bonehead he is, Dennis (Pegg) leaves pregnant Libby (Newton) at the altar for no good reason. Five years later, when he comes back into Libby and working as a security guard in a lingerie shop, Dennis desperately tries to win her back as she's about to marry Whit (Azaria), a rich American marathon runner. Of course, the way to win her heart is to challenge the fiance to a race. (Despite the fat jokes, Dennis is not fat. Out of shape and lazy, yes, but not fat.) Cute and charming, but never laugh-out-loud funny. **100m/C DVD.** *GB* Simon Pegg, Thandie Newton, Hank Azaria, Dylan Moran, Harish Patel, India de Beaufort, Matthew Festoon; *D:* David Schwimmer; *W:* Michael Ian Black, Michael Parker; *C:* Richard Greatrex; *M:* Alex Wurman.

Run for the Dream: The Gail Devers Story 🦴🦴½ **1996** (PG-13) Inspirational biopic on U.S. track star Devers (Woodard) who won a gold medal in the 100m sprint in the 1992 Olympics. But 17 months before, Devers suffers complications from a debilitating thyroid condition, Graves's Disease, which could not only cost her her career but her life. **99m/C VHS.** Alfre Woodard, Louis Gossett Jr., Robert Guillaume; *D:* Neema Barnette; *W:* Dianne Houston, Scott Abbott; *C:* Edward Pei; *M:* Pete Anthony. **CABLE**

Run for the Roses 🦴½ *(Thoroughbred)* **1978** (PG) "National Velvet" clone about a young Puerto Rican boy and a champion race horse in Kentucky. Cheery family fare. **93m/C VHS.** Lisa Eilbacher, Vera Miles, Stuart Whitman, Sam Groom; *D:* Henry Levin.

Run If You Can 🦴 **1987** (R) A woman sees a brutal murderer killing his victims on her TV. Will she be next? **92m/C** Martin Landau, Yvette Nipar, Jerry Van Dyke; *D:* Virginia Lively Stone.

Run Lola Run 🦴🦴🦴½ *(Lola Rennt)* **1998** (R) Berlin punkette Lola (Potente) receives a frantic phone call from her small-time criminal boyfriend Manni (Bleibtreu). He's lost a bag of money he was delivering to his boss and he's history. Lola then sprints off in a manic attempt to find the money needed to save her man. Lola then comes roaring to a halt, and is then repeated with different outcomes based on small changes in Lola's path, with different styles to match. Writer/director Tom Tykwer's energetic style helps push this creative and technically brilliant thriller across the winner's line. German with subtitles. **81m/C VHS, DVD.** *GE* Franka Potente, Moritz Bleibtreu, Joachim Krol, Herbert Knaup, Armin Rohde;

Run of the Arrow 1956 Rather than surrender to the end of the Civil War, an ex-Confederate soldier (Steiger) joins the Sioux nation, engaged in war against the white man. Steiger's Irish brogue is weird and distracting, and the intriguing premise fails to satisfy, and the cast is competent and interesting. 85m/C VHS. *D:* Samuel Fuller; *W:* Samuel Fuller; *C:* Joseph Biroc; *M:* Victor Young, Max Steiner; *V:* Angie Dickinson.

Run Silent, Run Deep 1958 Submarine commander Gable battles his officers, especially the bitter Lancaster who vied for the same command, while stalking the Japanese destroyer that sunk his former command. Top-notch WWII sub action, scripted from Commander Edward L. Beach's novel. 93m/B VHS, DVD. Burt Lancaster, Clark Gable, Jack Warden, Don Rickles, Brad Dexter, Nick Cravat, Joe Maross, Mary Laroche, Eddie Foy III, Rudy Bond, H.M. Wynant, Joel Fluellen, Ken Lynch, John Bryant; *D:* Robert Wise; *W:* John Gay; *C:* Russell Harlan; *M:* Franz Waxman.

Run, Rebecca, Run 1981 Interesting family adventure yarn for the family about a South American refugee who tries to stop a young girl from leaving from an Australian island where they are both stranded. She eventually befriends him, and attempts to get permission for him to enter the country. 90m/C VHS, AU Simore Buchanan; Henri Szeps; *D:* Peter Maxwell.

Run, Stranger, Run (Mother's Day, Love, George) 1973 (PG) The inhabitants of a seaside house in Nova Scotia are paralyzed with fear when a number of brutal murders occur. A couple of sicko slasher scenes, but hard to swallow. 110m/C VHS. Ron Howard, Patricia Neal, Cloris Leachman, Bobby Darin. *D:* Darren McGavin; *C:* Walter Lassally.

Runaway 1984 (PG-13) A cop and his sidekick track down a group of killer robots wreaking havoc. Self-serious, sorry sci-fi. Features Simmons of the rock group KISS. 100m/C VHS, DVD. Tom Selleck, Cynthia Rhodes, Gene Simmons, Stan Shaw, Kirstie Alley; *D:* Michael Crichton; *W:* Michael Crichton; *C:* John A. Alonzo; *M:* Jerry Goldsmith.

The Runaway 2000 Luke Winter (Newton) and Joshua Monroe (McLaughlin) are best friends growing up in 1940s rural Georgia despite the fact that one is black and one is white. While on an adventure, they make a discovery that leads new sheriff Frank Richards (Cain) into reopening the investigation into the unsolved murders of three local black men. The town wants to hush up the whole incident but the sheriff wants justice to prevail. 98m/C VHS, DVD. Dean Cain, Maya Angelou, Debbi (Deborah) Morgan, Pat Hinge, Karen Erbe, Cliff DeYoung, Cody Newton, Duane McLaughlin, Roxanne Hart, Sony Shroyer; *D:* Arthur Allan Seidelman; *W:* Ron Raley; *C:* Ron Garcia; *M:* Ernest Troost. TV

The Run of the Country 1995 (R) Amid the scenic splendor of a small town south of the North Irish border in County Cavan, Danny (Keeslar) comes of age, sometimes the hard way. His relationship with his bullying dad (Finney), the local Garda officer, begins to crumble after the tragic death of his mum. So he runs away to live with the town malcontent Prunty (Brophy) and falls in love with the beautiful Annagh (Smurfit), who lives north of the border. Life gets even more complicated when Annagh learns she's pregnant. Director Yates, reunited with Finney for the first time since they won Oscars for "The Dresser," sometimes digs too deep into a big crock of standard Irish stew, occasionally delivering Celtic melodrama instead of poignant slice of life. The usual themes of family dysfunction, religious rebellion and moral dilemma are augmented by the occasional appearance of the frustrated, violent father. Finney shines. In their debut, Keeslar and Smurfit are fine, but Brophy's Prunty is the one you'll remember. Adapted by Connaughton (who used similar geography for "The Playboys") from his novel. 109m/C VHS. Albert Finney, Matt Keeslar, Victoria Smurfit, Anthony Brophy, David Kelly; *D:* Peter Yates; *W:* Shane Connaughton; *C:* Mike Southon; *M:* Cynthia Millar.

Runaway Bride 1999 (PG) If you don't mind being manipulated by masters (and you real ly won't), the predictability of this romantic comedy won't bother you either. Hey, if you weren't looking for a happy ending, you wouldn't be watching a romantic comedy. New York columnist Ike Graham (Gere) gets into hot water (as in fired) when his story on Maggie Carpenter (Roberts), the boring local girl who's left several men at the altar (three trips down the aisle and no vows), is filled with errors. So Ike decides to go to Maggie's hometown, where she's on her fourth engagement, and get the real scoop. Of course, he falls for the would-be bride and she for him but things aren't all hearts and flowers. Appealing performances and boy, does Roberts know how to wear a wedding dress. 116m/C VHS, DVD. Julia Roberts, Richard Gere, Joan Cusack, Hector Elizondo, Christopher Meloni, Rita Wilson, Paul Dooley, Laurie Metcalf, Jean Schertler, Donal Logue, Reg Rogers, Yul Vazquez, Lisa Roberts Gillan, Sea Ward, Tom Mason; *D:* Garry Marshall; *W:* Josann McGibbon, Sara Parriott; *C:* Stuart Dryburgh; *M:* James Newton Howard.

The Runaway Barge 1975 Two western worm ranchers are kidnapped by a female gang whose members are trying to steal from organized criminals. Just another typical worm rancher flick. 104m/C VHS. Nick Nolte, Devon Ericson, Christina Hart, James Best; *D:* Boris Valletta; *M:* Christopher Young.

Runaway Daughters 1994 (PG-13) Part of Showtime's "Rebel Highway" remakes of '50s flicks, in this case the 1956 AIP juvie drama (although the similarities are minimal). Three small town teen babes (Bowen, Lewis, Fields) fake their own kidnappings so they can steal a car and head out on the highway to catch the runaway beau (Young) of one babe who's knocked up. 82m/C DVD. Julie Bowen, Holly Fields, Jenny Lewis, Paul Rudd, Chris Young, Dick Miller, Fabian, Joe Flaherty, Belinda Balaski, Robert Picardo, Dee Wallace Stone, *Cameos:* Cathy Moriarty; *D:* Joe Dante; *W:* Charles S. Haas; C.A.B.L.E.

Runaway Father 1991 Pat Bennett's husband takes his own death in an attempt to abandon his family. When Bennett discovers he's alive she works to set a legal precedent—17 years worth of back child support. Based on a true story. 94m/C VHS, DVD. Donna Mills, Jack Scalia, Chris Mulkey, Jenny Lewis; *D:* John Nicolella. TV

Runaway Jury 2003 (PG-13) John Grisham-penned legal thriller has the goods. Hot-shot jury consultant Rankin Fitch (Hackman) is hired by a gun manufacturer on trial after an office massacre. The unscrupulous Fitch spies on potential jurors and isn't above using blackmail in his quest to find a totally biased jury. His goal of a totally biased jury is endangered when he's forced to include Nicholas (Cusack), a man with a secret. A-list cast, interesting plot development and a less fully-realized plot development and a less than satisfying ending. This is the first on-screen pairing of former roommates Hackman and Hoffman, and they make the most of it. 127m/C VHS, DVD. US John Cusack, Gene Hackman, Dustin Hoffman, Rachel Weisz, Bruce Davison, Bruce McGill, Jeremy Piven, Nick Searcy, Stanley Anderson, Clifford Curtis, Nestor Serrano, Leland Orser, Jennifer Beals, Gerry Bamman, Joanna Going, Bill Nunn, Juanita Jennings, Marguerite Moreau, Nora Dunn, Guy Torry, Rusty Schwimmer; *D:* Gary Fleder; *W:* Brian Koppelman, David Levien, Rick Cleveland, Matthew Chapman; *C:* Robert Elswit; *M:* Christopher Young.

The Runaway Bus 1954 Filled with the requisite motley crew of passengers, including a gold-carrying thief and the ever-befuddled Margaret Rutherford, a bus gets lost between airports and ends up in a deserted village. Would-be wacky comedy. 78m/B VHS, GB Frankie Howerd, Margaret Rutherford, Petula Clark, George Coulouris, Belinda Lee, Reginald Beckwith, Terence Alexander, Toke Townley, John Horsley, Anthony Oliver, Stringer Davis, Lisa Gastoni, Frank Phillips; *D:* Val Guest; *W:* Val Guest; *C:* Stanley Pavey; *M:* Ronald Binge.

The Rundown 2003 (PG-13) Amusing buddy/action comedy works because of the Roc's self-deprecating charm (and physical abilities) and Scott's insolent exuberance. Bounty hunter Beck (Johnson) takes one last job—that of retrieving the wastrel son of his boss. Travis (Scott) is an archeology student who's in the Amazon seeking a priceless golden artifact, which is also sought by his ex-girl-friend Marianna (Dawson), who wants to use the treasure to free her people from the inhuman working conditions imposed by manic mine owner Hatcher (Walken, who's obviously having a good time playing another crazy bad guy). The action Hawaii's rain forests and the San Gabriel Mountains provide appropriate substitutes for the Amazon. Watch for the scene with the Rock and some amorous monkeys. 104m/C VHS, DVD, UMD, HD DVD. US Dwayne "The Rock" Johnson, Seann William Scott, Rosario Dawson, Christopher Walken, Ewen Bremner, Jonjathan Gries, William Lucking, Ernie Reyes Jr., Stuart Wilson; *Cameos:* Arnold Schwarzenegger; *D:* Peter Berg; *W:* R.J. Stewart, James Vanderbilt; *C:* Tobias Schliessler; *M:* Harry Gregson-Williams.

Runaway Train 1985 (R) A tough jailbird and his sidekick break out of the hoosegow and find themselves trapped aboard a brakeless freight train heading for certain derailment in northwestern Canada. Harrowing existential action drama based on a screenplay by Akira Kurosawa. Voight is superb. 112m/C VHS, DVD. Edward (Eddie) Bunker, Jon Voight, Eric Roberts, Rebecca De Mornay, John P. Ryan, T.K. Carter, Kenneth McMillan, John Bloom; *D:* Andrei Konchalovsky; *W:* Andrei Konchalovsky, Djordje Milicevic, Edward (Eddie) Bunker, Paul Zindel; *C:* Alan Hume; *M:* Trevor Jones, Golden Globes '86: Actor—Drama (Voight).

Runaway Nightmare 1984 Two worm ranchers are kidnapped by a female gang who find themselves and initiate them, then talk about their plan to steal from organized criminals. *D:* Michael Cartel.

Runaways (Fugitive Lovers) 1975 A corrupt politician's wife falls in love with the man who saved her when she attempted suicide. The two try to escape her husband's wrathful vengeance. 95m/C VHS. Steve Oliver, Sondra Currie, John Russell, Virginia Mayo, Doodles Weaver, Juanita Moore, Frankie Darro, Vincent Barbi; *D:* John Carr; *C:* Michael Mileham; *M:* Alex Barnhardt.

Running Away 1989 Bittersweet story of WWII romance, with a twist of adventure. Strong cast creates good chemistry, but somehow the story is not engaging. Loren and Penny are mother and daughter, leaving Rome for the hills and encountering dangers. 111m/C VHS. Sophia Loren, Sydney Penny, Robert Loggia, Andrea Occhipinti; *D:* Dino Risi.

Running Against Time 1990 (PG) A teacher tries to change history (and erase his brother's Vietnam War death) by time-warping back to 1963 and preventing JFK's murder. Cable TV movie takes an offhanded gee-whiz approach to a tantalizing premise, as temporal paradoxes multiply in "Back to the Future" style. No assassination-conspiracy theories, by the way, but Lyndon Johnson fans may not like his portrayal here. Based on the novel "A Time to Remember" by Stanley Shapiro. 93m/C VHS. Robert Hays, Catherine Hicks, Sam Wanamaker, James DiStefano, Brian Smiar; *D:* Bruce Seth Green; *W:* Robert Glass. CABLE

The Runnin' Kind 1989 (R) A yuppie expecting to inherit his father's Ohio law firm goes on a wild spree with an all-girl rock band. Sexy drummer Howard shows him the sights of certain parts of L.A. Original, fun comedy. Independent. 89m/C VHS, DVD. David Packer, Pleasant Gehman, Brie Howard, Susan Shrasberg; *D:* Max Tash.

The Runner Stumbles 1979 Dated melodrama about a priest who goes on trial for murdering the nun with whom he fell in love in a mining town in the 1920s. Based on a true incident, from the play by Milan Stiff. Van Dyke in an unwanted serious role is miserably out of place. 109m/C VHS. Dick Van Dyke, Kathleen Quinlan, Maureen Stapleton, Ray Bolger, Beau Bridges, Tammy Grimes, Ed Lauter; *D:* Stanley Kramer; *M:* Ernest Gold.

Running Blind 1978 Espionage/adventure thriller has a double agent on a beautiful woman on the run in Iceland. 120m/C VHS. GB George Sewell, Vladek Sheybal, Ian McCulloch, Richard Hurndall, Stuart Wilson, Heidi Steinschottir, William Marlowe; *M:* Jack Gerson; *D:* Christopher Guiming.

Running Cool 1993 (R) Two easy-going bikers join up with an old friend to protect his wetland's property from a lowlife developer and his stooges. Chicks (there's a romance with a local biker babe) motorcycles, fighting, and saving the environment—what more could you want? 106m/C VHS. Andrew Divoff, Tracy Sebastian, Dedee Pfeiffer, James Gammon, Paul Gleason, Arien Dean Snyder, Bubba Baker; *D:* Beverly Sebastian, Ferd Sebastian.

Running Brave 1983 (PG) The true story of Billy Mills, a South Dakota Sioux Indian who won the Gold Medal in the 10,000 meter run at the 1964 Tokyo Olympics. Not bad, but hokey in the way of many of these plodding true-story flicks. 90m/C VHS, DVD. Robby Benson, Claudia Cron, Pat Hingle, Denis Lacroix; *D:* D.S. Everett; *W:* Henry Bean.

Running Delilah 1993 Delilah (Cattrall) is a secret agent who is apparently killed by a vicious arms dealer. Only her fellow agent (Zane) resurrects her and Delilah is transformed into a cybernetic super agent. And her assignment is to go after a terrorist who's building a nuclear weapon with plutonium supplied by Delilah's killer. 90m/C VHS, DVD. Kim Cattrall, Billy Zane, Diana Rigg; *M:* Lee Holdridge; *D:* Richard Franklin; *W:*

The Runner 1999 (R) Eldard stars as a compulsive Vegas gambler who's so deeply in debt he agrees to his shady uncle's (Mantegna) offer to get him with gangster Goodman. Eldard places bets with sports bookies (with mob money) and falls for cocktail waitress Cox, using some of Goodman's money to buy her a diamond ring. The vengeful Goodman doesn't take kindly to this. 95m/C VHS, DVD. Ron Eldard, John Goodman, Courtenay Cox, Joe Mantegna, Bokeem Woodbine; *D:* Ron Moler. *W:* Anthony E. Zuiker, Dustin Lee Abraham; *C:* James Glennon; *M:* Anthony Marinelli.

The Runestone 1991 (R) After the eponymous viking relic is unearthed, an imprisoned wolf-beast that terrorizes New York. An adequate horror flick that taps the seldom-explored vein of Norse mythology. Based on a novel by Mark E. Rogers. 105m/C VHS. Peter Riegert, Joan Severance, William Hickey, Tim Ryan, Chris Young, Alexander Godunov; *D:* Willard Carroll; *W:* Willard Carroll; *M:* David Newman.

Running Free 1994 (PG) Sullen Garrett joins his naturist mother in the Alaskan wilderness and establishes a friendship with a wolverine cub (who's smarter than the kid). 90m/C VHS, DVD. Jesse Montgomery Sythe, Jayme Lee Misfeldt, Michael Perez; *D:* Steve Kroschel.

Running Free 2000 (G) Inspiring story of the friendship between an orphaned servant boy and an abandoned colt named Lucky who is destined for a life of hard labor. Their quest for freedom from their proscribed lives creates a visually stunning tale about the triumph of the human spirit. **85m/C DVD.** Chase Moore, Jan Decleir, Arie Verveen, Maria Geelboci, Lukas Haas; *D:* Sergei Bodrov; *W:* Jeanne Rosenberg; *C:* Dan Laustsen; *M:* Nicola Piovani.

Running Hot 🎬🎬½ **1983 (R)** Seventeen-year-old convicted murderer Stoltz gets love letter in prison from older woman Carrico. When he escapes, they flee the law together. Quick-paced and entertaining. **88m/C VHS.** Monica Carrico, Eric Stoltz, Stuart Margolin, Virgil Frye, Richard Bradford, Sorrels Pickard, Juliette Cummins; *D:* Mark Griffiths; *W:* Mark Griffiths.

The Running Man 🎬🎬½ **1987 (R)** Special-effects-laden adaptation of the Stephen King novel (under his Richard Bachman pseud) about a futuristic TV game-show. Convicts are given a chance for pardon—all they have to do is survive an on going battle with specially trained assassins in the bombed-out sections of Los Angeles. Sci-fi with an attitude. **101m/C VHS, DVD.** Edward (Eddie) Bunker, Arnold Schwarzenegger, Richard Dawson, Maria Conchita Alonso, Yaphet Kotto, Mick Fleetwood, Dweezil Zappa, Jesse Ventura, Jim Brown; *D:* Paul Michael Glaser; *W:* Steven E. de Souza; *C:* Thomas Del Ruth; *M:* Harold Faltermeyer.

Running Mates 🎬🎬🎬 **1986 (PG-13)** Occasionally intriguing drama of two teens who fall in love, but are kept apart by their fathers' local political rivalry. Director Johnny To employs some flashy visuals in this overachieving crime movie and he got first-rate performances from his leads, particularly Lau Ching Wan, a tremendous character actor. **89m/C DVD. HK** Andy Lau, Lau Ching Wan, Waise Lee, Hui Siu Hung, Yoyo Mung; *D:* Johnny To; *C:* Yau Nai Hoi; *C:* Cheng Siu Keung; *M:* Wong Ying Wah.

Running Mates 🎬🎬🎬 **1992 (PG-13)** Cynically amusing political satire about a bachelor politician and his too intelligent lady love. Harris is Hugh, a U.S. senator looking forward to the presidential primaries when he meets widowed children's novelist Aggie (Keaton). She hates politics and he's Mr. Slick, although decent enough behind the political expedience. Aggie, however, has a potentially damaging secret in her past which causes the scandal-scenting pack of press hounds to bay in salivating anticipation. Will Hugh stick by Aggie and will Aggie overcome her natural political distaste for everything to end happily? A well-played romp. **88m/C VHS, DVD.** Ed Harris, Diane Keaton, Ed Begley Jr., Ben Masters, Robert Harper, Brandon Maggart, Russ Tamblyn; *D:* Michael Lindsay-Hogg; *W:* A.L. Appling. **CABLE**

Running Mates 🎬🎬½ **2000** Liberal governor James Pryce (Selleck) is a shoo-in for the presidential nomination at the L.A. Democratic convention. But he still has to choose his veep running mate. And he's got four powerful women giving him opinions, including his wife Jenny (Travis), his campaign manager Lauren (Linney), his political fundraiser Shawna (Hatcher), and boozy socialite Meg (Dunaway), who's the wife of Pryce's mentor (Culp). So will he go with the idealistic senator (Gunton) or the power broker (McGill)? **90m/C VHS, DVD.** Tom Selleck, Laura Linney, Nancy Travis, Teri Hatcher, Bruce McGill, Bob Gunton, Faye Dunaway, Robert Culp, Caroline Aaron, Mat Malloy; *D:* Ron Lagomarsino; *W:* Claudia Salter; *C:* Alan Caso; *M:* John Debney. **CABLE**

Running on Empty 🎬🎬🎬 **1988 (PG-13)** Two 1960s radicals are still on the run in 1988 for a politically motivated Vietnam War-era crime. Though they have managed to stay one step ahead of the law, their son wants a "normal" life, even if it means never seeing his family again. Well-performed, quiet, plausible drama. **116m/C VHS, DVD.** Christine Lahti, River Phoenix, Judd Hirsch, Martha Plimpton, Jonas Arby, Ed Crowley, L.M. Kit Carson, Steven Hill, Augusta Dabney, David Margulies, Sidney Lumet; *D:* Sidney Lumet; *W:* Naomi Foner; *C:* Gerry Fisher; *M:* Tony Mottola. Golden Globes '89: Screenplay; L.A. Film Critics '88: Actress (Lahti); Natl. Bd. of Review '88: Support. Actor (Phoenix).

Running out of Luck 🎬½ **1986 (R)** A light, song-packed story about a rock star very much like Jagger who is abandoned in South America and believed dead, until he returns to his world. Features songs from Jagger's solo album "She's the Boss." **88m/C VHS.** Mick Jagger, Dennis Hopper, Jerry Hall, Rae Dawn Chong; *D:* Julien Temple.

Running Out of Time 🎬🎬 *Dias Contados; Numbered Days* **1994** Antonio (Gomez) is a Basque who belongs to a terrorist organization. He's sent to Madrid to carry out an assignment, winds up getting involved with drug-addicted prostitute Charo (Gabriel), and finds that his mission overlaps with his relationship. Spanish with subtitles. **93m/C VHS, DVD. SP** Carmelo Gomez, Ruth Gabriel, Javier Bardem, Karra Elejalde, Candela Pena; *D:* Imanol Uribe; *W:* Imanol Uribe; *C:* Javier Aguirresarobe; *M:* Jose Nieto.

Running out of Time 🎬🎬🎬 **1999** Jewel thief Andy (Lau) knows that he has only two weeks to live. He goes ahead and pulls a job that sets him against Sean (Wan), a canny police negotiator. Director Johnny To employs some flashy visuals in this overachieving crime movie and he got first-rate performances from his leads, particularly Lau Ching Wan, a tremendous character actor. **89m/C DVD. HK** Andy Lau, Lau Ching Wan, Waise Lee, Hui Siu Hung, Yoyo Mung; *D:* Johnny To; *C:* Yau Nai Hoi; *C:* Cheng Siu Keung; *M:* Wong Ying Wah.

Running Red 🎬🎬 **1999 (R)** Gregori was once a member of an elite Soviet commando team. Sickened by the corruption, he quits and eventually sets up a new life for himself in the U.S. But his past comes back when his ex-boss contacts him and threatens to kill his family unless Greg does an assassination job for him. **92m/C VHS, DVD.** Jeff Speakman, Angie Everhart, Stanley Kamel, Elya Baskin, Geoffrey Rivas, Bradley Matthews, Bart Braverman; *D:* Jerry P. Jacobs; *W:* David Stauffer; *C:* Ken Blakey; *M:* Jim Halfpenny. **VIDEO**

Running Scared 🎬🎬 **1979 (PG)** Two young men, returning from military service as stowaways aboard an Army cargo plane, are caught by an intelligence agent and thought to be spies, because Reinhold has unknowingly photographed a secret U.S. base with his stolen Army-issue camera. Not-bad spy thriller with a twist—the "spies" are hapless nobodies, now on the lam. **92m/C VHS,** Ken Wahl, Judge Reinhold, John Saxon, Annie McEnroe, Bradford Dillman, Pat Hingle; *D:* Paul Glickler.

Running Scared 🎬🎬½ **1986 (R)** Hip, unorthodox Chicago cops Hines and Crystal have to handle an important drug arrest before taking an extended vacation in Key West. Not as relentless as "48 Hrs," but more enjoyable in some ways. Ever wonder what it's like to ride in a car at high speed on the tracks? Find out here. **107m/C VHS, DVD.** Gregory Hines, Billy Crystal, Dan Hedaya, Jimmy Smits, Darlanne Fluegel, Joe Pantoliano, Steven Bauer; *D:* Peter Hyams; *W:* Gary De Vore; *C:* Peter Hyams.

Running Scared 🎬🎬½ **2006 (R)** Frenetic actioner has small-time hood Joe (Walker) charged with disposing of a gun for his Mob cronies after a drug deal gone bad. The reason it went bad is that some crooked cops crashed the party and a few of them ended up dead. When a neighbor kid takes the gun and uses it to shoot his Russian mob-affiliated, abusive stepdad, things go sideways for everyone in a big hurry. Joe must race the clock, the cops, his associates, and the Russians to find the kid and the gun, both of which change hands with astonishing regularity over the course of the night. What this one lacks in cohesion and plausibility, it makes up for in pacing (which rarely slackens) and urgency. **122m/C DVD. US** Paul Walker, Cameron Bright, Vera Farmiga, Karel Roden, Johnny Messner, Ivana Milicevic, Chazz Palminteri, Alex Neuberger, Michael Cudlitz, Bruce Altman, Elizabeth Mitchell, Arthur J. Nascarelli, John Noble, David Warshofsky, Idalis DeLeon; *D:* Wayne Kramer; *W:* Wayne Kramer; *C:* James Whitaker; *M:* Mark Isham.

Running Wild 🎬🎬 **1927** Early silent comedy starring mustachioed Fields as an eternal coward who suddenly turns into a lion by hypnosis. Odd, often unfunny Fields entry sometimes hits the mark. He's awfully mean, though. **68m/B VHS.** W.C. Fields, Mary Brian, Claud Buchanan; *D:* Gregory La Cava; *M:* Gaylord Carter.

Running Wild 🎬🎬½ **1973 (G)** A free-lance photographer becomes involved in a dispute to save a corral of wild mustang horses. The usual great Colorado scenery enhances a good, family-view story. **102m/C VHS.** Lloyd Bridges, Dina Merrill, Pat Hingle, Gilbert Roland, Morgan Woodward; *D:* Robert McCahon; *W:* Robert McCahon.

Running Wild 🎬 **1994 (R)** Beautiful woman abandons her much older fiance to go on a wild road trip with his son that includes sex and crime. **91m/C VHS.** Jennifer Barker, Daniel Dupont, Daniel Spector, Eliott Keener; *D:* Philippe Blot.

Running Wild 🎬🎬½ **1999** Harrison stars as Maj. Matt Robinson, a retired Air Force pilot who has taken a position with the U.N. to track elephant migrations in Africa. He takes his children Angela (Nevin) and Nicholas (Jones) with him. Once they arrive in Africa, Matt meets a pretty veterinarian, Rachel (Hallier) and a guide, Isaac (Kanaventi). They enjoy a great adventure until Matt realizes that there are many elephant-hunting poachers in the area, and when they threaten Angela and Nicholas, Matt and Rachel spring into action to rescue the children. Fun film for the entire family, although a bit too preachy at times concerning the plight of endangered animals. Contains fine performances, as well as breathtaking nature photography. Horror-industry vet Harry Alan Towers executive produced this family film, which was directed by the writer of the slasher classic "Happy Birthday to Me"! **92m/C VHS, DVD.** Gregory Harrison, Lori Hallier, Cody Jones, Brooke Nevin, Munyaradzi Kanaventi; *D:* Timothy Bond.

Running with Scissors 🎬🎬 **2006 (R)** Sex, drugs, and insanity are manifest in the debuting Murphy's adaptation of Augusten Burrough's memoirs of his screwed-up adolescence. Narcissist monster mom Deirdre (Bening) has divorced son Augusten's (Cross) alcoholic father Norman (Baldwin) and is in therapy with bizarre shrink Dr. Finch (Cox). The two adults decide Augusten will live with Finch's family in their ramshackle Victorian house, where he is subjected to such eccentricities as the depressed, kibble-eating Mrs. Finch (Clayburgh) and adoptive son Neil (Fiennes), who seduces the willing teenager. Also ensconced are Bible-reading Hope Finch (Paltrow) and her rebellious youngest sister Natalie (Wood), who befriends Augusten. Cross has the least showy role as reactive narrator and the flick is more scenic than coherent. **121m/C DVD. US** Joseph Cross, Annette Bening, Brian Cox, Joseph Fiennes, Evan Rachel Wood, Alec Baldwin, Jill Clayburgh, Gwyneth Paltrow, Gabrielle Union, Kristin Chenoweth, Patrick Wilson, Jack Kaeding, Gabriel Guedj; *D:* Ryan Murphy; *W:* Ryan Murphy; *C:* Christopher Baffa; *M:* James Levine.

Running Woman 🎬🎬 **1998 (R)** Emily Russo (Russell) is accused of the mysterious death of her young son and goes on the lam to prove her innocence. With the police on her trail, Emily's quest leads her to a gang that's terrorizing some seedier parts of L.A. **84m/C VHS, DVD.** Theresa Russell, Andrew (Andy) Robinson, Gary (Rand) Graham, Eddie Velez, Anthony Crivello, Robert LaSardo, Chris Pennock; *D:* Rachel Samuels; *W:* Rachel Samuels; *C:* Chris Manley; *M:* Christopher Lennerz. **VIDEO**

Rupert's Land 🎬🎬½ **1998** British lawyer Rupert is reunited for the first time since childhood with his hard-living half-brother Dale, a British Columbia fisherman, at the funeral of their father. The Canadian side of Rupert's family seems to be Dale's mother Trudy, the keeper of the family's sordid secrets. Rupert and Dale suffer through a series of misadventures as they try to reunite as brothers and deal with their father's flawed legacy. **95m/C VHS. CA** Samuel West, Ian Tracey, George Wendt, Susan Hogan, Gabrielle Miller; *D:* Jonathan Tammuz; *W:* Graeme Manson; *C:* Gregory Middleton; *M:* Phil Marshall.

Rush 🎬 **1984** A post-nuclear world war movie in which a rebel named Rush battles the rulers of a slave colony. **83m/C VHS. IT** Conrad Nichols, Gordon Mitchell, Laura Trotter, Rita Furlan; *D:* Tonino Ricci.

Rush 🎬🎬 **1991 (R)** Texas drug culture, circa 1975, is portrayed in this bleak cop drama. Rookie narcotics officer Kristen Cates (Leigh) goes undercover with the experienced Raynor (Patric) to catch a big-time dealer, menancingly played by Allman, and their bosses don't much care how they do it. Cates falls in love with Raynor and is drawn ever deeper into the drug-addicted world they are supposed to destroy. Fine performances and a great blues score by Clapton. The directorial debut of Zanuck. Based on ex-narcotics cop Kim Wozencraft's autobiographical novel. **120m/C VHS, DVD.** Jason Patric, Jennifer Jason Leigh, Gregg Allman, Max Perlich, Sam Elliott, Tony Frank, William Sadler, Special K. McCray; *D:* Lili Fini Zanuck; *W:* Pete Dexter; *C:* Kenneth MacMillan; *M:* Eric Clapton.

Rush Hour 🎬🎬½ **1998 (PG-13)** Clichéd buddy film that's sauced up a bit with the unlikely pairing of loud-mouthed Tucker and swift-footed Chan. Motormouth L.A. detective James Carter (Tucker) is temporarily assigned to the FBI to babysit Hong Kong detective Lee (Chan) and keep him away from a kidnapping case that Lee is anxious to solve for personal reasons. Chan is more subdued stuntwise than in his own pictures but nonetheless a charmer against the abrasive Tucker. The culture clash scenes and some high gloss action moments make for a rousing action-comedy. Film was a surprise boxoffice smash. **98m/C VHS, DVD, UMD.** Jackie Chan, Chris Tucker, Tzi Ma, Julia Hsu, Philip Baker Hall, Rex Linn, Elizabeth Pena, Mark Rolston, Tom Wilkinson; *D:* Brett Ratner; *W:* Jim Kouf, Ross LaManna; *C:* Adam Greenberg; *M:* Lalo Schifrin. MTV Movie Awards '99: On-Screen Duo (Chris Tucker/Jackie Chan).

Rush Hour 2 🎬🎬 **2001 (PG-13)** Director Ratner and stars Tucker and Chan all reteam for the sequel to their $250 million 1998 comedy. Det. Carter (Tucker) travels to Hong Kong with his new buddy, Det. Lee (Chan), where they get involved in a criminal conspiracy. The jokes aren't as funny or fresh as in the original, and that situation isn't helped by the fact that before the movie's half over you just want Tucker to shut up. Chan does a fine job with his duties, which are to continue to amusingly mangle the English language, and do some more of those great martial-arts stunts. He gets some help in the acrobatic martial-arts department from Ziyi, Lone, and a nice cameo by Cheadle. They should stop now, but they won't. RH3 is almost guaranteed. **91m/C VHS, DVD, UMD. US** Chris Tucker, Jackie Chan, Harris Yulin, Zhang Ziyi, John Lone, Alan King, Roselyn Sanchez, Kenneth Tsang, Ernie Reyes Jr., Jeremy Piven, Saul Rubinek, Don Cheadle; *D:* Brett Ratner; *W:* Jeff Nathanson; *C:* Matthew F. Leonetti; *M:* Lalo Schifrin.

Rush Hour 3 🎬½ **2007 (PG-13)** Third in the franchise brings nothing fresh to the table except a new location, Paris, for Chan and Tucker's wacky culture clash schtick. After the attempted murder of the Chinese ambassador (Ma), the two travel to Paris to track the assassin, protect his daughter, and make a bunch of jokes that constantly refer back to the previous, better entries in the series. Chan and Tucker still have chemistry but director Ratner doesn't give them much to work with. The fight scenes seem slowed-down, shorter, and less fun, and even the standard end-of-movie blooper reel is a yawn. Roman Polanski cameos as a particularly nasty French cop. **91m/C DVD, Blu-ray Disc. US** Jackie Chan, Chris Tucker, Max von Sydow, Hiroyuki (Henry) Sanada, Yvan Attal, Roselyn Sanchez, Roman Polanski, Noemie Lenoir, Vinnie Jones, Tzi Ma, Julie Depardieu, Youki Kudoh, Dana Ivey, Zhang Jingchu; *D:* Brett Ratner; *W:* Jeff Nathanson; *C:* J. (James) Michael Muro; *M:* Lalo Schifrin.

Rush It 🎬½ **1977** Scriptwriters ponder possible plots over capucino: "I've got it! 'Bike Messengers in Love'!" "Nah. The title's too obvious. Why don't we call it

'Rush It?' Much hard work and many months later, the result is forgettable. 78m/C VHS. Tom Berenger, Jill Eikenberry, John Heard, Christina Pickles; **D:** Gary Youngman; **C:** Don Lenzer; **M:** Buzzy Linhart.

Rush Week ♂♂ **1988** (R) Dead coeds populate campus during frat week. Greg Allman has part and the Dickies perform two songs. 93m/C VHS, DVD. Dean Hamilton, Gregg Allman, Kathleen Kinmont, Roy Thinnes, Pamela Ludwig; **D:** Bob Bralver; **W:** Michael W. Leighton, Russell V. Manzatt; **C:** Jeff Mart.

Rushmore ♂♂♂½ **1998** (R) Fresh and original comedy from Wes Anderson follows 15-year-old Max (Schwartzman) to impress her, however, instigating a war of nasty tricks between the two quirky rivals. Murray drops his trademark smirk and gives his best performance to date. Also shining is newcomer Schwartzman, who is the son of Talia Shire. At this rate, the Coppola show biz clan may take over Hollywood by sheer population as well as talent. 93m/C VHS, DVD. Bill Murray, Jason Schwartzman, Olivia Williams, Seymour Cassel, Brian Cox, Mason Gamble, Sara Tanaka, Connie Nielsen, Kim Terry, Stephen McCole, Ronnie McCawley, Keith McCawley; **D:** Wes Anderson; **W:** Wes Anderson, Owen Wilson; **C:** Robert Yeoman; **M:** Mark Mothersbaugh. Ind. Spirit '99: Director (Anderson), Support. Actor (Murray); L.A. Film Critics '98: Support. Actor (Murray); N.Y. Film Critics '98: Support. Actor (Murray); Natl. Soc. Film Critics '98: Support. Actor (Murray).

VIDEO

Russell Mulcahy's Tale of the Mummy ♂♂ **1999** (R) Archeologists break open the sealed tomb of an Egyptian prince and are destroyed by the curse of Talos. Fifty years later, Samantha Turkel (Lombard) discovers her grandfather's logbook and decides to retrace the course of his deadly expedition. She recovers a sacred amulet and suddenly the power of Talos threatens again. The film was originally released at 119 minutes under the title "Talos the Mummy." 87m/C VHS, DVD. Jason Scott Lee, Louise Lombard, Sean Pertwee, Lysette Anthony, Michael Lerner, Jack Davenport, Honor Blackman, Christopher Lee, Shelley Duvall, Jon Polito; **D:** Russell Mulcahy; **W:** Russell Mulcahy, John Esposito; **C:** Gabriel Beristain.

Russian Dolls ♂♂♂½ **1990**, _Les Poupees Russes_ **2005** Set five years after Klapisch's 2002 comedy "L'Auberge Espagnole," the roommates of the Barcelona apartment are older but only a little wiser. Narrator Xavier (Duris) is now 30 and writing for a TV soap in Paris while maintaining a friendship with his exasperating ex Martine (Tautou). His co-writer is Brit Wendy (Reilly), whose brother William (Bishop) is engaged to Russian ballerina Natacha (Obraztsova). The friends are reuniting in St. Petersburg for the wedding. Generally picturesque froth. English, French, Spanish, and Russian with subtitles. 125m/C DVD, FR. Romain Duris, Audrey Tautou, Cecile de France, Kelly Reilly, Kevin Bishop, Lucy Gordon, Aissa Maiga, Evgenya Obraztsova; **C:** Dominique Colin; **M:** Loik Dury, Laurent Levesque.

The Russia House ♂♂ **1990** (R) Russian scientist Brandauer attempts to publish book debunking Soviet Union's claims of military superiority by passing it through ex-lover Pfeiffer to British editor Connery, apparently unaware of impending glasnost. Star-studded spy thriller aspires to heights it never quite reaches. Adapted from John Le Carre's novel. Stoppard's screenplay is very fine, actually making some aspects of the novel work better. 122m/C VHS, DVD. Sean Connery, Michelle Pfeiffer, Roy Scheider, James Fox, John Mahoney, Klaus Maria Brandauer, Ken Russell, J.T. Walsh, Michael Kitchen, David Thelfall, Ian McNeice, Christopher Lawford; **D:** Fred Schepisi; **W:** Tom Stoppard; **C:** Ian Baker; **M:** Jerry Goldsmith.

Russian Roulette ♂♂ **1975** The Russian premier is visiting Vancouver in 1970, and the Mounties must prevent a dissident KGB terrorist from assassinating him. Un-thrilling spy yarn fails to deliver on intriguing premise. 100m/C VHS. George Segal, Christina Raines, Bo Brundin, Denholm Elliott, Louise Fletcher; **D:** Lou Lombardo.

Russian Roulette ♂♂½ **1993** Routine story about an American woman on vacation in Russia who finds herself in the middle of a plot to locate a hidden Czarist artifact and smuggle it out of the country. Everyone on her tour group is suspect, an American businessman becomes involved, and a killer starts eliminating the number of players. Great location scenery. 88m/C VHS, DVD. Susan Blakely, Barry Bostwick, E.G. Marshall, Jeff Altman; **D:** Greydon Clark.

The Russian Terminator ♂ **1990** (R) An FBI agent is up against a one-man "death squad" in Helena, Michael son, Frederick Offrein, Harley Mein, Tina Tung; **D:** Mats Helge; **W:** Mats Helge.

The Russians Are Coming, the Russians Are Coming ♂♂♂ **1966** Based on the comic novel "The Off-Islanders" by Nathaniel Benchley, th-s is the story of a Russian sub which accidentally runs aground off the New England coast. The residents falsely believe that the nine-man crew is the beginning of a Soviet invasion, though the men are only looking for help. A memorable set of silly events follows the landing, engineered by a gung-ho police chief and a town filled with overactive imaginations. 126m/C VHS, DVD, Alan Arkin, Carl Reiner, Theodore Bikel, Eva Marie Saint, Brian Keith, Paul Ford, Jonathan Winters, Ben Blue, Tessie O'Shea, Doro Merande, John Phillip Law; **D:** Norman Jewison; **C:** Joseph Biroc; Golden Globes '67: Actor—Mus./Comedy (Arkin), Film—Mus./Comedy.

Russkies ♂♂½ **1987** (PG) A jolly comedy about three adorable American kids who capture, and eventually grow to like, a stranded Russian sailor. Friendly and peace-loving, but dull. 99m/C VHS, DVD. Joaquin Rafael (Leaf) Phoenix, Whip Hubley, Peter Billingsley, Stefan DeSalle, Susan Walters; **D:** Rick Rosenthal; **M:** James Newton Howard.

Rustin ♂♂ **2001** (PG-13) Every cliche possible appears in this cross between an afterschool special and a movie-of-the-week. Billy Stagen (Johnson) is a former pro football player who's becomes the sheriff of his Alabama hometown, Rustin. He slides by on charm and local celebrity until troubled teen Lee (Johnson) shows up, claiming to be his daughter. Now it's time to see if Billy can handle adult responsibilities. Meat Loaf is the current high school coach and Bryan is the latest football player-hero in case you're wondering why they're featured on the box cover. 100m/C VHS, DVD. Rick Johnson, Meat Loaf Aday, Ashley Johnson, Zachery Ty Bryan, Michael (Mike) Papajohn, Shawn Weatherly; **D:** Rick Johnson; **W:** Jon Lucas; **C:** Wally Pfister, Morgan Price.

Rustler's Hideout ♂ **1944** One of numerous westerns starring Crabbe as cowboy do-gooder Billy Carson, here plodding through standard histrionics against rustlers, a cardsharp, and a business fraud. 60m/C VHS. Buster Crabbe, Al "Fuzzy" St. John, Charles "Blackie" King, John Merton, Lane Chandler, Hal Price, Edward Cassidy, Bud Osborne; **D:** Sam Newfield.

Rustler's Paradise ♂ **1935** Carey seeks revenge on the man who stole his wife and daughter. 59m/B VHS. Harry Carey Sr., Gertrude Messinger, Edmund Cobb; **D:** Harry Fraser.

Rustler's Rhapsody ♂♂ **1985** (PG) A singing cowboy rides into a small western town and encounters all kinds of desperados in this earnest would-be satire

---

of '40s B-movie westerns. 88m/C VHS, DVD. Tom Berenger, Patrick Wayne, G.W. Bailey, Andy Griffith, Marilu Henner; **D:** Hugh Wilson; **W:** Hugh Wilson; **C:** Jose Luis Alcaine; **M:** Steve Dorff.

Rustler's Roundup ♂½ **1933** Mix rides to the rescue of Sinclair, whose daddy has been murdered by villains out to steal the ranch. 58m/B VHS. Tom Mix, Diane Sinclair, Noah Beery Jr., Douglass Dumbrille, Roy Stewart, Nelson McDowell, William Desmond, Franc Lackteen; **D:** Henry MacRae.

Rustler's Valley ♂½ **1937** Hopalong Cassidy is a ranch foreman who tries to save his employer from the clutches of a crooked lawyer. Pretty fun ordinary range-ridin' saga. 59m/B VHS. William Boyd, George "Gabby" Hayes, Lee J. Cobb; **D:** Nate Watt.

Rusty's Birthday ♂♂½ **1949** Danny searches for the lost Rusty who's long Cassidy is a ranch foreman who tries workers. When Danny discovers his pal, he finds the young son of the family doesn't want to give Rusty up. 61m/B VHS. Ted Donaldson, John Litel, Ann Doran, Jimmy Hunt, Ray Teal; **D:** Seymour Friedman; **W:** Brenda Weisberg.

The Rutanga Tapes ♂♂½ **1990** been taken in by a family of transient searches for the killer of his deputies. 98m/ C VHS. Earl Owensby; **D:** Thom McIntyre.

The Rutherford County Line ♂ **1987** A tough small-town sheriff DeVito and his mistress spend a romantic evening plotting his obnoxious wife's untimely demise. Before he can put his plan into action, he's delighted to discover she's been kidnapped by some very desperate people—who don't stand a chance with Bette. High farcical entertainment is a variation on the story "The Ransom of Red Chief" by O. Henry. 93m/C VHS, DVD. Bette Midler, Danny DeVito, Judge Reinhold, Helen Slater, Anita Morris, Bill Pullman; **D:** David Zucker, Jim Abrahams, Jerry Zucker; **W:** Dale Launer; **C:** Jan De Bont; **M:** Michel Colombier.

Ruby Gloom ♂♂♂ **1948** Revenge and romance beset the court of Charles II in this tale of mistaken identity (with Marais in a dual role). Based on the novel by Victor Hugo. 90m/B VHS, FR. Jean Marais, Daniele Darrieux; **D:** Pierre Billon; **W:** Jean Cocteau.

RV ♂♂ **2006** (PG) When Bob Munro (Williams) is forced to cancel a vacation for a business trip to Colorado he decides it's the perfect opportunity to reconnect with his over-scheduled family. Bob rents a hideously gaudy RV and tricks wife Jamie (Hines), grumpy teen daughter Cassie (Levesque), and macho, young son Carl (Hutcherson) into a road trip. Bob is basically clueless, and they run into various calamities (generally involving raw sewage) as well as the goofy, constantly upbeat Gornicke family, who live in their RV and really want to bond with the Munros. Headed by Daniels and Cheroweth, the Gornickes are a really s-ary/funny bunch. Williams does get stuck but at least the schmaltz is minimal. 99m/C DVD, Blu-ray Disc, UMD, US Robin Williams, Jeff Daniels, Cheryl Hines, Kristin Chenoweth, Joanna "JoJo" Levesque, Josh Hutcherson, Will Arnett, Brendan Fletcher, Brian Markinson, Barry Sonnenfeld, Hunter Parrish, Rob LaBelle, Chloe Sonnenfeld, Alex Ferris, Tony Hale, Brian Howe; **D:** Barry Sonnenfeld; **W:** Geoff Rodkey; **C:** Fred Murphy; **M:** James Newton Howard.

Rx ♂♂½ **2006** When his parents face financial ruin, Andrew "Balfour) decides to head south of the border with two friends, Jonny (Hanks) and Melissa (German), to pull off a big-money drug scheme. Things take a bad turn "or the twentysomethings, and their only escape is returning home from Mexico in the form of a perilous pact with gay German drug dealers—who enjoy partying dressed as Nazis—that also endangers their lives. Predictable but definitely not dull. 86m/C DVD. Eric Balfour, Colin Hanks, Lauren German, Danny Pino, Lola Molina; **D:** Ariel Vromen; **W:** Ariel Vromen, Morgan Land.

VIDEO

Ryan's Daughter ♂♂♂½ **1970** (PG) Irish woman (Miles) marries a man she does not love and then falls for a shell-shocked British major who arrives during the 1916 Irish uprising to keep the peace. Not surprisingly, she is accused of betraying the local IRA gunrunners to the British lover. Tasteful melodrama with lots of pretty scenery that goes on a bit too long. 194m/C VHS, DVD. GB Sarah Miles, Robert Mitchum, John Mills, Trevor Howard, Christopher Jones, Leo McKern; **D:** David Lean; **W:** Robert Bolt; **C:** Freddie Young; **M:** Maurice Jarre. Oscars '70: Cinematog., Support. Actor (Mills); Golden Globes '71: Support. Actor (Mills).

Ryder P.I. ♂ **1986** (PG-13) P.I Ryder and his sidekick fight crime and solve weird cases in the big city. 92m/C VHS, DVD. Bob Nelson, Dave Hawthorne, John Mulrooney, Howard Stern; **D:** Karl Hosch, Chuck Walker; **W:** Bob Nelson, Dave Hawthorne, Karl Hosch, Chuck Walker; **C:** Phil Arfman; **M:** Kevin Kelly.

Ryna ♂♂ **2005** In rural Romania, beautiful teenager Ryna (Petre) is forced to dress as a boy and work as a mechanic by her abusive father (Popescu). But she re-creations describe the painful technique used on prisoners. Director Ritty Panir (himself an inmate at S21) takes an unvarnished look at the horrors perpetrated in the name of the state. 106m/C DVD, FR. Ritty Panir; **W:** Ritty Panir; **C:** Ritty Panir; **D:** Prum Mesar; **M:** Mark Marder.

Sabaka ♂♂ **1955** Adventure set in India about a scary religious cult Karloff and the local band of stalwart "E" movie performers have fun with this re-creations describe the painful technique used on prisoners. Director Ritty you should too. 81m/C VHS, DVD. Boris Karloff, Reginald Denny, Victor Jory, Lisa Howard, Jeanne Bates, Jay Novello, June Foray; **D:** Frank Ferrin.

S21: The Khmer Rouge Killing Machine ♂♂♂ **1955** _The Hindu_ **1955** S21: La _Machine De Mort Khmere Rouge_. S21: The Khmer Rouge, led by Pol Pot, instituted a series of murderous purges that took place at S21, a high school turned interrogation and torture center in Phnom Penh where 17,000 prisoners were "processed." Only three lived to tell about it. Vann Nath, an artist, relates his story of survival by painting flattering portraits of the guards. Journals kept by guards and re-creations describe the painful technique used on prisoners. Director Ritty Panir (himself an inmate at S21) takes an unvarnished look at the horrors perpetrated in the name of the state. 106m/C DVD, FR. Ritty Panir; **D:** Ritty Panir.

Sabata ♂♂½ **1969** (PG-13) Van Cleef is the man in black as gunslinger Sabata in this exuberant, if confusing, spaghetti western. Sabata enters the town of Daughtery just after a robbery of Union Army funds. Sabata wants the reward but quickly discovers that three of the town's leaders funded the theft so he decides to blackmail them. They send numerous assassins after Sabata with no luck. 111m/C DVD, FR Lee Van Cleef, William Berger, Ignazio Spalla, Frank Ressel, Aldo Canti, Gianni Rizzo, Antonio Gradoli; **D:** Gianfranco Parolini; **W:** Gianfranco Parolini, Renato Izzo; **C:** Sandro Mancori; **M:** Marcello Giombini.

Sabotage ♂♂♂ **1936** A Woman Alone; Hidden Power **1936** Early Hitchcock thriller based on Conrad's "The Secret Agent." A woman who works at a movie theatre (Sidney) might be the terrorist planting bombs around London. Numerous sly touches of

---

the Master's signature humor. **81m/B VHS, DVD.** Oscar Homolka, Sylvia Sidney, John Loder, Desmond Tester, Joyce Barbour, Matthew Boulton, S.J. Warmington, William Dewhurst, Austin Trevor, Torin Thatcher, Aubrey Mather, Peter Bull, Charles Hawtrey, Martita Hunt, Hal Walters, Frederick Piper; *D:* Alfred Hitchcock; *W:* Charles Bennett, Ian Hay, Alma Reville, E.V.H. Emmett, Helen Simpson; *C:* Bernard Knowles.

Sabotage 1996 (R) A disgraced ex-Navy counterterrorism operative and bodyguard is on the trail of the man who murdered his boss, along with the FBI agent assigned to the case. Standard-issue shoot-em-up with decent action. **99m/C VHS, CA** Mark Dacascos, Carrie-Anne Moss, Tony Todd, Graham Greene, John Neville, James Purcell; *D:* Tibor Takacs; *W:* Michael Stokes; *C:* Curtis Petersen; *M:* Guy Zerata.

Saboteur 1942 A man wrongly accused of sabotaging an American munitions plant during WWII sets out to find the traitor who framed him. Hitchcock uses his locations, including Boulder Dam, Radio City Music Hall, and the Statue of Liberty, to greatly intensify the action. Stunning resolution. **108m/B VHS, DVD.** Priscilla Lane, Robert Cummings, Otto Kruger, Alan Baxter, Norman Lloyd, Charles Halton; *D:* Alfred Hitchcock; *W:* Alfred Hitchcock, Peter Viertel; *C:* Joseph Valentine; *M:* Frank Skinner.

Sabre Jet 1953 Run-of-the-mill wartime drama of hubbies flying combat missions in Korea and long-suffering spouses on the home front. **90m/C VHS.** Robert Stack, Amanda Blake, Louis King; *D:* Louis King.

Sabretooth WOOF! 2001 (R) Stupid scientist uses fossil DNA to genetically recreate the sabretooth tiger, loses control of the new beastie, which goes on a killing spree of campers no less). Supremely dumb, unintentionally humorous, with bad acting (by actors who certainly have done better work), bad special effects...well, if you like cheap horror flicks, this woof is for you. **90m/C VHS, DVD.** David Keith, Vanessa Angel, John Rhys-Davies, Lahmard Tate; *D:* James D.R. Hickox; *W:* Tom Woolsley; *C:* Christopher Pearson. VIDEO

Sabrina Two wealthy brothers, one an aging businessman (Bogart) and the other a dissolute playboy (Holden), vie for the attention of their chauffeur's daughter (Hepburn), who has just returned from a French cooking school. Typically acerbic, in the Wilder manner, with Bogart and Holden cast interestingly against type (but it's Hepburn's picture anyway). Based on the play "Sabrina Fair" by Samuel Taylor. **113m/B VHS, DVD.** Audrey Hepburn, Humphrey Bogart, William Holden, Walter Hampden, Francis X. Bushman, John Williams, Martha Hyer, Marcel Dalio; *D:* Billy Wilder; *W:* Billy Wilder, Ernest Lehman; *C:* Charles B(ryant) Lang Jr. Oscars '54: Costume Des. (B&W); Directors Guild '54: Director (Wilder); Golden Globes '55: Screenplay; Natl. Film Reg. '02. Support. Actor (Williams), Natl. Film Reg.

Sabrina 1995 (PG) Updated version of Billy Wilder's 1954 fairytale that starred a luminous Audrey Hepburn. This time around the pretty Ormond is the chauffeur's daughter who gets closely involved with the wealthy Larrabees. And this time the emphasis is more on workaholic business mogul Linus (Ford), who plays a dangerous game when he decides to transfer Sabrina's affections from his feckless engaged brother David (Kinnear) to himself in order to protect a business merger. Ford's a little too stodgy (you'll wonder why Sabrina bothers except she's probably suitably charming (in his film debut) and Marchand properly matriarchal. **127m/C VHS, DVD.** Harrison Ford, Julia Ormond, Greg Kinnear, Nancy Marchand, John Wood, Richard Crenna, Angie Dickinson, Lauren Holly, Fanny Ardant, Dana Ivey, Patrick Bruel, Miriam Colon, Elizabeth Franz; *D:* Sydney Pollack; *W:* David Rayfiel, Barbara Benedek; *C:* Giuseppe Rotunno; *M:* John Williams.

Sabrina the Teenage Witch 1996 (PG) Based on the Archie Comics, this lighthearted movie finds 16-year-old Sabrina (Hart) being told by her two eccentric aunts, Hilda (Miller) and Zelda (Fernetz), that she is a witch,

descended from a long line of good witches and warlocks. Sabrina's having enough trouble fitting in at Riverdale High without this kind of news but she does find that her magical powers have their advantages. Pilot for the TV series. **90m/C VHS, DVD.** Melissa Joan Hart, Charlene Fernetz, Sherry Miller, Michelle Beaudoin, Ryan Reynolds, Tobias Mehler, Lalainia Lindbjerg; *D:* Tibor Takacs; *W:* Barney Cohen, Kathryn Wallack, Nicholas Factor. CABLE

Sacco & Vanzetti *Sacco e Vanzetti* 1971 (PG) Two Italian immigrants and acknowledged anarchists are caught amidst communist witch-hunts and judicial negligence when they are tried and executed for murder in 1920s America. Based on the true-life case, considered by some a flagrant miscarriage of justice and political martyrdom, by others, honest American judicial-system proceedings. Well-made and acted. Joan Baez sings the title song "The Ballad of Sacco and Vanzetti." **120m/C VHS, DVD.** Gian Marie Volonte, Riccardo Cucciolla, Milo O'Shea, Cyril Cusack, Geoffrey Keen; *D:* Guiliano Montaldo; *M:* Ennio Morricone. Cannes '71: Actor (Cucciolla).

The Sacketts 1979 Follows the adventures of three Tennessee brothers who migrate to the West after the Civil War. Based on two Louis L'Amour novels. **198m/C VHS, DVD.** Jeffery Osterhage, Tom Selleck, Sam Elliott, Glenn Ford, Ben Johnson, Mercedes McCambridge, Ruth Roman, Jack Elam, Gilbert Roland; *D:* Robert Totten. TV

Sacred Ground 1983 (PG) A trapper and his pregnant Apache wife unknowingly build shelter on the Paiute Indians' sacred burial ground. When the wife dies in childbirth, the pioneer is forced to kidnap a Paiute woman who has just buried her own deceased infant. Average western drama. **100m/C VHS, DVD.** Tim McIntire, Jack Elam, L.Q. Jones, Mindi Miller; *D:* Charles B. Pierce; *W:* Charles B. Pierce.

The Sacrifice 1986 (PG) Tarkovsky's enigmatic final film, released after his death. Deals with a retired intellectual's spiritually symbolic efforts at self-sacrifice in order to save his family on the eve of a nuclear holocaust. Stunning cinematography by Nykvist. Acclaimed, but sometimes slow going; not everyone will appreciate Tarkovsky's visionary spiritualism. In Swedish and Russian with English subtitles. **145m/C VHS, DVD. FR SW** Erland Josephson, Susan Fleetwood, Valerie Mairesse, Allan Edwall, Gudrun Gisladottir, Sven Wollter, Filippa Franzen; *D:* Andrei Tarkovsky; *W:* Andrei Tarkovsky; *C:* Sven Nykvist. British Acad. '87: Foreign Film.

Sacrifice 2000 (R) Serial killer has murdered the daughter of felon Tyler Pearce, who escapes from prison to get revenge. He hooks up with an ex-prostitute (Luner) but he'll have to avoid an FBI agent who wants to put Tyler back behind bars. **91m/C VHS, DVD.** Michael Madsen, Bokeem Woodbine, Jamie Luner, Joshua Leonard; *D:* Mark L. Lester. VIDEO

Sacrilege 1986 A nun and a nobleman engage in a hot love affair that fosters scandal, murder and, revenge. Cynical case of religious theme masks otherwise ordinary sex/romance flick. Controversial Italian-made erotic drama. **104m/C VHS. IT** Myriem Roussel, Alessandro Gassman; *D:* Luciano Odorisio.

The Sad Sack 1957 A bumbling hero with a photographic memory winds up in Morocco as a member of the French Foreign Legion. Although a success at the box office, Lewis's second movie (without partner Dean Martin) seems jerky and out of sorts today. Based on the comic strip character by George Baker, but not effectively. **98m/B VHS.** Jerry Lewis, Phyllis Kirk, David Wayne, Peter Lorre, Gene Evans, Mary Treen; *D:* George Marshall; *C:* Loyal Griggs; *M:* Burt Bacharach, Hal David.

Sadat 1983 (PG) Gossett Jr. well plays his title role of Egyptian leader and Nobel Peace Prize-winner Anwar el Sadat. But the controversial life and peace efforts of the president (assassinated in 1981) are given a quick overview in this average drama. **195m/C VHS.** Louis Gossett Jr., John Rhys-Davies, Jeremy Kemp, Nehemiah

Persoff, Madolyn Smith, Anne Heywood, Jeffrey Tambor, Barry Morse; *D:* Richard Michaels; *M:* Charles Bernstein. TV

The Saddest Music in the World 2003 Arty but amusing take on the classic musicals and screwball comedies of the 1930s set in Depression era Winnipeg, Canada. Eccentric plot has legless beer baroness Lady Helen Port-Huntly (Rossellini) proclaiming she will offer a prize of $25,000 and a crown of frozen tears to any nation that comes up with the world's saddest music. Americans Chester Kent (McKinney), a failed Broadway producer and Canadian ex-pat, and Narcissa (de Medeiros), his amnesiac, nymphomanic muse, decide to take a crack at it. Truly stylish, madcap and clever, zaniness nonetheless wears thin by the conclusion. Appropriately eclectic soundtrack. Based on an original screenplay by Kazuo Ishigura. **99m/B DVD. CA** Isabella Rossellini, Mark McKinney, Maria De Medeiros, Ross McMillan, David Fox, Claude Dorge, Darcy Fehr; *D:* Guy Maddin; *W:* Guy Maddin, George Toles, Kazuo Ishiguro; *C:* Luc Montpellier; *M:* Christopher Dedrick.

Saddle Buster 1932 A rodeo cowboy loses his nerve after being thrown by a tough horse, but gets it back again by the end of the hour. Actual rodeo footage is incorporated into this low-budget bronco saga. **59m/B VHS.** Tom Keene, Helen Foster, Charles Quigley, Marie Quillen, Robert Frazer, Charles "Slim" Whitaker; *D:* Fred Allen.

Saddle Mountain Roundup 1941 The Range Busters are on the trail again when they smoke out a murderer. **61m/B VHS, DVD.** Ray Corrigan, John "Dusty" King, Max Terhune, Lita Conway, George Chesebro, Jack Mulhall, Willie Fung, John Elliott; *D:* S. Roy Luby; *W:* Earle Snell, John Vlahos; *C:* Robert E. Cline.

Sade 2000 Director Jacquot takes a low-key approach to a short period in the life of the notorious Marquis de Sade (Auteuil), who's depicted as a manipulative bon vivant rather than a sexual libertine, is one of many aristocrats imprisoned at a former convent called Picpus during the Reign of Terror. His relatively luxurious abode is thanks to the machinations of a former mistress he's nicknamed Sensible (Denicourt), which she is since she's now under the protection of Fournier (Colin), one of Robespierre's men. Sade enjoys his situation by staging sexual tableaus and plotting the seduction of virginal teen Emilie (Le Besco) by handsome gardener Augustin (Lespert). (All to save her life of course.) Based on the novel "La Terreur du Boudoir" by Serge Bramly. French with subtitles. **100m/C DVD. FR** Daniel Auteuil, Marianne (Cuau) Denicourt, Gregoire Colin, Isild Le Besco, Jeanne Balibar, Jean-Pierre Cassel, Jalil Lespert; *D:* Benoit Jacquot; *W:* Jacques Fieschi, Bernard Minoret; *C:* Benoit Delhomme.

Sadie McKee 1934 A melodrama with Crawford as a maid searching for love in the big city. She falls for a self-destructive ne'er-do-well, marries an alcoholic millionaire, and eventually finds true love with the wealthy Tone (who would become Crawford's third husband). Professional acting and directing elevate the story. **90m/B VHS.** Joan Crawford, Franchot Tone, Gene Raymond, Edward Arnold; *D:* Clarence Brown.

Sadie Thompson 1928 Swanson plays a harlot with a heart of gold, bawdy and good-natured, in the South Seas. A zealot missionary (Barrymore) arrives and falls in love with her. The last eight minutes of footage have been recreated by using stills and the original title cards, to replace the last reel which had decomposed. Remade as "Rain," "Dirty Gertie From Harlem," and "Miss Sadie Thompson." Based on W. Somerset Maugham's "Rain." **97m/B VHS, DVD.** Gloria Swanson, Lionel Barrymore, Raoul Walsh, Blanche Frederici, Charles Lane, James A. Marcus; *D:* Raoul Walsh; *W:* Raoul Walsh; *C:* George Barnes, Robert B. Kurtle, Oliver Marsh.

The Sadist 1963 *The Profile of Terror* 1963 Three teachers on their way to Dodger Stadium find themselves stranded at a roadside garage and terrorized by a snivelling lunatic. Tense and plausible. **95m/B VHS, DVD.** Arch Hall Jr., Helen Hovey, Richard Alden, Marilyn Manning; *D:* James Landis; *W:* James Landis; *C:* Vilmos Zsigmond.

Safari 3000 1982 (PG) "Playboy" writer is assigned to do a story on a three-day, 3,000 kilometer car race in Africa. Doesn't take itself too seriously, and neither should we. Dumb, dull, and disjointed. **91m/C VHS.** Stockard Channing, David Carradine, Christopher Lee; *D:* Harry Hurwitz; *M:* Ernest Gold.

Safe 1995 (R) Suburban California housewife Carol (Moore) literally becomes allergic to her environment and winds up seeking relief in a holistic center in Albuquerque, where director Haynes takes a shot at the New Age and finds a link to the AIDS crisis. Serious, stylistically detached look at a near future riddled with environmental toxins is led by Moore's performance as the sunny suburbanite undone by the unseen. **119m/C VHS, DVD.** Julianne Moore, Peter Friedman, Xander Berkeley, Susan Norman, James LeGros, Mary Carver, Kate McGregor-Stewart, Jessica Harper, Brandon Cruz; *D:* Todd Haynes; *W:* Todd Haynes; *C:* Alex Nepomniaschy; *M:* Ed Tomney.

Safe Harbour *Danielle Steel's Safe Harbour* 2007 (PG-13) Ophelie's (Gilbert) husband and son are killed in a plane crash and she retreats with 14-year-old daughter Pip (Liberato) to a rented beach house to grieve. While walking the beach, Pip meets artist Matt (Johnson) but Ophelie is horrified that her daughter is talking to strangers until Matt introduces himself. (Naturally, he has family problems of his own to work through.) Her best friend Andrea (Staab) urges Ophelie to have a little fun with Matt but she thinks it's too soon and then she finds out a secret. It's all really nice and stilted and passion-free (since the character in Danielle Steel's book was French) but doesn't pull it off. **101m/C DVD.** Melissa Gilbert, Brad Johnson, Rebecca Staab, Edithe Swensen, Liana Liberato, Katie Walder; *D:* William Corcoran; *C:* Curtis Petersen; *M:* Joey Newman. VIDEO

Safe House 1999 Comedy-thriller with a terrific lead performance by Stewart. A retiree succumbing to Alzheimer's, Mace Sowell's become increasingly paranoid and taken to carrying a gun and maintaining an elaborate security system around his L.A. home. Mace claims to be an ex-government agent, marked for death by his former boss who's now a presidential candidate. His fears are dismissed by his shrink (Elizondo) and his daughter forces him to get an in-home caregiver, Andi Travers (Williams). But soon Andi begins to think her charge may not be crazy after all. **125m/C VHS, DVD.** Patrick Stewart, Kimberly Williams, Hector Elizondo, Craig Shoemaker; *D:* Eric Steven Stahl; *W:* Eric Steven Stahl, Sean McLain; *C:* Vincent Donohue; *M:* Kevin Kiner. CABLE

Safe Men 1998 (R) Goofy, low-budget indie comedy whose pieces don't quite fit together. Set in Providence, R.I., talentless would-be singers Sam (Rockwell) and Eddie (Zahn) are mistaken by the local Jewish mafia for a pair of expert safecrackers. The inept duo are pressured by Big Fat Bernie Gayle (Lerner) and his henchman Veal Chop (Giamatti) to break into the home of Bernie's rival, Good Stuff Leo (Fierstein). Some dumb luck and a lot of coincidence work in the guys favor. But then the real safecracking team turns up. **89m/C VHS, DVD.** Sam Rockwell, Steve Zahn, Paul Giamatti, Michael Lerner, Harvey Fierstein, Mark Ruffalo; *D:* John Hamburg; *W:* John Hamburg; *C:* Michael Barrett; *M:* Theodore Shapiro.

Safe Passage 1994 (PG-13) Grueling family drama with Sarandon and Shepherd portraying an unhappily married couple who are the parents of seven sons, one of whom is missing and presumed dead in the Sinai Desert war. One by one the grown boys arrive home to await any further news. They rehash memories, watch old videos, open old wounds, and generally affirm life. None of the performances, with the exception of Sarandon, are truly believable. She is the only one that brings any depth to her character as the tough matriarch that holds the family together. Feels like a TV movie, albeit one with classier names. Based on the novel by Ellyn Bache. **96m/C VHS, DVD, Susan Sarandon, Jan Shepard, Robert Sean Leonard, Dean Astin, Mary Gay Harden, Nick Stahl, Jason London, Philip Bosco, Matt Keeslar; D:** Robert Allan Ackerman; **W:** Deena Goldstone; **C:** Raf Bode; **M:** Mark Isham.

The Safety of Objects ♦♦♦ 2001 (R) The lives of four suburban families intersect in Troche's third feature, based on stories by A.M. Homes. Esther Gold (Close) is committed to caring for her comatose son Paul (Jackson), who was the secret over of divorcee Annette (Clarkson), who makes a pass at lawn & pool guy Randy (Olyphant). Then there's Jim (Mulroney) who doesn't tell wife Susan (Kelly) he's left his job and whose young son is obsessed with his sister's Barbie-like doll. And Esther and Susan get involved in a contest to win an SUV and still the neighborhood's tentacles continue to spread among the inhabitants. **121m/C VHS, DVD, US** Glenn Close, Dermot Mulroney, Jessica Campbell, Patricia Clarkson, Joshua Jackson, Moira Kelly, Robert Klein, Timothy Olyphant, Mary Kay Place, Kristen Stewart, Alex House; **D:** Rose Troche; **W:** Rose Troche; **C:** Enrique Chediak.

Safety Last ♦♦♦ 1923 Lloyd silent comedy about an average guy who goes to the big city to become a success, and his misadventures. Hilarious and inspiring building climbing scene set new standards for movies and comedy-film stunts, which became Lloyd's trademark. **78m/B VHS, DVD, Harold Lloyd, Mildred Davis, Bill Strothers, Noah Young; D:** Fred Newmeyer, Sam Taylor; **W:** Sam Taylor, Jean C. Hayez, Tim Whelan Natl. Film Reg. '94.

Safety Patrol ♦♦½ 1998 Clumsy 11-year-old Scout (Hall) is determined to join his school's safety patrol team and instead winds up involved with a mother/son team of con artists. **92m/C VHS, Bug Hall, Leslie Nielsen, Lanie Kazan, Wink Martindale, Ed McMahon, Curtis Armstrong, Charlene Tilton, Alex McKenna, Kurtwood Smith, Stephanie Faracy; D:** Savage Steve Holland. **VIDEO**

Saga of Death Valley ♦♦½ 1939 Rogers battles a band of outlaws and discovers that their leader is his own brother. Exciting and likeable early Rogers western. **56m/B VHS, DVD, Roy Rogers, George "Gabby" Hayes, Donald (Don "Red") Barry, Doris Day; D:** Joseph Kane.

The Saga of the Draculas ♦ 1972 (R) An aging vampire wishes to continue his bloodline and seeks to convert his niece's baby to his blood-sucking ways. **90m/C VHS, DVD, SP** Narciso Ibanez Menta, Tina Sainz, Tony Isbert, Maria Koski, Cristina Suriani, Helga Line; **D:** Leon Klimovsky.

Saga of the Vagabond ♦♦♦ Seragoku Gunto-Den 1959 Arranged by master director Akira Kurosawa. A band of ruthless outlaws career across a civil war-torn countryside. With English subtitles. **115m/C VHS, JP** Toshiro Mifune, Michiyo Aratama, Misa(ko) Uehara; **D:** Toshio Sugie.

Sagebrush Law ♦♦½ 1943 Western yarn has Holt playing a young man trying to clear the name of his bank president father. Barclay serves as the love interest and "Ukulele Ike" Edwards provides needed comic and music relief. **56m/B VHS, Tim Holt, Cliff Edwards, Joan Barclay, Edward Cassidy, Karl Hackett, Roy Barcroft, Ernie Adams; D:** Sam Nelson; **W:** Bennet Cohen.

Sagebrush Trail ♦♦♦ 1933 Wayne's second-ever western, complete with all sorts of tumbleweed and white-hat cliches. Our hero is wrongly accused of killin' a man, and busts out of the hoosegow to clear his name. Interesting plot twists makes for fun, compelling viewing. **53m/B VHS, DVD, John** Wayne, Yakima Canutt.

Wally Wales; **D:** Armand Schaefer; **W:** Lindsay Parsons; **C:** Archie Stout.

Sahara ♦♦♦ 1943 A British-American unit must fight the Germans for their survival in the Libyan desert during WWII. Plenty of action and suspense combined with good performances makes this one a step above the usual war movie. **97m/B VHS, DVD, Humphrey Bogart, Dan Duryea, Bruce Bennett, Lloyd Bridges, Rex Ingram, J. Carrol Naish, Richard Nugent, Carl Harbord; D:** Zoltan Korda; **W:** Zoltan Korda, John Howard Lawson; **M:** Miklos Rozsa.

Sahara WOOF! 1983 (PG) Disappointing "Perils of Pauline" type adventure. Shields disguises herself as a man (sure) to complete a race across the desert in honor of her late father, and a sheik captures her. **111m/C VHS, Brooke Shields, Lambert Wilson, Horst Buchholz, John Rhys-Davies, Ronald Lacey, John Mills, Steve Forrest, Perry Lang, Cliff (Clifton) Potts; D:** Andrew V. McLaglen; **W:** James R. Silke; **M:** Ennio Morricone.

Sahara ♦♦½ 2005 (PG-13). Second attempt to construct a franchise around Clive Cussler's popular Dirk Pitt character (the first was 1980's "Raise the Titanic"). Pitt (McConaughey) and his buddy, Al Giordino (Zahn), are ex-Navy treasure-hunters searching for a lost Civil War battleship off the coast of West Africa. Cruz is a UN doctor who enlists Pitt in helping her find the source of a virulent African plague. The plot reeks of modern-day Indiana Jones and, thankfully, doesn't try to hide it, helped along by McConaughey and Zahn's boisterous chemistry. Eisner wisely chooses to keep things light throughout, which makes the film both charmingly self-aware and easily dismissible. **127m/C DVD, Blu-ray Disc, UMD, HD DVD, US** Matthew McConaughey, Steve Zahn, Penelope Cruz, Lambert Wilson, Glynn Turman, William H. Macy, Delroy Lindo, Lennie James, Rainn Wilson; **D:** Breck Eisner; **W:** John C. Richards, Thomas Dean Donnelly, Joshua Oppenheimer, James V. Hart; **C:** Seamus McGarvey; **M:** Clint Mansell.

Saigon Commandos ♦ 1988 (R) Commandos, on the eve of the fall of Saigon in the 1970s, attempt to prevent heroin dealers from toppling the already shaky government. So-so war/action flick. **84m/C VHS, Richard Young, P.J. Soles, John Allen Nelson, Jimi B Jr.; D:** Clark Henderson.

Saigon: Year of the Cat ♦ 1987 Drama about an American ambassador, a CIA operative, and a British bank clerk who try to leave Saigon in 1974 before the Vietcong enter the city. **106m/C VHS, DVD, GB** Frederic Forrest, E.G. Marshall, Judi Dench; **D:** Stephen Frears; **W:** David Hare; **M:** George Fenton. **TV**

Sailor Beware ♦♦ 1952 Naive Navy along with lothario singer Al Crowthers (Martin). In this typical slapstick mishmash of comedy and music, Lewis causes havoc aboard a submarine and becomes the judge of the most kissable girl contest in Hawaii while Martin romances singer Calvert (playing herself). Betty Hutton has a cameo as one of Dean's gals during the recruitment scene. **108m/B VHS, Jerry Lewis, Dean Martin, Marion Marshall, Robert Strauss, Corine Calvert, Leif Erickson, Don "The Dragon" Wilson, Vince Edwards; Cameos:** Betty Hutton; **C:** Daniel F. Fapp; **M:** Joseph J. Lilley.

Sailing Along ♦♦ 1938 British musical about a young starlet who sacrifices her career for true love. **80m/B VHS, Jessie Matthews, Barry Mackay, Jack Whiting, Roland Young, Noel Madison, Athene Seyler, Patrick Barr; D:** Sonnie Hale.

The Sailor Who Fell from Grace with the Sea ♦♦ 1976 (R) Perverse tale of a disillusioned sailor who rejects the sea for the love of a lonely young widow and her troubled son. Graphic sexual scenes. Based on the novel by Yukio Mishima, the film suffers from the transition of Japanese culture to an English setting. **105m/C VHS, DVD, GB** Sarah Miles, Kris Kristofferson, Jonathan Kahn, Margo Cunningham; **D:** Lewis John Carlino; **W:** Lewis John Carlino.

St. Benny the Dip ♦♦½ 1951 Three con-men evade police by posing as clergymen and end up going straight after a series of adventures in a skid row mission. Funny in parts but but a weak story wastes lots of talent and time. **110m/C VHS, DVD, Rob Lowe, Demi Moore, Andrew McCarthy, Judd Nelson, Ally Sheedy, Emilio Estevez, Mare Winningham, Martin Balsam, Jenny Wright, Joyce Van Patten, Andie MacDowell, Ana Maria Horsford; D:** Joel Schumacher; **W:** Carl Kurlander, Joel Schumacher; **C:** Stephen Burum; **M:** David Foster. Golden Raspberries '85: Worst Support. Actor (Lowe).

St. Elmo's Fire ♦♦½ 1985 (R) Seven Georgetown graduates confront adult problems during their first post-graduate year. Reminiscent of "The Big Chill," scenic. Templar's exploits are featured in a series of novels by Leslie Charteris, and previously appeared in earlier movies and on TV. **115m/C VHS, DVD, Val Kilmer, Elisabeth Shue, Rade Serbedzija, Valery (Valeri Nikolayev) Nikolaev, Henry Goodman, Alun Armstrong, Michael Byrne, Eugene (Yevgeny) Lazarev, Charlotte Cornwell, Irina Apeximova, Emily Mortimer; D:** Phillip Noyce; **W:** Jonathan Hensleigh, Wesley Strick; **C:** Phil Meheux; **M:** Graeme Revell.

Saint-Ex: The Story of the Storyteller ♦♦ 1996 (PG) Ambitious bio based on famous French aviator, and author of the children's classic "The Little Prince," Antoine de Saint-Exupery (Ganz). Flashbacks show his childhood obsession with flying that eventually lead to Saint-Exupery's perilous North African mail flights during WWII. Beyond his passion for flying is his marriage to Consuelo (Richardson), who comes to resent his frequent absences, and in later, more-supportive love of Genevieve (McTeer). Striking visuals but that's about all. **90m/C VHS, DVD, Bruno Ganz, Miranda Richardson, Janet McTeer, Ken Stott, Katrin Cartlidge, Eleanor Bron, Brid Brennan; D:** Anand Tucker; **W:** Frank Cottrell-Boyce; **C:** David Clark Johnson; **M:** Barrington Pheloung.

The Saint ♦♦½ 1997 (PG-13). The plot makes about as much sense as that average ego-driven bad guys, and Shue's naive scientist/babe is totally unbelievable (she's like a deer caught in a car's headlights). The only reason the movie works at all is due to the debonair, if wooden, charms of Kilmer as superthief and master of disguise Simon Templar. He's hired by Russian strongman Ivan Tretiak (Serbedzija) to steal the formula for cold fusion from scientist Emma Russell (Shue) so that Tretiak can save a Moscow winter by delivering cheap energy and thus make Russ a formidable power once again (with himself as leader, natch). Only problem is Templar, who names all his alter egos after saints, falls for Emma and tries to get them out of harm's way by double-crossing Tretiak. At least the Moscow and Oxford settings are extremely predictable. Still, good for a few laughs. **80m/B VHS, DVD, Val Kilmer, Elisabeth Shue, Rade Serbedzija, Valery (Valeri Nikolayev) Nikolaev, Henry Goodman, Alun Armstrong, Michael Byrne, Eugene (Yevgeny) Lazarev, Charlotte Cornwell, Irina Apeximova, Emily Mortimer; D:** Phillip Noyce; **W:** Jonathan Hensleigh, Wesley Strick; **C:** Phil Meheux; **M:** Graeme Revell.

The Saint ♦♦ 1968 Moore is Simon Templar, Leslie Charteris's mysterious British detective/hero in this adventure that takes him to Naples. Revival of and improvement on earlier British TV show, and based on the very popular British TV series. **98m/C VHS, DVD, Roger Moore, Ian Hendry.**

The Saint in London ♦♦ 1939 The Saint investigates a gang trying to pass counterfeit banknotes. The third in the "The Saint" series. **72m/B VHS, George Sanders, Sally Gray; D:** Jack Raddy Carstairs.

The Saint in New York ♦♦ 1938 The Saint, Simon Templar, turns Robin Hood to help the Civic Committee clean up a gang of desperados. First of "The Saint" series. **71m/B VHS, Louis Hayward, Kay Sutton, Jack Carson, Charles Halton; D:** Ben Holmes.

St. Ives ♦♦ 1976 (PG) Former police reporter Bronson agrees to recover some stolen ledgers and finds himself dealing with betrayal and murder. Bisset is sultry and the tale is slickly told, but dumb. Co-stars Travanti, later of TV's "Hill Street Blues." **94m/C VHS, DVD, Charles Bronson, Jacqueline Bisset, John Houseman, Jerry Guardino, Maximilian Schell, Harris Yulin, Elisha Cook Jr., Daniel J. Travanti; D:** J. Lee Thompson; **W:** Barry Beckerman; **M:** Lalo Schifrin.

St. Ives ♦♦ 1998 (R) Robert Louis Stevenson's St. Ives: All for Love 1998 (R) During the Napoleonic Wars, dashing French officer, Captain Jacques St. Ives (Barry), is captured during battle and sent to a POW camp in the Scottish Highlands that is run by Major Chevening (Grant) St. Ives and leading actress and chose the inexperienced Seborg (her screen debut). A good thing for her career, but not for this lil-begotten overambitious opus. Seborg doesn't fit. Also available colorized. **131m/C VHS, DVD, Jean Seberg, Anton Walbrook, Richard Widmark, John Gielgud, Harry Andrews, Felix Aylmer, Richard Todd; D:** Otto Preminger; **W:** Graham Greene; **C:** Georges Perinal.

Saint Jack ♦♦♦ 1979 (R) The story of a small-time pimp with big dreams working the pleasure palaces of late-night Singapore. Engrossing and pleasant. Based on Paul Theroux's novel. **112m/C VHS, DVD, Ben Gazzara, Denholm Elliott, Joss Ackland, George Lazenby, Peter Bogdanovich; D:** Peter Bogdanovich; **W:** Peter Bogdanovich; **C:** Robby Muller.

Saint Joan ♦♦ 1957 Film of the George Bernard Shaw play, adapted by Graham Greene, about the French Maid of Orleans at her trial. Otto Preminger went on a nationwide talent hunt for his leading actress and chose the inexperienced Seberg (her screen debut). A good thing for her career, but not for this lil-begotten overambitious opus. Seberg doesn't fit. Also available colorized. **110m/B VHS, DVD, Jean Seberg, Anton Walbrook, Richard Widmark, John Gielgud, Harry Andrews, Felix Aylmer, Richard Todd; D:** Otto Preminger; **W:** Graham Greene; **C:** Georges Perinal.

Saint Maybe ♦♦♦ 1998 Quietly affecting family saga adapted from the novel by Anne Tyler. Heedless Ian Bedloe (McCarthy) is disturbed when his older brother Danny (Nordling) impulsively marries scatty divorcee Lucy (Parker) who has two kids. When Lucy gets pregnant, Ian's interference results in a double tragedy. Seeking to atone for his mistake Ian discovers the Church of the Second Chance and he decides to raise his brother's three children. **96m/C VHS, Thomas (Tom) McCarthy, Blythe Danner, Edward Herrmann, Mary-Louise Parker, Jeffrey Nordling, Melina Kanakaredes, Glynnis O'Connor, Amy Hargreaves, Kristofer Ryan Winters, Denis O'Hare, Rene Auge; D:** Michael Pressman; **W:** Robert W. Lenski; **C:** Shelly Johnson. **TV**

The St. Francisville Experiment ♦ 2000 (PG-13) Psychic, amateur ghost hunter, history student, and filmmaker fly to Louisiana to investigate a haunted house plagued by the spirit of slaves. **79m/C VHS, DVD, Tim Baldini, Madison Charap, Ryan Larson, Paul Palmer, Paul James, Paul Salamoff, Troy Taylor; D:** Tim Thompson.

St. Helen's, Killer Volcano ♦♦½ 1982 A young man and an old man develop a deep friendship amid the devastation, fear, greed, and panic surrounding the eruption of the Mt. St. Helen's volcano. Based on the true story of Harry Truman (!), who refused to leave his home. Pretty good. **95m/C VHS.**

St. Michael Had a Rooster ♦♦ 1972 In 19th-century Italy, idealist anarchist Giulio Manieri (Brogi) hopes to inspire the local peasantry through armed raids. Imprisoned for his trouble, Manieri takes upon his release after 10 years that his political struggles have been forgotten to life on the outside. Based on the Leo Tolstoy story "The Divine and the Human." Italian with subtitles. **87m/C VHS, DVD, IT** Giulio Brogi, Danielle Dublino, Renato Scarpa; **D:** Paolo Taviani, Vittorio Taviani; **W:** Paolo Taviani, Vittorio Taviani; **C:** Mario Masini.

The Saint of Fort Washington 1993 (R) Sweetly naive and schizophrenic Matthew (Dillon) is homeless and through government screw-ups is sent to the Fort Washington Armory, which houses more than 700 homeless men. Harassed by others, Matthew is befriended by Jerry, a kindly Vietnam vet, who tries to care for him. Subject is taken seriously but slips into mawkishness; good performances by the leads. 104m/C VHS. Danny Glover, Matt Dillon, Rick Aviles, Nina Siemaszko, Ving Rhames, Joe Seneca; D: Tim Hunter; W: Lyle Kessler; C: Frederick Elmes; M: James Newton Howard.

St. Patrick: The Irish Legend 2000 Unfortunately neither the impressive cast, the beautiful scenery, or the special effects can transform this costumer from being bland and boring. Patrick (who allegedly drove all the snakes out of Ireland) was the privileged son of a nobleman in 5th century Britian, who suffered through six years as a slave before finding his religious calling. Over great opposition, he's eventually appointed as the first bishop of Ireland though he must still struggle with his enemies in the Church of England. 120m/C VHS, DVD. Patrick Bergin, Malcolm McDowell, Alan Bates, Susannah York, Luke Griffin, Eamon Owens, Shaun Brennan, Chris McHallen, Michael Caven; D: Robert C. Hughes; W: Robert C. Hughes, Martin Duffy; C: James Mathers.

St. Patrick's Day 1999 (PG-13) Widowed Mary McDonaugh (Laurie) is the matriarch of a dysfunctional Irish-American family. Four generations gather at her house for St. Patrick's Day where she announces she has taken the pledge and refuses to allows any whiskey in her home (which is ignored by certain family members). As the day progresses, family secrets are revealed, including romantic feelings finally acknowledged, divorcing spouses, extramarital affairs, and other sexual shenanigans. 106m/C VHS, DVD. Pippa Laurie, Joanne Baron, Jim Metzler, Julie Strain, Herta Ware, Redmond M. Gleeson, David Ault, Colleen (Ann) Fitzpatrick, Chris Valenti, Stephen O'Mahoney; D: Hope Perello; W: Hope Perello; C: Denise Brassard; M: Michael Muhlfriedel.

Saint Ralph 2004 (PG-13) With his mother in the hospital dying, young Ralph (Adam Butcher) decides that if he can pull off the miracle of winning the Boston Marathon, his mother will benefit from the overflow. Heartfelt story, but lacks grit and emotion, leading to a rather flat end. 98m/C VHS, DVD. Campbell Scott, Gordon Pinsent, Jennifer Tilly, Tamara Hope, Adam Butcher, Shauna Macdonald, Michael Kanev; C: Rene Ohashi; M: Andrew Lockington.

The Saint Strikes Back 1939 Sanders debuts as the mysterious Simon Templar in this competent series. On a trip to San Francisco, the Saint aims to clear the name of a murdered man. The second in the series. 67m/B VHS. George Sanders, Wendy Barrie, Jonathan Hale, Jerome Cowan, Neil Hamilton, Barry Fitzgerald, Edward (Ed) Gargan, Robert Strange; D: John Farrow.

The Saint Strikes Back: Criminal Court 1946 A suspense double feature: The Saint helps a daughter clear the name of her murdered father, a San Francisco police commissioner in "The Saint Strikes Back," and a young lawyer becomes involved in murder in "Criminal Court." 127m/B VHS. George Sanders, Wendy Barrie, Barry Fitzgerald, Tom Conway, Steve Brodie; D: John Farrow.

The Saint Takes Over 1940 More adventures with the British mystery man; this time involving racetrack gambling. An original story that wasn't based on a Leslie Charteris novel as were the others. 69m/B VHS. George Sanders, Jonathan Hale, Wendy Barrie, Paul Guilfoyle, Morgan Conway, Cy Kendall; D: Jack B. Hively.

The St. Tammany Miracle 1994 Predictable, good-natured sports film about young coach Lootie Pfannder (Luner) who takes the losing girls basketball team into winners. Her broadcaster boyfriend Carl (Gosselaar) thinks she's crazy but aided by her assis-

tant (Frye), Lootie is determined to prove everyone wrong. 90m/C VHS, DVD. Jamie Luner, Mark Paul Gosselaar, Soleil Moon Frye, Jeffrey Meek, Julie McCullough; Cameos: Steve Allen; D: Joy Houck Jr.; W: Jim McCullough Jr.; M: Jay Weigel.

The St. Valentine's Day Massacre 1967 Corman's big studio debut re-creates the events leading to one of the most violent gangland shootouts in modern history: the bloodbath between Chicago's Capone and Moran gangs on February 14, 1929. Uninspired and unremittingly violent. Watch for Jack Nicholson's bit part. 100m/C VHS, DVD. Jason Robards Jr., Ralph Meeker, Jean Hale, Joseph Campanella, Bruce Dern, Clint Ritchie, Richard Bakalyan, George Segal, Harold J. Stone, Jonathan Haze, Dick Miller, Barboura Morris, Jack Nicholson, Frank Silvera, Milton Frome, Alex Rocco, John Agar, Tom Signorelli; D: Roger Corman; W: Howard Browne; C: Milton Krasner; M: Lionel Newman.

A Saintly Switch 1999 Aging quarterback Grier has just moved his pregnant wife Fox and his kids to a New Orleans. Mom's very unhappy and the kids are worried that their parents are going to split up—at least until they manage to mysteriously swap their parents' bodies. So now dad gets to be pregnant and mom has to learn to score touchdowns. 90m/C VHS, DVD. David Alan Grier, Vivica A. Fox, Rue McClanahan, Al Waxman; D: Peter Bogdanovich. TV

Saints and Sinners 1995 (R) Street-smart "Pooch" Puccia (Chapa) returns to his 'hood as an undercover cop to set up childhood buddy, drug dealer Big Boy Baynes (Plank), and winds up getting involved with seductive bad girl Eve (Rubin), who's also bedding Baynes. Then Pooch discovers his police contact is in the pay of the mob. Lots of macho posturing (attractive actors). 95m/C VHS. Damian Chapa, Scott Plank, Jennifer Rubin, Damon Whitaker, Panchito Gomez, William Atherton; D: Paul Mones; W: Paul Mones; C: Michael Bonvillain.

Saints and Soldiers 2003 (PG-13) Ragtag group of G.I.s narrowly escapes a massacre during the Battle of the Bulge, only to find themselves stumbling around and philosophizing in No-Man's-Land. Mormon sponsored WWII film is surprisingly quiet and even-handed in dealing with big metaphysical conundrums, but pro-war theme may raise the hackles of some. 90m/C DVD. Corbin Allred, Peter Asle Holden, Alexander Polinsky, Kirby Heyborne, Larry Bagby, Ethan Vincent; D: Ryan Little; M: Bart Hendrickson.

The Saint's Double Trouble 1940 Leslie Charteris' suave detective becomes embroiled in another mystery, this one involving jewel thieves. Sanders plays a dual role as the hero and the crook. The fourth in the series. 68m/B VHS, George Sanders, Helene Whitney, Jonathan Hale, Bela Lugosi, Donald MacBride, John Hamilton; D: Jack B. Hively.

Salaam Bombay! 1988 A gritty film about a child street beggar in the slums of Bombay trying to raise enough money to return to his mother's house in the country. The boy experiences every variety of gutter life imaginable, from humiliation to love. Moving and searing. Filmed on location, with actual homeless children; Nair's first feature. In Hindi with subtitles. 114m/C VHS, DVD. IN GB Shafiq Syed, Hansa Vithal, Chanda Sharma, Nana Patekar, Aneeta Kanwar, Sarfuddin Quarassi, Raju Barnad, Raghuvir Yadav; D: Mira Nair; W: Sooni Taraporevala; C: Sandi Sissel; M: L. Subramaniam.

The Salamander 1982 (R) A French detective tries to find the assassin of the leaders of a neo-fascist underground movement in Italy and follows clues that lead back to WWII. Disappoint-

ing, overwrought adaptation of a Morris West novel. 101m/C VHS, DVD. GB Franco Nero, Anthony Quinn, Martin Balsam, Sybil Danning, Christopher Lee, Cleavon Little, Paul Smith, Claudia Cardinale, Eli Wallach; D: Peter Zinner; M: Jerry Goldsmith.

Salammbo 1914 An early silent epic in the grand Italian tradition. Loosely based on Flaubert's novel about ancient Carthage. 49m/B VHS. IT Ernesto Pagani; D: Giovanni Pastrone.

Salem's Lot 1979 (PG) Based on Stephen King's novel about a sleepy New England village which is infiltrated by evil. A mysterious antiques dealer takes up residence in a forbidding hilltop house—and it becomes apparent that a vampire is on the loose. Generally creepy; Mason is good, but Soul only takes up space in the lead as a novelist returning home. 112m/C VHS, DVD. David Soul, James Mason, Lance Kerwin, Bonnie Bedelia, Lew Ayres, Ed Flanders, Elisha Cook Jr., Reggie Nalder, Fred Willard, Kenneth McMillan, Marie Windsor; D: Tobe Hooper; W: Paul Monash; C: Jules Brenner; M: Harry Sukman. *Blood Thirst* TV

Salem's Lot 2004 Made-for-TNT remake of the 1979 miniseries based on Stephen King's novel, this time a bit more faithful to the book, but still using the miniseries format. Writer Ben Mears (Lowe) returns to his hometown to exorcise some personal demons, only to find a real-life demon, in the form of vampire Barlow (Hauer) taking over. Resurrects characters and subplots that the original ignored, but the pacing is too rushed to create any real atmosphere or genuine chills. Another in a long line of disappointing King adaptations. 180m/C DVD. Rob Lowe, Samantha Mathis, Andre Braugher, Donald Sutherland, Robert Mammone, Rutger Hauer, James Cromwell, Julia Blake, Dan Byrd, Andy Anderson, Robert Grubb, Steven Vidler, Elizabeth (Liz) Alexander, Nicholas Hammond, Tara Morice, Penny McNamee; D: Mikael Salomon; W: Peter Filardi; C: Ben Nott; M: Patrick Cassidy, Lisa Gerard, Christopher Gordon. TV

Sakharov 1984 The true story of the Russian physicist who designed the H-bomb and then rose to lead the Soviet dissident movement and win the Nobel Peace Prize. Robards is excellent. Topical and powerful. 120m/C VHS. CABLE Glenda Jackson, Jason Robards Jr., Michael Bryant; D: Jack Gold; M: Carl Davis. CABLE

finds herself stuck in a remote Eskimo community in Alaska where she becomes involved with Kotzebue (lang in her film debut), who poses as a man to work on the Alaskan pipeline. The title has something to do with preserved berries—don't bother, it makes about as much sense as the entire movie. English and German with English subtitles. 94m/C VHS, DVD. GE CA Rosel Zech, k.d. lang, Chuck Connors, Jane Lind, Oscar Kawagley, Christel Merian; D: Percy Adlon; W: Percy Adlon, Felix Adlon; C: Newton Thomas (Tom) Sigel.

Salo, or the 120 Days of Sodom 1975 Extremely graphic film follows 16 children (eight boys and eight girls) who are kidnapped by a group of men in Fascist Italy. On reaching a secluded villa in the woods, the children are told to follow strict rules and then subjected to incredible acts of sadomasochism, rape, violence, and mutilation. This last film of Pasolini's was taken from a novel by the Marquis de Sade. Viewers are strongly recommended to use their utmost discretion when watching this controversial film. In Italian with English subtitles. 117m/C VHS, DVD. IT FR Caterina Boratto, Giorgio Cataldi, Umberto P. Quintavalle, Paolo Bonacelli; D: Pier Paolo Pasolini; W: Pier Paolo Pasolini, Sergio Citti; C: Tonino Delli Colli; M: Ennio Morricone.

Salome 1922 Garish silent rendition of Oscar Wilde's scandalous story. 54m/B VHS, DVD. Alla Nazimova, Madame Rose (Dion) Dione, Mitchell Lewis, Earl Schenck; D: Charles Bryant. Natl. Film Reg. '00.

Salome 1953 An over-costumed version of Oscar Wilde's Biblical story about King Herod's lascivious stepdaughter who danced her way to stardom and tried to save the life of John the Baptist. Talented cast can't overcome hokey script. 103m/C VHS. Rita Hayworth, Stewart Granger, Charles Laughton, Judith Anderson, Cedric Hardwicke, Basil Sydney, Maurice Schwartz; D: William Dieterle; C: Charles B(ryant) Lang Jr.; M: George Duning.

Salome 1985 (R) An updated and graphic version of the Oscar Wilde historical fantasy about the temptress Salome who helped topple Herod's Biblical kingdom with her dance of the Seven Veils. Not really a remake of the 1953 film since this is set during the 1940s. 100m/C VHS. Jo Champa, Tomas Milian, Pamela Salem; D: Claude D'Anna; C: Pasqualino De Santis.

Salome, Where She Danced 1945 Set during the Franco-Prussian war. A European dancer helps an American reporter in a spy scheme. She eventually relocates to America and becomes the toast of San Francisco. Somehow, De Carlo managed to spring from this ridiculous camp outing to stardom. 90m/C VHS. Yvonne De Carlo, Rod Cameron, David Bruce, Walter Slezak; D: Charles Lamont; C: William Howard Greene, Hal Mohr.

Salome's Last Dance 1988 (R) A theatrical, surreal adaptation of the Wilde story. Typically flamboyant Russell. 113m/C VHS, DVD. Glenda Jackson, Stratford Johns, Nickolas Grace, Douglas Hodge, Imogen Millais Scott; D: Ken Russell; W: Ken Russell; C: Harvey Harrison.

The Salon 2005 (PG-13). The release was delayed until 2007, which makes this stereotypical comedy even more dated-(Ben Affleck/J.Lo jokes, anyone?). Lame rehash of "Barbershop" and "Beauty Shop" set in Baltimore, with Jenny (Fox) as the owner of the hair salon that's also the local meeting place filled with the usual eccentrics (both workers and customers). The shop's threatened by an urban renewal project but Jenny's determined to fight City Hall. Writer/director/ producer Brown, who also produced the "Barbershop" flicks, needs to find a new thematic. 92m/C DVD. US Vivica A. Fox, Kym E. Whitley, Brooke Burns, Darrin Dewitt Henson, Terrence Howard, Dondre T. Whitfield, Garrett Morris, Monica Calhoun, Taral Hicks, Greg Germann, D'Angelo Wilson, Sheila Kutchkov; D: Mark Brown; W: Mark Brown; C: Brandon Trost.

Salsa 🐾🐾 1988 (PG) An auto repairman would rather dance in this "Dirty Dancing" clone. Rosa was formerly a member of the pop group Menudo. 97m/C VHS, DVD. Robby Rosa, Rodney Harvey, Magali Alvarado, Miranda Garrison, Moon Orona, Kamar De Los Reyes; D: Boaz Davidson; W: Boaz Davidson, Tomas Benitez.

Salt of the Earth 🐾🐾🐾½ 1954 Finally available in this country after being suppressed for 30 years, this controversial film was made by a group of blacklisted filmmakers during the McCarthy era. It was deemed anti-American, communist propaganda. The story deals with the anti-Hispanic racial strife that occurs in a New Mexico zinc mine when union workers organize a strike. 94m/B VHS, DVD. Rosaura Revueltas, Will Geer, David Wolfe; D: Herbert Biberman; W: Michael Wilson; C: Stanley Meredith, Leonard Stark; M: Sol Kaplan. Natl. Film Reg. '92.

The Salton Sea 🐾🐾 2002 (R) 1954 Feature debut by helmer Caruso is very good at getting down into the sleaze and grime world of methedrine addicts, dealers, and victims. Maybe too good. The parade of degradation drowns out everything else; the performances of Kilmer as the nominal hero, and D'Onofrio as kingpin/sadist Pooh-Bear, the time-addled plot that begs for concentration, and any sense that anything good will come from viewing this film. What it does, it does well. The question is, does anyone have the stomach to see it done? 103m/C VHS, DVD. US Val Kilmer, Vincent D'Onofrio, Adam Goldberg, Luis Guzman, Doug Hutchison, Anthony LaPaglia, Glenn Plummer, Peter Sarsgaard, Deborah Kara Unger, Chandra West, B.D. Wong, R. Lee Ermey, Shalim Harlow, Shirley Knight, Meat Loaf Aday, Azura Skye, Danny Trejo, Josh Todd; D: D.J. Caruso; W: Tony Gayton; C: Amir M. Mokri; M: Thomas Newman.

Salty 🐾🐾 1973 A lovable but mischievous sea lion manages to complicate two brothers' lives when they volunteer to help a friend renovate a Florida marina, which is threatened by a mortgage foreclosure. Straightforward and inoffensive tale. 93m/C VHS. Clint Howard, Mark Slade, Nina Foch; D: Ricou Browning.

Salut l'Artiste 🐾🐾🐾 1974 Two tad actors try to make it in the industry. Delightfully funny with an excellent cast, especially Mastroianni. Snide and irreverant, yet loving and comic look at the world of acting in French with English subtitles. 96m/C VHS. FR Marcello Mastroianni, Jean Rochefort, Francoise Fabian, Carla Gravina; D: Yves Robert; M: Vladimir Cosma.

Salute John Citizen 🐾🐾½ 1942 The life of an average English family during the early days of WWII is depicted, focusing on the deprivation and horror of the Nazi blitzkrieg. Adapted from the novels "Mr. Bunting" and "Mr. Bunting at War" by Robert Greenwood. 74m/B VHS. GB Edward Rigby, Jimmy Hanley, Peggy Cummins, Mabel Constanduros, Eric Micklewood; D: Maurice Elvey; W: Clemence Dane, Elizabeth Baron; C: James Wilson.

Salvador 🐾🐾🐾½ 1986 (R) Photojournalist Richard Boyle's unflinching and sordid adventures in war-torn El Salvador. Boyle (Woods) must face the realities of social injustice. Belushi and Woods are hard to like, but excellent. Early critical success for director Stone. 123m/C VHS, DVD. James Woods, James Belushi, John Savage, Michael Murphy, Elpidia Carrillo, Cynthia Gibb, Tony Plana, Colby Chester, Will MacMillan, Jose Carlos Ruiz, Jorge Luke, Juan Fernandez, Valerie Wildman; D: Oliver Stone; W: Oliver Stone, Richard Boyle; C: Robert Richardson; M: Georges Delerue. Ind. Spirit '87. Actor (Woods).

Salvation! 🐾🐾 1987 (R) A mean-tempered, timely satire about a money-hungry TV evangelist beset by a family of fervent, equally money-hungry followers, who proceed to cheat, seduce and blackmail him. Occasionally quite funny, but sloppy and predictable. Underground director Beth B's first above-ground film. 80m/C VHS. Stephen McHattie, Exene Cervenka, Dominique Davalos, Viggo Mortensen, Rockets Redglare, Billy Bastiani; D: Beth B; W: Beth B.

The Salzburg Connection 🐾½ 1972 (PG) A list of Nazi collaborators is discovered in Austria. A vacationing American lawyer is caught up in the battle for its possession. Filmed on location, it's still a poor, cheesy adaptation of the Helen MacInnes novel. 103m/C VHS. Barry Newman, Anna Karina, Klaus Maria Brandauer, Karen Jensen; D: Lee H. Katzin.

Sam & Janet 🐾 2002 (PG-13) Sam (Brown) goes through a messy divorce and is reluctant to hook up again, until he meets Janet (Ferguson). What follows is a long and tedious courtship in which Janet hides her past, which includes a nasty ex-husband who causes trouble. Most of the movie is devoted to the growing relationship, which is realistic but gets boring. It's basically like seeing your most boring friends' stories about how they met played out on your TV. Should garner a strong following among the Lifetime set. 90m/C VHS, DVD. Gary Busey, Ryan Brown, Jennifer Ferguson, Anna Beck, Blake Woltney, George Back; D: Rick Walker; W: Rick Walker; C: Byron Werner; M: David Percefull.

Samantha 🐾🐾 1992 (PG) Twenty-one year-old Samantha discovers she was left on her parents' doorstep in a basket and decides to find out where she came from. Good cast and high charm quotient help this film along. 101m/C VHS, DVD. Martha Plimpton, Dermot Mulroney, Hector Elizondo, Mary Kay Place, Ione Skye; D: Steven La Rocque; W: John Golden, Steven La Rocque.

Samar 🐾🐾½ 1962 (PG) A liberal penal colony commandant rebels against his superiors by leading his prisoners through the Philippine jungles to freedom. Original action drama with an interesting premise. 89m/C VHS, DVD. George Montgomery, Gilbert Roland, Joan O'Brien, Ziva Rodann; D: George Montgomery.

Samaritan: The Mitch Snyder Story 🐾🐾🐾 1986 Effective TV drama based upon the true story of Vietnam vet Mitch Snyder (Sheen) who battles various government agencies and ultimately fasts to call national attention to his crusade against homelessness. (Snyder eventually committed suicide.) Tyson appears as a bag lady. 90m/C VHS. Martin Sheen, Roxanne Hart, Joe Seneca, Stan Shaw, Cicely Tyson; D: Richard T. Heffron. TV

Same Old Song 🐾🐾🐾 On Connait la Chanson 1997 Amusing melodrama that replaces some dialogue with lip-synched popular song lyrics ala Dennis Potter's "Pennies from Heaven" and "The Singing Detective." (Pic is dedicated to Potter). Camille (Jaoui) is helping her sister Odile (Azema) and brother-in-law Claude (Arditi) look for a new Paris apartment, while beginning an affair with real estate broker Marc (Wilson) and ignoring the overtures of love-sick Simon (Dussollier). Meanwhile, Nicolas (Bacri), Odile's now-married ex-flame is also apartment hunting and love her anymore. Everybody lies to everybody else (and themselves) and misinterprets all the situations. French with subtitles. 122m/C VHS. FR Agnes Jaoui, Jean-Pierre Bacri, Andre Dussollier, Sabine Azema, Lambert Wilson, Pierre Arditi, Jane Birkin, Jean-Paul Roussillon; D: Alain Resnais; W: Agnes Jaoui, Jean-Pierre Bacri; C: Renato Berta; M: Bruno Fontaine, Cesar '98: Actor (Dussollier), Film, Film Editing, Sound, Support. Actor (Bacri), Support. Actress (Jaoui), Writing.

Same River Twice 🐾🐾½ 1997 Four men who became friends while working as river rafting guides decide to have a reunion on the same river some 13 years

---

Sam Whiskey 🐾🐾½ 1969 (PG-13) Charming but uneven western/heist flick has widow Dickinson hire a motley group of misfits, led by Sam Whiskey (Reynolds) to retrieve her late husband's gold from the bottom of a river. Only she wants them to return it to the U.S. Mint from which they stole it. Quirky comedy has a great cast, but doesn't always equal the sum of its parts. 96m/C DVD. Burt Reynolds, Clint Walker, Ossie Davis, William Schallert, Angie Dickinson, Woodrow Parfrey, Anthony James, Del Reeves, William Boyett; D: Arno C. Laven; W: William W. Norton Sr.; M: Herschel Burke Gilbert.

Samson 🐾🐾 1961 Samson attempts to keep wits and and battles various. 90m/C VHS. DVD. /T Brad Harris, Luisella Boni, Alan Steel, Serge Gainsbourg, Mara Berni; D: Gianfranco Parolini.

Samson Against the Sheik 🐾 Maciste Contro lo Sceicco 1962 Samson survives long enough to battle a sheik in the Middle Ages. 106m/C VHS. /T Ed Fury, Carlo Latimer, Pierro Lulli, Adriano Micantoni; D: Domenico Paolella; W: Gian Paolo Callegari, Alessandro Ferrau; C: Carlo Bellero; M: Carlo Savina.

Samson and Delilah 🐾🐾 1950 The biblical story of the vindictive Delilah, who after being rejected by the mighty Samson, robbed him of his strength by shearing his curls. Delivered in signature DeMille style. Wonderfully fun and engrossing. Mature is excellent. 128m/ C VHS, DVD. Victor Mature, Hedy Lamarr, Angela Lansbury, George Sanders, Henry Wilcoxon, Olive Deering, Fay Holden; D: Cecil B. DeMille; C: George Barnes. Oscars '50: Art Dir/Set Dec, Color or Costume Des. (C).

Samson and Delilah 🐾🐾 1984 TV version of the biblical romance, semibased on DeMille's 1950 version. Original Samson (Mature) plays Samson's father. Too long but inoffensive; see the DeMille version instead. 95m/C VHS, DVD. Antony Hamilton, Belinda Bauer, Max von Sydow, Jose Ferrer, Victor Mature, Maria Schell; D: Lee Philips; M: Maurice Jarre. TV

Samson and Delilah 🐾🐾 1996 Another in TNT's biblical retellings, this time with Israelite shepherd Samson (Thai), who also the strongest man alive, falling for beautiful-but-treacherous Philistine Delilah (Hurley). Seems Samson is causing havoc with General Tariq's (Hopper) Philistine army and Delilah is to discover the secret of his strength. 180m/C VHS, DVD. Eric Thal, Elizabeth Hurley, Dennis Hopper, Michael Gambon, Diana Rigg, Ben Becker, Paul Freeman, Daniel Massey, Pinkas Braun, Debora Caprioglio, Alessandro Gassman, Mark

---

Same Time, Next Year 🐾🐾🐾 1978 A chance meeting between an accountant and a housewife results in a sometimes tragic, always sentimental 25-year affair in which they meet only one weekend each year. Well-cast leads carry warm, touching story based on the Broadway play by Bernard Slade. 119m/C VHS, DVD. Ellen Burstyn, Alan Alda; D: Robert Mulligan; C: Robert L. Surtees; M: Marvin Hamlisch. Golden Globes '78: Actress—Mus./Comedy (Burstyn).

Sammy & Rosie Get Laid 🐾🐾🐾 1987 An unusual social satire about a sexually liberated couple living in London whose lives are thrown into turmoil by the arrival of the man's father—a controversial politician in India. Provides a confusing look at sexual and class collisions. From the makers of "My Beautiful Laundrette." 97m/C V+S. GB Shashi Kapoor, Frances Barber, Claire Bloom, Ayub Khan-Din, Roland Gift, Wendy Gazelle, Meera Syal; D: Stephen Frears; W: Hanif Kureishi; C: Oliver Stapleton; M: Stanley Myers.

Sam's Son 🐾🐾 1984 (PG) Sentimental, autobiographical tale about how a young man's athletic prowess opens the door for an acting career in Hollywood. Good performance by Wallach as the boy's father. Self-indulgent, through entertaining. 107m/C VHS. Eli Wallach, Anne Jackson, Timothy Patrick Murphy, Hallie Todd, James Karen, Allan Hayes, Joanna Lee, Michael Landon; D: Michael Landon; W: Michael Landon.

Sammy, the Way-Out Seal 🐾 1962 Two young boys bring a mischievous seal to live in their beach house and try to keep it a secret from their parents. Disney in its early '60s phase. 89m/C VHS. Michael McGreevey, Billy Mumy, Patricia Barry, Robert Culp; D: Norman Tokar.

Samson in the Wax Museum 🐾½ 1961 Santo (here called Samson) the masked hero and athlete, battles the forces of darkness as a horde of female vampires attempt to make an unsuspecting girl their next queen. Not that if you're into the Mexican wrestling genre. 89m/B VHS, DVD, MX Santo, Lorena Lezlauzez, Jaime Fernandez, Maria Duval; D: Alfonso Corona Blake.

Samson vs. the Vampire Women 🐾½ 1961 Santo (here called Samson) the masked hero and athlete, battles the forces of darkness as a horde of female vampires attempt to make an unsuspecting girl their next queen. Not that if you're into the Mexican wrestling genre. 89m/B VHS, DVD, MX Santo, Lorena Lezlauzez, Jaime Fernandez, Maria Duval; D: Alfonso Corona Blake.

Samurai 3: Duel at Ganryu Island 🐾🐾🐾½ 1956 The final film of Inagaki's trilogy, in which Musashi Miyamoto confronts his lifelong enemy in a climactic battle. Depicts Miyamoto's spiritual awakening and realization that love and hatred exist in all of us. In Japanese with English subtitles. 102m/C VHS, DVD. JP Toshiro Mifune, Koji Tsuruta, Kaoru Yachigusa, Mariko Okada; D: Hiroshi Inagaki; W: Hiroshi Inagaki; C: Kazuo Yamada; M: Ikuma Dan.

Samurai Banners 🐾🐾½ Fūrin Kazan; Under the Banner of Samurai; Wind-Fire-Forest-Mountain 1969 In the 16th century, while working to advance the cause of a united Japan, a Samurai warrior and his master happens to be the daughter of a slain rival. Handsome production moves along well, balancing a complex story with grand battles and scenes of intimacy. 155m/C VHS, DVD. JP Toshiro Mifune, Yoshiko Sakuma, Kinnosuke Nakamura, Katsuo Nakamura, Masakazu Tamura, Yujiro Ishihara, Mayumi Ozora; C: Kazuo Yamada; M: Masaru Sato. VIDEO

Samson and the 7 Miracles of the World 🐾🐾 Maciste Alla Corte del Gran Khan; Maciste in the Great Khan; Goliath and the Golden City 1962 This rarely seen muscle epic. Hercules, Maciste, and Ursus all take part in a battle royale. 94m/C VHS. /T Allan Steel, Red Rossi; D: Giorgio Capitani.

Samson and His Mighty Challenge 🐾½ 1964 In this rarely seen muscle epic, Hercules, Maciste, McGann, Jonathan Rhys Meyers; D: Nicolas Roeg; W: Allan Scott; C: Raffaele Mertes; M: Marco Frisina. C.A.B.L.E.

Samson in the Wax Museum 🐾🐾 Santo en el Museo de Cera; Santo in the Wax Museum 1963 Masked Mexican wrestling hero Santo (here called Samson) does battle with a scientist who has discovered a way to make wax monsters come to life. 92m/B VHS, DVD. MX Santo, Claudio Brook, Ruben Roo, Norma Mora, Roxana Bellini; D: Alfonso Corona Blake.

Samson vs. the Vampire Women 🐾🐾 1961 Santo (here called Samson) the masked hero and athlete, battles the forces of darkness. 80m/C VHS, DVD. FR /T Santo, Scott, Yoko Tani, Gabriele Antonini, Leonardo Severini, Valeri Inkizhinov, Helene Chanel; D: Riccardo Freda; M: Les Baxter.

Samurai 1: Musashi Miyamoto 🐾🐾🐾½ 1955 The first installment in the film version of Musashi Miyamoto's life as he leaves his 17th-century village as a warrior in a local civil war only to return beaten and disillusioned. Justly award-winning. In Japanese with English subtitles. 92m/C VHS, DVD. JP Toshiro Mifune, Kaoru Yachigusa, Rentaro Mikuni, Eiko Miyoshi; D: Hiroshi Inagaki; W: Hiroshi Inagaki, Tokuhe Wakao; C: Jun Yasumoto; M: Ikuma Dan. Oscars '55: Foreign Film.

Samurai 2: Duel at Ichijoji Temple 🐾🐾🐾½ 1955 Inagaki's second film depicting the life of Musashi Miyamoto, the 17th century warrior, who wandered the disheveled landscape of feudal Japan looking for glory and love. In Japanese with English subtitles. 102m/C VHS, DVD. JP Toshiro Mifune, Akihiko Hirata, Daisuke Kato, Mariko Okada, Sachio Sakai, Kaoru Yachigusa; D: Hiroshi Inagaki; W: Hiroshi Inagaki; C: Jun Yasumoto; M: Ikuma Dan.

Samurai 3: Duel at Ganryu Island (see center column)

Samurai Cowboy 🐾½ 1993 Seto (Go) is a successful Japanese businessman who moves to Running Moose, Montana, and buying a cattle ranch. Talk about culture shock! Inoffensive fish-out-of-water comedy. Go is a popular singer in his native Japan. 101m/C VHS. Hiromi Go, Catherine

Samurai

Mary Stewart, Robert Conrad, Conchata Ferrell, Matt McCoy; **D:** Michael Keusch; **W:** Michael Keusch; **M:** Osamu Kitajima.

Samurai Rebellion ✓✓✓ *Rebellion* 1967 Isaburo (Mifune) is a reknowned swordsman in 18th-century Japan who is the model of loyalty until his overlord demands the return of a former mistress, who is now Isaburo's daughter-in-law. This insult to his family forces Isaburo to take a deadly stand, which turns out to be against his best friend (Nakadai) who's trying to uphold the feudal code. Lots of swordplay. Last in Kobayashi's trilogy following "Harakiri" (1962) and "Kwaidan" (1964). Japanese with subtitles. **121m/B VHS, DVD.** *JP* Toshiro Mifune, Tatsuya Nakadai; **D:** Masaki Kobayashi; **W:** Shinobu Hashimoto.

Samurai Reincarnation ✓✓ 1981 After the Shogunate government kills 38,000 Christian rioters in the revolt of 1638, and publicly beheads the leader Shiro Amakusa, Shiro reincarnates during a monstrous thunderstorm. Consumed with hatred, he discards the teachings of Jesus Christ and seeks revenge. In Japanese with English subtitles. **122m/C VHS, DVD.** *JP* Sonny Chiba, Kenji Sawada, Akiko Kana, Ken Ogata, Hiroyuki (Henry) Sanada; **D:** Kinji Fukasaku; **W:** Kiyoshi Hasegawa.

San Antonio ✓✓ 1945 A bad girl working in a dance hall turns over a new leaf on meeting the good guy. Trite plot, but good production. **105m/C VHS.** Errol Flynn, Alexis Smith, S.Z. Sakall, Victor Francen, Florence Bates, John Litel, Paul Kelly; **D:** David Butler; **M:** Max Steiner.

San Demetrio, London ✓✓ 1/2 1947 Set in 1940, the crew of a crippled tanker endures harrowing situations to reach port. Based on a true story, the plot sags with unbelievable scenes and holes on the plot side. **76m/B VHS.** Walter Fitzgerald, Mervyn Johns, Ralph Michael, Robert Beatty, Charles Victor, Frederick Piper; **D:** Charles Frend.

San Fernando Valley ✓✓ *San Fernando* 1944 Another lawman-in-evil-town epic. Rogers received his first on-screen kiss in 1944's biggest western. Fairly typical, pleasant cowboy tale. **54m/B VHS.** Jean Porter, Andrew Tombes, Edward (Ed) Gargan, Roy Rogers, Dale Evans; **D:** John English; **W:** Dorrell McGowan, Stuart E. McGowan; **C:** William Bradford; **M:** Gordon Jenkins.

San Francisco ✓✓✓1/2 1936 The San Francisco Earthquake of 1906 serves as the background for a romance between an opera singer and a Barbary Coast saloon owner. Somewhat overdone but gripping tale of passion and adventure in the West. Wonderful special effects. Finale consists of historic earthquake footage. Also available colorized. ♫"San Francisco; A Heart That's Free; Would You?; Air des Bijoux; Sempre Libera. **116m/B VHS, DVD.** Jeanette MacDonald, Clark Gable, Spencer Tracy, Jack Holt, Jessie Ralph, Al Shean, Ted Healy, Shirley Ross, Margaret Irving, Harold Huber, Edgar Kennedy, Kenneth Harlan, Roger Imhof, Russell Simpson, Bert Roach, Warren Hymer; **D:** Woodbridge S. Van Dyke; **W:** Anita Loos. Oscars '36: Sound.

San Franpsycho ✓ 2006 (R) Serial killer. Yawn. Two San Francisco detectives, a cop and a reporter hunt for a serial killer who has been sending the newshound letters after each slaying. **7m/ C DVD.** Joe Estevez, Jose Rosette, Todd Bridges, Eleni C. Krimiscos, Chris Angelo, Victor Zaragoza, Elias Castillo; **D:** Eduardo Quiroz, Jose Quiroz; **W:** Eduardo Quiroz, Jose Quiroz; **C:** Rocky Robinson; **M:** Eduardo Quiroz. VIDEO

San Quentin ✓✓1/2 1937 Former army officer Stephen Jameson (O'Brien) heads to San Q to try some reform work on the rowdy cons, including Red Kennedy (Bogart), who isn't buying his routine. Jameson has it bad for Red's singing sister May (Sheridan), who thinks he's okay for trying to help Red. Only Red, egged on by con Hanson (Sawyer), escapes the gang to have it out with May. Convinced it's real love, Red surrenders and makes a plea to give Jameson's methods a chance—which Red doesn't get. Much of the melodrama was shot in and around the prison itself. **70m/B DVD.** Pat O'Brien, Humphrey Bogart, Ann Sheridan, Barton MacLane, Joseph (Joe) Sawyer, Veda Ann Borg, Joe King, Gordon Oliver, Emmett Vogan, Garry Owen, Marc Lawrence, George Lloyd; **D:** Lloyd Bacon; **W:** John Bright, Peter Milne, Robert Tasker; **C:** Sid Hickox; **M:** Charles Maxwell, David Raksin, Heinz Roemheld.

Sanctimony woof! 2001 It's just like "American Psycho"... only much, much worse. Director Uwe Boll, the second worst thing that Germany's ever been responsible for, steals liberally from Bret Easton Ellis and David Fincher's "Se7en" in one of the clumsiest serial killer stories ever put to film. Two cops (Pare and Rubin) suspect that stock broker Tom Merrick (Van Dien) is really the psycho murderer known as the "Monkey Maker" (Worst. Villain. Name. Ever.) So what do they do about it? Not much. Boll's screenplay (He writes too!) is as aimless as friendly fire and just as entertaining. By the time you get to the inexplicable snuff film sequence, you'll be wondering if Boll had a stroke halfway through writing the script. **87m/C VHS, DVD.** *GE US* Casper Van Dien, Eric Roberts, Michael Pare, Jennifer Rubin, Catherine Oxenberg; **D:** Uwe Boll; **W:** Uwe Boll; **C:** Mathias Neumann; **M:** Uwe Spies. VIDEO

Sanctuary ✓✓ 1998 (R) A former government agent, Luke Connolly has completely changed his life by becoming a clergyman. However, when his old agency discovers his whereabouts, the deadly skills he's renounced may be all that can save him. **110m/C VHS, DVD.** Mark Dacascos, Kylie Travis, Jaimz Woolvett, Alan Scarfe; **D:** Tibor Takacs; **W:** Michael Stokes; **M:** Norman Orenstein. VIDEO

Sanctuary of Fear ✓1/2 *Girl in the Park* 1979 A priest in New York City helps an actress subjected to a series of terrorizing incidents. Uninspired would-be TV pilot based on Chesterton's "Father Brown" series. **98m/C VHS.** George Hearn, Barnard Hughes, Kay Lenz, Michael McGuire, Robert Schenkkan, David Rasche, Fred Gwynne, Elizabeth Wilson; **D:** John Llewellyn Moxey. TV

Sand ✓✓ 2000 Tyler Briggs (Vartan) wants to start over—away from his violent father (Quaid) and brothers. So after his mother's death, he heads to the quiet beach town where his mom grew up. There Tyler falls for Sandy (Wuhrer) and starts to make a peaceful new life but trouble and family follow. **90m/C VHS, DVD.** Michael Vartan, Denis Leary, Randy Quaid, Kari Wuhrer, Marshall Bell, Julie Delpy, Rodney Eastman, Bodhi (Pine) Elfman, Emilio Estevez, John Hawkes, Jon Lovitz, Norman Reedus, Peter Simmons, Harry Dean Stanton; **D:** Matt Palmieri; **W:** Matt Palmieri; **C:** John Skotchdopole.

Sand and Blood ✓✓1/2 *Blood and Sand; De Sable et de Sang* 1987 A young matador who wishes to escape poverty and a young, cultivated doctor, who despises bullfighting, meet and eventually become friends. A woman enters the picture and completes the love triangle. Widely praised by critics. Interesting and moving. In French with English subtitles. **101m/C VHS.** *FR* Sami Frey, Andre Dussollier, Clementine Celarie, Patrick Catalifo, Maria Casares, Catherine Rouvel; **D:** Jeanne Labrune; **W:** Jeanne Labrune.

Sand Trap ✓✓1/2 1997 (R) Wealthy businessman Nelson Yeager (Koepenick) gets pushed over a cliff by his best friend Jack (James). But when Jack and Nelson's not-so-grieving widow Margo (Morehead) report the accident and the local sheriff (Thompson) goes to find the body, it's not there. Now a murder plot turns into a desire for revenge. Low-budget modern noir. **99m/C VHS.** Elizabeth Morehead, David John James, Brad Koepenick, Bob Thompson; **D:** Harris Done; **W:** Harris Done; **C:** Mark W. Gray. VIDEO

Sandakan No. 8 ✓✓✓ *Brothel 8; Sandakan House 8* 1974 A Japanese woman working as a journalist befriends an old woman who was sold into prostitution in Borneo in the early 1900s. Justly acclaimed feminist story dramatizes the role of women in Japanese society. Japanese with English subtitles. **121m/C VHS.** *JP* Kinuyo Tanaka, Yoko Takakashi, Komake Kurihara, Eitaro (Sakae, Saka Ozawa) Ozawa; **D:** Kei Kumai. Berlin Intl. Film Fest. '75: Actress.

Sanders of the River ✓✓✓ *Bosambo* 1935 A British officer in colonial Africa must work with the local chief to quell a rebellion. Tale of imperialism. Dated but still interesting and of value. Robeson is very good; superb location cinematography. **80m/B VHS, DVD.** *GB* Paul Robeson, Leslie Banks, Robert Cochran; **D:** Zoltan Korda; **C:** Georges Perinal.

Sandflow ✓✓1/2 1937 Well-made Western with Jones playing a man whose father has cheated many ranchers. Jones is out to prove all of his father's misdeeds and build a new life for himself in this above-average oater. **58m/B VHS.** Buck Jones, Lita Chevret, Robert F. (Bob) Kortman, Arthur Aylesworth, Robert Terry, Enrique DeRosas; **D:** Lesley Selander.

The Sandlot ✓✓✓ 1993 (PG) Young Scotty (Guiry) moves to a new neighborhood in California in 1962 and tries to make friends despite not knowing anything about playing baseball. His scrappy teammates include the friendly Benny (Vitar), a chubby loud-mouthed catcher named Ham (Renna), and Squints (Leopardi), a would-be Lothario before his time. Action revolves around Scotty's attempt to get baseball autographed by Babe Ruth back from the clutches of giant killer junkyard dog owned by Jones before dad Leary discovers it's missing. Small wonder is nostalgic without being sentimental, and tells its tale with grace and humor, supported by a period soundtrack. **101m/C VHS, DVD.** Tom Guiry, Mike Vitar, Patrick Renna, Chauncey Leopardi, Marty York, Brandon Adams, Denis Leary, Karen Allen, James Earl Jones, Maury Wills, Art LaFleur, Marley Shelton, Brooke Adams, Robert Gunter; **C:** Anthony B. Richmond; **M:** David Newman; **V:** Arliss Howard.

The Sandpiper ✓✓ 1965 Free-spirited artist Taylor falls in love with Burton, the married headmaster of her son's boarding school. Muddled melodrama offers little besides starpower. Filmed at Big Sur, California. ♫The Shadow of Your Smile. **117m/C VHS.** Elizabeth Taylor, Richard Burton, Charles Bronson, Eva Marie Saint, Robert Webber, Morgan Mason; **D:** Vincente Minnelli; **C:** Milton Krasner; **M:** Johnny Mandel. Oscars '65: Song ("The Shadow of Your Smile").

Sandra of a Thousand Delights ✓✓✓1/2 *Sandra; Of a Thousand Delights; Vaghe Stelle Dell'Orsa* 1965 Haunting drama with strong women (and weak men). Sandra returns to Italy from her American home in order to attend a ceremony honoring her father—a Jewish scientist who died in a Nazi concentration camp. Back with her family, Sandra tries to deal with her past, including her mother's possible betrayal of her father and her brother's incestuous longings. Italian with subtitles. **100m/B VHS.** *IT* Claudia Cardinale, Jean Sorel, Marie Bell, Michael Craig, Renzo Ricci; **D:** Luchino Visconti; **W:** Luchino Visconti, Suso Cecchi D'Amico.

Sands of Iwo Jima ✓✓✓ 1949 Wayne earned his first Oscar nomination as a tough Marine sergeant, in one of his best roles. He trains a squad of rebellious recruits in New Zealand in 1943. Later they are responsible for the capture of Iwo Jima from the Japanese—one of the most difficult campaigns of the Pacific Theater. Includes striking real war footage. **109m/B VHS, DVD.** John Wayne, Forrest Tucker, John Agar, Richard Jaeckel, Adele Mara, Wally Cassell, James Brown, Richard Webb, Arthur Franz, Julie Bishop, William Murphy, George Tyne, Hal Baylor, John McGuire, Martin Milner, William (Bill) Self, Peter Coe, I. Stanford Jolley, Col. D.M. Shoup, Lt. Col. H.P. Crowe, Capt. Harold G. Shrier, Rene A. Gagnon, Ira H. Hayes, John H. Bradley; **D:** Allan Dwan; **W:** Harry Brown, James Edward Grant; **C:** Reggie Lanning; **M:** Victor Young.

Sands of Sacrifice ✓✓1/2 *Tangled Trails* 1921 Hart, a Northwest Mountie, seeks an unscrupulous promoter who's selling worthless mining stock. **56m/B VHS.** Neal Hart, Violet Palmer, Gladys Hampton, Jules Cowles, Jean Bary, Ed Roseman; **D:** Charles Bartlett.

The Sandy Bottom Orchestra ✓✓1/2 2000 Sandy Bottom, Wisconsin is a quaint small town that is resistant to change. Big city Ingrid (Headly), a former classical pianist, discovered this when she married local dairy farmer Norman (Irwin)—he wants to include a classical concert in the town's annual summer festival rather than the usual marching band and is meeting with opposition. Their daughter Rachel (Zima) also longs to fit in but her musical talent has outgrown the limited resources of the community and decisions must be made. **100m/C VHS, DVD.** Glenne Headly, Tom Irwin, Madeline Zima, Jane Powell, Richard McMillan, Tamara Hope, Roger Dunn, Bradley Reid; **D:** Bradley Wigor; **W:** Joseph Maurer; **C:** Robert Primes; **M:** David Bell. CABLE

Sanjuro ✓✓✓ *Tsubaki Sanjuro* 1962 In this offbeat, satiric sequel to "Yojimbo," a talented but lazy samurai comes to the aid of a group of naive young warriors. The conventional ideas of good and evil are quickly tossed aside; much less earnest than other Kurosawa Samurai outings. In Japanese with English subtitles. **96m/B VHS, DVD.** *JP* Toshiro Mifune, Tatsuya Nakadai, Yuzo Kayama; **D:** Akira Kurosawa; **W:** Akira Kurosawa, Ryuzo Kikushima, Hideo Oguni; **C:** Fukuzo Koizumi, Takao Saito; **M:** Masaru Sato.

Sans Soleil ✓✓✓ *Sunless* 1982 A female narrator reads and comments on the letters she receives from a friend, a freelance cameraman traveling through Japan, West Africa, and Iceland. The cameraman meditates on the cultural dislocation he feels and the meaning of his work and of life itself. Both narrator and cameraman remain unseen with the visuals being the cameraman's work in progress. **100m/C VHS.** *FR* **D:** Chris Marker; **W:** Chris Marker; **Nar:** Alexandra Stewart.

Sanshiro Sugata ✓✓✓ 1943 Kurosawa's first film. A young man learns discipline in martial arts from a patient master. Climactic fight scene is early signature Kurosawa. In Japanese with English subtitles. **82m/B VHS, DVD.** *JP* Denjiro Okochi, Yukiko Todoroki, Ranko Hanai, Ryonosuke Tsukigata, Sugisaku Aoyama, Kokuten Kodo, Susumo Fusuita, Takashi Shimura; **D:** Akira Kurosawa.

Sansho the Bailiff ✓✓✓ *The Bailiff; Sansho Dayu* 1954 A world masterpiece by Mizoguchi about feudal society in 11th century Japan. A woman and her children are sold into prostitution and slavery. As an adult, the son seeks to right the ills of his society. Powerful and tragic, and often more highly esteemed than "Ugetsu." In Japanese with English subtitles. **132m/B VHS, DVD.** *JP* Kinuyo Tanaka, Yoshiaki Hanayagi, Kyoko Kagawa, Eitaro Shindo, Ichiro Sugai; **D:** Kenji Mizoguchi; **W:** Yoshikata Yoda; **M:** Fumio Hayasaka.

Santa Baby ✓✓1/2 2006 (PG) Amusing comedy about finding the true spirit of Christmas. Mary (McCarthy) is a successful marketing exec who decides her dad's (Wendt) business needs to run more efficiently. And, of course, dad is Santa Claus. Mary returns to the North Pole when Santa has some heart trouble and tries to whip those elves into shape

Santa Claus Conquers the Martians 🎬 *Santa Claus Defeats the Aliens* 1964 A Martian spaceship comes to Earth and kidnaps Santa Claus and two children. It seems, are jealous that Earth tykes have Christmas. Features, then-child star Pia Zadora. 80m/C **VHS, DVD.** Dudley Moore, John Lithgow, David Huddleston, Judy Cornwell, Burgess Meredith; **D:** Jeannot Szwarc; **W:** David Newman; **M:** Henry Mancini.

Santa Claus WOOF! 1959 Santa Claus teams up with Merlin the Magician to fend off an evil spirit who would ruin everyone's Christmas. Mexican camp classic. 94m/C **VHS, DVD, MX** Jose Elias Moreno, Cesareo Quezada; **D:** Rene Cardona Sr.; **Nar:** Ken Smith.

Santa Claus: The Movie 🎬🎬½ 1985 (PG) A big-budgeted spectacle about an elf who falls prey to an evil toy maker and almost ruins Christmas and Santa Claus. Boring. 'Tis-the-season fantasy-drama, meant to warm our cockles. 112m/C **VHS, DVD, MX** Dudley Moore, John Lithgow, David Huddleston, Judy Cornwell, Burgess Meredith; **D:** Jeannot Szwarc; **W:** David Newman; **C:** Arthur Ibbetson; **M:** Henry Mancini.

The Santa Clause 🎬🎬½ 1994 (PG) If you like Allen, you'll enjoy this lightweight holiday comedy about divorced workaholic dad Scott Calvin and eight-year-old son Charlie (Lloyd). Seems Santa injures himself falling off the Calvin roof and dad winds up putting on Santa's suit. But as it turns out when you put on Santa's suit, you become Santa, including a noticeable weight gain, a fluffy beard, and all those reindeer and elves to deal with (but where's Mrs. Claus?). 97m/C **VHS, DVD.** Tim Allen, Eric Lloyd, Judge Reinhold, Wendy Crewson, David Krumholtz, Mary Gross; **D:** John Pasquin; **W:** Leo Benvenuti, Steve Rudnick; **C:** Walt Lloyd; **M:** Michael Convertino, Blockbuster '95. Male Newcomer, T. (Allen).

The Santa Clause 2 🎬🎬½ 2002 (G) Sequel to the 1994 film has Santa (Allen again) facing expulsion if he doesn't find himself a Mrs. Claus. He also has to deal with the fact that his son Charlie (Lloyd) just landed on the "naughty" list. When Santa/Scott heads back to the U.S. to help Charlie, he runs afoul of the school's female principal (can you see where this is going?). Back at the Pole, the clone Santa he left in charge is staging a coup, of sorts. Funnier, with more of an edge than the original; this one gives adults plenty to smirk at while the kids are distracted by all the yuletide yahooey. 99m/C **VHS, DVD.** US Tim Allen, Elizabeth Mitchell, David Krumholtz, Eric Lloyd, Judge Reinhold, Wendy Crewson, Spencer Breslin, Liliana Mumy, Art LaFleur, Kevin Pollak, Jay Thomas, Michael Dorn, Danielle Woodman, Aisha Tyler; **D:** Michael Lembeck; **W:** Don Rhymer, Cinco Paul, Ken Daurio; **C:** Adam Greenberg; **M:** George S. Clinton.

The Santa Clause 3: The Escape Clause 🎬½ 2006 (G) Tim Allen returns for a dead reindeer in this pointless sequel. Reprising his role as Scott/Santa, he's faced with a pregnant Mrs. Claus (Mitchell) and an uprising by Jack Frost (Short), who wants to turn the North Pole into Upper Vegas. Forced to deal with a visit by his in-laws (Arkin, Margret) and toy sabotage by Frost, he contemplates quitting his seasonal job. The anti-commercialism message is a little hypocritical for a movie that could have been called "Beclause We Want More of your Dough." 91m/C **DVD, Blu-ray Disc.** US Tim Allen, Elizabeth Mitchell, Martin Short, Spencer Breslin, Judge Reinhold, Wendy Crewson, Eric Lloyd, Liliana Mumy, Alan Arkin, Ann Margret, Cameos: Kevin Pollak, Jay Thomas, Peter Boyle, Aisha Tyler; **D:** Michael Lembeck; **W:** Edward Decter, John J. Strauss; **C:** Robbie Greenberg; **M:** George S. Clinton.

Santa Fe 🎬🎬 1951 Action-packed western with Scott playing a Confederate soldier who heads West to take a job with the Santa Fe Railroad. However, his brothers, with their wounded rebel pride, have different ideas for forgetting the defeat. Refusing to 'take money from Northern businesses, they become outlaws. Based on a story by Louis Stevens and the novel by James Marshall. 89m/C **VHS, DVD.** Randolph Scott, Janis Carter, Jerome Courtland, Peter Thompson, John Archer, Warner Anderson, Roy Roberts, Billy House; **D:** Irving Pichel; **W:** Kenneth Gamet.

Santa Fe 🎬🎬½ 1997 (R) Muddled romantic drama with an appealing cast. It's taken cop Paul Thomas (Cole) eight months to recover from bullet wounds suffered in a shoot-out with a local cult. In the meantime, wife Leah's (Kelley) distanced herself from the marriage but still urges Paul into group counseling with charismatic Eleanor (Davidovich). Despite Paul's mistrust of her guru-like status, he's naturally drawn to Eleanor (and she to him). There's some tedious subplot stuff but the leads do fine. 97m/C **VHS, DVD.** Gary Cole, Lolita (David) Davidovich, Sheila Kelley, Tina Majorino, Jere Burns, Pamela Reed, Phyllis Frelich, Mark Medoff, Tony Plana, Jeffrey Jones; **D:** Andrew Shea, Mark Medoff; **C:** Paul Elliott; **M:** Mark Governor.

Santa Fe Bound 🎬🎬 1937 Tyler must work to clear his name when he is falsely accused of having murdered a man. 58m/B **VHS.** Tom Tyler, Jeanne Martel, Richard Cramer, Charles "Slim" Whitaker, Edward Cassidy, Late (Lafayette) McKee, Dorothy Woods, Charles "Blackie" King; **D:** Harry S. Webb.

Santa Fe Marshal 🎬🎬 1940 The 27th Hopalong Cassidy movie, if anyone's counting. In the title job the Hopster goes undercover with a medicine show to smash a criminal gang. A little different of the crooked mastermind. 66m/B **VHS, MX** of the surprise identity William Boyd, Russell Hayden, Marjorie Rambeau, Bernadene Hayes, Earle Hodgins, Kenneth Harlan, Eddie Dean; **D:** Lesley Selander.

Santa Fe Stampede 🎬🎬½ 1938 The Three Mesquiteers join an old prospector in his claim but when he is killed, one of them (Wayne) is framed. The photography makes up for the weak storyline and direction. 58m/B **VHS, DVD.** John Wayne, Ray Corrigan, Max Terhune, William Farnum, June Martel, Leroy Mason, Yakima Canutt, Curley Dresden; **D:** George Sherman.

Santa Fe Trail 🎬🎬 1940 Historically inaccurate but entertaining tale about the pre-Civil War fight for "bloody Kansas." The action-adventure depicts future Civil War Generals J.E.B. Stuart (Flynn) and George Armstrong Custer (Reagan) as they begin their military career (although Custer was really just a youth at this time). Good action scenes. Also available colorized. 110m/B **VHS, DVD.** Errol Flynn, Olivia de Havilland, Ronald Reagan, Van Heflin, Raymond Massey, Alan Hale; **D:** Michael Curtiz; **W:** Robert Buckner; **C:** Sol Polito; **M:** Max Steiner.

Santa Fe Uprising 🎬🎬½ 1946 Red Ryder has to save Little Beaver from kidnappers. Good first entry for Lane in the "Red Ryder" series. 54m/B **VHS.** Allan "Rocky" Lane, Robert (Bobby) Blake, Martha Wentworth, Barton MacLane, Jack La Rue, Dick Curtis, Pat Michaels, Edythe Elliott, Tom London, Edmund Cobb; **D:** R.G. Springsteen; **W:** Earle Snell; **C:** Bud Thackery.

Santa Sangre 🎬🎬🎬 1990 (R) A circus in Mexico City, a temple devoted to a saint without arms, and a son who faithfully dotes upon his armless mother are just a few of the bizarre things in this wildly fantastic film. Fenix acts as his mother's arms, plays the piano for her, and carries out any wish she desires—including murder. Visually intoxicating but strange outing may prove too graphic for some viewers. Not as rigorous as other Jodorowsky outings. Also available in an NC-17 version. 123m/C **VHS, IT MX** Axel Jodorowsky, Blanca Guerra, Thelma Tixou, Adan Jodorowsky, Faviola Tapia, Jesus Juarez; **D:** Alejandro Jodorowsky; **W:** Robert Leoni, Claudio Argento, Alejandro Jodorowsky; **C:** Danielle Nannuzzi; **M:** Simon Boswell.

Santee 🎬🎬 1973 (PG) A father-son relationship develops between a bounty hunter and the son of a man he killed. Good, but not great, Western. 93m/C **VHS, DVD.** Glenn Ford, Dara Wynter, Jay Silverheels, John Larch, Michael Burns; **D:** Gary Nelson.

Santa with Muscles 🎬½ 1996 (PG) Cartoonish holiday-themed comedy finds the Hulkster as Scrooge-like millionaire Blake Thorne. Through a series of stupid circumstances, Thorne winds up in a Santa suit in a shopping mall hiding from the cops. But a blow to the head makes him believe he's the Jolly-Old-Elf himself and he comes to the aid of a local orphanage, whose tykes are about to be evicted. Silly's the kindest thing to say. 97m/C **VHS.** Hulk Hogan, Don Stark, Ed Begley Jr., Clint Howard, Robin Curtis, Garrett Morris, Adam Wylie; **D:** John Murlowski; **W:** Jonathan Bond, Fred Mata, Dorrie Krum Raymond; **C:** Michael Gleiner; **M:** James Covell.

The Santa Trap 🎬🎬½ 2002 Having just moved from snowy New England to the desert Southwest, it just doesn't feel like Christmas to the Emerson family. Young Judy is afraid Santa isn't real, so she sets a trap and captures a jolly intruder, who's arrested and thrown in jail. Now what'll happen to Christmas if Santa can't make his deliveries? And what about those embittered Emersons' roof? 92m/C **DVD.** Shelley Long, Robert Hays, Dick Van Patten, Stacy Keach, Sierra Abel, Corbin Bernsen, Amanda Pays, Steve Monroe; **D:** John Shepphird; **W:** Jom Shepphird; **C:** Neal Brown; **M:** Joseph Conlan. TV

Santitos 🎬🎬 1999 (R) Esperanza Diaz (Heredia) is a young Mexican widow whose 12-year-old daughter Blanca (Zapata) has supposedly died, although her mother never saw the child's body. When Esperanza's favorite saint, St. Jude the patron of lost causes, starts appearing to her, she begins a search for her lost child that takes her to the La Casa Rosa brothel in Tijuana. But faith and motherly love will help Esperanza survive anything. Disarmingly innocent film based on the novel by Escandon, who also wrote the screenplay. Spanish with subtitles. 99m/C **VHS, DVD, MX** Dolores Heredia, Fernando Torre Lazhari, Juan Duarte, Ana Bertha Espin, Meya Zamora, Roberto Cobo; **D:** Alejandro Springall; **W:** Mara Ampara Escandon; **C:** Xavier Perez Grobet; **M:** Carlo Nicolau, Rosino Serrano.

Sapphire 🎬🎬🎬 1959 Two Scotland Yard detectives seek the killer of a beautiful black woman who was passing for white. Good mystery and topical social comment; remains interesting and engrossing. Superbly acted all around. 92m/C **VHS.** GB Nigel Patrick, Yvonne Mitchell, Michael Craig, Paul Massie, Bernard Miles; **D:** Basil Dearden British Acad. '59. Film.

The Saphead 🎬🎬½ 1921 Keaton's first outing as the rich playboy has him playing the none-to-bright son of Wall Street mogul. Some great moments provide a glimpse of cinematic greatness to come from the budding comedic genius. Based on the play "The New Henrietta" by Winchell Smith and Victor Mapes. Silent. 70m/B **VHS, DVD.** William H. Crane, Buster Keaton, Carol Holloway, Edward Connelly, Irving Cummings; **D:** Herbert Blache; **W:** June Mathis; **C:** Harold Wenstrom.

Saps at Sea 🎬🎬½ 1940 A doctor advises Ollie to take a rest away from his job at a horn factory. He and Stan rent a boat, which they plan to keep tied to the dock, until an escaped criminal happens by and uses the boys (and their boat) for his getaway. Cramer is a good bad guy; Stan and Ollie cause too much trouble, as always. 57m/B **VHS.** Stan Laurel, Oliver Hardy, James Finlayson, Ben Turpin, Richard Cramer; **D:** Gordon Douglas.

Sara 🎬🎬½ 1997 A harsh winter in the 'Sarah' saga is set in 1918. **W** Saragossa 1965 Ambitious fantasy based

Sara Dane 🎬🎬 1981 A strong young woman in the 18th century rises in the world through marriage and business acumen. Interesting but imperfect and slow. 150m/C **VHS.** Juliet Jordan, Sean Scully; **D:** Rod Hardy.

The Santa Fe Trail 1951 (see above)

Sarabande 🎬🎬🎬½ 2003 (R) Bergman's final film has his "Scenes From a Marriage" (1974) characters reuniting after a 30-year separation. When Marianne (Ullmann) visits Johan (Josephson) she finds he is still bitter and full of hatred. Henrik (from another marriage) and granddaughter Karin who live in his guest house. When Karin is provided an opportunity to study music in Helsinki, an emotional confrontation comes to a head. Ex-captioned swan song. 107m/C **DVD, SWIT, GE FI, DK, AT** Erland Josephson, Liv Ullmann, Borje Ahlstedt, Julia Dufvenius, Gunne Fredt; **D:** Ingmar Bergman; **W:** Ingmar Bergman; **C:** Raymond Wemmenlov, Sofi Stridh, P.O. Lantto.

Sarafina! 🎬🎬🎬 1992 (PG-13) Part coming-of-age saga, part political drama, part musical, and all emotionally powerful. Sarafina is a young girl in a township school in Soweto, South Africa in the mid-'70s, gradually coming into a political awakening amid the Soweto riots. Khumalo recreates her stage role as the glowing and defiant Sarafina with both Goldberg and Makeba good in their roles as Sarafina's outspoken and inspirational teacher and her long-suffering mother, respectively. Adapted from Ngema's stage musical. 98m/C **VHS, DVD.** Leleti Khumalo, Whoopi Goldberg, Miriam Makeba, John Kani, Mbongeni Ngema, Wil-liam Ndlovu; **D:** Darrell Roodt; **W:** Mbongeni Ngema, William Nicholson; **M:** Stanley Myers.

The Saragossa Manuscript 🎬🎬🎬½ *Rekopis Znaleziony w Saragossie* 1965 Ambitious fantasy based on the 1813 novel "Sanatorium Under the Hourglass" by Bruno Schulz. A romantic Belgian army officer, travelling to Spain, meets two beautiful princesses who send him on a fantastic journey to prove himself worthy of their affections. Polish with subtitles. 174m/B **VHS, DVD.** PL Zbigniew Cybulski, Iga Cembrzynska, Joanna Jedryka, Slawomir Lindner; **D:** Wojciech Has; **W:** Tadeusz Kwiatkowski; **C:** Mieczyslaw Jahoda; **M:** Krzysztof Penderecki.

Sarah, Plain and Tall 🎬🎬🎬 1991 (G) New England school teacher (Close) travels to Kansas circa 1910 to care for the family of a widowed farmer who has advertised for a wife. Superior entertainment for the whole family. Adapted from Patricia MacLachlan's novel of the same name by MacLachlan and Carol Sobieski. Nominated for nine Emmy Awards. A "Hallmark Hall of Fame" presentation. 98m/C **VHS, DVD.** Glenn Close, Christopher Walken, Lexi (Fenn) Randall, Margaret Sophie Stein, Jon (John) DeVries, Christopher Bell; **D:** Glenn Jordan; **W:** Carol Sobieski; **C:** Mike Fash; **M:** David Shire. TV

Sarah, Plain and Tall: Skylark 🎬🎬½ *Skylark* 1993 (G) In a sequel to "Hallmark Hall of Fame's hugely successful "Sarah, Plain and Tall," the whole Kansas crew shows up for more of their little-farm-on-the-prairie life. After two years in America's squarest state, mail-order bride Sarah (Close) loves Jacob (Walken), but not the scenery and still yearns for the lush greenery of Maine. When drought and fire threaten the farm, Jacob fears for the "family's health and safety, and sends them back East for a visit. Close's "tough Yankee" expression grows a bit tiresome in a plot that is a tad predictable, yet the simplistic charm and nostalgia are irresistible and work to propel this quality Hallmark production. 98m/C **VHS, DVD.** Glenn Close, Christopher Walken, Lexi (Fenn) Randall, Christopher Bell, Tresa Hughes, Lois Smith, Lee Richardson, Elizabeth Wilson, Margaret Sophie Stein, Jon (John) DeVries, James Feltham, Woody Watson; **D:** Joseph Sargent; **W:** Patricia MacLachlan; **C:** Mike Fash; **M:** David Shire. TV

Sarah, Plain and Tall: Winter's End 🎬🎬🎬 *Winter's End* 1999 (G) The third installment of the "Sarah, Plain and Tall" saga takes a strange turn when Jacob's (Walken), and their three children Jacob's family knew Jacob was a boy, suddenly shows up on their farm. A devastating storm proves just as paralyzing as the unresolved feelings between Jacob and John, but Sarah is determined to do what's best for her family. **99m/C VHS, DVD.** Glenn Close, Christopher Walken, Jack Palance, Lexi (Faith) Randall, Christopher Bell, Emily Osment; **D:** Glenn Jordan; **C:** Ralf Bode; **M:** David Shire. **TV**

Sarah Silverman: Jesus Is Magic ♂♂½ 2005 Stand-up show performed by delightfully potty-mouthed comedian Silverman at North Hollywood's El Portal Theater, with a couple of offstage skits thrown in. Her routine is an equal opportunity offender of race, religion, sex, and current events as Silverman hypes her Jewish American Princess attractiveness and her nice-girl-gone-naughty persona. Best left to her fans. **72m/C DVD. US** Sarah Silverman; **D:** Liam Lynch; **C:** Rhet Baer. **M:** Sarah Silverman, Liam Lynch.

Sarah's Child ♂♂½ 1996 (PG-13) Sarah LaMere is devastated to learn that she can never have children. While husband Michael tries to accept, Sarah's upbringing has led her to believe that's her only purpose in life and she becomes increasingly unbalanced. Seemingly out of nowhere children's clothes and toys appear in their home and soon a strange young girl named Melissa appears, whom Sarah treats as her own child. When their landlady dies horribly after questioning Melissa, Michael is afraid the line between reality and fantasy has been breached but just how can he fight? **90m/C VHS, DVD.** Mary Parker Williams, Michael Berger, Ruth Hale, Bryce Chamberlain; **D:** Ron Beckstrom; **W:** Mufty Mead Thomas; **C:** Gregg Stouffer; **M:** Jim Ball, Glenn Workman.

Saratoga ♂♂½ 1937 Gable plays a bookie and Harlow the daughter of an impoverished horse breeder in this romantic comedy centered around the race tracks. This was the final film appearance for Harlow, who died before the film's completion. Mary Dees was chosen as her stand-in and had to finish many of the scenes. "Saratoga" was released just a month after Harlow's death and became one of the biggest moneymakers of the year. **94m/B VHS.** Jean Harlow, Clark Gable, Lionel Barrymore, Walter Pidgeon, Frank Morgan, Una Merkel, Cliff Edwards, George Zucco, Hattie McDaniel, Jonathan Hale; **D:** Jack Conway; **W:** Anita Loos, Robert Hopkins.

Saratoga Trunk ♂♂½ 1945 Lavish, if slow-moving, version of Edna Ferber's romance novel reteams Cooper and Bergman (who starred in "For Whom the Bell Tolls"). It's 1875 New Orleans and bitter Clio, the half-Creole illegitimate daughter of a local, is determined to marry rich. But first, she gets involved with Texas gambler Clint Maroon (Cooper). He's in a business deal with wealthy Van Steed (Warburton), about the Saratoga railroad line, and Clio decides to go after him. Of course, she really wants Clint and they go through lots of bother before ending up together. Filmed in 1943 but release was delayed because of WWII. **135m/B VHS.** Gary Cooper, Ingrid Bergman, John Warburton, Flora Robson, Florence Bates, Jerry Austin; **D:** Sam Wood; **W:** Casey Robinson; **C:** Ernest Haller; **M:** Max Steiner.

Sardinia Kidnapped ♂♂½ 1975 A beautiful girl is trapped in a clash between two powerful families while on vacation in Sardinia, where the peasants' custom is to kidnap a member of a rival family and then exchange the victim for land. Former documentary maker Mingozzi creates a realistic and uncompromising look at culture and change. In Italian; dubbed. **95m/C VHS. IT** Charlotte Rampling, Franco Nero; **D:** Gianfranco Mingozzi.

Sartana's Here... Trade Your Pistol for a Coffin ♂ 1970 A soldier of fortune searches for a missing shipment of gold in the Old West. **92m/C VHS, DVD. IT** George Hilton, Charles Southwood, Erika Blanc, Linda Sini; **D:** Giuliano Carnimeo; **W:** Tito Carpi; **C:** Stelvio Massi; **M:** Francesco De Masi.

S.A.S. San Salvador ♂ 1984 A CIA agent tries to prevent a psychotic from running amok in El Salvador. **95m/C VHS. FR GE** Raymond Harmstorf, Anton Diffring, Sybil Danning, Miles O'Keeffe, Dagmar Lassander,

Catherine Jarrett; **D:** Raoul Coutard; **W:** Gerard de Villiers; **C:** Georges Liron; **M:** Michel Magne.

Sasquatch woof! 1976 Purported "documentary" about the mythical creature Bigfoot. Includes pictures of the "actual" monster. For those real stupid moods. **94m/C VHS, DVD.** George Lauris; **D:** Ed Ragozzini.

Sasquatch ♂♂½ *The Untold* 2002 (R) Mogul Harlan Knowles (Henriksen) runs a bio-tech company and is frantic when one of the company's planes crashes in the forests of the Pacific Northwest. Not only is his daughter (Parker) aboard but so is the very expensive prototype of a DNA testing machine. So Knowles assembles a rescue team and heads into the woods—only to discover the plane's crew torn to shreds. **86m/C VHS, DVD. CA** Lance Henriksen, Andrea Roth, Erica Durance; **D:** Jonas Quastel; **W:** Jonas Quastel, Chris Lanning; **C:** Shaun Lawless; **M:** Tal Bergman, Larry Seymour. **VIDEO**

The Sasquatch Gang ♂ *The Sasquatch Dumpling Gang* 2006 Three mild-mannered loser buddies (Sumpter, Palmer, Pinkston) upset their stoner neighbor Zerk (Long) with their sword-and-fantasy fights. So he decides to play a trick by having the trio stumble over a faked Bigfoot site in the woods. Clumsy comedy. **86m/C DVD.** Jeremy Sumpter, Justin Long, Rob Pinkston, Joey Kern, Hubbel Palmer, Addie Land, Carl Weathers, Jon(athan) Gries, Stephen Tobolowsky, Michael Mitchell; **D:** Tim Skousen; **W:** Tim Skousen; **C:** Munn Powell; **M:** John Swihart. **VIDEO**

Satan in High Heels ♂½ 1961 Sordid show-biz tale of a carnival dancer (Myles) who dreams of making it big on Broadway. First she finagles her way into a position as a nightclub singer and the mistress of a convenient millionaire. But she loses it all for love when she falls for flamboyant performance by Hall as the lesbian nightclub owner. **90m/B VHS, DVD.** Meg Myles, Grayson Hall, Del Tenney, Mike Keene, Robert Yuro, Sabrina, Earl Hammond, Paul Scott; **D:** Jerald Intrator; **W:** John T. Chapman; **C:** Bernard Herschensen; **M:** Mundell Lowe.

The Satan Killer ♂♂½ 1993 A vicious serial killer is targeted by two tough police detectives. What makes it personal is Detective Stephen's fiance is one of the killer's victims and he's not going to let justice stand in the way of his revenge. **90m/C VHS.** Steve Sayre, Billy Franklin, James Westbrook, Belinda Creason, Cindy Healy; **D:** Stephen Calamari.

Satan Met a Lady ♂♂½ 1936 A weak adaptation of Dashiell Hammett's "Maltese Falcon." This version has Davis employing a private detective to track down a mysterious woman. The hunted woman is herself searching for a valuable collectible. **74m/B VHS.** Bette Davis, Warren William, Alison Skipworth, Arthur Treacher, Marie Wilson, Porter Hall, Olin Howlin; **D:** William Dieterle.

The Satanic Rites of Dracula ♂♂ *Count Dracula and His Vampire Bride; Dracula Is Dead and Well and Living in London* 1973 Count Dracula is the leader of a satanic cult of prominent scientists and politicians who develop a gruesome plague virus capable of destroying the human race. Preceded by "The 7 Brothers Meet Dracula." **88m/C VHS, DVD. GB** Christopher Lee, Peter Cushing, Michael Coles, William Franklyn, Freddie Jones, Joanna Lumley, Richard Vernon, Patrick Barr, Barbara Yu Ling; **D:** Alan Gibson; **W:** Don Houghton; **C:** Brian Probyn; **M:** John Cacavas.

Satanik ♂ 1969 (R) A hideous old hag is turned into a lovely young woman by a stolen potion, but it doesn't last long and she becomes a monster. **85m/C VHS, DVD. IT SP** Magda Konopka, Julio Pena, Luigi Montini, Armando Calvo, Umberto Raho; **D:** Piero Vivarelli.

Satan's Black Wedding ♂ 1975 (R) The ghouls arrive at a Monterey monastery in their Sunday best to celebrate devildom's most diabolical ritual, the "Black Wedding." **61m/C VHS, DVD.** Greg Braddock, Ray Miles, Lisa Milano; **D:** Steve Millard.

Satin's Blood ♂ *Escalofrio* 1977 Uncut version of the Spanish horror flick that was condemned upon its release for its sex and sadism (and 'nudity). A young married couple, visiting friends at their isolated country home, are influenced by occult forces to participate in Satanic rituals. Spanish with subtitles. **82m/C DVD. SP** Angel Aranda, Sandra Alberti, Mariana Karr, Jose Maria Guillen; **D:** Carlos Puerto; **W:** Eva Del Castillo; **C:** Andres Berenguer; **M:** Librado Pastor.

Satan's Brew ♂ *Satansbraten* 1976 Aspiring poet (Raab) murders his mistress and assumes the identity of 19th-century symbolist poet Stefan George, including his idol's homosexual tastes. Fassbinder at his most excessive. German with subtitles. **100m/C VHS, DVD. GE** Kurt Raab, Margit Carstensen, Volker Spengler, Ingrid Caven, Helen Vita; **D:** Rainer Werner Fassbinder; **W:** Rainer Werner Fassbinder; **C:** Michael Ballhaus; **M:** Peer Raben.

Satan's Cheerleaders woof! 1977 (R) A demonic high school janitor traps a bevy of buxom cheerleaders at his Satanic altar for sacrificial purposes. The gals use all of their endowments to escape the clutches of the evil sheriff and his fat wife. Is it ever campy! **92m/C VHS, DVD.** John Carradine, John Ireland, Yvonne De Carlo, Kerry Sherman, Jacqulin Cole, Hilary Horan, Alisa Powell, Sherry Marks, Jack Kruschen, Sydney Chaplin; **D:** Greydon Clark; **W:** Greydon Clark, Alvin L. Fast; **C:** Dean Cundey; **M:** Gerald Lee.

Satan's Harvest ♂½ 1965 American detective inherits estate in Johannesburg, only to find the place is being used by drug smugglers. Sidesteps the political climate and shows the despots of the land. And a good thing: the story is virtually nonexistent. **88m/C VHS.** George Montgomery, Tippi Hedren; **D:** Ferde Grofe Jr.

Satan's Little Helper ♂ 2004 (R) On Halloween, naive Doug befriends a masked serial killer, not realizing the carnage they leave behind is real, and takes him home to meet his family. His mom (Plummer) and sister (Winnick) must save the family from the maniac. Terrible genre spoof is cheap, distasteful, and pointless. **99m/C DVD.** Amanda Plummer, Alexander Brickel, Stephen Graham, Dan Ziskie, Katheryn Winnick, Joshua Annex; **D:** Jeff Lieberman; **W:** Jeff Lieberman; **C:** Dejan Georgevich; **M:** David Horowitz. **VIDEO**

Satan's Princess ♂ 1990 Satanic cult with a female leader runs amuck. Sloppy and forgettable. **90m/C VHS.** Robert Forster, Caren Kaye, Lydie Denier, Phillip Glasser, Michael (M.K.) Harris, Ellen Geer, Jack Carter; **D:** Bert I. Gordon; **W:** Stephen Katz.

Satan's Sadists ♂ 1969 (R) Tamblyn and his biker gang terrorize folks in the Southern California desert, including a retired cop, a Vietnam vet and a trio of vacationing coeds. Violent film will probably be best appreciated by Adamson completists. **88m/C VHS, DVD.** Russ Tamblyn, Regina Carrol, Gary Kent, Jackie Taylor, John Cardos, Kent Taylor, Robert Dix, Scott Brady, Evelyn Frank, Greydon Clark, Bill Bonner, Bobby Clark, Yvonne Stewart, Cheryl Anne, Randee Lynn, Bambi Allen, Breck Warwick; **D:** Al Adamson; **W:** Dennis Wayne; **C:** Gary Graver; **M:** Harley Hatcher.

Satan's School for Girls ♂ 1973 When a young woman investigates the circumstances that caused her sister's suicide, it leads her to a satanic girl's academy. Dumb and puerile made for TV "horror." **74m/C VHS, DVD.** Pamela Franklin, Roy Thinnes, Kate Jackson, Lloyd Bochner, Jamie Smith-Jackson, Jo Van Fleet, Cheryl Ladd, Gwynne Gilford, Bing (Neil) Russell; **D:** David Lowell Rich; **W:** Arthur Ross; **M:** Laurence Rosenthal. **TV**

Satan's Touch woof! 1984 (R) A simpleton worships the Devil and gets burned for his trouble. **86m/C VHS.** Paul Davies, James Lawless, Shirley Venard; **D:** John Goodell; **W:** John Goodell.

Satanwar woof! 1979 A fictional look at various forms of Satan worship. **95m/C VHS.** Bart LaRue, Sally Schemerhorn, Jimmy Drankovitch; **D:** Bart La Rue; **W:** Bart La Rue; **C:** Laura Andrus; **M:** William Eucker.

Satin Rouge ♂♂½ 2002 Lilia (Abbass) is a very proper widowed seamstress who lives with her in-laws and rebellious teenaged daughter Salma (El Fahem). Salma is taking belly-dancing classes and Lilia suspects the girl is flirting with musician Chokri (Kamoun), so she follows him to a club and is seduced by the exuberance of the dancers. One, Folla (Hichri), invites Lilia in and soon she is leading a double-life—grieving widow by day and costumer and part-time dancer by night. Arabic with subtitles. **95m/C VHS, DVD. FR** Hiam Abbass, Hend El Fahem, Maher Kamoun, Monia Hichri; **D:** Raja Amari; **W:** Raja Amari; **C:** Diane Baratier; **M:** Nawfel El Manaa.

Satisfaction ♂ 1988 (PG-13) An all-girl, high school rock band play out the summer before college. The Keatons should have sent Bateman to her room for this stunt. **93m/C VHS, DVD.** Justine Bateman, Trini Alvarado, Britta Phillips, Julia Roberts, Scott Coffey, Liam Neeson, Deborah Harry; **D:** Joan Freeman; **W:** Charles Purpura; **M:** Michel Colombier.

Saturday Night and Sunday Morning ♂♂♂½ 1960 This "kitchen sink" drama finds the 23-year-old Finney in star form as working-class Arthur Seaton, who's devoted to good times, spending his weekends with boozing, brawling, and willing women. He's having an affair with the older, married Brenda (Roberts) and pursuing the strictly moral Doreen (Field), who refuses to sleep with him without a commitment. Arthur thinks he's falling in love and is (eventually) ready for marriage but not without complications and not before warning Doreen that he's unlikely to completely change his carefree ways. Reisz's first feature film; Sillitoe adapted from his novel. Finney was voted the most promising newcomer at the British Academy's (BAFTA) awards. **90m/B VHS, DVD. GB** Albert Finney, Rachel Roberts, Shirley Anne Field, Bryan Pringle, Norman Rossington, Hylda Baker, Robert Cowdra, Elsie Wagstaff, Frank Pettitt; **D:** Karel Reisz; **W:** Alan Sillitoe; **C:** Freddie Francis; **M:** John Dankworth. British Acad. '61: Actress (Roberts); Film; Natl. Bd. of Review '61: Actor (Finney).

Saturday Night Fever ♂♂½ 1977 (R) Brooklyn teenager (Travolta), bored with his daytime job, becomes the nighttime king of the local disco. Based on a story published in "New York Magazine" by Nik Cohn. Acclaimed for its disco dance sequences, memorable soundtrack by the Bee Gees, and carefree yet bleak script; extremely dated, although it made its mark on society in its time. Followed by the sequel "Staying Alive." Also available in a 112-minute "PG" rated version. ♫Staying Alive; Night Fever; More Than a Woman; How Deep Is Your Love? **118m/C VHS, DVD.** John Travolta, Karen (Lynn) Gorney, Barry Miller, Donna Pescow, Joseph Call, Bruce Ornstein, Paul Pape, Fran Drescher; **D:** John Badham; **W:** Norman Wexler; **C:** Ralf Bode; **M:** David Shire. Natl. Bd. of Review '77: Actor (Travolta).

Saturday Night Special ♂½ 1992 (R) Country singer/songwriter Travis (played by Nashville stalwart Burnette) gets a job fronting the house band of Tennessee tavern owner T.J. (Dean). Travis also takes up with ambitious Darlene (Ford), who happens to be T.J.'s wife. But it's Darlene who has the brains in this unpleasant trio, she decides to get rid of hubby and sets Travis up to take the fall. It's all been done before (and better). **75m/C VHS, DVD.** Billy Burnette, Maria Ford, Rick Dean; **D:** Dan Golden; **W:** Jonathan Banks; **M:** Billy Burnette, Nicholas Rivera.

Saturday the 14th ♂½ 1981 (PG) A parody of the popular axe-wielding-maniac genre, about a family inheriting a haunted mansion. Poorly made; not funny or scary. Followed by even worse sequel "Saturday the 14th Strikes Back." **91m/C VHS, DVD.** Richard Benjamin, Paula Prentiss, Severn Darden, Jeffrey Tambor, Kari Michaelsen, Kevin Brando, Rosemary DeCamp, Stacy Keach; **D:** Howard R. Cohen; **W:** Howard R. Cohen; Jeff Begun; **C:** Daniel Lacambre; **M:** Parmer Fuller.

Saturday the 14th Strikes Back ♂ 1988 Continuing the name, but not the story line, cast, or characters of the original, this one concerns the invasion of a birthday party by a vampire (Stonebrook) and her monstrous friends. The monsters decide that they should be their new leader. Pretty lame, even by the original's standards. **91m/C VHS, DVD.** *Ray* Walston, Avery Schreiber, Patty McCormack, Julianne McNamara, Rhonda Aldrich, Daniel Will-Harris, Joseph Ruskin, Pamela Stonebrook, Phil Leeds, Jason Presson, Michael Berryman, Victoria Morsell; *D:* Howard R. Greenhalgh; *M:* Elmer Bernstein.

Saturn 3 1980 (R) Two research scientists create a futuristic Garden of Eden in an isolated sector of our solar system, but love story turns to horror story when a killer robot arrives. Sporadically promising, but ultimately lame; dumb ending. For Farrah fans only. **88m/C VHS, DVD.** *GB* Farrah Fawcett, Kirk Douglas, Harvey Keitel, Ed Bishop; *D:* Stanley Donen; *M:* Elmer Bernstein.

Saul and David *vd 1964* Beautifully filmed story of King Saul, the battle with Goliath, and the tragic end of Saul. From the "Bible" series. **120m/C VHS, DVD.** Norman Wooland, Gianni "John" Garko, Elisa Cegani, Virginio Teixeira; *D:* Marcello Baldi; *W:* Tonino Guerra; *C:* Juan Ruiz Romero, Marcelo Masciocchi; *M:* Teo Usuelli.

Savage! WOOF! *Black Valor 1973 (R)* A savage foreign mess with ex-baseball star Iglehart killing people with grenades and guns, abetted by an army full of murderous models. **81m/C VHS.** *MX* James Iglehart, Lada Edmund, Carol Speed, Rossana Ortiz, Sally Jordan, Aura Aurea, Vic Diaz; *D:* Cirio H. Santiago.

Savage 1996 (R) Mad scientist discovers the gateway to a future world, which unleashes a powerful guardian known known as the Savage (Gruner). The Savage must prevent the doorway between the worlds from exploding and causing an apocalypse, even as he hunts his nemesis. **103m/C VHS, DVD.** Oliver Gruner, Kario Salem, Jennifer Grant, Sam McMurray, Kristin Minter; *D:* Avi Nesher; *W:* Patrick Highsmith, Peter Segal; *C:* Peter Fernberger; *M:* Roger Neill.

Savage Abduction 1973 *Saul e David:* Two girls visiting Los Angeles are kidnapped by a bizarre man. **84m/C VHS, DVD.** Tom Drake, Stephen Oliver, Sean Kenney; *D:* John Lawrence.

Savage Attraction *Hostage: The Christine Maresch Story; Hostage 1583 (R)* True story of a 16-year-old girl forced to marry an ex-Nazi, and her hellish life thereafter. Frustrating because it could have been much better. **93m/C VHS, UMD.** *AU GB* Kerry Mack, Ralph Schicha; *D:* Frank Shields.

Savage Beach 1989 (R) A pair of well-endowed female federal agents battle assorted buccaneers on a remote Pacific isle over a rediscovered cache of gold from WWII. Exploitative, pornographic, and degrading to watch. Sequel to "Picasso Trigger." **90m/C VHS, DVD.** Dona Speir, Hope Marie Carlton, Bruce Penhall, Rodrigo Obregon, John Aprea, Teri Weigel, Lisa London; *D:* Andy Sidaris.

The Savage Bees 1976 A South American ship harbored at New Orleans during Mardi Gras unleashes killer bees into the celebratory crowds. Not bad, relatively exciting, TV thriller. **90m/C V-HS.** Ben Johnson, Michael Parks, Paul Hecht, Horst Buchholz, Gretchen Corbett, Bruce French, James Best; *D:* Bruce Geller; *W:* Guerdon Trueblood; *C:* Richard C. Glouner. **TV**

Savage Capitalism *Capitalismo Selvaje 1993* Melodramatic romance between a reporter and a mining company exec crumbles when the exec's presumed dead wife returns. Meanwhile, the reporter uncovers the truth behind the company's plans to mine in the interior of Brazil, which could cause ecological ruin. Portuguese with subtitles. **86m/C VHS, BR** Fernanda Torres, Jose Mayer, Marisa Orth, Marcelo Tass; *D:* Andre Klotzel; *W:* Andre Klotzel, Djalma Batista.

Savage Dawn 1984 (R) In yet another desert town, yet another pair of combat-hardened vets are confronted by a vicious motorcycle gang. Haven't we seen this one before? **102m/C VHS.** George Kennedy, Karen Black, Richard Lynch, Lance Henriksen, William Forsythe; *D:* Simon Nuchtern.

Savage Drums 1951 Sabu returns to his South Seas island to help end tribal warfare there. Dated and dumb, but fun-to-watch melodrama/action. **70m/B VHS.** Sabu, Lita Baron, H.B. Warner, Sid Melton, Steven Geray, Margia Dean, Paul Beaumont; *D:* Jack Greenhalgh; *W:* Fenton Earnshaw; *C:* Darrell Calker.

Savage Fury 1935 Feature-length version of the popular movie serial. **80m/B VHS.** Harry Woods, Bryant Washburn, Fred Mackaye, Noah Beery Jr., Dorothy Short; *D:* Lew Landers; *C:* Richard Fryer, William Sickner.

The Savage Girl 1932 A hunter journeys through the darkest jungle in search of a beautiful white jungle girl, falls in love with her and attempts to take her back with him. **64m/B VHS.** Rochelle Hudson, Walter Byron, Harry C. (Henry) Myers, Ted Adams, Adolph Milar, Floyd Schackleford; *D:* Harry Fraser.

Savage Harvest 2: October Blood 2006 Sequel that was 13 years in the making follows low-budget horror film director Tyge Murdock (Gaa) as he returns home to reassess his life after an actor is accidentally killed on one of his sets. But home is where the nightmares are. Reuniting with his high school flame (Haack) brings back remnants of a mass murder that took place ten years earlier and the old gang quickly finds themselves trapped in a demonic gore-spattered nightmare. Script is decent enough but the cast doesn't have the chops to pull it off. Haack being the exception as the deadly-intense Ashley Lomack. **119m/C DVD.** Benjamin Gaa, Emily Haack, Eric Stanze, David Propst, Jonathan Baker; *D:* Jason Christ; *W:* Jason Christ; *C:* Jason Christ; *M:* Shawn Donoho. **VIDEO**

Savage Hearts 1995 Terminally ill mob hitwoman Beatrice Baxter (D'Abo) has six months left to live and she wants her six days to be spent in style. So she steals $2 million from her mob employer Roger Focely (Harris)—who's determined to get the money back. **90m/C VHS.** Maryam D'Abo, Richard Harris, Myriam Cyr, Jerry Hall; *D:* Mark Ezra.

Savage Hunger 1984 Ten plane crash survivors struggle to survive in the Baja desert. **90m/C VHS.** Chris Makepeace, Scott Hylands, Anne Lockhart; *D:* Sparky Green.

Savage Instinct 1989 A woman stumbles across a drug ring and becomes a target when they fear she could expose them. Only Mongo and his crew are even more surprised when she decides to fight back. **95m/C VHS.** Debra Sweaney, Brian Oldfield; *D:* Patrick G. Donahue; *W:* Patrick G. Donahue; *C:* Mike Pierce; *M:* Emilio Kauderer.

Savage Intruder 1968 (R) A wardering opportunist worms his way into the heart and home of a rich ex-movie star. She soon discovers that he's a sexual deviant who mutilates and murders for fun. Twisted doings with Hopkins in her final role. **90m/C VHS.** John David Garfield, Miriam Hopkins, Gale Sondergaard, Florence Lake, Joe Besser, Minta Durfee; *D:* Donald Wolfe.

Savage Is Loose 1974 (R) Woman Drivel about a scientist, his wife, and their son stranded on a deserted island for 20 years. Not surprisingly, as junior matures he realizes there isn't a woman for him—or is there? Completely lacking in redeeming qualities. Absurd pseudo-Freudian claptrap produced by C. Scott. **114m/C VHS.** George C. Scott, Trish Van Devere, John David Carson, Lee Montgomery; *D:* George C. Scott.

Savage Island 1985 (R) Women in prison in the tropics sets the scene for the usual exploitative goings-on. Blair is actually in the film only for a few minutes. Chopped-up, even worse version of "Escape From Hell." **74m/C VHS, DVD, SP IT** Nicholas Beardsley, Linda Blair, Anthony Steffen, Ajita Wilson, Christina Lai, Leon Askin; *D:* Edward (Edoardo Mularigi) Muller; *W:* Nicholas Beardsley, Golden Raspberries '85. Worst Actress (Blair).

Savage Messiah 1972 (R) Bio of young French sculptor Henri Gaudier and his intense, though platonic, affair with a refined Polish woman 20 years his senior. Stylized drama is spared most of director Russell's noted excesses but he manages to believably show their magnetic attraction. Gaudier was killed in WWI at the age of 24. Based on the biography by H.S. Ede. **96m/C VHS, GB** Scott Antony, Dorothy Tutin, Helen Mirren, Lindsay Kemp, Peter Vaughan, Michael Gough; *D:* Ken Russell; *W:* Christopher Logue; *C:* Dick Bush.

Savage Run 1970 Reynolds as a Papago Indian framed and imprisoned for his brother's murder. Sprung from the pen, he heads back to the reservation to find the real killers and avenge his brother's death. Convincing drama. Stevens's last role before her suicide. **75m/C VHS, DVD.** Burt Reynolds, Inger Stevens, James Best, Rodolfo Acosta, Don Dubbins, Joyce Jameson, Barry Sullivan; *D:* Paul Wendkos; *W:* Serge Ladouceur; *M:* Frank DeVol. **AKA:** *Run, Simon, Run.*

Savage Sam 1963 Intended as a sequel to "Old Yeller," Sam, the offspring of the heroic dog named Old Yeller, tracks down some children kidnapped by Indians. Fun, but not fully successful. **103m/C VHS, DVD.** Tommy Kirk, Kevin Corcoran, Brian Keith, Dewey Martin, Jeff York, Marta Kristen; *D:* Norman Tokar; *C:* Edward Colman.

Savage Island 2003 Wanting to escape their troubled marriage, Steven and Julie seek refuge with their baby at her parents' remote island home. The serenity is squelched when they're held responsible for a horrible accident that claims the life of one of the island's other inhabitants—the rural Savage family—who will stop at nothing to avenge their loss. **90m/C VHS, DVD.** Winston Rekert, Brendan Beiser, Gregg Scott, Don S. Davis, Steven Man, Kristina Copeland, Beverley Breuer, Zoran Vukelic, Nahanni Arntzen; *D:* Jeffrey Scott Lando; *W:* Kevin Mosley; *C:* Geoff Rogers; *M:* Chris Nickel. **VIDEO**

Savage Journey 1983 (PG) A wagon train of pioneers has difficulty on its westward journey. Simple story with no real appeal. **99m/C VHS, DVD.** Richard Moll, Maurice Grandmaison, Faith Clift; *D:* Tom McGowan.

Savage Justice 1988 A young woman seeks revenge against leftist rebels (boo, hiss) in a Southeast Asian country who killed her parents and raped her. She hooks up with an ex-Green Beret, and they fight and love their way through the jungle. The usual nudity and violence derivative and dumb. **90m/C VHS, DVD.** Julia Montgomery, Steven Memel, Ken Metcalfe; *D:* Joey Romero.

Savage Land 1994 (PG) Family western finds a young brother and sister travelling by stage to meet up with their father. The stage is robbed by some bumbling bad guys, who then pursue the kids and two other passengers across the frontier. The kids, of course, are smarter than most of the adults, and manage to get the best of the bad hombres. **91m/C VHS, DVD.** Graham Greene, Corbin Bernsen, Vivian Schilling, Mercedes McNab, Corey Carrier, Brion James, Bo Svenson, Charlotte Ross; *D:* Dean Hamilton; *W:* Dean Hamilton; *C:* Roland Smith; *M:* Michael Conway Baker.

Savage Messiah 2002 (R) Canadian social worker Paula Jackson (Walker) discovers charismatic Roch Theriault (Picard), who calls himself Moses, maintains a backwoods commune/religious cult consisting of several women who think of themselves as his wives. When Paula tries to intercede on behalf of their children, she finds the cult leader will not give their kids up to social services than leave their leader despite their abuse at his hands. Based on a true story, which took place in Quebec. English and French with subtitles. **96m/C VHS, DVD, CA** Polly Walker, Luc Picard, Isabelle Blais, Isabelle Cyr, Pascale Montpetit, Donnin Blythe, Julia La Rochelle, Elizabeth Robertson; *D:* Mario Azzopardi; *W:* Sharon Riley; *C:* Serge Ladouceur; *M:* Frank Illiman. Genie '02: Actor. Adapt. Score, Support. Actress (Montpetit).

Savage Weekend WOOF! *The Upstate Murders 1980 (R)* A killer behind a ghoulish mask stalks human prey in the boonies, of course. As te rided rape scene betrays the exploitative intentions, though other bits are entertaining, in a trashy kind of way. **83m/C VHS, DVD.** Linda Blair, John Vernon, Sal Landi, Robert Dryer, Debra Blee, Linnea Quigley; *D:* Danny Steinmann; *M:* John D'Andrea. Golden Raspberries '85. Worst Actress (Blair).

Savage Wilderness 1955 When a trio of fur trappers lose a year's worth of skins to a band of marauding Indians, they decide to take scouting jobs at a cavalry outpost. But they find the new commander (Preston) hasn't gotten his nickname as the "Butcher of Shiloh" without reason. Adapted from the novel "The Gilded Rooster" by Richard Emery Roberts. **98m/C VHS, DVD.** Victor Mature, Robert Preston, Guy Madison, James Whitmore, Anne Bancroft, Russell Collins, Peter Whitney, Pat Hogan, Manuel Donde, Guy Williams; *D:* Anthony Mann; *W:* Philip Yordan, Russell S. Hughes; *M:* Leigh Harline.

The Savage Woman 1991 Marianna escapes from a desperate situation and is found unconscious in the woods by Elysee. He nurses her back to health, learns her terrible secret, and tries to help Marianna decide whether to turn herself into the police or keep running in. In French with English subtitles. **100m/C VHS, CA** Patricia Tulasne, Matthias Habich; *D:* Lea Pool.

The Savages 2007 (R) The Savages are a highly dysfunctional family consisting of middle-aged siblings savages and "civilized" men are really the same. **106m/C VHS, DVD.** Lewis J. Stadlen, Anne Francine, Thayer David, Salome Jens, Susan Blakely, Kathleen Widdoes, Sam Waterston; *D:* James Ivory; *C:* Walter Lassally.

The Savages The Savages are a highly dysfunctional family consisting of middle-aged siblings Wendy (Linney) and Jon (Hoffman) as well as their aging father Lenny (Bosco), who still lives in his recently deceased girlfriend's condo in Sun City, Arizona. After years of estrangement, two phone calls bring to light Lenny's advancing dementia, which reunites the three as they return Lenny to Buffalo. This task is complicated by the predictable but ridiculous humor that bubbles up through the cracks. A wholly worthwhile viewing experience. **113m/C DVD.** US Laura Linney, Philip Seymour Hoffman, Philip Bosco, Peter Friedman, Cara Seymour; *D:* Tamara Jenkins; *W:* Tamara Jenkins; *C:* Mott Hupfel III; *M:* Stephen Trask. Ind. Spirit '03: Actor (Hoffman), Screenplay.

The Savage Seven 1968 An underground classic where everyone loses. A motorcycle gang rides into an Indian town which is at the mercy of corrupt businessmen. The gang's leader becomes involved in the Indians' problems but trouble ensues and the cops cause trouble for all concerned. Less than memorable. Produced by Dick Clark. **96m/C VHS.** Larry Bishop, Joanna Frank, Adam Roarke, Robert Walker Jr.; *D:* Richard Rush.

Savage Streets 1983 (R) Blair seeks commando-style revenge on the street gang that raped her dead sister. Exploitative. **93m/C VHS, DVD.** Linda Blair, John Vernon, Robert Dryer; *M:* John D'Andrea.

Savages from Hell *Big Enough and Old Enough 1968 (R)* Greasy biker dude beats up a young black guy because he was flirting with the biker's woman. The biker also tries to rape a migrant farm-worker's daughter because he lusts after her. Trashy exploitation film. **79m/C VHS, DVD.** Bobbie Byers, Cyril Poitier, Diwaldo Myers, Viola Lloyd, William Kelley; **D:** Joseph Prieto; **W:** Joseph Prieto.

Savannah Smiles ✓✓½ 1982 (PG) Poor little rich girl Anderson runs away from home, into the clutches of two ham-handed crooks. She melts their hearts, and they change their ways. Decent, sentimental family drama. **104m/C VHS, DVD.** Bridgette Andersen, Mark Miller, Donovan Scott, Peter Graves, Chris Robinson, Michael Parks; **D:** Pierre De Moro.

Save Me ✓✓ 1993 (R) Jim Stevens' (Hamlin) wife has left him and his boss is involved in some dirty deals that could cost Jim his job. So things couldn't get worse, could they? Well, of course they could—and do. Because Jim meets Ellie (Anthony), a sexual adventuress just destined to bring trouble to a lonely guy. Also available in an unrated version. **89m/C VHS, DVD.** Harry Hamlin, Lysette Anthony, Michael Ironside, Olivia Hussey, Bill Nunn, Steve Railsback; **D:** Alan Roberts; **M:** Neil Ronco; **M:** Richard (Rick) Marvin.

Save the Lady ✓✓ 1982 Plucky kids fight city hall to save an old ferry, the Lady Hope, from the scrap heap. Nothing offensive here—just a pleasant family flick. **76m/C VHS.** Matthew Excell, Robert Clarkson, Miranda Cartledge, Kim Clifford; **D:** Leon Thau.

Save the Last Dance ✓✓½ 2001 (PG-13) "Fame" (or "Flashdance" or "Saturday Night Fever") meets "Romeo and Juliet" (or "West Side Story" or any trashy talk show) in this clearly not-so-original but solid teen drama. White, middle-class Sara (Stiles) adjusts to life and rediscovers her passion for dance in an all-black, inner-city Chicago high school when she must give up her dreams of attending Juilliard and move in with her down-on-his-luck father (Kinney) on the South Side. There, she befriends Chenille (Washington), who helps her get hip, and falls for her smart, ambitious brother Derek (Thomas), who helps her learn hip-hop. Stiles and Thomas turn in good performances despite somewhat stereotypical cast of characters. **112m/C VHS, DVD.** US Julia Stiles, Sean Patrick Thomas, Fredro Starr, Kerry Washington, Terry Kinney, Bianca Lawson, Garland Whitt, Vince Green; **D:** Thomas Carter; **W:** Duane Adler, Cheryl Edwards; **C:** Robbie Greenberg; **M:** Mark Isham.

Saved! ✓✓½ 2004 (PG-13) Uneven, subversive satire about teens at a fundamentalist Christian high school hits a lot of standard cliches and makes a plea for tolerance at the same time. Good girl Mary (Malone) finds out boyfriend Dean (Faust) is gay and has a vision of "curing" him through sex. She winds up pregnant, which puts Mary clearly on the side of the sinners as far as the school's self-righteous queen bee Hilary Faye (Moore) is concerned. Of course, the sinners seem to be having more fun. Mary's situation engages the sympathy of sweet believer Patrick (Fugit), the son of the school's zealous principal, Pastor Skip (Donovan). Moore and Malone well play the opposing force of their characters and are ably supported by the rest of the cast. **92m/C DVD.** Jena Malone, Mandy Moore, Macaulay Culkin, Patrick Fugit, Heather Matarazzo, Eva Amurri, Martin Donovan, Mary-Louise Parker, Chad Faust, Elizabeth Thai; **Cameos:** Valerie Bertinelli; **D:** Brian Dannelly, Michael Urban; **C:** Bobby Bukowski; **M:** Mark Isham.

Saved by the Light ✓✓½ 1995 On September 17, 1975, ruthless Dannion Brinkley's (Roberts) life was changed forever—he died. Struck by a bolt of lightning, Brinkley was declared dead, only to wake up 28 minutes later in the morgue. A changed man, which some of Brinkley's acquaintances find hard to believe, he becomes a public speaker, telling about his trip to heaven and his belief in love and salvation. TV movie based on Brinkley's book about his near-death experience. **95m/C VHS.** Eric Roberts, Lynette Walden, K. Callan; **D:** Lewis Teague. TV

Saving Face ✓✓½ 2004 (R) Director/writer Alice Wu's debut effort adeptly explores some familiar, and not so familiar, mother/daughter themes with a Chinese-American backdrop. Ma (Chen) is disappointed that her up-and-coming surgeon daughter, Wilhelmina (Krusiec), or Wil, isn't married yet as Ma is in denial over Wil's lesbianism. Just when Wil begins a hot, new, and still-closeted romance, the 48-year-old Ma (who has lived with her parents since her husband died, as is custom) moves in after being kicked out once her pregnancy by an unnamed man is revealed, which forces the pair to confront their issues. **90m/C DVD.** US Michelle Krusiec, Joan Chen, Lynn Chen, Li Zhiyu, Shen Gung Lan, Jessica Hecht, Ato Essandoh; **D:** Alice Wu; **W:** Alice Wu; **C:** Harlan Bosmajian; **M:** Anton Sanko.

Saving Grace ✓✓ 1986 (PG) A tale of the fictional youngest Pope of modern times, Pope Leo XIV (Conti). Beset by duty, he decides to shed his robes and get in touch with the world's peasantry. Improbable, but that's okay; the mortal sin is that it's improbable and slow and boring. **112m/C VHS.** Tom Conti, Fernando Rey, Giancarlo Giannini, Erland Josephson, Donald Hewlett, Edward James Olmos; **D:** Robert M. Young; **W:** David S. Ward; **M:** William Goldstein.

Saving Grace ✓✓½ 2000 (R) Widowed Blethyn finds out her late hubby has left her deeply in debt and in order to maintain her comfortable lifestyle, her gardener (Ferguson) suggests that she grow pot and sell it. Quaint comedy has the trademark quirky characters and gently bawdy humor you'd expect. Blethyn and Ferguson are fine, and it's all veddy cheerful. Low-key approach lends itself well to the small screen. **93m/C VHS, DVD.** GB Brenda Blethyn, Craig Ferguson, Martin Clunes, Tcheky Karyo, Jamie Foreman, Valerie Edmond, Tristan Sturrock; **D:** Nigel Cole; **W:** Craig Ferguson, Mark Crowdy; **C:** John de Borman.

Saving Private Ryan ✓✓✓✓ 1998 (R) Big-budget WWII Spielberg epic finds eight soldiers, led by army captain Hanks, forced to go behind enemy lines in order to rescue downed paratrooper James Ryan (Damon). He's the sole surviving brother of four soldier siblings and the government wants some good PR—thusiastic, however. Pick your favorite reviewer-speak word—gripping, moving, intense, masterpiece—any or all of them will work. The opening 25-minute graphic depiction of Omaha Beach on D-Day is, on its own, Oscar-worthy. Hanks and the rest of the cast (which included a few surprise cameos) are excellent. Spielberg deglamorizes war, without belittling the sacrifices made by those who fought. The actors (except Damon) went through boot camp in England in order to get the proper attitude. **175m/C VHS, DVD.** Tom Hanks, Edward Burns, Tom Sizemore, Jeremy Davies, Giovanni Ribisi, Adam Goldberg, Barry Pepper, Vin Diesel, Matt Damon, Ted Danson, Dale Dye, Dennis Farina, Harve Presnell, Paul Giamatti, Bryan Cranston, David Wohl, Leland Orser, Joerg Stadler, Maximilian Martini, Amanda Boxer, Harrison Young; **D:** Steven Spielberg; **W:** Robert Rodat, Frank Darabont; **C:** Janusz Kaminski; **D:** John G. Avildsen; **M:** Marvin Hamlisch. Oscars '98: Cinematog., Director (Spielberg), Film Editing, Sound, Sound FX Editing; British Acad. '98: Sound; Directors Guild '98: Director (Spielberg); Golden Globes '99: Director (Spielberg); L.A. Film Critics '98: Cinematog., Director (Spielberg); Film; N.Y. Film Critics '98: Film; Broadcast Film Critics '98: Director (Spielberg), Film, Score.

Saving Sarah Cain ✓✓½ 2007 (PG) Sarah (Pepper) is a struggling Portland newspaper columnist who travels back to her Pennsylvania Amish family for the funeral of her sister. Sarah learns that she is now the guardian of her sister's five children and she moves the kids back to the city with her, using their story as the topic of her columns. But Sarah soon realizes that she must choose between her own ambitions and what's best for the kids. Based on the novel "The Redemption of Sarah Cain" by Beverly Lewis. **103m/C DVD.** Elliott Gould, Tess Harper, Abigail Mason; **D:** Michael Landon Jr.; **W:** Brian Bird, Cindy Kelley; **C:** Matthew Williams; **M:** Mark McKenzie. CABLE

Saving Shiloh ✓✓½ 2006 (PG) The last of the trilogy based on the Phyllis Reynolds Naylor novels finds adorable beagle Shiloh and his master, Marty (Dolley), believing that their troubled neighbor Judd (Wilson) is sincere about becoming a better person. Marty continues to stand by Judd even when the man is accused of thievery and worse. But Judd isn't all they have to worry about—there's also a watery rescue and some escaped convicts to deal with. Wholesome without being too sweet. **90m/C DVD.** US Scott Wilson, Gerald McRaney, Jason Dolley, Ann Dowd, Jordan Garrett; **D:** Sandy Tung; **W:** Dale Rosenbloom; **C:** Lex du Pont; **M:** Adam Gorgoni.

Saving Silverman ✓ *Evil Woman* 2001 (PG-13) Testosterone-driven comedy has three buddies' bond threatened by ball-breaking fiancee of one of the boys. Peet is the whip-wielding control freak Judith Snodgrass-Fessbeggler, out to tame Neil Diamond-loving loser Darren (Biggs) and despised by best buds Wayne (Zahn) and J.D. (Black). The boys scheme to break up the duo by kidnaping Judith and re-acquainting Darren with his first love, now an aspiring nun. Black and Zahn provide much-needed comic relief, as do the scenes with their Diamond cover band. However, over-the-top characters and sophomoric humor mixed with increasingly gross gags ultimately not so much save but sink "Silverman." **90m/C VHS, DVD.** US Jason Biggs, Steve Zahn, Jack Black, Amanda Peet, R. Lee Ermey, Amanda Detmer, Neil Diamond; **D:** Dennis Dugan; **W:** Hank Nelken, Greg DePaul; **C:** Arthur Albert; **M:** Mike Simpson.

Savior ✓✓ 1998 (R) After his wife and son are killed in a terrorist bombing, an American officer (Quaid) turns mercenary and assumes a new identity. As Guy, he's a soulless killing machine, working for the Serbs in Bosnia. At a prisoner exchange, he is told to take a pregnant young Serbian woman, Vera (Ninkovic), back to her village. Guy winds up delivering the baby and protecting Vera on their hazardous (and ultimately tragic) journey as he slowly regains flickers of his own humanity. Excellent change-of-pace performance by Quaid in a gut-wrenching film inspired by a true story. **104m/C VHS, DVD.** Dennis Quaid, Natasa Ninkovic, Sergej Trifunovic, Stellan Skarsgard, Nastassja Kinski; **D:** Pedrag (Peter) Antonijevic; **W:** Robert Orr; **C:** Ian Wilson; **M:** David Robbins.

Saw ✓✓ 2004 (R) Splatter film finds a serial killer named Jigsaw playing sadistic games with two men he's kidnapped: doctor Lawrence Gordon (Elwes) and photog Adam (co-writer Whannell). They're chained on opposite corners of a filthy bathroom with a corpse between them, several other items, a couple of hacksaws, and a time limit. They have to collaborate and figure out the clues left them in order to free themselves before the doc's wife and child (oh, and the saws aren't strong enough to cut through metal but flesh and bone isn't a problem. Glover figures in as an obsessed ex-cop who's had previous dealings with Jigsaw). Lots of gruesome flashbacks and various cheap scares. **100m/C DVD, Blu-ray Disc, UMD.** US Leigh Whannell, Cary Elwes, Danny Glover, Ken Leung, Dina Meyer, Tobin Bell, Makenzie Vega; **D:** James Wan; **W:** Leigh Whannell; **C:** David Armstrong; **M:** Charlie Clouser.

Saw 4 woof! 2007 (R) John/Jigsaw (Bell) is at it again in this bloody mesh of soft-core porn and horror that "Saw" fans have come to expect from director Bousman, this time doling out his special brand of moral murder from the afterlife. At the autopsy, a tape recorder is found in John's stomach echoing the killer's words and setting the scene for the fourth installment as his murder-machines continue all that yucky butchering in his absence. Flashbacks are thrown in between the gore and the (ahem) plot, offering glimpses into just what made this formerly successful and previously normal guy into the film franchise he is today. Pop the corn and settle in if you must, but this "Saw" ends up being about as sharp as a butter knife. **108m/C DVD.** US Tobin Bell, Costas Mandylor, Scott Patterson, Betsy Russell, Lyriq Bent, Athena Karkanis, Billy Otis; **D:** Darren Lynn Bousman; **W:** Patrick Melton, Marcus Dunstan; **C:** David Armstrong; **M:** Charlie Clouser.

Saw II ✓✓ 2005 (R) Since the sequel is just more of the same, if you liked the first one, you'll find this outing equally sadistic, disgusting, and enjoyable. Sicko Jigsaw (Bell) has trapped eight victims in a house with a number of booby traps that will force them to play his life-or-death games. One victim is the teenaged son (Knudsen) of the detective (Wahlberg) who has captured the madman. Of course, the groundwork is laid for more sequels. **93m/C DVD, Blu-ray Disc, UMD.** US Tobin Bell, Shawnee Smith, Donnie Wahlberg, Erik Knudsen, Franky G., Glenn Plummer, Beverley Mitchell, Dina Meyer, Emmanuelle Vaugier; **D:** Darren Lynn Bousman; **W:** Darren Lynn Bousman, Leigh Whannell; **C:** David Armstrong; **M:** Charlie Clouser.

Saw III ✓✓½ 2006 (R) With death sequences so unnecessarily elaborate, even fans of the franchise may be tiring of the gore. Along with accomplice Amanda (Smith), a dying Jigsaw (Bell) kidnaps surgeon Lynn (Soomekh), with the hope that she can remove his brain tumor. A difficult procedure, especially when you're wearing an explosive neck brace that will detonate if your patient's heart rate flatlines. Distracting flashbacks supposedly offer motivations for the actions but, by now, the franchise lacks the surprise of the original. **107m/C DVD, Blu-ray Disc.** US Tobin Bell, Shawnee Smith, Angus MacFadyen, Dina Meyer, Bahar Soomekh, Mpho Koaho, Debra McCabe, Donnie Wahlberg, Barry Flatman, Lyriq Bent, Costas Mandylor, Betsy Russell; **D:** Darren Lynn Bousman; **W:** Leigh Whannell; **C:** David Armstrong; **M:** Charlie Clouser.

Sawbones ✓ 1995 (R) Medical school reject Willy Knapp (Harvey) takes out his frustrations by murdering people and then performing gruesome surgeries on the bodies. Cop But Miller (Baldwin) investigates. **78m/C VHS.** Don Harvey, Adam Baldwin, Barbara Carrera, Nina Siemaszko, Nicholas Sadler, Don Stroud; **D:** Catherine Cyran; **C:** Christopher Baffa. CABLE

Sawdust & Tinsel ✓✓✓ *The Naked Night; Sunset of a Clown; Gycklarnas Afton* 1953 Early Bergman film detailing the grisly, humiliating experiences of a traveling circus rolling across the barren Swedish countryside. Lonely parable of human relationships. In Swedish with English subtitles. **87m/B VHS.** SW Harriet Andersson, Ake Gronberg; **D:** Ingmar Bergman; **W:** Ingmar Bergman.

Say Anything ✓✓✓ 1989 (PG-13) A semi-mature, successful teen romance about an offbeat loner Lloyd Dobler (Cusack, in a winning performance), whose interested in the martial arts and going after the beautiful class brain, Diane Court (Skye), of his high school. Things are complicated when her father James (Mahoney) is suspected of embezzling by the IRS. Joan Cusack, John's real-life sister, also plays his sister in the film. Works well on the romantic level without getting too sticky. **100m/C VHS, DVD.** John Cusack, Ione Skye, John Mahoney, Joan Cusack, Lili Taylor, Richard Portnow, Pamela Segall, Jason Gould, Loren Dean, Bebe Neuwirth, Aimee Brooks, Eric Stoltz, Chynna Phillips, Joanna Frank, Jeremy Piven, Don "The Dragon" Wilson; **D:** Cameron

Crowe; **W:** Cameron Crowe. **C:** Laszlo Kovacs; **M:** Anne Dudley, Richard Gibbs, Nancy Wilson.

Say Goodbye, Maggie Cole 🐾½ 1972 A widow goes to work as a doctor in a Chicago street clinic and becomes emotionally involved with a dying child. Hayward's final role in moving made-for-TV drama. 78m/C VHS. Susan Hayward, Darren McGavin, Michael Constantine, Nichelle Nichols, Dane Clark; **D:** Jud Taylor.

Say Hello to Yesterday 🐾½ 1971 (PG) A May-December romance that takes place entirely in one day. An unhappy housewife meets an exciting young traveler while both are in London. Cast and director try hard but fail to get the point across to the audience. 91m/C VHS. Jean Simmons, Leonard Whiting, Evelyn Layer; **D:** Alvin Rakoff.

Say It Isn't So 🐾 2001 (R) The Farrelly brothers produced this tale of boy-meets-girl, boy-gets-girl, boy-finds-out-girl-is-his-sister. They shouldve kept their money and done it themselves, it mightve been a better movie. Klein stars as good-guy orphan Gilly, who meets cute with Jo (Graham), an inept hairdresser who cuts off more than a little off the top. Gilly sets out to set things right amid Farrelly-approved gross-out gags and humiliations galore. First-time helmer Rogers lacks the Farrelly sense of timing and sentiment, which results in most of the jokes falling flat. 95m/C VHS, DVD. US Chris Klein, Heather Graham, Orlando Jones, Sally Field, Richard Jenkins, John Rothman, Jack Plotnick, Eddie Cibrian, Mark Pellegrino, Richard Riehle, Brent Briscoe, Henry Cho, Suzanne Somers, Brent Hinkley, Gerry Swallow; **D:** James B. Rogers; **W:** Peter Gaulke, Gerry Swallow; **C:** Mark Irwin; **M:** Mason Daring.

Say Nothing 🐾🐾 2001 (R) While on vacation by herself, unhappy Grace (Kinski) has a one-nighter with wealthy Julian (Baldwin) who becomes obsessed and wants to get her away from her unemployed husband Matt (Bochner). He even hires Matt to work at his company—much to Grace's distress. A low-budget "Fatal Attraction" minus the boiled bunny. 94m/C VHS, DVD. Nastassja Kinski, William Baldwin, Hart Bochner, Michele Duquet; **D:** Allan Moyle; **W:** Madeline Sunshine; **C:** Walter Bal.

Say Uncle 🐾🐾 2005 (R) Paul (Paige) dotes excessively on his young godson and is devastated when he learns the boy and his family are moving to Japan. So he decides to take his surrogate parenting to the local park where the watchful mothers eye this man-child with suspicion, especially after he admits to mom Maggie (Najimy) that he's gay. Paul's actions may be misconstrued but he behaves stupidly as well, although Maggie is little more than a one-note hysteric. Paige's directorial debut. 91m/C DVD. Peter Paige, Kathy Najimy, Anthony Clark, Melanie Lynskey, Gabrielle Union, Lisa Edelstein; **D:** Peter Paige; **W:** Peter Paige; **C:** David Makin; **M:** Kurt Swinghammer.

Say Yes! 🐾½ 1986 (PG-13) A nutty millionaire (Winters) bets $250 million that his inept nephew cannot get married within 24 hours. Three times the length of usual wacky sitcom, alas. 87m/C VHS. Jonathan Winters, Art Hindle, Logan Ramsey, Lissa Layng; **D:** Larry Yust.

Sayonara 🐾🐾🐾 1957 An Army major is assigned to a Japanese airbase during the Korean conflict at the behest of his future father-in-law. Dissatisfied with his impending marriage, he finds himself drawn to a Japanese dancer and becomes involved in the affairs of his buddy who, against official policy, marries a Japanese woman. Tragedy surrounds the themes of bigotry and interracial marriage. Based on the novel by James Michener. 147m/C VHS, DVD. Marlon Brando, James Garner, Ricardo Montalban, Patricia Owens, Red Buttons, Miyoshi Umeki, Martha Scott, Kent Smith, Miiko Taka; **D:** Joshua Logan; **W:** Paul Osborn; **C:** Ellsworth Fredericks; **M:** Franz Waxman. Oscars '57: Art Dir/Set Dec., Sound Support, Actor (Buttons), Support. Actress (Umeki); Golden Globes '58: Support. Actor (Buttons).

Scalpel 🐾🐾 1976 (R) After his daughter's death, a plastic surgeon creates her image on another woman to get an inheritance. Violent and graphic, with a surprise ending. Not too bad; interesting premise. 95m/C VHS. Robert Lansing, Judith Chapman, Arlen Dean Snyder, Sandy Martin, David Scarroli; **D:** John Grissmer; **W:** John Grissmer.

Scalphunters 🐾🐾½ 1968 Semi-successful, semi-funny western about an itinerant trapper (Lancaster) who is forced by Indians to trade his pelts for an educated black slave (Davis); many chases and brawls ensue. Good performances. 102m/C VHS, DVD. Burt Lancaster, Ossie Davis, Telly Savalas, Shelley Winters, Nick Cravat, Dabney Coleman, Paul Picerni; **D:** Sydney Pollack; **W:** William W. Norton Sr.; **M:** Elmer Bernstein.

Scalps 🐾🐾 1983 (R) Hunted Indian princess and man whose family was killed by Indians form uneasy alliance in old West. 90m/C VHS, DVD. Karen Wood, Alberto Bravo, Vassili Garis; **C:** Werner Knox.

Scam 🐾🐾½ 1993 (R) Maggie and her partner Barry are con artists making their living scamming "high rollers in Miami Beach. Then Maggie tries to pull a con on the wrong man. Jack Shanks is an ex-FBI agent with a score to settle and he black-mails Maggie into helping him. 102m/C VHS. Christopher Walken, Lorraine Bracco, Miguel Ferrer; **D:** John Flynn.

Scandal 🐾🐾🐾 Snuban 1950 Handsome artist (Mifune) and beautiful concert singer (Yamaguchi) become the victims of a libelous article in a gossip magazine. The artist decides to sue but, being softhearted, chooses a questionable lawyer because the man's young daughter is dying. Then the unethical lawyer accepts a bribe to prejudice the case. Japanese with subtitles. 105m/B VHS. JP Toshiro Mifune, Takashi Shimura, Yoshiko (Shirley) Yamaguchi; **D:** Akira Kurosawa; **W:** Ryuzo Kikushima, Akira Kurosawa; **M:** Fumio Hayasaka.

Scandal 🐾🐾🐾 1989 (R) A dramatization of Britain's Profumo government sex scandal of the 1960s. Hurt plays a society doctor who enjoys introducing pretty girls to his wealthy friends. One of the girls, Christine Keeler, takes as lovers both a Russian government official and a British Cabinet Minister. The resulting scandal eventually overturned an entire political party, and led to disgrace, prison, and death for those concerned. Also available in an unedited 115-minute version which contains more controversial language and nudity. Top-notch performances make either version well worth watching. 105m/C VHS, DVD. GB John Hurt, Joanne Whalley, Ian McKellen, Bridget Fonda, Jeroen Krabbe, Britt Ekland, Roland Gift, Daniel Massey, Leslie Phillips, Richard Morant; **D:** Michael Caton-Jones; **W:** Michael Thomas; **C:** Mike Molloy; **M:** Carl Davis.

A Scandal in Paris 🐾🐾½ 1946 Based on the real-life escapades of 19th-century criminal Francois Eugene Vidocq, Vidocq (Sanders) escapes from prison, briefly joins Napoleon's army, and catches the eye of Therese (Hasso), whose father is an important official. Under an assumed name, Vidocq joins the Paris police force in order to

---

Scandalous 🐾 1988 A duke and his uncle work together to find a secretary who disappeared after witnessing a murder. 90m/C VHS. Albert Finney, Lauren Hutton, Ursula Carver, Capucine; **D:** Robert W. Young.

Scandalous John 🐾🐾 1971 (G) Comedy western about a last cattle drive devised by an aging cowboy (Keith) in order to save his ranch. Keith's shrewd acting as the ornery cattle man who won't sell to developers carries this one. 113m/C VHS. Brian Keith, Alfonso Arau, Michele Carey, Rick Lenz, John Ritter, Harry (Henry) Morgan; **D:** Robert Butler.

Scanner Cop 🐾½ 1994 (R) When deranged scientist Sigmund Glock escapes from prison, he's determined to take revenge on Peter Harrigan, the cop who put him behind bars. With the aid of an evil assistant and a mind-altering drug, Glock kidnaps and programs innocent citizens into cop-killing maniacs. Harrigan's only weapon is a rookie cop with the scanner power to read minds—and then destroy them. 94m/C VHS. Daniel Quinn, Darlanne Fluegel, Richard Lynch, Mark Rolston, Hilary Shepard, Gary Hudson, Cyndi Pass, Luca Bercovici, Brion James; **D:** Pierre David; **W:** John Bryant, George Saunders.

Scanner Cop 2: Volkin's Revenge 🐾🐾 1994 (R) Scanner cop Sam Staziak (Quinn) has become curious about his family, asking Carrie Goodart (Haje) to find out what she can. But Carrie's attacked by evil scanner Carl Volkin (Kilpatrick), whom Sam once sent to prison, and left in a coma. Then Sam discovers Volkin is draining the life force of other scanners in order to make himself invincible when he and Sam have their final showdown. 95m/C VHS. Daniel Quinn, Patrick Kilpatrick, Khrystyne Haje, Robert Forster, Stephen Mendel; **D:** Steve Barnett; **W:** Mark Sevi; **C:** Thomas Jewett.

A Scanner Darkly 🐾🐾½ 2006 (R) Trippy, faithful adaptation of Philip K. Dick's 1977 novel of the same name forecasts a blurry, drug-fueled world of paranoia in which the government not only listens to phone calls but watches its citizens through ambiguous undercover police whose identities are secret even to their bosses. Fred (Reeves) is one such agent,

---

The Scalawag Bunch 🐾 1975 Yet another retelling of Robin Hood and his Merry Men and their adventures in Sherwood Forest. 100m/C VHS. IT Mark Damon, Luis Davila, Silvia Dionisio; **D:** George Ferron.

Scalp Merchant 🐾 1977 Private investigator Cliff Rowan hunts for a missing payroll. Someone would rather see him dead than successful. 108m/C VHS. Cameron Mitchell, John Waters, Elizabeth (Liz) Alexander, Margaret Nelson; **D:** Howard Ruble.

Scandal 🐾🐾½ 1967 A French photographer gets in over his head when he snaps the daughter of an American can KKK leader embracing a black man in a nightclub. In French with English subtitles. 86m/C VHS. Josephine Chaplin, Vittorio De Sica, Raymond Pellegrin, Francis Blanche, Maurice Ronet; **D:** Richard Balducci; **W:** Richard Balducci.

Scandal Sheet 🐾🐾 1985 (PG) How low can you go? Writer Helen Grant (Reed) is a broke single mom working in New York, who is lured to la-la land by ruthless Harold Fallan (Lancaster), the publisher of a celebrity scandal rag. Helen learns her employment isn't random; Fallan wants her write a nasty piece on the attempted comeback of fresh-out-of-alcohol-rehab actor Ben Rowen (Urich) since she was the college roomie of his wife, actress Meg (Hutton). Helen tries to take the high road but Fallan puts the pressure on and Helen is soon down in the muck with the rest of the scavengers. 101m/C VHS. Burt Lancaster, Pamela Reed, Robert Urich, Lauren Hutton, Peter Jurasik; **D:** David Lowell Rich; **W:** Howard Rodman; **C:** Jacques "Jack" Marquette; **M:** Randy Edelman. TV

---

perpetrate his biggest crime. Instead, thanks to Therese's love, he goes straight. Sanders does an excellent job. 100m/B VHS, DVD. George Sanders, Signe Hasso, Akim Tamiroff, Carole Landis, Gene Lockhart, Alan Napier, Vladimir Sokoloff, Alma Kruger; **D:** Douglas Sirk; **W:** Ellis St. Joseph; **C:** Guy Roe; **M:** Hanns Eisler, Heinz Roemheld.

Scandal Man 🐾🐾½ 1967 A ...

Scanners 🐾🐾½ 1981 (R) "Scanners" are telepaths who can will people to explode. One scanner in particular has psychic abilities for his band of psychic gangsters. Gruesome but effective special effects. 102m/C VHS, DVD. CA Stephen Lack, Jennifer O'Neill, Patrick McGoohan, Lawrence Dane, Michael Ironside, Robert A. Silverman; **D:** David Cronenberg; **C:** Mark Irwin; **M:** Howard Shore.

Scanners 2: The New Order 🐾🐾½ 1991 (R) This not-bad sequel to the 1981 cult classic finds a power-mad police official out to build a psychic militia of captured scanners. More psychotic than the first two films. 104m/C VHS. Steve Parrish, Liliana Komorowska, Valentin Trujillo, Tom Butler, Vlasta Vrana, Dorothee Berryman, Raoul Trujillo; **C:** David Hew; **W:** B.J. Nelson; **M:** Marty Simon.

Scanners 3: The Takeover 🐾½ 1992 (R) The third sequel in which Scanner siblings battle for control of the world. Lacks the creativity and storyline of the first two films. 101m/C VHS. Steve Parrish, Liliana Komorowska, Valerie Valois; **D:** Christian Duguay.

The Scar 🐾🐾½ Hollow Triumph 1948 A cunning criminal robs the mob, then hides by "stealing" the identity of a look-alike psychologist. But he's overlooked one thing...or two. Farfetched film noir show-thing...or two. Based on a novel by Murray Forbes. 83m/B VHS, DVD. Paul Henreid, Joan Bennett, Eduard Franz, Leslie Brooks, John Qualen, Mabel Paige, Herbert Rudley; **D:** Steve Sekely.

Scar of Shame 🐾🐾 1927 Explores the ill-fated romance between a successful black concert pianist and the lower-class woman he marries. Gives a look at the color caste system and divisions within the black community of the era. 90m/B VHS. Harry Henderson, Lucia Lynn Moses, Ann Kennedy, Norman Johnstone; **D:** Frank Peregini.

Scaramouche 🐾🐾🐾½ 1952 Thrilling swashbuckler about a nobleman family during the French Revolution. To avenge the death of a friend, he joins a theatre troupe where he learns swordplay and becomes the character "Scaramouche." Features a rousing six-and-a-half-minute sword battle. 111m/C VHS, DVD. Stewart Granger, Eleanor Parker, Janet Leigh, Mel Ferrer, Henry Wilcoxon, Nina Foch, Richard Anderson, Robert Coote, Lewis Stone, Elisabeth Risdon, Howard Freeman; **D:** George Sidney; **C:** Charles Rosher.

Scarecrow 🐾🐾½ 1973 (R) Two homeless drifters (Hackman and Pacino) walk across America, heading toward a car wash business they never reach. An oft-neglected example of the early 70s extra-realistic subgenre initiated by "Midnight Cowboy." Engrossing until the end, when it falls flat. Filmed on location in De-

ordered to spy on his pill-popping friends (Downey Jr., Harrelson, Cochrane, and Ryder) and the owner of the house where they drop in to check out who happens to be another incarnation of himself. Confusing? That's the point. Director Linklater utilizes a technique known as "interpolated rotoscoping," essentially digitally adding a layer of animation over footage of live actors, which effectively enhances the altered-states feel. 102m/C DVD, Blu-ray Disc. Keanu Reeves, Winona Ryder, Robert Downey Jr., Woody Harrelson, Rory Cochrane, Melody Chase, Lisa Marie Newmyer; **D:** Richard Linklater; **W:** Richard Linklater; **C:** Shane Kelly; **M:** Graham Reynolds.

troit. 112m/C VHS, DVD. Gene Hackman, Al Pacino, Ann Wedgeworth, Eileen Brennan, Richard Lynch, Fredric Myrow, Penelope Allen, Dorothy Tristan, Rutanya Alda; C: Vilmos Zsigmond. Cannes '73: Film.

Scared Stiff 1953 Fleeing a murder charge, Martin and Lewis find gangsters and ghosts on a Caribbean island. Funny and scary, a good remake of "The Ghost Breakers," with cameos by Hope and Crosby. ♪San Domingo; Song of the Enchilada Man; Mama Yo Quiero; You Hit the Spot; I Don't Care If the Sun Don't Shine; I'm Your Pal; When Somebody Thinks You're Wonderful. 108m/B VHS. Dean Martin, Jerry Lewis, Lizabeth Scott, Carmen Miranda, Dorothy Malone; *Cameos:* Bob Hope, Bing Crosby; D: George Marshall.

Scared Stiff 1987 (R) Three people move into a mansion once owned by a sadistic slave trader. Once there, they become unwilling victims of a voodoo curse. Bad special effects and script, not redeemed by decent but unoriginal story. 85m/C VHS. Andrew Stevens, Mary Page Keller, David Ramsey; D: Richard Friedman, Mark Frost, Daniel F. Bacaner.

Scared to Death 1946 Begins with a woman dying of fright when shown the death mask of the man she framed. Dead woman then proceeds to narrate the remainder of the story, which focuses on events leading up to her unfortunate, untimely, and fairly uninteresting demise. Memorable as Lugosi's only color film. DVD version is paired with 1941's "The Devil Bat." 60m/C VHS, DVD. Bela Lugosi, George Zucco, Douglas Fowley, Nat Pendleton, Joyce Compton; D: Christy Cabanne.

Scared to Death 1980 (R) A scientific experiment goes awry as a mutation begins killing off the residents of Los Angeles. 93m/C VHS, DVD. John Stinson, Diana Davidson, David Moses, Kermit Eller; D: William Malone; M: Tom Chase.

Scarface *Scarface: The Shame of a Nation* 1931 The violent rise and fall of 1930s Chicago crime boss Tony Camonte—magnetically played by Muni—and based on the life of notorious gangster Al Capone. Release was held back by censors due to the amount of violence and its suggestion of incest between the title character and his sister (Dvorak). Morley is ice-cold at Tony's moll Poppy. Producer Howard Hughes recut and filmed an alternate ending, without director Hawks' approval, to pacify the censors, and both versions of the film were released at the same time. Remains brilliant and impressive. Remade in 1983. 93m/B VHS, DVD. Paul Muni, Ann Dvorak, Karen Morley, Osgood Perkins, George Raft, Boris Karloff, W.R. Burnett, Ben Hecht, John Lee Mahin, Seton I. Miller; D: Howard Hawks; W: Fred Pasley; C: Lee Garmes; M: Gus Arnheim, Adolph Tandler. Natl. Film Reg. '94.

Scarface 1983 (R) Al Pacino is a Cuban refugee who becomes powerful in the drug trade until the life gets the better of him. A remake of the 1932 classic gangster film of the same name, although the first film has more plot. Extremely violent, often unpleasant, but not easily forgotten. 170m/C VHS, DVD, UMD. Al Pacino, Steven Bauer, Michelle Pfeiffer, Robert Loggia, F. Murray Abraham, Mary Elizabeth Mastrantonio, Harris Yulin, Paul Shenar, Oliver Stone, Pepe Serna, Mark Margolis, Richard Belzer, Victor Campos, Gregg Henry; D: Brian De Palma; W: Oliver Stone; C: John A. Alonzo; M: Giorgio Moroder.

Scarface Mob 1962 This is the original TV pilot film for the popular series "The Untouchables," about Eliot Ness's band of good guys battling Chicago's crime lord, Al Capone. Still strong stuff. Narrated by Walter Winchell. 120m/B VHS. Robert Stack, Neville Brand, Barbara Nichols; D: Phil Karlson; W: Paul Monash; *Nar:* Walter Winchell. TV. *Tueur de Chicago*

The Scarlet & the Black 1983 A priest clandestinely works within the shield of the Vatican's diplomatic immunity to shelter allied soldiers from the Nazis in occupied Rome. His efforts put him at odds with the Pope and target him for Gestapo assassination. Swashbuckling adventure at its second-best. Based on the nonfiction book "The Scarlet Pimpernel of the Vatican" by J.P. Gallagher. 145m/C VHS, DVD. Gregory Peck, Christopher Plummer, John Gielgud, Raf Vallone; D: Jerry London; M: Ennio Morricone. TV.

The Scarlet Car 1917 Chaney is a bank cashier who discovers his boss has been embezzling funds. A fight causes Chaney to believe he has killed his employer and he hides out in a remote cabin where guilt preys on his mind. 50m/B VHS. Lon Chaney Sr., Franklyn Farnum, Edith Johnson, Sam De Grasse; D: Joseph DeGrasse.

Scarlet Claw *and the Scarlet Claw Sherlock Holmes* 1944 Holmes and Watson solve the bloody murder of an old lady in the creepy Canadian village of Le Mort Rouge. The best and most authentic of the Sherlock Holmes series. 74m/B VHS, DVD. Basil Rathbone, Nigel Bruce, Miles Mander, Gerald Hamer, Kay Harding; D: Roy William Neill.

The Scarlet Clue 1945 A better script and faster pacing improved this Monogram entry in the Chan series. Charlie investigates a series of mysterious deaths which lead to a plot to steal secret government radar plans. 65m/B VHS, DVD. Sidney Toler, Benson Fong, Mantan Moreland, Robert E. Homans, Helen Devereaux; D: Phil Rosen.

Scarlet Dawn 1932 Lavish sets and costumes abound in this romantic drama starring Fairbanks as a Russian aristocrat and Carroll as his maid servant. Together they flee Russia during the Revolution, marry, and settle into the life of the common working class. Restless under his new status, Fairbanks pursues Tashman and tries his hand at swindling. A slow but interesting love story. Adapted from the novel "Revolt" by Mary McCall. 58m/B VHS. Douglas Fairbanks Jr., Nancy Carroll and Alexander, Frank Reicher; D: William Dieterle; W: Douglas Fairbanks Jr., Niven Busch, Erwin Gelsey.

Scarlet Diva 2000 Writer/director/star Asia Argento, daughter of Italian horror director Dario Argento, explores the trappings of fame in her semi-autobiographical debut. As Anna Battista, Argento is an Italian actress tired of her success and looking for love and fulfillment. Anna's mother (Argento's real life mother, Nicolodi), glimpsed in flashbacks, died of a methadone overdose, and her childhood in general has clearly left her damaged. She becomes easy prey for Hollywood vultures like the lascivious producer (Coleman) who wants to cast her in a "Cleopatra" remake opposite Robert De Niro. Back in Rome, Anna's decadent lifestyle is briefly interrupted when she falls in love with an Australian rock star (Shepherd) who promptly leaves her pregnant and devastated. Strangely watchable, but wildly formless style and digital video format matches pic's equally rambling writing and acting. In English, French, and Italian. 91m/C VHS, DVD. IT Asia Argento, Daria Nicolodi, Joe Coleman, Francesca D'Aloja, Jean Shepard, Herbert Fritsch, Gianluca Arcopinto; D: Asia Argento; W: Asia Argento; C: Frederic Fasano.

Scarlet Empress 1934 One of Von Sternberg's greatest films tells the story of Catherine the Great and her rise to power. Dietrich stars as the beautiful royal wife who outwits her foolish husband Peter (Jaffe) to become empress of Russia. Incredibly rich decor is a visual feast for the eye, as perfectionist von Sternberg fussed over every detail. Dietrich is excellent as Catherine, and von Sternberg's mastery of lighting and camera work makes for a highly extravagant film. Based on the diary of Catherine the Great. 110m/B VHS, DVD. Marlene Dietrich, John Lodge, Sam Jaffe, Louise Dresser, Maria Sieber, Sir C. Aubrey Smith, Ruthelma Stevens, Olive Tell; D: Josef von Sternberg; W: Manuel Komroff; C: Bert Glennon.

The Scarlet Letter 1934 Unlikely comic relief provides only measure of redemption for this poorly rendered version of Hawthorne's classic novel about sin and Hester Prynne. 69m/B VHS, DVD. Colleen Moore, Hardie Albright, Henry B. Walthall, Alan Hale, Cora Sue Collins, Betty Blythe; D: Robert G. Vignola.

The Scarlet Letter 1973 A studied, thoughtful, international production of the Nathaniel Hawthorne classic about a woman's adultery which incites puritanical violence and hysteria in colonial America. Fine modernization by Wenders. In German with English subtitles. 90m/C VHS, DVD. SP GE Senta Berger, Lou Castel, Yella Rottlaender, William Layton, Yelena Samarina, Hans-Christian Blech; D: Wim Wenders.

The Scarlet Letter 1979 Faithful yet passionate TV adaptation of Hawthorne's classic novel of 17th-century New England. Hester Prynne (Foster) is condemned by her Puritan fellows for having a child out of wedlock and is forced to wear a scarlet letter A for adultery. Secretly sharing Hester's torment is the Rev. Arthur Dimmesdale (Heard), the baby's father, and Hester's vengeful back-from-the-dead husband, Roger Chillingsworth (Conway). 240m/C VHS, DVD. Meg Foster, John Heard, Kevin Conway, Josef Sommer; D: Rick Hauser; W: Allan Knee, Alvin Sapinsley; M: John Morris.

The Scarlet Letter 1995 (R) Ewwwwww—ego-driven stinker of '95 ("Showgirls" not-withstanding). Feisty Hester Prynne (Moore) is condemned to wear the scarlet letter "A" of adultery by her 17th-century Puritan neighbors because she bore a child out of wedlock. Oldman is the lusty Reverend Arthur Dimmesdale (her partner in illicit passion) while Duvall chews scenery as Hester's wronged hubby. This "freely adapted" version of the 1850 American classic should have set author Nathaniel Hawthorne spinning in his grave as his moral saga of sin and redemption meets 20th-century moviemaking by having the passion made explicit and a happy ending tacked on. 135m/C VHS, DVD. Demi Moore, Gary Oldman, Robert Duvall, Robert Prosky, Edward Hardwicke, Joan Plowright, Roy Dotrice, Dana Ivey, Sheldon Peters Wolfchild, Diane Salinger, Lisa Joliff-Andoh, Amy Wright, Tim Woodward; D: Roland Joffe; W: Douglas Day Stewart; C: Alex Thomson; M: John Barry. Golden Raspberries '95: Worst Remake/Sequel.

The Scarlet Pimpernel 1934 Sir Percy Blakeney (Howard) is a supposed dandy of the English court who assumes the identity of "The Scarlet Pimpernel" in order to outwit the French Republicans and aid innocent aristocrats during the French Revolution. The frustrated French send sinister ambassador Chauvelin (Massey) to discover the rogue's identity and involve Blakeney's French wife, Marguerite (Oberon) in their plot. Classic rendering of Baroness Orczy's novel, full of exploits, 18th century costumes, intrigue, damsels, etc. Produced by Alexander Korda, who fired the initial director, Rowland Brown. Remade twice for TV. 95m/B VHS, DVD. GB Leslie Howard, Joan Gardner, Merle Oberon, Raymond Massey, Anthony Bushell, Nigel Bruce, Bramwell Fletcher, Walter Rilla, O.B. Clarence, Ernest Milton, Edmund Breon, Melville Cooper, Gibb McLaughlin, Morland Graham, Allan Jeayes; D: Harold Young; W: Robert Sherwood, Arthur Wimperis, Lajos Biro; C: Harold Rosson; M: Arthur Benjamin.

The Scarlet Pimpernel 1982 Remake of the classic about a British dandy who saved French aristocrats from the Reign of Terror guillotines during the French Revolution. Almost as good as the original 1935 film, with beautiful costumes and sets and good performances from Seymour and Andrews. 142m/C VHS, DVD. GB Anthony Andrews, Jane Seymour, Ian McKellen, James Villiers, Eleanor David; D: Clive Donner; M: Nick Bicat. TV.

The Scarlet Pimpernel 1999 Wealthy, foppish English aristocrat, Sir Percy Blakeney (Grant), is not the fool many believe him to be. Indeed, he masquerades as the daring Scarlet Pimpernel, the rescuer of those persecuted by the French Revolution, and the bane of the French spy Chauvelin (Shaw). Why Percy has even managed to fool his lovely French wife, Marguerite (McGovern), who was once involved with Chauvelin, and who comes to see her husband in a more heroic light. Based on the novels by Baroness Emmuska Orczy. 120m/C VHS, DVD. Richard E. Grant, Elizabeth McGovern, Martin Shaw, Anthony Green, Ronan Vibert, Christopher Fairbank, Jonathan Coy, Emilia Fox, Dominic Mafham; D: Patrick Lau; W: Richard Carpenter; C: Simon Kossoff; M: Michael Pavlicek. CABLE.

The Scarlet Pimpernel 2: Mademoiselle Guillotine 1999 The Scarlet Pimpernel and wife Marguerite head to France to save the daughter of a French nobleman from the clutches of Gabrielle Damiens (Black), AKA Mademoiselle Guillotine, and her band of revolutionaries. The disgraced Chauvelin is also involved and then Marguerite gets captured, so quite a lot of rescuing needs to be done. Based on the books by Baroness Emmuska Orczy. 90m/C VHS, DVD. Richard E. Grant, Elizabeth McGovern, Martin Shaw, Anthony Green, Ronan Vibert, Christopher Fairbank, Jonathan Coy, Denise Black, James Callis, Peter Jeffrey, Julie Cox; D: Patrick Lau; W: Richard Carpenter; C: Simon Kossoff; M: Michael Pavlicek. CABLE.

The Scarlet Pimpernel 3: The Kidnapped King 1999 France's 10-year-old Dauphin is under the control of Robespierre when he is captured by a masked figure. As Sir Percy investigates, all clues point to legendary swordsman Chevalier D'Orly. Meanwhile, Marguerite has supposedly left Sir Percy and although Robespierre isn't convinced, Chauvelin is plotting to win back his former love. Based on the books by Baroness Emmuska Orczy. 90m/C VHS. Richard E. Grant, Elizabeth McGovern, Martin Shaw, Anthony Green, Ronan Vibert, Christopher Fairbank, Jonathan Coy, Suzanne Bertish, Jerome Willis, Bryce Engstrom, Dalibor Sipek; D: Edward Bennett; W: Richard Carpenter; C: John Hooper; M: Michael Pavlicek. CABLE.

Scarlet Spear 1954 Woof! Filmed in Nairobi National Park in Kenya. A great white hunter convinces a young African chief that the ancient practices of his people are uncivilized. Pathetically stated and culturally offensive by today's standards. 78m/C VHS. John Bentley, Martha Hyer, Morasi; D: George Breakston, C. Ray Stahl; W: George Breakston, C. Ray Stahl; M: Ivor Slaney.

Scarlet Street 1945 A mild-mannered, middle-aged cashier becomes an embezzler when he gets involved with a predatory, manipulating woman. Lang remake of Jean Renoir's "La Chienne" (1931). Set apart from later attempts on the same theme by excellent direction by Lang and acting. Also available Colorized. 95m/B VHS, DVD. Edward G. Robinson, Joan Bennett, Dan Duryea, Samuel S. Hinds; D: Fritz Lang; C: Milton Krasner.

The Scarlet Tunic 1997 Based on the novella "The Melancholy Hussar of the German Legion" by Thomas Hardy. It's 1802 in Hardy's fictional Wessex countryside where a light cavalry regiment of bored Germans, fighting with the British against Napoleon, has an encampment on the land of retired doctor Edward Groves (Shepherd). Groves' pretty daughter Frances (Fielding) is engaged to local businessman Humphrey Gould (Sessions) but, of course, she falls for dashing German hussar Matthaus Singer (Barr). Since this is a Hardy story, don't expect any happy endings. 101m/C VHS. GB Jean-Marc Barr, Emma Fielding, Simon Callow, John Sessions, Jack Shepherd, Andrew Tiernan, Thomas Lockyer; D: Stuart St. Paul; W: Stuart St. Paul, Mark Jenkins, Colin Clements; C: Malcolm McLean; M: John Scott. TV.

Scarlett 1994 (PG-13) Well, fiddle-dee-dee. While purists may object to any tampering of "Gone With the Wind," this epic TV miniseries, from the Alexandra Ripley novel, manages to be good if overlong fun for those willing to sit back and relax. Scarlett tries to get back Tara and Rhett (they divorce but still battle continuously); explores her Irish family ties and even moves to Ireland; then gets involved with the wrong man and is accused of murder so Rhett can save her and everything can turn out okay (there's lots more). The big budget is up on-screen ...

with lavish costumes and sets and a big cast—although why two Brits got the leads in this Southern melodrama is anyone's guess. *(Whalley and Dalton try hard).* **360m/C VHS, DVD.** *Joanne Whalley* (Faris), from the previous "Strays" ends up on the farm of Tom Logan (Rex) while tracking down to whoever watches. Machine-gun fire gags whiz by, missing most of the movies he spoofs and plays them for all they're worth, which isn't very much. Blond moment between Anderson and McCarthy is a highlight, as is Latifah in "Matrix" spoof. **90m/C VHS, DVD.** *US Anna Faris, Anthony Anderson, Leslie Nielsen, Carmyn Manheim, Simon Rex, George Carlin, Queen Latifah, Eddie Griffin, Denise Richards, Regina Hall, Charlie Sheen, Kevin Hart; Cameos: Pamela Anderson, Jenny McCarthy, Jeremy Piven, D.L. Hughley, Ja Rule, Master P, Marny Ray Redman, Raekwon, Pat Proft; C: Mark Irwin; M: James L. Venable.*

Scary Movie 4 🐾🐾½ 2006 (PG-13)
Critic-proof spoof has Zucker returning for a second director's stint and the formula staying the same. Nominal story involves Cindy (Faris) being a home care worker for an elderly woman (unbilled Leachman) and falling for divorced dad Tom (Bielko, doing that Cruise couch-jumping thing in front of a fake Oprah). Films spoofed include "Saw," "The Village," "War of the Worlds," and more. Some jokes hit, more miss, but the franchise made $41 million its opening weekend so it's likely to lead to a fifth go-round. **83m/C DVD, HD DVD.** *US Anna Faris, Regina Hall, Craig Bielko, Anthony Anderson, Carmen Electra, Chris Elliot, Kevin Hart, Cloris Leachman, Michael Madsen, Leslie Nielsen, Bill Pullman, Simon Rex, Charlie Sheen, Molly Shannon, Shaquille O'Neal, Bryan Callen, Dave Attell, Conchita Campbell, Debra Wilson, Patrice O'Neal; D: David Zucker; W: Craig Mazin, Jim Abrahams; C: Thomas Ackerman; M: James L. Venable; Nar: James Earl Jones.*

Scavenger Hunt 🐾 1979 (PG) Action begins when a deceased millionaire's will states that his 15 would-be heirs must compete in a scavenger hunt, and whoever collects all the items first wins the entire fortune. Big cast wanders about aimlessly. **117m/C VHS.** *Richard Benjamin, James Coco, Ruth Buzzi, Cloris Leachman, Cleavon Little, Roddy McDowall, Scatman Crothers, Tony Randall, Robert Morley, Richard Mulligan, Dirk Benedict, Willie Aames, Vincent Price; D: Michael A. Schultz; M: Billy Goldenberg.*

Scavengers 🐾 1987 (PG-13) A man and a woman become involved in a spy plot and wind up in all sorts of danger. Pathetic excuse for a "thriller." **94m/C VHS.** *Kenneth Gilman, Brenda Bakke, Ken Gampu, Norman Anstey, Crispin De N/s; D: Duncan McLachlan.*

Scenario du Film Passion 🐾🐾 1982 A classically self-analyzing video piece by Godard, in which he "recreates on tape the scenario for his film 'Passion,' resulting in a reflexive, experimental essay on the process of image-making and conceptualizing films, especially Godard's. In French with English subtitles. **54m/C VHS.** *D: Jean-Luc Godard; Anne-Marie Mieville, Bernard Menoud.*

Scene of the Crime 🐾🐾½ 1985 Three short mysteries, which the audience is asked to solve: "The Newlywed Murder," "Medium Is the Murder," and "Vote for Murder." **74m/C VHS; Merkle Post, Orson Welles. TV.**

Scene of the Crime 🐾🐾 1987 Beautiful widow, trapped in small French town, is sexually awakened by escaped convict hiding out near her home. Acclaimed, but sometimes distracting camera technique and slow pace undermine the film. In French with English subtitles. **90m/C VHS.** *FR Catherine Deneuve, Danielle Darrieux, Wadeck Stanczak, Victor Lanoux, Nicolas Giraudi, Jean Bousquet, Claire Nebout; D: Andre Techine; W: Olivier Assayas.*

The Scent of a Woman 🐾🐾 1975 Sweet Smell of Woman; Profumo di Donna 1975 An acclaimed dark comedy that may be an acquired taste for some. A blinded military officer and his valet take a sensual tour of Italy, the sightless man seducing beautiful women on the way. But at the real point of the tale, based on a novel by Giovanni Arpino, in Italian with English subtitles. Remade in 1992 as "Scent of a Woman." **103m/C VHS, DVD.** *IT Alessandro Momo, Agostina Belli, Moira Orfei, Franco Rico, Vittorio Gassman; D: Dino Risi; W: Ruggero Maccari, Dino Risi; C: Claudio Cirillo; M: Armando Trovajoli.*

Scenes from a Marriage 🐾🐾🐾 1973 (PG) Originally produced in six one-hour episodes for Swedish TV, this bold and sensitive film excruciatingly portrays the painful, unpleasant disintegration of a marriage. Ullmann is superb. Realistic and disturbing. Dubbed. **168m/C VHS, DVD, SW Liv Ullmann, Erland Josephson, Bibi Andersson, Jan Malmsjo, Anita Wall; D: Ingmar Bergman; W: Ingmar Bergman; Giorgio Piazza; D: Alberto De Martino.** *Film: N.Y. Film Critics '74; Actress (Ullmann), Screenplay; Natl. Soc. Film Critics '74: Actress (Ullmann), Film, Screenplay, Support. Actress (Andersson).*

Scenes from the Class Struggle in Beverly Hills 🐾🐾 1989 (R) Social satire about the wealthy, their servants, and the hangers-on in two Hollywood households. Two chauffeurs spend their spare time lusting after their lovely employers, and bet to see who can accomplish reality first. All kinds of erotic capers result. Usually funny and irreverent; occasionally misfires or takes itself too seriously. Reunites the trio from cult classic "Eating Raoul". **91m/C VHS.** *Jacqueline Bisset, Ray Sharkey, Mary Woronov, Robert Beltran, Ec Begley Jr., Wallace Shawn, Paul Bartel, Paul Mazursky, Amelia Walker, Rebecca Schaeffer, Edith Diaz; Cameos: Little Richard, Michael Feinstein; D: Paul Bartel; W: Bruce Wagner; C: Steven Fierberg; M: Stanley Myers.*

Scenes from a Murder 🐾½ 1972 A killer (Savalas) stalks a beautiful actress (Heywood). Dull excuse for a suspense flick. **91m/C VHS.** *IT Telly Savalas, Anne Heywood, Giorgio Piazza; D: Alberto De Martino.*

Scenes from the Goldmine 🐾½ 1987 (R) A young woman joins a rock band and falls in love with its lead singer. Realistic but bland, music not memorable (performed mostly by the actors themselves). **99m/C VHS.** *Catherine Mary Stewart, Cameron Dye, Joe Pantoliano, John Ford Coley, Steve Railsback, Timothy B. Schmit, Jewel Shepard, Alex Rozco, Lee Ving, Lesley-Anne Down; D: Marc Rocco.*

Scenes from a Sexual Nature 🐾 2006 (R) All talk and no action, in case you were wondering about that title. The relationships of seven couples are explored during one summer afternoon on London's Hampstead Heath. There's a gay couple, a divorced couple, one on a blind date, one couple arguing and breaking up, and one meeting accidentally years after their romance, among other moments. **92m/C DVD, GB Ewan McGregor, Eileen Atkins, Hugh Bonneville, Holly Aird, Douglas Hodge, Adrian Lester, Andrew Lincoln, Sophie Okonedo, Mark Strong, Catherine Tate, Eglantine Rembauville, Polly Walker, Benjamin Whitrow; D: Ed Blum; W: Aschlin Ditta; C: David Meadows; M: Dominik Scherrer.*

Scent of Green Papaya 🐾🐾🐾 Mui du Xanh 1993 Tranquil film, set in 1951 Vietnam, follows 10-year-old peasant girl Mui as she spends the next 10 years as a servant in a troubled family, gracefully accommodating herself to the small changes in her life. At 20, she finds a fairy-tale romance with her next employer, a young pianist. Presents a romanticized view of the stoicism of Vietnamese women but is visually beautiful. Directorial debut of Hung is based on his childhood memories of Vietnam, which he re-created on a soundstage outside Paris. In Vietnamese with English subtitles. **104m/C VHS, DVD, VT Tran Nu Yen-Khe, Lu Man San, Truong Thi Loc, Vuong Hoa Hoi, Tran Anh Hung; W: Tran Anh Hung, Patricia Petit; C: Benoit Delhomme; M: Ton That Tiet.*

Schemes 🐾🐾 1995 (R) Grieving widower Paul Stewart (McCaffrey) becomes interested in Laura Pierce (Hope), a lovely young woman who said she knew his late wife. Then, Paul's business partner Evelyn (Draper) discovers Laura's not on the up and up and is really interested in Paul's substantial insurance payoff. Laura's part of a con job set up by volatile Victor (Glover), but since Evelyn's also in love with Paul, things aren't all as they seem. **95m/C VHS, DVD.** *John Glover, Poly Draper, Leslie Hoze, James McCaffrey, John de Lancie, Allison Mackie; D: Derek Westervelt; W: Derek Westervelt; M: Mark Chait.*

Schindler's List 🐾🐾🐾🐾 1993 (R) Spielberg's staggering evocation of the Holocaust finds its voice in Oskar Schindler (Neeson), womanizing German businessman and aspiring war profiteer, who cajoled, bribed, and bullied the Nazis into allowing him to employ Jews in his factories during WWII. By doing so he saved over 1,000 lives. The atrocities are depicted matter of factly as a by-product of sheer Nazi evil. Shot in black and white for the story, sets of the Auschwitz concentration camp were reconstructed directly outside the camp after protests about "filming" on the actual site. A tour de force and labor of love for Spielberg, who finally garnered the attention and respect as a filmmaker he deserves. **195m/B VHS, DVD. Liam Neeson, Ben Kingsley, Ralph Fiennes, Embeth Davidtz, Caroline Goodall, Jonathan Sagalle, Mark Ivanir, Malgoscha Gebel, Shmulik Levy, Beatrice Macola, Andrzej Seweryn, Friedrich von Thun, Norbert Weisser, Michael Schneider, Anna Mucha; D: Steven Spielberg; W: Steven Zaillian; C: Janusz Kaminski; M: John Williams. Oscars '93: Adapt. Screenplay, Art Dir./Set Dec., Cinematog., Director (Spielberg), Film Editing, Picture, Orig. Score; AFI '98: Top 100; British A.awd. '93: Adapt. Screenplay, Director (Spielberg), Film, Support. Actor (Fiennes); Directors Guild '93: Director (Spielberg); Golden Globes '94: Director, Drama, Screenplay; L.A. Film Critics '93: Cinematog., Director (Spielberg), Film, Support. Actor (Fiennes); Natl. Bd. of Review '93: Film, Natl. Film Reg. '04; N.Y. Film Critics '93: Cinematog., Director (Spielberg), Film, Support. Actor (Fiennes); Natl. Film Critics '93: Cinematog., Director (Spielberg), Film, Support. Actor (Fiennes); Writers Guild '93: Adapt. Screenplay.*

Scary Movie 🐾🐾 2000 (R) If the last few Leslie Nielsen outings didn't convince you that the genre spoof was played out, this parody of "Scream" and all its progeny will. The Wayans brothers go for quantity of jokes and targets, and quality definitely suffers for it. Fart gags and gratuitous cussing (neither of which we often object to, but we have our limits) are substituted for focused satire. If you're looking for well-done genre spookery, rent "Airplane!" and "I'm Gonna Git You Sucka" and leave this one to the discount previously viewed bin. **85m/C VHS, DVD, Blu-ray Disc.** *Keenen Ivory Wayans, Marlon Wayans, Shawn Wayans, Carmen Electra, Jon Abrahams, Shannon Elizabeth, Lochlyn Munro, Cheri Oteri, Anna Faris, Regina Hall, Kurt Fuller, David Lander, Dave Sheridan, Dan Joffre; D: Keenen Ivory Wayans; W: Marlon Wayans, Shawn Wayans; C: Francois Kenny; M: David Kitay.*

Scary Movie 2 🐾 2001 (R) You knew they were lying when the tagline of this first film declared, "No mercy, no shame, no sequel." Especially since the spoof brought in more than $144 million worldwide. The plot, such as it is, consists of a spooky doctor (Curry) convincing the Wayans to parody a whole new batch of movies and do a lot (and we mean A LOT) of bodily fluid and sex jokes. Unfortunately, they don't do it any better than they did the first time, and whatever freshness the original had is long gone. **82m/C VHS, DVD.** *US Anna Faris, Shawn Wayans, Marlon Wayans, Chris Elliott, Tori Spelling, Christopher K. Masterson, Kathleen Robertson, Regina Hall, James Woods, David Cross, Andy Richter, Natasha Lyonne, Veronica Cartwright, Richard Moll; D: Keenen Ivory Wayans; W: Shawn Wayans, Marlon Wayans, Alyson Fouse, Greg Grabianski, Dave Polsky, Michael Anthony Snowden, Craig Wayans; C: Steven Bernstein; V: Coleen (Ann) Fitzpatrick.*

Scary Movie 3 🐾½ 2003 (PG-13) Zucker-directed spoof pushes the limits of parody in this Wayans-created franchise with rehashed gags and strained satire.

Scarred 🐾½ Street Love; Red on Red 1984 (R) Unwed teenage mother becomes prostitute to support baby. Predictable plot and acting pull this one down. **85m/C VHS.** *Jennifer Mayo, Jackie Berryman, David Dean; D: Rosemarie Turko.*

Scarred City 🐾🐾 1998 (R) Cliched and predictable actioner with a decent cast. Trigger-happy cop John Trace (Baldwin) is forced to join an elite crime unit, headed by Laine Devon (Palminteri), which uses any means necessary to get the job done. But Trace soon decides that his fellow cops are basically just fulfilling their own violent impulses. Then Trace saves hooker Candy (Carrere) from a mob hit and his buddies decide they'd be better off without him. **95m/C VHS, DVD.** *Chazz Palminteri, Stephen Baldwin, Tia Carrere, Gary Dourdan, Michael Rispoli, Steve Flynn; D: Ken Sanzel; W: Ken Sanzel; C: Michael Slovis; M: Anthony Marinelli.*

The Scars of Dracula 🐾🐾½ 1970 (R) A young couple tangles with Dracula in their search for the man's missing brother. Gory, creepy, violent, sexy tale from the dark side. Don't see it late at night. Preceded by "Taste the Blood of Dracula" and followed by "Dracula A.D. 1972." **96m/C VHS, DVD, GB Christopher Lee, Jenny Hanley, Dennis Waterman, Wendy Hamilton, Patrick Troughton, Michael Gwynn, Anoushka (Anouska) Hempel, Michael Ripper, Christopher Matthews, Delia Lindsay; D: Roy Ward Baker; W: John (Anthony Hinds) Elder; M: James Bernard.*

Scary City 🐾½ You knew they were lying when the tagline...

Mainly a send up of flicks "The Ring" and "Signs," TV reporter Cindy Campbell depth of talent of Allen and Midler. **87m/C VHS, DVD.** *Woody Allen, Bete Midler, Bill Irwin, Daren Firestone, Rebecca Nickels; Cameos: Father Murphy.*

(bottom column, Scent of a Woman 1992)
Scent of a Woman 🐾🐾🐾 1992 (R) Pacino is a powerhouse (verging on caricature) in a story that, with anyone else in the lead, would be your run-of-the-mill, overly sentimental coming of age/redemption flick. Blind, bitter, and semi-alcoholic Pacino is a retired army colonel being cared for in his married niece's home alone over Thanksgiving, under the

watchful eye of local prep school student Charlie (O'Donnell). Pacino's abrasive (though wonderfully intuitive and romantic) colonel makes an impact on viewers that lingers like a woman's scent long after the last tango. O'Donnell is competently understated in key supporting role, while the tango lesson between Pacino and Anwar dances to the tune of "classic." Boxoffice winner as a remake of 1975 Italian film "Profumo di Donna," the 1974 **157m/C VHS, DVD, HD DVD.** *Al Pacino, Chris O'Donnell, James Rebhorn, Gabrielle Anwar, Philip Seymour Hoffman, Richard Venture, Bradley Whitford, Rochelle Oliver, Margaret Eginton, Tom Riis Farrell, Frances Conroy, Ron Eldard; D: Martin Brest; W: Bo Goldman; C: Donald E. Thorin; M: Thomas Newman. Oscars '92: Actor (Pacino); Golden Globes '93: Actor—Drama (Pacino), Film—Drama, Screenplay.*

Schizo 1977 (R) Devious intentions abound as a middle-aged man is overcome by weird scenes and revelations, caused by the impending wedding of the figure skater he adores. Confusing tale of insanity, obsession, and skating. 109m/C VHS, DVD. *GB* Lynne Frederick, John Leyton, Stephanie Beacham, John Fraser, Jack Watson, John McEnery; *D:* Pete Walker; *W:* John M. Watson Sr.; *C:* Peter Jessop.

Schizo 2004 Set amid the dusty and desolate bleakness of rural Kazakhstan, film follows 15 year old Mustafa (Erailbeva), who has been given the nickname Schizo because of an apparent mental disorder. His mother's boyfriend, who he idolized, is a small time gangster whose racket is setting up illegal bare-fisted boxing matches. With little else to do in his dead-end town, Mustafa gets involved by recruiting men looking for a quick buck in the ring. When one combatant dies after an especially brutal fight, Mustafa is obliged to fulfill the man's dying wish to deliver his winnings to his girlfriend. This leads to an unlikely romantic involvement, which has the uneasy feel of Mustafa stepping into another man's shoes. 86m/C DVD. Olzhas Nusupaev, Eduard Tabychev, Olga Landina, Bakhytbek Baymukhambetov, Soukhorukov, Gulnara Jeraleva, Kanagat Nurtay; *D:* Gulshad Omarova; *W:* Sergei Bodrov, Gulshad Omarova; *C:* Khasan Kydyraliyev; *M:* Sig.

Schizoid 1980 (R) *Murder by Mail* 1980 (R) Advice-to-the-lovelorn columnist Hill receives a series of threatening letters causing her to wonder whether psychiatrist Kinski is bumping off his own patients. Boring blood dripper. 91m/C VHS. Klaus Kinski, Marianna Hill, Craig Wasson; *D:* David Paulsen.

Schizopolis 1997 Experimental, empty satire on modern spirituality and communication combines a number of weird and wacky devices that are not particularly entertaining. In an interesting premise, Soderbergh takes the lead in a dual role as Fletcher Munson, a manically neurotic employee of a self-help guru and his own look-alike, a ho-hum dentist having an affair with Fletcher's wife. Soderburgh's real-life ex, actress Brantley, plays his wife, who also has a double that shows up at the dentist. Things grow more bizarre for no apparent reason, as secondary cast members speak in other languages or just complete nonsense while strange sound effects confuse, in a film which also lists no credits (the title is shown in film on a character's t-shirt). Soderburgh, who wrote, directed and lensed this surrealist homage, shot on a superlow $250,000 budget as a way of expressing ideas not allowed in bigger budget, conventional films. To most, this just looks like expensive therapy. 96m/C VHS, DVD. Steven Soderbergh, Betsy Brantley, David Jensen; *D:* Steven Soderbergh; *W:* Steven Soderbergh.

Schlock 1973 *The Banana Monster* 1973 (PG) Accurately titled horror parody is first directorial effort for Landis, who does double duty as a missing link who kills people and falls in love with blind girl. Look for cameo appearance by Forrest J. Ackerman; ape-makeup by Rick Baker. 78m/C VHS, DVD. John Landis, Saul Kahan, Joseph Piantadosi, Eliza (Simons) Garrett, Emil Hamaty, Eric Allison; *Cameos:* Forrest J Ackerman; *D:* John Landis; *C:* Robert E. (Bob) Collins; *M:* David Gibson.

Schnelles Geld 1984 A mild-mannered guy gets involved with a prostitute, and is plunged into a world of crime and drugs. In German with English subtitles. 90m/C VHS. *GE* Dieter Schidor, Anne Bennent, Hub Martin, Gila von Weitershausen; *D:* George Moorse; *W:* George Moorse; *M:* Wolfgang Dickmann.

School Daze 1988 (R) Director/writer/star Lee's second outing is a rambunctious comedy (with a message, of course) set at an African-American college in the South. Skimpy plot revolves around the college's homecoming weekend and conflict among frats and sororities and African-Americans who would lose their racial identity and others who assert it. Entertaining and thought provoking. A glimpse at Lee's "promise," fulfilled in "Do the Right Thing." 114m/C VHS, DVD. Spike Lee, Laurence Fishburne, Giancarlo Esposito, Tisha Campbell, Ossie Davis, Joe Seneca, Art Evans, Ellen Holly, Branford Marsalis, Bill Nunn, Kadeem Hardison, Darryl M. Bell, Joie Lee, Tyra Ferrell, Jasmine Guy, Gregg Burge, Kasi Lemmons, Samuel L. Jackson, Phyllis Hyman, James Bond III; *D:* Spike Lee; *W:* Spike Lee; *C:* Ernest R. Dickerson; *M:* Bill Lee.

School for Scoundrels 2006 (PG-13) Remake of the 1960 British comedy about a student-teacher battle for the same girl. Wimp Roger (Heder) needs to man up so he signs on for a course on self-esteem taught by arrogant Dr. P (Thornton). Roger gains enough confidence to ask out pretty neighbor Amanda (Barrett), only to discover that the leering doc is after the same babe, who is too good for either of these losers. A comedy that's not at all funny degs itself from mean-spirited to mushy. 101m/C DVD. *US* Billy Bob Thornton, Jon Heder, Jacinda Barrett, Michael Clarke Duncan, Ben Stiller, Luis Guzman, Horatio Sanz, Sarah Silverman, David Cross, Todd Louiso, Steve Monroe; *D:* Todd Phillips; *W:* Todd Phillips, Scot Armstrong; *C:* Jonathan Brown; *M:* Christophe Beck.

School of Life 2006 (PG) Stodgy middle school biology teacher Matt Warner (Paymer) is bent on continuing his late dad's (Astin) "Teacher of the Year" legacy but he feels challenged when a young and hip history teacher, Mr. D (Reynolds), comes along and wows everyone. A little touchy-feely at times, though Reynolds is fun to watch. 100m/C DVD. David Paymer, Ryan Reynolds, John Astin, Andrew Robb, Kate Vernon; *D:* William Dear; *W:* Jonathan Kahn; *C:* Brian Pearson; *M:* Ari Wise. TV

School of Rock 2003 (PG-13) Substitute any other actor for Jack Black and this movie becomes a direct-to-video blip, or doesn't get made at all. Black is Dewey Finn, a life-long rocker and true believer who gets tossed by his band and forced to get a job. Dewey snakes a teaching gig from his roomie, ending up at an exclusive elementary school with a stuffy principal (Cusack). There he finds a classroom full of precocious kids with musical talent and an entire spectrum of self-esteem problems. He molds them into a rock band with the intention of entering the Battle of the Bands. Some plot points are treated casually (sometimes to the point of ignoring them), but Black's wild-eyed, fully-committed performance easily carries the day, and he's ably supported by the kids, all of whom can actually play and sing, and by a savvy script that takes the music seriously. 108m/C VHS, DVD. *US* Jack Black, Joan Cusack, Mike White, Sarah Silverman, Joey Gaydos, Miranda Cosgrove, Kevin Alexander Clark, Rebecca Julia Brown, Robert Tsai, Maryam Hassan, Caitlin Hale, Aleisha Allen, Brian Falduto, Zachary Infante, James Hosey, Angelo Massagli, Cole Hawkins, Nicole Afflerbach, Jordan-Claire Green, Adam Pascal, Chris Stack, Tim Hopper, Nicky Katt, Kate McGregor-Stewart; *D:* Richard Linklater; *W:* Mike White; *C:* Rogier Stoffers; *M:* Craig (Shudder to Think) Wedren.

School Spirit 1985 (R) A hormonally motivated college student is killed during a date. He comes back as a ghost to haunt the campus, disrupt the stuffy president's affair, and fall in love. Forgettable, lame, low-grade teen sex flick. 90m/C VHS, DVD. Tom Nolan, Elizabeth Foxx, Larry Linville; *D:* Allan Holleb; *W:* Geoffrey Baere; *M:* Tom Bruner.

School Ties 1992 (PG-13) Encino man Fraser does a dramatic turn as a talented 1950s quarterback who gets a scholarship to the elite St. Matthew prep school. To conform with the closed-mindedness of the McCarthy era, both his father and coach suggest that he hide his Jewish religion. Fraser's compliance results in his big-man-on-campus status, until his rival in football and his love interest both find out that he is Jewish, creating an ugly rift in the school. What easily could have been just another teen hunk flick looks at much more than just Fraser's pretty face in successful, unflinching treatment of anti-Semitism. 110m/C VHS, DVD. Brendan Fraser, Matt Damon, Chris O'Donnell, Randall Batinkoff, Andrew Lowery, Cole Hauser, Ben Affleck, Anthony Rapp, Amy Locane, Peter Donat, Zeljko Ivanek, Kevin Tighe, Michael Higgins, Ed Lauter; *D:* Robert Mandel; *W:* Darryl Ponicsan, Dick Wolf; *C:* Freddie Francis; *M:* Maurice Jarre.

School's Out 1999 (R) *Schrei - denn ich werde dich toten!* 1999 (R) At a high school graduation party/dance, some of the students wander off to pull pranks in the deserted school on the same night that a homicidal maniac who killed his last victim in the school escapes from an asylum. Bloody mayhem ensues. German import provides some first rate scares. 90m/C VHS, DVD. *GE* Katharina Wackernagel, Marlene Meyer-Dunker, Nils Nellessen, Niels Bruno Schmidt; *D:* Robert Sigl; *W:* Kai Meyer; *C:* Sven Kirsten.

Schtonk 1992 Hermann Willie is a down-and-out journalist who thinks he's come upon the find of the century when he's given what are supposedly Hitler's diaries. Based on the 1983 scandal when $5 million and printed what turned out to be not-very-clever forgeries. Director Dietl mocks the greedy gullibility of the journal, the ingenuity of the forger, as well as the nostalgia of the ex- and neo-Nazis in modern Germany. The title is a meaningless expletive uttered by Charlie Chaplin in "The Great Dictator." German with subtitles. 115m/C VHS, DVD. *GE* Goetz George, Uwe Ochsenknecht, Rolf Hoppe; *D:* Helmut Dietl; *W:* Helmut Dietl; Berlin Intl. Film Fest. '92: Actor (George), Director (Dietl), Film.

Schultze Gets the Blues 2003 (PG) Bittersweet, sentimental comedy finds hefty bachelor salt miner Schultze (Krause) pushed into early retirement and wondering what he's going to do besides play the accordion at his local polka club. One night, Schultze's world changes when he happens to catch a zydeco song on the radio. Amazed at how different an accordion can sound, he sets his familiar polkas to a zydeco beat. Schulze's friends are equally amazed and decide to take up a collection and send him to compete in a music festival in their sister city of Moulton, Texas. Adventure is just the liberating journey that shy Schultze needs. German with subtitles. 114m/C DVD. Horst Krause, Harald Warmbrunn, Karl-Fred Muller, Hannelore Schubert, Wolfgang Boos, Rosemarie Deibel, Wilhelmine Horschig, Anne V. Angelie, Ursula Schucht, Alozia St. Julien; *D:* Michael Schorr; *W:* Michael Schorr; *C:* Axel Schneppat; *M:* Thomas Wittenbecher.

Sci-Fighter 2004 *X-Treme Fighter* 2004 After playing a virtual reality game his grandpa designed, a teenager needs his father to join in to free him from the clutches of a vicious virus that won't let them leave without a fight. 90m/C VHS, DVD. Don "The Dragon" Wilson, Cynthia Rothrock, Aki Aleong, Lorenzo Lamas, Dan(eya) Mayid, Rebecca Chaney; *D:* Art Camacho; *W:* Tom Callicoat; *C:* Andrea V. Rossetto; *M:* Vince DiCola. VIDEO

Sci-Fighters 1996 (R) Renegade cop Cameron Grayson (Piper) is tracking rapist Adrian Dunn (Drago) in 2009 Boston and discovers that Dunn has been exposed to a deadly, mutating virus. It's actually changing the bad guy into an alien methane-breathing lifeform that, of course, wants to inhabit the earth. Appropriately gross alien makeup and some decent special effects. 94m/C VHS, DVD. Roddy Piper, Billy Drago, Jayne Heitmeyer; *D:* Peter Svatek; *W:* Mark Sevi; *C:* Barry Gravelle; *M:* Milan Kymlicka.

Science Crazed 1990 A scientist creates a monster who could conceivably destroy the world. 90m/C VHS. *CA* Tony Della Ventura, Robin Hartsell, Cameron Klein; *D:* Ron Switzer; *W:* Ron Switzer; *C:* Joe Maagdenberg.

The Science of Sleep 2006 (R) Fanciful and surreal effort will appeal most to fans of Gondry's previous work. Immature and hyper-imaginative graphic artist Stephane (Garcia Bernal) has just returned to Paris and his mother (Miou-Miou) after growing up in Mexico with his divorced dad. Maybe he's suffering from culture shock and maybe Stephane is more than a little weird but he's certainly more comfortable living in his own fantasies. Stephanie chums up with artist neighbor Stephanie (Gainsbourg) but pulls back from the romantic impulses he can't handle, going back into his dream world. Visually fascinating and sometimes funny, but the perpetual parade of dream sequences never pays off. 105m/C DVD. FR IT Gael Garcia Bernal, Charlotte Gainsbourg, Alain Chabat, Miou-Miou, Pierre Vaneck, Emma de Caunes, Sacha Bourdo, Alain de Noyencourt; *D:* Michel Gondry; *W:* Michel Gondry; *C:* Jean-Louis Bompoint; *M:* Jean-Michel Bernard.

Scissors 1991 (R) Yes, this Hitchcock imitation needs trimming. An unstable young woman contends with a rapist, devious lookalikes, birds, and a prison-like apartment, not all of which are relevant to the plot. An unsharp stab at suspense from novelist/filmmaker DeFelitta. 105m/C VHS. Sharon Stone, Steve Railsback, Michelle Phillips, Ronny Cox, Albert "Poppy" Popwell; *D:* Frank De Felitta; *W:* Frank De Felitta.

Scooby-Doo 2002 (PG) Zoinks! Everybody's favorite cartoon Great Dane comes to life in this live-action-plus-CGI summer blockbuster. Fred (Prinze) is out to debunk the apparent haunting of the theme-park Spooky Island, accompanied by Daphne (Gellar), Velma (Cardellini), Shaggy (Lillard), and Scooby, of course. The plot, which is shaky to begin with, goes against the theme of the cartoon, where there are no ghosts, and meddling kids overcome mean old men in wacky costumes. The movie only takes off when the inflated budget is on screen. Based on the 1969 cartoon, "Scooby-Doo, Where Are You?" 87m/C VHS, DVD, UMD. *US* Freddie Prinze Jr., Sarah Michelle Gellar, Matthew Lillard, Linda Cardellini, Rowan Atkinson, Miguel A. Nunez Jr., Stephen Grives, Isla Fisher, Sam Greco; *D:* Raja Gosnell; *W:* James Gunn, Craig Titley; *C:* David Eggby; *M:* David Newman.

Scooby-Doo 2: Monsters Unleashed 2004 (PG) Those meddling kids are at it again! During their enshrinement into the Coolsonian Criminology Museum for all their prior do-good acts, all the ghosts and goblins on display suddenly come back to life and the gang sets out to unmask the culprit responsible. Shaggy (Lillard) and the CGI Scooby do not disappoint but this second act is weighed down with special-effects action sequences that play more violently (cartoonish, but still) than its predecessor. Seth Green is fun to watch as the museum's curator and Velma's love interest. 93m/C DVD. *US* Freddie Prinze Jr., Sarah Michelle Gellar, Linda Cardellini, Matthew Lillard, Seth Green, Peter Boyle, Tim Blake Nelson, Alicia Silverstone; *D:* Raja Gosnell; *W:* James Gunn; *C:* Oliver Wood; *M:* David Newman; *V:* Neil Fanning, Ian Abercrombie. Golden Raspberries '04: Worst Remake/Sequel.

Scoop 2006 (PG-13) Allen's 35th directorial feature is evidence he should ease up on that yearly quota. This time the kvetching centers around a naive journalism student (Johansson) who is given the scoop of a lifetime by the ghost of a muckraking journalist (McShane), and must investigate with the help of a third-rate magician (Allen) on whose stage they first appeared. Feels like a patchwork collection of past Allen flicks with nothing new or interesting, including the requisite abundance of self-centered Judaic jokes. 96m/C DVD. *US* Woody Allen, Scarlett Johansson, Hugh Jackman, Ian McShane, Charles Dance, Romola Garai, Fenella Woolgar, Julian Glover, Victoria Hamilton, Anthony Head; *D:* Woody Allen; *W:* Woody Allen; *C:* Remi Adefarasin.

Scorched 2002 (PG-13) Tepid crime caper finds three disgruntled bank tellers—unbeknownst to each other—deciding to rob their bank branch on the same day. Sheila has just been dumped by bank manager/longtime boyfriend Rick (Leonard) and wants to rob the ATM so he'll lose his job. Milquetoast desert-dweller Jason (Harrelson) decides to steal the contents of the safety deposit box of evil millionaire Mr. Merchant (Cleese), who's caused him grief. And Stuart (Costanzo) has a Vegas get-rich-quick scheme that he decides to finance by taking the bank's ready cash. **94m/C DVD.** Alicia Silverstone, Woody Harrelson, John Cleese, Paulo Costanzo, Joshua Leonard, Rachael Leigh Cook, David Krumholtz; **D:** Gavin Grazer; **M:** John Cleese, Bruce Douglas Johnson; **M:** John (Gianni) Frizzell.

Scorched ♂️½ **2002 (R)** China sets off a series of underground nuclear explosions that cause tectonic plate shifts, earthquakes, volcanoes, and a rapid rise in global temperature. The only way to save the planet is a nuclear counterstrike—centered beneath L.A. in three days. So the city is evacuated and the usual team of misfits is assembled to do the impossible. At least this flick's fast-paced enough to run right over all those pesky plot holes. **87m/C VHS, DVD.** Mark Dacascos, Ruger Hauer, John Rhys-Davies, Mark Rolston, G.W. Bailey, Rayne Marcus, Tamara Davies; **D:** James Seale; **W:** Steve Latshaw, Rebecca Morrison; **C:** Maximo Munzi; **M:** Bill Brown.

VIDEO

Scorchers ♂️½ **1992 (R)** Back in the bayou, Splendid (Lloyd), a newlywed who won't sleep with her husband, and her cousin Talbot (Tilly), a preacher's daughter whose husband prefers the town whore Thais (Dunaway), find their lives intertwined because of their marital and sexual problems. A real "scorcher." **87m/C VHS, DVD.** Faye Dunaway, Denholm Elliott, James Earl Jones, Emily Lloyd, Jennifer Tilly, Leland Crooke, Anthony Geary; **D:** David Beaird; **W:** David Beaird.

Scorchy ♂️ **1976 (R)** Low-budget female cop action flick about a narcotics agent (Stevens) on the trail of a drug kingpin. Blood and guts, guns, and violence. Poor casting. **100m/C VHS,** Connie Stevens, William (Bill) Smith, Cesare Danova, Marlene Schmidt; **D:** Howard Avedis; **W:** Howard (Hikmel) Avedis

Score ♂️ **1972** Swinging marrieds Jack and Elvira turn their attention to a newlywed couple in order to indulge their sexual desires. Campy, cutely erotica. **89m/ C VHS, DVD.** Calvin Culver, Claire Wilbur, Lynn Lowry, Gerald Grant, Carl Parker; **D:** Radley Metzger; **W:** Jerry Douglas; **C:** Franco Vodopivec.

Score WOOF! **1995** If you've seen "Hard Boiled," "City on Fire," or "Reservoir Dogs," then you can skip this one. Chance (Ozawa) is released from prison and forced to return to work for his old crime boss. Chance recruits three other thieves to rip off a jewelry store. Following the robbery, distrust sets in amongst the crooks and a pair of hitchhikers interfere with their getaway plans. Borrows liberally from the films mentioned above and is never exciting or engaging. Instead, it's morally ambiguous and boring. Also, this film features some of the thinnest and reddest blood ever seen in a movie. **94m/C DVD.** JP Hitoshi Ozawa, Osamu Ebara, Ryuuji Mi-nakami, Kazuyoshi Ozawa, Miyuki Takano, Masahiro Yamashita; **D:** Atsushi Muroga.

The Score ♂️½ **2001 (R)** Slow-starting crime comedy with De Niro as a semi-retired thief, living a quiet life running a Montreal jazz club, until his fence (Brando) and a wannabe thief (Norton) talk him into pulling another job in Montreal's customs house. Bassett is DeNiro's squeeze (good taste there) who wants him out of the life. Painstaking but realistic in its portrayal of the preparation and events leading to the heist, but when things finally get going, it crackles with tense "will-they-get-caught" moments and double-crosses aplenty. De Niro is solid, as always, but he seems like he may be getting too old for this stuff. Norton gets most of the screen time, and uses it well. Brando is surprisingly understated in an amusing way. **124m/C VHS, DVD.** US Robert De Niro, Edward Norton, Marlon Brando, Angela Bassett, Gary Farmer, Paul Soles, Jamie Harrold; **D:** Frank Oz; **W:** Kario Salem, Scott Marshall Smith, Lem Dobbs; **C:** Rob Hahn; **M:** Howard Shore.

Scorned ♂️ **1993 (R)** Seductive Patricia Langley loves her husband Truman so much that she'll do anything to help him get that promotion, including seducing another man. Too bad Alex has ruined her life

and she's going to get revenge by running his. Also available in an unrated version. **100m/C VHS,** Shannon Tweed, Andrew Stevens, Michael D. Arenz, Kim Morgan Greene, Stephen Young, Daniel McVicar; **D:** Andrew Stevens; **M:** Barry Avrich.

Scorned 2 ♂️½ **1996 (R)** Amanda (McClure) seems happily married to psych prof Mark—even if she is having those bad dreams. But when her hubby is tempted by a pretty coed and Amanda finds out—well this is one woman that should never be scorned. **105m/C VHS, DVD.** Tane McClure, Wendy Schumacher, Myles O'Brien, John McCook, Andrew Stevens, Seth Jaffe; **D:** Rodney McDonald; **M:** Patrick Seymour.

Scorpio ♂️½ **1973 (PG)** Okay cat-and-mouse espionage tale about a wily, veteran CIA agent (Lancaster) who may have turned traitor. He's set up to be killed by a CIA boss but the assassin, code-name Scorpio (Delon), has some trouble fulfilling his assignment. Cross- and double-cross abound. **114m/C VHS, DVD.** Burt Lancaster, Alain Delon, Paul Scofield, John Colicos, Gayle Hunnicutt, J.D. Cannon, Joanne Linville, Melvin Stewart, James B. Sikking, Vadek Sheybal, William (Bill) Smithers, Celeste Yarnall; **D:** Michael Winner; **W:** David W. Rintels, Gerald Wilson.

The Scorpio Factor ♂️♂️ **1990** Murder and mayhem follow microchip heist. **87m/C VHS, DVD.** Attila Bertalan, David Nerman, Wendy Dawn Wilson; **D:** Michel Wachniuc; **W:** Carole Saure, June Pinheiro; **C:** Bruno Philip; **M:** Richard Gresko.

Scorpio One ♂️½ **1997 (R)** Scientists aboard spacestation Scorpio One have made a discovery that has cost them their lives and may now cause the destruction of earth. **92m/C VHS,** Jeff Speakman, Robert Carradine, Robin Curtis, Steve Kanaly; **er:** George Murdock, Judith Chapman; **D:** Worth Keeter; **W:** Steve Latshaw; **C:** Doyle Smith; **M:** Paul Wurst, Eric Wurst.

Scorpion ♂️ **1986 (R)** A karate-master and anti-terrorist expert defeases a skyjacking and infiltrates international assassination conspiracies. Ex-real life karate champ Tulleners is a ho-hum hero, and the story is warmed over. **98m/C VHS, DVD.** Tonny Tulleners, Allen Williams, Don Murray; **D:** William Reed.

The Scorpion King ♂️♂️ **2002 (PG-13)** Billed as a prequel to "The Mummy" series, this actioner is more in the "Sword 'n' Sandals" vein. The Rock is the title star, an assassin hired by a group of beleaguered tribes to defeat the evil warlord Memnon (Brand). The warlord is helped, somewhat unenthusiastically, by a sorceress (Hu) who can foresee the outcome of battles. Yes, it's cheesy, and downright silly at times, but it doesn't really strive for any more than that. The only motivation behind the whole endeavor seems to be to make The Rock a movie star, and if he sticks with action pics, he seems to be on his way. All the men do the requisite amount of killing, and discussing killing, and the women are all scantily clad. The target audience should be overjoyed. **94m/C VHS, DVD, HD DVD.** US Dwayne "The Rock" Johnson, Michael Clarke Duncan, Steven Brand, Kelly Hu, Bernard Hill, Grant Heslov, Peter Facinelli, Ralph (Ralf) Moeller, Branscombe Richmond, Roger Rees, Sherri Howard, Conrad Roberts; **D:** Chuck Russell; **W:** Stephen Sommers, William Osborne, David Hayter; **C:** John R. Leonetti; **M:** John Debney.

Scorpion Spring ♂️ **1996 (R)** Drug runner Astor (Morales) is on the lam through the desert with a beautiful hostage (Aviles) when two unsuspecting travelers (Molina and McGaw) offer the stranded duo a ride. But drug lord El Rojo (McConaughey) wants Astor dead and doesn't care who gets in his way and there's also a border patrol officer (Blades) on their trail as well. **89m/C VHS,** Matthew McConaughey, Argel Aviles, Ruben Blades, Miguel (Michael) Sandoval, Richard Edson, John Doe; **D:** Brian Cox; **W:** Brian Cox; **C:** Nancy Schreiber; **M:** Lalo Schifrin.

Scorpion with Two Tails ♂️ **1971** Graphic murder scenes rev up this early thriller by master filmmed with plot twists and visual games. Dubbed in English. **90m/C VHS, DVD.** IT SP Evelyn Stewart, Anita Strindberg, George Hilton, Luigi Pistilli, Janine Reynaud; **D:** Sergio Martino; **W:** Sauro Scavolini, Ernesto Gastaldi; **M:** Bruno Nicolai.

The Scorpion's Tail ♂️ **1971** Shakespeare's "Macbeth" meets Mojobs in director Morrissette's original black comedy set in 1970s rural Pennsylvania. Far from royalty, these McBeths, Slacker Mac (LeGros) and wife Pat (Tierney), are burger-flippers at Duncan's, toiling away on minimum wage. At Pat's urging, they off nepotistic restaurant owner Norm Duncan (Rebhorn) after a promotion goes to his two sons. After a fryer "mishap" and a cover-up, the power-hungry couple are then free to work their way, remodeling the restaurant and changing the name to McBeth's, complete with a (wink-wink) giant "M." However, vegetarian cop McDuff (Walken) is assigned to find Duncan's killer. Falls just short of reaching full potential, but Tierney is especially great and the black humor should drove enjoyable for both Shakespeare and non-Shakespeare fans alike. **102m/C VHS, DVD,** US Maura Tierney, James LeGros, Christopher Walken, Kevin Corrigan, James Rebhorn, Tom Guiry, Amy Smart, Andy Dick, Josh Pais, Geoff Dunsworth; **D:** Billy Morrissette; **W:** Billy Morrissette; **C:** Waly Pfister, **M:** Anton Sanko.

Scotland, PA ♂️♂️½ **2002 (R)** A female Viennese judge becomes entwined in an unusual case which partially parallels her own life. Her new young lover turns out to be bisexual. Not gripping. In German with English subtitles. **101m/C VHS,** GE Angelica Domrose, Fritz Hammel; **D:** Susanne Zanke.

The Scorpion Woman ♂️♂️ **1989** A female Viennese judge becomes entwined in an unusual case which partially parallels her own life. Her new young lover turns out to be bisexual. Not gripping. In German with English subtitles. **101m/C VHS,** GE Angelica Domrose, Fritz Hammel; **D:** Susanne Zanke.

Scott of the Antarctic ♂️♂️½ **1948** Drama of doomed British expedition of 1911 struggling to be the first group to reach the South Pole. Much of the stunning location filming was shot in the Swiss Alps. Story is authentic, but oddly uninvolving, due to stiff upper lip. **111m/C VHS, DVD.** GB John Mills, Christopher Lee, Kenneth More, Derek Bond; **D:** Charles Frend; **C:** Geoffrey Unsworth.

Scott Turow's The Burden of Proof ♂️♂️½ *The Burden of Proof* 1992 Attorney Alejandro "Sandy" Stern (Elizondo) struggles to discover the reasons behind his wife's baffling suicide and deal with the problems caused by the federal investigation of his brother-in-law's commodities business. The character of Stern was also featured in the film "Presumed Innocent" (played by Raul Julia). TV movie; on two cassettes. **184m/C VHS,** Hector Elizondo, Brian Dennehy, Mel Harris, Stefanie Powers, Victoria Principal, Adrienne Barbeau, Anne Bobby, Gail Strickland, Concetta Tomei, Jeffrey Tambor; **D:** Mike Robe; **C:** Kees Van Oostrum.

Scotland Yard Inspector ♂️♂️ *Lady in the Fog* 1952 An American newspaperman (Romero) in London looks for a killer. Nothing special. **73m/B VHS.** GB Cesar Romero, Bernadette O'Farrell, Lois Maxwell, Geoffrey Keen, Campbell Singer; **D:** Sam Newfield; **W:** Orville H. Hampton; **C:** Walter J. (Jimmy W.) Harvey; **M:** Ivor Slaney.

The Scout ♂️♂️ **1994 (PG-13)** Brooks is an about-to-be-canned scout for the New York Yankees who discovers a weird, though genuine, phenom pitcher (Fraser) on a trip to Mexico. He convinces the Yankees to take the phenom on though he's not sure whether Fraser isn't a few innings shy of a complete game. But with a 100 mph fast ball and a bat that would make Babe Ruth envious, who cares? Film straddles sports comedy and melodrama territories, satisfying in neither. Fraser plays variation on the script, Man. Brooks rewrote part of the script, adding much needed biting humor, but not

enough. Bombastic real-life team owner Steinbrenner plays himself. **101m/C VHS, DVD.** Albert Brooks, Brendan Fraser, Diane Wiest, Lane Smith, Michael Rapaport, Steve Garvey, Bob Costas, Roy Firestone, Anne Twomey, Tony Bennett; **D:** Michael Ritchie; **W:** Albert Brooks, Andrew Bergman, Monica Johnson; **Cameos:** Mr. Bill Conti.

Scout's Honor ♂️♂️ **1980** An orphan (Coleman) is determined to become the best Cub Scout ever when he joins a troop led by an executive who dislikes children. Harmless, enjoyable family tale includes several former child stars as Scout parents. **96m/C VHS.** Gary Coleman, Katharine Helmond, Wilfrid Hyde-White, Pat O'Brien, Joanna Moore, Meeno Peluce, Jay North, Harry (Henry) Morgan, Angela Cartwright; **D:** Henry Levin. TV

Scream ♂️♂️ **1983** Vacationers on a raft trip down the Rio Grande are terrorized by a mysterious murderer. Hopelessly dull. **86m/C VHS,** Pepper Martin, Hank Worden, Alvy Moore, Woody Strode, John Ethan Wayne; **D:** Byron Quisenberry.

Scream ♂️♂️½ **1996 (R)** Director Craven playfully tweaks the cliches of teen slasher pics (which he helped create with "Nightmare on Elm Street") with this tongue-in-cheek thriller. Yep, where there's a mad slasher on the loose, there must be a group of teenagers "just" out for a good time. The difference is both the killer and the victims have been raised on '80s splatter movies and, therefore, know all the rules. Sexual activity and/or substance abuse? Start picking out coffins. The stalker uses his cellular phone to terrorize his victims. He also uses it to ask his prey trivia questions or offer critiques of low-grade horror movies. Campbell plays the virginal heroine in the tight sweater, with Ulrich playing opposite as her sexually frustrated boyfriend. More fun than a bucket full of Karo syrup with red dye #3. **111m/C VHS, DVD.** Matthew Lillard, Drew Barrymore, Neve Campbell, Courteney Cox, David Arquette, Skeet Ulrich, Rose McGowan, Henry Winkler, Liev Schreiber, W. Earl Brown, Jamie Kennedy, Lawrence Hecht; **Cameos:** Wes Craven, Linda Blair; **D:** Wes Craven; **W:** Kevin Williamson; **C:** Mark Irwin; **M:** Marco Beltrami. MTV Movie Awards '97: Film.

Scream 2 ♂️♂️ *Scream Again* 1997 The filmmakers swear that this series is indeed only a trilogy. Good thing because, while entertaining enough, this third film is showing wear. Sidney is working as a crisis counselor and living in blessed anonymity in northern California. However, the actors involved in "Stab 3" are being offed and it ties in to her mother's mysterious past; so Sid is forced to resurface. Ambitious Gale (Cox Arquette) returns as does dopey Dewey (Arquette) and newcomer LAPD detective Kincaid (Dempsey) tries to figure out if there are any film rules that will help him catch a killer. **115m/C VHS, DVD.** Neve Campbell, David Arquette, Courteney Cox, Patrick Dempsey, Scott Foley,

Scream 3 ♂️♂️½ **2000 (R)** The filmmakers swear that this series is indeed only a trilogy. Good thing because, while entertaining enough, this third film is showing wear. Sidney is working as a crisis counselor and living in blessed anonymity in northern California. However, the actors involved in "Stab 3" are being offed and it ties in to her mother's mysterious past; so Sid is forced to resurface. Ambitious Gale (Cox Arquette) returns as does dopey Dewey (Arquette) and newcomer LAPD detective Kincaid (Dempsey) tries to figure out if there are any film rules that will help him catch a killer. **120m/C VHS.** Neve Campbell, Courteney Cox, Neve Campbell, David Arquette, Jada Pinkett Smith, Jamie Kennedy, Liev Schreiber, Sarah Michelle Gellar, Laurie Metcalf, Elise Neal, Lewis Arquette, Duane Martin, Omar Epps, David Warner, Timothy Olyphant, Rebecca Gayheart, Portia de Rossi, Heather Graham; **Cameos:** Tori Spelling; **D:** Wes Craven; **W:** Kevin Williamson; **C:** Peter Deming; **M:** Marco Beltrami. MTV Movie Awards '98: Female Perf. (Campbell).

Scream

Lance Henriksen, Matt Keeslar, Jenny McCarthy, Emily Mortimer, Parker Posey, Deon Richmond, Patrick Warburton, Liev Schreiber, Heather Matarazzo, Jamie Kennedy, Carrie Fisher, Kevin Smith; **W:** Wes Craven; **W:** Ehren Kruger; **M:** Marco Beltrami.

Scream and Scream Again 🦴🦴½ *Screamer* 1970 (PG) Price is a sinister doctor who tries to create a super race of people devoid of emotions. Cushing is the mastermind behind the plot. Lee is the agent investigating a series of murders. Three great horror stars, a psychedelic disco, great '60s fashions; it's all here. **95m/C VHS, DVD.** *GB* Vincent Price, Christopher Lee, Peter Cushing, Judy Huxtable, Alfred Marks, Anthony Newlands, Uta Levka, Judi Bloom, Yutte Stensgaard; **D:** Gordon Hessler; **W:** Christopher Wicking; **C:** John Coquillon.

Scream, Baby, Scream 🦴 *Nightmare House* 1969 An unsuccessful artist switches from sculpting clay to carving young models' faces into hideous deformed creatures. **86m/C VHS, DVD.** Ross Harris, Eugenie Wingate, Chris Martell, Suzanne Stuart, Larry Swanson, Brad Grinter; **D:** Joseph Adler.

Scream Blacula Scream 🦴🦴 1973 (R) Blacula returns from his dusty undoing in the original movie to once again suck the blood out of greater Los Angeles. A voodoo priestess (Grier) is the only person with the power to stop him. A weak follow up to the great "Blacula," but worth a look for Marshall and Grier. **96m/C VHS, DVD.** William Marshall, Don Mitchell, Pam Grier, Michael Conrad, Richard Lawson, Lynne Moody, Janee Michelle, Barbara Rhoades, Bernie Hamilton; **D:** Bob Kelljan.

Scream Bloody Murder woof! 1972 (R) A young boy grinds his father to death with a tractor but mangles his own hand trying to jump off. After receiving a steel claw and being released from a mental institution he continues his murderous ways in and around his home town. Inspiring. **90m/C VHS, DVD.** Fred Holbert, Leigh Mitchell, Robert Knox, Suzette Hamilton; **D:** Robert Emery.

Scream Dream 🦴 1989 (R) A beautiful rock star uses her supernatural powers to control her fans, turning them into revenge-seeking monsters when she wants to. Heavy on the blood and skin; heavily exploitative. **80m/C VHS.** Melissa Moore, Carole Carr, Nikki Riggins, Jesse Ray; **D:** Donald Farmer; **W:** Donald Farmer.

Scream for Help 🦴 1986 (R) A young girl discovers that her cheating stepfather is plotting to murder her mother, but no one will believe her. Is she paranoid? So bad it's funny; otherwise, it's just bad, and far too nutty to take seriously. **75m/C VHS.** Rachael Kelly, David Allan Brooks, Marie Masters; **D:** Michael Winner; **W:** Tom Holland.

Scream of Fear 🦴🦴🦴 *Taste of Fear* 1961 (R) A wheelchair-bound young woman goes to visit her father and new stepmother only to find her father is away on business. But she believes she sees her father's corpse. Is someone trying to drive her mad? Abounds in plot twists and mistaken identities. A truly spooky film, suspenseful, and well-made. **81m/B VHS.** *GB* Susan Strasberg, Ronald Lewis, Ann Todd, Christopher Lee; **D:** Seth Holt; **W:** Jimmy Sangster.

Scream of the Demon Lover woof! 1971 (R) A young biochemist has a busy day as she works for a reclusive Baron. She fantasizes about him, tries to track down a murderer, and eventually discovers a mutant in the cellar. About as bad as they come, but short! **75m/C VHS.** Jennifer Hartley, Jeffrey Chase; **D:** Jose Luis Merino.

Scream of the Wolf 🦴🦴 1974 Author and ex-hunter John (Graves) is called on to help the police in their investigation of a series of murders that seem to have been caused by a wolf (think Walker), an old friend and obsessive hunter (think Zaroff, in "The Most Dangerous Game") for help, but Byron refuses, arguing that the murders are making the people in the community feel more alive than ever. Byron involves Zaroff in a battle of brawn and

hunting skill that will ultimately reveal the truth behind the killings. Passable TV movie by director Curtis feels like another attempt to create a "Kolchak: The Night Stalker"-type TV series, complete with Graves's flashy red Corvette, and a jazzy '70s "wokka-chikka" soundtrack. **74m/C VHS, DVD.** Peter Graves, Clint Walker, JoAnn Pflug, Phil Carey, James Storm; **D:** Dan Curtis; **W:** Richard Matheson, David Case; **C:** Paul Lohmann; **M:** Robert Cobert. **TV**

Screamer 🦴 1974 A woman wants revenge after she is viciously attacked and raped. Now every man she sees is her attacker as she becomes more and more unbalanced. **71m/C VHS.** Pamela Franklin, Donal McCann; **D:** Shaun O'Riordan; **W:** Brian Clemens.

Screamers 🦴 *L'Isola Degli Uomini Pesce; Island of the Fishmen; Something Waits in the Dark* 1980 (R) A mad scientist on a desert island gleefully turns escaped convicts into grotesque monstrosities. Gory and gratuitous. **83m/C VHS.** Richard Johnson, Joseph Cotten, Barbara Bach; **D:** Dan T. Miller, Sergio Martino.

Screamers 🦴🦴 1996 (R) In the year 2078, Colonel Joe Hendricksson (Weller) and a small band of survivors fight a civil war on the radiation contaminated planet Sirius 6B. They run up against the screamers—mechanical creatures with razor-sharp claws, originally designed to protect humans. The screamers are bent on destroying all life in the universe while somehow mutating and breeding on their own. Unfortunately, director Duguay doesn't give any indication how this is taking place. Some fine stunt work and special effects redeem standard action adventure. Based on the novella "Second Variety" by Philip K. Dick ("Blade Runner"). **107m/C VHS, DVD.** Peter Weller, Jennifer Rubin, Andrew Lauer, Charles Powell, Ron White, Michael Caloz; **D:** Christian Duguay; **W:** Dan O'Bannon, Miguel Tejada-Flores; **C:** Rodney Gibbons; **M:** Normand Corbeil.

The Screaming Dead 🦴 *Dracula vs. Frankenstein* 1972 Monsters rise from the tomb to do battle with planet Earth and each other. Not to be confused with the Al Adamson epic "Dracula vs. Frankenstein." **84m/C VHS, DVD.** *SP* Dennis Price, Howard Vernon, Alberto Dalbes, Mary Francis, Genevieve Deloir, Josianne Gibert, Fernando Bilbao; **D:** Jess (Jesus) Franco.

Screaming Dead 🦴🦴 2003 (R) Satisfactory exploitation/horror flick has a fetish photographer, his assistant, and some models doing a shoot in an abandoned, possibly haunted hospital where hundreds of patients were tortured and killed in a basement dungeon. Not as much skin or gore as you'd expect from the set-up, and it takes a while to get going, but it's not too bad for fans of the genre. **95m/C DVD.** Misty Mundae, Rob Monkiewicz, Joseph Farrell, Rachael Robbins, Heidi Kristoffer; **D:** Bret Piper; **W:** Bret Piper; **M:** Jon Greathouse. **VIDEO**

The Screaming Skull 🦴½ 1958 Man redecorates house with skulls in attempt to drive already anxious wife insane. **68m/B VHS, DVD.** William (Bill) Hudson, Peggy Webber, Toni Johnson, Russ Conway, Alex Nicol; **D:** Alex Nicol; **M:** Ernest Gold.

Screams of a Winter Night 🦴 1979 (PG) Ghostly tale of an evil monster from the lake and the terror he causes. **92m/C VHS.** Matt Borel, Gil Glasco; **D:** Philippe Mora; **W:** Philippe Mora.

Screamtime 🦴 1983 (R) Two fiendish friends filch a trilogy of horror tapes for home viewing. After the show, real scary things happen. **89m/C VHS.** Jean Anderson, Robin Bailey, Dora Bryan, David Van Day; **D:** Al Beresford.

Screen Test woof! 1985 (R) Oversexed silly teenagers arrange fake screen tests in order to meet girls. **84m/C VHS.** Michael Allan Bloom, Mary Ellen Trainor, Paul Lueken, David Simpatico, Cynthia Kahn, Mari Laskarin, Katherine Sullivan, Monique Gabrielle, Michelle (McClellan) Bauer, Deborah Blaisdell; **D:** Sam Auster; **W:** Sam Auster; **C:** Jeffrey Jur.

Screw Loose 🦴🦴 *Svitati* 1999 (R) Bernardo's (Greggio) dying father (Barra) has one last request—he wants a reunion with his American WWII buddy Jake (Brooks). So being a dutiful son, Bernardo comes to America and discovers Jake is in an L.A. mental institution. Nevertheless, he breaks him out and flies Jake back to Italy with him—followed by Jake's doctor, Barbara (Condra). And it turns out maybe Jake isn't the only one with a few loose screws. Slapsticky, with a weak script. **85m/C VHS, DVD.** *IT* Mel Brooks, Ezio Greggio, Gianfranco Barra, Julie Condra, Randi Ingerman; **D:** Ezio Greggio; **W:** Rudy DeLuca, Steve Haberman; **C:** Luca Robecchi.

Screwball Academy 🦴½ 1986 (R) A beautiful female director makes a soft-core film on a secluded island, and gets trouble from thugs, evangelists, horny crew members and others. Former "SCTV" director John Blanchard understandably used a pseudonym to direct this lame effort. **90m/C VHS.** Colleen Camp, Kenneth Welsh, Christine Cattall; **D:** Reuben Rose.

Screwballs 🦴 1983 (R) Freewheeling group of high school boys stirs up trouble for their snooty and virginal homecoming queen. Another inept teen sex comedy with no subtlety whatsoever. Sequel: "Loose Screws." **80m/C VHS.** Peter Keleghan, Lynda Speciale; **D:** Rafal Zielinski; **W:** Jim Wynorski.

Screwed woof! 2000 (PG-13) Chauffeur MacDonald tries kidnapping his mean boss's dog for ransom but things get screwed up so badly that the boss thinks it's the chauffeur that's been kidnapped. Lame physical and gross-out "comedy" ensues. Just who the title refers to is never made clear, but it seems like it's the producers, who had to pay the actors and writer/directors for this, ahem, dog. DeVito is the only one on screen who seems to know what he's doing, and Alexander and Karaszewski look to be cashing in on some far superior prior screenwriting work. **82m/C VHS, DVD.** Norm MacDonald, Elaine Stritch, Danny DeVito, Dave Chappelle, Daniel Benzali, Sherman Hemsley, Malcolm Stewart; **D:** Scott M. Alexander, Larry Karaszewski; **W:** Scott M. Alexander, Larry Karaszewski; **C:** Robert Brinkmann; **M:** Michel Colombier.

Scrooge 🦴🦴🦴 1935 On Christmas Eve a miser changes his ways after receiving visits from the ghosts of Christmas past, present, and future. Co-scripter Hicks gives an interesting performance as Ebeneezer Scrooge. Based on the novel "A Christmas Carol" by Charles Dickens. **61m/B VHS, DVD.** *GB* Sir Seymour Hicks, Maurice Evans, Robert Cochran, Donald Calthrop, Mary Glynne, Oscar Asche; **D:** Henry Edwards; **W:** Sir Seymour Hicks; **C:** Sydney Blythe; William Luff.

Scrooge 🦴🦴½ 1970 (G) Well done musical version of Charles Dickens' classic "A Christmas Carol," about a miserly old man who is faced with ghosts on Christmas Eve. Finney is memorable in the title role. ♪The Beautiful Day; Happiness; Thank You Very Much; A Christmas Carol; Christmas Children; I Hate People; Father Christmas; See the Phantoms; December the 25th. **86m/C VHS, DVD.** *GB* Albert Finney, Alec Guinness, Edith Evans, Kenneth More; **D:** Ronald Neame; **W:** Leslie Bricusse; **C:** Oswald Morris; **M:** Leslie Bricusse. Golden Globes '71: Actor–Mus./Comedy (Finney).

Scrooged 🦴🦴 1988 (PG-13) Somewhat disjointed big-budgeted version of the hallowed classic. A callous TV executive staging "A Christmas Carol" is himself visited by the three ghosts and sees the light. Kane is terrific as one of the ghosts. Film is heavy-handed, Murray too sardonic to be believable. **101m/C VHS, DVD.** Bill Murray, Carol Kane, John Forsythe, David Johansen, Bob(cat) Goldthwait, Karen Allen, Michael J. Pollard, Brian Doyle-Murray, Alfre Woodard, John Glover, Robert Mitchum, Buddy Hackett, Robert Goulet, Jamie Farr, Mary Lou Retton, Lee Majors, Damon Hines, Mary Ellen Trainor, Mabel King, Wendie Malick, Joel Murray, John Houseman, Steve Kahan, Kate McGregor-Stewart; **D:** Richard Donner; **W:** Mitch Glazer, Michael O'Donoghue; **C:** Michael Chapman; **M:** Danny Elfman.

Scrubbers 🦴 1982 (R) Young girl is sent to reform school where she's forced to survive in a cruel and brutal environment. Low-budget "reform school" movie with no point, but lots of lesbianism. **93m/C VHS.** *GB* Amanda York, Chrissie Cotterill, Elizabeth Edmonds, Kate Ingram, Debbie Bishop, Dana Gillespie; **D:** Mai Zetterling.

Scruples 🦴🦴½ 1980 Set in the glamorous, jet-setting world of Beverly Hills, this top-rated miniseries follows the career of Billy Ikehorn (Wagner) as she weds a wealthy industrialist and opens a clothing boutique named "Scruples." She caters to high society's haute couture, and encounters unscrupulous individuals who threaten to dethrone her from her position of power and privilege. Based on the best-selling novel by Judith Krantz. **279m/C VHS.** Lindsay Wagner, Barry Bostwick, Kim Cattrall, Gavin MacLeod, Connie Stevens, Efrem Zimbalist Jr., Gene Tierney; **M:** Charles Bernstein.

The Sculptress 🦴🦴 1997 Troubled writer Rosalind Leigh (Goodall) prepares to interview convicted killer Olive Martin (Quirke), who five years before was found with the dead bodies of her mother and sister. Nicknamed "The Sculptress" for the gruesome nature of the murders, Olive is also a convincing liar. Although Olive says she's guilty, Roz is certain she's hiding something and becomes determined to discover the truth. Very creepy. Made for British TV, based on the novel by Minette Walters. **180m/C VHS, DVD.** *GB* Caroline Goodall, Pauline Quirke, Christopher Fulford, Dermot Crowley, David Horovitch, Jay Villiers, Lynda Rooke; **D:** Stuart Orme; **W:** Reg Gadney; **C:** Gavin Finney; **M:** Colin Towns. **TV**

Scum 🦴🦴🦴 1979 Adapted from Roy Minton's acclaimed play, this British production looks at the struggle among three young men in a British Borstal (a prison for young convicts.) Portrays the physical, sexual, and psychological violence committed. Horrifying and powerful. **96m/C VHS, DVD.** *GB* Phil Daniels, Mick Ford, Ray Winstone; **D:** Alan Clarke.

Scum of the Earth 🦴½ 1963 Early '60s skin flick about innocent young Kim (Miles), who is cruelly tricked into posing topless for a photographer and is then blackmailed into a downward spiral of sleaze that ends in murder and suicide. The film features much of the cast and crew of director Lewis's "Blood Feast." **73m/B DVD.** Vicki (Allison Louise Downe) Miles, Lawrence Wood, Mal Arnold, Thomas Sweetwood, Sandy Sinclair; **D:** Herschell Gordon Lewis; **W:** Herschell Gordon Lewis.

The Sea 🦴🦴 2002 A "King Lear" variation set in Iceland and concerned with fish. Fierce patriarch Thordur (Eyolfsson) summons his three adult children to discuss the family fishery. The kids are upset because dad never modernized the business and it can't compete with the larger corporations. His unhappy progeny want to sell out, divide the profits, and get on with their lives. Everyone enjoys spreading their own particular misery and angst around. Icelandic with subtitles. **109m/C DVD.** *IC* Gunnar Eyjolfsson, Kristbjorg Kjeld, Hilmir Snaer Gudnason, Gudrun S. Gisladottir, Sigurdur Skulason, Herdis Osvaldsdottir; **D:** Baltasar Kormakur; **W:** Baltasar Kormakur, Olafur Haukur Simonarson; **C:** Jean-Louis Vialard; **M:** Jon Asgeirsson.

Sea Chase 🦴🦴 1955 An odd post-war sea adventure, wherein a renegade German freighter captain is pursued by British and German navies as he leaves Australia at the outbreak of WWII. A Prussian Wayne rivaled only by his infamous Genghis Khan in "The Conqueror" for strange character selection. Turner is on board as Wayne's girlfriend. **117m/C VHS, DVD.** John Wayne, Lana Turner, Tab Hunter, James Arness, Lyle Bettger, David Farrar, Richard (Dick) Davalos, Claude Akins, John Qualen; **D:** John Farrow; **C:** William Clothier.

Sea Devils 🦴🦴 1931 Sentenced to prison for a crime he didn't commit, a man escapes and joins a boatload of treasure hunters, but mutiny is afoot. Don't get soaked by this cheapie. **77m/B VHS.** Walter

Sea Devils 🐶🐶 1937 The tale of a sea captain and his lovely daughter who have differing opinions on whom she should marry. While her father would like her to marry a tame gentleman under his command, she has her heart set on another, a torrid relationship with one of his suspects. Pacino doesn't stand a chance when Barkin heats up the screen. **113m/C VHS, DVD, HD DVD** *Al Pacino, Ellen Barkin, John Goodman, Michael Rooker, William Hickey, Richard Jenkins;* **D:** *Harold Becker;* **W:** *Richard Price;* **C:** *Ronnie Taylor;* **M:** *Trevor Jones.*

The Sea God 🐶 1930 Pink Barker's (Arlen) dive to come together during the Napoleonic Wars in this sea romance filled with intrigue and adventure. **86m/C VHS, GB** *Rock Hudson, Yvonne De Carlo, Maxwell Reed;* **D:** *Raoul Walsh.*

Sea Gypsies 🐶🐶 1978 (G) A smuggler and a beautiful spy come together during the Napoleonic Wars in this sea romance filled with intrigue and adventure. **86m/C VHS, GB** *Fay Wray, Eugene Pallette, Robert Gleickler, Ivan Simpson;* **D:** *George Abbott;* **W:** *Archie Stout.*

The Sea Hawk 🐶🐶🐶 1940 An English privateer learns the Spanish are going to invade England with their Armada. After numerous adventures, he is able to aid his queen and help save his country, finding romance along the way. One of Flynn's swashbuckling best. Available colorized. **128m/B VHS, DVD** *Errol Flynn, Claude Rains, Donald Crisp, Alan Hale, Flora Robson, Brenda Marshall, Henry Daniell, Gilbert Roland, James Stephenson, Una O'Connor;* **D:** *Michael Curtiz;* **W:** *Howard Koch.*

The Sea Inside 🐶🐶🐶 *Mar Adentro* 2004 (PG-13) Poignant, unsentimental, fact-based drama based on the life of Spanish quadriplegic Ramon Sampedro, who tried for some 30 years for the right to commit assisted suicide. Paralyzed in a diving accident, Ramon (Bardem) becomes a cause celebre as he lies bedridden, cared for by his religious family who are opposed to his decision. He builds his case with the help of his lawyer Julia (Rueda), who suffers herself from a degenerative disease. Ramon also inspires Rosa (Duenas), a neighbor who tries to convince the single-minded man to live and then falls in love with him. Bardem does an amazing job since, except for some brief flashbacks and fantasies, his movement is limited to his neck and head. The real Sampedro gave numerous interviews, and filmed his assisted suicide (in 1998) so it could be shown on TV. Spanish with subtitles. **125m/C DVD** *Javier Bardem, Celso Bugallo, Jose Maria Pou, Belen Rueda, Lola Duenas, Mabel Rivera, Clara Segura, Joan Dalmau, Alberto Jimenez, Tamar Novas, Francesc Garrido;* **D:** *Alejandro Amenabar;* **W:** *Alejandro Amenabar, Mateo Gil;* **C:** *Javier Aguirresarobe;* **M:** *Alejandro Amenabar. Oscars '04: Foreign Film; Golden Globes '05: Foreign Film; Ind. Spirit '05: Foreign Film.*

The Sea Lion 🐶 1921 A vicious sea captain, embittered by a past romance, becomes sadistic and intolerable, until the truth emerges. Lots of action, but plodding, rehashed plot. Silent. **50m/B VHS** *Hobart Bosworth, Emory Johnson, Bessie Love, Carol Holloway, Charles Clary, Jack Curtis;* **D:** *Rowland V. Lee;* **W:** *Joseph Poland;* **C:** *J.O. Taylor.*

Sea Hound 1947 A 15-part series set in the late 1940s that charts the voyage of a group of pirates searching for buried treasure. Everything goes well until Crabbe emerges to wreck their hopes. **?m/B VHS.** *Buster Crabbe, Jimmy Lloyd, Pamela Blake, Ralph Hodges, Bob (Robert) Barron;* **D:** *Walter B. Eason, Mack V. Wright.*

Sea Wife 🐶🐶½ 1957 Using nicknames and a newspaper's personal column to correspond, Sea Wife, Bulldog, and Biscuit are apparently rehashing a crime committed against a fourth person that's still haunting them. A flashback reveals three men and a woman in a lifeboat after their ship has been torpedoed by the Japanese in 1942. Only three ultimately survive their ordeal. Collins plays a nun of all things, although she keeps her calling a secret from the others. Rather drab adaptation of J.M. Scott's adventure/thriller "Sea-Wyf." **82m/C VHS, GB** *Richard Burton, Joan Collins, Basil Sydney, Ronald Squire, Cy Grant, Joan Hickson, Lloyd Lamble, Eileen Way;* **D:** *Bob McKnight;* **W:** *George K. Burke;* **C:** *Edward Scaife;* **M:** *Kenneth V. Jones, Leonard Salzedo.*

The Sea Serpent 🐶½ 1985 A young sea captain and a crusty scientist unite to search out a giant sea monster awakened by atomic tests. Not one of Milland's better films. **92m/C VHS, SP** *Timothy Bottoms, Ray Milland, Jared Martin;* **D:** *Gregory Greens.*

Sea Racketeers 🐶 1937 Soggy old tribute to the Coast Guard inadvertently makes them look like a bunch of bumblers, as they belatedly uncover a fur-smuggling racket working under their noses from a floating nightclub. **64m/B VHS.** *Weldon Heyburn, Jeanne Madden, Warren Hymer, Dorothy McNulty, J. Carrol Naish, Joyce Compton, Charles Trowbridge, Syd Saylor, Lane Chandler, Benny Burt;* **D:** *Hamilton MacFadden.*

The Sea Shall Not Have Them 🐶🐶 1955 A British bomber crashes into the North Sea during WWII. Film tells of the survivors' rescue by the Air-Sea Rescue Unit. Decent drama/adventure. **92m/B VHS.** *Michael Redgrave, Dirk Bogarde;* **D:** *Lewis Gilbert;* **M:** *Malcolm Arnold.*

The Sea Wolf 🐶🐶½ 1941 Jack London's adventure novel about brutal, canny Captain Wolf Larsen (Robinson), his rebellious crew, and some unexpected passengers. Knox and Lupino are shipwreck survivors, picked up by Robinson and forced into working aboard his ship, the aptly named "Ghost." Crewman Garfield falls for Lupino and tries to rally his shipmates into resisting the megalomaniacal Robinson. Fine performances by all, especially Robinson as the personification of malevolent ego. Screen debut of Knox. Director Curtiz filmed entirely in studio tanks, sets, and pervasive fog machines. Previously filmed three times; later remade as "Barricade" and "Wolf Larsen." **90m/C VHS.** *Edward G. Robinson, Ida Lupino, Gene Lockhart, Barry Fitzgerald, Stanley Ridges, Francis McDonald, David Bruce, Howard de Silva, Frank Lackteen, Ralf Harolde;* **D:** *Michael Curtiz;* **W:** *Robert Rossen.*

Sea of Dreams 🐶 1990 Don't expect much in the way of a script from this soft-core production. **80m/C VHS.** *Jon Rodgers, Chad Scott, Jacky Peel, Renee O'Neil.*

Sea of Love 🐶🐶🐶½ 1989 (R) A gripping, well-written thriller about an alcoholic cop with a mid-life crisis. While following the track of a serial killer, he begins a torrid relationship with one of his suspects. Pacino doesn't stand a chance when Barkin heats up the screen. **113m/C VHS, DVD, HD DVD** *Al Pacino, Ellen Barkin, John Goodman, Michael Rooker, William Hickey, Richard Jenkins;* **D:** *Harold Becker;* **W:** *Richard Price;* **C:** *Ronnie Taylor;* **M:** *Trevor Jones.*

Sea of Sand 🐶🐶½ 1958 Typical actioner set in WWII British desert patrol's latest mission is to blow up Rommel's fuel supply before the battle of El Alamein. Lots of heroics against the Nazis and stiff upper lips. **97m/B VHS.** *Richard Attenborough, John Gregson, Michael Craig, Vincent Ball, Ray McAnally;* **C:** *Guy Green;* **W:** *Robert Westerby;* **C:** *Wilkie Cooper;* **M:** *Clifton Parker.*

Sea People 🐶🐶 2000 Teen swimmer Amanda (Moss) rescues elderly John McRae (Cronyn) after he leaps from a bridge into the water. But she discovers that John wasn't trying to commit suicide and that he and his wife, Bridget (Gregan Moss, Joan Gregson, Ron Lea, Don McKellar, Cedric Smith;* **D:** *Vic Sarin.* **CABLE**

Sea Wolves 🐶🐶 1981 (PG) True WWII story about a commando-style operation undertaken by a group of middle-aged, retired British cavalrymen in India in 1943. Decent acting, though Peck's British accent fades in and out, with Moore as Bond. **120m/C VHS, GB** *Gregory Peck, Roger Moore, David Niven, Trevor Howard, Patrick Macnee, William Morgan Sheppard;* **D:** *Andrew V. McLaglen;* **W:** *Reginald Rose.*

Seabiscuit 🐶🐶🐶½ 2003 (PG-13) Equine Cinderella story of the legendary Seabiscuit—a funny-looking, ill-tempered thoroughbred—and the men who shaped him into a racing legend: owner Charles Howard (Bridges); partially blind, over-sized, luck-challenged jockey Red Pollard (Maguire); and trainer "Silent" Tom Smith (Cooper) who believed in the underdog horse. The ragtag trio eventually wrangles a race with the more-celebrated War Admiral, whose owner had previously refused to share a track with the far inferior Seabiscuit. Writer/director Ross delivers suitably rousing race scenes in this can't miss story of an unlikely champion who brought hope and inspiration to the Depression-era crowds and became a symbol of hope. All three leads are outstanding, as is Macy as the excitable radio announcer. Based on Laura Hillenbrand's best-seller "Seabiscuit: An American Legend." **140m/C VHS, DVD, HD DVD, US Today** *Tobey Maguire, Jeff Bridges, Chris Cooper, Elizabeth Banks, William H. Macy, Gary Stevens, Eddie Jones, Ed Lauter, Michael O'Neill, Royce D. Applegate, Annie Corley, Valerie Mahaffey;* **D:** *Gary Ross;* **W:** *Gary Ross;* **C:** *John Schwartzman;* **M:** *Randy Newman;* **Nar:** *David McCullough.*

The Seagull 🐶🐶½ 1975 Danner's sensitive performance as Nina, an aspiring actress with fragile emotions, highlights this filmed production of Chekhov's "The Seagull," originally staged by the Williamstown Theatre Festival. **117m/C VHS, DVD.** *Blythe Danner, Olympia Dukakis, Lee Grant, Frank Langella, Kevin McCarthy, Marian Mercer, Mikhail Sweitanod, Louis Zorich;* **D:** *John J. Desmond, Nikos Psacharopoulos.* **TV**

The Seagull 🐶🐶🐶 1971 A pensive, sensitive adaptation of the famed Chekhov play about the depressed denizens of an isolated country estates. In Russian with English subtitles. **99m/C VHS.** *Alla Demidova, Lyudmila Savelyeva, Yuri Yakovlev;* **D:** *Yuri Karasik.*

Seamless WOOF! 2000 (R) Overwrought, silly and senseless story about a group of rave-happy homeless kids who are offered work and a place to live by paternalistic J.B. (charmless Kenaro Seagal, Steven's son). Things don't work out as the kids wind up back on the street, resorting to drug dealing, prostitution and the like to get by, and that's bad but not nearly as bad as this dreck. **91m/C VHS, DVD.** *Shannon Elizabeth, Peter Alexander, Melinda Scherwinski, Broc Benedict;* **D:** *Denise Brassard;* **M:** *Memoru Mochizuki.* **VIDEO**

Seance 🐶 2006 (R) Typically dumb, low-budget teen slasher/horror flick. College student Lauren (Erickson) gets a nasty surprise when she sees the ghost of a young girl in her dorm room. Stuck on campus over Thanksgiving break, the remaining students decide to hold a seance and see if they can contact Cara, whom Lauren learned died suspiciously in their dorm. Instead, Spence (Paul) appears and they quickly discover that the former janitor was a serial killer who's not done yet. **88m/C DVD** *Adrian Paul, Kandis Erickson, A.J. Lamas, Tori White, Chauntal Lewis, Joel Geist, Bridget Shergalis;* **D:** *Mark Smith;* **C:** *Geoffrey Schaaf;* **M:** *Vincent Gillioz.* **VIDEO**

The Sea Wolf 🐶🐶 1993 Yet another tough, tightly wound thriller about an alcoholic cop with a mid-life crisis. While following the track of a serial killer, he begins hunters through sneer ruthlessness and ego. He rescues snobbish theatre critic Van Weyden (Reeve) and pretty scam artist Flaxen (Stewart) from a capsized ferry. The self-educated captain wants to test out his theories about survival of the fittest by making the rich Van Wayden his cabin boy (Flaxen gets leveled at). Lots of teeth-gnashing and bellowing in this turgid TV remake, although Revill has fun as the sniveling Cookie. See the Edward G. Robinson version instead. **120m/C VHS, Charles Bronson, Christopher Reeve, Catherine Mary Stewart, Clive Revill;* **D:** *Michael Anderson Sr.;* **W:** *Andrew J. Fenady;* **M:** *Charles Bernstein.*

Seance on a Wet Afternoon 🐶🐶🐶½ 1964 Dark, thoughtful film about a crazed pseudo-psychic who coerces her husband into a kidnapping so she can gain recognition by divining the child's whereabouts. Directed splendidly by Forbes, and superb acing from Stanley and Attenborough, who co-produced with Forbes. **111m/B VHS, DVD.** *Kim Stanley, Richard Attenborough, Margaret Lacey, Maria Kazan, Mark Eden, Patrick Magee;* **D:** *Bryan Forbes;* **W:** *John Barry, British Acad. '64;* **C:** *Attenborough;* **Natl. Bd. of Review '64; Actress (Stanley);* **N.Y. Film Critics '64;* Actress (Stanley).* **VIDEO**

The Search 🐶🐶🐶½ 1948 Clift, an American soldier stationed in post-WWII Berlin, befriends a homeless nine-year-old amnesiac boy (Jandl) and tries to find his family. Meanwhile, his mother has been searching the Displaced Persons camps for her son. The steps aside, and mother and son are finally reunited. Clift's first screen appearance, although this movie was actually filmed after his debut in "Red River," it was released first. **105m/B VHS, Montgomery Clift, Aline MacMahon, Ivan Jandl, Jarmila Novotna, Wendell Corey;* **D:** *Fred Zinnemann;* **W:** *Paul Jarrico.* Oscars '48: Story; Golden Globes '49: Screenplay.

Search and Destroy 🐶🐶 1988 (R) Sci-fi action flick about the capture of a secret biological warfare research station. **90m/C VHS.** *Perry King, Don Stroud, Fank Jong Soo, George Kennedy, Tisa Farrow, David Fruet.*

Search and Destroy 🐶🐶 1994 (R) Complex story finds bankrupt businessman Martin Mirtcheim (Dunne) trying to overcome his financial woes by making a film based on a book by self-help guru, Dr. Luther Waxling (Hopper). Of course, since Martin's broke, he first has to find someone willing to invest in his venture, and the shady duo (Walken and Turturro) he does just leave him with more problems. Tediously stagy adaptation of Howard Korders' play. Directorial debut by artist Salle at least looks great and provides some quirky moments. **91m/C VHS, DVD.** *Griffin Dunne, Dennis Hopper, Rosanna Arquette, Christopher Walken, John Turturro, Illeana Douglas, Ethan Hawke;* **D:** *John Salle;* **W:** *Michael Almereyda;* **C:** *Michael Spiller, Bobby Bukowski;* **M:** *Elmer Bernstein.*

The Search for Bridey Murphy 🐶🐶 1956 Long before channelers, Ramtha and New-Age profiteers, there was a Colorado housewife who, under hypnosis described a previous life as an Irish girl. Her famous claim was never proven—but that didn't stop this well-acted but dull dramatization. Neither sensationalist, nor likely to persuade skeptics. Based on the book by Morey Bernstein, hypnotist in the case. **84m/B VHS.** *Teresa Wright, Louis Hayward, Nancy Gates, Kenneth Tobey, Richard Anderson;* **D:** *Noel Langley.*

The Search for One-Eyed Jimmy 🦴🦴 1996 (R) Good-natured slice-of-life comedy about lowlife friends in the Brooklyn neighborhood of Red Hook. Film school grad Les (McCallany) returns to his old stomping grounds to make a documentary and decides missing local character Jimmy (Rockwell) will be his topic. Only no one except Jimmy's parents seem really concerned and Les' friends are such dimwits that they couldn't find a hole in the ground anyway. 86m/C VHS, DVD. Holt McCallany, Nicholas Turturro, Steve Buscemi, Michael Badalucco, Ray "Boom Boom" Mancini, Anne Meara, John Turturro, Samuel L. Jackson, Sam Rockwell; D: Sam Henry Kass; W: Sam Henry Kass; C: Charles Levey; M: William Bloom.

Search for Signs of Intelligent Life in the Universe 🦴🦴🦴 1991 (PG-13) Tomlin's brilliant one-woman show has been expanded into a wonderful film. As Tomlin's cast of 12 female and male characters meet and interact, they show every viewer his/her own humanity. 120m/C VHS, DVD. Lily Tomlin; D: John Bailey; W: Jane Wagner; M: Jerry Goodman.

Search for the Gods 🦴½ 1975 A dig in the Southwest turns interesting when one of the archeologists comes across an exquisite ancient medallion that could answer questions about alien visitors. Pilot for a TV series that didn't make it. 100m/C VHS, Kurt Russell, Stephen McHattie, Ralph Bellamy, Victoria Racimo, Raymond St. Jacques; D: Jud Taylor. TV

The Searchers 🦴🦴🦴🦴 1956 The classic Ford western, starring John Wayne as a hard-hearted frontiersman who spends years doggedly pursuing his niece, who was kidnapped by Indians. A simple western structure supports Ford's most moving, mysterious, complex film. Many feel this is the best western of all time. 119m/C VHS, DVD, Blu-ray Disc, HD DVD. John Wayne, Jeffrey Hunter, Vera Miles, Natalie Wood, Ward Bond, John Qualen, Harry Carey Jr., Olive Carey, Antonio Moreno, Henry (Kleinbach) Brandon, Hank Worden, Lana Wood, Dorothy Jordan, Patrick Wayne; D: John Ford; W: Frank Nugent; C: Winton C. Hoch; M: Max Steiner. AFI '98: Top 100, Natl. Film Reg. '89.

Searching for Bobby Fischer 🦴🦴🦴 1993 (PG) Seven-year-old Josh Waitzkin (Pomeranc, in his debut) shows an amazing gift for chess, stunning his parents, who must then try to strike the delicate balance of developing his abilities while also allowing him a "normal" childhood. Excellent cast features Mantegna and Allen as his parents, Kingsley as demanding chess teacher Pandolfini, and Fishburne as an adept speed-chess hustler. Pomeranc is great, and his knowledge of chess (he's a ranked player) brings authenticity to his role. Title comes from Pandolfini's belief that Josh may equal the abilities of chess whiz Bobby Fischer. Underrated little gem based on a true story and adapted from the book by Waitzkin's father. 111m/C VHS, DVD. Joe Mantegna, Max Pomeranc, Joan Allen, Ben Kingsley, Laurence Fishburne, Robert Stephens, David Paymer, William H. Macy, Hal Scardino; D: Steven Zaillian; W: Steven Zaillian; C: Conrad L. Hall; M: James Horner. MTV Movie Awards '94: New Filmmaker (Zaillian).

Searching for Bobby D 🦴 2005 (R) Lame wiseguy/showbiz comedy. Four bit part Brooklyn actors decide to make their own movie and, thanks to family mobster connections, wind up in Pennsylvania. There, Johnny's cousin Leo has lied to a financial backer by saying Robert De Niro is starring in their flick (they bring in a look-alike). Naturally, much stupidity follows. 105m/C DVD. William DeMeo, James Madio, Tyson Beckford, Louis Vanaria, Daniel Margotta, Tony Darrow, Carmen Electra; D: Paul Borghese; W: William DeMeo, Paul Borghese; C: George Mitas; M: Neil Berg.

Searching for Paradise 🦴½ 2002 (R) Gilda (Pratt) is obsessed with New York actor Michael De Santis (Noth). After her father dies (and she's disillusioned by some family skeletons), Gilda decides to take up her grandmother's offer to visit her in the Big Apple—the better to stalk De Santis. Hopelessly naive and a little unhinged, Gilda eventually poses as a journalist to meet her hero. Underdeveloped drama with little character development or explanation. Writer/director Paci's debut. 88m/C VHS, DVD. Susan May Pratt, Christopher Noth, Jeremy Davies, Mary Louise Wilson, Josef Sommer, Michele Placido, Laila Robins; D: Myra Paci; W: Myra Paci; C: Teodoro Maniaci; M: Carter Burwell.

Searching For Wooden Watermelons 🦴🦴½ 2001 A small-town woman with big-time dreams of becoming a television writer battles her trepidations about ditching her hum-drum life for the Hollywood hills in this poignant narrative drawn from star/co-producer/writer English's personal experiences. While the moral might be simplistic and overstated, the players are genuine. 86m/C VHS, DVD. Wendy English, Chad Safar, Scott M. Rudolph, Dixie Tucker, Victoria Anne LeBlanc; D: Bryan Goldsworthy; W: Wendy English; C: David M. Sammons; M: Andy Daniels. VIDEO

Seas Beneath 🦴🦴 1931 Commander Bob Kingsley and his men are sent on a secret mission to sink a German U-boat. Maria, whom Kingsley loves, turns out to be a German spy whose brother is the captain of the U-boat. She tries to sabotage Kingsley's mission but is thwarted. Shot off Catalina Island, Ford received naval assistance, including the use of two submarines and a mine sweeper. 90m/B DVD. George O'Brien, Mona Maris, Henry Victor, John Lodge, Marion Lessing, Steve Pendleton, Larry Kent; D: John Ford; W: Dudley Nichols; C: Joseph August.

Seaside Swingers 🦴½ Every Day's a Holiday 1965 A group of teenagers at a seaside resort work to win a talent competition on TV. But where is the real comedy? Dumb teen romance comedy with accidental plot. ♪All I Want Is You; A Girl Needs a Boy; Second Time Around; Indubitably Me; Love Me, Please; Now, Ain't That Somethin'—Caw Blimey; Romeo Jones; What's Cookin. 94m/C VHS. GB Michael Sarne, Grazina Frame, John Leyton; D: James Hill.

Season for Assassins 🦴½ 1971 Police commissioner Castroni is the only man who can stop a wave of violence enveloping Rome. 102m/C VHS. IT Magali Noel, Rossano Brazzi, Joe Dallesandro, Martin Balsam; D: Marcello Andrei; M: Alberto Verrecchia.

A Season for Miracles 🦴🦴 1999 Because their drug-addict mother, Berry (Derm), is in jail, Alanna (Whitman) and younger brother J.T. (Sabara) are about to be placed in foster care. Instead, they go on the lam with their devoted Aunt Emilie (Gugino), whose car breaks down (hey, it's a Christmas movie). The family are taken under the eccentric wing of a diner waitress (Duke) and the trio warily settle in—with Emilie even drawing the romantic interest of handsome cop Nathan (Conrad). Of course, trouble comes calling when their secret is exposed. (It's Christmas—there's a happy ending.) Adapted from the book by Marilyn Pappano. 90m/C VHS. Carla Gugino, David Conrad, Kathy Baker, Laura Dern, Patty Duke, Lynn Redgrave, Mae Whitman, Evan Sabara, Patti Prince, Mary Louise Wilson; D: Michael Pressman; W: Maria Nation; C: Shelly Johnson; M: Craig Safan. TV

Season of Change 🦴½ 1994 Tepid coming of age saga set in rural Montana, circa 1942. Thirteen-year-old Sally Mae (Tom) notices the tensions between her Bible-bound mother (Anderson) and war vet dad (Madsen), who's worried about finding a job to support his family. Sally Mae tries to understand all these adult notions even as she herself becomes attracted to teen mechanic Bobby (Randall). Cliched script and awkward performances don't help. 93m/C VHS, DVD. Nicholle Tom, Michael Madsen, Jo Anderson, Hoyt Axton, Ethan (Randall) Embry; D: Robin Murray; W: Shirley Hillard.

Season of Fear 🦴½ 1989 (R) A young man visits his estranged father's home. Abandoned as a child, he's embroiled in a murder scheme engineered by his father's beautiful young wife. Intriguing premise, forgettable execution. 89m/C VHS. Michael Bowen, Clancy Brown, Clare Wren, Ray Wise, Michael J. Pollard; D: Doug Campbell; W: Doug Campbell.

Season of the Witch 🦴½ 1973 (R) Hungry Wives; Jack's Wife 1973 (R) A frustrated housewife becomes intrigued with a neighboring witch and begins to practice witchcraft herself, through murder and seduction. Meant to be suspenseful, thrilling, and topical, it is none of these. Poorly acted at best. Originally 130 minutes! 89m/C DVD. Jan White, Ray Laine, Bill Thunhurst, Joedda McClain, Virginia Greenwald, Ann Muffly, Neil Fisher, Esther Lapidus, Dan Mallinger, Ken Peters; D: George A. Romero; W: George A. Romero; C: George A. Romero.

A Season on the Brink 🦴🦴½ 2002 (R) Indiana University basketball coach Bobby Knight (Dennehy) is determined that the 1985-86 season will be a winning one. But his constant tirades are beginning to negatively affect his players. Dennehy owns this role as the abusive blowhard but since there's nothing sympathetic about Knight, it's hard to get too involved. Based on the book by journalist John Feinstein. 87m/C VHS, DVD. Brian Dennehy, Al Thompson, James Lafferty, Michael James Johnson; D: Robert Mandel; W: David W. Rintels; C: Claudio Chea; M: Randy Edelman. Steve Porcaro. CABLE

Sebastian 🦴🦴½ Mr. Sebastian 1968 Mathematics whiz is employed by the British to decipher codes. He falls in love with York, another code breaker, and becomes involved in international intrigue. A bit too fast-paced and busy, but enjoyable spy drama. Sutherland has a small role. 100m/C VHS. GB Dirk Bogarde, Susannah York, Lilli Palmer, John Gielgud, Margaret Johnston, Nigel Davenport, Donald Sutherland; D: David Greene; M: Jerry Goldsmith.

Sebastiane 🦴🦴🦴 1979 An audacious film version of the legend of St. Sebastian, packed with homoerotic imagery and ravishing visuals. Honest, faithful rendering of the Saint's life and refusal to obey Roman authorities. Jarman's first film, in Latin with English subtitles. 90m/C VHS, DVD. GB Leonardo Treviglio, Barney James, Neil Kennedy, Richard Warwick, Lindsay Kemp; D: Derek Jarman, Paul Humfress; W: Derek Jarman, Paul Humfress; C: Peter Middleton; M: Brian Eno.

The Second Awakening of Christa Klages 🦴🦴🦴 Das Zweite Erwachen der Christa Klages 1978 Young divorced mother Christa (Engel) decides to finance her money-troubled day-care center by robbing a bank with her lover Werner (Muller-Westernhagen). Werner's killed and Christa becomes a fugitive, taking refuge with her friend Ingrid (Reize). German with subtitles. 90m/C VHS, DVD. GE Tina Engel, Sylvia Reize, Marius Muller-Westernhagen, Peter Schneider, Katharina Thalbach; D: Margarethe von Trotta; W: Margarethe von Trotta, Luisa Francia; C: Franz Rath; M: Klaus Doldinger.

Second Best 🦴🦴🦴 1994 (PG-13) Quiet, intimate drama about a lonely Welsh postmaster (Hurt) who decides to adopt a son (Miles). James, the 11-year-old boy he considers adopting, comes from a troubled background and is prone to violent outbursts. Graham, the village postmaster, is dealing with emotional demons of his own, and his problems are interwoven with those of the deprived, temperamental James. Although Hurt seems miscast as a shy, middle-aged Welshman, he turns in one of the best performances of his career. Richly acted and flawlessly directed, Menges has created a convincing and effective father-son drama. Based on David Cook's novel. 105m/C VHS. GB William Hurt, Chris Cleary Miles, Keith Allen, Prunella Scales, Jane Horrocks, Alan Cumming, John Hurt; D: Chris Menges; W: David Cook; M: Simon Boswell.

Second Best 🦴🦴 2005 In this 'guy flick' Elliot (Pantoliano) is the protagonist, emotionally dwelling a few levels below the incessant whinings of Woody Allen. Fired from a Manhattan publishing house for not producing best sellers, he now spends his days hosting a Web site for downcasts like himself and writing stories he never has the guts to submit to a publisher. When a longtime friend, now a hot shot movie producer (Gaines), returns greener pastures, Elliot is forced to seriously reassess his life. Directing is a bit laid back and the buddies' kvetch sessions become somewhat wearing, but it does make poignant observations amidst the wry humor. 86m/C DVD. US Joe Pantoliano, Boyd Gaines, Jennifer Tilly, Peter Gerety, Bronson Pinchot, Polly Draper, Barbara Barrie, James Ryan, Paulina Porizkova, Matthew Arkin, Fiona Gallagher; D: Eric Weber; W: Eric Weber; C: Christopher Norr; M: Tom O'Brien, Nathan Wilson, John Leccese, Joe Weber.

Second Best Secret Agent in the Whole Wide World 🦴🦴½ Licensed to Kill 1965 A klutzy agent attempts to prevent a Swedish anti-gravity formula from falling into Russian hands. Surprisingly good early spoof of the James Bond genre. 93m/C VHS. GB Tom Adams, Veronica Hurst, Peter Bull, Karel Stepanek, John Arnatt; D: Lindsay Shonteff.

Second Chance 🦴🦴 1953 A former prizefighter (Mitchum) travels to Mexico where he protects a gangster's moll (Darnell) targeted for murder. But Palance is on their tail. Originally released theatrically on a wide screen in 3-D. Good melodrama. 82m/C VHS. Robert Mitchum, Linda Darnell, Jack Palance, Reginald (Reggie, Reggy) Sheffield, Roy Roberts; D: Rudolph Mate; W: Robert Presnell Sr., Sydney (Sidney) Boehm; C: William E. Snyder; M: Roy Webb.

Second Chance 🦴🦴 1980 When a woman finds her husband is in love with another, her marital happiness is shattered. She leaves her betrayer and struggles to adapt to life as a single mother. 270m/C VHS. GB Susannah York, Ralph Bates; D: Gerry Mill, Richard Handford. TV

The Second Chance 🦴🦴 2006 (PG-13) Ethan (Smith) is a young pastor preaching the faith from his dad's ministry via a protected world of TV performances to mostly rich white folks. As a lesson, he's sent to work with the troubled members of an urban black church led by Jake (Carr), a move that he initially rebuffs, but eventually Jake makes him see the error of his state's/ways. Fans of popular Christian rock singer Smith will enjoy his first foray into film. 102m/C DVD. US Michael W. Smith, J. Don Ferguson, Lisa Arindell Anderson, David Alford, Jeff Obafemi Carr, Henry Haggard, Kenda Benward, Jonathan Thomas, Calvin Hobson, Bobby Daniels, Shirley Cody, Peggy Walton Walker, Vilia Steele; D: Steve Taylor; W: Steve Taylor, Henry O. Arnold, Ben Pearson; C: Ben Pearson; M: Michael W. Smith.

Second Chances 🦴🦴½ 1998 Think a family version of "The Horse Whisperer." 10-year-old Sunny is left unable to walk without crutches after a car accident and becomes emotionally withdrawn. She and her mom move next door to former rodeo champ Ben Taylor and Sunny develops a rapport with both Ben and a crippled horse named Ginger. 107m/C VHS. Tom Amandes, Kelsey Mulrooney, Isabel Glasser, Stuart Whitman, Theodore Bikel, Terry Moore, Madeline Zima; D: James Fargo. VIDEO

Second Chorus 🦴🦴½ 1940 Rivalry of two trumpet players for a girl and a job with Artie Shaw Orchestra. Music, dance, and romance. Nothing great, but pleasant. ♪Would You Like To Be the Love of My Life?; Poor Mr. Chisholm; (I Ain't Hep to That Step) But I'll Dig It; Sweet Sue; I'm Yours. Swing Concerto; 83m/B VHS, DVD. Fred Astaire, Paulette Goddard, Burgess Meredith, Artie Shaw, Charles Butterworth; D: H.C. Potter.

The Second Civil War 🦴🦴½ 1997 (R) Political satire falls apart at the end but until then manages to provide some dark comedy. In the near future, Idaho Governor Farley (Bridges) closes his state's borders to a planeload of refugee children from a Pakistan-India nuclear war. The President (Hartman), who wants to look tough, gives Farley 72 hours to change his mind and the media, led by executive producer Mel Burgess. (Hedaya), goes into a typical frenzy. **105m/C VHS, DVD.** Beau Bridges, Phil Hartman, James Coburn, Dan Hedaya, Elizabeth Peña, Kevin Dunn, Denis Leary, James Earl Jones, Ron Perlman, Joanna Cassidy; **D:** Joe Dante; **W:** Martyn Burke; **C:** Mac Ahlberg; **M:** Hummie Mann. **CABLE.**

Second Coming of Suzanne ♂1/2 1980 Young actress encounters a hypnotic film director. Her role: to star in a crucifixion—which may be more real than she imagines. Winner of two international film festivals. **90m/C VHS, DVD.** Sondra Locke, Richard Dreyfuss, Gene Barry, Paul Sand, Jared Martin; **D:** Michael Barry; **W:** Michael Barry; **M:** Isidore Mankofsky.

Second Fiddle ♂♂1/2 1939 Power is a studio flack who's hired to mount a huge talent search for a girl to star in a new film epic (very clear parallels to the Scarlett O'Hara 'Gone With the Wind' hunt). He's sent to smalltown Minnesota where he meets Henie, who doesn't want her forbidding aunt (Oliver), who lives with her niece to go to wicked Hollywood. Nevertheless, Henie gets the part, becomes a success, and falls for her co-star Vallee. But it's all a publicity stunt on his part and Power is the one who really loves the girl. Henie gets to do some skating. ♫Back to Back; I'm Sorry for Myself; I Poured My Heart Into Song; An Old-Fashioned Tune Is Always New; When Winter Comes; Song of the Metronome. **86m/B VHS.** Sonja Henie, Tyrone Power, Rudy Vallee, Edna May Oliver, Mary Healy, Lyle Talbot, Alan Dinehart, Minna Gombell; **D:** Sidney Lanfield; **W:** Harry Tugend; **M:** Irving Berlin.

Second Sight ♂ 1989 (PG) A detective (Larroquette) and a goofy psychic (Pinchot) set out to find a kidnapped priest. Flick is sidetracked along the way by such peculiarities as a pixieish nun for romantic, not religious, intrigue. Remember this one? No? That's because you blinked when it was released to theatres. Eminently missable. **84m/C VHS.** Dominic Chianese, John Larroquette, Bronson Pinchot, Bess Armstrong, James Tolkan, Christine Estabrook, Cora-Lee Guest, Stuart Pankin, William Prince, John Schuck; **D:** Joel Zwick; **W:** Patricia Resnick; Tom Schulman.

Second Sight ♂♂♂ 1999 Hard-charging Detective Chief Inspector Ross Tanner (Owen) is called to investigate the murder of a college student who was beaten death within yards of his family's home. But beyond the murder, Tanner has a serious personal problem—a rare eye disease is causing him to go blind. Trying to keep his condition a secret, Tanner is forced to rely on new Detective Inspector Catherine Tully (Skinner), who has her own reasons for keeping quiet. **180m/C VHS, DVD. GB** Clive Owen, Claire Skinner, Stuart Wilson, Phoebe Nichols, Tom Mullion, Louise Atkins, Eddie Marsan, Rebecca Egan, Benjamin Smith; **D:** Charles Beeson; **W:** Paula Milne; **C:** Rex Maidment. **TV**

Second in Command ♂♂ 2005 (R) Military attaché Sam Keenan (Van Damme) is assigned to the American embassy in a small East European country whose government is targeted by rebels. Keenan rescues the country's president and takes him to the embassy, which is now besieged by the rebel militia, leaving Keenan and a few Marines to hold their position. Routine actioner. **95m/C DVD. US** Jean-Claude Van Damme, Julie Cox, Velibor Topic, William Tapley, Alan McKenna, Serban Celea; **D:** Simon Fellows; **W:** David Corley, Jonathan Bowers, Jayson Rothwell; **C:** Doug Milsome; **M:** Mark Sayfritz. **VIDEO**

The Second Front ♂ 2005 (R) American agent Frank Hossom (Sheffer) must make certain that German Jewish scientist Nicky Raus doesn't fall into Nazi or Russian hands. But Frank makes the mistake of getting romantically interested in Nicky's lover, Olga (Metkina), who happens to be a KGB spy. Nonsensical melodrama enlivened by a certain amount of gunfire. **87m/C DVD.** Craig Sheffer, Ron Perlman, Svetlana Metkina; **D:** Dmitri Fiks; **C:** Goran Pavicenic; **M:** Igor Khoroshev, Sterzhen.

Second Victory ♂♂1/2 1987 (PG) Major Mark Hanlon has been appointed an Occupation Officer in the winter of 1945. He expects this will be his chance to brutally murdered all his thoughts turn to revenge. Based on the novel by Morris West. **95m/C VHS.** Anthony Andrews, Max von Sydow, Renee Soutendijk; **D:** Gerald Thomas.

Second Wind ♂♂ 1976 (PG) Wagner and Naughton are trying to settle into their new life together, but find they must make a variety of difficult choices. **93m/C VHS.** CA Ken Pogue, Teddie Moore, Tom Harvey, Lindsay Wagner, James Naughton; **C:** Donald Shebib; **W:** Hal Ackerman; **C:** Reginald Morris; **M:** Hagood Hardy.

The Second Woman ♂♂ *Here Lies Love; Twelve Miles Out* 1951 An architect, suffering from blackouts and depression, believes himself responsible for the death of his fiancee. Well-done psychodrama. **91m/B VHS, DVD.** Robert Young, Betsy Drake, John Sutton; **D:** James V. Kern; **W:** Mort Briskin, Robert Smith; **C:** Hal Mohr.

Secondhand Lions ♂♂♂ 2003 (PG) Timid Walter (Osment) is left with his eccentric uncles Hub (Duvall) and Garth (Caine) by his husband-seeking flaky mom Mae (Sedgewick). Finding no TV when he arrives, Walter becomes fascinated by the uncles' tales of an adventurous past, which are told in flashback in B-action movie style. Alternately syrupy and quirky, pic tries too much to be everything

Self-centered engineer Alberto (Molla) is married to the loving Elena (Gil) but is miserable. He hates "his job even though he's successful and is terrified that his wife will discover he's been unfaithful—with doctor Diego (Bardem) who doesn't know Alberto is even married. When Elena does find out, Alberto swears he's broken off the relationship but he's lying and his security continues to crumble since he won't make a choice between either of his lovers. Molla's a disappointment since it's not clear what either lover or wife sees in him but Bardem and Gil make up for his shortcomings. Spanish with subtitles. **104m/C VHS, DVD. SP** Javier Bardem, Jordi Molla, Ariadna Gil, Cecilia (Celia) Roth, Javier Albala, Mercedes Sampietro, Adrian Sac; **D:** Gerardo Vera; **W:** Angeles Gonzalez-Sinde; **C:** Julio Madurga; **M:** Foque Banos.

Second Skin ♂♂ 2000 (R) Sam Kane (MacFayden) falls in love with Crys (Henstridge), who's suffering from amnesia after a car crash. Sam tries to help her out and Crystal remembers that she has a previous and dangerous connection. **91m/C VHS, DVD.** Angus MacFadyen, Natasha Henstridge, Peter Fonda, Liam Waite; **D:** Darrell Roodt.

Second Thoughts ♂ 1983 (PG) Frustrated woman attorney divorces her stuffy husband and takes up with an aging hippie. She comes to regret her decision when it becomes obvious that her new man has his head firmly stuck in the 60s. Comedy-drama lacking real laughs or drama. **109m/C VHS.** Lucie Amaz, Craig Wasson, Ken Howard, Joe Mantegna; **D:** Lawrence Turman; **W:** Steve Brown; **M:** Henry Mancini.

Second Time Lucky ♂ 1984 The devil makes a bet with God that if the woman and the man fall for each other.
The Second Track ♂♂ *Zweite Gleis* 1962 Brock, a train inspector, witnesses a robbery at the railyard and recognizes one of the thieves from his wartime days, though' he hides the fact from the police. But Brock's daughter has become curious about her father's past and her investigation uncovers some Nazi-era secrets that the thief (and her father) want to stay hidden. German with subtitles. **80m/B DVD. GE** Walter Richter, Erik S. Klein, Albert Hetterle, Annekathrin Burger, Horst Jonischkan, Helga Goring; **D:** Joachim Kunert; **C:** Joachim Kunert, Gunter Kunart; **C:** Rolf Sohre; **M:** Pavol Simai.

The Secret Agent ♂♂ 1936 Presumed dead, a British Intelligence agent (Gielgud) reappears and receives a new assignment. Using h's faked death to his advantage, he easily journeys to Switzerland where he is to eliminate an enemy agent. Strange Hitchcockian melange of comedy and intrigue, atypical, but worthy offering from the Master. **83m/B VHS, DVD.** GB Madeleine Carroll, Peter Lorre, Robert Young, John Gielgud, Lilli Palmer, Percy Marmont, Charles Carson, Florence Kahn; **D:** Alfred Hitchcock; **W:** Charles Bennett; **C:** Bernard Knowles; **M:** Louis Levy.

The Secret Agent ♂♂ 1996 (R) Fain, rain go away. In this waterlogged adaptation of the Conrad novel, Hoskins plays Adolf Verloc, a cowardly agent provocateur who heads a group of anarchists in soggy Victorian England. His real mission, however, is to report the actions of the expatriates to the Russian government. After he is bullied into a terrorist attack on the Greenwich Observatory by his contact at the Russian embassy, the lives of Verloc, his wife Winnie (Arquette) and her mentally disabled brother Stevie (Bale) are blown to pieces (sometimes literally by the concussion). The only spark in the otherwise dank and gloomy production is Williams (listed as George Spelvin) as the demented explosives expert known only as

to everybody, and may not appeal to younger, jaded viewers. Their parents as grandparents, nostalgic for this kind of wholesome family entertainment, will be more receptive. Duvall and Caine make up for many of the flaws, but Osment doesn't 'register as strongly as hoped in his first post-child star role. **107m/C VHS, DVD. UMD.** US Michael Caine, Robert Duvall, Haley Joel Osment, Nicky Katt, Kyra Sedgwick, Emmanuelle Vaugier, Christian Kane, Josh Lucas, Adrian Pasdar; **D:** Tim McCanlies; **W:** Tim McCanlies; **C:** Jack N. Green; **M:** Patrick Doyle.

Seconds ♂♂♂ 1966 (R) Aging banker Arthur Hamilton (Randolph) is frantic to escape his dead-end existence and accepts an invitation from a mysterious organization to give him a second chance at life. Through surgery Arthur's transformed into handsome artist Tony Wilson (Hudson). Uncomfortably living in Malibu, he finds out all his new neighbors are also "seconds," who are afraid he'll betray their secret. Wilson decides he wants out of his new arrangement and back to his former life but it comes at a very high price. Eerie film manages to (mostly) overcome its plot problems, with a fine performance by Hudson. Based on the novel by David Ely. **107m/B VHS, DVD.** Rock Hudson, John Randolph, Salome Jens, Will Geer, Jeff Corey, Richard Anderson, Murray Hamilton, Karl Swenson, Khigh Dhiegh, Frances Reid, Wesley Addy; **D:** John Frankenheimer; **W:** Lewis John Carlino; **C:** James Wong Howe; **M:** Jerry Goldsmith.

Secre of the Andes ♂♂1/2 1998 (PG) Rebellious Ciana (Belle) travels to Argentina with her mother (Allen) to visit her estranged father (Keith). He's an archeologist searching for gold and Diana dabbles in the supernatural to help him out. **102m/C VHS, DVD.** David Keith, Nancy Allen, John Rhys-Davies, Camilla Belle, Jerry Stiller; **D:** Alejandro Azzano.

The Secret ♂♂1/2 1993 Businessman and political candidate Mike Dunsmore (Douglas) comes to terms with his lifelong battle with dyslexia when his grandson begins to show signs of the same affliction. Set in picturesque New England fishing village. **92m/C VHS, DVD.** Kirk Douglas, Bruce Boxleitner, Brock Peters, Laura Harrington; **D:** Karen Arthur.

Secret Admirer ♂♂ 1985 (R) A teenager's unsigned love letter keeps falling into the wrong hands. Intends to be funny, and sometimes is; too often, though, it surrenders to obviousness and predictability. **98m/C VHS, DVD.** C. Thomas Howell, Cliff DeYoung, Kelly Preston, Dee Wallace Stone, Lori Loughlin, Fred Ward, Casey Siemaszko, Corey Haim, Leigh Taylor-Young; **D:** David Greenwalt.

Secret Ballot ♂♂♂ *Raye Makfi* 2001 (G) Iranian road picture/comedy gets laughs and provokes thought as a macho soldier and a liberated female pollster travel around the desert. Brought together when a ballot box parachutes down from the sky, and onto the desolate beach that the soldier is guarding, the two are classic opposites. The reluctant, hardened soldier is eventually coerced by the hopeful electioneer (Abdi) into driving her to each city on her mission to collect every vote possible for the upcoming election. The journey proves useful to both as they get more than a glimpse of the other's point of view. Their radically different views are fertile soil for the ensuing comedy as well as food for thought. The personalities and culture of Iran are explored through their journey, sometimes whimsically, in the light of democracy. Charming score matches pic's equally winsome vision of the Middle East. **105m/C VHS, DVD. IA** Nassim Abdi, Cyrus Abidi; **D:** Babak Payami; **M:** Miklos Rozsa.

Secret Ceremony ♂♂ 1968 (R) An aging prostitute and a young, aimless waif resemble each other's dead mother and dead daughter, respectively, and the relationship goes on, strangely, from there. This original big-screen version is very good. Freudian psycho-drama; 101-minute TV version is unfortunately greatly diluted. **109m/C VHS.** Elizabeth Taylor, Robert Mitchum, Mia Farrow, Pamela Brown, Peggy Ash-

the Professor. Alfred Hitchcock also used blackmail in the western world and only specially in "Sabotage." **95m/C VHS, DVD. GB** Bob Hoskins, Patricia Arquette, Gerard Depardieu, Robin Williams, Jim Broadbent, Christian Bale, Elizabeth Spriggs, Peter Vaughan, Julian Wadham; **D:** Christopher Hampton; **W:** Christopher Hampton; **C:** Denis Lenoir; **M:** Philip Glass.

Secret Agent 00 ♂ *Operation Kid Brother* 1967 (R) A master criminal plans to blackmail the western world and only specially. Secret Agent 00 can stop him. Bad spy genre ripoff, interesting only as the screen debut of Sean Connery's brother. **97m/C VHS. IT** Neil Connery, Daniela Bianchi, Adolfo Celi; **D:** Alberto De Martino; **M:** Ennio Morricone.

The Secret Club ♂1/2 1989 International spy decides to fulfill his dream of opening a detective agency in his old neighborhood. Release of this direct-to-video mishmash was delayed until '95. **71m/C VHS.** Billy Dee Williams, Anthony Michael Hall, Lesley-Anne Down, Mathew McCurley, Richard Moll, James Hong, Barry Bostwick, Jack Nance; **D:** James A. Contner; **C:** S. Douglas Smith.

Secret Agent Super Dragon ♂1/2 *Super Dragon* 1966 The CIA calls in the agent known as "Super Dragon" when it is discovered that a Venezuelan drug czar plans to spike U.S. gum and candy with an LSD-like drug. Less than competent production offers some unintended laughter. Ferroni used the pseudonym Calvin Jackson Padget. **95m/C VHS.** FR IT GE Ray Danton, Marisa Mell, Margaret Lee, Jess Hahn, Carlo D'Angelo, Andriana Ambesi; **D:** Giorgio Ferroni.

Secret Agent 00-Soul ♂1/2 1966 The CIA calls in the agent known as "Super Dragon" when it is discovered... **90m/C VHS, DVD.** Hulk Hogan, Richard Moll, Lesley-Anne Down, Mathew McCurley, Edward Albert, Lyman Ward, James Hong, Barry Bostwick, Jack Nance; **D:** Julius Le Flore.

Secret Beyond the Door ♂♂♂ 1948 A wealthy heiress marries a widower and soon discovers that he murdered his first wife. Understandably, she wonders what plans he might have for her. Capably done chiller, but the plot is hackneyed pseudo-Hitchcock. **99m/B VHS, DVD.** Joan Bennett, Michael Redgrave, Barbara O'Neil, Anne Revere; **D:** Fritz Lang; **M:** Miklos Rozsa.

croft; **D**: Joseph Losey; **M**: Richard Rodney Bennett.

The Secret Code ♂♂ 1942 A 15-chapter serial with the Black Commando (Kelly) thwarting the Nazis' attempts at sabotage. After each chapter's cliffhanger ending a new form of secret code is explained and decoded. **315m/B VHS**. Paul Kelly, Anne Nagel, Clancy Cooper, Trevor Bardette, Gregory Gay, Ludwig Donath, Eddie (Ed, Eddy, Edwin) Parker; **D**: Spencer Gordon Bennet.

The Secret Diary of Sigmund Freud ♂♂ 1984 Spoofy look at the early years of Sigmund Freud, the father of modern psychoanalysis. Freud (Cort) has an affair with lisping nurse Kane while tending to patient Shawn and answering to mama Baker, who's carrying on with mad doctor Kinski. Talented cast falls asleep on couch. **129m/C VHS**. Bud Cort, Carol Kane, Carroll Baker, Klaus Kinski, Marisa Berenson, Dick Shawn, Ferdinand "Ferdy" Mayne; **D**: Danford B. Greene.

Secret File of Hollywood ♂½ *Secret File: Hollywood* 1962 A down-and-out private eye gets a job taking photos for a sleazy Hollywood scandal sheet and finds himself in the midst of a blackmail plot masterminded by his editor. An often childish potboiler, perhaps inspired by the once-feared Confidential Magazine. **85m/B VHS**. Robert Clarke, Francine York, Syd Mason, Maralou Gray, John Warburton; **D**: Ralph Cushman.

The Secret Four ♂♂ *The Four Just Men* 1940 Three young men seek to avenge the death of their friend at the hands of British traitors, and become involved in a plot to sabotage the Suez canal. Poorly adapted from the novel by Edgar Wallace. **79m/B VHS**. **GB** Hugh Sinclair, Griffith Jones, Francis L. Sullivan, Frank Lawton, Anna Lee, Alan Napier, Basil Sydney; **D**: Walter Forde.

Secret Games ♂½ 1992 (R) An unhappily married woman (Brin) is searching for relief from her restrictive marriage. At the "Afternoon Demitasse," an exclusive brothel where women are paid for fulfilling their ultimate fantasies, she meets a man (Hewitt) who pushes her beyond her sexual limits and threatens to totally possess her. **90m/C VHS, DVD**. Martin Hewitt, Michele Brin, Delia Sheppard, Billy Drago; **D**: Alexander Gregory (Gregory Dark) Hippolyte; **W**: Georges des Esseintes; **C**: Wally Pfister, Thomas Denove; **M**: Joseph Smith.

Secret Games 2: The Escort ♂½ 1993 (R) A performance artist (Hewitt) learns how to seduce women on from a beautiful escort (Rochele). However, he falls for his trainer despite being a star pupil who could have anyone he wanted. Plot conveniently lends itself to lots of steamy love scenes. Also available in an unrated version. **84m/C VHS**. Martin Hewitt, Amy Rochelle, Sara Suzanne Brown, Marie Leroux; **D**: Alexander Gregory (Gregory Dark) Hippolyte; **C**: Russell Lavalle; **M**: Ashley Irwin.

Secret Games 3 ♂½ 1994 (R) A bored doctor's wife gets her kicks by visiting a club catering to women's fantasies. But then she meets a criminal who wants her all to himself. An unrated version is available at 91 minutes. **82m/C VHS, DVD**. Woody Brown, Brenda Swanson, Rochelle Swanson; **D**: Alexander Gregory (Gregory Dark) Hippolyte; **C**: Wally Pfister; **M**: Ashley Irwin.

The Secret Garden ♂♂♂ 1949 Orphaned Mary Lennox (O'Brien) is sent to live with her cold and uncaring Uncle Archibald Craven (Marshall), who has never recovered from his wife's death. He keeps his crippled son, Colin (Stockwell), a virtual prisoner in the house until Mary discovers a neglected hidden garden, once the pride of Mrs. Craven, which Mary secretly begins to tend. Touching tearjerker based on the novel by Frances Hodgson Burnett. O'Brien leads an outstanding cast in one of her final juvenile roles. In black and white, with Technicolor for later garden scenes. **92m/B VHS**. Margaret O'Brien, Herbert Marshall, Dean Stockwell, Gladys Cooper, Elsa Lanchester, Brian Roper; **D**: Fred M. Wilcox; **C**: Ray June; **M**: Bronislau Kaper.

The Secret Garden ♂♂½ 1984 Orphaned Mary Lennox is sent to live with her mysterious uncle after her parents die. Mary is willful and spoiled and her uncle's house holds a number of secrets, including a crippled cousin. When Mary discovers a mysteriously abandoned locked garden she makes it her mission to restore the garden to life. Based on the children's classic by Frances Hodgson Burnett. **107m/C VHS, DVD**. **GB** Sarah Hollis Andrews; David Patterson; **D**: Katrina Murray. **TV**

The Secret Garden ♂♂♂ 1987 (PG) Lonely orphan Mary Lennox is sent to live with her uncle in England after her parent's deaths. Mary, who has grown up in India, is selfish and unhappy until she discovers two secrets on her uncle's estate. Class production of the children's classic by Frances Hodgson Burnett with wonderful performances; added prologue and afterword showing Mary as an adult are unnecessary, but don't detract either. Made for television as a "Hallmark Hall of Fame" special. **100m/C VHS, DVD**. Gennie James, Barret Oliver, Jadrien Steele, Michael Hordern, Derek Jacobi, Billie Whitelaw, Lucy Gutteridge, Julian Glover, Colin Firth, Alan Grint; **D**: Alan Grint; **W**: Blanche Hanalis; **C**: Robert Paynter; **M**: John Cameron. **TV**

The Secret Garden ♂♂♂½ 1993 (G) Rekindled interest in Frances Hodgson Burnett's classic tale has prompted a Broadway musical, two TV movies, and this latest big screen version. Befitting director Holland's reputation this version is beautiful but dark, with children prey to very adult anxieties. **102m/C VHS, DVD**. Kate Maberly, Maggie Smith, Haydon Prowse, Andrew Knott, John Lynch; **D**: Agnieszka Holland; **C**: Roger Deakins; **M**: Zbigniew Preisner. L.A. Film Critics '93: Score.

Secret Honor ♂♂♂ *Lords of Treason; Secret Honor: The Last Testament of Richard M. Nixon; Secret Honor: A Political Myth* 1985 Idiosyncratic, single-set, one-man film version adapted by Donald Freed and Arnold Stone from their stage play about Richard Nixon coping with the death of his presidency on the night he's decided to blow his brains out. Made with students at the University of Michigan, and carried by the ranting and raving of Hall as a tragic Shakespearean Nixon with plenty of darkly humorous lines. **90m/C VHS, DVD**. Philip Baker Hall; **D**: Robert Altman; **W**: Donald Freed, Arnold Stone; **C**: Pierre Mignot; **M**: George Burt.

The Secret Invasion ♂♂½ 1964 In 1943, British intelligence officer Major Richard Mace (Granger) offers pardons to five criminals (Vallone, Rooney, Byrnes, Silva, Campbell) in return for their expertise. Their mission is to rescue an Italian general who has promised that his troops will switch sides and fight for the allies. Said general is imprisoned by the Nazis in Dubrovnik, Yugoslavia. Only the general they rescue turns out to be an imposter, which sorta complicates things. Actioner was well-done by Corman before 1967's "The Dirty Dozen." **95m/C DVD**. Stewart Granger, Raf Vallone, Mickey Rooney, Edd Byrnes, William Campbell, Henry Silva, Spela Rozin, Helmo Kinderman, Enzo Fiermonte, Peter Coe; **D**: Roger Corman; **W**: Arthur E. Arling; **C**: Hugo Friedhofer.

Secret Life of an American Wife ♂♂ 1968 A bored housewife (Jackson) tries to seduce a client of her husband's, with less than hilarious results. Too much dialogue, not enough genuine humor. Disappointing inversion of director Axelrod's "The Seven Year Itch." **97m/C VHS**. Walter Matthau, Anne Jackson, Patrick

O'Neal, Edy Williams, John MacKay; **D**: George Axelrod; **W**: George Axelrod.

The Secret Life of Girls ♂♂½ 1999 Fifteen-year-old Natalie (Delfino) is caught in the midst of family turmoil when her unhappy mother, Ruby (Hamilton), reveals that Natalie's college professor father, Hugh (Levy), has been fooling around with one of his students. Natalie hides out in the university library where she shyly flirts with a cute boy, but the family chaos continues when Hugh suffers the pangs of conscience. **90m/C VHS**. Majandra Delfino, Linda Hamilton, Eugene Levy, Kate Vernon, Meagan Good, Aeryk Egan, Andrew Ducote; **D**: Holly Goldberg Sloan.

The Secret Life of Mrs. Beeton ♂♂½ 2006 Beginning in the 1850s, Isabelle Beeton writes domestic advice columns for her husband Sam's various London publications. She produces a collection of recipes (though she can't cook) and household management tips that become a best-selling sensation. However, her own marriage is fraught with secrets that include financial difficulties, many personal tragedies, and her own early death at the age of 28. **90m/C DVD**. J.J. Feild, Jim Carter, Anna Chancellor, Anna Madeley, Siobhan Hayes, Joseph Mawle, Andrea Riseborough; **D**: Jon Jones; **W**: Sarah Williams; **C**: Ian Moss; **M**: Charlie Mole. **TV**

The Secret Life of Walter Mitty ♂♂♂ 1947 An entertaining adaptation of the James Thurber short story about a meek man (Kaye) who lives an unusual secret fantasy life. Henpecked by his fiancee and mother, oppressed at his job, he imagines himself in the midst of various heroic fantasies. While Thurber always professed to hate Kaye's characterization and the movie, it scored at the box office and today stands as a comedic romp for Kaye. Available with digitally remastered stereo and original movie trailer. **110m/C VHS, DVD**. Danny Kaye, Virginia Mayo, Boris Karloff, Ann Rutherford, Fay Bainter, Florence Bates; **D**: Norman Z. McLeod; **W**: Everett Freeman, Ken Englund, Philip Rapp; **C**: Lee Garmes; **M**: Sylvia Fine, David Raksin.

The Secret Lives of Dentists ♂♂♂ 2002 (R) Rudolph's funny, dead-on take on married dentists in crisis. Mild-mannered David (Scott) suspects his wife and fellow dentist Dana (Davis) may be having an affair with a member of her community opera troupe when his imagination begins to go wild. His acerbic, misogynist patient (Leary in a no-brainer bit of casting) plays devil's advocate as David begins to see him everywhere, imparting advice on how to handle the situation. As the marriage continues to decay, David's hilarious waking dreams continue unabated and he is forced to deal with the darker side of his milquetoast persona. Refreshingly realistic, original, and well-acted. Based on the novel "The Age of Grief" by Jane Smiley. **104m/C VHS, DVD**. US Campbell Scott, Hope Davis, Denis Leary, Robin Tunney, Kevin Carroll; **D**: Alan Rudolph; **W**: Craig Lucas; **C**: Florian Ballhaus; **M**: Gary DeMichele. Ind. Spirit '04: Support. Actress (Davis); N.Y. Film Critics '03: Actress (Davis).

Secret Mission ♂♂½ 1942 Four British intelligence agents are sent into occupied France to assess the strength of Nazi forces. But after discovering the information, their cover is blown and it's a race to get the intelligence into the right hands before the Nazis get to them first. **94m/B VHS**. **GB** James Mason, Hugh Williams, Roland Culver, Michael Wilding, Carla Lehmann, Nancy Price, Percy Walsh, Karel Stepanek, Herbert Lom, Stewart Granger; **D**: Harold French; **W**: Anatole de Grunwald, Basil Bartlett; **C**: Bernard Knowles, Cyril Knowles; **M**: Mischa Spoliansky.

Secret Obsession ♂ 1988 (PG) A love triangle among a father, his illegitimate son, and the woman they both love, set in North Africa in 1955. Sounds intriguing, but don't be fooled. Slow, dull, and poorly acted. **82m/C VHS, DVD**. Julie Christie, Ben Gazzara, Patrick Bruel, Jean Carmet; **D**: Henri Vart.

The Secret of Dr. Kildare ♂♂ 1939 Badly dated but worth seeing for the era's familiar faces and the difference in medical attitudes. Grumpy Dr. Gillespie (Barrymore) is terminally ill and trying to continue his research into new treatments for pneumonia. He doesn't have time for wealthy Paul Messenger (Atwill) and his apparently neurotic debutante daughter Nancy's (Gilbert) health problems, so he sends young Dr. Kildare (Ayres) to look into the matter. The third in the MGM B-movie series. **84m/B DVD**. Lew Ayres, Lionel Barrymore, Lionel Atwill, Helen Gilbert, Walter Kingford, Samuel S. Hinds, Emma Dunn, Nat Pendleton, Laraine Day; **D**: Harold Bucquet; **W**: Harry Ruskin, Willis Goldbeck; **C**: Alfred Gilks; **M**: David Snell.

The Secret of El Zorro ♂½ 1957 Don Diego's friend, Don Ricardo, threatens to unmask Zorro's secret identity when he challenges the legendary swordsman to a duel. **75m/B VHS**. Guy Williams.

The Secret of My Success ♂♂ 1987 (PG-13) Country bumpkin Fox goes to the Big Apple to make his mark. He becomes the corporate mailboy who rises meteorically to the top of his company (by impersonating an executive) in order to win the love of an icy woman executive. He spends his days running frantically between his real job in the mailroom and his fantasy position, with various sexual shenanigans with the boss's wife thrown in to keep the viewer alert. Fox is charismatic while working with a cliche-ridden script that ties up everything very neatly at the end. **110m/C VHS, DVD**. Michael J. Fox, Helen Slater, Richard Jordan, Margaret Whitton, Fred Gwynne; **D**: Herbert Ross; **W**: Jim Cash, Jack Epps Jr., A.J. Carothers; **C**: Carlo Di Palma; **M**: David Foster.

The Secret of Navajo Cave ♂♂ *Legend of Cougar Canyon* 1976 (G) Fair family adventure. Two young friends explore the mysterious Navajo cave, where one can be assured that a secret awaits. **84m/C VHS, DVD**. Holger Kasper, Steven Benally Jr., Johnny Guerro; **D**: James T. Flocker; **Nar**: Rex Allen.

The Secret of NIMH ♂♂♂ 1982 (G) Animated tale, produced by a staff of Disney-trained artists led by "American Tail's" Bluth, concerns a newly widowed mouse who discovers a secret agency of superintelligent rats (they've escaped from a science lab) who aid her in protecting her family. As is usually the case with Bluth films, the animation is superb while the socially aware plot struggles to keep pace. That aside, it's still an interesting treat for the youngsters. Adapted from Robert C. O'Brien's "Mrs. Frisby and the Rats of N.I.M.H." **84m/C VHS, DVD**. **D**: Don Bluth; **W**: Don Bluth; **M**: Jerry Goldsmith; **V**: John Carradine, Derek Jacobi, Dom DeLuise, Elizabeth Hartman, Peter Strauss, Aldo Ray, Edie McClurg, Wil Wheaton.

The Secret of Roan Inish ♂♂♂½ 1994 (PG) Irish myth comes to life in this fantasy about the importance of family and place, seen through the eyes of 10-year-old Fiona Coneelly (newcomer Courtney) who's sent to live with her grandparents in post-WWII County Donegal. Fiona's drawn to her grandfather's stories about the family's ancestral home on the island of Roan Inish and the loss of her baby brother Jamie, who was carried out to sea. Another family tale is about a Selkie—a beautiful seal/woman captured by a Coneelly fisherman who eventually returned to her ocean home. When Fiona visits Roan Inish she becomes convinced that Jamie is alive and being cared for by the island's seals. Director Sayles keeps a firm grip on the cuteness factor while cinematographer Wexler works his usual magic on the sea, sky, and land of Ireland. Based on the 1957 novel "Secret of the Ron Mor Skerry" by Rosalie K. Fry. **102m/C VHS, DVD**. Jeni Courtney, Mick (Michael) Lally, Eileen Colgan, John Lynch, Richard Sheridan, Susan Lynch, Cillian Byrne; **D**: John Sayles; **W**: John Sayles; **C**: Haskell Wexler; **M**: Mason Daring.

The Secret of Santa Vittoria 🐾🐾½ 1969 (PG) Italo Bambolini (Quinn) is an amiable drunk who unexpectedly becomes the mayor of his wine-making village during WWII. Hearing the Nazis are headed toward Santa Vittoria to loot their supply of vintage wines, Italo and his savvy wife, Rosa (Magnani), enlist the villagers to hide most of the bottles in a cave outside of town, leaving a token amount to satisfy suspicious German Commander Von Prum (Kruger), who tries to learn the truth. Overly long but still amusing. Based on the novel by Robert Crichton. 139m/C VHS. Anthony Quinn, Anna Magnani, Hardy Kruger, Renato Rascel, Giancarlo Giannini, Valentina Cortese, Sergio Franchi; **D:** Stanley Kramer; **W:** William Rose, Ben Maddow; **C:** Giuseppe Rotunno; **M:** Ernest Gold.

Secret of Stamboul 🐾½ *The Spy in White* 1936 British take on Hollywood action films finds two soldiers thrown out of their regiment thanks to a slinky rebel plot to overthrow the Turkish government. 85m/B VHS. Valerie Hobson, Peter Haddon, Frank Vosper, Kay Walsh, Cecil Ramage, James Mason; **D:** Andrew Marton; **W:** Laszlo Benedek, George Hill. VIDEO

Secret of the Black Trunk 🐾🐾½ 1962 Chilling. Edgar Wallace story about a series of murders at a famed English hotel. Filmed in Great Britain. 96m/C VHS. GE Joachim Hansen, Senta Berger, Hans Reiser, Leonard Steckel, Peter Carsten; **D:** Werner Klingler.

Secret of the Cave 🐾🐾 2006 (PG) Fourteen-year-old American Roy Wallace is spending the summer with his aunt and uncle in the small Irish village where his father grew up. Rumors of ghosts have the villagers in a tizzy and Roy's investigations point to a nearby sea cave. Pretty scenery and a Christian message as the film was sponsored by Southern Adventist University. 89m/C DVD. Kevin Novotny, Josep Kelly, Patrick Bergin, Niall O'Brien, Niamh Finn, Noelle Brown; **D:** Zach C. Gray; **W:** Aaron Adams, Scott Fog; **C:** David George; **M:** John Carta.

The Secret of the Golden Eagle 🐾🐾 1991 A boy and his new adventurer friend are on a quest to find the strange "Golden Statue" that causes people to grow old before their time. They must take it from criminals who are using it for evil purposes. A good adventure/fantasy for the entire family. 90m/C VHS. Michael Moriarty, Sally Kellerman, David Mendenhall, Virgil Frye, Gerald Anthony, Norbert Weisser; **D:** Radu Gabrea.

The Secret of the Ice Cave 🐾 1989 (PG-13) A motley band of explorers, hijackers and mercenaries go after a secret treasure in the remote mountains. 106m/C VHS. Michael Moriarty, Sally Kellerman, David Mendenhall, Virgil Frye, Gerald Anthony, Norbert Weisser; **D:** Radu Gabrea.

The Secret of the Loch 🐾🐾 1934 Scottish scientist claims to have seen Loch Ness Monster but everyone thinks his bagpipe's blown a reed. 80m/B VHS. GB Seymour Hicks, Nancy O'Neil, Gibson Gowland, Frederick Peisley; **D:** Milton Rosmer.

The Secret of the Telegian 🐾🐾½ *The Telegian* 1961 Rare Japanese sci-fi flick about a soldier who uses a teleportation device to kill fellow soldiers who tried to kill him. He could find his victims wherever they hid. 85m/C VHS. JP Koji Tsuruta, Yumi Shirakawa, Akihiko Hirata, Tadao Nakamura; **D:** Jun Fukuda.

The Secret Passion of Robert Clayton 🐾 1992 (R) When Robert Clayton Jr. (Valentine) returns to his home town to take the position of D.A., he is forced to go head to head in a lurid murder trial with the defense attorney (Mahoney), who also happens to be his own father. 92m/C VHS. John Mahoney, Scott Valentine, Eve Gordon, Kevin Conroy; **D:** E.W. Swackhamer; **W:** Brian Ross; **C:** Billy Dickson.

Secret of Yolanda 🐾 *Mute Love; Atara Hemeth* 1982 (R) Steamy romance about a young deaf-mute whose guardian and riding instructor both fall for her. 90m/C VHS. IS Aviva Ger, Asher Tzarfati, Shraga Harpaz; **D:** Joel Silberg; **W:** Eli Tavor; **C:** David Gurfinkel; **M:** Kobi Oshrat.

Secret Passions 🐾½ 1978 A young couple are haunted by a dark, romance-novel-type secret. 99m/C VHS. John James, Susan Lucci; **D:** Michael Pressman. TV

Secret Places 🐾🐾 1985 (PG) On the brink of WWII, a German girl in an English school finds friendship with a popular classmate. Touching and involving, but somehow unsatisfying. 98m/C VHS. GB Maria Therese Relin, Tara MacGowan, Claudine Auger, Jenny Agutter; **D:** Zelda Barron; **W:** Zelda Barron.

The Secret Policeman's Other Ball 🐾🐾 1982 (R) Engaging live performance by most of the Monty Python troupe and guest rock artists, staged for Amnesty International. Follows 1979's "The Secret Policeman's Ball" and followed by 1987's "The Secret Policeman's Third Ball." 101m/C VHS. GB John Cleese, Graham Chapman, Michael Palin, Terry Jones, Pete Townshend, Sting, Bill Connolly, Bob Geldof; **D:** Julien Temple; **W:** Michael Palin.

Secret Policeman's Private Parts 🐾🐾½ 1981 Various sketches and performances from the various Secret Policeman occasions, featuring classic Python sketches including "I'm a Lumberjack and I'm OK." Also featured are performances by Phil Collins, Pete Townshend, Donovan, and Bob Geldof. Thank you very much. 77m/C VHS. GB John Cleese, Michael Palin, Terry Jones, Eric Idle, Graham Chapman, Phil Collins, Peter Cook, Donovan, Bob Geldof; **D:** Roger Graef, Julien Temple.

The Secret Rapture 🐾🐾 1994 (R) Two sisters clash in this family drama, adapted by Hare from his 1988 play. The bohemian Isobel (Stevenson) and her estranged sister, the forbidding Marion (Wilton), are brought together by their father's death. While Isobel grieves, Marion seeks to gain advantage in the family business, and both must deal with their young, alcoholic, and volatile stepmother Katherine (Whalley-Kilmer). Emotional intensity with good performances but abrupt shifts in tone. 96m/C VHS. GB Juliet Stevenson, Penelope Wilton, Joanne Whalley, Alan Howard, Neil Pearson, Robert Stephens, Hilton McRae; **D:** Howard Davies; **W:** David Hare; **C:** Ian Wilson; **M:** Richard Hartley.

Secret Society 🐾🐾 2000 Pleasingly plump Daisy gets a job in a canning factory and discovers that a group of her fellow buxom female workers are secretly meeting after work to train as Sumo wrestlers. As Daisy becomes more involved with the group, her husband Ken gets suspicious and then intervenes when he wants Daisy in a match. He winds up in the hospital and Daisy promises to quit until the women decide to accept the challenge of going public and fighting a group of male Japanese sumo wrestlers. 88m/C VHS, DVD. GB Charlotte Brittain, Lee Ross, Annette Badland, James Wooton; **D:** Imogen Kimmel, Catriona McGowan; **C:** Glynn Speeckaert; **M:** Paul Heanc.

A Secret Space 🐾🐾½ 1988 Story of a young man, born of secular parentage, searching for the meaning of his Jewish roots as he nears his Bar Mitzvah. He is helped along by a group of Jews who are also searching for this meaning, some in this dull, overwrought drama. 86m/C VHS. Robert Klein, Phyllis Newman, John Matthews, Sam Schacht, Virginia Graham; **D:** Roberta Hodes.

Secret Weapon 🐾🐾 1990 An Israeli technician flees this country with atomic secrets and a beautiful government agent is sent to induce him to return. Based on the true case of Mordecai Vanunu. Slow-paced and not very suspenseful. 95m/C VHS. Griffin Dunne, Karen Allen, Stuart Wilson, Jeroen Krabbe, Brian Cox, John Rhys-Davies, Ian Mitchell; **D:** Ian Sharp. CABLE

The Secret War of Harry Frigg 🐾½ 1968 (R) Non-conformist WWII Private Harry Frigg is promoted to general as part of a scheme to help five Allied generals escape from the custody of the Germans. Rare Newman bomb; dismal comedy. 123m/C VHS. Paul Newman, Sylva Koscina, John Williams, Tom Bosley, Andrew Duggan; **D:** Jack Smight; **C:** Russell Metty.

Secrets 🐾🐾 1971 (R) A wife, her husband, and her daughter each have a sexual experience which they must keep secret. Bisset's nude love scene is an eye-opener. Fast forward through the rest of this dull, disjointed drama. 86m/C VHS. Jacqueline Bisset, Per Oscarsson, Shirley Knight, Robert Powell, Tarka Kings, Martin C. Thuriey; **D:** Philip Saville; **M:** Michael Gibbs.

Secrets 🐾🐾 1977 An unhappy young bride starts having numerous affairs when her mother dies. Hardly worth the effort. 100m/C VHS. Susan Blakely, Roy Thinnes, Joanne Linville, John Randolph, Anthony Eisley, Andrew Stevens; **D:** Paul Wendkos. TV

Secrets 🐾🐾 1982 British drama about the confused life of an innocent schoolgirl who's the victim of a mess of authoritative misunderstandings. One of David Puttnam's "First Love" series. 79m/C VHS. Helen Lindsay, Anna Campbell-Jones, Daisy Cockburn; **D:** Gavin Millar. TV

Secrets 🐾🐾½ 1994 (PG-13) Teenager Anna Berter, growing up in turn-of-the-century Iowa, is told by her snobbish mother Etta (Hamel) not to befriend the boy, which include the woman who raised help.

Secret Weapons 🐾 *the Red Bedroom* 1985 Sexy Russian babes are KGB-trained to get any secret from any man. Strains credibility as well as patience. Made for TV. 100m/C VHS, DVD. Linda Hamilton, Sally Kellerman, Hunt Block, Viveca Lindfors, Christopher Atkins, Geena Davis, James Franciscus; **D:** Don Taylor; **M:** Charles Bernstein. TV

Secret Window 🐾🐾½ 2004 Wandering around with a wicked case of bed-head in a ratty old bathrobe and talking incessantly to himself, Johnny Depp cranks this ho-hum psycho-thriller up a notch with a typically quirky and suitably humorous performance as Mort Rainey, an eccentric mystery writer. After catching wife Amy (Bello) in the sack with another man (Hutton) Mort holes up in a remote lake cottage during his traumatic divorce only to be roused from his depression-induced torpor and writers block by Shooter (Turturro) a deranged hayseed in an Amish-looking hat who claims Mort stole his story. Mort, who is increasingly showing signs that he may not be playing with a full deck, is almost sure that isn't true and can prove it if he can only find the back issue of a magazine that published his story years before Shooter claims to have penned his. Adapted from a novella by Stephen King. 96m/C VHS, DVD, Blu-ray Disc. US Johnny Depp, John Turturro, Maria Bello, Timothy Hutton, Charles S. Dutton, Len Cariou, John Dunn-Hill, Vlasta Vrana; **D:** David Koepp; **W:** David Koepp; **C:** Fred Murphy; **M:** Philip Glass.

The Secretary 🐾½ 1994 (R) Another bland variation of "The Temp." Career woman Ellen Bradford (Harris) has a new fast-track job and a highly efficient secretary in Deirdre (Kelley). But it turns out Deirdre's also lethally efficient in disposing of co-workers through a series of inexplicable accidents and "suicides." So just what's Ellen going to do to show Deirdre who's boss? 94m/C VHS, DVD. Mel Harris, Sheila Kelley, Barry Bostwick, James Russo; **D:** Andrew Lane; **C:** Steven Bernstein. **M:** Louis Fabre.

Secretary 🐾🐾🐾 2002 (R) Lighter look at S&M conveniently hooks up submissive secretary Lee (Gyllenhaal, in a breakthrough role), with her obsessive perfectionist new boss, Edward. After too many misspelled words (bad secretary!) Lee discovers the dominant Edward is perfect at fulfilling her masochistic fantasies. With a sketchy (at best) romantic history, the plucky heroine tries a normal relationship with an old classmate, Peter (Davies) but still craves her kinky boss's brand of quiet discipline. Alternately poignant and funny, story is original and doesn't call prey to cliche or pathos. Adapted from a 1988 story by Mary Gaitskill. 104m/C VHS, DVD. US James Spader, Maggie Gyllenhaal, Lesley Ann Warren, Jeremy Davies, Patrick Bauchau, Stephen McHattie, Oz (Osgood) Perkins II, Jessica Tuck, Amy Locane, Michael Mantell; **D:** Steven Shainberg; **W:** Erin Cressida Wilson; **C:** Steven Fierberg; **M:** Angelo Badalamenti.

Secrets of a Married Man 🐾½ 1984 A married man's philandering ways are his ruination when he falls hard for a beautiful prostitute. Shatner and Shepherd contain their laughter as they make their way through this hyper-earnest family drama. 96m/C VHS, DVD. William Shatner, Cybill Shepherd, Michelle Phillips, Glynn Turman; **D:** William A. Graham.

Secrets of a Soul 🐾🐾½ 1925 A visually impressive presentation of Freudian psychoanalytic theory, in which a professor, wanting a child and jealous of his wife's childhood sweetheart, moves toward madness he did say Freudian and is cured through dream interpretation. Great dream sequences bring out the arm-chair psychoanalyst. Silent. 94m/E VHS. GE Werner Krauss, Ruth Weyher, Jack Trevor; **D:** G.W. Pabst.

Secrets of Sweet Sixteen WOOF! 1974 (R) Gag-fest about budding sexuality in high school. 84m/C VHS, DVD. GE Kristina Lindberg, Sasha Henn; **D:** Ernest Hofbauer; **W:** Erich Tomek; **M:** Gerhard Heinz.

Secrets of the Heart 🐾🐾🐾 *Secretos del Corazon* 1997 Javi (Erburu) grows up in a provincial town in Spain in the 1960s. Director Armendariz isn't as flamboyant as Fellini in "Amarcord" but his intentions are similar. 108m/C DVD. SP Carmelo Gomez, Charo Lopez, Andoni Erburu, Silvia Munt, Alvaro Nagore; **D:** Montxo Armendariz; **C:** Javier Aguirresarobe.

Secrets of Three Hungry Wives 🐾 1978 When a multi-millionaire is killed, the women with whom he was having affairs are suspected. Tacky TV flick. 97m/C VHS. Jessica Walter, Gretchen Corbett, Eve Plumb, Heather MacRae, James Franciscus, Craig Stevens; **D:** Gordon Hessler. TV

Secrets of Women 🐾🐾🐾 *Kvinnors Vanten; Waiting Women* 1952 A rare Bergman comedy about three sisters-in-law as they await their husbands at a lakeside resort. His first commercial success, though it waited nine years for release (1961). In Swedish with English subtitles. 114mB VHS, DVD. SW Anita Bjork, Karl Arne Holmsten, Eva Dahlbeck, Maj-Britt Nilsson, Jarl Kulle; **D:** Ingmar Bergman; **W:** Ingmar Bergman.

The Secrets of Wu Sin 🐾🐾 1932 A suicidal news writer in Chinatown is given a reason to live by a news editor who gives her a job. She starts investigating a ring smuggling Chinese workers, with the trail leading to, of course, China.

...Anna alongside her granddaughter Edwina. When Edwina is seduced by a Berber family friend and left pregnant, Etta decides to adopt her baby daughter—whether Edwina wants to or not. All this obsessive behavior leads Anna to discover some very unhappy family secrets surrounding their own birth. Made for TV. 92m/C VHS. Veronica Hamel, Julie Harris, Richard Kiley, Thomas Gibson, Shea D'Lyn, Jessica Bowman, Reed Edward Diamond; **D:** Jud Taylor. TV

Secrets and Lies 🐾🐾🐾 1995 (R) Too-long film focusing on family and identity, the adoptive parents of black Yuppie Londoner Hortense (Jean-Baptiste) have just died and she decides it's time to seek out her birth parents. She's warned about the emotional consequences, especially upon discovering her biological mother is white—factory worker Cynthia (Blethyn), who has another daughter, Roxanne (Rushbrook), who doesn't get along with mum. Naturally, when Hortense is introduced to Cynthia's family, there's lots of dysfunction to explore. Good performances, although Hortense's character is bland, but pacing drags. 142m/C VHS, DVD. GB Brenda Blethyn, Marianne Jean-Baptiste, Timothy Spall, Claire Rushbrook, Phyllis Logan, Lee Ross, Ron Cook, Lesley Manville; **Cameos:** Allison Steadman; **D:** Mike Leigh; **W:** Mike Leigh; **C:** Dick Pope; **M:** Andrew Dickson. Australian Film Inst. '97: Foreign Film; British Acad. '96: Actress (Blethyn), Film; Golden Globes '97: Actress (Blethyn); L.A. Film Critics '96: Actress (Blethyn), Director (Leigh), Film; Cannes '96: Actress (Blethyn), Film.

town. Low-budget crime thriller. **65m/B VHS.** Lois Wilson, Grant Withers, Dorothy Revier, Robert Warwick, Toshia Mori; **D:** Richard Thorpe.

Seduce Me: Pamela Principle 2 ♂½ *Pamela Principle 2* 1994 (R) Charles is a bored, married, architectural photographer who decides a change of pace is in order. So he starts shooting lingerie fashion spreads and gets seduced by model Pamela, who likes her men married. The only connection to the 1991 film is the married man/affair angle. **96m/C VHS.** Alina Thompson, Nick Rafter, India Allen; **D:** Edward Holzman. **TV**

Seduced ♂♂ 1985 When a rich businessman turns up dead, the ambitious politician who was involved with his wife must find the killer. Not memorable or exceptional, but not boring or offensive either. **100m/C VHS, DVD.** Gregory Harrison, Cybill Shepherd, Jose Ferrer, Adrienne Barbeau, Michael C. Gwynne, Karmin Murcelo, Paul Stewart; **D:** Jerrold Freedman. **TV**

Seduced and Abandoned ♂♂♂ *Sedotta e Abbandonata* 1964 A lothario seduces his fiancee's young sister. When the girl becomes pregnant, he refuses to marry her. Family complications abound. A comic look at the Italian code of honor. In Italian with English subtitles. **118m/B VHS, DVD.** *IT* Saro Urzi, Stefania Sandrelli, Aldo Puglisi, Leopoldo Trieste; **D:** Pietro Germi; **W:** Pietro Germi. Cannes '64: Actor (Urzi). **VIDEO**

Seduced by Evil ♂♂ 1994 A journalist (Somers) is investigating a story in a small Southwest town when she encounters a sorcerer (Vargas) who decides he wants her for himself alone. Even if it means destroying everyone she holds dear. Adapted from the novel "Brujo" by Jann Arrington Wolcott. **88m/C VHS, DVD.** Suzanne Somers, John Vargas, Julie Carmen, James B. Sikking, Mindy Spence, Nancy Moorves; **D:** Tony Wharmby; **W:** Bill Svanoe.

The Seducer ♂♂ *Some Like It Sexy* 1969 (R) Things get dangerous when a playboy's goals turn from love to death. **72m/C VHS.** *GB* Nicola Pagett, Erika Bergmann, Penny Riley, Christopher Mathews; **D:** Donovan Winter; **W:** Donovan Winter; **C:** Gus Coma.

The Seducers ♂ 1970 An acid-dropping mother takes her shy, withdrawn son on a Mediterranean cruise and asks some of her girlfriends in the hopes of stoking his libido. However, she finds it difficult to control her own impulses. The boy gets a chance when the ship runs aground on a remote island and he meets an innocent native girl. His mother, though, has designs of her own. Dubbed from Italian. **88m/C VHS.** *GE* Rosalba Neri, Edwige Fenech, Maud de Belleroche, Maurizio Bonuglia, Ruggero Miti, Ewa Thulin; **D:** Ottavio Alessi.

Seducers ♂ *Death Game* 1977 (R) Wealthy, middle-aged man unsuspecting: Wanda (O'Brien) is a black widow with fish-boarded doctor if it is to attract new factory owners. The villagers find a possible pigeon in a young Montreal plastic surgeon (Boutin) who comes for a visit. They pretend to love everything he does, from playing cricket rather than their favored hockey to throwing a beef stroganoff festival because it's

---

his favorite food. Very lightweight but enjoyable comedy in the style of "Waking Ned Devine." **110m/C VHS, DVD.** *CA* David Boutin, Lucie Laurier, Benoit Briere, Bruno Blanchet, Raymond Bouchard, Bruno Blanchet, Pierre Collin, Rita Lafontaine; **D:** Jean-François Pouliot; **M:** Jean-Marie Benoit.

Seducing Maarya ♂♂ 1999 Maarya is an East Indian/Canadian working in a Montreal restaurant. She agrees to an arranged marriage with the restaurant owner's son, even though he's gay, and then begins a romance with the sixty-something dad. No one seems too concerned by the situation until Maarya's violent brother turns up, exposing a family secret, and Maarya announces her pregnancy. Melodramatic. **107m/C VHS, DVD. CA** Nandana Sen, Mohan Agashe, Vijay Mehta, Ryan Hollyman, Cas Anwar; **D:** Hunt Hoe; **W:** Hunt Hoe; **C:** Michael Wees; **M:** Dino Giancola, Janet Lumb.

The Seduction of Joe Tynan ♂♂½ 1979 (R) Political drama about a young senator (Alda) torn between his family, his political career, and his mistress (Streep). Alda also wrote the thin screenplay, which reportedly is loosely based on the remarkable life of Ted Kennedy. Relatively shallow treatment of the meaty themes of power, hypocrisy, sex, and corruption in our nation's capital. **107m/C VHS.** Alan Alda, Meryl Streep, Melvyn Douglas, Barbara Harris, Rip Torn; **D:** Jerry Schatzberg; **W:** Alan Alda; **M:** Bill Conti. L.A. Film Critics '79: Support. Actor (Douglas), Support. Actress (Streep); Natl. Bd. of Review '79: Support. Actress (Streep); N.Y. Film Critics '79: Support. Actress (Streep); Natl. Soc. Film Critics '79: Support. Actress (Streep).

Seduction of Mimi ♂♂♂ *Mimi Metallurgico Ferito Nell'Onore* 1972 (R) Comic farce of politics and seduction about a Sicilian laborer's escapades with the Communists and the local Mafia. Giannini is wonderful as the stubborn immigrant to the big city who finds himself in trouble. One of the funniest love scenes on film. Basis for the later movie "Which Way is Up?" Italian with subtitles. **92m/C VHS, DVD.** *IT* Giancarlo Giannini, Mariangela Melato, Turi Ferro, Agostina Belli, Elena Fiore; **D:** Lina Wertmuller; **W:** Lina Wertmuller; **C:** Dario Di Palma; **M:** Piero Piccioni.

Seduction: The Cruel Woman ♂♂ 1989 A curiously uninvolving look at sexual games and fantasies. Wanda is a dominatrix, who also owns a sado-masochistic gallery where her various friends and current and former lovers act out their basest desires. Stylized, with some graphic sex. Based on the novel "Venus in Furs" by Leopold Sacher-Masoch. In German with English subtitles. **84m/C VHS, DVD. GE** Mechthild Grossmann, Carola Regnier, Udo Kier, Sheila McLaughlin; **D:** Elfi Mikesch, Monika Treut; **W:** Elfi Mikesch, Monika Treut.

The Seductress ♂♂½ 2000 Beautiful Alexis (O'Brien) is a black widow with a string of murdered wealthy husbands behind her. Kay Sanders (Hall) is a researcher obsessed with keeping tabs on each of Alexis's new identities, especially when the babe goes after Kay's boyfriend Paul (Smith). But it turns out that Kay and Alexis have a closer connection than that. The R-rated version is a mere 70 minutes. **82m/C VHS, DVD.** Shauna O'Brien, Gabriella Hall, Jonathan Smith; **D:** J Edie Martin. **VIDEO**

See How She Runs ♂ 1978 Running becomes a central and redefining experience for a 40-year-old divorced schoolteacher (Woodward). Her training culminates with a run in the Boston marathon. Her loved ones, though concerned for her health and sanity, cheer her on. Excellent made for TV drama. Screen daughter Newman is also Woodward's real-life daughter. **92m/C VHS.** Joanne Wood-

---

ward, John Considine, Lissy Newman, Barbara Manning; **D:** Richard T. Heffron. **TV**

See No Evil ♂♂♂ *Blind Terror* 1971 (PG) A blind girl gradually discovers the murdered bodies of her uncle's family. Trapped in the family mansion, she finds herself pursued by the killer. Chilling and well crafted. **90m/C VHS, DVD.** Mia Farrow, Dorothy Allison, Robin Bailey; **D:** Richard Fleischer; **W:** Brian Clemens; **M:** Elmer Bernstein.

See No Evil ♂ 2006 (R) Wrestling star Kane (7 feet tall and some 400 pounds) plays psycho Jacob Goodnight, who's living in an abandoned hotel. He's pleasantly surprised when his ex-cop nemesis (Vidler) and eight delinquents on a community service detail show up. And he welcomes them one-by-one (keeping eyeballs as souvenirs). Typically gory teen-slasher flick. **84m/C DVD, Blu-ray Disc.** *US* Michael J. Pagan, Christina Vidal, Steven Vidler, Penny McNamee, Glen "Kane" Jacobs, Samantha Noble, Luke Pegler, Rachael Taylor, Craig Horner; **D:** Gregory Brown; **W:** Dan Madigan; **C:** Ben Nott; **M:** Tyler Bates.

See No Evil, Hear No Evil ♂♂ 1989 (R) Another teaming for Pryor and Wilder, in which they portray a blind man and a deaf man both sought as murder suspects. Pryor and Wilder deserve better. **103m/C VHS, DVD.** Gene Wilder, Richard Pryor, Joan Severance, Anthony Zerbe, Kevin Spacey; **D:** Arthur Hiller; **W:** Andrew Kurtzman, Eliot Wald, Earl Barret, Anne Sultan, Gene Wilder, **C:** Victor Kemper; **M:** Stewart Copeland.

See Spot Run woof! 2001 (G) How can you not like a movie with dogs? Easy, put David Arquette in it. Spot, an FBI-trained dog, has a contract on his life after removing "one of the family jewels" of crime family boss Sonny Talia (Sorvino) and ends up in a doggie witness protection program. He lands in the possession of James (Jones), his mother (Bibb), and babysitter neighbor Gordon (Arquette). One may find the true essence of the movie in the middle of a large pile of Spot's morning business, where Gordon eventually finds himself. More scatological humor and other crass gags send "Spot" to the doghouse. Duncan is the sole high point as the dog's FBI handler. **97m/C VHS, DVD.** *US* David Arquette, Michael Clarke Duncan, Leslie Bibb, Angus T. Jones, Joe (Johnny) Viterelli, Paul Sorvino, Anthony Anderson; **D:** John Whitesell; **W:** George Gallo, Dan Baron, Chris Faber; **C:** John Bartley; **M:** John Debney.

See You in the Morning ♂½ 1989 (PG-13) Ill-conceived romantic comedy-drama about a divorced psychiatrist and a widow, both of whom had unhappy marriages, who meet and marry. They must cope with family expectations, and their own expectations, in order to make things right. Homicidal marriage work. **119m/C VHS.** Jeff Bridges, Alice Krige, Farrah Fawcett, Drew Barrymore, Lukas Haas, Macaulay Culkin, David Dukes, Frances Sternhagen, Theodore Bikel, George Hearn, Linda Lavin; **D:** Alan J. Pakula; **W:** Alan J. Pakula.

Seed of Chucky ♂½ 2004 (R) The fifth in the "Child's Play" series is filled with the usual camp and carnage, and a movie-within-a-movie premise. Tilly plays herself as an actress filming a "Chucky" movie as well as the voice of Chucky's doll bride. Tiffany. Homicidal dolls Chucky (voiced by Dourif) and Tiff are on-set and are eventually reunited with long-lost offspring Glen (voiced by Boyd), who has a gender crisis due to a lack of anatomical correctness and is sometimes Glenda (a nod to Ed Wood's 1953 masterpiece). Chucky thinks it would be swell if Glen/Glenda could have a sibling, with Tilly as the mom. The actress is nothing if not game for a variety of indignities and snarky one-liners. Waters appears briefly as a pesky paparazzo. **86m/C DVD, HD DVD.** *US* Jennifer Tilly, Hannah Spearritt, John Waters, Jason Flemyng, Keith-Lee Castle, Steve Lawton, Redman, Tony Gardner; **D:** Don Mancini; **W:** Don Mancini; **C:** Vernon Layton; **M:** Pino Donaggio; **V:** Jennifer Tilly, Brad Dourif, Billy Boyd.

Seedpeople ♂½ 1992 Mindless horror flick has bloodthirsty plants inhabiting peaceful Comet Valley after their seeds fall from outer space and germi-

---

nate. These "seedpeople" possess tremendous powers and soon have the rural residents transformed into zombies. Bears an uncanny resemblance to "Invasion of the Bodysnatchers," and is so bad it's almost good. Also available with Spanish subtitles. **87m/C VHS.** Sam Hennings, Andrea Roth, Dane Witherspoon, David Dunard, Holly Fields, Bernard Kates, Anne Betancourt, Sonny Carl Davis; **D:** Peter Manoogian; **W:** Jackson Barr; **M:** Bob Mithoff.

Seeds of Doubt ♂♂½ 1996 (R) Formula thriller finds reporter Jennifer Kingsley (Watson) working to free convicted murderer Crawford (Lando) from prison because she thinks he's innocent (and she's fallen for him). Detective Dexter (Coyote) is unsuccessful in convincing her otherwise but Jennifer begins to have her own doubts when a new series of killings begin after Crawford's release. **94m/C VHS.** Alberta Watson, Peter Coyote, Joe Lando; **D:** Peter Foldy.

Seeds of Evil ♂♂ *The Gardener* 1976 (R) Warhol alumnus Dallesandro is a strange gardener who grows flowers that can kill. He can also turn himself into a tree and figures to seduce rich and bored housewife Houghton (niece of Katharine Hepburn) after he finishes tending her garden. Strange, quirky horror flick. **97m/C VHS, DVD.** Katharine Houghton, Joe Dallesandro, Rita Gam; **D:** James H. Kay.

Seeing Other People ♂♂½ 2004 (R) About-to-be-married couple begin seeing other people in this fun, top-notch sex comedy romp. Ed (Mohr) and Alice (Nicholson) decide to sow some wild oats before settling down into marital bliss. Initially exciting for both, the affairs spark their own lagging passion. Soon, however, the two enter more dangerous territory when conquest Donald (Davis) begins obsessing over Alice and Ed meets waitress Sandy (Ritchie) and it's clear no good can come of this hair-brained experiment. Despite a rather worn-out premise, characters have wonderful chemistry and are likeable, unique and well-drawn. Able supports include Graham, as Alice's sister, and Richter as Ed's grounded best friend. **90m/C DVD.** *US* Jay Mohr, Julianne Nicholson, Lauren Graham, Bryan Cranston, Josh Charles, Andy Richter, Matthew Davis, Helen Slater, Jill Ritchie, Alex Borstein, Mimi Rogers, Nicole Marie Lenz, Jonathan Davis, Mike Faiola, Sheeri Rappaport, Liz Vassey; **D:** P. M. Wallace Wolodarsky; **W:** M. Wallace Wolodarsky, Maya Forbes; **C:** Mark Doering-Powell; **M:** Alan Elliott.

Seeing Red ♂♂½ 1999 British soap opera star Coral Atkins (Lancashire) is doing a charity event in the 1970s at a children's home where she finds the conditions untenable. Having survived a terrible childhood herself, Coral improbably decides to switch careers and open her own home for abused children, though British social bureaucracy thwarts her every decision. Based on Atkins' 1990 memoir. **100m/C VHS.** *GB* Nicholas Gecks, Sarah Lancashire; **D:** Graham Theakston; **W:** Christopher Monger. **TV**

The Seeker: The Dark Is Rising ♂½ 2007 (PG) Fourteen-year-old Will (Ludwig), transplanted from America to England, wakes up one day with magical powers and an important destiny in this all-too-familiar tale that is both a lousy adaptation of a 1973 book and a rip-off of comparable, contemporary stories. McShane, as Will's mentor Merriman, does his best with the poor script, but there's no saving this mess. Needlessly simplifies and Americanizes the original story until "Harry Potter" retread. **94m/C DVD.** *US* Christopher Eccleston, Ian McShane, Frances Conroy, Wendy Crewson, Alexander Ludwig, John Benjamin Hickey, Gregory Edward Smith, James Cosmo, Jim Piddock; **D:** David L. Cunningham; **W:** John Hodge; **C:** Joel Ransom; **M:** Christophe Beck.

The Seekers ♂♂ 1979 The story of the Kent family continues, as Abraham Kent, his wife and young son are forced to leave the safety of Boston for the rugged, untamed Pacific Northwest. TV movie based on the novel by John Jakes; pre-

---

ceded by "The Bastard" and "The Rebels." **200m/C** VHS. Randolph Mantooth, Edie Adams, Neville Brand, Delta Burke, John Carradine, George DeLoy, Julie Gregg, Roosevelt "Rosie" Grier, George Hamilton, Alex Hyde-White, Brian Keith, Ross Martin, Gary Merrill, Martin Milner, Vic Morrow, Timothy Patrick, Murphy, Hugh O'Brian, Robert Reed, Allan Rich, Barbara Rush, Sarah Rush, Stuart Whitman, Ed Harris, Jeremy Licht, Eric Stoltz; **D:** Sidney Hayers.

Seems Like Old Times ♂♂♂ **1980 (PG)** A sweet lawyer (Hawn) finds herself helping her ex-husband (Chase) when two robbers force him to hold up a bank. Grodin is the new spouse threatened by Chase's appearance and by the heavies's trying to escape. Better-than-average script, with funny and appealing characters. **102m/C** VHS, DVD. Goldie Hawn, Chevy Chase, Charles Grodin, Robert Guillaume, Harold Gould, George Grizzard, T.K. Carter; **D:** Jay Sandrich; **W:** Neil Simon; **C:** David M. Walsh; **M:** Marvin Hamlisch.

Seize the Day ♂♂♂ **1986** A man approaching middle age (Williams) feels that he is a failure. Brilliant performances by all, plus a number of equally fine actors in small roles. Based on the short novel by Saul Bellow. **93m/C** VHS, DVD, Robin Williams, Joseph Wiseman, Jerry Stiller, Glenne Headly, Tony Roberts; **D:** Fielder Cook.

Seizure ♂♂½ **1974 (PG)** Three demonic creatures from a writer's dreams come to life and terrorize him and his houseguests at a weekend party. Brilliant performances. Slick but disjointed; Stone's directorial debut. Interesting cast includes Tattoo from "Fantasy Island." **93m/C** VHS, CA Jonathan Frid, Hervé Villechaize, Christina Pickles, Martine Beswick, Joseph Sirola, Troy Donahue, Mary Woronov, Anne Meacham; **D:** Oliver Stone; **W:** Oliver Stone, Edward Andrew (Santos Alcocer) Mann; **C:** Roger Racine.

Seizure: The Story of Kathy Morris ♂♂ **1980** The real-life story and struggle of a young music student who must have brain surgery and comes out of it unable to read or count. Workaday cramatization. **104m/C** VHS. Leonard Nimoy, Penelope Milford; **D:** Gerald I. Isenberg.

Selena ♂♂½ **1996 (PG)** Lopez is appealing in the title role of the 23-year-old Tejano superstar singer who was just breaking into international prominence when she was murdered by the president of her fan club in 1995. Flashbacks show Abraham's (Olmos) dashed musical aspirations and he serves as a stage father to his children, recognizing his daughter Selena's exceptional voice. Film covers her marriage to guitarist Chris Perez (Seda) and her building success until the final tragedy (which isn't shown). Film concludes with concert footage of the real Selena. **127m/C** VHS, DVD. Jennifer Lopez, Edward James Olmos, Jon Seda, Constance Marie, Jacob Vargas, Lupe Ontiveros, Jackie Guerra, Sal Lopez, Rebecca Lee Meza; **D:** Gregory Nava; **W:** Gregory Nava; **C:** Edward Lachman; **M:** Dave Grusin.

Self-Defense ♂♂ **1983 (R)** When a city's police force goes on strike, the citizens band together into vigilante troops as the daffy politician. Powell is wonderful as the young man is studied by a psychiatrist. She discovers that her patient is a "sender" who can transmit his nightmares to other patients at a hospital. **92m/C** VHS, GB Kathryn Harrold, Zeljko Ivanek, Shirley Knight, Paul Freeman, Sean Hewitt, Harry Ditson, Marsha A. Hunt, Al Matthews, Angus MacInnes, Olivier Pierre; **D:** Roger Christian; **W:** Thomas Baum; **M:** Trevor Jones.

Send Me No Flowers ♂♂♂ **1964** Vintage Hudson-Day comedy. Hudson plays a hypochondriac who thinks his death is imminent. He decides to provide for his family's future by finding his wife a rich husband. She thinks he's feeling guilty for having an affair. **92m/C** VHS. Rock Hudson, Doris Day, Tony Randall, Paul Lynde; **D:** Norman Jewison; **W:** Julius J. Epstein.

The Sender ♂♂ **1982 (R)** An amnesiac young man is studied by a psychiatrist. She discovers that her patient is a "sender" who can transmit his nightmares to other patients at a hospital. **92m/C** VHS, GB Kathryn Harrold, Zeljko Ivanek, Shirley Knight, Paul Freeman, Sean Hewitt, Harry Ditson, Marsha A. Hunt, Al Matthews, Angus MacInnes, Olivier Pierre; **D:** Roger Christian; **W:** Thomas Baum; **M:** Trevor Jones.

A Self-Made Hero ♂♂♂ **1995** *Un Héros Tres Discret; A Very Discreet Hero* Albert Delhousse (Kassovitz) is a young Frenchman who manages to avoid military service in WWII. His one great talent is his confidence and his ability as a salesman. So, with some help from a true freedom fighter known as the Captain (Dupontel), he sells himself as a hero of the Resistance in 1945 Paris and manages to do so very effectively for the rest of his life. Kassovitz does an excellent job as the assured imposter. Based on the novel by Jean-Francoise Deniau; French with subtitles. **105m/C** VHS, FR Mathieu Kassovitz, Anouk Grinberg, Albert Dupontel, Sandrine Kiberlain, Jean-Louis Trintignant, Nadia Barentin; **D:** Jacques A. Tardif; **W:** Jacques Audiard, Alain Le Henry; **C:** Jean-Marc Fabre; **M:** Alexandre Desplat.

Selma, Lord, Selma ♂♂½ **1999** Civil rights drama focuses on the youngest two participants in a 1965 voting-rights march from Selma to Montgomery. Presented by Dr. Martin Luther King Jr.'s (Powell) message of nonviolent demonstration and becomes dedicated to the cause, along with her best friend Rachel Nelson (Peyton). Things come to a climax with the March 7th march to the Edmund Pettus Bridge in Selma, a day that became known as "Bloody Sunday" when state troopers attacked the demonstrators. Adapted from the book "Selma, Lord, Selma" by Webb-Christburg, Nelson, and Frank Sikora. **88m/C** VHS, DVD. Jurnee Smollett, Stephanie Zandria Feyton, Clifton Powell, Yolanda King; **D:** Charles Burnett; **W:** Cynthia Whitcomb. TV

Semi-Pro ♂ **2008 (R)** Faced with low fan turnout, the failing ABA of the '70s plans to dissolve the league and incorporate four of its best teams into the NBA. Owner/player Jackie Moon (a fully-freed Ferrell) rises to the occasion, pulling out all the stops to get his lousy Flint Tropics (that's Flint, Michigan nowhere near anything remotely tropical) on the map and into contention. He concocts aging star Ed Monix (Harrelson) and stages events like bear wrestling to get fans in the door. A funny premise that awwardly cuts-course itself with an actual underdog sports drama. As with most of Ferrell's co-stars, Harrelson and Benjamin (as Coffee Black) take a backseat to the SNL alum's outrageous antics, making this little more than a scattering of Will Ferrell sketches. **90m/C** VHS, DVD. Will Ferrell, Woody Harrelson, Andre Benjamin, Maura Tierney, Will Arnett, Andy Richter, David Koechner, Rob Corddry, Matt Walsh, Jackie Earle Haley, Andrew Daly; **D:** Kent Alterman; **W:** Scott Armstrong; **C:** Shane Hurlbut; **M:** Theodore Shapiro.

The Senator Was Indiscreet ♂♂♂ **1947** *Mr. Ashton was Indiscreet* A farcical comedy concerning a slightly loony senator with presidential aspirations. He thinks he can win the nomination because he keeps a diary that would prove embarrassing to numerous colleagues. The diary than falls into the hands of a journalist. Powell is wonderful as the daffy politician. Playwright Kaufman's only directorial effort. **75m/B** VHS. William Powell, Ella Raines, Hans Conried, Arleen Whelan, Ray Collins, Allen Jenkins, Charles D. Brown; **D:** George S. Kaufman; **C:** William Mellor. N.Y. Film Critics '47. Actor (Powell).

Semi-Tough ♂♂½ **1977 (R)** Likeable, still current social satire involving a couple of pro-football buddies and their mutual interest in their team owner's daughter. Romantic comedy, satire of the sports world, zany highjinks—it's all here, though not enough of any of these. Pleasant and enjoyable. Based on the novel by Dan Jenkins. **107m/C** VHS, DVD. Burt Reynolds, Kris Kristofferson, Jill Clayburgh, Lotte Lenya, Robert Preston, Bert Convy, Richard Masur, Carl Weathers, Brian Dennehy, John Matuszak, Ren Silver; **D:** Michael Ritchie; **W:** Walter Bernstein.

Sell Out ♂♂½ **1976 (PG)** A former spy living in Jerusalem is called out of retirement; his protege, who defected to the Soviets, now war's out. **102m/C** VHS, DVD. Richard Widmark, Oliver Reed, Gayle Hunnicutt, Sam Wanamaker; **D:** Peter Collinson; **W:** Judson Kinberg, Murray Smith; **C:** Arthur Ibbetson; **M:** Colin Frechter.

The Sender ♂♂½ **1998 (R)** Naval officer Dallas Grayson (Madsen) and his daughter Lisa are possessed of a mysterious power they may have inherited from Dallas' long-missing father, a Naval pilot shot down in the '60s. Whatever they have, the government wants, and they don't care how they get it. **98m/C** VHS, DVD. Michael Madsen, Dyan Cannon, Robert Vaughn, R. Lee Ermey, Steven Williams, Brian Bloom, Shelton Ray; **D:** Richard Pepin; **W:** Richard Preston Jr., Nathan Long; **C:** Michael Weaver.

Senior Trip ♂ **1981** N.Y.C. will never-be the same when a bunch of rowdy Midwestern high school seniors tear up the town on their graduation trip. **96m/C** VHS. James Carroll, Scott Baio, Mickey Rooney, Faye Grant, Vincent Spano, Jane Hoffman; **D:** Kenneth Johnson. TV

Senior Week WOOF! **1988** A batch of girl-hungry teens have a wacky time on their Florida vacation just before graduation. **97m/C** VHS. Michael St. Gerard, Devon Skye, Leesa Bryte; **D:** Stuart Goldman.

The Seniors ♂♂ **1978 (R)** A group of college students decide to open a phony sex clinic, but the joke is on them when the clinic becomes a success. Better than it sounds. Pretty good acting and much harmless goofiness. **87m/C** VHS, DVD. Dennis Quaid, Priscilla Barnes, Jeffrey Byron, Gary Imhoff; **D:** Rod Amateau.

Senora Tentacion ♂♂ **1949** Musical melodrama about a composer who falls in love with his mother, sister, and girlfriend in order to free with Hortensia, a famous singer. In Spanish with English subtitles. **82m/B** VHS. David Silva, Susana Guzar, Ninon Sevilla; **D:** Jose Diaz Morales; **W:** Jose Diaz Morales; **C:** Ezequiel Carresco; **M:** Antonio Diaz Conde.

Sensation ♂♂ **1994 (R)** A college co-ed agrees to participate in a professor's paranormal experiments in order to test her psychic abilities. Unfortunately, what she senses is her prof involved in the unsolved sex-murder of a former student. **102m/C** VHS. Kari Wuhrer, Eric Roberts, Ron Perlman, Ed Begley Jr., Paul LeMat, Claire Stansfield, Kieran Mulroney, Tracey Needham; **D:** Brian Grant; **W:** Doug Wallace; **M:** Arthur Kempel.

Sensations ♂♂ **1987 (R)** A woman and a man who aren't exceptionally ford of one another share a lottery ticket and win. Vincent becomes a former addict of porno flicks, and he manages to work in sexual overtones. **91m/C** VHS. Krista Lane, Blake Bahner, Jennifer Delora, Rick Savage, Loretta Palma, Frank Stewart; **D:** Chuck Vincent.

Sensations of 1945 ♂♂½ **1945** Sensations 1944 A press agent turns his firm over to one of his clients, a dancer with some wild promotional ideas. Brings together numerous variety and musical acts. W. C. Fields has a cameo in his last film role. Mostly unremarkable, occasionally fun musical. **86m/B** VHS. Eleanor Powell, Dennis O'Keefe, Sir C. Aubrey Smith, Eugene Pallette, Lyle Talbot, Marie Blake; **Cameos:** W.C. Fields; **D:** Lyle Talbot; **C:** Rodney Bennett. TV

Sense & Sensibility ♂♂ **1985** BBC miniseries adaptation of the Jane Austen's first novel concerning two sisters striving for happiness in their well-ordered lives. **174m/C** VHS, DVD. **GB** Irene Richard, Tracey Childs; **D:** Rodney Bennett. TV

Sense and Sensibility ♂♂♂ **1995 (PG)** Thanks to the machinations of greedy relatives, the impecunious Dashwood family is forced to move to a country cottage when father dies. Sensible Elinor (Thompson) looks after the household while overly romantic Marianne (Winslet) pines for passion—ignoring the noble attentions of middle-aged neighbor Brandon (Rickman) for the far more dashing Willoughby (Wise). Elinor has her own hopes for marriage with boyishly ineffectual Edward (Grant) but all three men have secrets that could crush romantic dreams (at least temporarily). Somewhat slow-paced but with adaptation (by Thompson) of Jane Austen's first novel, well-acted and beautifully photographed (oh, to be in the English countryside). **135m/C** VHS, DVD, Blu-ray Disc. **GB** Emma Thompson, Kate Winslet, Hugh Grant, Alan Rickman, Greg Wise, Robert Hardy, Elizabeth Spriggs, Emilie Francois, Gemma Jones, James Fleet, Harriet Walter, Imogen Stubbs, Imelda Staunton, Hugh Laurie, Richard Lumsden; **D:** Ang Lee; **W:** Emma Thompson; **C:** Michael Coulter; **M:** Patrick Doyle. Oscars '95. Adapt. Screenplay; British Acad. '95. Adapt. Screenplay; Golden Globes '95. Film, Support. Actress (Winslet); Natl. Bd. of Review '95. Actress (Thompson); Film—Drama, Screenplay; L.A. Film Critics '95. Screenplay; Natl. Bd. of Review '95. Actress (Thompson); Director (Lee); Film; N.Y. Film Critics '95. Director (Lee); Screen Actors Guild '95. Support. Actress (Winslet); Writers Guild '95. Adapt. Screenplay; Broadcast Film Critics '95.

Senseless ♂♂ **1998 (R)** Darryl (Wayans) is a poverty stricken college student trying to work his way through school while still supporting his family back home. He agrees to be a medical test subject for a procedure intended to heighten the senses. Unfortunately, as one sense is amplified, the others are drowned out, and Darryl becomes a flailing buffoon. Meanwhile he is in a competition against smarmy frat boy Scott (Spade, who looks about ten years late for his last Econ class) that would land him a job on Wall Street. After dealing with sounds that are too loud and smells that are too pungent, his body and senses itself. The slapstick bits are hit and miss, but the likable Wayans and dislikable Spade prop up the movie fairly well. **93m/C** VHS, DVD. Marlon Wayans, David Spade, Matthew Lillard, Rip Torn, Tamara Taylor, Brad Dourif, Ken Lerner, Ernie Lively, Richard McGonagle, Esther Scott, Kenya Moore; **D:** Penelope Spheeris; **W:** Greg Erb, Craig Mazin; **C:** Daryn Okada; **M:** Yello.

A Sense of Freedom ♂♂♂ **1978 (R)** A hopeless racketeering criminal is thrust from institution to institution until the Scottish authorities decide on an innovative style of reform. Based on Jimmy Boyle's autobiographical book. Excellent and disturbing. **81m/C** VHS. **GB** David Hayman, Alex Norton, Jake D'Arcy, Sean Scanlan, Fulton Mackay; **D:** John MacKenzie.

Senso ♂♂♂ **1954** *The Wanton Contessa* Tragic story of romance and rebellion as Italian patriots battle the Austro-Hungarian empire for independence in 1866. An Italian noblewoman betrays her marriage, and almost her country, to be with a cynical Austrian soldier in this visually stunning piece of cinematography. In Italian with English subtitles or dubbed. **125m/C** VHS, DVD. **IT** Alida Valli, Massimo Girotti, Heinz Moog, Farley Granger; **D:** Luchino Visconti; **C:** Robert Krasker.

The Sensual Man ♂½ **1974 (R)** Hot-blooded Italian falls in love and gets married only to find out that his wife cannot consummate their marriage. Exploitative, misogynistic, and unfunny. **90m/C** VHS. Giancarlo Giannini, Rossana Podesta, Lionel Stander; **D:** Marco Vicario.

Sensual Partners WOOF! **1987** Young actresses are lures to Tangier by a fake movie producer and sold as sex slaves. Emphasis on soft-focus, soft-core flesh. **87m/C** VHS. **GE** Josianne Gibert, Esther Studer, Jacques Stany, Gina Jansen, Eric Falk; **D:** Marco Vicario.

Jacques Guy; **W:** Jacques Guy; **C:** Alain Hardy; **M:** Walter Baumgartner.

The Sensuous Nurse WOOF! **1976 (R)** Italian comedy about a beautiful nurse hired by the greedy, treacherous relatives of a weak-hearted count in hopes that her voluptuousness will give him a heart attack. It doesn't, and she falls in love. Mindless, but fun and sexy. Dubbed in English. **79m/C VHS, DVD. IT** Ursula Andress, Mario Pisu, Duilio Del Prete, Jack Palance; **D:** Nello Rosatti.

Sensuous Summer 🐾½ **1993 (R)** When Bobby returns home to the town of Elk Lake he finds the family business, run by his brother Nick, is in deep trouble. It seems Alex, an unscrupulous banker, wants to foreclose. But business comes second to pleasure when Bobby is reunited with old flame Jill and Nick takes up again with old girlfriend Cindy. **80m/C VHS.** Tom Case, Christina Campbell, Brittany McGrea, Gina Jorand; **D:** Boots Rakely; **W:** Boots Rakely; **C:** Brett Webster; **M:** Gene Ober.

The Sensuous Teenager WOOF! *Libido; Forbidden Passions* **1970 (R)** Overwhelmingly erotic and uncontrollably seductive, a teenage girl aims to please by releasing all the sensuality within her. **80m/C VHS.** Sandra Julien, Janine Reynaud, Michel Lemoine; **D:** Max Pecas.

The Sentinel 🐾🐾 **1976 (R)** A model, who has moved into a New York City brownstone, encounters an aging priest and some unusual neighbors. When she investigates strange noises she finds out that the apartment building houses the doorway to hell—and that she's intended to be the next doorkeeper. Modest suspense film with a good cast and enough shock and special effects to keep the viewer interested. **92m/C VHS, DVD.** Chris Sarandon, Christina Raines, Ava Gardner, Jose Ferrer, Sylvia Miles, John Carradine, Burgess Meredith, Tom Berenger, Beverly D'Angelo, Jeff Goldblum, Arthur Kennedy, Deborah Raffin, Eli Wallach, Christopher Walken; **D:** Michael Winner; **W:** Michael Winner, Jeffrey Konvitz; **C:** Richard Kratina; **M:** Gil Melle.

The Sentinel 🐾🐾 **2006 (PG-13)** Veteran Secret Service agent Pete Garrison (Douglas) is in charge of guarding first lady Sarah Ballentine (Basinger), which is really convenient since they're having an affair. It's bad news though when Garrison gets blackmailed and learns that a presidential assassination is planned. Accused of treason and on the run, Garrison is pursued by his former protege-turned-enemy David Breckinridge (a grim Sutherland). Longoria provides supporting eye candy as rookie agent Jill Marin. Much like Harrison Ford, Douglas excels as a strong (ageless) man who can overcome any crisis and take on all his (younger) adversaries. **105m/C DVD, Blu-ray Disc. US** Michael Douglas, Kiefer Sutherland, Martin Donovan, Ritchie Coster, Eva Longoria, Kim Basinger, Blair Brown, David Rasche, Kristen Lehman, Raynor Scheine, Chuck Shamata, Paul Calderon, Clark Johnson; **D:** Clark Johnson; **W:** George Nolfi; **C:** Gabriel Beristain; **M:** Christophe Beck.

Separate but Equal 🐾🐾🐾½ **1991 (PG)** One of TV's greatest history lessons, a powerful dramatization of the 1954 Brown vs. the Board of Education case that wrung a landmark civil rights decision from the Supreme Court. Great care is taken to humanize all the participants, from the humblest schoolchild to NAACP lawyer Thurgood Marshall (Poitier). On two cassettes. **194m/C VHS, DVD.** Sidney Poitier, Burt Lancaster, Richard Kiley, Cleavon Little, John McMartin, Graham Beckel, Lynne Thigpen, Albert Hall; **D:** George Stevens Jr.; **W:** George Stevens Jr.

Separate Lives 🐾🐾½ **1994 (R)** Psych prof Lauren Porter (Hamilton) is in need of some counseling herself. Seems she has a sexy alter ego calling herself Lena and Lauren fears she may have killed someone in her Lena persona. So she turns to her student Tom (Belushi), who happens to be an ex-cop, for help. Sketchy characters and a tired formula make this one a yawner. **101m/C VHS.** Linda Hamilton, James Belushi, Vera Miles, Elisabeth (Elisabeth, Elizabeth, Liz) Moss, Drew Snyder, Mark Lindsay Chapman, Marc Poppel, Elizabeth Arlen; **D:** David Madden; **W:** Steven Pressfield; **M:** William Olvis.

A Separate Peace 🐾🐾 **1973 (PG)** Two young men in a New England prep school during WWII come to grips with the war, coming of age, and a tragic accident. Cheap rendition of a not-so-great novel by John Knowles. **104m/C VHS.** John Heyl, Parker Stevenson, William Roerick; **D:** Larry Peerce; **M:** Charles Fox.

A Separate Peace 🐾🐾 **2004 (R)** Uninspired coming of age story based on the John Knowles novel. In 1942, bookworm Gene (Barton) transfers to the all-male Devon prep school in New England. His roomie is campus jock/rule breaker Finny (Moore), who can't wait to enlist. Finny practices his paratrooper moves by jumping from a tree into the lake below. Gene is the only one who'll jump with him and they forge a bond until a questionable accident affects their friendship. **92m/C DVD.** J Barton, Toby Moore, Jason Ashmore, Danny Swerdlow, Alison Pill, Sean McCann, Hume Cronyn; **D:** Peter Yates; **W:** Wendy Kesselman; **C:** Checco Varese. CABLE

Separate Tables 🐾🐾🐾½ **1958** Adaptation of the Terence Rattigan play about a varied cast of characters living out their personal dramas in a British seaside hotel. Guests include a matriarch and her shy daughter, a divorced couple, a spinster, and a presumed war hero. Their secrets and loves are examined in grand style. Fine acting all around. **98m/B VHS, DVD.** Burt Lancaster, David Niven, Rita Hayworth, Deborah Kerr, Wendy Hiller, Rod Taylor, Gladys Cooper, Felix Aylmer, Cathleen Nesbitt, Audrey Dalton, May Hallatt, Priscilla Morgan, Hilda Plowright; **D:** Delbert Mann; **W:** John Gay; **C:** Charles B(ryant) Lang Jr.; **M:** David Raksin. Oscars '58: Actor (Niven), Support. Actress (Hiller); Golden Globes '59: Actor—Drama (Niven); N.Y. Film Critics '58: Actor (Niven).

Separate Tables 🐾🐾½ **1983 (PG)** A remake of the 1958 film adapted from Terence Rattigan's play. Separated into two parts, "Table by the Window" and "Table Number Seven." The lives of the lonely inhabitants of a hotel are dramatized through wonderful acting by Christie and Bates. **50m/C VHS.** Julie Christie, Alan Bates, Claire Bloom, Irene Worth; **D:** John Schlesinger. CABLE

Separate Vacations 🐾½ **1986 (R)** A married man leaves his wife and kids to take a separate vacation, hoping he'll find exciting sex. Wife and kids end up at a ski resort, where romance comes her way. A lightweight, old story. **90m/C VHS.** David Naughton, Jennifer Dale, Mark Keyloun; **D:** Michael Anderson Sr.

Separate Ways 🐾½ **1982 (R)** Unhappily married couple involved in various affairs split up in order to deal with themselves and their marriage. Good cast; bad script wandering down Maudlin Lane. **92m/C VHS.** Karen Black, Tony LoBianco, David Naughton, Sybil Danning; **D:** Howard (Hikmet) Avedis; **C:** Dean Cundey.

The Separation 🐾🐾 **1994** Emotions (and fine performances) rather than action move along this domestic drama. Anne (Huppert) and Pierre (Auteuil) are living together in Paris with their toddler son when Anne suddenly announces that she's involved with another man. Anne doesn't see why this this should cause any rift in their domestic arrangements but Pierre slowly falls to pieces. Adapted from the novel by Dan Franck; French with subtitles. **85m/C DVD. FR** Isabelle Huppert, Daniel Auteuil, Karin Viard, Jerome Deschamps; **D:** Christian Vincent; **W:** Christian Vincent, Dan Franck; **C:** Denis Lenoir.

Sepia Cinderella 🐾🐾 **1947** A songwriter, who finds himself with a hit, abandons his current life and love to try high society. He finds out it's not what he wants after all. **67m/B VHS.** Sheila Guyse, Rubel Blakely, Freddie Bartholomew, Sid Catlett, Deke Wilson; **D:** Arthur Leonard; **W:** Vincent Valentini; **C:** George Webber; **M:** Charlie Stavers.

September 🐾🐾½ **1988 (PG-13)** Woody does Bergman again with a shuttered, claustrophobic drama about six unhappy people trying to verbalize their feelings in a dark summer house in Vermont. Well-acted throughout and interesting at first, but the whining and angst attacks eventually give way to boredom. Of course, the Woodman went on to "Crimes and Misdemeanors," blending his dark and comedic sides masterfully, so the best way to look at this is as a training film. **82m/C VHS, DVD.** Mia Farrow, Dianne Wiest, Denholm Elliott, Sam Waterston, Elaine Stritch, Jack Warden; **D:** Woody Allen; **W:** Woody Allen; **C:** Carlo Di Palma; **M:** Art Tatum.

September Affair 🐾🐾½ **1950** A married engineer and a classical pianist miss their plane from Naples. When the plane crashes, they're presumed dead, and they find themselves free to continue their illicit love affair. They find they cannot hide forever and must make peace with their pasts. Features the hit "September Song," recorded by Walter Huston. **104m/B VHS.** Joseph Cotten, Joan Fontaine, Francoise Rosay, Jessica Tandy, Robert Arthur; **D:** William Dieterle; **C:** Charles B(ryant) Lang Jr. Golden Globes '52: Score.

September Dawn WOOF! **2007 (R)** Take a stock Old West setting, add a theme of religious intolerance, a "Romeo and Juliet" subplot, a ton of gratuitous violence, Jon Voight, and the label "based on a true story," and you have this truish fiasco about a Mormon militia massacring 120 settlers on September 11th, 1857. Bishop Jacob Samuelson (Voight) isn't pleased about a wagon train of non-Mormons and their worldly ways passing through his territory, but when his son (Ford) falls for one of the settlers (Hope), he goes berserk and decides to show them who's religion is right, after all. Mass-murder of the settlers (and the viewer's tolerance) ensues. Voight chews scenery while the movie collapses into a pit of one-dimensional characters, heavy-handed plotting, and made-for-TV level production values. Movie stirred controversy and accusations of anti-Mormon bias because of the implication that Mormon leader Brigham Young authorized the massacre. **110m/C DVD. US CA** Jon Voight, Trent Ford, Taylor Handley, Tamara Hope, Jon(athan) Gries, Shaun Johnston, Lolita (David) Davidovich, Dean Cain, Huntley Ritter, Terence Stamp; **D:** Christopher Cain; **W:** Christopher Cain, Carole Whang Schutter; **C:** Juan Ruiz-Anchia; **M:** William Ross.

September Gun 🐾🐾½ **1983** A nun hires an aging gunfighter to escort her and a group of Apache children to a church school 200 miles away. Preston is excellent as the ornery varmint in this enjoyable, pleasant western comedy. **94m/C VHS.** Robert Preston, Patty Duke, Christopher Lloyd, Geoffrey Lewis, Sally Kellerman; **D:** Don Taylor. TV

September 30, 1955 🐾🐾½ *9/30/55* **1977 (PG)** A college undergrad (Thomas) in a small Arkansas town is devastated when he learns of the death of his idol, James Dean. (The title refers to the day Dean died.) Jimmy gathers a group of friends together for a vigil which turns into a drinking-binge, resulting in police chases and, finally, tragedy. Film debut of Quaid. **107m/C VHS.** Richard Thomas, Lisa Blount, Deborah Benson, Tom Hulce, Dennis Christopher, Dennis Quaid, Susan Tyrrell; **D:** James Bridges; **W:** James Bridges.

Seraphim Falls 🐾🐾 **2006 (R)** Irishmen Neeson and Brosnan star as a couple of post-Civil War soldiers (film's set in 1868) in an old-fashioned and beautifully filmed tale of brutal revenge. Wounded Yankee Gideon (Brosnan) is being hunted by Confederate Carver (Neeson) and his four hired guns over a wartime horror, but he won't go easily. There are various showdowns as Gideon picks off the thugs while awaiting that inevitable final confrontation. **115m/C DVD. US** Liam Neeson, Pierce Brosnan, Anjelica Huston, Michael Wincott, Robert Baker, Ed Lauter, John Robinson, Tom Noonan, Kevin J. O'Connor; **D:** David Von Ancken, Abby Everett Jaques; **W:** David Von Ancken, Abby Everett Jaques; **C:** John Toll; **M:** Harry Gregson-Williams.

Serendipity 🐾🐾½ **2001 (PG-13)** Romance finds Jonathan (Cusack) and Sara (Beckinsale) falling in love one cold New York winter's night but then they part company because Sara believes if it's meant to be, fate will bring them back together. Sara's a twinkling twit. Ten years later both are engaged, but Jon and Sara also become separately convinced that they are destined to be together—if they can find each other again. Lots of near-misses and travel between New York and San Francisco until the inevitable happens. Swoony romanticism and more dippy than serendipitous but done in an expert manner. **87m/C VHS, DVD. US** John Cusack, Kate Beckinsale, Molly Shannon, John Corbett, Jeremy Piven, Bridget Moynahan, Eugene Levy; **D:** Peter Chelsom; **W:** Marc Klein; **C:** John de Borman; **M:** Alan Silvestri.

Serenity 🐾🐾🐾 **2005 (PG-13)** Failed TV shows usually make pretty crappy movies (remember "Mod Squad?"), but Joss Whedon's big-screen adaptation of his small-screen "Firefly" series is one of the coolest sci fi adventures in recent memory. Captain Mal Reynolds (Fillion) and the crew of his cargo ship, Serenity, attempt to hide River Tam (Glau), a waifishly good-natured super-assassin, from the evil government Alliance that created her. Things hit the fan when the coolly evil Operative (Ejiofor) gets on their trail, but that won't keep Mal from "aiming to misbehave." Imagine a movie based on everything you loved about Han Solo and the Millenium Falcon, and you'll get an idea of why so many fanboys worship at the altar of Whedon. **119m/C DVD, UMD, HD DVD. US** Nathan Fillion, Gina Torres, Alan Tudyk, Adam Baldwin, Sean Maher, Ron Glass, Chiwetel Ejiofor, Morena Baccarin, Jewel Staite, Summer Glau; **D:** Joss Whedon; **W:** Joss Whedon; **C:** Jack N. Green; **M:** David Newman.

Sgt. Bilko 🐾🐾½ **1995 (PG)** Popular '50s sitcom doesn't march so much as limp to the big screen with Martin leading the troops as the wise-cracking title character, crafted so brilliantly by Phil Silvers on the small screen. Martin films and flams with frenetic energy as he tries to save his base from Washington cutbacks and the film from utter disaster. Enter Major Thorn (Hartman), Bilko's old adversary, who's plotting revenge on the con artist sergeant. Aykroyd's Bilko's naive boss, Col. Hall, but has little to do. Director Lynn finds his usual comic flair on leave this time around—too few laughs, spread too thin. Sentimental stroke has Catherine-Silvers, Phil's daughter, playing Lt. Monday. **95m/C VHS, DVD.** Steve Martin, Dan Aykroyd, Phil Hartman, Glenne Headly, Daryl (Chill) Mitchell, Max Casella, Brian Leckner, Pamela Segall, Eric Edwards, Dan Ferro, John Marshall Jones, Brian Ortiz, Dale Dye; **D:** Jonathan Lynn; **W:** Andy Breckman; **C:** Peter Sova; **M:** Alan Silvestri.

Sgt. Kabukiman N.Y.P.D. WOOF! **1994** When New York cop Harry Griswold (Gianasi) investigates the death of a famous Japanese Kabuki actor, he suddenly finds himself in a kimono, having really bad hair-dos, and vesting into the powers of "Kabukiman". With the help of his beautiful teacher Lotus (Byun), he learns to channel his commmand of such amazing weapons as suffocating sushi rolls and lethal chopsticks into crime fighting. Stupid and insulting (deliberately so) all at the same time. A PG-13 version runs 95 minutes. **104m/C VHS, DVD.** Rick Gianasi, Susan Byun, Brick Bronsky, Bill Weeden, Thomas Crnkovich, Larry Robinson, Noble Lee Lester; **D:** Lloyd Kaufman, Michael Herz; **W:** Lloyd Kaufman, Andrew Osborn; **C:** Bob Williams; **M:** Bob Mithoff.

Sergeant Matlovich vs. the U.S. Air Force 🐾🐾½ **1978** A serviceman fights to remain in the Air Force after admitting his homosexuality. Compelling theme (from a true story) and good lead performance from Dourif are not enough to carry a rather flat made for TV script. **100m/C VHS.** Brad Dourif, Marc Singer, Frank Converse, William Daniels, Stephen Elliott, David Spielberg, Rue McClanahan, Mitchell Ryan, David Ogden Stiers; **C:** Paul Leaf. TV

Sgt. Pepper's Lonely Hearts Club Band WOOF! **1978 (PG)** "Ripoff" would be putting it kindly. A classic album by one of the greatest rock bands of all time deserves the respect of not having a star-studded extravaganza "filimization" made of it. Gratuitous, weird casting, bad acting give it a surreal feel. And the

Sergeant Rutledge ✶✶✶ 1960
The story of a court-martial, told in flashback, about a black cavalry officer on trial for rape and murder. A detailed look at overt and covert racism handled by master director Ford. It is always apparent Strode (as Rutledge) is a heroic, yet human, figure who refuses to be beaten down by circumstances. The courtroom setting is deliberately oppressive but does make the film somewhat static. Based on the novel "Captain Buffalo" by James Warner Bellah. 112m/C VHS, DVD. Woody Strode, Jeffrey Hunter, Constance Towers, Billie Burke, Juano Hernandez, Carleton Young, Charles Seel, Jan Styne, Mae Marsh; D: John Ford; W: Willis Goldbeck, James Warner Bellah; M: Howard Jackson.

Sergeant Ryker ✶✶½ 1968 Confident lead acting from Marvin as a U.S. serviceman accused of treason during the Korean War carries this otherwise blah courtroom drama. Remake of 1963 TV film "The Case Against Sergeant Ryker." Dillman is good as Marvin's energetic lawyer. 85m/C VHS. Lee Marvin, Bradford Dillman, Vera Miles, Peter Graves, Lloyd Nolan, Murray Hamilton; D: Buzz Kulik; M: John Williams.

Sergeant York ✶✶✶ 1941 Timely and enduring war movie based on the true story of Alvin York, the country boy from Tennessee drafted during WWI. At first a pacifist, Sergeant York (Cooper, who won an Oscar-winning role) finds justification for fighting and becomes one of the war's greatest heros. Gentle scenes of rural life contrast with horrific battlegrounds. York served as a consultant. 134m/B VHS, DVD. Gary Cooper, Joan Leslie, Walter Brennan, Dickie Moore, Ward Bond, George Tobias, Noah Beery Jr., June Lockhart, Stanley Ridges, Margaret Wycherly, James Anderson, David Bruce, Lane Chandler, Elisha Cook Jr., Erville Alderson, Howard da Silva, Donald Douglas, Frank Faylen, Pat Flaherty, Joseph Girard, Creighton Hale, Russell Hicks, George Irving, Selmer Jackson, Jack Pennick, Harvey Stephens, Kay Sutton, Clem Bevans, Charles Trowbridge, Guy Wilkerson, Gig Young; D: Howard Hawks; W: Abem Finkel, Harry Chandlee, Howard Koch, John Huston; C: Sol Polito; M: Max Steiner. Oscars '41: Actor (Cooper), Film Editing; N.Y. Film Critics '41: Actor (Cooper).

Sergio Lapel's Drawing Blood ✶ *Drawing Blood* 1999 ArtistVampire Diana (Spinella) fulfills her artistic visions with blood instead of oils or watercolors. Her human slave Edmond (Wilson) supplies a constant flow of "models" until he meets homeless prostitute Dee (Smith) and decides to take control of his life. Edmond also has his hands full keeping his ever-horny dad (Palatta) out of trouble. The Troma label says it all: non-existent production values, mediocre acting, plenty of flowing red stuff, and ample female exposure (although this time there's a genuine narrative logic to all the nudity). 90m/C DVD. Kirk Wilson, Larry Palatta, Dawn Spinella, Lee Otero, Erin Smith; D: Sergio Lapel; Act: Shawn Lewален.

Serial Bomber ✶✶ 1980 (R) Fun spoof of hyper-trendiness—open marriage, health foods, fad religions, navel-gazing—in Marin County, the really good place to live across the Golden Gate from San Francisco. Mull in his first lead is the oddly normal guy surrounded by fruits and nuts. Based on Cyra McFadden's novel. 90m/C VHS, DVD. Martin Mull, Sally Kellerman, Tuesday Weld, Tom Smothers, Bill Macy, Peter Bonerz, Barbara Rhoades, Christopher Lee; D: Bill Persky; W: Rich Eustis, Michael Elias.

Serial Bomber ✶✶ 1996 (R) A would-be bomber in Seattle targets his ex-girlfriend but his plan is foiled by an FBI agent. So he bombs other shifts targets. Based on the novel "Christmas Apocalypse" by Toshiyuki Tajima. 89m/C VHS.

Bee Gees? Please. A nadir of '70s popular entertainment. ♪♪Sgt. Pepper's Lonely Hearts Club Band; With a Little Help From My Friends; Fixing a Hole; Getting Better; Here Comes the Sun; I Want You; (She's So Heavy); Good Morning, Good Morning; Nowhere Man; Polythene Pam. 113m/C VHS, DVD. Takaaki Yamashita, Maurice Gibb, Peter Frampton, Barry Gibb, Steve Martin, George Burns, Donald Pleasence; D: Michael A. Schultz.

Serial Killer ✶✶ 1995 (R) Selby (Delaney) is able to think like a killer in order to catch them. That's how the beautiful cop captured serial killer William Lucian Morrano (Bell) who has now escaped—Selby's his ultimate target but friends as bait and leaves the bodies to first he wants revenge. So he uses her to discover. 84m/C VHS, DVD. Kim Delaney, Gary Hudson, Tobin Bell, Pam Grier, Marco Rodriguez, Lyman Ward, Cyndi Pass, Andrew Prine; D: Pierre David; W: Mark Sevi; C: Thomas Jewett; M: Louis Febre.

Serial Killing 101 ✶✶ *Serial Killing 4 Dummies* 2004 (R) Outcast high-school kid Casey decides that he wants to be a serial killer when he grows up. His suicidal (and presumably equally outcast) girlfriend thinks this is a great idea. At least they won't have to sweat the SATs. When a real serial killer shows up, guess who the cops suspect. Myriad problems (besides the tasteless premise) ensure a small audience for this one. 88m/C VHS, DVD. Thomas Haden Church, Justin Urich, Lisa Loeb, Rick Overton, George Murdock, Barbara Niven; D: Trace Slobotkin; W: Trace Slobotkin; C: John Tarver; M: Jeffrey Alan Jones. VIDEO

Serial Mom ✶✶✶ 1994 (R) June Cleaver-like housewife Turner is nearly perfect, except when someone disrupts her orderly life. Didn't rewind your video-tape? Chose the white shoes after Labor Day? Uh oh. Stardom reigns after she's caught and the murderer-as-celebrity phenomenon is exploited to the fullest. Darkly funny Waters satire tends toward the mainstream and isn't as perverse as earlier efforts, but still maintains a shocking edge (vital organs are good for an appearance or two). Turner's chameleonic performance as the perfect mom/crazed killer is right on target, recalling "The War of the Roses." Waterston, Lake, and Lillard are terrific as her generic suburban family. 93m/C VHS, DVD. Kathleen Turner, Sam Waterston, Ricki Lake, Matthew Lillard, Mink Stole, Traci Lords, Suzanne Somers, Scan Rivers, Patty (Patricia Campbell) Hearst, Mary Jo Catlett, Justin Whalin, Susan Lowe, Alan J. Wendl, Mary Vivian Pearce; D: John Waters; W: John Waters; C: Robert M. Stevens; M: Basil Poledouris; V: John Waters.

Serial Slayer ✶½ *Claustrophobia* 2003 (R) A serial killer hunts in the daylight. Three office workers are trapped in a suburban house trying to avoid being the next victims of the Crossbow Killer. Modestly suspenseful, although it can't avoid most of the genre's cliches. At least the three chicks don't run around screaming in their scanties (sorry, guys). 79m/C DVD. Melanie Lynskey, Sheeri Rappaport, Mary Lynn Rajskub, Judith O'Dea; D: Mark Tapio Kines; W: Mark Tapio Kines; C: Bevan Crothers; M: Christopher Farrell.

Series 7: The Contenders ✶✶½ 2001 (R) Reality TV takes to the big screen in this morbid but insightful portrayal of a fictional show called "The Contenders" in which the participants hunt each other down to their ultimate, televised, demise. Pic is presented which stars eight-month's pregnant Dawn in the form of a marathon of the show, who takes on five new challengers, including an 18-year-old girl (Weaver), a cancer victim and past who friend (Fitzgerald). Revealing portrayals make all the contestants sympathetic, but Dawn and Jeff's unique plight is the most interesting. A scene where Dawn casually guns people down in a convenience store while bystanders look on is a highlight in this interesting social satire. 86m/C VHS, DVD, US Brooke Smith, Glenn Fitzgerald, Merritt Wever, Michael Kaycheck, Richard Venture, Donna Hanover, Marylouise Burke, Nada Despotovich, Danton Stone, Jennifer Van Dyck, Angelina Phillips, Tanny McDonald; D: Daniel Minahan; W: Daniel Minahan; C: Randy Drummond; M: Girls Against Boys; Nar: Will Arnet.

The Serpent and the Rainbow ✶✶½ 1987 (R) A good, interesting book (by Harvard ethnobotanist Wade Davis) offering serious speculation on the possible existence and origin of

---

The Servant ✶✶✶½ 1963 A dark, intriguing examination of British class hypocrisy and the master-servant relationship. Wealthy, bored aristocratic playboy Tony (Fox) is ruined by his socially inferior but crafty and ambitious Cockney manservant Hugo (Bogarde). Playwright Harold Pinter wrote the adaptation of Robin Maugham's novel in his first collaboration with expatriate American director Losey. The best kind of British societal navel-gazing. 112m/B VHS, DVD. GB Dirk Bogarde, James Fox, Sarah Miles, Wendy Craig, Catherine Lacey, Richard Vernon; D: Joseph Losey; W: Harold Pinter; C: Douglas Slocombe; M: John Dankworth.

Servants of Twilight ✶✶ 1991 (R) Religious zealots target a small boy for assassination because their cult leader says he's the anti-Christ. Adaptation of the Dean R. Koontz novel. Packed with action, it's spell on the viewer hinges on a cruel shock ending that undercuts what came before. 95m/C VHS, DVD. Bruce Greenwood, Belinda Bauer, Grace Zabriskie, Richard Bradford, Jarret Lennon, Carel Struycken, Jack Kehoe, Kelli Maroney, Dale Dye; D: Jeffrey Obrow; W: Stephen Carpenter. CABLE

Service De Luxe ✶✶ 1938 Glamorous New York businesswoman Helen Murphy (Bennett) caters to a rich clientele by dealing with all the problems they don't wish to. Wealthy Scott Robinson (Ruggles) wants to prevent his country-bred nephew Robert Wade (Price, in his film debut) from bothering him. But Helen finds herself reluctantly in the eye of the media storm. The TV film won 3 EMMY awards: Best Actress for Close; Best Supporting Actress for Davis (as Margarethe's lover); and Best Screenplay. 92m/C VHS, DVD. Constance Bennett, Vincent Price, Charlie Ruggles, Helen Broderick, Mischa Auer; D: Rowland V. Lee; W: Gertrude Purcell, Leonard Spigelgass; C: George Robinson.

Serving Sara ✶ 2002 (PG-13) Unfunny comedy stars Perry as process server Joe Tyler, who is trying to serve divorce papers on flirty Englishwoman Sara Moore (Hurley), who's married to cheatin' Texas cattle baron Gordon (Campbell). But Sara turns the tables by bribing Joe to try to serve divorce papers to the elusive Gordon instead. Perry's trip to rehab during filming delayed production solely at the lack of laughs surely can't be laid new family is a bunch of do-dos. (literally), followed by a viridictive social worker, two schemers, new by promising to complete the work in such a week, although under ideal circumstances it should take a month. Unfortunately, "iced circumstances" are not about atmosphere soon gets to Gordon and his crew, who begin turning on each other at the discovery of nine audio tapes containing rumors of satanic rituals and tor-

Serving in Silence: The Margarethe Cammermeyer Story ✶✶½ 1995 Army nurse Margarethe Cammermeyer (Close) has had a distinguished career for 24 years, a bronze star earned in Vietnam, and obtained the rank of colonel. During a security clearance interview, she admits to the military that she is a lesbian and finds her self reluctantly in the eye of the media storm. The TV film won 3 EMMY awards: Best Actress for Close; Best Supporting Actress for Davis (as Margarethe's lover); and Best Screenplay. 92m/C VHS, Glenn Close, Judy Davis, Jan Rubes, Wendy Makkena, William Converse-Roberts, Susan Barnes, Colleen Flynn, William Allen Young; D: Jeff Bleckner; M: Allison Cross. TV

Sesame Street Presents: Follow That Bird ✶✶½ 1985 (G) Possibly the best children's TV show in the history of the medium makes a so-so transition to the big screen. Suffering an identity crisis, a lonely Big Bird allows himself to be adopted by a family of birds. Quickly realizing that his the big guys heads back to NYC, followed by carnival owners, and the assorted residents of Sesame Street. There are great moments (mostly involving Super-Grover and Ernie & Bert) and some fun cameos from Weylon Jennings and SCTV alumni, but it never lives up to the potential of the TV show. 92m/C VHS, DVD. Sandra Bernhard, John Candy, Chevy Chase, Joe Flaherty, Dave Thomas, Waylon Jennings; D: Ken Kwapis; W: Judy Freudberg, Tony Geiss; C: Curtis Clark; M: Lennie Niehaus; V: Carroll Spinney, Jim Henson, Frank Oz.

Session 9 ✶✶ 2001 (R) Hazardous materials contractor Gordon (Mullan) bids on a job to remove asbestos from a run-down insane asylum. He secures the contract by promising to complete the work in such a week, although under ideal circumstances it should take a month. Unfortunately, "iced circumstances" are not about in the creepy booby hatch. The oppressive

---

Serpent Island ✶½ 1954 Two seamen fight over a Caribbean woman amid voodoo rituals, sea monsters and buried treasure. 63m/C VHS. Mary Munday, Sonny Tufts, Tom Monroe, Rosalind Hayes, Don Blackman, Tom Monroe; D: Tom Gries; C: Bert I. Gordon; M: Domingo Rodriguez.

The Serpent's Egg ✶✶½ *Das Schlangenei* 1978 (R) Big disappointment from the great Bergman in his second film in English, Ullmann is not sultry and Carradine is horrible. Big budget matched by paranoid of himself. The plot concerns a pair of Jewish trapeze artists surviving in Berlin during Hitler's rise by working in a grisly and mysterious medical clinic. 119m/C VHS, DVD. GE David Carradine, Liv Ullmann, Gert Frobe, James Whitmore; D: Ingmar Bergman; W: Ingmar Bergman; C: Sven Nykvist.

The Serpent's Kiss ✶✶ 1997 (R) Great cast can't quite overcome the story's predicability. In 1699, young Dutch landscape artist Meneer Chrome (MacGregor) accepts a job at the remote English estate of Thomas Smithers (Postlethwaite) who wants a magnificent garden to present to his bored wife, Juliana (Scacchi). But Chrome is secretly employed by Juliana's scheming cousin, James Fitzmaurice (Grant), to bankrupt Smithers so that James can regain Juliana's affections. Of course, Juliana casts her eyes on the handsome gardener instead, and then there's the matter of the Smithers' teenaged daughter, Thea (Chaplin). Rousselot is better known as a cinematographer (this is his first directorial effort) and the film at least looks gorgeous. 119m/C VHS, DVD. GB FR Ewan McGregor, Greta Scacchi, Pete Postlethwaite, Richard E. Grant, Carmen Chaplin, Donal McCann, Charley Boorman; D: Philippe Rousselot; W: Tim Rose Price; C: Jean-François Robin; M: Goran Bregović.

The Serpent's Lair ✶✶ 1995 (R) Tom (Fahey) and Alex (Medway) have just moved into what's supposed to be their dream apartment in L.A. Too bad there's lots of secrets and Tom's soon drawn into the web of sultry beauty Lilith (Lisa B.), who's not just your average femme fatale. 90m/C VHS. Jeff Fahey, Heather Medway, Lisa Barbuscia, Anthony Palermo, Kathleen Noone, Taylor Nichols, Patrick Bauchau, Jack Kehoe; D: Jeff Reiner; M: Marc Rosenberg; C: Fallis Parnell.

Serpico ✶✶✶ 1973 (R) Based on Peter Maas's book about the true-life exploits of Frank Serpico, a New York undercover policeman who exposed corruption in the police department. Known as much for his nonconformism as for his honesty, the real Serpico eventually retired from the force and moved to Europe. South Bronx-raised Pacino gives the character reality and strength. Excellent New York's location photography. 130m/C VHS, DVD. Al Pacino, John Randolph, Jack Kehoe, Barbara Eda-Young, Cornelia Sharpe, F. Murray Abraham, Tony Roberts; D: Sidney Lumet; W: Waldo Salt, Norman Wexler; C: Arthur Ornitz; M: Mikis Theodorakis. Golden Globes '74: Actor—Drama (Pacino); Natl. Bd. of Review '73: Adapt. Screenplay.

---

zombies in Haiti was hacked and slashed into a cheap Wes Craven-ized screen semblance of itself. And a shame it is: the result is racist, disrespectful, exploitative, and superficial. 98m/C VHS, DVD, Paul Guilfoyle, Bill Pullman, Cathy Tyson, Zakes Mokae, Paul Winfield, Conrad Roberts, Badja (Medu) Djola, Theresa Merritt, Brent Jennings, Michael Gough; D: Wes Craven; W: Richard Maxwell, A.R. Simon; C: John Lindley; M: Brad Fiedel.

Serpent *[DVD. Jason London, Lori Petty, James LeGros, Yuki Amami; D: Keoni Waxman.]*

---

ture of patients. Somewhat married by editing that gives away the plot too early, and also by the fact that workers under a deadline, these guys stand around getting freaked out way too much. Shot using Sony's CineAlta HD digital video cameras instead of film. **100m/C VHS, DVD.** *US* Peter Mullan, David Caruso, Josh(ua) Lucas, Brendan Sexton III, Paul Guilfoyle, Stephen Gevedon; *D:* Brad Anderson; *W:* Brad Anderson, Stephen Gevedon; *C:* Uta Briesewitz; *M:* Climax Gold Twins.

A Session with The Committee 🎬🎬 **1968 (PG)** Comedy film of the seminal comedy troupe "The Committee," specialists in short, punchy satire. Dated, but of interest to comedy buffs. **88m/C VHS, DVD.** Wolfman Jack, Howard Hesseman, Barbara Bosson, Peter Bonerz, Garry Goodrow, Carl Gottlieb; *D:* Jack Del.

Sessions 🎬🎬 **1983** Mentally exhausted by her roles as sister, single parent, lover, exercise enthusiast, and high-priced prostitute, Leigh Churchill (Hamel) seeks professional counselling. Hamel's first role after "Hill Street Blues" is only average in this made for TV drama. **96m/C VHS.** Veronica Hamel, Jeffrey DeMunn, Jill Eikenberry, David Marshall Grant, George Coe, Henderson Forsythe, Deborah Hedwall; *D:* Richard Pearce. **TV**

Set It Off 🎬🎬🎬½ **1996 (R)** Lethal "Waiting to Exhale," finds four female friends in Los Angeles pushed over the edge and taking up bank robbery to escape poverty and strike a blow against "the man." The felonious, funky divas of crime include Stony (Pinkett), who seems to be having fun with this role) and Latifah as Cleo, in a powerhouse performance. Butt-kicking action scenes are entertaining combined with a soundtrack, including Seal, En Vogue, the Fugees and Brandy, to match. Melodramatic sequences, including Stony's romance with Keith (Underwood); drag. **123m/C VHS, DVD.** Jada Pinkett Smith, Queen Latifah, Vivica A. Fox, Kimberly Elise, Blair Underwood, John C. McGinley, Anna Maria Horsford, Ella Joyce, Charles Robinson, Chaz Lamar Shepherd, Vincent Baum, Van Baum, Thomas Jefferson Byrd, Samantha MacLachian; *D:* F. Gary Gray; *W:* Kate Lanier, Takashi Bufford; *C:* Marc Reshovsky; *M:* Christopher Young.

Set Me Free 🎬🎬½ **1999** *Emporte-Moi* Thirteen-year-old Hanna is trying to deal with her loneliness in 1963 Montreal. Her Polish immigrant father (Manojlovic) is a frustrated writer who takes his problems out on his family while takes his depressed wife (Pussieres) slaves in a garment factory to support them. Hanna tries to find solace at the cinema where she becomes enamored of actress Anna Karina, the sultry star of Jean-Luc Godard's "My Life to Live," in which she plays an independent prostitute (not a first-choice role model). Hanna's confusion and unhappiness go unresolved, but then she still has a lot of living to do. French with subtitles. **85m/C VHS.** *CA* S/Karine Vanasse, Miki (Pedrag) Manojlovic, Pascale Bussieres, Alexandre Merineau, Charlotte Christeler, Nancy Huston, Monique Mercure; *D:* Lea Pool; *W:* Lea Pool, Monique H. Messier, Nancy Huston; *C:* Jeanne Lapoirie.

The Set-Up 🎬🎬½ **1949** Excellent, original if somewhat overwrought morality tale about integrity set in the world of boxing. Filmed as a continuous narrative covering only 72 minutes in the life of aging fighter Stoker Thompson (Ryan). His manager (Tobias) takes a gangster's bribe for Thompson to throw the fight (without informing him), never believing the washed-up boxer has a chance to win. Powerful, with fine performances, especially from Ryan in the lead. Inspired by Joseph Moncure March's narrative poem. **72m/B VHS, DVD.** Robert Ryan, Audrey Totter, George Tobias, Alan Baxter, James Edwards, Wallace Ford; *D:* Robert Wise; *M:* Art Cohn; *C:* Milton Krasner.

The Set Up 🎬🎬½ **1995 (R)** Electronic engineer-turned-cat burglar Charlie Thorpe (Zane) is now apparently reformed after a prison stint and works designing and installing security systems. His latest job is for Chairman Jeremiah Cole (Coburn) at Charter Trust bank where he begins romancing the beautiful Gina (Sara). But she becomes the hostage of Charlie's ex-prison buddy Kliff (Russo), who wants Charlie's help in breaking into the bank. However, there's a doublecross (or maybe even a triplecross) that has Charlie scrambling to save his life. Based on the book "My Laugh Comes Last" by James Hadley Chase. **103m/C VHS, DVD.** Billy Zane, Mia Sara, James Coburn, James Russo; *D:* Strathford Hamilton; *W:* Michael Thoma; *C:* David Lewis; *M:* Conrad Pope.

The Settlement 🎬🎬 **1999** Con men Jerry and Pat try to make money by buying life insurance policies on the terminally ill. Unfortunately for them, their clients have been living a lot longer than anticipated. Then they meet the seriously ill Barbara and things begin to change. **92m/C VHS, DVD.** Kelly McGillis, John C. Reilly, William Fichtner, Dan Castellaneta, David Rasche; *D:* Mark Steilen; *C:* Judy Irola; *M:* Brian Tyler.

Seven 🎬🎬½ **1979 (R)** Freelance desperado Smith takes $7 million of your tax dollars at work from the feds to get rid of Hawaiian gangsters. Might be tongue in cheek, though sometimes it's hard to tell. Fun action pic unfortunately characterized by bad camera work and over-earnest direction. Features the original of a gag made famous in "Raiders of the Lost Ark." **100m/C VHS.** William (Bill) Smith, Barbara Leigh, Guich Koock, Art Metrano, Martin Kove, Richard Le Pore, Susan Kiger; *D:* Andy Sidaris.

Seven 🎬🎬🎬🎬 **1995 (R)** *Se7en* If this grim thriller can't make you jump, you're dead, and you won't be the only one. Arrogant, ignorant detective David Mills (Pitt) is newly partnered with erudite old-timer William Somerset (Freeman) and they're stuck with the bizarre case of a morbidly obese man who was forced to eat himself to death. The weary Somerset is certain it's just the beginning and he's right—the non-buddy duo are on the trail of a serial killer who uses the seven deadly sins (gluttony, greed, sloth, pride, lust, envy, and wrath) as his modus operandi. Since most of the film is shot in dark, grimy, and unrelentingly rainy circumstances, much of the grotesqueness of the murders is left to the viewer's imagination—which will be in overdrive. **127m/C VHS, DVD.** Brad Pitt, Morgan Freeman, Gwyneth Paltrow, Kevin Spacey, R. Lee Ermey, Richard Roundtree, John C. McGinley, Julie Araskog, Reg E. Cathey, Peter Crombie; *D:* David Fincher; *W:* Andrew Kevin Walker; *C:* Darius Khondji; *M:* Howard Shore. MTV Movie Awards '96: Film, Most Desirable Male (Pitt), Villain (Spacey); Natl. Bd. of Review '95: Support. Actor (Spacey); N.Y. Film Critics '95: Support. Actor (Spacey); Broadcast Film Critics '95: Support. Actor (Spacey).

Seven Alone 🎬🎬½ **1975 (G)** *House Without Windows* Family adventure tale (based on Monroe Morrow's book "On to Oregon," based in turn on a true story) about seven siblings who undertake a treacherous 2000-mile journey from Missouri to Oregon, after their parents die along the way. Inspiring and all that; good family movie. **85m/C VHS, DVD.** Dewey Martin, Aldo Ray, Anne Collins, Dean Smith, Stewart Petersen; *D:* Earl Bellamy.

Seven Beauties 🎬🎬🎬🎬 *Pasqualino: Settebellezze; Pasqualino: Seven Beauties* **1976** Very dark war comedy about a small-time Italian crook in Naples with seven ugly sisters to support. He survives a German prison camp and much else; unforgettably, he seduces the ugly commandant of his camp to save his own life. Good acting and tight direction. **116m/C VHS, DVD.** *IT* Giancarlo Giannini, Fernando Rey, Shirley Stoler, Elena Fiore, Enzo Vitale; *D:* Lina Wertmuller; *W:* Lina Wertmuller; *C:* Tonino Delli Colli.

Seven Brides for Seven Brothers 🎬🎬🎬 **1954** The eldest of seven fur-trapping brothers in the Oregon Territory brings home a wife. She begins to civilize the other six, who realize the merits of women and begin to look for romances of their own. Thrilling choreography by Michael Kidd—don't miss "The Barn Raising." Charming performances by Powell and Keel, both in lovely voice. Based on Stephen Vincent Benet's story. Thrills, chills, singin', dancin'—a classic Hollywood good time. 🎵When You're In Love: Spring, Spring, Spring; Sobbin' Women; Bless Your Beautiful Hide; Goin' Co'tin; Wonderful, Wonderful Day; June Bride; Lonesome Polecat Lament. **103m/C VHS, DVD.** Howard Keel, Jane Powell, Russ Tamblyn, Julie Newmar, Jeff Richards, Tommy (Thomas) Rall, Virginia Gibson; *D:* Stanley Donen; *W:* Albert Hackett, Frances Goodrich, Dorothy Kingsley; *C:* George J. Folsey. Oscars '54: Score (Musical); Natl. Film Reg. '04.

Seven Chances 🎬🎬🎬½ **1925** Silent classic that Keaton almost didn't make, believing instead that it should go to Harold Lloyd. Desperate lawyer Jimmie Shannon (Keaton) finds that he can inherit $7 million from his grandfather's estate if he marries by 7:00 p.m. on his 27th birthday, which is that day. After his girlfriend (Dwyer) turns down his botched proposal, chaos breaks loose when Jimmie advertises for someone—anyone—to marry him and make him rich. Suddenly he finds what seems to be hundreds of women willing to make the sacrifice, setting up one of the great film pursuits. Memorable boulder sequence was re-shot after preview audience indicated climax was lacking that certain something. Based on the play by David Belasco and remade with Chris O'Donnell as "The Bachelor" (1990). **60m/B VHS, DVD.** Buster Keaton, T. Roy Barnes, Snitz Edwards, Ruth Dwyer, Frankie Raymond; *D:* Buster Keaton; *W:* Clyde Bruckman, Jean C. Havez, Joseph A. Mitchell; *C:* Byron Houck, Elgin Lessley.

Seven Cities of Gold 🎬🎬 **1955** An expedition of Spanish conquistadors and missionaries descend on 18th-century California, looking for secret Indian caches of gold. Semi-lavish costume epic. **103m/C VHS.** Anthony Quinn, Michael Rennie, Richard Egan, Rita Moreno, Jeffrey Hunter, Eduardo Noriega, John Doucette; *D:* Robert D. Webb.

Seven Days Ashore 🎬½ **1944** Sailor Dan Arland (Oliver) wants to enjoy his shore leave in San Francisco only he has three girls waiting for him in port. So he pawns Carol (Mayo) and Lucy (Ward) off on his pals Monty (Brown) and Orval (Carney) so he can romance debutante Annabelle (Shepard). Only the girls find out what Dan's done and decide to pay him back. Brown and Carney were a popular comedy duo at the time. **74m/B VHS.** Gordon Oliver, Wally Brown, Alan Carney, Elaine Shepard, Virginia Mayo, Amelita Ward, Marcy McGuire, Dooley Wilson; *D:* John Houseman.

Seven Days in May 🎬🎬🎬½ **1964** Topical but still gripping Cold War nuclear-peril thriller. After President Jordan Lyman (March) signs a nuclear disarmament treaty with the Soviets, General James M. Scott (Lancaster), the leader of the Joint Chiefs of Staff, plans a military takeover because he considers the president's pacifism traitorous. Lyman learns of the potential coup and works to expose the plot before it's too late. Highly suspenseful, with a breathtaking climax. Based on a novel by Fletcher Knebel and Charles Waldo Bailey II. **117m/B VHS, DVD.** Burt Lancaster, Kirk Douglas, Edmond O'Brien, Fredric March, Ava Gardner, Martin Balsam, George Macready, Whit Bissell, Hugh Marlowe, Richard Anderson, Andrew Duggan, John Houseman; *D:* John Frankenheimer; *W:* Rod Serling; *C:* Ellsworth Fredericks; *M:* Jerry Goldsmith. Golden Globes '65: Support. Actor (O'Brien).

Seven Days' Leave 🎬🎬 **1942** Radio star-crammed musical comedy about a soldier who must marry a certain already betrothed gal (Ball) within a week so he can inherit a fortune. Songs include "Can't Get Out of this Mood," "A Touch of Texas," and "Baby, You Speak My Language." Following the completion of the film, Mature joined the Coast Guard. Lively but not memorable. **87m/B VHS.** Victor Mature, Lucille Ball, Harold (Hal) Peary, Mary Cortes, Ginny Simms, Marcy McGuire, Peter Lind Hayes, Walter Reed, Wallace Ford, Arnold Stang, Buddy Clark, Charles Victor; *D:* Tim Whelan.

Seven Days to Live 🎬🎬½ **2001 (R)** Ellen (Plummer) and her hubby Martin Shaw (Pertwee) move to a remote country house to recover from the death of their son. Of course, the house just happens to be built over a graveyard and Ellen is haunted by warnings that she has only, well, the title tells it all. Quite creepy. **96m/C VHS, DVD.** Amanda Plummer, Sean Pertwee, Nick Brimble, Gina Bellman; *D:* Sebastian Niemann.

Seven Days to Noon 🎬🎬½ **1950** Dated but still powerful story detailing the threat of a nuclear explosion. Unbalanced atomic scientist John Willingdon (Jones) threatens to blow up the center of London unless the Prime Minister (Adam) agrees to stop research into nuclear weapons. And Willingdon can do it, too, since he's stolen an atomic bomb. Scotland Yard has until noon of the following Sunday to find him. **94m/B VHS.** Barry Jones, Andre Morell, Ronald Adam, Olive Sloane, Joan Hickson, Hugh Cross, Sheila Manahan; *D:* John Boulting, Roy Boulting; *W:* Roy Boulting, Paul Dehn, James Bernard, Frank Harvey; *C:* Gilbert Taylor; *M:* John Addison.

Seven Deadly Sins 🎬🎬🎬 **1953** A collection of tales concerning destructive emotions and the downfalls they cause. Contains shorts from some of Europe's finest directors (five French and two Italian). Stories and their directors are "Avarice and Anger" (de Filippo); "Sloth" (Dreville); "Lust" (Allegret); "Envy" (Rossellini); "Gluttony" (Rim); "Pride" (Autant-Lara) and "The Eighth Sin" (Lacombe). **127m/B VHS.** *FR IT* Eduardo de Filippo, Isa Miranda, Jacqueline Plessis, Louis de Funes, Paolo Stoppa, Frank Villard, Jean Richard, Francoise Rosay, Jean Debucourt, Louis Seigner; *D:* Eduardo de Filippo, Jean Dreville, Yves Allegret, Roberto Rossellini, Carlo Rim, Claude Autant-Lara, Georges Lacombe.

Seven Deaths in the Cat's Eye 🎬🎬 **1972** A ravenous beast slaughters people in a small Scottish village. This flick reveals a little-known fact about felines. **90m/C VHS, DVD.** *IT* Anton Diffring, Jane Birkin; *D:* Anthony M. Dawson.

Seven Doors to Death 🎬 **1944** Young architect tries to solve a crime to avoid being placed under suspicion. He suspects are six shop owners in this low-budget attempt at a murder mystery. **70m/B VHS, DVD.** Chick Chandler, June Clyde, George Meeker, Gregory Gay, Edgar Dearing; *D:* Elmer Clifton.

7 Faces of Dr. Lao 🎬🎬🎬 **1963** Dr. Lao is the proprietor of a magical circus that changes the lives of the residents of a small western town. Marvelous special effects and makeup (Randall plays seven characters) highlight this charming family film in the Pal tradition. Charles Finney adapted from his novel. **101m/C VHS, DVD.** Tony Randall, Barbara Eden, Arthur O'Connell, Lee Patrick, Noah Beery Jr., John Qualen, John Ericson, Royal Dano; *D:* George Pal; *W:* Charles Beaumont; *C:* Robert J. Bronner; *M:* Leigh Harline.

Seven Girlfriends 🎬🎬 **2000 (R)** Melancholy romantic comedy has thirty-something bachelor Jesse (Daly) so disheartened by his string of failed romances that he seeks out seven ex-girlfriends to find out what went wrong. Good cast. **100m/C VHS, DVD.** Timothy Daly, Laura Leighton, Mimi Rogers, Olivia D'Abo, Jami Gertz, Elizabeth Pena, Melora Hardin, Arye Gross, Katy Selverstone; *D:* Paul Lazarus; *W:* Paul Lazarus, Stephen Gregg; *C:* Don E. Fauntleroy; *M:* Christopher Tyng.

The Seven Hills of Rome 🎬🎬½ **1958** Quiet story of a TV star (Lanza) who follows his girlfriend (Castle) to Rome after a lovers' quarrel, and there falls in love with Allasio. Fantastic music makes up for a weak plot. Based on a story by Giuseppi Amato. *Fantaserci Roma; Seven Hills of Rome; Never Till Now; Earthbound; Come Dance With Me; Lolita; There's Gonna Be a Party Tonight; Italian Calypso; Questa o Quella.* **107m/C VHS.** Mario Lanza, Peggy Castle, Renato Rascel, Marisa Allasio, Clelia Matania, Rosella Como; *D:* Roy Rowland; *W:* Giorgio Prosperi, Art Cohn; *M:* Georgie Stoll.

Seven Hours to Judgment 🎬🎬 **1988 (R)** When the punks who murdered his wife go free, a psychotic man (Leibman) decides to take justice into his own hands. He kidnaps the wife of the judge in charge (Bridges, who also directed) and leads him on a wild

Seven Keys to Baldpate 1917 Early version of the famous stage play by George M. Cohan in which George Washington Magee accepts a challenge that he can finish a novel in 24 hours while staying at the deserted Baldpate Inn. **66m/B VHS.** *C:* Hanana Beer. *M:* ...

Seven Keys to Baldpate 1929 Early talkie version of the film which was based on the famous stage play of the same name by George M. Cohan which follows an author into a deserted Baldpate Inn on a bet that he can't finish a novel in 24 hours while there are after an armored car chase which shows up to steal a Van Gogh that's also inside. During the melee, Jack gets away with the painting but most of his crew are after an armored car escape as a hostage. Now he must rescue his partner, aided or hindered by NATO cop Kelly Anders (Outhwaite). **90m/C DVD, UMD.** *US* Wesley Snipes, Pete Lee-Wilson, Dinoti Opar... *D:* Serge Sonic. *W:* Simon Fellows; *C:* Michael Slovis; *M:* Barry Taylor. VIDEO

The Seven Little Foys 1955 Enjoyable musical biography of Eddie Foy (played ebulliently by Hope) and his famed vaudevillian troupe. Cagney's appearance as George M. Cohan is brief, but long enough for a memorable dance duet with Hope. ♪*Mary's a Grand Old Name; I'm a Yankee Doodle Dandy; I'm the Greatest Father of Them All; Nobody; Chinatown, My Chinatown; My Comedy Ballet; I'm Tired; Chinatown, My Chinatown.* **95m/C VHS, DVD.** Bob Hope, Milly Vitale, George Tobias, Angela (Cark) Clarke, James Cagney; *D:* Melville Shavelson; *W:* Melville Shavelson, Jack Rose.

Seven Magnificent Gladiators 1984 (PG) Seven gladiators team up to save a peaceful Roman village from total annihilation. Seems like a remake of "The Seven Samurai"— see the original instead, please. Ferrigno was "The Incredible Hulk" on TV. **85m/C VHS.** Lou Ferrigno, Sybil Danning, Brad Harris, Dan Vadis, Carla Ferrigno; *D:* Bruno Mattei.

Seven Minutes in Heaven 1986 (PG) Sensitive love story about a 15-year-old girl who invites her platonic male friend to live in her house, and finds it disturbs her boyfriend as these things will. Ever so tasteful (unlike most other teen comedies), with gentle comedy—but forgettable. **90m/C VHS.** Jennifer Connelly, Byron Thames, Maddie Corman, Lauren Holly; *D:* Linda Feferman; *W:* Jane Bernstein.

The Seven-Per-Cent Solution 1976 (PG) Jr. Watson (Duvall) persuades Sherlock Holmes (Nicholson) to meet with Sigmund Freud (Arkin) to cure his cocaine addiction. Holmes and Freud then find themselves teaming up to solve a supposed kidnapping. Adapted by Nicholas Meyer from his own novel. One of the most charming Holmes films; well-cast, intriguing blend of mystery, drama, and fun. Title refers to the solution of cocaine Holmes injects. **113m/C VHS, DVD.** Alan Arkin, Nicol Williamson, Laurence Olivier, Robert Duvall, Vanessa Redgrave, Joel Grey, Samantha Eggar, Jeremy Kemp Charles Gray, Regine; *D:* Herbert Ross; *W:* Nicholas Meyer. *C:* Oswald Morris; *M:* John Addison.

Seven Samurai ♦♦♦♦ 1954 Kurosawa's masterpiece, set in 16th-century Japan. A small farming village, beset by marauding bandits, hires seven professional soldiers to rid itself of the scourge. Wanna watch a samurai movie? This is the one. Sweeping, complex human drama with all the ingredients: action, suspense, comedy. Available in several versions of varying length, all long—and all too short. Splendid acting. In Japanese with English subtitles. **204m/B VHS, DVD.** *JP* Toshiro Mifune, Takashi Shimura, Yoshio Inaba, Kumnori Kodo, Isao 'Ko' Kimura, Seiji Miraguchi, Minoru Chiaki, Daisuke Kato, Bokuzen Hidari, Kamaari (Keita) Fujiwara, Yoshio Kosugi, Yoshio Tsuchiya, Jun Tatara, Sojin, Kichijiro Ueda, Jun

Seven Seconds ♦ 2005 (R) Snipes career isn't helped by this confusing and lackluster actioner. Professional thief Jack Tolliver (Snipes) and his crew are after an armored car escape as a hostage. Now he must rescue his partner, aided or hindered by NATO cop Kelly Anders (Outhwaite). **90m/C DVD, UMD. Blu-Ray Disc.** Brad Pitt, David Thewis, B.D. Wong, Ingeborga Dapkounaite, Jean-Jacques Arnaud; *D:* Jean-Jacques Annaud; *W:* Becky Johnston; *C:* Robert Fraisse; *M:* John Williams.

Seven Sinners 1940 A South Seas cabaret singer (Dietrich) attracts sailors like flies, resulting in bar brawls, romance, and intrigue. Manly sailor Wayne falls for her. A good-natured, standard Hollywood adventure. Well cast; performed and directed with gusto. **83m/B VHS.** Marlene Dietrich, John Wayne, Albert Dekker, Broderick Crawford, Mischa Auer, Billy Gilbert, Oscar Homolka; *D:* Tay Garnett; *W:* John Meehan, Harry Tugend; *C:* Rudolph Mate; *M:* Frank Skinner.

Seven Thieves 1960 *Cafe al the winds up going to high school with lookalike granddaughter Sydney (Tia Mowry) and has a second chance with the teen-aged Gene. Meanwhile, Willie is searching for an antidote since his formula has some potentially serious flaws. That the story is silly isn't the problem—it's also incoherent.* **97m/C VHS, DVD.** Tia Mowry, Tamara Mowry, Hope Clarke, Robert Hooks; *D:* Jeff Byrd; *W:* Stewart St. John; *C:* John Tarver; *M:* Christopher Franke, Shawn Stockman. CABLE.

1776 ♦♦♦ 1972 (G) Musical comedy about America's first Continental Congress. The delegates battle the English and each other trying to establish a set of laws and the Declaration of Independence. Adapted from the Broadway hit with many members of the original cast. ♪*The Lees of Old Virginia; He Plays the Violin; But, Mr. Adams; Sit Down John; Till Then; Piddle, Twiddle and Resolve; Yours, Yours, Yours; Mama Look Sharp; The Egg.* **141m/C VHS, DVD.** William Daniels, Howard da Silva, Ken Howard, Donald Madden, Blythe Danner, Ronald Holgate, Virginia Vestoff, Stephen Nathan, Ralston Hill; *D:* Peter H. Hunt; *C:* Harry Stradling Jr.

The Seventeenth Bride ♦♦ 1984 Set in a Czechoslovakian town; a strong-willed young woman is slowly destroyed by the insanity of war and racism. **92m/C VHS, DVD.** Lisa Hartman Black, Rosemary Leach; *D:* Ismeli Nadav Levitan.

Seventh Cavalry ♦♦½ 1956 A somewhat different look at Custer's defeat at the Little Big Horn. A soldier who was branded a coward for not taking part in the festivities tries to assuage his guilt by heading up the burial detail. The muddled ending tries to tell us that the Indians were afraid of Custer's horse. **75m/C VHS, DVD.** Randolph Scott, Barbara Hale, Jay C. Flippen, Jeanette Nolan, Frank Faylen, Leo Gordon, Denver Pyle, Harry Carey Jr., Michael Pate, Donald Curtis, Frank Wilcox, Pat Hogan, Russell Hicks *D:* Joseph H. Lewis; *C:* Ray Rennahan.

The Seventh Coin ♦♦½ 1992 (PG-13) The legendary King Herod minted seven coins bearing this image which have become coin collector Emil Saber's (O'Toole) obsession. (He's a homicidal lunatic who thinks he's the reincarnation of Herod anyway.) Saber has found six of the coins but the seventh has fallen into the unsuspecting hands of Salim (Chowdhry), a pickpocket who has actually snatched it from the equally unsuspecting Ronnie (Powers), an American teenager visiting Jerusalem (good local color). The two become allies when Saber comes after them. They're an appealing couple; O'Toole camps it up shamelessly; and the movie is easygoing escapism. **92m/C VHS.** Alexandra Powers, Navin Chowdhry, Peter O'Toole, John Rhys-Davies, Ally Walker; *D:* Dror Soref; *W:* Michael Lewis, Dror Soref; *C:* Avi (Avraham) Karpik.

The 7th Commandment ♦♦½ 1961 Unlikely melodrama about a man afflicted with amnesia following an auto accident. He becomes a successful evangelist only to be blackmailed by an old girlfriend. Don't you just hate when that happens? **82m/B VHS.** Jonathan Kidd, Lynn Statten.

Seventeen Again ♦♦ 2000 Willie (Tahj Mowry) is doing a science project involving an anti-aging formula that accidentally gets mixed into some soap that his divorced grandparents, Cat (Clarke) and Gene (Hooks), wind up using. This turns them both in 17-year-olds (Tamara Mowry as Cat and Taylor as Gene), Cat

The Seventeenth Bride ♦♦

The Seventh Dawn ♦♦ 1964 Clichéd adventure romance set in Malaysia in 1945. Guerrilla fighter Ferris (Holden) decides to become a landowner and stay on with mistress Dhana (Capucine) after the war. Ferris's old buddy Ng (Tamba) takes off to Moscow and returns indoctrinated and determined to convert the country to Communism. Ng and his fighters exclude Ferris from their attacks until British governor Trumphrey (Goodliffe) accuses Dhana of treason and threatens to execute her. So Ferris has to get Ng or risk Dhana. The young York plays Candace, the governor's daughter who has a crush on Ferris and helps him out. Based on the novel "The Durian Tree" by Michael Keon. **123m/C VHS.** *GB US* William Holden, Capucine, Susannah York, Tetsuro Tamba, Michael Goodliffe, Allan Cuthbertson, Maurice Denham, Beulah Quo; *D:* Lewis Gilbert; *W:* Karl Tunberg; *C:* Frederick A. (Freddie) Young; *M:* Riz Ortolani.

The Seventh Floor ♦♦ 1993 (R) Kate's computer-controlled apartment becomes a psycho takes charge of the system. **99m/C VHS, DVD, AU** Brooke Shields, Masaya Kato, Craig Pearce, Linda Cropper; *D:* Ian Barry.

Seventh Heaven ♦♦ 1998 Married Mathilde (Kiberlain) is sunk in a serious depression that only begins to lessen when she meets a mysterious doctor (Berléand) who specializes in hypnosis and alternative medicine. He tells her that seven levels of heaven—the last a sort of self-fulfilled bliss. After a successful session with the doctor, Mathilde is suddenly sexually and emotionally rejuvenated—much to the consternation of her (til then) dominating spouse, Nico (Lindon). The more Mathilde takes control, the less Nico is able to cope with their role reversals and in desperation adopts some Bergman's master-piece. Von Sydow is stunning as the knight. In Swedish with English subtitles. **96m/B VHS, DVD.** *SW* Gunnar Bjornstrand, Max Von Sydow, Bibi Andersson, Bengt Ekerot, Nils Poppe, Gunnel Lindblom; *D:* Ingmar Bergman; *W:* Ingmar Bergman. Cannes '57: Grand Jury Prize.

The Seventh Seal As the plague sweeps through Europe a weary knight convinces "death" to play one game of chess with him. If the knight wins, he and his wife will be spared. The game leads to a discussion of religion and the existence of God. Considered by some Bergman's masterpiece. French with subtitles. **91m/C VHS, DVD, FR** Sandrine Kiberlain, Vincent Lindon, François Berléand; *D:* Benoit Jacquot; *W:* Benoit Jacquot, Jerome Beaujour; *C:* Romain Winding.

The Seventh Sign ♦♦ 1988 (R) A pregnant woman realizes that the mysterious stranger boarding in her house and her unborn child. Tries hard, but it's difficult to get involved in the supernatural goings-on. **105m/C VHS, DVD.** Demi Moore, Jurgen Prochnow, Michael Biehn, John Heard, Peter Friedman, Manny Jacobs, John Taylor, Lee Garlington, Akosua Busia; *D:* Carl Schultz; *W:* W. W. Wicket; *C:* Juan Ruiz-Anchia; *M:* Jack Nitzsche.

The Seventh Stream ♦♦½ 2001 Filmed on location in the west of Ireland and based on the Celtic legend of the selkies. Owen Quinn (Glenn) is a fisherman whose life is empty since the death of his wife. Then he comes to the rescue of Mairead (Burrows), a beautiful and myste-

Seven Year Itch ♦♦½ 1955 Classic, sexy Monroe comedy. Stunning blonde model (who else?) moves upstairs just as happily married guy Ewell's wife leaves for a long vacation. Under-standably, he gets itchy. Monroe's famous blown skirt scene is here, as well as funny situations and appealing performances. **105m/C VHS, DVD.** Marilyn Monroe Tom Ewell, Evelyn Keyes, Sonny Tufts, Victor Moore, Doro Merande, Robert Strauss, Oscar Homolka, Carolyn Jones; *D:* Billy Wilder; *W:* Billy Wilder, George Axelrod. *C:* Milton Krasner; *M:* Alfred Newman. Golden Globes '56: Actor—Mus./Comedy (Ewell).

Seven Years Bad Luck ♦♦♦ 1921 French comic Linder is at the proverbial seven years' bad luck all in one day (!) after he breaks a mirror. Original and quite funny; full of fetching sophisticated sight gags. Silent with music score. **67m/B VHS.** Max Linder, Thelma Percy, Alta Allen, Betty Peterson; *D:* Max Linder; *C:* Charles Van Enger.

Seven Years in Tibet ♦♦½ 1997 (PG-13) Big budget epic of a cold-hearted Austrian mountaineer Heinrich Harrer (Pitt) who becomes a WWII POW in a British internment camp in India. When he and fellow climber Peter Aufschnaiter (Thewlis) escape, they travel to Tibet where Harrer bonds with and becomes a tutor to the young Dalai Lama (Wangchuk). Sweeping vistas and snowcapped mountain scenery does little to aid the sluggish and unfocused narrative, which tries to cover too many subplots and doesn't really get going until halfway through. Pitt's screen presence is forceful but his performance capable but ham-pered by a somewhat labored Austrian accent. Based on Harrer's memoirs, film ran into numerous problems, including the revelation that Harrer had been a Nazi in the '30s, sensitivity to the storyline, and China's refusal to allow filming. Director Annaud wound up substituting the Argentine Andes for the Himalayas. **131m/C VHS, DVD. Blu-Ray Disc.** Brad Pitt, David Thewis, B.D. Wong, Ingeborga Dapkounaite; *D:* Jean-Jacques Annaud; *W:* Becky Johnston; *C:* Robert Fraisse; *M:* John Williams.

The Seven-Ups ♦♦½ 1973 (PG) An elite group of New York City detectives seeks to avenge the killing of a colleague and to bust crooks whose felonies are punishable by jail terms of seven years or more. Unoriginal premise portends ill; plotless cop action flick full of car chases. Schneider tries hard. Directed by the producer of "The French Connection." **109m/C VHS, DVD.** Roy Scheider, Tony LoBianco, Larry Haines, Jerry Leon; *D:* Philip D'Antoni.

The Seventh Cross ♦♦♦ 1944 Tracy stars as one of seven men who escape from a German concentration camp. When all is discovered they're gone, the commandant nails seven crosses to several trees, intending them for the seven escapees. Watch for Tandy ("Driving Miss Daisy") in her first screen appearance. Effective war-time drama. From the novel by Anna Seghers. **110m/B VHS.** Spencer Tracy, Signe Hasso, Hume Cronyn, Jessica Tandy, Ray Collins, Alexander Granach, George Macready, Steven Geray, Karen Verne, George Zucco, Katherine Locke, Paul Guilfoyle, Kurt Katch, Konstantin Shayne, John Wengraf, Elly Malyan; *D:* Fred Zinnemann; *W:* Helen Deutsch; *C:* Karl Freund; *M:* Roy Webb.

Sex Crimes 🦴🦴 **1992** A tough female judge is brutally raped and she keeps the attack a secret. However, she does ask a friendly police detective to teach her how to use a gun. He's suspicious of her reasons and decides to trail her as she sets out for revenge on her attacker. Predictable actioner. **90m/C VHS, DVD.** Jeffery Osterhage, Maria Richwine, Fernando Garzon, Craig Alan, Grace Morley; **D:** David Garcia.

Sex, Drugs, and Rock-n-Roll woof! **1984** Several girls frequent a rock club looking for all the action they can get their hands on. **90m/C VHS.** Jeanne Silver, Sharon Kane, Tish Ambrose, Josey Duval.

Sex, Drugs, Rock & Roll: Eric Bogosian 🦴🦴 **1991 (R)** Bogosian's 1990 concert performance, taped live at the Wilur Theatre in Boston, exhibits the electricity and finely nuanced characters for which he is justly famous. The characters share a depressingly negative side, however, which keeps this film from being strictly belly-laugh territory. **96m/C VHS.** Eric Bogosian; **D:** John McNaughton; **W:** Eric Bogosian.

Sex is Comedy 🦴🦴 **2002** Breillat's plot is a fictionalized re-creation of her own difficulties filming the crucial sex scene between a 15-year-old girl (Mesquida, reprising her role) and her older boyfriend (Colin) for her 2001 film "Fat Girl." Breillat's stand-in as director is the neurotic and demanding Jeanne (Parrillaud), whose troubles include lousy weather, leads who can't stand each other, and a problematic prosthetic penis. Jeanne irritates her actors and crew (and they her) and only finds a sympathetic ally in her smitten assistant Leo (Wanninger). Actors are always quick to say that filming sex scenes is not erotic and here's the proof. French with subtitles. **92m/C DVD.** Anne Parillaud, Ashley Wanninger, Dominique Colladant; **D:** Catherine Breillat; **W:** Catherine Breillat; **C:** Laurent Machuel.

Sex Is Crazy 🦴 **1979** A melange from Italian horror director Franco containing some epic, some horror, some sex, some sitcom, and some documentary. Little green aliens touch down and impregnate earth women in one skit. In another, a gambler's girlfriend demands two thugs ravage her for the sheer sexual thrill. And in a third, a severed hand commands a heroine to martyr herself to the great god Cucutat. Spanish with English subtitles. **81m/C VHS. SP** Lina Romay; Anthony (Jose, J. Antonio, J.A.) Mayans, Tony Skios; **D:** Jess (Jesus) Franco.

sex, lies and videotape 🦴🦴🦴 **1989 (R)** Acclaimed, popular independent film by first-timer Soderbergh, detailing the complex relations among a childless married couple, the wife's adulterous sister, and a mysterious college friend of the husband's obsessed with videotaping women as they talk about their sex lives. Heavily awarded, including first prize at Cannes. Confidently uses much (too much?) dialogue and slow (too slow?) pace. **101m/C VHS, DVD.** James Spader, Andie MacDowell, Peter Gallagher, Laura San Giacomo, Ron Vawter, Steven Brill; **D:** Steven Soderbergh; **W:** Steven Soderbergh; **C:** Walt Lloyd; **M:** Cliff Martinez. Cannes '89: Actor (Spader), Film; Ind. Spirit '90: Actress (MacDowell), Director (Soderbergh), Film, Support. Actress (San Giacomo); L.A. Film Critics '89: Actress (MacDowell), Natl. Film Reg. '06; Sundance '89: Aud. Award.

Sex, Love and Cold Hard Cash 🦴🦴½ **1993 (PG-13)** Sarah (Williams) is a high-priced hooker whose life savings ($20 million in stocks and bonds) have just been stolen. She hires an ex-con (Denison) to help recover the money on the wrong side of some Mob trouble as well. Enough twists to keep a viewer interested as well as the prerequisite amount of shootings and chase scenes. **86m/C VHS.** JoBeth Williams, Anthony John (Tony) Denison, Joel Swetow, Henry Brown, Bradford English, Robert Forster, Eric Pierpoint, Richard Sarafian, Tobin Bell; **D:** Harry S. Longstreet; **W:** Harry S. Longstreet; **C:** Rob Draper; **M:** John Keane.

Sex and the City: The Movie 🦴🦴🦴 **2008** The HBO show ended in 2004 and what's been happening to our gals? Happily married to Harry (Handler), adoptive mom Charlotte (Davis) finds out she's preggers; on the other hand, marrieds Miranda (Nixon) and Steve (Eigenberg) are troubled in Brooklyn with infidelity issues; sex bomb Samantha (Cattrall), who now lives in L.A., may not have stopped looking but maybe she's stopped touching since younger hottie Smith (Lewis) is still in the picture; and our beloved narrator Carrie Bradshaw (Parker) is about to marry Big (Noth) while wearing a a really ugly wedding ensemble. But will our perennial Manhattan single actually tie the knot? Not yet reviewed. **?m/C** Sarah Jessica Parker, Kim Cattrall, Kristen Davis, Cynthia Nixon, Christopher Noth, David Eigenberg, Jason Lewis, Evan Handler, Jennifer Hudson, Willie Garson, Mario Cantone, Lynn Cohen; **D:** Michael Patrick King; **W:** Michael Patrick King; **C:** John Thomas; **M:** Aaron Zigman.

Sex and the College Girl 🦴 **1964** Folks talk about their relationship problems while vacationing in Puerto Rico. Tame talkfest providing Grodin with his first role. Included as part of Joe Bob Brigg's "Sleaziest Movies in the History of the World" series, probably just for the title. **100m/C VHS.** Charles Grodin, Richard Arlen, Luana Anders; **D:** Joseph Adler.

Sex and the Other Man 🦴🦴 *Captive* **1995 (R)** Bill's (Eldard) having this little impotence problem, which girlfriend Jessica (Wuhrer) naturally finds frustrating. So much so that she succumbs to the charms of her married boss, Arthur (Tucci). But when Bill catches them together in bed, his reaction is something none of them expected. Based on the play "Captive" by Paul Weitz. **89m/C VHS, DVD.** Ron Eldard, Kari Slovin, Stanley Tucci; **D:** Karl Slovin; **W:** Karl Slovin; **C:** Frank Prinzi; **M:** Anton Sanko.

Sex and the Single Girl 🦴🦴½ **1964** Curtis is a reporter for a trashy magazine who intends to write an expose on "The International Institute of Advanced Marital and Pre-Marital Studies," an organization run by Wood. Curtis poses as a man having marital trouble, using his neighbor's name and marital problems, in order to get close to Wood. Things get sticky when Wood wants to meet Curtis' wife and three women show up claiming to be her. This confusing but amusing tale twists and turns until it reaches a happy ending. Loosely based on the book by Helen Gurley Brown. **114m/C VHS.** Tony Curtis, Natalie Wood, Henry Fonda, Lauren Bacall, Mel Ferrer, Fran Jeffries, Leslie Parrish, Edward Everett Horton, Larry Storch, Count Basie; **D:** Richard Quine; **W:** David R. Schwartz; **C:** Charles B(ryant) Lang Jr.; **M:** Neal Hefti.

Sex and the Single Parent 🦴🦴½ **1982** St. James and Farrell, both divorced, both with kids, have a relationship. Complications set in—just how does one be a single parent and have a fulfilling sex life in this day and age? **98m/C VHS.** Susan St. James, Mike Farrell, Dori Brenner, Warren Berlinger, Julie Sommars, Barbara Rhoades; **D:** Jackie Cooper. TV

Sex and Zen 🦴🦴 **1993** Softcore Hong Kong sex film based on the 17th century novel "Prayer Mat for the Flesh" by Li Yu. Mei Yang (Yip) gets married to beautiful Yuk Heung (Ng) but intends to commit adultery as often as possible. There's lots of bizarre sexual practices and Yuk ends up in a brothel while Mei finds his decadent lifestyle not quite as entertaining as he imagined. Cantonese with subtitles or dubbed. **99m/C VHS, DVD. HK** Lawrence Ng, Amy Yip, Kent Cheng, Isabella Chow, Lo Lieh, Carrie Ng; **D:** Michael Mak; **W:** Lee Ying Kit; **C:** Peter Ngor; **M:** Chan Wing Leung.

---

rious woman with strong ties to the sea. Owen opens his heart and home to her but will Mairead vanish as easily as she appeared? **98m/C VHS, DVD.** Scott Glenn, Saffron Burrows, John Lynch, Fiona Shaw, Eamon Morrissey; **D:** John Gray; **W:** John Gray; **C:** Seamus Deasy; **M:** Ernest Troost. TV

The Seventh Veil 🦴🦴🦴½ **1946** A concert pianist loses the use of her hands in a fire, and with it her desire to live. Through the help of her friends and a hypnotizing doctor, she regains her love for life. Superb, dark psycho-drama. Todd as the pianist and Mason as her guardian are both unforgettable. Wonderful music and staging. **91m/B VHS. GB** James Mason, Ann Todd, Herbert Lom, Hugh McDermott, Albert Lieven; **D:** Compton Bennett. Oscars '46: Orig. Screenplay.

The Seventh Victim 🦴🦴🦴 **1943** Another Val Lewton-produced low-budget exercise in shadowy suggestion, dealing with a woman searching for her lost sister, who'd gotten involved with Satanists. The Hays Office's squeamishness regarding subject matter makes the film's action a bit cloudy but it remains truly eerie. **71m/B VHS, DVD.** Kim Hunter, Tom Conway, Jean Brooks, Hugh Beaumont, Erford Gage, Isabel Jewell, Evelyn Brent; **D:** Mark Robson; **W:** "Blackie" O'Neal.

The Seventh Voyage of Sinbad 🦴🦴🦴 **1958 (G)** Sinbad seeks to restore his fiancee from the midget size to which an evil magician (Thatcher) has reduced her. Ray Harryhausen works his animation magic around a well-developed plot and engaging performances by the real actors. Great score and fun, fast-moving. **94m/C VHS, DVD.** Kerwin Mathews, Kathryn Grant, Torin Thatcher, Richard Eyer, Alec Mango, Danny Green, Harold Kasket, Alfred Brown; **D:** Nathan "Jerry" Juran; **W:** Kenneth Kolb; **C:** Wilkie Cooper; **M:** Bernard Herrmann.

The '70s 🦴🦴½ **2000** Follows "The '60s" miniseries with the same superficial exploration of the decade seen through the eyes of four friends and lots of music. (Disco rules!) Dexter (Torry), Byron (Rowe), Eileen (Shaw), and Christine (Smart) are all at Kent State on that fateful day when the National Guard and their lives continue through numerous hot-button issues, including Watergate, feminism, drugs, sex, the Black Panthers, the environment, and religious cults. Cast is surprisingly strong. **170m/C VHS, DVD.** Brad Rowe, Guy Torry, Vinessa Shaw, Amy Smart, Kathryn Harrold, Graham Beckel, Tina Lifford, Chandra West, Robert Joy, Jeanetta Arnette, Michael Easton, Peggy Lipton; **D:** Peter Werner; **W:** Mitch Brian, Kevin Willmott; **C:** Neil Roach; **M:** Peter Manning Robinson. TV

Severance 🦴🦴 **1988** An ex-pilot attempts to save his daughter from the world of drugs and violence. **93m/C VHS.** Lou Liotta, Lisa Nicole Wolpe, Linda Christian-Jones; **D:** David Max Steinberg.

Severance 🦴🦴 **2006 (R)** In a team-building exercise, the sales division of an international arms manufacturer heads for a weekend retreat at a desolate chalet located in a Hungarian forest. But it seems the woods are filled with booby-traps and crazed commandos determined to see them all dead. An extreme example of how team spirit and cooperation will save your life (not to mention your job). **96m/C DVD. GB** Tim (McInnerny) McInnery, Laura Harris, Toby Stephens, Danny Dyer, Claudie Blakley, Andy Nyman, Babou Ceesay; **D:** Chris Smith; **W:** Chris Smith, James Moran; **C:** Ed Wild; **M:** Christian Henson.

The Severed Arm woof! **1973 (R)** Trapped in a cave, five men are compelled to cut off the arm of a companion in order to ward off starvation. Then as luck would have it, they're rescued. Years later, one by one they meet a bloody demise. Is it the one-armed man? **89m/C VHS, DVD.** Deborah Walley, Marvin Kaplan, Paul Carr, John Crawford, David Cannon; **D:** Thomas Alderman.

Severed Ties 🦴½ **1992 (R)** Brilliant genetic scientist experiments with human limb regeneration in order to re-grow his accidentally severed arm. His strange mixture of lizard and serial-killer genes results in a repulsive reptilian limb with a nasty habit of slithering out of his shoulder. His mother discovers his experiments and tries to sell his discovery to the Nazis but her son escapes into a bizarre subterranean society and vows revenge. So bad it's just bad. **95m/C VHS.** Billy Morrissette, Elke Sommer, Oliver Reed, Garrett Morris; **D:** Damon Santostefano.

Sex 🦴🦴🦴 **1920** Interesting dated relic. Morality play about a Broadway star who uses her charms to destroy a marriage only to dump her lover for richer prospects. The businessman she lands then shamelessly betrays her. What a title, especially for its time! **87m/B VHS.** Adrienne Renault, Louise Glaum, Irving Cummings, Peggy Pearce, Myrtle Stedman; **D:** Fred Niblo.

Sex Adventures of the Three Musketeers woof! **1971** Soft-core spoof of the Dumas classic. Dubbed. **79m/C VHS. GE** Inga Steeger, Achim Hammer, Peter Graf, Jurg Coray; **D:** Erwin C. Dietrich; **W:** Erwin C. Dietrich; **C:** Peter Baumgartner; **M:** Walter Baumgartner.

Sex and Breakfast 🦴½ **2007 (R)** Having couples troubles, James (Culkin) and Heather (Dziena) and Ellis (Becker) and Renee (Dushku) experiment with group sex while trying to figure out what makes a relationship successful. But jealousy, confusion, and insecurity make things as difficult as you might expect. Not as sexual as you might think though, despite the title and rating. **81m/C DVD.** Macaulay Culkin, Alexis Dziena, Kuno Becker, Eliza Dushku, Joanna Miles, Eric Lively, Tracie Thoms, Jaime Ray Newman; **D:** Miles Brandman; **W:** Miles Brandman; **C:** Mark Schwartzband.

Sex and Buttered Popcorn 🦴🦴🦴 **1991 (R)** Stylish and entertaining documentary of the Hollywood sexploitation moguls, and their films, from the 1920s through the 1950s. These films shamelessly catered to audience's prurient interests, but typically delivered saccharin-coated morality messages and stock footage of routine baby births or the horrible effects of sexually transmitted diseases. Hosted by Ned Beatty, and featuring clips from the actual films, plus an interview with the widow of Kroger Babb, the most notorious of the exploiteers. A real hoot. **70m/C VHS, DVD.** David Friedman; **D:** Sam Harrison.

Sex and Lucia 🦴🦴 *Lucia y el Sexo* **2001** Sexually explicit, if confusing, story finds waitress Lucia (Vega) learning that her ex-boyfriend, writer Lorenzo (Ulloa), has supposedly died. So, she decides to revisit the island where they first met. Lucia meets scuba-diver Carlos (Freire) who lives with Elena (Nimri), who has ties to Lorenzo that Lucia never suspected. Elena's brother, Pepe (Camara), happens to be Lorenzo's best friend and introduces nanny Belen (Anaya) into the menage and it all just kinda goes 'round and 'round. Spanish with subtitles. **128m/C DVD. SP** Paz Vega, Tristan Ulloa, Najwa Nimri, Daniel Freire, Elena Anaya, Silvia Llanos, Javier Camara; **D:** Julio Medem; **W:** Julio Medem; **C:** Kiko de la Rica; **M:** Alberto Iglesias.

Sex & Mrs. X 🦴🦴 **2000** New York magazine journalist Joanna Scott (Hamilton) thought her marriage was as successful as her career—until husband Dale (Bick) leaves her for a younger woman. So Joanna is happy to go to Paris to interview the notorious Madame Simone (Bisset), but she winds up learning just as much about herself and how to face her new future. **91m/C VHS, DVD.** Linda Hamilton, Jacqueline Bisset, Paolo Seganti, Stewart Bick, Peter MacNeill, Tracy Bregman, Daniel Pilon; **D:** Arthur Allan Seidelman; **W:** Elisa Bell; **C:** Don E. Fauntleroy; **M:** Joseph Conlan. CABLE

The Sex Machine Woof! *Conviene far Bene l'Amore* 1975 (R) In the year 2037, a scientist finds two of the world's greatest lovers and unites them so he can transform their reciprocating motion into electricity. It worked on paper, Italian with subtitles. **80m/C VHS.** *I'T* Agostina Belli, Eleonora Giorgi, Christian de Sica, Gigi Proietti, Adriana Asti; *D:* Pasquale Festa Campanile; *W:* Pasquale Festa Campanile; *C:* Franco Di Giacomo; *M:* Fred Borgusto.

Sex with a Smile ♂ 1976 (R) Five slapstick episodes by five different directors with lots of sexual satire pointed at religion and politics in Italy. Don't know much about Italy? Then you'll be left out of the joke here. And really, only one episode is funny anyway (the one with Feldman of "Young Frankenstein" fame). **100m/C VHS.** *I'T* Marty Feldman, Edwige Fenech, Alex Marino, Enrico Monterano, Giovanna Ralli; *D:* Sergio Martino.

Sexpot ♂ 1988 (R) A voluptuous woman's rich husband mysteriously keep dying, but not before they leave their fortunes to her. **55m/C VHS.** Ruth (Coreen) Collins, Troy Donahue, Joyce Lyons, Gregory Patrick, Frank Stewart, Jack Carter; *D:* Chuck Vincent.

Sextette Woof! 1978 (PG) Lavish film about an elderly star who is constantly interrupted by former spouses and well-wishers while on a honeymoon with her sixth husband. West unwisely came out of retirement for this last film role, based on her own play. Exquisitely embarrassing to watch. Interesting cast. **91m/C VHS, DVD.** Mae West, Timothy Dalton, Ringo Starr, George Hamilton, Dom DeLuise, Tony Curtis, Alice Cooper, Keith Moon, George Raft, Rona Barrett, Walter Baker; *C:* James A. Crabe; *M:* Artie Butler.

Sexton Blake and the Hooded Terror ♂♂ 1938 Sexton Blake, a British private detective a la Holmes, is pitted against "The Snake," a master criminal, and his gang over "The Hooded Terror," who seduced and robbed more than 40 women. This con artist transformed himself into whatever kind of Mr. Right his victim needed—until he picked on the wrong woman. **70m/B VHS. GB** Tod Slaughter, Greta Gynt, George Curzzn; *D:* George King.

Sexual Intent ♂♂ 1994 (R) Based on the true story of pathological liar John Valsome, known as "the Sweetheart Scammer," who seduced and robbed women. **88m/C VHS.** *D:* Kurt MacCarley; *W:* Kurt MacCarley.

The Sexual Life of the Belgians ♂½ *La Vie Sexuelle des Belges* 1994 Autobiographical comedy of sexual manners covering 1950 to 1978. Jan Bucquoy (Compere) grows up with a...

The Sex Monster ♂♂ 1999 (R) Unhappy husband convinces reluctant wife to get involved in a menage-a-trois. Only she's more turned on by the other woman than he is. Not very funny for a comedy, and not very sexy for a flick with the word "sex" in the title. Binder does Woody Allen without the humor, but then, so does Woody lately. **97m/C VHS, DVD.** Mike Binder, Mariel Hemingway, Renee Humphrey, Taylor Nichols, Missy (Melissa) Crider, Stephen Baldwin; *D:* Mike Binder; *W:* Mike Binder; *C:* Keith L. Smith.

Sex Through a Window ♂ *Extreme Close-Up* 1972 (R) TV reporter becomes an obsessive voyeur after filing a report on high tech surveillance equipment. Flimsy premise is a yucky, lame excuse to show skin. **81m/C VHS.** James McMullan, James A. Watson Jr., Kate Woodville, Barbara Bynes, Al Checco, Antony Carbone; *D:* Jeannot Szwarc; *W:* Michael Crichton.

Sex on the Run Woof! *Casanova and Co.; Some Like It Cool* 1978 (R) Lovestarved wife of an oil-rich sheik, stimulated by the idea of having Casanova for her lover, teases her master into delivering him, but Casanova finds peace in the arms of three convent lovelies. Disgusting, amateurish, and offensive. **88m/C VHS, DVD.** Tony Curtis, Marisa Berenson, Britt Ekland; *D:* Francois Legrand.

Sexual Malice ♂♂ 1993 (R) Another erotic thriller finds a bored wife involved in an obsessive affair with a mystery man who has murder on his mind. Also available in an unrated version. **96m/C VHS, DVD.** Diana Barton, John Laughlin, Chad McQueen, Edward Albert, Don Swayze, Kathy Shower, Samantha (Sam) Phillips; *D:* Jag Mundhra; *W:* Carl Austin; *C:* James Mathers.

Sexual Response ♂♂ 1992 (R) Eve, a radio talk show "sexologist," is ironically unhappy in her marriage but scoffs at her producer's suggestion of an affair. That is until she meets a brash sculptor and they begin a torrid, and increasingly obsessive, romance. Her lover suggests that her husband have an "accident" with his hurting rifle, but Eve refuses and throws him out. The sculptor, however, breaks into the husband's loft to steal the rifle and finds some news clippings about the man's past that could ruin the lives of many. Little more than an excuse for torrid love scenes. Also available in an unrated version. **87m/C VHS.** Shannon Tweed, Catherine Oxenberg, Vernon Wells, Emile Levisetti; *D:* Yaky Yosha.

Sexual Roulette ♂ 1996 (R) A distaff and decidedly raunchier "Indecent Proposal." Jed and Sally wind up in monetary trouble and get in deeper by trying to recoup their loses (and losing bigtime) in a Vegas horse race. Then a rich blonde with some kinky preferences makes Jed an offer he can't afford to refuse. The unrated version is six minutes longer. **96m/C VHS, DVD.** Tane McClure, Tim Abell, Gabriella Hall, Richard Gabai, Myles O'Brien, G. Gordon Baer; *D:* Gary Graver; *W:* Sean McGinley; *C:* Gary Graver.

Sexus ♂½ *Nuit la Plus Longue; Enfer Dans la Peau* 1964 Beautiful Virginia (de Solen) is kidnapped by Blackie (Tissier) and his cohorts and held in an abandoned farmhouse until her father pays her ransom. In the meantime, he looks provoke both jealousy and passion. French with subtitles. **88m/B VHS.** *Fr* Willy Braque, Virginia De Solen, Yves Duffaut, Anna Jasse, Alain Tissier; *D:* Jose Benazeraf; *W:* Jose Benazeraf; *C:* Alain Derobe; *M:* Chet Baker.

Sexy Beast ♂♂½ 2000 (R) This British suspense/thriller is not only tense and caustically funny at times, it also has the guy who played Gandhi as a snarling, bad-ass gangster. Ben Kingsley plays Logan, who's sent to southern Spain to lure retired gangster "Gal" Dove (Winstone) back to England for "one last job." When Gal refuses, Logan threatens non-non-violence on Gal's wife Deedee (Redman) and pals Aitch (Kendall, in his last role) and Jackie (White). Gal is forced into accepting after some unfortunate events, and the plot, masterminded by Logan's boss Teddy (McShane), is carried out. After the caper is done, however, Gal will have a harder time relaxing poolside with the reminders of the "sexy beast" of his criminal life all too close. Kingsley dominates the movie as the profanity-spewing Logan, but the rest of the cast also turn in outstanding performances. **88m/C VHS, DVD. GB** Ray Winstone, Ben Kingsley, Ian McShane, Amanda Redman, James Fox, Robert Atiko, Julianne White, Cavan Kendall, Alvaro Monje; *D:* Jonathan Glazer; *W:* Louis Mellis, David Scinto; *C:* Ivan Bird; *M:* Roque Banos. Broadcast Film Critics '02: Support. Actor (Kingsley).

S.F.W. ♂♂ 1994 (R) Get out your cliche-o-meter for another look at Generation X. Suburban teen Cliff Spab (Dorff) unwillingly becomes a media sensation during a terrorist hostage crisis at a convenience store. The phrasemaking teen's apathetic words are adopted by his peers just as he realizes that there is something...

---

grim mother and immediately takes an interest in sex and beautiful women, which only heightens as he winds up in Brussels during the hedonistic '60s. He has a short, disastrous marriage, lots of affairs, no: much sense, and a mocking disregard for Belgian provincialism. French with subtitles. **80m/C VHS. BE** Jean-Henri Compere, Isabella Legros, Sophie Schneider, Michele Shor; *D:* Jan Bucquoy; *W:* Jan Bucquoy; *C:* Miche Baudour.

Shack Out on 101 ♂♂♂ 1955. A waitress (Moore) in an isolated cafe on a busy highway notices suspicious doings among her customers. What could they be up to? Communist subversion, of course. Of-its-era anti-pinko propoganda, but with a twist: Moore uncovers commie plots, pleases her customers, and fends off unwelcome lecherous advances all in 80 minutes, on a single set! **80m/B VHS.** Lee Marvin, Terry Moore, Keenan Wynn, Frank Lovejoy, Whit Bissell, Jess Barker, Donald Murphy, Frank De Kova, Len Lesser, Fred Gabourie; *D:* Edward Dein; *W:* Edward Dein, Mildred Dein; *C:* Floyd Crosby; *M:* Paul Dunlap, Louis Prima.

Shackleton ♂♂♂ 2002 Stirring adventure about the ill-fated expedition of Sir Ernest Shackleton (Branagh) to Antarctica in 1914. His ship, the Endurance, gets trapped in ice and eventually sinks, leaving Shackleton and his crew of 27 to set up camp on a nearby island. Shackleton and two of the crew set out for help to a whaling station on South Georgia Island—an unbelievably difficult journey of survival for those travelling and those left behind. **200m/C VHS, DVD.** Kenneth Branagh, Kevin McNally, Chris Larkin, Mark McGann, Lorcan Cranitch, Nicholas (Nick) Rowe, Pip Torrens, Shaun Dooley, Matthew Day; *D:* Charles Sturridge; *W:* Charles Sturridge; *C:* Henry Braham; *M:* Adrian Johnston. **C A B L E.**

Shade ♂♂ 2003 (R) Glamorous group of LA card sharks finds it's a very bad idea to scam the mob and need to take on ultimate legend "The Dean" (Stallone) to worm their way out of this. A nest of actors in his first directorial feature, shows that you can still flop with a winning hand as he leads the talent of this cast. Nieman goes down the river. **95m/C VHS, DVD.** Sylvester Stallone, Gabriel Byrne, Melanie Griffith, Hal Holbrook, Thandie Newton, Stuart Townsend, Jina Merrill, Bo Hopkins, Jamie Foxx, Patrick Bauchau, Louis Freese, Roger Guenveur Smith, Charles Rocket, Michael Dorn, Jack Conley, Frank Medrano, Glenr Plummer, Damien Nieman; *D:* Damien Nieman; *W:* Damien Nieman; *C:* Anthony B. Richmond; *M:* Christopher Young.

Shades of Black ♂♂ 1993 Young, small-town photographer/athlete Kate becomes the romantic obsession of charismatic, older artist Lilly. But Lilly's manipulations also hide the deeper secret of her mental instability, which soon proves dangerous to Kate. **115m/C VHS.** *D:* Mary Haverstick.

Shades of Darkness ♂♂½ 2000 (R) Stephen King sort of story has to do with a woman (Treblicock) who returns to her small hometown and finds that supernatural forces are at work. **90m/C DVD.** John Maczko, Annie Treblicock; *D:* Christopher Johnson.

Shades of Fear ♂♂ *Great Moments in Aviation* 1993 (R) Adventurous would-be aviatrix Gabriel Angel (Ayola), who's sailing from Grenada to England, is mistakenly assigned a room with Duncan (Pryce) and decides to pose as his wife to avoid a scandal. But a fellow passenger (Hurt) believes Duncan is also the art forger who ran off with his wife and caused her death. On their last night at sea, there's a final confrontation. **93m/C VHS, DVD. GB** Jonathan Pryce, Rakie Ayola, John Hurt, Vanessa Redgrave, Dorothy Tutin; *D:* Beeban Kidron. **TV**

Shadey ♂♂½ 1987 (PG-13). The premise for this oddball comedy came to someone in the wee hours: I've got it! Mid-mannered mechanic can film people's thoughts; wants to use his gift only for good, but needs money for a sexchange operation. Assorted bad guys want to use him for evil purposes.

---

he actually cares about—fellow hostage Wendy Pfister (Witherspoon), a cheerleader, who wouldn't have given him the time of day before. A somewhat heavy-handed commentary on "fame in our tabloid-intensive society." Title acronym stands for "So F***ing What." Many reviewers had a similar reaction. Based on the novel by Andrew Wellman. **92m/C VHS, DVD.** Stephen Dorff, Reese Witherspoon, Jake Busey, Joey Lauren Adams, Pernale Gidley, David Barry Gray, Jack Noseworthy, Richard Portnow; *D:* Jefery Levy; *W:* Jefery Levy, James Foley.

The Shadow ♂½ 1936 Scotland Yard pulls out all the stops to track down a murderous extortionist, enlisting the aid of a novelist in their efforts. Long on talk and short on action. **63m/B VHS, DVD. GB** Henry Kendall, Elizabeth Allan, Jeanne Stuart, Felix Aylmar, Cyril Raymond; *D:* George Cooper.

The Shadow ♂½ 1994 (PG-13) Who knows what evil lurks in the hearts of man? Why "The Shadow" of course, as is shown in this highly stylized big screen version of the '30s radio show that once starred Orson Welles. Billionaire playboy Lamont Cranston (Baldwin) is a master of illusion and defender of justice thanks to his alter ego. Aided by companion Margo Lane (Miller), da Shadow battles supercriminal Shiwan Khan (Lone), the deadliest descendant of Ghengis Khan. Numerous and elaborate special effects provide icing on the cake for those in the mood for a journey back to the radio past or a quick superhero fix. **112m/C VHS, DVD.** Alec Baldwin, John Lone, Penelope Ann Miller, Peter Boyle, Ian McKellen, Tim Curry, Jonathan Winters, Andre Gregory, James Hong, Sat Shimono, Max Wright, Aaron Lustig, Ethan Phillips, Larry Joshua, Al Leong, Abraham Benrubi, Armin Shimerman, Steve Hytner, Kate McGregor-Stewart; *D:* Russell Mulcahy; *W:* David Koepp; *C:* Stephen Burum; *M:* Jerry Goldsmith.

The Shadow Box ♂♂♂ 1980 Three terminally ill people at a California hospice confront their destinies. Pulitzer Prize-winning play by Michael Cristofer is actually improved by director Newman and a superb, well-chosen cast. Powerful. **96m/C VHS.** Joanne Woodward, Christopher Plummer, Robert Urich, Valerie Harper, Sylvia Sidney, Melinda Dillon, Ben Masters, John Considine, James Broderick; *D:* Paul Newman; *M:* Henry Mancini.

The Shadow Conspiracy ♂ 1996 (R) Laughable innocent-on-the-run tale of presidential advisor Bobby Bishop (Sheen), who finds himself smack in the middle of an assassination conspiracy against the Prez (Waterston). Accused of murder, Bishop hooks up with ex-gal pal, reporter Amanda Givens (Hamilton) to get to the truth before the police and the bad guys get to them. Hunting the duo is a pro known as "The Agent" (Lang). Lang's lethal Agent comes off as one of the only believable characters here, perhaps because his films has absolutely no dialogue to sabotage him. Sutherland fares better than most as Chief of Staff Conrac Jacob. Ludicrous plot twists and unconvincing performances by leads Sheen anc Hamilton. **123m/C VHS, DVD.** Charlie Sheen, Linda Hamilton, Stephen Lang, Donald Sutherland, Sam Waterston, Ben Gazzara, Nicholas Turturro, Charles Cioffi, Theodore Bikel, Stanley Anderson, Dey Young, Gore Vidal, Paul Gleason, Terry O'Quinn; *D:* George P. Cosmatos; *W:* Rick Gibbs, Wayne Beach; *C:* Buzz Feitshans IV; *M:* Bruce Broughton.

Shadow Creature ♂ 1996 (R) Detective investigating a series of grisly murders finds a mad scientist and a mysterious formula that could unlock the secrets of immortality. The downside being the entire mutation of all life on earth into monsters. **?m/C VHS.** Shane Minor, Dennis Keefe, Scott Heim; *D:* James Gribbins.

Shadow Dancer ♂♂ 1996 (F) Formulaic Corman exploitation. Beaumont Theater of Dance is haunted by the ghost of his former dancers who died unexpectedly during a performance of "Medusa." Now, over 50 years later, Jessica, the pick for the lead in the new production, begins to take on her predecessor's mannerisms and spirit as she "faces her impending doom. Surprisingly believable and sus-

---

Strange, but not bad; Helmont's character is memorable. **90m/C VHS. GB** Anthony Sher, Ellie Whitelaw, Patrick Macnee, Katherine Helmond, Leslie Ash, Larry Lamb, Bernard Hepton; *D:* Philip Saville; *W:* Snoo Wison; *C:* Roger Deakins; *M:* Colin Towns.

penseful—and scary! 100m/C VHS. Nadine Van Der Velde, James Kee, John Colicos, Shirley Douglas, Christopher Plummer; *D:* John Furey; *M:* Jay Gruska.

Shadow Force 🦴🦴½ **1992** Homicide detective Rick Kelly is investigating the murders of a district attorney and a police sergeant. With the help of Mary, the usual beautiful female journalist, he uncovers a plot to assassinate key law enforcement officers. 80m/C VHS. Dirk Benedict, Lance LeGault, Lise Cutter, Jack Elam, Glenn Corbett, Bob Hastings; *D:* Darrell Davenport.

Shadow Magic 🦴🦴½ **2000 (PG)** Englishman Raymond Wallace (Harris) turns up in Peking in 1902 with a hand-cranked, black and white, soundless camera and projector, thus bringing the first moving images to China. Local photographer Liu Jinglun (Yu), intrigued by the new technology, bridges the cultural barriers between Raymond and the community, causing problems of loyalty with his own family and friends and even jeopardizing his marriage chances. Mandarin with subtitles. 115m/C VHS, DVD. GE Jared Harris, Xia Yu, Peiqi Liu, Liping Lu, Xing Yufei, Wang Jingming, Li Yusheng; *D:* Ann Hu; *W:* Ann Hu, Huang Dan, Tang Louyi, Kate Raisz, Bob McAndrew; *C:* Nancy Schreiber; *M:* Zhang Lida.

The Shadow Man 🦴🦴 *Street of Shadows* **1953** A casino operator in London (Romero) is accused of killing a former girlfriend and works to clear himself. Familiarly conventional action mystery; nothing to write home about. 76m/B VHS. GB FR IT Jacques Champreux, Ugo Pagliali, Cesar Romero, Simone Silva, Kay Kendall, John Penrose, Edward Underdown, Victor Maddern; *D:* Richard Vernon, Georges Franju; *W:* Richard Vernon, Ugo Pagliali; *C:* Phil Grindrod, Guido Bertoni; *M:* Eric Spear, Georges Franju.

Shadow Man 🦴🦴 **1975 (PG)** A mysterious thief, a master of disguise, sets out to steal the Treasure of the Knights Templar and nothing will stand in his way. 89m/C VHS. Josephine Chaplin, Gert Frobe, Gayle Hunnicutt.

Shadow Man 🦴½ **2006 (R)** Mediocre adventure from Seagal. Jack Foster is a retired CIA agent who is taking his daughter (Bennett) to visit Bucharest, the home of her late mother. Only she gets kidnapped because the bad guys think Foster is in possession of a bio-weapon that he knows nothing about but rogue CIA agents do. 91m/C DVD. Steven Seagal, Werner Daehn, Imelda Staunton, Skye Bennett, Garrick Hagon; *D:* Michael Keusch; *W:* Steven Collins, Joc Halpin; *C:* Geoffrey Hall. VIDEO

Shadow of a Doubt 🦴🦴🦴🦴½ **1943** Uncle Charlie has come to visit his relatives in Santa Rosa. Although he is handsome and charming, his young niece slowly comes to realize he is a wanted mass murderer—and he comes to recognize her suspicions. Hitchcock's personal favorite movie; a quietly creepy venture into Middle American menace. Good performances, especially by Cronyn. From the story by Gordon McConnell. 108m/B VHS, DVD. Teresa Wright, Joseph Cotten, Hume Cronyn, MacDonald Carey, Henry Travers, Wallace Ford; *D:* Alfred Hitchcock; *W:* Thornton Wilder, Sally Benson, Alma Reville; *C:* Joseph Valentine; *M:* Dimitri Tiomkin. Natl. Film Reg. '91.

Shadow of a Scream 🦴🦴 **1997 (R)** Detective Alice Redmond (Massey) goes undercover to investigate a suspected killer (Chokachi) and discovers his rough sexual fantasies appeal to the less staid side of her nature. So good, that more and more of her clients tell her all their darkest secrets and fears, leaving Lily herself falling into such a deep depression that she wonders if she can go on. 84m/C VHS. Athena Massey, David Chokachi, Cyril O'Reilly, Timothy Busfield; *D:* Howard McCain.

Shadow of Angels *der Engel Schatten* **1976** Beautiful prostitute Lily Brest's (Caven) latest client, a wealthy real estate investor (Lowitsch), just wants to talk and Lily's a good listener. So good, that more and more of her clients tell her all their darkest secrets and fears, leaving Lily herself falling into such a deep depression that she wonders if she can go on. Based on Fassbinder's play "The Garbage, the City and Death"; Fassbinder himself appears as a pimp. German subtitles. 103m/C VHS. GE Ingrid Caven, Klaus Lowitsch; *Cameos:* Rainer Werner Fassbinder; *D:* Daniel Schmid; *W:* Rainer Werner Fassbinder, Daniel Schmid.

Shadow of Chikara 🦴 *Thunder Mountain; The Curse of Demon Mountain* **1977 (PG)** A Confederate Army Captain and an orphan girl encounter unexpected adventures as they search for a fortune in diamonds hidden in a river in northern Arkansas. 96m/C VHS, DVD. Joe Don Baker, Sondra Locke, Ted Neeley, Slim Pickens; *D:* Earl E. Smith; *W:* Earl E. Smith; *C:* Jim Roberson; *M:* Jaime Mendoza-Nava.

Shadow of China 🦴🦴🦴 **1991 (PG-13)** A young man struggles for power and love in Hong Kong, while an English beauty and an Asian activist hold the keys to his future and a past which could destroy him. Excellent acting, stunning location photography. Based on the Japanese best-seller "Snakehead" by Yves Theriault. 108m/C VHS. CA Lou Diamond Phillips, Donald Sutherland, Jennifer Tilly, Toshiro Mifune; *D:* Mitsuo Yanagimachi; *W:* Mitsuo Yanagimachi, Richard Maxwell.

Shadow of Chinatown 🦴🦴½ **1936** Mad scientist creates wave of murder and terror in Chinatown. Edited version of a 15-chapter serial. 70m/B VHS, DVD. Bela Lugosi, Bruce Bennett, Joan Barclay, Luana Walters, Maurice Liu, William Buchanan; *D:* Robert F. "Bob" Hill.

Shadow of Doubt 🦴🦴½ **1998 (R)** L.A. defense attorney Kitt Devereux (Griffiths) likes high-profile cases and her latest has the added tension of being prosecuted by ex-lover, Asst. D.A. Jack Campioni (Berenger). Kitt works with an investigator (Lewis) to prove a rapper (Dominguez) innocent of murder while being threatened by an accused rapist (Sheffer) and a prominent Senator, who's angling for a presidential nomination. How everything ties together is something Kitt will have to figure out if she wants to discover the truth. 103m/C VHS. Melanie Griffith, Tom Berenger, Craig Sheffer, Huey Lewis, John Ritter, Wade Dominguez; *D:* Randal Kleiser; *W:* Raymond De Felitta, Myra Byanka.

Shadow of the Eagle 🦴🦴 **1932** Former wartime flying ace Wayne is accused of being a criminal known as "The Eagle." He's using his flying skills (which include skywriting) to threaten a corporation which has stolen plans for a new invention. But can Wayne really be our villain? 12-chapter serial. 226m/B VHS, DVD. John Wayne, Dorothy Gulliver, Walter Miller; *D:* Ford Beebe.

Shadow of the Thin Man 🦴🦴🦴 **1941** In the fourth "Thin Man" film, following "Another Thin Man," Nick and Nora stumble onto a murder at the racetrack. The rapport between Powell and Loy is still going strong, providing us with some wonderful entertainment. Followed by "The Thin Man Goes Home." 97m/B VHS, DVD. William Powell, Myrna Loy, Barry Nelson, Donna Reed, Sam Levene, Alan Baxter, Dickie Hall, Loring Smith, Joseph Anthony, Henry O'Neill; *D:* Woodbridge S. Van Dyke.

Shadow of the Vampire 🦴🦴🦴 **2000** Behind the scenes look at what possibly went on during the making of the silent vampire classic, 1922's "Nosferatu." Director F.W. Murnau (Malkovich) and his crew head for Czechoslovakia for location shooting on his version of "Dracula" and the first meeting of the dedicated actor who will play the title role—a very eccentric Max Schreck (Dafoe). Only Murnau has struck a devil's bargain with Schreck, who is an actual vampire—the leading man gets leading lady Greta (McCormack) as a reward—and a snack. But it seems Schreck can't wait, as the crew starts to fall mysteriously ill. A little slow going but strangely compelling and the two lead performances are outstanding. 93m/C VHS, DVD. GB John Malkovich, Willem Dafoe, Catherine McCormack, Cary Elwes, Eddie Izzard, Udo Kier, Ronan Vibert, Aden (John) Gillett; *D:* Edmund Elias Merhige; *W:* Steven Katz; *C:* Lou Bogue; *M:* Dan (Daniel) Jones. L.A. Film Critics '00: Support. Actor (Dafoe).

Shadow of the Wolf 🦴🦴 *Agaguk; Shadow of the Wolf* **1992 (PG-13)** Phillips is Agaguk, the son of the village leader, in this epic saga of survival set against the wilderness of the Arctic. Agaguk decides he cannot accept the white man's intrusion, so he sets out on his own. His father believes his departure to be the ultimate betrayal and casts upon him the "curse of the white wolf." Now Agaguk and his companion (Tilly) must face the harsh tundra alone and struggle to stay alive in the Great White North. Based on the novel "Agaguk" by Yves Theriault. 108m/C VHS. CA Lou Diamond Phillips, Donald Sutherland, Jennifer Tilly, Toshiro Mifune; *D:* Jacques Dorfmann; *W:* Rudy Wurlitzer, Evan Jones. Genie '93: Art Dir/Set Dec., Costume Des.

Shadow on the Sun 🦴½ **1988** The life of Beryl Markham, pioneer female aviator and adventurer of the 1930s. Way too long and boring TV answer to "Out of Africa." 192m/C VHS. Stefanie Powers, Claire Bloom, Frederic Forrest, James Fox, John Rubinstein, Jack Thompson; *D:* Tony Richardson. TV

Shadow Play 🦴½ **1986 (R)** A successful female playwright is haunted by visions of a past lover. Her life slowly falls apart, but not before this film does. 98m/C VHS. Dee Wallace Stone, Cloris Leachman; *D:* Susan Shadburne; *W:* Susan Shadburne.

Shadow Puppets 🦴 **2007** Strangers wake up in some kind of dank medical facility/prison minus much of their clothes (they're in their underwear) and their memories. They try to figure out what's going on but something in the shadows is out to get 'em. Generally dopey psycho-thriller. 103m/C DVD. James Marsters, Jolene Blalock, Tony Todd, Jonathan Hale, Marc Winnick; *D:* Michael Winnick; *W:* Michael Winnick; *M:* Ross Nykiforuk. VIDEO

The Shadow Riders 🦴🦴 *Louis L'Amour's "The Shadow Riders"* **1982 (PG)** Two brothers who fought on opposite sides during the Civil War return home to find their brother's fiancee kidnapped by a renegade Confederate officer who plans to use her as ransom in a prisoner exchange. They set out to rescue the woman. Preceded by "The Sacketts" and based on the works of Louis L'Amour. 96m/C VHS, DVD. Tom Selleck, Sam Elliott, Ben Johnson, Katharine Ross, Jeffery Osterhage, Gene Evans, R.G. Armstrong, Marshall Teague, Dominique Dunne, Jeanetta Arnette; *D:* Andrew V. McLaglen; *W:* Jim Byrnes; *C:* Jack Whitman; *M:* Jerrold Immel. TV

The Shadow Strikes 🦴½ **1937** Adaptation of the radio serial. The sleuth pursues a killer and a gangster. Meanwhile, the police try to pin a robbery on the "Shadow." Who did it? The Shadow knows! 61m/B VHS, DVD. Rod La Rocque, Lynn Anders, James Blakely, Walter McGrail, Cy Kendall, Kenneth Harlan, John St. Polis, Wilson Benge; *D:* Lynn Shores; *W:* Al Martin; *C:* Marcel Le Picard.

Shadow Warriors 🦴½ **1995 (R)** *Assault on Devil's Island* **1997** Navy SEALS, led by Mike McBride (Hogan), plan an assault on the island hideaway of drug lord Gallindo (Drago). Lending assistance is undercover DEA agent Hunter Wiley (being that the part is played by Tweed she's never really covered, appearing in a variety of lingerie and bikinis while kicking butt). However, when the SEALS get Gallindo, his crew retaliates. 94m/C VHS, DVD. Hulk Hogan, Carl Weathers, Shannon Tweed, Martin Kove, Billy Drago, Trevor Goddard, Billy Blanks; *D:* Jon Cassar. CABLE

Shadow Warriors 2: Hunt for the Death Merchant 🦴🦴½ **1997 (R)** The elite commando unit of Hogan, Weathers, and Tweed return—and this time they must rescue a group of American gymnasts who are being held hostage. If you enjoyed the first movie, you'll enjoy this one since it's more of the action-filled same. 95m/C VHS. Hulk Hogan, Carl Weathers, Shannon Tweed, Martin Kove; *D:* Jon Cassar. CABLE

A Shadow You Soon Will Be 🦴🦴 *Una Sombra Ya Pronto Seras* **1994** An allegory of the emptiness of contemporary Argentinian society, following the end of military rule, and based on a 1990 novel by Soriano, who co-wrote the screenplay. A man known merely as "The Engineer" (Sola) returns from Europe where he's lived in exile during the military dictatorship. Without family or friends, he wanders through the southern pampas, briefly communicating with other eccentric travelers, and non-committally watching the world go by. Spanish with subtitles. 105m/C VHS, DVD. AR Miguel Angel Sola, Eusebio Poncela, Pepe Soriano, Alicia Bruzzo, Luis Brandoni, Diego Torres, Gloria Carra; *D:* Hector Olivera; *W:* Hector Olivera, Osvaldo Soriano; *C:* Felix Monti; *M:* Osvaldo Montes.

Shadowboxer 🦴½ **2006 (R)** Gratuitous, graphic sex and violence dominate a story about biracial assassins who are not only lovers but stepmother and stepson, played for some reason by the great Mirren and Gooding. Complications arise when a job doesn't go as planned and the odd couple find themselves on the lam with their target and her just-born infant. Add a half bone for somehow landing Oscar-caliber leads. 93m/C DVD. US Cuba Gooding Jr., Helen Mirren, Vanessa Ferlito, Macy Gray, Joseph Gordon-Levitt, Mo'Nique, Stephen Dorff; *D:* Lee Daniels; *W:* William Lipz; *C:* M. David Mullen; *M:* Mario Grigorov.

Shadowhunter 🦴🦴 **1993 (R)** Glenn stars as a burned-out big city detective who is sent to a Navajo reservation in Arizona to bring a murder suspect back to Los Angeles. When the alleged killer escapes custody Glenn must track him across forbidding desert territory and face his suspect's unusual mystical powers. 98m/C VHS. Scott Glenn; *D:* J.S. Cardone; *W:* J.S. Cardone; *C:* Dick Bush.

Shadowlands 🦴🦴🦴 *C.S. Lewis Through the Shadowlands* **1985** A look at the later life of bachelor-scholar C.S. Lewis (also the author of the "Chronicles of Narnia"). A devout proponent of Christianity, the middle-aged Lewis fell in love and married Joy Gresham, a divorced American poet with two young sons. Joy was diagnosed with cancer and her illness provided Lewis with the clearest test of his faith. Wonderful performances by both Ackland, Claire Bloom, Rupert Baderman; *D:* Norman Stone.

Shadowlands 🦴🦴🦴 **1993 (PG)** Touching, tragic story of the late-in-life romance between celebrated author and Christian theologian C.S. Lewis (Hopkins) and brash New York divorcee Joy Gresham (Winger). Attenborough's direction is rather stately and sweeping and Winger is really too young for her role but Hopkins is excellent as (another) repressed man who finds more emotions than he can handle. Critically acclaimed adaptation of Nicholson's play will require lots of kleenex. 130m/C VHS, DVD. GB Anthony Hopkins, Debra Winger, Edward Hardwicke, Joseph Mazzello, Michael Denison, John Wood, Peter Firth, Peter Howell; *C:* Richard Attenborough; *W:* William Nicholson; *C:* Roger Pratt; *M:* George Fenton. British Acad. '93: Film, L.A. Film Critics '93: Actor (Hopkins); Natl. Bd. of Review '93: Actor (Hopkins).

Shadows 🦴🦴🦴 **1922** A Chinese laundryman (Chaney) lives with a group of his countrymen in a New England seacoast village. All is peaceful until the local minister decides to convert the "heathen" Chinese. Ludicrous but worth seeing for Chaney's fun performance. Silent with music score. 70m/B VHS, DVD. Lon Chaney Sr., Harrison Ford; *D:* Tom Forman; *W:* Eve Unsell, Hope Loring; *C:* Harry Perry; *M:* Gaylord Carter.

Shadows 🦴🦴🦴 **1960** Director Cassavetes' first indie feature finds jazz playboy Hugh (Hurd) forced to play dives to support his brother Ben (Carruthers) and sis-

...ter Leila (Goldoni). Light-skinned enough to pass for white, Leila takes on the uptown New York art crowd and gets involved with the white Tony (Ray), who leaves when he finds out her true heritage. Meanwhile, Ben drifts along with his friends who abandon him when trouble finds them. Script was improvised by cast. **87m/B VHS, DVD.** Hugh Hurd, Lelia Goldoni, Ben Carruthers, Anthony Ray, Rupert Crosse, Tom Allen; **D:** John Cassavetes; **C:** Erich Kollmar; **M:** Charles Mingus, Shfi Hadi. Nat. Film Reg. '93.

Shadows and Fog ✔✔ 1992 (PG-13) Offbeat, unpredictable Allen film that is little more than an exercise in expressionistic visual stylings. The action centers around a haunted, alienated clerk (Allen) who is awakened in the middle of the night to join a vigilante group searching the streets for a killer. Although reminiscent of a silent film, Carlo DiPalma's black-and-white cinematography is stunning. Several stars appear briefly throughout this extremely unfocused comedy. **85m/B VHS, DVD.** Woody Allen, Kathy Bates, John Cusack, Mia Farrow, Jodie Foster, Fred Gwynne, Julie Kavner, Madonna, John Malkovich, Kenneth Mars, Kate Nelligan, Donald Pleasence, Lily Tomlin, Philip Bosco, Robert Joy, Wallace Shawn, Kurtwood Smith, Josef Sommer, David Ogden Stiers, Michael Kirby, Anne Lange; **D:** Woody Allen; **W:** Woody Allen; **C:** Carlo Di Palma, Jack Greenhalgh.

Shadows of Forgotten Ancestors ✔✔✔ Tini Zabutykh Pred-kiv; Shadows of Our Ancestors; Shadows of Our Forgotten Ancestors; Wild Horses of Fire 1964 Set in rural Russia in the early 20th century. Brings to expressive life the story of a man whose entire life has been overtaken by tragedy. Folk drama about a peasant who falls in with the daughter of his father's killer, then marries another woman. Strange, resonant and powerful with distinctive camera work. In Ukrainian with English subtitles. **99m/C VHS, RU** Ivan Micro-laichuk, Larisa Kadochnikova; **D:** Sergei Paradja-nov.

Shadows of the Orient 1937 Two detectives are out to smash a Chinese smuggling ring. **70m/B VHS, DVD.** J. Farrell MacDonald, Oscar Apfel, Sidney Blacmer, Regis Toomey, Esther Ralston; **D:** Burt Lynwood; **W:** Charles Francis Royal; **C:** James S. Brown Jr.

Shadows of Tombstone ✔✔ 1953 There's corruption in the western town of Shadow Rock as the crooked sheriff and saloonkeeper make things miserable for the inhabitants. Rex and Slim try to right the wrongs but take their time about it. **54m/B VHS.** Rex Allen, Slim Pickens, Roy Bancroft, Emory Parnell, Jeanne Cooper; **D:** William Witney; **W:** Gerald Geraghty; **C:** Bud Thackery; **M:** R. Dale Butts.

Shadows on the Stairs ✔✔ 1941 A creepy boarding house is the scene of a number of mystery-drenched murders. A bizarre assortment of suspects make things even crazer. **63m/B VHS, DVD.** Frieda Inescort, Paul Cavanagh, Heather Angel, Bruce Lester, Miles Mander, Lumsden Hare, Turhan Bey; **D:** David Ross Lederman.

Shadows over Shanghai ✔½ 1938 This adventure relic was set during the Japanese invasion of China prior to WWII and uses much newsreel footage of that infamy. As for the plot, it's a groaner about good guys and bad skulking around the eponymous port in search of a treasure. **66m/B VHS. D:** Charles Lamont.

Shadows Run Black ✔½ 1984 A police detective must save a college coed from the clutches of a maniac wielding a meat cleaver. Ordinary slash-em-up. Bet Costner's embarrassed now about this early role—like Stallone's porno role in "The Italian Stallion." **89m/C VHS, DVD.** William J. Kulzer, Elizabeth Trosper, Kevin Costner; **D:** Howard Heard.

Shadowzone ✔✔ 1989 (R) As a result of NASA experiments in dream travel, an interdimensional monster invades our world in search of victims. Begins well, generates into typical slasher flick. Good special effects. **88m/C VHS, DVD.** Louise Fletcher, David Beecroft, James Hong, Shawn Weatherly, Lu Leonard; **D:** J.S. Cardone.

ShadowZone: The Undead Express ✔✔½ 1996 (PG-13) Teen-aged Zach (Leopardi) winds up in New York's subway tunnels where he meets the vampire Valentine (Silver) and his fellow bloodsuckers. Based on the book by J.R. Black. **89m/C VHS, DVD.** Chauncey Leopardi, Ron Silver, Natavya Ross, Tony T. Johnson, Ron White; **Cameos:** Wes Craven; **C:** Stephen Williams; **W:** Roy Swallows; **C:** Curtis Petersen; **M:** Reg Powell. CABLE

Shadrach ✔✔½ 1998 (PG-13) The Dabneys run-down Depression Era southern farm was once a rich tobacco plantation and, as they learn, the former home to aged black man Shadrach (Sawyer) who returns in order to die on the land where he grew up. Flawed family patriarch Vernon (Keitel) gives his word to the ex-slave that he can be buried on the land, but learns otherwise from the local sheriff. Still, Vernon tries to fulfill his promise. Director Susanna Styron's lethargic adaptation of her father William's 1978 short story proves that the story should have stayed shorter than 90 minutes. Although the relatively small budget shows, the cast provides good performances. **88m/C VHS, DVD.** Edward (Eddie) Eunker, Harvey Keitel, John Franklin Sawyer, Andie MacDowell, Scott Terra, Monica Bugajski, Daniel Larson, Deborah Hedwall, Daniel Treat; **D:** Susanna Styron; **W:** Susanna Styron, Bridget Terry; **C:** Hiro Narita; **M:** Van Dyke Parks.

Shaft ✔✔✔ 1971 (R) A black private eye (Roundtree) is hired to find a Harlem gangster's (Gunn) kidnapped daughter. Lotsa sex and violence; suspenseful and well directed by notable "Life" photographer Parks. Great entry. Academy Award-winning theme song by Isaac Hayes, the first music award from the Academy to an African American. Followed by "Shaft's Big Score" and "Shaft in Africa." ♪ Theme From Shaft. **98m/C VHS, DVD.** Richard Roundtree, Moses Gunn, Charles Cioffi, Christopher St. John, Gwen Mitchell, Lawrence Pressman, Victor Arnold, Antonio Fargas, Drew "Bundini" Brown; **D:** Gordon Parks; **W:** John D.F. Black, Ernest Tidyman; **C:** Urs Furrer; **M:** Isaac Hayes, J.J. Johnson. Oscars '71: Song ("Theme from Shaft"); Golden Globes '72: Score. Natl. Film Reg. '00.

Shaft ✔✔✔ 2000 (R) Singleton's updated the 1971 blaxploitation flick with Jackson starring as the nephew of the coolest private dick ever (Roundtree has a cameo in his original role). But Jackson can more than hold his own in the cool department as he tracks down rich-kid murderer Walter Wade Jr. (Bale), who's after the only witness to his crime, a scared waitress (Collette). Wade hires a Latino drug dealer (Wright, in a standout performance almost equal to Jackson's) and a couple of bad cops to find the girl and kill Shaft, setting off much gunfire and snappy dialogue. Jackson has charisma to burn, but other characters, as well as potentially interesting plot points, get short shrift. This is most likely a result of Wright's part being (deservedly) beefed up from the original screenplay (about which Singleton and Jackson were said to be not entirely happy). **98m/C VHS, DVD.** Samuel L. Jackson, Christian Bale, Vanessa Williams, Jeffrey Wright, Philip Bosco, Toni Collette, Angela Pietropinto, Dan Hedaya, Josef Sommer, Richard Roundtree, Ruben Santiago-Hudson, Lynne Thigpen, Pat Hingle, Busta Rhymes, Mekhi Phifer, Zach Grenier, Catherine Kellner, Isaac Hayes, Lee Tergesen, Gloria Reuben, Gordon Parks, Daniel vor Bargen; **D:** John Singleton; **W:** Richard Price; **C:** Stuart Dryburgh; **M:** Isaac Hayes, David Arnold.

The Shaft 2001 (R) The express elevators in New York's Millennium Building start to malfunction (as in killing passengers) but no one senses it. Ex-mechanic Mark (Marshall) to fix the problem, by nosy reporter Jennifer (Watts), who learns. So Mark decides to investigate, aided by ... **98m/C VHS, DVD.** Michael Ironside, Edward Herrmann, Dan Hedaya, Ron Perlman; **D:** Dick Maas; **W:** Dick Maas; **C:** Marc Felperlaan.

Shaft in Africa ✔✔ 1973 (R) Violent action entry this detective Shaft forced into helping an African nation stop some modern-day slave trading. Second sequel, following "Shaft's Big Score." **112m/C VHS, DVD.** Richard Roundtree, Frank Finlay, Vonetta McGee, Neda Americ, Jacques Marin; **D:** John Guillermin; **W:** Stirling Silliphant.

Shaft's Big Score ✔✔½ 1972 (R) This first sequel to the extremely successful "Shaft" has Roundtree's detective trying to mediate between several mobsters while investigating a friend's murder. Lots of action and an exciting Brooklyn chase scene involving cars, helicopters, and boats but still routine when compared to the original. Followed by "Shaft in Africa." **105m/C VHS, DVD.** Richard Roundtree, Moses Gunn, Joseph Mascolo, Drew "Bundini" Brown, Wally Taylor, Kathy Imrie, Julius W. Harris, Rosalind Miles, Joe Santos; **D:** Gordon Parks; **W:** Ernest Tidyman; **M:** Gordon Parks.

Shag: The Movie ✔✔✔ 1989 (PG) The time is 1963, the setting Myrtle Beach, South Carolina, the latest craze shaggin' when four friends hit the beach for one last weekend together. Carson (Cates) is getting ready to marry staid Harley (Power); Melaina (Fonda) wants to be discovered in Hollywood; and Fudge (Gish) and Luanne (Hannah) are off to college. They encounter lots of music, boys, and dancing in this delightful 'teen' movies, this one boasts a good script and an above average cast. **96m/C VHS, DVD.** Phoebe Cates, Annabeth Gish, Bridget Fonda, Page Hannah, Scott Coffey, Robert Rusler, Tyrone Power Jr., Jeff Yagher, Carrie Hamilton, Shirley Anne Field, Leilan Sarelle Ferrer; **D:** Zelda Barron; **W:** Robin Swicord, Lanier Laney, Terry Sweeney; **C:** Peter Macdonald.

The Shaggy D.A. ✔✔ 1976 (G) Wilby Daniels is getting a little worried about his canine alter ego as he is about to run for District Attorney. Fun sequel to "The Shaggy Dog." **90m/C VHS, DVD.** Dean Jones, Tim Conway, Suzanne Pleshette, Keenan Wynn, Helene Winston; **D:** Robert Stevenson; **M:** Buddy (Norman Dale) Baker.

The Shaggy Dog ✔✔ 1959 (G) When young Wilby Daniels utters some magical words from the inscription of an ancient ring he turns into a shaggy dog, causing havoc on family and neighbors. Disney slapstick is on target at times, though it drags in places. Followed by "The Shaggy D.A." and "Return of the Shaggy Dog." **101m/B VHS, DVD.** Fred Mac-Murray, Jean Hagen, Tommy Kirk, Annette Funicello, Tim Considine, Kevin Corcoran; **D:** Charles T. Barton; **C:** Edward Colman.

The Shaggy Dog ✔✔ 2006 (PG) Allen goes from man to dogman after being bitten by a 300-year-old Tibetan collie with magical DNA in this remake of Disney's 1959 live-action blockbuster. Allen plays a district attorney and full-time dad now prone to loads of anthropomorphic shtick–barking, lifting his leg to pee, chasing cats, and, of course, sniffing rear-ends. Often comes across more creepy than goofy. Downey succeeds as the prototypical mad scientist villain. Strictly for the kiddies. **98m/C DVD. US** Tim Allen, Robert Downey Jr., Kristen Davis, Spencer Breslin, Joshua Leonard, Danny Glover, Jane Curtin, Zena Grey, Philip Baker Hall, Craig Kilborn, Annabelle Gurwitch, Bess Wohl, Shawn Python, Laura Kightlinger, Jarrad Paul; **D:** Brian Robbins; **W:** Cormac Wibberley, Marianne S. Wibberley, Geoff Rodkey, Jack Amiel, Michael Begler; **C:** Gabriel Beristain; **M:** Alan Menken.

Shaka Zulu ✔✔✔ 1983 British miniseries depicting the career of Shaka, king of the Zulus (Cele). Set in the early 19th century during British ascendancy in Africa. Good, absorbing cross-cultural action drama would have been better with more inspired directing by Faure. **300m/C VHS, DVD. GB** Edward Fox, Robert Powell, Trevor Howard, Christopher Lee, Fiona Fullerton, Henry Cele; **D:** William C. Faure. TV

Shake Hands with the Devil ✔✔✔ 1959 It's the Irish Rep. Army against the British Black and Tans as Ireland fights for independence in 1921. Cagney is a teaching surgeon who is secretly a militant, obsessed with the idea of gaining Irish freedom. He urges his students to join with him, which Irish-American Murray does. When Murray's peace treaty, he must decide whether to betray Cagney in order to stop further violence. Cagney is excellent as the hard-bitten revolutionary who can't see beyond his own ideals. Filmed on location in Dublin, which further heightens the film's tension. **110m/B VHS, DVD.** James Cagney, Don Murray, Dana Wynter, Glynis Johns, Michael Redgrave, Sybil Thorndike, Harry Brogan, Michael Brown; **D:** Michael Anderson Sr.; **W:** Ivan Goff.

Shake Hands With the Devil: The Journey of Roméo Dallaire ✔✔✔½ 2004 In 1992 Lt. Gen. Roméo Dallaire went to Rwanda to help save their international people only to find his pleas for humane intervention betray his words along with archival footage give a brutal recounting of atrocities that were given but a flash in Western news reports. Deserved winner of the Audience Best Film Documentary award at Sundance. **91m/C DVD. D:** Peter Raymont; **C:** John Westheuser; **M:** Mark Korven.

Shake, Rattle and Rock ✔✔½ 1957 A deejay goes to open a teen music club playing rock 'n' roll, which has all the conservative parents up in arms. A court case follows which plays to the great music by Fats Domino, Joe Turner, Annita Ray, and Tommy Charles. Songs include "Ain't It a Shame," "Honey Chile," "I'm in Love Again," "Feelin' Happy," and "Sweet Love on My Mind." **76m/C VHS, DVD.** Mike Connors, Lisa Gaye, Sterling Holloway, Margaret Dumont, Raymond Hatton, Douglas Dumbrille; **D:** Edward L. Cahn; **W:** Lou Russoff.

Shake, Rattle & Rock! ✔✔½ 1994 (PG-13) Remake of the 1957 flick. Teenager Susan (Zellweger) scandalizes her uptight mom (Dunn) and the other conservative adults in town because of her love of that evil rock 'n' roll music—and dad boy Lucky (Doe). Made as part of Showtime's "Rebel Highway" series **83m/C VHS, DVD.** Renee Zellweger, John Doe, Noa Dunn, Howie Mandel, Patricia Childress, Mary Woronov, Max Perlich, Dick Miller, William Schallert, Paul Anka; **D:** Allan Arkush; **M:** Trish Soodick; CABLE

Shakedown ✔✔½ Blue Jean Cop 1988 (R) Power-packed action film. An overworked attorney and an undercover cop work together to stop corruption in the N.Y.P.D. Although lacking greatly in logic or plot, the sensational stunts make this an otherwise entertaining action flick. **96m/C VHS, DVD.** Sam Elliott, Peter Weller, Patricia

Charbonneau, Antonio Fargas, Blanche Baker, Richard Brooks, Jude Ciccolella, George Loros, Tom Waits, Shirley Stoler, Rockets Redglare, Kathryn Rosseter; **D:** James Glickenhaus; **C:** John Lindley; **M:** Jonathan Elias.

Shakedown 2002 (R) Perlman is the leader of a doomsday cult that plans to steal a biological weapon and unleash it on the population. They take over the L.A. bank where the weapon is stored just at the same time that an earthquake hits, which traps the bad guys. When the military discovers the situation, a general (Dryer) decides to destroy the bank to prevent the virus from escaping. 92m/C VHS, DVD. Ron Perlman, Erika Eleniak, Fred (John F.) Dryer, Wolf Larson, Matt Westmore; **D:** Brian Katkin; **W:** Brian Katkin; **C:** Yoram Astrakhan; **M:** Chris Farrell. VIDEO

Shaker Run 1985 A stunt car driver and his mechanic transport a mysterious package. They don't know what to do—they're carrying a deadly virus that every terrorist wants! Car chases galore, and not much else. However, if you like chase scenes... 91m/C VHS, DVD. NZ Leif Garrett, Cliff Robertson, Lisa Harrow; **D:** Bruce Morrison.

Shakes the Clown 1992 (R) Chronicles the rise and fall of Shakes, an alcoholic clown wandering through the all-clown town of Palukaville. Framed for the murder of his boss by his archrival, Binky, Shakes takes it on the lam in order to prove his innocence, aided by his waitress girlfriend Judy, who dreams of becoming a professional bowler. Meant as a satire of substance-abuse recovery programs and the supposed tragedies of a performer's life, the film is sometimes zany, but more often merely unpleasant and unamusing. Williams has an uncredited role as a mime. 83m/C VHS, DVD. Bob(cat) Goldthwait, Julie Brown, Blake Clark, Adam Sandler, Tom Kenny, Sydney Lassick, Paul Dooley, Tim Kazurinsky, Florence Henderson, LaWanda Page; *Cameos:* Robin Williams; **D:** Bob(cat) Goldthwait; **W:** Bob(cat) Goldthwait; **C:** Bobby Bukowski, Elliot Davis.

Shakespeare in Love 1998 (R) Lively romantic comedy about a frustrated Elizabethan playwright suffering from writer's block—who just happens to be William Shakespeare (Fiennes). Will owes a comedy to bankrupt theatre manager Henslowe (Rush) but just can't come up with a suitable story. His creative (and other) juices are sparked by wealthy beauty Viola De Lesseps (Paltrow), who so loves the theatre that she disguises herself as a boy in order to act. (Women are forbidden to be seen on the stage.) But their affair is bittersweet since Viola is about to be married. Ah well, at least Will comes up with "Romeo and Juliet." Terrific acting, costumes and cinematography, and you don't have to be a Shakespeare scholar to enjoy yourself. 122m/C VHS, DVD. Joseph Fiennes, Gwyneth Paltrow, Ben Affleck, Geoffrey Rush, Colin Firth, Judi Dench, Simon Callow, Tom Wilkinson, Imelda Staunton, Jim Carter, Rupert Everett, Martin Clunes, Anthony Sher, Joe Roberts; **D:** John Madden; **W:** Marc Norman, Tom Stoppard; **C:** Richard Greatrex; **M:** Stephen Warbeck. Oscars '98: Actress (Paltrow), Art Dir/Set Dec, Costume Design, Orig. Screenplay, Picture, Support. Actress (Dench), Orig. Mus./Comedy Score; British Acad. '98: Film, Film Editing, Support. Actress (Dench), Support. Actor (Rush), Support. Actress (Dench); Golden Globes '99: Actress-Mus./Comedy (Paltrow), Film-Mus./Comedy, Screenplay; MTV Movie Awards '99: Kiss (Joseph Fiennes/Gwyneth Paltrow); N.Y. Film Critics '98: Screenplay; Natl. Soc. Film Critics '98: Support. Actress (Dench); Screen Actors Guild '98: Actress (Paltrow), Cast; Writers Guild '98: Orig. Screenplay; Broadcast Film Critics '98: Orig. Screenplay.

Shakespeare Wallah 1965 Tender, plausible drama of romance and postcolonial relations in India. A troupe of threadbare traveling Shakespeareans quixotically tours India trying to make enough money to return to England. Wonderfully acted and exquisitely and sensitively directed by Ivory. Based in part on the real-life experiences of the theatrical Kendal family. 120m/B VHS, DVD. Felicity Kendal, Shashi Kapoor, Madhur Jaffrey, Geoffrey Kendal, Laura Liddell; **D:** James Ivory; **W:** James Ivory, Ruth Prawer Jhabvala; **C:** Subrata Mitra; **M:** Satyajit Ray.

The Shakiest Gun in the West 1968 Remake of Bob Hope's "Paleface" has Philadelphia dentist Jesse W. Heywood (Knotts) heading off for a new practice in the wild west of Big Springs. There he unwittingly takes on bad guys and sultry Penny (Rhoades), an undercover government agent who ropes the nervous dentist into marriage for the sake of her job. 101m/C VHS, DVD. Helene Winston, Don Knotts, Barbara Rhoades, Jackie Coogan, Donald (Don "Red") Barry, Ruth McDevitt, Dub Taylor, Noriyuki "Pat" Morita; **D:** Alan Rafkin; **W:** James Fritzell, Everett Greenbaum.

Shaking the Tree 1992 (PG-13) Group of four high school buddies are still in quest of self-fulfillment ten years after high school as they grapple with problems in the real world of adulthood, seeking distraction in adventure, romance, friendship, and sex. 97m/C VHS, DVD. Arye Gross, Gale Hansen, Doug Savant, Steven Wilde, Courteney Cox, Christina Haag, Michael Arabian, Nathan Davis; **D:** Duane Clark; **W:** Duane Clark; **M:** David E. Russo.

Shakma 1989 A group of medical researchers involved with experiments on animal and human tendencies toward aggression take a night off to play a quiet game of "Dungeons and Dragons." The horror begins when their main experimental subject comes along and turns things nasty! 101m/C VHS. Roddy McDowall, Christopher Atkins, Amanda Wyss, Ari Meyers; **D:** Hugh Parks.

Shalako 1968 Connery/Bardot pairing promises something special, but fails to deliver. European aristocrats on a hunting trip in New Mexico, circa 1880, are menaced by Apaches. U.S. Army scout tries to save captured countess Bardot. Strange British attempt at a Euro-western. Poorly directed and pointless. Based on a Louis L'Amour story. 113m/C VHS, DVD. Brigitte Bardot, Sean Connery, Stephen Boyd, Honor Blackman, Woody Strode, Alexander Knox; **D:** Edward Dmytryk; **W:** Scott (Scot) Finch, James J. Griffith, Hal Hopper, Clarke Reynolds; **C:** Ted Moore; **M:** Robert Farnon.

Shall We Dance 1937 And shall we ever! Seventh Astaire-Rogers pairing has a famous ballet dancer and a musical-comedy star embark on a promotional romance and marriage, to boost their careers, only to find themselves truly falling in love. Score by the Gershwins includes memorable songs. Thin, lame plot—but that's okay. For fans of good singing and dancing, and especially of this immortal pair. ♪Slap That Bass; Beginner's Luck; Let's Call the Whole Thing Off; Walking the Dog; They All Laughed; They Can't Take That Away From Me; Shall We Dance. 116m/B VHS, DVD. Fred Astaire, Ginger Rogers, Edward Everett Horton, Eric Blore; **D:** Mark Sandrich; **M:** George Gershwin, Ira Gershwin.

Shall We Dance? *Shall We Dansu?* 1996 A timid Japanese businessman (Yakusyo) is lured to ballroom dancing when he glimpses a beautiful, sad-eyed teacher (Kusakari) through a window. As much commentary on controlled Japanese society as a spirited discovery of learning to live and dance. Well-drawn, quirky characters and good humor amid the observant social commentary should put this one at the top of the anyone's foreign film dance card. In Japanese with subtitles. 118m/C VHS, DVD. JP Koji Yakusho, Tamiyo Kusakari, Naoto Takenaka, Akira (Tsukamoto) Emoto, Eriko Watanabe, Yu Tokui, Hiromasa Taguchi, Reiko Kusamura; **D:** Masayuki Suo; **W:** Masayuki Suo; **C:** Naoke Kayano; **M:** Yoshikazu Suo. Natl. Bd. of Review '97: Foreign Film; Broadcast Film Critics '97: Foreign Film.

Shall We Dance? 2004 (PG-13) Well-to-do, attractive lawyer (Gere) with a beautiful, loving wife (Sarandon) and children suddenly faces a mid-life crisis and decides to ballroom dance his way out. Inoffensive, though forgettable, remake of a much better and more logical 1996 Japanese movie of the same name. Attractive leads are fine, as are the multitude of daffy supporting characters, but it all seem flimsy and one-dimensional. 106m/C VHS, DVD. US Richard Gere, Jennifer Lopez, Susan Sarandon, Stanley Tucci, Lisa Ann Walter, Richard Jenkins, Bobby Cannavale, Omar Benson Miller, Anita Gillette, Mya, Stark Sands, Tamara Hope, Nick Cannon; **D:** Peter Chelsom; **W:** Masayuki Suo; **C:** John de Borman; **M:** Gabriel Yared, John Altman.

Shallow Grave 1987 (R) Four coeds en route to Florida witness a murder in rural Georgia and then are pursued relentlessly by the killer, a local sheriff. Decent premise and talented cast could have offered something better, given a meatier script. 90m/C VHS. Tony March, Lisa Stahl, Tom Law, Carol Cadby; **D:** Richard Styles.

Shallow Grave 1994 (R) Juliet (Fox), David (Eccleston), and Alex (McGregor), three completely unlikable housemates, face a moral dilemma when their new roomie, Hugo (Allen), turns up dead of a drug overdose, leaving behind a suitcase stuffed with cash. Their decision to chop up the body, bury the bits, and keep the loot leads to a well-deserved dementia. Interesting character study in which the veneer of civility is totally destroyed at the first hint of temptation. Style wins out over substance as the characters are never humanized before they're demonized. 91m/C VHS, DVD. GB Kerry Fox, Christopher Eccleston, Ewan McGregor, Keith Allen, Ken Stott, Colin McCredie, John Hodge; **D:** Danny Boyle; **W:** John Hodge; **C:** Brian Tufano; **M:** Simon Boswell.

Shallow Ground 2004 (R) Unable to catch a serial killer, a small-town yokel sheriff is closing up shop a year later when—this just in!—a major break in the case appears in his doorstep in the form of a muted young man carrying the murder weapon and covered in the bloody stuff. Script, direction, music, and acting make for one bloody mess. 97m/C DVD. CA Timothy Murphy, Stan Kirsch, Patty McCormack, Natalie Avital, Myron Natwick, Rocky Marquette, Patty McCormack, Lindsey Stoddart; **D:** Sheldon Wilson; **W:** Sheldon Wilson; **M:** Steve London. VIDEO

Shallow Hal 2001 (PG-13) Dumpy loser Hal (Black), along with buddy Mauricio (Alexander), will only go after supermodel-perfect women (with predictable results), until self-help guru Tony Robbins hypnotizes him into seeing the inner beauty of the women he encounters. This leads him to meet and pursue Rosemary (Paltrow), who he sees as the physical ideal, but the rest of the world knows to be 300 pounds. The Farrellys try to have it both ways, making fat jokes while projecting the message that appearance shouldn't matter. They're only moderately and intermittently successful. Paltrow does a good job of showing Rosemary's wariness and self-acceptance, while Black at times seems to be trying a little too hard. 114m/C VHS, DVD, UMD. US Jack Black, Gwyneth Paltrow, Jason Alexander, Joe (Johnny) Viterelli, Bruce McGill, Susan Ward, Rene Kirby, Tony Robbins, Zen Gesner, Brooke Burns, Rob Moran, Nan Martin; **D:** Bobby Farrelly, Peter Farrelly; **W:** Bobby Farrelly, Peter Farrelly, Sean Moynihan; **C:** Russell Carpenter.

The Shaman 1987 (R) Members of a family succumb to the hypnotic spell of the Shaman as he searches for the perfect one to inherit his powers. 88m/C VHS. Michael Conforti, Eivind Harum, James Farkas, Lynn Weaver; **D:** Michael Yakub.

The Shame *The Intruder; I Hate Your Guts; The Stranger* 1961 Strangely unsuccessful low-budget Corman effort, starring pre-"Star Trek" Shatner as a freelance bigot who travels around Missouri stirring up opposition to desegregation. Moralistic and topical but still powerful. Adapted from the equally excellent novel by Charles Beaumont. Uses location filming superbly to render a sense of everydayness and authenticity. 84m/B VHS, DVD. William Shatner, Frank Maxwell, Jeanne Cooper, Robert Emhardt, Leo Gordon, Charles Beaumont, Beverly Lunsford, William F. Nolan, George Clayton Johnson; **D:** Roger Corman; **W:** Charles Beaumont; **C:** Taylor Byars; **M:** Herman Stein.

The Shame 1968 (R) A Bergman masterpiece focusing on the struggle for dignity in the midst of war. Married concert musicians Ullmann and von Sydow flee a bloody civil war for a small island off their country's coast. Inevitably, the carnage reaches them and their lives become a struggle to endure and retain a small measure of civilized behavior as chaos overtakes them. Deeply despairing and brilliantly acted. In Swedish with English subtitles. 103m/C VHS, DVD. SW Max von Sydow, Liv Ullmann, Gunnar Bjornstrand, Sigge Furst, Birgitta Valberg, Hans Alfredson, Ingvar Kjellson; **D:** Ingmar Bergman; **W:** Ingmar Bergman; **C:** Sven Nykvist. Natl. Soc. Film Critics '68: Actress (Ullmann), Director (Bergman), Film.

Shame 1987 (R) Strange Australian revenge drama about a female lawyer/biker who rides into a small town and finds herself avenging the rape of a 16-year-old girl. Is it a genuinely feminist movie about justice and a strong woman taking charge? Or is it exploitative trash using a politically correct theme and "message" as a peg for much—very much—gratuitous violence? Hard to tell. Cultish for sure; made on a B budget. 95m/C VHS. AU Deborra-Lee Furness, Tony Barry, Simone Buchanan, Gillian Jones; **D:** Steve Jodrell; **W:** Beverly Blakenship, Michael Brindley.

Shame 1992 In a small logging town a group of violent high school thugs get away with rape because the women are too terrified to go to the cops. Then lawyer Diana Cadell (Donohoe) gets stuck in town when her motorcycle breaks down. When she finds out what's been happening, she urges one victim (Balk) to speak out and suddenly they become the targets of both the vicious attackers and a town which would like to hush the entire mess up. Very strong performances by Donohoe and Balk. U.S. version of the same-titled 1987 Australian movie. 91m/C VHS. Amanda Donohoe, Fairuza Balk, Dean Stockwell, Dan Gauthier; **D:** Dan Lerner; **W:** Rebecca Soladay. CABLE

Shame of the Jungle 1975 (R) Animated spoof of Tarzan featuring the voices of John Belushi, Bill Murray, and Johnny Weissmuller Jr. 73m/C VHS. BE FR **D:** Jean-Paul Picha, Boris Szulzinger, Anne Beatts; **C:** Raymond Burlet; **V:** Johnny Weissmuller Jr., John Belushi, Bill Murray, Brian Doyle-Murray, Christopher Guest, Andrew Duncan.

Shame, Shame on the Bixby Boys 1982 Somewhere in the Old West, outside a small town, lives a band of misfits who persist in rustling cattle. The Bixby Boys and their Pa have made a bad habit into a family tradition. 90m/C VHS. Monte Markham, Sammy Jackson; **D:** Zalman King.

Shame, Shame, Shame 1998 (R) Pretty much lives up to its title. A Ph.D candidate working on her thesis asks her subjects to disrobe as part of her interviewing process and discovers as they shed their clothes they shed their secrets and inhibitions as well. 87m/C VHS. Heidi Schanz, Costas Mandylor, Audie England, Valerie Perrine, Olivia Hussey; **D:** Zalman King. VIDEO

Shameless *Mad Dogs and Englishmen* 1994 (R) Wealthy Antonia Dyer (Hurley) is the self-centered, drug addict daughter of aristocrat Sir Harry Dyer (Treves). Her boyfriend is upper-class Tony Vernon-Smith (Brett), who's involved with Sandy (Delamere), the daughter of corrupt narcotics cop Stringer (Ackland). Stringer discovers the two girls know each other and irrationally blames Antonia for his daughter's heroin habit. Meanwhile, American student Mike (Howell) has been trying to get girlfriend Antonia off the drugs. Hurley's properly snooty and manipulative while Howell seems out-of-place and uncomfortable. 99m/C VHS, DVD. GB Elizabeth Hurley, C. Thomas Howell, Joss Ackland, Jeremy Brett, Frederick Treves, Claire Bloom, Louise Delamere, Chris(topher) Adamson; **D:** Henry Cole; **W:** Tim Sewell; **C:** John Peters; **M:** Barrie Guard.

The Shaming ✗½ 1971 (R) *The Sin; Good Luck; Miss Wyckoff.* Puritanical schoolteacher is raped by a janitor, then develops a voracious sexual appetite. Horrible script, offensive premise can't be saved by good cast. Based on a novel by William Inge. 90m/C VHS. Anne Heywood, Donald Pleasence, Robert Vaughn, Carolyn Jones; *D:* Marvin J. Chomsky.

Shampoo ✓✓½ 1975 (R) A satire of morals (and lack thereof) set in Southern California, concerning a successful hairdresser (Beatty) and the many women in his life. A notable scene with the many women with Julie Christie is set at a 1968 presidential election-night gathering. Fisher's screen debut, only one year before "Star Wars" made her famous. Has a healthy glow in places and perky bounce, but too many split ends. *M:* John Barry. Oscars '75: Support. Actress (Grant); Natl. Soc. Film Critics '75: Screenplay; Writers Guild '75: Orig. Screenplay.

Shamus ✓✓ 1973 (PG) Private dick Reynolds investigates a smuggling ring, beds a sultry woman, gets in lotsa fights. Classic Burt vehicle meant as a send-up. Unoriginal but fun. 91m/C VHS, DVD. Burt Reynolds, Dyan Cannon, John P. Ryan; *D:* Buzz Kulik; *W:* Barry Beckerman; *M:* Jerry Goldsmith.

Shane ✓✓✓ 1953 A retired gunfighter, now a drifter, comes to the aid of a homestead family threatened by a land baron and his hired gun. Ladd is the mystery man who becomes a friend to the family's young son. Classic, flawless Western. Pulitzer prize-winning western novelist A.B. Guthrie Jr. adapted from the novel by Jack Schaefer. Long and stately; worth savoring. 117m/C VHS, DVD. Alan Ladd, Jean Arthur, Van Heflin, Brandon de Wilde, Jack Palance, Ben Johnson, Elisha Cook Jr., Edgar Buchanan, Ernie Meyer; *D:* George Stevens; *W:* Jack Sher. *C:* Loyal Griggs; *M:* Victor Young. Oscars '53: Color Cinematog; AFI '98: Top 100; Natl. Bd. of Review '53: Director (Stevens), Natl. Film Reg. '93.

The Shanghai Cobra ✓½ 1945 Below-average mystery has Chan hired by the government to investigate several supposed cobra bite murders. All motives lead to stealing a supply of radium. 64m/B VHS, DVD. Sidney Toler, Benson Fong, Mantan Moreland, Walter Fenner, James B. Cardwell, Joan Barclay, James Flavin; *D:* Phil Karlson.

Shanghai Express ✓✓✓½ 1932 Dietrich is at her most alluring in this mystical and exotic story that made legends out of both star and director. Dietrich plays Shanghai Lily, a woman of objectionable reputation, who has a reunion of sorts with ex-lover Brook aboard a slow-moving train through China. Remade as "Peking Express." Based on a story by Harry Hervey. 80m/B VHS. Marlene Dietrich, Clive Brook, Anna May Wong, Warner Oland, Eugene Pallette, Lawrence Grant, Louise Closser Hale; *D:* Josef von Sternberg; *W:* Jules Furthman; *C:* Lee Garmes. Oscars '32: Cinematog.

The Shanghai Gesture ✓✓✓½ 1942 A wildly baroque, subversive melodrama. An English financier tries to close a gambling den, only to be blackmailed by the female proprietor—who tells him not only is the man's daughter heavily indebted to her, but that she is the wife he abandoned long ago. Based on a notorious Broadway play. Von Sternberg had to make numerous changes to the script in order to get it past the Hays censors; the director's final Hollywood work, and worthy of his oeuvre, but oddly unsatisfying. 97m/B VHS, DVD. Walter Huston, Gene Tierney, Victor Mature, Ona Munson, Phyllis Brooks, Mike Mazurki; *D:* Josef von Sternberg; *W:* Josef von Sternberg, Jules Furthman, Geza Herczeg, Karl Vollmoller; *C:* Paul Ivano; *M:* Richard Hageman.

Shanghai Kiss ✓✓ 2007 Twenty-something Liam Liu (Leung) is a struggling Chinese-American actor in L.A. who befriends 16-year-old high school genius Adelaide (Panettiere). Imagine the complications when 'romance starts lurking, and Liam can't quite forget temptation when he decides to move to Shanghai after inheriting his grandmother's house. 106m/C VHS, DVD. Ken Leung, Hayden Panettiere, Kelly Hu, Joel David Moore, James Hong, Timothy Bottoms; *D:* Ken Konwiser, David Ren; *W:* David Ren; *C:* Alexander Buono; *M:* David Kitay. VIDEO

Shanghai Knights ✓✓½ 2003 (PG-13) Chon Wang (Chan) and Roy (Wilson) team up again when Wang's father is killed while guarding the Imperial Seal. Wang's sister Li (Fann) has witnessed the crime and followed the culprit to London, where the duo also converge. There they find a plot by frustrated royal heirs Fathbone (Gillen) and Wu Chan (Yen) to overthrow the British and Chinese thrones. Chan and Wilson still have their great chemistry, and the script gives them plenty of opportunities to show it. Chan choreographs the fight scenes like numbers in a musical to excellent effect, paying homage to "Singin' in the Rain" as well as some of his influences such as the Keystone Kops, Harold Lloyd, Abbott and Costello, and Charlie Chaplin. Victorian-era cultural references are fun to catalogue as well. 107m/C VHS, DVD. Jackie Chan, Owen Wilson, Aidan Gillen, Fann Wong, Donnie Yen, Gemma Jones, Kim Chan, Aaron Johnson, Thomas (Tom) Fisher, Oliver Cotton; *D:* David Dobkin; *W:* Alfred Gough, Miles Millar; *C:* Adrian Biddle; *M:* Randy Edelman.

Shanghai Noon ✓✓½ 2000 (PG-13) Goofy, good-natured, western action/comedy finds Chinese imperial guard Chon Wang (Chan) in trouble for not preventing Princess Pei Pei (Liu) from running off to America (circa 1880) with her American tutor (Connery). But it all turns out to be a kidnapping scheme and Wang winds up in Nevada, helping to deliver the ransom gold. Through some unlikely events, Wang hooks up with talkative, unsuccessful outlaw Roy O'Bannon (Wilson), learns some of the west's wilder ways, and the buds set out to rescue the damsel, who's no shrinking flower herself. Chan and Wilson are both throughly ingratiating and you've got the Chan sturts to look forward to as well. 110m/C VHS, DVD. Jackie Chan, Lucy Liu, Owen Wilson, Roger Yuan, Xander Berkeley, Jason Connery, Henry O, Walton Goggins, Russ Badger, Ratae Baez, Brandon Merrill; *D:* Tom Dey; *W:* Alfred Gough, Miles Millar; *C:* Dan Mindel; *M:* Randy Edelman.

Shanghai Surprise ✗½ 1986 (PG-13) The salesman Penn and missionary Madonna (yeah, right) are better than you'd think, and the story (of opium smuggling in China in the '30s) is intrepid and widly fun, but indifferently directed and unsure of itself. Executive producer George Harrison wrote the songs and has a cameo. 90m/C VHS, DVD. Sean Penn, Madonna, Paul Freeman, Richard Griffiths; *Cameos:* George Harrison; *D:* Jim Goddard; *W:* Robert Bentley; *M:* George Harrison. Golden Raspberries '86: Worst Actress (Madonna).

Shanghai Triad ✓✓✓½ 1995 Yeo a laboration of director Yimou and star Li takes place in violent crime dynasty of 1930s Shanghai. Here, eight days are seen through the eyes of a young boy (Cuihua) initiated into the Triad to be the lackey of the mob boss's arrogant mistress (Li). The trio and some trusty associates flee to the country after things heet up with a rival mob. Yimou subtly distinguishes the dichotory between the jaded criminals and the naive youth with the move from the city to the country and his use of color and tone while avoiding cliche. Plot twists are fresh and technical aspects impeccable. Chinese with subtitles. 108m/C VHS, DVD. FR:CH Gong Li, Baotian Li, Xuejian Li, Shun Chun Shusheng, Wang Xiaoxiao Cuihua, Jiang Baoying; *D:* Yimou Zhang; *W:* Bi Feiyu; *C:* Lu Yue; *M:* Zhang Guangtian.

Shanty Tramp ✗ 1967 Small-town tramp puts the moves on an evangelist, a motorcyle gang, and a young black man, who risks his life trying to save her from her loose morals. A nother cheesy flick made for the drive-in crowd. 72m/B VHS, DVD. Lee Holland, Bill Rogers, Lawrence Tolin; *D:* Joseph Prieto. TV

Shark Attack 3: Megalodon ✓½ 2002 (R) An amusing goof of a killer sea critter flick. A company lying cable on the ocean floor wakes up a prehistoric Megalodon shark that decides to snack on vacationers at a nearby resort min on Ben (Barrowman) and paleontologist Cataine (McShane) hunt the beastie down. And then find out they've only killed a baby. And boy is mama mad! 94m/C VHS, DVD. John Barrowman, Jenny (Jennifer) McShane, Ryan Cutrona, George Stanchev; *D:* David Worth; *W:* Scott Devine, William Hooke; *C:* David Worth; *M:* Bill Wandel. VIDEO

Shark Attack 2 ✓½ 2000 (R) Biological experiment on shark goes awry causing a shark to go on a particularly nasty tear. Yeah, some shark hunters go after the beastie but you know they're just as nasty. 93m/C VHS, DVD. Nikita Ager, Dan-iel Alexander, Thorsten Kaye, Danny Kei; *D:* David Worth, Yossi Wein; *W:* William Hooke, Scott Devine. *M:* Mark Morgan. VIDEO

Shark Attack ✓✓½ 1999 (R) A marine biologist investigates a rash of shark attacks terrorizing an African fishing village that have claimed the life of a friend. 95m/C VHS, DVD. SA Casper Van Dien, Ernie Hudson, Bentley Mitchum, Jenny (Jennifer) McShane; *D:* Bob Misiorowski; *W:* Scott Devine, William Hooke; *C:* Lawrence Sher. VIDEO

Shark! ✗½ *Man-Eater; Un Arma de Dos Filos* 1968 (PG) American gun smuggler Reynolds, stranded in a tiny seaport in Africa, joins the crew of a marine biologist's boat. He soon discovers the boat's owner and his wife are trying to retrieve gold bullion that lies deep in shark-infested waters. Typical Reynoldsian action-intrested dumbness. Like "Twilight Zone: The Movie," earned notoriety because of on-location tragedy: a stunt diver really was killed by a shark. Edited without the consent of Fuller, who disowned it. 92m/C VHS, DVD. Burt Reynolds, Barry Sullivan, Arthur Kennedy; *D:* Samuel Fuller; *M:* Samuel Fuller.

Shark Hunter ✗ *Deep; Il Cacciatore di Squali* 1979 Shark hunter gets ensnared in the mob's net off the Mexican coast as they race for a cache of sunken millions. The usual garden-variety B-grade adventure. 95m/C VHS. IT SP Franco Nero, Jorge Luke, Mike Forrest, Werner Pochath; *D:* Enzo G. Castellari; *W:* Tito Carpi; *C:* Pablo Cubero; *M:* Guido de Angelis, Maurizio de Angelis.

Shark River ✗½ 1953 A man attempts to get his brother, a Civil War veteran accused of murder, through the Everglades and send him to safety in Cuba. Good photography of the great swamp; disappointing story. 80m/C VHS. Steve Cochran, Carole Mathews, Warren Stevens; *D:* John Rawlins; *W:* Lewis Meltzer, Louis Lantz.

Shaolin Soccer ✓✓½ 2001 (PG-13) *Siulam Chukkau; Siu lam juk kau.* Wacky action-comedy about Sing (Chow), a kung fu expert and Shaolin monk, playing on a soccer team with other monks vying for Hong Kong's national championship against "Team Evil." Went on to become the highest-grossing film in Hong Kong's history. In Cantonese; with English subtitles. 87m/C DVD. Stephen (Chiau) Chow, Yin (Patrick) Tse; *D:* Stephen (Chiau) Chow; *W:* Stephen (Chiau) Chow, Kan-Cheung (Sammy) Tsang; *C:* Ting Wo Kwong, Pak-huen Kwan; *M:* Lowell Lo, Raymond Wong.

The Shape of Things ✓✓ 2003 (R) LaBute is back to his own skewed view of the world, taken from his 2001 play. Nebbishy Adam (Rudd) works as a guard at a college art museum. Evelyn (Weisz) is the art student who bedazzles him, and she begins to make him over into someone desirable, which angers his chauvinistic best friend Philip (Weller). But the "new" Adam sparks feeings in Philip's fiancee Jenny (Mol), who was once the object of Adam's unrecalled affection. Never subtle, LaBute's intention to leave no cruelty unexplored is blatant and wears quickly. Despite the best efforts of the actors invoved, the film's stage origins and LaBute's obvious direction combine to lessen the film's impact. 96m/C VHS, DVD. US Paul Rudd, Rachel Weisz, Gretchen Mol, Frederick Weller; *D:* Neil LaBute; *W:* Neil LaBute; *C:* James L. Carter; *M:* Elvis Costello.

Shark Tale ✓✓½ 2004 (PG) This animated underwater comedy has the taint smell of dead fish clinging to it—probably because it tries too hard. Boastful guppy Oscar (Smith) works at the mob-fronted Whale Wash and is in trouble with his boss Sykes (Scorsese), who thinks the kid should be taught a lesson. Teaching lessons is also on the mind of shark mob boss Lino (De Niro), who wants son Frankie (Imperioli) to straighten out his schnook who's gone vegetarian, Oscar takes the credit when Frankie accidentally gets killed and then must defend his reputation as a sharkslayer, aided by a reluctant Lenny. Longtime collaborators De Niro and Scorsese have a blast spoofing their director/producer past Wilde. 90m/C VHS, DVD. Will Smith, Robert De Niro, Renee Zellweger, Jack Black, Angelina Jolie, Martin Scorsese, Peter Falk, Mic'eal Imperioli, Vincent Pastore, Doug E. Doug, Ziggy Marley, Katie Couric, Jenifer Lewis, Lenny Venito, Phil LaMarr.

Sharks' Treasure ✓✓½ 1975 (PG) A band of escaped convicts commandeer a boat filled with gold. Old fashioned sunken-treasure tale unexceptional except as a virtual one man show by writer/actor/director/producer/fitness nut Wilde. 95m/C VHS. Cornel Wilde, Yaphet Kotto, John Neilson, Cliff Osmond, David Canary, David G.llam; *D:* Cornel Wilde.

Sharky's Machine ✓✓½ 1981 (R) A tough undercover cop (Reynolds) is hot on the trail of a crooked crime czar. Meanwhile he falls for a high-priced hooker. Well done but overdone action, with much violence. Based on the William Diehl novel. 119m/C VHS, DVD. Burt Reynolds, Rachel Ward, Vittorio Gassman, Brian Keith, Charles Durning, Bernie Casey, Richard Libertini, Henry Silva, John Fiedler, Earl Holliman; *D:* Burt Reynolds; *W:* Gerald Di Pego; *C:* William A. Fraker.

Sharma & Beyond ✗ 1984 A teenage would-be science fiction writer falls in love with the daughter of a famous sci-fi author. 85m/C VHS. Suzanne Burden, Robert Urquhart, Michael Maloney; *D:* Brian Gilbert; *M:* Rachel Portman.

Sharon's Secret ✗ 1995 (R) When the mutilated bodies of wealthy Richard Harty and his wife are discovered, investigating detective Thomas McGregor (Henry) looks to place the blame on their traumatized 16-year-old daughter Sharon (Cameron), who'll inherit a fortune. Psychiatrist Laurel O'Connor (Harris) is assigned to help Sharon recover and she's determined by family attorney Frank Bowdin (McArthur) that it seems everyone has something to hide. 91m/C VHS. Candace Cameron, Mel Harris, Gregg Henry, Alex McArthur, Paul Regina, Elaine Kagan, James Piccens Jr.; *D:* Michael Scott; *W:* Mark Horner. CABLE

Sharpe's Battle ✓✓½ 1994 Sharpe (Bean) must prepare the Royal Irish company, led by Lord Kiely (Durr) and used to only ceremonial duties, for their first battle. Meanwhile, Kiely's wife (Byrne) goes to Sharpe for help with a personal matter and there's more trouble with the friend Harper (O'Malley). 100m/C VHS, DVD. GB Sean Bean, Daragh O'Malley, Hugh Fraser, Jason Durr, Allie Byrne; *D:* Tom Clegg; *W:* Russell Lewis. TV

Sharpe's Challenge ✓✓½ 2006 After Waterloo, Richard Sharpe (Bean) is dispatched to India because a local Maharaja is threatening British interests. Things worsen when Sharpe discovers best friend Harper (O'Malley) is missing, a general's daughter (Brown) has been kidnapped, and the beautiful but scheming Madhuvanti (Lakshmi) wants to use Richard to further her own ambitions. Filmed in Rajasthan, India; based on the Bernard Cornwell novels. The first new TV Sharpe adventure since 1997. 138m/C DVD.

GB Sean Bean, Padma Lakshmi, Toby Stephens, Daragh O'Malley, Lucy Brown, Hugh Fraser, Michael Cochrane, Peter Symonds, Karan Panthaky; *D:* Tom Clegg. **TV**

Sharpe's Company 🦴🦴½ 1994 Sharpe (Bean) sets out to rescue Spanish lover Teresa (Serna) and his infant daughter, trapped in the French-held city of Badajoz, which is about to be stormed by British troops. To make matters worse, Sharpe must also deal with the machinations of underhanded madman Sergeant Obadiah Hakeswill (Postlethwaite), an old enemy with a grudge to settle. Based on the novel by Bernard Cornwell; made for British TV. 100m/C VHS, DVD. *GB* Sean Bean, Assumpta Serna, Daragh O'Malley, Pete Postlethwaite, Hugh Fraser, Clive Francis, Louise Germaine; *D:* Tom Clegg; *W:* Charles Wood. **TV**

Sharpe's Eagle 🦴🦴½ 1993 Sharpe (Bean) and his chosen band of sharpshooters are once again in the thick of battle against Napoleon's troops but this time they have the misfortune to be led by the imbecilic Sir Henry Simmerson (Cochrane). Thanks to Simmerson's cowardice, the regimental colors are captured and a heroic officer Sharpe admires is killed. Setting out for revenge, Sharpe is determined to capture the French eagle, a carved golden eagle carried into battle, and settle some personal scores. Based on the novel by Bernard Cornwell; made for British TV. 100m/C VHS, DVD. *GB* Sean Bean, Assumpta Serna, Brian Cox, David Troughton, Daragh O'Malley, Michael Cochrane, Katia Caballero; *D:* Tom Clegg; *W:* Eoghan Harris; *C:* Ivan Strasburg; *M:* Dominic Muldowney. **TV**

Sharpe's Enemy 🦴🦴½ 1994 Sharpe (Bean) is sent to a mountain stronghold, held by a band of deserters, to ransom Isabella (Hurley), the bride of English colonel, Sir Augustus Farthingdale (Child). But the evil Hakeswill (Postlethwaite) is leading the criminals and he refuses to make things easy for our hero—nor will the French troops leave the English soldiers in peace. Based on the novel by Bernard Cornwell; made for British TV. 100m/C VHS, DVD. *GB* Sean Bean, Assumpta Serna, Pete Postlethwaite, Daragh O'Malley, Hugh Fraser, Elizabeth Hurley, Michael Byrne, Jeremy Child, Nicholas (Nick) Rowe; *D:* Tom Clegg; *W:* Eoghan Harris. **TV**

Sharpe's Gold 🦴🦴½ 1994 Circa 1813 and Richard Sharpe (Bean) has now been promoted to Major—still leading his band of renegade sharpshooters. This time they're assigned to trade rifles for deserters held by the partisans and search for hidden Aztec gold, as Wellington (Fraser) prepares to push on into France. Sharpe must also protect Wellington's cousin Bess (Linehan) and her daughter Ellie (Ashbourne) as they search for Bess' missing husband. Based on the novel by Bernard Cornwell; made for British TV. 100m/C VHS, DVD. *GB* Sean Bean, Daragh O'Malley, Hugh Fraser, Rosaleen Linehan, Jayne Ashbourne, Abel Folk, Peter Eyre; *D:* Tom Clegg; *W:* Nigel Kneale. **TV**

Sharpe's Honour 🦴🦴½ 1994 Sharpe (Bean) becomes a pawn of French spy Pierre Ducos when he's forced to cross enemy lines, disguised as a Spanish rebel, in order to defend himself against allegations of dishonor. Sharpe's also unable to resist the attractions of the Marquesa Dorada (Krige), who's also part of Ducos' plan. Based on the novel by Bernard Cornwell; made for British TV. 100m/C VHS, DVD. *GB* Sean Bean, Daragh O'Malley, Hugh Fraser, Michael Byrne, Ron Cook; *D:* Tom Clegg; *W:* Colin MacDonald. **TV**

Sharpe's Justice 🦴🦴½ 1997 Having cleared his name, Richard Sharpe (Bean) returns to England and is ordered north where he's to command the local militia. But Sharpe soon has to decide whether to support the local gentry or the working class in a time of social unrest. Based on the novel by Bernard Cornwell. 100m/C VHS, DVD. *GB* Sean Bean, Daragh O'Malley, Abigail Cruttenden, Alexis Denisof, Douglas Henshall, Caroline Langrishe, Philip Glenister; *D:* Tom Clegg.

Sharpe's Legend 🦴🦴½ 1997 Highlights from the British TV series detailing the life, loves, and career of 19th-century British soldier/hero Richard Sharpe (Bean). Narrated by Rifleman Cooper (Mears). 90m/C VHS, DVD. *GB* Sean Bean, Michael Mears; *D:* Paul Wilmshurst. **TV**

Sharpe's Mission 🦴🦴½ 1996 Sharpe (Bean) joins with Colonel Brand (Strong) and his men to blow up an ammunition depot as Wellington continues his invasion of France. But Brand arouses Sharpe's suspicions that the supposedly heroic Colonel is actually a French spy. Based on the novel by Bernard Cornwell; made for British TV. 100m/C VHS, DVD. *GB* Sean Bean, Daragh O'Malley, Hugh Fraser, James Laurenson, Mark Strong, Abigail Cruttenden; *D:* Tom Clegg; *W:* Eoghan Harris. **TV**

Sharpe's Regiment 🦴🦴½ 1996 Wellington prepares for the invasion of France in June, 1813 but the South Essex battalion needs more men. So Sharpe (Bean) and Harper (O'Malley) are sent back to London for recruits and uncover corruption in high places. Based on the novel by Bernard Cornwell. 100m/C VHS, DVD. *GB* Sean Bean, Daragh O'Malley, Nicholas Farrell, Michael Cochrane, Abigail Cruttenden, Caroline Langrishe, James Laurenson; *D:* Tom Clegg; *W:* Eoghan Harris. **TV**

Sharpe's Revenge 🦴🦴½ 1997 The Penisular War is over but Sharpe (Bean) is accused of stealing Napoleon's treasures by old enemy Ducos. Abandoned by his wife when he's convicted of the crime, Sharpe escapes from prison and crosses postwar France in search of the truth. Based on the novel by Bernard Cornwell. 100m/C VHS, DVD. *GB* Sean Bean, Daragh O'Malley, Abigail Cruttenden, Feodor Atkine, Alexis Denisof, Cecile Paoli, Philip Whitchurch; *D:* Tom Clegg; *W:* Eoghan Harris. **TV**

Sharpe's Rifles 🦴🦴½ 1993 Swashbuckling heroics dominate as the Duke of Wellington's British soldiers battle Napoleon's French forces in the 1809 Peninsular War (fought in Spain and Portugal). Common soldier Richard Sharpe (Bean) has just been promoted and given the unenviable task of leading a group of malcontent sharpshooters on a secret mission to aid Britain's Spanish allies. But it's not all hard times for Sharpe since the Spanish commander happens to be a very lovely woman. Adapted from the novel by Bernard Cornwell; made for British TV. 100m/C VHS, DVD. *GB* Sean Bean, Assumpta Serna, Brian Cox, David Troughton, Daragh O'Malley, Julian Fellowes, Timothy Bentinck, Simon Andreu, Michael Mears, John Tams, Jason Salkey, Paul Trussell; *D:* Tom Clegg; *W:* Eoghan Harris; *C:* Ivan Strasburg; *M:* Dominic Muldowney. **TV**

Sharpe's Siege 🦴🦴½ 1996 In the winter of 1813, Napoleon Bonaparte sends his best spy, Major Ducos (Atkine), to find out where Wellington plans to invade France. The newly married Sharpe (Bean) is forced to leave his ill wife, Jane (Cruttenden), and capture a French fort while preventing Ducos' treachery. Based on the novel by Bernard Cornwell. 100m/C VHS, DVD. *GB* Sean Bean, Daragh O'Malley, Hugh Fraser, Abigail Cruttenden, James Laurenson, Feodor Atkine; *D:* Tom Clegg; *W:* Eoghan Harris. **TV**

Sharpe's Sword 🦴🦴½ 1994 Sharpe's (Bean) sent to protect Wellington's top spy, El Mirador, and finds himself up against Napoleon's top swordsman Colonel Leroux (Fierry). When Sharpe's wounded, it's up to Lass (Mortimer), a young mute convent girl, to save our hero's life. Based on the novel by Bernard Cornwell; made for British TV. 100m/C VHS, DVD. *GB* Sean Bean, Daragh O'Malley, Patrick Fierry, Emily Mortimer, John Kavanagh; *D:* Tom Clegg; *W:* Eoghan Harris. **TV**

Sharpe's Waterloo 🦴🦴½ 1997 Sharpe's (Bean) making a new life with new love Lucille (Paoli) at their French chateau. But when Napoleon returns from exile, Sharpe returns to the army and the Chosen Men to organize a defense before the battle of Waterloo. Based on the novel by Bernard Cornwell. 100m/C VHS, DVD. *GB* Sean Bean, Daragh O'Malley, Hugh Fraser, Cecile Paoli, Alexis Denisof, Paul Bettany; *D:* Tom Clegg. **TV**

Shattered 🦴🦴🦴 *Scherben* 1921 Key film in Germany's kammerspiel (chamber play) movement, which emphasized naturalism with a minimum number of characters. A railway worker's daughter is seduced by her father's supervisor. When the man abandons her, the girl's father takes revenge. 62m/B VHS. *GE* Werner Krauss, Edith Posca, Paul Otto; *D:* Lupu Pick; *W:* Carl Mayer.

Shattered 🦴🦴½ *Something to Hide* 1972 (R) Finch plays Harry, a man blamed for a failed marriage, held hostage in his home by his own paranoia, and driven to bouts of drinking. Slowly his tenuous grip on sanity slips and at any moment his fragile and crumbling life may be shattered. Tired, overwrought domestic drama. 100m/C VHS. *GB* Peter Finch, Shelley Winters, Colin Blakely; *D:* Alastair Reid.

Shattered 🦴🦴 1991 (R) An architect recovering from a serious automobile accident tries to regain the memory that he has lost. As he begins to put together the pieces of his life, some parts of the puzzle don't quite fit. For example, he recalls his now loving wife's affair as well as his own. He remembers that he hired a private detective to follow his wife and shockingly, he remembers that he once believed his wife had planned to kill him. Are these memories the real thing, or are they all part of some mad, recuperative nightmare? Who knows. 98m/C VHS, DVD. Tom Berenger, Bob Hoskins, Greta Scacchi, Joanne Whalley, Corbin Bernsen, Theodore Bikel; *D:* Wolfgang Petersen; *W:* Wolfgang Petersen.

Shattered 🦴🦴 *Butterfly on a Wheel* 2007 (R) Neil (Butler) and his wife Abby (Bello) must perform a series of nearly-impossible (and criminal) tasks around Chicago in order to save their young daughter, who's been kidnapped by sociopath Ryan (Brosnan). Implausible and unsubtle (with a twist ending) but that's one cool cast. 95m/C DVD. *CA* Pierce Brosnan, Gerard Butler, Maria Bello, Claudette Mink, Callum Keith Rennie, Nicholas Lea, Samantha Ferris; *D:* Mike Barker; *W:* Malia Nurmi; *C:* Ashley Rowe; *M:* Robert Duncan.

Shattered Dreams 🦴🦴½ 1990 TV movie about domestic violence finds Wagner as the battered wife of a prominent, high-profile government official. Based on a true story. 94m/C VHS, DVD. Georgann Johnson, James Karen, Lindsay Wagner, Michael Nouri; *D:* Robert Iscove; *W:* David Hill; *C:* John Beymer; *M:* Michael Convertino.

Shattered Glass 🦴🦴🦴½ 2003 (PG-13) Christensen loses the Jedi robes to take on a character lured by a less-mystical dark side. Wunderkind Stephen Glass, a young New Republic journalist, is found to have fabricated 27 of the 41 articles he'd published. He also goes to great lengths to give truth to the lies, falsifying phone numbers, creating a bogus website, keeping fake notes. First-time director Ray was in close council with the principals involved in the true tale and does a fabulous job keeping the depiction believable. Background as to what drove him to it is all that's missing in this journalist suspense story. 99m/C VHS, DVD. *US* Hayden Christensen, Peter Sarsgaard, Chloe Sevigny, Rosario Dawson, Melanie Lynskey, Steve Zahn, Hank Azaria, Luke Kirby, Cas Anvar, Ted Kotcheff, Mark Blum, Simone-Elise Girard, Chad E. Donella; *D:* Billy Ray; *W:* Billy Ray; *C:* Mandy Walker; *M:* Mychael Danna. Natl. Soc. Film Critics '03: Support. Actor (Sarsgaard).

Shattered Image 🦴🦴½ 1993 (R) Confusing thriller about the FBI's involvement in the kidnapping of the owner of a model agency, as well as plastic surgery, and a big money scam. 100m/C VHS, DVD. Bo Derek, Jack Scalia, John Savage, Dorian Harewood, Ramon Franco, Carol Lawrence, Michael (M.K.) Harris, David McCallum; *D:* Fritz Kiersch. CABLE

Shattered Image 🦴🦴½ 1998 Jessie (Parillaud) is either a cold-blooded hit woman dreaming she's a honeymooner, or a newlywed dreaming she's a psycho assassin. Or both. After whacking a businessman in the men's room at a Seattle restaurant, our heroine goes home to bed, and wakes up a different woman. Literally. On her way to Jamaica with her new husband (Baldwin), Jessie again nods off and she's back in Seattle on her next hit. Each reality features characters from the alternate one, although (like Jessie) each has a different personality. Ruiz fills the screen with stunning homages (Wellesian mirror shots and Hitchcockian split personalities), a truly outrageous ending, and the surrealistic feel of a dream, making for psychotic, if not completely convincing, fun. 102m/C VHS, DVD. Anne Parillaud, William Baldwin, Lisanne Falk, Graham Greene, Bulle Ogier, Billy Wilmott, O'Neil Peart, Leonie Forbes; *D:* Raul Ruiz; *W:* Duane Poole; *C:* Robby Muller; *M:* Jorge Arriagada.

Shattered Silence 🦴🦴½ *When Michael Calls* 1971 A woman is tormented by phone calls that seem to be coming from her dead son as her life is torn apart by divorce. Leaves unanswered the question: Will there be any suspense? Made for TV. Worthless and dumb. 73m/C VHS, DVD. Elizabeth Ashley, Ben Gazzara, Michael Douglas, Karen Pearson; *D:* Philip Leacock. **TV**

Shattered Spirits 🦴🦴½ 1986 (PG-13) Quiet family man cracks and goes on a rampage through his normally peaceful suburban neighborhood. Been done before and better. 93m/C VHS, DVD. Martin Sheen, Melinda Dillon, Matthew Laborteaux, Roxana Zal, Lukas Haas; *D:* Robert Greenwald; *W:* Gregory Goodell; *C:* John R. Jensen; *M:* Michael Hoenig.

Shattered Vows 🦴🦴 1984 A young nun struggles with her love for a priest and her desire for a child. Bertinelli is convincing as the confused teen in otherwise ordinary TV drama. Adapted from the true story of Dr. Mary Gilligan Wong as told in her book, "Nun: A Memoir." 95m/C VHS. Valerie Bertinelli, David Morse, Caroline McWilliams, Patricia Neal, Millie Perkins, Leslie Ackerman, Lisa Jane Persky; *D:* Jack Bender.

Shaun of the Dead 🦴🦴🦴 2004 (R) Brits Wright and Pegg's flick has been referred to as a "rom zom com" or romantic zombie comedy-certainly a cinematic rarity. Slacker clerk Shaun (Pegg), who lives with his loser chum Ed (Frost), is dumped by frustrated girlfriend Liz (Ashfield) and goes to his favorite pub to drown his sorrows. Because of his morning hangover, Shaun is unaware that London is suddenly overrun with the walking dead. It takes a zombie in the garden to get Shaun and Ed to take action—armed with a cricket bat, shovel, and unwanted vinyl discs from their record collection (the better to slice off a zombie's head). But there's an up side: the zombie crisis brings out the best in Shaun as the survivors retreat to the pub for a final stand, and more. 99m/C VHS, DVD, UMD, HD DVD. Kate Ashfield, Penelope Wilton, Bill Nighy, Simon Pegg, Nick Frost, Lucy Davis, Dylan Moran, Nicola Cunningham, Jessica Stevenson; *D:* Edgar Wright; *W:* Simon Pegg, Edgar Wright; *C:* David M. Dunlap; *M:* Daniel Mudford, Peter Woodhead.

The Shawshank Redemption 🦴🦴🦴½ 1994 (R) Bank veep Andy (Robbins) is convicted of the murder of his wife and her lover and sentenced to the "toughest prison in the Northeast." While there he forms a friendship with lifer Red (Freeman), experiences the brutality of prison life, adapts, offers financial advice to the guards, and helps the warden (Gunton) cook the prison books...all in a short 19 years. In his theatrical debut, director Darabont avoids belaboring most prison movie cliches while Robbins' talent for playing ambiguous characters is put to good use, and Freeman brings his usual grace to what could have been a thankless role. Adapted from the novella "Rita Hayworth and the Shawshank Redemption" by Stephen King. 142m/C VHS, DVD. Tim Robbins, Morgan Freeman, Bob Gunton, William Sadler, Clancy Brown, Mark Rolston, Gil Bellows, James Whitmore; *D:* Frank Darabont; *W:* Frank Darabont; *C:* Roger Deakins; *M:* Thomas Newman.

She 🐾🐾½ 1925 H. Rider Haggard's famous story about the ageless Queen Ayesha, (Blythe), who renews her life force periodically by walking through a pillar of cold flame. Story and titles by Haggard. Blythe is a stirringly mean queen. Silent film with music score. 69m/B VHS. Betty Blythe, Carlyle Blackwell, Mary Odette, Tom Reynolds; D: Leander De Cordova, (George) Blenthold) Samuelson; W: Walter Summers.

She 🐾🐾½ 1935 First sound version of H. Rider Haggard's popular 1887 adventure tale, although the film's location was changed from Africa to the frozen Arctic. Explorers Scott and Bruce are searching for a strangely mean queen, who doesn't return her love, and there's trouble. Fantastic Art Deco sets and special effects. 95m/B VHS, DVD. Helen Gahagan, Randolph Scott, Nigel Bruce, Helen Mack, Gustav von Seyffertitz; D: Irving Pichel, Lansing C. Holden; M: Max Steiner.

She 🐾🐾 1983 A beautiful female warrior rules over the men in a post-holocaust world. She is kidnapped by a wealthy merchant who uses her to fight evil mutants. Utter rubbish vaguely based on the Haggard novel. 90m/C VHS. Sandahl Bergman, Harrison Muller, Quin Kessler, David Goss; D: Avi Nesher.

S*H*E 🐾🐾 1979 A flashy made for TV spy thriller. The female agent S*H*E (Securities Hazards Expert) must save the world's oil; good locations, nifty plot and looker Sharpe as the she-Bond and a reasonaly fun time. Scripted by "Bond"-writer Maibaum. 100m/C VHS. Cornelia Sharpe, Robert Lansing, William Taylor, Isabella Rye, Anita Ekberg; Cameos: Omar Sharif; D: Robert Lewis; W: Richard Maibaum; M: Michael Kamen. TV

She and He 🐾🐾½ 1963 Hani's look at the oppression of women, marital and spiritual discontent, and class divisions. Naoko is a bored housewife, living in a sterile high-rise apartment with her equally dissatisfied husband, and yearning for something to express her inner feelings. She accidentally meets an intinctly unforgiving feminist fiction. Arnold is classmate of her husband's who has become a poor ragpicker and tries to aid him. But all her efforts only lead to further tragedies. In Japanese with English subtitles. 110m/C VHS. JP Sachiko Hidari, Eiji Okada, Kikuji Yamashita; D: Susumu Hani.

The She-Beast 🐾🐾½ 1965 Il Lago di Satana; The Revenge of the Blood Beast; La Sorella de Satan. The Sister of Satan 1965 Burned at the stake in 18th-century Transylvania, a witch returns in the body of a beautiful young English woman on her honeymoon fin Transylvania(?), and once again wreaks death and destruction. Caution. 74m/C VHS, DVD. IT YU Barbara Steele, Ian Ogilvy, Mel Welles, Lucretia Love; D: Michael Reeves; W: Michael Reeves; M: Ralph Ferraro.

She Came on the Bus Woof! 1969 Young thugs break into a well-kept suburban home and terrorize the housewife through rape and torture. Then they kidnap a bus and pose as the drivers until they can find more victims. Contains scenes of graphic violence which would be considered offensive even by today's standards. 58m/C VHS, DVD. D: Harry Vincent.

She Came to the Valley 🐾🐾 1952 A wealthy oil heiress (Simmons) with good intentions plans to give her money away to those friends who had helped her when she was struggling. Things don't go quite as planned; her philanthropy leads to unexpected mayhem in her Arkansas hometown. Passable, but not memorable comedy. 90m/C VHS. Robert Mitchum, Jean Simmons, Arthur Hunnicutt, Edgar Buchanan, Wallace Ford; D: Lloyd Bacon.

She Couldn't Say No 🐾🐾 Texas in Flames 1977 (PG) A tough pioneer woman becomes embroiled in political intrigue during the Spanish-American War. Based on Cleo Dawson's book. 90m/C VHS. DVD. Ronee Blakley, Dean Stockwell, Scott Glenn, Freddy Fender; D: Albert Band; C: Daniel Pearl; M: Tommy Lecnetti. Beautiful But Dangerous

She Creature 🐾🐾½ Mermaid Chronicles Part 1: She Creature 2001 (R) In 1905, carnival barker Angus Shaw (Liiy) is traveling in Ireland with his girlfriend Lily (Gugino) posing as a mermaid in a sideshow attraction. They meet drunken ex-sailor Woolrich (Morris) who takes them to his home where he has his own attraction—a real live mermaid (Kilhstech). Angus steals the mermaid and sails for America but the creature begins attacking crewman and Lily develops a symbiotic relationship with the creature. Very loosely based on the AIP 1956 B-movie of the same title, this was one of a series of cable remakes under the umbrella title "Creature Features." 91m/C VHS, DVD. Ru-tus Sewell, Carla Gugino, Rya Kihlstech, Aubrey Morris, Jim Piddock, Gil Bellows, Reno Wilson; D: Sebastian Gutierrez; W: Sebastian Gutierrez; C: Thomas Callaway; M: David Reynolds. CABLE

She Demons Woof! 1958 Pleasure craft loaded with babes crashes into a remote island controlled by a mad ex-Nazi scientist who transforms pretty girls into rubber-faced Frankensteins. Incomprehensible, to say the least. 68m/B VHS, DVD. Irish McCalla, Tod Griffin, Victor Sen Yung, Rudolph Anders, Gene Roth, Bill Coontz, Billy Dix; D: Richard Cunha; W: Richard Cunha, H.E. Barrie; C: Meredith Nicholson; M: Nicholas Carras.

She-Devil 🐾🐾½ 1989 (PG-13) A comic book version of the acidic Fay Weldon novel "The Life and Loves of a She-Devil"; a fat, dowdy, suburban wife (Arnold) becomes a vengeful beast when a smarmy romance novelist steals her husband. Uneven comedic reworking of a distinctly unforgiving feminist fiction. Arnold is given too much to do and she does-Streep's role is too slight, though she does great things with it. 100m/C VHS, DVD. Meryl Streep, Roseanne, Ed Begley Jr., Linda Hunt, Elizabeth Peters, Bryan Larkin, A. Martinez, Sylvia Miles; D: Susan Seidelman; W: Mark Burns, Barry Strugatz; C: Oliver Stapleton; M: Howard Shore.

She Devils in Chains 🐾🐾 American Beauty Hostages; Ebony, Ivory, and Jade; Foxforce 1976 (PG) A group of traveling female athletes are kidnapped by a groups of sadists who torture and beat them. In the end, however, the girls get their revenge. 82m/C VHS, DVD. Colleen Camp, Rosanne Katon, Sylvia Anderson, Ken Washington, Leo Martinez; D: Cirio H. Santiago; M: Eddie Nova.

She-Devils on Wheels Woof! 1968 Havoc erupts as an outlaw female motorcycle gang, known as "Maneaters on Motorbikes," terrorizes a town—especially the men. Really, really bad biker flick finely honed by Lewis. 83m/C VHS, DVD. Betty Connell, Christie Wagner, Pat Poston, Nancy Lee Noble, Ruby Tuesday, Roy Collodi, David Harris, Steve White; D: Herschell Gordon Lewis; W: Allison Louise Downe; C: Roy Collodi; M: Larry Wellington.

She Done Him Wrong 🐾🐾🐾 1933 Singer Lady Lou (West) fronts an 1890s Bowery saloon for her shady boss. Gus Jordan (Beery Sr.). Gus gives her diamonds but when she gets an eyeful of young Salvation Army Capt. Cummings (Grant), Lou starts to think there's other things in life worth having. West imparts the screen version of her Broadway hit "Diamond Lil" with her usual share of double entendres and racy comments. ♫ Silver Threads Among the Gold; Maisie, My Pretty Daisy; Easy Rider; I Like a Guy What Takes His Time; Frankie and Johnny. 66m/B VHS. Mae West, Cary Grant, Owen Moore, Noah Beery Sr., Gilbert Roland, Louise Beavers, Rafaela (Rafael, Raphaella) Ottiano; D: Lowell Sherman; W: Harvey Thew, John Bright; C: Charles Bryant) Lang Jr.; M: Ralph Rainger, David Landau. Natl. Film Reg. '96.

She Shall Have Music 🐾½ 1936 A magnate hires a dance band to broadcast from a cruise ship. Features music by Jack Hylton and his band, one of Britain's most popular orchestras of the 1930s. 75m/B VHS. GB Jack Hylton, June Clyde, Claude Dampler, Bryan Lawrence, Gwen Farrar; D: Leslie Hiscott; W: C. Denier Warren; C: Sydney Blythe; M: William Luff.

She Shoulda Said No 🐾 The Devil's Weed; Wild Weed; Marijuana the Devil's Weed 1949 Funny smelling cigarettes ruin the lives of a couple who inhale. Viewers advice: just say no. Leed's actual drug bust with Robert Mitchum got her the lead. 70m/B VHS, DVD. Lila Leeds, Alan Baxter, Lyle Talbot, Jack Elam, David Gorcey; D: Sam Newfield.

She Waits 🐾🐾 1971 When a newlywed couple moves into an old house, the bride becomes possessed by the spirit of her husband's first wife. Unoriginal and mediocre. 74m/C VHS. Dorothy McGuire, Patty Duke, David McCallum; D: Delbert Mann. TV

She Wolf of London 🐾½ 1946 In turn of the century London, Phyllis Allenby (Lockhart) learns that people are being murdered by a wolf in a nearby park. Since the Allenby family suffers from a werewolf curse, Phyllis decides that she must be the killer (though she doesn't remember doing anything). But her fiance Harry (Porter) is determined to prove her innocent. 62m/B VHS, DVD. June Lockhart, Don Porter, Sara Haden, Jan Wiley, Lloyd Corrigan, Dennis Hoey, Martin Kosleck, Eily Malyon, Frederick Worlock; D: Jean Yarbrough; W: George Bricker; M: William Lava; C: Maury Gertsman.

She Wore a Yellow Ribbon 🐾🐾🐾½ 1949 An undermanned cavalry outpost makes a desperate attempt to repel invading Indians. Wayne shines as an officer who shuns retirement in order to help his comrades. Still fun and compelling. The second chapter in director Ford's noted cavalry trilogy, preceded by "Fort Apache" and followed by "Rio Grande." 93m/C VHS, DVD. John Wayne, Joanne Dru, John Agar, Ben Johnson, Harry Carey Jr., Victor McLaglen, Mildred Natwick, George O'Brien, Arthur Shields, Noble Johnson, Harry Woods, Michael Dugan, Jack Pennick, Paul Fix, Francis Ford, Cliff Lyons, Tom Tyler, Chief John Big Tree; D: John Ford; W: Frank Nugent, Laurence Stallings; C: Winton C. Hoch, Charles P. Boyle; M: Richard Hageman. Oscars '49: Color Cinematog.

She Goes to War 🐾🐾 1929 King's first part-sound effort that takes place in the milieu of WWI. Boerdman plays a spoiled rich girl who grows up fast when confronted with the horrors of the frontline while working in a canteen. 50m/B VHS. Eleanor Boardman, Alma Rubens, Al "Fuzzy" St. John; D: Henry King.

She Hate Me 🐾½ 2004 (R) Spike Lee's latest film is about corporate whistle-blowers. No wait, it's about the AIDS epidemic. Hold on a second, it's about Watergate and lesbians and fatherhood and the Mafia. Confused? So is this movie. John Henry Armstrong is a vice-president of a drug company. After blowing the whistle and getting fired, Armstrong finds a second career as a stud for lesbians who want to be impregnated. While the movie touches on some very interesting material, Lee randomly jumps from one subject to the next, creating a rather schizophrenic hodge-podge of political rants. 138m/C VHS, DVD. US Anthony Mackie, Kerry Washington, Ellen Barkin, Monica Bellucci, Jim Brown, Ossie Davis, Jamel Debbouze, Brian Dennehy, Woody Harrelson, Bai Ling, Lonette McKee, Paula Jai Parker, Q-Tip, John Turturro, Chiwetel Ejiofor, Dania Ramirez, David Bennett, Isiah Whitlock Jr., Spike Lee; W: Spike Lee, Michael Genet; C: Matthew Libatique; M: Terence Blanchard.

She Must Be Seeing Things 🐾🐾 1987 Filmmaker Jo (Weaver) is making a picture about a 7th-century woman who lived her life as a man. Jo's lover Agatha (Dabney) becomes disturbed when she reads Jo's diary, learns she's been having affairs with men, and begins to fantasize about Jo's crew. Agatha's insecurities finally lead her to disguising herself as a man in order to spy on Jo's film. When she's happening in Jo's film, Agatha's insecurities finally lead her crew. 95m/C VHS. Sheila Dabney, Lois Weaver, Kyle DiCamp, John Erdman; D: Sheila McLaughlin; W: Sheila McLaughlin.

She-Freak 🐾 Alley of Nightmares 1967 Remake of Tod Browning's "Freaks." A cynical waitress burns everyone in a circus and gets mauled by the resident freaks. Pales beside its unacknowledged, classic original. 87m/C VHS, DVD. Claire Brennan, Lynn Courtney, Bill McKinney, Lee Raymond, Madame Lee, Claude Smith, Ben Moore; D: Byron Mabel; C: William G. Troiano; M: William Allen Castleman.

She Gods of Shark Reef 🐾 Shark Reef 1956 Typical no-budget Corman exploitation tale of two brothers shipwrecked on an island inhabited by beautiful pearl-diving women. Filmed in Hawaii. 63m/C VHS, DVD. Bill Cord, Don Durant, Lisa Montell, Carol Lindsay, Jeanne Gerson; D: Roger Corman.

Sheba, Baby 🐾🐾 1975 (PG) A female dick (Grier) heads to Louisville where someone is trying to threaten her rich father and his loan company. Oddly non-violent for action-flick vet Grier, poorly written and directed. 90m/C VHS, DVD. Pam Grier, Rudy Challenger, Austin Stoker, D'Urville Martin, Charles Kissinger; D: William Girdler; W: William Girdler; C: William Asher; M: Alex Brown.

Sheena, Baby Woof! 1984 (PG) "TV sportscaster aids a jungle queen in defending her kingdom from being overthrown by an evil prince. Horrid bubble-gum "action" fantasy. 117m/C VHS, DVD. GE FR Tanya Roberts, Ted Wass, Donovan Scott, Elizabeth Toro; D: John Guillermin; W: David Newman; C: Pasqualino De Santis.

The Sheep Has Five Legs 🐾🐾🐾½ 1954 Quintuplet brothers return from around the world for a reunion planned by their small French village. Fernandel plays the father and all five sons; otherwise, comedy is only average-to-good. In French with English subtitles. 96m/B VHS. French with English subtitles. FR Fernandel, Edouard Delmont, Louis de Funes, Paulette Dubost; D: Henri Verneuil.

Sheer Madness 🐾🐾 1984 Focuses on the intense friendship between a college professor and a troubled artist. Engrossing and subtle exposition of a relationship. Ambiguous ending underscores film's general excellence. Subtitled. 105m/C VHS. GE FR Hanna Schygulla, Angela Winkler; D: Margarethe von Trotta; W: Margarethe von Trotta; C: Michael Ballhaus.

The Sheik 🐾🐾 1921 High camp Valentino has English woman fall hopelessly under the romantic spell of Arab sheik who flares his nostrils. Followed by "Son of the Sheik." 80m/B VHS, DVD. Agnes Ayres, Rudolph Valentino, Adolphe Menjou, Walter Long, Lucien Littlefield, George Waggner, Patsy Ruth Miller; D: George Melford.

Sheitan 🐾½ Satan 2006 Beautiful Eve (Mesquida) invites a group of horny, drunken teens she met at the disco to join her at her isolated farmhouse on Christmas Eve. Strange servant Josep (Cassel) seems to have something sinister planned. Weird and creepy rather than horror gory. French with subtitles. 94m/C DVD. FR Vincent Cassel, Roxane Mesquida, Olivier Barthelemy, Leila Bekhti, Nico Le Phat Tan, Ladiy; D: Kim Chapiron; W: Kim Chapiron, Christian Chapiron; C: Alex Lamarque; M: Nguyen Le.

She'll Be Wearing Pink Pajamas 🐾🐾 1984 Eight women volunteer for a rugged survival course to test their mettle. The intense shared experience gives them all food for thought. Well acted from a pretty thin story. 90m/C VHS. Julie Walters, Anthony (Tony) Higgins; D: John Goldschmidt; M: John Du Prez.

The Shell Seekers 🐾🐾 1993 (PG) The widowed Penelope Keeling (Lansbury) is recovering from a heart attack and her three grown children want to make things easy. But the scare has convinced Penelope to revisit her past and the happiness she once knew. So she returns to her childhood home in Cornwall to see what she can discover. Fine cast in a heart-tugger (with some lovely scenery from Cornwall, England and the island of

Ibiza). Adapted from the novel by Rosamunde Pilcher. A Hallmark Hall of Fame presentation. **94m/C VHS, DVD. GB** Angela Lansbury, Sam Wanamaker, Anna Carteret, Michael Gough, Christopher Bowen, Patricia Hodge, Denis Quilley, Sophie Ward, Irene Worth; **D:** Waris Hussein; **W:** John Pielmeier. **TV**

Shell Shock *Betzilo Shel Helem Krav; China Ranch* **1963** Four GI's fight off the Germans and the longings for home during WWII. Hebrew with subtitles. **90m/C VHS, DVD. IS** Anat Atzmon, Gili Ben-Uzilo, Stanislav Chaplin, Dan Turgeman, Asher Tzafati; **D:** Yoel Sharon; **C:** Yoav Kosh; **M:** Edward Reyes, Arik Rudich.

Shelter **1998 (R)** ATF agent Martin Matthews (Allen) is set up by his commanding officer and has a bounty on his head. He takes refuge with a crime lord (Onorati), whom the bad guys feds as also after, and plans how to get even. **92m/C VHS, DVD.** John Allen Nelson, Peter Onorati, Brenda Bakke, Costas Mandylor, Charles Durning, Linden Ashby, Kurtwood Smith; **D:** Scott Paulin; **W:** Max Strom; **C:** Eric Goldstein; **M:** David Williams.

Shelter Island **2003 (R)** Lou (Sheedy) was leading the good life, but a brutal assault makes her and lesbian lover Alex (Kensit) run away to Lou's island digs. One dark and stormy night brings a creepy, uninvited guest (Baldwin) who gets grim with 'em when the lights go out. Familiar cast drifts aimlessly out to sea trying to create a tense erotic thriller. **83m/C VHS, DVD.** Ally Sheedy, Patsy Kensit, Stephen Baldwin, Mimi Langeland, Christopher Penn, Joey Gironda, Kathleen York; **D:** Geoffrey Schaaf; **W:** Paul Convino; **M:** Jeff Rona. **VIDEO**

The Sheltering Sky **1990 (R)** American couple Winger and Malkovich flee the plasticity of their native land for a trip to the Sahara desert where they hope to renew their spirits and rekindle love. Accompanied by socialite acquaintance Scott with whom Winger soon has an affair, their personalities and belief systems deteriorate as they move through the grave poverty of North Africa in breathtaking heat. Based on the existential novel by American expatriate Paul Bowles who narrates and appears briefly in a bar scene. Overlong but visually stunning, with cinematography by Vittorio Storaro. **139m/C VHS, DVD.** Debra Winger, John Malkovich, Campbell Scott, Jill Bennett, Timothy Spall, Eric Vu-An, Sotigui Koyate, Amina Annabi, Paul Bowles; **D:** Bernardo Bertolucci; **W:** Mark Peploe, Bernardo Bertolucci; **C:** Vittorio Storaro; **M:** Ryuichi Sakamoto, Richard Horowitz. Golden Globes '91: Score; N.Y. Film Critics '90: Cinematog.

Shenandoah **1965** A Virginia farmer (Stewart), in a top-notch performance) who has raised six sons and a daughter, tries to remain neutral during the Civil War. War takes its toll as the daughter marries a Confederate soldier and his sons become involved in the fighting. Screen debut for Ross. **105m/C VHS, DVD.** James Stewart, Doug McClure, Glenn Corbett, Patrick Wayne, Rosemary Forsyth, Katharine Ross, George Kennedy, Phillip Alford, James Best, Charles Robinson, James McMullan, Tim McIntire, Eugene Jackson, Paul Fix, Denver Pyle, Harry Carey Jr., Dabbs Greer, Strother Martin, Warren Oates, Kelly Thordsen; **D:** Andrew V. McLaglen; **W:** James Lee Barrett; **C:** William Clothier; **M:** Frank Skinner.

Shep Comes Home **1949** Shep the wonder canine accompanies an orphan through the Midwest where he nabs a band of bankrobbers. Sequel to "My Dog Shep." **62m/B VHS.** Robert Lowery, Sheldon Leonard, Billy Kimbley, Margia Dean, Martin Garralaga, Michael Whalen, J. Farrell MacDonald, Lyle Talbot, Frank Jenks, Edna Holland, Matt Willis; **D:** Ford Beebe; **W:** Ford Beebe; **C:** Ernest Miller; **M:** Walter Greene.

Shepherd **1999 (R)** Offers plenty of cheap thrills as long as you don't expect the plot to make any sense. You've got your basic futuristic nightmare world—this time ruled by rival religious cults until this guns to extend their power. Howell is a sharpshooting mercenary who decides not to follow orders anymore—and there's hell to pay. **86m/C VHS.** C. Thomas Howell, Roddy Piper, Robert Carradine, Heidi von Palleske; **D:** Peter Hayman.

The Shepherd of the Hills **1941** Young Ozark mountain moonshiner Matt Matthews (Wayne) vows to one day find and kill the unknown father who deserted his family, leading to the early death of Matt's mother. His hatred is so strong that his girlfriend Sammy (Field) refuses to marry him because of it. Then a stranger, Daniel Howitt (Carey Sr.), comes to town and his kind deeds have everyone calling him "The Shepherd." Even Matt warms to the man—until he discovers that Howitt is his father. Based on the novel by Harold Bell Wright. **98m/B VHS, DVD.** John Wayne, Harry Carey Sr., Betty Field, Beulah Bondi, James Barton, Marjorie Main, Ward Bond, Fuzzy Knight; **D:** Henry Hathaway; **W:** Grover Jones, Stuart Anthony; **C:** Charles B(ryant) Lang Jr., William Howard Greene; **M:** Gerard Carbonara.

The Sheriff of Fractured Jaw **1959** A spoof of the old west with More as a Londoner who inherits a gun company and decides to head to the Wild West to show of his wares. He is tricked into becoming the sheriff of a lawless town but never loses his British stiff-upper-lip. Mansfield is the tough-talking sharpshooter who sets out to get her man. **103m/C VHS, DVD. GB** Charles Farrell, Kenneth More, Jayne Mansfield, Henry Hull, William Campbell; **D:** Raoul Walsh; **W:** Howard Dimsdale; **C:** Otto Heller; **M:** Robert Farnon.

Sheriff of Tombstone **1941** Trouble begins when a "judge" takes a sharpshooter in a poker game. **60m/B VHS, DVD.** Roy Rogers, George "Gabby" Hayes, Elyse Knox, Addison Richards, Sally Payne, Harry Woods, Zeffie Tilbury, Wally Wales, Jay Novello, Jack Ingram; **D:** Joseph Kane; **W:** Olive Cooper; **C:** William Nobles.

Sherlock: Case of Evil *Case of Evil* **2002 (R)** A young Sherlock Holmes (D'Arcy) is out to make a name for himself in London where he is hired by drug lord Ben Harrington (Rodger) to discover who is killing the local dealers and introducing a new narcotic—heroin—in an effort to control the market. First will turn out to be Professor Moriarty (D'Onofrio); also in the mix is Mycroft Holmes (Grant), who here is a drug addict, and Dr. Watson (Morlidge), who is not Sherlock's confidante at this time. In fact, Holmes's assistant is actress Rebecca (Anwar), who has her own agenda. **100m/C VHS, DVD.** James D'Arcy, Vincent D'Onofrio, Gabrielle Anwar, Roger Morlidge, Struan Rodger, Nicholas Gecks, Richard E. Grant; **D:** Graham Theakston; **W:** Piers Ashworth; **C:** Lukas Strebel; **M:** Mike Moran. **CABLE**

Sherlock Holmes and the Deadly Necklace *Sherlock Holmes Und Das Halsband des Todes; Valley of Fear* **1962** Once again, Holmes and Watson are up against their old nemesis Moriarty. This time, Moriarty wants to get his hands on a necklace stolen from Cleopatra's tomb. Not only does Scotland Yard not consider him a suspect, they seek his advice. Enter Holmes and Watson, and the game's afoot. The offbeat casting and direction help make this one of the odder versions of Conan Doyle's work. **84m/B VHS, DVD. GE** Christopher Lee, Senta Berger, Hans Sohnker, Hans Nielsen, Ivan Desny, Leon Askin, Thorley Walters; **D:** Terence Fisher.

Sherlock Holmes and the Incident at Victoria Falls *Incident at Victoria Falls* **1991** A substandard Holmes excursion brings the Baker Street sleuth out of retirement to transport the world's largest diamond from Africa to London. The resulting mystery involves Teddy Roosevelt, the inventor of radio, and poor plotting. **120m/C VHS, DVD. GB** Christopher Lee, Patrick Macnee, Jenny Seagrove; **D:** Bill Corcoran.

Sherlock Holmes and the Secret Weapon *Secret Weapon* **1942** Based on "The Dancing Men" by Sir Arthur Conan Doyle. Holmes battles the evil Moriarty in an effort to save the British war effort. Good Holmes mystery with gripping wartime setting. Hoey is fun as bumbling Inspector Lestrade. Available colorized. **68m/B VHS, DVD.** Basil Rathbone, Nigel Bruce, Karen Verne, William Post Jr., Dennis Hoey, Holmes Herbert, Mary Gordon, Henry Victor, Philip Van Zandt, James Craven, Paul Fix, Hugh Herbert, Lionel Atwill; **D:** Roy William Neill; **W:** Scott Darling; **C:** Lester White; **M:** Frank Skinner.

Sherlock Holmes Faces Death **1943** Dead bodies are accumulating in a mansion where the detecting duo are staying. Underground tunnels, life-size dress boards, and unanswered mysteries... Top-notch Holmes. Peter Lawford appears briefly as a sailor. Also available with "Hound of the Baskervilles" on Laser Disc. **68m/B VHS, DVD.** Basil Rathbone, Nigel Bruce, Milburn Stone, Halliwell Hobbes, Arthur Margetson, Gavin Muir; **D:** Roy William Neill.

Sherlock Holmes in Washington **1943** A top-secret agent is murdered; seems it's those blasted Nazis again! Holmes and Watson rush off to Washington, D.C. to solve the crime and to save some vitally important microfilm. Heavily flag-waving Rathbone episode. Dr. Watson is dumbfounded by bubble gum. **71m/B VHS, DVD.** Basil Rathbone, Nigel Bruce, Henry Daniell, George Zucco, Marjorie Lord, John Archer; **D:** Roy William Neill.

Sherlock Holmes: The Voice of Terror **1942** Holmes and Watson try to decode German radio messages during WWII. First Rathbone-as-Holmes effort for Universal, and first in which we are asked to believe the Victorian sleuth and his hairdo could have lived in this century. Patriotic and all that—and lots of fun. **65m/B VHS, DVD.** Basil Rathbone, Nigel Bruce, Hillary Brooke, Reginald Denny, Evelyn Ankers; **D:** John Rawlins.

Sherlock, Jr. **1924** Keaton stars as a movie projectionist who's learning to be a detective by reading a how-to book. He delivers a box of candy to his girl McGuire only to be upstaged by rival Crane. Back at the movie theatre, Keaton falls asleep during the romantic film and dreams that he and his girl are the on-screen couple, still being beset by his rival, although the situations keep changing. He then dreams that he's the famous detective Sherlock, Jr. who must rescue a damsel from villains. Packs an amazing amount into 44 minutes, which came at a transitional point in Keaton's career when he had moved on from two-reel shorts to longer features. **44m/B VHS, DVD.** Buster Keaton, Kathryn McGuire, Ward Crane, Joe Keaton, Erwin Connelly; **D:** Buster Keaton; **W:** Clyde Bruckman, Jean C. Havez, Joseph A. Mitchell; **C:** Byron Houck, Elgin Lessley. Natl. Film Reg. '91.

Sherlock: Undercover Dog **1994 (PG)** Billy (Eroen) arrives on Catalina Island to spend the summer with his father, an eccentric inventor. He makes a human friend in Emma (Cameron) and a canine companion in Sherlock, a police dog who's able to talk but naturally only to the two kids. Seems Sherlock's policeman master has been kidnapped by bumbling smugglers and its up to the trio to come to the rescue. **80m/C VHS, DVD.** Benjamin Eroen, Brynne Cameron, Anthony Simmons, Margy Moore, Barry Philips; **D:** Richard Harding Gardner; **M:** Lou Forestieri.

Sherman's March **1986** Director Ross McElwee set out to re-trace Sherman's March through Georgia and document that event's lingering effect on the modern South. Instead, after his girlfriend left him shortly before filming began, he ended up documenting how the various southern women he encountered affected him. McElwee's self-deprecating manner and the interesting variety of women he meets keep things enjoyable. **157m/C DVD. Cameos:** Burt Reynolds; **C:** Ross McElwee; **W:** Ross McElwee.

Sherrybaby **2006** Gyllenhaal startles in the title role of this compelling but disturbing drama. Sherry is a needy, emotionally stunted and impulsive ex-heroin addict who has cleaned herself up and has just been paroled from prison. She desperately wants to regain custody of her young daughter Alexis (Simpkins), who's bonded with her surrogate family, Sherry's brother Bobby (Henke) and his wife Lynette (Barkan). They've got a right to be cautious of Sherry's plans since the only way she knows to get what she needs is by using her sexuality, and her temptation to slip back into her druggy ways is still strong. **95m/C DVD. US** Maggie Gyllenhaal, Brad William Henke, Danny Trejo, Giancarlo Esposito, Bridget Barkan, Ryan Simpkins, Sam Bottoms; **D:** Laurie Collyer; **W:** Laurie Collyer; **C:** Russell Fine; **M:** Jack Livesey.

She's All That **1999 (PG-13)** There are no surprises to be found in this formulaic Pygmalion-via-MTV teen comedy. Zack (Prinze Jr.) is the BMOC in yet another broadly drawn high school pecking order. After he's dumped by girlfriend Taylor (O'Keefe) in an amusing send-up of MTV's "The Real World"), he accepts a bet from a pal that he can make artsy wallflower Laney (Cook) into a prom queen. The intelligent Laney suspects his motives, but proceeds with the makeover with caution. When Taylor decides she wants her man back, the stage is set for a predictable prom night showdown. **97m/C VHS, DVD.** Rachael Leigh Cook, Freddie Prinze Jr., Matthew Lillard, Paul Walker, Jodi Lyn O'Keefe, Kevin Pollak, Anna Paquin, Kieran Culkin, Elden (Ratliff) Henson, Usher Raymond, Gabrielle Union, Dule Hill, Kimberly (Lil' Kim) Jones; **D:** Robert Iscove; **W:** R. Lee Fleming Jr.; **C:** Francis Kenny; **M:** Stewart Copeland.

She's Back **1988 (R)** Murderee Fisher pesters hubby Joy from beyond the grave to avenge her death at the hands of a motorcycle gang. Uneven, but occasionally funny. **89m/C VHS.** Bobby DiCicco, Carrie Fisher, Robert Joy; **D:** Tim Kincaid.

She's Dressed to Kill **1988 (R)** *Someone's Killing the World's Greatest Models* **1979** Beautiful models are turning up dead during a famous designer's comeback attempt at a mountain retreat. Who could be behind these grisly deeds? Suspenseful in a made for TV kind of way, but not memorable. **100m/C VHS.** Eleanor Parker, Jessica Walter, John Rubinstein, Connie Sellecca; **D:** Gus Trikonis. **TV**

She's Gotta Have It **1986 (R)** Lee wrote, directed, edited, produced and starred in this romantic comedy about an independent-minded black girl in Brooklyn and the three men and one woman who compete for her attention. Full of rough edges, but vigorous, confident, and hip. Filmed entirely in black and white except for one memorable scene. Put Lee on the film-making map. **84m/B VHS.** Tracy C. Johns, Spike Lee, Tommy Redmond Hicks, Raye Dowell, John Canada Terrell, Joie Lee, S. Epatha Merkerson, Bill Lee, Cheryl Burr, Aaron Dugger, Stephanie Covington, Renata Cobbs, Cheryl Singleton, Monty Ross, Lewis Jordan, Erik Todd Dellums, Reginald (Reggie) Hudlin, Eric Payne, Marcus Turner, Gerard Brown, Ernest R. Dickerson; **D:** Spike Lee; **W:** Spike Lee; **C:** Ernest R. Dickerson; **M:** Bill Lee. Ind. Spirit '87: First Feature.

She's Having a Baby **1988 (PG-13)** Newlyweds Bacon and McGovern tread the marital waters with some difficulty, when news of an impending baby further complicates their lives. Told from Bacon's viewpoint as the tortured young writer/husband, who wonders if the yuppie life they lead is trapping him. Hughes's first venture into the adult world isn't as satisfying as his teen angst flicks, although the charming leads help. Major drawbacks are the arguably sexist premise and dull resolution. Great soundtrack; observant viewers will notice the beemer's license plate is the title's acronym: "SHAB." **106m/C VHS, DVD.** Kevin Bacon, Elizabeth McGovern, William Windom, Paul Gleason, Alec Baldwin, Cathryn Damon, Holland Taylor, James Ray, Isabel Lorca, Dennis Dugan, Edie McClurg, John Ashton; **D:** John Hughes; **W:** John Hughes; **C:** Don Peterman; **M:** Stewart Copeland.

She's in the Army Now **1981** Farce about military life. Two bubbleheaded females undergo basic training. "Private Benjamin" ripoff was meant as a TV pilot. **97m/C VHS.** Jamie Lee Curtis, Kathleen Quinlan, Melanie Griffith, Susan Blanchard, Julie

Shifting Sands 1918 Compelling film tells the tale of a young girl looking to be a successful artist. Her landlord makes constant overtures 'towards her. She refuses, so he has her thrown in jail for prostitution as an act of revenge. She fears her past may prevent her from obtaining true love. *D:* Hy Averback. *M:* Artie Butler. **TV**

She's the Man ✓✓½ 2006 (PG-13) Get past the familiar story and the fact that adorable Bynes can in no way pass for a boy, and it's light-hearted teen comedy provides an amusing take on Shakespeare's "Twelfth Night." When the girls' soccer team is disbanded at her prep school, star soccer player Viola (Bynes) disguises herself as her twin brother Sebastian (Kirk) and takes his place at his new school. Her first problem is falling for handsome roomie/soccer captain Duke (Tatum), who has a crush on Olivia (Ramsey) who's crushing on Viola—ah, Sebastian. Confusion follows. 105m/C DVD. US Amanda Bynes, Channing Tatum, Laura Ramsey, Vinnie Jones, Robert Hoffman III, Julie Hagerty, David Cross, Alex Breckinridge, Jonathan Sadowski, Emily Perkins, James Kirk, Clifton McCabe Murray, Brendon Jay McLaren; *D:* Andy Fickman; *W:* Karen McCullah Lutz, Kirsten Smith, Ewan Leslie; *C:* Greg Gardiner; *M:* Nathan Wang.

She's the One ✓✓½ 1996 (R) Another Irish family saga from Burns covering lots of of the same territory as "The Brothers McMullen." Semi-slacker taxi driver Mickey Fitzpatrick (Burns) impulsively marries passenger Hope (Bahns), and their romance is contrasted with the disintegrating marriage of Mickey's younger brother, buttoned-down stockbroker Francis (McGlone) and his frustrated wife Renee (Aniston). No wonder she's frustrated, Francis is having an affair with slutty Heather (Diaz), who turns out to be Mickey's former flame. Mahoney offers a typically fine performance, along with bad mental advice as the boys' father. Again the blustering men don't have a clue about the usually smarter women. 95m/C VHS, DVD. Edward Burns, Mike McGlone, Jennifer Aniston, Cameron Diaz, Maxine Bahns, John Mahoney, Leslie Mann, George McCowan, Amanda Peet, Anita Gillette, Frank Vincent; *D:* Edward Burns; *W:* Edward Burns; *C:* Frank Prinzi; *M:* Tom Petty.

She's So Lovely ✓✓ *Love* 1997 (R) Troubled young alcoholic Eddie (Penn) disappears for three days on his pregnant wife Maureen (Wright), and returns to discover that she has been brutalized by a neighbor. Film revels in the style that made Penn as famous (or infamous), and is best appreciated as a tribute. Travolta and Penn play well off each other. 97m/C VHS, DVD, Sean Penn, Robin Wright Penn, John Travolta, Harry Dean Stanton, Debi Mazar, James Gandolfini, Gena Rowlands, Kelsey Mulroney, David Thornton, Susan Traylor, Chloe Webb, Burt Young; *D:* Nick Cassavetes; *W:* John Cassavetes, Cannes '97: Actor "Penn).

She's Out of Control ✓½ 1989 Dad Danza goes nuts when teen daughter Dolenz (real-life daughter of Monkee Mickey Dolenz) takes the advice of Dad's girlfriend on how to attract boys. Formulaic plot could almost be an episode of "Who's the Boss?" Danza is appealing, but not enough to keep this one afloat. 95m/C VHS, DVD. Tony Danza, Ami Dolenz, Catherine Hicks, Wallace Shawn, Dick O'Neill, Laura Mooney, Derek McGrath, Matthew Perry, Dana Ashbrook, Todd Bridges, Robb:s (Reist) Rist; *D:* Stan Dragoti; *C:* Don Peterman; *M:* Alan Silvestri, Alan Silvestri. **DVD**

Shiloh ✓✓½ 1997 (PG) Schmaltzy but redeeming story about small town West Virginia 11-year-old Marty (Heron), who seeks to rescue and care for mistreated hunting dog Shiloh, who belongs to mean hermit Judd (Wilson). Goes beyond the typical "boy and his dog" theme with moral and ethical issues that Marty faces when he takes the dog from its owner. Frannie (who plays Shiloh) is a very cute and expressive beagle. Adapted from the Newberry award-winning novel by Phyllis Reynolds Naylor. 93m/C VHS, DVD, Blake Heron, Michael Moriarty, Scott Wilson, Rod Steiger, Ann Dowd, Bonnie Bartlett; *D:* Dale Rosenbloom; *C:* Frank Byers; *M:* Joel Goldsmith.

Shiloh 2: Shiloh Season ✓✓½ 1999 Low-key rural drama finds 12-year-old Marty Preston (Browne) claiming responsibility for lovable beagle Shiloh from his hard-drinking owner, Judd Travers (Wilson). But when Travers is injured in an accident, the kid has enough compassion to ask his parents to help him with the ornery cuss. Adapted from the novel by Phyllis Reynolds Naylor. 96m/C VHS, DVD, Blake Browne, Scott Wilson, Michael Moriarty, Ann Dowd, Rod Steiger, Bonnie Bartlett, Joe Pichler; *D:* Sandy Tung; *W:* Dale Rosenbloom; *M:* Joel Goldsmith.

Shin Heike Monogatari ✓✓✓ *New Tales of the Taira Clan* 1955 Mizoguchi's second to last film, in which a deposed Japanese emperor in 1137 endeavor's to win back the throne from the current despot, who cannot handle the feudal lawlessness. Acclaimed; his second film in color. In Japanese with English subtitles. 106m/C VHS. JP Raizo Ichikawa, Ichijiro Oye, Michiyo Kogure, Eijiro Yanagi, Tatsuya Ishiguro, Yoshiko Kuga; *D:* Kenji Mizoguchi.

Shinbone Alley ✓✓½ 1970 (G) Animated musical about Archy, a free-verse poet reincarnated as a cockroach, and Mehitabel, the alley cat with a zest for life. Based on the short stories by Don Marquis. 83m/C VHS, DVD. *D:* John D. Wilson; *V:* Carol Channing, Eddie Bracken, John Carradine, Alan Reed.

Shine ✓✓✓ 1995 (PG-13) Astonishing true portrayal of musical genius and its cost. Teenaged pianist David Helfgott (Taylor) is a prodigy in his native Australia but is pushed to the limit by his authoritarian father Peter (Mueller-Stahl). Eventually defying his father's strictures, David accepts a scholarship to London's Royal College of Music where he triumphs under the tutelage of professor Cecil Parkes (Gielgud), but then collapses from strain. For 15 years, he is confined to psychiatric hospitals, unable to play the piano, until the now-adult David (Rush) has a chance meeting with the loving Gillian (Redgrave), whose support enables him to resume his career. Helfgott himself plays piano for his screen counterparts. 105m/C VHS, DVD. AU Geoffrey Rush, Noah Taylor, Armin Mueller-Stahl, Lynn Redgrave, John Gielgud, Google Withers, Chris Haywood, Sonia Todd, Alex Rafalowicz, Randall Berger; *D:* Scott Hicks; *W:* Jan Sardi; *C:* Geoffrey Simpson; *M:* David Hirschfelder. Oscars '96: Actor (Rush); Australian Film Inst. '96: Film (Rush); Golden Globes '97: Actor—Drama (Rush); L.A. Film Critics '96: Actor (Rush), Film; N.Y. Film Critics '96: Actor (Rush); Natl. Bd. of Review '96: Actor (Rush); Screen Actors Guild '96: Actor (Rush); Broadcast Film Critics '96: Actor (Rush).

Shiner ✓✓½ 2000 Caine delivers the goods as a small-time boxing promoter from London's East End on the brink of hitting it big. As Billy "Shiner" Simpson, Caine preps his son Eddie for a high-profile, possibly career-making match against 1938 Rogers brings a band of outlaws to justice and clears an old man suspected of being their accomplice. Title bears no relation to story line. 60m/B VHS. Roy Rogers, Lynne Roberts, Stanley Andrews.

Shine on, Harvest Moon ✓✓ 1938 Rogers brings a band of outlaws to justice and clears an old man suspected of being their accomplice. Title bears no relation to story line. 60m/B VHS. Roy Rogers, Lynne Roberts, Stanley Andrews.

Shining Through ✓✓½ 1992 (R) Baby-voiced Griffith as a spy sent behind enemy lines without training? Douglas as a spy sent behind enemy lines without speaking German? Old-fashioned blend of romance, espionage, and derring-do where a noble hero saves spunky heroine from nasty Nazis in WWII Germany works despite thin plot. Series of flash-forwards to an aged Griffith is annoying and tends to stop action cold, but everyone tries hard and period flavor is authentic. Adapted from best-selling Susan Isaacs novel, but bears little resemblance to book. 133m/C VHS, DVD. Michael Douglas, Melanie Griffith, Liam Neeson, Joely Richardson, John Gielgud, Francis Guinan, Patrick Winczenski, Sylvia Syms; *D:* David Seltzer; *W:* David Seltzer; *C:* Jan De Bont; *M:* Michael Kamen. Golden Raspberries '92: Worst Picture, Worst Actress (Griffith), Worst Director (Seltzer).

Ship Ahoy ✓✓½ 1942 Songs, comedy, a spy spoof, and some patriotism thrown in for good measure. Powell plays her pulp fiction writer boyfriend (Skelton, Emery, posing as an FBI man, convinces Powell to smuggle a package for him but he's really a spy and the whole thing's a con which turns out to be based on one of

Shining Star ✓½ *That's the Way of the World* 1975 (PG) A recording company is run by the mob. Potentially interesting film is hampered by quality of sound and photography and general lack of purpose or direction. 100m/C VHS, DVD, HD DVD. Harvey Keitel, Ed Nelson, Cynthia Bostick, Bert Parks; *D:* Sig Shore.

A Shining Season ✓✓✓ 1979 Tearjerker about a potential-packed long-distance runner, John Baker, stricken with cancer. He spends his last year training a girls' track team to a championship. Earnest, well-performed and involving. Based on a true story. Made for TV. 100m/C VHS. Timothy Bottoms, Rip Torn, Allyn Ann McLerie, Ed Begley Jr., Benjamin Bottoms, Mason Adams, Constance Forsund, Ellen Geer; *D:* Stuart Margolin; *M:* Richard Bellis. **TV**

The Shining Hour ✓✓ 1938 A compelling melodrama in which Crawford portrays a New York night club dancer who is pursued by the rather conservative Douglas. His brother tries to persuade him from marrying Crawford, but then he soon finds himself attracted to her. A devastating fire wipes out all problems of family dissension in this intelligent soap opera. 76m/B VHS. Joan Crawford, Margaret Sullavan, Melvyn Douglas, Robert Young, Fay Bainter, Allyn Joslyn; *D:* Frank Borzage; *W:* Ogden Nash, Jane Murfin; *C:* George J. Folsey.

The Shining ✓✓½ 1980 (R) Very loose adaptation of the Stephen King horror novel about a writer and his family, snowbound in a huge hotel, who experience various hauntings caused by either the hotel itself or the writer's dementia. Technically stunning, and pretty damn scary, but too long, pretentious and implausible. Nicholson is excellent as the failed writer gone off the deep end. 143m/C VHS, DVD, Blu-ray Disc, HD DVD. Jack Nicholson, Shelley Duvall, Danny Lloyd, Scatman Crothers, Joe Turkel, Barry Nelson, Philip Stone, Lia Beldam, Billie Gibson, Barry Dennen, David Baker, Lisa Burns, Alison Coleridge, Kate Phelps, Anne Jackson, Tony Burton; *D:* Stanley Kubrick; *W:* Stanley Kubrick, Diane Johnson; *C:* John Alcott; *M:* Walter (Wendy) Carlos, Rachel Elkind.

Ship of Fools ✓✓✓ 1965 A group of passengers sailing to Germany in the 1930s find mutual needs and concerns. Based on the Katherine Ann Porter novel. Leigh's last film role; she died two years later. Kramer grapples with civil rights issues in much of his work. 149m/B VHS, DVD, Vivien Leigh, Simone Signoret, Jose Ferrer, Lee Marvin, Oskar Werner, Michael Dunn, Elizabeth Ashley, George Segal, Jose Greco, Charles Korvin, Heinz Ruhmann; *D:* Stanley Kramer; *W:* Abby Mann; *C:* Ernest Laszlo; *M:* Ernest Gold. Oscars '65: Art Dir./Set Dec., B&W, B&W Cinematog.; Natl. Bd. of Review '65: Actor (Werner); N.Y. Film Critics '01: Support. Actress (Eland-vin).

The Shipping News ✓✓ 2001 (R) Spacey is Quoyle, a middle-aged life-time loser who returns to his childhood home of Newfoundland after his daughter and aunt (Dench) after his adulterous wife (Blanchett) dies. There, among the absurdly quirky citizenry, he meets Wavey (Moore) a widow who runs the day-care center and may hold the key to changing Quoyle's life around. Those who 'read the book (and there are many), will be deeply disappointed, and those who haven't may merely be deeply depressed. The desolate landscape is beautifully shot, but Spacey is badly miscast as the sad-sack loser, and subplots that could lead to some drama are dropped inexplicably. Banchett and Moore distinguish themselves nicely. 120m/C VHS, DVD. US Kevin Spacey, Judi Dench, Cate Blanchett, Julianne Moore, Pete Postlethwaite, Scott Glenn, Rhys Ifans, Gordon Pinsent, Jason Behr, Larry Pine, Jeanetta Arnette, Robert Joy, Alyssa Garner, Kaitlyn Gainer, Lauren Gainer; *D:* Lasse Hallstrom; *W:* Robert Nelson Jacobs; *C:* Oliver Stapleton; *M:* Christopher Young.

Ships in the Night ✓✓ 1928 Ships of the Night 1928 (PG) Kiddie swashbuckler (based sen 1994 (PG) Logan is the plucky heroine who is searching for her missing brother who has been captured by the hidden pirate island where he defends the hidden pirate treasure he finds by boobytrapping the island. 93m/C VHS. NO Gabriel Byrne, Shian Smestad, Louisa Haigh, Trond Munch, Bjorn Sundquist, Eva Von Hanno, Kjell Stormoen; *D:* Nils Gaup; *W:* Nils Gaup, Nick Thiel; *M:* Patrick Doyle.

Shipwrecked ✓✓½ 1990 Haakon Haakonsen 1994 (PG) Kiddie swashbuckler (based on the 1873 popular novel "Haakon Haakonsen." A cabin boy is marooned on an island where he defends the hidden pirate treasure he finds by boobytrapping the island. 93m/C VHS. NO Gabriel Byrne, Shian Smestad, Louisa Haigh, Trond Munch, Bjorn Sundquist, Eva Von Hanno, Kjell Stormoen; *D:* Nils Gaup; *W:* Nils Gaup, Nick Thiel; *M:* Patrick Doyle.

Shirley Valentine ✓✓½ 1989 A lively middle-aged English housewife gets a new lease on life when she travels to Greece without her husband. Collins recreates her London and Broadway stage triumph. The character frequently addresses the audience directly to explain her thoughts and feelings, but her spunk carry the day. Good script by Russell from his play. From the people who brought us "Educating Rita." 108m/C VHS, DVD. GB Pauline Collins, Tom Conti, Alison Steadman, Julia McKenzie, Joanne Lumley, Bernard Hill, Sylvia Syms; *D:* Lewis Gilbert; *W:* George Hedlin-assios, Willy Russell; *C:* Alan Hume; *M:* Willy Russell. British Acad. '89: Actress (Collins).

The Shock ✓✓½ 1923 Crippled low-life Chaney becomes restored spiritually by a small-town girl and rebels against his Chinese boss. This causes an unfortunate string of melodramatic tragedies, including the San Francisco earthquake of 1906. Silent. Odd, desultory tale with bad special effects is worth seeing for Chaney's

---

an American. The match has disaster written all over it early on, however, when Billy's daughter interrupts to bring up some past legal problems, Eddie doesn't perform as expected, and murder, betrayal, and doublecrosses rear their ugly heads. A showcase for Caine's talents, unfortunately the story around him loses it's luster after a solid first half turns disappointing. Borrows liberally from Shakespeare's "King Lear." 99m/C VHS, DVD. GB Michael Caine, Martin Landau, Matthew Marsden, Frances Barber, Frank Harper, Andy Serkis, Claire Rushbrook, Danny (Daniel) Webb, Kenneth Cranham, David Kennedy, Peter Wight, Nicola Walker; *D:* John Irvin; *W:* Scott Cherry; *C:* Mike Molloy; *M:* Paul Grabowsky.

Skelton's potboiler plots. An uncredited Frank Sinatra is the singer with the Dorsey band, along with drummer Buddy Rich and trumpeter Ziggy Elman who provide some great musical solos. ♪ Last Call For Love; Poor You; On Moonlight Bay; Tampico; I'll Take Tallulah; Cape Dance; Ship Ahoy. 95m/B VHS. Eleanor Powell, Red Skelton, Bert Lahr, Virginia O'Brien, John Emery, William Post Jr.; *D:* Edward Buzzell; *W:* Harry Kurnitz, Harry Clork, Irving Brecher.

Shock

ney's good acting. **96m/B VHS, DVD.** Lon Chaney Sr.; **D:** Lambert Hillyer.

Shock! 1946 A psychiatrist is called on to treat a woman on the edge of a nervous breakdown. He then discovers she saw him murder his wife, and tries to keep her from remembering it. Interesting premise handled in trite B style. Price's first starring role. **70m/B VHS, DVD.** Vincent Price, Lynn Bari, Frank Latimore, Anabel Shaw; **D:** Alfred Werker.

Shock *Beyond the Door 2; Shock (Transfer Suspense Hypnos); Suspense; Al 33 di Via Orologio fa Sempre Freddo* 1979 (R) Better treatment of the possession theme, but this time the door is to the home of a new family: Colin (from the original) plays a boy possessed by his dead father, who seeks revenge on his new husband. Director Bava's last feature. **90m/C VHS, DVD.** *IT* John Steiner, Daria Nicolodi, David Colin Jr., Ivan Rassimov, Nicola Salerno; **D:** Mario Bava; **W:** Lamberto Bava, Franco Barbieri, Dardano Sacchetti; **C:** Alberto Spagnoli.

Shock Corridor 1963 A reporter, dreaming of a Pulitzer Prize, fakes mental illness and gets admitted to an asylum, where he hopes to investigate a murder. He is subjected to disturbing experiences, including shock therapy, but does manage to solve the murder. However, he suffers a mental breakdown in the process and is admitted for real. Disturbing and lurid. **101m/B VHS, DVD.** Peter Breck, Constance Towers, Gene Evans, Hari Rhodes, James Best, Philip Ahn, Larry Tucker, Paul Dubov; **D:** Samuel Fuller; **W:** Samuel Fuller; **C:** Stanley Cortez; **M:** Paul Dunlap. Natl. Film Reg. '96.

Shock! Shock! Shock! 1987 Another low-budget slasher flick, with a homicidal lunatic wielding a butcher knife. Space alien jewel thieves add an element, for what it's worth. Makes one ponder the cosmic question: What's the diff between a bad slasher flick and a spoof of a bad slasher flick? Whichever this one is, it's really bad! **60m/B VHS.** Brad Isaac, Cyndy McCrossen, Allen Rickman, Brian Fluorry; **D:** Todd Rutt, Am McConnell.

A Shock to the System 1990 (R) Business exec. Caine is passed over for a long-deserved promotion in favor of a younger man. When he accidentally pushes a panhandler in front of a subway in a fit of rage, he realizes how easy murder is and thinks it may be the answer to all his problems. Tries to be a satire take on corporate greed, etc., but somehow loses steam. Excellent cast makes the difference; Caine adds class. Based on the novel by Simon Brett. **88m/C VHS.** Michael Caine, Elizabeth McGovern, Peter Riegert, Swoosie Kurtz, Will Patton, Jenny Wright, John McMartin, Barbara Baxley; **D:** Jan Egleson; **W:** Andrew Klavan; **C:** Paul Goldsmith; **M:** Gary Chang.

Shock to the System 2006 (R) In the second Donald Strachey mystery (following "Third Man Out"), the Albany PI (Allen) is suspicious when client Paul Hale allegedly commits suicide. He discovers Paul's homophobic mom (Fairchild) pushed him towards a gay conversion therapy group run by the shady Dr. Cornell (Woods). So Donald decides to go undercover to investigate, which may cost him his own life. Based on the series by Richard Stevenson. **95m/C DVD.** Chad Allen, Sebastian Spence, Michael Woods, Morgan Fairchild, Daryl Shuttleworth, Nelson Wong, Anne Marie Deluise; **D:** Ron Oliver; **W:** Ron McGee; **C:** C. Kim Miles; **M:** Peter Allen. **CABLE**

Shock Treatment *Traitement de Choc* 1981 (PG) Seldom-seen mediocre semi-sequel to the cult classic, "The Rocky Horror Picture Show" (1975). Brad and Janet, now married and portrayed by different leads, find themselves trapped on a TV gameshow full of weirdos. Same writers, same director, and several original cast members do make an appearance. **94m/C VHS, DVD.** Richard O'Brien, Jessica Harper, Cliff DeYoung, Patricia Quinn, Charles Gray, Ruby Wax, Nell Campbell, Rik Mayall, Barry Humphries, Darlene Johnson, Manning Redwood; **D:** Jim Sharman; **W:** Jim Sharman, Richard O'Brien; **C:** Mike Molloy; **M:** Richard Hartley, Richard O'Brien.

Shock Waves *Death Corps; Almost Human* 1977 (PG) Group of mutant-underwater-zombie-Nazi-soldiers terrorizes stranded tourists staying at a deserted motel on a small island. Cushing is the mad scientist intent on recreating the Nazi glory days with the seaweed-attired zombies. Odd B-grade, more or less standard horror flick somehow rises (slightly) above badness. Halpin's name was erroneously listed as Halpirn—even on the original movie poster! **90m/C VHS, DVD.** Peter Cushing, Brooke Adams, John Carradine, Luke Halpin, Jack Davidson, Fred Buch; **D:** Ken Wiederhorn; **W:** Ken Wiederhorn, John Kent Harrison; **C:** Reuben Trane; **M:** Richard Einhorn.

Shocker 1989 (R) Another Craven gore-fest. A condemned serial killer is transformed into a menacing electrical force after being fried in the chair. Practically a remake of Craven's original "Nightmare on Elm Street." Great special effects, a few enjoyable weird and sick moments. What's Dr. Timothy Leary doing here? **111m/C VHS, DVD.** Michael Murphy, Peter Berg, Camille (Cami) Cooper, Mitch Pileggi, Richard Price, Timothy Leary, Heather Langenkamp, Theodore (Ted) Raimi, Richard Brooks, Sam Scarber; **D:** Wes Craven; **W:** Wes Craven; **C:** Jacques Haitkin; **M:** William Goldstein.

The Shoes of the Fisherman 1968 (G) Morris West's interesting, speculative best seller about Russian Pope brought to the big screen at much expense, but with little care or thought. Siberian prison-camp vet Quinn, elected Pope, tries to arrest nuclear war. Director Anderson wasted the prodigious talents of Olivier, Gielgud, et al. Sloppy use of good cast and promising plot. **160m/C VHS, DVD.** Anthony Quinn, Leo McKern, Laurence Olivier, John Gielgud, Vittorio De Sica, Oskar Werner, David Janssen; **D:** Michael Anderson Sr.; **M:** Alex North. Golden Globes '69: Score; Natl. Bd. of Review '68: Support. Actor (McKern).

Shoeshine 1947 Two shoeshine boys struggling to survive in post-war Italy become involved in the black market and are eventually caught and imprisoned. Prison scenes detail the sense of abandonment and tragedy that destroys their friendship. A rich, sad achievement in neo-realistic drama. In Italian with English subtitles. **90m/B VHS, DVD.** *IT* Franco Interlenghi, Rinaldo Smordoni, Anniello Mele, Bruno Ortensi, Pacifico Astrologo; **D:** Vittorio De Sica; **W:** Cesare Zavattini, Sergio Amidei, Adolfo Franci, C.G. Viola.

Shogun *James Clavell's Shogun* 1980 Miniseries chronicling the saga of a shipwrecked English navigator who becomes the first Shogun, or Samurai warrior chief, from the Western world. Colorfully adapted from the James Clavell bestseller. Also released in a two-hour version, but this full-length version is infinitely better. **550m/C VHS, DVD.** Richard Chamberlain, Toshiro Mifune, Yoko Shimada, John Rhys-Davies, Damien Thomas, William Morgan Sheppard; **D:** Jerry London; **M:** Maurice Jarre; **Nar:** Orson Welles. **TV**

Shogun Assassin 1980 (R) Story of a proud samurai named Lone Wolf who served his Shogun master well as the Official Decapitator, until the fateful day when the aging Shogun turned against him. Extremely violent, with record-breaking body counts. Edited from two other movies in a Japanese series called "Sword of Vengeance": a tour de force of the cutting room. The samurai pushes his son's stroller through much of the film-sets it aside to hack and slash. **86m/C VHS, DVD.** *JP* Tomisaburo Wakayama, Kayo Matsuo, Shin Kishida, Masahiro Tomikawa; **D:** Robert Houston; **W:** Robert Houston, David Weisman, Kazuo Koike; **C:** Chishi Makiura; **M:** W. Michael Lewis, Mark Lindsay.

Shogun's Ninja 1983 In 16th-century Japan, an age-old rivalry between two ninja clans sparks a search for a dagger which will lead to one clan's hidden gold. Martial arts performed and directed by Sonny Chiba. In Japanese with usual poor English dubbing. **112m/C VHS, DVD.** *JP* Hiroyuki (Henry) Sanada, Etsuko (Sue) Shihomi, Sonny Chiba; **D:** Noribumi Suzuki.

Shoot 1985 (R) Five hunting buddies fall prey to a group of crazed killers after one man is shot by accident. What's the message: Anti-gun? Anti-hunting? Silly, unbelievable, irresponsibly moralistic, and gratuitously violent. **98m/C VHS.** *CA* Ernest Borgnine, Cliff Robertson, Henry Silva, Helen Shaver; **D:** Harvey Hart.

Shoot 1992 (R) Photographer Katie Tracy goes undercover to expose an illegal gambling ring fronted by an exotic nightclub. The latest gambling stakes involve the Emperor's pearls, offered in a private auction which could turn deadly, especially when Katie gets involved with her. **90m/C VHS.** Dedee Pfeiffer, Miles O'Keeffe, Christopher Atkins; **D:** Hugh Parks.

Shoot 'Em Up 2007 (R) Mystery man Smith (Owen) sees a pregnant woman being chased by a crew of thugs and decides to step in. The woman dies, but not before Smith delivers the baby and takes it under his protection, recruiting prostitute Donna (Bellucci) to help nurse it. Meanwhile he's got to fight off mercenary Hertz (Giamatti), who's determined to get the baby no matter what it takes. Inevitably, the bodies start to pile up as Smith shows that he's handled a gun or four in his past. Extraordinarily violent with a tongue-in-cheek attitude, owing much to John Woo and other Asian action directors (Davis cites "Hard Boiled" as his inspiration). Davis doesn't match other big guns/big explosion actioners in quality but it hits fairly often, although Davis doesn't have Woo's knack for story or breaking the tension between onslaughts of extreme violence. **87m/C DVD, Blu-ray Disc.** *US* Clive Owen, Paul Giamatti, Monica Bellucci, Daniel Pilon, Julian Fichings; **D:** Michael Davis; **W:** Michael Davis; **C:** Peter Pau; **M:** Paul Haslinger.

Shoot It Black, Shoot It Blue 1974 Rogue cop shoots a black purse snatcher and thinks he has gotten away with it. Unknown to him, a witness has filmed the incident and turns the evidence over to a lawyer. **93m/C VHS.** Michael Moriarty, Eric Laneuville, Paul Sorvino, Earl Hindman, Linda Scruggs; **D:** Dennis McGuire; **W:** Dennis McGuire; **C:** Bob Bailin; **M:** Terry Stockdale.

Shoot Loud, Louder, I Don't Understand! *Spara Forte, Piu Forte...Non Capisco* 1966 A sculptor who has a hard time separating reality from dreams thinks he witnessed a murder. Shenanigans follow. Meant to be a black comedy, but when not dull, it is confusing. Welch looks good, as usual, but doesn't show acting talent here. In Italian with English subtitles. **101m/C VHS, DVD.** *IT* Marcello Mastroianni, Raquel Welch; **D:** Eduardo de Filippo; **M:** Nino Rota.

Shoot or Be Shot 2002 (PG-13) Harvey Wilkes (Shatner) is a movie-lover who bolted from the psych ward with a script of his very own. As luck would have it, he happens upon a film crew shooting in the desert and usurps the production. Shatner is in great comedic form in this otherwise stale mockery of all that is Hollywood. **90m/C VHS, DVD.** William Shatner, Harry Hamlin, Tim Thomerson, James Healy Jr., Scott Rinker; **D:** Randy Argue; **C:** Ralph Linhardt; **M:** Joseph Alfuso. **VIDEO**

Shoot Out *Shootout* 1971 Hamfisted western based on Will James' novel "The Lore Cowboy" and previously filmed in 1934. Clay Lomax (Peck) gets out a prison and wants revenge on the partner, Sam Foley (Gregory), who doublecrossed him. So Foley hires a young gunslinger (Lyons) to take care of Lomax. In addition, Lomax gets stuck with an orphaned 8-year-old girl, who's the daughter of an ex-lover (and may be Lomax's flesh-and-blood). Peck's just too nice while Lyons chews all the scenery. **94m/C DVD.** Gregory Peck, Robert F. Lyons, Susan Tyrrell, Jeff Corey, James Gregory, Rita Gam, Pepe Serna, Nicolas Davis Chandler, Paul Fix, Arthur Hunnicutt, Nicolas Beaury; **D:** Henry Hathaway; **W:** Marguerite Roberts; **C:** Earl Rath; **M:** Dave Grusin.

Shoot the Living, Pray for the Dead *Prega il Morto e Ammazza il Vivo* 1970 While travelling through Mexico, the leader of a band of killers promises his guide half of a share in stolen gold if he can lead them to it. **90m/C VHS.** *IT* Klaus Kinski, Victoria Zinny, Paul Sullivan, Dino Stano; **D:** Giuseppe Vari; **C:** Franco Villa; **M:** Mario Migliardi.

Shoot the Moon 1982 (R) A successful writer, married and with four children, finds his life unrewarding and leaves his family to take up with a younger woman. The wife must learn to deal with her resentment, the fears of her children, and her own attempt at a new love. Fine acting but a worn-out story. **124m/C VHS.** Diane Keaton, Albert Finney, Karen Allen, Peter Weller, Dana Hill, Viveka Davis, Tracey Gold, Tina Yothers; **D:** Alan Parker; **W:** Bo Goldman.

Shoot the Piano Player *Tirez sur le Pianiste; Shoot the Pianist* 1962 Former concert pianist (Aznavour, spendidly cast) changes his name and plays piano at a low-class Paris cafe. A convoluted plot ensues; he becomes involved with gangsters, though his girlfriend wants him to try a comeback. Lots of atmosphere, character development, humor, and romance. A Truffaut masterpiece based on a pulp novel by David Goodis. In French with English subtitles. **92m/B VHS, DVD.** *FR* Charles Aznavour, Marie DuBois, Nicole Berger, Michele Mercier, Albert Remy; **D:** Francois Truffaut; **W:** Marcel Moussey, Francois Truffaut; **C:** Raoul Coutard; **M:** Georges Delerue.

Shoot the Sun Down 1981 (PG) Four offbeat characters united in a search for gold turn against each other. "Gilligan's Island"-style assortment of characters (Indian; gunfighter; girl; sea captain) are cast away in a pointless plot from which they never escape. Too bad: talented cast could have done better. **102m/C VHS.** Christopher Walken, Margot Kidder, Geoffrey Lewis, Bo Brundin, Sacheen Little Feather; **D:** David Leeds.

Shoot to Kill 1947 B-grade noir-esque mystery about a crooked D.A. and a gangster who bite the dust. Suspenseful, dark, street-level crime drama uncovered by ambitious journalist Ward. **64m/B VHS, DVD.** Russell Wade, Luana Walters, Nestor Paiva, Edmund MacDonald, Vince Barnett, Robert Kent, Charles Trowbridge, Harry Cheshire; **D:** William Berke; **W:** Edwin Westrate; **C:** Benjamin (Ben H.) Kline; **M:** Darrell Calker.

Shoot to Kill 1988 (R) A city cop (Poitier, better than ever after 10 years off the screen) and a mountain guide (Berenger) reluctantly join forces to capture a killer who is part of a hunting party traversing the Pacific Northwest and which is being led by the guide's unsuspecting girlfriend (Alley). Poitier may be a bit old for the role, but he carries the implausible plot on the strength of his performance. Good action. **110m/C VHS.** Sidney Poitier, Tom Berenger, Kirstie Alley, Clancy Brown, Richard Masur, Andrew (Andy) Robinson, Frederick Coffin, Kevin Scannell; **D:** Roger Spottiswoode; **W:** Michael Burton, Harv Zimmel, Daniel Petrie Jr.; **C:** Michael Chapman; **M:** John Scott.

Shoot to Kill *Disparan a Matar* 1990 An innocent young man is murdered during a police round-up while his mother watches helplessly. The victim a criminal—but she launches a long campaign for justice. Spanish with subtitles. **90m/C VHS, DVD.** *VZ* Amalia Perez Diaz, Jean Carlo Simancas, Dan Alvarado, Flor Nunez; **D:** Carlos Azpurua; **W:** David Suarez; **C:** Adriano Moreno; **M:** Waldemar D'Lima.

The Shooter 1997 The frontier town of Kingston is being terrorized by outlaw Krantz (Smith) and his gang until gunfighter Michael Atherton (Dudikoff) becomes their reluctant defender. Modest budget but lots of action. **93m/C VHS.** Mi-

Shooter 🐾🐾½ 2007 (R) Political conspiracy action thriller, based on the novel "Point of Impact" by Stephen Hunter. Former Marine sniper Bob Lee Swagger (Wahlberg), the perfect stoic hero) is living peacefully in a Wyoming cabin when he's approached by retired colonel Isaac Johnson (Glover), who tells Swagger his expertise is needed to prevent a president's assassination. Naturally, it's all a set-up and Swagger has to go on the run to counteract those government weasels. Pena and Mara serve as allies while Glover, Beatty, Koreas, and Sherbedgia are on the side of evil. 122m/C DVD, Blu-ray Disc, HD DVD. *US* Mark Wahlberg, Michael Pena, Danny Glover, Kate Mara, Elias Koreas, Rhona Mitra, Rade Serbedzija, Levon Helm, Ned Beatty, Tate Donovan, Justin Louis; *D:* Antoine Fuqua. **W:** Jonathan Lemkin; **C:** Peter Menzies Jr.; **M:** Mark Mancina.

Shooters 🐾🐾 1989 A wacky platoon of misfits is paired off against a group of vicious killers in a "war game" training session. Not completely unfunny or worthless. 84m/C VHS. *US* Mark Wahlberg, Michael Pena, Danny Aldo Ray; *D:* Glenn Dufori, Colin Paul Maibaum; **M:** Todd Hayen.

Shooters 🐾🐾 2000 (R) South London bad boy Gilly (Dempsey) is out on parole after six years. All he wants is his share from a long-ago heist with violent partner J (Howard) but J wants Gily to help him out on one last job that involves an arms dealer (Dunbar). Naturally, things go very wrong. Typical Cool Britannia crime actioner. 95m/C VHS, DVD, GB Louis Dempsey, Andrew Howard, Adrian Dunbar, Gerard Butler, Jason Hughes, Ioan Gruffudd, Melanie Lynskey; *D:* Glenn Dufori, Colin Teague; **W:** Louis Dempsey, Andrew Howard; **C:** Tom Erisman; **M:** Kemal Ulianur.

Shootfighter: Fight to the Death 🐾½ 1993 (R) Two boys become experts in the martial arts and confront rivals. Now grown-up they take their rivalry to a deadly level in a "shootfight," a game which has no 'rules and is so brutal it's banned as a sport. Not that this stops them. An unrated version is also available. 94m/C VHS. Bolo Yeung, Martin Kove, William Zabka, Michael Bernado, Maryam D'Abo, Edward Albert, Kenn Scott; *D:* Patrick Alien; **W:** Judd B. Lynn, Larry Feliz Jr., Peter Shaner.

Shootfighter 2: Kill or Be Killed! 🐾½ 1996 (R) The Miami underworld is placed on alert when a police chief, seeking to avenge the death of his son, joins with a martial arts master to recruit and train a group of fighters. Then they'll infiltrate the illegal spectator games of to-the-death-combat and see what mayhem they can cause. 90m/C VHS. Bolo Yeung, Michael Bernado, William Zabka; *D:* Paul Ziller; **W:** Peter Shaner, Greg Mellot.

The Shooting 🐾🐾🐾 1966 A mysterious woman, bent on revenge, persuades a former bounty hunter and his partner to escort her across the desert, with tragic results. Offbeat, small film filled with strong performances by Nicholson and Oates. Filmed concurrently with "Ride in the Whirlwind," with the same cast and director. Bang-up surprise ending. 82m/C VHS, DVD. Warren Oates, Millie Perkins, Jack Nicholson, Will Hutchins; *D:* Monte Hellman; **W:** Adrien (Carole Eastman) Joyce; **C:** Gregory San-do; **M:** Richard Markowitz.

Shooting 🐾 1982 Three boys run away when they think they have killed a man in a hunting accident. 60m/C VHS. Lynn Redgrave, Lance Kerwin, Barry Primus; *D:* Michael Ray Rhodes; **W:** Josef Anderson; **M:** John Cacavas.

Shooting Dogs 🐾🐾 *Beyond the Gates* 2005 (R) The Ecole Technique Officielle is a secondary school located in Kigali, Rwanda. Young British teacher Joe Connor (Dancy) is getting his feet wet by spending a year at the school, run by steadfast Father Christopher (Hurt). Tensions are building between the Hutu and Tutsi factions and the school eventually becomes an uncertain shelter amidst the genocide. Film comes off as well-intentioned but overly familiar, although Hurt is a high-...

Shooting Elizabeth 🐾½ 1992 (PG-13) A fed-up husband decides to shut his loudmouthed wife up—permanently. Only before he can kill her, she disappears. The police don't buy it and want to charge him with murder. Can he find his wife before things really get serious? 96m/C VHS, DVD. Jeff Goldblum, Mimi Rogers; *D:* Baz Taylor.

Shooting Fish 🐾🐾½ 1998 (PG) London con-artists Dylan (Futterman) and Jez (Townsend) are trying to figure out a way to save her retarded brother's home from her greedy fiance. Breezy, fun comedy benefits from a great chemistry between the likable leads, but suffers from plot overload near the end. 109m/C VHS, DVD. *GB* Dan Futterman, Stuart Townsend, Kate Beckinsale, Dominic Melham, Claire Cox, Nickolas Grace, Peter Capaldi, Annette Crosbie, Jane Lapotaire; *D:* Stefan Schwartz; **W:** Stefan Schwartz; Richard Holmes; **C:** Jenny Braham; **M:** Stanislas Syrewicz.

Shooting Livien 🐾🐾 2005 John Livien (Behr), named after John Lennon, is a self-destructive rock singer who is about to blow his band's big chance at success with his behavior, which endears him to no one but groupie Emi (Wynter). As Livien becomes increasingly unstable, he connects ever more dangerously with Lennon's life—and death. 94m/C VHS, DVD. Jason Behr, Sarah Wynter, Dominic Monaghan, Joshua Leonard, Ally Sheedy, Polly Draper, Jay O. Sanders; *D:* Rebecca Cook; **W:** Rebecca Cook; **C:** Harlan Bosmajian.

The Shooting Party 🐾🐾🐾 1977 Told in flashbacks, a story of a crime of passion, an innocent man, and guilty secrets. A magistrate cannot admit his love for a woodsman's daughter so she falls into a loveless marriage and a decadent affair. In a fit of passion, the magistrate kills her and then decides to prosecute her innocent husband for the crime. Based on a story by Chekhov. In Russian with English subtitles. 105m/C VHS, PU Oleg (Yankovsky) Jankovsky, Galina Belyaeva; *D:* Emil Loteanu.

The Shooting Party 🐾🐾🐾½ 1985 A group of English aristocrats assemble at a nobleman's house for a bird shoot on the eve of WWI. Splendid cast crowned Mason, in his last role. Fascinating crucible class anxieties, rich with social scheming, personality conflicts, and things left unsaid. Adapted from Isabel Colegate's novel. 97m/C VHS, DVD. *GB* James Mason, Dorothy Tutin, Edward Fox, John Gielgud, Robert Hardy, Cheryl Campbell, Judi Bowker; *D:* Alan Bridges; **W:** Julian Bond. L.A. Film Critics '85: Support, Actor (Gielgud); Natl. Soc. Film Critics '85: Support, Actor (Gielgud).

Shooting Stars 🐾 1985 Two actors who play private eyes on TV are pushed out of their jobs by a jealous co-star. They take to the streets as "real" crime-fighting dicks. Interesting premise goes nowhere. 96m/C VHS. Billy Dee Williams, Parker Stevenson, Efrem Zimbalist Jr., Edie Adams; *D:* Richard Lang. TV

Shooting the Past 🐾🐾½ 1999 Christopher Anderson (Cunningham) is a wealthy American developer who has just purchased an old London mansion, which he is intending to convert into a business school. The mansion presently houses the Fallon Photo Library, consisting of some 10 million historical pictures. The indifferent Anderson says the collection must be sold or destroyed within a week. But Anderson reckons without the library's imperious employees, who will do whatever is necessary to save their library. 180m/C VHS, DVD. *GB* Liam Cunningham, Lindsay Duncan, Timothy Spall, Emilie Fox; *D:* Stephen Poliakoff; **W:** Stephen Poliakoff. TV

Shopgirl 🐾🐾🐾 2005 (R) Writer/actor/director Steve Martin adapts his novella about a rather bland, disconnected and melancholy 20-something glove salesgirl, Mirabelle (Danes) shares an unemotional romance with older rich guy Ray Porter (Martin), then meets Jeremy (Schwartzman) who is perhaps a better (and younger) match. Martin doesn't depart from his previous films, again staying in his beloved L.A. Characters are a bit flat, but Martin's flair for words and setting the scene add an artsy, high-brow element that absolutely works. 116m/C DVD. *US* Steve Martin, Claire Danes, Jason Schwartzman, Bridgette Wilson-Sampras, Sam Bottoms, Frances Conroy, Rebecca Pidgeon, Samantha Shelton, Gina Doctor, Clyde Kusetsu, Romy Rosemont, Anne Marie Howard; *D:* Anand Tucker; **W:** Steve Martin; **C:** Peter Suschitzky; **M:** Barrington Pheloung.

Shopping 🐾🐾 1993 (R) A crumbling British industrial city (filmed at London's docklands) is the bleak setting for gangs of aimless youth who steal cars, crash into the windows of various shops, grab what-ever comes to hand, and then lead the police on high-speed chases. Adrenaline junkie Billy (Law) is accompanied by thrill-seeking girlfriend Jo (Frost) on one such escapade while fending off rival Tommy (Pertwee), who doesn't like his burgeoning criminal empire disturbed. Tries too hard for that rebel youth feeling. 86m/C VHS, DVD. *GB* Jude Law, Sadie Frost, Sean Pertwee, Fraser James, Sean Bean, Marianne Faithfull, Jonathan Pryce, Daniel Newman; *D:* Paul W.S. Anderson; **W:** Paul W.S. Anderson; **C:** Tony

Shooting Fish... light. 115m/C DVD. *GB* John Hurt, Hugh Dancy, Dominique Horwitz, Nicola Walker, Louis Mahoney, Steve Toussaint; *D:* Michael Caton-Jones; **W:** Richard Wolstencroft; **C:** Ivan Strasburg; **M:** Dario Marianelli.

Shooting Elizabeth...

Shop Angel 🐾🐾 1932 A department store dress designer encounters romance and scandal in this low-budget drama of intrigue and romance. She falls in love with the fiance of her boss's daughter, and schemes to blackmail him (the boss). Competently rendered if unexceptional tale. 66m/B VHS. Marion Shilling, Holmes Herbert, Creighton Hale; *D:* E. Mason Hopper.

The Shop Around the Corner 🐾🐾🐾½ 1940 A low-key romantic classic in which Stewart and Sullavan are feuding clerks in a small Budapest shop, who unknowingly fall in love via a lonely hearts club. Charming portrayal of ordinary people in ordinary situations. Adapted from the Nikolaus Laszlo's play "Parfumerie." Later made into a musical called "In the Good Old Summertime" and, on Broadway, "She Loves Me." 99m/B VHS, DVD. Margaret Sullavan, James Stewart, Frank Morgan, Joseph Schildkraut, Sara Haden, Felix Bressart, Charles Halton; *D:* Ernst Lubitsch; **W:** Samson Raphaelson; **C:** William H. Daniels; **M:** Werner R. Heymann. Natl. Film Reg. '99.

The Shop on Main Street 🐾🐾🐾🐾 *The Shop on High Street; Obch Od Na Korze* 1965 During WWII, a Slovak takes a job as an "Aryan comptroller" for a Jewish-owned button shop. The owner is an old deaf woman; they slowly build a friendship. Tragedy ensues when all of the town's Jews are to be deported. Sensitive and subtle. Surely among the most gutwrenching portrayals of human tragedy ever on screen. Exquisite plotting and direction. In Czechoslovakian with English subtitles. 111m/B VHS, DVD. *CZ* Ida Kaminska, Josef Krone; Hana Slivkova, Frantisek Holly, Martin Gregor; *D:* Jan Kadar, Elmar Klos; **W:** Jan Kadar, Elmar Klos; **C:** Vladimir Novotny; **M:** Zdenek Liska. Oscars '65: Foreign Film; N.Y. Film Critics '66: Foreign Film.

Short Cuts 🐾🐾🐾½ 1993 (R) Multi-storied, fish-eyed look at American culture with some 22 characters intersecting—profoundly or fleetingly—through each other's lives. Running the emotional gamut from disturbing to humorous, Altman's portrait of the contemporary human condition is nevertheless fascinating. Based on nine stories and a prose poem by Raymond Carver. 189m/C VHS, DVD. *US* Andie MacDowell, Jack Lemmon, Lily Tomlin, Tom Waits, Bruce Davison, Andie MacDowell, Jack Lemmon, Peter Gallagher, Lily Tomlin, Tom Waits, Frances McDormand, Peter Gallagher, Lily Tomlin, Robert Downey Jr., Jarrett Lennon, Zane Cassidy; *D:* Robert Altman; **W:** Frank Barhydt, Robert Altman; **C:** Walt Lloyd; **M:** Mark Isham. Ind. Sprit '94: Director (Altman). Film; Screenplay; Natl. Soc. Film Critics '93: Support. Actress (Stowe); Venice Film Fest. '93: Film.

Short Eyes 🐾🐾🐾½ 1993 (R) *The Slammer* 1979 (R) When a child molester (Davison) enters prison, the inmates act out their own 'orm of revenge against him. Filmed on location at New York City's Men's House of Detention. nicknamed "The Tombs." Script by Manuel Pinero from his excellent play; he also acts in the film. Top-notch performances and respectful direction from Young bring unsparingly realistic prison drama to the screen. Title is prison jargon for child molester. 100m/C VHS, DVD. Bruce Davison, Miguel Pinero, Nathan George, Donald Blakely, Curtis Mayfield, Jose Perez, Shawn Elliott; *D:* Robert M. Young.

The Shootist 🐾🐾🐾½ 1976 (PG) Wayne, in a supporting last role plays a legendary gunslinger afflicted with cancer who seeks peace and solace in his final days. Town bad guys Boone and O'Brian aren't about to let him rest and are determined to gun him down to avenge past deeds. One of Wayne's best and most dignified performances about living up to a personal code of honor. Stewart and Bacall head excellent supporting cast. Based on Glendon Swarthout's novel. 100m/C VHS, DVD. John Wayne, Lauren Bacall, Ron Howard, James Stewart, Richard Boone, Hugh O'Brian, Bill McKinney, Harry (Henry) Morgan, John Carradine, Sheree North, Scatman Crothers; *D:* Donald Siegel; **W:** Scott Hale, Miles Hood Swarthout; **C:** Bruce Surtees; **M:** Elmer Bernstein.

Shore Leave 🐾🐾🐾 1925 Dress-maker Mackaill isn't getting any younger. Tough-guy sailor Blige Smith (Barthelmess, in top form) meets her on shore leave; little does he realize her plans for him! She owns a dry-docked ship, you see, and if (and she) will be ready for him when he comes ashore next. Lovely, fun lowed two years later, save Sheedy and Guttenberg, by the lame "Short Circuit 2" (if rather plodding) romantic comedy. Later made into musicals twice, as "Hit the Deck" and "Follow the Fleet." 74m/B VHS. Richard Barthelmess, Dorothy Mackaill; *D:* John S. Robertson.

Short Circuit 🐾🐾 1986 (PG) A newly developed robot designed for the military is hit by lightning and begins to think it's alive. Sheedy and Guttenberg help it hide from the mean people at the weapons lab who want to take it home. Followed two years later, save Sheedy and Guttenberg, by the lame "Short Circuit 2" 98m/C VHS, DVD, UMD. Ally Sheedy, Austin Pendleton, Fisher Stevens, Brian McNamara; *D:* John Badham; **W:** S.S. Wilson; **C:** Nick McLean; **M:** David Shire.

Short Circuit 2 🐾🐾 1988 (PG) A sequel to the first adorable-robot-outwits-bad-guys tale. The robot, Number Five, makes his way through numerous plot turns without much human assistance or much purpose. Harmless (unless you have to spend time watching it) but pointless and juvenile. Very occasional genuinely funny moments. 95m/C VHS, DVD. Fisher Stevens, Cynthia Gibb, Michael McKean, Jack Weston, David Hemblen; *D:* Kenneth Johnson; **W:** Brent Maddock; **C:** Nick McLean; **M:** Charles Fox.

Shopworn Angel 🐾🐾🐾 1938 'Weepy melodrama about a sophisticated actress who leads on a naive Texas soldier who's in New York prior to being shipped out for WWI duty. Later, as they kiss she goes on stage, she learns he's been killed at the front. She rallys to sing "Pack Up your Troubles in Your Old Kit Bag and Smile, Smile, Smile." Lots of tears. Adapted from the story 'Private Pettigrew's Girl" by Dana Burnet. This remake of the same-titled 1929 film considerably softened the characters. Remade again in 1959 as "That Kind of Woman." 85m/B VHS. Margaret Sullavan, James Stewart, Walter Pidgeon, Nat Pendleton, Alan Curtis, Sam Lavene, Hattie McDaniel, Charley Grapewin, Charles D. Brown; *D:* H.C. Potter; **W:** Waldo Salt; **C:** Joseph Ruttenberg.

Short Fuse 🦴🦴½ *Good to Go* 1988 (R) A Washington, D.C. reporter uncovers the truth behind the rape and murder of a nurse. Interesting "go-go" music from the Washington D.C. ghetto aids an otherwise uninteresting film. **91m/C VHS.** Art Garfunkel, Robert DoQui, Harris Yulin, Richard Brooks, Reginald Daughtry; **D:** Blaine Novak.

Short Night of Glass Dolls 🦴🦴 *Corta Notte delle Bambole di Vetro; Paralyzed; Malastrana* 1971 Journalist Gregory Moore (Sorel) is found dead in a Prague square and taken to the morgue. Only he's not dead but paralyzed—he can't move or communicate but his brain works and through flashbacks he tries to remember what's happened to him. Gregory is investigating the disappearance of his girlfriend Mira (Bach) and learns that she is only one of many girls who have gone missing. The police are no help and Gregory's snooping leads to a sinister club and a secret society. Italian with subtitles. **97m/C DVD.** *IT* Jean Sorel, Ingrid Thulin, Mario Adorf, Barbara Bach, Fabian Sovagovic; **D:** Aldo Lado; **W:** Aldo Lado; **C:** Giuseppe Ruzzolini; **M:** Ennio Morricone.

Short Time 🦴🦴½ 1990 (PG-13) Somewhere between "Tango & Cash" and "Airplane" is where you'll find "Short Time." Non-stop action/comedy stars Dabney Coleman and Teri Garr as partners in crime and humor. Coleman is a cop days from retirement; wrongly told he is dying, he tries hard to get killed so his family will be provided for. Coleman is wonderful. Garr, no longer the long-suffering wife of "Oh, God" and "Close Encounters," is appealing here as the indulgent sidekick. **100m/C VHS.** Dabney Coleman, Teri Garr, Matt Frewer, Barry Corbin, Joe Pantoliano, Xander Berkeley, Rob Roy, Kaj-Erik Eriksen; **D:** Gregg Champion; **W:** John Blumenthal, Michael Berry; **M:** Ira Newborn.

The Shot 🦴🦴½ 1996 Shot in 14 days for $40,000 (and sometimes showing it), this independent release follows out-of-work actors Dern Reel (Bell) and Patrick St. Patrick (Rivkin) as they try to break into the movie business. They foil for the two sensitive artist-types is the shallow but successful director David Egoman. Offended by his brainless action movies, the duo decide to "kidnap" the only print of his latest epic. Although production values are low and the sound is a bit dicey, indie fans will probably like this depiction of Hollywood's shady side. Gained some publicity when ten reels of Kevin Spacey's "Albino Alligator" were swiped from an airport baggage claim shortly after its release. **84m/C VHS.** Dan Bell, Michael Rivkin, Mo Gaffney, Michael DeLuise, Vincent Ward, Jack Kehler, Theodore (Ted) Raimi, Jude Horowitz; *Cameos:* Dana Carvey; **D:** Dan Bell; **W:** Dan Bell; **C:** Alan Caudillo; **M:** Dan Sonis.

A Shot at Glory 🦴🦴 2000 (R) Scottish soccer saga starring Duvall as McLeod, the manager of a struggling local football club. Looking to launch the lads into stardom, the team's new American owner Cameron (Keaton) hires former star McQuillan (real-life player McCoist) against the wishes of McLeod. Despite McQuillan's drinking and carousing—which has cost him his marriage to none other than McLeod's daughter Kate (Mitchell)—the Knockies soon find their way into the Scottish Cup finals, where McLeod meets up with his old nemesis Smith (Cox), manager of the opposing Glasgow Rangers. Though thin on drama, well-shot soccer action will appeal to sports fans. Inside high profile and manufactured brogue bog down an otherwise solid performance. **115m/C VHS, DVD.** Robert Duvall, Michael Keaton, Brian Cox, Cole Hauser, Ally McCoist, Kirsty Mitchell, Morag Hood, Libby Langdon; **D:** Michael Corrente; **W:** Dennis O'Neill; **C:** Alex Thomson; **M:** Mark Knopfler.

A Shot in the Dark 🦴🦴½ 1933 A minister suspects murder when a despised miser is thought to have committed suicide. He takes it on himself to investigate in this routine mystery. **53m/B VHS.** *GB* Dorothy Boyd, O.B. Clarence, Jack Hawkins, Russell Thorndike, Michael Shepley; **D:** George Pearson.

A Shot in the Dark 🦴🦴 1935 When his son is murdered at a New England college, a distraught dad takes it on himself to investigate. Movie cowboy Starrett plays the sleuthing pop in this undistinguished mystery. **69m/B VHS, DVD.** Charles Starrett, Robert Warwick, Edward Van Sloan, Marion Shilling, Doris Lloyd, Helen Jerome Eddy, James Bush; **D:** Charles Lamont.

A Shot in the Dark 🦴🦴🦴½ 1964 Second and possibly the best in the classic "Inspector Clouseau-Pink Panther" series of comedies. The bumbling Inspector Clouseau (Sellers, of course) investigates the case of a parlor maid (Sommer) accused of murdering her lover. Clouseau's libido convinces him she's innocent, even though all the clues point to her. Classic gags, wonderful music. After this film, Sellers as Clouseau disappeared until 1975's "Return of the Pink Panther" (Alan Arkin played him in "Inspector Clouseau," made in 1968 by different folks). **101m/C VHS, DVD.** Peter Sellers, Elke Sommer, Herbert Lom, George Sanders, Bryan Forbes; **D:** Blake Edwards; **W:** William Peter Blatty, Blake Edwards; **C:** Christopher Challis; **M:** Henry Mancini.

Shot in the Heart 🦴🦴🦴 2001 (R) In 1977, shortly after the Supreme Court reinstated capital punishment, convicted murderer Gary Gilmore (Koteas) requested execution by a Utah firing squad, becoming the first person executed in a decade. But Gilmore's brothers, Frank Jr. (Tergesen), and his younger brother, writer Mikal (Ribisi), come to Draper Prison to plead with him to change his mind. Alienated for years, the brothers' uneasy reunion brings up lots of twisted family memories. Haunting movie about internal demons and brotherly ties; based on Mikal's 1994 memoir of the same name. **98m/C VHS, DVD.** Giovanni Ribisi, Elias Koteas, Lee Tergesen, Sam Shepard, Amy Madigan, Eric Bogosian; **D:** Agnieszka Holland; **W:** Frank Pugliese; **C:** Jacek Petrycki. CABLE

Shot Through the Heart 🦴🦴🦴 1998 (R) Based on a true story of the ethnic conflict that tore apart the former Yugoslavia and started a civil war between 1992 and 1995. Serbian Slavko (Perez) and Croat Vlado (Roache), whose childhood friends and former teammates on the Yugoslavian target-shooting team. Slavko is drafted into the Serbian army and urges his friend to flee Sarajevo. Instead, Vlado and his family are trapped in the city and Vlado is forced to take up his rifle in defense against deadly Serbian snipers. Which leads him to a final confrontation with Slavko. Filmed in Sarajevo and Budapest. **115m/C VHS, DVD.** Linus Roache, Vincent Perez, Lothaire Bluteau, Adam Kotz, Lia Williams, Karianne Henderson; **D:** David Atwood; **W:** Guy Hibbert; **M:** Ed Shearmur. CABLE

Shotgun 🦴🦴½ 1955 A sheriff on the trail of a killer is accompanied by a girl he's saved from Indians. Average western cowritten by western actor Rory Calhoun, who had hoped to star in the film, but was turned down by the studio. **81m/C VHS.** Sterling Hayden, Zachary Scott, Yvonne De Carlo; **D:** Lesley Selander; **C:** Ellsworth Fredericks.

The Shout 🦴🦴🦴 1978 (R) From a stranger Robert Graves story, an even stranger film. A lunatic befriends a young couple, moves in with them, and gradually takes over their lives. The movie's title refers to the man's ability to kill by shouting, a power he learned from his Australian aboriginal past. **88m/C VHS.** *GB* Alan Bates, Susannah York, John Hurt, Tim Curry; **D:** Jerzy Skolimowski; **W:** Michael Austin; **M:** Tony Banks. Cannes '78: Grand Jury Prize.

Shout 🦴🦴 1991 (PG-13) Romance and rebellion set in a sleepy Texas town during the 1950s. Jesse Tucker's (Walters) rebellious ways land him in the Benedict Home for Boys and he seems lost until Jack Cabe (Travolta) enters town. Jack introduces Jesse and the gang to the exciting new sounds of rock 'n' roll. Been done before and better. **93m/C VHS, DVD.** John Travolta, James Walters, Heather Graham, Richard Jordan, Linda Fiorentino, Scott Coffey; **D:** Jeffrey Hornaday; **C:** Robert Brinkmann; **M:** Randy Edelman.

Shout at the Devil 🦴½ 1976 (PG) English officer Moore and Irish-American adventurer Marvin seek to blow up a German battleship out for repairs in East Africa before the outbreak of WWI. There's also some intrigue about ivory smuggling. From the novel by Wilbur Smith and based on an actual incident, but that doesn't make the comedy adventure any more palatable. Marvin's hamming is ludicrous, Moore is unusually wooden, and the big budget permits any number of fairly pointless action-oriented excursions and explosions. **128m/C VHS.** *GB* Lee Marvin, Roger Moore, Barbara Parkins, Ian Holm; **D:** Peter Hunt; **M:** Maurice Jarre.

The Show 🦴🦴 1995 (R) Choppy and incoherent behind-the-scenes look at the attitude and people who make up the explosive hip-hop and rap scene. Mixes black and white concert footage and interviews with Russell Simmons, LL Cool J and Snoop Doggy Dogg, who discuss their music and fans. Will be a disappointment for those looking for a more in-depth study of the music, as this exercise merely scratches the surface. Includes an abundance of cameos from today's top hip hop artists such as Notorious B.I.G., Naughty by Nature and Wu-Tang Clan. **90m/B VHS, DVD.** Craig Mack, Dr. Dre, Run DMC, Slick Rick, Warren G, Kurtis Blow; **D:** Brian Robbins; **C:** Larry Banks, Steven Consentino, Ericson Core, John L. (Ndiaga) Demps Jr., Todd A. Dos Reis.

Show Boat 🦴🦴🦴🦴 1936 The second of three film versions of the Jerome Kern/Oscar Hammerstein musical (based on the Edna Ferber novel), filmed previously in 1929, about a Mississippi showboat and the life and loves of its denizens. Wonderful romance, unforgettable music. Director Whale also brought the world "Frankenstein." The laser edition includes a historical audio essay by Miles Kreuger, excerpts from the 1929 version, Ziegfeld's 1932 stage revival, "Life Aboard a Real Showboat" (a vintage short), radio broadcasts, and a 300-photo essay tracing the history of showboats. Remade 15 years later. ♫Ol' Man River; Ah Still Suits Me; Bill; Can't Help Lovin' Dat Man; Only Make Believe; I Have the Room Above Her; You Are Love; Gallivantin' Around; Cotton Blossom. **110m/B VHS.** Irene Dunne, Allan Jones, Paul Robeson, Helen Morgan, Hattie McDaniel, Charles Winninger, Donald Cook, Bobs Watson; **D:** James Whale; **W:** Oscar Hammerstein; **M:** Oscar Hammerstein, Jerome Kern. Natl. Film Reg. '96.

Show Boat 🦴🦴½ 1951 Third movie version of the 1927 musical about the life and loves of a Mississippi riverboat theatre troupe. Terrific musical numbers, with fun dance routines from Champion, who went on to great fame as a choreographer. Grayson is somewhat vapid, but lovely to look at and hear. Gardner didn't want to do the part of Julie, although she eventually received fabulous reviews—her singing was dubbed by Annette Warren. The 171-foot "Cotton Blossom" boat was built on the Tarzan lake on the MGM back lot at an astounding cost of $126,468. Warfield's film debut—his "Ole Man River"—was recorded in one take, excerpts from "Broadway," "Silent Film," and radio Version of "Show Boat," a documentary featuring life on a real show boat, and a commentary on the performers, the film, and the history of show boats. ♫Make Believe; Can't Help Lovin' Dat Man; I Might Fall Back On You; Ol' Man River; You Are Love; Why Do I Love You?; Bill; Life Upon the Wicked Stage; After the Ball. **115m/C VHS, DVD.** Kathryn Grayson, Howard Keel, Ava Gardner, William Warfield, Joe E. Brown, Agnes Moorehead, Gower Champion; **D:** George Sidney; **W:** George Wells, Jack McGowan; **C:** Charles Rosher; **M:** Oscar Hammerstein.

Show Business 🦴🦴🦴 1944 Historically valuable film record of classic vaudeville acts, especially Cantor and Davis. A number of vaudevillians re-create their old acts for director Marin—unforgettable slapstick and songs. All this pegged on a plot that follows Cantor's rise to fame with the Ziegfeld Follies. ♫Alabamy Bound; I Want a Girl (Just Like the Girl Who Married Dear Old Dad); It Had to Be You; Makin' Whoopee; Why Am I Blue; They're Wearing 'Em Higher in Hawaii; The Curse of an Aching Heart; While Strolling in the Park One Day; You May Not Remember. **92m/B VHS.** Eddie Cantor, Joan Davis, George Murphy; **D:** Edwin L. Marin.

Show Me 🦴½ 2004 (R) No, please don't. Sarah (Nolden) is carjacked and kidnapped by two homeless teens, Jenna (Isabelle) and Jackson (Turton), who force her to take them to her isolated cabin. Only Sarah decides to turn the tables on her captors and plays some mind games herself. Isabelle is frighteningly feral. **97m/C DVD.** *CA* Michelle Nolden, Katharine Isabelle, Kett Turton, Gabriel Hogan; **D:** Cassandra Nicolaou; **W:** Cassandra Nicolaou; **C:** Patrick Mcgowan; **M:** Evelyne Datl.

Show Me Love 🦴🦴 1999 Sixteen-year-old Agnes (Liljeberg) is the new girl in the boring, small Swedish town of Amal. Agnes isn't cool enough to be with the popular crowd (she's a brainy vegetarian) and she's rumored to be a lesbian as well. Agnes does have a crush on bored beauty, Elin (Dahlstrom), who goes to extremes to get her kicks, even making a bet with her sister Jessica (Carlson) about kissing Agnes. Then, shocked by her own reactions, Elin makes out with convenient Johan (Rust). But Elin's betrayal of self leads to self-discovery—for both girls. Swedish with subtitles. **89m/C VHS, DVD.** *SW* Rebecca Liljeberg, Alexandra Dahlstrom, Mathias Rust, Erica Carlson, Stefan Horberg, Ralph Carlsson, Maria Hedborg; **D:** Lukas Moodysson; **W:** Lukas Moodysson; **C:** Ulf Brantas.

A Show of Force 🦴🦴½ 1990 (R) Reporter Irving investigates the coverup of a murder with political ramifications. Brazilian director Barreto cast (surprise!) his girlfriend in the lead; she doesn't exactly carry the day. Phillips is good, but you'll see much of highly billed Duvall or Garcia. Based on a real incident of 1978, but hardly believable as political realism or even moralism. **93m/C VHS, DVD.** Erik Estrada, Amy Irving, Andy Garcia, Robert Duvall, Lou Diamond Phillips; **D:** Bruno Barreto; **W:** Evan Jones; **M:** Georges Delerue.

The Show-Off 🦴🦴½ 1926 Irresponsible Aubrey Piper (Sterling) incessant boasting wrecks havoc with his wife Amy (Wilson), and their life together. Brooks has a small role as the girl-next-door. **82m/B VHS, DVD.** Ford Sterling, Lois Wilson, Louise Brooks, Claire McDowell, C.W. Goodrich, Gregory Kelly; **D:** Malcolm St. Clair; **W:** Pierre Collins; **C:** Lee Garmes; **M:** Timothy Brock.

The Show-Off 🦴🦴½ 1946 Aubrey Piper (Skelton) has big dreams which far out weigh his modest talents. He tells outlandish tales to impress girlfriend Amy (Maxwell) and schemes to make them come true. Dated material which even gifted comedian Skelton can't rescue. Adapted from a play by George Kelly and previously filmed in 1926, 1929, and 1934. **83m/B VHS, DVD.** Red Skelton, Marilyn Maxwell, Marjorie Main, Virginia O'Brien, Eddie Anderson, George Cleveland, Leon Ames, Marshall Thompson, Jacqueline White, Lila Leeds, Emory Parnell; **D:** Harry Beaumont; **W:** George Wells.

Show People 🦴🦴🦴 1928 A pretty girl from the boonies tries to make it big in Tinseltown. But as a slapstick star?! She wanted to be a leading lady! Enjoyable, fun silent comedy shows Davies's true talents. Interesting star cameos, including director Vidor at the end. **82m/B VHS.** Marion Davies, William Haines, Dell Henderson, Paul Ral-

Show Them No Mercy 🐾🐾🐾 *Tainted Money* 1935 A couple and their baby out for a drive unwittingly stumble into a kidnapping that doesn't go as planned. Tense gangster drama reincarnated as the Western "Rawhide." **78m/B VHS.** Rochelle Hudson, Cesar Romero, Bruce Cabot, Edward Norris, Edward Brophy, Warren Hymer, Herbert Rawlinson; **D:** George Marshall.

The Showdown 🐾🐾 1940 The title actually refers to a tricky poker game, the highlight of yet another Hopalong Cassidy versus hoss thieves quickie epic. Kermit Maynard is the brother of cowboy hero Clayton Roy Barcroft, Kermit Maynard; **D:** Howard Bretherton.

The Showdown 🐾🐾½ 1950 Elliott plays cattle trail boss Shad Jones who knows one of his fellow cowhands has murdered his brother. Jones is determined to find out who it is and even the score. Brennan is cast against type as a greedy cattle baron. Elliott's last film for Republic. **86m/B VHS.** William (Wild Bill) Elliott, Walter Brennan, Marie Windsor, Harry (Henry) Morgan, Rhys Williams, Jim Davis, Leif Erickson, Yakima Canutt; **D:** Stuart E. McGowan, Dorrell McGowan; **W:** Stuart E. McGowan, Dorrell McGowan.

Showdown 🐾🐾½ 1973 (PG) Billy Massey (Martin) and Chuck Garvis (Hudson) had been friends since childhood, until they fell out over the attentions of pretty Kate (Clark), whom Chuck married. Chuck became the honest town sheriff while Billy took to train robbing. Now it's up to Chuck to bring Billy to justice. Director Seaton's final film. **99m/C VHS.** Dean Martin, Rock Hudson, Susan Clark, Donald Moffat, John McLiam, Ed Begley Jr.; **D:** George Seaton; **W:** Theodore Taylor; **C:** Ernest Laszlo; **M:** David Shire.

Showdown 🐾½ 1993 (R) A small southern town is taken over by a motorcycle gang whose leader, Kincade, decides to set up his fencing and drug operations there. But the local law enforcement has other ideas, calling in a martial arts expert who wants revenge against Kincade for the death of his partner. Richard Lynch, Leo Fong, Werner Hoezinger, Frank Marth, Tom MacDowell, Troy Donahue; **D:** Leo Fong; **W:** Leo Fong.

Showdown 🐾½ 1993 (R) Ken, the new kid in a particularly nasty high school, gets picked on by the martial-arts expert school bully. After getting beaten up a lot, Ken finds out the school janitor can help turn him into a high-kicking fighter. Lots of fast-paced fight scenes which is all the genre demands. An edited PG-13 version is also available. **90m/C VHS.** Kenn Scott, Billy Blanks, Patrick Kilpatrick, Kenneth McLeod; **D:** Robert Radler.

Showdown 🐾½ 1994 (R) New Yorker Vinny (Accovone) has left the family crime business and moved to California for a quieter life. But when his fast-living nephew Anthony (LeBlanc) moves in, Vinny reluctantly finds himself drawn back into violence. **90m/C VHS, DVD.** Jay Accovone, Matt LeBlanc, Lou Rawls, John Lamotta, Stephanie Richards, Real Andrews; **D:** Guy Magar; **C:** Gerry Lively; **M:** Jeff Beal.

Showdown at Boot Hill 🐾🐾 1958 A bounty hunter (Bronson) kills a wanted murderer but cannot collect the reward because the townspeople will not identify the victim. Rather ordinary plot is carried by Bronson's performance. **76m/B VHS.** Carole Mathews, Thomas Browne Henry, Charles Bronson, Robert Hutton, John Carradine; **D:** Gene Fowler Jr.; **W:** Louis Vittes; **C:** John M. Nicolaus Jr.

Showdown at Williams Creek 🐾🐾½ *Kootenai Brown* 1991 (R) A graphic Canadian Western set in the old Montana territory, where an outcast settler goes on trial for killing an old man. Testimony recounts a shocking history of greed and betrayal. The dark side of the Gold Rush, generally well-acted. Inspired by an actual incident. **97m/C VHS.** Tom Burlinson, Donnelly Rhodes, Raymond Burr, Michael Thrush, John Pyper-Ferguson, Alex Brulanski; **D:** Allen Kroeker; **W:** John Gray; **M:** Michael Conway Baker.

Showdown in Little Tokyo 🐾🐾 1991 (R) Lundgren stars as a martial arts master/L.A cop who was raised in Japan, and has all the respect in the world for his "ancestors" and heritage. Brandon Lee (son of Bruce) is Lundgren's partner, and he's a bona fide American-made, pop-culture, mall junkie. Together, they go after a crack-smuggling gang of "yakuza" (Japanese thugs). Lots of of high-kicking action and the unique angle on stereotypes make this a fun martial arts film. **78m/C VHS, DVD.** William Boyd, Russell Hayden, Britt Wood, Morris Ankrum, Jan Clayton Roy Barcroft, Kermit Maynard; **D:** Howard Bretherton.

Shower 🐾🐾 *Xizao* 2000 (PG-13) Da Ming (Xin) is a successful modern businessman who returns to Beijing after receiving alarming news from his retarded younger brother Er Ming (Wu) about their father, Liu (Xu). But the worst thing Liu has to worry about is the closure of the old-fashioned bathhouse he runs, which provides a quiet haven for its denizens. Da Ming slowly begins to reconnect to his family and working class roots but what will happen if the bathhouse really does close? Sentimental comic saga. Chinese with subtitles. **94m/C VHS, DVD, CH Zhu Xu, Jiang Wu, Pu Cun Xin; D:** Yang Zhang; **W:** Yang Zhang; **C:** Jian Zhang; **M:** Ye Xiao Gang.

The Showgirl Murders 🐾½ 1995 (R) Stripper Jessica (Ford) goes into management when she turns a failing Las Vegas bar into a money-maker but this femme fatale wants owner Mitch (Preston) wife Carolyn (Case). Meanwhile, black-mailing DEA agent Ridley (McFarland) and hitman Joey (Albar) cause problems. **84m/C VHS, DVD.** Maria Ford, Matt Preston, Jeff Douglas, D.S. Case, Kevin Alber, Bob McFarland; **D:** Gene Hertel; **W:** Christopher Wooden.

Showgirls woof! 1995 (NC-17) Long on ridiculous dialogue and bad acting and short on costumes, coming-of-age tale follows one young woman as she nakedly climbs the ladder of success as a Vegas showgirl. Oh, the things she must do to be headliner. Berkley makes the jump from TV's "Saved by the Bell" to portray Nomi, the young lap dancer with the grit of pelvic thrust and the will to succeed. Whether cavorting clothed or nude, Berkley is uniformly wooden, a mass of lip gloss and mascara struggling to emote. Gershon, as her sly nemesis, brings some wit and splash to her role as the jaded headliner. Eszterhas script descends below its makularly high. Titanic amount of female flesh on display fails to give film even a faint hint of sexuality, proof that there is a hell. Rent it, and be prepared to fast forward (to what, we're not sure, though there is a certain camp element that might have been amusing if not imprisoned here). Also available in "R" and unrated versions. **131m/C VHS, DVD.** Elizabeth Berkley, Gina Gershon, Kyle MacLachlan, Glenn Plummer, Alan Rachins, Robert Davi, Gina Ravera; **D:** Paul Verhoeven; **W:** Joe Eszterhas. **C:** Jost Vacano; **M:** David A. Stewart. Golden Raspberries '95: Worst Picture, Worst Actress (Berkley), Worst Director (Verhoeven), Worst Screenplay, Worst Song ("Walk into the Wind"), Worst New Star.

Showtime 🐾🐾 2002 (PG-13) Murphy hams and De Niro grimaces as they both plod through this lame buddy cop comedy. The odd couple are the fiery LAPD detective Preston (De Niro), who's forced to star in a reality-based TV cop show with beat copcrust[r]ated actor Sellers (Murphy) after Preston impulsively shoots out a law suit. Russo camera and must avoid a law suit. Russo is the show's producer and has little to do here. The rest of the action involves tracking down some robbers who are also the owners of a really, really big gun. Shatner briefly injects some life into the lackluster action as he coaches the boys on how to play to the camera. Although the two leads are unarguably cast correctly and easy to watch doing what they do best, the premise lets them, and the audience, down. **95m/C VHS, DVD, US** Robert De Niro, Eddie Murphy, Rene Russo, Frankie Faison, Mos Def, William Shatner, Pedro Damian, Nestor Serrano, Drena De Niro, Kadeem Hardison, TJ Cross, Judah Friedlander; **D:** Tom Dey; **W:** Alfred Gough, Miles Millard; **C:** Thomas Kloss; **M:** Alan Silvestri.

Shredder Orpheus 🐾 1989 Rock star Orpheus skateboards through hell to stop deadly TV transmissions and rescue his wife. **93m/C VHS.** Jesse Bernstein, Brandon McGinley, Vera McCaughan, Megan Murphy, Carlo Scandizzi; **D:** Robert McGinley.

Shrek 🐾🐾🐾 2001 (PG) Animated tale from DreamWorks about a grumpy green ogre, Shrek (Myers), who's upset when some annoying fairy types overrun his swamp. So he makes a deal with the local hotshot, Lord Farquaad (Lithgow), to save his home by rescuing Princess Fiona (Diaz) from a tower that's guarded by your not-so-basic dragon type so Farquaad can marry her. Along as Shrek's unwelcome sidekick is a smart-mouthed donkey (Murphy), who insists on helping the ogre out. This one has some eye-popping visuals as well as inside jokes (and digs at Disney) to keep the adults amused. Based (loosely) on the children's book by William Steig. **89m/C VHS, DVD, US D:** Andrew Adamson, Victoria Jenson; **W:** Ted Elliott, Terry Rossio, Roger S.H. Schulman, Joe Stillman; **M:** Harry Gregson-Williams, John Powell; **V:** Mike Myers, Cameron Diaz, Eddie Murphy, John Lithgow, Vincent Cassel, Kathleen Freeman, Conrad Vernon. Oscars '01: Animated Film; British Acad. '01: Adapt. Screenplay; L.A. Film Critics '01: Animated Film; Broadcast Film Critics '01: Animated Film.

Shrek 2 🐾🐾🐾 2004 (PG) Sequel picks up with Shrek (Myers) and Princess Fiona (Diaz) returning from their honeymoon. They are invited to visit Fiona's parents in the high-falutin' Kingdom of Far, Far Away and Shrek must deal with something more dangerous than dragons or diminutive evil kings—his in-laws, King Harold (Cleese) and Queen Lillian (Andrews), who don't much care to have an ogre in the family (let alone as a daughter). In fact, there's a plot to eliminate Shrek for Fiona's old beau Prince Charming (Everett). The King hires feline assassin Puss-in-Boots (Banderas, uproariously capitalizing on his Spanish hearttrob/Zorro image). Donkey's (Murphy) along as well. The film relies a little too hard in spots, but ya still gotta love the big guy. **92m/C DVD, US D:** Andrew Adamson, Kelly Asbury, Conrad Vernon; **W:** Andrew Adamson, Joe Stillman, J. David Stem, David N. Weiss; **M:** Harry Gregson-Williams; **V:** Mike Myers, Cameron Diaz, Eddie Murphy, John Cleese, Julie Andrews, Rupert Everett, Antonio Banderas, Jennifer Saunders, Larry King, Conrad Vernon.

Shrek the Third 🐾🐾 2007 (PG) Third time is not the charm in the latest tale of the cranky ogre, Shrek (Myers), Fiona (Diaz), and Donkey (Murphy) must find an heir by the name of Arthur (Timberlake) to replace Fiona's dying father (Cleese), prevent Prince Charming (Everett) from staging a coup, and deal with the idea of tiny baby ogres and donkey-dragon toddlers. Swashbuckling Kitty Puss (Banderas) is along for the ride, as well as the standard host of fairy tale and legendary characters, old and new. Potty gags as fresh or fun as in previous efforts. The all-star cast and some of the charm of the first two remains, but all in all the movie spends more time trying to be funny rather than actually being funny and doesn't bring anything fresh or new to the story. **92m/C DVD, HD DVD, US D:** Chris Miller, Raman Hui; **W:** Jeffrey Price, Peter S. Seaman, Jon Zack; **M:** Harry Gregson-Williams; **V:** Mike Myers, Cameron Diaz, Eddie Murphy, Antonio Banderas, John Cleese, Julie Andrews, Justin Timberlake, Rupert Everett, Amy Sedaris, Maya Rudolph, Cheri Oteri, Amy Poehler, John Krasinski, Ian McShane, Eric idle, Regis Philbin, Larry King, Conrad Vernon, Seth Rogen.

Shriek If You Know What I Did Last Friday the 13th 🐾🐾½ 2000 (R) If you're a member of the no joke is too cheap to laugh at club, you'll like this parody of parodies. There's a killer on the loose and he's tar-

geting a group of friends who go to Bullmia High. The humor may date quickly. **86m/C VHS, DVD.** Harley Cross, Tiffani-Amber Thiessen, Coolio, Tom Arnold, Julie Benz, Aimee Graham, Majandra Delfino, Shirley Jones, Rose Marie, Mink Stole, Simon Rex, Danny Strong; **D:** John Blanchard; **W:** Sue Baby, Joe Nelms; **C:** David J. Miller; **M:** Tyler Bates.

Shriek in the Night 🐾🐾 1933 Two rival reporters (Rogers and Talbot, previously paired in "The Thirteenth Guest") turn detective to solve a string of apartment murders. Made on a proverbial shoestring, but not bad. **66m/B VHS.** Ginger Rogers, Lyle Talbot, Harvey Clark; **D:** Albert Ray.

Shrieker 🐾 1997 (R) Six college students are squatting in an abandoned hospital that just happens to be the scene of a 50-year-old massacre. So, one gets the bright idea of conjuring up the creature that did the deed after learning that it will only kill five victims—and the sixth will become the creature's master. This one's really lame. **80m/C VHS, DVD.** Tanya Dempsey, Jamie Gannon, Parry Shen; **D:** Victoria Sloan; **M:** Richard Band.

The Shrieking 🐾 *Hex* 1973 (PG) Black magic women hang out with biker types in Nebraska in 1919. **93m/C VHS.** Keith Carradine, Christina Raines, Gary Busey, Robert Walker Jr., Dan Haggerty, John Carradine, Scott Glenn; **D:** Leo Garen; **M:** Charles Bernstein.

Shriek of the Mutilated woof! 1974 (R) An anthropological expedition on a deserted island turns into a night of horror as a savage beast kills the members of the group one by one. **85m/C VHS, DVD.** Alan Brock, Jennifer Stock, Michael (M.K.) Harris, Tawn Ellis, Darcy Brown; **D:** Michael Findlay; **W:** Ed Adlum, Ed Kelleher; **C:** Roberta Findlay.

The Shrimp on the Barbie 🐾½ 1990 (R) When daddy rejects her marriage to dim bulb boyfriend, Australian Samms hires L.A. low life Marin to pose as new beau. Another in a long line of pseudonymous Smithee efforts. **86m/C VHS, DVD.** Richard "Cheech" Marin, Emma Samms, Vernon Wells, Bruce Spence, Carole Raphaele) Davis; **D:** Alan Smithee.

Shrunken Heads 🐾🐾 1994 (R) Inspired by their comic book heroes three boys try to take on neighborhood thugs only to be gunned down. But along comes Mr. Sumatra, a retired voodoo specialist, who revives the three (in a somewhat smaller form) so they can fight the good fight once again. Title theme music by director Richard's brother, Danny Elfran. **86m/C VHS.** Aeryk Egan, A.J. Damato Bo Sharon, Darris Love, Leigh-Allyn Baker, Troy Fromin, **D:** Richard Elfman; **W:** Matthew Bright; **M:** Richard Elfman.

Shut Up and Kiss Me 🐾🐾 2005 Harmless, unremarkable romantic romp with best buds Ryan (Barnes) and Pete (Rowe) who see their 20s in the rearview mirror when true love finally catches up to them—at the same time (in the serious Ryan gets plowed over—literally—by Jessica (Richardson) while Pete is in over his head with Tiara (Allen), whose protective mobster uncle (Young) isn't too keen about the surfer dude. **101m/C DVD.** Christopher Daniel Barnes, Krista Allen, Brad Rowe, Burt Young, Kristin Richardson, Joan Capodice, Victoria Jackson, Frank Bonner, Yeiba Osario, Kevin Meaney; **D:** Gary Brockette; **W:** Alden "Steve" Chase, Howard Flamm; **C:** Jacques Haitkin; **M:** Andrew Gross. **VIDEO**

Shutter 🐾½ 2008 (PG-13) Another watered-down version of Asian horror, this time around the 2004 Thai chiller by the same name gets the Hollywood treatment. New bride Jane (Taylor) joins her photographer husband Benjamin (Jackson) on a business trip to Japan. One foggy night the couple accidentally hit a girl in the road. They assume she's okay and life goes on. However, her ghostly image begins appearing in Benjamin's photographs, tormenting the couple. Tame and tepid compared to the original, recycling the usual scare tactics now common in J-horror remakes. **85m/C DVD, US** Joshua Jackson, Rachael Taylor, Megumi Okina, David Denman, John Hensley, Maya Hazen, James Kyson

Lee; **D:** Masayuki Ochiai; **W:** Luke Dawson; **C:** Katsumi Yanagijima; **M:** Nathan Barr.

Shy People 🦴🦴🦴 1987 (R) An urbanized New York journalist and her spoiled daughter journey to the Louisiana bayou to visit long-lost relatives in order to produce an article for "Cosmopolitan." They find ignorance, madness, and ancestral secret's and are forced to examine their motives; their relationships and issues brought to light in the watery, murky, fantastic land of the bayous. Well-acted melodrama with an outstanding performance by Hershey as the cajun matriarch. 119m/C VHS. Edward (Eddie) Bunker, Jill Clayburgh, Barbara Hershey, Martha Plimpton, Mare Winningham, Merritt Butrick, John Philbin, Don Swayze, Pruit Taylor Vince; **D:** Andrei Konchalovsky; **W:** Gerard Brach, Marjorie David; **C:** Chris Menges; *M:* Tangerine Dream. Cannes '87: Actress (Hershey).

Siam Sunset 🦴🦴½ 1999 Mild fish-out-of-water comedy finds British chemist Perry (Roache), who works on devising new paint colors, caught up in every conceivable disaster while on an Australian holiday. The recent widower (his wife was crushed by a refrigerator) wins his vacation, which turns out to be a decidedly third-rate bus trip cross-country with a petty tyrant operator (Billing) and a number of Aussie eccentrics. Title refers to a particular shade of red that Perry is trying to develop. 91m/C VHS, DVD. *AU* Linus Roache, Danielle Cormack, Roy Billing, Alan Brough, Ian Bliss, Victoria Hill, Rebecca Hobbs; **C:** John Polson; **W:** Max Dann, Andrew Knight; **C:** Brian J. Breheny; **M:** Paul Grabowsky.

Siberiade 🦴🦴🦴 1979 Depicts life in a Siberian village from 1909 to 1969 for a wealthy family and a peasant clan and how Soviet society affects them. Rambling narrative with strong characters. In Russian with subtitles. 190m/C VHS, DVD. *RU* Vladimir Samoilov, Vitaly Solomin, Nikita Mikhalkov, Ludmila Gurchenko, Nathalia Andretchenko; **D:** Andrei Konchalovsky; **W:** Valentin Yezhov, Andrei Konchalovsky; **M:** Eduard Artemyev. Cannes '79: Grand Jury Prize.

Siberian Lady Macbeth 🦴🦴🦴½ *birska Ledi Magbet* 1961 A Polish version of Shakespeare's Macbeth which ranks with the greatest film translations of his work. In Czarist Russia the passionate wife of a plantation owner begins an affair with a farm hand, and poisons her father-in-law when he finds them out. As her madness grows, she plots the murder of the husband and other suspicious family members. In Serbian with English subtitles. 93m/B VHS, DVD. *RU* Olivera Markovic, Ljuba Tadic, Kapitalina Eric; **D:** Andrzej Wajda; **W:** Sveta Lukic; **C:** Aleksandar Sekulovic.

The Sibling 🦴🦴🦴 *So Evil, My Sister* 1972 (PG) Two sisters become involved in the accidental murder of a man who was a husband to one woman and lover to the other. Of course, one sister has just been released from the mental rehabilitation clinic. 85m/C VHS, DVD. Susan Strasberg, Faith Domergue, Sydney Chaplin, Steve Mitchell; **D:** Reginald LeBorg.

Sibling Rivalry 🦴🦴 1990 (PG-13) Repressed doctor's wife (redundant) Alley rolls in hay with soon to be stiff stranger upon advice of footloose sister. Stranger expires from heart attack in hay and Alley discovers that the corpse is her long-lost brother-in-law. Slapstick cover-up ensues. 88m/C VHS, DVD. Kirstie Alley, Bill Pullman, Carrie Fisher, Sam Elliott, Jami Gertz, Ed O'Neill, Scott Bakula, Frances Sternhagen, Bill Macy; **D:** Carl Reiner.

Siblings 🦴🦴 2004 (R) Toronto teen Joe (Alex Campbell) and his stepsiblings Margaret (Gadon), Pete (Chalmers), and Danielle (Weinstein) want their evil boozy stepmom (Smits) and evil lascivious stepdad (Nicholas Campbell) dead. And then the gruesome twosome die—kinda semi-accidentally. So now the sibs have to get rid of the bodies, claim their inheritance, and watch out for each other. Polley plays the wacky, helpful girl-next-door whom Joe has a crush on. 85m/C VHS, DVD. *CA* Alex Campbell, Andrew Chalmers, Sarah Polley, Sonja Smits, Nicholas (Nick) Campbell, Tom McCamus, Martha Burns, Sarah Gadon, Saman-

tha Weinstein; **D:** David Weaver; **W:** Jackie May; **C:** David (Robert) A. Greene; **M:** Ron Sures.

The Sicilian 🦴🦴½ 1987 (R) Adapted from the Mario Puzo novel and based on the life of Salvatore Giuliano. Chronicles the exploits of the men who took on the government, the Catholic Church, and the Mafia in an effort to make Sicily secede from Italy and become its own nation in the 1940s. Pretentious, overdone, and confused. This long, uncut version was unseen in America, but hailed by European critics; the 115-minute, R-rated American release is also available, but isn't as good. See "Salvatore Giuliano" (Francesco Rosi, 1962) instead of either version. 146m/C VHS, DVD. Christopher Lambert, John Turturro, Terence Stamp, Joss Ackland, Barbara Sukowa; **D:** Michael Cimino; **W:** Steve Shagan; **C:** Alex Thomson; **M:** David Mansfield.

Sicilian Connection 🦴🦴½ 1972 A narcotics agent poses as a nightclub manager to bust a drug-smuggling organization. 100m/C VHS. *IT* Ben Gazzara, Silvia Monti, Fausto Tozzi, Jess Hahn; **D:** Ferdinando Baldi; **C:** Aiace Parolini; **M:** Guido de Angelis, Maurizio de Angelis.

The Sicilian Connection 🦴🦴 *The Pizza Connection* 1985 (R) Two brothers in the mob serve out vendettas and generally create havoc wherever they go. 117m/C VHS. Michele Placido, Mark Switzer, Simona Cavallari, Luigi Burruano; **D:** Damiano Damiani; **W:** Damiano Damiani, Ernesto Gastaldi, Franco Marotta, Laura Toscano; **C:** Nino Celeste; **M:** Carlo Savina.

S.I.C.K. Serial Insane Clown Killer 🦴½ *Grim Weekend* 2003 Five unsympathetic characters travel to a remote cabin for a weekend of ghost stories and fun. Instead they find a decidedly unfunny clown, a high body count, and little dolls. Amateurish effort doesn't manage much to recommend it, unless you like evil clowns. 97m/C VHS, DVD. Ken Hebert, Amanda Watson, Melissa Bale, Chris Bruck, Hank Fields; **D:** Bob Williems; **W:** Ken Hebert; **C:** Jaroslav Vodehnal. VIDEO

Sicko 🦴🦴🦴 2007 (PG-13) Rabble-rousing Moore takes on the profit-driven U.S. health care industry. He showcases various Americans who have suffered (primarily because of being denied insurance coverage and/or claims) and looks at other countries with national health care services, including England, France, Canada—and most controversial—Cuba. It's still personal storytelling but less bombastic than Moore's usual rants, and the greed, double-dealing, and health concerns are easy for most Americans to follow. 113m/C DVD. *US* **D:** Michael Moore; **W:** Michael Moore; **M:** Erin O'Hara.

Sid & Nancy 🦴🦴🦴½ *Sid & Nancy; Love Kills* 1986 (R) The tragic, brutal, true love story of The Sex Pistols' Sid Vicious and American groupie Nancy Spungen, from the director of "Repo Man." Remarkable lead performances in a very dark story that manages to be funny at times. Depressing but engrossing; no appreciation of punk music or sympathy for the self-destructive way of life is required. Oldman and Webb are superb. Music by Joe Strummer, the Pogues, and Pray for Rain. 111m/C VHS, DVD. *GB* Gary Oldman, Andrew Webb, Debbie Bishop, David Hayman, Andrew Schofield, Tony London, Xander Berkeley, Biff Yeager, Courtney Love, Iggy Pop; **D:** Alex Cox; **W:** Alex Cox, Abbe Wool; **C:** Roger Deakins; **M:** The Pogues, Pray for Rain, Joe Strummer. Natl. Soc. Film Critics '86: Actress (Webb).

Siddhartha 🦴🦴 1972 Siddhartha (Kapoor), a wealthy young Brahmin, decides to become a wandering ascetic and follow holy teachings. But after several years, Siddhartha abandons himself to hedonism and the delights of courtesan Kamala (Garewal) until his ultimate decision to return to his search for inner peace. Based on the novel by Herman Hesse. 85m/C VHS, DVD. Shashi Kapoor, Simi Garewal; **D:** Conrad Rooks; **W:** Conrad Rooks; **C:** Sven Nykvist; **M:** Hemant Kumar.

Side by Side 🦴🦴 1988 In the same vein as "Cocoon," three senior citizens who aren't ready to retire decide to start their own business and launch a

sportswear company designed for seniors. A witty portrayal of graceful aging that is uneven at times. 100m/C VHS. Milton Berle, Sid Caesar, Danny Thomas; **D:** Jack Bender.

Side Effects 🦴🦴½ 2005 (R) Shrill comedy about corporate evils. Karly is a sales rep for an unscrupulous drug firm. She falls for fellow rep Zach, who wants to throw over corporate greed for country life. Karly decides to work six more months and suddenly the perks are rolling in, just as she learns about some shady dealings. So will Karly decide to listen to her conscience or her cash flow? 90m/C DVD. Katherine Heigl, Lucian McAfee, David Durbin, Dorian DeMichele; **D:** Kathleen Slattery-Moschkau; **W:** Kathleen Slattery-Moschkau; **C:** Carl F. Whitney; **M:** John Tanner, Ralph Bruner.

Side Out 🦴🦴 1990 (PG-13) The first major film about volleyball!? What a claim! What a bore. Midwestern college guy spends summer in Southern Cal. working for slumlord uncle; instead enters "the ultimate" beach volleyball touring. Bogus. Don't see it, dude. 100m/C VHS, DVD. C. Thomas Howell, Peter Horton, Kathy Ireland, Sinjin Smith, Randy Stoklos, Courtney Thorne-Smith, Harley Jane Kozak, Christopher Rydell; **D:** Peter Israelson.

Side Show 🦴🦴 1984 A runaway teen joins the circus, witnesses a murder, and must use his wits to stay out of reach of the killer. Forced "suspense" and "drama" of the bad made for TV ilk. 98m/C VHS. Lance Kerwin, Red Buttons, Anthony (Tony) Franciosa, Connie Stevens; **D:** William Conrad; **M:** Ralph Burns.

Side Street 🦴🦴 1950 Sweaty noir with young postman Joe Norson (Granger) giving into a momentary weakness and finding a world of hurt. He just wants to provide for pregnant wife Ellen (O'Connell), so when he sees a wad of cash in a lawyer's office, he takes it. But the tainted loot is part of a blackmail payoff tied to murder. Joe tries to return the dough but runs into problems and finds more trouble when the money (and the friend who was holding it for him) disappears. About this time Joe learns the greenbacks belonged to gangster Garsell (Craig). Joe has to go on the lam from Garsell and the cops, who now think the poor stooge is tied into the murder. 83m/B DVD. Farley Granger, Cathy O'Donnell, James Craig, Paul Kelly, Edmon Ryan, Paul Harvey, Jean Hagen, Charles McGraw, Nick Drumman; **D:** Anthony Mann; **W:** Sydney (Sidney) Boehm; **C:** Joseph Ruttenberg; **M:** Lennie Hayton.

Sideburns 🦴🦴 1991 The Pushkin Club, a group of reactionaries who try to remove the western influence from Russia, attack first a rock band, then innocent civilians as they act as a social cleaning service. Uses humor to try and warn people against the rising fascism in Russia because of the battle between conservative and reformist forces. In Russian with English subtitles. 110m/C VHS. *RU* Viktor Sukhonkov, Aleksandr Medvedev, Artur Vakha, Vladlen Binyukov, Aleksandr Lykov; **D:** Yuri Mamin; **W:** Vyacheslav Leikin; **C:** Sergei Nekrasov; **M:** Aleksei Zalivalov.

Sidekicks 🦴🦴 1993 (PG) Cutesy ego vehicle for executive producer Norris (Brandis) is bullied by the kids at school and doesn't find much support at home from his well-meaning but ineffectual dad. He has a severe case of hero-worship for Norris, who appears as himself in a series of daydream karate sequences, saving the good guy and maiming the bad. Predictable and sappy. 100m/C VHS. Chuck Norris, Jonathan Brandis, Beau Bridges, Mako, Julia Nickson-Soul, Danica McKellar, Richard Moll, Joe Piscopo; **D:** Aaron Norris; **W:** Donald W. Thompson, Lou Illar; **C:** Joao Fernandes; **M:** Alan Silvestri, David Shire.

Sidewalks of London 🦴🦴🦴 *St. Martin's Lane* 1938 Laughton's a sidewalk entertainer who takes in homeless waif Leigh and puts her in his act and in his heart. Harrison steals her away and before long she's a star in the music halls. Meanwhile, Laughton has fallen on hard times. Memorable performances. 86m/B VHS, DVD. *GB* Charles Laughton, Vivien Leigh,

Rex Harrison, Larry Adler, Tyrone Guthrie, Gus McNaughton, Bart Cormack, Edward Lexy, Maire O'Neill, Basil Gill, Claire Greet, David Burns, Cyril Smith, Ronald Ward, Romilly Lunge, Helen Haye, Jerry Verno; **D:** Tim Whelan; **W:** Clemence Dane; **C:** Jules Kruger; **M:** Arthur Johnston.

Sidewalks of New York 🦴🦴 1931 A hapless New York millionaire (Keaton) falls for tenement gal Page and tries to win her heart by saving her street urchin brother from joining the local gang of toughs. Keaton was a silent screen classic as a comedian but his talkie career was disappointing as he lost creative control and battled alcohol problems. 74m/B VHS. Buster Keaton, Anita Page, Cliff Edwards, Frank LaRue, Frank Rowan, Norman Phillips Jr.; **D:** Jules White, Zion Myers.

Sidewalks of New York 🦴🦴 2001 (R) Burns's lightweight comedy about various New Yorkers looking for sex and/or romance suffered from post-Sept. 11 disdain for anything frivolous. But it also suffers from weak writing, obvious "borrowing" from Woody Allen when he was still funny, and too few characters the audience can connect with. Burns is recently dumped TV producer Tommy, who hooks up with recently divorced teacher Maria (Rosario), whose ex, Ben (Crumholtz), thinks they can reunite, before he meets young waitress Ashley (Murphy), who's having an affair with a dentist (Tucci), who's married to Tommy's real-estate agent (Graham), in whom he naturally becomes interested. Oh, and they're all being interviewed for a documentary on love and sex in NYC. Even if it doesn't work on many levels, the performances are generally fine, with Tucci standing out in the meatiest role. 107m/C VHS, DVD. *US* Edward Burns, Heather Graham, Rosario Dawson, Dennis Farina, David Krumholtz, Brittany Murphy, Stanley Tucci, Callie (Calliope) Thorne, Aida Turturro, Nadia Dajani, Michael Leydon Campbell; **D:** Edward Burns; **W:** Edward Burns; **C:** Frank Pinzi.

Sideways 🦴🦴🦴½ 2004 (R) Open a bottle of pinot noir and enjoy the darkly comedic road trip of two self-absorbed, middle-aged buddies in denial. Divorced English teacher, failed novelist, and oenophile Miles (teddy-bearish Giamatti) decides that his lothario, D-list actor pal Jack (Church) deserves a weeklong send-off in the California wine country before his marriage. Naturally, they meet two women infinitely more self-aware and honest than themselves. For Miles, it's kindly blonde waitress Maya (Madsen) while Jack figures he can indulge in a pre-wedding fling with tart-tongued wine pourer Stephanie (Payne's wife Oh). Payne's film is for adults in the best possible way: it's intelligent, amusing, exasperating, and romantic—much like the characters themselves. Great performances by all; based on the novel by Rex Pickett. 124m/C DVD. *US* Paul Giamatti, Thomas Haden Church, Virginia Madsen, Sandra Oh, Marylouise Burke, Jessica Hecht, M.C. Gainey, Missy Doty; **D:** Alexander Payne; **W:** Alexander Payne; **C:** Phedon Papamichael; **M:** Rolfe Kent. Oscars '04: Adapt. Screenplay; British Acad. '04: Adapt. Screenplay; Golden Globes '05: Film—Mus./Comedy, Screenplay; Ind. Spirit '05: Actor (Giamatti), Director (Payne), Film, Screenplay, Support, Actor (Church), Support. Actress (Madsen); Screen Actors Guild '04: Cast; Writers Guild '04: Adapt. Screenplay.

Sidewinder One 🦴 1977 (PG) Motocross racing is the setting for a romance between a racer and an heiress. Good racing footage, but where's the plot? If you like cars a whole lot... 97m/C VHS, DVD. Michael Parks, Marjoe Gortner, Susan Howard, Alex Cord, Charlotte Rae; **D:** Earl Bellamy; **W:** Nancy Voyles Crawford.

Sidney Sheldon's Bloodline woof! 1979 (F) Wealthy businesswoman Hepburn finds she is marked for death by persons unknown. Exquisitely bad trash from another Sheldon bestseller. 116m/C VHS. Audrey Hepburn, Ben Gazzara, James Mason, Romy Schneider, Omar Sharif, Irene Papas, Beatrice Straight; **D:** Gert Frobe, Maurice Ronet, Beatrice Straight; **D:** Terence Young; **C:** Frederick A. (Freddie) Young; **M:** Ennio Morricone.

The Siege 🎬🎬½ 1998 (R) *Against All Enemies.* Controversial political suspense/action movie caused quite a ruckus when first released. Although protested by Arab-American groups for alleged negative stereotyping, it actually points the finger at the U.S. military as the bad guys. First half centers on the U.S. military (as the bad guys. First half centers on the U.S. military (Washington) and his prominently Lebanese-American partner Haddad (Shalhoub) as they try to stop terrorist bombings of New York. After the bombings escalate, martial law is declared in Brooklyn. Under semi-fascist Gen. Devereaux, all Constitutional rights are suspended and young Arab-Americans are rounded up and imprisoned and Hubbard forms a shaky alliance with shady CIA lady Elise Kraft to break the terrorist ring and restore freedom. Substitutes cardboard cutouts spouting political platitudes for characters. 116m/C VHS, DVD. **D:** Edward Zwick; **W:** Menno Meyjes, Lawrence Wright; **C:** Roger Deakins. '98: Worst Actor (Willis). **M:** Graeme Revell. **C:** Denzel Washington, Tony Shalhoub, Annette Bening, Bruce Willis, Sami Bouajila, David Proval, Jack Gwaltney, Chip Zien, Victor Slezak, Will Lyman, Dakin Matthews, E. Katherine Kerr, Jimmie Ray Weeks, Lance Reddick, Mark Valley, Liana Pai, Anno Salama; **D:** Edward Zwick; **W:** Menno Meyjes, Lawrence Wright; **C:** Roger Deakins.

The Siege of Firebase Gloria 🎬🎬 1989 Story of the Marines who risked their lives defending an outpost against overwhelming odds during the 1968 Tet offensive in Vietnam. Purportedly patriotic war drama made by an Australian director; lead Hauser is a disgusting sadist, and plot is hopelessly hackneyed. 95m/C VHS. Wings Hauser, R. Lee Ermey, Mark Neely, Gary Hershberger, Clyde Jones, Margi Gerard, Richard Kuhlman, David Anderson, Robert Arevalo, John Calvin, Albert "Poppy" Popwell; **D:** Brian Trenchard-Smith; **W:** Tony Johnston, William Nagle; **C:** Joe Batac; **M:** Paul Schutze.

Siegfried 🎬🎬🎬 *Siegfried's Death* 1924 Half of Lang's epic masterpiece "Der Niebelungen," based on German mythology. Title hero bathes in the blood of a dragon he has slain. He marries a princess, but wicked Queen Brunhilde has him killed. Part two, in which Siegfried's widow marries Attila the Hun, is titled "Kriemhild's Revenge." These dark, brooding, archetypal tours de force were patriotic tributes, and were loved by Hitler. Silent with music score. 100m/B VHS, DVD. **D:** Fritz Lang.

Siesta 🎬🎬½ 1987 (R) Barkin is a professional stunt woman who leaves her current lover/manager, played by Sheen, and returns to visit her former lover and trainer, Byrne, on the eve of his marriage to another woman. Her trip, marked by flashbacks and flights of seemingly paranoid fantasy, leads to the discovery of murder, but she cannot remember who, when, why, or where. The film distorts time, reality, and perception in a somepsychological mystery. Attractively filmed by video director Lambert. Barkin and Byrne were married in real life a year after the film's release. 97m/C VHS. Ellen Barkin, Gabriel Byrne, Jodie Foster, Julian Sands, Isabella Rossellini, Martin Sheen, Grace Jones, Alexei Sayle; **D:** Mary Lambert; **W:** Patricia Louisianna Knop; **M:** Miles Davis, Marcus Miller.

The Sign of Four 🎬🎬½ 1983 Sherlock Holmes and the ever-faithful Watson are hired by a young woman who has been anonymously sent an enormous diamond. An inept production which looks good but that's all. 97m/C VHS, DVD. GB Ian Lun:hi; **D:** Desmond Davis; **W:** Charles Edward Pogue; **C:** Denis Lewiston; **M:** Harry Rabinowitz.

The Sign of Four 🎬🎬 2001 Holmes (Frewer), Watson (Welsh), and the Baker Street Irregulars are involved in murder, poison darts, a fortune in Indian jewels, and much suspicious behavior. 120m/C VHS, DVD. CA Matt Frewer, Kenneth Welsh, Marcel Jeannin, Sophie Lorain, Edward Yankie, Michel Perron, Kevin Woodhouse; **C:** Eric Cayla; **M:** Marc Ouellette. **W:** Joe Wiesenfeld. **CABLE.**

The Sign of the Cross 🎬🎬½ 1933 Depraved Emperor Nero (Laughton) decides he wants a new city so he burns down Rome—blaming the fire on the Christians he also wants to get rid of (preferably by the lions in the arena). Meanwhile, Marcus (March), the Roman Prefect, has fallen for the virginal Christian Mercia (Landi) and risks his life to save her. Besides Laughton's overwhelmingly hammy performance, Colbert sinks seductively as the emperor's vixenish wife, Poppaea. Again, lots of crowd scenes on location in the Cotswold district of England, with music by the Czech Symphony Orchestra. 118m/C VHS, DVD. **D:** Cecil B DeMille. **W:** Rob Nilsson.

The Sign of Zorro 🎬🎬 1960 Adventures of the masked swordsman as he champions the causes of the oppressed in early California. Full-length version of the popular late-50s Disney TV series. 89m/C VHS. Guy Williams, Henry Calvin, Gene Sheldon, Romney Brent, Britt Lomond, George Lewis, Lisa Gaye; **D:** Norman Foster, Lewis R. Foster.

Signal 7 🎬🎬 1983 An improvised, neo-verite document of a night in the lives of two San Francisco taxi drivers. Nilsson's first major release and a notable example of his unique seriocless, tape-to-film narrative technique. 89m/C VHS, DVD. Bill Ackridge, Dan Leegant; **D:** Rob Nilsson.

Signs 🎬🎬🎬 2002 (PG-13) Shyamalan takes on crop circles in this eerily potent psycho-thriller. Widowed father Gibson, a lapsed minister, lives on a farm with children Culkin and Breslin, along with younger brother Phoenix when things start to get strange. Everything seems normal, but even simple everyday actions are steeped in the brand of moodiness and unspoken dread that Shyamalan does best. By the time mysterious circles appear in the cornfields, it's clear that the question of whether or not aliens are to blame for the crop circles is secondary to how the characters will react. Quiet and intense, what doesn't happen is as important as what does in this top-notch suspenser. Film was shot in the director's native Pennsylvania. 120m/C VHS, DVD. US Mel Gibson, Joaquin Rafael (Leaf) Phoenix, Rory Culkin, Abigail Breslin, Cherry Jones, Patricia Kalember; **W:** M Night Shyamalan; **D:** M Night Shyamalan; **C:** Tak Fujimoto; **M:** James Newton Howard.

Signs & Wonders 🎬🎬 2000 Commodities trader Alec (Skarsgard) has been living in Athens with wife Marjorie (Rampling) and their children. He begins an affair with sultry co-worker Katherine (Unger) and abandons his family to go to the States with her and then changes his mind. However, when he returns to Athens, Alec discovers Marjorie has moved on with her own lover, Andreas (Katalifos). But Alec isn't giving up and the consequences are unexpected. 108m/C VHS. Deborah Kara Unger, Charlotte Rampling, Stellan Skarsgard, Dimitris Katalifos, Ashley Remy, Michael Cook; **D:** Jonathan Nossiter; **W:** Jonathan Nossiter, James Lasdun; **C:** Yorgos Arvanitis; **M:** Adrian Utley.

Signs of Life 🎬🎬 *Lebenszeichen* 1968 German soldier Stroszek (Brogle), injured during the occupation of Crete, is sent to recuperate on the remote island of Kos. With his Greek wife Nora, Stroszek has nothing to do but guard a deserted fortress and a store of abandoned ammunition. But soon the suspicious natives and the isolation begin to drive Stroszek's madness and he decides to blow up the ammunition dump (and the island along with it). German with subtitles. 90m/B VHS, DVD. GE Peter Brogle, Wolfgang Reichmann, Athina Zacharopoulos, Wolfgang Stumpf; **D:** Werner Herzog; **W:** Werner Herzog; **C:** Thomas Mauch; **M:** Stavros Xarchacos.

Signs of Life 🎬🎬½ 1989 (PG-13) A boat-building company in Maine closes its doors after centuries in business; the employees and families whose lives have been defined by it for generations learn to cope. Wonderful performances compensate only partly for

---

a week script. An episode on PBS's "American Playhouse." 95m/C VHS. Beau Bridges, Arthur Kennedy, Vincent D'Onofrio, Kevin J. O'Connor, Will Patton, Kate Reid, Michael Lewis, Kathy Bates, Mary-Louise Parker, Georgia Engel; **D:** John David Coles; **W:** Mark Malone; **C:** Elliot Davis; **M:** Howard Shore.

Silas Marner 🎬🎬🎬 1985 Superb adaptation of the 1861 George Eliot classic about an itinerant weaver subjected to criminal accusation, poverty, and exile. Wonderful detail and splendid acting. Shot on location in the Cotswold district of England. 92m/C VHS, DVD. GB Ben Kingsley, Jenny Aguter, Patrick Ryecart, Patsy Kensit; **D:** Giles Foster; **M:** Carl Davis. **TV.**

The Silence 🎬🎬🎬 *Tystnaden* 1963 A brutal, enigmatic allegory about two sisters, one a nymphomaniac, the other a violently frustrated lesbian, traveling with the former's young son to an unnamed country beset by war. Fascinating and memorable but frustrating and unsatisfying: What is it about? What is it an allegory of? Where is the narrative? "The third in Bergman's crisis-of-faith trilogy following "Through a Glass Darkly" and "Winter Light." In Swedish with English subtitles or dubbed. 96m/B VHS, DVD. SW Ingrid Thulin, Gunnel Lindstrom, Birger Malmsten; **D:** Ingmar Bergman; **W:** Ingmar Bergman; **C:** Sven Nykvist.

Silence 🎬🎬 *Crazy Jack and the Boy* 1973 (G) An autistic boy gets lost in the wilderness and faces an array of difficulties while his foster parents search for him. 82m/C VHS, DVD. Will Geer, Ellen Geer, Richard Kelton, Ian Geer Flanders, Craig G. Kely; **D:** John Korty.

Silence Like Glass 🎬🎬½ 1990 (R) Diagnosed with life-threatening illness, two young women struggle to overcome their anger at their fate. They find friendship and together, search for reasons to live. Fine performances with pacing that keeps the melodrama to a minimum. 102m/C VHS, Jami Gertz, Martha Plimpton, George Peppard, Rip Torn, James Remar; **D:** Carl Schenkel; **M:** Anne Dudley.

The Silence of Neto 🎬🎬 *Siencio de Neto* 1994 A sheltered young boy comes of age in Guatemala during the early 1950s, a period marked by political upheaval and Cold War paranoia. His relationship with his socialist-leaning uncle causes family friction as it reflects on a repressive society and calls for reform. Spanish with subtitles. 106m/C VHS, DVD. **D:** Luis Arguera; **W:** Luis Arguela; **C:** Ramon Suarez.

Silence of the Hams 🎬½ 1993 (R) Very feeble parody of "The Silence of the Lambs" and others in the thriller/horror genre. Director/writer Greggio also stars as the murder victim, stabbed in the shower, who narrates the story in flashback. There's an eager FBI recruit, a femme fatale, assorted cameo turns, and DeLuise, chewing more scenery than even Anthony Hopkins could swallow, as nutcase Dr. Animal Cannibal Pizza. 85m/C VHS. Ezio Greggio, Dom DeLuise, Billy Zane, Joanna Pacula, Charlene Tilton, Martin Balsam, Wilhelm von Homburg; **Cameos:** Stuart Pankin, John Astin, Phyllis Diller, Bubba Smith, Larry Storch, Rip Taylor, Shelley Winters, Mel Brooks, John Landis, John Carpenter, Joe Dante; **D:** Ezio Greggio; **W:** Ezio Greggio; **C:** Jacques Haitkin.

Silence of the Heart 🎬🎬½ 1984 Mother copes with aftermath of suicide of teenage son following her recent divorce. Hartley is captivating in this gripping drama. 100m/C VHS, DVD. Mariette Hartley, Dana Hill, Howard Hesseman, Chad Lowe, Charlie Sheen; **D:** Richard Michaels; **W:** Phil Penningroth; **M:** Georges Delerue.

The Silence of the Lambs 🎬🎬🎬 1991 (R) Foster is FBI cadet Clarice Starling, a woman with ambition, a cum laude degree in psychology, and a traumatic childhood. When a serial killer begins his ugly rounds, the FBI wants psychological profiles from other serial killers and she's sent to collect a profile from one who's exceptionally clever—psychiatrist Hannibal Lecter, a vicious killer prone to dining on his victims. Brilliant performances from Foster and Hopkins, finely detailed supporting character-

Silence of the Palace 🎬🎬🎬 *Les Silences du Palais* 1994 Set in 1950s Tunisia at the end of the ruling monarchy. Twenty-five-year-old Alia (Lacroix) returns to the run-down palace where she was born and grew up as the daughter of a lifelong servant. Khedija (Hedhili), who was also the personal favorite of her master, Prince Sidi Ali (Fazaa). She remembers the limited, repressed existence they endured and realizes that ten years after leaving the palace, she has traded one form of subjugation for another. Arabic with subtitles. 116m/C VHS. FR Ghalia Lacroix, Amel Hedhili, Kamel Fazaa, Hend Sabri,

---

"Through a Glass Darkly" and "Winter Light." In Swedish with English subtitles or

Silence of the North 🎬🎬 1981 (PG) A widow (Burstyn) with three children struggles to survive under rugged pioneer conditions on the Canadian frontier. The scenery is, not surprisingly, stunning. Based on a true but generic story. 94m/C VHS. CA Ellen Burstyn, Tom Skerritt; **D:** Allan Winton King; **M:** Michael Conway Baker.

The Silencer 🎬🎬 1992 (R) Walden stars as Harley-riding Angel who is out to stop a slavery and prostitution ring that abuses young runaways. Video arcades hold the clues, and Angel must learn to kill without a conscience. Every time she kills, Angel seeks comfort in the arms of anonymous lovers. However, what she doesn't know is that her demented ex-boyfriend is watching. 85m/C VHS, DVD. Lynette Walden, Chris Mulkey, Paul Ganus, Morton Downey Jr.; **D:** Amy Goldstein; **W:** Amy Goldstein, Scott Kraft.

The Silencer 🎬🎬 1999 (R) FBI agent Jason Wells (Elliott) takes his own death in order to assume a new identity for a Citizen" by Donald Hamilton. Followed by "Murderer's Row" (1966), "The Ambushers" (1967), and "The Wrecking Crew" (1968). 103m/C VHS, DVD. Dean Martin, Victor Buono, Stella Stevens, Daliah Lavi, Arthur O'Connell, Robert Webber, James Gregory, Nancy Kovack, Roger C. Carmel, Cyd Charisse; **D:** Phil Karlson; **W:** Oscar Saul; **C:** Burnet Guffey; **M:** Elmer Bernstein.

The Silencers 🎬🎬½ 1995 (R) Secret Service agent Chuck Rafferty (Scala) discovers that his latest enemies, known as the Men in Black, are actually humanappearing aliens seeking to conquer Earth. Now Rafferty's only hope is to team up with inter-galactic peace officer Condor (Christopher) to defeat this evil. 103m/C VHS, DVD. Jack Scalia, Dennis Christopher Clarence Williams III, Carlos aaurchu, Lucinda Weist; **D:** Richard Pepin.

The Silencers 🎬🎬 1966 Rompy spy scoot is the first of Martin's Matt Helm films, made to take advantage of the James Bond craze. Sexy secret agent (missile system from sabotage by Big O. the organization headed by Tung-Tze (Buono). That is if Matt can stay away from the babes and the booze. Based on the novels "The Silencers" and "Death of all. 92m/C VHS, DVD. CA Michael Dudikoff, Brennan Elliott, Gabrielle Miller, Terence Kely, Peter Lacroix; **D:** Robert Lee; **M:** Peter Allen. **VIDEO**

Silence of the North 🎬🎬½ 1992 (R) Walden

Silences

Some brutal visual effects. Excellent portrayals of women who refuse to be victims. Based on the Thomas Harris novel. 118m/ C VHS, DVD. Dan E. Butler, Frankie Faison, Kasi Lemmons, Kathryn Witt, Tracey Water, Obba Babetunde, Ron Vawter, Brent Hinkley, Daniel von Bergen, Jodie Foster, Anthony Hopkins, Scott Glenn, Ted Levine, Brooke Smith, Charles Napier, Roger Corman, Anthony Heald, Diane Baker, Chris Isaak; **D:** Jonathan Demme; **W:** Ted Tally; **C:** Tak Fujimoto; **M:** Howard Shore. Oscars '91: Actor (Hopkins), Actress (Foster), Adapt. Screenplay, Director (Demme), Picture; AFI '98, 100; British Acad. '91: Actor (Hopkins), Actress (Foster); Directors Guild '91: Director (Demme); Golden Globes '92: Actress—Drama (Foster); Natl. Ed. of Review '91: Film Support Actor (Hopkins); N.Y. Film Critics '91: Actor (Hopkins), Actress (Foster), Director (Demme), Film; Writers Guild '91: Adapt. Screenplay.

Silences

Silent Assassins 1988 Fists and bullets fly when a scientist is kidnapped in order to gain secrets to biological warfare. Chong and Rhee, real-life owners of a martial arts studio, produced and choreographed the film. Blair is here, but doesn't figure much. A notch up from most similar martial arts pics. 92m/C VHS. Sam Jones, Linda Blair, Jun Chong, Phillip Rhee; *D:* Scott Thomas, Lee Doo-yong.

Silent Code 1935 A Mountie is framed for the murder of a young miner. 55m/B VHS. Tom Tyler, Blanche Mehaffey, Kane Richmond; *D:* Stuart Paton; *W:* George Morgan; *C:* Roland Price.

The Silent Enemy 1958 The true-life exploits of British frogmen battling Italian foes during WWII. Suspenseful and engrossing; good performances and good rendering of underwater action. Video release snips 20 minutes from the original and adds color. 91m/C VHS, DVD. *GB* Laurence Harvey, John Clements, Michael Craig, Dawn Addams, Sidney James, Alec McCowen, Nigel Stock; *D:* William Fairchild.

Silent Fall 1994 Grisly double murder of his parents is witnessed by autistic nine-year-old, Tim Warden (Faulkner), and his traumatized over-protective teenaged sister Sylvie (Tyler). Retired psychiatrist Jake Rainier (Dreyfuss) is reluctant to get involved, ever since an autistic child in his care died, but when authoritarian rival Dr. Harlinger (Lithgow) is called instead, Jake changes his mind. Second half of film takes a lurid turn as Jake probes Tim's damaged psyche to discover the killer. Trite, clueless whodunnit that generally wastes the talent involved; Tyler and Faulkner make their film debuts. 101m/C VHS, DVD. Richard Dreyfuss, Ben Faulkner, John Lithgow, Liv Tyler, Linda Hamilton, J.T. Walsh; *D:* Bruce Beresford; *W:* Akiva Goldsman; *C:* Peter James; *M:* Stewart Copeland.

Silent Hill 2006 Visually arresting but nonsensical adaptation of a videogame. Rose (Mitchell) and husband Christopher (a wasted Bean) find their young daughter Sharon (Ferland) sleepwalking, muttering about "Silent Hill." Rose researches the name and learns it's a West Virginia mining community that's been deserted since 1974 due to a devastating fire. Nevertheless, Rose grabs Sharon and heads for the town, only to become lost in some alternate existence where she runs around looking for the vanished Sharon and encounters various ghostly freaks, creepy religious fanatics, and a helpful motorcycle cop named Cybil (Holden). 127m/C DVD, Blu-ray Disc, UMD. *CA FR* Radha Mitchell, Sean Bean, Laurie Holden, Deborah Kara Unger, Jodelle Ferland, Alice Krige, Kim Coates, Tanya Allen; *D:* Christophe Gans; *W:* Roger Avary; *C:* Dan Laustsen; *M:* Jeff Danna.

Silent Hunter 1994 (R) Undercover cop Jim Paradine (O'Keeffe) retreats to a remote mountains cabin when his family is killed by a gang of bank robbers. Naturally, the thugs just happen to crash land on Paradine's mountain top with their stolen loot and he goes off to hunt them down. 97m/C VHS. Miles O'Keeffe, Fred Williamson, Lynne Adams, Peter Colvey, Jason Cavalier, Sabine Karsenti; *D:* Fred Williamson.

Silent Madness 1984 (R) A psychiatrist must stop a deranged killer, escaped from an asylum, from slaughtering helpless college coeds in a sorority house. Meanwhile, hospital execs send orderlies to kill the patient, to conceal their mistake. Ludicrous. 93m/C VHS. Belinda J. Montgomery, Viveca Lindfors, Sydney Lassick; *D:* Simon Nuchtern.

The Silent Mr. Sherlock Holmes 1912 These two silent shorts are a rare treat for Holmes fans. "The Copper Beeches" was produced with the "personal supervision of Arthur Conan Doyle." In "The Man with the Twisted Lip," Holmes is hired to find out whether a banker was murdered. 68m/B VHS. *GB* Ellie Norwood.

Silent Motive 1991 Laura is a Hollywood screenwriter who's shocked to discover that a killer is using her recent script as an outline for a series of film-industry murders. She's even more unnerved when a detective makes Laura his number one suspect. 90m/C VHS. Patricia Wettig, Mike Farrell, Ed Asner, Rick Springfield, David Packer; *D:* Lee Philips; *W:* William Bekkala.

Silent Movie 1976 (PG) A has-been movie director (Brooks) is determined to make a comeback and save his studio from being taken over by a conglomerate. Hilarious at times but uneven. An original idea; not as successful as it could have been. Has music and sound effects, but only one word of spoken dialogue by famous mime Marceau. 88m/C VHS, DVD. Mel Brooks, Marty Feldman, Dom DeLuise, Burt Reynolds, Anne Bancroft, James Caan, Liza Minnelli, Paul Newman, Sid Caesar, Bernadette Peters, Harry Ritz, Marcel Marceau; *D:* Mel Brooks; *W:* Mel Brooks, Ron Clark, Rudy DeLuca, Barry Levinson.

Silent Night, Bloody Night *Night of the Dark Full Moon; Death House* 1973 (R) An escaped lunatic terrorizes a small New England town, particularly a mansion that was once an insane asylum. Not great, but well done by director Gershuny, with some nail-biting suspense and slick scene changes. 83m/C VHS, DVD. Patrick O'Neal, John Carradine, Walter Abel, Mary Woronov, Astrid Heeren, Candy Darling; *D:* Theodore Gershuny.

Silent Night, Deadly Night 1984 (R) A psycho ax-murders people while dressed as jolly old St. Nick. Violent and disturbing, to say the least. Caused quite a controversy when it was released to theatres. Santa gimmick sold some tickets at the time, but resist the urge to rent it: it's completely devoid of worth, whatever the killer's outfit. As if one were not enough, we've been blessed with four sequels. 92m/C VHS, DVD. Lilyan Chauvin, Gilmer McCormick, Toni Nero; *D:* Charles E. Sellier; *M:* Perry Botkin.

Silent Night, Deadly Night 2 1987 (R) The psychotic little brother of the psychotic, Santa Claus-dressed killer from the first film exacts revenge, covering the same bloody ground as before. Almost half this sequel consists of scenes lifted whole from the original. 88m/C VHS, DVD. Eric Freeman, James Newman, Elizabeth Kaitan, Jean Miller; *D:* Lee Harry; *M:* Michael Armstrong.

Silent Night, Deadly Night 3: Better Watch Out! 1989 (R) The now grown-up psycho goes up against a young blind woman. Santa is no longer the bad guy, thank goodness. The least bad of the lot, with black humor—though not enough to make it worth seeing. 90m/C VHS. Richard Beymer, Bill Moseley, Samantha Scully, Eric (DaRe) Da Re, Laura Elena Harring, Robert Culp; *D:* Monte Hellman.

Silent Night, Deadly Night 4: Initiation 1990 (R) A secret L.A. cult of she-demons use the slasher Ricky for their own ends—making for more mayhem and horror. Has virtually nothing to do with the other "sequels"—which is not to say it's very good. 90m/C VHS. Maud Adams, Allyce Beasley, Clint Howard, Reggie Bannister; *D:* Brian Yuzna.

Silent Night, Deadly Night 5: The Toymaker 1991 (R) A young boy's Christmas is overrun by murderous Santas and vicious stuffed animals. Definitely for fans of the genre only. 90m/C VHS. Mickey Rooney, William Thorne, Jane Higginson; *D:* Martin Kitrosser; *W:* Martin Kitrosser, Brian Yuzna; *C:* James Mathers; *M:* Matthew Morse.

Silent Night, Lonely Night 1969 Two lonely middle-aged people (Bridges and Jones) begin an affair at Christmas to stem the pain of their separately disintegrating marriages. Poignant but not successfully credible. Based on the play by Robert Anderson. 98m/C VHS. Lloyd Bridges, Shirley Jones, Jeff Bridges, Cloris Leachman, Carrie Snodgress, Lynn Carlin; *D:* Daniel Petrie; *M:* Billy Goldenberg. TV

The Silent One 1986 Featuring underwater photography by Ron and Valerie Taylor, this is the odd story of a mysterious Polynesian boy who has a nautical relationship with a sea turtle. 96m/C VHS. *NZ* Telo Malese, George Henare; *D:* Yvonne Mackay.

The Silent Partner 1978 A bank teller (Gould) foils a robbery, but manages to take some money for himself. The unbalanced robber (Plummer) knows it and wants the money. Good script and well directed, with emphasis on suspense and detail. Unexpectedly violent at times. Early, non-comedic role for big guy Candy. 103m/C VHS, DVD. *CA* Elliot Gould, Christopher Plummer, Susannah York, John Candy; *D:* Daryl Duke; *W:* Curtis Hanson; *C:* Billy Williams.

Silent Partner 2005 (R) CIA desk jockey Gordon Patrick (Moran) is sent to Moscow to look into the suspicious death of a major political figure. He meets hooker Dina (Reid), who is in possession of a briefcase filled with incriminating files, which belonged to the dead man. Pop tart Reid is a natural in her role but this is a familiar story. 96m/C DVD. *US RU* Nick Moran, Tara Reid, Gregg Henry, Patrick Gallagher, Katrina M. Faessel; *D:* James D. Deck; *W:* James D. Deck; *C:* Mikhail Agranovich; *M:* Lawrence Brown.

VIDEO

The Silent Passenger 1935 Amateur sleuth Lord Peter Wimsey makes cinematic debut investigating murder and blackmail on the British railway. Dorothy Sayer's character later inspired BBC mystery series. 75m/B VHS. *GB* John Loder, Peter Haddon, Mary Newland, Austin Trevor, Donald Wolfit, Leslie Perrins, Aubrey Mather, Ralph Truman; *D:* Reginald Denham.

Silent Predators 1999 SNAKE! Of course, not any any snake but mean hybrid rattlesnakes who slither over a small California desert town when an explosion at a construction site disturbs their home. And it's up to fire chief Hamlin to save the town! If the snakes are half as creepy as the video box art, this is one seriously scary snake movie. 91m/C VHS, DVD. Harry Hamlin, Shannon Sturges, Patty McCormack, Jack Scalia, David Spielberg, Beau Billingslea; *D:* Noel Nosseck; *W:* John Carpenter, Matt Dorff; *C:* John Stokes; *M:* Michael Tavera.

CABLE

Silent Rage 1982 (R) Sheriff Norris of a small Texas town must destroy killer Libby who has been made indestructible through genetic engineering. Chuck Norris meets Frankenstein, sort of. Nice try, but still thoroughly stupid and boring. 100m/C VHS, DVD. Chuck Norris, Ron Silver, Stephen Furst, Toni Kalem, Ron Libby, Stephen Keats, Toni Kalem; *D:* Michael Miller; *W:* Joseph Fraley; *C:* Robert C. Jessup, Neil Roach; *M:* Peter Bernstein.

Silent Raiders 1954 A commando unit is sent to France in 1943 to knock out a Nazi communications center. 72m/B VHS. Richard Bartlett, Earle Lyon, Jeanette Bordeau; *M:* Elmer Bernstein.

Silent Rebellion *My Palikari* 1982 A Greek immigrant (Savalas) and his son return to Greece, where they reunite their heritage and each other. Cross-cultural misunderstandings abound; could have been interesting, but the story is just too generic and uninspired. 90m/C VHS. Telly Savalas, Keith Gordon, Michael Constantine, Yula Gavala; *D:* Charles S. Dubin; *W:* Leon Capetanos, George Kirgo; *C:* Ennio Guarnieri; *M:* John Cacavas.

Silent Running 1971 (G) Members of a space station orbiting Saturn care for the last vegetation of a nuclear-devastated earth. When orders come to destroy the vegetation, Dern takes matters into his own hands. Speculative sci-fi at its best. Trumbull's directorial debut; he created special effects for "2001" and "Close Encounters." Strange music enhances the alien atmosphere. 90m/C VHS, DVD. Bruce Dern, Cliff (Potter) Potts, Ron Rifkin; *D:* Douglas Trumbull; *W:* Michael Cimino, Deric Washburn, Steven Bochco; *C:* Charles F. Wheeler; *M:* Prof. Peter Schickele.

Silent Scream 1980 (R) College kids take up residence with the owner of an eerie mansion complete with obligatory murders. Obvious to the point of being gratuitous—and just plain uninteresting. 87m/C VHS, DVD. Rebecca Balding, Cameron Mitchell, Avery Schreiber, Barbara Steele, Steve Doubet, Brad Reardon, Yvonne De Carlo; *D:* Denny Harris; *W:* Wallace C. Bennett, Jim Wheat, Ken Wheat; *C:* Michael D. Murphy; David Shore.

Silent Scream 1984 A former Nazi concentration camp commandant collects unusual animals and humans as a hobby. 60m/C VHS, DVD. *GB* Peter Cushing, Brian Cox, Elaine Donnelly; *D:* Alan Gibson.

Silent Tongue 1992 (PG-13) Weird western finds the crazed Talbot Roe (Phoenix) alone in the wilderness, guarding the tree that is the burial place of his half-breed wife Awbonnie (Tousey). Roe's father (Harris) bought his son's bride from her greedy and abusive father McCree (Bates). In an effort to return Talbot to some semblance of normality, Roe offers to buy McCree's other daughter (Arredondo) for his son. But Talbot is haunted by his wife's angry ghost, who wants her spirit set free by ritual burning, and McCree himself fears the vengeance of his one-time Indian wife Silent Tongue (Cardinal). Messy, over-the-top plot with some poignant performances, especially Phoenix's. 101m/C VHS. River Phoenix, Sheila Tousey, Richard Harris, Alan Bates, Jeri Arredondo, Dermot Mulroney, Tantoo Cardinal; *Cameos:* Bill Irwin, David Shiner; *D:* Sam Shepard; *W:* Sam Shepard; *C:* Jack Conroy; *M:* Patrick O'Hearn.

The Silent Touch 1994 (PG-13) Irascible, aged composer Henry Kesdi (Von Sydow), living in Denmark with his long-suffering wife Helena (Miles), hasn't written a note in 40 years. Music student Stefan (Bluteau) dreams of a composition he believes Henry started but never completed. So Stefan naturally sets out to help Henry finish his symphony by mystically healing his composer's block. Yes, it does sound hokey but the fluff is saved by Von Sydow's buoyantly funny performance. 92m/C VHS. *PL DK GB* Max von Sydow, Lothaire Bluteau, Sarah Miles, Sofie Grabol, Aleksander Bardini, Peter Hesse Overgaard; *D:* Krzysztof Zanussi; *W:* Peter Morgan, Mark Wadlow; *M:* Wojciech Kilar.

Silent Trigger 1997 (R) Special Forces commando Shooter (Lundgren) becomes a paid assassin for an undercover agency but an ill-fated mission causes him and partner Spotter (Bellman) to question the agency, who then decide the duo are expendable. Fast-paced with some eye-catching action sequences. 94m/C VHS, DVD. Dolph Lundgren, Gina Bellman, Conrad Dunn; *D:* Russell Mulcahy; *W:* Sergio D. Altieri; *C:* David Franco; *M:* Stefano Mainetti.

Silent Valley 1935 Adventure of the Old West with American cowboy star Tom Tyler. 60m/B VHS. Tom Tyler, Alan Bridge, Wally Wales, Charles "Blackie" King, Charles "Slim" Whitaker, Murdock MacQuarrie, Nancy Deshon; *D:* Bernard B. Ray; *W:* Rose Gordon, Carl Krusada; *C:* J. Henry Kruse, Abe Scholtz.

Silent Victim 1992 (R) Greene stars as Bonnie Jackson, a Georgia housewife whose marriage has not only gone wrong but turned violent. She takes a drug overdose in a suicide attempt but it results only in a miscarriage. Her furious husband sues her for the murder of their unborn child while an ambitious district attorney petitions the state to charge Bonnie with committing an illegal abortion. Bonnie's torment soon becomes a media circus as she goes on trial. Made on a true story. 116m/C VHS. Michele Greene, Kyle Secor, Ely Pouget, Alex Hyde-White, Dori Bremner, Leann Hunley; *D:* Menahem Golan; *W:* Nelly Adnil, Jonathan Platnick; *M:* William T. Stromberg.

Silent Victory: The Kitty O'Neil Story 1979 Genuinely stirring real-life-overcoming-adversity story of the deaf woman who became a top stunt woman in Hollywood and holder of the land speed record for women. Channing is very good as O'Neil. Made for television. 96m/C Stockard Channing, Brian Den-

Silent Waters *⅔ Khamosh Pani 2003* When a young Muslim makes an all-too-quick conversion from his romance-filled life to militant indoctrination, it leads his mother to confront her haunted past. Geared primarily for the Pakistani audience, the story takes for granted that Western viewers have a background understanding of the 1947 partitioning of India and Pakistan. While Kirron Kher delivers a full-dimensional performance as the mother, other characters aren't as fleshed out. Teeters between doc and Bollywood display. Also available unrated. 70m/C VHS, DVD. Cherlyn Shea, Stephanie Champlin, Julie Skiru; **D:** Joe Gauley.

Silent Witness *⅔ 1985 (R)* A woman (Bertinelli) witnesses her brother-in-law and his friend rape a young woman. She must decide whether to testify against them or keep the family secret. Exploitative and weakly plotted. Rip-off of the much-discussed Massachusetts barroom rape case. 97m/C VHS, DVD. Valerie Bertinelli, Steven Williams; Jacqueline Brookes, Alex Hawkins; **M:** Ralph Netzer. **TV**

Silent Witness *⅔½ 1995 (R)* D: Arshad Mahmud, Kiron Kher, Aamir Ali Malik, Salman Shahid, Shilpa Shukla, Sarfaraz Ansari; **D:** Sabina Sumar; **C:** Ralph Netzer; **M:** Madan Gopal Singh, Arshad Mahmud.

Silent Witness *⅔½ 1991 (R)* Detained in a small Texas town, a woman witnesses the murder of a local girl—but in silhouette, so the killer's identity takes a feature-length running time to resolve. A fair but contrived thriller that the leading lady co-produced. 89m/C VHS. Faye Dunaway, David Rasche, John Terry, Carlos Gomez, Ron Campbell, Margaret Blye, Talisa Soto, Ritch Brinkley; **D:** Czel Schenkel. **W:** Victor Buell. **CABLE**

Silhouette *⅔⅔ 1991 (R)* Do Not Disturb 1999 (R) Walter Richmond (Hurt) and his wife Cathryn (Tilly) are in Amsterdam with their mute daughter Melissa so Walter can close a business deal. But Melissa witnesses a murder and then disappears, leaving her frantic parents to find her before the killers do. This one turns out to be more of a parody of the thriller genre than a serious example. 94m/C VHS, DVD. William Hurt, Jennifer Tilly, Denis Leary, Francesca Brown, Michael Chiklis, Michael Goorjian; **D:** Dick Maas.

Silicon Towers *⅔½ 1999* VIDEO Charlie Cook (Quint) is suddenly promoted to an executive position at Silicon Towers. But a mysterious e-mail warns him that the corporation is illegally accessing bank accounts worldwide and then contrived thriller that the leading lady co-leaves his wife Helene (Knightley) and to obtain silkworms from his boss (Molina), but ends up falling for a concubine (Ashi-ne) of the warlord who provides the silk-worms (Yakusho). Movie skips anything interesting about the historical period in which it's set and opts for tired clichés in Honolulu. Ludicrous plot, bad acting, lots of skin and violence—what more co.uld you want? Dreadful. 85m/C VHS. Monique Gabrielle, Peter Nelson, Jan Merlin, Maria Claire; **D:** Cirio H. Santiago.

Silk *⅔ 1986 (R)* A beautiful and blood-thirsty detective cuts a swath through local heroin rings. 84m/C VHS. Cec Verrell, Bill McLaughlin, Fred Bailey; **D:** Cirio H. Santiago.

Silk *⅔ 2007 (R)* Boring historical drama strives for epic romance but lacks appealing characters, convincing plot, or any chemistry between its leads. Herve (Pitt) leaves his wife Helene (Knightley) and to obtain silkworms from his boss (Molina), 109m/C DVD. CA IT JP Michael Pitt, Keira Knightley, Koji Yakusho, Alfred Molina, Kenneth Welsh, Sei Ashina; **D:** Francois Girard; **W:** Francois Girard, Michael Golding; **C:** Alai Dostie; **M:** Ryuichi Sakamoto.

Silk 2 *⅔ 1989 (R)* A foreign-made sequel, in which a beautiful cop stops crime. 85m/C VHS. Monique Gabrielle, Peter Nelson, Jan Merlin, Maria Claire; **D:** Cirio H. Santiago.

Silk Degrees *⅔½ 1994 (R)* Actress witnesses a murder and is targeted for elimination by the killer. She's supposed to be protected by the killer. It seems there's a traitor agents but it seems there's a traitor nehy, Colleen Dewhurst, Edward Albert, James Farentino; **D:** Lou Antonio. **TV**

Silk 'n' Sabotage *⅔½ Witchild 2 1994* Serious-minded Jamie comes up with a program for a new computer game. When it's stolen by a con artist, Jamie and her frivolous roommates team up to retrieve it. Since the roomies operate a large-scale business there's lots of pulchritude on display. 81m/C VHS. Deborah Shelton, Marc Singer, Mark Hamill, Michael Des Barres, Charles Napier, Gilbert Gottfried, Adrienne Barbeau; **D:** Armand Garabidian; **W:** Stuart Gibbs, Douglas J. Sloan, Robert Gottlieb; **M:** Larry Wolff.

The Silk Road *⅔⅔½ 1992 (PG-13)* In 11th-century China the ancient trading route leads to Dur Huang, a desert city that is the last Chinese outpost on the road. Zhao, a young scholar, travels in a caravan which is attacked by a neighbor. His life is spared and when his new home is attacked by a neighboring nation, he hides the city's treasures in nearby caves. Adapted from the novel by Yashushi Inoue, which was based on the Thousand Buddha Caves, where a treasure of Buddhist icons and scrolls were discovered in 1900. Billed as an epic, there's lots of pageantry and some impressive battle scenes but is too stately and overdone to be more than merely interesting. In Japanese with English subtitles. 99m/C VHS. CH JP Koichi Sato, Tsutiyuki Nishida, Anna Nakagawa, Tsunehiko Watase, Daijiro Harada, Takahiro Tamura; **D:** Junya Sato; **M:** Masaru Sato.

Silk Stockings *⅔⅔⅔ 1957* Splendidly musical comedy adaptation of "Ninotchka," with Astaire as a charming American movie man, and Charisse as the cold Soviet official whose commie heart he melts. Music and lyrics by Cole Porter highlight this film adapted from George S. Kaufman's hit Broadway play. Director Mamoulian's last film. ♪ Too Bad; Paris Loves Lovers; Fated to Be Mated; The Ritz Roll 'n Rock; Silk Stockings; Red Blues; All of You; Stereophonic Sound; Josephine. 117m/C VHS, DVD. Fred Astaire, Cyd Charisse, Janis Paige, Peter Lorre, George Tobias; **D:** Rouben Mamoulian; **M:** Andre Previn.

Silkwood *⅔⅔⅔ 1983 (R)* The story of Karen Silkwood, who died in a 1974 car crash under suspicious circumstances. She was a nuclear plant worker and activist who was investigating shoddy practices at the plant. Streep acts up a storm, disappearing completely into her character. Cher surprises with her fine portrayal of a lesbian co-worker, and Russell is also good. Nichols has a top grip time since we already know the ending, but he brings top-notch performances from his excellent cast. 131m/C VHS, DVD. Meryl Streep, Kurt Russell, Cher, Diana Scarwid, Bruce McGill, Fred Ward, David Strathairn, Ron Silver, Josef Sommer, Craig T. Nelson; **D:** Mike Nichols; **W:** Nora Ephron, Alice Arlen; **C:** Miroslaw Ondricek; **M:** Georges Delerue. Golden Globes '84: Support. Actress (Cher).

Silver Bandit *⅔ 1950* A bookkeeper is sent to investigate a mine theft. Along the way he finds romance and western songs. 54m/B VHS, DVD. Bob Gilbert, Virginia Jackson, Gene Gray, Richard Elliott, Spade Cooley; **D:** Elmer Clifton; **W:** Elmer Clifton; **C:** Harvey Hines.

Silver Bears *⅔⅔ 1978 (PG)* Las Vegas mobster Balsam hires con man Caine and sends him to Switzerland to buy a bank for laundering purposes. Only a bankrupt prince (Jourdan) entices Caine into a scheme to control the word's silver market and he ends up being swindled himself. So-so entry adapted from the novel by Paul Erdman. 114m/C VHS. Michael Caine, Cybill Shepherd, Louis Jourdan, Stephane Audran, David Warner, Tom Smothers, Martin Balsam, Jay Leno, Charles Gray, Joss Ackland; **D:** Ivan Passer; **M:** Claude Bolling.

The Silver Bullet *⅔⅔ 1934* Follows the adventures of Tom, the sheriff of a small gold mining town. 55m/C VHS. Tom Tyler, Jayne Regan, Late "Lafayette" McKee, Charles King, George Chesebro, Charles "Slim" Whittaker, Lew Meehan, Franklyn Farnum, Walt Williams; **D:** Bernard B. Ray.

The Silver Chalice *⅔ 1954* Newman's career somehow survived this movie debut in this bloated, turgid Biblical epic about the momentous events that befall a young Greek sculptor who fashions a holder for the cup that was used at the Last Supper. Newman later took out an ad in Variety to apologize for the film, in which Greene also made his debut. Based on the novel by Thomas Costain. 135m/C VHS. Paul Newman, Virginia Mayo, Pier Angeli, Jack Palance, Natalie Wood, Joseph Wiseman, Lorne Greene, E.G. Marshall; **D:** Victor Saville; **M:** Franz Waxman.

Silver City *⅔⅔ 1984 (PG)* A saga depicting the plight of Polish refugees who find their home in 1949. A pair of lovers find each other in a crowded refugee camp. He's married to her friend. Too-complex, slow but earnest effort. 110m/C VHS. AU Gosia Dobrowolska, Ivar Kants; **D:** Sophia Turkiewicz.

Silver City *⅔⅔ 2004 (R)* Surprisingly clumsy political drama finds Sayles pushing his ensemble in places they're not comfortable going. Conservative Richard "Dim Dickie" Pilager (Cooper) is the son of a U.S. senator (Murphy) and the current frontrunner in the Colorado governor's race. He's about to film a commercial on a very dead body instead of a trout. Savvy and suspicious campaign manager Chuck Raven (Dreyfuss) hires disgraced journalist-turned-PI Danny O'Brien (Huston) to investigate the three prime suspects: talk show host Castleton (Farren), environmental crusader Lyle (Waite), and Dickie's black sheep sister Maddy (Hannah). Disappointing tale of a conspiracy of corruption and all-too easy targets. 129m/C DVD. US Danny Huston, Maria Bello, Billy Zare, Chris Cooper, Richard Dreyfuss, Michael Murphy, Daryl Hannah, Kris Kristofferson, Mary Kay Place, David Clennon, Miguel Ferrer, Raph Waite, Sal Lopez, James Gammon, Tim Roth, Thora Birch, Luis Saguar, Alma Delfina, Aaron Vieyra, Hugo Carbajal; **D:** John Sayles; **W:** John Sayles; **C:** Haskell Wexler; **M:** Mason Daring.

Silver City Bonanza *⅔⅔½ 1951* Lots of action in this outrageous oater that includes a haunted ranch and an undersea battle as plot devices. Singing cowboy Allen and sidekick Ebsen use a a blind man. Since Roy Rogers and Republic parted company the year of this film's release, singing star Allen was groomed to become the new "King of the Cowboys." However, by this time, the singing-cowboy craze was almost out of hat. 67m/B VHS. Rex Allen, Buddy Ebsen, Mary Ellen Kay, Billy Kimbley, Alan B. Kennedy, Gregg Barton, Clem Bevans; **D:** George Blair; **W:** Bob Williams; **C:** John MacBurnie; **M:** Stanley Wilson.

Silver City Kid *⅔⅔ 1945* Two mine owners learn about a rich mineral vein under a rancher's land, kill him, and then try to steal the property from his sister. So it's up to ranch foreman Jack Adams (Lane) to expose the plot and bring the guilty to justice. 56m/B VHS. Peggy Stewart, Wally Vernon, Twinkle Watts, Harry Woods, Glenn Strange, Lane Chandler, Frank Jaquet, Allan "Rocky" Lane; **D:** John English; **C:** Reggie Lanning, Taylor Cavan; **M:** Joseph Dubin.

Silver Dream Racer *⅔½ 1983 (PG)* An English grease monkey wants to win the World Motorcycle Championship title away from an American biker. He's also after someone else's girlfriend. Boring, stilted, unoriginal "Big Race" flick. 103m/C VHS, DVD. Beau Bridges, David Essex, Christina Raines, Diane Keen, Harry H. Corbett; **D:** David Wickes; **M:** David Essex.

Silver Hawk *⅔⅔ 2004* Fei Ying (PG-13) Campy kung fu superhero adventure stars Yeoh as socialite Lulu Wong, whose inhabitants are being brutally murdered. It finally dawns on them the culprit is a werewolf. Action moves along at a good clip and the film has its share of suspense. 94m/C VHS, DVD. Ccrey Haim, Gary Busey, Megan Follows, Everett McGill, Robin Groves, Leon Russom, Terry O'Quinn, Bill Smitrovich, Kent Broadhurst, Lawrence Tierney; **D:** Daniel Attias; **W:** Stephen King; **C:** Armand6 Nannuzzi.

Silver Bullet *⅔⅔ 1985 (R)* Adapted from Stephen King's "Cycle of the Werewolf," about a town whose inhabitants are being brutally murdered. It finally dawns on them the culprit is a werewolf. Action moves along at a good clip and the film has its share of suspense. 95m/C VHS, DVD. Corey Haim, Gary Busey, Megan Follows, Everett McGill, Robin Groves, Leon Russom, Terry O'Quinn, Bill Smitrovich, Kent Broadhurst, Lawrence Tierney; **D:** Daniel Attias; **W:** Stephen King; **C:** Armand6 Nannuzzi.

Silver Lode *⅔⅔½ 1954* A man accused of murder on his wedding day attempts to clear his name while the law use the money to hunt for more silver. Ordinary story improved by good, energetic cast. 92m/C VHS, DVD. John Payne, Dan Duryea, Lizabeth Scott, Stuart Whitman; **D:** Allan Dwan.

Silver Queen *⅔⅔ 1942* A woman finds out her father has gambled away a silver mine and left her with debts. She opens a saloon, only to have her fiancé launches an intensive manhunt for him. 81m/3 VHS, DVD. Priscilla Lane, George Brent, Bruce Cabot, Eugene Pallette; **D:** Lloyd Bacon.

Silver River *⅔⅔ 1948* Average western that marked the final collaboration between director Walsh and star Flynn. It never even comes close to their previous works. Flynn plays a no-good, power-hungry cad who will stop at nothing to get what he wants. He happens to want Sheridan, who is married to Bennett, so Flynn schemes to get rid of him. Overall, Flynn acts as though he really isn't interested in the material and had to make a pact with Walsh that he would stay sober until five in the afternoon while filming. Based on an unpublished novel by Stephen Longstreet. 109m/B VHS. Errol Flynn, Ann Sheridan, Thomas Mitchell, Bruce Bennett, Tom D'Andrea, Barton MacLane, Monte Blue, Jonathan Hale; **D:** Raoul Walsh; **W:** Stephen Longstreet, Harriet Frank Jr., Finney.

Silver Spurs *⅔ 1943* Villain tries to get some oil-rich property by murdering the ranch's owner. Ranch foreman Rogers saves the day. 60m/B VHS. Roy Rogers, Jerome Cowan, John Carradine, Phyllis Brooks, Smiley Burnette, Joyce Compton; **D:** Joseph Kane.

Silver Stallion *⅔½ 1941* Thunder the Wonder Horse plays the title character, who fights rattlesnakes, wild dogs and triumphs over evil men, other horses, and the elements to become leader of the herd. Based on the Australian children's novel "The Silver Brumby" by Elyne Mitchell. 93m/C VHS, DVD. AU Caroline Goodall, Ami Daemion, Russell Crowe; **D:** John Tatoulis, John Stephens; **M:** Tassos Ioannidis.

The Silver Stallion: King of the Wild Brumbies *⅔½* The Silver Brumby 1993 (G) The adolescent Indi is enthralled as her writer-mother relates each new chapter in the saga of Thara, the amazing silver stallion. And she imagines each adventure as the horse tries to become leader of the herd and who fights the humans in this frat family. Pretty western with nice scenery and action scenes. 59m/C VHS. David Sharpe, Carol Hughes, Leroy Mason, Walter Long; **D:** Edward Finney.

Silver Star *⅔⅔ 1955* Man elected sheriff of a western town turns down the job because he is a pacifist. He changes his mind when this defeated opponent hires a trio of killers to come after him. 73m/B VHS, DVD. Edgar Buchanan, Marie Windsor, Lon Chaney Jr., Earle Lyon, Richard Bartlett, Barton MacLane, Morris Ankrum, Edith Evanson; **D:** Richard Bartlett; **W:** Richard Bartlett, Ian MacDonald; **C:** Guy Roe; **M:** Leo Klatzkin.

Silver Strand 🦴🦴½ **1995 (R)** Hunky Brian Del Piso (Bellows), a naval cadet in the S.E.A.L. training school, makes the big mistake of falling for sexy Michelle (Sheridan), who just happens to be an officer's wife. As if he didn't have enough challenges, should their affair be exposed Brian might just as well kiss his career goodbye. **104m/C VHS.** Gil Bellows, Nicolette Sheridan; **D:** George Miller; **W:** Douglas Day Stewart; **C:** David Connell; **M:** Joseph Conlan.

The Silver Streak 🦴🦴 **1934** The sickly son of a diesel train designer needs an iron lung—pronto. A rival's super-fast locomotive s the only hope for the boy. Murders, runaway engines, and a crew that would further walk enliven this race against time. **72m/B VHS, DVD.** Sally Blane, Charles Starrett, Arthur Lake, Edgar Kennedy, William Farnum; **D:** Thomas Atkins.

Silver Streak 🦴🦴🦴 **1976 (PG)** Pooped exec Wilder rides a train from L.A. to Chicago, planning to enjoy a leisurely, relaxing trip. Instead he becomes involved with murder, intrigue, and a beautiful woman. Energetic Hitchcock parody features successful first pairing of Wilder and Pryor. **113m/C VHS, DVD.** Gene Wilder, Richard Pryor, Jill Clayburgh, Patrick McGoohan, Ned Beatty, Ray Walston, Richard Kiel, Scatman Crothers; **D:** Arthur Hiller; **W:** Colin Higgins; **M:** Henry Mancini.

Silver Wolf 🦴🦴½ **1998** Jesse (Meier) and his dad head into the mountains on a snow board trip when a sudden storm hits. Jesse's dad is killed and he is injured. But he finds a companion, a wounded young wolf he names Silver. However, when Jesse is rescued, Silver disappears and Jesse is desperate to find him. Jesse gets his chance when he's taken in by his mountain man uncle (Biehn) but their search pits them against a villainous hunter (Schneider). **97m/C VHS, DVD.** Michael Biehn, Roy Scheider, Shane Meier, Kimberly Warnat; **D:** Peter Svatek; **W:** Michael Amo; **C:** Curtis Petersen; **M:** Robert Carli. **VIDEO**

Silverado 🦴🦴🦴 **1985 (PG-13)** Affectionate pastiche of western cliches has everything a viewer could ask for—except Indians. Straightforward plot has four virtuous cowboys rise up against a crooked lawman in a blaze of six guns. No subtlety from the first big Western in quite a while, but plenty of fun and laughs. **132m/C VHS, DVD.** Kevin Kline, Scott Glenn, Kevin Costner, Danny Glover, Brian Dennehy, Linda Hunt, John Cleese, Jeff Goldblum, Rosanna Arquette, Jeff Fahey; **D:** Lawrence Kasdan; **W:** Lawrence Kasdan; **C:** John Bailey; **M:** Bruce Broughton.

Simba 🦴🦴🦴 **1955** A young English man arrives at his brother's Kenyan farm to find him murdered in a local skirmish between the Mau Maus and white settlers. Well made, thoughtful look at colonialism, racial animosity, and violence. **98m/C VHS.** GB Dirk Bogarde, Donald Sinden, Virginia McKenna, Orlando Martins; **D:** Brian Desmond Hurst; **C:** Geoffrey Unsworth.

The Simian Line 🦴🦴½ **1999** Uneven but affecting look at several couples trying to define their romantic relationships. Middleaged divorcee Katharine (Redgrave) is jealousy in love with her younger live-in lover, Rick (Connick), and very fond of throwing dinner parties. But Katharine's latest soiree not only includes two other couples who are also romantically questionable but an eccentric psychic (Daly), who sees two ghosts in the house (Hurt, Mathis) and makes an ominous prediction. Too many stories clutter the film, particularly since the best performances come from Redgrave and Connick (with Daly offering comedic support). **106m/C VHS, DVD.** Lynn Redgrave, Harry Connick Jr., Jamey Sheridan, Cindy Crawford, Tyne Daly, Monica Keena, Dylan Bruno, Samantha Mathis, William Hurt, Eric Stoltz; **D:** Linda Yellen; **W:** Gisella Bernice; **C:** David Bridges; **M:** Patrick Seymour.

Simon 🦴🦴½ **1980 (PG)** A group of bored demented scientists brainwash a college professor into believing he is an alien from a distant galaxy, whereupon he begins trying to correct the evil in America. Screwball comedy, or semi-serious satire of some kind? Hard to tell. Some terrific set pieces but the movie as a whole doesn't quite hold together. Directorial debut of Brickman, who previously worked as a scriptwriter with Woody Allen ("Sleeper," etc.). **97m/C VHS.** Alan Arkin, Madeline Kahn, Fred Gwynne, Adolph Green, Wallace Shawn, Austin Pendleton; **D:** Marshall Brickman; **W:** Marshall Brickman; **C:** Thomas Baum.

Simon Birch 🦴🦴🦴 **1998 (PG)** *A Small Miracle* Young Simon Birch (Smith) believes he's destined to become a hero, and that his disability—dwarfism resulting from Morquio's syndrome—is actually a gift from God to facilitate his destiny. After his best friend Joe's idolized mother dies, the two decide to track down Joe's father, who hasn't been seen for years. The quest leads to the climactic disaster that is the impetus for the heroics Simon has been waiting for. Smith's onscreen presence is the main attraction, as most of the emotion and inspiration in the source material, John Irving's novel "A Prayer for Owen Meany," is absent. Irving demanded both the character name change (Meany to Birch) and a screen credit change—from "based on" to "suggested by." **110m/C VHS, DVD.** Ian Michael Smith, Joseph Mazzello, Ashley Judd, Oliver Platt, David Strathairn, Dana Ivey, Jan Hooks, Beatrice Winde, Ceciley Carroll, Sumela-Rose Keramidopolos, Sam Morton, John Robinson; **D:** Mark Steven Johnson; **W:** Mark Steven Johnson; **C:** Aaron Schneider; **M:** Marc Shaiman; **Nar:** Jim Carrey.

Simon Bolivar 🦴🦴½ **1969** The title character leads the Venezuelan revolution in 1817. **110m/C VHS.** IT SP VZ Maximilian Schell, Rosanna Schiaffino; **D:** Alessandro Blasetti; **W:** Joe Luis Dibildos; **C:** Manuel Berenguer; **M:** Aldemaro Romero.

Simon, King of the Witches 🦴🦴½ **1971 (R)** An L.A. warlock who lives in a sewer drain finds himself the center of attention when his spells actually work. This interesting hippie/witchcraft entry bogs down now and then but Prine's performance is droll and lively. **90m/C VHS.** Andrew Prine, Brenda Scott, George Paulsin, Norman Burton, Ultra Violet; **D:** Bruce Kessler; **W:** Robert Phippeny; **C:** David L. Butler.

Simon of the Desert 🦴🦴🦴½ *Simon del Desierto* **1966** Not Bunuel's very best, but worthy of the master satirist. An ascetic stands on a pillar in the desert for several decades—closer to God, farther from temptation. Pinal is a gorgeous devil that tempts Simon. Hilarious, irreverent, sophisticated. What's with the weird ending, though? In Spanish with English subtitles. **46m/B VHS.** Claudio Brook, Silvia Pinal, Enrique Alvarez Felix; **D:** Luis Bunuel; **W:** Luis Bunuel; **C:** Gabriel Figueroa; **M:** Raul Lavista.

Simon Sez 🦴½ **1999 (PG-13)** Convoluted spy thriller stars basketball bad boy Dennis Rodman as Simon, an Interpol agent on the trail of effete illegal arms dealer Ashton (Pradon). He must be posing undercover as a gigantic space-age punk rock coloring book, because the nose rings, tattoos and shock treatment hair don't exactly say "inconspicuous." He is approached for help by his old friend and colleague Nick (Cook), a private eye who's in over his head on a kidnapping case. The two cases just happen to be connected, but the plot is just an excuse to show car chases and shoot 'em up action sequences. Rodman shows some decent acting skills, and he's still as bad as he wants to be. Unfortunately, the movie is a lot worse than he wants it to be. **85m/C VHS, DVD.** Dennis Rodman, Dane Cook, Natalia Cigliuti, Filip Nicolic, John Pinette, Jerome Pradon, Ricky Harris; **D:** Kevin Elders; **W:** Andrew Miller, Andrew Lowery; **C:** Avi (Avraham) Karpik; **M:** Brian Tyler. **VIDEO**

Simon the Magician 🦴🦴½ *Simon Magus* **1999** At the beginning of the French police, Budapest magician Simon (Andorai) travels to Paris to solve a murder, although it doesn't seem very important to the plot. Instead, Simon falls in love with Jeanne (Delarme) and is challenged by rival Peter (Halasz) to a deadly duel—being buried alive for three days. References to the biblical story of Simon Magus and St. Peter. Hungarian and French with subtitles. **100m/B DVD.** FR HU Peter Andorai, Hubert Kounde, Julie Delarme, Peter Halasz, Mari Nagy; **D:** Ildiko Enyedi; **W:** Ildiko Enyedi; **C:** Tibor Mathe.

Simone 🦴🦴 **2002 (PG-13)** Part Hollywood send-up and part child of Hollywood, pic shows pitfalls of using gimmicks to sell movies and uses the same gimmick to sell the movie itself. Perfect Tinseltown logic. Pacino is Viktor, a has-been Pygmalion who becomes a high tech filmmaker when he creates an actress from scratch after inheriting a mad inventor's computer program. Solving his recent dilemma involving a temperamental star (Ryder), Viktor's digital thesp, Simone (short for simulated one) becomes a smash hit and revives his career in the process. Of course, the rabid tabloid press and public expect to see a real actress, not a synthespian, creating a host of publicity problems. Writer/director/producer Nicol is in familiar techno-wizardry territory here, but doesn't match his previous efforts. **117m/C VHS, DVD.** US Al Pacino, Catherine Keener, Jay Mohr, Jason Schwartzman, Pruitt Taylor Vince, Stanley Anderson, Evan Rachel Wood, Daniel von Bargen, Rachel Roberts, Elias Koteas, Rebecca Romijn; **Cameos:** Winona Ryder; **D:** Andrew Niccol; **W:** Andrew Niccol; **C:** Edward Lachman; **M:** Carter Burwell.

Simone Barbes 🦴🦴 *Simone Barbes ou la Vertu* **1980** Simone (Bourgoin) ushers at a porn theater where she likes to embarass the clientele. One Parisian night she visits the seedy nightclub where her lesbian lover performs burlesque and decides to embark on some of her own erotic adventures, which prove dangerous. French with subtitles. **80m/C VHS, DVD.** FR Ingrid Bourgoin, Michel Delahaye, Martine Simonet, Pascal Bonitzer; **D:** Marie-Claude Treilhou; **W:** Marie-Claude Treilhou, Michel Delahaye; **C:** Jean-Yves Escoffier.

Simpatico 🦴🦴½ **1999 (R)** Excellent performances and a disappointing script mark this adaptation of the Sam Shephard play. Nolte is Vinnie, who has evidence of horse breeder Carter's (Bridges) involvement in a past race fixing and blackmail scheme. Vinnie's been blackmailing Carter for years and summons him to California on the pretense of helping Vinnie out of a sexual misconduct rap. The supposed victim (Keener) of the misconduct is unaware that any took place and agrees to help Carter. Vinnie then steals Carter's I.D, car, and plane ticket and visits their old blackmail victim (Finney), and then Carter's wife Rosie (Stone), who was also in on the con. In a haze of confused motivations and implausible plot machinations, the three try to redeem their past deeds, with Vinnie and Carter seemingly switching places. **106m/C VHS, DVD.** Nick Nolte, Sharon Stone, Jeff Bridges, Catherine Keener, Albert Finney, Shawn Hatosy, Kimberly Williams, Liam Waite; **D:** Matthew Warchus; **W:** Matthew Warchus, David Nicholls; **C:** John Toll; **M:** Stewart Copeland.

Simple Justice 🦴½ **1989 (R)** Mindless, justice-in-own-hands anti-liberal hogwash. Overwrought, smug, and violent story of a young couple beaten by robbers who remain at large. **91m/C VHS, DVD.** Cesar Romero, John Spencer, Doris Roberts, Candy McClain; **D:** Deborah Del Prete.

The Simple Life of Noah Dearborn 🦴🦴½ **1999 (PG)** Simple morality tale with an affecting performance by Poitier. Noah Dearborn is a 91-year-old carpenter and farmer who refuses to sell his Georgia property to developers. So they try to declare the old man incompetent. **87m/C VHS, DVD.** Sidney Poitier, Mary-Louise Parker, Dianne Wiest, George Newbern; **D:** Gregg Champion. **TV**

Simple Men 🦴🦴🦴 **1992 (R)** Oddball brothers Bill (a petty criminal) and Dennis (a shy college student) decide to track down their missing father in this fractured comedy. Dad, a former big-league baseball player who bombed the Penta-gon in the '60s, is a long-time fugitive hiding out somewhere in the wilds of Long Island. Their search leads the two to equally opposite women, the wary Kate, whom Bill immediately falls for, and the sexy Elina, who turns out to know dear old dad quite well. Deliberately deadpan and cliched, Hartley's quirky style can either irritate or illuminate via the weird turnings of his characters' lives. **105m/C VHS, DVD.** Robert John Burke, William Sage, Karen Sillas, Elina Lowensohn, Martin Donovan, Mark Bailey, John MacKay, Jeffrey Howard, Holly Marie Combs; **D:** Hal Hartley; **W:** Hal Hartley; **C:** Michael Spiller; **M:** Hal Hartley.

A Simple Plan 🦴🦴🦴 **1998 (R)** Hank (Paxton), his "slow" brother Jacob (Thornton), and Jacob's best bud, alcoholic Lou (Briscoe) find the wreckage of a small plane in the snowy Minnesota woods. The pilot is dead and there's a bag filled with $4 million in cash, which they decide is drug money. The trio decide to keep quiet about the find and keep the money hidden until the plane is discovered by someone else. But having all that loot brings out the greed in everyone and soon nasty things begin to happen to all those involved. Adapted from the 1993 novel by Scott Smith. **121m/C VHS, DVD.** Bill Paxton, Billy Bob Thornton, Brent Briscoe, Bridget Fonda, Gary Cole, Becky Ann Baker, Chelsie Ross, Jack Walsh; **D:** Sam Raimi; **W:** Scott B. Smith; **C:** Alar Kivilo; **M:** Danny Elfman. L.A. Film Critics '98: Support. Actor (Thornton); Broadcast Film Critics '98: Adapt. Screenplay, Support. Actor (Thornton).

A Simple Promise 🦴🦴 **2007** Struggling artist Marcus and aspiring singer Madison get romantically involved and make a promise to help each other with their careers. But when one gets that longed-for big break, it causes a lot of friction and they have to figure out if their love can get them through. **95m/C DVD.** Ella Joyce, Layla Kayleigh, Wallace Demaria, Bobby Reed, Bobby Reed, Selwyn Ward, Glen Mac; **D:** Earnest Harris; **W:** Max Lucas; **C:** Andrew Giannetta, Gigi Malavasi; **M:** Matt Hamel.

A Simple Story 🦴🦴½ *Une Histoire Simple* **1979** A woman faces her 40th birthday with increasing uneasiness, though her life seems perfect from the outside. She evaluates her chances at love, childbearing, and friendship, after having an abortion and breaking up with her lover. Schneider's performance is brilliant in this gentle, quiet drama. In French with English subtitles. **110m/C VHS.** FR Romy Schneider, Bruno Cremer, Claude Brasseur; **D:** Claude Sautet.

A Simple Twist of Fate 🦴🦴½ **1994 (PG-13)** Comedy drama gives Martin chance to flex serious muscles with this update of George Eliot's "Silas Marner." Adoptive father Michael McMann wants to keep his daughter Mathilda (played by the prerequisite adorable twins) in the face of demands from her biological father (Byrne), who happens to be a local politician. Then revelations brought out at the custody hearing threaten the politician's career. Cuddly dad is hardly Martin's image (in spite of "Parenthood"), though strong cast limits the sugar. **106m/C VHS, DVD.** Steve Martin, Gabriel Byrne, Catherine O'Hara, Stephen Baldwin, Alana Austin, Alyssa Austin, Laura Linney, Anne Heche, Michael Des Barres, Byron Jennings; **D:** Gilles Mackinnon; **W:** Steve Martin; **M:** Cliff Eidelman.

A Simple Wish 🦴🦴½ **1997 (PG)** Equal employment opportunities now even extend to the fairy godmother realm. Anabel (Wilson) knows her dad (Pastorelli) wants to become a Broadway actor. So she wishes for a fairy godmother—and gets stuck with Murray (Short), the first affirmative-action male practitioner, who's really not very good at spellcasting. Both Anabel and Murray have bigger problems—evil fairy godmother Claudia (Turner) is after all the fairy godmothers' magic wands so she can rule the world's wishes. Short's brand of comic energy plays right into the kid audience, and Wilson lights up every scene she's in. **95m/C VHS, DVD.** Mara Wilson, Martin Short, Kathleen Turner, Robert Pastorelli, Amanda Plummer, Teri Garr, Francis Capra, Jonathan Hadary, Alan Campbell, Ruby Dee; **D:**

Michael Ritchie; **W:** Jeff Rothberg; **C:** Ralf Bode; **M:** Bruce Broughton.

Simply Irresistible 1999 (PG-13) Romantic comedy in which failing restaurant owner/chef Amanda Shelton (Gellar) falls for exec Tom Bartlett (Flanery). Thanks to the intervention of fairy-godmother O'Reilly (Durang) Amanda suddenly possesses a unique culinary ability—every emotion she's feeling goes into her food and winds up affecting her customers. Tries too hard (this kind of whimsical comedy should be lighter than a souffle) and the leads, appealing as they may be, don't generate any heat when together. The film also spends like an Americanized version of "Like Water for Chocolate," even if no one's admitting to the notion. **95m/C VHS, DVD.** Sarah Michelle Gellar, Sean Patrick Flanery, Patricia Clarkson, Dylan Baker, Betty Buckley; **D:** Mark Tarlov; **W:** Judith Roberts; **C:** Robert M. Stevens; **M:** Gil Goldstein.

The Simpsons Movie 2007 (PG-13) Best. Movie. Ever. Okay, maybe not, but it's pretty good; Homer's infatuation with a condemned pig sparks a near apocalyptic fate for Springfield and a cross-country trek to Alaska for the Simpson clan in their long-awaited big screen debut. All of the main characters, and many of the minor ones, get their shot in the spotlight, and the show's trademark sly humor, social commentary, and digs at popular culture are, thankfully, intact. Marge provides the voice of reason, and some surprising pathos along the way. **87m/C DVD, Blu-ray Disc. US D:** David Silverman; **W:** James L. Brooks, David Mirkin, Matt Groening, Mike Reiss, Al Jean, Ian Maxton-Graham, George Meyer, Mike Scully, Matt Selman, John Swartzwelder, Jon Vitti; **M:** Hans Zimmer; **V:** Dan Castellaneta, Julie Kavner, Nancy Cartwright, Yeardley Smith, Harry Shearer, Hank Azaria, Pamela Hayden, Tom Hanks.

Sin 2002 (R) Retired cop Eddie Burns (Rhames) searches for his missing sister Kassie (Washington) and discovers she's part of a twisted plot by crime boss Charlie Strom (Oldman) to get revenge on Burns for their shared past. Too many plot holes and unbelievable situations make it's revenge thriller less than scintillating despite the poor work of the leads. (Okay, so Oldman chews the scenery but you expect that.) **107m/C VHS.** Ving Rhames, Gary Oldman, Kerry Washington, Brian Cox, Alicia Coppola, William Sage, Gregg Henry, Arie Verveen, Chris Spencer; **D:** Michael Stevens; **W:** Tim Willocks; **C:** Zoran Popovic; **M:** Michael Giacchino.

Sin and Redemption 1994 (PG-13) Billie (Gibb) is raped by an unknown assailant and gives birth to a daughter from the attack. Several years later, she marries Jim (Grieco). But her daughter has an unusual medical condition that leads to Billie to believe her new husband was also her rapist. **94m/C VHS.** Cynthia Gibb, Richard Grieco, Concetta Tomei, Cheryl Pollak, Chapelle Jaffe, Ralph Waite; **D:** Neema Barnette. **TV**

Sin City 2005 (R) Rodriguez teamed with comic legend Frank Miller to co-direct this overly literal adaptation of Miller's black-and-white crime noir series. Set in the hellishly corrupt Basin City, the plot bounces between a menagerie of unsavory anti-heroes, including Marv (Rourke), a lovable thug bent on avenging a hooker's murder, Dwight (Owen), a moralistic man-with-a-past; and Hartigan (Willis), a cop who spent eight years in prison to protect a virtuous stripper (Alba). More o' a slideshow than a film, you'll marvel at how closely it resembles the comic, though the directors' fundamentalist zeal for their source material tests the audience's patience throughout. Acting and pacing are ignored while Rodriguez uses cheap-looking CGI to slavishly reproduce exact panels of Miller's art. Fanboy fervor gone too far. **124m/B DVD, UMD. US/**Jessica Alba, Devon Aoki, Alexis Bledel, Rosario Dawson, Benicio Del Toro, Michael Clarke Duncan, Carla Gugino, Josh Hartnett, Rutger Hauer, Jaime (James) King, Michael Madsen, Brittany Murphy, Clive Owen, Mickey Rourke, Nick Stahl, Bruce Willis, Elijah Wood, Marley Shelton, Powers Boothe, Nicky Katt, Makenzie Vega, Arie Verveen, Tommy Nix, Jude Ciccolella, Rick Gomez, Lisa Marie Newmyer, Nick Offerman; **D:** Robert Rodriguez, Frank Miller; **C:** Robert Rodriguez; **M:** Robert Rodriguez, Graeme Revell, John Debney.

Sin of Adam & Eve 1967 (R) El Pecado de Adán y Eva The story of Adam and Eve in the Garden of Eden and their fall from grace. Voice-over narrator is the only sound in this strange dialogue-less story of the Adam and Eve, how they got kicked out of the Garden of Eden, and how they lose and then find each other. The film also depicts it to say the least. **72m/C VHS.** Candy Wilson, Jorge (George) Rivero; **D:** Michael Zachary.

The Sin of Harold Diddlebock 1947 Mad Wednesday A man gets fired from his job, stumbles around drunk, and wins a fortune gambling. He then buys a circus and uses it to frighten investors into backing him. Inventive comedy, but missing the spark and timing of "The Freshman" (1925), of which it is a sequel. The final feature film for Lloyd (who did all his own stunts), made at the urging of director Sturges. **89m/B VHS, DVD.** Harold Lloyd, Margaret Hamilton, Frances Ramsden, Edgar Kennedy, Lionel Stander, Rudy Vallee, Franklin Pangborn; **D:** Preston Sturges.

The Sin of Madelon Claudet 1931 The Lullaby Hayes plays common thief who works her way into upper crust of Parisian society only to tumble back into the street, all in the name of making a better life for her illegitimate son. Very sudsy stuff, with an outstanding performance by Hayes. **74m/B VHS.** Helen Hayes, Lewis Stone, Neil Hamilton, Robert Young, Cliff Edwards, Jean Hersholt, Marie Prevost, Karen Morley, Charles Winninger, Alan Hale, Franklin Pangborn; **D:** Edgar Selwyn. Oscars '32: Actress (Hayes).

Sin Takes a Holiday 1930 A woman marries her boss to save him from his girl friend. On a trip to Paris, she is wooed by a refined European gentleman, but finds that she's really does love her husband. By today's standards, it doesn't sound like much, but in the '30s, it was pretty sophisticated stuff. **81m/B VHS.** Constance Bennett, Kenneth MacKenna, Basil Rathbone, Rita La Roy, Zasu Pitts, Fred Walton, Richard Carlé, Helen Johnson; **D:** Paul Stein.

Sin You Sinners 1963 Aging stripper gets ahold of an amulet that allows her to look youthful and manipulate the lives of others. When she loses the amulet, however, bad things happen. Twisted camp. **73m/B V-S, DVD.** June Colbourne, Dian Lloyd, Derek Murcott, Beverly Nazarow, Charles Clements; **D:** Anthony Farrar.

Sinai Commandos: The Story of the Six Day War. Ha'Mataa'ah Tiran 1968 The story of a group of commandos in the Israeli Six-Day War in 1967 and triumphant comeback with his first Arab radar installations. Includes actual combat footage. **99m/C VHS.** Robert Fuller; **D:** Raphael Nussbaum.

Sinbad 1971 A sardonic portrait of an aging hedonist as he tries to hold onto the pleasures of drink, sex and gluttony. In Magyar (Hungarian), with English subtitles. **98m/C VHS.** *HU* Zoltan Latinovits, Eva Ruttkai, Eva Leelossy, Marjit Dajkai; **D:** Zoltan Huszarik; **W:** Zoltan Huszarik; **C:** Sándor Sara; **M:** Zoltan Jeney.

Sinbad and the Eye of the Tiger 1977 (G) The swashbuckling adventures of Sinbad the Sailor as he encounters the creations of Ray Harryhausen's special effects magic. Don't see this one for the plot, which almost doesn't exist. Otherwise, mildly fun. **113m/C VHS, DVD.** Patrick Wayne, Jane Seymour, Taryn Power, Margaret Whiting; **D:** Sam Wanamaker; **M:** Roy Budd.

Sinbad: Legend of the Seven Seas 2003 (PG) Loose retelling of the "Arabian Nights" tale (so loose that it incorporates Greek and Roman legends and gods) from DreamWorks studio that's a combo of computer generated and hand-drawn animation. Sinbad the sailor/thief (voiced by Pitt) gets in trouble when Eris (Pfeiffer), the goddess of chaos, steals the Book of Peace and frames Sinbad for the crime. His best friend, Proteus (Fiennes) believes in Sinbad's innocence and stakes his life on Sinbad's return with the book. Proteus's fiancee Marina (Zeta-Jones) stows away to make sure Sinbad keeps his promises and to provide him with a foil. Jumbled story and inconsistent animation lead to ho-hum outing that the kids may enjoy, if they've tired of "Finding Nemo" after the umpteenth viewing. **86m/C VHS, DVD. US D:** Tim Johnson, Patrick Gilmore; **W:** John Logan; **M:** Harry Gregson-Williams; **V:** Brad Pitt, Catherine Zeta-Jones, Michelle Pfeiffer, Joseph Fiennes, Dennis Haysbert, Timothy West, Adriano Giannini.

Sinbad of the Seven Seas 1989 Italian muscle epic based on the ancient legends. Ferrigno isn't green, but he's still a hulk, and he still can't act. It's poorly dubbed, which makes little distracting...less. **90m/C VHS, DVD. IT** Lou Ferrigno, John Steiner, Leo Gullotta, Teagan Clive; **D:** Enzo G. Castellari.

Sinbad, the Sailor 1947 Fairbanks fits well in his luminent father's swashbuckling shoes, as he searches for the treasure of Alexander the Great. Self-mocking but hamhanded, and confusing if you seek the hidden plot. Still, it's all in fun, and it is fun. **117m/C VHS.** Douglas Fairbanks Jr., Maureen O'Hara, Anthony Quinn, Walter Slezak, George Tobias, Jane Greer, Mike Mazurki, Sheldon Leonard; **D:** Richard Wallace; **C:** George Barnes.

Since Otar Left... 2003 Depuis Qu'Otar est Parti Bittersweet, female-centric drama set in a rundown flat in Tbilisi, in the former Soviet Republic of Georgia. Domineering matriarch Eka (90-year-old Gorintin) dotes on her son who works illegally in Paris. Meanwhile, her middle-aged daughter Marina (Khomassouridze) resents her mother's obvious preference and her own daughter, Ada (Droukarova), tries to keep the peace between the two women. When Marina and Ada learn that Otar has been killed, they conspire to keep the truth from Eka through an elaborate ruse with unexpected consequences. Russian, Georgian and French with subtitles. **102m/C VHS, DVD. FR** Esther Gorintin, Nino Khomassouridze, Dinara Droukarova, Temour Kalandadze, Roussoudan Bolkvadze, Sacha Sarichvili, Douta Skhirtladze; **D:** Julie Bertucelli; **W:** Julie Bertucelli, Roger Bohbot, Bernard Renucci; **C:** Christophe Pollock.

Since You Went Away 1944 An American family copes with the tragedy, heartache and shortages of wartime in classic megatribute to the home front. Be warned: very long and though your hankies, Colbert is superb, as is the photography. John Derek unobtrusively made his film debut, as an extra. **172m/B VHS, DVD.** Claudette Colbert, Jennifer Jones, Shirley Temple, Joseph Cotten, Agnes Moorehead, Monty Woolley, Guy Madison, Lionel Barrymore, Robert Walker, Hattie McDaniel, Keenan Wynn, Craig Stevens, Albert Bassermann, Alla Nazimova, Lloyd Corrigan, Terry Moore, Florence Bates, Ruth Roman, Andrew V. McLaglen, Dorothy Dandridge, Rhonda Fleming, Addison Richards, Jackie Moran; **D:** John Cromwell; **W:** David O. Selznick; **C:** Stanley Cortez, Lee Garmes; **M:** Max Steiner; Oscars '44: Orig. Dramatic Score.

Since You've Been Gone 1998 The Clear View High School class of 1987 has their ten-year reunion and rivalries and romance are rediscovered. Grace (Boyle) has a penchant for nasty practical jokes she's never gotten over while Marie (Hatcher) is a self-important would-be exec who insults her one-time classmates and Rob (Schwimmer) is the still-loathed class president. **95m/C VHS, DVD.** David Schwimmer, Lara Flynn Boyle, Teri Hatcher, Joey Slotnick, Tom (Thomas E.) Hodges, Philip Rayburn Smith, Haidi Stillman, Jon Stewart, Lauren Graham, Molly Ringwald; **D:** David Schwimmer.

Sincerely Charlotte 1986 Signe Charlotte Huppert directs her sister in this film about a beautiful singer framed for her boyfriend's murder. She enlists an old lover to help her flee across the countryside. Love story/thriller is pleasingly odd and absorbing. In French with English subtitles. **92m/C VHS. FR** Isabelle Huppert, Niels Arestrup, Christine Pascal; **D:** Caroline Huppert; **C:** Bruno de Keyzer.

Sincerely Yours 1955 Liberace race wisely stayed away from acting after inauspiciously debuting in this horrible, maudlin remake of "The Man Who Played God." He plays a pianist who loses his hearing and decides to become a philanthropist to help those less fortunate than himself. Laughably cheesy. Thirty-one musical numbers, including Liberace's inimitable arrangement of "Chopsticks." **116m/C VHS.** Liberace, Joanne Dru, Dorothy Malone, William Demarest; **D:** Gordon Douglas; **W:** Irving Wallace.

Sinful Intrigue 1995 (R) Hardyman is main suspect in a series of attacks on women living in a wealthy neighborhood. **88m/C VHS, DVD.** Bobby Johnston, Beckie Mullen, Mark Zuericke, Griffin (Griffen) Drew; **D:** Edward Holzman; **M:** John Nelson; **C:** Harris Done; **M:** Patrick John Scott.

A Sinful Life 1989 (R) A strained, offbeat, B-grade comedy about an odd, infantile mother fighting to keep her unusual child from being taken away. Definitely not a must-see; can be irritating and obnoxious, depending on viewer and mood. Morris is at her oddball comedic best as the mother and former show dancer. Adult Tefkin plays her little girl. Based on the play "Just Like the Pom Pom Girls." **112m/C VHS,** Anita Morris, Rick Overton, Dennis Christopher, Blair Tefkin, Mark Rolston, Cynthia Szigeti; **D:** William Schreiner.

Sing 1989 (PG-13) The students in the real-life Brooklyn public school "Sing" program endure the trials of adolescence while putting together a musical revue. Hurtles over the edge into cheesiness from the start with way too much (cheesy) music. From the creator of "Fame" and "Footloose." **111m/C VHS.** Lorraine Bracco, Peter Dobson, Jessica Steen, Louise Lasser, George DiCenzo, Patti LaBelle; **D:** Richard Baskin; **M:** Jay Gruska.

Sing and Like It 1934 Goofy farce involving a tone-deaf songbird and a love-struck mobster boss. Annie Sirodograss (Pitts) has a voice that could make dogs howl, but moony-eyed gangster Fenny (Pendleton) hears it differently. He's going to make her a star, even threatening a top music critic at gunpoint to give her a glowing review. **72m/B VHS.** Zasu Pitts, Pert Kelton, Edward Everett Horton, Nat Pendleton, Ned Sparks; **D:** William A. Seiter; **W:** Marion Dix, Laird Doyle.

Sing, Cowboy, Sing 1937 Decent adventure story about a wagon train heading west that runs into a band of outlaws doing outlaw stuff and must somehow get through. **60m/B VHS, DVD.** Tex Ritter, Louise Stanley, Al "Fuzzy" St. John, Charles "Blackie" King, Karl Hackett, Horace Murphy; **D:** Robert North Bradbury; **W:** Robert Emmet Tansey; **C:** Gus Peterson.

Sing Me a Love Song 🦴🦴 1937 Jerry Haines (Melton) takes a job working incognito at his late father's department store to see how things are going in run. Music-counter clerk Jean (Ellis) falls for Jerry, especially when he helps her out by crooning the hit parade to her customers. But Jerry keeps getting into trouble (must be all that singing) and also discovers some of the store's executives are up to no good. 75m/B VHS. Patricia Ellis, Hugh Herbert, Zasu Pitts, Allen Jenkins, Nat Pendleton, Walter Catlett, James Melton; *D:* Ray Enright; *W:* Sid Herzig, Jerry Wald; *C:* Arthur L. Todd.

Sing Sing Nights 🦴½ *Reprieved* 1935 A world-famous journalist is killed with three bullets. Three men have confessed, but only one could have actually done it. A professor sets out to solve the case. 60m/B VHS. Conway Tearle, Mary Doran, Hardie Albright, Patricia "Boots" Mallory, Ferdinand Gottschalk, Berton Churchill, Jameson Thomas; *D:* Lewis D. Collins.

Sing Your Worries Away 🦴🦴 1942 Songwriter Ebsen inherits $3 million and finds the money causes him nothing but trouble. Band of crooks cause the requisite wacky complications. Fun, harmless musical comedy. ♪It Just Happened to Happen; Sally, My Dear Sally; Sing Your Worries Away; Cindy Lou McWilliams; How Do You Fall in Love. 71m/B VHS. Buddy Ebsen, Bert Lahr, June Havoc, Patsy Kelly, Margaret Dumont; *D:* Edward Sutherland.

Singapore 🦴🦴½ 1947 Rather boring romantic drama finds pearl smuggler Matt Gordon (MacMurray) returning to Singapore to resume his illegal trade at the end of WWII. He spots Linda (Gardner), the love of his life, but discovers she's suffering from amnesia and has married another man. Gangsters want Matt's hidden supply of pearls and kidnap Linda to get his cooperation. Remade with equal dullness in 1956 as "Istanbul." 80m/B VHS. Fred MacMurray, Ava Gardner, Roland Culver, Richard Haydn, Thomas Gomez, Spring Byington, Porter Hall; *D:* John Brahm; *W:* Seton I. Miller, Robert Thoeren; *C:* Maury Gertsman; *M:* Daniele Amfitheatrof.

Singin' in the Rain 🦴🦴🦴🦴 1952 One of the all-time great movie musicals—an affectionate spoof of the turmoil that afflicted the motion picture industry in the late 1920s during the changeover from silent films to sound. Don Lockwood (Kelly) and Lina Lamont (Hagen) are a popular romantic silent screen team when sound comes along. To continue, temperamental Lina must have her terrible voice dubbed by aspiring actress Kathy Selden (Reynolds), whom Don falls for. O'Connor's acrobatic marvel as Don's best pal, Cosmo Brown, and of course there's Kelly's classic, much-copied title dance. Later a Broadway musical. ♪All I Do is Dream of You; Should I?; Singin' in the Rain; Wedding of the Painted Doll; Broadway Melody; Would You; I've Got a Feelin' You're Foolin'; You Are My Lucky Star; Broadway Rhythm. 103m/C VHS, DVD. Gene Kelly, Donald O'Connor, Jean Hagen, Debbie Reynolds, Rita Moreno, King Donovan, Millard Mitchell, Cyd Charisse, Douglas Fowley, Madge Blake, Joi Lansing; *D:* Gene Kelly, Stanley Donen; *W:* Adolph Green, Betty Comden; *C:* Harold Rosson; *M:* Nacio Herb Brown, Lennie Hayton. AFI '98: Top 100; Golden Globes '53: Actor—Mus./Comedy (O'Connor), Natl. Film Reg. '89.

The Singing Blacksmith 🦴🦴½ 1938 A relic of American Yiddish cinema, adapting popular 1909 play by David Pinski. A married blacksmith is wooed by another woman and falls victim to alcoholism. Overlong, but Oysher and his rich baritone voice still shine. 95m/B VHS. *PL* Miriam Riselle, Florence Weiss, Moishe Oysher; *D:* Edgar G. Ulmer.

Singing Buckaroo 🦴🦴 1937 Dastardly bandits try to pilfer money from pretty blonde damsel and have to battle with yodelin' cowboy. B-level western good guy Scott belts out a few numbers and saves the day. Innocuously pleasant. 58m/B VHS. Fred Scott, Victoria Vinton, Cliff Nazarro; *D:* Tom Gibson.

The Singing Cowgirl 🦴 1939 Band of outlaws murder a ranch owner to get to a gold mine. Heroine Page rides in to save the day but gets shot when trying western stereotypes. 60m/B VHS, DVD. Dorothy Page, Dave O'Brien, Vince Barnett, Stanley Price; *D:* Samuel Diege; *W:* Arthur Hoerl.

The Singing Detective 🦴🦴🦴 1986 A musical/mystery/fantasy British miniseries, based on the work by Dennis Potter. Pulp fiction writer Phillip Marlowe (Gambon) is confined to his hospital bed, unable to move due to extreme psoriasis. In his lucid moments he tries to figure out his condition, but in his elaborate daydreams he's a detective (and big band singer) who's working to solve a series of murders. Six episodes: "Skin," "Heat," "Lovely Days," "Clues," "Pitter Patter," and "Who Done It." 420m/C VHS, DVD. Michael Gambon, Patrick Malahide, Janet Suzman, Joanne Whalley; *D:* Jon Amiel. TV

The Singing Detective 🦴🦴½ 2003 (R) Dan Dark (Downey) is a pulp crime novelist who suffers from a painful debilitating disease that leaves him confined to a hospital bed. As Dark drifts in and out of reality, his imagination fuses episodes from his novels with memories of his childhood. In his fantasies, Dark imagines himself as a detective of a '50s film noir. Real personas in his life begin to play characters in his fantasy and his delusions begin to bleed into his real life. Adding to the surreality is the slew of '50s pop songs that the characters sing at the slightest provocation. Visually stunning, and a bit convoluted. Downey delivers a solid performance, as do the supporting cast, including an almost unrecognizable Mel Gibson. Based on the BBC mini-series of the same name. 109m/C VHS, DVD. *US* Robert Downey Jr., Robin Wright Penn, Mel Gibson, Jeremy Northam, Katie Holmes, Adrien Brody, Jon Polito, Carla Gugino, Saul Rubinek, Alfre Woodard; *D:* Keith Gordon; *W:* Dennis Potter; *C:* Tom Richmond.

The Singing Nun 🦴🦴 1966 The true story of a Belgian nun who takes a liking to a motherless little boy. She writes a song for him, and a kind-hearted priest talks to a record producer to help getting the song to go somewhere. The song soon becomes an international hit, and the nun ends up on the "Ed Sullivan Show." Sentimental and sugary sweet, but a big boxoffice hit. 98m/C VHS. Debbie Reynolds, Ricardo Montalban, Greer Garson, Agnes Moorehead, Chad Everett, Katharine Ross, Juanita Moore, Ricky Cordell, Michael Pate, Tom Drake; *D:* Henry Koster; *C:* Milton Krasner.

Singing the Blues in Red 🦴🦴🦴 1987 Dark, pessimistic character study of a protest singer/songwriter who leaves his native East Germany to escape repression and finds his royalties divided. A moving personal story, as well as insightful, subtle social commentary, in English and German with subtitles. 110m/C VHS. *GE* Gerulf Pannach, Fabienne Babe, Cristine Rose, Trevor Griffiths; *D:* Ken Loach; *W:* Trevor Griffiths; *C:* Chris Menges.

Single Bars, Single Women 🦴🦴½ 1984 Utterly formulaic made for TV comedy-drama based on Dolly Parton's song is not entirely without merit. Lonely people gather in a local pickup joint and share their miseries and hopes. 96m/C VHS. Shelley Hack, Christine Lahti, Tony Danza, Mare Winningham, Keith Gordon, Paul Michael Glaser; *D:* Harry Winer; *M:* Basil Poledouris. TV

A Single Girl 🦴🦴½ *La Fille Seule* 1996 Follows, in real time, a young woman as she tells her boyfriend that she's pregnant, (Ledoyen) through her job handling room service at a Paris hotel, then again with her boyfriend after work. French with subtitles. Part sexual hotel fantasy, part observation of an ordinary couple going about daily life. 90m/C VHS, DVD. *FR* Virginie Ledoyen, Benoit Magimel, Vera Briole, Dominique Valadie; *D:* Benoit Jacquot; *W:* Benoit Jacquot, Jerome Beaujour; *C:* Caroline Champetier; *M:* Kvarteto Mesta Prahi.

Single Room Furnished 🦴🦴🦴 1968 The fall of a buxom blonde from uncorrupted innocence through pregnancies to desperate prostitution. Fails to demonstrate any range of talent in Mansfield, who died before it was completed. Exploitative and pathetic. 93m/C VHS, DVD. Jayne Mansfield, Dorothy Keller; *D:* Matt Cimber, Matteo Ottaviano.

The Single Standard 🦴🦴 1929 San Francisco deb Garbo flings with artsy Asther and finds out the Hayes Code is just around the corner. 93m/B VHS. Greta Garbo, Nils Asther, Johnny Mack Brown, Dorothy Sebastian, Lane Chandler, Zeffie Tilbury; *D:* John S. Robertson.

Single White Female 🦴🦴½ 1992 (R) Psycho thriller casts Fonda as chic Manhattan computer consultant Allison-Jones, who advertises for a roommate after a falling out with her boyfriend. Leigh is the frumpy, shy, bookstore clerk Hedra who answers the ad and moves into Allie's great Upper West Side apartment. They hit it off, that is until Allie notices Hedra's beginning to look and sound very familiar. Hmm... Derivative, though bonus points for creative murder implements and interesting performances throughout, including Friedman as Allie's gay upstairs neighbor. Based on the novel "SWF Seeks Same" by John Lutz. 107m/C VHS, DVD. Jessica Lundy, Bridget Fonda, Jennifer Jason Leigh, Steven Weber, Peter Friedman, Stephen Tobolowsky, Frances Bay, Renee Estevez, Kenneth Tobey; *D:* Barbet Schroeder; *W:* Don Roos; *C:* Luciano Tovoli; *M:* Howard Shore. MTV Movie Awards '93: Villain (Leigh). VIDEO

Single White Female 2: The Psycho woof! 2005 (R) So in the first movie she wasn't a psycho? Down-on-her-luck young woman moves into an apartment and soon discovers her new roomie has become fixated on her, later turning killer. Inept rehash of the original with all the thrills (and acting ability) removed. And still it took three writers to come up with this dreck. 93m/C DVD. Kristen Miller, Allison Lange, Brooke Burns, Todd Babcock, Francois Groday, Rif Hutton; *D:* Keith Samples; *W:* Andy Hurst, Ross Helford, Glenn Hobart; *C:* Thomas M. Harting; *M:* Steven Stern. VIDEO

Singles 🦴🦴🦴 1992 (PG-13) Seattle's music scene is the background for this lighthearted look at single 20-somethings in the '90s. Hits dead on thanks to Crowe's tight script and a talented cast, and speaks straight to its intended audience—the "Generation X" crowd. Real life band Pearl Jam plays alternative band Citizen Dick and sets the tone for a great soundtrack featuring the hot Seattle sounds of Alice in Chains, Soundgarden, and Mudhoney. The video contains six extra minutes of footage after the credits that was thankfully edited out of the final cut. Look for Horton, Stoltz (as a mime), Skerritt, and Burton in cameos. 100m/C VHS, DVD. Matt Dillon, Bridget Fonda, Campbell Scott, Kyra Sedgwick, Sheila Kelley, Jim True-Frost, Bill Pullman, James LeGros, Ally Walker, Devon Raymond, Camilo Gallardo, Jeremy Piven; *Cameos:* Peter Horton, Eric Stoltz, Tim Burton, Tom Skerritt; *D:* Cameron Crowe; *W:* Cameron Crowe; *C:* Ueli Steiger; *M:* Paul Westerberg.

Singleton's Pluck 🦴🦴🦴 *Laughterhouse* 1984 Touching British comedy about a determined farmer who must walk his 500 geese 100 miles to market because of a strike. He becomes a celebrity when the TV stations start covering his odyssey. 89m/C VHS. *GB* Ian Holm, Penelope Wilton, Bill Owen, Richard Hope; *D:* Richard Eyre.

The Sinister Invasion 🦴 *Alien Terror; The Incredible Invasion; Invasion Siniestra* 1968 A turn-of-the-century scientist (Karloff) discovers a death ray. Aliens, who would like a closer peek at what makes it work, use a sex-fiend's body to do so. One of Karloff's last four films, made simultaneously in Mexico. The great horror master's final offering. Excruciating. 95m/C VHS. *MX* Boris Karloff, Enrique Guzman, Jack Hill, Yerye Beirut, Maura Monti, Tere Valdez; *D:* Juan Ibanez, Jack Hill; *W:* Luis Enrique Vergara, Karl Schanzer; *C:* Raul Dominguez, Austin McKinney.

The Sinister Urge woof! *The Young and the Immortal; Hellbom* 1960 Vice cops Duncan and Moore search for the murderer of three women. Seems the disturbed slayer is unbalanced because he's been looking at pictures of naked ladies. Was this meant to be taken seriously at the time? The last film by camp director Wood, maker of the infamous "Plan 9 from Outer Space." A must see for Wood fans. 82m/B VHS. Kenne Duncan, Duke Moore, Jean Fontaine, Carl Anthony, Harvey B. Dunn, Dino Fantini, Reed Howes, Conrad Brooks; *D:* Edward D. Wood Jr.; *W:* Edward D. Wood Jr.; *C:* William C. Thompson.

Sink or Swim 🦴🦴½ *Hacks* 1997 (R) TV writer/producer Brian (a suitably hangdog Rea) is suffering from creative burnout and depression. His agent, Danny (Arnold), has just landed Brian a new job writing a TV series that he's dreading. His weekly poker buddies (and fellow writers) offer possible scenarios, amidst their backstabbing, but Brian may have reignited his creative spark after witnessing a romantic encounter between two silhouetted figures in a hotel window. He thinks the woman may be Georgia (Douglas), whom he meets in a bar, and Brian wants her story—at practically any price. 93m/C VHS, DVD. Stephen Rea, Illeana Douglas, Tom Arnold, John Ritter, Dave Foley, Richard Kind, Ryan O'Neal, Ricky Jay, Jason Priestley, Olivia D'Abo, Bob Odenkirk; *D:* Gary Rosen; *W:* Gary Rosen; *C:* Ralf Bode; *M:* Anthony Marinelli.

Sink the Bismarck 🦴🦴🦴 1960 British navy sets out to locate and sink infamous German battleship during WWII. Good special effects with battle sequences in this drama based on real incidents. One of the better of the plethora of WWII movies, with stirring naval battles and stylish documentary-style direction. 97m/B VHS, DVD. *GB* Kenneth More, Dana Wynter, Karel Stepanek, Carl Mohner, Laurence Naismith, Geoffrey Keen, Michael Hordern, Maurice Denham, Esmond Knight, Michael Goodliffe, Jack Watling, Jack (Gwyllam) Gwillim, Mark Dignam, Ernest Clark, John Horsley, Sydney Tafler, John Stuart, Walter Hudd, Sean Barrett, Peter Burton, Edward R. Morrow; *D:* Lewis Gilbert; *W:* Edmund H. North; *C:* Christopher Challis; *M:* Clifton Parker.

Sinners in Paradise 🦴🦴 1938 An assortment of trouble-plagued characters alternately hide and face up to their mysterious pasts when their plane crashes on a deserted island. Interesting "crucible" premise runs out of steam, but plucky, resourceful cast and competent direction keep it going. 64m/B VHS, DVD. Madge Evans, John Boles, Bruce Cabot, Marion Martin, Gene Lockhart, Dwight Frye, Charlotte Wynters, Nana Bryant, Milburn Stone, Donald (Don "Red") Barry, Morgan Conway; *D:* James Whale.

Sinner's Blood woof! 1970 (R) Bikers terrorize and torture a small town. 81m/C VHS. Stephen Jacques, Crusty Beal, Nancy Sheldon, Parker Herriott, Julie Connors; *D:* Neil Douglas.

Sinners in the Sun 🦴½ 1932 Proverbial love dilemma finds Carole Lombard as a New York fashion model caught between two loves, one a rich philanderer and the other a poor garage mechanic who truly has her heart. Film was nothing spectacular but interesting to see Grant in his "diamond in the rough" days. 70m/B VHS. Carole Lombard, Cary Grant, Chester Morris, Adrienne Ames; *D:* Alexander Hall; *W:* Samuel Hoffenstein, Vincent Lawrence, Waldemar Young. VIDEO

Sins 1985 On her way up the ladder of success in the fashion industry, Helene has stepped on a few toes. Those rivals seem to make this film an exciting one and her ever-increasing acquisition of power and money make this film an exciting drama. 336m/C VHS. Joan Collins, Timothy Dalton, Catherine Mary Stewart, Gene Kelly, James Farentino; **D:** Douglas Hickox.

Sins of Desire 1992 Highly erotic thriller with Roberts going undercover as a nurse in a sex therapy clinic. It seems her sister was a former patient at the clinic and has since died a mysterious death. Linking up with private eye Cassavetes, Roberts sets out to investigate the character's mirror image. Might have been intriguing and stylish; instead, only disappointing and incompetent. 95m/C VHS. Tanya Roberts, Jay Richardson, Delia Sheppard, Nick Cassavetes, Jan-Michael Vincent; **D:** Jim Wynorski; **W:** Mark Thomas McGee, Peter Paul Liapis.

The Sins of Dorian Gray 1982 (PG) A modernized adaptation of "The Portrait of Dorian Grey" by Oscar Wilde, with Dorian as a beautiful woman who remains young for 30 years, while a video screen test ages, like the original character's mirror image. Might have been intriguing and stylish; instead, only disappointing and incompetent. 95m/C VHS. Belinda Bauer, Joseph Bottoms, Anthony Perkins; **D:** Tony Maylam. TV

Sins of Jezebel 1954 Biblical epic about Jezebel, who worships an evil god. She marries the king of Israel and brings the kingdom nothing but trouble. 74m/C VHS, DVD. Paulette Goddard, George Nader, John Hoyt, Eduard Franz, John Shelton, Margia Dean, Joe Besser, Ludwig Donath; **D:** Reginald LeBorg; **W:** Richard H. Landau; **C:** Gilbert Warrenton; **M:** Bert Shefter.

Sins of Rome 1954 Spartacus risks it all in a bold attempt to free his fellow slaves. Not nearly the equal of Kirk Douglas's "Spartacus," but much better than later Italian adventure-epics. 75m/B VHS, DVD. /T Ludmilla Tcherina, Massimo Girotti, Gianna Maria Canale, Yves Vincent; **D:** Riccardo Freda.

Sins of the Father 1997 (R) Thomas Frank Cherry (Sizemore) is a middle-aged Texan who comes to believe that his father, Bobby Frank Cherry (Jenkins), was one of four KKK members who bombed the Sixteenth Street Baptist Church in Birmingham, Alabama, in 1963. Four young black girls were killed in the explosion and the investigation dragged on and off for 33 years. When the investigation is revived once again, Tom decides to give testimony before a grand jury that casts doubt on his father's original alibi. Cherry was convicted of murder in 2002. 95m/C VHS, DVD. Tom Sizemore, Ving Rhames, Richard Jenkins, Colm Feore; **D:** Robert Dornhelm; **W:** John Pielmeier; **C:** Tom Sigel. CABLE

Sins of the Mind 2001 (R) Michelle (Crider), the 25-year-old daughter of Eve (Clayburgh) and William (Farrell) Widener, awakens from a coma after a car accident and turns out to have psychological damage. Previously a conservative, hard-working artist, she's now a hedonist, given to erratic impulses and sexual compulsions. Michelle's actions threaten her family but her father is concerned he can still get his little girl back. 92m/C VHS. Missy (Melissa) Crider, Mike Farrell, Jill Clayburgh, Louise Fletcher, Michael Mantell, Richard Pine, Cyia Batten, Greyson McCourt; **D:** James Frawley. CABLE

Sins of the Night 1993 (R) An ex-con insurance investigator is hired to find a sultry exotic dancer. Also available in an unrated version. 82m/C VHS. Miles O'Keeffe, Richard Roundtree, Matt Roe, Nick Cassavetes, Deborah Shelton; **D:** Gregory Dark; **W:** Russell Lavalle; **C:** Glenn Kershaw; **M:** Ashley Irwin.

Sinthia: The Devil's Doll 1970 A little girl is thought to be possessed by a demon after she has horrible dreams about killing her father. 75m/C VHS, DVD. Shula Roan, Diane Webber; **D:** Ray Dennis Steckler.

Sioux City 1994 (PG-13) Jesse Rainfeather Goldman (Phillips) is a Lakota Sioux adopted away from the reservation of his birth and raised in Beverly Hills by a Jewish family. Jesse's curious when his birth mother suddenly contacts him, but when he arrives at the Sioux City reservation, he discovers she's suddenly died under mysterious circumstances. So Jesse sticks around to find out what's going on and discovers his heritage along the way. Well-meaning but dull. 102m/C VHS, DVD. Lou Diamond Phillips, Salli Richardson, Melinda Dillon, Ralph Waite, Adam Roarke, Bill Allen, Gary Farmer; **D:** Lou Diamond Phillips; **W:** L. Virginia Browne; **M:** Christopher Lindsey.

Sioux City Sue 1946 Talent scouts looking to cast a western musical find Autry, then trick him into being the voice of a singing conkey in an animated production. But, the yodelin cowboy belts out a number or two, and the poobahs give him the lead. Singin' and fancy ridin' abound in Autry's first post-WWII role. 69m/B VHS, DVD. Gene Autry, Lynne Roberts, Sterling Holloway, Richard Lane, Ralph Sanford, Kenneth Lundy, Pierre Watkin; **D:** Frank McDonald; **W:** Olive Cooper; **C:** Reggie Lanning; **M:** R. Dale Butts.

Siren of the Tropics 1927 In love with a French businessman, West Indies native girl Papitou (Baker) sneaks back to Paris with him—despite his engagement to another woman—but finds her true calling in life as a dancer in music halls. Memorable only as the legendary Baker's film debut, showcasing her stunning dancing abilities. Silent with French soundtrack added. 86m/B DVD. Josephine Baker, Pierre Batchelf, Georges Melchior, Regina Dalthy, Regina Thomas; **D:** Mario Nalpas, Henri Etievant; **W:** Maurice Dekobra.

Sir Arthur Conan Doyle's The Lost World 1998 *The Lost World* (R) In the '30s, zoologist George Challenger (Bergin) recruits a team of scientists to help him find a mythic land where dinosaurs and other prehistoric creatures exist. Lots of cliches although the special effects aren't bad. 96m/C VHS. Patrick Bergin, David Nerman, Jayne Heitmeyer, Julian Casey; **D:** Bob Keen; **W:** Jean LaFleur; **C:** Barry Gravelle; **M:** Milan Kymlicka. VIDEO

Sirens 1994 (R) Staid minister Anthony Campion (Grant) takes Australian artist Norman Lindsay to task for submitting scandalous works to public exhibitions. Noted by one reviewer as "Enchanted April with nipples," comedy of manners is witty but lacks plot and looks remarkably like a centerfold layout. Ample displays of nudity as the models (including supermodel MacPherson in her acting debut) frolic in the buff. Grant is terrific as the seemingly enlightened but easily shocked minister, but Neill's Lindsay is thinly written and too often takes a back seat to the vamping models. Fictionalized account of a true incident from the 1930s. Lindsay's home and some of his artworks were used. Check out writer/director Duigan as a pompous village minister. 98m/C VHS, DVD. AU GB Hugh Grant, Tara Fitzgerald, Sam Neill, Elle Macpherson, Kate Fischer, Portia de Rossi, Pamela Rabe, Ben Mendelsohn, John Polson, Mark Gerber, Julia Stone, Ellie MacCarthy, Vincent Ball; **Cameos:** John Duigan; **D:** John Duigan; **W:** John Duigan; **C:** Geoff Burton; **M:** Rachel Portman.

Sirens 1999 (R) The sirens in this case are those attached to police cars. Sally Rawlings (Delany) gets a big promotion and decides to share the good news with her ex-hubby (Curtis Hall). They wind up parked under a bridge, steaming up the windows, when a cop car comes along. Trigger-happy cop (Carradine) winds up shooting the unarmed ex dead and the police try to cover up the bad shooting. Of course, Sally wants justice—no matter what it costs. 102m/C VHS. Dana Delany, Keith Carradine, Vondie Curtis-Hall, Brian Dennehy, Jus in Theroux; **D:** John Sacret Young; **C:** Eagle Egilsson; **M:** Brian Tyler. CABLE

Sirens 2002 Detective Jay Pearson (Nardini) is investigating a London serial rapist while fending off the unwelcome advances of his boss (Gleinster). But

The Sisters 🦴🦴🦴 1938 Lavish film of three sisters and their marital problems in turn of the century San Francisco. Davis gives a great performance as the oldest sister with the most trouble—notably in the form of unreliable sports reporter Flynn. Look for Susan Hayward in a bit role, as well as Bogart's wife, Mayo Methot. Based on the bestselling novel by Myron Brinig. **98m/B VHS.** *C:* Bette Davis, Errol Flynn, Anita Louise, Jane Bryan, Ian Hunter, Henry Travers, Beulah Bondi, Donald Crisp, Dick Foran, Patric Knowles; *D:* Anatole Litvak; *M:* Max Steiner.

Sisters 🦴🦴🦴 1973 (R) Siamese twins are separated surgically, but one doesn't survive the operation. The remaining sister is scarred physically and mentally with her personality split into bad and good. And then things really get crazy. DePalma's first ode to Hitchcock, with great music by Bernard Herrmann. Scary and suspenseful. **93m/C VHS, DVD.** Margot Kidder, Charles Durning, Barnard Hughes, Jennifer Salt, William Finley, Lisle Wilson, Mary Davenport, Dolph Sweet; *D:* Brian De Palma; *W:* Brian De Palma, Louisa Rose; *C:* Gregory Sandor; *M:* Bernard Herrmann.

Sisters 🦴🦴 1997 (R) Sisters Phyllis and Elizabeth are both lonely but have always been jealous and afraid of each other. A look at their lives from childhood to adulthood reveals their fantasies, fears, and failures. **89m/C VHS.** Claudia Christian, Valerie Breiman, Peter Berg, Jeff Conaway, Sydney Lassick; *Nar:* Charlie Sheen.

The Sisters 🦴🦴1/2 2005 (R) Alfieri adapted his play, which was inspired by Anton Chekhov's "The Three Sisters." In this contemporary update, set in a Manhattan college faculty lounge, sisters Olga (Masterson), Marsha (Bello), and Irene (Christensen) gather with their brother Andrew (Nivola) and various lovers and colleagues, most of whom are an insufferable talky bunch. Irene's birthday seems to be just the right time to bring up family secrets and play psychological roulette. Unlike Chekov, this is overwrought yet boring. **113m/C DVD.** *US* Maria Bello, Mary Stuart Masterson, Erika Christensen, Eric McCormack, Chris O'Donnell, Tony Goldwyn, Steven Culp, Alessandro Nivola, Elizabeth Banks, Rip Torn; *D:* Arthur Allan Seidelman; *W:* Richard Alfieri; *C:* Chuy Chavez; *M:* Thomas Morse.

Sisters of Death 🦴🦴 1976 (PG) Five members of a sorority gather together for a reunion in a remote California town. Little do they know, a psychopath is stalking them, one by one. Could it have something to do with the terrible secret they each keep? Good, cheap thrills and some Bicentennial fashions to boot. **87m/C VHS, DVD.** Arthur Franz, Claudia Jennings, Cheri Howell, Sherry Boucher, Paul Carr; *D:* Joseph Mazzuca.

Sisters of Satan 🦴🦴1/2 1975 (R) The nuns of the infamous convent St. Archangelo choose to survive by trading God for the devil. **91m/C VHS, DVD.** *MX* Claudio Brook, David Silva, Tina Romero, Susana Kamini; *D:* Juan Lopez Moctezuma.

Sisters of the Gion 🦴🦴 1936 *Gion No Shimai* Story follows two geisha sisters, illuminating the plight of women in Japan. Elder sister Umekichi is traditional and dependent on her patrons while her modern younger sister Omocha exploits her customers as much as possible. But no matter the difference in their attitudes, both remain trapped by circumstances. Adapted from the novel "Yama" by Alexander Ivanovich Kuprin. Japanese with subtitles. **66m/B VHS, DVD.** *JP* Isuzu Yamada, Yoko Umemura, Eitaro Shindo, Benkei Shiganoya; *D:* Kenji Mizoguchi; *W:* Kenji Mizoguchi, Yoshikata Yoda; *C:* Minoru Miki.

Sisters, Or the Balance of Happiness 🦴🦴 1979 *Schwestern Oder die Balance des Glucks* Orderly Maria (Lampe) runs the household for her resentful, dependent sister Anna (Gabriel). Opposites in temperment, the dysfunctional duo can neither live with or without each other. When Anna commits suicide, Maria tries to makeover young typist Miriam (Fruh) to take her sister's place. German with subtitles. **97m/C VHS, DVD.** *GE* Jutta Lampe, Gudrun Gabriel, Jessica Fruh; *D:* Margarethe von Trotta; *W:* Margarethe von Trotta; *M:* Franz Rath; *C:* Konstantin Wecker.

Sitcom 🦴🦴 1997 Family dysfunction taken to the extreme. There's a pet rat, a new maid whose African husband seduces the son of the family, a daughter who becomes a paraplegic dominatrix, orgies, incest, and dad, who kills everyone when they throw him a surprise birthday party. Or does he? Or does it matter, anyway? French with subtitles. **80m/C VHS, DVD.** *FR* Evelyne Dandry, Francois Marthouret, Marina de Van, Adrien de Van, Stephane Rideau, Lucia Sanchez, Jules-Emmanuel Eyoum Deido; *D:* Francois Ozon; *W:* Francois Ozon; *C:* Yorick Le Saux; *M:* Eric Neveux.

Sitting Bull 🦴🦴 1954 Thanks to Cody acting as an advisor, this take on Little Big Horn was more sympathetic to the plight of the Native Americans than the typical western. Sioux chief Sitting Bull (Naish) calls for patience while Crazy Horse (Cody) wants war against the white interlopers. Maj. Bob Parrish (Robertson) gets court-martialed for siding with the Indians against bloodthirsty Col. Custer (Kennedy). President Grant (Hamilton) wants Parrish to pow-wow with Sitting Bull but there's more trouble coming. **105m/B DVD.** Dale Robertson, J. Carrol Naish, Iron Eyes Cody, Mary Murphy, Douglas Kennedy, John Litel, Josh Hamilton, Joel Fluellen, William Hopper; *D:* Sidney Salkow; *W:* Sidney Salkow, Jack DeWitt; *C:* Charles Van Enger; *M:* Raoul Kraushaar.

Sitting Ducks 🦴🦴🦴 1980 (R) Mildmannered accountant and lecherous pal rip off and then attempt to outrun the mob—all while swapping songs and confessions. Emil and Norman make it up as they go along; their hilarious repartee is largely improvised. They pick up a gorgeous lady (Townsend) and go about their way. **88m/C VHS, DVD.** Michael Emil, Zack Norman, Patrice Townsend, Richard Romanus, Irene Forrest, Henry Jaglom; *D:* Henry Jaglom; *W:* Henry Jaglom.

Sitting Pretty 🦴🦴🦴 1948 Webb is a delight in his Oscar-nominated role as the prissy Lynn Belvedere, who takes a job as a babysitter to the three hellion sons of Harry (Young) and Tacey (O'Hara) in their typical suburban community. Mr. Belvedere has soon wrangled the family in line but there's more to the man than his superior skills. It seems he's doing research and writing on expose on life in the suburbs, which becomes a best-seller and a local scandal. Followed by "Mr. Belvedere Goes to College" and "Mr. Belvedere Rings the Bell." Based on the novel "Belvedere" by Gwen Davenport. **84m/B VHS.** Clifton Webb, Robert Young, Maureen O'Hara, Richard Haydn, Louise Albritton, Randy Stuart, Ed Begley Sr.; *D:* Walter Lang; *W:* F. Hugh Herbert; *C:* Norbert Brodine; *M:* Alfred Newman.

Six Days, Seven Nights 🦴🦴1/2 1998 (PG-13) Brash magazine editor Robin Monroe (Heche) is working on a tropical vacation with fiance Frank (Schwimmer) when a deadline crisis forces her to ask gruff cargo pilot Quinn Harris (Ford) for a lift to Tahiti. A plane crash strands the incompatible duo on a remote island and naturally they need each other to survive. This started out as a routine romantic comedy but the action quotient was upped as filming progressed, thanks to a storyline involving modern-day pirates that's a waste of time. Also a waste are scenes involving Frank with Quinn's bodacious babe, Angelica (Obradors). Why does the only other woman with a significant part have to be a coochie-coo Charo impersonator? Thankfully, Ford and Heche do have considerable sass between them. Filmed on location in Kauai. **101m/C VHS, DVD.** Harrison Ford, Anne Heche, David Schwimmer, Temuera Morrison, Jacqueline Obradors, Allison Janney, Danny Trejo; *D:* Ivan Reitman; *W:* Michael Browning; *C:* Michael Chapman; *M:* Randy Edelman.

Six Days, Six Nights 🦴🦴 *A la Folie* 1994 (R) Two French sisters—the older and competitive Elsa (Dalle) and creative and evasive Alice (Parillaud)—move to New York with Alice's boxer boyfriend (Aurignac). Sex and heartbreak ensues, as it usually does. French with subtitles. **96m/C DVD.** *FR* Patrick Aurignac, Anne Parillaud, Beatrice Dalle; *D:* Diane Kurys; *W:* Diane Kurys, Antoine Lacomblez.

Six Degrees of Separation 🦴🦴1/2 1993 (R) Some believe that any two people, anywhere in the world, are connected by links to only six other people, hence the six degrees of separation. For the upper crust New Yorker Kittredges, Ouisa (Channing) and Flan (Sutherland), this becomes an issue when they encounter a charming young man (Smith) who claims to be Sidney Poitier's son and a friend of their children. The story unfolds as they realize they've been hustled—and don't understand why. Guare adapted his hit play, but what worked well there is almost too talky here. Channing, reprising her stage role, is very good as the stuffy Ouisa, with Sutherland delivering another interesting performance. Incredibly, the play was based on a true story. **112m/C VHS, DVD.** Stockard Channing, Will Smith, Donald Sutherland, Mary Beth Hurt, Bruce Davison, Ian McKellen, Richard Masur, Anthony Michael Hall, Heather Graham, Eric Thal, Anthony Rapp, Oz (Osgood) Perkins II, Kitty Carlisle Hart, Catherine Kellner; *D:* Fred Schepisi; *W:* John Guare; *C:* Ian Baker; *M:* Jerry Goldsmith.

Six Gun Gospel 🦴🦴 1943 Hatton masquerades as a preacher to investigate some shady dealings. Laughs come when the women of the congregation prevail upon him to sing, and he croons a ballad about Jesse James! **59m/B VHS.** Johnny Mack Brown, Raymond Hatton, Inna Gest, Eddie Dew, Roy Barcroft, Kenneth MacDonald, Bud Osborne; *D:* Lambert Hillyer.

Six Gun Rhythm 🦴1/2 1939 Novelty western plot has football player traveling to Texas to avenge his father's murder. **59m/B VHS.** Tex Fletcher, Joan Barclay, Ralph Peters, Reed Howes, Ted Adams, Malcolm "Bud" McTaggart, Kit Guard; *D:* Sam Newfield; *W:* Fred Myton; *C:* Arthur Reed; *M:* Lew Porter, Johnny Lange.

633 Squadron 🦴🦴1/2 1964 A skilled R.A.F. pilot attempts to lead his squadron on a mission deep into the fjords of Norway in search of a Nazi fuel plant. Robertson tries hard, as always, but is really not British officer material. Well-made war flick, based on a true story. **102m/C VHS, DVD.** Cliff Robertson, George Chakiris, Maria Perschy, Harry Andrews; *D:* Walter Grauman; *W:* James Clavell.

Six in Paris 🦴🦴1/2 *Paris vu Par* 1968 Six short films by acclaimed French New Wave directors, each depicting a different Parisian neighborhood. "Saint-Germaindes-Pres" finds an American girl disillusioned by two French boys. "Gare du Nord" has a woman meeting a handsome stranger who announces he's going to kill himself. A shy dishwasher brings a prostitute to his room in the "Rue Saint-Denis." When a salesman is accosted by a derelict in the "Place de l'Etoile" he hits him with his umbrella until he thinks he's killed the man. "Montparnasse-Levallois" has a woman thinking she's mixed-up her meetings with her two lovers. "La Muette" finds a small boy buying earplugs to shut out the noise of his parents constant arguing. In French with English subtitles. **93m/C VHS.** *FR* Barbara Wilkin, Jean-Francois Chappey, Jean-Pierre Andreani, Nadine Ballot, Barbet Schroeder, Gilles Queant, Micheline Dax, Claude Melki, Jean-Michel Rouziere, Marcel Gallon, Joanna Shimkus, Philippe Hiquilly, Serge Davri, Stephane Audran, Gilles Chusseau, Dinah Saril, Claude Chabrol; *D:* Jean Douchet, Eric Rohmer, Jean Rouch, Jean-Luc Godard, Claude Chabrol; *W:* Jean Douchet, George Keller, Jean Rouch, Jean-Daniel Pollet, Eric Rohmer, Jean-Luc Godard, Claude Chabrol; *C:* Nestor Almendros.

Six of a Kind 🦴🦴 1934 When Flora (Boland) and J. Pinkham Whinney (Ruggles) decide to drive to California for a second honeymoon, they advertise for another couple to share expenses. Unfortunately, it's Burns and Allen and their exceptionally large Great Dane that answer the ad. There's numerous complications, including bank clerk Whinney's being suspected of embezzlement, prompting Sheriff "Honest John" Hoxley (Fields) to go after the supposed criminals. Veteran comedy performers make this one a delight. **63m/B VHS, DVD.** Charlie Ruggles, Mary Boland, Gracie Allen, George Burns, W.C. Fields, Alison Skipworth; *D:* Leo McCarey; *W:* Walter DeLeon, Harry Ruskin; *C:* Henry Sharp; *M:* Ralph Rainger.

Six Pack 🦴1/2 1982 (PG) The Gambler goes auto racing. Rogers, in his theatrical debut, stars as Brewster Baker, a former stock car driver. He returns to the racing circuit with the help of six larcenous orphans that strip cars. Kinda cute if you're in the mood for sugar-powered race car story. **108m/C VHS, DVD.** Kenny Rogers, Diane Lane, Erin Gray, Barry Corbin, Anthony Michael Hall; *D:* Daniel Petrie; *M:* Charles Fox.

Six Shootin' Sheriff 🦴🦴 1938 A cowboy framed for bank robbery is released and seeks to rid his town of all evil. And he gets the girl. **59m/B VHS.** Ken Maynard, Marjorie Reynolds, Walter Long; *D:* Harry Fraser.

Six-String Samurai 🦴🦴 1998 (PG-13) In 1957 the USSR bombs and assumes control of the U.S., and Las Vegas is the only safe haven of freedom. Forty years later, a rock musician/samurai is on an odyssey across the desert to replace the recently deceased Elvis as king of the neon city; challenging his quest is another guitar-slinger, Death (Gauger), and his cronies. Our hero Buddy (played by martial artist Falcon as a cross between Buddy Holly and Yojimbo) and his sidekick The Kid (McGuire) must face all the bad guys we've come to expect in a post-apocalyptic adventure. Filled with campy dialogue and well-staged Hong Kong-style action (directed by Falcon), basically all the makings of a good midnight movie, but it doesn't quite come together. **89m/C VHS, DVD.** Jeffrey Falcon, Justin McGuire, Stephane Gauger, John Sakisian; *D:* Lance Mungia; *W:* Lance Mungia, Jeffrey Falcon; *C:* Kristian Bernier; *M:* Brian Tyler.

Six Ways to Sunday 🦴🦴 1999 (R) Weird mob drama about a hitman and his Oedipal relationship with mom. Passive, repressed teenager, Harry Odum (Reedus), lives with his domineering mother, Kate (Harry), who controls his life. That is, until Harry assists his hoodlum buddy Arnie (Brody) with a job and manages to impress Arnie's boss, Mr. Varga (Adler). Since Harry turns out to have a latent talent for violence, he's soon elevated to hit man—although mom's still a problem. Based on the 1962 novel "Portrait of a Young Man Drowning" by Charles Perry. **97m/C VHS, DVD.** Norman Reedus, Deborah Harry, Adrien Brody, Jerry Adler, Peter Appel, Elina Lowensohn, Isaac Hayes, Anna Thomson, David Ross; *D:* Adam Bernstein; *W:* Adam Bernstein, Marc Gerald; *C:* John Inwood; *M:* Theodore Shapiro.

Six Weeks 🦴🦴 1982 (PG) A young girl dying of leukemia brings together her work-driven mother and an aspiring married politician. Manipulative hanky-wringer has good acting from both Moores but oddly little substance. **107m/C VHS.** Dudley Moore, Mary Tyler Moore, Katherine Healy; *D:* Tony Bill; *M:* Dudley Moore.

Six Wives of Henry VIII 🦴🦴 1971 Michell has been called the definitive Henry VIII, and this BBC Classic (shown as part of "Masterpiece Theatre" on PBS) was perhaps the most praised series on

British TV. Henry's wives were: Catherine of Aragon, Anne Boleyn, Jane Seymour, Anne of Cleves, Catherine Howard, and Catherine Parr. Each episode tells of their (sometimes tragic) fates as pawns in Henry's quest for an heir, and his changes from an eager young man to aged, bitter monarch. **540m/C VHS, DVD, GB** Keith Michell, Annette Crosbie, Dorothy Tutin, Anne Stallybrass, Elvi Hale, Angela Pleasence, Rosalie Crutchley; **D:** John Glenister, Naomi Capon. **TV**

Sixteen 🦴🦴 *Like a Crow on a June Bug* 1972 (R) A naive country lass is attracted to the glitter and hum of the outside world. Her determination and optimism help her triumph. **84m/C VHS, DVD,** Mercedes McCambridge, Parley Baer, Ford Rainey, Beverly (Hills) Powers, John Lozier, Simone Griffith, Maddie Norman; **D:** Lawrence (Larry) Dobkin.

16 Blocks 🦴🦴🦴 2006 (PG-13) Willis lets himself go to seed as alcoholic NYPD detective Jack Moseley, a burnout who's been corrupted by the job and is just waiting to collect his pension. He's assigned to transport motor-mouthed witness Eddie Bunker (Mos Def) to a grand jury hearing 16 blocks from the station. Easy—until someone starts shooting at them. Jack calls for backup only to discover that Eddie is testifying about some bad cops, including Jack's ex-partner Frank Nugent (a menacing Morse), who isn't about to let that happen. Donner directed via the "Lethal Weapon" series, so he knows how to keep things moving. **105m/C DVD, Blu-ray Disc, HD DVD, US** Bruce Willis, Mos Def, David Morse, Cylk Cozart, Casey Sander, David Zayas, Jenna Stern, Robert Rack; **D:** Richard Donner; **W:** Richard Wenk; **C:** Glen MacPherson; **M:** Klaus Badelt.

Sixteen Candles 🦴🦴🦴 1984 (PG) Over a decade after hitting the theatres, "Sixteen Candles" is still popular—reaching near cult status among generation X-ers. Hilarious comedy of errors features the pouty Ringwald as an awkward teen who's been dreaming of her 16th birthday. But the rush of her sister's wedding causes everyone to forget, turning her birthday into her worst nightmare. Hughes may not be critically acclaimed, but his movies are so popular they nearly take on a life of their own. Ringwald and Hall are especially charming as the angst-ridden teens, encountering one trauma after another. Great soundtrack includes the title song by The Stray Cats. **93m/C VHS, DVD,** Molly Ringwald, Justin Henry, Michael Schoeffling, Anthony Michael Hall, Paul Dooley, Carlin Glynn, Blanche Baker, Edward Andrews, Carole Cook, Max (Casey Adams) Showalter, Liane (Alexandra) Curtis, John Cusack, Joan Cusack, Brian Doyle-Murray, Jami Gertz, Cinnamon Idles, Zelda Rubinstein, Billie Bird; **D:** John Hughes; **W:** John Hughes; **C:** Bobby Byrne; **M:** Ira Newborn.

Sixteen Fathoms Deep 🦴🦴 1934 A sponge fisherman risks it all, including his love, when a mean businessman threatens his operation. Good underwater photography, but otherwise undistinguished. **57m/B VHS,** Lon Chaney Jr., Sally O'Neil, George Regas, Maurice Black, Russell Simpson; **D:** Armand Schaefer.

The 6th Day 🦴🦴½ 2000 (PG-13) Arnold's a family guy in the near-future who finds out a clone has taken over his life. Not only that, but the evil corporation behind the clone doesn't want the original around to muck up their nefarious plans. Typical (although somewhat toned-down) Ah-nuld type mayhem ensues. Schwarzenegger has fun with his image, and the supporting players get some fine moments, too. Thought-provoking questions about human cloning add an interesting dimension, raising this one slightly above the genre-pic/star-vehicle level. **124m/C VHS, DVD,** Arnold Schwarzenegger, Tony Goldwyn, Sarah Wynter, Michael Rooker, Robert Duvall, Michael Rapaport, Wendy Crewson, Rodney Rowland, Ken Pogue, Wanda Cannon, Christopher Lawford, Terry Crews, Colin Cunningham, Taylor Anne Reid, Jennifer Gareis, Don McManus, Steve Bacic; **D:** Roger Spottiswoode; **W:** Cormac Wibberley, Marianne S. Wibberley; **C:** Pierre Mignot. **M:** Trevor Rabin.

16 Years of Alcohol 🦴🦴 2003 (R) Abandoned as a child and raised by an abusive, alcoholic father, Frankie grows up a drunk who leads a brutal gang in Edinburgh. But when he falls in love he decides to straighten up. Richard Jobson loosely adapts his life story. **96m/C VHS, DVD, GB** Kevin McKidd, Ewen Bremner, Laura Fraser, Susan Lynch, Stuart Sinclair Blyth, Lisa May Cooper, Lewis Macleod; **D:** Richard Jobson; **W:** Richard Jobson. **VIDEO**

The Sixth Man 🦴½ 1997 (PG-13) College basketball star Antoine Tyler (Hardison) dies but returns as a ghost to help his brother (Wayans) lead their team to the NCAA finals. Basketball seems to be the sport of choice for Hollywood lately so you'd think they'd be able to get one of these movies right. Once again, they bow to the layup. The first half relies on the requisite flashback and tearjerker death scene, both of which are surprisingly effective. But then the focus turns to "hilarious" on-court hijinks and the all-time sports cliche champion: the second-half rally from an impossible deficit. Hardison and Wayans are the bright spots, displaying fine comic and dramatic chemistry. **107m/C VHS, DVD,** Kadeem Hardison, Marlon Wayans, David Paymer, Michael Michele, Kevin Dunn, Gary Jones, Vladimir Cuk, Chris Spencer, Kirk Baily, Saundra McClain, Lorenzo Orr, Travis Ford, Harold Sylvester; **D:** Randall Miller; **W:** Christopher Reed, Cynthia Carle; **C:** Michael Ozier; **M:** Marcus Miller.

The Sixth Sense 🦴🦴🦴 1999 (PG-13) Creepy psycho thriller about a traumatized young boy who can communicate with the dead (this is not the film's big surprise). Failed child shrink Malcolm Crowe (Willis in an excellent subdued performance) takes on the case of 9-year-old Cole (a touching Osment, carrying the picture on frail shoulders), who's divorced mom, Lynn (Collette), is worried about her terrified son's nightmares and episodes of acting out. Well, if you saw dead people at the time, you'd be scared too. When Crowe (who's dealing with traumas of his own) finally believes Cole, it leads to a breakthrough and an unexpected twist on what's happened before. **107m/C VHS, DVD,** Bruce Willis, Haley Joel Osment, Toni Collette, Olivia Williams, Donnie Wahlberg, Glenn Fitzgerald, Trevor Morgan, Mischa Barton, Bruce Norris; **D:** M. Night Shyamalan; **W:** M. Night Shyamalan; **C:** Tak Fujimoto; **M:** James Newton Howard. MTV Movie Awards '00: Breakthrough Perf. (Osment); Broadcast Film Critics '99: Breakthrough Perf. (Osment)

The '60s 🦴🦴½ 1999 (PG-13) A quick trip through the decade of peace, love, and Vietnam, told with all the usual cliches. Film uses the parallel stories of two families to hit the high points—the white, middleclass Herlihy family of Chicago and the black Taylor family of Mississippi. You've got hippies, Black Panthers, civil rights, the war, the anti-war movement, drugs, and rock n' roll. The soundtrack may be the best thing the miniseries has going for it. **171m/C VHS, DVD,** Jerry O'Connell, Josh Hamilton, Julia Stiles, Bill Smitrovich, Annie Corley, Leonard Roberts, Charles S. Dutton, Jordana Brewster, David Alan Grier, Jeremy Sisto, Cliff Gorman, Donovan Leitch, Carmia Wilson, Rosanna Arquette; **D:** Mark Piznarski; **W:** Jeffrey Alladin Fiskin; **C:** Michael D. O'Shea. **TV**

61* 🦴🦴🦴 2001 Crystal's nostalgic and meticulous telling of the 1961 home run race between Mickey Mantle (Jane) and Roger Maris (Pepper) clears the fence. Pepper and Jane are excellent as the "M & M Boys", and the rest of the solid cast is up to the task as well. The fine script mixes the baseball action with the behind the scenes material well. Crystal and writer Steinberg take great pains to show the tremendous pressure and outside distractions with which both players had to contend. With the exception of a few sportswriters (the obligatory villains), most of the characters are fleshed out nicely, instead of becoming a checklist of familiar names. Baseball geeks will find nits to pick, but for the most part, the baseball scenes and historical facts are right on the mark. Crystal's daughter plays Mrs. Maris. **128m/C VHS, DVD,** Thomas Jane, Barry Pepper, Chris Bauer, Christopher McDonald, Anthony Michael Hall, Bob Gunton, Bruce McGill, Richard Masur, Bobby Hosea, Donald Moffat, Renee Taylor, Joe Grifasi, Michael Nouri, Paul Borghese, Jennifer Crystal Foley, Seymour Cassel, Peter Jacobson, Robert Joy, Patricia Crowley, Robert Costanzo; **D:** Billy Crystal; **W:** Hank Steinberg; **C:** Haskell Wexler; **M:** Marc Shaiman. **CABLE**

'68 🦴 1987 (R) A Hungarian family struggles with the generation gap in 1968 America. **99m/C VHS, DVD,** Eric Larson, Terra Vandergaw, Neil Young, Sandor Tecsy; **D:** Steven Kovacks; **C:** Daniel Lacambre; **M:** Shony Alex Braun, John Cipollinan.

Sizzle 🦴 1981 When her boyfriend is murdered by the mob, nightclub singer Anderson, newly arrived from Hicksville in the Roaring '20s Chicago, stoops at nothing to get revenge. Bad-guy gangster Forsythe falls for her charms. Fun but unsophisticated. Made for TV. **100m/C VHS,** Loni Anderson, John Forsythe, Leslie Uggams Roy Thinnes, Richard Lynch, Michael Goodwin; **D:** Don Medford; **M:** Artie Butler. **TV**

Sizzle Beach U.S.A. 🦴 *Malibu hot Summer* 1974 (R) Three aspiring young actresses want a shot at becoming famous and travel to Los Angeles where they spend their time at the beach with little budget and no particular purpose. Re-released and renamed in 1986 when Costner (in his film debut) became more well-known. **89m/C VHS, DVD,** Terry Congie, Leslie Brander, Roselyn Royce, Kevin Costner; **D:** Richard Brander.

Skag 🦴🦴 1979 Disabled following a stroke, a Pittsburgh steel worker confronts a change in family roles and long-ignored family problems during his convalescence. Malden is exceptional and believable as a steel TV outing, pilot for the NBC series. **145m/C VHS,** Karl Malden, Piper Laurie, Craig Wasson, Leslie Ackerman, Peter Gallagher, Kathryn Holcomb, Powers Boothe; **D:** Frank Perry. **TV**

Skateboard 🦴 1977 (PG) A down-and-out Hollywood agent creates a pro skateboarding team and enters them in a race worth $20,000. Quickie premise executed lamely. **97m/C VHS,** Allen (Goowitz) Garfield, Kathleen Lloyd, Chad McQueen, Leif Garrett, Richard Van Der Wyk, Tony Alva, Antony Carbone; **W:** Dick Wolf.

The Skateboard Kid 🦴 1993 Mystery creature helps Sammy build his dream skateboard, which turns out to have a mind of its own. **95m/C VHS,** Bess Armstrong, Trevor Knight, Dee Wallace Stone, Bruce Davison, Andrew Stevens; **D:** Andrew Stevens.

The Skateboard Kid 2 🦴½ 1993

Skeeter 🦴½ 1993 (R) Yes, it's the attack of the killer mosquito! Not just any mosquito of course, but a new gigantic species bred on toxic waste. They're invading the quiet desert town of Mesquite and they're out for blood! **95m/C VHS, DVD,** Tracy Griffith, Jim Youngs Charles Napier, Michael J. Pollard; **D:** Clark Brandon; **W:** Clark Brandon. Jenny Horn; **M:** David Lawrence.

Skeezer 🦴🦴½ 1982 A dog becomes a key factor in a sympathetic doctor's efforts to communicate with emotionally unstable children. Based on reality, and a good cast makes it believable and moving. Quality family fare. **100m/C VHS,** Karen Valentine, Dee Wallace Stone, Tom Atkins, Mariclare Costello, Leighton Greer, Justine Lord; **D:** Peter H. Hunt.

Skeleton Coast 🦴 *Fair Trade* 1989 (R) Borgnine plays a retired U.S. Marine colonel who organizes a Magnificent Seven-like group of tough mercenaries to go into eastern Africa to save hostages held by Angolan terrorists. Cliches abound, including a token large-breasted woman, Mutford, getting her t-shirt ripped open. No plot and a bad script. **94m/C VHS DVD,** Ernest Borgnine, Robert Vaughn, Oliver Reed, Herbert Lom, Daniel Greene, Nancy Mulford, Leon Isaac Kennedy; **D:** John Cardos.

The Skeleton Key 🦴🦴 2005 (PG-13) Caroline Ellis (Hudson) is a live-in nurse for a bayou stroke victim who finds herself creeping around in her underwear at night trying to uncover the hoodoo history of the cursed... Tight plot and just enough suspenseful garnish keep the journey engaging enough. **104m/C DVD, US** Kate Hudson, Gena Rowlands, John Hurt, Joy Bryant, Peter Sarsgaard; **D:** Iain Softley; **W:** Ehren Kruger; **C:** Dan Mindel; **M:** Ed Shearmur.

Skeletons 🦴🦴 1996 (R) Journalist Peter Crane (Silver) decides to leave New York after suffering a heart attack and moves his family to what he thinks will be the quiet of Saugatuck, Maine. They're settling in when Peter is approached by the mother of a young man, who's standing trial for murder, and who claims her son is innocent. When Peter investigates, the town's skeletons go back 100 years and the secrets are deadly. **91m/C VHS,** Ron Silver, James Coburn, Christopher Plummer, Dee Wallace Stone, Kyle Howard, Thomas Wilson; **D:** David DeCoteau.

Skeletons in the Closet 🦴🦴½ 2000 (R) Seth Reed (Jackson) is more than just a rebellious teenager. A loner, he's given to violent outbursts that have his widowed father, Will (Williams), worried. Especially when a series of murders are committed in their New Hampshire town. But since Will is still suffering from the aftermath of his wife's death in a fire, maybe it's his sanity that's in question. Creepy if sometimes clichéd thriller. **86m/C VHS DVD.** Treat Williams, Jonathan Jackson, Linda Hamilton, Schuyler Fisk, Gordon Clapp; **D:** Wayne Powers; **W:** Wayne Powers, Donna Powers; **C:** Michael Barrett; **M:** Christopher Stone. **VIDEO**

Sketch Artist 🦴🦴 1992 (R) Jack Whitfield (Fahey) is a police sketch artist whose latest rendering of a murder suspect looks suspiciously like his wife, Emmy. He decides to keep this information to himself while he does some quiet investigating but the may not have any time. The police have a new murder suspect in mind—Jack. **89m/C VHS,** Jeff Fahey, Courteney Cox, Jonathan Silverman, Drew Barrymore, Frank McRae, Tcheky Karyo, James Tolkan, Charlotte Lewis; **D:** Predon Papamichael; **W:** Michael Angeli. **CABLE**

Sketch Artist 2: Hands That See 🦴🦴½ 1994 Fahey returns as police sketch artist Jack Whitfield, who's asked to draw a sketch of a blind rape victim. Near-victim Emmy (Cox) just happens to be blind but describes to Jack how the rapist looked as she felt his face. Emmy's hubby, Glenn (Silverman) is concerned, especially when the creep warns Emmy about her trip to the cops. Solid characters build to good courtroom climax. **95m/C VHS,** Jeff Fahey, Courteney Cox, Jonathan Silverman, James Tolkan, Leila-ni Sarelle Ferrer, Michael Nicolosi, Scott Eunkholo; **D:** Jack Sholder; **W:** Michael Angeli; **M:** Tim Truman.

Sketches of a Strangler 🦴🦴 1978 A psychotic art student sketches, then murders prostitutes. Interesting lead character but hardly chilling—just horrible. Made for TV. **91m/C VHS,** Allen (Goowitz) Garfield, Meredith MacRae; **D:** Paul Leder. **TV**

Ski Bum 🦴 1975 (R) A ski bum discovers corruption and violence at a Colorado Rockies resort. Eminently forgettable. Based on a novel by Romain Gary. **94m/C VHS,** Charlotte Rampling, Zalman King, Dimitra Arliss, Anna Karina; **D:** Bruce (B.D.) Clark.

Ski Party 🦴🦴 1965 Slight and rather lame comedy. Ga... pals Deborah and Yvonne are off on a ski trip to Squaw Valley, leaving behind their clueless would-be boyfriends Frankie and Dwayne. The guys decide to follow and cross-dress, passing themselves off as a couple of English chicks to get a better understanding of the mysteries of women. This causes some confusion when Dwayne falls for their sexy Swedish ski instructor (Shaw) and Frankie gets hit on by the clueless Kincaid. Lesley Gore and James Brown and the Flames perform. **90m/C DVD.** Frankie Avalon, Dwayne Hickman, Deborah Walley, Yvonne Craig, Bobbi Shaw, Aron Kincaid, Robert Q. Lewis; **D:** Alan Rafkin; **W:** Robert Kaufman; **C:** Arthur E. Arling; **M:** Gary Usher.

Ski Patrol ♂♂ **1989 (PG)** Wacky ski groupies try to stop an evil developer. Good ski action in a surprisingly plotful effort from the crazy crew that brought the world "Police Academy." **85m/C VHS.** Roger Rose, Yvette Nipar, T.K. Carter, Leslie Jordan, Ray Walston, Martin Mull; **D:** Richard Correll.

Ski School ♂ **1991 (R)** Rival ski instructors compete for jobs and babes. Brow lowering. **89m/C VHS.** Ava Fabian, Dean Cameron, Tom Breznahan, Stuart Fratkin; **D:** Damian Lee.

Ski School 2 ♂½ **1994 (R)** Former ski instructor Dave finds that both his job and his ex-gal have been acquired by a jerk. So Dave decides to get them both back. **92m/C VHS, DVD.** Dean Cameron, Wendy Hamilton, Heather Campbell, Brent Sheppard, Bill Dwyer; **D:** David Mitchell; **W:** Jay Naples.

Skier's Dream **1988** This spectacular action-packed film focuses on a young executive in search of the ultimate run. Shot on the most exotic ski locations in the world; covers freestyle skiing, powder skiing, snowboarding, extreme skiing, cliff jumping, paragliding, and wave riding. **75m/C VHS.** John Eaves, Ian Boyt; **M:** Jimi Hendrix, Tom Cochrane.

Skin ♂½ **1993 (R)** Very offbeat character study focusing on Will, a tormented tattoo artist who specializes in decorating the backs of the young Asian prostitutes who work in a nearby brothel. Haunted by his memories as a Vietnam POW, Will decides to exorcise some demons on his latest female canvas. **90m/C VHS.** Kirk Baltz, Jake Weber, Nora Ariffin; **D:** William Daniels.

Skin Deep ♂½ **1989 (R)** A boyish Don Juan tries everything to win back his ex-wife. Ritter whines about his mid-life crisis and seduces women; this substitutes don't make this worth watching. **102m/C VHS, DVD.** John Ritter, Vincent Gardenia, Julianne Phillips, Alyson Reed, Nina Foch, Chelsea Field, Denise Crosby; **D:** Blake Edwards; **W:** Blake Edwards; **M:** Henry Mancini.

Skin Deep ♂½ **1994** Lesbian filmmaker Alex is obsessed with making her first feature, which is about the pleasure and pain associated with body art. She places an ad in a tattoo magazine for an assistant and is intrigued by respondent, Chris, who's still dealing with her transgendered experience. As Alex gets deeper into her movie, she fails to notice Chris' growing infatuation with her until Chris decides to do something desperate to gain Alex's attention. **82m/C VHS.** CA Natsuko Ohama, Keram Malicki-Sanchez, Dana Brooks, Melanie Nicholls-King, David Crean; **D:** Midi Onodera; **W:** Midi Onodera, Barbara O'Kelly.

Skin Game ♂½ **1931** Two British families feud over land rights. Not thrilling, not characteristic of working with Hitchcock. Way too much talking in excruciating, drawn-out scenes. Adapted from the play of the same name. **87m/B VHS, DVD.** GB Phyllis Konstam, Edmund Gwenn, Frank Lawton, C.V. France, Jill Esmond, Helen Haye; **D:** Alfred Hitchcock; **W:** Alfred Hitchcock; **C:** Jack Cox.

Skin Game ♂♂♂ **1971 (PG)** A fast talking con-artist (Garner) and his black partner (Gossett) travel throughout the antebellum South setting up scams—Gossett is sold to a new owner by Garner, who helps him escape. Garner and Gossett make a splendid comedy team in this different kind of buddy flick. All is well until Asner turns the tables on them. Finely acted comedy-drama. **102m/C VHS.** James Garner, Louis Gossett Jr., Susan Clark, Ed Asner, Andrew Duggan; **D:** Paul Bogart; **M:** David Shire.

Skinheads: The Second Coming of Hate ♂ **1988 (R)** Neofascists run rampant. Exploitative effort from schlock-doyen Clark. **93m/C VHS.** Chuck Connors, Barbara Bain, Brian Brophy, Jason Culp, Elizabeth Sagal; **D:** Greydon Clark; **W:** Greydon Clark.

Skinned Alive WOOF! **1989** A woman and her children travel cross-country to sell leather goods. When a detective discovers where the leather comes from he's hot on their trail. **90m/C VHS, DVD.** Mary Jackson, Scott Spiegel; **D:** Jon Killough; **W:** Jon Killough.

Skinner ♂ **1993 (R)** Psychopath Dennis Skinner (Raimi) more than lives up to his grisly name with his penchant for stalking hookers with carving knives and cleavers. Now he's going after his innocent landlady (Lake) and it's up to Heidi (Lords), a victim who managed to get away, to find him before he can kill again. Lords in lingerie (and nasty scars) and some really disgusting skinning scenes. **89m/C VHS, DVD.** Theodore (Ted) Raimi, Traci Lords, Ricki Lake; **D:** Ivan Nagy; **W:** Paul Hart-Wilden; **C:** Greg Littlewood.

Skinner's Dress Suit ♂♂½ **1926** Meek, hen-pecked office clerk tells domineering wife he got a raise so she'll get off his back. She quickly insinuates them into upper crusty social circle, where the fib pays off big. Remake of the 1917 version based on Henry Irving Dodge's novel. **79m/B VHS.** Reginald Denny, Laura La Plante, Arthur Lake, Hedda Hopper; **D:** William A. Seiter.

Skins ♂♂½ **2002 (R)** The Pine Ridge Indian Reseration in South Dakota is rife with unemployment, alcoholism, drug abuse, and violence, which native cop Rudy (Schweig) contends with on a daily basis. His older brother Mogie (Greene) is an embittered Vietnam vet and alcoholic who can't be a father to his own teenage son Herbie (Watts). While Rudy seems to have a better handle on life, in fact his frustrations lead to an act of destruction that has unexpected consequences. Based on the 1995 novel by Adrian C. Louis. **90m/C VHS, DVD.** US Eric Schweig, Graham Greene, Gary Farmer, Noah Watts, Lois Red Elk, Michelle Thrush, Nathaniel Arcand, Chaske Spencer; **D:** Chris Eyre; **W:** Jennifer D. Lyne; **C:** Stephen Kazmierski; **M:** B.C. Smith.

Skinwalker ♂♂½ **2002** Middle-aged Native American detective Joe Leaphorn has moved from the city to an Arizona Navajo reservation at the behest of his wife Emma (Tousey). He's finding it difficult to adjust, particularly when someone—or something—begins killing the local medicine men. His young partner, Officer Jim Chee (Beach) of the Navajo Tribal Police, thinks a skinwalker—an evil shape-shifting force—is at work but Leaphorn thinks the killer is more human than supernatural. Based on the mystery series by Tony Hillerman. **120m/C VHS, DVD.** Wes Studi, Adam Beach, Sheila Tousey, Alex Rice, Rupaul Charles; **D:** Chris Eyre; **M:** James Redford. **TV**

Skinwalkers ♂ **2007 (PG-13)** Timothy (Knight) is about to turn thirteen when he discovers that he, like his dead father, uncle, and extended family, is a werewolf—not a bad werewolf, but a good werewolf that fights bad werewolves. Plus, there's a mysterious prophecy about him, so he and Uncle Jonas (Koteas) must go on the run to avoid bad werewolf Varek (Behr) and his crew of motorcycle-riding henchmen. Embarrassing howler (despite Koteas's decent performance) sanitizes the lycanthropic sex and violence for the adolescent set, and the results are dull and silly. **110m/C DVD.** US CA GE Jason Behr, Elias Koteas, Rhona Mitra, Matthew Knight, Kim Coates, Tom Jackson, Barbara Gordon; **D:** James Isaac; **W:** James DeMonaco, James Roday, Todd Harthan; **C:** Adam Kane, David Armstrong; **M:** Barbara Carrera, Andrew Lockington.

Skipped Parts ♂½ **2000 (R)** Fourteen-year-old Sam Callahan (Hall) and his bad-girl mom, Lydia (Leigh), have been exiled to Wyoming in 1963 by Lydia's southern big daddy, Caspar (Ermey). Lydia promptly takes up with the wrong guy (Greyeyes) and encourages Sam in sexual experimentation with schoolmate Maurey (Barton), with unfortunate results. Based on Sandlin's coming-of-age trilogy, the film is flat and predictable. **93m/C VHS, DVD.** US Jennifer Jason Leigh, Bug Hall, Michael Greyeyes, Mischa Barton, Peggy Lipton, Brad Renfro, R. Lee Ermey, Angela Featherstone, Alison Pill, Drew Barrymore, Gerald Lenton-Young; **D:** Tamra Davis; **W:** Tim Sandlin; **C:** Claudio Rocha; **M:** Stewart Copeland.

Skirts Ahoy! ♂ **1952** Williams, Evans, and Blaine are three WAVES who have their eyes set on three handsome men. To get them, of course, they must sing and dance a lot, and Williams must perform one of her famous water ballets. ♫Oh By Jingo; Hold Me Close to You; What Makes a WAVE?; What Good is a Gal Without a Guy?; The Navy Waltz; I Get a Funny Feeling; We Will Fight. **109m/C VHS.** Esther Williams, Joan Evans, Vivian Blaine, Barry Sullivan, Keefe Brasselle, Billy Eckstine, Debbie Reynolds; **D:** Sidney Lanfield.

The Skull ♂♂ **1965** Horror abounds when Cushing gets his hands on the skull of the Marquis de Sade that has mysterious, murderous powers. Based on a story by Robert Bloch. **83m/C VHS.** Peter Cushing, Patrick Wymark, Christopher Lee, Nigel Green, Jill Bennett, Michael Gough, George Coulouris, Patrick Magee; **D:** Freddie Francis.

Skull: A Night of Terror ♂♂ **1988 (R)** A cop vows not to use guns after a tragic accident, then single-handed and unarmed, takes on terrorists who kidnap his family. **80m/C VHS.** Nadia Capone, Robert Bideman, Robbie Fox, Paul Sanders; **D:** Robert Bergman; **W:** Robert Bergman, Gerard Ciccoritti.

Skull & Crown ♂♂ **1935** Rin Tin Tin Jr. helps the hero break up a group of smugglers. A favorite of Tin fans everywhere. **58m/B VHS, DVD.** Jack Mower, Molly O'Day, Lois January, Regis Toomey, Jack Mulhall, James Murray; **D:** Elmer Clifton; **W:** Bennett Cohen, Carl Krusada; **C:** Piny Goodfriend.

Skullduggery ♂½ **1970 (PG)** When a peaceful race of blond ape-people are discovered in New Guinea, a courtroom battle ensues to prevent their slaughter at the hands of developers. Interesting premise sadly flops. **105m/C VHS.** Burt Reynolds, Susan Clark, Roger C. Carmel, Chips Rafferty, Edward Fox, Wilfrid Hyde-White, Rhys Williams; **D:** Gordon Douglas.

Skullduggery WOOF! Warlock **1979 (PG)** Costume-store minion Haverstock carries a curse that makes him kill and mutilate. The usual unspeakable horror ensues for a group of medieval-game players. **95m/C VHS.** Thom Haverstock, Wendy Crewson, David Calderisi; **D:** Ota Richter.

The Skulls ♂½ **2000 (PG-13)** Well, you just can't trust those darn secret societies. Teen star Jackson is Luke, an ambitious kid from the wrong side of the tracks at an "unnamed" Ivy League school that starts with "Y." Because he's the captain of the rowing team, he's asked to join the elite secret society the "Skulls." After the requisite hazing and initiation, Luke is showered with money and other perks. Membership has its privileges. But when his best friend Will (Harper) is found dead after snooping in Skull business, Luke suspects foul play and the movie goes from laughable to ludicrous. This secret society, led by evil judge Litten Mandrake (Nelson), does a lot of its business, including duels and car chases, out in the open. Another entry aping the teen-paranoia-adults-are-bad theme, which should, mercifully, help kill off the genre for a while. **106m/C VHS, DVD.** Joshua Jackson, Paul Walker, Hill Harper, Leslie Bibb, Christopher McDonald, Steve Harris, William L. Petersen, Craig T. Nelson; **D:** Rob Cohen; **W:** John Pogue; **C:** Shane Hurlbut; **M:** Randy Edelman.

The Skulls 2 ♂♂ **2002 (R)** College student Ryan (Dunne) becomes a member of the secret fraternity the Skulls but when he sees a girl fall off the fraternity's roof, the situation turns ugly. **100m/C VHS, DVD.** CA Robin Dunne, Aaron Ashmore, Ashley Lyn Catagna, Christopher Ralph, Nathan West, James Callanders, Lindy Booth; **D:** Joe Chappelle; **W:** Hans Rodionoff, Michele Colucci-Zieger; **C:** Steve Danyluk; **M:** Christophe Beck. **VIDEO**

The Sky Above, the Mud Below ♂½ Le Ciel et le Boue **1961** An acclaimed documentary following a band of explorers transversing New Guinea in 1959, and their confrontations with native rituals, heretofore unknown cannibal tribes and physical calamities. In HiFi. **90m/C VHS. D:** Pierre-Dominique Gaisseau. Oscars '61: Feature Doc.

Sky Bandits ♂½ **1940** Mounties uncover the mystery of a disappearing plane carrying gold from a Yukon mine. Last of the "Renfrew of the Mounties" pictures. **56m/B VHS, DVD.** James Newill, Dave O'Brien, Louise Stanley; **D:** Ralph Staub; **W:** Edward Halperin; **C:** Mack Stengler.

Sky Captain and the World of Tomorrow ♂♂½ **2004 (PG)** More of a film experiment from first-timer Conran (it looks stunning) than a truly engaging film—notable for being the first studio feature where the actors worked against backgrounds that were entirely created digitally. In a pulp wartime melodrama, a sleek, streamlined New York is under attack from giant robots; it must be saved from destruction by the dashing Joe Sullivan (Law) better known as Sky Captain. Former flame/ace girl reporter Polly Perkins (Paltrow) goes along for the ride as she investigates the disappearance of a number of German scientists. The winsome twosome work together, aided (briefly) by eye-patch-wearing British air Franky (Jolie), to uncover the sinister plot of evil Dr. Totenkopf (the long-deceased Olivier creepily resurrected via digitized stock footage). **107m/C DVD, Blu-ray Disc, HD DVD.** US Gwyneth Paltrow, Jude Law, Angelina Jolie, Giovanni Ribisi, Michael Gambon, Omid Djalili, Laurence Olivier, Trevor Baxter, Julian Curry; **D:** Kerry Conran; **W:** Kerry Conran; **C:** Eric Adkins; **M:** Ed Shearmur.

Sky Hei$t **1975** Criminals plan robbery of police helicopter carrying fortune in gold bullion. **96m/C VHS.** Stefanie Powers, Joseph Campanella, Don Meredith, Larry Wilcox, Frank Gorshin, Shelley Fabares, Ken Swofford, Ray Vitte, Nancy Belle Fuller, Suzanne Somers; **D:** Lee H. Katzin. **TV**

Sky High ♂♂ **1951** A spy at an Air Force base is trying to get hold of the plans to a secret plane. A GI is recruited to catch him. **60m/B VHS.** Sid Melton, Mara Lynn, Douglas Evans, Sam Flint, Fritz Feld, Margia Dean, Paul Bryar; **D:** Jack Newfield; **W:** Orville H. Hampton; **C:** Jack Greenhalgh; **M:** Bert Shefter.

Sky High ♂ **1984** Three college students become immersed in international intrigue when the C.I.A. and the K.G.B. pursue them through Greece looking for a secret Soviet tape. **103m/C VHS, DVD.** Daniel Hirsch, Clayton Norcross, Frank Schultz, Lauren Taylor; **D:** Nico Mastorakis.

Sky High ♂♂♂ **2005 (PG)** Will Stronghold (Angarano) is expected to follow in the footsteps of his superhero parents the Commander (Russell) and Jetstream (Preston) by attending Sky High School to learn the tricks of the trade. He is at first deemed a sidekick, which adds to his adolescence miseries, including a showdown against nemesis Warren Peace (Strait). Carries just the right mix of action, humor and gooeyness delivered by a top notch all-ages cast. **100m/C DVD,**

The Sky Is Falling 🎬🎬 *Il Cielo Cade 2000* In 1944, young orphaned sisters Penny (Niccoli) and Baby (Campoli) are sent to the Tuscan countryside to live with their Aunt Katchen (Roselli) and German-Jewish Uncle Wilhelm (Krabbe). Although they have managed to survive the war so far, things worsen as the retreating German Army closes in on their small town and the family is urged to make their way to Switzerland. But Uncle Wilhelm doesn't want to leave his home. Based on the autobiographical novel by Lorenza Mazzetti. Italian with subtitles. 102m/C VHS, DVD. *IT* Isabella Rosselini, Jeroen Krabbe, Veronica Niccolai, Lara Campoli; *D:* Andrea Frazzi; *W:* Suso Cecchi D'Amico; *C:* Franco Di Giacomo; *M:* Luis Bacalov.

Sky Liner 🎬 1949 An FBI agent is trailing a spy who has taken secret documents aboard a west-bound flight. 62m/B VHS. Richard Travis, Pamela Blake, Rochelle Hudson, Steven Geray, Greg McClure, Steve Pendleton, Michael Whalen, Ralph Peters; *D:* William Berke; *M:* Maurice Tombragel; *C:* Carl Berger; *M:* Raoul Kraushaar.

Sky Parade 🎬½ 1936 Three World War I buddies (Gargan, Taylor, Fiske) team up to run a commercial airline but don't realize that enemy spies are checking out their design for a new plane. Allen, at the time a well-known teenaged pilot in his only screen appearance, plays himself and comes to the save the day. 70m/B VHS. William Gargan, Kent Taylor, Robert (Fisk) Fiske, Katherine DeMille, Jimmie Allen, Grant Withers, Syd Saylor, Billie Lee; *D:* Otto Lovering; *W:* Arthur Beckhard, Robert Burtt; *C:* William Mellor, Alfred Gilks.

The Sky Pilot 🎬🎬½ 1921 Young clergyman sets up a parish on North Pacific coast and finds he must prove himself to the cowboys. He saves young woman from stampede, but her father blames himself for her maimed legs and sets the preacher's church on fire, providing girl with excuse to overcome handicap. 63m/B VHS. John Bowers, Colleen Moore, David Butler, Donald MacDonald; *D:* King Vidor.

Sky Pirates WOOF! 1987 Space epic deals about pieces of ancient stone left by prehistoric extraterrestrials, now lost in a time warp. Bad stunts, bad script and notably bad acting make it a woofer in any era. 88m/C VHS. *AU* John Hargreaves, Max Phipps, Meredith Phillips; *D:* Colin Eggleston.

Sky Riders 🎬🎬½ 1976 (PG) Hang-gliders risk it all to take on a group of political kidnappers. Fine hang-gliding footage and glorious Greek locations make up for garden-variety plot. 93m/C VHS. James Coburn, Susannah York, Robert Culp, Charles Aznavour, Harry Andrews, John Beck; *D:* Douglas Hickox; *W:* Jack DeWitt, Garry Michael White; *M:* Lalo Schifrin.

Skyline 🎬🎬 *La Linea Del Cielo 1984* (R) A Spanish photographer comes to New York City to work for a magazine and tries to adjust to his cultural dislocation. Quietly funny, with a startling ending. Partly in Spanish with English subtitles. 84m/C VHS. *SP* Antonio Resines, Beatriz Perez-Porro, Jaime Nos, Roy Hoffman; *D:* Fernando Colomo.

The Sky's the Limit 🎬🎬½ 1943 Astaire spends his leave in Manhattan and falls in love with fetching journalist Leslie. He's in civvies, so little does she know he's a war hero. Nothing-special semi-musical, with Fred-Ginger spark missing. 💿One For My Baby; My Shining Hour; I've Got a Lot in Common With You. 89m/B VHS, DVD. Fred Astaire, Joan Leslie, Robert Benchley, Robert Ryan, Elizabeth Patterson; *D:* Edward H. Griffith.

Skyscraper 🎬 1995 (R) Gun-wielding helicopter pilot/heroine Carrie Wink (Smith) must battle villainous mercenaries holding hostages in an LA skyscraper. But she still manages to find time to find lots of

steamy showers ('o best display the only assets she film has). 96m/C VHS, DVD. Anna Nicole Smith, Richard Steinmetz; *D:* Raymond Martino; *W:* William Applegate Jr.; *C:* Frank Harris; *M:* Jim Halfpenny.

Slacker 🎬🎬🎬 1991 (F) Defines a new generation: Overwhelmed by the world and its demands, "Slackers" react by retreating into lives of minimal expectations. Filmed as a series of improvisational stories about people living on the fringes of the working world and their reactions (or lack thereof) to the life swirling around them. First feature for writer/director Linklater on a budget of $23,000; filmed on location in Austin, Texas with a cast of primarily non-professional actors. 97m/C VHS, DVD. Richard Linklater, Rudy Basquez, Jean Caffeine, Jan Hockey, Stephan Hockey, Mark James, Samuel Dietert; *D:* Richard Linklater; *W:* Richard Linklater; *C:* Lee Daniel.

Slackers 🎬½ 2002 (R) Schwartzman is wasted as Ethan, a social outcast college student with his stalker-like eye on the prize—an intelligent college girl with model good looks (former model King). Nicknaming himself "Cool Ethan," our semi-delusional hero blackmails three of the campus's best and brightest, who have gotten that rep entirely through cheating. Ethan demands the boys use their unique methods of chicanery to get him his dream girl, or he'll get them all expelled. Leader of the gang Dave (Sawa) leads the fix-up charade but ends up falling for the cutie himself. Unlike esting, annoying characters, awkward piloting, and the requisite ton of sophomoric, sexual, and gross-out humor, including a gratuitous septuagenarian sponge bath. 86m/C VHS, DVD. *US* Devon Sawa, Jason Schwartzman, Jaime (James) King, Jason Segel, Michael Maronna, Laura Prepon, Mamie Van Doren, Joe Flaherty, Leigh Taylor-Young, Sam Anderson, Cameron Diaz; *D:* Dewey Nicks; *W:* David H. Steinberg; *C:* James R. Bagdonas; *M:* Joseph (Joey) Altruda.

Slam 🎬🎬 1998 (R) Levin makes his feature film debut with this part-prison, part-ghetto drama. Street-smart, low-level drug dealer Ray (Williams) is living in gang-ridden D.C. When he's busted for possession and suspicion of murdering his supplier. Jail's just as rough as the streets since two local inside gangs each want Ray's allegiance. Ray wants to keep to himself and work on his writing—the poetry he composes about bail and then has a lot of hard decisions to make. 100m/C VHS, DVD. Saul Williams, Sonia Sohn, Bonz Malone; *D:* Marc Levin; *W:* Marc Levin, Saul Williams, Sonia Sohn, Bonz Malone, Richard Stratton; *C:* Mark Benjamin. Sundance '98.

Slam Dunk Ernest 🎬 1995 (PG-13) Ernest (Varney) becomes a basketball star in a city league exhibition game when the Basketball Angel (Abdul-Jabbar) loans him his magic shoes. 93m/C VHS, DVD. Jim Varney, Kareem Abdul-Jabbar, Jay Brazeau; *D:* Jim R, Cherry III; *W:* John R. Cherry III, Daniel Butler; *M:* Mark Adler.

Slamdance 🎬½ 1987 (R) A struggling cartoonist is framed for the murder of a beautiful young woman while being victimized by the real killer. A complicated murder mystery with a punk beat and visual flash. But the tale is unoriginal—and where's the slamdancing? 99m/C VHS, DVD. Tom Hulce, Virginia Madsen, Mary Elizabeth Mastrantonio, Harry Dean Stanton, Adam Ant, John Doe; *D:* Wayne Wang.

Slammer Girls 🎬 1987 (R) In this sex-drenched, unfunny spoof on women's prison films, the inmates of Loch Ness Penitentiary try to break out using their

sexual wiles. The actresses are pseudonymous porn stars. 82m/C VHS. Jane (Veronica Hart) Hamilton, Jeff Eagle, Devon Jenkin; *D:* Chuck Vincent.

The Slap *La Gifle 1976* (PG) French teens learn about love this French way. 103m/C VHS. FR Isabelle Adjani, Lino Ventura; *D:* Claude Pinoteau; *M:* Georges Delerue.

Slap Shot 🎬🎬🎬 1977 (R) Profane satire of the world of professional hockey. Over-the-hill player-coach of the third-rate Charlestown Chiefs, Reggie Dunlop (Newman), gathers an odd-ball mixture of has-beens and young players and reluctantly initiates them, using violence on the ice to make his team win. The on-ice striptease by star player Ned Braden (Ontkean) needs to be seen to be believed. Charming in its own bone-crunching way. 123m/C VHS, DVD. Paul Newman, Strother Martin, Michael Ontkean, Jennifer Warren, Lindsay Crouse, Jerry Houser, Melinda Dillon, Swoosie Kurtz; *D:* Victor Kemper; *M:* Elmer Bernstein.

Slap Shot 2: Breaking the Ice 🎬🎬 2002 (R) Okay, it took 25 years to make a sequel—is this a record? Rude and crude hockey, 'comedy' finds the Charlestown Chiefs being sold to media mogul Busey, who moves the team to Omaha, Nebraska. But the team is not supposed to play 'real' hockey; they are only supposed to take the money and serve as cash fools to the geeky Hanson brothers and team captain Baldwin. 104m/C VHS, DVD. Stephen Baldwin, Jeff Carlson, Steve Carlson, Dave Hanson, Gary Busey, Callum Keith Rennie, Jessica Steen; *D:* Steve Boyum; *W:* Broderick Miller; *C:* Joel Ransom. VIDEO

Slappy and the Stinkers 🎬🎬½ 1997 (PG) Five young misfits, known as 'The Stinkers,' are constantly in trouble with their stuffy school principal Morgan Brinway (Wong). On a class trip to the acquarium, the Stinkers meet Slappy the sea lion and decide to liberate him (they think he looks unhappy), stowing Slappy in Mr. Erinway's hot tub. Then the kids find out evil animal thief Boccoli (McMurray) wants to steal the critter and sell him to a circus. Just as silly as it sounds but Slappy is really cute. 78m/C VHS, DVD. B.D. Wong, Bronson Pinchot, Sam Mcmurray, Joseph Ashton, Travis Tedford, Gary LeRoi Gray, Carl Michael Lindner, Scarlet Pomers, Jennifer Coolidge; *D:* Barnet Kellman; *W:* Michael Scott, Bob Wollerstoff.

Slapstick of Another Kind 🎬½ 1984 (PG) Lewis and Kahn play dual roles as an alien brother and sister and their adoptive Earth parents who are being pursued by U.S. agents. Rather miserable rendition of a Kurt Vonnegut novel. 85m/C VHS. Jerry Lewis, Madeline Kahn, Marty Feldman, Jim Backus, Noryuki "Pat" Morita, Samuel Fuller, Orson Welles; *D:* Steven Paul.

Slash 🎬½ 1987 Each of four people caught in a political takeover harbors a secret that could harm one of the others. Extremely violent. 90m/C VHS. Rorano Kristoff, Michael Monty, Gwen Hung; *D:* John Gale.

Slashdance WOOF! 1989 A really pathetic thriller follows a lady cop uncovering murdering the dancers. The acting is on the level of pro wrestling. Don't be fooled by the naked babes on the cassette box—there's no nudity. 83m/C VHS, DVD. Cindy Maranne, James Carroll Jordan, Deanra (Dee) Bocher, Joel von Omsteiner, Jay Richardson; *D:* James Shyman; *W:* James Shyman.

Slashed Dreams 🎬🎬 *Sunburst 1974* (R) Hippie couple travels to California wilderness in search of a friend. A pair of woodsmen assault them and rape the woman, which really messes with their heads. Retitled and packaged as slasher movie. 74m/C VHS. Peter Hooter, Kathrine Baumann, Ric Carrott, Anne Lockhart, Robert England, Rudy Valee, James Keach, David Pritchard, Peter Brown; *D:* James Polakof; *W:* James Keach, David Pritchard.

The Slasher WOOF! *Rivelazioni di un Maniaco Sessuale al Capo Della Scuaera Mobile; Revelations of a Sex Maniac to the Head of the Criminal Investigation Division; So Naked, So Dead; So Sweet, So Dead; Confessions of a Sex Maniac 1972* (R) A policeman must find the madman who has been killing off unfaithful married women. Miserably gory, pointless slasher (hence the title) interesting only as an early example of its kind. 88m/C VHS. IT Farley Granger, Sylva Koscina, Nieves Navarro, Annabella Incontrera, Femi Benussi, Jessica Dublin; *D:* Robert Bianchi Montero; *W:* Robert Bianchi Montero; *C:* Fausto Rossi; *M:* Giorgio Gaslini.

Slate, Wyn & Me 🎬 1987 (R) Two bank-robbing, kidnapping brothers flee cross-country from the law, and fall in love with the girl they've snatched. Pointless and pointlessly violent and vulgar. 90m/C VHS. Sigrid Thornton, Simon Burke, Martin Sacks; *D:* Don McLennan; *C:* David Connell.

Slaughter 🎬 1972 (R) After his parents are murdered, a former Green Beret goes after their killers. Plenty of brutality. Followed by "Slaughter's Big Ripoff." 92m/C VHS, DVD, Jim Brown, Stella Stevens, Rip Torn, Cameron Mitchell, Don Gordon, Marlene Clark, Robert Phillips; *D:* Jack Starrett; *W:* Mark Hanna, Don Williams; *C:* Rosalio Solano; *M:* Luchi De Jesus.

Slaughter High 🎬 1986 (R) A high school nerd is accidentally disfigured by a back-firing prank. Five years later, he returns to exact bloody revenge. Available in an unrated version. 90m/C VHS. Caroline Munro, Simon Scuddamore, Kelly Baker; *D:* George Dugdale.

Slaughter Hotel 🎬 *Asylum Erotica; La Bestia Uccide a Sangue Freddo 1971* (R) An asylum already inhabited by extremely bizarre characters is plagued by a series of gruesome murders. Lots of skin and lots of blood; Neri shines as a nymphomaniacal lesbian nurse. 72m/C VHS, DVD. Klaus Kinski, Rosalba Neri, Margaret Lee, John Ely; *D:* Fernando Di Leo.

Slaughter in San Francisco 🎬 *Chuck Norris vs. the Karate Cop; Yellow-Faced Tiger; Karate Cop 1981* (R) A Chinese-American cop leads a one-man fight against corruption in the department in Day City, near San Francisco. Norris is the bad guy, made in 1973 but not released until he had an established following (and he still had only some 18 minutes of film footage). Plenty of kicking and karate choos. 92m/C VHS. *CH* Chuck Norris, Don Wong; *D:* William Lowe.

Slaughter of the Innocents 🎬🎬 1993 (R) FBI agent Broderick (Glenn) is sent to Salt Lake City to investigate the murders of two children which are found to be connected to a series of bizarre killings that have occurred around Monument Valley. Unbeknownst to his associates, Broderick often uses his 11-year-old whiz-kid son Jesse's (Cameron-Glickenhaus) computer skills to aid his research. Only this time, his inquisitive son gets too close to a serial killer and unless Dad can figure things out or his own, Jesse will be the next victim. 104m/C VHS, DVD. Scott Glenn, Jesse Cameron-Glickenhaus, Sheila Tousey, Darlanne Fluegel, Zitto Kazann; *D:* James Glickenhaus; *W:* James Glickenhaus.

The Slaughter Rule 🎬🎬½ 2002 In rural Montana, high schooler Roy Chutney (Gosling) gets cut from the football team days after his estranged dad is killed in a train accident. With his divorced mom (Lynch) unable to cope, Roy finds some unexpected diversion when he joins the six-man football squad coached by eccentric loner Gideon Ferguson (Morse), Gideon has a dark past and a somewhat unsavory local reputation but Roy needs someone he can turn to, whatever the consequences. Performances by Gosling and

Skyscraper Souls 🎬🎬 1932 businessman who manipulates stock prices and double-crosses lovers in order to have complete control of a 100-story office building. He sacrifices everything and everyone in this story of big business. Based on the novel "Skyscraper" by Faith Baldwin. 98m/B VHS. Warren William, Maureen O'Sullivan, Gregory Ratoff, Anita Page, Verree Teasdale, Norman Foster, Jean Hersholt, Wallace Ford; *D:* Edgar Selwyn.

Morse are the reason to watch since the storytelling is uneven. **115m/C VHS, DVD.** Ryan Gosling, David Cale, Eddie Spears, Amy Adams; *D:* Alex Smith, Andrew Smith; *W:* Alex Smith, Andrew Smith; *C:* Eric Alan Edwards; *M:* Jay Farrar.

Slaughter Trail ♂♂ 1951 Ranch-er-turned-stage robber Young shoots two Indians and cavalry colonel Donlevy has to deal with the fallout. Peace returns when Young dies. Ordinary western with balladeer device helping the plot along, or trying to. **78m/C VHS.** Brian Donlevy, Gig Young, Virginia Grey, Andy Devine, Robert Hutton; *D:* Irving Allen.

Slaughterday ♂1/2 1977 (R) An innocent woman is caught in the middle of an ex-con's elaborate scheme to commit the largest heist of his life. **87m/C VHS.** Rita Tushingham, William Berger, Frederick Jaeger, Michael Hauseman, Gordon Mitchell; *D:* Peter Patzak.

Slaughterhouse woof! 1987 (R) A rotund, pig-loving country boy kills, maims, and eats numerous victims. Features the requisite dumb teens and plenty of blood. **87m/C VHS, DVD.** Joe Barton, Sherry Bendorf, Don Barrett, Bill Brinsfield; *D:* Rick Roessler; *W:* Rick Roessler; *C:* Richard Benda.

Slaughterhouse Five ♂♂ 1972 (R) A suburban optometrist becomes "unstuck" in time and flits randomly through the experiences of his life, from the Dresden bombing to an extraterrestrial zoo. Noticed at Cannes but not at theatres; ambitious failure to adapt Kurt Vonnegut's odd novel. **104m/C VHS, DVD.** Sharon Gans, Roberts Blossom, Michael Sacks, Valerie Perrine, Ron Leibman, Eugene Roche, Perry King; *D:* George Roy Hill; *W:* Stephen Geller; *C:* Miroslav Ondricek; *M:* Glenn Gould. Cannes '72: Special Jury Prize.

Slaughterhouse Rock woof! 1988 (R) The ghost of a sexy rock star draws a young man into a confrontation with a sadistic spirit that rules a deserted prison. There's also some cannibalism involved. Music group Devo did the score for this flick. **90m/C VHS.** Nicholas Celozzi, Donna Denton, Toni Basil, Hope Marie Carlton; *D:* Dimitri Logothetis.

Slaughter's Big Ripoff ♂1/2 1973 (R) Slaughter is back battling the Mob with guns, planes and martial arts. This undistinguished sequel features McMahon as a mob boss. **92m/C VHS, DVD.** Jim Brown, Brock Peters, Don Stroud, Ed McMahon, Art Metrano, Gloria Hendry; *D:* Gordon Douglas; *W:* Charles Johnson; *C:* Charles F. Wheeler; *M:* James Brown, Fred Wesley.

Slave Girls from Beyond Infinity ♂♂ 1987 (R) In this B-movie spoof, two beautiful intergalactic slave girls escape their penal colony, land on a mysterious planet, and meet a cannibalistic despot. Fun spoof of '50s "B" sci-fi movies. **80m/C VHS.** Elizabeth Kaitan, Cindy Beal, Brinke Stevens, Don Scribner, Carl Horner, Kirk Graves, Randolph Roehbling, Bud Graves; *D:* Ken Dixon; *W:* Ken Dixon; *C:* Thomas Callaway, Kenneth Wiatrak; *M:* Carl Dante.

A Slave of Love ♂♂♂ 1978 Poignant love story set in the Crimea as the Bolshevik Revolution rages around a film crew attempting to complete a project. Interesting as ideological cinema but also enjoyable romantic drama. In Russian with English subtitles. **94m/C VHS, DVD.** *RU* Elena Solovei, Rodion Nakhapetov, Alexander Kalyagin; *D:* Nikita Mikhalkov; *M:* Eduard Artemyev.

Slavers ♂♂ 1977 (R) Detailed depiction of the 19th century African slave trade with a little romance thrown in. **102m/C VHS.** *GE* Trevor Howard, Britt Ekland, Ron Ely, Cameron Mitchell, Ray Milland; *D:* Jurgen Goslar.

Slaves in Bondage ♂ 1937 Young country girls are lured into the big city and initiated into a life of ill repute in this exploitation classic. A must for camp fans of the '30s. **70m/C VHS, DVD.** Lona Andre, Wheeler Oakman, Donald Reed, Florence Dudley, Alison Merton, Richard Cramer; *D:* Elmer Clifton; *W:* Robert A.(R.A.) Dillon; *C:* Edward Linden.

Slaves of Hollywood ♂♂1/2 1999 Paulette (Morgan) is filming a documentary about five aspiring Hollywood wannabe execs as they work their way up

---

the Tinseltown ladder. Lots of stylish flourishes highlight a familiar tale of the backstabbing, schmoozing movie biz. **80m/C VHS, DVD.** Nicholas Worth, Katherin Morgan, Amy Lyndon, Tim Duquette, Hill Harper, Andre Barron, Rob Hyland, Elliot Markman; *D:* Terry Keefe, Michael J. Wechsler; *C:* David Alan Parks; *M:* Joseph (Joey) Altruda, Bradford T. Ellis.

Slaves of New York ♂1/2 1989 (R) Greenwich Village artists worry about life and love in the '80s and being artistic enough for New York. Adapted from the stories of Tama Janowitz, who also wrote the screenplay and appears as Abby. Disastrous adaptation of a popular novel. Directed by Olivia (O'Grady) who wants to get rid of her jealous hubby (Tobolowsky) and wants Hutch to aid her. But he's got bigger problems—Cotton is out of prison and out for revenge. Meanwhile, Hutch's faithful secretary (Kurtz) decides it's time to make her romantic feelings known to her boss. **115m/C VHS, DVD.** Bernadette Peters, Chris Sarandon, Mary Beth Hurt, Madeleine Potter, Adam Coleman Howard, Jsu Garcia, Mercedes Ruehl, Joe Leeway, Charles McCaughan, John Harkins, Anna (Katerina) Katarina, Tama Janowitz, Michael Schoeffling, Steve Buscemi, Anthony LaPaglia, Stanley Tucci; *D:* James Ivory; *W:* Tama Janowitz; *C:* Tony Pierce-Roberts; *M:* Richard Robbins.

Slaves to the Underground ♂1/2 1996 (R) Love affair between Seattle bandmates Shelly (Gross) and Suzy (Ryan) runs into problems when Shelly's ex-boyfriend Jimmy (Bortz) re-enters the picture and some old feelings are also re-ignited. Mediocre yet abrasive, with that dated postgrunge, Seattle-is-so-over feeling. **90m/C VHS, DVD.** Jason Bortz, Molly Gross, Marisa Ryan; *D:* Kristine Peterson; *W:* Bill Cody; *C:* Zoran Hochstatter; *M:* Mike Martt.

The Slayer woof! *Nightmare Island* 1982 (R) It's movies like this that give getting back to nature a bad name. That horrible monster is after three nice young people again! This time it's on an island off the coast of Georgia. **95m/C VHS, DVD.** Alan McRae, Sarah Kendall, Frederick Flynn, Carol Kottenbrook; *D:* J.S. Cardone; *W:* J.S. Cardone; *C:* Karen Grossman; *M:* Robert Folk.

Slayground ♂1/2 1984 (R) Man, distraught at the accidental death of his daughter, hires a hitman to exact revenge. Excruciating adaptation of the novel by Richard Stark (Donald E. Westlake). **85m/C VHS, DVD.** *GB* Peter Coyote, Mel Smith, Billie Whitelaw, Philip Sayer, Kelli Maroney; *D:* Terry Bedford; *M:* Colin Towns.

SLC Punk! ♂♂♂ 1999 (R) Lillard is Stevo, a punk rocker rebelling against "the establishment" in mid-'80s Salt Lake City, Utah before it's time to head off to Harvard Law. He and his friends wander aimlessly from fights with rednecks and hippies to trashy clubs to various girlfriends. Nothing really funny or particularly dramatic happens in the comedy-drama, which seems like an excuse for director/writer Merendino to relive his carefree college years. **97m/C VHS, DVD.** Matthew Lillard, Michael Goorjian, Annabeth Gish, Jennifer Lien, Christopher McDonald, Devon Sawa, James Duval, Til Schweiger, Kevin Breznahan, Jason Segel, Summer Phoenix; *D:* James Merendino; *C:* Greg Littlewood; *M:* Melanie Miller.

The Sleazy Uncle ♂♂ *Lo Zio Indegno* 1989 A successful but bored businessman is energized by an encounter with his vice-ridden uncle, a mooching, womanizing beatnik poet who knows how to enjoy life. An energetic but rather formulaic comedy. In Italian with English subtitles. **104m/C VHS, DVD.** *IT* Giancarlo Giannini, Vittorio Gassman, Andrea Ferreol, Stefania Sandrelli; *D:* Franco Brusati; *W:* Franco Brusati, Leonardo Benvenuti, Piero De Bernardi; *C:* Romano Albani.

Sledgehammer woof! 1983 A madman is wreaking havoc on a small town, annihilating young women with a sledgehammer. **87m/C VHS.** Ted Prior, Doug Matley, Steven Wright; *D:* David A. Prior; *W:* David A. Prior.

Sleep Easy, Hutch Rimes ♂♂ 2000 Insurance agent Hutch Rimes (Webber) may be a womanizer but he knows nothing about women. When abused wife (and Hutch's squeeze) Holly (Siemaszko) decides to murder hubby Cotton (Henry), she enlists Hutch's help. The plan is botched, Holly dies, and Cotton goes to prison. Ten years later, Hutch is now seeing Olivia (O'Grady) who wants to get rid of her jealous hubby (Tobolowsky) and wants Hutch to aid her. But he's got bigger problems—Cotton is out of prison and out for revenge. Meanwhile, Hutch's faithful secretary (Kurtz) decides it's time to make her romantic feelings known to her boss. **99m/C VHS, DVD.** Steven Weber, Swoosie Kurtz, Gail O'Grady, Gregg Henry, Gabriel Mann, Nina Siemaszko, Stephen Tobolowsky, Stacey Travis, Bonnie Somerville, Jack Johnson; *D:* Matthew Irmas; *W:* Michael O'Connell; *C:* Jerry Sidell; *M:* Alex Wurman. **CABLE.**

Sleep of Death ♂1/2 1979 Young Englishman's pursuit of a blue-blooded woman seems to set off a series of bizarre and mysterious murders. A gothic thriller based on Sheridan Le Fanu's short story. **90m/C VHS.** Brendan Price, Marilu Tolo, Patrick Magee, Curt Jurgens, Per Oscarsson; *D:* Calvin Floyd.

Sleep with Me ♂♂1/2 1994 (R) What happens when love comes between friendship? Sarah (Tilly), Joseph (Stoltz), and Frank (Sheffer) are about to find out. Sarah and Joseph are about to get married when they realize Frank realizes he's in love with Sarah. So he sets out to seduce her and when Joseph realizes what's going on, he not only questions Frank's friendship but wonders just what signals Sarah's been giving off (although Joseph's hardly blameless). Six writers each wrote one of the social scenes detailing their triangular troubles, including a party where Tarantino does a hilarious riff on the homoerotic subtext in "Top Gun." Kelly's directorial debut. **117m/C VHS, DVD.** Eric Stoltz, Meg Tilly, Todd Field, Craig Sheffer, Eric Stoltz, Meg Tilly, Todd Field, Adrienne Shelly, Lewis Arquette, Susan Traylor, Tegan West, Parker Posey, Dean Cameron, Thomas Gibson, June Lockhart, Quentin Tarantino, Joey Lauren Adams; *D:* Rory Kelly; *W:* Rory Kelly, Roger Hedden, Neal Jimenez, Michael Steinberg, Duane Dell'Amico, Joe Keenan; *M:* David Lawrence.

Sleepaway Camp ♂ 1983 Crazed killer hacks away at the inhabitants of a peaceful summer camp in this run-of-the-mill slasher. **88m/C VHS, DVD.** Mike Kellin, Jonathan Tiersten, Felissa Rose, Christopher Collet, Robert Earl Jones; *D:* Robert Hiltzik; *W:* Robert Hiltzik; *C:* Benjamin Davis; *M:* Edward Bilous.

Sleepaway Camp 2: Unhappy Campers ♂1/2 1988 (R) A beautiful camp counselor is actually a blood-thirsty, murdering madwoman. Sequel to the 1983 slasher, "Sleepaway Camp." **82m/C VHS, DVD.** Pamela Springsteen, Renee Estevez, Walter Gotell, Brian Patrick Clarke; *D:* Michael A. Simpson.

Sleepaway Camp 3: Teenage Wasteland woof! 1989 (R) This second sequel is as bad as the first two movies. Another disturbed camper hacks up another bevy of teenagers. Better luck at the Motel Six. **80m/C VHS, DVD.** Pamela Springsteen, Tracy Griffith, Michael J. Pollard; *D:* Michael A. Simpson.

Sleeper ♂♂♂1/2 1973 (PG) Hapless nerd Allen is revived two hundred years after an operation gone bad. Keaton portrays Allen's love interest in a futuristic land of robots and giant vegetables. He learns of the hitherto unknown health benefits of hot fudge sundaes; discovers the truth about the nation's dictator, known as the Leader, and gets involved with revolutionaries seeking to overthrow the government. Hilarious, fast-moving comedy, full of slapstick and satire. Don't miss the "orgasmatron." **88m/C VHS, DVD.** Woody Allen,

---

Diane Keaton, John Beck, Mary Gregory, Don Keefer, John McLiam; *D:* Woody Allen; *W:* Marshall Brickman, Woody Allen; *C:* David M. Walsh; *M:* Woody Allen.

Sleeper Cell ♂♂1/2 2005 Darwyn (Ealy) is a black Muslim FBI agent posing as a disgruntled ex-con to infiltrate an LA terrorist cell. Seems there's a plot by charismatic leader Farik (Fehr) to attack various city sites. Then Darwyn gets distracted from his work by getting involved with single mom Gayle (Saggemiller). Ten-episode miniseries suffers from a saggy middle and a rather bland lead. **600m/C DVD.** *US* Michael Ealy, Oded Fehr, Grant Heslov, Melissa Sagemiller, Alex Nesic, James LeGros, Henri Lubatti; *D:* Clark Johnson; *W:* Cyrus Voris, Ethan Reiff; *C:* Robert Primes; *M:* Paul Haslinger. **CABLE**

Sleepers ♂♂1/2 1996 (R) Tense, gritty drama based on Lorenzo Carcaterra's book about four teenaged friends from Hell's Kitchen who get into trouble and wind up being sent to a reform school, where they're brutalized by guards. John (Eldard) and Tommy (Crudup), who grow up to be men, recognize their chief abuser (Bacon) years later and kill him. Their trial is prosecuted by Michael (Pitt), another of the gang, who's now the assistant DA. It's supposed to be a true story (the book is published as non-fiction) but doubt has been cast on Carcaterra's veracity (his character is the fourth member, journalist Lorenzo, played by Patric). De Niro and Hoffman excel in relatively minor, but pivotal, roles. **150m/C VHS, DVD.** Brad Pitt, Jason Patric, Ron Eldard, Billy Crudup, Kevin Bacon, Robert De Niro, Dustin Hoffman, Vittorio Gassman, Minnie Driver, Terry Kinney, Brad Renfro, Jonathan Tucker, Joe Perrino, Geoff Wigdor, Bruno Kirby, Aida Turturro, Frank Medrano; *D:* Barry Levinson; *W:* Barry Levinson; *C:* Michael Ballhaus; *M:* John Williams.

Sleepers West ♂♂1/2 1941 Ah, the romance of the sleeper train! Only Shayne's (Nolan) on the job, transporting alcoholic ex-showgirl Helen (Hughes) from Denver to San Francisco so she can give her surprise testimony in a murder trial. Also aboard are Shayne's ex-girlfriend, snoopy reporter Kay Bentley (Bari), and her lawyer fiance (Douglas). Could they have anything to do with the attempts to prevent Helen from arriving safely at the station? **74m/B DVD.** Lloyd Nolan, Lynn Bari, Mary Beth Hughes, Donald Douglas, Louis Jean Heydt, Edward Brophy, Don Costello, Ben Carter; *D:* Eugene Forde; *W:* Lou Breslow, Stanley Rauh; *C:* J. Peverell Marley; *M:* Cyril Mockridge.

Sleeping Beauty ♂♂♂ 1959 (G) Classic Walt Disney version of the famous fairy tale as the princess put to sleep by the evil queen. Handsome prince Reeve comes to the rescue in this classy retelling of the Sleeping Beauty legend. Combines live action and animation. From Shelley Duvall's "Faerie Tale Theatre." **60m/C VHS, DVD.** Christopher Reeve, Bernadette Peters, Beverly D'Angelo; *D:* Jeremy Paul.

Sleeping Beauty ♂♂♂1/2 1983 Peters is the princess put to sleep by the evil queen in this live action version of the beloved fairy tale, with Welch in the title role. **92m/C VHS.** Tahnee Welch, Morgan Fairchild, Nicholas Clay, Sylvia Miles, Kenny Baker.

Sleeping Beauty ♂♂ 1989 Live action version of the beloved fairy tale, with Welch in the title role. **87m/C VHS.** David Naughton, Julie Aronson, Kevin McCarthy, Jeff Conaway, Dani Minnick, John Carl Buechler; *D:* Douglas Curtis.

The Sleeping Car ♂♂ 1990 A vindictive ghost haunts a group of people living in an old railway car. Fairly fun, fairly competent horror. **87m/C VHS.** David Naughton, Judie Aronson, Kevin McCarthy, Jeff Conaway, Dani Minnick, John Carl Buechler; *D:* Douglas Curtis.

Sleeping Car to Trieste ♂♂ 1945 Conspirators in the theft of a diplomat's diary ride the Orient Express, as a wily detective on board tries to piece together murder clues. Based on the story "Rome Express" by Clifford Grey. **95m/B**

The Sleeping Dictionary 🎬🎬½ 2002 (R) In the 1930s, young Englishman John Truscott (Dancy) is newly arrived to take up his government post in Sarawak, Malaysia (where the movie was filmed). Governor Henry Bullard (Hoskins) tells Truscott that he will only be able to educate the native Iban population by learning their language and customs, so he arranges for the beautiful half-breed Selima (Alba) to become John's tutor. But John is not suppose to fall in love with the girl. Beautiful but slow-moving and that's a body double in Alba's love scenes. 109m/C VHS, DVD, Hugh Dancy, Jessica Alba, Bob Hoskins, Brenda Blethyn, Emily Mortimer, Noah Taylor; C: Martin Fuhrer; M: Simon Boswell.

Sleeping Dogs 🎬🎬 1977 A man in near-future New Zealand finds it between a repressive government and a violent resistance movement. The first New Zealand film ever to open in the U.S., and a fine debut for director Donaldson. 107m/C VHS, DVD, NZ Sam Neill, Ian Mune, Nevar Rowe, Dona Akersten, Warren Oates; D: Roger Donaldson.

Sleeping Dogs Lie 🎬🎬 2006 (R) Should you be completely honest in any relationship? Goldthwait's answer is a firm "no" in this off-the-wall comedy. When she was a bored college student, Amy (Hamilton) got, uh, very friendly with her dog (it's implied, not shown). When her fiance John (Johnson) asks Amy to tell him her deepest, darkest secret, she does. He's repulsed. Unfortunately, this situation occurs during their meet-the-parents weekend and Amy's left to deal with the consequences. Hamilton's a sweetie and the low-budget indie is subversively engaging. 87m/C DVD, US Bryce Johnson, Melinda Page Hamilton, Colby French; D: Bob(cat) Goldthwait; W: Bob(cat) Goldthwait; C: Ian S. Takahashi; M: Jerry Brunskill.

The Sleeping Tiger 🎬🎬½ 1954 A thief breaks into the home of a psychiatrist, who captures him. In exchange for his freedom, the thief agrees to become a guinea pig for the doctor's rehabilitation theories with ultimately tragic results. Director Losey was originally compelled to release the film under a pseudonym, "Victor Hanbury," because he had been blacklisted by Hollywood during the 1950s red scare. First pairing of Losey and Bogarde, who collaborated on several later films, including "Modesty Blaise" (1966) and "Accident" (1967). 89m/B VHS, Alexis Smith, Alexander Knox, Dirk Bogarde, Hugh Griffith; D: Joseph Losey; W: Harold Buchman, Carl Foreman; M: Malcolm Arnold.

Sleeping with the Enemy 🎬🎬 1991 (R) Roberts escapes from abusive husband by taking death, flees to Iowa, falls for drama professor, and, gasp, is found by psycho husband. Occasionally chilling but oft predictable thriller based on novel by Nancy Price. 99m/C VHS, DVD, Julia Roberts, Kevin Anderson, Patrick Bergin, Elizabeth Lawrence, Kyle Secor, Claudette Nevins; D: Joseph Ruben; W: Ronald Bass; M: Jerry Goldsmith.

Sleepless 🎬🎬 2001 Argento, master of arty gore, returns in a familiar story. Retired inspector von Sydow is called back into service when a series of murders is identical to those of a spree committed by a dwarf) that the inspector solved 17 years earlier. Also becks is the only witness (Dionisi) from the earlier crimes. 117m/C VHS, DVD, IT Max von Sydow, Stefano Dionisi, Chiara Caselli; D: Dario Argento, Finlay Currie; D: Jack Paddy Carstairs.

Sleeping with Strangers 🎬🎬½ 1994 (R) Two hoteliers in a small British Columbia town find their rivalry increasing as one hotel gets a boost when a drunken rock star and his Hollywood starlet arrive with their entourage in tow. Of course, the media follows and so does the comedic hysteria. 103m/C VHS, Adrienne Shelly, Neil Duncan, Shawn Thompson, Kymberley Huffman, Scott McNeil; D: William T. Bolson; W: Joan Carr-Wiggin.

Sleepwalkers 🎬½ 1992 (R) Wher Mary and her son Charles arrive in the small town of Travis, Indiana, ugly things begin to happen. And no wonder, it seems the deadly duo are sleepwalkers—fiendish, cat-like vampire creatures who can only survive by sucking the life force out of virgins. Gory but not without some humor, particularly in Krige's portrayal of the sexy and too-loving mother. Not nearly as good as some of King's other horror classics. 91m/C VHS, DVD, Brian Krause, Madchen Amick, Alice Krige, Jim Haynie, Cindy Pickett, Lyman Ward, Ron Perlman, Stephen King, Tobe Hooper, Mark Hamill, Glenn Shadix, Joe Dante, Clive Barker, John Landis, Dan Martin; D: Mick Garris; W: Stephen King; C: Rodney Charters; M: Nicholas Pike.

Sleepwalk 🎬 1986 (R) Odd independent effort about a bored New York desk worker who is given an ancient text of Chinese fairy tales to translate, and finds they're manifesting themselves in dangerous ways in real life. 78m/C VHS, DVD, Jay Underwood, Michael (M.K.) Harris, Kathryn Morris; D: Tuli Meyer.

Sleepwalking 🎬½ 2008 (R) Down-and-out single mom Joleen (Theron) and her tween daughter Tara (Robb) are left homeless after Joleen's boyfriend is busted for drugs. The two drop in to visit Joleen's good-natured brother James (Stahl), but mom splits that night, leaving James stuck with the girl. Soon enough James loses his job and apartment, and James is taken away by Social Services. James then steals Tara back and they escape to the family farm house, still occupied by James and Joleen's villainous father (Hopper). A depressing, slow-moving indie flick appropriately titled. 101m/C DVD, Charlize Theron, Nick Stahl, AnnaSophia Robb, Dennis Hopper, Woody Harrelson, Deborah Kara Unger; D: William Maher; W: Zac Stanford; C: Juan Ruiz Anchia; M: Christopher Young.

Sleepstalker: The Sandman's Last Rites 🎬🎬 1994 (R) A serial killer known as the Sandman (Harris) is executed but returns as a shape-shifting horror who can strip the flesh off his victims with whirling sand. He haunts the nightmares of a reporter (Underwood), the only survivor of one of the killer's massacres (Moris) to learn the creature's origins and defeat him. Good special effects. 101m/C VHS, DVD, Jay Underwood, Michael Harris, Kathryn Morris; D: Turi Meyer.

Sleepover 🎬½ 2004 (PG) Light-weight teen comedy has outsider Julie (Vega) celebrating her graduation from junior high by hosting a sleepover with friends Hannah (Bocrem), Yancy (Chidress), and Farah (Taylor-Compton). Julie breaks parental rules and sneaks out (to a scavenger hunt—the winner gets to sit at "A, some scenes involving older men, bars, showers, and these girls are about 14, some scenes barely-there attire—are queasie-inducing if not downright sleazy, although the intended audience will no doubt think all the hijinks are great fun. 9mn/C VHS, DVD, Alexa Vega, Mika Boorem, Sam Huntington, Jane Lynch, Scout Taylor-Compton, Kallie Flynn Childress, Jeff Garlin, Sean Faris, Sara Paxton, Eileen April Boylan, Timothy Dowling, Brie Lawson; D: Joe Nussbaum; W: Elisa Bell; C: James L. Carter; M: Deborah Lurie.

The Sleepy Time Gal 🎬🎬 2001 Frances (Bissell), in her fifties and suffering from cancer, begins reflecting on her life and the daughter she gave up for adoption. Just about this time, her daughter, Rebecca (Plimpton) has been thinking out the her birth mother. Film follows both stories by showing parallels between Frances's youth and Rebecca's life. In a doctor's father) Bob, and ends up lonely close to TV disease-move-o-the-week territory, but impressive performance by Bisset helps it go. Interesting melodrama will do if the cable's out and you can't watch Lifetime. 94m/C VHS, DVD, US Jacqueline Bisset, Martha Plimpton, Nick Stahl, Amy Madigan, Frankie Faison, Carmen Zapata, Seymour Cassel, Peggy Gormey, Kate McGregor-Stewart; D: Christopher Munch; W: Christopher Munch; M:

The Slender Thread 🎬🎬 1965 Based on a true story. Poitier plays a college student who volunteers at a crisis center and must keep would-be suicide Bancroft on the phone until the police can find her. Filmed on location in Seattle. First film for director Pollack. 98m/C VHS, Sidney Poitier, Anne Bancroft, Telly Savalas, Steven Hill; D: Sydney Pollack; W: Stirling Silliphant; C: Loyal Griggs; M: Quincy Jones.

Sleuth 🎬🎬½ 1972 (PG) Milo (Caine), the owner of a chain of hair salons, is invited to the home of detective novelist Andrew Wyke (Olivier), who reveals that he and Wyke's wife Marguerite are lovers. He persuades Milo to assist him with a fake robbery and an insurance scam that will help them both. Of course, Shaffer's complex plot, taken from his play) reveals its every shifting, elaborate, and diabolical plots against each man, complete with red herrings, traps, and tricks. Playful, cerebral mystery thriller from top director Mankiewicz. 138m/C VHS, DVD, Laurence Olivier, Michael Caine, John Matthews, Alec Cawthorne, Teddy Martin; D: Joseph L. Mankiewicz; W: Anthony Shaffer; C:

Sleepless in Seattle 🎬🎬🎬½ 1993 (PG) Witty, sweet romantic comedy explores the differences between men and women when it comes to love and romance. When widower Sam Baldwin (Hanks) talks about his wife on a national talk show, recently engaged Annie Reed (Ryan) responds. Writer/director Ephron's humorous screenplay is brought to life by a perfectly cast ensemble, it also breathed new life into the classic weepie "An Affair to Remember," comparing it to "The Dirty Dozen" in an unforgettable scene. A movie is full of fine detail, from Sven Nykvist's camera work to the graphic layout of the opening credits to the great score. Captured millions at the boxoffice, coming in as the fourth highest grossing movie of 1993. 105m/C VHS, DVD, Tom Hanks, Meg Ryan, Bill Pullman, Ross Malinger, Rosie O'Donnell, Gaby Hoffman, Victor Garber, Rita Wilson, Barbara Garrick, Carey Lowell, Rob Reiner, Larry Atlas, David S. Ward, Nora Eshron; C: Sven Nykvist; M: Marc Shaiman.

Sleepover 🎬🎬½ 2004 (PG)

Sleepy Hollow 🎬🎬🎬 1999 (R) Gorgeous and grisly Burtonized version of Washington Irving's tale "The Legend of Sleepy Hollow." In this retelling, Ichabod Crane (Depp) is a New York constable who believes in reason and science, which won't do him much good when he's sent to investigate a series of decapitation murders. Crane is housed by wealthy Baltus Van Tassel (Gambon), whose somewhat shy daughter Katrina (Ricci) falls for the quaking Crane, who refuses to believe that a ghost is committing mayhem. He's soon confronted by the graphic evidence of his own eyes. (Heads do certainly roll). Landau has a wordless cameo as the man of victim. 105m/C VHS, DVD, Blu-ray Disc, UMD, Johnny Depp, Christina Ricci, Miranda Richardson, Michael Gambon, Christopher Walken, Casper Van Dien, Jeffrey Jones, Richard Griffiths, Ian McDiarmid, Michael Gough, Christopher Lee, Marc Pickering, Lisa Marie, Steven Waddington, Claire Skinner, Alun Armstrong, Marx Spalding, Jessica Oyelowo; Cameos: Martin Landau; D: Tim Burton; W: Andrew Kevin Walker; C: Emmanuel Lubezki; M: Danny Elfman. Oscars '99: Art Dir/Set Dec; British Acad. '99: Art Dir/Set Dec. Costume Des

Sleepy Eyes of Death: The Chinese Jade 🎬🎬🎬 1963 Master swordsman Nemuri Kyoshirou slaughters six would-be ambushers and has the sensuous enemy. Chen Sun, all for the sake of discovering the secret of the Chinese Jade. Adapted from the novel by Shibata Renzaburo. Japanese with subtitles. 82m/C VHS, JP Raizo Ichikawa, Tamao Nakamura, Jo Kenzaburo; D: Tokuzo Tanaka.

A Slight Case of Murder 🎬🎬 1938 Robinson spoofs his own tough-guy image in this screwy comedy. Remy (Robinson) and his gang made a fortune as bootleggers selling lousy beer. Now that Prohibition is over, Remy is nearly bankrupt trying to sell the same rotgut and needs cash fast. To top off the bad news, daughter Mary (Bryan) get engaged to state trooper Dick (Parker). The family heads to their summer home so Remy can think but he finds four dead gangsters and loot from a heist litering up the place while shooter Innocence (Downing) is lurking around. Oh, and company is coming. 85m/B DVD, Edward G. Robinson, Jane Bryan, Allen Jenkins, Ruth Donnelly, Willard Parker, John Litel, Edward Brophy, Harold Huber, Paul Harvey, Bobby Jordan, Margaret Hamilton, George E. Stone, Bert Hanlon, Betty Compson, John Harmon, Harry Tenbrook; D: Lloyd Bacon; W: Earl Baldwin, Joseph Schrank; C: Sic Hickox; M: Adolph Deutsch, Howard Jackson.

A Slight Case of Murder 🎬🎬½ 1999 Cable TV critic Terry Thorpe (Macy) is in a panic after accidentally killing one of his girlfriends. Instead of confessing, Terry tries to keep the truth from the cops (Arkin, Pickers Jr.) and his surviving gal pa (Huffman). Then along comes a suspicious PI (Cromwell) with a blackmail scheme. Goofy film noir that gets too complicated. Based on the novel "A Travesty" by Donald E. Westlake. 94m/C VHS, DVD, William H. Macy, Adam Arkin, Felicity Huffman, James Cromwell, James Cromwell, Paul Mazursky, Vincent Pastore; D: Steven Schachter; W: Neal Hamilton, George E. Stone, Bert Hanlon, Betty Compson, John Harmon; M: Macy, Steve?, Schachter; C: Andre Pienaar.

Slightly Honorable 🎬🎬½ 1940 A lawyer gets involved in political scandals and becomes a murder suspect. Snappy comedy-drama with good performances but too many subplots. Based on the novel "Send Another Coffin" by F. G. Presnell. 75m/B VHS, DVD, Pat O'Brien, Broderick

Slicing Doors 🎬🎬½ 1997 (R) The sliding doors are those of a London subway train. If Helen (Paltrow) makes it through before they close, her life (and loves) go one way. If she's just left on the plat-form, they go another, and the audience is let in on both options. She'll either glance or stick with cheating boyfriend Gerry (Lynch), who has been sleeping with ultrabitchy ex-girlfriend Lydia (Tripplehorn). And she will either strike up a relationship with a charming stranger (Hannah) on the train and become fabulously successful, or end up slinging hash in a diner while pregnant with her scumbag boyfriend's baby. The concept and story of the dual possibilities is pulled off well, although it is a bit too cute at times. Will you like it? Depends on if it's already been rented when you're at the video store. If it's not, be careful what you pick, because you may entirely the small stuff really does matter. 99m/C VHS, DVD, Gwyneth Paltrow, John Lynch, John Hannah, Jeanne Trippleson, Virginia McKenna, Zara Turner, Douglas McFerran, Paul Brightwell, Nina Young; D: Peter Howitt; W: Peter Howitt; C: Remi Adefarasin; M: David Hirschfelder.

Sleuth 🎬 2007 (R) You'd think that Law would've learned his lesson after trying to fill Caine's shoes in his "Alfie" remake. But no, here he remakes the 1972 pic, tackling the Caine role while Caine himself steps into Laurence Olivier's part. Working-class upstart Milo Tindle (Law) has been boffing the wife of rich mystery writer Andrew Wyke (Caine), and Andrew invites Milo to his ultra-modern manor to discuss the situation and says he'll give his wife a divorce if Milo will stage a jewel robbery so Andrew can claim the insurance. Pinter ups the homoerotic subtext and trims a lot of Anthony Shaffer's original dialogue, but it's all for naught as direct. However, Caine is as reliable as ever. 86m/C DVD, GB US Michael Caine, Jude Law; D: Kenneth Branagh; W: Harold Pinter; C: Haris Zambarloukos; M: Patrick Doyle.

Morris; M: John Addison. N.Y. Film Critics '72: Actor (Olivier).

VIDEO

Crawford, Edward Arnold, Eve Arden, Evelyn Keyes, Phyllis Brooks; **D:** Tay Garnett.

A Slightly Pregnant Man 🐾🐾 1979 (PG) Comic complications abound as a construction worker becomes the world's first pregnant man. Surprise ending saves this simple and not very exciting film. **92m/C VHS, DVD.** *FR IT* Catherine Deneuve, Marcello Mastroianni, Marisa Pavan, Micheline Presle, Claude Melki, Andre Falcon, Maurice Biraud, Alice Sapritch, Micheline Dax; **D:** Jacques Demy; **W:** Jacques Demy; **C:** Andreas Winding; **M:** Michel Legrand.

Slightly Scarlet 🐾🐾½ 1956 Small-time hood Payne carries out an assignment from boss DeCorsia to smear a law-and-order politico running for mayor. He falls in love with the candidate's secretary, tries to go straight, and ends up running the mob when DeCorsia flees town. A spiffy, low-budget noir crime drama based on the James M. Cain novel "Love's Lovely Counterfeit." **99m/C VHS, DVD.** Rhonda Fleming, Arlene Dahl, John Payne, Kent Taylor, Ted de Corsia; **D:** Allan Dwan; **W:** Robert Blees; **C:** John Alton; **M:** Louis Forbes.

Slightly Terrific 🐾½ 1944 A group of theatrical newcomers enlist the help of twin brothers (one a producer and the other a wealthy businessman) to help them put on a show. Mistaken identity and confusion follows. **65m/B VHS.** Leon Errol, Eddie Quillan, Richard Lane, Anne Rooney, Ray Malone, Betty Kean, Lorraine Krueger; **D:** Edward F. (Eddie) Cline; **W:** Stan Davis, Edward Dein; **C:** Paul Ivano.

Slime City 🐾 1989 The widow of an alchemist poisons her tenants so they will join her husband in the hereafter. Very low-budget; occasionally funny. **90m/C VHS, DVD.** Robert C. Sabin, Mary Huner, T.J. Merrick, Dick Biel; **D:** Gregory Lamberson.

The Slime People woof! 1963 Huge prehistoric monsters are awakened from long hibernation by atomic testing in Los Angeles. They take over the city, creating the fog they need to live. Thank goodness for scientist Burton, who saves the day. Filmed in a butcher shop in Los Angeles. **76m/B VHS, DVD.** Robert Hutton, Robert Burton, Susan Hart, William Boyce, Les Tremayne, John Close, Judee Morton; **D:** Robert Hutton; **W:** Vance Skarstedt; **C:** William G. Troiano.

Sling Blade 🐾🐾🐾½ 1996 (R) Mildly retarded killer Karl Childers (Thornton), making his feature directorial debut) is released from a mental hospital, where he was placed after killing his mother and her lover, after 25 years. Returning to his hometown, he befriends a boy (Black) with problems of his own. His mother is living with a mean, bullying drunkard (Yoakam, in a brilliant performance) who has no use for anyone, least of all mom's openly gay co-worker (Ritter). Thornton's excellent script moves at the slow pace of its hero, providing the superb cast plenty of opportunity to explore the rich characterization and dialogue. Filmed in Thornton's home state of Arkansas. **134m/C VHS, DVD.** Billy Bob Thornton, Dwight Yoakam, John Ritter, Lucas Black, Natalie Canerday, James Hampton, Robert Duvall, J.T. Walsh, Rick Dial, Brent Briscoe, Christy Ward, Col. Bruce Hampton, Vic Chesnutt, Mickey Jones, Jim Jarmusch, Ian Moore; **D:** Billy Bob Thornton; **W:** Billy Bob Thornton; **C:** Barry Markowitz; **M:** Daniel Lanois. Oscars '96: Adapt. Screenplay; Ind. Spirit '97: First Feature; Writers Guild '96: Adapt. Screenplay.

Slings & Arrows: Season 2 🐾🐾🐾½ 2005 Geoffrey Tennant (Gross) is the reluctant artistic director of the financially troubled New Burbage Theater Festival. This season's star-crossed production is that cursed Scottish play "MacBeth," which has Geoffrey clashing with pompous star Henry Breedlove (Wyn Davies) and still seeing his ghostly mentor, Oliver (Ouimette). Company diva Ellen (Burns) is being audited, pretentious director Darren Nichols (McKellar) is staging "Romeo and Juliet," and the festival's imexec (Feore), is being re-branded by a cut-throat ad exec (Feore). 6 episodes. **280m/C DVD.** *CA* Paul Gross, Martha Burns, Stephen Ouimette, Colm Feore, Geraint Wyn Davies, Don McKellar, Matt Fitzgerald, Mark McKinney, Susan Coyne; **D:** Peter Wellington; **W:** Mark McKinney, Susan Coyne, Bob Martin.

The Slingshot 🐾🐾🐾 1993 (R) Quirky coming-of-age tale, set in 1920s Stockholm, finds 12-year-old Roland (Salen) trying to survive childhood dilemmas. His mother (Frydman) is a Russian Jew (who sells condoms illegally) and his father (Skarsgard) is a zealous socialist, so Roland is subjected to unceasing bullying and prejudice. But the resourceful Roland doesn't let society get him down—he uses the contraband condoms in an inventive slingshot design that brings him an unwarranted amount of attention. Based on the novel by Roland Schutt. Swedish with subtitles. **102m/C VHS.** *SW* Jesper Salen, Stellan Skarsgard, Basia Frydman, Niclas Olund, Ernst-Hugo Jaregard, Jacob Leygraf; **D:** Ake Sandgren; **W:** Bjorn Isfalt, Ake Sandgren.

The Slipper and the Rose 🐾🐾½ 1976 (G) Lavish musical adaptation of the fairy tale "Cinderella." Chamberlain is a very princely prince and the lovely Craven makes a fine and spunky servant girl, whom he can't help falling in love with. Besides the lively musical numbers, viewers will also enjoy the beautiful Austrian scenery. **127m/C VHS, DVD.** *GB* Richard Chamberlain, Gemma Craven, Annette Crosbie, Edith Evans, Christopher Gable, Michael Hordern, Margaret Lockwood, Kenneth More, Julian Orchard, Lally Bowers, Sherrie Hewson, Rosalind Ayres, John Turner, Keith Skinner, Polly Williams, Norman Bird, Roy Barraclough, Peter Graves; *Cameos:* Bryan Forbes; **D:** Bryan Forbes; **W:** Bryan Forbes, Robert B. Sherman, Richard M. Sherman; **C:** Tony Imi; **M:** Robert B. Sherman, Richard M. Sherman.

A Slipping Down Life 🐾🐾½ 1999 (R) The often-quirky Taylor gives a quirky performance as meek and depressed Evie, who has a crummy amusement park job in a small town and nothing to look forward to. That is, until she begins obsessed with a struggling local musician called Drumstrings Casey (laconically played by Pearce). She carves his (last) name on her forehead, which at least gets Drumstrings attention and leads to some much-needed publicity. Evie begins to blossom under his interest, but is that all there is? You'll also be saying that about this indie. (Fans of Anne Tyler, on whose novel, her first, the film is based, may not be happy that the teenagers are now twenty-somethings). After showing at the Sundance Film Festival, litigation kept the film out of circulation for five years. **111m/C VHS, DVD.** *US* Lili Taylor, Guy Pearce, John Hawkes, Sara Rue, Irma P. Hall, Tom Bower, Shawnee Smith, Veronica Cartwright, Marshall Bell, Bruno Kirby; **D:** Toni Kalem; **W:** Toni Kalem; **C:** Michael Barrow; **M:** Peter Himmelman.

Slipping into Darkness 🐾🐾 1988 (R) Three spoiled, rich college girls are held responsible for a retarded local boy's death. Honest and overwrought. **86m/C VHS.** T.J. McFadden, Michelle Johnson, John DiAquino; **D:** Eleanor Gaver; **W:** Eleanor Gaver.

Slipstream 🐾🐾 1973 "Turgid" and "gloomy" are the words for this romantic drama set in remote Alberta. The minor plot concerns a young woman who teaches a lonely disc jockey a lesson about life and love. This film feels like a long Canadian winter. **93m/C VHS.** *CA* Luke Askew, Scott Hylands, Patti Oatman, Eli Rill; **D:** David Acomba; **W:** William Fruet; **C:** Marc Champion; **M:** Brian Ahern.

Slipstream 🐾🐾 1989 (PG-13) A sci-fi adventure set on a damaged Earthscape where people seek to escape a giant jetstream. While tracking down a bounty hunter gone bad, a futuristic cop follows his quarry into the dangerous river of wind. Ambitious "Blade Runner" clone with big names (Hamill is good) was never released theatrically in the US. **92m/C VHS, DVD.** *GB* Mark Hamill, Bill Paxton, Bob Peck, Eleanor David, Kitty Aldridge, Robbie Coltrane, Ben Kingsley, F. Murray Abraham; **D:** Steven Lisberger; **W:** Tony Kayden; **C:** Frank Tidy; **M:** Elmer Bernstein.

Slipstream 🐾 2007 (R) Hopkins is the star, writer, director, and composer of this self-indulgent, experimental fantasy. Early scenes turn out to be part of a movie script that is being rewritten by aging screenwri-

ter Felix—a production that is falling apart because its star (Slater) has suddenly died. Characters pop in and out of Felix's imagination offering suggestions and complaints while most viewers will wonder what the heck was going on in Hopkins' head. **96m/C DVD.** Anthony Hopkins, Christian Slater, John Turturro, Michael Clarke Duncan, S. Epatha Merkerson, Fionnula Flanagan, Jeffrey Tambor, Camryn Manheim, Gavin Grazer, Lana Antonova; **D:** Anthony Hopkins; **W:** Anthony Hopkins; **C:** Dante Spinotti; **M:** Anthony Hopkins.

Slither 🐾🐾🐾 1973 (PG) Caan and Boyle become wrapped up in a scheme to recover $300,000 in cash, stolen seven years previously. Along the way they pick up speed freak Kellerman, who assists them in a variety of loony ways. Frantic chase scenes are the highlight. **97m/C VHS, DVD.** James Caan, Peter Boyle, Sally Kellerman, Louise Lasser, Allen (Goorwitz) Garfield, Richard B. Shull, Alex Rocco; **D:** Howard Zieff; **W:** W.D. Richter.

Slither 🐾🐾🐾 2006 (R) Slime and disfiguration abound after a meteorite crashes to Earth, allowing a nasty little alien hitchhiker to burrow into the chest of a prominent businessman. From there, things get ugly. Literally. Picture the Elephant Man covered in snot, hungry for flesh, and stripped of his dashing good looks. Done with style, intelligence, and tongue firmly in cheek, it makes for a good of' fashioned popcorn n' mutations kind of flick. Tremendous props for ditching CGI and utilizing old-school make-up effects. These creatures pulsate and drip and shock better than any MPEG file. **95m/C DVD, HD DVD, DVD.** *US CA* Nathan Fillion, Elizabeth Banks, Gregg Henry, Michael Rooker, Brenda James, Don Thompson, Tania Saulnier, Jenna Fischer; **D:** James Gunn; **W:** James Gunn; **C:** Gregory Middleton; **M:** Tyler Bates.

Slithis woof! 1978 (PG) Slithis, the nuclear-waste creature, is the menace of Venice, California. Keep your pets (and yourself) indoors! **86m/C VHS.** Alan Blanchard, Judy Motulsky, Mello Alexandria, Dennis Lee Fait, Win Condict; **D:** Stephen Traxler; **W:** Stephen Traxler; **C:** Robert Caramico; **M:** Steve Zuckerman.

Sliver 🐾🐾½ 1993 (R) Another voyeuristic thriller starring Stone. She's Carly Norris, a lonely book editor who moves into one of Manhattan's toothpick thin buildings (the "sliver" of the title). She meets pulp novelist Jack (Berenger), whose libido is as overheated as his prose, but gets involved in a steamy affair with handsome neighbor Zeke (Baldwin), a computer whiz who also owns the building. Oh, by the way, he's installed video cameras in every unit that reveal many intimate secrets. Lots of sex and murders. Murky and underdeveloped and the ending, which was reshot, still leaves much to be desired. Lots of hype, little to recommend. **106m/C VHS, DVD.** Sharon Stone, William Baldwin, Tom Berenger, Martin Landau, Polly Walker, Colleen Camp, CCH Pounder, Nina Foch, Keene Curtis; **D:** Phillip Noyce; **W:** Joe Eszterhas; **C:** Vilmos Zsigmond; **M:** Howard Shore. MTV Movie Awards '94: Most Desirable Male (Baldwin).

Sloane woof! 1984 Typical sleazy sex and violence flick. For the record: organized crime baddies kidnap good guy Resnick's girlfriend and he seeks revenge. **95m/C VHS.** Robert Resnick, Debra Blee, Paul Aragon; **D:** Dan Rosenthal.

Slow Burn 🐾🐾 1986 An ex-reporter tries some detective work in the seamy side of Palm Springs, and becomes embroiled in the standard drug, kidnapping, murder routine. Based on the novel "Castle Burning" by Arthur Lyons. **92m/C VHS.** Eric Roberts, Beverly D'Angelo, Dan Hedaya, Dennis Lipscomb; **D:** Matthew Chapman; **W:** Matthew Chapman; **M:** Loek Dikker. CABLE

Slow Burn 🐾🐾½ 1990 (R) The Mafia and Chinese Triads are having troubles in the standard drug, kidnapping in the US. **92m/C VHS,** Anthony James, Ivan Rogers; **D:** John Eyres; **W:** Stephen Lister; **C:** Nathaniel Massey; **M:** Allan Gray.

Slow Burn 🐾🐾½ 2000 (R) Trina (Driver) is searching for a family heirloom—a box of missing diamonds—that were lost in the Mexican desert when her

grandmother died. While she hunts around, the goods have already been discovered by a couple of escaped cons (Spader and Brolin) who take Trina hostage and steal her car. But when her car is disabled, things in the desert start to steam, with Trina trying to play both men against one another so she can make off with the treasure. **97m/C VHS, DVD.** Minnie Driver, James Spader, Josh Brolin, Stuart Wilson; **D:** Christian Ford; **W:** Christian Ford, Roger Soffer; **C:** Mark Vicente; **M:** Anthony Marinelli. VIDEO

Slow Burn 🐾🐾 2005 (R) Filmed in 2003, did the festival circuit in '05, and finally saw a limited release in '07; the aging process didn't improve this confusing crime flick. DA Ford Cole (Liotta) is running for mayor but scandal threatens when ADA Nora Timmer (Blalock)—who's also Ford's occasional lover—is arrested for the death of her alleged rapist. But the case isn't so open-and-shut when Luther (LL Cool J) shows up, claiming Nora deliberately did the deed to cover up some secrets. The convoluted script just gets worse and the characters aren't interesting enough to make you care. **93m/C DVD.** *US* Ray Liotta, Jolene Blalock, LL Cool J, Mekhi Phifer, Bruce McGill, Chiwetel Ejiofor, Taye Diggs; **D:** Wayne Beach; **W:** Wayne Beach; **C:** Wally Pfister; **M:** Jeff Rona.

Slow Moves 🐾½ 1984 Slow story of slow people who meet slowly, have sluggish affair, and find tragedy eventually. **93m/C VHS.** Marshall Gaddis, Roxanne Rogers; **D:** Jon Jost; **W:** Jon Jost; **C:** Jon Jost; **M:** Jon Jost.

The Slugger's Wife 🐾½ *Neil Simon's The Slugger's Wife* 1985 (PG-13) The marriage between an Atlanta Braves outfielder and a rock singer suddenly turns sour when their individual careers force them to make some tough choices. **105m/C VHS, DVD.** Michael O'Keefe, Rebecca De Mornay, Martin Ritt, Randy Quaid, Loudon Wainwright III, Cleavant Derricks, Lynn Whitfield; **D:** Hal Ashby; **W:** Neil Simon; **C:** Caleb Deschanel.

Slugs woof! 1987 (R) A health inspector discovers that spilled toxic waste is being helpfully cleaned up by the slug population, saving Uncle Sam countless dollars. But wait! The slugs are mutating into blood-thirsty man-eaters. Is this the answer to military cut-backs? **90m/C VHS, DVD.** Michael Garfield, Kim Terry, Philip Machale, Alicia Moro, Santiago Alvarez, Emilio Linder, Concha Cuetos; **D:** (Juan) Piquer Simon; **W:** (Juan) Piquer Simon; **C:** Julio Bragado; **M:** Tim Souster.

Slumber Party '57 🐾½ 1976 (R) At a slumber party, six girls get together and exchange stories of how they lost their virginity. Lots of great music by the Platters, Big Bopper, Jerry Lee Lewis, the Crewcuts, and Paul and Paula but complete schlock otherwise. **89m/C VHS.** Noelle North, Bridget Holloman, Debra Winger, Mary Ann Appleseth, Cheryl "Rainbeaux" Smith, Janet Wood, R.L. Armstrong, Rafael Campos, Larry Gelman, Will Hutchins, Joyce Jillson, Victor Rogers, Joe E. Ross, Bill (Billy) Thurman; **C:** William A. Levey; **M:** Miles Goodman.

Slumber Party Massacre 🐾½ 1982 (R) A psychotic killer with a power drill terrorizes a high school girls' slumber party. Contrived and forced, but not always unfunny. **84m/C VHS, DVD.** Michele Michaels, Robin Stille, Andre Honore, Michael Villela, Debra Deliso, Gina Mari, Brinke Stevens, Jean Vargas, Rigg Kennedy; **D:** Amy Holden Jones; **W:** Rita Mae Brown; **C:** Stephen Posey; **M:** Ralph Jones.

Slumber Party Massacre 2 woof! 1987 Drowsy babes in lingerie are drilled to death by a perverse madman. Another disappointing sequel. **75m/C VHS, DVD.** Crystal Bernard, Kimberly McArthur, Juliette Cummins, Patrick Lowe; **D:** Deborah Brock; **W:** Deborah Brock; **C:** Thomas Callaway; **M:** Richard Ian Cox.

Slumber Party Massacre 3 woof! 1990 (R) Parents: Don't let your daughters have any slumber parties! Yes, it's a drill—for the third time. **76m/C VHS, DVD.** Keely Christian, Brittain Frye, Michael (M.K.) Harris, David Greenlie, Hope Marie Carlton, Maria Ford; **D:** Sally Mattison; **W:** Catherine Cyran; **C:** Jurgen Baum; **M:** Jaime Sheriff.

Slums of Beverly Hills ✗✗½ 1998 (R) Every few months, Murray Abromowitz (Arkin) packs up daughter Vivian (Lyonne) and sons Ricky (Marienthal) and Ben (Krumholtz) to sneak out of their current dumpy apartment (without paying the rent) and move on to the next one, always within Beverly Hills so the kids can stay in a good school. Murray takes her in. While Murray's main concern is the kids' education, Vivian is more obsessed with the size of her breasts and exploring her adolescent sexuality. Semi-autobiographical first film for Jenkins, who scripted while at the Sundance Institute, has lots of character and charm, and just enough bite. Lyonne has no trouble being the center of attention and injects comedy into the many awkward social situations that a teenage girl must endure. **91m/C VHS, DVD**, Natasha Lyonne, Alan Arkin, Marisa Tomei, Kevin Corrigan, David Krumholtz, Carl Reiner, Eli Marienthal, Jessica Walter, Rita Moreno; **D:** Tamara Jenkins; **W:** Tamara Jenkins; **C:** Tom Richmond; **M:** Rolfe Kent.

The Small Back Room ✗✗✗ 1949 A crippled WWII munitions expert leads a tormented existence and laments government bureaucracy. Powerfully presented adult storyline. **100m/B VHS**, David Farrar, Jack Hawkins, Cyril Cusack, Kathleen Byron, Anthony Bushell, Michael Gough, Robert Morley; **D:** Michael Powell, Emeric Pressburger.

Small Change ✗✗✗ L'Argent de Poche 1976 (PG) Pudgy, timid Desmouceaux and scruffy, neglected Goldman lead a whole pack of heartwarming tykes. A realistically presented adult storyline. Powerfully presented adult testament to the "great director's belief in childhood as a "state of grace." Criticized for sentimentality, "Small Change" followed Truffaut's gloomy "The Story of Adele H." Steven Spielberg suggested the English translation of "L'Argent de Poche." In French with English subtitles. **104m/C VHS, DVD, FR** Geory Desmouceaux, Philippe Goldman, Jean-Francois Stevenin, Chantal Mercier, Claudio Deluca, Frank Deluca, Richard Boffier, Sylvie Greze, Pascale Bruchon, Nicole Felix, Francis Truffaut; **D:** Francois Truffaut; **W:** Suzanne Schiffman, Francois Truffaut; **C:** Pierre William Glenn; **M:** Maurice Jaubert.

Small Faces ✗✗✗ 1995 (R) Semi-autobiographical account of three brothers growing up in a working class, gang-ridden section of Glasgow in 1968. Scottish lad Lex MacLean (Robertson) is at the crucial age of 13 and caught between two events, forcing him to ally with both brothers. Writer/director MacKinnon makes sure even the most tense situations are offset with dark humor, and stages the violent scenes beautifully. Garnering comparisons with other Scottish youth fables like "Trainspotting," film follows somewhat the same storytelling formula, but is much more low-key. Character and plot are giving an equal attention and film greatly benefits from an outstanding performance by Robertson. CNT Violence and language. **108m/C VHS, GB** Iain Robertson, Clare Higgins, Ian McElhinney, Kevin McKidd, Joseph McFadden, J.S. Duffy, Laura Fraser, Garry Sweeney, Mark McCrmochie, Steven Simpson, David Walker; **D:** Gilles Mackinnon; **W:** Gilles Mackinnon, Billy Mackinnon; **C:** John de Borman; **M:** John Keane.

A Small Circle of Friends ✗✗½ 1980 (R) Three Harvard students struggle with their shifting relationships during their college years in the 1960s. **112m/C VHS, DVD**, Brad Davis, Jameson Parker, Karen Allen, Shelley Long; **D:** Rob Cohen.

Small Soldiers ✗✗½ 1998 (PG-13) Why do kids today get all the really cool toys? G.I. Joe with the Kung Fu Grip never held any small Ohio towns under siege, and his fingers eventually fell off. But thanks to former defense supplier turned toy maker Globotech and its chairman Gil Mars (Leary), the residents of Winslow Corners receive a shipment of action figures called the Commando Elite. These toys are designed to interact with their owners. And do they ever—they take on a life of their own and wage war, thanks to being mistakenly implanted with military intelligence chips. Led by Chip Hazard (voice of Jones), these commandoes take on the previously quiet town in their quest to eradicate their toy rivals, the peaceful alien Gorgonites. Led by the gentle Archer (voice of Langella), the Gorgonites enlist the help of teens Alan (Smith) and Christy (Dunst) to battle this miniature menace. Combo of computer animation, Stan Winston's animatronic puppets, and live-action bring the toys to life. **110m/C VHS, DVD**, Gregory Smith, Kirsten Dunst, Phil Hartman, Ann Magnuson, Jay Mohr, Denis Leary, Kevin Dunn, Wendy Schaal, Dick Miller, David Cross, Robert Picardo; **D:** Joe Dante; **W:** Gavin Scott, Adam Rifkin, Ted Elliott, Terry Rossio; **C:** Jamie Anderson; **M:** Jerry Goldsmith; **V:** Tommy Lee Jones, Frank Langella, Ernest Borgnine, Jim Brown, Bruce Dern, George Kennedy, Clint Walker, Christopher Guest, Michael McKean, Harry Shearer, Sarah Michelle Gellar, Christina Ricci.

Small Time ✗✗ 1991 Chronicles the downfall of a young small-time Harlem thief. Vince knows nothing but the streets and peer pressure, indifference, and police abuse has put him inexorably to a fatal crime. Near documentary style only heightens the tensions. **33m/B VHS**, Richard Barboza, Carolyn Hinebrew, Keith Allen, Scott Ferguson, Jane Williams, Carolyn Smith; **D:** Norman Loftis; **W:** Norman Loftis; **M:** Arnold Bieber.

Small Time Crooks ✗✗✗ 2000 (PG) Ex-con dishwasher Allen and his manicurist wife Ullman decide to become rich by robbing a New York City bank. Problem is, they team up with three bumblers (Lovitz, Rapaport, Darrow) to pull off the heist. As a result of the mishaps, the couple accidentally gains fame and fortune only to find it doesn't suit them at all. Grant is a well-bred snob trying to teach the lower classes some couth. Ullman as usual, is endearing, while Allen is hard to

Small Hotel ✗✗ 1957 After discovering that he is to be replaced as head-waiter by a young woman, Harker plots to turn to his comedy stylings of old, the comedy in 'Small Time Crooks", actually just seems old and tired. Harker plots to save his job through espionage, blackmail and cajolery. Average comedy, adapted from a popular British stage play as a star vehicle for Harker. **59m/B VHS**, Gordon Harker, Marie Lohr, John Loder, Irene Handl, Janet Munro, Billie Whitelaw, Francis Matthews, Dora Bryan; **D:** David MacDonald.

A Small Killing ✗✗ 1981 An undercover cop and a college professor pose as a wino and a lady, when trying to put the tabs on a druglord. Made for TV mystery/romance based on "The Rag Bag Clan" by Richard Barth. **100m/C VHS**, Ed Asner, Jean Simmons, Sylvia Sidney, Andrew Prine, J. Pat O'Malley, Anne Ramsey; **D:** Steven Hilliard Stern. **TV**

Small Sacrifices ✗✗½ 1989 The true story of Diane Downs, an Oregon woman who may have murdered her own three children in 1983. Fine performance from Fawcett, who seems to like made for TV tales of true-life domestic violence as an antidote to her earlier ditzy persona as a Charlie's Angel. Gripping, with a superb script. **159m/C VHS**, Farrah Fawcett, Ryan O'Neal, John Shea, Emily Perkins, Gordon Clapp; **D:** David Greene; **W:** Joyce Eliason. **TV**

Small Kill ✗½ 1993 (R) Burghoff leaves his lovable MASH character far behind, testing his acting skills as a psycho who disguises himself as a female fortune teller to rob his victims of their life savings so he can become head druglord of his town (what a goal). Two cops try to stop him/her. **86m/C VHS**, Gary Burghoff, Rebecca Ferratti, Donnie Kehr, Jason Miller, Fred Carpenter; **D:** Robert M. Fresco; **W:** Fred Carpenter.

Small Town Girl ✗✗½ 1937 One Horse Town 1953 Typical romantic musical of the era, as a city slicker picked up for speeding in a hick town is pursued by the sheriff's daughter. Several Busby Berkeley blockbuster musical numbers are shoehorned incongruously into the rural doings. ♫Take Me To Broadway; I've Got To Hear That Beat; My Flaming Heart; Fine, Fine, Fine; The Fellow I'd Follow; Lullaby of the Lord; Small Towns Are Smile Towns; My Gaucho. **93m/C VHS**, Jane Powell, Farley Granger, Bobby Van, Ann Miller, Billie Burke, Robert Keith, S.Z. Sakall, Fay Wray, Nat King Cole, Chill Wills; **D:** Leslie Kardos; **M:** Andre Previn.

A Small Town in Texas ✗✗ 1976 (PG) An ex-con returns home looking for the sheriff who framed him on a drug charge, and who has stolen his woman. Not-too-violent, predictable revenge flick. **96m/C VHS**, Timothy Bottoms, Susan George, Bo Hopkins; **D:** Jack Starrett; **W:** William W. Norton Sr.; **M:** Charles Bernstein.

Small Vices: A Spenser Mystery ✗✗½ 1999 Robert B. Parker's erudite Boston sleuth, Spenser (Mantegna) makes a return appearance along with his associate, Hawk (Mahmud-Bey), and lover Susan Silverman (Harden). This time Spenser is asked to check out a possible miscarriage of justice—did a streetwise young black man actually rape and murder a white suburban college student. But as things turn increasingly dangerous, it's clear someone doesn't want Spenser snooping around. **100m/C VHS**, Joe Mantegna, Marcia Gay Harden, Shiek Mahmud-Bey, Eugene Lipinski, Wood Harris; **Cameos:** Robert B. Parker; **D:** Robert Markowitz; **W:** Robert B. Parker; **C:** Ron Garcia; **M:** David Shire. **CABLE**

The Smallest Show on Earth ✗✗½ 1948 A melodramatic tale about the son of an executed murderer who becomes the object of derision in the small town where he lives. One tormentor finally attacks him, and the young man must make a split-second decision that may affect his own mortality. **90m/B VHS**, Dane Clark, Gail Russell, Ethel Barrymore, Allyn Joslyn, Harry (Henry) Morgan, Lloyd Bridges, Selena Royle, Rex Ingram, Harry Carey Jr.; **D:** Frank Borzage.

The Smallest Show on Earth ✗✗✗ Big Time Operators 1957 A couple inherit not only an old movie house, but the three people who work there as well. Very funny and charming, with a wonderful cast. Sellers is delightful as the soused projectionist. **81m/B VHS, DVD, GB** Bill Travers, Virginia McKenna, Margaret Rutherford, Peter Sellers, Bernard Miles, Leslie Phillips, Stringer Davis, Francis De Wolff, Sidney James, June Cunningham; **D:** Basil Dearden; **W:** William Rose, John Eldridge; **C:** Douglas Slocombe.

Smalltime ✗½ 1990 (R) Mobster, The Dutchman, needs to deliver a bag full of drugs to a desolate ranch and then wait for someone to pick up the goods and pay him. He decides to pass the job along to lower-level goon, Ben, who figures this two friends should be in on the caper. They get bored waiting and decide to call some girls to have a party, during which time the drugs get used up. Now, they've got nothing to switch for the money. This is going to make a lot of people unhappy. **96m/C VHS, DVD**, Jeff Fahey, Glenn Plummer, Rae Dawn

Smart Alecks ✗✗½ 1942 The Bowery Boys get involved with gangsters when Jordan helps capture a crook. The usual wise-cracking from Hall and Gorcey helps keep things moving. **68m/B VHS, DVD**, Leo Gorcey, Huntz Hall, Gabriel Dell, Gale Storm, Roger Pryor Jr., Walter Wolf King, Herbert Rawlinson, Joe (Joseph) Kirk, Marie Windsor; **D:** Wallace Fox.

Smart House ✗✗ 200C Ben Ives with his widowed dad and his younger sister in a typical suburban house. But Ben likes to enter contests and actually wins a "Smart House," a house designed to take care of all those pesky daily choices thanks to a computer, for his family. Ben's dad persuades his dad to move in. But Ben's dad fails for the house's creator and the house itself gets jealous and decides to keep the family trapped inside. Although the premise has been used for horror movies, this one is strictly a comedy. **82m/C VHS, DVD**, Ryan Merriman, Kevin Kilner, Jessica Steen, Susan Haskell; **D:** LeVar Burton; **W:** Katey Segal. **CABLE**

Smart Money ✗✗½ 1931 Nick (Robinson) is a small-town barber who holds a poker game in his back room, helped by his assistant, Jack (Cagney). A consistent winner, Nick is encouraged to try his luck in a big-city game and loses everything, only to realize he's been set-up. So Nick sends for Jack and they work out their own scheme to get back at the crooked gamblers. The only time Robinson and Cagney were paired up onscreen. **90m/B VHS, DVD**, Edward G. Robinson, James Cagney, Boris Karloff, Noel Francis, Ben Taggart, Ralf Harolde, Evalyn Knapp; **D:** Alfred E. Green; **W:** Kubec Glasmon, Lucien Hubbard, John Bright, Joseph Jackson; **C:** Robert B. Kurle.

Smart Money ✗✗½ 1986 A wrongly jailed man enlists the help of his oddball pals to get revenge on the real thief who committed the computer fraud that put him behind bars. They get even while padding their pockets. **88m/C VHS, DVD**, Spencer Leigh, Alexandra Pigg, Ken Campbell; **D:** Bernard Rose; **W:** Matthew Jacobs.

Smart People ✗✗ 2008 (R) Who don't act like it and behave badly. Supercilious Lawrence Wetherhold (Quaid) is a widowed English literature professor at Carnegie Mellon who's bored and contemptuous of his students. His son James (Holmes) avoids the drama by living in the dorm and too closely in dad's footsteps. An accident that forbids Lawrence from driving brings doctor (and ex-student) Janet Hartigan (Parker) into Lawrence's life as well as his ne'er-co-well adoptive brother Chuck (Church), who moves in as temporary chauffeur. Church has the most fun with his stoner free spirit while everyone else does well enough by their stereotypes, but the plot falling in love. Adapted from the play "Nancy's Private Affair" by Myron C. Fagan. **95m/C DVD, US** Dennis Quaid, Sarah Jessica Parker, Thomas Haden Church, Ellen Page, Ashton Holmes; **D:** Noam Murro; **W:** Mark Jude Poirier; **C:** Toby Irwin.

Smart Woman ✗✗ 1931 If she's so smart how come she's married to such a louse? Nancy Gibson (Astor) is fed up with being blamed for womanizing hubby Don's (Ames) infidelities so she decides to start a flirtation with Guy (Halliday only to find herself falling in love. Adapted from the play "Nancy's Private Affair" by Myron C. Fagan. **68m/B VHS**, Mary Astor, Robert Ames, John Halliday, Edward Everett Horton, Noel Francis, Ruth Weston, Gladys Gale; **D:** Gregory La Cava; **W:** Salisbury Field; **C:** Nicholas Musuraca.

Smash Palace ✗✗✗ 1982 A compelling drama of a marriage jeopardized by his obsession with building a race car and her need for love and affection. Melodramatic, but worth watching. Rob Ames as their young daughter is wonderful. **100m/C VHS, DVD, NZ** Bruno Lawrence, Anna Maria Monticelli, Greer Robson, Keith Aberdein; **D:** Roger Donaldson; **W:** Bruno Lawrence.

Smash-Up: The Story of a Woman ✗✗ 1947 A Woman Destroyed 1947 A famous nightclub singer gives up her career for marriage and a family, only to

Chong, Daren McGavin; **D:** Jeff Reiner; **W:** Jeff Reiner, Pat Cupo; **C:** Felixs Parnell; **M:** Vinnie Golia.

Smash-Up

become depressed when her husband's career soars. She turns to alcohol and her life falls apart. When her husband sues for divorce and custody of their child, she fights to recover from alcoholism. Hayward's first major role. **103m/B VHS, DVD.** Susan Hayward, Lee Bowman, Marsha Hunt, Eddie Albert; **D:** Stuart Heisler; **W:** John Howard Lawson.

Smashing the Rackets 🦴🦴½ 1938 (R) FBI agent Jim Conway (Morris) is shunted into a job in the DA's office. He meets playgirl debutante Letty Lane (Johnson) and falls for her more sedate sister Susan (Mercer). Since Letty has a boyfriend (Cabot) who's involved with the mob, Jim decides to use his new position to go after racketeers. Inspired by the career of New York district attorney Thomas E. Dewey. **69m/B VHS.** Chester Morris, Frances Mercer, Rita Johnson, Bruce Cabot, Ben Welden; **D:** Lew Landers; **W:** Lionel Houser; **C:** Nicholas Musuraca.

Smashing Time woof! 1967 Abysmal British comedy was never widely released on this side of the Atlantic and it's easy to see why. The film follows two small-town girls—Brenda (Tushingham), who's mousy and bony, and Yvonne (Redgrave), who's loud and pushy—who come to London at the swinging '60s. Unfortunately, they are two of the most unattractive comic heroines ever to hit the screen, and apparently that's a choice the filmmakers made deliberately. Moreover, their accents are difficult to understand and their voices could blister an elephant's hide. **96m/C VHS, DVD.** *GB* Rita Tushingham, Lynn Redgrave, Michael York, Anna Quayle, Irene Handl, Ian Carmichael; **D:** Desmond Davis; **W:** George Melly; **C:** Manny Wynn; **M:** John Addison.

Smile 🦴🦴🦴 1975 (PG) Barbed, merciless send-up of small-town America focusing on a group of naive California girls who compete for "Young American Miss" crown amid rampant commercialism, exploitation and pure middle-class idiocy. Hilarious neglected '70s-style satire. Early role for Griffith. **113m/C VHS, DVD.** Bruce Dern, Barbara Feldon, Michael Kidd, Nicholas Pryor, Geoffrey Lewis, Colleen Camp, Joan Prather, Annette O'Toole, Melanie Griffith, Denise Nickerson, Titos Vandis; **D:** Michael Ritchie; **W:** Jerry Belson; **C:** Conrad L. Hall; **M:** Daniel Osborn, Leroy Holmes.

Smile, Jenny, You're Dead 🦴½ 1974 Janssen discovers that close friend's son-in-law has been murdered, and falls in love with the daughter, the main suspect. Pilot for Janssen's "Harry-O" detective series. **100m/C VHS.** David Janssen, John Anderson, Howard da Silva, Martin Gabel, Clu Gulager, Zalman King, Jodie Foster, Barbara Leigh; **D:** Jerry Thorpe. **TV**

A Smile Like Yours 🦴½ 1996 (R) Too-cute yuppie couple Danny and Jennifer (Kinnear and Holly) decide to start a family, only to discover that Danny's "boys" can't swim. Many formulaic and predictable gags about masturbation and the possibility of infidelity ensue. Unfortunately, laughs do not. Kinnear comes off as amiable enough, while Holly turns in an aggravating, over-the-top performance. Thomas and Cusack, as the couple's best friends, fare better than anyone, with the possible exception of scene-stealer Meullerleile as the cranky clinic nurse. Writer/director Samples is the former head of now-defunct Rysher Entertainment (flick's producing company). Coincidence? We think not. **99m/C VHS, DVD.** Greg Kinnear, Lauren Holly, Jill(ian) Hennessey, Christopher McDonald, Joan Cusack, Jay Thomas, Donald Moffat, France Nuyen, Marianne Muellerleile; **Cameos:** Shirley MacLaine; **D:** Keith Samples; **W:** Keith Samples, Kevin Meyer; **C:** Richard Bowen; **M:** William Ross.

Smiles of a Summer Night 🦴🦴🦴½ 1955 *Sommarnattens Leende* The best known of Bergman's rare comedies; sharp satire about eight Swedish aristocrats who become romantically and comically intertwined over a single weekend. Inspired Sondheim's successful Broadway musical "A Little Night Music," and Woody Allen's "A Midsummer Night's Sex Comedy." In Swedish with English subtitles. **110m/B VHS, DVD.** *SW* Gunnar Bjornstrand, Harriet Andersson, Ulla Jacobsson, Eva Dahlbeck, Jarl Kulle, Margit Carlquist; **D:** Ingmar Bergman; **W:** Ingmar Bergman.

Smiley Face 🦴🦴 2007 (R) Lame reefer comedy. Wannabe actress and chronic stoner Jane (Faris) starts off her day eating some pot-laced cupcakes baked by her roommate and then runs mundane errands like going to an audition, visiting her dentist, and paying off her drug dealer while experiencing life in a very high and happy place. However, it's not a place a viewer will care to experience with her unless they're in the same drug-induced state. **88m/C DVD.** Anna Faris, John Krasinski, Danny Masterson, Adam Brody, Ben Falcone; **D:** Gregg Araki; **W:** Dylan Haggerty; **C:** Shawn Kim; **M:** David Kitay.

Smiley's People 🦴🦴🦴 1982 George Smiley (Guinness) is once again retired from British Intelligence when he learns that the murder of a former colleague is linked to their Soviet spy rival, Karla (Stewart). Smiley doggedly pursues his information, despite opposition, while Karla seeks to cover his tracks. Based on the novel by John Le Carre; the sequel to "Tinker, Tailor, Soldier, Spy." **324m/C VHS, DVD.** *GB* Alec Guinness, Barry Foster, Patrick Stewart, Bernard Hepton, Eileen Atkins, Anthony Bate, Michael Byrne, Sian Phillips, Beryl Reid, Michael Gough, Curt Jurgens, Rosalie Crutchley; **D:** Simon Langton; **W:** John Hopkins; **C:** Kenneth Macmillan; **M:** Patrick Gowers. **TV**

Smilin' Through 🦴🦴🦴 1933 First sound version of this melodrama/romance which Franklin had directed as a silent in 1922. Shearer is set to marry Howard when jealous rival March shows up armed at the wedding and accidentally kills the bride. March escapes and Howard spends his years as a recluse until his young niece, the image of his dead fiance (naturally, since she's also played by Shearer) arrives to live with him. She meets a young man who turns out to be March's son (played again by March) and they fall in love. Pure sentiment done with high gloss. Remade in 1941. **97m/B VHS.** Norma Shearer, Fredric March, Leslie Howard, O.P. Heggie, Ralph Forbes, Beryl Mercer, Margaret Seddon; **D:** Sidney Franklin; **C:** Lee Garmes.

Smilin' Through 🦴🦴🦴 1941 Third filming, second with sound, first in color, of a popular melodrama. An embittered man whose wife was murdered on their wedding day raises an orphaned niece, only to have her fall in love with the son of her aunt's murderer. Songs include title tune and "A Little Love, a Little Kiss." **101m/C VHS.** Jeanette MacDonald, Brian Aherne, Gene Raymond, Ian Hunter, Frances Robinson; **D:** Frank Borzage.

Smiling Fish & Goat on Fire 🦴🦴½ 1999 (R) Title refers to the childhood nicknames that Chris Remi (Derick Martini) and his brother Tony (Steven Martini) were given by their Native American/Italian grandma. Accountant Chris and aspiring actor Tony share a house in L.A. and have trouble with women. Their current relationships are falling apart, but new ones are looming, and the confused bros get some sage advice from their elderly friend, Clive (Henderson). Low-budget, wry slice-of-life. **90m/C VHS, DVD.** Steven Martini, Derick Martini, Bill Henderson, Christa Miller, Amy Hathaway, Rosemarie Addeo, Heather Jae Marie, Nicole Rae, Wesley Thompson; **D:** Kevin Jordan; **W:** Kevin Jordan, Steven Martini, Derick Martini; **C:** Fred Iannone; **M:** Chris Horvath.

The Smiling Lieutenant 🦴🦴🦴½ 1931 Flirting at the wrong time/wrong place can get a guy into big trouble. Niki (Chevalier), an officer with Vienna's Royal Guards, is romancing violinist Franzi (Colbert). During a visit by King Adolf (Barbier), his plain daughter Princess Anna (Hopkins) mistakes a smile meant for Franzi to mean that Niki is interested in her. Duty-bound, Niki is forced into a royal marriage. So the worldly Franzi decides to help Anna win her reluctant new hubby's love by turning her into a knockout. **89m/B DVD.** Maurice Chevalier, Claudette Colbert, Miriam Hopkins, George Barbier, Charlie Ruggles, Robert Strange, Hugh O'Connell; **D:** Ernst Lubitsch; **W:** Ernst Lubitsch, Ernest Vajda, Samson Raphaelson; **C:** George J. Folsey; **M:** Oscar Straus.

Smilla's Sense of Snow 🦴🦴 1996 (R) Thriller starts off well but fails to sustain the suspense of the Peter Hoeg mystery on which it is based. Solitary scientist Smilla Jasperson (Ormond) is a half-Inuit, half-American (Danish in the book) resident of Copenhagen who's an expert on snow and ice. Born and raised in Greenland, Smilla is drawn back to her home when the body of six-year-old Isaiah (Miano), whom she's grudgingly befriended, is discovered at their apartment building. Smilla believes the boy was murdered and when she begins investigating it leads to the Greenland mining company where Isaiah's late father worked and which is run by the suspicious Tork (Harris). Location cinematography is particularly impressive. **121m/C VHS, DVD.** *GE DK SW* Julia Ormond, Gabriel Byrne, Richard Harris, Vanessa Redgrave, Robert Loggia, Jim Broadbent, Mario Adorf, Bob Peck, Tom Wilkinson, Peter Capaldi, Emma Croft, Clipper Miano; **D:** Bille August; **W:** Ann Biderman; **C:** Jorgen Persson; **M:** Hans Zimmer, Harry Gregson-Williams.

Smith! 🦴🦴½ 1969 (G) Naive but well intentioned look at present-day treatment of Native Americans. Rancher Ford becomes embroiled in the trial of murder suspect Ramirez. Based on Paul St. Pierre's novel "Breaking Smith's Quarter Horse." **101m/C VHS.** Glenn Ford, Frank Ramirez, Keenan Wynn; **D:** Michael O'Herlihy; **W:** Louis Pelletier; **M:** Robert F. Brunner.

Smithereens 🦴🦴🦴 1982 (R) Working-class girl leaves home for New York's music scene. Rugged, hip character study. Director Seidleman's first feature. **90m/C VHS, DVD.** Susan Berman, Brad Rijn, Richard Hell, Christopher Noth; **D:** Susan Seidelman; **W:** Ron Nyswaner, Peter Askin.

Smoke 🦴🦴½ 1970 A young boy nurses a lost German sheperd back to health with the help of his new stepfather, whom he learns to trust. Then he runs away with the dog when the original owners show up. Disney fare starring Opie/Richie (and later successful director) Howard. **89m/C VHS.** Earl Holliman, Ron Howard, Andy Devine, Jacqueline Scott, Shug Fisher, Pamelyn Ferdin, Kelly Thordsen; **D:** Vincent McEveety; **C:** William E. Snyder; **M:** Robert F. Brunner.

Smoke 🦴🦴 1993 Three days in the life of Michael, as he travels between fantasy and reality, past and present, searching for love with the perfect older man. **90m/C VHS.** Nick Discenza, Barbara Andrews, Mark D'Aria; **D:** Mark D'Aria; **M:** Arnold Bieber.

Smoke 🦴🦴🦴 1995 (R) Brooklyn slice of life centers around the local cigar store run by Auggie Wren (Keitel). An ensemble piece, divided into five chapters, which includes such characters as down-on-his luck novelist Paul (Hurt), troubled black teenager Rashid (Perrineau Jr.), Augie's ex-wife Ruby (Channing) and supposed daughter (Judd), and many more (some of whom get lost in the shuffle). Wonderfully acted but the stories tend to disappear in a wisp of smoke. Based on a story by Auster. Wang and Auster also made an impromptu companion film "Blue in the Face." **112m/C VHS, DVD.** Harvey Keitel, William Hurt, Stockard Channing, Forest Whitaker, Harold Perrineau Jr., Ashley Judd, Mary Ward, Victor Argo, Jared Harris, Giancarlo Esposito, Mel Gorham, Stephen Gevedon, Erica Gimpel, Malik Yoba, Jose Zuniga, RuPaul Charles; **D:** Wayne Wang; **W:** Paul Auster; **C:** Adam Holender; **M:** Rachel Portman.

Smoke in the Wind 🦴½ 1975 (PG) Subpar western about men accused of complicity with the Union in postbellum Arkansas. Minor role for Brennan was his last; also director Kane's last film. **93m/C VHS.** John Ashley, Walter Brennan, John Russell, Myron Healey; **D:** Joseph Kane.

Smoke Signals 🦴🦴 1998 (PG-13) Serious themes are treated in a deceptively simple and humorous manner, based on stories from Alexie's book "The Lone Ranger and Tonto Fistfight in Heaven." Geeky, orphaned Thomas (Adams) lives on the Coeur d'Alene reservation in Idaho where he's reluctantly looked after by stoic Victor (Beach), whose long-gone father Arnold (Farmer) saved Thomas from the fire that killed his parents. When Victor learns of Arnold's death in Phoenix, Thomas says he'll pay the expenses of the trip if he can accompany Victor. The young men reach an understanding during their travels, while Victor struggles to deal with his complicated feelings about his father and the past. **89m/C VHS, DVD.** Adam Beach, Evan Adams, Irene Bedard, Gary Farmer, Tantoo Cardinal, Michelle St. John, Robert Miano, Molly Cheek, Elaine Miles, Michael Greyeyes, Cody Lightning, Cynthia Geary, Simon Baker; **D:** Chris Eyre; **W:** Sherman Alexie; **C:** Brian Capener; **M:** B.C. Smith. Ind. Spirit '99: Debut Perf. (Adams). Sundance '98: Aud. Award, Filmmakers Trophy.

The Smokers 🦴 2000 (R) Bleech—this would-be revenge comedy is guaranteed to leave a bad taste in your mouth with its unappealing characters and storyline. Boarding school friends Jefferson (Swain), Karen (Phillips), and Lisa (Pratt) are sick of boys treating them wrong. So with a stolen gun, they are determined to have the miscreants make amends. **97m/C VHS, DVD.** Dominique Swain, Keri Lynn Pratt, Busy Philipps, Oliver Hudson, Ryan Browning, Joel West, Thora Birch, Nicholas M. Loeb; **D:** Christina Peters; **W:** Christina Peters, Kenny Golde; **C:** J.B. Letchinger; **M:** Lawrence Gingold.

Smokescreen 🦴🦴½ 1990 (R) A young ad exec meets the girl of his dreams, and finds himself working for her gangster boyfriend. Competently made and acted, but phoney ending wrecks it. **91m/C VHS.** Kim Cattrall, Dean Stockwell, Matt Craven, Kim Coates, Brian George, Michael Hogan; **D:** Martin Lavut.

Smokey and the Bandit 🦴🦴½ 1977 (PG) The first and best of the series about bootlegger Reynolds is one long car chase. Reynolds makes a wager that he can deliver a truckload of Coors beer—once unavailable east of Texas—to Atlanta from Texas in 28 hours. Gleason is a riot as the "smokey" who tries to stop him. Field is the hitchhiker Reynolds picks up along the way. Great stunts; director Needham was a top stunt man. **96m/C VHS, DVD.** Susan McIver, John Schneider, Hank Worden, Sonny Shroyer, Burt Reynolds, Sally Field, Jackie Gleason, Jerry Reed, Mike Henry, Paul Williams, Pat McCormick; **D:** Hal Needham; **W:** Hal Needham, Charles Shyer; **C:** Bobby Byrne; **M:** Bill Justis, Jerry Reed.

Smokey and the Bandit 2 🦴 1980 (PG) *Smokey and the Bandit Ride Again* Pathetic sequel to "Smokey and the Bandit" proved a boxoffice winner, grossing $40 million. The Bandit is hired to transport a pregnant elephant from Miami to the Republican convention in Dallas. Sheriff Buford T. Justice and family are in hot pursuit. **101m/C VHS, DVD.** David Huddleston, Burt Reynolds, Sally Field, Jackie Gleason, Jerry Reed, Mike Henry, Dom DeLuise, Pat McCormick, Paul Williams, John Anderson, Brenda Lee, Mel Tillis; **Cameos:** Joe "Mean Joe" Greene, Don Williams, Terry Bradshaw; **D:** Hal Needham; **W:** Jerry Belson, Michael Kane, Brock Yates; **C:** Michael C. Butler.

Smokey and the Bandit, Part 3 🦴 1983 (PG) You thought the second one was bad? Another mega car chase, this time sans Reynolds and director Needham. **88m/C VHS, DVD.** Jackie Gleason, Jerry Reed, Paul Williams, Pat McCormick, Mike Henry, Colleen Camp; **Cameos:** Burt Reynolds; **D:** Dick Lowry; **W:** Stuart Birnbaum, David Dashev.

Smokey & the Hotwire Gang ⭐½ 1979 A convoy of truckers try to track down a beautiful woman driving a stolen car. **85m/C VHS.** *D:* Anthony Cardoza. *C:* Gary Cardoza. *W:* Harry Hope, Dan Seeger. *C:* Dan Seeger. Stanley Livingston, Tony Lorea, Alvy Moore, George Barris. Cardoza.

Smokey & the Judge ⭐ 1980 (PG) Police officer has his hands full with a trio of lovely ladies. **90m/C VHS.** Gene Price, Wayne Preston, Juanita Curiel, Rory Calhoun. *D:* Mikhail Suslov; *M:* Bruce Stewart.

Smokey Bites the Dust ⭐ 1981 (PG) Car-smashing gag-fest about a sheriff's daughter kidnapped by her smitten beau. Near-plotless and literally unoriginal: lifted footage from several other Corman-produced flicks, a technique that can best be called garbage picking. **87m/C VHS.** Janet (Johnson) Julian, Jimmy (James Vincent) McNichol, Patrick Campbell, Karl Lizer, John Blyth) Barrymore Jr., Kedrick Wolfe, Walter Barnes. *D:* Charles B. Griffith. *W:* Max Apple; *C:* Gary Graver; *M:* Bent Myggen.

Smokey Smith ⭐½ 1936 Ubiquitous Hayes and steely Steele hunt down the slayers of an elderly couple. Ordinary oater directed by Steele's father, Bradbury. **59m/B VHS, DVD.** Bob Steele, George "Gabby" Hayes. *D:* Robert North Bradbury.

Smokin' Aces ⭐⭐ 2007 (R) Exhaustingly convoluted guy flick from Carnahan has sleazy nightclub magician Buddy "Aces" Israel (Piven) willing to turn FBI snitch on the Nevada mob. Naturally, the head gangster puts out a hit, attracting all sorts of other violent lowlifes, while the maybe one too many). Like its location, it's stylish but empty. **109m/C VHS, DVD, HD DVD, US** Jeremy Piven, Ben Affleck, Andy Garcia, Ray Liotta, Alicia Keys, Ryan Reynolds, Peter Berg, Taraji P. Henson, Martin Henderson, Chris Pine, Jason Bateman, Joseph Ruskin, Davenia McFadden, Nestor Carbonell, Tommy Flanagan, Alex Rocco, Vladimir Kulich, David Proval, Joel Edgerton, Matthew Fox, Common, Mike Falkow, Kevin Durand, Maury Sterling, Christopher Carlo. *D:* Joe Carnahan; *C:* Mauro Fiore; *M:* Clint Mansell.

Smoking/No Smoking ⭐⭐ 1994 Two linked films director Resnais adapted from writer Alan Ayckbourn's eight-play cycle "Intimate Exchanges" (although the screenwriters have only used six stories). Azema and Arditti plays nine characters in various tableaux on marriage and affairs set at a Yorkshire school. The opening sequence of each episode provides the title tie-in, as faculty wife Celia goes onto the terrace, finds a pack of cigarettes, and decides whether or not to light up. A studio set provides all the frankly fake backdrops. Very slight and very long. French with subtitles. **285m/C VHS, FR** Sabine Azema, Pierre Arditti; *D:* Alain Resnais; *W:* Jean-Pierre Bacri, Agnes Jaoui; Cesar '94: Actor (Arditti), Art Dir/Set Dec, Director (Resnais), Film, Writing.

A Smoky Mountain Christmas ⭐⭐ 1986. Dolly, gets away from it all in a secluded cabin that has been appropriated by a gang of orphans, and sings a half dozen songs. Innocuous seasonal country fun. Winkler's TV directing debut. **94m/C VHS.** Dolly Parton, Bo Hopkins, Dan Hedaya, Gennie James, David Ackroyd, Rene Auberjonois, John Ritter, Anita Morris, Lee Majors; *D:* Henry Winkler. **TV**

Smooth Talk ⭐⭐⭐ 1985 (PG-13) An innocent, flirtatious teenager catches the eye of a shady character, played by Williams. Disturbing and thought-provoking film that caused some controversy when it opened. Dern gives a brilliant performance as the shy, sheltered girl. Based on the Joyce Carol Oates story "Where Are You Going, Where Have You Been?" Made for PBS' "American Playhouse" series. **92m/C VHS, DVD.** Laura Dern, Treat Williams, Mary Kay Place, Levon Helm, William Ragsdale, Margaret Welsh, Sarah Inglis; *D:* Joyce Chopra; *W:* Tom Cole; *C:* James Glennon. Sundance '86: Grand Jury Prize. **TV**

Smooth Talker Woof! 1990 (R) A serial killer stalks the women of a 976 party line. Bad acting, bad dialog, not a scare to be found. **89m/C VHS.** Joe Guzaldo, Peter Crombie, Stuart Whitman, Burt Ward, Sydney Lassick, Blair Weickgenant; *D:* Tom Milo.

Smouldering Fires ⭐⭐½ 1925 A tough businesswoman falls in love with an ambitious young employee, who is 15 years her junior. After they marry, problems arise in the form of the wife's attractive younger sister. Surprisingly subtle melodrama, if that's not an oxymoron. **100m/B VHS.** Pauline Frederick, Laura La Plante, Malcolm McGregor, Wanda (Petit) Hawley, Helen Lynch. George Cooper, Bert Roach; *D:* Clarence Brown.

Smugglers ⭐ *Lover of the Great Bear* 1925 Opportunistic smugglers take advantage of the Russian Revolution to sack the land and make a bundle. **110m/C VHS. //** Senta Berger, Giuliano Gemma; *D:* Valentino Orsini.

Smugglers' Cove ⭐⭐⭐ 1948 Gorcey wrongly believes he has inherited a mansion. He and the Bowery Boys move in, only to stumble across a smuggling ring. Plenty of slapsticks; the boys at their best. **66m/B VHS.** Leo Gorcey, Huntz Hall, Gabriel Dell; *D:* William Beaudine.

Snake Eyes ⭐⭐½ 1998 (R) Stylish thriller with Nick Cage as the wild-eyed best Cage is corrupt Atlantic City cop Rick Santoro, investigating the bold assassination of Secretary of Defense Kirkland (Fabiani) during a heavyweight boxing match. The first half of the film packs a visual punch, with De Palma's trademark jazzy camera work, but shortly after Santoro Dunne (Sinise), and realizes nothing is what it seems, story is lost with a combination of implausibility and a lackluster climax. De Palma's first film since directing the b.o. smash "Mission Impossible." Shot exclusively in a Montreal skating arena. **99m/C VHS, DVD.** Nicolas Cage, Gary Sinise, Carla Gugino, John Heard, Stan Shaw, Kevin Dunn, Michael Rispoli, Joel Fabiani, Luis Guzman, Tamara Tunie; *D:* Brian De Palma; *M:* Ryuichi Sakamoto, Koepp; *C:* Stephen Burum; *M:* Ryuichi Sakamoto.

The Snake Hunter Strangler ⭐ 1966 A young girl is rescued after 15 years from an evil cult of snake people. **65m/C VHS.** Guy Madison, Ivan Desny; *D:* Luigi Capuano.

The Snake People ⭐ *Isle of the Snake People; Cult of the Living Dead; La Muerte Viviente; Isle of the Living Dead* 1968 A police captain investigates a small island littered with LSD-experimenting scientists, snake-worshippers, and voodoo. One of the infamous quartet of Karloff's final films, all made in Mexico. **90m/C VHS, DVD, MX** Boris Karloff, Julissa Carlos East; *D:* Enrique Vergara.

The Snake Pit ⭐⭐½ 1948 One of the first films to compassionately explore mental illness and its treatment. Following an emotional collapse Virginia (de Havilland) is placed in a mental institution by her husband, Robert (Stevens). The severity of her depression causes her sympathetic doctor (Genn) to try such treatments as electric shock, hydrotherapy, and drugs, along with the psychoanalysis which gradually allows her to accept her fears and make her recovery. Tour-de-force performance by de Havilland. Based on the novel by Mary Jane Ward. **108m/B VHS.** Olivia de Havilland, Mark Stevens, Leo Genn, Celeste Holm, Glenn Langan, Helen Craig, Leif Erickson, Beulah Bondi; *D:* Anatole Litvak; *W:* Frank Partos, Millen Brand; *C:* Leo Tover. Oscars '48: Sound; N.Y. Film Critics '48: Actress (de Havilland).

The Snake Woman ⭐ 1961 A herpetologist working in a small English village during the 1890s is conducting strange experiments to try to cure his wife's madness. He tries injecting his pregnant wife with snake venom and she gives birth to a cold-blooded daughter who, when she grows up, has the ability to change herself into a deadly snake. She promptly begins killing the local male populace until Scotland Yard is appropriately snakey but this movie is dull. **68m/C**

Snakeman Woof! *The Snake King* 2005 Sci-Fi channel cheesefest with lousy CGI. A group of scientists are tramping through the Amazon jungle and enco enter a gigantic, multi-headed snake that sees them as chow and a snake-worshiping tribe that would be happy to sacrifice the interlopers. **96m/C DVD.** Stephen Baldwin, Jayne Heitmeyer, Larry Day, Gary Hudson; *D:* Allan Goldstein, Declan O'Brien; *C:* Eric Moynier; *M:* Claude Daisy.

Snakes on a Plane ⭐⭐ 2006 (R) And the title says it all. An Internet fanphenom long before its opening, the studio was so taken by the buzz that they had director Ellis do some re-shoots to make the popcorn flick scarier (more snakes, more gore). FBI agent Neville Flynn (Jackson) is escorting a witness on a commercial flight from Hawaii to L.A. When the plane is halfway over the ocean, some 400 deadly snakes are let loose from a time-release crate into the cabin in an effort to eliminate the witness and apparently everyone else. Unfortunately, the flick doesn't live up to the buzz, failing to supply the gleeful camp and wink that the title suggests, and the audience expects. **105m/C DVD.** US Samuel L. Jackson, Julianna Margulies, Kenan Thompson, Nathan Phillips, Flex Alexander, Byron Lawson, Rachel Blanchard; *D:* David Koechner, Sunny Mabrey, Todd Louiso, Lin Shaye, Terry Chen, Elsa Pataky, Taylor Kitsch, Samantha McLeod, Byron Lawson, Rachel Blanchard; *D:* David R. Ellis; *W:* Sebastian Gutierrez, John Heffernan; *C:* Adam Greenberg; *M:* Trevor Rabin.

Snap Decision ⭐⭐½ 2001 Widowed mom Jen (Winningham) allows her friend Carrie (Huffman), a professional photographer, to take candid pictures of her three children when Carrie visits. But the owner of a photo-developing shop gets flustered by what she sees and contacts the police about the "obscene" material. The kids are taken away from Jen and she faces prison time for child pornography in this true story that is every parent's nightmare. Felicity Huffman, Chelcie Ross, Chuck Shamata, Megan Fahlenbock, Ronn Sarosiak, Robert Bockstael, Dan Jiliksowl; *C:* Rhett Morita; *M:* Ara Watson, Sam Blackwell; *C:* James Matters; *M:* Michael Linn.

Snapdragon ⭐⭐ 1993 (R) Police psychologist is led astray by his libido while investigating a lusciously amnesiac. His sensible vice cop girlfriend then discovers the sexpot is actually a psycho serial killer calling herself the Snapdragon who kept her boyfriend even care? **96m/C VHS, DVD.** Steven Bauer, Pamela Anderson, Chelsea Field; *D:* Worth Keeter; *W:* Gene Church; *C:* James Mathers; *M:* Michael Linn.

The Snapper ⭐⭐⭐ 1993 (R) Originally made for BBC TV, Frears creates a small comic gem based on the second novel of Doyle's Barrytown trilogy. Set in Dublin, 20-year-old Sharon Curley (Kellegher) finds herself unexpectedly

---

SnakeEater 2: The Drug Buster ⭐ 1989 (R) A cop goes nuts tracks down swine who killed his parents and kidnapped his sister. "Rambo" rip-off with little plot, but lots of action. Followed by two sequels. **89m/C VHS.** Lorenzo Lamas, Larry Csonka, Ron Palillo; *D:* George Erschbamer.

SnakeEater ⭐ 1989 (R) Loner cop tracks down swine who killed his parents and kidnapped his sister. "Rambo" rip-off with little plot, but lots of action. Followed by two sequels. **89m/C VHS.** Lorenzo Lamas, Larry Csonka, Ron Palillo; *D:* George Erschbamer.

SnakeEater 3: His Law ⭐ 1992 (R) Tough cop Jack Kelly (Lamas) aka SnakeEater, is out to avenge a woman's beating by a gang of thug bikers. Lots of action and violence, not much plot, based on W. Glenn Duncan's novel "Rafferty's Rules." **109m/C VHS.** Lorenzo Lamas, Minor Mustain, Tracy Cook, Holly Chester, Scott "Bam" Bigelow; *D:* George Erschbamer; *W:* John Dunning.

Snatch ⭐⭐⭐ 2000 (R) A a "Lock, Stock and 2 Smoking Barrels," director Ritchie's second film is another well-populated and disorganized crime caper, this time with descriptively named lowlifes trying to heist a stolen 84-carat diamond. Leading the mayhem are Turkish (Statham) and Tommy (Graham), two boxing promoters who sign Mickey (Pitt), an Irish Gypsy, to take a dive. Meanwhile, Franky Four Fingers (Del Toro) transports the red-hot rock to London and his boss Avi (Farina), when it promptly gets lifted. Enter Brick Top (Ford) and a host of others whose seemingly unrelated subplots eventually meet. Casting lots of action, and Ritchie's usual use of heavy Cockney accents are upstaged by Pitt's Gypsy pugilist and his much talked about thick-as-Guinness brogue which even the other characters can't decipher. The elaborate and sometimes confusing plotlines are aided by titles and narration and effective use of Ritchie's usual slo-mo, fast cutting, and split-screen. **104m/C VHS, DVD, UMD. GB** Benicio Del Toro, Dennis Farina, Brad Pitt, Vinnie Jones, Rade Serbedzija, Jason Statham, Lennie James, Ewen Bremner, Alan Ford, Mike Reid, Robbie Gee, Jason Flemyng, Sorcha Cusack, Stephen Graham; *D:* Guy Ritchie; *W:* Guy Ritchie; *C:* Tim Maurice-Jones; *M:* John Murphy.

Snatched ⭐⭐ 1972 The wives of three wealthy men are held for ransom, but one man doesn't want to pay, while one of the victims needs insulin. Standard TV fare. **73m/C VHS.** Howard Duff, Leslie Nielsen, Sheree North, Barbara Parkins, Robert Reed, John Saxon, Tisha Sterling; *D:* Sutton Roley; *M:* Randy Edelman. **TV**

Sneakers ⭐⭐½ 1992 (PG-13) Computer thriller about free computer hackers with questionable pasts and an equally questionable government job. Of course, nothing is as it seems. Rather slow-going considering the talents and suspense involved; but includes enough turns to keep a viewer's interest. **125m/C VHS, DVD.** Robert Redford, Sidney Poitier, River Phoenix, Dan Aykroyd, Ben Kingsley, David Strathairn, Mary McDonnell, Timothy Busfield, George Hearn, Eddie Jones, James Earl Jones, Stephen Tobolowsky, Donal Logue; *D:* Phil Alden Robinson; *W:* Lawrence Lasker, Walter F. Parkes, Phil Alden Robinson; *C:* John Lindley; *M:* James Horner, Branford Marsalis.

Sniper ⭐⭐⭐ *The Deadly Tower* 1975 Suspenseful drama based on true story of Charles Whitman, who shot at University of Texas students from Texas Tower one summer day in 1966. Disney alumnus Russel breaks type as mass killer, with

---

SnakeEater 2: The Drug Buster (duplicate)

Snapshots ⭐⭐½ 2002 (R) Aging expatriate in Amsterdam for the last 30 years. He runs a used bookstore and is attracted to young, free-spirited Aisha (Chaplin) when she comes into the shop. Eventually, Larry finds out that the girl is the daughter of his long-lost love Narma (Christie), whom he remembers from his visit to Morocco (shown in flashbacks) when circumstances bring them back together. **93m/C VHS, DVD.** Burt Reynolds, Carmen Chaplin, Julie Christie, Eric Michael Cole, Jemima Rooper; *D:* Rudolf Van Den Berg; *W:* Rudolf Van Den Berg, O'Loughlin; *C:* Gabor Szabo.

Snapshot ⭐ *Sweeter Song* 1977 ⭐½ Typical grade Z sex comedy; a free-lance photographer ogles lots of variously disrobed young women through his lens. **84m/C VHS.** Jim Henshaw, Susan Petrie; *D:* Jack Darcus, *M:* Jim Henshaw, Susan Petrie; *D:* Roddy Doyle. **TV**

pregnant and refuses to name the father. Family and friends are understanding—until they discover the man's identity. Affecting performances, particularly from Meaney as Sharon's dad who takes a much greater interest in the birth of his grandchild than he ever did with his own children. Cheerful semi-sequel to "The Commitments" serves up domestic upheavals graced with humor and a strong sense of family loyalty. **95m/C VHS, DVD.** IR Tina Kellegher, Colm Meaney, Ruth McCabe, Colm O'Byrne, Pat Laffan, Eanna MacLiam, Ciara Duffy; *D:* Stephen Frears; *W:* Roddy Doyle. **TV** fine support by Yniguez as a police officer on the scene and Beatty as the passerby who lends a hand. Finely crafted re-creation of disturbing, true event. **85m/C VHS, DVD.** Kurt Russell, Ned Beatty, Pernell Roberts, Clifton James, Paul Carr, Alan Vint, Pepe Serna; **D:** Jerry Jameson. **TV**

The Sniper ♂♂½ 1978 A law-abiding citizen becomes a vigilante killer after witnessing a violent crime. **90m/C VHS.** *IT* Stefano Satta Flores, Benedetta Fantoli, Claudia Cardinale; **D:** Pasquale Squitieri; **W:** Pasquale Squitieri; **C:** Giulio Albonico; **M;** Tullio De Piscopo.

Sniper ♂½ 1992 (R) Less than compelling shoot-'em-up set in Panama. Lead characters include Sgt. Beckett (Berenger), a seasoned assassin who gets a rush from killing. Also assigned to the case is Richard Miller (Zane), a newcomer who knows his guns but not his jungles. Together they go in search of their target, a politician planning a coup with the help of a druglord. Action is poorly choreographed and plot is cursory at best. **99m/C VHS, DVD.** Tom Berenger, Billy Zane, J.T. Walsh, Aden Young, Ken Radley, Reinaldo Arenas, Carlos Alvarez, Roy Edmonds, Dale Dye; **D:** Luis Llosa; **W:** Michael Frost Beckner, Crash Leyland; **C:** Bill Butler; **M:** Gary Chang.

Sniper 2 ♂½ 2002 (R) This sequel comes some 10 years after the first "Sniper" and you wonder why anyone would bother with such a familiar story. Marine sniper Beckett (Berenger) is called on for one last mission: to kill a Serbian general who's committing atrocities on the Muslim population. Beckett is teamed with soldier Cole (Woodbine), who's on death row and has a chance to earn his freedom if he survives. **91m/C VHS, DVD.** Tom Berenger, Bokeem Woodbine, Dan E. Butler, Erika Marozsan, Linden Ashby; **D:** Craig R. Baxley; **W:** Ron Mita, Jim McClain; **C:** David Connell; **M:** Gary Chang. **VIDEO**

Sniper 3 ♂ 2004 (R) An assassin's work is never done, so yet again, Beckett dusts off the old hardware to rub out a supposed terrorist for his new employer, the National Security Agency. Things go haywire, seeing as his prey is as old a chum and so his aim turns to tracking down the truth. **90m/C VHS, DVD.** Tom Berenger, Byron Mann, John Doman, Denis Arndt, Troy Winbush, Jeanetta Amette, William Duffy; **D:** P.J. Pesce; **W:** J.S. Cardone, Ross Helford; **C:** Michael Bonvillain; **M:** Timothy S. (Tim) Jones. **VIDEO**

Snipes ♂♂½ 2001 (R) Snipes are the posters you see plastered to walls and lampposts—in this case they're of up-and-coming Philly rapper Prolifik (Nelly), who's got a gangsta background and a shady record label owner, Bob by Starr (Winters), in hock to local mobster Johnnie Maradino (Vincent). When Prolifik gets kidnapped and the master tape of his recordings is also stolen, Starr, for some unknown reason, thinks that gofer/fan Erik (Jones) is somehow mixed up in the mess. Actually, there's a lot that's unclear since first-timer Murray overstuffs the plot. **113m/C VHS, DVD.** Sam Jones III, Dean Winters, Mpho Koaho, Nelly, Zoe Saldana, Frank Vincent; **D:** Rich Murray; **W:** Rich Murray, Rob Wiser; **C:** Alexander Buono.

Sno-Line ♂ 1985 (R) A New York gangster moves to Texas and begins to wipe out the competition on his way to building his drug and gambling dynasty. Bo-ring excuse for entertainment. No hope, no redemption, no titillation: just ultra-"realistic" depiction of organized crime, poorly acted. **89m/C VHS.** Vince Edwards, Paul Smith, June Wilkinson; **D:** Douglas F. Oneans.

Snow Angels ♂♂½ 2007 (R) Tragedy tolls with the sound of distant gunfire as a high school marching band rehearses on the football field, stunning the students into silence. Flash back several weeks to a dreary, snowy northwest small town, where newly divorced waitress (Annie) and her on-the-edge ex (Rockwell) navigate a tense trauma over the sad custody of their four-year-old child. Annie's sleeping with a co-worker's (Sedaris) husband, while another young co-worker Arthur (Angarano), who she used to babysit

is in the apprehensive beginning stages of a high school romance with Lila (Thirlby). Director Green likes to dump you into his films and let you figure out your emotions along with the characters, which sometimes makes for uncomfortable viewing, but the tactic works in this study of love and loss in a claustrophobic town. **106m/C DVD.** *US* Kate Beckinsale, Sam Rockwell, Michael Angarano, Jeanetta Amette, Griffin Dunne, Nicky Katt, Olivia Thirlby, Amy Sedaris, Tom Noonan, Connor Paolo, Hudson Grace; **D:** David Gordon Green; **W:** David Gordon Green; **C:** Tim Orr; **M:** Jeff McIlwain.

Snow Buddies ♂♂½ 2008 (G) Big on the awwwww factor since those "Air Bud" pups are as cute as ever. Budderball gets locked into an ice cream truck and when his four siblings try to rescue him, they all wind up in Alaska. (Right, like the plot should make sense.) They're befriended by a couple of sled dogs and before you know it, our cuties are mushing the trail in an effort to get home. **87m/C DVD.** Molly Shannon, Richard Karn, Cynthia Stevenson; **D:** Robert Vince; **W:** Robert Vince, Anna McRoberts; **M:** Brahm Wenger; **V:** Dylan Sprouse, James Belushi, Kris Kristofferson, Josh Flitter, Jimmy Bennett, Liliana Mumy, Skyler Gisondo, Lothaire Bluteau, Henry Hodges. **VIDEO**

Snow Cake ♂♂ 2006 Middle-aged Brit Alex (Rickman) is driving through Ontario and reluctantly offers a ride to hitchhiking teen Vivienne (Hampshire). She's killed in a crash and uninjured Alex decides he must convey his condolences to her mother, only to discover that Linda (Weaver) is autistic and doesn't process emotions. Alan decides to stay for the funeral and meets Linda's secretive neighbor Maggie (Moss), who offers her own personal brand of sympathy. Moss is best as a small-town femme but Rickman and Weaver are chilly and constricted. **112m/C DVD.** *GB CA* Sigourney Weaver, Alan Rickman, Carrie-Anne Moss, James Allodi, Emily Hampshire; **D:** Marc Evans; **W:** Angela Pell; **C:** Steve Cosens; **M:** Broken Social Scene.

Snow Country ♂♂½ 1957 Romantic drama of an unsuccessful, married artist from Tokyo who travels to a mountain resort to find himself. He requests a Geisha for the evening and, when none are available, the beautiful adopted daughter of the local music teacher is sent to him instead. Based on the Nobel Prize winner Yasunari Kawabata's. In Japanese with English subtitles. Remade in 1965. **104m/B VHS.** *JP* Ryo Ikebe, Keiko Kishi, Akira Kubo, Kaoru Yachigusa, Hisaya Morishige, Mineko Yorozuyo, Etsuko Ichihara, Noriko Sengoku, Kumeko Urabe, Eiko Miyoshi, Akira Tan, Chieko Naniwa, Daisuke Kato, Hanuo Tanaka; **D:** Shiro Toyoda.

The Snow Creature WOOF! 1954 Stupid troop of explorers bring back a snow creature from the Himalayas. Critter escapes in L.A. and terrorizes all in its path before blending in with club crowd. Very bad monster epic (the first about a snow monster) that strains credibility frame by frame. Occasionally, depending upon camera angle, light, and viewer mood, monster appears to be something other than guy in bad suit sweating. Directed by Billy Wilder's brother and another argument against genetic consistency. **72m/B VHS, DVD.** Paul Langton, Leslie Denison; **D:** W. Lee Wilder.

Snow Day ♂½ 2000 (PG) Goofy, innocuous family comedy may provide a distraction for the little monsters if you're stuck with a snow day of your own. Tom (Chase) is the hapless weatherman who's as surprised as anyone when the white stuff falls. Meanwhile, the neighborhood kids seek to foil the efforts of the evil Snowplowman (Elliott) who is out to destroy their dream of having more than one day off from school. **89m/C VHS, DVD.** Chevy Chase, Chris Elliott, Mark Webber, Jean Smart, Schuyler Fisk, Iggy Pop, Pam Grier, John Schneider, Emmanuelle Chriqui; **D:** Chris Koch; **W:** Will McRobb, Chris Viscardi; **C:** Robbie Greenberg; **M:** Steve Bartek.

Snow Dogs ♂♂ 2002 (PG) Gooding leads this kid flick as Ted Brooks, a dentist who only finds out about his adoption after his biological mom's death in Alaska.

Aside from a rather dilapidated house, mom's estate included a team of frisky Siberian husky sled dogs. Displaced city boy Ted, who's from Miami, hates the cold and the dogs but stays to take care of the estate, seek out his real father, and get better acquainted with friendly local bar owner Barb (Bacalso). Meanwhile, the grizzled Thunder Jack (Coburn) is on Ted's tail, trying to get him to sell the dogs. The expected Iditarod-type dog race ensues. Gooding mugs amiably and the good natured physical humor and action should amuse the young and undiscriminating. **99m/C VHS, DVD.** *US* Cuba Gooding Jr., James Coburn, Sisqo, Nichelle Nichols, M. Emmet Walsh, Graham Greene, Brian Doyle-Murray, Joanna Bascalso, Michael Bolton; **D:** Brian Levant; **W:** Jim Kouf, Tommy Swerdlow, Michael Goldberg, Mark Gibson, Philip Halprin; **C:** Thomas Ackerman; **M:** John Debney.

Snow Falling on Cedars ♂♂ 1999 (PG-13) Visually beautiful but remarkably dull adaptation of David Guterson's novel. In 1954, journalist and WWII vet, the portentiously named Ishmael Chambers (Hawke), confronts his past when he's assigned to report on the trial of Japanese-American Kazuo Miyamoto (Yune), who's accused of murdering a fellow fisherman (Thai) in a small community north of Puget Sound. Kazuo just happens to be married to Ishmael's former flame, Hatsue (Kudoh)—their romance having been thwarted by the prejudicial times. Lots of impressionistic flashbacks complicate matters while the story meanders along, not helped by Hawke's blank-faced performance. **128m/C VHS, DVD.** Ethan Hawke, Youki Kudoh, Rick Yune, Sam Shepard, Max von Sydow, James Cromwell, James Rebhorn, Richard Jenkins, Eric Thal, Celia Weston, Max Wright; **D:** Scott Hicks; **W:** Scott Hicks, Ronald Bass; **C:** Robert Richardson; **M:** James Newton Howard.

Snow in August ♂♂½ 2001 In the summer of 1947, young Michael Devlin's (Tambakis) friendship with immigrant Czech Rabbi Hirsch (Rea) brings on the wrath of the local Irish street gang. Michael witnesses the beating of a Jewish shopkeeper, loses his friends, and decides to turn to an ancient Jewish text to summon the protection of a Golem. Based on the novel by Pete Hamill. **104m/C VHS, DVD.** Peter Tambakis, Stephen Rea, Lolita (David) Davidovich; **D:** Richard Friedenberg; **W:** Richard Friedenberg. **CABLE**

Snow Kill ♂½ 1990 Five city-dwellers travel into the mountains for a fun survival training weekend, but the fun turns deadly when they accidentally come across a murderous drug gang. Pseudo-'30s suspense adventure fails to thrill or surprise. **90m/C VHS.** Terence Knox, Patti D'Arbanville, David Dukes; **D:** Thomas J. Wright; **W:** Harv Zimmel. **CABLE**

The Snow Queen ♂♂½ 1983 From "Fairie Tale Theatre" comes this adaptation of the Hans Christian Andersen tale. A boy and girl who grow up together are separated by evil when the boy is held captive in the icy palace of the Snow Queen. The girl sets out to rescue him. **60m/C VHS.** Lauren Hutton, Linda Manz, David Hemmings, Melissa Gilbert, Lee Remick, Lance Kerwin; **D:** Peter Medak. **CABLE**

The Snow Queen ♂♂ 2002 An updated reworking of the Hans Christian Andersen fairytale is visually splendid but overly long. Gerda (Hobbs) lives with her bitter father (Wisden) in a remote hotel in the snowy north country. She's attracted to bellboy Kai (Guilbat), who disappears after a beautiful but sinister guest (Fonda) also leaves. So Gerda decides to track them down and save Kai from the evil Snow Queen. **172m/C VHS, DVD.** Bridget Fonda, Robert Wisden, Jeremy Guilbat, Chelsea Hobbs; **D:** David Wu; **W:** Simon Moore; **C:** Gregory Middleton; **M:** Lawrence Shragge. **CABLE**

Snow: The Movie ♂ 1983 Rates creative zero for title, though there is snow, as well as skiing, growing up, romance, and good times among the young people involved. Filmed in Australia. **83m/C VHS.** David Argue, Lance Curtis; **D:** Robert Gibson.

Snow Treasure ♂ 1967 (G) With the help of an underground agent, Norwegian children smuggle gold out of the country right under the noses of the Nazis. Based on the novel by Marie McSwigan. **96m/C VHS.** James Franciscus, Paul Anstad; **D:** Irving Jacoby.

The Snow Walker ♂♂½ 2003 (PG) A pilot and his Inuit passenger struggle to conquer the elements and their cultural differences after they crash-land in the bitterly cold Canadian Arctic—if they want to survive. Drawn from Farley Mowat's short story "Walk Well My Brother." **109m/C VHS, DVD.** Barry Pepper, Annabella Piugattuk, James Cromwell, Kiersten Warren, Jon(athan) Oates, Robin Dunne, Greg Spottiswood, Samson Jorah, Michael Buble; **D:** Charles Martin Smith; **W:** Charles Martin Smith; **C:** David Connell, Jon Joffin, Paul Sarossy; **M:** Mychael Danna. **VIDEO**

Snow White: A Tale of Terror ♂♂ 1989 The incomparable Rigg stars in this witty retelling of the beautiful girl and her seven little friends. **86m/C VHS, DVD.** Diana Rigg, Sarah Patterson, Billy Barty; **D:** Michael Berz.

Snow White ♂♂ 1997 (R) *Grimm Brothers' Snow White Black Forest; Grimm Brothers' Snow White* This definitely puts the grim in the Grimm Brothers version of the fairy tale. In medieval Austria, beautiful Claudia (Weaver) marries widowed Frederick who, unfortunately, has an even-more beautiful daughter, Lilli (Keena), who's put out by this rival for her father's affections. The stepmom/stepdaughter battle increases when Claudia's own long-awaited baby is still-born and the wrathful and unbalanced Claudia orders Lilli's death. Only she's rescued by seven outcasts (only one of whom is a dwarf) living in the forest. The witchy Claudia does still like to talk to her mirror, however. Filmed in the Czech Republic. **101m/C VHS, DVD.** Sigourney Weaver, Sam Neill, Monica Keena, Gil Bellows, Taryn Davis; **D:** Michael Cohn; **W:** Thomas Szollosi, Deborah Serra; **C:** Mike Southon; **M:** John Ottman.

Snow White and the Seven Dwarfs ♂♂♂♂ 1937 (G) Classic adaptation of the Grimm Brothers fairy tale about the fairest of them all. Beautiful animation, memorable characters, and wonderful songs mark this as the definitive "Snow White." Set the stage for other animated features after Walt Disney took an unprecedented gamble by attempting the first animated feature-length film, a project which took over two years to create and $1.5 million to make, and made believers out of those who laughed at the concept. Lifelike animation was based on real stars; Margery Belcher (later Champion) posed for Snow, Louis Hightower was the Prince, and Lucille LaVerne gave the Queen her nasty look. ♫Some Day My Prince Will Come; One Song; With a Smile and a Song; Whistle While You Work; Bluddle-Uddle-Um-Dum; The Dwarfs' Yodel Song; Heigh Ho; I'm Wishing; Isn't This a Silly Song?. **83m/C VHS, DVD.** David Hand; **W:** Ted Sears, Otto Englander, Earl Hurd, Dorothy Blank, Richard Creedon, Dick Richard, Merrill De Maris, Webb Smith; **V:** Frank Churchill, Paul J. Smith, Larry Morey, Leigh Harline; **V:** Adriana Caselotti, Harry Stockwell, Lucille LaVerne, Moroni Olsen, Billy Gilbert, Pinto Colvig, Otis Harlan, Scotty Matraw, Roy Atwell, Stuart Buchanan, Marion Darlington, Jim Macdonald. AFI '98: Top 100, Natl. Film Reg. '89.

Snow White and the Seven Dwarfs ♂ 1983 From "Faerie Tale Theatre" comes the story of a princess who befriends seven little men to protect her from the jealous evil queen. **60m/C VHS, DVD.** Elizabeth McGovern, Rex Smith, Vincent Price, Vanessa Redgrave; **D:** Peter Medak. **CABLE**

Snow White and the Three Stooges ♂ *Snow White and the Three Clowns* 1961 The Stooges fill in for the Seven Dwarfs when they go off prospecting in King Solomon's mines. Alas, see any Stooge movie but this one. **107m/C VHS, DVD.** Moe Howard, Larry Fine, Joe DeRita, Carol Heiss, Patricia Medina, Edson Stroll; **D:** Walter Lang; **W:** Noel Langley, Elwood Ullman; **C:** Leon Shamroy; **M:** Lyn Murray.

Snow White: The Fairest of Them All 2002 Kreuk certainly looks the title part and Richardson makes a fine wicked stepmother and queen but this version of the fairy tale is lame. Snow's mother dies when she's a baby and her father (Irwin) unwittingly places his daughter under a curse when he marries the witchy Elspeth (Richardson). Oh, and the dwarves are rainbow-colored and named after the days of the week. But Snow still gets stuck in that glass coffin until the prince comes along. 90m/C VHS, DVD. Kristin Kreuk, Miranda Richardson, Tom Irwin, Vera Farmiga, Vincent Schiavelli, Warwick Davis, Michael J. Anderson, Clancy Brown, Tyron Leitso; *D:* Caroline Thompson; *W:* Caroline Thompson. TV

The Snows of Kilimanjaro 1952 Called by Hemingway "The Snows of Zanuck," in reference to the great producer, this film is actually an artful pastiche of several Hemingway short stories and novels. The main story, "The Snows of Kilimanjaro," acts as a framing device, in which the life of a successful writer is seen through his fevered flashbacks as he and his rich wife, while on safari, await as a doctor to save his gangrenous leg. 117m/C VHS, DVD. Gregory Peck, Susan Hayward, Ava Gardner, Hildegarde Kneef, Leo G. Carroll, Torin Thatcher, Ava Norring, Helene Stanley, Marcel Dalio, Vincente Gomez, Richard Allen, Leonard Carey; *D:* Henry King; *W:* Casey Robinson; *C:* Leon Shamroy; *M:* Bernard Herrmann.

Snowball Express 1972 (G) When a New York City accountant inherits a hotel in the Rocky Mountains, he decides to move his family west to attempt to make a go of the defunct ski resort, only to find that the place is falling apart. Run-of-the-mill Disney comedy, based on the novel "Chateau Bon Vivant" by Frankie and John O'Rear. 120m/C VHS, DVD. Dean Jones, Nancy Olson, Harry (Henry) Morgan, Keenan Wynn; *D:* Norman Tokar; *M:* Robert F. Brunner. TV

Snowballing 1985 (PG) *Apres-Ski* 1971 A ski instructor gives private lessons to a bunch of snow bunnies. 90m/C VHS, CA Mariette Levesque, Robert Arcand, Seline Lomez, Daniel Filion; *D:* Roger Cardinal; *W:* Roger Cardinal; *C:* Roger Racine; *M:* Mark Hamilton.

Part of the polluted wave of teen-sex flicks of the 1980s, this is very mild for the genre but still no prize. Lusty high schoolers at a skiing competition look for action on and off the slopes, and up exposing a fraud. 96m/C VHS, DVD. Mary (Elizabeth) McDonough, Bob Hastings; *D:* Charles E. Sellier; *W:* Thomas Chapman; *C:* Henning Schellerup; *M:* Larvan Whitley.

Snowbeast 1977 The residents of a ski resort are being terrorized by a half-human, half-animal beast leaving a path of dead bodies in its wake. "Jaws" hits the slopes. Not scary or even funny. Made for TV. 96m/C VHS, DVD. Bo Svenson, Yvette Mimieux, Sylvia Sidney, Clint Walker, Robert F. Logan; *D:* Herb Wallerstein. TV

Snowblind *Ski Lift to Death* 1978 Two ski groups are derail, placing the passengers in jeopardy. Among the passengers is a mobster being pursued by an assassin. 98m/C VHS, DVD. Deborah Raffin, Charles Frank, Howard Duff, Don Galloway, Gail Strickland, Don Johnson, Veronica Hamel, Clu Gulager, Lisa Reeves, Suzy Chaffee; *D:* William Wiard.

Snowboard Academy 1996 (PG) Chris Barry (Haim), the younger son of a ski resort owner, gets into trouble when his crazy snowboarder pals take over the slopes. Chris' older brother challenges him to start a school that will turn the bumblers into racers in just two weeks. Filmed at Le Chanticleer resort in the Laurentian Mountains near Montreal. 89m/C VHS, DVD. Corey Haim, Jim Varney, Brigitte Nielsen, Joe Flaherty, Paul Hospins, Brendan O'Toole; *D:* John Shepphird; *M:* Rudy Rupak, James Saliskoz; *C:* Bruno Philip; *M:* Ross Vannelli.

Snowbound: The Jim and Jennifer Stolpa Story 1994 Based on a true story, this TV drama finds Jim (Harris) Stolpa, his wife Jennifer (Williams), and their 5-month-old baby fighting for survival when they're trapped in the open by a Nevada snowstorm for eight days. 120m/C VHS, DVD. Neil Patrick Harris, Kelli Williams, Susan Clark, Michael Gross, Richard Cox; *D:* Christian Duguay; *W:* Jonathan Finkels; *C:* Peter Woeste; *M:* Lou Natale. TV

Snuffy Smith, Yard Bird *Private Snuffy Smith; Snuffy Smith* 1942 The pint-sized moonshiner finds himself in the Army, clashing with his sergeant. Followed by "Hillbilly Blitzkrieg" later the same year. 67m/B VHS, DVD. Bud Duncan, Edgar Kennedy, Sarah Padden, Doris Linden; *D:* Edward F. (Eddie) Cline.

So Close to Paradise *Biandan Guniang* 1998 Buddies Dong Zi and Geo Ping are farm workers who arrive in Shanghai for better lives. Dong gets a menial job on the docks while Gao turns to crime to survive. When a gang boss cheats Gao, he gets revenge by kidnapping the man's mistress, Vietnamese nightclub singer Ruan Hong. After some violence, Gao and Ruan fall in what passes for love but this story is not about to have a happy ending. A Chinese version of E-movie, Hollywood noir, Mandarin with subtitles. 90m/C VHS, DVD, Oi Guo, Tao Tong Wu, Xiaoshuai Wang, Pang Ming; *C:* Tao Yang; *M:* Lin Liu.

So Dear to My Heart 1949 A farm boy and his misfit black sheep wreak havoc at the county fair. Several sequences combine live action with animation. Heartwarming and charming straightforward and likeable but never sentimental. Wonderful, vintage Disney. ♪Sourwood Mountain; Billy Boy; So Dear To My Heart; County Fair; Stick-To-It-Ivity; Ol' Dan Patch; It's Whatcha Do With Watcha Got; Lavender Blue (Dilly Dilly). 82m/C VHS, DVD. Bobby Driscol, Burl Ives, Beulah Bondi, Harry Carey Sr., Luana Patten; *D:* Harold Schuster.

So Ends Our Night 1941 German scorns Nazi ideology, flees Austria, and meets young Jewish couple seeking asylum. Fine adaptation of Erich Maria Remarque's novel "Flotsam" with splendid performances from Sullavan (on loan from Universal) and young Ford. 117m/B VHS, DVD. Fredric March, Margaret Sullavan, Frances Dee, Glenn Ford, Anna Sten, Erich von Stroheim; *D:* John Cromwell; *C:* William H. Daniels.

So Fine 1981 (R) Absent-minded English professor O'Neal tries to rescue his father's clothing business from going bottom-up. He accidentally invents peek-a-boo bottomed jeans, which become an immediate hit and make him rich. Comedy smorgasbord, setting outing from sometime novelist Bergman, hits and misses. O'Neal is memorable, as is the ubiquitous Warden and his sidekick. 91m/C VHS, DVD. Ryan O'Neal, Jack Warden, Mariangela Melato, Richard Kiel; *D:* Andrew Bergman; *W:* Andrew Bergman; *M:* Ennio Morricone.

So I Married an Axe Murderer 1993 (PG-13) Combination comedy/romance/thriller. Charlie is a hip bookstore owner with a commitment problem. When he finally falls in love with a butcher, he comes to suspect she's a serial killer and he's in line as her next victim. "Saturday Night Live" star Myers has a dual role: as Charlie and as Scottish dad Stuart, allowing him to do "fanatically World" popularity, which didn't pan out at the boxoffice. Best appreciated by Myers fans, this one is better on the small screen. 92m/C VHS, DVD. Mike Myers, Nancy Travis, Anthony LaPaglia, Amanda Plummer, Brenda Fricker, Matt Doherty; *Cameos:* Charles Grodin, Phil Hartman, Steven Wright, Alan Arkin, Michael Richards; *D:* Thomas Schlamme; *W:* Robbie Fox, Mike Myers; *M:* Bruce Broughton.

So Proudly We Hail 1943 True story of the lives of three war-front nurses and their heroism under fire during WWII. Colbert is Lt. Davidson in charge of nine Red Cross Army nurses serving in the Pacific. Lake and Goddard play the other leads. With the popularity of its stars and the patriotic spirit of the film, the picture hit boxoffice gold. Critics praised its authenticity, as the film never fell victim to the usual standards of Hollywood glamour. Fans of Lake beware: she has short hair in this film because the government requested that she not appear as a servicewoman with her famous peek-a-boo hair style because female factory workers were getting their long Lake-inspired hair caught in the machinery. 126m/B VHS, DVD. Claudette Colbert, Paulette Goddard, Veronica Lake, George Reeves, Barbara Britton, Walter Abel, Sonny Tufts, John Litel, Mary Servoss, Ted Hecht, Mary Treen, Helen Lynd, Adrian Booth, Dorothy Adams, Ann Doran, Jean Willes, Jan Wiley, Lynn Walker, Joan Tours, Kitty Kelly, James Bell, Dick Hogan, Bill Goodwin, James Flavin; *D:* Mark Sandrich; *W:* Alan Scott; *C:* Charles Bryant; *M:* Miklos Rozsa.

So This Is Africa 1933 Spoof of Hollywood jungle pictures stars the comedy team of Wheeler and Woolsey. Wilbur (Wheeler) and Alexander (Woolsey) are a pack of broke vaudevillians with a lion act when they are told to make a jungle picture in Africa. Alexander becomes the plaything of Mrs. female slave of the Amazon queen (Torres), the duo dress as women to escape the Amazons only to be captured by a pack of jungle Tarzans. The original release ran 90 minutes but ran afoul of censors and was heavily edited for double entendres and sexual content. 61m/B VHS, DVD. Bert Wheeler, Raquel Torres, Esther Muir, Berton Churchill; *D:* Edward F. (Eddie) Cline; *W:* Norman Krasna; *C:* Leonard Smith.

So This Is Paris 1926 Roguish pre-Hayes Code dancing duo seeks spice through alternative love-mates. Classic sophisticated Lubitsch, with outstanding camera work and a bit of jazz. 68m/B VHS. Monte Blue, Patsy Ruth Miller, Lilyan Tashman, Andre de Beranger, Myrna Loy; *D:* Ernst Lubitsch.

So This Is Washington *Lum & Abner* 1943 The comedy team go to Washington with wacky inventions to help the war effort. Turns out there's too entirely too much nonsense going around, and the boys give 'em a piece of their mind. Fun, featherweight wartime comedy. 70m/B VHS, DVD. Alan Mowbray, Mildred Coles, Chester Lauck, Norris Goff; *D:* Ray McCarey; *W:* Leonard Praskins, Roswell Fogers; *C:* Harry Wild.

Soapdish 1991 (PG-13). The back stage lives of a daytime soap opera, "The Sun Also Sets," and its cast. When the soap's ratings fall, a character written out of series via decapitation is brought back to give things a lift. While the writer struggles to make the reincarnation believable, the cast juggles old and new romances, and professional jealousies abound. Some genuinely funny moments as film actors spoof the genre that gave many of them a start. 97m/C VHS, DVD. Sally Field, Kevin Kline, Robert Downey Jr., Cathy Moriarty, Whoopi Goldberg, Elisabeth Shue, Carrie Fisher, Garry Marshall, Teri Hatcher, Paul Johansson, Costas Mandylor, Stephen Nichols, Leeza Gibbons, John Tesh, Kathy Najimy, Sheila Kelley, Finola Hughes; *D:* Michael Hoffman; *W:* Andrew Bergman, Robert Harling; *C:* Ueli Steiger; *M:* Alan Silvestri.

...ver, Larry Storch, Jennifer Edwards, Robert Loggia, Rosanna Arquette, Marisa Berenson; *D:* Blake Edwards; *W:* Blake Edwards; *C:* Harry Stradling Jr.; *M:* Henry Mancini. Natl. Soc. Film Critics '81: Support. Actor (Preston).

Soccer Dog: The Movie 1998 (PG) Clay Newlin (Foley) discovers the small town he's just moved to doesn't seem very friendly. His joint is the local soccer team but isn't having much luck and Clay's only friend is stray dog Lincoln, who likes to watch the games. Then, when the team is short a player and in danger of forfeiting, the coach drafts Lincoln and the team actually wins. If you've seen this before, it's the "Air Bud" movie. 98m/C VHS, DVD, Jeremy Foley, James Marshall, Olivia D'Abo; *D:* Tony Giglio; *W:* Daniel Forman.

Social Error 1935 A college student gets expelled from college for various missteps and escapades, then becomes involved in the kidnapping of an heiress. Zany stunts highlight this hodge-podge. 60m/3 VHS. Gertrude Messinger, David Sharpe, Monte Blue, Lloyd Hughes, Sheila Terry, Matty Fain, Ted Adams, Roger Williams, Joseph Girard, Mickey Daniels, Fred "Snowflake" Toones; *D:* Harry Fraser; *W:* Charles E. Roberts; *C:* Arthur Brooks.

Social Intercourse Woof! 2001 Waste of celluloid concerning the social reclamation of cyber geek Todd (Taylor), who also edited, produced, directed, and co-scripted) at a friend's blow-out bash. If horny hijinks, tough-talking chicks, and water-balloon snicer constituted good plot elements, then "Social Intercourse" would be the "Citizen Kane" of party films. 38m/C DVD. Steve Taylor, Lee Abbott, Kim Little, Ashley Davis, Steve Grabowsky; *D:* Steve Taylor; *W:* Steve Taylor, Roger Kristian Jones; *C:* Armand Garab'an.

Social Misfits 2000 Twelve troubled teenagers, including our narrator Skylar (co-writter Tann), are sent to Camp Resurrection outside Fresno for a week-long psycho-drama as each of the kids tells his or her story. The whole thing is produced with more enthusiasm than experience or talent. (Note the visible zero-era s'adows.) Production values are minimal but adequate to the subject matter. 91m/C VHS, DVD. Boris Cabrera, Le'Mark Cruise, Gabriel Demon, Isall de la Fuente, Tyrcme Tann; Eric Gray, Paul Gleason, Tyrcme Tann; *D:* *W:* Le'Mark Cruise, Tyrone Tann; *C:* Eric Leach; *M:* William Richter.

The Social Secretary 1916 Driven from the rat race by lecherous men, Talmadge gets new job as minister's secretary, where she soon down-dresses to avoid further lewd encounters. She falls for her boss's son, but isn't considered marriage material until she proves herself. 56m/B VHS. Norma Tamadge, Kate Lester, Helen Weir, Gladden James, Herbert Frank; *D:* John Emerson.

Society 1992 (R) A teenager wonders if his visions are real or hallucinations when he believes his family, and everyone else around him, are flesh-eating predators. The puzzle isn't much but wait for the special-effects ladened ending to get your fill of gore. 99m/C VHS, DVD. Billy Warock, Devin Devasquez, Evan Richards; *D:* Brian Yuzna.

Sodbusters 1994 (PG-13) Western spoof about homesteaders versus a greedy cattle baron and the railroad in 1875 Colorado. A lascivious railroad wife and a mysterious gunslinger—as well as a couple of gay cowboys—are included for additional fun. 97m/C VHS, DVD. Kris Kristofferson, John Vernon, Fred Willard, Wendel Meldrum, Max Gail, Steve Landesberg, Don Lake, Adam Pickens Jr., John Hemphill; *D:* Eugene Levy. TV

Sodom and Gomorrah *Sodome e Gomorrah; The Last Days of Sodom and Gomorrah* 1962 The Italian-made, internationally produced epic about Lot, the Hebrews and the destruction of the two sinful biblical cities. Moderately entertaining but ponderous, to say the least, and very long. 154m/C VHS. IT Stewart Granger, Stanley Baker, Pier Angeli, Anouk Aimee, Rossana Podesta; **D:** Robert Aldrich; **M:** Miklos Rozsa.

Sofie 🦴🦴 1992 Sweet family melodrama about a late 19th Jewish family in Denmark. Sofie (Mynster) is the unmarried 28-year-old daughter of loving, protective parents. She has fallen in love with a gentile artist (Christensen) but gives him up to marry within her faith. Unsuited, Sofie and Jonas (Zeller) lead melancholy lives, which Sofie redeems through her joy in her son. Self-effacing drama is Ullmann's directorial debut. Adapted from the novel "Mendel Philipsen & Son" by Henri Nathansen. In Swedish with English subtitles. 145m/C VHS, DVD. SW Karen-Lise Mynster, Ghita Norby, Erland Josephson, Jesper Christensen, Henning Moritzen, Torben Zeller, Stig Hoffmeyer, Kirsten Rolffes, Lotte Herman; **D:** Liv Ullmann; **W:** Liv Ullmann, Peter Poulsen.

Soft and Hard 🦴🦴½ 1985 Video by Godard and Mieville intends to evaluate the role of media and television in everyday life via a seemingly informal look at the couple's daily existence and the propensity for image production in it. In French; subtitled. 48m/C VHS. FR Anne-Marie Mieville, Jean-Luc Godard. TV

Soft Deceit 🦴🦴½ 1994 (R) Master criminal Trent (Bergin) gets caught in the heist of $16 million in mob money. Then Anne (Vernon) shashays into prison in exchange for breaking him out. She succeeds but maybe a doublecross is next on the agenda. 95m/C VHS. Patrick Bergin, Kate Vernon, John Wesley Shipp, Gwynyth Walsh, Nigel Bennett, Damir Andrei; **D:** Jorge Montesi; **W:** Jorge Montesi.

Soft for Digging 🦴🦴½ 2001 Something evil is happening in the Maryland woods. Virgil (Mercier) is a hermit-like old man who believes he sees a man strangle a young girl (Ingerson) in the forest. Of course, when the cops arrive there's no body and nothing to indicate a crime happened. But Virgil knows it did—since the little girl is haunting him, demanding justice. Film is nearly without dialogue and title cards divide the scenes. It's an interesting but generally amateurish experiment. 78m/C DVD. Edmond Mercier, Sarah Ingerson, Andrew Hewitt, David Husko, Joshua Billings; **D:** J.T. Petty; **W:** J.T. Petty; **C:** Patrick McGraw; **M:** James L. Wolcott.

Soft Fruit 🦴🦴½ 1999 (R) Patsy (Drynan) is dying of cancer and, though her grumpy husband (Haft) isn't happy about it, her four children show up to care for her—the first time in 15 years that all the family has been together. The three sisters (Lemon, Horler, Talbot) have a long-standing case of sibling rivalry and son Bo (Dykstra) is only out on a prison parole because of his mother's condition. But Patsy has some definite ideas about how she wants to spend her last days, whatever her family thinks. 101m/C VHS. AU Jeanie Drynan, Genevieve Lemon, Sacha Horler, Linal Haft, Alicia Talbot, Russell Dykstra; **D:** Christina Andreef; **W:** Christina Andreef; **C:** Laszlo Baranyai; **M:** Antony Partos. Australian Film Inst. '99: Actor (Dykstra), Support. Actress (Horler).

The Soft Kill 🦴🦴 1994 (R) LA private eye Jack Ramsey (Bernsen) becomes the prime murder suspect when his girlfriend is strangled. Can he prove his innocence before more bodies pile up and the cops catch him? 95m/C VHS, DVD. Corbin Bernsen, Brion James, Matt McCoy, Michael (M.K.) Harris, Kim Morgan Greene, Carrie-Anne Moss; **D:** Eli Cohen.

The Soft Skin 🦴🦴🦴 1964 Le Peau Douce; Silken Skin 1964 A classic portrayal of marital infidelity by the master director. A writer and lecturer has an affair with a stewardess. After the affair ends, his wife confronts him, with tragic results. Cliche plot is forgivable; acted and directed to perfection. Frequent Truffaut star Jean-Pierre Leaud served here as an apprentice director. In French with English subtitles. 120m/B VHS, DVD. FR Jean Desailly, Nelly Benedetti, Francoise Dorleac, Daniel Ceccaldi; **D:** Francois Truffaut; **W:** Francois Truffaut, Jean-Louis Richard; **C:** Raoul Coutard; **M:** Georges Delerue.

Soggy Bottom U.S.A. 🦴🦴 1984 (PG) A sheriff has his hands full trying to keep the law enforced in a small Southern town. Quite-good cast keeps the plot from disappearing altogether. 90m/C VHS, DVD. Don Johnson, Ben Johnson, Dub Taylor, Ann Wedgeworth, Lois Nettleton, Anthony Zerbe; **D:** Theodore J. Flicker.

Soho Square 🦴½ 2000 (R) Meandering, low-budget, first-time effort from Rafn. A nameless detective (Biggs) is assigned to a serial killer case where the killer preys on young women in London's Soho district, setting them on fire. This detective may not have been the best choice since he's drinking too much and seeing visions of his dead wife. Then he meets Julia (Davenport), a woman who could be his dead wife's doppelganger, and she may be the big break in the case. 90m/C DVD. GB Lucy Davenport, Anthony Biggs, Livy Armstrong, Emma Poole, Sasha Lowenthal, Amanda Haberland, William Wilde; **D:** Jamie Rafn; **W:** Jamie Rafn; **C:** Brendan McGinty; **M:** Chris Read.

Sois Belle et Tais-Toi 🦴 Look Beautiful and Shut Up; Be Beautiful but Shut Up; Be Beautiful but Shut Up: Blonde for Danger 1958 A police detective tracks jewel thieves and falls in love with a young waif. Several interesting and later famous actors have small parts. Light-hearted adventure. Subtitled in English. 110m/B VHS. FR Henri Vidal, Mylene Demongeot, Jean-Paul Belmondo, Alain Delon, Hugh Brooks, Roger Hanin; **D:** Marc Allegret; **W:** Roger Vadim, Odette Joyeux, William Benjamin, Jean Marsan, Gabriel Arout; **C:** Armand Thirard.

Sol Goode 🦴🦴½ 2001 (R) Sol Goode (Getty) is a familiar character—a 20something wannabe actor who uses his looks and charm to bed the babes. But his best pal Chloe (Towne) knows there's a decent guy lurking somewhere underneath the hipster facade. When a series of minor misfortunes find Sol examining his life, he realizes that Chloe is the woman of his dreams—now he just has to convince her that he's sincere. 100m/C VHS, DVD. Balthazar Getty, Katharine Towne, Jamie Kennedy, Natasha Gregson Wagner, Tori Spelling, Cheri Oteri, Robert Wagner, Danny Comden, Carmen Electra, Johnathon Schaech, Christina Pickles, Max Perlich, Jason Bateman, China Chow; **D:** Danny Comden; **W:** Joe Gannon, Tedi Sarafian; **C:** Russell Carpenter; **M:** Maurice Jarre.

Solar Crisis 🦴🦴 1992 (PG-13) Eye-popping special effects highlight this Earth-on-the-edge-of-destruction sci-fier. In 2050 the sun has gone on self-destruct and begins throwing off giant solar flares which turn the Earth extra-crispy. A space team is sent to divert the flares but the mission may become a victim of sabotage. Director Sarafian actually forgoes credit for the standard Smithee pseudonym. 111m/C VHS, DVD. Tim Matheson, Charlton Heston, Peter Boyle, Annabel Schofield, Jack Palance, Corin "Corky" Nemec; **D:** Richard Sarafian, Alan Smithee; **W:** Joe Gannon, Tedi Sarafian; **C:** Russell Carpenter; **M:** Maurice Jarre.

Solar Force 🦴🦴 1994 (R) Cop (Pare), stationed on the moon, is sent to earth to find a stolen chemical that is capable of restoring a destroyed environment. But there are secrets behind the assignment which could cost him his life. 91m/C VHS, DVD. Michael Pare, Billy Drago, Walker Brandt; **D:** Boaz Davidson; **W:** Terrence Pare; **C:** Avi (Avraham) Karpik; **M:** Don Peake.

Solarbabies 🦴 1986 (PG-13) Rollerskating youths in a drought-stricken future vie for a mysterious power that will replenish the Earth's water. Shades of every sci-fi movie you've ever seen, from "Mad Max" to "Ice Pirates." Pathetic. 95m/C VHS, DVD. Richard Jordan, Sarah Douglas, Charles Durning, Lukas Haas, Jami Gertz, Jason Patric; **D:** Alan Johnson; **W:** Walon Green; **M:** Maurice Jarre.

Solaris 🦴🦴 1972 Solyaris 1972 With this the USSR tried to eclipse "2001: A Space Odyssey" in terms of cerebral science-fiction. Some critics thought they succeeded. You may disagree now that the lumbering effort is available on tape. Adapted from a Stanislaw Lem novel, it depicts a dilapidated space lab orbiting the planet Solaris, whose ocean, a vast fluid "brain," materializes the stir-crazy cosmonauts' obsessions—usually morose ex-girlfriends. Talk, talk, talk, minimal special effects. In Russian with English subtitles. In a two-cassette package, with a letterbox format presenting Tarkovsky's widescreen composition. 167m/C VHS, DVD. RU Donatas Banionis, Natalya Bondarchuk, Juri Jarvet, Vladislav Dvorzhetsky, Nikolai Grinko, Anatoli (Otto) Solonitzin, Sos Sarkisyan; **D:** Andrei Tarkovsky; **W:** Andrei Tarkovsky; **C:** Vadim Yusov; **M:** Eduard Artemyev. Cannes '72: Grand Jury Prize.

Solaris 🦴🦴½ 2002 (R) In the midst of grieving over his dead wife Rheya (McElhone), psychologist Chris Kelvin (Clooney) is summoned to help bring back the survivors of a failed mission aboard a space station orbiting the planet Solaris. Once there, he finds the commander dead and the remaining crewmembers in the grip of some planet-induced paranoia. He also finds his supposedly-dead wife in bed with him the next morning. Soderburgh's moody, claustrophobic, deliberately-paced space oddity offers up existential dread, regret, and search for redemption as the main foes for his characters, rather than some malevolent outside force. This will definitely put off those looking for "Star Wars/Alien" type thrills, but will satisfy those looking for a more cerebral exercise. 99m/C VHS, DVD. US George Clooney, Natascha (Natasha) McElhone, Jeremy Davies, Viola Davis, Ulrich Tukur, Morgan Rusler; **D:** Steven Soderbergh; **W:** Steven Soderbergh; **C:** Steven Soderbergh; **M:** Cliff Martinez.

Solas 🦴🦴½ 1999 (R) Hard-drinking, embittered Maria (Fernandez) moves into an apartment in a run-down Seville neighborhood and gets a job cleaning offices. Her abusive father (De Osca) is in a nearby hospital and Maria's patient mother Rosa (Galiana) temporarily moves in with her resentful daughter. Rosa has always made the best of what life has given her and she soon befriends Maria's courtly neighbor (Alvarez-Novoa) while Maria continues to get involved with the wrong men and make bad choices. Spanish with subtitles. 98m/C VHS, DVD. SP Maria Galiana, Ana Fernandez, Carlos Alvarez-Novoa, Paco De Osca; **D:** Benito Zambrano; **W:** Benito Zambrano; **C:** Tote Trenas; **M:** Antonio Meliveo.

Soldat Duroc... Ca Va Etre Ta Fete! 🦴🦴 Soldier Duroc 1975 Days after the 1944 liberation of Paris, a French soldier crosses back over the French lines to see his lover, and is caught as a German sympathizer by American troops. 105m/C VHS. FR Pierre Tornade, Robert Webber, Michel Galabru, Roger Carel; **D:** Michel Gerard.

The Soldier 🦴 Codename: The Soldier 1982 (R) The Russians are holding the world at ransom with a pile of stolen plutonium, and a soldier finds himself in the position to carry out an unauthorized and dangerous plan to preserve the balance of world power. Wildly implausible, gratuitously violent spy trash. 90m/C VHS. Ken Wahl, Klaus Kinski, William Prince, Alberta Watson; **D:** James Glickenhaus.

Soldier 🦴🦴 1998 (R) Steals trite scenes from other post-apolyptic sci-fi shoot-em-ups just to prove that 47-year-old Kurt Russell had been working out. Genetically engineered soldier Russell is discarded as obsolete on a garbage dump planet inhabited by a freedom-loving survivalist (Pertwee) and his band of human flotsam. When a force led by next-generation soldier Jason Scott Lee invades the planet, Russell helps save the skanky-looking group of squatters. Robbed of his hollow character smirk, Russell delivers a garbage planet set recycles props used in "Demolition Man," "Executive Decision," and "Event Horizon." The movie recycles ideas from every other sci-fi flick. 99m/C VHS, DVD. Kurt Russell, Jason Scott Lee, Gary Busey, Michael Chiklis, Sean Pertwee, Jason Isaacs, Connie Nielsen, Brenda Wehle, Mark Bringleson, K.K. Dodds; **D:** Paul W.S. Anderson; **W:** David Peoples; **C:** David Tattersall; **M:** Joel McNeely.

Soldier Blue 🦴🦴 1970 (R) Two survivors of an Indian attack make their way back to an army outpost. The cavalry then seeks revenge on the Cheyenne tribe accused of the attack. Gratuitously violent Vietnam-era western hits hard on racial themes. Based on the novel "Arrow in the Sun" by Theodore V. Olsen on the Sand Creek Indian massacre. 109m/C VHS, DVD. Candice Bergen, Peter Strauss, Donald Pleasence, Dana Elcar, Jorge (George) Rivero; **D:** Ralph Nelson; **W:** John Gay; **C:** Robert B. Hauser.

Soldier Boyz 🦴½ 1995 (R) Ex-Marine Major Howard Tolliver (Dudikoff), who now runs a high-security prison for youthful offenders, is called on to rescue a United Nations worker who's being held hostage by a group of revolutionaries in Vietnam. For help, he takes along six of his toughest prisoners. A variation of "The Dirty Dozen." 91m/C VHS. Michael Dudikoff, Cary-Hiroyuki Tagawa, Tyrin Turner, David Barry Gray, Channon Roe, Cedrick Terrell, Demetrius Navarro, Jacqueline Obradors; **D:** Louis Morneau; **W:** Darryl Quarles.

Soldier in Love 🦴🦴 1967 Teleplay from "George Schaefer's Showcase Theatre" is based on the life of John Churchill, first Duke of Marlborough, and his wife Sarah. The ambitious young couple held the favor of Queen Anne for a time, until political intrigue brought about their downfall. 76m/C VHS. Jean Simmons, Claire Bloom, Keith Michell; **D:** George Schaefer. TV

Soldier in the Rain 🦴🦴½ 1963 An unusual friendship develops between career sergeant Gleason and wheeler-dealer McQueen. Gleason is in good form, but McQueen is listless, and the story (set in a Southern army camp) is unsatisfying. Weld is the comely teen who makes for an intriguing love triangle. From the novel by William Goldman. 88m/B VHS. Steve McQueen, Jackie Gleason, Tuesday Weld, Tony Bill, Tom Poston, Ed Nelson; **D:** Ralph Nelson; **W:** Blake Edwards; **M:** Henry Mancini.

Soldier of Fortune 🦴🦴½ 1955 A woman (Hayward) enlists mercenaries to help find her lost husband in Red China. Late Gable vehicle with the formula beginning to feel the post-war strain and the star looking a trifle long in the tooth. Still, a fun adventure from a top star. Hayward had been among the myriad starlets vying for the Scarlett O'Hara role nearly two decades earlier. 96m/C VHS, DVD. Clark Gable, Susan Hayward, Gene Barry, Alexander D'Arcy, Michael Rennie, Tom Tully, Anna Sten, Russell Collins, Leo Gordon, Jack Kruschen, Robert Quarry; **C:** Edward Dmytryk; **W:** Ernest K. Gann; **C:** Leo Tower; **M:** Hugo Friedhofer.

Soldier of Fortune Inc. 🦴🦴 1997 (R) Retired Major Matt Shepherd (Johnson) is recruited by Washington insider Xavier Trout (Selby), who works for a mystery organization that handles covert operations, to extract American POWs from Iraq, Matt puts together a specialized and secret unit in order to accomplish his mission. Action-packed TV pilot of the syndicated series. 98m/C VHS, DVD. Brad Johnson, David Selby, Melinda (Mindy) Clarke, Tim Abell, Real Andrews, Mark Sheppard, Brian Cousins; **D:** Robert Radler. TV

Soldier of Orange 🦴🦴🦴 1978 Soldaat van Oranje 1978 The lives of six Dutch students are forever changed by the WWII invasion of Holland by the Nazis. Based on the true-life exploits of Dutch resistance leader Erik Hazelhoff. Exciting and suspenseful; cerebral; carefully made and well acted. Made Rutger Hauer an international star. 144m/C VHS, DVD. NL Derek de Lint, Rutger Hauer, Jeroen Krabbe, Edward Fox, Susan Penhaligon; **D:** Paul Verhoeven; **W:** Paul Verhoeven, Gerard Soeteman, Kees Hollierhoek; **C:** Jan De Bont; **M:** Roger van Otterloo. L.A. Film Critics '79: Foreign Film.

Soldier of the Night 🦴🦴 1984 (R) Toy-store worker by day, vigilante killer by night. Israeli thriller set in Tel Aviv lacks vim and is badly dubbed. 88m/C VHS. Yehuda Efroni, Iris Kraner, Sari Raz, Ytach Kataur; **D:** Dan Wolman; **W:** Dan Wolman; **C:** Yossi Wein; **M:** Alex Cagan.

A Soldier's Daughter Never Cries 🦴🦴½ 1998 (R) American novelist and WWII vet Bill Willis (Kristofferson) lives in 1960s Paris with his sexy, free-thinking and -drinking wife Marcella (Hershey), their adopted French son Billy (Gruen), and teenage daughter Channe, the center of the story. Her relationships with her brother and a rude (yet likable) classmate (Costanzo) provide much of the film's emotional punch. Bill develops heart problems and takes the family home to the States. Against the backdrop of social and political turmoil, Bill's core values help the family through their own challenges. Ivory and Merchant make an admirable leap into the 20th century. Unfortunately, the film's episodic jumps are too confusing to make it a complete success. Based on the 1990 book by Kaylie Jones, daughter of novelist James Jones. **128m/C VHS, DVD.** Kristofferson, Barbara Hershey, Leelee Sobieski, Jesse Bradford, Anthony Roth Costanzo, Dominique Blanc, Jane Birkin, Virginie Ledoyen, Isaach de Bankole, Samuel Gruen, Luisa Conlon; **D:** James Ivory; **W:** Ruth Prawer Jhabvala; **C:** Jean-Marc Fabre; **M:** Richard Robbins.

Soldier's Fortune ⭐½ 1991 (R)
A traveling gun for hire leaves the combat of Central America for the jungles of Los Angeles, only to find out that his daughter had been taken hostage. That's the last thing these kidnappers will ever do when they are found by this tough guy looking for his child. **96m/C VHS.** Gil Gerard, Charles Napier, Dan Haggerty, P.J. Soles, Barbara Bingham, Janus Blythe; **D:** Arthur N. Mele.

Soldier's Girl ⭐⭐⭐ 2003
First-rate drama takes some time to find its pace but boasts superior performances and a strong final act. Unsophisticated Army Pvt. Barry Winchell (Garity) is dragged as a joke to a gay bar in Nashville where he sees Calpernia Addams (Pace), a transgendered nightclub performer, who is taken with Barry's gentlemanly manners. They begin a tentative courtship that progresses from curiosity to love, which threatens the relationship between Barry and his unstable roommate Fisher (Halsyl), who begins spreading rumors about a gay soldier on base. The manipulative Fisher engineers a confrontation between Barry and a young Oklahoma redneck recruit that explodes into stunning violence. Based on the 1999 murder of a G.I. at a Kentucky military base. **112m/C VHS, DVD.** Troy Garity, Lee Pace, Andre Braugher, Shawn Hatosy, Philip Eddolls; **D:** Frank Pierson; **W:** Ron Nyswaner; **C:** Paul Sarossy; **M:** Jan A.P. Kaczmarek. **CABLE**

Soldiers of Change ⭐⭐⭐
Painting 2006 (PG-13) **VIDEO**

Soldier's Revenge ⭐⭐ 1984
Vent-grence of a Soldier 1984 A Vietnam vet has a hard time adjusting to life at home. **92m/C VHS, DVD.** Maria Socas, Paul Lambert, Edgardo Moreira, Francisco Cano, John Savage; **D:** David Worth; **W:** David Worth, Lee Stull; **C:** Leonardo Solis; **M:** Gary Reast.

A Soldier's Story ⭐⭐⭐ 1984 (PG)
A black army attorney is sent to a Southern base to investigate the murder of an unpopular sergeant. Features WWII, Louisiana, jazz and blues, and racism in and outside the corps. From the Pulitzer prize winning play by Charles Fuller, with most of the Broadway cast. Fine performances from Washington and Caesar. **101m/C VHS, DVD.** Howard E. Rollins Jr., Adolph Caesar, Denzel Washington, Patti LaBelle, Robert Townsend, Scott Paulin, Wings Hauser, Art Evans, Larry Riley, David Alan Grier; **D:** Norman Jewison; **W:** Charles Fuller; **C:** Russell Boyd; **M:** Herbie Hancock. **L.A. Film Critics '84:** Support. Actor (Caesar).

A Soldier's Sweetheart ⭐⭐½ 1998 (R)
Bored Vietnam soldier, Rat (Sutherland), narrates the unlikely story of Marianne (Gates). Her high school boyfriend, Fossie (Ulrich), is a lonely medic who manages to bring Marianne over to join him. All the guys in the squad fall for her, but Marianne falls in love with the excitement/uncertainty/terror of war. Adapted from the story "Sweetheart of the Song Tra Bong" by Tim O'Brien. **111m/C VHS.** Kiefer Sutherland, Skeet Ulrich, Georgina Cates, Daniel London, Larry Lawrence Gilliard Jr., Christopher Birt, Louis Vanaria; **D:** Thomas Michael Donnelly; **W:** Thomas Michael Donnelly; **C:** Jacek Laskus; **M:** Gary Chang. **CABLE**

A Soldier's Tale ⭐⭐ 1991 (R)
During WWII, a menage-a-trois develops that can only lead to tragedy, yet the participants find themselves unable to resist. When she's kicked out of the sole survivor of a plane crash. **85m/C VHS.** Anita Skinner, Leon Robinson; **D:** Thom Eberhardt; **C:** Russell Carpenter.

Sole Survivor ⭐½ 1984 (R)
A group of zombies are searching "for a living. When she's kicked out of the likes of which humanity has not yet seen. **91m/C VHS.** Ru, Mikhail Nojkine, Alexandre Fatiouchine; **D:** Mikhail Toumanichvili.

Solid Gold Cadillac ⭐⭐⭐ 1956
Holiday is a winning lead as Laura Partrige, an idealistic, small-time stockholder who discovers that the corporate board of directors are crooked. She makes waves at its stockholders meeting, gets noticed by the press, finds romance with former CEO Edward McKeever (Douglas), and works to oust the scalawags from power. The title comes from Laura's fervent desire to own a—you guessed it—solid gold cadillac. Based on the Broadway play by George S. Kaufman and Howard Teichmann. **99m/B VHS.** Judy Holliday, Paul Douglas, Fred Clark, Neva Patterson, Arthur O'Connell, Ray Collins; **D:** Richard Quine; **W:** Abe Burrows; **C:** Charles Bryant Lang Jr.; **M:** Cyril Mockridge; **Nar:** George Burns. **Oscars '56:** Costume Des. (B&W).

Solitaire for 2 ⭐⭐½ 1994 (R)
Sweet-natured romantic comedy about a rogue and a psychic. Handsome Daniel Becker (Frankel) is a behavioral psychologist who specializes in interpreting body language and using his expertise to bed as many beautiful women as happen his way. Uptight paleontologist Katie (Pays) has a problem with men—she can literally read their minds and gets angry at their lewd thoughts. So the path to true commitment is going to get a bit bumpy. **105m/C VHS.** 3B Mark Frankel, Amanda Pays, Roshan Seth, Maryam D'Abo, Jason Isaacs, Annette Crosbie; **D:** Gary Sinyor; **W:** Gary Sinyor; **C:** Henry Braham; **M:** David A. Hughes, John Murphy.

The Solitary Man ⭐⭐ 1982
Glum look at a family breakup, from the husband's point of view. Holliman is good, but the exercise at large is regularly blues-inducing, and not especially inspiring or artful. **96m/C VHS.** Earl Holliman, Carrie Snodgrass, Lara Parker, Lane Smith, Nicolas Coster, Michelle Pfeiffer; **D:** John Llewellyn Moxey. **TV**

Solo ⭐⭐ 1977 (PG)
Young hitchhiker Peers enters the lives of the patrol pilot Gil and his teenage son. A plotless thing develops, headed nowhere—like this movie. Great New Zealand scenery might be worth the price of rental. **90m/C VHS.** Vincent (Vince Gill) Gill, Perry Armstrong, Martyn Sanderson, Lisa Peers; **D:** Tony Williams.

Solo ⭐⭐ 1996 (PG-13)
Fast-paced actioner stars Van Peebles as Solo, an android assassin with a heart of gold. It seems the muscle-bound, computerized killer is programmed with not only amazing fighting skills but the ability to think and learn. Solo who, being naughty in the sight of one-dimensional government bigwigs, is scheduled for replacement by a fighting machine that won't be so fickle when it comes to pulling the trigger. The chase is on when Solo learns of their plot and takes to the jungles of Central America, where together with the local peasants, the rebellious robot fights to preserve this humanity and his life. Poor man's "Terminator" is sprinkled with the kind of glib one-liners usually reserved for Schwarzenegger, although Van Peebles' presence up a notch. Adapted from Robert Mason's novel "Weapon." **106m/C VHS.** Mario Van Peebles, William Sadler, Seidy Lopez, Barry Corbin, Adrien Brody, Abraham Verduzco, Jaime Gomez, Damian Bechir, Joaquin Garrido; **D:** Norberto Barba; **W:** David Corley; **C:** Chris Walling; **M:** Christopher Franke.

Some Call It Loving ⭐ 1973 (R)
Bad, pretentious modern version of Sleeping Beauty, set in L.A. King buys the sleeping girl (Farrow) from a carnival show, but she doesn't live up to his ideal. Strong performances by all. **136m/C VHS, DVD.** Frank Sinatra, Dean Martin, Shirley MacLaine, Martha Hyer, Arthur Kennedy, Nancy Gates; **D:** Vincente Minnelli; **C:** William H. Daniels; **M:** Elmer Bernstein.

The Sombrero Kid ⭐⭐ 1942
The Kid unwittingly gets involved in a murder and is nearly hanged before his friends help him discover the real culprits. Plenty of action in this straight forward, fun western. **54m/B VHS.** Donald (Don "Red") Barry, Lynn Merrick, Rand Brooks; **D:** George Sherman.

Some Came Running ⭐⭐⭐ 1958
James Jones's follow-up novel to "From Here to Eternity" does not translate nearly as well to the screen. Overlong and with little plot, the action centers around a would-be writer who returns to his floozy girlfriend, and is holier-than-thou characters which populate the town in which he grew up and to which he has now returned. Strong performances by all. **136m/C VHS, DVD.** Frank Sinatra, Dean Martin, Shirley MacLaine, Martha Hyer, Arthur Kennedy, Nancy Gates; **D:** Vincente Minnelli; **C:** William H. Daniels; **M:** Elmer Bernstein.

Some Mother's Son ⭐⭐⭐ Sons
and Warriors 1996 (R) Young IRA members Gerard Quigley (Gillen) and Frank Higgins (O'Hara) are sentenced to long prison terms after an attack on the British army. Tough, politically active Annie Higgins (Flanagan) has already lost one son to "The Troubles" and is willing to support Frank in whatever he does. But her son Gerard's involvement takes apolitical schoolteacher Kathleen (Mirren) completely by surprise. When their sons join in a prison hunger strike, the two mothers lose the choice of supporting their sons possible deaths by starvation or allowing the prison's officials to force-feed them. The leads give tough, terrific performances in a heartwrenching story. **112m/C VHS.** IR GB Helen Mirren, Fionnula Flanagan, Aidan Gillen, David O'Hara, John Lynch, Tim Woodward, Ciaran Hinds, Gerard McSorley, Geraldine

Sole Voyage: The Revenge ⭐⭐ 1990
A Russian "Rambo" goes on a murderous rampage, the likes of which humanity has not yet seen. **91m/C VHS.** Ru, Mikhail Nojkine, Alexandre Fatiouchine; **D:** Mikhail Toumanichvili.

Solo Sunny ⭐⭐ 1980
Pop singer Sunny (Krossner) is constantly on the road with a mediocre band, trying to make a living. When she's kicked out of the group for consistently resisting the leader's sexual advances, she tries her hand at work out well, and Sunny is getting increasingly desperate. German with subtitles. **102m/C VHS.** GE Renate Krossner, Alexander Lang, Dieter Montag, Heide Kipp, Klaus Brasch; **D:** Konrad Wolf; **W:** Wolfgang Kohlhaase; **C:** Eberhard Geick; **M:** Gunther Fischer.

Solomon ⭐⭐½ 1998
Solomon is crowned king of Israel and vows to build a temple to house the Ark of the Covenant. In return, he is granted the gift of wisdom, of which he doesn't seem to make much use at first. He falls deeply in love with the Queen of Sheba but when she is forced to return to her homeland, Solomon falls into such a depression that he neglects his kingdom and allows corruption to spread. **172m/C VHS, DVD.** Ben Cross, Vivica A. Fox, Anouk Aimee, Max von Sydow, Maria Grazia Cucinotta, Stefania Rocca, David Suchet, Richard Dillane; **D:** Roger Young. **CABLE**

Solomon and Gaenor ⭐⭐ 1998 (R)
Around 1911, a young Jewish peddler named Solomon (Gruffudd) meets Gaenor (Roberts), the daughter of Welsh mineworkers. Hiding his Orthodox Jewish origins, Solomon calls himself Sam and the young duo are soon in love. Gaenor winds up pregnant and her family wants to send her away and force her to give up the baby. She finally tracks down Solomon's family but they are equally upset that their son is involved with a gentile. Amidst all this family turmoil, is a violent dispute between the workers and the mine owners. Conventional tear-stained period piece. **103m/C VHS, DVD.** GB Ioan Gruffudd, Nia Roberts, Mark Lewis Jones, William Thomas, Maureen Lipman, David Horovitch; **D:** Paul Morrison; **C:** Nina Kellgren; **M:** Ilona Sekacz.

Solomon and Sheba ⭐⭐ 1959
King Solomon's brother and the Egyptian Pharaoh send the Queen of Sheba to Israel to seduce King Solomon so they may gain his throne. Tyrone Power had filmed most of the lead role in this silly, overwrought epic when he died of a heart attack. The role was reshot, with Brynner (with a full head of hair) replacing him. Director Vidor's unfortunate last film. Shot on location in Spain. **139m/C VHS.** Yul Brynner, Gina Lollobrigida, Marisa Pavan, George Sanders, Alejandro Rey; **D:** King Vidor; **C:** Frederick A. (Freddie) Young; **M:** Malcolm Arnold.

Some Girls ⭐⭐½ 1988 (R)
A young man goes to Quebec to see his college girlfriend who informs him that she is not in love with him anymore. But she has two sisters ready to comfort him! Strange black comedy; Gregory as the girl's father elevates so-so story. **104m/C VHS.** Patrick Dempsey, Andre Gregory, Lila Kedrova, Florinda Bolkan, Jennifer Connelly, Sheila Kelley; **D:** Michael Hoffman; **M:** James Newton Howard.

Some Kind of Hero ⭐⭐ 1982
A Vietnam prisoner of war returns home to a changed world. Pryor tries hard, but can't get above this poorly written, unevenly directed film. **97m/C VHS.** Richard Pryor, Margot Kidder, Ray Sharkey, Ronny Cox, Lynne Moody, Olivia Cole; **D:** Michael Pressman; **W:** Robert Boris.

Some Kind of Wonderful ⭐⭐ 1987 (PG-13)
A high-school tomboy has a crush on a guy who also happens to be her best friend. Her feelings go unrequited as he falls for a rich girl with snobbish friends. In the end, true love wins out. Flawless cast includes a fetching Masterson at her best; hilarious script. Curtis does his Cary Grant impression. Classic scenes between Lemmon in drag and Joe E. Brown as a smitten suitor. Brown also has the film's famous closing punchline. Monroe sings "I Wanna Be Loved By You," "Running Wild," and "I'm Through With Love." One of the very funniest movies of all time. **120m/B VHS, DVD.** Marilyn Monroe, Tony Curtis, Jack Lemmon, George Raft, Pat O'Brien, Nehemiah Persoff, Joe E. Brown, Joan Shawlee, Mike Mazurki; **D:** Billy Wilder; **W:** Billy Wilder, I.A.L. Diamond; **C:** Charles Bryant Lang Jr.; **M:** Adolph Deutsch. **Oscars '59:** Costume Des. (B&W); **AFI '98:** Top 100; **British Acad. '59:** Actor (Lemmon); **Golden Globes '60:** Actor—Mus./Comedy (Lemmon), Actress—Mus./Comedy (Monroe), Film—Mus./Comedy. **Natl. Film Reg. '89.**

Some Like It Hot ⭐⭐⭐⭐ 1959
Two unemployed musicians witness the St. Valentine's Day massacre in Chicago. They disguise themselves as women and join an all-girl band headed for Miami to escape the gangsters' retaliation.

Some Folks Call It a Sling Blade ⭐⭐⭐ 1994
The short film that became 1996's critically acclaimed "Sling Blade." This stark black-and-white short, penned by Billy Bob Thornton and directed by George Hickenlooper ("Hearts of Darkness: A Filmmaker's Apocalypse"), premiered at Sundance. The original version only involves a young reporter's (Ritgwald) interview with Karl Childers (Thornton), in which he recalls the events that led him to be in the institution. Also includes "The Making of 'Some Folks Call It a Sling Blade'" (color, 13 minutes) which comprises interviews the stars, director, and producer. **29m/B VHS, DVD.** Billy Bob Thornton, Molly Ringwald, J.T. Walsh, Jefferson Mays, Suzanne Dyer; **D:** George Hickenlooper; **W:** Billy Bob Thornton; **C:** Kent Wakeford; **M:** Billy Bob.

O'Rawe; **D:** Terry George; **W:** Jim Sheridan, Terry George; **C:** Geoffrey Simpson; **M:** Bill Whelan.

Some Prefer Cake 🦴🦴 **1997** Best friends Kira (Fontaine) and Sydney (Howley) are also roomies in San Francisco. Kira's stage fright prevents her from pursuing a career as a stand-up comedian and she's resentful when the material she wrote for her sister (Gonzalez) makes her a success. Kira's also got problems with a one-night stand turned stalker (Saito). Meanwhile, Syd is insisting everything is fine but she has career and boyfriend problems. Both women struggle with their co-dependency until realizing that the only way to move forward is to do it without clinging to each other. **95m/C DVD.** Kathleen Fontaine, Tara Howley, Mimi Gonzalez, Machiko Saito, Desi del Valle, Leon Acord; **D:** Heidi Arnesen; **W:** Jeannie Kahaney; **C:** Matt Siegel.

Somebody Has to Shoot the Picture 🦴🦴½ **1990 (R)** Photographer Scheider is hired by a convicted man to take a picture of his execution. Hours before the event, Scheider uncovers evidence that leads him to believe the man is innocent. He then embarks in a race against time to save him. Adapted by Doug Magee from his book "Slow Coming Dark." Unpretentious, tough drama. **104m/C VHS.** Roy Scheider, Bonnie Bedelia, Robert Carradine, Andre Braugher, Arliss Howard; **D:** Frank Pierson; **W:** Doug Magee; **C:** Bojan Bazelli; **M:** James Newton Howard. **C A B L E**

Somebody Is Waiting 🦴½ **1996 (R)** Charlotte Ellis (Kinski) tries to be the best mom she can to her five kids after her abusive, drunken husband Roger (Byrne) finally abandons them. Eighteen-year-old Leon (Whitworth) seems to be headed down the same dark road after being arrested for drunk driving. Charlotte agrees to set up a bank account for Leon, if he'll move out, and is then killed in a robbery, where Leon is injured. Roger then shows up to look after his shattered family but it's only a matter of time before things get even worse. Pros Byrne and Kinski do what they can but the script is certainly no help. **90m/C VHS.** Gabriel Byrne, Nastassja Kinski, Johnny Whitworth, Rebecca Gayheart, Shirley Knight, Brian Donovan; **D:** Martin Donovan; **C:** Greg Gardiner; **M:** Ella Cmiral.

Somebody to Love 🦴🦴½ **1994 (R)** Spunky taxi dancer Mercedes (Perez) wants to be an actress despite the bad luck actor/boyfriend Harry (a subdued Keitel) has. One of her clients is the impious Ernesto (De Lorenzo), who quickly becomes infatuated by Mercedes and to impress her, takes a job with local racketeer Emilio (Quinn). Ernesto even decides to take a contract hit to get the money Mercedes needs to help out Harry, leading to tragedy. Confusing look at the fringes of the L.A. showbiz scene, with lots of missed chances though Perez gets some flashy diva scenes. **103m/C VHS, DVD.** Edward (Eddie) Bunker, Rosie Perez, Harvey Keitel, Michael Delorenzo, Anthony Quinn, Steve Buscemi, Stanley Tucci, Gerardo Mejia, Paul Herman; **Cameos:** Angel Aviles, Quentin Tarantino; **D:** Alexandre Rockwell; **W:** Alexandre Rockwell, Sergei Bodrov.

Somebody Up There Likes Me 🦴🦴🦴 **1956** Story of Rocky Graziano's (Newman) gritty battle from his poor, street-wise childhood to his prison term (where he developed his boxing skills) and his eventual success as the middleweight boxing champion of the world. Adapted from Graziano's autobiography. Superior performance by Newman (in his third screen role, after the miserable "The Silver Chalice" and forgettable "The Rack"); screen debuts for McQueen and Loggia. **113m/B VHS, DVD.** Paul Newman, Pier Angeli, Everett Sloane, Eileen Heckart, Sal Mineo, Robert Loggia, Steve McQueen; **D:** Robert Wise; **W:** Ernest Lehman; **C:** Joseph Ruttenberg; **M:** Bronislau Kaper. Oscars '56: Art Dir./Set Dec., B&W, B&W Cinematog.

Someone at the Door 🦴🦴 **1950** Reporter Medwin arranges to be suspected of killing his sister, thus providing him with a good story and advancing his career. His plan almost backfires, when he is almost executed. Remake of a 1936 film of the same name. **65m/B VHS. GB** Michael Medwin, Garry Marsh, Yvonne Owen, Hugh Latimer; **D:** Francis Searle.

Someone Behind the Door 🦴🦴½ **1971 (PG)** Evil brain surgeon Perkins implants murderous suggestions into psychopathic amnesia victim Bronson's mind, then instructs him to kill the surgeon's wife and her lover. **97m/C VHS, DVD.** Charles Bronson, Anthony Perkins, Jill Ireland, Henri Garcin; **D:** Nicolas Gessner; **W:** Nicolas Gessner, Marc Behm; **C:** Pierre Lhomme; **M:** Georges Garvarentz.

Someone Else's America 🦴🦴🦴 **1996 (R)** "Grumpy Old Men" explores friendship and the modern immigrant experience in Brooklyn. Bayo (Manojlovic) is a comical, sad-sack Serb who works at the bar of Alonso (Conti), a Spaniard who immigrated with his blind mother (Casares). Story follows Bayo's family as they illegally immigrate to chase the American dream and adapt to life once they arrive. Touchingly funny highlight involves a scheme to help men which enables Alonso's homesick mother to revisit her village in Spain. Filmed in Germany with sets built to resemble Brooklyn, picture has an appealingly unreal quality. Cast and crew together formed its own melting pot, with over 20 nationalities contributing. English and Serbo-Croatian with subtitles. **116m/C VHS. FR GB GE** Tom Conti, Miki (Predrag) Manojlovic, Maria Casares, Zorka Manojlovic, Sergej Trifunovic, Chia-ching Niu, Andjela Stojkovic, Ananda Ellis; **D:** Goran Paskaljevic; **W:** Gordan Mihic; **C:** Yorgos Arvanitis; **M:** Andrew Dickson.

Someone I Touched 🦴🦴½ **1975** Way-overdone melodrama starring Leachman as a finally pregnant woman who learns her husband and a teenager he slept with have venereal disease. **74m/C VHS.** Cloris Leachman, James Olson, Glynnis O'Connor, Andrew (Andy) Robinson, Allyn Ann McLerie; **D:** Lou Antonio.

Someone Like You 🦴🦴½ **2001 (PG-13)** New Yorker Jane (Judd) is a talk-show talent booker who falls for the program's new exec, Ray (Kinnear), who seems to be about her too. In fact, Jane gives up her apartment expecting to move in with Ray, then is suddenly dumped. Homeless, Jane agrees to temporarily share the loft of co-worker Eddie (Jackman), a one-night only stud. What it does give Jane a chance to test her theory comparing men to bulls, who aren't interested in a cow (or girlfriend) they've had before. Gets by because the cast is so darn cute. Based on the novel "Animal Husbandry" by Laura Zigman. **97m/C VHS, DVD. US** Ashley Judd, Hugh Jackman, Greg Kinnear, Marisa Tomei, Ellen Barkin, Peter Friedman, Catherine Dent, Laura Regan; **D:** Tony Goldwyn; **W:** Elizabeth Chandler; **C:** Anthony B. Richmond; **M:** Rolfe Kent.

Someone to Die For 🦴🦴 **1995 (R)** Accused murderer (and cop) Bernsen is out to prove his innocence but teams that the real killer may be very close to home. **98m/C VHS.** Corbin Bernsen, Ally Walker, Robert Stewart; **D:** Clay Borris.

Someone to Love 🦴🦴 **1987 (R)** Rootless filmmaker gathers all his single friends together and interviews them about their failed love lives. Welles's last film as an actor. Wildly uneven, interesting experiment. **110m/C VHS, DVD.** Henry Jaglom, Orson Welles, Sally Kellerman, Andrea Marcovicci, Michael Emil, Oja Kodar, Stephen Bishop, Ronee Blakley, Kathryn Harrold, Monte Hellman; **D:** Henry Jaglom; **W:** Henry Jaglom; **C:** Hanania Baer.

Someone to Watch Over Me 🦴🦴🦴 **1987 (R)** After witnessing the murder of a close friend, beautiful and very wealthy Claire Gregory (Rogers) must be protected from the killer. Working-class New York detective Mike Keegan (Berenger), who's assigned the duty, is more than taken with her, despite the fact that he has both a wife (a knowing Bracco) and son at home. A highly watchable, stylish romantic crime thriller. **106m/C VHS, DVD.** Tom Berenger, Mimi Rogers, Lorraine Bracco, Jerry Orbach, Andreas Katsulas, Tony DiBenedetto, James Moriarty, John Rubinstein; **D:** Ridley Scott; **W:** Howard Franklin; **C:** Steven Poster; **M:** Michael Kamen.

Somersault 🦴🦴 **2004** Troubled Heidi (Cornish) is a luscious, 16-year-old blonde testing her sexuality on her mother's boyfriend, which gets her kicked out of the house. She travels to the ski resort town of Jindabyne, where she casually trades sex for a place to stay. Eventually Heidi lands a job at a convenience store and persuades motel owner Irene (Curran) to rent her a room. She also finds sparks with 20-something Joe (Worthington), the son of a wealthy local farmer, but he's got problems too, and her neediness frightens him off. Debut feature for Shortland skimps on the character details but Cornish is a real heartbreaker. **106m/C DVD. AU** Sam Worthington, Lynette Curran, Leah Purcell, Nathaniel Dean, Abbie Cornish, Erik Thomson, Hollie Andrew, Olivia Pigeot, Blake Pittman; **D:** Cate Shortland; **W:** Cate Shortland; **C:** Robert Humphreys.

Something About Sex 🦴🦴 *Denial* **1998 (R)** Acerbic bachelor Art (Alexander) broaches the subject of marital fidelity with three couples at a dinner party. All the couples publicly denounce flings while privately not practicing what they preach. **92m/C VHS, DVD.** Patrick Dempsey, Jonathan Silverman, Christine Taylor, Amy Yasbeck, Jason Alexander, Leah Lail, Ryan Alosio, Jessica Lundy, Charles Shaughnessy, Angie Everhart, Hudson (Heidi) Leick, Nicholas Worth, Jessica Capshaw, Steve Schirripa; **Cameos:** Adam Rifkin; **D:** Adam Rifkin; **W:** Adam Rifkin; **C:** Francis Kenny.

Something for Everyone 🦴🦴½ *The Rook; Black Flowers for the Bride* **1970 (R)** A corrupt footman uses sex and murder in an attempt to take over the estate of an aristocratic Bavarian family in post-WWII Germany. He nearly succeeds in marrying the countess (Lansbury), but someone has been keeping tabs on him. Funny, ambitious black comedy. From the novel "The Code" by Harry Kressing. **112m/C VHS.** Angela Lansbury, Michael York, Anthony (Conlan) Higgins, Heidelinde Weis; **D:** Harold Prince; **C:** Walter Lassally.

Something for the Boys 🦴🦴 **1944** Chiquita (Miranda), Blossom (Blaine), and Harry (Silvers) are distant cousins who inherit a run-down southern plantation. Army Sgt. Rocky Fulton (O'Shea), who's stationed nearby, convinces them to turn the place into a hotel for military wives and to raise the money needed for restoration, they decide to put on a show. Como's debut as a singing soldier. **87m/C DVD.** Carmen Miranda, Vivian Blaine, Phil Silvers, Michael O'Shea, Sheila Ryan, Perry Como, Glenn Langan, Thurston Hall, Clarence (C. William) Kolb; **D:** Lewis Seiler; **W:** Robert Ellis, Helen Logan, Frank Gabrielson, Frank Gabrielson; **C:** Ernest Palmer; **M:** Jimmy McHugh.

Something in Common 🦴🦴½ **1986** A woman discovers her 22-year-old son is having an affair with a woman her own age. Nicely done comedy; Burstyn and Weld both make good use of a solid script. Made for TV. **94m/C VHS.** Ellen Burstyn, Tuesday Weld, Don Murray, Patrick Cassidy, Eli Wallach; **D:** Glenn Jordan; **W:** Susan Rice; **M:** John Addison. **TV**

Something in the Wind 🦴🦴½ **1947** Mary Collins (Durbin) is a DJ having a sort of romance with Donald Read (Dall), who gets the mistaken idea that she was once his wealthy Uncle Chester's (Winninger) mistress and is still after the family money. O'Connor gets to steal the show as Durbin's ally, Charlie. ♫Something in the Wind; Turntable Song; It's Only Love; You Wanna Keep Your Baby Lookin' Right; Happy Go Lucky and Free. **89m/B VHS, DVD.** Deanna Durbin, Donald O'Connor, John Dall, Charles Winninger, Helena Carter, Margaret Wycherly; **D:** Irving Pichel; **W:** William Bowers, Harry Kurnitz; **C:** Milton Krasner; **M:** Johnny Green.

Something More 🦴🦴 **1999 (R)** Sam (Goorjian), the romantic loser, and best bud Jim (Lovgren), the obnoxious womanizer, both fall for Kelly (West). The usual romantic complications abound as do all the usual romantic cliches. Cute cast. **97m/C VHS, DVD.** Michael Goorjian, Chandra West, David Lovgren, Jennifer Beals, Tom Cavanagh; **D:** Rob King; **W:** Peter Bryant; **C:** Jon Kranhouse; **M:** Rob Bryanton.

Something New 🦴🦴½ **2006 (PG-13)** Interracial romance with two completely delectable leads. Kenya (Lathan) is a successful African-American accountant who's too busy for romance. She does agree to a blind date, only to discover it's the very white Brian (Baker), an affable landscape architect. She rejects him as boyfriend material but hires him to redo her pathetic backyard. Kenya then tries to resist his wooing, especially when her upscale family and friends don't approve. Then IBM (Ideal Black Man) Mark (Underwood) enters the picture and Kenya must decide if she can get past her own prejudices and find that happy ending. **100m/C DVD. US** Sanaa Lathan, Simon Baker, Mike Epps, Donald Adeosun Faison, Blair Underwood, Wendy Raquel Robinson, Golden Brooks, Taraji P. Henson, Earl Billings, Katharine Towne, Alfre Woodard; **D:** Sanaa Hamri; **W:** Kristopher Turner; **C:** Shane Hurlbut; **M:** Wendy Melvoin, Lisa Coleman, Paul Anthony Stewart.

Something of Value 🦴🦴🦴 **1957** Good ensemble performances in a serious colonial story about the Mau Mau rebellion in Kenya. Hudson and Poitier are torn between their friendship and their opposing loyalties. Drama solidly grounded in fact from the book by Robert Ruark. **113m/B VHS.** Rock Hudson, Sidney Poitier, Wendy Hiller, Dana Wynter, Juano Hernandez; **D:** Richard Brooks; **W:** Richard Brooks; **M:** Miklos Rozsa.

Something Short of Paradise 🦴½ **1979 (PG)** The owner of a Manhattan movie theatre has an on again/off again romance with a magazine writer. Would-be Allenesque romantic comedy is too talky and pretentious. **87m/C VHS, DVD.** David Steinberg, Susan Sarandon, Jean-Pierre Aumont, Marilyn Sokol; **D:** David Helpern; **W:** Fred Barron.

Something Special 🦴🦴½ *Willy/Milly; I Was a Teenage Boy* **1986 (PG-13)** A 14-year-old girl has her wish come true when she is turned into a boy. Charming, original fantasy-comedy is fun for young and old. **93m/C VHS.** Pamela Segall, Patty Duke, Eric Gurry, John Glover, Seth Green; **D:** Paul Schneider; **W:** Walter Carbone.

Something to Sing About 🦴🦴 *Battling Hoofer* **1936** Musical melodrama about a New York bandleader's attempt to make it big in Hollywood. Allows Cagney the opportunity to demonstrate his dancing talents; he also sings. Rereleased in 1947. Also available colorized. Frawley was Fred on "I Love Lucy." ♫Any Old Love; Right or Wrong; Loving You; Out of the Blue; Something to Sing About. **84m/B VHS, DVD.** James Cagney, William Frawley, Evelyn Daw, Gene Lockhart; **D:** Victor Schertzinger.

Something to Talk About 🦴🦴½ *Grace Under Pressure* **1995 (R)** Romantic comedy/drama finds Grace (Roberts) running her overbearing father Wyly's (Duvall) horsebreeding operation and learning that her husband Eddie (the ever-charming Quaid) is tomcatting around. So Grace tosses him out and makes a tearful move with daughter Caroline (Aull) back home. Tart-tongued sister Emma Rae (Sedgwick) is sympathetic but long-suffering mama Georgia (Rowlands) thinks Grace should make the best of things (the way she's done). Naturally, Eddie wants his family back but the frazzled Grace is just coming to terms with what she wants out of life. Star appeal from both leads lends this familiar plot some spark. **106m/C VHS, DVD.** Julia Roberts, Dennis Quaid, Robert Duvall, Gena Rowlands, Kyra Sedgwick, Brett Cullen, Haley Aull, Muse Watson, Anne Shropshire; **D:** Lasse Hallstrom; **W:** Callie Khouri; **C:** Sven Nykvist; **M:** Hans Zimmer.

Something Weird woof! **1968** McCabe is disfigured horribly in an electrical accident. A seemingly beautiful witch fixes his face, on condition that he be her lover. The accident also gave him ESP— and it gets cheesier from there. **80m/C VHS, DVD.** Tony McCabe, Elizabeth Lee, William Brooker, Mudite Arums, Taed Heil, Lawrence Wood, Larry Wellington, Roy Collodi, Jeffrey Allen, Stan Dale, Richard Nilsson, Carolyn Smith, Norm Lenet, Louis Newman, Dick Gatfield, Janet Charlton, Lee

Something Wicked This Way Comes 🐾🐾 1983 (PG) Two young boys discover the evil secret of a mysterious traveling carnival that visits their town. Bradbury wrote the screenplay for this much-anticipated expensive adaptation of his own novel. Good special effects, but disappointing. 94m/C VHS, DVD. Jason Robards Jr., Jonathan Pryce, Diane Ladd, Pam Grier, Richard (Dick) Davalos, James Stacy, Royal Dano; **W:** Ray Bradbury; **C:** Stephen Burum; **M:** James Horner.

Something Wild 🐾🐾 1986 (R) Mild-mannered business exec Daniels is picked up by an impossibly free-living vamp with a Louise Brooks hairdo, and taken for the ride of his up-till-then staid life, eventually leading to explosive violence. A sharp-edged comedy with numerous changes of pace. Too-happy ending wrecks it, but it's great either way. Look for cameos from filmmakers John Waters and John Sayles. 113m/C VHS, DVD, Jeff Daniels, Melanie Griffith, Ray Liotta, Margaret Colin, Tracey Walter, Dana Peru, Jack Gilpin, Su Tissue, Kenneth Utt, Sister Carol East, John Waters, Charles Napier; **D:** Jonathan Demme; **W:** E. Max Frye; **C:** Tak Fujimoto; **M:** Rosemary Paul, John Cale, Laurie Anderson; Golden Globes '04: Actress—Mus./Comedy (Keaton); Natl. Bd. of Review '03: Actress (Keaton).

Something's Gotta Give 🐾🐾🐾 2003 (PG-13) The title's bland but the film is anything but (particularly for the woman of a certain age). Harry Sanborn (Nicholson) is a legendary womanizer. Now 60-something, he's notorious for dating only much-younger chicks. Harry's current squeeze is Marin (Peet), who takes Harry to her mom's Hamptons beach house to consummate the relationship. Turns out mom, successful (if neurotic) divorced playwright Erica Barry (Keaton), and her sister, feminist professor Zoe (McDormand), are there as well. Harry has a real heart attack and his doctor, Julian Mercer (Reeves), says Harry can't travel, leading to changing ideas, beds, and relationships. It's Keaton's film all the way (she's a natural wonder) and even scene-stealer Nicholson concedes to her charm; McDormand provides some droll asides and Reeves is appropriately earnest. 124m/C DVD, US Diane Keaton, Jack Nicholson, Keanu Reeves, Amanda Peet, Frances McDormand, Rachel Ticotin, Paul Michael Glaser, Jon Favreau, KaDee Strickland; **D:** Nancy Meyers; **W:** Nancy Meyers; **C:** Michael Ballhaus; **M:** Hans Zimmer.

Sometimes a Great Notion 🐾🐾 1971 *Never Give an Inch* (PG) Trouble erupts in a small Oregon town when a family of loggers decide to honor a contract when the other loggers go on strike. Newman's first role as an old man. Based on the novel by Ken Kesey. 15m/C VHS, Paul Newman, Henry Fonda, Lee Remick, Richard Jaeckel, Michael Sarrazin; **D:** Paul Newman; **W:** John Gay; **M:** Henry Mancini.

Sometimes in April 🐾🐾🐾 2005 In 1994 almost one million citizens of Rwanda were massacred in 100 days. Focusing on two brothers, one a Rwandan Army officer and one a broadcaster at an extremist radio station, the film gives the country's genocide perspective and humanitarian faces. In the same vein as "Hotel Rwanda," filmed in Rwanda using the locals as extras. Paints a powerful picture of a genocide that may have otherwise gone unnoticed by most of the Western world. 140m/C DVD. Idris Elba, Debra Winger, Noah Emmerich, Oris Erhuero, Carole Karemara, Pamela Nomvete; **D:** Raoul Peck; **W:** Raoul Peck; **C:** Eric Guichard; **M:** Bruno Coulais. **TV**

Sometimes They Come Back 🐾🐾 1991 (R) Another Stephen King tale of terror. Matheson plays a man haunted by the tragedy in his past. A witness to his brother's death, he also witnesses the fiery crash of his brother's killers. Only now they have returned from the dead, to take their revenge on him. 97m/C VHS, DVD. Tim Matheson, Brooke Adams, Robert Rusler, William Sanderson; **D:** Tom

Ahlsmann, Roger Papsch, Daniel Carrington; **D:** Herschell Gordon Lewis; **W:** James F. Hurley; **C:** Herschell Gordon Lewis, Andy Romanoff.

Sometimes They Come Back... Again 🐾1/2 1996 (R) Psychologist John Porter (Gross) and his teenaged daughter (Swank) return to Porter's hometown after his mother's mysterious death. He should know you can never go home again since they're both soon threatened by a young man (Arquette) involved in the ritualistic murder of Porter's sister years before. Gruesome special effects are the highlight. 98m/C VHS, DVD. Michael Gross, Hilary Swank, Alexis Arquette, Jennifer Elise Cox, William Morgan Sheppard; **D:** Adam Grossman; **W:** Adam Grossman; **C:** Christopher Baffa; **M:** Peter Manning Robinson. **TV**

Sometimes They Come Back... For More 🐾🐾 1999 (R) Two military officers investigate the disappearance of crew members at a government outpost in Antarctica. 88m/C VHS, DVD. Clayton Rohner, Chase Masterson, Faith Ford, Max Perlich, Damian Chapa; **D:** Daniel Berk.

Somewhere I'll Find You 🐾🐾 1942 Clark and Turner heat up the screen as correspondents running all over the war-torn world in their second film together ("Honky Tonk" was their first). Notable mainly because Gable's beloved wife, Carole Lombard, was killed in a plane crash just three days into production. Gable forced himself to finish the film and it became one of the studio's biggest hits. Although critics applauded his determination to complete the film, many felt his performance was subdued and strained. Film debut of Wynn. Based on a story by Charles Hoffman. 108m/B VHS, Clark Gable, Lana Turner, Robert Sterling, Reginald Owen, Lee Patrick, Charles Dingle, Tamara Shayne, Leonid Kinskey, Diana Lewis, Molly Lamont, Patricia Dane, Sara Haden, Keenan Wynn; **D:** Wesley Ruggles; **W:** Walter Reisch, Marguerite Roberts.

Somewhere in Sonora 🐾🐾 1933 Early Wayne Western set in Old Mexico. Wayne plays a rodeo performer who joins an outlaw gang to save a friend when he stands up to a gang of gambling swindlers. Silent. Like most of the other films of the series, this was a remake of a Ken Maynard silent. Based on a story and the novel "Somewhere South in Sonora" by Will Levington Comfort. 59m/B VHS, DVD. John Wayne, Henry B. Walthall, Shirley Palmer, (John) Paterson) McGowan, Frank Rice, Billy Franey, Paul Fix, Ralph Lewis; **D:** Mack V. Wright; **W:** Joe Roach.

Somewhere in the City 🐾🐾1/2 1997 Covers the screwy lives of six tenants at a Lower East Side New York apartment building. Betty (a subdued Bernhard) is an unlucky-in-love therapist who's still neurotically trying. She agrees to help out Chinese exchange student Lu Lu (Ling) who's desperately seeking a green card marriage. Then there's unhappy wife Marta (Mutti), whose upstairs lover, Franke (Burke), is a gay actor. Graham crook. There's also gay actor Graham (Stormare), who's disappointed personally and professionally, and basement-dwelling Che (Stewart), a trust-fund baby who wants to be a radical revolutionary. Sporadically amusing with a talented cast. 93m/C VHS, DVD. Sandra Bernhard, Bai Ling, Ornella Muti, Robert John Burke, Peter Stormare, Paul Anthony Stewart, Bule Ogier, James Edward J. Koch; **D:** Ramin Niami; **W:** Ramin Niami, Patrick Dillon; **C:** Igor Sunara; **M:** John Cale.

Somewhere in Time 🐾🐾 1980 (PG) Playwright Reeve (in his first postcard role) falls in love with a beautiful woman in an old portrait. Through self-hypnosis he goes back in time to 1912 to discover what their relationship might have been. The film made a star of the Grand Hotel, located on Mackinac Island in Michigan, where it was shot. Drippy rip-off of the brilliant novel "Time and Again" by Jack Finney. Reeve is horrible, Seymour is undersexed. All in all, rather wretched. 103m/C VHS, DVD. Christopher Reeve, Jane Seymour, Christopher Plummer, Teresa Wright; **D:** Jeannot Szwarc; **W:** Richard Matheson; **C:** Isidore Mankofsky; **M:** John Barry.

Somewhere Tomorrow 🐾🐾1/2 1985 (PG) A lonely, fatherless teenage girl is befriended by the ghost of a young man killed in a plane crash. Charming and moving, if not perfect. 91m/C VHS, DVD, Sarah Jessica Parker, Nancy Addison, Tom Shea; **D:** Robert Wiemer.

Sommersby 🐾🐾1/2 1993 (PG-13) A too-good-to-be-true period romance based on the film "The Return of Martin Guerre." A Civil War veteran (Gere) returns to his wife's (Foster) less-than-open arms. She soon warms up to his kind, sensitive and caring manner, but can't quite believe the change that the war has wrought. Neither can the neighbors, especially the one (Pullman) who had his own eye on Laurel Sommersby. So is he really Jack Sommersby or an all too clever impostor? Lots of hankies needed for the tender-hearted. Strong performance by Foster. Filmed in Virginia (passing for the state of Tennessee). 114m/C VHS, DVD. Richard Gere, Jodie Foster, Bill Pullman, James Earl Jones, William Windom, Brett Kelley, Richard Hamilton, Maury Chaykin, Lanny Flaherty, Frank Faison, Wendell Wellman, Clarice Taylor, R. Lee Ermey; **D:** Jon Amiel; **W:** Nicholas Meyer, Sarah Kernochan; **C:** Philippe Rousselot; **M:** Danny Elfman.

Son-in-Law 🐾1/2 1993 (PG-13) Surfer-dude comic Shore's a laconic fish out of water as a city-boy rock 'n' roller who falls in love with a country beauty, marries her, and visits the family farm to meet the new in-laws. Once there, he weirds out everyone how to live, Pauly style. Silly entertainment best appreciated by Shore fans. 95m/C VHS, DVD. Pauly Shore, Carla Gugino, Lane Smith, Cindy Pickett, Mason Adams, Patrick Renna, Dennis Burkley, Dan Gauthier, Tiffani-Amber Thiessen; **D:** Steve Rash; **W:** Adam Small, Shawn Schepps, Fax Bahr; **C:** Peter Deming; **M:** Richard Gibbs.

Son of a Gun 🐾🐾1/2 1919 A lovable but ornery cowboy gets banished from the country for disturbing the peace. However, he wins the favor of the townspeople when he stands up to a gang of gambling swindlers. Silent. 60m/B VHS. "Broncho" Billy Anderson, Fred Church, Frank Whitson, Joy Lewis; **D:** "Broncho" Billy Anderson.

Son of Ali Baba 🐾🐾 1952 Keshma Baba, son of Ali Baba, enters the military academy to learn to withstand adversity. He has other ideas however, until he must suddenly fill his father's shoes and fight the evil Caliph. He fights bravely with the help of his childhood friend, a beautiful princess, in this swashbuckler. 85m/C VHS. Tony Curtis, Piper Laurie, Susan Cabot, Victor Jory, Hugh O'Brian, William Reynolds, Gerald Mohr; **D:** Ross Hunter.

Son of a Gun [see duplicate]

Son of God's Country 🐾1/2 1948 Utterly hackneyed, near-comic attempt at a western. Good-guy U.S. Marshal poses as a crook to get the lowdown on the varmints. 60m/B VHS, Monte Hale, Pamela Blake, Adrian Booth; **D:** R.G. Springsteen; **C:** John MacBurnie; **M:** R. Dale Butts.

Somewhere Tomorrow [see above]

Son of Dracula 🐾🐾 1943 In this late-coming sequel to the Universal classic, a stranger named Alucard is invited to America by a Southern belle obsessed with eternal life. It is actually Dracula himself, not his son, who wreaks havoc in this spine-tingling chiller. 80m/B VHS, DVD, Lon Chaney Jr., Evelyn Ankers, Frank Craven, Robert Paige, Louise Allbritton, J. Edward Bromberg, Samuel S. Hinds; **D:** Robert Siodmak; **W:** Eric Taylor; **C:** George Robinson.

Son of Flubber 🐾🐾1/2 1963 Sequel to "The Absent Minded Professor" finds Fred MacMurray still toying with his prodigious invention, Flubber, now in its form of Flubbergas, which causes those who inhale it to float away. Disney's first-ever sequel is high family wackiness. 96m/C VHS, DVD. Fred MacMurray, Nancy Olson, Tommy Kirk, Leon Ames, Joanna Moore, Keenan Wynn, Charlie Ruggles, Paul Lynde; **D:** Robert Stevenson; **C:** Edward Colman; **M:** George Bruns.

Son of Captain Blood 🐾1/2 *Figlio del Capitano Blood* 1962 (G) The son of the famous pirate meets up with his father's enemies on the high seas. The son plays the son of the character (the elder Flynn played in "Captain Blood." Let's just say the gimmick didn't work. 90m/C VHS. *SP* Sean Flynn, Ann Todd; **D:** Tulio Demicheli.

Son of Godzilla 🐾🐾 *Gojira no Musuko: Monster Island's Decisive Battle: Godzilla's Son* 1966 Dad and junior protect beauty Maeda from giant spiders on a remote island ruled by a mad scientist. Fun monster filck with decent special effects. 86m/C VHS, DVD. JP Akira Kubo, Beverly (Bihari) Maeda, Tadao Takashima, Akihiko Hirata, Kenji Sahara; **D:** Jun Fukuda; **W:** Shinichi Sekizawa, Kazue Shiba; **C:** Kazuo Yamada; **M:** Masaru Sato.

Son of Hercules in the Land of Darkness 🐾 1963 Argolis (Vadis) must rescue prisoners trapped in an underground city. 74m/B VHS, DVD. *IT* Dan Vadis, Carol Brown, Spela Rozin; **D:** Alvaro Mancori; **W:** Alvaro Mancori; **C:** Claude Haroy; **M:** Francesco De Masi.

Son of Ingagi 🐾🐾1/2 1940 Lonely ape-man kidnaps woman in search of romance. Early all-black horror film stars Williams of "Amos 'n' Andy." 70m/B VHS. Zack Williams, Laura Bowman, Alfred Grant, Spencer Williams Jr., Daisy Bufford, Arthur Ray; **D:** Richard C. Kahn; **W:** Spencer Williams Jr.; **C:** Roland Price, Herman Schopp.

Son of Frankenstein 🐾🐾🐾 1939 The second sequel (after "The Bride of Frankenstein") to the 1931 version of the horror classic. The good doctor's skeptical son returns to the family manse and becomes obsessed with his father's work and with reviving the creature. Full of memorable characters and brooding ambience. Karloff's last appearance as the monster. 99m/C VHS, DVD, Basil Rathbone, Bela Lugosi, Boris Karloff, Lionel Atwill, Josephine Hutchinson, Donnie Dunagan, Emma Dunn, Edgar Norton, Lawrence Grant, Lionel Belmore; **D:** Rowland V. Lee; **W:** Willis Cooper; **C:** George Robinson.

Son of Fury 🐾🐾 1942 Dashing Tyrone Power is left penniless when his sinister uncle (Sanders) wrongfully takes the family fortune. Ben escapes to sea and the while plotting his revenge. But he still finds time to fall for the zealous Tierney. Fine 18th-century costumer done in grand style. Based on the novel "Benjamin Blake" by Edison Marshall. 98m/C VHS, Tyrone Power, Gene Tierney, George Sanders, Frances Farmer, Roddy McDowall, John Carradine, Elsa Lanchester, Harry Davenport, Kay Johnson, Dudley Digges, Halliwell Hobbes, Marian Lamont, Arthur Hohl, Pedro de Cordoba, Dennis Hoey, Heather Thatcher; **D:** John Cromwell; **W:** Philip Dunne; **M:** Alfred Newman.

Son of Gascogne 🐾🐾1/2 *Les Fils de Gascogne* 1995 Offbeat comedy about identity, romance, and wish fulfillment. Gavicy Harvey (Colin) is serving as a travel guide to a group of Georgian folksingers when they are giving concerts in Paris. Harvey falls for their pretty teenaged interpreter, Dinara (Droukarova), who reciprocates. The duo meet Marco (Dreyfus), a chauffeur/con man, who insists that Harvey doesn't know who his father is) and insists on introducing him to his dad's cinematic colleagues (thus supplying cameos of numerous French cinema greats). French in with subtitles. 106m/C VHS, DVD. *FR* Gregoire Colin, Jean-Claude Dreyfus, Dinara Drukarova, Bernadette LaFont, Alexandre Stewart, Stephane Audran, Jean-Claude Briely, Bule Ogier, Marie-France Pisier, Anemone, Patrice Leconte, Marina Vlady; **D:** Pascal Aubier; **W:** Paul Gangelin; **C:** Jean-Jacques Flori; **M:** Angelo Zurzolo.

Son of Kong 🐾🐾1/2 1933 King Kong's descendant is discovered on an island amid prehistoric creatures in this ten-humorous sequel to RKO's immensely popular "King Kong." Hoping to capitalize on the enormous success of its predecessor, director Schoedsack quickly threw this together. As a result, its success at the boxoffice did not match the original's, and didn't deserve to. But it's fun. Nifty special effects from Willis O'Brien, the man who brought them to us the first time. 70m/B VHS, DVD. Robert Armstrong, Helen Mack; **D**: Ernest B. Schoedsack; **M**: Max Steiner.

The Son of Monte Cristo 🐾🐾½ 1940 Illegitimate offspring of the great swashbuckler with Robert Donat proves they made pathetic, pointless sequels even back then. 102m/B VHS, DVD. Louis Hayward, Joan Bennett, George Sanders, Florence Bates, Montagu Love, Ralph Byrd, Clayton Moore; **D**: Rowland V. Lee; **W**: George Bruce; **C**: George Robinson; **M**: Edward Ward.

Son of Paleface 🐾🐾🐾½ 1952 Hilarious sequel to the original Hope gagfest, with the Harvard-educated son of the original character (again played by Hope) heading west to claim an inheritance. Hope runs away with every cowboy cliche and even manages to wind up with the girl. Songs include "Buttons and Bows" (reprised from the original), "There's a Cloud in My Valley of Sunshine," and "Four-legged Friend." 95m/C VHS, DVD. Bob Hope, Jane Russell, Roy Rogers, Douglass Dumbrille, Iron Eyes Cody, Bill Williams, Harry von Zell; **D**: Frank Tashlin; **W**: Malcolm Stuart Boylan; **C**: Henry Freulich; **M**: Clarence Wheeler.

Son of Rusty 🐾🐾½ 1947 Danny and his friends are warned to stay away from the farm of suspicious Jed Barlow. But Rusty keeps running away to see Jed's dog Barb and Danny gets to know Jed. Then Danny must stand by his new friend when word of Jed's past turns folks against him. (Rusty and Barb have puppies too.) 70m/B VHS, Steve (Stephen) Dunne, Tom Powers, Ann Doran, Thurston Hall, Ted Donaldson; **D**: Lew Landers; **W**: Malcolm Stuart Boylan; **C**: Henry Freulich; **M**: Clarence Wheeler.

Son of Samson 🐾½ *Le Geant de la Vallee Das Rois* 1962 Man with large pectoral muscles puts an end to the evil Queen of Egypt's reign of terror 89m/C VHS, DVD. **FR IT TU** Mark Forest, Chelo Alonso, Angelo Zanolli, Vira (Vera) Silenti, Frederica Ranchi; **D**: Carlo Campogalliani.

Son of Sinbad 🐾🐾 *Nights in a Harem* 1955 Sinbad, captured by the Khalif of Baghdad, must bring him the secret of Greek fire to gain his freedom and free the city from the forces of mighty Tamerlane. About three dozen nubile young women wear very little and gambol with our hero herein; much-anticipated skinfest caused a scandal, nurtured by Howard Hughes for profit. 88m/C VHS. Dale Robertson, Sally Forrest, Vincent Price, Lili St. Cyr, Mari Blanchard, Joi Lansing; **D**: Ted Tetzlaff.

The Son of the Bride 🐾🐾½ *El Hijo de la Novia* 2001 (R) Middle-aged Rafael Belvedere (Darin) manages the Buenos Aires restaurant started by his father Nino (Alterio) and mother Norma (Aleandro). Rafael's workaholic behavior has cost him his marriage and estranged him from his daughter and his girlfriend Naty (Verbeke). After suffering a mild heart attack, Rafael is forced to slow down and take more of an interest in domestic matters, including Nino's decision to remarry his wife in the church service they never had, even though Norma is living in a nursing home because she suffers from Alzheimer's and is frequently unaware of what is going on around her. Spanish with subtitles. 123m/C DVD. **AR** Ricardo Darin, Hector Alterio, Norma Aleandro, Natalia Verbeke, Eduardo Blanco, Gimena Nobile, Claudia Fontan; **D**: Juan J. Campanella; **W**: Juan J. Campanella, Fernando Castets; **C**: Daniel Shulman; **M**: Angel Illaramendi.

animation company, finding the magical mask in time for his company's Halloween party. Of course he puts it on and gets transformed. Before the night is over, Avery gets a promotion and impregnates his wife (how's that for multitasking?). Soon after their son Alvey is born they realize that he's not like other kids. He has masklike powers and the ability to warp into a freakish tornado of cartoon characters. Flick wilts under the weight of the digital effects, which on a baby seem creepily misplaced. 86m/C DVD. Jamie Kennedy, Alan Cumming, Traylor Howard, Steven Wright, Liam Falconer, Ryan Falconer, Kal Penn, Bob Hoskins; **D**: Lawrence (Larry) Guterman; **W**: Lance Khazei; **C**: Greg Gardiner; **M**: Randy Edelman. Golden Raspberries '05: Worst Remake/Sequel.

Son of the Morning Star 🐾🐾🐾 1991 (PG-13) Lavish made for TV retelling of Custer's famed-butt kicking. Complex characterizations and unusual points of view, based on the book by Evan S. Connell. 186m/C VHS. Gary Cole, Rosanna Arquette, Dean Stockwell, Rodney A. Grant, Terry O'Quinn, David Strathairn, Stanley Anderson, George American Horse; **D**: Mike Robe. **TV**

Son of the Pink Panther 🐾½ *Blake Edwards' Son of the Pink Panther* 1993 (PG) Lame leftover from the formerly popular comedy series. Director Edwards has chosen not to resurrect Inspector Clouseau, instead opting for his son (Benigni), who turns out to be just as much of a bumbling idiot as his father. Commissioner Dreyfus (Lom), the twitching, mouth-foaming former supervisor of the original Clouseau is looking for a kidnapped princess (Farentino) along with Clouseau, Jr., who himself does not know he is the illegitimate son of his partner's dead nemesis. Many of the sketches have been recycled from previous series entrants. Rather than being funny, they seem used and shopworn like a threadbare rug. 115m/C VHS, DVD. Roberto Benigni, Herbert Lom, Robert Davi, Debrah Farentino, Claudia Cardinale, Burt Kwouk, Shabana Azmi; **D**: Blake Edwards; **W**: Blake Edwards; **C**: Dick Bush; **M**: Henry Mancini.

The Son of the Shark 🐾🐾🐾 *Le Fils du Requin* 1993 Simon (Da Silva) and Martin Vanderhoes (Vandendaele) have been abandoned by their mother and prefer to live as homeless delinquents rather than with their drunken father. The boys commit petty crimes and vandalism to survive (always escaping from foster homes and institutions) while Martin dreams of running away to his true home in the ocean—proclaiming himself to be "the son of a female shark." Depressing and casually cruel; based on a true story. French with subtitles. 88m/C VHS. **FR** Ludovic Vandendaele, Erick Da Silva, Sandrine Blancke, Maxime LeRoux; **D**: Agnes Merlet; **W**: Agnes Merlet; **C**: Gerard Simon; **M**: Bruno Coulais.

Son of the Sheik 🐾🐾🐾 1926 This sequel to Valentino's star-making "The Sheik" (1921) also turned out to be his last film. Ahmed (Valentino) falls in love with dancing girl Yasmin (Banky). He leader of a group of thieves, who tells the sheik's son that Yasmin has betrayed him. After his escape, Ahmed takes revenge by kidnapping Yasmin. Eventually, all the misunderstandings are resolved. Based on the novel by E.M. Hull. 62m/B VHS, DVD. Rudolph Valentino, Vilma Banky, Montagu Love, George Fawcett, Karl (Daen) Dane, Agnes Ayres; **D**: George Fitzmaurice; **W**: Frances Marion; **C**: George Barnes. Natl. Film Reg. 03.

Son of Zorro 🐾🐾 1947 Zorro takes the law into his own hands to protect ranchers from bandits. A serial in 13 chapters. 164m/B VHS. George Turner, Peggy Stewart, Roy Barcroft, Edward Cobb, Ernie Adams, Stanley Price, Edmund Cobb, Ken Terrell; **D**: Spencer Gordon Bennet, Fred Brannon; **W**: Frank (Franklyn) Adreon, Basil Dickey, Jesse Duffy; **C**: Bud Thackery.

Sonatine 🐾🐾 1996 (R) Middle-age Yakuza mobster Murakama (director Kitano, using his screen name Beat Takeshi) wishes to retire but is instead sent to mediate a low-level gang war. Upon arrival, an attempt is made on his life, so he and

his men hole up at a beach house. The young punks of the gang engage in horseplay and antics that indicate their violent natures and signal that all will not remain calm for long. Kitano's performance, writing, and direction are superb, understating the violence while not glamorizing it, and showing the effect it has on the man who carries it out. The relatively tranquil setting of the hideout allows some humor and character development, as well as preventing the cliches that usually pop up in this type of movie. Ever on the prowl for Far East gangster chic, Tarantino's Rolling Thunder brought this one to U.S. shores. Japanese with subtitles. 93m/C VHS, DVD. **JP** Takeshi "Beat" Kitano, Aya Kokumai, Tetsu Watanabe, Masanobu Katsumura, Susumu Terashima, Ren Osugi, Tonbo Zushi, Eiji Minakata, Kenichi Yajima; **D**: Takeshi "Beat" Kitano; **W**: Takeshi "Beat" Kitano; **C**: Katsumi Yanagishima; **M**: Jo Hasaishi.

A Song for Martin 🐾🐾🐾 *En Sang for Martin* 2001 (PG-13) Love found and lost but not in the usual way. Martin (Wolter) is a famous conductor/composer and Barbara (Seldahl) is his first violinist. Both are past middle-age and married but that doesn't stop them from falling deliriously in love, divorcing their spouses, and marrying each other. But Martin's memory soon begins to give him trouble and he is diagnosed with Alzheimer's, which causes him to push Barbara away. Swedish with subtitles. 118m/C VHS, DVD. **DK SW** Sven Wollter, Viveka Seldahl, Reine Brynolfsson, Linda Kallgren, Lisa Werlinder; **D**: Bille August; **W**: Bille August; **C**: Jorgen Persson; **M**: Stefan Nilsson.

A Song Is Born 🐾🐾 1948 A group of music professors try to trace the history of music. Kaye is in charge of a U.S. music foundation whose research has led him up to ragtime. He is soon, however, thrust into the sometimes seedy world of jazz joints and night spots, all in the name of research. Enter love interest Mayo, a woman on the run from her gangster boyfriend who hides out at the foundation. Not one of Kaye's funniest or best, but if you enjoy big band music, you'll love this. Includes music by Louis Armstrong and his orchestra, Tommy Dorsey and his orchestra, and Charlie Barnet and his orchestra. This was Kaye's last film for Goldwyn. 🎵 A Song is Born; Stealth Boogie; Anitra's Dance; I'm Getting Sentimental Over You; Blind Barnabas; Mockin' Bird; Redskin Rhumba; The Goldwyn Stomp; Daddy-O. 113m/B VHS. Danny Kaye, Virginia Mayo, Benny Goodman, Hugh Herbert, Steve Cochran, J. Edward Bromberg, Felix Bressart; **D**: Howard Hawks; **C**: Gregg Toland.

Song o' My Heart 🐾🐾🐾 1929 An early musical starring popular Irish tenor McCormack as a singer forced to abandon his career when he marries a woman he does not love. A tour de force for the lead in his movie debut. 🎵 Little Boy Blue; Paddy Me Lad; I Hear You Calling Me; A Fair Story by the Fireside; Just For a Day; Kitty My Love; The Rose of Tralee; A Pair of Blue Eyes; I Feel You Near Me. 91m/B VHS. John McCormack, Maureen O'Sullivan, John Garrick, J.M. Kerrigan, Tommy Clifford, Alice Joyce; **D**: Frank Borzage.

Song of Arizona 🐾🐾 1946 Rogers and the Sons of the Pioneers arrive to aid their pal Hayes against a gang of bank robbers in this modern-day oater. Eight songs perpetually punctuate the perfunctory plot, particularly "Will Ya Be My Darling," "Half-a-Chance Ranch," and the title tune. 54m/B VHS, DVD. Roy Rogers, Dale Evans, George "Gabby" Hayes, Lyle Talbot, Bob Nolan; **D**: Frank McDonald.

The Song of Bernadette 🐾🐾🐾 1943 Depicts the true story of a peasant girl who sees a vision of the Virgin Mary in a grotto at Lourdes in 1858. The girl is directed to dig at the grotto for water that will heal those who believe in its powers, much to the astonishment and concern of the townspeople. Based on Franz Werfel's novel. Directed with tenderness and carefully cast, and appealing to religious and sentimental susceptibilities, it was a boxoffice smash. 156m/B VHS, DVD. Charles Bickford,

Lee J. Cobb, Jennifer Jones, Vincent Price, Anne Revere, Gladys Cooper; **D**: Henry King; **C**: Arthur C. Miller; **M**: Alfred Newman. Oscars '43: Actress (Jones), B&W Cinematog., Orig. Dramatic Score; Golden Globes '44: Actress—Drama (Jones), Director (King), Film—Drama.

Song of Freedom 🐾🐾½ 1936 John Zinga (Robeson) is a British-born black dockworker whose vocal gifts are discovered by an opera impresario. After realizing a career as a concert performer, Zinga ventures to Africa to investigate his ancestry and finds he has royal roots, and that his tribe have fallen under the grip of corrupt spiritualists. Robeson turns in a fine performance in what is otherwise an average film. 🎵 Sleepy River; Lonely Road; Song of Freedom; The Black Emperor. 80m/B VHS, DVD. **GB** Paul Robeson, Elisabeth Welch, George Mozart; **D**: J. Elder Willis; **W**: Ingram D'Abbes, Fenn Sherie; **C**: Eric Cross, Harry Rose.

Song of Love 🐾🐾🐾 1947 Hepburn gracefully depicts the gifted 19th-century concert pianist Clara Wieck Schumann, who set aside her talents to be the wife of composer Robert Schumann and care for their seven children, which she did by herself after his untimely death in a mental facility. Clara shunned a marriage proposal from her deceased husband's star pupil, Johannes Brahms, who had long been infatuated with her, in order to dedicate her life to performing Schumann's works. 121m/B VHS, DVD. Katharine Hepburn, Paul Henreid, Robert Walker, Henry Daniell, Leo G. Carroll, Gigi Perreau, Ann Carter, Jimmy Hunt, Elsa (Else) Janssen, Janine Perreau, Ellene Janssen, Roman Bohnen, Ludwig Stossel, Tala Birell, Konstantin Shayne, Henry Stephenson; **D**: Clarence Brown; **W**: Robert Ardrey, Ivan Tors, Allen Vincent; **C**: Harry Stradling Sr.

Song of Nevada 🐾🐾 1944 Rogers woos the high-society daughter (Evans, of course) of a rancher (Hall). Quintessential Roy-n-Dale. 🎵 It's Love, Love, Love; New Moon Over Nevada; Hi Ho Little Dogies; The Harum Scarum Barber-O of the Harmonium; What Are We Going to Do?; A Cowboy Has to Yodel in the Morning. 60m/B VHS, DVD. Roy Rogers, Dale Evans, Thurston Hall; **D**: Joseph Kane.

Song of Norway 🐾🐾½ 1970 (G) A dramatization of the early life of the beloved Norwegian Romantic composer Edvard Grieg. Filmed against the beautiful mountains, waterfalls, and forests of Norway and based on the popular '40s stage production. The scenery is the best thing because Grieg's life was dull—even with cinematic liberties taken. 🎵 Strange Music; The Song of Norway; The Little House; Be a Boy Again; Three There Were; A Rhyme and a Reason; Wrong to Dream; I Love You; The Solitary Wanderer. 143m/C VHS. Toralv Maurstad, Florence Henderson, Edward G. Robinson, Christina Schollin, Frank Porretta, Oscar Homolka, Robert Morley, Harry Secombe; **D**: Andrew L. Stone.

Song of Old Wyoming 🐾½ 1945 Three of those songs are presented in the course of an ordinary western about a spunky widow driving badmen out of Wyoming territory. La Rue plays the villainous Cheyenne Kid; this was before he got his own series as the heroic "Lash" La Rue. 65m/C VHS. Eddie Dean, Sarah Padden, Lash LaRue, Jennifer Holt, Emmett Lynn, John Carpenter, Ian Keith, Bob (Robert) Barron; **D**: Robert Emmett Tansey.

Song of Scheherazade 🐾🐾 1947 Superficial musical bio of Russian composer Rimsky-Korsakov (Aumont) and his romance with dancer Cara de Talavera (De Carlo), who inspires him to write the "Song of Scheherazade." 106m/C VHS. Jean-Pierre Aumont, Yvonne De Carlo, Brian Donlevy, Eve Arden, Philip Reed, John Qualen; **D**: Walter Reisch; **W**: Walter Reisch; **C**: Hal Mohr, William V. Skall.

The Song of Songs 🐾🐾½ 1933 Orphaned Lily (Dietrich) is living with her elderly Aunt Rasmussen (Skipworth) in Berlin and falling for sculptor Richard (Aherne). He wants her to pose for a nude statue, based on the Song of Solomon, after getting a gander at Lily's legs. How-

Song of Texas 🐾🐾½ 1943 When a young woman journeys west to visit her father at "his" ranch, Roy and his pals must keep the father's secret that he is just another hired hand. Whenever possible, everyone breaks into song. **54m/B VHS, DVD.** Roy Rogers, Harry Shannon, Pat Brady, Barton MacLane, Arline Judge; **D:** Joseph Kane.

Song of the Exile 🐾🐾½ 1990 A Chinese/Japanese student living in London in the early 1970s faces racial discrimination and decides to return to her native Hong Kong. But on the home front, she and her family clash emotionally until daughter and mother come to a gradual understanding of how the past affects the present. In Cantonese and Japanese with English subtitles. **100m/C VHS.** Chi Maggie Cheung, Shwu-Fen Chang; **D:** Ann Hui.

Song of the Gringo 🐾🐾 1936 The Old Corral 1936 Tex Ritter stars in his first singing western as a sheriff going after a gang of claim jumpers. **57m/B VHS, DVD.** Tex Ritter, Richard Adams, Warner Richmond; **D:** John P. McCarthy.

Song of the Islands 🐾🐾½ 1942 Landing families in Hawaii feud over a beach, while the son of one (Mature) and the daughter of the other (Grable) fall in love. Plenty of songs, and dancing to display Grable's legs. Of course happiness and concord reign at the end. Songs include "O'Brien Has Gone Hawaiian," "Sing Me a Song of the Islands," "What's Buzzin', Cousin?" **75m/C VHS.** Betty Grable, Victor Mature, Jack Oakie, Thomas Mitchell, Billy Gilbert; **D:** Walter Lang.

The Song of the Lark 🐾🐾½ 2001 Thea Kronborg (Elliott) is a minister's daughter in 1890s Colorado who is encouraged by local doctor Howard Archie (Howard) to pursue her musical dreams. At first, Thea travels to Chicago to study piano but her teacher (Hulce) realizes that Thea's true gift is her voice. Handsome brewery heir Fred Ottenburg (Goldwyn) offers to sponsor her career but their romance is rocky and Thea must eventually make her own way. Based on the novel by Willa Cather. **120m/C VHS, DVD.** Alison Elliott, Arliss Howard, Tony Goldwyn, Maximilian Schell, Norman Lloyd, Robert Floyd, Endre Hules, Nan Martin, Christian Meoli; **D:** Karen Arthur; **W:** Joseph Maurer; **M:** Charles Fox. TV

Song of the Thin Man 🐾🐾½ 1947 The sixth and final "Thin Man" mystery. This time Nick and Nora Charles (Powell and Loy) investigate the murder of a bandleader. Somewhat more sophisticated than its predecessor, set partly in the jazz music world. Sequel to "The Thin Man Goes Home." **86m/B VHS, DVD.** William Powell, Myrna Loy, Keenan Wynn, Dean Stockwell, Philip Reed, Patricia Morison, Gloria Grahame, Jayne Meadows, Don Taylor, Leon Ames, Ralph Morgan, Warner Anderson; **D:** Edward Buzzell; **C:** Charles Rosher.

Song of the Trail 🐾🐾 1936 Our hero saves an old man hornswoggled at cards. **65m/B VHS.** Kermit Maynard, George "Gabby" Hayes, Fuzzy Knight, Wheeler Oakman, Evelyn Brent, Andrea Leeds; **D:** Russell Hopton.

Song Spinner 🐾🐾½ 1995 (G) In a mysterious land, a stranger gives a young girl the power of music, which she hopes to share with the king. But first she must get cast the kingdom's noise police. **95m/C VHS.** Meredith Henderson, Patti LuPone, John Neville; **D:** Randy Bradshaw.

A Song to Remember 🐾🐾🐾 1945 With music performed by Jose Iturbi, this film depicts the last years of the great pianist and composer Frederic Chopin, in-

cluding his affair with famous author George Sand, the most renowned French woman of her day. Typically manglec film biography. ♪Valse in D Flat (Minute Waltz); Mazurka in B Flat, Opus 7, No. 1; Fantasie Impromptu, Opus 66; Etude in A Flat, Opus 53 (partial); Polonaise in A Flat, Opus 25, No. 1 (partial); Scherzo in B Minor, Etude in C Minor, Opus 10, No. 12; Nocturne in E Flat, Opus 9, No. 2. **112m/C VHS.** Cornel Wilde, Paul Muni, Merle Oberon, Nina Foch, George Coulouris; **D:** Charles Vidor; **C:** Gaetano Antonio "Tony" Gaudio; **M:** Miklos Rozsa.

Songcatcher 🐾🐾🐾 1999 Turn-of-the-century musicologist Dr. Lily Penleric (McTeer) heads for Appalachia in a huff after the all-male review board of the East Coast university where she teaches refuses to grant her tenure. She begins teaching at her sister Elna's (Adams) mountain school, harboring a superior attitude toward the rubes she's teaching. She discovers to her amazement that the songs the rustic people sing, dance and live to are barely altered from the time they were brought over from Europe. She meets resistance from local Tom (Quinn), who feels that if the hillbillies have something civilized from the outside world, it'll be clear him win the real bad guys attack. **113m/C VHS, DVD.** Janet McTeer, Aidan Quinn, Pat Carroll, Jane Adams, Emmy Rossum, Mike Harding, Iris DeMent, Greg Cook, David Patrick Kelly, E. Katherine Kerr, Taj Mahal, Muse Watson, Stephanie Roth; **D:** Maggie Greenwald; **W:** Maggie Greenwald; **C:** Enrique Chediak; **M:** David Mansfield.

Songs and Bullets 🐾🐾½ 1938 Simple zen-like title sums it up. The songs total five in number, the bullets somewhat more as hero cowboy's battle rustlers in routine fashion. One of a handful of films (westerns and comedies) produced by funnyman Stan Laurel. **57m/B VHS.** Fred Scott, Al "Fuzzy" St. John, Alice Ardell, Charles "Blackie" King, Karl Hackett, Frank LaRue, Budd Buster; **D:** Sam Newfield.

Songwriter 🐾🐾½ 1984 (R) A high-falutin' look at the lives and music of two popular country singers with, aptly, plenty of country tunes written and performed by the stars. Singer-businessman Nelson needs Kristofferson's help keeping a greedy investor at bay. Never mind the plot; plenty of good music. ♪How Do You Feel About Foolin' Around?; Songwriter; Who'll Buy My Memories; Write Your Own Songs; Nobody Said It Was Going To Be Easy; Good Times; Eye of the Storm; Crossing the Border; Down to Her Socks. **94m/C VHS, DVD.** Willie Nelson, Kris Kristofferson, Rip Torn, Melinda Dillon, Lesley Ann Warren; **D:** Alan Rudolph.

Sonic Impact 🐾½ 1999 (R) Nutjob hijacks an airliner and threatens to crash it into the nearest large city. So a group of commandoes led by Nick Halton (Russo) makes plans to stop him. **94m/C VHS, DVD.** James Russo, Ice-T, Mel Harris; **D:** Rodney McDonal. VIDEO

Sons of Steel 🐾🐾 1935 Two brothers, owners of a steel mill, lead vastly different lives. They raise their sons in their own images, causing problems. **65m/B VHS.** Charles Starrett, Polly Ann Young William Bakewell, Walter Walker, Aileen Pringle, Holmes Herbert, Florence Roberts, Richard Carlyle, Lloyd Ingraham; **D:** Charles Lamont.

Sons of Katie Elder 🐾🐾🐾 1965 After their mother's death, four brothers are reunited. Wayne is a gunman; Anderson is a college graduate; silent Holliman is a killer; and Martin is a gambler. When they learn that her death might have been linked to their father's murder, they come together to devise a way to seek revenge on the killer. The town bullies complicate matters; the sheriff tells them to lay off. Especially strong screen presence by Wayne, in his first role following cancer surgery. One of the Duke's most popular movies of the '60s. **122m/C VHS, DVD.** John Wayne, Dean Martin, Earl Holliman, Michael Anderson Jr., Martha Hyer, George Kennedy, Dennis Hopper, Paul Fix, James Gregory; **D:** Henry Hathaway; **M:** Harry Essex, Allan Weiss, William Wright; **C:** Lucien Ballard; **M:** Elmer Bernstein.

Sons 🐾🐾 1989 Three sons decide to honor their father's last wish by taking him back to Normandy where he left behind a French girlfriend during WWII. He's hoping to see her again while his sons experience their own adventures in Paris. **88m/C VHS.** Stephane Audran, Jennifer Beels, Steve Axelrod, Elizabeth Bracco, William Forsythe, Bernard Fresson, Samuel Fuller, Judith Godeche, William Hickey, Robert Miranda, Shirley Stcler, D.B Sweeney; **D:** Alexandre Rockwell; **W:** Brandon Cole, Alexandre Rockwell; **C:** Stefan Czapsky; **M:** Mader.

Song Without End 🐾🐾½ 1950 This musical biography of 19th century Hungarian pianist/composer Franz Liszt is given the Hollywood treatment. The lavish production emphasizes Liszt's scandalous exploits with married women and his life among the royal courts of Europe rather than his musical talents. Features music from several composers including Handel, Beethoven, Bach and Schumann. This film marked the debut of Capucine. Director Vidor died during filming and Cukor stepped in, so there is a noticeable change in style. Although there is much to criticize in the story, the music is beautiful. ♪Mephisto Waltz; Sonata in B Minor, Un Sospiro; Fantasy on Themes From "Rigoletto"; Les Preludes; Piano Concerto No. 1. **130m/C VHS, DVD.** Dirk Bogarde, Capucine, Genevieve Page, Patricia Morison, Ivan Desny, Martita Hunt, Lou Jacobi; **D:** Charles Vidor, George Cukor; **C:** James Wong Howe; **M:** Morris Stoloff, Harry Sukman. Oscars '61: Film—Mus./Comedy.

Sonny Boy Woof! 1987 (R) A transvestite and a psychopath adopt a young boy, training him to do their bidding, which includes murder. **96m/C VHS.** David Carradine, Paul Smith, Brad Dourif, Conrad Janis, Sydney Lassick, Savina Gersak, Alexandra Powers, Steve Carlisle, Michael Griffin; **D:** Robert Martin Carroll; **W:** Graeme Whifler; **C:** Roberto D'Ettorre Piazzoli; **M:** Carlo Maria Cordio.

Sonny and Jed 🐾 La Banda J.&S. Cronaca Criminale del Far West 1973 (R) An escaped convict and a free-spirited woman travel across Mexico pillaging freely, followed determinedly by shiny-headed lawman Savalas. Lame rip-off of the Bonnie and Clyde legend. **89m/C VHS, DVD.** Tomas Milian, Telly Savalas, Susan George, Rosama Jarni, Laura Betti; **D:** Sergio Corbucci; **M:** Ennio Morricone.

Sonora Stagecoach 🐾🐾 1944 Okay sagebrush saga with an interesting lineup; two cowboys, a heroic Indian, and a tough gal pilot escort a murder suspect in the title conveyance and manage to clear him when the real bad guys attack. **61m/B VHS.** Hoot Gibson, Bob Steele, Chief Thundercloud, Rocky Cameron, Betty Miles, Glenn Strange, George Eldredge, Karl Hackett; **D:** Robert Emmett Tansey.

Sonny 🐾🐾 2002 (R) Cage's directorial debut is about one man's frustrated attempts at leaving a life of crime. In 1981 New Orleans, Sonny (Franco) is fresh out of the Army and hopeful about working in his buddy's Texas bookstore. His corrupt pimp mother Jewel (Blethyn) would rather him reenter the family business and attempts to fix him up with Carol (Suvari), one of her new "girls." The two fall in love and, after a disastrous encounter with the "straight" world, Sonny descends back into his element, under-good. Stanton is in 'his element, under-good. Stanton is the once despised for playing the good-hearted, drunk boyfriend of Jewel while Cage makes an amusing appearance as Acid Yellow, a gay pimp. Heavy handed and overly emotional (the hysterical Blethyn is practically unwatchable), with an uneven rhythm and not a lot of explanation. Cage falls victim to first-time indulgence, but respectable narrative debut nonetheless. **105m/C VHS, DVD. US** James Franco, Mena Suvari, Brenda Blethyn, Harry Dean Stanton, Nicolas Cage, Seymour Cassel, Brenda Vaccaro, Scott Caan; **D:** Nicolas Cage; **W:** John Carlen; **C:** Barry Markowitz; **M:** Clint Mansell.

Sons of Trinity 🐾🐾 1995 (PG) The two sons, Bambino (Neuberti) and Trinity (Kizzier), of legendary cowpokes first meet when Bambino is about to be hung for horse thieving in the town of San Clemen-tino. When Trinity gets his new friend off, they wind up as sheriff and deputy of the same town. Lots of physical comedy. **90m/C VHS.** Heath Kizzier, Keith Neuberti, Ronald Nitschke, Siegfried Rauch; **D:** E.B. (Enzo Barboni) Clucher; **C:** Juan Amoros; **M:** Stelano Manelli.

Sons of the Pioneers 🐾🐾 1942 Small town sheriff Hayes hires cowboy Roy to rid town of outlaws. **61m/B VHS, DVD.** Roy Rogers, George "Gabby" Hayes, Maris Wrixon, Forrest Taylor; **D:** Joseph Kane.

Sons of the Desert 🐾🐾🐾 Sons of the Legion; Convention City; Fraternally Yours 1933 Laurel and Hardy in their best-written film. The boys try to fool their wives by pretending to go to Hawaii to cure Ollie of a bad cold when in fact, they are attending their lodge convention in Chicago. Also included is a 1935 Thelma Todd/Patsy Kelly short, "Top Flat." **73m/B VHS, DVD.** Stan Laurel, Oliver Hardy, Mae Busch, Charley Chase, Dorothy Christy; **D:** William A. Seiter; **W:** Frank Craven; **C:** Kenneth Peach Sr.

Sophia Loren: Her Own Story 🐾🐾 1980 Bio of Sophia Loren, watching her grow from a spindly child in a local rock idol and must decide whether to go all the way. **100m/C VHS, DVD.** Rex Smith, Judd Hirsch, Denise Miller, Morey Amsterdam, Lynn Redgrave; **D:** Bruce Hart. TV

Sophie Scholl: The Final Days 🐾🐾🐾 Sophie Scholl: Die Letzten Tage 2005 Documentary traces the five days prior to the killing of University of Munich students Sophie Scholl (Jentsch) and her brother Hans (Hinrichs) in 1943 by German Nazis for their rebellious behavior in distributing anti-war literature at the school. Powerful interrogation scenes between Sophie and General Alexander Held (Mohr), as her quiet determination affects the general. Whatever empathy he feels can't change her inevitable fate. **117m/C DVD.** Julia Jentsch, Alexander Held, Fabian Hinrichs, Johanna Gastdorf, Andre Henricke, Florian Stetter; **D:** Marc Rothemund; **W:** Fred Breinersdorfer; **C:** Martin Langer; **M:** Johnny Klimek. Reinl-old Heil.

Sophie's Choice 🐾🐾🐾½ 1982 (R) A haunting modern tragedy about Sophie Zawistowska, a beautiful Polish Auschwitz survivor settled in Brooklyn after WWII. She has intense relationships with Southern writer. An artful, immaculately performed and resonant drama, with an astonishing, commencing performance by the versatile Streep, a chilling portrayal of the banality of evil. From the best-selling autobiographical novel by William Styron. **157m/C VHS, DVD.** Meryl Streep, Kevin Kline, Peter MacNichol, Rita Karin, Stephen D. Newman, Josh Mostel; **D:** Alan J. Pakula; **W:** Alan J. Pakula; **C:** Nestor Almendros; **M:** Marvin Hamlisch. Oscars

Sooner or Later 🐾½ 1978 13-year-old girl passes herself off as 16 with the family and surprisingly becomes a link to help heal. Italian with subtitles. **99m/C VHS, DVD.** IT Fil Nanni Moretti, Laura Morante, Giuseppe Sanfelice, Jasmine Trinca, Stefano Accorsi, Sofia Vigliar, Silvio Orlando, Claudia Della Seta; **D:** Nanni Moretti; **W:** Nanni Moretti, Linda Ferri, Heidrun Schleef; **C:** Giuseppe Lanci; **M:** Nicola Piovani. Cannes '01: Film.

The Son's Room 🐾🐾🐾 La Stanza del Figlio 2000 Giovanni (Moretti) is a psychiatrist in a provincial seaside town with a wife, Paola (Morante), and two teenage children—Irene (Trinca) and Andrea (San-felice). Their average lives are suddenly shattered when Andrea dies in a diving accident. The family falls apart and begins to distance themselves from each other and their grief. By accident, Arianna (Vigliar), a casual girlfriend of Andrea's who doesn't know about his death, contacts the family and surprisingly becomes a link to help heal.

'82: Actress (Streep); Golden Globes '83: Actress—Drama (Streep); L.A. Film Critics '82: Actress (Streep); Natl. Bd. of Review '82: Actress (Streep); N.Y. Film Critics '82: Actress (Streep); Cinematog.; Natl. Soc. Film Critics '82: Actress (Streep).

Sophisticated Gents 🦴🦴🦴 1981 Nine boyhood friends, members of a black athletic club, reunite after 25 years to honor their old coach and see how each of their lives has been affected by being black men in American society. Based on the novel "The Junior Bachelor Society" by John A. Williams. 200m/C VHS. Paul Winfield, Roosevelt "Rosie" Grier, Bernie Casey, Raymond St. Jacques, Thalmus Rasulala, Dick Anthony Williams, Ron O'Neal, Rosalind Cash, Denise Nicholas, Alfre Woodard, Melvin Van Peebles, Robert Earl Jones, Robert Hooks, Janet DuBois, Joanna Miles, Janet MacLachlan, Bibi Besch, Beah Richards, Albert Hall, Harry Guardino, John Zaremba, Al Fann, Matthew "Stymie" Beard, Mario Van Peebles; D: Harry Falk; W: Melvin Van Peebles. TV

Sorcerer 🦴🦴½ Wages of Fear 1977 (PG) To put out an oil fire, four men on the run in South America agree to try to buy their freedom by driving trucks loaded with nitroglycerin over dangerous terrain—with many natural and man-made obstacles to get in their way. Remake of "The Wages of Fear" is nowhere as good as the classic original, but has exciting moments. Puzzlingly retitled, which may have contributed to the boxoffice failure, and the near demise of Friedkin's directing career. 121m/C VHS, DVD. Roy Scheider, Bruno Cremer, Francesco Rabal, Soudad Amidou, Ramon Bieri; D: William Friedkin; W: Walon Green; C: Dick Bush, John Stephens; M: Tangerine Dream.

Sorceress WOOF! 1982 (R) The Harris girls are sisters who use their powers of sorcery and fighting skills to battle demons, dragons, and evil. Yeah, sure. Really, they're just a pair of babes parading for the camera. 83m/C VHS. Leigh Anne Harris, Lynette Harris, Bob Nelson, David Millbern, Bruno Rey, Anna De Sade; D: Brian Stuart; W: Jim Wynorski.

Sorceress 🦴🦴🦴 Le Moine et la Sorciere 1988 A friar in medieval Europe feels insecure in his woman who heals through ancient practices. Historically authentic and interestingly moody. Written, produced, and directed by two women: an art history professor and a collaborator of Francois Truffaut's. In French with English subtitles or dubbed. 98m/C VHS. FR Tcheky Karyo, Christine Boisson, Jean Carmet, Raoul Billerey, Catherine Frot, Feodor Atkine; D: Suzanne Schiffman; W: Pamela Berger, Suzanne Schiffman; C: Patrick Blossier.

Sordid Lives 🦴🦴 2000 Shores adapted his play but the comedy goes flat before the finale. Texas matriarch Peggy dies (under scandalous circumstances) and her dysfunctional family goes into hyperdrive. There's proper daughter Latrelle (Bedelia) who can't accept that her actor son Ty (Geiger) is gay, probably because her own brother—known only as Brother Boy (Jordan)—is a drag queen confined to a mental institution. But brassy sister LaVonda (Walker) still thinks he should come to the funeral. And there's Aunt Sissy (Grant) and G.W. (Bridges), who was having an affair with Peggy, and his wife Noleta (Burke), who's LaVonda's best friend and...it just kinda goes on and on. 111m/C VHS, DVD. Bonnie Bedelia, Beth Grant, Delta Burke, Ann Walker, Leslie Jordan, Beau Bridges, Kirk Giger, Rosemary Alexander, Olivia Newton-John; D: Del Shores; W: Del Shores; C: Max CiVon; M: George S. Clinton.

Sorority Babes in the Slimeball Bowl-A-Rama 🦴🦴 The Imp 1987 (R) An ancient gremlin-type creature is released from a bowling alley, and the great-looking sorority babes have to battle it at the mall, with the help of a wacky crew of nerds. Horrible horror spoof shows plenty of skin. 80m/C DVD. Linnea Quigley, Brinke Stevens, Andras Jones, John Wildman, Robin Rochelle, Michelle (McClellan) Bauer, George "Buck" Flower; D: David DeCoteau; W: Sergei Hasenecz; C: Scott Ressler, Stephen Blake; M: Guy Moon; V: Michael Sonye.

Sorority Boys 🦴 2002 (R) Three frat boys (Williams, Rosenbaum and Watson) become bosom buddies when they don girlish garb to pass as sorority sisters in this contrived campus comedy. After being accused of a theft in their frat house, the badly disguised trio head to the notorious loser Delta Omega Gamma (DOG) house to stay in school. The boys teeter in their high heels, can't find dresses big enough for their ample "cabooses," and generally begin to understand the drag of being a gal while the film continues to serve up a kegful of gross-out and misogynist humor. Another in a string of misguided homages to "Animal House," with alums Daughton, Metcalf, Furst, and Vernon showing up for paychecks. Although Williams is considered to be the best of the three leads, all are terrible. Tepid romantic subplot with DOG house president doesn't help matters any. 93m/C VHS, DVD. Barry Watson, Michael Rosenbaum, Harland Williams, Melissa Sagemiller, Tony Denman, Brad Beyer, Heather Matarazzo, Kathryn Stockwood, Yvonne Scio; D: M. Wallace Wolodarsky; W: Joe Jarvis, Greg Coolidge; C: Michael D. O'Shea; M: Mark Mothersbaugh.

Sorority Girl 🦴½ 1957 Camp classic in which beautiful co-ed Cabot is presented as a malicious rich kid involved in everything from petty fights to blackmail. Cheap production from the Corman factory. 60m/B VHS. Susan Cabot, Dick Miller, Barbara Crane, June Kenney, Fay Baker, Jeane Wood, Barbaura Morris; D: Roger Corman; W: Leo Lieberman, Ed Waters; C: Monroe Askins; M: Ronald Stein.

Sorority House Massacre WOOF! 1986 (R) A knife-wielding maniac stalks a sorority girl while her more elite sisters are away for the weekend. Yawn—haven't we seen this one before? Unfortunately for us we'll see it again because this one's followed by a sequel. 74m/C VHS, DVD. Angela O'Neill, Wendy Martel, Pamela Ross, Nicole Rio; D: Carol Frank; W: Carol Frank; C: Marc Reshovsky; M: Michael Wetherwax.

Sorority House Massacre 2: Nighty Nightmare WOOF! 1992 Another no-brainer with a different cast and director. This time around three lingerie-clad lovelies are subjected to the terrors of a killer their first night in their new sorority house. College just keeps getting tougher all the time. 80m/C VHS, DVD. Melissa Moore, Robin Harris, Stacia Zhivago, Dana Bentley, Shannon Wilsey; D: Jim Wynorski; W: James B. Rogers, Bob Sheridan; M: Chuck Cirino.

Sorority House Party 🦴 1992 (R) A famous rock guitarist is held against his will at the sexiest sorority house on campus. He definitely has mixed feelings about the experience considering the inhabitants saunter around in bikinis and "force" him to party with them. Anders and Attila are transplants from the modeling circuit. 95m/C VHS. Attila, April Lerman, Kim Little, Avalon Anders, Joe Mundi, Rachel Latt, Mark Stulce, Michael Xavier; D: David Michael Latt; W: John Murdy, Steve Taylor.

Sorority House Vampires 🦴½ 1995 Sexy college coed Buffy fights to save her man and her sorority from Count Vlad, Queen of Darkness, and Count Vlad. 90m/C VHS, DVD. Eugenie Bondurant, Robert Bucholz, Kathy Presgrave; D: Geoffrey De Valois. VIDEO

Sorrento Beach 🦴🦴 Hotel Sorrento 1995 (R) A beachside community outside Melbourne, Australia, Sorrento is home to the Moynihan sisters—Meg (Goodall), Hillary (Gillmer), and Pippa (Morice)—are reunited after 10 years by their father's sudden death. Lots of tensions, rivalries, and jealousies come to the surface as well as old secrets regarding a family tragedy. Talky film hasn't quite cast off its stage origins (it's adapted from a play by Hannie Rayson) but the performances are noteworthy. 112m/C VHS. AU Caroline Goodall, Caroline Gillmer, Tara Morice, Joan Plowright, John Hargreaves, Ray Barrett, Ben Thomas, Nicholas Bell; D: Richard Franklin; W: Richard Franklin, Peter Fitzpatrick, Hannie Rayson; C: Geoff Burton; M: Nerida Tyson-Chew. Australian Film Inst. '95: Adapt. Screenplay, Support. Actor (Barrett).

The Sorrow and the Pity 🦴🦴🦴½ 1971 A classic documentary depicting the life of a small French town and its resistance during the Nazi occupation. Lengthy, but totally compelling. A great documentary that brings home the atrocities of war. In French with English narration. 265m/B VHS, DVD. FR Pierre Mendes-France, Sir Anthony Eden, Dr. Claude Levy, Denis Rake, Louis Grave, Maurice Chevalier; D: Marcel Ophuls; C: Mandre Gazut, Jurgen Thieme.

Sorrowful Jones 🦴🦴½ 1949 A "Little Miss Marker" remake, in which bookie Hope inherits a little girl as collateral for an unpaid bet. Good for a few yuks, but the original is much better. 88m/B VHS, DVD. Bob Hope, Lucille Ball, William Demarest, Bruce Cabot, Thomas Gomez, Mary Jane Saunders; D: Sidney Lanfield; W: Jack Rose, Melville Shavelson; C: Daniel F. Fapp.

Sorrows of Gin 🦴🦴½ 1979 Eight-year-old girl searches for a sense of family amid her parents' lives. Her efforts to deal with alienation and emotional isolation lead her to run away from home. From a short story by John Cheever. 60m/C VHS. DVD. Edward Herrmann, Sigourney Weaver, Mara Hobel, Eileen Heckart, Rachel Roberts; D: Jack Hofsiss; W: Wendy Wasserstein. TV

The Sorrows of Satan 🦴🦴 1926 Dempster and Cortez star as writers in love with each other, but Cortez can't take his poverty and the rejection of publishers. As he is about to end it all, the devil appears to him in disguise and makes an offer he can hardly refuse. He is introduced to London society and winds up marrying a fortune hunter. When he discovers who still loves him, and vows to give up everything for her. Menjou then reveals himself to be the devil but Dempster's faith is so strong that the evil is vanquished. 111m/B VHS. Adolphe Menjou, Carol Dempster, Ricardo Cortez, Lya de Putti; D: D.W. Griffith.

Sorry, Haters 🦴🦴 2005 Behaving erratically, New York cable TV executive Phoebe (Wright Penn) hops into a cab driven by Ashade (Kechiche) to head to her ex-husband's house in Jersey seeking to get even with him for remarrying and taking everything. A chemist in his homeland, Ashade is suffering too, as the Syrian Muslim's brother is being unjustly held at Guantanamo, unable to enter the country. But his compassion for her and belief that she could help him are horribly misguided. Wright Penn and Kechiche are solid in this uneven look at post-9/11 culture and attitudes. 83m/C DVD. US Robin Wright Penn, Abdellatif Kechiche, Sandra Oh, Elodie Bouchez, Aasif Mandvi, Remy K. Selma, Fred Durst; D: Jeff Stanzler; W: Jeff Stanzler; C: Maurizio Rubinstein; M: Raz Mesinai.

Sorry, Wrong Number 🦴🦴🦴½ 1948 A wealthy, bedridden wife overhears two men plotting a murder on a crossed telephone line, and begins to suspect that one of the voices is her husband's. A classic tale of paranoia and suspense. Based on a radio drama by Louise Fletcher, who also wrote the screenplay. Remade for TV in 1989. 89m/B VHS, DVD. Barbara Stanwyck, Burt Lancaster, Ann Richards, Wendell Corey, Harold Vermilyea, Ed Begley Sr.; D: Anatole Litvak; W: Lucille Fletcher; C: Sol Polito; M: Franz Waxman.

Sorry, Wrong Number 🦴½ 1989 Cable remake of the 1948 Barbara Stanwyck thriller about a bed-ridden woman trying to get help after she realizes she's being stalked by a killer. Offers a new twist (drug dealing), but doesn't even approach the Stanwyck original. From the story by Lucille Fletcher. 90m/C VHS. Loni Anderson, Hal Holbrook, Patrick Macnee, Miguel Fernandes, Carl Weintraub; D: Tony Wharmby; M: Bruce Broughton. CABLE

Sorted 🦴½ 2004 Compelled by his brother's odd drowning death in London, Carl noses around only to become consumed with the same wild party scene that could lead him to a similar demise. 105m/C VHS, DVD. Matthew Rhys, Sienna Guillory, Fay Masterson, Tim Curry, Jason Donovan, Stephen Marcus; D: Alexander Jovy; W: Malcolm Campbell, Alexander Jovy; C: Mike Southon; M: Guy Farley. VIDEO

S.O.S. Coast Guard 🦴🦴½ 1937 A fiendish scientist creates a disintegrating gas and the U.S. Coast Guard must stop him from turning it over to unfriendly foreigners. Loads of action in this 12-part serial. 224m/B VHS, DVD. Ralph Byrd, Bela Lugosi, Maxine Doyle, Richard Alexander, Lawrence Grant, Thomas Carr, Lee Ford, John Picorri, George Chesebro; D: Alan James, William Whitney; W: Frank (Franklyn) Adreon, Winston Miller, Barry Shipman; C: William Nobles.

S.O.S. Pacific 🦴🦴 1960 A seaplane crashes on a nuclear-test island and the survivors find that they get nuked. Even though there is plenty of the usual action one would expect from such a film, the story really revolves around the characters. The British and U.S. versions have different endings. 91m/B VHS. GB Eddie Constantine, Pier Angeli, Richard Attenborough, John Gregson, Eva Bartok; D: Guy Green.

S.O.S. Titanic 🦴🦴½ 1979 The story of the Titanic disaster, recounted in flashback, in docu-drama style. James Costigan's teleplay of the familiar story focuses on the courage that accompanied the horror and tragedy. Thoroughly professional, absorbing TV drama. 102m/C VHS, DVD. GB Beverly Ross, David Janssen, Cloris Leachman, Susan St. James, David Warner, Ian Holm, Helen Mirren, Harry Andrews, David Battley, Ed Bishop, Peter Bourke, Shevaun Briars, Nick Brimble, Jacob Brooke, Catherine Byrne, Tony Caunter, Warren Clarke, Nicholas Davies, Deborah Fallender; D: William (Billy) Hale; W: James Costigan; C: Christopher Challis; M: Howard Blake. TV

Sotto, Sotto 🦴🦴½ 1985 (R) A minor Wermuller comedy about an Italian businessman who is constantly suspicious of his wife's fidelity. As it happens, she's attracted to another woman (de Santis). Massimo Wertmuller is Lina's nephew. Entertaining. In Italian with English subtitles. 104m/C VHS. IT Enrico Montesano, Veronica Lario, Massimo Wertmuller, Luisa de Santis; D: Lina Wertmuller; W: Lina Wertmuller.

Soul Assassin 🦴🦴 2001 (R) Kevin Burke (Ulrich) works for the security branch of an international investment bank in Rotterdam. He's been mentored by the bank's managing director, Karl Jorgensen (de Lint), much to the disgust of Jorgensen own son, Karl, Jr. (Kamerling). When Kevin's fiancee Rosalind (Lang) is assassinated, Kevin discovers he didn't know her as well as he thought. Seems she was involved in money laundering and corporate espionage. While Kevin seeks the truth, mystery woman Tessa (Swanson) is shadowing him—is she friend or foe? 97m/C VHS, DVD. NL Skeet Ulrich, Kristy Swanson, Derek de Lint, Antoine Kamerling, Rena Owen, Serge-Henri Valcke, Thom Hoffman, Katherine Lang, Pierre Allard; D: Laurence Malkin; W: Laurence Malkin, Chad Thurman; C: Lex Wertwijn; M: Alan Williams.

Soul-Fire 🦴🦴 1925 South Pacific high seas induce Cupid's arrow. Silent. 100m/B VHS. Richard Barthelmess, Bessie Love, Walter Long, Arthur Metcalfe; D: John S. Robertson.

Soul Food 🦴🦴½ 1997 (R) In between the mouth watering servings of fried-chicken, collard greens and catfish unfolds the lives of sisters Williams, Fox, and Long. They struggle to hold their family together by keeping up their mother's Sunday dinner tradition after she becomes ill. As mom's health deteriorates, so do the sisters' relationships with their significant others, turning things a bit soapy and pre-

Soul Hustler woof! 1976 (PG) A con man becomes rich and famous as a tent-show evangelist. Pathetic drivel. 81m/C VHS. Fabian, Casey Kasem, Larry Bishop, Nai Bonet. *D:* Burt Topper.

Soul Man 1986 (PG-13) Denied the funds he expected for his Harvard tuition, a young white student (Howell) masquerades as a black in order to get a minority scholarship. As a black student at Harvard, Howell learns about racism and bigotry. Pleasant lightweight comedy with romance thrown in (Chong is the black girl he falls for), and with pretensions to social satire that it never achieves. 112m/C VHS, DVD. *C:* Thomas Howell, Rae Dawn Chong, James Earl Jones, Leslie Nielsen, Arye Gross; *D:* Steve Miner. *W:* Carol Black; *C:* Jeffrey Jur; *M:* Tom Scott.

Soul of the Beast 1923 An elephant repeatedly saves Bellamy from the villainous Beery, with original organ score. 77m/B VHS. Madge Bellamy, Cullen Landis, Noah Beery Sr.; *D:* John Griffith Wray; *W:* Ralph Dixon; *C:* Henry Sharp.

Soul of the Game 1996 Cable movie follows the lives of three talented players in the Negro League during the 1945 season as they await the potential integration of baseball. Brooklyn Dodgers general manager Branch Rickey (Herrmann) has his scouts focusing on three men in particular: flashy, aging pitcher Satchel Paige (Lindo), mentally unstable catcher Josh Gibson (Williamson), and the young, college-educated Jackie Robinson (Underwood). Manages to resist melodrama through terrific performances. 105m/C VHS, DVD. Delroy Lindo, Mykelti Williamson, Blair Underwood, Edward Herrmann, R. Lee Ermey, Gina Ravera, Salli Richardson, Obba Babatunde, Brent Jennings, Edwin Morrow, Richard Riehle; *C:* Kevin Rodney Sullivan; *M:* David Himmelstein; *C:* Sandi Sissel. CABLE

Soul Patrol 1980 (R) Black newspaper reporter clashes with the all-white police department in a racist city. 90m/C VHS, DVD. Nigel Davenport, Ken Gampu, Peter Dyneley. *D:* Christopher Rowley.

Soul Plane 2004 (R) Nashawn Wade (Hart) wins a $100 million settlement after a near-disastrous flight and promptly creates a new airline for the "urban traveler." With a pimped out plane, lusty security officer (Mo'Nique) and a pilot (Snoop Dogg) who likes to get high, this one's doomed before the plane even takes off. What it lacks in entertainment, it more than makes up for in raunchiness, over-the-top stereotypes and sleazy sex jokes, making it a sure-fire cable and late night Comedy Central hit. Tom Arnold also makes an appearance as the token white guy. 86m/C VHS, DVD. US Kevin Hart, Tom Arnold, Method Man, Snoop Dogg, K.D. Aubert, Brian Hooks, D.L. Hughley, Mo'Nique, Chuck Wilson; *C:* Jonathan Sela; *M:* The RZA.

Soul Survivor 1995 (PG-13) Set in Toronto's Jamaican community, this urban drama focuses on twentysomething Tyrone (Williams) who's stuck in a custodial job and looking to make some easy money. He goes to work making collections for local gangster Winston (Harris), who tries to reassure his protege that money buys respect. But when Tyrone falls for straight-living social worker Annie (Scott), he begins to see the potholes in the path he's on. 85m/C VHS, DVD, CA Peter Williams, George Harris, Judith Scott, Clark Johnsen Williams; *C:* David Smith; *D:* Stephen Williams; *M:* Stephen Williams.

Souls at Sea 1937 Good buddy work by Cooper and Raft highlight this complicated seafaring yarn. In the 1840s sailor and abolitionist Nuggin Taylor (Cooper) is secretly sabotaging slave ships, working undercover for the British Navy. With loyal friend Powdah (Raft), Taylor tries to gather evidence against British officer Tarryton (Wilcoxon) even though he's fallen for Tarryton's sister Margaret (Dee). But after a sea disaster, Taylor's accused of murder and brought to trial. Will the truth come out in time to save him? 93m/B VHS. Gary Cooper, George Raft, Henry Wilcoxon, Frances Dee, Olympe Bradna, George Zucco, Harry Carey Sr., Robert Cummings, Porter Hall, Joseph Schildkraut; *D:* Henry Hathaway; *W:* Grover Jones, Dale Van Every; *C:* Charles Bryant, Lang Jr.

Soul's Midnight 2006 (R) So how do you feel about bloody cults in Texas? Charles (Floyd) and his pregnant wife Alicia (Bennett) have come home for his dad's funeral. The town is big on celebrating the feast of St. George and the defeat of that pesky dragon, which was posed to be a descendant of St. George and Alicia has weird dreams that hotel owner Simon (Assante) wants their unborn child to carry on the sacrificial ritual. 87m/C DVD. Armand Assante, Robert Floyd, Elizabeth Bennett, Miguel Perez, Lucia Sola, Joe Nipote; *D:* Harry Basil; *W:* Brian Cleveland, Jason Cleveland; *C:* Keith J. Duggan; *M:* Clint Torjussen. VIDEO

Soultaker ♂½ 1990 (R) The title spirit is after a young couple's souls, and they have just an hour to reunite with their bodies after a car crash. Meanwhile, they're in limbo (literally) between heaven and earth. The ending's OK, if you can make it that far. 94m/C VHS, DVD, CA Estevez, Vivian Schilling, Gregg Thomsen, David "Shark" Fralick, Jean Reiner, Chuck Williams, Robert Z'Dar; *D:* Michael Rissi; *W:* Vivian Schilling; *C:* James Rosenthal; *M:* Jon McCallum.

Soul Survivors woof! 2001 (R). Perhaps the worst slash and burn editing job in the history of film was used to chop this muddled horror flick from an R to a PG-13 rating. Cassie (Sagemiller) and her boyfriend Sean (Affleck) go to one last party with their friends Annabel (Dushku) and Matt (Bentley). The party is a nasty Goth rave held in a cathedral, seemingly gets upset when he misinterprets an innocent kiss between Cassie and Matt, who's also her ex. On the way home, a distracted Cassie crashes the car while trying to iron things out with Sean, killing him. Or not, as the case may be, because Cassie keeps seeing her dead boyfriend wherever she goes. Also, she keeps being chased by creepy Goth skanks. So is Cassie crazy? Is Sean alive? Frankly, you won't care even if you make it to the end of this contorted mess. 85m/C VHS, DVD, US Melissa Sagemiller, Wes Bentley, Casey Affleck, Eliza Dushku, Luke Wilson; *D:* Stephen Carpenter; *W:* Stephen Carpenter; *C:* Fred Murphy; *M:* Daniel Licht.

Soul Vengeance ♂ Welcome Home Brother Charles 1975 Black man is jailed and brutalized for crime he didn't commit and where women are concerned. 91m/C VHS, DVD. Marlo Monte, Reatha Grey, Stan Kamber, Tiffany Peters, Ven Bigelow, Jake Carter; *D:* Jamaa Fanaka; *M:* Jamaa Fanaka.

The Souler Opposite 1997 (R) Buddies Barry (Meloni) and Robert (Busfield) haven't grown up—especially where women are concerned. Most of struggling comic Barry's material is about his failed relationships while complacent, married Robert learns that his wife has departed she's a lesbian. Then sexist Barry meets feminist Thea (Moloney) and sparks fly—but can "souler" opposites really come together? First-time writer/director Kalmenson knows the territory since he's a stand-up comedian himself. 104m/C VHS, DVD. Christopher Meloni, Timothy Busfield, Janel Moloney, Allison Mack, John Putch, Rurary a Alda, Steve Landesberg; *D:* Bill Kalmenson; *W:* Bill Kalmenson; *C:* Amit Bhattacharya; *M:* Peter Himmelman.

Sound of Horror ♂ El Sonido de la Muerte; Sound From a Million years Ago, The Prehistoric Sound 1964 The Hound usually admires creative efforts to keep budgets down, but this is too much (o too little). A dinosaur egg hatches, and out lashes an invisible predator. Yes, you'll have to use your imagination as archaeologists are slashed to bits by the no-show terror. 85m/B VHS, DVD. SP James Philbrook, Arturo Fernandez, Soledad Miranda, Ingrid Pitt; *D:* Jose Antonio Neves-Conde.

The Sound and the Silence ♂♂½ 1993 Bio of inventor Alexander Graham Bell (Bach). The Scottish Bell's father was a speech specialist and his beloved mother Eliza (Fricker) was severely hearing impaired. Bell himself trained to work with the deaf in Boston was experimented with transmitting speech electronically—a project which only grew when Bell married the deaf Mabel Hubbard (Quinn), Bell's lifelong devotion lead to his development of the telephone as well as numerous other inventions (and his founding of "National Geographic" magazine). Bell was hardly a lively character but its his TV drama is lavishly done. In two parts. 93m/C VHS, John Bach, Elizabeth Quinn, Brenda Fricker, Ian Bannen; *D:* John Kent Harrison; *W:* Tony Foster, William Schmid, John Kent Harrison; *M:* John Charles. TV.

Sound of Love ♂ 1978 The mutual attraction between a deaf female hustler and a deaf race car driver leads to a deep relationship where they both learn about their own fears and desires. 74m/C VHS. Celia de Burgh, John Jarratt, George Ogilvie; *D:* John Power; *W:* John Power; *C:* Geoff Burton; *M:* Peter Best.

Sound of Murder 1982 A successful children's book writer wants to exact revenge on his adulterous wife, but is himself murdered before he can "execute" his plan. 114m/C VHS. Pippa Scott, Leonard Frey, David Ackroyd, Michael McHarty, Joanna Miles; *D:* Michael Lindsay-Hogg; *W:* William Fairchild.

The Sound of Music ♂♂♂ 1965 The classic film version of the Rodgers and Hammerstein musical based on the true story of the singing von Trapp family of Austria and their escape from the Nazis just before WWII. Beautiful Salzburg, Austria location photography and an excellent cast. Andrews, fresh from her Oscar for "Mary Poppins," is effervescent, in beautiful voice, but occasionally too good to be true. Not Rodgers & Hammerstein's most innovative score, but lovely to hear and see. Plummer's singing was dubbed by Bil Lee. Mami Nixon... behind-the-scenes songstress for "West Side Story" and "My Fair Lady," makes her on-screen debut as one of the nuns. ♫ I Have Confidence In Me; Something Good; The Sound of Music; Preludium; Morning Hymn; Alleluia; How Do You Solve A Problem Like Maria?; Sixteen, Going on Seventeen; My Favorite Things; 174m/C VHS, DVD. Julie Andrews, Christopher Plummer, Eleanor Parker, Peggy Wood, Charmian Carr, Heather Menzies, Marni Nixon, Richard Haydn, Anna Lee, Norma Varden, Nicholas Hammond, Angela Cartwright, Portia Nelson, Duane Chase, Debbie Turner, Kym Karath; *D:* Robert Wise; *W:* Ernest Lehman; *C:* Ted D. McCord. Oscars '65: Adapt. Score, Director (Wise), Film Editing, Picture, Sound; AFI '98: Top 100; Directors Guild '65: Director (Wise); Golden Globes '66: Actress—Mus./Comedy (Andrews), Film—Mus./Comedy, Natl. Film Reg. '01.

A Sound of Thunder ♂ 2005 (PG-13) Not much more needs to be said other than this is a summer flick, a time-traveling adventure, very loosely based on a Ray Bradbury story. The setting is 2055 Chicago, where folks with deep pockets get the opportunity to run with (okay, hunt) the dinosaurs, courtesy of a greedy entrepreneur (Kingsley). A snafu threatens to change the future, reverting Chicago (and the rest of the planet) back to prehistoric times. Loads and loads of special effects and well, that's about it. "The Simpsons" does a few years ago. 102m/C DVD. GE US Kingsley, Jemima Rooper, August Zimer, Corey Johnson, David Oyelowo, Wilfried Hochholdinger, *D:* Peter Hyams; *W:* Thomas Dean Donnelly, Joshua Oppenheimer; Gregory Poirier *C:* Peter Hyams; *M:* Nick Glennie-Smith.

Sounder ♂♂♂ 1972 (G) The struggles of a family of black sharecroppers in rural Louisiana during the Depression. When the father is sentenced to jail for stealing to feed his family, they must pull together even more, and one son finds education so the way out of poverty. Tyson brings strength and style to her role, with fine help from Winfield. Moving and well made, with little sentimentality. Adapted from the novel by William Armstrong. 105m/C VHS, DVD, Paul Winfield, Cicely Tyson, Kevin Hooks, Taj Mahal, Carmen Mathews, James Best, Janet MacLachlan; *D:* Martin Ritt; *M:* Lonne Elder III; *C:* John A. Alonzo; *M:* Taj Mahal. Natl. 3d. of Review '72: Actress (Tyson); Natl. Soc. Film Critics '72: Actress (Tyson).

Soundman ♂♂½ 1999 Very black showbiz comedy about obsessive sound engineer Igby Walters (Pere), who manages to piss off anyone with any clout on his current movie job. As his life just gets worse, Igby's behavior becomes increasingly violent, including his arranging a musical audition for his violin-playing next-door neighbor (Chappuis)—at gunpoint. 105m/C VHS, DVD. Wayne Pere, William Forsythe, Wes Studi, Eliane Chappuis, Nick Stahl, Tamlyn Tomita, Danny Trejo, John Koyama; *D:* Steven Ho; *W:* Steven Ho; *C:* David Aubrey.

Sounds of Silence ♂♂ 1991 A young deaf boy fears that a killer arsonist may be at large—but can he prove it? One of a number of obscure oddities featuring former youth idol Donahue. 106m/C VHS. Kristen Jensen, Dennis Castillo, Troy Donahue, Peter Nelson; *D:* Peter Borg; *W:* Peter Borg; *C:* Mats Hallesip; *M:* Martin Brandtveit.

Soup for One ♂♂ 1982 (R) Writer-director Kaufer's first film is a solid entry in the Woody Allen-esque Manhattanite's angst genre. Young Jewish guy Rubinek pines for the woman of his dreams, finds her, is rejected, persists, gets her, wonders if she's what he wants after all. If you like Woody Allen, this is worth seeing. 84m/C VHS. Saul Rubinek, Marcia Strassman, Gerrit Graham, Richard Libertini, Andrea Martin; *D:* Jonathan Kaufer.

Sour Grapes ♂♂ 1998 (R) "Seinfeld" co-creator David's feature directorial debut has cousins Evan and Richie (Weber and Bierko) feuding over an Atlantic City slot machine jackpot. Evan a successful neurosurgeon lends Richie, an extroverted loser, two quarters for one last pull on the slots. Of course, Richie wins the real-life daughter of J. Peterman, plays Fifi's girlfriend. If you liked "Seinfeld," this flick's for you. 91m/C VHS, DVD. Jack Kehler, Steven Weber, Craig Bierko, Karen Sillas, Matt Keeslar, Robyn Peterman, Jennifer Leigh Warren, Richard Gant, James MacDonald, Philip Baker Hall, Ann Guilbert; *D:* Larry David; *W:* Larry David; *C:* Victor Hammer.

Sourdough ♂♂ 1977 Fur trapper Perry escapes the hustle and bustle of modern life by fleeing to the Alaskan wilderness. Near-plotless film depends heavily on scenery—and the scenery is beautiful.

Sous Sol ♂♂ Not Me 1996 In 1967 Montreal, overly sensitive 11-year-old Rene (McWatt) spies on his parents while they make love and the next morning learns his father has died. Rene becomes certain that sex leads to death, which puts a crimp in his budding sexuality. As a matter of fact he literally refuses to grow up, remaining in his pre-adolescent state for several years while Mom Reine (Portal) eventually hooks up with a new boyfriend Roch (Godin), who moves in. This causes a few more problems for Rene. French with subtitles. **90m/C VHS.** *CA* Louise Portal, Richard Moffat, Isabelle Pasco, Lisa Blount, Joe Estevez, Lewis Van Bergen, Julia Montgomery, Brandis Kemp, Danitza Kingsley, Mary Grace Canfield, Bert Remsen; **D:** Mark Rezyka; **M:** Nigel Holton.

South Beach Academy ✗✗ 1996
(R) Eye candy focusing on a beach school that specializes in surfing, swimming, and volleyball rather than the usual academics. Maybe that's why the school's about to close—unless the lightly clad student body can come up with a plan to save their alma mater. **91m/C VHS.** Corey Feldman, Al Lewis, James Hong, Elizabeth Kaitan; **D:** Joe Esposito.

South Bronx Heroes ✗✗½ *The Runaways; Revenge of the Innocents* 1985 (R) A police officer helps two children when they discover their foster home is the headquarters for a pornography ring. **105m/C VHS, DVD.** Brendan Ward, Mario Van Peebles, Megan Van Peebles, Melissa Esposito, Martin Zurla, Jordan Abeles; **D:** William Szarka; **W:** William Szarka, Don Shifrin; **C:** Eric Schmitz; **M:** Al Zima.

South Central ✗✗ 1992 (R) A low-budget urban drama set in a gang-infested L.A. neighborhood. Bobby is a young black man, and former gang leader, who has spent ten years in prison for murder. His wife has become a drug addict and his young son Jimmie has begun running with his dad's old gang. Now paroled, Bobby hopes to re-establish the bond with his son—enough to protect him from following in his nowhere-to-go-but-down footsteps. Feature debut of director Anderson. Based on the novel "Crips" by Donald Bakeer. **99m/C VHS, DVD.** Glenn Plummer, Carl Lumbly, Christian Coleman, LaRita Shelby, Byron Keith Minns; **D:** Steve (Stephen M.) Anderson; **W:** Steve (Stephen M.) Anderson; **C:** Charlie Lieberman; **M:** Tim Truman.

South of Heaven, West of Hell ✗½ 2000 (R) A marshal (Yoakam), who once ran with an outlaw clan, must deal with his past when the bandits show up to terrorize the Arizona town he's sworn to protect. Yoakam's not much of a leading man and there's a lot of brutal violence to contend with. **133m/C VHS, DVD.** Dwight Yoakam, Bridget Fonda, Vince Vaughn, Billy Bob Thornton, Peter Fonda, Bud Cort, Michael Jeter, Paul (Pee-wee Herman) Reubens; **D:** Dwight Yoakam; **W:** Dwight Yoakam; **C:** James Glennon; **M:** Dwight Yoakam.

South of Hell Mountain ✗✗½ 1970 (R) On the run from a gold mine robbery where they left 20 dead, the McHenry brothers meet a mother-daughter team that slows them down. **87m/C VHS.** Ann Stewart, Sam Hall, Nicol Britton; **D:** William Sachs, Louis Leahman.

South of Monterey ✗✗½ 1947 Western adventure with the Cisco kid. **63m/B VHS.** Gilbert Roland, Martin Garralaga, Frank Yaconelli, Marjorie (Reardon) Riordan; **D:** William Nigh.

South of Pago Pago ✗✗ 1940 The unsuspecting natives of a tropical isle are exploited by a gang of pirates searching for a seabed of rare pearls. A notch up from most similar adventure outings, with great violent action and excellent cinematography. Leading lady Farmer was thought to be a rising star, but retired at 29 in 1942 because of alcoholism and spent some time in mental institutions. "Frances" (1982), with Jessica Lange, is based on her life. **98m/B VHS.** Victor McLa-

glen, Jon Hall, Frances Farmer, Gene Lockhart; **D:** Alfred E. Green.

South of Reno ✗✗ 1987 (R) A man living a secluded life in the desert dreams of moving to Reno and learns his wife is cheating on him. Odd, minimal plot. Impressive first feature for Polish director Rezyka, who cut his teeth on music videos. **98m/C VHS.** Jeffery Osterhage, Lisa Blount, Joe Estevez, Lewis Van Bergen, Julia Montgomery, Brandis Kemp, Danitza Kingsley, Mary Grace Canfield, Bert Remsen; **D:** Mark Rezyka; **M:** Nigel Holton.

South of St. Louis ✗✗½ 1948 A peaceful cattle rancher turns renegade gunrunner during the Civil War when his stock is destroyed by Union guerrillas. Overplotted but exciting and action-packed western, with Smith dazzling in a plethora of costumes. **88m/C VHS.** Joel McCrea, Zachary Scott, Victor Jory, Douglas Kennedy, Alexis Smith, Alan Hale, Dorothy Malone; **D:** Ray Enright; **C:** Karl Freund; **M:** Max Steiner.

South of Santa Fe ✗✗ 1932 Mexican rebels give the hero a hard time in this standard Western. **60m/B VHS.** Bob Steele, Janis Elliott, Chris-Pin (Ethier Crispin Martin) Martin, Jack Clifford, Eddie Dunn, Robert Burns, Hank Bell, Allan Garcia; **D:** Bert Glennon.

South of Santa Fe ✗✗ 1942 Rogers and friends take on the mob—yes, the mob, armed with machine guns and airplanes—after they are falsely implicated in a crime. In lulls between the rootin' tootin' gunfights, Rogers belts out "We're Headin' for the Home Corral," "Down the Trail," and "Open Range Ahead." **60m/B VHS.** Roy Rogers, George "Gabby" Hayes, Linda Hayes, Paul Fix, Judy Clark; **D:** Joseph Kane.

South of the Border ✗✗ 1939 Autry and Burnette are government agents sent to Mexico to investigate a possible revolution instigated by foreign agents. Propaganda-heavy singing western appeared just before the U.S. entered WWII; did well at the boxoffice and boosted Autry's career. **70m/B VHS, DVD.** Gene Autry, Smiley Burnette, June Storey, Lupita Tovar, Mary Lee, Duncan Renaldo, William Farnum, Frank Reicher; **D:** George Sherman; **W:** Betty Burbridge, Gerald Geraghty; **M:** William Nobles.

South of the Rio Grande ✗✗½ 1945 The Cisco Kid rides again as he comes to the aid of a rancher whose horses were stolen. Garden-variety law-and-order western. **60m/B VHS.** Duncan Renaldo; **D:** Lambert Hillyer.

South Pacific ✗✗✗½ 1958 A young American Navy nurse and a Frenchman fall in love during WWII. Expensive production included much location shooting in Hawaii. Based on Rodgers and Hammerstein's musical; not as good as the play, but pretty darn good still. The play in turn was based on James Michener's novel "Tales of the South Pacific." ♪My Girl Back Home; Dites-Moi; Bali Ha'i; Happy Talk; A Cockeyed Optimist; Soliloquies; Some Enchanted Evening; Bloody Mary; I'm Gonna Wash That Man Right Out of My Hair. **167m/C VHS, DVD.** Mitzi Gaynor, Rossano Brazzi, Ray Walston, France Nuyen, John Kerr, Juanita Hall, Tom Laughlin; **D:** Joshua Logan; **W:** Paul Osborn; **C:** Leon Shamroy; **M:** Richard Rodgers, Oscar Hammerstein; **V:** Giorgo Tozzi. **Oscars '58:** Sound.

South Park: Bigger, Longer and Uncut ✗✗✗ 1999 (R) The most unlikely critical darling of the summer of 1999 caught everyone's attention with it's MPAA-baiting language and sexual subject matter, and made audiences laugh—a lot—along the way. Stan, Kenny, Cartman, and Kyle sneak into an R-rated movie and shock their families with what they learn. So, concerned South Park parents form a censorship board to take on Canada (which results in a war, with enough bloody violence to make Sam Peckinpah sick, but didn't faze the MPAA), and the kids decide to fight back. Like most TV shows adapted for the big screen, this one flags at times, but has enough inspired comic moments to (mostly) justify the hype. The easily offended should definitely pass. **80m/C VHS, DVD.** Trey Parker, Matt Stone, Pam Brady; **W:** Marc Shaiman, Trey Parker; **V:** Trey Parker,

Matt Stone, Isaac Hayes, George Clooney, Minnie Driver, Mike Judge, Eric Idle, Mary Kay Bergman, Brent Spiner, Nick Rhodes, Stewart Copeland.

South Riding ✗✗½ 1937 Estate owner Robert Carne (Richardson) lives with teenaged daughter Midge (Johns) and has money woes from keeping ill wife Madge (Todd) in a mental hospital. A city councilman as well, Carne's drawn into a plan that will supposedly built decent housing for the lower classes but is actually a scam (which he discovers). Adapted from the novel by Winifred Holtby. **85m/B VHS.** GB Ralph Richardson, John Clements, Edna Best, Glynis Johns, Ann Todd, Edmund Gwenn, Marie Lohr, Milton Rosmer; **D:** Victor Saville; **W:** Ian Dalrymple; **C:** Harry Stradling Sr.; **M:** Richard Addinsell.

South Sea Sinner ✗✗½ 1950 Jake Davis (Carey) is wandering the South Seas after being framed on a gun-smuggling charge and comes across the bar of Coral (Winters), a gorgeous singer men can't keep their eyes off. Coral is forced by her boss to spy on Jake but the more time the two spend together the higher the flame grows and the more dangerous the game becomes. Respectable remake of Marlene Dietrich and John Wayne's "Seven Sinners." Features Liberace in his film debut as "Maestro." **88m/B VHS.** MacDonald Carey, Shelley Winters, Luther Adler, Frank Lovejoy; **D:** H. Bruce Humberstone; **W:** Oscar Brodney. **VIDEO**

South Sea Woman ✗✗½ 1953 Nightclub tootsie Ginger Martin (Mayo) testifies at the court-martial of Marine Sgt. James O'Hearn (Lancaster). Seems he and buddy Pvt. Davy White (Connors) met the stranded Ginger in Shanghai just before Pearl Harbor. O'Hearn tries to prevent the impulsive White from marrying her and the trio wind up on the Vichy French Island of Namou, where O'Hearn discovers some Nazis plotting evil. There's derring-do and various heroics but O'Hearn doesn't make it back to his unit in time and gets accused of desertion—hence the trial. Good action and a light touch—there's more comedy than angst. **99m/B DVD.** Burt Lancaster, Virginia Mayo, Chuck Connors, Barry Kelley, Hayden Rorke, Bob Sweeney, Leon Askin; **D:** Arthur Lubin; **W:** Earl Baldwin, Edwin Blum, Stanley Shapiro; **C:** Ted D. McCord; **M:** David Buttolph.

South Seas Massacre WOOF! *South Seas* 1974 A cop and a prisoner, shackled together, try to survive modern-day pirates, natives, and each other. They may make it through, but viewers may wish they didn't. **60m/C VHS.** PH Dania Ramirez, Juneo Jennings, Vic Vargas, Troy Donahue; **D:** Pablo Santiago; **W:** Leo Martinez; **C:** Joe Batac.

Southern Belles ✗✗ 2005 (R) Harebrained-but-likeable trailer park chicks Bell (Breckenridge) and Belle (Faris) want to escape their dull lives in rural Georgia to start anew in the "big city" of Atlanta. But they need some quick cash to get there so they concoct a half-baked plan that is interrupted by Bell's affections toward a policeman named Rhett Butler (Chambers). **90m/C DVD.** Anna Faris, Justin Chambers, Frederick Weller, Heather Goldenhersch, Laura Breckenridge; **D:** Paul S. Myers, Brennan Shroff; **W:** Paul S. Myers, Brennan Shroff. **VIDEO**

Southern Comfort ✗✗✗ 1981 (R) A group of National Guardsmen are on weekend maneuvers in the swamps of Louisiana. They run afoul of some of the local Cajuns, and are marked for death in this exciting and disturbing thriller. Boothe is excellent in a rare exploration of a little-understood way of life. Lots of blood. If you belong to the National Guard, this could make you queasy. **106m/C VHS, DVD.** Powers Boothe, Keith Carradine, Fred Ward, Franklyn Seales, Brion James, T.K. Carter, Peter Coyote, Ned Dowd, Lewis Smith, Les Lannom, Alan Autry, Sonny Landham; **D:** Walter Hill; **W:** Walter Hill, David Giler, Michael Kane; **C:** Andrew Laszlo; **M:** Ry Cooder.

Southern Man ✗✗ 1999 Turgid, undermotivated drama revolves around an actor (Withers) who goes back to Nashville from Los Angeles to work out childhood problems involving sexual abuse. **104m/C DVD.** Mark Withers, Ella Vier-

ling, Jesse Head, Leigh Rose, Jack Betts; **D:** Rick Rosenberg; **W:** Rick Rosenberg, Robert Northup; **C:** Ken Glassing; **M:** Matthew Ferrado.

A Southern Yankee ✗✗½ *My Hero* 1948 Skelton plays a bumbling bellboy who ends up as a Union spy during the Civil War. Enjoyable comedy, thanks largely to the off-screen input of Buster Keaton. **90m/B VHS.** Red Skelton, Brian Donlevy, Arlene Dahl, George Couloris, Lloyd Gough, John Ireland, Minor Watson, Charles Dingle, Art Baker, Reed Hadley, Arthur Space, Addison Richards, Joyce Compton, Paul Harvey, Jeff Corey; **D:** Edward Sedgwick.

The Southerner ✗✗✗✗ 1945 A man used to working for others is given some land by an uncle and decides to pack up his family and try farming for himself. They find hardships as they struggle to support themselves. A superb, naturalistic celebration of a family's fight to survive amid all the elements. From the story "Hold Autumn in Your Hand," by George Sessions Perry. Novelist Faulkner had an uncredited hand in the script. He thought Renoir the best contemporary director, and later said "The Southerner" gave him more pleasure than any of his other Hollywood work (though this is faint praise; Faulkner is said to have hated Hollywood). **91m/B VHS, DVD.** Zachary Scott, Betty Field, Beulah Bondi, Norman Lloyd, Bunny Sunshine, Jay Gilpin, Estelle Taylor, Blanche Yurka, Percy Kilbride, J. Carrol Naish; **D:** Jean Renoir; **W:** Jean Renoir, Hugo Butler, William Faulkner; **C:** Lucien N. Andriot; **M:** Werner Janssen. Natl. Bd. of Review '45: Director (Renoir); Venice Film Fest. '46: Film.

Southie ✗✗ 1998 (R) Another return of the native son drama offers some decent performances but nothing much that is new. Danny Quinn (Wahlberg) is a South Boston bad boy returning to home turf after a sojourn in New York. Danny's pals are tied up with one Irish gangster crew while his own family is involved with oldtimer Colie (Tierney) and Danny himself has a score to settle with longtime rival, Joey (Cummings). **95m/C VHS, DVD.** Donnie Wahlberg, Rose McGowan, Lawrence Tierney, James (Jimmy) Cummings, Anne Meara, Amanda Peet, John Shea; **D:** John Shea; **W:** James (Jimmy) Cummings, John Shea, Dave McLaughlin; **C:** Allen Baker; **M:** Wayne Sharp.

Southland Tales ✗½ 2006 (R) The U.S. is now monitored by a Big Brother-esque agency called US-IDENT, but revolutionaries in World War III-era Los Angeles are plotting to turn popular opinion against the government. Meanwhile, right-wing action star Boxer Santaros (Johnson) has lost his memory and has started an affair with porn actress-turned-talk show host Krysta Now (Gellar), which is somehow connected to the anti-government plot and the presidential election, in which his father-in-law (Osborne) is the Republican vice presidential candidate. Oh, and Justin Timberlake guards a pier against terrorist invaders while (mis)quoting T.S. Eliot and Revelations. Kelly's twisted, convoluted sci-fi black comedy is, at best, difficult to follow, with far more questions than it answers. When the movie works, it's an entertaining, absurdist post-9/11 farce; when it doesn't, it verges on incomprehensible. Kelly trimmed 19 minutes after the film was booed at Cannes. **144m/C DVD.** US Dwayne "The Rock" Johnson, Sarah Michelle Gellar, Seann William Scott, Curtis Armstrong, Nora Dunn, Wood Harris, John Larroquette, Mandy Moore, Holmes Osborne, Miranda Richardson, Justin Timberlake; **D:** Richard Kelly; **W:** Richard Kelly; **C:** Steven Poster; **M:** Moby.

Southward Ho! ✗✗ 1939 In the first western to team Rogers with sidekick Gabby Hayes, they portray ranchers investigating bloodshed in their valley. Roy meanwhile yodelin' four tunes. Fun outing. **56m/B VHS, DVD.** Roy Rogers, George "Gabby" Hayes, Lynne Roberts, Wade Boteler, Arthur Loft, Lane Chandler, Tom London; **D:** Joseph Kane; **W:** Gerald Geraghty; **C:** Jack Marta.

Souvenir ✗✗ 1988 (R) A German soldier returns to France after WWII to find the woman he left behind and the daughter he never saw. Might have been good, but too melodramatic and overwrought,

Soylent Green 🐾🐾½ **1973 (PG)** In the 21st Century, hard-boiled police detective Heston investigates a murder and discovers "what soylent green—the people's principal food—is made of. Robinson, in his final film, plays an uncharacteristically non-heavy role in this disappointing adaptation. Remains a provocative drama of a frightening future gone mad. **93m/C VHS, DVD.** Christopher Plummer, Catherine Hicks, Christopher Cazenove, Michael (Michel) Lonsdale. **D:** Geoffry Reeve.

Space: 1999—Alien Attack 🐾🐾🐾 **1979** After an explosion on the moon, Moonbase Alpha loses contact with Earth forever. Pilot episode of the popular British sci-fi series. **109m/C VHS. C:** Martin Landau, Barbara Bain, Barry Morse, Nick (Nichalas) Tate, Roy Dotrice, Philip Madoc, Lou Satton, Eric Carte. **D:** Lee H. Katzin.

Space Chimps 🐾🐾 **2008** Animated silliness about three NASA chimps (Warburton, Hines, Samberg) who are sent on a fat-off mission and find themselves on an uncharted planet where they must inspire the inhabitants to overcome their tyrant ruler (Daniels). Don't watch it with kids. **95m/C VHS, DVD. V:** Andy Samberg, Cheryl Hines, Patrick Warburton, Jeff Daniels, Stanley Tucci, Kristin Chenoweth, Kenan Thompson, Omid Abtahi, Patrick Breen, Kath Soucie, Jane Lynch.

Space Cowboys 🐾🐾🐾 **2000 (PG-13)** Eastwood, starring and directing again, plays a retired Air Force pilot who was passed over for the astronaut training program in the late 1950s. However, now NASA needs his expertise when an ailing 1960s satellite poses a threat if it crashes to Earth. He agrees to go into space and repair it only if he can bring his equally codgerly buddies, Sutherland, Jones, and Garner, to assist. Hey, if John Glenn can go back into space at age 77, why not Eastwood? Fun ensemble piece that succesfully weaves some action and thrills into the final act. **123m/C VHS, DVD, Blu-ray Disc, HD DVD. C:** Clint Eastwood, Tommy Lee Jones, James Garner, James Cromwell, Donald Sutherland, Marcia Gay Harden, Loren Dean, William Devane, Rade Serbedzija, Courtney B. Vance, Barbara Babcock, Blair Brown; **D:** Clint Eastwood; **W:** Ken Kaufman, Howard Klausner; **C:** Jack N. Green; **M:** Lennie Niehaus.

Space Jam 🐾🐾½ **1996 (PG)** Ex-pensive live action-animation combo finds basketball great Jordan forced to play ball against evil intergalactic invaders who are out to capture Bugs Bunny and the rest of the Looney Tunes characters. It's all fairly silly but the kids will enjoy it. **87m/C VHS, DVD.** Michael Jordan, Bill Murray, Wayne Knight, Theresa Randle; **D:** Joe Pytka; **W:** Leo Benvenuti; **C:** Michael Chapman; **M:** James Newton Howard; **V:** Danny DeVito.

Space Marines 🐾🐾 **1996 (R)** Cheesy cable thriller finds intergalactic marines battling 21st century space pirates who've stolen a nuclear cargo and taken hostages. **93m/C VHS.** Billy Wirth, John Pyper-Ferguson, Meg Foster, Edward Albert, James Shigeta, Cady Huffman; **D:** John Weidner.

Space Monster WOOF! First Woman into Space: Voyage beyond the Sun 1964 Really bad, low-budget flick with a rubber monster and a climactic crash into a "sea of monsters" which is really a fish tank full of crabs. Ultra cheap production with handled effects. Why bother? Who cares? **93m/C VHS.** Reb Brown, James Ryan, John Philip Law, Cameron Mitchell; **D:** David Winters; **W:** Maria Dante.

Space Mutiny 🐾 **1988 (PG)** Spaceship falls under the attack of the mutinous Kalgan. To keep everyone from being sold into slavery, a small band of loyal passengers strike back. Will they be successful in thwarting the attack? Who cares? **93m/C VHS, DVD. C:** Reb Brown, John Phillip Law, Cameron Mitchell, James Ryan, Cisse Cameron; **D:** David Winters.

Space Raiders 🐾 **Star Child 1983 (PG)** A plucky 10-year-old blasts off into a futuristic world of intergalactic desperados, crafty alien mercenaries, starship battles and cliff-hanging dangers. Recycled special effects (from producer Corman's movie factory) and plot (lifted near-whole from "Star Wars"). **84m/C VHS.** Vince Edwards, David Mendenhall; **D:** Howard R. Cohen.

Space Riders WOOF! **1983 (PG)** A rescue adventure about the world's championship motorcycle race, with a rock soundtrack featuring Duran Duran, Simple Minds and Melba Moore. **93m/C VHS.** Barry Sheene, Gavan O'Herlihy, Toshiya Ito, Stephanie McLean, Sayo Inaba; **D:** Joe Massot.

Space Soldiers Conquer the Universe 🐾🐾 **1940** Edited version of the Flash Gordon serial "Flash Gordon Conquers the Universe." The evil Emperor Ming introduces a horrible plague from outer space called "The Purple Death." Dr. Zarkov, Dale, and Flash Gordon travel from the frozen wastes of Frigia to the palaces of Mongo and must take risk after risk. Twelve chapters at 20 minutes each. **240m/B VHS.** Buster Crabbe, Charles Middleton, Carol Hughes; **D:** Ford Beebe, Ray Taylor; **W:** George Plympton, Basil Dickey, Barry Shipman; **C:** Jerome Ash, William Sickner.

Space Truckers 🐾🐾 **1997 (PG-13)** Sci-fi spoof about space haulage-truckers in the 21st century. Veteran hauler John Canyon (Hopper) accepts a dangerous assignment when he agrees to transport some sealed containers to Earth—no questions asked. Canyon, girlfriend Cindy (Mazar) and newbie driver Mike (Dorff) have their ship boarded by space pirates, led by Capt. Macanudo (Dance), who's part-machine. The cargo turns out to be murderous androids, sent to conquer Earth. Canyon and his crew must perform various heroics to save the planet! Lots of campy bad taste. **97m/C VHS, DVD, IR Dennis Hopper, Stephen Dorff, Charles Dance, Debi Mazar, George Wendt, Shane Rimmer, Vernon Wells, Barbara Crampton; **D:** Stuart Gordon; **W:** Ted Mann; **M:** Colin Towns.

Spaceballs 🐾🐾½ **1987 (PG)** A humorous Brooks parody of recent science fiction pictures, mostly notably "Star Wars," with references to "Alien," the "Star Trek series," and "The Planet of the Apes." Disappointingly tame and tentative, but chuckle-laden enough for Brooks fans. The great man himself appears in two roles, including puny wise man Yogurt. **96m/C VHS, DVD.** Mel Brooks, Rick Moranis, John Candy, Bill Pullman, Daphne Zuniga, Dick Van Patten, John Hurt, George Wyner, Joan Rivers, Lorene Yarnel, Sal Visuoso, Stephen Tcbolowsky, Dom DeLuise, Michael Winslow; **D:** Mel Brooks; **W:** Mel Brooks, Ronny Graham, Thomas Meehan; **M:** John Morris.

SpaceCamp 🐾🐾 **1986 (PG)** Gang of teens and their instructor at the U.S. Space Camp are accidentally launched on a space shuttle, and then must find a way to return to Earth. Hokey plot, subpar special effects; why bother? Well, it is "inspirational." **115m/C VHS, DVD.** Kate Capshaw, Tate Donovan, Joaquin Rafael (Leaf) Phoenix, Kelly Preston, Larry B. Scott, Tom Skerritt, Lea Thompson, Terry O'Quinn; **D:** Harry Winer; **M:** John Williams.

Spaced Invaders 🐾🐾 **1990 (PG)** Five ultra-cool aliens crash-land in a small midwestern town at Halloween. Local denizens mistake them for trick-or-treaters. Poorly made and a waste of time. **102m/C VHS, DVD.** Douglas Barr, Royal Dano, Ariana Richards, Kevin Thompson, Jimmy Briscoe, Tony Cox, Debbie Lee Carrington, Tommy Madden; **D:** Patrick Read Johnson; **W:** Scott Lawrence Alexander. **C:** James L. Carter.

Spaced Out WOOF! Outer Reach **1980 (R)** Naughty sci-fi sex comedy that parodies everything from "Star Wars" to "2001," though not very well. The sultry female aliens are visually pleasing.

Space Rage 🐾 Trackers **1986 (R)** A criminal sentenced to life on a prison planet leads a revolt of the inmates. Lame, formula western set in outer space. **78m/C VHS.** Michael Paré, Richard Farnsworth, John Laughlin, Lee Purcell; **D:** Conrad Parniseau.

Spacehunter: Adventures in the Forbidden Zone 🐾🐾½ **1983 (PG)** Galactic bounty hunter agrees to rescue three damsels held captive by a cyborg. Strauss ain't no Harrison Ford. Filmed in 3-D, but who cares? **90m/C VHS, DVD.** Peter Strauss, Molly Ringwald, Michael Ironside, Ernie Hudson, Andrea Marcovicci; **D:** Lamont Johnson; **W:** Len Blum; **C:** Frank Tidy; **M:** Elmer Bernstein.

Spacejacked 🐾½ **1998 (R)** In the future, the wealthy take pleasure trips to the Moon. Only greedy Barnes (Bernsen) sabotages the ship in order to extort money from the passengers—promising them a safe passage home in the escape pod. Of course, Barnes tries to double-cross everyone. Filled with low-budget clichés. Why should we suffer through it with him? **76m/B VHS, DVD.** Corbin Bernsen, Amanda Pays, Steve Bonc; **D:** Jeremiah Cullinane; **W:** Brendan Broderick, Daniella Purcell; **C:** Laurence Manly; **M:** Siobhan Cleary.

Spaceship 🐾½ **1983 Scientist Duff** is beset by all sorts of troubles: his experimental rockets explode, his wife has an affair with an ambitious scientist, and when they disappear together, he's accused of killing them and placing their bodies in the exploded rocket. All in all, a pretty bad (and long) day for our hero. Why not very funny, with the exception of the song-and-dance routine by the monster. **88m/C VHS, DVD.** Cindy Williams, Bruce Kimmel, Leslie Nielsen, Gerrit Graham, Patrick Macnee, Ron Kurowski; **D:** Bruce Kimmel.

Spaceways 🐾½ **1953 (R)** The Creature Wasn't Nice: Naked Space **1981 (PG)** Misguided attempt to spoof creature-features. Mad scientist tries to protect kindly monster from crazed crew. Not very funny, with the exception of the song-and-dance routine by the monster. **88m/C VHS, DVD.** Cindy Williams, Leslie Nielsen, Gerrit Graham, Patrick Macnee, Ron Kurowski; **D:** Bruce Kimmel.

Spaghetti House 🐾½ **1982** A handful of waiters are held hostage by ruthless killers in this innocuous but worthless Italian comedy. Dubbed. **103m/C VHS.** Nino Manfredi, Rita Tushingham; **D:** Giulio Paradisi.

Spaghetti Western 🐾½ **Cipolla Colt 1975 (PG)** A farmer and a publisher take on the vile oil baron who is taking over the town. A parody—or is it?—of Eastwoodian B-grade spaghetti westerns. No director credited. **92m/C VHS, IT SP Franco Nero, Martin Balsam, Sterling Hayden, Dick Butkus, Leo Anchoriz, Romano Puppo, Emma Cohen; **D:** Enzo G. Castellari; **W:** Sergio Donati, Luciano Vincenzoni; **C:** Alejandro Ulloa; **M:** Guido de Angelis, Maurizio de Angelis.

Spalding Gray: Terrors of Pleasure 🐾🐾🐾 **1988** The ultra-cool Gray tells the story of one man's dream to own land in his own inimitable way. HBO comedy special. **60m/C VHS.** Spalding Gray; **D:** Thomas Schlamme.

Spangles 🐾 **1926** Silent circus drama. **58m/B VHS.** Marion (Mirian) Nixon, Hobart Bosworth, Pat O'Malley, Gladys Brockwell; **D:** Frank O'Connor.

Spanglish 🐾½ **2004 (PG-13)** Sandler plays a sweetheart of a hubby in Brooks's problematic social comedy. As celebrity chef John Clasky, he's loving and supportive despite the complete self-absorption of his disturbing/unpleasant wife, Deborah (Leoni). Even Deborah's live-in lush of a mother (Leachman) knows what a horror her daughter is. Into this unhappy household comes lovely Flor (V'ega). A Mexican who doesn't yet speak English/illegal (who doesn't yet speak English) who takes the job as housekeeper because it will offer a better life for her own daughter, Cristina (Bruce). Given John's marital circumstances, is it any wonder that he and Flor become increasingly simpatico? Sandler's sincere and Leoni is nothing if not gutsy but it hardly seems worth the effort. **129m/C VHS, DVD. US** Adam Sandler, Tea Leoni, Paz Vega, Cloris Leachman, Thomas Haden Church, Shelbie Bruce, Sarah Steele, Ian Hyland, Victoria Luna; **D:** James L. Brooks; **W:** James L. Brooks; **C:** John Seale; **M:** Hans Zimmer.

Spanking the Monkey 🐾🐾🐾 **1994 (R)** "What'd ya do on your summer vacation"? Ray Aibelli (Davies) has an interesting answer in this dark comedy about family dysfunction, sexual politics, incest and masturbation, topics which, surprising attention on the story and characters rather than the delicate subject matter at hand. M.I.T. Ray learns he must give up a prestigious internship to care for his bedridden mother (Watson) while Dad goes on an extended "business" trip. Much sexual and emotional confusion follows. Mom, it seems, is rather attractive, controlling, and in need of hands-on assistance. Black comedy is understated and sensitive, focusing attention on the story and characters rather than the delicate subject matter. Sharp directorial debut by Russell features fine performances by mostly unknown cast, elevating low-budget feel. See it with a relative. **99m/C VHS, DVD.** Jeremy Davies, Alberta Watson, Benjamin Hendrickson, Carla Gallo, Matthew Puckett; **D:** David O. Russell; **W:** David O. Russell; **C:** Mike Mayers, Ind. Spirit '95: First Feature, First Screenplay Sundance '94; Aud. Award.

The Spaniard's Curse 🐾🐾½ **1958** When a man is convicted for a murder he did not commit, he puts a curse on the judge and jury responsible. Mysteriously, the marked people begin dying; is he responsible? Then he dies and the A.J. Cronin novel, turned into a showcase for Bocgarde in the title role. **95m/C VHS.** Dirk Bogarde, Jon Whiteley, Michael Horden, Ralph Truman.

The Spanish Gardener 🐾🐾🐾 **1957** A boy in a prominent family spends more time with the gentle gardner than with the domineering father, so dad arranges for his rival to be framed and sent to prison. An affecting British adaptation of the A.J. Cronin novel, turned roughly like the plot to "The Mexican" but this film is much worse. **98m/C VHS.** Dirk Bogarde, Jon Whiteley, Michael Hordern, Cyril Cusack, Maureen Swanson, Lyndon Brook, Josephine Griffin, Bernard Lee; **D:** Philip Leacock.

The Spanish Main 🐾🐾 **1945 (PG)** Typical, gusto-laden swashbuckler. RKO's first in Technicolor. Evil Spanish governor Slezak captures Dutch crew led by Henreid. They escape and kidnap his fiancée (O'Hara) off a ship coming from Mexico. Henreid forces her to marry him, but his crew uses the might of the armada, and returns O'Hara to Slezak behind Henreid's back. Wow! **100m/C Paul Henreid, Maureen O'Hara, Walter Slezak, Binnie Barnes, John Emery, Barton MacLane; **D:** Frank Borzage; **M:** George Barnes.

The Spanish Prisoner 🐾🐾🐾 **1997 (PG)** Playwright-filmmaker Mamet goes Hitchcockian in thriller involving an elaborate con game. Naive inventor Joe Ross (Scott) develops a formula for some corporate employers. No one is what they appear to be (if they were, it wouldn't be much of a thriller) in this unpredictable and seductive puzzle. Although the staccato dialogue is grating at times, and the emotional payoff is slight, there's enough twists throughout to keep you intrigued. Title comes from an old scam that feeds on the greed and lust of the mark. **112m/C VHS, DVD.** Campbell Scott, Steve Martin, Rebecca Pidgeon, Ben Gazzara, Ricky Jay, Felicity Huffman; **D:** David Mamet; **W:** David Mamet; **C:** Gabriel Beristain; **M:** Carter Burwell.

Spanish Judges 🐾½ **1999 (R)** Boring crime drama set in L.A. finds three criminals—muscle Max (D'Onofrio), brains Jack (Lillard), and vamp Jamie (Golino)—looking to steal a couple of valuable Spanish pistols. Yes, it does sound roughly like it. **95m/C VHS, DVD.** Matthew Lillard, Valeria Golino, Sam Hiona; **D:** Oz Scott; **W:** William Rehor; **C:** Stephen McNutt.

Spare Me 🐾🐾½ **1992** Family and personal dysfunction mark the long-awaited home video debut of Harrison's cult fave "bowling noir" film. Theo (Paseka) is put on suspension from the Pro Bowler's Tour for attacking an opponent with his bowling ball. He searches out his bowling-legend father, Buzz (Alfred), who might be able to help him out. Along the way he meets and falls for a pyromaniac waitress (MacFayden), whose father is evil bowling kingpin Miles Kastle, and brother is escaped psycho patient Junior. When Theo finds Pop, he's in cahoots with Miles, helping him run an illegal midget bowling circuit. Harrison's excellent low-budget direction, and a hilarious, if completely twisted script, enables this one to pick up the difficult 7-10 split of cinematic success. **85m/C VHS.** Mark Alfred, Christopher Cooke, Lawton Paseka, Christopher Grimm, Christie MacFadyen, Richard W. Sears Jr., Bill Christ, Sean Haggerty; **D:** Matthew Harrison; **W:** Christopher Grimm; **C:** Mike Mayers; **M:** Danny Brenner.

Spare Parts WOOF! **1979** Guests at a remote hotel discover that it is run by black marketeers who kill guests and sell the body parts. Of course, they don't bother signing out. **108m/C VHS.** *GE* Judith Speidel, Wolf Roth; **D:** Rainer Erler; **W:** Rainer Erler; **C:** Wolfgang Grasshoff; **M:** Eugen Thomass.

Spark 🐾🐾 **1998** Quarreling lovers Byron and Nina are stranded when their car breaks down in nowheresville. Stuck in a redneck dump while their ride is being fixed, the couple learns too many ugly lovely secrets. **102m/C DVD.** Terrence Howard, Nicole Ari Parker, Brendan Sexton III, Sandra Ellis Lafferty, Timothy McNeil; **D:** Garret Williams; **W:** Garret Williams; **C:** Samuel Ameen; **M:** Marc Anthony Thompson.

Sparkle 🐾🐾½ **1976 (PG)** The saga of three singing sisters struggling to rise to the top of the charts in the 1950s. Sound familiar? Well done but cliched fictional version of the Supremes' career. McKee shines. Alcohol, drugs, and mobsters get in the way. Excellent musical score. **98m/C VHS, DVD.** Irene Cara, Lonette McKee, Dwan Smith, Philip Michael Thomas, Mary Alice, Dorian Harewood, Tony King; **D:** Sam O'Steen; **W:** Joel Schumacher; **M:** Curtis Mayfield.

Sparkler 🐾🐾½ **1999 (R)** Effervescent Melba May (Overall) is a trailer-park wife, living just off the highway to Vegas. She leaves her husband, Flint (Harvey), for cheating on her and eventually winds up in Vegas with three young men she met and her old high-school buddy Dottie (Cartwright), who's now a stripper. And everybody gets an education of sorts. Doesn't have a consistent tone, with Overall and Cartwright providing the best performances. **96m/C VHS, DVD.** Park Overall, Veronica Cartwright, Jamie Kennedy, Steven Petrarca, Freddie Prinze Jr., Don Harvey, Grace Zabriskie, Sandy Martin; **D:** Darren Stein; **W:** Darren Stein; **C:** Rodney Taylor; **M:** David E. Russo.

Sparrows 🐾🐾🐾 **1926** Hidden in a southern swamp, the evil Grimes (von Seyffertitz) runs a baby farm, where unwanted children are sent and used as slave labor. The eldest, nicknamed Mama Mollie (Pickford), tries to protect the others from Grimes's cruelty. They eventually plan their escape but must cross treacherous quicksand with Grimes in pursuit. Silent melodrama features a notable performance by Pickford. **109m/B VHS, DVD.** Mary Pickford, Gustav von Seyffertitz, Charlotte Mineau, Roy Stewart, Mary Louise Miller, "Spec" (Walter) O'Donnell, Mary Frances McLean, Camilla Johnson; **D:** William Beaudine; **W:** C. Gardner Sullivan, Winifred Dunn; **C:** Charles Rosher, Karl Struss, Hal Mohr; **M:** William Perry.

Spartacus 🐾🐾🐾½ **1960 (PG-13)** The true story of a gladiator who leads other slaves in a rebellion against the power of Rome in 73 B.C. The rebellion is put down and the rebels are crucified. Douglas, whose political leanings are amply on display herein, also served as executive producer, surrounding himself with the best talent available. Magnificent climactic battle scene features 8,000 real, live Spanish soldiers to stunning effect. A version featuring Kubrick's "director's cut"

is also available, featuring a restored, controversial homoerotic bath scene with Olivier and Curtis. Anthony Mann is uncredited as co-director. A boxoffice triumph that gave Kubrick much-desired financial independence. **196m/C VHS, DVD, HD DVD.** Vinton (Hayworth) Haworth, Kirk Douglas, Charles Laughton, Laurence Olivier, Jean Simmons, Tony Curtis, Charles McGraw, Herbert Lom, Nina Foch, Woody Strode, Peter Ustinov, John Gavin, John Ireland, Charles McGraw, Joanna Barnes; **D:** Stanley Kubrick; **W:** Dalton Trumbo; **C:** Russell Metty; **M:** Alex North. Oscars '60: Art Dir/Set Dec., Color, Color Cinematog., Support. Actor (Ustinov); Golden Globes '61: Film—Drama.

Spartan 🐾🐾🐾 **2004 (R)** The president's daughter has been kidnapped—possibly by a Middle Eastern group of woman slave traders—and cagey special ops agent Robert Scott (Kilmer) is entrusted with the task of bringing her home. But, as with any Mamet venture, what seems to be the reality might not be and the deeper Scott gets into the job the less he can be certain of. His dilemma and the questions that swirl around make for high-octane action-thriller fun...until it sadly runs out of gas toward the end. Kilmer seizes the character along with the fundamentals of the smart, fast-paced language; Luke has a good turn (as Scott's trainee) as do perpetual Mamet performers Macy and O'Neill. **107m/C DVD.** *US* Val Kilmer, Derek Luke, Tia Texada, Kristen Bell, Johnny Messner, Lionel Mark Smith, Tony Mamet, Clark Gregg, Steven Culp, Aaron Stanford, Geoffrey Pierson, William H. Macy, Ed O'Neill, Andrew Davoli, Said Taghmaoui, Matt Malloy, Kick (Christopher) Gurry, David Paymer; **D:** David Mamet; **W:** David Mamet; **C:** Juan Ruiz-Anchia; **M:** Mark Isham.

Spasms WOOF! *Death Bite* **1982 (R)** Reed is the unfortunate big game hunter who encounters The Demon Serpent, known as N'Gana Simbu, the deadliest snake in the world. Lame-brained horror fantasy; the producers should have released the nifty Tangerine Dream soundtrack and chucked the movie. Based on the novel "Death Bite" by Michael Maryk and Brent Monahan. **92m/C VHS.** *CA* Peter Fonda, Oliver Reed, Kerrie Keane, Al Waxman, Miguel Fernandes, Marilyn Lightstone, Laurie Brown, Gerard Parkes; **D:** William Fruet; **W:** Don Enright.

Spawn 🐾🐾🐾 **1997 (PG-13)** Government agent Al Simmons (White) returns to earth, six years after being murdered, in the form of Spawn, a hell-born creature with supernatural powers. He wants to avenge his death and also save his loved ones from the evil Violator (Leguizamo). With green eyes and a friendship with Satan, Spawn's more of a lethal weapon and way more sinister looking than the villain. An unrecognizable Leguizamo and sleazy Sheen team up as adequate adversaries. Extravagant special effects, and a complex, dark story put a unique spin on the over-exposed superhero premise. Adapted from the best-selling comic book. An R-rated director's cut, which includes a "making of" feature and an interview with Todd McFarlane, is also available. **97m/C VHS, DVD.** Michael (Mike) Papajohn, Michael Jai White, John Leguizamo, Martin Sheen, Theresa Randle, D.B. Sweeney, Nicol Williamson, Melinda (Mindy) Clarke, Miko Hughes; **D:** Mark Dippe; **W:** Alan B. McElroy; **C:** Guillermo Navarro; **M:** Graeme Revell.

Spawn of the North 🐾🐾🐾 **1938** Alaska's the final frontier in the early 1900s as fisherman Jim Kimmerlee (Fonda) tries to earn an honest buck. But former friend Tyler Dawson (Raft) has joined a group of Russian pirates who plunder the nets of others and the two men are forced into a deadly confrontation. Solid cast, weak script, and a special Oscar for photographic and sound effects (a glacier's birth!). Based on the novel by Barrett Willoughby; remade in 1954 as "Alaska Seas." **110m/B VHS.** Henry Fonda, George Raft, Dorothy Lamour, John Barrymore, Akim Tamiroff, Louise Platt, Fuzzy Knight, Duncan Renaldo; **D:** Henry Hathaway; **W:** Jules Furthman, Talbot Jennings; **C:** Charles (Bryant) Lang Jr.; **M:** Dimitri Tiomkin.

Speak 🐾🐾🐾 **2004 (PG-13)** Stewart gives an amazingly touching performance as Melinda Sordino, a high school freshman who has retreated into selective mutism after being raped at a summer party. Having called the cops on a popular senior, Melinda is now a social pariah, with her parents (Perkins, Sweeney) too preoccupied to recognize her anguish. But over the school year, her unconventional art teacher, Mr. Freeman (Zahn), shows Melinda that expressing herself is a way to confront her experience. Based on the novel by Laurie Halse Anderson. **93m/C DVD.** Kristen Stewart, Steve Zahn, Elizabeth Perkins, D.B. Sweeney, Hallee Hirsh, Eric Lively, Michael Angarano, Robert John Burke, Allison Siko; **D:** Jessica Sharzer; **W:** Jessica Sharzer, Annie Young; **C:** Andrij Parekh. **CABLE**

Speak Easily 🐾🐾½ **1932** Keaton is bored with his dull life as a college professor. Durante tries to spice things up with a phony inheritance letter, and Keaton decides to spend his supposed money backing a stage show. Keaton is the star, but Durante steals the show. Great supporting cast. **82m/B VHS, DVD.** Buster Keaton, Jimmy Durante, Ruth Selwyn, Thelma Todd, Hedda Hopper, Sidney Toler, Lawrence Grant, Henry Armetta, Edward Brophy; **D:** Edward Sedgwick.

Speak of the Devil 🐾 **1990** A New Orleans evangelist who seduces his followers moves to Los Angeles and strikes a bargain with Satan. Exploitative, unthinking spoof of Swaggart/Bakker scandals of recent years. **99m/C VHS.** Gil Bottcher, Robert Elarton, Jean Miller, Bernice Tamara Goor, Louise Sherill, Walter Kay, Shawn Patrick Greenfield; **D:** Raphael Nussbaum; **W:** Raphael Nussbaum; **C:** Chuck Colwell.

Speak Up! It's So Dark 🐾🐾 *Tala! Det ar sa Mork!* **1993** Soren (Norrthon) is a skinhead who gets beaten up at a neo-Nazi rally. He meets Jewish shrink Jacob (Glaser) on a train and Jacob offers to tend to Soren's wounds. Although Soren continually parrots hateful doctrine, Jacob (whose family died at Auschwitz) tries to help him and Soren slowly begins to see he's wrong. Swedish with subtitles. **83m/C VHS.** *SW* Etienne Glaser, Simon Norrthon; **D:** Suzanne Osten; **W:** Niklas Radstrom; **C:** Peter Mokrosinski.

Speaking Parts 🐾🐾🐾 **1989** VCR-obsessed laundry worker and another woman battle for the attention of bit-part actor McManus who works in ritzy hotel. A telling picture of the inextricable nature of modern technology. **92m/C VHS, DVD.** *CA* Michael McManus, Arsinee Khanjian, David Hemblen, Gabrielle Rose, Tony Nardi, Patricia Collins, Gerard Parkes; **D:** Atom Egoyan; **W:** Atom Egoyan; **C:** Paul Sarossy; **M:** Mychael Danna.

Special Bulletin 🐾🐾🐾 **1983** A pacifistic terrorist threatens to blow up Charleston, South Carolina, with a nuclear warhead. Done quite well in docu-drama style as a TV news bulletin. Interesting examination of the media's treatment of dramatic events. Top-notch made-for-TV fare. **105m/C VHS.** Ed Flanders, Christopher Allport, Kathryn Walker, Roxanne Hart; **D:** Edward Zwick; **W:** Marshall Herskovitz, Edward Zwick. **TV**

A Special Day 🐾🐾🐾 *Una Giornata Speciale; The Great Day* **1977** The day of a huge rally celebrating Hitler's visit to Rome in 1939 serves as the backdrop for an affair between weary housewife Loren and lonely, unhappy homosexual radio announcer Mastroianni. Good performances from two thorough pros make a depressing film well worth watching. In Italian with English subtitles or dubbed. **105m/C VHS, DVD.** *IT* Sophia Loren, Marcello Mastroianni, John Vernon, Francoise Berd; **D:** Ettore Scola; **W:** Ettore Scola, Ruggero Maccari, Maurizio Costanzo; **C:** Pasqualino De Santis; **M:** Armando Trovajoli. Golden Globes '78: Foreign Film.

Special Delivery 🐾🐾½ **1976 (PG)** Three unemployed Vietnam veterans decide to rob a bank but their getaway plans go awry. Svenson, the only robber who escapes, stashes the cash in a mailbox only to have it discovered by nutty artist, Shepherd, and crooked barkeep Gwynne. **99m/C VHS.** Bo Svenson, Cybill Shepherd, Vic Tayback, Michael C. Gwynne, Tom Atkins, Sorrell Booke, Deidre Hall, Gerrit Graham, Jeff Goldblum; **D:** Paul Wendkos; **C:** Harry Stradling Jr.; **M:** Lalo Schifrin.

Special Effects 🐾🐾 **1985 (R)** A desperate movie director murders a young actress, then makes a movie about her death. Solid, creepy premise sinks in the mire of flawed execution; a good film about Hollywood ego trips and obsession is lurking inside overdone script. **103m/C VHS, DVD.** *GB* Zoe Tamerlis, Eric Bogosian, Kevin J. O'Connor, Brad Rijn, Bill Oland, Richard Greene; **D:** Larry Cohen; **W:** Larry Cohen.

Special Forces 🐾 *Hell in Normandy* **1968** Eight specially trained soldiers drop behind enemy lines to rescue prisoners of war in WWII. **90m/C VHS, DVD, IT** Peter Lee Lawrence, Guy Madison, Erika Blanc, Tony Norton; **D:** Alfonso Brescia; **W:** Maurice De Vries, Lorenzo Gicca Palli; **C:** Fausto Rossi; **M:** Italo Fischetti.

Special Investigator 🐾🐾½ **1936** Dix is a criminal attorney who specializes in getting his mob clients freed. Then his FBI brother gets killed by the same criminals he's been defending. So Dix becomes a special agent and sets out to get the mob boss responsible for his brother's murder. Climax is the big shootout at the gang's hideaway. Based on the novel by Earle Stanley Gardner. **60m/B VHS.** Richard Dix, J. Carrol Naish, Margaret Callahan, Erik Rhodes, Owen Davis Jr., Ray Mayer, Joseph (Joe) Sawyer; **D:** Louis King.

Special Olympics 🐾 **1978** A father attempts to cure his three sons, one of whom is mentally retarded, following the death of his wife. **104m/C VHS.** Charles Durning, Philip Brown, George Parry, Irene Tedrow, Mare Winningham, Herb Edelman, Debra Winger, Constance McCashin; **D:** Lee Philips. **TV**

Special Police 🐾🐾½ **1985** Police inspector protecting old friend's murder-witnessing sister learns that important politicians are involved with a seedy underground political movement. French thriller also available dubbed. **92m/C VHS.** *FR* Richard Berry, Carole Bouquet, Fanny Cottencon; **D:** Michael Vianey; **W:** Michael Vianey.

The Specialist 🐾🐾½ **1975 (R)** Lawyer West thinks he has seduced stunning Capri, but she has lured him into her clutches—she's been hired to kill him. Campy crud. It's old home week for '60s TV alums: West was Batman; bailiff Moore was Mr. Kimbell on Green Acres. **93m/C VHS, DVD.** Adam West, John Anderson, Anna Capri, Alvy Moore; **D:** Howard (Hikmet) Avedis; **W:** Howard (Hikmet) Avedis, Marlene Schmidt, Ralph B. Potts; **C:** Massoud Joseph; **M:** Shorty Rogers.

The Specialist 🐾½ **1994 (R)** Buffed bods do not a movie make—at least not in this mechanical actioner featuring Stone as the revenge-minded May Munro. Seems May's parents were killed by Cuban gangsters, led by father/son thugs Joe (Steiger) and Tomas Leon (Roberts), and she decides ex-CIA bomb specialist Ray Quick (Stallone) is just the man she needs to settle the score. But Quick has his own reasons for accepting—his ex-partner is nutball Ned Trent (Woods), who's now working for the Leons. Things blow up a lot, the two leads show off their toned flesh (but not much acting), and Woods gets to steal the movie with his amusing scenery chewing. **110m/C VHS, DVD.** Sylvester Stallone, Sharon Stone, James Woods, Eric Roberts, Rod Steiger; **D:** Luis Llosa; **W:** Alexandra Seros; **C:** Jeffrey L. Kimball; **M:** John Barry. Golden Raspberries '94: Worst Actress (Stone).

The Specials 🐾🐾🐾 **2000** This is the movie that "Mystery Men" wanted to be. It's a smart comic book spoof that depends on good acting and well-written characters. The Specials are the sixth or seventh greatest team of superheroes in the business. Headquarters is a suburban house in Silver Lake. Their immediate goal—if they can quit bickering among themselves—it to get a line of action figures on the market. **89m/C DVD.** Rob Lowe, Jamie Kennedy, Thomas Haden Church, Paget Brewster, Judy Greer, James Gunn, Sean Gunn, Jordan Ladd, Kelly Coffield; **D:** Craig Mazin; **W:** James Gunn; **C:** Eliot Rockett; **M:** Brian Langsbard, Spring Aspers.

Species 🐾🐾½ 1995 (R) A "friendly" galactic message containing a recipe on how to combine extraterrestrial DNA with human DNA is sent to scientists on Earth. The scientists, led by Fitch (Kingsley), whip up a batch of genetic material resulting in a sexy half alien, half human procreating/killing machine named Sil, who escapes from the lab, leaving the scientists with the unenviable task of catching her/it. All-star special effects team, including "Alien" designer H.R. Giger, create over-the-top, stomach-churning thrills. Dips literally into the tricks of many sci-fi classics. For avid gore-meisters only. **108m/C VHS, DVD, Blu-ray Disc, UMD.** Ben Kingsley, Michael Madsen, Alfred Molina, Forest Whitaker, Marg Helgenberger, Natasha Henstridge, Michelle Williams; **D:** Roger Donaldson; **W:** Christopher Leon; **M:** Christopher Young, MTV Movie Awards '96: Kiss (Natasha Henstridge/Anthony Guidera).

Species 2 🐾½ 1998 (R) Genetic scientists, in their quest to see an actual babe who will talk to genetic scientists, create a clone named Eve (Henstridge) from the monster in the original movie. Meanwhile, the U.S. has managed to successfully put an underwater model who can't act on Mars. Astronaut Patrick Ross (Lazard) has been infected with spores of alien DNA. Soon Ross' urge to procreate takes over and nasty alien babies are exploding out of screaming women all over town. Government assassin Press Lennox (Madsen) and Dr. Laura Baker (Helgenberger) are once again called in to track down the new species, with the help of Eve. Can they stop Ross and his brood before they mature? Can they stop Eve and Ross from making the beast with several scaly slimy multi-appendaged backs? Can they please stop making this movie again? **95m/C VHS, DVD.** Natasha Henstridge, Michael Madsen, Marg Helgenberger, Mykelti Williamson, George Dzundza, James Cromwell, Myriam Cyr, Baxter Harris; **D:** Peter Medak; **W:** Chris Brancato; **C:** Matthew F. Leonetti; **M:** Ed Shearmur.

Specimen 🐾½ 1997 (R) Twenty-four years ago, aliens impregnated Carol Hillary and she gave birth to a son, Mark. Now, the aliens have returned to claim him, only he doesn't want to go. **95m/C VHS, DVD, CA Mark Paul Gosselaar, Doug O'Keefe, Michelle Johnson, Andrew Jackson; D:** Domenic Keating, Helena Mattsson, Marco Bacuzzi; **D:** Nick Lyon; **W:** Ben Ripley; **C:** Jaime Reynoso; **M:** Paul Cristo, Kevin Haskins. **VIDEO**

The Speckled Band 🐾🐾🐾 1931 Set in 1930, this early talkie is a Sherlock Holmes adventure wherein the great detective must solve the mysterious death of a young woman. Massey makes his screen debut as Holmes, making the sleuth cynical, unhappy and pessimistic. Interesting prototypical Holmes case, faithful to the like-titled Conan Doyle story. **84m/B VHS, DVD.** Raymond Massey, Lyn Harding, Athole Stewart, Angela Baddeley, Nancy Price; **D:** Jack Raymond; **C:** Frederick A. (Freddie) Young.

Species 4: The Awakening 🐾 2007 Same old, same old. Miranda (Mattsson) discovers she's teen cloned from both human and alien DNA. She awakens from a blackout and learns she's probably a murderer after her alien side goes on the hunt for a mate. **103m/C** Natasha Henstridge, Ben Cross, Domenic Keating, Helena Mattsson, Marco Bacuzzi.

The Spectator 🐾🐾 La Spettatrice 2001 Lonely 20-something Valeria (Bobulova), a translator in Turin, becomes obsessed with her middle-aged neighbor Massimo (Renzi), a doctor whose work she translates. When he moves to Rome, Valeria follows. When he becomes her companion, Flavia (Catillon). After befriending Flavia, Valeria discovers that Massimo is now also interested in her. Romantic tribulations ensue. Italian with subtitles. **98m/C DVD.** Barbara Bobulova, Andrea Renzi, Brigitte Catillon; **D:** Paolo Franchi; **W:** Paolo Franchi; **C:** Giuseppe Lanci, Stefano Francini; **M:** Carlo Crivelli.

Specters 🐾 Spettri 1987 Archaeologists excavating the Roman catacombs break open the gates of hell. Hellishly confused plot is unoriginal, but decent production values hardly compensate. **95m/C VHS.** Donald Pleasence, John Pepper, Erna Schurer, Katrine Michelsen; **D:** Marcello Avallone; **W:** Marcello Avallone, Andrea Purgatori, Dardano Sacchetti, Maurizio Tedesco.

Spectre 🐾 House of the Damned Forger Corman Presents; House of the Damned 1996 (R) Maura South (Paul) is the heiress to a old mansion in Ireland and when she, husband Will (Evigan), and their young daughter Aubrey (played by Evigan's daughter Briana) move in they discover it's haunted by the vengeful spirit of a young girl. When they discover the girl's body, the family hope a proper burial will set her spirit to rest but the ghost has other ideas. Filmed in Ireland. **82m/C VHS, DVD.** Alexandra Paul, Briana Evigan, Robert Draper, Dick Donaghue; **D:** Scott Levy; **W:** Brendan Broderick; **C:** Christopher Baffa; **M:** Christopher Lennertz. **C.A.B.L.E.**

The Spectre of Edgar Allen Poe 🐾½ 1973 The horridly fictionalized writer of horror fiction visits the asylum where his love Lenore is being held, and discovers murder and torture. Based very loosely on Poe's own torments. **90m/B VHS.** Cesar Romero, Robert Walker Jr., Tom Drake; **D:** Mohy Quandour.

Spectre of the Rose 🐾🐾½ 1946 Strange film set in the world of ballet. An impresario contends with an over-the-hill ballerina and a young male dancer with a deadly affinity for knives. **90m/B VHS.** Judith Anderson, Michael Chekhov, Ivan Kirov, Viola Essen, Lionel Stander; **D:** Ben Hecht; **W:** Ben Hecht.

Speechless 🐾🐾½ 1994 (PG-13) Cute romantic comedy about sparring speechwriters who fall in love, and then briefly turn enemies when they discover they're working at professional odds. Davis is the idealistic liberal working for senatorial candidate Wannamaker, while Keaton is a TV sitcom writer doing a one-shot deal for a millionaire businessman, Republican Garvin. Both stars do a likable job; this one's supporting cast fares better with Reeve as an egotistical TV reporter, as well as Davis's fiance, and Bedelia as Keaton's ex-wife/campaign press secretary. Although the film parallels the real-life romance of rival Bush-Clinton spin doctors Mary Matalin and James Carville, it was written prior to the 1992 presidential race. **99m/C VHS, DVD.** Michael Keaton, Geena Davis, Christopher Reeve, Bonnie Bedelia, Ernie Hudson, Charles Martin Smith, Gailard Sartain, Ray Baker, Mitchell Ryan; **D:** Ron Underwood; **W:** Robert King; **C:** Don Peterman; **M:** Marc Shaiman.

Speed 🐾🐾🐾½ 1994 (R) Excellent dude Reeves has grown up (and bulked up) as Los Angeles SWAT cop Jack Traven, up against bomb expert Howard Payne (Hopper, more maniacal than usual), who's after major ransom money. First it's a rigged elevator in a very tall building. Then it's a rigged bus— if it slows, it will blow, bad enough any day, but a nightmare in LA traffic. And that's still not the topper for cinema. Smart-assed but believable action from both. Terrific directorial debut for cinematographer De Bont, who certainly knows how to keep the adrenaline pumping. Fine support work by Daniels, Bullock, and Morton and enough wit in Yost's script to keep you chuckling. Great nonstop action-er from the "Die Hard" school. **115m/C VHS, DVD, Blu-ray Disc, UMD.** Keanu Reeves, Dennis Hopper, Sandra Bullock, Joe Morton, Jeff Daniels, Alan Ruck, Glenn Plummer, Richard Lineback, Beth Grant, Hawthorne James, David Kriegel, Carlos Carrasco, Natsuko Ohama, Daniel Villarreal; **D:** Jan De Bont; **W:** Graham Yost; **C:** Andrzej Bartkowiak; **M:** Mark Mancina. Oscars '94: Sound, Sound FX Editing; MTV Movie Awards '95: Female Perf. (Bullock), Most Desirable Female (Bullock), On-Screen Duo (Keanu Reeves/Sandra Bullock), Villain (Hopper), Action Seq.; Blockbuster '95: Movie V., Action Actress, T. (Bullock), Action Actress. V. (Bullock).

Speed 2: Cruise Control 🐾 1997 (PG-13) Bigger's certainly not better in this lame sequel. Annie's (Bullock) got a new beau, hot-headed cop Alex (Patric), and the twosome decide to go on a Caribbean cruise for a little romance. Annie's luck with transportation holds as the ship is taken over by villainous computer geek with-a-grudge John Giger (a particularly wild-eyed Dafoe), who sends the liner on a collision course with an oil tanker. Since Alex is off performing heroics, there's not much togetherness and Annie's left to get taken hostage (again)). De Bont spent $25 million on the ship's endless crash into a Caribbean island, which still manages to lock fake and only elicits "you've got to be kidding me" disappointment. Bullock's feisty but powerless to save the sinking flick. Patric's bland and Dafoe is never menacing enough to create any thrills. This sea disaster crashes against the rocks of high expectations and poor execution. **123m/C VHS, DVD.** Sandra Bullock, Jason Patric, Willem Dafoe, Temuera Morrison, Brian McCardie, Glenn Plummer, Royale Watkins, Colleen Camp, Lois Chiles, Michael G. (Mike) Hagerty, Kimmy Robertson, Christine Firkins, Bo Svenson, Patrika Darbo; **Cameos:** Tim Conway; **D:** Jan De Bont; **W:** Jeff Nathanson, Randall McCormick; **C:** Jack N. Green; **M:** Mark Mancina. Golden Raspberries '97: Worst Remake/Sequel.

The Speed of Life 🐾½ Saturn 1999 (R) Although Drew (Caan) loves his father (Burmester), he would prefer to be doing anything else instead of having the emotional and physical burden of caring for the terminally-ill man. Meeting drug-addicted Sarah (Kirshner) only hastens his desire to flee. Slow-moving and shallow. **95m/C VHS, DVD.** Scott Caan, Mia Kirshner, Leo Burmester, Anthony Michael Ruivivar; **D:** Ron Schmidt; **W:** Rob Schmidt; **C:** Matthew Lhabique; **M:** Ryeland Allison. **VIDEO**

The Speed Lovers 🐾 1968 Stock car driver Lorenzen plays himself as an inspiration to a young man to join the auto racing circuit. More of a pat on the industry's back than a serious drama. Features footage from a number of race tracks around the country although shot principally in Atlanta. **90m/C** Fred Lorenzen, William F. McCara, Peggy O'Hara, David Marcus, Caro Street, Glenda Brunson; **D:** William F. McGaha; **W:** William F. McGaha, Elaine Wilkerson, Fred Tuch.

Speed Racer 2008 Go Speed Racer! Fearless Speed (Hirsch) is loyal to his racing family and the memory of his dead brother Rex whom he idolized. Speed turns down an offer to drive for Royalton Industries, angering its owner (Allam) so that he blacklists Speed, who has also uncovered a race-fixing secret. Aided by his one-time rival, the mysterious Racer X (Fox), Speed and his Mach 5 are going all out to win the Crucible, the cross-country racing rally that already claimed his brother's life. Based on the 1960s Japanese animated TV series and the first directorial venture from the Wachowski brothers since 2003's "The Matrix Reloaded." Not yet reviewed. **?m/C** Emile Hirsch, Christina Ricci, Matthew Fox, John Goodman, Susan Sarandon, Roger Allam, Hiroyuki (Henry) Sanada, Richard Roundtree, Paulie (Lirowsy) Litt, Benno Furmann, Scott Porter, Christian Oliver; **C:** Andy Wachowski, Larry Wachowski; **W:** Andy Wachowski; **C:** David Tattersall; **M:** Michael Giacchino.

Speed Reporter 🐾 1936 A newshound is the intrepid reporter investigating a photo reform movement that's really a front for a gang of criminals. Mediocre drama with Talmadge's thick German accent a hindrance. **56m/B VHS, DVD.** Richard Talmadge, Luana Walters, Richard Cramer; **D:** Bernard B. Ray.

Speed Zone 🐾 1988 (PG) Comic celebrities take over a high speed auto race when a redneck cop locks up the real drivers. Unfunny sequel to "Cannonball Run." **96m/C VHS.** Melody Anderson, Peter Boyle, Tim Matheson, Donna Dixon, John Candy, Eugene Levy, Joe Flaherty, Matt Frewer, Shari Belafonte, Tom Smothers, Dick Smothers, Brooke Shields, Lee Van Cleef, Jamie Farr, John Schneider, Michael Spinks; **D:** Jim Drake. Golden Raspberries '89: Worst Support. Actress (Shields).

The Speed Spook 🐾 1924 Silent ghost races car and steals documents. **85m/B VHS.** Johnny Hines, Warner Richmond; **D:** Charles Hines.

Speedway 🐾 1968 (G) Elvis the stock car driver finds himself being chased by Nancy the IRS agent during an important tax race. Will Sinatra keep to the business and comes to the attention of seasoned hustler Eric (Brower) who offers to teach Johnny the ropes. Johnny agrees but will only deal with women clients— at a stop in Vegas, naive Johnny gets robbed and comes to the business. **90m/C VHS, DVD.** Elvis Presley, Nancy Sinatra, Bill Bixby, Gale Gordon, William Schallert, Carl Ballantine, Ross Hagen; **Cameos:** Jordan Brower, Jonathan Taylor Thomas, Dany Hannan, Patsy Kensit, Tiffani-(Amber) Thiessen; **D:** Nicholas Perry; **W:** Nickolas Perry; **C:** Steve Adcock; **M:** Stan Ridgway.

Speedtrap 🐾🐾 1978 (PG) Typical chase scenes and cross-gender sparring characterize this tale of a private detective and a police officer pursuing car thieves. Good cast and fun chemistry between the leads; weak, typical script. **101m/C VHS, Joe Don Baker, Tyne Daly, Richard Jaeckel, Robert Loggia, Morgan Woodward, Timothy Carey; D:** Earl Bellamy.

Speeding Up Time 🐾 1971 (R) An angry man wants to ice the dudes who torched his mother's tenement. **90m/C VHS.** Winston Thrash, Pamela Donegan; **D:** John Evans.

Speedway Junky 🐾🐾½ 1999 Army brat Johnny (Bradford) dreams of being an auto racing champion. So he runs away from his home in California and gets a job with driver Richard Petty's crew. At a stop in Vegas, naive Johnny gets teamed to make it to North Carolina and get a job with driver Richard Petty's crew. **96m/C VHS, DVD.** Jesse Bradford, Jonathan Taylor Thomas, Daryl Hannah, Patsy Kensit, Tiffani-(Amber) Thiessen; **D:** Nicholas Perry; **W:** Nickolas Perry; **C:** Steve Adcock; **M:** Stan Ridgway.

Speedy 🐾🐾🐾 1928 Lloyd comes to the rescue when the last horse car in NYC, operated by his fiance's grandfather (Rigg), is stolen by a gang. Thoroughly pleasing, fun pursuit/action comedy shot on location. Look for a brief appearance by Babe Ruth. **72m/B VHS, DVD.** Harold Lloyd, Ann Christy; **D:** Ted Wilde.

Speedy Death 🐾🐾🐾 The Mrs. Bradley Mysteries: Speedy Death 1999 Gladys Mitchel wrote some 66 mysteries starring the witty and clever Mrs. Adela Bradley (Rigg). A wealthy divorcee, Mrs. Bradley has a knack for investigations and a helpful chauffeur, George Moody (Dudgeon). In 1929, Adela is invited to the country estate of friends to celebrate Eleanor Bing's (Fielding) engagement. Only her fiance is murdered and then doesn't turn out to be what he seemed. But then, nor ther does anyone else. **90m/C VHS, DVD, GB** Diana Rigg, Neil Dudgeon, John Alderton, Emma Fielding, Tristan Gemmill, Tom Butcher, Sue Devaney, John Conroy, Michael Troughton; **D:** Audrey Cooke; **W:** Simon Booker. **TV**

The Spell 🐾🐾 1977 An obese 15-year-old girl has the power to inflict illness and death on the people she hates. Necessarily mean-spirited, if we're being asked to sympathize with the main character. Therein lies the rub. Made for TV. **86m/C VHS.** Lee Grant, James Olson, Susan Myers, Barbara Bostock, Lelia Goldoni, Helen Hunt; **D:** Lee Philips. **TV**

The Spellbinder 🐾🐾 1988 (R) L.A. lawyer Daly falls in love with a woman he saves from an attacker, then discovers she's a "fugitive from a satanic cult that wants her back. Unoriginal, but slickly made. **96m/C VHS.** Timothy Daly, Kelly Preston, Rick Rossovich, Audra Lindley; **D:** Janet Greek; **W:** Tracy Torme; **M:** Basil Poledouris.

Spellbound 🐾🐾 The Spell of Amy Nugent 1941 Broken-hearted over dead girlfriend, young college student attempts to contact her through spiritualism, succeeds, and suffers nervous breakdown. **75m/B VHS, DVD, GB** Derek Farr, Vera Lindsay, Frederick Leister; **D:** Hay Petrie, Felix Aylmer; **D:**

Spellbound ♪♪½ 1945 Peck plays an amnesia victim accused of murder who uncovers this past through Freudian analysis and ends up falling in love with him. One of Hitchcock's finest films of the 1940s, with a riveting dream sequence designed by Salvador Dali. Full of classic Hitchcock plot twists and Freudian imagery. Based on Francis Beeding's novel "The House of Dr. Edwardes." **111m/B VHS, DVD.** Ingrid Bergman, Gregory Peck, Leo G. Carroll, Michael Chekhov, Wallace Ford, Rhonda Fleming, Regis Toomey; **D:** Alfred Hitchcock; **W:** Ben Hecht; **C:** George Barnes; **M:** Miklos Rozsa. Oscars '45: Orig. Dramatic Score; N.Y. Film Critics '45: Actress (Bergman).

Spellbound ♪♪♪ 2002 (G) Excellent documentary follows a group of teenagers and their families as they compete in the 1999 National Spelling Bee. Shows the preparation and competition the students go through to make it to the Nationals. **97m/C VHS, DVD. D:** Jeffrey Blitz; **C:** Jeffrey Blitz; **M:** Daniel Hulsizer.

Spellbreaker: Secret of the Leprechauns ♪♪½ 1996 (G) Youngster Mike Dennehy (Smith) is on summer vacation in Fairyhill, Ireland where he meets, what else, a band of leprechauns. He finds out the wee folk are battling sinister sorceress Nula, Queen of the Dead, who wants to seize the leprechauns power and destroy them. But not if Mike can stop her! **85m/C VHS.** Gregory Edward Smith, Madeleine Potter, Godfrey James, Tina Martin, Sylvester McCoy, James Ellis; **D:** Ted Nicolaou; **W:** Ted Nicolaou; **C:** Adolfo Bartoli; **M:** Richard Kosinski.

Spellcaster ♪ 1991 (R) An evil wizard invites a DJ and a band of rock 'n' roll fanatics to his 1000-year-old Italian castle for an evil and bloodcurdling treasure hunt. **83m/C VHS.** Richard Blade, Gail O'Grady, Harold P. Pruett, Bunty Bailey, Rafal Zielinski, Adam Ant; **D:** Rafal Zielinski.

Spencer's Mountain ♪♪½ 1963 Fonda plays the larger-than-life patriarch of nine (with O'Hara as his wife), who's inherited the Wyoming mountain land claimed by his father. Fonda's dream is to build a new house large enough to contain his brood but something always gets in his way. This time it's eldest son MacArthur's dream of a college education. Sentimental family fare based on a novel by Earl Hammer Jr., which also became the basis for the TV series "The Waltons." **118m/C VHS.** Henry Fonda, Maureen O'Hara, James MacArthur, Donald Crisp, Wally Cox, Mimsy Farmer, Virginia Gregg, Lillian Bronson, Whit Bissell, Hayden Rorke, Dub Taylor, Veronica Cartwright; **D:** Delmer Daves; **W:** Delmer Daves; **M:** Max Steiner.

Spenser: A Savage Place ♪♪½ 1994 PI Spenser (Urich) is lured to Toronto by an old flame who wants him to help her expose a racketeering scam in the city's film industry. **91m/C VHS, DVD.** Robert Urich, Cynthia Dale, Avery Brooks, Ross Petty, Wendy Crewson; **D:** Joseph L. Scanlan; **W:** Donald Martin; **C:** Vic Sarin; **M:** Brad MacDonald.

Spenser: Ceremony ♪♪½ 1993 Urich resumes his role as Robert B. Parker's Boston PI, which he played in the TV series "Spenser: For Hire." This time around Spenser is searching for a troubled runaway who's gotten involved in prostitution. But her suburban dad, who has political aspirations, seems reluctant to have her found. Brooks returns as Spenser's menacing associate Hawk. Toronto stands in for Boston. Based on Parker's novel "Ceremony." **95m/C VHS, DVD.** Robert Urich, Avery Brooks, Barbara Williams, Tanya Allen, David Nichols, Lynne Cormack; **D:** Paul Lynch; **W:** Joan H. Parker, Robert B. Parker. **CABLE**

Spenser: Pale Kings & Princes ♪♪ 1994 Spenser's (Urich) new case involves the murder of a reporter who was investigating a drug-ridden small New England town. But was the journalist killed for what he found out about a Colombian cocaine connection or did his womanizing have deadly consequences? Adapted from Robert B. Par-

ker's novel. **95m/C VHS, DVD.** Robert Urich, Avery Brooks, Barbara Williams; **D:** Vic Sarin; **W:** Joan H. Parker, Robert P. Parker; **C:** Vic Sarin; **M:** Paul Zaza. **CABLE**

Spenser: The Judas Goat ♪♪½ 1994 Boston PI Spenser (Urich) is hired by billionaire mining exec Hugh Dixon (Pownall) and sent to Ottawa, Canada to investigate the deadly car bombing that killed his wife and children. Seems black African political leader Boyko (Bess) was the true target and the assassin hasn't given up. Adapted from the Robert B. Parker novel; made for cable TV. **95m/C VHS, DVD.** Robert Urich, Avery Brooks, Leon Pownall, Ardon Bess, Georgie Johnson, Natalie Radford, Wendy Crewson; **D:** Joseph L. Scanlan. **CABLE**

Spent ♪♪½ 2000 Gambling addict/occasional actor Max (London) has a girlfriend, Brigette (Spradling), who has a drinking problem, and a roommate, Grant (Park), who won't admit he's gay although his crush on Max seems pretty obvious. In fact, any communication is a big problem, since no one really wants to see their lives for what they are. Film coasts along without much happening. **90m/C VHS, DVD.** Jason London, Charlie Spradling, James Parks, Phill Lewis, Richmond Arquette, Barbara Barrie, Gilbert Cates, Rain Phoenix, Margaret Cho; **D:** Gil Cates Jr.; **C:** Robert D. Tomer; **M:** Stan Ridgway.

Spetters ♪♪½ 1980 (R) Four Dutch teenagers follow the motorcycle racing circuit and motocross champ Hauer. Misdirected youth comes along with this spicy performance from Soutendijk. Plenty of violence, sex, and gripping photography. Verhoeven went on to direct "Robocop" and "Total Recall." **108m/C VHS, DVD. NL** Rutger Hauer, Renee Soutendijk; **D:** Paul Verhoeven; **C:** Jan De Bont.

Sphere ♪♪½ 1997 (PG-13) It must've looked good on paper, but bringing Michael Crichton's decade-old novel to the screen turned out to be a big mistake for all involved. Hoffman, Jackson, and Stone are a team of researchers sent underwater to investigate a mysterious 300-year-old space ship. After realizing the ship has American origins, they stumble across a huge liquid metal sphere that can make their deepest fears come true, in the form of huge squids and sea snakes. Never lives up to the promising premise or high-class looks. Despite three mega-stars and an A-list director, it's a hollow excursion low on thrills and originality, but there's plenty of existential ramblings about the power of the mind. **152m/C VHS, DVD.** Dustin Hoffman, Sharon Stone, Samuel L. Jackson, Peter Coyote, Queen Latifah, Liev Schreiber; **D:** Barry Levinson; **W:** Paul Attanasio, Stephen Hauser; **C:** Adam Greenberg; **M:** Elliot Goldenthal.

The Sphinx ♪♪½ 1933 A murderer causes havoc for his deaf-mute twin (Atwill), good in a dual role) when he frames him for his own crimes. Remade as "The Phantom Killer." **63m/B VHS, DVD.** Lionel Atwill, Theodore Newton, Sheila Terry, Paul Hurst, Luis Albemi, George "Gabby" Hayes; **D:** Phil Rosen.

Sphinx woof! 1981 (PG) Woman archaeologist searches for hidden riches in the tomb of an Egyptian king. The scenery is impressive, but otherwise, don't bother. Based on the novel by Robin Cook. **117m/C VHS, DVD.** Lesley-Anne Down, Frank Langella, John Gielgud, Maurice Ronet, John Rhys-Davies; **D:** Franklin J. Schaffner; **W:** John Byrum.

Spice World: The Movie ♪½ 1997 (PG) Clear some space on the video rack next to "Cool as Ice," the Spice Girls made a movie! Stretching their acting ability, the pop group plays a band of marginally talented singers who are inexplicably thrown to the top of the charts by a bitter twist of pop culture fate. What passes for the plot is stolen from "A Hard Day's Night," by the Beatles, depicting five days before a sellout concert at Albert Hall. The courageous champions of girl power do battle with the hassles of fame, bossy managers, and the media in their quest to get to the show. They find the time to visit around the babe of his dreams—Mary Jane Watson (Dunst). His life changes—not necessarily for the better—when he

themselves along the way. Unfortunately (at least for those over 13) they're not poked with anything really sharp. Loads of celebrity cameos (Elton John, Elvis Costello, Bob Hoskins), some of whom run off screen faster than if they were on fire. **92m/C VHS, DVD. GB** Emma (Baby Spice) Bunton, Geri (Ginger Spice) Halliwell, Victoria (Posh Spice) Adams, Melanie (Sporty Spice) Chisholm, Melanie (Scary Spice) Brown, Richard E. Grant, Alan Cumming, George Wendt, Claire Rushbrook, Mark McKinney, Richard O'Brien, Roger Moore, Barry Humphries, Jason Flemyng, Meat Loaf Aday, Bill Paterson, Stephen Fry, Hugh Laurie, Jennifer Saunders; *Cameos:* Elvis Costello, Bob Geldof, Bob Hoskins, Elton John; **D:** Bob Spiers; **W:** Kim Fuller, Jamie Curtis; **C:** Clive Tickner; **M:** Paul Newcastle. Golden Raspberries '98: Worst Actress (The Spice Girls).

Spices ♪♪♪ 1986 Poor woman Sonbai revolts against the sexist mores of rural colonial India in the 1940s. Features actress Patil in her final role. In Hindi with English subtitles. **98m/C VHS. IN** Naseeruddin Shah, Om Puri, Sureh Oberoi, Deepti Naval, Smita Patil; **D:** Ketan Mehta; **W:** Ketan Mehta; **M:** Rajat Dholakia.

Spider ♪♪♪ 2002 (R) Gripping and well-directed psychodrama tells the story of Spider, a paranoid-schizophrenic, as he tries to resolve his convoluted memories and emotions. After being released from a mental hospital, Spider (Ralph Fiennes) lives in an eerie halfway house for mental patients. There he recounts the events of his life that led to his tortured state of mind. Yet, since the film is told entirely from Spider's perspective it's impossible to distinguish between reality and the blurred fiction of a madman, making the entire film both illusionary and fascinatingly real. Stellar performances from Fiennes, Miranda Richardson, Gabriel Byrne, and Bradley Hall in an amazing turn as the young Spider. Cronenberg's most polished drama to date shows that he's successfully outgrown the moniker of Canada's "baron of blood." **98m/C VHS, DVD. CA GB** Ralph Fiennes, Miranda Richardson, Gabriel Byrne, Bradley Hall, Lynn Redgrave, John Neville, Gary Reineke, Sara Stockbridge, Philip Craig; **D:** David Cronenberg; **W:** Patrick McGrath; **C:** Peter Suschitzky; **M:** Howard Shore. Genie '02: Director (Cronenberg).

The Spider and the Fly ♪♪ 1949 A quilting of catch and catch-can, have and have-not stitches together this WWI romantic charade known as "The Game." Their latest unsuspecting patsy is crime writer Michael Moore (Shackelford)—who falls for Diahna bigtime. Then their publisher is killed—in the same sort of murder scenario one of them devised. **87m/C VHS.** Mel Harris, Ted Shackleford, Kim Coates, Colm Feore, Frankie Faison, Cynthia Belliveau, Kenneth Welsh, Peggy Lipton; **D:** Michael Katleman; **W:** Robert Pucci, Alanna Hamill; **M:** Richard Bellis. **CABLE**

Spider Baby ♪ *The Liver Eaters; Spider Baby, or the Maddest Story Ever Told; Cannibal Orgy, or the Maddest Story Ever Told* 1964 A tasteless horror-comedy about a chauffeur who takes care of a psychotic family. Theme song sung by Lon Chaney. **86m/B VHS, DVD.** Lon Chaney Jr., Mantan Moreland, Carol Ohmart, Sid Haig, Beverly Washburn, Jill Banner, Quinn; **C:** Alfred Taylor; **M:** Ronald Stein.

Spider-Man ♪♪♪ 2002 (PG-13) Raimi does a little 21st-century updating of the Marvel comic hero, who first made his appearance back in 1962, but remembers to keep the heart along with the action. Peter Parker (Maguire) is a nerdy teenager who gets tongue-tied every time he's around the babe of his dreams—Mary Jane Watson (Dunst). His life changes—not necessarily for the better—when he

gets bitten by a genetically altered spider and takes on weird arachnid traits, such as strength, agility, wall crawling, web shooting, and swinging. After a family tragedy, the newly monickered Spider-Man becomes a crime fighter. His nemesis is, of course, the Green Goblin (Dafoe), who himself has a dual identity. **121m/C VHS, DVD, Blu-ray Disc. US** Tobey Maguire, Willem Dafoe, Kirsten Dunst, James Franco, Cliff Robertson, Rosemary Harris, J.K. Simmons, Gerry Becker, Bill Nunn, Jack Betts, Joe Manganiello, Stanley Anderson, Ron Perkins, Theodore (Ted) Raimi, Larry Joshua, Michael (Mike) Papajohn, Joseph (Joe) D'Onofrio; *Cameos:* Bruce Campbell, Lucy Lawless; **D:** Sam Raimi; **W:** David Koepp; **C:** Don Burgess; **M:** Danny Elfman.

Spider-Man 2 ♪♪♪½ 2004 (PG-13) Spidey's back, with more to worry about than ever. Mary Jane's engaged, Harry Osborne is out to avenge the death of his father (Green Goblin), and there's a new villain in town: Doctor Octopus (Molina). Raimi's first installment was the best comic book adaptation in a while, and he's managed to top it here. Peter Parker's angst over Spidey's affect on his life, romantic conflict over MJ, and guilt over his uncle's death provide more depth than any comic book character has previously been granted on screen. Even Doc Ock is three dimensional and somewhat sympathetic, in no small part because of Molina's portrayal. The effects are again top-notch and non-intrusive. Raimi shows enough humor to remind everybody why the super-called comic books. **127m/C DVD, UMD.** Tobey Maguire, Kirsten Dunst, Alfred Molina, James Franco, Elizabeth Banks, Rosemary Harris, J.K. Simmons, Vanessa Ferlito, Bill Nunn, Theodore (Ted) Raimi, Dylan Baker, Donna Murphy, Bruce Campbell, Aasif Mandvi, Willem Dafoe, Cliff Robertson, Daniel Gillies; **D:** Sam Raimi; **W:** Alvin Sargent, Alfred Gough, Miles Millar; Michael Chabon; **C:** Bill Pope; **M:** Danny Elfman. Oscars '04: Visual FX.

Spider-Man 3 ♪♪½ 2007 (PG-13) Raimi's sublime superhero series falters in this third chapter, thanks largely to the director's cheeseball sensibilities. Spider-Man (Maguire) is enjoying a brief period of popularity, which only makes things worse with his fading star girlfriend MJ (Dunst) and his vengeance-minded pal Harry (Franco). Adding to the mix is a nasty rival photographer (Grace), the powerful excon Sandman (Church), and Venom, an evil alien parasite that gives Spidey a black suit and makes him act like a jerk. There's a lot of blockbuster fun, but you'll spend half the movie rolling your eyes at the unconvincing love quadrangle and Raimi's attempts to turn Spidey into the messiah of New York. Still, much better than the third chapters of the X-Men, Superman, or Batman franchises. **139m/C DVD, Blu-ray Disc. US** Tobey Maguire, Kirsten Dunst, James Franco, Thomas Haden Church, Topher Grace, Bryce Dallas Howard, James Cromwell, Rosemary Harris, J.K. Simmons, Dylan Baker, Bill Nunn, Theresa Russell, Theodore (Ted) Raimi, Cliff Robertson, Elizabeth Banks, Perla Haney-Jardine, Michael (Mike) Papajohn, Joe Manganiello, Lucy Gordon, Bruce Campbell, Daniel Gillies; **D:** Sam Raimi; **W:** Sam Raimi, Alvin Sargent, Ivan Raimi; **C:** Bill Pope; **M:** Christopher Young.

Spider Woman ♪♪♪ *Sherlock Holmes and the Spider Woman* 1944 A modernized Holmes and Watson adventure as the duo track down a woman responsible for a series of murders. His adversary uses poisonous spiders to do her work. Zestful, superior Holmes. **62m/B VHS, DVD.** Basil Rathbone, Nigel Bruce, Gale Sondergaard, Dennis Hoey; **D:** Roy William Neill.

Spiderman: The Deadly Dust ♪♪♪ 1978 A live-action episode of Spiderman, from the TV series, as he attempts to prevent a city-destroying plutonium accident. **93m/C VHS.** Nicholas Hammond, Robert F. Simon, Chip Fields; **D:** Ron Satlof. **TV**

Spiders ♪♪♪ 1918 One of the earliest surviving films by director Lang, and predates Indiana Jones by almost 60 years. In these first two chapters ("The Golden Lake" and "The Diamond Ship") of an unfinished 4-part thriller, Carl deVogt battles with the evil Spider cult for a mystically powerful Incan diamond. Restored

Spiders 🐾🐾½ **2000 (R)** Throwback to the "big bug" sci-fi horrors of the 1950s also borrows heavily from "The X-Files." College reporter Marci (Parrilla) and a couple of her pals sneak into a desert military base in time to witness the secret landing of a space shuttle. On board is a spider that has been injected with alien DNA and is doing absolutely disgusting things. It all ends with an arachnid attack on Phoenix! Can the city be saved? **93m/C VHS, DVD.** David Carpenter, Lana Parrilla; **D:** Gary Jones. **DVD. VIDEO**

Spiders 2: Breeding Ground 🐾½ **2001 (R)** Alexandra (Niznik) and hubby Jason (Cromer) are enjoying a boating holiday when a storm capsizes their craft and they are rescued by freighter captain Bigelow (Quinn). The ship's doctor, Gabac (Mol), gives Jason a shot of "antibiotics," which give him hallucinations about giant spiders that incubate in human bodies. Alex thinks this is nuts until she finds some spiders and realizes that Jason has been infected. She then proceeds to kicks butt 'cause nobody messes with her man! **96m/C VHS, DVD.** Stephanie Niznik, Daniel Quinn, Richard Moll, Greg Cromer; **D:** Sam Firstenberg; **W:** Stephen Brooks; **C:** Peter Belcher, Plamen Somov; **M:** Serge Colbert. **VIDEO**

The Spiderwick Chronicles 🐾🐾🐾 **2008 (PG)** Jared (Highmore), his twin Simon, and sister Mallory (Bolger) move into a rural mansion with their mom (Parker) and discover that their new home is a gateway into a world of magical creatures, some of which aren't so nice. Evil Mulgarath (Nolte) wants a magic book written by Jared's ancestor, and it's up to Jared to protect it while convincing his siblings that the charmed world outside their door is real. Well-written, ably directed adaptation of the bestselling children's series. **97m/C DVD.** US Freddie Highmore, Sarah Bolger, Mary-Louise Parker, David Strathairn, Joan Plowright, Andrew McCarthy; **D:** Mark S. Waters; **W:** Karey Kirkpatrick, David Berenbaum, John Sayles; **C:** Caleb Deschanel; **M:** James Horner; **V:** Nick Nolte, Seth Rogen, Martin Short.

Spider's Stratagem 🐾🐾🐾 **1970** Thirty years after his father's murder by the facists, a young man returns to a small Italian town to learn why his father was killed. The locals resist his efforts, and he is trapped in a mysterious web where history and lies exert a stranglehold on the truth. Intriguing, high literate thriller. Based on a short story by Jorge Luis Borges. In Italian with English subtitles. **97m/C VHS.** *IT* Giulio Brogi, Alida Valli; **D:** Bernardo Bertolucci.

Spider's Web 🐾🐾 **2001 (R)** Investment banker Baldwin is seduced into stealing $40 million from his politically connected father but betrayal follows. **87m/C VHS, DVD.** Stephen Baldwin, Kari Wuhrer, Michael Gregory, George Lazenby, Benjamin King, Scott Williamson, George Murdock; **D:** Paul Levine; **W:** D. Alveio, David Lloyd, Robert Stitt; **M:** Michael Cohen.

Spies 🐾🐾½ **1928** A sly criminal poses as a famous banker to steal government information and create chaos in the world in this silent Lang masterpiece. Excellent entertainment, tight plotting and pacing, fine performances. Absolutely relentless intrigue and tension. **89m/B VHS, DVD.** *GE* Rudolf Klein-Rogge, Lupu Pick, Fritz Rasp, Gerda Maurus, Willy Fritsch; **D:** Fritz Lang.

Spies, Lies and Naked Thighs 🐾½ **1991** A pair of crackpot CIA agents find themselves in a whirlpool of comedic madness when they are assigned to track down a deadly assassin. The problem? The assassin happens to be the ex-wife of one of the guys. Can he come out on top? Who cares? **90m/C VHS, DVD.** Harry Anderson, Ed Begley Jr., Rachel Ticotin, Linda Purl, Wendy Crewson; **D:** James Frawley.

Spies Like Us 🐾🐾½ **1985 (PG)** Chase and Aykroyd meet while taking the CIA entry exam. Caught cheating on the old seaside home, where he hopes to find artistic inspiration. Instead, he finds an attractive ghost, Arabella (Williams), who has been hanging around for 200 years after her over's betrayal. And the jealous Arabella wants to get her new lover's wife out of the way. Yes, ghosts CAN do it. moderately close. Lost for several campaigns by film directors. **103m/C VHS, DVD.** Chevy Chase, Dan Aykroyd, Steve Forrest, Bruce Davison, William Prince, Bernie Casey, Tom Hatten, Donna Dixon, Frank Oz, Michael Apted, Constantin Costa-Gavras, Terry Gilliam, Ray Harryhausen, Joel Coen, Martin Brest, Bob Swaim; **D:** John Landis; **C:** Robert Paynter; **M:** Elmer Bernstein.

Spin 🐾🐾 **2004 (PG-13)** Orphaned by his parents deaths, young Eddie's cold uncle passes him off to one of his Hispanic ranch hands and his wife who, despite their best efforts, have difficulty keeping the teenager on the right track. Based on Donald Everett Axinn's novel. **107m/C VHS, DVD.** Ryan Merriman, Stanley Tucci, Dana Delany, Paula Garces, Ruben Blades; **D:** James Redford; **W:** James Redford; **C:** Paul Ryan; **M:** Todd Boekelheide. **VIDEO**

Spin the Bottle 🐾🐾 **1997** Jonah (Graham) invites four childhood friends, whom he hasn't seen in 10 years, for a weekend reunion at his Vermont lakefront summer house, which leads to sexual hijinks and sweet revenge. Yerkes's debut feature. **83m/C VHS, DVD.** Holter Graham, Jessica Faller, Mitchell Riggs, Kim Winter, Heather Goldenhersch; **D:** Jamie Yerkes; **C:** Stephen Lighthill; **M:** David Nichtern.

Spinout 🐾🐾 **1966** A pouty traveling singer decides to drive an experimental race car in a rally. Usual Elvis fare with the King being pursued by an assortment of beauties. **90m/C VHS.** Elvis Presley, Shelley Fabares, Carl Betz, Diane McBain, Cecil Kellaway, Jack Mullaney, Deborah Walley, Una Merkel, Warren Berlinger, Will Hutchins, Dodie Marshall; **D:** Norman Taurog.

Spiral 🐾🐾 **2007** Pathologically shy and delusional, artist Mason (Moore) gets a job at an insurance company, thanks to his only friend Berkeley (Levi). Fellow new employee Amber (Tamblyn) bonds with Mason over their work and she agrees to pose for a portrait. And then the trouble really begins. **91m/C DVD.** Joel David Moore, Amber Tamblyn, Zachary Levi, Tricia Helfer, David Muller, Annie Neal; **D:** Joel David Moore, Adam Green; **W:** Joel David Moore, Jeremy Danial Boreing; **C:** Will Barratt; **M:** Todd Baldwin, Michael "Fish" Herring.

The Spiral Staircase 🐾🐾🐾 **1946** A mute servant, working in a creepy Gothic mansion, may be the next victim of a murderer preying on women afflicted with deformities, especially when the next murder occurs in the mansion itself. Great performance by McGuire as the terrified victim. Remade for TV in 1975. **83m/B VHS, DVD.** Dorothy McGuire, George Brent, Ethel Barrymore, Kent Smith, Rhonda Fleming, Gordon Oliver, Elsa Lanchester, Sara Allgood; **D:** Robert Siodmak; **W:** Mel Dinelli; **C:** Nicholas Musuraca; **M:** Roy Webb.

Spiral Staircase 🐾½ **1975** Mild TV remake of the 1946 classic about a mute servant who is menaced by a psychopathic killer. Why didn't they just show the original? **99m/C VHS.** *GB* Jacqueline Bisset, Christopher Plummer, John Philip Law, Mildred Dunnock, Sam Wanamaker, Gayle Hunnicutt; **D:** Peter Collinson; **W:** Allan Scott, Chris Bryant.

Spirit Rider 🐾🐾🐾 **1993** Jesse Threeoaks is a sullen 16-year-old Ojibway who has been shuttled from foster homes since the age of six. Repatriated to his family's Canadian reservation, he's left in the care of his grandfather, Joe Moon. When he's knocked down, 'ris gal appears at ringside to inspire him, and does. **70m/B VHS, DVD.** Joe Louis, Mantan Moreland, Clarence Muse, Edna Mae Harris, Mae Turner, Cleo Desmond, Jewel Smith, Jesse Lee Brooks; **D:** Harry Fraser; **W:** Arthur Hoerl; **C:** Roger E. Cline; **M:** Clarence Muse, Elliot Carpenter.

The Spirit of Youth 🐾🐾 **1937** Joe Louis supports his family with menial jobs until he shows his knack as a fighter. When he's knocked down, 'ris gal appears at ringside to inspire him, and does. **70m/B VHS, DVD.** Joe Louis, Mantan Moreland, Clarence Muse, Edna Mae Harris, Mae Turner, Cleo Desmond, Jewel Smith, Jesse Lee Brooks; **D:** Harry Fraser; **W:** Arthur Hoerl; **C:** Roger E. Cline; **M:** Clarence Muse, Elliot Carpenter.

The Spirit of West Point 🐾½ **1947** The true story of West Point's two All-American football greats, Doc Blanchard and Glenn Davis (who play themselves), while on leave after graduation from the little school. **77m/B VHS.** Felix "Doc" Blanchard, Glenn Davis, Tom Harmon, Alan Hale Jr., Anne Nagel, Robert Shayne; **D:** Ralph Murphy.

Spirit of the West 🐾½ **1932** Rodeo star Gibson and his ranch foreman brother work together to save a fair damsel's land from a gang of 'rustlers. Routine western of its era. **61m/B VHS.** Hoot Gibson, Hooper Atchley; **D:** Otto Brower.

Spirit of the Eagle 🐾🐾 **1990 (PG)** Man and young son wander in mountain's and make friends with feathered creature. Then boy is kidnapped, creating problems for dad. Somnolent family fare. **93m/C VHS, DVD.** Dan Haggerty, William (Bill) Smith, Don Shanks, Jeri Arredondo, Trevor Yarrish; **D:** Boon Collins; **C:** Lew V. Adams; **M:** Parmer Fuller.

Spirit of the Beehive 🐾🐾🐾 **1973** An acclaimed and haunting film about a young Spanish girl enthralled by the 1931 "Frankenstein," embarking on a journey to find the creature in the Spanish countryside. One of the best films about children's inner life, in Spanish with subtitles. **95m/C VHS, DVD.** *SP* Fernando Fernan-Gomez, Teresa Gimpera, Ana Torrent, Isabel Telleria, Laly Soldevila; **D:** Victor Erice; **W:** Victor Erice; **C:** Luis Cuadrado; **M:** Luis Ennio de Pablo.

Spirit of St. Louis 🐾🐾🐾 **1957** A lavish Hollywood biography of famous aviator Charles Lindbergh and his historic transatlantic flight from New York to Paris of American culture. Now time travelers must return to 1776 to reacquire the Constitution to fix things up. But when their computer goes on the blink, the do-gooders land, not in 1776, but in 1976 at the boxoffice. **137m/C VHS, DVD.** James Stewart, Patricia Smith, Murray Hamilton, Marc Connelly; **D:** Billy Wilder; **W:** Billy Wilder, Wendell Mayes; **C:** Robert Burks; **M:** Franz Waxman.

Spirit Lost 🐾🐾 **1996 (R)** John (Leon) and wife Willy (Tayor) move to an old seaside home, where he hopes to find artistic inspiration. Instead, he finds an attractive ghost, Arabella (Williams), who has been hanging around for 200 years after her over's betrayal. And the jealous Arabella wants to get her new lover's wife out of the way. Yes, ghosts CAN do it. **137m/C VHS, DVD.** Leon, Regina Taylor, Cynda Williams, James Avery, Juanita Jennings; **D:** Neema Barnette; **W:** Joyce Renee Lewis; **C:** Yuri Neyman; **M:** Lionel Cole.

Spirit of '76 🐾½ **1991 (PG-13)** In the 22nd century, the Earth faces certain disaster as a magnetic storm wipes out all of American culture. Now time travelers must return to 1776 to reacquire the Constitution to fix things up. But when their computer goes on the blink, the do-gooders land, not in 1776, but in 1976 at the boxoffice. **82m/C VHS, DVD.** David Cassidy, Olivia D'Abo, Leif Garrett, Geoff Hoyle, Jeff (Jeffrey) McDonald, Steve McDonald, Liam O'Brien, Barbara Bain, Julie Brown, Thomas Chong, Iron Eyes Cody, Don Novello, Carl Reiner, Rob Reiner, Moon Zappa, Mark Mothersbaugh, Lucas Reiner; **C:** Stephen Lightfill; **M:** David Nichtern.

Spiritism 🐾🐾 *Espiritismo* **1961** Mother uses one of her three wishes to bring back her dead son. Dubbed from the "Monkey's Paw." **85m/B VHS.** *MX* Nora Veryan, Jose Luis Jimenez, Jorge Mondragon, Rene Cardona Jr.; **D:** Benito Alazraki.

Spirits of the Dead 🐾🐾🐾 *Histoires Extraordinaires; Tre Passi nel Delirio; Tales of Mystery and Imagination; Trois Histoires Extraordinaires d'Edgar Poe* **1969 (R)** Three Edgar Allan Poe stories adapted for the screen and directed by three of Europe's finest. "Metzengerstein," directed by Roger Vadim stars the Fonda siblings in a tale of incestuous lust. "William Wilson" fincs Louis Malle directing Delon and Bardot in the story of a vicious Austrian army officer haunted by a murder victim. Finally, Fellini directs "Never Bet the Devil Your Head" or "Toby Dammit" in which Stamp plays a drunken British film star who has a gruesome date with destiny. Although Fellini's segment is generally considered the best (and was released on its own) all three provide an interesting atmospheric vision of Poe. French and Italian with subtitles. **117m/C VHS, DVD.** *IT FR* Jane Fonda, Peter Fonda, Carla Marlier, Francoise Prevost, James Robertson Justice, Brigitte Bardot, Alain Delon, Katia Christine, Terence Stamp, Salvo Randone; **D:** Roger Vadim, Louis Malle, Federico Fellini; **W:** Roger Vadim, Louis Malle, Federico Fellini, Daniel Boulanger, Bernardino Zapponi; **C:** Torino Delli Colli, Claude Renoir, Giuseppe Rotunno; **M:** Nino Rota, Diego Masson; **Nar:** Vincent Price, Clement Biddle Wood.

Spirits 🐾½ **1990 (R)** A priest tormented by his lust-filled dreams breaks his vows of chastity with a woman who turns out to be a murderer. Bad luck. **88m/C VHS.** Erik Estrada, Carol Lynley, Robert Quarry, Brinke Stevens, Oliver Darrow, Kathrin Lautner; **D:** Fred Olen Ray.

Spirited Away 🐾🐾🐾½ *Sen to Chihiro—No Kamikakushi* **2001 (PG)** Bratty 10-year-old Chihiro (voiced by Chase) is upset that her family is moving. What's worse is when they get lost and discover what appears to be an abandoned Japanese theme park. Her greedy parents get turned into pigs and Chihiro is trapped inside the park's palace. She earns that it is a resting place for millions of spirits and is run by a sorceress who makes Chihiro work for her and wants the girl to renounce her identity and never return to the human world. Also available in the original Japanese language version. **124m/C VHS, DVD.** *JP* *D:* Hayao Miyazaki; *W:* Hayao Miyazaki; *M:* Joe Hisaishi; *V:* Daveigh Chase, Suzanne Pleshette, Jason Marsden, Susan Egan, David Ogden Stiers, Lauren Holly, Michael Chiklis, John Ratzenberger, Tara Strong Oscars '02: Animated Film.

Spirit: Stallion of the Cimarron 🐾🐾 **2002 (G)** Spirit is a wild stallion and leader of his herd, who is captured and treated badly by a Cavalry Co-onel (Cromwell) until he escapes with the help of a young Lakota brave, Little Creek (Studi). Action sequences are impressive, even breathtaking, but the simplistic story and constant musical cues to the moods expressed on screen wear quickly. Combination of traditional 2-D and computer-generated 3-D elements does-n't always work, either. On the other hand, the animals don't speak (except for some of Spirit's thoughts in a voiceover provided by Damon), and there are no wacky sidekicks to clutter what is a pretty serious story for an animated feature. **85m/C VHS, DVD.** US *D:* Kelly Asbury, Lorna Cook; *W:* John Fusco; *M:* Hans Zimmer, Bryan Adams; *V:* Matt Damon, James Cromwell, Daniel Studi.

Spite Marriage 🐾🐾🐾 **1929** When Sebastian's lover dumps her like yesterday's garbage, she marries Keaton out of spite. Much postnuptual levity follows. Keaton's final silent. **82m/B VHS, DVD.** Buster Keaton, Dorothy Sebastian, Edward Earle, Leila Hyams, William Bechtel, Hank Mann; **D:** Edward Sedgwick.

Spitfire 🐾🐾🐾 1934 Sentimental comedy-drama starring Hepburn as a hillbilly faith healer from the Ozarks who falls into a love affair. One in a string of early boxoffice flops for Hepburn. She wanted to play a role other than patrician Eastern Seaboard, and did, but audiences didn't buy it. **90m/B VHS.** Katharine Hepburn, Robert Young, Ralph Bellamy, Sidney Toler, Martha Sleeper, Sara Haden, Virginia Howell, Will Geer; **D:** John Cromwell; **W:** Jane Murfin; **C:** William Cronjager; **M:** Max Steiner.

Spitfire 🐾🐾½ 1942 *The First of the Few* True story of Reginald J. Mitchell, who designed "The Spitfire" fighter plane, which greatly enabled the Allies during WWII. Howard's last film. Heavily propagandist but enjoyable and uncomplicated biography, with a splendid score. **88m/B VHS, DVD. GB** Leslie Howard, David Niven, Rosamund John, Roland Culver, David Horne, J.H. Roberts, Patricia Medina; **D:** Leslie Howard; **C:** Georges Perinal; **M:** William Walton.

The Spitfire Grill 🐾🐾½ 1995 (PG-13) Newly released from prison, Perry Talbott (Elliott) moves to smalltown Gilead, Maine, and gets a waitressing job at the Spitfire Grill, run by the cranky Hannah (Burstyn). Perry's upfront about her jail time, which doesn't endear her to the regulars. Particularly censorious is businessman Nahum Goddard (Patton), who sends his downtrodden wife Shelby (Harden) to keep an eye on Perry. There are a number of personal dilemmas that take their toll in this familiar setting—redeemed by strong performances. **117m/C VHS, DVD.** Alison Elliott, Ellen Burstyn, Marcia Gay Harden, Will Patton, Kieran Mulroney, Gailard Sartain, Louise De Cormier, John M. Jackson; **D:** Lee David Zlotoff; **W:** Lee David Zlotoff; **C:** Rob Draper; **M:** James Horner. Sundance '96: Aud. Award.

Spittin' Image 🐾 1983 After falling from her mean-spirited father's wagon, a young girl befriends a kind mountain man. She learns the ways of the wilderness and tobacco spitting. **92m/C VHS.** Lloyd "Sunshine" Parker, Trudi Cooper, Sharon Barr, Karen Barr; **D:** Russell Kern.

Splash 🐾🐾½ 1984 (PG) A beautiful mermaid ventures into New York City in search of a man she's rescued twice when he's fallen overboard. Now it's her turn to fall in love. Charming performances by Hanks and Hannah. Well-paced direction from Howard, with just enough slapstick. Don't miss the lobster scene. **109m/C VHS, DVD.** Tom Hanks, Daryl Hannah, Eugene Levy, John Candy, Dody Goodman, Shecky Greene, Richard B. Shull, Bobby DiCicco, Howard Morris; **C:** Don Peterman; **D:** Ron Howard; **W:** Babaloo Mandel, Lowell Ganz; **M:** Lee Holdridge. Natl. Soc. Film Critics '84: Screenplay.

Splatter University woof! 1984 A deranged killer escapes from an asylum and begins to slaughter and mutilate comely coeds at a local college. Abysmally motiveless killing and gratuitous sex. Also available in a 78-minute "R" rated version. **79m/C VHS, DVD.** Francine Forbes, Dick Biel, Cathy Lacommare, Ric Randing, Dan Eaton, Denise Texeira, Mary Ellen David, Joanna Mihalakis; **D:** Richard W. Haines; **W:** Richard W. Haines, John Michaels, Michael Cunningham; **M:** Chris Burke.

Splendor 🐾🐾½ 1935 Typical romantic weepie finds beautiful-but-poor Phyllis (Hopkins) marrying into the snobby clan of Brighton Lorrimore (McCrea). His family (whose fortunes are sliding) want to break the duo up and push Phyllis towards an affair with wealthy broker Martin (Cavanagh). There's a scandal and the Lorrimore's separate but true love conquers all, as you expect. **77m/B VHS.** Miriam Hopkins, Joel McCrea, Paul Cavanagh, Helen Westley, Billie Burke, Katherine Alexander, David Niven,

Arthur Treacher, Ruth Weston; **D:** Elliott Nugent; **W:** Rachel Crothers; **C:** Gregg Toland.

Splendor 🐾🐾½ 1999 (R) A '90s screwball comedy about an unconventional sexual arrangement. Veronica (Robertson) is an aspiring L.A. actress who enjoys her sexual exploits and who falls for two men on the opposite ends of the romantic spectrum. Abel (Schaech) is a freelance music critic who's intelligent and handsome while punk rock drummer Zed (Keeslar) is dumb but really sexy. Veronica refuses to choose between the two, so both move in with her (and prove to be more immature than the lady herself). Then Veronica meets successful and wealthy TV director, Ernest (Mabius), and wonders if it's time for a real adult relationship. Surprisingly sweet and stylish fluff from Araki. **93m/C VHS, DVD.** Kathleen Robertson, Johnathon Schaech, Matt Keeslar, Eric Mabius, Kelly Macdonald; **D:** Gregg Araki; **W:** Gregg Araki; **M:** Daniel Licht.

Splendor in the Grass 🐾🐾🐾 1961 A drama set in rural Kansas in 1925, concerning a teenage couple who try to keep their love on a strictly intellectual plane and the sexual and family pressures that tear them apart. After suffering a mental breakdown and being institutionalized, the girl returns years later in order to settle her life. Film debuts of Beatty, Dennis, and Diller. Inge wrote the screenplay specifically with Beatty in mind, after the actor appeared in one of Inge's stage plays. Filmed not in Kansas, but on Staten Island and in upstate New York. **124m/C VHS, DVD.** Natalie Wood, Warren Beatty, Audrey Christie, Barbara Loden, Zohra Lampert, Phyllis Diller, Sandy Dennis; **D:** Elia Kazan; **W:** William Inge; **C:** Charles Durham; **M:** David Amram. Oscars '61: Story & Screenplay.

Spliced 🐾🐾 2003 (R) Slick slasher that may be derivative but still manages some shudders. High school senior Mary Ryan (Balaban) is obsessed with horror movies and much too suggestible. She becomes convinced that the mad slasher character in one of her faves is not only real but offing her classmates. School doctor Morgan Campbell (Silver) first thinks Mary is merely crazy but then comes to change his mind. **86m/C VHS, DVD.** Liane Balaban, Ron Silver, Sin Baruc, Drew Lachey; **D:** Gavin Wilding; **W:** Ellen Cook. **VIDEO**

Splinter 🐾🐾 2006 (R) L.A. gangbanger brothers Dreamer (Almeida) and Dusty (Guglielmi) are looking for their older brother's killer. Someone is also torturing and killing fellow gang members (Atis), brings in rookie detective Gramm (Atis), who's teamed up with corrupt, unstable veteran Cunningham (Sizemore, perhaps typecast). Maybe someone just wants to expand their turf or maybe a serial killer is targeting the gangs. Olmos plays a police captain and yeah, that's his kid helming this familiar pic. **90m/C VHS.** Tom Sizemore, Edward James Olmos, Noel Guglielmi, Resmine Atis, Enrique Almeida, Dallas Page; **D:** Michael D. Olmos; **W:** Michael D. Olmos; **C:** Bridger Nielson; **M:** Jae Chong. **VIDEO**

Split 🐾 1990 Humanoids from another dimension manipulate earth activity. **85m/C VHS.** John Flynn, Timothy Dwight, Chris Shaw, Joan Bechtel; **D:** Chris Shaw.

Split Decisions 🐾🐾 1988 (R) An Irish family of boxers, dad and his two sons, slug it out emotionally and physically, as they come to terms with career choices and each other. Good scenes in the ring but the drama leans toward melodrama. Decent family drama, but somewhat of a "Rocky" rip-off. **95m/C VHS, DVD.** Gene Hackman, Craig Sheffer, Jeff Fahey, Jennifer Beals, John McLiam, Eddie Velez, Carmine Caridi, James Tolkan; **D:** David Drury; **W:** David Fallon; **M:** Basil Poledouris.

Split Image 🐾🐾½ 1982 (R) An all-American boy comes under the spell of a cult. His parents then hire a deprogrammer to bring the boy back to reality. Exceptional performances by Dennehy and Woods. This is a worthwhile film that spent far too little time in theatres. **113m/C VHS.** Michael O'Keefe, Karen Allen, Peter Fonda, Brian

Dennehy, James Woods; **D:** Ted Kotcheff; **W:** Robert Mark Kamen; **M:** Bill Conti.

Split Second 🐾🐾 1953 An escaped prisoner holds hostages in a Nevada atomic bomb testing area. McNally's excellent performance as the kidnapper, in addition to strong supporting performances, enhance a solid plot. Powell's directorial debut. **85m/B VHS.** Paul Kelly, Richard Egan, Jan Sterling, Alexis Smith, Stephen McNally; **D:** Dick Powell; **W:** William Bowers, Irving Wallace.

Split Second 🐾🐾½ 1992 (R) Hauer is a futuristic cop tracking down a vicious alien serial killer in London in the year 2008. The monster rips out the hearts of his victims and then eats them in what appears to be a satanic ritual in this bloodsoaked thriller wanna-be. Hauer gives a listless performance and overall, the action is quite dull. The music soundtrack also manages to annoy with the Moody Blues song "Nights in White Satin" playing at the most inappropriate times. A British/American co-production. **91m/C VHS, DVD.** Rutger Hauer, Kim Cattrall, Neil Duncan, Michael J. Pollard, Alun Armstrong, Pete Postlethwaite, Ian Dury, Roberta Eaton; **D:** Tony Maylam; **W:** Gary Scott Thompson; **C:** Clive Tickner; **M:** Francis Haines, Stephen Parsons.

Split Second 🐾🐾½ 1999 Corporate lawyer Michael Anderson (Owen) is fed up with both his work and home lives. A road rage incident leaves a cyclist dead and Michael fleeing the scene. He tries to repress the incident but it only leads to further angst and anger. Owen is a champion brooder but this is a routine diversion. **90m/C DVD. GB** Clive Owen, Helen McCrory, John Bowe, James Cosmo, Tony Curran; **D:** David Blair. **TV**

Splitting Heirs 🐾🐾½ 1993 (PG-13) Idle stars as the offspring of titled parents who is accidentally abandoned in a restaurant as an infant and raised by poor Pakistanis. (His mother winds up claiming the wrong abandoned baby.) When he discovers he's actually the 15th Duke of Bournemouth he plots, ineffectually, to kill off the present unknowing imposter, a nitwit American (Moranis). Cleese pops in as a shabby lawyer hired by Idle to help him claim the title with Hershey as Idle's real mother, the addle-brained and sexstarved Duchess. Convoluted plot, bland comedy. **87m/C VHS, DVD.** Eric Idle, Rick Moranis, Barbara Hershey, John Cleese, Catherine Zeta-Jones, Sadie Frost, Stratford Johns, Brenda Bruce; **D:** Robert M. Young; **W:** Eric Idle; **M:** Michael Kamen.

Splitz woof! 1984 (PG-13) An all-girl rock band agrees to help out a sorority house by participating in a series of sporting events. **85m/C VHS, DVD.** Robin Johnson, Patti Lee, Shirley Stoler, Raymond Serra; **D:** Domonic Paris.

Spoiled Children 🐾🐾½ 1977 *Les Enfants Gates* A famous film director (Piccoli) tries to work on his new script at home but is too distracted by his family life. So he rents a high-rise apartment for peace and quiet but winds up involved in a tenant/landlord dispute and with a girl half his age. In French with English subtitles. **113m/C VHS. FR** Michel Piccoli, Christine Pascal, Michel Aumont, Gerard Jugnot, Arlette Bonnard; **D:** Bertrand Tavernier; **W:** Christine Pascal, Charlotte Dubreuil, Bertrand Tavernier; **M:** Philippe Sarde.

Spoiler 🐾🐾½ 1998 Wrongly convicted Daniels is stuck in a sadistic 21st-century prison with just one aim—to escape and reunite with his young daughter. **100m/C VHS, DVD.** Gary Daniels, Meg Foster, Bryan Genesse, Jeffrey Combs, Arye Gross, Duane Whitaker, David Groh; **D:** Carmen Von Daacke; **W:** Michael Kalesniko; **C:** Philip Lee. **VIDEO**

The Spoilers 🐾🐾 1914 Virtually unstaged account of gold hunting in the Alaskan wilderness enhanced by gritty film quality. Was a gold mine when released. **110m/B VHS.** William Farnum, Thomas Santschi, Kathlyn Williams, Bessie Eyton, Frank Clark, Wheeler Oakman; **D:** Colin Campbell.

The Spoilers 🐾🐾½ 1942 Two adventurers in the Yukon are swindled out of their gold mine and set out to even the score. A trademark scene of all versions of

the movie (and there are many) is the climactic fistfight, in this case between hero Wayne and bad-guy Scott. One of the better films adapted from the novel by Rex Beach. William Farnum, who starred in both the 1914 and the 1930 versions, has a small part. **88m/B VHS, DVD.** John Wayne, Randolph Scott, Marlene Dietrich, Margaret Lindsay, Harry Carey Sr., Richard Barthelmess, Charles Halton; **D:** Ray Enright; **C:** Milton Krasner.

The SpongeBob SquarePants Movie 🐾🐾½ 2004 (PG) Nickelodeon's animated series (equally popular with kiddies, college students, and wannabe hipsters) makes its debut on the big screen with all its bright colored frivolity intact. Our peppy yellow sea sponge and his dim-witted best pal, starfish Patrick, must save their home of Bikini Bottom from the evil Plankton, who steals the crown of King Neptune. You weren't honestly expecting more of a plot, were you? Hasselhoff appears in all his "Baywatch" glory to save our watery heroes from a desperate dry land fate. **90m/C VHS, DVD, UMD.** *US Cameos:* David Hasselhoff; **D:** Stephen Hillenburg; **W:** Derek Drymon, Tim Hill; Stephen Hillenburg, Paul Tibbett; **C:** Jerzy Zielinski; **M:** Gregor Narholz; **V:** Tom Kenny, Bill Fagerbakke, Clancy Brown, Roger Bumpass, Alec Baldwin, Scarlett Johansson, Jeffrey Tambor, Carolyn Lawrence, Mary Jo Catlett, Mr. Lawrence, Jill Talley; **C:** Levie Isaacks; **M:** Graeme Revell.

Spontaneous Combustion 🐾🐾 1989 (R) A grisly horror film detailing the travails of a hapless guy who has the power to inflict the title phenomenon on other people. **97m/C VHS, DVD.** Brad Dourif, Jon Cypher, Melinda Dillon, Cynthia Bain, William Prince, Dey Young, Dick Butkus, John Landis, Dale Dye; **D:** Tobe Hooper; **W:** Tobe Hooper, Howard Goldberg; **C:** Levie Isaacks; **M:** Graeme Revell.

Spook Busters 🐾🐾½ 1948 The Bowery Boys take jobs as exterminators, only to find themselves assigned the unenviable task of ridding a haunted house of ghosts. To make matters worse, the resident mad scientist wants to transplant Sach's brain into a gorilla. Essential viewing for anyone who thought "Ghostbusters" was an original story. **68m/B VHS.** Leo Gorcey, Huntz Hall, Douglass Dumbrille, Bobby Jordan, Gabriel Dell, William Benedict, David Gorcey, Bernard Gorcey, Tanis Chandler, Maurice Cass, Charles Middleton; **D:** William Beaudine.

The Spook Who Sat by the Door 🐾🐾½ 1973 (PG) A black CIA agent organizes an army of inner-city youths and launches a revolution. Based on the novel by Sam Greenlee. **95m/C VHS, DVD.** Lawrence Cook, Paula Kelly, J.A. Preston; **D:** Ivan Dixon; **M:** Herbie Hancock.

Spookies woof! 1985 (R) An old master sorcerer who lives in a run-down haunted house sacrifices humans to give eternal life to his unconscious bride. He needs only a few more victims when a group of teenagers come to explore the house. **85m/C VHS.** Felix Ward, Dan Scott, Maria Pechukas, Brendan Faulkner, Eugene Joseph; **D:** Thomas Doran.

Spooks Run Wild 🐾🐾½ 1941 The East Side Kids seek refuge in a spooky mansion owned by the eerie Lugosi. A fun horror-comedy with the Kids' antics playing off Lugosi's scariness quite well. Co-scripter Carl Foreman later co-wrote "High-Noon," "The Bridge on the River Kwai," and "The Guns of Navarone." Not the same movie as "Ghosts on the Loose" which followed in '43 and also featured Lugosi and the Kids. **64m/B VHS, DVD.** Huntz Hall, Leo Gorcey, Bobby Jordan, Sammy (Earnest) Morrison, Dave O'Brien, Dennis Moore, Bela Lugosi; **D:** Phil Rosen; **C:** Carl Foreman.

Spooky Encounters 🐾🐾½ 1980 *Encounters of the Spooky Kind* Writer/director/star Samo Hung is Cheung, a simple-minded braggart who takes a bet to spend one night in a haunted temple. But it's a set-up. His unfaithful wife's lover hires an evil sorcerer to raise the dead. The film covers practically the entire palette of Chinese horror, including hopping vampires and flesh-eating zombies, along with flying undead and plenty of black magic. Samo pulls the film off easily, using his trademark humor to soften the horrific edge.

94m/C DVD. *HK* Sammo Hung, Chung Fat. *D:* Sammo Hung; *W:* Sammo Hung.

The Sporting Club woofl 1972 (R) A semi-gothic melodrama about a strict all men's club which, during a 100th anniversary party, reverts to savagery and primitive rites. 104m/C VHS. Robert Fields, Margaret Blye, Nicolas Coster, Ralph Waite, Jack Warden, Linda Blair; *D:* Larry Peerce.

Spotlight Scandals 1943 A barber and his eccentric aunt put the moves on a doctor who may have committed murder. Served as a TV pilot for a series that never materialized. 78m/C VHS. Billy Gilbert, Frank Fay, Bonnie Baker; *D:* William Beaudine; *C:* Mack Stengler.

Review: Spotlight on Scandals

Sprague 1984 A Boston professor and his eccentric aunt... 104m/C VHS. Robert Fields, Margaret Blye, Nicolas Coster, Ralph Waite, Jack Warden, Linda Blair; *D:* Larry Peerce.

The Spree 1996 Cliched crime thriller with wooden dialogue has cat burglar Xina (Baals) luring cop Hatcher (Boothe) into the nasty side of life. 98m/C VHS. Jennifer Beals, Powers Boothe, Gary Chalk, John Cassini, Nathaniel DeVeaux, Rita Moreno; *D:* Tommy Lee Wallace; *W:* Livia Linden, Percy Angress; *C:* Richard Leiterman; *M:* Peter Manning Robinson. CABLE.

The Spring 1989 Two archaeologists search Florida for the fountain of youth after they find new clues to its whereabouts. However, a greedy industrialist and an evil priest are both on their trail, fighting to keep the secret for themselves at any cost. 110m/C VHS. Dack Rambo, Gedde Watanabe, Shari Shattuck, Steven Keats; *D:* John D. Patterson.

The Spring 2000 (PG-13) Widower Dennis Conway (MacLachlan) and his son Nick (Cross) stop in the small town of Springville when traveling and Nick has an accident. The kid has to spend some time in the hospital where Dennis becomes involved with his son's doctor, Sophie Weston (Eastwood). But the town hides a secret—the residents are much older than they appear, and none can ever leave. Based on the novel by Clifford Irving. 90m/C VHS, DVD. Kyle MacLachlan, Alison Eastwood, Joseph Cross, George Eads, Zachary Ansley, Aaron Pearl; *D:* David Jackson; *W:* J.B. White. TV

Spring Fever 1981 Heartaches of the junior tennis circuit are brought to the screen in this sports comedy. Previews promised a lot more than the film could ever hope to deliver. Even tennis fans will be disappointed. 93m/C VHS. Susan Anton, Frank Converse, Jessica Walter, Stephen Young; *D:* Joseph L. Scanlan; *W:* Stuart Gillard; *C:* Donald Wilder; *M:* Fred Mollin.

Spring Break 1983 (R) Four college students go to Fort Lauderdale on their spring vacation and have a wilder time than they bargained for, though viewers are deprived of excitement, too. 101m/C VHS. David Knell, Steve Bassett, Paul Land, Jayne Modean, Corinne Alphen; *D:* Sean S. Cunningham.

Springtime in the Rockies 1942 A Broadway duo Vicky (Grable) and Dan (Payne) just can't get along despite being in love with each other. So Vicky decides to partner up with Victor (Romero) while Dan tries to make Vicky jealous by dating his Brazilian secretary Rosita (Miranda). Top-notch musical, with a touch of romantic tension and comedy. Beautifully filmed in the Canadian Rockies. ♪I Had the Craziest Dream; Run Little Raindrop Run; A Poem Set to Music; Pan American Jubilee; I Like to Be Love by You; Chattanooga Choo Choo; Tic Tac Do Meu Coracao. 91m/C VHS. Betty Grable, John Payne, Carmen Miranda, Cesar Romero, Charlotte Greenwood, Edward Everett Horton, Jackie Gleason; *D:* Irving Cummings; *W:* Ken Englund, Walter Bullock; *C:* Ernest Palmer.

Spring Symphony 1986 (PG-13) Fruhlingssinfonie 1986 (PG-13) A biography of composer Robert Schumann, concentrating on his rhapsodic love affair with pianist Clara Weick. Kinski is very good as the rebellious daughter, while the music is even better. Reasonably accurate in terms of history, dubbed. 102m/C VHS, DVD. GE Nastassia Kinski, Rolf Hoppe, Herbert Gronemeyer; *D:* Peter Schamoni; *W:* Peter Schamoni; *C:* Gerard Vandenburg.

Springfield Rifle 1952 Autry is a cattle-ranch foreman whose employer decides to try raising sheep. This doesn't set well with the other ranchers, but Autry manages to save the day and sing a little too. 60m/B VHS, DVD. Gene Autry, Polly Rowles, Smiley Burnette. *D:* Joseph Kane.

Springtime in the Sierras 1947 *Song of the Sierra* 1947 Rogers and Devine band together to fight a gang of poachers who prey on the wildlife of a game preserve. Features a number of songs by Rogers and The Sons of the Pioneers. 54m/B VHS, DVD. Roy Rogers, Andy Devine, Jane Frazee, Stephanie Bachelor. *D:* William Witney.

The Sprinter 1984 A young homosexual, while trying to submerge his confusion in professional track and field, gets to know a homely shot-putter and is seduced by her. In German with English subtitles. 90m/C VHS, DVD. GE Dieter Eppler, Jurgen Mikol, Renate Muri; *D:* Christoph Boll; *W:* Christoph Boll; *C:* Peter Gauhe.

Sprung 1996 (R) The dating scene among four young African-Americans is examined in this well-intended, yet untocused romantic comedy. Couple A are Brandy (Campbell) and Montel (Cundieff) who realize that they have a chance at true love. Couple B are their friends Adi-

na (Parker) and Clyde (Torry) who try to sabotage Brandy and Montel's happiness in order to save them from being "sprung" (in love) with each other. The camaraderie between the couples is funny, some of the humor often turns from vulgar to juvenile and scenes drag on a bit, comedic find who makes the film tolerable. Cundieff and Campbell are too bland to carry over the used plot but Torry is a comedic find who makes the film tolerable. 105m/C VHS, DVD. Tisha Campbell, Paula Jai Parker, Rusty Cundieff, Joe Torry, John Witherspoon, Clarence Williams III; *D:* Rusty Cundieff; *W:* Darin Scott, Rusty Cundieff; *C:* Joao Fernandes; *M:* Stanley Clarke.

Spring, Summer, Fall, Winter... and Spring 2003 (R) *Bom Yeorum Gaeul Gyeoul Geurigo... Bom* 2003 (R) Telling his tale in five segments as the title suggests, writer-director-actor Ki-Duk describes a Buddhist monk—from his beginnings as a mischievous boy to a troubled adult running from the law and his demons—and his relationship with an older monk serving as his mentor. All scenes take place in a floating monastery (created specifically for the film) in a breathtaking Korean lake that truly reflects the drama's elegance and stark simplicity. In Korean, with English subtitles. 102m/C VHS, DVD, KN Young Soo, Kim Ki Duk, Kim Young Min, Seo Jae Kyung, Ha Yeo Jin, Kim Jong Ho, Kim Jung Young, Ji Dae Han, Cho Min, Park Ji A, Song Min Young; *D:* Kim Ki Duk, Kim Ki Duk; *C:* Baek Dong Hyun; *M:* Bark Jee Woong.

Spurs 1930 A rodeo star takes on a whole gang of rustlers and their imposing machine gun. This transitional western was made both with and without sound. 60m/B VHS. Hoot Gibson, Robert E. Homans; *D:* B. Reeves Eason.

Spy 1989 A former spy who knows too much becomes the target of a renegade agency. 88m/C VHS. Ned Beatty, Tim Choate, Bruce Greenwood, Catherine Hicks, Jameson Parker, Michael Tucker; *D:* Philip Frank Messina. TV

Spy Game 2001 (R) It's 1991, and cagey veteran spy Nathan Muir (Redford) is on the verge of retirement, when he discovers that former protege Tom Bishop (Pitt) is to be executed in a Chinese prison for espionage. Muir has 24 hours to rescue Bishop, and to do it, he would rather lose the rogue agent than risk damaging an international trade agreement. Story's core is implausible but script is dense with information and drama, and the ultra-brisk editing leaves little time to consider the inadequacies. The use of geopolitical atrocities to add weight to a romantic subplot between Bishop and a British foreign-aid worker (McCormack) feels forced and, at times, insensitive. But Redford's cool and sarcastic performance, recalling his role in "Three Days of the Condor," makes up for some deficiencies and anchors the film nicely. 127m/C VHS, DVD, HD DVD, US Robert Redford, Brad Pitt, Catherine McCormack, Stephen (Dillon) Dillane, Larry Bryggman, Michael Paul Chan, Marianne Jean-Baptiste, David Hemmings, Matthew Marsh, Todd Boyce, Charlotte Rampling; *D:* Tony Scott; *W:* Michael Frost Beckner, David Arata; *C:* Dan Mindel; *M:* Harry Gregson-Williams.

Spy Games 2001 (R) *History is Made at Night* 1999 CIA agent Harry (Pullman) and Russian SVR agent Natasha (Jacob) dash around Helsinki chasing a videotape that contains U.S. satellite codes and spatting romantically. Old-fashioned and lame. 94m/C VHS, DVD. GB Bill Pullman, Irene Jacob, Bruno Kirby, Glenn Plummer, Udo Kier, Andre Oumansky, Feodor Atkine; *D:* Ilkka Jarvilaturi; *W:* Patrick Amos; *C:* Michel Amathieu; *M:* Courtney Pine.

Spy Hard 1996 (PG-13) Nielsen does yet another genre spoof—this time a combo of "Die Hard" meets James Bond. Agent Dick Steele aka WD40 (Nielsen) is brought out of retirement to thwart the plans of crazed General Rancor (Griffith) for world domination. Not much else plotwise, which ropes Nielsen in domino-fashion through the myriad of unimaginative spoots on such films as "Speed" and "Pulp Fiction." Minus the charm and pace

Spun 2002 A bleached-out, grunge look at meth heads, Ross 'Schwartzman' hooking up with dealer Spider Mike (Leguizamo). Film lurches along from user to dealer to addict and from one in disgust to another. Who cares. 96m/C VHS, DVD. Jason Schwartzman, John Leguizamo, Mena Suvari, Patrick Fugit, Brittany Murphy, Mickey Rourke, Peter Stormare, Alexis Arquette, Eric Roberts; *D:* Jonas Akerlund; *W:* Will De Los Santos, Creighton Vero; *C:* Eric Broms; *M:* Billy Corgan.

Sputnik 1961 *A Dog, a Mouse, and a Sputnik* 1961 A Frenchman, amnesiac after a car crash, comes up against Russian scientists, space-bound dogs, and weightlessness. Pleasant and charming family fun though clearly dated. Another fine performance from Auer. Dubbed. 80m/B VHS, DVD. FR Noella Noel, Mischa Auer, Denise Grey; *D:* Jean Dreville.

Spy in Black 1939 *U-Boat 29* 1939 A German submarine captain returns from duty at sea during WW I and is assigned to infiltrate one of the Orkney Islands and obtain confidential British information in the U.S. as "U-Boat 29," this film is based on a J. Storer Clouston novel. 82m/B VHS. GB Conrad Veidt, Valerie Hobson, Sebastian Shaw, Marius Goring, June Duprez, Helen Haye, Cyril Raymond, Hay Petrie; *D:* Michael Powell; *M:* Miklos Rozsa.

Spy Kids 2001 (PG) Rare live-action kids movie that doesn't talk down to its target audience has pre-teens Carmen (Vega) and Juni Cortez (Sabara) being troublesome bullies until their parents disappear. It seems that Mom (Gugino) and Dad (Banderas) are retired super-spies who get kidnapped while on one last mission. It's up to the kids, along with perennial sidekick Marin, to show their folks (and that he'd be proud to show his children/the world) from evil kid-show host Fegan Floop (Cumming, bidding for the title of world's busiest screen villain) and Minion (Shalhoub). Director/writer/editor/composer Rodriguez makes a concerted effort to provide family entertainment with zero objectionable material but plenty of gee-whiz gadgetry, fanciful set design, and exciting action. He said he wanted to make a movie that he'd be proud to show his children. Nearly as good as the original. 88m/C VHS, DVD. US Alexa Vega, Daryl Sabara, Antonio Banderas, Carla Gugino, Alan Cumming, Tony Shalhoub, Teri Hatcher, Richard "Cheech" Marin, Robert Patrick, Danny Trejo, George Clooney; *D:* Robert Rodriguez; *W:* Robert Rodriguez; *C:* Guillermo Navarro; *M:* John Debney.

Spy Kids 2: The Island of Lost Dreams 2002 (PG) Worthy sequel finds Carmen (Vega) and Juni (Sabara) fighting rival kid spies when they take on a distant island. Vexing blond siblings Gary and Gerti Giggles (O'Leary and Osment) take credit for any turn. Meanwhile, super-sleuthing all of the Cortez's super-sleuthing at every turn. Meanwhile, Cortez patriarch Gregorio (Banderas) has his own problems with the Giggles' dad Donnagon (Judge), as they battle for OSS leadership. Life in a spy family isn't always easy. All that aside, the newly minted junior OSS agents must do their third and latest role in saving the day, traveling to the mutant-animal-populated island of mad scientist Romero. Neatly as good as the original. Montalban and Taylor as good as mom Ingrid's disappointing folks are a highlight. 86m/C VHS, DVD. US Antonio Banderas, Carla Gugino, Alexa Vega, Daryl Sabara, Mike Judge, Steve Buscemi, Danny Trejo, Richard "Cheech" Marin, Ricardo Montalban, Holland Taylor, Matt O'Leary, Emily Osment; *D:* Robert Rodriguez; *W:* Robert Rodriguez; *C:* Robert Rodriguez; *M:* John Debney, Robert Rodriguez.

Spy Kids 3-D: Game Over 2003 (PG) Yes, in order to see the film, you need the funny glasses. Despite that bit of amusing nostalgia, George Clooney as the President of the United States and Sylvester Stallone in four different roles, this third and latest addition to director Rodriguez's "Spy Kids" franchise still doesn't manage to make much of an impression. The evil villain Toymaker (Stallone) and his three super-spies Juni (Sabara) and Carmen Gugino) and grandpa (Montalban) to the rescue. With a tired plot, lackluster pacing, unimaginative visuals, and wooden acting,

of parody, pioneers Zucker/Abrahams/ Zucker, this latest entry should retire the whole genre. Directorial debut of Friedberg. 80m/C VHS, DVD. Leslie Nielsen, Nicolette Sheridan, Andy Griffith, Charles Durning, Marcia Gay Harden, Barry Bostwick; *D:* Rick Friedberg; *W:* Rick Friedberg, Dick Chudnow, Jason Friedberg, Aaron Seltzer; *C:* John R. Leonetti; *M:* Bill Conti.

can't save this chapter from virtual obscurity. **85m/C VHS, DVD.** *US* Antonio Banderas, Carla Gugino, Daryl Sabara, Alexa Vega, Ricardo Montalban, Sylvester Stallone, Holland Taylor, Danny Trejo, Mike Judge, Emily Osment, Matt O'Leary, Salma Hayek, Richard "Cheech" Marin, Bobby Edner, Courtney Jines, Alan Cumming, Tony Shalhoub, Steve Buscemi, Bill Paxton, George Clooney, Elijah Wood; *D:* Robert Rodriguez; *W:* Robert Rodriguez; *C:* Robert Rodriguez; *M:* Robert Rodriguez. Golden Raspberries '03: Worst Support. Actor (Stallone).

Spy of Napoleon *1936* A French aristocrat agrees to marry the illegitimate daughter of Emperor Napoleon III and finds himself working to uncover traitors to the throne. Based on Baroness Orczy's novel. **77m/B VHS.** *GB* Richard Barthelmess, Dolly Haas, Francis L. Sullivan, Frank Vosper, Joyce Bland, Lyn Harding, Henry Oscar, Marjorie Mars; *D:* Maurice Elvey; *W:* Fred V. Merrick; *C:* Curt Courant.

The Spy Ring *International Spy; Somewhere in Paris 1938* Captain Todd Hayden (Hall) is the top player on an army-camp polo team. What he doesn't know might kill him—some of the players are evil spies, looking to steal plans for a new anti-aircraft gun. Will Hayden have to throw the big polo match to catch the bad guys? **61m/B VHS.** William Hall, Jane Wyman, Esther Ralston, Robert Warwick, Leon Ames; *D:* Joseph H. Lewis; *W:* George Waggner, Francis Van Wyck Mason.

Spy Smasher *1942* A war reporter uses his supposed death (and a convenient twin brother) to go underground and fight Nazi counterfeiters trying to wreck the economy. 12-episode serial. **185m/B VHS.** Kane Richmond, Marguerite Chapman, Sam Flint, Hans Schumm, Tristram Coffin; *D:* William Witney.

Spy Smasher Returns *1942* The exciting 12-part serial "Spy Smasher" was cut and edited into feature length and released under this title. The masked marvel and his twin brother battle enemy agents during WWII. This new version is just as exciting as the original cliffhanger. **100m/B VHS.** Kane Richmond, Marguerite Chapman, Sam Flint, Hans Schumm, Tristram Coffin; *D:* William Witney.

Spy Trap *1992* Four junior-high school friends concoct bogus military plans using futuristic toys for blueprints. The "secret" plans get sold to the Russians and the kids find themselves chased by the unhappy KGB and the CIA. Family adventure. **96m/C VHS.** Elya Baskin, Danielle Du Clos, Jason Kristofer, Cameron Johann, Devin Ratray, Kimble Joyner; *D:* Arthur Sherman.

The Spy Who Came in from the Cold *1965* The acclaimed adaptation of the John Le Carre novel about an aging British spy who attempts to infiltrate the East German agency. Prototypical Cold War thriller, with emphasis on de-glamorizing espionage. Gritty and superbly realistic with a documentary style which hampered it at the boxoffice. **110m/B VHS, DVD.** Richard Burton, Oskar Werner, Claire Bloom, Sam Wanamaker, Peter Van Eyck, Cyril Cusack, Rupert Davies, Michael Hordern; *D:* Martin Ritt; *W:* Paul Dehn, Guy Trosper; *C:* Oswald Morris; *M:* Sol Kaplan. British Acad. '66: Film; Golden Globes '66: Support. Actor (Werner).

The Spy Who Loved Me *1977 (PG)* James Bond teams up with female Russian Agent XXX to squash a villain's plan to use captured American and Russian atomic submarines in a plot to destroy the world. The villain's henchman, 7'2" Kiel, is the steel-toothed Jaws. Carly Simon sings the memorable, "Nobody Does It Better." **136m/C VHS, DVD.** *GB* Roger Moore, Barbara Bach, Curt Jurgens, Richard Kiel, Caroline Munro, Walter Gotell, Geoffrey Keen, Valerie Leon, Bernard Lee, Lois Maxwell, Desmond Llewelyn; *D:* Lewis Gilbert; *W:* Christopher Wood, Richard Maibaum; *C:* Claude Renoir, Lamar Boren; *M:* Marvin Hamlisch, Paul Buckmaster.

Spy with a Cold Nose *1966* A sporadically funny spy spoof about a bugged dog passed between British and Soviet intelligence. Hard-working cast keeps it from collapsing. **93m/C VHS.** *GB* Laurence Harvey, Daliah Lavi, Lionel Jeffries; *D:* Daniel Petrie.

The Spy Within *Flight of the Dove 1994 (R)* Spy Alex (Russell) is working undercover as a call girl and Will (Glenn) is an explosives expert on the run from his past. The two share more than a mutual attraction since a covert organization wants them both dead. Confusing plot but fast-paced action. Railsback's directorial debut. **92m/C VHS, DVD.** Theresa Russell, Scott Glenn, Lane Smith, Terence Knox, Katherine Helmond, Alex Rocco, Joe Pantoliano, Rudy Ramos; *D:* Steve Railsback; *W:* Lewis Green.

Spymaker: The Secret Life of Ian Fleming *Spymaker 1990* Fictionalized account of the creator of the ultimate spy, James Bond, and his early days in the British Secret Service. Fans of the Bond movies will appreciate the numerous inside jokes. Connery is the son of Sean. **96m/C VHS.** *GB* Jason Connery, Kristin Scott Thomas, Joss Ackland, Patricia Hodge, David Warner, Fiona Fullerton, Richard Johnson; *D:* Ferdinand Fairfax. **TV**

S*P*Y*S *1974 (PG)* An attempt to cash in on the success of "M*A*S*H," this unfunny spy spoof details the adventures of two bumbling CIA men who botch a Russian defection, and get both sides after them. Usually competent director Kershner had a bad day. **87m/C VHS, DVD.** Donald Sutherland, Elliott Gould, Joss Ackland, Zouzou, Shane Rimmer, Vladek Sheybal, Nigel Hawthorne; *D:* Irvin Kershner; *W:* Malcolm Marmorstein, Lawrence J. Cohen; *M:* Jerry Goldsmith.

Squanto: A Warrior's Tale *1994 (PG)* Family adventure fare about 17th-century Massachusetts brave Squanto (Beach), who's captured by English traders and taken to Plymouth, England for display as a "savage." He manages to escape, eventually hiding aboard a trading vessel bound for America, and on returning home even brings about a peace between fearful Pilgrims and a neighboring tribe (which culminates in the first Thanksgiving feast). It may be history lite but it's also a thoughtful, adventurous saga with good performances, and Cape Breton, Canada. **101m/C VHS, DVD.** Adam Beach, Mandy Patinkin, Michael Gambon, Nathaniel Parker, Eric Schweig, Donal Donnelly, Stuart Pankin, Alex Norton, Irene Bedard; *D:* Xavier Koller; *W:* Darlene Craviotto; *M:* Joel McNeely.

Square Dance *Home is Where the Heart Is 1987 (PG-13)* A Texas teenager leaves the farm where she's been raised by her grandfather to live in the city with her promiscuous mother (Alexander, cast against type) where she befriends a retarded young man (yes, it's Lowe, also cast against type). Too slow, but helped by good acting. **118m/C VHS, DVD.** Jane Alexander, Jason Robards Jr., Rob Lowe, Winona Ryder, Deborah Richter, Guich Koock, Elbert Lewis; *D:* Daniel Petrie; *W:* Alan Hines; *M:* Bruce Broughton.

Square Dance Jubilee *1951* TV scouts hit Prairie City in search of cowboy stars, and stumble onto cattle rustlers; 21 C&W tunes support a near-invisible plot, suitable for fridge runs. **78m/B VHS.** Mary Beth Hughes, Donald (Don "Red") Barry, Wally Vernon, John Eldridge; *D:* Paul Landres; *W:* William Nolte, Ron Ormond, Daniel Ullman; *C:* Ernest Miller; *M:* Walter Greene.

Square Shoulders *1929* Adventures of young military school student with geometric anatomy (Coghlan). **58m/B VHS.** Frank "Junior" Coghlan, Louis Wolheim, Anita Louise, C. Montague Shaw; *D:* E. Mason Hopper.

The Squeaker *Murder on Diamond Row 1937* Good Edgar Wallace mystery about a disgraced inspector trying to clear his name. **77m/C VHS.** Edmund Lowe, Sebastian Shaw; *M:* Miklos Rozsa.

The Squeaker *1965* Complicated but interesting thriller about the underworld goings-on after a big-time diamond heist. German remake of an early (1930) British talkie, also done in 1937, based on the Edgar Wallace novel. **95m/B VHS.** *GE* Heinz Drache, Eddi Arent, Klaus Kinski, Barbara Rutting; *D:* Alfred Vohrer.

The Squeeze *1977 (R)* Scotland Yard detective Keach, fired for drunkenness, gets a chance to reinstate himself when his ex-wife is caught up in a brutal kidnapping scheme. Slim script gives good cast uphill work. Ordinary thriller. Available with Spanish subtitles. **106m/C VHS, DVD.** Stacy Keach, Carol White, David Hemmings, Edward Fox, Stephen Boyd; *D:* Michael Apted.

The Squeeze *The Heist; Rip-Off 1980* An aging safecracker is hired for a final job, but learns that his cohorts plan to kill him when the heist is finished. Blah revenge thriller. **93m/C VHS, DVD.** *IT* Lee Van Cleef, Karen Black, Edward Albert, Lionel Stander, Robert Aida; *D:* Anthony M. Dawson; *W:* Paul Costello; *C:* Sergio d'Offizi; *M:* Paolo Vasile.

The Squeeze WOOF! *1987 (PG-13)* Keaton is wasted in this attempt at a comedy about a small-time con artist who discovers a Mafia plan to f*x a lottery electromagnetically. **101m/C VHS, DVD.** Michael Keaton, Rae Dawn Chong, John Davidson, Ric Abernathy, Bobby Bass, Joe Pantoliano, Meat Loaf Aday, Paul Herman; *D:* Roger Young; *C:* Arthur Albert; *M:* Miles Goodman.

Squeeze *1997 (R)* Self-conscious but not unappealing first effort made on a shoestring budget, with a director who teaches acting at a Boston youth center and who wrote his script based on the lives of his three teenaged lead actors. Tyson (Burton), Hector (Cutanda) and Boa (Duong) lead aimless lives on Boston's meaner streets where trouble finds them despite their efforts to stay (more-or-less) clear. **96m/C VHS, DVD.** Tyrone Burton, Eddie Cutanda, Phuong Duong, Geoffrey Rhue, Russell Jones, Leigh Williams; *D:* Robert Patton-Spruill; *W:* Robert Patton-Spruill; *C:* Richard Moos; *M:* Bruce Flowers.

Squeeze Play WOOF! *1979* Group of young women star a softball team and challenge the boyfriends to a game. Standard battle of the sexes takes places, with a wet T-shirt contest thrown in for good measure. Cheap, plotless, offensive trash from Troma. **92m/C VHS, DVD.** Al Corley, Jennifer Hetrick, Jim Metzler, Jim Harris, Rick Gitlin, Helen Campitelli, Rick Kahn, Diana Valentien; *D:* Lloyd Kaufman; *W:* Charles Kaufman, Haim Pekelis; *C:* Lloyd Kaufman.

The Squid and the Whale *2005 (R)* Writer-director Baumbach's semiautobiographical tale of two adolescent brothers struggling to cope with their self-centered parents' divorce. Set in Brooklyn in 1986, Walt (Eisenberg) and Frank (Kline) are the progeny of pompous writer Bernard (Daniels), whose career is faltering, and unfaithful writer Joan (Linney), whose career is on the rise. The title refers to a popular exhibit at the Natural History Museum and its significance arguably becomes clear. Expert acting by all concerned; newcomer Kline is the son of actors Kevin Kline and Phoebe Cates. **88m/C DVD.** *US* Jeff Daniels, Laura Linney, Jesse Eisenberg, Owen Kline, Anna Paquin, William Baldwin, Halley Feiffer, David Benger; *D:* Noah Baumbach; *W:* Noah Baumbach; *C:* Robert Yeoman; *M:* Britta Phillips, Dean Wareham. L.A. Film Critics '05: Screenplay; Natl. Bd. of Review '05: Screenplay; N.Y. Film Critics '05: Screenplay; Natl. Soc. Film Critics '05: Screenplay; *W:* Jeff Lieberman.

Squirm *1976 (R)* Storm disrupts a highly charged power cable, electrifying a host of garden-variety worms. The worms then turn themselves into giant monsters that terrorize a small town in Georgia. The opening credits claim it's based on an actual 1975 incident. Yeah, right. Okay entry in the giant worm genre. **92m/C VHS, DVD.** Don Scardino, Patricia Pearcy, Jean Sullivan; *D:* Jeff Lieberman; *W:* Jeff Lieberman.

Squizzy Taylor *1984* The rise and fall of real-life Australian mob boss Squizzy Taylor in the 1920s. Colorful period gangster drama loses steam about halfway through. **82m/C VHS.** *AU* Jacki Weaver, Alan Cassell, David Atkins; *D:* Kevin James Dobson; *C:* Dan Burstall.

SS Girls WOOF! *Casa Privata per le SS; Private House of the SS 1977* After the assassination attempt of July 1944, Hitler does not trust the Wehrmacht and extends the power of the SS over Germany. General Berger entrusts Hans Schillemberg to recruit a specially chosen group of prostitutes who must test the fighting spirit and loyalty of the generals. Seedy exploitation. **82m/C VHS, DVD.** *IT* Gabriele Carrara, Marina Daunia, Vassili Karis, Macha Magal, Thomas Rudy, Lucio Bogoljub Benny, Ivano Staccioli; *D:* Bruno Mattei; *W:* Bruno Mattei; *C:* Emilio Giannini; *M:* Gianni Marchetti.

Sssssss *1973 (PG-13)* Campy, creepy story of snake expert Carl Stoner (Strother Martin) who's developed a serum from cobra venom that just happens to turn human beings into snakes. His latest unwitting guinea pig is reasearch assistant David Blake (Benedict). Cool makeup effects. **99m/C VHS, DVD.** Strother Martin, Dirk Benedict, Heather Menzies, Richard B. Shull, Tim O'Connor, Jack Ging; *D:* Bernard L. Kowalski; *W:* Hal Dresner; *C:* Gerald Perry Finnerman; *M:* Patrick Williams.

Stacey *Stacey and Her Gangbusters 1973 (R)* Ex-Playmate Randall stars as Stacey Hansen, a beautiful, implausibly talented private detective. Hyper-convoluted plot, too much sex and violence detract from a potentially not-wretched whodunit. **87m/C VHS.** Anne Randall, Marjorie Bennett, Anitra Ford, Alan Landers, James Westmoreland; Christina Raines; *D:* Andy Sidaris.

Stacking *Season of Dreams 1987 (PG)* In the 1950s, a Montana family is threatened with losing their farm. Typical, boring '80s farmland tragedy with coming of age tale. **95m/C VHS.** Christine Lahti, Megan Follows, Frederic Forrest, Peter Coyote, Jason Gedrick; *D:* Martin Rosen; *W:* Victoria Jenkins; *C:* Richard Bowen, Paul Elliott; *M:* Patrick Gleeson.

Stacy's Knights *1997 (R)* *Double Down 1983 (PG)* A seemingly shy girl happens to have an uncanny knack for blackjack. With the odds against her and an unlikely group of "knights" to aid her, she sets up an implausible "sting" operation. Blah TV fodder for the big screen. **95m/C VHS, DVD.** Kevin Costner, Andra Millian; *D:* Jim Wilson; *W:*

Stag *1997 (R)* Bachelor party goes out of control and it's every guy for himself. Best man Michael (Van Peebles) surprises groom-to-be Victor (Stockwell) by inviting guys to his bachelor party that he hasn't seen in years—for good reason—such as drug dealer Pete (McCarthy). But when stripper Kelly (McShane) is accidentally killed, Pete's the only one to keep his cool and lay out their options. And this group is a lot more interested in self-preservation than in doing the right thing. **92m/C VHS, DVD.** Mario Van Peebles, Andrew McCarthy, John Stockwell, Kevin Dillon, Taylor Dane, William McNamara, Jerry Stiller, Ben Gazzara, John Henson, Jenny (Jennifer) McShane; *D:* Gavin Wilding; *W:* Evan Tylor; *C:* Maryse Alberti; *M:* Paul Zaza.

Stage Beauty *2004 (R)* Set in London during the 1660s, this entertaining but sometimes stiff drama centers on gender identity. Actor Ned Kynaston (Crudup) is renowned for his female roles (his Desdemona is legendary) at a time when women were banned from the stage. But that does not stop his devoted dresser Maria (Danes) from appearing in the same part in an illegal production that comes to the attention of flamboyant King Charles II (Everett), who is then persuaded that only women should now play female parts. This turn of events makes Ned's life a misery since he doesn't know how to play the man—either on or off the stage. Danes is somewhat mediocre playing a mediocre actress but Crudup is eye-catching as he plays vain, charming, desperate, and, finally, resilient. Adapted by Hatcher from his play "Compleat Female Stage Beauty." **105m/C DVD.** *GB US* Billy Crudup, Claire Danes, Rupert Everett, Tom Wilkinson, Ben Chaplin, Edward Fox, Zoe Tapper; *D:* Richard Eyre; *W:* Jeffrey Hatcher; *C:* Andrew Dunn; *M:* George Fenton.

Stage Door *1937* An energetic ensemble peek at the women of the theatre. A boarding house for potential actresses houses a wide variety of talents and dreams. Patrician Hepburn and wise-cracking Rogers make a good team in a

Stage Door Canteen ✓✓½ 1943 The Stage Door Canteens were operated by the American Theatre Wing during WWII for servicemen on leave. They were staffed by some of the biggest stars of the day, 65 of whom are featured here. The slight, hickey plot concerns three soldiers who fall for canteen workers while on furlough in NYC. Many musical numbers, cameos, and walk-ons by a plethora of stars. ⅛We Mustn't Say Goodbye; Bombshell From Brooklyn; The Machine Gun Song; Sleep, Baby, Sleep in Your Jeep; Quick Sands; You're Pretty Terrific Yourself; Don't Worry Island; We Meet in the Funniest Places; A Rookie and His Rhythm. **135m/C VHS, DVD.** Cheryl Anken, William Terry, Marjorie (Reardon) Riordan, Lon (Bud) McCallister, Sunset Carson, Tallulah Bankhead, Merle Oberon, Katharine Hepburn, Paul Muni, Ethel Waters, Judith Anderson, Ray Bolger, Helen Hayes, Harpo Marx, Gertrude Lawrence, Ethel Merman, Edgar Bergen, George Raft, Benny Goodman, Peggy Lee, Count Basie, Kay Kyser, Guy Lombardo, Xavier Cugat, Johnny Weissmuller; **D:** Frank Borzage; **W:** Delmer Daves; **C:** Harry Sweet; **M:** Brian May.

Stage Fright ✓✓✓ 1950 Wyman will stop at nothing to clear her old boyfriend, who has been accused of murder. Disguised as a maid, she "falls in love with the investigating detective. Dietrich sings "The Laziest Gal in Town." The Master's last film made in England until "Frenzy" (1971). **110m/B VHS, DVD.** GB Jane Wyman, Marlene Dietrich, Alastair Sim, Sybil Thorndike, Michael Wilding, Kay Walsh; **D:** Alfred Hitchcock.

Stage Fright ✓ 1983 Bashful actress is transformed into a homicidal killer after a latent psychosis in her becomes active. **82m/C VHS.** Jenny Neumann, Gary Sweet; **M:** Brian May.

Stage Struck ✓✓½ 1936 Broadway show dance director George Randall (Powell) gets stuck working with no-talent star Peggy Revere (Blondell), who's only cast because she has deep pockets are backing the whole show. George and Peggy are constantly butting heads, but show producer Fred Harris (Williams) smoothes things out by telling Peggy that George is secretly in love with her-and telling George that Peggy is secretly in love with her! **9m/B VHS.** Dick Powell, Joan Blondell, Frank McHugh, Charles Adler; **D:** Busby Berkeley; **W:** Robert Lord, Tom Buckingham.

Stage Struck ✓✓ 1957 Strasberg reprises the role made famous by Katharine Hepburn as a determined, would-be actress in this mediocre remake of "Morning Glory" (1933). Christopher Plummer's screen debut shows little of his later talent. **95m/B VHS.** Henry Fonda, Susan Strasberg, Christopher Plummer, Herbert Marshall, Joan Greenwood; **D:** Sidney Lumet; **M:** Alex North.

Stage to Mesa City ✓✓ 1948 Marshal LaRue must find out who is behinc the pesky attacks on the stage line to Mesa City. A "Fuzzy" St. John, George Chesebro, ...eenifer Holt, Russell Arms; **D:** Ray Taylor.

Stagecoach ✓✓✓✓ 1939 Varied group of characters with nothing in common are stuck together inside a coach besieged by bandits and Indians. Considerec structurally perfect, with excellent direction by Ford. It's the film that made Wayne a star as the Ringo Kid, an outlaw looking to avenge the murder of his brother and father. The first pairing of Ford and Wayne changed the course of the modern western. Stunning photography by Bert Glennon and Ray Binger captured the mythical air of Monument Valley, a site that Ford was often to revisit. Based on the story "Stage to Lordsburg" by Ernest Haycox. Remade miserably with in 1966 and again—why?—as a TV movie in 1986. **100m/B VHS, DVD.** John Wayne, Claire Trevor, Thomas Mitchell, George Bancroft, John Carradine, Andy Devine, Donald Meek, Louise Platt, Berton Churchill, Tim Holt, Tom Tyler, Chris Pin (Ether Crispin Martin) Martin, Francis Ford, Jack Pennick; **D:** John Ford; **W:** Dudley Nichols; **C:** Bert Glennon, Ray Binger; **Score;** AFI '98: Top 100; Nat'l Film Reg. '95; N.Y. Film Critics '39: Director (Ford), Actor (Mitchell), Score; AFI '98: Top 100; Nat'l Film Reg. '95; N.Y. Film Critics '39: Director (Ford), Actor (Mitchell), Score.

Stagecoach ✓ 1986 A forgettable remake of the classic. 1939 western about a motley crew of characters in a cross-country coach beset by thieves and Indians. **95m/C VHS, DVD.** Willie Nelson, Waylon Jennings, Johnny Cash, Kris Kristofferson, John Schneider, Elizabeth Ashley, Mary Crosby, Anthony (Tony) Franciosa; **D:** Ted Post; **M:** Willie Nelson. **TV**

Stagecoach to Denver ✓✓ 1946 Lane as Red Ryder investigates a stagecoach wreck and uncovers a landgrabbing plot led by who else?—the pillar of the community (Barcroft). Well-directed "Red Ryder" episode. **53m/B VHS, DVD.** Allan Lane, Roy Barcroft, Robert (Bobby) Blake, Peggy Stewart, Martha Wentworth; **D:** R.G. Springsteen.

Stagefright ✓ 1987 A maniacal serial killer tries to cover his trail by joining the cast of a play about mass murder. The other actors soon have more to worry about than remembering their lines. Typical low-grade horror. **95m/C VHS, DVD.** David Brandon, Barbara Cupisti, Robert Gligorov; **D:** Michele (Michael) Soavi; **W:** Luigi Montefiore.

Stairway to Heaven ✓✓✓½ 1946 (PG) Wonderful romantic fantasy features Niven as RAF pilot Peter D. Carter, who falls in love with American WAC June (Hunter). Forced to bail out during a mission, Peter is rescued and must undergo a risky operation. What's riskier is an angel (Goring) has made a mistake and realizes that Peter should have died. While on the operating table, Peter's spirit travels to Heaven and pleads his case for life against a harsh prosecutor (Massey) and a group of judges. Terrific work by cinematographer Cardiff. **104m/C VHS, DVD.** GB David Niven, Kim Hunter, Marius Goring, Raymond Massey, Roger Livesey, Robert Coote, Kathleen Byron, Richard Attenborough; **D:** Michael Powell, Emeric Pressburger; **W:** Michael Powell, Emeric Pressburger; **C:** Jack Cardiff; **M:** Allan Gray.

Stakeout ✓✓✓ 1962 An ex-con tries to start life anew, but every time he finds a good job, his past catches up with him. A return to the life of crime looks tempting. Predictable and familiar plot, but performances are sincere. **81m/B VHS.** Bing (Neil) Russell, Billy Hughes, Bill Hale, Jack Harris, Eve Brent; **D:** James Landis; **M:** James Landis.

Stakeout ✓✓½ 1987 (R) A sometimes violent comedy-thriller about a pair of detectives who stake out a beautiful woman's apartment, hoping for a clue to the whereabouts of her psycho boyfriend who has broken out of prison. One of them (Dreyfuss) then begins to fall in love with her. Natural charm among Estevez, Dreyfuss, and Stowe that adds to the proceedings, which are palpably implausible and silly. Slapstick sequel "Another Stakeout" followed in 1993. **117m/C VHS, DVD.** Richard Dreyfuss, Emilio Estevez, Madeleine Stowe, Aidan Quinn, Forest Whitaker, Dan Lauria, Earl Billings; **D:** John Badham; **W:** Jim Kouf; **M:** Arthur B. Rubinstein.

Stalag 17 ✓✓✓ 1953 A group of American G.I.s in a German POW camp during WWII suspects the spy in their midst. One of the very best American movies of the 1950s, adapted from the play by Donald Bevan and Edmund Trzcinski. Wilder, so good at comedy, proved himself equally adept at drama, and brought a top-drawer performance out of Holden. **120m/B VHS, DVD.** William Holden, Don Taylor, Peter Graves, Otto Preminger, Harvey Lembeck, Robert Strauss, Sig Rumann, Richard Erdman, Neville Brand, Gil Stratton, Robinson Stone, Robert Shawley, Jay Lawrence; **D:** Billy Wilder; **W:** Billy Wilder, Edwin Blum; **C:** Ernest Laszlo; **M:** Franz Waxman. Oscars '53: Actor (Holden).

Stalag Luft ✓✓ 1993 Senior British officer James Forrester (Fry) is regarded by fellow POWs as a first-class idiot, since he has a record 23 escapes and re-captures. But he's determined to break all 327 prisoners out of their Nazi camp while the nervous German Kommandant keeps one eye on the advancing Allies army and the other on his prisoners. **100m/C VHS, DVD.** Stephen Fry, Geoffrey Palmer, Nicholas Lyndhurst, David Bamber, Hugh Bonneville; **D:** Adrian Shergold. **TV**

Stalin ✓✓✓½ 1992 The story of the leader of the Soviet Union who ruled with an iron fist from 1924-53. One of the most feared men of the 20th century, he wrenched the largest country in the world singlehandedly from a backward, pastoral farmland to a industrial landscape. He was also responsible for the teared purges in the late 1930s where more than a million people were executed. Also explored is the dictator's relationships with his family, including how marriage to a cunning, sadistic, paranoid tyrant affected his wife. Filmed at actual historical locations in Russia. **173m/C VHS.** Robert Duvall, Julia Ormond, Jeroen Krabbe, Joan Plowright, Maximilian Schell, Frank Finlay, Roshan Seth, Daniel Massey, Miriam Margoyes, Jim Carter, Joanna Roth, Andras Balint; **D:** Ivan Passer; **W:** Paul Monash; **C:** Vilmos Zsigmond. **CABLE**

Stalingrad ✓✓✓ 1994 Group of German stormtroopers fall victim to the brutal war of attrition over Stalingrad in 1942 and 1943. Realistic depiction of war is not for kiddies; German with subtitles. **150m/C VHS, DVD.** GE Dominique Horwitz, Thomas Kretschmann, Jochen Nickel; **D:** Joseph Vilsmaier; **W:** Joseph Vilsmaier; **C:** Joseph Vilsmaier; **M:** Norbert J. Schneider.

Stalk the Wild Child ✓✓½ 1976 Well-intentioned but unconvincing American remake of Truffaut's "The Wild Child," about a child psychologist's efforts to rehabilitate a boy raised by wolves. TV pilot inspired "Lucan," a short-lived series. **78m/C VHS.** David Janssen, Trish Van Devere, Benjamin Bottoms, Joseph Bottoms; **D:** William Hale. **TV**

Stalked ✓½ 1994 (R) Daryl Gleeson can remake of Truffaut's "The Wild Child." Naturally, she's grateful—only Daryl takes her gratitude for something more intimate and becomes fixated on her every move. **95m/C VHS.** Maryam D'Abo, Jay Underwood, Tod Fennell, Lisa Blount, Alex Karzis, Karen Robinson, Vivian Reis; **D:** Douglas Jackson.

Stalked woof! 1999 Macedonian transplant Aleksandr (Ognenovski) wakes up to an American nightmare, firding himself the target: of a small town's wrath when framed for murder. Mayhem ensues, but not without: those forced moments of pathos, romance, and testos:erone-infused male bonding. Writer/director/star Ognenovski retreads the formula from early Stallone, Schwarzenegger, and Van Damme films: an outsider trapped in a hostile environment with only his wits and a few hundred rounds to protect him. Here, the cliches pile up faster than the body count. Add abysmal dialog, casting misfires (like the actor with a smell American accent playing the mayor of a small American town), and fight scenes rife with punches that don't connect, and we are in the presence of a potential Ed Wood for the action crowd. Sublime schlock, any way you slice it. **93m/C DVD.** Jorgo ,Ognenovski; **W:** Jorgo ,Ognenovski; **D:** Jorgo ,Ognenovski; **C:** Ricardo Jacques Gale.

Stalker ✓✓✓ 1979 A meteorite, crashing to Earth, has caused a wasteland area known as the Zone. The Zone is forbidden to anyone except special guides called Stalkers. Three Stalkers enter the region searching for its center, which contains a room that supposedly reveals fantasies. From the Soviet team that made "Solaris." Filmed with both color and black-and-white sequences. Suspenseful atmosphere due to the director's use of long takes, movement, and color. In Russian with English subtitles. **160m/C VHS.** RU Alexander Kaidanovsky, Nikolai Grinko, Anatoli (Otto) Solonitzin, Alice Freindlich; **D:** Andrei Tarkovsky; **M:** Eduard Artemyev.

Stalker ✓½ 1998 (R) And what a very dumb, psychological stalker he is too. 'Family' man Mack Maddox (Howell) is selected for jury duty and realizes that the murder victim is a woman with whom he had an affair. What's worse is the accused killer (Underwood) finds out that Maddox was involved with his wife and begins, well, stalking him and his family, even though Maddox has confessed his involvement to the cops. The plot never does make any sense and the flat performances don't help either. **93m/C VHS, DVD.** C.A:C Thomas Howell, Jack Scalia, William Friedkin; **D:** Marc S. Grenier; **W:** Michael Ract; **C:** Georges Archambault; **M:** Normand Corbeil. **VIDEO**

Stalking Danger ✓✓ 1986 C.A.T. Squad. A secret government group must team its assassination plot by a terrorist organization. **97m/C VHS.** Joe Cortese, Steve James, Patricia Charbonneau, Jack Youngblood; **D:** William Friedkin; **M:** Ennio Morricone.

Stalking Laura ✓✓½ 1993 Laura Black (Shields) has just landed her first job at a California engineering firm where she meets co-worker Richard Farley (Thomas). He asks her out—she turns him down—he starts harassing her. Laura reports it to the company, and he eventually gets Farley fired. Fact-based TV movie with ominous obsessive. **90m/C VHS, DVD.** Brooke Shields, Richard Thomas, Viveka Davis, William Allen Young, Richard Yniguez, Scott Bryce; **D:** Michael Switzer; **W:** Frank Abatemarco; **C:** Rob Draper.

The Stalking Moon ✓✓½ 1969 (G) Indian scout Peck, ready to retire, meets a woman and her half-breed son who need protection in the morning and meets woman who's fled from her murderous Apache husband who then comes looking for them. Kidnapped by infamous outlaws, he pledges allegiance to their dreams. **109m/C VHS, DVD.** Gregory Peck, Eva Marie Saint, Robert Forster, Noland Clay; **D:** Robert Mulligan; **W:** Alvin Sargent.

Stamp of a Killer ✓✓ 1987 (PG) A tough cop tries to decipher the pattern of a rampaging serial killer. **95m/C VHS.** Jimmy Smits, Judith Light, Audra Lindley, Michael Parks, Rhea Perlman; **D:** Larry Elikann. **TV**

Stand Alone ✓✓ 1985 (R) WWII vet Durning battles local dope dealers in his New York neighborhood. Self-serious anti-drug flick miscasts Durning rover-weight and looking silly in fight scenes) and Grier. **94m/C VHS.** Charles Durning, Pam Grier, James Keach; **D:** Alan Beattie; **W:** Roy Carlson.

Stand and Deliver ✓✓✓ 1988 (PG) A tough teacher inspires students in an East L.A. barrio to 'ake the Advanced Placement Test in calculus. A superb, inspirational true story, with a wonderful performance from Olmos. **105m/C VHS, DVD.** Edward James Olmos, Lou Diamond Phillips, Rosanna Desoto, Andy Garca, Will Gotay, Ingrid Oliu, Virginia Paris, Mark Eliot, Eugene Robert Glazer; **D:** Ramon Menendez; **W:** Ramon Menendez; Tom M.ssai; **C:** Tom Richmond; **M:** Craig Safan. Ind. Spirt '89: Actor (Olmos), Director (Menendez.

dez), Film, Screenplay, Support. Support. Actor (Phillips), Support. Actress (Desoto).

Stand by Me 🐾🐾🐾 1986 (R) A sentimental, observant adaptation of the Stephen King novella "The Body." Four 12-year-olds trek into the Oregon wilderness to find the body of a missing boy, learning about death and personal courage. Told as a reminiscence by narrator "author" Dreyfuss with solid performances from all four child actors. Too much gratuitous obscenity, but a very good, gratifying film from can't-miss director Reiner. **87m/C VHS, DVD.** River Phoenix, Wil Wheaton, Jerry O'Connell, Corey Feldman, Kiefer Sutherland, Richard Dreyfuss, Casey Siemaszko, John Cusack; **D:** Rob Reiner; **W:** Raynold Gideon; **C:** Thomas Del Ruth; **M:** Jack Nitzsche.

Stand-In 🐾🐾🐾 1937 When a Hollywood studio is threatened with bankruptcy, the bank sends in timid efficiency expert Howard to save it. Satire of studio executives and big-budget movie making. Bogart is interestingly cast and effective in his first comedy role, playing a drunken producer in love with star Shelton. **91m/B VHS, DVD.** Humphrey Bogart, Joan Blondell, Leslie Howard, Alan Mowbray, Maria Shelton, Jack Carson; **D:** Tay Garnett.

Stand-Ins 🐾 1985 A strange comedyaction film that takes a behind-the-scenes look at sleaze films and organized crime. **87m/C VHS.** Danny Glover; **D:** Robert Zagone.

Stand-Ins 🐾🐾½ 1997 Would-be actresses in pre-WWII Hollywood find themselves looking for fame and unwillingly settling for stand-in status. The girls all hang out at Jack's (Mandylor) bar, where Greta Garbo-double, druggie Shirley (Zuniga), battles with cynical Bette Davis stand-in, Monica (Ladd), as they celebrate the birthday of Jean Harlowish Martha Anne (Davis), along with Mae West clone Peggy (Chatton) and Marlene Dietrich stand-in Rhonda (Crider). This desperate gang are bitchy and frustrated and, of course, theatrical. Based on Kelleher's one-act play. **89m/C VHS, DVD.** Daphne Zuniga, Jordan Ladd, Sammi Davis, Missy (Melissa) Crider, Charlotte Chatton, Costas Mandylor, Katherine Heigl; **D:** Harvey Keith; **W:** Harvey Keith, Ed Kelleher; **C:** Andrzej Sekula; **M:** Bill Elliott.

Stand Off 🐾½ 1989 Two young hoodlums with guns take 18 girls hostage in a dormitory. In Hungarian with English subtitles. **97m/C VHS.** HU Ary Beri, Gabor Svidrony, Zbigniew Zapasiewicz, Istvan Szabo; **D:** Gyula Gazdag.

Stand Off 🐾🐾½ April One 1993 (PG-13) Dramatization of a 14-hour hostage incident that took place at the Bahamian High Commission in Ottawa on April Fools Day in 1986. Ex-con David Maltby (Shellen) politely demands that an empty firehall become a shelter for women by taking the High Commissioner for the Bahamas, Jane Briscoe (Sears), as a hostage. Somewhat flawed but psychologically interesting. **90m/C VHS.** CA Stephen Shellen, Djanet Sears, David Strathairn, Gordon Clapp, Pierre Curzi, Wayne Robson; **D:** Murray Battle; **W:** Murray Battle; **M:** Jonathan Goldsmith.

Stand Up and Cheer 🐾🐾½ 1934 (PG) The new federal Secretary of Entertainment organizes a huge show to raise the country's depressed spirits. Near-invisible plot, fantastic premise are an excuse for lots of imagery, dancing, and comedy, including four-year-old Temple singing "Baby Take a Bow." Also available colorized. 🎵"I'm Laughing; We're Out of the Red; Broadway's Gone Hillbilly; Baby Take a Bow; This Is Our Last Night Together; She's Way Up Thar; Stand Up and Cheer. **80m/B VHS.** Shirley Temple, Warner Baxter, Madge Evans, Nigel Bruce, Stepin Fetchit, Frank Melton, Lila Lee, James Dunn, John Boles, Scotty Beckett; **D:** Hamilton MacFadden; **W:** Will Rogers, Ralph Spence; **C:** Ernest Palmer.

Stander 🐾🐾½ 2003 (R) Set in 1976 in South Africa, the volatile antihero of the title (played with bravado by Jane) is the youngest police capitain in Johannesburg during a Soweto protest march that quickly turns violent. Guilt-stricken after killing an unarmed black youth, Andre Stander realizes that the police are so busy enforcing apartheid that a white criminal can get away with anything. To test his theory, he robs a bank, and then another bank, and then more. Eventually arrested, Stander, along with mates McCall (Fletcher) and Heyl (O'Hara), breaks out of prison and goes on another bank-robbing spree and into the annals of folk hero notoriety. Loosely based on a true story. **111m/C DVD.** GB CA SA GE Thomas Jane, Dexter Fletcher, Deborah Kara Unger, Marius Weyers, David O'Hara, Ashley Taylor; **D:** Bronwen Hughes; **C:** Jess Hall; **M:** Bronwen Hughes, Bima Stagg; **C:** Jess Hall; **M:** David Holmes, Steve Hilton.

Standing in the Shadows of Motown 🐾🐾🐾 2002 (PG) Director Justman and writer Slutsky (who wrote the book of the same name) reveal the behind-the-scenes story of the "Funk Brothers," the musicians who backed-up Motown's best and were unknown to anyone but their peers and music fanatics. There's archival footage, interviews with the remaining "Brothers," and a concert performance with contemporary singers doing the Motown standards accompanied by these living legends. **108m/C VHS, DVD.** **D:** Paul Justman; **W:** Ntozake Shange, Walter Dallas; **C:** Doug Milsome, Lon Stratton. N.Y. Film Critics '02: Feature Doc.

Standing on Fishes 🐾🐾 1999 (R) With their relationship already on the rocks, Caleb, an aspiring sculptor, pushes Erica's feminist ideals to the limit by taking an odd job of designing a fake vagina for a film. So when an adoring kindred soul makes moves on him, he's more than tempted. Writing/directing team Tatum and Scott Lynn also star in the lead roles. **89m/C VHS, DVD.** Bradford Tatum, Meredith Scott Lynn, Jason Priestley, Lauren Fox, Kelsey Grammer, Pamela Reed, James Black; **D:** Bradford Tatum; **W:** Meredith Scott Lynn; **W:** Bradford Tatum; **C:** Mark Mervis; **M:** Juliet Prater. **VIDEO**

Standing Still 🐾🐾 2005 (R) Talented cast is wasted in an all-too-familiar story about a post-collegiate reunion of 20-somethings who find adulthood a generally bewildering trial. Los Angeles couple Michael (Garcia) and Elise (Adams) gather their friends together for their wedding. Among them are best man Rich (Stanford) and his girlfriend Samantha (Sagemiller), sarcastic Lana (Suvari) and oddball Pockets (Abrahams), movie star Simon (Van Der Beek), agent Quentin (Hanks), and outspoken lesbian Jennifer (German), who has issues with the bride, who's not the only one keeping secrets. **90m/C VHS, DVD.** US Adam Garcia, Amy Adams, Aaron Stanford, Melissa Sagemiller, Mena Suvari, Jon Abrahams, Xander Berkeley, Lauren German, Colin Hanks, Roger Avary, Ethan (Randall) Embry, James Van Der Beek; **D:** Michael Cole Weiss; **W:** Timm Sharp, Matthew Perniciaro; **C:** Robert Brinkmann; **M:** B.C. Smith.

Standing Tall 🐾🐾 1978 A small-time cattle rancher takes on a high-class land baron in this average, made-for-TV western set during the Depression. Playing a "half-breed," Forster carries an otherwise mediocre effort. **100m/C VHS.** Robert Forster, Linda Evans, Will Sampson, L.Q. Jones; **D:** Harvey Hart.

Standoff 🐾🐾½ 1997 (R) A botched FBI raid on a Texas cult stronghold lead the four fed survivors to seek shelter in an abandoned farmhouse. Surrounded by gunfire, they're soon not any safer inside, especially when they capture two of the cult's female recruits. **91m/C VHS, DVD.** Chris Robinson, Alex Rocco, Susan Carroll; **D:** William Grefe.

Stanley 🐾½ 1972 (PG) Seminole Vietnam veteran Robinson uses rattlesnakes as his personal weapon of revenge against most of mankind. Thoroughly wretched effort in the gross-pets vein of "Willard" and "Ben." **108m/C VHS, DVD.** Chris Robinson, Alex Rocco, Susan Carroll; **D:** William Grefe.

Stanley and Iris 🐾🐾½ 1990 (PG-13) Blue collar recent widow Fonda meets co-worker De Niro, whose illiteracy she helps remedy. Romance follows, inevitably but excruciatingly. Leads' strong presence helps along a very slow, under-

---

developed plot. **107m/C VHS, DVD.** Jane Fonda, Robert De Niro, Swoosie Kurtz, Martha Plimpton, Harley Cross, Jamey Sheridan, Feodor Chaliapin Jr., Zohra Lampert, Loretta Devine, Julie Garfield; **D:** Martin Ritt; **W:** Harriet Frank Jr., Irving Ravetch; **M:** John Williams.

Stanley and Livingstone 🐾🐾🐾 1939 The classic Hollywood kitsch version of the Victorian legend-based-on-fact. American journalist Tracy sets out into darkest Africa to locate a long lost Brisith explorer. Lavish, dramatically solid fictionalized history. The real Stanley did not become a missionary—but hey, this is the movies). Tracy is excellent, as usual, and low-key. **101m/B VHS.** Spencer Tracy, Cedric Hardwicke, Nancy Kelly, Walter Brennan, Richard Greene, Charles Coburn, Henry Hull, Henry Travers, Miles Mander, Holmes Herbert, Paul Stanton, Brandon Hurst, Joseph Crehan, Russell Hicks; **D:** Henry King; **C:** George Barnes; **M:** Alfred Newman.

The Star 🐾🐾🐾 1952 A washed-up and self-destructive former Hollywood star (Davis, who allegedly took the role to lampoon rival Joan Crawford) gets, and blows, one last chance at a comeback and finds love with a former protege (Hayden) who gave up stardom for the simple life. To the chagrin of both him and her daughter (Wood), she can't quite give up the siren song of her past glory and continues to sabotage what could be a happy life. Gut-wrenching and squirmy for the scenes in which Davis's character, for which she received an Oscar nomination, debases herself personally and professionally. **89m/B VHS, DVD.** Bette Davis, Sterling Hayden, Natalie Wood, Warner Anderson, Minor Watson, June Travis, Paul Frees, Herb Vigran, Barbara Lawrence, Fay Baker, Katherine Warren, Stuart Heisler; **W:** Katherine Albert, Dale Eunson; **C:** Ernest Laszlo; **M:** Victor Young.

Star! 🐾🐾🐾 Those Were the Happy Times 1968 Campy showbiz extravaganza based on the life of famed musical comedy performer Gertrude Lawrence (Andrews), star of the London and Broadway stage. Film follows Lawrence's adventures from the British music halls to her fateful meeting with Noel Coward (Massey), who would not only become her dearest friend but perform with and write for her as well. A tumultuous private life is also on display. 17 lavishly staged musical numbers helped boost the cost of the film to $14 million—big bucks in '68. Movie was a colossal flop on opening and was recut, deleting 50 minutes, but still didn't recoup its losses. Has gained a cult following. 🎵Down at the Old Bull and Bush; Piccadilly; Star!; Oh, It's a Lovely War; In My Garden of Joy; Forbidden Fruit; Parisian Pierrot; Someday I'll Find You; Has Anybody Seen Our Ship? **172m/C VHS, DVD.** Julie Andrews, Daniel Massey, Richard Crenna, Michael Craig, Robert Reed, Bruce Forsyth, Beryl Reid, John Collin, Alan Oppenheimer, Anthony Eisley, Jenny Agutter, J. Pat O'Malley, Richard Karlan, Lynley Laurence, Harvey Jason, Elizabeth St. Clair; **D:** Robert Wise; **W:** William Fairchild; **C:** Ernest Laszlo.

The Star Chamber 🐾🐾 1983 (R) A conscientious judge (Douglas) sees criminals freed on legal technicalities and wonders if he should take justice into his own hands. He finds a secret society that administers justice extra-legally. Implausible yet predictable. **109m/C VHS, DVD.** Michael Douglas, Hal Holbrook, Yaphet Kotto, Sharon Gless, James B. Sikking; **D:** Peter Hyams; **W:** Peter Hyams, Roderick Taylor.

Star Crash 🐾🐾½ Stella Star 1978 (PG) Trio of adventurers (woman, man, and robot) sent by emperor Plummer square off against interstellar evil (Spinell) by using their wits and technological wizardy. Semi-funny and cheesy sci-fi, done with style beyond its limited budget. **92m/C VHS, DVD.** IT Caroline Munro, Marjoe Gortner, Christopher Plummer, David Hasselhoff, Robert Tessier, Joe Spinell, Nadia Cassini, Judd Hamilton; **D:** Lewis (Luigi Cozzi) Coates; **W:** Lewis (Luigi) Coates; **M:** John Barry.

Star Crystal 🐾🐾 1985 (R) Aboard a spaceship, an indestructible alien hunts down the human crew. Cheap imitation of "Alien." **93m/C VHS, DVD.** C. Judson Campbell, Faye Bolt, John W. Smith; **D:** Lance Lindsay.

Star 80 🐾🐾½ 1983 (R) Based on the true-life tragedy of Playmate of the Year Dorothy Stratten and Paul Snider as they battle for control of her body, her mind, and her money, with gruesome results. Roberts is overpowering as the vile Snider, but the movie is generally unpleasant. Fosse's last film. **104m/C VHS, DVD.** Mariel Hemingway, Eric Roberts, Cliff Robertson, David Clennon, Josh Mostel, Roger Rees, Carroll Baker; **D:** Bob Fosse; **W:** Bob Fosse; **C:** Sven Nykvist; **M:** Ralph Burns.

Star Hunter 🐾½ 1995 (R) When a bus filled with football players and cheerleaders takes a wrong turn, it winds up in an intergalatic hunting ground where the humans become the prey. Lots of lame chase and would-be action scenes. **80m/C VHS, DVD.** Roddy McDowall, Stella Stevens, Ken Stott, Zack (Zach) Ward, Wendy Schumacher; **D:** Cole McKay.

A Star Is Born 🐾🐾🐾½ 1937 A movie star declining in popularity marries a shy girl and helps her become a star. Her fame eclipses his and tragic consequences follow. Shows Hollywood-behind-the-scenes machinations. Stunning early color, one last dramatic turn at a comeback and is based on the real-life tragedy of silent film star Wallace Reid, who died of a morphine overdose in 1923 at age 31. Remade twice, in 1954 and 1976. **111m/C VHS, DVD.** Janet Gaynor, Fredric March, Adolphe Menjou, May Robson, Andy Devine, Lionel Stander, Franklin Pangborn; **D:** William A. Wellman; **W:** William A. Wellman, Dorothy Parker; **C:** William Howard Greene; **M:** Max Steiner. Oscars 37: Story.

A Star Is Born 🐾🐾🐾½ 1954 (PG) Aging actor helps a young actress to fame. She becomes his wife, but alcoholism and failure are too much for him. She honors his memory. Remake of the 1937 classic was Garland's triumph, a superb and varied performance. Newly restored version reinstates over 20 minutes of long-missing footage, including three Garland musical numbers. 🎵I'll Get By; You Took Advantage of Me; Black Bottom; Peanut Vendor; My Melancholy Baby; Swanee; It's a New World; Gotta Have Me Go with You; Somewhere There's Someone. **175m/C VHS, DVD.** Judy Garland, James Mason, Jack Carson, Tommy Noonan, Charles Bickford, Emerson Treacy, Charles Halton; **D:** George Cukor; **W:** Moss Hart; **C:** Sam Leavitt; **M:** Harold Arlen, Ira Gershwin. Golden Globes 55: Actor--Mus./Comedy (Mason), Actress--Mus./Comedy (Garland), Song ("Evergreen"), Score.

A Star Is Born 🐾🐾🐾 1976 (R) Miserable update of the 1937 and 1954 classics permitting Ms. Streisand to showcase her hit song "Evergreen." The tragic story of one rock star (the relentlessly un-hip Streisand) on her way to the top and another (good old boy Kristofferson) whose career is in decline. Kristofferson is miscast, Streisand eventually numbing, but film may irritate those looking into big-budget, big-star misfires. 🎵Watch Closely Now; Spanish Lies; Hellacious Acres; With One More Look At You; Woman in the Moon; Queen Bee; Everything; Crippled Cow; I Believe in Love. **140m/C VHS, DVD.** Barbra Streisand, Kris Kristofferson, Paul Mazursky, Gary Busey, Sally Kirkland, Oliver Clark, Marta Heflin, Robert Englund; **D:** Frank Pierson; **W:** Frank Pierson, Joan Didion, John Gregory Dunne; **C:** Robert L. Surtees; **M:** Paul Williams. Oscars '76: Song ("Evergreen"); Golden Globes '77: Actor--Mus./Comedy (Kristofferson), Actress--Mus./Comedy (Streisand), Film--Mus./Comedy, Song ("Evergreen").

Star Kid 🐾🐾🐾 The Warrior of Waverly Street 1997 (PG) Twelve-year-old Spencer Griffith (Mazzello) is the new wimp in town, with a face that immediately attracts the fists of the biggest bully around, Turbo Bradley (Simmin). On the run from Turbo, Spencer encounters Cy, an experimental cyber-battlesuit built by cutesy good aliens to save themselves from reptilian bad aliens. After inserting himself into Cy, and solving a few problems common to boy-inside-alien relationships, Spencer takes his first awkward steps, gets some humorous revenge on Turbo, and learns some lessons about confronting one's fears and accepting responsibility. Film delivers enough action and effects to keep every-

Star Knight ♂ one happy. **101m/C VHS, DVD.** Joseph Mazzel-lo, Alex Daniels, Richard Gilliland, Joey Simmrin, Brian Simpson, Danny Masterson, Corinne Bohrer, Arthur Burghardt, Ashlee Levitch, Heidi Lenhart; **D:** Manny Coto; **C:** Manny Coto; **M:** Nicholas Pike.

The Star Maker ♂♂ *L'Uomo delle Stelle* 1995 (R) Con man Joe Morelli (Castellitto) travels through the villages of 1950s Sicily claiming to be a movie talent scout. For a fee, he offers the locals a chance to shoot a screen test, which reveals various bits and pieces of their lives. There's a brief romance and Joe's scam eventually comes to light but the story's more nostalgia than narrative. Italian with subtitles. **107m/C VHS, DVD. IT** Sergio Castellitto, Tiziana Lodato; **D:** Giuseppe Tornatore; **W:** Giuseppe Tornatore, Fabio Rinau-do; **C:** Dante Spinotti; **M:** Ennio Morricone.

Star Maps ♂♂ 1997 (R) Ambitious and ambiguous effort from first-time director Arteta has boyish Carlos (Spain) chase his dreams of movie stardom on the streets of Hollywood. Pimped by his manipulative and brutal father Pepe (Figueroa), Carlos sells "maps of the stars' homes" as a cover for his real job, male prostitute. Dad's hooker mistress (Murphy) mentors 'im in the family business. Add in a mother (Velez) "recovering" from a nervous breakdown by talking to long-dead Mexican comedy star Cantinflas, and a brother (Chandler) who acts out scenes from Mexican wrestling movies, and it's a wonder he doesn't make his screen debut on Jerry Springer. Despite fine performances and a solid debut effort from Arteta, the tragic elements don't fit well with the attempted comic tone of the rest of the movie. **80m/C VHS.** Douglas Spain, Efrain Figueroa, Lysa Flores, Kandeyce Jensen, Martha Velez, Annette Murphy, Vincent Chandler, Al Vincente, Herbert Siguenza, Robin Thomas, Lalo Pardo; **D:** Miguel Arteta. **W:** Miguel Arteta; **C:** Chuy Chavez; **M:** Lysa Flores.

Star of Midnight ♂♂ 1935 A lawyer/detective becomes involved in the disappearance of the leading lady in a Broadway show and the murder of a columnist. Powell and Rogers take on characters similar to Nick and Nora Charles, but the pizazz of the "Thin Man" series is missing. **90m/B VHS.** Ginger Rogers, William Powell. **K+y: D:** Stephen Roberts.

The Star Packer ♂♂ 1934 Wayne puts on a marshal's badge, straightens out a gang of crooks, and still finds time for romance. Implausible and kind of dull early Wayne vehicle. **53m/B VHS, DVD.** John Wayne, George "Gabby" Hayes, Earl Dwire, Yakima Canutt; **D:** Robert North Bradbury. **W:** Robert North Bradbury; **C:** Archie Stout.

Star Portal ♂♂ 1997 (R) Alien Fera (Massey) comes to Earth seeking blood to help her dying race. Assuming the form of a babe, she falls in love with a hematologist (Bauer), and must battle a law-enforcer from her own planet. **83m/C VHS.** Athena Massey, Steven Bauer, Stephen Davies, Anthony Crivello; **D:** Jon Purdy. **VIDEO**

Star Quest ♂ *Beyond the Rising Moon; Space 2074* 1989 A genetically engineered woman fights for freedom from her corporate creators. Mediocre effects and some pointless action; done much better by Ridley Scott in "Blade Runner." **90m/C VHS.** Tracy Davis, Hans Bachman, Michael Mack; **D:** Philip Cook.

Star Quest ♂♂½ 1994 (R) Eight astronauts, suspended in a cryogenic sleep for nearly 100 years, awaken to find the human race has been destroyed by a nuclear holocaust. **95m/C VHS, DVD.** Steven Bauer, Emma Samms, Alan Rachins, Brenda Bakke, Ming Na, Gregory McKinney, Cliff DeYoung; **D:** Rick Jacobson.

Star Reporter ♂½ 1939 A son takes over his father's newspaper when dad is killed by gangsters. The son uses the paper in an attempt to destroy the underworld, but stumbles on some startling personal information that could drastically backfire on him. Generally interesting plot, but has some implausibility and too-broad characterization. **62m/B VHS, DVD.** Warren Hull, Marsha Hunt, Morgan Wallace, Clay Clement, Wallis (Clarke) Clark, Virginia Howell, Paul Fix, Joseph Crehan; **D:** Howard Bretherton.

Star Slammer ♂½ 1987 (R) A beautiful woman is unjustly sentenced to a brutal intergalactic prison ship. She leads the convicts to escape amid zany situations. Unevenly funny sci-fi comedy. **85m/C VHS, DVD.** Ross Hagen, John Carradine, Sandy Brooke, Aldo Ray; **D:** Fred Olen Ray; **W:** Michael Sonye; **C:** Paul Elliot; **M:** Anthony Harris.

Star Spangled Girl ♂½ 1971 (G) One of Neil Simon's lesser plays, one of his least movies. A pert, patriotic young lady captures the hearts of two left-wing alternative-newspaperguys, next door; their political conflicts never rise above bland sitcom level. **94m/C VHS, DVD.** Sandy Duncan, Tony Roberts, Todd Susman, Elizabeth Allen; **D:** Jerry Paris; **W:** Neil Simon; **C:** Sam Leavitt; **M:** Charles Fox.

Star Spangled Rhythm ♂♂♂ 1942 Movie studio guard (Moore) has told his son (Bracken), a sailor, that he's actually the head of the studio in this WW2 musical/comedy. When he learns his son pals are coming for a visit, he enlists the aid of a friendly studio switchboard operator (Hutton) to pull a fast one. (Luckily, the real studio boss is out of town.) Plot doesn't matter anyway since its just an excuse for a lot of studio stars to show up and perform. ♪A Sweater, a Sarong and a Peek-a-Boo Bang; That Old Black Magic; Hit the Road to Dreamland; Old Glory; On the Swing Shift; Doing It for Defense; Sharp as a Tack; He Loved Me Till the All-Clear Came. **99m/B VHS, DVD.** Betty Hutton, Eddie Bracken, Victor Moore, Bing Crosby, Ray Milland, Bob Hope, Veronica Lake, Dorothy Lamour, Susan Hayward, Dick Powell, Mary Martin, Alan Ladd, Paulette Goddard, Cecil B. DeMille, Arthur Treacher, Preston Sturges, Eddia Anderson, William Bendix; **D:** George Marshall; **W:** Melvin Frank, George S. Kaufman, Norman Panama, Arthur Ross, Harry Tugend; **C:** Theodore Sparkuhl; Leo Tover.

Star Time ♂½ 1992 Henry is a mentally ill loser who wants to be as happy and famous as his favorite TV stars. Deciding to kill himself, Henry is stopped by the mysterious Sam Bones, who offers him TV stardom—at a steep price. Henry achieves his 15 minutes of fame as a serial killer and his only link to reality is a female social worker. **85m/C VHS.** Michael St. Gerard, John P. Ryan, Maureen Teefy; **D:** Alexander Cassini; **C:** Fernando Argueles.

Star Trek: The Motion Picture ♂♂½ 1979 (PG) The Enterprise fights a strange alien force that threatens Earth in this first film adaptation of the famous TV series. Shatner's Kirk has been promoted to admiral and is called to take command of the vessel. He gets his old crew to tag along as well. Underrated at its theatrical release, but has benefitted from time, re-evaluation, and a director's cut. **136m/C VHS, DVD.** William Shatner, Leonard Nimoy, DeForest Kelley, James Doohan, Stephen Collins, Persis Khambatta, Nichelle Nichols, Walter Koenig, George Takei, Majel Barrett, Mark Lenard, Grace Lee Whitney; **D:** Robert Wise. **W:** Harold Livingston; **C:** Richard H. Kline; **M:** Jerry Goldsmith.

Star Trek 2: The Wrath of Khan ♂♂♂ 1982 (PG) Picking up from the 1967 Star Trek episode "Space Seed," Admiral James T. Kirk and the crew of the Enterprise must battle Khan, an old foe out for revenge. Warm and comradly in the nostalgic mode of its successors. Introduced Kirk's former lover and unknown son to the series plot, as well as Mr. Spock's "death," which led to the next sequel (1984's "The Search for Spock"). **113m/C VHS, DVD.** William Shatner, Leonard Nimoy, Ricardo Montalban, DeForest Kelley, Nichelle Nichols, James Doohan, George Takei, Walter Koenig, Kirstie Alley, Merritt Butrick, Paul Winfield, Bibi Besch; **D:** Nicholas Meyer; **C:** Gayne Rescher; **M:** James Horner.

Star Trek 3: The Search for Spock ♂♂½ 1984 (PG) Captain Kirk hijacks the USS Enterprise and commandeers the aging crew to go on a mission to the Genesis Planet to discover whether Mr. Spock still lives (supposedly he died in the last movie). Klingons threaten, as usual. Somewhat slow and humorless, but intriguing. Third in the series. **105m/C VHS, DVD.** William Shatner, Leonard Nimoy, DeForest Kelley, James Doohan, George Takei, Walter Koenig, Mark Lenard, Robin Curtis, Merritt Butrick, Christopher Lloyd, Judith Anderson, John Larroquette, James B. Sikking, Nichelle Nichols, Catherine Shirtliff, Miguel Ferrer, Grace Lee Whitney; **D:** Leonard Nimoy; **W:** Harve Bennett; **C:** Charles Correll; **M:** James Horner.

Star Trek 4: The Voyage Home ♂♂♂ 1986 (PG) Kirk and the gang go back in time to the 1980s, conveniently to save the Earth of the future from destruction. Filled with hilarious moments and exhilarating action; great special effects enhance the timely conservation theme. Watch for the stunning going-back-in-time sequence. Spock is particularly funny as he tries to fit in and learn the '80s lingo! Also available as part of Paramount's "director's series," in which Nimoy discusses various special effects aspects in the film series. The six-part (so far) series. **119m/C VHS, DVD.** William Shatner, DeForest Kelley, Catherine Hicks, Walter Koenig, Mark Lenard, Leonard Nimoy, DeForest Kelley, George Takei, Walter Koenig, Nichelle Nichols, James Doohan, Majel Barrett, Brock Peters, John Schuck, Jane Wyatt; **D:** Leonard Nimoy; **W:** Steve Meerson; **C:** Don Peterman; **M:** Leonard Rosenman.

Star Trek 5: The Final Frontier ♂½ 1989 (PG) A renegade Vulcan kidnaps the Enterprise and takes it on a journey to the mythic center of the universe. Shatner's big-action directorial debut (he also co-wrote the script) is a poor follow-up to the Nimoy-directed fourth entry in the series. Heavy-handed and pretentiously pseudo-theological. **107m/C VHS, DVD.** William Shatner, Leonard Nimoy, DeForest Kelley, James Doohan, Laurence Luckinbill, Walter Koenig, George Takei, Nichelle Nichols, David Warner, Melanie Shatner, Harve Bennett; **D:** William Shatner; **W:** David Loughery, William Shatner; **C:** Andrew Laszlo; **M:** Jerry Goldsmith; Golden Raspberries '89; Worst Director; Worst Picture, Worst Director (Shatner).

Star Trek 6: The Undiscovered Country ♂♂½ 1991 (PG) The final chapter in the long-running Star Trek series is finally here. The Federation and the Klingon Empire are preparing a much-needed peace summit but Captain Kirk has his doubts about the true intentions of the Federation's long-time enemies. When a Klingon ship is attacked, Kirk and the crew of the Enterprise, who are accused of the misdeed, must try to find the real perpetrator. Has an exciting, climactic ending. As is typical of the series, the film highlights current events—glasnost—in its plotlines. Meyer also directed Star Trek movie 2 ("The Wrath of Khan") and wrote the screenplay for 4 ("The Voyage Home"). **110m/C VHS, DVD.** William Shatner, Leonard Nimoy, DeForest Kelley, James Doohan, George Takei, Walter Koenig, Nichelle Nichols, Christopher Plummer, Kim Cattrall, Iman, David Warner, Mark Lenard, Grace Lee Whitney, Brock Peters, Kurtwood Smith, Rosanna Desoto, John Schuck, Michael Dorn, Christian Slater; **D:** Nicholas Meyer; **W:** Nicholas Meyer, Denny Martin Flinn; **C:** Hiro Narita; **M:** Cliff Eidelman.

Star Trek: First Contact ♂♂♂ 1996 (PG-13) The eighth big-screen Trek saga is firmly in the hands of the "Next Generation" cast as Picard and the Enterprise cross paths with the Borg and their sinister Queen. It's hard to tell where the cry "Resistance is Futile" is coming from the Borg, or the Trek franchise itself, as this installment may well bring in new "Trekkers" with its "less techo-babble, more action" approach and the fact that this crew can act. The Borg attempt to change history by traveling back in time (to 2063) to prevent scientist Cromwell from inventing warp drive. While the lesser interesting members of the crew stay on Earth to put up with the launch, the battle for the Enterprise rages on in space. Trademark effects, humor, and idealism are in abundant supply and should please the long-time fan as well as the neophyte. Captain Kirk is propelled into the future thanks to an explosion and manages to hook up with current starship captain, Picard. Of course, just in time to save the galaxy from the latest space icon, the villainous Dr. Soren (McDowell), renegade Klingons, and your basic mysterious space entity. For comic relief, android Data gets an emotion chip. Terrific special effects (courtesy of Industrial Light and Magic) and yes, the heroic Kirk receives his mandatory grandiose death scene. Other original characters making a brief appearance are Scotty and Chekov. An entertaining romp through time and space. **117m/C VHS, DVD.** William Shatner, Patrick Stewart, Malcolm McDowell, Whoopi Goldberg, Jonathan Frakes, Brent Spiner, LeVar Burton, Michael Dorn, Antony Zerbe, Gates (Cheryl) McFadden, Marina Sirtis, Gregg Henry, Daniel Hugh-Kelly, Claudette Nevins; **D:** Jonathan Frakes; **W:** Michael Piller; **C:** Matthew F. Leonetti; **M:** Jerry Goldsmith.

Star Trek: Generations ♂♂♂ 1996 (PG) The sci-fi phenomena continues from one film into the recently departed "Star Trek: The Next Generation" TV series and the adventures of the Enterprise crew. **117m/C VHS, DVD.** Patrick Stewart, Jonathan Frakes, Brent Spiner, LeVar Burton, Michael Dorn, Marina Sirtis, Gates (Cheryl) McFadden, Alfre Woodard, James Cromwell, Alice King, Neal McDonough, Robert Picard, Dwight Schultz, Jonathan Frakes; **W:** Brannon Braga, Ronald D. Moore; **C:** Matthew F. Leonetti; **M:** Jerry Goldsmith.

Star Trek: Insurrection ♂♂½ 1998 (PG) In the ninth film, Captain Picard (Stewart) goes to Data's (Spiner) rescue when the android seemingly goes berserk while on a scientific mission to investigate Ba'ku. What Picard discovers is a planet that's virtually a fountain of youth and a dastardly plan by the Federation and an evil Son'a, led by bitter Ru'afo (Abraham), to gain the secret even though it means destroying the planet to do so. More humor and romance than usual done in the typical professional manner of the franchise. After crew members Riker and Troi get hitched, the Enterprise heads to a celebration, but is sidetracked by the discovery of a dismantled prototype of Data. Picard then receives word of the Romulans' intention to negotiate a peace with the Federation. He smells a rat, and he's right. The leader of the Romulans is actually from Romulus's hard-core Trekkers. **116m/C VHS, DVD, LMD** US Patrick Stewart, Jonathan Frakes, Brent Spiner, LeVar Burton, Michael Dorn, Marina Sirtis, Gates (Cheryl) McFadden, Donna Murphy, F. Murray Abraham, Jonathan Frakes, LeVar Burton, Michael Dorn, Anthony Zerbe; **D:** Jonathan Frakes; **W:** Michael Piller; **C:** Matthew F. Leonetti; **M:** Jerry Goldsmith.

Star Trek: Nemesis ♂♂ 2002 (PG-13) The venerable (some may say dusty) franchise ends(?) its "Next Generation" incarnation with this disappointing outing. After crew members Riker and Troi get hitched, the Enterprise heads to her homeworld for a celebration, but is sidetracked by the discovery of Pi-card, he's a clone of Picard, even he can't save this snooze-fest that even tried the patience of the hard-core Trekkers. **116m/C VHS, DVD.** US Patrick Stewart, Jonathan Frakes, Brent Spiner, LeVar Burton, Thomas (Tom) Hardy, Ron Perlman, Shannon Cochran, Dina Meyer, Jude Ciccolella, Kate Mulgrew, Wil Wheaton; **D:** Stuart Baird; **W:** John Logan; **C:** Jeffrey L. Kimball; **M:** Jerry Goldsmith; **V:** Majel Barrett.

Star Wars ♂♂♂♂ *Star Wars: Episode 4—A New Hope* 1977 (PG) First entry in the Lucas's "Star Wars" trilogy proved to be one of the biggest boxoffice hits of all time. A young hero, a captured princess, and a hot-shot pilot, even the cute robots, a vile villain, and a heroic and mysterious Jedi knight blend together with marvelous special effects in a fantasy tale about rebel forces engaged in a life or death struggle with the tyrant leaders of the Galactic Empire. Set a new cinematic standard for realistic special effects, making many pre-"Star Wars" effects seem almost laughable in retrospect. Followed by "The Empire Strikes Back" (1980) and "Return of the Jedi" (1983). **121m/C VHS, DVD.** Mark Hamill, Carrie Fisher, Harrison Ford, Alec Guinness, Peter Cushing, Kenny Baker, James Earl Jones, David Prowse, Anthony Daniels, Peter Mayhew; **D:** George Lucas; **W:** George Lucas; **C:** Gilbert Taylor; **M:** John Williams. Oscars '77: Art Dir./Set Dec., Costume Des., Film Editing, Sound, Visual FX, Orig. Score; AFI '98: Top 100; Golden Globes '78: Score; L.A. Film Critics '77: Film, Natl. Film Reg. '89.

Star Wars: Episode 1—The Phantom Menace 1999 (PG) Lucas' first "Star Wars" film in 16 years is also the beginning of his prequel trilogy. Jedi Master Qui-Gon Jinn (Neeson) and rebellious apprentice Obi-Wan Kenobi (McGregor) are sent to the peaceful planet Naboo to aid young Queen Amidala (Portman), who is being forced to sign a Trade Federation treaty. When the Jedis escape to Tatooine with Amidala, they encounter a slave boy, Anakin (Lloyd), whom Jinn realizes is empowered by the Force, and are pursued by the Federation and evil Dark Lord, Darth Maul (Park). The special effects are all they're cracked up to be (practically the whole thing is computer generated, but doesn't look it), and the action scenes have the zip and excitement you'd expect. The characters and story may aim a little more at kids than some would like, but those kids will be the teenagers that flock to see the next two. Some plot holes, but that's to be expected in the first installment of a trilogy. **130m/C VHS, DVD.** Liam Neeson, Ewan McGregor, Natalie Portman, Jake Lloyd, Ian McDiarmid, Samuel L. Jackson, Ray Park, Pernilla August, Terence Stamp, Brian Blessed, Oliver Ford Davies, Hugh Quarshie, Ralph Brown, Sofia Coppola; **D:** George Lucas; **W:** George Lucas; **C:** David Tattersall; **M:** John Williams. MTV Movie Awards '00: Action Seq.

Star Wars: Episode 2—Attack of the Clones 2002 (PG) Ambitious Jedi knight Anakin (Christensen) goes further on his journey to the dark side while Obi-Wan (McGregor) tries to reign him in. He and Amidala (Portman), who's now a senator, have a forbidden romance, and the Republic continues to be plagued by enemies from within and without. The romance angle, so touted in the pre-release hype, seems forced due to a lack of chemistry (and some ridiculous dialogue) between the two leads, but everything else is spectacular. The exposition is handled much better than in Episode 1, (and really whets the appetite for Episode 3) and the action set pieces are (as expected) well done, and superbly choreographed. Christensen shows brief flashes of the personality changes to come in Anakin, but his performance is uneven. Jackson finally gets to show what he's got as the baddest Jedi this side of Yoda. **124m/C VHS, DVD.** US Ewan McGregor, Hayden Christensen, Natalie Portman, Ian McDiarmid, Temuera Morrison, Samuel L. Jackson, Christopher Lee, Pernilla August, Jimmy Smits, Jack Thompson, Rose Byrne, Oliver Ford Davies, Leanna (Leeanna) Walsman, Anthony Daniels, Kenny Baker, Ronald Falk; **D:** George Lucas; **W:** George Lucas, Jonathan Hales; **C:** David Tattersall; **M:** John Williams; **V:** Frank Oz, Ahmed Best, Andrew Secombe. Golden Raspberries '02: Worst Support. Actor (Christensen).

Star Wars: Episode 3—Revenge of the Sith 2005 (PG-13) After three years of fighting, the Clone Wars are finally ending; the Jedi dispatch Obi-Wan (McGregor) to bring General Grievous to justice; Supreme Chancellor Palpatine (McDiarmid) seeks to consolidate power and bring Anakin Skywalker (Christensen) to the dark side (thus turning him into Darth Vader); the Republic is transformed into the Galactic Empire and the last of the Jedi go into hiding. The end chapter of Lucas' prequel trilogy is appropriately dark, with Lucas's trademark great battle scenes (especially Anakin and Obi-Wan going at it) and at times laughable dialogue and direction. Wraps some elements up neatly, but leaves some major logic holes as well. **140m/C DVD.** US Ewan McGregor, Hayden Christensen, Natalie Portman, Samuel L. Jackson, Ian McDiarmid, Peter Mayhew, Christopher Lee, Ahmed Best, Oliver Ford Davies, Temuera Morrison, Keisha Castle-Hughes, Bruce Spence, Silas Carson, Jay Laga'aia, Wayne Pygram, David Bowers; **D:** George Lucas; **W:** George Lucas; **C:** David Tattersall; **M:** John Williams. Golden Raspberries '05: Worst Support. Actor (Christensen).

Starbird and Sweet William 1973 (G) On a solo plane flight, a young Native American crashes in the wilderness. He must fight for survival in the harsh woods with his only friend, a bear cub. Good family fare. **95m/C VHS.** A. Martinez, Louise Fitch, Dan Haggerty, Skip Homeier; **D:** Jack B. Hively.

Starchaser: The Legend of Orin 1985 (PG) Animated fantasy about a boy who must save the world of the future from malevolent hordes. **107m/C VHS, DVD. D:** Steven Hahn; **W:** Jeffrey Scott; **M:** Andrew Belling; **V:** Joe Colligan, Carmen Argenziano, Anthony DeLongis, Tyke Caravelli, Dennis Alwood, Daryl Bartley.

Stardom 2000 (R) Price of fame, media-obsessed drama set in the world of modeling. Sultry teen Tina (Pare) is playing on a women's hockey team in smalltown Ontario when she's discovered. French photog Phillipe (Berling) puts her on the road to stardom, American manager Renny (Gibson) moves her career forward, but her success causes trouble for the older man she becomes involved with—celebrity restauranteur Barry Levine (Aykroyd) until Tina moves on. All the while she's part of the disposable, instant celeb culture but you're never too sure who's doing the manipulating and how much Tina is complicit in her own exploitation. **102m/C VHS, DVD.** FR CA Jessica Pare, Dan Aykroyd, Thomas Gibson, Charles Berling, Frank Langella, Robert Lepage; **D:** Denys Arcand; **W:** Denys Arcand, Jacob Potashnik; **C:** Guy Dufaux; **M:** Francois Dompierre.

Stardust 2007 (PG-13) Tristan (Cox) wants to win the love of cold-hearted Victoria (Miller) by promising that he'll retrieve a star that's fallen into the magical realm bordering their village. But he discovers that the star has transformed into the lovely Yvaine (Danes)—and Tristan isn't the only one who wants the prize. Among the others are Lamia the witch (Pfeiffer) and cross-dressing pirate Shakespeare (De Niro). The mix of epic magical fable, swashbuckling adventure, romance, and "Princess Bride"-style irreverence doesn't always mesh, but eventually settles into an involving and satisfying tale. Based on the novel by Neil Gaiman. **128m/C DVD, HD DVD, Blu-ray Disc.** GB US Charlie Cox, Claire Danes, Robert De Niro, Sienna Miller, Michelle Pfeiffer, Peter O'Toole, Jason Flemyng, Rupert Everett, Mark Strong, Henry Cavill, Ricky Gervais, Nathaniel Parker, David Walliams, Kate Magowan, David Kelly, Sarah Alexander; **D:** Matthew Vaughn; **W:** Matthew Vaughn, Jane Goldman; **C:** Benjamin Davis; **M:** Ilan Eshkeri; **N:** Ian McKellen.

Stardust Memories 1980 (PG) Allen's "8 1/2." A comic filmmaker is plagued with creative blocks, relationships, modern fears and fanatical fans. The last film in Allen's varying self-analysis, with references to Fellini and Antonioni. **88m/B VHS, DVD.** Woody Allen, Charlotte Rampling, Jessica Harper, Marie-Christine Barrault, Tony Roberts, Helen Hanft, Cynthia Gibb, Amy Wright, Daniel Stern; **D:** Woody Allen; **W:** Woody Allen; **C:** Gordon Willis.

The Starfighters 1963 Air Force Lieutenant Dornan must prove his courage to his disapproving war hero Congressman father. Dornan flies his F-104 through a dangerous storm, thereby earning his father's respect, which leads them to form a bond. **84m/C VHS.** Robert Dornan, Richard Jordahl, Shirley Olmstead; **D:** Will Zens; **W:** Will Zens; **C:** Leif Rise.

Starflight One Starflight: the Plane that Couldn't Land 1983 A space shuttle is called on to save the world's first hypersonic airliner trapped in an orbit above earth. The film features good special effects, but also a predictable "rescue-mission" plot. **155m/C VHS.** Ray Milland, Lee Majors, Hal Linden, Lauren Hutton, Robert Webber, Terry Kiser; **D:** Jerry Jameson.

Stargate 1994 (PG-13) U.S. military probe of a ring-shaped ancient Egyptian artifact (your tax dollars at work) sends he-man colonel Russell and geeky Egyptologist Spader into a parallel universe. There they meet the builders of the pyramids who are enslaved by an evil despot (Davidson) posing as a sun god. Ambitious premise zapped from prepubescent imaginations gets an A for effort, but a silly plot that jumbles biblical epic panoramas and space odyssey special effects with otherworldly mysticism and needless emotional hang-ups trade shlock for style. Spader's shaggy scholar is neurotically fun, Russell's jarhead a bore, and Davidson's vampy villain an unintended hoot. **119m/C VHS, DVD, Blu-ray Disc, UMD.** Kurt Russell, James Spader, Jaye Davidson, Viveca Lindfors, Alexis Cruz, Leon Rippy, John Diehl, Erik Avari, Mili Avital; **D:** Roland Emmerich; **W:** Dean Devlin, Roland Emmerich; **C:** Jeff Okun; **M:** David Arnold.

Stargate: The Ark of Truth 2008 Direct-to-video movie finishes off most of the story left dangling when "Stargate: SG-1" ended its 10th TV season. In this adventure (think "Raiders of the Lost Ark" with some "Terminator" thrown in), Daniel Jackson, Teal'c, and Vala are continuing their planetary search for the Merlin weapon that will defeat the fanatical Ori before they have a chance to attack Earth. Meanwhile, Mitchell and Sam are aboard the Odyssey dealing with a double-crossing official, Ori motherships, and a lot of replicators. A nice bonus for fans of the series. **102m/C DVD.** Ben Browder, Amanda Tapping, Christopher Judge, Michael Shanks, Claudia Black, Beau Bridges, Currie Graham, Tim Guinee, Morena Baccarin, Sarah Strange, Julian Sands, Michael Beach, Spencer Maybee; **D:** Robert Cooper; **W:** Robert Cooper; **C:** Peter Woeste; **M:** Jeff Goldsmith. VIDEO

Starhops 1978 (R) A trio of buxom young women attract business to their drive-in restaurant by wearing skimpy outfits. Surprisingly inoffensive for an "R" rated plot. **92m/C VHS.** Dorothy Buhrman, Sterling Frazier, Jillian Kesner, Peter Paul Liapis, Paul Ryan, Anthony Mannino, Dick Miller; **D:** Barbara Peeters; **W:** Stephanie Rothman.

Stark 1985 Wichita detective journeys to Las Vegas in an effort to locate his missing sister. During his search, he finds himself taking on the mob. Pilot for a TV series that never happened, and Tidyman's first screenplay. A sequel, "Stark: Mirror Image," was made in 1986. **94m/C VHS.** Nicolas Surovy, Dennis Hopper, Marilu Henner, Seth Jaffe; **D:** Rod Holcomb; **W:** Ernest Tidyman. TV

Stark Raving Mad 2002 (R) Likeable hood Ben (Scott) inherits a big debt to gangster Mr. Gregory (Phillips) after his brother is murdered. His chance to clear it is by stealing a valuable statue from a bank vault located next to a Chinese nightclub that will be hosting a loud and crowded rave. Of course there's all kinds of complications, including a potential double-cross, a local Triad member who wants the statue for himself, and a couple of feds working a drug operation on the club. Scott maintains his goofy charm and adds some physical action to the mix but there's nothing new about this tired plot. **98m/C DVD.** Seann William Scott, Lou Diamond Phillips, Patrick Breen, Terry Chen, Monet Mazur, Suzy Nakamura, Timm Sharp, John Crye, Adam Arkin, Dave Foley, Kavan Smith; **D:** David Schneider, Drew Drywall; **W:** David Schneider, Drew Drywall; **C:** Chuck Cohen; **M:** John Digweed, Nick Muir.

Starkweather 2004 (R) Humdrum retelling of 19-year-old Charlie Starkweather's (Taylor) 1958 murder spree across Nebraska in the company of his 14-year-old sweetie Carli-Ann Fugate (Lucio). See "Badlands" instead. **90m/C DVD.** Lance Henriksen, Jerry Kroll, Brent Taylor, Shannon Lucio; **D:** Byron Werner; **W:** Stephen Johnston; **C:** Byron Werner. VIDEO

Starlight 1997 Alien envoy searches for a genetic component (found in a half-alien/half-human hybrid) that will allow her people to live in a post-apocalyptic Earth's polluted atmosphere. **100m/C VHS.** Rae Dawn Chong, Willie Nelson, Billy Wirth, Jim Byrnes, Deborah Wakeham; **D:** Jonathan Kay.

Starlight Hotel 1990 (PG) An unhappy teenage girl sets off to find her father, with the help of a shellshocked veteran wrongly accused of a crime. Set in New Zealand during the Depression. Lovely scenery and good acting highlight nice story of odd friendship. **90m/C VHS.** NZ Greer Robson, Peter Phelps, Marshall Napier, Pat Smythe, Alice Fraser; **D:** Sam Pillsbury.

Starman 1984 (PG) An alien from an advanced civilization lands in Wisconsin. He hides beneath the guise of a grieving young widow's recently deceased husband. He then makes her drive him across country to rendezvous with his spacecraft so he can return home. Well-acted, interesting twist on the "Stranger in a Strange Land" theme. Bridges is fun as the likeable starman; Allen is lovely and earthy in her worthy role. **115m/C VHS, DVD.** Jeff Bridges, Karen Allen, Charles Martin Smith, Richard Jaeckel; **D:** John Carpenter; **W:** Bruce A. Evans, Raynold Gideon; **C:** Donald M. Morgan; **M:** Jack Nitzsche.

Starry Night 1999 (PG-13) So what would artist Vincent Van Gogh do if he suddenly found himself alive (a century after his death) in modern-day Los Angeles and happens on a bizarre backwoods family marginally run by Stanley (Phillips). Stereotypical pursuit of humor teeters precariously on the edge of black comedy without actually being funny. Stinky script dooms fine cast to just acting weird in a "Deliverance" sort of way. Based on the novel by William Boyd. **95m/C VHS.** Daniel Day-Lewis, Harry Dean Stanton, Jim Cusack, Joan Cusack, Spalding Gray, Will Patton, Martha Plimpton, Glenne Headly, Laurie Metcalf, Maury Chaykin; **D:** Pat O'Connor; **W:** William Boyd.

Stars and Bars 1988 (R) O'Connor misfire strands Day-Lewis in the midst of hillbillies. A stuffy English art expert travels from New York to Georgia to price a Renoir, and happens on a bizarre backwoods family marginally run by Stanley.

Stars and Stripes Forever Marching Along 1952 Sumptuous, Hollywoodized bio of composer John Phillip Sousa, based on his memoir "Marching Along," but more concerned with the romantic endeavors of young protege Wagner. Accuracy aside, it's solid entertainment even if you're not mad about march music. ♫Stars and Stripes Forever; El Capitan; Washington Post; King Cotton; The Battle Hymn of the Republic; Dixie; Light Cavalry; Turkey in the Straw; Hail to the Chief. **89m/C VHS.** Clifton Webb, Debra Paget, Robert Wagner, Ruth Hussey, Finlay Currie; **D:** Henry Koster.

The Stars Fell on Henrietta 1994 (PG) Down-on-his-luck wildcatter Mr. Cox (Duvall) searches for oil and redemption. He's looking for it on the failing farm of couple Don and Cora Day (Quinn and Fisher) in the middle of the 1930s Texas dustbowl with the reluctant backing of more successful oil man (Dennehy). Quiet character study of an obsessed wheeler-dealer playing with his luck poker chip verges on the romantic in its quest for black gold, true to its message about never giving up hope. Directorial debut for Keach is led by

Stars in My Crown 🎬🎬🎬 **1950** McCrea provides a moving performance as the pistol-wielding preacher who helps the residents of a 19th-century small town battle a typhoid epidemic and KKK terrorism. Adapted from the novel by Joe David Brown. **89m/B VHS.** Joel McCrea, Ellen Drew, Dean Stockwell, Alan Hale, Lewis Stone, Amanda Blake, Juano Hernandez, Charles Kemper, Connie Gilchrist, Ed Begley Sr., James Arness, Jack Lambert, Arthur Hunnicutt; **D:** Jacques Tourneur; **W:** Margaret Fitts; **M:** Adolph Deutsch; **Nar:** Marshall Thompson.

The Stars Look Down 🎬🎬🎬 **1939** A mine owner forces miners to work in unsafe conditions in a Welsh town and disaster strikes. Redgrave is a miner's son running for office, hoping to improve conditions, and to escape the hard life. Forceful, well-directed effort suffered at the box-office, in competition with John Ford's similar classic "How Green Was My Valley." From the novel by A.J. Cronin. The original British version was released at 110 minutes. **96m3 VHS, DVD, GB** Michael Redgrave, Margaret Lockwood, Emlyn Williams, Cecil Parker; **D:** Carol Reed.

Starship 🎬 **(PG)** British sci-fi seems to be an oxymoron. To wit, this lame 'Star Wars' ripoff is about human slaves on a planet run by evil robots. **91m/C VHS, GB** John Tarrant, Cassandra Webb, Donough Rees, Deep Roy, Ralph Cotterill; **D:** Roger Christian.

Starship Invasions 🎬 **1977 (PG)** Lee leads a group of bad aliens seeking to take over the Earth. He's thwarted by UFO expert Vaughn, who is aided by a group of good aliens. Cheesy special effects have this one looking like a bad sci-fi serial from the '40s. **89m/C VHS, CA** Christopher Lee, Robert Vaughn, Daniel Pilon, Helen Shaver, Henry Ramer, Victoria (Vicki) Johnson; **D:** Edward Hunt; **W:** Edward Hunt.

Starship Troopers 🎬🎬🎬 **1997** As Bugs Bunny would say, "Of course you know, this means war!" Giant arachnids prove to be an invincible opponent for things with less than four legs in Verhoeven's comic-book styled, epic slaughter fest. The futuristic, fascist, co-ed Mobile Infantry, led by renegade Commander Rasczak (Ironside), does battle with the sinister arthropods, usually resulting in much human bloodshed. The 'high body count includes many young actors, but unlike Verhoeven's "Showgirls," their careers should remain relatively unscathed. The acting is straight out of a Mattel toy factory, but the action and confrontations with the enemy insects are a thrill thanks to computer animated special effects. Cheesy, bloody good fun, if you can ignore the 'fact that fascists are portrayed as the good guys. Based on the 1959 novel by Robert A. Heinlein. **129m/C VHS, DVD, UMD.** Casper Van Dien, Michael Ironside, Neil Patrick Harris, Clancy Brown, Denise Richards, Dina Meyer, Jake Busey, Patrick Muldoon, Seth Gilliam, Rue McClanahan, Marshall Bell, Eric B-ukorter, Blake Lindsley, Anthony Michael Ruivivar, Dean Norris, Dale Dye, Amy Smart; **D:** Paul Verhoeven; **W:** Edward Neumeier. **C:** Jost Vacano; **M:** Basil Poledouris.

Starsky & Hutch 🎬🎬½ **2004 (PG-13).** The big-screen adaptation with Ben Stiller (as Starsky) and Owen Wilson (as Hutch) spoofs everything the TV show took so seriously, and to good effect. In this outing, we find out how the duo became partners, and why. It seems both are misfits, with the opposing personality traits of the originals exaggerated to an almost-impossible level, giving them a very high-energy odd-couple buddy vibe as they chase aspiring drug kingpin Reese Feldman (Vaughn). Of course, Huggy Bear is there to assist (in the person of

---

Start the Revolution without Me 🎬🎬🎬 **1970 (PG)** Hilarious, Molliere-esque farce about two sets of identical twins (Wilder and Sutherland) separated at birth, who meet 30 years later, just before the French Revolution. About as harmy as they come; Wilder is unforgettable. Neglected when released, but now deservedly a cult favorite. **91m/C VHS, DVD, AU** Jo Kennedy, Ross O'Donovan, Pat Evison; **D:** Gillian Armstrong; **C:** Russell Boyd.

Starter for Ten 🎬🎬½ **2006 (PG-13)** Title refers to the number of points given for starter questions on popular British TV quiz show "University Challenge." In 1985, working-class Brian (McAvoy) crosses the social barrier when he's accepted at Bristol University and meets posh blonde Alice (Eve) while trying out for the quiz team. Appealingly geeky, Brian is too starry-eyed to realize he's better suited to firebrand Rebecca (Hall) as he tries to reconcile his past with the potential of his future. **96m/C VHS, DVD, US GB** James McAvoy, Rebecca Hall, Dominic Cooper, Charles Dance, Alice Eve, Catherine Tate, Benedict Cumberbatch, Mark Gatiss, Lindsay Duncan; **D:** Tom Vaughan; **W:** David Nicholls; **C:** Ashley Rowe; **M:** John Addison.

The Starter Wife 🎬🎬½ **2007** Hollywood wife Molly Kagan (Messing) gets discarded by her studio honcho louse of a hubby, Kenny (Jacobson), for an ambitious younger bimbo. Her status suddenly gone, Molly is given the loan of boozy buddy Joan's (Davis) beach house where she can lick her wounds and plan for her future. Which may just include suave but depressed movie mogul Lou (Mantegna) or hunky, secretive beach bum Sam (Moyer). Showbiz fluff based on the insider novel by Gigi Levangie Grazer. **276m/C DVD.** Debra Messing, Judy Davis, Stephen Moyer, Peter Jacobson, Lou Mantegna, Miranda Otto, Anika Noni Rose, Aden Young, Chris Diamantopoulos; **D:** Jon Avnet; **W:** Josann McGibbon, Sara Parriot; **C:** Geoffrey Simpson; **M:** Ed Shearmur. **CABLE**

Starting Out in the Evening 🎬🎬½ **2007 (PG-13)** Leonard Schiller (Langella) is a 70-year-old, still-respected writer whose books are out of print and who has been working on his latest novel for more than 10 years. Ambitious grad student Heather Wolfe (Ambrose) insists on making Leonard the subject of her master's thesis and also hopes to inspire him to complete his book. She wants to shake up his life; he insists on maintaining his dignity. Meanwhile, Ambrose tries to hold her own against a riveting performance by Langella. **111m/C DVD.** Frank Langella, Lauren Ambrose, Lili Taylor, Adrian Lester, Jessica Hecht; **D:** Andrew Wagner; **W:** Andrew Wagner, Fred Parnes; **C:** Harlan Bosmajian; **M:** Adam Gorgoni.

Starting Over 🎬🎬🎬 **1979 (R)** His life 'racked by divorce, Phil Potter learns what it's like to be single, self-sufficient, and lonely once again. When a blind date grows into a serious affair, the romance is temporarily halted by his 'nang-up for his ex-wife. Enjoyable love-triangle comedy loses direction after a while, but Reynolds is subtle and charming and Bergen good as his ex, a very bad songwriter. Based on a novel by Dan Wakefield. **106m/C VHS, DVD.** Burt Reynolds, Jill Clayburgh, Candice Bergen, Frances Sternhagen, Austin Pendleton, Mary Kay Place, Kevin Bacon, Daniel Stern; **D:** Alan J. Pakula; **W:** James L. Brooks; **C:** Sven Nykvist; **M:** Marvin Hamlisch.

Starstruck 🎬🎬½ **1982 (PG)** Fun-loving folly about a teen who tries to help his talented cousin make it as a singer. Playfully tweaks Hollywood musicals. Enjoyable and fresh. **91m/C VHS, DVD, AU** Jo Kennedy, Ross O'Donovan, Pat Evison; **D:** Gillian Armstrong; **C:** Russell Boyd.

Starved 🎬🎬 **1997** Monica (Beaman) thinks she's found a terrific guy in Scott Dawson (Adams). He gives her flowers, writes her romantic notes, and offers her candle lit dinners. So naturally, Monica falls in love. Too bad, Scott's a sociopath. He takes her prisoner, keeps her in his basement, and uses mind games and starvation to try and break Monica's will. Monica's best friend Jane (Zobel) continues to search for her, even after the police have let the case go. But can she find her in time? Based on a true story. **90m/C VHS, DVD.** Lee Ann Beaman, Hal Adams, Toni Zobel; **D:** Guy Crawford, Yvette Hoffman.

State and Main 🎬🎬 **2000 (R)** Hollywood filmmakers descend on a small New England town, which promptly becomes dazzled by all the showbiz glitter. Much of the story rotates around Hoffman, who plays the down-to-earth writer forced to rewrite his script entitled "The Old Mill" after the crew discovers the town's old burned down years ago. Meanwhile, he becomes concerned when he realizes the film's star (Baldwin) has become involved with a local teenaged girl. Macy and Lu-Pone, Mamet regulars, also enliven the cast. Entertaining, satirical look at Holly-wood egos bumping up against middle America. Not too many guffaws, but nice comedy. **90m/C VHS, DVD.** Alec Baldwin, Philip Seymour Hoffman, William H. Macy, Julia Stiles, David Paymer, Rebecca Pidgeon, Sarah Jessica Parker, Charles Durning, Patti LuPone; **D:** David Mamet; **W:** David Mamet; **C:** Oliver Stapleton; **M:** Theodore Shapiro.

State Department File 649 🎬🎬½ **1949** Insipid spy drama set in northern China. Mongolian rebels hold U.S. agent Lundigan captive; he hopes to capture a Chinese warlord. **87m/C VHS, DVD.** Virginia Bruce, William Lundigan; **D:** Sam Newfield.

State Fair 🎬🎬🎬 *It Happened One Summer* 1945 The second version of the glossy slice of Americana about a family at the Iowa State Fair, featuring plenty of great songs by Rodgers and Hammerstein. Adapted from the 1933 screen version of Phil Stong's novel. Remade again in 1962. ⌐It Might as Well Be Spring; It's a Grand Night for Singing; That's For Me; Isn't It Kinda Fun?; All I Owe Iowa; Our State Fair. **100m/C VHS, DVD.** Charles Winninger, Jeanne Crain, Dana Andrews, Vivian Blaine, Dick Haymes, Fay Bainter, Frank McHugh, Percy Kilbride, Donald Meek, William Marshall, Harry (Henry) Morgan; **D:** Walter Lang; **W:** Oscar Hammerstein; **C:** Leon Shamroy; **M:** Richard Rodgers, Oscar Hammerstein, Oscars '45: Song ("I Might as Well Be Spring").

State Fair 🎬🎬 **1962** The third film version of the story of a 'farm family who travel to their yearly state fair and experience life. The original songs are still there, but otherwise this is a letdown. Texas setting required dropping the song "All I Owe Iowa." ⌐Our State Fair; It's a Grand Night for Singing; That's for Me; It Might as Well Be Spring; Isn't It Kinda Fun?; More Than Just a Friend; It's the Little Things in Texas; Willing and Eager; This Isn't Heaven. **118m/C VHS, DVD.** Pat Boone, Ann-Margret, Bobby Darin, Tom Ewell, Alice Faye, Pamela Tiffin, Wally Cox; **D:** Jose Ferrer; **C:** William Mellor.

State of Emergency 🎬🎬½ **1994 (R)** John Novelli (Mantegna) is a cynical, overworked emergency-room doctor for an over-crowded, underequipped big-city hospital. His latest casualty is a head trauma case the hospital is ill-prepared to handle and as the patient's condition worsens both doctor and hospital are put at risk. **97m/C VHS, DVD.** Joe Mantegna, Lynn Whitfield, Paul Dooley; **D:** Lesle Linka Glatter; **W:** Susan Black, Lance Gentile. **TV**

State Property 2 WOOf! **2005 (R)** Rappers who think they can act glamorize their world of drugs and violence in a most reprehensible way. Jail time, scores to settle, double- and tripe-crossing, homicidal fantasies and plenty of actual death. Everything you don't want your kids to see. Come to think of it, you probably don't want to see it either. **94m/C DVD.** Beanie Sigel, Michael Bentt, Victor NORE Santiago, Damon Dash, Omillio Sparks, Oschino; **D:** Damon

---

Snoop Dogg, who is spot-on). Stiller and Wilson have this act down, and they never linger on a gag too long. One of the better '70s show spoofs (which may seem like damning with faint praise). Paul Michael Glaser and David Soul have a quick cameo near the end. **97m/C VHS, DVD.** Ben Stiller, Owen Wilson, Snoop Dogg, Fred Williamson, Vince Vaughn, Juliette Lewis, Amy Smart, Carmen Electra, Jason Bateman, Will Ferrell, Christopher Penn, Richard Edson, George Kee Cheung, Jeffrey Lorenzo, Molly Sims, Patton Oswalt; **Cameos:** Paul Michael Glaser, David Soul; **D:** Todd Phillips; **W:** Todd Phillips, John O'Brien, Scot Armstrong; **C:** Barry Peterson; **M:** Theodore Shapiro.

State of Grace 🎬🎬🎬 **1990 (R)** Irish hood Penn returns to old NYC neighborhood as undercover cop and becomes involved with an Irish Westies mob in a fight for survival as urban renewal encroaches on their Hell's Kitchen turf. Shrinking client base for shakedown schemes and protection rackets forces them to become contract killers for the Italian mafia. Fine performances, with Penn tense but restrained, gang honcho Harris intense, and Oldman chewing up gritty urban scenery as psycho brother of Harris, but the story is long and meandering. Well-choreographed violence. **134m/C VHS, DVD.** Sean Penn, Ed Harris, Gary Oldman, Robin Wright Penn, John Turturro, Burgess Meredith, John C. Reilly; **D:** Phil Joanou; **W:** Dennis McIntyre; **C:** Jordan Cronenweth; **M:** Ennio Morricone.

State of Play 🎬🎬🎬 **2003** Ambitious MP Stephen Collins (Morrissey) learns that his research assistant Sonia has died in a suspicious accident. Could her death be in any way connected to the execution-style murder of a teenaged thief and drug dealer? Newspaper editor Cameron Foster (Nighy) assigns reporters Cal (Simm), Della (Macdonald), and Dan (McAvoy) to chase leads and soon dirty secrets, political and private, start spilling out. Complex miniseries with notable performances. **350m/C DVD, GB** David Morrissey, Bill Nighy, Kelly Macdonald, James McAvoy, John Simm, Polly Walker, Amelia Bullmore, Philip Glenister, Marc Warren, Benedict Wong; **D:** David Yates; **W:** Paul Abbott; **C:** Chris Seager; **M:** Nicholas Hooper. **TV**

State of Siege 🎬🎬🎬 *Etat de Siege* **1973** Third pairing of Montand and Costa-Gavras, about the real-life death of USAID employee Daniel Mitrione, suspected to be involved in torture and murder in Uruguay in the '60s. Quietly suspenseful, with snazzy editing; conspiracy-theory premise is similar to Stone's "JFK," and similarly disturbing, whether you believe it or not. Dubbed. **119m/C VHS, FR** Yves Montand, Renato Salvatori, O.E. Hasse, Jacques Perrin; **D:** Constantin Costa-Gavras.

State of the Union 🎬🎬🎬 **1948** Liberal multimillionaire Tracy is seeking the Republican presidential nomination. His estranged wife (Hepburn) is asked to return so they can masquerade as a loving couple for the sake of his political career. Hepburn tries to help Tracy, as the backstage political machinations erode his personal convictions. Adapted from a highly successful, topical Broadway play; the writers changed dialogue constantly to reflect the news. Capra and his partners at Liberty Pictures originally hoped to cast Gary Cooper and Claudette Colbert; Hepburn and Menjou were at odds politically (over communist witch hunts in Hollywood) but are fine together onscreen. **124m/B VHS, DVD.** Spencer Tracy, Katharine Hepburn, Angela Lansbury, Van Johnson, Adolphe Menjou, Lewis Stone, Howard Smith; **D:** Frank Capra; **C:** George J. Folsey.

State of Things 🎬🎬🎬 **1982** Ostensibly a mystery involving a film crew trying to remake a B-movie, "The Most Dangerous Man On Earth," but also an in-depth look at the process of filmmaking, a scathing look at nuclear warfare and an homage to Roger Corman and Hollywood at large. An enigmatic, complex film from Wenders prior to his American years. In German with English subtitles; some dialogue in English. **120m/B VHS, GF** Patrick Bauchau, Allen (Goowitz) Garfield, Isabelle Weingarten, Viva, Samuel Fuller, Paul Getty III, Roger Corman; **D:** Wim Wenders. Venice Film Fest. '82.

Dash; **W:** Adam Moreno; **C:** Tom Houghton; **M:** Kerry Muzzey.

The State Within 🐾🐾½ **2006** A very complicated political conspiracy entangles British ambassador to the U.S., Sir Mark Brydon (Isaacs), with terrorists, corporate hijinks, and the tough-talking U.S. secretary of defense (Gless). When a British airliner is blown up over D.C., the bomb is traced to a British Muslim suicide bomber with apparent ties to a Central Asian nation in political turmoil. Then there's British national Luke Gardner (James), who's on Florida's death row, and is tied into the players in unexpected ways. Isaacs and Gless are outstanding, but the story has too many shadowy characters and subplots for its own good. **360m/C DVD. GB** Jason Isaacs, Sharon Gless, Ben Daniels, Eva Birthistle, Lennie James, Neil Pearson, Alex Jennings, Noam Jenkins, Genevieve O'Reilly, Nigel Bennett; **D:** Daniel Percival; **W:** Daniel Percival, Elizabeth (Lizzie) Mickery; **C:** David Perrault; **M:** Jennie Muskett. **CABLE**

Stateline Motel 🐾½ **1975 (R)** *Last Chance for a Born Loser* 1975 (R) Cheap Italian ripoff of "The Postman Always Rings Twice," with a surprise ending but little of great interest. **86m/C VHS, DVD.** *IT* Eli Wallach, Ursula Andress, Fabio Testi, Barbara Bach; **D:** Maurizio Lucidi.

The Statement 🐾🐾 **2003 (R)** Michael Caine plays Pierre Brossard, a Frenchman who helped the Nazis in the execution of several Jews during World War II. As a wanted war criminal, Brossard has been eluding authorities for years with the help of arch-conservative extremists within the Catholic church. While an interesting story, the movie is schizophrenic and leaves a lot of questions unanswered. Adapted from the novel by Brian Moore, it is actually based on the true story of Paul Touvier. **120m/C VHS, DVD. CA GB FR** Michael Caine, Tilda Swinton, Jeremy Northam, Alan Bates, Charlotte Rampling, John Neville, Ciaran Hinds, Frank Finlay, William Hutt, Matt Craven, Noam Jenkins, Peter Wight, Colin Salmon, David de Keyser; **D:** Norman Jewison; **W:** Ronald Harwood; **C:** Kevin Jewison; **M:** Normand Corbeil.

State's Attorney 🐾🐾½ *Cardigan's Last Case* 1931 Mob attorney Barrymore finds trouble after his boss sets him up as District Attorney and he decides to go after his old cronies. His ex-prostitute lover gets caught in the middle after he dumps her for a powerful politico's daughter. Contrived, improbable story succumbs to star-quality ham acting from Barrymore. Remade in 1937 with Lee Tracy as "Criminal Lawyer." **79m/B VHS.** John Barrymore, Jill Esmond, William "Stage" Boyd, Helen Twelvetrees, Mary Duncan, Ralph Ince, Albert Conti, C. Henry Gordon, Leon Ames; **D:** George Archainbaud; **W:** Gene Fowler Sr., Rowland Brown; **C:** Leo Tover; **M:** Max Steiner.

Stateside 🐾🐾 **2004 (R)** Romantic soap opera that writer/director Anselmo says is based on a true story. The movie starts in 1984 with hospitalized Marine Mark (Tucker) flashing back to 1980. While drunk, high schooler Mark gets into a serious car accident that his wealthy dad (Mantegna) fixes by having Mark enlist in the Corps rather than doing jail time. On leave, Mark visits gal pal Sue (Bruckner) in a mental hospital and meets her schizophrenic ex-actress/singer roomie Dori (Cook). They immediately fall for each other and the drama ensues. Tucker fares best as his character matures from boy to man under Kilmer's tough drill instructor, while Cook is playing standard Hollywood crazy. Movie might have benefited from a longer run time since the overstuffed plot doesn't have time to develop. Penny Marshall has an uncredited cameo as a nurse. **96m/C VHS, DVD.** *US* **GE** Rachael Leigh Cook, Jonathan Tucker, Agnes Bruckner, Val Kilmer, Joe

Mantegna, Carrie Fisher, Diane Venora, Ed Begley Jr., Michael Goduti, Daniel Franzese, Penny Marshall; **D:** Reverge Anselmo; **W:** Reverge Anselmo; **C:** Adam Holender; **M:** Joel McNeely.

Static 🐾🐾½ **1987 (PG-13)** A strange, disquieting independent film about an eccentric youth who claims to have built a machine through which one can see heaven. Uneven, with some dull stretches. **88m/C VHS.** Keith Gordon, Amanda Plummer, Bob Gunton, Jane Hoffman, Barton Heyman, Lily Knight; **D:** Mark Romanek; **W:** Keith Gordon, Mark Romanek.

Station 🐾🐾½ **1981** A Japanese detective's love affair is corrupted by his ruthless search for a bloodthirsty cop killer. With English subtitles. **130m/C VHS.** *JP* Ken Takakura, Chieko Baisho; **D:** Yasuo Furuhata.

The Station 🐾🐾 **1992** A sophisticated woman, who has just abandoned her fiancee, waits in a tiny station for an early train. The only person around is the young and ordinary stationmaster. Gradually the two are drawn together in a number of charming and comic romantic fantasies. In Italian with English subtitles. **92m/C VHS.** *IT* Margherita Buy, Ennio Fantastichini; **D:** Sergio Rubini; **W:** Sergio Rubini.

The Station Agent 🐾🐾🐾 **2003 (R)** Reclusive train enthusiast dwarf, Fibar McBride (Dinklage) takes up residence in an abandoned rural New Jersey train station he inherited in writer/director McCarthy's funny and poignant first film. Finbar's seemingly happy solitude is intruded upon by incurably outgoing local coffee cart owner Joe (Cannavale) who is fascinated by the strange newcomer. Among the other lonely locals is the downtrodden Olivia (Clarkson) who is dealing with the death of her child and a divorce. Finbar's passion for trains soon takes a back seat to some regular human contact. Dinklage is a standout in the title role, while Clarkson, Williams and Cannavale are equally excellent in this well-crafted dramedy. **88m/C VHS, DVD.** *US* Peter Dinklage, Patricia Clarkson, Bobby Cannavale, Raven Goodwin, Paul Benjamin, Michelle Williams; **D:** Thomas (Tom) McCarthy; **W:** Thomas (Tom) McCarthy; **C:** Oliver Bokelberg; **M:** Stephen Trask. Boldface Acad. '03: Orig. Screenplay; Ind. Spirit '04: First Screenplay; Natl. Bd. of Review '03: Support. Actress (Clarkson); Natl. Soc. Film Critics '03: Support. Actress (Clarkson).

Station Jim 🐾🐾½ **2001** In the 1890s, a performing circus dog escapes its abusive master and is found by railway station porter Bob (Creed-Miles), who names the terrier Jim. Jim becomes a favorite of the Luke Short story, especially young Henry (Sangster). Jim and Bob soon find themselves in a battle to save the orphanage from closure, even as the pooch helps Bob with romancing schoolteacher Harriet (Fraser) and thwarts a plot to kill Queen Victoria. **87m/C DVD. GB** Charlie Creed-Miles, George Cole, Laura Fraser, Thomas Sangster, Frank Finlay, David Haig, Celia Imrie, Prunella Scales, Timothy West, David Ross; **D:** John Roberts; **W:** Mark Wallington; **C:** Vernon Layton. **TV**

Station West 🐾🐾🐾 **1948** A disguised Army officer is sent to uncover a mystery of hijackers and murderers. Along the way, he meets up with and falls for a beautiful woman who may be involved in the treachery. Good, solid western with a fine cast and plenty of fun action shot against the requisite beautiful western landscapes. Based on the Luke Short story. Also available colorized. **92m/B VHS, DVD.** Dick Powell, Jane Greer, Agnes Moorehead, Burl Ives, Tom Powers, Raymond Burr; **D:** Sidney Lanfield.

The Stationmaster's Wife 🐾🐾🐾½ **1977** In Germay's Weimar Republic a provincial stationmaster's wife expresses her boredom with her pleasant but ineffectual husband by having numerous meaningless affairs. Meant to invoke postwar German dread and the fake bourgeois morality which covered political and social resentments. Originally shown as a 200-minute miniseries for German TV; subtitled. **111m/C VHS, DVD. GE** Elisabeth Trissenaar, Kurt Raab, Gustal Bayrhammer, Bernard Helfrich, Udo Kier, Volker Spengler; **D:** Rainer Werner

Fassbinder; **W:** Rainer Werner Fassbinder; **C:** Michael Ballhaus; **M:** Peer Raben. **TV**

The Statue 🐾🐾 **1971 (R)** Famed sculptress unveils a nude rendering of her Nobel Prize-winning husband. Much hilarity in the British vein is meant to ensue, but doesn't. Niven is OK, but this empty, plotless farce should have been much shorter. **84m/C VHS. GB** David Niven, Virna Lisi, Robert Vaughn, Ann Bell, John Cleese; **D:** Rod Amateau.

Stavisky 🐾🐾🐾 **1974** Sumptuously lensed story of Serge Stavisky, a con-artist and bon-vivant whose machinations almost brought down the French government when his corruption was exposed in 1934. Belmondo makes as charismatic an antihero as you could find. Excellent score complements the visuals. In French with English subtitles. **117m/C VHS, DVD.** Jean-Paul Belmondo, Anny (Annie Legras) Duperey, Charles Boyer, Francois Perier, Gerard Depardieu; **D:** Alain Resnais; **W:** Jorge Semprun; **C:** Sacha Vierny; **M:** Stephen Sondheim. N.Y. Film Critics '74: Support. Actor (Boyer).

Stay 🐾🐾½ **2005 (R)** Confusing psychological thriller finds compassionate shrink Sam Foster (McGregor) trying to prevent his patient Henry (Gosling) from committing suicide. Distracting and oblique things happen and Sam begins to question whether what he sees is real or part of a nightmare. ou probably won't be able to understand what you're seeing either. Good cast, good director, but too artsy by far. **99m/C DVD.** *US* Ewan McGregor, Naomi Watts, Ryan Gosling, Janeane Garofalo, B.D. Wong, Bob Hoskins, Kate Burton, Michael Gaston, Mark Margolis, Elizabeth Reaser, Sherriff Kennelly; **D:** Marc Forster; **W:** David Benioff; **C:** Roberto Schaefer; **M:** Asche & Spencer.

Stay Alive 🐾 **2006 (PG-13)** Hackneyed horror. The title refers to a video-game that was being tested by players who subsequently died. The game is then passed on to Hutch (Foster). When he and his fellow gamers play, more teens die and Hutch finally realizes that when a player dies in the game, they die exactly the same way in real life. Their nemesis (for no good reason) turns out to be sadistic, blood-bathing 16th-century Hungarian countess Elizabeth Bathory, who is now occupying a Louisiana plantation. Apparently the deaths keep her young and beautiful. Makes about as much sense as it sounds like it would. **85m/C DVD.** *US* Jon Foster, Samaire Armstrong, Frankie Muniz, Jimmi Simpson, Wendell Pierce, Sophia Bush, Adam Goldberg; **D:** William Brent Bell; **W:** William Brent Bell, Matthew Peterman; **C:** Alejandro Martinez; **M:** John (Gianni) Frizzell.

Stay As You Are 🐾½ **1978** Aging French architect Mastroianni has designs on a teenager who may be his illegitimate daughter from an earlier affair. **90m/C VHS, DVD.** *SA* Shirley Jane Harris, Tanya Gordon, Jayne Hutton, Heath Porter; **D:** John Bernard.

Stay Away, Joe 🐾 **1968 (PG)** The King is a singing half-breed rodeo star who returns to his reservation where he finds love and trouble. Utterly cliche, embarrassing, and stupid even by Elvis-movie standards. **98m/C VHS, DVD.** Elvis Presley, Burgess Meredith, Joan Blondell, Thomas Gomez, L.Q. Jones, Katy Jurado, Henry Jones; **D:** Peter Tewkesbury.

Stay Hungry 🐾🐾🐾 **1976 (R)** A wealthy southerner (Bridges) is involved in a real estate deal which depends on the sale of a gym where a number of body builders hang out. He becomes immersed in their world and finds himself in love with the working-class Field. Big Arnold's first speaking role in his "Hercules in New York" (this first role in "Hercules in New York" was dubbed.) Offbeat and occasionally uneven comedy-drama is a sleeper. **102m/C VHS, DVD.** Jeff Bridges, Sally Field, Arnold

Schwarzenegger, Robert Englund, Scatman Crothers; **D:** Bob Rafelson; **W:** Bob Rafelson.

Stay Tuned 🐾🐾 **1992 (PG-13)** Suburban yuppie couple buys a large-screen TV and satellite dish from Hellvision salesman, are sucked into their dish, and wind up starring in hellish TV shows such as "Wayne's Underworld," "Northern Overexposure," "Sadistic Home Videos," and "My Three Sons of Bitches." If they can survive for 24 hours, they'll be able to return to their normal lives. Clever idea for a film is wasted as this one never really gets off the ground; viewers may not want to stay tuned to the low comedy and frantic yucks. **90m/C VHS, DVD.** John Ritter, Pam Dawber, Jeffrey Jones, Eugene Levy, David Tom, Heather McComb; **D:** Peter Hyams; **W:** Tom S. Parker; **C:** Peter Hyams; **M:** Bruce Broughton.

Stay Tuned for Murder 🐾🐾½ **1988** A sexy news reporter gets caught in a web of financial wrongdoings and corruption. The financiers, lawyers, and other sinister types she's investigating decide to give her a story she will never forget—if she ever gets the chance to tell it! **92m/C VHS.** Terry Reeves Wolf, Christopher Ginnaven; **D:** Gary Jones.

Staying Alive 🐾½ **1983 (PG)** "Saturday Night Fever" was the ultimate cheesy '70s musical, hence likeable in a dorky way. This pathetic sequel (directed by Stallone from a Rocky-esque script about beating the odds, etc.) is utterly predictable and forgettable. Music mostly by Frank Stallone, the great heir to Rodgers and Hammerstein. ("The Woman in You; I Love You Too Much; Breakout; Someone Belonging to Someone; Life Goes On; Far From Over; Devils and Seducers; (We Dance) So Close to the Fire; Hope We Never Change. **96m/C VHS, DVD.** John Travolta, Cynthia Rhodes, Finola Hughes, Norma Donaldson; **D:** Sylvester Stallone; **W:** Sylvester Stallone; **M:** Frank Stallone.

Staying On 🐾🐾½ **1980** Based on the Paul Scott novel, this English drama follows the life of a post-colonial British colonel and his wife who chose to remain in India. **87m/C VHS, DVD.** *GB* Trevor Howard, Celia Johnson; **D:** Irene Shubik.

Staying Together 🐾½ **1989 (R)** Three midwestern brothers go into a panic when their father decides to sell the restaurant they've worked at all their adult lives. Somehow they manage the transition and learn about life. Sloppy comedy-drama with way too many unresolved subplots. **91m/C VHS, DVD.** Dermot Mulroney, Tim Quill, Sean Astin, Stockard Channing, Melinda Dillon, Daphne Zuniga; **D:** Lee Grant; **W:** Monte Merrick; **C:** Dick Bush; **M:** Miles Goodman.

The Steagle 🐾 **1971 (R)** The threat of the Cuban missile crisis lets a fantasizing professor loose to enact his wildest dreams. Odd Mitty-esque fantasy comedy might have worked, but ends up confusing and frustrating. **101m/C VHS.** Richard Benjamin, Cloris Leachman; **D:** Paul Sylbert.

Steal Big, Steal Little 🐾🐾 **1995 (PG-13)** Twins Robby and Reuben Martinez (Garcia) battle over the California ranch land left to Reuben by their mother. Evil, manipulative Robby, all fancy suits and slicked-back hair, wants to build condos while gentle, less-fashionable Reuben can't fight to fulfill his dream of building a home for the migrant workers he employs. Yawn. Writer/director Davis' flashy action movie technique doesn't fit into the dramatic social commentary—it's too fast and forced to work. Garcia's radical character changes are impressive though. Arkin provides comic relief as the good-hearted used-car dealer who tries to save the day, if not the film. **130m/C VHS, DVD.** Andy Garcia, Alan Arkin, Rachel Ticotin, Joe Pantoliano, David Ogden Stiers, Charles Rocket, Holland Taylor; **D:** Andrew Davis; **W:** Lee Blessing, Jeanne Blake, Terry Kahn, Andrew Davis; **C:** Frank Tidy; **M:** William Olvis.

Steal the Sky 🐾🐾 **1988** Israeli agent Hemingway seduces Iraqi pilot Cross and persuades him to steal a Soviet MIG jet and defect to Israel. Unlikely plot but swell flying scenes. Hemingway is poorly cast, as she often is. **110m/C VHS,**

DVD. Mariel Hemingway, Ben Cross, Etai Ankri; *D:* John Hancock. CABLE.

Steal This Movie! 🦴🦴 *Abbie* 2000 (R) Bio of anti-war activist and Yippie founder Abbie Hoffman tries to explore the counterculture of the 60s but bites off more than it can chew. Film's fragmented by its structure of using the flashback re-collections of Abbie's (D'Onofrio) first wife Anita (Garofalo) and lawyer Gerry Lefcourt (Pollak) to explain the manic and charismatic Hoffman, who wound up spending most of the 70s an underground fugitive and who died a suicide. Garity, who's the son of Tom Hayden and Jane Fonda, plays his activist dad. 111m/C VHS, DVD. Vincent D'Onofrio, Janeane Garofalo, Jeanne Tripplehorn, Donal Logue, Kevin Pollak, Kevin Corrigan, Troy Garity, Alan Van Sprang; *D:* Robert Greenwalt; *W:* Bruce Graham; *C:* Denis Lenoir; *M:* Mader.

Stealing Beauty 🦴🦴 1996 (R) The film's main asset, besides the beautiful Tuscan scenery, is the coltish charm of Tyler, who stars as virginal teenager Lucy Harmon. An innocent abroad, she's spending the summer with family friends after her mother's suicide. Ostensibly artist Ian Grayson (McCann) is doing her portrait but Lucy's more interested in finding romance with neighbor lad Niccolo (Zibetti), who bestowed her first kiss on a previous visit. Lucy's sunny appeal doesn't go unnoticed by the villa's other inhabitants, including dying playwright Alex (Irons), but it seems Lucy's growing up won't be easy on anyone (nor even herself). 118m/C VHS, DVD. IT GB FR Liv Tyler, Jeremy Irons, Donal McCann, Sinead Cusack, Jean Marais, D.W. Moffett, Stefania Sandrelli, Carlo Cecchi, Roberto Zibetti, Joseph Fiennes, Jason Flemyng, Leonardo Treviglio, Rachel Weisz; *D:* Bernardo Bertolucci; *W:* Bernardo Bertolucci, Susan Minot; *C:* Darius Khondji; *M:* Richard Hartley.

Stealing Candy 🦴🦴 2004 (R) Two ex-cons and a computer whiz team up to kidnap a movie star Candi (Lano) so they can stage a pay-per-view internet sex session with her. Predictable thriller piles on the non-stop action and plays on the promise of sex. 83m/C VHS, DVD. Jenya Lano, Daniel Baldwin, Coolio, Alex McArthur, Julie St. Claire; *D:* Mark L. Lester; *W:* C. Courtney Joyner. VIDEO

Stealing Harvard 🦴 2002 (PG-13) Prince of low-brow Green adds another tarnished jewel to his crown with this tired, inane crime caper comedy. As Duff, Green is teamed with Jason Lee as John, who needs to raise $30,000 to finance the Harvard education he promised his niece. That should take care of her first semester. His fiancee (Mann), also wants John to bankroll their future together, and won't marry him until he has the exact amount in the bank. What follows are the disastrous duo's clumsy attempts to steal the money. Largely unfunny, with small chunks of mild humor. 83m/C VHS, DVD. US Tom Green, Jason Lee, Leslie Mann, Megan Mullally, Dennis Farina, Richard Jenkins, John C. McGinley, Christopher McCulloch; *D:* Bruce McCulloch; *W:* Peter Tolan; *C:* Jeff Steiger; *D:* Christophe Beck.

Stealing Heaven 🦴🦴 1988 (R) Based on the lives of Abelard and Heloise. In 12th-century Paris, a theologian and teacher falls in love with a beautiful young woman, and the two must defend their bond from all comers, including her righteous uncle. Steamy; trimmed to 108 minutes after threatened X rating. Attractive and cerebral. Available in a 115 minute uncut, unrated version. 108m/C VHS, GB YU Derek de Lint, Kim Thomson, Denholm Elliott, Mark Jax, Bernard Hepton, Kenneth Cranham, Angela Pleasence, Rachel Kempson; *D:* Clive Donner; *W:* Chris Bryant; *M:* Nick Bicat.

Stealing Home 🦴🦴 1988 (PG-13) A washed-up baseball player learns his former babysitter (who was also his first love and inspiration), has committed suicide. Their dysfunctional relationship is told through flashbacks as Foster's superb performance steals the show in this quiet sleeper. 98m/C VHS, DVD. Mark Harmon, Jodie Foster, William McNamara, Blair Brown, Harold Ramis, Jonathan Silverman, John Shea, Helen Hunt, Richard Jenkins, Ted Ross, Thatcher Goodwin, Yvette Croskey; *D:* Steven Kampmann, Will Aldis; *W:* Steven Kampmann, Will Aldis; *M:* David Foster.

Stealing Sinatra 🦴🦴½ 2004 (R) Telling of the screwy but true details behind the 1963 botched kidnapping of Frank Sinatra Jr. by three amateurs trying to score some quick dough from his renowned father, Frank Sinatra. 95m/C VHS, DVD. David Arquette, William H. Macy, Ryan Browning, Sam McMurray, Thomas Ian Nicholas, Gillian Barber, Colin Cunningham, Brandy Hedrick, Catherine Barroll, Matthew Bennett, Johnathan Brownlee, Ron Chartier, Michael Coristine; *D:* Ron Underwood; *W:* Howard Korder; *C:* Brian Pearson; *M:* John Powell, James McGee Smith. TV

Stealth 🦴½ 2005 (PG-13) Dumb, loud, mindless entertainment category. Three elite Navy pilots (Lucas, Biel, Foxx)—who all look really good in their dress whites—are chosen to test the latest stealth aircraft, with a fourth jet as wingman. This is a pilot-less craft controlled by an artificial intelligence known as EDI. Naturally, EDI goes haywire and must be stopped by those puny humans. Director Cohen likes action, and the actors are just along for the ride. 121m/C DVD, Blu-ray Disc, UMD. US Josh(ua) Lucas, Jamie Foxx, Jessica Biel, Sam Shepard, Joe Morton, Richard Roxburgh, Ian Bliss, Nicholas Hammond, Ebon Moss-Bachrach; *D:* Rob Cohen; *W:* W.D. Richter; *C:* Dean Semler; *M:* BT (Brian Transeau); *V:* Wentworth Miller.

Stealth Fighter 🦴½ 1999 (R) Naval pilot Owen Turner (Ice-T) fakes his own death and goes to work for the bad guys in South America. Then he steals a stealth fighter from a U.S. military base and starts bombing foreign military installations. So naval officer Ryan Mitchell (Mandylor) is sent to stop him. Wynorski directed under the pseudonym "Jay Andrews." 87m/C VHS, DVD. Ice-T, Costas Mandylor, Ernie Hudson, Erika Eleniak, Andrew Divoff, John Enos, Steve Eastin; *D:* Jim Wynorski; *W:* Lanny Juliano; *C:* J.E. Bash; *M:* K. Alexander (Alex) Wilkinson. VIDEO

Steam: A Turkish Bath 🦴🦴🦴 *Hamam: Il Bagno Turco* 1996 Francesco (Gassman) is a young Italian businessman married to the equally busy Marta (c'Aloja) and living a fashionable life in Rome. When he learns an aunt has left him a building in Istanbul, he leaves to check out his inheritance. What Francesco discovers is that he now possesses a traditional Turkish bath and that the family his aunt lived with and employed is eager for him to stay. Mysterious Istanbul begins to work its magic as does Francesco's unexpected (and mutual) growing attraction to the family's son, Mehmet (Gunsur). Of course, Marta does eventually show up. Italian and Turkish with subtitles. 96m/C VHS, DVD, TU IT SP Alessandro Gassman, Francesca D'Aloja, Carlo Cecchi, Mehmet Gunsur, Serif Sezer, Basak Kockukaya, Halil Ergun, Alberto Molinari; *D:* Ferzan Ozpetek; *W:* Ferzan Ozpetek, Stefano Tunmolini; *C:* Pasquale Mari; *M:* Aldo De Scalzi.

Steamboat Bill, Jr. 🦴🦴🦴½ 1928 City-educated student returns to his small home-town and his father's Mississippi river boat, where he's an embarrassment to dad. But bond they do, to ward off the owner of a rival riverboat, whose daughter Keaton falls for. Engaging look at small-town life and the usual wonderful Keaton antics, including braving the big tornado. 75m/B VHS, DVD. Buster Keaton, Ernest Torrence, Marion Byron, Tom Lewis; *D:* Charles Reisner; *W:* Carl Harbaugh; *C:* Bert Haines, Devereaux Jennings.

Steamboat Round the Bend 🦴🦴½ 1935 Snake oil salesman Dr. John Pearly (Rogers) is traveling to meet his nephew Duke (McGuire) so they can go into the riverboat business together. But Duke has been falsely convicted of murder and will hang unless Pearly and Duke's girlfriend Fleety Belle (Shirley) can find the only witness to the crime. A big steamboat race is part of the plot. The last film that Rogers shot, although "In Old Kentucky" was released after. 81m/B DVD. Will Rogers, Anne Shirley, John McGuire, Eugene Pallette, Berton Churchill, Stepin Fetchit, Francis Ford, Irvin S. Cobb, Roger Imhof, Hobart Bosworth, Raymond Hatton; *D:* John Ford; *W:* Lamar Trotti, Dudley Nicholas; *C:* George Schneiderman; *M:* Samuel Kayin.

Steamboy 🦴🦴 2005 (PG-13) Generational conflict explodes into epic machine war above the streets of an alternate Victorian London. It all revolves around something called the steamball, a dangerous revolutionary new form of power created by a father-son pair of mad scientists (Stewart and Molina) who battle for the loyalty of its grandson (Paquin) and the proper use of their invention. Overwrought, over-thought anime spectacle with some absolutely mind-blowing visuals from the mind of "Akira" creator Otomo. Could have benefited from some wise surgical editing. Original and English language versions available. 125m/C DVD, Blu-ray Disc, UMD. JP Katsuhiro Otomo; *M:* Steve Jablonsky; *V:* Anne Suzuki, Masane Tsukayama, Katsuo Nakamura, Manami Konishi, Kiyoshi Kobayashi, Susumu Terajima, Anna Paquin, Alfred Molina, Patrick Stewart, Kari Wahlgren, Robin Atkin Downes, David Lee.

Steaming 🦴🦴 1986 (R) Six women get together in a London bathhouse and review their various troubles with men. Unfortunate adaptation of the good play by Neil Dunn. Where are the laughs—and what happened to the dramatic tension? The last film of Dors and director Losey. 102m/C VHS, GB Vanessa Redgrave, Sarah Miles, Diana Dors; *D:* Joseph Losey.

Steel 🦴🦴 *Look Down and Die, Men of Steel* 1980 (R) Construction workers on a mammoth skyscraper face insurmountable odds and strong opposition. Will they finish their building? Worth watching, if you don't have anything else to do. 100m/C VHS. Lee Majors, Jennifer O'Neill, Art Carney, George Kennedy, Harris Yulin, Terry Kiser, Richard Lynch, Roger E. Mosley, Albert Salmi, R.G. Armstrong; *D:* Steve Carver; *W:* Leigh Chapman; *M:* Michel Colombier.

Steel 🦴½ 1997 (PG-13) Metal specialist John Henry Irons (O'Nea) has designed a top-secret military weapon that falls into the hands of a street gang. Donning a suit of armor he designed, he becomes super hero Steel and sets out to end the reign of former childhood-chum-turned super villain Burke (Nelson). Adaptation of popular DC comic keeps target audience in mind with lots of action and plenty of humor. Shaq proves once again that as an actor he's a pretty good basketball player. 97m/C VHS, DVD. Shaquille O'Neal, Judd Nelson, Annabeth Gish, Richard Roundtree, Irma P. Hall, Charles Napier, Kerrie Keane, Hill Harper, Thom Barry; *D:* Kenneth Johnson; *W:* Kenneth Johnson; *C:* Mark Irwin; *M:* Mervyn Warren.

Steel and Lace 🦴🦴 1990 (R) Davison is the scientist brother of a classical pianist who commits suicide after being raped. He revives her as a cyborg which promptly sets out to enact its revenge. Depressingly, morbid sci-fi. 92m/C VHS. Bruce Davison, Clare Wren, Stacy Haiduk, David Naughton, David Lander; *D:* Ernest Farino; *W:* Joseph Dougherty, Dave Edison; *C:* Thomas Callaway.

Steel Arena 🦴 1972 (PG) Several real life stunt-car drivers appear in this action-packed film, crammed with spins, jumps, explosions and world-record-breaking, life risking stunts. 99m/C VHS. Dusty Russell, Gene Drew, Buddy Love; *D:* Mark L. Lester.

Steel City 🦴🦴 2006 (R) Blue-collar angst and family dysfunction in a low-key drama. Alcoholic Carl (Heard) abandoned his family long ago and is presently jailed for vehicular homicide. Younger son PJ (Guiry) is trying to man up but he's scared and confused and tends to make bad choices while his repentant father offers advice during prison visits and conceals a secret. Debut feature from Jun was shot in his Alton, Illinois hometown. 95m/C DVD. John Heard, Tom Guiry, America Ferrera, Clayne Crawford, James McDaniel, Laurie Metcalf, Heather McComb, Raymond J. Barry; *D:* Brian Jun; *W:* Brian Jun; *C:* Ryan Samul; *M:* Mark Geary.

The Steel Claw 🦴🦴 1961 One-handed ex-Marine Montgomery organizes guerilla forces against the Japanese in the Philippines in WWII. Good location shooting and plenty of action. 95m/C VHS. George Montgomery, Charito Luna, Mario Barri; *D:* George Montgomery.

Steel Cowboy 🦴🦴 1978 With his marriage, sanity, and livelihood on the line, an independent trucker agrees to haul a hot herd of stolen steers. Passable made-for-TV macho adventure. 100m/C VHS. James Brolin, Rip Torn, Jennifer Warren, Strother Martin, Melanie Griffith, Lou Frizzell; *D:* Harvey Laidman; *M:* Charles Bernstein.

Steel Dawn 🦴🦴½ 1987 (R) Another "Mad Max" clone. A leather-clad warrior wields his sword over lots of presumably post-apocalyptic desert terrain. Swayze stars with his real-life wife Niemi, in unfortunate follow-up to "Dirty Dancing". 90m/C VHS, DVD. Patrick Swayze, Lisa Niemi, Christopher Neame, Brett Hool, Brion James, Anthony Zerbe; *D:* Lance Hool; *W:* Doug Lefler; *C:* Jiri (George) Tirl; *M:* Brian May.

Steel Frontier 🦴🦴 1994 (R) Post-apocalypse actioner finds a group of survivors trying to make a new life in a town they call New Hope. But then a group of bandit soldiers take over—until a lone hero comes along to save the day. 94m/C VHS, DVD. Joe Lara, Brion James, Bo Svenson, Stacie Foster; *D:* Paul G. Volk, Jacobsen Hart.

The Steel Helmet 🦴🦴🦴½ 1951 Hurriedly made Korean War drama stands as a top-notch war film. Brooding and dark, Gis don't save the world for democracy or rescue POWs; they simply do their best to survive a horrifying situation. Pointless death, confused loyalties and cynicism abound in writer-director Fuller's scathing comment on the madness of war. Screenplay by R. Harling, based on lives. 84m/B VHS. Gene Evans, Robert Hutton, Steve Brodie, William Chun, James Edwards, Richard Loo, Harold Fong, Neyle Morrow, Sid Melton, Richard Monahan, Lynn Stalmaster; *D:* Samuel Fuller; *C:* Ernest Miller; *M:* Paul Dunlap.

Steel Magnolias 🦴🦴🦴 1989 (PG) Shelby Eatenton (Roberts) is a young woman stricken with severe diabetes who chooses to live her life to the fullest despite her bad health. Much of the action centers around a Louisiana beauty shop (run by Parton) where the women get together to discuss the goings-on of their lives. Screenplay by R. Harling, based on his partially autobiographical play. Sweet, poignant, and often hilarious, yet just as bitter divorcee; Parton is sexy and fun as the hairdresser; but Field and Roberts (as mother and daughter) go off the deep end and make it all entirely too weepy. 118m/C VHS, DVD. Sally Field, Dolly Parton, Shirley MacLaine, Daryl Hannah, Olympia Dukakis, Julia Roberts, Tom Skerritt, Sam Shepard, Dylan McDermott, Kevin J. O'Connor, Bill McCutcheon, Ann Wedgeworth, Janine Turner; *D:* Herbert Ross; *W:* Robert Harling; *C:* John A. Alonzo; *M:* Georges Delerue. Golden Globes '90: Support. Actress (Roberts).

Steel Sharks 🦴🦴 1997 (R) A military coup in Iran finds chemical weapons expert Cr. Van Tasset (Livingston) kidnapped by revolutionaries. Members of an elite squad of Navy SEALs are sent to rescue him, aided by a U.S. sub. But the good guys wind up prisoners on an Iranian sub and a deadly game of underwater hide-and-seek follows. 94m/C VHS, DVD. Billy Dee Williams, Gary Busey, Tim Loundos, Barry Livingston, Billy Warlock, Gary Poindexter, Tim Abell, Robert Miranda, David Roberson, Matthew St. Patrick; *D:* Rodney McDonald; *W:* Rodney McDonald, William Martell; *C:* Bryan Greenberg; *M:* David Lawrence. VIDEO

Steel Toes 🦴🦴 2006 (R) Jewish liberal lawyer Danny Dunkleman (Strathairn) becomes the court-appointed attorney for skinhead Mike Downey (Walker), who's confessed to murdering an East Indian immigrant in a Montreal alley. Danny is trying to find Michael a defense end make him confront what he has done, without much cooperation. Lots of jailhouse talk gets an extra half a bone for Strathairn's compelling performance. 9cm/

c DVD. **CA** Marina Orsini, David Strathairn, Andrew W. Walker, Ivan Smith; **D:** David Gow, Mark Adam; **C:** Mark Adam; **M:** Benoit Groulx.

Steele Justice ♂ 1987 (R) A tough 'Nam vet takes on the whole Vietnamese Mafia in Southern California after his friend is murdered. One of those headscratchers: Should I laugh, or be offended? **96m/C VHS.** Martin Kove, Sela Ward, Ronny Cox, Bernie Casey, Joseph Campanella, Sarah Douglas; **D:** Robert Boris; **W:** Robert Boris.

Steele's Law ♂♂ 1991 (R) A loner cop is forced to take the law into his own hands in order to track down an insane international assassin. **90m/C VHS, DVD.** Fred Williamson, Bo Svenson, Doran Ingram, Phyllis Cicero; **D:** Fred Williamson; **W:** Charles Eric Johnson; **C:** David Blood; **M:** Mike Logan.

Steelyard Blues ♂♂½ 1973 (PG) A motley-crew comedy about a wacky gang that tries to steal an abandoned WW II airplane. Zany pranks abound. Technically flawed direction from Myerson mars a potentially hilarious story. **93m/C VHS, DVD.** Jane Fonda, Donald Sutherland, Peter Boyle, Howard Hesseman, John Savage, Garry Goodrow; **D:** Alan Myerson; **W:** David S. Ward; **M:** David Shire.

Stella ♂♂½ 1955 Mercouri's film debut has her as a free-spirited bar singer who gets involved in a tragic romantic triangle with a middle-class writer and a local football hero. Melodramatic but Mercouri's earthy joie de vivre is already apparent. In Greek with English subtitles. **94m/B VHS, DVD. GR** Melina Mercouri, Yiorgo Fountas, Alekos Alexandrikis, Sophia Vembo; **D:** Michael Cacoyannis; **W:** Michael Cacoyannis; **C:** Costa Theodorides; **M:** Manos Hadjidakis.

Stella ♂♂ 1989 (PG-13) Anachronistic remake update of "Stella Dallas" casts Midler as a single mother who sacrifices everything to give her daughter a better life. Barbara Stanwyck did it much better in 1937. Based on Olive Higgins Prouty's novel. **106m/C VHS, DVD.** Bette Midler, Trini Alvarado, Marsha Mason; **D:** John Erman; **W:** Robert Getchell; **C:** Billy Williams.

Stella Dallas ♂♂♂ 1937 Uneducated Stella (Stanwyck) lets go of her daughter (Shirley) she loves when she realizes the girl more advantages. What could be sentimental turns out believable and worthwhile under Vidor's steady hand. Stanwyck never makes a wrong move. From a 1923 novel by Olive Higgins Prouty. Remade in 1989 as "Stella," starring Bette Midler. **106m/B VHS, DVD.** Barbara O'Neil, Tim Holt, Barbara Stanwyck, Anne Shirley, John Boles, Alan Hale, Marjorie Main; **D:** King Vidor; **W:** Sarah Y. Mason, Victor Heerman; **C:** Rudolph Mate; **M:** Alfred Newman.

Stella Does Tricks ♂♂ 1996 Stella (Macdonald) is a teen runaway, working as a prostitute in London for pimp Mr. Peters (Bolam). She was abused by her dad (Stewart) and has revenge fantasies—some of which she takes out on clients, which leads to punishment by her boss. She briefly gets free of Peters and gets a legit job, but Stella has also become involved with junkie Eddie (Matheson) and his drug needs have him betraying Stella. No Cinderella stories here—Stella's life is bleak and violent, with Macdonald giving a powerhouse performance. **97m/C VHS, DVD. GB** Kelly Macdonald, James Bolam, Ewan Stewart, Hans Matheson, Andy Serkis, Paul Chahidi; **D:** Coky Giedroyc; **W:** A.L. Kennedy; **C:** Barry Ackroyd; **M:** Nick Bicat.

Stella Maris ♂♂♂ 1918 Pickford inspiringly plays two difficult roles. As Stella Maris, she's a wealthy orphaned cripple who's in love with the married John Risca (Tearle), while Unity Blake (Pickford's second role). When Unity is eventually rescued by John, she also falls in love with him. Brimming with the tragic consequences of love. **100m/B VHS, DVD.** Mary Pickford, Conway Tearle, Camille Ankewich, Ida Waterman, Herbert Standing; **D:** Marshall Neilan; **W:** Frances Marion; **C:** Walter Stradling.

The Stendahl Syndrome ♂♂ *La Sindrome di Stendhal* 1995 Psycho serial-killer thriller about a Rome police detective, Anna (Argento), who has an extreme hallucinatory reaction to artwork after his syndrome). While visiting an art gallery, she collapses and is assisted by Alfredo (Kretschmann), who turns out to be the very rapist-killer whom she's hunting. Anna escapes from him once (after being tortured) but is captured again. However, she manages to fight back in ways squeamish viewers may want to avoid watching. Inspired by Graziella Magherini's novel "La Sindrome di Stendhal." **118m/C VHS, DVD. IT** Asia Argento, Thomas Kretschmann, Marco Leonardi, Luigi Diberti, Paolo Bonacelli, John Quentin; **D:** Dario Argento; **W:** Dario Argento; **C:** Giuseppe Rotunno; **M:** Ennio Morricone.

Step Brothers ♂♂½ 2008 Ferrell, Reilly, and director McKay re-team (after 2006's "Talladega Nights") for what we hope is a yuk fest. Middle-aged Brennan Huff (Ferrell) is still living with his mother, Nancy (Steenburgen). Equally useless Dale Doback (Reilly) lives with dad, Robert (Jenkins). After Nancy and Robert marry, they inform the competitive step-siblings that they must get jobs and move out, causing the immature duo to form an unlikely bond. Not yet reviewed. **?m/C** Will Ferrell, John C. Reilly, Mary Steenburgen, Richard Jenkins, Adam Scott, Kathryn Hahn; **D:** Adam McKay; **W:** Will Ferrell, Adam McKay; **C:** Oliver Wood.

Step Into Liquid ♂♂♂ 2003 Brown is the son of surf-documentary pioneer Bruce "Endless Summer" Brown, so he knows his way around visuals. Brown takes on the positive energy of surfing around the world with the sport's top competitors, including Laird Hamilton, Kelly Slater, and Taj Burrow, as well as a number of ordinary folks who just like to catch the wave. **87m/C DVD, Blu-ray Disc. US D:** Dana Brown; **W:** Dana Brown; **C:** John-Paul Beeghly; **M:** Richard Gibbs; **Nar:** Dana Brown.

Step Lively ♂♂½ 1944 A convoluted plot doesn't slow down the enjoyment of this musical comedy. Naive Glen (Sinatra) writes a dramatic play and sends it—along with his life savings—to slick NY producer Miller (Murphy). When he shows up to see how things are progressing, Glen learns that Miller has used his dough to help finance a new musical, so Miller has showgirl Christine (DeHaven) keep Glen occupied. But the show is in trouble without a male lead—and then Miller hears Glen sing. And the rest is showbiz, folks. ♫Some Other Time; As Long As There's Been Music; Where Does Love Begin?; Come Out, Come Out, Wherever You Are; Why Must There Be an Opening Song; And Then You Kissed Me; Ask the Madame. **88m/B DVD.** Frank Sinatra, George Murphy, Adolphe Menjou, Walter Slezak, Anne Jeffreys, Eugene Pallette, Gloria DeHaven; **D:** Tim Whelan; **W:** Peter Milne, Warren Duff; **C:** Robert De Grasse.

Step Up ♂♂ 2006 (PG-13) Tyler Gage (Tatum) is from the wrong side of the Baltimore line. He's assigned to do community service at the elite Maryland School of the Arts after he helps trash their auditorium. Beautiful ballet dancer Nora (Dewan) needs a partner for an important recital and, with her encouragement, Ty discovers his inner Fred Astaire. Dance sequences are excellent, and the cast is appropriately beautiful, but you've seen the rest of the plot before, especially if you've seen writer Adler's "Save the Last Dance." **88m/C DVD. US** Channing Tatum, Rachel Griffiths, Damaine Radcliff, Jenna Dewan, Dwight "Heavy D" Myers, De'Shawn Washington, Josh Henderson, Deirdre Lovejoy; **D:** Anne Fletcher; **W:** Duane Adler, Melissa Rosenberg; **C:** Michael Seresin; **M:** Aaron Zigman.

The Stepdaughter ♂♂½ 2000 (R) After years of abuse in foster homes, Susan (Roth) wants to strike back at the birth mother who abandoned her. She tracks down the now happily married woman (Pickett), gets a job on the ranch where she lives, and plans her next deadly move. **92m/C VHS, DVD.** Andrea Roth, Lisa Dean Ryan, Jaimz Woolvett, Cindy Pickett, Gary

Hudson, Gil Gerard, Matt Farnsworth, Lee Dawson; **D:** Peter Paul Liapis; **W:** Richard Dana; **C:** Maximo Munzi. **VIDEO**

The Stepfather ♂♂♂ 1987 (R) Creepy thriller about a seemingly ordinary stepfather who is actually a homicidal maniac searching for the "perfect family." An independently produced sleeper tightly directed and well written. Followed by two inferior sequels. **89m/C VHS.** Terry O'Quinn, Shelley Hack, Jill Schoelen, Stephen Shellen, Charles Lanyer, Stephen E. Miller; **D:** Joseph Ruben; **W:** Donald E. Westlake; **C:** John Lindley; **M:** Patrick Moraz.

Stepfather 2: Make Room for Daddy ♂½ 1989 (R) A poor sequel to the suspenseful sleeper, wherein the psychotic family man escapes from an asylum and woos another suburban family, murdering anyone who may suspect his true identity. Followed by yet another sequel. **93m/C VHS, DVD.** Terry O'Quinn, Meg Foster, Caroline Williams, Jonathan Brandis, Henry Brown, Mitchall Laurance; **D:** Jeff Burr; **W:** John P. Auerbach; **C:** Jacek Laskus.

Stepfather 3: Father's Day ♂ 1992 (R) The father from Hell is back! Escaping from the loony bin with a surgically altered face, the stepfather settles in a small town and gets a job at a nursery (he's a favorite gardening tool fast becomes the mulch machine, and soon locals are fertilizing the garden. Well below the original, but it may please fans of this genre. **110m/C VHS.** Robert Wightman, Priscilla Barnes, Season Hubley; **D:** Guy Magar; **C:** Alan Caso.

The Stepford Wives ♂♂♂ 1975 Joanna (Ross) and husband Walter (Masterson) move from bustling Manhattan to the supposedly idyllic Connecticut town of Stepford. Joanna gets suspicious when she notices all the wives are strangely content and subservient and when she meets fellow newcomer, Bobby (Prentiss), they decide to investigate. Creepy adaptation of the Ira Levin novel. **115m/C VHS, DVD.** Katharine Ross, Paula Prentiss, Peter Masterson, Nanette Newman, Patrick O'Neal, Tina Louise, Dee Wallace Stone, William Prince, Mary Stuart Masterson, Carol Rossen; **D:** Bryan Forbes; **W:** William Goldman; **C:** Owen Roizman; **M:** Michael Small.

The Stepford Wives ♂♂½ 2004 (PG-13) Remake of the spooky 70's classic. Joanna Eberhart (Kidman) is a successful television network executive fired after a reality show disaster. Joanna, her husband Walter (Broderick) and their family move to the seemingly perfect Connecticut town of Stepford. Strangely enough, the impeccably perfect bombshell women of Stepford have no other interests than housecleaning and making their rat-nerdy-looking husbands happy. Trades eerie suspense of the original for campy comedy. While there are some well placed barbs and one-liners, plot holds no surprises and loses the satirical edge of the source material. Walker, as the community leader who holds the secret to Stepford, and Midler as a fellow outsider, do well in their respective roles. **93m/C DVD. US** Nicole Kidman, Matthew Broderick, Christopher Walken, Glenn Close, Bette Midler, Jon Lovitz, Roger Bart, David Marshall Grant, Faith Hill; **D:** Frank Oz; **W:** Paul Rudnick; **C:** Rob Hahn; **M:** David Arnold.

Stephanie Daley ♂♂ 2006 (R) Disturbing talky drama with flashbacks depicting what happened to a pregnant teen. 16-year-old Stephanie (Tamblyn) gives birth on a school ski trip and is brought up on criminal charges when the baby is found dead. She claims not to have known she was pregnant and that the infant was stillborn. Forensic psychologist Lydie Crane (Swinton) is called in to examine Stephanie, but the situation may be too close for Lydie to be objective. She is pregnant again after suffering a stillbirth herself and both Lydie and Stephanie have a lot of unresolved feelings. Strong performances by both leads in a story with no easy answers. **91m/C DVD. US** Amber Tamblyn, Tilda Swinton, Timothy Hutton, Denis O'Hare, Jim Gaffigan, Deirdre O'Connell, Melissa Leo, Halley Feiffer, Kel O'Neill; **D:** Hilary Brougher; **W:** Hilary Brougher; **C:** David Rush Morrison; **M:** David Mansfield.

Stephano Quantestorie ♂♂ 1993 Walter Mitty-ish story about daydreaming cop Stephano (Nichetti) who falls for the prime suspect in a robbery he's investigating. He escapes his conflicting feelings by imagining himself living other lives—as a math professor, airline pilot, saxophone player, and thief, but soon all these alter ego are intruding into his work. Italian with subtitles. **90m/C VHS. IT** Maurizio Nichetti; **D:** Maurizio Nichetti; **W:** Maurizio Nichetti.

Stephen King's Golden Years ♂½ *Golden Years* 1991 Stephen King creates a chilling vision of scientific progress gone awry in this shocking techno-thriller. After being accidentally exposed to exotic chemicals in a lab explosion, an aging janitor undergoes an extraordinary transformation and the government will sacrifice anything to learn more about it. **232m/C VHS, DVD.** Keith Szarabajka, Frances Sternhagen, Ed Lauter, R.D. Call, Stephen King, Felicity Huffman, Stephen (Steve) Root; **D:** Kenneth Fink, Stephen Tolkin, Allen Coulter; **M:** Michael G. Gerrick; **W:** Stephen King, Josef Anderson. **TV**

Stephen King's It ♂♂½ 1990 A group of small town children, who were terrorized by an evil force in their youth, are traumatized again some 30 years later, when they learn a new series of child murders occurred in their Eastern home town. The adults, who now all have successful and diverse careers, must come to terms with the terrible secret they share, as "IT" has returned to wreak havoc in their New England home town. Based on horror master King's bestselling novel of the same name. **193m/C VHS, DVD.** Tim Reid, Richard Thomas, John Ritter, Annette O'Toole, Richard Masur, Dennis Christopher, Harry Anderson, Olivia Hussey, Tim Curry, Jonathan Brandis, Michael Cole; **D:** Tommy Lee Wallace; **W:** Stephen King. **TV**

Stephen King's Rose Red ♂♂ *Rose Red* 2002 (PG-13) The fictional memoir "The Diary of Ellen Rimbauer" was released shortly before the miniseries aired, rather than the movie being based on an already successful novel. The "Diary's" editor, Dr. Joyce Reardon (Travis), is a college professor looking for the supernatural inside Rose Red, a decaying mansion known for its strange history. She gathers together various paranormals, including autistic teenager Annie (Brown) who has strong telekinetic powers. The house begins to feed off Annie's energy and all hell breaks loose. Last role for Dukes (as Joyce's nemesis Professor Miller) who died during filming. **254m/C VHS, DVD.** Nancy Travis, Kimberly J. Brown, Matt Keeslar, David Dukes, Julian Sands, Judith Ivey, Melanie Lynskey, Matt Ross, Kevin Tighe, Julia Campbell, Jimmi Simpson; **D:** Craig R. Baxley; **W:** Stephen King; **C:** David Connell; **M:** Gary Chang. **TV**

Stephen King's The Langoliers ♂♂½ *The Langoliers* 1995 (PG-13) Bloated variation of "Ten Little Indians" finds 10 airline passengers dozing off on their L.A.-to-Boston flight and awakening to find their fellow passengers and the crew have vanished. Of course, one passenger (Morse) is a pilot and he gets them to Bangor, Maine (where the miniseries was filmed), only to discover the airport is deserted and very weird things are going on. Oh yeah, the "langoliers" look like flying cannonballs with piranha teeth and have something to do with neurotic Pinchot's character. Not that you'll care much. **180m/C VHS, DVD.** David Morse, Bronson Pinchot, Patricia Wettig, Dean Stockwell, Kate Maberly, Christopher Collet, Kimber Riddle, Mark Lindsay Chapman, Frankie Faison, Baxter Harris, Stephen King, Tom Holland; **D:** Tom Holland; **C:** Paul Maibaum; **M:** Vladimir Horunzhy. **TV**

Stephen King's The Night Flier ♂♂ *The Night Flier* 1996 (R) Portrays blood-sucking beings that prey upon the weakness of mortal men in order to survive. And besides tabloid journalists, there's vampires in it, too! Richard Dees (Ferrer) is a reporter/photographer for a National Enquirer-like paper who is not above staging lurid photos to grab Page

One. His editor pits him in a contest with rookie paparazzo Katherine (Entwistle) for a story about a murderer who wears a black cape and tricorn hat, flies into small airports in a sinister black plane. Dees follows the killer's trail in his own plane, stopping to ruthlessly grill his victims' blood. Genuinely spooky show-down will leave only one monster stand-ing. Who is it? Inquiring minds want to know. **97m/C VHS, DVD.** Michael H. Moss, Migu-el Ferrer, Julie Entwisle, Dan Monahan, John Ben-nes, Beverly Skinner, Rob Wilds, Richard Olsen, Elizabeth McCormick; **D:** Mark Pavia; **W:** Mark Pa-via, Jack O'Donnell; **C:** David Connell; **M:** Brian Keane. **CABLE**

Stephen King's The Stand 🐾🐾½ *The Stand* 1994

Ghoulish made for TV adaptation of the King novel about a superflu/plague that decimates the U.S. population. The few survivors are soon divided into two camps—those dreaming of a godly old black woman known as Mother Abigail and others of the satanic Randall Flagg, the Walkin' Dude. Boulder, Colorado (where King was living when he wrote the novel) serves as head-quarters for Abigail's brood while Las Vegas (where else) is Flagg territory. It all comes down to a battle of good vs. evil, with the future of mankind at stake. Reli-gious allegory can get tedious but it's a varied cast with some scenes not for those with queasy stomachs. On four cas-settes. **360m/C VHS, DVD.** Jamey Sheridan, Ruby Dee, Gary Sinise, Molly Ringwald, Miguel Ferrer, Laura San Giacomo, Rob Lowe, Adam Storke, Matt Frewer, Corin "Corky" Nemec, Ray Walston, Bill Fagerbakke, Ossie Davis, Shawnee Smith, Rick Aviles, John (Joe Bob Briggs) Bloom; **D:** Mick Garris; **W:** Stephen King; **C:** Edward Pei; **M:** W.G. Snuffy Walden. **TV**

Stephen King's The Storm of the Century 🐾🐾½ *Storm of the Cen-tury* 1999 (PG-13)

Little Tall Island, Maine, is under siege—and not just from the most ferocious storm the island has seen in years. No, there's madness and murder afoot in the form of demonic stranger An-dre Linoge (Feore). He seems to know ev-eryone's secrets but what he wants is any-body's guess. Now it's up to amiable con-stable Michael Anderson (Daly) to control the rising hystera and come up with a so-lution. **247m/C VHS, DVD.** Colm Feore, Timothy Daly, Debrah Farentino, Casey Siemaszko, Jeffrey DeMunn, Richard Blackburn; **D:** Craig R. Baxley; **W:** Stephen King; **C:** David Connell; **M:** Gary C-ang. **TV**

Stephen King's The Tommyknockers 🐾🐾 *The Tom-myknockers* 1993 (R)

Another of King's creepy tales, adapted for TV. Bobbi (Hel-genberger) and Gard (Smits) live in the small town of Haven, Maine (actually filmed on New Zealand's North Island). She's an aspiring writer; he's a fading poet with a drinking problem and a metal plate in his head (this is important). Walking in the woods, Bobbi stumbles over a long-buried spaceship which begins to take possession of the townspeople—their eyes shine green, their teeth fall out, and they act out their (often violent) fanta-sies—all but Gard. The whole thing's more silly than scary. The title comes from an old children's rhyme. **120m/C VHS, DVD.** Jim-my Smits, Marg Helgenberger, Joanna Cassidy, E.G. Marshall, Traci Lords, John Ashton, Allyce Beasley, Cliff DeYoung, Robert Carradine, Leon Woods, Paul McIver; **D:** John Power; **W:** Lawrence D. Cohen; **M:** Christopher Franke. **TV**

Stephen King's Thinner 🐾🐾 *Thinner* 1996 (R)

Holland takes all the meat out of this supernatural horror by turning it into a formulaic pursuit-of-justice bore. Porcine lawyer Billy Halleck (Burke) acci-dentally hits a gypsy with his car and is cursed with a case of perpetual weight loss. Conveniently for Billy, the client he has just gotten an acquittal for is local monster Richie "The Hammer" Ginelli (Mantegna) who is now determined to save him. Ponderous plot and lackluster-looking latex make his requisite cameo as

Stephen King's The Tommyknockers

knockers 1993 (R)...

Steppenwolf 🐾🐾½ 1974 (PG)

Stat-ic, enigmatic film version of the famous Herman Hesse novel about a brooding writer searching for meaning and self-worth. Interesting to watch, but the offbeat novel doesn't translate to the screen; leaves you flat. **105m/C VHS, DVD. SI** Max von Sydow, Dominique Sanda, Pierre Clementi, Carla Romanelli, Roy Bosier; **D:** Fred Haines; **W:** Fred Haines. **C:** Tomislav Pinter. **M:** George Gruntz.

Stepping Out 🐾🐾½ 1991 (PG)

Minnelli stars as a would-be Broadway dancer who gives tap dancing lessons in an old church to an assortment of offbeat and interesting characters. When the troupe is asked to perform for a local char-ity. A warm and touching ensemble piece that avoids over-sentimentalizing and uti-lizes its cast to best advantage. **113m/C VHS.** Liza Minnelli, Shelley Winters, Bill Irwin, Ellen Greene, Julie Walters, Robyn Stevan, Jane Kra-kowski, Sheila McCarthy, Andrea Martin, Carol Woods, Nora Dunn, Eugene Robert Glazer; **D:** Lewis Gilbert; **W:** Richard Harris; **M:** Peter Matz.

Steps from Hell 🐾 1992

Vaid Tempest is an evil immortal in control of a cult of zombie women. He's stolen a sa-cred map that will lead to a gateway which, when opened, will unleash a su-preme evil on the world. Unless the heroic John Clark can find a way to prevent it, of course. **90m/C VHS.** Bernardo Rosa, Rocky Tucker, Ron Odell, Philip Cable, Liz Stoeckel, Steve Quimby, Lisa Lund; **D:** James Tucker; **W:** James Tucker.

The Stepsister 🐾🐾 1997 (PG-13)

Pediatrician Donna Canfield is lured to her death by one of her young patients. When daughter Darcy (Sofer) comes home to console her dad, Dr. Derek (Rachins), she finds her place usurped by the widowed Melinda (Wilson). Married in unseemly haste, the wealthy Derek dies equally quickly, leaving Darcy suspicious of her new stepfamily. **91m/C VHS.** Rena Sofer, Brid-gette Wilson-Sampras, Linda Evans, Alan Rachins; **D:** Matt Dorff; **W:** Matt Dorff; **C:** Laszlo George; **M:** Peter Manning Robinson.

Dr. Bangor (get it, Maine?) Originally pub-lished in 1984 under Bachman's pseudonym Richard Bachman. **92m/C VHS, DVD.** Robert John Burke, Joe Mantegna, Lucinda Jenney, Mi-chael Constantine, Kari Wuhrer, Elizabeth Franz, Joy Lentz, Jeff Ware; **Cameos:** Stephen King; **D:** Tom Holland; **W:** Michael McDowell, Tom Holland; **C:** Kees Van Oostrum; **M:** Daniel Licht.

Stepmom 🐾🐾🐾 1998 (PG-13)

The opening scenes make it hard to like a comed-ic catfight-filled ride. Harris is a divorced dad with two kids, a glamorous new girl-friend (Roberts), whose career seems more important than the kids. Jibes and glares are traded by the two women until mom is stricken with some form of untreat-able terminal cancer. This changes the story from broad comedy to emotional dra-ma as Sarandon must train the younger woman to be the new mom. Columbus seems comfortable with the shift, and manages to keep everything upbeat. The script, penned by five writers, becomes more clichéd as the film goes on, but stays just this side of chick-flick. **124m/C VHS.** Jena Malone, Liam Aiken, Lynn Whitfield, Darrell Larson, Mary Louise Wilson; **D:** Chris Columbus; **W:** Gigi Levangie, Karen Leigh Hopkins, Ronald Bass, Gigi Levangie, Karen Leigh Hopkins; **C:** Donald McAlpine; **M:** John Williams, Natl. Bd. of Review '98. Support; Actor (Harris).

The Stepmother 🐾🐾½ 1972 (PG-13)

A new stepmother is a monster—literally. Doesn't work any better than "My Step-mother Is an Alien." **85m/C VHS, DVD.** Alan Arkin, Robin Riker, Corey Feldman, John Astin, Ami Dolenz, George Gaynes; **D:** Jeremy Stanford.

Stepmonster 🐾🐾 1992 (PG)

Yet another Hitchcock ripoff story involving an evil stepmother. Rey is passable, but there's not much else to recommend this dredge. **100m/C VHS.** Alejandro Rey, John An-derson, Katherine Justice, John David Garfield, Marlene Schmidt, Claudia Jennings, Larry Linville; **D:** Howard (Hikmet) Avedis.

The Stepfather 🐾🐾🐾 1992

A toy tries to convince his father that his new stepmother is a monster—literally. Doesn't work any better than "My Step-mother Is an Alien."

The Stick-Up 🐾 *Mad* 1977

In 1935, a young American traveling in Great Britain is introduced to some rather illegal fun. Rather sorry attempt at romance/comedy/ adventure. **101m/C VHS.** David Soul, Pamela McMyler; **D:** Jeffrey Bloom; **W:** Jeffrey Bloom.

Stickfighter 🐾 1989 (PG)

The op-pressive reign of an evil Spanish ruler of the Philippines is challenged by the world's best stickfighter. **102m/C VHS. PH** Dean Stockwell, Nancy Kwan, Alejandro Rey, Ro-land Dantes; **D:** Luis Nepomuceno.

Stickmen 🐾🐾½ 2001 (R)

Bar owner Dave talks three regulars into entering a pool tournament to get him out of debt. The three pals are more than willing, but their relationship problems keep popping up. Not especially original concept is helped by the chemistry of the buddies and some amusingly quirky subplots. **94m/C VHS, DVD. NZ** Paolo Rotondo, Robbie Magasiva, Scott Wills, Anne Nordhaus, John Leigh, Simone Kes-sel, Emma Rotwell; **W:** Nick War; **D:** Hamish Rothwell.

Sticks 🐾🐾 1998 (R)

Who knew cigars could cause so much trouble? Lenny (Brancato) discovers that an illicit ship-ment of Cuban cigars, the special private label of Castro himself, have been stolen. Maria (Machado) wants to swap the cigars for weapons to help liberate Cuba while

Stewardess School 🐾 *WOOF!* 1986

(R) Airline spoof aims at wackiness, but misses the runway. Generic title betrays probable badness which turns out to be all too real. An utter woofer. **84m/C VHS.** San-dahl Bergman, Corinne Bohrer; **D:** Ken Blancato. **to:** **W:** Ken Blancato; **M:** Steve Doff.

Stick 🐾🐾 1985 (R)

Ex-con Stick (Reynolds) walked away from a promising gymnastics career and into trouble. Thanks to her latest run-in with the law. Haley is sentenced to attend a gymnastics academy run by gruff coach Burt Vickerman (Bridges). The other girls dislike her attitude, but training and com-petition bring them closer as Haley to-gether did the similarly girl-powered Bendinger did the similarly girl-powered cheerleading comedy "Bring It On." **105m/ C DVD. US** Missy Peregrym, Jeff Bridges, Vanes-sa Lengies, John Patrick Amedori, Nikki Soohoo, Maddy Curley, Kellan Lutz, Svetlana Efremova, Mio Drakula, Jon(athan) Gries, Gia Carides, Polly Holliday, Julie Warner, John Kapelos, "arah Paiga'; **Cameos:** Bart Conner; **D:** Jessica Bendinger; **W:** Jessica Bendinger; **C:** Daryn Okada; **M:** Mike Simpson.

Stick It 🐾🐾 2006 (PG-13)

Teenager Haley (Peregrym) walked away from a promising gymnastics career and into trouble. Thanks to her latest run-in with the law. Haley is sentenced to attend a new life for himself in Miami. Lots of drug dealers and guns don't help the interest level in this dull underworld tale. Based upon the Elmore Leonard novel. **109m/C VHS.** Burt Reynolds, Candice Bergen, George Se-gal, Charles Durning, Dar Robinson; **D:** Ken Blanca-to. **W:** Elmore Leonard; **M:** Steve Dorff.

Stepsisters *WOOF!* 1974

Murderous double-crosses occur among a pilot, his wife, and her sister. **75m/C VHS.** Hal Fletcher, Sharyn Talbert, Bond Gideon; **D:** Perry Tong; **W:** Perry Tong; **M:** Sandy Pinkard

The Sterile Cuckoo 🐾🐾🐾 *Pook-ie* 1969 (PG)

An aggressive co-ed pursues a shy freshman who seems to embody her romantic ideal. Minnelli's performance is outstanding; Burton as the naive young man is also fine. Pakula's splendid first directing job. **108m/C VHS.** Liza Minnelli, Wen-dell Burton, Tim McIntire; **D:** Alan J. Pakula; **W:** Alvin Sargent; **C:** Milton Krasner.

Stevie 🐾🐾 1978

Jackson brings her flawless skill to the role of British poet Stevie Smith. Excellent performance from Washbourne as Stevie's spinster aunt. Hugh Whitemore stage play is helped greatly by good performances, but is too talky and, frankly, rather dull and self-ab-sorbed. **102m/C VHS, GB** Glenda Jackson, Mona Washbourne, Alec McCowen, Trevor Ho-ward; **D:** Robert Enders; **C:** Frederick A. (Freddie) Young, L.A. Film Critics '78. Support. Actress (Washbourne); Montreal World Film Fest. '78: Ac-tress (Jackson); N.Y. Film Critics '78: Support. Ac-tress (Washbourne).

[sixth column]

her boyfriend Mark (Brunsmann) just wants some cold hard cash by selling the merchandise to a private Hollywood club frequented by high rollers. And Lenny sees a chance to make his own score. Too bad the m:os and the feds have their own ideas. **94m/C VHS, DVD.** Lilo Brancato, Leri Rossi, Justina Machado, Keith Brunsmann; **D:** Bret Mayer; **W:** Brett Mayer; **C:** Nils Erickson; **M:** Bill Elliott. **VIDEO**

Sticks and Stones 🐾🐾 1996 (PG-13)

Three high school friends are ha-rassed by the local bully and the situation gets tragically out of control. **96m/C VHS, DVD.** James Spader, Leslie Stefanson, David Keith, John Livingston, Robert Miano, Alf Hun-phreys; **D:** Rowdy Herrington; **W:** Rowdy Herring-ton; **C:** Chris Manley; **M:** David Kitay. **VIDEO**

The Stickup 🐾🐾 2001 (R)

Burned-out cop Parker (Spader) travels to a small resort town and promptly gets involved with the wrong woman (Stefanson), a bank robbery, and the feds. This one is tricker than it seems at first. **97m/C VHS, DVD.** James Spader, Leslie Stefanson, David Matthews, James Urbaniak, Belinda Becker, Ni-cole Zaray, Samantha Buck; **D:** Hilary Brougher; **W:** Hilary Brougher; **C:** Ethan Maass; **M:** Miki Nava-zio.

Sticky Fingers 🐾 1988 (PG-13)

Two female musicians, asked to watch nearly a million bucks in drug money, go on a mega shopping spree. Completely incredi-ble, unlikeable and mean-spirited attempt at zany comedy. **95m/C VHS.** Melanie Mayron, Helen Slater, Eileen Brennan, Carol Kane, Christo-pher Guest, Danitra Vance, Gwen Walles, Stephen McHattie, Shirley Stoler; **D:** Catlin Adams; **W:** Cat-lin Adams, Melanie Mayron; **C:** Gary Thielges; **M:** Gary Chang.

The Sticky Fingers of Time 🐾🐾 1997

New York writer Tuck-er (Mathews) is not having your average day. She goes out for coffee in 1953 and winds up in 1997 (thanks to some kind of atom-bomb mutation in her DNA). Turns out she's not the only time traveler, ac-cording to fellow freak Isaac (Urbaniak). In fact, Isaac was responsible for bringing Tucker (who's a pulp novelist) out of her own time and later to 1997 New York. This one is tricker than it seems at first. Turns everything that happens with chain-smoking aplomb. **81m/B VHS, DVD.** Teruni takes a restorative trip to Italy and later to India, where Aunt Agnes herself is sub-jected to a leering tea-planter. **Horace** (Ustinov). Meanwhile, Edward and Cedric are exploring their own "strange feelings" for one another. As with any film in this genre some gags work better than others. **85m/C VHS, DVD. GB** Samuel West, Robert Por-tal, Georgina Cates, Sean Pertwee, Prunella Scales, Peter Ustinov, Brian Glover, Frank Finlay, Simon Archer; **D:** Gary Sinyor; **W:** Gary Sinyor; **C:** **D:** Gary Sinyor; **M:** David A. Hughes, John Murphy.

Stigma 🐾½ 1973

"Miami Vice" star Thomas (then 23; later to restore his mid-dle name, Mike) is a young doctor who treats a syphilis epidemic in a small town. He's indistinguishable, but better than anything else here. Ever seen close-ups of advanced syphilis? Here's your chance—but it's not pretty. **93m/C VHS.** Phil-ip Michael Thomas, Harlan Cary Poe; **D:** David E. Durston.

Stiff Upper Lips 🐾🐾½ 1996

Spoof of all the upper-crusty British cos-tume dramas replete with sexual innuen-does and enlightening travel to hot climes. Twittish Edward (West) tries to pair off best chum Cedric (Portal) with his virgin sister, Emily (Cates). Only Emily prefers nearly servant, George (Pertwee). Snooty Aunt Agnes 'Scales) decides everyone should take a restorative trip to Italy and later to

Stigmata 🐾½ 1999 (R)

Disappointing horror flick that's campy instead of creepy. Airhead Pittsburgh beautician Frankie (Ar-quette) doesn't even believe in God, so why is she suddenly afflicted with visions and seizures that leave her with Christ-like wounds? Could it have anything to do with the rosary her vacationing mom sent her from Braz'l? When the media picks up the story, the Vatican decides to send Father Kiernan (Byrne), who makes a very sexy priest) to check things out. Lots of hokey mumbo-jumbo ensues. **103m/C VHS, DVD.** Patricia Arquette, Gabriel Byrne, Jonathan Pryce, Portia de Rossi, Patrick Muldoon, Nia Long, Thomas Kopache, Rade Serbedzija, Enrico Colantoni, Dick Latessa, Ann Cusack; **D:** Rupert Wainwright; **W:** Rick Ramage, Tom Lazarus; **C:** Jeffrey L. Kimball; **M:** Elia Cmiral.

Stiletto 1969 (R) Good cast is wasted in this mediocre depiction of the trouble encountered by a general Mafia assassin when he decides to change careers. Based on the usual pulp cheese by Harold Robbins. **101m/C VHS.** Alex Cord, Britt Ekland, Patrick O'Neal, Joseph Wiseman, Barbara McNair, Roy Scheider, M. Emmet Walsh, Raul Julia; **D:** Bernard L. Kowalski; **C:** Jack Priestley.

Stiletto Dance 2001 (R) Anton (Doyle) is the head of the Russian mob in Buffalo, NY, who plans to sell a nuclear device to the Albanians. Undercover cop Kit Adrian (Roberts) has other ideas—before he makes the mistake of falling for a mob enforcer's wife (Laurier). **97m/C VHS, DVD.** Eric Roberts, Shawn Doyle, Brett Porter, Romano Orzari, Lucie Laurier, Yaphet Kotto, Mark Camacho, Justin Louis; **D:** Mario Azzopardi; **W:** Alfonse Ruggiero; **C:** Pierre Jodoin. **CABLE**

Still Breathing 1997 (PG-13) Romance with elements of the fantastical. Fletcher (Fraser) is an eccentric street performer in San Antonio, who dreams of a woman he knows will become his wife (it's a family thing). This turns out to be tough L.A. con woman Rosalyn (Going), whose next sting just happens to involve a Texan. When Fletcher flies to L.A. to find his would-be lady love, they meet cute and have a lot of mistaken assumptions before things come out right. Fraser's character may be wide-eyed but he's no fool and Going displays a needed touch of vulnerability for her manipulative bad girl. **109m/C VHS, DVD.** Brendan Fraser, Joanna Going, Ann Magnuson, Celeste Holm, Lou Rawls, Angus MacFadyen, Paolo Seganti; **D:** James F. Robinson; **C:** John Thomas; **M:** Paul Mills.

Still Crazy 1998 (R) Twenty years after the breakup of his band Strange Fruit, Tony (Rea) is ready to give it a go again. With the Wisbech rock festival beckoning, he rounds up the others: lead singer Ray (Nighy), still a musician living in a mansion; drummer Beano (Spall), a gardener on the run from the tax collector; and singer-bassist Les (Nail), who runs a roofing business. One glitch: lead guitarist Brian (Robinson), the most popular band member, is supposedly dead. Luckily, love of the music (and money) forces the band to get it together. Inspired by a reunion tour of the Animals, but has more "Full Monty" fun and heart than "Spinal Tap" parody to it. The cast is superb and the actual concert makes you want to stand up and cheer, when you're done laughing. **96m/C VHS, DVD. GB** Stephen Rea, Billy Connolly, Jimmy Nail, Timothy Spall, Bill Nighy, Juliet Aubrey, Helena Bergstrom, Bruce Robinson, Hans Matheson, Rachael Stirling, Phil Daniels, Frances Barber, Philip Davis; **D:** Brian Gibson; **W:** Dick Clement, Ian La Frenais; **C:** Ashley Rowe; **M:** Clive Langer.

Still Life 1992 (PG-13) The press has dubbed him "the Art Killer," a serial murderer who makes sculptures out of his victims. He's a sensation—and not ready to stop. This sicko's next "Still Life" may just be a struggling young musician. **83m/C VHS.** Jason Gedrick, Jessica Steen, Stephen Sheller; **D:** Graeme Campbell; **M:** Mychael Danna.

The Still Life 2007 Julian Lamont (Barry) is a reclusive, alcoholic artist who developed a new art genre called destructionism, which brings surprising commercial success, which he has not handled well. Struggling to regain his identity, once past the self-loathing and deep-rooted inner-hatred, he comes to realize the first step. Too much angst, not enough substance. **155m/C DVD.** Jason Barry, Rachel Miner; **D:** Terry Moore, Don S. Davis, Robert Miano; **C:** Joel Miller; **W:** Joel Miller; **C:** Richard Barbadillo.

Still Not Quite Human 1992 Teenage android Chip must do battle with unscrupulous industrialists and their robot weapon Spartacus to rescue his inventor father from their deadly clutches. **84m/C VHS.** Alan Thicke, Christopher Neame, Betsy Palmer, Adam Philipson, Rosa Nevin, Ken Pogue, Jay Underwood; **D:** Eric Luke; **W:** Eric Luke.

Still of the Night 1982 (PG) A Hitchcock-style thriller about a psychiatrist infatuated with a mysterious woman who may or may not be a killer. **91m/C VHS.** Meryl Streep, Roy Scheider, Jessica Tandy, Joe Grifasi, Sara Botsford, Josef Sommer; **D:** Robert Benton; **W:** Robert Benton, David Newman; **C:** Nestor Almendros.

The Stilts 1984 From modern Spanish cinema's preeminent director, this is a study of sexual dynamics revolving around a doomed love triangle. Aging professor Gomez wants young Del Sol to commit to him, but she won't; she has another, younger lover. Overwrought at times, but well acted. In Spanish with English subtitles. **95m/C VHS. SP** Laura Del Sol, Francesco Rabal, Fernando Fernan-Gomez; **D:** Carlos Saura.

The Sting 1973 (PG) Newman and Redford together again in this sparkling story of a pair of con artists in 1930s Chicago. They set out to fleece a big-time racketeer, pitting brain against brawn and pistol. Very inventive, excellent acting. Scott Joplin's wonderful ragtime music adapted by Marvin Hamlisch. The same directorial and acting team from "Butch Cassidy and the Sundance Kid" triumphs again. **129m/C VHS, DVD, HD DVD.** Paul Newman, Robert Redford, Robert Shaw, Charles Durning, Eileen Brennan, Harold Gould, Ray Walston, Dana Elcar, Jack Kehoe, Dimitra Arliss, Robert Earl Jones, Sally Kirkland; **D:** George Roy Hill; **W:** David S. Ward; **C:** Robert L. Surtees; **M:** Marvin Hamlisch. Oscars '73: Art Dir/Set Dec, Costume Des., Director (Hill), Film Editing, Picture, Story & Screenplay, Orig. Song Score and/or Adapt.; Directors Guild '73: Director (Hill), Natl. Film Reg. '05.

The Sting 2 1983 (PG) Complicated comic plot concludes with the final con game, involving a fixed boxing match where the stakes top $1 million and the payoff could be murder. Lame sequel to "The Sting" (1973). **102m/C VHS, DVD.** Jackie Gleason, Mac Davis, Teri Garr, Karl Malden, Oliver Reed; **D:** Jeremy Paul Kagan; **W:** David S. Ward; **C:** Bill Butler; **M:** Lalo Schifrin.

Stingray 1978 (PG) Two guys buy a Corvette, not knowing it's loaded with stolen heroin. Gangsters with an interest in the dope come after them, and the chase is on. Very violent and not all that funny. **105m/C VHS, DVD.** Chris Mitchum, Sherry Jackson, Les Lannom; **D:** Richard Taylor.

Stir 1998 Scientist about to reveal a medical discovery is murdered in his hotel room. Months later, his wife and young son return to the hotel and the son, while sleeping, sees the night of the murder through his father's eyes. **100m/C VHS.** Tony Todd, Traci Lords, Daniel Roebuck, Seth Adkins, Karen Black, Michael J. Pollard, Andrew Heckler; **D:** Rodion Nakhapetov; **W:** Rodion Nakhapetov; **C:** Darko Suvak; **M:** Keith Bilderbeck. **VIDEO**

Stir Crazy 1980 (R) Two down-on-their luck losers find themselves convicted of a robbery they didn't commit and sentenced to 120 years behind bars with a mean assortment of inmates. Wilder and Pryor's second teaming isn't quite as successful as the first go-round, but still provides plenty of laughs. **111m/C VHS, DVD.** Richard Pryor, Gene Wilder, Nicolas Coster, Lee Purcell, Craig T. Nelson, JoBeth Williams; **D:** Sidney Poitier; **W:** Bruce Jay Friedman; **C:** Fred Schuler; **M:** Tom Scott, Michael Masser.

Stir of Echoes 1999 (R) The kid in "The Sixth Sense" isn't the only one seeing dead people, although blue-collar Tom Witzky (Bacon) really doesn't have a clue as to what's happening to him. After being hypnotized at a party by his witchy sister-in-law, Lisa (Douglas), Tom winds up with some very scary clairvoyant abilities, which link him to a neighborhood teenaged girl who's presumed missing but has, in fact, been murdered. Naturally, Tom's visions and obsessions lead to some problems with his family and friends. Based on the novel by Richard Matheson. **110m/C VHS, DVD, Blu-ray Disc.** Kevin Bacon, Illeana Douglas, Kathryn Erbe, Liza Weil, Kevin Dunn, Conor O'Farrell, Zachary David Cope, Jenny (Jennifer) Morrison, Eddie Bo Smith Jr.; **D:** David Koepp; **W:** David Koepp; **C:** Fred Murphy; **M:** James Newton Howard.

Stir of Echoes 2: The Homecoming 2007 (R) Another of those mostly-in-name-only sequels. Army Captain Ted Cogan (Lowe) and his unit erroneously fire upon a van of civilians (who die) in Iraq, which leads to an insurgent attack that wounds Cogan. After coming out of his coma, Cogan is discharged and returns home to Chicago, where his wife and kid are having their own problems. Cogan starts suffering disturbing flashbacks that include ghosts who seemingly are trying to communicate with him. **89m/C DVD.** Rob Lowe, Marnie McPhail, Katya Gardner, Zachary Bennett, Ben Lewis; **D:** Ernie Barbarash; **W:** Ernie Barbarash; **C:** Francois Dagenais; **M:** Norman Orenstein. **CABLE**

Stitches 1985 (R) Adolescent comedy about med students playing practical jokes on the dean using laboratory specimens. So bad the director (actually Rod Holcomb) allegedly did not want his name associated with it. **92m/C VHS.** Eddie Albert, Parker Stevenson, Geoffrey Lewis, Brian Tochi; **D:** Alan Smithee; **W:** Michael Choquette.

Stolen Childhoods 2005 Presents footage shot over seven years in eight different countries of the deplorable conditions and horrific practices under which youths are forced to work. Castigates governments for not enforcing child labor laws, blames the rising frenzy for cheap consumer goods in the Western markets, and praises programs that rehabilitate children and save them from servitude. Well-intentioned premise feels unfocused, losing much of its punch. **83m/C US D:** Len Morris; **W:** Georgia Morris; **C:** U. Roberto Romano; **M:** Miriam Cutler.

The Stolen Children Ladro di Bambini 1992 Highly acclaimed Italian neo-realist film that tells the story of a shy carabiniere and two children who have been placed in his care. They are an emotionally battered 11-year-old girl who was forced into prostitution by her mother and her sullen 9-year-old brother. As they journey from Milan to Sicily and gradually get to know each other, all three of the characters undergo a slight transformation. Gracefully executed, this haunting masterpiece explores the overriding themes of guilt and innocence and keeps you thinking about them long after the movie's over. Italian with subtitles. **108m/C VHS. IT** Enrico Lo Verso, Valentina Scalici, Giuseppe Ieracitano, Florence Darel, Marina Golovine, Fabio Alessandrini; **D:** Gianni Amelio; **W:** Gianni Amelio, Sandro Petraglia, Stefano Rulli; **M:** Franco Piersanti. Cannes '92: Grand Jury Prize.

A Stolen Face 1952 Creepy, implausible drama of a plastic surgeon, spurned by a beautiful concert pianist, who transforms a female convict to look just like her. The convict runs away, but perhaps there's hope in the future with the pianist. **71m/B VHS. GB** Paul Henreid, Lizabeth Scott, Andre Morell, Susan Stephen, Everley Gregg, Cyril Smith; **D:** Terence Fisher; **W:** Martin Berkeley, Richard H. Landau; **C:** Walter J. (Jimmy W.) Harvey; **M:** Malcolm Arnold.

Stolen Hearts Two If By Sea 1995 (R) Instead of reporting to the cops after he takes Keyes (Finiani) to the cops after he takes her money, bar owner Dana Andrews (Aletonis) hires PI Justin Gibbons (Dale) to get back her savings. Justin happens to work with a psychic, Tess (Hall), and the twosome have a mutual attraction. They find the sleaze and get back the dough. Very boring. **82m/C VHS, DVD.** Landon Hall, Vincent Dale, Jim Finiani, Paula Aletonis; **D:** Ralph Portillo.

Stolen Hours 1963 Inferior remake of Bette Davis's "Dark Victory" casts Hayward as an oil-rich heiress who learns she has a fatal illness. Bring the tissues for this tearjerker. Based on the play "Dark Victory" by George Emerson Brewer Jr. and Bertram Block. **100m/C VHS.** Susan Hayward, Michael Craig, Diane Baker, Edward Judd, Paul Rogers; **D:** Daniel Petrie; **W:** Jessamyn West, Joseph Hayes.

Stolen Identity 1953 A Viennese cabbie sees his American dream dashed for lack of the proper papers. When an American businessman is murdered in his cab he is quick to seize the moment...and the dead man's identity. In no time at all he finds himself involved with the widow, entangled with the murderer and under suspicion for the killing. Predictable and sluggish, the story inches its way to the foregone conclusion. **81m/B VHS.** Francis Lederer, Donald Buka, Joan Camden, Adrienne Gessner; **D:** Gunther Fritsch.

Stolen Kisses Baisers Voles 1968 Sequel to "The 400 Blows," the story of Antoine Doinel; his unsuccessful career prospects as a detective in Paris, and his initially awkward but finally successful adventures with women. Made during Truffaut's involvement in a political crisis involving the sack of Cinematique Francais director Henri Langlois. Truffaut dedicated the film to Langlois and the Cinematique, but it is a thoroughly apolitical, small-scale, charming (some say too charming) romantic comedy, Truffaut-style. Followed by "Bed and Board." **90m/C VHS, DVD. FR** Jean-Pierre Leaud, Delphine Seyrig, Michael (Michel) Lonsdale, Claude Jade; **D:** Francois Truffaut; **W:** Francois Truffaut, Claude de Givray; **C:** Denys Clerval; **M:** Antoine Duhamel. Natl. Soc. Film Critics '69: Director (Truffaut).

A Stolen Life 1946 Remake of a 1939 film of the same title starring Elisabeth Bergner. Oddly, Davis chose this as her first and last producing effort. Implausible tale of an evil twin (Davis) who takes her sister's (Davis) place so she can have the man they both love. Davis pulls it off as both twins; Ford is good as the hapless hubby. **107m/B VHS.** Bette Davis, Glenn Ford, Dane Clark, Walter Brennan, Charlie Ruggles, Bruce Bennett, Esther Dale, Peggy Knudsen; **D:** Curtis Bernhardt; **M:** Max Steiner.

Stolen Summer Project Greenlight's Stolen Summer 2002 (PG) The background of the film (first-timer Jones won a national competition sponsored by Ben Affleck and Matt Damon) may be more interesting than this decidedly old-fashioned story. It's a Chicago summer in 1976 with young Irish Catholic Pete O'Malley (Stein) deciding that he, in order to get to heaven, he needs to convert his Jewish friend Danny Jacobsen (Weinberg). Danny's father (Pollak), who happens to be a rabbi, takes the news benignly while Pete's dad, Joe (Quinn), has some trouble believing that his family is not being condescended to. The performances are appealing and there's a good lesson about the acceptance of another's religion. **95m/C VHS, DVD. US** Adi Stein, Mike Weinberg, Aidan Quinn, Kevin Pollak, Bonnie Hunt, Eddie Kaye Thomas, Brian Dennehy; **D:** Pete Jones; **W:** Pete Jones; **C:** Pete Jones; **M:** Danny Lux.

Stomp the Yard 2007 (PG-13) The yard in question would be a highly competitive step dancing war between two rival black fraternities. L.A. teen DJ (Short) lands in a major beef and is shipped off to his Uncle Nate (Lennix) in Atlanta to be enrolled at historic Truth University. The brash freshman immediately pisses off Mu Gamma Xi hotshot Grant (Henson), but his street moves win DJ a place at rival frat Theta Nu Theta. They want to win that national championship (yes, there's a dance-off). Oh so predictable plot but the dancing is impressive. **114m/C DVD. US** Columbus Short, Meagan Good, Brian White, Laz Alonso, Ne-Yo, Yun Qu, Valarie Pettiford, Harry J. Lennix, Allan Louis; **D:** Sylvain White; **W:** Robert Adetuyi; **C:** Scott Kevan; **M:** Sam Retzer, Tim Boland.

The Stone Boy ✱✱✱½ 1984 (PG) A boy accidentally kills his older brother on their Montana farm. The family is torn apart by sadness and guilt. Sensitive look at variety of reactions during a crisis, with an excellent cast led by Duvall's crystal-clear performance. 95m/C VHS, DVD, Mary Ellen Trainor, Glenn Close, Robert Duvall, Jason Presson, Frederic Forrest, Wilford Brimley, Linda Hamilton; D: Christopher Cain; W: Gina Berriault; C: Juan Ruiz-Anchia; M: James Horner, John Beal.

Stone Cold Dead woof! 1991 (R) Flamboyant footballer Bosworth made his acting debut in this sensitive human document, playing the usual human documentary around him. 91m/C VHS, DVD, Brian Bosworth, Lance Henriksen, William Forsythe, Arabella Holzbog, Sam McMurray; D: Craig R. Baxley; W: Walter Doniger; C: Alexander Gruszynski; M: Sylvester Levay.

Stone Fox ✱✱ 1990 (R) Rugged cop Crenna battles crime lord Williams (Paul Williams? Yeah, sure) over a prostitution ring. Based on John Reynolds Gardner's book. 96m/C VHS, Buddy Epsen, Joey Cramer, Belinda J. Montgomery, Gordon Tootoosis; D: Harvey Hart.

The Stone Killer ✱✱½ 1973 (R) 1987 Heartwarming family drama in which a young man must win a dogsled race to save the family farm. Based on John Reynolds Gardiner's popular children's book. 96m/C VHS, Buddy Epsen, Joey Cramer, Belinda J. Montgomery, Gordon Tootoosis; D: Harvey Hart.

The Stone Merchant ✱✱½ Il Mercante di Pietre 2006 Unhappy Leda (March) in this action-packed drama about a Mafia plot to use Vietnam vets in a mass killing. Violent but terse and action-packed revenge adventure set in the underworlds of New York and Los Angeles. 95m/C VHS, Charles Bronson, Martin Balsam, Norman Fell, Ralph Waite, John Ritter; D: Michael Winner.

Stone of Silver Creek ✱✱ 1935 The owner of the Bonanza saloon, T. William Stone (Jones), discovers some of his unsavory patrons are planning to rob him. After a friend is shot trying to help him, Stone decides to even the score. Chapter 3 of "Gordon of Ghost City" finds Mary and Gordon entering a mine owned by Mary's grandfather, which turns out to be rich in gold. A figure sets an explosion and Mary and Gordon get trapped in the mine! 87m/B VHS, Buck Jones, Noel Francis, Niles Welch, Marion Shilling, Peggy Campbell, Harry Semels, Madge Bellamy, Walter Miller; D: Grinda, Ray Taylor.

Stone Reader ✱✱✱ 2002 (PG-13) Mark Moskowitz searches for "The Stones of Summer" author Dow Mossman. He also interviews critic Leslie Fiedler and editor Robert Gottlieb, who edited "Catch-22." 128m/C VHS, DVD, US D: Mark Moskowitz; W: Mark Moskowitz; C: Mark Moskowitz, Joseph Vardaregast, Jeffrey Conter; M: Michael Mandrell.

Stonebrook ✱✱ 1998 (PG-13) Two college roommates at a private university gamble to make their tuition money and wind up drawing the attention of a detective who wants to use their illegal activities to incriminate the mob. 90m/C VHS, DVD, Seth Green, Brad Rowe, Zoe McLellan, William Mesnik, Stanley Kamel; D: Bryn W. Thompson.

Stoned ✱✱ 2005 A muddled and unenlightening account of the final months of drug addicted Rolling Stones guitarist Brian Jones (Gregory), who was found dead in his swimming pool in 1969. Although "death by misadventure" is the official cause, a 1994 deathbed confession by Frank Thorogood (Considine) allegedly reveals that Frank admitted drowning Jones. Flashbacks linger on the guitarist's hedonistic lifestyle while, before his death, lethargically stirs himself to torment those around him. Woolley's directorial debut. 102m/C DVD, GB Leo Gregory, Paddy Considine, David Morrissey, Ben Whishaw, Amelia Warner, Monet Mazur, David Williams, Tuva Novotny, Luke De Woolfson, Melanie Ramsay, Ruediger Rudoiph; D: Stephen Woolley; W: Robert Wade, Neal Purvis; C: John Mathieson; M: David Arnold.

The Stoned Age ✱ 1994 (R) Budding look to get wasted and find some chicks. Set in the '70s. 90m/C VHS, DVD, Michael Kopelow, China Kantner, Renee Griffer; D: James Melkonian.

Stones of Death ✱ 1988 (R) An aboriginal curse is invoked when a subdivision is built too close to an ancient burial site. Teenagers begin having all-too-real nightmares about death. 90m/C VHS, Tom Jennings, Natalie McCurry, Zoe Carides, Eric Oldfield; D: James Bogle.

Stonewall ✱✱✱ 1995 (R) Fictional account of the June, 1969 police raid on Greenwich Village gay bar the Stonewall Inn, which is considered to have launched the modern gay rights movement. White-bread, midwestern activist Matty Dean (Weller) arrives in New York and gets thrown in jail for defending streetwise drag queen LaMiranda (Daz) from harassing cops. They become lovers but Matty is also involved with conservative prepster Ethan (Corbalis), who thinks the flamboyant queens give the drag movement a bad name. Meanwhile, the drag queens at the Stonewall are getting fed up with police raids and brutal treatment. Adapted from Martin Duberman's social history "Stonewall." Director Finch died during the final editing stages of the film. 93m/C VHS, DVD, Frederick Weller, Guillermo Diaz, Brendan Corbalis, Bruce MacVittie, Duane Boutte, Peter Ratray, Luis Guzman; D: Nigel Finch; W: Rikki Beadle Blair; C: Chris Seager; M: Michael Kamen.

The Stooge ✱✱½ 1951 Singer Bill Miller (Martin) asks the antic Ted Rogers (Lewis) to join him in his vaudeville act, where Rogers' clowning has them on the road to success. But then Miller decides he wants to go solo. Sounds more fun little autobiographical. ♪A Girl Named Mary and a Boy Named Bill; Who's Your Little Whozis?; Just One More Chance; With My Eyes Wide Open I'm Dreaming; I'm Yours. 100m/B VHS, DVD, Dean Martin, Jerry Lewis, Polly Bergen, Marion Marshall, Eddie Mayehoff, Richard Erdman, Frances Bavier; D: Norman Taurog; W: Martin Rackin, Fred Finklehofe, Elwood Ullman; C: Daniel F. Fapp.

Stoogemania ✱ 1985 A nerd becomes so obsessed with the Three Stooges that they begin to take over his life and ruin it. Harmless except as a waste of time. Includes actual Stooge footage including some colorized—but see an ole Stooges movie instead. 95m/C VHS, Josh Mostel, Melanie Chartof, Sid Caesar, Mark Holton, Patrick DeSantis, Armin Shimerman, Thom Sharp, Joshua John Miller, Victoria Jackson, Ron House, Alan Shearman, Diz White; D: Chuck Workman; W: Chuck Workman, Jim Geoghan; C: Christopher Tufty; M: Hummie Mann, Gary Tigerman.

Stop-Loss ✱✱½ 2008 (R) Fresh from duty in Iraq, Sgt. Brandon King (Phillippe) and his buddy Sgt. Steve Shriver (Tatum) return home to Texas only to struggle with assimilation and strained relationships due to the war experiences. Suddenly, Brandon is ordered to return to Iraq (the title refers to the military term for extending a soldier's enlistment contract without consent or even a heads-up), setting off a bomb of emotion and leading to an AWOL escape that puts him, his

Stop Making Sense ✱✱✱½ 1984 The Talking Heads perform 18 of their best songs in this concert filmed in Los Angeles. Considered by many to be the best concert movie ever made. The band plays with incredible energy and imagination, and Demme's direction and camera work is appropriate ly frenzied and original. Features such Talking Heads songs as "Burning Down the House," "Psycho Killer," and "Once in a Lifetime." Band member Tina Weymouth's Tom Tom Club also performs for the audience. 99m/C VHS, DVD, D: Jonathan Demme; C: Jordan Cronenweth.

Stop! or My Mom Will Shoot ✱ 1992 (PG-13) Getty is an overbearing mother paying a visit to her cop son (Stallone) in Los Angeles. When mom witnesses a crime she has to stay in town longer than intended, which gives her time to meddle in her son's work and romantic lives. If Stallone would actually change his image, this so-called comedy isn't the way to do it—because the joke is only on him. Viewers who'll rent this may find the joke is on them. 87m/C VHS, DVD, Sylvester Stallone, Estelle Getty, JoBeth Williams, Roger Rees, Martin Ferrero, Gailard Sartain, Dennis Burkley; D: Roger Spottiswoode; W: William Osborne, William Davies, Blake Snyder; M: Alan Silvestri. Golden Raspberries '92: Worst Actor (Stallone), Worst Support. Actress (Getty), Worst Screenplay.

Stop That Cab ✱ 1951 Sloppy crooks accidentally leave precious jewels in the back seat of a taxi, and pursue and torture the cabby who found and hid them. Rather mean-spirited, uninteresting comedy. 56m/B VHS, Sid Melton, Iris Adrian, Tom Neal, Marjorie Lord, Greg McClure; C: Carl Berger.

Stopover Tokyo ✱ 1957 An American intelligence agent uncovers a plot to assassinate the American ambassador while on leave in Japan. Nice location shooting and scenery; limp story and characters. Based on a novel by John P. Marquand. 100m/C VHS, DVD, Robert Wagner, Joan Collins, Edmond O'Brien, Ker Scott, Larry Keating, Sarah Selby, Reiko Oyama, Solly Nakamura; D: Richard L. Breen; W: Richard L. Ereen, Walter Reisch, Frances Clarke; M: Paul Sawtell.

The Stork Club ✱✱ 1945 A little song, a little dance, will Betty Hutton find romance? The actors manage to rise above the script in this silly, overdone fable. Hutton stars as the poor but spunky hatcheck girl who unwittingly saves the life of a cynical gazillionaire. His expressions of gratitude are less than appreciated by her G.I. beau. Dcne mainly as a vehicle for Hutton's promotion, so Betty's die-hard fans may find it is their liking. ♪Doctor, Lawyer, Indian Chief; Baltimore Oriole; I'm a Dozen Hearts; Love Me; China Boy; If I Had a Shade of the Old Apple Tree. 99m/B VHS, DVD, Betty Hutton, Barry Fitzgerald, Don DeFore, Robert Benchley, Bill Goodwin, Iris Adrian; D: Hal Walker.

Storm ✱✱ 1987 (PG-13) Uneven thriller finds college students on a camping trip who must fight for their lives when they are confronted by killer thieves. Somewhat contrived but interesting ending to this low-budget outing. 99m/C VHS, CA David Palfy, Stan Kane, Harry Freedman, Lawrence Elion, Tom Schioler; D: David Winning; M: Amin Bhatia.

Storm and Sorrow ✱✱ 1990 Molly Higgins is known as the "Spider-woman of the Rockies" for her legendary mountain climbing abilities. Then she joins a team looking to scale the 24,000-foot peaks of Russia's Pamir Mountains. The group meets deadly hazards—both natu-

friends, and his family in jeopardy. Director and co-writer Kimberly Pierce, whose brother had been stop-lossed by the army, brings honesty and humanity to a subject close to her heart, and the lead performances are grippingly spot-on. 112m/C DVD, US Ryan Phillippe, Abbie Cornish, Channing Tatum, Joseph Gordon-Levitt, Ciaran Hinds, Timothy Olyphant, Josef Scmmer, Victor Rasuk, Rob Brown, Mamie Gummer; D: Kimberly Pierce; W: Kimberly Pierce, Mark Richard; C: Chris Menges; M: John Powell.

ral and those caused by the ego-driven rivalries of the group's mentcers. A fact-based drama based on the novel by Richard and Craig. 96m/C VHS, DVD, Lor Singer, Todd Allen, Steve (Stephen M.) Anderson, Jay Baker; W: Leigh Chapman.

Storm Catcher ✱✱ 1999 (R) Air Force pilot Jack Holloway (Lundgren) is falsely convicted of stealing a prototype military aircraft. He manages to escape in order to find the real culprits, which also puts Holloway's family in danger. 95m/C VHS, DVD, Dolph Lundgren, Mystro Clark, Yvonne Zima, Kylie Bax; D: Anthony Hickox; W: Bill Gucwa, Ed Masterson. VIDEO

Storm Chasers; Revenge of the Twister ✱✱½ 1998 Having lost her husband in a plane crash, "storm chaser" Jaime (McGillis) throws herself into her work. Sent to Colorado to investigate a tornado, she hooks up with hunky FEMA coordinator, Will (Larson). There are some severe disturbances in the atmosphere causing problems—and disturbances on a more personal level as well. Dul and dumb. 96m/C VHS, DVD, Kelly McGillis, Wolf Larson, Liz Torres, Adrian Zmed, James MacArthur; D: Mark Sobel. VIDEO

Storm in a Teacup ✱✱✱½ 1937 A reporter starts a campaign to save a sheepdog that the town magistrate has ordered killed because the owner can't pay the license tax. 87m/B VHS, Vivien Leigh, Rex Harrison, Cecil Parker, Sara Allgood; D: Victor Saville.

Storm over Asia ✱✱✱½ The Heir to Genghis Khan 1928 A Mongolian trapper is discovered to be descended from Genghis Khan and is made puppet emperor of a Soviet province. Beautiful and evocative. Silent masterpiece. 70m/B VHS, DVD, RU I. Inkizhinov, Valeri Inkizhinov, A. Chris tiakov, A. Dedinstev, V. Tzoppi, Paulina Belinskaya; D: Vsevolod Pudovkin; C: Anatoli Golovnya.

Storm over Wyoming ✱✱ 1950 Holt and Martin find themselves haplessly embroiled in a Wyoming range war. Action-packed but thin, ordinary western. 60m/B VHS, Tim Holt, Richard Martin, Noreen Nash, Tom Keene, Bill Kennedy, Kenneth Mac-Donald, Holly (Mike Ragan) Bane; D: Lesley Selander; W: Ed Earl Repp; C: J. Roy Hunt; M: Paul Sawtell.

Storm Rider ✱✱ 1957 A gunman hired to protect a group of ranchers from a powerful rancher falls in love with a local widow. After his job is done, however, he leaves her behind. Typical western fare. 70m/B VHS, DVD, Scott Brady, Mala Powers, Bill Williams, Olin Howlin, William "Bill" Fawcett, John Goddard; D: Edward L. Bemds; W: Les Baxter.

Storm Tracker ✱✱ 1999 (PG-13) Meteorologist Ron Young (Perry) develops a method of controlling the path of deadly storms and is recruited by General Roberts (S'neen) to perfect his storm-tracking system for government use. Naturally, this isn't altruistic, the General wants to turn the violent storms on his enemies. 90m/C VHS, DVD, Luke Perry, Martin Sheen, Alexandra Powers, David Moses, Renee Estevez; D: Harris Dona. CABLE

Storm Trooper ✱✱ 1998 Abused wife Grace Tolson (Alt) is just cleaning up after killing her husband when the mysterious Stark (Laughlin) shows up at her back door. Closely following are a group of armed men who manage to wound the stranger, exposing wires and circuitry. Stark the cyborg gets Grace into a car of danger but she's got a gun and she's not gonna take it anymore. 89m/C VHS, Carol Alt, John Laughlin, Zach Galligan, Corey Feldman, Richard (Frick) Hill, Kool Moe Dee; D: Jim Wynorski; W: T.L. Lankford; C: J.E. Bash; M: Terry Plumeri. VIDEO

Storm Warning ✱✱ 1951 New York model Martha (Rogers) visits her sister Lucy (Day, in a non-singing role), who's living in a small southern town. She's barely off the bus before Martha witnesses a murder committed by the KKK and sees two men's faces and when she does get to Lucy's, Martha sees that her brutish brother-in-law Hank (Cochran) was one of the killers and the other is his boss, Charlie (Sanders). When prosecutor Burt Rainey (Reagan) learns that Martha was a witness, he tries to get her to testify but she clams up. But her silence doesn't do her any good. Hard-hitting for its time although there are no black characters in the story; the dead man is a white reporter writing an expose. Film was shot in Corona, California and an occasional palm tree incongruously appears. **93m/B DVD.** Ronald Reagan, Ginger Rogers, Doris Day, Steve Cochran, Hugh Sanders, Raymond Greenleaf, Lloyd Gough; **D:** Stuart Heisler; **W:** Richard Brooks, Daniel Fuchs; **C:** Carl Guthrie; **M:** Daniele Amfitheatrof.

The Storm Within ♪♪♪½ *Les Parents Terribles* **1948** Based on Cocteau's play, many consider this domestic drama of a troubled family's tortured existence to be his finest work. De Bray plays the domineering mother, Marais plays the son, and Day is the woman he (and his father) love in this complex story of sexuality, parental rivalry and jealousy. With the film set in only two locations, Cocteau creates a claustrophobic intimacy within the walls of De Bray's family apartment and Day's apartment. An inferior remake, "Intimate Relations" was released in Britain in 1953. In French with English subtitles. **98m/B VHS.** *FR* Jean Marais, Yvonne de Bray, Gabrielle Dorziat, Marcel Andre, Josette Day; **D:** Jean Cocteau; **W:** Jean Cocteau; **Nar:** Jean Cocteau.

Stormquest *woof!* **1987** Deep in the jungle, a band of women warriors live without men. When it is discovered that one of the group has a male lover, she is sentenced to death. Her man tries to rescue her, and it turns into a war of the sexes—literally. In Spanish with subtitles. **90m/C VHS.** *SP* Kai Baker, Brent Huff; **D:** Alex Sessa.

Stormswept ♪½ **1995** Actress Brianna (Hughes) rents a haunted Louisiana mansion housing the spirit of a slave master. When a storm strands Brianna and friends, the spirit causes everyone to give up to all sorts of sexual escapades. **94m/C VHS, DVD.** Julie Hughes, Melissa Moore, Kathleen Kinmont, Justin Carroll, Lorissa McComas, Ed Wasser, Kim Kopf, Hunt Scarritt; **D:** David Marsh; **M:** David Marsh.

Stormy Monday ♪♪♪ **1988 (R)** An American developer conspires to strike it rich in Newcastle, England real estate by resorting to violence and political manipulations. Sting plays the jazz club owner who opposes him. Slow plot, but acted and directed well; interesting photography. **108m/C VHS, DVD.** *GB* Melanie Griffith, Tommy Lee Jones, Sting, Sean Bean, James Cosmo, Mark Long, Brian Lewis; **D:** Mike Figgis; **W:** Mike Figgis; **C:** Roger Deakins; **M:** Mike Figgis.

Stormy Nights ♪½ **1997 (R)** Femme fatale Nicole (Spaulding) worms her way into the lives of Jennifer McCormick (Tweed) and her weak-willed hubby (Clark), leading to seduction and betrayal. **90m/C VHS.** Shannon Tweed, Tracy Spaulding, Brett (Baxter) Clark; **D:** Alberto Vidaurri; **W:** Michael Meyer; **C:** S. Douglas Smith; **M:** Jay Bolton.

Stormy Trails ♪♪ **1936** Bell battles bellicose bad guys who are after his property. At least all the gunfights should keep a viewer awake! **59m/B VHS, DVD.** Rex Bell, Bob Terry, Lois Wilde, Lane Chandler, Earl Dwire, Lloyd Ingraham, Karl Hackett, Murdock MacQuarrie, Jimmy Aubrey, Roger Williams; **D:** Sam Newfield; **W:** Phil Dunham; **C:** Robert E. Cline.

Stormy Waters ♪♪½ *Remorques* **1941** A romantic French drama about a sea captain falling in love with a woman he rescues from a storm. He goes back to his wife, however, when she becomes critically ill. Director Gremillon insisted on realistic footage of storms at sea; production was delayed because of the difficulties of the German occupation. Dubbed. **75m/B VHS.** *FR* Jean Gabin, Michele Morgan, Madeleine Renaud; **D:** Jean Gremillon.

Stormy Weather ♪♪♪ **1943** In this cavalcade of black entertainment, the plot takes a back seat to the nearly nonstop array of musical numbers, showcasing this stellar cast at their performing peak. ♪There's No No Two Ways About Love; Stormy Weather; Ain't Misbehavin'; Rhythm Cocktail; Rang Tang Tang; Dat, Dot, Dah; That Ain't Right; I Can't Give You Anything But Love, Baby; Digga Digga Doo. **77m/B VHS, DVD.** Lena Horne, Bill Robinson, Fats Waller, Dooley Wilson, Cab Calloway; **D:** Andrew L. Stone; **C:** Leon Shamroy. Natl. Film Reg. '01.

The Story Lady ♪♪½ **1993** A retiree uses her story-telling abilities as a hostess on a public-access children's program. She becomes so popular that two network execs want to exploit her as a spokesperson for a toy company. Only a young girl can help her find a way to resist going commercial. **120m/C VHS, DVD.** Jessica Tandy, Lisa Jakub, Ed Begley Jr., Charles Durning, Stephanie Zimbalist; **D:** Larry Elikann; **M:** Lee Holdridge. **TV**

The Story of a Cheat ♪♪♪ **1936** The hero of the film discovers at an early age that dishonesty is probably the best policy and he sets out to put this theory into use. Director/writer Guitry also turns in a great performance as the central character. Guitry was a major influence on such different directors as Welles, Resnais and Truffaut. Based on Guitry's novel "Memoires d'Un Tricheur." In French with English subtitles. **83m/B VHS.** *FR* Sacha Guitry; **D:** Sacha Guitry; **W:** Sacha Guitry.

Story of a Cowboy Angel ♪ *Christmas Mountains* **1981** On the Christmas Mountain Ranch, a cowboy angel descends to Earth to bestow various beneficences. **90m/C VHS.** Fran Ryan, Mark Miller, Barbara Stanger, Brian Poelman, Slim Pickens; **D:** Pierre De Moro; **M:** Mark Miller.

Story of a Love Affair ♪♪ *Cronaca di un Amore* **1950** Paola (Bose) is the young wife of wealthy industrialist Enrico (Sarmi), who swiftly married her during the war. Now curious about her unknown past, Enrico hires a detective (Rossi) to investigate. This results in reuniting Paola with her ex-lover Guido (Girotti). Both are afraid that questions will be raised about the suspicious death of Guido's fiancee and, as the two rekindle their involvement, they consider getting rid of Enrico to preserve their secrets. Antonioni's first dramatic feature; Italian with subtitles. **98m/B DVD.** *IT* Lucia Bose, Massimo Girotti, Gino Rossi; **D:** Michelangelo Antonioni; **W:** Michelangelo Antonioni, Francesco Maselli, Daniele D'Anza, Silvio Giovannetti; **C:** Enzo Serafin; **M:** Giovanni Fusco.

The Story of a Love Story ♪♪½ *Impossible Object* **1973** Bates plays a writer whose imagination gets the better of him when he attempts an extra-marital affair. Was he with her or not? Unusual concept doesn't stand up in the long run. Fine cast is under-utilized. **110m/C VHS.** *FR* Alan Bates, Dominique Sanda, Evans Evans, Lea Massari, Michel Auclair, Laurence De Monaghan; **D:** John Frankenheimer; **W:** Alan Bates.

Story of a Prostitute ♪♪ *Joy Girls; Shunpuden* **1965** Lurid film adapted from a novel by Taijiro Tamura. A betrayed woman volunteers to become a prostitute for a garrison of soldiers stationed on the Manchurian front in WWII. Soon, the commander takes the woman as his sole property, though she has fallen for one of his junior officers. Japanese with subtitles. **96m/B VHS.** *JP* Yumiko Nogawa, Tamio Kawaji, Isao Tamagawa; **D:** Seijun Suzuki.

The Story of a Three Day Pass ♪♪½ *La Permission* **1968** A black American GI falls in love with a white French girl he meets in peacetime Paris. Based on Van Peebles book "La Permission." With English subtitles. Made on a low budget and flawed, but poignant and impressive. **87m/B VHS, DVD.** Harry Baird, Nicole Berger, Pierre Doris; **D:** Melvin Van Peebles; **W:** Melvin Van Peebles.

The Story of Adele H. ♪♪♪ *L'Histoire d'Adele H* **1975 (PG)** The story of Adele Hugo, daughter of Victor Hugo, whose love for an English soldier leads to obsession and finally to madness after he rejects her. Sensitive and gentle unfolding of characters and story. Beautiful photography. In French with English subtitles. **97m/C VHS, DVD.** *FR* Isabelle Adjani, Bruce Robinson, Sylvia Marriott; **D:** Francois Truffaut; **W:** Suzanne Schiffman, Jean Gruault; **C:** Nestor Almendros; **M:** Maurice Jaubert. Natl. Bd. of Review '75: Actress (Adjani); N.Y. Film Critics '75: Actress (Adjani), Screenplay; Natl. Soc. Film Critics '75: Actress (Adjani).

The Story of Alexander Graham Bell ♪♪♪ **1939** Lavish Fox biography on the inventor of the telephone provided Ameche with his most popular role. He's a serious Scot who comes to Boston to teach speech to the deaf and falls in love with the rich, beautiful and hearing impaired Young (whose three sisters, Georgianna, Polly Ann, and Sally are also in the film). Thanks to Young's rich daddy (Coburn), Bell gets the money to work on his invention, aided by enthusiastic assistant Watson (Fonda). No, it's not an undone. **97m/B VHS.** Don Ameche, Loretta Young, Henry Fonda, Charles Coburn, Spring Byington, Gene Lockhart, Sally Blane, Polly Ann Young, Georgianna Young, Bobs Watson, Jonathan Hale, Harry Davenport; **D:** Irving Cummings; **W:** Lamar Trotti; **C:** Leon Shamroy.

The Story of an African Farm ♪♪½ *Bustin' Bonaparte: The Story of an African Farm* **2004 (PG)** Grant stars as a gleeful villain named Bonaparte Benkins, who invades the lives of young cousins Em (Weidemann) and Lydall (Kropinski). It's 1870, and the two orphaned girls are stuck on the remote African farm of their strict Aunt Sannie (Van der Laag), whom drifter Bonaparte proceeds to charm into letting him stay. The children are plucky and the adults are generally foolish but the experience is only mildly entertaining. Based on the 1883 children's book by South African Olive Schreiner. **97m/C DVD.** *SA* Richard E. Grant, Armin Mueller-Stahl, Kasha Kropinski, Anneke Weidemann, Karin van der Laag, Luke Gallant; **D:** David Lister; **W:** Bonnie Rodini, Thandi Brewer, Peter Tischhauser; **M:** J.B. Arthur.

The Story of Boys & Girls ♪♪♪ *Storia de Ragazzi e di Ragazze* **1991** Two very different families come together for the wedding feast of their children, during which family secrets are revealed and we come to know and care for everyone present. A 20-course meal rivals the food scenes in "Babette's Feast" and is guaranteed to make your mouth water. Fine ensemble of actors, well directed, with a vivid evocation of 1930s Italy. In Italian with English subtitles. **92m/C VHS.** *IT* Lucrezia Lante della Rovere, Massimo Bonetti, Davide Bechini, Enrica Maria Modugno, Valeria Bruni Tadeschi, Lina Bernardi, Anna Bonaiuto, Alessandro Haber; **D:** Pupi Avati; **W:** Pupi Avati; **M:** Riz Ortolani.

The Story of David ♪♪♪ **1976 (PG)** Well-done Old Testament Bible drama about the shepherd boy who slew Goliath, overcame the Philistines, and united Israel. Then, as King David, he winds up involved in an illicit love affair with Bathsheba that threatens to destroy his kingdom. Fine acting and a literate script highlight this TV production. **192m/C VHS.** Timothy Bottoms, Anthony Quayle, Jane Seymour, Keith Michell, Susan Hampshire; **D:** Alex Segal; **W:** Ernest Kinoy. **TV**

The Story of Dr. Wassell ♪♪♪ **1944** Courageous true story of Corydon M. Wassell (Cooper), who won the Navy Cross for humanitarianism in WWII. Stationed in Java when the Japanese overrun the island, Wassell's placed in charge of evacuating the wounded. When he learns that stretcher cases must be left behind, he disobeys orders to rescue some badly wounded soldiers and get them to safety. (Naturally, there has to be some romance, so Cooper's paired with Day as a Red Cross nurse). Based on the book by James Hilton. **137m/C VHS.** Gary Cooper, Laraine Day, Signe Hasso, Dennis O'Keefe, Carol Thurston, Carl Esmond, Stanley Ridges, Paul Kelly, Elliott Reid, Philip Ahn, Barbara Britton; **D:** Cecil B. DeMille; **W:** Charles Bennett, Alan LeMay; **C:** Victor Milner; **M:** Victor Young.

The Story of Esther Costello ♪♪½ *Golden Virgin* **1957** Rich American Margaret Landi (Crawford) is visiting her Irish homeland when she meets Esther (Sears), a young girl rendered deaf, mute, and blind by a childhood trauma. The childless Margaret is persuaded to take Esther in as a surrogate daughter and the waif gradually begins to respond to her care, sparking a media frenzy over the inspirational saga. This brings Carlo (Brazzi), Margaret's estranged and money-grubbing husband, out of the woodwork, with some get-rich-quick schemes. Well-done melodrama adapted from the book by Nicholas Monsarrat. **102m/B VHS.** *GB* Joan Crawford, Heather Sears, Rossano Brazzi, Lee Patterson, Ron Randell, Fay Compton, John Loder, Denis O'Dea; **D:** David Miller; **W:** Charles A. Kaufman; **C:** Robert Krasker; **M:** Georges Auric.

The Story of Fausta ♪♪½ *Romance da Empregada* **1988 (R)** An unhappily married cleaning woman in the slums of Rio entices all the money and gifts she can out of an elderly widower. Decidedly grim comedy-drama, well-done but unsentimental. In Portuguese with English subtitles. **90m/C VHS.** *BR* Betty Faria, Daniel Filho, Brandao Filho; **D:** Bruno Barreto; **M:** Ruben Blades.

The Story of G.I. Joe ♪♪♪½ **1945** Grunt's-eye-view of the European theatre in WWII, based on the columns of war correspondent Ernie Pyle. Follows an infantry unit through Italy and concentrates on the everyday experiences of the soldiers, registering genuine emotion and realism. Mitchum's breakthrough role. Most of the actual unit played themselves. Pyle was killed by a sniper shortly before the film's release. **109m/B VHS, DVD.** Burgess Meredith, William Murphy, Wally Cassell, William Benedict, William (Bill) Self, Jack Reilly, Tito Renaldo, Hal Boyle, Chris Cunningham, Jack Foisie, George Lah, Bob Landry, Clete Roberts, Robert Rueben, Don Whitehead; **D:** William A. Wellman; **W:** Leopold Atlas, Guy Endore, Philip Stevenson; **C:** Russell Metty; **M:** Louis Applebaum, Ann Ronell.

The Story of Jacob & Joseph ♪♪ **1974 (R)** Fine biblical drama finds brothers Jacob and Esau fighting over their birthright, tearing apart their family for 20 years. When the brothers finally reconcile, it's only to cast an envious eye on youngest brother Joseph, whom they sell into slavery. Taken to Egypt Joseph uses his talents to become the Pharoah's chief advisor but he can never forget his family or what was done to him. All-around good acting, directing, and writing. **96m/C VHS, DVD.** Keith Michell, Tony LoBianco, Julian Glover, Colleen Dewhurst, Herschel Bernardi, Harry Andrews; **D:** Michael Cacoyannis; **W:** Ernest Kinoy; **M:** Mikis Theodorakis.

The Story of Louis Pasteur ♪♪♪ **1936** Formulaic Hollywood biopic raised a notch or two by Muni's superb portrayal of the famous scientist and his career leading up to his most famous discoveries. Acclaimed in its time; excellent despite low budget. **85m/B VHS.** Paul Muni, Josephine Hutchinson, Anita Louise, Fritz Leiber, Donald Woods, Porter Hall, Akim Tamiroff, Walter Kingsford; **D:** William Dieterle; **C:** Gaetano Antonio "Tony" Gaudio. Oscars '36: Actor (Muni), Story.

The Story of O ♪♪ **1975 (NC-17)** A young woman's love for one man moves her to surrender herself to many men, in order to please him. Soft-core porn with bondage and S&M beautified by camera work. Based on the classic Freudian-erotic novel by Pauline Reage. **105m/C VHS, DVD.** Corinne Clery, Anthony Steel, Udo Kier, Jean Gaven, Christiane Minazzoli, Martine Kelly, Nadine Perles; **D:** Just Jaeckin; **W:** Sebastien Japrisot; **C:** Robert Fraisse, Yves Rodallec; **M:** Pierre Bachelet.

The Story of O, Part 2 ♪ **1987** A sort-of sequel to the erotic classic, in which the somewhat soiled vixen seducing everyone in it. **107m/C DVD.** *FR* Sandra Wey, Carole James; **D:** Eric Rochat; **M:** Hans Zimmer.

The Story of Qiu Ju ♪♪♪ *Qiu Ju Da Guansi* **1991 (PG)** A simple story, beautifully directed and acted, about a peasant woman's search for justice. The pregnant

Qiu Ju's husband is assaulted and injured by the head of their village. Outraged, Qiu Ju slowly climbs the Chinese administrative ladder from official to higher official as she insistently seeks redress. Presents a close observance of daily life and customs with a strong female lead. Adapted from the novel "The Wan Family's Lawsuit" by Chen Yuan Bin. In Mandarin Chinese with English subtitles. **100m/C VHS, DVD, CH** Gong Li, Lei Lao Sheng, Liu Pei Qu, Ge Zhi Jun, Ye Jun, Yang Liu Xia, Zhu Qianqing, Cui Luowen, Yang Huiqin, Wang Jianfa, Lin Zi; **D:** Yimou Zhang; **W:** Liu Heng; **C:** Chi Xiaolin, Yu Xiaoqun; **M:** Jiping Zhao. San. Soc. Film Critics '93; Foreign Film; Venice Film Fest. '92: Actress (Li). Film.

The Story of Robin Hood & His Merrie Men 🐾🐾 1952
The Story of Robin Hood 1952 Richard Todd was Disney's swashbuckler based on the English legend. Almost but not quite, as memorable as the 1938 Michael Curtiz' version had Errol Flynn, after all. **83m/C VHS, DVD** Richard Todd, Joan Rice, Peter Finch, Martita Hunt; **D:** Ken Annakin.

The Story of Ruth 🐾🐾 1960
Biblical saga of adventures of Ruth as she denounces her pagan gods and flees to Israel. Typically "epic" with overwrought performances. Alternately not too bad to downright boring. **132m/C VHS, DVD** Elana Eden, Viveca Lindfors, Peggy Wood, Tom Tryon, Stuart Whitman, Jeff Morrow, Thayer David, Eduard Franz; **D:** Henry Koster.

The Story of Seabiscuit 🐾🐾 1949
Pride of Kentucky The famous racing winner Seabiscuit is featured in a fluffy story of a racetrack romance. Temple is in love with a jockey (McCallister) but wants him to give up racing. Her uncle (Fitzgerald), who is Seabiscuit's trainer, has other things in mind. **93m/C VHS, DVD.** Shirley Temple, Barry Fitzgerald, Lon (Bud) McCallister, Rosemary DeCamp; **D:** David Butler.

The Story of the Late Chrysanthemum 🐾🐾½ 1939
Die Geschichte vom Wein- enden Kamel 2003 *(PG)* Tale of animal estrangement and reconciliation combining reality situations. Follows a family trife of shepherds through the camel's birthing season, a way of life that is slowly being eliminated. When one camel mother rejects her white calf, a musician from the village is sent to perform a musical ceremony using a two-stringed, boxlike violin and soothing, hypnotic melodies to reunite calf and mother. Some may argue the re-created sequences are out of balance or perhaps unnecessary, but the story is presented in a thoughtful, honest manner. In Mongolian with English subtitles. **90m/C DVD, GE** Odgerel Ayush, Ikhbayar Amgaabazar, Guntbaatar Ikhbayar, Enkhtuya Ikhbayar, Uuganbaatar Ikhbayar, Chimed Ohin, Janchiv Ayurzana, Amgaabazar Gonzon, Zeveljamz Nyam, Guntbaatar Nyam, Munkbayar, Amirjargal Adiya, Dago Rolav, Chulu..rezeg Gur; **D:** Byambasuren Davaa, Luigi Falorni; **C:** Luigi Falorni; **M:** Marcel Lenz. Directors Guild '04: Feature Doc.

The Story of Us 🐾🐾 1999 *(R)*
Hey attraction is easy but sustaining a relationship is hard—particularly after 15 years in a marriage of opposites. Crossword puzzle editor Katie (Pfeiffer) is a planner and organizer while hubby Ben (Willis), a TV comedy writer, is a spontaneous free-spirit. The kids are away at summer camp when the constantly bickering duo decide on a trial separation as they wonder what went wrong. Appealing leads but story is repetitive and sentimental. **96m/C VHS, DVD.** Bruce Willis, Michelle Pfeiffer, Rita Wilson, Paul Reiser, Rob Reiner, Tim Matheson, Jeff Morrow, Jayne Meadows, Tom Poston, Betty White, Julie Hagerty, Jayne Meadows, Red Buttons; **D:** Rob Reiner.

The Story of Vernon and Irene Castle 🐾🐾 1939
In this, a beautiful and mysterious young woman. Gray is separated from his family are strong candidates for the film and exasperated everyone on the set by insisting that Rogers be a brunette. Still fun, vintage Fred and Ginger. *Only When You're in My Arms; Missouri Waltz; Oh, You Beautiful Doll; Nights of Gladness; By the Beautiful Sea; Glow, Little Glow Worm; Destiny Waltz; Row, Row, Row; The Yama Yama Man.* **93m/B VHS, DVD.** Fred Astaire, Ginger Rogers, Edna May Oliver, Lew Fields, Jack Perrin, Walter Brennan; **D:** H.C. Potter.

The Story of Women 🐾🐾🐾
Une Affaire de Femmes 1988 Riveting factual account of a woman (Huppert) who was guillotined for performing abortions in Nazi-occupied France. In French with English subtitles. **110m/C VHS, FR** Isabelle Huppert, Francois Cluzet, Marie Trintignant, Nils Tavernier, Louis Ducreux; **D:** Claude Chabrol; **C:** Jean Rabier; **M:** Matthieu Chabrol. L.A. Film Critics '89: Foreign Film; N.Y. Film Critics '89: Foreign Film; Venice Film Fest. '88: Actress (Huppert).

The Story of Xinghua 🐾🐾🐾 1993
Obedient wife Xinghua (Wenli) endures the cruelty of her greedy husband (Guoli) in a northern Chinese village, built within the shadow of the Great Wall. Xinghua is drawn to his gentleness and the two become lovers. When her husband hears that gold may be buried beneath one of the wall's watchtowers, he persuades his fellow villagers to help him dig beneath the stones—a decision that leads to tragedy. Mandarin with subtitles. **88m/C VHS, CH** Jiang Wenli, Zhang Guoli, Tian Shaojun; **D:** Yin Li.

Storybook 🐾🐾½ 1995 *(G)*
Eight-year-old Brandon finds a magic storybook and enters into a realm of fantasy. He discovers the only way to return home from Storyland is to save the kingdom from the rule of Queen Evilla and along with Woody the Woodsman, Pouch the Boxing Kangaroo, and Hoot the Wise Owl, Brandon just may succeed. **86m/C VHS, DVD.** Sean Fitzgerald, William McNamara, Swoosie Kurtz, Robert Costanzo, James Doohan, Brenda Epperson, Gary Morgan, Richard Moll, Jack Scalia, Milton Berle; **D:** Lorenzo Doumani; **W:** Lorenzo Doumani, Susan Bowen.

Storytelling 🐾🐾 2001 *(R)*
Anthology explores the roles that sex and dysfunction play in creativity. First story, "Fiction" explores the complex relationship of writing student Vi (Blair) and her boyfriend Marcus (Fitzpatrick), who has cerebral palsy. The two are using each other for different ends, most notably to read each other's writing. Vi moves on to an intense one-night stand with her formidable black writing professor (Wisdom). Shaken, Vi weaves the graphic, brutal, but fascinating encounter into a story of her own. In "Non-fiction," feature documentarian Toby (Giamatti) goes to the burbs to document the life of a teen, his characteristic dysfunctional family, and their Salvadoran maid. Solondz's characteristic black humor and social satire offers a range of hot topics, including homosexuality, political correctness, social stereotypes, the Holocaust, race, poverty, and the disabled. **87m/C VHS, DVD.** *US* Selma Blair, Leo Fitzpatrick, Aleksa Palladino, Robert Wisdom, Noah Fleiss, Paul Giamatti, John Goodman, Julie Hagerty, Lupe Ontiveros, Franka Potente, Mike Schank, Mark Webber, Jonathan Osser; **D:** Todd Solondz; **W:** Todd Solondz; **M:** Belle & Sebastian, Nathan Larsor.

Storyville 🐾🐾½ 1974 *(PG)*
Love and music overcome prostitution and poverty in this turn-of-the-century New Orleans jazz drama, but tragedy prevails. **96m/C VHS.** Tim Rooney, Jeannie Wilson, Butch Benit, Wayne Mack, Bond Gideon, Oley Sassone; **D:** Jack Weis.

The Story of Vernon and Irene Castle 🐾🐾 1939
W: Alan Zweibel, Jessie Nelson; **C:** Michael Chapman; **M:** Eric Clapton, Marc Shaiman.

Storyville 🐾🐾 1992 *(R)*
Southern Gothic tale set in New Orleans about a feckless young lawyer running for a local congressional seat. Neither Cray nor his values vote. Cray is separated from his wife and willingly indulges in an affair with This leads to a blackmail plot when he finds out his lover has been videotaping their antics. There's also a murder investigation and a host of family skeletons rattling around. Robards is the crafty uncle but Spader's low-key attitude works against the story. Directorial debut of Frost. **111m/C VHS, DVD.** James Spader, Joanne Whalley, Jason Robards Jr., Charlotte Lewis, Michael Warren, Piper Laurie, Michael Parks, Chuck McCann, Woody Strode, Charles Haid; **D:** Mark Frost; **W:** Mark Frost, Lee Reynolds; **M:** Carter Burwell.

Stowaway 🐾🐾🐾 1936 *(G)*
After her missionary parents are killed in a Chinese revolution, Shirley stows away on a San Francisco-bound liner and pays cupid to a bickering young couple who adopt her. *Good Night, My Love; One Never Knows, Does One; You Gotta S-M-I-L-E to Be H-A-P-P-Y; I Wanna Go To the Zoo; That's What I Want For Christmas.* **86m/B VHS.** Shirley Temple, Robert Young, Alice Faye, Eugene Pallette, Helen Westley, Arthur Treacher, Astrid Allwyn; **D:** William A. Seiter; **C:** Arthur C. Miller.

Straight for the Heart 🐾🐾
Corps Perdu 1988 Photojournalist Pierre returns to Montreal after a harrowing assignment in Nicaragua. His homecoming is less than happy when he discovers both his lovers, David and Sarah, have deserted him. Pierre takes to wandering the Montreal streets, taking pictures, hoping they will help him have some sense of this life and help him re-establish a connection with beauty and humanity. In French with English subtitles. **92m/C VHS, CA** Matthias Habich, Johanne-Marie Tremblay; **D:** Lea Pool.

Straight into Darkness 🐾🐾½ 2004 *(R)*
Privates Losey (Francis) and Deming (MacDonald) go AWOL in Nazi-occupied France, eventually finding shelter at an abandoned hotel. The hotel also houses Deacon (Warren), Maria (Thorson), and a brood of orphans who have been trained to fight. The numerous flashbacks are confusing and the fate of the child soldiers disturbing. **94m/C DVD, Ryan** Francis, James LeGros, Daniel Roebuck; **D:** Jeff Burr; **W:** Jeff Burr; **C:** Viorel Sergovici Jr.; **M:** Michael Convertino.

Straight Line 🐾🐾 1988 T.S. Turner
is a private investigator who goes after street gangs in order to prevent further violence in this action-packed story. **95m/C VHS.** Mr. T, Sean Roberge, Ron Ryan, Ken Walsh; **D:** George Mihalka.

Straight out of Brooklyn 🐾🐾 1991 *(R)*
A bleak, nearly hopeless look at a struggling black family in a Brooklyn housing project. The son seeks escape through crime, his father in booze. An up-close and raw look at part of society seldom shown in mainstream film, its undeniable power is sapped by ragged production values and a loose narrative prone to melodrama. Rich (seen in a supporting role) was only 19 years old when he completed this, funded partly by PBS-TV's "American Playhouse." **91m/C VHS, DVD.** George T. Odom, Ann D. Sanders, Larry (Lawrence) Gilliard Jr., Mark Malone, Reana E. Drummond, Barbara Sanon, Matty Rich; **D:** Matty Rich; **W:** Matty Rich; **C:** John Rosnell; **M:** Harold Wheeler. Ind. Spirit '92: First Feature; Sundance '91: Special Jury Prize.

Straight out of Compton 🐾🐾½ 1999
Stereotype-riddled saga of a tough Compton local, Henry "Hen" Alabaster, and his plan to score some big time cash and start his own record company. He targets a racist politician named Drake Norelli, who's made a fortune laundering mob money. The whole thing seems to want to deliver the meaningful message that "you can't escape your past," but it's lost amidst a mess of cliches and offensive stereotypes. **?m/C DVD.** Ryan Combs, Johnny JeaRenzo.

Straight Shooter 🐾🐾 1999 *(R)*
Former Foreign Legionnaire Volker Breitz (Farch) seeks revenge for his daughter's death by killing the politicians he thinks are responsible. Frank Hector (Hopper), his former trainer, may be the only one who can stop him but will he? Hopper's the only English-speaking actor in this German thriller—the other actors are dubbed. **98m/C VHS, DVD, GE** Dennis Hopper, Heino Ferch, Ulrich Muhe; **D:** Thomas Bohn.

Straight Shootin' 🐾🐾½ 1917
Ford's first major effort launched both Carey and Gibson to national fame. Prototypical western; great action, great scenery. Silent. **53m/B VHS.** Harry Carey Sr., Hoot Gibson, Mollie Melone; **D:** John Ford.

The Straight Story 🐾🐾🐾½ 1999 *(G)*
Surprisingly sweet true story from the generally eccentric Lynch. Septugenarian Alvin Straight (Farnsworth), who lives in an Iowa town, is determined to visit his ailing, estranged brother Lyle (Stanton), even though he can no longer drive a car. So, he hitches a small trailer to his riding mower and heads off at a stately 6 miles per hour—to Wisconsin (a 300 mile trip). Alvin realizes this is his last chance at 20th freedom and family and he's determined to make the most of it. Farnsworth plays Straight as a gruff, straight-talking old geezer and there's little or no sentimental anew. She finds a job as a receptionist at WNCY radio, but is mistaken for the new radio psychologist. Her homespun advice ("Get off the cross, Somebody needs the wood.") becomes hugely popular and soon "Dr. Shirlee is the toast of the town. Parton's advice is the funniest part of this filmsy movie, but she is helped immensely by Dunne and Orbach. Woods, however, is not in his element in a romantic comedy, and holds the movie down. **91m/C VHS, DVD.** Dolly Parton, James Woods, Griffin Dunne, Michael Madsen, Deirdre O'Connell, John J Sayles, Teri Hatcher, Spalding Gray, Jerry Orbach, Philip Bosco, Charles Fleischer, Jay Thomas; **D:** Barnet Kellman; **W:** Craig Bolotin, Patricia Resnick; **M:** Brad Fiedel.

Straight Talk 🐾🐾½ 1992 *(PG)*
Shirlee (Parton), a down-home gal from Arkansas, heads for Chicago to start life anew.

Straight Time 🐾🐾🐾 1978 *(R)*
Ex-con Hoffman hits the streets for the first time in six years and finds himself again falling into a life of crime. Well-told, sober-ing story flopped at the boxoffice and has never received the recognition it deserves. Convincing, realistic portrayal of a criminal. Hoffman was the original director, but gave the reins to Grosbard. Based on the novel "No Beast So Fierce" by Edward Bunker. **114m/C VHS, DVD.** Dustin Hoffman, Harry Dean Stanton, Gary Busey, Theresa Russell, M. Emmet Walsh, Kathy Bates, Edward Bunker; **D:** Uli Grosbard; **W:** Jeffrey Boam, Alvin Sargent, Edward (Eddie) Bunker; **C:** Owen Roizman; **M:** David Shire.

Straight to Hell 🐾🐾 1987 *(R)*
A wildly senseless, anachronistic western spoof about a motley, inept gang of frontier thieves. An overplayed, indiscriminating junk spaghetti oat-opera. **86m/C VHS, DVD.** Dennis Hopper, Joe Strummer, Elvis Costello, Grace Jones, Jim Jarmusch, Dick Rude, Courtney Love, Sy Richardson, Xander Berkeley, Shane McGowan; **D:** Alex Cox; **W:** Alex Cox, Dick Rude; **C:** Tom Richmond; **M:** The Pogues, Pray for Rain.

Straight Up 🐾🐾½ 1990
A musical for x-ridden attempts to warn MTV-era children about drugs, but visual gimmicks often spoof about a mother, inept gang of frontier thieves. An overplayed, indiscriminating junk spaghetti oat-opera. The smartest segment lambasts cigarette and alcohol ads. **75m/C VHS.** Chad Allen, Louis Gossett Jr.

Jules Dupree, Sean Epps; D: Ryan Combs; **W:** Ryan Combs; **C:** Eric Green.

Strait-Jacket 🦴🦴½ 1964 After Crawford is released from an insane asylum where she was sent 20 years for axing her husband and his mistress, mysterious axe murders begin to occur in the neighborhood. Coincidence? Aging axist Crawford is the prime suspect, and even she cannot say for sure who's doing it. Daughter Baker is there to help her adjust. Moderately creepy grade B+ slasher is lifted somewhat by Crawford ("Psycho"). Never one to miss a gimmick, director Castle arranged for the distribution of cardboard "bloody axes" to all theatre patrons attending the movie. **89m/B VHS, DVD.** Joan Crawford, Leif Erickson, Diane Baker, George Kennedy, Howard St. John, Rochelle Hudson, Edith Atwater, Lee Majors, John Anthony Hayes, Mitchell Cox, Lee Yeary, Patricia Krest; **D:** William Castle; **W:** Robert Bloch; **C:** Arthur E. Arling; **M:** Van Alexander.

Stranded 🦴🦴 1987 (PG-13) A group of aliens escaping interplanetary persecution land on Earth and enlist the aid of an Earth family. Solid characters make it more than sci-fi; sort of a parable of intolerance, human (and alien) goodness, etc. **80m/C VHS.** Maureen O'Sullivan, Ione Skye, Cameron Dye; **D:** Tex Fuller; **W:** Alan Castle.

The Strange Affair of Uncle Harry 🦴🦴½ *Uncle Harry* 1945 Small-town gothic with fine acting by Sanders, an aging bachelor who plots murder when his romance is threatened by a jealous sister. A title card asks you not to reveal the 'surprise' ending—a hackneyed twist that appeased the censors but made producer Joan Harrison resign in protest. Based on a play by Robert Job. Tape suffers from poor film-video transfer. **80m/B VHS.** George Sanders, Geraldine Fitzgerald, Ella Raines, Sara Allgood, Moyna MacGill, Samuel S. Hinds, Harry von Zell; **D:** Robert Siodmak.

A Strange and Deadly Occurrence 🦴½ 1974 Strange things start to happen to a family when they move to a house in a remote area. **74m/C VHS.** Robert Stack, Vera Miles, L.Q. Jones, Herb Edelman; **D:** John Llewellyn Moxey. **TV**

Strange Awakening 🦴 1958 Traveling in France while recuperating from amnesia, Barker is trapped in a plot of fraud and theft. Confused and contrived. **75m/B VHS.** Lex Barker, Carole Mathews, Nora Swinburne, Richard Molinos, Peter Dyneley; **D:** Montgomery Tully.

Strange Bedfellows 🦴🦴½ 1965 Within 24 hours of Carter Hudson (Hudson) arriving to work in London, he's met and married eccentric Italian Toni Vincent (Lollobrigida). Complete opposites, the marriage is soon over and Carter returns to the States. Seven years later, he's back in London, ready to officially divorce Toni but learns from company PR whiz Dick Bramwell (Young) that his big promotion is contingent on his happy marriage. Carter courts Toni again, and tries to support her liberal causes and friends, but it turns out her latest stunt is aimed at his firm. Supposedly a check of the closing credits shows the film was shot on a Universal back lot and not on location. **104m/C VHS, DVD.** Rock Hudson, Gina Lollobrigida, Gig Young, Edward Judd, Howard St. John, Nancy Kulp, Bernard Fox, Terry-Thomas; **D:** Melvin Frank; **W:** Melvin Frank, Michael Pertwee; **C:** Leo Tover; **M:** Leigh Harline.

Strange Bedfellows 🦴🦴½ 2004 (R) Because of financial problems, lifelong buddies Vince (Hogan) and Ralph (Caton) pose as a gay couple to get a newly-enacted tax break. But suspicious auditor Russell McKenzie (Postlethwaite) comes to their small town to check out their story. Surprisingly charming, though predictable, comedy plays up the outrageous aspects of the deception while still maintaining its heart. **100m/C VHS, DVD.** AU Paul Hogan, Michael Caton, Pete Postlethwaite, Alan Cassell, Kestie Morassi, Roy Billing, Glynn Nicholas, Amanda Monroe; **D:** Dean Murphy; **W:** Dean Murphy, Stewart Faichney; **C:** Roger Lanser; **M:** Dale Cornelius.

Strange Behavior 🦴🦴 *Dead Kids; Small Town Massacre* 1981 (R) In a small Midwestern town, the police chief follows the clues from a series of murders to the experimental lab of the local college. Seems there's a mad scientist involved... Grisly and creepy, but unduly ballyhooed when it appeared. Shot on location in New Zealand. **105m/C VHS, DVD.** Michael Murphy, Louise Fletcher, Dan Shor, Fiona Lewis, Arthur Dignam, Marc McClure, Scott Brady, Dey Young, Charles Lane; **D:** Michael Laughlin; **W:** Michael Laughlin, Bill Condon; **C:** Louis Horvath.

Strange Brew 🦴🦴½ 1983 (PG) The screen debut of the SCTV alumni's characters Doug & Bob MacKenzie, the Great White North duo. They do battle with a powerful, megalomaniacal brew master over—what else?—a case of beer. Dumb, but what did you expect? Watch it, or be a hoser. **91m/C VHS, DVD.** C4 Rick Moranis, Dave Thomas, Max von Sydow, Paul Dooley, Lynne Griffin, Angus MacInnes; **D:** Rick Moranis, Dave Thomas; **W:** Steve DeJarnatt, Rick Moranis, Dave Thomas; **C:** Steven Poster; **M:** Charles Fox; **V:** Mel Blanc.

Strange Cargo 🦴🦴½ 1940 Convicts escaping from Devil's Island are mystically entranced by a Christ-like fugitive en route to freedom. An odd, pretentious Hollywood fable waiting for a cult following. Gable and Crawford's eighth and final pairing. Adapted by Anita Loos from the book "Not Too Narrow...Not Too Deep" by Richard Sale. **128m/C VHS, DVD.** Jack Palance, Leo Genn, Clark Gable, Joan Crawford, Ian Hunter, Peter Lorre, Paul Lukas, Albert Dekker, J. Edward Bromberg, Eduardo Ciannelli, Frederick Worlock; **D:** Frank Borzage; **W:** Lesser Samuels; **C:** Robert Planck; **M:** Franz Waxman.

Strange Case of Dr. Jekyll & Mr. Hyde 🦴🦴 1968 An adaptation of the classic Robert Louis Stevenson book about a scientist who conducts experiments on himself to separate good from evil. Palance is oddly but appealingly cast; Made for TV. Oscar Homolka, Billie Whitelaw, Denholm Elliott; **D:** Charles Jarrott; **M:** Robert Cobert. **TV**

Strange Case of Dr. Jekyll & Mr. Hyde 🦴🦴 1989 The Robert Louis Stevenson classic, with Hyde portrayed as an icy, well-dressed sociopath. An entry in Shelley Duvall's "Nightmare Classics" series. More psychological than special effect-y. **60m/C VHS.** Anthony Andrews, Laura Dern, George Murdock, Nicholas Guest; **D:** Charles Jarrott; **M:** Ivor Slaney. **CABLE**

The Strange Case of the End of Civilization As We Know It 🦴🦴½ 1993 Cleese stars as the detective grandson of Sherlock Holmes, who also has a reputation for making a mockery of police investigations. Nevertheless, the police commissioner summons him to capture that diabolical criminal Professor Moriarty. **55m/C VHS, DVD.** GB Ron Moody, Joss Ackland, Holly Palance, John Cleese, Stratford Johns, Connie Booth, Arthur Lowe; **D:** Joseph McGrath; **W:** Joseph McGrath, John Cleese; **C:** Kenneth Higgins; **M:** Ivor Slaney.

Strange Confession 🦴🦴½ 1945 Contains one of the truly rare Inner Sanctum Mysteries from Universal. A scientist working for an unscrupulous pharmaceutical company takes revenge on his boss when the premature release of an untested flu medicine results in the death of his son. **62m/C VHS.** Lon Chaney Jr., Brenda Joyce, J. Carrol Naish, Milburn Stone, Lloyd Bridges; **D:** John Hoffman; **W:** M. Coates Webster.

The Strange Countess 🦴🦴 1961 A girl is almost murdered and no apparent motive can be found until a 20-year-old murder is uncovered in this Edgar Wallace story. **96m/C VHS.** GE Joachim Fuchsberger, Lil Dagover, Marianne Hoppe, Brigitte Grothum; **D:** Josef von Baky.

Strange Days 🦴🦴½ 1995 (R) It's 1999 in volatile L.A. and vice cop-turned-street-hustler Lenny Nero (Fiennes) is plying his SQUID trade—discs that offer the wearer the chance to experience any vice. The seedily likeable Lenny draws the line at peddling snuff clips until one capturing the murder of his friend, hooker Iris (Bako), shows up. Lenny's in way over his head and turns to self-sufficient security agent Mace (Bassett) to save him. The phenomenal Bassett heats up the screen (and kicks major butt) while the generally cerebral Fiennes shows why someone could care about his desperate lowlife. Bigelow's an action expert and struts on the film's dark visuals while offering some emotional impact with her society-on-the-eve-of-destruction saga. **145m/C VHS, DVD.** Kelly Hu, Michael Jace, Ralph Fiennes, Angela Bassett, Juliette Lewis, Tom Sizemore, Michael Wincott, Brigitte Bako, Vincent D'Onofrio, William Fichtner, Richard Edson, Glenn Plummer, Josef Sommer; **D:** Kathryn Bigelow; **W:** James Cameron, Jay Cocks; **C:** Matthew F. Leonetti; **M:** Graeme Revell.

The Strange Door 🦴🦴 1951 Laughton hams it up as the evil Alan de Maletroit (Laughton), who's imprisoned his brother Edmond (Cavanagh) over the crime of marrying Alan's one love. Now Maletroit wants to destroy his niece Blanche (Forrest) as well. But Edmond's faithful retainer Voltan (Karloff) is determined to stop the evil. Low-budget hokum adapted from the Robert Louis Stevenson story "The Sire de Maletroit's Door." **81m/B VHS, DVD.** Charles Laughton, Boris Karloff, Paul Cavanagh, Sally Forrest, Richard Stapley, Michael Pate, Alan Napier; **D:** Joseph Pevney; **W:** Jerry Sackheim; **C:** Irving Glassberg.

Strange Fits of Passion 🦴🦴½ 1999 Low-budget comedy/drama is McCredie's directorial debut. A nameless overly romantic young woman (Noonan) is convinced that she has just let the perfect man (Finsterer) slip away and she becomes obsessive about finding him again. Her search does not stop her, however, from having some alternative romantic prospects in mind. **83m/C VHS, DVD.** AU Michela Noonan, Mitchell Butel, Samuel Johnson, Steve Adams, Anni Finsterer, Jack Finsterer; **D:** Elise McCredie; **W:** Elise McCredie; **C:** Jaems Grant; **M:** Cezary Skubiszewski.

Strange Frequency 2 🦴🦴 2001 (R) Anthology consisting of four episodes from the title TV series: "Soul Man," "Instant Karma," "Cold Turkey," and "Don't Stop Believing." They each have a musical premise and a frequently supernatural twist about the price of fame and success. **84m/C VHS, DVD.** Roger Daltrey, Jason Gedrick, Patsy Kensit, Wendie Malick, James Marsters, Peter Strauss; **D:** Jeff Woolnough. **TV**

Strange Fruit 🦴🦴 2004 Intriguing premise is done in by a sluggish production (although the performances are generally strong). Gay black lawyer William Boyals (Faulcon) reluctantly leaves New York to return to the Louisiana bayou town he left years before after an old friend is found lynched. He needs to conduct his own investigation since the local sheriff (Jones) is a homophobic bigot. **115m/C DVD.** Sam Jones, Cecile Johnson, Kent Faulcon, Berlinda Tolbert, David Raibon; **D:** Kyle Schickner; **W:** Kyle Schickner; **C:** David Oye; **M:** Sidney James.

Strange Illusion 🦴🦴½ *Out of the Night* 1945 Unbalanced teen Lydon believes his mother, about to remarry, was responsible for his father's death. He feigns insanity in a plan to catch her, but is sent to an asylum, where he nearly goes insane for real. Slow and implausible, but creepy enough to hold your interest. **87m/B VHS, DVD.** Jimmy Lydon, Warren William, Sally Eilers, Regis Toomey, Charles Arnt, George Reed, Jayne Hazard; **D:** Edgar G. Ulmer; **W:** Adele Comandini; **C:** Philip Tannura; **M:** Leo Erdody.

Strange Impersonation 🦴🦴 1946 Dreamy noir has chemist Nora Goodrich (Marshall) injecting herself in order to test a new anesthetic she's developing. (This is never a good idea.) Then her life goes nuts when she can't separate reality from her dreams. **68m/B VHS, DVD.** Brenda Marshall, William Gargan, Hillary Brooke, George Chandler, Ruth Ford, H.B. Warner, Lyle Talbot, Mary Treen; **D:** Anthony Mann; **W:** Mindret Lord; **C:** Robert Pittack.

Strange Interlude 🦴🦴🦴 *Strange Interval* 1932 Shearer is at her best in screen adaptation of talky Eugene O'Neill play in which she portrays a young wife who wants a child, but discovers that insanity runs in her husband's family. Doing the only sensible thing, she decides to have a child by another man (Gable). Interesting because the characters' thoughts are revealed to the audience through voice-overs. **110m/B VHS.** Norma Shearer, Clark Gable, May Robson, Ralph Morgan, Robert Young, Mary Alden, Maureen O'Sullivan, Henry B. Walthall; **D:** Robert Z. Leonard; **C:** Lee Garmes.

Strange Interlude 🦴🦴½ 1990 Slow PBS production of Eugene O'Neill's famous drama covering two decades of the lives and loves of an upper-class family. Excellent performances help to make up for talkiness. On two cassettes. **190m/C VHS.** Glenda Jackson, Jose Ferrer, David Dukes, Ken Howard, Edward Petherbridge; **D:** Herbert Wise.

Strange Invaders 🦴🦴🦴 1983 (PG) Body-snatchers-from-space sci-fi with an attitude—fun spoof of '50s alien flicks. Space folks arrive in a midwestern town in the '50s, assuming the locals' appearance and attire before returning to their ship. Seems one of them married an earthling—but divorced and moved with her half-breed daughter to New York City. So the hicksters from space arrive in Gotham wearing overalls... **94m/C VHS, DVD.** Jack Kehler, Paul LeMat, Nancy Allen, Diana Scarwid, Michael Lerner, Louise Fletcher, Wallace Shawn, Fiona Lewis, Kenneth Tobey, June Lockhart, Charles Lane, Dey Young, Mark Goddard; **D:** Michael Laughlin; **W:** Bill Condon; **C:** Louis Horvath; **M:** John Addison.

Strange Justice: The Clarence Thomas and Anita Hill Story 🦴🦴½ 1999 (R) Someone must have lied at the 1991 confirmation hearings for Supreme Court Justice Clarence Thomas (Lindo) and this cable drama takes a look at playing hardball politics. Lobbyist Kenneth Duberstein (Patinkin) is assigned by the Bush White House to get Thomas appointed. But he doesn't anticipate the testimony of Anita Hill (Taylor) and her claims that her former boss sexually harassed her. Based on the nonfiction account by Jane Mayer and Jill Abramson. **111m/C VHS.** Delroy Lindo, Regina Taylor, Mandy Patinkin, Paul Winfield, Louis Gossett Jr.; **D:** Ernest R. Dickerson; **W:** Jacob Epstein. **CABLE**

The Strange Love of Martha Ivers 🦴🦴🦴 1946 Douglas is good in his screen debut as the wimpy spouse of unscrupulous Stanwyck. Stanwyck shines as the woman who must stay with Douglas because of a crime she committed long ago... Tough, dark melodrama; classic film noir. **117m/B VHS, DVD.** Barbara Stanwyck, Van Heflin, Kirk Douglas, Lizabeth Scott, Judith Anderson; **D:** Lewis Milestone; **W:** Robert Rossen; **C:** Victor Milner; **M:** Miklos Rozsa.

The Strange Love of Molly Louvain 🦴🦴½ *Molly Louvain* 1932 Unwed mother Dvorak finds herself in hiding, after her criminal beau fatally shoots a police officer. She falls in love with the unsuspecting newsman (Tracy) hot on her trail. Good performance from Dvorak but the film in general lacks sparkle. Adapted from the play "Tinsel Girl" by Maurine Watkins. **70m/B VHS.** Ann Dvorak, Lee Tracy, Richard Cromwell, Guy Kibbee, Leslie Fenton, Frank McHugh, Evalyn Knapp, Charles Middleton, Mary Doran, C. Henry Gordon; **D:** Michael Curtiz; **W:** Erwin Gelsey, Brown Holmes.

Strange New World 🦴🦴½ 1975 Three astronauts awake from 188 years in the fridge to find cloning has arrived. Made for TV as a pilot for a hoped-for series that might have been even worse. **100m/C VHS.** John Saxon, Kathleen Miller, Keene Curtis, Martine Beswick, James Olson, Catherine Bach, Richard Farnsworth, Ford Rainey; **D:** Robert Butler. **TV**

The Strange One 🦴🦴½ 1957 Appropriate title for this dank drama based on Willingham's novel and play "End As a Man." Jacko De Paris (Gazzara) is the student leader at a Southern military school, who uses his power to intimidate and brutalize fellow cadets, aided by minions Knoble (Hingle) and Gatt (Olson). Finally a group of younger students, led by Marquales (Peppard, in his film debut) go after the tyrant. Also filmed as 1957's "Sorority Girl." **100m/B VHS.** Ben Gazzara, Pat Hingle, James Olson, George Peppard, Peter Mark Richman, Larry Gates, Clifton James, Arthur

Strange Planet 🦴🦴½ **1999** Romantic comedy that follows six characters (three young women who share a house and three male buddies) from one New Year's Eve to the next. They have affairs, fall in love, breakup, and get together with different partners over the span of time. It's not new but it's sweet and Watts, Karvan, and Williamson are standouts. **95m/C VHS, DVD.** AU Claudia Karvan, Naomi Watts, Alice Garner, Tom Long, Hugo Weaving, Marshall Napier, Aaron Jeffrey, Felix Williamson; *D:* Emma-Kate Croghan; *W:* Emma-Kate Croghan, Stavros Kazantzidis; *C:* Justin Brickle.

Strange Relations 🦴🦴 **2002** New York shrink Jerry Lipman (Reiser) is diagnosed with leukemia and needs a bone marrow transplant. His mother Esther (Dukakis) finally confesses that Jerry was adopted in England and he heads to Liverpool to find his biological mother. That would be tough-talking, working class Sheila (Walters), who has a soft heart and is eager to welcome Jerry into the family. Jerry keeps his cancer a secret—not wanting to admit that's why he sought out his new relatives, especially as he gets closer to them. Walters is the one to watch but Reiser's sarcasm does help to keep the sentiment at bay. **107m/C VHS, DVD.** Paul Reiser, Julie Walters, George Wendt, Olympia Dukakis, Amy Robbins, Tony Maudsley, Suzanne... ; *W:* Tim Kazurinsky; *C:* Lawrence Jones; *M:* Rupert Gregson-Williams. **CABLE.**

Strange Shadows in an Empty Room 🦴🦴 **1976 (R)** *Blazing Magnums.* ...Whitman wants answers about the murder of his kid sis. He beats lots of people up, and the viewer leaves the empty living room to look at the inside of the fridge, which is more interesting. De Martino used the pseudonym Martin Herbert. **97m/C VHS.** Stuart Whitman, John Saxon, Martin Landau, Tisa Farrow, Carole Laure, Gayle Hunnicutt; *D:* Alberto De Martino.

Strange Wilderness 🦴 **2008 (R)** Peter Gaulke (Zahn) takes over as host of his dead father's popular wildlife show, but his inept stoner on-air persona pushes it to the brink of cancellation. Desperate, Peter and his loyal soundman Fred Wolf ['Covert; note that the dopey script names the two main characters after themselves] hatch a plan to showcase their search for Bigfoot in Ecuador, with their merry band of dudes in tow. Lots of herbally enhanced gags and goof-ups ensue, none of them particularly amusing (unless you're equally medicated). Given the funny-guy cast, what could have been a clever send-up of nature documentaries is all but wasted (in more ways than one) by the dopey script. **85m/C DVD.** US Steve Zahn, Allen Covert, Jonah Hill, Kevin Heffernan, Ashley Scott, Justin Long, Peter Dante, Harry Hamlin, Robert Patrick, Joe Don Baker, Jeff Garlin, Ernest Borgnine; *D:* Fred Wolf; *W:* Fred Wolf, Peter Gaulke; *C:* David Henings; *M:* Waddy Wachtel.

The Strange Woman 🦴🦴 **1946** Lamarr stalks man after man, but never creates much excitement in spite of Ulmer's fancy camera work and intense pace. **100m/B VHS, DVD.** Hedy Lamarr, George Sanders, Louis Hayward, Gene Lockhart, Hillary Brooke, June Storey; *D:* Edgar G. Ulmer; *W:* Herb Meadow; *C:* Lucien N. Andriot; *M:* Carmen Dragon.

Strange World of Coffin Joe 🦴 *O Estranho Mundo de Ze do Caixao* **1968** A collection of three shocking horror episodes about a truly disgusting dollmaker who becomes tempted by his humanlike creations, a balloon seller's repulsive necrophiliac impulses, and a doctor (the disguised Coffin Joe) with a sadistic gift for excruciating torture. In Portuguese with English subtitles. **80m/B VHS, BR VHS.** BR Jose Mojica Marins; *D:* Jose Mojica Marins.

The Strangeness WOOF! **1985** Miners in search of gold release a "strange" creature from far beneath the earth—eek! Made on a negative budget.

The Stranger and the Gunfighter 🦴🦴 **1976** The baddest spaghetti western of all time—or is it a kung fu movie? Alcoholic cowpoke Van Cleef and kung fu master Lieh pair up to find hidden treasure. There is a map, but parts are printed on the assorted fannies of various women. **106m/C VHS.** IT Patty (Patti) Shepard, Lee Van Cleef, Lo Lieh; *D:* Anthony M. Dawson.

Stranger by Night 🦴 **1994 (R)** Detective Bobby Corcoran and his partner are hunting a mutilating serial killer. Since Corcoran suffers from black-outs and fits of rage the evidence begins pointing very close to home. **96m/C VHS, DVD.** Steven Bauer, William Katt, Jennifer R.... ; *D:* Michael Parks.

A Stranger Among Us 🦴🦴 **1992 (PG-13)** A missing jeweler turns up dead and more than $1 million in diamonds has disappeared. NYPD Detective Emily Eden (Griffith) is called in to solve the case, and she decides she must go undercover in a community of Hasidic Jews to find the perpetrator. She not only finds the criminal, but she also falls in love with one of the group's most devout residents. Griffith is out of her element as a tough cop with her baby voice and cutesy style, but other actors, including Thal pin this movie debut) and Sara, perform splendidly, even though they're held back by a cumbersome script with many similarities to "Witness." **109m/C VHS, DVD.** James Gandolfini, Melanie Griffith, Eric Thal, John Pankow, Tracy Pollan, Lee Richardson, Mia Sara, Jamey Sheridan; *D:* Sidney Lumet; *W:* Robert J. Avrech; *C:* Andrzej Bartkowiak; *M:* Jerry Bock. Golden Raspberries '92: Worst Actress (Griffith).

The Stranger Woman (Long) 🦴½ **1995 (R)** Mystery woman (Long) rides into small town and rids it of a vicious motorcycle gang. Femme version of the lone hero saga. **98m/C VHS.** Kathy Long, Andrew Divoff, Eric Pierpoint, Robin Lynn Heath; *D:* Fritz Kiersch; *W:* Gregory Poirier.

The Stranger 🦴½ **1973** Corbett crash-lands on a planet an awful lot like Earth—and must stay on the run. Uneven fugitive thriller in sci-fi drag. Made for TV. **100m/C VHS.** Cameron Mitchell, Glenn Corbett, Sharon Acker, Lew Ayres, George Coulouris, Dean Jagger; *D:* Lee H. Katzin. TV

The Stranger 🦴🦴🦴 **1946** Notably conventional for Welles, but swell entertainment nonetheless. War crimes tribunal sets Shayne free hoping he'll lead them to his quarry, Robinson trails Shayne through Europe and South America to a small town in Connecticut. Tight suspense made on a tight budget saved Welles's directorial career. **95m/B VHS, DVD.** Edward G. Robinson, Loretta Young, Martha Wentworth, Konstantin Shayne, Richard Long, Orson Welles; *D:* Orson Welles; *W:* Victor Trivas; *C:* Russell Metty; *M:* Bronislau Kaper.

The Stranger 🦴🦴 **1987 (R)** Amnesiac car-wreck victim Bedelia begins regaining her memory, and realizes she witnessed several grisly murders. Is he shrink (Riegert) helping her remember, o keeping something from her? Good, neglected thriller. **93m/C VHS.** AR Bonnie Bedelia, Peter Riegert, Barry Primus, David Spielberg; *D:* Adolfo Aristarain; *W:* Dan Gurskis; *M:* Craig Safan.

VIDEO

A Stranger in the Kingdom 🦴🦴 **1998 (R)** Walt Andrews (Hudson) has been hired right unseen to be the new minister in a small Vermont community in the '50s. The unseen part is a problem since the townspeople are shocked when Walt turns out to be black. Then Walt gets arrested for the murder of a young housekeeper, Claire's (Bayma), whom he was sheltering from her abusive employer and the town seems determined to make him the scapegoat. Based on a novel by Howard Frank Mosher. **111m/C VHS, DVD.** Ernie Hudson, David Lansbury, Jean (Louisa) Kelly, Martin Sheen, Sean Nelson, Jordan Bayne, Bill Raymond, Henry Gibson, Larry Pine, Tom Aldredge, Carrie Snodgrass; *D:* Jay Craven; *W:* Jay Craven, Don Bredes; *C:* Philip Holahan.

A Stranger in Town 🦴🦴 **1957** A young journalist looks into the murder of an American composer in a sleepy English village. He discovers blackmail and intrigue. So-so thriller. Based on the novel "The Uninvited" by Frank Chittenden. 73m/B VHS. GB Alex Nicol, Ann Page, Mary Laura Wood, Mona Washbourne, Charles Lloyd-Pack; *D:* George Pollock.

A Stranger in Town 🦴🦴 **1995** Single mom lets Kay Tarses (Smart) has relocated to a small, quiet town with her infant son. But her peace is disturbed by menacing Barnes (Hines), a stranger who seems to know Kay has been lying about her past—and her child. When he seems determined to take her child, Kay has to decide whether to run, accept her fate, or fight. **93m/C VHS, DVD.** Jean Smart, Gregory Hines, Jeffrey Nordling, Lucinca Jenney, Richard Riehle; *D:* Peter Levin; *M:* Mark Snow. TV

The Stranger: Kabloonak 🦴½ *Kabloonak* **1995** Pioneering filmmaker Robert Flaherty (Dance) premieres his documentary "Nanook of the North" in 1922 and recalls (in flashback) the difficulties in making the film. History has been tweaked but the cinematography is gorgeous and Dance's...

A Stranger Is Watching 🦴½ **1982 (R)** Rapist-murderer Torn holds his victim's 10-year-old child hostage, along with a New York TV anchorwoman. Complicated and distasteful. **92m/C VHS.** DVD. Rip Torn, Kate Mulgrew, James Naughton; *D:* Sean S. Cunningham. TV

Stranger in Paso Bravo 🦴 **1968** A distraught drifter returns to a strange Italian town to avenge the murders of his wife and daughter years before. Dubbed. **92m/C VHS.** IT Anthony Steffen, Giulia Rubini, Eduardo Fajardo, Andriana Ambesi; *D:* Salvatore Rosso; *W:* Lucio Battistrada; *C:* Alfonso Nieva; *M:* Angelo Francesco Lavagnino.

Stranger in the House 🦴🦴 **1997 (R)** Jack (Railsback) hid a diamond necklace in an old house after his heist went bad. When he gets out of prison and goes to retrieve his loot, he discovers the house is now occupied by Joanna (Greene) and Dan (Dinsmore). Turns out Dan wants to kill Joanna for her money, and Jack's being pursued by an insurance adjuster (Vrana) after the necklace. **94m/C VHS.** Michele Greene, Steve Railsback, Bruce Dinsmore, Vlasta Vrana; *D:* Rodney Gibbons; *W:* Peter Paul Liapis, Steve Pesce; *M:* Marty Simon.

The Stranger from Venus WOOF! *Immediate Disaster; The Venusian* **1954** "The Day the Earth Stood Still" warmed over. Venusian Dantine tells earth lady Neal he's worried about the future of our planet. Real low budget. Includes previews of coming attractions from classic sci-fi. **78m/B VHS, DVD.** Patricia Neal, Helmut Dantine, Derek Bond; *D:* Burt Balaban; *W:* Hans Jacoby; *C:* Ken Talbot; *M:* Eric Spear.

The Stranger from Pecos 🦴🦴 **1945** Brown fights a cheater who swindles people at poker and then uses the money to buy their mortgages. Meanwhile, his pal Hatton finds a novel way to help a robbery victim buy back his property. **55m/B VHS.** Johnny Mack Brown, Raymond Hatton, Kirby Grant, Christine McIntyre, Steve Clark, Kermit Maynard; *D:* Lambert Hillyer.

Stranger on the Third Floor 🦴🦴🦴 **1940** Reporter McGuire's testimony helped convict cabbie Cook of murder, but he begins to have doubts. Odd, shadowy psycho-thriller considered by some the first film noir. The reporter comes to be suspected of the crime, and his fiancee pounds the pavement to prove him innocent. Average acting, but great camera work gives the whole a deliciously menacing feel. **64m/B VHS.** Peter Lorre, John McGuire, Elisha Cook Jr., Margaret Tallichet, Charles Halton; *D:* Boris Ingster.

Stranger than Fiction 🦴🦴½ **1999 (R)** Would-be horror thriller wastes its talented cast. Jared (Astin) arrives, hysterical, at the home of his best friend, Austin (Field), with some confusing tale about a murder in his apartment. Austin, Jared and their friends Emma (Meyer) and Violet (Wagner) return to the scene of the crime, only to discover that Jared has been less than honest with them. **100m/C VHS, DVD.** MacKenzie Astin, Todd Field, Dina Meyer, Natasha Gregson Wagner; *D:* Eric Bross; *W:* Tim Garrick, Scott Russell; *C:* Horacio Marquinez; *M:* Larry Seymour.

Stranger Than Paradise 🦴🦴🦴 **1984 (R)** Would-be New York hipster Willie (Lurie) is a Hungarian emigre who is asked to look after his newly arrived teenaged cousin Eva (Balint). They develop a weird affectionate relationship before Eva heads to Cleveland to live with an aunt (Stark). When Willie realizes he misses her, he and buddy Eddie (Edson) drive to visit her and the threesome then decide to head to Florida for some fun in the sun. The thinking person's mindless flick. Inventive independent comedy made on quite a low budget was acclaimed at Cannes. **90m/B VHS, DVD.** GE John Lurie, Eszter Balint, Richard Edson, Cecillia Stark, Danny Rosen; *D:* Jim Jarmusch; *W:* Jim Jarmusch; *C:* Tom DiCillo; *M:* John Lurie. Natl. Soc. Film Critics '84: Film.

The Stranger Who Looks Like Me 🦴🦴 **1974** Adoptees Baxter and Bridges set out to find their real parents. Not-bad TV fare. Meredith is the real-life mom. Look for a young Patrick Duffy. **74m/C VHS.** Meredith Baxter, Beau Bridges, Whitney Blake; *D:* Larry Peerce. TV

The Stranger Within 🦴½ **1974** Made-for-TV "Rosemary's Baby" rip-off. Black mark against his name, Jeff Travis (Scott) goes to Arizona and ends up billing Grizzard is impotent. The stranger within begins commanding her to do its bidding. just as if she were a genie. **74m/C VHS.** Barbara Eden, George Grizzard, Joyce Van Patten, Nehemiah Persoff; *D:* Lee Philips; *M:* Charles Fox. TV

The Stranger Wore a Gun 🦴🦴 **1953** Hoping to remove as a stagecoach robbery. Features a great action sequence in a burning saloon. Originally shot in 3-D, this is based on the novel "Yankee Gold" by John M. Cunning... lead performance is strong. **185m/C VHS.** CA FR Charles Dance; *D:* Claude Massot; *C:* Jacques Loiseleux, François Protat, Sebastian Regnier.

Stranger on the Third Floor ... (see above)

Stranger Than Fiction 🦴🦴½ **2006 (PG-13)** Ferrell stars as milquetoast everyman Harold Crick, a Chicago IRS agent living a tiny little life, which he suddenly starts hearing his life narrated by a British-accented woman. Harold appears to be a character in writer Kay Eiffel's (Thompson) latest book in which she plans to kill him. Harold, real or imaginary, doesn't want to die and seeks the services of literature professor Jules Hilcert (Hoffman) who advises Harold to do what he's always wanted to do, prompting Harold to turn to feisty baker Ana (Gyllenhaal). Good move, Harold. Cast is first-rate but, remember, Ferrell is supposed to be low-key. **113m/C DVD, Blu-ray Disc.** US Will Ferrell, Maggie Gyllenhaal, Dustin Hoffman, Emma Thompson, Queen Latifah, Tony Hale, Tom Hulce, Linda Hunt; *D:* Marc Forster; *W:* Zach Helm; *C:* Roberto Schaefer; *M:* Brian Reitzell, Britt Daniel.

ham. **83m/C VHS, DVD.** Randolph Scott, Claire Trevor, Joan Weldon, George Macready, Alfonso Bedoya, Lee Marvin, Ernest Borgnine, Pierre Watkin, Joseph (Joe) Vitale; **D:** Andre de Toth.

Strangers 🎬🎬 **1990** Australian horror film revolves around a man in a troubled marriage who fools around with another woman, only to realize she is dead set on mating for life. When he hesitates, she vows to murder his wife. Very similar to the smash hit "Fatal Attraction." **83m/C VHS. AU** James Healey, Anne Looby; **D:** Craig Lahiff.

Strangers 🎬🎬 **1991 (R)** Features three provocative vignettes that take place far from home. Fiorentino, Chen, and Hutton each star in an erotic story played out in a foreign land. **85m/C VHS.** Linda Fiorentino, Joan Chen, Timothy Hutton; **D:** Joan Tewkesbury.

The Strangers 🎬 **1998** Seems Trent doesn't know as much about his lover Jade as he thinks—until she turns him into a werewolf. He gets away and hides out in the small town of Pine Fork, even beginning to fall in love. Then Jade shows up with her new boyfriend—looking for revenge and fresh meat. **90m/C VHS, DVD.** Richard Bent, Shanna Betz, Victoria Hunter, Jennifer Marks, Matt Martin, Jimmy Lord, J.J. Denton, Joe Durrenberger; **D:** Charles Solomon Jr., Peter Cohl, Steven Weller; **C:** Anthony Moncado. **VIDEO**

Strangers in Good Company 🎬🎬🎬 **1991 (PG)** A loving metaphor to growing older. Director Scott uses non-actors for every role in this quiet little film about a bus-load of elderly women lost in the Canadian wilderness. They wait for rescue without hystrionics, using the opportunity instead to get to know each other and nature. Beautifully made, intelligent, uncommon and worthwhile. **101m/C VHS, DVD. CA** Alice Diabo, Mary Meigs, Cissy Meddings, Beth Webber, Winifred Holden, Constance Garneau, Catherine Roche, Michelle Sweeney; **D:** Cynthia Scott; **W:** Cynthia Scott, Gloria Demers, Sally Bochner; **M:** Marie Bernard.

Strangers in Love 🎬½ **1932** Routine melodrama. Evil twin (March) cheats his brother out of his share of their father's inheritance by faking the will. But when he suddenly dies, nice bro assumes his identity, makes amends for his wickedness, and gets the girl (Francis). **76m/B VHS.** Fredric March, Kay Francis, Stuart Erwin, Sidney Toler, Juliette Compton, George Barbier; **D:** Lothar Mendes; **W:** Grover Jones, William Slavens McNutt; **C:** Henry Sharp.

Strangers in Paradise 🎬½ **1984** A scientist who had cryogenically frozen himself to escape the Nazis is thawed out in the present, and his powers are used by a delinquent-obsessed sociopath. **81m/C VHS.** Ulli Lommel, Ken Letner, Geoffrey Barker, Thom Jones; **D:** Ulli Lommel; **W:** Ulli Lommel; **M:** William Pettijohn.

Strangers in the City 🎬🎬 **1962** Puerto Ricans newly arrived in New York try to make their way. Serious but slightly overwrought immigrant-family melodrama. **80m/B VHS.** Robert Gentile, Camilo Delgado, Rosita De Triana; **D:** Rick Carrier.

Strangers Kiss 🎬🎬½ **1983 (R)** Hollywood director encourages his two leads to have an off-screen romance to bring reality to his film. Conflict arises when the leading lady's boyfriend, the film's financier, gets wind of the scheme. Intriguing, fun, slightly off-center. Based on Stanley Kubrick's film "Killer's Kiss." **93m/C VHS.** Peter Coyote, Victoria Tennant, Blaine Novak, Dan Shor, Richard Romanus, Linda Kerridge, Carlos Palomino; **D:** Matthew Chapman; **W:** Blaine Novak, Matthew Chapman; **M:** Gato Barbieri.

Strangers of the Evening 🎬🎬 **1932** In its day this dark comedy/mystery caught flak for its gruesomeness. There's been a mixup at the undertaker's, and the wrong body was buried—possibly alive. Good photography and acting make the humor work, intentionally or not. Based on the novel "The Illustrious Corpse," by Tiffany Thayer. **70m/B VHS.** Zasu Pitts, Eugene Pallette, Lucien Littlefield, Tully Marshall, Miriam Seegar, Theodore von Eltz; **D:** H. Bruce Humberstone.

Strangers on a Train 🎬🎬🎬🎬 **1951** Long before there was "Throw Momma from the Train," there was this Hitchcock super-thriller about two passengers who accidentally meet and plan to "trade" murders. Amoral Walker wants the exchange and the money he'll inherit by his father's death; Granger would love to end his stifling marriage and wed Roman, a senator's daughter, but finds the idea ultimately sickening. What happens is pure Hitchcock. Screenplay co-written by murder-mystery great Chandler. Patricia Hitchcock, the director's only child, plays Roman's sister. The concluding "carousel" scene is a masterpiece. From the novel by Patricia Highsmith. **101m/B VHS, DVD.** Farley Granger, Robert Walker, Ruth Roman, Leo G. Carroll, Patricia Hitchcock, Marion Lorne; **D:** Alfred Hitchcock; **W:** Raymond Chandler; **C:** Robert Burks; **M:** Dimitri Tiomkin.

Strangers: The Story of a Mother and Daughter 🎬🎬🎬 **1979** Rowlands is the long-estranged daughter of Davis, who won an Emmy for her portrayal of the embittered widow. The great actress truly is at her recent best in this made-for-TV tearjerker, and Rowlands keeps pace. **88m/C VHS.** Bette Davis, Gena Rowlands, Ford Rainey, Donald Moffat; **D:** Milton Katselas.

Strangers When We Meet 🎬🎬½ **1960** A married architect and his equally married neighbor begin an affair. Their lives become a series of deceptions. Lavish but uninvolving soaper. Written by Evan Hunter and based on his novel. **117m/B VHS, DVD.** Kirk Douglas, Kim Novak, Ernie Kovacs, Walter Matthau, Barbara Rush, Virginia Bruce, Kent Smith; **D:** Richard Quine; **W:** Charles B(ryant) Lang Jr.

Strangers with Candy 🎬🎬 **2006 (R)** Sedaris takes her Comedy Central series to the big screen with all its crude tackiness on display. Jerri is a middle-aged ex-junkie, ex-hooker, ex-con who goes back to high school and meets to win the science fair to make her comatose dad proud. Calling her dim-witted would be kind. But she's in good company because mostly everyone around her falls into freak territory. It's one over-extended sketch with a lead you don't really want to spend time with unless you're already a fan. **97m/C DVD. US** Amy Sedaris, Paul Dinello, Stephen Colbert, Deborah Rush, Greg Hollimon, Dan Hedaya, Allison Janney, Philip Seymour Hoffman, Kristen Johnston, Justin Theroux, Matthew Broderick, Sarah Jessica Parker, Ian Holm, Carlo Alban, Maria Thayer, Elisabeth Harnois, Chris Pratt, Elisabeth Harnois, Joseph Cross, David Pasquesi, Alicia Ashley, Ryan Donowho; **D:** Paul Dinello; **W:** Amy Sedaris, Paul Dinello, Stephen Colbert; **C:** Oliver Bokelberg.

Stranglehold 🎬½ **1994 (R)** The executive assistant of Congresswoman Fillmore (McWhirter), who becomes the hostage of a nerve gas holding nutcase (Wells). Cooper manages to evade the nutcase's thugs while using his martial arts prowess to rescue his boss. **73m/C VHS, DVD. AU** Jerry Trimble, Jillian McWhirter, Vernon Wells; **D:** Cirio H. Santiago.

The Strangler 🎬½ **1964** A confused, mother-fixated psychopath strangles young women. Made at the time the Boston Strangler was terrorizing Beantown. The film slayer strangles ten lasses before his love of dolls gives him away. **89m/B VHS, DVD.** Victor Buono, David McLean, Diane Sayer, Ellen Corby, Jeanne Bates, James B. Sikking; **D:** Burt Topper.

Strangler of Blackmoor Castle 🎬🎬 **1963** Someone is murdering people at an old English castle and Scotland Yard sends an investigator to track down the killer. **87m/B VHS, DVD. GE** Karin Dor, Ingmar Zeisberg, Harry Riebauer, Rudolf Fernau, Hans Nielsen, Dieter Eppler; **D:** Harald Reinl; **W:** Ladislas Fodor; **C:** Ernst W. Kalinke; **M:** Oskar Sala.

Strangler of the Swamp 🎬½ **1946** The ghost of an innocent man wrongly hanged for murder returns to terrorize the village where he was lynched. Decidedly B-grade horror features an out-of-focus ghost and Edwards—on the other side of the camera—as one of his would-be victims. **60m/B VHS, DVD.** Rosemary La Planche, Blake Edwards, Charles Middleton, Robert Barrat; **D:** Frank Wisbar; **W:** Frank Wisbar; **C:** James S. Brown Jr.

Strapless 🎬🎬½ **1990 (R)** Just-turned-40 American doctor Brown lives and works in London. She has just ended a long-term romance, and takes up with suave foreigner Ganz. Her young sister Fonda, arrives for a visit. Good, interesting if sometimes plodding story of adult relationships. **99m/C VHS, DVD. GB** Blair Brown, Bridget Fonda, Bruno Ganz, Alan Howard, Michael Gough, Hugh Laurie, Suzanne Burden, Camille Coduri, Alexandra Pigg, Billy Roch, Gary O'Brien; **D:** David Hare; **W:** David Hare; **C:** Andrew Dunn; **M:** Nick Bicat.

Strapped 🎬🎬½ **1993** Earnest urban drama about a young man who needs quick cash and turns to selling guns to get it. ("Strapped" in street lingo means both carrying a gun and needing money.) Diquan's (Woodbine) pregnant girlfriend is in jail for selling crack and he doesn't have the bail money. So he and a partner begin selling guns but it turns out Diquan has also doesn't stay a secret for long. Whitaker's directorial debut. **102m/C VHS, DVD.** Bokeem Woodbine, Kia Joy Goodwin, Fred "Fredro" Scruggs, Michael Biehn, Craig Wasson; **D:** Forest Whitaker; **W:** Dena Kleiman. **CABLE**

Strategic Air Command 🎬🎬 **1955** A classic post-WWII chunk of Air Force patriotism. Veteran third baseman Stewart is recalled to flight duty at the hint of a nuclear war. He's already put in his time in the Big One and thinks he's being singled out now, but he answers his Uncle Sam's call. Allyson plays Stewart's wife for the third time. **114m/C VHS.** James Stewart, June Allyson, Frank Lovejoy, Barry Sullivan; **D:** Anthony Mann; **C:** William H. Daniels.

The Stratton Story 🎬🎬🎬 **1949** Stewart and Allyson teamed up for the first of the three pictures they'd make together in this true story of Monty Stratton, the Chicago White Sox pitcher. A baseball phenom, Stratton suffers a devastating hunting accident which leads to the amputation of one leg. Learning to walk with an artificial limb, Stratton also struggles to resume his baseball career. Stewart's fine as always, with Allyson lending noble support as the loving wife. Chisox manager Jimmy Dykes played himself as did pitcher Gene Bearden, lending further authenticity to an excellent production. **106m/B VHS, DVD.** James Stewart, June Allyson, Frank Morgan, Agnes Moorehead, Bill Williams, Bruce Cowling; **D:** Sam Wood; **W:** Guy Trosper, Douglas S. Morrow. Oscars '49: Story.

The Strauss Family 🎬🎬½ **1973** British miniseries covers the drama and scandal surrounding 85 years in the lives of the musical Strauss family of 19th-century Vienna. Woolfe is patriarch Johann Strauss, whose son Schanni (Wilson) will exclipse his egotistical father's talents. Music performed by the London Symphony Orchestra. On 4 cassettes. **390m/C VHS, DVD. GB** Eric Woolfe, Stuart Wilson, Anne Stallybrass, Derek Jacobi, Jane Seymour; **D:** David Giles, Peter Potter, David Reid; **W:** David Butler, David Reid, Anthony Skene. **TV**

Straw Dogs 🎬🎬🎬 **1972 (R)** An American mathematician, disturbed by the predomance of violence in American society, moves with his wife to an isolated Cornish village. He finds that primitive savagery exists beneath the most peaceful surface. After his wife is raped, Hoffman's character seeks revenge. A violent, frightening film reaction to the violence of the 1960s. **118m/C VHS, DVD. GB** Sally Thomsett, Colin Welland, Peter Arne, Dustin Hoffman, Susan George, Peter Vaughan, T.P. McKenna, David Warner; **D:** Sam Peckinpah; **W:** Sam Peckinpah, David Zelag Goodman; **C:** John Coquillon; **M:** Jerry Fielding.

Strawberry and Chocolate 🎬🎬🎬 *Fresa y Chocolate* **1993 (R)** Sex, politics, and friendship set in 1979 Havana. University student David (Cruz) is sitting morosely in a cafe eating chocolate ice cream when he's spotted by strawberry-eating Diego (Perugorria), who manages to persuade David to visit him at his apartment. Resolutely hetero (and communist), David is appalled not only by Diego's sexuality but by his subversive politics. But gradually David's seduced by Diego's ideas and friendship into questioning the regime's harsh policies (and homophobia). Satiric and sympathetic—not only to the characters but to Cuba itself. Ill with cancer, Gutierrez Alea finished the film with the aid of Tabio. From the short story "The Wolf, the Forest and the New Man" by screenwriter Paz. Spanish with subtitles. **110m/C VHS, DVD. CU** Jorge Perugorria, Vladimir Cruz, Mirta Ibarra, Francisco Gattorno, Jorge Angelino, Marilyn Solaya; **D:** Tomas Gutierrez Alea, Juan Carlos Tabio; **W:** Tomas Gutierrez Alea, Senel Paz; **C:** Mario Garcia Joya; **M:** Jose Maria Vitier.

Strawberry Blonde 🎬🎬🎬 **1941** A romantic comedy set in the 1890s, with Cagney as a would-be dentist infatuated with money-grubbing Hayworth (the strawberry blonde of the title), who wonders years later whether he married the right woman (chestnut brunette de Havilland). Attractive period piece remade from 1933's "One Sunday Afternoon," and revived yet again in 1948 by Raoul Walsh. **100m/B VHS.** James Cagney, Olivia de Havilland, Rita Hayworth, Alan Hale, George Tobias, Jack Carson, Una O'Connor, George Reeves; **D:** Raoul Walsh; **W:** Julius J. Epstein, Philip G. Epstein; **C:** James Wong Howe.

Strawberry Fields 🎬🎬 **1997** Rebellious teenaged Japanese-American Irene (Nakamura) takes off on a road trip of self-discovery with her boyfriend, whom she soon dumps to spend quality time alone in the Arizona desert figuring out life. Ambitious period piece remade from **86m/C VHS, DVD.** Suzy Nakamura, James Sie, Chris Tashima, Marilyn Tokuda, Reiko Mathieu, Peter Yoshida, Heather Yoshimura, Takayo Fischer; **D:** Rea Tajiri, Kerri Sakamoto; **C:** Zack Winestine; **M:** Bundy Brown.

Strawberry Roan 🎬🎬 **1933** Maynard plays a stubborn rodeo cowboy, out to prove he ain't whipped yet. One of Maynard's most popular films. Gene Autry bought the story to help him out in later years; the 1948 Autry "remake" uses only the title. **59m/B VHS.** Ken Maynard, Ruth Hall; **D:** Ken Maynard.

The Strawberry Statement 🎬🎬 **1970 (R)** Dated message film about a campus radical who persuades a college student to take part in the student strikes on campus during the '60s. Ambitious anti-violence message is lost in too many subplots. Soundtrack features songs by Crosby, Stills, Nash and Young and John Lennon. **109m/C VHS.** Kim Darby, Bruce Davison, Bud Cort, James Coco, Kristina Holland, Bob Balaban, David Dukes, Jeannie Berlin; **D:** Stuart Hagmann; **W:** Israel Horovitz. Cannes '70: Special Jury Prize.

The Stray 🎬🎬 **2000 (R)** When Vonna Grayson (Everhart) accidentally hits a homeless man (Lysenko) when she's driving home, she insists on having him recover at her ranch. Soon the relationship becomes romantic, and her "stray" has a hidden agenda and Vonna winds up in danger. **98m/C VHS, DVD.** Angie Everhart, Stefan Lysenko, Michael Madsen, Frank Zagarino, Seidy Lopez; **D:** Kevin Mock; **W:** Terry Cunningham; **C:** Ken Blakey; **M:** John Sponsler. **VIDEO**

Stray Bullet 🎬 **1998 (R)** Attorney John Burnside (Carradine) mistakenly picks up the luggage of fellow traveler Stella Crosby (Staab), who invites him to her home for a party. But John gets kidnapped from the party by some thugs who are owed money by Stella's husband, who they have mistaken John for. Instead of setting things straight, Stella persuades John to pose as her husband until she can works things out. John agrees because he has the hots for Stella. John's very dumb. **86m/C VHS.** Robert Carradine, Rebecca Staab, Fred (John F.) Dryer, Ian Beattie; **D:** Robert Spera; **W:** Christopher Wood; **C:** Jules Labarthe; **M:** Arthur Kempel. **VIDEO**

Stray Dog 🎬🎬🎬 **1949** A tense, early genre piece by Kurosawa, about a police detective who has his revolver picked from his pocket on a bus, and realizes soon after it's being used in a series of

Strayed ✓✓✓ *Les Egares* 2003 Set in the chaotic summer of 1940, when the Germans invaded France. Film follows the flight of recently widowed schoolteacher Odile (Beart) and her children, 13-year-old Philippe (Leprince-Ringuet) and 7-year-old Cathy (Meyer), out of Paris. Part of a stream of refugees heading south, the family is forced into the countryside, where they meet 17-year-old Yvan (Ulliel), who's illiterate but skilled at survival. Stumbling across an abandoned villa, the foursome set aside their uncertainties to manage a precarious semblance of family life as the sexual tension between Odile and Yvan grows. Since 'echine specializes in character studies, this is as much about conflict and desire, civilization versus savagery. Based on the 1983 novel, "The Boy With Grey Eyes," by Gilles Perrault. French with subtitles. **95m/C VHS, DVD.** *FR* Emmanuelle Beart, Samuel Labarthe, Gaspard Ulliel, Gregoire Leprince-Ringuet, Clemence Meyer, Jean Fornerod; *D:* Andre Techine; *W:* Andre Techine, Gilles Taurand; *C:* Agnes Godard; *M:* Philippe Sarde.

Streamers ✓✓ 1983 (R) Six young soldiers in a claustrophobic army barracks tensely await the orders that will send them to Vietnam. Written by Rabe from his play. Well acted but downbeat and drawn out. **118m/C VHS, Bill Allen, Matthew Modine, Michael Wright, Mitchell Lichtenstein, George Dzundza; *D:* Robert Altman; *W:* David Rabe.

The Street ✓✓ 1923 A dark classic of German Kammerspiel film, notable for its expressionist treatment of Paris street life. A middle-aged man decides to abandon his wife and job to see what exc'rement he can find. He is duped by a prostitute, accused of murder, imprisoned, and nearly commits suicide before being rescued. Silent. **87m/B VHS.** *GE* Max Schreck, Karl Grune; *C:* Karl Hasselmann.

Street Asylum ✓ 1990 (R) Real-life Watergate spook Liddy is pathetically bad as an evil genius who cooks up a scheme to rid the streets of deadbeats and scum-bags by implanting cops with a gizmo that makes them kill. Also available in a 94-minute unrated version. **94m/C VHS.** Wings Hauser, Alex Cord, Roberta Vasquez, G. Gordon Liddy, Marie Chambers, Sy Richardson, Jesse Doran, Jesse Aragon, Brion James; *D:* Gregory Brown.

Strays ✓✓ 1991 (R) Here kitty kitty! A young couple move into their dream home, convinced it is the perfect place to raise their daughter. What they don't know is that the area is populated by a pack of dirty work and wild cats. Before they can get rid of the kitties, one has marked their bedroom as his territory and they find themselves battling a swarm of mean kitties during a bad storm. **83m/C VHS.** Kathleen Quinlan, Timothy Busfield, Claudia Christian; *D:* John McPherson; *W:* Shaun Cassidy.

Street Corner Justice ✓✓ 1996 Typical vigilante action movie features ex-cop Mike Justus (Singer), who's possessed of a short fuse and a strong sense of justice. He inherits a house in a crime-ridden L.A. neighborhood and finds himself coming to the aid of merchants who are being terrorized by the local drug-dealing gangs. **102m/C VHS, DVD.** Marc Singer, Steve Railsback, Kim Lankford, Willie Gee; *D:* Charles "Chuck" Bail, "Chuck" Bail, Gary Kent, Stan Berkowitz; *C:* Doug O'Neons, David Golia; *M:* K. Alexander (Alex) Minnion.

Street Crimes ✓✓ 1992 (R) A street-wise cop convinces gang members to put down their weapons and settle their grudges in the boxing ring. But when a gang leader starts shooting down the police and civilians, the cop and his young partner must work together to keep the neighborhood safe. **93m/C VHS, DVD.** Dennis

murders. Technically somewhat flawed, but tense and intense. Mifune's pursuit of the criminal with his gun becomes metaphorically compelling. In Japanese with English subtitles. **122m/B VHS, DVD.** *JP* Toshiro Mifune, Takashi Shimura, Isao Kimura; *D:* Akira Kurosawa.

Farina, Max Gail, Mike Worth; *D:* Stephen Smoke; *M:* John Gonzalez.

The Street Fighter ✓✓ 1974 *Satsujin-ken* 1974 Fast-paced martial arts action finds freelance fighter Terry Tsuguri (Chiba), hired to spring a convicted killer from prison. But after he succeeds, his employers renege on their payment. Big mistake. Dubbed from Japanese. Three sequels: "Return of the Street Fighter," "The Street Fighter's Last Revenge," and "Sister Street Fighter." **91m/C VHS, DVD.** *JP* Sonny Chiba, Gerald (Walchi) Yamada, Tony Cetera, Doris (Yutaka) Nakajima; *D:* Shigehiro (Sakael) Ozawa; *W:* Motohiro Torii, Koji Takada; *C:* Ken Tsukakoshi; *M:* Toshiaki Tsushima.

Street Fighter ✓½ 1994 (PG-13) Yes, it's a movie based on a popular video game (guess no one worried about the colossal flop of "Super Mario Bros"). Van Damme is action-minded Colonel Guile who is assigned to defeat crazed dictator General Bison (Julia, in one of his last roles) in order to rescue kidnapped relief workers. Yes, there's lots of cartoon action. Shot on location in Australia and Bangkok. **101m/C VHS, DVD.** Jean-Claude Van Damme, Raul Julia, Wes Studi, Ming Na, Damian Chapa, Simon Callow, Roshan Seth, Kylie Minogue, Byron Mann; *D:* Steven E. de Souza; *W:* Steven E. de Souza; *C:* William A. Fraker; *M:* Graeme Revell.

The Street Fighter's Last Revenge ✓ *Revenge; The Killing Fist, Street Fighter Counterattacks* 1974 Third in the martial arts series finds Terry Tsuguri (Chiba) hired by a mob boss to do some dirty work and then getting double-crossed—resulting in the deaths of Terry's girl. So, Terry hunts his miscreants down one by one. Lots of action, not much acting. Followed by "Sister Street Fighter." **79m/C VHS, DVD.** *JP* Sonny Chiba, Etsuko (Sue) Shihomi; *D:* Teru Ishii.

Street Girls ✓ 1975 (R) A father enters the world of urban drugs and prostitution to find his runaway daughter. **77m/C.** Carol Case, Christine Souder, Paul Pompian; *D:* Michael Miller.

Street Gun ✓ 1996 Small-time hood Joe Webster (Pageli) pines for some sense of accomplishment in his life. A tip from his 'hustler-friend lands Joe in the good graces of the local crime boss. As he ingratiates himself into his new malevolent world, the shadows yield betrayal, murder, and no place to hide. Potentially interesting premise is botched, with cowriter/director Milloy aping John Woo gun pyrotechnics and "Reservoir Dogs" attitude (a Woo rip-off once removed). There is also the thorny dilemma of 'rooting for a hero who aspires to be an exceptional thug. **92m/C VHS, DVD.** Justin Pagel, Scott Cooke, Michael Egan; *D:* Travis Milloy; *W:* Travis Milloy, Timothy Lee; *C:* Joel King.

Street Heart ✓✓ *Le Coeur au Poing* 1998 Louise has structured a very sheltered, controlled (if lonely) word for herself that gradually comes undone as both her sister and her lover abandon her. Feeling the need to reconnect with life, Louise goes about making contact in a dangerous manner. She begins to stop strangers on the street and offers to do whatever they would like for one hour. French with subtitles. **100m/C VHS, CA** Pascale Montpetit, Anne-Marie Cadieux, Guy Nadon, Guylaine Tremblay; *D:* Charles Biname; *W:* Monique Proulx, Charles Biname; *C:* Pierre Gill; *M:* Richard Gregoire, Yves Desrosiers.

Street Hero woof! 1984 A young thug is torn between 'amilial common sense and Mafia connections. **102m/C VHS.** Vince Colosimo, Sigrid Thornton, Sandy Gore; *D:* Michael Pattinson; *W:* Jan Sardi; *C:* Vincent Monton.

Street Hunter woof! 1990 (R) Former cop turned freelance fighter quit the force when his integrity was questioned, but he still helps out now and then. Scum-bag drug dealers line up a thug to waste him; epic kung fu battle ensues. **120m/C VHS.** Steve James, Reb Brown, John Leguizamo, Valarie Pettiford, Frank Vincent, Richie Havens; *D:* John A. Gallagher; *C:* Phil Parmet.

Street Justice ✓✓ 1989 (R) Overcomplex tale of a CIA agent on the lam. Returning from years of Russian imprisonment, Ontkean finds his wife remarried, his daughter grown and both battling the corrupt town government. Good performances can't help the confusion of too many characters too flatly developed. **94m/C VHS.** Michael Ontkean, Joanna Kerns, Catherine Bach, J.C. Cannon, Jeanette Nolan, Richard Cox, William Windom; *D:* Richard Sarafian.

The Street King ✓✓ 2002 (R) *King Rikki* 2002 Rikki Ortega (Seda) wants to be top dog on the gang-ravaged streets of East L.A. And the one man to oppose him is his childhood buddy turned cop, Juan Vallejo (Lopez). It's alleged to be a modern reworking of Shakespeare's "Richard III." **90m/C VHS, DVD.** Jon Seda, Mario Lopez, Timothy Paul Perez, Jill-Michele Melean; *D:* James Gavin Bedford; *W:* Jesse Graham; *C:* Rob Sweeney.

Street Kings ✓✓ 2008 (R) Ellroy, who had a hand in the script (adapted from his novel) but this over-the-top violent melodrama more closely resembles what director Ayers did as a writer with the equally preposterous "Training Day." Widowed vice cop Tom Ludlow (Reeves) drinks on the job and is possibly more violent than the L.A. criminals he's after. Ludlow's commanding officer Wander (Whitaker), practically pop-eyed and frothing) seems to have his back until Tom's ex-partner Washington ('Crews) is gunned down after he talks to Internal Affairs, which puts a bullseye on Ludlow's back. **109m/C DVD.** *US* Keanu Reeves, Forest Whitaker, 'Hugh Laurie, Chris Evans, Jay Mohr, John Corbett, Amaury Nolasco, Cedric the Entertainer, Terry Crews, Naomie Harris, Common, The Game, Martha Higareda; *D:* David Ayer, James Moss; *W:* Kurt Wimmer, James Ellroy; *C:* Gabriel Beristain; *M:* Graeme Revell.

Street Knight ✓✓ 1993 (R) Gang warfare in L.A. in a routine actioner. Jake is an ex-cop who gets drawn into a battle between two rival gangs when their truce is broken by mysterious murders on both sides. Seems there's an unsuspected third party involved—a para-military band of professional killers that want the gang violence to divert police interest from their own nefarious operations. **88m/C VHS.** Jeff Speakman, Christopher Neame, Lewis Van Bergen, Bernie Casey, Jennifer Gatti, Richard Coca; *D:* Albert Magnoli.

Street Law ✓ *The Citizen Rebels; Il Cittadino si Ribella* 1974 (R) Vivid and violent study of one man's frustrated war on crime. **77m/C VHS, DVD.** *IT* Franco Nero, Barbara Bach, Renzo Palmer, Giancarlo Prete; *D:* Enzo G. Castellari; *W:* Massimo De Rita, Arduino G. Mauri; *C:* Carlo Carlini; *M:* Guido de Angelis, Maurizio de Angelis.

Street Law ✓✓½ 1995 (R) John Ryan (Wincott) is a down-on-his-luck trial lawyer whose childhood buddy Luis Calderone ('Prieto) is willing to lend a helping hand. Too bad Luis is an ex-con who hasn't left his dangerous street ways behind him and now John is caught up in some unsavory action. **98m/C VHS, DVD.** Jeff Wincott, Paco Christian Prieto, Christina Cox; *D:* Damian Lee; *W:* Damian Lee; *C:* Gerald F. Gozzie; *M:* Ronald C. Weiss.

Street Music ✓✓ 1981 The elderly people living in an old hotel join forces that may save their building. Well-directed urban comedy-drama; good location shooting in San Francisco's Tenderloin. **88m/C VHS.** Larry Breeding, Elizabeth (E.G. Daily) Daily, Ned Glass, Marjcie Eaton, D'Alan Moss, David Parr; *D:* Jenny (H. Anne Riley) Bowen; *W:* Jenny (H. Anne Riley) Bowen; *C:* Richard Bowen. Sundance '82; Grand Jury Prize.

Street War ✓ *Paura in citta* 1976 A cop pursues the Mob in the name of revenge as well as duty. **90m/C VHS, DVD.** *IT* Maurizio Merli, Silvia Dionisio, Fausto Tozzi, James Mason, Cyril Cusack, Raymond Pellegrin; *D:* Giuseppe Rosati; *W:* Giuseppe Rosati, Giuseppe Pulieri; *C:* Giuseppe Bernardini; *M:* Gianpaolo Chiti.

Street Warriors woof! 1987 Ostensibly "serious" look at juvenile crime. Actually miserable, exploitative, offensive junk. **105m/C VHS.** Christa Leem, Nada Windell, Victor Pett, Francisco (Frank) Brana; *D:* Jose Antonio De la Loma.

Street Warriors, Part 2 woof! 1987 Even worse than its predecessor, and that's saying something. Horrible dubbing from Spanish would be laughable, if

---

Street of Forgotten Women ✓ 1925 Hollywood, in one of its periodic morality binges, came up with this 'purported exposé on prostitution. An innocent girl is seduced and brutalized by a theatrical agent and eventually finds herself walking the pavement for less than moral purposes. Lots of shots of scantily clad show-girls and our heroine in her undies. **55m/B VHS.**

Street of Shame ✓✓½ *Akasen Chitai* 1956 A portrayal of the abused lives of six Tokyo prostitutes. Typically sensitive to the roles and needs of women and critical of the society that dor gave it direction. **88m/B VHS, DVD.** Sylvia Beulah Bondi, David Landau; *D:* King Vidor; *W:* Elmer Rice; *C:* George Barnes; *M:* Alfred Newman.

The Street King ✓✓ 2002 (R) See The Street King.

Street People woof! 1976 (R) Gratuitous car chases and violence do not a movie make, as in this case in point. Utter inanity. **92m/C VHS.** Roger Moore, Stacy Keach, Ivo Garrani, Ettore Manni; *D:* Maurizio Lucidi.

Street Scene ✓✓✓ 1931 Life in a grimy New York tenement district, circa 1930. Audiences nationwide ate it up when Elmer Rice adapted his own Pulitzer Prize-winning play and top helmsman Vidor gave it direction. **80m/B VHS, DVD.** Sylvia Sidney, William "Buster" Collier Jr., Estelle Taylor, Beulah Bondi, David Landau; *D:* King Vidor; *W:* Elmer Rice; *C:* George Barnes; *M:* Alfred Newman.

Street Smart ✓✓ 1987 (R) Reeve was billed as Superman (let's be frank), and he's bland here as a desperate New York freelance writer who fakes a dramatic story about prostitution. When his deception returns to haunt him, he's in trouble with pimps and murderers, as well as the D.A. Freeman and Baker are both superb. Based on screenwriter David Freeman's own experience with "New York" magazine. **97m/C VHS, DVD.** Christopher Reeve, Morgan Freeman, Kathy Baker, Mimi Rogers, Andre Gregory, Jay Patterson, Anna Maria Horsford; *D:* Jerry Schatzberg; *W:* David Freeman; *C:* Adam Holender; *M:* Miles Davis. Ind. Spirit '88: Support. Actor (Freeman); L.A. Film Critics '87, N.Y. Film Critics '87: Support. Actor (Freeman); Natl. Soc. Film Critics '87: Support. Actor (Freeman); Support. Actress (Baker).

Street Soldiers ✓½ 1991 (R) Martial artists are out to take back the streets from the punks and scum who now rule them. **98m/C VHS.** Jun Chong, Jeff Rector, David Homb, Jonathan Gorman, Joon Kim, Katherine Armstrong, Joel Weiss; *D:* Lee Harry.

Street Trash woof! 1987 In Brooklyn, a strange poisonous liquor is being sold cheap to bums, making them melt and explode. A gross, cheap, tongue-in-cheek shocker. **91m/C VHS, DVD.** Vic Noto, Mike Lackey, Bill Chepil, R.L. Ryan, James Lorinz, Miriam Zucker; *D:* J. (James) Michael Muro; *W:* Roy Frumkes; *C:* David Sperling.

Street Vengeance woof! 1995 Drug lord seeks vengeance against cop for death of brother. No-budget shot-on-video flick is atrocious in every way. **85m/C DVD.** Merl Blackwell, Michael Eugene; *D:* Rene Migliaccio; *W:* Michael Farakash.

the rapes weren't so graphic. **105m/C VHS.** Angel Luis Fernandez, Paul Ramirez, Teresa Giminez, Veronica Mirel, Conrad Tortosa; **D:** Jose Antonio De La Loma.

Street Wars 1991 (R) Violent low-budget drama of 17-year-old Sugarpop, who takes over older brother Frank's Los Angeles drug operation, after Frank is murdered, and finds himself battling a rival gang. **90m/C VHS, DVD.** Alan Joseph, Bryan O'Dell, Clifford Shegog, Jean Pace, Vaughn Cromwell, Cardella Demilo; **D:** Jamaa Fanaka; **W:** Jamaa Fanaka; **C:** John L. (Ndiaga) Demps Jr.; **M:** Michael Dunlap, Yves Chicha.

The Street with No Name 1948 In his follow-up to "Kiss of Death," Widmark confirms his rep as one disturbed guy playing psychotic career criminal whose life is a grisly trail of murder and brutality. **93m/B VHS, DVD.** Mark Stevens, Richard Widmark, Lloyd Nolan, Barbara Lawrence, Ed Begley Sr., Donald Buka, Joseph Pevney; **D:** William Keighley.

A Streetcar Named Desire 1951 (PG) Powerful film version of Tennessee Williams' play about a neurotic southern belle with a hidden past who comes to visit her sister and is abused and driven mad by her brutal brother-in-law. Grim New Orleans setting for terrific performances by all, with Malden, Leigh, and Hunter winning Oscars, and Brando making highest impact on audiences. Brando disliked the role, despite the great impact it had on his career. **122m/ B VHS, DVD.** Vivien Leigh, Marlon Brando, Kim Hunter, Karl Malden; **D:** Elia Kazan; **W:** Tennessee Williams; **C:** Harry Stradling Sr.; **M:** Alex North. Oscars '51: Actress (Leigh), Art Dir./Set Dec., B&W, Support. Actor (Malden), Support. Actress (Hunter); AFI '98: Top 100; British Acad. '52: Actress (Hunter), Natl. Film Reg. '99; N.Y. Film Critics '51: Actress (Leigh), Director (Kazan). **Film.**

A Streetcar Named Desire 1984 Excellent TV adaptation of the Tennessee Williams drama about fading southern belle Blanche du Bois (Ann-Margret in a terrific performance). D'Angelo is her plain sister Stella who lives with brutish husband Stanley Kowalski and fragile Southern belle Blanche DuBois from the Broadway revival of Tennessee Williams 1947 Pulitzer Prize-winning play. This TV version is truer to the dialogue and situations of the original production than the censored '51 film. **156m/C VHS.** Jessica Lange, Alec Baldwin, Diane Lane, John Goodman, Frederick Coffin; **D:** Glenn Jordan; **C:** Ralf Bode; **M:** David Mansfield. **TV**

Streetfight 1975 (R) *Coonskin* Semi-animated racist exploitation from the creator of "Fritz the Cat." Features some superb animation. **89m/C VHS.** Philip Michael Thomas, Scatman Crothers, Barry White, Charles Gordone; **D:** Ralph Bakshi; **W:** Ralph Bakshi; **C:** William A. Fraker; **M:** Chico Hamilton.

Streets 1990 (R) Applegate (of Fox TV's "Married...With Children") is believable as an illiterate runaway teen. Good drama set in Venice, California about life on the streets is flawed by near-gratuitous pairing with story of a crazy prostitute-killing cop. **90m/C VHS.** Christina Applegate, David Mendenhall, Eb Lottimer; **D:** Katt Shea, Andy Ruben; **W:** Andy Ruben.

Streets of Fire 1984 A soldier of fortune rescues his ex-girlfriend, now a famous rock singer, after she's been kidnapped by a malicious motorcycle gang. Violently energetic in its insistent barrage of imagery, Director Hill's never-never land establishes a retro-futuristic feel and is beautifully photographed, however vacuous the ending may be. **93m/C VHS, DVD, HD DVD.** Michael Pare, Diane Lane, Rick Moranis, Amy Madigan, Willem Dafoe, Deborah Van Valkenburgh, Richard Lawson, Rick Rossovich, Bill Paxton, Lee Ving, Stoney Jackson, Robert Kevin Townsend, Grand L. Bush, Mykelti Williamson, Elizabeth (E.G. Dailey) Daily, Lynne Thigpen, Marine Jahan, Ed Begley Jr., John Dennis Johnston, Olivia Brown; **D:** Walter Hill; **W:** Walter Hill, Larry Gross; **C:** Andrew Laszlo; **M:** Ry Cooder.

Streets of Gold 1986 (R) Brandauer is good as a Soviet boxer who defected and now washes dishes in Brooklyn. He trains a pair of street youngsters in the hope of beating his old coach in the Olympics. "Rocky"-like in the boxing, and in the rags-to-riches optimism. **94m/C VHS.** Klaus Maria Brandauer, Adrian Pasdar, Wesley Snipes; **D:** Joe Roth; **W:** Richard Price, Heywood Gould, Tom Cole; **C:** Arthur Albert; **M:** Jack Nitzsche.

The Streets of L.A. 1979 A frustrated middle-aged woman teaches some punks from an L.A. barrio a thing or two about pride and motivation when she demands reimbursement for the tires they slashed. Without thoroughly professional Woodward to carry it, there would not be much of a movie. Woodward's character is resourceful, and so is the actress. Made for TV. **94m/C VHS.** Joanne Woodward, Robert Webber, Michael C. Gwynne; **D:** Jerrold Freedman; **C:** Allen Daviau. **TV**

The Streets of San Francisco 1972 The pilot that spawned the popular TV series. A streetwise old cop and his young college-boy partner (who else but Malden and Douglas as Stone and Keller) investigate the murder of a young woman. Adapted from "Poor, Poor Ophelia" by Carolyn Weston. **120m/C VHS.** Karl Malden, Robert Wagner, Michael Douglas, Andrew Duggan, Tom Bosley, Kim Darby, Mako; **D:** Walter Grauman. **TV**

Streets of Sin 1949 *Not Wanted* Written and produced by movie star Lupino (who also took over directing when credited director Clifton became ill), this morality play tells the story of a naive girl's tribulations when she becomes infatuated with a musician and then becomes pregnant by him. Shunned by the musician, she enters a home for unwed mothers to sort out her life and feelings for a crippled veteran who wants to marry her. **91m/B VHS.** Sally Forrest, Keefe Brasselle, Leonard Penn, Dorothy Adams, Rita Lupino; **D:** Elmer Clifton; **W:** Ida Lupino.

Streetwalkin' 1985 (R) Life in the Big Apple isn't always rosy for a brother and sister who must contend with prostitutes, drug dealers, and tough cops. She turns to prostitution to get by. Miserable, exploitative trash. **86m/C VHS.** Melissa Leo, Dale Midkiff, Leon Robinson, Julie Newmar, Randall Batinkoff, Annie Golden, Antonio Fargas; **D:** Joan Freeman; **W:** Joan Freeman, Robert Alden; **C:** Steven Fierberg.

Streetwise 1984 Eye-opening and candid documentary inspired by a "Life" magazine article. Frank and honest look at homeless children making a living on the streets. Seattle provides the backdrop to the story of a life, earning their trust, and receive the truth from them. Crudely, funny, enraging, but always sobering look into a population of homeless in America. A deservedly acclaimed, terrifying vision of urban America. **92m/C VHS.** **D:** Martin Bell; **W:** Cheryl McCall; **M:** Tom Waits.

Stricken 1998 Six college buddies become obsessed with practical jokes that becomes more and more vicious—all of which are orchestrated by Guffy (Gunn). The butt of most of the gags, Banyon (Kennedy), has certainly had enough and helps play one last joke on Guffy that leads to his accidental death. Everyone but Banyon begins to panic and turn on each other but Banyon sees his chance to get back at everyone who humiliated him. Offers low-budget tension. **90m/C VHS, DVD.** Jamie Kennedy, Sean Gunn, Judy Green, Tait Smith, Kevin Patrick Walls; **D:** Paul Chilsen; **W:** William W. Vought; **C:** Maida Sussman; **M:** Todd Scales.

Strictly Ballroom 1992 (PG) Offbeat, cheerfully tacky dance/romance amusingly turns every movie cliche slightly askew. Scott (Mercurio) has been in training for the Pan-Pacific ballroom championships since the age of six. While talented, he also refuses to follow convention and scandalizes the stuffy dance establishment with his new steps. When his longtime partner leaves him, Scott takes up with a love-struck beginner (Morice), with some surprises of her own. Ballet dancer Mercurio (in his film debut) is appropriately arrogant yet vulnerable, with Morice as the plain Jane turned steel butterfly. Wonderful supporting cast; great debut for director Luhrmann. **94m/C VHS, DVD. AU/**Paul Mercurio, Tara Morice, Bill Hunter, Pat Thomsen, Barry Otto, Gia Carides, Peter Whitford, John Hannan, Sonia Kruger-Tayler, Kris McQuade, Pip Mushin, Leonie Page, Antonio Vargas, Armonia Benedito; **D:** Baz Luhrmann; **W:** Baz Luhrmann, Craig Pearce; **C:** Steve Mason; **M:** David Hirschfelder. Australian Film Inst. '92: Costume Des., Director (Luhrmann), Film, Film Editing, Screenplay, Support. Actor (Otto), Support. Actress (Thomsen).

Strictly Business 1991 (PG-13) An upwardly mobile black broker has his career aspirations in order until he meets a beautiful club promoter who finds him square and boring. Wanting to impress her he asks the advice of a young man who works in the mail room for the proper way to dress and talk. A low-rent Pygmalion story. **83m/C VHS.** Halle Berry, Tommy Davidson, Joseph C. Phillips; **D:** Kevin Hooks; **M:** Michel Colombier.

Strictly G.I. 1944 A collection of war-time patriotic shorts, including "All Star Bond Rally." The support and perception of WWII is historically intriguing. **45m/B VHS.** Bing Crosby, Frank Sinatra, Betty Grable, Judy Garland, Harpo Marx, Harry James, Bob Hope, Jerry Colonna.

Strictly Sinatra *Cocozza's Way* 2001 (R) Sinatra cover song act Toni Cocozza (Hart) plys his trade in the local pubs of Glasgow, dreaming about making it as big as Old Blue Eyes himself. The Scottish-Italian crooner's tiny faction of fans under 65 includes some local mobsters. When one claims he met Sinatra himself in Vegas, Toni, who's only truly comfortable on-stage, finds himself intrigued and drawn in to their gang, who shower him with the attention and respect he craves. Underworld mayhem complicates a potentially interesting comedy/thriller that doesn't fully live up to either. Technically adroit, with top-notch songs and arrangements and a stunning performance by Hart. **97m/C VHS, DVD, GB** Ian Hart, Kelly Macdonald, Brian Cox, Alun Armstrong, Tommy Flanagan, Iain Cuthbertson, Jimmy Chisholm, Jimmy Yuill; **Cameos:** Richard E. Grant; **D:** Peter Capaldi; **W:** Peter Capaldi; **C:** Stephen Blackman; **M:** Stanislas Syrewicz.

Strike 1924 Eisenstein's debut, and a silent classic. Stirring look at a 1912 clash between striking factory workers and Czarist troops. **94m/B VHS, DVD, RU** Alexander Antonov, Yudif Glizer, Ivan Klyukvin, Grigori Aleksandrov; **D:** Sergei Eisenstein; **W:** Grigori Aleksandrov, Sergei Eisenstein; **C:** Eduard Tisse.

Strike a Pose 1993 (R) Erotic thriller finds international model-turned-fashion photographer Miranda Cross, her boyfriend LAPD detective Nick Carter, and Miranda's model friends stalked by a revenge-minded killer. Also available in an unrated version. **75m/C VHS, DVD.** Margie Peterson, Robert Eastwick, Michelle LaMothe; **D:** Dean Hamilton.

Strike Back 1980 A convict escapes from prison to find the girl he loves, and is hounded by both the police and the mob. **89m/C VHS.** Dave Balko, Brigette Wollner; **D:** Carl Schenkel.

Strike Commando woof! 1987 (R) Cheap, exploitative ripoff of the expensive, exploitative mega-action thriller "Rambo." Sleepwalking actors; horrible, overwrought script. Mattei used the pseudonym Vincent Dawn. **92m/C VHS.** Reb Brown, Christopher Connelly, Locs Kamme; **D:** Bruno Mattei.

Strike Force *Crack* 1975 A New York City cop, a Federal agent and a state trooper work together to battle a large drug ring. Failed made-for-TV pilot. Early Gere appearance; not related to later Robert Stack film with the same title. **74m/C VHS, DVD.** Cliff Gorman, Richard Gere, Donald Blakely; **D:** Barry Shear. **TV**

Strike Force 1981 The jurors on an embezzlement case turn up bloody and headless around town, so a special criminal strike force is brought in to solve the murders. Why do the murders happen only on Tuesdays? Made for TV. **90m/C VHS.** Robert Stack, Dorian Harewood, Herb Edelman; **D:** Richard Lang. **TV**

Strike It Rich *Loser Take All* 1990 (PG) A honeymooning couple find themselves resorting to the Monte Carlo gambling tables in order to raise money for the ride home. Lightweight fluff unfortunately adapted from Graham Greene's short novel "Loser Takes All." Only for hard-core Gielguddies. **86m/C VHS, DVD.** Molly Ringwald, Robert Lindsay, John Gielgud, Max Wall, Simon de la Brosse; **D:** James Scott; **W:** James Scott; **M:** Cliff Eidelman.

Strike Me Pink 1936 Shy Eddie Pink (Cantor) decides to change his ways after reading a self-help book and takes on the management of the ocal amusement park. Then some crooks want to muscle in on the action and Eddie must prove his mettle. Merman as girlfriend Joyce gets to belt out a few songs. ♪The Lady Dances; Shake It Off with Rhythm; You Have Me High, You Have Me Low; Calabash Pipe. **100m/B VHS.** Eddie Cantor, Ethel Merman, Sally Eilers, William Frawley, Parkyakarkus (Harry Einstein), Brian Donlevy, Jack La Rue; **D:** Norman Taurog; **W:** Frank Butler, Walter DeLeon, Francis Martin; **C:** Gregg Toland, Merritt B. Gerstad; **M:** Harold Arlen.

Strike Up the Band 1940 A high school band turns to hot swing music and enters a national radio contest. Rooney and Garland display their usual charm in this high-energy stroll down memory lane. ♪Over the Waves; The Light Cavalry Overture; Walkin' Down Broadway; Five Foot Two, Eyes of Blue; After the Ball; Nobody; Strike Up the Band. **120m/B VHS.** Judy Garland, Mickey Rooney, Paul Whiteman, William Tracy, June Preisser; **D:** Busby Berkeley. Oscars '40: Sound.

Striker 1988 (R) Mercenary John "Striker" Slade is sent to Nicaragua to free a captured American journalist, not knowing his superiors have betrayed him to the Contras and the Sandinistas. He battles it out with both groups while seeking revenge on the businessmen who set him up. **90m/C VHS.** Frank Zagarino, Melanie Rogers, Paul Werner; **D:** Stephen M. Andrews.

Striker's Mountain 1987 Story of a sports enthusiast who creates heliskiing and builds it into a business. Great ski scenes, but skip the rest. **99m/C VHS.** Bruce Greenwood, Mimi Kuzyk, Leslie Nielsen, August Schellenberg, Jessica Steen; **D:** Allen Simmonds.

Striking Distance 1993 (R) Tom Hardy (Willis) is a hard-nosed fifth-generation Pittsburgh homicide cop whose police detective father (Ma-honey) is killed, apparently by a serial killer. Hardy insists the perp was really a fellow cop and winds up on the River Rescue squad (at least his partner is the fetching Parker). When the serial killer starts striking at women with some connection to Hardy, he finds scant support from his fellow cops. High action quotient backed by a fine cast, but the killer's identity won't be a ny surprise. **101m/C VHS, DVD.** Bruce Willis, Sarah Jessica Parker, Dennis Farina, Tom Sizemore, Brion James, Robert Pastorelli, Timothy Busfield, John Mahoney, Andre Braugher; **D:** Rowdy Herrington; **W:** Marty Kaplan, Rowdy Herrington; **C:** Mac Ahlberg; **M:** Brad Fiedel.

Striking Point 1994 (R) Police detectives are determined to stop ex-KGB commandoes from smuggling high-tech weapons into the country. **96m/C VHS.** Chris Mitchum, Tracy Spaulding; **C:** Tony Browning; **M:** Thomas Fenton; **C:** Thomas Fenton; **W:** Laura Porter.

Strip Search ✍✍½ 1997 (R) Police detective Robby (Pare) gets seduced by easy money and sex when he gets involved with sex clubs and underworld gangs. 90m/C VHS, DVD, CA Michael Pare, Pam Grier, Caroline Neron, Lucie Laurier, Maury Chaykin, Heidi von Palleske, MacKenzie Gray; D: Rod Hewitt.

Stripes ✍✍½ 1981 (R) Feeling like losers and looking to straighten out their lives, two friends enlist in the Army under the mistaken impression that military life is something like a summer camp for grownups. A boxoffice success (despite a weak script) due in large part to Murray's charm and his verbal and sometimes physical sparring with Oates, who is good as the gruff-tempered platoon sergeant. Features humorous stints from va-ous "Second City" players, including Candy, whom Murray turns into a "ean, mean fighting machine." 105m/C VHS, DVD, UMD, Bill Murray, Harold Ramis, P.J. Soles, Warren Oates, John Candy, John Larroquette, Judge Reinhold, Sean Young, Dave Thomas, Joe Flaherty, Lance Le-Gault; D: Ivan Reitman; W: Len Blum, Harold Ramis; C: Bill Euler; M: Elmer Bernstein.

Stripped to Kill ✍✍ 1987 (R) A female cop goes undercover to lure a psycho killing strippers. Not-bad entry from Corman and cohorts. Followec by—you guessed it—"Stripped to Kill II." 88m/C VHS, DVD, Kay Lenz, Greg Evigan, Norman Fell, Pia Kamakahi, Tracy Crowder, Debana Shelton, Lucia Nagy Lexington, Carlye Byron, Athena Worthy, Michelle Foreman, Diana Bellamy; D: Katt Shea; W: Len Blum, Harold Ramis; C: Bill Euler; M: John O'Kennedy.

Stripped to Kill II: Live Girls ✍ 1989 A young woman with extra-sensory powers dreams of murders which she discovers are all too real. A weak sequel, despite the interesting premise. 83m/C VHS, DVD, Maria Ford, Ed Lottimer, Karen Mayo-Chandler, Marjean Holden Birke Tan, Debra Lamb; D: Katt Shea; W: Katt Shea.

The Stripper ✍✍½ 1963 Woman of Summer 1963 A middl-e-aged stripper in a traveling show returns to the small Kansas town of her youth. Left stranded, she moves in with an old friend whose teenage son promptly falls in love with her. Based on the play "A Loss of Roses" by William Inge. 95m/B VHS, Janette Boyd, Sara Costa, Kimberly Holcomb; D: Jerome Gary; M: Jack Beymer, Claire Trevor, Carol Lynley, Robert Webber, Gypsy Rose Lee; D: Franklin J. Schaffner; M: Jerry Goldsmith.

Striptease ✍✍½ 1996 (R) Single mcm Erin Grant (Moore) loses custody of her daughter Angela (Moore's real-life offspring, Rumer) to her lowlife ex, Darrell (Patrick). In order to raise the money for an appeal, she dances at a Miami strip club, where she runs across politician David Dilbeck (Reynolds), who has a thing for both vaseline and Erin. Unlike "Showgirls," this one's intentionally funny and features some fine script work and performances, which got overlooked almost all the hype, including Moore's record-setting (for an actress) $12 million paycheck, 4 mil of which reportedly was for agreeing to dance nude. Based on the novel by Carl Hiaasen. 115m/C VHS, DVD, Demi Moore, Armand Assante, Ving Rhames, Robert Patrick, Burt Reynolds, Rumer Willis, Paul Guilfoyle, Dina Spybey; D: Andrew Bergman; W: Andrew Bergman; C: Stephen Goldblatt; M: Howard Shore. Golden Raspberries '96: Worst Director (Bergman), Worst Picture, Worst Actress (Moore), Worst Screenplay, Worst Song ("Pussy, Pussy, Pussy (Whose Kitty, Cat, Are You?)").

Stripshow ✍ 1995 (R) Veteran Vegas stripper shows the ropes to newcomer and then must vie with the upstart for her boyfriend's interest. 96m/C VHS, DVD. Monique Parent, Tane McClure, Steven Trefson; D: Gary Orona; W: Gary Orona.

Stripteaser ✍ 1995 (R) Sicko psycho Dean holds dancers and patrons hostage in an L.A. strip joint where he provides various humiliations for his captives. Ford's the beautiful ecdysiast whose been the object of the fellow's secret obsessions. Also available unrated. 82m/C VHS, DVD, Rick Dean, Maria Ford, Lance August; D: Dan Golden.

Stroke of Midnight ✍✍½ 1990 (PG) Souped-up Cinderella with Lowe as egotistic high fashion designer, Grey as struggling shoe designer and a pumpkin-colored VW Bug. 102m/C VHS, Rob Lowe, Jennifer Grey, Andrea Ferreol; D: Tom Clegg.

Stroker Ace WOOF! 1983 (PG) Flamboyant stock car driver tries to break an iron-clad promotional contract signed with a greedy fried-chicken magnate. Off duty, he ogles blondes as dopey as he is. One of the worst from "Reynolds—and that's saying something. 96m/C VHS, DVD, Burt Reynolds, Ned Beatty, Jim Nabors, Parker Stevenson, Loni Anderson, Bubba Smith; D: Hal Needham; W: Hal Needham, Hugh Wilson; C: Nick McLean; M: Al Capps. Golden Raspberries '83: Worst Support. Actor (Nabors).

Stromboli ✍✍½ 1950 Bergman is a Czech refugee who marries an Italian fisherman in order to escape from her displaced persons camp. He brings her to his home island of Stromboli where she finds the life bleak and isolated and her marriage a trial. In Italian with English subtitles. The melodrama was even greater offscreen than on its set. Rossellini and Bergman scandalous affair. 107m/B VHS, IT Ingrid Bergman, Mario Vitale, Renzo Cesana; D: Roberto Rossellini.

Strong Man ✍✍✍ 1926 A WWI veteran, passing himself off as an American circus strongman, searches an American city for the girl whose letters gave him hope during the war. Perhaps Langdon's best full-length film. 73m/B VHS, DVD, Harry Langdon, Gertrude Astor, Tay Garnett; D: Frank Capra, Natl. Film Reg. '07.

Strong Medicine ✍✍½ 1984 Strange, avant-garde film about a strange, off-written young woman. Cleverly directed experiment that's not for everyone. 84m/C VHS, Carol Kane, Raul Julia, Wallace Shawn, Kate Manheim, David Warrilow; D: Guy Green.

The Strongest Man in the World ✍✍½ 1975 (G) Another crazy mix-up involves Dexter Riley (Russell) and his friends at Medfield College in wacky adventures. One of their experiments gets mixed up with one of the students' breakfast cereal and turns cut to give humans super-strength for a short time. The dean may provide fun for the young 'uns, and will definitely bring back fond memories for their parents. 92m/C VHS, DVD, Kurt Russell, Joe Flynn, Eve Arden, Cesar Romero, Phil Silvers, Dick Van Patten, Harold Gould, Richard Bakalyan, Michael McGreevey, William Schallert, Benson Fong, James Gregory, Don Carter, John Debney, Fritz Feld, Roy Roberts, Kathleen Freeman; W: Joseph L. McEveety, Herman Groves; C: Andrew Jackson; M: Robert F. Brunner.

Structure of Crystals ✍✍½ 1969 Struktura Krysztalu 1969 A member of the scientific elite meets with an old friend who has moved to a remote meteorological station and tries to persuade him to return to the city and resume his work. Zanussi's cerebral first feature was also the first of a series of films to explore the scientific community. In Polish with English subtitles. 76m/B VHS.

Stroszek ✍✍½ 1977 Three German misfits—a singer, a prostitute and an old man—tour the U.S. in search of their dreams. Touching, hilarious comedy-drama with a difference and an attitude. One of Herzog's easiest and also best films. In English and German with English subtitles. 108m/C VHS, DVD, GE Wilhelm von Homburg, Eva Mattes, Bruno S., Clemens Scheitz; D: Werner Herzog; W: Werner Herzog; C: Thomas Mauch; M: Chet Atkins, Tom Paxton.

Struggle ✍ 1931 Unfortunately Griffith's final directorial effort is a ludicrous melodrama about the evils of alcohol. Because of Prohibition, working man Jimmie Wilson (Skelly) takes to illegal booten, which turns out to be tainted, causing Jimmie to abuse his wife and daughter and destroy their formerly happy home. 87m/B VHS, Hal Skelly, Zita Johann, Evelyn Baldwin, Charlotte Wynters, Helen Mack, Kate Bruce, Jack Lipson, Charles Richman, Scott Moore, Arthur Lipson; D: D.W. Griffith, W: D.W. Griffith, Anita Loos, John Emerson; C: Joseph Ruttenberg; M: D.W. Griffith, Philip A. Scheib.

Stryker ✍½ 2004 Just your typical Canadian gangster and transvestite flick. Stryker is a speechless 14-year-old boy on the lam after burning down a church near his Indian reservation. He hops a train and finds himself a bla-k observer, wandering the seedy underbelly Winnipeg. After witnessing the warring Indian Posse and the Asian Bomb Squad, he finds protection in a home of transvestite prostitutes and then under the wing of the police. Low budget flair that tries to be quirky and fresh, but suffers from stiff performances and amateur theatrics. Fans of early John Waters may be amused. 93m/C DVD, Kyle Henry, Ryan Black, Deena Fontaine, Joseph Mesiano, Nick Ouilette, Nancy Sanderson; D: Noam Gonick; W: Noam Gonick, David Macintosh; C: Edward Lachman; M: Karman Omsopoos.

Stuart Bliss ✍✍ 1998 Curious little comedy mixes elements of "The X-Files" and "The Truman Show." Stuart Bliss (Zelniker) is an ordinary guy who slowly succumbs to paranoia and apocalyptic religious visions. Of course, the question is: Is he crazy or well-informed? 88m/C VHS, DVD, Michael Zelniker, Dea Lawrence, Derek McGrath, Ania Suli, Mark Fite; D: Neil Grieve; W: Michael Zelniker, Neil Grieve; C: Jens Sturup.

Stuart Little ✍✍½ 1999 (PG) This bigscreen adaptation of E.B. White's 1945 children's classic is hardly faithful but has its own charms. Mr. (Laurie) and Mrs. (Davis) Little decide to expand their family through adoption and wind up with a tiny, talking, clothes-wearing, white mouse named Stuart (Fox). Their scn George (Lipnicki) has a hard time thinking of a mouse as his little brother and family cat Snowbell (Lane) thinks the rodent is snack food. When his attempt to eat Stuart fails, Snowbell turns to kidnapping. The array of digital effects is amazing. 92m/C VHS, DVD, UMD, Geena Davis, Hugh Laurie, Jonathan Lipnicki, Brian Doyle-Murray, Estelle Getty, Julia Sweeney, Dabney Coleman; D: Rob Minkoff; W: M. Night Shyamalan, Greg Booker; C: Guillermo Navarro; M: Alan Silvestri; V: Michael J. Fox, Nathan Lane, Chazz Palminteri, Bruno Kirby, Jennifer Tilly, David Alan Grier, Jim Doughan.

Stuart Little 2 ✍✍✍ 2002 (PG) Amazingly good sequel finds Stuart tooling around Manhattan in his miniature red sport car with a new, similar-sized friend: a cute, yellow bird named Margalo (Griffith). Stuart is smitten with his fine-feathered friend, taking her on a very PG date to a drive-in movie (his car parked in front of the TV set). Unbeknownst to Stuart, Margalo is actually n cahoots with a scheming Falcon (Woods) who sets off numerous adventures out in the big city for Stuart and a reluctant and even snarkier Snowball (Lane). New York looks just as idyllic as it is even better, and the animation blended with live-action is even better than the first, on which both films were based. 78m/C VHS, DVD, UMD, US Geena Davis, Hugh Laurie, Jonathan Lipnicki, Brad Garrett; D: Rob Minkoff; W: Bruce Joel Rubin; C: Steven Poster; M: Alan Silvestri; V: Michael J. Fox, Nathan Lane, Melanie Griffith, James Woods, Steve Zahn.

Stuart Saves His Family ✍✍ 1994 (PG-13) Fired from his self-help TV show on a Chicago public-access station, New-Age advice guru Smalley (Franken) returns home to his pathetically dysfunctional family sort out their problems the endless parade of mediocre "Saturday Night Live" sketches stretched for the big screen that takes a few surprisingly maudlin turns. Based on Franken's book of Smalley's "daily affirmations." "I'm Good Enough, I'm Smart Enough, and Doggone It, People Like Me!" 97m/C VHS, DVD, Al Franken, Laura San Giacomo, Vincent D'Onofrio, Shirley Knight, Harris Yulin, Julia Sweeney, Aaron Lustig, Darrell Larson Camille Saviola, Gerrit Graham, Theodore (Ted) Raimi, Joe Flaherty; D: Harold Ramis; W: Al Franken; C: Lauro Escorel; M: Marc Shaiman.

Stuck on You ✍ 1984 (R) Couple engaged in a palimony suit takes their case to a judge to work out their differences. Wing-clipped angel Gabriel (Corey) comes to earth to help them patch it up. Never mind. 90m/C VHS, DVD, Prof. Irwin Corey, Virginia Penta, Mark Mikulski; D: Lloyd Kaufman, Michael Herz; W: Lloyd Kaufman, Mi...

Stuck On You ✍✍½ 2003 (PG-13) Surprisingly sentimental movie for the Farrelly brothers. Damon and Kinnear play conjoined twins Bob and Walt Tenor who've adapted to their rather unusual living arrangement with ease. Wa-t, however, has caught the acting bug and wants to make it big in Hollywood. As fate would have it, Walt becomes an unlikely star. While the movie borders on being a one-joke premise, it does have its sincere moments. 118m/C VHS, DVD, US Matt Damon, Greg Kinnear, Eva Mendes, Wen Yann Shih, Pat Crawford Brown, Jean-Pierre Cassel, Cher, Ray "Rocket" Valliere; Cameos: Jay Leno; D: Bobby Farrelly, Peter Farrelly; W: Bobby Farrelly, Peter Farrelly; C: Dan Mindel.

Stuckey's Last Stand ✍ 1980 A group of camp counselors prepare to take 22 children on a nature hike they will never forget. Mindless teen fodder. Faithfully adapted by sister Jackie Collins from her novel. 90m/C VHS, DVD, GB Joan Collins, Oliver Tobias; D: Quentin Masters; W: Jackie Collins.

The Stud ✍ 1978 (R) Owner of a fashionable "after hours" dance spot hires a young, handsome stud to manage the club and attend to her personal needs. Low-budget look and seemingly scoreless. 94m/C VHS, GB Joan Collins, Oliver Tobias; D: Quentin Masters.

The Student Affair ✍ The Lay of the Land 1997 (R) Larr'e would-be comedy based on Shapiro's stage play, which also starred Kellerman. She's college prof M.J. Dankworth, who suspects hubby Harvey (Begley Jr.) is tossing their tired marriage aside to shtupp his well-endowed grad student Muriel (Taylor). So she hires a P.I. (Margolin) to snoop out he's more interested in his client. Then the married's seek out (different) psychiatrists for help and M.J. indulges her rage in silly fantasy scenes. Don't waste your time. 94m/C VHS, CA Sally Kellerman, Ed Begley Jr., Sandra Taylor, Stuart Margolin, Tyne Daly, Rance Howard, Avery Schreiber; D: Larry Arrick; W: Mel Shapiro; C: Frederic Goodich; M: Jeff Lass.

Student Affairs WOOF! 1988 (R) A bunch of highschool misfits vie for roles in a movie about a bunch of high school misfits. 92m/C VHS, Louie Bonanno, Jim Abele Alan Fisler, Deborah Blaisdell; D: Chuck Vincent.

Student Bodies WOOF! 1981 (R) A "Halloween"-style spoof of high-school horror films, except it's not funny. And what's sc funny about bloody murder anyway? Wren the on-the-set problems and strife arose (which they did), why didn't everyone just cut their losses and go home? 86m/C VHS, DVD, Kristen Riter, Matthew...

Goldsby, Richard Brando, Patrick O'Neal, Alexander Scourby, Scott Bloom, James Dixon, Tammy Grimes; D: Mickey Rose; W: Mickey Rose.

Student Confidential 1987 (R) A Troma-produced spoof of seedy high school youth movies, new and old, involving four students who are led into the world of adult vices by a mysterious millionaire. Badly made and dull. Douglas and Jackson both have brothers named Michael. 99m/C VHS, DVD. Eric Douglas, Marion Jackson, Susie Scott, Ronee Blakley, Elizabeth Singer; D: Richard Horian

The Student Nurses 1970 (R) The adventures, amorous and otherwise, of four last-year nursing students. Followed by four sequels: "Private Duty Nurses," "Night Call Nurses," "The Young Nurses," and "Candy Stripe Nurses." Better than average exploitation fare. First release from Roger Corman's New World studios; it goes down hill from there. 89m/C VHS, DVD. Elaine Giftos, Karen Carlson, Brioni Farrell, Barbara Leigh, Reni Santoni, Richard Rust, Lawrence Casey, Darrell Larson, Paul Camen, Richard Stahl, Scottie MacGregor, Pepe Serna; D: Stephanie Rothman; W: Don Spencer; C: Stevan Larner.

Student of Prague 1913 Early silent classic based on the German Faust legend: a student makes a pact with the devil to win a beautiful woman. Poor fellow. With either German or English title cards. Music track. 60m/B VHS, DVD. GE Lothar Koerner, Grete Berger, Paul Wegener; D: Paul Wegener; Stellan Rye.

The Student Prince 1954 Delightful rendition of Sigmund Romberg's famous operetta in which Purdom stars as the Prince of Heidelberg who falls for barmaid Blyth. Lanza recorded the soundtrack, but could not star in this film because of his weight problem. Previously filmed in 1919 and 1927 without music. ♪Golden Days; Serenade; Deep in My Heart; To the Inn We're Marching; Drink, Drink; Come Boys, Let's All Be Gay, Boys; Summertime in Heidelberg; Beloved; I Walk With God. 107m/C VHS, DVD. GE Ann Blyth, Edmund Purdom, John Ericson, Louis Calhern, Edmund Gwenn, S.Z. Sakall, Betta St. John; D: Richard Thorpe; C: Paul Vogel.

The Student Prince in Old Heidelberg Old Heidelberg 1927 Prince Karl Heinrich silently falls in love with lowly barmaid. 102m/B VHS. Ramon Novarro, Norma Shearer; D: Ernst Lubitsch.

The Student Teachers 1973 Yet another soft-core Corman product. Three student teachers sleep around, on screen. 79m/C VHS, DVD. Susan Damante-Shaw, Brooke Mills, Bob Harris, John Cramer, Chuck Norris; D: Jonathan Kaplan.

Studs Lonigan 1960 Drifting, too artsy rendering a James T. Farrell's trilogy about an Irish drifter growing up in Chicago in the '20s. Good period detail, but oddly off-kilter and implausible as history. 96m/B VHS, DVD. Christopher Knight, Frank Gorshin, Jack Nicholson, Jay C. Flippen, Katherine Squire, Dick Foran, Carolyn Craig; D: Irving Lerner; W: Philip Yordan; C: Haskell Wexler; M: Jerry Goldsmith.

A Study in Scarlet 1933 Owen played Watson the previous year in "Sherlock Holmes"; here he's miscast as Holmes, and the plot differs from the Doyle story of the same title. 77m/B VHS, DVD. Reginald Owen, Alan Mowbray, Anna May Wong, June Clyde, Alan Dinehart; D: Edwin L. Marin; W: Reginald Owen.

A Study in Terror Sherlock Holmes Grosster Fall; Fog 1966 A well-appointed Sherlock Holmes thriller, and the second one in color. Premise has a young, athletic Holmes in pursuit of an educated Jack the Flipper in 1880s London. 94m/C VHS. GE GB John Neville, Donald Houston, Judi Dench, Anthony Quayle, Robert Morley, Frank Finlay, Cecil Parker; D: James Hill.

The Stuff 1985 (R) Surreal horror semi-spoof about an ice cream mogul and a hamburger king who discover that the new, fast-selling confection in town zombifies its partakers. Forced, lame satire from producer/director/writer Cohen. 93m/C VHS, DVD. Michael Moriarty, Andrea Marcovicci, Garrett Morris, Paul Sorvino, Danny Aiello, Brooke Adams, Patrick O'Neal, Alexander Scourby, Scott Bloom, James Dixon, Tammy Grimes; D: Mickey Rose; W: Larry Cohen; C: Paul Glickman; M: Anthony Guefen.

Stuff Stephanie in the Incinerator 1987 (R) In Deadly Heat 1989 (PG-13) A Troma gagfest about wealthy cretins who torture and kill young women. "Funny" title betrays utter, exploitive mindlessness. 97m/C VHS, DVD. Catherine Dee, William Dame, M.R. Murphy, Dennis Cunningham; D: Don Nardo.

The Stunt Man 1980 (R) A marvelous and unique exercise in metacinematic manipulation. O'Toole, in one of his very best roles, is a power-crazed movie director; Railsback is a fugitive sheltered by him from sheriff Rocco. When a stunt man is killed in an accident, O'Toole prevails on Railsback to replace him, leading Railsback to wonder if O'Toole wants him dead. A labor of love for director-producer Rush, who spent nine years working on it, and waited two years to see it released, by Fox. Based on the novel by Paul Brodeur. 129m/C VHS, DVD. Peter O'Toole, Steve Railsback, Barbara Hershey, Charles "Chuck" Bail, Alex Rocco, Allen Goorwitz (Goorwitz), Garfield, Adam Roarke, Sharon Farrell, Philip Bruns; D: Richard Rush; W: Richard Rush, Lawrence B. Marcus; C: Mario Tosi; M: Dominic Frontiere. Golden Globes '81: Score; Montreal World Film Fest. '80: Film; Natl. Soc. Film Critics '80: Actor (O'Toole).

Stunt Pilot 1939 A young man takes a job at a film studio as a stunt pilot and finds mayhem and romance on and off the ground. One in the "Tailspin Tommy" series. Well-paced and fun to watch. 61m/C VHS, John Trent, Marjorie Reynolds, Milburn Stone, Jason Robards Sr., Pat O'Malley; D: George Waggner; W: George Waggner, Scott Darling; C: Fred H. Jackman Jr.; M: Frank Sanucci.

Stunts 1977 (PG) See "The Stunt Man" instead. OK script hides near-invisible plot; stunt man engages in derring-do. 90m/C VHS, DVD. Robert Forster, Fiona Lewis, Joanna Cassidy, Darrell Fetty, Bruce Glover, James Luisi; D: Mark L. Lester; M: Michael Kamen.

Stuntwoman 1981 Welch plays a stuntwoman whose death-defying job interferes with her love life. What ever shall she do? 95m/C VHS. Raquel Welch, Jean-Paul Belmondo; D: Claude Zidi.

The Stupids 1995 (PG) In the tradition of "Dumb and Dumber," the aptly named Stupids--dad Stanley (Arnold), mom Joan (Lundy), brother Buster (Hall), and sis Petunia (McKenna)--blunder unwittingly into and out of dangerous adventures involving their garbage. Landing Arnold for the lead seems like the casting coup of the decade but the movie itself is shaky and uninspired. Based on the children's best-selling books. Keep a lookout for Captain Kangaroo (Keeshan) and numerous other cameos. 93m/C VHS, DVD. Tom Arnold, Jessica Lundy, Bug Hall, Alex McKenna, Mark Metcalf, Matt Keeslar, Frankie Faison, Christopher Lee, Bob Keeshan; Cameos: Robert Wise, Norman Jewison, Constantin Costa-Gavras, David Cronenberg, Atom Egoyan, Gillo Pontecorvo; D: John Landis; W: Brent Forrester; C: Manfred Guthe; M: Christopher Stone. Golden Raspberries '96: Worst Actor (Arnold).

Styx 2000 (R) Nelson (Weller) decides to get out of the safecracking trade after his brother Mike (MacFadyen) rescues him from a botched bank heist that leaves several accomplices unaccounted for. Nelson tries to go straight but Mike is a losing gambler with a big debt to some loan sharks. Nelson agrees to do a diamond heist only to learn that his not-so-missing partner Art (Brown) is the mastermind and Art just may be holding a grudge. Pro cast can't save this fast-paced action take this above the usual heist flicks. 94m/C VHS, DVD. Peter Weller, Bryan Brown, Angus MacFadyen, Adrienne Pierce, Anthony Bishop, Nan Hamilton, Shane Howarth, Gerard Rudolf; D: Alexander Wright; W: George Ferris; C: Russell Lyster; M: Roy Hay.

Sub Down 1997 (PG-13) Silly underwater saga about a submarine trapped under the polar ice cap in the Bering Strait. Scientists Baldwin, Conti, and Anwar are aboard the USS Portland when it manages to collide with a Russian sub and sink. So they're running out of air and have to figure out a way to survive. Director Gregg Champion took his name off, so be warned. 91m/C VHS, DVD. Stephen Baldwin, Gabrielle Anwar, Tom Conti, Chris Mulkey, Tony Plana, Joel Thomas Traywick, Doug McKeon; D: Alan Smithee; W: Howard Chesley; C: Hiro Narita; M: Stefano Mainetti. CABLE

Subhuman Shelf Life 2004 (R) Psycho bounty hunter Martin (McDonald) is going around decapitating people when he's accidentally run over by Ben (McLaughlin) and Julie (Kramer). He convinces them not to take him to a hospital; instead they take him to their home (because they're really stupid). Martin tells them he's hunting blood-sucking parasites that can only be destroyed by decapitating the host, which turns out to be true as the couple soon finds out. 90m/C DVD. CA William McDonald, Earl Pastko, Bryce McLaughlin, Courtney Kramer; D: Mark Tuit; W: Mark Tuit; C: Craig Powell; M: Stephen Bukat, Jeff Tymoschuk.

Subject Two 2006 (R) A claustrophobic "Frankenstein" variation. In a remote Rocky Mountain cabin, scientist Dr. Vick (Stapleton) uses his new assistant, Adam (Oliver), as a guinea pig in his controversial research on death and resurrection. He kills Adam and revives him, over and over again. 93m/C DVD. US Dean Stapleton, Christian Oliver, Courtney Mace, Jurgen Jones; D: Philip Chidel; W: Philip Chidel; C: Rich Confalone; M: Erik Godal.

The Subject Was Roses 1968 Outstanding story of family dysfunction and love based on Gilroy's Pulitzer Prize-winning play. Timmy Cleary (Sheen) returns from WWII to find that his parents' marriage has disintegrated into open hostility. Formerly mom Nettie's (Neal) favorite, Timmy finally starts to learn about blustery dad John (Albertson) and attempts to moderate between the rancorous duo. But he quickly discovers that each of his parents will use him against the other and Timmy decides the best thing for everyone would be if he strikes out on his own. First film for Neal following a series of strokes. 107m/C VHS. Martin Sheen, Patricia Neal, Jack Albertson; D: Ulu Grosbard; W: Frank D. Gilroy; C: Jack Priestley; M: Lee Pockriss. Oscars '68: Support. Actor (Albertson).

Sublime 2007 (R) George Grieves (Cavanagh) goes to the hospital for a routine procedure and doctors mistakenly perform a different surgery that results in George contracting a flesh-eating bacteria. This results in more surgeries and a series of flashbacks concerning George's anxieties, including his health concerns (guess he was right about that). 113m/C DVD. Tom Cavanagh, Kathleen York, Lawrence-Hilton Jacobs, Kyle Gallner, Katherine Cunningham-Eves, Paget Brewster, Shanna Collins; D: Tony Krantz; W: Erik Jendresen; C: Dermott Downs; M: Peter Golub. VIDEO

Subliminal Seduction Roger Corman Presents: Subliminal Seduction; The Corporation 1996 (R) Videogame designer Ziering realizes that mind-control messages have been coded into CD-ROMS. 81m/C VHS. Ian Ziering, Diane de Wallace Stone, Kin Shriner, Stella Stevens, Katherine Kelly Lang, Larry Manetti, Andrew Stevens; D: Andrew Stevens. CABLE

Submarine Attack Torpedo Zone; The Great Hope; La Grande Speranza 1954 Unconventional war story posits an Italian submarine captain (Baldini) who decides to rescue the survivors of a Danish freighter that he has sunk. 92m/B VHS, DVD. IT Renato Baldini, Lois Maxwell, Folco Lulli, Carlo Bellini, Earl Cameron; D: Duilio Coletti; C: Leonida Barboni; M: Nino Rota.

Submarine Seahawk 1959 When a group of Japanese warships mysteriously disappear, allied intelligence suspect a big battle is brewing. An inexperienced commander who has been tracking the movement of the submarine Seahawk, even though the crew lacks faith in his command abilities. His own men may prove a bigger obstacle than any of the Japanese. Lots of action and stock WWII footage. 83m/B VHS. John Bentley, Brett Halsey, Wayne Heffley, Steve Mitchell, Henry McCann, Frank Gerstle; D: Spencer Gordon Bennet.

Submerged 2000 (R) Terrorists hijack a commerical airliner carrying a computer decoder that controls a national defense satellite capable of launching nuclear weapons. The hijackers deliberately plunge the plane into the Pacific Ocean and while the passengers struggle to survive, a team of Nacy SEALS attempt a rescue mission and a strike against the bad guys. 95m/C VHS, DVD. Coolio, Nicole Eggert, Fred William, Dennis Weaver, Maxwell Caulfield, Brent Huff, Tim Thomerson, Stacey Travis, Yvette Nipar; D: Fred Olen Ray; W: Steve .atshaw; C: Thomas Callaway. VIDEO

Submerged 2005 (R) Cookie-cutter Steven Seagal action flick has the fading star as a notorious "freelance" anti-terrorist agent sprung from prison to help end a US government conspiracy and fight terrorists aboard a nuclear sub. 96m/C DVD. Steven Seagal, Vinnie Jones, Nick Brimble, William Hope, Christine Adams; D: Anthony Hickox; W: Anthony Hickox, Paul DeSouza; C: David Bridges; M: Guy Farley. VIDEO

Subspecies 1990 (R) New improved vampire demons descend on earth. The first full-length feature film shot on location in Transylvania. For horror buffs only. 90m/C VHS, DVD. Laura Tate, Michael Watson, Anders (Tofting) Hove, Michelle McBride, Irina Movila, Angus Scrimm; D: Ted Nicolaou.

Submission 1977 (R) A pharmacist's sensuality is reawakened when she has a provocative affair with a clerk in her shop. 107m/C VHS. IT Franco Nero, Lisa Gastoni; D: Salvatore Samperi.

The Substance of Fire 1996 (R) Publisher Isaac Geldhart (Rifkin) is an autocrat in both his business and his personal life, which may be why he's having so much trouble with both. A Holocaust survivor, Geldhart's obsessive about publishing a lavish four-volume history of Nazi medical experiments that will bankrupt the family firm. So his children wind up ousting him from the company and Isaac slowly slips over the edge into madness. Very King Lear, with an astonishing performance by Rifkin who also played the character in Baitz's 1991 Off-Broadway play. 100m/C VHS, DVD. Ron Rifkin, Tony Goldwyn, Timothy Hutton, Sarah Jessica Parker, Ronny Graham, Elizabeth Franz, Gil Bellows; D: Daniel Sullivan; W: Jon Robin Baitz; C: Robert Yeoman; M: Joseph Vitarelli.

The Substitute 1993 (R) Donohue plays a sexy high-school substitute teacher who turns out to have homicidal tendencies, which she decides to take out on her students. Film debut for rapper/underwear model Mark. 86m/C VHS. Amanda Donohoe, Dalton James, Natasha Gregson Wagner, Eugene Robert Glazer, Mark Wahlberg; D: Martin Donovan; W: Cynthia Verlaine; M: Gerald Gouriet.

The Substitute 1996 (R) Berenger plays a Vietnam vet mercenary who poses as a substitute teacher to uncover a drug ring after his girlfriend (Venora) is roughed up by the gang. At one point, he displays his unique teaching style by throwing some unruly students out of the second floor window. Hmm...wonder if that was on the test. Being a concerned teacher, he decides to uncover the kingpin of the unruly drug gang. Being an unruly drug gang, they decide to shoot at him...a lot. Unless you're a fan of heavy weaponry, banal one liners or yelling at the screen in frustration, substitute another movie for this one. 114m/C VHS, DVD. Tom Berenger, Ernie Hudson, Diane Venora, Marc Anthony, Glenn Plummer, Cliff DeYoung, William Forsythe, Raymond Cruz, Sharron Corley, Richard Brooks, Rodney A. Grant, Luis Guzman; D: Robert Mandel; W: Alan Ormsby, Roy Frumkes, Rocco Simonelli; C: Bruce Surtees; M: Gary Chang.

The Substitute 2: School's Out 1997 (R) Mercenary Carl Thomasson (Williams) poses as a high school substitute teacher to hunt down the New York gang bangers who murdered his brother during a carjacking. But his plans for revenge out innocent schoolchildren at risk as well. **90m/C VHS, DVD.** Treat Williams, B.D. Wong, Angel David, Michael Michele, Larry (Lawrence) Gilliard Jr.; **D:** Steven Pearl; **W:** Roy Frumkes, Rocco Simonelli; **C:** Larry Banks; **M:** Joe Delia. VIDEO

The Substitute 3: Winner Takes All ✶✶½ 1999 (R) Mercenary Karl Thomasson (Williams) visits Nicole, the daughter of a dead friend who's a teacher at an eastern college. After Nicole is badly beaten, Karl takes over as a substitute and has his fellow mercenaries investigate. They discover members of the football team are on steroids, thanks to an in with the scn of the local crime boss, so Karl and his buddies decide to clean things up. **90m/C VHS, DVD.** Treat Williams, Rebeca Staab, Claudia Christian, James Black, Richard Portnow; **D:** Robert Radler; **W:** Roy Frumkes, Rocco Simonelli; **C:** Barry M. Wilson; **M:** Tor Hyams. VIDEO

The Substitute 4: Failure is Not an Option ✶1½ 2000 (R) Undercover cop Karl Thomason (Williams) poses as a teacher at a military academy and discovers a group of neo-Nazi cadets whose aims are supported by members of the staff. The more sequels, the less steam this series has—this one is definitely running on Icw. **91m/C VHS, DVD.** Treat Williams, Angie Everhart, Bill Nunn, Tim Abell, Simon R-ree, Patrick Kilpatick, Michael Weatherly, Grayson Fricke; **D:** Robert Radler; **M:** Stephen (Steve) Edwards. VIDEO

The Substitute Wife ✶✶½ 1994 (PG-13) Dying Nebraska frontier woman Amy Hightower (Thompson) decides to find her husband Martin (Weller) a new wife to help on the farm and look after their four children. But women are so scarce (and the farm is so isolated) that the only one willing to give it a try is prostitute Pearl (Fawcett), who's fed up with her profession but isn't exactly the motherly type (at least not at first). Amusing relationships develop between the two women and the bewildered husband. Made for TV. **92m/C VHS, DVD.** Farrah Fawcett, Lea Thompson, Peter Weller; **D:** Peter Werner; **W:** Stan Daniels; **C:** Neil Roach; **M:** Mark Snow. TV

Subterano ✶ 2001 (R) The low-budget sci-fier... underground parking garage. But they get problems—a crazy videogame designer uses the garage as a set-up for the life-size version of his virtual reality game Subterano and they've just become his new players. **95m/C VHS, DVD,** Au Alex Dimitrades, Tasma Walton, Alison Whyte, Kate Sherman, Jason Stojanovski; **D:** Esben Storm; **W:** Esben Storm; **C:** Graeme Wood.

Subterfuge ✶✶ 1968 When a special American security agent goes to England for a "vacation," rebel leader Conrad (Dimitriades) and fellow dissident Stone (Walton) ... causes speculation and poses several serious questions for both British Intelligence and the underworld. Nothing special, with the occasional suspenseful moment. **89m/C VHS.** GB Tom Adams, Joan Collins, Gene Barry, Richard Todd; **D:** Peter Graham Scott.

Subterfuge ✶✶ 1998 (R) When a plane explodes over the Black Sea, the CIA, Russian spies, and drug runners are all after the black box. **95m/C VHS, DVD.** Matt McColm, Amanda Pays, Glynn Turman, Jason Gould, Richard Brake, Ben -Hammer; **D:** Herb Freed; **W:** Marion Segal; **C:** Irek Hartowicz; **M:** Jim Halfpenny.

Suburban Commando ✶✶ 1991 (PG) A goofy, muscular alien mistakenly lands on Earth while on vacation. He does his best to remain inconspicuous, resulting in numerous hilarious situations. Eventually, he is forced to confront his arch, interstellar nemesis in order to defend the family who befriended him. A harmless, sometimes cute vehicle for wrestler Hogan, which will certainly entertair his younger fans. **88m/C VHS, DVD.** Hulk Hogan, Christopher Lloyd, Shelley Duvall, Larry Miller, William Ball, JoAnn Dearing, Jack Elam;

Suburbia ✶ 1983 (R) When a group of punk rockers move into a condemned suburban development, they become the targets of a vigilante group. Low budget, needless violent remake of anyone of many '50s "rebellion flicks that tries to have a "message." **99m/C VHS, DVD.** Chris Pederson, Bill Coyne, Jennifer Clay, Timothy Eric O'Brien, Andrew Pece, Don Allen; **D:** Penelope Spheeris; **W:** Penelope Spheeris; **C:** Tim Suhrstedt; **M:** Alex Gibson.

subUrbia ✶✶ 1996 (R) Ensemble piece featuring three aimless post-high school friends, Jeff (Ribisi), Buff (Zahn), and Tim (Katt) who spend their time hanging out in the parking lot of a convenience store. What's different about this night is that they're joined by Jeff's girlfriend Sooze (Carey), and her friend Bee-Bee (Spybey), and they actually have a purpose for waiting around. The guys are expecting a visit from their old buddy Pony (Eartok), a rock musician just finding success. But when Pony does appear, the fact that he has done something to get out ... succeed turns the meeting hostile. Based on the play by Eric Bogosian. **118m/C VHS.** Giovanni Ribisi, Steve Zahn, Nicky Katt, Jayce Bartok, Amie Carey, Dina Spybey, Parker Posey, Ajay Naidu, Samia Shoaib; **D:** Richard Linklater; **W:** Eric Bogosian; **C:** Lee Daniel.

Subway ✶1½ 1985 (R) Surreal, MTV-esque vision of French fringe life from the director of "Le Dernier Combat". A spike-haired renegade escapes the law by plunging into the Parisian subway system. Once there, he encounters a bizarre sub-culture living under the city. Plenty of angry-youth attitude, but where's the point? And frankly, too much bad New Wave music. **103m/C VHS, DVD.** FR Christopher Lambert, Isabelle Adjani, Jean-Hugues Anglade, Jean Reno, Richard Bohringer, Michel Galabru, Eric Serra, Arthur Simms; **D:** Luc Besson; **W:** Luc Besson, Pierre Jolivet, Alain Le Henry, Marc Perrier, Sophie Schmit; **C:** Carlo Varini; **M:** Rickie Lee Jones, Eric Serra, Cesar '86. Actor (Lambert), Art Dir/Set Dec. Sound.

Subway Stories ✶✶ 1997 (R) Ten short films based on actual experiences on the New York subway system featuring such topics as harassment, flirtation, sex, food, and money. **82m/C VHS.** Bill Irwin, Kris Parker, Denis Leary, Christine Lahti, Steve Zahn, Roy Dotrice, Christopher Neame, Tony Longo; Jerry Stiller, Bonnie Hurt, Lili Taylor, Michael Rapaport Mercedes Ruehl, Santa Choudhury, Taral Hicks, Danny Hoch, Mike McGlone, Rosie Perez, Gregory Hines, Anne Heche; **D:** Ted (Edward) Demme, Abel Ferrara, Jonathan Demme, Julie Dash, Seth Zvi Rosenfeld, Bob Balaban, Alison Maclean, Lucas Platt, Patricia Benoit, Craig McKay; **W:** Danny Hoch, John Guare, Alison Maclean, Lucas Platt, Patricia Benoit, Craig McKay, Seth Zvi Rosenfeld, Joe Viola, Albert Innaurato, Angela Todd; **C:** Ken Kelsch, Adam Kimmel, Tom Hurwitz, Anthony Jannelli.

Suburban Girl ✶✶ 2007 (PG-13) Naive NYC associate book editor Brett (Gellar) is overwhelmed by her new job. Then she meets lecherous star publisher Archie Knox (Baldwin), who offers to show her how to fit in. The mismatched love affair works kinda well, basically because Baldwin knows how to sell his somewhat smarmy charm. Gellar seem's a little out of her depth. Based on two stories from "The Girls' Guide to Hunting and Fishing" by Melissa Grant. **97m/C DVD, Blu-ray Disc.** Sarah Michelle Gellar, Alec Baldwin, James Naughton, Maggie Grace, Chris Carmack; **D:** Marc Klein; **W:** Marc Klein; **C:** Steven Fierberg; **M:** Heitor Pereira.

Suburban Roulette ✶ 1967 "Adults only" feature from splattermaster Lewis caters to the prurient. Groovy themes like wife swapping and other very daring subjects. Totally '60s. Presented as part of Joe Bob Briggs "Sleaziest Movies in the History of the World" series. **81m/C VHS.** Elizabeth Wilkinson, Ben Moore, Tony McCabe, Debbie Grant; **D:** Herschell Gordon Lewis; **W:** Herschell Gordon Lewis; **C:** Roy Collodi.

The Suburbans ✶1½ 1999 (R) Bland and not very funny ensemble comedy. The Suburbans were an '80s one-hit wonder band who reunite 18 years later at member Gil's (Ferrell) wedding. Their impromptu reunion draws the attention of a likely record company talent scout Kate (Hewitt), who decides she wants to resurrect their would-be music careers. The music satire is funny but the domestic angst is boring. **81m/C VHS, DVD.** Jennifer Love Hewitt, Will Ferrell, Donal Lardner Ward, Craig Bierko, Amy Brenneman, Bridgette Wilson-Sampras, Tony Guma, Robert Loggia, Antonio Fargas, Ben Stiller, Jerry Stiller; **D:** Donal Lardner Ward; **W:** Donal Lardner Ward, Tony Guma; **C:** Michael Barrett; **M:** Robbia Mowry.

Sucker Free City ✶✶✶ 2005 Three young men of different ethnicities turn to crime as the answer to surviving their rough lives in San Francisco. (Crowley) steals credit card data in his office mailroom job; K-Luv (Mackie) is part of a black gang but wants out; and Chinese mafia member Lincoln (Leung) is moving up the ranks. Eventually tensions arise and an explosive showdown unfolds. Showtime original movie was directed by Spike Lee as a series pilot, though it wasn't picked up. **116m/C DVD.** Ken Leung, Anthony Mackie, Darris Love, Laura Allen, Ben Crowley, Kathy Eaker; **D:** Spike Lee; **W:** Alex Tse. CABLE

Sucker Money ✶1½ 1933 Newspaper reporter works to expose phony spiritualist. Good title; little else. Boring. **59m/B VHS.** Mischa Auer, Phyllis Barrington, Earl McCarthy, Ralph Lewis, Mae Busch, Alan Bridge, J. Frank Glendon, Harry Troc; **D:** Dorothy Davenport Reid, Melville Shyer; **W:** Willis Kent; **C:** James Diamond, William Nobles.

Suckerfish ✶✶ 1999 Veteran pet supply salesmen Alan (Donovan) and Dick (Orr) resent that a retiring colleague's lucrative territory is being given to ambitious newbie Ken (Bodden). So they set out to sabotage him. When Ken finds out why he's not making any sales, he plans revenge—starting with the knowledge that Dick's wife Elizabeth (Lawlor) is having an affair with Alan. **88m/C VHS, DVD.** Dan Donovan, Tim Orr, Kurt Bodden, Gerri Lawler; **D:** Brien Burroughs; **C:** Christopher Braun; **M:** Joshua Raoul Brody.

The Sucker ✶✶ 1965 Le Corniaud 1965 Antoine Maréchal (Bourvil) is on his way to an Italian vacation when his car is wrecked in an accident. The businessman who smashed his car offers Antoine a Cadillac to drive but this turns him into a smuggler. However, Antoine isn't as dumb as he may appear and he makes the most of his unusual situation. French with subtitles. **90m/C VHS.** FR Amae Bourvil, Louis de Funes; **D:** Gérard Oury.

Such a Long Journey ✶✶✶ 1998 Bank clerk Gustad Noble has a modest life that is beginning to fall apart. First his young daughter becomes very ill and then his son defies Gustad's ambitions for him. Finally, he receives a letter from an old friend asking for his help and Gustad finds himself caught up in unexpected danger and deception. Set in Bombay in 1971, as India prepares for war, and based on the novel by Rohinton Mistry. **110m/C VHS.** CA GB Roshan Seth, Om Puri, Kurush Deboo, Naseeruddin Shah, Ranjit Chowdhari; **D:** Sturla Gunnarsson; **W:** Soon Ta'apeviela; **C:** Jan Kiesser. Genie '98. Actor (Seth), Film Editing.

Success Is the Best Revenge ✶✶½ 1984 A Polish film director living in London struggles with his rebellious teenage son. Both struggle with questions of exile and identity. Uneven but worthwhile and based on Skolimowski's own experiences. His better earlier film is "Moonlighting." **95m/C VHS.** Gä Michael York, Michel Piccoli Anouk Aimee, John -rut, Jane Asher, Joanna Szerbic, Michael Lyndon, George Skolimowski; **D:** Jerzy Skolimowski; **M:** Hans Zimmer.

Subway to the Stars ✶✶½ Un Trem Para as Estrelas 1987 Young saxophonist Fontes searches the back streets of Rio for his missing girlfriend. Realistic and sometimes depressing, if aimless at times. Overall, an intriguing "underworld" flick from Brazil. Portuguese with subtitles. **103m/C VHS.** Guilherme Fontes, Milton Goncalves, Taumaturgo Ferrira, Ze Trirdade, Ana Beatriz Willgen; **D:** Carlos Diegues.

Sudden Death ✶ 1977 (R) Fast on the Draw cowboys posing as hired gunmen in order to kill a wealthy, homesteader-hating land baron. **55m/B VHS.** James Ellison, Russell Hayden, Fuzzy Knight, Raymond Hatton, Julie Adams, Tom Tyler, John Cason, Stanley Price; **D:** Thomas Car; **W:** Ron Ormond, Maurice Tombragel; **C:** Ernes: Miller.

Sudden Death ✶ 1985 (R) Two professional violence merchants put themselves up for hire. **84m/C VHS, DVD.** Robert Conrad, Felton Perry, Don Stroud, Bill Raymond, Ron Vawter, Harry Rosloenko; **D:** Richard Forenes; Miller.

Sudden Death ✶✶ 1995 (R) A beautiful businesswoman decides to kill every rapist she can find after she herself has been - attacked. Exploitative in its own fashion; fueled and fueled by rage. **95m/C VHS.** Denise Coward, Frank Runyeon, Jamie Tirelli; **D:** Sig Shore.

Sudden Death ✶✶ 1995 (R) Terrorists invade a hockey arena where the Vice President and 17,000 fans, including Fire Marshal Jean-Claude and his kids, are watching the seventh game of the Stanley Cup Finals. The latest in the "Die Hard in a..." genre covers the territory with the row-standard lack of characterization, family member in peril, and ever-increasing body count. Boothe (playing A an Rickman playing a bad guy) does most of the talking while Van Damme kicks people in the head and plays goalie. Producer Howard Baldwin owns the Pittsburgh Penguins, coincidentally one of the teams on the ice for the second pairing of "Time-cop" vets Hyams and Van Damme. **110m/C VHS, DVD.** Jean-Claude Van Damme, Powers Boothe, Ross Malinge-, Whittni Wright, Raymond J. Barry, Dorian Harewood, Kate McNeil, Audra Lindley; **D:** Peter Hyams; **W:** Gene Quirano; **C:** Peter -hyams; **M:** John Debney.

Sudden Fear ✶✶✶ 1952 Successful playwright/heiress Myra Hudson (Crawford) has a whirlwind romance leading to marriage, with oh-so-charming actor Lester Blaine (Palance). But Les s more interested in Myra's money and gets together with former flame Irene (always the bad girl Grahame) to get rid of his new bride and inherit her fortune. But Myra finds out about the plot and puts her writing talent to work in coming up with a new scenario. Good suspenser with fine performances. Adapted from the book by Edna Sherry. **111m/B VHS, DVD.** Joan Crawford, Jack Palance, Gloria Grahame, Bruce Bennett, Virginia Huston, Mike Conners; **D:** David Miller; **W:** Lenore Coffee, Robert Smith; **C:** Charles (Bryant) Lang Jr.; **M:** Elmer Bernstein.

Sudden Impact ✶✶½ 1983 (R) Eastwood directs himself in this formula thriller, the fourth "Dirty Harry" entry. This time "Dirty Harry" Callahan tracks down a revenge-obsessed murderess and finds he has more in common with her than he expected. Meanwhile, local mobsters come gunning for him. This is the one where he says, "Go ahead. Make my day." Followed by "The Dead Pool." **117m/C VHS, DVD.** Clint Eastwood, Sondra Locke, Pat Hingle, Bradford Dillman, Albert "Popry" Popwell; **D:** Clint Eastwood; **W:** Joseph C. Stinson; **C:** Bruce Surtees; **M:** Lalo Schifrin.

Sudden Manhattan ✶✶ 1996 Unemployed single Donna (Shelly) thinks she witnesses a murder—over and over again. Of course, no one believes her and she tries to figure out the truth. Shelly's directorial debut. **80m/C VHS, DVD.** Adrienne Shelly, Tim Guinee, Roger Rees, Louise Lasser, Hynden Walch; **D:** Adrienne Shelly; **W:** Adrienne Shelly; **C:** Jim Denault; **M:** Pat Irwin.

Suddenly ✶✶✶ 1954 Crazed gunman John Baron (Sinatra) holds a family hostage in the hick town of Suddenly, California, as part of a plot to kill the president, who's stopping at the local train station. As things begin to go wrong, Baron begins to unravel. Tense thriller with a good display for Sinatra's acting talent. Unfortunately hard to find because of distribution after hearing that Kennedy's assassin Lee Harvey Oswald had watched "Suddenly" only days before November

22, 1963. Really, Ol' Blue Eyes should have stuck with making top-notch thrillers like this one, instead of degenerating into the world's greatest lounge singer. 75m/B VHS, DVD. Frank Sinatra, Sterling Hayden, James Gleason, Nancy Gates, Paul Frees, Willis Bouchey, Kim Charney, Christopher Dark; *D:* Lewis Allen; *W:* Richard Sale; *C:* Charles Clarke; *M:* David Raksin.

Suddenly, Last Summer ✓✓✓½ 1959 Brain surgeon is summoned to the mansion of a rich New Orleans matron who wishes him to perform a lobotomy on her niece, supposedly suffering from a mental breakdown. Based on the play by Tennessee Williams. Softened for the censors, though the themes of homosexuality, insanity, and murder, characterizations of evil, and unusual settings presage many movies of the next two decades. Extremely fine performances from Hepburn and Taylor. Clift never completely recovered from his auto accident two years before and does not come across with the strength of purpose really necessary in his character. Still, fine viewing. 114m/B VHS, DVD. Elizabeth Taylor, Katharine Hepburn, Montgomery Clift, Mercedes McCambridge, Albert Dekker; *D:* Joseph L. Mankiewicz; *W:* Gore Vidal; *C:* Jack Hildyard; *M:* Malcolm Arnold. Golden Globes '60: Actress—Drama (Taylor).

Sudie & Simpson ✓✓✓ 1990 Heart-tugging tale of friendship set in rural 1940s Georgia. Twelve-year-old white Sudie's forbidden friendship with the adult black Simpson provides a lot of talk in their small town. Racial barriers finally cause Simpson to be accused of child molestation and the odds of his survival, despite his innocence, don't seem great. Based on Sara Flanigan Carter's autobiographical novel. 95m/C VHS, DVD. Sara Gilbert, Louis Gossett Jr., Frances Fisher, John M. Jackson, Paige Danahy, Ken Strong; *D:* Joan Tewkesbury; *W:* Sara Flanigan Carter, Ken Koser; *C:* Mario DiLeo; *M:* Michel Colombier. CABLE

Suds ✓✓½ 1920 Pickford is tragic laundress with major crush on a guy who left his shirt at the laundry. 75m/B VHS, DVD. Mary Pickford, William Austin, Harold Goodwin, Madame Rose (Dione) Dione, Theodore Roberts; *D:* John Francis Dillon.

Sueno ✓✓ 2005 (PG-13) Simple rags-to-riches musical saga follows Antonio (Leguizamo), a Mexican-born singer-musician who moves to LA to find success in the city's Latino music scene. He's got big dreams that may come true if he can overcome some predictable hardships. Pena is a delightful surprise as Mirabela, a recently divorced mother who regains her confidence when she begins singing with Antonio. 108m/C DVD. John Leguizamo, Ana Claudia Talancon, Elizabeth Pena, Nestor Serrano, Jsu Garcia, Jose Maria Yazpik; *D:* Renee Chabria; *W:* Renee Chabria; *C:* Eric Moynier; *M:* Joselo Rangel.

Suffering Bastards ✓✓½ 1990 Buddy and Al have never worked a day in their lives—Mom's nightclub always gave them something to do and a regular paycheck. But when Mom's swindled out of the family business, they decide it's time to take charge. Soon they're caught between bullets, babes, and belly laughs in this action-filled comedy. 95m/C VHS. Eric Bogosian, John C. McGinley, David Warshofsky; *W:* Bernard McWilliams; *C:* Neil Hodges; *M:* Danny Di Paola.

Sugar & Spice ✓✓✓ 2001 (PG-13) If there is such a thing as a smart cheerleader teen pic, this is it. Satire of offbeat pep squadders who cheer by day and rob banks by night includes Suvari's rebellious Kansas and Shelton's permanently upbeat Diane. Diane meets Jack (Marsden), and two American kids do the best they can when they learn Diane is pregnant. They decide to marry, move into a seedy apartment, and take up work at a local fast food joint. After losing said employment, the motivation becomes clear for the girls' ensuing illegal capers. Littered with pop culture references: the girls rent "Reservoir Dogs" to prepare for the heist, rob the banks in "Betty" masks, and deal with one of the girls' hots for Conan O'Brien. 81m/C VHS, DVD. US Marley Shelton, James Marsden, Mena Suvari, Maria Sokoloff, Rachel Blanchard, Melissa Georgem Alexandra Holden, Sara Marsh, Sean Young; *D:* Francine McDougall; *W:* Mandy Nelson; *C:* Robert Brinkmann; *M:* Mark Mothersbaugh.

Sugar Cane Alley ✓✓✓ *Rue Cases Negres* 1983 (PG) After the loss of his parents, an 11-year-old orphan boy goes to work with his grandmother on a sugar plantation. She realizes that her young ward's only hope is an education. Set in Martinique in the 1930s among black workers. Poignant and memorable. French with subtitles. 106m/C VHS, DVD. FR Garry Cadenat, Darling Legitimus, Douta Seck; *D:* Euzhan Palcy; *W:* Euzhan Palcy; *C:* Dominique Chapuis.

Sugar Cookies WOOF! 1977 (R) Erotic horror story in which young women are the pawns as a satanic satyr and an impassioned lesbian play out a bizarre game of vengeance, love, and death. 89m/C VHS, DVD. Mary Woronov, Lynn Lowry, Monique Van Vooren; *D:* Michael Herz.

Sugar Hill ✓✓ 1994 (R) Two brothers (Wright & Snipes) are heroin dealers who have built their own crime empire in the Sugar Hill section of Harlem. Snipes is moved to reconsider his career options when he falls for an aspiring actress (Randle). Jarring editing sequence recaps the seminal event in the brothers' upbringing and serves to explain how the wide-eyed boys became cold-blooded pushers. Good performances by all, but formulaic plot will leave viewers asking themselves if they haven't seen it before and why it was they saw it then. 123m/C VHS, DVD. Wesley Snipes, Michael Wright, Theresa Randle, Clarence Williams III, Abe Vigoda, Ernie Hudson, Larry Joshua, Leslie Uggams, Khandi Alexander, Raymond Serra, Joe Dallesandro, Vondie Curtis-Hall, Steve Harris, Kimberly Russell, Dule Hill, Donald Adeosun Faison, Nick(y) Corello; *D:* Leon Ichaso; *W:* Barry Michael Cooper; *C:* Bojan Bazelli; *M:* Terence Blanchard.

Sugar Sweet ✓✓½ 2002 Amusing, if slight, Japanese lesbian romantic comedy. Struggling filmmaker Naomi is trying to pay the bills by shooting lesbian porn but the producers protest that she's being too "arty." Frazzled, Naomi confides her troubles to an online friend named Sugar. Then, Naomi gets the chance to direct a girl-meets-girl match-making TV show and casts her pal Azusa and an exotic dancer named Miki to play the romantic couple. Azusa is willing but Miki turns out to be more interest in romancing Naomi. Japanese with subtitles. 67m/C VHS, DVD. JP Saori Kitagawa, Saki, C Snatch Z; *D:* Desiree Lim; *W:* Desiree Lim, Carole Hisasue; *C:* Natsuyo Nakamura; *M:* Masan Tahara, Katsuharu Imano.

Sugar Town ✓✓ 1999 (R) Ambitions collide in this saga of the L.A. music scene. Savvy and unscrupulous young singer Gwen (Gordon) is determined to land a recording contract while a group of middle age rock stars (Taylor, Des Barres, and Kemp) want to recapture their fame—with music producer Burt (Klein) as their catalyst. There's also struggling studio musician Carl (Doe) and his woes with Latina singer, Rosio (Cavazos) and various other subplots—one of which hangs together terribly well. 92m/C VHS. Michael Des Barres, Jade Gordon, John Taylor, Martin Kemp, Larry Klein, John Doe, Lumi Cavazos, Lucinda Jenney, Rosanna Arquette, Ally Sheedy, Beverly D'Angelo, Richmond Arquette, Jeff (Jeffrey) McDonald, Vincent Berry, Polly Platt, Chris Mulkey; *D:* Allison Anders, Kurt Voss; *W:* Allison Anders, Kurt Voss; *C:* Kristian Bernier; *M:* Larry Klein.

Sugarbaby ✓✓ *Zuckerbaby* 1985 (R) An acclaimed German film about a fat mortuary attendant living in Munich who transforms herself (but doesn't lose weight) in order to seduce a young, handsome subway conductor. Touching and warm film that introduced Sagebrecht to American audiences. A bit too cutting-edge cinematographically. In German with English subtitles. Remade as "Babycakes." Sagebrecht and director Adlon team up again for "Bagdad Cafe" and "Rosalie Goes Shopping." 103m/C VHS, GE Marianne Saegebrecht, Eisi Gulp, Toni Berger, Will Spendler, Manuela Denz; *D:* Percy Adlon; *W:* Percy Adlon.

The Sugarland Express ✓✓✓ 1974 (PG) To save her son from adoption, a young woman helps her husband break out of prison. In their flight to freedom, they hijack a police car, holding the policeman hostage. Speilberg's first feature film is a moving portrait of a couple's desperation. Based on a true story, adapted by Hal Barwood and Matthew Robbins. 109m/C VHS, DVD. Goldie Hawn, Ben Johnson, Michael Sacks, William Atherton; *D:* Steven Spielberg; *W:* Steven Spielberg, Matthew Robbins, Hal Barwood; *C:* Vilmos Zsigmond; *M:* John Williams.

Sugartime ✓✓✓½ 1995 (R) Based on the true-life romance of '60s Chicago mobster Sam Giacana (Turturro) and song bird Phyllis Maguire (Parker), one of the wholesome Maguire Sisters. Naturally, getting involved with a crime boss did little for her image and Maguire's career hit the skids while Giacana's volatile jealousy brought unwanted attention from both fellow gangsters and the feds. (He was murdered in 1975 but had broken off with Phyllis before that). The real Maguire denounced the inaccuracy of the TV production. Suggested by William F. Roemer Jr.'s book "Roemer: Man Against the Mob." 108m/C VHS, DVD. John Turturro, Mary-Louise Parker, Elias Koteas, Maury Chaykin, Louis Del Grande, Christopher Barry, Richard Blackburn; *D:* John N. Smith; *W:* Martyn Burke; *C:* Pierre Letarte.

Suicide Club ✓✓ *Jisatsu Sakuru* 2002 Fifty-four high school girls join hands and leap to their deaths from a subway platform into the path of an oncoming train. Police detective Kuroda (Ishibashi) receives a message from a mystery girl who informs him of a website that predicts the deaths even before they happen. With a continuing rash of suicides in Tokyo, the police are baffled—are the jumpers part of a cult and does a teen-girl pop group have some strange influence? Very bloody, very surreal, and a wicked social critique of disaffected Japanese youth. Japanese with subtitles. 92m/C VHS, DVD. JP Ryo Ishibashi, Takashi Nomura, Masatoshi Nagas, Tamao Sato, Mai Housyou; *D:* Sono Sion; *W:* Sono Sion; *C:* Kazuto Sato.

Suicide Fleet ✓ 1931 When three playboy sailors aren't fighting German U-boats aboard a decoy ship they're fighting to win the affections of a young woman (Rogers) working on the Coney Island midway. Some great shots of WWI vessels but a poor overall effort. 87m/B VHS. William Boyd, Robert Armstrong, James Gleason, Ginger Rogers; *D:* Albert Rogell; *W:* Herbert A. Jones, Lew Lipton. VIDEO

Suicide Kings ✓✓ 1997 (R) When the sister of one of four prep school friends is kidnapped, the guys decide to take retired mobster Charlie Barrett (Walken) hostage so he'll help them. The wanna-be "Reservoir Pups" lose control almost as soon as the caper begins, and the savvy Barrett takes advantage to turn his captors against each other with news that the girl's abduction may have been an inside job. Maze of a plot, which wanders into "Usual Suspects" is-this-all-real? territory, does nothing to help any of the young actors, who are clearly overmatched by Walken. Not much here for anyone except fans of Walken's patented Gangster Cool. 106m/C VHS, DVD. Louis Lombardi, Christopher Walken, Jay Mohr, Henry Thomas, Sean Patrick Flanery, Denis Leary, Jeremy Sisto, Johnny Galecki, Cliff DeYoung, Laura San Giacomo, Laura Harris; *D:* Peter O'Fallon; *W:* Josh McKinney, Gina Goldman, Wayne Rice; *C:* Christopher Baffa; *M:* Graeme Revell, Tim Simonec.

Suicide Ride ✓✓ 1997 Action-movie junkie Barney's (Quill) life is going nowhere, so looking for some real adventure he decides to hire a hitman (Hues) to off him. Only the hitman wants to retire and instead offers Barney his job, which he takes. This causes him lots of trouble. Quirky low-budgeter. 86m/C VHS. Tim Quill, Mathias Hues, Frank Adonis; *D:* Samer Daboul, Trevor Sands.

Suite 16 ✓ 1994 (R) A penthouse suite in a French Riviera hotel is occupied by rich, manipulative, wheelchair-bound Glover (Postlethwaite). Young gigolo/thief Chris (Kamerling), who believes he's killed his latest trick, is given refuge by Glover in exchange for allowing the aging voyeur to watch Chris (via camera) perform with a succession of prostitutes. Finally, Chris wants to leave but Glover offers him a huge amount of money for one final vicarious—and deadly—thrill. Eurotrash, with corny dialogue, but Postlethwaite's chillingly creepy. Also available in an R-rated version. 93m/C VHS, DVD. BE GB Pete Postlethwaite, Antoine Kamerling, Geraldine Pailhas, Thom Jansen; *D:* Dominique Deruddere; *W:* Charles Higson, Lise Mayer; *C:* Jean-Francois Robin; *M:* Walter Hus.

The Suitors ✓ 1988 When a group of Iranians decide to sacrifice a lamb in their apartment, the New York police send in SWAT team assuming they're terrorists. First time effort by Ebrahimian, in Farsi with English subtitles. 106m/C VHS, DVD. Pouran Esrafily, Assurbanipal Babila, Shahab Navab, Ali Azizian; *D:* Ghasem Ebrahimian; *W:* Ghasem Ebrahimian; *C:* Manfred Reiff.

Sullivan's Travels ✓✓✓✓ 1941 Sturges's masterpiece is a sardonic, whip-quick romp about a Hollywood director tired of making comedies who decides to make a serious, socially responsible film and hits the road masquerading as a hobo in order to know hardship and poverty. Beautifully sustained, inspired satire that mercilessly mocked the ambitions of Depression-era social cinema. Gets a little over-dark near the end before the happy ending; Sturges insisted on 20-yea-old Lake as The Girl; her pregnancy forced him to rewrite scenes and design new costumes for her. As ever, she is stunning. 90m/B VHS, DVD. Joel McCrea, Veronica Lake, William Demarest, Robert Warwick, Franklin Pangborn, Porter Hall, Eric Blore, Byron Foulger, Robert Greig, Torben Meyer, Jimmy Conlin, Margaret (Maggie) Hayes, Chester Conklin, Alan Bridge; *D:* Preston Sturges; *W:* Preston Sturges; *C:* John Seitz; *M:* Leo Shuken. Natl. Film Reg. '90.

The Sum of All Fears ✓✓½ 2002 (PG-13) Affleck takes over as Jack Ryan, who's now just an analyst, and has a girlfriend (Moynihan) who's a young doctor (hmmm...), but the film is still set in the present-day. That's just the first confusing element of this complicated spy thriller. The first half is spent on set pieces that seem to have no connection, until a climactic event (which takes place an hour in). Ryan is trying to prevent a nuclear war between the U.S. and Russia. Neo-Nazis are the baddies who put the world on the brink, and give the audience a safe, cartoony villian to make up for the now all-too-possible nuclear scenario. Affleck shows signs of growing into the role if the franchise continues, but he's not there yet. Pic is at its best when in the conference rooms of the White House and Kremlin, with each leader's advisors pressing their agendas. 118m/C VHS, DVD. US Ben Affleck, Morgan Freeman, James Cromwell, Bridget Moynahan, Liev Schreiber, Ron Rifkin, Alan Bates, Ciaran Hinds, Philip Baker Hall, Bruce McGill, Colm Feore, Josef Sommer, Ken Jenkins, Michael Byrne, John Beasley, Jamie Harrold, Richard Marner, Lee Garlington, Eugene (Yevgeny) Lazarev, Sven-Ole Thorsen, Lisa Gay Hamilton, Lisa Bronwyn Moore; *D:* Phil Alden Robinson; *W:* Paul Atanasio, Daniel Pyne; *C:* John Lindley; *M:* Jerry Goldsmith.

The Sum of Us ✓✓✓ 1994 (R) Sweet and faithful adaptation of David Stevens' stage play about a father and his gay son. Widowed Harry Mitchell (Thompson) shares his house with son Jeff (Crowe), who's never made a secret of his sexual orientation. Affable Harry only wants what's best for his boy, including his over-enthusiastic welcome to Jeff's potential new boyfriend (Polson). Too bad Harry's not so lucky in love—his new woman friend Joyce (Kennedy) has problems with Jeff's sexuality. Well, she just has to adjust. Pervasive feel-good message may leave less well-adjusted viewer amused. Sensitive performances, though the film's antecedents as a play are highlighted by

Summer 🎬🎬🎬 *Green Ray* 1986 (R) The fifth and among the best of Rohmer's "Comedies and Proverbs" series. A romantic but glum young French girl finds herself stuck in Paris during the tourist season searching for true romantic love. Takes time and patience to seize the viewer; moving ending makes it all worthwhile. In French with English subtitles. 98m/C VHS, DVD. *FR* Marie Riviere, Lisa Heredia, Beatrice Romand, Eric Hamm, Rosette, Isabelle Riviere; *D:* Eric Rohmer; *W:* Eric Rohmer. 🎬

Summer Affair 🎬½ 1979 Two young lovers run away from their bickering parents and get shipwrecked on a desert island. 90m/C VHS. *I:* Ornella Muti, Les Rannow; *D:* George S. Casorati.

Summer and Smoke 🎬🎬½ 1961 Repressed, unhappy Page falls for handsome doctor Harvey. A tour de force for Page, but that's all; adapted clumsily from the overwrought Tennessee Williams clay. 118m/C VHS. Laurence Harvey, Geraldine Page, Rita Moreno, Una Merkel, John McIntire, Thomas Gomez, Pamela Tiffin, Lee Patrick, Max Shannon, Pattee Chapman; *D:* Peter Glenville. *C:* Charles Bronard; Lang Jr.; *M:* Elmer Bernstein. Golden Globes '62: Actress (Page); Natl. Bd. of Review '61: Actress (Page).

Summer Camp Nightmare 🎬½ 1986 (PG-13) See "Lord of the Flies" instead. A young fascist incites children at two summer camps to overthrow and imprison the adults. Barbarism rears its ugly head. Self-serious and anticlimactic. Based on the novel "The Butterfly Revolution" by William Butler. 89m/C VHS, Chuck Connors, Charles Stratton, Harold P. Pruett, Tom Fridley, Adam Carl; *D:* Bert L. Dragin. *C:* Don Burgess.

Summer Catch 🎬½ 2001 (PG-13) Freddie Prinze, Jr. is really gonna have to learn to shake off some of the signs his agent is giving him, in this rip-off of every baseball movie of the last decade. Prinze plays underdog pitcher Ryan, on his last chance in his hometown Cape Cod league. Complicating matters are his flamboyant rival Eric (Pearson) and upperclass babe Tenley (Biel), who he falls for while curing lawns for his irascible father (Ward). Can Ryan make it to the big leagues with help from grizzled manager Schiffner (Dennehy)? Will he win the bodacious babe despite protests from her bluebood father (Davison)? Will Lillard make another appearance in a Freddie Prinze, Jr. movie? If you can't know the answers to those questions, you deserve to watch this bush-league flick. 108m/C VHS, DVD. *US* Freddie Prinze Jr., Jessica Biel, Matthew Lillard, Brian Dennehy, Fred Ward, Jason Gedrick, Brittany Murphy, Marc Blucas, Bruce Davison, Wilmer Valderrama, Christian Kane, Gabriel Mann, Cedric Pendleton, Zena Grey, Corey Pearson; *D:* Mike Tollin. *W:* Kevin Falls, John Gatins; *C:* Tim Suhrstedt; *M:* George Fenton.

Summer City 🎬 1977 *Coast of Terror* Fun-and-sun surfing movie complete with romance, hot rods, murder and great shots of the sea; features Gibson in his debut. Ever wonder what Australian surf bums do on weekends? The same as their California counterparts—except they talk funny. 83m/C VHS, DVD. *AU* Me Gibson, Phillip Avalon, John Jarratt, Christopher Fraser; *D:* Christopher Fraser; *W:* Phillip Avalon; *C:* Jerry Marek.

Summer Fantasy 🎬 1984 Mindless TV surf saga about a curvy teen who would rather watch the beach hunks then go to medical school. 96m/C VHS, Julianne Phillips, Ted Shackleford, Michael Gross, Dorothy Lyman; *D:* Noel Nosseck; *M:* Phil Butkis.

---

having the main characters talk directly to the camera. Aussie slang provides a challenge. 99m/C VHS, DVD. *AU* Jack Thompson, Russell Crowe, John Polson, Deborah Kennedy, Mitch Mathews, Julie Herbert, Joss Moroney. Rebekah Elmaloglou; *D:* Kevin Dowling, Geoff Burton; *W:* David Stevens; *C:* Geoff Burton; *M:* Dave Bates; *D:* Michie Gleason; *C:* Elliot Davis. play, Montreal World Film Fest. '94: Adapt. Screenplay, Australian Film Inst. '94: Actress (Page).

Summer Holiday 🎬½ 1948 Rooney comes of age with a vengeance during summer vacation in musical rendition of "Ah, Wilderness." Undistinguished, but jazzy Technicolor cinematography. Ended up in the red by over $1.5 million. Songs: Afraid to Fall in Love; All Hail, Danville High; The Stanley Steamer; It's Independence Day; I Think You're the Sweetest Kid I've Ever Known; Weary Blues. 92m/C VHS, Mickey Rooney, Gloria De Haven, Walter Huston, Frank Morgan, Jackie "Butch" Jenkins, Marilyn Maxwell, Agnes Moorehead, Selena Royle, Anne Francis; *D:* Rouben Mamoulian.

The Summer House 🎬🎬½ 1994 Comedy of manners set in 1959 England about the manipulations of three middle-aged women (Moreau, Plowright, Walters) over the impending marriage of one's dreamy young daughter (Headey) to a dolt (Threlfall). Moreau stirs things up as the spirited and skeptical friend of Walters, the deluded bride's mother whom she must interrupt her busy nuptial preparations and somehow communicate the obvious. Plowright is perfectly cast as the gimlet-eyed groom's mother, well aware of her son's flaws, who achieves an odd alliance with polar opposite Moreau. Strong performances from all the veterans carry the day. Based on the novel by Alice Thomas Ellis. 85m/C VHS. *GB* Jeanne Moreau, Joan Plowright, Julie Walters, Lena Headey, David Threlfall, Padraig Casey, Britta Smith, John Wood; *D:* Waris Hussein; *W:* Martin Sherman; *M:* Stanley Myers.

Summer Interlude 🎬🎬½ *Illicit Interlude; Sommarlek 1950* A ballerina recalls a summer spent with an innocent boy, who was later tragically killed. Contains many earmarks and visual ideas of later Bergman masterpieces. In Swedish with English subtitles. 95m/B VHS, DVD. *SW* Maj-Britt Nilsson, Birger Malmsten, Alf Kjellin; *D:* Ingmar Bergman; *W:* Ingmar Bergman.

Summer Lovers 🎬 1982 (R) Summer vacation finds young couple traveling to the exotic Greek island of Santorini. They meet up with a fun-loving woman and discover three-way sexual tension, but little in the way of plot, dialogue, or acting. From the director of "Grease" and "Blue Lagoon" and best watched late at night while half conscious. 98m/C VHS, DVD. Peter Gallagher, Daryl Hannah Valerie Quennessen; *D:* Randal Kleiser; *M:* Basil Poledouris.

Summer Magic 🎬🎬 1963 An impecunious recent widow is forced to leave Boston and settle her family in a small town in Maine. Typical, forgettable Disney drama; early Mills vehicle. A remake of "Mother Carey's Chickens." 116m/C VHS, DVD. Hayley Mills, Burl Ives, Dorothy McGuire, Deborah Walley, Una Merkel, Eddie Hodges; *D:* James Neilson; *M:* Buddy (Norman Dale) Baker.

Summer Night with Greek Profile, Almond Eyes & Scent of Basil 🎬🎬 1987 A wealthy woman tycoon hires an ex-CIA man to kidnap a high-priced, professional terrorist and hold him for ransom. An ironic battle of the sexes follows. In Italian with English subtitles. 94m/C VHS, DVD. *IT* Mariangela Melato, Michele Placido, Roberto Herlitzka, Massimo Wertmuller; *D:* Lina Wertmuller; *W:* Lina Wertmuller.

Summer Heat 🎬½ 1987 (R) In rural, mid-Depression North Carolina, a young, lonely wife and mother is seduced by a drifter and together they plot murder. Her husband neglects her, and you should neglect to see this utter yawner. Based on a Louise Shivers novel. 80m/C VHS, Lori Singer, Anthony Edwards, Bruce Abbott, Kathy Bates; *D:* Michie Gleason; *C:* Elliot Davis.

The Summer of Ben Tyler 🎬🎬½ 1996 (R) Temple Rayburn (Woods) is an up-and-coming lawyer in a small southern town in 1942 and the protege of influential Spencer Marland (Cariou). Before his family's black housekeeper dies, Rayburn agrees to take in her mentally handicapped teenaged son, Ben (Mattocks), to the dismay of the white community. Then Maitland insists Rayburn defend his son Junius (Isola) against a drunk driving charge when a woman was killed. TV movie. 134m/C VHS, James Woods, Len Cariou, Elizabeth McGovern, Charles Mattocks, Kevin Isola, Julia McIvaine, Clifton James; *D:* Arthur Allan Seidelman; *W:* Robert Inman; *C:* Neil Roach; *M:* Van Dyke Parks; *Nar:* Judith Ivey. TV

Summer of Fear 🎬🎬 *Stranger in Our House* 1978 A happy young woman (Blair) must overcome evil forces when her cousin (a teenage witch not akin to Sabrina) comes to live with—and control—her family. Based on a novel by Lois Duncan, who also wrote the source novel for 1997's "I Know What You Did Last Summer." Pretty scary if ordinary, made-for-TV horror from later-famous Craven. 94m/C VHS, DVD. Linda Blair, Lee Purcell, Jeremy Slate, Carol Lawrence, MacDonald Carey, Jeff McCracken, Jeff East, Fran Drescher; *D:* Wes Craven; *M:* Tom D'Andrea. TV

Summer of '42 🎬🎬 1971 (R) Touching if sentimental story about 15-year-old Hermie's (Grimes) sexual coming of age during his summer vacation on an island off New England. While his friends are fumbling with girls their own age, he falls in love with a beautiful 22-year-old woman (O'Neill) whose husband is off fighting in the war. 102m/C VHS, DVD, Jennifer O'Neill, Gary Grimes, Jerry House, Oliver Conant; *D:* Robert Mulligan; *W:* Herman Raucher; *C:* Robert L. Surtees; *M:* Michel Legrand. Oscars '71: Orig. Dramatic Score.

The Summer of Miss Forbes 🎬🎬 1988 *El Verano de la Senora Forbes* A governess rules over two young boys with an iron hand by day and cavorts nude and drunk by night. The young boys fantasize about her murder, but fate has different plans. In Spanish with English subtitles. 85m/C VHS. *SP* Hanna Schygulla, Alexis Castaneres, Victor Cesar Villalobos, Guadalupe Sandoval, Fernando Balzaretti, Yuriria Munguia; *D:* Jaime Humberto Hermosillo.

The Summer of My German Soldier 🎬🎬 1978 A young Jewish girl befriends an escaped German prisoner of war in a small town in Georgia during WWII. Occasionally sentimental but more often genuinely moving TV drama. Rolle won a deserved Emmy as the housekeeper. Adapted from Bette Green's novel. 98m/C VHS, Kristy McNichol, Esther Rolle, Bruce Davison; *D:* Michael Tuchner. TV

Summer of Sam 🎬🎬½ 1999 (R) Spike Lee's take on the summer of 1977, when serial killer Son of Sam traumatized New York City. The plot does not center on the actual crimes of David Berkowitz, but on the repercussions they had in the neighborhoods of New York. Leguizamo and Sorvino play a married Bronx couple who grow to question pal Ritchie (Brody), a newly converted punk rocker who leads a double life as a gay dancer. As the killer's attacks continue, fear begins to rise along with the temperature, and the neighborhood begins to tear itself apart. Lee's film drew highly publicized protests from the families of Berkowitz's victims. 142m/C VHS, DVD, Adrien Brody, John Leguizamo, Spike Lee, Mira Sorvino, Jennifer Esposito, Michael Badalucco, Anthony LaPaglia, Patti LuPone, Ben Gazzara, Bebe Neuwirth, John Savage, Roger Guenveur Smith, Michael Rispoli; *D:* Spike Lee; *W:* Spike Lee, Michael Imperioli; *C:* Ellen Kuras; *M:* Terence Blanchard.

Summer of the Monkeys 🎬½ 1998 (G) Fairly sappy family pic set in rural America. John Lee (Ontkean) is a hard-working farmer with a caring wife, Sara (Hope), precocious son Jay Berry (Sevier) and a crippled daughter, Daisy (Stuart). Gramps (Brimley) runs the local general store and

---

Tree." 95m/C VHS. *IS* Kaipo Cohen, Gila Almagor; *D:* Eli Cohen; *W:* Eli Cohen, Gila Almagor.

The Summer of Ben Tyler *(duplicate header)*

burn (Woods) is an up-and-coming lawyer

Summer Palace 🎬🎬🎬 *Yihe Yuan* 2006 The lives of Yu Hong (Hao) and her lover Zhou Wei (Guo)are traced from their first and get the reward for their return. 101m/C VHS, *CA* Michael Ontkean, Leslie Hope, Corey Sevier, Katie Stuart, Wilford Brimley, Don Francks, B.J. McLellan; *D:* Michael Anderson Sr.; *W:* Greg Taylor, Jim Strain; *C:* Michael Storey; *M:* George Blondheim.

Jay works there, hoping to save money to buy Daisy a pony. When a nearby train wreck leads to the escape of a foursome of circus monkeys, Jay aims to find them first and get the reward for their return. enrollment at Beijing University in 1988 and subsequently involvement in the demonstrations at Tiananmen Square, into adulthood, which never seems to match the promise of their youth. Frank and explicit in both its sexuality and its examination of the changes China has undergone since 1989. Director Ye was banned from filmmaking for five years by the Chinese government after showing this at Cannes without permission. 140m/C DVD, *CH* FR Lei Hao, Xiaodong Guo, Ling Hu, Xiannin Zhang; *D:* Ye Lou; *W:* Ye Lou, Mei Feng, The Range Busters; *C:* Qing Hua; *M:* Peyman Yazdanian.

A Summer Place 🎬🎬🎬 1953 Melodrama about summer liaisons amid the young and middle-aged rich on an island off the coast of Maine. Too slick; romantic drama is a little more than skin-deep, and dialogue is excruciating. Donahue's first starring role. Based on the Sloan Wilson novel. Featuring "Theme from a Summer Place," which was a number-one hit in 1959. 130m/C VHS, DVD. Troy Donahue, Richard Egan, Sandra Dee, Dorothy McGuire, Arthur Kennedy, Constance Ford, Beulah Bondi; *D:* Delmer Daves; *W:* Delmer Daves; *C:* Harry Stradling Sr.; *M:* Max Steiner.

Summer Rental 🎬🎬 1985 (PG) That John Candy just can't win, can he? Here, as a hopeless, harried air traffic controller, he tries to have a few days to relax in sunny Florida. Enter mean rich guy Crenna (Candy can add something to the lowest of plots, and does so here. Watch the first hour for yech, then rewind. 87m/C VHS, DVD. John Candy, Rip Torn, Richard Crenna, Karen Austin, Kerri Green, John Larroquette, Pierrino Mascarino; *D:* Carl Reiner; *W:* Mark Reisman, Jeremy Stevens; *C:* Ric Waite; *M:* Alan Silvestri.

Summer School 🎬🎬½ 1987 (PG-13) A high-school teacher's vacation plans are ruined when he gets stuck teaching remedial English in summer school. It seems all these students are interested in is re-enacting scenes from "The Texas Chainsaw Massacre," learning to drive, and surfing. Actually, one of the better films of this genre, thanks mostly to Harmon's likeability. 98m/C VHS, DVD, Mark Harmon, Kirstie Alley, Courtney Thorne-Smith, Shawnee Smith, Robin Thomas, Dean Cameron, Gary Riley, Kelly Jo Minter, Fabiana Udenio, Patrick Labyorteaux, Duane Davis, Nels Van Patten; *D:* Carl Reiner; *W:* Jeff Franklin; *Cameos:* Carl Reiner; *D:* Carl Reiner; *W:* Jeff Franklin; *C:* David M. Walsh; *M:* Danny Elfman.

Summer School Teachers WOOF! 1975 (R) Three sultry femmes bounce about Los Angeles high school and make the collective student body happy. Typical Corman corn; sequel to "The Student's Teachers." 87m/C VHS, Candice Rialson, Pat Anderson, Rhonda Leigh Hopkins, Christopher Wales; *D:* Barbara Peeters.

Summer Snow 🎬🎬 *Nuiyan, Seisegi Woman, Forty* 1994 Broad comedy mixed (not always successfully) with family drama. May (Siao) is forced to take in her father-in-law Sun (Chiao) after his wife dies. The old man immediately causes chaos with his habit of wandering off and bizarre behavior, which is finally diagnosed as being Alzheimer's disease. Working mother May tries to find a practical way to deal with her dilemmas but the strains are beginning to crack the family apart. Cantonese with subtitles. **106m/C VHS.** *HK* Josephine Siao, Roy Chiao, Law Karying, Allen Ting; *D:* Ann Hui; *W:* Chan Man-keung; *C:* Mark Lee Ping-Bin; *M:* Yoshihide Otomo. Berlin Intl. Film Fest. '94. Foreign Film.

Summer Solstice ✶✶½ **1981**
Fonda and Loy are splendid as a couple married half a century who revisit the beach where they first met. Fonda especially shines, as a crusty old artist. Yes, it is an awful lot like "On Golden Pond." **75m/C VHS, DVD.** Henry Fonda, Myrna Loy, Lindsay Crouse, Stephen Collins; *D:* Ralph Rosenblum. TV

Summer Stock ✶✶✶ **1950** *Like Singing* Garland plays farm owner Jane Falbury whose sister, Abigail (DeHaven) arrives with a summer stock troupe, led by Joe Ross (Kelly), to rehearse a show in the family barn. Jane agrees, if the troupe will help her with the farm's harvest. When Abigail decamps for New York, leaving the leading lady role open, guess who steps into the breach. Slim plot papered over with many fun song-and-dance numbers. Also features Garland's first MGM short, "Every Sunday," made in 1936 with Deanna Durbin. ♫Friendly Star; Mem'ry Island; Dig-Dig-Dig For Your Dinner; If You Feel Like Singing, Sing; Howdy Neighbor; Blue Jean Polka; Portland Fancy; You, Wonderful You; Get Happy. **109m/ C VHS, DVD.** Judy Garland, Gene Kelly, Gloria De Haven, Carleton Carpenter, Eddie Bracken, Phil Silvers, Hans Conried, Marjorie Main, Ray Collins; *D:* Charles Walters; *W:* George Wells, Sy Gomberg.

A Summer Story ✶✶✶ **1988**
Superbly acted, typically British period drama about beautiful farm girl Stubbs and city lawyer Wilby, who fall in love. But can they overcome difference of social class? From the story "The Apple Tree" by John Galsworthy. **97m/C VHS.** *GB* James Wilby, Imogen Stubbs, Susannah York, Sophie Ward, Kenneth Colley, Jerome Flynn; *D:* Piers Haggard; *W:* Penelope Mortimer; *M:* Georges Delerue.

A Summer to Remember ✶✶✶ *Seryozha* **1961** A five-year-old boy spends a summer with his stepfather on a Soviet collective farm. The two become deeply attached. Scenes of collective life will be of more interest to Westerners than the near-sentimental story. Star Bondarchuk later directed the epic, award-winning "War and Peace." **80m/B VHS, DVD.** *RU* Borya Barkhazov, Sergei Bondarchuk, Irana Skobtseva; *D:* Igor Talankin, Georgi Daneliya; *W:* Igor Talankin, Georgi Daneliya; *C:* Anatoli Nitochkin; *M:* Boris Chaikovsky.

A Summer to Remember ✶✶½ **1984 (PG)** A deaf boy (played by Gerlis, himself deaf since birth) develops a friendship with an orangutan through sign language. Bad guys abduct the friendly ape—but all is right in the end. Nice, innocuous family viewing. Based on a story by Scott Swanton and Robert Lloyd Lewis. **93m/C VHS, DVD.** Tess Harper, James Farentino, Burt Young, Louise Fletcher, Sean Gerlis, Bridgette Andersen; *D:* Robert Lewis; *C:* Stephen W. Gray; *M:* Charles Fox. TV

Summer Vacation: 1999 ✶✶ *1999–Nen No Natsu Yasumi* **1988** Four boys are left behind at boarding school during their summer vacation. They experience all the early pangs of adolescence from love to jealousy. Their summer is then disturbed by the arrival of another boy who appears to be the reincarnation of a dead friend. Romantic look at youth caught between innocence and awareness. In Japanese with English subtitles. **90m/C VHS.** *JP* Eri Miyajima, Miyuki Nakano, Tomoko Otakra, Rie Mizuhara; *D:* Shusuke (Shu) Kaneko.

Summer Wishes, Winter Dreams ✶✶✶ **1973 (PG)** Woodward and Balsam are a materially prosperous middle-aged couple with little but tedium in their lives—a tedium accurately replicated in what feels like real life, in this slow, dull film. The two leads and Sidney—in her first screen role in 17 years—are all excellent, but the story of regret and present unhappiness wears the viewer down. **95m/ C VHS.** Joanne Woodward, Martin Balsam, Sylvia

Sidney, Dori Brenner, Ron Richards; *D:* Gilbert Cates; *W:* Stewart Stern. British Acad. '74: Actress (Woodward); Natl. Bd. of Review '73: Support. Actress (Sidney); N.Y. Film Critics '73: Actress (Woodward).

Summerdog ✶✶ **1978 (G)** Harmless family tale about vacationers who rescue a cheerful, lovable mutt named Hobo. And a good thing they found him: He saves them from many perils. Thanks, Hobo! **90m/C VHS.** James Congdon, Elizabeth Eisenman, Oliver Zabriskie, Tavia Zabriskie; *D:* John Clayton.

Summer's Children ✶ **1979** Man who suffers from amnesia as a result of a car crash becomes the target of a mysterious killer. Forget about it. **83m/C VHS.** *CA* Tom Haoff, Paully Jardine, Kate Lynch, Don Francks, Kate Lynch, Ken James, Patricia Collins, Wayne Best; *D:* Julius Kohanyi; *W:* Jim Osborne; *C:* Josef Seckeresh; *M:* Chris Stone.

Summer's End ✶✶½ **1999** In 1983, physician William Blakely (Jones) decides to move to the small Georgia town where he grew up. But the lakeside community is lilywhite and hostile (Blakely's family was originally driven out by racial violence). However, fatherless 12-year-old Jamie (LeDoux) and the doc become friends, despite pressures on the boy to toe the racist line. **101m/C VHS, DVD.** James Earl Jones, Wendy Crewson, Brendan Fletcher, Jake LeDoux; *D:* Helen Shaver. **CABLE**

A Summer's Tale ✶✶½ *Conte d'Été* **1996** Talky and slow-moving vacation comedy is the third in Rohmer's "Tales of the Four Seasons" series. Young Gaspard (Poupaud) is spending a month in a borrowed flat in the seaside resort of Dinard. He becomes friendly with waitress Margot (Langlet) while he waits for his girlfriend Lena (Nolin) to join him; but is also introduced to Margot's friend Solene (Simon), who's interested in a quick fling with Gaspard. When all three women agree to accompany him on a sightseeing trip, he's got more a than a little maneuvering to do. French with subtitles. **133m/C VHS, DVD.** *FR* Melvil Poupaud, Amanda Langlet, Aurelia Nolin, Gwenaelle Simon; *D:* Eric Rohmer; *W:* Eric Rohmer; *M:* Sebastien Erms, Philippe Eidel.

Summertime ✶✶✶ *Summer Madness* **1955** Spinster Hepburn vacations in Venice and falls in love with Brazzi. She is hurt when inadvertently she learns he is married, but her life has been so bleak she is not about to end her one great romance. Moving, funny, richly photographed in a beautiful Old World city. From Arthur Laurents' play "The Time of the Cuckoo." **98m/ C VHS, DVD.** Katharine Hepburn, Rossano Brazzi, Isa Miranda, Darren McGavin, Mari Aldon, MacDonald Parke, Jeremy Spenser; *D:* David Lean; *W:* David Lean, H.E. Bates; *C:* Jack Hildyard; *M:* Alessandro Cicognini. N.Y. Film Critics '55: Director (Lean).

Summertree ✶✶ **1971 (PG)** Douglas stars as a young musician in the 1960s trying to avoid the draft and the wrath of his parents. Contrived and heavy-handed. Produced by Douglas pere, Kirk. Adapted from the play by Ron Cower. **88m/C VHS.** Michael Douglas, Jack Warden, Brenda Vaccaro, Barbara Bel Geddes, Kirk Calloway, Bill Vint; *D:* Anthony Newley; *M:* David Shire.

The Sun Comes Up ✶✶ **1949** MacDonald, in her last screen appearance, plays a bitter widow whose life is changed by an orphan's love for a collie. Songbird MacDonald manages to sing a number of songs, some of them backed by a chorus of "orphans." Based on short stories by Marjorie Kinnan Rawlings. **93m/ C VHS.** Jeanette MacDonald, Lloyd Nolan, Claude Jarman Jr., Lewis Stone, Dwayne Hickman; *D:* Richard Thorpe; *W:* William Ludwig; *M:* Andre Previn.

Sun Ra & His Intergalactic Solar Arkestra: Space Is the Place ✶✶ **1974** Space age flick starring most appropriately Sun Ra, space age prophet/jazz musician. Sun Ra returns from a space odyssey and embarks on saving black youth from the world's oppressive control by bringing them back into space with him. The shaman's philosophy on film. ♫Watusi; Outer Spaceways

Inc.; The Satellites are Spinning. **63m/C VHS, DVD.** *D:* John Coney; *W:* Joshua Smith.

The Sun Shines Bright ✶✶✶ **1953** Heavily stereotyped, contrived tale of a Southern judge with a heart of gold who does so many good deeds (defending a black man accused of rape; helping a desperate prostitute) that he jeopardizes his re-election. Set during Reconstruction. An unfortunate remake of Ford's own 1934 "Judge Priest," starring Will Rogers. **92m/B VHS.** Charles Winninger, Arleen Whelan, John Russell, Stepin Fetchit, Milburn Stone, Russell Simpson; *D:* John Ford; *C:* Archie Stout.

Sun Valley Serenade ✶✶½ **1941** Wartime musical fluff about a band that adopts a Norwegian refugee waif as a publicity stunt. She turns out to be a full-grown man-chaser who stirs up things at a ski resort. Fun, but it ends abruptly—because, they say, Henie fell during the huge skating finale, and Darryl Zanuck wouldn't greenlight a reshoot. One of only two feature appearances by Glenn Miller and his Orchestra (the other was "Orchestra Wives"), on video with a soundtrack restored from original dual-track recordings. ♫Chattanooga Choo Choo; I Know Why and So Do You; It Happened In Sun Valley; The Kiss Polka; In the Mood. **86m/C VHS.** Sonja Henie, John Payne, Glenn Miller, Milton Berle, Lynn Bari, Joan Davis, Dorothy Dandridge; *D:* H. Bruce Humberstone.

Sunburn ✶✶ **1979 (PG)** Insurance investigator Grodin hires model Fawcett to pretend to be his wife to get the scoop on a suicide/murder case of a rich guy in Acapulco. Made-for-TV drivel. **110m/C VHS.** Farrah Fawcett, Charles Grodin, Joan Collins, Art Carney, William Daniels; *D:* Richard Sarafian; *W:* James Booth. TV

Sunchaser ✶✶½ **1996 (R)** Mishmash of medicine and mysticism focuses on yuppie UCLA oncologist Dr. Michael Reynolds (Harrelson) who's kidnapped by 16-year-old patient, Brandon "Blue" Monroe (Seda). Blue is a half-Navajo gangbanger whose cancer is inoperable and he needs the doc to drive him to a reservation in Arizona where he feels a medicine man and the waters of a supposedly magical lake can cure him. Reynolds naturally discovers some humanity on the trip and decides to help his truculent patient. Leads give sincere performances but film has nebaked at best. **123m/C VHS.** Woody Harrelson, Jon Seda, Anne Bancroft, Alexandra Tydings, Matt Mulhern, Talisa Soto, Lawrence Pressman, Michael O'Neill, Harry Carey Jr.; *D:* Michael Cimino; *W:* Charles Leavitt; *C:* Doug Milsome; *M:* Maurice Jarre.

Sundance and the Kid ✶✶ **1976 (PG)** Two brothers try to collect an inheritance against all odds. Originally known as "Sundance Cassidy and Butch the Kid." **84m/C VHS.** John Wade, Karen Blake; *D:* Arthur Pitt.

Sunday ✶✶ **1996** Basically a two-character study of mistaken identity among lonely, middleaged people. On a winter's Sunday morning in Queens, depressed Oliver (Suchet) is greeted by failing British actress Madeleine (Harrow), who mistakes him for a director she once met. She invites him to lunch and Oliver, who's actually a homeless former accountant, struggles to maintain the charade. The unstable Madeleine's bitter when she discovers his deception but is also unwillingly to let the connection between them die. **93m/C VHS, DVD.** David Suchet, Lisa Harrow, Larry Pine, Jared Harris, Joe Grifasi; *D:* Jonathan Nossiter; *W:* Jonathan Nossiter, James Lasdun; *C:* Michael Barrow, John Foster; *M:* Jonathan Nossiter. Sundance '97: Screenplay, Grand Jury Prize.

Sunday, Bloody Sunday ✶✶✶ **1971 (R)** Adult drama centers around the interwined love affairs of the homosexual Finch, the heterosexual Jackson, and self-centered bisexual artist Head, desired by both. Fully drawn characters brought to life by excellent acting make this difficult story well worth watching—though Head's central character is sadly rather dull. Day-Lewis makes his first (brief) screen appearance as a car vandalizing teenager. Powerful, sincere, and sensitive. **110m/C**

VHS, DVD. *GB* Glenda Jackson, Peter Finch, Murray Head, Peggy Ashcroft, Tony Britton, Maurice Denham, Vivian Pickles, Bessie Love, Daniel Day-Lewis; *D:* John Schlesinger; *W:* Penelope Gilliatt; *C:* Billy Williams; *M:* Ron Geesin. British Acad. '71: Actor (Finch), Actress (Jackson), Director (Schlesinger); Film; Golden Globes '72: Foreign Film; N.Y. Film Critics '71: Screenplay; Natl. Soc. Film Critics '71: Actor (Finch), Screenplay; Writers Guild '71: Orig. Screenplay.

Sunday Daughters ✶✶✶ **1980** A teenage girl kept in a detention home constantly tries to escape and find some kind of familial love. Stronge performances mix with keen direction. In Hungarian with English subtitles. **100m/C VHS.** *HU* Julianna Nyako; *D:* Janosz Rozsa.

Sunday in New York ✶✶ ½ **1963** Distraught Eileen (Fonda) heads to New York to seek counsel from her airline pilot brother Adam (Robertson) after she breaks up with fiance Russ (Wilson). Adam is in the middle of setting up a much-interrupted date with sometime-girlfriend Mona, so Eileen wanders around NYC. Soon she meets cute with suave fella Mike on the bus. Romantic comedy complications follow as Russ comes back into the picture. Amusing look at the changing sexual mores of the time must've seemed mildly shocking then, but now seems quaint. Robertson stands out among great cast. **105m/C VHS, DVD.** Rod Taylor, Jane Fonda, Cliff Robertson, Robert Culp, Jo Morrow, Jim Backus, Rayford Barnes, Jim Hutton; *Cameos:* Peter Nero; *D:* Peter Tewkesbury; *C:* Leo Tover; *M:* Peter Nero.

A Sunday in the Country ✶✶✶ ½ *Un Dimanche a la Campagne* **1984 (G)** A lush, distinctively French affirmation of nature and family life. This character study with a minimal plot takes place during a single summer day in 1910 France. An elderly impressionist painter-patriarch is visited at his country home by his family. Highly acclaimed, though the pace may be too slow for some. Beautiful location photography. In French with English subtitles. **94m/C VHS, DVD.** *FR* Louis Ducreux, Sabine Azema, Michel Aumont; *D:* Bertrand Tavernier; *W:* Bertrand Tavernier, Colo Tavernier O'Hagan; *C:* Bruno de Keyzer. Cannes '84: Director (Tavernier); Cesar '85: Actress (Azema), Cinematog., Writing; Natl. Bd. of Review '84: Support. Actress (Azema); N.Y. Film Critics '84: Foreign Film.

Sunday in the Park with George ✶✶✶ **1986** Taped theatrical performance of the Tony, Grammy, and Pulitzer Prize-winning musical play, which is based upon impressionist George Seurat's painting "A Sunday Afternoon on the Island of Grande Jatte." Features a celebrated music score by Sondheim. **120m/C VHS, DVD.** Mandy Patinkin, Bernadette Peters, Barbara Byrne, Charles Kimbrough; *D:* James Lapine; *M:* Stephen Sondheim.

Sunday Too Far Away ✶✶✶ **1974** The rivalries between Australian sheep shearers and graziers leads to an ugly strike at a remote outback area in 1955. An uncomplicated story and a joy to watch. **100m/C VHS.** *AU* Max Cullen, Robert Bruning, Jerry Thomas, Jack Thompson; *D:* Ken Hannam; *W:* John Dingwall; *C:* Geoff Burton; *M:* Patrick Flynn. Australian Film Inst. '74: Actor (Thompson), Film.

Sundays & Cybele ✶✶✶ ½ *Les Dimanches de Ville d'Avray; Cybele* **1962** A ragged war veteran and an orphaned girl develop a strong emotional relationship, which is frowned upon by the townspeople. Warm and touching. In French with English subtitles. Also available in a letterboxed edition. **110mB VHS.** *FR* Hardy Kruger, Nicole Courcel; *D:* Serge Bourguignon; *M:* Maurice Jarre. Oscars '62: Foreign Film.

Sunday's Children ✶✶✶ **1994** Lyrical exploration of childhood continues trilogy that includes "Fanny and Alexander" and "Best Intentions." Wistful childhood memoir takes up the story of Ingmar Bergman's eight years after the director was born. Many of the same familial issues surface, but story soon narrows its focus to the relationship between little Ingmar, whom everyone calls Pu, and his stern father Henrik. Deeply emotional and intense, film represents the steps

Sundown *♂* The elder Bergman is finally able to take regarding the
painful relationship he had with his own
father. Father-son theme made more poignant with Ingmar's son Daniel making his
feature debut as director. 118m/C VHS, SW
Thommy Berggren, Lena Endre, Henrik Linnros,
Jacob Leygraf, Maria Bolme, Börje Ahlstedt, Per
Myrberg; **D:** Daniel Bergman; **W:** Ingmar Bergman.

Sundown *♂♂½* **1941** In Africa at
the beginning of WWII, a local girl aids the
British against a German plot to run guns
to the natives and start a rebellion. Engaging performances and efficient direction
keep it above the usual cliches. Also available in a colorized version. 91m/B VHS,
DVD. Gene Tierney, Bruce Cabot, George Sanders, Harry Carey Sr., Cedric Hardwicke, Joseph
Calleia, Dorothy Dandridge, Reginald Gardiner; **D:**
Henry Hathaway; **C:** Charles Bryant) Lang Jr.; **M:**
Miklos Rozsa.

Sundown *♂♂½* **1991 (R)** An ambitious shot at a vampire western fails because it drains almost all vampire lore and
winds up resembling a standard oater.
Carradine plays a reformed vampire king
(guess who) running a desert clinic that
weans bloodsuckers away from preying
on humans. But undead renegades attack
using sixguns and wooden bullets. The climax may outrage horror purists. 104m/C
VHS. David Carradine, Bruce Campbell, Deborah
Foreman, Maxwell Caulfield, Morgan Brittany; **D:**
Anthony Hickox.

Sundown Fury *♂* **1942** Young cowboy fights against a group
of bandits to hold a telegraph office. 56m/B
VHS. Donald (Don "Red") Barry, Lynn Merrick, Al
"Fuzzy" St. John, Douglas Walton, Karl Hackett,
Lee Shumway, Stanley Blystone, Frank Brownlee,
George Chesebro; **D:** George Sherman; **W:** Doris
Schroeder, Richard Murphy. **C:** John MacBurnie;
M: Cy Feuer.

Sundown Kid *♂♂* **1943** A Pinkerton agent goes undercover to break up a
counterfeiting operation. Routine western.
55m/B VHS. Ian Keith, Helen MacKellar, Emmett
Lynn, Linda Leighton, Donald (Don "Red") Barry;
D: Elmer Clifton; **W:** Norman S. Hall; **C:** Ernest
Miller; **M:** Mort Glickman.

Sundown Riders *♂* **1948** Cowhands are victimized by noose-happy outlaws. Filmed in just over a week on a
$30,000 budget and originally shot on
16mm to make it accessible to hospitals
and schools with basic viewing equipment. The lesson here: it takes time and
money to make a good western. 56m/B
VHS. Russell Wade, Andy Clyde, Jay Kirby; **D:**
Lambert Hillyer.

Sundown Saunders *♂* **1936** A
standard oater about a cowboy whose
prize for winning a horse race is a ranch.
Trouble is, an outlaw wants the homestead as well. 64m/B VHS. Bob Steele; **D:** Robert North Bradbury.

The Sundowners *♂♂♂½* **1960**
Slow, beautiful, and often moving epic
drama about a family of Irish sheepherders in Australia during the 1920s who
must continually uproot themselves and
migrate. They struggle to save enough
money to buy their own farm and wind up
training a horse they hope will be a mon-
ey-winner in racing. Well-acted by all, with
Johns and Ustinov providing some humorous moments. Adapted from the novel by
Jon Cleary. Filmed in Australia and London studios. 133m/C VHS, DVD. Deborah Kerr,
Robert Mitchum, Peter Ustinov, Glynis Johns, Dina
Merrill, Chips Rafferty, Michael Anderson Jr., Lola
Brooks, Wylie Watson; **D:** Fred Zinnemann; **C:**
Jack Hildyard; **M:** Dimitri Tiomkin. Nat. Bd. of Re-
view '60. Actor (Mitchum); Natl. Film Critics '60:
Actress (Kerr).

Sunny *♂♂* **1941** Another glossed-
over, love-conquers-all musical with Neagle as a circus star who falls for a wealthy
car maker's son. Dad and crew disapprove, putting a damper on the romance.
In spite of the weak storyline and flat direction, Kerns' music and Bolger's dancing make it enjoyable. *♪Who?; D'ya Love
Me?; Sunny; Two Little Bluebirds. 98m/B
VHS. Anna Neagle, Ray Bolger, John Carroll, Edward Everett Horton, Frieda Inescort, Helen Westley, Fanny Rubin, Richard Lane, Martha Tilton; **D:**
Herbert Wilcox.

Sunny Side Up *♂♂½* **1928** As
stress of pickle factory work takes toll on
woman's friend, she makes heroic effort to
help her to the country to recover. 66m/B
VHS. Vera Reynolds, ZaSu Pitts, Edmund Burns,
Sally Rand; **D:** Donald Crisp.

Sunny Skies *♂* **1930** Bargain-base-
ment retread has Lease donating a pint of
blood. *♪Sunny Days; I Must Have You;
Wanna Find a Boy; Must Be Love. 75m/B
VHS. Benny Rubin, Marceline Day, Rex Lease,
Marjorie "Babe" Kane, Wesley Barry; **D:** Norman
Taurog.

Sunnyside *woc!f* **1979 (R)** Travolta
plays a street kid trying to bring an end to
the local gang warfare so he can move to
Manhattan. Features a host of pop tunes
in an attempt to ride the coattails of brother John's successful 'Saturday Night Fever.' Laughably bad. 100m/C VHS, Joey Travolta, John Lansing, Stacey Pickren, Andrew Rubin, Michael Tucci, Talia Balsam, Joan Darling; **D:**
Timothy Galfas.

Sunrise *♂♂♂* **1927** Magnificent silent story of
a simple country boy who, prodded by an
alluring city woman, tries to murder his
wife. Production values wear their age
well. Gaynor won an Oscar for her stunning performance. Remade in Germany
as "The Journey to Tilsit." Based on a story by Hermann Suderman. 110m/B VHS,
DVD. George O'Brien, Janet Gaynor, Bodil Rosing,
Margaret Livingston, J. Farrell MacDonald, Carl
Mayer; **D:** F.W. Murnau; **C:** Charles Rosher, Karl
Struss. Oscars '28: Actress (Gaynor), Cinematog,
Natl. Film Reg. '89.

Sunrise *♂♂♂* **1960** A successful adaptation of the Tony
award-winning play by Schary, who wrote
the screenplay and also produced the film.
In 1921, the Roosevelt family is vacationing at Campobello when Franklin (Bellamy,
re-creating this stage role) becomes ill with
what turns out to be polio. His formidable
mother Sara (Shoemaker) wants her paralyzed so to give up his political aspirations
but politico pal Louis Howe (Cronyn) insists Franklin get on with living, aided by
the strength of wife Eleanor (an excellent
performance by Garson). 143m/C VHS.
Ralph Bellamy, Greer Garson, Hume Cronyn, Jean
Hagen, Jack Perrin, Lyle Talbot, Ann Shoemaker,
Tim Considine, Zena Bethune, Pat Close; **D:** Vincent J. Donehue; **W:** Dore Schary; **C:** Russell Harlan; **M:** Franz Waxman. Golden Globes '61: Actress—Drama (Garson); Natl. Bd. of Review '60:
Actress (Garson).

Two Humans *Sunrise—A Song of*

Sunrise at Campobello *♂♂♂*

Sunrise Trail *♂♂½* **1931** Lots of
action with Steele working undercover for
the sheriff, trying to stop a rustler. He also
finds the time to fall for Lamaid Mehaffey.
65m/B VHS. Bob Steele, Blanche Mehaffey, Jack
Clifford, Eddie Dunn; **D:** John P. McCarthy.

The Sun's Burial *♂♂* **1960**
Oshima's stylized and violent drama depicts life in Osaka's worst slum—a teenage underworld populated by teen gangs,
prostitutes, and criminals. All want control
of the area's most profitable business, an
illegal blood-selling operation. In Japanese with English subtitles. 87m/C VHS. JP
Kayoko Honoo, Koji Nakahara, Masahiko Tsugawa; **D:** Nagisa Oshima.

Sunset *♂♂½* **1988 (R)** Edwards wanders the range in this soft-centered farce
about a couple of Western legends out to
solve a mystery. On the backlots of Hollywood, silent screen star Tom Mix (Willis)
meets aging marshal Wyatt Earp (Garner)
and participates in a fire-e-warp western
circa 1927. They encounter a series of misadventures while trying to finger a murderer. Garner ambles enjoyably, lifting him
a level above the rest of the cast. 107m/C
VHS, DVD. Bruce Willis, James Garner, Mariel
Hemingway, Darren McGavin, Jennifer Edwards,
Malcolm McDowell, Kathleen Quinlan, M. Emmet
Walsh, Patricia Hodge, Richard Bradford, Joe Dallesandro, Dermot Mulroney; **D:** Blake Edwards; **W:**
Blake Edwards, Rod Amateau; **C:** Anthony B.
Richmond; **M:** Henry Mancini. Golden Raspberries
'88: Worst Director (Edwards).

Sunset Boulevard *♂♂♂♂½* **1950**
Famed tale of Norma Desmond (Swanson), aging silent film queen, who refuses
to accept that stardom has ended for her
and hires young down-on-his-luck screen-

writer Joe Gillis (Holden) to help engineer
her movie comeback. The screenwriter,
who becomes the actress' kept man, assumes he can manipulate her, but finds
out otherwise. Reality was almost too
close for comfort, as Swanson, von Stroheim (as her major domo Max), and others
very nearly play themselves. A darkly humorous look at the legacy and loss of
fame with witty dialog, stellar performances, and some now-classic scenes.
Based on the story "A Can of Beans" by
Brackett and Wilder. 110m/B VHS,
DVD. Gloria Swanson, William Holden, Erich von Stroheim,
Nancy Olson, Buster Keaton, Jack Webb, Cecil B.
DeMille, Fred Clark; **D:** Billy Wilder; **W:** Billy Wilder,
Charles Brackett, D.M. Marshman Jr.; **C:** John
Seitz; **M:** Franz Waxman. Oscars '50: Art Dir/Set
Dec., B&W, Story & Screenplay, Orig. Dramatic
Score; AFI '98: Top 100; Golden Globes '51: Ac-
tress—Drama (Swanson), Director (Wilder), Film—
Drama, Score, Natl. Film Reg. '89.

Sunset Grill *♂♂* **1992 (R)** While investigating his wife's murder, detective
Ryder Hart (Weller) discovers a pattern of
grisly killings. Sexy singer Loren Du-
quesne (Singer) leads him south of the
border to her boss and his bloody money-
making scheme. Unrated version also
available. 105m/C VHS, DVD. Peter Weller, Lori
Singer, Alexandra Paul, John Rhys-Davies, Michael Anderson Jr., Stacy Keach; **D:** Kevin Connor.

Sunset Heat *♂♂* *Midnight Heat* **1992**
(R) Former drug dealer (Paré) returns to
his home in Los Angeles with a legit job as
a photojournalist. He stays with an old
friend who turns out to be involved with
the obsessed drug czar that Paré used to
work for. Trouble comes along when the
drug lord is robbed and blames Paré for
the crime. Action-packed, with some good
plot twists. An unrated version contains
two additional minutes of footage. 94m/C
VHS. Michael Paré, Dennis Hopper, Adam Ant,
Daphne Ashbrook, Charlie Schlatter; **D:** John Nicolella.

Sunset in El Dorado *♂♂* **1945**
Roy and Dale thwart a villainous scheme
to defraud farmers of their land. 56m/B
VHS, DVD. Roy Rogers, Dale Evans, George
"Gabby" Hayes, Hardie Albright, Roy Barcroft,
Tom London, Edmund Cobb; **D:** Frank McDonald.

Sunset in the West *♂♂* **1950**
Deputy sheriff Rogers figures out that local gunrunners are using the railroad to
help them move their merchandise and he
sets out to stop them. 67m/C VHS. Roy Rogers, Gordon Jones, Penny Edwards, Estelita Rodriguez; **D:** William Witney; **W:** Gerald Geraghy; **C:**
Jack Marta.

Sunset Limousine *♂♂½* **1983**
An out-of-work stand-up comic gets
thrown out by his girlfriend, then takes a
job as a chauffeur. Standard vehicle with
occasional bursts of speed. 92m/C VHS,
DVD. Charles Lane, John Ritter, Martin Short, Susan Dey, Paul Reiser, Audrie Neenan, Lainie Kazan; **D:** Terry Hughes.

Sunset Park *♂♂* **1996 (R)** Brooklyn
phys ed teacher Phyllis Saroka (Perriman)
becomes the coach of a high school basketball team that, despite her total lack of
knowledge about the game, gives them to
the city championships. The cast's excellent performances hold interest, even
though the predictable storyline gives
away all of its moves before it gets near
the hoop. Star of the rap group Onyx) is
outstanding as the most talented (and
most troubled) member of the team. 100m/
C VHS, DVD. Rhea Perlman, Carol Kane, Terrence Howard, Camille Saviola, Fredro Starr,
James Harris, Antwon Tanner, Shawn Michael Howard, De'Aundre Bonds; **D:** Steve Gomer; **W:** Seth
Zvi Rosenfeld, Kathleen McGee-Anderson; **C:**
Robbie Greenberg; **M:** Kay Gee, Miles Goodman.

Sunset on the Desert *♂♂½*
1942 Rogers gets to wear a white hat and
a black hat as both the leader of a gang of
outlaws and the hero who brings them to
justice. A poor man's Western omelette.
54m/B VHS, DVD. Roy Rogers, George "Gabby"
Hayes, Lynne Carver, Frank M. Thomas Sr., Bob
Nolan, Beryl Wallace, Glenn Strange, Douglas
Fowley, Roy Barcroft, Pat Brady; **D:** Joseph Kane.

Sunset Range *♂♂½* **1935** The
"World's All-Around Champion Cowboy"
of 1912 stars in this chaps-slappin', shit-
chompin', dust-raisin' saga of the plains.
59m/B VHS, DVD. Hoot Gibson, Mary Doran, Walter McGrail, James Eagles, John Elliott, Ralph
Lewis; **D:** Ray McCarey; **W:** Paul Schofield; **C:** Gilbert Warrenton.

Sunset Serenade *♂♂* **1942** Roy
and Gabby outwit murderous duo who
plan to eliminate the new heir to a ranch.
66m/B VHS, DVD. Roy Rogers, George "Gabby"
Hayes, Helen Parrish; **D:** Joseph Kane.

Sunset Strip *♂♂* **1985** A photographer investigates a friend's murder, and
enters the seamy world of drugs and rock
and roll in L.A. 83m/C VHS, Tom Elpin, Cheri
Cameron Newell, John Mayall; **D:** William Webb;
W: William Webb; **C:** Erich Anderson.

Sunset Strip *woc!f* **1991 (R)** A
young dancer finds a job in a strip club
and competes against the other women
there to find the man of her dreams. The
women take their jobs very seriously—
ever attending ballet classes to improve
their performances. However, the viewer
probably won't take this movie very seriously since it is just another excuse to
show women in as little clothing as possible. 95m/C VHS, DVD. Jeff Conaway, Michelle
Foreman, Shelley Michelle; **D:** Paul G. Volk; **M:**
John Gonzalez.

Sunset Trail *♂* **1932** Routine Maynard sagebrush saga with the hero protecting a woman rancher from outlaws.
60m/B VHS. Ken Maynard, Ruth Hiatt, Frank Rice, Philip
P.H. (P.M.) McCullough, Buddy Hunter, Ken Maynard; **D:** B. Reeves Eason; **W:** Bennett Cohen; **C:**
Arthur Reed.

Sunshine *♂♂* **1999 (R)** Sprawling
look at four generations of an assimilated
Hungarian-Jewish family covers a lot of
time at the expense of cohesiveness and
character. Title refers to the health tonic
that makes the family fortune and is a pun
on the family's original name, Sonnen-
schein. Fiennes turns up in three roles as
the family prospers in Budapest by changing their name to avoid the anti-Semitic
society—eventually converting to Catholicism. It will not protect them, however,
from the Nazi holocaust and the turbulent
postwar period that leads to the Hungarian
Revolution of 1956. 180m/C VHS, DVD, CA
HU Ralph Fiennes, Rosemary Harris, Rachel
Weisz, Jennifer Ehle, Molly Parker, Deborah Kara
Unger, James Frain, William Hurt, John Neville,
Miriam Margolyes, Mark Strong; **D:** Istvan Szabo;
W: Istvan Szabo, Israel Horovitz; **C:** Lajos Koltai;
M: Maurice Jarre. Genie '99: Film.

Sunshine *♂♂½* **2007 (R)** The year
is 2057, and the sun is dying. A previous
mission to reignite it has failed, and the
pluckiest, prettiest crew of scientists ever
assembled is sent with a massive nuclear
bomb to do the job, and of course, technical and human calamities seemingly cobbled from other big-screen space odys-
seys ensure. Stunning visuals and lots of
claustrophobic suspense mix with metaphysical ookiness, and the cast is crack,
but even sci-fi fans who can forgive the
deja vu will be tested by the "what-planet-
are-you-on?" ending. 107m/C DVD, Blu-ray
Disc. GB US Cillian Murphy, Chris Evans, Rose
Byrne, Michelle Yeoh, Hiroyuki (Henry) Sanada,
Cliff Curtis, Troy Garity, Benedict Wong, Mark
Strong; **D:** Danny Boyle; **W:** Alex Garland; **C:** Alwin
Kuchler; **M:** John Murphy.

The Sunshine Boys *♂♂♂½*
1975 (PG) Two veteran vaudeville partners,
who have shared a love-hate relationship
for decades, reunite for a TV special.
Adapted by Neil Simon from his play. Matthau was a replacement for Jack Benny,
who died before the start of filming. Burns,
in 1939, won an Oscar. Since his "Honolu"
for his first starring role since "Honolu"
in 1939, won an Oscar. 111m/C VHS, DVD.
George Burns, Walter Matthau, Richard Benjamin,
Lee Meredith, F. Murray Abraham, Carol Arthur,
Howard Hessaman; **D:** Herbert Ross; **W:** Neil Simon. Oscar's '75: Support. Actor (Burns); Golden
Globes '76: Actor—Mus./Comedy (Matthau),
Film—Mus./Comedy, Support. Actor (Benjamin);
Writers Guild '75: Adapt. Screenplay.

The Sunshine Boys *♂♂♂* **1995**
TV version of the Neil Simon play about
two old vaudevillians is updated, not necessarily for the better. The feuding duo are

a formerly popular 50s TV comedy team whose breakup was not amicable (Think Lewis and Martin. Go ask your folks, we'll wait). They are persuaded to reunite for a special appearance, but the old grudges come back. Suffers by comparison to the original, with Allen and Falk unable to duplicate the chemistry of Burns and Matthau. **90m/C VHS, DVD.** Woody Allen, Peter Falk, Sarah Jessica Parker, Michael McKean, Liev Schreiber, Edie Falco, Kirk Acevedo, Michael Badalucco, Jennifer Esposito, Whoopi Goldberg; **D:** John Erman; **W:** Neil Simon. **TV**

Sunshine Run *Black Rage* **1979 (PG)** Two escaped slaves and a young widow search for Spanish treasure in the Everglades. **102m/C VHS.** Chris Robinson, Ted Cassidy, David Legge, Phyllis Robinson; **D:** Chris Robinson.

Sunshine State **2002 (PG-13)** Sayles returns with a tale of developers invading a northern Florida resort island and the effect on the locals. Of the excellent ensemble, a superb Falco is the standout, as is her Jack (Hutton), one of the pack of real estate sharks after her property. Bassett is Desiree, who returns to her hometown in an attempt to reconcile with her mother (Alice), whose own island dream home was a nightmare for Desiree growing up. Not so much big biz vs. the little people as a coming to terms with life, family and the past. **141m/C VHS, DVD.** *US* Edie Falco, Angela Bassett, Timothy Hutton, James Alexander, Ralph Waite, Mary Alice, Bill Cobbs, Alex Lewis, Gordon Clapp, Richard Edson, Tom Wright, Perry Lang, Miguel Ferrer, Michael Greyeyes, Alan King, Charlaine Woodard; **D:** John Sayles; **W:** John Sayles; **C:** Patrick Cady; **M:** Mason Daring. L.A. Film Critics '02: Support. Actress (Falco). **VIDEO**

Sunstorm **2001 (R)** Four sisters who've never met unite to find out who killed their father (Keach), who was an important general. When the same people come after the sisters, the stage is set for a ridiculously confused plot and plenty of fight scenes between the sisters and numerous henchmen. Sets out as exploitation, but plays it too seriously and even disappoints in the eye candy department. **94m/C VHS, DVD.** Stacy Keach, Bo Derek, Geoffrey Lewis, Margaret Scarborough, Ray Raglin, Ron Hale, Rebecca Stauber, Michael Manasseri; **D:** Mike Marvin; **C:** Steve (Steven) Shaw.

Sunstroke **1992 (R)** Seymour plays a desperate mother searching for her kidnapped child through the Arizona desert. Framed for murder, she cannot contact the police but must track the kidnappers herself, until she meets a drifter with secrets of his own. **91m/C VHS.** Jane Seymour, Stephen Meadows, Steve Railsback, Ray Wise, Don Ameche; **D:** James Keach; **W:** Duane Poole.

The Super **1991 (R)** Pesci stars as a slumlord who faces a prison sentence thanks to his terminal neglect. The option given to him is to live in his own rat hole until he provides reasonable living conditions. This he does, and predictably learns a thing or two about his own greed and the people who suffer as a result of it. Pesci as always gives an animated performance but poor scripting laden with stereotypes and cliches successfully restricts effort. **86m/C VHS, DVD.** Joe Pesci, Vincent Gardenia, Madolyn Smith, Ruben Blades, Stacey Travis; **D:** Rod Daniel; **C:** Bruce Surtees.

Super Bitch *Mafia Junction* **1973** Nasty, cold, and uncaring woman uses men to keep up her expensive habits, then ruthlessly tosses them aside when she is done. She purposely entangles them in the drug trade and thinks nothing of their deaths. Proving once again that you get what you pay for. **90m/C VHS.** Stephanie Beacham, Patricia Hayes, Gareth Thomas; **D:** Massimo Dallamano.

Super Brother *Black Jesus* **1968 (R)** The feared and respected leader of an oppressed people is imprisoned, much to everyone's regret. **90m/C VHS.** *IT* Jean Servais, Franco Citti, Pier Paolo Capponi, Woody Strode; **D:** Valerio Zurlini; **W:** Valerio Zurlini; **C:** Alace Parolini; **M:** Ivan Vandor.

Super Force **1990** When astronaut Zach Stone (Olandt) returns from an assignment on Mars he finds his policeman brother has been murdered. He quits NASA and joins the force to get revenge, battling evil crime boss Tao Satori (Liddy). Stone also moonlights as a vigilante, complete with motorcycle and high-tech armoured suit. It's dumb but there's lots of action. **92m/C VHS.** Ken Olandt, G. Gordon Liddy, Larry B. Scott, Lisa Niemi, Marshall Teague; **Cameos:** Patrick Macnee; **D:** Richard Compton.

Super Fuzz *Supersnooper* **1981 (PG)** Rookie policeman develops super powers after being accidentally exposed to radiation. Somewhat ineptly, he uses his abilities to combat crime. Somewhat ineptly acted, written, and directed as well. **97m/C VHS, DVD.** Terence Hill, Joanne Dru, Ernest Borgnine; **D:** Sergio Corbucci; **W:** Sergio Corbucci.

Super Mario Bros. **1993 (PG)** $42 million adventure fantasy based on the popular Nintendo video game. The brothers are in hot pursuit of the Princess Daisy who's been kidnapped by evil slimebucket Hopper and taken to Dinohattan, a fungi-infested, garbage-strewn, rat-hole version of Manhattan. Hopper will amuse the adults, doing a gleeful reptilian version of Frank Booth from "Blue Velvet." Hoskins and Leguizamo act gamely in broad Nintendo style, and directed the many gags. Hits bullseye of target audience—elementary and junior high kids—with frenetic pace, gaudy special effects, oversized sets, and animatronic monsters. **104m/C VHS, DVD.** Bob Hoskins, John Leguizamo, Samantha Mathis, Fisher Stevens, Richard Edson, Dana Kaminsky, Dennis Hopper, Fiona Shaw, Mojo Nixon, Lance Henriksen; **D:** Rocky Morton, Annabel Jankel; **W:** Edward Solomon, Parker Bennett, Terry Runte; **M:** Alan Silvestri.

Super Seal **1977 (G)** An injured seal pup disrupts a family's normal existence after the young daughter adopts him. **95m/C VHS.** Foster Brooks, Sterling Holloway, Sarah Brown; **D:** Michael Dugan.

Super Size Me **2004** Director Spurlock becomes a human guinea pig in his cautionary tale/experiment into the apparently very dangerous world of fast food. Vowing to eat three meals a day at McDonald's for a full 30 days, Spurlock also had a strict "always say yes" policy when asked by a Mickey D's employee if he wanted to super size. The result was a 30-pound weight gain, severely declining health, and a film so controversial it caused McDonald's to stop their super size promotion months after the film debuted at the Sundance Film Festival. Gross-out doc mixes comedy with concern. Watching this one might even have die hard fast food freaks munching salad. Includes interviews with ice cream lover John Robbins, former surgeon general David Sacher, and Subway poster-boy Jared. **98m/C DVD.** **D:** Morgan Spurlock; **W:** Morgan Spurlock; **C:** Scott Ambrosy; **M:** Steve Horowitz, Michael Parrish.

Super Sucker **2003 (R)** Daniels wrote, directed, and starred in this sometimes sleazy and intermittently funny comedy. Fred Barlow (Daniels) works for Johnson City Super Sucker Vacuums as a salesman, only his career is in trouble. The company has launched a sales contest to see (essentially) who will remain employed and who will get the boot. Fred is despondent until he discovers his wife using one of the vacuum's attachments for personal satisfaction that has nothing to do with household cleaning. Suddenly Fred has the proper gimmick to sell the vacuum to the city's lonely housewives. **95m/C VHS, DVD.** Jeff Daniels, Matt Letscher, Harve Presnell, Guy Sanville, Sandra Birch, John Seibert, Kate Peckham, Dawn Wells; **D:** Jeff Daniels; **W:** Jeff Daniels; **C:** Richard Brauer.

Super Troopers *Broken Lizard's Super Troopers* **2001 (R)** Vermont is the setting for this snobs vs. slobs comedy that pits wacky state troopers facing a budget-forced shutdown against the local cops, who curry favor with the politicians. Plot involving a jurisdictional fight over a murder and a drug bust only occasionally interferes with the drug, sex, and grossout humor that carries the pic to a satisfying conclusion. Cox is hilarious as the barely-in-control commander of the station, while Von Bargen does a great job as his nemesis. **100m/C VHS, DVD, UMD.** Jay Chandrasekhar, Kevin Heffernan, Steve Lemme, Paul Soter, Erik Stolhanske, Brian Cox, Daniel von Bargen, Marisa Coughlan, Kevin Weaver, Jim Gaffigan, John Bedford Lloyd, Lynda Carter; **D:** Jay Chandrasekhar; **W:** Jay Chandrasekhar, Kevin Heffernan, Steve Lemme, Paul Soter, Erik Stolhanske; **C:** Joaquin Baca-Asay.

Superargo *Il Re Dei Criminali; Superargo the Giant; The King of Criminals* **1967** A wrestler becomes a superhero with psychic powers and a bulletproof leotard, fighting a madman who is turning athletes into robots. Successful Italian hero who wouldn't last two minutes in the ring with Batman. **95m/C VHS.** *IT SP* Guy Madison, Ken Wood, Liz Barrett, Diana Loris; **D:** Paul Maxwell.

Superbabies: Baby Geniuses 2 woof! **2004 (PG)** A super stupid waste of time. The who cares follow-up to the 1999 release pits evil German media mogul Biscane (Oscar-winner Voight, who once had a real career) against four toddlers who have a super ability to communicate with each other via really bad dubbing and Kahuna (the Fitzgerald triplets). Biscane's diabolical plan is to control the minds of children by brainwashing them via subliminal messages through the TV. Wait, hasn't that already been done? Baio and Angel pop in as the owners of an L.A. daycare center. **90m/C VHS, DVD.** *GE GB* Jon Voight, Scott Baio, Vanessa Angel, Peter Wingfield, Justin Chatwin, Gerry Fitzgerald, Leo Fitzgerald, Myles Fitzgerald, Skyler Shaye, Max Scheideman, Maia Bastidas, Keana Bastidas, Joshua Lockhart, Maxwell Lockhart; **D:** Bob (Benjamin) Clark; **W:** Gregory Poppen; **C:** Maher Maleh; **M:** Paul Zaza, Helmut Zerlett.

Superbad **2007 (R)** Seth (Hill) and Evan (Cera) are crude, socially inept, and sex-obsessed, like most teenage boys. When the girls they have crushes on ask them to buy booze for a graduation party, Seth sees this as their last chance to woo their beloveds the best way he knows how—by getting them drunk. Roping their fake-ID wielding friend Fogell (Mintz-Plasse) into Seth's scheme, every night becomes an odyssey of cops, robbers, crazed bums, cokeheads, violent thugs, party-crashing losers, vomit, and facing fears about their futures. Unapologetically teens with both raunch and heart. Hill and Cera shine as the hapless leads (named after writers Rogan and Goldberg, who penned the original version of the project while in junior high), but newcomer Mintz-Plasse steals every scene as the hopeless geek who renames himself "McLovin." **112m/C DVD, Blu-ray Disc.** *US* Jonah Hill, Michael Cera, Bill Hader, Seth Rogen, Christopher Mintz-Plasse, Aviva, Stacy Edwards, Kevin Corrigan, Emma Stone, Martha MacIsaac; **D:** Greg Mottola; **W:** Seth Rogen, Evan Goldberg; **C:** Russ T. Alsobrook; **M:** Lyle Workman.

Superbug Super Agent **1976** Dodo, the wonder car puts the brakes on crime in this silly action-adventure tale. A lemon in a lot full of Herbies. **90m/C VHS.** *GE* Robert Mark, Heidi Hansen, George Goodman; **D:** Rudolf Zehetgruber; **W:** Rudolf Zehetgruber; **C:** Hannes Staudinger; **M:** Jurgen Elert.

Superchick woof! **1971 (R)** Mild-mannered stewardess by day, sexy blonde with karate blackbelt by night. In addition to stopping a skyjacking she regularly makes love to men around the world. A superbomb that never gets off the ground. **94m/C VHS, DVD.** Joyce Jillison, Louis Quinn, Thomas Reardon, Uschi Digart; **D:** Ed Forsyth; **W:** Gary Crutcher; **C:** Paul Hipp; **M:** Allan Alper.

Supercop *Police Story 3: Supercop* **1992 (R)** Super Hong Kong cop Kevin Chan (Chan) heads to China to assist the authorities in cracking an international drug ring. He's partnered with disciplined-but-beautiful Director Yang (Yeoh), who's also a terrific fighter, and the duo go undercover (as a married couple) to infiltrate the operation, which takes them to a Malaysian resort. Then Chan's girlfriend shows up, blowing their cover. Lots of action-packed fighting and wild chases. The 1996 American release loses about a half-hour of run time from the original. Dubbed from Cantonese. **93m/C VHS, DVD. HK** Jackie Chan, Michelle Yeoh, Maggie Cheung, Kenneth Tsang, Yuen Wah; **D:** Stanley Tong; **W:** Edward Tang, Fibe Ma, Lee Wai Yee; **C:** Ardy Lam; **M:** Joel McNeely.

Supercop 2 *Police Story 3, Part 2* **1993 (R)** Rising star Inspector Jessica Yang (Yeoh) has her life disrupted when her boyfriend David is dishonorably discharged from the police force and leaves town. Several months later, Jessica is assigned to stop a crime ring that turns out to be headed by David. Chan has a brief cameo (in drag). **94m/C VHS, DVD. HK** Michelle Yeoh, Yukari Oshima, Eric Tsang, Rongguang Yu, Athene Chu, Siu-wong Fan, Jackie Chan, Emile Chau, Chu Yan; **D:** Stanley Tong; **W:** Stanley Tong, Mok Tang Han, Sui Lai Kang.

Supercross: The Movie **2005 (PG-13)** In case you are unaware, supercross is an offshoot of motocross racing but is held on indoor tracks equipped with gravity-defying jumps. Brothers KC (Howey) and Trip (Vogel) want to become champs but, for now, they are underdogs. KC has to play second bike to corporate sponsor star Rowdy (Tatum), so Trip decides he'd be better off going it alone and gets his own sponsor, Earl Cole (Patrick, the only one with actual acting ability). Richardson and Bush are the chicks the brothers get involved with. The plot may be clunky but director Boyum cranks up the racing thrills and noise level. **98m/C VHS** Mike Vogel, Channing Tatum, J.D. Pardo, Robert Carradine, Steve Howey, Cameron Richardson, Sophia Buh, Aaron Carter, Carolina Garcia, Ryan Locke; **D:** Steve Boyum; **W:** Ken Solarz, Bart Baker; **C:** William Wages.

Superdad **1973 (G)** A middle-aged parent is determined to bridge the generation gap by trying his hand at various teenage activities. Disney family fare that's about as complicated as a TV commercial. The adolescents are two-dimensional throwbacks to the fun-loving '50s. **94m/C VHS.** Bob Crane, Kurt Russell, Joe Flynn, Barbara Rush, Kathleen (Kathy) Cody, Dick Van Patten; **D:** Vincent McEveety; **M:** Buddy (Norman Dale) Baker.

SuperFire **2002 (PG-13)** Hackneyed heroes story. Jim Merrick (Sweeney) is a disgraced fire-fighter tanker pilot whose mistakes cost the lives of 12 smokejumpers. So no one is ready to listen when Jim says an enormous superfire is forming that will obliterate the local community. Then the wildfire gets out of control and it's up to Jim to save the day. **99m/C VHS, DVD.** D.B. Sweeney, Wes Studi, Chad E. Donella, Diane Farr, Ellen Muth, Katrina Hobbs; **D:** Steven Quale; **W:** Michael Vickerman; **C:** William Wages. **TV**

Superfly **1972 (R)** Controversial upon release, pioneering blaxploitation has Harlem dope dealer finding trouble with gangs and police as he attempts to establish retirement fund from one last deal. Excellent period tunes by Curtis Mayfield. Two lesser sequels. **98m/C VHS, DVD.** Ron O'Neal, Carl Lee, Sheila Frazier, Julius W. Harris, Charles McGregor; **D:** Gordon Parks Jr.; **W:** Phillip Fenty; **C:** James Signorelli; **M:** Curtis Mayfield. **TV**

Superfly T.N.T. woof! *Super Fly T.N.T* **1973 (R)** This confusing sequel to "Superfly" finds O'Neal returning as Youngblood Priest. The now ex-drug dealer has retired with his girlfriend to Rome where he is approached by an African gun-runner (Browne) for help in a revolution against an oppressive government. Cheap

Supergirl 🐾🐾 1984 (PG) Big-budget bomb in which Slater made her debut and nearly killed in her career, with the help of Kryptonite. Unexciting and unsophisticated story of a young woman, cousin to Superman, with super powers, based on the comic book series. She's in pursuit of a magic paperweight, but an evil sorceress wants it too. Dunaway is a terrifically vile villainess with awesome black magic powers. Slater is great to look at, but is much better in almost any other film. 114m/C VHS, DVD, GB Faye Dunaway, Helen Slater, Peter O'Toole, Mia Farrow, Brenda Vaccaro, Marc McClure, Simon Ward, Hart Bochner, Maureen Teefy; David Healy, Matt Frewer; D: Jeannot Szwarc; W: David Odell; C: Alan Hume; M: Jerry Goldsmith.

SuperGuy: Behind the Cape 🐾½ 2002 Leaping into a thin plot with a single bound, this comic-book farce exposes the increasingly mortal superhero SuperGuy who fights having his super-image tarnished as humanlike weaknesses are revealed and his once-adoring fans afford him no pity. 74m/C VHS, DVD. Charles Dierkop, Katherine Victor; Peter Stacker, David Anthony Hernandez; D: Bill La; C: Mike Ziemkowski. VIDEO

Superhero Movie 🐾 2008 (PG-13) Holy send-up, Batman! In this swing at blockbuster superhero flicks, wreaking havoc with comic-book lore, likable teen dream Bell is bitten by a genetically altered dragonfly and transforms into a dragonfly superhero, possessing all manner of super powers—except he can't fly. Dragonfly then has a showdown with power-crazed CEO turned-villainous-arch enemy Hourglass (McDonald). Strings together the usual lazy jabs at pop-culture targets and D-list cameos, the irony of which will be lost on the target teenybopper audience. Another waste of time and effort. 86m/C DVD, US Drake Bell, Marion Ross, Sara Paxton, Christopher McDonald, Leslie Nielsen, Ryan Hansen; Thomas Ackerman; M: James L. Venable.

Superman: The Movie 🐾🐾🐾½ 1978 (PG) The DC Comics legend comes alive in this wonderfully entertaining saga of Superman's life from a baby on the doomed planet Krypton (Reeve is Superman's dad) to Earth's own Man of Steel (a chiseled Reeve). Hackman and Beatty pair marvelously as super criminal Lex Luthor and his bumbling sidekick Otis, while Kidder is an intelligent Lois Lane. Award-winning special effects and a script that doesn't take itself too seriously make this great fun. Followed by three sequels. 152m/C VHS, Blu-ray Disc, HD DVD. Christopher Reeve, Margot Kidder, Marlon Brando, Gene Hackman, Glenn Ford, Susannah York, Ned Beatty, Valerie Perrine, Jackie Cooper, Marc McClure, Trevor Howard, Sarah Douglas, Terence Stamp, Jack O'Halloran, Phyllis Thaxter, Marc Newman; C: Mario Puzo, Robert Benton, David Newman; C: Geoffrey Unsworth; M: John Williams. Oscars '78: Visual FX.

Superman 2 🐾🐾🐾 1980 (PG) The sequel to "the movie" about the Man of Steel. This time, he has his hands full with three super-powered villains from his home planet of Krypton. The romance between reporter Lois Lane and our superhero is made believable and the story line has more pace to it than the original. A sequel that often equals the first film—leave it to Superman to pull off the impossible. 128m/C VHS, DVD, Blu-ray Disc, HD DVD. Christopher Reeve, Margot Kidder, Gene Hackman, Ned Beatty, Jackie Cooper, Sarah Douglas, Terence Stamp, Jack O'Halloran, Susannah York, Marc Do gas; M: John Williams.

The Supernaturals 🐾½ 1986 (R) Confederate Civil War-era ghosts, bent on avenging their deaths, haunt a wooded area in which modern Yar-kee army maneuvers are practiced. Antebellum boredom. 85m/C VHS. Bobby DiCicco, Maxwell Caulfield,

Supergrass 🐾🐾 1987 (R) A low-brow British farce about a nebbish who poses as a drug smuggler to impress his girlfriend, and is then mistaken for a real one by the authorities. 105m/C VHS, GB Adrian Edmondson, Peter Richardson, Leslie Phillips, Jennifer Saunders, Ronald Allen, Dawn French; D: Peter Richardson.

Superman 3 🐾🐾 1983 (PG) Villainous businessman Ross Webster (Vaughn) tries to conquer Superman (Reeve) via the expertise of bumbling computer expert Gus Gorman (Pryor) and the judicious use of an artificial form of Kryptonite. Superman explores his darker side after undergoing transformation into sleaze ball. Promising satiric start ultimately defeated by uneven story and direction and boring physical comedy. Notable is the absence of Lois Lane as a main character; instead the big guy takes up with former flame Lana Lang (O'Toole). Followed by "Superman 4." 123m/C VHS, DVD. Christopher Reeve, Richard Pryor, Annette O'Toole, Jackie Cooper, Margot Kidder, Marc McClure, Annie Ross, Robert Vaughn; D: Richard Lester; W: David Newman; C: Robert Paynter; M: John Williams.

Superman 4: The Quest for Peace 🐾🐾 1987 (PG) The third sequel, in which the Man of Steel endeavors to rid the world of nuclear weapons, thereby pitting himself against nuclear-entrepreneurs. Nuclear Man. Special effects are dime-store quality and it appears that someone may have walked off with parts of the plot. Reeve deserves credit for remaining true to character through four films. 90m/C VHS, DVD. Christopher Reeve, Gene Hackman, Jon Cryer, Marc McClure, Margot Kidder, Mariel Hemingway, Sam Wanamaker; D: Sidney J. Furie; W: Mark Rosenthal; M: Alexander Courey; D: Lee Sholem. TV

Superman Returns 🐾🐾½ 2006 (PG-13) Over-hyped and overlong return of the Man of Steel, last seen on the big screen in 1987's "Superman IV." Christopher Reeve look-alike Routh fills out the spandex but lacks a certain superhero charm as Supes returns to Earth five years after the events of "Superman 2" (like everyone else, they pretend that "III" and "IV" never happened). Clark Kent heads back to the "Daily Planet" where he discovers that Lois is a mother, shacked up on an anti-Superman rant she works on and a fiance. Lex Luthor (Spacey) wants to take over the world—again. Superman comes to the rescue—again. Singer plays the story straight and there's not a lot of gee-whiz joy to be found. 140m/C DVD, Blu-ray Disc, HD DVD. US Brandon Routh, Kate Bosworth, Kevin Spacey, James Marsden, Eva Marie Saint, Parker Posey, Frank Langella, Sam Huntington, Kal Penn, Noel Neill, Jack Larson, Marlon Brando, Tristan Lake Leabu, David Fabrizio; D: Bryan Singer; W: Bryan Singer, Michael Dougherty, Daniel P. "Dan" Harris; C: Newton Thomas (Tom) Sigel; M: John Ottman.

Supernatural 🐾🐾½ 1933 Roma (Lombard) falls prey to a phony medium (Dinehart) who promises to call up the spirit of her recently murdered twin brother. At the same moment of the seance a murderess dies in the electric chair and her body is used in Dr. Houston's (Warner) life-after-death experiment. Too bad his girlfriend is used in Dr. Houston's experiment. Roma becomes possessed by the woman's evil spirit. Now the doctor and Roma's fiance (Scott) must undo the curse. A hokey B-grade movie disliked by Lombard. 78m/B VHS. Carole Lombard, Randolph Scott, H.B. Warner, Alan Dinehart, Vivienne Osborne, Beryl Mercer, William Farnum, Willard Robertson; D: Victor Halperin; W: Harvey Thew, Brian Marlow; C: Arthur Martinelli.

Supervixens 🐾🐾 1975 Russ Meyer's Supervixens; Supervixens Eruption; Vixens 1975 True to Meyer's low-rent exploitation film canon, this wild tale is filled with characteristic Amazons, sex and violence. A gas station attendant is framed for the grisly murder of his girlfriend and hustles out of town, meeting a succession of well-endowed women during his travels. As if it needed further problems, it's hampered by a tasteless storyline and incoherent writing. 105m/C VHS, DVD. Shari Eubank, Charles Napier, Uschi Digart, Charles Pitts, Henry Rowland, Sharon Kelly, Haji; D: Russ Meyer; W: Russ Meyer; C: Russ Meyer; M: William Loose.

Support Your Local Gunfighter 🐾🐾 1971 (G) Garner plays a western con man with his tongue firmly in his cheek. He comes to the small town of Purgatory and is thought to be a notorious gunfighter. He decides to go with the mistaken identity and use it to his

---

Marshall; D: Richard Lester; W: Mario Puzo, David Newman; C: Robert Paynter; M: John Williams.

Supernova 🐾½ 1996 (PG-13) This one got stuck on the studio shelf for awhile and didn't improve with age, in fact, director Walter Hill was so incensed over studio re-editing that he removed his name, leaving the pseud. "Thomas Lee" to grace this space mishmash. Nick Vanzant (Spader) is stuck piloting a 22nd-century medical vessel after the captain (Forster) is killed. The craft receives a distress call and makes the mistake of rescuing Karl (Facinelli), an odd duck who proves to be dangerous. You'll wonder what got left on the cutting-room floor. 91m/C VHS, DVD. James Spader, Angela Bassett, Robin Tunney, Peter Facinelli, Lou Diamond Phillips, Wilson Cruz, Robert Forster; D: Walter Hill; W: David Campbell Wilson; C: Lloyd Ahern II; M: David Williams.

Supersonic Man woof! 1978 (PG) Incoherent shoestring-budget Superman spoof with a masked hero fighting to save the world from the evil intentions of a mad scientist. 85m/C VHS, SP Michael Coby, Cameron Mitchell, Diana Polakov; D: J(uan) Piquer Simon.

Superstar 🐾🐾 1999 (PG-13) Yet another SNL skit tries to stretch to feature film length and remain funny. Don't these people ever give up?! What's next? "Weekend Update: The Movie"? This time producer Lorne Michaels showcases klutzy Catholic schoolgirl Mary Katherine Gallagher (Shannon) as she tries to win a school talent contest and a kiss from the campus hunk (Ferrell). Of course it's really about her strange armpit sniffing technique and pasty-flashing behavior. The material doesn't translate well to movie length (shocking!), and the "teenagers" look like they're about 20 years late for homeroom. There are some funny bits, however, and if you like the character on the show you'll probably like the movie. Warning: There are scenes where Ms. Gallagher french kisses a tree, which sounds a lot funnier than it actually is. 82m/C VHS, DVD. Molly Shannon, Will Ferrell, Elaine Hendrix, Glynis Johns, Mark Mckinney, Harland Williams, Emmy Laybourne; D: Bruce McCulloch; W: Steve Koren; C: Walt Lloyd; M: Michael Gore.

Superstar: The Life and Times of Andy Warhol 🐾🐾🐾 1990 Even if you didn't grok Andy's 'pop' artwork and self-created celebrity persona, this ironic, kinetic, oft-rollicking documentary paints a vivid picture of the wild era he inspired and exploited. Interviewees range from Warhol cohorts like Dennis Hopper to proud executives at the Campbell Soup plant. One highlight: a Warhol guest shot on "The Love Boat." 87m/C VHS, DVD. Tom Wolfe, Sylvie Miles, David Hockney, Taylor Mead, Dennis Hopper, Viva, Allen Ginsberg, Ultra Violet, Paul Morrissey, Sally Kirkland, Fran Lebowitz, Lou Reed, Shelley Winters, Holly Woodlawn; D: Chuck Workman; W: Chuck Workman; C: Burleigh Wartes.

Superstition 🐾½ 1982 The Witch 1982 A reverend and his family move into a vacant house despite warnings about a curse from the townsfolk. Some people never learn. 85m/C VHS, DVD. James Hough ton, Albert Salmi, Lynn Carlin; D: James Robertson.

Sure Fire 🐾🐾 1990 Wes (Blair) is a mercurial entrepreneur who thinks he has found the financial ticket to paradise and chagrin of his wife Ellen (Dezina), he refuses to let anything stand in the way of his sure-fire fortune, even his family. Wes develops a little self-control as he realizes he's beginning to flake out, but it may be too late. Director Jost has put together a surprisingly unpretentious film with a virtually no-name cast, speaking volumes on the American condition while unfolding in the bleak Utah desert. 86m/C VHS, DVD. Tom Blair, Kristi Hager, Robert Ernst, Kate Dezina, Phillip R. Brown; D: Jon Jost; W: Jon Jost.

The Sure Thing 🐾🐾🐾 1985 (PG-13) College students who don't like each other end up traveling to California together, and of course, falling in love. Charming performances make up for predictability. Can't-miss director (and ex-Meathead) Reiner's second direct hit at the boxoffice. 94m/C VHS, DVD. John Cusack, Daphne Zuniga, Anthony Edwards, Boyd Gaines, Lisa Jane Persky, Viveca Lindfors, Nicolette Sheridan, Tim Robbins; D: Rob Reiner; W: Jonathan Roberts, Steven L. Bloom; C: Robert Elswit; M: Tom Scott.

Surabaya Conspiracy 🐾🐾 1975 Mystery and intrigue surround a quest for gold in Africa. 90m/C VHS. Michael Rennie, Richard Jaeckel, Barbara Bouchet, Mike (Michael) Preston; D: Roy Davis.

Sure Nazis Must Die 🐾 1987 A piece cf deliberate camp in the Troma mold, about a group of psychotic neo-Nazi surfers 'aking over the beaches of California in the wake of a devastating earthquake. Tongue-in-cheek, tasteless and cheap, but intentionally so. 83m/C VHS, DVD. Barry Brenner, Gail Neely, Michael Sonye, Dawn Widsmith, Tom Shell, Bobbie Bresee; D: Peter George; W: John Ayre; C: Rolf Kesterman; M: Jon McCallum.

Supreme Sanction 🐾🐾 1999 (R) An assassin (Swanson) working for a cowl government agency decides not to kill the journalist who's threatening to expose the corrupt organization that trained her. This doesn't please her bosses and they mark 'er for death. 95m/C VHS, DVD. Michael Madsen, Kristy Swanson, David Dukes, Donald Adeosun Faison, Tommy (Tiny) Lister, Ron Perlman; D: John Terlesky; W: John Terlesky; M: Don Aneche; D: Hy Averback; W: Don McGuire.

Suppose They Gave a War and Nobody Came? 🐾🐾½ 1969 (R) Wer Games 1970 (G) A small Southern town battles into a gold rush town, he winds up becoming an unwitting sheriff. Gamer is perfect es scion where he convinces Dern to remain in jail, in spite of the lack of bars. Neatly subverts every western cliche it encounters, yet keeps respect for formula western. Followed by "Support Your Local Gunfighter." 92m/C VHS, James Garner, Joan Hackett, Walter Brennan, Bruce Dern, Jack Elam, Harry (Henry) Morgan; D: Burt Kennedy; W: William Bowers; C: Harry Stradling Jr.

Support Your Local Sheriff 🐾🐾🐾½ 1969 (G) Amiable, reverent western spoof with more than its fair share of laughs. When a stranger stumbles into a gold rush town, he winds up becoming sheriff. Gamer is perfect es scion where he convinces Dem to remain in jail, in spite of the lack of bars. Neatly subverts every western cliche it encounters, yet keeps respect for formula western. Followed by "Support Your Local Gunfighter." 92m/C VHS, James Garner, Joan Hackett, Walter Brennan, Bruce Dern, Jack Elam, Harry (Henry) Morgan; D: Burt Kennedy; W: William Bowers; C: Harry Stradling Jr.

profitable advantage. Elam is his bumbling sidekick and Pleshette the love interest. A delightful, deliberately cliche-filled western. A follow-up, not a sequel, to "Support Your Local Sheriff" (1969). 92m/C VHS, DVD. James Gamer, Jack Elam, Suzanne Pleshette, Harry (Henry) Morgan, Dub Taylor, John Dehner, Joan Blondell, Ellen Corby, Henri Jones; D: Burt Kennedy; W: James Edward Grant; C: Harry Stradling Jr.; M: Jack Elliott, Allyn Ferguson.

Surf Ninjas 1993 (PG) Action comedy for the kiddies finds two young surfer dudes who are actually the long-lost crown princes of the obscure nation of Patu San. The country's incompetent (what a surprise, it's Nielsen) warlord wants the boys to stay lost. Lame jokes and tame martial arts sequences. **87m/C VHS, DVD.** Kelly Hu, Ernie Reyes Jr., Nick Cowen, Leslie Nielsen, Tone Loc, Rob Schneider, John Karlen, Ernie Reyes Sr.; **D:** Neal Israel; **W:** Dan Gordon; **C:** Arthur Albert; **M:** David Kitay.

Surf Party 1964 Romance among the sands of Malibu with Vinton as the owner of a surf shop. Risque in 1964; utterly campy today. ♪If I Were an Artist; That's What Love Is; Pearly Shells. **68m/C VHS.** Bobby Vinton, Jackie DeShannon, Patricia Morrow, Kenny (Ken) Miller; **D:** Maury Dexter.

Surf 2 woof! 1984 *Surf 2: The End of the Trilogy* (R) A most excellent group of surfers get sick from drinking tainted Buzz Cola concocted by demented chemist Deezen in most heinous effort to obliterate surfer population from Southern California. Bogus, dude. No, you didn't miss "Surf 1" (there's not one), the title is the sort of in-joke this exercise in mental meltdown perpetuates as comedy. Ha. **91m/C VHS.** Morgan Paull, Cleavon Little, Lyle Waggoner, Ruth Buzzi, Linda Kerridge, Carol Wayne, Eddie Deezen, Eric Stoltz, Brandis Kemp, Terry Kiser; **D:** Randall Badat; **W:** Randall Badat; **M:** Peter Bernstein.

Surface to Air 1998 (R) Naval pilot Steven Madison (McQueen) is estranged from half-brother Zach (Madsen), who's in the Marines. But both wind up in Persian Gulf. Steve and fellow pilot Lori (Shatner) are captured by Iraqi terrorists and face certain death—unless Zach can come to the rescue. **93m/C VHS.** Michael Madsen, Chad McQueen, Melanie Shatner, Larry Thomas; **D:** Rodney McDonald. **VIDEO**

Surfacing woof! 1984 A girl braves the hostile northern wilderness to search for her missing father. This pseudo-psychological, sex-driven suspense flick makes little sense. **90m/C VHS.** Joseph Bottoms, Kathleen Beller, R.H. Thomson, Margaret Dragu; **D:** Claude Jutra.

Surf's Up 2007 ♪♪½ (PG) Dude! Penguins march, tap dance, and now they surf. Young Cody Maverick (LaBeouf) is an outcast among his peers with his surfer dreams. He follows a scout to the surfer Pen Gu Island, the home of a championship contest, and finds a mentor in laid-back legend Big Z (Bridges). Cody even gets a much more competent potential love interest in lifeguard Lani (Deschanel). Sidekick Chicken Joe (Heder) provides some diversion. Not ground-breaking in the animation department (although the look of the waves is impressive), but the story is fun and the vocal work just right. **85m/C DVD, HD DVD.** US **D:** Chris Buck, Ash Brannon; **W:** Lisa Addario, Joe Syracuse, Christian Darren, Don Rhymer; **V:** Shia LaBeouf, Jeff Bridges, Zooey Deschanel, Jon Heder, James Woods, Diedrich Bader, Mario Cantone, Jane Krakowski, Brian Benben, Michael McKean, Dana Belben.

The Surgeon 1994 ♪ *Exquisite Tenderness* (R) Routine hospital horror finds Dr. Theresa McCann (Glasser) caught up in murder when patients and doctors become poison victims. Aided by toxicologist Benjamin Hendricks (Remar), McCann finds a lollipop left behind and realizes the killer is ex-boyfriend/doctor Julian Matar (Haberle), whose unlawful experiments in tissue regeneration got him suspended. Now he's hiding out in the hospital and killing to get the pituitary glands necessary for his miracle serum. Film's original title "Exquisite Tenderness" is a term for the point when pain becomes so extreme it turns to pleasure—the film merely turns grisly. **100m/C VHS, DVD.** GE Isabel Glasser, James Remar, Sean Haberle, Charles Dance, Peter Boyle, Malcolm McDowell, Charles Bailey-Gates, Gregory West, Mother Love; **D:** Carl Schenkel; **C:** Patrick Cirillo; **C:** Thomas Burstyn; **M:** Christopher Franke.

Surprise Attack 1970 The Spanish Civil War forms the backdrop for this action opus. **124m/C VHS.** Simon Andreu, Dan (Daniel, Danny) Martin, Patty (Patti) Shepard; **D:** Jose Antonio De La Loma.

Surrender 1987 (PG) A struggling woman artist and a divorced author fall in love but won't admit it for fear of being hurt again. Jumbled plot, unfortunate casting. Available in a Spanish-subtitled version. **95m/C VHS.** Michael Caine, Sally Field, Steve Guttenberg, Peter Boyle, Jackie Cooper, Julie Kavner, Louise Lasser, Iman; **D:** Jerry Belson; **W:** Jerry Belson; **C:** Juan Ruiz-Anchia; **M:** Michel Colombier.

Surrender Dorothy ♪½ 1998 Weird psychosexual drama focuses on 26-year-old sexually confused Trevor (Pryor), who's afraid of women. He offers drugs and a place to crash to heroin addict Lahn (Di Novis) but their arrangement soon turn bizarre when Trevor desires Lahn to cross-dress as Dorothy, his concept of the ideal girlfriend, and then wants to take his obsession even farther. **97m/B VHS, DVD.** Kevin Di Novis, Peter Pryor, Jason Centeno, Elizabeth Casey; **D:** Kevin Di Novis; **W:** Kevin Di Novis; **C:** Jonathan Kovel; **M:** Christopher Matarazzo.

Surrogate ♪♪ 1988 A young couple fights to keep their marriage afloat by turning to a sex surrogate. Strong cast helps carry odd, confusing script, with plenty of (you guessed it) sex, and a mystery to solve. **100m/C VHS.** CA Art Hindle, Shannon Tweed, Carole Laure, Michael Ironside, Marilyn Lightstone; **D:** Don Carmody.

Surveillance 24/7 2007 Low-budget thriller that doesn't quite hang together. Gay teacher Adam heads off to London to party and get laid. He picks up Jake and his life goes to hell, especially when Jake turns up dead. Why? Well, although Adam was unaware, Jake gave him some evidence that a British royal is involved in a gay affair and no one wants the truth to come out. **87m/C DVD.** GB Simon Callow, Tom Harper, Dawn Steele, Sean Brosnan; **D:** Paul Oremland; **W:** Kevin Sampson; **C:** Alistair Cameron; **M:** Helen Jane Long.

Survival Game 1987 A young combat expert (Chuck Norris's son) gets involved with some ex-hippies in search of a $2 million cache. High-kickin' action. **91m/C VHS.** Mike Norris, Deborah Goodrich, Seymour Cassel; **D:** Herb Freed.

Survival Island ♪♪ *Demon Island; The Pinata: Survival Island* 2002 (R) Kinda cheesy horror fun. Group of college students are on a Cinco de Mayo treasure hunt on a tropical island when something evil turns up—a killer pinata! Actually, it's a demon hidden inside the pinata that starts picking off the clueless one by gory one. What a way to get voted off the island. **90m/C VHS, DVD.** Nicholas Brendon, Jaime Pressly, Garrett Wang, Eugene Byrd, Daphne Lynn Duplaix; **D:** David Hillenbrand, Scott Hillenbrand; **W:** David Hillenbrand, Scott Hillenbrand; **C:** Philip D. Schwartz; **M:** David Hillenbrand. **VIDEO**

Survival Quest ♪♪½ 1989 (R) Students in a Rocky Mountain survival course cross paths with a band of bloodthirsty mercenaries-in-training. A battle to the death ensues; you'll wish they'd all put each other out of their misery a lot sooner. **90m/C VHS, DVD.** Lance Henriksen, Dermot Mulroney, Mark Rolston, Steve Antin, Paul Provenza, Ben Hammer, Traci Lind, Catherine Keener, Reggie Bannister; **D:** Don A. Coscarelli; **W:** Don A. Coscarelli.

Survival Run ♪ 1980 (R) Six California teenagers become stranded in the Mexican desert, where they witness Graves and Milland making a shady deal. The chase is on, the story is lame, the gory parts aren't gory—so why bother? **90m/C VHS.** Peter Graves, Ray Milland, Vincent Van Patten; **D:** Larry Spiegel; **W:** Gerard M. Cahill.

Survival Zone woof! 1984 (R) Nuclear holocaust survivors battle a violent band of marauding motorcyclists on the barren ranches of the 21st century. Advice to director Rubens and cohorts: Next time, find a plot that's not growing mold. **90m/C VHS.** Gary Lockwood, Morgan Stevens, Camilla Sparv; **D:** Percival Rubens.

The Survivalist 1987 (R) An arms-ready survivalist nut defends his family and supplies against a panicked society awaiting nuclear war. Poorly acted, little tension, and ineffective plotting make boredom seem a more critical issue than survival. **96m/C VHS.** Steve Railsback, Susan Blakely, Marjoe Gortner, David Wayne, Cliff DeYoung; **D:** Sig Shore; **W:** Robert Dillon.

Surviving Christmas 2004 (PG-13) Affleck finds himself stuck in another boxoffice disaster as wealthy yuppie Drew, who plans to reconnect with his past by visiting his boyhood home. The house is now occupied by working-class grump Tom Valcos (Gandolfini), his frustrated wife Christine (O'Hara), their porn-obsessed teen son Brian (Zuckerman) and serious daughter Alicia (Applegate). For $250,000, the Valcos agree to be Drew's rented relatives and indulge his Christmas dreams. Comedic embarrassment follows resulting in a few, brief, reluctant chuckles. **92m/C VHS, DVD.** US Ben Affleck, James Gandolfini, Christina Applegate, Catherine O'Hara, Josh Zuckerman, Bill Macy, Jennifer Morrison, Stephen (Steve) Root; **D:** Mike Mitchell; **W:** Deborah Kaplan, Harry Elfont, Jeffrey Ventimilia, Joshua Sternin; **C:** Peter Collinson, Tom Priestley; **M:** Randy Edelman.

Surviving Desire ♪♪♪ 1991 Donovan plays Jude, a neurotic, romantic English professor who falls madly in love with an independently minded student, Sophie. Unfortunately, Sophie is more interested in how the seduction will advance her writing than how it will affect her life. The lovers explore their brief affair by analyzing every emotion and motive in a series of quirky conversations. Intelligent, amusing, and stylized film from director Hartley. The tape also includes two Hartley shorts: "Theory of Achievement" and "Ambition." **86m/C VHS, DVD.** Martin Donovan, Mary B. Ward, Matt Malloy, Rebecca Nelson; **D:** Hal Hartley; **M:** Randy Edelman.

Surviving Picasso ♪♪½ 1996 (R) Merchant-Ivory team takes time off from bodice-rippers to tear into the personal life of the Cubist legend, Pablo Picasso. Takes an unglamourous look at the mythically famous artist, focusing on the rocky ten-year affair with Françoise Gilot (newcomer McElhone), who met the artist in Nazi-occupied Paris when she was 22 and he was 62. Hopkins is well-cast as the insufferable senior and adds a strong dose of charm to soften his portrayal. Scores high tech credits, especially production design and frequent collaborator Luciana Arrighi. Unfortunately adapted from the decidedly one-sided biography "Picasso: Creator and Destroyer" by controversial author Arianna Huffington. Denied use of the artist's works by his estate, the filmmakers settled for some "work in progress" replicas. **126m/C VHS.** Anthony Hopkins, Natascha (Natasha) McElhone, Julianne Moore, Joss Ackland, Joan Plowright, Diane Venora, Peter Eyre, Jane Lapotaire, Joseph Maher, Bob Peck; **D:** James Ivory; **W:** Ruth Prawer Jhabvala; **C:** Tony Pierce-Roberts; **M:** Richard Robbins.

Surviving the Game ♪ 1994 (R) Poorly made hunt-the-human story. Homeless Ice-T is hired by a group of men to assist them on their annual hunt. But wait, he's the prey. Unbelievable premise pits the streetwise, down and out Ice-T against the savvy and weapons rich group—and he beats them at their own game. Few high-impact action sequences. The violence, although there isn't as much as might be expected, is graphic. **94m/C VHS, DVD.** Rutger Hauer, Ice-T, F. Murray Abraham, Gary Busey, Charles S. Dutton, John C. McGinley, William McNamara, Jeff Corey; **D:** Ernest R. Dickerson; **W:** Eric Bernt; **C:** Bojan Bazelli; **M:** Stewart Copeland.

Survivor ♪ 1980 A jetliner crashes, leaving but one survivor, the pilot, who is then plagued by visions, tragedies, and ghosts of dead passengers. Viewers also suffer. **91m/C VHS, DVD.** AU Robert Powell, Jenny Agutter, Joseph Cotten, Angela Punch McGregor; **D:** David Hemmings; **W:** David Ambrose; **M:** Brian May.

Survivor ♪♪ 1987 (R) A lone warrior on a post-nuclear holocaust wasteland battles a megalomaniac ruler. Moll as the evil villian is watchable, but overall the film is a wasteland, too. **92m/C VHS.** Chip (Christopher) Mayer, Richard Moll, Sue Kiel; **D:** Michael Shackleton.

The Survivor ♪♪ 1998 (R) Yet another evil-warrior sci-fi where Earth is a mess—this time it's a rainforest-covered penal colony run by the violent Kyla (Moll) and his vicious minions. When the president's (Herd) spaceship crashes, convicted murderer Tarkin (Declle) tries to save him from Kyla. Not bad special effects and lots of action. **95m/C VHS.** Richard Moll, Xavier Declle, Richard Herd; **D:** Nick Davis. **VIDEO**

Survivors ♪♪ 1983 (R) Two unemployed men find themselves the target of a hit man, whom they have identified in a robbery attempt. One of the men goes gun-crazy protecting himself. Uneven comedy with wild Williams and laid-back Matthau. **102m/C VHS, DVD.** Robin Williams, Walter Matthau, Jerry Reed, John Goodman, James Wainwright, Kristen Vigard; **D:** Michael Ritchie; **W:** Michael Leeson; **C:** Billy Williams; **M:** Paul Chihara.

Susan and God ♪♪ 1940 *The Gay Mrs. Trexel* 1940 A selfish socialite returns from Europe and starts practicing a new religion, much to the dismay of her friends and family. Despite her preaching, her own domestic life is falling apart and she realizes that her preoccupation and selfish ways have caused a strain on her marriage and her relationship with her daughter. An excellent script and a fine performance from Crawford make this a highly satisfying film. **115m/B VHS.** Joan Crawford, Fredric March, Ruth Hussey, John Carroll, Rita Hayworth, Nigel Bruce, Bruce Cabot, Rose Hobart, Rita Quigley, Marjorie Main, Gloria De Haven; **D:** George Cukor; **W:** Anita Loos.

Susan Lenox: Her Fall and Rise ♪♪ 1931 *The Rise of Helga; Rising to Fame* 1931 Garbo, the daughter of an abusive farmer, falls into the arms of the handsome Gable to escape an arranged marriage. Both stars are miscast, but the well-paced direction and **84m/B VHS.** Greta Garbo, Clark Gable, Jean Hersholt, John Miljan, Alan Hale, Hale Hamilton; **D:** Robert Z. Leonard; **C:** William H. Daniels.

Susana ♪♪♪ 1951 Minor though still interesting Bunuel, in which a sexy delinquent young girl is rescued from vagrancy by a Spanish family, and how she subsequently undermines the family's structure through sexual allurement and intimidation. In Spanish with English subtitles. **87m/B VHS.** MX Rosita Quintana, Fernando Soler, Victor Manuel Mendoza, Matilde Palou; **D:** Luis Bunuel.

Susan Slept Here ♪♪½ 1954 While researching a movie on juvenile delinquents, a Hollywood script writer (Powell) is given custody of a spunky 18-year-old delinquent girl (Reynolds) during the Christmas holidays. Cute sex comedy. Based on the play "Susan," by Alex Gottlieb and Steve Fisher. **98m/C VHS.** Dick Powell, Debbie Reynolds, Anne Francis; **D:** Frank Tashlin.

Susanna Pass ♪♪ 1949 Oil deposits underneath a fish hatchery lake attract bad guys. They set off explosions to destroy the fishery, but game warden Rogers investigates. Minor outing for Roy. **67m/C VHS, DVD.** Roy Rogers, Dale Evans, Estelita Rodriguez, Martin Garralaga, Robert Emmett Keane, Lucien Littlefield, Douglas Fowley; **D:** William Witney.

Susannah of the Mounties ♪♪½ 1939 (PG) An adorable young girl is left orphaned after a wagon train massacre and is adopted by a Mountie. An Indian squabble gives Shirley a chance to play little peacemaker and teach Scott how to tap dance, too. Could she be any cuter? Available colorized. **78m/B VHS.** Shirley Temple, Randolph Scott, Margaret Lockwood, J. Farrell MacDonald, Moroni Olsen, Victor Jory; **D:** William A. Seiter; **C:** Arthur C. Miller.

Suspect 🐾🐾½ 1987 (R) An overworked Washington, DC, public defender (Cher) is assigned to a controversial murder case in which her client is a deaf-mute, skid-row bum. A cynical lobbyist on the jury illegally researches the case himself. They work together to uncover a far-reaching conspiracy. Unrealistic plot, helped along by good performances and tight direction. 101m/C VHS, DVD. Dennis Quaid, Cher, Liam Neeson, E. Katherine Kerr, Joe Mantegna, John Mahoney, Philip Bosco; D: Peter Yates; W: Eric Roth; C: Billy Williams; M: Michael Kamen.

Suspect Device 🐾½ 1995 Roger Corman Presents: Suspect Device 1995 Nonsensical (R) Cop with a past is assigned to a task force that's hunting down a sadistic vigilante. 97m/C VHS, Richard Grieco, Nick Mancuso, Jim Byrnes; D: Clay Borris; M: Kevin Kiner.

Suspect Zero 🐾½ 2004 (R) Maverick FBI agent Thomas Mackelway (Eckhart) has been demoted to a backwater bureau just in time to discover a serial killer whose M.O. is that he kills other serial killers and likes to taunt the fed via fax. Soon, Mackelway is joined by no-nonsense former partner/lover Fran Kulok (Moss in a thankless role). Eckhart's generally wasted as the standard troubled good guy (he works better in edgier roles) while Kingsley does what a professional does—make the most of an absurd movie. Merrige apparently prefers to set an artistic moodiness rather than worry about pace, plot, or coherence. 99m/C DVD. Aaron Eckhart, Ben Kingsley, Carrie-Anne Moss, Harry J. Lennix, William Mapother, Ellen Bake, Chloe Russell, Kevin Chamberlin; D: E. Elias Merhige; W: Zak Penn, Billy Ray; C: Michael Chapman; M: Clint Mansell.

Suspended Alibi 🐾½ 1956 British crime-drama about an adulterous man unjustly accused when his alibi is murdered. Overlock the convenient coincidence. 64m/B VHS, GB Patrick Holt, Honor Blackman, Andrew Keir, Valentine Dyall; D: Alfred Shaughnessy.

Suspended Animation 🐾🐾 2002 Animator Thomas Kempton (McArthur) takes a break from his work to go snowmobiling with some buddies. He gets separated from the group and taken captive by a couple of crazy sisters who have a hatred of men and a love of cannibalism. Menacing and engaging script mixes the "It seny" with comic spatterings. Hancock goes old-school but fails to overcome structural flaws. 114m/C DVD. US Alex McArthur, Sage Allen, Rebecca Harrell, Laura Esterman, Maria Cina; D: John Hancock; W: Dorothy Tristan; C: Misha (Mikhail) Suslov; M: Christopher Lennerz. CABLE

Suspicion 🐾🐾🐾½ 1941 Alfred Hitchcock's suspense thriller about a woman who gradually realizes she is married to a killer and may be next on his list. An excellent production unravels at the end due to RKO's insistence that Grant retain his "attractive" image. This forced uncertainness to leave his guilt or innocence undetermined. Available colorized. 99m/B VHS, DVD. Cary Grant, Joan Fontaine, Cedric Hardwicke, Nigel Bruce, May Whitty, Leo G. Carroll, Heather Angel; D: Alfred Hitchcock; C: Harry Stradling Sr.; M: Franz Waxman. Oscars '41: Actress (Fontaine); N.Y. Film Critics '41: Actress (Fontaine).

Suspicion 🐾🐾 1987 Remake of the chilling Hitchcock tale. Newlywed bride is consumed with fears about her wealthy new husband. The suspense builds as she comes to suspect that she is married to a cold-blooded killer. Curtin in way over her head. 97m/C VHS, Jane Curtin, Anthony Andrews, Jeremy Northam, Ron Pember, Betsy Blair, Michael Siberry, Vivian Pickles, Jo Anderson; D: Andrew Grieve. ·

Suspicion 🐾🐾 2003 Carol Finnegan (Redman) is celebrating her 20th wedding anniversary to husband Mark (Dunbar) when she begins receiving a series of anonymous emails accusing Mark of having an affair with his secretary. She tells Mark, who dismisses them as the work of a disgruntled ex-employee, but Carol's suspicions grow. Then the secretary is murdered and Carol who is accuser of the crime. 150m/C DVD, GB Amanda Redman, Adrian Dunbar, Saskia Reeves, Adam Kotz; D: Barney McCall.

Suspicious Agenda 🐾🐾½ 1994 Leila's answer to a stale marriage and the small-town blues? Start hooking with guests at the seedy motel job of course! And wait for that very special lunatic to come along and steal her heart and put her up a time or two. 92m/C VHS, DVD, Molly Parker, Callum Keith Rennie, Mary Kate Walsh, Joel Bissonnette, Deanna Milligan, Sarah Jane Redmond, Norman Armour, Byron Lucas, Michael Shanks, Don S. Davis, Jay Brazeau, Gillian Barber, Paul Jarrett, Bruno Verdoni, Ingrid Tesch, Bill Dow; D: Lynne Stopkewich; W: Lynne Stopkewich; C: Gregory Middleton; M: Don MacCollad. VIDEO

Suspiria 🐾🐾🐾 1977 (R) An American dancer enters a weird European ballet academy and finds they teach more than movement as bodies begin piling up. Sometimes weak plot is aided by great, but gory special effects, fine photography, good music, and a chilling opening sequence. Also available in unrated version. 99m/C VHS, DVD. IT Jessica Harper, Joan Bennett, Alida Valli, Udo Kier, Stefania Casini, Flavio Bucci, Barbara Magnolfi, Rudolf Schneider; D: Dario Argento; W: Dario Argento, Daria Nicolodi; C: Luciano Tovoli; M: Dario Argento, The Goblins.

Suture 🐾🐾 1993 Quirky thriller is a homage to late '50s melodramas with its strange tale of mistaken identity. Vincent wants to hide his unsavory past by assuming the identity of his estranged half-brother, Clay, which should be difficult since Vincent is white and Clay is black but the movie's premise is that everyone confuses the two. Vincent tries to kill Clay in an explosion but he survives—with amnesia and with everyone in the hospital assuring him he's Vincent. Shifting points of view as the viewer as well. Perfect film debut for the directors. 96m/B VHS, DVD. Dennis Haysbert, Sab Shimono, Mel Harris, Michael (M.K.) Harris, Dina Merrill, David Graf, Fran Ryan; D: Scott McGehee, David Siegel; W: Scott McGehee, David Siegel; C: Greg Gardner; M: Sundance '94: Cinematog.

Suzanne 🐾½ 1980 (R) Set in 1950s Quebec, the story of a good woman whose criminal boyfriend leaves her pregnant when he is sent to prison. Ten years later, he returns, threatening their happy marriage. Confused script can't be saved by valiant cast. 103m/C VHS, CA Jennifer Dale, Gabriel Arcand, Winston Rekert, Ken Pogue; D: Robin Spry; W: Robin Spry; C: Miklos Lente; M: François Cousineau.

Suzy 🐾🐾½ 1936 Harlow's fourth film and her only one with Grant is a mixture of romance, action, and comedy set during WWI. Grant plays a French flier who falls in love with Harlow, although she is married to Tone. Excellent air footage and some good funny scenes keep this film moving right along. Even has Grant singing hit song, "Did I Remember?" 99m/B VHS, Jean Harlow, Franchot Tone, Cary Grant, Benita Hume, Lewis Stone, Inez Courtney; D: George Fitzmaurice.

Svengali 🐾 1931 A music teacher uses his hypnotic abilities to manipulate one of his singing students and make her a star. Soon the young woman is singing for sell-out crowds, but only if her teacher is present. Barrymore in a hypnotic performance. Adapted from "Trilby" by George Du Maurier. Remade in 1955 and 1983. 76m/B VHS, DVD. John Barrymore, Marian Marsh, Donald Crisp; D: Archie Mayo; W: J. Grubb Alexander; C: Barney McGill.

Svengali 🐾🐾½ 1955 Limp remake of the 1931 film about Trilby, an artist's model, falling under the mesmerizing spell of the title character, who is determined to make her into a famous singer. Chiefly notable for its visuals which were based on the illustrations from the original novel "Trilby" by George du Maurier. 82m/C VHS. GB Hildegarde Knef, Donald Wolfit, Terence Morgan, Paul Rogers, David Kossoff; D: Noel Langley; W: Noel Langley.

Svengali 🐾🐾½ 1983 Flamboyant but faded music star O'Toole mentors Foster, a young pop singer looking for stardom. Boring remake of the Barrymore classic. 96m/C VHS, DVD. Peter O'Toole, Jodie Foster, Elizabeth Ashley, Larry Joshua, Pamela Blair, Barbara Byrne, Holly Hunter; D: Anthony Harvey; M: John Barry. TV

Swamp Fire 🐾🐾½ 1946 Mississippi river-boat captain Weissmuller, wrestles alligators and battles with Crabbe for the woman he loves in this turgid drama. Look for Janssen in an early screen performance. 69m/B VHS, DVD. Johnny Weissmuller, Virginia Grey, Buster Crabbe, Carol Thurston, Edwin Maxwell, Pedro de Cordoba, Pierre Watkin, David Janssen; D: William H. Pine; W: Daniel Mainwaring; C: Fred H. Jackman Jr.; M: Rudolph (Rudy) Schrager.

Swamp of the Lost Monster 🐾 1965 An incredible Mexican horror/western/musical that features a mucose-like monster that'll scare the cheese out of you. 88m/B VHS, MX Gaston Santos, Sarah Cabrera, Manuel Donde; D: Rafael Baledon Sr.

Swamp Thing 🐾🐾½ 1982 (PG) Overlooked camp drama about scientist accidentally turned into tragic half-vegetable half-man swamp creature, with government agent Barbeau caught in the middle, occasionally while topless. A vegetarian nightmare or ecology propaganda? You be the judge. Adapted from the comic book by Craven. 91m/C VHS, DVD. Adrienne Barbeau, Louis Jourdan, Ray Wise, Dick Durock; D: Wes Craven; W: Wes Craven; C: Robbie Greenberg; M: Harry Manfredini.

Swamp Women 🐾 words: Cruel Swamp 1955 Four escaped women convicts, known as the "Nardo Gang," chase after a stash of diamonds in this super cheap, super bad action adventure from cult director Corman. 73m/C VHS, Carole Mathews, Susan Cummings, Jonathan Haze, Jill Jarmyn, Ed Nelson, Lou Place; D: Roger Corman; W: David Stern; M: Elil Holman.

The Swan 🐾🐾½ 1925 Princess' arranged marriage with a prince is complicated by a poor man also in love with her. Classic romantic comedy of the silent era. Remade in 1956. Based on a play by Ferenc Molnar. 50m/B VHS. Adolphe Menjou, Ricardo Cortez, Frances Howard; D: Dimitri Buchowetzki.

The Swan 🐾🐾🐾 1956 A twist on the Cinderella story with Kelly (in her last film before her marriage) as the charming beauty waiting for her prince. Both Guinness, as the crown prince, and Jourdan, as her poor tutor, want her hand (and the rest of her.) Attractive cast, but story gets slow from time to time. Remake of a 1925 silent film. 112m/C VHS. Grace Kelly, Louis Jourdan, Alec Guinness, Jessie Royce Landis, Brian Aherne, Estelle Winwood; D: Charles Vidor; C: Joseph Ruttenberg, Robert L. Surtees.

The Swan Princess 🐾🐾 1994 (G) Formulaic prince-and-princess love story based loosely on "Swan Lake" takes a modern twist: Princess Ocette, offended by the emphasis her intended, Prince Derek, places on her beauty, flees the kingdom. She's kidnapped by the evil Rothbart, an enchanter who turns her into a swan able to take human form only when touched by moonlight. A snappy tro animal staff eventually helps Odette reunite with her newly P.C. love, with lots of zesty musical numbers and various Disney-inspired plot points along the way. Adults may yawn, but kiddies will be charmed just the same. 90m/C VHS, DVD. D: Richard Rich; W: Richard Rich, Brian Nissen; M: Lex de Azevedo; V: Jack Palance, Michelle Nicastro, Howard McGillin, Liz Callaway, John Cleese, Steven Wright, Steve Vinovich, Dakin Matthews, Sandy Duncan, Mark Harelik, James Arrington, Davis Gaines, Joel McKinnon Miller.

The Swan Princess 2: Escape from Castle Mountain 🐾🐾½ 1997 (G) Heroine Odette changes into a swan to help husband Derek defeat evil magician Clavius. Some humor, decent animation, some nice tunes, and decent animation should keep the kids happy. It "That's What You Do for a Friend; The Magic of Love; You Gotta Love It." 75m/C VHS. DVD. D: Richard Rich; W: Brian Nissen; M: Lex de Azevedo; V: Michelle Nicastro, Douglas Sills, Jake Williamson, Christy Landers.

Swann 🐾½ 1996 Too many loose ends and weak direction from Benson Gyles (in her feature film debut) waste the efforts of a talented cast. Chicago-based writer Sarah Maloney (Richardson) is writing a biography of Mary Swann, whose murder victim of a backwater Ontario farmer, who secretly wrote poetry (and gets compared to Emily Dickinson). Sarah heads to Nadeau to meet with Mary's friend Rose (Fricker) and discovers she may have altered some of the published poetry but there's not much there to really care about. Based on a novel by Carol Shields. 98m/C VHS. GB CA Miranda Richardson, Brenda Fricker, Michael Ontkear, Sean McCann, John Neville, Sean Hewitt, Kyra Harper, David C.ibitt, Gerry Walter; D: Anna Benson Gyles; W: David Young; C: Gerald Packer; M: Richard Rodney Bennett.

Swann in Love 🐾🐾½ 1984 (R) A handsome, wealthy French aristocrat makes a fool of himself over a beautiful courtesan who cares nothing for him. Elegant production lacks spark. Based upon a section of Marcel Proust's "Remembrance of Things Past." In French with English subtitles or an English language version. 110m/C VHS, DVD. FR GE Jeremy Irons, Ornella Muti, Alain Delon, Fanny Ardant, Marie-Christine Barrault; D: Volker Schlondorff; W: Peter Brook, Jean-Claude Carrieradopoulos; C: Alex Phillips Jr.; M: Gershon Kingsley.

Swap Meet 🐾 1979 (R) Wacky teen sex comedy about shenanigans at a small town swap meet. Strictly bargain basement. 86m/C VHS, Ruth Cox, Deborah Richter, Danny Goldman, Cheryl Rixon, Jonathan) Gries; D: Brice Mack.

The Swap 🐾½ 1971 (R) Sam's Song Ex-con searches for his brother's killer. Muddled story uses clips from early De Niro film. 120m/C VHS DVD. Robert De Niro, Jared Martin, Sybil Danning, Terrayne Crawford, Martin Kelley; D: Jordan Leondopoulos; C: Alex Phillips Jr.; M: Gershon Kingsley.

The Swarm 🐾 1978 (PG) Low-brow insect contest as scientist Caine fends off a swarm of killer bees when they attack metro Houston. The bees are really just black spots painted on the film. And the acting is terrible. "B" movie on film, but it's still better than "The Bees." 115m/C VHS, DVD. Michael Caine, Katharine Ross, Richard Widmark, Lee Grant, Richard Chamberlain, Olivia de Havilland, Henry Fonda, Fred MacMurray, Patty Duke, Ben Johnson, Jose Ferrer, Slim Pickens, Bradford Dillman, Cameron Mitchell; D: Irwin Allen; W: Stirling Silliphant; C: Fred W. Koenekamp; M: Jerry Goldsmith.

Swashbuckler 🐾🐾 1976 (PG) Jaunty pirate returns from sea to find his friends held captive by dastardly dictator for their political views. He resorts them, and helps free an erstwhile despot. 101m/C VHS, DVD. Robert Shaw, James Earl Jones, Peter Boyle, Genevieve Bujold, Beau Bridges, Geoffrey Holder; D: James Goldstone; W: Jeffrey Bloom; C: Philip Lathrop; M: John Addison.

Swashbuckler ♂♂½ *The Scarlet Buccaneer* 1984 Eighteenth-century pirate farce that can't compete with Errol Flynn. **100m/C VHS.** *FR* Jean-Paul Belmondo, Marlene Jobert, Laura Antonelli, Michel Auclair, Julien Guiomar. *D:* Jean-Paul Rappeneau.

S.W.A.T. ♂♂½ **2003 (PG-13)** Hondo (Jackson) is the leader of the elite LAPD Special Weapons and Tactics unit. He and his crew have to guard captured drug lord Alex (Martinez) and move him into federal custody. Only Alex has an open offer of $100 mil to anyone who can free him. Above-average big screen version of the mid-seventies TV series provides the correct summer blockbuster mix of action, stunts, and humor, with just enough character development to make you care about the outcome, but not so much that you get bored. **111m/C VHS, DVD, Blu-ray Disc, UMD.** *US* Samuel L. Jackson, Colin Farrell, LL Cool J, Josh Charles, Michelle Rodriguez, Olivier Martinez, Jeremy Renner, Brian Van Holt, Reg E. Cathey, Larry Poindexter, Domenick Lombardozzi, Lucinda Jenney, Reed Edward Diamond; *Cameos:* Clark Johnson, Steve Forrest; *D:* Clark Johnson; *W:* David Ayer, David McKenna; *C:* Gabriel Beristain; *M:* Elliot Goldenthal.

Sweater Girls woof! 1978 (R) Sex comedy about two girls starting their own club called the "Sweater Girls." Terrible teen exploitaiton film. **90m/C VHS.** Charlene Tilton, Harry Moses, Meegan King, Noelle North, Kate Sarchet, Carol Selfinger, Tamara Barkley, Julie Parsons; *D:* Donald M. Jones.

Swedenhielms ♂♂½ 1935 A poor Swedish scientist struggles to support his family while hoping to win a Nobel prize, while his two sons get involved in a moneylending scandal. Bergman is the rich fiance of one son, to whom poverty is a puzzlement. Fine performances by Ekman and the 20-year-old Bergman (in her third film). In Swedish with English subtitles. **92m/B VHS.** *SW* Gosta Ekman, Karin Swanstrom, Bjorn Berglund, Hakan Westergren, Tutta Rolf, Ingrid Bergman, Sigurd Wallen; *D:* Gustaf Molander.

Sweeney Todd: The Demon Barber of Fleet Street ♂♂½ 1984 A filmed performance of Sondheim's Tony-winning Broadway musical. Creepy thriller about a demon barber, his razor, and his wife's meatpies. **139m/C VHS, DVD.** *GB* Angela Lansbury, George Hearn; *D:* Harold Prince; *M:* Stephen Sondheim.

Sweeney Todd: The Demon Barber of Fleet Street ♂♂♂ 2007 (R) Some critics seemed to think that this adaptation of the Stephen Sondheim Broadway musical was too gory. Well, it's true, it's a lot harder to deal with buckets of blood onstage than in the movies, and Burton does seem to revel in his subject matter, which happens to be a singing, throat-slitting serial killer whose victims get turned into meat pies in dank, 19th-century London. A real toe-tapper that is. Sweeney (Depp) was unfairly transported to Australia when corrupt judge Turpin (Rickman) coveted his wife and daughter. Now years later, barber Sweeney has returned (unrecognizable) to exact his revenge, partnered in crime by his equally corpse-like (and ever-loving) landlady Mrs. Lovett (Bonham Carter). Not a direct adaptation (Burton omits and abridges songs and does some reshaping) and neither the Depp nor Bonham Carter are singers, but you have to admire the sheer chutzpah. **117m/C DVD.** *US* Johnny Depp, Helena Bonham-Carter, Alan Rickman, Timothy Spall, Sacha Baron Cohen, Jayne Wisner, Jamie Campbell Bower, Edward Sanders; *D:* Tim Burton; *W:* John Logan; *C:* Darius Wolski; *M:* Stephen Sondheim. *Oscars '07:* Art Dir./Set Dec.; *Golden Globes '08:* Actor—Mus./Comedy (Depp), Film—Mus./Comedy.

The Sweeper ♂♂½ 1995 (R) LA cop Mark Goddard (Howell) has a problem—his suspects have a bad habit of dying in his custody. Then he's recruited by a secret police organization whose aim is to dispense their own brand of deadly justice and Mark discovers a key to his troubled past and the murder of his cop father (Fahey). **101m/C VHS, DVD.** *C:* Thomas Howell, Ed Lauter, Cynda Williams, Jeff Fahey; *D:* Joseph Merhi; *W:* William Applegate Jr.; *C:* Ken Blakey; *M:* K. Alexander (Alex) Wilkinson.

Sweepers ♂♂ 1999 (R) Former land mine sweeper Christian Erickson (Lundgren) is called out of retirement to help bomb expert Michelle Flynn (Stansfield) uncover a terrorist plan to plant landmines in the U.S. **96m/C VHS, DVD.** Dolph Lundgren, Claire Stansfield, Bruce Payne; *D:* Darby Black; *W:* Darby Black, Kevin Bernhardt. **VIDEO**

Sweet Adeline ♂♂ 1926 Small-time hayseed makes it big in the music business while brother steals his girl back home. Not easily put off, young songster perseveres. **60m/B VHS.** Charles Ray, Gertrude Olmstead, Jack Clifford, Ida Lewis; *D:* Jerome Storm.

Sweet Adeline ♂♂½ 1935 Dunne attracts all the men in her father's Hoboken beer garden but Woods plays the songwriter with whom she finds real love. Wonderful score. ♪Play Us a Polka, Dot; Here Am I; We Were So Young; Why Was I Born?; Mollie O'Donahue; Lonely Feet; 'Twas Not So Long Ago; Don't Ever Leave Me. **87m/B VHS.** Irene Dunne, Donald Woods, Hugh Herbert, Ned Sparks, Joseph Cawthorn, Louis Calhern; *D:* Mervyn LeRoy; *M:* Jerome Kern, Oscar Hammerstein.

Sweet and Lowdown ♂♂♂½ 1999 (PG-13) Slight jazzy comedy, set in the '30s, traces the up-and-down career of fictional musician Emmet Ray (Penn), who's haunted by the fact that he's the second-best jazz guitarist in the world (Django Reinhardt is the first). However talented Emmet is musically, he's scum as a human being, abandoning Hattie (Morton), the mute laundress who turns out to be the love of his life in favor of wealthy writer Blanche (Thurman). Fine cast, good look, great music. **95m/C VHS, DVD.** Sean Penn, Samantha Morton, Uma Thurman, Brian Markinson, Anthony LaPaglia, Gretchen Mol, Vincent Guastaferro, John Waters, Kellie Overbey, Michael Sprague, Woody Allen; *D:* Woody Allen; *W:* Woody Allen; *C:* Fei Zhao; *M:* Dick Hyman.

Sweet Beat ♂ *The Amorous Sex* 1959 A young woman gets a chance to become a singer when she reaches the finals of a British beauty contest. Pedestrian story enlivened by music from popular British bands of the time. **66m/B VHS.** *GB* Julie Amber, Sheldon Lawrence, Iv Bauer, Billy Myles; *D:* Ronnie Albert; *C:* S.D. Onions.

Sweet Bird of Youth ♂♂♂ 1962 An acclaimed adaptation of the Tennessee Williams play. A handsome drifter who travels with an aging movie queen to help him small Florida hometown, hoping she'll get him into a movie career. However, coming home turns into a big mistake, as the town boss wants revenge on Chance for seducing his daughter. Heavenly. Williams's original stage ending was cleaned up, providing a conventional "happy" movie ending for the censors. Remade for TV in 1989 with Elizabeth Taylor and Mark Harmon in the lead roles. **120m/C VHS, DVD.** Paul Newman, Geraldine Page, Ed Begley Sr., Mildred Dunnock, Rip Torn, Shirley Knight, Madeleine Sherwood, Kelly Thordsen; *D:* Richard Brooks; *W:* Richard Brooks; *C:* Milton Krasner. *Oscars '62:* Support. Actor (Begley); *Golden Globes '63:* Actress—Drama (Page).

Sweet Bird of Youth ♂♂♂ 1989 (R) TV remake of the Tennessee Williams's play, which was filmed for the big screen in 1962, with Harmon and Taylor having the unenviable task of following in the roles played by Paul Newman and Geraldine Page. She is an egotistical, has-been movie star and he is her ambitious gigolo who wants a movie career of his own. Unfortunately, the trouble that drove him from his Florida hometown is still there when he reappears, actress in tow. Things don't bode well. The TV production uses Williams's original ending, which was cleaned up for a "happier" version in the '62 film. **97m/C VHS.** Elizabeth Taylor, Mark Harmon, Rip Torn, Valerie Perrine, Ruta Lee, Seymour Cassel, Kevin Geer, Michael Wilding Jr.; *D:* Nicolas Roeg; *W:* Gavin Lambert; *M:* Ralph Burns. **TV**

Sweet Charity ♂♂♂ 1969 An ever-optimistic dime-a-dance girl has a hard time finding a classy guy to marry. MacLaine is appealing in this big-budget version of the popular Broadway musical by Neil Simon (derived from Fellini's "Notti di Cabiria"). Fosse's debut as film director. ♪My Personal Property; It's a Nice Face; Hey, Big Spender; Rich Man's Frug; If My Friends Could See Me Now; There's Gotta Be Something Better Than This; Rhythm of Life; Sweet Charity; I'm a Brass Band. **148m/C VHS, DVD.** Shirley MacLaine, Chita Rivera, John McMartin, Paula Kelly, Sammy Davis Jr., Ricardo Montalban, Bud Cort; *D:* Bob Fosse; *C:* Robert L. Surtees; *M:* Cy Coleman.

Sweet Country ♂♂½ 1987 (R) During the overthrow of the Allende government in Chile, the lives of a Chilean family and an American couple intertwine. Heavy-going propaganda is a cross between tragedy and unintentional comedy. Made by the director of "Zorba the Greek." **147m/C VHS.** Jane Alexander, John Cullum, Carole Laure, Franco Nero, Joanna Pettet, Randy Quaid, Irene Papas, Jean-Pierre Aumont, Pierre Vaneck, Katia Dandoulaki; *D:* Michael Cacoyannis.

Sweet Country Road ♂♂½ 1983 A rock singer journeys to Nashville to try to cross over into country music. **95m/C VHS.** Buddy Knox, Kary Lynn, Gordy Trapp, Johnny Paycheck, Jeanne Pruett; *D:* Jack McCallum; *W:* Gordy Trapp; *C:* Cyrus Black.

Sweet Creek County War ♂ 1979 (PG) Retired sheriff must leave his quiet ranch to battle a greedy businessman. **90m/C VHS.** Richard Egan, Albert Salmi, Nita Talbot, Slim Pickens; *D:* J. Frank James; *W:* J. Frank James; *C:* Gregory von Berblinger; *M:* Richard Bowden.

Sweet Dreams ♂♂½ 1985 (PG-13) Biography of country singer Patsy Cline (Lange), who is struggling until her recording of "Walking After Midnight" becomes a hit. Her second marriage to fan Charlie Dick (Harris) begin to unravel as his drinking and her success both increase and Charlie turns abusive. Patsy's rise to stardom ended in an early death. Fine performances thoughout, with Lange lip-synching to Cline's original recordings. ♪Walking After Midnight; Crazy; Sweet Dreams; San Antonio Rose; Blue Moon of Kentucky; Lovesick Blues; Seven Lonely Days; Foolin' Around; Your Cheatin' Heart. **115m/C VHS, DVD.** Jessica Lange, Ed Harris, Ann Wedgeworth, David Clennon, John Goodman, James Staley, Gary Basaraba, P.J. Soles; *D:* Karel Reisz; *W:* Robert Getchell; *C:* Robbie Greenberg; *M:* Charles Gross.

Sweet Ecstasy ♂½ *Douce Violence;* *Sweet Violence* 1962 Wealthy shenanigans on the French Riviera. Olivier (Pezy) is the upright young man who can't sleep with anyone unless he's in love, much to sex bomb Elke's (Sommer) dismay. **75m/B VHS, DVD.** *FR* Elke Sommer, Pierre Brice, Christian Pezy, Claire Maurier; *D:* Max Pecas; *M:* Charles Aznavour. **VIDEO**

Sweet Evil ♂ 1995 (R) Naomi and Mike seek the help of a surrogate after a number of failed fertility treatments. Jenny seems to be perfect but after she moves into their home, they learn Jenny's got a nasty secret. **92m/C VHS, DVD.** Bridgette Wilson-Sampras, Peter Boyle, Scott Cohen, Eiko Matsuda, Claudette Nevins; *D:* Rene Eram. **VIDEO**

Sweet Evil ♂ 1998 Anthony Thurman is the owner of a club that specializes in exotic dancers and sometimes the married Anthony gets a little too involved with the entertainment. His wife knows about his habits and doesn't mind until one of Anthony's affairs uncovers an old secret that was better left hidden. **87m/C VHS, DVD.** Al Sapienza, Andrea Rlave, Douglas De Marco; *D:* Michael Paul Girard; *W:* Michael Paul Girard; *C:* Luis Escobar; *M:* Michael Paul Girard. **VIDEO**

Sweet 15 1990 A young Hispanic girl learns that there is more to growing up than parties when she learns her father is an illegal alien. Originally aired on PBS as part of the "Wonderworks" family movie series. **120m/C VHS, DVD.** Karla Montana, Panchito Gomez, Tony Plana, Jenny Gago, Susan Ruttan; *D:* Victoria Hochberg.

Sweet Georgia ♂ 1972 Soft-core star Jordan is a lusty wife whose husband is an alcoholic, so she has a roll in the hay with almost every other cast member. Lots of action, too, including a pitchfork fight. Ride 'em cowboy. **80m/C VHS, DVD.** Marsha Jordan, Barbara Mills, Gene Drew, Chuck Lawson; *D:* Edward Boles; *W:* Ron Hennessy; *M:* Hal Southern.

Sweet Hearts Dance ♂♂ 1988 (R) Parallel love stories follow two long-time friends, one just falling in love, the other struggling to keep his marriage together. Charming performances from all, but a slow pace undermines the film. **95m/C VHS, DVD.** Don Johnson, Jeff Daniels, Susan Sarandon, Elizabeth Perkins, Justin Henry, Holly Marie Combs; *D:* Robert Greenwald; *W:* Ernest Thompson; *C:* Tak Fujimoto; *M:* Richard Gibbs.

The Sweet Hereafter ♂♂♂½ 1996 (R) A schoolbus crash kills 14 children in the small town of Sam Dent, British Columbia. Big city lawyer Mitchell Stephens (Holm) arrives to persuade the townspeople to begin a class-action suit targeting city authorities and the bus manufacturer, while struggling to deal with his drug-addicted daughter Zoe (Banks). Paralyzed teenaged survivor Nicole Burnell (Polley) tries to cope with the aftermath of the tragedy as does widower Billy Ansell (Greenwood), whose two children died in the crash. But the case soon begins to tear the reeling town apart as everyone struggles with loss and fate. Egoyan's intimate, lyrical adaptation of the novel by Russell Banks is filled with wonderful performances, particularly by Polley. **110m/C VHS, DVD.** *CA* Ian Holm, Sarah Polley, Bruce Greenwood, Tom McCamus, Arsinee Khanjian, Alberta Watson, Gabrielle Rose, Maury Chaykin, David Hemblen, Earl Pastko, Peter Donaldson, Caerthan Banks, Brook Johnson, Stephanie Morgenstern; *D:* Atom Egoyan; *W:* Atom Egoyan; *C:* Paul Sarossy; *M:* Mychael Danna. *Cannes '97:* Grand Jury Prize; *Genie '97:* Actor (Holm), Cinematog., Director (Egoyan), Film, Film Editing, Sound, Score; *Ind. Spirit '98:* Foreign Film; *Toronto-City '97:* Canadian Feature Film.

Sweet Home Alabama ♂♂½ 2002 (PG-13) Rich hot city guy or hot poor country guy? That's the choice NYC fashion designer Melanie (Witherspoon) has to make in this amiable romantic comedy. The dueling beaus are Andrew (Dempsey), son of NYC mayor Bergen, and Jake (Lucas), Melanie's high school sweetheart (and current husband) back home in Alabama who still has the hots for her. When Andrew pops the question in high style, Melanie accepts and then races off to Alabama to finalize matters with Jake, who hasn't given her a divorce. Complications abound where sparks fly with Jake and Mel's snooty city friends discover her well-hidden, trailer-trash upbringing. Witherspoon plays her trademark plucky act well, elevating a so-so vehicle. **105m/C VHS, DVD.** *US* Reese Witherspoon, Josh(ua) Lucas, Patrick Dempsey, Candice Bergen, Mary Kay Place, Fred Ward, Jean Smart, Ethan (Randall) Embry, Melanie Lynskey, Courtney Gains, Rhona Mitra, Mary Lynn Rajskub, Nathan Lee Graham, Dakota Fanning; *D:* Andy Tennant; *W:* C. Jay Cox; *C:* Andrew Dunn; *M:* George Fenton.

Sweet Hostage ♂♂♂ 1975 Escaped mental patient kidnaps uneducated farm girl and holds her captive in a remote cabin. Blair and Sheen turn in good performances. Adaptation of Nathaniel Benchley's "Welcome to Xanadu." **93m/C VHS.** Linda Blair, Martin Sheen, Jeanne Cooper, Lee DeBroux, Dehl Berti, Bert Remsen; *D:* Lee Philips. **TV**

Sweet Insanity woof! 2006 (R) Despite being troubled by nightmares (no doubt caused by a series of local murders), high schooler Stacey (Hoyle) invites strange transfer student Christina (Firgens) to her party when her parents go out of town for the weekend. Boring and stupid even by teen slasher standards. **87m/C DVD.** *US* Rebekah Hoyle, MacKenzie Firgens, David Fine, Josh McRae; *D:* Daniel Hess; *W:* Daniel Hess, Adam Weis; *C:* Kenn Ferro, Virgil Harper; *M:* Jesper Kyd.

Sweet Jane 🎬🎬½ 1998 Teenaged Tony (Gordon-Levitt) has AIDS and no family. He becomes initiated with HIV-positive heroin addict Jane (Mathis), whom he sees in the hospital, and follows her into a dangerous street life. Although Jane treats him badly, Tony sticks around to "protect" her and they slowly establish a mutually dependent relationship that offers surrogate family ties and solace for them both. **83m/C VHS, DVD.** Joseph Gordon-Levitt, Sue Gayton; Samara MaryWronov; **D:** Joe Gayton; **W:** Joe Gayton; **C:** Greg Littlewood; **M:** Walter Werzowa.

Sweet Justice 🎬🎬 1992 (R) This time its the women who get to be commandos, have all the adventures, and get revenge on various scum. The nominal plotline has Sunny Justice (Carter) and her group of gal-warriors avenging the sadistic murder of a friend. Martial arts, weapons, and action galore. **92m/C VHS, DVD.** Finn Carter, Kathleen Kinmont, Marc Singer, Frank Gorshin, Mickey Rooney; **D:** Allen Plone; **W:** Allen Plone.

Sweet Killing 🎬🎬 1993 (R) A banker murders his shrewish wife to be with another woman. He thinks he has the perfect alibi, but then it his fictitious excuse comes to life when a mysterious stranger begins stalking him. Based on the novel "Quatthrough" by Agnes Hall. **87m/C VHS, DVD.** Anthony (Corlan) Higgins, F. Murray Abraham, Leslie Hope, Michael Ironside, Andrea Ferreol; **D:** Eddy Matalon; **W:** Eddy Matalon.

Sweet Land 🎬🎬½ 2005 (PG) Inge Oltenberg (Reaser) becomes a mail-order bride for Norwegian-American farmer Olaf (Guinee) in Minnesota just after WWI. But the fact that she is German (and knows minimal English) causes strong feelings within the community and the local minister (Heard) refuses to marry them. Olaf moves into the barn to preserve decorum while Inge tries to settle in, but they fall in love. Sweet story, told in flashbacks. **110m/C DVD.** Elizabeth Reaser, Tim Guinee, Alan Cumming, John Heard, Alex Kingston, Ned Beatty, Lois Smith, Paul Sanc; **D:** Ali Selim; **W:** Ali Selim; **C:** David Tumbley; **M:** Mark Orton.

Sweet Liberty 🎬🎬 1986 (PG) Alda's hometown is overwhelmed by Hollywood chaos during the filming of a movie version of his novel about the American Revolution. Pleasant but predictable. **107m/C VHS, DVD.** Alan Alda, Michael Caine, Michelle Pfeiffer, Bob Hoskins, Lillian Gish; **D:** Alan Alda; **W:** Alan Alda; **M:** Bruce Broughton.

Sweet Lies 🎬🎬 1988 (R) An insurance investigator tracking a scam artist in Paris is preyed upon by a group of single women betting one another that any man can be seduced. Slow comedy. **96m/C VHS.** Treat Williams, Joanna Pacula, Julianne Phillips, Laura Manszky, Norbert Weisser, Marilyn Dodds Frank; **D:** Nathalie Delon; **M:** Trevor Jones.

Sweet Light in a Dark Room 🎬🎬🎬 Julia a Tma; Romeo, Julieta a Tma; Romeo, Juliet and Darkness 1960 A student in Prague during the Nazi Occupation hides a Jewish girl. He falls in love with her but becomes the suspect in the murder of a Nazi officer. Directed by the great Czech filmmaker Weiss who was himself forced to leave his country during Nazi occupation. In Czech with English subtitles. **93m/B VHS. CZ** Ivan Mistrik, Dana Smutna; **D:** Jiri Weiss.

Sweet Lorraine 🎬🎬🎬 1987 (PG-13) A bittersweet, nostalgic comedy about the staff and clientele of a deteriorating Catskills hotel on the eve of its closing. **91m/C VHS, DVD.** Maureen Stapleton, Lee Richardson, Trini Alvarado, Freddie Roman, John Bedford Lloyd, Giancarlo Esposito, Edie Falco, Todd Graff, Evan Handler; **D:** Steve Gomer; **M:** Michael Zeller, Shelly Altman; **M:** Richard Robbins.

Sweet Love, Bitter 🎬🎬🎬 It Won't Rub Off, Baby; Black Love, White Love 1967 The downfall of a black jazz saxophonist in the 1950s. The character is loosely based on the life of legendary musician Charlie "Bird" Parker. Alto sax man Charles McPherson dubs Gregory's solos. Adapted from the novel "Night Song" by John A. Williams. **92m/C VHS.** Dick Gregory, Don Murray, Diane Varsi, Robert Hooks; **D:** Herbert Danska; **W:** Lewis Jacobs, Herbert Danska; **M:** Mal Waldron.

Sweet Movie 🎬🎬 1975 A provocative cult classic concerning a South African tycoon who purchases a virgin bride and then exploits her sexually. In English and French with subtitles. **120m/C VHS, DVD. CA FR GE** Carole Laure, Pierre Clementi, Sami Frey, Anna Prucnal, Jane Mallet, John Vernon; **D:** Dusan Makavejev; **W:** Dusan Makavejev; **C:** Pierre Lhomme; **M:** Manos Hadjidakis.

Sweet Murder WOOF! 1993 (R) 'Single White Female' rip-off features Udy allowing Davidtz to share her apartment— with nasty consequences. **101m/C VHS.** Helene Udy, Embeth Davidtz, Russel Todd; **D:** Perceval Rubens.

Sweet Nothing 🎬🎬🎬 1996 (R) Wall Street up-and-comer Angel (Imperioli) is given some crack by a buddy (Calderon) to celebrate the birth of his child. This starts a downward spiral into addiction and dealing. At first, his wife Monika (Sorvino) goes along, but as Angel deteriorates, she learns not to trust him. Excellent performances by Imperioli and Sorvino—no avoid over-the-top theatrics. Script provides a realistic look at how addiction affects real people, and steers clear of obvious cliches. Based on diaries found in a Bronx apartment building. Film's producers tracked down the author and paid for his rehab. **89m/C VHS.** Michael Imperioli, Mira Sorvino, Paul Calderon, Billie Neal; **D:** Gary Winick; **W:** Lee Drysdale.

Sweet November 🎬🎬 1968 Tearjerker stars Dennis as Sara Deever, a terminally ill woman who shares her apartment with a different lover each month. She helps the guy with his particular hang-up and he helps her, well, live. That is until Mr. November (Newley) refuses to leave when his month is up because he's fallen in love. Remade in 2001. **113m/C VHS.** Sandy Dennis, Anthony Newley, Theodore Bikel, Burr de Benning, Sandy Baron, Marj Dusay, Martin West, Virginia Vincent, King Moody; **D:** Robert Ellis Miller; **W:** Herman Raucher; **C:** Daniel F. Fapp; **M:** Michel Legrand.

Sweet November 🎬🎬½ 2001 (PG-13) Stale and contrived remake of the 1968 film stars Theron as a kooky, carefree boho looking to rehabilitate uptight businessmen one month at a time, until her inevitable demise from a mysterious illness. Nelson Moss (Reeves) is Mr. November, who is invited to live with Sara in exchange for losing his cell phone, monk-lysuit, and too-tense attitude for a day at the beach (literally). As the November holiday looms and Sara's secret is sappily revealed, we can give thanks that the movie is almost over. Improbable story with decent performance by Theron, while Reeves is just so-so, shocking no one. **114m/C VHS, DVD.** Keanu Reeves, Charlize Theron, Jason Isaacs, Greg Germann, Liam Aiken, Lauren Graham, Michael Rosenbaum, Robert Joy, Jason Kravits, Frank Langella; **D:** Pat O'Connor; **W:** Kurt Voelker; **C:** Edward Lachman; **M:** Christopher Young.

Sweet Perfection 🎬🎬 The Perfect Model 1990 (R) Jackson plans a big promotion for her beauty contest. Who will be voted the "Perfect Woman?" Tired premise, but it has its moments. **90m/C VHS, DVD.** Stoney Jackson, Anthony Norman McKay, Catero Colbert, Liza Cruzat, Reggie Theus, Tatiana Tumbtzen; **D:** Darryl Roberts; **C:** Sam Sako.

Sweet Poison 🎬🎬 1991 (R) Bobby Stiles is a ruthless criminal who has just broken out of prison. He wants to get home and settle the score with his brother, who actually committed the crime Bobby was imprisoned for. Henry and Charlene are traveling cross-country when Bobby crosses their path and forces them to drive him home. Bobby's not too busy eluding the police to notice that his captives' marriage is a little shaky—and that Charlene is attractive and sexy. As Bobby and Charlene get closer husband Henry just becomes another problem. **101m/C VHS.** Steven Bauer, Patrice Healy, Edward Herrmann; **D:** Brian Grant.

Sweet 16 🎬🎬 1981 (R) Serial killings in Texas town begin to set off muffled alarms in big head of sheriff Hopkins. Six-teen-year-old Melissa has recently moved into town. She's beautiful, mysterious, and promiscuous, and she has a big problem—all her boyfriends end up dead. No real puzzle. **90m/C VHS.** Susan Strasberg, Bo Hopkins, Don Stroud, Dana Kimmel, Patrick Macnee, Larry Storch; **D:** Jim Sotos.

Sweet Sixteen 🎬🎬🎬 2002 (R) Compston is exceptional in his debut role of teenaged Liam, who lives in Greenock, Scotland where unemployment and violence are rampant. Liam's one wish is to buy a trailer he can move his mother Jean (Coulter) into when she's released from prison in time for his 16th birthday. In order to get the money, petty criminal Martin and his friend Pinball (Ruane) steal the heroin stash of Jean's dealer boyfriend Stan (McCormack). Selling 't puts the boys in opposition to local gangster Tony (McCardie), who decides to hire Martin himself. Then, things go from bad to worse. Film is melancholy, humorous, tender, and subtitled because of the thick Scottish accents. **106m/C VHS, DVD. GB GE SF** Martin Compston, William Ruane, Annmarie Fulton, Michelle Coulter, Gary McCormack, Martin McCardie, Michelle Abercromby, Tommy McKee; **D:** Ken Loach; **W:** Paul Laverty; **C:** Barry Ackroyd; **M:** George Fenton. Cannes '03: Screenplay.

Sweet Smell of Success 🎬🎬🎬½ 1957 Powerful and ruthless New York City gossip columnist J.J. Hunsecker (Lancaster) writes a syndicated newspaper column that pandering press agent Sidney Falco (Curtis)

Sweet Revenge 🎬🎬 1990 When a judge tells a divorced couple that the many must pay the man alimony, she hires an investigator to dig up dirt on her ex. The tables are turned in this way-out marriage flick, reminiscent of the screwball comedies of the 1940s. **82m/C VHS.** Rosanna Arquette, Carrie Fisher, John Sessions; **D:** Charlotte Brandstrom; **W:** Janet Brownell; **M:** Hubert Bougis.

Sweet Revenge 🎬½ The Revengers' Comedies 1998 Even this professional cast can't rescue this predictable black comedy that is condensed from two 1991 Alan Ayckbourn plays, "The Revengers' Comedies." After saving each other from committing suicide, depressed businessman Henry Bell (Neill) and orphaned aristocrat Karen Knightly (Bonham Carter) agree on reciprocal revenge plots. Karen will punish the guy (Coogan) who stole Henry's job while Henry will destroy the neurotic wife (Scott Thomas) whose husband was once Karen's lover. Then Henry discovers Karen hasn't been telling him the truth. Too much seems to be lost from the original source. **82m/C VHS, DVD, GB FR** Sam Neill, Helena Bonham-Carter, Kristin Scott Thomas, Martin Clunes, Rupert Graves, Steve Coogan, John Wood, Liz Smith, Charlotte Coleman; **D:** Malcolm Mowbray; **W:** Malcolm Mowbray; **C:** Romain Winding; **M:** Alexandre Desplat.

Sweet Rosie O'Grady 🎬🎬½ 1943 Musical-comedy star Grable has returned to New York after success in England, where she caught the eye of nobleman Gardiner. Ex-boyfriend Young is a tabloid reporter who's expected by editor Menjou to get the scoop on her past. Seems she used to perform in Bowery saloons although that's not what Grable's been telling everyone. Slight story, charming performances, and lots of songs. Remade in 1948 as "The Wonderful Urge." ♪ My Heart Tells Me; My Sam; Oh Where is the Groom?; The Wishing Waltz; Going to the Country Fair; Get Your Police Gazette; Battle Cry; Sweet Rosie O'Grady; Two Little Girls in Blue. **74m/C VHS.** Betty Grable, Robert Young, Adolphe Menjou, Reginald Gardiner, Virginia Grey, Phil Regar, Sig Rumann, Alan Dinehart; **D:** Irving Cummings; **C:** Ernest Palmer.

Sweet Revenge 🎬🎬 1987 (R) TV journalist kidnapped by a white slavery ring in the Asian jungles. After escaping, she returns for vengeance. Meek drama. **79m/C VHS.** Ted Shackleford, Nancy Allen, Martin Landau; **D:** Mark Sobel.

Sweet Sugar 🎬½ Chaingang Girls; Captive Women 3: Sweet Sugar 1972 (R) Slave labor on a Costa Rican sugar-ar cane plantation and its cruel owner. Needless to say, vulgar exploitation runs hither and yon in this film. **90m/C VHS.** Phyllis E. Davis, Ella Edwards, Pamela Collins, Cliff Osmond, Timothy Brown; **D:** Michel Levesque.

Sweet Spirits 186° Soft-sell European fluff about a modern mannequin having a raucous affair with an artist. **87m/C VHS.** It Erika Blanc, Farley Granger; **D:** Renzo Russo; **W:** Renzo Russo.

Sweet Talker 🎬🎬 1991 (PG) Following his release from prison, a charming con man shows up in a small coastal village, thinking the townsfolk will be ripe for the ficking. What he doesn't know is they can do some sweet talking of their own, and he soon finds himself caring for a pretty widow and her son. Enjoyable light comedy works thanks to likable leads. **91m/C VHS, DVD. AU** Bryan Brown, Karen Allen, Chris Haywood, Bill Kerr, Bruce Spence, Bruce Myles, Paul Chubb, Peter Hehir, Justin Rosniak; **D:** Michael Jenkins; **W:** Tony Morphett; **C:** Russell Boyd; **M:** Richard Thompson, Peter Filleul.

Sweet Thing 🎬🎬 2000 (R) Well-constructed tale concerning a troubled young artist, Sean Fields (Fox), who begins a potentially meteoric rise with a series of controversial paintings. His abusive stepfather, Ray Fields (Lunning), a district judge, has announced his intention to run for U.S. Congress and his campaign success is mirrored by the growing popularity of Sean's work, although the graphic nature of the paintings sparks a warped media frenzy. **115m/C DVD.** Jeremy Fox, Amalia Stifter, Ev Lunning Jr.; **D:** Mark David; **W:** Mark David, Mark Spacek; **C:** Mark David, Levy Castleberry; **M:** Marc Wiskemann.

Sweet Trash WOOF! 1970 (R) A vice cop, naving an affair with a 17-year-old prostitute, is blackmailed by an underworld figure. Lives up to its name. **80m/C VHS.** Anthony (Tony) Vorno, Sharon Matt, Luke Perry, Bonnie Carr, Gene Blackey; **D:** John Hayes.

Sweet William 🎬🎬🎬 1979 (R) A philandering and seemingly irresistible school teacher seeks all sorts of attention from young man finds that one sensitive womanhasn't the patience or time for his escapades. Adult comedy concerned with sex without displaying any on the screen. **88m/C VHS. GB** Sam Waterston, Jenny Agutter, Anna Massey, Arthur Lowe; **D:** Claude Whatham; **W:** Beryl Bainbridge.

Sweet Young Thing Monique and Julie 1973 Young students at a French girls' school receive all sorts of attention from the male staff. **83m/C VHS. FR** Germaine Dhont, Hugette Parmair, Rudy Lenoir, Jean-Louis Cabula, Jean Tolzac, Bernard Musson; **D:** Alain Payet; **C:** Maurice Felcous; **M:** Philippe Brejean.

The Sweetest Gift 🎬🎬½ 1998 Two Florida neighbors (Carroll and Shaver) turn out to have many of the same problems—they're both single parents trying to raise their kids as best they can

is desperate to have his clients be a part of. Hunsecker only cares about the welfare of his younger sister, Susan (Harrison), and is outraged over her budding romance with jazz musician Steve Dallas (Milner). So he strong arms Falco into breaking up the relationship, with unexpected consequences. Engrossing performances, great dialogue. **96m/C VHS, DVD.** Burt Lancaster, Tony Curtis, Martin Milner, Barbara Nichols, Sam Levene, Susan Harrison; **D:** Alexander Mackendrick; **W:** Ernest Lehman, Clifford Odets; **C:** James Wong Howe; **M:** Elmer Bernstein; **Natl Film Reg** '93.

Sweet Sweetback's Baadasssss Song 🎬🎬🎬 1971 A black pimp kills two policemen who beat up a black militant. He uses his street-wise survival skills to allude his pursuers and escape to Mexico. A thriller, but racist, sexist, and violent. **97m/C VHS, DVD.** Melvin Van Peebles, Simon Chuckster, Hubert Scales, John Dullaghan, Rhetta Hughes, Jon Amos, West Gale, Niva Rochelle, Nick Ferrari, Mario Van Peebles; **D:** Melvin Van Peebles; **W:** Melvin Van Peebles; **C:** Robert Maxwell; **M:** Melvin Van Peebles.

while dealing with poverty and prejudice. And despite the racial differences, their kids become friends. **90m/C VHS.** Helen Shaver, Diahann Carroll, Tisha Campbell; **D:** Stuart Margolin; **W:** Rosa Jordan; **C:** Ron Stannett; **M:** Lawrence Shragge. **CABLE**

The Sweetest Thing ♂♂ 2002
(R) Girls can be just as sex-obsessed and disgusting as boys as this raunchy comedy sets out to prove. San Francisco party girl Christina Walters (Diaz) isn't looking for Mr. Right—just Mr. Right Now. And she thinks she's met him when Christina and gal pal Courtney (Applegate) take the third of the Musketeer trio—the just-dumped Jane (Blair)—out to a dance club to drink and flirt. Christina meets cute with Peter (Jane) but doesn't follow through. After getting ragged on by Courtney, the babe duo decide to track him down at the oh-so-genteel wedding that they're attending. Havoc ensues. Film's both giddy and sleazy but if you like Diaz at her daffiest, you'll sit through the tacky situations. **84m/C VHS, DVD.** US Cameron Diaz, Christina Applegate, Thomas Jane, Selma Blair, Jason Bateman, Parker Posey; **D:** Roger Kumble; **W:** Nancy M. Pimental; **C:** Anthony B. Richmond; **M:** Ed Shearmur.

Sweetheart of the Navy ♂1/2
1937 Sailors help a cafe singer out of a jam, with one of them almost giving up his career for the romance. Standard fare, but Parker is well worth listening to. **63m/B VHS.** Eric Linden, Cecilia Parker, Roger Imhof, Bernadene Hayes, Jason Robards Sr., Don Barclay; **D:** Duncan Mansfield.

Sweethearts ♂♂♂ 1938 MacDonald and Eddy star as married stage actors trying to get some time off from their hectic schedule in this show-within-a-show. Trouble ensues when their conniving producer begs, pleads and tricks them into staying. Lots of well-staged musical numbers. ♪Wooden Shoes; Every Lover Must Meet His Fate; Sweethearts; Pretty as a Picture; Summer Serenade; On Parade.♪ **114m/C VHS.** Jeanette MacDonald, Nelson Eddy, Frank Morgan, Florence Rice, Ray Bolger, Mischa Auer; **D:** Woodbridge S. Van Dyke.

Sweethearts ♂♂1/2 1997 (R) Manic-depressive Jasmine (Garofalo) responds to a personal ad placed by Arliss (Rouse), so she'll have a date for her 31st birthday. When the experience goes badly, Jasmine prevents Arliss from leaving by pulling a gun on him. Offbeat and downbeat. **85m/C VHS.** Janeane Garofalo, Mitch Rouse, Margaret Cho, Bob(cat) Goldthwait; **D:** Aleks Horvat; **W:** Aleks Horvat; **C:** John Peters; **M:** Carl Schultz.

Sweetie ♂♂♂ 1989 (R) Bizarre, expressive Australian tragicomedy about a pair of sisters—one a withdrawn, paranoid Plain Jane, the other a dangerously extroverted, overweight sociopath who re-enters her family's life and turns it upside down. Campion's first feature. **97m/C VHS, DVD.** AU Genevieve Lemon, Karen Colston, Tom Lycos, Jon Darling, Dorothy Barry, Michael Lake, Andre Pataczek; **D:** Jane Campion; **W:** Gerard Lee, Jane Campion; **M:** Martin Armiger.

Sweetwater: A True Rock Story ♂♂1/2 1999 (PG-13) TV music journalist Cami Carlson (Williams) gets out of drug rehab and learns her new assignment is a "where are they now" story about '60s band Sweetwater, the opening act at Woodstock. Teenaged singer Nansi Nevins (Johnson) disappeared after the festival and the band soon broke up. Cami tracks down ex-band members and flashbacks show how the band started and what caused Nansi to take off. **95m/C VHS.** Kelli Williams, Amy Jo Johnson, Kurt Max Runte, Robert Moloney, Frederic Forrest, Michelle Phillips, Terry David Mulligan, Nancy Warren; **D:** Lorraine Senna; **W:** Victoria Wozniak; **C:** Bernard Couture. **CABLE**

Swept Away... ♂♂♂ Swept Away...By an Unusual Destiny in the Blue Sea of August 1975 (R) A rich and beautiful Milanese woman is shipwrecked on a desolate island with a swarthy Sicilian deck hand, who also happens to be a dedicated communist. Isolated, the two switch roles, with the wealthy woman dominated by the crude proletarian. Sexy and provocative. Italian with subtitles. **116m/C VHS, DVD.** IT

Giancarlo Giannini, Mariangela Melato; **D:** Lina Wertmuller; **W:** Lina Wertmuller; **C:** Julio Battiferri; **M:** Piero Piccioni.

Swept Away ♂ 2002 (R) Guy Ritchie directs his wife Madonna in this ill-advised remake of Lina Wertmuller's politically charged romantic comedy. Amber (Madonna) arrives with her husband (Greenwood) as part of a group of ugly Americans taking a tour of the Greek islands on a yacht. A demanding prima (Ma)donna, she is especially rude to first mate Giuseppe (Giannini), whom she calls either "Guido" or "Pee Pee." Amber demands that Guiseppe take her out in the dinghy and they run out of gas and are forced to drift. They end up on a deserted island where Giuseppe now has the upper hand and begins to dominate Amber. Despite the fact that these actors fail at chemistry worse than remedial students, we're supposed to believe that they fall in love. "Gilligan's Island" is more believable, with more romantic sparks. Adriano Giannini reprises the role his father Giancarlo played in the original. **93m/C VHS, DVD.** US Madonna, Adriano Giannini, Jeanne Tripplehorn, Bruce Greenwood, David Thornton, Yorgo Voyagis, Elizabeth Banks, Michael Beattie; **D:** Guy Ritchie; **W:** Guy Ritchie; **C:** Alex Barber; **M:** Michel Colombier. Golden Raspberries '02: Worst Picture, Worst Actress (Madonna), Worst Director (Ritchie).

Swept from the Sea ♂♂1/2
Amy Foster 1997 (PG-13) Shipwrecked foreigner (Perez) and ostracized servant girl (Weisz) are star-crossed lovers in 19th century Cornwall. Told in flashback by Dr. Kennedy (McKellen) to Kathy Bates' invalid Miss Swaffer, he recalls how the native Ukrainian Yanko, who could speak no English, was thought to be an idiot by all in town, except the kind and gentle Amy, who found him washed up on the shore. Kennedy and Yanko bond through a game of chess, and the kindly doctor teaches him English. Armed with the native words of love, Yanko goes a courtin' Miss Amy. Definitely for die-hard romantics, the film throws in all the melodrama it can muster and then some, but performances are worthy (especially McKellen's). Based on a short story by Joseph Conrad. **115m/C VHS, DVD, GB** Vincent Perez, Rachel Weisz, Kathy Bates, Ian McKellen, Joss Ackland, Tom Bell, Zoe Wanamaker, Tony Haygarth, Fiona Victory; **D:** Beeban Kidron; **W:** Tim Willocks; **C:** Dick Pope; **M:** John Barry.

Swift Justice ♂♂ 1988 Mayor of a small town thinks he's gotten away with murder after leaving a young girl for dead in a junk yard. However, the mayor and his violent pals are soon hunted by an ex-Green Beret with a penchant for justice. **90m/C VHS.** Jon Greene, Cindy Rome, Cameron Mitchell, Aldo Ray, Chuck "Porky" Mitchell, Wilson Dunster, Ted Leplat; **D:** Harry Hope.

Swifty ♂1/2 1935 A cowpoke is accused of murder but escapes to track down the real culprit and win the hand of the girl he loves. **60m/B VHS.** Hoot Gibson, June Gale, George "Gabby" Hayes, Ralph Lewis, Late (Lafayette) McKee, Robert F. (Bob) Kortman, William (Bill) Gould, Wally Wales; **D:** Alan James; **W:** Roger Allman, Walter Farrar; **C:** Arthur Reed.

Swim Team ♂ 1979 New coach for a terminally inept school swimming team whips them into shape. Doesn't hold much water. **81m/C VHS.** Stephen Furst, James Daughton, Jenny Neumann, Kim Day, Buster Crabbe; **D:** James Polakof.

Swimfan ♂♂ 2002 (PG-13) Watered down, teen "Fatal Attraction." Ben Cronin (Bradford) is a suburban NYC high school swimming star, and Madison Bell (Christensen) a new girl in town who looks the studly jock and reels him in. Otherwise involved, the promising athlete allows Madison to seduce him in the pool on one occasion, which automatically sets off her crazy mechanism. She immediately begins to run the well-worn stalker playbook. Ben's life begins to unravel due to Madison's devious designs and after a face-off with his psycho one-night-stand, he's forced to fight back with the help of her cousin, the class nerd. Mildly thrilling pic suffers from editing and continuity gaffes. **93m/C VHS, DVD.** US Erika Christensen, Jesse Bradford, Shiri Appleby, Kate Burton, Clayne

---

Crawford, Jason Ritter, Kia Joy Goodwin, Dan Hedaya, Michael Higgins, Nick Sandow, James DeBello, Pamela Isaacs, Phyllis Somerville; **D:** John Polson; **W:** Charles F. Bohl, Phillip Schneider; **C:** Giles Nutgens; **M:** Louis Febre.

The Swimmer ♂♂♂1/2 1968 (PG)
A lonely suburbanite swims an existential swath through the pools of his neighborhood landscape in an effort at self-discovery. A surreal, strangely compelling work based on a story by John Cheever. **94m/C VHS, DVD.** Burt Lancaster, Janice Rule, Janet Landgard, Marge Champion, Kim Hunter, Rose Gregorio, John David Garfield; **D:** Frank Perry; **M:** Marvin Hamlisch.

Swimming ♂♂1/2 2000 Teenaged tomboy Frankie (Ambrose) works in the family diner in the resort town of Myrtle Beach, S.C., alongside her older brother Neil (Pais). Her best friend is extroverted body piercer Nicola (Dundas Lowe), who is somewhat overprotective of the inexperienced Frankie. This shows when Neil hires slinky, confident Josee (Carter) as a waitress and Josee makes a pass at Frankie, who doesn't know how to react. Frankie also catches the eye of newcomer Heath (Harrold) to whom she is drawn, although he makes her no romantic promises. Coming-of-ager with an appealing performance by Ambrose. **98m/C VHS, DVD.** Lauren Ambrose, Joelle Carter, Jennifer (Jennie) Dundas Lowe, Jamie Harrold, Josh Pais, Anthony Michael Ruivivar; **D:** Robert Siegel; **W:** Robert Siegel, Liza Bazadona, Grace Woodard; **C:** John Leuba; **M:** Mark Wike.

Swimming Pool ♂♂1/2 1970 (PG)
Two men and two women spend a weekend in a villa on the French Riviera, manipulating each other, playing sexual games, and changing partners. Their escapades end in murder. Romantic melodrama is sensuous if slow-moving. French film dubbed in English. **85m/C VHS.** FR Romy Schneider, Alain Delon, Maurice Ronet, Jane Birkin; **D:** Jacques Deray.

Swimming Pool ♂♂ 2003 (R)
Sophisticated, tricky thriller stars Rampling as successful British crime writer Sarah Morton—who's suffering from writer's block. Sarah complains to her publisher, John (Dance), and he offers her his summer house in the South of France. She accepts, thinking a change of scene will be inspiring and hoping John will visit. Instead, Sarah's quiet vacation is rudely interrupted by the arrival of John's uninhibited French daughter from his first marriage, Julie (Sagnier). The neglected teen moves in, flaunts her sexuality (and body) in front of the repressed Englishwoman, and brings home a series of one-night stands. Sarah surreptitiously watches Julie and begins a novel about her. Then, when one of Julie's lovers disappears, and makes ironic observations about modern life. It works. **87m/C VHS.** Spalding Gray; **D:** Jonathan Demme; **C:** John Bailey; **M:** Laurie Anderson.

has occurred. A surprise denouncement may leave viewers frustrated but there's an uneasy seduction to the film, with both actresses giving their roles edge and vulnerability. **102m/C VHS, DVD.** FR GB Charlotte Rampling, Ludivine Sagnier, Charles Dance, Marc Fayolle, Jean-Marie Lamour; **D:** Francois Ozon; **W:** Francois Ozon, Emmanuele Bernheim; **C:** Yorick Le Saux; **M:** Philippe Rombi.

Swimming to Cambodia ♂♂♂ 1987 Gray tells the story of his bit part in "The Killing Fields," filmed in Cambodia, and makes ironic observations about modern life. It works. **87m/C VHS.** Spalding Gray; **D:** Jonathan Demme; **C:** John Bailey; **M:** Laurie Anderson.

Swimming Upstream ♂♂ 2003 (PG-13) Dysfunctional family drama with a sports twist based on a true story. Screenwriter/exec producer Anthony Fingleton fictionalizes his own story of competitive swimming during the 50s and 60s in Brisbane, Australia. His career did not reach true heights due to an overbearing and increasingly violent alcoholic father. Perhaps this poorly executed film had a more cathartic effect on the creator than it does on an audience. **113m/C DVD.** Geoffrey Rush, Judy Davis, Jesse Spencer, Deborah Kennedy, Mark Hembrow, Melissa Thomas, Tim Draxl, David Hoflin, Craig Horner, Brittany Byrnes, Mitchell Dellevergin, Thomas Davidson, Kain O'Keefe, Robert Quinn, Keeara Byrnes, Des Drury, Dawn Fraser,

---

Remi Broadway, Murray Rose; **D:** Russell Mulcahy; **W:** Anthony Fingleton; **C:** Martin McGrath; **M:** Reinhold Heil, Johnny Klimek.

Swimming with Sharks ♂♂♂
The Buddy Factor 1994 (R) Budding screenwriter Guy (Whaley) goes to work for notoriously insulting movie producer Buddy (Spacey). Soon, Guy grows tired of his boss's demeaning treatment and cruel means of communication and devises a scheme which would even the score. Hollywood satire has more bite than "The Player," and a devious climax, but it's mostly an opportunity for Spacey to hang his hams, which he does with glee. Debut for director Huang, who based his script on his experience as a production assistant. See it with your boss. **93m/C VHS, DVD.** Kevin Spacey, Frank Whaley, Michelle Forbes, Benicio Del Toro; **D:** George Huang; **W:** George Huang; **C:** Steven Finestone; **M:** Tom Heil. N.Y. Film Critics '95: Support. Actor (Spacey).

Swimsuit ♂1/2 1989 A young ad executive decides to revitalize a swimsuit company's failing business by sponsoring a contest for the perfect swimsuit model in this TV fluff. **100m/C VHS, DVD.** William Katt, Catherine Oxenberg, Cyd Charisse, Nia Peeples, Tom Villard, Cheryl Pollak, Billy Warlock, Jack Wagner; **D:** Chris Thomson; **W:** Robert Schiff; **C:** Laszlo George; **M:** John D'Andrea. **TV**

Swindle ♂ 1992 Two life-long friends set up scam after scam in their quest for sex and money. Their latest scam involves a phony marriage broker business, which provides the opportunity to meet a lot of lovely ladies. Only it turns out the hustlers may be the ones getting hustled. **85m/C VHS.** Robby West, Britt Houston, Elaina Dunn, Samantha Fong, Bobby Tess, Donna Thomas; **D:** Jason Holt.

The Swindle ♂♂ Rien ne va plus 1997 Chabrol's 50th film deals with femme fatale con woman Betty (Huppert) and her older partner, Victor (Serrault). Their modus operandi is for Betty to pick up a businessman, go to his hotel room, and after he passes out from the mickey she's put in his drink, Betty and Victor steal just enough to make it worth their time without raising immediate suspicions. But Betty wants to go for higher stakes and works her own scam with shady Maurice (Cluzet), which has unexpected consequences for the trio. French with subtitles. **105m/C VHS, DVD.** FR Isabelle Huppert, Michel Serrault, Francois Cluzet, Jean-Francois Balmer; **D:** Claude Chabrol; **W:** Claude Chabrol; **C:** Eduardo Serra; **M:** Matthieu Chabrol.

Swindle ♂♂1/2 2002 (R) One-dimensional heist flick. Seth George (Sizemore) is a New York undercover cop who's maybe been undercover a little too long. He's investigating a crime syndicate run by nightclub owner Sophie (Fenn), who's planning a bank heist using Seth as muscle. Since his superiors decide Seth is untrustworthy, they try to shut down his operation, but, having fallen for Sophie, Seth is determined to see her plans through. **93m/C VHS, DVD.** Tom Sizemore, Sherilyn Fenn, Dave Foley, Conrad Pla; **D:** K.C. Bascombe; **W:** K.C. Bascombe; **C:** Bruce Chun.

Swindled ♂♂ Incautos 2004 Young con man Ernesto (Altiero) partners up with older Marco (Luppi) for a potentially lucrative real estate swindle. However, they need the help of sexy Pilar (Abril), a former lover of Federico's who has double-crossed him before. Can they trust each other enough to work together? Or will the temptation of the con be too much for the shady partners? Spanish with subtitles. **107m/C DVD.** SP Ernesto Alterio, Victoria Abril, Federico Luppi, Manuel Alexandre; **D:** Miguel Bardem; **W:** Miguel Bardem, Carlos Martin; **C:** Thierry Arbogast; **M:** Juan Bardem.

Swing ♂♂♂1/2 1998 (R) Martin Luxford (Speer) is out on parole, having learned to play the sax in the slammer from his cellmate Jack (Clemons), who does the sax solos). So he decides to put together a neo-40s swing band in Liverpool (with his sultry ex-girlfriend, singer Joan (Stansfield), who's now married to jealous cop, Andy (McCall). Martin has to recruit musicians, get them gigs, and manage to avoid

Swing, High, Swing Low ☆☆½ 1937 A trumpet player gets put in jail (and win back Joan). It's an amusing "let's put on a show" flick style. Solid drama. From the stage play "Burlesque." Made first as "The Dance of Life," then as "When My Baby Smiles At Me." 98m/C VHS. Carole Lombard, Fred MacMurray, Charles Butterworth, Dorothy Lamour. D: Mitchell Leisen.

Swing It, Professor ☆☆½ 1937 A stodgy music professor refuses to recognize jazz as a valid musical form and subsequently loses his job. During his unemployment, he wanders into a nightclub and discovers jazz isn't so bad after all. Nice camera work. 62m/B VHS. Pinky Tomlin, Paula Stone, Mary Kornman, Milburn Stone, Pat Gleason. D: Marshall Neilan.

Swing It, Sailor! ☆☆ 1937 Two footloose sailors go after the same woman while on shore leave. Decent screwball comedy. 61m/B VHS, DVD. Wallace Ford, Ray Mayer, Isabel Jewell, Mary Treen. D: Raymond Cannon.

Swing Kids ☆☆ 1993 (PG-13) In 1939 in Germany, big band of "swing" music is the instrument enjoyed by a group of young people to rebel against the conformity demanded by Hitler. Highlights the politics of the era, but concentrates mainly on three teenagers and the strains that Nazi power put on their friendship. Although there is still something disturbingly silly about the entire production. Dance sequences are lively and well-choreographed. Branagh (in an uncredited role) plays a smooth-talking Gestapo chief. Filmed on location in Prague, Czechoslovakia (as a substitute for Hamburg, Germany). 114m/C VHS, DVD. Robert Sean Leonard, Christian Bale, Frank Whaley, Barbara Hershey, Tushka Bergen, David Tom, Kenneth Branagh, Noah Wyle. D: Thomas Carter. W: Jonathan Marc Feldman. C: Jerzy Zielinski. M: James Horner.

Swing Parade of 1946 ☆☆ 1946 One of the multitude of 1940s musicals. Young songwriter falls in love with club owner. Highlights include an appearance by the Three Stooges. ♫Stormy Weather, Just a Little Fond Affection, On the Sunny Side of the Street, Oh, Brother, After All This Time, Caledonia. 74m/B VHS. Gale Storm, Phil Regan, Mae Howard, Edward Brophy, Connee Boswell. D: Phil Karlson.

Swing Shift ☆☆½ 1984 (PG) When Hawn takes a job at an aircraft plant after her husband goes off to war, she learns more than riveting. Lahti steals the film as her friend and co-worker. A detailed reminiscence of the American home front during WWII that never seems to gel. Produced by Hawn. 100m/C VHS, DVD. Goldie Hawn, Kurt Russell, Ed Harris, Christine Lahti, Holly Hunter, Chris Lemmon, Belinda Carlise, Fred Ward, Roger Corman, Lisa Pelikan. D: Jonathan Demme. W: Ron Nyswaner, Bo Goldman. C: Tak Fujimoto. N.Y. Film Critics '84. Support. Actress (Lahti).

Swing Time ☆☆☆ 1936 Astaire, a dancer who can't resist gambling, is engaged to marry another woman, until he meets Ginger. One of the team's best efforts. ♫Swing Time; Never Gonna Dance; Pick Yourself Up; A Fine Romance; Bojangles of Harlem. 103m/B VHS, DVD. Fred Astaire, Ginger Rogers, Helen Broderick, Betty Furness, Eric Blore, Victor Moore, Dorothy Fields. Oscars '36: Song ("The Way You Look Tonight"). Natl Film Reg. '04.

Swing Vote 2008 Small-town loser Bud Johnson (Costner) has one good thing in his life—his precocious 12-year-old daughter Molly (Carroll). But the overachieving youngster sets in motion an unlikely series of events on Election Day that results in the presidential election coming down to a single deciding vote—Bud's. A cinema fairytale indeed since the first thing a candidate would scream for is a recount (and isn't there that whole electoral college thing going on?). Hey, it's gotta be more fun than the actual 2008 presidential race. Not yet reviewed. ?m/C Kevin Costner, Dennis Hopper, Nathan Lane, Kelsey Grammer, Madeline Carroll, Stanley Tucci, George Lopez, Judge Reinhold, Paula Patton, Mare Winningham, Joshua Michael Stern. D: Joshua Michael Stern. W: Jason Richman, Joshua Michael Stern. C: Shane Hurlbut. M: John Debney.

Swingers ☆☆☆ 1996 (R) Hip, hilarious, and highly entertaining low-budget comedy features five young showbiz wanna-bes on the prowl for career breaks and beautiful "babies" in the Hollywood retro club scene. Mike (screenwriter Favreau) is a struggling actor/comedian from New York who's having trouble getting over his ex. His slick, handsome friend Trent (Vaughn, in a star-making turn) and the rest of his neo-Rat Pack buddies try to get him back in the game with nightly parties and lounge-hopping. Witty script and clever, camera work make this one "money, baby, money!" 96m/C VHS, DVD, UMD, Jon Favreau, Vince Vaughn, Ron Livingston, Patrick Van Horn, Alex Desert, Brooke Langton, Heather Graham, Deena Martin, Katherine Kendall, Blake Lindsley. D: Doug Liman. W: Jon Favreau. C: Doug Liman. M: Justin Reinhard. MTV Movie Awards '97: New Filmmaker (Liman).

A Swingin' Summer ☆☆ 1965 A bunch of groovy guys and gals go-go to the beach for a vacation of fun and sun and end up starting a rock 'n' roll concert series. Everybody gets part of the action...even the bespectacled Welch, who gets a chance to sing. Performances from the Righteous Brothers and rock semi-legends Donnie Brooks, Gary Lewis and the Playboys, Justine, Penny the Fool, Out to Lunch, Nitro, Ready to Groove. 81m/C VHS. James Stacy, William Wellman Jr., Quinn O'Hara, Martin West, Mary Mitchell, Allan Jones, Raquel Welch. D: Robert Sparr. W: Leigh Chapman.

The Swinging Cheerleaders ☆½ 1974 (PG) A group of amorous cheerleaders turn on the entire campus in this typical sexploiter. 90m/C VHS, DVD. Cheryl "Rainbeaux" Smith, Colleen Camp, Rosanne Katon, Jo Johnston, Mae Mercer, Bob Minor, George D. Wallace. D: Jack Hill. W: Betty Conklin. C: Alfred Taylor. M: William Allen Castleman, William Loose.

Swingtime Johnny ☆☆ 1943 Typical wartime musical fare. The Andrews Sisters forgo their showbiz careers to help out the war effort by taking factory work making artillery shells. But they still find time to harmonize. 61m/B VHS. The Andrews Sisters, Harriet Hilliard Nelson, Peter Cook. F. (Eddie) Cline. W: Clyde Bruckman. C: Jerome Coldinger.

Swiss Conspiracy ☆☆ Per Saldo Mord 1977 (PG) Against the opulent background of the world's richest financial capital and playground of the wealthy, one man battles to stop a daring and sophisticated blackmailer preying on the secret bank account set. Fast-paced, if sometimes confusing. 92m/C VHS, DVD. GE David Janssen, Senta Berger, John Saxon, Ray Milland, Elke Sommer. D: Jack Arnold. W: Norman Klein. M: Klaus Doldinger.

The Swiss Family Robinson ☆☆½ 1960 A family, seeking to escape Napoleon's war in Europe, sets sail for New Guinea, but shipwrecks on a deserted tropical island. There they build an idyllic life, only to be confronted by a band of pirates. Lots of adventure for family viewing. Filmed on location on the island of Tobago. Based on the novel by Johann Wyss. 126m/C VHS, DVD. John Mills, Dorothy McGuire, James MacArthur, Tommy Kirk, Janet Munro, Sessue Hayakawa, Kevin Corcoran. D: Ken Annacin. W: Lowell S. Hawley. C: Harry Waxman. M: William Alwyn.

Swiss Miss ☆☆½ 1938 Stan and Ollie are mousetrap salesmen on the job in Switzerland. Highlights include Stan's tuba serenade and the gorilla-on-the-bridge episode. Also included on this tape is a 1935 Thelma Todd/Patsy Kelly short, "Hot Money." 97m/B VHS. Stan Laurel, Oliver Hardy, Della Lind, Walter Woolf King, Eric Blore, Patsy Kelly. D: John Blystone.

The Switch ☆☆☆ The Con Artists; Bluff Storia di Truffe e di Imbroglioni 1976 (R) An escaped convict takes the place of a talented conman and chaos ensues. 105m/C VHS, DVD. IT Anthony Quinn, Adriano Celentano, Corinne Cléry. D: Sergio Corbucci. W: Massimo De Rita. C: Marcello Gatti. M: Lelio Luttazzi.

Switch ☆☆☆ 1991 (R) A chauvinist louse, slain by the girlfriends he misused, is sent back to Earth as an a luring female to learn the other side's point of view. The plot may lack urgency, but this is a sparkling adult comedy that scores as it pursues the gimmicky concept to a logical, outrageous and touching conclusion. Barkin's act as swaggering male stuck in a woman's body is as swaggering mae stuck in a humor. 104m/C VHS, DVD. Ellen Barkin, Jimmy Smits, JoBeth Williams, Lorraine Bracco, Perry King, Bruce Payne, Tony Roberts. D: Blake Edwards. W: Blake Edwards. C: Dick Bush. M: Henry Mancini.

Switchback ☆☆ 1997 (R) FBI agent Frank Lacrosse (Quaid) pursues the serial killer who kidnapped his son. Against the backdrop of a snowstorm, the killer, who may or may not be a former rail worker (Glover) or the hitchhiking ex-doctor (Leto) he picked up, leads Lacrosse on a convoluted cat-and-mouse game with no apparent logic or motive. First-time director Stuart, who wrote "Die Hard" and "The Fugitive," wrote this one in film school, and it shows. Connect-the-dots set pieces and plot twists only provide Quaid more time to perfect his Harrison Ford impression and Glover more scenery and dialogue to chew. Ermey is impressive as the put-upon small-town sheriff. Stunt work is well done and the Colorado countryside looks great. 120m/C VHS, DVD Dennis Quaid, Danny Glover, Jared Leto, R. Lee Ermey, William Fichtner, Ted Levine, Leo Burmester, Merrle Kennedy. D: Jeb Stuart. W: Jeb Stuart. C: Oliver Wood. M: Basil Poledouris.

Switchblade Sisters WOOf! The Jezebels; Playgirl Gang 1975 Crime gang of female ex-cons wreaks pseudo-feminist havoc. Bruce is Lenny Bruce's daughter. 91m/C VHS, DVD. Robbie Lee, Joanne Nail, Monica Gayle, Kitty Bruce, Asher Brauner, Chase Newhart, Marlene Clark, Janice Karman, Don Stark, Kate Murtagh, Bill Adler. D: Jack Hill. W: F.X. Maier. C: Stephen M. Katz. M: Les Baxter, Medusa, Chuck Day, Richard Person.

Switched at Birth ☆☆½ 1991 (PG) A fact-based drama about two girls, switched in a hospital nursery at birth. Only when one girl dies, a decade later, do her parents discover that she could not have been their biological child. How one family's search for their daughter leads to an emotional conflict between the the man that raised her, and the biological parents who seek to claim her. Beware of the sappy Hollywood ending; five years later the story of Kimberly Mays was still going through the U.S. judicial system. 200m/C VHS. Bonnie Bedelia, Brian Kerwin, Ed Asner, Caroline McWilliams, John M. Jackson, Lois Smith, Eve Gordon, Judith Hoag, Ariana Richards. D: Waris Hussein. TV

Switching Channels ☆☆½ 1988 (PG) A modernized remake of "His Girl Friday," and therefore the fourth version of "The Front Page." Beautiful TV anchorwoman (Turner) wants to marry handsome tycoon (Reeve), but her scheming ex-husband (Reynolds) gets in the way. Weak performances from everyone but Beatty and lackluster direction render this oft-told story less funny than usual. 108m/C VHS. Burt Reynolds, Kathleen Turner, Christopher Reeve, Ned Beatty, Henry Gibson, George Newbern, Al Waxman, Ken James, Joe Silver, Charles Kimbrough, Tony Rosato. D: Ted Kotcheff. W: Jonathan Reynolds. M: Michel Legrand.

Swoon ☆☆☆ 1991 Kalin's directorial debut is a stylish rendering of the sensational 1924 kidnapping and murder of Bobby Franks by Richard Loeb and Nathan Leopold Jr. and their subsequent trial and imprisonment. Core elements of the case remain but Kalin imposes contemporary styles and morals on the past, particularly his protest against the homophobic attitudes influencing the trial while acknowledging the jaded and dispassionate behavior of the two young men. Previous cinematic versions of the murder case in clude "Rope" and "Compulsion" but Kalin graphically portrays the characters' homosexuality, which was only hinted at in the earlier films. 95m/B VHS, DVD. Daniel Schlachet, Craig Chester, Ron Vawter, Michael Kirby, Michael Stumm, Valda Z. Drabla, Natalia Stanford. D: Tom Kalin. W: Tom Kalin. C: Ellen Kuras. M: James Bennett. Sundance '92: Cinematog.

Sword & the Dragon ☆☆ Ilya Mourametz 1956 A young warrior must battle any number of giant mythical creatures. 81m/C VHS. Yvonne De Caro, Jorge Mistral. D: Carlo L. Bragaglia.

The Sword and the Cross ☆½ 1958 A grade-B adventure about the life of Mary Magdalere a. 93m/B VHS. Yvonne De Caro, Jorge Mistral. D: Carlo L. Bragaglia.

Sword & the Sorcerer ☆☆½ 1982 (R) Young prince strives to regain control of his kingdom, now ruled by an evil king and an evil wizard, with the help of the world by Merlin and Archimedes the owl. Although not in the Disney master-piece fold, boasts the usual superior animation and a gripping mythological tale. 79m/C VHS, DVD. D: Wolfgang Reitherman. W: Bill Peet. M: George Bruns. V: Ricky Sorenson, Sebastian Cabot, Karl Swenson, Junius Matthews, Alan Napier, Norman Alden, Martha Wentworth, Barbara Jo Allen.

The Sword & the Rose ☆☆½ 1953 Mary Tudor, sister of King Henry VIII, shuns the advances of a nobleman for the love of a commoner. Johns is an obstinate princess. Justice, a fun animated production with the help of Merlin and Archimedes the owl. 91m/C VHS. Richard Todd, Glynis Johns, Michael Gough, Jane Barrett, James Robertson Justice. D: Ken Annakin. C: Geoffrey Unsworth.

The Sword in the Stone ☆☆☆ 1963 (G) The Disney version of the first volume of T.H. White's "The Once and Future King" wherein King Arthur, as a boy, is instructed in the ways of the world by Merlin and Archimedes the owl. Although not in the Disney masterpiece fold, boasts the usual superior animation and a gripping mythological tale. 80m/C VHS, DVD. D: Wolfgang Reitherman. W: Bill Peet. M: George Bruns. V: Ricky Sorenson, Sebastian Cabot, Karl Swenson, Junius Matthews, Alan Napier, Norman Alden, Martha Wentworth, Barbara Jo Allen.

Sword of Doom ☆☆½ Daibosatsu Toge 1967 A rousing samurai epic detailing the training of an impulsive, bloodlusting warrior by an elder expert. In Japanese with English subtitles. 120m/B VHS, DVD. JP Tatsuya Nakadai, Toshiro Mifune. D: Kihachi Okamoto.

The Sword of El Cid ☆½ La Spada del Cid 1962 Not much dash and very little daring-do in this poorly plotted, overly dramatic saga of good vs. evil. Spanish style. Rightful heir to the crown threatens, with the pretender to his throne. Costume mavens may find something to tickle their interest. 86m/C VHS. SP IT Roland Carey, Sandro Moretti, Chantal Deberg, Iliana Grimaldi, Jose Luis Pelicena, Daniela Bianchi. D: Miguel Iglesias.

Sword of Gideon ☆☆½ 1986 An action-packed and suspenseful TV film about an elite commando group who set out to avenge the Munich Olympic killings of 1972. Adapted from "Vengeance" by George Jonas. 148m/C VHS. Steven Bauer, Michael York, Rod Steiger, Colleen Dewhurst, Robert Joy, Laurent Malet, Lino Ventura, Leslie Hope. D: Michael Anderson. TV

Sword of Honor 1994 (R) Undercover cop and martial arts expert Johnny Lee (Leigh) investigates his partner's mysterious death amidst the tawdry glamor of Vegas. 97m/C VHS, DVD, Steven Leigh, Sophia Crawford, Angelo Tiffe, Jerry Tiffe, Jeff Pruitt, Debbie Scofield; D: Robert Tiffe; W: Robert Tiffe, Clay Ayers; M: David Rubinstein. **VIDEO**

Sword of Honour 2001 After a divorce, 35-year-old Guy Crouchback (Craig) finds new resolve by joining up (although his unit is composed of misfits) and battling the Nazis—until the absurdities of war cause cracks in his idealism. Based on Evelyn Waugh's WWII trilogy. 200m/C DVD. *GB* Daniel Craig, Katrin Cartlidge, Megan Dodds, Robert Pugh, Guy Henry, Nicholas Boulton; D: Bill Anderson; W: William Boyd; C: Daf Hobson; M: Nina Humphreys. **TV**

Sword of Lancelot *Lancelot and Guinevere* 1963 A costume version of the Arthur-Lancelot-Guinevere triangle, with plenty of swordplay and a sincere respect for the old legend. 115m/C VHS, DVD. *GB* Cornel Wilde, Jean Wallace, Brian Aherne, George Baker; D: Cornel Wilde.

Sword of Sherwood Forest 1960 The Earl of Newark plots the murder of the Archbishop of Canterbury in yet another rendition of the Robin Hood legend. Cushing is truly evil as the villain. 80m/C VHS. *GB* Richard Greene, Peter Cushing, Niall MacGinnis, Richard Pasco, Jack (Gwillam) Gwillim, Sarah Branch, Nigel Green, Oliver Reed; D: Terence Fisher.

Sword of the Valiant 1983 (PG) The Green Knight arrives in Camelot to challenge Gawain. Remake of "Gawain And The Green Knight." Connery adds zest to a minor epic. 102m/C VHS, DVD. *GB* Sean Connery, Miles O'Keeffe, Cyrielle Claire, Leigh Lawson, Trevor Howard, Peter Cushing, Wilfrid Brambell, Lila Kedrova, John Rhys-Davies; D: Stephen Weeks; W: Philip M. Breen; C: Frederick A. (Freddie) Young.

Sword of Venus *Island of Monte Cristo* 1953 Uninspired production finds the son of the Count of Monte Cristo the victim in a scheme to deprive him of his wealth. 73m/B VHS, DVD. Robert Clarke, Catherine McLeod, Dan O'Herlihy, William Schallert; D: Harold Daniels.

Swordfish 2001 (R) CIA operative Gabriel Shear (Travolta) uses associate Ginger (Berry) to coerce a computer hacker (Jackman) who's just been released from prison, to steal nine billion dollars from a DEA slush fund. In return, the hacker gets a fresh start with his wife and daughter. The plot goes on from there, but it's too convoluted and pointless to bother with. As is usually the case with anything directed by Sena or produced by Joel Silver, the emphasis is on flash, high-energy action set pieces, and collateral damage, all of which is well done, if eventually repetitive, here. Travolta is wasted at playing the smirking supervillain, but it does wear. Jackman and Cheadle give better performances than the flick deserves, and Berry has fun with her obligatory femme fatale role. 99m/C VHS, DVD, Blu-ray Disc, UMD, HD DVD. *US* John Travolta, Hugh Jackman, Halle Berry, Don Cheadle, Vinnie Jones, Sam Shepard, Zach Grenier, Camryn Grimes, Rudolf Martin, Drea De Matteo; D: Dominic Sena; W: Skip Woods; C: Paul Cameron; M: Christopher Young.

Swords of Death 1971 Final film by Uchida, released posthumously, deals with the adventurous period exploits of the irrepressible Miyamoto Musashi. With English subtitles. 76m/C VHS, DVD. JP Kinnosuke Nakamura, Rentaro Mikuni; D: Tomu Uchida.

The Swordsman 1992 (R) The quest to return the stolen sword of the legendary Alexander the Great to a museum is muscular detective Lamas' assignment. Turns out the detective and the evil millionaire antagonist have been chasing each other through time in their endless quest for revenge and power. 98m/C VHS, DVD. Lorenzo Lamas, Claire Stansfield, Michael Champion; D: Michael Kennedy; W: Michael Kennedy.

Swordsmen in Double Flag Town 1991 Stylized martial arts flick best-appreciated by aficionados. Young Hei Ge (Gao) enters the village of Double Flag Town to claim his promised bride. He kills a man trying to rape his intended and provokes the wrath of the man's brother, a well-known killer called the Lethal Swordsman. Naturally, there's the Chinese equivalent of a showdown at high noon. Mandarin with subtitles. 90m/C DVD. *CH* Wei Gao, Mana Zhao, Jiang Chang, Haiying Sun, Gang Wang; D: Ping He; W: Ping He, Zhangquang Yang; C: Deling Ma; M: Long Tao.

Sworn Enemies 1996 (R) Clifton Santier (Greene) goes on a killing spree in a small town where the local sheriff turns out to be his ex-partner, Pershing Quinn (Pare). Now the two enemies decide that only death will settle their old (and new) scores. 101m/C VHS, DVD. *CA* Peter Greene, Michael Pare, Macha Grenon; D: Shimon Dotan; W: Rod Hewitt; C: Sylvain Brault; M: Walter Christian Rothe, Richard Anthony Boast.

Sworn to Justice 1997 (R) Psychologist Jana Dane (Rothrock) wakes up with psychic powers after sustaining a serious head injury from the burglars who killed her sister and nephew. Jana then decides to put her new abilities to work for her by becoming a night time avenger. 90m/C VHS, DVD. Cynthia Rothrock, Kurt McKinney, Tony LoBianco, Brad Dourif, Mako, Kenn Scott; D: Paul Maslak; W: Robert Easter; C: Richard Benda; M: John Coda.

Sybil 1976 Fact-based story of a woman who developed 16 distinct personalities, and the supportive psychiatrist who helped her put the pieces of her ego together. Excellent production featuring Field's Emmy-winning performance. 122m/C VHS, DVD. Sally Field, Joanne Woodward, Brad Davis, Martine Bartlett, Jane Hoffman; D: Daniel Petrie. **TV**

Sydney White 2007 (PG-13) Hi ho, hi ho, it's off to college we go. Shut out of her dead mother's sorority, Sydney (Bynes) ends up living with seven, ahem, dorks and must find a way to defeat "fairest-of-them-all" sorority president Rachel (Paxton), win the heart of dreamy Tyler Prince (Long), and teach the entire campus to appreciate the diverse assortment of nerds she calls sidekicks. Bynes has ample charm and talent, but that can't overcome the failings of this modern-day retelling of the Snow White story, whose message is undercut by the fact that it mocks a lot of the characters as much as it uplifts them. 105m/C DVD. *US* Amanda Bynes, Matt Long, Sara Paxton, John Schneider, Crystal Hunt, Jack Carpenter, Jeremy Howard; D: Joe Nussbaum; W: Chad Gomez Creasy; C: Mark Irwin; M: Deborah Lurie.

Sylvester 1985 (PG) A 16-year-old girl and a cranky stockyard boss team up to train a battered horse named Sylvester for the National Equestrian trials. Nice riding sequences and good performances can't overcome familiar plot, but the kids will enjoy this one. 104m/C VHS, DVD. Melissa Gilbert, Richard Farnsworth, Michael Schoeffling, Constance Towers; D: Tim Hunter.

Sylvia 2003 (R) Paltrow gamely takes on the life of the talented but tortured American poet Sylvia Plath in Jeffs' bummer biopic. Following Plath's seven-year marriage to English poet Ted Hughes (Craig) until her 1963 suicide in London at 30, pic deals impartially with the details of the affair that caused Plath to jettison Hughes. Also explores her mental illness and long-time grief over her father's death, as well as her conflicted feelings over the dueling roles of artist and wife/mother, and icon for budding feminist issues. Thoughtfully directed, although Paltrow doesn't quite get her teeth into the challenging role. 110m/C VHS, DVD. *GB* Gwyneth Paltrow, Daniel Craig, Jared Harris, Amira Casar, Andrew Havill, Sam Troughton, Anthony Strachan, Lucy Davenport, Blythe Danner, Michael Gambon, David Birkin, Michael Mears; D: Christine Jeffs; W: John Brownlow; C: John Toon; M: Gabriel Yared.

Sylvia and the Phantom *Sylvia and the Ghost* 1945 A charming French comedy about a lonely young girl who is befriended by the ghost of a man killed decades earlier in a duel over the girl's grandmother. Based on the play by Alfred Adam. In French with English subtitles. 88m/B VHS. *FR* Odette Joyeux, Jacques Tati, Francois Perier; D: Claude Autant-Lara.

Sylvia Scarlett 1935 An odd comedy/drama about a woman who masquerades as a boy while on the run with her father, who causes all kinds of instinctive confusion in the men she meets. 94m/B VHS, DVD. Katharine Hepburn, Cary Grant, Brian Aherne, Edmund Gwenn, Natalie Paley, Dennie Moore, Lennox Pawle, Daisy Belmore, Nola Luxford; D: George Cukor; W: John Collier, Gladys Unger, Mortimer Offner; C: Russell Metty.

Sympathy for the Devil *One Plus One* 1970 Rolling Stones provide music for confused, revolutionary documentary. Episodic jumble is odd, sometimes fascinating. 110m/C VHS. *FR* Mick Jagger, Rolling Stones; D: Jean-Luc Godard.

Sympathy for the Underdog *Bakuto Gaijin Butai: Gamblers in Okinawa* 1971 Old-fashioned yakuza Masuo Gunji (Tsuruta) is released after a 10-year prison stint and discovers that all the dock action has been commandeered by the Daitokai crime syndicate. So he gets his former crew together and tells them he wants to muscle in on the black market in Okinawa instead. This doesn't prove to be so easy. There's a suitably bloody final showdown between the criminal gangs. Japanese with subtitles. 93m/C DVD. *JP* Koji Tsuruta, Tomisaburo Wakayama, Tsunehiko Watase, Noboru Ando, Kenji Imai, Akiko Kudo; D: Kinji Fukasaku; W: Kinji Fukasaku, Hiro Matsuda, Fumio Konami; C: Hanjiro Nakazawa; M: Takeo Yamashita.

Synapse 1995 (R) Black-marketeer Andre (Makepeace) is doublecrossed by a partner and arrested by Life Corp., which runs this futuristic civilization. As an experimental punishment, his mind is implanted into the body of Celeste (Duffy), who manages to escape and join up with a band of revolutionaries determined to destroy the evil corporation. Fast-paced story and good special effects. 89m/C VHS, DVD. Karen Duffy, Saul Rubinek, Matt McCoy, Chris Makepeace; D: Allan Goldstein.

Syngenor 1990 (R) Syngenor stands for Synthesized Genetic Organism, to differentiate it from all other organisms. Created by science, it escapes, and a crack team of scientists and gung-ho military types are mobilized to track it down. 98m/C VHS, DVD. Starr Andreeff, Mitchell Laurance, David Gale, Charles Lucia, Riva Spier, Jeff Doucette, Bill Gratton, Lewis Arquette, Jon Korkes, Melanie Shatner; D: George Elanjian Jr.; M: Tom Chase, Steve Rucker.

The Syrian Bride 2004 Mona (Khoury) isn't thrilled about her arranged marriage to her Syrian cousin since it means she can't return to visit her family in the Golan Heights because of the political situation. But Mona, accompanied by her older sister Amal (Abbass), prepares to fulfill her family's wishes despite endless red tape at the border crossing. Arabic and Hebrew with subtitles. 97m/C VHS, DVD. *IS FR GE* Hiam Abbass, Ashraf Barhoum, Clara Khoury, Eyad Sheety, Derar Sliman; D: Eran Riklis; W: Eran Riklis, Suha Arraf; C: Michael Wiesweg; M: Cyril Morin.

Syriana 2005 (R) Gaghan once again uses multiple storylines to tackle a major social issue (after his excellent "Traffic"). This time he studies the interactions of foreign and U.S. governments, Wall Street, the CIA, energy companies, ordinary workers, and lawyers that control the flow of oil to consumers. Dense narrative follows a displaced oil field worker, corporate troubleshooting lawyer (Wright), an energy analyst (Damon) who suffers a tragic loss, a betrayed CIA operative (Clooney), an oil-rich prince (Siddig), and a behind-the-scenes power broker (Plummer) as they maneuver to, intentionally or not, affect who controls the energy market, through backroom deals, terrorism (or the threat of it), and even lesspleasant methods. Well-done, if confusing film will generate discussion and reflection. 126m/C DVD, Blu-ray Disc, HD DVD. *US* George Clooney, Matt Damon, Jeffrey Wright, Chris Cooper, William Hurt, Tim Blake Nelson, Amanda Peet, Christopher Plummer, Alexander Siddig, Akbar Kurtha, Max Minghella, David Clennon, Robert Foxworth, Mark Strong, Mazhar Munir, Khan Shadid Ahmed, William C. Mitchell, Dadral Sonnell; D: Stephen Gaghan; W: Stephen Gaghan; C: Robert Elswit; M: Alexandre Desplat, Cynthia Weil. Oscars '05: Support. Actor (Clooney); Golden Globes '06: Support. Actor (Clooney); Natl. Bd. of Review '05: Adapt. Screenplay.

T-Bird Gang 1959 A high school student goes undercover to infiltrate a teen gang. When his cover is blown, things get hairy. Laughable sleaze-bag production. 75m/B VHS, DVD. Ed Nelson, John Brinkley, Pat George, Beach Dickerson, Tony Miller; D: Richard Harbinger; M: Shelley Manne.

T Bone N Weasel 1992 (PG-13) Hines and Lloyd play not-so-excons who steal a car and try to lead a life of ease. Crime doesn't pay. 94m/C VHS. Gregory Hines, Christopher Lloyd, Ned Beatty, Larry Hankin, Graham Jarvis, Rusty Schwimmer, Rip Torn, Sam Whipple; D: Lewis Teague; C: Thomas Del Ruth; M: Steve Tyrell. **CABLE**

T-Force 1994 (R) T-Force is a successful cybernetic law enforcement team set up in the year 2007. But when innocent people get caught in the T-Force crossfire, a team shutdown is ordered, causing the members to turn renegade and fight for their survival instead. The plot rarely gets in the way of the hard-hitting action. 101m/C VHS, DVD. Jack Scalia, Erin Gray, Evan Lurie, Daron McBee; D: Richard Pepin.

T-Men 1947 Treasury Department agents Dennis O'Brien (O'Keefe) and Tony Genaro (Ryder) infiltrate a mob counterfeiting gang. Filmed in semi-documentary style, exciting tale serves also as an effective commentary on the similarities between the agents and those they pursue. Mann and cinematographer Alton do especially fine work here. 96m/B VHS, DVD. Alfred Ryder, Dennis O'Keefe, June Lockhart, Mary Meade, Wallace Ford, Charles McGraw; D: Anthony Mann; W: John C. Higgins; C: John Alton; M: Paul Sawtell.

Table for Five 1983 (PG) A divorced father takes his children on a Mediterranean cruise and while sailing, he learns that his ex-wife has died. The father and his ex-wife's husband struggle over who should raise the children. Sentimental and well-acted. 120m/C VHS, DVD. Jon Voight, Millie Perkins, Richard Crenna, Robbie Kiger, Roxana Zal, Son Hoang Bui, Marie-Christine Barrault, Kevin Costner; D: Robert Lieberman; W: David Seltzer; M: Miles Goodman.

Table One 2000 (R) Mildly amusing but too familiar comedy finds Norman (Herman) and his buddies deciding to open a restaurant/bar in Manhattan so they can meet chicks. But they can't quite raise enough money, so Norman gets a local mobster to become a partner, only the mobster sends along his right-hand man Jimmy (Baldwin) to keep an eye on his investment. 84m/C VHS, DVD. David Herman, Stephen Baldwin, Michael Rooker, Luis Guzman, Burt Young, Ben Shenkman; D: Michael Scott Bregman; W: Michael Scott Bregman.

Table Settings 1984 A taped performance of James Lapines' comedy about the lives of three generations of a Jewish family. 90m/C VHS, Robert Klein, Stockard Channing, Dinah Manoff, Eileen Heckart; D: Trevor Evans; W: James Lapine.

Tabloid! 1988 Unorthodox woman prints and sells racy trash for enquiring minds. 99m/C VHS. Scott Davis, Glen Coburn; D: Bret McCormick, Matt Shaffen.

Taboo *Gohatto* 1999 In Kyoto, the Shogunate is crumbling and Japanese politics are turbulent. Two new recruits join a strict samurai academy—the rugged Tashiro (Asano) and a delicate teenager named Kano (Matsuda). Kano soon proves his worth to the commander, Kondo (Sai), and Captain Hijikata (Kitano), but his androgynous beauty begins to cause dissension—leading Kondo to forbid any relations between his men. Japanese with subtitles. 100m/C VHS, DVD. *JP* Takeshi "Beat" Kitano, Ryuhei Matsuda, Shinji Takeda, Tadanobu Asano; *D:* Nagisa Oshima; *W:* Nagisa Oshima; *M:* Ryuichi Sakamoto.

Taffin 1988 (R) An Irish bill collector battles a group of corrupt businessmen who want to replace the local soccer field with a hazardous chemical plant. Pretty dull fare, overall, with Brosnan much less charismatic than usual. 96m/C VHS, DVD. *GB* Pierce Brosnan, Ray McAnally, Alison Doody, Patrick Bergin; *D:* Francis Megahy; *W:* David Ambrose.

Tactical Assault 2002 (PG-13) During the Gulf War, Air Force pilot John Holiday (Hauer) loses it under pressure and nearly shoots down an unarmed passenger jet. Pilot Lee Banning (Patrick) is forced to shoot down Holiday's plane instead to save the situation. But Holiday doesn't see things that way and decides to get revenge on Lee. Good action in what's really a revenge thriller. 89m/C VHS, DVD. Rutger Hauer, Robert Patrick, Isabel Glasser, Ken Howard; *D:* Mark Griffiths. **VIDEO**

Tadpole 2002 (PG-13) You know you've hit a chord when your movie's title has been adopted as a verb (tadpoling) for the trend of older women cruising younger men. Precocious, prep-schooler Oscar Grubman (Stanford) comes home to Manhattan to spend the holidays with his remarried dad (Ritter) and his new stepmom (Weaver) on whom he promptly develops a crush. Soon the unrequited love for his new mum, the aptly named Eve, is soothed instead by her crackle-robbing best friend (a show-stealing Neuwirth). Stanford shines, even through the drab digital camerawork, in this witty new millennium "Graduate." 77m/C VHS, DVD. *US* Aaron Stanford, Sigourney Weaver, John Ritter, Bebe Neuwirth, Peter Appel, Adam LeFevre; *D:* Gary Winick; *W:* Heather McGowan, Niels Mueller; *C:* Hubert Taczanowski.

Tae Guk Gi: The Brotherhood of War 2004 (R) Two brothers are dragged into the ugly chaos of the Korean War when they're conscripted into the South Korean army after North Korea invades. Elder brother Jin-tae does what he can to protect his promising younger brother Jin-seok from the conflict, but both are swept up in the carnage and blood lust. Graphic and powerful anti-war film that puts the viewer in the center of what for most Americans is a historical footnote. Dizzyingly violent battle scenes may make some queasy. 140m/C DVD. *KN* Dong-Kun Jang, Won Bin, Lee Eun-joo; *D:* Kang Je-gyu; *W:* Kang Je-gyu; *C:* Hong Kyung-Pyo; *M:* Lee Dong-Jun.

Tabu: A Story of the South Seas 1931 Fascinating docudrama about a young pearl diver's ill-fated romance. The gods have declared the young woman he desires "taboo" to all men. Filmed on location in Tahiti. Authored and produced by Murnau and Flaherty. Flaherty left in mid-production due to artistic differences with Murnau, who was later killed in an auto accident one week before the premiere of film. 81m/B VHS, DVD. *D:* Robert Flaherty, F.W. Murnau; *C:* Floyd Crosby. Oscars '31: Cinematog, Natl. Film Reg. '94.

Taboo 2002 (R) Mish-mash horror/psycho-thriller flick. Six college friends gather at a remote mansion to play a provocative game of "taboo" involving a sex question. The following New Year's Eve they gather again and each receives an anonymous note condemning their previous answer. Then the killings start. 80m/C VHS, DVD. Nick Stahl, Eddie Kaye Thomas, January Jones, Lori Heuring, Derek Hamilton, Amber Benson; *D:* Max Makowski; *W:* Chris Fisher; *M:* Ryan Beveridge.

Tail Lights Fade 1999 (R) Angie (Allen) is living in Toronto when she learns her marijuana-dealing brother has been busted. So she convinces boyfriend Cole (Meyer) that they should drive to Vancouver in order to destroy his greenhouse crop before the cops discover it. And for some reason, Cole decides this would be a perfect opportunity to convince their friends Bruce (Busey) and Wendy (Richards) that they should indulge in a cross-country relay race. Dumb. Title comes from a Buffalo Tom song. 87m/C VHS, DVD. *CA* Tanya Allen, Breckin Meyer, Jake Busey, Denise Richards, Lisa Marie, Elizabeth Berkley, Jaimz Woolvett; *D:* Malcolm Ingram; *W:* Matthew Gissing; *C:* Brier Pearson.

The Tailor of Panama 2000 (R) British spy Andrew Osnard (Brosnan) threatens to expose the shady past of society tailor Harry Pendel (Rush) unless Harry passes on information about the political situation in Panama. But since Harry doesn't really know anything, he just makes up plausible lies. Le Carre and Boorman create a smart, cynical film from Le Carre's 1996 novel, utilizing Brosnan's not-so-famous alter-ego and expose the corruption of post-Cold War espionage and Western foreign affairs. Well-written, with believable characterizations and subtle, consistent plotting, and as an added bonus, the performances match the high standards of the writing. 109m/C VHS, DVD. *US IR* Pierce Brosnan, Geoffrey Rush, Jamie Lee Curtis, Brendan Gleeson, Catherine McCormack, Leonor Varela, Harold Pinter, Daniel Radcliffe, David Hayman, Mark Margolis, Martin Ferrero, John Fortune; *D:* John Boorman; *W:* John Boorman, Andrew Davies, John Le Carre; *C:* Philippe Rousselot; *M:* Shaun Davey.

Tails You Live, Heads You're Dead 1995 (R) Cable thriller features Bernsen as psycho Neil Jones, who kills at random—and tells a stranger, Jeff Quint (McGinley), whom he met at a bar that the man is his next victim. After an unsuccessful attempts on his life, Quint turns to private detective McKinley (Matheson) for help. Based on the short story "Liar's Dice" by Bill Pronzini. 91m/C VHS. Corbin Bernsen, Tec McGinley, Tim Matheson; *W:* Miguel Tejada-Flores; *D:* Tim Matheson; *M:* Michael Frank. **CABLE**

Tag: The Assassination Game 1982 (PG) An exciting new game has been discovered by a group of university students. Players act as spies and assassins. "killing" each other to make points. But a school newspaper sportswriter finds the game has become more real than make-believe. Timely topic in the early '80s when Dungeons and Dragons and other "war" games were popular on college campuses across the nation. 92m/C VHS, Robert Carradine, Linda Hamilton, Michael Winslow, Kristine DeBell, Perry Lang; *D:* Nick Castle; *W:* Nick Castle.

Tagget 1990 (PG-13) A former CIA operative who has erased his nightmarish stint in Vietnam gradually begins to recall his past. When pieces of the puzzle begin to come together, he remembers a few things that the government would prefer he forget. Soon, CIA men are on his trail and their mission is to see that he forgets his past—permanently. 89m/C VHS, Daniel J. Travanti, William Sadler, Roxanne Hart, Stephen Tobolowsky, Peter Michael Goetz, Sarah Douglas, Noel Harrison; *D:* Richard T. Heffron. **CABLE**

Tai-Pan 1986 (R) A 19th century Scottish trader and his beautiful Chinese mistress are the main characters in this confusing attempt to dramatize the story of Hong Kong's development into a thriving trading port. Too many subplots and characters are introduced in a short time to do justice to James Clavell's novel of the same name, the basis for the movie. The first American production completely filmed in China. 130m/C VHS, DVD. Bryan Brown, Joan Chen, John Stanton, Kyra Sedgwick, Tim Guinee, Russell Wong, Bert Remsen; *D:* Daryl Duke; *W:* John Briley; *C:* Jack Cardiff; *M:* Maurice Jarre.

Tainted 1988 Small-town woman tries to endure after being raped. Both her husband and the attacker are killed, and she is forced to conceal their deaths. Poorly scripted. 90m/C VHS, Shari Shattuck, Park Overall, Gene Tootle, Magilla Schaus, Blaque Fowler; *D:* Orestes Matacena.

Tainted Blood 1993 (R) Welch stars as an investigative reporter who latest story has her attempting to find the teenage twin of a psychotic killer. 86m/C VHS, Raquel Welch, Alley Mills, Kerri Green, Natasha Gregson Wagner, Joan Van Ark; *D:* Matthew Patrick; *W:* Kathleen Rowell, Ginny Cerrella; *C:* Billy Dickson.

Tainted Image 1991 Artist woman starts to lose sanity with help of boyfriend, psycho neighbor and rash of bizarre deaths. She turns to canvas for solace and decides she needs secret ingredient that can't be found in art supply store to complete masterpiece. 95m/C VHS, Tom Saunders, Sandra Frances, Annetta Arpin, Ken La Motte, Heidi Emerich, Steve Kornacki; *D:* Steve Kornacki.

The Take 1990 (R) Recovering alcoholic cop faces wrath of drug lord and marriage on the rocks. 91m/C VHS, Ray Sharkey, R. Lee Ermey, Lisa Hartman Black, Larry Manetti, Joe Lala; *D:* Leon Ichaso; *W:* Edward Anhalt, Hancel Glassberg; *M:* David 3eal.

The Take 2007 (R) Armored car driver Felix (Leguizamo) works hard to support his wife Marina (Perez) and their kids in L.A.'s tough Boyle Heights neighborhood. Felix barely survives a hijacking, carried out by vicious Adell Baldwin (Gibson). Shot in the head, Felix struggles with memory loss and anger issues and then learns the bad guys are trying to frame him for their crimes, but not if he gets to them first. 91m/C DVD. John Leguizamo, Rosie Perez, Tyrese Gibson, Bobby Carnevale, Yul Vazquez, Carlos Sanz, Roger Guenveur Smith, Matthew Hatchette, Jake Muxworthy; *D:* Brad Furman; *W:* Jonas Pate, Josh Pate; *C:* Lukas Ettlin; *M:* Chris Hajian. **VIDEO**

Take a Hard Ride 1975 (PG) Dull spaghetti western about a cowboy transporting money to Mexico, evading bandits and bounty hunters. 103m/C VHS, DVD. */T* Jim Brown, Lee Van Cleef, Fred William-

Tailspin: Behind the Korean Airline Tragedy 1989 Made-for-TV docudrama on the 1983 downing of Korean Aire flight 007 in Soviet airspace. Purports to show the U.S. government's reaction to what became a major international incident. 95m/C VHS, Michael Moriarty, Chris Sarandon, Harris Yulin, Gavin O'Herlihy, Ed O'Rose; *D:* David Darlow; *M:* David Ferguson.

Tailspin Tommy 1934 Features 12 chapters of the great action serial. Intrepid pilot helps a small airline win a mail contract then must battle an unscrupulous rival to keep it. 248m/B VHS, Maurice Murphy, Noah Beery Jr., Walter Miller, Patricia Farr, Grant Withers, John Davidson, William Desmond, Charles A. Browne; *D:* Lew Landers.

Take 2007 Nicolas Beauvy, Stephen Furst, Kevin Hooks; *D:* Keith Merrill.

Take Down *Evil: The Taking of Alta View* 1992 (PG-13) Rick Worthington (Hamlin) takes hostages in a Utah hospital maternity ward, seeking revenge on the doctors who sterilized his wife. He threatens to detonate a bomb ever as a hostage negotiator (O'Quinn) tries to defuse the situation. 95m/C VHS, DVD. Harry Hamlin, Teri Garr, Terry O'Quinn, Gary Frank, Keith Coulouris; *D:* Peter Levin; *W:* John Miglis; *C:* Fred Ovieux; *M:* John Mills. **TV**

Take It Big 1944 Uninspired B-musical starring the Tin Man from "Wizard of Oz." Haley is an impoverished actor who inherits a ranch and saves it by—surprise—putting on a show. 75m/B VHS, Jack Haley, Harriet Hilliard Nelson, Mary Beth Hughes, Arline Judge, Nils T. Granlund, Fuzzy Knight, Ozzie Nelson; *D:* Frank McDonald; *W:* Howard J. Green; *C:* Fred H. Jackman Jr.

Take It to the Limit 2001 Jack and Kay Chambers move to a new community in hopes of saving their marriage but all their neighbors are wife-swappers and the Chambers are soon joining in. Then there's a problem with a murder and the dull overextended sexcapades turn into a dull overextended thriller. 300m/C DVD. *GB* Robson Green, Beth Goddard, Danny (Daniel) Webb, Keith Barron, Olga Sosnovska; *D:* Alex Pillai; *W:* Caleb Ranson; *C:* Simon Meggs; *M:* Louis Gabriel Cowan. **TV**

Take Me 2001 Troubled teen Rick (Fitzpatrick) is sent to stay with his uncle (Mario) in hopes that it'll straighten him out. But that happens when Jill (Roenfeld), a cute girl, introduces him to rock climbing. This is a pretty good movie for kids. It's a bit obvious, but it treats the characters seriously. 87m/C DVD. Leo Fitzpatrick, John Mario, Grethel Roenfeld, Jason Bortz, Christin Coutz; *D:* Sam Klett; *W:* Arthur Jeon; *C:* Michael Anderson; *M:* Louis Gabriel Cowan.

Take Me Back to Oklahoma 1940 Musical western with comedy. 64m/B VHS, DVD. Tex Fitter, Terry Walker, Karl Hackett, George Eldredge; *D:* Albert Herman.

Take Me Home: The John Denver Story 2000 Biopic of the 70s country-folk crooner hits the high points and explores the lows, but it's typical TV movie fare, made quickly after Denver's death in a plane crash. Although he bares no physical resemblance to the singer, Lowe does a fine job. Based on the autobiography Denver co-wrote with Arthur Tobier. 90m/C VHS, DVD. Chad Lowe, Kristen Davis, Gerald McClaney, Brian Markinson, Susan Hegan, Garry Chalk; *D:* Jerry London; *W:* Stephan Harrigan; *C:* Mike Fash; *M:* Lee Holdridge. **TV**

Take Me Out to the Ball Game 1949 *Everybody's Cheering* Williams manages a baseball team, locks horns with players Sinatra and Kelly, and wins them over with song. Naturally, there's a water ballet scene. Contrived and forced, but enjoyable. ♪Take Me Out to the Ball Game; The Hat My Father Wore on St. Patrick's Day; O'Brien to Ryan to Goldberg; The Right Girl for Me; It's Fate, Baby, It's Fate; Yes, Indeedy; Strictly U.S.A. 93m/C VHS, DVD. Frank Sinatra, Gene Kelly, Esther Williams, Jules Munshin, Betty Garrett, Edward Arnold, Tom Dugan, Richard Lane; *D:* Busby Berkeley; *W:* Harry Tugend, George Wells; *C:* George J. Folsey; *M:* Roger Edens.

Take My Eyes *Te Day Mis Ojos* 2003 Pilar takes her young son Juan and hides out at her sister Ana's to escape violent husband Antonio. He, of course, can't understand what he did wrong and insists Pilar come back, but Ana has gotten her a job that gives her a little independence and self-esteem. When Antonio goes into counseling, Pilar reluctantly agrees to return but things are soon back to their nasty routine. Spanish with subtitles. 106m/C DVD. *SP* Laia Marull, Luis Tosar, Candela Pena, Rosa Maria Sarda, Sergi Calleja;

D: Iciar Bollain; **W:** Iciar Bollain, Alicia Luna; **C:** Carlos Gusi; **M:** Alberto Iglesias.

Take the Lead 🐾🐾½ **2006 (PG-13)** Charming Banderas dances with happy feet in this cliched, inspirational saga based on a true story. The instructor-owner of a Manhattan ballroom dance academy, Pierre Dulaine offers his services to Principal James (Woodard) in an effort to teach her South Bronx high school detention students some discipline and manners. The kids are reluctantly impressed by a smoldering tango, and Dulaine is equally intrigued when they add their hiphop moves to his formal steps. Everyone is gradually won over and, yes, it all leads up to a big "I've had the time of my life" dance competition. **117m/C DVD.** *US* Antonio Banderas, Alfre Woodard, Jenna Dewan, Dante Basco, Rob Brown, Yaya DaCosta, Lauren Collins, John Ortiz, Brandon D. Andrews; **D:** Liz Friedlander; **W:** Dianne Houston; **C:** Alex Nepomniaschy; **M:** Aaron Zigman.

Take the Money and Run 🐾🐾 **1969 (PG)** Allen's directing debut; he also co-wrote and starred. "Documentary" follows a timid, would-be bank robber who can't get his career off the ground and keeps landing in jail. Little plot, but who cares? Nonstop one-liners and slapstick. **85m/C VHS, DVD.** Woody Allen, Janet Margolin, Marcel Hillaire, Louise Lasser, Jacquelyn Hyde, Lonny (Lonnie) Chapman, Jan Merlin, James Anderson, Jackson Beck, Howard Storm; **D:** Woody Allen; **W:** Mickey Rose, Woody Allen; **C:** Lester Shorr; **M:** Marvin Hamlisch.

Take This Job & Shove It 🐾🐾 **1981 (PG)** The Johnny Paycheck song inspired this story of a hot-shot efficiency expert who returns to his hometown to streamline the local brewery. Encounters with old pals inspire self-questioning. Alternately inspired and hackneyed. Cameos by Paycheck and other country stars. **100m/C VHS, DVD.** Robert Hays, Art Carney, Barbara Hershey, David Keith, Martin Mull, Eddie Albert, Penelope Milford; **Cameos:** Johnny Paycheck, David Allan Coe, Charlie Rich, Lacy J. Dalton; **D:** Gus Trikonis; **W:** Barry Schneider.

Take Two 🐾 **1987 (R)** A woman has an affair with her husband's twin brother. Interesting metaphysically: Are you my husband or my lover? But is an adultery/murder drama with Frank Stallone worth 101 minutes of your time? **101m/C VHS.** Grant Goodeve, Robin Mattson, Frank Stallone, Warren Berlinger, Darwyn Swalve, Nita Talbot; **D:** Peter Rowe.

Taken 🐾🐾½ **1999 (R)** Businessman Coleman gets kidnapped along with his wife and business partners see a financial opportunity and decide not to pay the ransom. When he realizes this, Coleman thinks it prudent to befriend kidnapper Boutsikaris and hope that something can be worked out. **96m/C VHS, DVD.** *CA* Dabney Coleman, Dennis Boutsikaris, Linda Smith, Dorothee Berryman, Carl Alacchi; **D:** Max Fischer; **W:** Pierre Lapointe.

Taken 🐾🐾½ *Steven Spielberg Presents: Taken* **2002** There was nothing "mini" about this 10-part series shown on the Sci Fi Channel. It's a classic saga of alien abductions over 60 years and three generations, beginning in 1947. Series is narrated by 10-year-old Allie Keys (Fanning), the granddaughter of WWII fighter pilot Russell (Burton), who is taken by mysterious blue lights. There's also that Roswell incident and contact with aliens and strange powers and, well, a lot. **900m/C DVD.** Steve (Stephen) Burton, Julie Benz, Joel Gretsch, Michael Moriarty, Tina Holmes, Catherine Dent, Eric Close, Ryan Hurst, Chad Morgan, Willie Garson, Matt Frewer, James McDaniel, Emily Bergl, Dakota Fanning; **D:** Tobe Hooper, Bryan Spicer, Felix Alcala, Thomas J. Wright, Jeremy Paul Kagan, Jeff Woolnough, John Fawcett, Breck Eisner, Sergio Mimica-Gezzan, Michael Kattleman; **W:** Leslie Bohem; **C:** Jonathan Freeman, Joel

---

Ransom; **M:** Laura Karpman; **Nar:** Dakota Fanning. **CABLE**

Taken Alive 🐾🐾½ **1995 (PG-13)** Secret agent working for the U.S. government winds up in Italy to help a presidential candidate whose mistress has been kidnapped. In a case of mistaken identity, she hires a local sculptor (whom she believes is a professional assassin) to help her out. **92m/C VHS.** Franco (Columbo) Columbu, Barbara Niven, Frank Stallone, Robert Ginty, William (Bill) Smith; **D:** Christopher Holmes; **W:** Franco (Columbo) Columbu.

Taken Away 🐾🐾½ **1989** Struggling young divorcee Stephanie Monroe waits tables during the day and studies to be a computer tech at night in order to provide her eight-year-old daughter Abby with a better life. Unable to afford child care, Stephanie leaves Abby alone in the afternoon until she can get home from work. But when the welfare system finds out Stephanie is accused of child neglect and must fight a bureaucratic nightmare in order to get her child back. **94m/C VHS.** Valerie Bertinelli, Kevin Dunn, Joshua Maurer, Anna Maria Horsford, Juliet Sorcey, Nada Despotovich, Matthew Faison, James Arone; **D:** John D. Patterson; **W:** Robert Freedman, Selma Thomson. **TV**

The Takeover 🐾🐾½ **1994 (R)** East coast crime boss Danny Stein (Drago) decides to take over the L.A. operations of rival Tony Valachi (Mancuso). Lots of mayhem ensues. **91m/C VHS.** Billy Drago, Nick Mancuso, John Savage, Eric (Dafie) Da Re, Cali Timmins, David Amos, Gene Mitchell; **D:** Troy Cook; **W:** Gene Mitchell; **M:** Jimmy Lifton.

Taking Care of Business 🐾🐾½ *Filofax* **1990 (R)** Too familiar tale of switched identity has crazed Cubs fan Belushi find Grodin's Filofax, allowing him to pose as businessman and a story full of potholes. Old jokes and a story full of potholes. **108m/C VHS, DVD.** James Belushi, Charles Grodin, Anne DeSalvo, Loryn Locklin, Veronica Hamel, Hector Elizondo, Mako, Gates (Cheryl) McFadden, Stephen Elliott; **D:** Arthur Hiller; **W:** J.J. (Jeffrey) Abrams; **C:** David M. Walsh; **M:** Stewart Copeland.

Taking Lives 🐾🐾 **2004 (R)** Illeana Scott (Jolie), a sexy FBI profiler with an affinity for the macabre, is called in by the Montreal police to use her "special" skills to track down a serial killer who assumes the identity of his victims. Since the heroine cannot be without a love interest, along comes art gallery owner James Costa (Hawke) who, naturally, is a witness...no, wait, he's a suspect...oh, now he's a target. Keep your scorecards handy, folks. Caruso strives to craftily overwhelm his audience with loads of gruesome gore, and perhaps if the plot weren't as mangled as the victims it would have succeeded. Sutherland bears little more than play the convenient scapegoat while Rowlands masters the role of the alleged slayer's surly novel. Adapted from Michael Pye's novel where, interestingly, Jolie's character didn't exist. **103m/C VHS, DVD.** *US* Angelina Jolie, Ethan Hawke, Kiefer Sutherland, Gena Rowlands, Olivier Martinez, Tchéky Karyo, Jean-Hugues Anglade, Paul Franklin Dano, Justin Chatwin; **D:** D.J. Caruso; **W:** Jon Bokenkamp; **C:** Amir M. Mokri; **M:** Philip Glass.

The Taking of Beverly Hills 🐾 **1991 (R)** Deranged billionaire Bat Masterson designs a bogus toxic spill that leaves the wealth of Beverly Hills his for the taking. Football hero Boomer Hayes teams up with renegade cop Ed Kelvin to try and stop Masterson and save the city of Beverly Hills. **96m/C VHS.** Ken Wahl, Matt Frewer, Robert Davi, Harley Jane Kozak, Lee James, Branscombe Richmond, Lyman Ward, Michael Bowen, William Prince, Ken Swofford, George Wyner; **D:** Sidney J. Furie; **W:** Sidney J. Furie, David Burke.

The Taking of Flight 847: The Uli Derickson Story 🐾🐾 *The Flight* **1988** Wagner plays the stewardess who acted as a go-between for the passengers during a 1985 terrorist hijacking, saving all but one life. True-story drama is suspenseful and entertaining, nominated for several Emmys. **100m/C VHS.** Lindsay Wagner, Sandy McPeak, Ray Wise, Laurie Walters, Eli Danker, Joseph Nasser; **D:** Paul Wendkos; **W:** Norman Merrill. **TV**

The Taking of Pelham One Two Three 🐾🐾🐾 **1974 (R)** A hijack team, lead by the ruthless Shaw, seizes a NYC subway car and holds the 17 passengers for $1 million ransom. Fine pacing keeps things on the edge. New cinematic techniques used by cameraman Owen Roizman defines shadowy areas like never before. **105m/C VHS, DVD.** Robert Shaw, Walter Matthau, Martin Balsam, Hector Elizondo, Earl Hindman, Dick O'Neill, Jerry Stiller, Tony Roberts, Doris Roberts, Kenneth McMillan, Julius W. Harris, Sal Viscuso; **D:** Joseph Sargent; **W:** Peter Stone; **C:** Owen Roizman; **M:** David Shire.

Taking Sides 🐾🐾½ *Der Fall Furtwängler* **2001** Szabo again looks at Nazi-era Germany, this time in the story of famed conductor Wilhelm Furtwängler, who stayed in Germany as conductor of the Berlin Philharmonic under the Nazis. The film concentrates on Furtwängler's (Skarsgaard) pre-trial interrogation by American Denazification Committee officer Steve Arnold (Keitel), whose aides, both of German and Jewish descent, have some sympathy for Furtwängler. Arnold is caustic and unrelenting in his mission to get to the bottom of the conductor's collaboration, while Furtwängler refuses to believe he has anything to apologize for, invoking his allegiance to his art, and his professed belief that he was making a difference. Both performances are magnificent and aid greatly in Szabo and Harwood's ability to let you know where they stand, yet be balanced in their portrayal of both views of the man. **105m/C DVD.** *FR GE GB AT* Harvey Keitel, Stellan Skarsgard, Moritz Bleibtreu, Birgit Minichmayr, Oleg Tabakov, Ulrich Tukur, Hanns Zischler, August Zirner, R. Lee Ermey, Robin Renucci; **D:** Istvan Szabo; **W:** Ronald Harwood; **C:** Lajos Koltai.

Taking the Heat 🐾🐾½ **1993 (R)** When mobster Arkin kills a sporting-goods dealer with a golf club the murder is witnessed by yuppie Goldwyn. Whitfield is the ambitious cop who wants Goldwyn to testify against the gangster—if she can keep him alive long enough to get him to court. One long chase scene. **91m/C VHS.** Lynn Whitfield, Tony Goldwyn, Alan Arkin, George Segal, Peter Boyle; **D:** Tom Mankiewicz; **W:** Dan Gordon. **CABLE**

Tale of a Vampire 🐾🐾½ **1992 (R)** In present day London, ageless vampire Alex (Sands) still mourns his long-lost vampiric love, Virginia, when he meets Anne (Hamilton) (who resembles Virginia). Alex doesn't know he's being stalked by Virginia's husband, Edgar (Cranham), also a vampire. Edgar decides to use Anne (with whom Alex has fallen in love) as bait, in a revenge plot. A tiny budget and slow pacing mar the film's fine visual style and good work by the two male leads. Film debut for director Sato. **93m/C VHS.** *GB* Julian Sands, Kenneth Cranham, Suzanna Hamilton; **D:** Shimako Sato; **W:** Jane Corbett, Shimako Sato; **M:** Julian Joseph.

The Tale of Ruby Rose 🐾🐾 **1987 (PG)** Living in the mountains of Tasmania, Ruby Rose, her husband Henry, and their adopted son Gem, struggle to survive the '30s depression by hunting and trapping. Having spent all her life in the mountains, Ruby Rose has a very superstitious view of life and a terror of nightfall. But after an argument with her husband, Ruby Rose sets out on a cross-country journey to find her grandmother and discover the secrets of her past. **101m/C VHS.** *AU* Melita Jurisic, Chris Haywood; **D:** Roger Scholes; **W:** Roger Scholes; **M:** Paul Schutze.

A Tale of Springtime 🐾🐾½ **1989 (PG)** Comedy-romance is the first film in Rohmer's planned new series, the "Tales of the Four Seasons," not to be confused with his "Six Moral Tales" or his "Comedies and Proverbs." Centers around Jeanne, a high school philosophy teacher; Natacha, a young student; and Igor, Natacha's father. As characteristic of Rohmer films, texture and character largely overshadow linear plots and social messages. However, the efficiency and directness of his camera work make it a pleasure to watch. **107m/C VHS, DVD.** *FR*

Anne Teyssedre, Hugues Quester, Florence Darel, Eloise Bennett, Sophie Robin; **D:** Eric Rohmer; **W:** Eric Rohmer; **C:** Luc Pages; **M:** Robert Schumann.

The Tale of the Frog Prince 🐾🐾½ **1983** Superb edition of Shelley Duvall's "Faerie Tale Theatre" finds Williams the victim of an angry fairy godmother's spell. Garr to the rescue as the self-centered princess who saves him with a kiss. Directed and written by Idle of Monty Python fame. **60m/C VHS, DVD.** Robin Williams, Teri Garr; **D:** Eric Idle; **W:** Eric Idle.

A Tale of Two Cities 🐾🐾🐾 **1936** Lavish production of the Dickens' classic set during the French Revolution, about two men who bear a remarkable resemblance during the Revolution, both in love with the same girl. Carefree lawyer Sydney Carton (Colman) roused to responsibility, makes the ultimate sacrifice. A memorable Madame DeFarge from stage star Yurka in her film debut, with assistance from others. Dickens' film stars Rathbone, Oliver, and Walthall. **128m/B VHS, DVD.** Ronald Colman, Elizabeth Allan, Edna May Oliver, Reginald Owen, Isabel Jewell, Walter Catlett, H.B. Warner, Donald Woods, Basil Rathbone, Blanche Yurka, Henry B. Walthall; **D:** Jack Conway; **W:** W.P. Lipscomb, S.N. Behrman; **M:** Herbert Stothart.

A Tale of Two Cities 🐾🐾🐾 **1958** A well-done British version of the Dickens' classic about a lawyer who sacrifices himself to save another man from the guillotine during the French Reign of Terror. The sixth remake of the tale. **117mB VHS, DVD.** *GB* Dirk Bogarde, Dorothy Tutin, Christopher Lee, Donald Pleasence, Ian Bannen, Cecil Parker; **D:** Ralph Thomas.

A Tale of Two Cities 🐾🐾½ **1980** Impressive looking but bloodless adaptation of the Dickens novel set in the French Revolution. Saradon takes on the dual role of sacrificing English lawyer Carton and French nobleman Darnay, with Krige as the lovely woman caught between the two. **156m/C VHS.** Chris Sarandon, Alice Krige, Peter Cushing, Kenneth More, Barry Morse, Flora Robson, Billie Whitelaw; **D:** Jim Goddard; **W:** John Gay. **TV**

A Tale of Two Pizzas 🐾🐾 **2003 (PG)** Predictable family comedy with some charm. Rival Yonkers pizzeria owners Vito (Pastore) and Frank (Vincent) are constantly at odds over whose secret recipe is best. However, their kids, Angela (Paul) and Tony (Dubin), have more than sauce and crust on their minds. **82m/C DVD.** Vincent Pastore, Frank Vincent, Conor Dubin, Patti D'Arbanville, Robin Paul, Angela Pietropinto, Louis Guss; **D:** Vincent Sassone; **W:** Vincent Sassone; **C:** Peter Nelson; **M:** Peter Fish.

Tale of Two Sisters 🐾🐾🐾 **1989** Sheen narrates sensual drama about two beautiful, ambitious sisters. **90m/C VHS, DVD.** Valerie Breiman, Claudia Christian, Sydney Lassick, Jeff Conaway, Peter Berg; **D:** Adam Rifkin; **W:** Charlie Sheen; **C:** John Parenteau; **M:** Marc David Decker; **Nar:** Charlie Sheen.

A Tale of Two Sisters 🐾🐾🐾 **2003** *Janghwa, Hongryeon* Two sisters return home after a mysterious absence to the cold attentions of a near-psychotic stepmother and emotionally impotent father. A horrid tragedy occurred in this house, revealed piece by piece: sometimes slowly and indirectly, sometimes shockingly and brutally. Creepy Korean horror film works its way under the skin, sometimes borrowing the style of recent Japanese shockers. Actually reaches level of Greek tragedy through powerful ending. **115m/C DVD. KN** Jung-ah Yum, Su-jeong Lim, Geun-yeong Mun, Kap-su Kim; **D:** Ji-woon Kim; **W:** Ji-woon Kim; **C:** Mo-gae Lee; **M:** Byung-woo Lee.

A Tale of Winter 🐾🐾½ **1992** *Conte D'Hiver* Portrays the romantic trials of a young French woman who cannot choose between her two smitten lovers and her

---

one true love, the lord disappeared after one tried love, the lord disappeared father of her child. Felicie (Very) hopelessly loves Charles (Van Den Driessche), whom she met five years before, but mistakenly gave the wrong address. Rohmer's trademark conversation-filled scenas find her brooding over her predicament, running from one lover and back again, until a revelation during a viewing of Shakespeare's "The Winter's Tale." A charming cast carries the story to a surprise twist of an ending. Second in the series "Tales of the Four Seasons." In French with English subtitles. **114m/C VHS.** *FR* Charlote Very, Frederic Van Drer Driessche, Michel Voletti, Herve Furic, Ava Loraschi, Jean-Luc Revol, Haydee Caillot, Claude Bilette, Rosette, Mare Riviere; *D:* Eric Rohmer. *W:* Eric Rohmer; *C:* Luc Pages; *M:* Sebastien Erms.

Talent for the Game ⊘⊘½
1991 (PG) A slight but handsomely produced baseball pleasantry about a talent scout who recruits a phenomenal young pitcher, then sees the kid exploited by the team owner. More like an anecdote than a story, with an ending that aims a little too hard to please. Good for sports fans and family audiences. **91m/C VHS, DVD.** Edward James Olmos, Lorraine Bracco, Jeff Corbett, Jamey Sheridan, Terry Kinney; *D:* Robert M. Young; *W:* David Himmelstein, Thomas Michael Donnelly, Larry Ferguson; *M:* David Newman.

The Talent Given Us ⊘⊘⊘
2004 Writer/director/producer Andrew Wagner gives this road trip story a quasi-reality twist by casting his father Allen, mother Judy and sisters Emily and Maggie as, well, themselves. The Wagners have not seen their elusive son Andrew (Wagner) in several years, and embark on a cross-country drive from Manhattan to Los Angeles to catch up with him, picking up family friend Bumby (Dixon) en route. The miles are filled with unfiltered and sometimes unflattering discussion of everything from driving habits to sex to prescription drugs to thoughts of infidelity. The unnerving fascination with the line between real life and fantasy is a major draw. **97m/C DVD.** *US* Billy Wirth, Judy Wagner, Allen Wagner, Emily Wagner, Maggie Wagner, Judy Dixon; *D:* Andrew Wagner; *W:* Andrew Wagner; *C:* Andrew Wagner; *M:* David Dryas.

The Talented Mr. Ripley ⊘⊘½
1999 (R) Beautiful but ultimately hollow adaptation of Patricia Highsmith's chiller, which was previously filmed as 1960's "Purple Noon." This time around Damon takes on the title role as a poor nobody who is sent to Italy in 1958 to persuade rich playboy Dickie Greenleaf (Law), to return to the bosom of his family in New York. Only the more the emotionally needy Ripley sees of Dickie's sybaritic lifestyle—the more he wants it for himself, even if it means killing Dickie and literally assuming his identity. Law is the draw and the movie suffers a letdown after his death. **139m/C VHS, DVD.** Matt Damon, Jude Law, Gwyneth Paltrow, Cate Blanchett, Philip Seymour Hoffman, Jack Davenport, James Rebhorn, Stefania Rocca; *D:* Anthony Minghella; *W:* Anthony Minghella; *C:* John Seale; *M:* Gabriel Yared. British Acad. '99: Support. Actor (Law); Natl. Bd. of Review '99: Director (Minghella), Support. Actor (Hoffman).

Tales from a Parallel Universe: Eating Pattern ⊘⊘
Eating Pattern **1997 (R)** The *Lexx* space cruiser is part machine and part organic matter, so it needs nourishment, as does its crew. But Zev and Stanley make a big mistake stopping for food at the planet Klaagya. Seems the inhabitants are controlled by parasitic worms that feed on their brains and they're always interested in a fresh meal. Now it's up to Kai to come to the rescue. Third episode in the series. **93m/C VHS.** Brian Downey, Eva Habermann, Michael McManus, Rutger Hauer; *D:* Rainer Matsutani; *W:* Paul Donovan; *C:* Les Krizsan; *M:* Marty Simon.

Tales from a Parallel Universe: Giga Shadow ⊘⊘
Giga Shadow **1997 (R)** The Lexx crew must make a dangerous attempt to replenish Kai's supply of proto-blood, which brings them perilously near their arch-enemy. His

Shadow. The fourth (and last) film of the series. **93m/C VHS.** Brian Downey, Eva Habermann, Michael McManus, Malcolm McDowell; *D:* Robert Sigl; *W:* Paul Donovan; *C:* Les Krizsan; *M:* Marty Simon. **C.A.B.L.E.**

Tales from the Crypt Presents Bordello of Blood ⊘⊘
Bordello of Blood **1996 (R)** Detective Rafe Guttman (Miller) is on the case of a Bible thumper's (Eleniak) missing brother (Feldman). The trail leads him to a unique establishment, a brothel presided over by vampire queen Lilith (Everhart), whose clients all wind up dead (but probably with smiles on their faces), and the strange Reverend Current (Sarandon), who made a fine vampire himself in "Fright Night." Crypt Keeper's second big screen outing showcases Miller's slant on the leading man gig and serves up campy fun with the blood. **87m/C VHS, DVD.** Dennis Miller, Angie Everhart, Chris Sarandon, Corey Feldman, Erika Eleniak; *D:* Gilbert Adler; *W:* Gilbert Adler, A.L. Katz; *C:* Tom Priestley; *M:* Chris Boardman.

Tales from the Crypt Presents Demon Knight ⊘⊘
Demon Knight; Demon Keeper **1994 (R)** Gruesomely garish big-screen version of the TV series that was inspired by the lurid 1950s E.C. comics. Horrormeister Crypt Keeper offers his usual pun-filled introduction to a tale spun in a seedy boarding-house. Brayker (Sadler) is the guardian of an ancient key that keeps the forces of darkness from overwhelming mankind, a key desired by the charismatic Collector (Zane), who unleashes a disgusting mix of demons against the house's inhabitants. Curious hybrid of spook/splatter pic that doesn't quite work in either genre. **93m/C**

Tales from a Parallel Universe: Super Nova ⊘⊘
per Nova **1997 (R)** A continuation of the '*I Worship His Shadow*" episode, which finds the rebels in possession of the mile-long spacecraft known as The Lexx, which also happens to be the most destructive weapon in the universe. But they don't want to destroy the craft, instead they use the Lexx to visit the lost planet of Brunnis in hopes of restoring their lost leader to life. Only the rebels get captured by the Poet Man (Curry), and their deaths could lead to the total annihilation of the universe. **93m/C VHS.** Brian Downey, Eva Habermann, Michael McManus, Ellen Dubin, Tim Curry; *D:* Ron Oliver; *W:* Paul Donovan; *C:* Les Krizsan *M:* Marty Simon. **C.A.B.L.E.**

Tales from the Crypt ⊘⊘⊘
1972 (PG) A collection of five scary stories from the classic EC comics that bear the movie's title. Richardson tells the future to each tale involving misfortune and, of course, gore. **92m/C VHS, GB** Ralph Richardson, Joan Collins, Peter Cushing, Richard Greene, an Hendry; *D:* Freddie Francis.

Tales from the Crypt ⊘⊘⊘
1989 Three contemporary tales of the macabre, "The Man Who Was Death," "The Night Before," and "Dig That Cat. He's Real Gone," linked together by a special-effects host. Ry Cooder provides the musical score for the second episode. Based on stories published by William M. Gaines in EC Comics. **81m/C VHS.** William Sadler, Mary Ellen Trainor, Larry Drake, Joe Pantoliano, Robert Wuhl, Gustav Vintas; *D:* Richard Donner, Walter Hill, Robert Zemeckis; *M:* Ry Cooder, Alan Silvestri. **C.A.B.L.E.**

Tales of Erotica ⊘⊘
Die Erotische Geschichten **1993 (R)** Four stories made for German TV. "The Dutch Master" finds New Yorker Teresa (Sorvino) becoming obsessed with a Vermeer-style painting at a museum. She begins to dress like the lively characters and eventually disappears into the picture itself. "The Insatiable Mrs. Kirsch" finds a vacationing writer (Shepherd) becoming fascinated by a fellow guest (Baynes), who seems to be having something. In "Vroom Vroom Vroom" luckless Leroy (Barboza) asks a voodoo doctor for help with the girls and winds up with a motorcycle that transforms itself into a beautiful woman when ridden. "Wet" has bathroom-fixture salesman Bruce (Howard) enticed by persistent customer Davida (Williams), who insists they both try out the showroom hot tub before she'll consider buying. **104m/C VHS, DVD.** Melvin Van Peebles, Simon Shepherd, Hetty Baynes, Ken Russell, Richard Barboza, Ariliss Howard, Cynda Williams; *D:* Ken Russell, Susan Seidelman, Melvin Van Peebles, Bob Rafelson; *W:* Susan Seidelman, Melvin Van Peebles, Bob Rafelson, Jonathan Brett; *C:* Maryse Alberti, Hong Manley, Igor Sunara; *M:* Melvin Van Peebles, Wendy Blackstone, David Mc-Hugh. **TV**

The Tales of Hoffmann ⊘⊘½
195? A ballet-opera consisting of three stories by Jacques Offenbach covering romance, magic and mystery arising out of a poet's misadventures in love. Lavishly designed and highly stylized. **135m/C VHS,**

Tales from a Parallel Universe: I Worship His Shadow ⊘⊘
I Worship His Shadow **1997 (R)** Space rebels try to unseat a tyrannical ruler known as His Shadow, in this first of a four-part series. A prophecy states that the ruler will be defeated by a dying race and aiding that prediction are rebel leader Thodin (Bostwick), cowardly Stanley Tweedle (Downey), warrior Kai (McManus), and Zev (Habermann). His Shadow's unwilling love slave. Followed by the "Super Nova" episode. **95m/C VHS.** Brian Downey, Eva Habermann, Michael McManus, Barry Bostwick, Ellen Dubin; *D:* Paul Donovan; *W:* Paul Donovan, Lex Gigeroff; *M:* Marty Simon. **C.A.B.L.E.**

Tales from the Darkside: The Movie ⊘⊘
1990 (R) Three short stories in the tradition of, the ghoulish TV show are brought to the big screen, with mixed results. The plot centers around a boy who is being held captive by a cannibal, in order to prolong his life, he tells her horror stories. The tales were written by such famous writers as Sir Arthur Conan Doyle, Stephen King and Michael McDowelI. **93m/C VHS, DVD.** Deborah Harry, Christian Slater, David Johansen, William Hickey, James Remar, Rae Dawn Chong, Julianne Moore, Robert Klein, Steve Buscemi, Matthew Lawrence; *D:* John Harrison; *M:* George A. Romero, Michael McDowell; *C:* Rob Draper.

Tales from the Gimli Hospital ⊘⊘
1988 A smallpox outbreak at the turn of the century finds Einar and Gunnar sharing a hospital room. They begin telling each other increasingly bizarre personal secrets and develop a serious rivalry. Sharp dialogue with some equally grotesque imagery. Director Maddin's first feature film. **68m/B VHS, DVD.** *CA* Kyle McCulloch, Michael Gottli, Angela Heck, Margaret Anne McLeod; *D:* Guy Maddin; *W:* Guy Maddin. *C:* Guy Maddin.

Tales from the Hood ⊘⊘
1995 (R) Horror anthology with that urban twist. Three young thugs search for lost drugs inside a funeral parlor run by creepy Mr. Simms (Williams III) and instead walk into a world of four chilling and funny stories of fright dealing with racism and black on black crime Tales aren't very original and are often too preachy for true enjoyment, but its nice to see someone attempt to breath life into an old and familiar genre. **97m/C VHS; DVD.** Lamont Bentley, De'Aundre Bonds, Tom Wright, Michael Massee, Duane Whitaker, Brandon Hammond, Paula Jai Parker, Roger Guenveur Smith, Art Evans, Clarence Williams III, Corbin Bernsen, David Alan Grier, Wings Hauser, Rosalind Cash, Rusty Cundieff, Joe Torry, Antony Griffith, Darin Scott; *D:* Rusty Cundieff; *W:* Rusty Cundieff, Darin Scott; *C:* Anthony B. Richmond; *M:* Christopher Young.

Tales of Beatrix Potter ⊘⊘½
Beatrix Potter and Tales of Potter **1971 (G)** The Royal Ballet Company of England performs in this adaptation of the adventures of Beatrix Potter's colorful and memorable creatures. Beautifully done. **90m/C VHS, DVD, GB** *D:* Reginald Mills.

Tales of the Kama Sutra 2: Monsoon ⊘
1998 Naval officer Kenneth Blake (Tyson) and his fiancee Sally (McShane) travel to the island of Goa, off the coast of India, to enjoy a resort vacation. But Blake is drawn into an affair with Leela (Brodie), who tells him that they are the reincarnation of legendary lovers who leaped to their death from the island's lighthouse 500 years before. It's one way to get a man interested. **96m/C VHS, DVD.** Richard Tyson, Helen Brodie, Jenny (Jennifer) McShane, Matt McCoy, Doug Jeffery, Gulshan Grover; *D:* Jag Mundhra. **VIDEO**

Tales of the Kama Sutra: The Perfumed Garden ⊘
The Perfumed Garden **1998 (R)** Not particularly erotic story centers on Americans Michael and Lisa, who have a rocky romantic relationship. Lisa follows Michael to India where he is helping to restore the erotic sculptures of Khajuraho. However, Michael's lust is aroused by a mysterious Indian woman (Kumar), who happens to resemble the statue he's repairing, which leads to a retelling of one Kama Sutra story about a royal courtesan set 1000 years earlier. **104m/C VHS, DVD.** Pravesh Kumar, Ivan Bacarra, Amy Lindsey, Rajeshwari Sachdev, Bhupinder Singh, Nasser; *D:* Jag Mundhra.

Tales of the Klondike: In a Far Country ⊘⊘
1987 An adaptation of Jack London's story exploring the fears, dangers, and joys experienced by prospectors in the harsh wilderness of northwest Canadian gold country. **60m/C VHS.** Robert Carradine, Scott Hylands; *D:* Janine Manatis; *Nar:* Orson Welles. **TV**

Tales of the Klondike: Race for Number One ⊘⊘
1987 Two men compete in a highly contested dogsled race—the goal of which is to be first to reach a tract of gold-laden land. Adapted from a story by Jack London. **60m/C VHS.** David Ferry, John Ireland; *D:* David Cobham; *Nar:* Orson Welles. **TV**

VHS, DVD. Billy Zane, William Sadler, Jada Pinkett Smith, Brenda Bakke, CCH Pounder, Dick Miller, Thomas Haden Church; *D:* Ernest R. Dickerson; *W:* Ethan Reiff, Cyrus Voris, Mark Bishop; *C:* Rick Bota; *M:* Ed Shearmur; *V:* John Kassir.

Tales of Manhattan ⊘⊘⊘
1942 Star-studded anthology about a tailor who curses a tailcoat that then travels, with varying degrees of good and bad fortune, from owner to owner. There's a love triangle, a love match, a concert appearance, a down-on-his-luck lawyer, a swanky party, a crook, and a windfall for some share-croppers. Fields' party episode ("he wears the coat to give a lecture and winds up wreaking havoc) was cut out of the original theatrical release. **118m/C VHS.** Charles Boyer, Rita Hayworth, Thomas Mitchell, Ginger Rogers, Henry Fonda, Cesar Romero, Elsa Lanchester, Charles Laughton, Edward G. Robinson, George Sanders, James Gleason, J. Carrol Naish, Paul Robeson, Ethel Waters, Eddie Anderson, W.C. Fields, Margaret Dumont; *D:* Julien Duvivier; *W:* Ben Hecht, Donald Ogden Stewart, Samuel Hoffenstein, Ferenc Molnar, Alan Campbell; *C:* Joseph Walker; *M:* Sol Kaplan.

Tales of Ordinary Madness ⊘
1983 Gazzara as a poet who drinks and sleeps with assorted women. Based on the stories of Charles Bukowski. Pretentious and dull. **107m/C VHS, DVD.** Ben Gazzara, Ornella Muti, Susan Tyrrell, Tanya Lopert, Roy Brocksmith, Katya Berger; *D:* Marco Ferreri; *W:* Marco Ferreri, Sergio Amidei, Anthony Foutz; *C:* Tonino Delli Colli; *M:* Philippe Sarde.

Tales of Robin Hood ⊘⊘
1952 A low-budget depiction of the Robin Hood legend. **59m/B VHS.** Robert Clarke, Mary Hatcher, Paul Cavanagh, Wade Crosby, Whit Bissell, Ben Welden, Robert Bice, Bruce Lester, Margia Dean, Lester Matthews; *D:* James Tinling; *W:* George Robinson.

Tales of Terror ⊘⊘
1962 Three tales of terror based on Poe's *Tales of Terror* **1962** Three tales of terror based on stories by Edgar Allan Poe: "Morella," "The Black Cat," and the "The Case of M. Valdemar." Price stars in all three segments and is excellent as the bitter and resentful husband in "Morella." **90m/C VHS, DVD.** Vincent Price, Peter Lorre, Basil Rathbone, Debra Paget, Joyce Jameson, Maggie Pierce, Leona Gage, Edmund Cobb; *D:* Roger Corman; *W:* Richard Matheson; *C:* Floyd Crosby; *M:* Les Baxter.

Tales of the Klondike: The Scorn of Women ✓✓ *1987* An available man is enthusiastically courted by every single woman in Dawson City, Alaska. From a story by Jack London. **60m/C VHS.** Tom Butler, Eva Gabor; **D:** Claude Fournier; **Nar:** Orson Welles. **TV**

Tales of the Klondike: The Unexpected ✓✓ *1987* Five gold prospectors grow rich, but lose all that is most valuable through overwhelming greed. Adapted from a story by Jack London. **60m/C VHS.** John Candy, Cherie Lunghi; **D:** Peter Pearson; **Nar:** Orson Welles. **TV**

Tales of the Unexpected ✓✓1/2 *1991* Four tales designed to startle the senses and provoke the imagination. Episodes include "People Don't Do Such Things," about a marriage gone awry; "Youth from Vienna," about a weird fountain of youth; "Skeleton in the Cupboard," which tells of a man desperately trying to hide some strange secret and finally, "Bird of Prey," in which a pet parrot leaves its owners an enormous egg before dying. **101m/C VHS.** Arthur Hill, Samantha Eggar, Don Johnson, Dick Smothers, Sharon Gless, James Carroll Jordan, Charles Dance, Zoe Wanamaker, Sondra Locke, Frank Converse; **D:** Gordon Hessler, Norman Lloyd, Paul Annett, Ray Danton.

Tales That Witness Madness ✓✓1/2 *1973* (R) An asylum is the setting for four tales of horror, as a doctor tells a visitor how four patients ended up in his clinic. Stories are "Mr. Tiger," "Penny Farthing," "Mel" and "Luau." At the time this was Novak's first film appearance in four years. **90m/C VHS, DVD, GB** Jack Hawkins, Donald Pleasence, Suzy Kendall, Joan Collins, Kim Novak, Mary Tamm, Georgia Brown, Donald Houston; **D:** David Wood, Peter McEnery; **D:** Freddie Francis.

Talion ✓✓ *An Eye for an Eye 1966* (PG) A western revenge movie that features two disabled men, a rancher and a bounty hunter, who team up to find the gang that slaughtered the rancher's family. **92m/C VHS.** Robert Lansing, Slim Pickens, Patrick Wayne; **D:** Michael D. Moore.

Talisman ✓1/2 *1998* (R) Theriel, the Black Angel, has been fused to an ancient Talisman for centuries. Summoned from his rest, he must offer seven human sacrifices to complete an evil ritual that will open the gates of hell and usher in the end of the world. Two teenagers are chosen to help Theriel but they've got other things in mind. Director DeCoteau used the pseud "Victoria Sloan" for this venture. **90m/C VHS.** Walter Jones, Jason Adelman, Billy Parish, Ilinca Goia; **D:** David DeCoteau; **W:** Benjamin Carr. **VIDEO**

Talk of Angels ✓✓ *1996* (PG-13) Young Irish aristocrat Mary (Walker) leaves her homeland for Spain to serve as governess for a wealthy family, just as the country is about to erupt into civil war. She ignites passion in everyone she encounters, especially her married employer and his married son. This forbidden relationship serves as the crux of the story. Unfortunately, good looks alone (which both stars have) don't create chemistry, and Walker and Perez simply fizzle on screen. The film and its leads are certainly nice to look at, but there's something missing: an interesting story. With wartime love story thefts from the ultimate wince factor. This "Gone With the Wind" (including a blatant rip-off of the famous scene where Scarlett walks among the sea of dead soldiers),

the story is hardly original. **97m/C VHS, DVD.** Polly Walker, Vincent Perez, Frances McDormand, Franco Nero, Marisa Paredes, Penelope Cruz, Ruth McCabe, Francesco Rabal, Ariadna Gil, Rossy de Palma; **D:** Nick Hamm; **W:** Ann Guedes, Frank McGuinness; **C:** Alexei Rodionov; **M:** Trevor Jones.

Talk of the Town ✓✓✓ *1942* A brilliantly cast, strange mixture of screwball comedy and lynch-mob melodramatics. An accused arsonist, a Supreme Court judge and the girl they both love try to clear the former's name and evade the cops. **118m/B VHS, DVD.** Ronald Colman, Cary Grant, Jean Arthur, Edgar Buchanan, Glenda Farrell, Rex Ingram, Emma Dunn; **D:** George Stevens.

Talk Radio ✓✓✓ *1988* (R) Riveting Stone adaptation of Bogosian's one-man play. An acidic talk radio host confronts America's evil side and his own past over the airwaves. The main character is loosely based on the life of Alan Berg, a Denver talk show host who was murdered by white supremacists. **110m/C VHS, DVD.** Eric Bogosian, Alec Baldwin, Ellen Greene, John Pankow, John C. McGinley, Michael Wincott, Leslie Hope; **D:** Oliver Stone; **W:** Eric Bogosian, Oliver Stone; **C:** Robert Richardson; **M:** Stewart Copeland.

Talk to Her ✓✓✓1/2 *Hable con Ella 2002* (R) Powerful entry from director Almodovar about the bond of two men caring for comatose women. Marco (Grandinetti), a travel writer, in the early stages of dating Spain's most famous female bullfighter Lydia (Flores), finds himself looking after her after she is gored by a bull. Benigno (Camara) is a male nurse who looks after the comatose Alicia (Watling), a ballerina he has only seen from afar but loves. The two men meet in the hospital and, sharing similar experiences, come to know one another in their grief. While both men are truly caring during their bedside vigils, a slightly disturbing, kinky undercurrent is also at work, and strange and shocking events will occur before film fully unspools. Refusing to judge these actions, however, Almodovar artfully offers some alternate motivations for his characters' seemingly anti-social behaviors and takes material that could have easily been a soap opera in lesser hands, and elevates it to a new level. Silent fantasy sequence depicts director's signature sexual exploration. **112m/C VHS, DVD, SP** Javier Camara, Dario Grandinetti, Rosario Flores, Leonor Watling, Geraldine Chaplin; **D:** Pedro Almodovar; **W:** Pedro Almodovar; **C:** Javier Aguirresarobe; **M:** Alberto Iglesias; **Cam:** Javier Aguirresarobe; **A:** Foreign Film, Orig. Screenplay; British Acad. '02: Foreign Film, Orig. Screenplay; Golden Globes '03: Foreign Film; L.A. Film Critics '02: Director (Almodovar); Natl. Soc. of Review '02: Foreign Film.

Talk to Me ✓✓ *1984* A successful New York accountant checks into the Hollins Communication Institute to cure his stuttering. While there, he meets and falls in love with a squirrel-hunting stuttering woman from Arkansas. **90m/C VHS.** Austin Pendleton, Michael Murphy, Louise Fletcher, Brian Backer, Clifton James; **D:** Julius Potocsny; **W:** Nelson Breen; **C:** Julius Potocsny; **M:** Coleridge-Taylor Perkinson.

Talk to Me ✓✓1/2 *2007* (R) Back when radio personalities had, well, personality, ex-con turned DJ Ralph Waldo "Petey" Greene Jr. (Cheadle) used his outlandish on- and off-air presence to lend a voice to the simmering racial and social unrest in 1960s Washington DC. Cheadle is magnetic as Greene battles both his uptight station director (the excellent Ejiofor) and his own personal demons during his tumultuous flash of fame. Director Lemmons explores both the hilarity and gravity of Greene's complex story, resisting the need to tie it up with a neat, triumphant bow. **118m/C DVD, HD DVD, US Don Cheadle, Chiwetel Ejiofor, Martin Sheen, Taraji P. Henson, Cedric the Entertainer, Ellie Downs, Mike Epps, Vondie Curtis-Hall; **D:** Kasi Lemmons; **W:** Michael Genet, Rick Famuyiwa; **C:** Stephane Fontaine; **M:** Terence Blanchard. Ind. Spirit '08: Support. Actor (Ejiofor).

Talkin' Dirty after Dark ✓✓ *1991* (R) Sexy comedy starring Lawrence as a suave comedian who will do anything to get a late-night spot at Dukie's comedy club. **88m/C VHS, DVD.** Martin Lawrence, Jedda

Jones, Phyllis Stickney, Darryl Sivad; **D:** Topper Carew; **W:** Topper Carew.

Talking about Sex ✓✓✓ *1994* Publishing party for a shrink's self-help manual sparks many conversations about sex and romance among a group of fashionable Los Angelenos. The breezy party chatter is broken up by B&W pseudo-documentary interludes of women exchanging confidences. **83m/C VHS.** Kim Wayans, Marcy Walker, Daniel Beer, Randy Powell, Kerry Ruff, Joe Richards, Daria Lynn; **D:** Aaron Speiser; **W:** Aaron Speiser, Carl Nelson; **M:** Tim Landers.

Talking Walls ✓1/2 *Motel Vacancy 1985* A college sociology student uses high-tech surveillance equipment to spy on the clients of a seedy motel, in order to complete his thesis on human sexuality. **85m/C VHS.** Stephen Shellen, Marie Laurin, Barry Primus, Sally Kirkland; **D:** Stephen Verona.

The Tall Blond Man with One Black Shoe ✓✓✓ *Le Grand Blond avec une Chaussure Noire 1972* (PG) A violinist is completely unaware that rival spies mistakenly think he is also a spy, and that he is the center of a plot to booby-trap an overly ambitious agent at the French Secret Service. A sequel followed called "Return of the Tall Blond Man with One Black Shoe" which was followed by a disappointing American remake, "The Man with One Red Shoe." In French with English subtitles or dubbed. **90m/C VHS, FR** Pierre Richard, Bernard Blier, Jean Rochefort, Mireille Darc, Jean Carmet; **D:** Yves Robert; **W:** Francis Veber; **M:** Vladimir Cosma.

Tall, Dark and Deadly ✓✓ *1995* (R) Roy (Scalia) romances Maggie (Delaney), a young woman he's met in a bar. The viewer's already clued in that Roy's a bad 'un (seein' as how he's killed one woman) and when he chains Maggie to a sink, she picks up on the idea that he's a wacko. Basic damsel-in-distress with a cast that manages to keep straight faces in the most preposterous of circumstances. **88m/C VHS.** Jack Scalia, Kim Delaney, Todd Allen, Gina Mastrogiacomo, Ely Pouget; **D:** Kenneth Fink; **W:** MaryAnne Kasica, Michael Scheff; **M:** Joseph Vitarelli. **CABLE**

The Tall Guy ✓✓✓ *1989* (R) Goldblum is a too-tall actor who tries the scene in London and falls the lead in a musical version of "The Elephant Man," becoming an overnight success. Not consistently funny, but good British comedy, including an interesting sex scene. **92m/C VHS, DVD.** John Wayne, Ella Raines, George "Gabby" Hayes, Ward Bond; **D:** Edwin L. Marin.

Tall in the Saddle ✓✓1/2 *1944* A misogynist foreman (Wayne) finds himself accused of murder. Meanwhile, he falls in love with his female boss's niece. An inoffensive and memorable western. **79m/B VHS, DVD.** John Wayne, Ella Raines, George "Gabby" Hayes, Ward Bond; **D:** Edwin L. Marin.

Tall Lie ✓✓ *For Men Only 1953* A student quits a fraternity hazing exercise. He's pursued by a psychotic bunch of his fraternity brothers and is killed in a smashup. A local doctor goes onto an anti-hazing campaign in the aftermath. **93m/B VHS.** Paul Henreid, Robert Sherman; **D:** Paul Henreid.

The Tall Men ✓✓ *1955* Standard western features frontier hands on a rough cattle drive confronting Indians, outlaws, and the wilderness while vying with each other for the love of Russell. **122m/C VHS.** Clark Gable, Jane Russell, Robert Ryan, Cameron Mitchell, Mae Marsh; **D:** Raoul Walsh; **W:** Sydney (Sidney) Boehm, Frank Nugent; **C:** Leo Tover; **M:** Victor Young.

Tall Story ✓✓ *1960* Perkins is a star basketball player who must pass a crucial test in order to continue to play the game. In addition to the pressure of the exam, he is being pressured by gamblers to throw a game against the Russians. Fonda makes her screen debut as a cheerleader who is so awe-struck by Perkins that she takes the same classes just to be close to him. Based on the play by Howard Lindsay and Russel Crouse, and the novel "The Homecoming Game" by Howard Nemerov. **91m/C VHS.** Anthony Per-

kins, Jane Fonda, Ray Walston, Marc Connelly, Anne Jackson, Tom Laughlin, Gary Lockwood, Elizabeth Patterson, Barbara Darrow; **D:** Joshua Logan; **W:** Julius J. Epstein; **C:** Ellsworth Fredericks; **M:** Cyril Mockridge.

The Tall T ✓✓1/2 *1957* A veteran rancher (Pat) stumbles onto big trouble when by chance he catches a stage coach that is eventually overrun by an evil band of cut-throats. After killing everyone on the coach except Pat and the daughter of a wealthy copper mine owner (Doretta), the renegades decide to leave the scene with the unfortunate two as hostages. Pat and Doretta, although in dire straits, find time to fall in love and devise an intricate plan for their escape. Regarded in certain western-lover circles as a cult classic. **77m/B VHS.** Randolph Scott, Richard Boone, Maureen O'Sullivan, Arthur Hunnicutt, Skip Homeier, Henry Silva, Robert Burton, Robert Anderson; **D:** Budd Boetticher; **W:** Burt Kennedy. Natl. Film Reg. '00.

Tall Tale: The Unbelievable Adventures of Pecos Bill ✓✓ *1995* (PG) Having trouble with greedy land owners out for his pa's land, Daniel Hackett (Stahl) summons the help of three Old West legends: Pecos Bill (Swayze), John Henry (Brown), and Paul Bunyan (Platt) to face off with the evil industrialist J.P. Stiles (Glenn). Disney's variation on the "Wizard of Oz" is riddled with cartoonish characters and sleep-inducing dialogue. It would truly be a tall tale if it were said that this movie was any good. **98m/C VHS.** Patrick Swayze, Oliver Platt, Roger Aaron Brown, Nick Stahl, Scott Glenn, Stephen Lang, Jared Harris, Catherine O'Hara; **D:** Jeremiah S. Chechik; **W:** Steven L. Bloom, Robert Rodat; **C:** Janusz Kaminski.

Tall, Tan and Terrific *1946* Things really go crazy when the owner of a nightclub in Harlem is accused of murder. **40m/C VHS.** Mantan Moreland, Monte Hawley, Francine Everett, Dots Johnson; **D:** Bud Pollard.

Tall Texan ✓✓1/2 *1953* A motley crew seeks gold in an Indian burial ground in the desert. Flawed but interesting and suspenseful. Greed, lust, Indians and desert heat. **82m/B VHS, DVD.** Lloyd Bridges, Lee J. Cobb, Marie Windsor, George Steele; **D:** Elmo Williams; **C:** Joseph Biroc.

Talladega Nights: The Ballad of Ricky Bobby ✓✓ *2006* (PG-13) It's a no-brainer concept—Will Ferrell as a NASCAR driver—but Ferrell's talented enough that he could probably make "Will Ferrell as a stamp collector" pretty entertaining. Race car legend Ricky Bobby is the oblivious king of his racing circuit until French Formula-1 driver Jean Girard (Baron Cohen) bests him and ruins Ricky's confidence. There are lots of laughs as Ricky claws his way back on top, but the scenario is so similar to Ferrell and director Adam McKay's previous effort, "Anchorman", that the whole affair has a "been there, done that" vibe. McKay's inability to ever yell "cut" during Ferrell's increasingly tedious tangents doesn't help either. **108m/C DVD, Blu-ray Disc, UMD, US** Will Ferrell, John C. Reilly, Sacha Baron Cohen, Michael Clarke Duncan, Leslie Bibb, Amy Adams, Gary Cole, Molly Shannon, Jane Lynch, Andy Richter, Houston Tumlin, Grayson Russell; **D:** Adam McKay; **W:** Will Ferrell, Adam McKay; **C:** Oliver Wood; **M:** Alex Wurman.

Talons of the Eagle ✓✓ *1992* Martial arts adventure centers around three undercover agents who go up against crimelord Mr. Li (Hong). To impress Li, martial arts champion Tyler Wilson (Blanks) and vice detective Michael Reeds (Merhi) enter a deadly martial arts tournament. They later hook up with beautiful agent Cassandra Hubbard (Barnes), who has already investigated Li's drug, gambling, and prostitution rings. Features the most advanced fighting techniques ever filmed. **96m/C VHS, DVD.** Billy Blanks, Jalal Merhi, James Hong, Priscilla Barnes, Matthias Hues; **D:** Michael Kennedy; **W:** J. Stephen Maunder.

Tamango ✓✓ *1959* A confusing drama set on a slave ship travelling from Africa to Cuba in 1830. Jurgens is the ship's captain who takes the black Dandridge as his mistress. Meanwhile, the slaves are plotting a revolt, with Dandridge as a conspirator. The interracial romance does take a secondary role to the racial conflicts. The title refers to the leader of the slave revolt, played by Cressan. Filmed in both English- and French-language versions. 98m/C VHS, FR Curt Jurgens, Dorothy Dandridge, Jean Servais, Alex Cressan; *D:* John Berry.

The Tamarind Seed 🦴1/2 **1974** Andrews and Sharif are star-crossed lovers kept apart by Cold War espionage. Dated, dull and desultory. 123m/C VHS, Julie Andrews, Omar Sharif, Anthony Quayle, Dan O'Herlihy, Sylvia Syms; *D:* Blake Edwards; *W:* Blake Edwards; *C:* Frederick A. (Freddie) Young; *M:* John Barry.

The Taming of the Shrew 🦴🦴1/2 **1929** Historically interesting early talkie featuring sole (if perhaps unfortunate) pairing of Pickford and Fairbanks. Features the legendary credit line "By William Shakespeare, with additional dialogue by Sam Taylor." Re-edited in 1966; 1967 Zeffirelli remake featured Taylor and Burton. 66m/B VHS, DVD, Mary Pickford, Douglas Fairbanks Sr., Edwin Maxwell, Joseph Cawthorn; *D:* Sam Taylor; *C:* Karl Struss.

The Taming of the Shrew 🦴🦴🦴1/2 **1967** A lavish screen version of the classic Shakespearean comedy. Burton and Taylor are violently physical and perfectly cast as the battling Katherine and Petruchio. At the time the film was made, Burton and Taylor were having their own marital problems, which not only added an inner fire to their performances, but sent the interested movie-goers to the theatres in droves. 122m/C VHS, DVD, IT Elizabeth Taylor, Richard Burton, Michael York, Michael Hordern, Cyril Cusack; *D:* Franco Zeffirelli; *W:* Franco Zeffirelli; *C:* Oswald Morris; *M:* Nino Rota.

Tammy and the Bachelor 🦴🦴1/2 **1957** A backwoods Southern girl becomes involved with a romantic pilot and his snobbish family. They don't quite know what to make of her but she wins them over with her down-home philosophy. Features the hit tune, "Tammy." Charming performance by Reynolds. 89m/C VHS, Debbie Reynolds, Leslie Nielsen, Walter Brennan, Fay Wray, Sidney Blackmer, Mildred Natwick, Louise Beavers; *D:* Joseph Pevney; *W:* Oscar Brodney.

Tammy and the Doctor 🦴🦴1/2 **1963** Sandra Dee reprises Debbie Reynolds's back-woods gal ("Tammy and the Bachelor"). Dee becomes a nurse's aide and is wooed by doctor Fonda, in his film debut. 88m/C VHS, Sandra Dee, Peter Fonda, MacDonald Carey; *D:* Harry Keller; *W:* Oscar Brodney.

Tammy and the T-Rex 🦴🦴1/2 **1994 (PG-13)** All Michael (Walker) wanted was a date with the lovely Denise (Richards)—he didn't expect to almost die for her. Nor did he expect a mad scientist to transplant his brain into a mechanical three-ton dinosaur. Part teen angst—part camp horror—all good-natured hooey. 82m/C VHS, Paul Walker, Denise Richards, Terry Kiser, John Franklin; *D:* Stewart Raffill.

Tampopo 🦴🦴🦴 Dandelion **1986** A hilarious, episodic Japanese comedy. Young restaurant hostess Tampopo (Miyamoto) is coached by 10 gallon-hatted stranger Goro (Yamazaki) in how to make the perfect noodle so she can open her own successful shop. There's also a loving gangster (Yakusho) who serves as an occasional narrator and gourmet. Popular, free-form hit that established Itami in the West. Japanese with subtitles. 114m/C VHS, DVD, JP Ken(saku) Watanabe, Tsutomu Yamazaki, Nobuko Miyamoto, Koji Yakusho, Rikiya Yasuoka, Kinzo Sakura, Hideji Otaki; *D:* Juzo Itami; *W:* Juzo Itami; *C:* Masaki Tamura; *M:* Kunihiko Murai.

Tangled 🦴1/2 **2001 (R)** After being found on a country road badly beaten, David (Hatosy) struggles to remember and explain what happened to a detective (Bracco) who is also investigating the disappearance of David's friend Jenny (Cook). Jenny was swept off her feet by David's old roommate Alan (Rhys-Meyers), who was strictly bad news. When Alan gets into trouble for drug possession, he blames David and Jenny and is determined to get revenge. Too tangled for its own good. 89m/C VHS, DVD, Shawn Hatosy, Rachael Leigh Cook, Jonathan Rhys Meyers, Lorraine Bracco, Estella Warren; *D:* Jay Lowi; *W:* Jeffrey Lieber; *C:* Bobby Bukowski; *M:* Reinhold Heil, Johnny Klimek.

Tangled Destinies 🦴🦴1/2 **1932** Old dark house thriller involving a desert mansion, murder, and faux diamonds. Good acting and a decent storyline make it one of the few successful independently made films of its time. 64m/B VHS, DVD, Lloyd Whitlock, Glenn Tryon, Vera Reynolds, Doris Hill, Sidney Bracy; *D:* Frank Strayer; *W:* Edward T. Lowe.

Tanglers 🦴 **1983** The disappearance of a British intelligence agent in Gibraltar sets off a chain-reaction of violent incidents. 82m/C VHS, Billie Whitelaw, Glynis Barber, Oscar Quitak, Ronald Lacy, Ronny Cox; *D:* Michael E. Briant; *W:* Michael Russell; *C:* Ernest Vincze; *M:* Paul Reade.

Tango 🦴1/2 **1936** An early melodrama that follows the ups and downs of a chorus girl and the guy who sticks with her through thick and thin and poorly filmed dance routines. Based on a novel by Vida Hurst. 66m/B VHS, Marion (Marian) Nixon, Chick Chandler, Matty Kemp, Mere Prevost, Warren Hymer, Herman Bing, Franklin Pangborn, George Meeker; *D:* Phil Rosen.

Tango 🦴🦴 **1998 (PG-13)** There's not much plot and it's not really needed when cinematographer Storaro so stunningly lenses Saura's semi-documentary look at Argentina's national dance. Middleaged Buenos Aires director Mario Suarez (Scla) is depressed after being abandoned by his wife, Laura (Narova), and decides to throw himself into making a movie about the tango. The film's shady investor, Angelo Larroca (Gallardo), insists Mario hire his young dancer mistress, Elena (Maestro), with whom Mario unwisely starts to 'fail in love. Spanish with subtitles. 115m/C VHS, DVD, SP Miguel Angel Sola, Juan Luis Gallardo, Mia Maestro, Cecilia Narova; *D:* Carlos Saura; *W:* Carlos Saura; *C:* Vittorio Storaro; *M:* Lalo Schifrin.

Tango and Cash 🦴🦴 **1989** Stallone and Russell are L.A. cops with something in common: they both think they are the best in the city. Forced to work together to beat drug lord Palance, they flex their muscles a lot. Directing completed by Albert Magnoli, after Andrei Konchalovsky left in a huff. 104m/C VHS, DVD, Sylvester Stallone, Kurt Russell, Jack Palance, Brion James, Teri Hatcher, Michael J. Pollard, James Hong, Marc Alaimo, Robert Z'Dar, Edward (Eddie) Bunker, Clint Howard, Lewis Arquette, Michael Jeter, Glenn Morshower, Geoffrey Lewis; *D:* Andrei Konchalovsky; *W:* Randy Feldman; *C:* Donald E. Thorin; *M:* Harold Faltermeyer.

Tango Bar 🦴🦴1/2 **1988** A romantic triangle between a tango dancer who leaves Argentina during a time of political unrest, his former partner, and his wife, who both stay behind. They are reunited after years of separation. Gives the viewer a detailed vision of the historical and cultural significance of the tango. Charming, interesting and very watchable. In Spanish with English subtitles. 90m/C VHS, AR Raul Julia, Valeria Lynch, Fuben Juarez; *D:* Marcos Zurinaga.

The Tango Lesson 🦴🦴1/2 **1997 (PG)** Semiautobiographical tale of director/star/writer and former dancer Potter ("Orlando" director), as Sally, who finds love and the meaning of life in the tango while living in Paris. While penning a noncommercial script called "Rage" about a paraplegic designer who stalks leggy models, Sally meets a partner, and soon the two are doing more than just the tango. Sally grooms Pablo to star in her upcoming pic as long as he allows the headstrong director to take the lead while they dance. Occasionally departs from the story to the "Rage" script, played out in color. While light on their toes, performances by the real-life director and real-life star are as heavy and stilted as some of the dialogue. Using dance as the metaphor for control and power in relationships, Potter falls flat in a pretentious "Lesson." 101m/B VHS, GB Sally Potter, Pablo Veron, Gustavo Naveira, Fabian Salas, David Toole, Carolina Iotti, Carlos Copello, Peter Eyre, Heathcote Williams; *D:* Sally Potter; *W:* Sally Potter; *C:* Robby Muller; *M:* Fred Frith, Sally Potter.

Tank 🦴1/2 **1983 (PG)** Retired Army officer Garner's son is thrown into jail on a trumped-up charge by a small town sheriff. Dad comes to the rescue with his restored Sherman tank. Trite and unrealistic portrayal of good versus bad made palatable by Garner's performance. 113m/C VHS, James Garner, Shirley Jones, G.D. Spradlin, C. Thomas Howell, Mark Herrier, Sandy Ward, Jenilee Harrison, Dorian Harewood; *D:* Marvin J. Chomsky; *W:* Dan Gordon; *C:* Donald Brinkant; *M:* Lalo Schifrin.

Tank Commando 🦴🦴1/2 **1959** Mediocre WWII actioner, set in Italy, about a demolition squad of battle-hardened Americans trying to locate a secret German crossing point. It turns out to be an underwater bridge and an Italian orphan is the only one, besides the Germans, to know its location. Can the Americans persuade the kid to talk? 79m/3 VHS, Bcb Robert, Wally Campo, Maggie Lawrence, Donato Farretta, Leo V. Metranga, Jack Sowards, Anthony Rich, Larry Hudson; *D:* Burt Topper; *W:* Burt Topper.

Tank Girl 🦴🦴 **1994 (R)** Big-budget adaption of the underground British comic book about a brash punker chick (Petty), who lives in the post-apocalyptic future. The heavily armed pixie battles the tyrannical Department of Water and Power, run by evil Dr. Kesslee (McDowell), for control of the world's water supply in the year 2033. Straying a bit too far from its source comic, the plot (such as it is) is crammed into a frantic action-movie structure that lacks excitement. Plays like a cheap Gen-X marketing ploy with its bizarre mixture of pop culture references and a hipper-than-thou soundtrack coordinated by Courtney Love. 104m/C VHS, DVD, Lori Petty, Malcolm McDowell, Ice-T, Naomi Watts, Jeff Kober, Reg E. Cathey, Scott Coffey, Ann Cusack, Don Harvey, Brian Wimmer, Stacey Linn Ramsower, Iggy Pop, Ann Magnuson; *D:* Rachel Talalay; *W:* Tedi Sarafian; *C:* Gale Tattersall; *M:* Graeme Revell.

Tanks a Million 🦴🦴 **1941** Despite the title, tanks aren't even mentioned in this. Tracy stars as a wacky genius who gets drafted. His excellent memory keeps getting him into one predicament after another. Though he gets promoted quickly, he shows himself no leader. Lots of time-worn gags, but they still work. 50m/B VHS, William Tracy, James Gleason, Noah Beery Jr., Joseph (Joe) Sawyer, Elyse Knox, Douglas Fowley, Frank Faylen, Dick Wessel, Frank Melton, Harold Goodwin, William (Bill) Gould, Norman Kerry; *D:* Fred Guiol.

Tanner '88 🦴🦴🦴 Tanner: A Political Fable **1988** Murphy is excellent as a long-shot politician on the trail of the Democratic presidential nomination. Precise political satire from a story by Gary "Doonesbury" Trudeau. 120m/C VHS, DVD Michael Murphy, Pamela Reed, Cynthia Nixon; *D:* Robert Altman. CABLE

Tanner on Tanner 🦴🦴 **2004** Trudeau's Tanner (Murphy) returns sixteen years later with Alex (Nixon) struggling to make a documentary of her dad's crashed presidential dreams while her own life is unraveling. Meanwhile, he's busily inflating his prominence within the party during the national convention. 120m/C VHS, DVD Michael Murphy, Cynthia Nixon, Pamela Reed, Matt Malloy, Ilana Levine, Jim Fyfe, Avery Clyde; *Cameos:* Tom Brokaw, Steve Buscemi, Mario Cuomo, Howard Dean, Michael Dukakis; *D:* Robert Altman; *W:* Garry Trudeau; *C:* Robert Altman; *M:* Richmond. TV.

Tanya's Island 🦴🦴1/2 **1981 (R)** Abused girlfriend fantasizes about life on deserted island and romance with an ape. Vanity billed as D.D. Winters. 100m/C VHS, DVD, Vanity, Dick Sargent, Mariette Lesequeue, Don McCleod; *D:* Alfred Sole.

The Tao of Steve 🦴🦴🦴 **2000 (R)** Overweight, intelligent kindergarten teacher Dex (Logue) is a hit with the ladies, but feels a vague sense of wanting something more. The title of the film comes from Dex's personal philosophy of such icons as Steve McQueen, Steve McGarrett, and Steve Austin—but is also tossed with ecual parts Kierkegaard and Aquinas. He's ripe for some growing up, and only needs to find the perfect mate, who comes along in the form of Syd (played by Greer Goodman, sister of the director and one of the film's three screenwriters), one of Dex's one-night stands. A sweet romantic comedy that can thank Logue 'or much of its charm. 87m/C VHS, DVD, Donal Logue, Greer Goodman, Kimo Wills, Ayelet Kaznelson, David Aaron Baker, Nina Jaroslaw; *D:* Jennifer Goodman; *W:* Greer Goodman, Jennifer Goodman, Duncan North; *C:* Teodoro Maniaci; *M:* Joe Delia.

Tap 🦴🦴1/2 **1989 (PG-13)** The son of a famous tap dancer, a dancer himself, decides to try to get away from his former life of crime by helping an aging hoofer revitalize the art of tap dancing. Fun to watch for the wonderful dancing scenes. Davis' last big screen appearance. Hines is sincere in this old-fashioned story, and dances up a storm. Captures some never-before filmed old hoofers. 106m/C VHS, DVD, Gregory Hines, Sammy Davis Jr., Suzzanne Douglass, Joe Morton, Terrence McNally, Steve Condos, Jimmy Slyde, Harold Nicholas, Etta James, Savion Glover, Dick Anthony Williams, Howard "Sandman" Sims, Bunny Briggs, Pat Rico, Arthur Duncan; *D:* Nick Castle; *W:* Nick Castle; *M:* James Newton Howard.

Tape 🦴🦴🦴 **2001 (R)** Director Linklater makes digital technology an asset in this intriguing, claustrophobic character study based on a play by Stephen Belber. Johnny (Leonard) pays a visit to high school churn Vince (Hawke), who's working as a low-level drug dealer. Their casual conversation becomes increasingly hostile as Vince begins making accusations involving Johnny and his first love, Amy (Thurman), who soon pays a visit herself. Despite a tiny cast and only one location, story stays stimulating throughout, as the script deftly shifts viewer allegiance between characters and explores interesting themes of memory, subjectivity and ownership of one's past. Linklater's use of high-definition video gives the film a vitality and spontaneous feel that suits the material. 86m/C VHS, DVD, US Ethan Hawke, Robert Sean Leonard, Uma Thurman; *D:* Richard Linklater; *W:* Stephen Belber; *C:* Maryse Alberti.

Tapeheads 🦴🦴1/2 **1999 (R)** Silly, sophomoric, sexy comedy starring Cusack and Robbins as young wanna-be rock-video producers who get mixed up with performers, conniving music-industry types, and asinine bands looking for MTV stardom before they eventually strike it big helping their childhood idols, The Swanky Modes. Many big-name music industry cameos and a great soundtrack help keep things lively when the plot goes out of control. Sam Moore and Junior Walker are the Sam & Dave-esque Modes. 93m/C VHS, DVD, Courtney Love, Ebbe Roe Smith, Lee Arenberg, Rocky Giordani, John Marshall Jones, Jessica Walter; *Cameos:* Tom Brokaw, Steve Allen, Sy Richardson, Coati Mundi, John Fleck, John Cusack, Tim Robbins, Mary Crosby, Connie Stevens, Susan Tyrrell, Lyle Alzado, Don Cornelius, Katy Boyer, Doug McClure, Clu Gulager, Jessica Walter, Stiv Bators, Sam Moore, Junior Walker, Martha Quinn, Ted Nugent, Weird Al Yankovic, Bobcat Goldthwait, Michael Nesmith, Xander Berkeley; *D:* Bill Fishman; *W:* Bill Fishman, Peter Mccarthy; *C:* Bojan Bazelli.

Taps 🦴🦴1/2 **1981 (PG)** Military academy students led by Hutton are so true to their school they lay siege to it to keep it from being closed. An antiwar morality play about excesses of zeal and patriotism. Predictable but impressive. 126m/C VHS, DVD, Timothy Hutton, George C. Scott, Ronny Cox, Sean Penn, Tom Cruise, Giancarlo Esposito, Evan Handler, Brendan Ward, John P. Navin Jr., Earl Hindman; *D:* Harold Becker; *W:* Darryl Ponicsan, Robert Mark Karren; *C:* Owen Roizman; *M:* Maurice Jarre.

Tara 🦴🦴 **1997** Female cop Prescott and crook Thigpen are high school sweethearts who went their separate ways. But they're reunited when Thigpen hijacks a squad car that just happens to be driven by guess who. There's also a story involving a group of black nationalists who kidnap white businessman and cover them in—you guessed it—tar. Likeable leads, improbable characters. **90m/C VHS, DVD.** Kevin Thigpen, Nicole Prescott, Seth Grissman; Ron Brice, Frank Minucci; *D:* Goetz Grossmann; *W:* Goetz Grossmann; *C:* Lloyd Handwerker; *M:* John Hill.

Tara Road 🦴🦴½ **2005 (PG)** American Marilyn's (MacDowell) son dies in an accident and she can't recover from her grief, while Irish Ria (Williams) is told by her husband (Glen) that he's leaving her to marry his pregnant girlfriend. Through a series of coincidences, the unhappy women decide to switch houses for two months and see if it will change their lives. Bland adaptation of the novel by Maeve Binchy. **97m/C DVD.** *IR* Andie MacDowell, Olivia Williams, Iain Glen, Stephen Rea, Brenda Fricker, Jean-Marc Barr; *D:* Gilles Mackinnon; *W:* Shane Connaughton; *C:* John de Borman; *M:* John Keane.

Tarantella 🦴🦴🦴 **1995** Aspiring New York photographer Diane DiSorella (Sorvino) gets a shock when her mother dies suddenly. After returning to the New Jersey home and Italian-American community she rejected, Diane is given a journal her mother secretly kept by old family friend Pina (Gregorio). Small-scale story with Diane's big change being learning to accept where she came from. **84m/C VHS, DVD.** Mira Sorvino, Rose Gregorio, Stephen Spinella, Matthew Lillard, Antonia Rey, Frank Pellegrino; *D:* Helen DeMichiel; *W:* Helen DeMichiel; Richard Hoblock; *C:* Teodoro Maniaci; *M:* Norman Moll.

Tarantula 🦴🦴🦴 **1955** If you're into gigantic killer insect movies this is one of the best with nifty special effects and some good action. Carroll plays a scientist working on a growth formula which he's testing on a spider when it accidentally gets loose. This eight-legged horror grows to 100 feet high and causes havoc in the Arizona desert until the Air Force napalms the sucker. Look for Eastwood in the final sequence as an Air Force pilot. **81m/B VHS, DVD.** Leo G. Carroll, John Agar, Mara Corday, Nestor Paiva, Ross Elliott, Clint Eastwood; *D:* Jack Arnold; *W:* Robert M. Fresco, Martin Berkeley, Jack Arnold.

Tarantulas: The Deadly Cargo 🦴🦴 **1977** Eeki! Hairy spiders terrorizing our sleepy town and destroying our orange crop! Made-for-TV cheapie not creepy; will make you sleepy. **100m/C VHS, DVD.** Claude Akins, Charles Frank, Deborah Winters, Pat Hingle, Sandy McPeak, Bert Remsen, Howard Hesseman, Tom Atkins, Charles Siebert, Matthew Laborteaux, Pepe Serna; *D:* Stuart Hagmann; *W:* Guerdon (Gordon) Trueblood; *C:* Robert L. Morrison; *M:* Mundell Lowe. **TV**

The Target 🦴½ *The Piano Player* **2002 (R)** Mercenary Alex Laney (Lambert) goes to South Africa to protect wealthy businessman Robert Nile (Hopper) from the crime boss (Majiba) who's now in jail thanks to Nile's promised testimony. But those who attempt to testify soon wind up dead, so after some near-misses, Niles, his daughter (Kruger), and Laney wind up in a small town with the bad guy (freed from prison) still on their trail. Typical "B" movie action. **94m/C VHS, DVD.** Christopher Lambert, Dennis Hopper, James Faulkner, Diane Kruger, Simon Majiba; *C:* Larry Smith.

Target Eagle 🦴🦴 **1984** Spanish police chief von Sydow hires mercenary Rivero to infiltrate drug-ring. Good performances; ho-hum story. **99m/C VHS. SP MX** Max von Sydow, George Peppard, Maud Adams, Chuck Connors, Jorge (George) Rivero, Susana Dosamantes; *D:* Jose Antonio De La Loma.

Target: Favorite Son 🦴🦴 **1987 (R)** An attractive, ammunition-laden woman sharp-shoots her way to power in this made-for-TV movie. **115m/C VHS.** Linda Kozlowski, Harry Hamlin, Robert Loggia, Ronny Cox, James Whitmore; *D:* Jeff Bleckner; *W:* Steve Sohmer; *C:* Bradford May; *M:* John Morris.

Target for Killing 🦴 **1966** Mediocre thriller about a secret agent who must protect a young heiress from a Lebanese syndicate that's out to kill her. **93m/C VHS.** Stewart Granger, Curt Jurgens, Molly Peters, Adolfo Celi, Klaus Kinski, Rupert Davies; *D:* Manfred Kohler.

Target of Opportunity 🦴🦴½ **2004 (R)** Rousing action tale hits the mark. Jim Jacobs (Cochran) is a former CIA guy who heads to Eastern Europe to rescue childhood buddy Nick Carlton (Jensen), an agent jailed for being on the wrong side of some spy games. But in the process Jim finds himself on his old employer's most wanted list. **91m/C VHS, DVD.** Todd Jensen, Hristo Naumov Shopov, Dean Cochran, Nadia Konakchieva, Bashar Rahal; *D:* Dan Lerner; *W:* Les Weldon. **VIDEO**

Targets 🦴🦴🦴 **1968 (PG)** Bogdanovich's suspenseful directorial debut. An aging horror film star plans his retirement, convinced that real life is too scary for his films to have an audience. A mad sniper at a drive-in movie seems to prove he's right. Some prints still have anti-gun prologue, which was added after Robert Kennedy's assassination. **90m/C VHS, DVD.** Boris Karloff, James Brown, Tim O'Kelly, Peter Bogdanovich, Mary Jackson, Sandy Baron, Monte Landis, Mike Farrell, Nancy Hsueh, Arthur Peterson, Tanya Morgan, Randy Quaid; *D:* Peter Bogdanovich; *W:* Peter Bogdanovich; *C:* Laszlo Kovacs.

Tarnation 🦴🦴½ **2003** Feature debut of Caouette is an experimental documentary constructed from home movies, photographs, letters, phone messages, and created video footage that Caouette edited on his home computer and layered with appropriate songs. It follows the emotional journey of Caouette and his mentally ill mother from a Texas childhood legacy of abuse, neglect, and an escape into a self-created fantasy world, to their lives 20-odd years later. **88m/C DVD.** *D:* Jonathan Caouette; *W:* Jonathan Caouette; *C:* Jonathan Caouette; *M:* John Califra, Max Lichtenstein.

Tarnished Angels 🦴🦴🦴 **1957** Reporter Burke Devlin (Hudson) is writing a story for the local New Orleans paper about a tormented trio of air circus performers. A former WWI ace, Roger Shumann (Stack) cares more about flying than he does his sizzling wife Laverne (Malone), who's loved-from-afar by loyal mechanic Jiggs (Carson). When Roger's plane cracks up, he uses his wife to obtain use of an experimental aircraft in order to win a race—and brings disaster crashing around them all. Good action, fine cast. Based on William Faulkner's 1930 novel "Pylon." **91m/B VHS.** Rock Hudson, Robert Stack, Dorothy Malone, Jack Carson, Robert Middleton, Troy Donahue, Alan Reed, Robert J. Wilke, William Schallert; *D:* Douglas Sirk; *W:* George Zuckerman; *C:* Irving Glassberg; *M:* Frank Skinner.

Tart 🦴🦴 **2001 (R)** Cat Storm (Swain) is desperate to belong to the in-crowd at her New York prep school even if it means dumping her best friend, Delilah (Phillips). But privilege has its price. **94m/C VHS, DVD.** Dominique Swain, Brad Renfro, Bijou Phillips, Mischa Barton, Lacey Chabert, Alberta Watson, Myles Jeffrey, Scott Thompson, Melanie Griffith; *D:* Christina Wayne; *W:* Christina Wayne; *C:* Stephen Kazmierski; *M:* Jeehun Hwang.

Tartuffe 🦴🦴½ **1984** Popular French leading man Depardieu makes directorial debut with Moliere classic about religious hypocrisy and an imposter taking advantage of a wealthy merchant and his family. In French with English subtitles. **140m/C VHS.** *FR* Gerard Depardieu, Francois Perier, Elisabeth Depardieu; *D:* Gerard Depardieu.

Tartuffe 🦴🦴½ **1990** Moliere's famous comedy has Tartuffe posing as a holy man who has attracted the incredulous merchant Orgon. Orgon is willing to give Tartuffe anything—money, social position, even his daughter—and Tartuffe is more than happy to accept. **110m/C VHS.** Anthony Sher, Nigel Hawthorne, Alison Steadman; *D:* Bill Alexander.

Tarzan 🦴🦴🦴 **1999 (G)** Disney animated film finds baby Tarzan lost in the jungle and raised by a gorilla family—patriarch Kerchak (Henriksen), nurturing mom Kala (Close), and bossy big sister Terk (O'Donnell). But, years later, a now grownup Tarzan's (Goldwyn) life is thrown into chaos when he first encounters humans—and realizes he is one. Eccentric gorilla scientist Professor Porter (Hawthorne) and his lovely daughter Jane (Driver) are willing to help, but jungle guide Clayton (Blessed) is the villain on the scene. Disney's animation is even more amazing than usual thanks to some new computer software that gives the jungle background unbelievable depth and Tarzan glides, surfs, and jumps in a wow! look! manner. **88m/C VHS, DVD.** *D:* Kevin Lima, Chris Buck; *V:* Tony Goldwyn, Minnie Driver, Rosie O'Donnell, Glenn Close, Lance Henriksen, Wayne Knight, Brian Blessed, Nigel Hawthorne, Alex D. Linz. Oscars '99: Song ("You'll Be In My Heart"); Golden Globes '00: Song ("You'll Be In My Heart").

Tarzan 2 🦴🦴½ **2005** Animated prequel to the 2004 Disney flick finds young Tarzan (Chad) upset that he's not as strong or as fast as his ape foster family. When his human weakness puts - his mom's (Close) life in danger, Tarzan leaves the tribe and seeks out a cranky, old hermit ape (Carlin) for advice. Lots of fun for the pee-wee set (and their parents will enjoy the Carlin humor). **72m/C DVD.** *D:* Brian J. Smith; *W:* Bob Tzudiker, Noni White; *M:* Mark Mancina; *V:* Harrison Chad, Glenn Close, George Carlin, Brad Garrett, Lance Henriksen, Ron Perlman, Estelle Harris. **VIDEO**

Tarzan and His Mate 🦴🦴🦴 **1934** Second entry in the lavishly produced MGM Tarzan series. Weissmuller and O'Sullivan cohabit in unmarried bliss before the Hays Code moved them to a tree house with twin beds. Many angry elephants, nasty white hunters, and hungry lions. **93m/B VHS, DVD.** Johnny Weissmuller, Maureen O'Sullivan, Neil Hamilton, Paul Cavanagh; *D:* Jack Conway; *W:* Leon Gordon, James Kevin McGuinness, Howard Emmett Rogers; *C:* Clyde De Vinna, Charles Clarke; *M:* William Axt.

Tarzan and the Green Goddess 🦴½ *New Adventures of Tarzan* **1938** Tarzan searches for a statue that could prove dangerous if in the wrong hands. AKA Tarzan (Van Dien). **72m/B VHS, DVD.** Bruce Bennett, Ula Holt, Frank Baker; *D:* Edward Kull.

Tarzan and the Lost City 🦴🦴 **1998 (PG)** *Tarzan and Jane; Greystoke 2:* Gorgeous locations in South Africa are a decided plus in this routine hero/adventure story. Lord Greystoke, AKA Tarzan (Van Dien), returns to Africa from England in order to save his future city of Opar. Spunky fiance Jane (March) heads to the jungle after her Ape Man and gets into (and out of) trouble with bad guy Nigel Ravens (Waddington). Not very convincing special effects but Van Dien looks good in his loincloth and has the action moves down cold. **84m/C VHS, DVD.** Casper Van Dien, Jane March, Steven Waddington, Winston Ntshona, Rapulana Seiphemo, Ian Roberts; *D:* Carl Schenkel; *W:* Bayard Johnson, J. Anderson Black; *C:* Paul Gilpin; *M:* Christopher Franke.

Tarzan and the Trappers 🦴🦴½ **1958** Bad-guy trappers and would-be treasure-seekers wish they hadn't messed with the ape man. **70m/B VHS, DVD.** Gordon Scott, Eve Brent, Ricky Sorenson, Maurice Marsac; *D:* Charles F. Haas, H. Bruce Humberstone, Sandy Howard.

Tarzan Escapes 🦴🦴🦴 **1936** Jane is tricked by evil hunters into abandoning her fairy tale life with Tarzan, so the Ape Man sets out to reunite with his one true love. The third entry in MGM's Weissmuller/O'Sullivan series is still among the better Tarzan movies thanks to the leads, but the Hays Office made sure Jane was wearing a lot more clothes this time around. **95m/B VHS, DVD.** Johnny Weissmuller, Maureen O'Sullivan, John Buckler, Benita Hume, William Henry; *D:* Richard Thorpe.

Tarzan Finds a Son 🦴🦴🦴 **1939** Weissmuller and O'Sullivan returned to their roles after three years with the addition of the five-year-old Sheffield as Boy. He's an orphan whose awful relatives hope he stays lost so they can collect an inheritance. Jane and Tarzan fight to adopt the tyke and when the new family are captured by a wicked tribe only an elephant stampede can save them! **90m/B VHS, DVD.** Johnny Weissmuller, Maureen O'Sullivan, John(ny) Sheffield, Ian Hunter, Henry Stephenson, Frieda Inescort, Henry Wilcoxon; *D:* Richard Thorpe.

Tarzan of the Apes 🦴🦴 **1917** Brawny Lincoln is the original screen Tarzan. Silent film well done and more faithful to the book than later versions. **63m/B VHS, DVD.** Elmo Lincoln, Enid Markey; *D:* Scott Sidney.

Tarzan, the Ape Man 🦴🦴🦴 **1932** The definitive Tarzan movie; the first Tarzan talkie, the original of the long series starring Weissmuller. Dubiously faithful to the Edgar Rice Burroughs story, but recent attempts to remake, update or improve it (notably the pretentious 1984 Greystoke) have failed to near the original's entertainment value or even its technical quality. O'Sullivan as Jane and Weissmuller bring style and wit to their classic roles. **99m/B VHS, DVD.** Johnny Weissmuller, Maureen O'Sullivan, Neil Hamilton; *D:* Woodridge S. Van Dyke; *C:* Clyde De Vinna.

Tarzan, the Ape Man woof! **1981 (R)** Plodding, perverted excuse to see Derek cavort nude in jungle. So bad not even hard-core Tarzan fans should bother. **112m/C VHS, DVD.** Bo Derek, Richard Harris, John Phillip Law, Miles O'Keeffe, Wilfrid Hyde-White, Akushula Selayah, Steven Strong, Laurie Main, Harold Ayer; *D:* John Derek; *W:* Gary Goddard; *C:* John Derek; *M:* Perry Botkin. Golden Raspberries '81: Worst Actress (Derek).

Tarzan the Fearless 🦴½ **1933** Tarzan (Crabbe) helps a young girl find her missing father. **84m/B VHS, DVD.** Buster Crabbe, Julie Bishop, E. Alyn (Fred) Warren, Edward (Eddie) Woods, Philo (Philip, P.H., P.M.) McCullough, Matthew Betz; *D:* Robert F. "Bob" Hill; *W:* Walter Anthony; *C:* Joseph Brotherton, Harry Neumann.

Tarzan the Tiger 🦴🦴🦴 **1929** Series of 15 chapters is loosely based on the Edgar Rice Burroughs novel entitled "Tarzan and the Jewels of Opar." These chapters were filmed as silent pieces, and were later released with a musical score and synchronized sound effects. Here Merrill is the first to sound the cry of the bull ape, Tarzan's trademark. **?m/B VHS, DVD.** Frank Merrill, Natalie Kingston, Lilian Worth, Al Ferguson; *D:* Henry Neumann.

Tarzana, the Wild Girl 🦴 **1969** Jungle cheapie about an expedition that finds a beautiful, scantily clad girl living wildly in the jungle. **87m/C VHS.** Ken Clark, Franca Polesello, Frank Ressel, Andrew Ray, James Reed; *W:* Philip Shaw.

Tarzan's New York Adventure 🦴🦴½ **1942** O'Sullivan's final appearance as Jane is a so-so adventure with some humorous moments when Tarzan meets the big city. When Boy is kidnapped by an evil circus owner, Tarzan, Jane, and Cheta head out to rescue him. Tarzan shows off his jungle prowess by climbing skyscrapers and diving off the Brooklyn Bridge into the East River. Lincoln, the screen's first Tarzan, has a cameo. **70m/B VHS, DVD.** Johnny Weissmuller, Maureen O'Sullivan, John(ny) Sheffield, Virginia Grey, Charles Bickford, Paul Kelly, Chill Wills, Russell Hicks, Cy Kendall; *Cameos:* Elmo Lincoln; *D:* Richard Thorpe.

Tarzan's Revenge ✗ 1938 Morris is a better Olympic runner than actor, Holm is horrible. Only for serious Tarzan fans. 70m/B VHS, DVD. *Glenn Morris, Eleanor Holm, Hedda Hopper; D:* David Ross Lederman.

Tarzan's Secret Treasure ✗✗½ 1941 Tarzan saves an expedition from a savage tribe only to be repaid by having the greedy hunters hold Jane and Boy hostage. They want Tarzan's help in finding a secret cache of gold. But Tarzan doesn't take kindly to those evil-doers a lesson! 81m/B VHS, DVD. *Johnny Weissmuller, Maureen O'Sullivan, John(ny) Sheffield, Reginald Owen, Barry Fitzgerald, Tom Conway, Phillip Dorn; D:* Richard Thorpe.

Task Force ✗✗½ 1949 History of naval aviation and the development of the combat carrier highlighted by actual WWII naval battles and Cooper's very effective in Pacific battles and Cooper is finally vindicated. 116m/B VHS. *Gary Cooper, Jane Wyatt, Wayne Morris, Walter Brennan, Julie London, Bruce Bennett, Jack Holt, Stanley Ridges, John Ridgely, Richard Rober, Art Baker, Moroni Olsen; D:* Delmer Daves; *W:* Delmer Daves.

A Taste for Killing ✗✗ 1992 (R) A monster from outer space comes to earth and is delight-ed with the easy pickings for his insatiable appetite. A brave boy and girl, and a summer of adventure awaits them; how-ever, they are made miserable by their blue-collar boss, who is resentful of their high society background. Then they meet Bo Landry, who befriends them and helps them survive. Unfortunately, Bo turns out to be anything but a friend as he reveals himself as a deadly con-artist in this intense psycho-logical thriller. 87m/C VHS. *Jason Bateman, Henry Thomas, Michael Biehn, Edward "Blue" Deckert, Helen Cates; D:* Lou Antonio; *W:* Dan Bronson.

A Taste of Blood ✗✗ 1967 Gore-meister Lewis's vampire film is actu-ally fairly restrained when compared to "2000 Maniacs" and "Blood Feasts." When John Stone (Rogers) drinks brandy con-taining the blood of Count Dracula, he turns into a green-faced killer bent on re-venge against the teachings of Islam. Final-ly, one old Turkish man relates his own story of attempted suicide and seemingly persuades Bacili to rethink his actions. 118m/C DVD. *Bill Rogers, Elizabeth Wilkinson, William Kerwin, Lawrence Tobin; D:* Herschell Gordon Lewis; *W:* Donald Stanford; *C:* Andy Romanoff.

The Taste of Cherry ✗✗ 1996 *Ta'm e Guilass, Taste of Cherries* Despairing, middle-aged Mr. Badii (Ershadi) is con-templating suicide and looking for some-one who will bury his corpse discreetly. (He's already dug his own shallow grave in the countryside.) He drives through the streets and picks up several different men—all of whom remind him that suicide goes against the teachings of Islam. Final-ly, one old Turkish man relates his own story of attempted suicide and seemingly persuades Badii to rethink his actions. 95m/C VHS, DVD. *[A Homayon Ershadi, Abdolrah-ma Bagheri, Afshin Bakhtiari; C:* Homayun Payvar. Cannes '97; Film; Natl. Soc. Film Critics '98: Foreign Film.

Taste of Death ✗ 1968 A youth discovers his courage within when he stands up to the bandits invading his vil-lage. 90m/C VHS. *T Faymond Pellegrin, Bruno Corazzari, Andrea Giordana, John Ireland; D:* Sergio Merolle; *W:* Biagio Proietti; *C:* Benito Frattari; *M:* Francesco De Masi.

A Taste for Flesh and Blood ✗✗ 1990 (R) A monster from... 84m/C VHS. Rubin Disbrow.

Taste the Blood of Dracula ✗✗½ 1970 (PG) Lee's Dra-cula only makes a brief appearance in this Hammer horror film which has three chil-dren taking over from the bloodsucker. Three Victorian dandies have killed the wizard who revived Dracula and he seeks their deaths by using their own children as the means of his revenge. Not enough Lee but still creepy. Preceded by "Dracula Has Risen from the "Grave" and followed by "Scars of Dracula." 91m/C VHS, DVD, GB *Christopher Lee, Ralph Bates, Geoffrey Keen, Gwen Watford, Linda Hayden, John Carson, Peter Sallis, Isla Blair, Martin Jarvis, Roy Kinnear, Antho-ny (Corbari) Higgins, Michael Ripper; D:* Peter Sasdy; *W:* John (Anthony Hinds) Elder; *C:* Arthur Grant; *M:* James Bernard.

Tatie Danielle ✗✗ 1991 Pitch-black comedy from the director of "Life is a Long Quiet River" sees a bitter, elderly widow moving in with her young nephew and making his life a hell. In French with yellow English subtitles. 114m/C VHS, FR *Tsilla Chelton, Catherine Jacob, Isabelle Nanty, Neige Dolsky, Eric Prat, Laurence Fevrier; D:* Eti-enne Chatiliez; *W:* Etienne Chatiliez.

The Tattered Web ✗✗ 1971 A police sergeant confronts and accidently kills the woman with whom his son-in-law has been cheating. He's then assigned the case. When he tries to frame a wino for the murder, things get more and more messy. Fine performances. 74m/C VHS, DVD. *Lloyd Bridges, Frank Converse, Broderick Crawford, Murray Hamilton, Sallie Shockley; D:* Paul Wendkos; *M:* Robert Jackson Drasnin. TV

Tattle Tale ✗½ 1992 (PG) Vindictive ex-wife writes book accusing her actor ex of abusing her and he loses out on his career-breaking role. So he decides to dis-guise himself and seduce her into telling the truth. Even dumber than it sounds. 96m/C VHS. *C. Thomas Howell, Ally Sheedy; D:* Baz Taylor.

Tattoo ✗✗ 1981 (R) A model be-comes the object of obsession for a crazy tattoo artist. He relentlessly pursues her, leaving behind all his other more illus-

A Taste of Hell ✗ 1973 (PG) Two American soldiers fight a guerilla outfit in the Pacific during WWII. A low-budget film with few redeeming characteristics. 90m/C VHS. *Liza Lorena, William (Bill) Smith, John Gar-wood; D:* Neil Yarema; *C:* Fred Conde; *M:* Nestor Robles.

A Taste of Honey ✗✗✗ 1961 A plain working-class girl falls in love with a black sailor. When she becomes preg-nant, a homosexual friend helps her out. A moving film with strong, powerful perfor-mances. Based on the London and Broad-way hit play by Shelagh Delaney. 100m/B VHS, GB *Rita Tushingham, Robert Stephens, Dora Bryan, Murray Melvin, Paul Danquah; D:* Tony Richardson; *W:* Tony Richardson, Shelagh Delaney; *C:* Walter Lassally; *M:* Johnny Addison. British Acad. '61: Film, Support. Actress (Bryan), British Acad. '62: Screenplay; Cannes '62: Actor (Melvin), Actress (Tushingham).

The Taste of Others ✗✗✗ 2000 *Le Gout des Autres* This classy import is a hard sell to American audiences; first, it's in French, and second, it begins as if the first reel is missing—the low-key action opens with two banal conversations in separate tables. Actress/writer Jaoui, in her directorial debut, takes time in sorting out relationships. Eventually it becomes clear that married boorish businessman Castella (Bacri) is falling for 40-year-old actress Clara (Alvaro), who's fretting about aging and her uncertain prospects, and who has been hired to teach Castella English. He pursues, she resists—at first. Meanwhile, Castella's tough bodyguard Moreno (Lanvin) is involved with Clara's free-spirited barmaid friend Manie (Jaoui). For fans of Rohmer, it works. The characters are engagingly different and in-teresting. The film looks as sharp and pol-ished as a comparable Hollywood ensem-ble comedy. French with subtitles. 112m/C DVD, FR *Jean-Pierre Bacri, Christiane Millet, Agnes Jaoui, Anne Alvaro, Gerard Lanvin, Wied-mir Yordanoff, Brigitte Catillon, Xavier De Guille-bon, Alain Chabat, Raphaël Defour; D:* Agnes Jaoui; *W:* Jean-Pierre Bacri, Agnes Jaoui; *C:* Lau-rent Dailland; *M:* Jean-Charles Jarrell.

The Tavern ✗✗ 2000 Ronnie (Dye) is a bartender who wants to buy a Manhat-tan watering hole from its alleged Florida bound owner, Kevin (Zitte). He borrows the money from a number of people, in-cluding his best friend Dave (Geer), who becomes his partner. But they're underfi-nanced and beset by competition and nu-merous other problems soon surface threatening their business survival. Un-sentimental and downbeat. 86m/C VHS, DVD. *Cameron Dye, Kevin Geer, Margaret Cho, Greg Zittel, Nancy Ticotin, Steven Marcus, Caro Alban, Kyr Austin, Gary Perez; D:* Walter Foote; *W:* Walter Foote; *C:* Kurt Lennig; *M:* Bill Lacey; Loren Toolajian.

Tattoo, a Love Story ✗✗½ 2002 Sara's perfectly planned future crum-bles when she's dumped by her groom-to-be, but the elementary school teacher lets loose after her "not-her-type" tattoo artist Vir-gil pops in for show-and-tell. Predictable yet pleasing indie romance. 95m/C VHS, DVD. *Megan Edwards, Stephen Davies, India Al-len, Virgil Mignanelli, Benjamin Burdick, Kathryn Cherasano, Gordon Reinhart, Stitch Marker, Sta-cey Bean, Nick Garcia, Tom Willmorth, Ben Lamed, Tyler Maier, Christina Lang, E.J. Pettinger, Travis Swartz, Sara Bruner, Gene Bickley, Amy Krengal, Jim Agenbroad, Eryn Spaeth, Ariel gia Lachapelle, Nick Halfrich, Curtis Stigers, Dave Yasuda, Carlie Powell, Walter Ragen, Jordan Gore, Joel Hawkins; D:* Richard W. Bean; *W:* Rich-ard W. Bean, Gregg Sacon; *C:* David Klein; *M:* Pete Droge, Pete Droge. VIDEO

Tax Season ✗✗ 1990 (PG-3) A small-time businessman buys a Holly-wood tax service sight-unseen, and finds it employing a hooker, a bookie and a vari-ety of other unconventional types. 93m/C VHS, DVD. *Fritz Bronner, James Hong, Jana Grant, Tony Tanaka, Dorie Krum, Sam Kaplan, Arte John-son; D:* Rob Slyker; *D:* Tom Law.

Taxi ✗✗½ 2004 (PG-13) Nowhere come-dy loosely based on director Luc Besson's 1998 French film. Stripped of its driver's license, inept New York cop Andy Wash-burn (Fallon, a negligible screen pres-ence) enlists the aid of cyrnamo cabbie Belle Williams (Queen Latifah) to drive him to the scene of a bank robbery. The heist turns out to have been committed by a quartet of gorgeous Brazilian gals who are also supermodels (led by Bundchen in her, um, acting debut). Ann-Margaret lends support in a winning comic turn as Andy's lush of a mother. The Queen, as always, is an irrepressible delight and the only reason to spend any time with this hack. 97m/C VHS, DVD. *US Jimmy Fallon, Jeni-fer Esposito, Ann-Margret, Henry Simmons, Chris-tian Kane, Queen Latifah, Gisele Bundchen, Ana Cristine de Oliveira, Ingrid Vandebosch, Magali Amadei; D:* Tim Story; *W:* Ben Garant, Thomas Lennon, Jim Kouf; *C:* Vance Barbery; *M:* Chris-tophe Beck.

Taxi Blues ✗✗½ 1990 A politi-cal allegory with the two protagonists re-presenting the new and old Soviet Union. A hard-working, narrow-minded cabdriver keeps the saxophone of a westernized, Jewish, jazz-loving musician who doesn't repay his fare. The two strike up a wary friendship as each tries to explain his view of life to the other. Good look at the street life of Moscow during drunks, punks, and black marketeers. Directorial debut of Lounguine. In Russian with En-glish subtitles. 110m/C VHS, RU *Piotr Mamo-nov, Piotr Zaitchenko, Natalia Koliakanova, Vladi-mir Kachpour; D:* Pavel (Lungin) Lounguine; *W:* Pavel (Lungin) Lounguine. Cannes '90: Director (Lounguine).

Taxi Dancers ✗✗ 1993 Smalltown Billie arrives in Hollywood with dreams of becoming an actress. Naturally, her dreams turn to despair and she resorts to "dancing" at the Shark Club where she owes money to the wrong people. 97m/C VHS. *Sonny Landham, Robert Mano, Brittany*

The Taxing Woman's Return ✗✗✗ 1988 *Marusa No Onna II* Maru-sa No Onma II Funny, sophisticated, action-packed. Mi-yamoto returns as the dedicated tax inves-tigator to fight industrialists, politicians, and other big swindlers, who have con-trived to inflate Tokyo's real estate values. Sequel to "A Taxing Woman." In Japa-nese with English subtitles. 127m/C VHS. *JP Nobuko Miyamoto, Renaro Mikuni, Masahiko Tsu-gawa, Tetsuro Tamba, Toru Masuoka, Takeya Na-kamura, Hosei Komatsu, Mihoko Shibata; D:* Juzo Itami; *W:* Juzo Itami; *C:* Yonezo Maeda; *M:* Toshiyuki Honda.

A Taxing Woman ✗✗✗½ 1987 *Marusa No Onna II* 1987 Satiric Japanese comedy about a woman tax collector in pursuit of a crafty millionaire tax cheater. Followed by the equally hilarious "A Taxing Woman's Return." In Japanese with English subti-tles. 127m/C VHS, DVD. *JP Nobuko Miyamoto, Tsutomu Yamazaki, Hideo Murota, Shuji Otaki; D:* Juzo Itami; *W:* Juzo Itami; *C:* Yonezo Maeda; *M:* Toshiyuki Honda.

The Taxman ✗✗ 1998 (R) Al Ben-jamin (Pantoliano) is an obsessive New York State tax investigator who stumbles across six dead bodies in a Brighton Beach gasoline company while on the job. He teams up with a pain-in-the-butt cop, Joseph Romero (Dominguez), who's profi-cient in Russian—a necessity in the immi-grant community. Their sleuthing leads them to uncover a scheme that utilizes... 105m/C VHS, DVD. *Joe Pantoliano, Wade Domin-guez, Elizabeth Berkley, Michael Chiklis, Robert Kevin Townsend; D:* Avi Nesher; *W:* Avi Nesher, Roger Berger; *D:* Jim Denault; *M:* Roger Neill.

Taxi to the Dark Side ✗✗✗✗ 2007 (R) Grim, disturbing documentary about government-sanctioned torture in the war on terror. The film centers around the brutal treatment and murder of a taxi driver named Dilawar in Afghanistan while in American custody, but does not limit it-self to the one incident. Instead, it uses tucies towards torture since 9/11. Director Gibney occasionally indulges in some gimmicky but overall presents a doggedly investigated film that asks harc questions and doesn't back down from brutal an-swers, including those provided through interviews with the men who killed Dila-war. 106m/C DVD. *US D:* Alex Gibney; *W:* Alex Gibney; *C:* Maryse Alberti, Greg Andracke; *M:* Ivor Guest, Robert Logan; *Nar:* Alex Gibney.

The Taxi Mystery ✗✗ 1926 Guy saves Broadway star from band of ne'er-do-wells thanks to his knowledge then tries to figure out who she is, una-ware that her sinister understudy plans to do her in. 50m/B VHS. *Edith Roberts, Robert Agnew, Virginia Pearson, Phillips Smalley; D:* Fred Windemere.

Taxi zum Klo ✗✗ 1981 An au-tobiographical semi-documentary about the filmmaker's aimless existence and at-tempts at homosexual affairs after being fired from his job as a teacher. Explicit in German with English subtitles. Sordid sex-ual situations. 98m/C VHS, DVD. *GE Bernd Broadkamp, Frank Rippioh; D:* Frank Rippioh

Taxi Driver ✗✗✗½ 1976 (R) A psy-chotic NYC taxi driver tries to save a child prostitute and becomes infatuated with an educated political campaigner. He goes on a violent rampage when his dreams do't work out. Repellant, frightening vi-sion of alienation. On-target performances from Foster and De Niro. 112m/C VHS, DVD. *Robert De Niro, Jodie Foster, Harvey Keitel, Cybill Shepherd, Peter Boyle, Albert Brooks, Leonard Harris, Joe Spinell, Martin Scorsese; D:* Martin Scorsese; *W:* Paul Schrader; *C:* Michael Chap-man; *M:* Bernard Herrmann. AFI '98: Top 100; Brit-ish Acad. '76: Support. Actress (Foster); Cannes '76 Film; L.A. Film Critics '76: Actor (De Niro), Natl. Film. Reg. '94;; N.Y. Film Critics '76: Actor (De Niro); Natl. Soc. Film Critics '76: Actor (De Niro), Director (Scorsese), Support. Actress (Foster).

McCrena, Tina Fita, Mirage Michaeux, Michele Hess, Randall Imir; *D:* Norman Thaddeus Vane; *W:* Norman Thaddeus Vane; *M:* Larry Blank.

TC 2000 🐾½ **1993 (R)** Jason Storm and Zoey Kinsella are cops working for The Controller, who has the unenviable task of protecting the community from roving gangs of vicious punks. When Zoey is killed, The Controller converts her into a super-cybernetic killing machine unleashed on the gangs. Meanwhile Jason is considered a liability and must battle the gangs, The Controller, and cyber-Zoey to save himself. Oh, there's also something about saving the Earth's atmosphere from nuclear destruction. Lots of action. **92m/C VHS.** Billy Blanks, Bobbie Phillips, Jalal Merhi, Bolo Yeung, Matthias Hues; **D:** T.J. Scott; **W:** T.J. Scott.

Tchaikovsky 🐾🐾½ **1971** The glorious music is all that saves this pedestrian biography of the 19th century Russian composer, which ignores his homosexuality and glosses over the dissolution of his marriage. Lead performance by Smoktunovsky does manage to rise above the moribund script. Originally released at 191 minutes. In Russian with English subtitles. **153m/C VHS, DVD.** *RU* Innokenti Smoktunovsky, Antonina Shuranova, Yevgeny Leonov, Maya Plisetskaya, Vladislav Strzelchik, Alla Demidova, Kirill Lavrov; **D:** Igor Talankin; **W:** Igor Talankin, Yuri Nagibin; Budimir Metalnikov; **C:** Margarita Pilikhina.

Tchao Pantin 🐾🐾🐾 **1984** An acclaimed French film noir about an ex-cop drawn into drug smuggling underground via a young Arab. English subtitles. Finely drawn characters skillfully portrayed make this a winner. **100m/C VHS.** *FR* Coluche, Richard Anconina, Agnes Soral; **D:** Claude Berri; **Cast '84:** Actor (Coluche), Cinematog., Sound. Support: Actor (Anconina).

Tea and Sympathy 🐾🐾🐾 **1956** A young prep school student, confused about his sexuality, has an affair with an older woman, his teacher's wife. The three leads recreate their Broadway roles in this tame adaption of the Robert Anderson play which dealt more openly with the story's homosexual elements. **122m/C VHS.** Deborah Kerr, John Kerr, Leif Erickson, Edward Andrews, Darryl Hickman, Norma Crane, Dean Jones; **D:** Vincente Minnelli; **W:** Robert Anderson; **C:** John Alton.

Tea for Three 🐾🐾 **1984 (R)** Sexual trio develops and seeks therapy after a fledgling doctor has been having sexual relationships with two women, and the females finally meet. **89m/C VHS.** Iris Berben, Mascha Gonska, Heinz Marecki; **D:** Gerhard Janda.

Tea for Two 🐾🐾🐾 **1950** This take-off on the Broadway play "No, No, Nanette" features Day as an actress who takes a bet that she can answer "no" to every question for 24 hours (life was less complex back then). If she can, she gets to finance and star in her own Broadway musical. ♫ I Know That You Know; Crazy Rhythm; Charleston; I Only Have Eyes For You; Tea For Two; I Want to be Happy; Oh Me, Oh My; The Call of the Sea; Do Do Do. **98m/C VHS.** Doris Day, Gordon MacRae, Gene Nelson, Patrice Wymore, Eve Arden, Billy DeWolfe, S.Z. Sakall, Bill Goodwin, Virginia Gibson, Crawford Kent, Harry Harvey; **D:** David Butler.

Tea with Mussolini 🐾🐾 **1999 (PG)** Semiautobiographical account of director Zeffirelli's own childhood in fascist Italy. In 1935, young Luca (Lucas) is abandoned by his mother and his neglectful father is happy when the boy is taken in by a group of middleaged, eccentric Englishwomen, including Mary (Plowright), Lady Hester (Smith), and Arabella (Dench). Soon, their group is joined by flamboyantly wealthy (and Jewish) American Elsa (Cher). But as Mussolini consolidates his power and WWII begins, Luca is sent away to school, and the women find themselves unwelcome foreigners. **116m/C VHS, DVD.** *IT GB* Joan Plowright, Maggie Smith, Judi Dench, Cher, Baird Wallace, Charlie Lucas, Lily Tomlin, Paolo Seganti, Massimo Ghini, Claudio Spadaro; **D:** Franco Zeffirelli; **W:** Franco Zeffirelli, John Mortimer; **C:** David Watkin; **M:** Alessio Vlad, Stefano Arnaldi. British Acad. '99: Support. Actress (Smith).

Teach Me 🐾🐾½ **1997 (R)** Erotic romance novelist Sara Kane gets a story idea from observing a troubled couple at a restaurant. Janine's got some sexual fears that are causing problems in her marriage but Sara's willing to intercede and help ease her tensions. **90m/C VHS.** Shannon Leahy, Raasa Leela Shields, Greg Provance; **D:** Gary Definer. **VIDEO**

The Teacher 🐾🐾 **1974 (R)** TV's "Dennis the Menace" (North) has an affair with his high school teacher; the pair is menaced by a deranged killer. Cheap but enjoyable. **97m/C VHS, DVD.** Angel Tompkins, Jay North, Anthony James; **D:** Howard (Hikmet) Avedis.

Teachers 🐾🐾 **1984 (R)** A lawsuit is brought against a high school for awarding a diploma to an illiterate student. Comedy-drama starts slowly and seems to condemn the school system, never picking up strength or resolving any issues, though Nolte is fairly intense. Shot in Columbus, Ohio. **106m/C VHS.** Nick Nolte, JoBeth Williams, Lee Grant, Judd Hirsch, Ralph Macchio, Richard Mulligan, Royal Dano, Morgan Freeman, Laura Dern, Crispin Glover, Madeline Sherwood, Zohra Lampert; **D:** Arthur Hiller.

Teacher's Pet 🐾🐾🐾 **1958** Cynical newspaper editor Jim Gannon (Gable) enrolls in a night college journalism course, believing that it won't teach anything of substance. But that's before he gets an eyeful of teacher Erica Stone (Day). Gannon decides to continue to pose as a student but watch the sparks fly when Erica finds out about his deception. Charming comedy with a well-written script and a superb comic performance by Young as Day's lovelorn suitor. **120m/B VHS, DVD.** Clark Gable, Doris Day, Mamie Van Doren, Gig Young, Nick Adams, Marion Ross, Jack Albertson, Charles Lane; **D:** George Seaton; **W:** Fay Kanin, Michael Kanin; **C:** Haskell Boggs; **M:** Roy Webb.

Teaching Mrs. Tingle 🐾🐾 **1999 (PG-13)** Williamson delivers a disappointing directorial debut in this teen horror/comedy adapted from one of his first scripts. Wrong-side-of-the-tracks Leigh Ann (Holmes) is anticipating being high school valedictorian until her sadistic English teacher Mrs. Tingle (Mirren) mistakenly accuses her of cheating. Leigh Ann and friends Jo Lynn (Coughlan) and Luke (Watson) go to Mrs. Tingle's house to plead their case and beg for mercy, but the heartless old hag refuses to listen to them. During an argument, Mrs. Tingle is knocked unconscious and the teens decide to tie her up and exact their revenge. **96m/C VHS, DVD.** Katie Holmes, Helen Mirren, Liz Stauber, Barry Watson, Jeffrey Tambor, Vivica A. Fox, Marisa Coughlan, Molly Ringwald, Michael McKean; **D:** Kevin Williamson; **W:** Kevin Williamson; **C:** Jerzy Zielinski; **M:** John (Gianni) Frizzell.

Team America: World Police 🐾🐾 **2004 (R)** The guys behind "South Park" take on Osama Bin Laden, Kim Jong Il, America's "bull-in-a-china-shop" foreign relations, the Hollywood Left, the Far Right, Jerry Bruckheimer movies, and (especially, to be exact) the MPAA with...puppets (marionettes, to be exact). With a truly heroic commitment to over-the-top satire, they tell the story of America's elite anti-terrorist force, the World Police, a gung-ho, if collateral damage-intensive band of action flick archetypes. New member Gary is recruited for his acting ability and goes through the usual conflicts before battling terrorists, the aforementioned North Korean dictator, and actor/activists such as Alec Baldwin. It's all pretty ridiculous, but that's the point. Add or subtract bones depending on your tolerance for puppet sex, vomit, and intention-

ally horrible dialogue. **98m/C DVD, UMD, US DVD.** **W:** Trey Parker, Matt Stone, Pam Brady; **C:** Bill Pope; **M:** Harry Gregson-Williams; **V:** Trey Parker, Matt Stone, Masasa, Maurice LaMarche, Kristen Miller, Daran Norris, Phil Hendrie.

Teamster Boss: The Jackie Presser Story 🐾🐾🐾 **1992 (R)** Well-done cable movie powered by a riveting performance by Dennehy. Presser followed Jimmy Hoffa as president of the Teamsters and was equally caught between the mob and the government as he tried to do what he considered best for the union. **111m/C VHS, DVD.** Brian Dennehy, Jeff Daniels, Maria Conchita Alonso, Eli Wallach, Robert Prosky, Donald Moffat, Tony LoBianco, Kate Reid, Henderson Forsythe, Al Waxman; **D:** Alastair Reid. **CABLE**

Tearaway 🐾½ **1987 (R)** Australian story of a street punk with an alcoholic father. Story has potential, but ends up going nowhere. **100m/C VHS.** *NZ AU* Matthew Hunter, Mark Pilisi, Peter Bland, Kim Willoughby, Rebecca Saunders; **D:** Bruce Morrison.

Tears in the Rain 🐾🐾 **1988** Casey Cantrell (Stone) travels to London to deliver a deathbed letter from her mother to Lord Richard Bredon. While in England, she is pursued by two men, an heir to the Bredon fortune, and his wealthy friend. After she finds a love which is forbidden, she makes a bizarre discovery that changes her life forever. **100m/C VHS, DVD.** *GB* Sharon Stone, Christopher Cazenove, Leigh Lawson, Paul Daneman; **D:** Don Sharp. **TV**

Tears of the Sun 🐾🐾½ **2003 (R)** Navy SEAL team, led by Lt. Waters (Willis), is sent into the middle of a Nigerian civil war to rescue Americans at a missionary hospital. When they get there, the doctor (Bellucci) refuses to go without the people she's been treating, who will surely be slaughtered by the rebels in the area. Waters defies orders to lead them all on a hazardous journey out of the country. Fuqua follows up "Training Day" with this visually stunning, almost thoughtful battle picture. Until the film degenerates into standard action fare at the end, it aspires to answer questions about the difficulty of America's role as world cop and what makes a hero. Fuqua is aided immensely by Willis's stoic performance and the work of editor Conrad Buff. **121m/C VHS, DVD, Blu-ray Disc.** *US* Bruce Willis, Monica Bellucci, Cole Hauser, Tom Skerritt, Eamonn Walker, Nicholas Chinlund, Fionnula Flanagan, Malick Bowens, Paul Francis, Johnny Messner, Akosua Busia, Peter Mensah, Chad Smith, Charles Ingram; **D:** Antoine Fuqua; **W:** Alex Lasker, Patrick Cirillo; **C:** Mauro Fiore; **M:** Hans Zimmer.

Tecumseh: The Last Warrior 🐾🐾½ **1995** Oh-so-noble TV biography of the Shawnee leader (1768-1813) and his refusal to give up the battle against white settlement of the Indiana Territory. North Carolina substitutes for Ohio and Indiana. Based on the book "Panther in the Sky" by James Alexander Thom. **90m/C VHS.** Jesse Borrego, David Clennon, Tantoo Cardinal, David Morse, Holt McCallany, August Schellenberg, Jimmie F. Skaggs, Jeri Arredondo; **D:** Larry Elikann; **W:** Paul F. Edwards; **M:** David Shire.

Ted & Venus 🐾½ **1991 (R)** Cort plays Ted, an oddball cult poet in love with Linda, a beach beauty who finds him repulsive. The more she rejects him, the more obsessed about her Ted gets, especially when his equally oddball friends offer him romantic advice. **100m/C VHS, DVD.** Bud Cort, Kim Adams, Rhea Perlman, James Brolin, Carol Kane; **Cameos:** Gena Rowlands, Martin Mull, Woody Harrelson, Andrea Martin, Timothy Leary, Cassandra Peterson; **D:** Bud Cort; **W:** Bud Cort, Paul Ciotti.

Teddy at the Throttle 🐾🐾🐾½ **1916** Teddy, the Great Dane, must rescue Gloria Swanson from a villain who has tied up her boyfriend. Silent. **20m/B VHS, DVD.** Bobby Vernon, Gloria Swanson, Wallace Beery; **D:** Clarence Badger.

Teen Alien 🐾 *The Varrow Mission* **1978 (PG)** On Halloween, a young boy and his friends run into a hostile alien. It could happen. **88m/C VHS.** Michael Dunn, Keith Nelson, Dan Harville, Vern Adix; **D:** Peter Semelka; **W:** Peter Semelka.

Teen Vamp 🐾 **1988** Dorky high schooler is bitten by a prostitute; becomes a cool vampire. Mindless "comedy." **87m/C VHS.** Clu Gulager, Karen Carlson, Angela Brown; **D:** Samuel Bradford.

Teen Witch 🐾🐾 **1989 (PG-13)** A demure high schooler uses black magic to woo the most popular guy in school. **94m/C VHS, DVD.** Robin (Robyn) Lively, Zelda Rubinstein, Dan Gauthier, Joshua John Miller, Dick Sargent; **D:** Dorian Walker; **W:** Robin Menken.

Teen Wolf 🐾🐾½ **1985 (PG)** A nice, average teenage basketball player begins to show werewolf tendencies which suddenly make him popular at school when he leads the team to victory. The underlying message is to be yourself, regardless of how much hair you have on your body. Lighthearted comedy carried by the Fox charm; followed by subpar "Teen Wolf Too." **92m/C VHS, DVD.** Michael J. Fox, James Hampton, Scott Paulin, Susan Ursitti; **D:** Rod Daniel; **M:** Miles Goodman.

Teen Wolf Too 🐾🐾½ **1987 (PG)** The sequel to "Teen Wolf" in which the Teen Wolf's cousin goes to college on a boxing scholarship. More evidence that the sequel is rarely as good as the original. **95m/C VHS, DVD.** Jason Bateman, Kim Darby, John Astin, Paul Sand; **D:** Christopher Leitch; **W:** Timothy King.

Teenage Bad Girl 🐾🐾½ *Bad Girl; My Teenage Daughter* **1959** A woman who edits a magazine for teenagers can't control her own daughter. The kid does time in the pen after staying out all night and generally running around with the wrong crowd. Syms's first lead performance is memorable in an otherwise routine teen-exploitation flick. **100m/B VHS.** Anna Neagle, Sylvia Syms, Norman Woolland, Wilfrid Hyde-White, Kenneth Haigh, Julia Lockwood; **D:** Herbert Wilcox.

Teenage Bonnie & Klepto Clyde 🐾½ **1993 (R)** Like their '30s namesakes, Clyde Barrow and Bonnie Parker are just two high-spirited kids who let their need for excitement get in the way of their better judgment (ha!). Bonnie and Clyde meet in a fast-food joint, become shoplifting buddies, fall in love, graduate to armed robbery, try to run for the border, and die. **90m/C VHS.** Bentley Mitchum, Tom Bower, Maureen Flannigan, Scott Wolf; **Cameos:** Don Novello; **D:** John Shepphird; **W:** John Shepphird; **M:** Terry Plumeri.

Teenage Catgirls in Heat 🐾🐾 **2000** On their lighthearted commentary track, the filmmakers admit that they had originally titled this Texas-produced horror simply "Catgirls." It was the good folks at Troma who came up with the modifiers that turns it into an inspired piece of exploitation. If the film doesn't quite live up (or down) to it, that's not too surprising. It involved takes it very seriously. **90m/C DVD.** Gary Graves, Carrie Vanston, Dave Cox; **D:** Scott Perry; **W:** Scott Perry, Grace Smith; **C:** Thad Halcli; **M:** Randy Buck, Nenad Vugrinec.

Teenage Caveman 🐾🐾 *Out of the Darkness; Prehistoric World* **1958** A teenage boy living in a post-apocalypse yet prehistoric world journeys across the river, even though he was warned against it, and finds an old man who owns a book about past civilizations in the 20th Century. Schlocky, and one of the better bad films around. The dinosaur shots were picked up from the film "One Million B.C." **66m/B VHS.** Robert Vaughn, Darrah Marshall, Leslie Bradley, Frank De Kova, Jonathan Haze, Beach Dickerson, Marshall Bradford, Robert Shayne, Joseph H. Hamilton, June Jocelyn, Charles P. Thompson; **D:** Roger Corman; **W:** Robert W(right) Campbell; **C:** Floyd Crosby; **M:** Albert Glasser.

Teenage Caveman 🐾 **2001 (R)** Post-apocalyptic nightmare world has a small group of cave dwellers, led by elders who ban sex to keep the population down. But teenage hormones will out and David leads girlfriend Sarah and a group of friends into the wilderness where they meet Neil and Judith, who are the result of genetic experimentation that has some unpleasant side effects for our little band of survivors (think sex). A "Creature Features" remake of the 1958 movie. **100m/C VHS, DVD.** Andrew Keegan, Tara Subkoff, Richard Hillman, Shari Elliot, Tiffany Limos, Stephen Jasso, Crystal Grant, Hayley Keenan, Paul Hipp; **D:** Larry Clark; **W:** Christos Ni Gage; **C:** Steve Gainer; **M:** Zoe Poledouris. C.A.B.L.E.

Teenage Crime Wave ✕ 1955
Route 66 provides thrills for a couple of teen punks, but things get out of hand when they blow a sheriff's head off. They scoop up a couple of babes and hightail it with the police close behind ultimately confronting their destiny at a mountain top observatory. **77m/B VHS.** Tommy Cook, Mollie McCart, Sue England, Frank Griffin, James Bell, Kay Riehl; **D:** Fred F. Sears.

Teenage Devil Dolls ✕ 1953 A cheap exploitation teenage flick wherein an innocent girl is turned on to reefer and goofballs, and eventually ends up on the street. **70m/C VHS, DVD.** Barbara Marks, Bramlel L. Price Jr.; **D:** B. Lawrence Price.

Teenage Doll ✕✕ 1957 Good old Corman teen exploitation pic features a good girl who's tired of being good and gets mixed up with some street punks. She even manages to set off a gang war by accidentally killing a beat girl from a rival group. **71m/B VHS, DVD.** Fay Spain, John Brinkley, June Kenney, Collette Jackson, Barbara Wilson, Ed Nelson, Richard Devon, Ziva Rodann, Barbora Morris, Bruno VeSota; **D:** Roger Corman; **W:** Charles B. Griffith; **C:** Floyd Crosby; **M:** Walter Greene.

Teenage Exorcist ✕½ 1993
Tired horror spoof finds the Grim Diane (Stevens) renting a creepy house from an equally creepy real estate agent (Berryman). After she moves in, Diane begins having horrible nightmares and calls her family for help. When they arrive Diane has turned into a chainsaw-wielding seductress. The family is so distressed that they misdial the phone and wind up with a pizza delivery geek (Deezen) instead of the exorcist they need. **90m/C VHS, DVD.** Brinke Stevens Eddie Deezen, Michael Berryman, Robert Quarry, Jay Richardson, Tom Shell, Elena Sahagun; **D:** Grant Austin Waldman; **W:** Brinke Stevens.

Teenage Frankenstein ✕½
1958 A descendent of Dr. Frankenstein makes his own scramble-faced monster out of a teenage boy. Lurid '50s drive-in fare (companion to "I Was a Teenage Werewolf") is campy fun in small doses only. **72m/B VHS.** Whit Bissell, Phyllis Coates, Robert Burton, Gary Conway, George Lynn, John Cliff; **D:** Herbert L. Strock.

Teenage Gang Debs ✕ 1966
These chicks throw a sleazy coming out party the likes of which defy description. Simply the most important social function of 1966. **77m/B VHS, DVD.** Diane Conti, Linda Gale, Eileen Scott, Sandra Kane, Robin Nolan, Linda Cambi, Sue McManus, Geri Tyler, Joey Naudic, John Batis, Tom Youck, Thomas Andrisano, George Winship, Doug Mitchel, Tom Eldred, Frank Spinella, Alec Primrose, Gene Marrir, Lyn Kennedy, Janet Banzet; **D:** Sande N. Johnsen; **W:** Hy Cahl; **C:** Harry Petricek; **M:** Steve Karmen.

Teenage Monster WOOF! 1967 A Swedish sex education teacher comes to town and poisons the minds of the local high school kids. Naturally one becomes pregnant and has to try to trick the father into marrying her. More awful stuff from the director of "Girl On a Chain Gang." **78m/C VHS.** Arlene Sue Farber, Frederick Riccio, Julie Ange, Howard Le May, George Peters; **D:** Jerry Gross; **W:** Jerry Gross; **C:** Richard Brooks; **M:** Steve Karmen.

Teenage Mother WOOF! 1967 A young boy is hit by a meteor and is somehow transformed into a raving, slime-covered maniac. **65m/B VHS, DVD.** Gilbert Perkins, Stephen Parker, Anne Gwynne, Stuart Wade, Gloria Castillo, Chuck Courtney; **D:** Jacques "Jack" Merquette; **W:** Ray Buffum; **C:** Taylor Byars.

Teenagers from Outer Space WOOF! 1959
Low-budget sci-fi effort finds extraterrestrial youngsters visiting earth to conquer it and find food for their "monstrous pets" (they're really lobster shadows.) So cheaply made and melodramatic that it just may be good for a laugh. **86m/B VHS, DVD.** Tom Graeff, Dawn Anderson, Harvey B. Dunn, Bryant Grant, Thomas Lockyer, King Moody, Bob Williams; **D:** Tom Graeff; **W:** Tom Graeff; **C:** Tom Graeff; **M:** Tom Graeff.

Teeth ✕✕½ 2007 (R) A darkly comic horror take on vagina dentate. Good girl Dawn (Weixler) preaches abstinence to her classmates in her little town next to a nuclear power plant, but when her

Teenage Mutant Ninja Turtles: The Movie ✕✕½ 1990 (PG) Four sewer-dwelling turtles that have turned into warrior ninja mutants due to radiation exposure take it upon themselves to rid the city of crime and pizza. Aided by a television reporter and their ninja master, Splinter the Rat, the turtles encounter several obstacles, including the evil warlord Shredder. A most excellent live-action version of the popular comic book characters which will hold the kids' interest. Much head-kicking and rib-crunching action as Leonardo, Donatello, Raphael, and Michelangelo fight for the rights of pre-adolescents everywhere. Combines real actors with Jim Henson creatures. **95m/C VHS, DVD.** Judith Hoag, Elias Koteas; **D:** Steven Barron; **W:** Todd W. Langen; **C:** John Fenner; **M:** John Du Prez; **V:** Robbie (Reist) Rist, Corey Feldman, Brian Tochi, Kevin Clash, David McCracken.

Teenage Mutant Ninja Turtles 2: The Secret of the Ooze ✕✕ 1991 (PG) Amphibious pizza-devouring mutants search for the toxic waste that turned them into marketable martial artist ecologically correct kid idols. Same formula as the first go-round with some new characters tossed in. Animatronic characters from the laboratory of Jim Henson, first screen appearance by rapper Vanilla Ice. Marked end of pre-teen turtle craze. **88m/C VHS, DVD.** Francois Chau, David Warner, Paige Turco, Ernie Reyes Jr., Vanilla Ice; **D:** Michael Pressman.

Teenage Mutant Ninja Turtles 3 ✕✕ 1993 (PG) Check it out dudes: the Teenage Mutant Ninja Turtles hit 17th century Japan to rescue loyal friend reporter April O'Neil. Plenty of smoothly executed, blood-free martial arts moves keep the pace rolling, while the turtles battle an evil lord and English pirates. Seeing the TMNT's use a little more of their reptilian grey matter, and smart a little less pizza should contribute to a relatively high adult tolerance level (considering the genre), and loads of good clean fun for the kiddies. **95m/C VHS.** Elias Koteas, Paige Turco, Stuart Wilson, Sab Shimono, Vivian Wu; **D:** Stuart Gillard; **W:** Stuart Gillard; **M:** John Du Prez; **V:** Rardi Mayem Singer, Matt Hill, Jim Razosa, David Fraser.

Teenage Strangler WOOF! 1964 A homicidal teen terrorizes his school. Cheap film features drag races, rumbles, dances, babes, rock 'n' roll and more. One for the "bad enough to be fun" category. **61m/C VHS, DVD.** Bill A. Bloom, Jo Canterbury, John Ensign, Jim Asp, Johnny Haymer, Bill Mills, Ron Ormond; **D:** Bill Fosner; **W:** Clark Davis; **C:** Fred Singer; **M:** Danny Dean.

Teenage Wolfpack ✕✕½ 1957
Boring film about German juvenile delinquents: robbery, violence, and murder. **90m/C VHS, DVD. GE** Horst Buchholz, Karin Baal, Christian Doermer; **D:** Georg Tressler.

Teenage Zombies WOOF! 1958
Mad scientist on remote island kidnaps teenagers and uses her secret chemical formula to turn them into zombies as part of her plan to enslave the world. Not as good as it sounds. **73m/C VHS, DVD.** Don Sullivan, Katherine Victor, Chuck Niles; **D:** Jerry Warren; **C:** Allen Chandler.

Teenager ✕✕ 1974 (R) "Three desperate, reckless individuals, all caught up in making a low budget movie, interact and eventually self-destruct. **91m/C VHS.** Andrea Cagan, Reid Smith, Susan Bernard; **D:** Gerald Seth Sindel.

Tell It to the Judge ✕✕½
1949 Russell plays the exuberant ex-wife of lawyer Cummings. They repeatedly try reconciling but ditzy blonde McDonald always manages to catch Cummings' eye. Fed up Russell takes off for a holiday in the mountains where she meets Young. When her ex-hubby follows her, she decides to try and make him jealous using Young as the bait. **87m/B VHS.** Rosalind Russell, Robert Cummings, Gig Young, Marie McDonald, Harry Davenport, Louise Beavers; **D:** Norman Foster.

Tell Me a Riddle ✕✕½ 1980 (PG) A dying woman attempts to reconcile with her family in this poignant story about an elderly couple rediscovering their mutual love after 47 years of marriage. Fine acting; Grant's directorial debut. **94m/C VHS.** Melvyn Douglas, Lila Kedrova, Eelinda J. Montgomery; **D:** Tzipi Trope.

Tell Me That You Love Me ✕½ 1984 (R) A tear-jerking portrait of a disintegrating modern marriage. **88m/C VHS.** Nick Mancuso, Barbara Williams, Eelinda Adams, Peter Coyote; **D:** Lee Grant; **W:** Joyce Eliason.

Tell Me Where It Hurts ✕✕ 1974 A middle-aged housewife changes her life when she forms a women's consciousness-raising group with her friends. The script won an Emmy. Stapleton's performance is redeeming in this otherwise slow movie. **78m/C VHS.** Maureen Stapleton, Paul Sorvino; **D:** Paul Bogart; **M:** David Shire. **TV.**

TekWar ✕✕½ 1994 It's 2044 and society is plagued by "Tek," an illegal addictive drug-like computer disk that creates powerful but destructive virtual-reality fantasies. Jake Cardigan (Enigan) is an cop framed on drug and murder charges, fresh out of prison, who's trying to both clear his name and find out what happened to his now ex-wife and son. Shatner, who wrote the Tek novels, guests as Walter Bascom, the head of a detective agency who promises to help Cardigan if Jake helps find a missing scientist. Made for TV. **92m/C VHS.** Greg Evigan, Eugene Clark, Torri Higginson, William Shatner; **D:** William Shatner. **TV.**

Telefon ✕✕ 1977 (PG) Suspenseful, slick spy tale. Soviet agents battle a lunatic comrade who tries to use hypnotized Americans to commit sabotage. Daly, later of TV's "Cagney and Lacey," is memorable. **102m/C VHS.** Charles Bronson, Lee Remick, Donald Pleasence, Tyne Daly, Patrick Magee, Sheree North; **D:** Donald Siegel; **W:** Stirling Silliphant, Peter Hyams; **M:** Lalo Schifrin.

Telegraph Trail ✕✕ 1933 Weak Wayne entry about an Army scout who helps some workers complete the first transcontinental wire line. Of course, Wayne errds up getting tough with some Indians. Cheaply made, with most of the action footage lifted from the 1926 silent, "The Red Raiders." **60m/B VHS, DVD.** John Wayne, Maceline Day, Frank McHugh, Otis Harlan, Yakima Canutt, Late (Lafayette) McKee; **D:** Tenny Wright; **M:** Kurt Kempler.

The Telephone WOOF! 1987 (R) A neurotic out-of-work actress begins a comedic chain of events via a few prank phone calls. Goldberg has managed to salvage some bad material with the strength of her comedic prowess, but not so here. In fact, she sued to prevent this version from ever seeing the light of day. Too bad she didn't have a better lawyer. Tom's directorial debut. **96m/C VHS.** Whoopi Goldberg, Elliott Gould, John Heard, Amy Wright; **D:** Rip Torn; **W:** Terry Southern.

The Tell-Tale Heart ✕✕½ The Hidden Room of 1,000 Horrors 1960 Daydreaming author fantasizes about falling for major babe and killing his best friend for her. Adapted Poe tale. **78m/B VHS, DVD, GB** Laurence Payne, Adrienne Corri, Dermot Walsh, Selma Vaz Dias, John Scott, John Martin, Annette Carall, David Lander; **D:** Ernest Morris; **W:** Brian Clemens.

Tell Them Who You Are ✕✕½ 2005 (R) Mark Wexler's documentary about his cinematographer father Haskell Wexler is not so much about the man's award-winning movie work as it is an examination of their father-son relationship. Acknowledged for his work and political endeavors, Haskell is undeniably witty, ego-tistical and outspokenly blunt. "I don't think there's a movie that I've been on that I wasn't sure I could direct better," he says after Willie kills his wife's father in self-defense. This was once-blacklisted Polonsky's first film in 21 years. **96m/C VHS.** Robert DeMaio; **C:** Mark S. Wexler; **W:** Mark S. Wexler, Robert DeMaio; **C:** Mark S. Wexler.

Tell Them Willie Boy Is Here ✕✕½ 1969 (R) Western drama set in 1909 California about a Paiute Indian named Willie Boy and his white bride. (led by the reluctant local sheriff, Redford) the twist is that there's a movie that includes his son's defense. Universally acclaimed performance by Bacon, who takes a one-dimensional persona and runs with it. Flockhart plays the "it" girl of Karchy's dreams. Smoothly told story suffers from a few of the usual clichés, but makes up for it heart. **101m/C VHS, DVD.** Kevin Bacon, Brad Renfro, Maximilian Schell, Calista Flockhart, Paul Guy Ferland; **W:** Joe Eszterhas; **D:** Abraham Polonsky; **W:** Abraham Polonsky; **C:** Conrad L. Hall; **M:** Dave Grusin.

Telling Lies in America ✕✕ 1996 (PG-13) Semiautobiographical Esterhaus-penned coming-of-ager allies a star-struck and naïve Hungarian immigrant teen with dirty deejay on the take in early 60s Cleveland. Karchy Jones (Renfro) worships the slick polyester prince of the airwaves Billy Magic (Bacon), and through a contest at school, wins a chance to become his eager-beaver lackey. The twist and rock-n-roll mentor shows Karchy the own, highly cynical version of attaining the American Dream which, naturally, leads to trouble. **101m/C VHS, DVD.** Kevin Bacon, Brad Renfro, Maximilian Schell, Calista Flockhart, Paul Dooley, Jonathan Rhys Meyers, Luke Wilson; **D:** Guy Ferland; **W:** Joe Eszterhas; **M:** Nicholas Pike.

Telling You ✕✕½ 1998 (R) Buddies Phil (Facinelli) and Dennis (Mihok) work at the local pizzeria and try to score, but don't have much success since they're, basically, amiable losers. Fluff and Hewitt's role is small as Phil's ex-girlfriend. **94m/C VHS, DVD.** Peter Facinelli, Dash Mihok, Matthew Lillard, Jennifer Love Hewitt, Richard Lineback, Robert DeFranco, Frank Medrano, Jennifer Josyin, Rick Rossovich, Jennie Garth; **D:** Robert DeFranco; **W:** Robert DeFranco, Marc Palmieri; **C:** Mark Doering-Powell; **M:** Russ Landau.

The Temp WOOF! 1993 (R) Unbelievably bad attempt at office horror. Beautiful, mysterious Kris temps for Hutton, a junior exec at the Mrs. Appleby baked goods company. She's almost too good to be true with unbelievable organizational skills and her dead serious ambition to climb the corporate ladder. Pyscho-drama has psychic, but lacks drama, direction, plot development, intelligent dialogue, and anything resembling motive. While Hutton is tolerable, we nominate ex-Twin Peaker Boyle for the bad acting hall of shame as the conniving psycho. **99m/C VHS, DVD.** Timothy Hutton, Lara Flynn Boyle, Faye Dunaway, Dwight Schultz, Oliver Platt, Steven Weber, Scott Coffey, Colleen Flynn, Dakin Matthews, Maura Tierney; **D:** Tom Holland; **W:** Kevin Falls; **C:** Steve Yaconelli; **M:** Frederic Talgorn; **Worst Support. Actress (Dunaway).

The Tempest ✕✕ 1928 A Russian peasant soldier rises through the ranks to become an officer, only to be undone by his love for the daughter of his commanding officer. Silent with musical score. **105m/B VHS, DVD.** John Barrymore, Louis Wolheim; **D:** Sam Taylor; **C:** Charles Rosher.

The Tempest ⚗️⚗️½ 1963 Shakespeare's classic tale of the fantasy world of spirits, sorcerers, maidens, monsters, and scheming noblemen is brought to life in George Schaefer's ethereal production. **76m/C VHS.** Maurice Evans, Richard Burton, Roddy McDowall, Lee Remick, Tom Poston; **D:** George Schaefer. **TV**

The Tempest ⚗️⚗️⚗️ 1982 (PG) New York architect Phillip (Cassavetes), fed up with city living, chucks it all and brings his daughter Miranda (Ringwald in her screen debut), and singer Aretha (Sarandon) to live with him on a barren Greek island where they encounter a hermit named Kalibanos (Julia). Then, thanks to Phillip's life, including his unfaithful wife Antonia (Rowland), show up to complicate his midlife crisis. Loosely based on the Shakespeare play of the same name. Well-written, thoughtfully acted, and beautifully filmed. **140m/C VHS, DVD.** John Cassavetes, Gena Rowlands, Susan Sarandon, Vittorio Gassman, Molly Ringwald, Paul Stewart, Sam Robards, Raul Julia; **D:** Paul Mazursky; **W:** Paul Mazursky, Leon Capetanos; **C:** Donald McAlpine; **M:** Stomu Yamashta.

The Tempest ⚗️⚗️½ 1999 (PG-13) This time around the Shakespeare fantasy is transported to a Civil War-era Mississippi bayou, which is where magic-studying Gideon Prosper (Fonda) is living with his daughter, Miranda (Heigl), and a runaway slave, Ariel (Perrineau). Into this secluded world stumbles young Union soldier, Frederick Allen (Mills), with whom the lonely Miranda immediately falls in love, while Gideon is finally forced to reckon with the world in the form of his unscrupulous brother, Anthony (Glover). **90m/C VHS.** Peter Fonda, John Glover, Harold Perrineau Jr., Katherine Heigl, Eddie Mills, John Pyper-Ferguson, Dennis Redfield; **D:** Jack Bender; **W:** James Henerson; **C:** Steve (Steven) Dubin. **TV**

Temptation of a Monk ⚗️⚗️ 1994 Costume drama about China's 7th-century Tang Dynasty finds General Shi (Hsin-kuo) duped into an assassination plot against the crown prince. After a massacre, the General flees and finds sanctuary with a group of Buddhist monks at a remote temple. There's also the General's sometime lover and a mystery woman (both played by Chen). Sometimes slow-moving and confusing but with exotic visuals. Based on a novel by Lilian Lee. Mandarin with subtitles. **118m/C VHS, DVD.** CH Wu Hsin-kuo, Joan Chen, Fengyi Zhang, Michael Lee; **D:** Clara Law; **W:** Eddie Ling-Ching Fong; **C:** Andrew Lesnie; **M:** Tats Lau.

Temptation ⚗️⚗️ 1994 (R) Ex-con Eddie (Fahey) gets hired to work on a luxury yacht, which helps him keep track of his double-crossing former partner. Too bad for Eddie that the guy's wife is such a distraction. **91m/C VHS.** Jeff Fahey, Alison Doody, Philip Casnoff, David Keith, Patricia Durdin, W. Paul Bodie; **D:** Stratford Hamilton.

Tempted ⚗️⚗️ 2001 (R) Wealthy builder Charlie LeBlanc (Reynolds) hires college student Jimmy Mulante (Facinelli) to do some carpentry work—and test the fidelity of his beautiful young wife Lilly (Burrows). Charlie heads out of town after offering Jimmy much bucks to seduce Lilly but Jimmy confesses the scheme to her

The Temptations ⚗️⚗️½ 1998 Miniseries bio of the Motown group from its high school beginnings in 1958 (under various names) through a meeting with Motown founder Berry Gordy (Babatunde) and major success in the '60s. Told from the viewpoint of the last original Temp, Otis Williams (Whitfield), as he and buddies Melvin Franklin (Woodside) and Paul Williams (Payton) hook up with first lead singer Eddie Kendricks (Brooks). When Kendricks goes solo it's the turn of David Ruffin (Leon) but the group suffers various ego traumas and tragedies. Naturally, the music's the real highlight. **150m/C VHS, DVD.** Charles Malik Whitfield, DB Woodside, Terron Brooks, Christian Payton, Leon, Alan Rosenberg, Gina Ravera, Vanessa Bell Calloway, Chaz Lamar Shepherd; **D:** Allan Arkush; **W:** Kevin Arkadie, Robert P. Johnson; **C:** Jamie Anderson. **TV**

instead and she decides to use the stud for her own purposes. **95m/C VHS, DVD.** Burt Reynolds, Peter Facinelli, Saffron Burrows, Mike Starr; **D:** Bill Bennett; **C:** Tony Clark; **M:** David Bridie.

The Tempter ⚗️ L'Anticristo; The Antichrist 1974 (R) Mirrors the gruesomeness of "The Exorcist" with story following an invalid's adventures with witchcraft, bestiality, and Satanism. **96m/C VHS, DVD.** IT Mel Ferrer, Carla Gravina, Arthur Kennedy, Alida Valli, Anita Strindberg, George Coulouris; **D:** Alberto De Martino; **M:** Ennio Morricone.

The Temptress ⚗️⚗️½ 1949 A doctor attempting to find a cure for polio is coerced by an irresistible woman into murder and blackmail. Well-hold story, if somewhat grim. **85m/B VHS. GB** Joan Maude, Arnold Bell, Don Stannard, Shirley Quentin, John Stuart, Ferdinand "Ferdy" Mayne; **D:** Oswald Mitchell.

Temptress ⚗️⚗️ 1995 (R) Photographer Karin Swann (Delaney) returns from a spiritual retreat in India obsessed with the deadly goddess Kali. Karin's new overtly sexual personality startles lover Matthew (Sarandon) while her work has also undergone some changes. When a friend is murdered, Matthew begins to wonder if Kali's evil powers have overtaken Karin. **93m/C VHS.** Kim Delaney, Chris Sarandon, Corbin Bernsen, Dee Wallace Stone, Jessica Walter, Ben Cross; **D:** Lawrence Lanoff; **M:** Melissa Mitchell.

Temptress Moon ⚗️⚗️ Feng Yue 1996 (R) 1920s Shanghai is displayed in all its decadence with opium-addicted Ruyi (Li) forced to officially head the Pang family after the death of her father. Power actually lies with distant male cousin Duanwen (Lin), who manages the household and is drawn to his cold relative. Ruyi's childhood playmate and fellow addict, Zhongliang (Cheung), is now a professional gigolo and blackmailer, working for a gangster (Tian) who wants him to seduce Ruyi and steal the Pang fortune. What happens is an obsessive affair between two beautiful manipulators. Chilly high-style soap opera. Mandarin with subtitles. **113m/C VHS, DVD. HK** Gong Li, Leslie Cheung, Kevin Lin, Xie Tian, Zhou Jie, Saifei He; **D:** Chen Kaige; **W:** Shu Kei; **C:** Christopher Doyle; **M:** Jiping Zhao.

10 ⚗️⚗️½ 1979 (R) A successful song-writer who has everything finds his life is incomplete without the woman of his dreams, the 10 on his girl-watching scale. His pursuit brings surprising results. Also popularizes Ravel's "Bolero." **121m/C VHS, DVD.** Dudley Moore, Julie Andrews, Bo Derek, Dee Wallace Stone, Brian Dennehy, Robert Webber; **D:** Blake Edwards; **W:** Blake Edwards; **C:** Frank Stanley; **M:** Henry Mancini.

The Ten ⚗️⚗️ 2007 (R) Number eleven must be "thou shalt be funny," because the lack of laughs in this collection of ten irreverent sketch-style short films based on the Ten Commandments is surely a sin of omission. Rudd plays the tablet-toting narrator who introduces each vignette, played out by a slew of Hollywood B-listers. Yeah, a "thou shalt not steal" tale starring Winona Ryder is kinda clever, but the rest of the warped jokes have narrow appeal—some hit, others miss, and most are too smug to gauge when a gag has gone on too long. **93m/C DVD.** US Paul Rudd, Jessica Alba, Adam Brody, Bobby Cannavale, Famke Janssen, Gretchen Mol, Justin Theroux, Winona Ryder, Rob Corddry, Oliver Platt, Ron Silver, Ken Marino; **D:** David Wain; **W:** Ken Marino, David Wain; **C:** Yaron Orbach; **M:** Craig (Shudder to Think) Wedren.

Ten Benny ⚗️⚗️ Nothing to Lose 1998 (R) Frustrated New Jersey shoe salesman Ray (Brody) borrows $10,000 from a local wiseguy in order to win enough money at the track to set himself up in business. Bad idea. As his luck continues a downward spiral, he abuses his wife (Temchen) into the arms of his buddy (Gallagher) and becomes more desperate to climb out of the hole he's dug for himself. First-time director Bross has obviously studied the Scorsese school of filmmaking, but must've skipped the classes on originality,

subtlety, and characterization. Not much going on here that hasn't been done (better) somewhere else, but Brody turns in a fine performance. **98m/C VHS, DVD.** Adrien Brody, Sybil Temchen, Michael Gallagher, Tony Gillan, James Moriarty, Frank Vincent; **D:** Eric Bross; **W:** Eric Bross, Tom Cudworth; **C:** Horacio Marquinez; **M:** Chris Hajian.

The Ten Commandments ⚗️⚗️½ 1923 The silent epic that established DeMille as a popular directorial force and which he remade 35 years later as an even bigger epic with sound. Follows Moses' adventures in Egypt, plus a modern story of brotherly love and corruption. Features a new musical score by Gaylord Carter. Remade in 1956. **146m/B VHS, DVD.** Theodore Roberts, Richard Dix, Rod La Rocque, Edythe Chapman, Nita Naldi; **D:** Cecil B. DeMille; **C:** Archie Stout; **M:** Gaylord Carter.

The Ten Commandments ⚗️⚗️⚗️ 1956 (G) DeMille's remake of his 1923 silent classic (and his last film) is a lavish Biblical epic that tells the life story of Moses, who turned his back on a privileged life to lead his people to freedom outside of Egypt. Exceptional cast, with Fraser Heston (son of Charlton) as the baby Moses. Parting of Red Sea rivals any modern special effects. A 35th Anniversary Collector's Edition is available uncut at 245 minutes, in widescreen format and Dolby Surround stereo, and 1,000 copies of an Autographed Limited Edition that includes an engraved bronze plaque and an imprinted card written and personally signed by Charlton Heston are also available. **219m/C VHS, DVD.** Charlton Heston, Yul Brynner, Anne Baxter, Yvonne De Carlo, Nina Foch, John Derek, H.B. Warner, Henry Wilcoxon, Judith Anderson, John Carradine, Douglass Dumbrille, Cedric Hardwicke, Martha Scott, Vincent Price, Debra Paget; **D:** Cecil B. DeMille; **W:** Aeneas MacKenzie, Jesse Lasky Jr., Frederic M. Frank, Jack Gariss; **C:** Loyal Griggs; **M:** Elmer Bernstein. **Family Reg. '99.**

Ten Days That Shook the World ⚗️⚗️½ October; Oktyabr 1927 Silent masterpiece based on American author John Reed's book of the same name. Eisenstein, commissioned by the Soviet government, spared no expense to chronicle the Bolshevik Revolution of 1917 (in a flattering Communist light, of course). He was later forced to cut his portrayal of Leon Trotsky, who was then an enemy of the state. Includes rare footage of the Czar's Winter Palace in Leningrad. Haunting score, combined with some of Eisenstein's most striking work. See Warren Beatty's "Reds" for a fictional look at Reed and the Russian Revolution. **104m/B VHS, DVD.** RU Nikandrov, N. Popov, Boris Livanov; **D:** Sergei Eisenstein, Grigori Alexandrov; **W:** Sergei Eisenstein, Grigori Alexandrov; **C:** Vladimir Popov, Eduard Tisse; **M:** Edmund Meisel.

Ten Days Wonder ⚗️⚗️½ La Decade Prodigieuse 1972 (PG) Mystery/drama focuses on the patriarch of a wealthy family (Welles), his young wife, and his adopted son (Perkins), who is having an affair with his stepmother. It also turns out that Perkins is certifiable and is trying to break all of the Ten Commandments, which he succeeds in doing before killing himself (gruesomely). Based on the mystery novel by Ellery Queen. **101m/C VHS, DVD.** FR Orson Welles, Anthony Perkins, Marlene Jobert, Michel Piccoli, Guido Alberti; **D:** Claude Chabrol.

10 Items or Less ⚗️⚗️ 2006 (R) Minimalist flick that focuses on a nameless big-time actor (Freeman) venturing into method territory. He travels outside LA in order to spend time at a local downscale grocery store to study how his store-manager character would behave, but instead observes all-business checkout clerk Scarlet (Vega) at work. When he's left stranded, Scarlet agrees to drive him home and he offers to help her prepare for a secretarial job interview she may deny the warmth of either Freeman or Vega but even for an indie this is slight material. **81m/C DVD.** US Morgan Freeman, Paz Vega, Bobby Cannavale, Anne Dudek, Jonah Hill, Danny DeVito, Rhea Perlman; **D:** Brad Silberling;

W: Brad Silberling; **C:** Phedon Papamichael; **M:** Antonio Pinto.

Ten Little Indians ⚗️⚗️ And Then There Were None 1975 (PG) Ten people are gathered in an isolated inn under mysterious circumstances. One by one they are murdered, each according to a verse from a children's nursery rhyme. British adaptation of the novel and stage play by Agatha Christie. **98m/C VHS, DVD. GB** Herbert Lom, Richard Attenborough, Oliver Reed, Elke Sommer, Charles Aznavour, Stephane Audran, Gert Frobe, Adolfo Celi, Orson Welles; **D:** Peter Collinson.

Ten Little Indians ⚗️⚗️ Agatha Christie's Ten Little Indians 1989 (PG) A group of prize-winning vacationers find themselves embarking on an African adventure. They all wind up at the same camp, and realize that they are being murdered one by one. Based on the work of Agatha Christie. **100m/C VHS.** Donald Pleasence, Brenda Vaccaro, Frank Stallone, Herbert Lom, Sarah Maur-Thorp; **D:** Alan Birkinshaw.

The Ten Million Dollar Getaway ⚗️⚗️ 1991 (PG-13) True story of the 1978 Lufthansa robbery at Kennedy Airport in which the criminals were forced to leave 10 of their $20 million heist behind when a pick-up van didn't show. Standard cable fare produced to cash in on the same scenario played out in "Goodfellas." **93m/C VHS.** John Mahoney, Karen Young, Tony LoBianco, Gerry Bamman, Joseph Carberry, Terrence Mann, Kenneth John McGregor, Christopher Murney; **D:** James A. Contner; **W:** Christopher Canaan. **CABLE**

Ten Nights in a Bar-Room ⚗️⚗️ 1931 A turn-of-the-century mill owner succumbs to alcoholism and ruins his life and family. Later, he sees the error of his ways and gives up drinking. This was one of many films made during this era that chronicled the evils of alcohol and fanned the flames of the prohibition debate. Remake of the 1913 silent film. **60m/B VHS.** William Farnum, Thomas Santschi, John Darrow, Robert Frazer; **D:** William A. O'Connor.

Ten Nights in a Barroom ⚗️⚗️ 1913 The evils of alcohol are dramatized when they ruin a man's life. One of many propaganda films about alcohol and the problems that it caused that were made during the prohibition era. Silent, with a musical score. Remade in 1931. **68m/B VHS.** Robert Lawrence, Marie Trado, Gladys Egan, Violet Horner, Jack Regan; **D:** Lee Beggs; **W:** Lee Beggs.

Ten North Frederick ⚗️⚗️⚗️ 1958 A shrewish wife (Fitzgerald) forces her gentle lawyer husband (Cooper) into cut-throat politics. He consoles himself in the arms of a much younger woman. Good performances, hokey script, based on the John O'Hara novel. **102m/B VHS.** Gary Cooper, Diane Varsi, Suzy Parker, Geraldine Fitzgerald, Tom Tully, Stuart Whitman; **D:** Philip Dunne; **W:** Philip Dunne.

10 Rillington Place ⚗️⚗️⚗️ 1971 (PG) A grimy, upsetting British film about the famed serial killer John Christie and the man wrongly hanged for his crimes, the incident that led to the end of capital punishment in England. Impeccably acted. **111m/C VHS. GB** Richard Attenborough, John Hurt, Judy Geeson, Gabrielle Daye, Andre Morell, Bernard Lee, Isobel Black, Pat Heywood; **D:** Richard Fleischer; **W:** Clive Exton; **C:** Denys Coop; **M:** John Dankworth.

Ten Speed ⚗️ 1976 Two advertising executives compete in a 400-mile bicycle race from San Francisco to Malibu. **89m/C VHS.** William Woodbridge, Patricia Hume, David Clover; **D:** Steven A. Hull.

Ten Things I Hate about You ⚗️⚗️⚗️ 1999 (PG-13) This Bill Shakespeare guy must be raking in the royalties, dude! The Bard is once again adapted for teens in this update of his very un-PC comedy "The Taming of the Shrew." Obstetrician and single dad Walter (Miller) has seen enough teen pregnancies to fear all adolescent boys who show up with flowers. He decrees that his ultra-popular daughter Bianca (Oleynik) cannot date before her man-hating sister Kat (Stiles) does. Two lovesick suitors,

Ten Who Dared 🐾 1960 Ten Civil War heroes brave the Colorado River in an effort to chart its course. Although it's based on an actual historic event, the film is poorly paced and lacks suspense. **92m/C VHS.** Brian Keith, John Beal, James Drury; **D:** William Beaudine.

Ten Wanted Men 🐾 1954 A successful cattle baron is confronted by a pistol-wielding landowner determined to ruin him. Standard fare, better than average performances from Scott and Boone. **80m/C VHS, DVD.** Randolph Scott, Jocelyn Brando, Richard Boone, Skip Homeier, Leo Gordon, Jack Perrin, Donna (Dona Martel) Martell; **D:** H. Bruce Humberstone; **W:** Harriet Frank Jr., Irving Ravetch.

10 Violent Women Woof! 1979 (R) Ten women who take part in a million dollar jewelry heist are tossed into a women's prison where brutal lesbian guards subject them to degradation and punishment. **97m/C VHS, DVD.** Sherri Vernon, Dixie Lauren, Sally Gamble; **D:** Ted V. Mikels; **W:** Ted V. Mikels; **C:** Yuval Shousterman; **M:** Nicholas Carras.

Ten to Midnight 🐾🐾 1983 (R) Vigilante Bronson is on the prowl again, this time as a police officer after a kinky serial murderer. The psychotic killer stalks his daughter and Dad's gonna stop him at any cost. **101m/C VHS, DVD.** Charles Bronson, Wilford Brimley, Lisa Eilbacher, Andrew Stevens; **D:** J. Lee Thompson; **W:** William Roberts.

10,000 B.C. 🐾 2008 (PG-13) In some prior "mythical age" on earth, tribal peoples (who all speak different languages; lucky for us one of them is English) live on a land ruled by nature and spirits. D'Leh (Strait), a young hunter, and Evolet (Belle), the blue-eyed beauty, are lovers in a remote mountain tribe. Evolet is kidnapped by a band of raiders and D'Leh heads out to save her. D'Leh and his small crew meet up with other civilizations along the way and soon there's an army behind him. Good thing as it turns out that his mission isn't just to save Evolet, but civilization, too. All of which sounds okay in theory, but on screen it falls especially flat in all its cheesy computer-generated glory. The special effects are cheap, the supposedly prehistoric actors too gorgeous, and the whole thing doesn't even try to make sense, with woolly mammoths trotting about at the same time pyramids are being erected. Stick with "The Flintstones." **109m/C DVD.** *US* Steven Strait, Camilla Belle, Clifford Curtis, Joel Virgel, Ben Badra; **D:** Roland Emmerich; **W:** Roland Emmerich, Harald Kloser, Thomas Wander; **C:** Ueli Steiger; **M:** Harald Kloser, Thomas Wander. **Narr:** Omar Sharif.

Ten 'Til Noon 🐾🐾 2006 (R) Low-budget but ingenious thriller that shows a ten-minute period (11:50 to noon) from several different viewpoints. Tech tycoon Larry Taylor (Wasserman) is rudely awakened by hitman Mr. Jay (Freeman) and his associate (Lano), who announce his murder. Maybe his unfaithful wife (Guest) has something to do with it, maybe it's the someone else is pulling the strings. Or maybe someone else is pulling the strings. **88m/C DVD.** Jenya Lano, Dylan Kussman, Thomas Kopache, Danie Nathan Spector, Rick D. Wasserman, Alfonso Freeman, Rayne Guest, Jason Hamer, Daniel Hagen, George Williams; **D:** Scott Storm; **W:** Paul Osborne; **C:** Alice Brooks; **M:** Joe Kraemer.

The Tenant of Wildfell Hall 🐾🐾½ 1996 Anne Bronte gets her turn in the spotlight with this TV adaptation of her 1848 novel. When the mysterious Helen Graham (Fitzgerald) and her young son become the new tenants of decaying Wildfell Hall, they naturally elicit lots of gossip in their rural community. Then young farmer Gilbert Markham (Stephens) becomes romantically interested in Helen and she's run away from her alcoholic and abusive husband Arthur Huntingdon (Graves), who has now kidnapped their son to force Helen to return. **180m/C VHS.** *GB* CA Tara Fitzgerald, Toby Stephens, Rupert Graves, Beatie Edney, James Purefoy, Jonathan Cake, Kenneth Cranham, Janet Dale; **D:** Mike Barker. **W:** Janet Barron, David Nokes; **C:** David G. Mitchell. **TV**

The Tenants 🐾½ 2006 (R) Adaptation of Bernard Malamud's 1972 novel, helmed by first-time director Green, is a small, grim drama about the failure to bridge racial and ethnic divides. Landlord Levenspiel (Cassel) is trying to force Henry (McDermott), his last legal tenant, to vacate his crumbling Brooklyn tenement so it can be torn down. But the obsessive writer refuses to go until he can finish his third novel; squatter Willie (Snoop Dogg) is an unpublished writer also working on his opus. The two meet, but racial tensions and mistrust eventually erupt. Snoop is convincing (in a stereotypical role) but the movie isn't. **97m/C DVD, DVD.** *US* Dylan McDermott, Snoop Dogg, Rose Byrne, Seymour Cassel, Niki J. Crawford, Laz Alonso; **D:** Danny Green; **W:** David Diamond, Danny Green; **C:** David W. Dubois; **M:** Leigh Gorman.

The Tender Age 🐾🐾 The Little Sister 1984 Troubled 18-year-old girl gets out of a detention home and is put on probation. She captivates her idealistic probation officer, whose interest may extend beyond professional concern. Fine idea, but under-played. **103m/C VHS.** John Savage, Tracy Pollan, Roxanne Hart, Richard Jenkins; **D:** Jan Egleson; **W:** Jan Egleson.

The Tenant 🐾🐾½ Le Locataire 1976 (R) Disturbing story of a hapless office worker who moves into a spooky Paris apartment house. Once lodged inside its walls, he becomes obsessed with the previous occupant, who committed suicide, and the belief that his neighbors are trying to kill him. Based on a novel by Roland Topor. **126m/C VHS, DVD, FR** Lila Kedrova, Claude Dauphin, Michel Blanc, Roman Polanski, Isabelle Adjani, Melvyn Douglas, Jo Van Fleet, Bernard Fresson, Shelley Winters; **D:** Roman Polanski; **W:** Gerard Brach, Roman Polanski; **C:** Sven Nykvist; **M:** Philippe Sarde.

Tender Comrade 🐾🐾 1943 Flag-waving, violin-accompanied tearjerker about five women who live together to make ends meet while their men do manly things during WWII. Intended to puff your heart up with patriotic gusto. Ironically, thanks to the girls' communal living arrangement, director Dmytryk was later accused of un-American activities. **101m/B VHS.** Ginger Rogers, Robert Ryan, Ruth Hussey, Patricia Collinge, Mady Christians, Kim Hunter.

Tenderness of the Wolves 🐾🐾 De Zärtlichkeit der Wölfe 1973 Inspired by Fritz Lang's film "M" but sticking closer to its source material, the case of real-life mass murderer Peter Kürten, known as the Dusseldorf Vampire. Lommel's film is also given the "Fassbinder" spin (he's in the cast as well as the producer and editor). In 1925, black marketeer Fritz Haarmann (Raab) lures job, only to seduce and murder them—and sell their remains as meat. Raab rather resembles the Peter Lorre character but all surface quiet and seething madness underneath. Very chilling, German with subtitles. **86m/C VHS, DVD. GE** Kurt Raab, Jeff Roden, Margit Carstensen, Rainer Werner Fassbinder, Wolfgang Schenck, Brigitte Mira, Ingrid Caven, Jürgen Prochnow; **D:** Ulli Lommel; **W:** Kurt Raab; **C:** Jürgen Jürges; **M:** Peer Raben.

The 10th Kingdom 🐾🐾½ 2000 Overly long but visually impressive fairy-tale extravaganza. New Yorkers Virginia (Williams) and her father Tony (Larroquette) find themselves magically transported into an alternate universe that consists of nine kingdoms filled with trolls, evil queens, human/beast hybrids, and all sorts of adventures. Their quest to return home (to what they learn is their own hometown, i.e. the 10th kingdom) is consistently thwarted until they clear up a little good vs. evil battle that's raging. **350m/C VHS, DVD.** Kimberly Williams, John Larroquette, Scott Cohen, Ann-Margret, Rutger Hauer, Camryn Manheim, Ed O'Neill, Dianne Wiest, Daniel Lapaine, Dawnn Lewis, Jimmy Nail, Warwick Davis, Timothy Bateson, Robert Hardy, Aiden (John) Gillett, Moira Lister; **D:** David Carson, Herbert Wise; **C:** Lawrence Jones, Chris Howard; **M:** Anne Dudley. **TV**

Tenacious D in the Pick of Destiny 🐾🐾½ 2006 (R) Big screen story of one guitar pick, two rockers and quite a bit of mind-altering substances. JB (Black) and KG (Gass) are Tenacious D, the hard-rockin' duo that simultaneously pays tribute to and pokes fun at the cliches of the world of hard rock. This hit-and-miss comedy traces the origins of the band and their experiences with talking Dio posters, Sasquatch and a musical duel with the Devil (Grohl). A must-see for fans of the band (however, it does not have powers comparable to Wonderboy), your Goblet of Rock and lower your cognitive capacity for this one. **93m/C DVD, US** Jack Black, Kyle Gass, Troy Gentile, Ben Stiller, Jason (JR) Reed, Tim Robbins, Meat Loaf Aday, Amy Poehler, Paul F. Tompkins, David Krumholtz, John C. Reilly, Fred Armisen, Ned Bellamy; **D:** Liam Lynch; **W:** Jack Black, Kyle Gass, Liam Lynch; **C:** Robert Brinkmann; **M:** Tenacious D.

Tender Flesh Woof! 1997 Unashamed exercise in sleaze from the prolific Jess Franco is worth noting for only one scene wherein a woman urinates on camera. Beyond that dubious distinction, it's yet another unfocused variation on "The Most Dangerous Game". **90m/C DVD, SP** Lina Romay, Amber Newman, Monique Parent; **D:** Jess (Jesus) Franco; **W:** Jess (Jesus) Franco.

Tender Is the Night 🐾🐾½ 1955 A TV adaptation of the F. Scott Fitzgerald classic, set in the roaring '20s, in which a psychiatrist marries one of his patients and then heads down the road to ruin, driven by his marriage and the times. An entry from the "Front Row Center" series. **60m/B VHS.** Mercedes McCambridge, James Daly. **TV**

Tender Loving Care 🐾 1973 Three nurses dispense hefty doses of T.L.C. in their hospital, and the patients aren't the only ones on the receiving end. **72m/C VHS, DVD.** Don a Desmond, Leah Simon, Anita King; **D:** Don Edmonds.

Tender Mercies 🐾🐾 1983 (PG) Down-and-out country singer Mac Sledge (Duvall) gets roaring drunk after breaking up with his wife Dixie (Buckley) andfinds himself waking up at a motel/gas station run by religious widow, Rosa Lee (Harper); mac sticks arounds and finds his life redeemed by the love of a good woman and he also decides to attempt a comeback. Aided by Horton Foote's script, Duvall, Harper, and Barkin (as Mac's daughter Sue Anne) keep this from being simplistic and sentimental. Duvall wrote as well as performed the songs in his Oscar-winning performance. Wonderful, life-affirming flick. **88m/C VHS, DVD.** Robert Duvall, Tess Harper, Betty Buckley, Ellen Barkin, Wilford Brimley, Lenny Von Dohlen, Allan Hubbard; **C:** Bruce Beresford; **W:** Horton Foote; **C:** Russell Boyd; **M:** George Dreyfus, Oscars '83: Actor (Duvall), Orig. Screenplay; Golden Globes '83: Actor-Drama (Duvall); L.A. Film Critics '83: Actor (Duvall); N.Y. Film Critics '83: Actor (Duvall); Writers Guild '83: Orig. Screenplay.

The Tender Trap 🐾🐾 1955 Charlie Reader (Sinatra) is a bachelor not content with the many women in his life. He meets the innocent Julie Gillis (Reynolds) and falls head over heels for her. He then torments himself over a marriage proposal, unwilling to let go of his free-wheeling lifestyle. **111m/C VHS.** Frank Sinatra, Debbie Reynolds, Celeste Holm, David Wayne, Carolyn Jones, Lola Albright, Tom Helmore, Howard St. John, Willard Sage, James Drury, Benny Rubin, Frank Sully, David White; **D:** Charles Walters; **W:** Julius J. Epstein; **C:** Paul Vogel.

The Tender Years 🐾🐾 1947 Sentimental drama of a minister trying to outlaw cog fighting, spurred on by his son's fondness for a particular dog. **81m/B VHS.** Joe E. Brown, Richard Lyon, Noreen Nash, Charles Drake, Josephine Hutchinson; **D:** Harold Schuster.

The Tender Warrior 🐾🐾 1971 (G) A beautifully photographed animal adventure with Haggerty as the woodsman. **85m/C VHS.** Dan Haggerty, Charles Lee, Liston Elkins; **D:** Stewart Raffill.

Tennessee's Partner 🐾🐾 1955 Enjoyable, unexceptional buddy Western. Reagan intervenes in an argument and becomes Payne's pal. Adapted from a story by Bret Harte. **87m/C VHS, DVD.** Ronald Reagan, Rhonda Fleming, John Payne; **D:** Allan Dwan; **W:** D.D. Beauchamp, Milton Krims, Teddi Sherman, Graham Baker; **C:** John Alton; **M:** Louis Forbes.

Tennessee Stallion 🐾 1978 A low-class horse-trainer breaks into the world of aristocratic thoroughbred racing. **87m/C VHS.** Audrey Landers, Judy Landers, James Van Patten; **D:** Don Hulette.

Tension 🐾🐾 1950 Nice guy Warren Quimby (Basehart) has modes; ambitions; a steady job, a house, and a loving wife. Well, two out of three...seems sultry Mrs. Q (Totter) is bored, so she finds a wealthy beachboy brute (Gough) to satisfy her itch. When Warren finds out, he plots to assume a new identity, kill the interloper, and get the missus back. But things don't work out as intended—putting Warren in the crosshairs of cynical detective Bonnabel (Sullivan). **95m/B VHS.** Richard Basehart, Audrey Totter, Barry Sullivan, Cyd Charisse, Lloyd Gough, William Conrad; **D:** John Berry; **W:** Allen Rivkin; **C:** Harry Stradling Sr.; **M:** Andre Previn.

Tension at Table Rock 🐾🐾 1956 Accused of cowardice, a lone gun-man must prove he's killed in self-defense. Well-cast serious Western. **93m/C VHS.** Richard Egan, Dorothy Malone, Cameron Mitchell; **D:** Charles Marquis Warren.

Tentacles Woof! Tentacoli 1977 (PG) Cheesy Italian version of "Jaws" lacking only the suspense and cogent storytelling. Huston slums as the investigator charged with finding the octopus gone mad, while Fonda collects checks and makes a quick exit. Hopkins is in charge of the killer whale-director is devoured by sea beast. From director of the aptly named "Beyond the Door" (that's not a recommendation). **90m/C VHS, DVD.** JT John Huston, Shelley Winters, Bo Hopkins, Henry Fonda, Cesare Danova, Delia Boccardo, Alan Boyd, Claude Akins; **D:** Ovidio G. Assonitis; **W:** Steven W. Carabatsos, Tito Carpi, Sonia Molteni; **C:** Roberto D'Ettorre Piazzoli; **M:** Stelvio Cipriani.

Tentacles of the North 🐾🐾 1926 Two ships are trapped in the ice of the Arctic with the only survivor of one ship being a fearful young girl. Tinted print. **54m/B VHS.** Gaston Glass, Alice Calhoun, Al Ferguson, Joseph Girard; **D:** Louis Chaudet.

10th & Wolf 🐾🐾½ 2006 (R) In 1991, ex-Marine Tommy Santoro (Marsden) returns to his Pittsburgh 'hood, and finds out that his cousin Joey (Ribisi) and younger bro Vincent (Renfro) are heavily involved in the family's mob business. Tommy cuts a deal with FBI agent Horvath (Dennehy) to wear a wire and get the goods on the deal between Joey and the drug ord gangland clichés. **107m/C VHS, DVD.** James Marsden, Giovanni Ribisi, Brad Renfro, Brian Dennehy, Piper Perabo, Lesley Ann Warren, Dash Minok, Dennis Hopper, Francesco Salvi, Tommy Lee Val Kilmer; **D:** Robert Moresco; **W:** Robert Moresco; **C:** Alex Nepomniaschy; **M:** Aaron Zigman.

The Tenth Man ✒✒½ 1988 Hopkins stars as a wealthy French lawyer, captured by the Nazis and sentenced to death. He discovers a fellow prisoner who is willing to take his place in exchange for Hopkins's wealth going to support the man's family. After his release, Hopkins returns to his old home, now occupied by the dead man's family, but doesn't reveal his true identity. When an imposter appears, claiming to be Hopkins, another twist is added. Slow-going but the usual excellent performances by Hopkins and Jacobi. Based on a novella by Graham Greene. **99m/C VHS.** Anthony Hopkins, Kristin Scott Thomas, Derek Jacobi, Cyril Cusack, Brenda Bruce, Paul Rogers; **D:** Jack Gold. **TV**

Tenth Month ✒✒ 1979 Carol Burnett plays a divorced, middle-aged woman who becomes pregnant by a married man. She refuses help, choosing instead to live alone and keep an ever-hopeful vigil for the birth of her child. Sappy but touching TV drama. **123m/C VHS.** Carol Burnett, Keith Michell, Dina Merrill; **D:** Joan Tewkesbury.

10th Victim ✒✒✒ 1965 *La Decima Vittima; La Dixieme Victime* 1965 Sci-fi cult film set in the 21st century has Mastroianni and Andress pursuing one another in a futuristic society where legalized murder is used as a means of population control. Intriguing movie where Andress kills with a double-barreled bra, the characters hang out at the Club Masoch, and comic books are considered literature. Based on "The Seventh Victim" by Robert Sheckley. **92m/C VHS, DVD.** *IT* Ursula Andress, Marcello Serani, Elsa Martinelli, Salvo Randone, Massimo Serato; **D:** Elio Petri; **W:** Elio Petri, Tonino Guerra, Ennio Flaiano, Giorgio Salvioni; **C:** Gianni Di Venanzo; **M:** Piero Piccioni.

Teorema ✒✒ 1968 Scathing condemnation of bourgeois complacency. Stamp, either a devil or a god, mysteriously appears and enters into the life of a well-to-do Milanese family and raises each member's spirituality by sleeping with them. Ultimately, the experience leads to tragedy. In Italian with English subtitles. **98m/C VHS, DVD.** *IT* Terence Stamp, Silvana Mangano, Massimo Girotti, Anna Wiazemsky, Laura Betti, Andres Jose Cruz; **D:** Pier Paolo Pasolini; **M:** Ennio Morricone.

Tequila Body Shots ✒ 1999 (R) Low-budget nightmare is suffered not just by the portentously named main character, Johnny Orpheus (Lawrence). Johnny is convinced by some buddies to attend a Day of the Dead party held on a Mexican beach where he imbibes some whacked Tequila that enables him to read women's thoughts and experience some afterlife horrors, courtesy of evil spirit Hector (Moreno). Turns out Hector is after his reincarnated wife who just happens to be the girl (Mouser) that Johnny is interested in. Oh yeah, and its all played for laughs (but you won't be). **94m/C VHS, DVD.** Joey Lawrence, Dru Mouser, Rene L. Moreno, Nathan Anderson, Josh Marchette, Jennifer Lyons, Henny Darrow; **D:** Tony Shyu; **W:** Tony Shyu; **C:** Lawrence Schweich; **M:** Shayne Fair, Larry Herbstritt.

Tequila Sunrise ✒✒½ 1988 (R) Towne's twisting film about two lifelong friends and a beautiful woman. Gibson is a (supposedly) retired drug dealer afraid of losing custody of his son to his nagging ex-wife. Russell is the cop and old friend who's trying to get the lowdown on a drug shipment coming in from Mexico. Pfeiffer runs the poshest restaurant on the coast and is actively pursued by both men. Questions cloud the plot and confuse the viewer; loaded with double-crosses, intrigue and surprises around every corner, still the photogenic leads are pleasant to watch. Steamy love scene between Pfeiffer and Gibson. **116m/C VHS, DVD.** Mel Gibson, Kurt Russell, Michelle Pfeiffer, Raul Julia, Arliss Howard, Ayre Gross, J.T. Walsh, Ann Magnuson; **D:** Robert Towne; **W:** Robert Towne; **C:** Conrad L. Hall; **M:** Dave Grusin.

Teresa Venerdi ✒✒ *Doctor Beware* 1941 An unusual Italian comedy about a man and his financial difficulties. His mistress, his fiance and a young girl make his troubles more confusing. Unusually sweet and humorous DeSica. **90m/B VHS.** *IT* Vittorio De Sica, Irasema Dilian, Anna Magnani, Adriana Benetti, Arturo Bragaglia, Olga Vittoria Gentilli; **D:** Vittorio De Sica; **W:** Vittorio De Sica; **C:** Vincenzo Seratrice; **M:** Renzo Rossellini.

Teresa's Tattoo ✒ 1994 A bimbo (Shelly) with a Chinese dragon tattoo somehow obtains a pair of earrings containing details of the U.S. space program. She's kidnapped by inept thugs and dies in a freak accident. Her kidnappers need a look-alike for their extortion scheme so they kidnap another girl (Shelly again) and drug and tattoo her. Naturally, when she wakes up she manages to escape. Thin farce striving too hard to be madcap and whimsical. **88m/C VHS.** Adrienne Shelly, C. Thomas Howell, Nancy McKeon, Lou Diamond Phillips, Casey Siemaszko, Jonathan Silverman, Diedrich Bader; **Cameos:** Majel Barrett, Anthony Clark, Nanette Fabray, Tippi Hedren, k.d. lang, Joe Pantoliano, Mary Kay Place, Mare Winningham, Kiefer Sutherland, Melissa Etheridge; **D:** Julie Cypher; **W:** Georgie Huntington; **C:** Sven Kirsten; **M:** Melissa Etheridge.

Tereza ✒✒✒ 1961 In politically chaotic Czechoslovakia, a female police detective tries to solve an intricate murder mystery. In Czech with English subtitles. **91m/B VHS.** *CZ* Jirina Svorcova; **D:** Pavel Blumenfeld.

The Terminal ✒✒ 2004 (PG-13) Viktor Navorski (Hanks), traveling to New York, must stay in the airport's international zone because his home country has fallen into civil war and technically no longer exists. With plucky resolve Navorski creates a makeshift life for himself while winning allies among the terminal's workforce. Central players are good: Tucci as cruel airport overseer; Zeta-Jones as love interest; and Hanks always appealing as the confused but intrepid traveler. Often clever, but basically cotton candy: sweet, but way too fluffy. Based on the true story of an Iranian immigrant who got stuck in Charles de Gaulle Airport in Paris. **128m/C VHS, DVD.** *US* Tom Hanks, Catherine Zeta-Jones, Stanley Tucci, Chi McBride, Diego Luna, Barry Shabaka Henley, Zoe Saldana, Eddie Jones, Michael Nouri, Kumar Pallana, Jude Ciccolella, Corey Reynolds, Guillermo Diaz, Rini Bell, Stephen Mendel, Valery Nikolayev Nikolaev; **D:** Steven Spielberg; **W:** Andrew Niccol, Jeff Nathanson, Sacha Gervasi; **C:** Janusz Kaminski; **M:** John Williams.

Terminal Bliss ✒½ 1991 (R) Teen heartthrob Perry stars as a spoiled rich druggie in this "Less Than Zero" knockoff. Perry and childhood pal Owen grow up sharing everything—lacrosse, girlfriends, and drugs. However, their friendship is really put to the test when a beautiful new girl (Chandler) moves to town just before graduation. Release was delayed, but obviously wants to capitalize on Perry's popularity. **94m/C VHS.** Luke Perry, Timothy Owen, Estee Chandler, Sonia Curtis, Micah Grant, Alexis Arquette; **D:** Jordan Alan; **W:** Jordan Alan; **C:** Greg Smith; **M:** Frank Becker.

Terminal Choice ✒½ 1985 (R) Staff at a hospital conduct a betting pool on patients' life expectancies. Someone decides he should win more often and is trying to hedge his bets. Wasted cast on this unsuspenseful and bloody film. **98m/C VHS.** Joe Spano, Diane Ventora, David McCallum, Ellen Barkin; **D:** Sheldon Larry; **M:** Neal Bell.

Terminal Entry ✒½ 1987 (R) Teen computer geeks accidentally find a terrorist online network, and inadvertently begin transmitting instructions to destroy U.S. targets. The premise is intriguing but poorly done. **95m/C VHS.** Edward Albert, Yaphet Kotto, Kabir Bedi; **D:** John Kincade; **C:** James L. Carter.

Terminal Error ✒ *Peace Virus* 2002 (PG-13) Disgruntled businessman cripples his old company with a computer virus to settle the score but the bug happens to spill out into the city and spells doom unless the CEO and his smarty-pants son can stop it. **90m/C VHS, DVD.** Robert Casey, Marina Sirtis, Michael Nouri, Timothy Busfield; **D:** John Murlowski; **C:** Philip Lee; **M:** James T. Sales. **VIDEO**

Terminal Exposure ✒½ 1989 (R) Predictable but likeable comedy-mystery. A pair of Venice, CA, beach denizens capture a murder on film and try to solve it. **105m/C VHS.** Steve Donmyer, John Vernon, Ted Lange, Joe Estevez, Hope Marie Carlton, Mark Hennessy, Scott King; **D:** Nico Mastorakis.

Terminal Force ✒ *Rescue Force* 1988 (R) Stupid, poorly executed story of kidnapping and the mob. So bad it never saw the inside of a theatre; went straight to video. **83m/C VHS, DVD.** Troy Donahue, Richard Harrison, Dawn Wildsmith; **D:** Fred Olen Ray. **VIDEO**

Terminal Impact ✒✒ 1995 (R) Bounty hunters Saint (Zagarino) and Max (Genesse) agree to a high-paying assignment at Delta Tech Labs without asking any questions. They discover that the lab's chairman Sheen (Roberts) is messing around with DNA and has been implanting insect DNA into unwilling human subjects, which turns them into killer cyborgs as well. **94m/C VHS.** Bryan Genesse, Frank Zagarino, Jenny (Jennifer) McShane, Ian Roberts; **D:** Yossi Wein; **W:** Jeff Albert, Dennis Dimster-Denk; **C:** Rod Stewart.

Terminal Island ✒½ 1973 (R) Tough southern California penal colony is crowded with inmates from death row. When prison becomes coed, violence breaks out. Exploitative and unappealing. **88m/C VHS, DVD.** Phyllis E. Davis, Tom Selleck, Don Marshall, Ena Hartman, Marta Kristen; **D:** Stephanie Rothman.

Terminal Justice: Cybertech P.D. ✒½ 1995 (R) Cop Bobby Chase (Lamas) is assigned to protect VR sex babe, Pamela Travis (Wuhrer). Turns out wealthy VR game manufacturer, Reginald Matthews (Sarandon) has teamed up with sicko doctor, Deacon (Vivyan), to clone beautiful women so they can be used in snuff films. And Matthews wants Pam's DNA to begin the process. **95m/C VHS, DVD.** Lorenzo Lamas, Chris Sarandon, Karl Wuhrer, Peter Coyote; **D:** Rick King; **W:** Frederick Bailey; **C:** Chris Holmes Jr.; **M:** Michael Hoenig. **VIDEO**

The Terminal Man ✒✒½ 1974 (R) A slick, visually compelling adaptation of the Michael Crichton novel. A scientist plagued by violent mental disorders has a computer-controlled regulator implanted in his brain. The computer malfunctions and he starts a murdering spree. Futuristic vision of man-machine symbiosis gone awry. Well acted, but still falls short of the novel. **107m/C VHS.** George Segal, Joan Hackett, Jill Clayburgh, Richard Dysart, James B. Sikking, Norman Burton; **D:** Mike Hodges; **W:** Mike Hodges.

Terminal Rush ✒✒ 1996 (R) Army Ranger Johnny Price (Wilson) is thrown out of the service after being framed for a crime. But when terrorists (led by Piper) take over Hoover Dam, Price is the one person with the necessary skills to thwart this vindictive madman. **94m/C VHS, DVD.** Don "The Dragon" Wilson, Roddy Piper; **D:** Damian Lee. **VIDEO**

Terminal Velocity ✒✒ 1994 (PG-13) Skydiving instructor Ditch Brodie (Sheen) thinks he sees student Chris Morrow (Kinski) plummet to her death, only it turns out she's not dead and certainly not a beginner. Upon further investigation, he finds the usual web of international intrigue descending upon him, and that the KGB definitely wants to mind his own business. Still, he pushes on. Another nobrainer actioner with few surprises satisfies the guilty pleasures of action addicts only. **132m/C VHS, DVD.** Charlie Sheen, Nastassja Kinski, James Gandolfini; Christopher McDonald, Melvin Van Peebles; **D:** Deran Sarafian; **W:** David N. Twohy; **C:** Oliver Wood; **M:** Joel McNeely.

Terminal Virus ✒✒ 1996 (R) A deadly sexually trasmitted disease has made reproduction impossible, so humanity is on the verge of extinction. It's up to an outlaw and a scientist to convince a suspicious population that a new serum is the cure everyone's been waiting for. **74m/C VHS.** James Brolin, Richard Lynch, Bryan Genesse; **D:** Dan Golden.

Termination Man ✒½ 1997 (R) Serbian terrorist blackmails NATO and the United Nations with a nerve gas threat and genetically enhanced agent Dylan Pope (Railsback), who may be immune to the gas, must lead a covert squad to save the day. Action by the numbers. **92m/C VHS, DVD.** Steve Railsback, Athena Massey, James Farentino, Eb Lottimer; **D:** Fred Gallo; **W:** Fred Gallo, Charles Philip Moore; **C:** Eugeny Guslinsky; **M:** Deddy Tzur. **VIDEO**

The Terminator ✒✒✒ 1984 (R) Futuristic cyborg (Schwarzenegger, suitably robotic and menacing) is sent to present-day Earth. His job: kill the woman, Sarah Connor (Hamilton), who will conceive the child destined to become the great liberator and arch-enemy of the Earth's future rulers. The cyborg is also pursued by another futuristic visitor, Kyle Reese (Biehn), who falls in love with the intended victim. Cameron's pacing is just right in this exhilarating, explosive thriller which displays Arnie as one cold-blooded villain who utters a now famous line: "I'll be back." Followed by "Terminator 2: Judgment Day." **108m/C VHS, VHS, DVD, Blu-ray Disc.** Arnold Schwarzenegger, Michael Biehn, Linda Hamilton, Paul Winfield, Lance Henriksen, Bill Paxton, Rick Rossovich, Dick Miller, Earl Boen; **D:** James Cameron; **W:** James Cameron; **M:** Brad Fiedel.

Terminator 2: Judgment

Day ✒✒✒½ 1991 (R) He said he'd be back and he is. Schwarzenegger is back to protect the boy who will be mankind's post-nuke resistance leader. But the T-1000, a shape-changing, ultimate killing machine, is also on the boy's trail. Twice the mayhem, ten times the special effects, ten times the budget of the first, but without Arnold it'd be half the movie. The word hasn't been invented to describe the special effects, particularly THE scariest nuclear holocaust scene yet. Worldwide megahit, but the $100 million budget nearly ruined the studio; Arnold accepted his $12 million in the form of a jet. **139m/C VHS, DVD, Blu-ray Disc.** Arnold Schwarzenegger, Linda Hamilton, Edward Furlong, Robert Patrick, Earl Boen, Joe Morton; **D:** James Cameron; **W:** James Cameron; **C:** Adam Greenberg; **M:** Brad Fiedel. Oscars '91: Makeup, Sound, Sound FX Editing, Visual FX; MTV Movie Awards '92: Film, Male Perf. (Schwarzenegger), Female Perf. (Hamilton), Breakthrough Perf. (Furlong), Most Desirable Female (Hamilton), Action Seq.

Terminator 3; Rise of the Machines ✒✒½ 2003 (R) Satisfying third chapter does not suffer from the absence of James Cameron or Linda Hamilton. This time around, the new bad Terminator is the female T-X (Loken) but the job is the same—kill future resistance leader John Connor (Stahl). Arnold's again sent back to protect him, as well as future cohort Kate (Danes). Solid script provides plenty of action, some inside humor, and (perhaps most importantly) a logical progression from the first two movies. Stahl does a good job as Connor, and Arnold proves he's still got the goods after a few disappointing outings. The special effects are, thankfully, seamless enough not to distract from the action at hand. **110m/C VHS, DVD, Blu-ray Disc, UMD, HD DVD.** *US* Arnold Schwarzenegger, Nick Stahl, Claire Danes, Kristanna Loken, David Andrews, Mark Famiglietti; **D:** Jonathan Mostow; **W:** John Brancato, Michael Ferris; **C:** Don Burgess; **M:** Marco Beltrami.

Termini Station ✒✒½ 1989 Dewhurst gives an excellent performance as the alcoholic matriarch of a small-town Canadian family. She drinks all day and dreams of traveling to Italy, while her children work and believe there is something more to life than their mundane existence. When they finally do leave, they discover an intriguing new world. Dewhurst and Follows also appear together in "Anne of Green Gables" and "Anne of Avonlea." **105m/C VHS.** *CA* Colleen Dewhurst, Megan Follows, Gordon Clapp, Hannah Lee, Leon Pownall, Debra McGrath, Elliott Smith, Norma Dell'Agnese; **D:** Allen King; **M:** Mychael Dana.

Terms of Endearment ✒✒✒ 1983 (PG) A weeper following the changing relationship between a young woman and her mother, over a 30-year period. Beginning as a comedy, turning serious as the years go by, this was Brooks' debut as screenwriter and director. Superb supporting cast headed by Nicholson's slyly charming neighbor/astronaut, with stunning performances by Winger and MacLaine as the two women who often know and love each other too well. Adapted from Larry McMurtry's novel. **DVD.** Shirley MacLaine, Jack Nicholson, Debra Winger, John Lithgow, Jeff Daniels, Danny DeVito; **D:** James L. Brooks; **W:** James L. Brooks. **C:** Michael Gore. Oscars '83: Actress (MacLaine), Picture, Support. Actor (Nicholson), Adapt. Screenplay, Director (Brooks); Golden Globes '84: Actress—Drama (MacLaine), Film—Drama, Screenplay, Support. Actor (Nicholson); Directors Guild '83: Director (Brooks); L.A. Film Critics '83: Actress (MacLaine), Director (Brooks), Film, Screenplay, Support. Actor (Nicholson); Natl. Bd. of Review '83: Actor (Nicholson); N.Y. Film Critics '83: Actress (MacLaine), Film, Support. Actor (Nicholson); Natl. Soc. Film Critics '83: Actress (Winger), Support. Actor (Nicholson); Writers Guild '83: Adapt. Screenplay.

Terraces 1977 TV series pilot about high-rise tenants whose balconies are their only common ground. Good performances. 90m/C VHS. Lloyd Bochner, Eliza...

Terranova 1991 Six characters in search of themselves, with the profound changes in their lives coming through an unlikely friendship. Rosetta is the poor matriarch of an Italian immigrant family while wealthy Noemi is an aristocratic landowner. But they share similar frustrations and the desire to change their lives. Set in a rural Venezuelan town in the 1950s. Spanish with subtitles. 96m/C VHS. /T Marisa Laurito, Mimi Lazo, Antonio Banderas, Patrick Bauchau, Massimo Bonetti, Nathalia Martinez; **D:** Calogero Salvo. **TV**

Terrified 1994 (R) Erotic thriller about a nympho being stalked by a mystery assailant. Genuinely creepy. 90m/C VHS, DVD. Heather Graham, Lisa Zane, Rustam Branaman, Tom Breznahan, Max Perlich, Balthazar Getty, Richard Lynch, Don Calfa; **D:** James Merendino; **W:** James Merendino, Megan Heath.

The Terror 1938 A hostelry is the scene of a number of brutal murders. Remake of a 1928 film and based on a play by Edgar Wallace. Good story, but weak version of it. 63m/B VHS, DVD, GB Wilfred Lawson, Bernard Lee, Arthur Wontner, Linden Travers, Henry Oscar, Alastair Sim; **D:** Richard Bird.

The Terror 1963 A lieutenant in Napoleon's army chases a lovely maiden and finds himself trapped in a creepy castle by a mad baron. Movie legend has it Corman directed the movie in three days at the sets from his previous movie ("The Raven") were being torn down around them. 81m/C VHS, DVD. Boris Karloff, Jack Nicholson, Sandra Knight, Dick Miller, Dorothy Neumann, Jonathan Haze; **D:** Roger Corman, Jack Hill, Francis Ford Coppola, Monte Hellman, Dennis Jacob, Jack Nicholson; **W:** Roger Corman, Leo Gordon, Jack Hill; **C:** John M. Nickolaus Jr.; **M:** Ronald Stein.

The Terror woof! 1979 (R) After 100 years, a man reveals in a film that his family killed a witch. Friends who see the film are attacked by supernatural forces. Originally double-billed with "Dracula's Dog." 86m/C VHS, DVD. John Nolan, Carolyn Courage, James Aubrey, Glynis Barber, Sarah Keller, Tricia Walsh; **D:** Norman J. Warren; **W:** Lester Young; **M:** Ivor Slaney.

Terror at London Bridge *Bridge Across Time; Arizona Ripper* 1985 London Bridge is transported brick by brick to Arizona. It carries its history with it including the havoc-wreaking spirit of Jack the Ripper. Campy made-for-TV effort. 96m/C VHS. David Hasselhoff, Stephanie Kramer, Adrienne Barbeau, Randolph Mantooth, Clu Gulager; **D:** E.W. Swackhamer; **C:** Gil Hubbs.

Terror at Red Wolf Inn *Club Dead; Terror House; The Folks at Red Wolf Inn* 1972 (R) Young woman wins a vacation; finds she's been invited for dinner, so to speak. Not campy enough to overcome stupidity. 90m/C VHS. Linda Gillin, Arthur Space, John Nielson, Mary Jackson, Janet Wood, Margaret Avery; **D:** Bud Townsend; **W:** Allen Actor.

Terror at Tenkiller 1986 Two girls vacationing in the mountains are seemingly surrounded by a rash of mysterious murders. 90m/C VHS. Stacey Logan; **D:** Ken Meyer; **M:** Robert Farrar. **VIDEO**

Terror Beach 1975 A doctor and his bride move to a coastal village, only to find themselves enmeshed in witchcraft and devil worship. 90m/C VHS, SP Victor Petit, Julie James, Maria Costi, Sandra Mozorovic; **C:** Francisco Sanchez; **M:** Armando de Ossorio.

Terror Beneath the Sea 1966 A mad scientist wants to rule the world with his cyborgs. American and Japanese scientists unite to fight him. Fine special effects, especially the transformation from human to monster. 85m/C VHS, DVD, JP Sonny Chiba, Peggy Neal, Franz Gruber, Gunther Braun, Andrew Hughes, Mike Daneen; **D:** Hajime Sato.

Terror by Night 1946 Holmes and Watson attempt to solve the murder of the owner of a gigantic, beautiful jewel. Their investigator must be completed before their train arrives at its destination, where the murderer can escape. 60m/B VHS, DVD. Basil Rathbone, Nigel Bruce, Alan Mowbray, Dennis Hoey, Renee Godfrey, Roy William Neill; **W:** Frank Gruber; **C:** Maury Gertsman.

Terror Creatures from the Grave 1966 Husband summons medieval plague victims to rise from the grave to drop in on his unfaithful wife. Should've been better. 85m/C VHS, DVD, /T Barbara Steele, Riccardo Garrone, Walter Brandi; **D:** Ralph Zucker.

Terror Eyes 1987 (PG-13) Spoof-thriller revolves around an "agent from Hell," sent to Earth to recruit writers for a horror film. 90m/C VHS Daniel Roebuck, Vivian Schilling, Dan Bell, Lance August; **D:** Eric Parkinson, Stephen Sommers, Vivian Schilling; **C:** Robert Grant, Mark Irwin; **M:** Jon McCallum.

Terror House woof! 1997 There's this creepy house, see, that's got an ugly family secret—in this case it's half-human and lives on warm blood. So these three college students think they have a chance at some big money if they can stay in the house, and they have visions of this beautiful woman, and night's coming, and you get the idea. 80m/C VHS, DVD. Jon McBride, Mark Alan Polonia, Clyde Burroughs, Holly Harrington; **D:** Jon McBride, Mark Alan Polonia; **W:** Mark Alan Polonia; **C:** Artur Daniels.

Terror in a Texas Town 1958 George Hansen (Hayden) is a Swedish seaman who returns home to discover his farmer father has been gunned down by the greedy Johnny Crale (Young), who's after the land so he can drill for oil. So Hansen's out for revenge. There's a final showdown that only includes six-shooters but a harpoon. 120m/B VHS, DVD. Sterling Hayden, Nedrick Young, Sebastian Cabot, Victor Millan; **D:** Joseph H. Lewis; **W:** Dalton Trumbo; **C:** Ray Rennahan; **M:** Gerald Fried.

Terror in Beverly Hills woof! 1990 When the President's daughter is kidnapped, it's up to an ex-marine to save her. The trouble is, the marine's guts as he blames him for the deaths of his wife and children. So incredibly bad it's campy and fun. 88m/C VHS. Frank Stallone, Cameron Mitchell, (Bill) Smith; **D:** John Myhers; **W:** John Myhers.

Terror in Paradise 1990 (R) Jason and Vickie think they're going to have a romantic holiday on a beautiful island paradise. But they've picked the wrong spot to vacation. It seems the island harbors a terrorist group and when they see more than they should the lovers become the next targets. 53m/C VHS. Joanna Pettet, Gary Lockwood, David Anthony Smith, Leslie Ryan; **D:** Peer J. Oppenheimer.

Terror in the Haunted House *My World Dies Screaming* 1958 Newlyweds move into an old house. The bride remembers it from her nightmares. First release featured the first use of Psychorama, a technique in which scary words or advertising messages were flashed on the screen for a fraction of a second—just long enough to cause subliminal response. The technique was banned later in that year. 90m/C VHS. Gerald Mohr, Cathy O'Connell, William Ching, John Qualen, Barry Bernard; **D:** Harold Daniels; **C:** Frederick E. West; **M:** Darrell Calker.

Terror in the Jungle 1968 (PG) Plane crashes in Peruvian wilds and young boy survivor meets Jivaro Indians who think he's a god. Much struggling to survive and battling with 'horrible script. 95m/C VHS, Jimmy Angle, Fawn Silver; **D:** Tom De Simone; **M:** Les Baxter.

Terror in the Swamp 1985 (PG) When not hanging out in the local murky waters, a swamp creature 'terrorizes the residents of a small town. 89m/C VHS, Billy Holliday; **D:** Joe Catalanotto.

Terror in the Wax Museum woof! 1973 (PG) The owner of a wax museum is killed while mulling over the sale of the museum. The new owner has little better luck as the bodies continue to pile up. Production uses every out-of-work horror film actor of the time. 93m/C VHS, DVD. Ray Milland, Broderick Crawford, Elsa Lanchester, Louis Hayward, Maurice Evans, John Carradine; **D:** Georg Fenady; **W:** Jameson Brewer.

Terror Is a Man *Blood Creature* 1959 A mad scientist attempts to turn a panther into a man on a secluded island. Early Filipino horror attempt inspired by H.G. Wells' "The Island of Doctor Moreau." 89m/B VHS, DVD, PH Francis Lederer, Greta Thyssen, Richard Derr, Oscar Keesee; **D:** Gerardo (Gerry) De Leon; **W:** Harry Paul Harber; **C:** Emmanuel I. Rojas; **M:** Ariston Avelino.

Terror of Mechagodzilla *Megagodzilla; Monsters from the Unknown Planet; The Escape of Megagodzilla; Mekagojira No Gyakushu* 1978 (G) It's Godzilla vs. machine in the heavyweight battle of the universe as a huge mechanical Godzilla built by aliens is pitted against the real thing. The last Godzilla movie made until "Godzilla 1985." 79m/C VHS, DVD, JP Katsuhiko Sasaki, Tomoko Ai; **D:** Inoshiro Honda; **W:** Yukiko Takayama; **C:** Motoaka Tomioka; **M:** Akira Ifukube.

Terror of Rome Against the Son of Hercules 1964 Muscle-bound gladiators battle it out in this low-budget Italian action flick. Dubbed. 100m/C VHS, FR /T Mark Forest, Marisa Tolo; **D:** Mario Caiano.

Terror of the Bloodhunters 1962 A French author is sentenced to Devil's Island for a crime he didn't commit. The warden's daughter takes a liking to him and arranges for him and a friend to escape, but numerous perils await them in the jungle. 60m/B VHS, DVD. Robert Clarke, Steve Conte, Dorothy Haney; **D:** Jerry Warren.

Terror of the Steppes 1964 Yet another sword and sandal extravaganza in which a musclebound hero conquers all. 97m/C VHS. /T Kirk Morris, Moira Orfei; Daniele Vargas, Furio Meniconi, Ombretta Colli; **D:** Tanio Boccia; **W:** Tanio Boccia; **M:** Carlo Rustichelli.

Terror of Tiny Town 1938 Main characteristic of this musical/western is its entire midget cast, all members of Jed Buell's Midgets. Otherwise the plot is fairly average and features a bad guy and the good guy who finally teaches him a lesson. Newfield plays up the cast's short stature—they walk under saloon doors and ride Shetland ponies. 63m/B VHS, DVD. Billy Curtis, Yvonne Moray, "Little Billy" Rhodes, Billy Platt, John Bambury, Charles Becker; **D:** Sam Newfield; **W:** Fred Myton, Clarence Marks; **C:** Mack Stengler.

Terror on Alcatraz 1986 The only prisoner to successfully escape from Alcatraz Island returns to retrieve the safety deposit box key he needs to get his stolen loot. And anyone who gets in his way is in for trouble. 56m/C VHS. Veronica Porsche Ali, Sandy Brooke, Aldo Ray, Scott Ryder; **D:** Philip Marcus.

Terror on the 40th Floor 1974 Seven people make an attempt to escape from the 40th floor of an inflamed skyscraper. Poorly done re-hash of "Towering Inferno." Unispired story. 93m/C V-HS, DVD. John Forsythe, Anjanette Comer, Don Meredith, Joseph Campanella; **D:** Jerry Jameson.

Terror on Tour woof! 1983 Clowns, a rock group on their way up, center their stage performance around sadistic, mutilating theatrics. When real murders begin, they become prime suspects. Exploitive, bloody, disgusting. 90m/C VHS, Dave Galluzzo, Richard Styles, Rick Pemberton; **D:** Don Edmonds.

Terror Out of the Sky *Revenge of the Savage Bees* 1978 A scientist must disguise herself as one of the killing bees from a busload of elementary children. Sub-par sequel to "The Savage Bees." 95m/C VHS, DVD. Efrem Zimbalist Jr., Dan Haggerty, Tovah Feldshuh, Lonny (Lonnie) Chapman, Ike Eisenmann, Steve Franken, Bruce French, Richard Herd, Philip Baker Hall; **D:** Lee H. Katzin; **W:** Guerdon (Gordon) Trueblood; **C:** Michael Hugo; **M:** William Goldstein. **TV**

Terror Ship 1954 Three people find an abandoned yacht which they believe was used for smuggling. While searching it, they find that it was used to transport stolen uranium. Before the police can arrive, the thieves show up. Not a very good handling of what was actually an interesting idea. Released as "Dangerous Voyage" in Great Britain. 72m/B VHS. GB William Lundigan, Naomi Chance, Vincent Ball, Jean Lodge, Richard Stewart; **D:** Vernon Sewell.

Terror Squad 1987 An unsuspecting high school population is put under the siege by Libyan terrorists. The students get a hands-on lesson in revolution and guerilla war tactics. 95m/C VHS. Kerry Brennan, Bill Calvert, Chuck Connors, Greer Brodie; **D:** Peter Maris.

Terror Stalks the Class Reunion 1993 (PG-13) Kay (Nelligan) is a teacher who disappears at a class reunion. Police dismiss the case as a runaway wife, except for Virginia, a young detective (Beals) who doesn't accept that theory. And she's right—Kay is held hostage in a remote cabin by an obsessed former student (Davies). Kay needs all her wits to fend off her deranged and possibly deadly suitor while Virginia races to find her. Based on the novel by Mary Higgins Clark. 95m/C VHS. Kate Nelligan, Jennifer Beals, Geraint Wyn Davies; **D:** Clive Donner; **W:** Marc Frinci; **C:** Gerrot Roll; **M:** Carlo Siliotto.

Terror Street *36 Hours* 1953 An Air Force pilot's wife is murdered. He has 36 hours to clear his name and find the killer. 97m/C VHS, DVD. Dan Duryea, Elsy Albiin, Ann Gudrun, Eric Pohlmann, Marianne Stone; **D:** Montgomery Tully; **W:** Steve Fisher; **C:** Walter J. (Jimmy W.) Harvey; **M:** Ivor Slaney.

Terror Tract 2000 (R) Real estate agent Bob (Ritter) takes newlyweds Allen (DeLuise) and Mary Ann (Smith) to three homes he has for sale. But each home was the site of some horrible evil: in one a wife kills her abusive husband, only to fear he's not really dead; in the second, a father tries to stop the mischief caused by his daughter's evil pet monkey; and in the third house, a teenage boy finds himself psychically linked to a killer who blames the teen for his crimes. Comfortably scary fun. 97m/C VHS, DVD. John Ritter, Will Estes, Brenda Strong, Rachel York, Allison Smith, Carmine D. Giovinazzo, David DeLuise, Wade Andrew Williams, Frederic Lehne; **D:** Lance Dreesen; **C:** Clint Hutchison; **W:** Geoffrey Wright; **M:** Brian Tyler. **VIDEO**

Terror Trail 1933 As usual, Mix uses guns and fists to bring bad guys to justice, and gets the girl in the bargain. 62m/B VHS. Tom Mix, Naomi Judge, Arthur (L.) Rankin, Raymond Hatton, Francis McDonald, Robert F. (Bob) Kortman, John St. Polis, Lafe (Lafayette) McKee, Buffalo Bill Jr.; **D:** Armand Schaefer.

Terror Train 1980 (R) A masquerade party is held on a chartered train. But someone has more than mask-wearing in mind as a series of dead bodies begin to appear. Copperfield provides magic, Curtis provides screams in this semi-scary slasher movie. 97m/C VHS, DVD. Jamie Lee Curtis, Ben Johnson, Hart Bochner, David Copperfield, Vanity, Howard Busgang, Michael Shanks, Amanda Tapping, Troy Kennedy-Martin, Anthony Sherwood, Timothy Webber; **D:** Roger Spottiswoode; **W:** Alec Curtis; **C:** John Alcott.

Terror 2000 *Intensivstation Deutschland* 1992 Satire/exploitation/slapstick and gross-out humor converge in a story about a husband and wife detective team sent to a German refugee camp to investigate the disappearance of a Polish family seeking asylum. The detectives discover the family has been kidnapped by a group of neo-Nazis. Have the Teenage Mutant Ninja Turtles grown up? 79m/C VHS. **GE** Margit Carstensen, Alfred Edel, Udo Kier, Peter Kern, Gary Indiana; **D:** Christoph Schlingensief; **W:** Christoph Schlingensief.

The Terror Within 1988 (R) Reptilian mutants hit the streets searching for human women to breed with. Have the human women grown up? 90m/C VHS, DVD. George Kennedy, Andrew Stevens, Starr Andreeff, Terri Treas; **D:** Thierry Notz; **W:** Thomas McKelvey Cleaver; **C:** Ronn Schmidt; **M:** Rick Conrad.

The Terror Within 2 1991 (R) In a world destroyed by biological warfare, a warrior and the woman he rescued traverse the badlands occupied by hideous mutants. What they don't know is that the real terror comes from within. How can they possibly survive? Not without decent dialogue, that's for sure. 90m/C VHS. Andrew Stevens, Stella Stevens, Chick Vennera, R. Lee Ermey; **D:** Andrew Stevens.

Terrorgram 1990 (R) Not a very special delivery. An offscreen James Earl Jones introduces three lesser tales of terror. Best seg: a sleazy filmmaker gets trapped in the world of his own exploitation scripts. The other two are bloody but negligible revenge-from-the-grave yarns. All start off with the receipt of a sinister package, hence a postal motif. 88m/C VHS. Michael Hartson, J.T. Wallace; **D:** Stephen Kienzle; **W:** Stephen Kienzle; **C:** Gregory Irwin; **M:** Roy J. Ravio; **Nar:** James Earl Jones.

The Terrorist *Malli* 1998 Malli (Dharkar) is a 19-year-old terrorist trained to kill from an early age and to die if necessary. She lives with her fellow militants in a camp and is chosen to kill a politician by detonating a bomb that will be strapped to her waist. But when Malli is forced to wait in the city for her victim, she begins to question her mission and her cause. Inspired by the 1991 assassination of Indian prime minister Rajiv Gandhi although the film itself never mentions country, group, or politics specifically. 95m/C VHS, DVD. **IN** Ayesha Dharker; **D:** Santosh Sivan; **W:** Santosh Sivan; **C:** Santosh Sivan; **M:** Sonu Sisupal.

Terrorists 1974 (PG) Just as later known as a Scottish Lithuanian sub-commander in "The Hunt for Red October" (1990), here Connery is forced to stop it. Brutal action. 81m/C VHS. Nick Millard, Marland Proctor, Irmgard Millard; **D:** Nick Millard; **W:** Nick Millard.

The Terrornauts WOOF! 1967 When man begins space exploration, Earth is attacked by aliens. The defenders are taken to an out-dated fortress where they learn that their forebears were similarly attacked. Juvenile, lackluster, contrived, and really dumb. 77m/C VHS. **GB** Simon Oates, Zena Marshall, Charles Hawtrey, Stanley Meadows; **D:** Montgomery Tully.

Terrorvision WOOF! 1986 (R) OUR TV GAVE BIRTH TO SPACE ALIENS! It's amazing what modern technology can do: Suburban family buys a fancy satellite dish; bad black comedy and gory special effects result. 84m/C VHS. Gerrit Graham, Mary Woronov, Diane Franklin, Bert Remsen, Alejandro Rey; **D:** Ted Nicolaou; **W:** Ted Nicolaou; **M:** Richard Band.

The Terry Fox Story 1983 In the spring of 1980, a young man who had lost his right leg to cancer dipped his artificial limb into the Atlantic Ocean and set off on a fund-raising "Marathon of Hope" across Canada, drawing national attention. Inspiring true story is well-scripted and avoids corniness. Good acting from Duvall, Reid (Fryer) and, as usual, from Duvall. 97m/C VHS. Eric Fryer, Robert Duvall, Chris Makepeace, Michael Zelniker, Rosalind Chao; **D:** Ralph L. (R.L.) Thomas; **M:** Bill Conti. Genie '84: Actor (Fryer), Film, Support. Actor (Zelniker). **TV**

Tess 1979 (PG) Sumptuous adaptation of the Thomas Hardy novel "Tess of the D'Urbervilles." Kinski is wonderful as an innocent farm girl who is seduced by the young aristocrat she works for and then finds marriage to a man of her own class only brings more grief. Polanski's direction is faithful and artful. Nearly three hours long, but worth every minute. 170m/C VHS, DVD. **GB FR** Nastassja Kinski, Peter Firth, Leigh Lawson, John Collin; **D:** Roman Polanski; **W:** Roman Polanski, Gerard Brach; **C:** Ghislan Cloquet, Geoffrey Unsworth. Oscars '80: Art Dir/Set Dec., Cinematog., Costume Des.; Cesar '80: Cinematog., Director (Polanski), Film; Golden Globes '81: Foreign Film; L.A. Film Critics '80: Cinematog., Director (Polanski); N.Y. Film Critics '80: Cinematog.

Tess of the D'Urbervilles 1998 Thomas Hardy's rural Victorian England is the setting for romantic tragedy. Tess Durbeyfield (Waddell) is a poor, naive 16-year-old who's unwillingly sent to work for the wealthy D'Urbervilles, whom her family believes are distant relatives. There, Tess becomes the target of wastrel Alec's (Flemyng) desires and he takes advantage of her. Several years later, Tess is now working as a dairymaid and falls in true love with Angel Clare (Milburn), but he can't accept her soiled past even though they've married. Heartbroken Tess falls deeper into hardship until Alec suddenly reappears in her life—and so does Angel. 180m/C VHS. **GB** Justine Waddell, Jason Flemyng, Oliver Milburn, John McEnery, Lesley Dunlop, Gerald James, Debbie Chazen; **D:** Ian Sharp; **W:** Ted Whitehead; **C:** Richard Greatrex; **M:** Alan Lisk. **TV**

Tess of the Storm Country 1922 Pickford remade her own 1914 film for the better, starring as poor Tessibel Skinner, who takes on her lover Frederick Graves' (Hughes) pregnant sister, Teola (Hope), and then says the child is hers to protect the unwed mom from her ruthless father (Torrence). Tessibel temporarily loses Frederick until the truth comes out. 120m/C VHS, DVD. Mary Pickford, Lloyd Hughes, David Torrence, Gloria Hope, Jean Hersholt; **D:** John S. Robertson; **W:** Elmer Harris; **C:** Charles Rosher, Paul Eagler; **M:** Jeffrey Mark Silverman.

The Tesseract 2003 (R) The lives of four folks—a psychologist, drug gopher, female assassin, and bellboy—each of whom has found at the same ratty Bangkok hotel. Wanders around in a "hopefully hip" kind of way. Based on Alex Garland's novel. 96m/C VHS, DVD. Jonathan Rhys Meyers, Saskia Reeves, Carlo Monni, Alexander Rendel, Lene Christensen, Veradis Vinyarath; **D:** Oxide Pang Chun; **W:** Alex Garland, Oxide Pang Chun; **C:** Decha Srimantra. **VIDEO**

Test of Donald Norton 1926 Good early Western. A young man raised by Indians finds work with the Hudson's Bay Company and does well, but is haunted by suspicions that he has a half-breed. 68m/B VHS. George Walsh, Tyrone Power Sr., Eugenia Gilbert, Robert Graves, Virginia True Boardman; **D:** B. Reeves Eason.

A Test of Love *Annie's Coming Out* 1984 (PG) Incorrectly diagnosed as retarded, a young woman with cerebral palsy struggles to adjust to life outside an institution. Predictable but touching and well-acted. 93m/C VHS. **AU** Angela Punch McGregor, Drew Forsythe, Tina Arnondis; **D:** Gil Brealey; **W:** Chris Borthwick. Australian Film Inst. '84: Film.

Test Pilot 1938 Gable and devoted mechanic respectively. When Gable has to land his experimental craft in a Kansas cornfield, he meets and falls in love with farm girl Loy. The two marry and raise a family, all the while she worries over his dangerous profession. When the Air Force asks him to test their new B-17 bomber, she refuses to watch, thinking the test will end in tragedy. Superb aviation drama featuring excellent cast. 118m/B VHS. Clark Gable, Myrna Loy, Spencer Tracy, Lionel Barrymore, Samuel S. Hinds; **D:** Victor Fleming.

Test Tube Babies WOOF! *Sins of Love; The Pill* 1948 A married couple's morals begin to deteriorate as they mourn the fact they can't have a child. The day is saved, however, when they learn about the new artificial insemination process. Amusing, campy propaganda in the vein of "Reefer Madness." Rereleased in 1967 as "The Pill" with extra scenes featuring Monica Davis and John Maitland. 83m/B VHS, DVD. Dorothy Dube, Timothy Farrell, William Thomason; **D:** W. Merle Connell; **W:** Richard McMahan.

Test Tube Teens from the Year 2000 *Virgin Hunters* 1993 (R) When sex is banned in the year 2000, horny teenagers are left with no choice but to travel through time for some action. 74m/C VHS. Morgan Fairchild, Ian Abercrombie, Brian Bremer, Christopher Wolf, Michelle Matheson, Sara Suzanne Brown, Don Dowe, Chuck Borden, Robin Joi Brown, Conrad Brooks; **D:** David DeCoteau; **W:** Kenneth J. Hall; **M:** Reg Powell.

The Testament of Dr. Cordelier *Testament in Evil; Le Testament du Docteur Cordelier* 1959 A strange, experimental fantasy about a Jekyll and Hyde-type lunatic stalking the streets and alleys of Paris. Originally conceived as a TV play, Renoir attempted to create a new mise-en-scene, using multiple cameras covering the sequences as they were performed whole. French with English subtitles. 95m/C VHS. **FR** Jean-Louis Barrault, Michel Vitold, Teddy Bilis, Jean Topart, Micheline Gary; **D:** Jean Renoir; **W:** Jean Renoir; **C:** Georges Leclerc; **M:** Joseph Kosma.

Testament 1983 (PG) Well-made and thought-provoking story of the residents of a small California town struggling to survive after a nuclear bombing. Focuses on one family who tries to accept the reality of post-holocaust life. We see the devastation but it never sinks into sensationalism. An exceptional performance from Alexander. 90m/C VHS, DVD. Jane Alexander, William Devane, Rossie (Ross) Harris, Roxana Zal, Kevin Costner, Rebecca De Mornay, Lukas Haas, Mako, Philip Anglim, Lilia Skala, Leon Ames, Lurene Tuttle; **D:** Lynne Littman; **W:** John Sacret Young; **M:** James Horner.

The Testament of Dr. Mabuse *The Crimes of Dr. Mabuse; The Last Will of Dr. Mabuse* 1962 The director of an asylum is controlled by the evil genius, Dr. Mabuse, who hypnotizes him in this well-done remake of Lang's 1933 classic. 88m/B VHS, DVD. Gert Frobe, Wolfgang Preiss, Senta Berger; **D:** Werner Klingler; **W:** Ladislas Fodor, Robert A. Stemmle; **C:** Albert Benitz; **M:** Raimund Rosenberger.

The Testament of Orpheus *Le Testament d'Orphée* 1959 Superb, personal surrealism; writer-director Cocteau's last film. Hallucinogenic, autobiographical dream-journey through time. Difficult to follow, but rewarding final installment in a trilogy including "The Blood of the Poet" and "Orpheus." In French with English subtitles. 80m/B VHS, DVD. **FR** Jean Cocteau, Edouard Dermithe, Maria Casares, Francois Perier, Yul Brynner, Jean-Pierre Leaud, Daniel Gelin, Jean Marais, Pablo Picasso, Charles Aznavour; **D:** Jean Cocteau; **W:** Jean Cocteau; **C:** Roland Pointoizeau; **M:** Georges Auric.

Testament of Youth 1979 Based on the autobiography of British feminist, author, and pacifist Vera Brittain (Campbell). Vera is enjoying herself at Oxford University in 1913 until war is declared. Vera then becomes a nurse on the frontlines in France and her experiences eventually shatter her, leading her to painfully change her life. 200m/C VHS, DVD. **GB** Cheryl Campbell, Rupert Frazer, Emrys James, Rosalie Crutchley, Joanna McCallum, Michael Troughton, Peter Woodward; **D:** Moira Armstrong; **W:** Elaine Morgan. **TV**

Testosterone 2003 Lurid black comedy about unrequited love, obsession, and revenge. When Pablo (Sabato) leaves Dean (Sutcliffe) without explanation after a torrid affair, Dean follows him to Argentina. There he gets mixed up with Pablo's intense circle of family and admirers. Some hinder Dean in his attempt to confront his errant lover. Wicked take on gay romance with some tasty over-the-top performances, especially Braga as Pablo's mother. 105m/C DVD. **US AR** David Sutcliffe, Jennifer Coolidge, Sonia Braga, Celia Font, Antonio Sabato Jr., Leonardo Brezicki, Dario Dukah; **D:** David Moreton; **W:** David Moreton, Dennis Hensley; **C:** Ken Kelsch; **M:** Marco d'Ambrosio.

Tetsuo: The Iron Man *The Ironman* 1992 A weird live-action science-fiction cartoon about a white-collar Japanese worker who finds himself being gradually transformed into a walking metal collection of cables, drills, wires, and gears. The newly formed metal creature then faces off with an equally bizarre metals fetishist (played by the director). In Japanese with English subtitles. 67m/B VHS, DVD. **JP** Tomoroh Taguchi, Kei Fujiwara, Shinya Tsukamoto; **D:** Shinya Tsukamoto; **M:** Chu Ishikawa.

Tetsuo 2: Body Hammer 1997 Taniguchi (Yaguchi) strikes back at the cyborgs who kidnapped and killed his young son by transforming himself into a killer robotic machine man. Japanese with subtitles. 83m/C VHS, DVD. **JP** Tomoroh Taguchi; **D:** Shinya Tsukamoto; **W:** Shinya Tsukamoto; **C:** Shinya Tsukamoto.

Tevye *Tevye the Milkhiker* 1939 Sholom Aleichem's story of Jewish family life, intermarriage, and turmoil in Poland. When Khave, the daughter of Tevye the dairyman, seeks to marry a Ukrainian peasant, Tevye must come to terms with his love for his daughter and his faith and loyalty to tradition. Also the basis for the musical "Fiddler on the Roof." In Yiddish with English subtitles. 96m/B VHS. Maurice Schwartz, Miriam Riselle; **D:** Maurice Schwartz. Natl. Film Reg. '91.

Tex 1982 (PG) Fatherless brothers in Oklahoma come of age. Dillon is excellent. Based on the novel by S.E. Hinton. 103m/C VHS, DVD. Matt Dillon, Jim Metzler, Meg Tilly, Bill McKinney, Frances Lee McCain, Ben Johnson, Emilio Estevez, Charles S. Haas; **D:** Tim Hunter; **W:** Tim Hunter, Charles S. Haas; **C:** Ric Waite; **M:** Pino Donaggio.

Tex Rides with the Boy Scouts 1937 Scouts and Ritter in capturing gold bandits with a little bit of singing thrown in for good measure. 60m/B VHS. Tex Ritter, Marjorie Reynolds, Horace Murphy, Charles "Blackie" King, Snub Pollard, Tommy Bupp, Karl Hackett, Forrest Taylor; **D:** Ray Taylor; **C:** Edmond Kelso; **C:** Gus Peterson.

The Texans 1938 Ex-Confederate soldier Kirk Jordan (Scott) struggles to make a new life for himself as a trail boss, aiming to get 10,000 head of cattle to the railroad in Abilene. But there's temptation in the form of Ivy Preston (Bennett) and a scheme to reignite the war. Remake of 1924 silent "North of '36." 93m/B VHS, DVD. Randolph Scott, Joan Bennett, Walter Brennan, May Robson, Robert Cummings, Raymond Hatton, Robert Barrat, Harvey Stephens, Chris-Pin (Ether Crispin Martini) Martin, Francis Ford; **D:** James Hogan; **W:** Bertram Millhauser, Paul Sloane, William Wister Haines.

Texas ✔✔✔ 1941 Two friends wander through the West after the Civil War, getting into scrapes and eventually drifting apart. Ford takes a job on a cattle ranch run by Trevor and discovers Holden has joined a gang of rustlers aiming to steal her herd. The two men vie for Trevor's affections. Although friends, a professional rivalry also existed between the two leading actors and their own stunts during filming. Well-acted, fun, and enthusiastic Western. 94m/B VHS, DVD. *William Holden, Glenn Ford, Claire Trevor, Edgar Buchanan, George Bancroft; D: George Marshall.*

Texas Across the River ✔✔½ 1966 James A. Michener's Texas is a wise-cracking gun runner who, along with Indian sidekick Kronk (Bishop), is recruiting settlers to become Mexican citizens. Eventually, calls for statehood become a mysterious hitchhiker. Made for TV miniseries adapted from Michener's novel. Filmed on location in Del Rio, Texas. 180m/C VHS, DVD. *Patrick Duffy, Stacy Keach, David Keith, Maria Conchita Alonso, Anthony Michael Hall, Rick Schroder, Benjamin Bratt, Chelsea Field, John Schneider, Giant Show, Randy Travis, Woody Watson; D: Richard Lang; W: Sean Meredith; M: Lee Holdridge.* TV

Texas, Adios ✔✔½ 1966 The Avenger. Curious spaghetti western stars Franco Nero as a sheriff who goes to Texas with his kid brother Jim (Dell'Acqua) to get the man who murdered their father. The action has all of the affectations of this rarified branch of the genre, and that makes it lots of fun for fans and virtually unwatchable for everyone else. 92m/C VHS, DVD. /I *Franco Nero, Alberto Dell'Acqua, Cole Kitosch, Elisa Montes, Josa Suarez; D: Ferdinando Baldi; W: Ferdinando Baldi; C: Russell Mery.*

Texas Bad Man ✔✔½ 1932 Sheriff Mix goes undercover to get in with Koh-ler's gang of outlaws and bring them to justice. 60m/B VHS. *Tom Mix, Fred Kohler Sr., Lucille Powers Ed LeSaint, Richard Alexander; D: Edward Laemmle.*

Texas Buddies ✔½ 1932 Steele plays a former military pilot who uses his trusty monoplane to round up outlaws. Interesting twist on standard oater, but suffers from poor execution. 57m/B VHS, DVD. *Bob Steele, Nancy Drexel, George "Gabby" Hayes, Francis McDonald, Harry Semels; D: Robert North Bradbury.*

Texas Carnival ✔✔ 1951 Williams and Skelton star as carnival performers who operate the dunk tank. When Skelton is mistaken for an oil tycoon, he lives high on the hog until the mistake is discovered. Believe it or not, this musical has only one water ballet sequence. Songs include "It's Dynamite," "Whoa! Emma," and "Young Folks Should Get Married." 77m/C VHS. *Esther Williams, Red Skelton, Howard Keel, Ann Miller, Paula Raymond, Keenan Wynn, Tom Tully; D: Charles Walters.*

The Texas Chainsaw Massacre ✔✔½ 1974 (R) The movie that put the "power" in power tools. An idyllic summer afternoon drive becomes a nightmare for a group of young people pursued by a chainsaw-wielding maniac. Made with tongue firmly in cheek, this is nevertheless a mesmerizing saga of gore, flesh, mayhem, and violence. 86m/C VHS, DVD. *Marilyn Burns, Allen Danziger, Paul A. Partain, William Vail, Teri McMinn, Edwin Neal, Jim Siedow, Gunnar Hansen, John Dugan, Jerry Lorenz; D: Tobe Hooper; W: Tobe Hooper, Kim Henkel; C: Daniel Pearl; M: Tobe Hooper, Wayne Bell; Nar: John Larroquette.*

The Texas Chainsaw Massacre ✔ 2003 (R) Rancid remake of Hooper's 1974 classic horror original stars Biel and much more blood and gore than actual chills. Once again five teenagers take a journey across Texas and pick up a mysterious hitchhiker who blows her brains out in their van after uttering a prophetic warning that they will all die. Enter Leatherface (Bryniarski) and his famously phallic chainsaw hacking up the horny teens to his evil heart's delight. Gruesome highlight as Leatherface has a literal face-off with Biel. Director Nispel, weaned on music videos, has a slicker looking product than the micro-budget original but far less of the palpable tension and shocking originality of its predecessor. 98m/C VHS, DVD, UMD, US Jessica Biel, Jonathan Tucker, Erica Leerhsen, Mike Vogel, Andrew Bryniarski, R. Lee Ermey, David Dorfran, Eric Balfour, Terrence Evans; D: Marcus Nispel; W: Scott Kosar; C: Daniel Pearl; M: Steve Jablonsky; Nar: John Larroquette.*

The Texas Chainsaw Massacre 2 WOOF! 1986 (R) A tasteless, magnified sequel to the notorious blood-bucket extravaganza about a cannibalistic family in southern Texas who kill and eat passing travelers. Followed by "Leatherface: The Texas Chainsaw Massacre 3." 90m/C VHS, DVD. *Dennis Hopper, Caroline Williams, Bill Johnson, Jim Siedow, Bill Moseley, Lou Perry, John (Joe Bob Briggs) Bloom; D: Tobe Hooper; W: L.M. Kit Carson; C: Richard Kooris; M: Tobe Hooper.*

The Texas Chainsaw Massacre 4: The Next Generation ✔✔ 1995 (R) Return of the Texas Chainsaw (Zellweger) and her three friends take a wrong turn down a dark country road and wind up in the nightmare clutches of homicidal tow-truck driver Vilmer (McConaughey), his accomplice Darla (Perenski), and the infamous Leatherface (Jacks). No restraint here—as the borderline sadism and tension builds to, unfortunately, something of a letdown. Feature debut for Henkel, who co-wrote Tobe Hooper's 1977 horror classic. Film finally got a release in 1997 after both McConaughey and Zellweger became stars in more mainstream films. Pay attention to "Love Theme from Texas Chainsaw Massacre," sung by Debbie Harry and Leatherface himself. 94m/C VHS, DVD, Renee Zellweger, Matthew McConaughey, Robert Jacks, Tony Perenski, Lisa Marie Newmyer, John Dugan Mary Burns; D: Kim Henkel; W: Kim Henkel; C: Levie Isaacks; M: Wayne Bell.*

The Texas Chainsaw Massacre: The Beginning WOOF! 2006 (R) Ugly is okay, ugly and dull is not. Contrary to what the title suggests, this is a prequel to the 2003 remake, although it provides flashbacks to Leatherface's origins, which include being born, hideously deformed, in a slaughterhouse. Ermey reprises his role as psycho cop/cannibal Hoyt, who becomes proud papa to his newly adopted gutter-child. As usual, a group of over-sexed teens are offered up for bloody sacrifice. With its unrelenting gore and sadism, flick's not for the squeamish. 84m/C VHS, DVD, Jordana Brewster, Andrew Bryniarski, Diora Baird, Taylor Handley, Matt Bomer, Lee Tergesen, Lew Temple; D: Jonathan Liebesman; W: Sheldon Turner; C: Lukas Ettlin; M: Steve Jablonsky.*

Texas Detour ✔✔ 1977 On a trip across country, a trio of young California teens have their van stolen. They decide to take the law into their own hands when the stranger rides into a town that turns out to be incredibly friendly. Later he realizes the entire town thinks he is a prominent citizen who disappeared years ago. 58m/B VHS, DVD. *Tim McCoy, Wheeler Oakman, Shirley Grey, Walter Brennan, John Wayne, Wallace MacDonald, Vernon Dent, Mary Gordon; D: David Ross Lederman.*

Texas Cyclone ✔✔ 1932 A stranger rides into a town that turns out to be incredibly friendly. Later he realizes the entire town thinks he is a prominent citizen who disappeared years ago. 58m/B VHS, DVD. *Tim McCoy, Wheeler Oakman, Shirley Grey, Walter Brennan, John Wayne, Wallace MacDonald, Vernon Dent, Mary Gordon; D: David Ross Lederman.*

A Texas Funeral ✔✔ 1999 (R) Sheen is a Texas patriarch, seen only in flashbacks since it's his funeral that's being attended by his crazy family, which has a long tradition of dysfunction. Set in the late-'60s. 98m/C VHS, DVD. *Martin Sheen, Woods, Jim Mason, Ken Maxwell; D: Phil Rosen.*

Texas Guns ✔✔ 1990 (PG) A gritty western about an old-time gunman (Nelson) and his quest for one last robbery, killing those who stand in his way and some just for fun. Also watch for Cassidy's comeback. 86m/C VHS, DVD. *Willie Nelson, Richard Widmark, Shaun Cassidy, Angie Dickinson, Kevin McCarthy, Royal Dano, Chuck Connors, Ker Curtis, Bo Taylor; D: Burt Kennedy; W: Burt Kennedy; C: Ken Lamkin; M: Arthur B. Rubinstein.*

Texas Jack ✔✔½ 1935 The head of a medicine show tries to trace the disappearance of his sister. 55m/B VHS. Jack Perrin, Jayne Fegan, Nelson McDowell, Budd Buster, Lew Meehan; D: Bernard B. Ray.

Texas John Slaughter: Geronimo's Revenge ✔✔ 1960 An Indian-loving rancher frets and fights when Geronimo attacks innocent settlers. Compiled from Disney TV episodes. 77m/C VHS. *Tom Tryon, Darryl Hickman, Betty Lynn; D: Harry Keller.* TV

Texas John Slaughter: Stampede at Bitter Creek ✔✔ 1962 Good guy Texas John Slaughter meets a variety of threatening obstacles when he tries to move his cattle herd into New Mexico. Originally from the "Walt Disney Presents" TV series. 90m/C VHS. *Tom Tryon; D: Harry Keller.* TV

Texas Justice ✔✔ 1942 The "Lone Rider" cavorts around in the desert, dispensing justice in the guise of a monk. 60m/B VHS. *George Houston, Al "Fuzzy" St. John, Dennis Moore, Wanda McKay, Clare Rochelle; D: Sam Newfield.*

Texas Kid ✔✔½ 1943 A typical western. Hero helps a vengeance-minded kid catch the robber-gang who robbed and killed his father. Yee-Haw. 53m/B VHS. *Johnny Mack Brown, Kermit Maynard, Raymond Hatton, Shirley Patterson, Edmund Cobb, Charles "Blackie" King; D: Lambert Hillyer.*

Texas Lady ✔✔ 1956 When a woman wins $50,000 gambling, she buys a Texas newspaper on the stipulation that she can edit it in this standard fare western. Good vehicle for Colbert to look beautiful, but the plot and script are average and uninspired. 86m/C VHS. *Claudette Colbert, Barry Sullivan, Gregory Walcott; D: Tim Whelan.*

Texas Legionnaires ✔✔ 1943 Men from Music Mountain. Roy comes back to his home town and gets caught between feuding cattle and sheep herders. 71m/B VHS, DVD. *Roy Rogers, Ruth Terry, Paul Kelly, Ann Gillis, George Cleveland, Bob Nolan; W: Betty Burbridge, Lucille Ward; C: Jack Marta.*

Texas Lightning ✔✔½ 1981 (R) Innocuous B-grade touching movie about a father and son and their family woes. 93m/C VHS, DVD. *Cameron Mitchell, Channing Mitchell, Maureen McCormick, Peter Jason; D: Gary Graver; W: Gary Graver; C: Gary Graver; M: Tommy Vig.*

Texas Masquerade ✔✔ 1944 Standard good cowboys versus land-grabbers action filler. William Boyd plays Hopalong Cassidy, Andy Clyde plays California Carson, Jimmy Rogers plays... Jimmy Rogers. 59m/B VHS, DVD. *William Boyd, Andy Clyde, Jimmy Rogers, Mady Correll, Don Costello, Russell Simpson, Nelson Leigh, Francis McDonald, J. Farrell MacDonald; D: George Archainbaud.*

Texas Gunfighter ✔✔ 1932 Your basic western from the Maynard series, with everything a western could have. 60m/B VHS. *Sheila Bromley, Lloyd Ingraham, Harry Woods, Jim Mason, Christopher Nash, Isaiah Washington IV, Joanne Whalley, Grace Zabriskie, Oliva D'Abo, Quinton Jones; D: William Blake Herron; W: William J Blake Herron; M: James Legg.*

Texas Rangers ✔✔ 2001 (PG-13) Western featuring Van Der 3eek and Kutcher (theyre dreamy!) as greenhorns who volunteer to fight bandits along the Ric Grande in 1875 Texas. McDermott's Ranger is the demanding mentor who teaches them a'ropin' and a'shootin'. All guys, and there is a passel of gunfights, are robbed of their families by the bad guys, and there's a passel of gunfights, but taming the West takes a backseat to ailing McNelly's fate in this revenge actioner. Cast is good but hindered by a weak script and direction. After sitting on the shelf for two years, yella-belied studio execs denied the state oater a't an advance screening, well aware of its weak appeal. 90m/C VHS, DVD, US James Van Der Beek, Dylan McDermott, Ashton Kutcher, Usher Raymond, John Howard, Broderick Crawford, May Robson, Ellen Drew, Anthony Quinn, Akim Tamiroff, Charley Grapewin, Harvey Stephens; D: James Hogan; W: William R. Lipman, Horace McCoy.*

The Texas Rangers ✔✔½ 1936 Two Texas lawmen are assigned to find and capture the notorious Sam Bass gang in exchange for their freedom. Good E Western; lot sa shootin'. 68m/C VHS. *Fred MacMurray, Jack Oakie, Lloyd Nolan, Jean Parker, Edward Ellis, Fred Kohler Sr., George "Gabby" Hayes; D: King Vidor; W: Louis Stevens.*

The Texas Rangers ✔✔½ 1951 A Western cattle keep disappearing from the Dangerfield ranch, owner Robson secretly calls in the Texas Rangers to find out what's going on. Howard and Crawford work undercover to root out the criminals while Howard also finds the time to make goo-goo eyes at Robson's granddaughter Drew. 66m/B VHS, DVD. *Fred MacMurray, Jack Oakie, Lloyd Nolan, Jean Parker, Edward Ellis, Fred Kohler Sr., George "Gabby" Hayes; D: King Vidor; W: Louis Stevens.*

Texas Payback ✔✔ 1995 (R) Convicted Killer Cody Giles (Hudson) busts out of prison in order to get revenge now-retired-and-working-in-Vegas Texas Ranger Louis Gentry (Jones) who put him away. 96m/C VHS. *Sam Jones, Gary Hudson, Kathleen Kinmont, Bo Hopkins; D: Richard W. Murchkin; W: Brian Page; C: Mark Morris; M: Jim Halfpenny.*

Texas Pioneers ✔✔ 1932 The Blood Brother 1932 A frontier scout is sent to an outpost town besieged by crooks. 54m/B VHS. *Bill Cody, Sheila (Manors) Mannors, Frank Lackteen, Iron Eyes Cody; D: Harry Fraser, W: Harry Fraser, Wellyn Totman; C: Faxon M. Dean.*

Texas to Bataan ✔½ 1942 The "Range Busters" ship horses to the Philippines and encounter enemy spies. Part of the "Range Busters" series. 56m/B VHS. *John "Dusty" King, David Sharpe, Max Terhune; D: Robert Emmett Tansey.*

Texas Terror ✔✔ 1935 Young Wayne resigns his badge when he mistakenly believes he has shot and killed his friend. He later rescues his friend's sister, learns the truth, and (naturally) finds true love. 50m/B VHS, DVD. *John Wayne, George "Gabby" Hayes, Lucille Browne, Leroy Mason, Fern Emmett; D: Robert North Bradbury; W: Robert North Bradbury.*

The Texas Rangers Ride Again ✔✔ 1940 When cattle keep disappearing from the Dangerfield ranch, owner Robson secretly calls in the Texas Rangers to find out what's going on. Howard and Crawford work undercover to root out the criminals while Howard also finds the time to make goo-goo eyes at Robson's granddaughter Drew. 66m/B VHS. *John Howard, Broderick Crawford, May Robson, Ellen Drew, Anthony Quinn, Akim Tamiroff, Charley Grapewin, Harvey Stephens; D: James Hogan; W: William R. Lipman, Horace McCoy.*

Texas Trouble ✔✔ 1942 Billy the Kid's Range War 1941 Hackett is out to stop Barclay's road building by using a Billy the Kid imposter to halt construction. But the real Billy is ticked off and comes to the rescue. 57m/B VHS. *Bob Steele, Al "Fuzzy" St. John.*

Texas

Carleton Young, Joan Barclay, Karl Hackett, Rex Lease; **D:** Sam Newfield; **W:** William Lively; **C:** Jack Greenhalgh; **M:** Lew Porter.

Texas Wildcats 1939 A cowboy helps make sure that sinister adversaries are brought to justice on the American Frontier. 60m/B VHS. Joan Barclay, Ben (Benny) Corbett, Forrest Taylor, Ted Adams, Tim McCoy; **D:** Sam Newfield; **W:** George Plympton.

Texasville 1990 (R) Sequel to "The Last Picture Show" finds the characters still struggling after 30 years, with financial woes from the energy crisis, mental illness inspired by the Korean War, and various personal tragedies. Lacks the melancholy sensitivity of its predecessor, but has some of the wit and wisdom that comes with age. Based again on a Larry McMurtry novel. Not well received during its theatrical release. 120m/C VHS, DVD. Timothy Bottoms, Jeff Bridges, Annie Potts, Cloris Leachman, William McNamara; **D:** Peter Bogdanovich; **W:** Peter Bogdanovich.

The Texican 1966 Former sheriff Jess Carlin (Murphy) is living in Mexico but must return to the Texas town of Rim Rock when his newspaperman brother is murdered. Town boss Luke Starr (Crawford) is behind the crime but the townspeople are too scared to help Carlin out—except for saloon gal Kit (Lorys). 86m/C VHS, DVD. Audie Murphy, Broderick Crawford, Diana Lorys, Aldo Sambrel, Antonio Casas; **D:** Lesley Selander; **W:** John C. Champion; **C:** Francis Marin.

Thank God It's Friday 1978 (PG) Episodic and desultory disco-dancing vehicle which won the Best Song Oscar for Donna Summer's rendition. Life is irony. Co-produced by Motown. ♫Last Dance; After Dark; Find My Way; It's Serious; Let's Make A Deal; Romeo and Juliet; You're the Reason I Feel Like Dancing; From Here to Eternity; Dance All Night. 100m/C VHS, DVD. Valerie Landsburg, Teri Nunn, Chick Vennera, Jeff Goldblum, Debra Winger; **D:** Robert Klane; **W:** Armyan Bernstein. Oscars '78: Song ("Last Dance").

Thank You & Good Night 1991 Director Oxenberg gathers members of her own family around a purple armchair of grandma's to talk about life, love, and family memories, including grandma's illness and recent death. 81m/C VHS. **D:** Jan Oxenberg; **W:** Jan Oxenberg; **C:** Claudia Raschke.

Thank You for Smoking 2006 (R) Smooth satire, based on the novel by Christopher Buckley, where no one onscreen is actually shown smoking. But if they want to, they have that right, which is what slick tobacco lobbyist Nick Naylor (Eckhart) is paid to defend. No surprise then that his friends are fellow "Merchants of Death," alcohol lobbyist Polly Bailey (Bello) and firearms lobbyist Bobby Jay Bliss (Koechner). Divorced Nick would like to be a good guy—he tries hard to be a concerned dad—but the game is just too enticing, even when it means bribing former cowboy icon (think Marlboro Man) Lorne Lutch (Elliott), who's dying of lung cancer, to stop attacking cigarette smoking. His opponents don't stand a chance and Eckhart plays Nick with outlandish, glib charm and confidence. 92m/C DVD. US Aaron Eckhart, Maria Bello, Cameron Bright, Adam Brody, Sam Elliott, David Koechner, Katie Holmes, Rob Lowe, William H. Macy, J.K. Simmons, Robert Duvall, Kim Dickens, Connie Ray, Todd Louiso; **D:** Jason Reitman; **W:** Jason Reitman; **C:** James Whitaker; **M:** Rolfe Kent. Ind. Spirit '07: Screenplay.

Thank you, Mr. Moto 1937 A series of Chinese scrolls reveal the hidden location of the treasure-laden tomb of Genghis Khan. Mr. Moto (Lorre) and his friend, Prince Chung (Ahn), are determined to protect the tomb from treasure hunters. 2nd in the series. 67m/B DVD. Peter Lorre, Jayne Regan, Sidney Blackmer, John Carradine, Sig Rumann; **D:** Norman Foster; **W:** Norman Foster, Willis Cooper; **C:** Virgil Miller; **M:** Samuel Kaylin.

Thank Your Lucky Stars 1943 A lavish, slap-dash wartime musical that emptied out the Warner celebrity turns. Features Shore in her movie debut. ♫They're Either Too Young or Too Old; Blues in the Night; Hotcha Cornia; Ridin' For A Fall; We're Staying Home Tonight; Goin' North; Love Isn't Born, It's Made; No You, No Me; Ice Cold Katie. 127m/B VHS. Eddie Cantor, Dinah Shore, Joan Leslie, Errol Flynn, Bette Davis, Edward Everett Horton, Humphrey Bogart, John Garfield, Alan Hale, Ann Sheridan, Ida Lupino, Jack Carson, Dennis Morgan, Olivia de Havilland; **D:** David Butler; **W:** Norman Panama.

Thanks for Everything 1938 Promoters Harcourt (Menjou) and Bates (Oakie) set up a radio contest to find the average American to use in their ads. The contest is won by grocery clerk Henry Smith (Haley) who is promptly put to work as a spokesman. Henry falls for small-town Madge (Whelan), who upsets everybody's plans when she realizes that Henry is being exploited. 70m/B VHS. Adolphe Menjou, Jack Oakie, Jack Haley, Arleen Whelan, Tony Martin, Binnie Barnes, George Barbier; **D:** William A. Seiter; **W:** Curtis Kenyon, Harry Tugend; **C:** Lucien N. Andriot; **M:** Louis Silvers.

Thanks for the Memory 1938 After Hope and Ross sang "Thanks for the Memory" in "The Big Broadcast of 1938," Paramount decided to capitalize on its popularity in this lame comedy. Steve Merrick (Hope) tends to the house while Anne (Ross) is working as a model to support the couple. Steve rebels against being a "kept man" and their marriage enters shaky ground until they come to their senses. 79m/B VHS. Bob Hope, Shirley Ross, Charles Butterworth, Otto Kruger, Hedda Hopper, Laura Hope Crews, Eddie Anderson; **D:** George Archainbaud; **W:** Lynn Starling; **C:** Karl Struss.

Tharus Son of Attila 1987 A couple of sword-wielding barbarians battle each other and an evil emperor. 89m/C VHS. Jerome Courtland, Rik van Nutter, Lisa Gastoni; **D:** Robert Bianchi Montero.

That Beautiful Somewhere 2006 (R) Two lost souls bond in this dreary thriller. Troubled Ontario police detective Conk Adams (Dupuis) gets help from equally unhappy forensic archeologist Catherine Nyland (McGregor) when a body is found in a bog. Catherine must determine if the corpse is new or old but the bog is thought to have special curative properties by members of the local native tribe, and they don't want it disturbed. 93m/C DVD. CA Roy Dupuis, Jane McGregor, Gordon Tootoosis, David Fox; **D:** Robert Budreau; **W:** Robert Budreau; **C:** Andrew Watt; **M:** Steve London.

That Brennan Girl 1946 A maudlin soap opera about how a girl's upbringing by an inconsiderate mother makes her a devious little wench. Fortunately her second husband had a better mom, and redemption is at hand. 95m/B VHS. James Dunn, Mona Freeman, William Marshall, June Duprez, Frank Jenks, Charles Arnt; **D:** Alfred Santell.

That Certain Age 1938 Alice (Durbin) is charmed by her newspaper-owning father's houseguest, older and sophisticated journalist Vincent Bullitt (Douglas). She gets a big crush and dumps boyfriend Ken (Cooper), causing much consternation to all. ♫That Certain Age; You're as Pretty as a Picture; Be a Good Scout; Has Anybody Ever Told You Before?; My Own. 101m/B VHS, DVD. Deanna Durbin, Melvyn Douglas, Jackie Cooper, John Halliday, Irene Rich, Nancy Carroll, Jackie Searl, Charles Coleman; **D:** Edward Ludwig; **W:** Bruce Manning; **C:** Joseph Valentine.

That Certain Thing 1928 Very early silent Capra comedy about a bachelor with a silver spoon in his mouth who loses his inheritance when he marries for love. It's got that certain Capra screwball feeling. 65m/B VHS. Viola Dana, Ralph Graves, Burr McIntosh, Aggie Herring, Syd Crossley; **D:** Frank Capra.

That Certain Woman 1937 Sentimental drama with Davis portraying a gangster's widow who wants to make a new life for herself. Fonda plays the rich playboy with whom she falls in love. Because of Davis' star power, she demanded that Fonda play opposite her. It seems Davis had a real life crush on him when they were both players in a stock company several years earlier. Remake of Goulding's "The Trespasser" which starred Gloria Swanson. 91m/B VHS. Bette Davis, Henry Fonda, Ian Hunter, Anita Louise, Donald Crisp, Katherine Alexander, Minor Watson; **D:** Edmund Goulding; **W:** Edmund Goulding; **M:** Max Steiner.

That Championship Season 1982 (R) Long-dormant animosities surface at the reunion of a championship basketball team. Unfortunate remake of Miller's Pulitzer-prize winning play, with none of the fire which made it a Broadway hit. 110m/C VHS, DVD. Martin Sheen, Bruce Dern, Stacy Keach, Robert Mitchum, Paul Sorvino, Jason Miller; **D:** Jason Miller; **C:** John Bailey; **M:** Bill Conti.

That Championship Season 1999 (R) Tom Daley (Sinise) returns to his hometown for the 20th anniversary of his high-school basketball team's championship victory. A night of nostalgia with Daley, his brother (Kinney), some friends (Shalhoub, D'Onofrio), and their coach (Sorvino, who directed this remake), turns into a drunken rehash of old grievances and the airing of some dirty laundry. Miller adapted his 1973 Pulitzer Prize-winning play, which he also directed for the big screen in 1982. 126m/C VHS. Gary Sinise, Terry Kinney, Vincent D'Onofrio, Tony Shalhoub, Paul Sorvino; **D:** Paul Sorvino; **W:** Jason Miller; **C:** Bruce Surtees; **M:** Larry Blank. CABLE

That Cold Day in the Park 1969 (R) Early Altman. An unhappy woman takes in a homeless young man from the park near her home. The woman (Dennis) is obsessive and odd; so is the film. Dennis is excellent. Reminiscent of "The Collector." 91m/C VHS. Sandy Dennis, Michael Burns, Susanne Benton, Michael Murphy, John David Garfield; **D:** Robert Altman.

That Darn Cat 1965 (G) Vintage Disney comedy about a Siamese cat that helps FBI Agent Jones thwart kidnappers. Could be shorter, but suspenseful and funny with characteristic Disney slapstick. Based on the book "Undercover Cat" by The Gordons. 115m/C VHS, DVD. Hayley Mills, Dean Jones, Dorothy Provine, Neville Brand, Elsa Lanchester, Frank Gorshin, Roddy McDowall; **D:** Robert Stevenson; **C:** Edward Colman; **M:** Robert F. Brunner.

That Darn Cat 1996 (PG) Innocuous Disney remake of the 1965 Disney comedy falls into the "why bother" category. Ricci's appealing as the sarcastic teen and Elvis the cat has a certain scrappy charm as well. Based on the novel "Undercover Cat" by Mildred and Gordon Gordon. 89m/C VHS, DVD. Christina Ricci, Doug E. Doug, Dean Jones, George Dzundza, Peter Boyle, Michael McKean, Bess Armstrong, Dyan Cannon, John Ratzenberger, Estelle Parsons, Rebecca Schull, Thomas F. Wilson, Brian Haley, Mark Christopher Lawrence; **D:** Bob Spiers; **W:** Scott M. Alexander, Larry Karaszewski; **C:** Jerzy Zielinski; **M:** Richard Gibbs.

That Darn Sorceress 1988 A child witch has grown up, and so has her power. To keep her disciples, she must perform increasingly horrible feats. 89m/C VHS. Pauline Adams, Bettie (Betty) Page; **D:** Whitney Bain.

That Eye, the Sky 1994 Alice (Harrow) and Sam (Fairall) Flack live on a small farm with their two children and senile grandmother. Sam's in a serious car crash and is eventually returned home still in a deep coma. Alice, who's having trouble coping, is grateful when wandering evangelist Harry Warburton (Coyote) shows up on her doorstep offering his help. But is this mystery man offering a miracle or more heartache? Based on the book by Tim Winton. 105m/C VHS. AU Lisa Harrow, Peter Coyote, Mark Fairall, Jamie Croft, Amanda Douge, Alethea McGrath; **D:** John Ruane; **W:** John Ruane, Jim Barton; **C:** Ellery Ryan; **M:** David Bridie. Australian Film Inst. '95: Support. Actress (Douge).

That Forsyte Woman 1950 Based on the novel "A Man of Property" by John Galsworthy, a married Victorian woman falls for an architect engaged to be wed. Remade later (and better) for BBC-TV as "The Forsythe Saga." 112m/C VHS, DVD. Errol Flynn, Greer Garson, Walter Pidgeon, Robert Young, Janet Leigh, Harry Davenport, Stanley Logan, Lumsden Hare, Aubrey Mather, Matt Moore; **D:** Compton Bennett; **C:** Joseph Ruttenberg.

That Funny Feeling 1965 Lightweight romantic comedy has freelance maid Joan (Dee) meeting and falling for businessman Tom (Darin). Instead of bringing him to her small apartment, which she shares with a roommate, she takes him to a client's place, unaware that it's Tom's. He goes along since he wants to get to know her better. Humor ensues as she tries to keep up appearances by keeping the place clean. 93m/C DVD. Sandra Dee, Bobby Darin, Donald O'Connor, Nita Talbot, Larry Storch, Leo G. Carroll, James Westerfield, Robert Strauss, Arte Johnson, Kathleen Freeman, Ben Lessy; **D:** Richard Thorpe; **W:** David R. Schwartz; **C:** Clifford Stine; **M:** Bobby Darin.

That Gang of Mine 1940 "East Side Kids" episode about gang member Mugg's ambition to be a jockey. Good racing scenes. 62m/B VHS, DVD. Bobby Jordan, Leo Gorcey, Clarence Muse, Dave O'Brien; **D:** Joseph H. Lewis.

That Girl from Paris 1936 An opera singer from Paris stows away on an ocean liner to be near the swing bandleader she has fallen in love with. An entertaining film with many songs; remade as "Four Jacks and a Jill." ♫Una Voce Poco Fa; The Blue Danube; Love and Learn; The Call to Arms; Seal It With A Kiss; My Nephew From Nice; Moon Face; Tarantella. 105m/B VHS. Lily Pons, Gene Raymond, Jack Oakie, Herman Bing, Lucille Ball, Mischa Auer, Frank Jenks; **D:** Leigh Jason.

That Hamilton Woman 1941 Screen biography of the tragic 18th-century love affair between British naval hero Lord Nelson and Lady Hamilton. Korda exaggerated the film's historical distortions in order to pass the censor's production code about adultery. Winston Churchill's favorite film which paralleled Britain's heroic struggles in WWII. 125m/B VHS. Laurence Olivier, Vivien Leigh, Gladys Cooper, Alan Mowbray, Sara Allgood, Henry Wilcoxon; **D:** Alexander Korda; **M:** Miklos Rozsa. Oscars '41: Sound.

That Long Night in '43 1960 *The Long Night of '43; La Lunga Notte del '43* Young married woman has an affair with an Army deserter during WWII while the local fascist leader makes a power grab by executing his opposition, including the deserter's father. Italian with subtitles. 110m/B VHS. IT Belinda Lee, Gabriele Ferzetti, Enrico Maria Salerno; **D:** Florestano Vancini; **W:** Florestano Vancini, Ennio de Concini, Pier Paolo Pasolini; **C:** Carlo Di Palma; **M:** Carlo Rustichelli.

That Lucky Touch 1975 York is a reporter covering NATO games; Moore is Bond warmed over as an arms dealer. Sexual and professional tension becomes unlikely romance. Slight and dull. Cobb's last film. 92m/C VHS. Roger Moore, Susannah York, Shelley Winters, Lee J. Cobb, Jean-Pierre Cassel, Raf Vallone, Sydne Rome; **D:** Christopher Miles; **W:** John Briley.

That Man Bolt ✓✓ 1973 Jefferson Bolt (Williamson) is a kung fu expert who agrees to carry $1 million from Hong Kong to Mexico City while being pursued by a government agent. Typical blaxploitation feature. **102m/C VHS, DVD.** Teresa Graves, Byron Webster, Miko Mayama, Satoshi Nakamura, Jack Ging, Vassili Lambrinos, John Orchard; **D:** Henry Levin, David Lowell Rich; **W:** Quentin Werty; **C:** Gerald Perry Finnerman; **M:** Charles Bernstein.

That Midnight Kiss ✓✓½ 1949 Glossy production of a musical romance featuring Lanza in his film debut. Thin plot has Lanza starring as a singing truck driver who is discovered by opera diva Grayson. ♪They Didn't Believe Me; I Know; I Know; Three O'Clock in the Morning; Santa Lucia; Down Among the Sheltering Palms; Revolutionary Etude; Caro Nome; Celeste Aida; Una Furtva Lacrima. **96m/C VHS.** Kathryn Grayson, Jose Iturbi, Ethel Barrymore, Mario Lanza, Keenan Wynn, J. Carrol Naish, Jules Munshin; **D:** Norman Taurog; **C:** Robert L. Surtees.

That Naughty Girl ✓✓ 1958 The bored daughter of a nightclub owner decides to experience all life has to offer. **77m/C VHS, DVD.** FR Brigitte Bardot, Jean Bretonniere, Francoise Fabian; **D:** Michel Boisrond.

That Night ✓✓ 1993 (PG-13) A view of romance through the eyes of a young girl, circa 1961. Ten-year-old Alice (Dushku) is the confidant of rebellious 17-year-old neighbor Cheryl (Lewis), who enlists the young girl's aid as a go-between with her wrong-side-of-the-tracks boyfriend Rick (Howell), 21 soundtrack oldies are featured. Directorial debut for screenwriter Bobrin. Based on a novel by Alice McDermott. **89m/C VHS.** C. Thomas Howell, Juliette Lewis, Eliza Dushku, Helen Shaver, John Dossett; **D:** Craig Bolotin; **W:** Craig Bolotin.

That Night in Rio ✓✓½ 1941 Ameche plays a dual role as entertainer Larry Martin and wealthy Baron Duarte, who's in financial trouble because of his failing airline. Needing to discreetly leave town to take care of business, the Baron asks Larry to step in, but he can't fool Duarte's wife, Cecilia (Faye), while Larry's singer girlfriend Carmen (Miranda) doesn't know what's going on. Remake of 1935's "Folies Bergere." **91m/C DVD.** Don Ameche, Alice Faye, Carmen Miranda, S.Z. Sakall, J. Carrol Naish, Curt Bois, Leonid Kinskey; **D:** Irving Cummings; **W:** Bess Meredyth, George Seaton, Hal Long; **C:** Ray Rennahan, Leon Shamroy; **M:** Mack Gordon, Harry Warren.

That Obscure Object of Desire ✓✓✓ 1996 Cet Obscur Objet du Desir 1977 (R) Buñuel's last film, a comic nightmare of sexual frustration. A rich Spaniard obtains a beautiful girlfriend who, while changing physical identities, refuses to sleep with him. Based on a novel by Pierre Louys, which has been used as the premise for several other films, including "The Devil is a Woman," "La Femme et le Pantin," and "The Female." Available with subtitles or dubbed. **100m/C VHS, DVD. SP** Fernando Rey, Carole Bouquet, Angela Molina, Julian Bertheau; **D:** Luis Buñuel; **W:** Jean-Claude Carriere; **C:** Edmond Richard. L.A. Film Critics '77; Foreign Film. Natl. Bd. of Review '77. **Director** (Buñuel), Natl. Soc. Film Critics '77.

That Old Feeling ✓✓ 1996 (PG-13) Bitter ex-spouses Lilly (Midler) and Dan (Farina) are reunited at the wedding of their daughter and things turn ugly. They cause a scene and are sent out of the reception to cool down. Instead, their

old passion flares up and they're found reeling in that old feeling in the back seat of a Porshe. After leaving to see where their whirlwind of romance takes them, they are trailed by their daughter (Marshall), her weenie husband (Denton), and their respective current spousal units Rowena (O'Grady) and Alan (Rasche). Fluffy romantic comedy carried mostly by gets a girlfriend. **105m/C VHS, DVD.** Bette Midler, Dennis Farina, Danny Nucci, Paula Marshall, Gail O'Grady, David Rasche, Jayne (Jane) Eastwood; **D:** Carl Reiner; **W:** Leslie Dixon; **C:** Steve Mason; **M:** Patrick Williams.

That Russell Girl ✓✓ 2008 Sarah Russell (Tamblyn) left her hometown the only outlet for a frustrated young working-class Brit. Prequel to "Stardust," DeKay, Henry Czerny, Paul Wesley, Max Morrow, Daniel Clark, Richard Leacock, Ben Lewis **D:** Jeff Bleckner; **W:** Jill Blotevogel; **C:** Charles Minsky; **M:** Jeff Beal. **TV**

That Sinking Feeling ✓✓✓ 1979 (PG) A group of bored Scot teenagers decide to steal 90 sinks from a plumber's warehouse. Their well received early film from Forsyth is genuinely funny as the boys try to get rid of the sinks and turn a profit. **82m/C VHS.** GB Robert Buchanan, John Hughes, Billy Greenlees, Alan Love; **D:** Bill Forsyth; **W:** Bill Forsyth.

That Summer of White Roses ✓✓½ 1990 (R) Compelling action drama about a lifeguard working at a resort in Nazi-occupied Yugoslavia and his love for a woman resistance fighter and her child. **98m/C VHS.** Tom Conti, Susan George, Rod Steiger; **D:** Rajko Grlić.

That Thing You Do! ✓✓✓ 1996 (PG) The Wonders, a small-town foursome, hit the big time in 1964 after a substitute drummer (like that could ever happen) adds some kick to the band's new song and sets the local kids a-truggin'. Developed by freshman director/screenwriter Hanks (who also plays the band's Svengali-like record exec) as a diversion from Oscar hype, it's nostalgic and uncomplicated to a fault, but engaging nonetheless. Hanks clone Scott puts the beat into the charmingly wholesome quartet, while the underused Tyler is disarming as the put-upon girlfriend. Look quick or you'll miss bosom buddy Scorsi as a TV host. Can't-get-it-out-of-your-head title track (played 11 times in the film) was selected from over 300 submissions after Hanks put out the call to music publishers. **110m/C VHS, DVD.** Johnathon Schaech, Tom Hanks, Liv Tyler, Tom Everett Scott, Steve Zahn, Ethan (Randall) Embry, Obba Babatunde, Charlize Theron, Peter Scolari, Alex Rocco, Bill Cobbs, Rita Wilson, Chris Isaak, Kevir Pollak, Giovanni Ribisi, Bryan Cranston, Holmes Osborne, Dawn Maxey, Sean M. Whalen, Clint Howard, Kathleen Kinmont, Barry Sobel, Gedde Watanabe, Jonathan Demme, Marc McClure, Colin Hanks; **D:** Tom Hanks; **W:** Tom Hanks; **C:** Tak Fujimoto; **M:** Howard Shore.

That Touch of Mink ✓✓½ 1962 In New York City, an unemployed secretary finds herself involved with a business tycoon. On a trip to Bermuda, both parties get an education as they play their game of "cat and mouse." Enjoyable romantic comedy. **99m/C VHS, DVD.** Cary Grant, Doris Day, Gig Young, Audrey Meadows, John Astin, Dick Sargent; **D:** Delbert Mann; **W:** Stanley Shapiro, Nate Monaster; **C:** Russell Metty; **M:** George Duning. Golden Globes '63. Film—Mus./Comedy.

That Uncertain Feeling ✓✓½ 1941 Light comedy about a couple's marital problems increasing when she develops the hiccups and a friendship with a flaky piano player. A remake of the earlier Lubitsch silent film, "Kiss Me Again." Available colorized. **86m/B VHS, DVD.** Merle Oberon, Melvyn Douglas, Burgess Meredith, Alan Mowbray, Eve Arden, Sig Rumann, Harry Davenport; **D:** Ernst Lubitsch; **W:** Donald Ogden Stewart, Walter Reisch; **C:** George Barnes; **M:** Werner R. Heymann.

That Was Then... This Is Now ✓✓ 1985 (R) Lame adaptation of S.E. Hinton teen novel about a surly kid who is attached to his adoptive brother and becomes jealous when the brother **96m/C VHS, DVD.** Ringo Starr, Keith Moon, David Essex, Rosemary Leach, James Booth, Billy Fury, Rosalind Ayres, Robert Lindsay, Brenda Bruce, Verna Harvey, James Ottaway, Deborah Watling, Beth Morris, Daphne Oxenford, Kim Braden, Ron Hackett, Johnny Shannon, Susan Holderness, The Debonairs; **D:** Claude Whatham; **W:** Ray Connolly; **C:** Peter Suszitzky.

That'll Be the Day ✓✓½ 1973 (PG) The early rock 'n' roll of the 1950s is

and loved ones behind after a tragedy for which she still blames herself. Having been diagnosed with leukemia, Sarah decides to return home to tell her family, only to find that the past will not leave her alone when she gets an antagonistic reception from depressed neighbor Lorraine (Ehle). Instead of making the story about Sarah's illness, the TV pic focuses on her past trauma and how to forgive, with mixed results. **96m/C DVD.** Amber Tamblyn, Jennifer Ehle, Mary Elizabeth Mastrantonio, Tim

That's Adequate ✓✓ 1990 (R) Mock documentary about a fictional film studio. Lampoons just about every movie ever made in the last 60 years. Premise might have been adequate for a sketch, but hardly for a feature-length film. Zaniness gets old quickly. **82m/C VHS.** Tony Randall, Robert Downey, Rocky Aoki, Bruce Willis, Robert Kevin Townsend, James Coco, Jerry Stiller, Peter Vaughn, Renee Taylor, Stuart Pankin, Robert Theodore, Anne Bloom, Chuck McCann, Anne Meara; **D:** Harry Hurwitz; **W:** Harry Hurwitz.

That's Dancing! ✓✓✓ 1985 (G) This anthology features some of film's finest moments in dance from classical ballet to break-dancing. **104m/C VHS, DVD.** Fred Astaire, Ginger Rogers, Ruby Keeler, Cyd Charisse, Gene Kelly, Shirley MacLaine, Liza Minnelli, Sammy Davis Jr., Mikhail Baryshnikov, Ray Bolger, Jennifer Beals, Dean Martin; **D:** Jack Haley Jr.; **M:** Henry Mancini.

That's Entertainment ✓✓✓ 1974 (G) A compilation of scenes from the classic MGM musicals beginning with "Gigi" (1958). Great fun, especially for movie buffs. **132m/C VHS, DVD.** Judy Garland, Fred Astaire, Frank Sinatra, Gene Kelly, Esther Williams, Bing Crosby; **D:** Jack Haley Jr.; **M:** Henry Mancini.

That's Entertainment, Part 2 ✓✓✓ 1976 (G) A cavalcade of great MGM musicals and comedy sequences from the past. Also stars Jeanette MacDonald, Nelson Eddy, the Marx Brothers, Laurel and Hardy, Jack Buchanan, Ann Miller, Mickey Rooney, Louis Armstrong, Oscar Levant, Cyd Charisse, Elizabeth Taylor, Maurice Chevalier, Bing Crosby, Jimmy Durante, Clark Gable, and the Barrymores, but as unified as its predecessor, but priceless nonetheless. **129m/C VHS, DVD.** Fred Astaire, Gene Kelly; **D:** Gene Kelly; **W:** Leonard Gershe; **C:** George J. Folsey; **M:** Nelson Riddle; **Nar:** Fred Astaire, Gene Kelly.

That's Entertainment, Part 3 ✓✓ 1993 (G) Third volume contains 62 MGM musical numbers from over 100 films, hosted by nine of the original stars, and is based on outtakes and unfinished numbers from studio archives. One new technique used here is a split-screen showing both the actual film with a behind-the-scenes shot that incudes cameramen, set designers, and dancers scurrying around. Although it has its moments, TE3 doesn't generate the same reverence for Hollywood's Golden Age that its predecessors managed to do. That 18-year gap between sequels may say something about what the studio execs thought of their film vault's remainders. **113m/C VHS, DVD. D:** Bud Friedgen, Michael J. Sheridan; **W:** Bud Friedgen, Michael J. Sheridan; **M:** Marc Shaiman.

That's Life! ✓✓ 1986 (PG-13) A lackluster semi-home movie starring Edwards' family and friends. A single weekend in the lives of a writer who's turning 60, his singer wife who has been diagnosed with cancer, and their family. **102m/**

That's Entertainment (see above duplicate) — [omitted]

Theatre of Death ✓✓½ 1967 Blood Fiend; Female Fiend Horror master Lee is back, this time as a theatre director in Paris. Meanwhile, police are baffled by a series of mysterious murders, each begun ning a trace of vampirism. Well-plotted suspense. A racy voodoo dance sequence, often cut, is available on some video versions. **90m/C VHS, DVD.** Christopher Lee, Lelia Goldoni, Julian Glover, Evelyn Laye, Jenny Till, Ivor Dean; **D:** Samuel Gallu; **W:** Ellis Kadison, Roger Marshall; **C:** Gilbert Taylor.

Thelma & Louise ✓✓✓ 1991 (R) Hailed as the first "feminist-buddy" movie, Sarandon and Davis bust out as best friends who head directly into one of the better movies of the year. Davis is the ditzy Thelma, a housewife rebelling against her dominating, unfaithful, abusive husband (who, rather than being disturbing, provides some of the best comic relief in the film). Sarandon is Louise, a hardened and world-weary relationship. They hit the road for a respite from their mundane lives, only to find violence and a part of themselves they never knew existed. Outstanding performances from Davis and especially Sarandon, with Pitt notable as the stud who gets Davis' motor revved. Directors cut has a fine eye for set details **130m/C VHS, DVD.** Susan Sarandon, Geena Davis, Harvey Keitel, Christopher McDonald, Michael Madsen, Brad Pitt, Timothy Carhart, Stephen Tobolowsky, Lucinda Jenney; **D:** Ridley Scott; **W:** Callie Khouri; **C:** Adrian Biddle; **M:** Hans Zimmer. Oscars '91; Orig. Screenplay; Natl. Bd. of Review '91: Actress (Sarandon); Actress (Davis); Nat. Soc. Film Critics '91: Support. Actor (Keitel); Writers Guild '91: Orig. Screenplay.

Them! ✓✓✓ 1954 A group of mutated giant ants wreak havoc on a southwestern town. The first of the big-bug movies, and far surpassing the rest, this is a classic fun flick. See how many names you can spot among the supporting cas. **93m/B VHS, DVD.** James Whitmore, Edmund Gwenn, Fess Parker, James Arress, Onslow Stevens, Jack Perrin, Joan Weldon, Sean McClor, Sandy Descher, Dub Taylor, William Schallert, Leonard Nimoy; **D:** Gordon Douglas; **W:** Richard Deacon; **D:** Gordon

That's My Baby! ✓✓ 1988 (PG-13) A man wants his girlfriend to have their baby, but the only thing she wants is her career. War between the sexes, poorly done. **97m/C VHS.** Sonja Smits, Timothy Webber; **D:** Edie Yolles, John Bradshaw.

That's the Way I Like It ✓✓½ 1999 (PG-13) Homage to the disco era, set in the East rather than the West. It's 1977 and Singapore clerk Hock (Pang) wants to win a disco tournament so he can buy a motorcycle. He drops his usual partner (Tang) for the flashier Julie (Francis) and the rivalry between the dance teams gets intense. But Hock just happens to have the spirit of the legendary "Saturday Night Fever" studster himself, struttin' his stuff (Pace), to give him that extra dance fever. **92m/C VHS, DVD.** Adrian Pang, Anna Belle Francis, Dominic Pace, Madeline Tang, Caleb Goh; **D:** Glen Goei; **W:** Glen Goei; **C:** Brian J. Breheny; **M:** Guy Gross.

Theatre of Blood ✓✓✓ 1973 Much Ado about Murder 1973 (R) Shakespearean ham actor Edward Lionheart (Price) committed suicide after losing an award and being ridiculed by the critics. Now those same critics are being murdered in bizarre ways—in fact, their deaths parallel those in the plays of the Bard. Well, it's no big surprise to discover that Lionheart is in deed alive and committing the inventive crimes with the assistance of his lovely daughter, Edwina (Rigg). Top drawer comedy noir with a great supporting cast of Britain's best (and quite a bit of gore). **104m/C VHS, DVD.** GB Vincent Price, Diana Rigg, Ian Hendry, Robert Morley, Dennis Price, Diana Dors, Milo O'Shea, Harry Andrews, Coral Browne, Robert Coote, Jack Hawkins, Michael Hordern, Arthur Lowe; **D:** Douglas Hickox; **W:** Anthony Greville-Bell; **C:** Wolfgang Suszitzky; **M:** Michael Lewis.

Douglas; **W:** Ted Sherdeman; **C:** Sid Hickox; **M:** Bronislau Kaper.

The Theme ☆☆☆ *Tema* 1979 Esenin is a mediocre middle-aged playwright who knows his success comes from kowtowing to the party line. Trying to find inspiration he visits his native village where he meets the young Sasa, an artist who has refused to compromise. Although Esenin falls for her, Sasa has only contempt for his lack of principles and stays with her poet/lover, who is reduced to digging graves and has decided to emigrate to Israel. The film went unreleased for years because of its themes of artistic freedom and emigration. In Russian with English subtitles. 100m/C VHS. *RU* Mikhail Ulyanov, Inna Churikova, Stanislav Lyubshin, Evgeny Vesnik, Sergei Nikonenko, Natalya Selezneva; **D:** Gleb Panfilov. Berlin Intl. Film Fest. '79: Golden Berlin Bear.

Theodora Goes Wild ☆☆☆ 1936 Tiny, priggish Lynnfield, Connecticut is shocked to discover that a scandalous best seller about smalltown life has been written pseudonymously by their very own Theodora Lynn (Dunne). When Theodora gets a chance to meet sophisticated New Yorker Michael Grant (Douglas), who did the illustrations for her book, she falls for him. But both must throw aside their own (and everyone else's) expectations and limitations for them to be happy. Dunne's first comedic lead role. 94m/B VHS. Irene Dunne, Melvyn Douglas, Thomas Mitchell, Thurston Hall, Rosalind Keith, Spring Byington, Elisabeth Risdon, Margaret McWade; **D:** Richard Boleslawski; **M:** Sidney Buchman; **C:** Joseph Walker; **M:** Morris Stoloff.

Theodore Rex ☆☆½ 1995 (PG) Futuristic comedy finds cynical, seasoned cop Katie Coltrane (Goldberg) furious at being teamed with Teddy, who just happens to be an eight-foot-tall, three-ton, returned-from-extinction Tyrannosaurus Rex (who has a taste for cookies). A comedy's not exactly the brightest dinosaur on the block, which makes Katie's job all the harder when they stumble across a major crime caper. 92m/C VHS, DVD. Whoopi Goldberg, Armin Mueller-Stahl, Richard Roundtree, Juliet Landau; **D:** Jonathan Betuel; **W:** Jonathan Betuel; **C:** David Tattersall; **M:** Robert Folk.

The Theory of Flight ☆☆ 1998 (R) Awkward film reflects the relationship between Jane Hatchard (Bonham Carter), a wheelchair-bound woman suffering from a motor-neurological disease, and her eccentric, reluctant caregiver, Richard (Branagh). Richard is an artist who dreams of human flight, and one of his attempts gets him assigned to community service and to being teamed with Jane. Her one wish is to lose her virginity but Richard won't oblige, although he's willing to set her up with a gigolo (Stevenson). Flints with bad taste and is generally worth watching because of Bonham Carter's fierce performance. 98m/C VHS. *GB* Helena Bonham-Carter, Kenneth Branagh, Gemma Jones, Holly Aird, Ray Stevenson; **D:** Paul Greengrass; **W:** Richard Hawkins; **C:** Ivan Strasburg; **M:** Rolfe Kent.

The Theory of the Leisure Class ☆☆ 2001 Kids on a field trip discover the murdered bodies of several children, missing from a small western community. City reporter Callie (Knight) shows up and begins snooping around, uncovering the town's secrets. Based on a true story. 108m/C VHS, DVD. Tuesday Knight, Michael Massee, Christopher McDonald, Brad Renfro; **D:** Gabriel Bologna; **W:** Amber Benson, Gabriel Bologna; **C:** Christopher Tuffy; **M:** Howard Drossin.

There Goes Barder ☆☆ *Ca Va Barder* 1954 Constantine plays a con-man who's hired by a crooked ship owner to be a security agent. 90m/B VHS. *FR* Eddie Constantine, May Britt, Jean Carmet, Jean Danet, Monique Van Vooren; **D:** John Berry; **W:** John Berry; **C:** Jacques Lemare.

There Goes Kelly ☆½ 1945 Moran and Miller are page boys at a radio station who try to get the station receptionist a singing job. When the vocalist on a popular show is murdered, the duo not only get their protege a break but get themselves a mystery to solve as well. 62m/B VHS. Jackie Moran, Sidney Miller, Wanda McKay, Ralph Sanford, Jan Wiley, Anthony Warde; **D:** Phil Karlson.

There Goes My Baby ☆☆½ 1992 (R) Eight California high school grads confront their futures on two nights in '65 (as the Watts riots ignite). There are Vietnam protests, flower children, would-be rock stars, friendships, and romantic complications. Yes, it sounds a lot like "American Graffiti" but the cast are winning and there's a good deal of affection without sinking to mawkishness. 99m/C VHS, DVD. Dermot Mulroney, Rick Schroder, Kelli Williams, Jill Schoelen, Noah Wyle, Kristin Minter, Lucy Deakins, Kenny Ransom, Seymour Cassel, Paul Gleason, Frederick Coffin, Andrew (Andy) Robinson, Shon Greenblatt, J.E. Freeman; **D:** Floyd Mutrux; **W:** Floyd Mutrux.

There Goes the Neighborhood ☆☆½ 1992 (PG-13) A dying convict tells prison psychiatrist Daniels where he has buried $8.5 million—under the home of neighbor O'Hara. Daniels and O'Hara try to discreetly dig up the fortune but the neighborhood finds out everyone wants a chance at the cash. 88m/C VHS. Jeff Daniels, Catherine O'Hara, Dabney Coleman, Hector Elizondo, Judith Ivey, Rhea Perlman, Harris Yulin, Jonathan Banks, Chazz Palminteri, Mary Gross; **D:** Bill Phillips; **M:** David Bell.

There Was a Crooked Man ☆☆☆½ 1970 (R) An Arizona town adds new ideas about law and order when an incorruptible and innovative warden takes over the town's prison. The warden finds he's got his hands full with one inmate determined to escape. Offbeat western black comedy supported by an excellent and entertaining production, with fine acting all around. 123m/C VHS, DVD. Kirk Douglas, Henry Fonda, Warren Oates, Hume Cronyn, Burgess Meredith, John Randolph, Arthur O'Connell, Alan Hale Jr., Lee Grant; **D:** Joseph L. Mankiewicz; **W:** Robert Benton, David Newman; **M:** Harry Stradling Jr.

There Will Be Blood ☆☆☆☆½ 2007 (R) Director Anderson ventures from the contemporary to a saga that covers some 30 years (from 1898 to the 1920s) following the fortunes of silver prospector turned oil magnate Daniel Planview (Day-Lewis). Misanthrope Planview wheels, deals, and cheats his way to a fortune, dogged by evangelical preacher Eli Sunday (Dano), whose family Plainview took advantage of to get his oil derricks gushing. Plainview's one human contact is the orphan H.W. (Freasier), whom he adopts (and later dismisses) in his obsessive quest for power and wealth. Foreboding, with a powerful performance from Day-Lewis as an egotist driven mad by his ambitions. Loosely based on Upton Sinclair's 1927 novel, "Oil!" 158m/C DVD. *US* Daniel Day-Lewis, Paul Franklin Dano, Kevin J. O'Connor, Ciaran Hinds, Dave Willis, Dillon Freasier, Russell Harvard, Sydney McCallister, Colleen Foy; **D:** Paul Thomas Anderson; **W:** Paul Thomas Anderson; **C:** Robert Elswit; **M:** Johnny Greenwood. Oscars '07: Actor (Day-Lewis), Cinematog.; British Acad. '07: Actor (Day-Lewis); Golden Globes '08: Actor (Day-Lewis); Screen Actors Guild '07: Actor (Day-Lewis).

Theremin: An Electronic Odyssey ☆☆☆ 1995 (PG) Profiles the life of Russian scientist Leon Theremin (who died in 1993), founder of electronic music, and his revolutionary musical invention, the Theremin. Martin located the 95-year-old Theremin in Moscow in 1991, interviewed him on camera, then brought him back to the U.S. to film reunions with friends and colleagues he hadn't seen in 50 years. Martin's focus is on the impact of the Theremin on Hollywood movie scores heard in '50s sci-fi and thriller classics ("The Day the Earth Stood Still") and in popular music (The Beach Boys' "Good Vibrations" is commented on by Brian Wilson). Theremin's life proves as curious as his instrument, with his controversial interracial marriage to a ballet star, abduction by Russian agents, and imprisonment in a Soviet mental hospital. "Theremin" provides a fascinating and heartfelt tribute to the man's work and life. 84m/C VHS, DVD. **D:** Steven M. Martin; **W:** Steven M. Martin; **C:** Robert Stone, Edward Lachman, Chris Lombardi; **M:** Hal Willner.

There's a Girl in My Soup ☆☆ 1970 (R) Sellers is a gourmet who moonlights as a self-styled Casanova. Early post "Laugh-In" Hawn is the young girl who takes refuge at his London love nest when her boyfriend dumps her. Lust ensues. Has its funny parts, but not a highlight of anyone's career. Based on the hit play. 95m/C VHS, DVD. *GB* Peter Sellers, Goldie Hawn, Diana Dors; **D:** Roy Boulting.

There's No Business Like Show Business ☆☆☆ 1954 A top husband and wife vaudevillian act make it a family affair. Filmed in CinemaScope, allowing for full and lavish musical numbers. Good performances and Berlin's music make this an enjoyable film. ♪When the Midnight Choo-Choo Leaves for Alabam; Let's Have Another Cup of Coffee; Play a Simple Melody; After You Get What You Want You Don't Want It; You'd Be Surprised; A Sailor's Not a Sailor; A Pretty Girl is Like a Melody; If You Believe Me; A Man Chases a Girl Until She Catches Him. 117m/C VHS, DVD. Charlotte Austin, Ethel Merman, Donald O'Connor, Marilyn Monroe, Dan Dailey, Johnny Ray, Mitzi Gaynor, Frank McHugh, Hugh O'Brian; **D:** Walter Lang; **W:** Phoebe Ephron, Henry Ephron; **C:** Leon Shamroy; **M:** Irving Berlin, Lionel Newman, Alfred Newman.

There's Nothing out There ☆☆ 1990 A group of seven teenagers spends Spring Break at a secluded mountain cabin. It sounds wonderful, but one of the boys (who claims to have seen every horror movie on video) knows the signs of a horror movie just waiting to happen. 91m/C VHS, DVD. Craig Peck, Wendy Bednarz, Mark Collver, Bonnie Bowers, John Carhart III, Claudia Flores, Jeff Dachis, Lisa Grant; **D:** Rolfe Kanefsky; **W:** Rolfe Kanefsky; **C:** Ed Hershberger; **M:** Christopher Thomas.

There's Something about Mary ☆☆☆ 1998 (R) Outrageously funny comedy that only veers from the gutter when it feels like taking a dip in the sewer. Set in 1985, the prologue introduces us to geeky Ted (Stiller), who gets a prom date with class knockout Mary (Diaz) after sticking up for her retarded brother Warren (Brown). The big date is not to be, however, for a vicious tuxedo zipper to the privates incapacitate Ted. Thirteen years later, Ted is still depressed over the incident, and still carries a torch for Mary. He hires Pat (Dillon), an oily detective with enormous choppers, to find her. Unfortunately for Ted, Pat is instantly smitten with Mary and lies. Ted learns the truth and heads to Miami for love from the gutter to this lowbrow masterpiece. 118m/C VHS, DVD, UMD. Ben Stiller, Matt Dillon, Cameron Diaz, Chris Elliott, Lee Evans, Lin Shaye, Jeffrey Tambor, Markie Post, Keith David, Jonathan Richman, W. Earl Brown, Khandi Alexander, Richard Tyson, Rob Moran, Lenny Clarke, Zen Gesner, Harland Williams, Richard Jenkins; *Cameos:* Brett Favre; **D:** Bobby Farrelly, Peter Farrelly; **W:** Bobby Farrelly, Peter Farrelly, Edward Decter, John J. Strauss; **C:** Mark Irwin; **M:** Jonathan Richman. MTV Movie Awards '99: Film, Female Perf. (Diaz), Villain (Dillon), Fight; N.Y. Film Critics '98: Actress (Diaz).

Therese ☆☆☆ 1986 Stylish biography of a young French nun and her devotion to Christ bordering on romantic love. Explores convent life. Real-life Therese died of TB and was made a saint. A directorial tour de force for Cavalier. In French with English subtitles. 90m/C VHS, DVD. *FR* Catherine Mouchet, Aurore Prieto, Sylvie Habault, Ghislaine Mona; **D:** Alain Cavalier; **W:** Alain Cavalier; **C:** Isabelle Dedieu. Cannes '86: Special Jury Prize; Cesar '87: Cinematog. Director (Cavalier), Film, Writing.

Therese & Isabelle ☆☆½ 1967 Story of growing love and physical attraction between two French schoolgirls. On holiday together, they confront their mutual desires. Richly photographed soft porn based on the novel by Violet Leduc. Not vulgar, but certainly not for adults. French with subtitles. 118m/B VHS, DVD. Essy Persson, Anna Gael, Barbara Laage, Anne Vernon; **D:** Radley Metzger; **W:** Jesse Vogel; **C:** Hans Jura; **M:** Georges Auric.

Therese Raquin ☆☆½ 1980 Therese Raquin (Nelligan)is a young woman unhappily married to mama's boy Camille (Cranham). She has an affair with Laurent (Cox) and the lovers do away with the inconvenient spouse. But their guilt turns to loathing for each other and haunts them into further acts of betrayal and violence. Based on the novel by Emile Zola. 173m/C VHS, DVD. *GB* Kate Nelligan, Brian Cox, Mona Washbourne, Kenneth Cranham, Alan Rickman, Richard Pearson; **D:** Simon Langton; **W:** Philip Mackie; **M:** Patrick Gowers. TV

Therese: The Story of Saint Therese of Lisieux ☆☆ 2004 Therese is born into a privileged French family but begs to follow her older sister into a Carmelite convent though she has self-doubts, which she describes in her journals. She becomes more and more of an ascetic, following a life of simplicity, humility, and compassion, which is revealed when her writings are published after her early death. 90m/C DVD. Linda Hayden, Lindsay Younce, Samantha Kramer, Judith Kaplan, Leonardo Defilippis; **D:** Leonardo Defilippis; **W:** Patti Defilippis; **C:** Lourdes Ambrose; **M:** Sister Marie Therese Sokol.

These Foolish Things ☆☆½ 2006 A sentimental and predictable wisp of a melodrama set in 1930s London. The orphaned daughter of a stage star, Diana (Tapper) decides to follow her mother's profession. She falls in love with ambitious playwright Robin (Leon), whose new play stars Douglas (Umbers), who wants to personally work with Robin offstage as well. Stamp's an all-knowing butler, Huston's the American financing the play, and Bacall plays another star. Based on the novel by Noel Langley. 107m/C DVD. Zoe Tapper, David Leon, Mark Umbers, Lauren Bacall, Anjelica Huston, Terence Stamp, Joss Ackland, Andrew Lincoln, Julia McKenzie; **D:** Julia Taylor-Stanley; **W:** Julia Taylor-Stanley; **C:** Gavin Finney; **M:** Ian Lynn.

These Girls ☆☆ 2005 (R) Best teen friends Keira (Dhavernas), Lisa (Lewis), and Glory (Walsh) all have a crush on married 30-year-old pot dealer Keith (Boreanaz). After discovering that Glory is already having a fling with Keith, her gal pals decide they should share the unwillingly stud equally, using blackmail about Glory's underage tryst as leverage. Since none of the attractive actresses can remotely pass for teenagers, this slight comedy is already at a disadvantage. Based on a play by Vivienne Laxdal. 92m/C DVD. *CA* Caroline Dhavernas, David Boreanaz, Holly Lewis, Amanda Walsh; **D:** John Hazlett; **W:** John Hazlett; **C:** Alex. Vendler; **M:** Ned Bouhalassa. VIDEO

These Old Broads ☆☆½ 2001 Three actresses—Addie Holden (Collins), Kate Westbourne (MacLaine), and Piper Grayson (Reynolds)—starred in a '60s musical that over the years has become a cult hit. A TV exec (Carbonell) wants to engineer a TV reunion special but the trio hate each other. Maybe the agent (Taylor) they all share can persuade them. 95m/C VHS, Debbie Reynolds, Joan Collins, Shirley MacLaine, Elizabeth Taylor, Jonathan Silverman, Peter Graves, Gene Barry, Pat Harrington; **D:** Matthew Diamond; **W:** Carrie Fisher, Elaine Pope; **C:** Eric Van Haren Noman; **M:** Guy Moon, Steve Tyrell. TV

These Three ☆☆☆½ 1936 A teenaged girl ruins the lives of two teachers by telling a malicious lie. Excellent cast. Script by Lillian Hellman, based on her play "The Children's Hour." Remade by the same director as "The Children's Hour" in 1961. 92m/B VHS. Miriam Hopkins, Merle Oberon, Joel McCrea, Bonita Granville, Marcia Mae Jones, Walter Brennan, Margaret Hamilton, Catherine Doucet, Alma Kruger, Carmencita Johnson, Mary Ann Durkin, Frank McGlynn; **D:** William Wyler; **W:** Lillian Hellman; **C:** Gregg Toland; **M:** Alfred Newman.

Thesis ☆☆☆ *Tesis; Snuff* 1996 (R) Angela (Torrent) is a university student writing her thesis on violence in the media. She comes across a snuff film that shows a girl being tortured to death. While trying to discover if the film is real, Angela finds out that the girl was a university student and that the film was actually shot on campus.

They 🐾 *Invasion from Inner Earth; Hell Fire* 1977 Beings from beneath the earth's crust take their first trip to the surface. *88m/C VHS, DVD, Paul Dentzer, Debbie Pick, Nick Holt; D: Ito Rebane.*

They All Kissed the Bride 🐾🐾½ 1942 Tough cookie Margaret Drew (Crawford) must take over the family's trucking business when dad dies and support her ditzy mother (Burke) and younger sister Vivian (Parrish). Crusading newspaperman Michael Holmes (Douglas) blasts Margaret's business practices in print but when they finally meet, the sparks fly. Crawford manages the physical comedy well and Douglas is suitably charming. *87m/B VHS. Joan Crawford, Melvyn Douglas, Billie Burke, Helen Parrish, Roland Young, Allen Jenkins, Emory Parnell; D: Alexander Hall. W: Andrew Solt, P.J. Wolfson; C: Joseph Walker; M: Werner R. Heymann.*

They All Laughed 🐾🐾 1981 (PG) Three detectives become romantically involved with the women they were hired to investigate. Essentially light-hearted fluff with little or no script. Further undermined by the real-life murder of Stratten before the film's release. *115m/C VHS, DVD. Ben Gazzara, John Ritter, Audrey Hepburn, Colleen Camp, Patti Hansen, Dorothy Stratten, Elizabeth Pena; D: Peter Bogdanovich.*

They Bite WOOF! 1995 (R) A pornographic filmmaker's latest epic about lustful girl-men is filming at the same Florida beach where a corpse found floating in a swimming pool. The characters are based on Erie Stanley Gardner (Hutton) and "Mr. Right." Young is a zoologist who is investigating reports of "man-alike fish monsters killing swimmers. Just a coincidence? Ultra-(and deliberately) cheesy; an unrated version is also available. *96m/C VHS. Donna Frotscher, Nick Baldasare, Charlie Barnet, Ron Jeremy; D: Robert Jackson Drasnin.* TV

They Call It Murder 🐾🐾 1971 D.A. Doug Selby (Hutton) investigates the matter of a corpse found floating in a swimming pool. *120m/C DVD. Jim Hutton, Lloyd Bochner, Jessica Walter, Leslie Nielsen, JoAnn Pflug, Nita Talbot, Bill Elliott, Vic Tayback; D: Walter Grauman; W: San Rolfe.* T.V.

They Call It Sin 🐾🐾 *The Way of Life* 1932 Often told story of a young country girl heading to the Big Apple in search of her big break and "Mr. Right." Young is a chorus line girl romantically involved with her married producer (Calhern) while faithful admirer Brent waits nearby. Predictable plot adapted from the novel. *68m/B VHS, DVD. Loretta Young, George Brent, David Manners, Louis Calhern, Una Merkel, Joseph Cawthorn, Helen Vinson; D: Thornton Freeland; W: Lillie Hayward, Howard J. Green.*

They Call Me Bruce? 🐾🐾 *Full of Chopsticks* 1982 (PG) A bumbling Bruce Lee look-alike meets a karate-chopping Mafia moll in this farce. Silly premise creates lots of laughs. Followed by a sequel, "They Still Call Me Bruce." *88m/C VHS, DVD. Johnny Yune, Margaux Hemingway; D: Elliot Hong; W: Tim Clawson.*

They Call Me Mr. Tibbs! 🐾🐾½ 1970 (R) Lieutenant Virgil Tibbs (Poitier) investigates the murder of a prostitute. The prime suspect is his friend, the Reverend Logan Sharpe (Landau). He is torn between his duty as a policeman, his concern for the reverend, and the turmoil of his domestic life. Less tense, less compelling sequel to "In the Heat of the Night." *108m/C VHS. Sidney Poitier, Barbara McNair, Martin Landau, Juano Hernandez, Anthony Zerbe, Ed Asner, Norma Crane, Jeff Corey; D: Gordon Douglas; W: Alan R. Trustman; C: Gerald Perry Finnerman; M: Quincy Jones.*

They Call Me Sirr 🐾🐾 2000 Based on the true story of Sirr Parker (Scott), a talented but poverty-stricken high school football player in South Central L.A. After Sirr and his younger brother

Now it's Angela's life in danger. Suspenseful with a shocker ending. Spanish gangs to look after his family (including an ailing grandmother) while keeping his place on the team. But the teen is finally forced to turn to his coach (Duncan) for help. *97m/C VHS, DVD, Kente Scott, Michael Clarke Duncan; D: Robert Munic; M: Robert Munic. CABLE*

They Call Me Trinity 🐾🐾½ *Lo Chiamavano Trinita Trinita* 1972 (G) Lazy drifter-gunslinger and his outlaw brother join forces to rout bullying cutlaws. Spoofs every western cliche with relentless comedy, parodying "The Magnificent Seven" and gibing the spaghetti western. Followed by "Trinity is Still My Name." Dubbed. *110m/C VHS, DVD. Terence Hill, Bud Spencer, Steffen Zacharias; D: E.B. (Enzo Barboni) Clucher.*

They Came Back 🐾🐾½ *Les Revenants* 2004 Warning: this is not your normal zombie-eats-people movie. Instead, thousands of the dead have shuffled back to their small French village to just live out their old lives. Sort of. As the living must work to deal with the sudden population explosion, the now-dimwitted undead have been holding secret nightly meetings. First-time director Campillo goes for a quiet look at society's reaction to the walking dead's return rather than a gorefest, a la George Romero. In French with English subtitles. *102m/C VHS, DVD, FR. Geraldine Pailhas, Jonathan Zaccai, Frederic Pierrot, Victor Garrivier, Catherine Samie; D: Robin Campillo; W: Robin Campillo, Brigitte Tijou; C: Jeanne Lapoirie; M: Martin Wheeler.* VIDEO

They Came from Beyond Space 🐾 1967 Aliens invade the earth and possess the brains of humans. They only want a few slaves to help them repair their ship which crashed on the moon. They raise a satiric parasite. Queasy, sleazy and weird. First major film by Cronenberg. *87m/C VHS, DVD. CA Paul Hampton, Joe Silver, Lynn Lowry, Barbara Steele, Susan Petrie, Allan Migicovsky, Ronald Mlodzik; D: David Cronenberg; W: David Cronenberg; C: Robert Saad; M: Ivan Reitman.*

They Came from Within 🐾🐾 *Shivers; The Parasite Murders; Frissons* 1975 (R) The occupants of a high-rise building go on a sex and violence spree when stricken by an aphrodisiac parasite. Queasy, sleazy and weird. First major film by Cronenberg. *87m/C VHS, DVD. CA Paul Hampton, Joe Silver, Lynn Lowry, Barbara Steele, Susan Petrie, Allan Migicovsky, Ronald Mlodzik; D: David Cronenberg; C: Robert Saad; M: Freddie Francis.*

They Came to Cordura 🐾🐾½ 1959 Mexico, 1916: a woman and six American soldiers—five heroes and one who has been branded a coward—begin a journey to the military headquarters in Cordura. Slow journey brings out personalities. Look for "Bewitched" hubby Dick York. Based on Glendon Swarthout's best-seller. *123m/C VHS, DVD. Gary Cooper, Rita Hayworth, Van Heflin, Tab Hunter, Dick York, Richard Conte; D: Robert Rossen; M: Ivan Moffat.*

They Crawl 🐾🐾 *Crawlers* 2001 (R) More complicated than usual for the creepy crawlie genre. Ted Gage (Cosgrove) learns his biophysicist brother has been electrocuted and all his organs removed. Ted teams up with cop Gina (Davies) to figure out what's going on and finds connections behind the murder, a homicidal cult, and lethal cockroaches linked to a government surveillance project. Everybody looks convinced that this makes some kind of sense. *93m/C VHS, DVD. Daniel Cosgrove, Dennis Boutsikaris, Tim Thomerson, Tamara Davies, Tone Loc, Mickey Rourke, Grace Zabriskie; D: John Allardice; M: Curtis Joseph, David Mason; C: John Allardice.* VIDEO

They Died with Their Boots On 🐾🐾🐾 1941 The Battle of Little Big Horn is re-created Hollywood style. Takes liberties with historical fact, but still an exciting portrayal of General Custer's last stand. The movie also marks the last time de Havilland worked with Flynn. Also available colorized. *141m/B VHS. Errol Flynn, Sydney Greenstreet, Anthony Quinn, Hattie McDaniel, Arthur Kennedy, Gene Lockhart, Regis Toomey, Olivia de Havilland, Charley Grapewin, G.P. (Tim) Huntley Jr., Frank Wilcox, Joseph (Joe)

are abandoned by their mother, Sirr struggles to look after his family (including an ailing grandmother)...

Sawyer, Eddie Acuff, Minor Watson, Tod Andrews, Stanley Ridges, John Litel, Walter Hampden, Joseph Crehan, Selmer Jackson, Gig Young, Dick Wessel; D: Raoul Walsh; W: Aeneas MacKenzie; C: Bert Glennon; M: Max Steiner.*

They Drive by Night 🐾🐾🐾½ 1940 Two truck-driving brothers break away from a large company and begin independent operation. After an accident that costs one brother his arm, the other goes back to the company where Lupino, the boss's wife, becomes obsessed with him and win Raft. When he rejects her, she accuses him of the murder. Well-plotted film with great dialogue. Excellent cast gives it their all. *97m/B VHS, DVD. Humphrey Bogart, Ann Sheridan, George Raft, Ida Lupino, Alan Hale, Gale Page, Roscoe Karns, Charles Halton; D: Raoul Walsh.*

They Got Me Covered 🐾🐾 1943 Two WWII-era journalists get involved in a comic web of murder, kidnapping and romance. Hope is very funny and carries the rest of the cast. Look for Do's Day in a bit part and listen for Bing Crosby singing whenever Hope opens his cigarette case. *95m/B VHS, DVD. Bob Hope, Dorothy Lamour, Otto Preminger, Eduardo Ciannelli, Donald Meek, Walter Catlett; D: David Butler; W: Harry Kurnitz; C: Rudolph Mate; M: Leigh Harline; V: Bing Crosby.*

They Knew What They Wanted 🐾🐾 1940 A lonely San Francisco waitress begins a correspondence romance with a grape grower and agrees to marry him after he sends her a photo which shows him as being young and handsome. She arrives to discover Laughton had sent her a picture of another man. An accident, an affair, and a pregnancy provide further complications before a satisfactory ending is suggested. Flawed adaptation of Sidney Howard's play still has strong performances from Lombard and Laughton. *96m/B VHS Charles Laughton, Carole Lombard, Harry Carey Sr., Karl Malden, William Gargan; D: Garson Kanin; C: Harry Stradling Sr.*

They Live 🐾🐾½ *Creepers* 1988 (R) A semi-serious science-fiction spoof about a drifter who discovers an alien conspiracy. They're taking over the country under the guise of Reaganism, capitalism and yuppiecom. Screenplay written by Carpenter under a pseudonym. Starts out fun, deteriorates into cliches and bad special effects makeup. *88m/C VHS, DVD. Roddy Piper, Keith David, Meg Foster, George "Buck" Flower, Peter Jason, Raymond St. Jacques, John Lawrence, Sy Richardson, Jason Robards III, Larry Franco, Wendy Brainard, Dana Bratton; D: John Carpenter; W: John Carpenter, Alan Howarth.*

They Live by Night 🐾🐾🐾½ *The Twisted Road; Your Red Wagon* 1949 Bowie joins a prison break with hardened cons Chickamaw (da Silva) and T-Dub (Flippen) who then use him as an extra pair of hands in a bank heist. Bowie tries to go straight by marrying young Keechie (O'Donnell) but gets sucked back in by his criminal compatriots and winds up a fugitive with no hope. Classic film noir was Ray's first attempt at directing. Based on Edward Anderson's novel "Thieves Like Us," under which title it was remade in 1974. Compelling and suspenseful. *95m/B VHS, DVD. Cathy O'Donnell, Farley Granger, Howard da Silva, Jay C. Flippen, Helen Craig, Will Wright; D: Nicholas Ray; W: Charles Schnee; C: George E. Diskant; M: Leigh Harline.*

They Made Me a Criminal 🐾🐾½ *I Became a Criminal; They Made Me a Fugitive* 1939 A champion prizefighter, believing he murdered a man in a drunken brawl, runs away. He finds refuge with the Dead End Kids. Remake of "The Life of Jimmy Dolan." Berkeley was best-known for directing and choreographing musicals and surprisingly did very well with this movie. *92m/B VHS, DVD. John Garfield, Ann Sheridan, Claude Rains, Leo Gorcey, Huntz Hall, Gabriel Dell, Bobby Jordan, Billy Halop; D: Busby Berkeley; W: Sid Herzig; C: James Wong Howe; M: Max Steiner.*

They Made Me a Fugitive 🐾🐾½ *I Became a Criminal; They Made Me a Criminal* 1947 Former RAF officer Clem Morgan (Howard) gets drawn into the excitement of the black market after the war but then is framed by his gang boss Narcey (Jones) when Morgan won't deal drugs. After he gets out of jail, Morgan heads back to Soho to get his revenge. Based on the novel "A Convict Has Escaped" by Jackson Budd. *96m/B VHS, DVD, GB Trevor Howard, Griffith Jones, Sally Gray, Rene Ray, Mary Merrall, Vida Hope, Charles Farrell, Ballard Berkeley; D: Alberto Cavalcanti; W: Noel Langley; C: Otto Heller; M: Marius Francois Gaillard.*

They Meet Again 🐾🐾 1941 The final segment of the Dr. Christian series. The country doctor sets out to prove the innocence of a man who has been wrongly accused of stealing money. Slow moving and not particularly exciting. *68m/B VHS, DVD. Jean Hersholt, Dorothy Lovett; D: Erie C. Kenton.*

They Met in Bombay 🐾🐾½ 1941 Two jewel thieves team up in this romantic action-comedy, complete with exotic locations and two big boxoffice stars. A Japanese invasion makes Russell reconsider her life of crime and gives Gable a chance to play hero. Look for Alan Ladd in a bit part in his pre-"This Gun for Hire" days. Based on a story by John Kafka. *86m/B VHS. Clark Gable, Rosalind Russell, Peter Lorre, Jessie Ralph, Reginald Owen, Eduardo Ciannelli, Alan Ladd; D: Clarence Brown; W: Anita Loos, Edwin Justus Mayer, Leon Gordon.*

They Might Be Giants 🐾🐾🐾 1971 (G) Woodward is a woman shrink named Watson who treats retired judge Scott for delusions that he is Sherlock Holmes. Scott's brother wants him committed so he can take him over. They fall in love, but boxoffice apathy kept this film in pieces. Woodward and Scott highlight a solid cast. *88m/C VHS, DVD. George C. Scott, Joanne Woodward, Jack Gilford, Eugene Roche, Kitty Winn, F. Murray Abraham, M. Emmet Walsh; D: Anthony Harvey; W: James Goldman; C: Victor Kemper; M: John Barry.*

They Never Come Back 🐾🐾 1932 A boxer breaks his arm in the ring, retires from a job as a wild beach town resident. *90m/B VHS. Regis Toomey, Dorothy Sebastian, Edward (Eddie) Woods, Greta Granstedt, Earle Foxe, Gertrude Astor, Jack (H.) Richardson; D: Fred Newmeyer; W: Arthur Hoerl, Sherman Lowe; C: James Diamond.*

They Only Kill Their Masters 🐾🐾½ 1972 (PG) Garner plays a California police chief investigating the death of a woman killed by her doberman pinscher. He discovers the woman was actually drowned and there are any number of secrets to uncover. Mild whodunit with a host of familiar faces. *98m/C VHS, DVD. James Garner, Katharine Ross, June Allyson, Hal Holbrook, Harry Guardino, Christopher Connelly, Tom Ewell, Peter Lawford, Edmond O'Brien, Arthur O'Connell, Ann Rutherford, Art Metrano; D: James Goldstone; M: Ferry Botkin.*

They Paid with Bullets: Chicago 1929 🐾🐾½ *Tempo di Charleston - Chicago 1929* 1969 The story of one man's rise to power, and eventual downfall as a Mafia consigliatore. *88m/C VHS. SP Peter Lee Lawrence, Ingrid Schoeler, William Bogart; D: Julio Diamante; W: Gonzalo Florj; C: Emilio Foriscot; M: Enrico Simonetti.*

They Saved Hitler's Brain WOOF! *Madmen of Mandoras; The Return of Mr. H* 1964 Fanatical survivors of the Nazi holocaust gave eternal life to the brain of their leader in the last hours of the war. Now it's on a Caribbean island giving orders again. One of the truly great "bad" movies. Shot in pieces in the U.S., the Philippines, and elsewhere, with chunks of other films stuck in to hold the "story" together. **91m/B VHS, DVD.** Walter Stocker, Audrey Caire, Nestor Paiva, Carlos Rivas, Dani Lynn, Bill Freed, John Holland, Scott Peters, Marshall Reed; **D:** David Bradley; **W:** Richard Miles, Steve Bennett; **C:** Stanley Cortez; **M:** Don Hulette.

They Shall Have Music 🦴🦴🦴
Melody of Youth; Ragged Angels **1939** A poverty-stricken child hears a concert by violinist Heifetz and decides to become a musician. He joins Brennan's nearly bankrupt music school and persuades Heifetz to play at a benefit concert. Hokey but enjoyable Goldwyn effort to bring classical music to the big screen. ♪Rondo Capriccioso; Hora Staccato; Estrellita; Melody; Concerto in E Minor for Violin and Orchestra; Waltz in D Flat, Opus 64, No. 1; Cara Nome; Casta Diva. **101m/B VHS.** Walter Brennan, Joel McCrea, Gene Reynolds, Jascha Heifetz, Marjorie Main, Porter Hall, Andrea Leeds, Terence (Terry) Kilburn; **D:** Archie Mayo; **W:** Robert Presnell Sr.; **C:** Gregg Toland; **M:** Alfred Newman.

They Shoot Horses, Don't They? 🦴🦴½ **1969 (R)** Powerful period piece depicting the desperation of the Depression Era. Contestants enter a dance marathon in the hopes of winning a cash prize, not realizing that they will be driven to exhaustion. Fascinating and tragic. **121m/C VHS, DVD.** Jane Fonda, Michael Sarrazin, Susannah York, Gig Young, Red Buttons, Bonnie Bedelia, Bruce Dern, Allyn Ann McLerie, Severn Darden, Al Lewis, Michael Conrad; **D:** Sydney Pollack; **W:** James Poe; **C:** Philip Lathrop; **M:** Johnny Green. Oscars '69: Support. Actor (Young); British Acad. '70: Support. Actress (York); Golden Globes '70: Support. Actor (Young); N.Y. Film Critics '69: Actress (Fonda).

They Still Call Me Bruce 🦴
1986 (PG) A Korean searches for the American who saved his life when he was young and instead becomes big brother to an orphan. Supposedly a sequel to "They Call Me Bruce," but has little in common with it. Poorly done and not particularly entertaining. **91m/C VHS.** Johnny Yune, Robert Guillaume, Pat Paulsen; **D:** Johnny Yune.

They Watch 🦴🦴½ *They* **1993 (PG-13)** Workaholic Bergin neglects his family and suffers the consequences when his young daughter dies in an auto accident. In fact, he's so distressed that he relies on blind psychic Redgrave to get in touch with his little girl's spirit. Based on the story "They" by Rudyard Kipling. **100m/C VHS.** Patrick Bergin, Vanessa Redgrave, Valerie Mahaffey; **D:** John Korty; **C:** Edithe Swensen; **M:** Gerald Gouriet. TV

They Went That-a-Way & That-a-Way WOOF! **1978 (PG)** Two bumbling deputies pose as convicts in this madcap prison caper. Terrible re-hash of Laurel-and-Hardy has nothing going for it. **96m/C VHS, DVD.** Johnny Yune, Robert Kiel, Chuck McCann; **D:** Edward Montagne; **W:** Tim Conway.

They Were Expendable 🦴🦴🦴½ **1945** Two American captains pit their PT boats against the Japanese fleet. Based on the true story of a PT boat squadron based in the Philippines during the early days of WWII. One of the best (and most underrated) WWII films. Also available in a colorized version. **135m/B VHS, DVD.** Robert Montgomery, John Wayne, Donna Reed, Jack Holt, Ward Bond, Cameron Mitchell, Leon Ames, Marshall Thompson, Paul Langton, Donald Curtis, Jeff York, Murray Alper, Jack Pennick, Alex Havier, Charles Trowbridge, Robert Barrat, Bruce Kellogg, Louis Jean Heydt, Russell Simpson, Philip Ahn, Betty Blythe, William B. Davidson, Pedro de Cordoba, Arthur Walsh, Harry Tenbrook, Tim Murdock, Vernon Steele; **D:** John Ford; **W:** Frank Wead; **C:** Joseph August; **M:** Herbert Stothart, Eric Zeisl.

They Were So Young 🦴🦴½
1955 European models become the pawns of wealthy Brazilian magnates when they are sent to South America. They are threatened with death if they do not cooperate. The scenes were shot in Italy and Berlin. Well acted and believable, although rather grim story. **78m/B VHS, DVD.** *GF* Scott Brady, Johanna (Hannerl) Matz, Raymond Burr; **D:** Kurt Neumann.

They Were Ten 🦴🦴½ **1961** Ten Soviet Jews make Palestine their home in the 1800s despite Arab and Turkish persecution and pressures among themselves. In Hebrew with English subtitles. **105m/B VHS.** *IS* Ninette, Oded Teomi, Leo Filer, Yosef Safra; **D:** Baruch Dienar.

They Won't Believe Me 🦴🦴🦴
1947 A man plots to kill his wife, but before he does, she commits suicide. He ends up on trial for her "murder." Interesting acting by Young and Hayward against type. Surprising, ironic ending. **95m/B VHS.** Robert Young, Susan Hayward, Rita Johnson, Jane Greer; **D:** Irving Pichel.

They Won't Forget 🦴🦴🦴½
1937 When a young girl is murdered in a southern town, personal interests take precedence over justice. Turner is excellent in her first billed role, as are the other actors. Superb script, and expert direction by LeRoy pulls it all together. Based on Ward Greene's "Death in the Deep South." **95m/B VHS.** Claude Rains, Otto Kruger, Lana Turner, Allyn Joslyn, Elisha Cook Jr., Edward Norris; **D:** Mervyn LeRoy; **W:** Robert Rossen, Aben Kandel.

They're Playing with Fire WOOF! **1984 (R)** An English teacher seduces a student and gets him involved in a murder plot to gain an inheritance. Turns out someone else is beating them to the punch. Sleazy semi-pornographic slasher. **96m/C VHS, DVD.** Sybil Danning, Eric Brown, Andrew Prine, Paul Clemens, K.T. Stevens, Alvy Moore; **D:** Howard (Hikmet) Avedis; **W:** Howard (Hikmet) Avedis.

Thick as Thieves 🦴🦴½ **1999 (R)** Master thief Mackin (Baldwin) likes to get the job done and then return to his quietly sophisticated private life. Pointy (White) is the arrogant up-and-comer, with mob ties, who wants to eliminate the competition by setting Mackin up for a crime. The dual between the duo upsets mob boss Sal Capetti (Byrd) and has police officer Petrone (DeMornay) also very interested. **93m/C VHS, DVD.** Alec Baldwin, Michael Jai White, Rebecca De Mornay, Andre Braugher, Bruce Greenwood, David Byrd, Richard Edson, Khandi Alexander, Robert Miano, Janeane Garofalo, Julia Sweeney, Ricky Harris, Michael Jace; **D:** Scott Sanders; **W:** Scott Sanders, Arthur Krystal; **C:** Chris Walling; **M:** Christophe Beck. CABLE

Thicker Than Water 🦴🦴 **1993** Eerie psychological thriller exploring the relationship between identical twins. Sam Crawford (Pryce) is a successful doctor, happily married to Jo (Russell), whose sister Debbie (Russell again) is completely different in temperament. The two share a strong psychic bond, however, and when Jo dies in a suspicious hit-and-run accident Debbie feels compelled to return to claim her own. Based on the novel by Dylan Jones. **150m/C VHS, DVD.** *GB* Theresa Russell, Jonathan Pryce, Robert Pugh; **M:** Dave Evans; **W:** Trevor Preston.

Thicker than Water 🦴½ **1999 (R)** Typical urban gangsta flick. Two rival LA gang leaders, DJ and Lonzo, want to get into the music biz. They decide to put their rivalries aside and get the money for their venture by organizing their hometown boys and pushing product for drug kingpin Gator. But just when the money starts rolling in, Gator pulls a doublecross and the gang rivalries explode again. **90m/C DVD.** Mack-10, Fat Joe, Ice Cube, Kidada Jones, CJ Mac, MC Eight, Louis Freese, Flesh N Bone, Big Pun; **D:** Richard Cummings Jr.; **W:** Ernest Nyle Brown; **C:** Robert Benavides; **M:** Tyler Bates, Quincey Jones III.

The Thief 🦴🦴 **1952** An American commits treason and is overcome by guilt. Novel because there is not one word of dialogue, though the gimmick can't sustain the ordinary story. A product of the Communist scare of the 1950s, it tends to be pretentious and melodramatic. **84m/B VHS, DVD.** Ray Milland, Rita Gam, Martin Gabel, Harry Bronson, John McKutcheon; **D:** Russell Rouse; **W:** Russell Rouse, Clarence Greene; **C:** Sam Leavitt; **M:** Herschel Burke Gilbert.

Thief 🦴🦴½ **1971** A successful businessman (Crenna) attempts to put his criminal past behind him. He's trapped when looking for a quick way to get some money to pay off a gambling debt. Well-written and -directed drama with tepid acting. **74m/C VHS.** Richard Crenna, Angie Dickinson, Cameron Mitchell, Hurd Hatfield, Robert Webber; **D:** William A. Graham. TV

Thief 🦴🦴🦴 *Violent Streets* **1981 (R)** A big-time professional thief likes working solo, but decides to sign up with the mob in order to make one more big score and retire. He finds out it's not that easy. Taut and atmospheric film debut. **126m/C VHS, DVD.** James Caan, Tuesday Weld, Willie Nelson, James Belushi, Elizabeth Pena, Robert Prosky, Dennis Farina; **D:** Michael Mann; **W:** Michael Mann; **C:** Donald E. Thorin; **M:** Tangerine Dream.

The Thief 🦴🦴🦴 *Vor* **1997 (R)** Postwar Russian drama set in 1952. Katya (Rednikova) is a young widow with a six year-old-son, Sanya (Philipchuk). She's traveling by train when a handsome soldier named Tolyan (Mashkov) enters their compartment. But the end of the trip, Katya's decided to go off with Tolyan and the threesome become a family. But Tolyan harbors a violent streak and Katya also discovers that Tolyan is an imposter--he's not a soldier but a thief. Still, she loves him and soon becomes his accomplice. Russian with subtitles. **92m/C VHS, DVD.** *RU* Vladimir Mashkov, Yekaterina Rednikova, Misha Philipchuk; **D:** Pavel Chukhrai; **W:** Pavel Chukhrai; **C:** Vladimir Klimov; **M:** Vladimir Dashkevich.

The Thief and the Cobbler 🦴🦴½ **1996 (G)** Musically animated fairy tale about Tack, a humble cobbler (Broderick) who aids the clever and beautiful Princess Yum Yum (Beals) when their town's golden treasures are stolen. Legendary villain Price lends his voice as the evil Zig Zag. Three time Oscar winning director Williams (of "Who Framed Roger Rabbit?" fame), and a team of animators led by Harris (part of the team that created Bugs Bunny) created sophisticated optical illusions that the team dubbed "two and a half dimensional." Incorporating intricate lighting, shadows and smooth motion, the project took almost three decades to complete. Soundtrack performed by the London Symphony Orchestra. **72m/C VHS, DVD. D:** Richard Williams; **W:** Richard Williams; **C:** John Leatherbarrow; **M:** Robert Folk; **V:** Vincent Price, Matthew Broderick, Jennifer Beals, Eric Bogosian, Toni Collette, Jonathan Winters, Clive Revill, Kenneth Williams, Clinton Sundberg, Thick Wilson.

The Thief Lord 🦴🦴 **2006 (PG)** Fantasy set on a popular children's book by Cornelia Fulke, around the Venice setting is gorgeous, but it's best seen by undemanding kiddies who won't mind its contrivances. Orphaned brothers Prosper and Bo are befriended by teenaged Scipio, the self-proclaimed Thief Lord, who cares for a group of child thieves living in an abandoned cinema. Scipio is hired by a greedy dealer to find a mysterious antique that can allegedly reverse time and the brothers get caught up in the adventure. **98m/C DVD.** *GB GE LU* Aaron Johnson, Rollo Weeks, Jim Carter, Caroline Goodall, Jasper Harris, Alexei Sayle, Richard Bathurst; **D:** Richard Claus; **W:** Richard Claus, Daniel Musgrave; **C:** David Slama; **M:** Nigel Clarke, Michael Csanyi-Wills.

The Thief of Bagdad 🦴🦴🦴½ **1940** A wily young thief enlists the aid of a powerful genie to outwit the Grand Vizier of Baghdad. An Arabian Nights spectacular with lush photography, fine special effects, and striking score. Outstanding performance by Ingram as the genie. **106m/C VHS, DVD.** *GB* Sabu, Conrad Veidt, June Duprez, Rex Ingram, John Justin, Miles Malleson, Morton Selten, Mary Morris; **D:** Tim Whelan, Michael Powell, Ludwig Berger, Alexander Korda, Zoltan Korda, William Cameron Menzies; **W:** Lajos Biro, Miles Malleson; **C:** Georges Perinal; **M:** Miklos Rozsa. Oscars '40: Color Cinematog.

The Thief of Baghdad 🦴🦴🦴 **1924** The classic silent crowd-pleaser, about a roguish thief who uses a genie's magic to outwit Baghdad's evil Caliph. With famous special effects in a newly struck print, and a new score by Davis based on Rimsky-Korsakov's "Scheherezade." Remade many times. **153m/B VHS, DVD.** Douglas Fairbanks Sr., Snitz Edwards, Charles Belcher, Anna May Wong, Etta Lee, Brandon Hurst, Sojin, Julanne Johnston; **D:** Raoul Walsh; **M:** Carl Davis. Natl. Film Reg. '96.

Thief of Baghdad 🦴🦴 *Il Ladro Di Bagdad; Le Voleur De Bagdad* **1961** An Arabian Nights fantasy about a thief in love with a Sultan's daughter who has been poisoned. He seeks out the magical blue rose which is the antidote. Not as lavish as the previous two productions by this title, nor as much fun. **89m/C VHS.** *IT* Georgia Moll, Steve Reeves; **D:** Arthur Lubin.

The Thief of Baghdad 🦴🦴½ **1978 (G)** A fantasy-adventure about a genie, a prince, beautiful maidens, a happy-go-lucky thief, and magic. Easy to take, but not an extraordinary version of this oft-told tale. Ustinov is fun as he tries to marry off his daughter. **101m/C VHS.** Peter Ustinov, Roddy McDowall, Terence Stamp, Frank Finlay, Ian Holm; **D:** Clive Donner. TV

Thief of Hearts 🦴🦴 **1984 (R)** A thief steals a woman's diary when he's ransacking her house. He then pursues the woman, using his secret knowledge. Slick, but too creepy. Re-edited with soft porn scenes in some video versions. Stewart's first film. **101m/C VHS, DVD.** Steven Bauer, Barbara Williams, John Getz, Christine Ebersole, George Wendt; **D:** Douglas Day Stewart; **W:** Douglas Day Stewart; **C:** Andrew Laszlo; **M:** Harold Faltermeyer.

A Thief of Time 🦴🦴½ **2004** Navaho tribal policemen Joe Leaphorn and Jim Chee suspect a missing anthropologist was selling Anasazi pottery on the black market. This leads them to rival colleagues, poachers, and shady collectors, as well as dead bodies. Based on the novel by Tony Hillerman. **95m/C DVD.** Wes Studi, Adam Beach, Gary Farmer, Graham Greene, Sheila Toussey, Peter Fonda, Lee Tergesen, James Pollard; **D:** Chris Eyre; **W:** Alice Arden; **C:** Roy Wagner; **M:** B.C. Smith. TV

The Thief Who Came to Dinner 🦴🦴 **1973 (PG)** A computer analyst and a wealthy socialite team up to become jewel thieves and turn the tables on Houston's high society set. Comedy plot gets complex, though O'Neal and Bisset are likeable. Early Clayburgh role as O'Neal's ex. Based on a novel by Terence Lore Smith. **103m/C VHS.** Ryan O'Neal, Jacqueline Bisset, Warren Oates, Jill Clayburgh, Ned Beatty, Gregory Sierra, Michael Murphy, Austin Pendleton, John Hillerman, Charles Cioffi; **D:** Bud Yorkin; **W:** Walter Hill; **M:** Henry Mancini.

Thieves Like Us 🦴🦴🦴 **1974 (R)** Story of doomed lovers during the Depression is thoughtfully told by Altman. Older criminals Remsen and Schuck escape from jail with young killer Carradine. They only know one way to make a living--robbing banks--and it isn't long before they're once more working at their trade. They get a lot of press but they have a distinct problem. They're not really very good at what they do. Cops on their trail, the gang tries, unsuccessfully, to survive. Fletcher's film debut as Remsen's sister-in-law. Good period atmosphere and strong characters. Based on the novel by Edward Anderson and previously filmed as "They Live by Night." **123m/C VHS, DVD.** Keith Carradine, Shelley Duvall, Bert Remsen, John Schuck, Louise Fletcher, Anne Latham, Tom Skerritt; **D:** Robert Altman; **W:** Joan Tewkesbury, Calder Willingham, Robert Altman.

Thieves of Fortune WOOF! **1989 (R)** Former Miss Universe stars as a contestant in a high stakes fortune hunt that spans half the globe. She meets with more than her share of action-packed encounters among the ruffians who compete for the $28 million purse. Implausible; horrible script; clichéd. **100m/C VHS, DVD.** Michael Nouri, Lee Van Cleef, Shawn Weatherly; **D:** Michael Maccarone; **W:** Michael Maccarone; **C:** James Robb.

Thin Air 🦴🦴 *Robert B. Parker's Thin Air* **2000** Frank Belson (Ferry) didn't know much about his pretty new wife Lisa (Butler) before he married her. So when she suddenly disappears, he hires Spenser (Mantegna) to locate her and the PI also uncovers some secrets from her past. Based on the novel by Robert B. Parker. **90m/C DVD.** Joe Mantegna, Marcia Gay Harden, David Ferry, Yancy Butler, Luis Guzman, Jon

The Thin Blue Line 🌂🌂½ 2000 (R) Based on a real-life police corruption scandal that took place in the '70s in Philadelphia. Jonathan Neumann (Morrow) takes over the court beat for the Philadelphia Examiner and is soon wallowing in cases of police abuse, which he promptly documents in print. He's soon threatened by the cops and gets on the bad side of blustery mayor Frank Rizzo (Sorvino). Docudrama's kinda blustery itself. 97m/C VHS, DVD. Rob Morrow, Randy Quaid, Paul Sorvino, Cynthia (Cyndy) Preston, G.W. Bailey, Al Waxman, Beau Starr, Chuck Shamata; D: Roger Young; W: Daniel Helfgott; C: Donald M. Morgan; M: Patrick Williams. CABLE

The Thin Blue Line 🌂🌂🌂½ 1988 The acclaimed docudrama about the 1977 shooting of a cop in Dallas County, and the incorrect conviction of Randall Adams for the crime. A riveting, spellbinding experience. Due to the film's impact and continued lobbying by Morris, Adams is now free. 101m/C VHS, DVD. D: Errol Morris; W: Philip Glass; C: Robert Chappell, Stefan Czapsky. M: Philip Glass. Natl. Film Reg. '01.

Thin Ice 🌂🌂🌂 1937 Successful musical romance featuring European prince Power falling for commoner Henie. A fine score, solid script, and Henie's excellent ice skating routines make this her best film. Based on the play "Der Komet" by Attila Obok. 🎵I'm Olga from the Volga; My Secret Love Affair; Over Night. 78m/B VHS. Sonja Henie, Tyrone Power, Arthur Treacher, Raymond Walburn, Joan Davis, Alan Hale, Sig Rumann, Melville Cooper, Maurice Cass, George Givot, Torben Meyer; D: Sidney Lanfield; W: Boris Ingster, Milton Sperling.

A Thin Line Between Love and Hate 🌂 1996 (R) Writer/director/star Lawrence shows that there's no line between a crude, foulmouthed ego trip and an unfunny, unsuspenseful film. Darnell Wright is a smooth talker constantly on the lookout for women to conquer and discard. Eventually, he meets the wrong lady (Whitfield), a classic movie psycho who turns his life upside down. Drawing heavily from "Fatal Attraction," this half-hearted effort offers bad pacing, a weak script, and totally unsympathetic characters, which could almost be overlooked if it was at all funny. Whitfield holds the flick's only redeeming value as the femme fatale. 106m/C VHS, DVD. Tracy Morgan, Martin Lawrence, Lynn Whitfield, Regina King, Bobby Brown, Della Reese, Roger E. Mosley, Malinda Williams, Daryl (Chill) Mitchell, Simbi Khali; D: Martin Lawrence; W: Martin Lawrence, Bentley Kyle Evans, Kenny Buford, Kim Bass; C: Francis Kenny; M: Roger Troutman.

The Thin Man 🌂🌂🌂½ 1934 Married sleuths Nick (Powell) and Nora (Loy) Charles investigate the mysterious disappearance of a wealthy inventor. Charming and sophisticated, this was the model for husband-and-wife detective teams that followed. Don't miss Asta, their wire-hair terrier. Based on the novel by Dashiell Hammett. Its enormous popularity triggered five sequels, starting with "After the Thin Man." 90m/B VHS, DVD. William Powell, Myrna Loy, Maureen O'Sullivan, Cesar Romero, Porter Hall, Nat Pendleton, Minna Gombell, Natalie Moorhead, Edward Ellis; D: Woodbridge S. Van Dyke; W: Albert Hackett, Frances Goodrich; C: James Wong Howe. Natl. Film Reg. '97.

The Thin Man Goes Home 🌂🌂½ 1944 Married sleuths Nick and Nora Charles solve a mystery with Nick's disapproving parents looking on in the film from the "Thin Man" series. Despite a three-year gap and slightly less chemistry between Powell and Loy, audiences welcomed the skinny guy. Sequel to "Shadow of the Thin Man"; followed by "Song of the Thin Man". 100m/B VHS, DVD. William Powell, Myrna Loy, Lucile Watson, Gloria De Haven, Anne Revere, Harry Davenport, Helen Vinson, Lloyd Corrigan, Donald Meek, Edward Brophy, Charles Halton; D: Richard Thorpe.

The Thing 🌂🌂🌂 1982 (R) A team of scientists at a remote Antarctic outpost discover a buried spaceship with an unwelcome alien survivor still alive. Bonbas-tic special effects overwhelm the suspense and the solid cast. Less a remake of the 1951 science fiction classic than a more faithful version of John Campbell's short story "Who Goes There?," since the seeds/spores take on human shapes. Available colorized. 109m/C VHS, DVD, HD DVD, Kurt Russell, Wilford Brimley, T.K. Carter, Richard Masur, Keith David, Richard Dysart, David Clennon, Donald Moffat, Thomas G. Waites, Charles Hallahan; D: John Carpenter; W: Bill Lancaster; C: Dean Cundey; M: Ennio Morricone.

The Thing: About My Folks 🌂🌂½ 2005 (PG-13) What happens when an old man on the brink of a divorce drops into his adult son's life? You get a vehicle for Peter Falk's patented crusty lovability. Sam Kleinman (Falk), after a lifetime spent buried in his work, is alone and unfulfilled after his wife Muriel (Dukakis) walks out. Son Ben (Reiser), a successful New York professional who is happily married to Rachel (Perkins), is considering a move to the country. Ben takes his father to inspect a property and the two are plunged into an adventure

The Thing 🌂🌂½ 1951 One of the best of the Cold War allegories and a potent lesson to those who won't eat their vegetables. Sci fi classic about an alien craft and creature (Arness in monster drag), discovered by an Arctic research team. The critter is accidentally thawed and then wreaks havoc, sucking the blood from sled dog and scientist alike. It's a giant seed-dispersing vegetable run amuck, unaffected by missing body parts, bullets, or cold. In other words, Big Trouble. Excellent direction assisted substantially by producer Hawks. Loosely based on "Who Goes There?" by John Campbell. Also known as "The Thing from Another World." 87m/B VHS, DVD. James Arness, Kenneth Tooey, Margaret Sheridan, Dewey Martin, Robert Cornthwaite, Douglas Spencer, James L. Young, Robert Nichols, William (Bill) Self, Eduard Franz, Sally Creighton, John Dierkes, George Fenneman; D: Christian Nyby, Howard Hawks; W: Charles Lederer, Ben Hecht; C: Russell Harlan; M: Dimitri Tiomkin. Natl. Film Reg. '01.

Things Behind the Sun 🌂🌂½ 2001 (R) Writer/director Anders partially takes on her own traumatic past to tell a story of rape and its long aftermath. Troubled singer-songwriter Sherry McGrale (Dickens) has a radio hit with a song about being raped as a girl in her Florida hometown. Music reporter Owen (Mann) gets the assignment to interview Sherry after

---

The Thin Red Line 🌂🌂🌂½ 1964 First adaptation of the James Jones novel about the fight for Guadalcanal focuses on the relationship between Sgt Welsh (Warden) and Pvt. Doll (Dullea). As battle experience hardens Doll, the mutual hatred the two have changes to a grudging respect. Effectively portrays the dehumanizing psychological effects of war. 99m/B VHS, DVD. Keir Dullea, Jack Warden, James Philbrook, Kieron Moore, Ray Daley, Merlyn Yordan, Bob Kanter, Stephen Levy; D: Andrew Marton; W: Bernard Gordon; C: Manuel Berenguer. M: Malcolm Arnold.

The Thin Red Line 🌂🌂🌂 1998 (R) After a long hiatus, director Malick returns in this epic WWII saga about a rifle company fighting at Guadalcanal. Visually stunning and focused on the inner thoughts, feelings, and philosophical leanings of the soldiers, the film sacrifices plot and continuity to study the questions of Man vs. Nature and the Origin of Evil. Plot similarities are highlighted by the physical and Caviezel. Combat scenes are, naturally, beautifully shot and effective, while the relationship between Penn and Caviezel makes the biggest impression among the many subplots (some of which go nowhere) and the star-laden, large cast. Based on the 1962 novel by James Jones. 170m/C VHS, DVD. Kirk Acevedo, Miranda Otto, Nick Stahl, James (Jim) Caviezel, Adrien Brody, Sean Penn, Nick Nolte, John Cusack, George Clooney, Woody Harrelson, Ben Chaplin, Elias Koteas, Jared Leto, John Travolta, Tim Blake Nelson, John C. Reilly, John Savage, Arie Verveen, David Harrod, Thomas Jane, Paul Gleason, Penelope Allen, Don Harvey, Shawn Hatosy, Donal Logue, Dash Mihok, Larry Romano; D: Terrence Malick; W: Terrence Malick (John Toll; M: Hans Zimmer. N.Y. Film Critics '98. Cinematog.

The Thing with Two Heads 🌂🌂½ 1972 (PG) The inspired box copy says it all: "They share the same body...but hate each other's guts" Max Kirshner (Milland), a white racist surgeon, plans to cheat death by having his head attached to another body, imagine his surprise when he finds his noggin stitched onto black Jack Moss (Grier), right next to the original head. Nobody involved is taking the material too seriously. 93m/C DVD. Ray Milland, Roosevelt "Rosie" Grier, Don Marshall, Roger Perry, Kathrine Baumann, Lee Frost, Wes Bishop, Rick Baker; D: Lee Frost; W: James Gordon White; C: Jack Steely; M: Robert O. Ragland.

Things 🌂 1987 A man creates a monster during his freakish experiments with artificial insemination. The monster "returns to his house seeking revenge, and the man's visiting brother and a friend disappear, probably a clever move given their lackluster circumstances. 90m/C VHS. Barry Gillis, Amber Lynn, Doug Bunston, Bruce Roach; D: Andrew Jordan.

Things 🌂🌂🌂 1993 Two horror tales told by a jilted wife who's holding her husband's mistress hostage. "The Box" finds evil Mayor Black (Delania) incensed about a newly opened brothel in his hick Nevada town. So he decides to teach the nookers a lesson with the help of a bizarre, boxed creature that's with him at all times. "Thing in a Jar" finds an abusive husband and his mistress plotting to kill his mousy wife. Only the murder victim comes back to haunt the deadly duo—at least parts of her do. Nicely grotesque special effects courtesy of Mike Tristano. 85m/C VHS. Neil Delama, Trey Howard, Debra Stevens, Courtney Lercara, Kinder Hunt; Cameos: Jeff Burr; D: Dennis Devine, Jay Woelfel; W: Dennis Devine, Steve Jarvis, Mike Bowler.

Things 2 🌂🌂½ 1997 Sequel to 1993's "Things." When a pizza delivery girl gets stranded at the creepy home of a strange horror novelist she entertains her with two tales of terror. Oh yes, if the girl can solve the mysteries within the stories, she gets to live, if not, well... The first has a cheating wife plotting to rid herself of her command. But the creature has other ideas. The second story finds a fashion photographer suspecting that a serial killer stalking her neighborhood may not be human. 85m/C VHS. Angela Eads, David Hussey, Rich Ward, Margie Rey; D: Steve Jarvis, Dennis Devine, Mike Bowler; W: Steve Jarvis, Dennis Devine, Mike Bowler; C: Craig Incadrone; M: Adam Karpel.

The Thing Called Love 🌂🌂½ 1993 (PG-13) Take last year's surprise hit "Singles" and replace grunge rock and Seattle with Country/Western and Nashville for the plot comes from the real-life Bluebird Cafe—the place where all aspiring singers and songwriters want to perform. Phoenix, Mathis, Mulroney, and Bullock did their own singing; look for Oslin as the Cafe owner. Phoenix's last completed film role. 116m/C VHS. River Phoenix, Samantha Mathis, Sandra Bullock, Dermot Mulroney, K.T. Oslin, Anthony Clark, Webb Wilder, Cameos, Trisha Yearwood; D: Peter Bogdanovich; W: Allan Moyle, Carol Heikkinen; C: Peter James.

Things Change 🌂🌂🌂 1988 (PG) An old Italian shoeshine guy agrees, for a fee, to be a fall guy for the Mafia. A lower-echelon mob hood, assigned to watch over him, decides to give the old guy a weekend of fun in Vegas before going to jail. Director Mamet co-wrote the screenplay with Silverstein, best-known for the children's books ("Where the Sidewalk Ends," "The Giving Tree"). Combines charm and menace with terrific performances, especially from Ameche and Mantegna. 114m/C VHS, DVD. Joe Mantegna, Don Ameche, Robert Prosky, J.J. Johnston, Ricky Jay, Mike Nussbaum, Jack Wallace, Dan Conway, J.T. Walsh, William H. Macy; D: David Mamet; W: David Mamet, Shel Silverstein; M: Alaric Jans. Venice Film Fest. '80: Actor (Ameche); Venice Film Fest. '88: Actor (Mantegna).

Things Happen at Night 🌂 1948 Scientist and insurance investigator determine that friendly ghost has possessed a family's youngest daughter. Not much happens. 79m/B VHS, GB Gordon Harker, Alfred Drayton, Robertson Hare, Olga Lindo, Wylie Watson; D: Francis Searle.

Things I Never Told You 🌂 1996 Over-educated clerk Ann's (Taylor) just been dumped long-distance by her boyfriend. After a half-hearted suicide attempt, she calls a hot line and is connected to Don (McCarthy), who's equally depressed about the way his life is going. He discovers who Ann is and tentatively begins to court her, without revealing his true identity. The entire movie is tentative (including most of the performances). 93m/C VHS, DVD. Lili Taylor, Andrew McCarthy, Debi Mazar, Alexis Arquette, Leslie Mann, Richard Edson, Seymour Cassel; D: Isabel Coixet; W: Isabel Coixet; C: Teresa Medina; M: Alfonso Vilallonga.

Things in Their Season 🌂🌂½ 1974 Melodrama about the imminent death of the mother of a Wisconsin farm family who makes those around her realize the value of happiness. Neal is excellent, rest of cast better than average in a well-told and sincere film. 79m/C VHS. Patricia Neal, Ed Flanders, Marc Singer, Meg Foster; D: James Goldstone. TV

The Things of Life 🌂🌂🌂 Les Choses De La Vie 1970 A car crash makes a man re-evaluate his life, goals, and loves. French with English subtitles. 89m/C VHS, FR Romy Schneider, Michel Piccoli, Lea Massari; D: Claude Sautet.

Things to Come 🌂🌂🌂 1936 Dissatisfied 25-year-old Adam (Stansko) quits his office job and moves back home for the summer. He comes up with a list of things he's always wanted to do and decides to see what he can accomplish before ultimately returning to adult responsibility. He enlists eccentric high-school buddy Mac (Wilson) to help him out. Of course, things don't always work out as expected. 85m/C DVD. CA Daniel Wilson, Michael Stansko, Amy Ballantyne, Paul McManus, Joanne Oke, Santic D'Asaro; D: Theodore Bezaire; W: Michael Stansko; C: Eric Schiller; M: Michael Bliss.

---

which includes a classic car, a billiard hall in school and a fishing trip, all of which serve as a framework for unraveling the meaning of life. Totally worth seeing Falk's magic. When Owen finally meets Sherry again, the circumstances of the past are revealed to them both. 117m/C VHS, DVD, Kim Dickens, Gabriel Mann, Don Cheadle, Eric Stoltz, Elizabeth Peña, Rosanna Arquette, Alison Folland, Patsy Kensit, CCH Pounder; D: Allison Anders; W: Allison Anders, Kurt Voss; C: Terry Stacey.

revealing that he and Sherry were friends in school and he knows who "raped" her.

Things to Do in Denver When You're Dead 🐾🐾🐾 1995

(R) Jimmy the Saint (Garcia) is an ex-mobster gone straight who is called upon by his former boss, the Man With the Plan (Walken), to do one last easy-money job. Jimmy agrees and rounds up his old gang, a colorfully off-color group which includes Pieces (Lloyd), a porn movie projectionist and Critical Bill (Williams), a hair-trigger psycho who works in a funeral parlor. The job goes awry and the group becomes a target of hitman Mr. Shhh (Buscemi). Hipster dialogue, crime-gone-wrong formula, and the presence of Buscemi instantly scream Tarantino rip-off, but the performances make it a worthwhile genre entry. 115m/C VHS, DVD. Andy Garcia, Christopher Lloyd, William Forsythe, Bill Nunn, Treat Williams, Jack Warden, Steve Buscemi, Fairuza Balk, Gabrielle Anwar, Christopher Walken, Glenn Plummer, Don Cheadle, Bill Cobbs, Josh Charles, Michael Nicolosi, Marshall Bell, Sarah Trigger, Jenny McCarthy, Tommy (Tiny) Lister; *D:* Gary Fleder; *M:* Michael Convertino.

Things We Lost in the Fire 🐾🐾½ 2007

(R) Audrey Burke (Berry) is the widow of murdered husband Brian (Duchovny—who, for a dead character has a lot of screen time). Although she's left financially sound, she is now a grieving single mother to two young children. Audrey invites Brian's best friend, heroin addict Jerry Sunborne (Del Toro), to the funeral and something makes the two of them put aside their obvious and seemingly overwhelming differences to cling together in their grief. What works is the emotional interplay between the two, as Jerry struggles to kick his habit and Audrey struggles to rebuild a new life for herself and her children; both Del Toro and Berry shine. What doesn't is that too many elements—the differing ethnic backgrounds, Jerry's addiction, Audrey's acceptance of Jerry—simply beg questions, and at times the study of grief overpowers and feels manufactured. 118m/C DVD. *US* Halle Berry, Benicio Del Toro, David Duchovny, Alison Lohman, Omar Benson Miller, John Carroll Lynch, Robin Weigert, Alexis Llewellyn, Micah Berry; Paula Newsome; *D:* Suzanne (Susanne) Bier; *W:* Allan Loeb; *C:* Tom Stern; *M:* Johan Soderqvist.

Things You Can Tell Just by Looking at Her 🐾🐾½ 2000

(PG-13) Ensemble female cast tells five stories that intersect in odd ways. Dr. Keener (Close) gets unhappy romantic Rose Baker), who becomes intrigued by her new neighbor—a dwarf (Woodburn), and finally staid Kathy (Brenneman) and her exuberantly sexy blind sister Carol (Diaz). 106m/C VHS, DVD. Cameron Diaz, Glenn Close, Calista Flockhart, Holly Hunter, Amy Brenneman, Kathy Baker, Valeria Golino, Matt Craven, Gregory Hines, Noah Fleiss, Miguel (Michael) Sandoval, Danny Woodburn, Roma Maffia; *D:* Rodrigo Garcia; *W:* Rodrigo Garcia; *C:* Emmanuel Lubezki; *M:* Ed Shearmur.

Think Big 🐾🐾½ 1990

(PG-13) Former professional wrestlers, the Pauls are truck drivers in this silly, enjoyable comedy. When a brilliant teenager runs... running from bad guys. Mayhem ensues. 86m/C VHS. Peter Paul, David Paul, Martin Mull, Ari Meyers, Richard Kiel, David Carradine, Richard Moll, Peter Lupus; *W:* Jim Wynorski, R.J. Robertson.

Think Dirty 🐾🐾 1970

Every Home Should Have One 1970 Lascivious comedy about ad exec Feldman's attempt to develop a series of sexy commercials to sell cereal. At the same time his wife forms a "clean up TV" group. Not very interesting or funny. 93m/C VHS. *GB* Marty Feldman, Judy Cornwell, Shelley Berman; *D:* Jim Clark.

Think Fast, Mr. Moto 🐾🐾½ 1937

Japanese sleuth Mr. Moto (Lorre) is trailing diamond smugglers and boards a ship bound for Shanghai. He befriends Robert Hitchings (Beck), the son of the ship's owner. Robert has fallen for singer Gloria (Field) who's tied in with the smugglers (and, upon their arrival, Moto must sort out the criminals from the patsies. More action-packed than the Charlie Chan mysteries although Mr. Moto is inscrutable. Based on the J.P. Marquand novels. First in the series. 66m/B DVD. Peter Lorre, Thomas Beck, Virginia Field, Lee Phelps, Sig Rumann, John Rogers, Murray Kinnell; *D:* Norman Foster; *W:* Norman Foster, Charles Kenyon, Howard E. Smith; *C:* Harry Jackson; *M:* Samuel Kaylin.

Think Tank 🐾 2006

(PG) Four 20-something uber-nerds are horrified when their favorite hang-out—the local pool hall—is in danger of closing. So they use their smarts to come up with a solution. Goofy and gross-free dumb comedy. 90m/C DVD. Tina Majorino, Eric Artell, Keith Paugh, Greg Neil, Michael Miranda, Gordon Goodman, Brian Petersen; *D:* Brian Petersen; *W:* Brian Petersen; *M:* John Swihart. VIDEO

Thinkin' Big 🐾 1987

(R) Guys and gals cavort on the Texas coast, except for one lonely fat guy who tries to increase his sexual prowess. The usual teen sex frenzy. 96m/C VHS. Bruce Anderson, Kenny Sargent, Randy Jandt, Nancy Buechler, Darla Ralston; *D:* S.F. Browning.

The Third 🐾🐾 *Der Dritte; Her Third* 1972

Margit (Hoffmann) has two children and two divorces after marrying men who wanted her more than she wanted them. So when Margit decides to take a third chance on love, she resolves to do the choosing. She picks unsuspecting colleague Hrdlistchka (Ludwig) and is determined to get him to say yes. German with subtitles. 107m/C VHS. *GE* Jutta Hoffmann, Rolf Ludwig, Armin Mueller-Stahl, Peter Kohnke, Barbara Dittus; *D:* Egon Gunther; *W:* Gunther Rucker; *C:* Erich Gusko; *M:* Karl-Ernst Sasse.

Third Degree Burn 🐾🐾 1989

Mystery about a small-time detective hired by a businessman to follow a woman, only to become a suspect when the woman's real husband is killed. 97m/C VHS. Treat Williams, Virginia Madsen, Richard Masur; *D:* Roger Spottiswoode. CABLE

The Third Key 🐾🐾½ *The Long Arm* 1957

A solid British crime drama follows a dogged detective as he probes serial safe-crackings, with a climax set at London's Festival Hall. Based on the book by Robert Barr, who co-scripted. 96m/B VHS. Jack Hawkins, Dorothy Allison, Geoffrey Keen, Richard Leech, Ian Bannen; *D:* Charles Frend.

The Third Man 🐾🐾🐾🐾 1949

An American writer of pulp westerns (Cotten) arrives in post-war Vienna to take a job with an old friend, but discovers he has been murdered. Or has he? Based on Graham Greene's mystery, this classic film noir plays on national loyalties during the Cold War. Welles is top-notch as the manipulative Harry Lime, black-market drug dealer extraordinaire. The underground sewer sequence is not to be missed. With a haunting (sometimes irritating) theme by Anton Karas on unaccompanied zither. 104m/B VHS, DVD. *GB* Joseph Cotten, Orson Welles, Alida Valli, Trevor Howard, Bernard Lee, Wilfrid Hyde-White, Ernst Deutsch, Erich Ponto, Siegfried Breuer, Frederick Bielbtrau, Paul Hoerbiger, Herbert Halbik, Frederick Schreiber, Jenny Werner, Nelly Arno, Alexis Chesnakov, Leo Bieber, Paul Hardtmuth, Geoffrey Keen, Annie Rosar; *D:* Carol Reed; *W:* Graham Greene; *C:* Robert Krasker; *M:* Anton Karas. Oscars '50: B&W Cinematog.; AFI '98: Top 100; British Acad. '49: Film; Cannes '49: Film; Directors Guild '49: Director (Reed).

Third Man on the Mountain 🐾🐾½ *Banner in the Sky* 1959

(G) A family epic about mountain climbing, shot in Switzerland and based on James Ramsey Ullman's "Banner in the Sky." A young man is determined to climb the "Citadel" as his ancestors have. He finds their "Citadel" as his ancestors have. imagined. Look for Helen Hayes (MacArthur's mother) in a cameo. Standard Disney adventure drama. 106m/C VHS, DVD. James MacArthur, Michael Rennie, Janet Munro, James Donald, Herbert Lom, Laurence Naismith; *Cameos:* Helen Hayes; *D:* Ken Annakin.

Third Man Out: A Donald Strachey Mystery 🐾🐾½ 2005

Donald Stachey (Allen) is a semi-successful gay PI who works in Albany, New York and lives with his politico lover, Tim Callahan (Spence). Donald reluctantly takes the case of hectoring gay activist John Rutka (Wetherall), whose tabloid outings have made him a target for violence. When Rutka winds up dead, Donald has a long list of suspects but things aren't always what they appear to be. Adapted from Richard Stevenson's 1992 mystery. 98m/C DVD. *US* Chad Allen, Sebastian Spence, Jack Wetherall, Sean Young, Woody Jeffreys; *D:* Ron Oliver; *W:* Mark Saltzman. CABLE

The Third Miracle 🐾🐾🐾½ 1999

(R) Harris makes for one sexy and dynamic priest. He's Father Frank Shore who is struggling with his faith and is in a kind of voluntary retirement. However, he's summoned by power player, Bishop Cahill (Haid), to investigate the purported miracles of the late Helen O'Regan (Sukowa). A cult is growing up around her memory and the mention of sainthood (which requires three proven miracles) has the church wary. Film is set in Chicago in 1979 and based on the book by Richard Vetere. 119m/C VHS, DVD. Ed Harris, Anne Heche, Charles Haid, Armin Mueller-Stahl, Michael Rispoli, Jean-Louis Roux, Ken James, James Gallanders, Barbara Sukowa; *D:* Agnieszka Holland; *W:* John Romano, Richard Vetere; *C:* Jerzy Zielinski; *M:* Jan A.P. Kaczmarek.

The Third Sex 🐾🐾 *Anders Als du und Ich* 1957

One of the first films to deal with homosexuality in which parents try to "straighten out" their gay son. German with subtitles. 90m/C VHS. *GE* Paul Dahlke, Paula Wesley, Hans Nielsen, Christian Wolff, Friedrich Joloff, Hilde Korber, Gunther Theil; *D:* Veit Harlan; *W:* Felix Lutzkendorff; *C:* Kurt Grigoleit; *M:* Erwin Halletz.

Third Solution 🐾🐾 *Russicum* 1989

(R) An Italian-made film about the discovery of a secret pact made between the Kremlin and the Vatican that may start WWIII. Well-cast, but poorly conceived spook drama, with music by Vangelis. 93m/C VHS. *IT* Treat Williams, F. Murray Abraham, Danny Aiello, Nigel Court, Rita Rusic, Rossano Brazzi; *D:* Pasquale Squitieri; *M:* Vangelis.

Third Walker 🐾 1979

A desperate woman sacrifices her marriage to immerse herself in efforts to reunite her twin sons, who were inadvertently separated at birth. An original and intriguing directorial debut by McLuhan. 85m/C VHS. *CA* William Shatner, Colleen Dewhurst, Marshall McLuhan, Monique Mercure, Andree Pelletier; *D:* Teri McLuhan; *W:* Teri McLuhan, Robert Thom.

The Third Wheel 🐾🐾 2002

(PG-13) Shy businessman Stanley finally gets up the nerve to ask out coworker Diana (Richards) after pining for her for a year. The night of the date, he hits a homeless guy Phil (screenwriter Lacopo) with his car, so Phil tags along. Stan also has to deal with a bunch of co-workers who've wagered on the outcome of the date, and are secretly monitoring the proceedings. Damon and Affleck's planned follow-up to "Good Will Hunting" sat on a shelf at Miramax for over two years, probably because of the inconsistent laughs and direction. Good cast does what it can with what it has to work with. 90m/C DVD. Luke Wilson, Denise Richards, Ben Affleck, Jay Lacopo, Matt Damon, Meredith Salenger, Bobby Slayton, Lauren Graham, Nicole Sullivan; *D:* Jordan Brady; *W:* Jay Lacopo; *C:* Jonathan Brown; *M:* Lisa Coleman, Wendy Melvoin. VIDEO

Third World Cop 🐾🐾 1999

(R) Detective Capone (Campbell) returns to his childhood home in Kingston and discovers that his best bud Ratty (Danvers) is the right-hand man for local crime boss One Hand (Bradshaw). Their friendship leaves the gangsters suspicious that Ratty is a police informer but even when he finally agrees to help Capone, things go wrong. Straight-ahead crime story does have the advantage of the Jamaican settings to take it out of the norm. 98m/C VHS, DVD. *JM* Paul Campbell, Carl Bradshaw, Mark Danvers, Audrey Reid; *D:* Christopher Browne; *W:* Christopher Browne, Suzanne Fenn, Chris Salewicz; *C:* Richard Lannaman; *M:* Sly Dunbar, Robbie Shakespeare.

Thirst 🐾🐾 1987

(R) A girl is abducted by a secret society that wants her to become their new leader. There is just one catch: she has to learn to like the taste of human blood. Chilling but weakly plotted. 96m/C VHS, DVD. David Hemmings, Henry Silva, Chantal Contouri; *D:* Rod Hardy.

The Thirst 🐾🐾½ 2006

Since Lisa (Kramer) has terminal cancer, she doesn't ask a lot of questions when Mariel (Scott Thomas) offers a chance at life—even if it's the undead kind. Naturally, ex-beau Maxx (Keeslar) is confused to see her out clubbing, but Lisa soon turns him and they join Eurotrash Darius (Sisto and his wandering accent) and his blood crew. Eventually the reunited lovebirds find out they don't really enjoy swilling human red. 88m/C DVD. Matt Keeslar, Clare Kramer, Jeremy Sisto, Serena Scott Thomas, Neil Jackson, Adam Baldwin, Erik Palladino, Charlotte Ayanna; *D:* Jeremy Kasten; *W:* Jeremy Kasten; *C:* Raymond N. Stella; *M:* Joe Kraemer. VIDEO

The Thirsty Dead woof! *The Blood Cult of Shangri-La; Blood Hunt* 1974

(PG) Maybe they could learn to like Gatorade. An eternally young jungle king is looking for a wife. She can be young forever too, if she's not overcome vampirism and sacrificing virgins. In spite of the jungle vampire slant, this Filipino-made movie is a woofer. 90m/C VHS, DVD. *PH* John Considine, Jennifer Billingsley, Judith McConnell, Fredricka Meyers, Tani Phelps Guthrie; *D:* Terry Becker.

Thirteen 🐾🐾🐾 2003

(R) Genuinely original indie probes the transformation of Tracy (Wood) a well-behaved, slightly nerdy, L.A. teen who, practically overnight, becomes a ragingly rebellious, boy-crazy shoplifter, thanks to psychologically scarred but savvy schoolmate Evie (co-writer Reed), who invites Tracy into her world of popularity, piercings, and partying. As Tracy's mom Melanie, a recovering alcoholic, frets over Tracy's disturbing personality makeover, Evie begins to bond with her. Performances are uniformly sparkling. Spot-on characters and all-too-real details come from director/co-writer Hardwicke's collaboration with the then 13-year-old Reed—whom she met while dating Reed's father—the real-life good girl of the story. 95m/C VHS, DVD. *US* Evan Rachel Wood, Nikki Reed, Holly Hunter, Jeremy Sisto, Deborah Kara Unger, Kip Pardue, Brady Corbet, Sarah Clarke, D.W. Moffett; *D:* Catherine Hardwicke; *W:* Nikki Reed, Catherine Hardwicke; *C:* Elliot Davis; *M:* Mark Mothersbaugh. Ind. Spirit '04: Debut Perf. (Reed); Sundance '03: Director (Hardwicke).

Thirteen Conversations About One Thing 🐾🐾🐾½ 2001

(R) "We plan, God laughs," as the saying goes. Smart, literary indie offers a fresh take on the familiar theme of destiny and the forms it takes. Focuses on the intersecting lives of five New Yorkers: college physics professor Turturro wants to change his boring life; housewife Irving confronts her hubby about his infidelity; lawyer McConaughey's life suddenly takes a wrong turn; housekeeper DuVall waits for something wonderful to happen; and cynical businessman Arkin is disturbed by his relentlessly upbeat coworker. Director Jill Sprecher and her sister, cowriter Karen, illustrates (in 13 sections), how even the smallest actions can have enormous consequences. Detailed omens arise everywhere, foreshadowing events to come in this karma chameleon of a movie. Well written, deftly directed and smartly written. 104m/C VHS, DVD. *US* Matthew McConaughey, Alan Arkin, John Turturro, Clea DuVall, Amy Irving, Barbara Sukowa, Tia Texada, Frankie Faison, William Wise, Shawn Elliott, David Connolly, Alex Burns; *D:* Jill Sprecher; *W:* Jill Sprecher, Karen Sprecher; *C:* Dick Pope; *M:* Alex Wurman.

Thirteen Days 🐾🐾🐾½ 2000

(PG-13) The Cuban Missile Crisis seen through the eyes of President JFK, Attorney General Robert Kennedy, and presidential aide Kenny O'Donnell (Costner). Director Donaldson wisely opts not to over-dramatize what was clearly a suspenseful story to begin with (and realizes, as well, that we know the outcome). The few sacrifices of historical accuracy are basically harmless. Greenwood and Culp ably handle the often difficult task of portraying the brothers Kennedy, and Costner is solid as the brothers' trusted confidante. Together on 1987's "No Way Out." **145m/C VHS, DVD.** Kevin Costner, Bruce Greenwood, Steven Culp, Dylan Baker, Michael Fairman, Kevin Conway, Tim Kelleher, Len Cariou, Bill Smitrovich, Dakin Matthews, Madison Mason, Christopher Lawford, Ed Lauter, Elya Baskin, Boris Krutonog, Peter White, James Karen, Tim Jerome, Olek Krupa, Lucinda Jenney, Henry Strozier, Frank Wood, Stephanie Romanov; **D:** Roger Donaldson; **W:** David Self; **C:** Andrzej Bartkowiak; **M:** Trevor Jones.

13 Going on 30 🐾🐾½ **2004 (PG-13)** Broadly appealing Garner makes the successful leap to bona fide big screen lead in this harmless body-switch comedy. Jenna (Allen) is an insecure 13-year-old who magically becomes the "30"-year-old and thriving" fashion magazine editor played by Garner. Comedy ensues when she is forced to deal with adult concerns foreign to a 13-year-old, including work at the magazine; her new, mature body; and her hockey player boyfriend, all of which she does with an endearing childlike zeal. Along with the perks, Jenna's transformation has also alienated her former best friend Matt (Marquette), once a chubby nerd who is now, 17 years later, a handsome and engaged hunk (Buffalo). Of course, Jenna would like to get reacquainted. Garner and Ruffalo elevate a so-so vehicle into an appealing romantic comedy. **97m/C DVD.** US Jennifer Garner, Mark Ruffalo, Judy Greer, Andy Serkis, Christa B. Allen, Kathy Baker, Phil Reeves, Joe Grifasi, Courtney Chase, Maz Jobrani, Robine Lee, Jim Gaffigan, Sean Marquette, Alex Black, Alexandra Kyle, Renee Olstead; **D:** Gary Winick; **W:** Josh Goldsmith, Cathy Yuspa; **C:** Don Burgess; **M:** Theodore Shapiro.

13 Moons 🐾🐾 **2002 (R)** Only a full moon in Los Angeles could pull together several intertwining yet divergent storylines to tell what really is a simple tale of a man, Mo (Proval), whose son, Timmy (Wolff), will die without a kidney transplant. Problem is the donor is a drug addict who flees the hospital. Along with a rag-tag group of otherwise-afflicted folks (including a fired TV clown, a stripper, and a rap executive), Mo must find him...and fast! While the performances evoke a sense of sincerity, the backbone is too weak to support them. **94m/C VHS, DVD.**

13 Ghosts 🐾🐾½ **1960** A dozen ghosts need another member to round out their ranks. They have four likely candidates to choose from when a family moves into the house inhabited by the ghoulish group. Originally viewed with "Illusion-O," a technology much like "3-D," which allowed the viewing of the ghosts only through a special pair of glasses. **88m/C VHS, DVD.** Charles Herbert, Jo Morrow, Martin Milner, Rosemary DeCamp, Donald Woods, Margaret Hamilton, John van Dreelen; **D:** William Castle; **W:** Robb White; **C:** Joseph Biroc; **M:** Von Dexter.

13 Ghosts 🐾🐾 **2001 (R)** Another attempt to meld humor and horror in a William Castle remake a/a/a "House on Haunted Hill" and it's up to Arthur to stop it. The special effects are above average, which is good, because the main attraction powered by ghosts complete with whirling gears and sliding glass panels that attack the inhabitants. It seems that crazy Uncle Cyrus built the house to open the Eye of Hell. Arthur (Shalhoub) inherits a weird glass mansion from his shadowy Uncle Cyrus (Abraham). He moves into the house with his kids Kathy (Elizabeth) and Bobby (Roberts) and their nanny Maggie (Digga). Along for kicks is spastic psychic Rafkin (Lillard). **91m/C VHS, DVD.** US Tony Shalhoub, Embeth Davidtz, Matthew Lillard, Shannon Elizabeth, Alec Roberts, Rah Digga, J.R. Bourne, F. Murray Abraham; **D:** Steve Beck; **W:** Richard D'Ovidio, Neal Marshall Stevens; **C:** Gale Tattersall; **M:** John (Gianni) Frizzell.

Steve Buscemi, Karyn Parsons, Peter Dinklage, David Proval, Austin Wolff, Deryl (Chili) Mitchell, Rose Rollins, Peter Stormare, Pruitt Taylor Vince, Gareth Williams, Francesco Messina, Jennifer Beals, Elizabeth Bracco, Matthew Sussman, Michael Badalucco, Danny Trejo; **D:** Alexandre Rockwell; **W:** Alexandre Rockwell; **C:** Phil Parmet; **M:** Brian Kelly, Kevin Salem. VIDEO

13 Rue Madeleine 🐾🐾 **1946** Cagney plays a WWII spy who infiltrates Gestapo headquarters in Paris in order to find the location of a German missile site. Actual OSS footage is used in this fast-paced early postwar espionage propaganda piece. Rex Harrison rejected the part taken by Cagney. **95m/B VHS, DVD.** James Cagney, Annabella, Richard Conte, Frank Latimore, Walter Abel, Sam Jaffe, Melville Cooper, E.G. Marshall, Karl Malden, Red Buttons, Blanche Yurka, Peter Von Zerneck, Marcel Rousseau, Dick Gordon, Alfred Linder; **D:** Henry Hathaway; **W:** Sy Bartlett, John Monks Jr.; **C:** Norbert Brodine; **M:** David Buttolph.

Thirteenth Day of Christmas 1985 A psychotic boy is left alone by his parents on Christmas night. **60m/C VHS, GB** Patrick Allen, Elizabeth Spriggs; **D:** Patrick Lau. TV

The 13th Floor 🐾🐾½ **1988 (R)** A young girl fuses with the spirit of a young boy her father ruthlessly killed years before, and together they wreak havoc. **86m/C VHS, DVD.** Lisa Hensley, Tim McKenzie, Miranda Otto; **D:** Chris Roach.

The Thirteenth Floor 🐾🐾 **1999 (R)** Silly sci-fier with a confusing virtual-reality plot and a lot of visual effects. An investigation into the mysterious death of tycoon Hannon Fuller (Mueller-Stahl) leads to the realization that he lived in parallel worlds—one in the present and one in 1937. Exec Douglas Hall (Bierko) stands to inherit, which raises the suspicious of cop McBain (Haysbert) while claiming to be Fuller's daughter. And then there's Hall's colleague Whitney (D'Onofrio), who also exists in the 1937 as a barkeep with a very important letter. Not only does this turns out to be particularly interesting. **100m/C VHS, DVD.** Craig Bierko, Vincent D'Onofrio, Armin Mueller-Stahl, Gretchen Mol, Dennis Haysbert, Steven Schub, Jeremy Roberts, Tia Texada, Alison Lohman; **D:** Josef Rusnak; **W:** Josef Rusnak; **C:** Wedigo von Schultzendorff; **M:** Harald Kloser.

13th Guest 🐾🐾 **1932** Two people try to solve a murder that occurred at a dinner party. An incredibly creaky early talk-ie melodrama that has all the clichés of the genre. **70m/B VHS, DVD.** Ginger Rogers, Lyle Talbot, J. Farrell MacDonald, Paul Hurst; **D:** Albert Ray.

The Thirteenth Man 🐾½ **1937** When a journalist investigating the murder of a district attorney is also killed, the paper's gossip columnist takes the case. Entertaining, fast-paced mystery. **70m/B VHS.** Weldon Heyburn, Inez Courtney, Selmer Jackson, Milburn Stone, Matty Fain; **D:** William Nigh.

The 13th Mission 🐾½ **1991** A low-budget overseas combat adventure, no better than the first 12. **95m/C VHS.** Robert Marius, Jeff Griffith, Mike Monty, David Morrison, Paul Holme, Jim Falch, Albert Bronski, Chantal Manz; **D:** Antonio Perez.

Thirteenth Reunion 🐾 **1981** A newspaperwoman uncovers a bizarre secret society when she does a routine story on a health spa. **60m/C VHS.** Julia Foster, Dinah Sheridan, Richard Pearson; **D:** Peter Sasdy.

The 13th Warrior 🐾🐾 *Eaters of the Dead* **1999 (R)** Banderas stars as Ahmed Ibn Fahdlan, a sophisticated Arabian poet and lover-turned-reluctant-warrior, who gets exiled from his homeland and caught up in a quest with a bunch of uncouth, slaughter-loving Vikings. Based on the 1976 book by Michael Crichton, this one has been sitting on the shelf a while after a rocky filming history. However, if you like bloody, action-packed epics it will satisfy your cravings. **103m/C VHS, DVD.** Antonio Banderas, Vladimir Kulich, Clive Russell, Omar Sharif, Diane Venora, Sven Wollter, Dennis Storhoi, Anders T. Anderson, Richard Bremmer, Neil Maffin, Tony Curran, Mischa Hausserman, Asbjorn Riis, Daniel Southern, Oliver Sveinall, Altie Wood-ington; **D:** Michael Crichton, John McTiernan; **W:** Michael Crichton; **C:** Peter Menzies Jr.; **M:** Jerry Goldsmith.

Thirty Day Princess 🐾🐾½ **1934** Princess Catterina (Sidney) comes to New York, immediately gets sick, and is unable to fulfill her royal obligations. Bankrupt in struggling actress Nancy (Sidney again), but newspaper publisher Porter Madison (Grant) gets suspicious, despite failing for the dame. There are a few more comedic plot points but Sidney and Grant carry through the familiarity with loads of charm. **74m/B DVD.** Cary Grant, Sylvia Sidney, Edward Arnold, Vince Barnett, Henry Stephenson, Edgar Norton; **D:** Marion Gering; **W:** Preston Sturges, Frank Partos, Sam Hellman, Edwin Justus Mayer; **C:** Leon Shamroy.

30 Days of Night 🐾🐾½ **2007 (R)** Vampires have discovered that Barrow, Alaska, offers the perfect combination of human flesh and 30-day absence of sunlight, so they descend upon the town like the darkness they require, devouring all but a small number of survivors, among them two sheriffs, Eban Oleson (Hartnett) and his estranged wife Stella (George). The story, based on a graphic novel series, unfolds as a horrible game of hide-and-seek, with the town's surviving inhabitants eventually discovering how to rid themselves of the bloodthirsty pestilence. The biggest problem is the predictability and repetition of the storyline, but with no shortage of stylized violent horror for those with an unquenchable thirst for such things. A great twist on the classic vampire story not to be missed by admirers of the genre. **113m/C DVD.** US Josh Hartnett, Melissa George, Danny Huston, Ben Foster, Mark Boone Jr., Mark Rendall; **D:** David Slade; **W:** Stuart Beattie, Steve Niles, Brian Nelson; **C:** Jo Willems; **M:** Brian Reitzell.

The 30-Foot Bride of Candy Rock 🐾 **1959** A junk dealer invents a robot, catapults into space and causes his girlfriend to grow to 30 feet in height. Lightweight, whimsical "fantasy was Costello's only solo starring film, and his last before his untimely death. **73m/B VHS.** Lou Costello, Dorothy Provine, Gale Gordon; **D:** Sidney Miller.

30 Is a Dangerous Age, Cynthia 🐾🐾½ **1968** Dudley Moore stars as a nightclub pianist who spends a lot of his time daydreaming about being rich, famous, and married to a beautiful woman. Moore determines to attain all these dreams before his 30th birthday, which is only six weeks away. **85m/C VHS. GB** Dudley Moore, Suzy Kendall, Eddie Foy Jr.; **D:** Joseph McGrath; **W:** Dudley Moore.

Thirty Seconds Over Tokyo 🐾🐾½ **1944** Dated but still interesting classic wartime flagwaver details the conception and execution of the first bombing raids on Tokyo by Lt. Col. James Doolittle and his men. Look for Blake Edwards, as well as Steve Brodie in his first screen appearance. Based on a true story. **139m/B VHS, DVD.** Spencer Tracy, Van Johnson, Robert Walker, Robert Mitchum, Phyllis Thaxter, Scott McKay, Stephen McNally, Louis Jean Heydt, Leon Ames, Paul Langton, Don DeFore, Tim Murdock, Alan Napier, Dorothy Morris, Jacqueline White, Selena Royle, Bill Philips, Donald Curtis, Gordon McDonald, John R. Reilly, Douglas Cowan, Ann Shoemaker, Steve Brodie; **D:** Mervyn LeRoy; **W:** Dalton Trumbo; **C:** Robert L. Surtees; **M:** Herbert Stothart.

30 Years to Life 🐾🐾 **2001 (R)** Six friends try to cope with the reality of turning 30, and the re-evaluation of their lives that the milestone brings. Natalie, a Wall Street success, pretends to be domesticated to attract a conservative doctor. Commitment-averse Leland is forced to propose to his live-in girl Joy because of a jewelry shop mix-up; Troy, a stand-up comedian who... and Malik quits his job to become a model. It all has a very sitcomy feel, but the writing is good enough to make the various lessons learned more palatable. **110m/C VHS, DVD.** Erika Alexander, Melissa De Sousa, Tracy Morgan, Kadeem Hardison, Paula Jai Parker, Allen Payne, T.E. Russell, Eddie Brill, Janet Hubert-Whitten, Jim Gaffigan; **D:** Vanessa Middleton; **W:** Vanessa Middleton; **C:** Cliff Charles; **M:** Timbaland. VIDEO

32 Short Films about Glenn Gould 🐾🐾🐾 **1993** Perceptive documentary-drama about the iconoclastic Canadian classical pianist who secluded himself in the studio, forsaking live performances for much of his career. A combination of dramatic recreation, archival material, and interviews depict the biographical details of the driven artist who died at the age of 50. Feore is memorable in the title role, especially since he's never actually shown playing the piano. Title and film structure refer to Bach's "Goldberg" Variations, a recording which made Gould's reputation. **94m/C VHS, DVD. CA** Colm Feore, Gale Garnett, David Hughes, Katya Ladan, Gerry Quigley, Carlo Rota, Peter Millard, Yehudi Menuhin, Bruno Monsaingeon; **D:** Francois Girard; **W:** Don McKellar, Francois Girard; **C:** Alan Dostie, Genie '93; Cinematog., Director (Girard), Film, Film Editing.

36 Fillete 🐾🐾 **1988** Lili, an intellectually precocious 14-year-old French girl who's literally bursting out of her children's dress size 36 fillette, discovers her sexuality. So while on vacation with her family she becomes determined to see if she can seduce a middle-aged playboy in French with English subtitles. **88m/C VHS. DVD. FR** Delphine Zentout, Etienne Chicot, Olivier Parniere, Jean-Pierre Leeud; **D:** Catherine Breillat; **W:** Catherine Breillat, Roger Salloch; **C:** Laurent Dailland.

36 Hours 🐾🐾🐾 **1964** Maj. Pike (Garner) is a high-ranking WWII Army officer with knowledge of top secret invasion plans who wakes up in an Army hospital with amnesia, a wife (Saint) he didn't know he had, and a shrink telling him that the war's been over for some time. But Pike's not sure what's real and what isn't, especially when the doc asks him to explain, in great detail, what happened just before he lost his memory. Are they telling the truth, or is this an elaborate hoax? Tight, suspenseful plot, and fine performances all around make this an enjoyable thriller even after that question is answered. Remade for TV in 1989 with Corbin Bernsen in the Garner role. **115m/B VHS, DVD.** James Garner, Eva Marie Saint, Rod Taylor, Werner Peters, John Banner, Russ Thorson, Alan Napier, Oscar Beregi, Edmund Gilbert, Sig. Rumann, Celia Lovsky, Karl Held, Marjorie Bennett, Martin Kosleck, Henry Rowland, Hilda Plowright, Joseph Mell, Rudolph Anders, James Doohan; **D:** George Seaton; **W:** George Seaton, Roald Dahl, Carl K. Hittleman; **C:** Philip Lathrop; **M:** Dimitri Tiomkin.

Thirty-Six Hours of Hell 🐾½ **1977** A troop of Marines battle Japanese forces in the South Pacific during WWII. Dubbed. **95m/C VHS.** Richard Harrison, Pamela Tudor; **D:** Roberto Montero.

36 Hours to Die 🐾🐾½ **1999** Noah Stone (Williams) is a brewery owner recovering from heart bypass surgery. As if he doesn't have enough to worry about, a crime syndicate wants to use his business as a front in an extortion scam and he's got a day-and-a-half to make up his mind (hence the title). Stone's wife (Cattrall), her ex-cop uncle (O'Connor), and even Stone's bowling team unite to take on the bad guys. **96m/C VHS.** Treat Williams, Saul Rubinek, Kim Cattrall, Carroll O'Connor, George Touliatos, Scott Hylands; **D:** Yves Simoneau; **W:** Robert Rodat. CABLE

'38: Vienna before the Fall 🐾🐾½ **1988** Wartime Vienna explodes with love and politics. Academy Award nominee for Best Foreign Language Film. In German with English subtitles. **97m/C VHS. GE** Tobias Engel, Sunnyi Melles; **D:** Wolfgang Gluck.

39 Pounds of Love 🐾🐾½ **2005** Ami Anklewicz, now living in Israel and working as a computer animator, celebrates his 34th birthday by traveling back to the hometown of his youth in Texas where at 18 months old he was diagnosed with spinal muscular atrophy, a condition, which was expected to shorten his life to no more than 6 years. Ami wishes to confront the doctor who predicted his early death, reconnect with his estranged brother and her Oscar and ride a Harley. Intercut with scenes from Anklewitz's animated work, which provides insight into much of his inner thinking—a good portion of which revolves around the unrequited love he holds for his former caregiver Christina. **70m/C DVD.** *US D:* Dani Menkin; *M:* Chris Gubisch.

The 39 Steps ✶✶✶✶ **1935** The classic Hitchcock mistaken-man-caught-in-intrigue thriller, featuring some of his most often copied set-pieces and the suriest visual flair of his pre-war British period. Remade twice, in 1959 and 1979. **81m/B VHS, DVD.** *GB* Robert Donat, Madeleine Carroll, Godfrey Tearle, Lucie Mannheim, Peggy Ashcroft, John Laurie, Wylie Watson, Helen Haye, Frank Cellier, Gus McNaughton, Jerry Verno, Peggy Simpson, Hilda Trevelyan, John Turnbull, Elizabeth Inglis, Wilfrid Brambell; *D:* Alfred Hitchcock; *W:* Charles Bennett, Alma Reville, Ian Hay; *C:* Bernard Knowles; *M:* Louis Levy.

The Thirty-Nine Steps ✶✶✶ ½ **1979** Hitchcock remake is a visually interesting, but mostly uninvolving, mystery. Powell is the man suspected of stealing plans to begin WWI. Above average, but not by much. **98m/C VHS, DVD.** *GB* Robert Powell, David Warner, Eric Porter, Karen Dotrice, John Mills, Andrew Keir; *D:* Don Sharp.

This Boy's Life ✶✶✶ **1993 (R)** In 1957, Carolyn (Barkin) and her teenage son Toby (DiCaprio) are in search of a new life, far from her abusive ex-boyfriend. In the town of Concrete, just outside Seattle, she meets ex-military man Dwight (De Niro), a slick but none too suave mechanic who may be the answer to her dreams, but then again, he might not. Nicely crafted performances from all, but keep your eye on DiCaprio (great in his first major role) as the confused and abused teen divided between dreams of prep school and the allure of the going-nowhere crowd. Based on the memoirs of Tobias Wolff; director Caton-Jones sensitively illustrates the skewed understanding of masculinity in the 1950s. Vintage soundtrack makes you back. **115m/C VHS, DVD.** Robert De Niro, Ellen Barkin, Leonardo DiCaprio, Jonah Blechman, Eliza Dushku, Chris Cooper, Carla Gugino, Zachary Ansley, Tracey Ellis, Kathy Kinney, Gerrit Graham; *D:* Michael Caton-Jones; *C:* Robert Getchell; *M:* Carter Burwell.

This Christmas ✶✶ **2007 (PG-13)** After several years apart, the Whitfields are reunited for the holidays at the solidly upper-middle-class family home in L.A. Ma'Dere (Devine) is the matriarch of this African American family whose members include the military son Quentin (Elba), oldest daughter Lisa (King), workaholic Kelli (Leal), college student Mel (London), and Baby (Brown), who announces his plan to follow their long-absent father into the jazz world. His is not the only bombshell to fall as everyone has a turn having his or her buttons pushed. Ma'Dere's long-time boyfriend Joe (Lindo) does a great job of holding everyone together long enough for them to realize what a treasure they have in each other. A tad overdone and over the top but still a fun holiday romp. **117m/C DVD.** *US* Delroy Lindo, Idris Elba, Loretta Devine, Sharon Leal, Lauren London, Reina King, Columbus Short, Mekhi Phifer; *D:* Preston A. Whitmore II; *W:* Preston A. Whitmore II; *C:* Alexander Grusynski.

This Could Be the Night ✶✶ ½ **1957** Rocco and Tony are two small-fry gangsters who run a nightclub. Anne is a prim schoolteacher who takes a part-time job as their secretary. She falls for the handsome Tony much to the dismay of Rocco who knows his partner's less-than-sterling character. Sweet but minor comedy. Franciosa's first film. ♪This Could Be The Night; Hustlin' News Gal; I Got It Bad; I'm Gonna Live Till I Die; Taking a Chance on Love; Trumpet Boogie; Mamba Combo; Blue Moon; Dream Dancing. **105m/B VHS.** Jean Simmons, Paul Douglas, Anthony (Tony) Franciosa, Joan Blondell, Julie Wilson, Neile Adams, J. Carrol Naish, Rafael

Campos, Zasu Pitts, Tom Helmore; *D:* Robert Wise.

This England ✶✶ ½ **1942** Patriotic morale booster is a rather dull jog through Britain's fight for freedom as an American journalist, visiting England, learns a village's history from a country squire, including surviving the Norman conquest, Spanish Armada, Napoleonic Wars, WWI, and the 1940 air attacks. **84m/B VHS.** *GB* Emlyn Williams, John Clements, Constance Cummings; *D:* David MacDonald.

This Film Is Not Yet Rated ✶✶ ½ **2006** Veteran filmmaker Kirby Dick tackles the secrecy surrounding the MPAA ratings board, with Dick out to illustrate their nonsensical approach to the process. Created in 1968, its anonymous panel (which Dick aims to identify) is frequently accused of being lenient towards violence and uptight about sex. Filmmakers generally have no way of knowing just what the board objects to since they don't offer specific criticism because that would be counterproductive. Kirby uses some question-and-answer methods to get board members on camera and he has no particular suggestions about reform, but if you're interested in filmmaking, the documentary and its revealing interviews makes for compelling viewing. **97m/C DVD.** *US D:* Kirby Dick; *C:* Shana Hagan, Kristen Johnson, Amy Vincent.

This Girl's Life ✶✶ **2003 (R)** Moon (knockout Marquis in her film debut) is a forthright beauty who likes sex and makes her living in the porn industry. Film is matter-of-fact about her life, which includes caring for her Pops (Woods), who has Parkinson's, worrying about an AIDS scare, and wondering about a budding relationship with a non-industry boyfriend (Pardue). Kudos to director/writer Ash for making a flick that's compelling without being violent or exploitative despite its subject matter. **101m/C DVD.** James Woods, Kip Pardue, Tomas Arana, Michael Rapaport, Juliette Marquis, Rosario Dawson, Ioan Gruffudd, Isaiah Washington IV, Cheyenne Silver, Kam Heskin, Natalie Taylor; *D:* Ash; *W:* Ash; *C:* Alessandro Zezza; *M:* Agatha Halou.

This Gun for Hire ✶✶ ½ **1942** In his first major film role, Ladd plays a hired gun seeking retribution from a client who betrays him. Preston is the cop pursuing him and hostage Lake. Ladd's performance as the cold-blooded killer with a soft spot for cats is stunning; his train-yard scene is an emotional powerhouse. Based on Graham Greene's novel "A Gun for Sale." Remade as "Short Cut to Hell." The first of several films using the Ladd-Lake team, but the only one in which Ladd played a villain. **81m/B VHS, DVD.** Alan Ladd, Veronica Lake, Robert Preston, Laird Cregar, Tully Marshall, Marc Lawrence, Yvonne De Carlo; *D:* Frank Tuttle; *W:* Albert (John B. Sherry) Maltz, W.R. Burnett; *C:* John Seitz; *M:* David Buttolph.

This Gun for Hire ✶✶✶ **1990 (R)** A professional assassin finds that he has been duped into killing a powerful political figure, whom he was told was a New Orleans mobster. Now on the run, he takes a nightclub performer hostage, unaware that she is the fiance of the FBI agent who is after him. All odds are against him, but the special relationship he forms with the woman may just be his ticket out. Adapted from novel by Graham Greene. **89m/C VHS.** Robert Wagner, Nancy Everhard, Frederic Lehne, John Harkins; *D:* Lou Antonio.

This Happy Breed ✶✶✶ ½ **1947** A celebrated film version of Noel Coward's classic, play depicts the changing fortunes of a large family in England between the world wars. Happiness, hardships, triumph and tragedy mix a series of memorable episodes, including some of the most cherished moments in popular British cinema, though its appeal is universal. **114m/C VHS.** *GB* Robert Newton, Celia Johnson, John Mills, Kay Walsh, Stanley Holloway, Amy Veness, Alison Leggatt, Eileen Erskine, John Blythe, Guy Verney, Betty Fleetwood, Merle Tottenham; *D:* David Lean; *W:* David Lean, Noel Coward, Ronald Neame; *C:* Ronald Neame; *M:* Noel Coward, Muir Mathieson; *Nar:* Laurence Olivier.

This Happy Feeling ✶✶ ½ **1958** Reynolds is a young woman who is romantically attracted to both Jurgens, a sophisticated retired actor, and Saxon, a younger suitor who is Jurgens' neighbor. Good acting all around. Charming telling of old tale. **83m/C VHS.** Curt Jurgens, Debbie Reynolds, John Saxon, Alexis Smith, Mary Astor, Estelle Winwood; *D:* Blake Edwards; *W:* Blake Edwards.

This Is a Hijack ✶ **1973 (PG)** Gambler hijacks the plane carrying his wealthy boss to help pay his debts. What it lacks in suspense, it lacks in performance and direction as well. **90m/C VHS.** Adam Roarke, Neville Brand, Jay Robinson, Lynn Borden, Dub Taylor; *D:* Barry Pollack; *C:* Bruce Logan; *M:* Charles Alden.

This Is Elvis ✶✶ **1981 (PG)** The life of Elvis, combining documentary footage with dramatizations of events in his life. Includes more than three dozen songs. Generally seen as an attempt to cash in on the myth, but was well-received by his fans. **144m/C VHS.** Elvis Presley; *D:* Malcolm Leo, Andrew Solt; *W:* Malcolm Leo, Andrew Solt; *C:* Gil Hubbs.

This Is England ✶✶ **2006** Meadows' autobiographical film about a lonely 12-year-old who is befriended by local skinheads in 1983 Britain. Shaun (non-pro Turgoose), whose soldier dad was killed in the Falklands, lives with his mum in a run-down community. He stands up to the teasing of the (essentially harmless) neighborhood gang and earns the respect of young leader Woody (Gilgun). Things change when older Combo (Graham) gets out of prison. A supporter of the National Front, Combo's racist rhetoric causes a split, but Shaun sticks with him since he sees Combo as a surrogate dad. **98m/C DVD.** *GB* Stephen Graham, Thomas Turgoose, Joe Gilgun, Vicky McClure, Andrew Shim, Jo Hartley; *D:* Shane Meadows; *W:* Shane Meadows; *C:* Danny Cohen; *M:* Ludovico Einaudi.

This Is My Father ✶✶ ½ **1999 (R)** Teacher Kieran Johnson (Caan) decides to research his Irish roots after discovering a photo of his mother with a mystery man who may have been his father. Told in flashback, it portrays the class differences in rural Ireland in the '30s and the doomed romance between wealthy, teenaged Fiona Flynn (Farrelly) and Kieran O'Dea (Quinn), a poor tenant farmer who works for the Flynn family. Affecting role for Aidan Quinn, who worked with brothers Paul and Declan. Script is based on a story Theresa Quinn told her children. **120m/C VHS, DVD.** Aidan Quinn, James Caan, Stephen Rea, Moya Farrelly, John Cusack, Jacob Tierney, Colm Meaney, Donal Donnelly, Brendan Gleeson; *D:* Paul Quinn; *W:* Paul Quinn; *C:* Declan Quinn; *M:* Donal Lunny.

This Is My Life ✶✶ **1992 (PG-13)** The story of a working mother torn between her skyrocketing career as a stand-up comic and her two daughters. Kavner plays the divorced mom who is determined to chuck her cosmetic sales job for comic success. Her career starts to really take off; she hires an agent and makes appearances on talk shows. As offers pour in, she eventually realizes that her girls are suffering as a result of her success. Good performances highlight an otherwise average drama. **105m/C VHS.** Julie Kavner, Samantha Mathis, Carrie Fisher, Dan Aykroyd, Gaby Hoffman; *D:* Nora Ephron; *W:* Nora Ephron, Delia Ephron.

This Is Not a Love Song ✶✶ **2002** Petty criminal Heaton (Glenaan) has just picked up his pal Spike (Colgan) who was doing a short stint in a Glasgow prison. When their car runs out of gas on a lonely country road, they hike to the nearest farm in search of help. Too bad the farmer thinks these ruffians are there to rob the place. In the ensuing confusion, Spike accidentally shoots and kills the farmer's daughter. Now the two friends take off across the moors—pursued not only by the police but by a vigilante group of locals. Title is taken from the Public Image Ltd. song that is heard in various versions. **92m/C VHS, DVD.** *GB* Michael Colgan, Kenny Glenaan, David Bradley, John Henshaw; *D:*

Bille Eltringham; *W:* Simon Beaufoy; *C:* Robbie Ryan; *M:* Adrian Johnston, Mark Rutherford.

This Is Not a Test ✶✶ **1962** When news comes of an impending nuclear attack, a state trooper at a roadblock offers sanctuary to passing travellers. The effectiveness of the film's social commentary is hindered by its small budget. **72m/B VHS, DVD.** Seamon Glass, Mary Morlass, Thayer Roberts, Aubrey Martin; *D:* Frederic Gadette; *W:* Frederic Gadette, Peter Abenheim, Betty Laskey; *C:* Brick Marquard; *M:* Greig McRitchie.

This Is Spinal Tap ✶✶✶ ½ *Spinal Tap* **1984 (R)** Pseudo-rockumentary about heavy-metal band Spinal Tap, profiling their career from "England's loudest band" to an entry in the "where are they now file." Hilarious satire, featuring music performed by Guest, McKean, Shearer, and others. Included are Spinal Tap's music video "Hell Hole," and an ad for their greatest hits album, "Heavy Metal Memories." Features great cameos, particularly David Letterman's Paul Shaffer as a record promoter and Billy Crystal as a surly mime. First feature for Reiner [Meathead on "All in the Family"]. Followed by "The Return of Spinal Tap." **82m/C VHS, DVD.** Michael McKean, Christopher Guest, Harry Shearer, Tony Hendra, Bruno Kirby, Rob Reiner, June Chadwick, Howard Hesseman, Billy Crystal, Dana Carvey, Ed Begley Jr., Patrick Macnee, Fran Drescher, Paul Shaffer, Anjelica Huston, Fred Willard, Paul Benedict, Archie Hahn; *D:* Rob Reiner; *W:* Michael McKean, Christopher Guest, Harry Shearer, Rob Reiner; *C:* Peter Smoker; *M:* Michael McKean, Christopher Guest, Harry Shearer, Rob Reiner. Natl. Film Reg. '02.

This Is the Army ✶✶ ½ **1943** A robust tribute to the American soldier of WWII based on the hit play by Irving Berlin. Murphy, who later was a senator from California, played Reagan's father. ♪Your Country and My Country; My Sweetie; Poor Little Me, I'm on K.P.; We're On Our Way to France; What Does He Look Like?; This Is the Army, Mr. Jones; I'm Gettin' Tired So I Can Sleep; Mandy; Ladies of the Chorus. **105m/C VHS, DVD.** George Murphy, Joan Leslie, Ronald Reagan, Alan Hale, Kate Smith, George Tobias, Irving Berlin, Joe Louis; *D:* Michael Curtiz; *M:* Max Steiner. Oscars '43: Scoring/Musical.

This Is the Sea ✶✶ ½ **1996 (R)** Belfast Protestant teenager Hazel Stokes (Morton) falls in love with Catholic boy, Malachy McAliskey (McDade), with trouble sure to follow. Interesting cast but the film winds up being simplistic and cliched. Director McGuckian also appears as Cathy, Padhar McAliskey's girlfriend, who is played by McGuckian's husband, Lynch. Title comes from a 1985 Waterboys song. **104m/C VHS.** *IR* Mary McGuckian, Samantha Morton, Ross McDade, Richard Harris, John Lynch, Gabriel Byrne, Marc O'Shea, Des McAleer; *D:* Mary McGuckian; *W:* Mary McGuckian; *C:* Des Whelan.

This Island Earth ✶✶✶ ½ **1955** The planet Metaluna is in desperate need of uranium to power its defense against enemy invaders. A nuclear scientist and a nuclear fission expert from Earth are kidnapped to help out. The first serious movie about interplanetary escapades. Bud Westmore created pulsating cranium special effects make-up. **86m/C VHS, DVD.** Jeff Morrow, Faith Domergue, Rex Reason, Russell Johnson; *D:* Joseph M. Newman; *M:* Herman Stein.

This Land Is Mine ✶✶✶ **1943** A timid French schoolteacher gathers enough courage to defy the Nazis when they attempt to occupy his town. Laughton's characterization is effective as the meek fellow who discovers the hero within himself in this patriotic wartime flick. **103m/B VHS.** Charles Laughton, Maureen O'Hara, George Sanders, Walter Slezak, George Coulouris, Una O'Connor; *D:* Jean Renoir. Oscars '43: Sound.

This Lightning Always Strikes Twice ✶ **1985** An elegant murder mystery made for British television. **60m/C VHS.** *GB* Amanda Root, Julia Goodman, Claire Bloom, Trevor Howard, Charles Dance; *D:* David Carson; *W:* Michael Robson. **TV**

This Man Must Die 🦴🦴½
Que La Bete Meure; Uccidero Un Uomo; Killer! 1970 (PG) A man searches relentlessly for the driver who killed his young son in a hit-and-run. When found, the driver engages him in a complex cat-and-mouse chase. Another stunning crime and punishment tale from Chabrol. 112m/C VHS, DVD, FR Michel Duchaussoy, Caroline Cellier, Jean Yanne, Anouk Ferjac, Maurice Pialat; *D:* Claude Chabrol; *W:* Paul Gegauff; *C:* Jean Rabier.

This Property Is Condemned 🦴🦴 1966 It's a hot-time down south once again in this adaptation of the Tennessee Williams play. Wood is the overly flirtatious southern charmer who takes a shine to the latest tenant of her loathsome mama's boarding-house. And since it's Redford, who can blame her. Things steam up when he returns her interest but there's trouble a'brewin'. Both leads are lovely but the film itself is overly southern-fried. Williams was reportedly unhappy with the script film. 109m/C VHS, DVD, Robert Redford, Natalie Wood, Charles Bronson, Kate Reid, Mary Badham, Jonathan Provost, Robert (Bobby) Blake, John Harding; *D:* Sydney Pollack; *W:* Francis Ford Coppola, Edith Sommer, Fred Coe.

This Revolution 🦴 2005 An action-addict network TV reporter (Crooker) covers the street protests that preceded the NYC-GOP convention. The blending of real footage with fictional is most effective and difficult to distinguish. Gives a relatively interesting twist on a topic covered in documentaries like "Fahrenheit 9/11" and "Bush's Brain." Movie became part of the story when Dawson was arrested at one of the rallies being filmed. 95m/C DVD, Nathan Crooker, Rosario Dawson, Amy Redford, Brennan Sexton III, Brett DelBuono; *D:* Stephen Marshall; *W:* Stephen Marshall; *C:* Brian Jackson.

This Special Friendship 🦴🦴½
Les Amities Particulieres 1967 Powerful, if overdone French drama about an emotionally sensitive young man at a Catholic boarding school. His sexual relationship with another boy leads to tragedy. Based on the novel by Roger Peyrefitte. 99m/B VHS, FR Francis Lacombrade, Didier Haudepin, Lucien Nat, Louis Seigner, Michel Bouquet, Francois Leccia; *D:* Jean Delannoy.

This Sporting Life 🦴🦴🦴 1963 A gritty, depressing portrait of former coal miner Frank Machin (Harris), who breaks into the violent world of professional rugby, and whose inability to handle social differences causes problems. He begins an affair with his widow Mrs. Hammond (Roberts), from whom he rents a room, but finds they are capable of only a physical attachment. One of the best of the British melodramas. 134m/B VHS, DVD, GB Richard Harris, Rachel Roberts, Alan Badel, William Hartnell, Colin Blakely, Vanda Godsell, Arthur Lowe; *D:* Lindsay Anderson; *W:* David Storey; *C:* Denys Coop; *M:* Roberto Gerhard. British Acad. '63: Actor (Harris); Cannes '63.

This Stuff'll Kill Ya! WOOF! 1971 (PG) A backwoods preacher who believes in free love and moonshining runs into trouble with the locals when a series of gruesome religious murders are committed. Southern drive-in material from one of the genre's masters. Holt's last film. 100m/C VHS, DVD, Jeffrey Allen, Tim Holt, Gloria King, Ray Sager; *D:* Herschell Gordon Lewis; *W:* Herschell Gordon Lewis; *C:* Alex Ameri; *M:* Herschell Gordon Lewis.

This Sweet Sickness 🦴🦴½
Dites-Lui Que Je L'Aime 1977 Destructive passion and sexual delusion is explored in this adaptation of the Patricia Highsmith novel. David seems to be a hardworking loner who is loved by the sweet Juliette. Rejected by him, Juliette then discovers chalet for the woman he does love, Lise, who's married and unaware of David's obsessional devotions. Extravagant emotions lead to tragedy. In French with English subtitles. 107m/C VHS, FR Gerard Depardieu, Miou-Miou, Dominique Laffin, Claude Pieplu.

This Thing of Ours 🦴 2003 Lame wiseguy movie hits all the cliches as broadly as possible. Ambitious hood Nick Santini (Provenzano) wants to impress the old New Jersey mobsters so he schemes with some pals to use computers to siphon off money from bank accounts worldwide and stash the cash offshore. Provenzano went to prison for tax evasion and racketeering so you'd think his experience would make the flick more compelling—no dice. 100m/C DVD, US Christian Maelen, Louis Vanaria, Frank Vincent, James Caan, Danny Provenzano, Vincent Pastore; *D:* Danny Provenzano; *C:* Tewc A. Bohus.

This Time I'll Make You Rich 🦴 1975 (R) Two American hoodlums work out a drug-ring heist in the Far East. Parolini used the pseudonym Frank Kramer. 97m/C VHS, Antonio (Tony) Sabato, Robin McDavid; *D:* Gianfranco Parolini.

This World, Then the Fireworks 🦴🦴½ 1997 (R) Long on style but short on substance, overwrought neo-noir tells the tragic tale of traumatized twins living a totally debauched life. After seeing their father murdered in a romantic triangle, which left their mother (McClanahan) with physical and emotional scars, brother Marty (Zane) and sister Carol (Gershon) cling to each other as they grow up and engage in an implied incestuous relationship. The duo winds up with grifters, murdering and pillaging their way through a small coastal town in the 1950s. Lee plays a messed-up cop who, tragically, becomes an easy mark for Marty. Based on a 1935 short story by Jim Thompson, director Oblowitz's debut gets too caught up in the excesses of pulp and focuses on slick visuals and dramatic style over a coherent story. Well-cast performances are universally solid and engaging. 100m/C VHS, Billy Zane, Gina Gershon, Sheryl Lee, Rue McClanahan, Seymour Cassel, Will Patton, Richard Edson, William Hootkins; *D:* Michael Oblowitz; *W:* Larry Gross; *C:* Tom Priestley; *M:* Pete Rugolo.

Thomas and the Magic Railroad 🦴🦴 2000 (G) Thomas, a spunky blue steam engine, is bullied by big bad engine, Diesel, and aided by Mr. Conductor (Baldwin), as well as young Lily (Wilson) who also come to Thomas' rescue. Part live-action, part animation adaptation of the British children's series will be fine for the kids but parents will over-dose on the whimsy factor. 84m/C VHS, DVD, Mara Wilson, Alec Baldwin, Peter Fonda, Didi Conn; *C:* Britt Allcroft; *M:* Hummie Mann.

The Thomas Crown Affair 🦴🦴🦴 *Thomas Crown and Company; The Crown Caper* 1968 (R) A multi-millionaire (McQueen) decides to plot and execute the perfect theft, a daring daylight robbery of a bank. Dunaway is the gorgeous and efficient insurance investigator determined to nab him. One of the best visual scenes is the chess match between the two as they begin to fall in love. Strong production with "Oscar-winning" theme "The Windmills of Your Mind." 🎵The Windmills of Your Mind. 102m/C VHS, DVD, Steve McQueen, Faye Dunaway, Jack Weston, Yaphet Kotto, Gordon Pinsent; *D:* Norman Jewison; *W:* Alan R. Trustman; *C:* Haskell Wexler. Oscars '68: Song ("The Windmills of Your Mind"); Golden Globes '69: Song ("The Windmills of Your Mind").

The Thomas Crown Affair 🦴🦴🦴 1999 (R) Slick, lavish, updated, and loose adaptation of the 1968 Steve McQueen/Faye Dunaway caper. Thomas Crown (Brosnan) is a self-made New York billionaire, who just can't resist pulling off the perfect crime by stealing a Monet from the Metropolitan Museum of Art. Catherine Banning (Russo) is the gorgeous insurance investigator on his trail, who can't help falling for the very charming criminal. The fortysomething duo sizzle (how fantastic to see two age-appropriate lovers for a change) and if the ending has a tacked-on feel, it doesn't really matter. Dunaway makes a cameo appearance as Crown's therapist. 111m/C VHS, DVD, Pierce Brosnan, Rene Russo, Denis Leary, Frank Keating, Mark Margolis, Faye Dunaway, Charles Keating, Ben Gazzara, Fritz Weaver, Esther Canadas; *D:* John McTiernan; *W:* Leslie Dixon, Kurt Wimmer; *C:* Tom Priestley; *M:* Bill Conti.

Thomas Graal's Best Film 🦴🦴 1917 The famous comical adventures of a film scriptwriter wooing his secretary, followed by "Thomas Graal's First Child." Silent. 70m/B VHS, Slv Victor Sjostrom, Karin Molander; *D:* Mauritz Stiller.

Thomas Graal's First Child 1918 The sequel to "Thomas Graal's Best Film." The comical screenwriter and actress couple attempt to raise a baby. Silent. 70m/B VHS, Victor Sjostrom, Karin Molander; *D:* Mauritz Stiller.

Thomas in Love 🦴🦴 *Thomas Est Amoureux* 2001 Oddball Belgian drama set slightly in the future where agoraphobic Thomas (Verhaert) spends all his time on his computer—living his life through the screen. In fact, the viewer never sees what he sees, including his arrangements for therapy and cybersex. French with subtitles. 97m/C VHS, DVD, 5E Benoit Verhaert, Aylin Yay, Magali Pinglaut, Micheline Hardy, Alexandre von Sivers, Frederic Topart, Serge Lariviere, Virginie Saint-Martin; *D:* Pierre-Paul Renderss; *W:* Philippe Blasband; *C:* Virginie Saint-Martin; *M:* Igor Sterpin.

Thompson's Last Run 🦴½ 1990 Boyhood friends grow up on either side of the law. They come face-to-face, though, when one is assigned to transport the other to prison. 95m/C VHS, DVD, Robert Mitchum, Wilford Brimley, Kathleen York, Susan Tyrrell; *D:* Jerrold Freedman; *M:* Miles Goodman.

Thor and the Amazon Women 🦴 *Women Gladiators* 1960 The mighty Thor leads his enslaved men on an attack against the evil Queen Nera and her female-dominated Amazon society. 85m/C VHS, DVD, IT Harry Baird, Maria Fiore, Claudia Capone, Alberto Cerenini, Antonio Leonviola, Jannin Hendy, Jce Robinson, Susy Andersen; *W:* Fabio Piccioni; *C:* Guglielmo Mancori; *M:* Roberto Nicolosi.

The Thorn 🦴½ 1974 (R) The Virgin Mary and Joseph try to raise Jesus Christ in the modern world. 90m/C VHS, Bette Midler, John Bassberger; *D:* Peter Alexander.

The Thorn Birds 🦴🦴🦴 1983 Pioneers find danger and romance in the Australian outback as they struggle to begin a dynasty. Charismatic priest sometimes hints, sometimes helps them. One of Stanwyck's last performances; Ward's American TV debut. Originally a ten-hour TV miniseries based on Colleen McCullough novel. Emmy nominations for actor Chamberlain, supporting actors Brown and Plummer, supporting actress Laurie, direction, photography, music, costume design, and editing. 486m/C VHS, DVD, Rachel Ward, Richard Chamberlain, Jean Simmons, Ken Howard, Mare Winningham, Richard Kiley, Piper Laurie, Bryan Brown, Christopher Plummer, Barbara Stanwyck; *D:* Daryl Duke; *C:* Bill Butler; *M:* Henry Mancini. TV

The Thorn Birds: The Missing Years 🦴🦴½ 1996 Follow-up to the critically acclaimed miniseries "The Thorn Birds." Fills in the 19-year gap since the original romantic melodrama aired. 178m/C DVD, Richard Chamberlain, Amanda Donohoe, Julia Blake, Olivia Burnette, Michael Caton, Zach English, Peter Ford, Jonathan Hardy, Ingrid Mason, Maximilian Schell, Jack Thompson, Simon Westaway, Paul Bertram, Rob Coran, Christopher Gabardi, Adam Grossetti, John Heywood, Phillip Hinton, Enrico Mammarella, Marjirie Mann, Todd Schulberg; *D:* Kevin James Dobson; *W:* David Stevens, Colleen McCullough; *C:* Ross Berryman; *M:* Garry McDonald, Lawrence Stone. TV

Thoroughbreds Don't Cry 🦴🦴½ 1937 Rooney plays a jockey who throws a race so his no-good family can win enough money to pay for his supposed medical problems. The owner of the horse then drops dead from a heart attack. Rooney feels guilty, so he asks his father to loan the owner's grandson $1,000 to run in another race. His father says no, so Rooney steals the money from him, and when the father finds out he tells the track officials that Rooney threw the race. Garland is Rooney's best friend and moral support, and she sings a few songs too! A fairly good horse racing story. 80m/B VHS, Judy Garland, Mickey Rooney, Sophie Tucker, Sir C. Aubrey Smith, Ronald Sinclair, Forrester Harvey; *D:* Alfred E. Green.

Thoroughly Modern Millie 🦴🦴½ 1967 (G) Andrews is a young woman who comes to New York in the early 1920s where she meets another newcomer, the innocent Moore. Andrews decides to upgrade her image to that of a "modern" woman, a flapper, and sets out to realize her ambition, to become a stenographer and marry the boss. Meanwhile, Moore has become an object of interest to Lillie, who just happens to run a white-slavery ring. Lots of frantic moments and big production numbers in this campy fun. 🎵Thoroughly Modern Millie; The Tapioca; Jimmy; The Jewish Wedding Song; Baby Face; Do It Again; Poor Butterfly; Rose of Washington Square; I Can't Believe That You're In Love With Me. 138m/C VHS, DVD, Julie Andrews, Carol Channing, Mary Tyler Moore, John Gavin, Beatrice Lillie, James Fox, Noriyuki "Pat" Morita; *D:* George Roy Hill; *W:* Richard Morris; *C:* Russell Metty; *M:* Elmer Bernstein. Oscars '67: Orig. Score; Golden Globes '68: Support. Actress (Channing).

Those Calloways 🦴🦴½ 1965 (PG) A small town family attempts to establish a sanctuary for the flocks of wild geese who fly over the woods of Swiftwater, Maine. Fine Disney family fare, with good cast. Based on Paul An nixter's novel "Swiftwater." 131m/C VHS, DVD, Brian Keith, Vera Miles, Brandon de Wilde, Walter Brennan, Ed Wynn, John Qualen, Linda Evans; *D:* Norman Tokar; *W:* Louis Pelletier; *C:* Edward Colman; *M:* Max Steiner.

Those Daring Young Men in Their Jaunty Jalopies 🦴🦴 *Monte Carlo or Bust; Quei Temerari Sulle Loro Pazze, Scatenate, Scalcinate Carriole* 1969 (G) Daring young men in noisy slow cars trek 1500 miles across country in the 1920s and call it a race. 125m/C VHS, Tony Curtis, Susan Hampshire, Terry-Thomas, Eric Sykes, Gert Frobe, Peter Cook, Dudley Moore, Jack Hawkins; *D:* Ken Annakin; *W:* Ken Annakin, Jack Davies.

Those Endearing Young Charms 🦴🦴 1945 Romance develops between a young Air Corps mechanic and a salesgirl. Complications arise when another man enters the scene. Light to romantic comedy. Based on the play by Edward Chodorov. 82m/B VHS, Robert Young, Laraine Day, Anne Jeffreys, Lawrence Tierney, Lewis Allen.

Those Fantastic Flying Fools 🦴½ *Blast-Off; Jules Verne's Rocket to the Moon* 1967 A mad race to be the first on the moon brings hilarious results. Loosely based on a Jules Verne story. 95m/C VHS, GB Burl Ives, Troy Donahue, Gert Frobe, Terry-Thomas, Hermione Gingold, Daliah Lavi, Lionel Jeffries; *D:* Don Sharp.

Those Glory, Glory Days 🦴½ 1983 An English woman, secure in her position as an outstanding sports journalist, reminisces about the days when she and her friends idolized the boys on the soccer team. Nothing extraordinary, but nicely made. 92m/C VHS, DVD, GB Zoe Nathenson, Liz Campion, Cathy Murphy; *D:* Philip Saville; *M:* Trevor Jones.

Those Lips, Those Eyes 🦴🦴½ 1980 (R) A pre-med student takes a job as a prop boy in a summer stock company and winds up falling in love with the company's lead dancer. Subplot about aging actor is more interesting, better played by Langella. O'Connor is appropriately lovely. Nicely made, charming sleeper of a film. 106m/C VHS, Frank Langella, Tom Hulce, Glynnis O'Connor, Jerry Stiller, Kevin McCarthy; *D:* Michael Pressman.

Those Magnificent Men in Their Flying Machines 🐾🐾

1965 In 1910, a wealthy British newspaper publisher is persuaded to sponsor an air race from London to Paris. Contestants come from all over the world and shenanigans, hijinks, double-crosses, and romance are found along the route. Skelton has fun in prologue, while Terry-Thomas is great as the villain. Fun from start to finish. **138m/C VHS, DVD.** *GB* Stuart Whitman, Sarah Miles, Robert Morley, Alberto Sordi, James Fox, Gert Frobe, Jean-Pierre Cassel, Flora Robson, Sam Wanamaker, Terry-Thomas, Irina Demick, Benny Hill, Gordon Jackson, Millicent Martin, Red Skelton; *D:* Ken Annakin; *W:* Ken Annakin, Jack Davies.

Those Who Love Me Can Take the Train 🐾🐾 *Ceux Qui M'Aiment Prednont le Train* **1998** Bisexual artist Jean-Baptiste Emmerich (Trintignant) has died in Paris but wished to be buried in his hometown of Limoges—a four-hour train trip for his motley group of mourners, which include friends, relatives, and former lovers of both sexes. Things don't calm down at the cemetery where yet more relatives await, including the artist's estranged twin brother. Rather than bonding in grief, the trip and funeral succeed in bringing out old hurts and rivalries and causing the shakeup of more than one relationship. French with subtitles. **122m/C VHS, DVD.** *FR* Jean-Louis Trintignant, Pascal Gregory, Charles Berling, Bruno Todeschini, Valeria Bruni-Tedeschi, Vincent Perez, Dominique Blanc, Sylvain Jacques, Marie Daems; *D:* Patrice Chereau; *W:* Patrice Chereau, Daniele Thompson, Pierre Trividic; *C:* Eric Gautier. *Cesar '99:* Cinematog, Director (Chereau), Support. Actress (Blanc).

Thou Shalt Not Kill...Except 🐾🐾 *Stryker's War* **1987** A Vietnam vet seeks revenge on the violent cult who kidnapped his girlfriend. **84m/C VHS, DVD.** Brian Schulz, Robert Rickman, John Manfredi, Tim Quill, Cheryl Hansen, Sam Raimi, Perry Mallette, Theodore (Ted) Raimi, Glenn Barr, Scott Spiegel, Bruce Campbell, Paul Grabke; *D:* Josh Becker; *W:* Josh Becker, Scott Spiegel; *C:* Josh Becker; *M:* Joseph LoDuca.

Though None Go With Me 🐾🐾 **2006** While Elizabeth (Grabow) is growing up during the 1950s, she devotes herself to a life of service to God. But over the years, the many hardships that follow have her questioning her faith even when she's courted by both Ben (Rowe) and Will (Narona). Ladd plays the older Elizabeth who recounts her story to her granddaughter. Based on the inspirational novel by Jerry B. Jenkins. **100m/C DVD.** Cheryl Ladd, Brad Rowe, Denise Grayson, Christopher Allport, Amy Grabow, David Narona; *D:* Armand Mastroianni; *W:* Pamela Wallace; *C:* Amit Bhattacharya; *M:* Nathan Furst. **C A B L E**

Thoughts Are Free 🐾🐾 ½ **1997** (R) **1984** (PG) A young soldier, wounded in WWII, escapes from the train that is transporting him and his comrades to a Soviet labor camp and rejoins his family. Under the repressive communist regime, he plots his family's escape to the West but his plans are thwarted when the Berlin Wall is erected, leaving him in the West and his wife and daughter in the East. As the years go by, they can get together only by outwitting the bureaucrats. The film's title is taken from an old German folk song "Die Gedanken sind frei." **93m/C VHS.** Herbert Ludwig, Kathrin Kratzer; *D:* Josef Sommer.

A Thousand Acres 🐾🐾 **1997** (R) Based on Jane Smiley's Pulitzer Prize-winning novel, it's "King Lear" set on an Iowa farm. Sisters (Pfeiffer, Lange, and Leigh) discover that their father has decided to divide the family's thousand-acre farm amongst the three of them. Then stranger Firth comes to town and divides an interest in both of them. Melodramatic and contrived, with every hot-button women's issue imaginable thrown into the mix. Director Moorhouse purportedly considered removing her name from the picture. **105m/C VHS, DVD.** Jessica Lange, Michelle Pfeiffer, Jennifer Jason Leigh, Colin Firth, Jason Robards Jr., Keith Carradine, Pat Hingle, Kevin Anderson, John Carroll Lynch, Anne Pitoniak, Vyto Ruginis, Michelle Williams, Elisabeth (Elizabeth, Liz) Moss; *D:* Jocelyn Moorhouse; *W:* Laura Jones; *C:* Tak Fujimoto; *M:* Richard Hartley.

A Thousand and One Nights 🐾🐾 ½ **1945** Handsome Aladdin (Wilde) falls in love with beautiful Princess Armina (Jergens) but fate steps in and Aladdin and sidekick Abdullah (Silvers) are off in search of a magic lamp. This time around the genie is a beautiful woman (Keyes), who falls for Aladdin herself and tries to thwart his would-be romance. Clever fun. **92m/C VHS.** Cornel Wilde, Evelyn Keyes, Adele Jergens, Phil Silvers, Rex Ingram, Dennis Hoey, Philip Van Zandt, Gus Schilling; *D:* Alfred E. Green; *W:* Jack Henley, Richard English; *C:* Ray Rennahan; *M:* Martin Skiles.

A Thousand Clowns 🐾🐾🐾 **1965** A nonconformist has resigned from his job as chief writer for an obnoxious kiddie show in order to enjoy life. But his independence comes under fire when he becomes guardian for his young nephew and social workers take a dim view of his lifestyle. Balsam won an Oscar for his role as Robard's agent brother. Adapted from Herb Gardner's Broadway comedy. **118m/B VHS, DVD.** Jason Robards Jr., Barry J. Gordon, William Daniels, Barbara Harris, Gene Saks, Martin Balsam; *D:* Fred Coe; *W:* Herb Gardner; *C:* Arthur Ornitz. *Oscars '65:* Support. Actor (Balsam).

The Thousand Eyes of Dr. Mabuse 🐾🐾 ½ *The Secret of Dr. Mabuse; The Diabolical Dr. Mabuse; The Shadow Versus the Thousand Eyes of Dr. Mabuse* **1960** Lang's last film is a return to his pre-war German character, the evil Dr. Mabuse. A series of strange murders occur in a Berlin hotel and police believe the killer thinks he's a reincarnation of the doctor. Disorienting chiller. German with subtitles. **103m/B VHS, DVD.** *GE* Dawn Addams, Peter Van Eyck, Gert Frobe, Wolfgang Preiss; *D:* Fritz Lang; *W:* Fritz Lang, Jan Fethke, Heinz Oskar Wuttig; *C:* Karl Lob; *M:* Gerhard Becker, Bert Grund.

A Thousand Heroes 🐾🐾 ½ *Crash Landing: The Rescue of Flight 232* **1992** (PG) Based on the true story of United Airlines Flight 232 which took off on a flight from Denver to Chicago and then suffered engine explosions over Iowa. The jumbo jet crashed in a fiery explosion but some 200 people survived. **95m/C VHS.** Leon Russom, John M. Jackson, Tom O'Brien, Philip Baker Hall, Richard Thomas, Charlton Heston, James Coburn; *D:* Lamont Johnson; *W:* Harve Bennett; *C:* William Wages; *M:* Charles Fox.

Thousand Pieces of Gold 🐾🐾🐾 **1991** (PG-13) A young Chinese woman is sold by her father to a marriage broker, but instead of a respectable marriage she is shipped to America and expected to work as a prostitute in an Idaho mining town. Instead she works taking in laundry as she tries to make her way in a man's world, finding a sweet romance of opposites along the way. Based on a true story. Excellent performances by Chao and Cooper. **105m/C VHS.** Rosalind Chao, Chris Cooper, Michael Paul Chan, Dennis Dun, Michael Paul Chan, Jimmie F. Skaggs, William Oldham, David Hayward, Beth Broderick; *D:* Nancy Kelly; *W:* Anne Makepeace; *C:* Bobby Bukowski; *M:* Gary Remal Malkin.

Thousands Cheer 🐾🐾 ½ **1943** A flag-waving wartime musical about a tap-dancing Army private who falls in love with the colonel's daughter, culminating with an all-star (MGM) USO show. Songs include "Honeysuckle Rose," sung by Home, and "The Joint Is Really Jumping Down at Carnegie Hall," sung by Garland. **126m/C VHS, DVD.** Gene Kelly, Kathryn Grayson, Judy Garland, Mickey Rooney, Mary Astor, John Boles, Lucille Ball, Eleanor Powell, Virginia O'Brien, Margaret O'Brien, Red Skelton, Lionel Barrymore, June Allyson, Frank Morgan, Kay Kyser, Bob Crosby, Lena Home, Donna Reed; *D:* George Sidney; *W:* Paul Jarrico; *C:* George J. Folsey.

Thrashin' 🐾 **1986** (PG-13) A new-to-L.A. teen must prove himself to a tough gang on skateboards by skateboarding a certain treacherous race. For skateboarding fans only. **93m/C VHS, DVD.** Josh Brolin, Pamela Gidley, Robert Rusler, Chuck McCann; *D:* David Winters; *M:* Paul Bown; *M:* Barry Goldberg.

Threads 🐾🐾🐾 **1985** The famed dramatic re-creation of the effects of nuclear war on a British city and two of its families. A disturbing, uncompromising, and somewhat plausible drama. **110m/C VHS.** *GB* Karen Meagher, Rita May, David Brierly, Reece Dinsdale, Harry Beety; *D:* Mick Jackson. **TV**

Threat 🐾🐾 ½ **1949** A killer escapes from jail and returns to settle the score with those who convicted him. Tense, fast-moving thriller. **66m/B VHS.** Michael O'Shea, Virginia Grey, Charles McGraw; *D:* Felix Feist.

Threat of Exposure 🐾 ½ **2002** (R) Hypnotherapist Dr. Daryl Sheleigh (Young) is having a problem with her patients—they keep disappearing. Dr. Badger Kari Welldon (Schaub) goes undercover as a patient to investigate since one of the missing is his younger brother. But disturbing secrets emerge from Badger's past, including an abusive childhood and his own violent nature, and evidence begins to point to Daryl as the prime suspect. It's all too easy to see where this wannabe thriller is headed. **90m/C DVD.** *US* Sean Young, William Devane, Will Schaub; *D:* Paul Thomas, Sara Crawford; *D:* Tom Whitus; *W:* Frederick Bailey, Jeno Hodi; *C:* Fred Paddock; *M:* Jamie Howarth, Kinny Landrum. **V I D E O**

Thr3e 🐾 ½ **2007** (PG-13) Plodding Christian psycho-thriller features Seattle seminary student Kevin Parsons (Blucas) being targeted by a serial bomber known as the Riddle Killer. He calls his victims, accuses them of getting away with a crime, and then threatens to set off a bomb unless they confess. Except RK doesn't even play by his own rules. Adapted from the book by Ted Dekker. **101m/C DVD.** *US* Marc Blucas, Justine Waddell, Max Ryan, Priscilla Barnes, Laura Jordan, Tom Bower, Bill Moseley, Jeff Hollis, Philip Dunbar; *D:* Robby Henson; *W:* Alan B. McElroy; *C:* Sebastian Milaszewski; *M:* David Bergeaud.

Three Ages 🐾🐾🐾 **1923** A parody of D.W. Griffith's 1916 film "Intolerance." Keaton's first feature film casts him in prehistoric days, ancient Rome, and in modern times. Silent with musical score. **59m/B VHS, DVD.** Wallace Beery, Oliver Hardy, Buster Keaton; *D:* Buster Keaton, Edward F. (Eddie) Cline.

3 A.M. 🐾🐾🐾 **2001** Slice-of-life ensemble drama traces the doings of NYC cabbies over 36 hours. The struggling cab company, run by the owner's daughter Box (Choudhury), is on the verge of bankruptcy and her drivers are spooked by a serial killer targeting cabbies. Meanwhile, Hershey (Glover) is stretching the patience of girlfriend George (Grier); Latina Salgado (Rodriguez) is tired of being sexually harassed; Bosian refugee Rasha (Tifunovic) is on the brink of being fired; and ambitious Jose (Cannavale) finds a brief-case of stolen money. **92m/C VHS, DVD.** Danny Glover, Pam Grier, Michelle Rodriguez, Santa Choudhury, Sergei Trifunovic, Bobby Cannavale, Isaach de Bankole, Mike Starr, Paul Calderon; *D:* Lee Davis; *W:* Lee Davis; *C:* Enrique Chediak; *M:* Branford Marsalis. **C A B L E**

Three Amigos 🐾🐾 **1986** (PG) Three out-of-work silent screen stars are asked to defend a Mexican town from bandits; they think it's a public appearance stint. Spoof of The Three Stooges and Mexican bandito movies that at times falls short, given the enormous amount of comedic talent involved. Generally enjoyable with some very funny scenes. Co-written by former "Saturday Night Live" producer Michaels. Short's first major film appearance. **105m/C VHS, DVD.** Chevy Chase, Steve Martin, Martin Short, Joe Mantegna, Patrice Martinez, Jon Lovitz, Phil Hartman, Randy Newman, Alfonso Arau; *D:* John Landis; *W:* Lorne Michaels, Steve Martin, Randy Newman; *C:* Ronald W. Browne; *M:* Elmer Bernstein.

The Three Avengers 🐾🐾 ½ *Enter Three Dragons* **1980** (R) Hung Tack (Lee) is the master of a kung fu school in a town plagued by two evil businessmen, who force Hung to take on the local gangs. During a fight, he's spotted by a talent scout and starts a career in the movies but is around to rescue a friend who's gotten into trouble. Hey, the fighting's the important part anyway. **93m/C VHS.** *HK* Dragon Lee, Bolo Yeung, Bruce Li, Bruce Lee; *D:* Wah Kay Wong; *W:* Wah Kay Wong; *C:* Chin Chiang Ma; *M:* Chao Wah Li.

Three Bad Men 🐾 **2005** (PG-13) Dull, incompetent western. Three bank robbers are heading for the Colorado border when they come across a dying man whose wife has been kidnapped. He begs them to rescue his missus and the outlaws must decide whether to risk their own lives or keep on riding. **118m/C DVD.** Mike Moroff, George Kennedy, Peter Brown, John Dixon, Chris Gann; *D:* Jeff Hathcock; *W:* Jeff Hathcock; *M:* Tom Crosby.

Three Blind Mice 🐾 ½ **2002** (R) Hacker Thomas Cross (Furlong) is obsessed with Internet webcam sites. One night, he witnesses a grisly murder at his favorite website, but when he contacts the police, Thomas realizes he doesn't know the victim's real name or address. He's soon involved in the investigation by cop Claire (Fox). Mild and implausible thriller wannabe. **92m/C VHS, DVD.** *FR GB* Edward Furlong, Emilia Fox, Chiwetel Ejiofor, Ben Miles, Elsa Zylberstein, James Laurenson; *D:* Mathias Ledoux; *W:* Mikael Ollivier; *C:* Stephane Le Parc; *M:* Eric Neveux.

Three Broadway Girls 🐾🐾🐾 *The Greeks Had a Word for Them* **1932** Three gold-diggers go husband-hunting. Well-paced, very funny telling of this old story. Remade many times, including "How to Marry a Millionaire," "Three Blind Mice," "Moon Over Miami," and "Three Little Girls in Blue." **78m/B VHS, DVD.** Joan Blondell, Ina Claire, Madge Evans, David Manners, Lowell Sherman; *D:* Lowell Sherman.

Three Brothers 🐾🐾🐾 *Tre Fratelli* **1980** (PG) An acclaimed Italian film by veteran Rosi about three brothers summoned to their small Italian village by a telegram saying their mother is dead. Sensitive and compassionate. In Italian with English subtitles. Adapted from Platonov's story "The Third Son." **113m/C VHS, DVD.** *IT* Philippe Noiret, Charles Vanel, Michele Placido, Vittorio Mezzogiorno, Andrea Ferreol; *D:* Francesco Rosi; *W:* Francesco Rosi; *C:* Pasqualino De Santis; *M:* Piero Piccioni.

Three Bullets for a Long Gun 🐾 ½ **1973** (PG) Two prairie renegades battle bandits as they search for an inherited gold mine. **89m/C VHS.** Keith Van Der Wat, Patrick Munhardt; *D:* Peter Henkel; *W:* Keith Van Der Wat.

The Three Burials of Melquiades Estrada 🐾🐾🐾 **2005** (R) Powerful meditation on the brutality of the U.S.-Mexico border region. Rancher Pete Perkins (Jones) forces Mike Norton (Pepper) to carry the body of Pete's friend Melquiades Estrada (Cedillo) from their dusty Texas border town to the dead man's home in Mexico for burial in his family cemetery. But the bigger story is how their journey acts as a metaphor for the all-too human boundaries of wealth, sex, race, and religion. Norton, a racist patrol officer (and Estrada's murderer) is transformed from a thug with a badge into a man who must seek redemption after his eyes are opened to the weight of his actions. Amazing performances are buoyed by Arriaga's knowing script. **120m/C DVD.** Tommy Lee Jones, Barry Pepper, Dwight Yoakam, January Jones, Melissa Leo, Levon Helm, Vanessa Bauche, Julio Cesar Cedillo, Mel Rodriguez, Cecilia Suarez, Ignacio Guadalupe; *D:* Tommy Lee Jones; *W:* Guillermo Arriaga; *C:* Chris Menges; *M:* Marco Beltrami.

Three by Hitchcock 🐾🐾 **1928** Condensed versions of three of Hitchcock's early films (1927-28). Consists of "The Ring," "Champagne," and "The Manxman," his last silent film. **90m/B VHS.** *D:* Alfred Hitchcock.

The Three Caballeros 🐾🐾 ½ **1945** (G) Donald Duck stars in this journey through Latin America. Full of music, variety, and live-action/animation segments. Stories include "Pablo the Penguin," "Little Gauchito," and adventures with Joe Carioca, who was first introduced in Disney's "Saludos Amigos." Today this film stands as one of the very best pieces of animation ever created. Great family fare. ♫ **71m/C VHS.** Baia. ♫The Three Caballeros; Baia.

DVD. D: Norman Ferguson; **V:** Sterling Holloway, Aurora Miranda.

Three Came Home 🎬🎬🎬 1950 Colbert is an American married to a British administrator in the Far East during WWII. Conquering Japanese throw the whole family into a brutal POW concentration camp, and their ordeal is recounted in harrowing and unsparing detail. Superior drama, also laudable for a fairly even-handed portrayal of the enemy captors. Based on an autobiographical book by Agnes Newton-Keith. 106m/B VHS, DVD. **C:** Claudette Colbert, Patric Knowles, Sessue Hayakawa, Florence Desmond, Sylvia Andrew, Mark Keuning; Phyllis Morris, Howard Chuman; **D:** Jean Negulesco; **W:** Nunnally Johnson; **M:** Hugo Friedhofer.

Three Cases of Murder 🎬🎬 1955 Three fast-paced tales of mayhem. "In the Picture" features a deranged taxidermist, a creepy house, and a hapless museum guide. From a story by Roderick Wilkinson. Two friends are in love with the same girl in "You Killed Elizabeth" and when she turns up dead it's clear one of them is guilty. From a story by Brett Halliday. The best features Welles as "Lord Mountdrago," who destroys the career of a fellow Parliament Member and is haunted by fears of retaliation. Based on a story by W. Somerset Maugham. 99m/B VHS, GB **C:** Alan Badel, John Gregson, Orson Welles, Elizabeth Sellars, Hugh Pryse, Jack Lambert; **D:** Wendy Toye, David Eady, George More O'Ferrall; **W:** Donald Wilson, Sidney Carroll, Ian Dalrymple; **C:** Georges Perinal; **M:** Doreen Carwithen.

Three Charlies and One Phoney! 1918 Three of Charlie Chaplin's best comedy shorts, plus one feature-length imitation—Billy West. Included are "Recreation" ("Fun is Fun") ("Spring Fever"), "The Piano Movers") ("Musical Tramps") "The Bond" (featuring Charlie in a Liberty Bond appeal) and "His Day Out" with Billy West imitating Chaplin. All but "His Day Out" were written and directed by Chaplin. 65m/B VHS. **C:** Charlie Chaplin, Mack Swain, Charley Chase, Edna Purviance, Sydney Chaplin, Albert Austin; **D:** Charlie Chaplin; **W:** Charlie Chaplin.

Three Coins in the Fountain 🎬🎬½ 1954 Three women throw money into fountain and get romantically involved with Italian men. Outstanding CinemaScope photography captures beauty of Italian setting. Sammy Cahn theme song sung by Frank Sinatra. 🎵 "Three Coins in the Fountain". 102m/C VHS, DVD. **C:** Clifton Webb, Dorothy McGuire, Jean Peters, Louis Jourdan, Maggie McNamara, Rossano Brazzi; **D:** Jean Negulesco; **C:** Milton Krasner; **M:** Victor Young. *(Three Coins in the Fountain")*

Three Comrades 🎬🎬🎬 1938 Taylor, Tone, and Young are three friends, reunited in bleak, post-WWI Germany, who meet and befriend Sullavan, a tubercular beauty. Reluctant to face an uncertain future. Bleak but forceful and passionate drama. Sullavan's performance is superb. Based on the novel by Erich Maria Remarque. Fitzgerald's script was heavily re-written because both Sullavan and producer Mankiewicz found his approach too literary with unspeakable dialogue. 99m/B VHS. **C:** Robert Taylor, Margaret Sullavan, Robert Young, Franchot Tone, Lionel Atwill, Guy Kibbee, Henry Hull, George Zucco, Monty Woolley, Charley Grapewin, Spencer Charters, Sarah Padden; **D:** Frank Borzage. **W:** F. Scott Fitzgerald, Edward Paramore. **C:** Joseph Ruttenberg; **M:** Franz Waxman. N.Y. Film Critics '38: Actress (Sullavan).

Three Daring Daughters 🎬🎬½ 1948 When her husband leaves her and she almost misses her daughter's graduation due to a fainting spell, MacDonald takes hiatus on a cruise ship where she meets and marries pianist Iturbi. Unknowing, the three daughters at home conspire to get Dad back in the family. Enraged when Mom returns with newfound hubby, the three

some do all in their power to make the newlyweds as miserable as possible. Happily ended musical-comedy is chock full of memorable tunes. Based on the play "The Bees and the Flowers" by Kohner and Albert Manning. 🎵 "Route 66; The Dickey Bird Song; Alma Mater; Fleurette; Passe-Dance; Where There's Love; Ritual Fire Dance; You Made Me Love You; Happy Birthday. 115m/C VHS. **C:** Jeanette MacDonald, Jose Iturbi, Jane Powell, Edward Arnold, Harry Davenport, Moyna MacGill, Elinor Donahue, Ann E. Todd; **D:** Fred M. Wilcox; **W:** Sonya Levien, John Meehan, Albert Mannheimer, Frederick Kohner.

Three Days of Rain 🎬½ 2002 Based on six loosely-connected short stories by Chekov, and set in Cleveland under a brooding rain. Director Michael Meredith attempts to highlight the small ways in which people reveal both cruelty and kindness. A wife's indifference toward a homeless person's hunger triggers a man's reevaluation of his life. A taxi driver has just lost his son, but his passenger tries to talk to his son. A lonely taxi driver is horrified when his wife behaves unkindly to a homeless man. A heroin addict trades sexual favors with a judge in order to see her daughter. A charming drunk manipulates his son for financial support. A mildly retarded man refuses to be pushed out of his job. Based on six stories by Anton Chekhov. 94m/C DVD. **C:** Blythe Danner, Bill Stockton, Merle Kennedy, Penny Allen, Michael Santoro, Heather Kafka, Maggie Walker; **D:** Michael Meredith; **W:** Michael Meredith; **C:** Cynthia Pusheck; **M:** Bob Belden.

Three Days of the Condor 🎬🎬🎬 1975 (R) CIA researcher Joe Turner (Redford) leaves the office to get some lunch and returns to find all his colleagues murdered. He calls for help but learns his own organization is responsible for the slaughter. So Joe goes on the run until he can expose the conspiracy. Good performances by Dunaway as photographer Kathy Hale, who is forced by Joe to help him but then becomes a willing accomplice. A post-Watergate tale of paranoia and suspense. Based on "Six Days of the Condor" by James Grady. 118m/C VHS, DVD. **C:** Robert Redford, Faye Dunaway, Cliff Robertson, Max von Sydow, John Houseman; **D:** Sydney Pollack; **W:** David Rayfiel; **C:** Owen Roizman; **M:** Dave Grusin.

Three Days to a Kill 🎬🎬 1991 (R) Calvin Sims is a mercenary hired to rescue a kidnapped ambassador—by any means necessary. 90m/C VHS, Fred Williamson, Bo Svenson, Henry Silva, Chuck Connors, Van Johnson, Sonny Landham; **D:** Fred Williamson.

Three Desperate Men 🎬🎬 1950 Three brothers accused of murder become outlaws. Not innovative, but satisfactory tale of the Old West. 71m/B VHS. Preston Foster, Virginia Grey, Jim Davis; **D:** Sam Newfield.

Three ... Extremes 🎬🎬 2004 (R) Twisted horror trilogy from Hong Kong, Korea, and Japan. Chan's truncated "Dumplings" (also a 90-minute feature) finds a vain former actress (Yeung), desperate to keep her looks and husband, partaking of the titular food prepared by Mei (Ling) with a secret ingredient and serious side effects. Park's "Cut" centers on

set Maugham play "Too Many Husbands" and filmed under the title in 1940. 🎵 "Someone to Watch Over Me; Which One?; Down Boy!; I've Been Kissed Before; I've Got a Crush on You; How Come You Like Me Like You Do?; Three for the Show. 93m/C VHS, Betty Grable, Jack Lemmon, Gower Champion, Marge Champion, Myron McCormick, Paul Harvey; **D:** H.C. Potter; **W:** Leonard Stern, Edward Hope; **C:** Arthur E. Arling; **M:** George Duning.

Three Fugitives 🎬🎬 1989 (PG-13) An ex-con holdup man (Nolte) determined to go straight is taken hostage by a bungling first-time 'bank robber, who is only attempting the holdup in order to support his withdrawn young daughter. Nolte winds up on the lam with the would-be robber and his daughter. The comedy is fun, the sentimental moments too sweet and slow. Remake of French "Les Fugitifs." 96m/C VHS, DVD. Nick Nolte, Martin Short, James Earl Jones, Kenneth McMillan, Sarah Rowland Doroff, Alan Ruck, Bruce McGill, Sy Richardson, Larry Miller, Lee Garlington, John Aylward, Kathy Kinney; **D:** Francis Veber; **W:** Francis Veber; **C:** Haskell Wexler; **M:** David McHugh.

Three Godfathers 🎬🎬🎬 1948 A sweet and sentimental western has three half-hearted outlaws on the run, taking with them an infant they find in the desert. Dedicated to western star and Ford alumni Harry Carey Sr. (whose son is one of the outlaws in the film) who died of cancer the year before, Ford had first filmed the tale with Carey Sr. as "Marked Men" in 1919. 82m/C VHS, DVD. John Wayne, Pedro Armendariz Sr., Harry Carey Jr., Ward Bond, Mae Marsh, Jane Darwell, Ben Johnson, Mildred Natwick, Guy Kibbee; **D:** John Ford; **C:** Winton C. Hoch.

Three Guys Named Mike 🎬🎬 1951 Wyman plays an overly enthusiastic airline stewardess who finds herself the object of affection from three guys named Mike, including an airline pilot, an advertising man, and a scientist. A cute comedy. 90m/B VHS, DVD. Jane Wyman, Van Johnson, Barry Sullivan, Howard Keel, Phyllis Kirk, Jeff Donnell; **D:** Charles Walters; **W:** Sidney Sheldon.

300 🎬🎬🎬 2007 (R) Blood, brutality, and buff bodies with the stylized action all done against bluescreen. Adaptation of Frank Miller's graphic novel follows the historical Battle of Thermopylae in 480 B.C. Sparta's King Leonidas (Butler) refuses to bow to the rule of the Persians and takes 300 of his best warriors to battle bejeweled and multi-pierced Xerxes (Santoro) and his hordes. Meanwhile, back at Sparta, the unfortunately-named Queen Gorgo (Headey) is battling sniveling politicos to get her hubby some reinforcements. This time Internet fanboy enthusiasm translated into blockbuster boxoffice bucks. 116m/C DVD, Blu-ray Disc, HD DVD, UHD. Gerard Butler, Lena Headey, Dominic West, David Wenham, Rodrigo Santoro, Andrew Tiernan, Tom Wisdom, Vincent Regan, Michael Fassbender, Stephen Mchattie; **D:** Zack Snyder; **W:** Zack Snyder, Kurt Johnstad, Michael B. Gordon; **C:** Larry Fong; **M:** Tyler Bates.

365 Nights in Hollywood 🎬🎬 1934 With stars in her eyes, Alice (Faye) comes to Hollywood to work in the movies but is snookered into attending a fraudulent acting school run by Delmar (Mitchell) and his partner Almont (Bradford). Delmar persuades wealthy Frank Young (Medford) to bankroll a film starring Alice, intending to sabotage the production and pocket the cash. Only desperate director Jimmy Dale (Dunn) is determined to make the most of his last opportunity and make Alice a star. 86m/B DVD, Alice Faye, James Dunn, Grant Mitchell, Frank Mitchell, John Bradford, Frank Melton, Jack Durant, John Qualen; **D:** George Marshall; **W:** William Conselman, Harry Jackson, Henry Johnson; **M:** Samuel Kaylin.

The 300 Spartans 🎬½ 1962 Typical sword-and-sandal epic (surprisingly, if not of the Italian muscleman variety) that's big on battles and small on character development. Sparta's King Leonidas (Egan) and his band of 300 warriors defend the mountain pass at Thermopylae against the much larger force of effete Persian King Xerxes (Farrar) in 480 B.C. Richardson is dignified as an Athenian military advisor but Egan is as stiff as the

the revenge taken on horror director Ryu (Lee) and his wife (Gang) by a resentful extra (Lim). Miike's "Box" has successful novelist Kyoko (Hasegawa) haunted by the death of her twin sister in childhood and forced to continually relive her part in the tragedy. Japanese, Cantonese, and Korean with subtitles. 126m/C DVD, Eai Ling, Tony Leung Ka-Fai, Pauline Lau, Meme Tian, Miriam Yeung, Chin Wan, Sum-Yeung Wong, Wai-sik Wong, Ka-Piu Yau, Kam-Mui Fung, Byung-hun Lee, Won-hie Lim, Hye-eong Kang, Jeong-yun Yun, Dae-yeon Lee, Gene Woo Park, Mi Mi Lee, Gyu-Suzuki, Yuu Suzuki, Mitsuru Akashodi; **D:** Fruit Chan, Takeshi Miike, Chan-wook Park; **W:** Nunnally Johnson; **C:** Stanley Cortez; **M:** Robert Emmett Dolan; **Nar:** Alistair Cooke. Oscars '57: Actress (Woodward); Golden Globes '58: Actress—Drama.

The Three Faces of Eve 🎬🎬½ 1957 Emotionally disturbed Eve (Woodward) seeks the help of psychiatrist Dr. Luther (Cobb), who eventually discovers she has three distinct personalities: a downtrodden housewife, a party girl, and a well-educated, well-balanced woman. So Luther decides to integrate all three into one Eve. Although Woodward gives a powerful performance, the film has dated badly particularly the narration by Cooke, which gives the film a now-stilted air. Although the film is fact-based, the story was deemed too implausible for the public to believe at the time without the assurances of the narrator. 91m/B VHS, DVD, Joanne Woodward, David Wayne, Lee J. Cobb, Nancy Kulp, Edwin Jerome, Vince Edwards; **D:** Nunnally Johnson; **W:** Nunnally Johnson; **C:** Stanley Cortez; **M:** Robert Emmett Dolan; **Nar:** Alistair Cooke.

Three Faces West 🎬🎬 1940 *The Refugee* 1940 A dust bowl community is helped by a Viennese doctor who left Europe to avoid Nazi persecution. He's aided by Duke in this odd combination of Western frontier saga and anti-Nazi propaganda. Works only part of the time. 79m/B VHS. **C:** John Wayne, Charles Coburn, Sigrid Gurie, Spencer Charters, Roland Varno; **D:** Bernard Vorhaus.

357 Magnum 🎬 1979 Jonathan Hightower, the CIA's special investigator in the Far East, speaks softly and carries a very big gun. 85m/C VHS, MX Mario Almada, Rene Auberjonois, Danny De La Paz; **D:** Larry Gross; **W:** Sam Bernard; **M:** Gary Chang.

3:15—The Moment of Truth 🎬🎬 1986 (R) A vicious high school gang is confronted by an angry ex-member in this so-so teen delinquent film. 86m/C VHS, Adam Baldwin, Deborah Foreman, Rene Auberjonois, Danny De La Paz, Gina Gershon; **W:** Sam Bernard; **M:** Gary Chang.

Three for Bedroom C 🎬🎬 1952 A movie star and a scientist make romance on a train bound for Los Angeles. Swanson's follow-up to "Sunset Boulevard." 74m/C VHS, Gloria Swanson, Fred Clark, Steve Brodie, Hans Conried, Margaret Dumont; **D:** Milton Bren.

Three for the Road 🎬🎬 1987 (PG) A young aspiring political aide and his roommate must escort a Senator's illmannered and spoiled daughter to a reform institution. On the road, they run into more than a few obstacles. Good performances elevate a bland script. Sheen made this movie before his riveting performance as a young GI in "Platoon". 98m/C VHS, Charlie Sheen, Kerri Green, Alan Ruck, Sally Kellerman; **D:** Bill W.L. Norton; **W:** Tim Metcalfe; **M:** Barry Goldberg.

Three for the Show 🎬🎬½ 1955 Julie (Grable) is a song-and-dance queen whose husband, Marty (Lemmon), was presumed dead in WWII. After she marries his songwriting partner, Vernon (Champion), Marty naturally shows up. Because she loves both men, Julie decides to set-up a household threesome until she can make up her mind. Champion's real-life spouse and dance partner, Marge, plays Grable's best friend. Some good dance numbers don't make up for the weak script. Based on the W. Somerset brush in that Spartan helmet. **108m/C DVD.** Richard Egan, Ralph Richardson, David Farrar, Barry Coe, Diane Baker, Kieron Moore, Donald Houston; **D:** Rudolph Maté; **C:** Geoffrey Unsworth; **M:** Manos Hadjidakis.

Three Legionnaires *𝄞𝄞½* 1937 Three Allied *Three Crazy Legionnaires* 1937 Three Allied soldiers in post-WWI Russia become involved in the Russian Revolution when they fall in love with a small village. **67m/B VHS.** Robert Armstrong, Lyle Talbot, Fifi d'Orsay, Anne Nagel, Donald Meek, Lyle Talbot, Stanley Fields, Maurice Black, Man Mountain Dean; **D:** Hamilton MacFadden; **W:** Carl Harbaugh, George Waggner; **C:** Ira Morgan.

The 300 Year Weekend *𝄞½* 1971 Ten people gather for a weekend-long group therapy session, led by Dr. Marshall (Tolan), that reveals what troubles them. You won't be interested. **123m/ C VHS.** Michael (Lawrence) Tolan, William Devane, Gabriel Dell, Dorothy Lyman, James Congdon, Sharon Laughlin, Roy Cooper, Mel Dowd, Bernard Ward, Carole Demas; **D:** Victor Stoloff; **W:** William Devane, Victor Stoloff; **C:** Joseph Brun; **M:** Gilber Fuller.

The 317th Platoon *𝄞𝄞𝄞* 1965 An emotionally gripping war drama of the French-Vietnamese War in which the 317th Platoon of the French Army, consisting of four French commanders and 41 Laotians, is ordered to leave Luong Ba, Cambodia and retreat to Tao Tsai. The men begin their march and slowly succumb to the elements and ambushes. Days later, when what is left of the platoon finally reaches Tao Tsai, the camp is in enemy hands and the remnants of the 317th Platoon are killed in cold blood. Director Schoendoerffer portrays this struggle, conflict, and the quiet haunting tension of war with great skill. In French with English subtitles. **100m/B VHS.** *FR* Jacques Perrin, Bruno Cremer, Pierre Fabre, Manuel Zarzo; **D:** Pierre Schoendoerffer; **W:** Pierre Schoendoerffer; **C:** Raoul Coutard; **M:** Gregorio Garcia Segura, Pierre Jansen.

Three Husbands *𝄞𝄞½* 1950 A deceased playboy leaves letters for the title characters incriminating their wives in extramarital affairs. The men's reactions are pure farce—even though this same concept was played straight with a sex change in the earlier "A Letter to Three Wives." **79m/B VHS, DVD.** Eve Arden, Ruth Warrick, Vanessa Brown, Howard da Silva, Shepperd Strudwick, Jane Darwell; **D:** Irving Reis.

Three in the Attic *𝄞½* 1968 (R) A college student juggles three girlfriends at the same time. When the girls find out they are being two-timed, they lock their boyfriend in an attic and exhaust him with forced sexual escapades. Then they talk. Limited trashy and foolish appeal. **92m/C VHS.** Christopher Jones, Yvette Mimieux, John Beck; **D:** Richard Wilson.

Three in the Cellar *𝄞𝄞* *Up in the Cellar* 1970 (R) A disgruntled college student seeks revenge on the school president by seducing his wife, daughter and mistress. Good screenplay helps carry it off. **92m/C VHS.** Wes Stern, Joan Collins, Larry Hagman, Judy Pace; **D:** Theodore J. Flicker.

Three in the Saddle *𝄞½* 1945 Ritter and the Texas Rangers fight for law and order. **61m/B VHS, DVD.** Tex Ritter, Dave O'Brien, Charles "Blackie" King; **D:** Harry Fraser; **C:** Robert E. Cline.

Three Kinds of Heat *𝄞* 1987 (R) Three Interpol agents track down a warring Asian crime lord. Alternately tongue-in-cheek and silly. Never released in theatres—it found it's home on video. Stevens created "The Outer Limits" for TV. **88m/C VHS.** Robert Ginty, Victoria Barrett, Shakti; **D:** Leslie Stevens. **VIDEO**

Three Kings *𝄞𝄞𝄞* 1999 (R) Director Russell turns the war movie genre on its ear with his subversive, chaotic, and ultimately satisfying studio film debut. At the end of the Gulf War, Special Forces Major Gates (Clooney) recruits three Army reservists to join him on an illegal mission to steal gold bullion which Hussein's troops had stolen from Kuwait. They wind up learning too much about U.S. policies and broken promises in the Middle East. Clooney is perfect as the pragmatic Gates, and Russell supplies the right mix of cynicism, dark humor, and action-movie heroism. **115m/C VHS, DVD.** George Clooney, Mark Wahlberg, Ice Cube, Spike Jonze, Nora Dunn, Jamie Kennedy, Mykelti Williamson, Clifford Curtis, Said Taghmaoui, Judy Greer, Liz Stauber, Holt McCallany; **D:** David O. Russell; **W:** David O. Russell; **C:** Newton Thomas (Tom) Sigel; **M:** Carter Burwell. Broadcast Film Critics '99: Breakthrough Perf. (Jonze).

---

the deaths. Common bloody revenge tale includes bits of dark humor. In Portuguese, with English subtitles. **90m/C VHS, DVD.** *PT* Maria Luisa Mendonca, Marieta Severo, Julia Lemmertz, Luiza Mariani, Carlos Vereza; **D:** Aluisio Abranches; **W:** Heitor Dhalia, Wilson Friere; **C:** Marcelo Durst. **VIDEO**

Three Men and a Baby *𝄞𝄞* 1987 (PG) The arrival of a young baby forever changes the lives of three sworn bachelors living in New York. Well-paced, charming and fun, with good acting from all. A remake of the French movie "Three Men and a Cradle." **102m/C VHS, DVD.** Tom Selleck, Steve Guttenberg, Ted Danson, Margaret Colin, Nancy Travis, Philip Bosco, Celeste Holm, Derek de Lint, Cynthia Harris, Lisa Blair, Michelle Blair, Paul Guilfoyle; **D:** Leonard Nimoy; **W:** James Orr, Jim Cruickshank; **C:** Adam Greenberg; **M:** Marvin Hamlisch.

Three Men and a Cradle *𝄞𝄞𝄞½* *Trois Hommes et un Coufin* 1985 (PG-13) Three carefree bachelors, Jacques (Dussollier), Pierre (Giraud), and Michel (Boujenah), find a baby girl in a basket outside the door of the home they share. One is the father—although none of the men are sure which one it is. After the initial shock of learning how to take care of a child, they fall in love with her and won't let her go. There's a strange subplot about Jacques hiding heroin in the baby's diapers that gets them all involved with drug dealers. Still, everything is played for laughs and the film has heaps of charm. French with subtitles. Remade in 1987 as "Three Men and a Baby." **100m/ C VHS, DVD.** *FR* Roland Giraud, Michel Boujenah, Andre Dussollier, Phillippe Leroy-Beaulieu, Martine Villalonga, Dominque Lavanant; **D:** Coline Serreau; **W:** Coline Serreau; **C:** Jean-Yves Escoffier. Cesar '86: Film, Support. Actor (Boujenah), Writing.

Three Men and a Little Lady *𝄞𝄞½* 1990 (PG) In this sequel to "Three Men and a Baby," the mother of the once abandoned infant decides that her child needs a father. Although she wants Selleck, he doesn't get the message and so she chooses a snooty British director. The rest of the movie features various semi-comic attempts to rectify the situation. **100m/C VHS, DVD.** Tom Selleck, Steve Guttenberg, Ted Danson, Nancy Travis, Robin Weisman, Christopher Cazenove, Fiona Shaw, Sheila Hancock, John Boswall, Jonathan Lynn, Sydney Walsh; **D:** Emile Ardolino; **W:** Charlie Peters, Sara Parriott, Josann McGibbon; **C:** Adam Greenberg; **M:** James Newton Howard.

Three Men on a Horse *𝄞𝄞* 1936 Comedy classic about mild-mannered McHugh's ability to predict horse races and the bettors that try to take advantage of him. Blondell is great as the Brooklynese girlfriend of one of the bettors. Lots of laughs, but don't watch for the horse-racing scenes, because there aren't many. **88m/B VHS.** Frank McHugh, Joan Blondell, Carol Hughes, Allen Jenkins, Guy Kibbee, Sam Levene; **D:** Mervyn LeRoy.

The Three Musketeers *𝄞𝄞* *D'Artagnan* 1916 One of the many movie adaptation of Alexandre Dumas' adventure, but this one comes from the hand of famed movie pioneer Ince. D'Artagnan joins the title characters in saving France's Queen Anne from a nefarious plot. Silent with the original organ score. **74m/B VHS.** Orin Johnson, Dorothy Dalton, Louise Glaum, Walt Whitman; **D:** Charles Swickard.

The Three Musketeers *𝄞𝄞𝄞½* 1921 D'Artagnan swashbuckles silently amid stylish sets, scores of extras and exquisite costumes. Relatively faithful adaptation of Alexandre Dumas novel, slightly altered in favor of D'Artagnan's lover. Classic Fairbanks, with the energetic stunts. **120m/B VHS, DVD.** Douglas Fairbanks Sr., Leon Bary, George Siegmann, Eugene Pallette, Boyd Irwin, Thomas Holding, Sidney Franklin, Charles Stevens, Nigel de Bruiler, Willis Robards, Mary MacLaren; **D:** Fred Niblo; **W:** Lotta Woods, Douglas Fairbanks Sr.; **C:** Arthur Edeson; **M:** Louis F. Gottschalk.

The Three Musketeers *𝄞𝄞𝄞* 1933 Modern adaptation of the classic tale by Alexander Dumas depicts the three friends as members of the Foreign Legion. Weakest of Wayne serials, in 12 parts. **215m/B VHS, DVD.** John Wayne, Jack Mulhall, Raymond Hat-

---

ton, Lon Chaney Jr., John Wayne, Francis X. Bushman, Ruth Hall, Noah Beery Jr., Al Ferguson; **D:** Colbert Clark, Armand Schaefer; **W:** Colbert Clark, Bennett Cohen, Wyndham Gittens, Norman S. Hall; **C:** Tom Galligan, Ernest Miller.

The Three Musketeers *𝄞𝄞* 1935 Three swordsmen, loyal to each other, must battle the corrupt Cardinal Richelieu. Generally regarded as the least exciting adaptation of Alexander Dumas' classic tale. The first talking version. **95m/B VHS.** Walter Abel, Paul Lukas, Moroni Olsen, Ian Keith, Margot Grahame, Heather Angel, Onslow Stevens, Miles Mander; **D:** Rowland V. Lee; **M:** Max Steiner.

The Three Musketeers *𝄞𝄞𝄞* 1939 Musical-comedy version of the famed Alexandre Dumas swashbuckling saga. Ameche is a singing D'Artagnan and the three Ritz brothers are the inept and cowardly Musketeers (who turn out to be phonies, after all). Silly fun. *♪* My Lady, Song of the Musketeers; Voila; Chicken Soup. **73m/B VHS, DVD.** Don Ameche, Al Ritz, Harry Ritz, Jimmy Ritz, Binnie Barnes, Lionel Atwill, Miles Mander, Gloria Stuart, Pauline Moore, Joseph Schildkraut, John Carradine, Douglass Dumbrille; **D:** Allan Dwan; **W:** M.M. Musselman, William A. Drake, Sam Hellman.

The Three Musketeers *𝄞𝄞𝄞½* 1948 The three musketeers who are "all for one and one for all" join forces with D'Artagnan to battle the evil Cardinal Richelieu in this rambunctious adaptation of the classic tale by Alexander Dumas. Good performances by the cast, who combined drama and comedy well. Turner's first color film. **126m/C VHS, DVD.** Lana Turner, Gene Kelly, June Allyson, Gig Young, Angela Lansbury, Van Heflin, Keenan Wynn, Robert Coote, Reginald Owen, Frank Morgan, Vincent Price, Patricia Medina; **D:** George Sidney.

The Three Musketeers *𝄞𝄞½* 1974 (PG) Extravagant and funny version of the Dumas classic. Three swashbucklers (Reed, Chamberlain, Finlay) and their country cohort (York), who wishes to join the Musketeers, set out to save the honor of the French Queen (Chaplin). To do so they must oppose the evil cardinal (Heston) who has his eyes on the power behind the throne (Dunaway). Welch is amusing as clumsy lady-in-waiting Constance. A strong cast leads this winning combination of slapstick and high adventure. Followed by "The Four Musketeers" and "The Return of the Musketeers." **105m/C VHS, DVD.** Richard Chamberlain, Oliver Reed, Michael York, Raquel Welch, Frank Finlay, Christopher Lee, Faye Dunaway, Charlton Heston, Geraldine Chaplin, Simon Ward, Jean-Pierre Cassel, William Hobbs; **D:** Richard Lester; **W:** George MacDonald Fraser; **C:** David Watkin; **M:** Michel Legrand. Golden Globes '75: Actress—Mus./Comedy (Welch).

The Three Musketeers *𝄞𝄞* 1993 (PG) Yet another version of the classic swashbuckler with Porthos, Athos, Aramis, and the innocent D'Artanan banding together against the evil Cardinal Richelieu and the tempting Milady DeWinter to save France. Cute stars, a little swordplay, a few jokes, and cartoon bad guys. Okay for the younger crowd. **105m/C VHS, DVD.** Kiefer Sutherland, Charlie Sheen, Chris O'Donnell, Oliver Platt, Rebecca De Mornay, Tim Curry, Gabrielle Anwar, Julie Delpy, Michael Wincott; **D:** Stephen Herek; **W:** David Loughery; **C:** Dean Semler; **M:** Michael Kamen.

3 Ninjas *𝄞𝄞½* 1992 (PG) Lively kid's actioner about three brothers who are trained as ninjas by their grandpa. When a group of bad guys tries to kidnap the boys, they're in for trouble. Sort of a cross between "The Karate Kid" and "Home Alone" that is suitable for family viewing. Followed by "3 Ninjas Kick Back." **84m/C VHS, DVD.** Victor Wong, Michael Treanor, Max Elliott Slade, Chad Power, Rand Kingsley, Alan McRae, Margarita Franco, Toru Tanaka, Patrick Laborteaux; **D:** Jon Turteltaub; **W:** Edward Emanuel; **M:** Richard (Rick) Marvin.

3 Ninjas: High Noon at Mega Mountain *𝄞𝄞* 1997 (PG) *Three Ninjas: Showdown at Mega Mountain* 1997 (PG) Fourth installment of the kid-fantasy franchise finds brothers Rocky (Botuchis), Colt (O'Laskey), and Tum-Tum (Roeske) in the

---

The Three Little Pigs *𝄞𝄞½* 1984 From "Faerie Tale Theatre" comes the story of three little pigs, the houses they lived in and the wolf that tried to do them in. **60m/C VHS, DVD.** Billy Crystal, Jeff Goldblum, Valerie Perrine; **D:** Howard Storm. **CABLE**

Three Little Words *𝄞𝄞𝄞* 1950 A musical biography of songwriting team Harry Ruby and Bert Kalmar, filled with Kalmar-Ruby numbers. Helen Kane (famous for her boop-boop-de-boops) dubbed "I Wanna Be Loved By You" for Reynolds. A musical in the best MGM tradition. *♪* I Wanna Be Loved By You; Who's Sorry Now?; Three Little Words; I Love You So Much; She's Mine, All Mine; So Long, Oo-Long; Hooray for Captain Spaulding; Up In the Clouds; All Alone Monday. **102m/C VHS, DVD.** Fred Astaire, Red Skelton, Vera-Ellen, Arlene Dahl, Keenan Wynn, Gloria De Haven, Debbie Reynolds, Gale Robbins; **D:** Richard Thorpe; **M:** Andre Previn. Golden Globes '51: Actor—Mus./Comedy (Astaire).

Three Lives and Only One Death *𝄞𝄞½* *Trois Vies et Une Seule Mort* 1996 Surrealist film where Mastroianni in four roles. Salesman Mateo Strano walks out on his wife Maria (Paredes) and doesn't see her for 20 years. When he finally returns, Mateo wants her back, although Maria's got a new husband, Andre (Atkine). Then there's Georges Vickers, negative anthropology professor-turned street tramp who takes up with hooker Tania (Galiena), who also has another identity. Then he's a butler who's trying to murder a young couple and steal their child and finally, Mastroianni's a rich industrialist who seems to be suffering from multiple personalities. And yes, somehow all the stories do tie together. French with subtitles. **124m/C VHS.** *FR* Marcello Mastroianni, Anna Galiena, Marisa Paredes, Melvil Poupaud, Chiara Mastroianni, Arielle Dombasle, Feodor Atkine, Jean-Yves Gautier, Pierre Bellemare, Lou Castel, Jacques Pieller; **D:** Raul Ruiz; **W:** Raul Ruiz, Pascal Bonitzer; **C:** Laurent Machuel; **M:** Jorge Arriagada.

The Three Lives of Karen *𝄞𝄞½* 1997 (PG-13) Thriller finds Karen Winthrop (O'Grady) engaged to state trooper Matt (Guinee) and seemingly happy until Paul Riggs (Boutsikaris) shows up. He has proof that Karen is actually his wife Emily who disappeared four years before, abandoning him and their daughter Jessica (Bugajski). So the confused Karen returns with Paul to try and remember what happened to her. She learns that she's actually disappeared twice before and the flashbacks Karen has of her past are terrifying. **88m/C VHS.** Gail O'Grady, Dennis Boutsikaris, Tim Guinee, Monica Bugajski; **D:** David Burton Morris; **W:** David Chisholm; **C:** John L. (Ndiaga) Demps Jr. **CABLE**

The Three Lives of Thomasina *𝄞𝄞* 1963 (G) A turn-of-the-century Scotland, a veterinarian orders his daughter's beloved cat destroyed when the pet is diagnosed with tetanus. After the cat's death (with scenes of kitty heaven), a beautiful and mysterious healer from the woods is able to bring the animal back to life and restore the animal to the little girl. Lovely Disney fairy tale with good performances by all. **95m/C VHS, DVD.** Patrick McGoohan, Susan Hampshire, Karen Dotrice, Matthew Garber; **D:** Don Chaffey; **V:** Elspeth March.

The 3 Marias *𝄞½* *As Tres Marias* 2003 Three decades after Filomena (Severo) dumped Guerra (Vereza) and married his rival, Guerra murders her husband and sons in cold blood. Things get messy when Filomena conspires with her three daughters—all named Maria—to avenge

---

3 Ninjas Kick Back 🐾🐾½ **1994** (PG) Sequel to the popular "3 Ninjas." Three brothers help their grandfather protect a ceremonial knife won in a ninja tournament in Japan 50 years earlier. Gramps' ancient adversary in that tournament, now an evil tycoon, wants the sword back and he's willing to enlist the aid of his three American grandchildren, members of garage band Teenage Vomit, to get it. The showdown eventually heads to Japan, where "Kick Back," unlike predecessors, dispenses with the Japan-bashing. High-spirited action fare that kids will enjoy. **95m/C VHS, DVD.** Victor Wong, Max Elliot Slade, Sean Fox, Evan Bonifant, Sab Shimono, Dustin Nguyen, Jason Schombing, Caroline Junko King, Angelo Tiffe; **D:** Simon S. Sheen; **W:** Alex S. Kim; **C:** Eugene Shlugleit; **M:** Gary Stevan Scott.

3 Ninjas Knuckle Up 🐾🐾½ **1995** (PG-13) Brothers Rocky (Treanor), Tum Tum (Power), and Colt (Slade) spend their summer vacation with ever-wise Grandpa Mori (Wong) and get to practice their martial arts skills on a variety of villains. Seems a waste management company has been illegally dumping toxins onto the nearby Indian reservation where the boys' friend Jo (Lightning) lives and have even kidnapped her dad (Shanks) to keep him silent. So it's our pint-sized heroes to the rescue. Filmed in '92 but released after "3 Ninjas Kick Back," which explains why Treanor and Power are missing from the second film. **84m/C VHS, DVD.** Victor Wong, Michael Treanor, Chad Power, Crystle Lightning, Patrick Kilpatrick, Don Shanks, Charles Napier, Nick Ramus, Vincent Schiavelli; **D:** Christopher Falcona; **M:** Richard (Rick) Marvin.

Three Nuts in Search of a Bolt 🐾½ **1964** (R) Three neurotics send a surrogate to a comely psychiatrist for help, but the shrink mistakes the surrogate's a three-way multiple personality. Raunchy monkey-shines ensue. Includes Van Doren's infamous beer bath scene. **78m/C VHS, DVD.** Mamie Van Doren, Tommy Noonan, Paul Gilbert, Alvy Moore; **D:** Tommy Noonan.

301, 302 🐾 **1994** Confusing horror story told in flashbacks focuses on two women in neighboring high-rise apartments. A young policeman is investigating the disappearance of the woman from apartment 302 (Hwang). He questions the tenant across the hall in 301 (Pang), an obsessive cook who tries to share her culinary results with Hwang, who happens to be an anorexic writer. Both have dark secrets in their pasts, which they share, leading to a grotesque resolution of their friendship. **99m/C VHS, DVD.** KiYeun-Jin Bang, Sin-Hye Hwang, Chu-Ryun Kim; **D:** Chul-Soo Park; **W:** Suh-Goon Lee.

Three o'Clock High 🐾🐾½ **1987** (PG) A nerdy high school journalist is assigned a profile of the new kid in school, who turns out to be the biggest bully, too. He approaches his task with great unease. Silly teenage farce is given souped-up direction by Spielberg protege Joanou. Features decent work by the young cast. **97m/C VHS, DVD.** Casey Siemaszko, Anne Ryan, Stacey Glick, Jonathan Wise, Richard Tyson, Jeffrey Tambor, Philip Baker Hall, John P. Ryan; **D:** Phil Joanou.

middle of a takeover at an amusement park. The ninja trained brothers, along with a computer-whiz neighbor (Early-wine) and reffing action hero Dave Dragon (Hogan) must save the day when Medusa (Anderson) and her henchmen ransom the park and its guests. Typically, the adults are incompetent when they're not busy being nasty. Pre-pubescent kids are the only ones likely to find this entertaining—if they're not too discriminating. The "action" is somewhere between cartoon Medusa's lead henchman. **93m/C VHS, DVD.** Hulk Hogan, Loni Anderson, Jim Varney, Victor Wong, Mathew Botuchis, Michael J. O'Laskey II, J.P. Roeske II, Chelsey Earlywine, Alan McRae, Margarita Franco, Kirk Baily; **D:** Sean McNamara, Jeff Phillips; **C:** Blake T. Evans; **W:** Sean McNamara, Jeff Phillips.

tian Matheson, Thomas Szolosi; **M:** Tangerine Dream.

Three of Hearts 🐾½ **1993** (R) Slick look at love in contemporary downtown New York. The triangle consists of sisters believe all their problems are caused by living in the provinces and their childhood home in Moscow, and their plan to marry a gold digger, 15-year-old singing sensation Durbin made her debut by bisexual Connie (Lynch), just dumped by girlfriend Ellen (Fenn), who in turn seduced by hired escort Joe (Baldwin), who will break her heart causing her to turn back to the sympathetic Connie. But guess what happens. Hiply superficial plot is transparent although the three leads are likeable, especially Lynch as the lanky lovelorn Connie. Don't reac further if you don't want to know what happens since the film was shot with two endings. U.S. release pairs Joe and Ellen for a typically American happy ending; the European release doesn't. **102m/C VHS, DVD.** Kelly Lynch, William Baldwin, Sherilyn Fenn, Joe Pantoliano Gail Strickland, Cec Verrell, Claire Callaway, Tony Amendola; **D:** Yurek Bogayevicz; **W:** Adam Greenman; **M:** Richard Gibbs.

Three on a Match 🐾🐾🐾 **1932** An actress, a stenographer and a society woman get together for a tenth year reunion. They become embroiled in a world of crime when Blondell's gangster boyfriend takes a liking to Dvorak. She leaves her husband and takes up with the crook. The results are tragic. Bogart's first gangster role. **64m/B VHS.** Joan Blondell, Warren William, Ann Dvorak, Bette Davis, Lyle Talbot, Humphrey Bogart, Patricia Ellis, Grant Mitchell; **D:** Mervyn LeRoy.

Three on a Meathook Woof! **1972** When a young man and his father living on an isolated farm receive female visitors, bloodshed is quick to follow. Essentially a remake of "Psycho," and very loosely based on the crimes of Ed Gein. Filmed in Louisville, Kentucky. **85m/C VHS, DVD.** Charles Kissinger, James Pickett, Sherry Steiner, Carolyn Thompson; **D:** William Girdler; **W:** William Girdler; **C:** William Asman; **M:** William Girdler.

Three on the Trail 🐾🐾🐾 **1935** This fifth entry in the "Hopalong Cassidy" series is one of the more ambitious. The fast-moving plot concerns Hoppy's (Boyd) efforts to help young schoolmarm Mary Stevens (Evans) from the clutches of an evil saloon keeper. Includes "The Threepenny Opera" (1931). **124m/B VHS.** GF Curt Jurgens, Hildegarde Knef, Gert Frobe, June Ritchie, Lino Ventura, Sammy Davis Jr.; **D:** Wolfgang Staudte; **W:** Wolfgang Staudte; **C:** Archie Stout.

The Three Penny Opera 🐾🐾 **1931** Mack the Knife presides over an exciting world of thieves, murderers, beggars, prostitutes and corrupt officials in a seedy section of London. Based on the opera by Kurt Weill and Bertold Brecht, which was based on "The Beggar's Opera" by John Gay. Remake of "The Threepenny Opera" (1931). **124m/B VHS.** GF Curt Jurgens, Hildegarde Knef, Gert Frobe, June Ritchie, Lino Ventura, Sammy Davis Jr.; **D:** Wolfgang Staudte; **W:** Wolfgang Staudte; **C:** Archie Stout.

Three Seasons 🐾🐾 **1998** (PG-13) First American indie production to be shot in Vietnam with native-speaking actors since the war (by Vietnam-born, U.S.-raised director Bui in his feature debut) has a number of beautiful shots but not much story to back it up. Bustling Ho Chi Minh City (Saigon) sets the stage for the intertwining fortunes of five characters: young flower seller Kien An (Hiep); street kid Woody (Cuoc), cyclo driver Hai (Duong), prostitute Lan (Bui), and ex-Marine Hager (Keitel), who's searching for his Amer-Asian daughter. **110m/C VHS.** Harvey Keitel, Don Duong, Nguyen Ngoc Hiep, Zoe Bui, Nguyen Huu Duoc, Tran Manh Cuong; **D:** Tony Bui; **W:** Tony Bui, Timothy Linh Bui; **C:** Lisa Rinzler; **M:** Richard Horowitz. Ind. Spirit '00. Cinematog.; Sundance '99. Cinematog., Aud. Award, Grand Jury Prize.

Three Secrets 🐾🐾½ **1950** A plane crashes and the only survivor is a five-year-old boy. Three women, each with a secret, seek to claim him as the child filled with fart jokes and little else would have it, his buddy picks him up from jail in each gave up for adoption five years before. Tearjerker with good cast. **98m/B VHS.** Eleanor Parker, Patricia Neal, Ruth Roman, Frank Lovejoy, Leif Erickson; **D:** Robert Wise.

Three Sovereigns for Sarah 🐾🐾🐾 **1985** Witch-hunters tortured and toasted Sarah's two sisters for practicing witchcraft in the past. Now, accused of witchery herself, she struggles to prove the family's innocence. Excellent, made-for-PBS. Fine performances from all, especially Redgrave. **152m/C VHS, DVD.** Vanessa Redgrave, Phyllis Thaxter, Patrick McGoohan; **D:** Philip Leacock.

Three Stooges in Orbit 🐾🐾½ **1962** Three TV performers (you know who) looking for a shtick and a place to live, encounter a crazy scientist with a rocket-like invention. In a shocking plot twist, the boys accidentally launch the rocket and must battle Martians to save the world and their TV career. **87m/B VHS, DVD.** Moe Howard, Larry Fine, Joe DeRita, Vicki Trickett, Quinn (K.) Redeker, Samson Burke, Lewis Charles, Martin McKeever, Michael McKeever, John Cliff, George Neise; **D:** Edward L. Bernds; **M:** Paul Dunlap.

The Three Stooges Meet Hercules 🐾🐾½ **1961** The Three Stooges are transported back to ancient Ithaca by a time machine with a young scientist; and his girlfriend. When the girl is captured, they enlist the help of Hercules to rescue her. **80m/B VHS, DVD.** Moe Howard, Larry Fine, Joe DeRita, Emil Sitka, Carol Christensen, Edson Stroll; **D:** Edward L. Bernds; **C:** Charles S. Welbourne; **M:** Paul Dunlap.

Three Stops to Murder 🐾 **Blood Orange 1953** An FBI agent investigates the murder of a beautiful model in this early, unspectacular Hammer production. **76m/B VHS.** GB Tom Conway, Mila Parely, Naomi Chance, Eric Pohlman, Andrew Osborn, Richard Watts, Eileen Way, Delphi Lawrence; **D:** Terence Fisher; **W:** Jan Read; **C:** Walter J. (Jimmy W.) Harvey; **M:** Ivor Slaney.

Three Strange Loves 🐾🐾🐾 **Thirst 1949** Men and women struggle with loneliness, old age, and sterility. Sometimes disjointed, but for the most part, well-made. Finely acted in Swedish with English subtitles. **88m/B VHS.** SW Eva Henning, Birgit Tengroth, Birger Malmsten; **D:** Ingmar Bergman.

Three Strikes Woof! **2000** (R) Two-time loser Rob is released from jail determined to stay straight and thus avoid the harsh sentencing of California's "Three Strikes" law. But as luck and a lame script would have it, his first day as a free man throughout, highlighted by the Elvis strutting through town in a "Reservoir Dogs" homage. Gratuitous violence and cliched action doesn't help movie's one-note appeal but the look is slick and the boys drive cool cars. **125m/C VHS, DVD, US Kevin**

3000 Miles to Graceland 🐾½ **2001** (R) Shockingly original olic sets Elvis impersonators in Vegas, only three Presley's wanna rob, not rock. Ex-cellmates Russell and Costner are the lead Kings, Michael and Murphy, who team up with Arquette, Slater, and Woodbine, and head to the quaint desert burg to relieve its wagering establishments of some extra cash. After a strong opening segment, any moments of comic relief are scattered throughout, highlighted by the Elvis strutting through town in a "Reservoir Dogs" homage. Gratuitous violence and cliched action doesn't help movie's one-note appeal. **125m/C VHS, DVD, US Kevin** Costner, Kurt Russell, Courteney Cox Arquette, Christian Slater, Bokeem Woodbine, David Arquette, Jon Lovitz, Howie Long, Thomas Haden Church, Kevin Pollak, Ice-T, Paul Anka; **D:** Demian Lichtenstein; **C:** David Franco; **M:** George S. Clinton.

Three Smart Girls 🐾🐾½ **1936** Fast-moving musical features three high-spirited sisters who attempt to bring their divorced parents back together. Their plan is thwarted when they learn of their father's plan to marry a gold digger, 15-year-old singing sensation Durbin made her debut but in this film. Based on a story by Cornmandini. Followed by "Three Smart Girls Grow Up." **84m/B VHS, DVD.** Deanna Durbin, Binnie Barnes, Alice Brady, Ray Milland, Charles Winninger, Mischa Auer, Nan Grey, Barbara Read; **D:** Henry Koster; **W:** Adele Commandini, Austin Parker; **C:** Joseph Valentine.

Three Smart Girls Grow Up 🐾🐾🐾 **1939** Durbin once again plays matchmaker, this time for her two older sisters and their fellas. A delightful mix of comedy and song, this lighthearted sequel turned out to be one of the top-grossing films of the year. Durbin sings "Because," which became one of her biggest hits. **88m/B VHS.** Deanna Durbin, Charles Winninger, Nan Grey, Helen Parrish, Robert Cummings, William Lundigar, Ernest Cossart; **D:** Henry Koster; **W:** Felix Jackson, Bruce Manning.

The Three Sisters 🐾🐾½ **1965** A stage production from the Actor's Studio of Chekhov's play about unhappy siblings in turn-of-the-century Russia. The three sisters believe all their problems are caused by living in the provinces and their childhood home in Moscow, and their plan to marry a gold digger, 15-year-old singing sensation Durbin made her debut but in this film. Based on a story by Cornmandini. Followed by "Three Smart Girls Grow Up." **167m/B VHS.** Shelley Winters, Sandy Dennis, Geraldine Page, Kevin McCarthy, Kim Stanley, Luther Adler, Robert Loggia, James Olson, Gerald Hiken; **D:** Paul Bogart.

Three Texas Steers 🐾½ **1939** Danger along the Range 1939 A circus owner inherits some land that the government wants for a water project and her manager tries to get it for himself. Enter the terrific trio to set things right. Last of the series for Terhune. The scenes of the circus tire were taken from "Circus Girl" (1937). **59m/B VHS.** John Wayne, Ray Corrigan, Max Terhune, Carole Landis, Ralph Graves, Roscoe Ates; **D:** George Sherman.

Three the Hard Way 🐾🐾½ **1974** (R) An insane white supremacist has a plan to eliminate blacks by contaminating water supplies. A big blaxploitation money maker and the first to team Brown, Williamson, and Kelly, who would go on to make several more pictures together. **93m/C VHS, Jim Brown, Fred Williamson, Jim Kelly,** Sheila Frazier, Jay Robinson, Alex Rocco; **D:** Gordon Parks.

3:10 to Yuma 🐾🐾½ **1957** (R) In order to collect $200 he desperately needs, a poor cattle rancher (Heflin) has to hold a dangerous killer at bay while waiting to turn the outlaw (Ford) over to the authorities arriving on the 3:10 train to Yuma. Stuck in a hotel room with the outlaw's gang gathering outside, the question arises as to who is the prisoner. Heflin is continually worked on by the outlaw Ford, it's gunplay. Crippled by war injury and bettin a drought, Evans struggles to keep his ranch and the respect of his wife (Mo) and son (Lerman). When Wade is captured and crime spree, Evans joins the posse that will transport him to the titular train. Wade quickly recognizes the weaknesses of the men guarding him and turns them to his advantage, leaving Evans to defend himself and his son against legendary outlaw Ben Wade (Crowe) against madman second-in command C'arlie Prince (Foster), in a career-making battle that's as much about psychology as it's gunplay. Masterfully explores the grey area between good and bad, and Vangold infuses the genre with a level of energy and excitement that hasn't been seen in a while. **120m/C VHS.** Glenn Ford, Van Heflin, Felicia Farr, Richard Jaeckel, Leora Dana, Robert Emhardt, Henry Jones, Ford Rainey; **D:** Delmer Daves; **W:** Halsted Welles; **C:** Charles Lawton Jr.; **M:** George Duning.

3:10 to Yuma 🐾🐾½ **2007** (R) Remake of the 1957 classic western pits rancher Dan Evans (Bale) against outlaw Ben Wade (Crowe). Evans, a down-on-his-luck rancher with more than its share of great dialogue. The two leads are exceptional, with Ford making the most of his character's cunning charm. Suspenseful, well-made action western adapted from an Elmore Leonard story. **122m/C VHS, DVD, Blu-ray Disc, US** Russell Crowe, Christian Bale, Ben Foster, Logan Lerman, Peter Fonda, Gretchen Mol, Dallas Roberts, Alan Tudyk, Vinessa Shaw, Kevin Durand, Johnny Whitworth; **D:** James Mangold; **W:** Halsted Welles, Michael Brandt, Derek Haas; **C:** Phedon Papamichael; **M:** Marco Beltrami.

Three Smart Girls ... find a way to clear himself and get home. There's not much to redeem this disaster of a flick, unless you find embarrassingly stereotypical characters and "In Living Color" reject jokes amusing. **83m/C VHS, DVD.** Brian Hooks, N'Bushe Wright, Faizon Love, Starletta DuPois, David Alan Grier, Dean Norris, Meagan Good, De'Aundre Bonds, Antonio Fargas, Vincent Schiavelli, David Leisure, Gerald S. O'Loughlin, George Wallace, E40, Barima McNight, Mo'Nique, Shawn Fonteno; **D:** DJ Pooh; **W:** DJ Pooh; **C:** Johnny (John W.) Simmons; **M:** Aaron Anderson, Andrew Slack.

Costner, Kurt Russell, Christian Slater, Bokeem Woodbine, David Arquette, Courteney Cox, Kevin Pollak, Jon Lovitz, Howie Long, Thomas Haden Church, Ice-T, David Kaye, Louis Lombardi; *D:* Demian Lichtenstein; *W:* Demian Lichtenstein, Brett and Recco; *C:* David Franco; *M:* George S. Clinton.

Three Times 🦴🦴 2005 *Zuihaode Shiguang* A trio of linked stories (about romantic longing) set in three time periods with Qi Shu and Chen Chang playing the leads. "A Time for Love" (1966) has a young soldier romancing a pool-hall hostess. "A Time for Freedom" (1911) is a silent drama with a courtesan in a brothel hoping a client will purchase her freedom. "A Time for Youth" (2005) finds a bisexual singer in Taipei drifting into an affair with a photographer. Mandarin and Taiwanese with subtitles. 139m/C DVD. *TW* Shu Qi, Chang Chen; *D:* Hou Hsiao-Hsien; *W:* Chu Tien-Wen; *C:* Mark Lee Ping-Bin.

Three to Tango 🦴½ 1999 (PG-13) Dopey would-be romantic comedy only demonstrates that actors who make it big in TV series think about sticking to the small screen. (Or being more careful about their big screen choices.) Married tycoon Charles Newman (McDermott) has it in his power to award a lucrative contract to struggling architect Oscar Novak (Perry) and his partner, Peter Steinberg (Peter). Somehow, Newman gets the impression that Oscar is gay and would be the perfect guy to spy on Newman's young mistress, Amy (Campbell), whom he fears is about to wander. Naturally, Oscar falls for the girl and then must work around all the mistaken assumptions. Yawn. 96m/C VHS, DVD. Dylan McDermott, Neve Campbell, Matthew Perry, Oliver Platt, Cylk Cozart, John C. McGinley, Bob Balaban, Kelly Rowan, Deborah Rush, Rodney Vaccaro, Aline Brosh McKenna; *C:* Loyal Griggs; *M:* Walter Scharf.

Three Violent People 🦴🦴 1957 Family feud set in post-Civil War Old West features Heston and Baxter impulsively marrying and returning to run the family ranch. Heston's brother (Tryon) wants to sell the ranch in order to get his share of the inheritance and then Heston finds out Baxter was once a prostitute. In this case family squabbles don't make for an exciting film. 100m/C VHS, DVD. Charlton Heston, Anne Baxter, Gilbert Roland, Tom Tryon, Forrest Tucker, Elaine Stritch, Bruce Bennett, Barton MacLane; *D:* Rudolph Mate; *W:* James Edward Grant; *C:* Loyal Griggs; *M:* Walter Scharf.

3-Way 🦴🦴 *Three Way Split* 2004 (R) Sure it can be fun to watch the pretty people double-cross each other in this adaptation of Gil Brewer's 1963 novel "Wild to Possess" but even that wears thin. A philandering hubby and his girlfriend plot to kidnap his rich wife (Gershon) then bump her off after they get the ransom. Enter Lew (Purcell)—a troubled soul (with a heart)—who overhears the scheme and sees an easy score; however a blackmailer (Yoakam) arrives just in time to foul things up. Too few degrees of separation among the players make for far-fetched scenarios that deflate potentially intriguing plot twists. 88m/C VHS, DVD. Joy Bryant, Gina Gershon, Dwight Yoakam, Desmond Harrington, Ali Larter, Dominic Purcell; *D:* Scott Ziehl; *W:* Russell P. Marleau; *C:* Antonio Calvache; *M:* Christopher Hoag. VIDEO

Three Way Weekend 🦴 1981 (R) Two young gals set off on a back-packing trip through the mountains of Southern California to enjoy camping and romance. 78m/C VHS. Dan Diego, Jody Lee Olhava, Richard Blye, Blake Parrish; *D:* Emmett Alston.

The Three Weird Sisters 🦴🦴 1948 The three weird sisters from "Macbeth" strive to maintain their life of luxury by plotting to kill their half-brother for the inheritance. Not a bad effort for Birt's first time out as director; script co-written by his wife, Louise and poet Thomas. 82m/B VHS. *GB* Nancy Price, Mary Clare; *D:* Daniel Birt; *W:* Dylan Thomas, Louise Birt.

Three Wishes 🦴🦴 1995 (PG) Mysterious—and perhaps mystical—stranger Jack (Swayze) moves into the lives of a 1950s suburban widow (Mastrantonio) and her kids (Mazzello and Mumy) after she hits him with her car. Jack proceeds to use Zen philosophy, stories of a genie disguised as a dog, and nude sunbathing to help the kids' Little League team, make a boy fly, and scandalize the neighborhood. Adults will recognize the beatnik, Kerouac-influenced philosophy of nonconformity. They'll also recognize the sellout of that ideal with the sickeningly sappy ending. Mumy is the son of former "Lost in Space" child star Billy Mumy. 115m/C VHS, DVD. Patrick Swayze, Mary Elizabeth Mastrantonio, Joseph Mazzello, David Marshall Grant, Michael O'Keefe, John Diehl, Jay O. Sanders, Diane Venora, Seth Mumy; *D:* Martha Coolidge; *W:* Elizabeth Anderson; *C:* Johnny E. Jensen; *M:* Cynthia Millar.

3 Women 🦴🦴 1977 (PG) Altman creates a surreal, dreamlike, sometimes creepy tale of women's relationships with each other. Shy reserved Pinky (Spacek) gets a job in a senior care center where she meets Millie (Duvall), a therapist who doesn't seem to acknowledge her invisibility. She immediately idolizes and moves in with Millie, following in Millie's wannabe modern woman footsteps, and slowly begins to take over her life. The two are friends with Willie (Rule), the morose, pregnant artist wife of their landlord who paints frightening figures in the bottom of the building's pool. Admittedly influenced by Ingmar Bergman, Altman deftly handles tragedy, questions of identity, and our dreams' relationship to our waking lives. 124m/C DVD. Shelley Duvall, Sissy Spacek, Janice Rule, Robert Fortier, Ruth Nelson, John Cromwell, Sierra Pecheur, Craig Richard Nelson, Maysie Hoy, Dennis Christopher; *D:* Robert Altman; *W:* Robert Altman, Patricia Resnick; *C:* Charles Rosher Jr.

Three Word Brand 🦴🦴 1921 Hart plays three roles in this film, a homesteader who is killed by Indians and his twin sons, who are separated after their father's death and reunited many years later. Silent with musical score. 75m/B VHS. William S. Hart, Jane Novak, S.J. Bingham; *D:* Lambert Hillyer.

The Three Worlds of Gulliver 🦴🦴½ 1977 *The Worlds of Gulliver* 1959 A colorful family version of the Jonathan Swift classic about an Englishman who discovers a fantasy land of small and giant people. Visual effects by Ray Harryhausen. 100m/C VHS, DVD. Kerwin Mathews, Jo Morrow, Basil Sydney, Mary Ellis; *D:* Jack Sher; *W:* Jack Sher, Arthur Ross; *C:* Wilkie Cooper; *M:* Bernard Herrmann.

The Threepenny Opera 🦴🦴 *Die Dreigroschenoper; L'Opera De Quat'Sous; Beggars' Opera* 1931 A musical about the exploits of gangster Mack the Knife. Adapted from Bertolt Brecht's play and John Gay's "The Beggar's Opera." In German with English subtitles. 107m/B VHS. Rudolph Forster, Lotte Lenya, Carola Neher, Reinhold Schunzel, Fritz Rasp, Valeska Gert, Ernst Busch; *D:* G.W. Pabst; *W:* Ladislao Vajda, Bela Balazs, Leo Lania; *C:* Fritz Arno Wagner; *M:* Kurt Weill.

Three's Trouble 🦴🦴 1985 A middle-class family erupts when a young male babysitter enters to care for its three mischievous sons. 93m/C VHS. *AU* John Waters, Jacki Weaver, Steven Vidler; *D:* Chris Thomson.

Threesome woof! 1994 (R) Another Generation X movie that tries hard to be hip, but fails miserably. Due to a college administrative error, Alex (Boyle) winds up sharing a suite with two male roommates, Eddy (Charles) and Stuart (Baldwin). Despite having completely different personalities, they soon become best friends and form one cozy little group, with cozy being the key word. Sexual tension abounds—Alex wants Eddy who wants Stuart who wants Alex. Filled with pathetic dialogue (most of it relating to bodily functions and body parts) and shallow, obnoxious characters, this menage a trois film is a flop. 93m/C VHS, DVD. Lara Flynn Boyle, Stephen Baldwin, Josh Charles, Alexis Arquette, Mark Arnold, Martha Gehman, Michelle Matheson; *D:* Andrew Fleming; *W:* Andrew Fleming; *C:* Alexander Gruszynski; *M:* Thomas Newman.

Threshold 🦴🦴½ 1983 (PG) An internationally acclaimed research biologist is frustrated by his inability to save a dying 20-year-old woman born with a defective heart. She becomes the recipient of the first artificial heart. Solid performances. 97m/C VHS. *CA* Donald Sutherland, Jeff Goldblum, John Marley, Mare Winningham; *D:* Richard Pearce. Genie '83: Actor (Sutherland).

The Thrill Killers woof! *The Monsters Are Loose; The Maniacs Are Loose* 1965 Young murderous thugs rampage through Los Angeles suburbs, killing indiscriminately. Pretentious and exploitative. Sometimes shown with Hallucinogenic Hypno-Vision—a prologue announcing the special effect would be shown before the film, and on cue, hooded ushers would run through the theatre with cardboard axes. Weird. 82m/C VHS, DVD. Ray Dennis Steckler, Liz Renay, Brick Bardo, Ron Haydock, Atlas King, Gary Kent, Carolyn Brandt, Herb Robins, Ron Burr, George Morgan, Arch (Archie) Hall Sr.; *D:* Ray Dennis Steckler; *W:* Gene Pollock, Ray Dennis Steckler; *C:* Joseph Mascelli; *M:* Andre Brummer.

Thrill of a Romance 🦴🦴 1945 Johnson, an Army hero, meets Williams, a swimming instructor of all things, at a resort in the Sierra Nevadas. The only problem is that she's married. Typical swim-romance vehicle. ♪Please Don't Say No, Say Maybe; I Should Care; Lonely Night; Vive L'Amour; Schubert's Serenade; The Thrill of a Romance. 105m/C VHS. Esther Williams, Van Johnson, Frances Gifford, Henry Travers, Spring Byington, Lauritz Melchior; *D:* Richard Thorpe.

The Thrill of It All! 🦴🦴½ 1963 An average housewife becomes a star of TV commercials, to the dismay of her chauvinist husband, a gynecologist. Fast and funny, with numerous acidic jokes about television sponsors and programs. 108m/C VHS, DVD. James Garner, Doris Day, Arlene Francis, Edward Andrews, Carl Reiner, Elliott Reid, Reginald Owen, Zasu Pitts; *D:* Norman Jewison; *W:* Carl Reiner; *C:* Russell Metty.

Thrill Seekers 🦴🦴½ *The Timeshifters* 1999 (PG-13) Fast-pace helps overcome the plot holes in this sci-fi thriller. Merrick is searching great past catastrophes. He discovers that aliens are traveling back in time (to earth's present) to take part in disasters of their own contrivance. Trying to prevent an arena fire, Merrick teams up with another reporter, Elizabeth (Bell), and they run into a couple of alien assassins (Saldana, Outerbridge). 90m/C VHS, DVD. Casper Van Dien, Catherine Bell, Peter Outerbridge, Theresa Saldana, Martin Sheen, Mimi Kuzyk, Lawrence Dane, Catherine Van Dien; *D:* Mario Azzopardi; *W:* Kurt Inderbitzin, Gay Walch; *C:* Derick Underschultz; *M:* Fred Mollin. CABLE

Thrilled to Death 🦴½ 1988 (R) An utterly naive husband and wife get caught in the middle of a lethal game when they befriend a scheming couple. 90m/C VHS. Blake Bahner, Krista Lane, Richard Maris, Christine Moore; *D:* Chuck Vincent.

Thrillkill 🦴 1984 A young girl is enmeshed in a multi-million-dollar burglary scheme after her computer-whiz/embezzler sister disappears. 88m/C VHS. Robin Ward, Gina Massey, Anthony Kramreither; *D:* Anthony D'Andrea.

Throne of Blood 🦴🦴🦴🦴 *Kumonosujo, Kumonsu-djo; Cobweb Castle; The Castle of the Spider's Web* 1957 Kurosawa's masterful adaptation of "Macbeth" transports the story to medieval Japan and the world of the samurai. Mifune and Chiaki are warriors who have put down a rebellion and are to be rewarded by their overlord. On their way to his castle they meet a mysterious old woman who prophesizes that Mifune will soon rule—but his reign will be short. She is dismissed as crazy but her prophesies come to pass. So steeped in Japanese style that it bears little resemblance to the Shakespearean original, this film is an incredibly detailed vision in its own right. In Japanese with English subtitles. 105m/B VHS, DVD. *JP* Toshiro Mifune, Isuzu Yamada, Takashi Shimura, Minoru Chiaki, Akira Kubo; *D:* Akira Kurosawa; *W:* Hideo Oguni, Shinobu Hashimoto, Ryuzo Kikushima, Akira Kurosawa; *C:* Asakazu Nakai; *M:* Masaru Sato.

Throne of Fire woof! 1982 A mighty hero battles the forces of evil to gain control of the powerful Throne of Fire. Dubbed. 91m/C VHS. *IT* Peter McCoy, Sabrina Siani; *D:* Franco Prosperi.

Through a Glass Darkly 🦴🦴🦴 *Sasom I En Spegel* 1961 Oppressive interactions within a family sharing a holiday on a secluded island: a woman recovering from schizophrenia, her husband, younger brother, and her psychologist father. One of Bergman's most mysterious, upsetting and powerful films. In Swedish with English subtitles. Part of Bergman's Silence-of-God trilogy followed by "Winter Light" and "The Silence." 91m/B VHS, DVD. *SW* Harriet Andersson, Max von Sydow, Gunnar Bjornstrand, Lars Passgard; *D:* Ingmar Bergman; *W:* Ingmar Bergman; *C:* Sven Nykvist. Oscars '61: Foreign Film.

Through Naked Eyes 🦴🦴½ 1987 Thriller about two people who spy on each other. They witness a murder and realize that someone else is watching them. What a coincidence. 91m/C VHS. David Soul, Pam Dawber; *D:* John Llewellyn Moxey. TV

Through the Breakers 🦴🦴½ 1928 Heartbroken woman suffers silently on South Pacific isle. 55m/B VHS. Margaret Livingston, Holmes Herbert, Clyde Cook, Natalie Joyce; *D:* Deborah Schwartz; *W:* Harold Shumate; *C:* Ray June.

Through the Eyes of a Killer 🦴🦴½ 1992 (R) Laurie Fisher (Helgenberger) has dumped cheating boyfriend Jerry (Pantoliano) and has declared her independence by finding a spacious but crummy New York apartment in desperate need of renovation. Enter handsome handyman Ray Bellano (Anderson), who's happy to work on the apartment—and Laurie as well. But where Laurie sees a fling, Ray sees true love, and since brooding Ray's got the prerequisite mystery past, you know Laurie's in for the shock of her life. Long-time nice guy Anderson does a credible turn as an obsessive psycho. Based on the short story "The Master Builder" by Christopher Fowler; made for TV. 94m/C VHS. Richard Dean Anderson, Marg Helgenberger, Joe Pantoliano, David Marshall Grant, Melinda Culea, Tippi Hedren; *D:* Peter Markle; *W:* John Pielmeier; *M:* George S. Clinton. TV

Through the Fire 🦴🦴🦴 2005 In a sort of mini-"Hoop Dreams," director Hock engagingly follows 18-year-old basketball player Sebastian Telfair during his senior year at Coney Island's Lincoln High School. A surprisingly level-headed Telfair debates whether to play college ball or risk jumping into the uncertainties of the NBA draft as his brother unsuccessfully did a few years before. But his path becomes clear when violence erupts at his family's projects and his chance to escape rests on him. 103m/C DVD. *US* *D:* Jonathan Hock; *C:* Alastair Christopher; *M:* Duncan Sheik, Pete Miser.

Through the Olive Trees 🦴🦴🦴 *Under the Olive Trees; Zire Darakhtan Zeyton* 1994 (G) Film-within-a-film is the last of a trilogy concerned with Persian village life. "Where Is My Friend's House?" and "And Life Goes On." Director, filming in an earthquake-ravaged village, discovers that the young bricklayer playing the bridegroom in his film is actually in love with the local girl who's playing the bride. However, she's turned down his real-life marriage proposal, feeling that the uneducated man is beneath her. Farsi with subtitles. It may be rated G but considering the subject matter and the fact that the film is subtitled, don't consider this one for the kiddies. 104m/C VHS. *IA* Hossein Rezai, Mohamad Ali Keshavarz, Taherek Ladania, Zarifeh Shivati; *D:* Abbas Kiarostami; *W:* Abbas Kiarostami; *C:* Hossein Jafarian, Farhad Saba.

Throw Down ✄ 2000 Ex-Marine martial artist Max Finister (Wingster) comes home to find that drug pushers have taken over the neighborhood. The rest of the story follows the familiar formula. This is an unusually inept action picture. The fights (directed by Wingster) tend to be slow and clumsy. 𝄞 **DVD.** La'Ward J. Wingster, Mark G. Young. Maribel Velez, Wendy Fajardo, John "Kato" Hollis, Patrick "Gun" Ryan; **D:** Cyrus Beyzavi; **C:** Mike Dolgetta.

Throw Momma from the Train ✄✄✄ 1987 [PG-13] DeVito plays a man, henpecked by his horrific mother, who tries to persuade his writing professor (Crystal) to exchange murders. DeVito will kill Crystal's ex-wife and Crystal will kill DeVito's mother. Only mama isn't going to be that easy to get rid of. Fast-paced and entertaining black comedy. Ramsey steals the film, inspired by "Hitchcock's 'Strangers on a Train.'" 88m/C VHS, DVD, Danny DeVito, Billy Crystal, Anne Ramsey, Kate Mulgrew, Kim Greist, Branford Marsalis, Rob Reiner, Bruce Kirby; **D:** Danny DeVito; **W:** Stu Silver; **C:** Barry Sonnenfeld; **M:** David Newman.

The Throwback ✄✄½ 1935 When Jones was a lad the townspeople accused his father of cattle rustling. When he returns as an adult he sets out to clear his father's name. 61m/B VHS. Buck Jones, Muriel Evans, Eddie Phillips, George "Gabby" Hayes, Bryant Washburn, Paul Fix, Frank LaRue; **D:** Ray Taylor.

Thumb Tripping ✄✄ 1972 (R) A dated '60s/hippie film. Two flower children hitchhike and encounter all kinds of strange people in their travels on the far-out roads. Loose adaptation of Hans Christian Andersen. 94m/C VHS. Meg Foster, Michael Burns, Bruce Dern, Marianna Hill, Michael Conrad, Joyce Van Patten; **D:** Quentin Masters.

Thumbelina ✄✄½ 1982 From "Faerie Tale Theatre" comes the story of a tiny girl who gets kidnapped by a toad and a mole, but meets the man of her dreams in the nick of time. Adapted from the classic tale by Hans Christian Andersen. 60m/C VHS, DVD. Carrie Fisher, William Katt, Burgess Meredith; **D:** Michael Lindsay-Hogg. **CABLE.**

Thumbelina ✄✄½ *Hans Christian Andersen's Thumbelina* 1994 (G) Ornery little girl named Mia gets magically sucked into the pages of the "Thumbelina" storybook she's reading and finds all sorts of adventures. Loose adaptation of Hans Christian Andersen fairy tale from Disney animated features, but pleasant enough for the kids. 86m/C VHS, DVD. **D:** Don Bluth, Gary Goldman; **V:** Don Bluth; **M:** William Ross, Barry Manilow, Barry Manilow. Jaime Luke, Jack Feldman, Bruce Sussman; **V:** Jodi Benson, Gary Imhoff, Charo, Gilbert Gottfried, Carol Channing, John Hurt, Will Ryan, June Foray, Kenneth Mars; Golden Raspberries '94: Worst Song ("Mary the Mole").

Thumbsucker ✄✄½ 2005 (R) Seventeen year old Justin's (Pucci) underachieving, unfulfilled parents (D'Onofrio) and Audrey (Swinton), saddled with their own baggage, are incapable of dealing with their son's embarrassing thumb-sucking habit. Justin's habit lands him in the office of the orthodontist/new-age guru Dr. Perry Lyman (Reeves), who uses hypnosis to break Justin's habit. But now without a coping mechanism Justin suffers from ADD. Newly armed with Ritalin and a pharmaceutical-enhanced self-confidence, he becomes an arrogant, bullying monster. The beauty of this film is in the way Justin relates to the adults around him—all of whom range from ec-centric to obscure and are played to perfection. 97m/C DVD. *US* Lou Taylor Pucci, Tilda Swinton, Vince Vaughn, Vincent D'Onofrio, Keanu Reeves, Benjamin Bratt, Kelli Garner, Chase Offerle; **D:** Mike Mills; **W:** Mike Mills; **C:** Joaquin Baca-Asay.

Thunder Alley ✄✄½ 1967 Annette teams up with Fabian again in this AIP stock car story. Daytona driver Fabian has a blackout during a race and causes a fatal crash. He and girlfriend McBain go on a thrill driving circuit, run by Murray. Annette is Murray's daughter and a swell...

---

stunt driver herself. To ingratiate himself with Annette, Fabian agrees to teach her boyfriend (Beringer) how to be a pro racer and they become rivals. Annette's last role for AIP was a bit more mature than what she'd previously done and the flick overall is geared more towards action than the girl fun in the sun. 90m/C DVD. Fabian, Annette Funicello, Diane McBain, Warren Beringer, Jan Murray, Stanley Adams; **D:** Richard Rush; **W:** Sy Salkowitz; **C:** Monroe Askins; **M:** Michael Curb.

Thunder Alley ✄½ 1985 In middle America, two friends and their rock group struggle for success. One of the friends dies after an accidental overdose and the other's group propels him to stardom. 𝄞 Can't Look Back; Just Another Pretty Boy; Sometimes in the Night; Heart to Heart; Can You Feel My Heart Beat; Do You Feel Alright?; Danger, Danger; Surrender; Gimme Back My Heart. 102m/C VHS. Roger Wilson, Jill Schoelen, Clancy Brown, Scott McGinnis, Cynthia Eilbacher, Phil Brock; **D:** J.S. Cardone; **W:** J.S. Cardone.

Thunder and Lightning ✄✄ 1977 (PG) A mismatched young couple chase a truckload of poisoned moonshine. Action-packed chases ensue. Nice chemistry between Carradine and Jackson. 94m/C VHS, DVD. David Carradine, Kate Jackson, Roger C. Carmel, Sterling Holloway, Eddie Barth; **D:** Corey Allen.

Thunder Bay ✄✄ 1953 Stewart and Duryea are a pair of Louisiana wildcat oil drillers who believe there is oil at the bottom of the Gulf of Mexico off the coast of the town of Port Felicity. They decide to construct an oil platform which the town's fisherman of the town believe will interfere with their livelihoods. Tensions rise between the two groups and violence seems likely. Action packed, with timely storyline as modern oil drillers fight to put wells in waters that have historically been off-limits. 82m/C VHS. James Stewart, Joanne Dru, Dan Duryea, Gilbert Roland, Marcia Henderson; **D:** Anthony Mann; **W:** John Michael Hayes; **C:** William H. Daniels.

Thunder Birds ✄✄½ 1942 Combat flight instructor Steve Britt (Foster) trains Brit cadet Stackhouse (Sutton) to become an ace fighter pilot in spite of the fact that they love the same woman (Tierney). Fine performances and an interesting story keep this from being just another WW2-era flag-waver. 78m/C DVD. Gene Tierney, Preston Foster, John Sutton, Jack Holt, May Whitty, George Barbier, Richard Haydn, Reginald Denny, Ted North, C. Montague Shaw, Peter Lawford; **D:** William A. Wellman; **W:** Lamar Trotti; **C:** Ernest Palmer; **M:** David Buttolph.

Thunder County ✄ 1974 Federal agents and drug runners are after a group of four convicts who have just escaped from prison. 78m/C VHS, DVD. Mickey Rooney, Ted Cassidy, Chris Robinson; **D:** Chris Robinson.

Thunder in God's Country ✄ 1951 A dishonest gambler eyes a peaceful western town as the next Vegas-like gambling capital. Before this occurs he is exposed as a cheat. 67m/B VHS. Buddy Ebsen, Ian MacDonald, Paul Harvey, Harry Lauter, Rex Allen, Mary Ellen Kay; **D:** George Blair; **W:** Arthur Orloff; **C:** John MacBurnie; **M:** Stanley Wilson.

Thunder in Paradise ✄½ 1993 (PG-13) R.J. Hurricane Spencer (Hogan) is a soldier of fortune who heads into Cuba to help a woman and child escape political imprisonment, using his high-tech, weapon-filled speedboat. He has to fight off a small army and manages to find a buried treasure as well. Simple-minded TV pilot. 104m/C VHS. Hulk Hogan, Robin Weisman, Chris Lemmon, Carol Alt, Patrick Macnee, Sam Jones, Charlene Rae; **D:** Douglas Schwartz. TV

Thunder in Paradise 2 ✄½ 1994 (PG) Damsel sends up a distress signal and it's the Hulkster and his pal to the rescue. Unfortunately, their commendo raid fails and now they need an escape plan. From the syndicated TV series...

C VHS, DVD. Hulk Hogan, Chris Lemmon, Carol Alt, Patrick Macnee; **D:** Douglas Schwartz.

Thunder in Paradise 3 ✄½ 1994 (PG-13) Hogan is on a top secret mission to capture a drug lord who's holding his daughter hostage. 88m/C VHS, DVD. Hulk Hogan, Carol Alt, Ashley Gorrell, Hulk Hogan; **D:** Douglas Schwartz; **W:** Deborah Schwartz.

Thunder in the City ✄✄ 1937 Robinson is an intense American promoter in the sales game who is sent to London by his employers to learn a more subdued way of doing business. Instead, he meets a pair of down-on-their-luck aristocrats whose only asset is an apparently worthless Rhodesian mine. Robinson, however, comes up with a way to promote the mine and get enough capital together to make it profitable. Good satire with Robinson wasn't taken with the script in its original form and persuaded his friend, playwright Robert Sherwood, to re-write it. 85m/B VHS, DVD. Edward G. Robinson, Nigel Bruce, Ralph Richardson, Constance Collier; **D:** Marion Gering; **M:** Miklos Rozsa.

Thunder in the Desert ✄ 1938 A cowhand joins an outlaw gang in order to catch his uncle's killer. 56m/B VHS, DVD. Bob Steele, Louise Stanley, Don Barclay, Charles "Blackie" King, Lew Meehan, Budd Buster; **D:** Sam Newfield.

Thunder in the Pines ✄ 1949 Two lumberjack buddies send for the same French girl to marry, unbeknownst to each other. When she arrives, the dismayed men agree to a contest to see who will marry her. Meanwhile the French girl jilted girlfriend vows to get even. She does, with the help of the lumberjacks. 61m/B VHS, DVD. Denise Darcel, George Reeves, Ralph Byrd, Lyle Talbot, Michael Whalen, Roscoe Ates, Vince Barnett; **D:** Robert Edwards.

Thunder Mountain ✄½ 1935 Zane Grey's novel about two prospectors who are bushwhacked on their way to file a claim comes to life on the screen. 56m/B VHS. George O'Brien, Frances Grant, Morgan Wallace, Barbara Fritchie, William Norton Bailey, Edward LeSaint; **D:** David Howard; **W:** Daniel Jarrett, Don Swift; **C:** Frank B. Good.

Thunder Over Texas ✄ 1934 The cowboy hero gets embroiled in a railroad scandal that involves a kidnapping. Directed by Edgar G. Ulmer, who used the alias John Warner because he was moonlighting. His first western, previously he was best known for "The Black Cat." 52m/B VHS. Marion Shilling, Helen Westcott, Victor Potel, Tiny Skelton; **D:** Edgar G. Ulmer.

Thunder Pass ✄✄ 1937 Gold and greed are the motives for murder as two young brothers become separated when their wagon train is attacked and their family's slaughtered. One brother searches for the other and finds him several years later. Based on the novel "Arizona Ames" by Zane Grey. Also released as "Thunder Trail." 58m/B VHS. Charles Bickford, Marsha Hunt, Gilbert Roland, Monte Blue; **D:** Charles T. Barton.

Thunder Pass ✄✄ 1954 Routine story about a wagon train threatened by hostile Indians and the Army officer who leads them to safety. Based on a story by George Van Marter. 76m/B VHS. Dane Clark, Dorothy Patrick, Andy Devine, Raymond Burr, John Carradine, Mary Ellen Kay; **D:** Frank McDonald; **W:** Tom Hubbard, Fred Eggers.

Thunder River Feud ✄✄ 1942 The Rangebusters help two ranchers avoid a range war. Part of "The Rangebusters" series. 58m/B VHS. Ray Corrigan, John "Dusty" King, Max Terhune, Jan Wiley, Carleton Young, George Chesebro, Budd Buster, Jack Holmes, Rick Anderson; **D:** S. Roy Luby; **W:** Earle Snell, John Vlahos; **C:** Robert E. Cline; **M:** Jean George.

Thunder Road ✄✄ 1958 (PG) Luke Doolin (Mitchum) is a Tennessee moonshiner who comes home to family moonshine business, fighting both mobsters and federal agents. An exciting chase between Luke and the feds ends the movie with the appropriate bang. Robert Mitchum not only produced, wrote and...

---

starred in this best of the moonshine-running films, but also wrote the theme song "Whippoorwill" (which later became a radio hit). Mitchum's teenaged son, James, made his film debut as his brother Robin Doolin, and later starred in a similar movie, "Moonrunners." A cult favorite. 92m/B VHS, DVD. Robert Mitchum, Jacques Aubuchon, Gene Barry, Keely Smith, Trevor Bardette, Sandra Knight, Jim Mitchum, Betsy Holt, Frances Koon, Mitchell Ryan, Peter Breck; **D:** Arthur Ripley; **W:** Walter Wise, Robert Mitchum; **C:** Alan Stensvold; **M:** Jack Marshall.

Thunder Run ✄ 1986 (PG-13) When a load of uranium needs to be transferred across Nevada, a retired trucker takes on the job. The trip is made more difficult since terrorists are trying to hijack the shipment to use for a bomb. 84m/C VHS. Forrest Tucker, John Ireland, John Shepherd, Jill Whitlow, Wally Langham, Cheryl Lynn; **D:** Gary Hudson; **W:** Charles Davis.

Thunder Trail ✄✄ 1937 Set of twins, separated by a wagon trail massacre, meet years later in opposite sides of the law. 58m/C VHS, Gilbert Roland, Charles Bickford, Marsha Hunt, J. Carrol Nash, James Craig, Monte Blue; **D:** Charles T. Barton.

Thunder Warrior 2 ✄ 1985 ✄ *Thunder* 1985

Thunder Warrior ✄ *Thunder* 1985

Thunder Warrior 3 ✄ 1988 The Indian Thunder has vowed to live in peace, but forswears the oath when his wife is kidnapped and family is terrorized. Revenge is the top priority as he torments the bad guys. De Angelis used the pseudonym Larry Ludman. 90m/C VHS. Mark Gregory, John Phillip Law, Ingrid Lawrence, Werner Pochath, Horst Schön; **D:** Fabrizio de Angelis.

Thunderball ✄✄✄ 1965 (PG) The fourth installment in Ian Fleming's James Bond series finds 007 on a mission to thwart SPECTRE, which has threatened to blow up Miami by atomic bomb if 100 million pounds in ransom is not paid. One of the more tedious Bond entries but a big boxoffice success. Tom Jones sang the title song. Remade as "Never Say Never Again" in 1983 with Connery reprising his role as Bond after a 12-year absence. 125m/C VHS, DVD. GB Sean Connery, Claudine Auger, Adolfo Celi, Luciana Paluzzi, Rik van Nutter, Martine Beswick, Molly Peters, Guy Doleman, Bernard Lee, Lois Maxwell, Desmond Llewelyn; **D:** Terence Young; **W:** John Hopkins, Richard Maibaum; **C:** Ted Moore; **M:** John Barry. Oscars '65: Visual FX.

Thunderbirds ✄½ 2004 (PG) Thunderbirds are go! Nobody's really sure why, since it's a 40-year-old British TV show about creepy puppets (remember "Super-marionation"?) rescuing other, equally creepy puppets. This version is live-action but it's still wooden. Billionaire ex-astronaut Jeff Tracy (Paxton) lives on an island in the South Pacific with his five sons (all named after astronauts) and a specially designed aircraft. He uses the Thunderbirds to run international rescue. Telekinetic evil guy, The Hood (Kingsley), is bent on world domination (what else?) and strands Dad and the four older boys on their orbiting space station, leaving young-est wannabe Thunderbird Alan (Corbett) and a couple of his pals to save the day. The 10-and-under crowd may be persuaded to sit through this harmless but lackluster adventure. 94m/C DVD. *US* Bill Paxton, Brady Corbet, Ben Kingsley, Anthony Edwards, Sophia Myles, Ron Cook, Gene Francis, Lou Hirsch, Nicola Walker, Jonannes Zaddcrzny, Soren Fulton, Vanessa Anne Hudgens, Philip Winchester, Dhobi Oparei, Kyle Herbert, Dominic Colenso, Ben Torgersen, Lex Shrapnel; **D:** Jonathan Frakes; **W:** Peter Hewitt; **C:** William Osborne, Michael McCullers; **M:** Hans Zimmer.

Thunderbolt & Lightfoot 🦴🦴🦴 1974 (R) Eastwood is an ex-thief on the run from his former partners (Kennedy and Lewis) who he's made off with the loot from their last job, the robbery of a government vault. He joins up with drifter Bridges, who helps him to escape. Later, Eastwood manages to convince Kennedy he doesn't know where the money is. Bridges then persuades the men that they should plan the same heist and rob the same government vault all over again, which they do. But their getaway doesn't go exactly as planned. All-around fine acting; notable is Bridges' scene dressed in drag. First film for director Cimino. 115m/C VHS, DVD. Clint Eastwood, Jeff Bridges, George Kennedy, Geoffrey Lewis, Gary Busey; D: Michael Cimino; C: Frank Stanley; M: Dee Barton.

Thunderground 🦴 1989 (R) A beautiful con artist teams with a fighter and together they travel to New Orleans to arrange a bout with the king of bare-knuckled fighting. 92m/C VHS. Paul Coufos, Margaret Langrick, Jesse Ventura, M. Emmet Walsh; D: David Mitchell.

Thunderheart 🦴🦴🦴 1992 (R) Young FBI agent Kilmer is sent to an Oglala Sioux reservation to investigate a murder. He is himself part Sioux, but resents being chosen for the assignment because of it. Aided by a veteran partner (Shepard), Ray learns, professionally and personally, from a shrewd tribal police officer (well played by Greene). Set in the late '70s, the film is loosely based on actual events plaguing the violence-torn Native American community at that time. Great cinematography by Roger Deakins. Filmed on the Pine Ridge Reservation in South Dakota. Director Apted deals with the actual incidents this film is based on in his documentary about Leonard Peltier, "Incident at Oglala." 118m/C VHS, DVD. Val Kilmer, Sam Shepard, Graham Greene, Fred Ward, Fred Dalton Thompson, Sheila Tousey, Chief Ted Thin Elk, John Trudell, Dennis Banks, David Crosby; D: Michael Apted; W: John Fusco; C: Roger Deakins; M: James Horner.

Thundering Forest 🦴🦴 1941 Australian actioneer pitting loggers against saboteurs. ?m/C VHS. AU Frank Leighton.

Thundering Gunslingers 🦴 1944 A group of gunmen terrorizing townspeople finally meet their match in this Western. 91m/B VHS. Al "Fuzzy" St. John, Frances Gladwin, Charles "Blackie" King, Jack Ingram, Kermit Maynard, Karl Hackett, Buster Crabbe; D: Sam Newfield; W: Fred Myton; C: Robert Cline.

Thundering Trail 🦴 *Thunder on the Trail* 1951 Two cowboys encounter plenty of trouble before they take the President's newly appointed territorial governor to his office. 55m/B VHS. Lash LaRue, Al "Fuzzy" St. John, Sally Anglim, Archie Twitchell, Ray Bennett; D: Ron Ormond; W: Ira Webb; C: Ernest Miller; M: Walter Greene.

Thursday 🦴🦴½ 1998 (R) Familiarity does breed something close to contempt in this comic crime thriller. Ex-drug dealer Casey Wells (Jane) has left L.A. for the straight and narrow life of a married Houston architect. That is until his lowlife ex-partner Nick (Eckhart) turns up one Thursday with a briefcase full of dope and some gangster problems. A succession of other nasty characters then proceeds to darken Casey's doorway and his efforts to get his life back just cause things to spin further out of control. The leads do a good job but it's nothing you haven't seen before. Also available in an unrated version. 82m/C VHS. Thomas Jane, Aaron Eckhart, Paulina Porizkova, James LeGros, Paula Marshall, Michael Jeter, Glenn Plummer, Mickey Rourke; D: Skip Woods; W: Skip Woods; C: Denis Lenoir.

Thursday's Child 🦴🦴 1943 A child's success in films causes trouble for her family. Melodramatic and sappy, but Howes, as the kid, is excellent. One of Granger's early supporting roles. 95m/B VHS. GB Stewart Granger, Sally Ann Howes, Wilfred Lawson, Kathleen O'Regan, Eileen Bennett, Marianne Davis, Gerhard Kempinski, Felix Aylmer, Margaret Yarde, Vera Bogetti, Percy Walsh, Ronald Shiner; D: Rodney Ackland; W: Rodney Ackland, Donald Macardle; C: Desmond Dickinson.

Thursday's Game 🦴🦴🦴 1974 (PG) Two crisis-besieged businessmen meet every Thursday, using poker as a ruse to work on their business and marital problems. Wonderful cast; intelligently written. 99m/C VHS. Gene Wilder, Ellen Burstyn, Bob Newhart, Cloris Leachman, Nancy Walker, Valerie Harper, Rob Reiner; D: James L. Brooks; W: James L. Brooks. TV

THX 1138 🦴🦴🦴 1971 (PG) In the dehumanized world of the future, people live in underground cities run by computer, are force-fed drugs to keep them passive, and no longer have names—just letter/number combinations (Duvall is THX 1138). Emotion is also outlawed and when the computer-matched couple THX 1138 and LUH 3417 discover love, they must battle the computer system to escape. George Lucas' first film, which was inspired by a student film he did at USC. 88m/C VHS, DVD. Robert Duvall, Donald Pleasence, Maggie McOmie; D: George Lucas; W: George Lucas; M: Lalo Schifrin.

Tiara Tahiti 🦴🦴 1962 Intrigue, double-cross, romance, and violence ensue when two old army acquaintances clash in Tahiti. Very fine performances from the two leading men. 100m/C VHS. James Mason, John Mills, Claude Dauphin, Rosenda Monteros, Herbert Lom; D: Ted Kotcheff.

The Tic Code 🦴🦴½ 1999 (R) Twelve-year-old Miles (Marquette) aspires to be a jazz pianist but must practice at the local bar because his single mom Laura (Draper) can't afford a piano. But Miles has a bigger problem—he suffers from the misunderstood Tourette's syndrome, which brings him close to his idol, sax player Tyrone (Hines), who is similarly afflicted. Soon Tyrone is also playing some sweet music with Laura but can't deal with his illness. 91m/C VHS, DVD. Gregory Hines, Polly Draper, James McCaffrey, Christopher Marquette, Carol Kane, Bill Nunn, Tony Shalhoub, Desmond Robertson, Fisher Stevens, Camryn Manheim, David Johansen; D: Gary Winick; W: Polly Draper; C: Wolfgang Held; M: Michael Wolff.

Tick Tock 🦴🦴🦴 2000 (R) In Bakersfield, California, trophy wife Rachel (Ward) and her pal Carla (Minter) plot to get rid of wealthy hubby (Dukes). That's only the beginning of a plot that stacks trick upon trick, double-cross upon double-cross. Think "Blood Simple" lite. It's a delightful guilty pleasure made all the more enjoyable by polished production values. 93m/C DVD. Megan Ward, Kristin Minter, Linden Ashby, John Ratzenberger, David Dukes; D: Kevin S. Tenney; W: Kevin S. Tenney; C: Jack Conroy; M: Dennis Michael Tenney.

Ticker 🦴½ 2001 (R) San Francisco detective Sizemore is tracking mad bomber Hopper (reprising his "Speed" role to little effect) aided by bomb squad leader Seagal. Nothing that hasn't been done a zillion times before (and much better). 92m/C VHS, DVD. Tom Sizemore, Steven Seagal, Nas, Jaime Pressly, Dennis Hopper, Chilli, Peter Greene; Cameos: Ice-T; D: Albert Pyun; W: Paul B. Margolis. VIDEO

The Ticket 🦴 1997 (PG-13) Keith Reiker (Marshall) works as a pilot for a financially ailing charter company. His marriage to CeCe (Doherty) is rocky but when Keith wins a lottery worth $123 million, he's certain his life has finally turned around. He persuades CeCe and their 13-year-old son to fly with him and collect the money but the plane is sabotaged. Now they must not only survive the wilderness but whoever is out to steal the ticket and make certain the Reickers don't get out alive. 88m/C VHS. James Marshall, Shannen Doherty, Heidi Swedberg, Al Mancini, John Tench; D: Stuart Cooper; W: David Alexander; C: Curtis Petersen; M: Charles Bernstein. CABLE

Ticket of Leave Man 🦴🦴 1937 London's most deadly organized killer fronts a charitable organization designed to help reform criminals. It actually steers them into a crime syndicate that cheats philanthropists out of their fortunes. 71m/B VHS. GB Tod Slaughter, John Warwick, Marjorie Taylor, Robert Adair, Peter Gawthorne, Jenny Lynn, Norman Pierce; D: George King; W: H.F. Maltby, A.R. Rawlinson; C: Hone Glendinning; M: Jack Beaver.

Ticket to Heaven 🦴🦴🦴 1981 (PG) A young man, trying to deal with the painful breakup of a love affair, falls under the spell of a quasi-religious order. His friends and family, worried about the cult's influence, have him kidnapped in order for him to be de-programmed. Mancuso is excellent, as are his supporting players Rubinek and Thomson. 109m/C VHS, DVD. CA Nick Mancuso, Meg Foster, Kim Cattrall, Saul Rubinek, R.H. Thomson, Jennifer Dale, Guy Boyd, Paul Soles; D: Ralph L. (R.L.) Thomas; W: Anne Cameron; C: Richard Leiterman; M: Micky Erbe. Genie '82: Actor (Mancuso), Film, Support. Actor (Rubinek).

Ticket to Tomahawk 🦴🦴½ 1950 A gunslinger is hired by a stagecoach company to sabotage a railroad. Look for Marilyn Monroe as a chorus girl in a musical number. 90m/C VHS. Dan Dailey, Anne Baxter, Rory Calhoun, Walter Brennan, Charles Kemper, Connie Gilchrist, Arthur Hunnicutt, Victor Sen Yung, Marilyn Monroe, Jack Elam; D: Richard Sale; W: Richard Sale, Mary Loos; C: Harry Jackson; M: Cyril Mockridge.

Tickle Me 🦴½ 1965 An unemployed rodeo star finds work at an all-girl health spa and dude ranch. He falls in love with a young lady who has a treasure map and keeps her safe from the evil men who want her fortune. ♫ (It's a) Long, Lonely Highway; Night Rider; It Feels So Right; Dirty, Dirty Feeling; (Such an) Easy Question; Put the Blame on Me; I'm Yours; I Feel That I've Known You Forever; Slowly but Surely. 90m/C VHS, DVD. Elvis Presley, Julie Adams, Jack Mullaney; D: Norman Taurog.

Ticks 🦴½ *Infested* 1993 (R) Mammoth mutant killer insects terrorize a Northern California campground! The predatory woodticks are the victims of steroids dumped in the water supply and a group of unwary teen campers fall prey to their deadly venom! And if that's not bad enough, a forest fire breaks out, trapping the teens! 85m/C VHS. Ami Dolenz, Rosalind Allen, Alfonso Ribeiro, Peter Scolari; D: Tony Randel.

Tidal Wave 🦴 *Nippon Chinbotsu*; *The Submersion of Japan*; *Japan Sinks* 1975 (PG) Scientists discover that Japan is slowly sinking and order the island to be evacuated. Originally a popular Japanese production, the American version is a poorly dubbed, re-edited mess. 82m/C VHS. JP Lorne Greene, Keiju Kobayashi, Rhonda Leigh Hopkins, Hiroshi Fujioka, Shiro Moriana; D: Andrew Meyer.

Tideland 🦴 2005 (R) First 10-year-old Jeliza-Rose's (Ferland) junkie mom (Tilly) overdoses in L.A., prompting her junkie dad (Bridges) to drag her to a middle-of-nowhere Texas farmhouse where he, of course, overdoses, leaving the girl to retreat into a not-so-pleasant fantasy world. When not conversing with her headless dolls, she wanders the grassy fields near the train tracks, where she runs into some odd neighbors—a taxidermist who, um, helps Jeliza-Rose with the dead dad problem, and the woman's brother, a mentally-challenged man-child whose relationship with the young Jeliza-Rose gets a little creepy. Ferland's excellent performance stands out in what is otherwise an unredeemable mess. Based on Mitch Cullin's 2005 novel. 122m/C DVD. CA GB Jodelle Ferland, Janet McTeer, Brendan Fletcher, Jeff Bridges, Jennifer Tilly; D: Terry Gilliam; W: Terry Gilliam, Tony Grisoni; C: Nicola Pecorini; M: Mychael Danna, Jeff Danna.

Tides of War 🦴 1990 In the twilight of WWII, a German officer begins to question his role in a proposed missile attack on Washington in light of the S.S. brutality he witnesses. 90m/C VHS. Yvette Heyden, Rodrigo Obregon, David Soul, Bo Svenson; D: Neil Rossati.

Tidy Endings 🦴🦴½ 1988 A man who died from AIDS leaves behind his male lover and his ex-wife. The two form a friendship as they both try to cope with the man's death. Based on the play by Fierstein. 54m/C VHS. Harvey Fierstein, Stockard Channing; D: Gavin Millar; W: Harvey Fierstein.

Tie Me Up! Tie Me Down! 🦴🦴½ *Atame!* 1990 (NC-17) A young psychiatric patient kidnaps a former porno actress he has always had a crush on, and holds her captive, certain that he can convince her to love him. Black comedy features a fine cast and is well directed. At least one fairly explicit sex scene and the bondage theme caused the film to be X-rated, although it was originally re-leased unrated by the distributor. In Spanish with English subtitles. 105m/C VHS, DVD. SP Victoria Abril, Antonio Banderas, Loles Leon, Francesco Rabal, Julieta Serrano, Maria Barranco, Rossy de Palma; D: Pedro Almodóvar; W: Pedro Almodóvar; C: Jose Luis Alcaine; M: Ennio Morricone.

The Tie That Binds 🦴 1995 (R) Insipid thriller is a cheap imitation of its cousin, "The Hand that Rocks the Cradle" (made by the same producers), but what the former movie did to the nanny business, this flick does to a whole genre. Leanne and John Netherwood (Hannah and Carradine) are psycho parents out to reclaim their daughter from the lame-brain yuppie couple (Spano and Kelly) who adopted her. Out of all the children there, they choose the one who likes to sleep with a butcher knife under her pillow. Duh! Every "family in danger from psychotic" cliche is employed in a vain attempt to build suspense for the silly conclusion. Dismal directorial debut of screenwriter Strick. 98m/C VHS, DVD. Daryl Hannah, Keith Carradine, Moira Kelly, Vincent Spano, Julia Devin, Ray Reinhardt, Cynda Williams; D: Wesley Strick; W: Michael Auerbach; C: Bobby Bukowski; M: Graeme Revell.

Tiefland 🦴🦴 1944 Melodrama based on the libretto for D'Albert's opera about a gypsy dancer and her loves. Unreleased until 1954, this film is the last of Riefenstahl's career; she subsequently turned to still photography. In German with English subtitles. 98m/B VHS, DVD. GE Leni Riefenstahl, Franz Eichberger, Bernard Minetti, Maria Koppenhofer, Luise Rainer; D: Leni Riefenstahl.

Tierra 🦴🦴 *Earth* 1995 Metaphysical messiness. Mystery exterminator Angel (Gomez) comes to Aragon, a land of red soil and lightning strikes, to fumigate the woodlice infesting the vineyards. He recruits some locals and gypsies to help him out while becoming involved with a couple of women—shy Angela (Suarez) and hot Mari (Klein). But Angel is also literally haunted by an alter ego—a situation that no doubt has some deep meaning that is never very clear. But neither is the rest of the movie. Spanish with subtitles. 122m/C VHS, DVD. SP Carmelo Gomez, Emma Suarez, Silke Klein, Karra Elejalde, Nancho Novo, Txema Blasco; D: Julio Medem; W: Julio Medem; C: Javier Aguiresarobe; M: Alberto Iglesias.

Tieta of Agreste 🦴🦴 1996 After many years, wealthy Tieta (Braga) returns to her village with her stepdaughter and immediately causes havoc for her greedy family. Based on a novel by Jorge Amado. Portuguese with subtitles. 140m/C VHS, DVD. BR Sonia Braga, Marilia Pera, Zeze Motta, Jorge Amado; D: Carlos Diegues; W: Terry Gilliam; M: Caetano Veloso.

Tiffany Jones 🦴 1975 (R) Tiffany Jones is a secret agent who has information that presidents and revolutionaries are willing to kill for. 90m/C VHS. Anouska Hempel, Ray Brooks, Eric Pohlmann, Martin Benson, Susan Sneers; D: Pete Walker.

Tiger and the Pussycat 🦴🦴½ *Il Tigre* 1967 (R) A successful Italian businessman's infatuation with an attractive American art student leads him to marital and financial woes. 110m/C VHS, DVD. Ann-Margret, Vittorio Gassman, Eleanor Parker; D: Dino Risi.

The Tiger and the Snow 🐾🐾½ *La Tigre e la Neve* 2005 First it was the Holocaust and now Benigni uses the backdrop of the war in Iraq, circa 2003, for his absurdist tragicomedy romance. Exuberant family problems. Muddled and sappy. 92m/ C VHS, DVD, Patrick Swayze, Barbara Williams, Piper Laurie, Bobby DiCicco, Kaye Ballard, Lee Richardson, Mary McDonnell; *D:* Amin Qamar Chaudhri.

self off as an aid worker and heads to Baghdad when he discovers Vittoria (Braschi), the woman he loves, has been seriously injured in a bombing. Italian with subtitles. 110m/C DVD. *T* Roberto Benigni, Nicoletta Braschi, Jean Reno, Tom Waits, Emilia Fox; *D:* Roberto Benigni; *W:* Roberto Benigni, Vincenzo Cerami; *C:* Fabio Cianchetti; *M:* Nicola Piovani.

Tiger Bay 🐾🐾🐾 1959 A young Polish sailor, on leave in Cardiff, murders his unfaithful girlfriend. Lonely ten-year-old Gillie sees the crime and makes her more popular with her peers. Confronted by a police detective, she convincingly lies but eventually the sailor finds Gillie and kidnaps her, hoping to keep her quiet until he can get aboard his ship. A delicate relationship evolves between the child and the killer as she tries to help him escape and the police close in. Marks Hayley Mills' first major role and one of her finest performances. 107m/B VHS, DVD, GB John Mills, Hayley Mills, Yvonne Mitchell, Megs Jenkins, Anthony Dawson, Kenneth Griffith, Michael Anderson Jr.; *D:* J. Lee Thompson; *W:* Laurie Johnson.

Tiger Claws 🐾½ 1991 (R) The pretty, petite Rothrock has been called the female Bruce Lee. Perhaps, but at least he got a good script every once in a while. This time Rothrock's a kung-fu cop investigating the strange ritual-murders of martial-arts champions. 95m/C VHS, DVD, Cynthia Rothrock, Bolo Yeung, Jalal Merhi; *D:* Kelly Makin; *W:* J. Stephen Maunder; *C:* Curtis Petersen, Mark Willis.

Tiger Fangs 🐾½ 1943 When Nazis threaten the Far East rubber production with man-eating tiger's, real-life big game hunter Frank Buck comes to the rescue. 57m/B VHS, DVD, Frank Buck, June Duprez, Duncan Renaldo; *D:* Sam Newfield.

Tiger Heart 🐾½ 1996 (PG-13) Teenaged karate champ Eric Chase (Robertson) is looking forward to a lazy summer with girlfriend Stephanie (Lyons) before heading off to college. Instead his neighborhood comes under attack from an unscrupulous developer and Stephanie runs afoul of his goons. Eric decides to take action. 90m/C VHS, DVD, Ted Jan Roberts, Jennifer Lyons, Robert LaSardo, Carol Potter, Timothy Williams; *D:* Georges Chamchoum; *W:* William Applegate Jr.; *M:* John Gonzalez.

Tiger Joe 🐾 1985 There's trouble in Southeast Asia, and the U.S. military confuses things even more. 96m/C VHS, Alan Collins, David Warbeck; *D:* Anthony M. Dawson.

Tiger of the Seven Seas 🐾🐾 1962 A female pirate takes over her father's command and embarks on adventures on the high seas. Generous portions of action, intrigue, and romance. Sequel to "Queen of the Pirates." 90m/C VHS. *IT FR* Gianna Maria Canale, Anthony Steel, Maria Grazia Spina, Ernesto Calindri; *D:* Luigi Capuano.

Tiger Town 🐾🐾½ 1983 (G) A baseball player, ending an illustrious career with the Detroit Tigers, sees his chance of winning a pennant slipping away. A young fan, however, proves helpful in chasing that elusive championship. 76m/C VHS, Roy Scheider, Justin Henry, Ron McLarty, Bethany Carpenter, Noah Moazezi; *D:* Alan Shapiro; *C:* Robert Elswit. **CABLE**

A Tiger Walks 🐾🐾½ 1964 A savage tiger escapes from a circus and local children start a nationwide campaign to save its life. Notable for its unflattering portrayal of America's heartland and small town dynamics. Radical departure from most Disney films of the period. 88m/C VHS, Sabu, Pamela Franklin, Brian Keith, Vera Miles, Kevin Corcoran, Peter Brown, Una Merkel, Frank McHugh, Edward Andrews; *D:* Norman Tokar; *M:* Buddy (Norman Dale) Baker.

Tiger Warsaw 🐾½ 1988 *The Tiger* 1937 (R) A young man returns to the town where he once lived, before he shot his father, plies actually meet each other before the end of the movie. Not here. That's one of the reasons this one isn't even good. Ghostwriter Gwen (Tripplehorn) and architect Nick (McDermott), although seemingly destined for one another, have more near-misses than a drunken, near-sighted airline pilot. They're shown in the same room, in adjoining rooms, leaving a room as soon as the other enters, etc., etc. Meanwhile, minor characters appear, speak some ham-fisted dialogue and then disappear. This happens for 20 years. Then they meet and the movie is (thankfully) over. Parker, however, does an excellent job as a rehab-addicted former child star who has ties to both characters. Feature directorial debut for Yinant. 113m/ C VHS, DVD, Dylan McDermott, Sarah Jessica Parker, Jeanne Tripplehorn, Jennifer Aniston, Ken Olin, Craig Bierko, Nina Foch, Alice Drummond, Christine Ebersole, Michael Tucker, Patrick Malahide, Kasi Lemmons, Karen Allen; *D:* Scott Winant; *W:* Winnie Holzman; *C:* Bobby Bukowski; *M:* Miles Goodman, Terence Blanchard.

The Tiger Woods Story 🐾🐾½ 1998 (PG-13) Kain stars as the young man who, at 21, became the youngest player ever to win the Masters Golf Tournament. Based on the book "Tiger" by John Strege. 103m/C VHS, Khalil Kain, Keith David, Freda Foh Shen; *D:* LeVar Burton; *W:* Takashi Bufford. **CABLE**

Tigerland 🐾🐾🐾 2000 (R) Irish newcomer Farrell made a big (and deserved) splash as Army draftee Roland Bozz, one of a group of grunts at the final stage of infantry training at Fort Polk, Louisiana in 1971. The title refers to the wilderness area designed for jungle combat simulation before the newbies are shipped out to Nam. But the rebellious, cynical Bozz gets away with defying every rule thrown at him to the disbelief of the others in the platoon. Familiar story but the ensemble cast is right on the mark and director Schumacher keeps tight control in this old-fashioned low-budget drama. 101m/C VHS, DVD, US Colin Farrell, Matthew Davis, Clifton (Gonzalez) Collins Jr., Tom Guiry, Russell Richardson, Cole Hauser, Shea Whigham; *D:* Joel Schumacher; *W:* Ross Klaven, Michael McGruther; *C:* Matthew Libatique; *M:* Nathan Larson.

Tigers in Lipstick 🐾½ 1980 (R) Seven short vignettes featuring the beautiful actresses as aggressive women and the men that they influence. *Wild Beds* 88m/C VHS. *IT* Laura Antonelli, Monica Vitti, Ursula Andress, Sylvia Kristel; *D:* Luigi Zampa.

A Tiger's Tale 🐾½ 1987 (R) A middle-aged divorced nurse begins an affair with her daughter's ex-boyfriend. 97m/C VHS, Ann-Margret, C. Thomas Howell, Charles Durning, Kelly Preston, Ann Wedgeworth, Tim Thomerson, Steven Kampmann, Traci Lind, Angel Tompkins, William Zabka; *D:* Peter Douglas; *C:* Tony Pierce-Roberts.

Tigershark 🐾 1987 (R) A martial arts expert goes to Southeast Asia to rescue his girlfriend, who has been kidnapped by communist forces and held captive for arms and ammunition. Strictly for fans of the martial arts. 97m/C VHS, Mike Stone, John Quade, Pamela Bryant; *D:* Emmett Alston; *W:* Ivan Rogers.

Tight Spot 🐾🐾🐾 1955 Been-around-the-block model Sherry Conley (Rogers) is serving time for a crime she didn't commit when she's offered a deal by U.S. attorney Lloyd Hallett (Robinson) if she'll testify against mob boss Benjamin Costain (Greene). But since no other political witness lived to the trial date, Sherry's against cooperating. However, Hallett puts her up in a hotel with bodyguard Vince Striker (Keith), in hopes she'll change her mind. But Costain has a lot of clout and is determined to get to Sherry. Rogers gives an excellent performance in a dramatic role with fine support from the rest of the cast. 97m/B VHS, Ginger Rogers, Edward G. Robinson, Brian Keith, Lorne Greene, Katherine Anderson; *D:* Phil Karlson; *W:* William Bowers; *C:* Burnett Guffey; *M:* George Duning.

Tightrope 🐾🐾 1984 (R) Police inspector Wes Block pursues a killer of prostitutes in New Orleans' French Quarter. The film is notable both as a thriller and as a fascinating vehicle for Eastwood, who experiments with a disturbing portrait of a cop with some peculiarities of his own. 115m/C VHS, DVD, Clint Eastwood, Genevieve Bujold, Dan Hedaya, Jennifer Beck, Alison Eastwood, Randi Brooks, Regina Richardson, Jamie Rose; *D:* Richard Tuggle; *C:* Bruce Surtees; *M:* Lennie Niehaus.

The Tigress 🐾½ 1993 (R) In 1920s Berlin two con artists set out to scam a rich American using sex as a lure. Things don't go as planned. Also available in an unrated version. 89m/C VHS, DVD, GE Valentin Baxter, Stephen Collins, Michelle Johnson, Kelli

Till Death Do Us Part 🐾½ 1972 (PG) Three married couples spend a weekend at a counseling retreat, unaware that the proprietor is a murderous maniac. 77m/C VHS, James Keach, Claude Jutra, Matt Craven; *D:* Timothy Brand.

Till Death Do Us Part 🐾🐾 1992 (R) An ex-cop turns into an evil killer who seduces unsuspecting women and murders them for their insurance money. Contains footage not seen in the TV movie. Based on a true story and the book by Vincent Bugliosi. 93m/C VHS, Treat Williams, Arliss Howard, Rebecca Jenkins; *D:* Yves Simoneau.

Till Human Voices Wake Us 🐾½ 2002 (R) Confusing romantic drama about memory. Psych professor Sam Franks (Pearce) is going home for his dad's funeral. He has an odd encounter with Ruby (Bonham Carter), rescues her from a suicide leap off a bridge, and discovers she has amnesia. Efforts to unlock Ruby's memories help Sam with his own teenaged tragedy that revolves around his girlfriend drowning. However, the story never does make much sense. 97m/C VHS, DVD, AU Guy Pearce, Helena Bonham-Carter, Frank Gallacher, Lindley Joyner, Brooke Harman, Peter Curtin, Margot Knight, Anthony Martin, Dawn Klingberg; *D:* Michael Petroni; *C:* Roger Lanser; *M:* Dale Cornelius.

Till Marriage Do Us Part 🐾🐾½ *Dio Mio, Come Sono Caduta in Basso; How Long Can You Fall?* 1974 (R) An innocent couple discovers on their wedding night that they are really brother and sister. Since they can't in good conscience get a divorce or consummate their marriage, they must seek sexual gratification elsewhere. Antonelli is deliciously tantalizing in this silly satire. In Italian with English subtitles. 97m/C VHS. *IT* Laura Antonelli, Alberto Lionello, Jean Rochefort, Michele Placido, Karin Schubert; *D:* Luigi Comencini.

Till Murder Do Us Part 🐾½ *A Woman Scorned: The Betty Broderick Story* 1992 (PG-13) Based on the true story of Betty Broderick, an obsessively devoted wife and mother whose husband leaves her for another woman. Even after a bitter divorce, Betty refuses to let go. Until she commits murder. 95m/C VHS, DVD, Meredith

Til There Was You 🐾½ 1996 (PG-13) You know what most great romance movies have in common? The cou-

Williams, Stephen (Steve) Root; *D:* Dick Lowry. **TV**

Till the Clouds Roll By 🐾🐾½ 1946 An all-star, high-gloss musical biography of songwriter Jerome Kern, that, in typical Hollywood fashion, bears little resemblance to the composer's life. Filled with wonderful songs from his Broadway hit. ♪ Showboat Medley; Till the Clouds Roll By; Howja Like to Spoon with Me?; The Last Time I Saw Paris; They Didn't Believe Me; I Won't Dance; Why Was I Born?; Who?; Sunny. 137m/C VHS, DVD, Robert Walker, Van Heflin, Judy Garland, Frank Sinatra, Lucille Bremer, Kathryn Grayson, June Allyson, Dinah Shore, Lena Horne, Virginia O'Brien, Tony Martin; *D:* Richard Whorf; *W:* Myles Connolly, Jean Holloway; *C:* Harry Stradling Sr.; *M:* Conrad Salinger, Roger Edens, Lennie Hayton.

Till the End of Time 🐾🐾½ 1946 Three GIs have trouble adjusting to civilian life in their home town after WWII. Fine performances and excellent pacing. Popular title song. Adapted from "They Dream of Home" by Niven Busch. 105m/C VHS, Robert Mitchum, Guy Madison, Bill Williams, Dorothy McGuire, William Gargan, Tom Tully; *D:* Edward Dmytryk.

Till There Was You 🐾 1991 (PG-13) A struggling musician travels to a faraway tropical isle to solve the mystery of his brother's death. 94m/C VHS, Mark Harmon, Deborah Kara Unger, Jeroen Krabbe, Shane Briant; *D:* John Seale; *M:* Graeme Revell.

Tillie Wakes Up 🐾🐾½ 1917 Third in the Tillie series, following "Tillie's Punctured Romance" and "Tillie's Tomato Surprise," and "Tillie Wakes Up," which starred Dressler but not Chaplin. 73m/B V+S, DVD, Charlie Chaplin, Marie Dressler, Mabel Normand, Mack Swain, Chester Conklin; *D:* Mack Sennett; *W:* Hampton Del Ruth, Frank D. Williams.

Tillie's Punctured Romance 🐾🐾🐾½ 1914 The silent comedy which established Chaplin and Dressler as comedians. Chaplin, out of his Tramp character, is the city slicker trying to con one over on farm girl Dressler, who pursues revenge. First feature length comedy film. Followed by "Tillie's Tomato Surprise." and "Tillie Wakes Up." 73m/B Marie Dressler, Charlie Chaplin, Mabel Normand, Mack Swain, Chester Conklin, Charley Chase; *D:* Mack Sennett; *W:* Hampton Del Ruth; *C:* Frank D. Williams.

Tilt 🐾 1978 (PG) Flimsy storyline concerns a young runaway's adventures, with an aspiring rock star. Shields' pinball expertise eventually leads her to a match against pinball champ Durning. 111m/C VHS, Brooke Shields, Geoffrey Lewis; *D:* Rudy Durand; *C:* Paul Onorato; *M:* Eric Jupp, Rudy Durand, Donald Cammel.

Tim 🐾🐾½ 1979 Follows the relationship between a handsome, mentally retarded young man and an attractive older businesswoman. Sappy slow, line is redeemed by Gibson's fine performance in one of his first roles. Based on Colleen McCullough's first novel. 94m/C VHS, DVD, AU Mel Gibson, Piper Laurie, Peter Gwynne, Alwyn Kurts, Pat Evison; *D:* Michael Pate; *W:* Michael Pate; *C:* Paul Onorato; *M:* Eric Jupp. Australian Film Inst. '79: Actor (Gibson).

Tim Burton's Corpse Bride 🐾🐾½ *Corpse Bride* 2005 (PG) The magnificent visual and animation and a lead character voiced by Johnny Depp. What more could you want? Well what you get is a sweet story of love lost with a nether-worldly twist or two. Victor Van Dort (Depp) is set to marry Victoria Everglot (Watson) in a parentally-arranged union. Nervous and awkward, Victor retreats to the nearby graveyard, practicing the vows he has struggled to memorize, where he accidentally slips the ring on the finger (which he takes for a twig) of the long dead Corpse Bride (Carter). She comes to life and insists she is now his wife, and he is then plunged into the much brighter world of the dead. **75m/C DVD, Blu-ray Disc, HD DVD. GB US** *D:* Michael Johnson, Tim Burton; *W:* John August, Caroline Thompson, Pamela Pettler; *C:* Pete Kozachik; *M:* Danny Elfman; *V:* Johnny Depp, Helena Bonham-Carter, Emily Watson, Tracey Ullman, Joanna Lumley, Albert Finney, Richard E. Grant, Michael Gough, Christopher Lee, Jane Horrocks, Deep Roy, Danny Elfman, Paul Whitehouse, Enn Reitel, Stephen Ballantyne, Lisa Kay. Natl. Bd. of Review '05: Animated Film.

Tim Tyler's Luck 1937 Lost but not forgotten serial in its 12-chapter entirety. The fearless Tim Tyler uses whatever he can to do battle with the sinister Spider Web gang. **235m/B VHS, DVD.** Frankie Thomas Jr., Frances Robinson, Al Shean, Norman Willis, Earl Douglas, Jack Mulhall, Frank Mayo, Pat J. O'Brien; *D:* Ford Beebe, Wyndham Gittens.

Timber Queen 1944 A WWII flier comes home and aids his best friend's widow, who must make a quota of timber or lose her sawmill to gangsters. Old-fashioned. **66m/B VHS.** Richard Arlen, Mary Beth Hughes, June Havoc, Sheldon Leonard, George E. Stone, Dick Purcell; *D:* Frank McDonald.

Time 2006 After two years, pathologically jealous She-hee believes her lover Ji-woo no longer finds her attractive, so she disappears for six months. After undergoing extensive plastic surgery, she returns with a new identity to woo him again, only to find she's competing with the memory of herself. Korean with subtitles. **97m/C DVD. JP KN** Heyon-a Seong, Jungwoo Ha, Ji-yeon Park; *D:* Ki-Duk Kim; *W:* Ki-Duk Kim; *C:* Jong-mu Seong; *M:* Hyeong-woo Noh.

Time After Time 1979 (PG) In Victorian London, circa 1893, H.G. Wells is experimenting with his time machine. He discovers the machine has been used by an associate, who turns out to be Jack the Ripper, to travel to San Francisco in 1979. Wells follows to stop any further murders and the ensuing battle of wits is both entertaining and imaginative. McDowell is charming as Wells and Steenbergen is equally fine as Wells's modern American love interest. **112m/C VHS, DVD.** Malcolm McDowell, David Warner, Mary Steenbergen, Patti D'Arbanville, Charles Cioffi; *D:* Nicholas Meyer; *W:* Nicholas Meyer; *M:* Miklos Rozsa.

Time and Tide 2000 *Seunlau Ngaklau* 2000 Non-stop action from Hark with the usual convoluted plot. Tyler (Tse) is working as a bodyguard for a client who turns out to be a Triad boss. Tyler's friend Jack (Bai) is an ex-mercenary whose pregnant wife, Hui (Lo), is the criminal's estranged daughter. And then Jack's former South American colleagues show up in Hong Kong with a plan to assassinate the Triad boss, among other gun battles. Oh, and Tyler is also about to become a father, courtesy of a one-night stand who doesn't want anything to do with him. Chinese with subtitles. **113m/C VHS, DVD. HK** Nicholas Tse, Wu Bai, Anthony Wong, Candy Lo, Cathy Chui, Joventino Couto Remotigue; *D:* Tsui Hark; *W:* Tsui Hark, Koan Hui; *C:* Herman Yau, Ko Chiu-lam; *M:* Tommy Wai.

Time at the Top 1999 Fourteen-year-old Susan Shawson travels back in time (via her apartment's elevator) from the Philadelphia of the present to the same city in 1881. There Susan befriends Victoria Walker and her younger brother Robert, who need help with their family troubles. The trio manage to time travel back and forth and the change both the past and the present. Based on the book by Edward Ormondroyd. **96m/C VHS.** Timothy Busfield, Elisha Cuthbert, Gabrielle Boni, Matthew Harbour, Lynne Adams, Denys Chapdelaine; *D:* Jim Kaufman; *W:* Linda Brookover; *C:* Francois Protat; *M:* Simon Carpenter. **CABLE**

Time Bandits 1981 (PG) A group of dwarves help a young boy to travel through time and space with the likes of Robin Hood, Napoleon, Agamemnon, and other time-warp playmates. Epic fantasy from Monty Python alumni. **110m/C VHS, DVD, UMD. GB** John Cleese, Sean Connery,

that causes amnesia—so Clay is really confused about why people keep trying to kill him. **88m/C VHS, DVD.** Roy Scheider, William McNamara, Dina Meyer, Henry Rollins; *D:* David Worth. **VIDEO**

Time Chasers 1995 Nick Miller (Burch) invents a device that permits his airplane to travel through time. But, after selling his invention, he soon discovers that it has turned the future into a desolate wasteland. Now Nick must try to regain control and put things back to normal. **90m/C VHS.** Matthew Burch, Bonnie Pritchard, Peter Harrington; *D:* David Giangola.

Time Code 2000 (R) *Timecode* 2000 (R) Figgis shot this film in one day, using four digital video cameras and 28 actors to tell four separate (though inter-connected) stories that were shown simultaneously onscreen in four rectangular quadrants. The stories center around a film production company headed by producer Alex Green (Skarsgard), whose wife Emma (Burrows) plans to leave him because he is having an affair with actress Rose (Hayek), whose own relationship with Lauren (Tripplehorn) is falling apart. Then there's various producers, directors, and actors pitching ideas or auditioning for parts. It's not as confusing as might be imagined although how it will play on video is a challenge. **97m/C VHS, DVD.** Stellan Skarsgard, Saffron Burrows, Salma Hayek, Jeanne Tripplehorn, Richard Edson, Julian Sands, Xander Berkeley, Glenne Headly, Holly Hunter, Danny Huston, Kyle MacLachlan, Alessandro Nivola, Steven Weber, Viveka Davis, Aimee Graham, Andrew Heckler, Daphna Kastner, Leslie Mann, Mia Maestro; *D:* Mike Figgis; *W:* Mike Figgis; *C:* Patrick Alexander Stewart; *M:* Mike Figgis, Anthony Marinelli.

A Time for Dancing 2000 (PG-13) Jules and Sam grew up best friends and shared a love for dancing that was to lead the girls to Juilliard College. When Jules learns that she has late-stage cancer, their life plans take a tragic shift. **94m/C VHS, DVD.** Larisa Oleynik, Shiri Appleby, Peter Coyote, Amy Madigan, Shane West, Lynn Whitfield, Patricia Kalember, Anton Yelchin; *D:* Peter Gilbert; *W:* Kara Lindstrom; *C:* Alex Nepomniaschy. **TV**

A Time for Miracles 1980 Dramatic biography of the first native-born American saint, Elizabeth Bayley Seton, who was canonized in 1975. **97m/C VHS.** Kate Mulgrew, Lorne Greene, Rossano Brazzi, John Forsythe, Jean-Pierre Aumont, Milo O'Shea; *D:* Michael O'Herlihy. **TV**

Time for Revenge 1982 A demolitions worker attempts to blackmail his corrupt employer by claiming a workplace explosion made him speechless. He finds himself in a contest of silence and wits. In Spanish with English subtitles. **112m/C VHS. AR** Federico Luppi, Haydee Padilla, Julio de Grazia, Ulises Dumont; *D:* Adolfo Aristarain. Montreal World Film Fest. '82: Film.

The Time Guardian 1987 (PG) Time-travelers of the future arrive in the Australian desert in 1988, intent on warning the local populace of the impending arrival of killer cyborgs from the 40th century. Muddled and confusing. **89m/C VHS.** Tom Burlinson, Carrie Fisher, Dean Stockwell, Nikki Coghill; *D:* Brian Hannant; *W:* Brian Hannant, John Baxter; *C:* Geoffrey Burton.

Time Indefinite 1993 Cinema verite effort once again follows filmmaker McElwee who returns to his Southern roots to confront personal tragedy by recording every moment on film. It is an emotional journey in which he discovers that his camera may not be enough to protect him from his own feelings. Moving, with occasional lapses into self-absorption. Companion film to McElwee's "Sherman's March." **117m/C VHS, DVD.** *D:* Ross McElwee; *W:* Ross McElwee.

Time Lapse 2001 (PG-13) Agent Clay Pierce (McNamara) is a member of a U.S. antiterrorist unit who unknowingly prevents an attempt to sell a nuclear device to the Iraquis. Too bad Clay is the only one who makes it back alive (more or less). He's got a lot of questions for his boss LaNova (Scheider), who turns out to be a double-dealer. And he deals with Clay by giving him an experimental drug

Shelley Duvall, Katherine Helmond, Ian Holm, Michael Palin, Ralph Richardson, Kenny Baker, Peter Vaughan, David Warner, Craig Warnock; *D:* Terry Gilliam; *W:* Terry Gilliam, Michael Palin; *C:* Peter Biziou; *M:* Mike Moran, George Harrison.

Time Lock 1957 An expert safecracker races against time to save a child who is trapped inside a bank's presest time-locked vault. Canada is the setting, although the film was actually made in England. Based on a play by Arthur Hailcis. **73m/B VHS. GB** Robert Beatty, Betty McDowall, Vincent Winter, Lee Patterson, Sandra Francis, Alan Gifford, Robert Ayres, Victor Wood, Jack Cunningham, Peter Mannering, Gordon Tanner, Larry Cross, Sean Connery; *D:* Gerald Thomas; *W:* Peter Rogers; *C:* Peter Hennessy; *M:* Stanley Black.

The Time Machine 1960 English scientist living near the end of the 19th century invents time travel machine and uses it to travel into various periods of the future. Rollicking version of H.G. Wells' classic cautionary tale boasts Oscar-winning special effects. Remade in 1978. **103m/C VHS, DVD.** Rod Taylor, Yvette Mimieux, Whit Bissell, Sebastian Cabot, Alan Young, Paul Frees, Bob Barran, Doris Lloyd; *D:* George Pal; *W:* David Duncan; *C:* Paul Vogel; *M:* Russell Garcia.

Time Machine 1978 (G) Yet another adaptation of H.G. Wells' classic novel about a scientist who invents a machine that enables him to travel through time. Inferior remake of the 1960 version. **99m/C VHS.** John Beck, Priscilla Barnes, Andrew Duggan; *D:* Henning Schellerup.

The Time Machine 2002 (PG-13) Well, the special effects are pretty cool but this sci-fi adventure has little to do with H.G. Wells' 1894 novel. Eccentric scientist Alexander Hartdegen (an anorexic-looking Pearce) lives in New York, circa 1900. He's devastated when his fiance Emma (Guillory) is killed and is determined to change fate by building a time machine. But going back in time changes nothing so Hartdegen goes forward to discover why he can't change things. He accidentally winds up in 800,000 when the Earth is once again pastoral and its inhabitants are divided into the gentle surface-dwelling Elois and the monstrous, cannibalistic subterranean Morlocks. Irish singer Mumba debuts as Mara, whom Hartdegen falls for, and a heavily made-up Irons is the Uber-Morlock. Unfortunately, the story is dull rather than what it should be—rousing in a who-cares-about-logic, B-movie way. **96m/C VHS, DVD. US** Guy Pearce, Samantha Mumba, Mark Addy, Sienna Guillory, Omera Mumba, Jeremy Irons, Orlando Jones, Phyllida Law, Yancey Arias; *Cameos:* Alan Young; *D:* Simon Wells; *W:* John Logan; *C:* Donald McAlpine; *M:* Klaus Badelt.

A Time of Destiny 1988 (PG-13) During WWII, an American soldier vows to kill his brother-in-law, who he believes caused his father's death. Meanwhile, the two men have become good friends in the army, never realizing their connection. A strange, overblown family saga from the director of "El Norte." Beautiful photography, terrific editing. **118m/C VHS,** William Hurt, Timothy Hutton, Melissa Leo, Stockard Channing, Megan Follows, Francesco Rabal; *D:* Gregory Nava; *W:* Gregory Nava, Anna Thomas; *M:* Ennio Morricone.

Time of Favor 2000 Military commander Meanchem (Avril) and best friend Pini (Alterman) have a falling out over Michal (Tinkerbell), the disillusioned daughter of radical Orthodox Rabbi Meltzer (Dayan), whom the men follow. But when Pini is rejected, he decides to channel his frustrations into self-abnegation. Hebrew with subtitles. **98m/C DVD. IS** Aki Avni, Tinkerbell, Edan Alterman, Assi Dayan, Micha Selektar, Amnon Volf; *D:* Joseph Cedar; *W:* Joseph Cedar; *C:* Ofer Inov; *M:* Jonathan Bar-Girora.

Time of Indifference 1964 *Gil Indifferenti; Les Deux Rivales* 1964 Based on the novel by Alberto Moravia. Tale of the disintegration of values in 1920s Italy is unable to take full advantage of its fine cast or potentially thought-provoking themes. **84m/B VHS. IT** Rod Steiger, Shelley Winters,

Claudia Cardinale, Paulette Goddard, Tomas Milian; *D:* Francesco Maselli.

Time of the Gypsies 1990 (R) *Dom Za Vesanje* 1990 (R) Acclaimed Yugoslavian saga about a homely, unlucky Gypsy boy who sets out to steal his way to a dowry large enough to marry the girl of his dreams. Beautifully filmed, magical, and very long. In the Gypsy language. Romany, it's the first feature film made in the Gypsy tongue. **136m/C VHS. YU** Davor Dujmovic, Sinolicka Trpkova, Ljubica Adzovic, Husnija Hasimovic, Bora Todorovic; *D:* Emir Kusturica. Cannes '89: Director (Kusturica).

Time of the Wolf 2003 (R) *Le Temps du Loup* 2003 (R) City family on a weekend outing to their country home discover it occupied by squatters after an unspecified widespread disaster. Dad (Duval) tries to dispel any potential violence but is shot dead for his trouble, with the rest of the family escaping to find a suddenly very different, very dangerous outside world. They set out on a nightmarish journey across desolate and unfamiliar landscape where survival is never certain. Harsh apocalyptic vision is reminiscent of "Night of the Living Dead" and Godard's "Weekend." Austrian director Haneke is great at creating a very realistic and claustrophobic atmosphere. **113m/C DVD. FR AT GE** Isabelle Huppert, Maurice Benichou, Lucas Biscombe, Patrice Chereau, Beatrice Dalle, Daniel Duval, Olivier Gourmet, Rona Hartner, Anais Demoustier, Maryline Even, Brigitte Rouan, Florence Loiret-Caille; *D:* Michael Haneke; *W:* Michael Haneke; *C:* Jurgen Jurges.

The Time of Their Lives 1946 *The Ghost Steps Out* 1946 A pair of Revolutionary War-era ghosts haunt a modern country estate. One of the best A & C comedies. **82m/B VHS, DVD.** Bud Abbott, Lou Costello, Marjorie Reynolds, Binnie Barnes, Gale Sondergaard, John Shelton; *D:* Charles T. Barton.

The Time of Your Life 1948 The only Cagney film that ever lost money. A simple but engaging story of people trying to live their dreams. Cagney is delightful as a barroom philosopher who controls the world around him from his seat in the tavern. Although it was not very popular with audiences at the time, the critics hailed it as an artistic achievement. Based on William Saroyan's play. **109m/B VHS, DVD.** James Cagney, William Bendix, Jeanne Cagney, Broderick Crawford, Ward Bond, James Barton, Paul Draper, Natalie Schafer; *D:* H.C. Potter.

Time Out for Love 1961 *Les Grandes Personnes; The Five Day Lover* 1961 An American girl travels to Paris in search of romance, but discovers more than she bargained for. In French with English subtitles. **91m/B VHS. IT FR** Jean-Seberg, Micheline Presle, Maurice Ronet, Francoise Prevost, Annibale Ninchi, Nando (Fernando) Bruno; *D:* Jean Valere; *M:* Georges Delerue.

Time Regained 1999 (R) *Le Temps Retrouve* 1999 (R) Based on Marcel Proust's final volume of "Remembrance of Things Past," this ambitious adaptation is a sweeping and sometimes surreal saga of an elderly man's life and memories. Concentrating on turn of the century Paris, period piece time travels around the world inhabited by Marcel (Mazzarella), based on the author himself, who mingles with the wealthy and beautiful. Legendary French beauties litter the screen in supporting roles, including Deneuve, as

Odette, who used her looks to get ahead and Beart, as Gilberte, her stepdaughter trapped in an unhappy marriage. Greggory is Saint-Loup, Gilberte's philandering, bisexual husband who cheats on her with naughty Zylberstein and Perez, while Malkovich does a turn as his even more depraved uncle. Worthy performance from Proust look-alike Mazzarella. In French with subtitles. **165m/C VHS, DVD, FR/IT** Marcello Mazzarella, Catherine Deneuve, Emmanuelle Beart, Vincent Perez, John Malkovich, Pascal Greggory, Marie-France Pisier, Chiara Mastroianni, Arielle Dombasle, Edith Scob, Elsa Zylberstein, Philippe Morier-Genoud, Melvil Poupaud, Mathilde Seigner; Jacques Pieiller, Laurence Fevrier, Jean-Francois Balmer, Jerome Prieur; **D:** Raul Ruiz; **W:** Raul Ruiz, Gilles Taurand; **C:** Ricardo Aronovich; **M:** Jorge Arriagada; **V:** Patrice Chereau.

Time Runner 1992 (R) It's 2022 and the Earth is being used as target practice by alien invaders. Space captain Hamill manages to find a hole in time and slip back to 1992 where he can battle the first of the alien infiltrators and maybe change Earth's destiny. The time-travel theme (including Hamill watching his own birth) is fun and the special effects are well done. **90m/C VHS,** Mark Hamill, Brion James, Rae Dawn Chong; **D:** Michael Mazo.

Time Served 1999 (R) Typically sleazy women-in-prison movie. Sarah McKinney (Oxenberg) is wrongly convicted by a psycho judge and sent to the slammer where she faces a crooked warden and lecherous guards. Sarah also disgram means stripping at an underground sex club frequented by the judge and his cronies. Sarah tries to expose more than just herself and tries to get the truth out. **94m/C VHS,** Catherine Oxenberg, Louise Fletcher, Jeff Fahey, Bo Hopkins, James Handy; **D:** Glen Pitre. **CABLE**

Time Stands Still Megall Az ido 1982 Two brothers experience troubled youth in Budapest. Artful, somberly executed, with American pop soundtrack. Subtitled in English. **99m/C VHS, HU** Istvan Znamenak, Henrik Pauer, Aniko Ivan, Sandor Soth, Peter Galfy; **D:** Peter Gothar; **W:** Peter Gothar; **C:** Lajos Koltai; **M:** Gyorgy Selmeczi; N.Y. Film Critics '82: Foreign Film.

Time to Die Az ido 1982 Two brothers experience troubled youth in Budapest. Artful, somberly executed... Rogan 1983 (R) WWII victim of heinous war crimes, obsessed with revenge, stalks his prey for a final confrontation, while eluding U.S. intelligence. Disappointing despite good cast working with Mario Puzo story. **88m/C VHS, DVD,** Edward Albert, Rex Harrison, Rod Taylor, Raf Vallone; **D:** Matt Cimber; **M:** Ennio Morricone.

A Time to Die 1991 (R) Lords plays a police photographer who, well, photographs on the side. But her camera catches one in the act of murder. Routine crime thriller. **93m/C VHS, DVD,** Traci Lords, Jeff Conaway, Richard Roundtree, Bradford Bancroft, Nitchie Barrett; **D:** Charles Kanganis; **W:** Charles Kanganis; **M:** Ennio Morricone.

Time to Kill Tempo di Uccidere 1989 (R) A young soldier in Africa wanders away from his camp and meets a woman whom he rapes and kills. When he returns to his outfit he finds he can't escape his torment. **110m/C VHS, DVD,** Nicolas Cage, Giancarlo Giannini, Robert Liensol; **D:** Guiliano Montaldo; **M:** Ennio Morricone.

A Time to Kill 1996 (R) Powerful story of revenge, racism, and the question of justice in the "new south." John Grisham had a lot of clout when he finally sold his first and favorite novel to the movies, including veto power over the leading man—director Schumacher was for Woody Harrelson, Grisham was opposed but both finally agreed on newcomer McConaughey. He's outstanding as idealistic smalltown Mississippi lawyer Jake Brigance, called to defend anguished father Carl Lee Hailey (Jackson), who's accused of killing daughter's rednecks who raped his young daughter. Jake's assisted by former mentor Lucien Wilbanks (Sutherland) and ambitious northern law student Ellen Roark (Bullock) against ruthless prosecutor Rufus Buckley (Spacey). Is it emotionally manipulative? You betcha. But Grisham's done well on screen and Schumacher (who also did "The Client") knows how to get that "from his cast and script. **150m/C VHS, DVD,** Matthew McConaughey, Samuel L. Jackson, Sandra Bullock, Kevin Spacey, Donald Sutherland, Brenda Fricker, Oliver Platt, Charles S. Dutton, Kiefer Sutherland, Chris Cooper, Ashley Judd, Patrick McGoohan, Rae'Ven (Alvia Larrymore) Kelly, John Diehl, Tonea Stewart, M. Emmet Walsh, Anthony Heald, Kurwood Smith; **D:** Joel Schumacher; **W:** Akiva Goldsman; **C:** Peter Menzies Jr.; **M:** Elliot Goldenthal. MTV Movie Awards '97: Breakthrough Perf. (McConaughey).

A Time to Remember 2003 Maggie (Roberts) has been diagnosed with Alzheimer's. A family Thanksgiving reunites her with her very different daughters. At one point the kid loses his voice—he probably choked on the pathos. **90m/C VHS,** Ruben Gomez, Raymond Serra, Dominic O'Connor, Morgana King; **D:** Thomas Travers; **W:** Thomas Travers; **C:** Richie Lee; **M:** Bill Grabowski.

A Time to Remember 1987 Sticky with sentiment, this family film tells of a boy with a gift for singing, encouraged by a priest, discouraged by his father. At one point the kid loses his voice (Delaney), who must learn to forgive old hurts in order to deal with the present. Vaietta (Gallagher) and Brit Thanksgiving. **88m/C DVD,** Doris Roberts, Megan Gallagher, Louise Fletcher, Rosemary Forsyth, Dana Delany, James W. Wrenn; **M:** Joe Kraemer. **CABLE**

A Time to Live and a Time to Die Tong Nien Wang Shi 1985 Family from southern mainland China emigrate to Taiwan in the '40s to escape from hardship and are unable to return after the communist takeover. They find themselves cut off from their cultural heritage and though the years pass, everyone still thinks of the mainland as home. Taiwanese with subtitles. **137m/C VHS, CH** Yu-Yuen Yang, Feng Tien, Shufen Xin, An-Shuin Yiu Mei Feng; **D:** Hsiao-Hsien Hou; **C:** Pin Bing Lee.

A Time to Love & a Time to Die 1958 Lush adaptation of Erich Maria Remarque novel about WWII German soldier who falls in love with a young girl during furlough. The two are married, only to be separated when he is forced to return to the Russian front. Sympathetic treatment of Germans opposed to Hitler's policies. Hutton's first film, credited to his real name, Dana J. Hutton. **133m/C VHS,** John Gavin, Lilo (Liselotte) Pulver, Jock Mahoney, Keenan Wynn, Klaus Kinski, Don DeFore, Thayer David, Dieter Borsche, Erich Maria Remarque, Barbara Rutting, Charles Regnier, Dorothea Wieck, Kurt Meisel, Clancy Cooper, John van Dreelen, Dana J. Hutton; **D:** Douglas Sirk; **W:** Orin Jannings; **C:** Russell Metty; **M:** Miklos Rozsa.

Time to Leave Les Temps Qui Reste 2005 French flick takes an unflinching look at death and dying from the perspective of a narcissistic young photographer who learns that he has terminal cancer and reacts in a very realistic, unHollywood way. First he has sex with his live-in lover and then immediately kicks him out; he insults and further alienates his single-mother sister during a family dinner while telling no one about his illness except for his outcast grandmother "because you're like me, you'll be dying soon," he bluntly tells her. An absence of melodrama and an interesting subplot involving a childless waitress followed by a genuinely moving and makes for a fine French import. **85m/C DVD, FR** Melvil Poupaud, Jeanne Moreau, Valeria Bruni-Tedeschi, Daniel Duval, Marie Riviere, Christian Sengewald, Louise-Anne Hippeau, Walter Pagano, Ugo Soussan, Ugo Trabelsi; **D:** Francois Ozon; **W:** Francois Ozon; **C:** Jeanne Lapoirie.

Time to Live 1985 Adaptation of Mary Lou Weisman's "Intensive Care" about a family's ordeal with Muscular Dystrophy. Minnelli's first appearance in a TV movie. **97m/C** Liza Minnelli, Jeffrey DeMunn, Swoosie Kurtz, Corey Haim, Scott Schwartz; **D:** Rick Wallace; **M:** Georges Delerue. **TV**

Time Trackers 1988 (PG) A Roger Corman cheapie about a race through time, from present-day New York to medieval England, to recover a time machine before it alters the course of history. **87m/C VHS,** Kathleen Beller, Ned Beatty, Will Shriner, Parley Baer, Robert Cornthwaite, Bridget Hoffman, Alex Hyde-White; **D:** Howard R. Cohen; **W:** Howard R. Cohen; **C:** Rorn Schmidt.

The Time Travelers Time Trap 1964 Scientists discover and pass through a porthole leading to earth's post-armageddon future where they encounter unfriendly mutants. Frightened they make a serious effort to return to the past. Remade as "Journey to the Center of Time." **82m/C VHS,** Preston Foster, Phil Carey, Merry Anders, John Hoyt, Joan Woodbury, Dolores Wells, Dennis Patrick; **D:** Ib Melchior.

Time Tracers 1997 A group of scientists, detectives, and a reporter time travel back to the Civil War and the Jurassic period to correct a glitch that could alter earth's future. El tacky production reminiscent of Saturday matinee filler that uses stock footage for its monster's. **93m/C VHS,** Jeffrey Combs, Rocky Patterson, T.J. Myers, Mason; **D:** Bret McCormick.

Time Troopers Morgan Grauer; Morning Terror 1989 (R) In another post-nuke society, special police must execute anyone who has misused their allotted "energy clips" for illicit behavior. Dime-store budget sci-fi. **90m/C VHS, AT** Albert Fortell, Hannelore Elsner; **D:** L.E. Neiman.

Time Walker 1932 (PG) An archaeologist unearths King Tut's coffin in California. An alien living inside is unleashed and terrorizes the public. **86m/C VHS,** Ben Murphy, Nina Axelrod, Kevin Brophy, James Karen, Austin Stoker; **D:** Tom Kennedy; **W:** Tom Friedman, Karen Levitt; **M:** Richard Band.

Time Without Pity 1957 Anti-capital punishment plea finds desperate alcoholic David Graham (Redgrave) discovering that his son Alec (McCowen) is about to be executed for murder. But David doesn't believe in the boy's guilt and has 24 hours to find the real killer. The audience knows Alec is innocent from the get-go, making for a certain suspense. Based on the play "Someone Waiting" by Emlyn Williams. **88m/B VHS, DVD, GB** Michael Redgrave, Alec McCowen, Ann Todd, Leo McKern, Peter Cushing, Renee Houston, Paul Daneman, Lois Maxwell, Richard Wordsworth, George Devine, Joan Plowright; **D:** Joseph Losey; **W:** Ben Barzman; **C:** Freddie Francis; **M:** Tristram Cary.

Timebomb 1991 (R) When someone attempts to kill Biehn, he turns to a beautiful psychiatrist for help. She triggers flashbacks that send her hunted patient on a dangerous, perhaps deadly, journey into his past. **96m/C VHS,** Michael Biehn, Patsy Kensit, Tracy Scoggins, Robert Culp, Richard Jordan, Raymond St. Jacques, Jim Maniaci, Billy Blanks, Ray "Boom Boom" Mancini, Steven J. Oliver; **D:** Avi Nesher; **M:** Patrick Leonard.

Timecop 1994 (R) "Terminator" rip-off is fodder for Van Damme followers with lots of action and special effects (you weren't expecting acting too?). In 2004 policeman Max Walker (Van Damme) must travel back in time to prevent corrupt politician Aaron McComb (Silver) from altering history for personal gain. It's also Walker's chance to alter his personal history since his wife Melissa (Sara) was killed in an explosion he can now prevent. "Futuristic thriller based on a Dark Horse comic. **98m/C VHS, DVD,** Jean-Claude Van Damme, Ron Silver, Mia Sara, Bruce McGill, Scott Lawrence, Kenneth Welsh, Gabrielle Rose, Duncan Fraser, Ian Tracey, Gloria Reuben, Scott Bellis, Jason Schombing, Kevin McNulty, Sean O'Byrne, Malcolm Stewart, Alfonso Quijada, Gina Road, Theodore Thomas; **D:** Peter Hyams; **W:** Mark Verheiden, Gary De Vore; **C:** Peter Hyams; **M:** Mark Isham.

Timecop 2: The Berlin Decision 2003 (R) Convoluted, confusing actioner. Timecop Ryan Chang (Lee) is sent to 1940s Germany where colleague Miller Branson (Griffith) is about to alter history by killing Hitler. While he stop... ping Branson, Chang inadvertently kills Branson's wife, which means the guy wants revenge. Branson keeps on hopping through time trying to change situations to correct a glitch that could affect history's future. El tacky production keeps care—best to stick with the Van Damme original if you like this sort of thing. **81m/C VHS, DVD,** Jason Scott Lee, Thomas Ian Griffith, Mary Page Keller, John Beck, Tava Smiley; **D:** Steve Boyum; **W:** Gary Scott Thompson; **C:** Cres-cano G.P. Notaile. **M:** Andy Gray. **VIDEO**

Timeless 1996 Hart's experimental feature debut uses Super-8, 16mm, and 35mm formats to tell a story. Eighteen-year-old Terry (Byrne) hangs out on the streets of Queens doing various odd jobs for a variety of small-time gamblers, dealers and mobsters. He falls for Lyrica (Duge) and gets her away from her abusive lover and the teen twosome head out of town, hoping for a better life. **90m/C VHS, DVD,** Peter Byrne, Michael Griffiths, Melissa Duge; **D:** Chris Hart; **W:** Chris Hart.

Timeline 2003 (PG-13) Weak big screen adaption of Michael Crichton's novel of the same name. Archaeologists travel back in time to medieva France to rescue a colleague. Features some of the most wooden performances since Pinnochio. While it's easy to blame the actors for their lackluster performance, a decent script would have helped them out a lot. **116m/C VHS, DVD, US** Paul Walker, Frances O'Connor, Gerard Butler, Billy Connolly, David Thewlis, Anna Friel, Neal McDonough, Matt Craven, Ethan (Randall) Embry, Michael Sheen, Lambert Wilson, Marton Csokas; **D:** Richard Donner; **W:** Jeff Maguire, George Nolfi; **C:** Caleb Deschanel; **M:** Brian Tyler.

Timelock 1999 In the 23rd century, asteroid Alpha 4 serves as a maximum security prison for the most dangerous criminals. However, the inmates have now gained controlled and its up to the reluctant heroics of a petty thief and a shuttle pilot to get the bad guys back in their cages. **100m/C VHS, DVD,** Maryam D'Abo, Arye Gross, Jeff Speakman, Jeffrey Meek, Martin Kove; **D:** Robert Munic; **W:** Joseph John Barnett; **C:** Larry Pizer; **M:** Michael Hoenig.

Timemaster 1995 (PG-13) The orphaned 12-year-old Jesse (Cameron-Glickenhaus) dreams his parents are alive in another time, so he asks inventor Isaiah (Morita) for help. The duo discover Jesse's parents are being held hostage by a galactic dictator (Dorn), who's using them in sinister virtual-reality games and Jesse must time-travel to rescue them. Co-written and co-produced by Michael Nesmith, best known for his days with the rock group "The Monkees." **93m/C VHS, DVD,** Jesse Cameron-Glickenhaus, Pat Morita, Joanna Pacula, Michael Dorn, Duncan Regehr, Michelle Williams; **D:** James Glickenhaus; **W:** James Glickenhaus.

Timerider The Adventure of Lyle Swan 1983 (PG) Motorcyclist riding through the California desert is accidentally thrown back in time to 1877, the result of a scientific experiment that went awry. There he finds no gas stations and lots of cowboys. Nesmith (yes, of the Monkees) co-wrote the film score with the rock group "The Monkees." **90m/C VHS,** Fred Ward, Belinda Bauer, Peter Coyote, Richard Masur, Ed Lauter, L.Q. Jones, Tracey Walker; **D:** William Dear; **W:** Michael Nesmith, William Dear; **C:** Larry Pizer; **M:** Michael Nesmith. **TV**

Times Have Been Better Le Ciel Sur la Tete 2006 Successful Jeremy is his parents' golden first-born, much to the dismay of younger brother Robin, who's the only one to know that Jeremy is gay. That changes when Jeremy announces his mom and dad aren't as liberal or progressive as they imagined when they decide to figure out what when "wrong" with their son. French with subtitles. **90m/C DVD, FR** Bernard Le Coq, Arnaud Binard, Olivier Guerriez, Charlotte de Turckheim, Stephane Boucher, Thierry Desroses, Pierre Deny; **D:** Regis Musset; **M:** Nicolas Mercier.

Times of Harvey Milk 1983 A powerful and moving documentary about the life and career of San Francisco supervisor and gay activist Harvey Milk. The film documents the assassination of Milk and Mayor George Moscone by Milk's fellow supervisor, Dan White. Highly acclaimed by both critics and audiences, the film gives an honest and direct look at the murder and people's reactions. News footage of the murders and White's trial is included. **90m/C VHS, DVD. D:** Robert Epstein. Oscars '83: Feature Doc.

Times Square 🐾🐾½ **1980 (R)** A 13-year-old girl learns about life on her own when she teams up with a defiant, anti-social child of the streets. Unappealing and unrealistic, the film features a New Wave music score. **111m/C VHS, DVD.** Tim Curry, Trini Alvarado, Robin Johnson, Peter Coffield, Elizabeth Pena, Anna Maria Horsford; **D:** Allan Moyle; **W:** Jacob Brackman; **C:** James A. Contner.

Times to Come 🐾🐾🐾 *Lo Que Vendra* **1981** Taut thriller reminiscent of bleak futuristic movies like "Clockwork Orange." Three people try to survive in a desolate, aggressive, and unstable future. In Spanish with English subtitles. **98m/C VHS. AR** Hugo Soto, Juan Leyrado, Charly Garcia; **D:** Gustavo Mosquera.

Timestalkers 🐾🐾½ **1987** A college professor's infatuation with a young woman is complicated by their pursuit of a criminal from the 26th century into the past. Mildly entertaining adventure. Tucker's last film. **100m/C VHS.** William Devane, Lauren Hutton, Klaus Kinski, John Ratzenberger, Forrest Tucker, Gail Youngs; **D:** Michael A. Schultz. **TV**

Tin Cup 🐾🐾🐾 **1996 (R)** You've got your romantic triangle, you've got your sports, you've got Costner reteamed with Shelton—"Bull Durham"—on a golf course? Can lightning strike twice? Ron "Tin Cup" McAvoy (Costner) is a West Texas golf hustler who has the ability but not the steadiness to be on the pro tour. When McAvoy decides on a last-ditch effort to qualify for the U.S. Open, he turns to psychologist Dr. Molly Griswold (Russo) to get his game together. And the fact that Molly is the girlfriend of McAvoy's longtime rival—and successful PGA player—Don Simms (Johnson), well Tin Cup isn't adverse to playing for the lady's affections either. The U.S. Open scenes were filmed at Houston's Kingwood Country Club and the actors did their own shots. **133m/C VHS, DVD.** Kevin Costner, Don Johnson, Rene Russo, Richard "Cheech" Marin, Linda Hart, Dennis Burkley, Rex Linn, Lou Myers, Richard Lineback, Mickey Jones; **D:** Ron Shelton; **W:** Ron Shelton, John Norville; **C:** Russell Boyd; **M:** William Ross.

Tin Man 🐾🐾 **2007** Surreal use of L. Frank Baum's "The Wizard of Oz" that can't really offer much in the way of heart or brain. The Outer Zone (or O.Z.) is an alternative universe ruled by evil sorceress Azkadellia (Robertson) and her heaving bosom. Our Dorothy is glowering tomboy D.G. (Deschanel), who still arrives by tornado, and meets her posse: Glitch (Cumming), whose brain has been removed; psychic beastie Raw (Trujillo); shape-shifting Toto (Mankuma); and grieving Wyatt Cain (McDonough), who's

called a "tin man" because he was a cop. And they have to find some emerald that will free O.Z. from Azkadellia's rule. And yes, there's a sorta druggie wizard/magician (Dreyfuss). A Sci-Fi Channel miniseries. **360m/C DVD.** Zooey Deschanel, Neal McDonough, Kathleen Robertson, Alan Cumming, Raoul Trujillo, Blu Mankuma, Richard Dreyfuss, Callum Keith Rennie, Nick Willing, Anna Galvin; **W:** Steve Mitchell, Craig W. Van Sickle; **C:** Thomas Burstyn; **M:** Simon Boswell.

Tin Men 🐾🐾½ **1987 (R)** Set in Baltimore in the 1960s, this bitter comedy begins with two aluminum-siding salesmen colliding in a minor car accident. They play increasingly savage pranks on each other until one seduces the wife of the other, ruining his marriage. Like "Diner," the movie is full of Levinson's idiosyncratic local Baltimore color. **112m/C VHS, DVD.** Richard Dreyfuss, Danny DeVito, Barbara Hershey, John Mahoney, Jackie Gayle, Stan Brock, Seymour Cassel, Bruno Kirby, J.T. Walsh, Michael Tucker; **D:** Barry Levinson; **W:** Barry Levinson; **C:** Peter Sova; **M:** David Steele.

Tin Pan Alley 🐾🐾½ **1940** Tin Pan Alley songwriters Oakie and Payne meet singing sisters Faye and Grable, who agree to plug their material. At first their music business thrives but when the women head off to sing in a hit London show, the business goes downhill. Since WWI has been declared, the boys enlist and wind up in England, where they get a second chance to see their gals. The first teaming of Faye and Payne, who would star together in three more films. Remade as "I'll Get By." 🎵"The Sheik of Araby; You Say the Sweetest Things, Baby; America I Love You; Goodbye Broadway; Hello France; K-K-K-Katy; Moonlight Bay; Honeysuckle Rose; Moonlight and Roses. **92m/B VHS.** Alice Faye, John Payne, Betty Grable, Jack Oakie, Allen Jenkins, Esther Ralston, John Loder, Elisha Cook Jr., Fred Keating, Billy Gilbert; **D:** Walter Lang; **W:** Robert Ellis, Helen Logan; **C:** Leon Shamroy; **M:** Alfred Newman. Oscars '40: Score.

The Tin Soldier 🐾🐾½ **1995 (PG)** Updated version of the Hans Christian Andersen story finds 12-year-old Billy (Knight) moving with his widowed mom (Sheedy) to a tough L.A. neighborhood. He's intimidated by the school bully to join a gang and smitten by a pretty girl who doesn't like his new friends. What's a guy to do? Why meet a mysterious toy shop owner (DeLuise), who gives Billy a tin soldier that magically transforms into a very real medieval knight named Yarik (Voight). Good intentions—no subtlety. Voight's directorial debut. **99m/C VHS.** Trenton Knight, Ally Sheedy, Dom DeLuise, Jon Voight; **D:** Jon Voight.

The Tin Star 🐾🐾🐾 **1957** Perkins is the young sheriff who persuades veteran bounty hunter Fonda to help him rid the town of outlaws. Excellent Mann western balances humor and suspense. **93m/B VHS, DVD.** Henry Fonda, Anthony Perkins, Betsy Palmer, Neville Brand, Lee Van Cleef, John McIntire, Michel Ray; **D:** Anthony Mann; **C:** Loyal Griggs; **M:** Elmer Bernstein.

The Tingler 🐾🐾🐾 **1959** Coroner Price discovers that a creepy creature is capable of growing on the human spine and increasing in size through fear. The only way to get rid of it is through constant screaming. Price takes what is probably the screen's first LSD trip and a partial color sequence fights nice red blood pouring from a faucet. One of Castle's cheesy best that originally wowed movie audiences in "Percepto" format, which consisted of installing electric buzzers under the seats for that true tingling sensation. **82m/B VHS, DVD.** Vincent Price, Darryl Hickman, Judith Evelyn, Philip Coolidge, Patricia Cutts, Pamela Lincoln; **D:** William Castle; **W:** Robb White; **C:** Wilfred M. Kline; **M:** Von Dexter.

Tinker, Tailor, Soldier, Spy 🐾🐾🐾 **1980** Guinness is brilliant as world-weary spy master George Smiley, who has been somewhat forcibly retired from British Intelligence, better known as "The Circus," after a change at the top. But when a mole is discovered operating at the very highest levels, Smiley is approached on the quiet to root him

out without giving the game away. Complex and sometimes confusing espionage drama based on the novel by John Le Carre. Followed by "Smiley's People." **324m/C VHS, DVD. GB** Alec Guinness, Michael Aldridge, Ian Bannen, Bernard Hepton, Ian Richardson, Terence Rigby, Anthony Bate, Hywel Bennett, Michael Jayston, Joss Ackland, Warren Clarke, Beryl Reid, Sian Phillips, Patrick Stewart; **D:** John Irvin; **W:** Arthur Hopcraft; **C:** Tony Pierce-Roberts; **M:** Geoffrey Burgon. **TV**

Tinseltown 🐾🐾 **1997 (R)** Two broke screenwriters, who are living in a self-storage facility, suspect that the man who rents the space next to them is an infamous L.A. serial killer. Naturally, the desperate duo are inspired by his deeds to write a screenplay, which could make them his next victims. Based on the play "Self-storage" by Tony Spiridakis and Shem Bitterman. **84m/C VHS, DVD.** Arye Gross, Joe Pantoliano, Ron Perlman, Tom Wood, Kristy Swanson, Rebecca Gray, John Considine, David Dukes; **D:** Tony Spiridakis; **W:** Tony Spiridakis.

Tintorera... Tiger Shark Woof! *Tintorera...Bloody Waters* **1978 (R)** Three shark hunters attempt to discover why buxom swimmers are disappearing. Phony takeoff of "Jaws." **91m/C VHS, DVD. GB MX** Susan George, Fiona Lewis, Jennifer Ashley; **D:** Rene Cardona Jr.

Tiny Toon Adventures: How I Spent My Vacation 🐾🐾 **1991** How the tiny toons of Acme Acres spend their summer vacation in this animated adventure that spoofs several popular films and amusements. Plucky Duck and Hampton Pig journey to "Happy World Land" (a takeoff on Walt Disney World), Babs and Buster Bunny's water adventure parodies "Deliverance," there's a spoof of "The Little Mermaid," and the Road Runner even makes a cameo appearance. Parents will be equally entertained by the level of humor and the fast-paced action. Based on the Steven Spielberg TV cartoon series, this is the first made-for-home-video animated feature ever released in the United States. **80m/C VHS, DVD.** Rich Arons; **V:** Charles Adler, Tress MacNeille, Joe Alaskey, Donald E. Messick, Jonathan Winters, Edie McClurg.

The Tioga Kid 🐾½ **1948** Dean takes on two roles here, that of a Texas Ranger and an outlaw who goes by the name of "The Tioga Kid." Andy Parker and the Plainsmen provide the cowboy tunes. **54m/B VHS, DVD.** Eddie Dean, Roscoe Ates, Jennifer Holt, Dennis Moore, William "Bill" Fawcett; **D:** Ray Taylor; **W:** Ed Earl Repp.

The Tip-Off 🐾🐾½ **1931** Lovable boxer (Armstrong) and vivacious girlfriend (Rogers) save less-than-bright friend from getting involved with mean mobster's girlfriend. Major chemistry between Rogers and Armstrong. **75m/B VHS.** Eddie Quillan, Robert Armstrong, Ginger Rogers, Joan Peers, Ernie Adams; **D:** Albert Rogell.

Tipping the Velvet 🐾🐾½ **2002** Provocative miniseries based on the Sarah Waters novel. Set in the 1890s, it takes a look at the unconventional life of male impersonator and music hall star Nan Astley (Stirling), who takes up her profession after becoming infatuated with cross-dressing performer Kitty Butler (Hawes). Hired as Kitty's assistant, Nan eventually reveals her love and the duo become partners on and off the London stage. But Nan's life takes a turn for the dark side when she turns to prostitution, gets involved with dominating aristocrat, Diana (Chancellor), and seeks help from potential new love, Florence (May). **180m/C DVD. GB** Rachael Stirling, Keeley Hawes, Anna Chancellor, Jodhi May, Hugh Bonneville, Alexei Sayle, John Bowe, Sally Hawkins; **D:** Geoffrey Sax; **W:** Andrew Davies; **C:** Cinders Forshaw; **M:** Adrian Johnston. **TV**

Tiptoes 🐾🐾 **2003 (R)** Rolfe (Oldman) and Steven (McConaughey) are brothers. Rolfe is a dwarf, and Steven isn't, which causes some worry for Steven's girlfriend Carol (Beckinsale) when she becomes pregnant and worries that her child will get the dwarf gene. In a twist, she falls for Rolfe, and comedy, drama, and romance ensues. Director Bright had a falling out

with the producers and was fired during the shoot, resulting in an uneven film and Bright issuing a scathing monologue against the producers at the film's debut at the Sundance Film Festival. Performances are good but can't save the film from falling flat. **90m/C DVD.** Gary Oldman, Matthew McConaughey, Kate Beckinsale, Peter Dinklage, Patricia Arquette, Debbie Lee Carrington; **W:** Bill Weiner; **C:** Sonja Rom. **VIDEO**

'Tis a Pity She's a Whore 🐾🐾½ *Addio, Fratello, Crudele* **1973 (R)** A brother and sister engage in an incestuous affair. She becomes pregnant and is married off. Her husband, however, becomes infuriated when he learns of his wife's pregnancy. Photography is by Vittorio Storaro in this highly stylized drama set in Renaissance Italy. **102m/C VHS, DVD. IT** Charlotte Rampling, Oliver Tobias, Fabio Testi, Antonio Falsi, Rick (Rik) Battaglia, Angela Luce, Rino Imperio; **D:** Giuseppe Patroni-Griffi; **M:** Ennio Morricone.

Titan A.E. 🐾🐾½ **2000 (PG)** Animated adventure set after Earth is destroyed by aliens. Young Cale begins a journey through space to find a legendary lost ship—The Titan—that holds the secret to mankind's salvation. Visuals—both computer-generated and traditionally drawn—are breathtaking, but the script is earthbound. Dialogue too often falls flat, and the story, aimed at teen boys, never lives up to the epic visual dazzle. **95m/C VHS, DVD. D:** Don Bluth, Gary Goldman; **W:** Ben Edlund, John August, Joss Whedon; **M:** Graeme Revell; **V:** Matt Damon, Drew Barrymore, Bill Pullman, Nathan Lane, Janeane Garofalo, John Leguizamo, Tone Loc, Ron Perlman, Alex D. Linz, Jim Breuer.

Titanic 🐾🐾🐾 **1953** Hollywoodized version of the 1912 sinking of the famous luxury liner sets the scene for the personal drama of a mother (Stanwyck) who wants to flee her husband (Webb) for a new life in America. Story gets a little too melodramatic, but it's not a bad retelling of the sea tragedy. Film is quite effective in conveying the panic and the calm of the actual sinking. A 20-foot-long model of the ship was built for the re-creation of that fateful moment when the "Titanic" hit the inevitable iceberg. **98m/B VHS, DVD.** Clifton Webb, Barbara Stanwyck, Robert Wagner, Richard Basehart, Audrey Dalton, Thelma Ritter, Brian Aherne; **D:** Jean Negulesco; **W:** Charles Brackett, Walter Reisch, Richard L. Breen. Oscars '53: Story & Screenplay.

Titanic 🐾🐾½ **1996 (PG-13)** Dull and draggy TV version of the 1912 tragedy between the luxury liner and an iceberg that resulted in the deaths of more than 1000 passengers. There are the usual romantic subplots, villains, and heroes, and Scott is properly noble as the veteran captain making his last voyage before retirement. Otherwise you've seen this many times before. **165m/C VHS, DVD.** George C. Scott, Peter Gallagher, Catherine Zeta-Jones, Eva Marie Saint, Tim Curry, Roger Rees, Harley Jane Kozak, Marilu Henner, Felicity Waterman, Scott Hylands, Kevin McNulty, Malcolm Stewart; **D:** Robert Lieberman; **W:** Ross LaManna, Joyce Eliason; **C:** David Hennings; **M:** Lennie Niehaus.

Titanic 🐾🐾🐾 **1997 (PG-13)** Skipper Cameron's mega-budget three-hour tour had its own brushes with disaster with a mammoth budget and delays. A love story that happens to have the sinking of the historic ship as a backdrop, real and fictional characters are blended for a detailed re-enactment of the luxury liner's only voyage. The two lovebirds, Jack Dawson (DiCaprio) and debutante Rose Bukater (Winslet) are from different ends of the economic and social ladder. DiCaprio and Winslet are dynamic and make the running time less of a chore. The special effects are impressive, with a life-size version of the ship built just for the film. Cameron's prowess as a storyteller keeps the outcome of the ship suspenseful and tense even though the ending is no secret. **197m/C VHS, DVD.** Kate Winslet, Leonardo DiCaprio, Billy Zane, Kathy Bates, Frances Fisher, Gloria Stuart, Jonathan Hyde, Danny Nucci, David Warner, Bill Paxton, Bernard Hill, Victor Garber, Suzy Amis, Bernard Fox; **D:** James Cameron; **W:** James Cameron; **C:** Russell Carpenter; **M:** James Horner. Oscars '97: Art Dir./Set Dec., Cinematog.,

Left box middle column:

The Tin Drum 🐾🐾🐾🐾 *Die Blechtrommel* **1979 (R)** German child in the 1920s wills himself to stop growing in response to the increasing Nazi presence in Germany. He communicates his anger and fear by pounding on a tin drum. Memorable scenes, excellent cast. In German with English subtitles. Adapted from the novel by Gunter Grass. **141m/C VHS, DVD. GE** David Bennent, Mario Adorf, Angela Winkler, Daniel Olbrychski, Katharina Thalbach, Heinz Bennent, Andrea Ferreol, Charles Aznavour; **D:** Volker Schlondorff; **W:** Jean-Claude Carriere, Volker Schlondorff; **C:** Igor Luther; **M:** Maurice Jarre. Oscars '79: Foreign Film; Cannes '79: Film; L.A. Film Critics '80: Foreign Film.

Title Shot ♂ 1981 (R) A crafty manager convinces a millionaire to bet heavily on the guaranteed loss of his heavyweight contender in an upcoming fight. He doesn't realize the boxer is too stupid to throw the fight. **88m/C VHS** Tony Curtis, Richard Gabourie, Susan Hogan, Robert Delbert; **D:** Les Rose.

Tito and Me ♂♂♂ 1992 Ten-year-old Zoran lives in 1954 Belgrade and is fascinated by Yugoslavian leader Marshall Tito. Crowded into a flat with his extended family, Zoran learns about volatility firsthand. Then there's romance—he has a crush on a classmate who breaks up with him when she is chosen as one of Tito's Young Pioneers, which means a two-week trip to the country. Political indoctrination means nothing but love—ahh. Debut role for the young Vojnov, who carries the weight of the movie with perfect aplomb. In Serbo-Croatian with English subtitles. **104m/C VHS, DVD, YU** Dimitrie Vojnov, Lazar Ristovski, Anica Dobra, Miki Manojlovic, Olivera Markovic; **D:** Goran Markovic; **W:** Goran Markovic; **C:** Radoslav Vladic; **M:** Zoran Simjanovic.

Titus ♂♂♂ 1999 (R) Flashy version of a lesser-known early Shakespearean play, the gory "Titus Andronicus." Theatrical director Taymor makes her film debut with verve and a wild mixture of styles. Victorius Roman general Titus (Hopkins) has just defeated the Goths and has captured Tamora (Lange), the Goth Queen and her sons, one of whom Titus promptly sacrifices to appease the gods. Decadent Emperor Saturninus (Cumming) claims Tamora for his queen; her daughter Lavinia (Fraser) suffers a fate worse than death; Tamora wants revenge. Titus wants revenge; there's a villainous Moor, Aaron (Lennix); and a lot of campy fantasy and blood. **162m/C VHS, DVD** Anthony Hopkins, Jessica Lange, Alan Cumming, Harry J. Lennix, Colm Feore, Laura Fraser, James Frain, Angus MacFadyen, Jonathan Rhys Meyers, Geraldine McEwan, Matthew Rhys, Bruno Bilotta; **D:** Julie Taymor; **W:** Julie Taymor; **C:** Luciano Tovoli; **M:** Elliot Goldenthal.

TMNT (Teenage Mutant Ninja Turtles) ♂♂ 2007 (PG) Our hard-shelled heroes haven't hit the big screen since 1993; maybe the producers are hoping to entice a new generation with improved CGI and (basically) the same old story. Well, not quite, since bad guy Shredder isn't around and the turtle quartet spent more time squabbling among themselves than being a team. That is until evil cosmic forces align to destroy mankind, like they do. There's a few jokes and a few fights and not enough pizza. **86m/C DVD, HD DVD, US HK D:** Kevin Munroe; **W:** Kevin Munroe; **C:** Steve Jones; **M:** Klaus Badelt. **V:** Chris Evans, Sarah Michelle Gellar.

T.N.T. ♂♂ 1998 (R) Gruner's managed to extricate himself from a covert fighting force but now they're threatening his family unless he does what he's told. **87m/C VHS, DVD** Olivier Gruner, Eric Roberts, Randy Travis, Sam Jones, Rebecca Staab; **D:** Robert Radler; **C:** Bryan Duggan; **M:** Stephen Edwards. **VIDEO**

TNT Jackson WOOF! 1975 (R) A kung fu mama searches for her brother while everyone in Hong Kong tries to kick her out of town. **73m/C VHS, DVD** Stan Shaw, Pat Anderson, Ken Metcalfe, Jeannie Bell; **D:** Cirio H. Santiago; **W:** Dick Miller; **C:** Felipe Sacdalan.

To All a Goodnight 1980 (R) Five young girls and their boyfriends are planning an exciting Christmas holiday until a mad Santa Claus puts a damper on things. Total gorefest, with few, if any, redeeming virtues. **90m/C VHS** Jennifer Runyon,

Costume Des., Director (Cameron), Film Editing, Picture, Song ("My Heart Will Go On"), Sound, Sound FX Editing, Visual FX, Orig. Score; Director (Cameron); Golden Globes '98; Director (Cameron), Film-Drama, Song ("My Heart Will Go On"), Score; MTV Movie Awards '98; Male Perf. (DiCaprio); Screen Actors Guild '97; Support. Actress (Stuart); Broadcast Film Critics '97; Director (Cameron).

To All My Friends on Shore ♂♂♂ 1971 Drama about a father dealing with his young son's sickle cell anemia. Fine performances, realistic script make this an excellent outing. **74m/C VHS, DVD** Bill Cosby, Gloria Foster, Dennis Hines; **D:** Gilbert Cates. **TV**

To Be or Not to Be ♂♂♂½ 1942 Sophisticated black comedy set in wartime Poland. Lombard and Benny are Maria and Josef Tura, the Barrymores of the Polish stage, who use the Warsaw Resistance against the invading Nazis. The opening sequence is regarded as a cinema classic. One of Benny's finest film performances, the movie marks Lombard's final screen appearance—she was killed in a plane crash druing a war bond drive shortly after completing the film. Classic Lubitsch. Remade in 1983 with Mel Brooks and Anne Bancroft. **102m/B VHS, DVD** Carole Lombard, Jack Benny, Robert Stack, Sig Ruman, Lionel Atwill, Felix Bressart, Stanley Ridges, George Lynn, Halliwell Hobbes, Miles Mander, Henry Victor, Leslie Denison, Frank Reicher, Charles Dunning, Jose Perez, Tim Ryan; **D:** Ernst Lubitsch; **W:** Ernst Lubitsch, Edwin Justus Mayer, Melchior Lengyel; **C:** Rudolph Mate; **M:** Werner R. Heymann, Miklos Rozsa. Nat. Film Reg. '96.

To Be the Best ♂♂ 1993 (R) Eric, a member of the U.S. Kickboxing Team, lets his love for the beautiful Cheryl and his hot temper get the best of him. When a ruthless gambler threatens to kill Cheryl if Eric doesn't throw his big match, he joins with his family, fellow teammates, and most feared opponent, to set things right. **99m/C VHS, DVD** Mike Worth, Martin Kove, Phillip Troy, Brittney Powell, Alex Cord Steven Leigh; **D:** Joseph Merhi; **M:** Michael January.

To Be or Not to Be ♂♂♂½ 1983 (PG) In this remake of the 1942 film, Bancroft and Brocks are actors in Poland during WWII. They accidently become involved with the Polish Resistance and work to thwart the Nazis. Lots of laughs, although at times there's a little too much slapstick. **108m/C VHS, DVD** Mel Brooks, Anne Bancroft, Charles Durning, Jose Ferrer, Tim Matheson, Christopher Lloyd; **D:** Alan Johnson; **W:** Ronny Graham.

To All a Goodnight — continued...

To Catch a King ♂♂ 1984 Garr is a singer working in Wagner's nightclub in 1940s' Lisbon. The pair becomes involved in trying to foil the Nazi plot to kidnap the vacationing Duke and Duchess of Windsor. Average cable fare. **120m/C VHS, DVD** Robert Wagner, Teri Garr, Horst Janson, Barbara Parkins, John Standing; **D:** Clive Donner; **M:** Nick Bicat. **CABLE, TV**

To Catch a Killer ♂♂ 1992 A chilling performance by Dennehy highlights this true-crime tale of a detective's relentless pursuit of serial killer John Wayne Gacy, who preyed on young men and hid the bodies in his home. Made for television. **95m/C VHS, DVD** Brian Dennehy, Michael Riley, Margot Kidder, Meg Foster, Ja-Till, **W:** Judson Kinberg; **C:** Rene Ohashi; **M:** Paul Zaza. **TV**

To Catch a Thief ♂♂♂ 1955 On the French Riviera, a reformed jewel thief falls for a wealthy American woman, who suspects he's up to his old tricks when a rash of jewel thefts occur. Oscar-winning photography by Robert Burks, a notable change of pace for Hitchcock, this charming comedy-thriller proved to be as popular as his other efforts. Based on the novel by David Dodge. Kelly met future husband Prince Rainier during a photo shoot while she was attending the Cannes Film Festival. **103m/C VHS, DVD** Cary Grant, Grace Kelly, Jessie Royce Landis, John Williams, Charles Vanel, Brigitte Auber; **D:** Alfred Hitchcock; **W:** John Michael Hayes; **C:** Robert Burks. Oscars '55; Color Cinematog.

To Catch a Yeti ♂½ 1995 (PG) Big game hunter Meat Loaf is all set for a trip to the Himalayas when the Yeti winds up being spotted in the canyons of Manhattan (and it turns out to be very tiny).

Forrest Swanson, Linda Gentle, William Lover, **D:** Paul Alexander) Hess.

To Die For ♂♂♂ 1995 (R) Beauteous, manipulative Suzanne Stone (Kidman) wants to be somebody—preferably a big TV personality—and nothing will stop her. She recruits a scruffy threesome to help her ice sweet-but-dim hubby. Larry (Dillon) even if it does means seducing aimless teenager Jimmy (Phoenix). Black comedy, loosely based on the "Pamela Smart" murder case and adapted from the media-obsessed culture with a wicked grin. Van Sant retains his fresh and hip storytelling in his first film for a major studio. Backed by Henry's zesty script, all the actors shine—with standout performances from Kidman as the monstrous Suzanne and Phoenix (River's younger brother) as the lost/horny Jimmy. Shot entirely in Canada. **103m/C VHS, DVD** Nicole Kidman, Matt Dillon, Joaquin Rafael (Leaf) Phoenix, Casey Affleck, Alison Folland, Illeana Douglas, Dan Hedaya, Wayne Knight, Kurtwood Smith, Holland Taylor, Maria Tucci, Susan Traylor; **Cameos:** George Segal, Buck Henry; **D:** Gus Van Sant; **W:** Buck Henry, Joyce Maynard; **C:** Eric Alan Edwards; **M:** Danny Elfman. Golden Globes '96; Actress—Mus.Comedy (Kidman); Broadcast Flim Critics '95; Actress

To Die For ♂♂½ 1989 (R) A vampire stalks, woos, and snacks on a young real estate woman. **99m/C VHS, DVD** Brendan Hughes, Scott Jacoby, Duane Jones, Steve Bond, Sydney Walsh, Amanda Wyss, Ava Fabian; **D:** Deran Sarafian; **W:** Leslie King; **C:** Jacques Haitkin; **M:** Cliff Eidelman.

To Die For 2: Son of Darkness ♂½ Son of Darkness: To Die For 2 1991 (R) This far outclasses part one in terms of acting and production values, but the plot still isn't back from the grave. Strange, because all the vampires are, despite their fiery deaths last time they flock around the adoptive mother of a baby secretly sired by a bloodsucker. **95m/C VHS, DVD** Rosalind Allen, Steve Bond, Scott Jacoby, Michael Praed, Jay Underwood, Amanda Wyss, Remy O'Neill, Vince Edwards; **D:** David F. Price.

To Die Standing ♂½ 1991 (R) Two mavericks team up to do what the D.E.A. and cops simply cannot...capture a dangerous international drug lord. High-action. **87m/C VHS** Cliff DeYoung, Robert Beltran, Jamie Rose, Gerald Anthony, Orlando Sacha, Michael Ford; **D:** Louis Morneau; **W:** Ross Bell, Daryl Haney.

To Each His Own ♂♂♂ 1946 Top-notch melodrama finds middle-aged businesswoman Josephine Norris (de Havilland) recalling her fast as she carries on through London's blitz. As a young woman, Josephine fell in love with a dashing WWI pilot (Lund), became pregnant, and had her lover killed in action. To avoid scandal, she gives the baby up for adoption, although she stays in touch with his

To Dance with the White Dog ♂♂♂ 1993 (PG) Robert Samuel Peek (Cronyn) is a pecan-tree grower from rural Georgia who has been married to Cora (Tandy) for 57 years. Then she dies and other fussing daughters (Baranski and Wright) wonder how their father will survive. But Sam's increasing loneliness is checked when he befriends a stray white dog that it seems no one else can see. Based on the novel by Terry Kay. **98m/C VHS, DVD** Hume Cronyn, Jessica Tandy, Christine Baranski, Amy Wright, Esther Rolle, Harley Cross, Frank Whaley, Terry Beaver, Dan Albright, David Dwyer; **D:** Glenn Jordan; **M:** Susan Cooper; **C:** Neal Roach. **TV**

To Cross the Rubicon ♂♂ 1991 Romantic comedy finds Kendall (Royce) getting dumped by David (Southern), her boyfriend of eight years, who then reconciles with former flame, Claire (DeVon). Meanwhile, Kendall involves herself with James (Burke), a young musician, and becomes new best friends with—you guessed it—Claire. But will David and Kendall's previous relationship cause friction? **120m/C VHS, DVD** Patricia Royce, J.D. Souther, Lorraine Devon, Billy Burke; **D:** Barry Caillier; **W:** Patricia Royce, Lorraine Devon; **C:** Christopher Tufty; **M:** Paul Speer, David Lanz.

88m/C VHS, Chantellese Kent, Jim Gordon, Richard Howland, Meat Loaf Aday; **D:** Bob Keen; **W:** Paul Adam; **C:** David Perrault.

To End All Wars ♂♂ 2001 (R) Based on Ernest Gordon's autobiographical 1962 novel "Through the Valley of the Kwai," bares the horrors that a group of WWII Allied soldiers suffered at the hands POWs during the erecting of the so-called "Railway of Death" in the nasty Burmese jungle. Related to events depicted in "The Bridge of the River Kwai" but not nearly so well imitated. **117m/C VHS, DVD** Robert Carlyle, Kiefer Sutherland, Ciaran McMenamin, Mark Strong, Masayuki Yui, James Cosmo, John Gregg, Pip Torrens, Sakae Kimura, Shu Nakajima, Yugo Saso, Greg Ellis, Adam Sinclair, Winton Nicholson, James McCarthy, Brendan Cowell, Duff Armour, Sergio Jones, Christopher White, Jeremy Pippin, Robert Jobe; **Cameos:** Ernest Gorcon, Takashi Nagase; **C:** Greg Gardiner; **M:** John Cameron, Mare Brennan. **VIDEO**

To Forget Venice ♂♂ 1979 Portrays the sensitive relationships among four homosexuals, and their shared fears of growing older. Dubbed in English. **90m/C VHS** IT Erland Josephson, Mariangela Melato, David Pontremoli, Eleanora Giorgi; **D:** Franco Brusati.

To Gillian on Her 37th Birthday ♂♂ 1996 (PG-13) Overly sentimental weeper explores the effects of a mother's death on the ones she's left behind. Gillian's been dead for two years but widower David Lewis (Gallagher) hasn't been able to let her spirit go and daughter Rachel (Danes) is having trouble growing up with a father who spends more time on the beach with his dead wife's ghost than with her. Enter nosy sister-in-law Esther (Baker) and annoying husband (Altman) who try to set him up on the anniversary of Gillian's death and you've got a mental family breakdown coming. Pfeiffer appears as Gillian in this script by husband Kelley, based on the play by Michael Brady. **92m/C VHS, DVD** Peter Gallagher, Claire Danes, Kathy Baker, Wendy Crewson, Bruce Altman, Michelle Pfeiffer, Freddie Prinze Jr., Laurie Fortier, Seth Green, Kate Olsen, Cynthia Geary, Rhea Perlman, Lori Loughlin; **D:** Jeff Franklin; **W:** Jeff Franklin.

To Grandmother's House We Go ♂♂½ 1994 The Olsen twins want to give mom a restful Christmas vacation so they decide to visit Grandma (on their own) and wind up in the hands of a pair of bumbling kidnappers. Made for TV movie. **89m/C VHS, DVD** Ashley (Fuller) Olsen, Kate Olsen, J. Eddie Peck, Stuart Margolin, Cynthia Geary, Rhea Perlman; **D:** Jeff Franklin; **W:** Jeff Franklin; **C:** Bob Saget. **TV**

To Have & Have Not ♂♂♂½ 1944 Martinique charter boat operator gets mixed up with beautiful woman and French resistance fighters during WWII. Top-notch production in every respect. Classic dialogue and fiery romantic bouts between Bogart and Bacall. Bacall's first film. Based on a story by Ernest Hemingway. Remade in 1950 as "The Breaking Point" and in 1958 as "The Gun Runners." **100m/B VHS, DVD** Humphrey Bogart, Lauren Bacall, Walter Brennan, Hoagy Carmichael, Marcel Dalio, Dolores Moran, Sheldon Leonard, Dan Seymour; **D:** Howard Hawks; **W:** Jules Furthman, William Faulkner.

To Heal a Nation ♂♂ 1988 The story of veteran Jan Scruggs, who spearheaded the movement to build the Vietnam Veterans memorial. The then little-known Ross Perot provided major financial support for Scruggs' dream. **100m/C VHS, DVD** Eric Roberts, Conrad Bachmann, Glynnis O'Connor, Marshall Colt, Scott Paulin, Lee Purcell, Laurence Luckinbill, Linden Chiles, Brock Peters; **D:** Michael Pressman; **W:** Lionel Chetwynd. **TV**

To Hell and Back ♂♂½ 1955 Adaptation of Audie Murphy's autobiography. Murphy plays himself from his unpromising as the son of Texas sharecroppers to his Army career in WWII, where he was the most-decorated American soldier. Murphy won more than 20 medals, including the Congressional Medal of Honor. Features realistic battle sequences punctuated with grand heroics. **106m/C VHS, DVD.** Audie Murphy, Marshall Thompson, Jack Kelly, Charles Drake, Gregg (Hunter) Palmer, Paul Picerni, David Janssen, Bruce Cowling, Paul Langton, Art Aragon, Felix Noriego, Denver Pyle, Brett Halsey, Susan Kohner, Anabel Shaw, Mary Field, Gordon Gebert, Rand Brooks, Richard Castle, Gen. Walter Bedell Smith; **D:** Jesse Hibbs; **W:** Gil Doud; **M:** Maury Gertsman;

To Joy ♪♪♪ *Till Gladje* 1950 The rocky marriage of a violinist and his wife illuminate the problems of the young in Swedish society. Early Bergman. In Swedish with English subtitles or dubbed. **90m/B VHS.** *SW* Maj-Britt Nilsson, Birger Malmsten, Margit Carlquist, Stig Olin, John Ekman, Victor Sjostrom; **D:** Ingmar Bergman; **W:** Ingmar Bergman; **C:** Gunnar Fischer.

To Kill a Clown ♪♪ 1972 (R) Painter and his wife working to save their marriage are trapped on an isolated island and terrorized by a crazed Vietnam veteran. This helps pull them together. Some holes in the plot, but generally effective. **82m/C VHS.** Alan Alda, Blythe Danner, Heath Lamberts; **D:** George Bloomfield.

To Kill a Mockingbird ♪♪♪♪ 1962 Faithful adaptation of powerful Harper Lee novel, with an evocative portrayal of childhood innocence and a denunciation of bigotry. Peck's performance as southern lawyer Atticus Finch defending black Tom Robinson (Peters), who's accused of raping a white woman, is flawless. Duvall debuted as the dim-witted Boo Radley. Lee based her characterization of "Dill," the Finch children's "goin' on seven" friend, on Truman Capote, her own childhood friend. **129m/B VHS, DVD.** Gregory Peck, Brock Peters, Phillip Alford, Mary Badham, Robert Duvall, Rosemary Murphy, William Windom, Alice Ghostley, John Megna, Frank Overton, Paul Fix, Collin Wilcox-Paxton; **D:** Robert Mulligan; **W:** Horton Foote; **C:** Russell Harlan; **M:** Elmer Bernstein; **Nar:** Kim Stanley. Oscars '62: Actor (Peck), Adapt. Screenplay, Art Dir./Set Dec.; AFI '98: Top 100; Golden Globes '63: Actor—Drama (Peck), Score, Natl. Film Reg. '95.

To Kill a Priest ♪♪ 1989 (R) Based on the true story of Father Jerzy Popieluszko, a young priest in 1984 Poland who defies his church and speaks out publicly on Solidarity. He is killed by the government as a result. Harris is good as the menacing police official. **110m/C VHS.** Christopher Lambert, Ed Harris, David Suchet, Tim Roth, Joanne Whalley, Pete Postlethwaite, Cherie Lunghi, Joss Ackland; **D:** Agnieszka Holland; **W:** Agnieszka Holland; **C:** Adam Holender; **M:** Georges Delerue.

To Live ♪♪♪♪ *Huozhe* 1994 Superb drama follows the lives of one family—weak but adaptable Fugui (You), his strong-willed wife Jiazhen (Li), and their young daughter and son—from prerevolutionary China in the 1940s through the '60s Cultural Revolution. Fugui loses the family fortune in the gambling houses, actually a blessing when the Communists come to power, and the family must struggle to survive financial and increasingly difficult political changes, where fate can change on a whim. Subtle saga about ordinary human lives reacting to terrifying conditions boasts extraordinary performances and evocative imagery. Adapted from the novel "Lifetimes" by Yu Hua. Chinese with subtitles. **130m/C VHS, DVD.** *CH* Ge You, Gong Li, Niu Ben, Guo Tao, Jiang Wu; **D:** Yimou Zhang; **W:** Lu Wei, Yu Hua; **C:** Lu Yue; Jiping Zhao. British Acad. '94: Foreign Film; Cannes '94: Actor (You), Grand Jury Prize.

To Live and Die in Hong Kong ♪½ 1989 Two sailors arrive in Hong Kong for a little R & R, until they are mistaken for spies by both the Hong Kong police and the Chinese mob. Action-packed tale. **98m/C VHS.** Rowena Cortes, Lawrence Jan, Mike Kelly, Laurens C. Postma; **D:** Lau Shing Hon.

To Live & Die in L.A. ♪♪ 1985 (R) Fast-paced, morally ambivalent tale of cops and counterfeiters in L.A. After his partner is killed shortly before his retirement, a secret service agent sets out to track down his ruthless killer. Lots of violence; some nudity. Notable both for a riveting car chase and its dearth of sympathetic characters. **114m/C VHS, DVD, UMD.** William L. Petersen, Willem Dafoe, John Pankow, Dean Stockwell, Debra Feuer, John Turturro, Darlanne Fluegel, Robert Downey; **D:** William Friedkin; **W:** William Friedkin.

To Love Again ♪½ 1980 A middle-aged love story about a reclusive college professor and the campus handyman. **96m/C VHS.** Lynn Redgrave, Brian Dennehy, Conchata Ferrell; **D:** Joseph Hardy.

To Paris with Love ♪♪½ 1955 A British man and his son fall in love with a shop girl and her boss while on vacation in Paris. Charming and humorous, with a witty performance from Guinness. **75m/C VHS.** Alec Guinness, Odile Versois, Vernon Gray; **D:** Robert Hamer; **M:** Edwin Astley.

To Play or to Die ♪♪ 1991 The introverted Kees attends an all-boy school where powerful bullies and sadomasochistic games are the rule. Kees is fascinated by the handsome Charel, the bullies leader. He invites Charel to his home, intending to turn the tables on his tormentor, but nothing goes as planned. Intense and controversial look at gay teens. Directorial debut of Krom. In Dutch with English subtitles. **50m/C VHS, DVD.** *NL* Geert Hunaerts, Tjebbo Gerritsma; **D:** Frank Krom; **W:** Anne Van De Putte, Frank Krom; **C:** Nils Post; **M:** Kim Hayworth, Ferdinand Bakker.

To Play the King ♪♪♪ 1993 Sequel to "The House of Cards" finds Francis Urquhart (Richardson), having murdered his way to the Prime Ministery, now bored with his political situation. But things may be changing—the Queen has been succeeded by her liberal son (Kitchen) and Francis, goaded by his equally vicious wife (Fletcher), plots treachery to bring down the monarchy. Followed by "The Final Cut", adapted from the novel by Michael Dobbs. **212m/C VHS, DVD.** *GB* Ian Richardson, Michael Kitchen, Diane Fletcher, Kitty Aldridge, Bernice Stegers, Colin Jeavons, Rowena King, Erika Hoffman, Nicholas Farrell; **D:** Paul Seed; **W:** Andrew Davies.

To Please a Lady ♪♪½ 1950 *Red Hot Wheels* Romantic comedy-drama about race car driver Gable and reporter Stanwyck. Although leads do their best with the script, they're unable to generate any sparks. However, race track scenes are excellent. Filmed at the Indianapolis Speedway, the spectacular racing footage makes up for overall average film. **91m/B VHS.** Clark Gable, Barbara Stanwyck, Adolphe Menjou, Will Geer, Roland Winters; **D:** Clarence Brown; **W:** Barre Lyndon, Marge Decker.

To Protect and Serve ♪♪ 1992 (R) When crooked cops start getting killed, two young cops are assigned to investigate. Suspicion points to a rookie (Howell), who just may have decided to clean things up his own way. **93m/C VHS.** C. Thomas Howell, Lezlie (Dean) Deane, Richard Romanus, Joe Cortese; **D:** Eric Weston.

To Race the Wind ♪♪ 1980 Blind man wants to be treated like a normal person as he struggles through Harvard Law School. Based upon Harold Krents's autobiography "Butterflies Are Free." **97m/C VHS.** Steve Guttenberg, Lisa Eilbacher, Randy Quaid, Barbara Barrie; **D:** Walter Grauman. TV

To See Paris and Die ♪♪ *Uvidet Parizh i Umeret* 1993 Elena Orekhova (Vasilyeva) is a Russian stage mother who will do absolutely anything to ensure pianist son Yuri gets chosen for a prestigious competition in Paris—even though she knows secrets from her past could place a blight on his career. Russian with subtitles. **110m/C VHS.** *RU* Tatyana Vasilyeva, Dmitry Malikov, Stanislav Lyubshin, Vladimir Steklov, Nina Usatova; **D:** Alexander Proshkin; **W:** Georgi Brenev; **C:** Boris Brozhovsky.

To Sir, with Love ♪♪♪ 1967 Teacher in London's tough East End tosses books in the wastebasket and proceeds to teach his class about life. Skillful and warm performance by Poitier as idealistic teacher; supporting cast also performs nicely. Based on the novel by E.R. Braithwaite. LuLu's title song was a big hit in 1967-68. **105m/C VHS, DVD.** *GB* Sidney Poitier, Lulu, Judy Geeson, Christian Roberts, Suzy Kendall, Faith Brook; **D:** James Clavell; **W:** James Clavell; **C:** Paul Beeson; **M:** Ron Grainer.

To Sleep with a Vampire ♪♪ 1992 (R) A Los Angeles bloodsucker is tired of his violent existence and craves the one thing he can't have—daylight. As he stalks his latest victim, a stripper, he decides to take her home and have her tell him about living in daytime. When she realizes what's going on, the intended victim decides to fight for her life. Action and eroticism raises this one above the norm. Remake of "Dance of the Damned." **90m/C VHS, DVD.** Scott Valentine, Charlie Spradling, Richard Zobel, Ingrid Vold, Stephanie Hardy; **D:** Adam Friedman; **W:** Patricia Harrington.

To Sleep with Anger ♪♪♪½ 1990 (PG) At first a comic, introspective look at a black middle-class family going about their business in the heart of Los Angeles. Sly charmer Glover shows up and enthralls the entire family with his slightly sinister storytelling and a gnawing doom gradually permeates the household. Insightful look into the conflicting values of Black America. Glover's best performance. **105m/C VHS.** Danny Glover, Mary Alice, Paul Butler, Sheryl Lee Ralph; **D:** Charles Burnett; **W:** Charles Burnett; **C:** Walt Lloyd. Ind. Spirit '91: Actor (Glover), Director (Burnett), Screenplay, Support. Actress (Ralph); Natl. Soc. Film Critics '90: Screenplay; Sundance '90: Special Jury Prize.

To the Death ♪♪½ 1993 (R) A kickboxer wants to retire from the boxing tournaments but the corrupt promoters refuse to let him go unless he manages to kill his rivals in the ring. **90m/C VHS.** John Barrett, Michael Quissi; **D:** Darrell Roodt.

To the Devil, a Daughter ♪♪ *Child of Satan* 1976 (R) A nun is put under a spell by a priest who has been possessed by Satan. She is to bear his child. A writer on the occult intervenes. Based on the novel by Dennis Wheatley. One of Kinski's early films. **93m/C VHS, DVD.** Richard Widmark, Christopher Lee, Nastassia Kinski, Honor Blackman, Denholm Elliott, Michael Goodliffe; **D:** Peter Sykes; **W:** Christopher Wicking; **C:** David Watkin.

To the Last Man ♪ 1933 An early Scott sagebrush epic, about two feuding families. Temple is seen in a small role. Based on Zane Grey's novel of the same name. **70m/B VHS, DVD.** Randolph Scott, Esther Ralston, Jack La Rue, Noah Beery Sr., Buster Crabbe, Gail Patrick, Barton MacLane, Fuzzy Knight, John Carradine, Jay Ward, Shirley Temple; **D:** Henry Hathaway.

To the Lighthouse ♪♪ 1983 The Ramsay family's annual proper British holiday at their Cornwall home turns into a summer of disillusionment in this adaptation of the Virginia Woolf novel. Made for British TV. **115m/C VHS, DVD.** Rosemary Harris, Michael Gough, Suzanne Bertish, Lynsey Baxter, T.P. McKenna, Kenneth Branagh; **D:** Colin Gregg. TV

To the Limit ♪ 1995 (R) Actioner finds the pulchritudinous Colette (Smith) revealing to mobster Frank (Travolta) that she's a CIA agent (and if you believe that I have a bridge in Brooklyn to sell you) and that they are the targets of a rogue agent (Richmond). No, Smith can't act but since she takes lots of showers and is supported by spies on trash value alone. **96m/C VHS, DVD.** Anna Nicole Smith, Joey Travolta, Michael Nouri, Branscombe Richmond, John Aprea, Kathy Shower, Rebecca Ferratti, David Proval; **D:** Raymond Martino; **W:** Raymond Martino, Joey Travolta; **C:** Henryk Cymerman; **M:** Jim Halfpenny.

To the Shores of Hell ♪♪ 1965 Leaving his sweetheart behind, Major Greg Donahue attacks Da Nang and plots to rescue his brother from the Viet Cong. **82m/C VHS.** Marshall Thompson, Richard Arden, Richard Jordahl, Kiva Lawrence; **D:** Will Zens; **W:** Will Zens; **C:** Leif Rise; **M:** William Schaefer.

To the Shores of Tripoli ♪♪½ 1942 Wartime propaganda in the guise of drama, in which a smarmy playboy is transformed into a Marine in boot camp. **82m/C VHS, DVD.** John Payne, Maureen O'Hara, Randolph Scott, Nancy Kelly, Harry (Henry) Morgan, Maxie "Slapsie" Rosenbloom, William Tracy, Minor Watson, Alan Hale Jr., Hugh Beaumont, Hillary Brooke; **D:** H. Bruce Humberstone.

To Walk with Lions ♪♪½ 1999 (PG) Continues the story of lion expert George Adamson, told previously in "Born Free" and "Living Free." Tony Fitzjohn (Michie) takes what he thinks will be a temporary job with Adamson (Harris) and his brother Terence (Bannen) in Kenya in the 1980s. The brothers are running a private wildlife preserve that rehabilitates zoo lions for life in the wild. Tony is naturally wary of his new employment and his curmudgeonly new employers but comes to value them all, even falling in love with anthropologist Lucy (Fox) who's working with the local tribes. Has some disturbing violence (both animal and human). **108m/C VHS, DVD.** *CA GB* Richard Harris, Ian Bannen, Kerry Fox, John Michie, Hugh Quarshie, Honor Blackman, Geraldine Chaplin; **D:** Carl Schultz; **W:** Keith Ross Leckie; **C:** Jean Lepine; **M:** Alan Reeves.

To Wong Foo, Thanks for Everything, Julie Newmar ♪♪½ 1995 (PG-13) Hot on the high heels of "The Adventures of Priscilla, Queen of the Desert," comes the sanitized for your protection Yankee version. And its all about hanging on to your dreams and how we're all the same inside, with politically correct gay drag queens doing the sermonizing. Yes, this is the feel-good drag road movie for the 90s. Den mother Vida (Swayze), tough beauty queen Noxeema (Snipes), and hot-blooded Chi Chi (Leguizamo doing his best Rosie Perez) head to Hollywood in a 1967 Cadillac convertible that inconveniently breaks down in a tiny Nebraska town. The "girls" work their magic, and presumably the people of this uncultured, anachronistic backwater will never be the same. One-dimensional characters, flat direction, and inconsistent script undercut exceptional efforts by Swayze and Leguizamo. **108m/C VHS, DVD.** Wesley Snipes, Patrick Swayze, John Leguizamo, Stockard Channing, Blythe Danner, Melinda Dillon, Arliss Howard, Jason London, Christopher Penn, RuPaul Charles; **Cameos:** Julie Newmar, Robin Williams; **D:** Beeban Kidron; **W:** Douglas Carter Beane; **M:** Rachel Portman.

The Toast of New Orleans ♪♪♪ 1950 A poor fisherman rises to stardom as an opera singer. Likable, though fluffy production features a plethora of musical numbers. ♫Be My Love; Tina Lina; I'll Never Love You; The Toast of New Orleans; Song of the Bayou; Boom Biddy Boom Boom. **97m/C VHS.** Kathryn Grayson, Mario Lanza, David Niven, Rita Moreno, J. Carrol Naish; **D:** Norman Taurog.

Toast of New York ♪♪♪ 1937 Arnold plays Jim Fisk, a New England peddler who rises to become one of the first Wall Street giants of industry. Atypical Grant performance. **109m/B VHS.** Edward Arnold, Cary Grant, Frances Farmer, Jack Oakie, Donald Meek, Billy Gilbert; **D:** Rowland V. Lee.

Tobor the Great ♪♪½ 1954 Sentimental and poorly executed, this film tells the tale of a boy, his grandfather, and Tobor the robot. Villainous communists attempt to make evil use of Tobor, only to be thwarted in the end. **77m/B VHS.** Charles Drake, Billy Chapin, Karin (Karen, Katharine) Booth, Taylor Holmes, Joan Gerber, Steven Geray, Helen Winston; **D:** Lee Sholem.

Tobruk ♪♪ 1966 American GI's endeavor to knock out the guns of Tobruk, to clear the way for a bombing attack on German fuel supply depots of North Africa in this WWII actioner. **110m/C VHS.** Rock Hudson, George Peppard, Guy Stockwell, Nigel Green; **D:** Arthur Hiller.

Toby McTeague 1987 (PG) A story about an Alaskan family that breeds Siberian Huskies. When his father is injured, the youngest son tries to replace him in the regional dog-sled race. 94m/C VHS, DVD. Winston Rekert, Warwick Bisson, Timothy Webber; *D:* Jean-Claude Lord; *W:* Djordje Milicevic, Jamie Brown.

Toby Tyler 1959 (G) A boy runs off to the circus, and teams up with a chimpanzee. A timeless and enjoyable Disney film that still appeals to youngsters. Good family-fare. 93m/C VHS, DVD. Kevin Corcoran, Henry Calvin, Gene Sheldon, Bob Sweeney; *D:* Charles T. Barton.

Today I Hang 1942 A man is framed for murder and sentenced to hang. His buddies on the outside do their best to prove his innocence. Meanwhile, in prison, the accused encounters any number of interesting characters. 67m/B VHS. Walter Woolf King, Mona Barrie, William Farnum, Harry Woods, James Craven; *D:* Oliver Drake.

Today We Kill, Tomorrow We Die 1971 (PG) A rancher is unjustly sent to prison; when his sentence is over he hires a gang to relentlessly track down the culprit who framed him. 95m/C VHS, DVD. Montgomery Ford, Bud Spencer, William Berger, Tatsuya Nakadai, Wayde Preston; *D:* Tonino Cervi.

Today We Live 1933 Triangle love story set in WWI. Crawford is a hedonistic Brit having a fling with her naval brother's (Tone) friend (Young). When American flyer Cooper appears she sets her sights on him but soon he's off to combat in France where he's reported killed. Crawford returns to Young but, naturally, reports of Cooper's death have been greatly exaggerated and the two eventually reunite. Faulkner co-scripted from his story "Turn About" which had no female character and concerned the rivalry between naval officers and fly boys. 113m/B VHS. Gary Cooper, Joan Crawford, Franchot Tone, Robert Young, Roscoe Karns, Louise Closser Hale; *D:* Howard Hawks; *W:* Dwight Taylor, William Faulkner, Edith Fitzgerald.

The Todd Killings 1971 (R) *A Dangerous Friend. Skipper* 1971 (R) A psychotic young man commits a series of murders involving young women. Sleazy, forgettable picture wastes a talented cast. 93m/C VHS. Robert F. Lyons, Richard Thomas, Barbara Bel Geddes, Ed Asner, Sherry Miles, Gloria Grahame, Belinda J. Montgomery; *D:* Barry Shear; *W:* Joel Oliansky.

Todd McFarlane's Spawn 1997 McFarlane's comic book creation makes his cable TV animated debut. Hellspawn was once human CIA assassin Al Simmons, murdered in the line of duty, who sold his soul to see his wife one last time. When he comes back from the grave with superhuman powers it's again as a killer with attitude, who leaves a high body count. A PG-13 version clocks in at 90 minutes. 147m/C VHS, DVD, UMD. *D:* Eric Radomski; *W:* Alan B. McElroy, Gary Hardwick; *V:* Keith David, Richard Dysart, Ronny Cox. CABLE.

Toga Party 1977 (R) Fraternity house throws a wild toga party in this raunchy low-rent depiction of college life. 82m/C VHS, DVD. Luther Bud Whaney, Mary Mitchell; *D:* Robert T. Megginson; *W:* Straw Weisman; *C:* Lloyd Freidus.

Together? 1979 (R) Divorced woman and a male chauvinist test the limits of their sexual liberation as well as viewer patience. 91m/C VHS. *IT* Maximilian Schell, Jacqueline Bisset, Terence Stamp, Monica Guerritore; *D:* Armenia Balducci; *M:* Burt Bacharach.

Together *He Ni Zaiyiqi* 2002 (PG) Sentimental story about a musical prodigy, his dad, and the "new China." With many of the restrictions of the Cultural Revolution a thing of the past, Western classical music is once more taught and performed. Violin prodigy Liu Xiaochun (Tang, who does his own playing) is 13 and his father Li Cheng (Liu) is determined to make the most of the boy's talents though the family is poor. Cheng and Xiaochun head to Beijing for an important musical competition and the boy makes an impressive showing. So much so, that his talent teacher (Wang) is able to persuade a cranky but talent teacher (Wang) to mentor Xiaochun. While in the big city, the lad also becomes infatuated with beautiful new neighbor Lili (Chen), a model with a consumer-oriented lifestyle from whom he receives important lessons about sacrifice and friendship. Mandarin with subtitles. 116m/C VHS, DVD. *CH KN* Yun ang, Peiqi Liu, Zhiwen Wang, Hong Chen, Chen Kaige; *D:* Chen Kaige; *W:* Chen Kaige, Xiaolu Xue; *C:* Hyung-koo Kim; *M:* Lin Zhao.

The Toilers and the Wayfarers 1997 New Ulm, Minnesota is an ultraconservative German-American community where the teenaged Dieter (Kemp) is the object of affection for best friend Phillip (Woodhouse). Although Dieter thinks he might be gay, he rejects Phillip, who soon takes off for Minneapolis. This leaves Dieter open to the attentions of slightly older, free-spirited Udo (Schirg). Dieter's father strongly disapproves and the young man leaves to join Phillip in the big bad city, with Udo in tow. But since none of the boys have any money, they're soon working the streets to survive. English and German with subtitles. 85m/C VHS, DVD. Matt Klemp, Ralf Schirg, Andrew Woodhouse; *D:* Keith Froelich; *W:* Keith Froelich; *C:* Jim Tittle; *M:* Chan Poling.

Togetherness 1970 Two wealthy, good-for-nothing playboys chase after the same blonde, a Communist, in Greece. 99m/C VHS. George Hamilton, Peter Lawford, Olinka (Schobrova) Benova, John Banner, Jesse White; *D:* Arthur Marks.

Tokyo Cowboy 1994 Tokyo burger flipper No Ogawa (Ida) dreams of the wild west and becoming a cowboy, inspired by the letters of his childhood pen pal Kate (Hirt). So he decides to head for Kate's small Canadian hometown and realize his fantasies. Kate's meddling mom makes him welcome but Kate herself, only recently returned home, is hiding the fact that her friend Shelly (Mortil) is also her lover. Both have some unrealistic expectations to overcome in their quest for happiness. 94m/C VHS, DVD. Hiromoto Ida, Christianne Hirt, Larry Musser, Michael Ironside; *D:* Kathy Garneau; *W:* Caroline Adderson; *C:* Kenneth Hewlett; *M:* Art Wise.

Tokyo Decadence 1991 (NC-17) Ai is a high-paid prostitute working in Tokyo for an agency that specializes in sado-masochism. Film follows her various sexual escapades in humiliating detail as well as her drug-addled search for a client Ai thinks she's in love with. Since Ai remains a cipher, the film also remains unfocused except for its creepy and explicit sex scenes. Adaptation of director Murakami's novel "Topaz." In Japanese with English subtitles or dubbed. 92m/C VHS, DVD. *JP* Miho Nikaido, Tenme Kano, Yayoi Kusama, Sayoko Amano; *D:* Ryu Murakami; *W:* Ryu Murakami; *C:* Tadashi Aoki; *M:* Ryuichi Sakamoto.

Tokyo Drifter 1966 Surreal yakuza film follows an honorable gangster hunted by both his own bosses and a rival mob, who chase him across Japan. Lots of camera trickery. Japanese with subtitles. 83m/C VHS, DVD. *JP* Eiji Go, Chieko Matsubara, Tetsuya Watari, Tamio Kawaji, Hideaki Nitani, Ryuji Kita; *D:* Seijun Suzuki; *W:* Yasunori Kawauchi; *C:* Shigeyoshi Mine; *M:* So Kaburagi.

Tokyo-Ga 1985 Impelled by his love for the films of Yasujiro Ozu, Wenders traveled to Tokyo and fashioned a caring document of both the city and of Ozu's career, using images that recall and comment on Ozu's visual motifs. 88m/B VHS, DVD. *D:* Win Wenders.

Tokyo Joe 1949 A war hero/nightclub owner returns to Tokyo and becomes ensnared in blackmail and smuggling while searching for his missing wife and child. Slow-moving tale has never been considered one of Bogart's better movies. 88m/B VHS, DVD. Humphrey Bogart, Florence Marly, Alexander Knox, Sessue Hayakawa, Jerome Courtland, Lora Lee Michel; *D:* Stuart Heisler.

Toll of the Desert 1935 A law-man learns that his father is a ruthless, back-stabbing renegade. Now he must try and catch him. 58m/B VHS. Roger Williams, Ted Adams, Edward Cassidy, Tom London, John Elliott, Earl Dwire, Betty Mack, Fred Kohler Jr.; *D:* William Berke.

The Toll Gate 1920 Quick on the draw outlaw Black Deering (Hart) is betrayed by one of his own men but manages to escape the authorities. He heads into the wilderness and finds shelter with an abandoned young mother (Nilsson). But the law is on his trail. 73m/B VHS, DVD. William S. Hart, Anna Q. Nilsson, Jack (H.) Richardson, Joseph Singleton; *D:* Lambert Hillyer; *W:* Lambert Hillyer; *C:* Joseph August.

Toll'able David 1921 A simple tale of mountain folk, done in the tradition of Mark Twain stories. A family of hillbillies is embroiled in a feud with a clan of outlaws. When the community's mail is stolen by the troublesome ruffians, the family's youngest member, who harbors dreams of becoming a mail driver, comes to the rescue. Silent film. 99m/B VHS, DVD. Richard Barthelmess, Gladys Hulette, Ernest Torrence; *C:* Henry Crotajer. Natl. Film Reg. '07.

Tokyo Olympiad 1966 A monumental sports documentary about the 1964 Olympic Games in its entirety. Never before available for home viewing. Letterboxed with digital sound. In Japanese with English subtitles. 170m/C VHS, DVD. *JP D:* Kon Ichikawa; *W:* Kon Ichikawa, Kazuo Miyagawa.

Tokyo Pop 1988 (R) A punk rocker travels to Japan to find stardom and experiences a series of misadventures. Enjoyable in its own lightweight way. Hamilton is the daughter of Carol Burnett. 99m/C VHS. Carrie Hamilton, Yutaka Tadokoro, Tetsuro Tamba, Taiji Tonoyama, Masumi Harukawa; *D:* Fran Rubel Kuzui; *W:* Lynn Grossman, Fran Rubel Kuzui; *M:* Alan Brewer.

Tokyo Raiders 2000 (PG-13) Remarkably stylish Hong Kong action flick. Director Jingle Ma brings a music video sensibility to the proceedings. The plot concerns a detective (Tony Leung) and his hunt for a gangster, but that's a negligible excuse for a series of cleverly choreographed action scenes. The physical violence is carefully modulated for a young audience, and many gadgets are employed. 100m/C VHS. *HK* Tony Leung Chiu-Wai, Ekin Cheng, Toru Nakamura, Hiroshi Abe, Kelly Chen, Kumiko Endo, Minami Shirakawa, Maiyu Ozawa, Cecilia Cheung; *D:* Jingle Ma; *W:* Susan Chan, Felix Chong; *C:* Jingle Ma, Chan Chi Ying; *M:* Peter Kam.

Tokyo Story 1953 Poignant story of elderly couple's journey to Tokyo where they receive little time and less respect from their grown children. Masterful cinematography, and sensitive treatment of universally appealing story. In Japanese with English subtitles. 134m/B VHS, DVD. *JP* Chishu Ryu, Chieko Higashiyama, So Yamamura, Haruko Sugimura, Setsuko Hara; *D:* Yasujiro Ozu; *W:* Yasujiro Ozu; *C:* Yuuharu Atsuta; *M:* Kojun Saito.

Tollbooth 1994 (R) Romantic dreamer Jack (Von Dohlen) mans a tollbooth on a stretch of Florida Keys highway while his equally longing honey Doris (Balk) works at a nearby gas station and has a thing going on the side with bait salesman Dash (Patton). The return of Doris' long-gone daddy, Leon (Cassel) causes some family problems while Jack's new associate Vic (Wilder) has a scam that's drawing interest from the state police. Thin plot but lots of charm from the two leads helps build interest in this first film. 108m/C VHS. Fairuza Balk, Lenny Von Dohlen, Will Patton, Seymour Cassel, James Wilder, Louise Fletcher, William Katt; *D:* Salome Breziner; *W:* Salome Breziner; *C:* Henry Vargas; *M:* Adam Gorgoni.

The Tollbooth 2004 Earnest, cliched comedy follows 22-year-old Sarabeth Cohen (Sokoloff) as she tries to escape what she sees as her smothering Brooklyn Jewish family 'or the life of a rebellious artist in Manhattan. She even gets a sweet goy boyfriend, Simon (McElhenney), but familial problems interfere while Sarabeth decides where her life should truly be going. 85m/C DVD. *US* Marla Sokoloff, Liz Stauber, Rob McElhenney, Idina Menzel, Jayce Bartok, Ronald Guttman, Tovah Feldshuh; *D:* Debra Kirschner; *W:* Debra Kirschner; *C:* Stefan Forbes; *M:* David Shire.

Tom and Francie 2005 Spinal Tap meets Sesame Street in this fabulous spoof on low-budget TV kids' shows. Twelve years after Tom and Francie's children show "The Flower Shop" is cancelled, they plan a comeback with their new show "Accepting Everyone Through Music." They are joined by a prop master who expresses his hostility through his puppets and a lawyer who smells a post-Barney gravy train. Apple-cheeked Goldie is a standout as kid-show trouper Francie. They must decide to come forward, expose the true fiend, and risk their own hides or run away and let an innocent man hang. 85m/C DVD. Annie Golden, Chris Fields, Steven Skybell, Tara O'Boyle; *D:* Patrick Michael Denny; *W:* Patrick Michael Denny; *M:* Annie Golden, Chris Fields, Patrick Michael Denny. VIDEO.

Tom and Huck 1995 (PG) Tom Sawyer and pal Huck Finn are the only witnesses to a murder. Tom's friend Muff is framed for the crime and the boys are being tracked by the real killer, Injun Joe. They must decide to come forward, expose the true fiend, and risk their own hides or run away and let an innocent man hang. True to the Twain story, Thomas plays a mischievous Tom to Renfro's troublesome Huck. Film was shot in Mooresville, Alabama, population 69, just down the road a piece from the Hannibal, Missouri of Twain fame. 91m/C VHS, DVD. Jonathan Taylor Thomas, Brad Renfro, Eric Schweig, Charles Rocket, Amy Wright, Michael McShane, Marian Seldes, Rachael Leigh Cook, Larry Flanery, Courtland Mead, Peter M. MacKenzie, Heath Lamberts; *D:* Peter Hewitt; *W:* Stephen Sommers, David Loughery; *C:* Bobby Bukowski; *M:* Stephen Endelman.

Tom and Jerry: The Movie 1993 (G) Everybody's favorite animated cat/mouse duo (who began life in a 1940 MGM short "Puss Gets the Boot") hit the big screen, in this talk-y, moralistic vehicle. Rather than cartoon mayhem our two protagonists are goody-two-shoes (with songs yet!) but still retain their charm. Kids will like it, but true "Tom and Jerry" fans should probably stick to the original cartoons. 84m/C VHS. *D:* Phil Roman; *W:* Dennis Marks; *M:* Henry Mancini, Leslie Bricusse; *V:* Richard Kind, Dana Hill, Charlotte Rae, Henry Gibson, Rip Taylor, Howard Morris, Edmund Gilbert, David Lander.

Tom & Viv 1994 (PG-13) American T.S. Eliot (Dafoe) is an Oxford student in 1914 when he meets the moody, monied Vivien Haigh-Wood (Richardson). After a whirlwind courtship, they marry—disastrously. Eliot begins to establish himself as a poet, while Vivien serves as muse/typist and unsuccessfully battles her misdiagnosed illnesses with too much drinking and drugs, as well as embarrassing public scenes. As Eliot gains success, he increasingly distances himself from the unhappy Viv, until finally committing her to an asylum. Dafoe is fine as the chilly, withdrawn poet but Richardson steals the film as his flamboyant, lost wife. Based on the play by Michael Hastings, who co-wrote the screenplay. 115m/C VHS, DVD, GB William Dafoe, Miranda Richardson, Rosemary Harris, Tim Dutton, Nickolas Grace, Philip Locke, Clare Holman, Joanna McCallum; *D:* Brian Gilbert; *W:* Michael Hastings, Adrian Hodges; *M:* Debbie Wiseman; Nat'l. Bd. of Review '94; Actress (Richardson).

Tom Brown's School Days 1940 *Adventures at Rugby* 1940 Depicts life among the boys in an English school during the Victorian era. Based on the classic novel by Thomas Hughes. Remade in 1951. 86m/B VHS, DVD. *GB* Cedric Hardwicke, Jimmy Lydon, Freddie Bartholomew; *D:* Robert Stevenson.

Tom Brown's School Days 1951 Tom enrolls at Rugby and is beset by bullies in classic tale of English school life. British remake of the 1940 version. Based on the novel by Thomas Hughes. 93m/B VHS. *GB* Robert Newton...

Tom

Newton, John (Howard) Davies, James Hayter; *D:* Gordon Parry.

Tom Clancy's Netforce 🐾🐾 *Netforce* 1998 (R) In 2005, technology has become so advanced that a special unit of the FBI, known as Netforce, has been established to police the Internet. Alex Michaels (Bakula) heads the unit after the murder of predecessor Steve Day (Kristofferson), leading Michaels to believe that criminals are trying to cause a global computer crash. Michael's two prime suspects are computer mogul Will Stiles (Reinhold) and crime boss Leong Cheng (Tagawa). Based on a story co-written by Clancy. **90m/C VHS, DVD.** Scott Bakula, Joanna Going, Brian Dennehy, Kris Kristofferson, Judge Reinhold, Cary-Hiroyuki Tagawa, CCH Pounder, Paul Hewitt, Chelsea Field, Frank Vincent, Alexa Vega, Victor Raider-Wexler; *D:* Robert Lieberman; *M:* Jeff Rona. TV

Tom, Dick, and Harry 🐾🐾½ 1941 Dreamy girl is engaged to three men and unable to decide which to marry. It all depends on a kiss. Remade as "The Girl Most Likely." **86m/B VHS.** Ginger Rogers, George Murphy, Burgess Meredith, Alan Marshal, Phil Silvers; *D:* Garson Kanin; *W:* Paul Jarrico.

Tom Horn 🐾🐾 1980 (R) The final days of one of the Old West's legends. Gunman Tom Horn, hired by Wyoming ranchers to stop cattle rustlers, goes about his job with a zeal that soon proves embarrassing to his employers. Beautifully photographed and authentic in its attention to details of the period, the film nonetheless takes liberties with the facts of Horn's life and is lacking in other aspects of production. **98m/C VHS, DVD.** Steve McQueen, Linda Evans, Richard Farnsworth, Billy Green Bush, Slim Pickens; *D:* William Wiard; *W:* Thomas McGuane; *C:* John A. Alonzo; *M:* Ernest Gold.

Tom Jones 🐾🐾🐾 1963 Bawdy comedy based on Henry Fielding's novel about a rustic playboy's wild life in 18th century England. Hilarious and clever with a grand performance by Finney. One of the sexiest eating scenes ever. Redgrave's debut. Theatrically released at 129 minutes, the film was recut by the director, who decided it needed tightening before its 1992 re-release on video. **121m/C VHS, DVD.** *GB* Albert Finney, Susannah York, Hugh Griffith, Edith Evans, Joan Greenwood, Diane Cilento, George Devine, David Tomlinson, Joyce Redman, Lynn Redgrave, Julian Glover, Peter Bull, David Warner; *D:* Tony Richardson; *W:* John Osborne; *C:* Walter Lassally; *M:* John Addison. Oscars '63: Adapt. Screenplay, Director (Richardson), Picture, Orig. Score; British Acad. '63: Film, Screenplay; Directors Guild '63: Director (Richardson); Golden Globes '64: Film—Mus./Comedy, Foreign Film; Natl. Bd. of Review '63: Director (Richardson); N.Y. Film Critics '63: Actor (Finney), Director (Richardson), Film.

Tom Jones 🐾🐾🐾 1998 Miniseries based on the Henry Fielding novel goes further than the hit 1963 movie by including Fielding (Sessions) as the narrator of Tom's bawdy adventures. Tom (Beesley) is an 18th-century orphan with a heart of gold, an affinity for trouble, and an eye for the ladies. His true love is Sophie (Morton), the daughter of the boisterous Squire Western (Blessed). But of course, the path of true love never runs smooth. Lavish adaptation and lots of fun. **300m/C VHS.** *GB* Max Beesley, Samantha Morton, Brian Blessed, John Sessions, Benjamin Whitrow, Frances de la Tour; *D:* Metin Huseyin; *W:* Simon Burke. CABLE

Tom Sawyer 🐾🐾🐾 1930 Winning adaptation of Mark Twain's oft told tale of boyhood in Hannibal, Missouri. Cast reprised their roles the following year in "Huckleberry Finn." **86m/B VHS.** Jackie Coogan, Mitzie Green, Lucien Littlefield, Tully Marshall; *D:* John Cromwell; *C:* Charles B(yam) Lang Jr.

Tom Sawyer 🐾🐾½ 1973 (G) Musical version of the Mark Twain tale of the boisterous Tom, his friend Becky Thatcher, and various adventures, including the fence whitewashing. Amusing kid fare shot on location in Missouri. 🎵River Song; Gratification; Tom Sawyer; Freebootin'; Aunt Polly's Soliloquy; If'n I Was God; A Man's Gotta Be What He's Born To Be; How Come?; Hannibal, Mo. **104m/C VHS,**

DVD. Johnny Whitaker, Jodie Foster, Celeste Holm, Warren Oates, Jeff East; *D:* Don Taylor; *M:* John Williams.

Tom Thumb 🐾🐾🐾 1958 Diminutive boy saves village treasury from bad guys. Adapted from classic Grimm fairy tale. Special effects combine live actors, animation, and puppets. **92m/C VHS, DVD.** *GB* Russ Tamblyn, Peter Sellers, Terry-Thomas; *D:* George Pal; *W:* Ladislas Fodor; *C:* Georges Perinal; *M:* Douglas Gamley.

Tomahawk 🐾🐾½ 1951 Indian sympathizer Jim Bridger (Heflin) is a local scout who anticipates trouble when the government decides to build a wagon route straight through Sioux hunting grounds in order to reach Montana's gold mines. The touchy situation is made worse by cavalry officer Dancy (Nicol) who thinks the only good Indian is a dead one. **82m/C VHS.** Van Heflin, Preston Foster, Yvonne De Carlo, Alex Nicol, Jack Oakie, Tom Tully, Rock Hudson, Ann Doran; *D:* George Sherman; *W:* Maurice Geraghty, Silvia Richards; *C:* Charles P. Boyle; *M:* Hans J. Salter.

Tomb 🐾🐾 1986 Fortune seekers disturb the slumber of a magical, sadistic princess much to their everlasting regret. Adapted from a Bram Stoker novel. **106m/ C VHS.** Cameron Mitchell, John Carradine, Sybil Danning, Richard Hench, Michelle (McClellan) Bauer, Susan Stokey, David Pearson, Francesca "Kitten" Natividad; *D:* Fred Olen Ray; *C:* Paul Elliott.

Tomb of Ligeia 🐾🐾🐾 *Tomb of the Cat* 1964 The ghost of a man's first wife expresses her displeasure when groom and new little missus return to manor. One of the better Corman adaptations of Poe. Also available with "The Conqueror Worm" on Laser Disc. **82m/C VHS, DVD.** *GB* Vincent Price, Elizabeth Shepherd, John Westbrook, Oliver Johnston, Richard Johnson, Derek Francis, Richard Vernon, Ronald Adam, Frank Thornton, Penelope Lee, Denis Gilmore; *D:* Roger Corman; *W:* Robert Towne; *C:* Arthur Grant; *M:* Kenneth V. Jones.

Tomb of the Undead 🐾½ 1972 The sadistic guards of a prison camp are rudely awakened by the prisoners they tortured to death when they return as flesh-eating zombies looking to settle the score. **60m/C VHS.** *GB* Duncan McLeod, Lee Frost, John Dennis; *D:* John Hayes.

Tomb of Torture Woof! *Metempsycose* 1965 Murdered countess is reincarnated in the body of a newspaperman's mistress. Together they investigate monster reports in a murder-ridden castle. The butler may have something to do with it. Filmed in Sepiatone and dubbed. **88m/B VHS, DVD.** Annie Albert, Thony Maky, Mark Marian; *D:* William Grace.

The Tomboy 🐾½ 1924 A young woman behaves boyishly in Colonial America. **64m/B VHS.** Dorothy Devore, Lotta Williams, Herbert Rawlinson, Harry Gribbon, Lee Moran; *D:* David Kirkland.

Tomboy Woof! 1985 (R) A pretty auto mechanic is determined to win not only the race but the love and respect of a superstar auto racer. **91m/C VHS, DVD.** Betsy Russell, Eric Douglas, Jerry Dinome, Kristi Somers, Richard Erdman, Toby Iland; *D:* Herb Freed.

Tomboy & the Champ 🐾🐾 1958 Despite many obstacles, a music-loving calf becomes a prize winner with the help of its loving owner. Kids will love it, but adults will find this one a little sugary. **82m/C VHS.** Candy Moore, Ben Johnson, Jesse White; *D:* Francis D. Lyon.

Tombs of the Blind Dead 🐾🐾½ *The Blind Dead; La Noche del Terror Ciego; La Noche de la Muerta Ciega; Crypt of the Blind Dead; Night of the Blind Dead* 1972 (PG) Blinded by crows for using human sacrifice in the 13th century, zombies rise from the grave to wreak havoc upon 20th-century Spaniards. Atmospheric chiller was extremely popular in Europe and

spawned three sequels. The sequels, also on video, are "Return of the Evil Dead" and "Horror of the Zombies." **102m/C VHS, DVD.** *SP PT* Caesar Burner, Lone Fleming, Helen Harp, Joseph Thelman, Rufino Ingles, Maria Silva; *D:* Alando de Ossorio; *W:* Armando de Ossorio; *C:* Pablo Ripoll; *M:* Anton Abril.

Tombstone 🐾🐾🐾 1993 (R) Saga of Wyatt Earp and his band of law-abiding large moustaches beat the Kasdan/Costner vehicle to the big screen by several months. Legendary lawman Wyatt (Russell) moves to Tombstone, Arizona, aiming to start a new life with his brothers, but alas, that's not to be. The infamous gunfight at the OK Corral is here, and so is best buddy Doc Holliday, gunslinger and philosopher, a role designed for scenery chewing (Kilmer excels). Romance is supplied by actress Josephine, though Delany lacks the necessary romantic spark. Russell spends a lot of time looking troubled by the violence while adding to the body count. Too self-conscious, suffers from '90s western revisionism, but blessed with a high energy level thanks to despicable villains Lang, Biehn, and Boothe. **130m/C VHS, DVD.** Kurt Russell, Val Kilmer, Michael Biehn, Sam Elliott, Dana Delany, Bill Paxton, Powers Boothe, Stephen Lang, Jason Priestley, Dana Wheeler-Nicholson, Billy Zane, Thomas Haden Church, Joanna Pacula, Michael Rooker, Harry Carey Jr., Billy Bob Thornton, Charlton Heston, Robert John Burke, John Corbett, Buck Taylor, Terry O'Quinn, Pedro Armendariz Jr., Chris Mitchum, Jon Tenney; *D:* George P. Cosmatos; *W:* Kevin Jarre; *C:* William A. Fraker; *M:* Bruce Broughton; *Nar:* Robert Mitchum.

Tombstone Canyon 🐾½ 1932 Death rides the range until Maynard and his horse Tarzan put a halt to it. **60m/B VHS, DVD.** Ken Maynard, Sheldon Lewis, Cecilia Parker, Lafe (Lafayette) McKee, Frank Brownlee; *D:* Alan James; *W:* Earle Snell, Claude Rister; *C:* Ted D. McCord.

Tombstone Terror 🐾 1934 A cowboy is beleaguered by a case of mistaken identity. **55m/B VHS.** George "Gabby" Hayes, Earl Dwire, Kay McCoy, Bob Steele; *D:* Robert North Bradbury; *W:* Robert North Bradbury; *C:* Harry Forbes.

Tomcat: Dangerous Desires 🐾🐾 1993 (R) Tom (Grieco) suffers from a rare degenerative condition and agrees to become a guinea pig in a secret, genetic imprinting experiment that has him injected with feline RNA. Tom's health is restored but the side effects give him the predatory instincts of a cat and the need to kill to stay alive. **96m/C VHS.** Richard Grieco, Maryam D'Abo, Natalie Radford; *D:* Paul Donovan; *W:* Paul Donovan; *C:* Peter Wunstorf; *M:* Graeme Cleman.

Tomcats Woof! 2001 (R) Writer/director Pourl takes a half-step down from his previous occupation of porn screenwriter with this steaming pile of misogyny. Michael (O'Connell) is a basically decent guy up to his ethics in gambling debt. The only way out is to marry off his last single friend, Kyle (Busey), in order to win a bet made with their other buddies. He tracks down Natalie (Elizabeth), the only one of Kyle's conquests who agrees, for half the dough and a measure of revenge, but soon the plotters fall in love. Every woman here is depicted as some form of evil, and humiliated accordingly. This isn't new, but it would help if something was at least chuckle-worthy. There's no such relief here, unless you find renegade cancerous sex organs amusing. **94m/C VHS, DVD, UMD.** *US* Jerry O'Connell, Shannon Elizabeth, Jake Busey, Jaime Pressly, Bernie Casey, David Ogden Stiers, Travis Fine, Heather Stephens, Horatio Sanz, Julia Schultz; *D:* Gregory Poirier; *W:* Gregory Poirier; *C:* Charles Minsky; *M:* David Kitay.

Tommy 🐾🐾 *The Who's Tommy* 1975 (PG) Peter Townsend's rock opera as visualized in the usual hyper-Russell style about the deaf, dumb, and blind boy who becomes a celebrity due to his amazing skill at the pinball machines. A parade of rock musicians perform throughout the affair, with varying degrees of success. Despite some good moments, the film ultimately fails prey to ill-conceived production concepts and miscasting. 🎵Under-

ture; Captain Walker Didn't Come Home; It's a Boy; '51 Is Going to Be a Good Year; What About the Boy?; The Amazing Journey; Christmas; See Me, Feel Me; Eyesight to the Blind. **108m/C VHS, DVD.** *GB* Ann-Margret, Elton John, Oliver Reed, Tina Turner, Roger Daltrey, Eric Clapton, Keith Moon, Pete Townshend, Jack Nicholson, Robert Powell, Paul Nicholas, Barry Winch, Victoria Russell, Ben Aris, Mary Holland, Jennifer Baker, Susan Baker, Arthur Brown, John Entwhistle; *D:* Ken Russell; *W:* Ken Russell, Keith Moon, John Entwhistle; *C:* Ronnie Taylor, Dick Bush; *M:* Pete Townshend, John Entwhistle. Golden Globes '76: Actress—Mus./Comedy (Ann-Margret).

Tommy Boy 🐾🐾 1995 (PG-13) Not-too-bright rich kid Tommy (Farley) teams up with snide, officious accountant Richard (Spade) to save the family auto parts business after dad (Dennehy) buys the farm. Tommy and Richard must deal with a conniving stepmom and stepbrother (Derek and Lowe), a ruthless rival (Aykroyd), and a road trip from hell to drum up some new business. Not as bad as it sounds, but inconsistent direction and too-familiar characters offset the amusing chemistry between Farley and Spade. **98m/C VHS, DVD.** Chris Farley, David Spade, Brian Dennehy, Bo Derek, Dan Aykroyd, Julie Warner, Rob Lowe; *D:* Peter Segal; *W:* Bonnie Turner, Terry Turner; *C:* Victor Kemper; *M:* David Newman. MTV Movie Awards '96: On-Screen Duo (Chris Farley/David Spade).

Tomorrow at Seven 🐾🐾½ 1933 A mystery writer is determined to discover the identity of the Ace of Spades, a killer who always warns his intended victim, then leaves an ace of spades on the corpse as his calling card. **62m/B VHS, DVD.** Chester Morris, Vivienne Osborne, Frank McHugh, Allen Jenkins, Henry Stephenson; *D:* Ray Enright.

Tomorrow Is Forever 🐾🐾½ 1946 Welles and Colbert marry shortly before he goes off to fight in WWI. Badly wounded and disfigured, he decides to stay in Europe while Colbert, believing Welles dead, eventually marries Brent. Fast forward to WWII when Brent, a chemical manufacturer, hires a new scientist to work for him in the war effort (guess who). This slow-moving melodrama wastes a good cast. Six-year-old Wood debuts as Welles' adopted daughter. **105m/B VHS.** Claudette Colbert, Orson Welles, George Brent, Lucile Watson, Richard Long, Natalie Wood; *D:* Irving Pichel; *C:* Joseph Valentine; *M:* Max Steiner.

The Tomorrow Man 🐾 2001 (R) Just go with the flow, cause this time travel adventure yarn doesn't make a whole lot of sense. Larry Mackey (Bernsen) is your average joe, living an average life in the 1970s with his son Bryon. Then Mackey's son is kidnapped by notorious criminal Mac (Rusler) who happens to have time-traveled from 30 years in the future. Larry gets together with a time cop (Kennedy) to get the kid back and discovers that Byron actually grows up to be Mac—and dad needs to figure out why. **95m/C VHS, DVD.** Corbin Bernsen, Zach Galligan, Beth Kennedy, Morgan Rusler, Adam Sutton; *D:* Doug Campbell. VIDEO

Tomorrow Never Comes 🐾½ 1977 When he discovers his girlfriend has been unfaithful, a guy goes berserk and eventually finds himself in a stand-off with the police. Violent. **109m/C VHS.** Oliver Reed, Susan George, Raymond Burr, John Ireland, Stephen McHattie, Donald Pleasence; *D:* Peter Collinson.

Tomorrow Never Dies 🐾🐾 1997 (PG-13) 18th installment of the James Bond series is all style and little else packaged in a tedious action adventure. Our villain is a media mogul (Pryce) who plans to start WWIII in order to increase his newspaper revenues. (Rupert Murdoch, start your lawyers!) In between the blatant product placements (from Heineken

Tonight for Sure 🎬 1961 Coppola made this nudie, his first film, as a student at UCLA. Two men, one who spies on women and the other who imagines nude women everywhere, plan an escapade. **66m/B** VHS. **D:** Francis Ford Coppola. **W:** Francis Ford Coppola.

Tonight and Every Night 🎬🎬½ 1945 Cabaret singer and RAF pilot fall in love during WWII. Her music hall post puts her in the midst of Nazi bombing, and her dedication to her song and dance career puts a strain on the romance. Imaginative production numbers outweigh pedestrian storyline. ♪Cry and You Cry Alone; What Does an English Girl Think of a Yank; Anywhere; The Boy I Left Behind; You Excite Me; Tonight and Every Night. **92m/C** VHS. Rita Hayworth, Lee Bowman, Janet Blair, Marc Platt, Leslie Brooks, Shelley Winters; **D:** Victor Saville.

Toni 🎬🎬🎬 1934 An Italian worker falls for his landlady and they make plans to marry. A grim turn of events, however, brings tragic consequences. Based on the lives of several townsfolk in the village of Les Marques, the film was shot in the town and members of the local populace were used as characters. In French with English subtitles. **90m/B** VHS. FR Charles Blavette, Jenny Hélia, Edouard Delmont, Celia Montalvan; **D:** Jean Renoir; **W:** Jean Renoir. **C:** Claude Renoir; **M:** Paul Bozzi.

Tongs: An American Nightmare 🎬 1988 (R) Chinese-American street gangs in Chinatown battle over turf and drug shipments. **80m/C** VHS. Ian Anthony Leung, Christopher O'Conner, Simon Yam; **D:** Philip Chan.

The Tong Man 🎬🎬½ 1919 Robbins owes the tong money and Hayakawa, as the tong's executioner, is sent to kill him when he won't pay up. Only it turns out Hayakawa is in love with Eddy, Robbins daughter, and refuses. Then the tong decide to kill him for disobeying their orders. **58m/B** VHS. Sessue Hayakawa, Helen Jerome Eddy, Marc Robbins, Toyo Fujita; **D:** William Worthington.

Tomorrow's Children 🎬 1934 An alarmist melodrama warning against the threat of government-induced female sterilization asks the question: if a woman's family is weird, should her tubes be tied? **55m/B** VHS, DVD. Sterling Holloway, Diana Sinclair, Sarah Padden, Don Douglas; **D:** Crane Wilbur.

Tomorrow's Child 🎬🎬 1982 TV drama about in vitro fertilization (test-tube babies) and surrogate motherhood. **100m/C** VHS. Stephanie Zimbalist, William Atherton, Bruce Davison, Ed Flanders, Salome Jens, James Shigeta, Susan Oliver, Arthur Hill; **D:** Joseph Sargent. TV

Tomorrow the World 🎬🎬 1944 This bizarre little wartime drama is dated in almost every respect. Emil Bruckner (Homeier) is a Hitler Youth who's sent to live with his uncle (March) in America. The conflict between a fascist mindset and liberal tolerance is painted with very broad strokes. Both acting and writing have an extravagant quality that contemporary audiences will have trouble accepting. **86m/B** DVD. Fredric March, Betty Field, Agnes Moorehead, Skip Homeier, Joan Carroll, Boots Brown, Edit Angold, Rudy Wissler, Marvin Davis, Patsy Ann Thompson, Mary Newton, Tom Fadden; **D:** Leslie Fenton; **W:** Ring Lardner Jr., Leopold Atlas; **C:** Henry Sharp.

Tonio Kroger 🎬🎬 1965 A young intellectual travels through Europe in search of intellectual and sensual relationships and a home that will suit him. He must balance freedom and responsibility. Works best if one is familiar with the Thomas Mann novel on which film is based. In German with English subtitles. **91m/B** C VHS, DVD. FR Gérard Depardieu, Josiane Balasko, Carole Bouquet, Roland Bertin; **D:** Bernard Blier; **W:** Bertrand Blier; **C:** Philippe Rousselot, Cannes '89: Grand Jury Prize, Cesar '90: Actress (Bouquet), Director (Blier), Film, Writing.

Tonka 🎬🎬½ 1958 A children's story about a wild horse tamed by a young Indian, only to have it recruited for the Battle of Little Bighorn. Mineo is fine as the Indian brave determined to be reunited with his steed. The film also makes a laudable effort to portray the Indians as a dignified race. The movie, however, stumbles at its conclusion and is contrived throughout. **97m/C** VHS. Sal Mineo, Phil Carey, Jerome Courtland; **D:** Lewis R. Foster.

Tonto Basin Outlaws 🎬 1941 The Range Busters team up with Teddy Roosevelt's Rough Riders in order to stop a gang of cattle rustlers. Standard oater material. Based on the story by Earle Snell. **60m/B** VHS, DVD. Ray Corrigan, John "Dusty" King, Max Terhune, Jan Wiley, Tristram Coffin, Edmund Cobb; **D:** S. Roy Luby; **W:** John Vlahos.

The Tonto Kid 🎬 1935 Action-packed western featuring Rex Bell. **56m/B** VHS. Rex Bell, Ruth Mix, Buzz Barton, Joseph Girard, Jack Rockwell, Murdock MacQuarrie; **D:** Harry Fraser.

Tony Draws a Horse 🎬🎬 1951 An eight-year-old draws an anatomically correct horse on the door of his father's office, leading to a rift between the parents as they argue how to handle the heartbreak of precociousness. Somewhat uneven but engaging comedy, based on a play by Lesley Storm. **90m/B** VHS. Cecil Parker, Anne Crawford, Derek Bond, Barbara Murray, Mervyn Johns, Barbara Everest, David Hurst; **D:** John Paddy Carstairs.

Tony Rome 🎬🎬½ 1967 Tony Rome (Sinatra) is a P.I. living the good life on his boat in Miami. He's hired by wealthy builder Rudolph Kosterman (Oakland) to keep an eye on his erratic daughter, Diana (Lyons). Turns out there's organized crime and blackmail involved as well—oh, and a babe named Ann (St. John). An entertaining diversion based on the novel "Miami Mayhem" by Marvin H. Albert. Followed by "The Lady in Cement" (1968). **110m/C** VHS, DVD. Frank Sinatra, Jill St. John, Simon Oakland, Gena Rowlands, Richard Conte, Lloyd Bochner, Jeffrey Lynn, Sue Lyon; **D:** Gordon Douglas; **W:** Richard L. Breen; **C:** Joseph Biroc; **M:** Billy May.

Too Bad She's Bad 🎬🎬½ 1954 Wide-eyed cab driver Paolo (Mastroianni) can't help but desire sexy Lina (Loren) with a blonde 'do) despite her attempt to swipe his ride. Later he realizes that thievery is her family's business and believes marrying her will turn her around. First of thirteen films starring the Italian acting legends. In Italian, with subtitles. **96m/B** VHS, DVD. Vittorio De Sica, Sophia Loren, Marcello Mastroianni, Memmo Carotenuto, Giorgio Sanna, Michael Simone, Margherita Bagni, Wanda Benedetti, Mara Berni, Paradisi; **D:** Alessandro Blasetti; **W:** Giulio Tomasini, John Stacy, Walter Bartoletti, Mauro Sacripanti. [Che Che una Canaglia]

Too Late for Tears 🎬🎬🎬 1949 Killer wife will stumble on a load of mob-stolen cash and become entangled in a web of deceit and murder as the wife resorts to increasingly desperate measures to keep her newfound fortune. Atmospheric and entertaining film noir albeit sometimes confusing. **99m/B** VHS, DVD. Lizabeth Scott, Dan Duryea, Arthur Kennedy, Kristine Miller, Barry Kelley, Denver Pyle, Jimmy Ames, Billy Halop, Jimmie Dodd; **D:** Byron Haskin; **W:** Roy Huggins; **C:** William Mellor; **M:** R. Dale Butts.

Too Late the Hero 🎬🎬🎬 1970 (PG) Unlikely band of allied soldiers battle Japanese force entrenched in the Pacific during WWII. Rousing adventure. Fine cast. **133m/C** VHS, DVD. Michael Caine, Cliff Robertson, Henry Fonda, Ian Bannen, Harry Andrews, Denholm Elliott, William Beckley, Ronald Fraser, Percy Herbert, Patrick Jordan, Harvey Jason, Sam Kydd, Ken Takaura; **D:** Robert Aldrich; **W:** Robert Aldrich, Lukas Heller; **C:** Joseph Biroc; **M:** Gerald Fried.

Too Many Crooks 🎬🎬 1959 A British spoof of crime syndicate films. Crooks try to extort, but bungle the job. **85m/B** VHS. GB Terry-Thomas, George Cole; **D:** Mario Zampi.

Too Many Girls 🎬🎬½ 1940 Beautiful heiress goes to a small New Mexico college to escape from a cadre of gold-digging suitors. Passable adaptation of the successful Rodgers and Hart Broadway show, with many original cast members and the original stage director. Lucy and Desi met while making this film, and married shortly after. ♪Spic and Spanish; Heroes in the Fall; Pottawatomie; 'Cause We All Got Cake; Love Never Went to College; Look Out I Didn't Know What Time It Was; The Conga; You're Nearer. **85m/B** VHS, DVD. Lucille Ball, Richard Carlson, Eddie Bracken, Ann Miller, Desi Arnaz Sr., Hal LeRoy, Libby Bennett, Frances Langford, Van Johnson; **D:** George Abbott; **M:** George Bass-man, Richard Rodgers, Lorenz Hart.

Too Much Sun 🎬½ 1990 (R) A dying man can inherit his fortune from his father only if he has two children simply by having one of his two children produce an heir. The problem is, his both gay! **97m/C** VHS, DVD. Robert Downey Jr., Ralph Macchio, Eric Idle, Andrea Martin, Laura Ernst, Jim Haynie, Allan Arbus; **D:** Robert Downey.

Too Pretty to Be Honest 🎬🎬 [Trop jolie pour être honnête] 1972 Four women sharing an apartment witness a robbery and begin to suspect that their neighbor is the culprit. So they decide to steal the money from him. In French with subtitles. **95m/C** VHS. FR Jane Birkin, Bernadette LaFont, Jeanne Jo Starck; **D:** Richard Balducci; **M:** Serge Gainsbourg.

Too Scared to Scream 🎬🎬 [Trop jolie pour être honnête] 1972 1985 (R) Policeman and an undercover agent team up to solve a bizarre series of murders at a Manhattan apartment house. **104m/C** VHS. Mike Connors, Anne Archer, Leon Isaac Kennedy, John Heard, Ian McShane, Maureen O'Sullivan, Murray Hamilton; **D:** Tony LeBlanc; **W:** Neal Barbera.

Too Shy to Try 🎬🎬 1982 (PG) A incredibly shy man meets his dream girl, and enrolls in a psychology course to overcome his ineptitude. A comedy, slapstick French comedy. **89m/C** VHS. FR Pierre Richard, Aldo Maccione; **D:** Pierre Richard.

Too Smooth 🎬🎬 [Hairshirt 1998 (R)] Danny (Paras) is a smooth-talking actor wannabe who lies to every woman he knows—until he meets naive Corey (Wright), whom he thinks is the girl of his dreams. But when his vindictive starlet ex (Campbell) learns about Corey's new romance, she becomes determined to expose him for the lying dog she's sure he remains. **91m/C** VHS, DVD. Dean Paras, Neve Campbell, Katie Wright, Rebecca Gayheart, Christian Campbell, David DeLuise, Stefan Brogren, Adam Carolla, Marley Shelton; **D:** Dean Paras; **W:** Dean Paras; **M:** Nathan Barr.

Too Wise Wives 🎬🎬 1921 A story of would-be marital infidelity and misunderstandings. Silent. **90m/C** VHS. Louis Calhern, Claire Windsor; **D:** Lois Weber.

Too Young to Die 🎬🎬 1990 (R) Teenager Amanda (Lewis) hooks up with the wrong guy in sleazy Billy (Pitt), who hooks her on drugs and turns her into a prostitute. She meets nice guy Mike (O'Keefe), who briefly takes her away from the life but when their relationship falls apart, Amanda winds up on trial for murder. Fact-based TV movie. **92m/C** VHS, DVD. Juliette Lewis, Brad Pitt, Michael Tucker, Michael O'Keefe, Emily Longstreth, Alan Fudge; **D:** Robert Markowitz; **W:** David Hill; **C:** Eric Van Haren Noman; **M:** Charles Bernstein.

The Toolbox Murders 🎬 1978 (R) Unknown psychotic murderer brutally claims victims one at a time, leaving a police mystified and townsfolk terrified. Sick and

Tonight or Never 🎬🎬 1931 Nella (Swanson) is a young opera singer whose Venice debut is criticized for her lack of passion. So she spends the night with a nameless handsome admirer (Douglas), which does the trick. Nella is suddenly offered a contract with the Metropolitan Opera and learns that her new lover is a talent scout who arranged the whole thing. Film is adapted from a play by Lili Hatvany, in which Douglas also starred. **80m/B** C VHS, DVD. FR Gloria Swanson, Melvyn Douglas, Ferdinand Gottschalk, Alison Skipworth, Boris Karloff, Robert Greig; **D:** Mervyn LeRoy; **W:** Ernest Vajda, Frederic Hatton, Fanny Hatton; **C:** Gregg Toland; **M:** Alfred Newman.

Too Beautiful for You 🎬🎬 [Trop Belle pour Toi] 1988 (R) A successful car salesman, married for years to an extraordinarily beautiful woman, finds himself head over heels for his frumpy secretary. Depardieu plays the regular guy who finds he's never believed in the love and fidelity of a woman he thinks is too beautiful for him. In French with English subtitles. **91m/C** VHS, DVD. FR Gerard Depardieu, Josiane Balasko, Carole Bouquet, Roland Bertin, Francois Cluzet; **D:** Bertrand Blier; **W:** Bertrand Blier; **C:** Philippe Rousselot, Cannes '89: Grand Jury Prize, Cesar '90: Actress (Bouquet), Director (Blier), Film, Writing.

Too Busy to Work 🎬🎬½ 1932 Hobo Jubilo (Rogers) has been searching for the man who ran off with his wife and daughter long ago. He becomes a reluctant handyman at Judge Hardy's (Burton) and discovers his daughter Rose (Nixon) is happy and living the good life and that his wife has died. Jubilo decides to keep his identity a secret and encourages marriage of not-so-proper New England-ers Danner and Hardy's daughter. **76m/B** VHS. Will Rogers, Marian Nixon, Dick Powell, Frederick Burton, Daniel Cosgrove, Louise Beavers, Charles Middleton, Bert Hanlon, Constantine Romanoff; **D:** John Blystone; **W:** Barry Connors, Philip Klein; **C:** Charles Clarke.

Too Fast, Too Young 🎬 1996 (R) L.A. police captain Floyd Anderson (Ironside) finds himself shouldering the blame when violent offender Dalton (Tiller) escapes from prison and goes on a cop-killing spree. **90m/C** VHS. Michael Ironside, Patrick Kilpatrick, James Wellington, Kasia (Kataizyfa) Figura, Marshall Bell; **D:** Tim Everitt; **W:** Tim Everitt.

Too Good to Be True 🎬½ 1979 Terrific TV adaptation of a series of John Updike stories focusing on the rocky longtime marriage of Blythe Danner, Michael Moriarty, Glenn Close, Ken Kercheval. **98m/C** VHS, DVD. Blythe Danner, Michael Moriarty, Glenn Close, Ken Kercheval; **W:** William Hanley.

Too Hot to Handle 🎬🎬 1938 Two rival photographers searching for a beautiful lady-pilot's missing brother wind up in Brazil, where they encounter a dangerous tribe of voodoo types. Amusing, if exaggerated, picture of the lengths to which reporters will go to for a story. Classic Gable. **105m/B** VHS. Clark Gable, Myrna Loy, Walter Pidgeon, Walter Connolly, Leo Carrillo, Virginia Weidler; **D:** Jack Conway.

Too Hot to Handle 🎬 1976 Voluptuous lady contract killer fights against the mob with all the weapons at her disposal. Filmed on location in Manila. **88m/C** VHS. Cheri Caffaro, Aharon Ipale, Corinne Calvet, Butz Aquino, Subas Herrero; **D:** Don Schain; **W:** Michael Sherman, Albert (Don) Buday; **C:** Fred Conde. VIDEO

Too Far to Go 🎬🎬 1979 (PG) L.A. police captain ... Terrific TV adaptation of a series of John Updike stories focusing on the rocky longtime marriage of not-so-proper New Englanders Danner and Hardy's daughter. **98m/C** VHS, DVD. Blythe Danner, Michael Moriarty, Glenn Close, Ken Kercheval; **W:** William Hanley.

Tooth and Nail 🐾 2007 (R) You've got your post-apocalyptic world, you've got your struggle to survive, you've got roving gangs of cannibals... Civilization collapses and chaos rules when the world runs out of oil. One struggling group has taken over an abandoned hospital, working together to stay alive, which is hard enough—and it only gets worse when a gang of marauding cannibals comes along, looking for their next meal. **94m/C DVD.** Rachel Miner, Rider Strong, Michael Kelly, Robert Carradine, Vinnie Jones, Michael Madsen, Gregg Easterbrook; **D:** Mark Young; **W:** Mark Young; **C:** Ella Cmiral.

The Tooth Fairy 🐾 2006 Peter (Munro) is renovating an old house, and his girlfriend Darcy (West) and her 12-year-old daughter Pamela (Munoz) come to help out. While looking around, Pam meets young Emma (Ballard), who tells her that the house was owned by an old woman named Elizabeth Craven (Konoval), who lured neighborhood kids inside with the promise of presents if they would give her their baby teeth. Instead, she killed them. Apparently, renovating the house has stirred up "The Tooth Fairy" and when Pam's last baby tooth happens to fall out, the horrors begin again. Silly rather than scary. **89m/C DVD.** Lochlyn Munro, Chandra West, Karin Konoval, P.J. Soles, Steve Bacic, Nicole Munoz, Jianna Ballard; **D:** Chuck Bowman; **W:** Stephen J. Cannell, Corey Strode, Cookie Rae Brown; **C:** David Pelletier; **M:** Richard John Baker, Jon Lee. **VIDEO**

Toothless 🐾½ 1997 Katherine Lewis (Alley) is a work-obsessed dentist who is struck by a car and wakes up in Limbo Land (yes, she's dead). The supervisor, Ms. Rogers (Redgrave), informs Katherine that because she had no emotional connections in life her entry into heaven will have to wait—and she's going to do her time as the Tooth Fairy. Katherine is not supposed to intervene with her charges but this sarcastic lady, who doesn't much care for her princess-like Tooth Fairy attire, gets involved with 12-year-old Bobby (Mallinger) and his widowed dad (Midkiff). **85m/C VHS, DVD.** Kirstie Alley, Ross Malinger, Dale Midkiff, Lynn Redgrave, Daryl (Chill) Mitchell, Melanie Mayron, Kimberly Scott, Helen Slater; **W:** Mark S. Kaufman. **TV**

Tootsie 🐾🐾🐾 1982 (PG) Stubborn, unemployed actor Michael Dorsey (Hoffman) disguises himself as a woman named Dorothy Michaels to secure a part on a soap opera. As his popularity on TV mounts, his love life becomes increasingly soap operatic. Hoffman is delightful, as is the rest of the stellar cast, especially Lange as the cast member he falls in love with. Debut of Davis; Murray's performance was unbilled. Director Pollack plays Michael's put-upon agent, George Fields. **110m/C VHS, DVD.** Dustin Hoffman, Jessica Lange, Teri Garr, Dabney Coleman, Bill Murray, Charles Durning, Geena Davis, George Gaynes, Estelle Getty, Christine Ebersole, Sydney Pollack; **D:** Sydney Pollack; **W:** Larry Gelbart, Murray Schisgal, Don McGuire; **C:** Owen Roizman; **M:** Dave Grusin. Oscars '82: Support. Actress (Lange); AFI '98: Top 100; British Acad. '83: Actor (Hoffman); Golden Globes '83: Actor—Mus./Comedy (Hoffman), Film—Mus./Comedy, Support. Actress (Lange); L.A. Film Critics '82: Director (Pollack), Screenplay, Support. Actress (Lange); Natl. Film Reg. '98; N.Y. Film Critics '82: Director (Pollack), Screenplay, Support. Actress (Lange); Natl. Soc. Film Critics '82: Actor (Hoffman), Film, Screenplay, Support. Actress (Lange); Writers Guild '82: Orig. Screenplay.

Top Dog 🐾½ 1995 (PG-13) Another cop-and-dog-team-up-to-get-the-bad-guys flick. This one, however, is meant to appeal to the kids who liked "Sidekicks." That raises a problem with the unfortunately topical right-wing-hate-group-bombing plot. Jake (Norris), a beer-swillin' karate-choppin' loner cop, teams up with canine Reno, whose ex-partner was killed by the neo-Nazi terrorists. Weak script and erratic storyline can't find a comfortable balance between the too-cute pooch scenes and the (admittedly toned-down) violence. Reno steals every scene he's in, and provides the flick's few redeeming moments. **93m/C VHS, DVD.** Chuck Norris, Clyde Kusatsu, Michele Lamar Richards, Carmine Caridi, Peter Savard Moore, Erik von Detten, Herta Ware, Kai Wulff, Francesco Quinn, Timothy Bottoms; **D:** Aaron Norris; **W:** Ron Swanson; **C:** Joao Fernandes.

Top Gun 🐾🐾½ 1986 (PG) Young Navy pilots compete against one another on the ground and in the air at the elite Fighter Weapons School. Cruise isn't bad as a maverick who comes of age in Ray Bans, but Edwards shines as his buddy. Awesome aerial photography and high-cal beefcake divert from the contrived plot and stock characters. The Navy subsequently noticed an increased interest in fighter pilots. Features Berlin's Oscar-winning song "Take My Breath Away." ♪Take My Breath Away; Danger Zone; Destination Unknown; Heaven in Your Eyes; Hot Summer Nights; Mighty Wings; Playing with the Boys; Through the Fire; Top Gun Anthem. **109m/C VHS, DVD, HD DVD.** Tom Cruise, Kelly McGillis, Val Kilmer, Tom Skerritt, Anthony Edwards, Meg Ryan, Rick Rossovich, Michael Ironside, Barry Tubb, Whip Hubley, John Stockwell, Tim Robbins, Adrian Pasdar; **D:** Tony Scott; **W:** Jim Cash, Jack Epps Jr.; **C:** Jeffrey L. Kimball; **M:** Harold Faltermeyer. Oscars '86: Song ("Take My Breath Away"); Golden Globes '87: Song ("Take My Breath Away").

Top Hat 🐾🐾🐾🐾 1935 Ginger isn't impressed by Fred's amorous attentions since she's mistaken him for a friend's other half. Many believe it to be the duo's best film together. Choreography by Astaire and score by Berlin makes this one a classic Hollywood musical. Look for a young Lucille Ball as a clerk in a flower shop. ♪Cheek to Cheek; Top Hat, White Tie and Tails; Isn't This A Lovely Day; The Piccolino; No Strings. **97m/B VHS, DVD.** Fred Astaire, Ginger Rogers, Erik Rhodes, Helen Broderick, Edward Everett Horton, Eric Blore, Lucille Ball; **D:** Mark Sandrich; **W:** Dwight Taylor, Allan Scott; **M:** Irving Berlin, Max Steiner. Natl. Film Reg. '90.

Top of the Heap 🐾 1972 (R) A cop is denied a promotion and gets angry. Deciding to chuck the laws of due process, he goes on a criminal-killing rampage. **91m/C VHS.** Christopher St. John, Paula Kelly, Patrick McVey; **D:** Christopher St. John.

Top of the World 🐾½ 1997 (R) Newly released con Ray Mercer (Weller) travels to Vegas with his estranged wife, Rebecca (Carrere), who wants a quickie divorce. She's got a new boyfriend, casino manager Steve Atlas (Hopper). But Ray just happens to get caught in the middle of a heist planned by Atlas to cover up his embezzling at the casino. Sounds like it should be entertaining but it's not. **98m/C VHS, DVD.** Peter Weller, Tia Carrere, Dennis Hopper, Joe Pantoliano, Martin Kove, Peter Coyote, David Alan Grier, Cary-Hiroyuki Tagawa; **D:** Sidney J. Furie; **W:** Bart Madison; **C:** Alan Caso; **M:** Robert O. Ragland.

Top Secret! 🐾🐾🐾 1984 (PG) Unlikely musical farce parodies spy movies and French intelligence agent combine forces to thwart information about Russian espionage in Cuba. Cerebral and intriguing, but not classic Hitchcock. Based on the novel by Leon Uris. **126m/C VHS, DVD.** John Forsythe, Frederick Stafford, Philippe Noiret, Karin Dor, Michel Piccoli; **D:** Alfred Hitchcock; **W:** Samuel A. Taylor; **C:** Jack Hildyard; **M:** Maurice Jarre. Natl. Bd. of Review '69: Director (Hitchcock), Support. Actor (Noiret).

Topaz 🐾🐾🐾 1969 (PG) American CIA agent and French intelligence agent combine forces to thwart information about Russian espionage in Cuba. Cerebral and intriguing, but not classic Hitchcock. Based on the novel by Leon Uris. **126m/C VHS, DVD.** John Forsythe, Frederick Stafford, Philippe Noiret, Karin Dor, Michel Piccoli; **D:** Alfred Hitchcock; **W:** Samuel A. Taylor; **C:** Jack Hildyard; **M:** Maurice Jarre. Natl. Bd. of Review '69: Director (Hitchcock), Support. Actor (Noiret).

Topaze 🐾🐾🐾 1933 A shy, depressed teacher is fired from his job at a private school and takes a new job, unaware that his boss is using him in a business scam. From the French play by Marcel Pagnol. An American version was also filmed in 1933; Pagnol produced his own version in '51. In French with English subtitles. **92m/B VHS.** FR Louis Jouvet, Edwige Feuillere, Marcel Vallee; **D:** Louis Gasnier; **W:** Marcel Pagnol; **M:** Max Steiner.

Topaze 🐾🐾🐾 1933 American adaptation of the Marcel Pagnol play, about an innocent, doltish schoolmaster who becomes the unknowing front for a baron's illegal business scam. Remade in two French versions, in 1933, and in 1951 by Pagnol. **127m/B VHS.** John Barrymore, Myrna Loy, Jobyna Howland, Jackie Searl; **D:** Harry D'Abbadie D'Arrast.

Topaze 🐾🐾½ 1951 After losing his job, a pathetic school teacher gets involved with the mob and winds up a powerful businessman. Remake of two earlier versions, one French and one American. Based on the play by director Pagnol. In French with English subtitles. **95m/B VHS.** FR Fernandel, Helen Perdriere, Pierre Larquey; **D:** Marcel Pagnol.

The Topeka Terror 🐾 1945 Lane stars as a federal agent who joins forces with a frontier lawyer to stop greedy land-grabber Barcroft from ripping off a group of homesteaders. Based on a story by Patricia Harper. **55m/B VHS.** Allan "Rocky" Lane, Linda Stirling, Roy Barcroft, Earle Hodgins, Bud Geary; **D:** Howard Bretherton; **W:** Patricia Harper, Norman S. Hall.

Topkapi 🐾🐾🐾 1964 An international bevy of thieves can't resist the treasures of the famed Topkapi Palace Museum, an impregnable fortress filled with wealth and splendor. Comic thriller based on Eric Ambler's "The Light of Day." **122m/C VHS, DVD.** Melina Mercouri, Maximilian Schell, Jess Hahn, Gilles Segal; **D:** Jules Dassin; **W:** Monja Danischewsky; **C:** Henri Alekan; **M:** Manos Hadjidakis. Oscars '64: Support. Actor (Ustinov).

Topper 🐾🐾½ 1937 Wealthy, madcap George (Grant) and Marion (Bennett) Kerby return as ghosts after a fatal car accident, determined to assist their morose banker pal Cosmo Topper (Young) to enjoy life. Of course, since Cosmo is the only one who can see the ghostly Kerbys his life becomes very complicated. Immensely popular at the boxoffice; followed by "Topper Takes a Trip" (1939) and "Topper Returns" (1941). The series uses trick photography and special effects to complement the comedic scripts. Based on Thorne Smith's novel, "The Jovial Ghosts." Inspired a TV series and remade in 1979 as TV movie. **97m/B VHS, DVD.** Cary Grant, Roland Young, Constance Bennett, Billie Burke, Eugene Pallette, Hoagy Carmichael; **D:** Norman Z. McLeod.

Topper Returns 🐾🐾🐾 1941 Cosmo Topper helps ghost find the man who mistakenly murdered her and warns her friend, the intended victim. Humorous conclusion to the trilogy preceded by "Topper" and "Topper Takes a Trip." Followed by a TV series. **87m/B VHS, DVD.** Roland Young, Joan Blondell, Dennis O'Keefe, Carole Landis, Eddie Anderson, H.B. Warner, Billie Burke; **D:** Roy Del Ruth; **W:** Gordon Douglas, Jonathan Latimer; **C:** Norbert Brodine.

Topper Takes a Trip 🐾🐾🐾 1939 Cosmo Topper and his wife have fallen out and ghosts Kerby help them get back together. The special effects sequences are especially funny. Also available colorized. **85m/B VHS.** Constance Bennett, Roland Young, Billie Burke, Franklin Pangborn, Alan Mowbray; **D:** Norman Z. McLeod.

Topsy Turvy 🐾🐾½ 1984 (R) A comedy about reckless romance and not much else. **90m/C VHS.** Lisbet Dahl, Ebbe Rode; **D:** Edward Fleming.

Topsy Turvy 🐾🐾🐾½ 1999 (R) The very contemporary Leigh takes a pass at Victorian England for his very long and chatty look at life in the theatre. His focus is on the comic-opera partnership of irascible lyricist W.S. Gilbert (Broadbent) and pleasure-loving composer, Sir Arthur Sullivan (Corduner). Their latest creation (after 10 hits) is a flop, causing a serious rift but Gilbert, after a visit to a Japanese art exhibit, is inspired to write "The Mikado" and pulls Sullivan back in. The film then follows the production of the opera from rehearsal to the 1885 premiere with all its difficulties and triumphs. **160m/C VHS, DVD.** GB Jim Broadbent, Allan Corduner, Leslie Manville, Eleanor David, Ron Cook, Timothy Spall, Kevin McKidd, Mark Benton, Shirley Henderson, Martin Savage, Jessie Bond; **D:** Mike Leigh; **W:** Mike Leigh; **C:** Dick Pope; **M:** Carl Davis. Oscars '99: Costume Des., Makeup; British Acad. '99: Makeup; N.Y. Film Critics '99: Director (Leigh); Film; Natl. Soc. Film Critics '99: Director (Leigh); Film.

Tor 🐾½ 1964 Medieval barbarian endeavors to free an enslaved village from a band of murderous hoodlums. **94m/C VHS.** Joe Robinson, Bella Cortez, Harry Baird; **D:** Antonio Leonviola.

Tora! Tora! Tora! 🐾🐾 1970 (G) The story of events leading up to December 7, 1941, is retold by three directors from both Japanese and American viewpoints in this tense, large-scale production. Well-documented and realistic treatment of the Japanese attack on Pearl Harbor that brought the U.S. into WWII; notable for its good photography but lacks a story line equal to its epic intentions. **144m/C VHS, DVD.** Martin Balsam, So Yamamura, Joseph Cotten, E.G. Marshall, Tatsuya Mihashi, Wesley Addy, Jason Robards Jr., James Whitmore, Leon Ames, George Macready, Takahiro Tamura, Eijiro Tono, Shogo Shimada, Koreya Senda, Jun Usami, Richard Anderson, Kazuo Kitamura, Keith Andes, Walter Brooke, Norman Alden, Ron Masak, Edmon Ryan, Asao Uchida, Frank Aletter, Jerry Fogel; **D:** Richard Fleischer, Toshio Masuda, Kinji Fukasaku; **W:** Ryuzo Kikushima, Hideo Oguni, Larry Forrester; **C:** Sinsaku Himeda, Charles F. Wheeler, Osami Furuya; **M:** Jerry Goldsmith. Oscars '70: Visual FX.

The Torch 🐾🐾 1950 Mexican revolutionary restores law and order when he captures a small town but then finds himself in turmoil as he falls for an aristocratic young woman. **90m/C VHS, DVD.** MX Gilbert Roland, Paulette Goddard, Pedro Armendariz Sr., Walter Reed; **D:** Emilio Fernandez.

Torch Song 🐾🐾 1953 In this muddled melodrama, a tough, demanding Broadway actress meets her match when she is offered true love by a blind pianist. Contains a couple of notoriously inept musical numbers. Made to show off Crawford's figure at age 50. Crawford's singing in the movie is dubbed. **90m/C VHS.** Joan Crawford, Michael Wilding, Marjorie Rambeau, Gig Young, Harry (Henry) Morgan, Dorothy Patrick, Benny Rubin, Nancy Gates; **D:** Charles Walters.

Torch Song Trilogy 🐾🐾½ 1988 (R) Adapted from Fierstein's hit Broadway play about a gay man who "just wants to be loved." Still effective, but the rewritten material loses something in the translation to the screen. Bancroft heads a strong cast with a finely shaded performance as Fierstein's mother. **126m/C VHS, DVD.** Anne Bancroft, Matthew Broderick, Harvey Fierstein, Brian Kerwin, Karen Young, Charles Pierce; **D:** Paul Bogart; **W:** Harvey Fierstein; **C:** Mikael Salomon; **M:** Peter Matz.

Torchlight 🐾 1985 (R) A young couple's life begins to crumble when a wealthy art dealer teaches them how to free base cocaine. Heavy-handed treatment of a subject that's been tackled with more skill elsewhere. **90m/C VHS, DVD.** Pamela Sue Martin, Steve Railsback, Ian McShane, Al Corley, Rita Taggart; **D:** Thomas J. Wright.

Torero 🐾 Bullfighter 1956 A young man becomes a bullfighter to overcome his fear of bulls. **89m/B VHS.** MX Luis Procuna, Manolete, Dolores Del Rio, Carlos Arruza; **D:** Carlos Velo; **W:** Carlos Velo, Hugo Butler.

Torment 🐾🐾🐾 Hets; Frenzy 1944 Tragic triangle has young woman in love with fellow student and murdered by sadistic teacher. Atmospheric tale hailed by many as Sjoberg's finest film. Ingmar Bergman's first filmed script. In Swedish with English subtitles. **90m/B VHS, DVD.** SW Alf Kjellin, Mai Zetterling, Stig Jarrel, Olof Winnerstrand, Gunnar Bjornstrand; **D:** Alf Sjoberg; **W:**

exploitative, with predictably poor production values. **93m/C VHS, DVD.** Cameron Mitchell, Pamelyn Ferdin, Wesley Eure, Nicolas Beaury, Aneta Corsaut, Tim Donnelly, Evelyn Guerrero; **D:** Dennis Donnelly; **W:** Robert Easter, Ann Kindberg; **C:** Gary Graver.

Torment ♂ 1985 (R) A mild-mannered fellow is secretly a mass murderer specializing in young lovers. He struggles to hide his secret as his daughter approaches dating age and a relentless detective gets closer to the truth. A low-budget slasher. **85m/C VHS.** Taylor Gilbert, William Witt, Eve Brenner. *D:* Samson Aslanian, John Hopkins.

Tormented ♂ 1960 Man pushes his mistress out of a lighthouse, killing her. Her returned body parts return to haunt him. **75m/B VHS, DVD.** Richard Carlson, Susan Gordon, Juli Reding; *D:* Bert I. Gordon; *W:* Bert I. Gordon, George Worthing Yates; *C:* Ernest Laszlo; *M:* Albert Glasser, Calvin Jackson.

The Tormentors WOOF! 1971 (R)

Torn Apart ♂ 1989 (R) Traditional Middle East hatreds undermine the love affair between two young people. Excellent performances highlight this drama. Adapted from the Chayim Zeldi's novel "A Forbidden Love." **95m/C VHS.** Adrian Pasdar, Cecilia Peck, Machram Huri, Arnon Zadok, Barry Primus; *D:* Jack Fisher; *M:* Peter Arnow.

Torn Between Two Lovers ♂♂ 1979 A beautiful married woman has an affair with an architect while on a trip. Remick is enjoyable to watch, but it's a fairly predictable yarn. **100m/C VHS, DVD.** Lee Remick, Joseph Bologna, George Peppard, Giorgio Tozzi; *D:* Delbert Mann. TV

Torn Curtain ♂♂½ 1966 American scientist poses as a defector to East Germany in order to uncover details of the Soviet missile program. He and his fiancee, who follows him behind the Iron Curtain, attempt to escape to freedom. Derivative and uninvolving. **125m/C VHS, DVD.** Paul Newman, Julie Andrews, Lila Kedrova, David Opatoshu; *D:* Alfred Hitchcock; *W:* Brian Moore; *C:* John F. Warren. *M:* John Addison.

Tornado ♂ 1983 An army sergeant revolts against his superiors and the enemy when his captain leaves him stranded in Vietnam. **90m/C VHS.** Giancarlo Prete, Tony Marsina, Alan Collins; *D:* Anthony M. Dawson.

Tornado! ♂½ 1996 (PG) TV movie with cheesy special effects chronicles a week when a pair of competing storm-chasing meteorologist Hudson, and government accountant Sturges who wants to stop funding for Hudson's new storm-warning device. Lame attempt to capture some of the "Twister" audience falls miserably. **90m/C VHS, DVD.** Bruce Campbell, Ernie Hudson, Shannon Sturges, L.Q. Jones, Bo Eason; *D:* Noel Nosseck; *W:* John Logan; *C:* George Law.

Torpedo Alley ♂♂ 1953 A guilt-ridden WWII Navy pilot feels responsible for the deaths of his crew. After the war, he joins a submarine crew and gradually learns to deal with his guilt. Average drama with plenty of submarine footage. **84m/B VHS.** Dorothy Malone, Mark Stevens, Charles Winninger, Bill Williams; *D:* Lew Landers.

Torpedo Attack ♂ 1972 Greek sailors, in an outdated submarine, bravely but hopelessly attack Mussolini's Italy during WWII. **88m/C VHS.** GR John Ferris, Sidney Kazan; *D:* George Law.

Torpedo Run ♂♂ 1958 Standard submarine melodramatics, about a U.S. sub that must torpedo a Japanese aircraft carrier which holds some of the crew's family members. Sometimes slow, generally worthwhile. **95m/C VHS.** Glenn Ford, Ernest Borgnine, Dean Jones, Diane Brewster, L.Q. Jones; *D:* Joseph Pevney; *C:* George J. Folsey.

Torque ♂♂ 2004 (PG-13) "The Fast and the Furious" on crotch rockets. Cary Ford (Henderson) is a tough-guy rider who's looking to patch things up with his girlfriend (Mazur) while trying to dodge the wrath of local gang leader Trey Wallace (Ice Cube). Turns out, Cary's been framed

for the murder of Trey's brother by evil crimelord Henry James (Schulze), who's mad at Cary over the loss of a couple bikes full of crystal meth. Music video director Joseph Kahn's first feature is jam-packed with videogame action and lots of CGI effects, but the screenplay is mostly brainless with only occasional funny moments (like Ice Cube quoting his own minute chase scene). **81m/C DVD.** Ice Cube, Martin Henderson, Ice Cube, Monet Mazur, Adam Scott, Matt Schulze, Jaime Pressly, Jay Hernandez, Will Yun Lee, Fredro Starr, Justina Machado, John Doe, Faizon Love; *D:* Joseph Kahn; *W:* Matt Johnson; *C:* Peter Levy; *M:* Trevor Rabin.

Torremolinos 73 ♂♂½ 2003 Alfredo (Camara) is a struggling encyclopedia salesman in Spain during the waning days of Franco's puritanical regime. Desperate for money, he and his wife Carmen (Pena) are initially reluctant partners in his boss, Don Carlos' (Diego), latest scheme: producing "educational" Super-8 sex films for the Scandinavian market. They turn out to be naturals, with Alfredo directing and Carmen starring. Then Alfredo gets ambitious and decides he wants to be the next Ingmar Bergman, writing a script (the movie's title) and persuading a disillusioned Carmen to go along with his idea. Spanish and Danish with subtitles. **91m/C DVD.** Javier Camara, Candela Pena, Juan Diego, Malena Alterio, Fernando Tejero; *D:* Pablo Berger; *W:* Pablo Berger; *C:* Kiko de la Rica.

Torrents of Spring ♂♂ 1990 (PG-13) Based on an Ivan Turgenev story, this lavishly filmed and costumed drama concerns a young Russian aristocrat circa 1840 who is torn between two women. Predictably, one is a good-hearted innocent, the other a scheming seductress. **102m/C VHS, DVD.** Timothy Hutton, Nastassja Kinski, Valeria Golino, William Forsythe, Urbano Barberini, Francesca Da Sapio, Jacques Herlin. *D:* Jerzy Skolimowski.

Torrid Zone ♂♂ 1940 Nick (Cagney) is the former manager of a Central America banana plantation (set up on Warner's back lot) who's about to head for Chicago and a new job. But owner Steve Case (O'Brien) is in a bind since he thinks new manager Anderson (Cowan) is incompetent and a local revolutionary (Tobias) wants to take back the plantation land. Throw in Nick's hot to trot wife Gloria (Vinson), and Nick's got his fair share of trouble. Sounds kinda like 1932's "Red Dust." **88m/B DVD.** James Cagney, Ann Sheridan, Pat O'Brien, Helen Vinson, Andy Devine, Jerome Cowan, George Reeves, George Tobias; *D:* William Keighley; *W:* Richard Macaulay, Jerry Wald; *C:* James Wong Howe. *M:* Adolph Deutsch.

Torso WOOF! 1973 [Corpi Presentano Tracce Di Violenza Carnale; Bodies Bear Traces of Carnal Violence] (R) Crazed psychosexual killer stalks beautiful women and dismembers them. Fairly bloodless and uninteresting, in spite of lovely Kendall. Italian title translates: The Bodies Showed Signs of Carnal Violence—quite an understatement for people missing arms and legs. **91m/C VHS, DVD.** IT Suzy Kendall, Tina Aumont, John Richardson; *D:* Sergio Martino; *W:* Sergio Martino, Ernesto Gastaldi; *C:* Giancarlo Ferrando; *M:* Maurizio de Angelis, Guido de Angelis.

Tortilla Flat ♂♂½ 1942 Based on the John Steinbeck novel of the same name, two buddies, Tracy and Garfield, struggle to make their way on the wrong side of the tracks in California. Garfield

is a butchered torso in Hamilton, Ontario, a streetcar conductor husband. Evelyn ad-mits to numerous affairs with wealthy and powerful men and a desire to lead the good life but did she really commit murder? **90m/C VHS, DVD.** Kathleen Robertson, Victor Garber, Callum Keith Rennie, Brenda Fricker, Jonathan Potts, John Henry Canavan; *D:* Alex Chapelle; *W:* Dennis Foon; *C:* Nikos Evdemon; *M:* Christopher Dedrick.

Tortilla Flat ♂♂½ 1942 Based on the John Steinbeck novel of the same name, two buddies, Tracy and Garfield, struggle to make their way on the wrong side of the tracks in California. Garfield and Lamarr provide the love interest. **105m/B VHS.** Spencer Tracy, Hedy Lamarr, John Garfield, Frank Morgan, Akim Tamiroff, Sheldon Leonard, John Qualen, Donald Meek, Connie Gilchrist; *D:* Victor Fleming; *C:* Karl Freund.

Tortilla Soup ♂♂½ 2001 (PG-13) Widower Martin Naranjo (Elizondo) is a Mexican-American patriarch trying to control the lives of his three grown daughters. Great performances from all, especially Schoolteacher Leticia (Pena) fears love has passed her by; successful Carmen (Obradors) questions her career choice; and Maribel (Mello) has graduated from high school. Martin is a chef who's lost his sense of taste and smell and is just eager to leave home. Meanwhile, Martin is a chef who's being pursued by divorced Hortensia (Welch). Food and family dinners bring the various crises out in the open. And yes, it's the American version of the 1994 Taiwanese film "Eat, Drink, Man, Woman" with an Hector Elizondo, Jacqueline Obradors, Elizabeth Pena, Tamara Mello, Nikolai Kinski, Raquel Welch, Paul Rodriguez, Joan, Constance Marie; *D:* Maria Ripoll; *W:* Tom Musca, Ramon Menendez, Vera Blasi; *C:* Xavier Perez Grobet; *M:* Bill Conti.

Torture Chamber of Baron Blood ♂♂½ Baron Blood; Gli Orrori del Castello di Norimberga; The Blood Baron; Chamber of Tortures; The Thirst of Baron Blood 1972 (PG) Baron with gorgeous thirst for the red stuff is reanimated and icts of innocent bystander's meet a grisly fate in this spaghetti gorefest. Familiar story has that certain Bava feel. **90m/C VHS, DVD.** IT Joseph Cotten, Elke Sommer, Massimo Girotti, Rada Rassimov, Antonio Cantafora; *D:* Mario Bava; *W:* Vincent Fotre, Christiane Rucker, Dieter Eppler; *D:* Harald Reinl.

The Torture Chamber of Dr. Sadism ♂ [Blood Demon; Die Schlangengrube und das Pendel; The Walking Dead; Die Schlangengrube und das Pendel 1569 (R) Director Milligan tortures audience with more mindless medieval pain infliction from Staten Island. **80m/C VHS.** Jeremy Brooks, Susan Cassidy; *D:* Andy Milligan.

Torture Dungeon ♂ 1970 (R) Director Milligan tortures audience with more mindless medieval pain infliction from Staten Island. **80m/C VHS.** Jeremy Brooks, Susan Cassidy; *D:* Andy Milligan.

Torture Garden ♂♂ 1967 A sinister man presides over an unusual sideshow where people can see what's in store if they allow the evil side of their personality to take over. Written by Bloch ("Psycho") and based on four of his short stories. **93m/C VHS, DVD.** GB Jack Palance, Burgess Meredith, Peter Cushing, Beverly Adams; *D:* Freddie Francis; *W:* Robert Bloch; *M:* Don Banks.

The Torture of Silence ♂♂½ Mater Dolorosa 1917 A simple little drama about a doctor's neglected wife seeking out the doctor's best friend for love, remade by Gance in 1932. **55m/B VHS, FR** Emmy Lynn, Firmin Gemier, Armand Tallier, Anthony Gildes, Paul Vermoyal; *D:* Abel Gance; *C:* Leonce-Henri Burel.

Torture Ship ♂½ 1939 Director Halperin, who earlier made the minor horror classic "White Zombie," was all at sea in this becalmed thriller about a mad doctor who uses convicts for glandular experiment in his shipboard laboratory. Based on the short story, "A Thousand Deaths," by Jack London. **57m/B VHS, DVD.** Lyle Talbot, Irving Pichel, Julie Bishop, Sheila Mannors; *D:* Victor Halperin.

Torture Train ♂½ 1975 (R) Mayhem, murder, and knife-wielding psychosis occurs on board a train. **78m/C VHS, DVD.** IT Marina Berti, Irene Miracle, Laura D'Angelo, Mecha Menil, Enrico Maria Salerno, Flavio Bucci, Gianfranco de Grassi; *D:* Aldo Lado; *W:* Aldo Lado; *C:* Gabor Pogany; *M:* Ennio Morricone.

Total Eclipse ♂ 1995 (R) Unfortunate look at the mutually destructive relationship between 19th-century French poets Arthur Rimbaud (DiCaprio) and Paul Verlaine (Thewlis). Rimbaud was a 16-year-old Parisian sensation for his iconoclastic work but what's presented is an obnoxious showoff, while the older, married Verlaine is a drunken lout who abuses his teenaged wife Mathilde (Bohringer). There's lots of dissolute, violent behavior and absolutely no insight into their work (which is the only reason to care). Ugly film wastes a lot of talent. **111m/C VHS, DVD.** Leonardo DiCaprio, David Thewlis, Romane Bohringer, Dominique Blanc; *D:* Agnieszka Holland; *W:* Christopher Hampton; *C:* Yorgos Arvanitis; *M:* Jan A.P. Kaczmarek.

Total Exposure ♂ 1991 (R) Total idiocy involving uncled babes and hormonally imbalanced men in blackmail and murder. 1990 Playboy Playmate Deborah Driggs proves there is of sorts after destruction of the universe. **97m/C VHS, DVD.** David Bradley, Thomas Kretschmann, Ely Pouget, Bill Shaw, Misa Koprova; *D:* Phillip J. Roth; *W:* Phillip J. 3oth, Robert Tossberg; *C:* Andres Garreton. VIDEO

Total Force ♂ 1998 Two men team up to destroy a weapon that uses satellite technology to turn ordinary citizens into killers. **100m/C VHS.** Timothy Bottoms, Frank Stallone, Richard Lynch; *D:* Steven Kamar; *M:* Barry Cotting. VIDEO

Total Reality ♂½ 1997 (R) In order to escape execution, disgraced soldier Anthony Rand (Bradley) agrees to follow renegade general Tunis (Kretschmenn) back through time and prevent the colonization of Mars, so he decides to visit a travel service that specializes in implanting vacation memories into its clients' brains and buy a memory trip to the planet. Only during the implant Quaid discovers his memories have been artificially altered and he must find out just what's real and what's not. Intriguing plot and spectacular special effects. Laced with graphic violence. Based on Phillip K. Dick's "We Can Remember It for You Wholesale." **113m/C VHS, DVD.** Arnold Schwarzenegger, Rachel Ticotin, Sharon Stone, Michael Ironside, Ronny Cox, Roy Brocksmith, Marshall Bell, Mel Johnson Jr.; *D:* Paul Verhoeven; *W:* Gary Goldman, Dan O'Bannon; *C:* Jost Vacano; *M:* Jerry Goldsmith. Oscars '90: Visual FX.

Total Recall ♂♂♂ 1990 (R) Mind-bending sci-fi movie set in the 21st century. Construction worker Quaid (Schwarzenegger) dreams every night of Mars and decides to visit a travel service that specializes in implanting vacation memories into its clients' brains and buy a memory trip to the planet. Only during the implant Quaid discovers his memories have been artificially altered and he must find out just what's real and what's not. Intriguing plot and spectacular special effects. Laced with graphic violence. Based on Phillip K. Dick's "We Can Remember It for You Wholesale." **113m/C VHS, UMD, DVD.** Arnold Schwarzenegger, Rachel Ticotin, Sharon Stone, Michael Ironside, Ronny Cox, Roy Brocksmith, Marshall Bell, Mel Johnson Jr.; *D:* Paul Verhoeven; *W:* Gary Goldman, Dan O'Bannon; *C:* Jost Vacano; *M:* Jerry Goldsmith. Oscars '90: Visual FX.

Total Recall 2070: Machine Dreams ♂♂½ 1999 (R) Pilot movie for the brief series that had only a tentative connection to the Arn-uld movie and the short stories of Philip K. Dick. David Hume (Easton) is a 21st century cop who is supposed to keep an eye on the Consortium, the group of private companies that unofficially now run the world. They create mayhem and he tries to clean it up. **89m/C VHS.** Michael Easton, Karl Prunell, Cynthia (Cyndy, Cindy) Preston, Judith Krant, Nick Mancuso; *D:* Mario Azzopardi; *C:* Peter Wunstorf. CABLE

Totally Blonde ♂♂ 2001 (PG-13) Brunette Meg (Allen) is having trouble finding Mr. Right, so she decides to hit the peroxide bottle and see if blondes really do have more fun. Of course, club owner Van (Buble) already thinks Meg is hot but she's been looking at him as just a friend. Instead, Meg hooks up with mister hot (and rich) body Brad (Hutzler). Funny thing, Meg gets green-eyed when her pal Liv (Quinlan) decides to go after Van for herself. **98m/C VHS, DVD.** Krista Allen, Maeve Quinlan, Michael Buble, Brody Hutzler, Mindy Sterling, Charlene Tilton; *D:* Andrew Van Slee; *W:* Andrew Van Slee; *C:* Jim Orr; *M:* Andrew Van Slee Miles Hill, Ian Putz. VIDEO

Totally F***ed Up ♂♂ 1994 The first of director Araki's teen trilogy, followed by "The Doom Generation" and "Nowhere," concerns itself with the teen angst experienced by a loose group of friends—four gays and a lesbian couple. In short chapters, they meet, talk, and wander through a soulless L.A. as one of their group, film school student Steven (Luna), makes a video documentary about their situation (footage of which in intercut throughout the film). **80m/C VHS, DVD.** James Duval, Gilbert Luna, Lance May, Roko Belic, Susan Behshid, Jenee Gill, Alan Boyce; **D:** Gregg Araki; **W:** Gregg Araki; **C:** Gregg Araki.

Toto le Heros ♂♂♂ 1991 (PG-13) *Toto the Hero* Bitter old man, who as a child fantasized that he was a secret agent named Toto, harbors deep resentment over not living the life he's convinced he should have had. He maintains a childhood fantasy that he and his rich neighbor were switched at birth in the confusion of a fire at the hospital. Series of flashbacks and fast forwards show glimpses of his life, not necessarily as it was, but how he perceived it. Sounds complex, but it's actually very clear and fluid. Mix of comedy and tragedy, with lots of ironic twists, and precise visuals. In French with English subtitles. **90m/C VHS, DVD.** *FR* Michel Bouquet, Jo De Backer, Thomas Godet, Mireille Perrier, Sandrine Blancke, Didier Femey, Hugo Harold Harrisson, Gisela Uhlen, Peter Bohlke; **D:** Jaco Van Dormael; **W:** Jaco Van Dormael; **C:** Walther Vanden Ende; **M:** Pierre Van Dormael. Cesar '91: Foreign Film.

The Touch ♂♂½ 1996 (R) Straightforward story of a woman who is satisfied with her husband until the arrival of a stranger. The stranger soon has her yearning for a life she never had. Bergman's first English film lacks the sophistication of his earlier work. **112m/C VHS.** *SW/Bibi* Andersson, Elliott Gould, Max von Sydow; **D:** Ingmar Bergman; **W:** Ingmar Bergman; **C:** Sven Nykvist.

Touch ♂♂½ 1996 (R) Sleazebags, fundamentalists, and a maybe saint would seem to make for a surefire success in this easygoing adaptation of the offbeat Elmore Leonard novel. And while individual scenes and performances shine, the film doesn't completely hang together. Young Juvenal (Ulrich) is a former monk, now working at an L.A. alcohol rehab center, who possesses the stigmata and seems to have an authentic gift for healing. Naturally, this brings the crazies and the scammers out of the woodwork, including former preacher Bill Hill (Walken), whose partner (Fonda) falls for the lad, and paramilitary religious fanatic August Murray (Arnold). **96m/C VHS.** Skeet Ulrich, Bridget Fonda, Christopher Walken, Tom Arnold, Gina Gershon, Lolita (David) Davidovich, Paul Mazursky, Janeane Garofalo, John Doe, Conchata Ferrell, Mason Adams, Breckin Meyer, Anthony Zerbe; **D:** Paul Schrader; **W:** Paul Schrader; **C:** Edward Lachman; **M:** David Grohl.

Touch & Go ♂♂ 1980 (PG) Three beautiful women commit grand larceny in order to raise funds for underprivileged children. **92m/C VHS.** *AU* Wendy Hughes; **D:** Peter Maxwell; **W:** Alan Ormsby.

Touch and Go ♂♂½ 1986 (R) Sentimental drama about a self-interested hockey pro who learns about love and giving through a young delinquent and his attractive mother. **101m/C VHS.** Michael Keaton, Maria Conchita Alonso, Ajay Naidu, Maria Tucci, Max Wright, John C. Reilly; **D:** Robert Mandel; **W:** Harry Colomby.

A Touch of Class ♂♂♂ 1973 (PG) Married American insurance adjustor working in London plans quick and uncommitted affair but finds his heart doesn't obey the rules. Jackson and Segal create sparking record of a growing relationship. **105m/C VHS, DVD.** George Segal, Glenda Jackson, Paul Sorvino, Hildegard(e) Neil, K. Callan, Mary Barclay, Cec Linder; Melvin Frank; **W:**

Jack Rose; **C:** Austin Dempster; **M:** John Cameron. Oscars '73: Actress (Jackson); Golden Globes '74: Actor—Mus./Comedy (Segal), Actress—Mus./Comedy (Jackson); Writers Guild '73: Orig. Screenplay.

Touch of Evil ♂♂♂♂ 1958 (PG-13) Stark, perverse story of murder, kidnapping, and police corruption in a Mexican border town. Welles portrays a police chief who invents evidence to convict the guilty. Filled with innovative photography reminiscent of "Citizen Kane," as filmed by Russell Metty. In 1998, Walter Murch restored the film working from Welles's notes, re-editing the work to what Welles had originally envisioned before studio intervention; this version is 101 minutes and is unrated. **108m/B VHS, DVD.** Charlton Heston, Orson Welles, Janet Leigh, Joseph Calleia, Akim Tamiroff, Marlene Dietrich, Valentin de Vargas, Dennis Weaver, Joanna Moore, Mort Mills, Victor Millan, Ray Collins; **Cameos:** Joi Lansing, Zsa Zsa Gabor, Mercedes McCambridge, Joseph Cotten; **D:** Orson Welles; **W:** Orson Welles; **C:** Russell Metty; **M:** Henry Mancini. Natl. Film Reg. '93.

Touch of Pink ♂♂ 2004 (R) Kyle MacLachlan plays the ghost of Cary Grant as he advises Alim (Mistry), a gay Pakistani film studio photographer. It seems Alim needs the advice, as his conservative mother (Mathew), whom he has yet to tell him. Of course, Alim, who lives with his British lover Giles (Holden-Ried), decides to hide the fact with just a fiancee. The usual hijinx occur. Mostly unremarkable except for a great performance by MacLachlan. **92m/C VHS, DVD.** Jimi Mistry, Kyle MacLachlan, Kris Holden-Ried, Brian George, Lisa Ray, Suleka Mathew, Veena Sood, Raoul Bhaneja; **D:** Ian Iqbal Rashid; **W:** Ian Iqbal Rashid; **C:** David Makin; **M:** Andrew Lockington.

The Touch of Satan ♂ *The Touch of Melissa; Night of the Demon; Curse of Melissa* 1970 (No) Lost on the road, a young man meets a lovely young woman and is persuaded to stay at her nearby farmhouse. Things there are not as they seem, including the young woman—who turns out to be a real witch. **90m/C VHS.** Michael Berry, Emby Mallay, Lee Amber, Yvonne Wilson, Jeanne Gerson; **D:** Don Henderson.

Touchdown ♂♂½ 1931 (No) College football coach Dan Curtis (Arlen) is a winat-all-costs kind of guy, that is until one of players is seriously injured after Curtis pushes him too hard. Things come to a head when the team is set to play their arch-rival, and Curtis has to decide which is more important—his team or the win? **m/B VHS.** Richard Arlen, Peggy Shannon, Jack Oakie, Regis Toomey, George Barbier, J. Farrell MacDonald, George Irving; **D:** Norman Z. McLeod; **W:** Grover Jones, William Slavens McNutt.

Touched ♂♂ 1982 (R) Two young people struggle with the outside world after their escape from a mental institution. Although melodramatic and poorly scripted, the film is saved by fine performances by Hays and Beller. **89m/C VHS.** Robert Hays, Kathleen Beller, Ned Beatty, Gilbert Lewis; **D:** John Flynn.

Touched ♂♂ 2005 (R) A terrible car accident claims the life of Scott Davis' (Batinkoff) young son and leaves Scott in a coma for two years. He awakens in a long-term care facility under the supervision of nurse Angela Martin (Elfman). Scott's wealthy parents (Venora, Davidson) decide to bring him home but since it appears that Scott has lost his sense of touch and is suffering hallucinations, they hire Angela as a live-in nurse. Scott and Angela fall in love. It's not quite as sappy as it sounds and it's refreshing to see the sunny Elfman try her talents in a drama. **90m/C DVD.** Jenna Elfman, Randall Batinkoff, Samantha Mathis, Diane Venora, Frederick Koehler, Mina (Badiyi) Badie, Bruce Davidson; **D:** Timothy Scott Bogart; **W:** Timothy Scott Bogart; **C:** Irv Goodnoff. **VIDEO**

Touched by Love ♂♂½ 1980 (PG) *To Elvis, With Love* The true story of a handicapped child who begins to communicate when her teacher suggests she write to Elvis Presley. Sincere and well performed. **95m/C VHS.** Deborah Raffin, Diane Lane, Christina Raines, Clu Gulager, Diane Amos;

D: Gus Trikonis; **W:** Hesper Anderson; **M:** John Barry.

Touching Evil ♂♂♂ 1997 London police detective Dave Creegan (Green) and his fellow cops at the (fictional) Organized and Serial Crime Unit investigate three creepy cases in this three-tape series. The first concerns the kidnapping of three small boys; the second involves patients being drugged and killed while in hospital; and the third involves corpses. The detectives are a fine, flawed unit and make for some interesting company. Followed by two sequels. **360m/C VHS, GB** Robson Green, Ian McDiarmid, Nicola Walker, Michael Feast, Adam Kotz, Kenneth MacDonald, Antony Byrne, Shaun Dingwall; **D:** Julian Jarrold, Marc Munden; **W:** Paul Abbott, Russell T. Davies; **C:** David Odd; **M:** Adrian Johnston. **TV**

Touching the Void ♂♂♂ 2003 Documentarian Macdonald turns to reenactments to provide a dramatic narrative for this saga of two British climbers whose adventure in the Peruvian Andes in 1985 goes horribly wrong. Simpson (Mackey) and Yates (Aaron), both in their early twenties, decide to test their abilities on the previously unclimbed west face of Siula Grande. They make it to the top but are beset by a storm during their descent when Simpson breaks his leg. Yates attempts to lower his partner down the mountain but Simpson goes into a crevasse. Uncertain if Simpson is still alive, Yates must then decide whether to cut the rope binding them together and make his way alone back to base camp or risk dying himself. How they both survive constitutes the rest of this harrowing story of survival. Simpson and Yates provide their own narration; based on the book by Simpson. **106m/C VHS, DVD.** Brendan Mackey, Nicholas Aaron; **D:** Kevin MacDonald; **C:** Mike Eley; **M:** Alex Heffes.

Tough and Deadly ♂♂ 1994 (R) CIA agent teams up with bounty hunter to stop a drug ring. **92m/C VHS.** Richard Norton, James Karen, Charles Kahlenberg, Billy Blanks, Roddy Piper; **D:** Steve Cohen; **W:** Steve Cohen; **C:** James Roberson; **M:** William Kidd.

Tough Assignment ♂ 1949 A reporter in the West discovers and infiltrates a gang of organized rustlers who are forcing butchers to buy inferior meat. **64m/B VHS, DVD.** Donald (Don "Red") Barry, Marjorie Steele, Steve Brodie, Marc Lawrence, Ben Welden, Sid Melton, John Cason, Fred Kohler Jr., Michael Whalen, Stanley Price, Leander De Cordova, William Bradcow, Wilford Brimley, Bob Watson; **D:** Richard Fleischer.

Tough Enough ♂♂ 1983 (PG) A country-western singer and songwriter decides to finance his fledgling singing career by entering amateur boxing matches. Insipid and predictable, with fine cast wasted. **107m/C VHS, DVD.** Dennis Quaid, Charlene Watkins, Warren Oates, Pam Grier, Stan Shaw, Bruce McGill, Wilford Brimley, Bob Watson; **D:** Richard Fleischer.

Tough Guy ♂ 1953 Based on the play by Bruce Walker, a London hood carouses, mugs, breaks hearts and personifies his generation's anxiety. **73m/B VHS, GB** James Kenney, Hermione Gingold, Joan Collins; **D:** Lewis Gilbert.

Tough Guy ♂ *Kung Fu: The Head Crusher* 1970 Two undercover policemen battle local gangsters in a bid to smash their crime ring. **90m/C VHS, DVD.** Chen Ying, Charlie Chung; **D:** Chieng Hung.

Tough Guys ♂♂½ 1986 (PG) Two aging ex-cons, who staged America's last train robbery in 1961, try to come to terms with modern life after many years in prison. Amazed and hurt by the treatment of the elderly in the 1980s, frustrated with their inability to find something worthwhile to do, they begin to plan one last heist. Tailor-made for Lancaster and Douglas, who are wonderful. Script becomes clichéd at end. **103m/C VHS.** Burt Lancaster, Kirk Douglas, Charles Durning, Eli Wallach, Jake Steinfeld, Dana Carvey, Alexis Smith, Darlanne Fluegel, Billy Barty, Monty Ash; **D:** Jeff Kanew; **W:** James Orr, Jim Cruickshank; **M:** James Newton Howard.

Tough Guys Don't Dance ♂♂½ 1987 (R) Mailer directed this self-satiric mystery thriller from his own novel. A writer may have committed murder—but he can't remember. So he searches for the truth among various friends, enemies, lovers, and cohorts. Poor production all around. **110m/C VHS, DVD.** Ryan O'Neal, Isabella Rossellini, Wings Hauser, Debra Sandlund, John Bedford Lloyd, Lawrence Tierney, Clarence Williams III, Penn Jillette, Frances Fisher; **D:** Norman Mailer; **W:** Norman Mailer; **C:** John Bailey; **M:** Angelo Badalamenti. Golden Raspberries '87: Worst Director (Mailer).

Tough Kid ♂ 1939 A bad kid with gang connections attempts to shield his boxer brother from corruption at the hands of the same gang. Poor production all around. **61m/B VHS.** Frankie Darro, Dick Purcell, Judith Allen, Lillian Elliot; **D:** Howard Bretherton.

Tough to Handle ♂½ 1937 ...And no picnic to watch, either. A reporter cracks a criminal racket that rips off lottery sweepstakes winners. A laughably inept production. **58m/B VHS.** Frankie Darro, Kane Richmond, Phyllis Fraser, Harry Worth; **D:** S. Roy Luby.

Tougher Than Leather ♂ 1988 (R) The rap triumvirate battles criminals, vigilante-style, in their hood neighborhood. Poorly executed and exploitative fare. **92m/C VHS.** Run DMC, The Beastie Boys, Slick Rick, Richard Edson, Jenny Lumet; **D:** Rick Rubin.

Toughlove ♂ 1985 The parents of a juvenile delinquent organize a support group for other parents having a difficult time with their teens. **100m/C VHS.** Lee Remick, Bruce Dem, Piper Laurie, Louise Latham, Dana Elcar, Jason Patric, Eric Schiff, Dedee Pfeiffer; **D:** Glenn Jordan. **TV**

Touki Bouki ♂♂ *Journey of the Hyena* 1973 Feeling alienated from their African society, Mory and Anta see freedom in the flashy consumerism of European culture and embark on a quest to meet happiness in Paris. A Bonnie & Clyde-like story symbolizing Africa's advancement toward a technological civilization. In Wolof with English subtitles. **85m/C VHS, DVD.** Ter-ence Knox, Stephen Caffrey, Joshua Maurer, Ramon Franco; **D:** Bill W.L. Norton. **TV** Magaye Niang, Mareme Niange, Aminata Fall, Ousseynou Diop; **D:** Djibril Diop Mambety; **W:** Djibril Diop Mambety; **C:** Georges Bracher.

Tour of Duty ♂♂½ 1987 Follows the trials that the members of an American platoon face daily during the Vietnam war. Pilot for the TV series. **93m/C VHS, DVD.** Tanya Roberts, Chuck Connors, Robin Sherwood, Jocelyn Jones, Jon Van Ness, Dawn Jeffory, Keith McDermott; **D:** David Schmoeller; **W:** David Schmoeller; **C:** Nicholas Josef von Sternberg; **M:** Pino Donaggio.

Tourist Trap ♂♂½ 1979 (PG) While traveling through the desert, a couple's car has a flat. A woman's voice lures the man into an abandoned gas station, where he discovers that the voice belongs to a mannequin. Or is it? Not very interesting or suspenseful. **90m/C VHS, DVD.** Chuck Connors, Jon Van Ness, Dawn Jeffory, Keith McDermott; **D:** David Schmoeller; **W:** David Schmoeller; **C:** Nicholas Josef von Sternberg; **M:** Pino Donaggio.

Tournament ♂♂ 1998 *Le Tournoi dans la Cite* 1929 Renoir's second-to-last silent film, in which Protestants and Catholics joust out their differences in era of Catherine de Medici. **90m/B VHS.** *FR* Enrique Rivero, Suzanne Despress, Blanche Bernis, Gerard Mack, Jackie Monnier, Aldo Nadi; **D:** Jean Renoir; **W:** Jean Renoir.

Tous les Matins du Monde ♂♂ *All the Mornings of the World* 1992 Haunting tale of two 17th-century French baroque composers and their relationship with each other and their music. Gerard Depardieu plays Marin Marais

Toute Une Nuit 🐾🐾🐾 *All Night Long* 1982 Assorted people stumble melo-dramatically in and out of one another's lives on steamy summer night in Brussels. Fine combination of avant-garde tech-nique and narrative. In French with En-glish subtitles. 90m/C **VHS, DVD.** BE FR Aurora Clement, Tcheky Karyo, Veronique Silver, Angelo Abazoglou, Natalia Ackerman. **D:** Chantal Aker-man. **W:** Andre Akers.

Toward the Terra 🐾🐾 1980 In the distant future mankind is forced to evacuate Earth and settles on the planet Atarakusha. Society ruthlessly sup-presses anything which could destabilize the population's mistakes the mistakes which destroyed the Earth. The most des-perate presence is the MU, a new race with incredible mental powers, who are ruthlessly hunted and eliminated. But the leader of the MU reaches out to a human with his own inexplicable powers to aid in establishing a new world. In Japanese with subtitles. 112m/C **VHS. JP D:** Hideo Onchi; **M:** Masaru Sato; **V:** Toru Furuya, Yasuo Hisamitsu, Taro Shigaki, Masako Ikeda.

Tower of Evil WOOF! *Horror on Snape Island; Beyond the Fog* 1972 (R) Anthro-pologists and treasure hunters unite in search of Phoenician hoard on Snape Island. Suddenly, inanimate bodies mate-rialize. Seems the island's single inhabi-tant liked it quiet. Cult favorite despite uneven performances. So bad it's not bad. 86m/C **VHS, DVD.** GE Bryant Haliday, Jill Ha-worth, Jack Watson, Mark Edwards, George Coul-ouris; **D:** James O'Connolly; **W:** James O'Connolly; **C:** Desmond Dickinson; **M:** Kenneth V. Jones.

Tower of London 🐾🐾 1939 Tells the story of Richard III (Rath-bone), the English monarch who brutally executed the people who tried to get in his way to the throne. This melodrama was considered extremely graphic for its time, and some of the torture scenes had to be cut before it was released. 93m/B **VHS.** Basil Rathbone, Boris Karloff, Barbara O'Neil, Ian Hun-ter, Vincent Price, Nan Grey, John Sutton, Leo G. Carroll, Miles Mander. **D:** Rowland V. Lee; **W:** Robert Frank Skinner.

Tower of London 🐾🐾 1962 A deranged lord (Price) murdering his way to the throne of England is eventually crowned Richard III. Sophisticated and well-made Poe-like thriller. More interest-ing as historic melodrama than as horror film. A remake of the 1939 version starring Basil Rathbone, in which Price played a supporting role. 79m/B **VHS, DVD.** Vincent Price, Michael Pate, Joan Freeman, Robert Brown, Sandra Knight, Justice Watson; **D:** Roger Corman; **W:** Leo Gordon, F. Amos Powell, James B. Gor-don; **C:** Arch R. Dalzell; **M:** Michael Anderson.

Tower of Screaming Virgins 🐾 1968 The Queen of France maintains a tower in which she has her lovers killed—after she makes love to them. An extremely loose adaptation of a Dumas novel; with English subtitles. 89m/C **VHS.** GE Uschi Glas, Marie-Ange Aries, Terry Tor-day, Jean Pat; **D:** Franz Antel; **W:** Kurt Nachmann; **C:** Oberdan Troiani; **M:** Mario Migliardi.

Tower of Terror 🐾🐾½ 1942 (NC-17) Woman escapes from a German concen-tration camp and takes refuge in a light-house. The proprietor sees in her an un-canny resemblance to his late wife, whom

who eventually becomes a court compos-er at Versailles. As a young man, he stud-ies under Sainte Colombe, a private and soulful musician, about whom little is known even today. Depardieu's son Guil-laume (in his film debut) plays the young Marais, who startles the quiet Sainte Co-lombe home and has an affair with one of his daughters. Filmmaker Cor-neau lends a quiet austere tone which parallels the life and music of Sainte Co-lombe. In French with English subtitles. 114m/C **VHS, DVD. FR** Gerard Depardieu, Guil-laume Depardieu, Jean-Pierre Marielle, Anne Bro-chet, Caroline Sihol, Carole Richert, Violaine La-croix, Nadege Teron, Miriam Boyer, Michel Bou-quet, Myriam Boyer; **D:** Alain Corneau; **W:** Pascal Quignard, Alain Corneau; **C:** Yves Angelo; **M:** Jordi Savall, Cesar '92: Cinematog, Director (Corneau), Film, Support. Actress (Brochet), Score.

Tower of Terror 🐾🐾½ 1997 This Disney TV movie really isn't very scary and is related to the thrill ride located at Disney World. Disgraced reporter Buzzy (Guttenberg) and his niece (Dunst) investi-gate the 60-year-old child star in a suppos-edly haunted hotel. 89m/C **VHS, DVD.** Steve Guttenberg, Kirster Dunst, Nia Peeples; **D:** D.J. MacHale. **TV**

The Towering Inferno 🐾🐾 1974 (PG) Raging blaze engulfs the world's tallest skyscraper on the night of its glam-orous dedication ceremonies. Allen had invented the disaster the night of two years earlier with "The Poseidon Adven-ture." Features a new but equally note-worthy cast. "We May Never Love Like This Again." 165m/C **VHS. DVD.** Steve McQueen, Paul Newman, William Holden, Faye Dunaway, Fred Astaire, Jennifer Jones, Richard Chamberlain, Susan Blakely, O.J. Simpson, Rob-ert Vaughn, Robert Wagner; **D:** John Guillermin, Irwin Allen; **W:** Stirling Silliphant; **C:** Joseph Biroc; Fred W. Koenekamp; **M:** John Williams. Oscar's '74: Cinematog., Film Editing, Song ("We May Never Love Like This Again"); British Acad. '75: Support. Actor (Astaire); Golden Globes '75; Sup-port. Actor (Astaire).

Town and Country 🐾 2001 (R) Yep, it's as bad as you've heard. The oft-delayed and much-discussed romantic-comedy features characters you don't care about (rich Manhattanites with more money than they need) in situations that've been done to death (bed-hopping amidst middle age angst and closet-hid-ing). Shandling and Beatty are the cad husbands who decide to risk 25-year mar-riages in the name of fighting boredom. Keaton and Hawn are the revenge-fueled wives. All are upstaged by Heston and Seldes as the gun-toting, four-mouthed parents of one of Beatty's dalliances (McDowell). 104m/C **VHS, DVD.** US Warren Beatty, Diane Keaton, Goldie Hawn, Andie MacDo-well, Jenna Elfman, Garry Shandling, Charlton He-ston, Marian Seldes, Tricia Vessey, Josh Hartnett, Nastassia Kinski, Katharine Towne, Buck Henry; **D:** Peter Chelsom; **W:** Buck Henry, Michael Laugh-lin; **C:** William A. Fraker; **M:** Rolfe Kent.

A Town Called Hell 🐾 *A Town Called Bastard* 1972 (R) Two men hold an en-tire town hostage while looking for "Agui-la," the Mexican revolutionary. Greed, evil, and violence take over. Shot in Spain. Whatever you call it, just stay out of it. 95m/C **VHS, DVD.** GB SP Robert Shaw, Stella Stevens, Martin Landau, Telly Savalas, Fernando Rey; **D:** Robert Parrish.

A Town Has Turned to Dust 🐾½ 1998 Lame remake of a 1958 Rod Serling script for "Playhouse 90." Serling's story was set in the South-west; this version goes for sci-fi and a fu-turistic desert town called Carbon, run by mob boss Perlman who controls the water supply and the main industry, which is mining. But when Perlman hangs an inno-cent man, he finally provoking drunken sheriff Lang to take action. 91m/C **VHS, DVD.** Ron Perman, Stephen Lang, Gabriel Olds, Judy Collins; **W:** Roc Serling. CABLE

The Town Is Quiet 🐾🐾½ *La Vi-le Est Tranquille* 2000 This town isn't quiet at all. Michele (Ascaride) works in a Mar-seilles fish market and then returns to her dingy apartment to care for her junkie prostitute daughter and her own alco-holic husband (Banderel). Taxi driver Paul (Darroussin) pays Michele for sex so she can buy drugs for her daughter from her former lover Gerard (Meylan). There's several subplots, murders, and a suicide. Don't watch if you're prone to depression. French with subtitles. 132m/C **VHS, DVD. FR** Ariane Ascaride, Gerard Meylan, Jean-Pierre Dar-roussin, Julie-Marie Par-mentier, Pierre Banderel, Pascale Roberts, Jacques Piel-er, Christine Brucher, Alexandre Ogou; **D:** Robert Guediguian; **W:** Robert Guediguian, Jean-Louis Milesi; **C:** Bernard Cavalie.

he killed, and soon plots to do away with her. Story hampered by poor acting. 62m/B **VHS.** GB Wilfred Lawson, Movita, Michael Rennie, Morland Graham, John Longden, George Wood-bridge; **D:** Lawrence Huntington.

Town That Dreaded Sundown 🐾🐾 1976 (R) A mad kill-er is on the loose in a small Arkansas town. Based on a true story this famous 1946 murder spree remains an unsolved mystery. 90m/C **VHS.** Ben Johnson, Andrew Prine, Dawn Wells, Jimmy Clem, Charles B. Pierce; **D:** Charles B. Pierce; **W:** Earl E. Smith; **C:** Jim Roberson.

Town without Pity 🐾🐾½ *Stadt ohne Mitleid* 1961 Though the subject of this courtroom drama remains far too timely, its treatment is dated in some key scenes. Of course, being 40 years old and based on novel "The Verdict" by Gene Pitney his biggest hit with the Academy Award-nominated title song. 103m/B **VHS, DVD.** GE Kirk Douglas, E.G. Marshall, Robert (Bobby) Blake, Richard Jaeckel, Frank Sutton, Alan Gifford, Barbara Rutting, Christine Kaufman; **W:** Silvia Reinhardt, Georg Hurdalek; **C:** Kurt Hasse; **M:** Dimitri Tiom-kin. Golden Globes '61: Song ("Town without Pity").

The Toxic Avenger 🐾🐾½ 1986 (R) Tongue-in-cheek, cult fave has 98-pound weakling Melvin (Torgl) fall into barrel of toxic waste to emerge as Toxie (Cohen), a crime-fighting, bloodthirsty hulk of sludge and mire. He falls for blind babe Sara (Maran-da) and sets out to do good (and get re-venge). Set in the legendary city of Tro-maVille. Billed as "The first Super-Hero from New Jersey." Followed by: "The Tox-ic Avenger, Part 2," "The Toxic Avenger, Part 3: The Last Temptation of Toxie," and "Citizen Toxie: The Toxic Avenger, Part 4." 90m/C **VHS, DVD, UMD.** Mitchell Co-hen, Andree Maranda, Jennifer Baptist, Robert Prichard, Cindy Manion, Mark Torgl, David Weiss; **D:** Michael Herz, Lloyd Kaufman; **W:** Lloyd Kaufman; James London.

The Toxic Avenger, Part 2 🐾½ 1989 (R) Sequel to "Toxic Aven-ger." Hulky slimer targets Japanese cor-porations that built toxic chemical dump in TromaVille. Followed by "The Toxic Aven-ger, Part 3: The Last Temptation of Tox-ie." 90m/C **VHS, DVD.** Ron Fazio, Phoebe Leg-ere, Rick Collins, John Altamura, Rikiya Yasuoka, Lisa Gaye, Mayako Katsuragi; **D:** Michael Herz, Lloyd Kaufman; **W:** Lloyd Kaufman, Gay Parting-ton Terry; **C:** James London; **M:** Barrie Guard.

The Toxic Avenger, Part 3: The Last Temptation of Toxie 🐾½ 1989 (R) Unemployed su-perhero is tempted to sell out to greedy capitalists when his cutie Claire needs an eye operation. Also available in an unrat-ed version. 102m/C **VHS. DVD.** Ron Fazio, Phoebe Legere, John Altamura, Rick Collins, Lisa Gaye, Jessica Dublin; **D:** Michael Herz, Lloyd Kaufman; **W:** Gay Partington Terry, Lloyd Kauf-man; **C:** James London; **M:** Christopher DeMarco.

The Toy 🐾½ 1982 (PG) Fenniless reporter finds himself the new "toy" of the spoiled son of a multimillionaire oil man. Unfortunate casting of Pryor as the toy owned by Gleason, with heavy-handed lecturing about earning 'friends. Slow and terrible remake of the Pierre Richard com-edy "Le Jouet." 102m/C **VHS, DVD.** Richard Pryor, Jackie Gleason, Ned Beatty, Wilfred Hyde-White, Scott Schwartz; **D:** Richard Donner; **W:** Carol Sobieski; **C:** Laszlo Kovacs; **M:** Patrick Wil-liams.

A Town Like Alice 🐾🐾½ 1985 An Australian miniseries based on a novel by Nevil Shute. The story follows women prisoners of war during WWII. Jean Paget is a British prisoner in the camps of Mala-ya when she meets and falls in love with a fellow prisoner, the rugged Australian, Joe. Separated by their captors, they reunite years later and try to see if their love has survived. Remake of a 1951 film of the same name that is also known as "Rape of Malaya." 301m/C **VHS, DVD.** AU Bryan Brown, Helen Morse, Gordon Jackson; **D:** David Stevens. **TV**

Toy Soldiers 🐾🐾 1991 (R) This un-likely action tale stops short of being laughable but still has a fair share of sil-liness. South American narco-terrorists seize an exclusive boys school. The mis-chievous students turn their talent for practical jokes to resistance-fighting. Or-dinary but unaffected cameo. Based on a novel by William P. Kennedy. 104m/C **VHS, DVD.** Sean Astin, Wil Wheaton, Keith Coo-gan, Andrew Divoff, Denholm Elliott, Louis Gossett Jr., Shawn (Michael) Phelan; **Cameos:** Jerry Or-bach; **D:** Daniel Petrie Jr.; **W:** Daniel Petrie Jr.; **C:** Thomas Burstyn; **M:** Robert Folk.

Toy Soldiers 🐾🐾 1984 (R) A group of college students are held for ransom in a war-torn Central American country. When they escape, they join forces with a seasoned mercenary who leads them as a vigilante force. 85m/C **VHS, DVD.** Cleavon Lit-tle, Jason Miller, Tim Robbins, Tracy Scoggins; **D:** David Fisher.

Toy Story 🐾🐾🐾 1995 (G) First feature length, wholly computer animated film confirms what we suspected all along—toys do have lives of their own, along with a posse of his own. Buzz Rickles berating an actual hockey puck. Woody (Hanks), a favorite toy, presides over his fellow playthings in Andy's room. Enter new toy on the block, Buzz Ligh-tyear (Allen), a space ranger action figure who thinks he's real, Jealous Woody and his delusional, high-tech companion soon find themselves in the outside world, where they must join forces to survive. Furry, intelligent script and voice charac-terizations that many live-action movies could take lessons from. All this, and Don Rickles berating an actual hockey puck. 81m/C **VHS, DVD, UMD. D:** John Lasseter; **W:** Joss Wheaton, Joel Cohen, Alec Sokolow; **V:** Ran-dy Newman; **V:** Tom Hanks, Tim Allen, Annie Potts, John Ratzenberger, Wallace Shawn, Jim Varney, Don Rickles, John Morris, R. Lee Ermey, Laurie Metcalf, Erik von Detten. Natl. Film Reg. '05.

Toy Story 2 🐾🐾🐾 1999 (G) Woody is kidnapped by a greedy toy col-lector and finds out that he was the star of a popular '50s children's show (think How-dy Doody) with a posse of his own. Buzz and the other denizens of Andy's room set out to save him, and in the process meet up with Buzz's arch-nemesis Emperor Zurg. All of the original cast members re-turn to their now-classic characters, and tributes to other movies keep this install-ment just as entertaining for kids and adults as the original. This one actually has more depth than the first, dealing with issues such as mortality and the meaning of a toy's life. Watch for the outtakes reel while the final credits roll. 92m/C **VHS, DVD. D:** John Lasseter, Lee Unkrich, Ash Brannon; **W:** Andy Stanton; **M:** Randy Newman; **V:** Tom Hanks, Tim Allen, Joan Cusack, Don Rickles, John Ratzenberger, Annie Potts, Wayne Knight, Laurie Metcalf, Jim Varney, Estelle Harris, Kelsey Grammer, Wallace Shawn, John Morris, R. Lee Ermey, Jodi Benson, Jonathan Harris, Joe Ranft, Andrew Stanton, Robert Goulet. Golden Globes '00: Film—Mus./Comedy.

Toys 🐾½ 1992 (PG-13) Disappointingly earnest comedy about Leslie (Williams), the whimsical son of a toy manufacturer who must fight to keep the playful spirit of the factory alive after it passes into the hands of his deranged uncle (Gamcon). This uncle is a general who attempts to transform the factory into an armaments plant. Leslie receives assistance in this battle from his sister Alsatia (Cusack) and his cousin Patrick (L.L. Cool J). Flat char-acters; generally falls short of trying too hard to send a message to viewers about the folly of war. Does have extremely vivid and intriguing visuals and special effects. 121m/C **VHS, DVD.** Robin Williams, Joan Cusack, Michael Gambon, L.L. Cool J, Robin Wright Penn, Donald O'Connor; **D:** Barry Levinson; **W:** Valerie Curtin, Barry Levinson; **C:** Adam Greenberg.

Toys in the Attic 🐾🐾 1963 A man returns to his childhood home with his child bride, where they will live with his two impoverished, spinster sis-ters. Toned-down version of the Lillian Hellman play. 88m/B **VHS.** Dean Martin, Geral-dine Page, Yvette Mimieux, Wendy Hiller, Gene

Tierney, Nan Martin, Larry Gates, Frank Silvera; *D:* George Roy Hill; *W:* James Poe; *C:* Joseph Biroc.

Trace of Stones *Spur der Steine* 1966 Building construction foreman Hannes Balla benevolently rules over a mammoth building site where he's supported by his workers because things run smoothly. Until, that is, a young female engineer, Kati Klee, and the new Party Secretary Werner Horrath show up. Balla soon isn't the top man anymore and, what's worse, he finds himself in a romantic triangle with Kati and Horrath. Based on the novel by Erik Neutsch. German with subtitles. 138m/B VHS. *GE* Manfred Krug, Krystyna Stypulkowska, Eberhard Esche; *D:* Frank Beyer; *W:* Karl-Georg Egel; *C:* Gunter Marczinkowski.

Traces of Red *⁇* 1992 Set in affluent Palm Beach, and filled with dead bodies, colorful suspects, and red herrings. The complex plot, often so serious it's funny, leads viewers through a convoluted series of events. Cop Jack Dobson (Belushi) is found dead in the opening scene, in homage to "Sunset Boulevard," his corpse acts as the narrator, a vehicle which unfortunately doesn't work as well here. He promises to recount the events leading up to his death which circle around a series of murders, and the people in his life who are possible suspects. Although Belushi's performance is average, Goldwyn, as Dobson's partner, shows off the talent he displayed in "Ghost." 105m/C VHS, DVD. James Belushi, Lorraine Bracco, Tony Goldwyn, William Russ, Michelle Joyner, Joe Lisi, Jim Piddock; *D:* Andy Wolk; *W:* Jim Piddock; *C:* Tim Suhrstedt; *M:* Graeme Revell.

Track of the Moonbeast *⁇* 1976 An American Indian uses mythology to capture the Moonbeast, a lizard-like creature that is roaming the deserts of New Mexico. 90m/C VHS, DVD. Chase Cordell, Donna Leigh Drake; *D:* Richard Ashe.

Track of the Vampire *⁇½* *Blood Bath* 1966 Half an hour of leftover footage from a Yugoslavian vampire movie stuck into the story of a California painter who kills into the story of a California painter who kills his models. Gripping and atmospheric, but disjointed. 80m/B VHS, DVD. *YU* William Campbell, Jonathan Haze, Sid Haig, Marissa Mathes, Lori Saunders, Sandra Knight; *D:* Stephanie Rothman, Jack Hill.

Track 16 *⁇½* 2002 Paul, the lead singer of a small-town rock band, gets mistakenly mixed up in the investigation of a murdered woman. Now the real killer is out for Paul's blood. Not cool, especially when he's got a gig the next night! Dopey rock soundtrack goes great with a lot of dopey action, reaching its embarrassing (ahem) climax with a song called "Sex with Someone You Love," during, yup, a sex scene. Mini-budget thriller that looks and sounds more like a demo tape. 90m/C DVD. Billy Frank, Bobbi Ashton, Alan Pratt; *D:* Michael (Mick) McCleery; *W:* Michael (Mick) McCleery; *C:* Michael (Mick) McCleery; *M:* Billy Frank. VIDEO

Track 29 *⁇½* 1988 (R) A confusing black comedy about a lonely woman, her husband who has a model train fetish, and a stranger who claims to be her son. Filmed in North Carolina. 90m/C VHS. Theresa Russell, Gary Oldman, Christopher Lloyd, Colleen Camp, Sandra Bernhard, Seymour Cassel, Leon Rippy, Vance Colvig; *D:* Nicolas Roeg; *W:* Dennis Potter.

Tracked *⁇* *Dogboys* 1998 Prisoner Julian Taylor (Cain) is sent to the patrol-dog training detail and discovers that the twisted department head (Brown) "rents" out his dogs and prisoners to hunters who want human prey. Carrere is the beautiful D.A. who investigates the rash of inmate deaths and discovers Julian is the next quarry. 92m/C VHS. Bryan Brown, Dean Cain, Tia Carrere, Ken James, Von Flores, Richard Chevolleau, Sean McCann; *D:* Ken Russell; *W:* David Taylor; *C:* Jamie Thompson; *M:* John Altman. CABLE

The Tracker *⁇½* 1988 HBO western about a retired gunman/tracker who must again take up arms. His college-educated son joins him as he searches for a murdering religious fanatic. Fairly decent for the genre. 102m/C VHS, DVD. Kris Kristofferson, Scott Wilson, Mark Moses, David Huddleston, John Quade, Don Swayze, Brynn Thayer; *D:* John Guillermin; *M:* Sylvester Levay. CABLE

The Trackers *⁇* 1971 A frontier marshal searches for the people who kidnapped his daughter and killed his son. He is joined by a cocky black tracker as the rancher seeking revenge. 73m/C VHS. Sammy Davis Jr., Ernest Borgnine, Julie Adams, Connie Kreski, Jim Davis; *D:* Earl Bellamy. TV

Tracks *⁇½* 1976 (R) Vietnam veteran accompanies the body of a buddy on a long train ride home. He starts suffering flashbacks from the war and begins to think some of the passengers are out to get him. 90m/C VHS, DVD. Dennis Hopper, Dean Stockwell, Taryn Power, Zack Norman, Michael Emil, Barbara Flood; *D:* Henry Jaglom; *W:* Henry Jaglom; *C:* Paul Glickman.

Tracks *⁇½* 2005 (R) Dull prison flick based on a true story. Fifteen-year-old Peter Madigan and his buds get wasted along some New Jersey train tracks and come up with a dumb prank that results in the derailing of a commuter train, killing the conductor. Peter and his pals become the first juveniles in New Jersey history to be sentenced to an adult maximum security facility. Follows Peter's adjustment to prison life as corrections officer Clark (Ice-T) takes a concerned interest in the young man, although Peter stays a pretty unsympathetic character. 92m/C DVD. Ice-T, John Heard, Chris Gunn, Barbara Christie; *D:* Peter Wade; *W:* Peter Wade; *C:* Jesse Weathington. CABLE

Tracks of a Killer *⁇* 1995 (R) Hawker (Vacation) and Clair (LeBrock) Hawker are vacationing at their isolated winter retreat with corporate climber Patrick (Larsen) and his wife Bella (Taylor). When Bella is killed on David's snowmobile in an accident—that's-no-accident, it turns out Patrick is after David's company in the worst possible way. 100m/C VHS. Kelly Le Brock, James Brolin, Wolf Larson, Courtney Taylor, George Touliatos; *D:* Harvey Frost; *W:* Michael Cooney; *C:* Bruce Worrall; *M:* Barron Abramovitch.

Trade *⁇* 2007 (R) Truth-based expose of human slave trafficking is more lurid and sleazy than illuminating. Thirteen-year-old Adriana (Gaitan) is kidnapped and taken from Mexico to New Jersey to be sold into sex slavery on the internet. Her brother Jorge (Ramos) and investigator Ray (Kline) pursue, then infiltrate the operation. Director Kreuzpaintner cranks up every sleazy detail, dwelling extensively on the abuse heaped on Adriana and her fellow victims by cruel captor Manuelo (Perez). The result is more sensational than condemning, however, and it's topped off with a cop-out happy ending to make you feel less icky for watching it. 119m/C DVD. *US* Kevin Kline, Paulina Gaitan, Marco Perez; *D:* Marco Kreuzpaintner; *W:* Jose Rivera; *C:* Daniel Gottschalk; *M:* Jacobo Lieberman, Leonardo Heiblum.

Trade Off *⁇* 1995 (R) Beautiful, unhappily married Jackie (Russell) seduces equally miserable married businessman Thomas (Baldwin) and jokes about getting rid of their respective spouses. Then Thomas' wife is killed in a car crash and Thomas learns Jackie caused the "accident." He should have watched "Strangers on a Train" to see where trading murders can get you. 92m/C VHS. Theresa Russell, Adam Baldwin, Megan Gallagher, Barry Primus, Pat Skipper; *D:* Andrew Lane.

Trade Secrets *⁇* *Flagrant Desir* 1986 Special investigator Jerry Morrison is assigned to probe the mysterious death of an heiress to a wine fortune. His investigation leads to the secrets and private fantasies of the woman's family and friends. 91m/C VHS. Sam Waterston, Marisa Berenson, Lauren Hutton, Arielle Dombasle, Anne Roussel; *D:* Claude Faraldo; *W:* Claude Faraldo; *C:* Willy Kurant; *M:* Gabriel Yared. TV

Trader Horn *⁇½* 1931 Early talkie was the first Hollywood picture to be filmed in Africa. Carey and Renaldo are traders who tangle with a native tribe while searching for the long-lost daughter of a missionary, who turns out to be a tribal goddess. Based on a novel by Alfred Aloysius Horn and Ethelreda Lewis. Boring remake in 1973. 105m/B VHS. Harry Carey Sr., Duncan Renaldo, Edwina Booth, Sir C. Aubrey Smith, Mutia Omoolu, Olive Carey; *D:* Woodbridge S. Van Dyke; *W:* Cyril Hume, Richard Schayer, Dale Van Every, John Thomas "Jack" Neville; *C:* Clyde De Vinna.

Trader Tom of the China Seas *⁇* 1954 A young island trader and a shipwrecked beauty get involved in espionage while helping the UN to safeguard the Asian corridor. A 12-part serial on two cassettes. 167m/B VHS. Harry Lauter, Aline Towne, Lyle Talbot, Fred Graham; *D:* Franklin (Franklyn) Adreon; *W:* Ronald Davidson; *C:* Bud Thackery; *M:* R. Dale Butts.

Trading Favors *⁇* 1997 (R) Seductress Alex (Arquette) talks eager high-school student Lincoln (Gummersall) into giving her a ride, not knowing she's trying to escape from her violent boyfriend (Greene). But that's only the beginning of the trouble. 103m/C VHS. Rosanna Arquette, Devon Gummersall, George Dzundza, Peter Greene, Julie Ariola, Alanna Ubach, Jason Henvey, Craig Nigh, Mary Jo Catlett, Lin Shaye, Richard Riehle, William Frankfather, Frances Fisher, Chad Lowe; *D:* Sondra Locke; *W:* Timothy Albaugh, Tag Mendillo; *C:* Jerry Sidell; *M:* Jeff Rona.

Trading Hearts *⁇* 1987 (PG) Over-the-hill baseball player falls for an unsuccessful singer and single mom at a Florida training camp set in the 1950s. 88m/C VHS. Beverly D'Angelo, Raul Julia, Jenny Lewis, Parris Buckner, Robert Gwaltney; *D:* Neil Leifer; *W:* Frank Deford.

Trading Mom *⁇½* 1994 (PG) Harried single parent Spacek is erased from the lives of her three kids, who decide they want a parent who's more fun. So, thanks to some magic, they head off to the Mommy Mart to try out a trio of bizarre choices. This gives Spacek a chance at three more roles before the kids come to their senses. Based on "The Mommy Market" by Nancy Brelis; directorial debut for daughter Tia. 82m/C VHS. Sissy Spacek, Anna Chlumsky, Aaron Michael Metchik, Asher Metchik, Maureen Stapleton; *D:* Tia Brelis; *W:* Tia Brelis; *M:* David Kitay.

Trading Places *⁇½* 1983 (R) Two elderly businessmen wager that environment is more important than heredity in creating a successful life, using a rich nephew and an unemployed street hustler as guinea pigs. Curtis is winning as a hooker-with-a-heart-of-gold who helps the hapless Aykroyd. Oft-told tale succeeds thanks to strong cast. Murphy's second screen appearance. 118m/C VHS, DVD, Blu-ray Disc. Eddie Murphy, Dan Aykroyd, Jamie Lee Curtis, Ralph Bellamy, Don Ameche, Denholm Elliott, Paul Gleason, James Belushi, Al Franken, Tom Davis, Giancarlo Esposito, Kristin Holby, Stephen Stucker, Nicholas Guest, Robert Earl Jones, Bill Cobbs; *D:* John Landis; *W:* Herschel Weingrod, Timothy Harris; *M:* Elmer Bernstein. British Acad. '83: Support. Actor (Elliott), Support. Actress (Curtis).

Traffic *⁇½* 1971 Eccentric auto designer Monsieur Hulot tries to transport his latest contraption from Paris to Amsterdam for an international auto show. As usual, everything goes wrong. Tati's last feature film and his fifth to feature Hulot. French with subtitles. 89m/C VHS. *FR* Jacques Tati, Maria Kimberly, Marcel Fraval; *D:* Jacques Tati; *W:* Jacques Lagrange, Jacques Tati; *C:* Eddy van der Enden, Marcel Weiss; *M:* Charles Dumont.

Traffic *⁇⁇* 2000 (R) Based on the 1990 British miniseries "Traffik," Soderbergh's film about the drug trade: Supreme Court Justice Douglas is appointed as head of the National Drug Task Force but learns his own daughter is a heroin addict; San Diego socialite wife Zeta-Jones learns the drug trade when her drug lord hubby gets busted; and Mexican border cop Del Toro works on his power base. Soderbergh takes on a large, complex subject with a large, uniformly excellent cast. The outcomes of the various storylines may not end happily or neatly (just like in real life), but the characters and ideas are explored along the way, are compelling. 147m/C VHS, DVD, HD DVD. Michael Douglas, Catherine Zeta-Jones, Benicio Del Toro, Dennis Quaid, Benjamin Bratt, Albert Finney, Amy Irving, Don Cheadle, Luis Guzman, Steven Bauer, James Brolin, Erika Christensen, Clifton (Gonzalez) Collins Jr., Miguel Ferrer, Tomas Milian, D.W. Moffett, Marisol Padilla Sanchez, Peter Riegert, Jacob Vargas, Rena Sofer, Stacey Travis, Salma Hayek, Topher Grace, Beau Holden, Enrique Murciano, Jsu Garcia; *D:* Steven Soderbergh; *W:* Stephen Gaghan; *C:* Steven Soderbergh; *M:* Cliff Martinez. Oscars '00: Adapt. Screenplay, Director (Soderbergh), Film Editing, Support. Actor (Del Toro); British Acad. '00: Adapt. Screenplay, Support. Actor (Del Toro); Golden Globes '01: Screenplay, Support. Actor (Del Toro); L.A. Film Critics '00: Director (Soderbergh); Natl. Bd. of Review '00: Director (Soderbergh); N.Y. Film Critics '00: Director (Soderbergh); Film. Support. Actor (Del Toro); Natl. Soc. Film Critics '00: Director (Soderbergh), Support. Actor (Del Toro); Screen Actors Guild '00: Cast; Writers Guild '00: Adapt. Screenplay; Broadcast Film Critics '00: Adapt. Screenplay, Director (Soderbergh).

Traffic in Souls *⁇½* 1913 Silent melodrama dealing with white slavery. Immigrants and gullible country girls are lured into brothels where they are trapped with no hope of escape until, in a hail of bullets, the police raid the dens of vice and rescue them. 74m/B VHS. Matt Moore, Jane Gail, William Welsh; *D:* George Tucker. Natl. Film Reg. '06.

Traffic Jam *⁇½* *Jutai* 1991 A light comedy about a Japanese family's attempt to travel on a holiday weekend. Tokyo couple and their two young children decide to visit the husband's family who happen to live on a distant island. Naturally, traffic's horrendous, they have very little time, and things continuously go wrong. Japanese with subtitles. 108m/C VHS. *JP* Kenichi Hagiwara, Hitomi Kuroki, Ayako Takarada, Shingo Yazawa, Eiji Okada; *D:* Mitsuo Kurotsuchi.

Traffik *⁇⁇* 1990 A tense, unnerving look at the international world of heroin smuggling. The British drama follows the lives of three men involved in the drug trade: a farmer in the poppy fields of Pakistan, a drug smuggler in Hamburg, and a Tory cabinet minister who heads his government's anti-drug cabinet and then comes to realize his own daughter is an addict. The basis for Steven Soderbergh's much-lauded 2000 film "Traffic". 360m/C VHS, DVD. *GB* Lindsay Duncan, Bill Paterson, Jamal Shah, Talat Hussain, Fritz Muller-Scherz, Julia Ormond, Knut Hinz, Feryal Gauhar Shah, Peter Lakenmacher, Vincenzo Benestante; *D:* Alastair Reid; *W:* Simon Moore; *C:* Clive Tickner; *M:* Tim Souster. TV

The Tragedy of a Ridiculous Man *⁇* *La Tragedia di un Uomo Ridicolo* 1981 (PG) The missing son of an Italian cheese manufacturer may or may not have been kidnapped by terrorists. Lesser Bertolucci effort may or may not have a point. In Italian with English subtitles. 116m/C VHS, DVD. *IT* Ugo Tognazzi, Anouk Aimee, Victor Cavallo, Ricky Tognazzi, Laura Morante; *D:* Bernardo Bertolucci; *W:* Bernardo Bertolucci; *C:* Carlo Di Palma; *M:* Ennio Morricone. Cannes '81: Actor (Tognazzi).

Tragedy of Flight 103: The Inside Story *⁇* 1991 (PG) Dramatization of the events surrounding the destruction of Pan Am flight 103 over Lockerbie, Scotland, due to a terrorist-planted bomb. 89m/C VHS. Ned Beatty, Peter Boyle, Vincent Gardenia, Timothy West, Michael Wincott, Harry Ditson, Aharon Ipale, John Shrapnel; *D:* Leslie Woodhead.

Trahir *⁇* *Betrayal* 1993 In 1948 Romania journalist George Vlaicu (Leysen) writes a controversial article on the death of democracy in his country and is imprisoned for 11 years. In 1959 he's offered a deal, go free as long as he talks weekly to a police inspector (Repan). He begins a new career as a poet and marries his former typist, Laura (Perrier), but after a tragedy learns that his meetings with the inspector aren't as innocuous as they've

Trail Beyond 🐾½ **1934** A cowboy and his sidekick go on the trek to the northwest to find a girl and a gold mine. **57mB VHS, DVD.** *J:* John Wayne, Noah Beery Sr., Verna Hillie, Noah Beery Jr.; *D:* Robert North Bradbury; *W:* Lindsley Parsons; *C:* Archie Stout.

Trail Drive 🐾 **1933** Adventures of a cowboy during a big cattle drive. **53mB VHS.** Ken Maynard, Cecilia Parker, Jack Rockwell.

Trail of a Serial Killer 🐾🐾 **1998** *(R)* FBI agent Jason Enola (Penn) and detective Brad Abraham (Madsen) team up to find a serial killer leaving a trail of dismembered corpses. **95mC VHS, DVD.** Christopher Penn, Michael Madsen, Jennifer Dale, Chad McQueen; *D:* Damian Lee. **VIDEO**

Trail of Robin Hood 🐾🐾 **1950** Rogers sees an escaped convict to get Christmas trees, in spite of the fact that a big business wants to raise the prices. Features a number of western stars, including Holt playing himself. **67mC VHS, DVD.** Roy Rogers, Penny Edwards, Gordon Jones, Jack Holt, Clifton Young, Monte Hale, Allan "Rocky" Lane, Emory Parnell, Rex Allen, Kermit Maynard, Tom Keene, Ray Corrigan, William Farnum; *D:* William Witney.

Trail of Terror 🐾 **1935** G-Man poses as an escaped convict to get the goods on a gang. **60mB VHS, DVD.** Bob Steele, Beth Marion, Forrest Taylor, Charles "Blackie" King, Lloyd Ingraham, Charles French; *D:* Robert North Bradbury.

Trail of the Hawk 🐾 **1937** Saga of frontier justice and love on the plains. **50mB VHS.** Yancey Lane, Betty Jordan, Dick(ie) Jones; *D:* Edward Dmytryk.

The Trail of the Lonesome Pine 🐾🐾 **1936** The first outdoor film to be shot in three-color Technicolor. Two backwoods Kentucky clans, the Tolliver and the Falins, have been feuding so long no one remembers what started the fuss. But young engineer Jack Hale (MacMurray) gets stuck in the middle when he comes to build a railroad through the Blue Ridge Mountains. Hale saves the life of Dave Tolliver (Fonda) but Dave's not happy when the city slicker starts mooning over Dave's sister, June (Sidney). And the Falins aren't happy about the railroad, which leads to even more fighting. Based on the novel by John Fox Jr. and previously filmed in 1916 and 1923. **102mC VHS.** Henry Fonda, Fred MacMurray, Sylvia Sidney, Robert Barrat, Fred Stone, Nigel Bruce, Beulah Bondi, George "Sparky" McFarland, Fuzzy Knight; *D:* Henry Hathaway; *W:* Grover Jones, Horace McCoy, Harvey Thew; *C:* William Howard Greene, Robert C. Bruce.

Trail of the Mounties 🐾 **1947** A Mountie gallops smack into a murdering slew of fur thieves, which includes his ne'er-do-well twin brother. **41mB VHS.** Russell Hayden, Emmett Lynn, Terry Frost, Harry Cording, Jennifer Holt; *D:* Howard Bretherton; *W:* Betty Burbridge; *C:* Benjamin (Ben H.) Kline.

Trail of the Pink Panther 🐾🐾 **1982** *(PG)* The sixth in Sellers' "Pink Panther" series. Inspector Clouseau disappears while he is searching for the diamond known as the Pink Panther. Notable because it was released after Sellers' death, using clips from previous movies to fill in gaps. Followed by "Curse of the Pink Panther." **97mC VHS, DVD.** Peter Sellers, David Niven, Herbert Lom, Capucine, Burt Kwouk, Robert Wagner, Robert Loggia; *D:* Blake Edwards; *W:* Blake Edwards, Frank Waldman; *C:* Dick Bush; *M:* Henry Mancini.

Trail of the Silver Spurs 🐾½ **1941** A lone man remaining in a ghost town discovers gold and becomes rich. Part of the "Range Busters" series. **57mB**

seemed. Excellent performances and a cold look at how a police state is able to control its artists and writers. Filmed primarily in Romania. Director Mihaileanu's first feature film. French with subtitles. **104mC VHS, FR SI SP RO** Johan Leysen, Mireille Perrier, Alexandru Repan, Razvan Vasilescu, Maia Morgenstern, Radu Beligan; *D:* Radu Mihaileanu, Maia Morgenstern; *W:* Laurent Moussard, Radu Mihaileanu. **Tribeca Film Fest. '93; Actor.** [Istoile Popa, Montreal World Film Fest. '93; Actor (Leysen).]

Trail Riders 🐾½ **1942** The Range Busters set a trap to capture a gang of outlaws who killed the son of the town marshal during a bank robbery. Part of the "Range Busters" series. **55mB VHS, DVD.** John "Dusty" King, David Sharpe, Max Terhune, Evelyn Finley, Forrest Taylor, Charles "Blackie" King, Kermit Maynard; *D:* Robert Emmett Tansey; *W:* Frances Kavanaugh; *C:* Robert E. Cline.

Trail Street 🐾½ **1947** Scott is Bat Masterson, the western hero. He aids the struggle of Kansans as they conquer the land and local ranchers. **84mB VHS.** Randolph Scott, Robert Ryan, Anne Jeffreys, George "Gabby" Hayes, Madge Meredith, Jason Robards Sr.; *D:* Ray Enright.

Trail to San Antone 🐾½ **1947** Gene trades the prairie for the racetrack when he helps out an injured jockey, whom Autry wants to ride for him in the big race. **67mB VHS.** Gene Autry, Peggy Stewart, Sterling Holloway, William Henry; *D:* John English; *W:* Jack Natteford; *C:* William Bradford.

Trailer, the Movie 🐾🐾 **1999** Goofy experimental comedy combines elements of "Last Action Hero" and "Purple Rose of Cairo." In a black-and-white introduction, two lonely guys (McCrudden and Pope) sneak into a theatre one night and fall in love with two actresses (Hicks and Crigler) they see in a trailer. After the guys are tossed out, they wish their way into a color world where the rules of movies apply. Unfortunately, this well-meaning independent production lacks the wit to make full use of the engaging premise. **101mC DVD.** Ian McCrudden, Will Pope, Miranda Hicks, Marjorie Crigler; *D:* Ian McCrudden; *C:* Matthew Uhry.

Trailin' 🐾🐾 **1921** Mix stars as a cowboy in this portrayal of his parentage. Based on the Max Brand story. **58mB VHS.** Tom Mix, Eva Novak, James Gordon; *D:* Lynn F. Reynolds.

Trailing Double Trouble 🐾½ **1940** A corrupt attorney murders a rancher to pursue a business scheme. Three ranch hands kidnap the rancher's orphaned baby to keep her safe from the attorney. The second entry in the "Range Busters" series. **56mB VHS.** Ray Corrigan, John "Dusty" King, Max Terhune; *D:* S. Roy Luby; *W:* Oliver Drake; *C:* Edward Linden.

Trailing Trouble 🐾½ **1930** Gibson is a cowpoke who gets robbed of the money he received for a cattle sale. When he rescues a Chinese girl from danger she helps him recover the money. He also has to battle a rival for his girlfriend's affections. He should have battled for a better script. **58mB VHS.** Hoot Gibson, Olive Young, Margaret Quimby, Pete Morrison, William (Bill Billy) McCall; *D:* Arthur Rosson.

The Train 🐾🐾🐾 **1965** Le Train II Treno During the German occupation of Paris in 1944, a German colonel (Scofield) is ordered to ransack the city of its art treasures and put them on a train bound for Germany. Word gets to the French Resistance who then persuade the train inspector (Lancaster) to sabotage the train. A battle of wills ensues between Scofield and Lancaster as each becomes increasingly obsessed with outwitting the other—though the cost to all turns out to be as irreplaceable as the art itself. Filmed on location in France. Frankenheimer used real locomotives, rather than models, throughout the film, even in the spectacular crash sequences. **133mC VHS, DVD, FR** /T Burt Lancaster, Paul Scofield, Jeanne Moreau, Michel Simon, Suzanne Flon, Wolfgang Preiss, Albert Rémy, Charles Millot, Jacques Marin, Donald O'Brien, Jean-Pierre Zola, Arthur Brauss, Howard Vernon, Richard Munch, Paul Bonifas, Jean-Claude Bercq; *D:* John Frankenheimer; *W:* Franklin Coen; *C:* Jean Tournier, Walter Wottitz; *M:* Maurice Jarre.

The Train Killer 🐾 **1983** A mad Hungarian is bent on destroying the Orient Express. **90mC VHS.** Michael Sarrazin; *D:* Sandor Simo.

Train of Events 🐾🐾½ **1949** An interesting look at lives affected by a train wreck just outside London, taking the form of four short episodes. Three are fairly somber, depressing tales of the ill-fated train driver, a murderer and an escaped prisoner-of-war. The fourth segment is a refreshingly lighthearted piece about romantic jealousies in a traveling orchestra. A precursor to the later swarm of crass disaster movies, except here emphasis is on character over special effects. **89mB VHS.** Jack Warner, Gladys Henson, Susan Shaw, Patric Doonan, Miles Malleson, Leslie Phillips, Joan Dowling, Laurence Payne, Valerie Hobson, John Clements, Peter Finch, Mary Morris, Laurence Naismith, Michael Hordern; *D:* Sidney Cole, Basil Dearden, Charles Crichton.

Train of Life 🐾🐾 **1998** *Train de Vie* **(R)** Theatrical fable set in 1941 in a mountainous village shtetl near the Russian border. Schlomo the fool (Abelanski) tells the village elders that the Nazis are on their way. So the Rabbi (Harari) and the villagers decide to construct their own mock deportation train and make their way to Palestine. Mordechai (Rufus) plays the role of the Nazi commandant (a little too well), while the train begins to roll out, with any number of comic complications. French with subtitles. **103mC VHS, FR** Rufus, Clement Harari, Agathe de la Fontaine, Lionel Abelanski, Michel Muller; *D:* Radu Mihaileanu; *W:* Radu Mihaileanu; *C:* Yorgos Arvanitis, Laurent Dailland; *M:* Goran Bregovic.

Train Robbers 🐾🐾 **1973** *(PG)* A widow employs the services of three cowboys to help her recover some stolen gold in order to clear her late husband's name. At least that's what she says. **92mC VHS, DVD.** John Wayne, Ann-Margret, Rod Taylor, Ben Johnson, Christopher George, Ricardo Montalban, Bobby Vinton, Jerry Gatlin; *D:* Burt Kennedy; *W:* Burt Kennedy; *C:* William Clothier.

Train Station Pickups 🐾 **1977** Trashy film about young girls who hook at a local train depot, until something goes wrong. **96mC VHS.** Marco Kroger, Katja Carrol, Ingeborg Steinbach, Benjamin Canwath; *D:* Walter Boos.

Train to Hollywood 🐾🐾🐾 **1986** Marilyn Monroe-obsessed young Polish girl daydreams incessantly as she works on dining car. Funny and surreal. Polish dialogue with English subtitles. **96mC VHS.** Halina Gallova, Piotr Siwkiewicz, P.L. Kasa (Katarzyna) Figura, Piotr Siwkiewicz, Rafal Wegrzyniak, Grazyna Krukowna; *D:* Radoslaw Piwowarski; *W:* Radoslaw Piwowarski; *C:* Wieslaw Zdort; *M:* Jerzy Matula.

Train to Tombstone 🐾 **1950** A train running from Albuquerque to Tombstone carries a motley mob of the usual characters. **60mB VHS.** Don(ald) (Don "Red") Barry, Judith Allen, Robert Lowery, Tom Neal; *D:* William Beaudine.

Trained to Kill 🐾½ **1988** Two brothers seek revenge on the mean streets of L.A. **94mC VHS.** Frank Zagarino, Glen Eaton, Lisa Aliff, Marshall Teague, Robert ZDar, Henry Silva, Arnie Goionka, Fon O'Neal, Harold Diamond; *D:* H. Kaye Dyal; *W:* H. Kaye Dyal, Arthur Webb.

Trained to Kill, U.S.A. 🐾½ **2001** *(R)* **No Mercy Man 1975 (R)** Vietnam veteran relives his war experiences when a gang of terrorists threaten his hometown. **88mC VHS.** Stephen Sander, Heidi Vaughn, Rockne Tarkington, Richard X. Slattery; *D:* Daniel Vance; *W:* Daniel Vance; *D:* Dean Cundey.

Training Day 🐾🐾½ **2001** *(R)* Until the script finally goes completely off the rails, this cop corruption tale is worth watching for the ferocious performance of Washington alone. He's veteran undercover narc Alonzo Harris, who's been for so long, he's become morally bankrupt and works on the L.A. streets for so long, that might undermine whatever suspense that might have been. **89mC VHS.** Opposing him is rookie Jake Hoyt (Hawke), who first wants to be a part of Harris's team and then learns just what it will cost him. Fuqua shot on location so you can definitely feel the grit. **120mC VHS, Blu-ray Disc, UMD, HD DVD, US DVD.** Denzel Washington, Ethan Hawke, Scott Glenn, Clifford Curtis, Dr. Dre, Snoop Dogg, Tom Berenger, Harris Yulin, Raymond J. Barry, Charlotte Ayanna, Macy Gray, Eva Mendes, Nicholas Chinlund, Jaime Gomez, Raymond Cruz; *D:* Antoine Fuqua; *W:* David Ayer; *C:* Mauro Fiore; *M:* Mark Mancina. Oscars '01: Actor (Washington); L.A. Film Critics '01: Actor (Washington).

Trainspotting 🐾🐾🐾 **1995** *(R)* From the same team who offered the violently comedic "Shallow Grave," comes an equally destructive look at a group of Edinburgh junkies and losers. Heroin-user Mark Renton (McGregor) once again decides to sort it all out to do so he has to get away from his friends: knife-wielding psycho Begbie (Carlyle), Sick Boy (Miller), Spud (Bremner), and Tommy (McKidd). He heads for a semi-respectable life in London but Begbie and Spud wind up involving him in a serious money drug deal that spells trouble. Strong fantasy visuals depict drug highs and lows while heavy Scottish accents (and humor) may prove difficult. Based on the 1993 cut novel by Irvine Welsh. Film drew much controversy for supposedly being pro-heroin but the junkie's life is hardly portrayed as being attractive in any way. **94mC VHS, DVD, GB** Ewan McGregor, Ewen Bremner, Jonny Lee Miller, Robert Carlyle, Kevin McKidd, Kelly Macdonald, Shirley Henderson, Paulina Lynch, Peter Mullan, Keith Allen, Eileen Nicholas; *D:* Danny Boyle; *W:* John Hodge; *C:* Brian Tufano; *M:* Leftfield. British Acad. '95: Adapt. Screenplay.

The Traitor 🐾🐾½ **1936** Undercover man joins a gang of bandits. **57mB VHS, DVD.** Tim McCoy, Frances Grant, Frank Melton, Karl Hackett, Pedro Regas; *D:* Sam Newfield; *C:* Jack Greenhalgh.

Tramp at the Door 🐾🐾½ **1987** Delightful drama about a wandering, magical man who enters the lives of an embittered family. He helps them sort the shelters in their closets, and works wonders for them. **84mC VHS, DVD.** Ed McNamara, August Schellenberg, Monique Mercure, Eric Peterson; *D:* Allen Kroeker.

Tramp, Tramp, Tramp 🐾🐾½ **1926** Langdon's first feature-length comedy, produced by his own company, features the silent star as the hapless son of a shoemaker who is facing bankruptcy. (Wealthy rival shoe manufacturer John Burton (Davis) has offered substantial prize money for a coast-to-coast walking race and Harry is persuaded to enter the contest in order to save the family business. Naturally, there are many obstacles to overcome—he almost falls from a precipice, must escape from a chain gang and is nearly killed by a cyclone. The plot is merely a series of sketches but Langdon is cheery and fearless. Crawford has an early role as his girlfriend. Langdon used numerous (uncredited) gag men for his film, including Frank Capra. The DVD also includes the Langdon short, "All Night Long." **84mB VHS, DVD.** Harry Langdon, Joan Crawford, Alec B. Francis, Edwards Davis; *D:* Harry Edwards; *C:* Elgin Lessley.

Tramplers 🐾 **1966** A rebel father and son split over the hanging of a Yankee during the Civil War. Italian made spaghetti western without much plot and lots of gratuitous gunplay. **103mC VHS.** Joseph Cotten, Gordon Scott; *D:* Albert Band, Mario Sequi.

Trancers 🐾🐾 **1985** *Future Cop* **1984 (PG-13)** A time-traveling cult from the future goes back in time to 1985 to meddle with fate. Only Jack Deth, defender of justice, can save mankind. Low-budget "Blade Runner." Followed by two sequels. **76mC VHS, DVD.** Tim Thomerson, Helen Hunt, Art LaFleur, Telma Hopkins, Michael Stefcio, Helen Band; *W:* Danny Bilson.

Trancers 2 🐾½ **1990** *(R)* Retro cop is back from the future again, but seems to have lost his wit and nerve in between sequels. Ward is miscast and the pacing undermines whatever suspense that might have been. **85mC VHS.** Tim Thomerson, Helen Hunt, Megan Ward, Biff Manard, Martine Beswick, Jeffrey Combs, Barbara Crampton, Richard Lynch; *D:* Charles Band.

Trancers 3: Deth Lives 🐾½ **1992** *(R)* In the third film of the "Trancers" series, time-traveling cop Jack Deth fights the deadliest form of government-sponsored Trancer yet—it has a brain. **83mC VHS.** Tim Thomerson, Melanie Smith, Andrew

(Andy) Robinson, Tony Pierce, Dawn Ann Billings, Helen Hunt, Megan Ward, Stephen Macht, Telma Hopkins; **D:** C. Courtney Joyner; **W:** C. Courtney Joyner; **M:** Richard Band.

Trancers 4: Jack of Swords 🦴🦴½ 1993 (R) Time-traveling cop Jack Deth finds himself in a mystical new dimension where he enslaved the local population as feeders. If Jack expects to conquer he'll first need to survive an ancient wizard's prophecy of death. Filmed on location in Romania. 74m/C VHS. Tim Thomerson, Stacie Randall, Ty Miller, Terri Ivens, Mark Arnold, Clabe Hartley, Alan Oppenheimer, Stephen Macht, David Nutter; **W:** Peter David; **M:** Gary Fry.

Trancers 5: Sudden Deth 🦴🦴½ 1994 (R) Irreverant time-travelling cop Jack Deth (Thomerson) returns to help the Tunnel Rats occupy the castle of Caliban. But the evil Lord Caliban is resurrected and his only desire is to destroy Jack. This is supposedly the final chapter of Deth's saga. 73m/C VHS. Tim Thomerson, Stacie Randall, Ty Miller, Terri Ivens, Mark Arnold, Clabe Hartley, Alan Oppenheimer, Jeff Moldovan, Lochlyn Munro, Stephen Macht; **D:** David Nutter; **W:** Peter David; **M:** Gary Fry.

Transamerica 🦴🦴🦴 2005 (R) Bree (Huffman) is a transsexual formerly known as Stanley on the brink of completing her male to female transformation through gender reassignment surgery. (S)he lives in Los Angeles, but just prior to her long-awaited surgery she receives a call from New York street hustler Toby (Zegers). Toby is looking for Stanley, who, as a result of a brief affair with his late mother, he believes to be his father. Because her therapist insists she must come to terms with this before her surgery, Bree heads to New York. From this point the film becomes a funny and touching road trip flick, as Bree and Toby drive back to L.A. learning about each other. 104m/C DVD. US Felicity Huffman, Kevin Zegers, Fionnula Flanagan, Elizabeth Pena, Graham Greene, Burt Young, Carrie Preston; **D:** Duncan Tucker; **W:** Duncan Tucker; **C:** Stephen Kazmierski; **M:** David Mansfield. Golden Globes '06: Actress—Drama (Huffman); Ind. Spirit '06: Actress (Huffman), First Screenplay; Natl. Bd. of Review '05: Actress (Huffman).

Transatlantic Merry-Go-Round 🦴🦴 1934 An early semi-musical mystery about an eclectic assortment of passengers aboard a luxury liner. ♪It Was Sweet of You; Rock and Roll; Moon Over Monte Carlo; Oh Leo, It's Love; If I Had a Million Dollars. 94m/B VHS. Jack Benny, Nancy Carroll, Boswell Sisters, Ralph Morgan, Sidney Blackmer; **D:** Ben Stoloff.

Transfixed 🦴🦴½ Bad Genres; Mauvais Genres 2001 A whodunnit set in the seamy side of Brussels. Cross-dressing Bo (Stevenin) sees police inspector Paul Huysmans (Bohringer) arrest his father for pedophilia. Does this crime tie into a serial killer who's going after the local transvestites and prostitutes? Muddled wannabe Hitchcock, although Stevenin gives a stellar performance. Based on the novel "Transfixions" by Brigitte Aubert. French with subtitles. 109m/C DVD. BE FR Robinson Stevenin, Richard Bohringer, Micheline Presle, Stephane Metzger; **D:** Francis Girod; **W:** Francis Girod, Philippe Cougrand; **C:** Thierry Jault; **M:** Alexandre Desplat.

Transformations 🦴🦴½ 1988 (R) An interplanetary pilot battles a deadly virus that threatens life throughout the universe. Obscure space jetsam. 84m/C VHS. Rex Smith, Patrick Macnee, Lisa Langlois, Christopher Neame; **D:** Jay Kamen; **W:** Mitch Brian.

Transformers 🦴🦴 2007 (PG-13) The Autobots wage their battle to destroy the evil forces of... heck, if you were alive during the 1980s, you know how the song goes. Bombast specialist Bay brings the successful toy/TV show franchise to the big screen, with this tale of transforming robots from outer space whom travel to Earth in search of the mythical Allspark cube. There's lots of rock 'em-sock-'em action, but the whole movie isn't nearly as big, dumb, or fun as it should be, though LaBeouf's "boy and his robot" storyline is the best of the multiple plotlines. 140m/C DVD, HD DVD, Blu-ray Disc. US Shia LaBeouf, Megan Fox, Josh Duhamel, Tyrese Gibson, Anthony Anderson, John Turturro, Jon Voight, Rachael Taylor, Glenn Morshower, Bernie Mac, Amaury Nolasco, Kevin Dunn, Zack (Zach) Ward, Michael O'Neill, Julie White, Travis Van Winkle, Peter Jacobson, William Morgan Sheppard; **D:** Michael Bay; **V:** Peter Cullen, Hugo Weaving, Keith David, Robert Foxworth, Reno Wilson, Darius McCrary, Mark Ryan.

Transformers: The Movie 🦴 1986 (G) A full-length animated film featuring the universe-defending robots fighting the powers of evil. These robots began life as real toys, so there's some marketing going on. 85m/C VHS, DVD. **D:** Nelson Shin; **M:** Vince DiCola; **V:** Orson Welles, Eric Idle, Judd Nelson, Leonard Nimoy, Robert Stack.

Transmutations 🦴 Underworld 1985 (R) Mad scientist Elliott develops a mind-altering drug which is tested by a group of young people. They find out too late that the drug causes horrible facial disfigurement, as well as leaving them hopelessly addicted, and they hide out underground, plotting their revenge. Cowper, a young hooker in the group, turns out to be immune to the side effects and works with her ex-mobster boss to get help. Confusing. Barker co-scripted from one of his stories but later disowned the film. 103m/C VHS. GB Denholm Elliott, Steven Berkoff, Miranda Richardson, Nicola Cowper, Larry Lamb, Art Malik, Ingrid Pitt, Irina Brook, Paul Brown; **D:** George Pavlou; **W:** Clive Barker, James Caplin; **C:** Syd Macartney.

Transport from Paradise 🦴🦴½ Transport Z Raje 1965 Follows the story of Jewish life in the Terezin ghetto during World War II. Inhabitants are imprisoned and shipped off to Auschwitz as part of Hitler's final solution. Based on a novel by Arnold Lustig. In Czech with English subtitles. 93m/B VHS. CZ Zdenek Stepanek, Ilja Prachar, Jiri Vrstala, Cestmir Randa; **D:** Zbynek Brynych; **W:** Zbynek Brynych; **C:** Jan Curik; **M:** Jiri Sternwald.

The Transporter 🦴🦴 2002 (PG-13) Short on plot but long on action, this product of the Luc Besson action factory is yet another of the producer's efforts to bring kung-fu fightin' to France. Mercenary "delivery man" Frank Martin (Statham) lives by three simple rules: Never change the deal, never exchange names and never look in the package. When one of his packages starts squirming, however, he breaks one of his rules. He opens a duffel bag and discovers beautiful Taiwanese girl Lai (Qi Shu), who reveals a slave labor. This angers the bad guys, an evil American known as Wall Street (Schulze) and Lai's creepy father Kwai (Young). They send countless henchmen after the heroes, and Martin delivers large amounts of bullets and kicks to the head without once asking anyone to sign for them. Directed by veteran Hong Kong fight choreographer Corey Yuen. 92m/C VHS, DVD, UMD, Blu-ray Disc, UMD. Jason Statham, Shu Qi, Francois Berleand, Matt Schulze, Ric Young; **D:** Corey Yuen; **W:** Luc Besson, Robert Mark Kamen; **C:** Pierre Morel; **M:** Stanley Clarke.

Transporter 2 🦴🦴½ 2005 (PG-13) Second in what appears will be a series. This time Frank (Statham) is in Miami, working as a driver for one very wealthy family's young son, Jack (Clary). Jack is kidnapped in a sinister plot to bilk his parents out of beaucoup bucks. Powerful dad (Modine) and distraught mom (Valletta) are really just along for the ride. Even hard-core action fans might balk at some of the implausible scenes (one involving a jet ski on a highway is particularly goofy), though the commitment to jam-packing action into the film is impressive. Plot is eerily similar to "Man on Fire" although the execution is not. 88m/C DVD, Blu-ray Disc, UMD. US FR Jason Statham, Alessandro Gassman, Amber Valletta, Matthew Modine, Jason Flemyng, Keith David, Kate Nauta, Francois Berleand, Jeffrey Chase, Hunter Clary; **D:** Louis Leterrier; **W:** Luc Besson, Robert Mark Kamen; **C:** Mitchell Amundsen; **M:** Alexandre Azaria.

Transylvania 6-5000 🦴 1985 (PG) Agreeably stupid horror spoof about two klutzy reporters who stumble into modern-day Transylvania and encounter an array of comedic creatures. Shot in Yugoslavia. 93m/C VHS, DVD. Jeff Goldblum, Joseph Bologna, Ed Begley Jr., Carol Kane, John Byner, Geena Davis, Jeffrey Jones, Norman Fell, Michael Richards; **D:** Rudy DeLuca; **W:** Rudy DeLuca; **C:** Tomislav Pinter; **M:** Lee Holdridge.

Transylvania Twist 🦴🦴½ 1989 (PG-13) Moronic comedy about vampires, teenage vampire hunters and half-naked babes. 90m/C VHS, DVD. Robert Vaughn, Teri Copley, Steve Altman, Ace Mask, Angus Scrimm, Jay Robinson, Brinke Stevens; **D:** Jim Wynorski; **W:** R.J. Robertson.

The Trap 🦴🦴 1922 Chaney kidnaps the son of a man he's sent to prison on false charges. Rather than give up the kid when the man is released, he plans a trap. ?m/B VHS. Lon Chaney Sr., Alan Hale, Irene Rich; **D:** Robert Thornby; **W:** George C. Hall; **C:** Virgil Miller.

The Trap 🦴🦴½ The Baited Trap 1959 In trying to escape justice, a ruthless crime syndicate boss holds a small desert town in a grip of fear. 84m/C VHS. Richard Widmark, Tina Louise, Lee J. Cobb, Earl Holliman, Lorne Greene, Carl Benton Reid; **D:** Norman Panama; **W:** Norman Panama.

Trap 🦴🦴 L'Aventure Sauvage 1966 A trapper buys a mute girl as his wife. Together they try to make a life for themselves in the Canadian wilderness. Fine telling of interesting western tale. Unusual and realistic. 106m/C VHS. GB CA Rita Tushingham, Oliver Reed, Rex Sevenoaks; **D:** Sidney Hayers; **C:** Robert Krasker.

Trap on Cougar Mountain 🦴 1972 (G) A young boy begins a crusade to save his animal friends from the traps and bullets of hunters. 97m/C VHS. Eric Larsen, Keith Larsen, Karen Steele; **D:** Keith Larsen.

Trap Them & Kill Them 🦴 Emanuelle and the Last Cannibals; Emanuelle's Amazon Adventure; Emanuelle e Gli Ultimi Cannibali 1977 American group traveling through the Amazon jungle encounter a terrifying aborigine tribe. Point of trip undergoes considerable reexamination. 90m/C VHS, DVD. IT Laura Gemser, Gabriele Tinti, Nieves Navarro, Donald O'Brien, Monica Zanchi; **D:** Joe D'Amato; **W:** Joe D'Amato; **C:** Joe D'Amato; **M:** Nico Fidenco.

Trapeze 🦴🦴 1956 Lancaster is a former trapeze artist, now lame from a triple somersault accident. Curtis, the son of an old friend, wants Lancaster to teach him the routine. Lollobrigida, an aerial acrobat, is interested in both men. Exquisite European locations, fine camera work. The actors perform their own stunts. 105m/C VHS. Burt Lancaster, Tony Curtis, Gina Lollobrigida, Katy Jurado, Thomas Gomez; **D:** Carol Reed; **C:** Robert Krasker; **M:** Malcolm Arnold.

Trapped 🦴🦴½ 1949 Semi-documentary crime drama shows in semi-documentary style how the feds hunt down a gang of counterfeiters by springing one of their comrades from prison. Well-paced, suspenseful and believable. 78m/B VHS. Lloyd Bridges, Barbara Payton, John Hoyt, James Todd; **D:** Richard Fleischer.

Trapped 🦴🦴½ 1989 (R) A woman working late in her high-rise office is stalked by a killer and must rely on her ingenuity to outwit him. 93m/C VHS. Kathleen Quinlan, Bruce Abbott, Katy Boyer, Ben Loggins; **D:** Fred Walton. **CABLE**

Trapped 🦴🦴 24 Hours 2002 (R) Heavy on torture, light on revenge thriller tears a perfect family's lives apart when serial kidnappers snatch their only child. Trapped in different cities at the same time, parents Will (Townsend) and Karen (Theron) Jennings are at the mercy of extortionists Bacon, Love and Vince. Vince babysits the child; Love takes on the out-of-town Townsend; while Bacon terrorizes mom at their picturesque seaside home. To make matters worse, it is revealed the child is a severe asthmatic. Bacon's efforts to seduce Theron don't help matters. Overly sadistic, pointless, and painfully unwatchable despite slick production values and creepily winning performance by vet Bacon. Based upon Iles's novel "24 Hours." 105m/C VHS, DVD. US Stuart Townsend, Charlize Theron, Kevin Bacon, Courtney Love, Pruitt Taylor Vince, Dakota Fanning, Colleen Camp; **D:** Luis Mandoki; **W:** Greg Iles; **C:** Frederick Elmes, Piotr Sobocinski; **M:** John Ottman.

Trapped Alive 🦴½ 1993 Robin and Monica are abducted by three escaped convicts who want their car as a getaway vehicle. Trying to avoid a police roadblock the car crashes through the cover of a long-abandoned mine. When the group try to find their way out of the maze of tunnels they realize they're not down there alone. 92m/C VHS. Alex Kubik, Elizabeth Kent, Michael Nash, Randolph Powell, Mark Witsken, Sullivan Hester, Laura Kallison, Cameron Mitchell; **D:** Leszek Burzynski; **W:** Leszek Burzynski.

Trapped by the Mormons 🦴🦴 1922 Mormons seduce innocent young girls to add to their harems. The Mormon Peril An interesting piece of paranoid propaganda. Silent with original organ music. 97m/B VHS. Olive Sloane, Ward McAllister, Olaf Hytten, George Wynn, Evelyn Brent, Lewis Willoughby; **D:** H.B. Parkinson; **W:** Frank Miller.

Trapped in Paradise 🦴🦴 1994 (PG-13) Three bungling brothers make off with a bundle of cash from the Paradise—the town, not the afterlife—bank on Christmas Eve. The locals, naive refugees from a Rockwell painting, don't recognize the buffoons as criminals, and reward their crime with hospitality, that would make Frank Capra proud. Chase scenes and subplots abound as the boys spend what seems an eternity trying to make their getaway. Routine, humdrum comedy is hampered by an obvious plot. Watchable only because of Carvey, Lovitz, and Cage. 111m/C VHS, DVD. Nicolas Cage, Jon Lovitz, Dana Carvey, John Ashton, Madchen Amick, Donald Moffat, Richard Jenkins, Florence Stanley, Angela Paton, Vic Manni, Frank Pesce, Sean McCann, Kathryn Witt, Richard B. Shull; **D:** George Gallo; **W:** George Gallo; **M:** Robert Folk.

Trapped in Silence 🦴🦴 1986 Young Sutherland, abused since childhood, stops speaking to protect himself mentally and physically. Psychologist Mason is determined to break down the walls to help him confront his pain. Interesting cameo by Silver as a gay counselor forced out of his job when his sexual preference is discovered. Mildly melodramatic made-for-TV message drama. 94m/C VHS, DVD. Marsha Mason, Kiefer Sutherland, John Mahoney, Amy Wright; **Cameos:** Ron Silver; **D:** Michael Tuchner.

Trapped in Space 🦴½ 1994 (PG-13) On a mission to Venus a space shuttle is damaged by a meteor strike, leaving only enough oxygen for one person to rescue a young woman held captive by a backwoods clan. 98m/C VHS, DVD. Robert Estes, Bo Hopkins, Ernie Hudson, Betsy Russell, Don Swayze, Noah Blake; **D:** Worth Keeter; **M:** Russell V. Manzatt; **C:** Irl Dixon; **M:** Shuki Levy.

Trapper County War 🦴 1989 (R) A city boy and a Vietnam vet band together to rescue a young woman held captive

Traps 🦴🦴 1993 (R) Australian journalist Michael Duffield (Reynolds) and his English photographer wife Louise (Reeves) arrive for an assignment in 1950 French Indochina. Michael is to write about life on a French-owned rubber plantation, managed by Daniel (Frey), who lives with his rather peculiar daughter Violette (McKenzie). The plantation is troubled by the increasingly militant Viet-Minh rebels and it becomes clear that the four characters all have their own emotional difficulties to deal with, as well. Loosely adapted from the novel "Dreamhouse" by

Kate Grenville. Feature film directing debut for Chan. **95m/C VHS, AU** Saskia Reeves, Robert Reynolds, Sami Frey, Jacqueline McKenzie; **D:** Pauline Chan; **C:** Kevin Hayward; **M:** Douglas Stephen Rae.

Trash 🐾🐾 1970 Andy Warhol's profile of a depraved couple (Warhol-veteran Dallesandro and female impersonator Woodlawn) living in a lower east side basement and scouting the streets for food and drugs. Not for those easily offended by nymphomaniacs, junkies, lice, and the like; a must for fans of underground film and the cinema verité style. **110m/C VHS, DVD, AU** Dallesandro, Holly Woodlawn, Jane Forth, Michael Sklar, Geri Miller, Bruce Pecheur, Andrea Feldman; **D:** Paul Morrissey; **W:** Paul Morrissey; **C:** Paul Morrissey.

Travelling North 🐾🐾 1987 (PG-13) A belligerent retiree falls in love with a divorcee and they move together to a rustic retreat. They have an idyllic existence until the man discovers he has a serious heart condition. Adaptation of David William-

The Travelling Saleswoman 🐾½ 1950 Western comedy in which Mabel (Davis) becomes a travelling saleswoman for King Soap to help her father save the company from bankruptcy. But Mabel manages to get herself in trouble with rustlers and gunfights. **75m/B VHS, DVD,** Joan Davis, Andy Devine, Adele Jergens, Joseph (Joe) Sawyer, Dean Reisner, John Cason; **D:** Charles Reisner; **W:** Howard Dimsdale; **C:** George E. Diskant.

Traveller 🐾🐾🐾 1996 (R) Deriving its name from the real-life group of wily Irish-American con men who prowl the Southeast, this view into the lives and clannish ways of its members may have you check-ing that brand-spankin' new driveway sealant. Their basic philosophy is: if you're not one of us, we're allowed to take all of your money. Bokky (Paxton) is the jack-of-all-tricks who takes the younger Pat (Wahlberg) under his wing after the boy is shunned by the rest of the group. Pat's father married outside the clan, and that's not allowed. Bokky falls into the same trap, however, when a beautiful bartender (Marguiles), who he has just fleeced, steals his heart. Rather violent ending dims the good feeling that builds and may leave you feeling...well, cheated. Directorial debut of long-time Clint Eastwood cinematographer Jack Green, who also shot "Twister" with Paxton. **100m/C VHS, DVD,** Bill Paxton, Mark Wahlberg, Julianna Margulies, James Gammon, Luke Askew, Michael Shaner, Nikki Deloach, Danielle Wiener; **D:** Jack N. Green; **W:** Jim McGlynn; **C:** Jack N. Green; **M:** Andy Paley.

Traveling Companion 🐾🐾 Compagna di Viaggio 1996 Cora (Argento) is a somewhat unstable teenager who makes a living with a variety of jobs, including dog-walking. One of her clients, Ada (Cohen), hires Cora to follow Ada's elderly father, Cosimo (Piccoli). A retired professor, Cosimo has become forgetful and gets lost while wandering around Rome. When embarks on a series of encounters that lead to a journey of self-discovery. Italian with subtitles. **104m/C VHS, DVD, IT** Asia Argento, Miche Piccoli, Lino Capolicchio, Silvia Cohen, Max Malatesta; **D:** Peter Del Monte; **W:** Gloria Malatesta, Peter Del Monte, Claudia Sbarigia; **C:** Giuseppe Lanci; **M:** Dario Lucantoni.

Traveling Man 🐾🐾 1989 Drama about a veteran insurance salesman who's assigned an eager young apprentice when his sales go down. Littgow gives a great performance as the burnt-out travel-ing salesman. **105m/C VHS, DVD,** John Lithgow, Jonathan Silverman, Margaret Colin, John Glover; **D:** Irvin Kershner; **M:** Miles Goodman. **CABLE.**

Trauma 🐾½ 1962 A girl suffers amnesia after the trauma of witnessing her aunt's murder. She returns to the mansion years later to piece together what happened. A sometimes tedious psychological thriller. **93m/C VHS, DVD,** John Conte, Lynn Bari, Lorrie Richards, David Garner, Warren Kemmerling, William Bissell, Bond Blackman, William Justine; **D:** Robert M. Young.

Traveling Players 🐾 o Thiassos 1975 Slow-going for those unfamiliar with Greek myths and modern Greek history as the country is continually oppressed and betrayed. A travelling company of provincial actors ply their trade over some 16 years (1936-1952) while their country experiences the upheavals of a fascist dictatorship, WWII, occupation, civil war, and repression by the right-wing regime. The focus is on ordinary people in ordinary surroundings (with Angelopoulos leaning towards the communist sensibility). Greek with subtitles. **230m/C VHS, GR** Eva Kotamanidou, Maria Vassilou, Petros Zarkadis, Aliki Georgouli, Stratos Pahis; **D:** Theo Angelopoulos; **W:** Theo Angelopoulos; **C:** Yorgos Arvanitis; **M:** Loukianos Kilaidonis.

Travels with My Aunt 🐾🐾½ 1972 (PG) A banker leading a mundane life is taken on a wild, whirlwind tour of Europe by an eccentric woman claiming to be his aunt. Based on Graham Greene's best-selling novel. **109m/C VHS, GR** McCowen, Louis Gosset Jr., Robert Stephens, Cindy Williams; **D:** George Cukor; **W:** Jay Presson Allen. Oscars '72: Costume Des.

Traxx 🐾 1987 (R) Satire about an ex-cop soldier of fortune. Not surprisingly, Stevens doesn't do much with this lame script. **88m/C VHS,** Shadoe Stevens, Priscilla Barnes, Willard Pugh, John Hancock, Robert Davi, Rick Overton; **D:** Jerome Gary; **W:** Gary De V'ore; **M:** Jay Gruska.

Treacherous Crossing 🐾🐾 1992 (PG) When her husband disappears on their honeymoon cruise heiress Wagner is taken on a wild ride to help her. They think she's crazy, but aided by new friend Dickinson, Wagner intends to find out just what's going on. Based on the radio play "Cabin B-13" by John Dickson Carr. **88m/C VHS,** Lindsay Wagner, Angie Dickinson, Grant Show, Joseph Bottoms, Karen Medak, Charles Napier, Jeffrey DeMunn, Erik Avari; **D:** Tony Wharmby; **W:** Elisa Bell; **C:** Brian Avari; **M:** Curt Sobel.

Treasure Island 🐾🐾🐾½ 1934 Fleming's adaptation of Robert Louis Stevenson's 18th-century English pirate tale of Long John Silver is a classic. Beery is great as the pirate; Cooper has trouble playing the boy. Also available colorized. Multitudinous remakes. **102m/B VHS, DVD,** Wallace Beery, Jackie Cooper, Lionel Barrymore, Lewis Stone, Otto Kruger, Douglass Dumbrille, Charles "Chic" Sale, Nigel Bruce; **D:** Victor Fleming; **C:** Clyde De Vinna.

Treasure Island 🐾🐾½ 1950 (PG) Spine-tingling Robert Louis Stevenson tale of pirates and buried treasure, in which young cabin boy Jim Hawkins matches wits with Long John Silver. Some editions excise extra violence. Stevenson's ending is revised. Full Disney treatment, excellent casting. **96m/C VHS, DVD,** Bobby Driscoll, Robert Newton, Basil Sydney, Walter Fitzgerald, Denis O'Dea, Ralph Truman, Finlay Currie; **D:** Byron Haskin; **C:** Frederick A. (Freddie) Young.

Treasure Island 🐾🐾½ 1989 Excellent cable version of the classic Robert Louis Stevenson pirate tale with Heston as Long John Silver. Written, produced, and directed by Fraser Heston, son of and starring Charlton Heston. **131m/C VHS,** Charlton Heston, Christian Bale, Julian Glover, Richard Johnson, Oliver Reed, Christopher Lee, Clive Wood, Nicholas Amer, Michael Halsey; **D:** Fraser Heston; **W:** Fraser Heston. **CABLE.**

Treasure Island 🐾🐾 La Isla Del Tesoro 1972 (G) Unexceptional British reheat of familiar pirate tale. Welles' interpretation of Long John Silver. He encounters every obstacle in the West while on his way to obtain the Mexican rebel treasure. Instead, she finds love and mystery. **79m/B VHS, DVD, GP** Adele Jergens, Steve Brodie, Glenn Langan; **D:** William Berke.

Treasure of Pancho Villa 🐾½ 1955 An American adventurer plots a gold heist to help Villa's revolution. He encounters every obstacle in the South American jungles. Silly and unnecessarily violent. **96m/C VHS, DVD,** Rory Calhoun, Shelley Winters, Gilbert Roland; **D:** George Sherman.

Treasure Island 🐾½ 1999 (PG) Appropriately adventurous version of Robert L. Stevenson's often-filmed tale of young Jim Hawkins, who has a treasure map and a boatload of pirates eager for

Treasure Island 🐾🐾½ 1999 Near the end of WWII, two officers of the fiction-al intelligence compound called "Treasure Island" are given a dead body and a covert assignment: construct a fake "backstory." When dumped in the ocean, it's hoped that the false information will send the Japanese in the wrong direction. The two officers find themselves consumed by visions of the body, which seems to show coded messages, encrypted dialogue, and implied meanings. Certainly not for all audiences, but a funny and fascinating exercise in style and cinematic invention. **83m/B DVD,** Lance Baker, Axel Nilsson, Hjalmar Selander, Phillip Glaur; **D:** Scott King; **W:** Scott King; **C:** Scott King.

The Treasure of Bengal 🐾½ 1953 Sabu attempts to stop his chief from looting the village's precious gem (the largest ruby in the world) for firearms. **72m/C VHS,** Sabu; **D:** Gianni Vernuccio; **W:** Gian Paolo Callegari; **C:** Renaman Jr.

Treasure of Arne 🐾½ 1919 A 16th century Scottish mercenary kills and loots the estate of rich, well-to-do property owner Sir Arne. Famous early Swedish silent that established Stiller as a director. **78m/B VHS, DVD, SW** Erik Stocklassa, Bror Berger, Richard Lund, Axel Nilsson, Hjalmar Selander; **D:** Mauritz Stiller; **C:** Julius Jaenzon.

The Treasure of Jamaica Reef 🐾½ 1974 (PG) Adventurers battle sharks and other nasty fish as they seek a sunken Spanish galleon and its cache of golden treasure. **96m/C VHS, DVD,** Cheryl Ladd, Stephen Boyd, Roosevelt Grier, David Ladd, Darby Hinton; **D:** Virginia Lively Stone.

The Treasure of Matecumbe 🐾🐾 1976 (G) A motley crew of adventurers led a young boy search for buried treasure as they are pursued by Indians and other foes. Filmed in the Florida Key Islands. **107m/C VHS, DVD,** Vic Morrow; **D:** Vincent McEveety; **M:** Buddy (Norman Dale) Baker.

Treasure of Fear 🐾½ Scared Stiff 1945 A bungling newspaper reporter gets involved when four jade chessmen once owned by Kubla Khan. A few laughs in this contrived haunted house story. **66m/B VHS, DVD,** Jack Haley, Barton MacLane, Ann Savage, Vede Ann Borg, Arthur Aylesworth, Lucian Littlefield, George E. Stone, Paul Hurst, Frank McDonald; **W:** Maxwell Shane, Daniel Mainwaring; **C:** Fred H. Jackman Jr.

Treasure of Monte Cristo 🐾🐾 1950 A woman marries a seaman said to be an ancestor of the Count for his inheritance. Instead, she finds love and mystery. **79m/B VHS, DVD, GP** Adele Jergens, Steve Brodie, Glenn Langan; **D:** William Berke.

The Treasure of the Amazon 🐾½ El Tesoro del Amazones 1984 Three fortune hunters embark on a perilous search for wealth in the South American jungles. Silly and unnecessarily violent. **105m/C VHS, DVD, MX** Stuart Whitman, Donald Pleasence, Ann Sydney, Bradford Dillman, John Ireland; **D:** Rene Cardona Jr.

Treasure of the Four Crowns 🐾 1982 (PG) Aging history professor hires a team of tough commandos to recover four legendary crowns containing the source of mystical powers. The crowns are being held under heavy guard by a crazed cult leader. **97m/C VHS, SP** Tony Anthony, Ana (Ana Garcia) Obregon, Gene Quin-

the riches hidden on Treasure Island! Parlance is notably snarly as peg-legged Long John Silver. **95m/C VHS, DVD, CA** Jack Palance, Kevin Zegers, Patrick Bergin; **D:** Peter Rowe; **W:** Peter Rowe; **C:** Marc Charlebois.

Treasure of the Moon Goddess 🐾 1988 (R) A dizzy nightclub singer is mistaken by Central American pirates and natives for the earthly manifestation of their Moon Goddess. **90m/C VHS,** Don Calfa, Joern Ayres, Asher Brauner; **D:** Joseph Louis Agraz.

Treasure of the Sierra Madre 🐾🐾🐾🐾 1948 Three prospectors in search of gold in Mexico find suspicion, treachery and greed. Bogart is superbly believable as the paranoid, and ultimately homicidal, Fred C. Dobbs. Huston directed his father and wrote the screenplay, based on a B. Traven story. **126m/B VHS, DVD,** Humphrey Bogart, Walter Huston, Tim Holt, Bruce Bennett, Barton MacLane, Robert (Bobby) Blake, Alfonso Bedoya; **D:** John Huston; **W:** John Huston; **C:** Ted D. McCord; **M:** Max Steiner. Oscars '48: Director (Huston), Screenplay, Support. Actor (Huston); AFI '98: Top 100; Golden Globes '49: Director (Huston), Film—Drama, Support. Actor (Huston); Natl. Bd. of Review '48: Actor (Huston), Natl. Film Reg. '90; N.Y. Film Critics '48: Director (Huston), Film.

Treasure of the Yankee Zephyr 🐾🐾½ 2002 (PG) Race for the Yankee Zephyr 1983 (PG) Trio joins in the quest for a plane that has been missing for 40 years...with a cargo of $50 million. They have competition in the form of Peppard and cronies. Decent cast muddles through the predictable plotting. **108m/C VHS, DVD, AU NZ** Ken Wahl, George Peppard, Donald Pleasence, Lesley Ann Warren, Bruno Lawrence, Grant Tilly; **D:** David Hemmings; **M:** Brian May.

Treasure Planet 🐾🐾½ 2002 (PG) Futuristic fairy tale has pirate ships in space gracing this awkwardly mod animated update of Robert Louis Stevenson's classic "Treasure Island." Jim Hawkins (voiced by Gordon-Levitt, with singing voice of Rzeznik), the troubled teen hero, and a trio of irritating sidekicks take to the skies in their souped-up space galleon to find buried treasure on (where else?) Treasure Planet. Mutiny and other problems, including a looming black hole and space storms just as scary as the ones at sea, show up to threaten the mission. Innovative mix of hand drawn and computer animation is visually rich, even magical, at times but fails to fully delight. **95m/C VHS, DVD, US D:** John Musker, Ron Clements; **W:** James Newton Howard; **V:** Joseph Gordon-Levitt, Brian Murray, Emma Thompson, David Hyde Pierce, Michael Wincott, Martin Short, Laurie Metcalf, Patrick McGoohan, Roscoe Lee Browne, Corey Burton, Michael McShane, Dane A. Davis, Austin Majors; **Nar:** Tony Jay.

The Treasure Seekers 🐾 1979 Four rival divers set off on a perilous Caribbean expedition in search of the legendary treasure of Morgan the Pirate. **88m/C VHS,** Rod Taylor, Stuart Whitman, Elke Sommer, Keenan Wynn, Jeremy Kemp; **D:** Henry Levin; **W:** Rod Taylor; **C:** Joe Jackman; **M:** Bruno Nicolai.

The Treat 🐾½ 1998 (R) Smalltown prostitutes get invited to work the mayor's birthday party where a disaster leaves them struggling to get out alive. **87m/C VHS, DVD,** Julie Depp, Georgina Cates, Pamela Gidley, Daniel Baldwin, Patrick Dempsey, Seymour Cassel, Vincent Perez, Alfred Molina, Michael York, Yancy Butler, Mark Boone Jr., Richmond Arquette, Larry Drake; **D:** Jonathan Gems; **W:** Jonathan Gems; **C:** Joey Forsyte; **M:** Stephen Croes.

The Treatment 🐾🐾½ 2006 Slight romantic comedy set mainly in New York's Upper West Side finds angst-ridden English teacher Jake (Eigeman) trying to

tano; **D:** Ferdinando Baldi; **W:** Lloyd Battista, James Bryce; **M:** Ennio Morricone.

Treasure of the Golden Condor 🐾🐾½ 1953 A swashbuckler heads to the jungles of 18th-century Guatemala in search of ancient treasure. Contains interesting footage of Mayan ruins, but otherwise ordinary. A remake of "Son of Fury." **93m/C VHS,** Cornel Wilde, Constance Smith, Fay Wray, Anne Bancroft, Lee G. Carroll, Robert (Bobby) Blake; **D:** Delmer Daves.

Treasure of the Lost Desert 🐾½ 1983 A Green Beret crushes a terrorist detachment in the Middle East. **93m/C VHS,** Bruce Miller, Susan West, Larry Finch; **D:** Tony Zarindast.

deal with his romantic travails in his weekly sessions with demanding Freudian shrink, Dr. Morales (Holm). When Jake becomes interested in wealthy and recently widowed Allegra (Janssen), Morales encourages a fling but no deep involvement; advice Jake promptly ignores. A generally smart take on NY neuroses, with performances and a script to match. Adapted from Daniel Menaker's 1998 novel. **86m/C DVD. US** Christopher Eigeman, Famke Janssen, Harris Yulin, Stephanie March, Blair Brown, Roger Rees, Stephen Lang; **D:** Oren Rudavsky; **W:** Oren Rudavsky, Daniel Housman; **C:** Andrij Parekh; **M:** John Zorn.

A Tree Grows in Brooklyn 🎬🎬🎬½ 1945 (PG)
Sensitive young Irish lass growing up in turn-of-the-century Brooklyn tries to rise above her tenement existence. Based on the novel by Betty Smith. Kazan's directorial debut. **128m/B VHS, DVD.** Peggy Ann Garner, James Dunn, Dorothy McGuire, Joan Blondell, Lloyd Nolan, Ted Donaldson, James Gleason, John Alexander, Charles Halton; **D:** Elia Kazan; **C:** Leon Shamroy; **M:** Alfred Newman. Oscars '45: Support. Actor (Dunn).

The Tree of Wooden Clogs 🎬🎬🎬½ 1978 *L'Albero Degli Zoccoli*
Epic view of the lives of four peasant families working on an estate in turn of the century Northern Italy. The title comes from the shoes the peasants wear. When a young boy breaks a shoe, his father risks punishment by cutting down one of his landlord's trees to make a new pair of clogs. Slow moving and beautiful, from former industrial filmmaker Olmi. In Italian with English subtitles. **185m/C VHS, DVD. IT** Luigi Omaghi, Francesca Moriggi, Omar Brignoli, Antonio Ferrari; **D:** Ermanno Olmi; **W:** Ermanno Olmi. Cannes '78: Film; N.Y. Film Critics '79: Foreign Film.

Treehouse Hostage 🎬🎬 1999 (PG)
Timmy needs a reat current-events project if he doesn't want to get stuck in summer school. Fortunately, he and some friends manage to capture an escaped counterfeiter, Banks (Varney), and turn him in for a grade. Only it turns out that the school principal is actually the head of the counterfeiting ring. **90m/C VHS, DVD.** Jim Varney, Joey Zimmerman, Richard Kline, Todd Bosley, Mark Moses, Debbie Boone, Jack McGee, Aria Noelle Curzon, Vincent Schiavelli; **D:** Sean McNamara; **W:** Jeff Phillips; **C:** Mark Doering-Powell; **M:** John Coda.

Tree's Lounge 🎬🎬½ 1996 (R)
First time director/writer Buscemi takes a look at the downward spiraling life of Tommy Basilio (Buscemi), a working-class misfit who loses his job and then spends most of his time hanging out at the dreary local bar. He finally winds up driving an ice cream truck, only leading to more trouble when his teenaged helper, Debbie (Sevigny), develops a crush on him—a situation her hot-headed father Jerry (Baldwin) takes exception to. And the irresponsible Tommy is finally forced to realize that his ill-concerned actions have consequences. **94m/C VHS, DVD.** Steve Buscemi, Chloe Sevigny, Daniel Baldwin, Elizabeth Bracco, Anthony LaPaglia, Debi Mazar, Carol Kane, Seymour Cassel, Mark Boone Jr., Eszter Balint, Mimi Rogers, Kevin Corrigan, Samuel L. Jackson; **D:** Steve Buscemi; **W:** Steve Buscemi; **C:** Lisa Rinzler; **M:** Evan Lurie.

Tremors 🎬🎬½ 1989 (PG-13)
A tiny desert town is attacked by giant man-eating worm-creatures. Bacon and Ward are the handymen trying to save the town. Amusing, with good special effects. **96m/C VHS, DVD, HD DVD.** Kevin Bacon, Fred Ward, Finn Carter, Michael Gross, Reba McEntire, Bibi Besch, Bobby Jacoby, Charlotte Stewart, Victor Wong, Tony Genaros, Ariana Richards; **D:** Ron Underwood; **W:** S.S. Wilson, Brent Maddock; **M:** Alexander Grusynski; **M:** Ernest Troost.

Tremors 2: Aftershocks 🎬🎬 1996 (PG-13)
They're baaaaack! The Graboids have resurfaced to eat their way through Mexican oil fields and it's up to tough guys Earl Bassett (Ward) and Burt Gummer (Gross) to get rid of the toothy worms once and for all. Same mix of tongue-in-cheek humor and special effects as the first film. **100m/C VHS, DVD.** Fred Ward, Michael Gross, Helen Shaver, Christopher Gartin, Marcelo Tubert; **W:** S.S. Wilson; **M:**

Wilson, Brent Maddock; **C:** Virgil Harper; **M:** Jay Ferguson.

Tremors 3: Back to Perfection 🎬🎬 2001 (PG-13)
Gross returns to his hometown of Perfection, Nevada, and sees a cheesy theme park based on the real Graboids return to wreck havoc again. Then real Graboids return to wreck havoc again. **104m/C VHS, DVD.** Michael Gross, Charlotte Stewart, Shawn Christian, Ariana Richards, Susan Chung, Helen Shaver, Christopher Gartin; **D:** Brent Maddock; **W:** John Whelpley; **C:** Virgil Harper; **M:** Kevin Kiner. **VIDEO**

The Trench 🎬🎬½ 1999
A sober look at the two-day buildup to the catastrophic Battle of the Somme in 1916 from the point of view of teenaged British Army soldier Billy Macfarlane (Nicholls). His tough sargeant, Telford Winter (Craig), tries to prepare the raw recruits for battle as they hunker down in their damp, vermin-infested trench but nothing can prepare them for the senseless carnage to come. Familiar cliches abound but the performances are strong. **90m/C VHS, DVD.** GB Paul Nicholls, Daniel Craig, Julian Rhind-Tutt, Danny Dyer, James D'Arcy, Ciaran McMenamin, Tam Williams, Anthony Strachan; **D:** William Boyd; **W:** William Boyd; **C:** Tony Pierce-Roberts; **M:** Evelyn Glennie, Greg Malcangi.

Trenchcoat 🎬½ 1983
Aspiring mystery writer travels to Malta to research her new novel and is drawn into a real-life conspiracy. Silly and contrived spoof of the detective genre. **95m/C VHS.** Margot Kidder, Robert Hays; **D:** Michael Tuchner; **W:** Jeffrey Price, Peter S. Seaman; **M:** Charles Fox.

Trespass 🎬🎬 1992 (R) *Looters*
Violent crime tale set in East St. Louis, Illinois. Two redneck firemen learn of stolen gold artifacts supposedly hidden in an abandoned building and go on a treasure hunt. When they witness a murder they also get involved in a battle between two crime lords—who want these interlopers dead. What follows is a deadly game of cat-and-mouse. Lots of action but it's all fairly routine. Original release date of summer 1992 was delayed until the winter because of unfortunate similarities to the L.A. riots. **104m/C VHS, DVD.** Ice Cube, Ice-T, William Sadler, Bill Paxton, Art Evans; **D:** Walter Hill; **W:** Robert Zemeckis, Bob Gale; **C:** Lloyd Ahern II; **M:** Ry Cooder.

Trespasser 🎬🎬 1981
A painter has an affair with a young woman. He comes to regret destroying his family and their life together. Based on a D.H. Lawrence novel. **90m/C VHS.** GB Alan Bates, Dinah Stabb, Pauline Morgan, Margaret Whiting; **D:** Colin Gregg; **W:** Hugh Stoddart; **C:** John Metcalfe; **M:** Julian Dawson-Lyell.

Trespasses 🎬 1986 (R)
Couple of drifters wander into a Texas town where they rape a local woman and kill a local rancher's son. So the fathers of the victims decide to get revenge. Brutal and tedious. **90m/C VHS.** Lou Diamond Phillips, Robert Kuhn, Ben Johnson, Adam Roarke, Mary Pillot, Van Brooks; **D:** Adam Roarke, Lauren Bivens; **W:** Lou Diamond Phillips.

The Trial 🎬🎬🎬 1963 *Le Proces; Der Prozess; Il Processo*
Expressionistic Welles adaptation of classic Kafka novella about an innocent man accused, tried, and convicted of an unknown crime in an unnamed exaggeratedly bureaucratic country. Another Welles project that met with constant disaster in production, with many lapses in continuity. **118m/B VHS, DVD.** FR Anthony Perkins, Jeanne Moreau, Orson Welles, Romy Schneider, Akim Tamiroff, Elsa Martinelli; **D:** Orson Welles; **W:** Orson Welles; **C:** Edmond Richard; **M:** Jean Ledrut.

The Trial 🎬🎬 1993
Spare adaptation of Franz Kafka's novel finds Prague bank clerk Joseph K (MacLachlan) arrested on unknown charges. His increasing guilt and paranoia fit well into a world where the most illogical things happen in the most matter of fact way. Good visuals. **120m/C VHS, DVD.** Kyle MacLachlan, Anthony Hopkins, Jason Robards Jr., Polly Walker, Juliet Stevenson, Alfred Molina; **D:** David Hugh Jones; **W:** Harold Pinter; **C:** Phil Meheux; **M:** Carl Davis.

Trial & Error 🎬🎬½ 1962 *The Dock Brief*
Comedic satire, based on the play by John Mortimer, finds hapless lawyer Morgenhall (Sellers) thinking he's finally got his big chance when he defends wife murderer Fowle (Attenborough). Fowle wants to plead guilty but Morgenhall dreams of being a court star and insists on pleading his client innocent. It's a disaster just waiting to happen. **78m/B VHS, DVD.** GB Peter Sellers, Richard Attenborough, Beryl Reid, David Lodge, Frank Pettingell, Eric Woodburn; **D:** James Hill; **W:** Pierre Rouve; **C:** Edward Scaife; **M:** Ron Grainer.

Trial and Error 🎬🎬 1992
Peter Hudson (Matheson) is an overly zealous prosecutor who successfully convicts a small time criminal of murder, sending him to death row. This launches Hudson's political career and five years later he's about to be nominated for Lieutenant Governor, just as the felon's execution draws near. Suddenly, new evidence points to the man's innocence, but if Hudson investigates it could ruin his political future. But he's got a bigger problem—the real killer decides to make Hudson's wife his next victim. **91m/C VHS.** Tim Matheson, Helen Shaver, Sean McCann, Eugene Clark; **D:** Mark Sobel.

Trial and Error 🎬🎬½ 1996 (PG-13)
Courtroom comedy may remind you of another law oriented movie. No, not "Kramer vs. Kramer," It's "My Cousin Vinny," also directed by Lynn. Both feature fake lawyers defending hopeless clients in small towns. In this case, lawyer Charles Tuttle (Daniels) is too messed up from his bachelor party to make it to court for a case in which the defendant Benny (Tom), a relative of Chuck's big-wig future father-in-law, is accused of selling mail-order "commemorative copper Lincoln engravings" which are actually pennies. His best bud Richard (Richards), an actor, decides to stand in for him, and the legal slip-and-pratfalls ensue. Richards as the physical comedian and Daniels as the white bread straight man have great comic chemistry, but the plot won't surprise you much. **98m/C VHS, DVD.** Michael Richards, Jeff Daniels, Rip Torn, Charlize Theron, Jessica Steen, Austin Pendleton, Alexandra Wentworth, Lawrence Pressman, Dale Dye, Max Casella, Jennifer Coolidge; **D:** Jonathan Lynn; **W:** Sarah Bernstein, Gregory Bernstein; **C:** Gabriel Beristain; **M:** Phil Marshall.

Trial by Jury 🎬🎬½ 1994 (R)
Strong cast, lame script. Idealistic single mother Valerie Alston (Whalley-Kilmer) winds up on the jury trying notorious mobster Rusty Pirone (Assante). Rusty's henchman, Tommy Vesey (Hurt), lets Valerie know that her son is in mortal danger if she doesn't find his boss innocent. Of course DA Daniel Graham (Byrne) is equally adamant about a conviction and is willing to use Valerie any way he has to. **107m/C VHS, DVD.** Joanne Whalley, William Hurt, Gabriel Byrne, Armand Assante, Kathleen Quinlan, Stuart Whitman, Margaret Whitton, Ed Lauter, Joe Santos, Richard Portnow, Beau Starr, Mike Starr, John Capodice, Lisa Arrindell Anderson; **D:** Heywood Gould; **W:** Heywood Gould, Jordan Katz; **C:** Frederick Elmes; **M:** Terence Blanchard.

Trial by Media 🎬🎬½ 2000 *An American Daughter*
Lyssa Dent Hughes (Lahti) is a prominent D.C. doctor (and senator's daughter) who has been nominated to become surgeon general. But thanks to media scrutiny, and some careless remarks, she becomes a target and her nomination is in jeopardy. Wasserstein scripted from her 1997 play "American Daughter." **92m/C VHS, DVD.** Christine Lahti, Tom Skerritt, Jay Thomas, Mark Feuerstein, Lynne Thigpen, Stanley Anderson, Blake Lindsley; **D:** Sheldon Larry; **W:** Wendy Wasserstein; **C:** Albert J. Dunk; **M:** Phil Marshall. **CABLE**

The Trial of Billy Jack **WOOF!** 1974 (PG)
Billy Jack takes on the feds and beats the hell out of a lot of people to prove that the world can live in peace. Awful, pretentious film. **175m/C VHS, DVD.** Tom Laughlin, Delores Taylor, Victor Izay, Teresa Laughlin, William Wellman Jr., Russell Lane, Michelle Wilson, Geo Ann Sosa, George Aguilar, Sacheen Little Feather; **D:** Frank Laughlin, Tom Laughlin; **W:** Tom Laughlin, Delores Taylor; **C:** Jack Marta; **M:** Elmer Bernstein.

The Trial of Lee Harvey Oswald 🎬🎬 1977
What would've happened if Jack Ruby had not shot Oswald. Oswald's trial and its likely results are painstakingly created. **192m/C VHS, DVD.** Ben Gazzara, Lorne Greene, John Pleshette, Lawrence Pressman; **D:** Gordon Davidson. **TV**

The Trial of Old Drum 🎬🎬½ 2000 (PG)
Set in 1955 and based on a true story. 11-year-old Charlie (Edner) lives in a small farming community with his widowed father Charles (Perlman). His best friend is his golden retriever Drum, who was trained by his late mother to protect the boy. The duo's problems lie with his surly maternal Uncle Lon (Schuck), who dislikes the dog and says Drum is a sheep-killer. Lon shoots the dog for being on his property and the sheriff sends poor Drum to the pound before his case goes to court. Charlie and his father enlist the services of lawyer George Graham Vest (Bakula) and Drum's trial is both humorous and touching. **88m/C VHS, DVD.** Bobby Edner, Ron Perlman, John Schuck, Scott Bakula, Randy Travis, David Graf, Dick Martin, Alia Shawkat; **D:** Sean McNamara; **W:** Ralph Gaby Wilson; **C:** Mark Doering-Powell.

The Trial of the Catonsville Nine 🎬🎬½ 1972 (PG)
Riveting political drama that focuses on the trial of nine anti-war activists, including Father Daniel Berrigan, during the Vietnam War days of the late 1960s. Imperfect, but involving. **85m/C VHS,** Ed Flanders, Douglas Watson, William Schallert, Peter Strauss, Richard Jordan; **D:** Gordon Davidson.

The Trial of the Incredible Hulk 🎬🎬 1989
The Hulk returns to battle organized crime and is aided by his blind superhero/lawyer friend Daredevil. Followed by "The Death of the Incredible Hulk." **96m/C VHS, DVD.** Bill Bixby, Lou Ferrigno, Rex Smith, John Rhys-Davies, Marta DuBois, Nancy Everhard, Nicholas Hormann; **D:** Bill Bixby. **TV**

The Trials of Oscar Wilde 🎬🎬 1960 *The Man with the Green Carnation; The Green Carnation*
Finch is the highlight as playwright/wit Wilde, who illadvisedly sues the Marquis of Queensbury (Jeffries) for libel when the peer accuses him of being a sodomite. Wilde is, in fact, having an affair with the Marquis's son, Lord Alfred Douglas (Fraser), which eventually leads to Wilde's imprisonment and the destruction of his life. Based on the play "The Stringed Lute" by John Furnell and the book "The Trials of Oscar Wilde" by Montgomery Hyde. **123m/C VHS.** GB Peter Finch, John Fraser, Lionel Jeffries, Nigel Patrick, James Mason, Yvonne Mitchell, Maxine Audley, James Booth, Paul Rogers, Ian Fleming, Laurence Naismith; **D:** Ken Hughes; **W:** Ken Hughes; **C:** Ted Moore; **M:** Ronald Goodwin.

The Triangle 🎬🎬½ 2001
This triangle is the Bermuda kind as friends charter a boat for their annual Caribbean fishing trip and instead discover the Queen of Scots, a ghostly luxury liner that has been missing for 60 years. Boarding the ship turns out to be a big mistake since the tragedy that overtook the lives of the passengers and crew lingers and begins to affect the present. **92m/C VHS, DVD.** Luke Perry, Dan Cortese, Olivia D'Abo, Dorian Harewood, Polly Shannon, David Hewlett; **D:** Lewis Teague; **W:** Ted Humphrey; **C:** Ric Waite; **M:** Lawrence Shragge. **CABLE**

The Triangle Factory Fire Scandal 🎬🎬 1979
Based on the true-life Triangle fire at the turn of the century. The fire killed 145 garment workers and drastically changed industrial fire and safety codes. **100m/C VHS, DVD.** Tom Bosley, David Dukes, Tovah Feldshuh, Janet Margolin, Stephanie Zimbalist, Lauren Frost, Stacey Nelkin, Ted Wass, Charlotte Rae, Milton Selzer, Valerie Landsburg; **D:** Mel Stuart. **TV**

Tribes 🎬🎬½ 1970
When a hippie is drafted into the Marines, despite the furious efforts of his drill sergeant, he refuses to conform to military life. Soon his boot-camp mates are trying his methods of defiance and survival. Well-made mix of comedy and social commentary. **90m/C VHS.** Jan-Michael

Vincent., Darren McGavin, Earl Holliman: **D:** Joseph Sargent. **TV**

Tribulation ♂ 2000 Police detective er accomplice search for husband's murderer. Racy **TV** fodder. 100m/C VHS, Cindy Williams, Markie Post, Chris Mulkey, James Whitmore Jr., J. Scott Paulin, John Ritter Apollonia: **D:** Jack Bender. **TV**

Tribute to a Bad Man ♂♂♂ 1956 Hard-nosed rancher Cagney will stop at nothing to retain his worldly possessions in this 1870s Colorado territory western. His ruthless behavior drives girlfriend Papas into the arms of hired hand Dubins. Spencer Tracy and Grace Kelly were originally cast for the roles of Jeremy Rodock and Jocasta Constantine, but Kelly backed out and Tracy was fired due to differences with director Wise. Based on the short story by Jack Schaefer. 95m/C VHS. James Cagney, Don Dubbins, Stephen McNally, Irene Papas, Vic Morrow, Royal Dano, Lee Van Cleef, James J. Griffith, Onslow Stevens, James Bell, Jeanette Nolan; **D:** Robert Wise. **W:** Michael Blankfort.

Trick ♂♂ 1999 (R) Cheery gay romantic comedy. Quiet Gabriel (Campbell) is a struggling Broadway composer with a humdrug straight roommate (Beyer) who is constantly taking over their apartment for his one-nighters (and locking Gabe out). Which leaves Gabriel in a dilemma when he meets hunky go-go boy, Mark (P'tiok), and the duo can't find a place to be alone. But as the night wears on, they discover that lust may be taking a backseat to some deeper feelings. Sweet but also quite scary. 97m/C VHS, DVD, Tori Spelling, Brad Beyer, Christian Campbell, John Paul (J.P.) Pitoc, Steve Hayes; **D:** Jim Fall; **M:** Jason Schafer. **C:** Terry Stacey;

Trick or Treat ♂♂½ 1986 (R) A high school student is helped to exact violent revenge against his bullying contemporaries. His helper is the spirit of a violent heavy metal rock star who he raises from the dead. Sometimes clever, not terribly scary. 97m/C VHS, DVD, Tony Fields, Marc Price, Ozzy Osbourne, Gene Simmons, Elaine Joyce, Glenn Morgan, Lisa Orgolini, Doug Savant; **D:** Charles Martin Smith; **W:** Joe Soisson, Michael S. Murphy, Rhet Topham; **C:** Robert Elswit.

Trick or Treats WOOF! 1982 (R) Young boy's pranks on his terrified babysitter backfire on Halloween night. His deranged father, escaped from an asylum, shows up to help him "scare" her. Giroux doesn't look very frightened in this extremely tedious film from Welles' best camera man. 90m/C VHS, Carrie Snodgress, David Carradine, Jackie Giroux, Steve Railsback, Chris Graver, Peter Jason, Jillian Kesner, Paul Bartel. **D:** Gary Graver.

Tricks ♂♂ 1997 (R) Once a Las Vegas showgirl, Jackie (Rogers) is now a gift shop clerk in Reno, making some extra dough by turning tricks at night. After being beaten by a john, Jackie loses her job and has trouble finding work. Her roommate Sarah (Daly) introduces her to old-time gangster Big Sam (Walston), who often tries to help her get even with the guys who beat her but it's not that easy. 96m/C VHS. Mimi Rogers, Tyne Daly, Ray Walston, Callum Keith Rennie, Kevin McNulty; **D:** Kenneth Fink; **W:** Deborah Amelon. **CABLE**

Tricheurs ♂♂ Cheaters 1984 Scam artists hit largest casino in the world and look forward to golden years of retirement. From the director of "Reversal of Fortune." In French with English subtitles. 94m/C VHS. **FR** Jacques Dutronc, Bulle Ogier, Kurt Raab, Virgilio Taixeira, Steve Baes; **D:** Barbet Schroeder.

Trident Force ♂ 1988 International counter-terrorism team is ordered to destroy the Palestinian Revolutionary Legion by any means possible. 90m/C VHS, Anthony Alonzo, Mark Gil, Nanna Anderson, Steve Rogers.

The Trigger Effect ♂♂½ 1996 (R) Nightmare in yuppiedom when a suspicious electromagnetic pulse knocks out all electrical power, telephone and broadcast signals for hundreds of miles around a tranquil southern California community, which becomes increasingly unsettled. Matt (MacLachlan), wife Annie (Shue), and friend Joe (Mulroney) hang out together during the mystery power outage with lots of mounting tension both within and without. Film, however dread-producing, doesn't really make that much sense. Based on a knowingly cool story but isn't Vic's about to get out of the loony bin and hes informed his enforcer, Ben London (Byrne), to get rid of his rivals and disloyal fellow mobsters in time for his return. Meanwhile, his chief of staff, Mickey (Goldblum), has been romancing both Vic's gal Grace (Lane) and her jealous older sister, Rita (Barkin). This situation does not make Vic happy. The movie won't make you happy either. 93m/C VHS, DVD, Richard Dreyfuss, Gabriel Byrne, Jeff Goldblum, Diane Lane, Ellen Barkin, Gregory Hines, Kyle MacLachlan, Larry Bishop, Burt Reynolds, Henry Silva, **Cameos:** Joey Bishop, Angie Everhart, Michael J. Pollard, Richard Pryor, Rob Reiner, Billy Idol; **D:** Larry Bishop; **W:** Larry Bishop; **C:** Frank Byers; **M:** Earl Rose.

Trigger, Jr. ♂♂½ 1950 Rogers and his Western Show find themselves in the middle of a dispute between intimidated ranchers and an evil local range patrol office. When Trigger is injured by a killer stallion, Roy turns to two unlikely allies—a 10-year-old boy who's scared of horses and frisky Trigger Jr. 67m/B VHS, DVD, Roy Rogers, Dale Evans, Grant Withers, Pat Brady, Gordon Jones, Peter Miles, George Cleveland; **D:** William Witney; **W:** Gerald Geraghty.

Trigger Men ♂½ Billy the Kid's Fighting Pals 1941 Steele, Young, and St. John ambushed by the villainous Peil. Seems Peil and his gang have taken over a small border town in order to set up a smuggling operation with Mexico. So the trio avenge the marshal by putting a stop to the nefarious doings. Newfield directed under the pseudonym Sherman Scott. 59m/B VHS, Bob Steele, Al "Fuzzy" St. John, Carleton Young, Edward Peil Sr., Phyllis Adair, Charles "Blackie" King, Curley Dresden, Hal Price, George Cheseboro, Forrest Taylor, Budd Buster; **D:** Sam Newfield.

Trigger Pals ♂½ 1939 Jarrett stars in this basic oater about bringing a gang of rustlers to justice. Besides the usual gunplay, he also attempts to sing a few songs. 58m/B VHS, Art Jarrett, Lee Powell, Al "Fuzzy" St. John, Dorothy Fay, Charles "Black-ie" King, Frank LaRue; **D:** Sam Newfield.

Trigger Tricks ♂½ 1930 Gibson's brother becomes the victim of a vicious cattleman and Hoot is cut for revenge. 60m/B VHS, Hoot Gibson, Sally Eilers, Neal Hart, Monte Montague, Pete Morrison, Robert E. Homans, Jack (H.) Richardson; **D:** B. Reeves Eason.

The Trigger Trio ♂♂ 1937 Rancher with diseased cattle kills a ranch inspector. The Three Mesquiteers are called in to crack the case. 54m/B VHS, Ray Corrigan, Max Terhune, Ralph Byrd, Robert Warwick, Cornelius Keefe, Wally Wales; **D:** William Witney.

Tricks of the Trade ♂♂ 1988 (R) Goody-two-shoe housewife and hooker con men in the jackpot after slipping of Two inept con men hit the jackpot after slipping of a cash-packed suitcase—problem is it's an advance to two hit men to snuff out a mob boss. Naturally they don't split the scene right away and the hit men catch up to them, but the hoopla doesn't end there in this mildly amusing farce. 96m/C VHS, DVD, Pete Postlethwaite, Neil Morrissey, Dornie Wahlberg, Adrian Dunbar, Amanda Plummer, Saul Rubinek; **D:** John Bradshaw; **W:** Tony Johnson; **C:** Barry Stone; **M:** Terence Gowan, Blair Packham.

Trilby ♂♂♂ 1917 Original screen production of Du Maurier's classic tale of Svengali. 59m/B VHS, Clara Kimball Young, Wilton Lackaye, Chester Barnett; **D:** Maurice Tourneur. **VIDEO**

Trilogy of Terror ♂♂½ 1975 Curtis follows up his 1975 TV movie with an okay sequel headed by Anthony Curtis. Black shows her versatility as she plays a tempting seductress, a mousy school-teacher, and the terrified victim of an African fetish doll in three horror shorts. Curtis' best story, "Bobby," and the deadly African Zuni fetish doll returns in "He Who Kills." 90m/C VHS, DVD, Lysette Anthony, Richard Fitzpatrick, Geraint Wyn Davies, Matt Clark, Geoffrey Lewis, Blake Heron; **D:** Dan Curtis; **W:** Dan Curtis, William F. Nolan, Richard Matheson; **C:** Elemer Ragalyi; **M:** Robert Cobert. **CABLE**

Trilogy of Terror 2 ♂♂ 1996 (R) tor Lackaye, Chester Barnett; **D:** Maurice Tourneur. Second sequel. Black shows her versatility as she plays a mousy school-teacher, and the terrified victim of an African fetish doll in three horror shorts. 78m/C VHS, DVD, Karen Black, Robert (Skip) Burton, John Karlen, Gregory Harrison, George Gaynes, James Storm, Kathryn Reynolds, Tracy Curtis; **D:** Dan Curtis; **W:** Richard Matheson, Paul Lohmann; **M:** Robert Cobert. **TV**

Trinity Is Still My Name ♂♂½ Continuavamo a Chiamarlo Trinita 1975 (G) Sequel to "They Call Me Trinity." Insouciant bumbling brothers Trinity and Bambino, oblivious to danger and hopeless odds, endure mishaps and adventures as they try to right wrongs. A funny parody of Western cliches that has become state. 117m/C VHS, DVD, Terence Hill, Harry Carey Jr.; **D:** E.B. (Enzo Barboni) Clucher.

Trio ♂♂♂ 1950 Sequel to "Quartet," featuring the W. Somerset Maugham stories "The Verger," "Mr. Knowall," and "Sanatorium Acclaimed"; 88m/B VHS, Jean Simmons, Michael Rennie, Bill Travers, James Hayter, Kathleen Harrison, Felix Aylmer, Nigel Patrick, Finlay Currie, John Laurie; **D:** Ken Annakin, Harold French; **C:** Geoffrey Unsworth, Reg Wyer.

The Trio ♂♂ 1997 Unconvincing German sex comedy finds gay middle-aged Zobel (George) and his daughter Lizzie (Hain) constantly on the move as they exercise their pickpocketing profession, along with Zobel's lover Karl (Redl). After Karl dies in an auto accident, Lizzie recruits hunky drifter Rudolf (Elner) to take his place. Which Rudolf does in more ways than one, since he soon becomes the lover of both father and daughter. German with subtitles. 97m/C VHS, DVD, GE Goetz George, Jeanette Hain, Felix Eitner, Christian Redl; **D:** Hermine Huntgeburth; **W:** Hermine Huntgeburth, Horst Sczerba, Volker Einrauch; **C:** Martin Kukula. **M:** Niki Reiser.

The Trip ♂♂ 1967 A psychedelic journey to the world of inner consciousness, via drugs. A TV director, unsure where his life is going, decides to try a "trip" to expand his understanding. Hopper is the drug salesman Dern, the tour guide for Fonda's trip through sex, witches, torture chambers, and more. Great period music. 85m/C VHS, DVD, Peter Fonda, Susan Strasberg, Bruce Dern, Dennis Hopper, Salli Sachse, Barbara Morris, Judith Lang, Luana Anders, Beach Dickerson, Dick Miller, Michael Nader, Michael Blodgett, Caren Bernsen, Katherine Walsh, Peter Bogdanovich, Tom Signorelli; **D:** Roger Corman; **M:** Barry Goldberg.

The Trip ♂♂ 2002 (R) In 1973 Los Angeles, young Republican Alan Oakley (Sullivan) is working for an establishment newspaper and cerving the fact that he's

Triggermen ♂♂ 2002 (R) Two inept

gay. In fact, Alan's writing a book that's a conservative attack on gay rights. When Alan meets gay rights activist Tommy (Braun), things change personally and professionally. Too bad Alan's manuscript gets published anonymously by envious wannabe lover, Peter (Baker). Film eventually makes its way to 1984 when Alan learns ex-lover Tommy is dying of AIDS in Mexico but would like to see Aan one more time. Not quite as sappy as you may think, since writer/director Swain is certainly sincere, but it's also bas:c melodrama. 93m/C VHS, DVD, Larry Sullivan, Steve Braun, Ray Baker, Art-Hindle, Jill St. John, Alexis Arquette; **D:** Miles Swain; **W:** Miles Swain; **C:** Charles L. Barbee, Scott Kevan; **M:** Steven Chesne.

Triple Agent ♂♂ 2004 Richmer enters murky political territory in this moral spy yarn based on a true crime, in 1936, Tsarist sympathizer Fiodor Voronin (Renko) is living in exile in Paris with his Greek-born wife Arsinoe (Didaskalou). His frequent business trips arouse Arsinoe's suspicions, but Fiodor is not having an affair. he's a spy playing the White Russians against the communists and the fascists in a dangerous and increasingly complicated triple-cross. French, Russian, and German with subtitles. 115m/C DVD, FR/IT/GR/RU/SP Serge Renko, Amanda Langlet, Katerina Didaskalou, Cyrielle Clair, Grigori Manoukov; **D:** Eric Rohmer; **W:** Eric Rohmer; **C:** Diane Baratier.

Triple Cross ♂♂♂ 1967 Plummer is a British safecracker imprisoned on the channel islands at the outbreak of WWII. When the Germans move in, he offers to work for them if they set him free. The Germans buy his story and send him to England, but once there he offers his services to the British as a double agent. Based on the exploits of Eddie Chapman, adapted from his book, "The Eddie Chapman Story." 91m/C VHS, FR GB Christopher Plummer, Romy Schneider, Trevor Howard, Gert Frobe, Yul Brynner, Claudine Auger, Georges Lycan, Jess Hahn, Howard Vernon; **D:** Terence Young.

Triple Echo ♂♂½ 1985 Soldier in Skirts 1977 (R) A young woman falls for an army deserter who is hiding from the military police by dressing as a woman. Mistrust and deception get the best of some of the involved parties. 90m/C VHS, GB Glenda Jackson, Oliver Reed, Brian Deacon; **D:** Michael Apted; **W:** Robin Chapman.

Triple Impact ♂ 1992 Hall, Cook, and Riley are three martial-arts experts who join forces against illegal gambling syndicates who are staging full-contact bloodmatches. Their alliance leads them to Asia w're're the prize is death—or a fortune in gold. 97m/C VHS, Dale "Apollo" Cook, Ron Hall, Bridget "Baby Doll" Riley, Brett Marius, Steve Rogers, Nick Nicholson, Ned Houani, Mike "Cobra" Cole; **W:** Steve Rogers.

TripleCross ♂♂ 2002 (R) Three former cops strike it rich and although they love the money, they miss the game. So they get involved in a murder case. Three wealthy detectives encounter high-level

The Trip to Bountiful ♂♂♂ 1985 (PG) An elderly widow, unhappy living in her son's fancy modern home, makes a pilgrimage back to her childhood home in Bountiful, Texas. Based on the Horton Foote play. Fine acting with Oscar-winning performance from Page. 112m/C VHS, DVD, Geraldine Page Rebeca De Mornay, John Heard, Carlin Glynn, Richard Bradford; **D:** Peter Masterson; **W:** Horton Foote; **C:** Fred Murphy Oscars '85: Actress (Page); Ind. Spirit '86: Actress (Page).

TripFall ♂♂½ 2000 (R) Tom Williams (Ritter) decides he, wife Gina (Hunter), and their kids need some family time, so they head off on a backpacking and nightmare of Eddie (Roberts) and his gang of kidnappers. With his wife and kids in Eddie's slimy hands, Tom has one day to think he wants them back alive. 95m/C VHS, DVD, John Ritter, Eric Roberts, Rachel Hunter; **D:** Serge Rodnunsky; **W:** Serge Rodnunsky; **C:** Greg Patterson; **M:** Evan Evans. **VIDEO**

gangsters, a baseball scandal, and a hit man in their race to solve the perfect crime. **97m/C VHS.** Ted Wass, Markie Post, Gary Swanson; **D:** David Greene.

The Triplets of Belleville *Les Triplettes de Belleville; Belleville Rendez-Vous* 2002 (PG-13) Surreal French animated tale of a joyless bicycle racer and his eccentric grandmother charms, surprises, and confounds with flights of fancy and wonderfully imaginative scenarios. Champion is a sad little boy who doesn't respond to anything until his grandmother buys him a tricycle. This leads him to become a top-level bike racer who is eventually kidnapped by French mobsters. His stalwart grandma stops at nothing to rescue him. **91m/C DVD.** *FR BE CA* **D:** Sylvain Chomet; **W:** Sylvain Chomet; **M:** Benoit Charest. L.A. Film Critics '03: Animated Film, Score.

Tripods: The White Mountains 1984 Sci-fi thriller about the takeover of earth by alien tripods. The conquerors start controlling human minds, but not until after they are 16 years old. Two boys seek to end the terror. **150m/C VHS.** John Shackley, Jim Baker, Carl Seel; **D:** Graham Theakston.

The Tripper 2006 (R) Arquette's directorial debut is a lame horror satire that makes you wonder if everyone on set was maybe tripping. Three hippie couples are driving through a North Carolina forest when they're attacked by a psycho wearing a Ronald Reagan mask and fondling sharp and deadly implements. **93m/C DVD.** Thomas Jane, Jaime (James) King, Richmond Arquette, Paz de la Huerta, Balthazar Getty, Lukas Haas, Jason Mewes, Paul (Pee-wee Herman) Reubens, David Arquette; **D:** David Arquette; **W:** David Arquette, Joe Harris; **C:** Bobby Bukowski; **M:** Jimmy Haun, Dave Wittman.

Trippin' 1999 (R) Gregory (Richmond) is a daydreamer who can't keep his mind on his studies until he finds out that the prom queen, Cinny (Campbell), goes for the brainy type. Between fantasies of fame, fortune, and exotic locales, Gregory, with the help of his ne'er-do-well buddies Fish (Torry) and June (Faison), tries to improve his grades and get her to the prom. Likeable cast and a nice message about the importance of getting an education balance out a gratuitous subplot about a local crime boss recruiting June. Lightweight but amusing. **92m/C VHS, DVD.** Deon Richmond, Maia Campbell, Donald Adeosun Faison, Guy Torry, Harold Sylvester, Stoney Jackson, Michael Warren, Aloma Wright, Bill Henderson; **D:** David Raynr; **W:** Gary Hardwick; **C:** John Aronson.

Tripwire 1989 (R) A vengeance-crazed government agent tracks down a terrorist who murdered his wife. **120m/C VHS.** Terence Knox, David Warner, Charlotte Lewis, Isabella Hofmann, Yaphet Kotto, Thomas Chong, Meg Foster; **D:** James (Momel) Lemmo.

Tristan & Isolde 2006 (PG-13) Pretty actors play tragic lovers in a romantic drama based on a Celtic legend. Dark Ages Irish princess Isolde (Myles) is the marriageable bargaining chip for her scheming father (O'Hara), whose aim is to rule the squabbling English tribes. Isolde rescues, and falls in love with, injured warrior Tristan (Franco), who happens to be the champion of powerful Briton Lord Marke (Sewell). Unbeknownst to the lovers, Isolde has been promised to Marke; they try to do the right thing. It's appropriately swoony and teary and noble. **125m/C DVD.** *GB GE US* James Franco, Sophia Myles, Rufus Sewell, David O'Hara, Mark Strong, Henry Cavill, Bronagh Gallagher, Roman Vibert, Lucy Russell, Thomas Sangster, JB Blanc, Graham Mullins; **D:** Kevin Reynolds; **W:** Dean Georgaris; **C:** Arthur Reinhart; **M:** Anne Dudley.

Tristana 1970 (PG) Allegorical tale of a beautiful girl (Deneuve) who moves in with a hypocritical benefactor following the death of her mother. She is quickly exploited and seduced by the one who would protect her, but runs away with an artist in pursuit of love. Searing in its commentary on Catholicism, death, lust, and the woebegone place of humanity in the world, the movie is also widely seen as a depiction of fascist Spain's attempt to find its place in the 20th century. Based on the novel by Benito Perez Galdos. In Spanish with English subtitles. **98m/C VHS.** *SP IT FR* Catherine Deneuve, Fernando Rey, Franco Nero, Lola Gaos, Antonio Casas, Jesus Fernandez, Vincent Solder; **D:** Luis Bunuel; **W:** Julio Alejandro, Luis Bunuel; **C:** Jose F. Aguayo.

Tristram Shandy: A Cock and Bull Story 2005 (R) Peculiar film-within-a-film follows Brit comedian Coogan playing an exaggerated version of "Steve Coogan" as he takes the title role in the filming of the eccentric 18th-century novel "The Life and Opinions of Tristram Shandy." Insecure and vain, Coogan annoys the director (Northam) and screenwriter (Hart), while childishly sparring with his primary co-star (Brydon) and ignoring his visiting girlfriend (Macdonald) and their baby. Best for Coogan fans or those interested in movie minutia. **91m/C DVD.** Steve Coogan, Rob Brydon, Keeley Hawes, Shirley Henderson, Dylan Moran, Jeremy Northam, Naomie Harris, Kelly Macdonald, James Fleet, Ian Hart, Kieran O'Brien, Stephen Fry, Gillian Anderson, David Williams, Anthony H. Wilson; **D:** Michael Winterbottom; **W:** Martin Hardy; **C:** Marcel Zyskind; **M:** Michael Nyman, Edward Nogria.

The Triumph of Hercules *Il Trionfo di Ercole; Hercules and the Ten Avengers; Hercules vs. the Giant Warriors* 1966 Hercules gets stripped of his powers by a peeved Zeus and must try to battle a sorceress and 10 giant bronze warriors without them, until Zeus reconsiders. **94m/C VHS, DVD.** *IT FR* Dan Vadis, Moira Orfei, Pierre Cressoy, Marilu Tolo, Pierro Lulli; **D:** Alberto De Martino; **W:** Robert Gianviti; **C:** Pier Ludovico Pavoni; **M:** Francesco De Masi.

The Triumph of Love 2001 (PG-13) Not much of a triumph but not a complete waste of time either. Adapted from Pierre Marivaux's 18th-century play, Sorvino plays Princess Leonide, who knows that her family usurped their throne and she is determined to see its rightful owner, Prince Agis (Rodan), returned to power. Of course, he's a handsome prince and the princess has fallen in love but there are complications that involve her disguising herself and insinuating herself into his guardians' (Kingsley, Shaw) austere lives. Deceptions abound. **107m/C VHS, DVD.** *IT GB* Mira Sorvino, Ben Kingsley, Fiona Shaw, Jay Rodan, Rachael Stirling, Ignazio Oliva; **D:** Clare Peploe; **W:** Clare Peploe, Bernardo Bertolucci, Marilyn Goldin; **C:** Fabio Cianchetti; **M:** Jason Osborn.

The Triumph of Sherlock Holmes 1935 Wontner and Fleming teamed for an early series of Holmesian romps. In one of their best outings, Sherlock Holmes comes out of retirement as a series of bizarre murders of Pennsylvania coal miners lure him: back into action. From "The Valley of Fear" by Sir Arthur Conan Doyle. **84m/B VHS, DVD.** *GB* Arthur Wontner, Ian Fleming; **D:** Leslie Hiscott.

Triumph of the Spirit 1989 (R) Gritty account of boxer Salamo Arouch's experiences in Auschwitz. The boxer became champion in matches between prisoners conducted for the amusement of Nazi officers. Filmed on location in Auschwitz. **115m/C VHS, DVD.** Willem Dafoe, Robert Loggia, Edward James Olmos, Wendy Gazelle, Kelly Wolf, Costas Mandylor, Kario Salem; **D:** Robert M. Young; **W:** Robert M. Young, Shimon Arama, Andrzej Krakowski, Laurence Heath, Arthur Coburn, Millard Lampell; **M:** Cliff Eidelman.

Triumph of the Will 1934 Director Riefenstahl's formidable, stunning film, documenting Hitler and the Sixth Nazi Party Congress in 1934 in Nuremberg, Germany. The greatest and most artful propaganda piece ever produced. German dialogue. Includes English translation of the speeches. **115m/B VHS, DVD.** *GE* **D:** Leni Riefenstahl; **C:** Sepp Algeier; **M:** Herbert Windt.

Triumphs of a Man Called Horse 1983 (R) An Indian must save his people from prospectors in order to keep his title as Peace. Chief of the Yellow Hand Sioux. Inadequate sequel to two previous films: "A Man Called Horse." and "The Return of a Man Called Horse." **91m/C VHS.** *MX* Richard Harris; **D:** John Hough; **W:** Carlos Aured, Jack DeWitt, Kenneth G. Blackwell.

Trixie 2000 (R) Performances by a fine ensemble cast are mangled almost as badly as the English language in this wandering comedy-mystery. Trixie (Watson) is a malaprop-spouting security guard at a resort casino who wants to be a detective. She stumbles onto a murder mystery involving bombastic Senator Avery (Nolte) and decides that if she solves the crime, a career as a detective will surely follow. Many false leads are chased, and the theme that not everyone is as they appear is hammered home time and time again. Among the list of usual suspects are a golddigging barfly (Murphy), a washed-up lounge singer (Warren), an impressionist/singer with a shady past (Lane). **117m/C VHS, DVD.** Emily Watson, Nick Nolte, Dermot Mulroney, Nathan Lane, Brittany Murphy, Lesley Ann Warren, Will Patton, Stephen Lang; **D:** Alan Rudolph; **W:** Alan Rudolph; **C:** Jan Kiesser; **M:** Mark Isham, Roger Neill.

Trois Couleurs: Blanc *White; Three Colors: White* 1994 (R) Bittersweet comedic rags-to-riches tale spiced with revenge and lasting love. "White" focuses on equality and begins when a bewildered Polish hairdresser is divorced by his disdainful French wife, who takes him for everything he has. Returning to his family in Poland, Karol doggedly works his way into wealth. Then he decides to take his death loves—or does he? In Polish and French with English subtitles. Part 2 of Kieslowski's trilogy, following "Trois Couleurs: Bleu" and followed by "Trois Couleurs: Rouge." **92m/C VHS, DVD.** *FR SI PL* Zbigniew Zamachowski, Julie Delpy, Janusz Gajos, Jerzy Stuhr, Aleksander Bardini, Grzegorz Warchol, Cezary Harasimowicz, Jerzy Nowak, Jerzy Trela, Cezary Pazura, Michel Lisowski, Philippe Morier-Genoud; **Cameos:** Juliette Binoche, Florence Pernel; **D:** Krzysztof Kieslowski; **W:** Krzysztof Kieslowski, Krzysztof Piesiewicz; **C:** Edward Klosinski; **M:** Zbigniew Preisner. Berlin Intl. Film Fest. '94: Director (Kieslowski).

Trois Couleurs: Bleu *Three Colors: Blue; Blue* 1993 (R) First installment of director Kieslowski's trilogy inspired by the French tricolor flag. "Blue" stands for liberty—here freedom is based on tragedy as Julie (Binoche) reshapes her life after surviving an accident which killed her famous composer husband and their young daughter. Excellent performance by Binoche, which relies on the internalized grief and brief emotion which flits across her face rather than over-whelming displays for expression. In French with English subtitles. **98m/C VHS, DVD.** *FR* Juliette Binoche, Benoit Regent, Florence Pernel, Charlotte Very, Helene Vincent, Philippe Volter, Claude Duneton, Hugues Quester, Florence Vignon, Jacek Ostaszewski; **Cameos:** Emmanuelle Riva; **D:** Krzysztof Kieslowski; **W:** Krzysztof Kieslowski, Krzysztof Piesiewicz, Slawomir Idziak, Agnieszka Holland, Edward Zebrowski; **C:** Slawomir Idziak; **M:** Zbigniew Preisner. Cesar '94: Actress (Binoche), Film Editing, Sound; L.A. Film Critics '93: Score, Venice Film Fest. '93: Actress (Binoche), Film.

Trois Couleurs: Rouge *Three Colors: Red; Red* 1994 (R) "Red" is for fraternity in the French tricolor flag and, in director Kieslowski's last film in his trilogy, emotional connections are made between unlikely couples. There's law student Auguste and his girlfriend Karin, young fashion model Valentine, and a nameless retired judge, brought together by circumstance and destined to change each other's lives. Subtle details make for careful viewing but it's a rewarding watch and a visual treat (keep an eye on cinematographer Sobocinski's use of the color red). Binoche and Delpy, who starred in the earlier films, also make an appearance, as Kieslowski uses the finale to tie up loose ends. In French with English subtitles. **99m/C VHS, DVD.** *FR PL SI* Irene Jacob, Jean-Louis Trintignant, Frederique Feder, Jean-Pierre Lorit, Samuel Le Bihan, Marion Stalens, Teco Celio, Bernard Escalon, Jean Schlegel, Elzbieta Jasinska; **Cameos:** Juliette Binoche, Julie Delpy, Benoit Regent, Zbigniew Zamachowski; **D:** Krzysztof Kieslowski; **W:** Krzysztof Kieslowski, Krzysztof Piesiewicz; **C:** Piotr Sobocinski; **M:** Zbigniew Preisner. Cesar '94: Score; Ind. Spirit '95: Foreign Film; L.A. Film Critics '94: Foreign Film; N.Y. Film Critics '94: Foreign Film; Natl. Soc. Film Critics '94: Foreign Film.

Trojan Eddie 1996 Stephen Rea puts his perpetual hangdog mug to good use as the hapless Trojan Eddie, so named for the make of the van in which he transports and sells stolen goods. He is married to the shrewish town tramp, who helps little in raising their two girls and makes fun of his dream of opening his own business. His boss is John Power (Harris), leader of a group of clannish con men. He is teamed with Power's nephew Dermot (Townsend), who's secretly romancing his uncle's much younger wife-to-be. The young lovers take off with the cache of wedding loot on the night of the nuptials, and Power involves Eddie in an all-out search for the couple. After they're caught and pardoned by Power, however, the spiral of betrayal and violence spins faster than ever, with Eddie always eyeing the chance to escape. Excellent rapport between Rea and Harris as their fortunes shift and reverse. **103m/C VHS, DVD.** Stephen Rea, Richard Harris, Brendan Gleeson, Sean McGinley, Angeline Ball, Brid Brennan, Stuart Townsend, Aislin McGuckin; **D:** Gilles Mackinnon; **W:** Billy Roche; **C:** John de Borman; **M:** John Keane.

The Trojan Horse *The Trojan War; The Mighty Warrior* 1962 Greek warrior Aeneas (Reeves), under the command of Ulysses (Barrymore), gets to hide out in the Trojan horse with his fellow fighters and then get those Trojans when they take the wooden beast into their city. When they're successful, Aeneas takes his guys and decides to go off and found the city of Rome. You were maybe expecting historical or mythological accuracy? **105m/C VHS, DVD.** *IT FR* Steve Reeves, John Drew (Blythe) Barrymore Jr., Juliette Mayniel, Edy Vessel, Lidia Alfonsi, Luciana Angiolillo, Arturo Dominici, Mimmo Palmara, Carlo Tamberlani, Nando Tamberlani; **D:** Giorgio Ferroni; **W:** Ugo Liberatore; **C:** Rino Filippini; **M:** Giovanni Fusco.

Trojan War 1997 (PG-13) Yes, the title does refer to the condom brand. High schooler Brad Kimble (Friedle) has finally convinced dream girl Brooke (Shelton) to get romantic—if he has the proper protection, of course. But as his search is continually thwarted, this gives his best gal Leah (Hewitt)—who would like to be something more—the chance to show who really loves him. Harmless, although sexually overt, teen fluff. **90m/C VHS.** Lee Majors, Wendie Malick, David Patrick Kelly, Anthony Michael Hall, Jennifer Love Hewitt, Will Friedle, Marley Shelton; **D:** George Huang; **W:** Andy Burg, Scott Myers; **C:** Dean Semler; **M:** George S. Clinton.

Trojan Women 1971 (G) Euripides' tragedy on the fate of the women of Troy after the Greeks storm the famous city. The play does not translate well to the screen, in spite of tour-de-force acting. **86m/C VHS, DVD.** Katharine Hepburn, Vanessa Redgrave, Irene Papas, Genevieve Bujold, Brian Blessed, Patrick Magee; **D:** Michael Cacoyannis. Natl. Bd. of Review '71: Actress (Papas).

Troll 1986 (PG-13) A malevolent troll haunts an apartment building and possesses a young girl in hopes of turning all humans into trolls. Sometimes imaginative, sometimes embarrassing. Followed by a sequel. **86m/C VHS, DVD.** Noah Hathaway, Gary Sandy, Anne Lockhart, Sonny Bono, Shelley Hack, June Lockhart, Michael Moriarty,

Troll 2 ✗½ **1992 (PG-13)** A young boy can only rely on his faith in himself when no one believes his warnings about an evil coming to destroy his family. Entering into a nightmare world, Joshua must battle witches' spells and the evil trolls who carry out their bidding. **95m/C VHS, DVD**, Michael Stephenson, Connie McFarland, Gavin Reed; *D:* Drago Floyd; *W:* Clyde (Claudio Fragasso) Anderson.

Troma's War woof! **1988 (R)** The survivors of an air crash find themselves amid a tropical terrorist-run civil war. Also available in a 105-minute, unrated version. Devotees of trash films shouldn't miss this one. **90m/C VHS, DVD**, Carolyn Beauchamp, Sean Bowen, Michael Ryder, Jessica Dublin, Steven Crossley, Lorayn Lane DeLuca; *D:* Michael Herz, Lloyd Kaufman; *W:* Lloyd Kaufman, Mitchell Harz, Eric Hattler, Thomas Martinek; *C:* James London; *M:* Christopher De Marco.

Tromba, the Tiger Man ✗ Tromba **1952** A circus tiger tamer uses a special drug that hypnotizes his every whim. When he tries the same drug on women, things get out of hand. **82m/B VHS, GE** Rene Deltgen, Angelika Hauff, Gustav Knuth, Hilde Weissner, Gretha Weiser, Gardy Granass, Adrian Hoven; *D:* Helmut Weiss.

Tromeo & Juliet ✗✗ **1995 (R)** There've been many versions of Shakespeare, but the Bard may never recover from being "Tromatized." On the outskirts of New York City, teenaged Tromeo Que (Keenan) falls in lust with babe Juliet Capulet (Jensen), but the family feud is still around to cause major disharmony. There's lots of profanity, perversity, and gore to keep your interest. As the movie's tagline says, "Body Piercing, Kinky Sex, Dismemberment. The things that made Shakespeare great." The unrated version is 105 minutes. **95m/C VHS, DVD**, Will Keenan, Jane Jensen, Debbie Rochon, Lemmy, Valentine Miele, Sean Gunn; *D:* Lloyc Kaufman; *W:* James Gunn; *C:* Brendan Flynt; *M:* Willie Wisely.

Tron ✗✗ **1982 (PG)** A video game designer enters into his computer, where he battles the computer games he created and seeks revenge on other designers who have stolen his creations. Sounds better than it plays. Terrific special effects, with lots of computer-created graphics. **96m/C VHS, DVD, UMD**, Jeff Bridges, Bruce Boxleitner, David Warner, Cindy Morgan, Barnard Hughes, Dan Shor, Peter Jurasik, Tony Stephano; *D:* Steven Lisberger; *W:* Steven Lisberger; *C:* Bruce Logan; *M:* Walter (Wendy) Carlos.

Troop Beverly Hills ✗ **1989 (PG)** Spoiled housewife Long isn't really spoiled, just misunderstood. She takes over leadership of her daughter's Wilderness Girls troop and finds the opportunity to redeem herself by offering her own unique survival tips to the uncooperative little brats who make up the troop. Everyone learns meaningful life lessons. Long is finally understood, and everyone lives happily ever after in posh Beverly Hills. Sheer silliness makes this one almost careful to watch, a shame since it boasts a good cast whose talent is totally wasted. **105m/C VHS, DVD**, Shelley Long, Craig T. Nelson, Betty Thomas, Mary Gross, Stephanie Beacham, Audra Lindley, Edd Byrnes, Ami Foster, Jenny Lewis, Kellie Martin; *D:* Jeff Kanew; *W:* Pamela Norris, Margaret Grieco Oberman; *M:* Randy Edelman.

A Troll in Central Park ✗✗½ **1994 (G)** Animated fantasy about Stanley the troll, who is cast out of his kingdom (because he's a good guy) and winds up in New York's Central Park. There, Stanley brings happiness to a little girl and her skeptical brother, all the while battling the evil troll queen. Strictly average family fare. **76m/C VHS, DVD**, *D:* Don Bluth; *V:* Dom DeLuise, Cloris Leachman, Jonathan Pryce, Hayley Mills, Charles Nelson Reilly, Phillip Glasser, Robert Morley, Sy Gonaeb, Tawney Sunshine Glover, Jordan Metzner.

Tropic Thunder **2008 (R)** Five actors are on location in Vietnam filming a war movie with things constantly going wrong. They wind up alone on a remote jungle location where they're mistaken for DEA agents by the local drug lords and suddenly find that pre-filming boot camp training is coming in handy. Stiller's the action star, Black's a druggie comedian, and Downey Jr. plays an Oscar-winning Method actor who dyes his skin black when the car trunk, drug character was supposed to accuse some controversy. This also caused some controversy offscreen when Stiller was filming a comedy highlighting showbiz cliches. Tom Cruise cameos in a fat suit as a foul-mouthed studio exec. Not yet reviewed. **?m/C** Ben Stiller, Robert Downey Jr., Jack Black, Jay Baruchel, Danny McBride, Bill Hader, Steve Coogar, Nick Nolte, Brandon T. Jackson, Tom Cruise, Matthew McConaughey, Tobey Maguire, Justin Theroux; *D:* Ben Stiller; *W:* Ben Stiller, Justin Theroux, Etan Cohen; *C:* John Toll; *M:* Theodore Shapiro.

Tropic of Cancer ✗✗ **1970 (NC-17)** Based on Henry Miller's once-banned, now classic novel, this film portrays the sexual escapades of the expatriate author living in 1920s Paris. Torn stars as the carefree, loose-living writer and Burstyn plays his disgusted wife. **87m/C VHS, DVD**, Rip Torn, James Callahan, Ellen Burstyn, David Bauer, Phil Brown; *D:* Joseph Strick.

Tropical Heat ✗✗ **1993 (R)** When the Maharajah is killed on safari, his grieving widow (D'Abo) files a $5 million insurance claim before returning to India. She's followed by an investigator (Rossovich) who becomes infatuated with the lovely D'Abo. Through palaces, primitive villages, and ancient jungle temples, they are drawn into a mystery involving black-mail and murder. Based on a story by Jag Mundhra, Michael W. Potts, and Simon Levy. **86m/C VHS**, Rick Rossovich, Maryam D'Abo, Lee Ann Beaman, Asha Silverkumar; *D:* Jag Mundhra; *W:* Michel W. Potts; *M:* Del Casher.

Tropical Malady ✗✗½ Sud praad **2004** Maybe it makes more sense to a Thai audience, in present-day Thailand, soldier Keng (Larmoi) meets country boy Tong (Kaewbuadee) and the two fall in love. Then we go from the natural to the supernatural world and something involving a Thai legend about a shaman who can transform himself into animals. Keng encounters a tiger in the jungle or maybe it's just a spirit tiger and Tong disappears except maybe he's the animal—or maybe not. And there's a talking monkey and the ghost of a dead cow. Thai with subtitles. **120m/C DVD, TH** Banlop Lomnoi, Sakda Kaewbuadee; *D:* Apichatpong Weerasethakul; *W:* Apichatpong Weerasethakul; *C:* Jean-Louis Vialard, Vichet Tanapanitch, Jarin Pengpanitch.

Tropical Snow ✗ **1988 (R)** A pair of lovers living poorly in Colombia decide to enter the drug trade in exchange for passage to the U.S. offered to them by drug kingpin Carradine. Unfortunately, they get more than they bargained for. Shot on location. **87m/C DVD**, David Carradine, Madeleine Stowe, Jsu Garcia, Argemiro Catibanco; *D:* Ciro Duran.

Tropix ✗½ **2002** Poor Corrine thinks her hubby whisked her to Costa Rica to salvage their wreck of a marriage only to realize that the no-good cad actually has crooked business dealings on the agenda. When things go haywire she's kidnapped and spends most of her time struggling to cut loose from her captors in the jungle. **99m/C VHS, DVD**, Keith Erunsmann, Ryan Barton-Grimley, Danielle Bisutti, Michelle Jones, Thomas Scott-Stanton; *D:* Percy Angress, Liva Linden; *D:* Luc G. Nickmair.

VIDEO

Trouble along the Way ✗✗½ **1953** Wayne is a once big-time college football coach who takes a coaching job at a small, financially strapped Catholic college in an effort to retain custody of his young daughter. His underhanded recruiting methods result in his firing—and the probable loss of his daughter. Unusual and sentimental role for Wayne proves he can handle comedy as well as action.

Trouble Bound ✗✗ **1992 (R)** Madsen is Harry, a guy just out of prison, on his way to Nevada with trouble dogging his every step. He's got a dead body in the car trunk, drug dealers after him, and a waitress (Arquette) his luck only gets worse. She plans to kill a Mob boss and it's no secret. Chases and violence. **90m/C VHS, DVD**, Michael Madsen, Patricia Arquette, Florence Stanley, Seymour Cassel, Sal Jenco; *D:* Jeff Reiner; *W:* Darrell Fetty, Francis Delia; *M:* Vinnie Golia.

Trouble Busters ✗ **1933** Troubled locals worry about who to call when oil is discovered in their town, bringing evil profiteers with it. The Trouble Busters come into town to set things straight. **51m/B VHS**, Jack Hoxie, Lane Chandler; *D:* Lewis D. Collins.

Trouble Chasers ✗½ **1945** Two crooks screw up the heist of a valuable necklace and frame an innocent man for the crime. Then, they get involved in a fist game, where they discover a link between a boxer and their patsy. **63m/B VHS**, Billy Gilbert, Maxie "Slapsie" Rosenbloom, Shemp Howard, Gloria Marlen; *D:* Lew Landers; *W:* Andre Lamb, George Plympton; *C:* Marcel Le Picard.

Trouble in Mind ✗✗ **1986 (R)** Stylized romance is set in the near future in a rundown diner. Kristofferson is an ex-cop who gets involved in the lives of a young couple looking for a better life. Look for Divine in one of her/his rare appearances outside of John Waters's works. **111m/C VHS**, Kris Kristofferson, Keith Carradine, Genevieve Bujold, Lori Singer, Divine, Joe Morton, George Kirby, John Considine; *D:* Alan Rudolph; *W:* Alan Rudolph; *C:* Toyomichi Kurita; *M:* Mark Isham. Ind. Spirit '86: Cinematography.

Trouble in Paradise ✗✗✗ **1932** Oh-so-assured sophisticated comedy finds gentleman jewel thief Gaston (Marshall) meeting his match in upscale pickpocket Lily (Hopkins). Even though they team up, their personal relationship doesn't get in the way of their professional ambitions. Gaston cons his way into the graces of wealthy widow Mariette Colet (Francis), who's well-aware she'd being used but is more amused than outraged. The same can't be said of her two devoted and dull suitors (Ruggles, Horton), who don't like the competition. Anc maybe Gaston is getting a little too interested in Mariette for even Lily's piece of mind. Both leading actresses are flirty and lovely and Marshall is suave and gallant. Because this is a pre-Production Code film, there's lots of sexual innuendo (both visual and verbal) and comes without punishment. **83m/B VHS, DVD**, Herbert Marshall, Miriam Hopkins, Kay Francis, Charlie Ruggles, Edward Everett Horton, Sir C. Aubrey Smith, Robert Greig; *D:* Ernst Lubitsch; *W:* Grover Jones, Samson Raphaelson; *C:* Victor Milner; *M:* W. Franke Harling.

Trouble in Paradise ✗✗ **1988** Welch stars as a widow stranded in a tropical island paradise with an Australian sailor. The two must struggle as they are stalked by a gang of drug smugglers, hence the title. **92m/C VHS, DVD**, Raquel Welch, Jack Thompson, Nicholas Hammond, John Gregg; *D:* Di Drew. **TV**

Trouble in Store ✗✗½ **1953** A bumbling department store employee stumbles on a gangster's plot. Fun gags and a good cast. **85m/B VHS, GB** Margaret Rutherford, Norman Wisdom, Moira Lister, Megs Jenkins; *D:* Jack Paddy Carstairs.

Trouble in Texas ✗✗ **1937** Outlaws go to a rodeo and try to steal the prize money. Tex wants to find out who killed his brother and in his spare time, sings and tries to stop the crooks. Notable because it is the last film Hayworth made under her original stage name (Rita Cansino). **65m/B VHS, DVD**, Tex Ritter, Rita Hayworth, Earl Dwire, Yakima Canutt; *D:* Robert North Bradbury.

Trouble in the Glen ✗✗½ **1954** A Scottish-American soldier returns to his ancestral home and becomes involved in a dispute between the town residents and a lord over a closed road. Uneven script undermines comic idea. **91m/C VHS, GB** Orson Welles, Victor McLaglen, Forrest Tucker, Margaret Lockwood; *D:* Herbert Wilcox.

The Trouble with Angels ✗✗½ **1966 (PG)** Two young girls turn a convent upside down with their endless practical jokes. Russell is everything a Mother Superior should be: understanding, wise, and kind. **112m/C VHS, DVD**, Hayley Mills, June Harding, Rosalind Russell, Gypsy Rose Lee, Binnie Barnes; *D:* Ida Lupino; *C:* Lionel Lindon; *M:* Jerry Goldsmith.

The Trouble with Dick ✗ **1988 (R)** An ambitious young science fiction writer's personal troubles begin to appear in his writing. Although the box cover displays a "Festival Winner" announcement, no one is as much singing as his earlier. Not good attention is paid to details. **86m/C VHS**, Tom Villard, Susan Dey, Elizabeth Gorcey, David Clennon, Marianne Muellerleile; *D:* Gary Walkow; *C:* Elaine Gittos, Daryl Studebaker; *W:* Roger Bourland. Sundance '87: Grand Jury Prize.

The Trouble with Girls (and How to Get into It) ✗ The Chautauqua **1969 (G)** A 1920s traveling show plays a Vermont town, it causes all kinds of problems for the community. No one is sure who killed Harry and what to do with the body. MacLaine's film debut and Herrmann's first musical score for Hitchcock. **90m/C VHS, DVD**, John Forsythe, Shirley MacLaine, Edmund Gwenn, Jerry Mathers, Mildred Dunnock, Mildred Natwick, Royal Dano; *D:* Alfred Hitchcock; *W:* John Michael Hayes; *C:* Robert Burks; *M:* Bernard Herrmann.

The Trouble with Harry ✗✗✗ **1955 (PG)** When a little boy finds a dead body in a Vermont town, it causes all kinds of problems as they try to solve a local murder. Made in 1984, not one bothered to release it for three years. **99m/C VHS, DVD**, Elvis Presley, Marlyn Mason, Nicole Jaffe, Sheree North, Edward Andrews, John Carradine, Vincent Price, Joyce Van Patten, Dabney Coleman, John Rubinstein, Anthony Teague, Helene Winston; *D:* Peter Tewkesbury.

The Trouble with Spies ✗ **1987 (PG-13)** A bumbling British spy goes to Ibiza to locate a Russian agent, makes a million mistakes and wins anyway. A loser of a film, wasted a fine cast. Made in 1984, no one bothered to release it for three years. **91m/C VHS, DVD**, Donald Sutherland, Ned Beatty, Michael Hordern, Robert Morley, Lucy Gutteridge, Ruth Gordon; *D:* Burt Kennedy; *W:* Burt Kennedy.

Troublemakers ✗½ **1994 (PG)** Travis (Hill) is the fastest gun in the west—but his brother Moses (Spencer) is the country's meanest bounty hunter. But their mother loves them, and wants both her boys home for Christmas. So she leaves it up to Travis to lure Moses back to the homestead. **98m/C VHS, DVD**, Terence Hill, Bud Spencer, Anne Kasprik, Ruth Bzzi, Ron Carey; *D:* Terence Hill; *W:* Terence Hill.

Troubles ✗✗½ **1988** In 1919, Major Brendan Archer arrives on the coast of Wicklow, Ireland to be reunited with his fiancee, Angela Spencer, at the family hotel, the decaying Majestic. Brendan is puzzled by the changes in both the hotel and Angela and begins to turn his interests to her friend, Sarah Devlin, who is a passionate Irish nationalist. But volatile Irish politics puts the romance in danger. Based on the 1970 novel by J.G. Farrell. **208m/C VHS, DVD, GB** Ian Charleson, Ian Richardson, Sean Bean, Emer Gillespie, Susannah Harker; *D:* Christopher Morahan; *W:* Charles Sturidge. **TV**

The Troubles We've Seen ✗✗✗ Veillees d'armes **1994** Footage of old and recent war coverage and journalist Marcel Ophuls' own work while in Sarajevo is woven together with interviews of various war correspondents as they provide an insider's view of the ethical and philosophical difficulties of covering the insanity of war while clinging to one's own precarious grip on sanity. This in-depth...

documentary explores topics as diverse as a reporter revealing his own opposition to the war he's covering to the dark truth that, as one subject puts it, "the more horrible the situation, the more successful we become." **224m/C DVD. D:** Marcel Ophuls; **W:** Marcel Ophuls; **C:** Pierre Milon, Pierre Boffety.

Troy 🦴🦴½ **2004 (R)** Petersen's epic telling of the Trojan War finally hit the screen after many delays (including Pitt injuring his Achilles tendon, oh the irony!) and budget-busting incidents. Merely inspired by Homer's "The Iliad," it dispenses with all those pesky Greek gods and makes it all about the warriors. When beautiful Helen (Kruger) flees her Spartan husband Menelaus (Gleeson) with prettyboy lover Paris (Bloom), her greedy brother-in-law Agamemnon (Cox) decides Troy's wealth is worth a little fighting. Arrogant Achilles (Pitt) is persuaded to join in, and while Paris is no fighter, big brother Hector (Bana) is. Naturally, Achilles and Hector will have to go mano-a-mano (in one of the film's best scenes). Also around to show those youngsters what acting's all about is O'Toole as aging King Priam. It's all handled professionally but it's just not terribly compelling. **162m/C DVD, Blu-ray Disc, HD DVD, GB** Brad Pitt, Orlando Bloom, Eric Bana, Peter O'Toole, Diane Kruger, Brendan Gleeson, Brian Cox, Sean Bean, Julian Glover, Julie Christie, Saffron Burrows, John Shrapnel, James Cosmo, Rose Byrne, Garrett Hedlund, Nathan Jones, Vincent Regan, Trevor Eve, Tyler Mane; **D:** Wolfgang Petersen; **W:** David Benioff; **C:** Roger Pratt; **M:** James Horner.

The Truce 🦴🦴 **1996** *La Tregua* Adaptation of the novel by Primo Levi, based on his true account of traveling home across Europe after the liberation of Auschwitz at the end of WWII. Tells the story of Levi's arduous journey home to Turin through Eastern Europe, as well as his slow rediscovery of life and hope. Has the trappings of a grand historical epic, but works best as a quiet introspective look at a man trying to reclaim his humanity after experiencing unimaginable horror. Flashback scenes in the camp are appropriately harrowing, but the film loses focus when joining Levi and his ragtag compadres on the road home, sometimes slipping into banal sentimentality or outright melodrama, two things a story this powerful doesn't need. Turturro, who committed to the project several years ago, gives the performance of his career, understated and convincing, and after giving Rosi's adaptation his blessing, **117m/C VHS, DVD. IT FR GE SI** John Turturro, Rade Serbedzija, Massimo Ghini, Stefano Dionisi, Teco Celio, Claudio Bisio, Roberto Citran, Andy Luotto, Agnieszka Wagner; **D:** Francesco Rosi; **W:** Stefano Rulli, Sandro Petraglia, Tonino Guerra, Francesco Rosi; **C:** Pasqualino De Santis, Marco Pontecorvo; **M:** Luis Bacalov.

Truck Stop 🦴 **19??** This truck stop has all a trucker needs—including the owner, voluptuous Pamela. **80m/C VHS.** Nikki Gentile, Elizabeth Turner; **D:** Jean Marie Pallardy.

Truck Stop Women 🦴🦴 **1974 (R)** Female truckers become involved in smuggling and prostitution at a truck stop. The mob wants a cut of the business and will do anything to get their way. Better than it sounds. **88m/C VHS.** Claudia Jennings, Lieux Dressler, John Martino, Dennis Fimple, Dolores Dorn, Gene Drew, Paul Carr, Jennifer Burton; **D:** Mark L. Lester.

Truck Turner 🦴🦴½ **1974 (R)** He's a bounty hunter, he's black and he's up against a threadbare plot. Hayes methodically eliminates everyone involved with his partner's murder while providing groovy soundtrack. Quintessential blaxploitation. **91m/C VHS, DVD.** Isaac Hayes, Yaphet Kotto, Annazette Chase, Nichelle Nichols, Scatman Crothers, Dick Miller; **D:** Jonathan Kaplan; **W:** Leigh Chapman; **C:** Charles F. Wheeler; **M:** Isaac Hayes.

Trucker's Woman 🦴 **1983 (R)** Man takes a job driving an 18-wheel truck in order to find the murderers of his father. **90m/C VHS.** Michael Hawkins, Mary Cannon; **D:** Will Zens.

Trucks 🦴🦴 **1997 (R)** A group of residents are terrorized by driverless trucks going on a rampage through their small town, which happens to be located in Area 51. Based on the short story by Stephen King and previously filmed as 1986's "Maximum Overdrive." **95m/C VHS, DVD.** Timothy Busfield, Brenda Bakke, Brendan Fletcher, Jay Brazeau, Amy Stewart; **D:** Chris Thomson; **W:** Brian Taggert; **C:** Rob Draper; **M:** Michael Richard Plowman. **CABLE**

The True and the False 🦴½
Den Undenbara Lognen **1955** Two stories haunt the dreams of young bride-to-be Josephine (Hasso). When she falls asleep reading Balzac's "La Grande Breteche," Josephine dreams that she and fiance Louis (Langford) are living out the story of infidelity and revenge. In Guy de Maupassant's "The Old Maid" a disfigured young girl loves a soldier who doesn't love her—until she inherits a fortune. In Swedish with subtitles; also available in an English-language version. **95m/B VHS.** Signe Hasso, William Langford, Ragnor Arvedson, Ann Bibby; **D:** Schamyl Bauman, Mike Road; **W:** Bob Condon; **C:** Sven Nykvist; **M:** Jules Sylvain.

True Believer 🦴🦴½ **1989 (R)** Cynical lawyer, once a '60s radical, now defends rich drug dealers. Spurred on by a young protege, he takes on the hopeless case of imprisoned Asian-American accused of gang-slaying. Tense thriller with good cast. **103m/C VHS, DVD,** James Woods, Robert Downey Jr., Yuji Okumoto, Margaret Colin, Kurtwood Smith, Tom Bower, Miguel Fernandes, Charles Hallahan; **D:** Joseph Ruben; **W:** Wesley Strick; **C:** John Lindley; **M:** Brad Fiedel.

True Blood 🦴🦴 **1989 (R)** A man returns to his home turf to save his brother from the same ruthless gang who set him up for a cop's murder. **100m/C VHS, DVD.** Chad Lowe, Jeff Fahey, Sherilyn Fenn; **D:** Peter Maris.

True Blue 🦴🦴 **2001 (R)** Rem Macy (Berenger) is supposed to be a seasoned NYPD detective. So why does he behave like a hormonally challenged rookie? He's investigating a severed hand found floating in a Central Park pond that turns out to belong to the roommate of Nikki (Heuring). Nikki begs protection from Macy and he lets her stay in his apartment—which the Hound is sure is standard police procedure. Naturally, this is a really dumb move. **101m/C VHS, DVD.** Tom Berenger, Lori Heuring, Barry Newman, Pamela Gridley, Soon-Teck Oh, Richard Chevolleau, Leo Lee; **D:** J.S. Cardone; **W:** J.S. Cardone; **C:** Darko Suvak; **M:** Timothy S. (Tim) Jones. **VIDEO**

True Colors 🦴🦴½ **1987 (PG-13)** A woman fights for her homeland of France in order to save the country from being taken over by Hitler. **160m/C VHS.** Noni Hazlehurst, John Waters, Patrick Ryecart, Shane Briant, Alan Andrews; **D:** Pino Amenta.

True Colors 🦴🦴 **1991 (R)** Law school buddies take divergent paths in post grad real world. Straight and narrow Spader works for Justice Department while dropout Cusack manipulates friends and acquaintances to further his position as Senator's aid. Typecast, predictable and, moralizing. **111m/C VHS, DVD.** Paul Guilfoyle, Dina Merrill, Philip Bosco, Brad Sullivan, Don McManus, John Cusack, James Spader, Imogen Stubbs, Mandy Patinkin, Richard Widmark; **D:** Herbert Ross.

True Confessions 🦴🦴🦴 **1981 (R)** Tale of corruption pits two brothers, one a priest and the other a detective, against each other. Nice 1940s period look, with excellent performances from De Niro and Duvall. Based on a true case from the Gregory Dunne novel. **110m/C VHS, DVD.** Robert De Niro, Robert Duvall, Kenneth McMillan, Charles Durning, Cyril Cusack, Ed Flanders, Burgess Meredith, Louisa Moritz; **D:** Ulu Grosbard; **W:** John Gregory Dunne, Joan Didion; **C:** Owen Roizman; **M:** Georges Delerue.

True Crime 🦴🦴½ **1995** *Dangerous Kiss* High school student turns detective when a classmate is killed, hooks up with a police cadet, and finds herself on the trail of a serial killer. **94m/C VHS, DVD.** Alicia Silverstone, Kevin Dillon, Bill Nunn, Michael Bower; **D:** Pat Verducci; **W:** Pat Verducci; **C:** Chris Squires; **M:** Blake Leyh.

True Crime 🦴🦴 **1999 (R)** Eastwood, who directs and stars, does a good job developing his character Steve Everett, a flawed reporter who has boozed and womanized his way out of the top of his profession. He is given the assignment to interview death row inmate Frank Beachum (Washington), who is scheduled to die in 24 hours. Everett becomes convinced that Beachum is innocent, and the plot erodes into a trite race against time to save the innocent man. Clint shows his acting chops before the story deflates, however, and his fans will certainly enjoy this one. **127m/C VHS, DVD.** Jack Kehler, Clint Eastwood, James Woods, Isaiah Washington IV, Denis Leary, Frances Fisher, Diane Venora, Mary McCormack, Lisa Gay Hamilton, Bernard Hill, Michael McKean, Michael Jeter, Hattie Winston, Laila Robins, Christine Ebersole, Anthony Zerbe, John Finn, Marissa Ribisi, Erik King, Graham Beckel, Sydney Tamiia Poitier, Penny Rae Bridges; **D:** Clint Eastwood; **W:** Larry Gross, Paul Brickman; **C:** Jack N. Green; **M:** Lennie Niehaus.

True Friends 🦴🦴 **1998 (R)** Amateurish but earnest effort by the three lead actors (who also wrote, directed, and produced in various combinations). In 1980, three 12-year-old Bronx buddies witness local mob boss, Big Tony, kill a man. They've stayed friends and kept the secret for 15 years but now the crime comes back to haunt them. **98m/C VHS, DVD.** James Quattrochi, Loreto Mauro, Rodrigo Botero, Dan Lauria, MacKenzie Phillips, John Capodice, Peter Onorati, Bentia Damas, Leo Rossi; **D:** James Quattrochi; **W:** James Quattrochi, Rodrigo Botero; **C:** Jeff Baustert; **M:** Charles Dayton.

True Grit 🦴🦴🦴 **1969 (G)** Hard-drinking U.S. Marshal Rooster Cogburn (Wayne) is hired by a young girl (Darby) to find her father's killer. Won Wayne his only Oscar. Based on the Charles Portis novel. Prompted sequel, "Rooster Cogburn." **128m/C VHS, DVD.** Jeremy Slate, Dennis Hopper, Alfred Ryder, Strother Martin, Jeff Corey, Ron Soble, John Fiedler, James Westerfield, John Doucette, Donald Woods, Edith Atwater, Carlos Rivas, Wilford Brimley, Jay Silverheels, Hank Worden, John Wayne, Glen Campbell, Kim Darby, Robert Duvall; **D:** Henry Hathaway; **W:** Marguerite Roberts; **C:** Lucien Ballard; **M:** Elmer Bernstein. Academy Awards '69: Actor (Wayne); Golden Globes '70: Actor—Drama (Wayne).

True Heart Susie 🦴🦴½ **1919** A simple, moving story about a girl who is in love with a man who marries another girl from the city. Silent. **87m/B VHS, DVD.** Lillian Gish, Robert "Bobbie" Harron; **D:** D.W. Griffith.

True Identity 🦴🦴 **1991 (R)** Henry, a comic superstar in England, stars as an innocent black man marked for death by the Mafia. He hides by disguising himself as white and gets a taste of life on the other side of the color line. The interesting premise was based on a classic Eddie Murphy sketch on "Saturday Night Live," but isn't treated with sufficient imagination or humor here. **94m/C VHS.** Lenny Henry, Frank Langella, Anne-Marie Johnson, Charles Lane; **D:** Charles Lane; **M:** Andy Breckman.

True Lies 🦴🦴½ **1994 (R)** Brain candy with a bang offers eye popping special effects and a large dose of unbelievability. Sort of like a big screen "Scarecrow and Mrs. King" as supposed computer salesman Harry Trasker (Ah-nuld) keeps his spy work secret from mousy, neglected and bored wife Helen (Curtis), who has a few secrets of her own and inadvertently ends up right in the thick of things. Raunchy and extremely sexist, but not without charm; the stupidity is part of the fun. Perfectly cast sidekick Arnold holds his own as a pig, but Heston is wasted as the head honcho. Tons of special effects culminate in a smashing finish. Very loosely adapted from the 1991 French comedy "La Total." **114m/C VHS, DVD.** Arnold Schwarzenegger, Jamie Lee Curtis, Tom Arnold, Bill Paxton, Tia Carrere, Art Malik, Eliza Dushku, Charlton Heston, Grant Heslov; **D:** James Cameron; **W:** James Cameron; **C:** Russell Carpenter; **M:** Brad Fiedel. Golden Globes '95: Actress—Mus./Comedy (Curtis); Blockbuster '96: Action Actress, V. (Curtis).

True Love 🦴🦴🦴 **1989 (R)** Low-budget, savagely observed comedy follows the family and community events leading up to a Bronx Italian wedding. Authentic slice-of-life account of two young people with very different ideas about what marriage and commitment mean. Acclaimed script and performances. **104m/C VHS, DVD.** Annabella Sciorra, Ron Eldard, Aida Turturro, Roger Rignack, Michael J. Wolfe, Star Jasper, Kelly Cinnante, Rick Shapiro, Suzanne Costallos, Vincent Pastore; **D:** Nancy Savoca; **W:** Nancy Savoca, Richard Guay; **C:** Lisa Rinzler. Sundance '89: Grand Jury Prize.

True Romance 🦴🦴🦴½ **1993 (R)** Geeky Clarence (Slater) and wide-eyed call girl Alabama (Arquette) meet and fall instantly in love (and marriage). The inept duo inadvertently steals her pimp's coke and they head to L.A. with the mob in pursuit. Gem performances in small roles include Walken's icily debonair mafioso; Clarence's dad (Hopper), an ex-cop who runs afoul of Walken; Pitt's space-case druggie; Oldman's crazed pimp; and the ghost of Elvis (Kilmer), whom Clarence talks to in times of stress. Horrific violence mixed with very black humor clicks most of the time. Tarantino helped finance "Reservoir Dogs" when he sold this script, his first. Unrated version also available. **116m/C VHS, DVD, UMD.** Christian Slater, Patricia Arquette, Gary Oldman, Brad Pitt, Val Kilmer, Dennis Hopper, Christopher Walken, Samuel L. Jackson, Christopher Penn, Bronson Pinchot, Michael Rapaport, Saul Rubinek, Conchata Ferrell, James Gandolfini, Tom Sizemore, Ed Lauter, Maria Pitillo, Gregory Sporleder, Kevin Corrigan, Michael Beach, Frank Adonis, Victor Argo, Paul Ben-Victor, Paul Bates; **D:** Tony Scott; **W:** Quentin Tarantino; **C:** Jeffrey L. Kimball; **M:** Hans Zimmer, Mark Mancina.

True Stories 🦴🦴🦴½ **1986 (PG)** Quirky, amusing look at the eccentric denizens of a fictional, off-center Texas town celebrating its 150th anniversary. Notable are Kurtz as the Laziest Woman in America and Goodman as a blushing suitor. Directorial debut of Byrne. Worth a look. **89m/C VHS, DVD.** David Byrne, John Goodman, Swoosie Kurtz, Spalding Gray, Annie McEnroe, Pops Staples, Tito Larriva, Alix Elias, Scott Valentine, Jo Harvey Allen; **D:** David Byrne; **W:** Beth Henley, Stephen Tobolowsky, David Byrne; **C:** Edward Lachman; **M:** David Byrne.

True Vengeance 🦴🦴 **1997 (R)** Navy operative firds himself on the run from a group of bounty hunters. **90m/C VHS.** Daniel Bernhardt, Miles O'Keeffe, Beverly Johnson; **D:** David Worth; **W:** Kurt Johnstad; **C:** David Worth.

True West 🦴🦴🦴 **1986** Filmed performance of the acclaimed Sam Shepard play about two mismatched brothers. **110m/C VHS.** John Malkovich, Gary Sinise; **D:** Allan Goldstein. **TV**

True Women 🦴🦴½ **1997 (PG-13)** Sarah McClure (Delany) leaves Georgia with husband Bartlett (Boothe), settles in Texas, and raises her orphaned sister Euphemia (Majorino and Gish), as well as her own family, while Bartlett's off being a Texas Ranger. Euphemia's eventually reunited with her best friend, southern plantation beauty Georgia (Jolie), who's trying to hide the fact that she's part-Cherokee. The ladies suffer through Comanche attacks, the Alamo and the Mexican Army, the Civil War, Reconstruction, and various romantic trials and tribulations, all while being gosh-darn heroic. TV miniseries based on the historical novel by Janice Woods Windle. **170m/C VHS, DVD.** Dana Delaney, Annabeth Gish, Angelina Jolie, Powers Boothe, Tina Majorino, Michael Greyeyes, Tony Todd, Terrence Mann, Michael York, Salli Richardson, Irene Bedard, Charles S. Dutton, Julie Carmen, Matthew Glave, John Schneider, John Terry; **D:** Karen Arthur; **W:** Chris-

Truly, Madly, Deeply ✓✓✓ 1991 (PG) The recent death of her lover Jamie (Rickman) drives Nina (Stevenson) into despair and anger, until he turns up at her apartment one day. And decides to bring some of his ghostly buddies and hang out. Tender and well written tale of love and the supernatural, with believable characters and plot-line. Playwright Minghella's directorial debut. 107m/C VHS, DVD, GB Juliet Stevenson, Alan Rickman, Bill Paterson, Michael Maloney, Christopher Rozycki, Keith Bartlett, David Ryall, Stella Maris; D: Anthony Minghella; C: Remi Adefarasin; M: Barrington Pheloung. Australian Film Inst. '92: Foreign Film; British Acad. '91: Orig. Screenplay.

Trumps ✓✓ Last Minute 1983 (R) Enormous Changes at the 1983 (R) Three dramas about women and contemporary relationships in New York City. Based on three stories—"Faith's Story," "Virginia's Story," and "Alexandra's Story."—by Grace Paley. 90m/C C: Thomas Neuwirth; M: Bruce Broughton. TV

The Trumpet of the Swan ✓½ 2001 (G) Disappointing animated adaptation of E.B. White's 1970 children's book has Louis, a mute trumpeter swan, trying to overcome his disability. Louis befriends a human boy who persuades him to learn to read and write, which doesn't help him much in the animal world, but brings him fame in the human one. His father, distraught over his son's "defect," steals a trumpet for him, and Louis learns to play, becoming famous enough to assuage his father's guilt over the theft by paying for the instrument. The animation, story, and (surprisingly) the score, all seem flat, while the script provides nothing in the way of magic. Only the youngest (under 5) of viewers will be distracted, but probably not for very long. 75m/C VHS, DVD, US D: Richard Rich, Terry L. Noss; W: Judy Rothman Rofé; V: Dee Baker, Jason Alexander, Mary Steenburgen, Reese Witherspoon, Seth Green, Carol Burnett, Joe Mantegna, Sam Gifaldi.

The Truth About Charlie ✓✓½ 2002 (PG-13) Jonathan Demme's remake of the Cary Grant-Audrey Hepburn vehicle "Charade" has the same Paris setting and convoluted plot, but not much of the carefree attitude of the original. Regina (Newton) comes home from a vacation and finds that her husband Charlie has been murdered, and that he was more than he seemed, as the police produce several passports that show Charlie with a different name and disguise. She also discovers that she now has a trio of her husband's former colleagues following her, looking for his hidden six million dollars. As an homage to the French New Wave cinema that was

Truman ✓✓✓½ 1995 (PG) Cable bio follows "Give 'em Hell" Harry (Sinise) from 1917 to 1968. The 33rd U.S. President, derided as a political hack, was determined to prove himself against the odds and by making the tough decisions, including authorizing use of the A-bomb on Japan. Sinise gives the appropriate no-nonsense performance, matched by Scarwid as ever-loyal wife Bess. Based on David McCullough's Pulitzer Prize-winning book. 135m/C VHS, DVD, Gary Sinise, Diana Scarwid, Colm Feore, Richard Dysart, James Gammon, Tony Goldwyn, Pat Hingle, Harris Yulin, Leo Burmester, Zeljko Ivanek, David Lansbury, Marian Seldes, Lois Smith, Richard Venture, Daniel von Bargen; D: Frank Pierson; W: Thomas Rickman; C: Paul Elliott; M: David Mansfield. CABLE

The Truman Show ✓✓✓✓ 1998 (PG) Flawless execution of an eerie, yet fantastical premise, marked by outstanding performances, make this surreal fable a joy to watch from start to finish. Unbeknownst to insurance salesman Truman Burbank, (Carrey) his entire life has been broadcast live on TV in a 24-hour soap opera. When evidence of Truman's fabricated life begs to surface, he plans his escape, upsetting the grand scheme of producer, director and charismatic artist Christof (Harris) in a stand-out performance). Carrey's sympathetic, low-key portrayal will make people forget the dis-appointment of "Cable Guy." Weir handles his satirical theme with craftmen-like precision, never letting his commentary on the power of the tube become too heavy-handed. Carrey reportedly took a pay cut from his $20 million fee in order to star. 102m/C VHS, DVD, Jim Carrey, Ed Harris, Laura Linney, Noah Emmerich, Natascha (Natasha) McElhone, Holland Taylor, Paul Giamatti, Philip Baker Hall, Brian Delate, Una Damon; D: Peter Weir; W: Andrew Niccol; C: Peter Biziou; M: Philip Glass, Burkhard Dallwitz; British Acad. '98: Director (Weir), Orig. Screenplay; Golden Globes '99: Actor—Drama (Carrey), Support. Actor (Harris), Score; MTV Movie Awards '99: Male Perf. (Carrey); Natl. Bd. of Review '98: Support. Actor (Harris).

Trust ✓✓ 1991 (R) An obnoxious girl, tossed out by her family after becoming pregnant, forms a loving bond with a strange, possibly deranged guy from an abusive household. Similar in style and theme to Hartley's "The Unbelievable Truth"—a peculiar sardonic comedy/drama not for every taste. 107m/C VHS, Adrienne Shely, Martin Donovan, Merritt Nelson, Edie Falco, John MacKay, Matt Malloy; D: Hal Hartley; W: Hal Hartley; C: Michael Spiller; M: Phil Reed.

Trust Me ✓✓ 1989 (R) A cynical L.A. art dealer decides to promote a young artist's work and then kill him off to increase the value of his paintings. Satirical view of the Los Angeles art crowd. 94m/C VHS, Adam Ant, Talia Balsam, David Packer, Barbara Bain, Joyce Van Patten, William De Acutis; D: Bobby Houston.

Trust the Man ✓✓ 2006 (R) Relationship flick finds two Manhattan couples examining the state of their love. Tobey (Crudup), a commitment-phobic but cute schlub. Everyone ponders the state of their unions while dabbling in infidelity and self-pity, and despite a few too many moments that are cloying, cliched, or contrived, the leads are good and make things watchable. Tom and Rebecca's two kids are played by Moore and Freundlich's real offspring. 103m/C DVD, US Julianne Moore, David Duchovny, Billy Crudup, Maggie Gyllenhaal, Garry Shandling, Eva Mendes, Ellen Barkin, James LeGros, Liam Broggy, Dagmara Dominczyk, Justin Bartha; D: Bart Freundlich; W: Bart Freundlich; C: Tim Orr; M: Clint Mansell.

Trust the Man ... continued

Trusting Beatrice ✓✓½ 1992 (PG) Larse comedy finds feckless landscaper Claude (Jacobs) the bewildered caretaker of Beatrice (Jacob), a Frenchwoman stranded in America without a green card and with a young Cambodian refugee girl. So Claude decides to take Beatrice home to his determinedly eccentric family. Tries for quirky but falls miserably. 86m/C VHS, Irene Jacob, Mark Evan Jacobs, Leonardo Cimino, Charlotte Moore, Steve Buscemi, Pat McNamara; D: Cindy Lou Johnson; W: Cindy Lou Johnson.

The Truth about Cats and Dogs ✓✓✓ 1996 (PG-13) Funny, intelligent Abby (Garofalo) hosts a popular radio call-in show for pet lovers. When a handsome Brit photographer (Chaplin) phones in with a Great Dane problem, he becomes intrigued by her voice, and asks for a date. Insecure about her looks, Abby asks her beautiful-but-dim girlfriend Noelle (Thurman) to fill in. Naturally, both women fall for the shy Englishman. Charming, updated version of "Cyrano de Bergerac" theme works because of strong lead performances, especially Garofalo, who steals the show with her dry, self-effacing wit. Entertaining romantic comedy features some nice scenes of Santa Monica, too. 97m/C VHS, DVD, Bob Odenkirk, Janeane Garofalo, Uma Thurman, Ben Chaplin, Jamie Foxx, Richard Coca, Stanley DeSantis; D: Michael Lehmann; W: Audrey Wells; C: Robert Brinkmann; M: Howard Shore.

Truth or Dare ✓✓½ 1991 (R) A quasi-concert-documentary—here is music superstar Madonna tarted up in fact, fiction, and fantasy—self-consciousness, and ultimately, if you are a Madonna fan, moving. On camera Madonna sings ex-boyfriend Warren Beatty, disses admirer Kevin Costner, quarrels with her father, reminisces and does sexy things with a bottle. Oh yes, she occasionally sings and dances. Both those who worship and dislike the Material Girl will find much to pick apart here. 118m/C VHS, DVD, Madonna; D: Alek Keshishian.

Truth or Dare? ✓ 1986 The childhood game of truth or dare turns deadly in this violent thriller. 87m/C VHS, John Brace, Mary Fanaro, Geoffrey Lewis Miller; D: Yale Wilson.

Truth or Die ✓✓ Doing Life 1986 In Bed with Madonna; Madonna Truth or Dare 1991 (R) ...

Tuck Everlasting ✓✓½ 2002 (PG) Director Jay Russell does an admirable job adapting the beloved 1975 children's novel by Natalie Babbitt into a feature film. Winnie (Bledel) is chafing under the strict discipline of her parents, particularly the rule that forbids her from playing in the nearby woods. One day, while sneaking into the forbidden forest, she meets Jesse, a boy from the rough and tumble Tuck clan. He tells her not to drink from a certain spring, but immediately after the warning she is abducted by Jesse's brother Miles (Bairstow). At the Tuck resi-

The Truth About Jane ✓✓½ 2000 Fifteen-year-old Jane (muth) is experiencing her first love. Unfortunately for her family and friends, it's with another girl and they just can't cope. Her mom, Janice (Channing), is especially upset and may lose Jane if she can't find a way to accept her. 91m/C VHS, DVD, Stockard Channing, Ellen Muth, James Naughton, RuPaul Charles, Noah Fleiss, Kelly Rowan, Jenny O'Hara, Alicia Lagano; D: Lee Rose; W: Lee Rose; C: Eric Van Haren Noman; M: Terence Blanchard. CABLE

The Truth About Love ✓✓ 2004 Prudish and plain nurse Alice (Hewitt) gets an anonymous Valentine's Day card and assumes it's meant for her philandering husband. Alice and sister Felicity (Miles) conspire, cooking up their own anonymous love letter to Alice's husband Sam (Misry) in hopes of proving his infidelity. Twists and turns are plentiful in this Brit love caper along the lines of Bridget Jones or Love Actually. 90m/C VHS, DVD, GB Jennifer Love Hewitt, Kate Miles, Jimi Mistry, Dougray Scott, Branka Katic; D: John Hay; W: John Hay, Peter Blore, William Johnston, Rik Carmichael; C: Graham Frake; M: Debbie Wiseman. VIDEO

Truth about Women ✓✓ 1958 An old aristocrat recounts his youthful adventures to his son-in-law. A pale British comedy of manners. 107m/C VHS, GB Laurence Harvey, Julie Harris, Mai Zetterling, Eva Gabor, Wilfrid Hyde-White, Derek Farr; D: Muriel Box.

Truth or Consequences, N.M. ✓ 1997 (R) Yes, the name of the town is real. No, Bob Barker is not the mayor. Dim parolee Raymond (Gallo) and his even dimmer girlfriend Addy (Dickens) are reunited and just want to settle down, but to tell the truth. Instead, they fall immediately back into a life of crime. Along with their accomplices Marcus (Williamson) and Curtis (Sutherland), they plan to rip off a drug dealer for big bucks (no whammies!). The heist, of course, goes bad; they steal an RV and kidnap its owners Gordon (Pollack) and Donna (Phillips). An attempt to unload the crooks on a powerful Mafia boss (Steiger) also goes awry, and that starts a real family feud. As the mob hit man (Sheen), the cops, and the crooks all converge on the eponymous New Mexico town, everyone is in jeopardy. Not logical, not original and not good. Directorial debut for Sutherland, who should really quit playing coked-up psychopaths; murderers. 106m/C VHS, DVD, Vincent Gallo, Kim Dickens, Kiefer Sutherland, Kevin Pollak, Martin Sheen, Rod Steiger, Rick Rossovich, John C. McGinley, Max Perlich; D: Kiefer Sutherland; W: Brad Mirman; C: Ric Waite; M: Jude Cole.

Tube ✓✓ Tyubeu 2003 (R) After suffering a shocking personal loss, police detective Jay (Kim) finds himself relegated to the ranks of subway cop. He told asleep until that fateful day when the good-guy-gone-bad (Park) takes control of the train and terrorizes the community, giving Jay the chance to be a hero again and save the day. While the action in director Woon-hak's Seoul-based debut zips along; the effort lacks the "certain something" (like a well-developed plot) that made its obvious inspirations—"Die Hard" and "Speed"—smash hits. Korean, with English subtitles. 112m/C VHS, DVD, Seok-hun Kim, Du-na Bae, Sang-min Park, Byeong-ho Son, Oh-jung Gweon; D: Woon-hak Baek; W: Woon-hak Baek, Weon-mi Byeon, Jeong-min Kim, Min-ju Kim; C: Hong-shik Yun; M: Saeng-jun Hwang. VIDEO

Tsui Hark's Vampire Hunters ✓ Vampire Hunters; The Era of the Vampires 2002 (R) Don't expect any sense past watch the kung fu sequences. There are four vampire hunters named Wind, Thunder, Lightning, and Rain who are assigned by their master to find and destroy the zombie-like vampires. They have several sword fights with some humanoid opponents as well. Cantonese with subtitles. 90m/C VHS, DVD, HK JP Lam Suet, Kwok-Kwan Chan, Ken Chang, Michael Chow Man-Kin; D: Wellson Chin; W: Tsui Hark; C: Herman Yau, Joe Chan, Sunny Tsang Tat Sze; M: J.M. Logan.

Tsotsi ✓✓✓ 2005 (R) Young Tsotsi and his gang of urban thugs pillage their shantytown-turf outside Johannesburg, South Africa. After stealing a BMW from a wealthy black woman, Tsotsi discovers he's also nabbed her infant son in the backseat. The child's affect on this criminal becomes the centerpiece and eventual redemption behind the story. Unpredictable, violent, and compassionate, Director Gavin Hood constructs a world foreign to most Western audiences, in every sense of the word. 94m/C DVD, Kenneth Nkosi, Zenzo Ngqobe, Presley Chweneyagae, Terry Pheto, Mothusi Magano, Israel Makoe, Percy Matsemela, Benny Moshe, Benny Moshe, Nambitha Mpumlwana, Rapulana Seiphemo, Ian Roberts, Jerry Mofokeng; D: Gavin Hood; W: Gavin Hood; C: Lance Gewer; M: Mark Kilian, Paul Hepker; Oscars '05: Foreign Film.

The Tsar's Bride ✓✓✓ Tsarskaya Nevesta 1966 A lovely young woman is chosen to be the bride of the horrible Tsar Glebov, but when the Tsar's bodyguard falls for her, romantic difficulties ensue. A hybrid of the 1849 Rimsky-Korsakov opera and an 1849 play. 95m/B VHS, Ru Raisa Nedashkovskaya, Natalya Rudnaya, Otar Koberidze; D: Vladimir Gorikker.

Tryst ✓✓½ 1994 (R) Julia plots to kill her husband with the help of a detective. Suspenseful melodrama analyzes mob rule and the criminal mind. 91m/B VHS, Lloyd Bridges, Kathleen Foster, Richard Carlson; Frank Lovejoy, Katherine Locke; D: Cy Endfield, Jo Pagano; C: Guy Roe.

Try and Get Me ✓✓ Sound of Fury 1950 A small town is incited into a manhunt for kidnappers who murdered their victim. 96m/C VHS, DVD, Tony Danza, Jon (John) DeVries, Lisa Langlois, Rocco Sisto; D: Gene Reynolds.

his cell. Still, an uncharacteristic role for sitcom guy Shatz. Based on Rosenberg's book "Doing Life." 104m/C VHS, DVD, US Mark Wahlberg, Thandie Newton, Tim Robbins, Joong-Hoon Park, Ted Levine, Lisa Gay Hamilton, Christine Boisson, Stephen (Dillon) Dillane; Cameos: Charles Aznavour, Anna Karina; D: Jonathan Demme; W: Jonathan Demme, Steven Schmidt, Jessica Bendinger; C: Tak Fujimoto; M: Rachel Portman.

dence. Jesse's parents inform her that the spring is a fountain of youth and that she is not allowed to return home with that knowledge. She begins to fall for young Jesse although she discovers that he is actually 104 years old. **90m/C VHS, DVD. US** Alexis Bledel, Jonathan Jackson, Sissy Spacek, William Hurt, Scott Bairstow, Ben Kingsley, Amy Irving, Victor Garber; **D:** Jay Russell; **W:** James V. Hart, Jeffrey Lieber; **C:** James L. Carter; **M:** William Ross; **Nar:** Elisabeth Shue.

Tucker: The Man and His Dream ✓✓✓
1988 (PG) Portrait of Preston Tucker, entrepreneur and industrial idealist, who in 1946 tried to build the car of the future and was effectively run out of business by the powers-that-were. Ravishing, ultra-nostalgic lullaby to the American Dream. Watch for Jeff's dad, Lloyd, in a bit role. **111m/C VHS, DVD.** Jeff Bridges, Martin Landau, Dean Stockwell, Frederic Forrest, Mako, Joan Allen, Christian Slater, Lloyd Bridges, Elias Koteas, Nina Siemaszko, Corin "Corky" Nemec, Marshall Bell, Don Novello, Peter Donat, Dean Goodman, Patti Austin; **D:** Francis Ford Coppola; **W:** Arnold Schulman, David Seidler; **M:** Joe Jackson, Carmine Coppola. Golden Globes '89: Support. Actor (Landau); N.Y. Film Critics '88: Support. Actor (Stockwell).

Tuesdays with Morrie ✓✓½
1999 Detroit sportswriter Mitch Albom (Azaria) spots his old college prof, 78-year-old Morrie Schwartz (Lemmon), on ABC's "Nightline" discussing his battle with ALS and his thoughts on death. The workaholic Albom, who has not seen Morrie in 16 years, decides to pay his one-time mentor a visit in Boston. The relationship rekindles and they begin to meet every Tuesday, with Albom coming to question the path his life is taking. Based on Albom's best-selling book. **89m/C VHS, DVD.** Jack Lemmon, Hank Azaria, John Carroll Lynch, Wendy Moniz, Bonnie Bartlett, Caroline Aaron, Aaron Lustig, Bruce Nozick; **D:** Mick Jackson; **W:** Thomas (Tom) Rickman; **C:** Theo van de Sande; **M:** Marco Beltrami. TV

Tuff Turf ✓✓
1985 (R) The new kid in town must adjust to a different social lifestyle and a new set of rules when his family is forced to move to a low-class section of Los Angeles. He makes enemies immediately when he courts the girlfriend of one of the local toughs. Fast-paced with a bright young cast. Music by Jim Carroll, Lene Lovich, and Southside Johnny. **113m/C VHS, DVD.** James Spader, Kim Richards, Paul Mones, Matt Clark, Olivia Barash, Robert Downey Jr., Catya (Cat) Sassoon, Claudette Nevins; **D:** Fritz Kiersch; **W:** Jette Rinck; **C:** Willy Kurant; **M:** Jonathan Elias.

Tulips ✓½
1981 (PG) Would-be suicide takes a contract out on himself, and then meets a woman who makes life worth living again. Together they attempt to evade the gangland hit man. Limp comedy. **91m/C VHS.** CA Gabe Kaplan, Bernadette Peters, Henry Gibson; **D:** Stan Ferris.

Tully ✓✓½
What Happened to Tully; Tully. 2000 (R) Quiet and convincing adaptation of Tom Neal's 1992 short story is set on a Nebraska dairy farm owned by taciturn Tully Coates Sr. (Burrus), who is hiding family secrets from his two sons. Handsome Tully Jr. (Mount) is the local womanizer while younger brother Earl (Fitzgerald) is shy and sensitive. Both have a soft spot for recently-returned neighbor Ella Smalley (Nicholson), who is too smart to fall for Tully's lines even as their friendship veers toward romance. **107m/C VHS, DVD.** US Anson Mount, Julianne Nicholson, Glenn Fitzgerald, Bob Burrus, Catherine Kellner, Natalie Canerday, John Diehl, V. Craig Heidenreich; **D:** Hilary Birmingham; **W:** Hilary Birmingham, Matt Drake; **C:** John Foster; **M:** Marcelo Zarvos.

Tulsa ✓✓✓
1949 High-spirited rancher's daughter begins crusade to save her father's oil empire when he's killed. Having become ruthless and determined to succeed at any cost, she eventually sees the error of her ways. Classic Hayward. **90m/C VHS, DVD.** Susan Hayward, Robert Preston, Chill Wills, Ed Begley Sr., Pedro Armendariz Sr.; **D:** Stuart Heisler; **C:** Winton C. Hoch.

Tumbledown Ranch in Arizona ✓
1941 After a rodeo accident, an unconscious college student dreams of adventure out west. Part of the "Range Busters" series. **60m/B VHS.** Ray Corrigan, John "Dusty" King, Max Terhune, Sheila Darcy, Marian Kerby; **D:** S. Roy Luby.

Tumbleweed Trail ✓✓½
1942 Action-packed thundering western. **57m/B VHS.** William Boyd, Art Davis, Lee Powell, Jack Rockwell; **D:** Sam Newfield.

Tumbleweeds ✓✓✓
1925 William S. Hart's last western. Portrays the last great land rush in America, the opening of the Cherokee Strip in the Oklahoma Territory to homesteaders. Preceded by a sound prologue, made in 1939, in which Hart speaks for the only time on screen, to introduce the story. Silent, with musical score. **114m/B VHS, DVD.** William S. Hart, Lucien Littlefield, Barbara Bedford; **D:** King Baggot.

Tumbleweeds ✓✓½
1998 (PG-13) Mary Jo Walker (McTeer) has been married numerous times and begins in even more relationships. 12-year-old daughter Ava (Brown) knows that when things go wrong with mom's romantic prospects they pack up and hit the road, which is why they're on their way to San Diego. Of course, Mary Jo meets trucker Jack (O'Connor) along the way and decides to shack up with him when they reach their destination, while the remarkably resilient Ava settles into another new life. But since Mary Jo has such lousy judgment (except about her love for Ava) this mother-daughter duo is headed for rocky times ahead. **104m/C VHS, DVD.** Janet McTeer, Kimberly J. Brown, Gavin O'Connor, Jay O. Sanders, Lois Smith, Laurel Holloman, Michael J. Pollard, Noah Emmerich; **D:** Gavin O'Connor; **C:** Dan Stoloff; **M:** Angela Shelton, Gavin O'Connor. Golden Globes '00: Actress—Mus./Comedy (McTeer); Ind. Spirit '00: Debut Perf. (Brown); Natl. Bd. of Review '99: Actress (McTeer); Sundance '99: Filmmakers Trophy.

Tundra ✓✓½
The Mighty Thunder. 1936 Quasi adventure-drama/documentary set in the Alaskan tundra. A young man, known only as the "Flying Doctor," tends to the sick in small villages throughout the wilderness. But his own survival is at stake when his small plane crashes. Filmed on location. **72m/B VHS.** Del Cambre; **D:** Norman Dawn.

The Tune ✓✓
1992 30,000 ink and watercolor drawings make up this animated gem which tells the story of Del (Neiden), a failed songwriter who gets a fresh start when he makes a wrong turn on the freeway and winds up in Flooby Nooby. The strange inhabitants of this town teach Del to throw out his rhyming dictionary and write about his experiences. Plymton's first full-length animated feature. Also includes "The Making of The Tune" and the animated short "Draw." **80m/C VHS, DVD.** D: Bill Plympton; **V:** Maureen McElheron, Bill Plympton, P.C. Vey; **C:** John Donnelly; **M:** Maureen McElheron; **V:** Daniel Neiden, Maureen McElheron, Marty Nelson, Emily Bindiger, Chris Hoffman.

Tune in Tomorrow ✓✓
1990 (PG-13) Lovesick young Martin (Reeves) wants to woo divorced older babe aunt-by-marriage Julia (Hershey) and is romantically counseled by wacky soap opera writer Pedro (Falk). Seems even soap operas draw on real life, and Martin's story is immortalized on the airwaves, circa 1951 New Orleans. The story-within-a-story also features Pedro's radio characters coming to hammy life. Sometimes funny, sometimes tiresome. Adapted from the novel "Aunt Julia and the Scriptwriter" by Mario Vargas Llosa. **90m/C VHS, DVD.** Barbara Hershey, Keanu Reeves, Peter Falk, Bill McCutcheon, Patricia Clarkson, Peter Gallagher, Dan Hedaya, Buck Henry, Hope Lange, John Larroquette, Elizabeth McGovern, Robert Sedgwick, Henry Gibson; **D:** Jon Amiel; **W:** William Boyd; **C:** Robert M. Stevens; **M:** Wynton Marsalis.

Tunes of Glory ✓✓✓
1960 Guinness and Mills are wonderful in this well made film about a brutal, sometimes lazy colonel and a disciplined and educated man moving up through the ranks of the British military. York's film debut. From

---

the novel by James Kennaway, who adapted it for the screen. **107m/C VHS, DVD.** GB Alec Guinness, John Mills, Dennis Price, Kay Walsh, Susannah York; **D:** Ronald Neame; **M:** Malcolm Arnold.

The Tunnel ✓✓½
1989 (R) Obsessive romance film with a trace of suspense. Artist sees the woman of his dreams at a showing of his work. Her marriage, and her trepidation, don't keep his obsession from consuming him. **99m/C VHS.** Jane Seymour, Peter Weller, Fernando Rey; **D:** Antonio Drove.

The Tunnel ✓✓✓½
Der Tunnel. 2001 Originally produced for German television broadcast. Based on the true story of Harry Melchior (Ferch), an East German swimming champ who fled to West Berlin in 1961 as the wall was going up. Melchior is so committed to getting his sister Lotte (Lara) and her family out of East Berlin that he hatches a plan to dig a tunnel under the wall. Naturally the tunnel becomes a massive undertaking requiring the clandestine enlistment of other West Berliners with loved ones behind the wall. This tense drama is packed with story lines and looming disaster—a rare gem with top notch production values. **157m/C DVD.** GE Heino Ferch, Nicolette Krebitz, Sebastian Koch, Mehmet Kurtulus, Alexandra Maria Lara, Felix Eitner; **D:** Roland Suso Richter; **W:** Johannes W. Betz; **C:** Martin Langer; **M:** Harald Kloser, Thomas Wanker. TV

The Tunnel of Love ✓✓½
1958 Day and Widmark are a married couple who find themselves over their heads in red tape when they try to adopt a baby. A beautiful, disapproving adoption investigator also causes more problems for the couple when she believes Widmark is less than ideal father material. Widmark is not in his element at comedy but Day and Young (as their next-door neighbor) are fine in this lightweight adaptation of the Joseph Fields-Peter DeVries play. **98m/B VHS.** Doris Day, Richard Widmark, Gig Young, Gia Scala, Elisabeth Fraser, Elizabeth Wilson; **D:** Gene Kelly; **M:** Jerome Chodorov.

Tunnel Vision ✓✓½
1995 (R) Detective Kelly Wheatstone (Kensit) and her partner Frank Yanovitch (Reynolds) are after a serial killer whose victims are all beautiful women killed in a ritualistic fashion. But all the clues begin to point to Yanovitch as the one committing the crimes. This one is routine all the way. **100m/C VHS, DVD.** AU Patsy Kensil, Robert Reynolds, Rebecca Rigg, Shane Briant; **D:** Clive Fleury; **W:** Clive Fleury; **C:** Paul Murphy; **M:** David Hirschfelder.

Tunnelvision ✓✓
1976 (R) A spoof of TV comprised of irreverent sketches. Fun to watch because of the appearances of several now-popular stars. **70m/C VHS, DVD.** Chevy Chase, John Candy, Laraine Newman, Joe Flaherty, Howard Hesseman, Gerrit Graham, Al Franken, Tom Davis, Ron Silver; **D:** Neal Israel.

Turbo: A Power Rangers Movie ✓
1996 (PG) The Power Rangers must battle the evil Divatox (Turner), who's kidnapped the wizard Lerigot so she can use his power to free her even more evil boyfriend Maligore. It's all around cheesy but if you're a five-year-old you may still enjoy the action. **99m/C VHS, DVD.** Jason David Frank, Stephen Antonio Cardenas, John Yong Bosch, Catherine Sutherland, Nakia Burrise, Blake Foster, Paul Schrier, Jason Narvy, Amy Jo Johnson, Austin St. John, Hilary Shepard Turner, Jon Simanton; **D:** David Winning, Shuki Levy; **W:** Shuki Levy, Shell Danielson; **C:** Ilan Rosenberg; **M:** Shuki Levy.

Turbulence ✓✓½
1996 (R) When you fly, it's usually the turbulence that makes you throw up. Well, this movie isn't that bad, but you may experience a touch of nausea. Flight attendant Teri (Holly) is pushing the drink cart on a strangely vacant New York to L.A. Christmas Eve run. Among the passengers are convicted felons Ryan (Liotta) and Stubbs (Gleeson), who are either on their way to serve prison or fulfilling the "consumption of airline food" portion of their sentence. The prisoners seize a gun from the marshals and accidentally rub out the cockpit crew. With all the passengers locked

---

away, Teri must battle the serial rapist/killer Ryan as well as learn to fly the plane through a horrible storm. Passengers on the left of the screen may look out and see "Passenger 57," while those on the right can see the ancient monument of "Airport 75." **103m/C VHS, DVD.** Ray Liotta, Lauren Holly, Hector Elizondo, Brendan Gleeson, Ben Cross, Rachel Ticotin, Jeffrey DeMunn, John Finn, Catherine Hicks; **D:** Robert Butler; **W:** Jonathan Brett; **C:** Lloyd Ahern II; **M:** Shirley Walker.

Turbulence 2: Fear of Flying ✓✓
1999 Group of scared to fly passengers try to overcome their fears aboard a jumbo 747. They will never set foot off the ground again after severe turbulence damages the plane and a nerve gas-carrying terrorist commandeers it. **100m/C VHS, DVD.** Tom Berenger, Craig Sheffer, Jennifer Beals, Jeffrey Nordling; **D:** David Mackay; **W:** Kevin Bernhardt, Brendan Broderick, Rob Kerchner. VIDEO

Turbulence 3: Heavy Metal woof!
2000 (R) Wannable shock rocker Slade Craven (Mann) wants to make his last concert a spectacular affair, so he has a passenger jet modified so he can give his performance, which will be broadcast over the Internet, in mid-air to a select audience. But the plane is hijacked and FBI agent Kate Hayden (Anwar), who just happens to be on board, and hacker Nick Watts (Sheffer) try to prevent a disaster. Stupid plot, stupid characters—all around cheese. **96m/C VHS, DVD.** Craig Sheffer, Gabrielle Anwar, Monica Schnarre, Rutger Hauer, Joe Mantegna, John Mann; **D:** Jorge Montesi; **W:** Wade Ferley; **C:** Philip Linzey; **M:** John McCarthy. VIDEO

Turf Boy ✓✓
Mr. Celebrity 1942 Desperate for cash, a boy and his uncle try to get an old horse into prime condition for racing. A minor equine melodrama, just the right length for an old-time matinee double-feature. **68m/B VHS.** Robert "Buzzy" Henry, James Seay, Doris Day, William (Bill) Halligan, Gavin Gordon; **D:** William Beaudine.

Turistas ✓
2006 (R) Young, sexy, and often-naked travelers are stuck in Brazil after a bus accident. That doesn't stop them from partying, however, until they wake up the next morning to the not-so-shocking realization that they've been drugged and robbed. The overly-friendly locals aren't what they seem, and soon a crazed surgeon straight out of the book of urban legends is blathering about economic inequality and carving out the visitors' vital organs. Dopey, dull, and not very scary (unless xenophobia counts). **89m/C DVD.** US Josh Duhamel, Melissa George, Olivia Wilde, Desmond Askew, Beau Garrett, Max Brown, Agles Steib, Miguel Lunardi; **D:** John Stockwell; **W:** Michael Arlen Ross; **C:** Enrique Chediak; **M:** Paul Haslinger.

Turk 182! ✓½
1985 (PG-13) The antics of a disabled fireman takes on City Hall in order to win back the pension that he deserves. He attacks through his graffiti art. Hutton is too heavy for the over-all comic feel of this mostly silly film. **96m/C VHS, DVD.** Timothy Hutton, Robert Culp, Robert Urich, Kim Cattrall, Peter Boyle, Darren McGavin, Paul Sorvino; **D:** Bob (Benjamin) Clark.

Turkish Delight ✓✓½
1973 Free spirit sculptor falls in love with free spirit gal from bourgeois family and artsy soft porn ensues. That is until a brain tumor puts an end to their fun, and he's left to wallow in flashbacks and more artsy soft porn. Dubbed. Verhoeven later became big boxoffice in the U.S. with "Total Recall." **100m/C VHS, DVD.** NL Monique Van De Ven, Rutger Hauer, Tonny Huurdeman, Wim Van Den Brink; **D:** Paul Verhoeven; **W:** Gerard Soeteman; **C:** Jan De Bont.

Turn It Up ✓½
2000 (R) Diamond (Pras) is a talented musician who's involved in the drug trade with childhood friend Gage (Ja Rule). He wants to go legit so he can pursue his music dreams but Gage is a hothead who gets them into more trouble. Then Diamond's girlfriend announces she's pregnant, his mother unexpectedly dies, and his estranged father (Curtis-Hall) turns up. **87m/C VHS, DVD.** Pras, Vondie Curtis-Hall, Ja Rule, Tamala Jones, Jason Statham, Eugene Clark; **D:** Robert Adetuyi;

W: Robert Adetuyi; C: Hubert Taczanowski; M: Gary Jones, Happy Walters.

Turn of the Blade 🐾 1997 Predictable thriller finds photographer Sam Peyton (Christensen) upset that his wife Kelly (Owens) is more interested in her acting career than in having a baby. It may be safer to have the kid, since Kelly's the lust object for a seedy film director and a dangerous stalker. Meanwhile, Sam has his own problems with his associate Wendy, who wants their relationship to get personal and is willing to kill out of the way. 91m/C VHS, DVD. **C:** David Keith Miller, Julie Horvath; **D:** Bryan Michael Stoller. **W:** Mark Berk; **C:** Richard A. Jones.

The Turn of the Screw 🐾 1989 (R) The young charges of a nanny are sought for their souls by a dark, unimaginable evil in the mansion. 60m/C version of the Henry James story. 120m/C VHS, DVD. **C:** Lynn Redgrave, Jasper Jacobs, Eva Griffith; **D:** Dan Curtis.

The Turn of the Screw 🐾 1992 (R) Yet another version of the Henry James classic as a young governess struggles with sexual obsession for the two children in her care who are possessed by evil. 95m/C VHS. **C:** Julian Sands, Patsy Kensit, Stephane Audran, Marianne Faithfull; **D:** Rusty Lemorande.

The Turn of the Screw 🐾🐾½ 1999 Solid TV adaptation of the Henry James novel boasts some fine performances in a now familiar story. Miss (May) comes to a remote manor, whose charges are the overly well-behaved Miles (Sowerbutts) and his younger sister, Flora (Robinson). Soon Miss is seeing ghosts—those of the former governess and another servant, Peter Quint (Salkey), whom she believes are corrupting her innocent children. But maybe the emotional young woman is simply crazy. 80m/C VHS, DVD, GB Jodhi May, Pam Ferris, Colin Firth, Joe Sowerbutts, Grace Robinson, Jason Salkey, Caroline Pegg, Jenny Howe. **D:** Ben Bolt. **W:** Nick Dear; **C:** David Odd; **M:** Adrian Johnston. **TV**

Turnaround 🐾 1987 (R) Unusual action/suspense film set in a small town. Relentless gang rampages the citizens. Finally, a man decides he's had enough, and turns on the heathens with his knowledge of magic. 97m/C VHS. **C:** Doug McKeon, Tim Maier, Eddie Albert, Gaye Hunnicutt; **D:** Ole Solum, Jack Epps Jr. **C:** Adam Greenberg; **M:** Charles Gross.

Turner and Hooch 🐾🐾 1989 (PG) A dog witnesses a murder, and a fussy cop is partnered with the drooling mutt and a weak script in his search for the culprit. Drool as a joke will only go so far, but Hanks is his usual entertaining self. 99m/C VHS. **C:** Tom Hanks, Mare Winningham, Craig T. Nelson, Scott Paulin, J.C. Quinn; **D:** Roger Spottiswoode; **W:** Michael Blodgett, Jim Cash, Jack.

The Turning 🐾🐾 1992 Twenty-two-year-old Cliff Harnish (Dolan) returns home after a four-year absence to shock his family with his strident Neo-Nazi beliefs. May be of curiosity value to Anderson's "X-Files" fans, since she appears (relatively briefly and partially nude) as the guy's girlfriend in a kitchen sex scene. Based on the play by Ceraso. 92m/C VHS, DVD. Michael Dolan, Raymond J. Barry, Karen Allen, Tess Harper, Gillian Anderson; **D:** L.A. Puopolo; **W:** L.A. Puopolo, Chris Ceraso; **C:** J. Michael McClary.

The Turning Point 🐾🐾½ 1977 (PG) A woman who gave up ballet for motherhood must come to terms as her daughter launches a ballet career and falls for the lead male dancer. The mother finds herself threatened by her daughter's affection toward an old friend who sacrificed a family life for the life of a ballerina. Baryshnikov's film debut. Melodramatic ending.

The Tuskegee Airmen 🐾🐾🐾 1995 (PG-13) Cable drama based on the formation and WWII achievements of the U.S. Army Air Corps' first squadron of black combat flyers. They get a 99m/C of the 332nd Fighter Group. They were nicknamed after they trained in Tuskegee, Alabama and distinguished themselves in combat, never losing a single bomber, and receiving more than 800 medals. Cast all do a fine job in what turns out to essentially be a standard action/war movie. Based on a story by former Tuskegee airman, Robert W. Williams. 107m/C VHS, DVD. Laurence Fishburne, Cuba Gooding Jr., Allen Payne, Malcolm Jamal Warner, Courtney B. Vance, Andre Braugher, John Lithgow, Rosemary Murphy, Christopher McDonald, Vivica A. Fox, Daniel Hugh-Kelly, David Harrod Eddie Braun, Bennet Guillory; **D:** Robert Markowitz; **W:** Paris Qualles, Ron Hutchinson, Trey Ellis; **C:** Ronald Orieux; **M:** Lee Holdridge. **CABLE**

Tusks 🐾½ 1989 (R) A ruthless hunter tries to kill elephants. 99m/C VHS, DVD. Andrew Stevens, John Rhys-Davies, Lucy Gutteridge, Julian Glover; **D:** Tara Hawkins Moore.

Tut & Tuttle 🐾½ 1981 Young dabbler in magic is transported to ancient Egypt where he is able to demonstrate courage and wits against the evil Horembed, who has kidnapped Prince Tut. 97m/C VHS, James Hampton, Kario Salem, Jo Anne Worley, Sydney Penny, Olivia Barash, Elaine Giftos, Chris Barnes, Eric Greene, Hans Conried, Vic Tayback; **D:** Ron Howard; **W:** Rance Howard; **C:** Gary Graver; **M:** Joe Renzetti. **TV**

The Tuttles of Tahiti 🐾🐾 1942 The Tuttles lead a life of leisure in the South Seas. Laughton's child becomes enamoured of his rival's offspring, causing problems between the two families. More interesting than it sounds. 91m/C VHS. Charles Laughton, Jon Hall, Peggy Drake, Victor Francen, Gene Reynolds, Florence Bates, Mala, Alma Ross, Curt Bois; **D:** Charles Vidor.

12 and Holding 🐾🐾🐾 2005 (R) Rudy (Donovan) and his fat buddy Leonard (Camacho) spend the night in their tree house, which is torched by bullies. Leonard is injured (he loses his sense of taste) but Rudy dies. His twin Jacob is barely able to cope (he already has self-esteem issues since a birthmark covers half his face), especially when confronted with his parents' grief and rage. Leonard's survival inspires him to lose weight and get in shape, much to the resentment of his obese parents. Meanwhile, their friend

Turtles Can Fly 🐾🐾🐾½ 2004 Lak-poshtna ham parvaz mikonand Director Ghobadi's stark and engrossing tale of the unending daily sufferings of refugee children living on the Iraq-Turkey border as they await the U.S.-led invasion in early 2003. Essentially absent of adults, Ghobadi centers on 13-year-old Satellite (Ebrahim)—who uses his technical savvy to bring TV to the camp so they can watch news channels—along with his rival Henkov, disfigured by landmines, and Henkov's withdrawn sister Agrin who rebuffs Satellite's romantic advances. In Kurdish, with English subtitles. 95m/C DVD. FR IA IQ Soran Ebrahim, Avaz Latif, Hirsh Feyssal, Saddam Hossein Feysal, Hiresh Feysal Rahman, Abdol Rahman Karim, Ajil Zibari; **D:** Bahman Ghobadi; **W:** Bahman Ghobadi; **C:** Shahriar Assadi; **M:** Hossein Alizadeh.

Turumba 🐾🐾🐾 1984 A quiet satire about a family of papier-mâché animal makers in a Philippine village who get a gargantuan order in time for the Turumba galop with English subtitles. 94m/C VHS, PH Claudia Azires, Johnny Ching, Mara Penipol; **D:** Kidlat Tahimik; **W:** Kidlat Tahimik.

Tuxedo Warrior 🐾½ 1982 Set in South Africa, this film involves the adventures of a well-dressed mercenary who is caught between the police, diamond thieves, and an old girlfriend's bank robbers. 87m/C DVD. David Duchovny, Sigourney Weaver, Ioan Gruffudd, Judy Greer, Fran Kranz, Lindsay Sloane, Justine Bateman, Lucy Davis; **D:** Jake Kasdan; **W:** Jake Kasdan; **C:** Uta Briesewitz.

Tweek City 🐾½ 2005 Bumpy indie follows San Francisco drug dealer Bill, who has a crystal meth problem that fuels his insecurities about his half-Latino heritage, his sexuality, and his troubled childhood. Bill can't get past his ex-high school girlfriend getting married and goes on a bender before crashing the wedding. Writer/director Johnson ultimately doesn't know where to take his character or story. 96m/C DVD. Giuseppe Andrews, Keith Brunsmann, Elizabeth Bogush, Eva Fisher; **D:** Eric Johnson; **W:** Eric Johnson; **C:** Barry Stone; **M:** Jim Latham.

Twelfth Night 🐾🐾½ 1996 (PG) Director Nunn's take on Shakespeare's gender-bending, romantic-comedy, which is now set in the 1890s. Shipwrecked on an unfriendly Illyrian shore, Viola (Stubbs), believing twin brother Sebastian (Mackintosh) to be dead, disguises herself in male attire and joins the retinue of the lovesick Duke Orsino (Stephens). He's pining for the Countess Olivia (Bonham Carter) and decides to use Viola-turned-Cesario as a surrogate wooer. Too bad Olivia's becoming more interested in her effeminate pseudo-suitor and that Orsino's having a few sexual quandries of his own. 133m/C VHS, DVD, GB Imogen Stubbs, Helena Bonham-Carter, Toby Stephens, Steven Mackintosh, Richard E. Grant, Nigel Hawthorne, Ben Kingsley, Imelda Staunton, Mel Smith, Nicholas Farrell; **D:** Trevor Nunn; **C:** Clive Tickner; **M:** Shaun Davey.

Turtle Diary 🐾🐾🐾 1986 (PG) Two lonely Londoners collaborate to free giant turtles from the city aquarium with the aid of a zoo-keeper, and the turtles' freedom somehow frees them as well. Jackson and Kingsley are stunning. Adapted by Harold Pinter from the Russell Hoban book. 90m/C VHS, GB Ben Kingsley, Glenda Jackson, Richard Johnson, Michael Gambon, Rosemary Leach, Jeroen Krabbe, Eleanor Bron; **D:** John Irvin; **W:** Harold Pinter; **M:** Geoffrey Burgon.

The Tuxedo 🐾½ 2002 (PG-13) After an unusual opening non sequiter, movie pits kickmaster Chan against the evil Banning (Coster) out to dehydrate the world by all, with much uncomfortably honest depiction of adolescent bewilderment and via a deadly ingredient in the water supply. Mild-mannered taxi driver Jimmy (Chan) takes a job chauffeuring Clark Devlin (Isaacs), a wealthy spy with a secret weapon: the title's near-magical tuxedo that turns the wearer into a martial arts fighting machine. After Devlin's injured, Jimmy dons the supersuit and joins agent Del (Hewitt) in the fight against Banning. 98m/C VHS, DVD. US Jackie Chan, Jennifer Love Hewitt, Jason Isaacs, Debi Mazar, Ritchie Coster, Peter Stormare, Romany Malco, Mia Cottet; **D:** Kevin Donovan; **W:** Michael J. Wilson, Michael Leeson; **C:** Stephen Windon; **M:** John Debney, Christophe Beck.

The TV Set 🐾🐾½ 2006 (R) Art vs. commerce in an amusing satire. Writer Mike (Duchovny) is trying to sell a personal project for TV development to a network headed by the predatory Lenny (Weaver), maybe too well for the show who aren't insiders. 87m/C DVD. David Duchovny, Sigourney Weaver, Ioan Gruffudd, Judy Greer, Fran Kranz, Lindsay Sloane, Justine Bateman, Lucy Davis; **D:** Jake Kasdan; **W:** Jake Kasdan; **C:** Uta Briesewitz.

The Twelve Days of Christmas Eve 🐾½ 2004 (PG) Take-off on Russian folktale first filmed in Yugoslavia in 1927. A rich magnate admits on her deathbed that she has hidden her jewels in the upholstery of one of 12 chairs that are no longer in her home. A Brooklsian treasure hunt ensues. 94m/C VHS, DVD. Mel Brooks, Dom Deluise, Frank Langella, Ron Moody, Bridget Brice; **D:** Mel Brooks, John Morris.

The Twelve Dogs of Christmas 🐾🐾 2005 Sappy Christmas story set in the Depression. 12-year-old Emma O'Connor (Green) is sent to live with her aunt in a small town and finds out about the town's ban on owning more than one dog, and sends the whole community (grrrr). So it's up to Emma, a large number of pooches, and a school holiday pageant to make everything right. Cute dogs, cute kid—probably tolerable for the younger set. Based on the book by Emma Kragen. 107m/C DVD. Jordan-Claire Green, John Billingsley, Richard Riehle, Eric Lutes, Bonita Friederichy, Mindy Sterling, John-Kevin Hilbert; **C:** Keith Merrill; **M:** Keith Merrill, Emma Kragen; **C:** Michael Fimognari. **VIDEO**

12 Monkeys 🐾🐾🐾 1995 (R) Forty years after a plague wipes out 99 percent of the human population and sends the survivors underground, scientists send prisoner James Cole (Willis) to the 1990s to investigate the connection between a virus and seriously deranged fanatic Jeffrey Goines (Pitt), whose father happens to be a renowned virologist. Director Gilliam's demented vision is a bit tougher and less capricious than usual, and the convoluted plot and accumulated detail require a keen attention span, but as each piece of the puzzle falls into place the story

Twelve Angry Men 🐾🐾🐾 1957 Fonda sounds the voice of reason as a jury inclines toward a quick-and-dirty verdict against a boy on trial. Excellent ensemble work. Lumet's feature film debut, based on a TV play by Reginald Rose. 95m/B VHS, DVD. Henry Fonda, Martin Balsam, Lee J. Cobb, E.G. Marshall, Jack Klugman, Robert Webber, Ed Begley Sr., John Fiedler, Jack Warden, George Voskovec, Edward Binns, Joseph Sweeney; **D:** Sidney Lumet; **W:** Reginald Rose; **C:** Boris Kaufman; **M:** Kenyon Hopkins, Berlin Intl. Film Fest. '57: Golden Berlin Bear; British Acad. '57: Actor (Fonda), Natl. Film Reg. '07.

Twelve Angry Men 🐾🐾½ 1997 (PG-13) Cable TV update of the 1954 "Studio One" teleplay/1957 movie (both written by Rose) that brings together an all-male jury (now with four black jurors) to decide the fate of a Latino murder suspect. Lemmon has the Henry Fonda role mined to provide a fair hearing. 117m/C VHS. George C. Scott, Jack Lemmon, Hume Cronyn, Tony Danza, Mykelti Williamson, Edward James Olmos, Courtney B. Vance, Ossie Davis, Armin Mueller-Stahl, Dorian Harewood, James Gandolfini, William L. Petersen, Mary McDonnell, Douglas Spain; **D:** William Friedkin; **W:** Reginald Rose. **CABLE**

The Twelve Chairs 🐾🐾🐾 1970

Malee (Weizenbaum) becomes preciously interested in one of her therapist mom's (Sciorra) patients, a hunky construction worker (Rennen). First-rate work. 95m/C DVD. US Zoe Weizenbaum, Jeremy Renner, Conor Donovan, Jesse Camacho, Annabella Sciorra, Linus Roache, Jayne Atkinson, Marcia DeBonis, Michael Fuchs; **D:** Michael Cuesta; **C:** Romeo Tirone; **M:** Pierre Foldes.

ry becomes a fascinating sci-fi spectacle. Pitt drops the pretty-boy image with a nutzoid performance that'll make revelers stop swooning in a heartbeat. Inspired by the 1962 French short "La Jetee." **131m/C VHS, HD DVD.** Bruce Willis, Madeleine Stowe, Brad Pitt, Christopher Plummer, David Morse, Frank Gorshin, Jon Seda; **D:** Terry Gilliam; **W:** David Peoples, Janet Peoples; **C:** Roger Pratt; **M:** Paul Buckmaster. Golden Globes '96: Support. Actor (Pitt).

Twelve o'Clock High 🦴🦴🦴🦴½
1949 Epic drama about the heroic 8th Air Force, with Peck as bomber-group commander sent to shape up a hard-luck group, forced to drive himself and his men to the breaking point. Compelling dramatization of the strain of military command. Includes impressive footage of actual WWII battles. Best-ever flying fortress movie. **132m/B VHS, DVD.** Gregory Peck, Hugh Marlowe, Gary Merrill, Millard Mitchell, Dean Jagger, Paul Stewart, Robert Arthur, John Kellogg, Sam Edwards, Russ Conway, Lawrence (Larry) Dobkin; **D:** Henry King; **W:** Sy Bartlett, Beirne Lay Jr.; **C:** Leon Shamroy; **M:** Alfred Newman. Oscars '49: Sound, Support. Actor (Jagger). Natl. Film Reg. '98.

12:01 🦴🦴🦴
1993 (PG-13) It's the "Groundhog Day" premise played for thrills. Barry Thompson (Silverman) is an employee at a scientific research firm who finds himself reliving the same 24-hour period over and over again. And what a day it is—he discovers a secret project is causing the mysterious time warp, falls in love with beauteous scientist Lisa (Slater) and watches as she gets murdered. Can Barry figure out how to stop what's going on and change things enough to save her? Adaptation of the short story "12:01" by Richard Lupoff, which was previously made into a short film. **92m/C VHS, DVD.** Jonathan Silverman, Helen Slater, Martin Landau, Nicolas Surovy, Jeremy Piven; **D:** Jack Sholder. **TV**

12 Plus 1 🦴🦴
1970 (R) *The Thirteen Chairs* A man sells 13 chairs left to him by his aunt, only to find that one of them contained a hidden fortune. He chases across Europe in search of each of them. Some good cameos help move this re-make of a Russian folk-tale along, but it remains lightweight. Tate's last movie, before her death at the hands of Manson and his "family." **94m/C VHS.** *FR/IT* Sharon Tate, Orson Welles, Vittorio Gassman, Mylene Demongeot, Terry-Thomas, Tim Brooke; *Cameos:* Vittorio De Sica; **D:** Nicolas Gessner.

Twenty Bucks 🦴🦴🦴
1993 (R) Whimsical film follows a $20 bill from its "birth" at a cash machine to its "death" as it is returned to the bank, tattered and torn, for shredding. The bill is passed from owner to owner, sometimes simply and briefly, sometimes altering fate. The original screenplay is nearly 60 years old: Endre Bohem originally drafted it in 1935, and his son revised and updated it. Clever transitions allow the various stories and characters to blend almost seamlessly. The strongest character is Shue's, a young waitress and aspiring writer. Rosenfeld's directorial debut is worth a look. Filmed in Minneapolis. **91m/C VHS, DVD.** Linda Hunt, David Rasche, George Morfogen, Brendan Fraser, Gladys Knight, Elisabeth Shue, Steve Buscemi, Christopher Lloyd, Sam Jenkins, Kamal Holloway, Melora Walters, William H. Macy, Diane Baker, Spalding Gray, Matt Frewer, Concetta Tomei, Nina Siemaszko; **D:** Keva Rosenfeld; **W:** Leslie Bohem, Endre Bohem; **C:** Emmanuel Lubezki; **M:** David Robbins. Ind. Spirit '94: Support. Actor (Lloyd).

20 Dates 🦴🦴½
1999 (R) Writer/director Myles Berkowitz, recently divorced and having career problems, decided to combine these two problems into one. He filmed himself going on 20 dates, sometimes without the dates' knowledge (until he sprung the release form on 'em at the end of the night). Some of it's real, some staged, but all of it focuses on Berkowitz. He talks about himself, and the project, incessantly, which gets annoying after awhile, but the film has its moments. When one of the dates actually works out, and turns into a budding romance, he has to tell the girl that he's still obligated to play out the string. Some of the funnier moments are his conversations with his financial backer, who thought he was getting a sex romp flick. **88m/C VHS. D:** Myles Berkowitz; **W:** Myles Berkowitz; **C:** Adam Biggs. **M:** Bob Mann, Steve Tyrel.

Twentieth Century 🦴🦴🦴🦴
1934 Maniacal Broadway director Barrymore transforms shop girl Lombard into a smashing success adored by public and press. Tired of Barrymore's manic-excessive ways, she heads for the Hollywood hills, pursued by the Profile in fine form. **91m/B DVD.** Carole Lombard, John Barrymore, Walter Connolly, Roscoe Karns, Edgar Kennedy, Ralph Forbes, Charles Lane, Etienne Girardot, Snow Flake; **D:** Howard Hawks; **W:** Charles MacArthur, Ben Hecht.

fighting. Look for newly mastered edition. **105m/B VHS, DVD.** Matt Moore, Allen Holubar, June Gail, William Welsh, Chris Benton, Dan Hanlon; **D:** Stuart Paton; **W:** Stuart Paton; **C:** Eugene Gaudio.

20,000 Leagues under the Sea 🦴🦴🦴🦴½
1954 From a futuristic submarine, Captain Nemo wages war on the surface world. A shipwrecked scientist and sailor do their best to thwart Nemo's dastardly schemes. Buoyant Disney version of the Jules Verne fantasy. **127m/C VHS, DVD.** James Mason, Kirk Douglas, Peter Lorre, Paul Lukas, Robert J. Wilke, Carleton Young, **D:** Richard Fleischer; **W:** Earl Felton; **C:** Franz Planer; **M:** Paul J. Smith. Oscars '54: Art Dir./Set Dec., Color.

20,000 Leagues Under the Sea 🦴½
1997 Silly TV version of the oft-told Verne tale finds marine biologist Aronnax (Crenna) and his assistant/daughter Sophie (Cox) prisoners on Captain Nemo's (Cross) submarine. In the original Verne version, Sophie was a young man—the sex change now means there's lots of boring eye-batting between Sophie, harpoonist Ned Land (Gross), and the jealous Nemo. The underwater photography is nifty but the fish also provide more excitement than the cast. **91m/C VHS, DVD.** Ben Cross, Richard Crenna, Paul Gross, Julie Cox, Michael Jayston; **D:** Michael Anderson Sr.; **W:** Joe Wiesenfeld; **C:** Alan Hume; **M:** John Scott. **TV**

Twenty Dollar Star 🦴½
1991 (R) Steamy thriller about an prominent actress who leads a double life as a cheap hooker, and consequent occupational hazards. The title may as well refer to the budget. **92m/C VHS.** Rebecca Holden, Bernie (Bernard) White, Eddie Barth, Marilyn Hassett, Dick Sargent; **D:** Paul Leder.

25th Hour 🦴🦴
2002 (R) Moody, atmospheric character study follows the last 24 hours of freedom for convicted drug dealer Monty Brogan (Norton) before he begins a seven-year sentence. Brogan says his goodbyes to his father, a retired firefighter who now runs a bar paid for with Monty's drug money; his longtime buddies Frank (Pepper), a Wall Street shark, and Jacob (Hoffman), a high school teacher with low self-esteem and a crush on one of his students (Paquin); and girlfriend Naturelle (Dawson), whom he suspects of turning him in. All feel different levels of guilt over letting Monty become involved in "the life." If Lee had stuck to these stories, it would've worked much better, but instead he lays the spectre of 9/11 over the proceedings, creating jarring scenes that sometimes work, but mostly distract from some impressive performances. **132m/C VHS, DVD.** *US* Edward Norton, Philip Seymour Hoffman, Barry Pepper, Rosario Dawson, Anna Paquin, Brian Cox, Isiah Whitlock Jr., Michael Genet, Tony Siragusa, Levani Outchanechvili, Misha Kuznetsov; **D:** Spike Lee; **W:** David Benioff; **C:** Rodrigo Prieto; **M:** Terence Blanchard. Golden Globes '03: Score.

The 24th Day 🦴🦴½
2004 (R) Tom learned 24 days ago that he and his wife are infected with HIV and Tom blames Dan—a man whom he had a one-night-stand with five years before. Off he goes to not merely confront Dan—who doesn't even remember Tom—but to take him hostage while his blood is tested with plans for a slow, painful death if it comes back positive. Adapted from writer-director Piccirillo's own stage play—where it should have stayed. **92m/C VHS, DVD.** Sofia Vergara, James Marsden, Scott Speedman; **D:** Tony Piccirillo; **W:** Tony Piccirillo; **C:** Alan Hostetter; **M:** Kevin Manthei. **VIDEO**

20 Million Miles to Earth 🦴🦴½
1957 A spaceship returning from an expedition to Venus crashes on Earth, releasing a fast-growing reptilian beast that rampages throughout Athens. Another entertaining example of stop-motion animation master Ray Harryhausen's work, offering a classic battle between the monster and an elephant. **82m/B DVD, Blu-ray Disc.** William Hopper, Joan Taylor, Frank Puglia, John Zaremba, Thomas B(rowne). Henry, Jan Arvan; **D:** Nathan "Jerry" Juran; **W:** Christopher Knopf, Bob Williams; **C:** Irving Lippman; **M:** Mischa Bakaleinikoff.

29th & Gay 🦴🦴
2005 A year in the life of a 29-year-old gay man, James Sanchez, who longs for love and success. But the average-looking, unemployed actor is trapped by his own idea of what his life should be. Charming if clichéd. **87m/C DVD.** James Vasquez, Mike Doyle, Kal Rocha, Michael Emerson, Nicole Marcks, David McBean, Annie Hinton; **D:** Carrie Preston; **C:** Mark Holmes; **M:** John Avila.

20,000 Leagues under the Sea 🦴🦴🦴
1916 Outstanding silent adaptation of Jules Verne's "20,000 Leagues Under the Sea" and "The Mysterious Island" filmed with a then revolutionary underwater camera. Much octopus Knight, Franco Nero, Anthony Quayle, Noel Willman; **D:** William A. Graham.

2103: Deadly Wake 🦴🦴
1997 A cargo ship is carrying deadly waste, unbeknownst to its crew, which is also unaware that the ship is intended to be sunk (with the crew). **100m/C VHS, DVD. CA GB** Malcolm McDowell, Michael Pare, Heidi von Palleske, Gwynth Walsh, Hal Eisen; **D:** G. Philip Jackson; **W:** Timothy Lee, Andrew Dowler, Doug Bagot. **VIDEO**

23 1/2 Hours Leave 🦴🦴
1937 Amusing WWI service comedy as a barracks wiseacre bets that by the following morning he'll be breakfasting with a general. It's a song-filled remake of a 1919 film, whose star Douglas MacLean later produced this. **73m/B VHS.** James Ellison, Terry Walker, Morgan Hill, Arthur Lake, Paul Harvey; **D:** John Blystone.

Twenty-Four Eyes 🦴🦴🦴
1954 *Nijushi No Hitomi* Miss Oishi (Takamine), a teacher on a remote Japanese island in the 1920s, attempts to transmit peaceful values to her 12 pupils amidst the clamor of a nation gearing up for war. As she watches them grow up over time, a few are doomed to an early death, she remains a pillar of quiet strength. In Japanese with English subtitles. **158m/B VHS. JP** Hideko Takamine, Chishu Ryu, Toshiko Kobayashi; **D:** Keisuke Kinoshita.

24 Hour Party People 🦴🦴
2001 (R) Winterbottom's tribute to the late '70s through early '90s punk rock/rave/acid culture of his native Manchester as seen through the bleary eyes of real-life figure Tony Wilson (Coogan). Wilson is a presenter for Granada TV when he's inspired by a Sex Pistols performance to open a club, the Hacienda, to showcase local bands, including Joy Division (which morphs into New Order) and the Happy Mondays. He also starts Factory Records—both of which eventually fail, thanks to drugs and general craziness. Filmed in a semi-documentary style with Wilson's asides to camera commenting on the scenes. **115m/C VHS, DVD. GB** Steve Coogan, Lennie James, Shirley Henderson, Paddy Considine, Andy Serkis, John Simm, Danny Cunningham, Keith Allen, Sean Harris, Chris Coghill, Paul Popplewell; **D:** Michael Winterbottom; **W:** Frank Cottrell-Boyce; **M:** Robby Muller.

Twenty-One 🦴🦴½
1991 (R) Modern morality tale of a young English woman who moves to the U.S. to make a new start, but falls into the same old habits. Kensit is frank and charming, in spite of difficulties with her drug addict boyfriend and the illegal alien she marries. Director Boyd leaves it to the viewer to decide between right and wrong and where Kensit fits. **92m/C VHS. GB** Patsy Kensit, Jack Shepherd, Patrick Ryecart, Maynard Eziashi, Rufus Sewell, Sophie Thompson, Susan Wooldridge, Julia Goodman; **D:** Don Boyd; **W:** Don Boyd; **C:** Keith Goddard; **M:** Michael Berkeley.

21 🦴🦴½
2008 (PG-13) 122m/C DVD. US Jim Sturgess, Kevin Spacey, Kate (Catherine) Bosworth, Aaron Yoo, Jacob Pitts, Laurence Fishburne, Liza Lapira; **D:** Robert Luketic; **W:** Peter Steinfeld, Allan Loeb; **C:** Russell Carpenter; **M:** David Sardy.

21 Days 🦴🦴½
1991 *Twenty-One Days Together; The First and the Last* **1937** Dull film somewhat redeemed by its stars. **75m/C VHS, DVD. GB** Vivien Leigh, Laurence Olivier, Leslie Banks, Francis L. Sullivan, Hay Petrie, Esme Percy, Robert Newton; **D:** Basil Dean; **W:** Graham Greene, Basil Dean.

21 Grams 🦴🦴🦴½
2003 (R) In his second film (his first in English), Inarritu takes what could have, in the wrong hands, become a trite Lifetime movie, and elevates it in an unusual and compelling fashion. Jack (DelToro), is imprisoned and born-again. Paul (Penn) has a terminal heart disease and needs a transplant. Christina (Watts), a recovering addict, mourns the loss of her family. Of course, the lives of these characters collide. Stellar performances by an excellent cast combine with beautiful cinematography to create a powerful film. Title refers to amount of weight a body loses upon death. **125m/C VHS, DVD. US** Sean Penn, Benicio Del Toro, Naomi Watts, Charlotte Gainsbourg, Melissa Leo, Clea DuVall, Danny Huston, Paul Calderon; **D:** Alejandro Gonzalez Inarritu; **W:** Guillermo Arriaga; **C:** Rodrigo Prieto; **M:** Gustavo Santaolalla. LA Film Critics '03: Actress (Watts); Natl. Bd. of Review '03: Actor (Penn).

21 Hours at Munich 🦴🦴🦴
1976 Made-for-TV treatment of the massacre of Israeli athletes by Arab terrorists at the 1972 Olympics. Well-done. The film was produced using the actual Munich locations. **100m/C VHS, DVD.** William Holden, Shirley

The 24 Hour Woman 🦴🦴½
1999 (R) Perez is Grace, a morning TV talk show producer who has her pregnancy announced on the air, to the surprise of the baby's father (and the show's co-host) Serrano. Heartless executive producer LuPone milks the pregnancy for every ratings point, then callously turns her back on her employee's problems once the demands of her job and motherhood, Grace has a major mental meltdown in which she confronts her harpy boss on air. Perez shows a more mature side while still retaining her Latina buzzsaw comic gifts. **93m/C VHS.** Rosie Perez, Marianne Jean-Baptiste, Patti LuPone, Karen Duffy, Wendell Pierce, Melissa Leo, Aida Turturro, Diego Serrano, Rosanna Desoto, Alicia Renee Washington; **D:** Nancy Savoca; **W:** Nancy Savoca, Richard Guay; **C:** Teresa Medina; **M:** Louis Vega, Kenny Gonzalez.

24 Hours in a Woman's Life 🦴🦴
2002 A girl in love with an irresponsible guy hears a cautionary tale from grandma Bergman, who once had a whirlwind romance with a young gambler and naively thought she could reform him. A static TV adaptation of an oft-filmed Stefan Zweig novel, unusually lavish for its time but on the dull side. **90m/C VHS.** Ingrid Bergman, Rip Torn, John Williams, Lili Darvas, Jerry Orbach; **D:** Alexander Finbow; **W:** John Mortimer.

24 Hours in London 🦴🦴
2000 (R) In 2009's London, organized crime openly vies with the police for control of the streets. Mob boss Christian (Olsen) has just 24 hours to prevent witness Martha (Smith) from testifying against him for murder or watch his criminal empire vanish. Violent. **91m/C VHS. GB** Gary Olsen, Tony London, Anjela Lauren Smith, David Sonnethal, Wendy Cooper, Sara Stockbridge, Luke Garrett; **D:** Alexander Finbow; **W:** Alexander Finbow; **C:** Chris Plevin; **M:** Edmund Butt.

24 Hours to Midnight ⌐⌐½ 1992 A widow uses her ninja skills to wipe out the crime bosses and henchmen who killed her husband. 91m/C VHS, DVD . C: Shack Pierce; D: Leo Fong.

24 Nights ⌐⌐½ 1999 Twenty-four-year-old Jonathan Parker has never stopped believing in Santa Claus after a magical encounter at the age of four. Now after an accident and finds the building deserted. London seems deserted as well—until he nearly becomes a victim of Christmas wish. 97m/C VHS, DVD. C: Kevin Isola, Aida Turturro, Steven Maillet, David Burtka, Mary Louise Wilson; D: Kieran Turner; W: Kieran Turner.

24-7 ⌐⌐ 1997 (R) Title is local Middlands English slang for 24 hours a day, seven days a week. And in this case it refers to the boredom suffered by the aimless, unemployed youth who live in the local housing estates in Thatcher's depressed '80s England. Middle-aged ex-boxer Alan Darcy (Hoskins) in a sincere and sweet performance) decides to help the ads by reviving the amateur boxing club which saved him in his youth. Although it seems to work for a time, things slide downward as, eventually, does the distraught Darcy himself. Meadows' feature directorial debut. 96m/B VHS, DVD. C: Bob Hoskins, Danny Nussbaum, James Hooton, Darren O. Campbell, Mat Hand, Jimmy Hynd, Justin Brady, Karl Collins, Johann Myers, Anthony Clarke, Bruce Jones, Frank Harper, Pamela Cundell; D: Shane Meadows; W: Shane Meadows; Paul Fraser; C: Ashley Rowe; M: Neil MacColl, Boo Heverdine.

25 Fireman's Street ⌐⌐⌐ Allmok a hazrol: Tuzolto utca 25 1973 An evocative drama about the residents of an old house in Hungary which s about to be torn down, and their evening of remembrances of life before, during and after WWII. In Hungarian with English subtitles. 97m/C VHS, DVD. Hu Rita Beres, Peter Muller, Lucyna Winnicka, Andras Balint; D: Istvan Szabo; W: Istvan Szabo, Luca Karall; C: Sanoor Sara.

27 Dresses ⌐⌐½ 2008 (PG-13) You know the drill: Hopeless romantic Jane (Heigl) simply adores weddings but is the perennial bridesmaid—literally—with 27 (oft hideous) bridesmaid dresses to prove it. Jane crushes on her boss George (Burns), but he has eyes for her sister Tess (Akerman). In the meantime perennial cynic Kevin (Marsden) has a thing for Jane, but she's too hooked on her boss to pay any attention. What she doesn't realize is that Kevin is actually the writer of a marriage column that Jane has been clipping for years. What ensues is pure romantic-comedy rehash. Heigl's adorable, but alas, this silly chick flick is much less so. 107m/C DVD. US Katherine Heg., James Marsden, Malin Akerman, Judy Greer, Edward Burns, Melora Hardin, Brian Kerwin, Maulik Pancholy; D: Anne Fletcher; W: Aline Brosh McKenna; C: Peter James; M: Randy Edelman.

The 27th Day ⌐⌐½ 1957 Temperate cold war allegory has aliens deliver five mysterious capsules to five Earthlings from different countries. Each capsule, if opened, is capable of decimating the population of the entire planet, but is rendered ineffective after 27 days or upon the death of the holder. Wild ending. Based on John Mantley novel. 75m/B VHS. C: George Voskovec, Arnold Moss, Stefan Schnabel, Ralph Clanton, Friedrich Ledebur, Mari Tsien; D: William Asher; W: John Mantley; C: Henry Freulich; M: Mischa Bakaleinikoff.

28 Days ⌐⌐½ 2000 (PG-13) Hard-partying New York journalist Gwen (Bullock) manages to destroy her sister's wedding reception when she gets drunk and manages to get arrested for DUI. The film's title refers to the amount of time Gwen must spend at a rehab clinic. Naturally, Gwen doesn't really believe she has a problem and that's the first attitude adjustment she has to make. Cliches galore although Bullock is welcoming), spiky rather than sweet. 103m/C VHS, DVD. Sandra Bullock, Viggo Mortensen, Dominic West, Diane Ladd, Elizabeth Perkins, Steve Buscemi, Alan Tudyk, Reni Santoni, Marianne Jean-Baptiste, Michael O'Malley, Azura Skye, Margo Martindale, Betty Thomas; W: Susannah Grant; C: Declan Quinn; M: Richard Gibbs.

28 Days Later ⌐⌐½ 2002 (R) Jim (Murphy) wakes up in a London hospital happens until they get hit from behind by a strange vehicle which sets off horrific violence. Seemingly pointless exercise in blood-drinking zombies. Rescued by Selena (Harris) and Mark (Huntley), Jim learns that animal rights activists released lab chimps who carried a blood-transmitted plague that decimated the population within 28 days. The infected survivors have banded together and decide to head to Manchester, where a military installation is said to be a safe haven. Ick and gore galore. 108m/C VHS, DVD, GB US Cillian Murphy, Megan Burns, Brendan Gleeson, Naomie Harris, Christopher Eccleston, Noah Huntley; D: Danny Boyle; W: Alex Garland; C: Anthony Dod Mantle; M: John Murphy.

28 Weeks Later ⌐⌐½ 2007 (R) Sequel to '28 Days Later' serves up new flawed protagonists and same old angry zombies ravaging Britain. Don (Carlyle), attacked by a horde infected by the rage virus, leaves his wife Alice (McCormack) behind. Reunited in an American-run safe zone in London, Alice infects Don and all hell breaks loose and several innocents must fight for their lives, sometimes at the expense of morality. Brutally terrifying and relentlessly paced, director Fresnadillo also injects wit and allegory, although both get buried as the movie progresses into a full-blown bloodfest. 99m/C DVD, GB US Robert Carlyle, Rose Byrne, Jeremy Renner, Harold Perrineau Jr., Catherine McCormack, Idris Elba; D: Juan Carlos Fresnadillo; W: Juan Carlos Fresnadillo, Rowan Joffe, Jesus Olmo, Enrique Lopez Lavigne; C: Enrique Chediak.

29th Street ⌐⌐½ 1991 (R) Compelling comedy-drama based on the true story of Frank Pesce, a New York actor who won $6 million in that state's first lottery. Great performance from Aiello, as usual, but the direction falters in the dramatic sequences. Based on the book by Frank Pesce and James Franciscus. 101m/ C VHS, DVD. Danny Aiello, Anthony LaPaglia, Lainie Kazan, Frank Pesce, Donna Magnani, Rick Aiello, Vic Manni, Ron Karabatsos, Robert Forster, Joe Franklin, Pete Antico; D: George Gallo; W: George Gallo; C: Steven Fierberg; M: William Olvis.

2046 ⌐⌐½ 2004 (R) Wong's quasi-sequel to 2001's "In the Mood for Love" is a swoony, hopeless romance about lovers who meet each other at the wrong time to fall in love. Womanizing Chow (Leung Chiu-wai) is a pulp fiction writer who moves into Room 2047 of Hong Kong's Hotel Oriental and gets involved with the beautiful women who briefly occupy Room 2046 ("2046" is also the name of the sci-fi novel Chow is writing). There are two ex-girlfriends named Su Li (Gong Li / Cheung), whom he left behind in Singapore; Lulu/Mimi (Lau), who is murdered; prostitute Bai Ling (Zhang), who becomes Chow's confidante; and Jing (Wong), the daughter of the hotel's owner who's in love with a man her father disapproves of. It certainly looks gorgeous. Japanese and Mandarin with subtitles. 129m/C DVD, CH HK FR GB Tony Leung Chiu-Wai, Gong Li, Takuya Kimura, Faye Wong, Zhang Ziyi, Carina Lau, Chang Chen, Maggie Cheung, Wang Sum, Lam Suping; Thongchai McIntyre, Dong Jie; D: Wong Kar-Wai; W: Wong Kar-Wai; C: Christopher Doyle, Lai Yiu-fai, Kwan Pun-leung; M: Peer Raben, Shingeru Umebayashi; N.Y. Film Critics '05: Cinematog; Natl. Soc. Film Critics '05: Cinematog.

Twentynine Palms ⌐⌐ 2003 Director Dumont's first feature made in the U.S. is a grim, moody thriller than grinds on monotonously until a twist near the end triggers an intense situation. L.A. residents David (Wissak) and his French-speaking girlfriend Katia (Golubeva) embark on a trip to the California desert locale of the title. The action mostly consists of motel stops where the eerily laconic couple, who mostly just drive around and bicker, copulate graphically and frequently out of boredom. David accidentally hits a dog, to Katia's horror, but not much else happens until they get hit from behind by a strange vehicle which sets off horrific violence. Seemingly pointless exercise in gratuitous sex and violence. Mostly in English with some French dialogue. 119m/C VHS, DVD. GE FR Yekaterina (Katia) Golubeva, David Wissak; D: Bruno Dumont; W: Bruno Dumont; C: Georges Lechaptois; M: Takashi Hirayasu, Bob Brozman.

Twice a Judas ⌐ Dos Veces Judas; Due Volte Giuda 1969 An amnesiac is swindled and has his family killed by a ruthless renegade. He wants to get even, even through he can't remember who anyone is. 90m/C VHS. IT SP Klaus Kinski, Antonio (Tony) Sabato, Emma Baron, Franco Beltramme, Jose Calvo; D: Nando Cicero; W: Jaime Jesus Balcazar; C: Franco Manni; M: Carol Pes.

Twice a Woman ⌐ Twee Vrouwen 1979 (R) Man and woman divorce, and then both fall in love with the same provocative young woman. It's complicated. 90m/C VHS, NL 3ibi Andersson, Anthony Perkins, Sandra Dumas, Charles Gormley; D: George Sluizer; M: Willem Breuker.

Twice Dead Woof! 1988 A family moves into a ramshackle mansion haunted by a stage actor's angry ghost. The ghost helps them battle some attacking delinquent boys. Uninteresting story, poorly cast. Unreleased in theatres. 94m/C VHS. Tom Breznahan, Jill Whitlow, Sam Melville, Brooke Bundy, Todd Bridges, Jonathan Chapin, Christopher Burgard; D: Bert L. Dragin; M: David Bergeaund.

Twice in a Lifetime ⌐⌐⌐ 1985 (R) Middle-aged man takes stock of his life when he's attracted to Ann-Margret. Realizing he's married in name only, he moves in with his new love while his former wife and children struggle with shock, disbelief, and anger. Well-acted, realistic, and unsentimental. 117m/C VHS, DVD. Gene Hackman, Ellen Burstyn, Amy Madigan, Ann-Margret, Brian Dennehy, Ally Sheedy; D: Bud Yorkin; W: Colin Weland.

Twice-Told Tales ⌐⌐⌐ Nathaniel Hawthorne's "Twice Told Tales" 1963 Horror trilogy based loosely on three Nathaniel Hawthorne tales. "Dr. Heidegger's Experiment," "Rappaccini's Daughter," and "The House of Seven Gables." Price is great in all three of these well-told tales. 120m/C VHS, DVD. Beverly Garland, Richard Denning, Vincent Price, Sebastian Cabot, Brett Halsey; D: Sidney Salkow; W: Robert E. Kent; C: Ellis W. Carter; M: Richard LaSalle.

Twice upon a Yesterday ⌐⌐ 1998 (R) Struggling London actor Victor (Henshall) is a romantic swine. He two-timed girlfriend Sylvia (Headey) and she wisely dumped him and found another guy, Dave (Strong), and they're going to get married. Through some time-travelling magic, Victor is able to relive his fateful moment and prevent Sylvia's going. But she winds up meeting Dave anyway while she unravels her convoluted romantic trials. Things are just a little too sappy and meandering but the cast is worth watching. 94m/C VHS, DVD. GB Douglas Henshall, Lena Headey, Mark Strong, Penelope Cruz, Elizabeth McGovern, Eusebio Lazaro, Charlotte Coleman, Gustavo Salmeron, Neil Stuke; D: Maria Ripoll; W: Rafa Russo; C: Javier Salmones.

Twilight ⌐⌐⌐ The Magic Hour 1998 (R) It's a pleasure to see pros at work, even if the story is a familiar one. In the noir world of L.A. ex-cop, ex-drunk, ex-P.I. Harry Ross (Newman) is living around the garage at the estate of movie star marrieds Jack (Hackn'an) and Catherine (Sarandon) Ames, for whom Harry has done several jobs. The cancer-stricken Jack asks Harry to handle a blackmail payoff, which seems to resurrect the circumstances of femme fatale Catherine's first husband's alleged suicide. Also involved is Harry's colleague Raymond Hope (Garner)and Harry's ex-flame, Verna (Channing), a cop investigating a murder with ties to the entire ugly situation. 94m/C VHS, DVD. Paul Newman, Susan Sarandon, Gene Hackman, James Garner, Stockard Channing, Reese Witherspoon, Giancar-lo Esposito, Liev Schreiber, Margo Martindale, John Spencer, M. Emmet Walsh; D: Robert Benton; W: Robert Benton, Richard Russo; C: Piotr Sobocinski; M: Elmer Bernstein.

The Twilight Girls ⌐⌐ Les Collegiennes 1957 Escaping a family scandal, Catherine Royner (Arnaud) enters an exclusive girls boarding school and is immediately introduced to a clique of wealthy girls—one of whom, Monica (Laurent) develops a amourous attraction to the newcomer. Film was originally banned in the New York because of the frankness of its lesbian scenes. Deneuve's film debut (under the family name Dorleac) as Adelaide. Her scenes were a cut in the version originally released in the U.S. but are restored on the DVD. 83m/B VHS, DVD. FR Marie-Helene Arnaud, Agnes Laurent, Elga Andersen, Henri Guisol, Estella Blain, Catherine Deneuve; D: Andrew Hunebelle; W: Jean Lambertie, Jacques Landeri; C: Paul Cotteret.

Twilight in the Sierras ⌐⌐½ 1950 Lots of heroics and music in this action-packed western. An ex-outlaw gone straight is kidnapped and even a killer and criminal finesse. Rogers must come to rescue. 99m/C VHS, Tim Matheson, Dean Stockwell, L. Scott Caldwell, Yvette Nipar, Georgann Johnson; D: Craig R. Baxley; W: Pablo F. Fenjves, Jim Korris; C: David Connell; M: Gary Chang.

Twilight Man ⌐⌐½ 1996 (R) University professor and novelist Jordan Cooper (Matheson) finds his great life turned upside down when a brief altercation with a stranger turns into a nightmare. Turns out the stranger is very strange indeed—computer hacker Hollis Dietz (Stockwell) has made Cooper his own deadly obsession. Suddenly his medical records say he's schizophrenic and even a killer and Cooper must elude police to clear his name. 99m/C VHS, Tim Matheson, Dean Stockwell, L. Scott Caldwell, Yvette Nipar, Georgann Johnson; D: Craig R. Baxley; W: Pablo F. Fenjves, Jim Korris; C: David Connell; M: Gary Chang.

Twilight of the Cockroaches ⌐⌐½ Gokiburi 1990 Mr. Saito is a slovenly bachelor who winds up leaving the remains of his meals for the anthropomorphic cockroaches that infest his apartment. The cockroaches have had it so good for so long that they don't know that is, until Mr. Saito's fastidious new girlfriend will finally see and declares war on the vermin. A lifelessly animated tale too dumb for both children and adults and with decidedly unpleasant subjects matter, despite the singing, dancing insects. In Japanese with English subtitles. 105m/C VHS. JP D: Hiroaki Yoshida; V: Kaoru Kobayashi, Setsuko Karasumaru.

The Twilight of the Golds ⌐⌐½ 1997 (PG-13) The upper-middle class Jewish Gold family seem conventional if fretful; there's doctor dad Walter (Marshall), concerned mom Phyllis (Beals), and aspiring theatrical producer son David (Fraser), who's gay. It seems everyone's deal with David's homosexuality until Suzanne's (Tenney) pregnant wife that tests on their unborn son show genes statistically link to him being gay. (The theory is unproven.) Suzanne considers abortion and David is understandably upset when no one tries to talk her out of it, beginning a family estrangement. Based on the play by Tolins. 90m/C VHS, DVD. Garry Marshall, Faye Dunaway, Jennifer Beals, Brendan Fraser, Jon Tenney, Jack Klugman, Sean O'Bryan, Rosie O'Donnell; D: Ross Kagan Marks; W: Jonathan Tolins, Seth Bass; C: Tom Richmond; M: Lee Holdridge. C.A.B.L.E.

The Twilight of the Ice Nymphs ⌐⌐ 1997 Welcome once again to filmmaker Maddin's weird world. Peter Glahn (Whitney) is released from prison and travels back to his mythical home in Mandragora, where the sun never sets. At the family ostrich farm, his sister Amelia (Duvall) is smitten with Dr. Solti (Thompson) who has unearthed a mysterious statue of Venus that apparently has strange powers. And Peter gets involved with two women, Zephyr (Krige) and Juliana (Bussieres), who also have ties to the doctor. Deliberately artificial and hallucinatory. **91m/C VHS, DVD.** *CA* Pascale Bussieres, R.H. Thomson, Alice Krige, Nigel Whitney, Shelley Duvall, Frank Gorshin, Ross McMillan; *D:* Guy Maddin; *W:* George Toles; *C:* Michael Marshall; *M:* John McCulloch.

Twilight on the Rio Grande 🦴 **1941** Autry runs into a female knife thrower and some jewel smugglers in this far-fetched western. **54m/B VHS.** Gene Autry, Sterling Holloway, Adele Mara, Bob Steele; *D:* Frank McDonald.

Twilight on the Trail 🦴🦴 **1941** Cattle rustlers disappear and Hopalong Cassidy and his sidekicks become "dude" detectives to solve the crime. **54m/B VHS, DVD.** William Boyd, Brad King, Andy Clyde, Jack Rockwell, Wanda McKay, Howard Bretherton; *D:* Howard Bretherton; *W:* J. Benton Cheney, Ellen Corby, Cecile Kramer; *C:* Russell Harlan; *M:* John Leipold.

Twilight People woof! *Beasts* **1972** (PG) When a mad scientist's creations turn on him for revenge, he runs for his life. Boring, gory, with bad make-up and even poorer acting. This one should fade away into the night. **84m/C VHS, DVD.** *PH* John Ashley, Patricia] Woodell, Jan Merlin, Pam Grier, Eddie Garcia; *D:* Eddie Romero.

The Twilight Samurai 🦴🦴🦴½ *Tasogare Seibei* **2002** Director Yamada's long-awaited foray into samurai cinema that was definitely worth the wait. Story takes place in mid-19th century feudal Japan and centers on Seibei (Sanada), a very capable but low-level samurai who must single-handedly take care of his aged, senile mother and two young daughters after the recent death of his wife. The hard-working Seibei makes very little from his clan-appointed jobs and spends the rest of his time doing household chores. Still grieving his wife, the staunchly single Seibei slowly begins to soften to the idea of love until suddenly being dispatched by the clan to take on the rebel Yogo (Tanaka), a master swordsman. Yamada lets the human drama takes center stage over the spectacular swordfighting usually found in this genre. Based on a novel by Shuhei Fujiwara. **129m/C DVD.** *JP* Hiroyuki (Henry) Sanada, Ren Osugi, Miki Ito, Rie Miyazawa, Nenji Kobayashi, Mitsuru Fukikoshi, Hiroshi Kanbe, Min Tanaka, Erina Hashiguchi; *D:* Yoji Yamada; *W:* Yoji Yamada, Yoshitaka Asama; *M:* Mutsuo Naganuma; *M:* Isao Tomita.

Twilight Zone: The Movie 🦴🦴½ **1983** (PG) Four short horrific tales are anthologized in this film as a tribute to Rod Serling and his popular TV series. Three of the episodes, "Kick the Can," "It's a Good Life" and "Nightmare at 20,000 Feet," are based on original "Twilight Zone" scripts. Morrow was killed in a helicopter crash during filming. **101m/C VHS, Blu-ray Disc, HD DVD.** Steven Williams, Dan Aykroyd, Albert Brooks, Vic Morrow, Kathleen Quinlan, John Lithgow, Billy Mumy, Scatman Crothers, Kevin McCarthy, Bill Quinn, Selma Diamond, Abbe Lane, John Larroquette, Jeremy Licht, Patricia Barry, William Schallert, Burgess Meredith, Cherie Currie, Nancy Cartwright, Dick Miller, Stephen Bishop; *D:* John Landis, Steven Spielberg, George Miller, Joe Dante; *W:* John Landis, George Clayton Johnson, Richard Matheson; *C:* Allen Daviau, John Hora, Stevan Larner; *M:* Jerry Goldsmith.

Twilight's Last Gleaming 🦴🦴½ **1977** (R) A maverick general takes a SAC missile silo hostage, threatening to start WWIII if the U.S. government doesn't confess to its Vietnam policies and crimes. Gripping film, with good performances. Based on a novel by Walter Wager, "Viper Three." **144m/C VHS.** Burt Lancaster, Charles Durning, Richard Widmark, Melvyn Douglas, Joseph Cotten, Paul Winfield, Burt Young, Roscoe Lee Browne, Richard Jaeckel, William Marshall, Vera Miles, Leif Erickson, Charles McGraw, William (Bill) Smith, John Ratzenberger; *D:* Robert Aldrich; *W:* Ronald M. Cohen; *C:* Robert B. Hauser; *M:* Jerry Goldsmith.

Twin Beds 🦴🦴½ **1942** Screwball comedy has newlyweds Mike and Julie Abbott (Brent and Bennett) trying to get a little alone time away from their overly friendly neighbors. The interruptions include Julie's ex-boyfriend Larky (Truex) who's on the lookout for imaginary burglars, and an inebriated Russian (Auer) who can't find his own room. Both of their wives just add to the fun. Provides plenty of laughs, especially when Auer's on screen. Adapted from the Margaret Mayo/Salisbury Field play. **85m/B VHS.** Joan Bennett, George Brent, Mischa Auer, Glenda Farrell, Ernest Truex, Una Merkel, Margaret Hamilton, Charles Arnt, Charles Coleman, Cecil Cunningham, Thurston Hall; *D:* Tim Whelan; *W:* Eddie Moran, Kenneth Earl, Curtis Kenyon; *C:* Hal Mohr; *M:* Dimitri Tiomkin.

Twin Dragons 🦴🦴 *Shuang Long Hui* **1992** (PG-13) Re-edited and redubbed English version of the Asian all-star film "Seung Lung Wui," a benefit for the Director's Guild of Hong Kong. Stealing the plot from Jean-Claude Van Damme of all people, Chan plays a dual role as twins separated at birth (as if there were any other kinds of twins in movie scripts) who grow up and cross paths. Chan's likable personality saves the trite, allegedly funny comedy jokelets from bouncing too hard, and the action is chop-sockety good. Cameos from Hong Kong big shots like Tsui Hark, Ringo Lam and John Woo. **89m/C VHS, DVD.** *HK* Jackie Chan, Maggie Cheung, Anthony Chan, Philip Chan, Nina Li Chi, Sylvia Chang, James Wong, Kirk Wong, Ringo Lam, Tsui Woo, Tsui Hark, Teddy Robin; *D:* Ringo Lam, Tsui Hark; *W:* Barry Wong, Tsui Hark; *C:* Wing-Hung Wong, Wong Ngor Tai; *M:* Michael Wandmacher, Phe Loung.

Twin Falls Idaho 🦴🦴🦴 **1999** (R) Eerie romantic drama about a lonely pair of conjoined twins, Francis (Michael Polish) and Blake (Mark Polish) Falls. The handsome 25-year-olds are celebrating their birthday in a shabby hotel room on Idaho Street, which is where hooker Penny (Hickey) shows up. Blake (the strong twin) intends Penny as a present for his fragile brother Francis, whose weakened heart is seemingly kept beating by Blake's sheer will. Initially repulsed, Penny begins to feel for Blake. But just what will happen if Francis does indeed die? The talented Polish brothers are identical but not "Siamese" twins. **110m/C VHS, DVD.** Michael Polish, Mark Polish, Michele Hicks, Jon(athan) Gries, Patrick Bauchau, Garrett Morris, William Katt, Lesley Ann Warren, Teresa Hill, Holly Woodlawn; *D:* Michael Polish; *W:* Michael Polish, Mark Polish; *C:* M. David Mullen; *M:* Stuart Matthewman.

Twin Peaks: Fire Walk with Me 🦴🦴 **1992** (R) Prequel to the cult TV series is weird and frustrating, chronicling the week before Laura Palmer's death. Suspense is lacking since we know the outcome, but Lynch manages to intrigue with dream-like sequences and interestingly offbeat characters. On the other hand, it's exploitative and violent enough to alienate series fans. Includes extremely brief and baffling cameos by Bowie as an FBI agent and Stanton as the manager of a trailer park. Several of the show's regulars are missing, and others appear and disappear very quickly. On the plus side are the strains of Badalamenti's famous theme music and Isaak as an FBI agent with amazingly acute powers of observation. **135m/C VHS, DVD.** *FR* Kyle MacLachlan, Sheryl Lee, Moira Kelly, David Bowie, Chris Isaak, Harry Dean Stanton, Ray Wise, Kiefer Sutherland, Peggy Lipton, Dana Ashbrook, James Marshall, David Lynch, Catherine Coulson, Julee Cruise, Eric (DaRe) Da Re, Miguel Ferrer, Heather Graham, Madchen Amick, Jurgen Prochnow, Grace Zabriskie; *D:* David Lynch; *W:* David Lynch; *C:* Ron Garcia; *M:* Angelo Badalamenti.

Twin Sisters 🦴½ **1991** Woman discovers her missing twin sister was a high-priced prostitute and a detective tries to protect the lowlifes sister was involved with. **92m/C VHS, DVD.** Stephanie Kramer, Susan Almgren, Frederic Forrest, James Brolin; *D:* Tom Berry; *M:* Lou Forestieri.

Twin Town 🦴🦴½ **1997** Dark comedy about class warfare, escalating revenge, and drug abuse in a small seaside Welsh town features sharp, profane, and very funny dialogue, well-developed and played characters, and uneven direction. Brothers Julian (Evans) and Jeremy (fans) like to steal expensive cars and get high on any substance they can find and control. They live with their handyman dad Fatty (Ceredig) and massage parlor receptionist sister (Scorgie) on the wrong side of the tracks. Dad falls off a roof while working for the local contractor/drug kingpin (Thomas); and is not fairly compensated. This starts a cycle of revenge that begins with public urination and gets nasty from there. Sort of a Welsh "Trainspotting," which featured a cameo by "Twin" writer/director Allen. Some scenes may be too much for some viewers (especially animal lovers). **101m/C VHS.** *GB* Llyr Evans, Rhys Ifans, Huw Ceredig, William Thomas, Dorien Thomas, Dougray Scott; *D:* Kevin Allen; *W:* Kevin Allen, Paul Durden; *C:* John Mathieson; *M:* Mark Thomas.

Twin Warriors 🦴🦴½ *The Tai-Chi Master; Tai ji Zhang San Feng* **1993** (R) Junbao (Li) and Tianbao (Siu-hou) grow up together in a Shaolin temple where they secretly learn kung fu by observing the monks in training. Eventually, they're kicked out and Junbao joins a group of rebels while Tianbao enlists in the imperial army. He betrays the rebels and Junbao works to become a Tai Chi master in order to defeat his old friend. Dubbed from Cantonese. **91m/C VHS, DVD.** *HK* Jet Li, Chin Siu-hou, Michelle Yeoh; *D:* Woo-ping Yuen; *W:* Kwong Kim Yip; *C:* Tom Lau; *M:* Wai Lap Wu.

Twins 🦴🦴 **1988** (PG) A genetics experiment gone awry produces twins rather than a single child. One is a genetically engineered superman, the other a short, lecherous petty criminal. Schwarzenegger learns he has a brother, and becomes determined to find him, despite their having been raised separately. The two meet and are immediately involved in a contraband scandal. Amusing pairing of Schwarzenegger and DeVito. **107m/C VHS, DVD.** Arnold Schwarzenegger, Danny DeVito, Kelly Preston, Hugh O'Brian, Chloe Webb, Bonnie Bartlett, Marshall Bell, Trey Wilson, Nehemiah Persoff; *D:* Ivan Reitman; *W:* William Davies, William Osborne, Timothy Harris, Herschel Weingrod; *C:* Andrzej Bartkowiak; *M:* Georges Delerue, Randy Edelman.

Twins of Evil 🦴🦴 *The Gemini Twins; Twins of Dracula; The Virgin Vampires* **1971** Beautiful female twins fall victim to the local vampire, and their God-fearing uncle is out to save/destroy them. Hammer sex and blood-sucking epic starring the Collinsons, who were featured in the October 1970 issue of "Playboy" as the first twin Playmates. **86m/C VHS.** *GB* Madeleine Collinson, Mary Collinson, Peter Cushing, Kathleen Byron, Dennis Price, Damien Thomas, David Warbeck, Katya Wyeth, Maggie Wright, Luan Peters, Kristen Lindholm, Judy Matheson; *D:* John Hough; *W:* Tudor Gates; *C:* Dick Bush.

Twinsanity 🦴 *Goodbye Gemini* **1970** (R) Evil twins are charged with the murder of a man who attempted to blackmail them. **91m/C VHS.** *GB* Judy Geeson, Martin Potter, Alexis Kanner, Michael Redgrave, Freddie Jones, Peter Jeffrey; *D:* Alan Gibson; *W:* Edmund Ward; *M:* Christopher Gunning.

Twinsitters 🦴🦴½ **1995** (PG-13) Twins Peter and David Falcone (Peter and David Paul) find themselves unexpectedly saving the life of corrupt businessman Frank Hillhurst (Martin). Hillhurst is turning state's evidence on his crooked operations and his disturbed partners have threatened both his life and the lives of his twin 10-year-old nephews. So Hillhurst hires the Falcones to protect his hellacious pint-sized relatives—who manage to get themselves kidnapped. **93m/C VHS, DVD.** Peter Paul, David Paul, Christian Cousins, Joseph Cousins, Jared Martin, George Lazenby, Rena Sofer, Mother Love; *D:* John Paragon; *W:* John Paragon.

Twirl 🦴🦴 **1981** Satirical look at the cutthroat world of baton twirling. Parents apply relentless pressure on their daughters to win a contest. Decent made-for-TV movie. **100m/C VHS.** Stella Stevens, Charles Haid, Lisa Whelchel, Erin Moran, Edd Byrnes, Sharon Spelman, Matthew Yuen, Heather Locklear, Deborah Richter, Jamie Rose, Tracy Scoggins; *D:* Gus Trikonis.

Twist 🦴🦴½ *Folies Bourgeoises* **1976** A tepid French drama chronicling the infidelities of various wealthy aristocrats. The aristocrats are boring, as is the film. In French with English subtitles or dubbed. **105m/C VHS.** *FR* Bruce Dern, Stephane Audran, Ann-Margret, Sydne Rome, Maria Schell, Charles Aznavour, Curt Jurgens, Jean-Pierre Cassel, Claude Chabrol; *D:* Manuel De Sica.

Twist 🦴🦴🦴 **2003** Dark adaption of the Charles Dicken's Oliver Twist novel set amongst the street hustlers and heroin junkies of Toronto's streets. Oliver (Close), a teenage runaway meets up with Dodge (Stahl), a young prostitute. Dodge introduces him to the life of street hustling and the protective wing of Fagin (Farmer), the local pimp. A mindful presence, but not seen on screen is Bill the drug dealer, who controls both Fagin and his lover Nancy (Pelletier), a waitress at the diner where Fagin's boys often hang out. Despite what the title would suggest, the focus of the movie is Dodge as he plies his trade to further his heroin addiction. Works mainly because the young actors are so genuine and compelling. **97m/C DVD.** *CA* Nick Stahl, Gary Farmer, Michelle-Barbara Pelletier, Joshua Close, Brigid Tierney, Stephen McHattie, Gary Farmer, Tygh Runyan; *D:* Jacob Tierney; *W:* Jacob Tierney; *C:* Gerald Packer; *M:* Ron Froux.

Twist & Shout 🦴🦴🦴 *Hab Og Karighed* **1984** (R) Sequel to the popular Danish import "Zappa," in which two teenage lovers discover sex and rock and roll. Transcends the teens discovering sex genre. Danish with English subtitles. Profanity, nudity, and sex. **107m/C VHS, DVD.** *DK* Lars Simonsen, Adam Tonsberg, Ulrikke Juul Bondo, Camilla Soeberg; *D:* Bille August; *W:* Bille August; *C:* Jan Weincke, Aldo (G.R. Aldo) Graziati.

Twisted 🦴🦴 **1986** (R) This curio from Slater's early career came out on tape to take advantage of his rising stardom. He's properly creepy as a brilliant but evil teen using electronics, psychology, and swordplay to terrorize victims. The suspense isn't too bad when direction doesn't go overboard, which unfortunately is half the time. Based on the play "Children! Children!" by Jack Horrigan. **87m/C VHS.** Lois Smith, Christian Slater, Tandy Cronyn, Brooke Tracy, Dina Merrill, Dan Ziskie, Karl Taylor, Noelle Parker, John Cunningham, J.C. Quinn; *D:* Adam Holender.

Twisted 🦴🦴 **1996** Apt title for a contemporary gay version of "Oliver Twist" set in New York. Homeless 10-year-old orphan Lee (Graves) is brought into the seedy world of brothel owner Andre (Hickey). The youngster is befriended by Angel (Norona) a drug-addicted hustler who's under the sway of abusive pimp Eddie (Crivello). Along with big-hearted drag queen Shiniqua (Porter), Angel tries to rescue Lee from a sordid life. A stylized, operatic melodrama. **100m/C VHS, DVD.** Kelyn McNeil Graves, William Hickey, David Norona, Anthony Crivello, Billy Porter; *D:* Seth Michael Donsky; *W:* Seth Michael Donsky; *C:* Hernan Oto.

Twisted 🦴🦴 **1996** (PG-13) Four people become trapped in a fantasy world where nothing is as it seems. An airline passenger loses his identity, a housewife finds romance, a con man find a new mark, and a hired killer decides to retire—or at least that's what they believe. From the Australian TV series "Twisted Tales." **86m/C VHS, DVD.** *AU* Geoffrey Rush, Rachel Ward, Bryan Brown, Kimberly Davies, Shane Briant; *D:* Samantha Lang, Christopher Robbin Collins, Gregor Jordan, Catherine Millar; *C:* James Bartle; *M:* Nerida Tyson-Chew; *Nar:* Bryan Brown.

Twisted 🦴🦴½ **2004** (R) Judd stars as police detective Jessica Shepard in a sleazy, predictable thriller. Jessica likes to drink herself into blackout stupors and have one-night stands, until her hook-ups start turning up dead. Somehow, she ends up in charge of the murder investigation and must hunt down the killer while wondering what she has to do with the crimes. Partner Mike (Garcia) and Police Commissioner Mills (Jackson) are there to keep the pressure on. Oh yeah, and her father

Twisted Brain ♂ *Horror High* 1974 (R)
An honor student develops a serum that makes him half man and half beast. Now he can exact revenge on all the jocks and cheerleaders who have humiliated him in the past. Cardi is okay, the rest of the cast is awful. Silly, horrific teen monster epic. 89m/C VHS, DVD. Austin Stoker, Rosie Holotik, John Niland, Joye Hash, Jeff Alexander, Luana Anders, John Stephenson. *D:* Larry N. Stouffer; *M:* Mark Isham.

Twisted Justice ♂♂ 1989 Set in 2020, Heavener is a cop determined to stop a ruthless killer. Matte's become complicated, however, when his gun is taken away. Now he's forced to rely on his cunning to outwit his sadistic opponent. "Misery" to me. Sounds like "Misery" to me. 90m/C VHS, DVD. David Heavener, Erik Estrada, Jim Brown, Shannon Tweec, James Van Patten, Don Stroud, Karen Black, Lori Warner. *D:* David Heavener; *C:* David Hue; timer.

Twisted Love ♂½ 1995 (R) Wallflower becomes obsessed with the most popular guy in school. He has a motorcycle accident-that-was-no-accident and winds up in her tender care. 90m/C VHS, DVD. Liza Walker, Jerome Natali, Ariale Dombasle. *D:* Fernando Trueba; *C:* Jose Luis Alcaine; *M:* Antone Duhamel.

Twisted Nightmare ♂ 1987 (R) The people responsible for a young retarded boy's death are hunted by a strange figure lurking in the shadows. 95m/C Rhonda Gray, Cleve Hall, Angelia High, Robert Padilla. *D:* Paul Hunt.

Twisted Obsession ♂♂ 1990 (R) A man becomes passionately obsessed with a woman, and it leads to murder. 109m/C VHS, DVD. Jeff Goldblum, Miranda Richardson, Anemone, Dexter Fletcher, Daniel Ceccaldi, Liza Walker, Jerome Natali, Ariale Dombasle; *D:* Fernando Trueba; *C:* Jose Luis Alcaine; *M:* Antone Duhamel.

Twister ♂♂ 1989 (PG-13) An intriguing independent feature about a bizarre midwestern family, its feverish eccentricities and eventual collapse. Awaiting a cult following. 93m/C VHS, DVD. Dylan McDermott, Crispin Glover, Harry Dean Stanton, Suzy Amis, Jenny Wright, Lindsay Christman, Lois Chiles, William S. Burroughs, Tim Robbins; *D:* Michael Almereyda; *W:* Michael Almereyda; *C:* Renato Berta; *M:* Hans Zimmer.

Twister ♂♂ 1996 (PG-3) Director De Bont's sophomore directorial effort is another non-stop adrenaline drive, but instead of a mad bomber, nature is the bad guy. Hunt leads a 'eam of storm chasing scientists through Oklahoma in hopes of placing robotic sensors inside a tornado. Hunt's soon-to-be ex-husband Paxton rejoins the chase, to spice things up when the skies clear. There's a lot of things flying around, including trucks, houses, cows and the plausibility of the plot. Some nice chemistry between Hunt and Paxton, apparently the only people who can still look attractive in high winds and blowing debris. 105m/C VHS, DVD, Blu-ray Disc. Bill Paxton, Helen Hunt, Cary Elwes, Jami Gertz, Alan Ruck, Lois Smith, Sean M. Whalen, Gregory Sporleder, Abraham Benrubi, Jake Busey, Joey Slotnick, Philip Seymour Hoffman, Jeremy Davies, Zach Grenier, Richard Lineback, Rusty Schwimmer, Alexa Vega. *D:* Jan De Bont; *W:* Michael Crichton, Anne-Marie Martin; *C:* Jack N. Green; *M:* Mark Mancina. MTV Movie Awards '97: Action Seq.

Twists of Terror ♂♂½ 1996 Three horror stories narrated by an agoraphobic Los Angelenos. In "The People You Meet," a couple are terrorized while in the country; "The Clinic" has Mancuso confined to a hospital after a vicious dog attack, but the patient learns he can't check out; while "Stolen Moments" finds one young woman and two playboys with murder on their minds. 90m/C VHS. Jennifer

want, crazy and killed a bunch of people, too. Convoluted backstory, lame plot, and yet another "Ashley Judd in trouble" role acts up to a mediocre turkey and a precipitous step down for director Kaufman. 96m/C DVD. *US* Ashley Judd, Samuel L. Jackson, Andy Garcia, Russell Wong, David Strathairn, Camryn Manheim, Mark Pellegrino, Titus Welliver, D.W. Moffett, Richard T. Jones, Leland Orser; *D:* Philip Kaufman; *W:* Sarah Thorp; *C:* Peter Deming; *M:* Mark Isham.

Twitch of the Death Nerve ♂ *Bay of Blood; Last House on the Left, Part 2; Carnage* 1971 (R) Four vacationers are relentlessly pursued by a homicidal maniac armed with a sickle, bent on decapitation. Supposedly the inspiration for the "Friday the 13th" series. 87m/C VHS, DVD. *IT* Claudine Auger, Chris Avram, Isa Miranda, Laura Betti, Luigi Pistilli, Sergio Canvari, Anna Maria Rosati; *D:* Mario Bava; *W:* Mario Bava, Filippo Ottoni, Joseph McLee, Gene Luotto; *C:* Mario Bava; *M:* Stelvio Cipriani.

Twitches ♂♂½ 2005 (PG) Tweener girls should enjoy the fantasy adventures of twins Camryn and Alex (Tamera & Tia Mowry) who were separated at birth and raised under very different circumstances. Meeting at 21, the twins learn that they were spirited away from their magical kingdom for their own safety and that they are powerful witches. Now they must learn to use their abilities and work together to defeat their evil uncle, Thantos (Fabian). 86m/C VHS, DVD. Tamera Mowry, Tia Mowry, Jessica Grieco, Karen Holness; *D:* Stuart Gillard; *W:* Daniel Berendsen, Patrick Fabian, Patrick Kelly, Arnold Pinnock, Leslie Seiler; *C:* Manfred Guthe; *M:* John Van Tongeren. C.A.B.L.E.

Twitches Too ♂♂½ 2007 Our twin witches return—continuing to learn to control their magical abilities while dealing with living as a family and other girl stuff. But the darkness follows Alex and Camryn into the mortal world, so they must return to Coventry to defeat it once and for all. 83m/C DVD. Tamera Mowry, Tia Mowry, Kristen Wilson, Patrick Kelly, Kevin Jubinville, Arnold Pinnock, Leslie Seiler, Patrick Fabian, Karen Holness, Chris Gallinger, Nathan Stephenson; *D:* Stuart Gillard; *W:* Daniel Berendsen; *C:* Manfred Guthe; *M:* John Van Tongeren.

2 by 4 ♂♂ 1998 Johnnie (Smalhome) is an Irish construction worker employed by his hard-living Uncle Trump (O'Neill) in New York. Though he's got a steady job, good friends, and a loving girlfriend in Maria (Topper), Johnnie's plagued by nightmares of something that happened in his childhood. And his apparent childhood abuse leads him to drugs, drink, and a certain sexual ambiguity as his repressed memories try to force their way to the surface. 90m/C VHS, DVD. Jimmy Smalhome, Chris O'Neill, Bradley, Fitts, Joe Holyoake, Terrence McGoff, Michael Liebman, Ronan Carr, Leo Hamill, Seamus McDonagh, Kimberly Topper; *D:* Jimmy Smalhome; *W:* Fergus Tighe, Jimmy Smalhome, Terrence McGoff. *C:* Declan Quinn. Sundance '98: Cinematog.

Two Alone ♂½ 1934 Romantic melodrama. Orphaned Mazie (Parker) is mistreated by farmer Slag (Byron) and his wife (Bondi). When reform school runaway Adam (Brown) shows up, he suffers similar abuse but does have Mazie's love. The lovebirds are rescued from despair by farmhand Marshall (Robertson) who has a secret of his own. Adapted from the play "Wild Birds" by Dan Totheroh. 75m/B VHS. Jean Parker, Tom Brown, Arthur Byron, Beulah Bondi, Willard Robertson, ZaSu Pitts, Charley Grapewin; *D:* Elliott Nugent; *W:* Joseph Moncure March, Joseph Lovett; *C:* Lucien N. Andriot.

Two Bits ♂♂½ *A Day to Remember* 1996 (PG-13) Depression-era drama tells the story of a 12-year-old boy and his emotional coming of age. Title refers to a quarter Gennaro (Barone), in his film debut) seeks in order to attend the grand opening of a glamorous, air-conditioned movie palace. A heavily made-up Pacino (looking suspiciously like Marlon Brando in the garden scene of "The Godfather"), costars as the boy's grandfather, who leaves his last quarter. Gramps promises that he can collect later that day, when, he says, he will die. Fine performances all around and some powerful scenes go a long way toward masking the fact that the material is a bit too thin to stretch over an entire feature film. 85m/C VHS, DVD. Al Pacino, Jerry Barone, Mary Elizabeth Mastrantonio, Joe Grifasi, Joanna Merlin, Andy Romano, Ron McLary, Donna Mitchell, Patrick Borriello, Mary Lou Rosato, Rosemary DeAngelis; *D:* James Foley; *W:* Joseph Stefano; *C:* Juan Ruiz-Anchia; *M:* Jane Musky; *V:* Alec Baldwin.

Two Bits & Pepper ♂♂½ 1995 (PG) Bumbling criminals (both played by Piscopo) still manage to kidnap a young girl and her friend and it's up to the title characters, a pet horse and a pony, to attempt a daring rescue. 90m/C VHS, DVD. Joe Piscopo, Lauren Eckstrom, Rachel Crane, Perry Stephens, Kathrin Lautner, Dennis Weaver; *D:* Corey Michael Eubanks; *W:* Corey Michael Eubanks; *C:* Jacques Haitkin; *M:* Louis Febre.

Two Brothers ♂♂♂½ 2004 (PG) Kiddy fare about tiger brothers whose happy cubhood is shattered by the intrusion of Man. Great White Hunter (Pearce) guns down their father, and the cubs are snatched away into captivity. One cub is bought by a cruel circus owner (Scattini); the other becomes a child's (Highmore) pet. Neither can be tamed though, and circumstances reunite them with predictably tender results. Set in Indochina in the 1920s, with gorgeous backdrops of crumbling temples and lush jungles. The tigers are great, but human characters are exaggerated and unbelievable. Director Annaud shows great talent working with animals, as in previous work, "The Bear." Perhaps next time he'll leave out the humans. 109m/C VHS, DVD, *FR GB* Guy Pearce, Jean-Claude Dreyfus, Freddie Highmore, Philippine Leroy-Beaulieu, Moussa Maaskri, Vincent Scarito, Mai Anh Le, Oanh Nguyen, Stephanie Lagarde; *D:* Jean-Jacques Annaud; *W:* Jean-Jacques Annaud, Alain Godard; *C:* Jean-Marie Dreujou; *M:* Stephen Warbeck.

2 Brothers & a Bride ♂♂½ *A Foreign Affair* 2003 (PG-13) Simple-minded siblings Jake (Arquette) and Josh (Nelson) need to find a good (yet equally simpleminded) woman to tend to the chores on the farm since dear old mom passed away. They figure they'll find that lucky girl waiting for them somewhere in Russia. 92m/C DVD. David Arquette, Tim Blake Nelson, Emily Mortimer, Larry Pine, Lois Smith, Allyce Beasley, Megan Follows, Redmond M. Gleeson; *D:* Helmut Schleppi; *W:* Geert Heetebrij; *C:* M. David Mullen; *M:* Todd Holden Capps.

Two by Forsyth ♂♂ *No Come-backs* 1986 Two short films based on stories by Frederick Forsyth, one dealing with a dying millionaire's clever efforts to prevent his fortune from being inherited by greedy relatives, the other about a mild-mannered nasty, gossip columnist. 60m/C VHS. Dan O'Herlihy, Cyril Cusack, Miki O'Shea, Shirley Anne Field; *D:* Michael O'Herlihy; *W:* Michael Callan; *C:* Jack Conroy, *M:* Bill Whelan.

Two Can Play That Game ♂½ 2001 (R) Upwardly mobile Shante (Fox) seems to be the fountain of knowledge on relationships for her romantically challenged girlfriends D'edre (Mo'Nique), Karen (Robinson) and Trayce (Jones) on the subject of how to keep a man in line. When she sees her boyfriend Keith (Chestnut) grinding on another woman at a nightclub, however, her credibility takes a blow. She decides on a 10-day plan of action to force Keith back under her thumb. Clued in by his worldly wise buddy Tony (Anderson), however, Keith is well versed in the battle tactics of the opposite sex. Familiar material (director Brown also wrote "How to Be a Player"), spotty performances and the incessant narration by Fox's character make this a game you may want to quit halfway through. 90m/C VHS, DVD, *US* Vivica A. Fox, Morris Chestnut, Anthony Anderson, Gabrielle Union, Wendy Raque Robinson, Tamala Jones, Mo'Nique, Ray Wise, Bobby Brown, Dondre T. Whitfield; *D:* Mark Brown; *W:* Mark Brown; *C:* Alexander Grusynski; *M:* Marcus Miller.

Two Daughters ♂♂♂ *Teen Kanya* 1961 Director Ray wrote the scripts for two stories based on the writings of Nobel Prize winner Rabindranath Tagore. "The Postmaster" covers the relationship between an ambitious young man who becomes friends with his servant without realizing the consequences of his actions. "The Conclusion" finds a solemn young scholar declining to marry the girl arranged to be his intended and instead marrying a high-spirited young woman who doesn't want to give up her freedoms. Bengali with English subtitles. 114m/B VHS. *IN* Chandana Banerjee Anil Chatterjee, Soumitra Chatterjee; *D:* Satyajit Ray; *W:* Satyajit Ray; *C:* Soumendu Roy; *M:* Satyajit Ray.

Two Days ♂♂ 2003 (R) What could be more depressing than being a dejected wanna-be actor? Apparently, not much as Paul Miller (Rudd) decides life isn't much worth living if he can't make it there (or, anywhere). In typical Hollywood fashion, he clings to his last 15 minutes (er, 48 hours) of fame by having his final two days put down on film. Will the filmmaking family, or his friends try to stop him? While Rudd tries his best to breathe life into it, this unconventional journey and its requisite destination proves too haphazardly constructed for anyone to truly care. 87m/C DVD. Paul Rudd, Paul Logue, Mackenzie Astin, Adam Scott, Joshua Leonard, Caroline Aaron, Graham Beckel, Marguerite Moreau, Stacey Travis; *D:* Sean McGinly; *W:* Sean McGinly; *C:* Julie Delpy; *C:* Lubomir Bakchev.

2 Days in Paris ♂♂♂ 2007 (R) Film adds two days with ten characters in one locale and one half dozen separate plots and tries to come up with a dark comedy/thriller and winning debut for Herzfeld. It succeeds, mostly. San Fernando Valley is the backdrop, with a diverse ensemble of disturbed characters thrown together by the murder of a philandering spouse. Disjointed, and some plot threads are eft hanging, but there's some fine comic moments and interesting character development, especially Aiello's culinary hitman. 90m/C *FR* Julie Delpy, Adam Goldberg, Albert Delpy, Marie Pillet, Adam Jodorowsky, Daniel Bruehl, Alexia Landeau, Alex Nahon; *D:* Julie Delpy; *W:* Julie Delpy; *C:* Lubomir Bakchev.

Two Days in the Valley ♂♂♂ 1996 (R) Film adds two days with ten characters in one locale and one half Jozen separate plots and tries to come up with a dark comedy/thriller and winning debut for Herzfeld. It succeeds, mostly. San Fernando Valley is the backdrop, with a diverse ensemble of disturbed characters thrown together by the murder of a philandering spouse. Disjointed, and some plot threads are eft hanging, but there's some fine comic moments and interesting character development, especially Aiello's culinary hitman. Dosmo Pizzo. Theron's Helga acts eye candy for, for those too young to remember "Dynasty," you may want to check out the intense cat-fight between Hatcher's Becky Foxx and Helga. 95m/C VHS, DVD. Danny Aiello, Jeff Daniels, Marsha Mason, Teri Hatcher, Glenne Headly, James Spader, Eric Stoltz, Greg Cruttwell, Peter Horton, Charlize Theron, Keith Carradine, Louise Fletcher, Austin Pendleton, Paul Mazursky, Kathleen Luong; *D:* John Herzfeld; *W:* John Herzfeld; *C:* Oliver Wood; *M:* Anthony Marinelli.

Two Deaths ♂♂ 1994 (R) Sex, brutality, power, madness, death, revolution—sounds like a Roeg concoction. In 1989 Romania, the Ceausescu government is under siege and a civil war rages outside. But inside the opulent apartment of cynical Dr. Daniel Pavenic (Gambon) an odd but annual reunion of friends join him for their annual reunion dinner. Dinner is served by Pavenic's housekeeper Ana (Braga), who has a strange, disturbing relationship with the doctor, and the relationship with the doctor that he relates to his friends. His candor leads to similar revelations by his companions. Based on the novel "The Two Deaths of Senora Puccini" by Stephen Dobyns. 102m/C VHS, DVD. *GB* Michael Gambon, Sonia Braga, Patrick Malahide, Nickolas Grace, John Shrapnel, Ion Caramitru; *D:* Nicolas Roeg; *W:* Allan Scott; *C:* Witold Stok; *M:* Hans Zimmer.

Two Drifters ♂ *Odete* 2005 Overwrought tearjerker. Rui is devastated when his lover Pedro is killed in a car accident. This leaves him vulnerable when he meets Odete, whose obsession to have a baby has left her unringed. She happens to know Pedro's mother Teresa and claims she's carrying Pedro's child and things just go downhill from there. Portuguese with subtitles. 98m/C DVD. *PT* Ana Cristine de Oliveira, Teresa Madruga, Nuno Gil,

---

Joao Carreira; **D:** Joao Pedro Rodrigues; **W:** Joao Pedro Rodrigues, Paulo Rebelo; **C:** Rui Pocas; **M:** Frank Beauvais.

Two English Girls 🦴🦴🦴½ *Les Deux Anglaises et le Continent; Anne and Muriel* 1972 (R) A pre-WWI French lad, with a possessive mother, loves two English sisters, one an impassioned, reckless artist, the other a repressed spinster. Tenderly delineates the triangle's interrelating love and friendship over seven years. Based on the novel "Les Deux Anglaises et le Continent" by Henri-Pierre Roche. In French with English subtitles. **130m/C VHS, DVD, FR** Jean-Pierre Leaud, Kika Markham, Stacey Tendeter, Sylvia Marriott, Marie Mansert, Philippe Leotard; **D:** Francois Truffaut; **W:** Francois Truffaut; **C:** Nestor Almendros; **M:** Georges Delerue.

Two Evil Eyes 🦴🦴½ *Due Occhi Diabolici* 1990 (R) Horror kings Romero and Argento each direct an Edgar Allan Poe tale in this release, hence the title. Barbeau, the scheming younger wife of a millionaire, hypnotizes her husband with the help of her lover in "The Facts in the Case of M. Valdemar." When hubby dies too soon to validate changes made in his will, the lovers decide to freeze him for two weeks in order that death can be recorded in the correct time. In "Black Cat" a crime photographer used to photographing gore adopts a feline friend and starts getting sick on the job. **121m/C VHS, DVD. IT** Adrienne Barbeau, Ramy Zada, Harvey Keitel, Madeleine Potter, Bingo O'Malley, E.G. Marshall, John Amos, Sally Kirkland, Kim Hunter, Martin Balsam, Tom Atkins; **D:** George A. Romero, Dario Argento; **W:** George A. Romero, Dario Argento, Franco Ferrini; **C:** Giuseppe Maccari, Peter Reniers; **M:** Pino Donaggio.

Two-Faced Woman 🦴🦴🦴 1941 Garbo, in her last film, attempts a ruse when she finds her husband may be interested in an old flame. Pretending to be her twin sister in an attempt to lure Douglas away from the other woman, she's fooled a little herself. Romantic comedy unfortunately miscasts Garbo as an American-ized ski bunny. **90m/B VHS.** Greta Garbo, Melvyn Douglas, Constance Bennett, Roland Young, Ruth Gordon, Robert Sterling, George Cleveland, Frances Carson; **D:** George Cukor; **C:** Joseph Ruttenberg.

The Two Faces of Dr. Jekyll 🦴🦴½ *House of Fright; Jekyll's Inferno* 1960 Henry Jekyll's (Massie) experiments lead to the release of his suave alter ego Edward Hyde. Suffering wife has taken up with his best friend. Hyde pits everyone against each other, while Jekyll struggles to retain control over his insidious other half. **87m/C VHS. GB** Paul Massie, Dawn Addams, Christopher Lee, David Kossoff, Francis De Wolff, Oliver Reed, Norma Marla, Terry Quinn; **D:** Terence Fisher; **W:** Wolf Mankowitz; **C:** Jack Asher.

The Two Faces of Evil 🦴 1982 A family's vacation turns into a night of unbearable terror when they pick up a sinister hitchhiker. **60m/C VHS, DVD.** Anna Calder-Marshall, Gary Raymond, Denholm Elliott, Pauline Delany, Philip Latham; **D:** Peter Sasdy, Alan Gibson.

Two Family House 🦴🦴½ 1999 (R) The '50s aren't exactly a time of happiness and prosperity for factory worker Buddy Rispoli. He's a frustrated singer, still haboring dreams of the big time, with a number of failed moneymaking schemes behind him. His latest venture is buying a two-family house where he and his family can live upstairs while he turns the downstairs into a bar. But the current tenants, a pregnant Irish teen and her abusive husband, have other ideas. **109m/C VHS, DVD.** Michael Rispoli, Kelly Macdonald, Katherine Narducci, Matt Servitto, Kevin Conway, Michele Santopietro; **D:** Raymond De Felitta; **W:** Raymond De Felitta; **C:** Mike Mayers; **M:** Stephen Endelman. Sundance '00: Aud. Award.

2 Fast 2 Furious 🦴🦴 (PG-13) 2003 2 dumb 2 believe, but no one seems to care. Walker reprises his role as now-disgraced undercover cop Brian O'Connor, and he's being upstaged by his co-star. This time it's Tyrese, as childhood pal and new partner-in-under-cover-crime Roman. It doesn't really matter, though, because everyone is upstaged by the lovingly photographed cars and the chaos they cause. The continuous action is now in Miami, as the buddies infiltrate the street-racing circuit to bust a Colombian drug ring and some bad cops. **94m/C VHS, DVD, UMD, HD DVD. US** Paul Walker, Tyrese Gibson, Cole Hauser, Eva Mendes, Ludacris, Devon Aoki, James Remar, Thom Barry, Michael Ealy, Mark Boone Jr.; **D:** John Singleton; **W:** Derek Haas, Michael Brandt; **C:** Matthew F. Leonetti; **M:** David Arnold.

Two Fathers' Justice 🦴🦴 1985 Two dads, one tough and one a wimp, seek revenge on the men who killed their kids. **100m/C VHS.** Robert Conrad, George Hamilton, Brooke Bundy, Catherine Corkill, Whitney Kershaw, Greg Terrell; **D:** Rod Holcomb. **TV**

Two Fisted Justice 🦴 1931 A cowboy protects a town against a daring and deadly Indian attack. **45m/B VHS.** Tom Tyler, Barbara Weeks, Bobby Nelson, William Walling, Yakima Canutt, John Elliott; **D:** George Arthur Durlam; **W:** George Arthur Durlam; **C:** Archie Stout.

Two-Fisted Justice 🦴 1943 The Range Busters do their part to maintain law and order in the old West. **55m/B VHS.** John "Dusty" King, David Sharpe, Max Terhune, Gwen Gaze, John Elliot, Charles "Blackie" King, George Chesebro, Frank Ellis; **D:** Robert Emmett Tansey; **W:** William Nolte; **C:** Robert E. Cline.

Two-Fisted Law 🦴½ 1932 McCoy plays a rancher who borrows big bucks from the corrupt Oakman, who's actually a land grabber. McCoy then teams up with a posse to bring the evildoer to justice. Early (and small) screen roles for Wayne and Brennan. **58m/B VHS, DVD.** Tim McCoy, Tully Marshall, Wheeler Oakman, Alice Day, Wallace MacDonald, John Wayne, Walter Brennan; **D:** David Ross Lederman; **W:** Kurt Kempler; **C:** Benjamin (H.) Kline.

Two for Texas 🦴🦴½ 1997 Young buck Holland (Bairstow) and grizzled adventurer Allison (Kristofferson) manage to escape from a Louisiana chain gang and decide to head to Texas so they can join in the Texas Volunteer Army under Sam Houston (Skerritt). Soon, they're part of a group sent to San Jacinto in order to avenge the massacre at the Alamo. Kind of plodding western based on the novel by James Lee Burke. **96m/C VHS.** Kris Kristofferson, Scott Bairstow, Tom Skerritt, Peter Coyote, Irene Bedard, Marco Rodriguez, Richard Jones; **D:** Rod Hardy; **W:** Larry Brothers; **C:** David Connell; **M:** Lee Holdridge. **CABLE**

Two for the Money 🦴🦴 2005 (R) Another bigger-than-life role for Al Pacino who plays "blackie" King, the owner of a sports betting advice empire. Walter takes on Brandon Lang (McConaughey) after his incredible football game-picking accuracy gains notice. Brandon, whose NFL hopes were shot down by a career-ending knee injury, moves to Manhattan where under the mentoring of Walter he becomes a game-picking superstar, rocketing into a world of wealth and glamour. Predictably Brandon's hot streak cools, plunging him back to earth. If you can't get enough of Pacino's "Hoo-WAH!" roles, you'll love this one, which borders on self-parody. **124m/C DVD. US** Al Pacino, Matthew McConaughey, Rene Russo, Armand Assante, Jeremy Piven, Jaime (James) King, Kevin Chapman, Gedde Watanabe, Carly Pope; **D:** D.J. Caruso; **W:** Dan Gilroy; **C:** Conrad W. Hall; **M:** Christophe Beck.

Two for the Road 🦴🦴🦴½ 1967 On a road trip to the French Riviera, Mark (Finney) and Joanna (Hepburn) look back on more than a decade of their relationship. Flashbacks to their first meeting and subsequent vacations detail what when wrong and if their love is worth saving. Mancini score adds poignancy to the couple's reflections on their stormy life. Well-acted but the very sixties look has dated badly. **112m/C VHS, DVD. GB** Audrey Hepburn, Albert Finney, Eleanor Bron, William Daniels, Claude Dauphin, Nadia Gray, Jacqueline Bisset, Georges Descrieres, Gabrielle Middleton, Judy Cornwell, Irene Hilda, Roger Dann, Libby Morris, Yves Barsac; **D:** Stanley Donen; **W:** Frederic Raphael; **C:** Christopher Challis; **M:** Henry Mancini.

Two for the Seesaw 🦴🦴🦴 1962 Mitchum stars as a Nebraska attorney who comes to New York and gets involved with MacLaine. Humorous and touching comedy-drama worked better on stage, because the large screen magnified the talkiness of Gibson's play. Unusual casting of Mitchum as a Midwest lawyer and MacLaine as a New York Jewish bohemian. **119m/B VHS, DVD.** Robert Mitchum, Shirley MacLaine, Edmon Ryan, Elisabeth Fraser, Eddie Firestone, Billy Gray, Vic Lundin; **D:** Robert Wise; **W:** Isobel Lennart; **M:** Andre Previn.

Two Friends 🦴🦴 1986 Campion's first feature, made for Australian TV, depicts the severing of the friendship between 15-year-olds Kelly (Bidenko) and Louise (Coles). Separated physically and emotionally as they begin growing up and attending different schools, the film flashes back to moments in their once inseparable friendship. **76m/C VHS, DVD. AU** Kris Bidenko, Emma Coles; **D:** Jane Campion; **W:** Helen Garner; **C:** Julian Penney; **M:** Martin Armiger.

Two Girls and a Guy 🦴🦴🦴 1998 (R) Graham and Wagner find out that Downey's been two-timing them and they confront him at his apartment. Only don't expect the usual revenge scenario. Yeah, it's talky, but the dialogue (much of it improvised) is great. Downey is at his best, playing an irresistibly charismatic actor backed into a (real and figurative) corner by his lifestyle while Graham and Wagner avoid the wronged-woman cliches. In one of the all-time male fantasies ever, Downey's character still gets to have sex with one of the women even after his lie has been exposed. The MPAA had a little problem with that, since that scene, like most of the rest of the movie, was shot in real time. The uncut NC-17 version is also available. **92m/C VHS, DVD.** Robert Downey Jr., Heather Graham, Natasha Gregson Wagner, Angel David, Frederique van der Wal; **D:** James Toback; **W:** James Toback; **C:** Barry Markowitz.

Two Girls and a Sailor 🦴🦴🦴 1944 Wartime musical revue loosely structured around a love triangle involving a sailor on leave. Vintage hokum with lots of songs. ♫Paper Doll; The Young Man with a Horn; Concerto for Index Finger; Take it Easy; Ritual Fire Dance; Inka Dinka Doo; My Mother Told Me; A Love Like Ours; In search of Madness. **124m/B VHS.** June Allyson, Gloria De Haven, Van Johnson, Xavier Cugat, Jimmy Durante, Tom Drake, Lena Horne, Harry James, Gracie Allen, Virginia O'Brien, Jose Iturbi, Carlos Ramirez, Donald Meek, Ben Blue; **Cameos:** Buster Keaton; **D:** Richard Thorpe; **C:** Robert L. Surtees.

The Two Great Cavaliers 🦴 1973 A Ming warrior has a hard time with the Manchurian army, fending it off as he must with only his bare instep, heel, and wrist. **95m/C VHS, DVD.** Chen Shing, Mao Ying; **D:** Yeung Ching Chen.

Two Gun Man 🦴½ 1931 America's first singing cowboy, Ken Maynard, performs hair-raising stunts in this old oater. One of the first "talkies!" **60m/B VHS, DVD.** Ken Maynard, Lafe (Lafayette) McKee, Charles "Blackie" King, Tom London, Lucille Powers; **D:** Phil Rosen.

Two-Gun Man from Harlem 🦴 1938 Big city guy travels to the wild West in search of a little truth. **60m/B VHS.** Herbert Jeffries, Marguerite Whitten, Mantan Moreland, Matthew "Stymie" Beard; **D:** Richard C. Kahn.

Two-Gun Troubador 🦴 *The Lone Troubador* 1937 A masked singing cowboy struggles to uncover his father's murderer. **59m/B VHS.** Fred Scott, Claire Rochelle, John Merton; **D:** Bernard B. Ray; **W:** Phil Dunham, Richard Bare; **C:** Walter Bluemel.

Two Hands 🦴🦴 1998 Black comedy/thriller stars Aussie heartthrob Ledger as teen Jimmy who's got a nothing job in Sydney and would like to improve his prospects. So he agrees to deliver a cash-filled envelope for local gang boss, Pando (Brown), and then promptly loses the money. This sends Jimmy on the run to avoid Pando's retribution. (But the kid still finds some time to romance naive Alex (Byrne).) **104m/C VHS, DVD. AU** Heath Ledger, Bryan Brown, David Field, Rose Byrne, Susie Porter, Tom Long, Steven Vidler; **D:** Gregor Jordan; **W:** Gregor Jordan; **C:** Malcolm McCulloch; **M:** Chris Gough. Australian Film Inst. '99: Director (Jordan), Film, Film Editing, Orig. Screenplay, Support. Actor (Brown).

200 Cigarettes 🦴🦴 1998 (R) Directorial debut from former casting director Garcia follows the adventures of various self-absorbed hipsters on New Year's Eve in early '80s New York. The excellent ensemble cast is given spotty material, however. The primary goal of all these rather unlikable characters is to find someone (or anyone) to sleep with before the night is over. They all hook up in this ode to the high life of pre-AIDS promiscuity, but you don't really care about them at all. Chapelle provides the most entertainment as a philosophy-spouting disco cabbie who schleps the shallow partygoers to and fro. **101m/C VHS, DVD.** Ben Affleck, Casey Affleck, Jay Mohr, Dave Chappelle, Gaby Hoffman, Courtney Love, Christina Ricci, Paul Rudd, Catherine Kellner, Martha Plimpton, Janeane Garofalo, Guillermo Diaz, Angela Featherstone, Brian McCardie, Nicoe Ari Parker, Kate Hudson, Elvis Costello; **D:** Risa Bramon Garcia; **W:** Shana Larsen; **C:** Frank Prinzi; **M:** Mark Mothersbaugh, Bob Mothersbaugh.

200 Motels 🦴½ 1971 (R) Rambling, non-narrative self-indulgent video album by and about Frank Zappa and the Mothers of Invention, as they document a long and especially grueling road tour. For fans only. **99m/C VHS.** Ringo Starr, Theodore Bikel, Keith Moon, Janet Ferguson, Lucy Offerall; **D:** Frank Zappa; **W:** Frank Zappa; **C:** Gillian Lynne; **M:** Frank Zappa.

Two If by Sea 🦴½ *Stolen Hearts* 1995 (R) Small-time hood Frank (Leary) and his girlfriend Roz (Bullock) hole up in a New England mansion after Frank steals a valuable Matisse painting. Between verbal sparring matches, the two try to mingle with the upper crusty residents with predictable results. Pursuing the pair are the FBI, led by the deluded O'Malley (Kotto), and Frank's bonehead cousin Beano (Robson) and his trio of dim henchmen. Tries to be a caper/romantic comedy but fails to deliver on all fronts. The usually caustic Leary takes some of the edge off of his trademark bitter humor, and the alleged witty repartee is just plain annoying as a result. Nova Scotia turns in a fine performance as New England. **96m/C VHS, DVD.** Denis Leary, Sandra Bullock, Stephen (Dillon) Dillane, Yaphet Kotto, Wayne Robson, Jonathan Tucker, Mike Starr, Michael Badalucco, Lenny Clarke, John Friesen; **D:** Bill Bennett; **W:** Denis Leary, Mike Armstrong; **C:** Andrew Lesnie.

The Two Jakes 🦴🦴 1990 (R) Ten years have passed and Jake Gittes is still a private investigator in this sequel to 1974's "Chinatown." When a murder occurs while he's digging up dirt on an affair between the wife of a real estate executive and the executive's partner, Jake must return to Chinatown to uncover the killer and face the painful memories buried there. Despite solid dialogue and effective performances, it's unreasonably difficult to follow if you haven't seen "Chinatown." Outstanding photography by Vilmos Zsigmond. **137m/C VHS, DVD.** Jack Nicholson, Harvey Keitel, Meg Tilly, Madeline Stowe, Eli Wallach, Ruben Blades, Frederic Forrest, David Keith, Richard Farnsworth, Tracey Walter; **D:** Jack Nicholson; **W:** Robert Towne; **C:** Vilmos Zsigmond; **M:** Van Dyke Parks.

Two Kinds of Love 🦴🦴 1985 Adapted from Peggy Mann's novel "There Are Two Kinds of Terrible," this is the story of a young boy who learns to love his distant, workaholic father after his protective mother suddenly dies. **94m/C VHS.** Rick Schroder, Lindsay Wagner, Peter Weller, Rossie (Ross) Harris; **D:** Jack Bender. **TV**

Two Lane Blacktop 🦴🦴🦴 1971 Counterculture critics darling that failed at the box-office but has since developed a cult following. The Driver (Taylor) and the Mechanic (Wilson) are car freaks in a '55 Chevy, driving the southwestern backroads looking for a race. They meet up with Oates who's at the wheel of a brand-new G.T.O. He proposes they cross-country to D.C. and the winner gets 'he loser's car. Along the way, everyone's enthusiasm wanes and they part, with wilson and ... as the film literally melts into a bright light. Music includes The Doors, Kris Kristofferson, and Ray Charles. **103m/C VHS, DVD.** James Taylor, Dennis Wilson, Warren Oates, Laurie 3rd, Harry Dean Stanton; **D:** Monte Hellman; **W:** Rudy Wurlitzer, Will Corry. **C:** Jackson Browne.

Two Men Went to War ♂♂ 1950 A young hero battles monstrous dinosaurs, pirates, and more in this drama set ... **W:** Tom Hutchard. **C:** Harry Neumann.

The Two Mrs. Carrolls ♂♂½ 1947 Bogart is a psycho-killer/artist who paints portraits of his wives as the Angel of Death—and then kills them. The married Bogart falls for Stanwyck and devises to rid himself of Stanwyck in the same manner as his first killing. Stanwyck, however, becomes increasingly suspicious and calls on an old beau for help. Melodrama cast Bogart against type (not always successfully). Filmed in 1945, but was unreleased until 1947. **99m/B VHS.** Humphrey Bogart, Barbara Stanwyck, Alexis Smith, Nigel Bruce, Pat O'Moore, Ann Carter; **D:** Peter Godfrey.

Two Minute Warning ♂ 1976 (R) A sniper plans to take out the president of the United States at an NFL playoff game in this boring, pointless disaster film that goes on forever. Features all the ready-made characters inherent in the genre, but, until its too late, precious little of the mayhem. To get caught watching the TV version, which features more characters and an additional subplot, would be truly disastrous. **116m/C VHS, DVD.** Charlton Heston, John Cassavetes, Martin Balsam, Beau Bridges, Marilyn Hassett, David Janssen, Jack Klugman, Walter Pidgeon, Gena Rowlands; **D:** Larry Peerce; **W:** Ed Hume. **C:** Gerald Hirschfeld; **M:** Charles Fox.

Two Moon Junction ♂ 1988 A soon-to-be-wed Southern debutante enters into a wild love affair with a rough-edged carnival worker. Poorly acted, wildly directed, with many unintentional laughs. **104m/C VHS, DVD.** Sherilyn Fenn, Richard Tyson, Louise Fletcher, Burl Ives, Kristy McNichol, Millie Perkins, Don Galloway, Herve Villechaize, Dabbs Greer, Milla Jovovich, Screamin' Jay Hawkins; **D:** Zalman King. **C:** Mark Plummer. **M:** Jonathan Elias.

Two Much ♂½ 1996 (PG-13) Banderas does double duty as a con man pretending to be twins in order to romance two sisters (Griffith and Hannah). Embarrassingly light comedy suffers from a convoluted plot (which still manages to leave holes), weak or non-existent characterization, and a general lack of humor. About the only thing it has going for it is Cusack as a wisecracking secretary. It was on the set of this film that Banderas and Griffith started their real-life romance. While that may have helped the boxoffice and gossip columns in Banderas's homeland, the works didn't find their way to the screen. Based on a Donald E. Westlake story. **118m/C VHS, DVD.** Antonio Banderas, Daryl Hannah, Joan Cusack, Danny Aiello, Eli Wallach, Vincent Schiavelli, Gabino Trueba; **W:** Fernando Trueba, David Trueba. **C:** Jose Luis Alcaine. **M:** Michel Camilo.

Two Lost Worlds Woof! 1950 A young hero battles monstrous dinosaurs, pirates, and more in this drama set ... uncharted island. Don't miss the footage from "Captain Fury," "One Billion B.C.," and "Captain Caution" and Arness long before his role in "The Thing." **63m/B VHS.** James Arness, Laura Elliot, Bill Kennedy; **D:** Norman Dawn. **W:** Tom Hutchard. **C:** Harry Neumann.

Two Mules for Sister Sara ♂♂ 1970 (PG) American mercenary in 19th century Mexico gets mixed up with a cigar-smoking nun and the two make plans to capture a French garrison. Based on a Boetticher story. MacLaine and Eastwood are great together. **105m/C VHS, DVD.** Shirley MacLaine, Clint Eastwood, Manolo Fabregas; **D:** Don Siegel; **W:** Albert (John B. Sherry) Maltz. **M:** Ennio Morricone.

Two Nights with Cleopatra ♂½ 1954 *Due Notti Con Cleopatra* A piece of Italian pizza involving Cleopatra's double (also played by Loren) falling in love with one of the guards. Notable only for the 19-year-old Sophia's pre-nudity. **77m/C VHS.** Sophia Loren, Ettore Manni, Alberto Sordi, Paul Muller, Alberto Talegalli, Rolf Tasna, Gianni Cavalieri, Nando (Fernando) Bruno, Riccardo Garrone, Carlo Dale; **D:** Mario Mattoli; **W:** Nino Maccari, Ettore Scola.

Two Ninas ♂♂ 2000 (R) Dreary romantic comedy finds mopey aspiring writer Marty (Livingston) meeting sarcastic Nina Cohen (Buono) at a party. The two hit it off but then Marty literally runs into Nina 2, i.e. wealthy Nina Harris (Peet), while rollerblading in Central Park. He keep his stories straight and hope the two Ninas never meet, which, of course, they do. **90m/C VHS, DVD.** US Ron Livingston, Cara Buono, Amanda Peet, Bray Poor, Jill(ian) Hennessey; **D:** Neil Turitz; **W:** Neil Turitz. **C:** Joaquin Baca-Asay; **M:** Joseph Saba.

Two of a Kind ♂½ 1982 In his TV movie debut, Burns plays an elderly man whose mentally handicapped grandson helps him put the starch back in his shirt. Sensitively produced and performed. **88m/C VHS, DVD.** George Burns, Robby Benson, Cliff Robertson, Barbara Barrie, Frances Lee McCain, Geri Jewell, Ronny Cox; **D:** Roger Young. **TV**

Two of a Kind ♂ 1983 (PG) Angels make a bet with God—two selfish people will redeem themselves or God can blow up the Earth. Bad acting, awful direction, and the script needs divine intervention. **88m/C VHS.** John Travolta, Olivia Newton-John, Charles Durning, Beatrice Straight, Scatman Crothers, Oliver Reed; **D:** John Herzfeld; **C:** Fred W. Koenekamp.

The Two of Us ♂♂½ 1968 *Le Vieil Homme Et L'Enfant; Claude; The Old Man and the Boy* 1968 Young Jewish boy flees Nazi-occupied Paris to live in the country with an irritable, bigoted guardian. Sensitive, eloquent movie about racial prejudice and anti-Semitism. In French with English subtitles. **86m/B VHS.** FR Michel Simon, Alain Cohen, Luce Fabiole, Roger Carel, Paul Preboist, Charles Denner; **D:** Claude Berri; **W:** Claude Berri; **C:** Jean Penzer. **M:** Georges Delerue.

Two of Us ♂♂ 2000 (PG-13) A "what-if" look at the friendship between ex-Beatles Paul McCartney and John Lennon in 1976. Paul (Quinn) is in New York to publicize a concert with his band Wings and he decides to visit estranged mate John (Harris) at the Dakota in a bittersweet effort to make peace with their relationship. **90m/C VHS, DVD.** Aidan Quinn, Jared Harris; **D:** Michael Lindsay-Hogg; **W:** Mark Stanfield; **C:** Miroslaw Baszak; **M:** David Schwartz. **CABLE**

Two or Three Things I Know about Her ♂♂ 1966 *Deux ou Trois Choses Que Je Sais d'Elle* 1966 Inspired by a magazine article about housewife-prostitutes, Godard takes on the bourgeoise. Juliette (Vlady) is a wife and mother who lives in the suburbs of Paris and goes into the city once a week to work as a prostitute. French with subtitles ... a grim vision of the future, the special effects and music are still stunning. Critically acclaimed and well accepted by some, simply confusing to others. Seen by some as a grim vision of man's historical use of machinery and by others an ... once a week to work as a prostitute. French with ... From Arthur C. Clarke's short story.

2000 Maniacs ♂♂½ 1964 One of cult director Lewis' most enjoyably watchable films. A literal Civil War "ghost town" takes its revenge 100 years after being slaughtered by renegade Union soldiers by luring unwitting "yankee" tourists to their centennial festival. The hapless Northerners are then chopped, crushed, ripped apart etc. while the ghostly rebels party. Quite fun in a cartoonishly gruesome sort of way. Filmed in St. Cloud, FL. **75m/C VHS, DVD.** William Kerwin, Connie Mason, Jeffrey Allen, Ben Moore, Gary Bakeman, Jerome (Jerry Stallion) Eden, Shelby Livingston, Michael Korn, Yvonne Gilbert, Mark Douglas, Linda Cochran, Vincent Santo, Andy Wilson; **D:** Herschell Gordon Lewis; **C:** Herschell Gordon Lewis; **M:** Herschell Gordon Lewis.

2001: A Space Odyssey ♂♂♂♂ 1968 Space voyage to Jupiter turns chaotic when a computer, HAL 9000, takes over. Seen by some as a mirror of man's historical use of machinery and by others an ... 1968 Space voyage to Jupiter turns chaotic when a computer, HAL 9000, takes over. Seen by some as a mirror of man's historical use of machinery and by others an ... well accepted by some, simply confusing ... the voice of HAL, but was replaced by Rain. From Arthur C. Clarke's short story.

Two Plus One 1995 Triangular drama about Yuppie relationships, set in Philadelphia. Romantic couple searches for happiness and decides to invite a third person to join their relationship. Newcomer Lewis is the sister of actress Julietta. **85m/C VHS.** William Sage, Deirdre Lewis, Tony Vinto; **D:** Eugene Merlan.

Two Rode Together ♂♂½ 1961 A Texas marshal and an army lieutenant negotiate with the Comanches for the return of captives, but complications ensue. **109m/C VHS.** James Stewart, Richard Widmark, Shirley Jones, Linda Crista, Andy Devine, John McIntire; **D:** John Ford.

2 Seconds ♂♂ 1998 *Deux Secondes* 1998 (R) Laurie (Laurier) has spent most of her life as a mountain bike racer but a two second hesitation costs her a race and second her retirement. She returns to Montreal and meets Lorenzo (Tavarone), a cantankerous, elderly former racer who runs a bike shop. Laurie gets a job as a bike courier and starts to re-evaluate her life. French with subtitles. **101m/C VHS, DVD.** CA Charlotte Laurier, Suzanne Clement, Yves Pelletier, Dino Tavarone; **D:** Manon Briand; **W:** Manon Briand. **C:** Louise Archambault, Pierre Crepo; **M:** Domine Grand Sylvain-Charles Grand.

The Two Sisters 1937 Goldstein, in her only film role, plays an older sister who sacrifices everything for the younger. The appearance of two young children, suspecting their mother Eileen may have murdered them. Two character study set in Eileen's home with both verbally revealed and physically possible the crime. Based on the play by Neal Bell. **85m/C VHS.** GE Fridr. Ward, Suzy Amis; **D:** Beth B; **W:** Beth B, Neal Bell. **C:** Phil Parmel.

Two Shades of Blue ♂½ 1998 (R) Surprisingly dull erotic thriller. Writer-Hunter is framed for the murder of fiancee Busey, so she assumes the alter ego identity of her novel's sexy heroine in order to hunt for the killer herself. She takes a job as a relay telephone operator for the deaf so she can contact deaf D.A. Matlin, a voyeuristic delight in their conversations. **103m/C VHS, DVD.** Rachel Hunter, Mariee Matlin, Eric Roberts, Gary Busey; **D:** James D. Deck; **W:** Ted Williams. **VIDEO**

Two Small Bodies ♂♂ 1993 Police detective Brann investigates the disappearance of two young children, suspecting their mother Eileen may have murdered them. Two character study set in Eileen's home with both verbally revealed and physically possible the crime. Based on the play by Neal Bell. **85m/C VHS.** GE Fridr. Ward, Suzy Amis; **D:** Beth B; **W:** Beth B, Neal Bell. **C:** Phil Parmel.

2010: The Year We Make Contact ♂♂♂ 1984 (PG) Based on Arthur C. Clarke's novel, which is his sequel to "2001: A Space Odyssey." American and Russians unite to investigate the abandoned starship Discovery's decaying orbit around Jupiter and try to determine why the HAL9000 computer sabotaged its mission years before, while signs of cosmic change are detected on and around the giant planet. **116m/C VHS, DVD.** Roy Scheider, John Lithgow, Helen Mirren, Bob Balaban, Keir Dullea, Madolyn Smith, Mary Jo Deschanel; **D:** Peter Hyams; **W:** Peter Hyams, Arthur C. Clarke; **C:** Peter Hyams; **M:** David Shire; **V:** Douglas Rain, Candice Bergen.

2020 Texas Gladiators Woof! 1985 (R) In the post-nuclear holocaust world, two groups, one good, one bad, get themselves on Bob Crosby's TV show. **91m/C VHS.** Al Cliver, Daniel Stephen, Peter Hooten, Sabrina Siani; **D:** Kevin Mancuso.

2069: A Sex Odyssey ♂½ 1978 (R) Team of beautiful, sensuous astronauts are sent to Earth to obtain male sperm which they must bring back to Venus. Tongue-in-cheek soft core sci-fi spoof. **73m/C VHS, DVD.** Alena Penz, Nina Frederic, Gerti Snelder, Raoul Retzer, Catherine Conti, Heidi Hammer, Michael Main, Herb Heesel; **D:** George Keil; **W:** Will Frisch; **C:** Michael Maaszalek, George Mondi; **M:** Hans Hammerschmid.

Two Tickets to Broadway ♂♂½ 1951 A small-town singer and a crooner arrange a hoax to get themselves on Bob Crosby's TV show. Appealing but lightweight. "Let the Worry Bird Worry For You; Pagliacci; There's No Tomorrow; Manhattan; Big Chief Hole in the Ground; The Closer You Are, Baby; You'll Never Be Sorry; Pelican Falls High; It Began In Yucatan." **106m/C VHS.** Tony Martin, Janet Leigh, Gloria De Haven, Joi Lansing; **D:** James V. Kern; **M:** Leo Robin, Jule Styne.

Two to Tango ♂½ 1988 (R) A hired assassin goes to Buenos Aires to kill a crime boss, and falls in love with his tango-dancing mistress. Based on the novel by J.P. Feinman. **87m/C VHS.** AR Don Stroud, Adrienne Sachs; **D:** Hector Olivera.

Two Tough Guys ♂♂½ 1960 *Dos Tipos Duros* 2003 Spanish hitman Paco (Resines) owes money to his boss Don Rodrigo (Alexandre) so he's willing to help out by any means necessary. Unfortunately Paco doesn't think this should mean that she can tag along on their next job. Uneasy mix of comedy and violence. Spanish with subtitles. **100m/C VHS, DVD.** SP Antonio Resines, Jordi Vilches, Elena Anaya, Rosa Maria Sarda, Manual Alexandre; **D:** Juan Martinez Moreno; **W:** Juan Martinez Moreno; **C:** Gonzalo F. Berridi; **M:** Alex Martinez.

Two-Way Stretch ♂♂♂ 1960 Three prison inmates in a progressive jail plan to break out, pull a diamond heist, and break back in, all in the same night. Fast-paced slapstick farce. **84m/B VHS, DVD.** GB Peter Sellers, Wilfrid Hyde-White, Liz Fraser, David Lodge; **D:** Robert Day.

2001: A Space Travesty ♂½ 2000 (R) Nielsen continues his tradition of parodies starring as none-too-bright Marshal "Dick" Dix who must rescue the U.S. president who has been kidnapped by aliens and replaced by a clone. He joins forces with sexy Cassandra (Winter) and heads to planet Vegan on his mission. **99m/C VHS, DVD.** Leslie Nielsen, Ezio Greggio, Peter Egan, Ophelie Winter; **D:** Allan Goldstein; **W:** Alan Shearman; **C:** Sylvain Brault; **M:** Claude Foisy.

"The Sentinel." Followed by a sequel "2010: The Year We Make Contact." **139m/C VHS, DVD, Blu-ray Disc, HD DVD, GB.** Keir Dulea, Gary Lockwood, William Sylvester, Dan Richter, Leonard Rossiter, Margaret Tyzack, Robert Beatty, Vivian Kubrick; **D:** Stanley Kubrick; **W:** Stanley Kubrick, Arthur C. Clarke; **C:** Geoffrey Unsworth; **M:** John Alcott; **V:** Douglas Rain, Douglas Rain. '68. Visual FX; AFI '98: Top 100, Natl. Film Reg. '91.

Two Weeks 🎬½ *2006 (R)* Wan and predictable family drama with a lot of unlikable characters (but not our Sally!). Four squabbling siblings unexpectedly find themselves together for two weeks in order to deal with their mother's upcoming death. Filmmaker Keith (Chaplin) decides to record interviews with mom Anita (Field) while the others cope (or not) in their own ways. **102m/C DVD.** Sally Field, Ben Chaplin, Julianne Nicholson, Glen Howerton, Thomas Cavanaugh, Clea DuVall, James Murtaugh; **D:** Steve Stockman; **W:** Steve Stockman; **C:** Stephen Kazmierski; **M:** Heitor Pereira.

Two Weeks in Another Town 🎬🎬 *1962* Douglas and Robinson are a couple of Hollywood has-beens who set out to make a comeback picture but meet with adversity at every turn. Extremely sappy melodrama is based on Irwin Shaw's trashy novel and represents one of director Minnelli's poorer efforts. **107m/C VHS.** Kirk Douglas, Edward G. Robinson, Cyd Charisse, George Hamilton, Daliah Lavi, Claire Trevor, James Gregory, Rosanna Schiaffino, George Macready, Stefan Schnabel, Vito Scotti, Leslie Uggams; **D:** Vincente Minnelli; **C:** Milton Krasner.

Two Weeks Notice 🎬🎬 *2002 (PG-13)* We know that Bullock and Grant are master charmers and they've both done romantic comedies, so perhaps our slight disappointment in this routine pairing can be understood. Irresponsible New York playboy and real estate developer George Wade (Grant) has a history of hiring female attorneys based on looks and not professional ability. Environmental activist Lucy Kelson (Bullock) is somehow roped in as George's latest lawyer/babysitter but she eventually has enough and hands in her, well, the title says it all. Of course, the ditzy duo need to figure out that they're made for each other. **100m/C VHS, DVD.** *US* Sandra Bullock, Hugh Grant, Alicia Witt, Dana Ivey, Robert Klein, Heather Burns, David Haig, Dorian Missick; **D:** Marc Lawrence; **W:** Marc Lawrence; **C:** Laszlo Kovacs; **M:** John Powell.

Two Weeks to Live 🎬½ *1943* The comedy team inherits a railroad line, only to find it's a pile of junk. **60m/B VHS, DVD.** Franklin Pangborn, Kay Linaker, Irving Bacon, Chester Lauck, Norris Goff; **D:** Malcolm St. Clair; **W:** Roswell Rogers, Michael L. Simmons; **C:** Jack MacKenzie; **D:** Marc Lawrence.

Two Weeks with Love 🎬🎬 *1950* Reynolds and family wear funny bathing suits in the early 1900s while the Debster sings songs and blushes into young adulthood. 🎵 Aba Daba Honeymoon; The Oceana Roll; A Heart That's Free; By the Light of the Silvery Moon; My Hero; Row, Row, Row; That's How I Need You; Beautiful Lady. **92m/C VHS.** Debbie Reynolds, Jane Powell, Ricardo Montalban, Louis Calhern, Ann Harding, Phyllis Kirk, Carleton Carpenter, Clinton Sundberg, Gary Gray; **D:** Roy Rowland.

The Two Worlds of Jenny Logan 🎬🎬½ *1979* A woman travels back and forth in time whenever she dons a 19th century dress she finds in her old house. She is also able to fall in love twice, in different centuries. Adapted from "Second Sight," a novel by David Williams. Stylish and well made. **97m/C VHS.** Lindsay Wagner, Marc Singer, Alan Feinstein, Linda Gray, Constance McCashin, Henry Wilcoxon, Irene Tedrow, Joan Darling, Allen Williams, Pat Corley, Gloria Stuart; **D:** Frank De Felitta. **TV**

Two Wrongs Make a Right 🎬 *1989* A quiet nightclub owner beats and clubs his way through his tough neighborhood to protect himself and his woman. Low budget actioner with standard plot and cool, atmospheric tone. **85m/C VHS.** Ivan Rogers, Ron Blackstone, Rich Komenich; **D:** Robert Brown; **W:** Ivan Rogers.

Two Years before the Mast 🎬🎬 *1946* Charles Stewart (Ladd) is the privileged son of a ship owner who discovers just how difficult a sailor's life in the 1840s can be. Drinking in a Boston waterfront dive, he's shanghaied and pressed into service aboard the S.S. Pilgrim, which is bound for California. Sadistic Captain Thompson (da Silva) brutalizes the men in an effort to set a record time for the voyage. Stewart and the crew eventually mutiny and face trial back in Boston. Based on the novel by Richard Henry Dana. **98m/B VHS.** Alan Ladd, Howard da Silva, Brian Donlevy, William Bendix, Barry Fitzgerald, Albert Dekker, Darryl Hickman, Esther Fernandez; **D:** John Farrow; **W:** George Bruce, Seton I. Miller; **C:** Ernest Laszlo; **M:** Victor Young.

2B Perfectly Honest 🎬½ *2B Perfectly Honest 2004* Frank and Josh try to strike it rich on the Internet but their agency sinks, making Frank ditch his posh Manhattan digs and—gulp—move back in with ma and pa. Another shot at success appears doomed when they find out their new investors are up to no good. **88m/C VHS, DVD.** Adam Trese, Andrew McCarthy, John Turturro, Hayley Mills, Mark Margolis, Robert Vaughn, Hayley Mills, Mark Margolis, Kathleen Chalfant, Bruce MacVittie; **D:** Randel Cole; **W:** Randel Cole; **D:** Christopher La Vasseur; **M:** Jason Frederick. **VIDEO**

Twogether 🎬🎬½ *1994 (R)* Struggling artist Jake (Cassavetes) and environmentalist Allison (Bakke) have this lust thing going on. It leads to a drunken Las Vegas wedding and a quickie divorce but they still don't keep their hands off of each other (or any other body parts) and Allison gets pregnant. They decide to become partners in raising the baby but first they'll have to do some growing up of their own. Also available unrated. **108m/C VHS.** Brenda Bakke, Nick Cassavetes, Jeremy Piven, Jim Beaver; **D:** Andrew Chiaramonte; **W:** Andrew Chiaramonte; **C:** Eugene Shuglejt; **M:** Nigel Holton.

Tycoon 🎬🎬 *1947* Wayne goes to Latin America to build a road for an American industrialist. When the industrialist insists on a shorter but more dangerous route, Wayne must satisfy his own sense of honor. Meanwhile, he's found romance with the industrialist's half-Spanish daughter. Long, but well-acted. **129m/C VHS.** John Wayne, Laraine Day, Cedric Hardwicke, Judith Anderson, James Gleason, Anthony Quinn, Jan Sterling, Grant Withers, Paul Fix, Charles Trowbridge; **D:** Richard Wallace; **W:** Borden Chase, John Twist; **C:** William Howard Greene, Harry Wild; **M:** Leigh Harline.

Tycus 🎬🎬 *1998 (R)* Journalist Jake Lowe (Onorati) investigates a suspicious mining company and discovers that visionary Peter Crawford (Hopper) has been building his own vast underground city as a modern-day Noah's Ark. Seems the Tycus comet is on a destructo course with Earth and not much is expected to survive. And when the rest of the world finds out, it'll be a race against time. **94m/C VHS, DVD.** Dennis Hopper, Peter Onorati, Finola Hughes, Chick Vennera; **D:** John Putch; **W:** Kevin Goetz; **C:** Ross Berryman; **M:** Alexander Baker, Clair Marlo. **VIDEO**

Tyler Perry's Meet the Browns 🎬½ *Meet the Browns 2008 (PG-13)* Single mother Brenda (Bassett) learns that her father, a man she's never met, has died, so she packs up the family and heads to Georgia for the funeral. There, she and her three children are greeted with varying degrees of Southern hospitality by a batch of half-siblings she never knew existed. Brenda then meets Harry (Fox, in a role not far from home), a handsome retired basketball player who sweeps Brenda off her feet (surprise, surprise). Typical Perry fare, loaded with racial commentary, monologues on family values, and conversations about econom-

ic struggle. **101m/C DVD.** *US* Angela Bassett, Rick Fox, Margaret Avery, Frankie Faison, Jenifer Lewis, Sofia Vergara, Lamman Rucker, Irma P. Hall, Tyler Perry, Lance Gross, David Mann, Tamela Mann, Judy Rhee; **D:** Tyler Perry; **W:** Tyler Perry; **C:** Sandi Sissel; **M:** Aaron Zigman.

Tyler Perry's Why Did I Get Married? 🎬🎬 *Why Did I Get Married? 2007 (PG-13)* Four couples—all friends who met as undergrads at a historically black college—navigate the rollercoaster of marriage as they gather for their annual couples retreat. Each is successful (there's a psychologist, lawyer, and pediatrician), but each relationship hides secrets and they begin to unfold over the retreat. One couple argues over having a second child; someone's sleeping with his wife's best friend; another couple fights about everything. Perry, with God's help (a theme throughout most of his work), wraps things up a bit too neatly by the end of the retreat. Despite the drama, though, the characters are both smart and refreshing. **113m/C DVD.** *US* Tyler Perry, Janet Jackson, Jill Scott, Malik Yoba, Richard T. Jones, Michael Jai White, Lamman Rucker, Sharon Leal, Tasha Smith, Denise Boutte; **D:** Tyler Perry; **W:** Tyler Perry; **C:** Toyomichi Kurita; **M:** Aaron Zigman.

Typhoon 🎬🎬 *Taepung 2006 (R)* Melodramatic action flick, filmed in Korea, Russia, and Thailand, follows North Korean exile Myong-jin (Jang), who's plotting to unleash chemical weapons during a typhoon on both South and North Korea. His family was betrayed and murdered while trying to escape the oppressive regime and he wants payback. Kang (Lee) is the military officer who must stop him. Korean with subtitles. **103m/C DVD.** *KN* Dong-kun Jang, Lee Mi-yeon, Lee Jung-jae; **D:** Kwak Kyung-taek; **W:** Kwak Kyung-taek; **C:** Hong Kyeng-pyo.

Typhoon Treasure 🎬 *1939* Whilst recovering his sunken treasure, the hero battles bad guys, savage natives and a crocodile, all of whom could probably have made a more sophisticated film. **68m/B VHS.** *AU* Campbell Copelin, Gwen Munro, Joe Valli, Douglas Herald; **D:** Noel Monkman.

Tyson 🎬🎬 *1995* Based on the life of former World Heavyweight Champion, Mike Tyson (White) who rose from the streets of Brownsville to a million dollar lifestyle and a spectacular fall to a rape conviction and a prison term (which are handled in voiceover). Story begins with trainer Cus D'Amato (Scott) finding unpolished and troubled young Tyson and training him for the Junior Olympics. When promoter Don King (Winfield) enters the picture, Tyson's career really takes off. Pulls no punches about Tyson's short fuse and brutal abilities. Based on the book "Fire and Fear: The Inside Story of Mike Tyson" by Jose Torres. **90m/C VHS.** Michael Jai White, Paul Winfield, George C. Scott, Malcolm Jamal Warner, Tony LoBianco, James B. Sikking, Clark Gregg, Kristen Wilson, Sheila Wills, Holt McCallany, Lilyan Chauvin, Georg Stanford Brown, Joe Santos, Charles Napier; **D:** Uli Edel; **W:** Robert P. Johnson; **M:** Stewart Copeland.

U-Boat Prisoner 🎬 *1944* Bennett is an American sailor who's captured by a Nazi U-boat. He promptly defeats the crew, leaving the U-boat to the mercy of a U.S. destroyer. Silly, silly, silly. **65m/B VHS.** Bruce Bennett, John Abbott, John Wengraf, Kenneth MacDonald, Erik Rolf; **D:** Lew Landers.

U-571 🎬🎬½ *2000 (PG-13)* U.S. sub crew is sent to steal an Enigma encryption device from a disabled Nazi U-boat before the Germans can send help. When their own sub is sunk, the Americans, led by Lt. Tyler (McConaughey), take over the German sub and try to make their way back home through enemy destroyers. Long on loud and impressive action sequences, but short on characterization and good dialogue, this one'll work best for adrenaline junkies and those who like theatre-quality entertainment systems. **116m/C VHS, DVD, HD DVD.** Matthew McConaughey, Bill Paxton, Harvey Keitel, Jon Bon Jovi, Jake Weber, David Keith, Terrence "T.C." Carson, Jack Noseworthy, Tom Guiry, Thomas Kretschmann, Erik Palladino, Will Estes, Matthew Settle, Dave Power, Derk Cheetwood; **D:** Jonathan Mostow; **W:** Jonathan Mostow, David Ayer, Sam Montgomery; **C:** Oliver Wood; **M:**

Richard (Rick) Marvin. Oscars '00: Sound FX Editing.

U-Turn 🎬🎬½ *Stray Dogs 1997 (R)* Bobby (Penn) is a two-bit gambler on his way to pay off the balance of a debt in Las Vegas (the down payment was two of his fingers) when he is stranded in the town of Superior, Arizona. He becomes mixed up with a married couple (Nolte and Lopez), each of whom want Bobby to kill the other. Adding to the fun in this Mayberry on mescaline are the walking grease pit of a mechanic (Thornton) and a local tough guy named TNT (Phoenix), who thinks Bobby is making a play for his nymphet girlfriend (Danes). Also appearing is the stock issue Oliver Stone wise old Indian who dispenses wisdom, or something like it. The characters meet for the predestined showdown in the desert, with predictable results. Stone has a good time taking steretypical noir characters and putting his unique twist on them, although you may not have as much fun watching them. **125m/C VHS, DVD.** Sean Penn, Jennifer Lopez, Claire Danes, Nick Nolte, Joaquin Rafael (Leaf) Phoenix, Powers Boothe, Billy Bob Thornton, Jon Voight, Abraham Benrubi, Julie Hagerty, Bo Hopkins, Valery (Valeri Nikolayev) Nikolaev, Aida Linares, Laurie Metcalf, Liv Tyler; **D:** Oliver Stone; **W:** John Ridley; **C:** Robert Richardson; **M:** Ennio Morricone.

UFO: Target Earth 🎬 *1974 (G)* Scientist attempts to fish flying saucer out of lake and costs studio $70,000. **80m/C VHS.** Nick Plakias, Cynthia Cline, Phil Erickson; **D:** Michael de Gaetano.

Uforia 🎬🎬 *1981* Two rival evangelists meet up with a UFO-infatuated girl. Under her guidance, they wait for UFO encounters they intend to use to milk their revivalist audiences. Sometimes clumsy, but more often fun. **92m/C VHS.** Cindy Williams, Harry Dean Stanton, Fred Ward, Hank Worden, Beverly Hope Atkinson, Harry Carey Jr., Diane Adair, Robert Gray, Ted Harris; **D:** John Binder; **W:** John Binder; **C:** David Myers; **M:** Richard Baskin.

Ugetsu 🎬🎬½ *Ugetsu Monogatari 1953* The classic film that established Mizoguchi's reputation outside of Japan. Two 16th century Japanese peasants venture from their homes in pursuit of dreams, and encounter little more than their own hapless folly and a bit of the supernatural. A wonderful mix of comedy and action with nifty camera movement. Based on the stories of Akinara Ueda. In Japanese with English subtitles. **96m/B VHS, DVD.** *JP* Machiko Kyo, Masayuki Mori, Kinuyo Tanaka, Eitaro (Sakae, Saka Ozawa) Ozawa; **D:** Kenji Mizoguchi; **W:** Yoshikata Yoda; **C:** Kazuo Miyagawa; **M:** Fumio Hayasaka. Venice Film Fest. '53: Silver Prize.

The Ugly 🎬🎬½ *1996* Confessed serial killer Simon (Rotondo) has celebrity shrink Karen (Hobbs) evaluate him to determine whether he's cured or has to stand trial for his crimes. Through flashbacks, dream sequences, and fantasies (both Simon's and the doc's), Simon's screwed-up past is revealed: mentally and physically abused by an unstable mother (Ward-Leeland) and picked on by bullies, he commits his first murder at 13. First-time director Reynolds' use of red herrings, alternate points of view, and mixing of perspectives can be hard to follow, but they do ratchet up the suspense. He also doesn't scrimp on the gore, which is highly stylized and effective. **93m/C VHS, DVD.** *NZ* Paolo Rotondo, Rebecca Hobbs, Jennifer Ward-Lealand, Roy Ward, Vanessa Byrnes; **D:** Scott Reynolds; **W:** Scott Reynolds; **C:** Simon Raby; **M:** Victoria Kelly.

The Ugly American 🎬🎬½ *1963* A naive American ambassador to a small, civil-war-torn Asian country fights a miniature Cold War against northern communist influence. Too preachy, and the "Red Menace" aspects are now very dated, but Brando's performance is worth watching. Based on the William J. Lederer novel. **120m/C VHS, DVD.** Marlon Brando, Sandra Church, Eiji Okada, Pat Hingle, Arthur Hill; **D:** George Englund; **W:** Stewart Stern.

The Ugly Dachshund ✗✗ 1965 Jones and Pleshette are married dog lovers who raise Dachshunds. When Ruggles convinces them to take a Great Dane puppy, the fun begins! The Great Dane thinks he is a Dachshund because he has been raised with such a large dog acts as if he is small! Kids will love this wacky Disney film. 93m/C VHS, DVD. Dean Jones, Suzanne Pleshette, Charlie Ruggles, Kelly Thordsen, Parley Baer, Mako; D: Norman Tokar; W: Albert Aley; C: Edward Colman; M: George Bruns.

The Ultimate Gift ✗✗1/2 2007 (PG) Sentimental sometimes preachy drama based on Jim Stovall's novel. Trust-fund twentysomething Jason (Ste-vens (Fuller) expects nothing from his estranged grandfather Red's (Garner) will. But Red, via videotaped messages, leaves Jason a fortune—with stipulations that are intended to teach him to be a better person, including bonding with young cancer patient Emily (Breslin). Pic veers off track when Jason goes to Ecuador and gets kidnapped by bandits but manages to get itself. And it's a pleasure to see old pros like Garner, Dennehy, and Cobb at work. 114m/C VHS, DVD. US Drew Fuller, James Garner, Ali Hillis, Abigail Breslin, Lee Meriwether, Bill Cobbs; D: Michael O. Sajbel; W: Cheryl McKay; C: Brian Baugh; M: Mark McKenzie, Anthony Short.

The Ultimate Imposter ✗ 1979 A secret agent acquires voluminous knowledge through a computer brain link-up, but can only retain the knowledge for 72 hours. In that timespan he has to rescue a detecting Russian from hordes of assassins. 97m/C VHS, Keith Andes, Erin Gray, Joseph Hacker, Macon McCalman; D: Paul Stanley. TV

The Ultimate Thrill ✗ 1974 84m/C VHS, Britt Ekland, Barry Brown, Michael Blodgett, John Davis Chandler, Eric (Hans Gudegast) Braeden; D: Robert Butler.

The Ultimate Warrior ✗✗1/2 1975 (R) Yul Brynner must defend the plants and seeds of a pioneer scientist to help replenish the world's food supply in this thriller set in 2012. 92m/C VHS, Yul Brynner, Max von Sydow, Joanna Miles, Richard Kelton, Lane Bradbury, William (Bill) Smith; D: Robert Clouse; W: Robert Clouse.

The Ultimate Weapon ✗✗ 1997 (R) Mercenary Hogan destroys an IRA base camp when he realizes he's been doublecrossed. 110m/C VHS, DVD. Hulk Hogan, Carl Marotte, Cynthia (Cyndy, Cindy) Pre-ston; C: Bert Tougas; M: Marty Simon. VIDEO

Ulee's Gold ✗✗✗ 1997 (R) Slow-paced, deliberate character study, set in the Florida panhandle. Ulysses "Ulee" Jackson (Fonda) is a widowed, middle-aged Vietnam vet who puts most of his energies into his work as a beekeeper, much to the detriment of his family. Son Jimmy (Wood) is in prison and druggie daughter-in-law Helen (Dunford) has disappeared, leaving the taciturn Ulee to care for his troubled granddaughters, teenaged Casey (Biel) and nine-year-old Penny (Zima). But their ordinary lives change when Helen turns up in Orlando with two violent hoods from Jimmy's past and Ulee must not only rescue her but find the emotional release to make them all a home. Splendidly moving performance from Fonda. 111m/C VHS, DVD. Peter Fonda, Tom Wood, Jessica Biel, Christine Dunford, Patricia Richardson, Vanessa Zima, Jessica Eie, J. Kenneth Campbell; D: Victor Nunez; W: Victor Nunez; C: Virgil Marcus Mirano; M: Charles Engstrom, Golden Globe '98; Actor—Drama (Fonda); N.Y. Film Critics '97; Actor (Fonda).

Ulterior Motives ✗1/2 1992 (R) P.I. Jack Blaylock agrees to protect a pretty reporter from Japanese gangsters. He finds himself caught up in deception and betrayal and uses all his considerable, and violent, skills to make certain he does his job. 90m/C VHS, Thomas Ian Griffin, Mary Page Keller, Joe Yamanaka, Ellen Crawford, Ken Howard, Tyra Ferrel; D: James Becket.

Ultimate Desires ✗✗ 1991 (R) When a high class hooker is brutally killed, beautiful Scoggins puts on what there is of the victim's clothes in order to solve the mystery. But trouble lies in wait as she actually begins to enjoy her funky new double life. Can she solve the crime before becoming lost in her own hot fantasy world? 93m/C VHS, Tracy Scoggins, Brion James, Marc Singe; Marc Baur, Marc Bennett, Suzy Joachim, Jason Scott, John Wood; D: Lloyd A. Simandl.

UKM: The Ultimate Killing Machine ✗ 2006 Action trash. After turning war hero Dodds (Northwood) into an uncontrollable killing machine, the army decides to experiment on a group of misfits instead, in an effort to turn them into super-soldiers. The side-effects are uncontrollable rage and uncontrollable lust and since this is a co-ed group, the latter wouldn't appear to be a problem. But the human guinea pigs escape, as does the raging Dodds, and the hunt is on! 90m/C DVD. CA Michael Madsen, John Evans, Simon Northwood, Erin Mackennon, Deanna Dezmari; D: David Mitchell; W: Tyler Levine, Tim McGregor; C: Marcus Elliott; M: Craig McConnell. VIDEO

UHF ✗✗ 1989 (PG-13) A loser is appointed manager of a bargain-basement UHF television station. He turns it around via bizarre programming ideas. Some fun spoofs of TV enhance this minimal story. Developed solely as a vehicle for Yankovic. 97m/C VHS, DVD. Weird Al Yankovic; C: David Lewis; M: John Du Prez.

Ultra Warrior ✗1/2 Welcome to Oblivion 1992 (R) A basic post-apocalyptic adventure tale of a radioactive earth, mutants, and various battles by the good guys to save the planet. 80m/C VHS, Dack Rambo, Meshach Taylor, Clare Beresford; D: Kevin Tent, Augusto Tamayo San Roman; W: Len Jenkin, Dan Kleinman; C: Cusi Barrio; M: Kevin Klingler.

Ultrachrist! ✗✗ 2003 It's the 21st century and Jesus is back in town—New York City, to be exact—but soon realizes that the old ways of getting his word out aren't cutting. So he dons a skin-tight superhero suit and assumes the alias Ultrachrist. But Dad isn't thrilled with this new-fangled approach and Christ must prove himself, while battling his archenemy the Antichrist. Further proof that crude and blasphemy is another's fun. 92m/C VHS, DVD. Jonathan C. Green, Celia A. Montgomery, Dara Shindler, Jordan Hoffman, Danielle Langlois, Samantha Dark, Nathaniel Graves, Bob Cohen, Jurgen Fauth, Marty Grillo, Rob Haussman, Ryan V. McCallum, Steve Montague, Leila Nelson, Mark Morales, Stephen Meadows, Patricia Healy; D: Douglas Dye, Jordan Hoffman; C: Kerry Howard Leshaw. VIDEO

Ultraviolet ✗1/2 1991 (R) Another warning against playing the good samaritan. Young couple on vacation in Death Valley try to help a stranded stranger only to have him turn on them. 80m/C VHS, Esai Morales, Stephen Meadows, Patricia Healy; M: Mark Griffiths.

Ultraviolet ✗✗1/2 1998 (R) Vampires walk among us. Humans are their food source and now they are threatened by humanity's ability to destroy itself and the ultraviolet light that vamps want to take control. The CIB, a secret government operation, is determined to prevent that situation. Atmospheric British miniseries in which the term "vampire" is never used—the bloodsuckers are referred to as Code Fives and the title refers to the ultraviolet light that the CIB uses in its work. 360m/C VHS, DVD. GB Jack Davenport, Susannah Harker, Philip Quast, Idris Elba, Corin Redgrave Stephen Moyer, Thomas Lockyer, Colette Brown, Fiona Dolman; D: Joe Ahearne; W: Joe Ahearne; C: Peter Greenhalgh.

Ultraviolet ✗ 2006 (PG-13) After being given a virus by the military to create a group of superhumans, sexy vamp Violet (Jovovich) must kick some major butt to save their lives when the powers-that-be decide to terminate them. Their ultimate survival rests within a boy named Six (Bright), whom Violet must protect. Set in a "Matrix"-like future world—a world where no shirt exists that Violet seems proud to crudely rip off a mishmash of other such action flicks as "Tomb Raider" and "Kill Bill," not to mention "Resident Evil." 89m/C DVD, Blu-ray Disc, UMD. US Milla Jovovich, Cameron Bright, Nicholas Chinlund, William Fichtner, Sebastien Andrieu; D: Kurt Wimmer; W: Kurt Wimmer; C: Arthur Wong Ngok Ta; M: Klaus Badelt.

Ulysses ✗✗1/2 Ulisse 1955 An Italian made version of the epic poem by Homer as the warrior returns to his homeland and the ever-faithful Penelope after the Trojan war. Ambitious effort provides for the ultimate mixed review. Douglas is good in the role and his stops along the ten-year way are well visualized. Sometimes sluggish with poor dubbing. Seven writers helped bring Homer to the big screen. 104m/C VHS, Kirk Douglas, Silvana Mangano, Anthony Quinn Rossana Podesta; D: Mario Camerini.

Ulysses ✗✗1/2 1967 James Joyce's probably unfilmable novel was given a noble effort in this flawed film covering a day in the life of Leopold Bloom as he wanders through Dublin. Shot in Ireland with a primarily Irish cast. 140m/B VHS, DVD. Milo O'Shea, Maurice Roeves, T.P. McKenna, Martin Dempsey, Sheila O'Sullivan, Barbara Jefford; D: Joseph Strick; W: Joseph Strick, Fred Haines; C: Wolfgang Suschitzky; M: Stanley Myers.

Ulysses' Gaze ✗✗ To Vlemma Tou Odyssea; The Gaze of Ulysses 1995 Nameless Greek-American filmmaker (Keitel) journeys across the Balkans from Athens to Sarajevo while making a documentary on pioneer filmmakers, the Manakia brothers, who ignored national and ethnic strife in order to record the lives of ordinary people. Keitel has heard that some undeveloped film shot by the brothers has turned up in Sarajevo and he's determined to see it despite the turmoil in Bosnia. Moving and pessimistic depiction of the Balkan conflict seen through a filmmaker's eyes. English with subtitles. 173m/C VHS, DVD. GR FR IT Harvey Keitel, Maia Morgenstern, Erland Josephson, Thanassis Vengos, Yorgos Michalakopoulos, Dora Volonaki; D: Theo Angelopoulos; W: Theo Angelopoulos, Tonino Guerra, Petros Markaris; C: Yorgos Arvanitis; M: Eleni Karaindrou. Cannes '95; Grand Jury Prize.

Uizana's Raid ✗✗✗ 1972 (R) An aging scout and an idealistic Cavalry lieutenant lock horns on their way to battling a vicious Apache chieftain. A violent, gritty western that defied critical re-evaluation years after its first release. 103m/C VHS, DVD. Burt Lancaster, Bruce Davison, Richard Jaeckel, Lloyd Bochner, Jorge Luke; D: Robert Aldrich; W: Alan Sharp; C: Joseph Biroc; M: Frank DeVol.

Umberto D ✗✗✗ 1955 A government pensioner, living alone with his beloved dog, struggles to keep up a semblance of dignity on his inadequate pension. De Sica considered this his masterpiece. A sincere, tender treatment of the struggles involved with the inevitability of aging. In Italian with English subtitles. Laser edition features letterboxed print. 89m/B VHS, DVD. IT Carlo Battista Maria Pia Casilio, Lina Gennari; D: Vittorio De Sica; W: Cesare Zavattini, Vittorio De Sica; M: Alessandro Cicognini. N.Y. Film Critics '55; Foreign Film.

Umbrellas of Cherbourg ✗✗✗1/2 Les Parapluies de Cherbourg; Die Regenschirme von Cherbourg 1964 A bittersweet film operetta with no spoken dialog. Genevieve (Deneuve) is the teenaged daughter of a widow (Vernon) who owns an umbrella shop. She and her equally young boyfriend Guy (Castelnuovo) are separated by his military duty in Algeria. Finding she is pregnant, Genevieve marries the wealthy Roland (Michel), and when her former lover returns he too marries someone else. But when they meet once again will their love be rekindled? Lovely photography and an evocative score enhance the story. French with subtitles; also available dubbed in English (not with the same effectiveness). 90m/C VHS, DVD. FR Catherine Deneuve, Nino Castelnuovo, Anne Vernon, Ellen Farner, Marc Michel, Mireille Perrey, Jean Champion, Alfred Wolf, Dorothee Blanck; D: Jacques Demy; W: Jacques Demy; C: Jean Rabier; M: Michel Legrand. Cannes '64; Film.

Un Air de Famille ✗✗ Respectable Families; Family Resemblances 1996 Comedy, adapted from a play, about a dysfunctional family. They're meeting at the family's rundown bar to celebrate the birthday of son Philippe's (Yordanoff) silly wife, Yolande (Frot). The bar is run by his brother Henri (Bacri), whose wife calls to say she's left him, while their tactless mother (Maurier) frets over their sister, Betty (Jaoui), who's 30 and still single. What no one knows is that Betty has been secretly seeing Denis (Darroussin), the bartender, whom everyone thinks is simple but is actually the only one with any clue to the family's hypocrisy. French with subtitles. 107m/C VHS, DVD. FR Jean-Pierre Bacri, Agnes Jaoui, Jean-Pierre Darroussin, Catherine Frot, Claire Maurier, Wladimir Yordanoff; D: Cedric Klapisch; W: Jean-Pierre Bacri, Agnes Jaoui, Jean-Pierre Bacri; C: Benoit Delhomme, Cesar '97; Support. Actor (Darroussin), Support. Actress (Frot), Writing.

Un Chien Andalou ✗✗✗ An Andalusian Dog 1928 Masterful surrealist short features a host of classic sequences, including a razor across an eye, a severed hand lying in a man's hand, priests dragged across a room. A classic. Score features both Wagner and tango. 20m/B VHS, DVD. FR Pierre Batcheff, Simone Mareuil, Jaime Miravilles, Luis Bunuel, Salvador Dali; D: Luis Bunuel, Salvador Dali; W: Luis Bunuel, Salvador Dali.

Un Coeur en Hiver ✗✗✗1/2 A Heart in Winter 1993 An anti-romance romantic drama where passion is frozen and real emotion is reserved for the inanimate. Stephane (Auteuil) is a master craftsman at repairing violins; his partner Maxime (Dussollier) runs the business side and deals with the musicians, including beautiful violinist Camille (Beart) with whom he has fallen in love. Camille is single-mindedly fixated on her career and she recognizes a kindred spirit in Stephane but their calculated emotional seduction causes problems for all. Can be frustrating since the smooth surface of the characters is rarely cracked. In French with English titles. 100m/C VHS, DVD FR Emmanuelle Beart, Daniel Auteuil, Andre Dussollier, Elisabeth Bourgine, Brigitte Cattillon, Maurice Garrel, Miriam Boyer; D: Claude Sautet; W: Jacques Fieschi, Jerome Tonnerre; C: Yves Angelo; M: Cesar '93; Director (Sautet), Support. Actor (Dussollier).

Un Singe en Hiver ✗✗1/2 A Monkey in Winter; It's Hot in Hell 1962 A young warderier (Belmondo) befriends a crusty old alcoholic (Gabin) who has kept his vow to abstain since his village survived the German bombing of WWII. Moving tale of regret and the passage of time. In French with English subtitles. 105m/B VHS. Jean-Paul Belmondo, Jean Gabin, Suzanne Flon, Paul Frankeur; D: Henri Verneuil.

Unaccompanied Minors ✗✗1/2 2006 (PG) Mildly goofy holiday comedy meant for the pre-adolescent crowd finds a disparate group of kids left by various adults at a midwestern airport to begin their solo travels on Christmas Eve. Only there's a blizzard and all flights are cancelled, leaving the little darlings to plot their escape from the control of airport stooge Mr. Porter (Black) and more sympathetic staffer Zach (Valderrama). May-hem ensues. 87m/C DVD. US Brett Kelly, Lewis Black, Wilmer Valderrama, Paget Brewster, Tyler James Williams, Dyllan Christopher, Gina Mantegna, Quinn Shephard, Dominique Saldana, Jessica Water, David Koechner, Rob Corddry, Teri Garr, Michelle Sandler; D: Paul Feig; W: Jacob Meszaros, Mya Stark; C: Christopher Baffa; M: Michael Andrews.

The Unapproachable 🦴🦴½ 1982 A rendition of the Polish director's two one-act plays concerning a reclusive aging stage star being manipulated by her hangers-on. 92m/C VHS. *PL* Leslie Caron, Danny (Daniel) Webb, Leslie Malton; *D:* Krzysztof Zanussi.

The Unbearable Lightness of Being 🦴🦴🦴½ 1988 (R) Tomas (Day Lewis), a young Czech doctor in the late 1960s, leads a sexually and emotionally carefree existence with a number of women, including provocative artist Olin. When he meets the fragile Binoche, he may be falling in love for the first time. On the eve of the 1968 Russian invasion of Czechoslovakia the two flee to Switzerland, but Binoche can't reconcile herself to exile and returns, followed by the reluctant Tomas who has lost his position because of his new-found political idealism. They lead an increasingly simple life, drawn ever closer together. The haunting ending caps off superb performances. Based on the novel by Milan Kundera. 172m/C VHS, DVD. Daniel Day-Lewis, Juliette Binoche, Lena Olin, Derek de Lint, Erland Josephson, Pavel Landovsky, Donald Moffat, Daniel Olbrychski, Stellan Skarsgard, Tomek Bork, Bruce Myers, Pavel Slaby, Pascale Kalensky, Jacques Ciron, Anne Lonnberg, Laszlo Szabo, Vladimir Valenta, Clovis Cornillac, Leon Lissek, Consuelo de Havilland; *D:* Philip Kaufman; *W:* Jean-Claude Carriere, Philip Kaufman; *C:* Sven Nykvist; *M:* Mark Adler, Ernie Fosselius, Leos Janacek. British Acad. '88: Adapt. Screenplay; Ind. Spirit '89: Cinematog.; Natl. Soc. Film Critics '88: Director (Kaufman), Film.

The Unbelievable Truth 🦴🦴½ 1990 (R) Ex-con Robocop-to-be Burke meets armageddon-obsessed model and sparks fly until bizarre murder occurs. Quirky black comedy shot in less than two weeks. 100m/C VHS, DVD. Adrienne Shelly, Robert John Burke, Christopher Cooke, Julia Mueller, Julia McNeal, Mark Bailey, Gary Sauer, Katharine Mayfield; *D:* Hal Hartley; *W:* Hal Hartley; *C:* Michael Spiller; *M:* Jim Coleman.

The Unborn 🦴½ 1991 (R) An infertile wife gets inseminated at unorthodox clinic. But once pregnant she suspects that her unborn baby is a monstrous being. Tasteless B-movie with A-performance from Adams; if the rest had been up to her standard this could have been another "Stepford Wives." Instead it cops out with cheap gore. 85m/C VHS, DVD. Brooke Adams, Jeff Hayenga, James Karen, K. Callan, Jane Cameron; *D:* Rodman Flender; *W:* John Brancato; *C:* Wally Pfister; *M:* Gary Numan, Michael R. Smith.

The Unborn 2 🦴 1994 (R) Greene's blood-craving baby thinks nothing of feasting on the babysitter until a gun-wielding avenger comes to the rescue. Some notably gross scenes. 84m/C VHS, DVD. Michele Greene, Scott Valentine, Robin Curtis; *D:* Rick Jacobson.

Unbreakable 🦴🦴½ 2000 (PG-13) Willis reteams with "The Sixth Sense" writer/director Shyamalan for another spooky saga. He's not only the sole survivor of a train crash but he emerged without a scratch, which intrigues Jackson, who suffers from brittle bone disease. Shyamalan still knows how to hold attention, and the look and feel of the movie are mesmerizing, but this time the story doesn't quite hold up. You'll either find this one a keeper or a head-scratcher. 107m/C VHS, DVD. Bruce Willis, Samuel L. Jackson, Robin Wright Penn, Spencer (Treat) Clark, Charlaine Woodard, James Handy, Elizabeth Lawrence, Leslie Stefanson, Eamonn Walker; *D:* M. Night Shyamalan; *W:* M. Night Shyamalan; *C:* Eduardo Serra; *M:* James Newton Howard.

Uncaged 🦴 Angel in Red 1991 (R) Five beautiful young prostitutes hit Sunset Strip, each of them dreaming of a better life. When a crazy pimp brutally murders one of their friends, they set out to avenge that girl, and her broken dreams. 78m/C VHS. Leslie Bega, Jeffrey Dean Morgan, Pamella D'Pella, Gregory Millar, Henry Brown, Jason Oliver, Elena Sahagun; *D:* William Duprey; *W:* Robert Alden, Joan Freeman, Catherine Cyran.

The Uncanny WOOF! 1978 Horror anthology of three tales concerned with feline attempts to control the world. Waste of good cast and cats on silly stories. Not released in the U.S. 85m/C VHS. *GB* Peter Cushing, Ray Milland, Samantha Eggar, Donald Pleasence; *D:* Denis Heroux.

Uncertain Glory 🦴🦴 1944 Errol plays a French thief who's willing to pretend to be a saboteur and die for his country. Based on a story by Joe May and Laszlo Vadnay. 102m/B VHS. Errol Flynn, Paul Lukas, Jean Sullivan, Lucile Watson, Faye Emerson, James Flavin, Douglass Dumbrille, Dennis Hoey, Sheldon Leonard; *D:* Raoul Walsh; *W:* Laszlo Vadnay, Max Brand.

The Unchastened Woman 🦴🦴 1925 A married couple is torn apart by infidelity despite their impending parenthood, and wife Bara heads overseas to run wild and have the baby. She returns with a foreign flame, whom she dumps when erstwhile husband finds fatherly feelings in his heart. One of Bara's last films. 52m/B VHS. Theda Bara, Wyndham Standing, Dale Fuller, John Miljan; *D:* James L. Young.

Uncivilized 🦴🦴 Endangered 1994 Young couple, on a vacation in the mountains, run into a gang of drug runners who don't want their whereabouts revealed. So, the duo have to play a deadly game of hide-and-seek to survive. 90m/C VHS. Sandra Hess, Dale Dye, Renee Estevez, Richard Hench, Martin Kove, Rick Aiello; *D:* Nick Kellis; *W:* Nick Kellis; *C:* Arnold Peterson; *M:* Peter Waldman.

Uncle Buck 🦴🦴🦴 1989 (PG) When Mom and Dad have to go away suddenly, the only babysitter they can find is good ol' Uncle Buck, a lovable lout who spends much of his time smoking cigars, trying to make up with his girlfriend, and enforcing the teenage daughter's chastity. More intelligent than the average slob/teen comedy with a heart, due in large part to Candy's dandy performance. Memorable pancake scene. 100m/C VHS, DVD. John Candy, Amy Madigan, Jean (Louisa) Kelly, Macaulay Culkin, Jay Underwood, Gaby Hoffman, Laurie Metcalf, Elaine Bromka, Garrett M. Brown; *D:* John Hughes; *W:* John Hughes; *C:* Ralf Bode; *M:* Ira Newborn.

Uncle Moses 🦴🦴½ 1932 The clash of old-world values and new-world culture in a story of East European Jewish immigrants transplanted to turn of the century New York's Lower East Side. Patriarch Uncle Moses struggles to keep traditional family values as romantic difficulties and labor union struggles intrude. Based on the novel by Sholem Asch. In Yiddish with English subtitles. 87m/B VHS. Maurice Schwartz, Rubin Goldberg, Judith Abarbanel, Zvee Scooler; *D:* Sidney Goldin, Aubrey Scotto.

Uncle Nino 🦴🦴½ 2003 (PG) Financially comfortable, but mildly dysfunctional, family headed by clueless dad (Mantegna) gets an unexpected visit from their colorful Italian uncle (Mascarino). He injects a little chaos into their lives, helping them to relax and smell the roses. Saccharin sweet family movie destined to please the masses. 104m/C *US* Joe Mantegna, Anne Archer, Pierrino Mascarino, Trevor Morgan, Gina Mantegna; *D:* Robert Shallcross; *W:* Robert Shallcross; *C:* Hugo Cortina; *M:* Larry Pecorella.

Uncle Sam 🦴 1996 (R) The box art is cool but this is basically a video horror. Desert Storm hero Sam Harper (Fralick) returns home—in a coffin. Only he doesn't stay dead and decides to liven up his small town's Fourth of July celebration by dressing up as Uncle Sam and going on a killing spree. 91m/C VHS, DVD. David "Shark" Fralick, Timothy Bottoms, Robert Forster, Isaac Hayes, Bo Hopkins; *D:* William Lustig; *W:* Larry Cohen; *C:* James Lebovitz; *M:* Mark Governor. VIDEO

Uncle Tom's Cabin 🦴🦴½ 1914 Satisfying version of Harriet Beecher Stowe's tale from the view of a founder of the underground railroad. Lucas was the first black actor to garner a lead role. 54m/C VHS. Mary Eline, Irving Cummings, Sam Lucas; *D:* William Robert Daly.

Uncle Tom's Cabin 🦴🦴½ 1927 Universal Studios' $2 million production was one of the costliest of the silent era, with more than 2400 actors, and a shooting schedule of 19 months. It follows Harriet Beecher Stowe's abolitionist novel about a black family torn apart by slavery. This version contains heroine Eliza's (Fischer) flight across the ice floes, which was borrowed by D.W. Griffith for his film "Way Down East." 112m/B VHS, DVD. James B. Lowe, Margarita Fischer, George Siegmann, Virginia Grey; *D:* Harry A. Pollard; *W:* Harry A. Pollard, Harvey Thew; *C:* Charles Stumar, Jacob Kull; *M:* Erno Rapee.

Uncle Tom's Cabin 🦴🦴½ Onkel Toms Hutte; La Case de L'Oncle Tom; Cento Dollari D'Odio; Cica Tomina Koliba 1969 (G) Ambitious adaptation of Harriet Beecher Stowe's stirring book about the Southern slavery and the famous underground railroad devised to aid those most determined to reach freedom. The film has the habit of drifting away from the facts. Though set in Kentucky, the picture was filmed in Yugoslavia with an international cast. 120m/C VHS. *FR IT YU GE* Herbert Lom, John Kitzmiller, Otto Wilhelm Fischer, Eleanora Rossi-Drago, Mylene Demongeot, Juliette Greco; *D:* Geza von Radvanyi; *V:* Ella Fitzgerald.

Uncle Tom's Cabin 🦴🦴½ 1987 The first American sound version of this film. Excellent cast and interestingly adapted script are perfect for a message that is still socially relevant today. Based on the novel by Harriet Beecher Stowe. 110m/C VHS. Avery Brooks, Kate Burton, Bruce Dern, Paula Kelly, Phylicia Rashad, Kathryn Walker, Edward Woodward, Frank Converse, George Coe, Albert Hall; *D:* Stan Lathan. TV

Uncle Was a Vampire 🦴🦴 Tempi Duri per I Vampiri; Hard Times for Vampires 1959 An impoverished Italian count has turned his castle into a hotel. But staying there could be hazardous to a guest's health since the count was bitten by a vampire. 85m/C VHS. *IT* Christopher Lee, Kai (Kay) Fischer, Renato Rascel, Sylva Koscina, Lia Zoppelli, Susanne Loret; *D:* Steno; *W:* Edoardo Anton; *C:* Marco Scarpelli.

Uncommon Valor 🦴🦴 1983 (R) After useless appeals to the government for information on his son listed as "missing in action" in Vietnam, Colonel Rhodes takes matters into his own hands. Hackman is solid and believable as always, surrounded with good cast in generally well-paced film. 105m/C VHS, DVD. Gene Hackman, Fred Ward, Reb Brown, Randall "Tex" Cobb, Robert Stack, Patrick Swayze, Harold Sylvester, Tim Thomerson; *D:* Ted Kotcheff; *C:* Stephen Burum; *M:* James Horner.

Unconditional Love 🦴🦴 2003 (PG-13) Watch it for Bates's performance because otherwise there's not much here (or maybe there's too much going on). Chicago housewife Grace Beasley (Bates) is abruptly dumped by hubby Max (Aykroyd) who needs his space. Meanwhile, a Chicago serial killer has just offed closeted lounge singer Victor Fox (Pryce), leaving his on-the-skids lover Dirk (Everett) to battle with Victor's sister Nola (Redgrave) over his estate. Fan Grace meets Dirk at Victor's funeral, they bond, and decide to hunt for Victor's killer together. Hey, it's one way to deal with unresolved feelings. 122m/C VHS, DVD. Kathy Bates, Rupert Everett, Lynn Redgrave, Meredith Eaton, Dan Aykroyd, Jonathan Pryce, Peter Sarsgaard, Stephanie Beacham, Richard Briers, Jack Noseworthy, Daniel Mofrey; *D:* P.J. Hogan; *W:* P.J. Hogan, Jocelyn Moorhouse; *C:* Remi Adefarasin; *M:* James Newton Howard.

Unconquered 🦴🦴½ 1947 Silly epic about America finds indentured servant Abby (Goddard), meeting Virginia militia man Christopher Holden (Cooper). He nobly buys her contract and frees her but scurvy trader Martin Garth (da Silva) manages to get Abby working in his saloon. Garth also illegally sells guns to the local Seneca Indian tribe and persuades their chief, Guyasuta (Karloff), to attack the colonists. Cooper has to keep rescuing Goddard throughout the movie, as well as battling da Silva and helping the settlers fight Indians. Based on the novel "The Judas Tree" by Neil H. Swanson. 147m/C VHS, DVD. Gary Cooper, Paulette Goddard, Howard da Silva, Boris Karloff, Cecil Kellaway, Ward Bond, Katherine DeMille, Henry Wilcoxon, Sir C. Aubrey Smith, Victor Varconi, Virginia Grey, Mike Mazurki, Porter Hall; *D:* Cecil B. DeMille; *M:* Charles Bernett, Jesse Lasky Jr., Frederic M. Frank; *C:* Ray Rennahan; *M:* Victor Young.

Uncorked 🦴🦴 At Sachem Farm; Higher Love 1998 (PG) British ex-pats gather together in Simi Valley, California to essentially drive each other crazy. Ross (Sewell) is visiting his family in order to close a deal on selling some rare wines so he can get the money to support another get-rich-quick scheme. But he's thwarted by his eccentric Uncle Cullen (Hawthorne) who wants Ross to do something he passionately believes in (which happens to be music). Ross also has a reclusive, nutty brother Paul (Rodgers), and then there's his snooty girlfriend Kendal (Driver) who really wants her ex-boyfriend, Tom (Sporleder) back. It's predictable but pleasant. 95m/C VHS, DVD. Rufus Sewell, Nigel Hawthorne, Minnie Driver, Michael E. Rodgers, Gregory Sporleder, Amelia Heinle, Keone Young; *D:* John Huddles; *C:* Mark Vicente; *M:* Jeff Danna.

Uncovered 🦴🦴 La Tabla de Flandes 1994 (R) Julia (Beckinsale at the beginning of her career) is restoring a 500-year-old painting of a chess game when she discovers an inscription hidden on the painting that says "Who killed the knight?". Some investigation indicates the painter was telling the story of a series of killings that followed the pattern of play in the painting, and that pattern is being duplicated in the present day. Complex and interesting story is undermined by poor acting (Beckinsale's inexperience shows) and inconsistent direction. 112m/C VHS, DVD. GB SP Kate Beckinsale, John Wood, Sinead Cusack, Peter Wingfield, Helen McCrory, Michael Gough, Art Malik, James Villiers, Paudge Behan; *D:* Jim McBride; *W:* Jim McBride, Jack Baran, Michael Hirst; *C:* Alfonso Beato; *M:* Philippe Sarde. VIDEO

Uncovered: The War on Iraq 🦴🦴 2004 Documentary presents case against Bush administration's decision to go to war with Iraq through interviews with authorities ranging from weapons inspectors and C.I.A. analysts to ex-military and diplomatic figures. Another in a slew of anti-Bush documentaries released in election year of 2004. Driven and less theatrical than political heavyweight Michael Moore, but the straightforward style make it effective and convincing. 83m/C DVD. *D:* Robert Greenwald; *C:* Richard Perez, Glen Pearcy, Bob Sullivan, Scott Williams, Hamish Campbell, Marc Levy, Bob Seeberger; *M:* Jim Ervin, Brad Chiet, Mars Lasar.

The Undead 🦴 1957 A prostitute is accidentally sent back to the Middle Ages as the result of a scientific experiment and finds herself condemned to die for witchcraft. Early Corman script filled with convoluted storylines, laughable characters, violence, and heaving bosoms. 75m/B VHS, DVD. Paul Blaisdell, Pamela Duncan, Richard Garland, Allison Hayes, Mel Welles, Richard Devon, Billy Barty, Dick Miller, Val Dufour, Dorothy Neumann, Aaron Saxon, Bruno VeSota; *D:* Roger Corman; *W:* Charles B. Griffith, Mark Hanna; *C:* William Sickner; *M:* Ronald Stein.

Undead 🦴🦴 2005 (R) A freakish meteor shower falls upon the residents of Berkeley, Queensland, tainting the water supply and causing the locals to morph into brain-munching zombies, except, of course, for a few lucky(?) unaffected folks who band together at an outback farmhouse with the area's resident kooky gun nut. As they try to fend off the mutants some aliens arrive. Not much of a point, but then it is a zombie flick. If you like your zombies with an Aussie accent, give this one a try, but don't say you weren't warned. 100m/C DVD. Felicity Mason, Mungo McKay, Lisa Cunningham, Dirk Hunter, Emma Randall, Steve Greig, Noel Sheridan, Gaynor Wensley, Eleanor Stillman, Peter Spierig; *D:* Peter Spierig, Michael Spierig; *W:* Peter Spierig, Michael Spierig; *C:* Andrew Strahorn; *M:* Cliff Bradley.

Undead or Alive 🦴 2007 (R) Unlikely cowboy Luke (Kattan) and his new partner, army deserter Elmer (Denton), run a con on a corrupt sheriff and escape into the desert. Only they're pursued by angry Sheriff Claypool (Bessen) and his posse. The duo meets up with Native

Undeclared War 🐾🐾 1991 (R) Suspenseful espionage thriller that takes as a mercenary. Interesting view of American media and its political necessities. **128m/C VHS, DVD.** Gene Hackman, Nick Nolte, Joanna Cassidy, Ed Harris, Richard Masur, Hamilton Camp, Jean-Louis Trintignant; **D:** Roger Spottiswoode; **W:** Clayton Frohman, Ron Shelton; **C:** John Alcott; **M:** Jerry Goldsmith.

American Sue (Rawal) and learn that be- cause of Geronimo's curse all the local zombies. About as dumb as you can imagine. **91m/C VHS.** Chris Katan, James Denton, Navi Rawat, Matt Besser, Christopher Coppola; **D:** Glasgow Phillips; **W:** Glasgow Phillips; **C:** Thomas Callaway; **M:** Ivan Koutikov.

Under Fire 🐾🐾½ 1983 (R) Three foreign correspondents, old friends from the past working together, find themselves in Managua, witnessing the 1979 Nicaraguan revolution. In a job requiring objectivity, but a situation requiring taking sides, they battle with their ethics to do the job right. Fine performances, including Harris coincidentally, happens to be CIA. Martial arts expert. You watch for Cynthia to kick butt not for plot anyway. **88m/C VHS.** Cynthia Rothrock, Don Nian, John Miller, Donna Jason; **D:** Andrew V. McLaglen; **C:** William Clothier. VIDEO

Under Heavy Fire 🐾½ Going graphic violence. In 1968, the Marines put in the Astoria neighborhood is a crazed killer. His cool lover Facula turns out to be the prime suspect. Who's deceiving who? **94m/C VHS,** Harry Hamlin, Joanna Pacula, Ed Lauter, Richard Beymer, Lydie Denier; **D:** Kevin Meyer; **W:** Kevin Meyer.

Under Satan's Sun 🐾🐾🐾 Under the Sun of Satan; Sous le Soleil de Satan 1987 A rural priest is tortured by what he sees his sins and failings to his parishioners. He is further tempted from the straight path by a beautiful murderess, a worldly priest, and perhaps by Satan in disguise. Stylized film is not easily accessible, but Depardieu's performance is worth the effort. Based on the Georges Bernanos book. "Diary of a Country Priest." In French with English subtitles. **97m/C VHS,** Gérard Depardieu, Sandrine Bonnaire, Yann Dedet, Alain Artur, Maurice Pialat; **D:** Maurice Pialat; **W:** Maurice Pialat. Cannes '87. Film.

Not much tension in what aims to be a tension-filled thriller. Hackman is accused of raping and murdering several Puerto Rican women and spends the film being interrogated by detectives Freeman and Jane, both of talk but little to connect with in this remake of Claude Miller's very well respected "Garde a Vue." Both Hackman and Freeman co-executive produced. **111m/C VHS, DVD.** Morgan Freeman, Gene Hackman, Thomas Jane, Monica Bellucci; **D:** Stephen Hopkins; **W:** Peter Iliff, Tom Provost; **C:** Peter Levy.

Under the Biltmore Clock 🐾🐾 1985 F. Scott Fitzgerald's story, "Myra Meets His Family," is the basis for this American Playhouse installment for PBS. It is outwit or be outwitted in this tale of a fortune-hunting '20s flapper who sets her sights on marriage by the man she has set her eyes on. "Sometimes It Snows in April," and "Anotherloverholenyohead." **DVD.** Prince, Jerome Benton, Francesca Annis, Kristin Scott Thomas; **D:** Prince; **C:** Michael Ballhaus. Golden Raspberries '86. Worst Picture, Worst Actor (Prince), Worst Director (Prince), Worst Song ("Love or Money").

Under the Boardwalk 🐾½ 1989 (R) A pair of star-crossed teenage lovers struggle through familial and societal differences in 1980s California. This is like, bogus, ya know. **102m/C VHS.** Keith Coogan, Danielle von Zerneck, Richard Joseph Paul, Hunter von Leer, Tracey Walter, Roxana Zal, Dick Miller, Sonny Bono, Corky Carroll; **D:** Neal Miller. **TV**

ley Hawes, Ben Miles, Tony Haygarth, James Murray, Steve Pemberton; D: Nicholas Laughland; W: Ashley Pharoah; C: John Aspinall; M: John Lunn, Jim Williams. TV

Under the Gun 1988 (R) A cop recruits a lawyer to help him find the man who murdered his brother. Action drives this formulaic plot along. 88m/C VHS. Sam Jones, Vanessa (Lynne) Williams, John Russell, Michael Halsey; D: James Sbardellati; W: James Sbardellati, Aimer John Davis.

Under the Gun 1995 (R) Debt-ridden club owner Frank Torrance (Norton) is in trouble with everyone he knows. But he can't clear his debts just by quitting the business, so he decides to fight back. 90m/C VHS, DVD. Jane Badler, Peter Lindsey, Richard Norton, Kathy Longi; D: Matthew George; W: Matthew George; C: Dan Burstall; M: Frank Strangio.

Under the Hula Moon 1995 (R) Buzzard (Baldwin) and Betty (Lloyd) are living unhappily in the charmless desert town of Cactus Gulch. Their trailer home is festooned in faux-Hawaiian finery and the duo dream of the day they can actually move to their island paradise. Buzz's invented an ultraprotective sunscreen that may be their ticket out, if his prison-escapee, trigger-happy half-brother Turk (Penn), who's also kidnapped Betty, doesn't get them all killed first. Charming lead performances—very lightweight story. 94m/C VHS. Stephen Baldwin, Emily Lloyd, Christopher Penn, Musetta Vander, Edie McClurg, Pruitt Taylor Vince, Billy Campbell, Carel Struycken, R. Lee Ermey; D: Jeff Celentano; W: Jeff Celentano; C: Phil Parmet.

Under the Lighthouse Dancing 1997 What began as a vacation for six friends on a picturesque Australian island turns into a mad scramble to fulfill Emma's dying wish to marry Harry. Flat, despite being drawn from actual events. 96m/C VHS, DVD. AU Jack Thompson, Jacqueline McKenzie, Naomi Watts, Aden (John) Gillett, Philip Holder, Zoe Bertram; D: Graeme Rattigan; W: David Giles, Graeme Rattigan; C: Paul Murphy; M: Nerida Tyson-Chew. VIDEO

Under the Moonlight 2001 A young seminary students gets the education he truly needs to serve the people when, after his vestments are stolen by a hustling street kid, he must enter the homeless subculture to retrieve them. In Farsi with English subtitles. 96m/C VHS. Hossein Parastar, Hamad Rajabali; D: Seyyed Reza Mir-Karimi; W: Seyyed Reza Mir-Karimi; C: Hamid Khozui-Abyaneh; M: Mohammad Reza Alighori. VIDEO

Under the Pampas Moon 1935 Rakish gaucho Cesar (Baxter) heads to Buenos Aires in search of his stolen horse and discovers beautiful singing senorita Yvonne (Gallian) instead. He figures out that her manager may also be a horse thief. Features Rita Hayworth (credited under Rita Cansino) as a dancehall girl. 78m/B VHS. Warner Baxter, Ketti Gallian, J. Carrol Naish, John Miljan, Jack LaRue, Ann Codee; D: James Tinling; W: Bradley King, Ernest Pascal; C: Chester Lyons.

Under the Pear Tree woof! 1981 Unterm Birnbaum 1973 Classic crime based on a novella by Theodor Fontane. Bankrupt restaurant owner Hradschek and his wife come up with a plan to foil the debt collector at their door. But when the man's carriage is found—empty—by the river, the neighbors remember Hradschek digging under the pear tree the night before. German with subtitles. 86m/C VHS. GE Angelica Domrose, Manfred Karge, Erik S. Klein, Agnes Kraus, Norbert Christian; D: Ralf Kirsten; W: Ralf Kirsten.

Under the Rainbow woof! 1981 (PG) Comic situations encountered by a talent scout and a secret service agent in a hotel filled with Munchkins during filming of "The Wizard of Oz." Features midgets, spies, and a prevailing lack of taste. International intrigue adds to the strange attempt at humor. 97m/C VHS. Chevy Chase, Carrie Fisher, Eve Arden, Joseph Maher, Zelda Rubinstein; D: Steve Rash; W: Pat McCormick, Martin Smith, Harry Hurwitz, Fred Bauer, Pat Bradley.

Under the Red Robe 1936 A French soldier of fortune is trapped into aiding Cardinal Richelieu in his persecution of the Huguenots and winds up falling in love with the sister of his intended victim. Good costume adventure-drama. 82m/B VHS, DVD. GB Raymond Massey, Conrad Veidt, Annabella, Romney Brent; D: Victor Sjostrom; C: James Wong Howe.

Under the Roofs of Paris Sous les Toits de Paris 1929 An early French sound film about the lives of young Parisian lovers. A gentle, highly acclaimed melodrama. In French with English subtitles. 95m/B VHS, DVD. FR Albert Prejean, Pola Illery, Gaston Modot, Edmond T. Greville; D: Rene Clair; W: Rene Clair; C: Georges Perinal; M: Armand Bernard.

Under the Same Moon La Misma Luna 2007 (PG-13) A heart-tugger that usually stays just this side of sentimentality. Young Carlitos (Alonso) lives in Mexico with his grandma while his mother Rosario (del Castillo) works illegally as a maid in L.A. Every Sunday she calls him from the same pay phone. When grandma dies, Carlitos decides to cross the border to reunite with his mom. He makes it to Texas but it's a problematic journey from there to California that may be for naught since the fed-up Rosario is deciding whether to return home. English and Spanish with subtitles. 109m/C DVD. US Adrian Alonso, Maya Zapata, Kate del Castillo, Eugenio Derbez, Gabriel Porras; D: Patricia Riggen; W: Ligiah Villalobos; C: Checco Varese; M: Carlo Siliotto.

Under the Sand Sous le Sable 2000 Middleaged Marie (Rampling) has been married for many years to Jean (Cremer). They are vacationing at their summer house and Jean goes for a swim while Marie takes a nap. When she awakens, he has disappeared. A search reveals nothing and Marie must eventually return to Paris and try to go on with her life. But Marie is deep in denial—she speaks as if Jean were still alive and, in fact, she continues to see and interact with—well, whatever spirit of Jean that she has conjured up. Bravura performance from Rampling. French with subtitles. 95m/C VHS. FR Charlotte Rampling, Bruno Cremer, Jacques Nolot, Alexandra Stewart, Pierre Vernier, Andree Tainsey; D: Francois Ozon; W: Francois Ozon, Marina de Van, Emmanuele Bernheim, Marcia Romano; C: Jeanne Lapoirie, Antoine Heberle; M: Philippe Rombi.

Under the Skin 1997 After their mother's unexpected death, 19-year-old Iris (Morton) and her married, pregnant older sister Rose (Rushbrook) deal with their grief in very different ways. The dreamy Iris decides to explore all her sexual fantasies after she has a spontaneous sexual encounter with a stranger, Tom (Townsend), and drifts into promiscuity. The fragile Iris pushes her limits to find some kind of comfort while her remaining family ties steadily disintegrate. Astonishing no-holds-barred performance by Morton. 81m/C VHS. GB Samantha Morton, Claire Rushbrook, Rita Tushingham, Stuart Townsend, Christine Tremarco, Mark Womack, Odette Springer; D: Carine Adler; W: Carine Adler; C: Barry Ackroyd; M: Ilona Sekacz.

Under the Sun Under Solen 1998 In 1956, 40-year-old virgin, Olof (Lassgard), who is rather rundown farm in western Sweden—his only friend being the younger Erik (Widerberg), who takes advantage of Olof's generosity. Then Ellen (Bergstrom) turns up in answer to Olof's ad for a housekeeper and the unlikely duo become a romantic couple much to Erik's dismay. So he decides to find out what a beautiful city girl is doing on a remote farm. Based on a short story by H.E. Bates. Swedish with subtitles. 118m/C VHS, DVD. SW Rolf Lassgard, Helena Bergstrom, Johan Widerberg, Jonas Falk, Linda Ulvaeus; D: Colin Nutley; W: Colin Nutley; C: Jens Fischer; M: Paddy Moloney.

Under the Tuscan Sun 2003 (PG-13) Very loose adaptation of the Frances Mayes bestseller has beautiful scenery—both from its leads and Italy. Still in shock from her recent divorce, writer Frances (Lane) is given a change-of-scenery trip by her lesbian best friend Patti (Oh). While traveling in Tuscany, Frances comes across a rundown villa, which she impulsively buys and proceeds to renovate with the aid of some displaced Polish workmen. She begins to make friends with the locals, including handsome Marcello (Bova), with whom she is soon getting romantic. Lane is exuberant as the newly risk-taking Frances but Oh supplies much humor when Patti shows up, pregnant and deserted by her lover, to join Frances's new household. 113m/C VHS, DVD. US Diane Lane, Sandra Oh, Lindsay Duncan, Raoul Bova, Vincent Riotta, Giulia Steigerwalt, Pawel Szajda, Valentine Pelka, Sasa Vulicevic, David Sutcliffe, Kate Walsh; D: Audrey Wells; W: Audrey Wells; C: Geoffrey Simpson; M: Christophe Beck.

Under the Volcano 1984 An alcoholic British ex-consul finds his life further deteriorating during the Mexican Day of the Dead in 1939. His half-brother and ex-wife try to save him from himself, but their affair sends him ever-deeper into his personal hell. Finney's performance is pathetic and haunting. Adapted from the novel by Malcolm Lowry. 112m/C VHS. Albert Finney, Jacqueline Bisset, Anthony Andrews, Katy Jurado; D: John Huston; M: John Beal, Alex North. L.A. Film Critics '84: Actor (Finney).

Under the Yum-Yum Tree 1963 When womanizing landlord Hogan's (Lemmon) ex-fiance Irene (Adams) moves out, he doesn't pine. Instead he plots to romance her niece Robin (Lynley) who's just moved into his building. But it's romantic shenanigans are thwarted by the presence of fiance David (Jones), who's living platonically with Robin to test their compatibility. Silly sex comedy based on the play by Roman. 110m/C VHS. Jack Lemmon, Carol Lynley, Dean Jones, Edie Adams, Imogene Coca, Paul Lynde, Robert Lansing, Bill Bixby; D: David Swift; W: David Swift, Lawrence Roman; C: Joseph Biroc; M: Frank DeVol.

Under Western Stars 1938 Roy's first starring vehicle. A newly elected congressman goes to Washington and fights battles for his constituents, caught in the middle of the Dust Bowl and drought. 83m/B VHS, DVD. Roy Rogers, Smiley Burnette; D: Jean Yarbrough.

The Underachievers 1988 (R) A night school is the scene for typical libido-oriented gags, but this time instead of teenagers it's adult education providing the plot. Only a few real laughs in this one. 90m/C VHS. Barbara Carrera, Edward Albert, Michael Pataki, Vic Tayback, Garrett Morris, Susan Tyrrell; D: Jackie Kong.

Underclassman woof! 2005 (PG-13) Venice beach bike cop, Tre (Cannon), gets assigned to prep school to investigate a murder. Sounds like it might have promise, but nope. Even the juxtaposition of Tre—the only African American on the starkly white prep school campus—falls flat amidst cheap jokes and predictably cliched circumstances. Poor Cheech Marin, who plays Tre's boss, adds another thankless role to his resume. Why Tre, a cop in the first place, is beyond logic. 95m/C DVD. US Nick Cannon, Shawn Ashmore, Roselyn Sanchez, Kelly Hu, Ian Gomez, Hugh Bonneville, Richard "Cheech" Marin, Mary Pat Gleason, Angelo Spizzirri, Kaylee DeFer; D: Marcos Siega; W: David T. Wagner, Brent Goldberg; C: David Hennings; M: BT (Brian Transeau).

Undercover 1987 (R) Routine cop action film in which an eastern detective finds himself undercover in a southern high school in search of a cop-murdering drug ring. Plagued with cliches. Director Stockwell is appropriately better known for his role as "Cougar" in "Top Gun." 92m/C VHS. David Neidorf, Jennifer Jason Leigh, Barry Corbin, David Harris, Kathleen Wilhoite; D: John Stockwell; M: Bruce Smeaton.

Undercover 1994 (R) Police detective (and hot babe) Cindy Hanen (Massey) gets an undercover assignment to capture a murderer who's targeted an upscale brothel. It's an excuse for interesting undies (or less). 93m/C VHS, DVD. Athena Massey, Tom Tayback, Anthony Guidera, Rena Riffel, Jeffrey Dean Morgan, Meg Foster; D: Alexander Gregory (Gregory Dark) Hippolyte; W: Oola Bloome, Lalo Wolf; C: Philip Hurn; M: Ashley Irwin.

Undercover Angel 1999 (PG-13) Predictably cheesy but still entertaining movie that features the chubby-cheeked blonde girl from the Welch's Juice TV commercials. Six-year-old Young is left in the care of struggling writer Winters, her mom's old boyfriend. He's attracted to Bleeth and the little moppet charges into the woman's life in order to get the duo together. Oh yeah, and then Young and Winters discover that he's actually her biological father. 93m/C VHS, DVD. Yasmine Bleeth, Dean Winters, Emily Mae Young, Lorraine Ansell, Casey Kasem, Richard Eden, James Earl Jones; D: Bryan Michael Stoller; W: Bryan Michael Stoller; C: Bruce Alan Greene; M: Greg Edmonson. VIDEO

Undercover Blues 1993 (PG-13) Comedy-thriller starring Turner and Quaid as married spies Jane and Jeff Blue, on parental leave from the espionage biz, who are on vacation with their 11-month-old daughter in New Orleans. But the holiday is interrupted when they're recruited by their boss to stop an old adversary from selling stolen weapons. The leads play cute together and the baby is adorable but this is strictly routine escapism. Stick with "The Thin Man" instead. 90m/C VHS, DVD. Kathleen Turner, Dennis Quaid, Fiona Shaw, Stanley Tucci, Larry Miller, Obba Babatunde, Park Overall, Tom Arnold, Saul Rubinek, Michelle Schuelke; D: Herbert Ross; W: Ian Abrams; M: David Newman.

Undercover Brother 2002 (PG-13) Funny but padded spoof of secret agents and blaxploitation movies. Brother (Griffin) is a secret agent from the B.R.O.T.H.E.R.H.O.O.D. sent to rescue a black war hero turned presidential candidate (the always-cool Williams) who has been brainwashed in a plot by The Man to destroy African-American culture. More-hit-than-miss comedy finds many targets of all stripes to lampoon, and does so with just the right amount of funk. 85m/C VHS, DVD. US Eddie Griffin, Chris Kattan, Denise Richards, Dave Chappelle, Chi McBride, Aunjanue Ellis, Neil Patrick Harris, Billy Dee Williams, Jack Noseworthy, Gary Anthony Williams, James Brown, Robert Trumbull; D: Malcolm Lee; W: John Ridley, Michael McCullers; C: Tom Priestley; M: Stanley Clarke; Nar: J.D. Hall.

Undercover Cop 1994 True story of Sergeant George Aguilar and the high-speed chase that left one dead and the police dealing their revenge on all the offenders. 90m/C VHS. Danny Trejo, Kevin Anthony Cole; D: Martin Greene; W: Glenn A. Bruce; M: Randall Kent Heddon.

The Undercover Kid 1995 (PG) Ten-year-old Max Anderson's (Pierce) dog has told him that the President is going to be assassinated. Can he get anyone to believe him? Harmless action adventure for the kiddies. 81m/C VHS. Bradley Michael Pierce, Melora Hardin, Nicolas Surovy, Erik Avari, Trishalee Hardy, Sven-Ole Thorsen; D: Linda Shayne; W: Dennis Carr; C: Jack Laskus; M: Steve Dorff; V: Robert Knepper, Victoria Jackson.

Undercover Man 1936 A Wells Fargo agent goes undercover to expose a crooked sheriff. 57m/B VHS. Johnny Mack Brown, Suzanne Kaaren, Ted Adams, Lloyd Ingraham, Horace Murphy; D: Albert Ray.

Undercurrent 1946 Minnelli's only foray into film noir is high-gloss melodrama based on the novel "You Were There" by Thelma Strabel. Innocent Ann (Hepburn) marries Alan (Taylor) after a whirlwind romance and then discovers he's not the man she thinks. He may be a murderer and there's some chicanery involving his brother Michael (Mitchum) and the family business. Taylor's in a rare bad guy role while Hepburn seems too sophisticated for her naive wife and Mitchum just seems tired. 116m/B VHS, DVD. Katharine Hepburn, Robert Mitchum, Edmund Gwenn, Marjorie Main, Clinton Sundberg, Dan Tobin, Jayne Cotter; D: Vincente Minnelli; W: Marguerite Roberts, Edward Chodorov, George Oppenheimer; C: Karl Freund; M: Herbert Stothart.

Undercurrent 🎬🎬 1999 (R) Ex-cop Lamas arrives in Puerto Rico to run a nightclub and is blackmailed into an affair transforms a sheik into an attendant in order to help him meet the girl of his dreams. A bad "Car Wash" spinoff. 93m/C VHS, DVD. *D:* Frank Kerr. *C:* Carlos Gaviria; *M:* Christopher Lennertz. VIDEO

The Underdog 🎬🎬½ 1943 After the bank forecloses, a farm family must move to the city. The family's young son has eavesdropping at a defense plant. He vents a scrambler that confuses the Axis and then rounding up a gang of spies piloting some WWII sabotage. Believe it if you dare. 65m/B VHS. *D:* William Nigh.

Underdog 🎬 2007 (PG) Live-action/ CGI combo finds the TV cartoon character making his feature film debut. Beagle Underdog (Lee) goes from ordinary to extraordinary, thanks to an accident in the lab of Dr. Simon Barsinister (Dinklage). He can even talk, which is a big surprise to his young owner Jack Unger (Neuberger). Now Underdog's new mission is to protect the citizens of Capitol City, especially lovely spaniel "Sweet" Polly Purebred (Adams), from Barsinister's...well...sinister plans to take over. With a dog as a superhero, there's no way this should have missed. Unfortunately, a handful of inspired moments aren't enough to overcome the generally disjointed and rushed feel of the whole thing. 84m/C DVD, Blu-ray Disc, UMD. *D:* Frederick Du Chau; *W:* Adam Rifkin, Joe Piscatella, Craig A. Williams; *V:* Jason Lee, Amy Adams.

Undergrads 🎬🎬 1985 A bright generational Disney comedy with Carney, estranged from his stick-in-the-mud son, deciding to attend college with his freethinking grandson. 102m/C VHS, DVD. *D:* Steven Hilliard Stern. TV

Underground 🎬🎬🎬 1941 Eric (Dorn) is a member of the German underground working against the Nazis. But he must conceal his activities from his loyal soldier brother Kurt (Lynn). Topical wartime drama still hits home with its freedivided loyalties. 95m/B VHS, DVD. *D:* Vincent Sherman; *W:* Charles Grayson; *C:* Sid Hickox. *M:* Adolph Deutsch.

Underground 🎬🎬🎬 *Once Upon a Time There Was a Country. Il Etait une Fois un Pays* 1995 Exhausting black comedy, set in Yugoslavia from '41 to 1992, follows the adventures of Marko (Manojlovic) and his best friend Blacky (Ristovski). They run a black-market operation and lead Communist Party meetings while trying to avoid the Gestapo in WWII Belgrade. Hiding out in a cellar, where refugees have put together a munitions factory, the treacherous Marko manages to convince everyone that the war is still going on—20 years later. But in fact—until the truth unexpectedly comes out (thanks to a pet monkey). The final section sees Marko unscrupulously dealing arms and drugs amidst the breakup of Yugoslavia in a civil war and the violence on all sides. 192m/C VHS, DVD, FR GE HU Miki (Predrag) Manojlovic, Lazar Ristovski, Mirjana Jokovic, Slavko Stimac, Ernst Stotzner, Srdan Todorovic, Mirjana Karanovic, Milena Pavlovic, Danilo Stojkovic, Bora Todorovic, Davor Dujmovic, Branislav Lecic, Dragan Nikolic, Hark Bohm; *Cameos:* Emir Kusturica, Dusan Kovacevic; *C:* Vilko Filac. *M:* Emir Bregovic. Can='95. Film.

The Underground 🎬🎬 1997 (R) A rap artist is gunned down by a gang and Sgt. Brian Donnigan (Fahey) and his partner Scully (Tiga) are on the case. But when Scully is killed by the same scum, Donnegan is partnered with a rookie (McFall) and the duo must infiltrate L.A.'s music scene to get their suspects. 92m/C VHS, DVD. *D:* Jeff Fahey, Ken Tigar, Michael Blakey; *M:* Cole McKay; *W:* William Lawlor; *C:* Ken Blakey.

Underground Aces WOOF! 1980 A group of parking lot attendants

Underground Agent 🎬🎬½ 1942 WWII release timeframe than it will for modern sensibilities. Government agent Lee Graham (Bennett) is hired to stop enemy

Underground Rustlers 🎬 1941 The Range Busters are commissioned by the government to stop unscrupulous gold-marketeers. 58m/B VHS. Ray Corrigan, Rhys Williams, Henry Victor, Addison Richards, Hans Conried; *D:* Michael Gordon; *C:* L.W. O'Connell.

Underground Terror 🎬 1988 A gang of murderers, organized by a psychopath, rampages through the New York City subway system. One cop enthusiastically tries to snuff out each one. 91m/C VHS. Doc Dougherty, Lenny Y. Lofrin; *D:* James McCalmont.

Underground U.S.A. 🎬 1984 Street hustler picks up a has-been underground movie star at the chic New York new wave disco, The Mudd Club. 85m/C VHS. Patti Astor, Eric Mitchell; *D:* Eric Mitchell.

Undermind 🎬½ 2003 Dissolute corporate lawyer Derrick (Trammell) wakes up in an altered reality as a low-life criminal named Zane. While Zane's enjoying the perks of Derrick's life, Derrick's finding it hard to manage Zane's bottom-feeder existence. Everything gets tied up neatly. Dwek's debut effort. 113m/C DVD. Sam Trammell, Erik Jensen, Susan May Pratt, Tara Subkoff, Celia Weston, Ellen Pompeo, Aasif Mandal, Michael Ryan Segal; *D:* Nevil Dwek; *W:* Nevil Dwek; *C:* Wolfgang Held; *M:* Joel Goodman.

The Underneath 🎬🎬 1995 (R) Recovering gambling addict Michael Chambers (Gallagher) returns home after skipping out on his debts and his wife Rachel (sultry newcomer Elliott) several years before. Old passions ignite in more ways than one, and Michael's lust for his ex, now married to a hot-tempered hoodlum, leads him to risk it all for a final big score. Moody and tense study of the complexities of emotion is capped by smart lead performances but style wins out over substance and the finale definitely leaves more questions than answers. Remake of the 1949 film noir classic "Criss Cross," based on Don Tracy's novel of the same name. 99m/C VHS, DVD. Peter Gallagher, Alison Elliott, William Fichtner, Elisabeth Shue, Adam Trese, Paul Dooley, Joe Don Baker, Anjanette Comer, Harry Goz, Vincent Gaskins, Tony Perenski, Helen Cates, John Martin, David Jensen, Joseph Chrest; *D:* Steven Soderbergh; *W:* Steven Soderbergh, Daniel Fuchs; *C:* Elliott Davis; *M:* Cliff Martinez.

Undersea Kingdom 🎬🎬 1936 Adventure beneath the ocean floor. In 12 chapters of 13 minutes each; the first chapter runs 20 minutes. Later re-edited into one film, "Sharad of Atlantis." 226m/B VHS, DVD. Ray Corrigan, Lon Chaney Jr., Lois Wilde, Monte Blue, William Farnum, Smiley Burnette; *D:* B. Reeves Eason.

Understudy: The Graveyard Shift 2 🎬½ 1988 (R) Vampire survives poorly directed cliche-riddled original to be cast as a vampire again in a horror movie within a horrible sequel. 88m/C VHS. CA Wendy Gazelle, Mark Soper, Silvio Oliviero, Ilse von Glatz, Tim Kelleher; *D:* Gerard Ciccoritti; *C:* Barry Stone.

The Undertaker and His Pals 🎬 1967 Undertaker teams up with diner owners in murder scheme to improve mortician's business and expand restaurateurs' menu. Pretty violent stuff, but not for every one's palate. 70m/C VHS.

Underwater! 🎬🎬 1955 A team of skin divers faces danger when they try to retrieve treasure from a Spanish galleon. 99m/C VHS, DVD. Jane Russell, Richard Egan, Gilbert Roland, Jayne Mansfield; *D:* John Sturges.

Underworld 🎬🎬🎬 1927 Inspired gangster saga finds bank robber Bull Weed (Bancroft) befriending a genteel bum, known as Rolls Royce (Brook), and taking him into his gang. The bum has brains and soon makes Weed king of the underworld but there's jealousy when Weed's moll Feathers (Brent) falls for Royce. Climactic shootout set a standard for the genre. 85m/B VHS. George Bancroft, Clive Brook, Evelyn Brent, Larry Semon, Fred Kohler Sr.; *D:* Josef von Sternberg. Oscars '28: Story.

Underworld 🎬🎬 1996 (R) Considering the on-screen talent, this crime comedy/thriller is a disappointment. Ex-wiseguy Johnny Crown (Leary), studied psychotherapy in the joint and when he's released, decides to put his new knowledge to work on bossman Frank Gavilan (Mantegna), who may be behind the hit on Johnny's old man. Contrived dialogue and story but a sleek-looking production. 95m/C VHS, DVD. Denis Leary, Joe Mantegna, Annabella Sciorra, Larry Bishop, Abe Vigoda, James Tolkan, Robert Costanzo; *D:* Roger Christian; *W:* Larry Bishop; *C:* Steven Bernstein; *M:* Anthony Marinelli.

Underworld 🎬🎬 2003 (R) Vampires and Lycans (werewolves) wage a century-old battle of survival. The aristocratic vampires have been in control, but it's the ly... Head vampire warrior Selene (Beckinsale) inexplicably falls in love with him, precipitating a final showdown.

DVD. Ray Dannis, James Westmoreland, Larrene Ott, Robert Lowery, Sally Frei; *D:* Andrew Janczak.

The Undertaker's Wedding 🎬🎬 1997 (R) Undertaker Mario Bellini (Brophy) takes the death and burial of mob boss Rocco (Wincott) to heart when a local mob war for him makes the big mistake of falling in love with the new "widow," Maria (Smith). 89m/C VHS, DVD. Adrien Brody, Jeff Wincott, Kari Wuhrer, Burt Young, Holly Gagnier, Nicholas Pasco; *D:* John Bradshaw; *C:* Edward T. Lowe, Kristen Overbren, Gladys Atwater; *C:* L.W. O'Connell.

Undertow 🎬½ 1930 Lighthouse keeper Paul (Brown) marries Sally (Nolan), but when he goes blind she's ripe for romance... Coast Guardsman Jim's (Ellis) attentions. Robert Ellis, Churchill Ross, Audrey Ferris; *D:* Harry A. Pollard; *W:* Edward T. Lowe, Kristen Overbaugh.

Undertow 🎬🎬 1996 (R) Drifter Jack Ketchum (Phillips) loses control of his car in a storm and wakes up in the secluded cabin of paranoid Lyle Yates (Dance) and his terrified wife, Willie (Sara). Since the storm's worse, Jack can't leave—too bad for him that Willie's so darn attractive and Lyle's so crazy. 90m/C VHS, Lou Diamond Phillips, Mia Sara, Charles Dance; *D:* Eric Red; *W:* Kathryn Bigelow, Eric Red; *C:* Geza Sinkovics; *M:* John (Gianni) Frizzell. CABLE.

Undertow 🎬🎬 2004 (R) Over-heated southern gothic. Rebellious teen Chris (Bell) lives on a ramshackle hog farm with widowed dad John (Mulroney) and sickly 10-year-old bro Tim (Alan). Then wicked Uncle Deel (Lucas) shows up, fresh outta prison and with a lot of pent-up resentment and anger toward John (seems John's late wife was Deel's gal first). He demands his share of some rare gold coins bequeathed to him and John, which John believes are cursed. Deel gives all Cain and Abel which forces the younger duo to grab the gold and take off running. Brit boy Bell manages his Southern twang with aplomb. Filmed on location around Savannah, Georgia. 107m/C DVD. US Jamie Bell, Joshua Lucas, Dermot Mulroney, Shiri Appleby, Patrica Healy, Bill McKinney, Aan Devon; *C:* Tim Orr; *M:* Philip Glass.

Underworld: Evolution 🎬🎬½ 2005 (R) Selene and Michael are still on the run and still trying to figure out the depths of the various betrayals and who, if anyone, they can trust. This time our little vampire and werewolf duo have to deal with the O.G. vampire and werewolf, then a few family issues to work out. There's also plenty of backstory, and more of what made the first installment a hit: Beckinsale in black leather, frenetic vampire-on-werewolf battle action, blood and gunplay. As a bonus, there's a much better villain and script that brings everything home (but don't rule out another sequel). 106m/C DVD, Blu-ray Disc, UMD. Kate Beckinsale, Scott Speedman, Tony Curran, Shane Brolly, Derek Jacobi, Bill Nighy, Steven Mackintosh, Brian Steele, John Mann, Michael Sheen, Sophia Myles, Richard Cetrone; *D:* Len Wiseman, Danny McBride; *C:* Simon Duggan; *M:* Marco Beltrami.

Underworld, U.S.A. 🎬🎬🎬 1960 A man infiltrates a tough crime syndicate to avenge his father's murder, which winds up with him caught between the mob and the feds. A well-acted and directed look at the criminal underworld. 99m/B VHS. Cliff Robertson, Dolores Dorn, Beatrice Kay, Robert Emhardt, Larry Gates, Paul Dubov; *D:* Samuel Fuller; *W:* Samuel Fuller; *C:* Hal Mohr.

The Underworld Story 🎬🎬½ 1950 Big city journalist at large moves to smalltown New England after losing job for unethical reporting and uncovers scheme to frame innocent man for murder. Solid performances. 90m/B VHS, Dan Duryea, Herbert Marshall, Gale Storm, Howard da Silva, Michael O'Shea, Mary Anderson, Gar Moore, Melville Cooper, Frieda Inescort, Art Baker, Harry Shannon, Alan Hale Jr., Steve (Stephen) Dunne, Roland Winters; *D:* Cy Endfield.

Underworld Scandal 🎬🎬 *Big Town Scandal* 1947 An editor attempts to break up a ring of basketball game fixers. Based on the radio program "Big Town." 61m/C VHS, Philip Reed, Hillary Brooke, Stanley Clements, Darryl Hickman, Carl "Alfalfa" Switzer; *D:* William C. Thomas; *W:* Milton Raison; *C:* Ellis W. Carter; *M:* Darrell Calker.

Undesirable 🎬 *With a Vengeance* 1992 Dull thriller-wannabe. Annesiesic Jenna King (Gilbert) has no memory of her childhood and only knows that she alone survived the murder of her family. Now working as a nanny, Jenna's life is in danger when that same killer finally decides to finish the job. 93m/C VHS, Melissa Gilbert, Jack Scala, Matthew Lawrence, Michael Gross, Roger Aaron Brown, John Cullum, Russell Johnson, Robert Donner; *D:* Walter Hill; *C:* David Gilgr; *M:* Stanley Clarke.

Undisputed 🎬🎬½ 2002 (R) Champicn boxer James "Ice Man" Chambers is locked up in Sweetwater maximum-security prison for rape, which he claims he didn't commit. Snipes is Monroe Hutchens, a lifer at Sweetwater and fellow boxing champ of the illegal boxing matches set up by a rough prison guard (Rooker). Smacking of real-life boxer Tyson, Chambers desperately tries to find honor in his unhappy situation and wants to be the first to break Hutchen's winning streak, but Monroe has his chambers on dialogue, pic is a well-cast, lean, mean movie machine. 96m/C VHS, DVD. US Wesley Snipes, Ving Rhames, Peter Falk, Michael Rooker, Jon Seda, Wes Studi, Fisher Stevens, Deyton Callie, Amy Aquino, Nils Allen Stewart, Denis Arndt, Rose Rollins; *D:* Walter Hill; *W:* Walter Hill, David Gilgr; *C:* Lloyd Ahern II; *M:* Stanley Clarke.

Undisputed II: Last Man Standing 2006 (R) An unnecessary sequel that has few ties to the first pic. Ex-boxing champ George Chambers (White) is making vodka commercials in Russia when he lands in prison on trumped-up charges. Seems the Russian mob wants to pit Chambers against the prison's best fighter, Uri Boyka (Adkins), in a televised match they expect will bring in big gambling bucks. The fights between the leads are impressive but scant as the rest of the action. 98m/C DVD. Michael Jai White, Eli Danker, Ben Cross, Scott Adkins; D: Isaac Florentine; W: David White, James Townsend; C: Ross Clarkson; M: Stephen (Steve) Edwards. VIDEO

The Undying Monster The Hammond Mystery 1942 Upper crusty Brit is werewolf with insatiable appetite. Familial story with lots of atmosphere and style. 63m/B VHS. James Ellison, Heather Angel, John Howard, Bramwell Fletcher, Heather Thatcher, Aubrey Mather, Halliwell Hobbes, Heather Wilde; D: John Brahm; M: Lillie Hayward, Michael Jacoby; C: Lucien Ballard; M: Cyril Mockridge, David Raksin, Arthur Lange. *

Une Parisienne 1958 Gallic fluff stars sex kitten Bardot finds her an unhappy newlywed whose husband (Vidal) is enjoying being a bon vivant a little too much. So she decides to make him jealous by heading off to the Riviera with an aging Prince (Boyer). French with subtitles. 85m/C VHS. FR Brigitte Bardot, Charles Boyer, Henri Vidal, Andre Luguet, Nadia Gray, Madeleine LeBeau, Noel Roquevert; D: Michel Boisrond; W: Michel Boisrond, Annette Wademant, Jean Aurel; C: Marcel Grignon; M: Hubert Rostaing.

Unearthed 2007 (R) It should be reburied as soon as possible. In this cliched creature feature an alien being, buried during the Anasazi tribe centuries ago, is unearthed during an archeological dig near a small New Mexico town. And now that it's awake it's angry and hungry. The beautiful Vaugier plays the town's troubled, alcoholic sheriff. 93m/C DVD. Emmanuelle Vaugier, Luke Goss, Charlie (Charles Q.) Murphy, Beau Garrett, M.C. Gainey, Russell Means; D: Matthewr Leutwyler; W: Matthewr Leutwyler; C: Ross Richardson, Ross Richardson.

The Unearthing 1993 (R) An unwanted pregnancy seems to find a happy solution when a woman decides to marry the heir to a wealthy estate and pass off her child as his. Not a fairy tale, it winds up with is a basement full of mutants. When his two latest about-to-be victims fall in love, the doctor's mutant assistant decides enough is enough and things come to an unpleasant end. Carradine is typecast. Absurd, but fun. 76m/B VHS, DVD. John Carradine, Tor Johnson, Allison Hayes, Myron Healey, Karl Johnson; D: Boris L. Petroff.

The Unearthly Stranger 1957 A mad scientist marries woman and decides she's from another planet. Not a nineties style gender drama; seems she's part of an invading alien force, but really does love her earth man. Surprisingly good low-budget sci-fi. 75m/B VHS. GB John Neville, Gabriella Licudi, Philip Stone, Patrick Newell, Jean Marsh, Warren Mitchell; D: John Krish.

Uneasy Terms 1948 Rennie is a detective investigating the murder of one of his own clients. Evidence points to stepchildren and inheritance money but things may not be as they seem. Written for the screen by Peter Cheyney, adapted from his own novel. 91m/B VHS. GB Michael Rennie, Moira Lister, Faith Brook, Joy Shelton, Patricia Goddard, Barry Jones, Nigel Patrick, Paul Carpenter, Marie Ney, Sydney Tafler, J.H. Roberts, John Robinson; D: Vernon Sewell; M: Peter Cheyney; C: Ernest Palmer.

An Unexpected Family 1996 (PG) Barbara Whitney (Channing) is a Manhattan career woman who is unwillingly thrust into the role of surrogate mom when her irresponsible sister, Ruth (Ebersole), dumps her two children at Barbara's door. Along with her friend Sam (Collins), Barbara and the children slowly make a new family but, after a year, Ruth returns, demanding her children back. Predictable plot is redeemed by good performances from Channing and Ebersole. 93m/C VHS. Stockard Channing, Stephen Collins, Christine Ebersole, Noah Fleiss, Chelsea Russo; D: Larry Elikann; W: Lee Rose; C: Eric Van Haren Noman; M: Tom Scott. CABLE

An Unexpected Life 1997 (PG) Sequel to 1996's "An Unexpected Family." Barbara Whitney (Channing) has moved to the country and is raising her niece Megan (Russo) and nephew Matt (Fleiss) with the help of boyfriend Sam (Collins). Then Babs discovers she's pregnant—not altogether welcome news. Neither is Barbara's sister Ruth (Ebersole) deciding her life is back on track and she wants to regain custody of her kids or Sam's estrangement from his own visiting mother (Stritch). This blended family needs a good therapist. 92m/C VHS. Stockard Channing, Stephen Collins, Christine Ebersole, Elaine Stritch, Noah Fleiss, Chelsea Russo, Russell Paul Charles; D: David Hugh Jones; W: Lee Rose. CABLE

Unexplained Laughter 1989 A cynical journalist vacations in Wales with her timid vegetarian friend and stumbles across a mystery in this darkly comic British TV-movie. 85m/C VHS. GB Diana Rigg, Elaine Page, Jon Finch; D: Gareth Davies; W: Alun Owen; C: Ashley Rowe.

Unfaithful 2002 (R) Director Lyne may be known for such hot-blooded features as "9 1/2 Weeks," "Fatal Attraction," and "Lolita" but he takes a cooler approach to adultery in this melodrama, which was inspired by Claude Chabrol's 1969 film "La Femme Infidele." Connie (a luscious Lane) is a suburban mom, complacently married to regular guy Edward (Gere), who cannot resist having a hot, hot, hot affair with French bookseller Paul (Martinez), whom Connie meets cute while shopping in New York. Edward gets suspicious, Connie tries to break things off, and it turns out there's nothing like a MAN who gets scorned to bring trouble. 123m/C VHS, DVD. US Richard Gere, Diane Lane, Olivier Martinez, Erik Per Sullivan, Dominic Chianese, Zeljko Ivanek, Kate Burton, Chad Lowe, Gary Basaraba, Margaret Colin; D: Adrian Lyne; W: Alvin Sargent, William Broyles Jr.; C: Peter Biziou; M: Jan A.P. Kaczmarek. N.Y. Film Critics '02: Actress (Lane), Actress (Lane).

Unfaithfully Yours 1948 A conductor suspects his wife is cheating on him and considers this course of action. He imagines classical scenarios while directing three classical works. Well-acted by all, but particularly by Harrison as the egotistical and jealous husband. Another of Sturges' comedic gems. Remade in 1984. 105m/B VHS, DVD. Rex Harrison, Linda Darnell, Kurt Kreuger, Rudy Vallee, Lionel Stander, Edgar Kennedy; D: Preston Sturges; C: Victor Milner.

Unfaithfully Yours 1984 (PG) A symphony conductor suspects his wife of fooling around with a musician; in retaliation, he plots an elaborate scheme to murder her with comic results. No match for the 1948 Preston Sturges film it's based on. 96m/C VHS, DVD. Dudley Moore, Nastassja Kinski, Armand Assante, Albert Brooks, Cassie Yates, Richard Libertini, Richard B. Shull; D: Howard Zieff; W: Valerie Curtin, Barry Levinson; Robert Klane; M: Bill Conti.

The Unfaithfuls Le Infedeli 1960 Infidelity among upper-class Italian society couples leads to divorce, blackmail, suicide, and (amazingly enough) some laughs. One philandering husband tries to catch his wife fooling around so he can get a divorce and hook up with his girlfriend. 89m/B VHS. IT Gina Lollobrigida, May Britt, Irene Papas, Pierre Cressoy, Marina Vlady, Franco Rossi; D: Mario Monicelli, Steno; W: Mario Monicelli, Steno, Franco Brusati, Ivo Perilli; C: Aldo Tonti; M: Armando Trovajoli.

Unfinished Business 1989 A 17 year-old girl leads a troubled adolescent life with her divorced parents. She decides running away will ease her problems—not a smart move. Sequel to "Nobody Waved Goodbye." 88m/C VHS. CA Isabelle Mejias, Peter Kastner, Leslie Toth, Peter Spence, Chuck Shamata, Julie Biggs; D: Don Owen.

An Unfinished Life 2005 (PG-13) Crusty Wyoming rancher Einar Jean Gilkyson (Lopez), Einar's widowed daughter-in-law has been abused by her lowlife boyfriend Gary (Lewis) for the last time and unwillingly seeks shelter at the ranch with her tough-talking, 11-year-old daughter Griff (Gardner). Einar, who blames Jean for his son's death, grudging allows them to stay temporarily and gradually thaws towards his spunky granddaughter. Much gruff bonding and a family reconciliation finally ensue (with the bear playing its part). Tomboyish Gardner is a delight, though Lopez has little to do and makes an equally slight impression. Best are the interactions between pros Redford and Freeman, whose characters squabble and fuss like a longtime married couple. Co-writer Spragg adapted from his novel. 107m/C DVD. US Robert Redford, Morgan Freeman, Jennifer Lopez, Josh(ua) Lucas, Damian Lewis, Camryn Manheim, Becca Gardner; D: Lasse Hallstrom, Andrew Mondshein; W: Mark Spragg; C: Oliver Stapleton; M: Christopher Young.

An Unfinished Piece for a Player Piano 1977 A general's widow invites family and friends to a weekend house party in 1910 Russia. Romantic and familial entanglements begin to intrude in a lyrical adaptation of Chekov's play "Platonov." In Russian with English subtitles. 100m/C VHS, DVD. RU Alexander Kalyagin, Elena Solovei, Antonina Shuranova, Oleg Tabakov, Yuri Bogatyrev, Nikita Mikhalkov; D: Nikita Mikhalkov.

Unforgettable 1996 (R) Unfortunately, the film doesn't live up to its title. On-the-edge medical examiner David Krane (Liotta) has barely escaped conviction for his wife's brutal murder. Living under a cloud of suspicion, he turns to university researcher Martha Briggs (Fiorentino, wasted as a nerdy scientist), whose experiments in memory transference lead David to believe he can uncover the killer. But, like a Chinese puzzle box, one discovery only leads to a further complication. Too many, in fact, for the story to stay focused (and the ending is less than satisfying). 116m/C VHS, DVD. Ray Liotta, Linda Fiorentino, Peter Coyote, Christopher McDonald, Kim Cattrall, David Paymer, Kim Coates, Duncan Fraser, Garwin Sanford; D: John Dahl; W: Bill Geddie; C: Jeffrey Jur; M: Christopher Young.

An Unforgettable Summer 1994 The elegant Marie-Therese Dumitriu (Scott Thomas) has married Army officer Petre (Bleont) and tried to focus on maintaining a serene life, following the Communist takeover of Romania. When Petre is transferred to an isolated border town, he and his family are caught between what the Army demands and what is just. The local Bulgarian peasants are accused of atrocities against the soldiers and Petre is ordered to execute a group of them as an example—guilty or not. Set in 1925 and based on the short story "La Salade" by Petru Dumitriu. English, French, and Romanian with subtitles. 82m/C VHS. RO Kristin Scott Thomas, Claudiu Bleont, Olga Tudorache, George Constantin; D: Lucian Pintilie; W: Lucian Pintilie; C: Calin Ghibu; M: Anton Suteu.

The Unforgiven 1960 A western family is torn asunder when it is suspected that the eldest daughter is of Indian birth. Film takes place in 1850s' Texas. One of Huston's weakest ventures, but viewed in terms of 1950s' prejudices it has more resonance. Fine acting from all the cast, especially Gish. Watch for the stunning Indian attack scene. 123m/C VHS, DVD. Burt Lancaster, Audrey Hepburn, Lillian Gish, Audie Murphy, John Saxon, Charles Bickford, Doug McClure, Joseph Wiseman, Albert Salmi; D: John Huston.

Unforgiven 1992 (R) Will Munny (Eastwood) lives a quiet life with his stepchildren on his failing pig farm, but his desperado past catches up with him when the Schofield Kid invites him to a bounty hunt. Munny reluctantly agrees, mistakenly believing that once the killing is through he can take up his peaceful ways again. Enter sadistic sheriff Little Bill Daggett (Hackman), who doesn't want any gunmen messing up his town. Eastwood uses his own status as a screen legend to full advantage as the aging gunman who realizes too late that his past can never be forgotten. Director Eastwood is also in top form with his well-seasoned cast and myth-defying Old West realism. Surprising critical and boxoffice hit. 131m/C VHS, DVD, Blu-ray Disc. Clint Eastwood, Gene Hackman, Morgan Freeman, Richard Harris, Jaimz Woolvett, Saul Rubinek, Rob Campbell, Anthony James; D: Clint Eastwood; W: David Peoples; C: Jack N. Green; M: Lennie Niehaus. Oscars '92: Director (Eastwood), Film Editing, Picture, Support. Actor (Hackman); AFI '98: Top 100; British Acad. '92: Director (Eastwood), Film, Support. Actor (Hackman); Directors Guild '92: Director (Eastwood); Golden Globes '93: Director (Eastwood), Support. Actor (Hackman); L.A. Film Critics '92: Actor (Eastwood), Director (Eastwood), Film, Screenplay, Support. Actor (Hackman); N.Y. Film Critics '92: Support. Actor (Hackman); Nat. Soc. Film Critics '92: Director (Eastwood), Film, Screenplay, Support. Actor (Hackman).

The Unholy 1988 (R) A New Orleans priest battles a demon that's killing innocent parishioners. Confusing and heavy-handed. 100m/C VHS. Ben Cross, Hal Holbrook, Trevor Howard, Ned Beatty, William Russ, James Dennis (Jim) Carroll; D: Camilo Vila; W: Philip Yordan; M: Roger Bellon.

Unholy Four A Stranger Came Home 1954 An amnesiac returns home after three years to attempt to find out which of his three fishing buddies left him for dead. Confusing at times, but has some suspenseful moments. 80m/B VHS. GB Paulette Goddard, Paul Carpenter, William Sylvester, Patrick Holt, Russell Napier; D: Terence Fisher; W: Michael Carreras; C: Walter J. (Jimmy W.) Harvey; M: Ivor Slaney, Leonard Salzedo.

Unholy Rollers Leader of the Pack 1972 (R) Jennings stars as a factory worker who makes it big as a tough, violent roller derby star. Typical "Babes-on-Wheels" film that promises nothing and delivers even less. 88m/C VHS. Claudia Jennings, Louis Quinn, Betty Anne Rees, Roberta Collins, Alan Vint, Candice Roman; D: Vernon Zimmerman.

The Unholy Three 1930 Chaney remade his silent hit of 1925 for his first and only talking picture (he died before the film was released). The story is essentially the same. Chaney is a ventriloquist who, with his circus friends, work as scam artists and thieves. When an innocent man is accused of their crimes Chaney tries his ventriloquist tricks to come to

The Unholy Three 1925 Ventriloquist Chaney, working with other carnival cohorts, uses his talent to gain entrance to homes which he later robs. Things go awry when two of the gang strike out on their own and the victim is killed. When the wrong man is accused, his girl, one of Chaney's gang, begs Chaney to get him free, which he does by using his vocal talents. Chaney decides being a criminal is just too hard and goes back to his ventriloquism. 70m/B VHS. Lon Chaney Sr., Harry Earles, Victor McLaglen, Mae Busch, Matt Moore, Matthew Betz, William Humphreys; D: Tod Browning.

his aid, only in this version Chaney is exposed as a fraud and is sent to prison. Rumors that Chaney was a nut had him agreeing to appear in a "talkie" and he actually used five a different voices for his various roles. **75m/B VHS**, Lon Chaney Sr., Lila Lee, Elliot Nugent, Harry Earles, John Miljan; **D:** Jack Conway.

Unholy Wife ⅛½ 1957 A young woman plans to murder her wealthy husband, but her plan goes awry when she accidentally kills someone else. Muddled scenery. **94m/C VHS**, Rod Steiger, Diana Dors, Tom Tryon, Marie Windsor, Beulah Bondi; **D:** John Farrow.

Unhook the Stars ⅛⅛½ 1996 (R) Director Cassavetes does mom Rowlands proud (and she him) with the lead role of widowed Mildred, who discovers there's life after the kids leave the nest. At loose ends, Mildred befriends her wild young neighbor Monica (Tomei), who conveniently needs a babysitter for her solemn six-year-old son J.J. (Lloyd). Monica also tries to get Mildred to loosen up by taking her to a local joint, where French-Canadian trucker Tommy (Depardieu) knows a good woman when he sees one. Mildred makes some tentative steps towards independence and ve get to enjoy the stellar Rowlands once again. **105m/C VHS, DVD**, Gena Rowlands, Marisa Tomei, Gerard Depardieu, Moira Kelly, Jake Lloyd, David Sherrill, David Thornton; **D:** Nick Cassavetes; **W:** Nick Cassavetes, Helen Caldwell; **C:** Phedon Papamichael; **M:** Steven Hufsteter.

Unidentified Flying Oddball ⅛⅛½ 1979 (G) An astronaut and his robotic buddy find their spaceship turning into a time machine that throws them back into Arthurian times and at the mercy of Merlin the magician. Futuristic version of Twain's "A Connecticut Yankee at King Arthur's Court." **92m/C VHS, DVD**, Dennis Dugan, Jim Dae, Ron Moody, Kenneth More, Rodney Bewes; **D:** Russ Mayberry; **W:** Don Tait; **C:** Paul Beeson; **M:** Ronald Goodwin.

Uniform ⅛⅛ Zhitu 2003 A young man goes to work in the family shop in order to help pay his father's medical bills. When a policeman leaves his uniform to be tailored, the young man puts it on and gains instant respect, especially from Zheng, who is also leading another life—as a prostitute. Mandarin with subtitles. **92m/C DVD**, Ch'Kai Han, Hengli Liang, Hue Qin; **D:** Diao Yinan; **W:** Diao Yinan; **C:** Jingso'g Dong; **M:** Zi Wan.

The Uninvited ⅛⅛⅛ 1944 Roderick Fitzgerald (Milland) and his sister Pamela (Hussey) buy a house in Cornwall, only to find it is haunted. Doors open and close by themselves, strange scents fill the air, and they hear sobbing during the night. Soon they are visited by a woman (Russell) with an odd link to the house—her mother is the spirit who haunts the house. Chilling and unforgettable, this is one of the first films to deal seriously with ghosts. Based on the novel by Dorothy Macardle. **99m/B VHS**, Ray Milland, Ruth Hussey, Donald Crisp, Cornelia Otis Skinner, Gail Russell, Alan Napier, Dorothy Stickney; **D:** Lewis Allen; **W:** Dodie Smith, Frank Partos; **C:** Charles Bryant; **M:** Victor Young.

The Uninvited WOOF! 1988 A mutant cat goes berserk onboard a luxury yacht, killing the passengers one by one with big, nasty, pointy teeth. **89m/C VHS**, George Kennedy, Alex Cord, Clu Gulager, Toni Hudson, Eric Larson, Shari Shattuck, Austin Stoker; **D:** Greydon Clark.

Uninvited ⅛⅛½ 1992 (R) Grady is a mysterious old man who leads eight misfits to the top of a sacred mountain with the promise of finding gold. But the fortune hunters have trespassed in a sacred Indian burial ground and find their nightmares becoming a violent reality. **90m/C VHS, DVD**, Jack Elam, Christopher Boyer, Erin Noble, Bari Buckner, Jerry Rector, Zane Pradc, Dennis Gibbs, Ted Haler, Eno Brotto; **D:** Michael Derek Bohusz; **W:** Michael Derek Bohusz.

Uninvited Guest ⅛⅛½ 1999 (R) Smooth-talking Silk (Phifer) comes to the suburban home of Howard (Jackson) and Debbie (McCrow) and asks

---

to use their phone. The couple agree and let the stranger in and he promptly takes them and their friends captive. A twist these sorts of movies. Terrorist Casper has promised to sell a cluster bomb to some renegades, although he doesn't have it yet. A team of Navy SEALs is assigned to locate and take possession of the bomb before Casper gets to it. **93m/C VHS, DVD**, Tyler Christopher, Bentley Mitchum, John Simon Jones, Gary Murphy; **D:** Franklin A. Vallette; **W:** Steve Latshaw; **C:** Don E. Fauntleroy. **VIDEO**

Union City ⅛⅛ 1981 (R) Deborah Harry of "Blondie" fame gets a little edgy when someone steals the milk from the law. Intended as a film noir spoof, and not without some good moments. **87m/C VHS, DVD**, Deborah Harry, Everett McGill, Dennis Lipscomb, Pat Benatar, Irina Maleeva, Terina Lewis, Sam McMurray, Paul Andor, Tony Azito, CCH Pounder; **D:** Mark Reichert; **W:** Mark Reichert; **C:** Edward Lachman; **M:** Chris Stein.

Union Pacific ⅛⅛⅛ 1939 Full DeMille treatment highlights this saga about the building of America's first transcontinental railroad. Jeff Butler (McCrea) is the construction overseer who must battle saboteurs and Indians (although the U.S. Cavalry does arrive to save the day). He also gets to fall for self-sufficient postmistress Mollie Monahan (Stanwyck). DeMille borrowed the actual golden spike used to drive in the last rail in 1869 for his reenactment of the completion celebration. Based on the book "Trouble Shooters" by Ernest Haycox. **136m/B VHS, DVD**, Joel McCrea, Barbara Stanwyck, Robert Preston, Brian Donlevy, Akim Tamiroff, Lynne Overman, Robert Barrat, Anthony Quinn, Stanley Ridges, Henry Kolker, Evelyn Keyes, Regis Toomey; **D:** Cecil B. DeMille; **W:** Walter DeLeon, Jesse Lasky Jr., C. Gardner Sullivan; **C:** Victor Milner.

Union Station ⅛⅛ 1950 Holden plays the chief of the railway police for Chicago's Union Station. He learns the station is to be used as a ransom drop in a kidnapping; but for all his security, the main thug gets away with the money, and the hunt is on. Good acting raises this film above the ordinary. **80m/B VHS**, William Holden, Barry Fitzgerald, Nancy Olson, Jan Sterling, Lee Marvin, Allene Roberts, Lyle Bettger; **D:** Rudolph Maté; **C:** Daniel F. Fapp.

United 93 ⅛⅛⅛ 2006 (R) Greengrass' intense, emotional drama covers the hijacking of United Airlines Flight 93 on September 11, 2001. Events alternate between what is happening onboard as the passengers and crew try to disarm the hijackers and what is happening at the FAA, air defense headquarters, and airport control towers as realization dawns about the scope of the disaster and what, if anything, can be done. The Boeing 757 eventually crashed near Shanksville, Pennsylvania, with a total loss of life. Greengrass filmed in the U.K., and a number of the cast are nonprofessionals playing themselves. **111m/C DVD, US** David Alan Basche, Richard Bekins, Susan Blommaert, Christian Clemenson, Ray Charleson, Gregg Henry, Polly Adams, Denny Dillon, Khalid Abdalla, Lewis Alsamari, Ben Sliney, Maj. James Fox, Trish Gates, Cheyenne Jackson; **D:** Paul Greengrass; **W:** Paul Greengrass; **C:** Barry Ackroyd; **M:** John Powell, British Acad. '06: Director (Greengrass), Film Editing.

U.S. Marshals ⅛⅛ 1998 (PG-13) Jones reprises his Oscar-winning role from "The Fugitive" as the hound dog U.S. Marshal Sam Gerard in this lackluster sequel. Gerard tracks down Sheridan (Snipes) who is framed for a double homicide of two federal agents. Gerard's probing reveals that Sheridan really isn't the average joe he seems, and the presence of shifty agent Downey Jr. further confirms Gerard's suspicions of a government cover-up. Jones remains solid in a popular role, supported well by his sidekick Cosmo (Pantolino). The stunts equal if not better its predecessor, yet a poorly developed Sheridan, compounded by Snipes's lack of intensity drag this chase movie down to a slow crawl. **133m/C VHS, DVD**, Tommy Lee Jones, Robert Downey Jr., Wesley Snipes, Joe Pantoliano, Kate Nelligan, Irene Jacob, Daniel Roebuck, Tom Wood, LaTanya Richardson Jackson, Michael Paul Chan; **D:** Stuart Baird; **W:** John Pogue; **C:** Andrze Bartkowiak; **M:** Jerry Goldsmith.

U.S. Navy SEALS: Dead or Alive ⅛½ 2002 (R) Lots of action, not much plot, which doesn't really matter with these sorts of movies. Terrorist Casper has promised to sell a cluster bomb to some renegades, although he doesn't have it yet. A team of Navy SEALs is assigned to locate and take possession of the bomb before Casper gets to it. **93m/C VHS, DVD**, Tyler Christopher, Bentley Mitchum, John Simon Jones, Gary Murphy; **D:** Franklin A. Vallette; **W:** Steve Latshaw; **C:** Don E. Fauntleroy. **VIDEO**

U.S. Seals ⅛⅛ 1998 (R) Absolutely undistinguished action flick pits a team of Navy SEALs against pirates from Kazakhstan. The heroes are jut-jawed guys with crewcuts and cute kids. Lots of stuff blows up. Production values are strictly of the made-for-cable quality. **90m/C DVD**, Jim Fitzpatrick, Greg Collins, J. Kenneth Campbell, Marshall Teague, Sophia Crawford; **D:** Isaac Florentine; **W:** Stephen (Steve) Edwards. **VIDEO**

U.S. Seals 2 ⅛½ 2001 (R) An ex-SEAL is planning to launch a nuclear strike on the U.S. from a secret Russian missile base unless the good guys can stop him. **95m/C VHS, DVD**, Damian Chapa, Mike Worth, Marshall Teague, Sophia Crawford; **D:** Isaac Florentine; **W:** Stephen (Steve) Edwards. **VIDEO**

The U.S. Vs. John Lennon ⅛⅛ 2006 (PG-13) A look at peace advocate John Lennon's post-Beatles contributions to music and popular culture that leaves out the man's dark edges (the documentary was made with the cooperation of Yoko Ono, so no surprise there). The focus is on the Nixon's administration paranoid view of Lennon as an enemy to national security and his subjection to wiretapping, surveillance, and deportation order. Music from Lennon's solo career highlights the visuals and it features an odd group of talking heads, from Geraldo Rivera to Gore Vidal. **95m/C DVD. US** David Lead, John Scheinfeld; **W:** David Leaf, John Scheinfeld; **C:** James Mathers.

Universal Soldier ⅛⅛ 1992 (R) A reporter discovers a secret government project to design perfect robo-soldiers by using the bodies of dead GIs, including tough guys Lundgren and Van Damme who were killed in Vietnam. But the knowledge is going to get her killed until Van Damme has flashbacks of his past (the soldier's memories have supposedly been erased) and agrees to help her. Lundgren doesn't have the same compassion and goes after them both. Big-budget thriller with some good action sequences and a lot of violence. **98m/C VHS, DVD, UMD**, Jean-Claude Van Damme, Dolph Lundgren, Ally Walker, Ed O'Ross, Jerry Orbach; **D:** Roland Emmerich; **W:** Dean Devlin, Christopher Leitch, Richard Rothstein; **C:** Karl Walter Lindenlaub; **M:** Christopher Franke.

Unknown Origin ⅛⅛ The Alien Within; Roger Corman Presents: The Alien Within 1995 (R) Scientific crew is stuck in an underwater installation with a deadly parasite. It's "Aliens" under the sea but a few twists will tweak your interest. **75m/C VHS, DVD**, Roddy McDowall, Melanie Shatner, Alex Hyde-White, Don Stroud; **D:** Scott Levy; **W:** Alex Simon; **M:** Christopher Lennertz. **CABLE**

Unknown Powers WOOF! 1980 (PG) Science and drama are combined to examine ESP and magic. Are they gifts or curses, and how are peoples' lives affected by them? Members of the cast introduce various sections of this totally inept film. **97m/C VHS, DVD**, Samantha Eggar, Jack Palance, Will Geer, Roscoe Lee Browne; **D:** Don Como.

The Unknown Ranger WOOF! ⅛½ 1936 Allen's first cowboy role has him toiling a gang of rustlers. The real highlight turns out to be the battle between his horse and a wild stallion. Eat your heart out, Trigger! **57m/B VHS**, Robert "Tex" Allen, Harry Woods, Martha Tibbetts, Hal Taliaferro, Robert "Buzzy" Henry; **D:** Spencer Gordon Bennet.

United States of Leland ⅛⅛ 2003 (R) Low-key high school student Leland (Gosling) senselessly stabs his ex-girlfriend's autistic brother to death at the beginning of this bleak flick. Director Hoge then spends the rest of his cebut film juggling the pieces attempting to define Leland's motivation. Was it his heroin-addicted girlfriend (Malone) who left him for her dealer? Or his emotionally absent novelist father, Albert (Spacey)? Or something else? Meanwhile, Pearl (Cheadle), an aspiring but struggling writer, is Leland's juvenile detention counselor who sees in him an opportunity for his first novel and some lively scenes, and Spacey, Cheadle, and Malone give capable performances, there's no sustaining this disjointed piece, which never encounters province quences. While those encounters province the hidden agenda has its own consequences. **108m/C DVD. US** Ryan Gosling, Don Cheadle, Chris Klein, Jena Malone, Lena Olin, Kevin Spacey, Michelle Williams, Martin Donovan, Ann Magnuson, Kerry Washington, Sherilyn Fenn, Matt Malloy, Michael Pena, Fon Canada, Troy Winbush, Yolonda Ross, Jim Haynie, Kimberly Scott, Angela Paton, Michael Welch; **D:** Matthew Ryan Hoge; **W:** Matthew Ryan Hoge; **C:** James Glennor; **M:** Jeremy Enigk.

Universal Soldier 2: Brothers in Arms ⅛⅛ 1998 (R) Cable actioner not to be confused with the 1999 big-screen sequel "Universal Soldier: The Return" starring Jean-Claude Van Damme. Here, Luc Devereaux (Battaglia), who works for the top-secret UniSol military operation, teams up with journalist Veronica Roberts (West) to expose UniSol's re-animate dead soldiers into unstoppable killing machines. **93m/C VHS, Matt Battaglia, Chandra West, Gary Busey, Jeff Wincott; **D:** Jeff Woolnough; **W:** Peter M. Lenkov; **C:** Russ Goozee; **M:** Ivan Doroschuk, John Kastner, Steve Pecile. **CABLE**

Universal Soldier 3: Unfinished Business ⅛½ 1998 (R) An ex-soldier and a journalist try to stop a billion-dollar robbery and discover the deadly (and dead) military men are acting once again. **95m/C VHS, Matt Battaglia, Chandra West, Burt Reynolds, Jeff Wincott; **D:** Jeff Woolnough; **W:** Peter M. Lenkov; **C:** Russ Goozee; **M:** Ivan Doroschuk, John Kastner, Steve Pecile. **CABLE**

Universal Soldier: The Return ⅛⅛ 1999 (R) The creators of superwarrior Van Damme have double-crossed him and he's out to get even in this sequel (although technically it's the fourth installment after two straight-to-cable releases). After Defense Department cutbacks short circuit the Universal Soldier program, the cyborgs start a rebellion led by an evil computer. Van Damme must battle the renegade warriors while attempting to not muss his hair. The Muscles from Brussels goes back to a proven winner after a series of boxoffice stinkers in hopes that he can kick-start his flagging career. **82m/C VHS**, Jean-Claude Van Damme, Bill White, Daniel von Bargen, Heidi Schanz, Xander Berkeley, Justin Lazard; **D:** Mic Rodgers; **W:** John Fasano, William Malone; **C:** Michael A. Benson; **M:** Don Davis.

The Unkissed Bride ⅛ Mother Goose A Go-Go 1966 (PG) A young newlywed couple are driven to distraction by the husband's inexplicable fainting spells and his strange obsession with Mother Goose, plots to kill the object of her intentions. Ghoulish as it is, the picture is really top-notch. **60m/B VHS, DVD**, Tommy Kirk, Anne Helm, Danica D'Hondt, Henny Youngman; **D:** Jack H. Harris.

The Unknown ⅛⅛½ 1927 Typically morbid Chaney fare has him working as a circus freak while trying to win the heart of his assistant. After drastic romancing he's still rejected by her, so he plots to kill the object of her intentions. Ghoulish as it is, the picture is really top-notch. **60m/B VHS, DVD**, Lon Chaney Sr., Norman Kerry, Joan Crawford, Nick De Ruiz, Frank Lanning, John St. Polis; **D:** Tod Browning.

Unknown Island ⅛½ 1948 Scientists travel to a legendary island where dinosaurs supposedly still exist. Bogus dinosaurs and cliche script. **76m/C VHS, DVD**, Virginia Grey, Philip Reed, Richard Denning, Barton MacLane; **D:** Jack Bernhard; **W:** Jack Harvey, Robert T. Shannon; **C:** Fred W. Jacman; **M:** Ralph Stanley.

The Unknown Soldier ⚔️⚔️½
1998 Fine performances in an ultimately depressing drama, with some unexpected twists, focusing on the tragedy of war. When aristocratic Sophia Carey's (Aubrey) ancestral home is turned into a private hospital for WWI soldiers, she seriously takes up her nursing duties. One of her latest patients is an amnesiac, initially mute soldier nicknamed Angel (Mavers) by the men who rescued him in France. Sophia falls hopelessly in love with the traumatized Angel but the working-class Jenny (McGuckin) claims Angel is actually her fiance John and the military police believe he's a deserter wanted for murder. **180m/C VHS, DVD.** *GB* Juliet Aubrey, Gary Mavers, Aislin McGuckin; *D:* David Drury; *W:* Peter Barwood. **TV**

Unknown White Male ⚔️⚔️⚔️½
2005 (PG-13) Spellbinding documentary following the lost life of Doug Bruce, a man with retrograde amnesia. Two years prior Doug took a subway trip to Coney Island; once he arrived he didn't know where he was or why he was there. Since that time, for reasons no one knows, his entire memory has been wiped out. His family, his girlfriend, his home have become pieces in a puzzle he's unable to fit back together. Completely absorbing and provocative. Would make for a wicked psycho-drama. **88m/C DVD.** *US* *D:* Rupert Murray; *C:* Orlando Stuart; *M:* Mukul.

Unknown World ⚔️
1951 A group of scientists tunnel to the center of the Earth to find a refuge from the dangers of the atomic world. Big start winds down fast. Director Terry Morse sometimes credited as Terrell O. Morse. **73m/B VHS, DVD.** Bruce Kellogg, Marilyn Nash, Victor Kilian, Jim Bannon; *D:* Terry Morse; *M:* Ernest Gold.

Unlawful Entry ⚔️⚔️
1992 (R) After a break-in, Karen and Michael Carr naturally call the cops. Handsome, polite policeman Pete Davis responds to the call and agrees to help burglar-proof their home. But Pete has some definite quirks—he falls for the beauteous Karen and begins stalking the couple, deciding to get rid of Michael in order to have his wife. A lurid combination of the worst moments of "Internal Affairs" and "Fatal Attraction" undermines this usually talented cast. **107m/C VHS, DVD.** Kurt Russell, Ray Liotta, Madeleine Stowe, Roger E. Mosley, Ken Lerner, Deborah Offner, Carmen Argenziano, Andy Romano, Barry W. Blaustein, Dick Miller; *D:* Jonathan Kaplan; *W:* Lewis Colick; *C:* Jamie Anderson; *M:* James Horner.

Unlawful Passage ⚔️⚔️
1994 (R) Vacation turns into a nightmare when a man's wife is kidnapped. **?m/C VHS.** Lee Horsley, William Zabka, Felicity Waterman; *D:* Camilo Vila; *W:* Peter Dixon; *C:* Henry Vargas.

Unleashed ⚔️⚔️
Danny the Dog **2005 (R)** Fight scenes are taken to seat-jolting heights by renowned martial-arts choreographer Yuen Wo Ping in this live-action cyberpunk cartoon starring Jet Li as Danny the human pit bull. Enslaved from childhood and conditioned to kill without conscience by his ruthless London mobster "owner" Bart (Hoskins), Danny maims and mutilates delinquent debtors when his collar is removed. With the collar he's passive and docile. His accidental liberation sends him to the only person who was ever kind to him, a blind piano tuner (Freeman), who through piano music helps connect him with his humanity. The gangster, alas, returns for Danny resulting in one last showdown of canine love and loyalty. **102m/C DVD, UMD, HD DVD.** *US FR GB HK* Jet Li, Morgan Freeman, Bob Hoskins, Michael Jenn, Kerry Gordon, Christian Gazio, Carole Ann Wilson; *D:* Louis Leterrier; *W:* Luc Besson; *C:* Pierre Morel; *M:* Massive Attack.

Unlikely Angel ⚔️⚔️½
1997 Brassy singer Ruby Diamond (Parton) dies suddenly in an accident but is having some trouble entering heaven. St. Peter (McDowall) thinks she's a likely prospect but Ruby needs a few more good deeds before she can get her wings. So she's sent to help a frazzled widower (Kerwin) who's the father of two lonely preteens.

92 *VideoHound's Golden Movie Retriever*

90m/C VHS, DVD. Dolly Parton, Roddy McDowall, Brian Kerwin; *D:* Michael Switzer.

An Unmarried Woman ⚔️⚔️⚔️
1978 (R) Suddenly divorced by her husband of 17 years, a woman deals with change. She enters the singles scene, copes with her daughter's growing sexuality, and encounters a new self-awareness. Mazursky puts real people on screen from start to finish. **124m/C VHS, DVD.** Jill Clayburgh, Alan Bates, Cliff Gorman, Michael Murphy; *D:* Paul Mazursky; *W:* Paul Mazursky; *M:* Bill Conti. Cannes '78: Actress (Clayburgh); L.A. Film Critics '78: Screenplay; N.Y. Film Critics '78: Screenplay; Natl. Soc. Film Critics '78: Screenplay.

Unmasked Part 25 ⚔️½
1988 A second-generation serial killer takes up where dad left off. This one is intended to be a parody of slasher films, but it's still very bloody. **85m/C VHS.** *GB* Gregory Cox, Fiona Evans, Edward Brayshaw, Debbie Lee London; *D:* Anders Palm.

Unmasking the Idol ⚔️
1986 A suave hero with tongue firmly in check battles Ninja warlords. Sequel to "Order of the Black Eagle." **90m/C VHS.** *GB* Ian Hunter, William T. Hicks, Charles K. Bibby; *D:* Worth Keeter.

The Unnamable ⚔️
1988 The adaptation of the H.P. Lovecraft story about a particular New England ancestral home haunted by a typically Lovecraftian bloodthirsty demon borne of a woman hundreds of years before. College students, between trysts, investigate the myths about it. Uncut version, unseen in theatres, available only on video good for a few giggles and thrills. **87m/C VHS.** Charles King, Mark Kinsey Stephenson, Alexandra Durrell, Laura Albert, Eben Ham, Blane Wheatley, Mark Parra, Katrin Alexandre; *D:* Jean-Paul Ouellette; *W:* Jean-Paul Ouellette; *C:* Tom Fraser.

The Unnamable 2: The Statement of Randolph Carter ⚔️½
H.P. Lovecraft's The Unnamable Returns; The Unnamable Returns **1992 (R)** Randolph Carter is investigating a series of murders at Miskatonic University. Evidence leads Carter back to a 17th-century warlock who had the misfortune to summon an evil creature known as Alyda. The half-demon, half-woman now wants to permanently return to the mortal plane and every new victim just helps her evil purpose along. Based on a story by H.P. Lovecraft. **104m/C VHS, DVD.** Mark Kinsey Stephenson, John Rhys-Davies, David Warner, Julie Strain, Maria Ford, Charles Klausmeyer; *D:* Jean-Paul Ouellette; *W:* Jean-Paul Ouellette; *C:* Greg Gardiner.

Unnatural ⚔️⚔️½
1952 A mad scientist creates a souless child from the genes of a murderer and a prostitute. The child grows up to be the beautiful Neff, who makes a habit of seducing and destroying men. Dark, arresting film from a very popular German story. **90m/B VHS, DVD.** Hildegarde Knef, Erich von Stroheim, Karl-Heinz Boehm, Harry Meyen, Harry Helm, Denise Vernac, Julia Koschka; *D:* Arthur Maria Rabenalt.

Unnatural Causes ⚔️⚔️⚔️
1986 A dying Vietnam vet believes that his illness is the result of exposure to Agent Orange. With the help of a VA counselor, they lobby for national programs to assist other veterans who have been exposed to the chemical and together bring publicity to the issue. A TV drama that is exceptionally well-acted. **96m/C VHS, DVD.** John Ritter, Patti LaBelle, Alfre Woodard, John Sayles, Sean McCann, John Vargas, Gwen E. Davis; *D:* Lamont Johnson; *W:* John Sayles; *M:* Charles Fox. **TV**

Unnatural Pursuits ⚔️⚔️
1991 Playwright Simon Gray's black comic look at a British playwright's sojourn from London to L.A., Dallas, and New York and the Broadway debut of his new work. Alcoholic Hamish Partt (Bates), in the throes of a midlife crisis, is plagued by ego, indignities, and hostile actors, audiences, and critics as he tries desperately to work. Made for British TV. **60m/C VHS.** *GB* Alan Bates, Keith Szarabajka, Deborah Rush, John Mahoney, Tom Hickey, Richard Wilson, David Healy, Jack Gilpin, Paul Zimet, Bob Balaban; *W:* Simon Gray. **TV**

Uno ⚔️⚔️½
2004 Living in Oslo with his dying father, withdrawn mother, and mentally-challenged brother proves too much for 25-year-old David (Hennie) who seeks refuge with the wrong crowd at the local gym and ends up under arrest. The distasteful change of scenery makes him grasp the meaning of life so he rats out the bad guys to get out of jail and rushes to his dad's deathbed to make amends. Unfortunately the crooks aren't so forgiving and unleash an overwhelming wave of violence that's not for the meek. Lead actor Hennie also wrote and directed. In Norwegian with English subtitles. **99m/C DVD.** Bjorn Floberg, Aksel Hennie, Nicolai Cleve Broch, Espen Juul Kristiansen, Ahmed Zeyan, Martin Skaug; *D:* Aksel Hennie; *W:* Aksel Hennie; *C:* John Andreas Andersen; *M:* Tom McRae. **VIDEO**

An Unreasonable Man ⚔️⚔️⚔️
2006 Straightforward look at the career of crusading consumer advocate Ralph Nader and his presidential aspirations. The self-righteous workaholic frequently exasperated his colleagues and was heavily criticized for siphoning votes away from Al Gore during the contested 2000 election. Documentary is a mix of contemporary interviews and archival footage. **122m/C DVD.** *US* Ralph Nader; *D:* Henriette Mantel, Stephen Skrovan; *C:* Mark Raker; *M:* Joe Kraemer.

An Unremarkable Life ⚔️⚔️
1989 (PG) Two aging sisters live symbiotically together, until one views the other's romantic attachment to a charming widower as destructive to her own life. **97m/C VHS, DVD.** Shelley Winters, Patricia Neal, Mako, Rochelle Oliver, Charles S. Dutton, Lily Knight; *D:* Amin Qamar Chaudhri.

The Unsaid ⚔️⚔️½
The Ties That Bind **2001 (R)** After psychologist Michael Hunter's (Garcia) teenaged son commits suicide, he becomes estranged from his wife and daughter and gives up hands-on therapy. But he's persuaded by his former student, Barbara (Polo), to look into one of her social work cases. Now nearly-18, Tommy (Kartheiser) discovered the body of his murdered mother when he was a boy and his father (Bottoms) is in prison for the crime. But Tommy has been keeping a lot of secrets. **110m/C DVD.** *US CA* Andy Garcia, Vincent Kartheiser, Teri Polo, Linda Cardellini, Sam Bottoms, August Schellenberg, Chelsea Field, Trevor Blumas, Brendan Fletcher; *D:* Tom McLoughlin; *W:* Miguel Tejada-Flores, Scott Williams; *C:* Lloyd Ahern II; *M:* Don Davis.

Unsane ⚔️⚔️
dell'Assassino; Tenebrae; Sotto gli Occhi dell'Assassino; Tenebrae; Terenbre **1982** A mystery novelist realizes that a series of bizarre murders strangely resembles the plot of his latest book. Bloody fun from Argento. **91m/C VHS, DVD.** *IT* Anthony (Tony) Franciosa, John Saxon, Daria Nicolodi, Giuliano Gemma, Christian Borromeo, Mirella D'Angelo, Veronica Lario, Ania Pieroni, Carola Stagnaro, John Steiner, Lara Wendel; *D:* Dario Argento; *W:* Dario Argento; *C:* Luciano Tovoli; *M:* The Goblins, Claudio Simonetti.

The Unseen ⚔️½
1980 Three young women from a TV station are covering a story in a remote area of California. Before nightfall, two are horribly killed, leaving the third to come face to face with the terror. **91m/C VHS.** Barbara Bach, Sydney Lassick, Stephen Furst; *D:* Peter Foleg.

Unseen Evil ⚔️
1999 (R) A group of archeological students accompany their professor to an ancient burial ground for a dig. Unfortunately, the prof wants to uncover a powerful alien force and is prepared to sacrifice anyone necessary. **90m/ C VHS, DVD.** Richard Hatch, Tim Thomerson, Robbie (Reist) Rist, Cindi Braun, Frank Ruotolo, Jere Jon, Cindy Pena; *D:* Jay Woelfel; *W:* Scott Spears. **VIDEO**

Unsettled Land ⚔️⚔️
1988 (PG) Young Israeli settlers try to survive the elements and Bedouin attackers in Palestine during the 1920s. **109m/C VHS.** *IS* Kelly McGillis, John Shea, Amon Zadok, Christine Boisson; *D:* Uri Barbash.

Unshackled ⚔️⚔️½
2000 (PG-13) Slightly overdone melodrama tells the true story of Harold Morris, who was sentenced to life at 20 for armed robbery and murder and later helped organize the first interracial basketball team at Georgia

---

State Prison. The team led the way to fully integrating the prison. Eventually paroled, Morris goes on to steer kids away from drugs and crime. Often heavy-handed, but the message is supposed to be inspirational (hence the PG13 rating), and it will be, to some. **106m/C VHS, DVD.** Burgess Jenkins, James Black, Stacy Keach, Morgan Fairchild; *D:* Bart Patton; *W:* Harold Morris; *C:* Paul Varrieur; *M:* Jeffrey Scott Pearson.

The Unsinkable Molly Brown ⚔️⚔️⚔️
1964 A spunky backwoods girl is determined to break into the upper crust of Denver's high society and along the way survives the sinking of the Titanic. This energetic version of the Broadway musical contains many Meredith Willson ("Music Man") songs and lots of hokey, good-natured fun. ♫Colorado Is My Home; Leadville Johnny Brown (Soliloquy); I Ain't Down Yet; Belly Up to the Bar, Boys; He's My Friend; I've Already Started; The Beautiful People of Denver; I May Never Fall in Love with You; Up Where the People Are. **128m/C VHS, DVD.** Debbie Reynolds, Harve Presnell, Ed Begley Sr., Martita Hunt, Hermione Baddeley; *D:* Charles Walters; *C:* Daniel F. Fapp; *M:* Meredith Willson.

Unspeakable ⚔️⚔️½
2000 James (Cline) and Alice Fheliepps have a nasty, unsatisfying marriage until a car accident turns their life together into a true horror. From that premise, Chad Ferrin spins out a relatively realistic tale of madness and murder. For hard-core horror fans only. **81m/C DVD.** Robert Cline, Timothy Muskatell, Tina Birchfield, Wolf Dangler; *D:* Chad Ferrin; *W:* Chad Ferrin; *C:* Nicholas Loizides.

Unspeakable ⚔️½
2002 (R) A shrink is sickened when her fancy-pants mind machine shows lots of icky and—could it be?—inhuman stuff going on inside the serial killer's head. Things get funky when he files the coop after outlasting the electric chair, making the hotheaded warden (Hopper) lose face (really). **109m/C VHS, DVD.** Michele J. Wolff, Marco Rodriguez, Dina Meyer, Lance Henriksen, Dennis Hopper, Luke McCoubrey, Jim Helton, Jonah Moran, Ron Pantane, Adam Zuckerman; *D:* Thomas J. Wright; *W:* Luke McCoubrey; *C:* Antonio Calvache; *M:* Jeff Marsh. **VIDEO**

The Unstoppable Man ⚔️½
1959 The son of an American businessman is kidnapped while they are in London. No pushover he, dad develops his own plan to destroy the criminals, eventually pursuing them with a flame thrower. **68m/B VHS.** *GB* Cameron Mitchell, Marius Goring, Harry H. Corbett, Lois Maxwell, Denis Gilmore; *D:* Terry Bishop.

Unstrung Heroes ⚔️⚔️½
1995 (PG) Semi-autobiographical tale of Steven Lidz (Watt), growing up in 1960s California with a mother who is dying of cancer (MacDowell) and a nutty professor-type father (Turturro) who refuses to accept her illness. A desperate Steven goes to live with his two oddball uncles (Richards and Chaykin) who provide understanding and insight for the youngster, as well as a new name, Franz. Moving and quirky without being sappy. Keaton's feature debut avoids what would've been easy stereotypes. Based on the autobiography by Franz Lidz. **93m/C VHS, DVD.** Andie MacDowell, John Turturro, Maury Chaykin, Nathan Watt, Kendra Krull; *D:* Diane Keaton; *W:* Richard LaGravenese; *C:* Phedon Papamichael; *M:* Thomas Newman.

Unsuitable Job for a Woman ⚔️⚔️
1982 Independent Cordelia Gray, following the death of her boss, takes over his detective agency and gets involved with murder. Based on the novel by P.D. James. **94m/C VHS.** *GB* Pippa Guard, Paul Freeman, Billie Whitelaw; *D:* Christopher Petit.

The Untamable ⚔️⚔️
1923 Unusual silent about volatile woman suffering from schizophrenia. **65m/B VHS.** Gladys Walton, Malcolm McGregor, John St. Polis, Etta Lee; *D:* Herbert Blache.

Untamed Heart ⚔️⚔️½
(PG-13) Adam (Slater), the painfully shy busboy with a heart condition, loves Caroline (Tomei), the bubbly waitress, from afar. She doesn't notice him until he saves

her from some would-be rapists and their love blooms in the coffee shop where they both work. Tomei and Slater are both strong in the leads and Perez, as Caroline's best buddy Cindy, hurls comic barbs with ease. Charmingly familiar surroundings help set this formulaic romance apart. Filmed on location in Minneapolis. **102m/C VHS, DVD.** Christian Slater, Marisa Tomei, Rosie Perez, Kyle Secor, Willie Garson; *D:* Tony Bill; *W:* Tom Sierchio. *C:* Jost Vacano. *M:* Cliff Eidelman. MTV Movie Awards '93: Most Desirable Male (Slater), Kiss (Christian Slater/Marisa Tomei); John Barry.

Until September 🐾🐾 1984 (R) An American tourist becomes stranded in Paris. She meets and falls in love with a married banker while she is stuck in her hotel. Routine romance. **96m/C VHS, DVD.** Karen Allen, Thierry Lhermitte, Christopher Cazenove, Johanna Pavlis; *D:* Richard Marquand; *M:* John Barry.

Until the End of the World 🐾🐾🐾½ *Bis ans Ende der Welt* 1991 (R) Convoluted road movie set in 1999 follows the travails of Sam Farber (Hurt) through 15 cities in eight countries on four continents as he is chased by Dommartin, her lover (Neill), a bounty hunter, a private detective, and tank robbers, until all wind up in the Australian outback. And this is only the first half of the movie. Visually stunning, unexpectedly humorous, with excellent performances from an international cast. Footage created with high definition (HDTV) video technology is a technological first. The soundtrack features Lou Reed, David Byrne, U2, and others. **158m/C VHS, AU GE FR** William Hurt, Solveig Dommartin, Sam Neil, Max von Sydow, Ruediger Vogler, Ernie Dingo, Jeanne Moreau, David Gulpilil; *D:* Wim Wenders; *W:* Wim Wenders, Peter Carey; *C:* Robby Muller; *M:* Graeme Revell.

Until They Get Me 🐾½ 1918

Until They Sail 🐾🐾½ 1957 Soap opera set in New Zealand during WWII. Plot centers around the lives of four sisters involved in love and murder. Dee's film debut. Based on a story by James Michener. **95m/B VHS.** Jean Simmons, Joan Fontaine, Paul Newman, Piper Laurie, Charles Drake, Sandra Dee, Wally Cassel, Alan Napier; *D:* Robert Wise; *W:* Robert Anderson.

Untold Scandal 🐾🐾 *Joseon Namnyeo Sangyeol Ji Sa* 2003 The scandalous 18th-century French novel "Les Liaisons Dangereuses" is transported to Korea during the publicly conservative (and privately wicked) Chosun dynasty. Jo Weon (Bae) is a pleasure-seeking artist whose manipulative cousin, Lacy Jo (Mi-suk Lee), wants him to seduce virginal teen Soh-ok (So-yeon Lee), who's about to become her husband's concubine. Jo Weon is more interested in the virtuous Catholic widow, Lady Jeong (Jeon), as a challenge. If you've seen any of the other film versions of the novel, you know what's coming. Korean with subtitles. **124m/C DVD.** KN Bae Yong-jun, Lee Mi-suk, Jeon Do-yeon; *D:* Je-yong Lee; *C:* Kim Byeong-il.

The Untold Story 🐾🐾 *Story: Human Meat/Roast Pork Buns; Ba Xian Fan Dian Zhi Ren Rou Cha Shao Bao; Bunman; Human Meat Pies* 1993 New restaurant owner Wong discovers the previous owner and his family mysteriously disappeared. Then the police detective (Lee) on the case makes a very shocking discovery. Modern cult classic includes footage cut from the original Hong Kong release and its violence is not for the squeamish. Cantonese with subtitles. **96m/C VHS, DVD. HK** Anthony Wong, Danny Lee, Er'ily Kwan, Fui-On Shing; *D:* Herman Yau, Danny Lee.

The Untold Story of Emmett Louis Till 🐾🐾🐾 2005 (PG-13) Documentary was released to coincide with the 50th anniversary of the 1955 murder of Till, a 14-year-old African American from Chicago who went to visit his grandfather in Money, Mississippi, where he was tortured and killed for allegedly whistling at a white woman. Till's murder became a pivotal moment in the civil rights movement. The Justice Department reopened the case when new evidence came to light, thanks to the years-long investigation of director Beauchamp. Includes TV and newsreel footage and numerous interviews. **70m/C DVD.** *D:* Keith Beauchamp; *C:* Rondrick Cowins, Skay Tang; *M:* Jim Papoulis.

The Untouchables 🐾🐾🐾½ 1987 (R) Big-budget, fast-paced, and exciting re-evaluation of the popular TV series about the real-life battle between Treasury officer Eliot Ness (Costner) and crime boss Al Capone (De Niro) in 1920s Chicago. History sometimes takes a back seat to Hollywood's imagination in the screenplay, but it doesn't really matter since there are splendid performances by De Niro and Connery as Ness' mentor Jimmy Malone to fine job showing the change in Ness from naive idealism to steely conviction. Beautifully filmed with excellent special effects. Note DePalma's long train station "Battleship Potemkin." **119m/C VHS, DVD, Blu-ray Disc, HD DVD.** Kevin Costner, Sean Connery, Robert De Niro, Andy Garcia, Charles Martin Smith, Billy Drago, Richard Bradford, Jack Kehoe; *D:* Brian De Palma; *W:* David Mamet; *C:* Stephen Burum; *M:* Ennio Morricone. Oscars '87: Support. Actor (Connery); Golden Globes '88: Support. Actor (Connery); Natl. Bd. of Review '87: Support.

Untraceable 🐾½ 2008 (R) Agent Jennifer Marsh (Lane) is an FBI "cyber-crime" expert who must find a killer whose elaborate, torturous murders are broadcast live on the Internet. The twist? The more hits the killer's website gets, the faster he kills his victims. Eventually, Marsh must work to stop the killer and protect her own family as well. Cynical movie that aspires to condemn people's love of exploitative violence while serving up lots of violent exploitation without a shred of irony to redeem it. **100m/C DVD. US** Diane Lane, Billy Burke, Colin Hanks, Joseph Cross, Mary Beth Hurt, Tyrone Giordano, Perla Haney-Jardine, Peter Lewis, Tim De Zarn; *D:* Gregory Hoblit; *W:* Allison Burnett, Robert Fyvolent, Mark R. Brinker; *C:* Anastas Michos; *M:* Christopher Young.

Unveiled 🐾🐾 *Fremde Haut; Foreign Skin* 2005 Translator Fariba (Tabatabai) is persecuted in Iran because she's a lesbian. She flees the country and takes the identity of male refugee Siamak (Akhavan), who commits suicide before learning that the he has been granted temporary asylum in Germany. Passing herself off as a young man, Fariba gets a job in a factory where she meets Anne (Samsa), who seemingly never realizes that the male she is infatuated with is actually a woman. But then Fariba's ruse begins to unravel. Farsi and German with subtitles. **97m/C DVD. GE** Jasmin Tabatabai, Anneke Kim Samsa, Navid Akhavan, Hinnerk Schoenemann, Jens Munchow; *D:* Angelina Maccarone; *W:* Judith Kaufmann, Angelina Maccarone; *C:* Judith Kaufmann; *M:* Hartmut Ewert, Jacob Hansons.

Unveiled 🐾🐾½ 1994 (R) Stephanie Montgomery's (Zane) friend falls victim to a killer in Marrakesh. So Steph sets out to trap the killer, with the help of government official Peter (Hubley). **103m/C VHS.** Lisa Zane, Whip Hubley, Nicholas Cinlund, Martha Gehman; *D:* William Cole; *W:* Michael Diamond, Roger Kumble; *M:* Christopher Tyng.

Unzipped 🐾🐾🐾 1994 (R) Witty, behind-the-scenes look at whiz-kid fashion designer Isaac Mizrahi as he prepares for the showing of his 1994 collection. Alternately filmed in black-and-white and color in a variety of film stocks, Keeve (Mizrahi's former lover) captures Mizrahi's varying moods from his creative struggles to his unique sense of humor and gift for mimicry. Highlights include scenes with Mizrahi's doting mother. Fashionphiles will enjoy every minute, and strictly off-the-rack viewers can enjoy the supermodels on parade. **76m/C VHS, DVD.** *D:* Douglas Keeve; *C:* Ellen Kuras. Sundance '95. Aud. Award.

Up and Down 🐾🐾 *Horem Pedem* 2004 (R) Oversized character drama begins with a couple of Czech truck drivers, who are transporting a group of illegal immigrants from India. They discover a baby they sell to a pawnshop owner who in turn sells the infant to a desperate childless couple who deserve their lives (breaking off from their hooligan friends) to try starting over as a family. Then there's a second storyline involving a man who's visiting his divorced parents for the first time in 20 years (he'd immigrated to Australia). Czech with subtitles. **108m/C DVD.** Jan Triska, Jaroslav Dusek, Petr Forman, Emilia Vasaryova, Jiri Machacek, Natasa Burger, Ingrid Timkova, Kristyna Liska-Bokova, Pavel Liska, Marek Daniel, Jan Budar, Zdenek Suchy; *Cameos:* Vaclav Havel; *D:* Jan Hrebejk; *W:* Jan Hrebejk; *C:* Jan Malir; *M:* Ales Brezina.

Up at the Villa 🐾🐾½ 2000 (PG-13) The British and American expatriate community in 1938 Florence is the setting for the unlikely romantic travails of respectable British widow Mary Panton (Scott Thomas). She is courted by long-time (and older) friend/diplomat Sir Edgar (Fox) who will offer her a comfortable if dull life in India. But at a party, Mary is paired off with confident American Rowley Flint (Penn), who must unexpectedly help Mary out of a jam involving a dead body. However, politics also plays its part with the rise of fascism. Scott Thomas and Penn may not have any romantic sparks but they do well individually and Bancroft is an amusing scene stealer as a wealthy socialite. Based on a novella by W. Somerset Maugham. **115m/C VHS, DVD, GB** Kristin Scott Thomas, Sean Penn, Anne Bancroft, Derek Jacobi, Jeremy Davies, James Fox, Massimo Ghini; *D:* Philip Haas; *W:* Belinda Haas; *C:* Maurizio Calvesi; *M:* Pino Donaggio.

Up Close and Personal 🐾🐾🐾 1996 (PG-13) Ambitious Reno card dealer Tally Atwater (Pfeiffer) wants to get into broadcasting and finds her chance at a Miami TV station where she's mentored by successful veteran-reporter-turned-producer Warren Justice (Redford). They fall in love but find their careers clashing as Tally climbs the media success ladder. Originally inspired by the tragic life of NBC reporter Jessica Savitch, whose problems with drugs and abusive relationships led to a sad ending, film turned into a star-powered romance with media trappings and another variation of "A Star is Born." It's now "suggested" by Alanna Nash's book "Golden Girl." **124m/C VHS, DVD.** Michelle Pfeiffer, Robert Redford, Kate Nelligan, Stockard Channing, Joe Mantegna, Glenn Plummer, James Rebhorn, Noble Willingham, Scott Bryce, Raymond Cruz, Dedee Pfeiffer, Miguel Sandoval, James Karen; *D:* Jon Avnet; *W:* Joan Didion, John Gregory Dunne; *C:* Karl Walter Lindenlaub; *M:* Thomas Newman.

Up Against the Eight Ball 🐾½ 2004 (R) Best friends Monique (Dahl) and Krista (La'Shawn) need money for their last year of college tuition. So they take their pool-hustling skills to a tournament in Vegas with various troubles (romantic and otherwise) accompanying them. Way too predictable in a you-go-girl way. **90m/C VHS, DVD.** Kym E. Whitley, Iva La'Shawn, Tawny Dahl, Jay Cooper, T. Ashanti Mozelle; *D:* Miguel A. Nunez Jr., Troy Curvey Jr.; *W:* Keith Sapere. VIDEO

Up Against the Wall 🐾🐾 1991 A black kid from the Chicago projects attends school in the affluent suburbs, but there too he must resist temptation, crime and violence. A well-intentioned but didactic cautionary drama. **103m/C VHS.** Marla Gibbs, Stoney Jackson, Catero Colbert, Ron O'Neal, Salli Richardson; *D:* Ron O'Neal.

Up for Grabs 🐾🐾½ 2005 The story of the controversy over ownership of Barry Bonds's record-setting home is actually more interesting than all the hype leading up to the history-making hit. Following the frenzied scramble for the ball, two men stepped forward into the spotlight—one with the ball and the other claiming he had caught it first, only to have it ripped from his hand in the ensuing struggle. Using news footage of the event as well as eyewitness accounts, documentarian Michael Wranovics shines a light on the absurd issue, which ends up in court. **86m/C DVD. US** *D:* Michael Wranovics; *C:* Zack Richard, Josh Kappel.

Up from the Depths 🐾½ 1979 Something from beneath the ocean is turning the paradise of Hawaii into a nightmare. Prehistoric fish are returning to the surface with one thing on their minds—lunch. "Jaws" rip-off played for humor. **85m/C VHS.** Sam Bottoms, Suzanne Reed, Virgil Frye; *D:* Charles B. Griffith; *W:* Alfred Sweeney; *M:* James Horner.

Up in Arms 🐾🐾 1944 Danny Kaye's first film presents a typical Kaye scenario: he plays a twitching hypochondriac who is drafted into the Army and sneaks his girlfriend aboard the troopship bound for the Pacific. **106m/C VHS, DVD.** Danny Kaye, Dinah Shore, Constance Dowling, Dana Andrews, Margaret Dumont, Lyle Talbot, Louis Calhern, Charles Halton; *D:* Elliott Nugent; *C:* Ray Renahan.

Up in Central Park 🐾🐾½ 1948 Poor adaptation of the hit Broadway musical (the studio removed much of Romberg's score) about Irish immigrant lass Rosie Moore (Durbin), who teams up with New York reporter John Matthews (Haymes) to expose corrupt politician Boss Tweed (Price). Without the songs, the plot is shown to be water-thin. ♫ When She Walks in the Room; Carousel in the Park; Oh Say Do You See What I See?; Pace, Pace Mio Dio. **88m/B VHS.** Deanna Durbin, Dick Haymes, Vincent Price, Albert Sharpe, Tom Powers, Hobart Cavanaugh, Thurston Hall; *D:* William A. Seiter; *W:* Dorothy Fields, Herbert Fields, Karl Tunberg; *C:* Milton Krasner; *M:* Sigmund Romberg.

Up in the Air 🐾🐾 1940 Darro and Moreland have ambitions as radio comedians, and their friend Reynolds wants to be a singer. Their break comes when other performers are murdered on the air. First, though, they must solve the killings. **62m/B VHS, DVD.** Frankie Darro, Marjorie Reynolds, Mantan Moreland, Gordon Jones, Tristram Coffin, Jon Holland, Carleton Young; *D:* Howard Bretherton; *W:* Edmond Kelso; *C:* Fred H. Jackman Jr.; *M:* Edward Kay, Johnny Lange, Lew Porter.

Up Periscope 🐾🐾½ 1959 Garner is a demolitions expert unwillingly assigned to a submarine commanded by O'Brien. His mission: to sneak onto a Japanese-held island and steal a top-secret code book. Trouble is, O'Brien may not wait for Garner to complete his mission before taking the sub back underwater. A routine submarine film. **111m/C VHS, DVD.** James Garner, Edmond O'Brien, Andra Martin, Alan Hale Jr., Carleton Carpenter, Frank Gifford, Richard Bakalyan; *D:* Gordon Douglas.

Up/Down/Fragile 🐾🐾 *Haut, Bas Fragile* 1995 New Wavish musical following the fortunes of three young women in Paris. Louise (Denicourt) has just emerged from a coma after several years and is living in a tiny apartment she has inherited the antiques-filled home of an aunt; Ninon (Richard) has fled from her gangster boyfriend and gotten a job as a delivery girl; and the adopted Ida (Cote) has become obsessed with learning the identities of her biological parents. Their link is Roland (Marcon) who knows all three. The mood's more important than the plot anyway. French with subtitles. **169m/C VHS, FR** Marianne (Quau) Denicourt, Laurence Cote, Nathalie Richard, Andre Marcon, Anna Karina; *D:* Jacques Rivette; *C:* Christophe Pollock; *M:* Francois Breant.

Up River 🦴 **1979** Wealthy land baron rapes and murders the wife of a simple pioneer, who is beaten and whose homestead is burned by the baron as well. The pioneer lives to seek terrible vengeance. 90m/C VHS. Jeff Corey, Morgan Stevens, Debbie AuLuce; **D:** Carl Kitt.

Up the Academy 🦴 *Mad Magazine's Up the Academy; The Brave Young Men of Weinberg* **1980 (R)** Four teenaged delinquents are sent to an academy for wayward boys where they encounter a sadistic headmaster and a gay dance instructor. Sometimes inventive, often tasteless fare from "Mad" magazine. 88m/C VHS, DVD. Ron Leibman, Ralph Macchio, Barbara Bach, Tom Poston, Stacey Nelkin, Wendell Brown, Tom Citera; **D:** Robert Downey.

Up the Creek 🦴🦴 **1958** Crazy antics abound in this tale of an old British destroyer, a black-market scheme run by the crew, and the new skipper whose hobby is rocket building. Followed by "Further Up the River." 83m/B VHS. *GB* David Tomlinson, Wilfrid Hyde-White, Peter Sellers, Vera Day, Michael Goodliffe, Lionel Jeffries; **D:** Val Guest.

Up the Creek 🦴🦴½ **1984 (R)** Four college losers enter a whitewater raft race to gain some respect for their school. The soundtrack features songs by Heart, Cheap Trick and The Beach Boys. Routine. 95m/C VHS. Tim Matheson, Jennifer Runyon, Stephen Furst, John Hillerman, James B. Sikking, Julia Montgomery, Jeana Tomasina; **D:** Robert Butler; **M:** William Goldstein.

Up the Down Staircase 🦴🦴🦴 **1967** A naive, newly trained New York public school teacher is determined to teach the finer points of English literature to a group of poor students. She almost gives up until one student actually begins to learn. Good production and acting. Based on Bel Kaufman's novel. 124m/C VHS. Sandy Dennis, Patrick Bedford, Eileen Heckart, Ruth White, Jean Stapleton, Sorrell Booke; **D:** Robert Mulligan.

Up the River 🦴🦴½ **1930** Tracy's film debut as convict St. Louis. He breaks out of jail with sidekick Dan (Hymer) and the two go their separate ways but can't keep out of trouble. They wind up back in the joint, this time sharing a cell with rich boy Steve (Bogart). Steve gets blackmailed after his release and his two prison buddies break out again to come to his aid. Ford reworked the original dramatic script into a comedy and shot the film in two weeks. 90m/B VHS, DVD. Spencer Tracy, Warren Hymer, Humphrey Bogart, Morgan Wallace, Robert Emmett O'Connor, Clare Luce, Joan Lawes; **D:** John Ford; **W:** Maurine Watkins, William "Buster" Collier Jr.; **C:** Joseph August.

Up the Sandbox 🦴🦴 **1972 (R)** A bored housewife fantasizes about her life in order to avoid facing her mundane existence. Fine acting from Streisand, with real problems of young mothers accurately shown. 98m/C VHS, DVD. Barbra Streisand, David Selby, Jane Hoffman, Barbara Rhoades; **D:** Irvin Kershner; **W:** Paul Zindel; **C:** Gordon Willis; **M:** Billy Goldenberg.

Up Your Alley 🦴🦴 **1989 (R)** A female reporter, pursuing a story on homelessness, and a skidrow bum find romance. Langston, who produced and cowrote the film, is better known as "The Unknown Comic." 90m/C VHS. Linda Blair, Murray Langston, Ruth Buzzi, Johnny Dark, Bob Zany, Yakov Smirnoff; **D:** Bob Logan.

Uphill All the Way 🦴🦴 **1985** A couple of card-cheatin' good old boys are pursued by posses and cavalry alike, and end up killing real outlaws. 91m/C VHS. Roy Clark, Mel Tillis, Glen Campbell, Trish Van Devere, Burl Ives, Burt Reynolds; **D:** Frank Q. Dobbs. TV

The Uppercrust 🦴½ *Den Tuchtigen Gehart die Welt* **1981** Boring tale of corruption and greed that takes place at the highest levels of American business and government. 95m/C VHS. *AT* Frank Gorshin, Broderick Crawford, Pavel Landovsky, Franz Buchrieser; **D:** Peter Patzak; **W:** Peter Patzak, Helmut Zenker; **C:** Walter Kinder.

The Uprising 🦴🦴 **1981** A Nicaraguan drama filmed just months after the 1979 Sandinista revolution, wherein a young guard of Somoza retains his job for the money, while his father is active in the revolutionary forces. In Spanish with English subtitles. 96m/C VHS. *SP* Oscar Castillo, Carlos Catania, Augustin Pereira, Guido Sanz; **D:** Peter Lilienthal; **W:** Peter Lilienthal; **C:** Michael Balhaus; **M:** Claus Bantzer.

Uprising 🦴🦴🦴 **2001** Well-done, realistic miniseries depicts the Warsaw Ghetto uprising of 1943, when Polish Jews, facing deportation to death camps, held off the Nazis for a month using guerrilla tactics. Solid script, which avoids melodrama and over-sentimentality, leaves room to show the politics and motivations involved between the people who wanted to negotiate with the Nazis, those who collaborated for self-preservation, and the fighters. Though the whole cast is up to the task, Sobieski's performance stands out, and Schwimmer makes a better showing here than he did in "Band of Brothers." 177m/C VHS, DVD. Leelee Sobieski, Hank Azaria, David Schwimmer, Jon Voight, Donald Sutherland, Cary Elwes, Stephen Moyer, Sadie Frost, Radha Mitchell, Mili Avital, Alexandra Holden, John Ales, Eric Lively, Jesper Christensen; **D:** Jon Avnet; **W:** Jon Avnet, Paul Brickman; **C:** Denis Lenoir; **M:** Maurice Jarre. TV

The Upside of Anger 🦴🦴🦴 **2005** Allen gives new meaning to term ferocious as betrayed suburban Detroit wife Terry Wolfmeyer. Her husband has apparently left Terry and their four beautiful daughters (Witt, Christensen, Russell, Wood) for his secretary. Terry takes to alcohol, anger, and rebellion while the girls run the household. When neighbor Denny (Costner) finds out about her plight, he's eager to make Terry a drinking buddy and possible romantic partner. Genial Denny, who's bored and lonely, is a retired Detroit Tigers pitcher turned radio talk show host. (He's also entranced by the sheer femaleness of the Wolfmeyer home.) There's a certain comfortable, angsty camaraderie to the whole situation that's appealing. Writer/director Binder also takes a small role as Denny's lecherous producer. 118m/C DVD. *US* Joan Allen, Kevin Costner, Erika Christensen, Evan Rachel Wood, Keri Russell, Alicia Witt, Mike Binder, Dane Christensen, Holt McCallany; **D:** Mike Binder; **W:** Mike Binder; **C:** Richard Greatrex; **M:** Alexandre Desplat, Stephen (Steve) Edwards.

Uptown Angel 🦴🦴 **1990 (R)** A young woman is determined to work her way out of her home on the wrong side of town. Black cast brings new life to old premise. 90m/C VHS. Caron Tate, Cliff McMullen, Gloria Davis Hill, Tracy Hill; **D:** Joy Shannon; **W:** Joy Shannon.

Uptown Girls 🦴½ **2003 (PG-13)** Cloying female buddy comedy pits a ditsy, down-on-her-luck socialite against an extremely precocious and well-off 8-year-old with annoying results. After her financial manager embezzles her inheritance, spoiled New York trust-fund kid Molly (Murphy) is forced to get a (shudder!) job. She becomes a nanny to young Ray (Fanning), who is largely abandoned by her record exec mum (Locklear in an especially unappealing performance.) The two butt heads immediately, but through a series of uninspired events predictably do the role reversal bit—learning from each other how to act more their own ages. Murphy's performance is forced and just plain weird at times. Fanning holds her own against her flaky co-star and dismal script. 93m/C VHS, DVD. *US* Brittany Murphy, Dakota Fanning, Heather Locklear, Donald Adeosun Faison, Marley Shelton, Austin Pendleton, Jesse Spencer, Polly Adams; **D:** Boaz Yakin; **W:** Mo Ogrodnik, Julia Dahl, Lisa Davidowitz; **C:** Michael Ballhaus; **M:** Joel McNeely.

Uptown New York 🦴🦴 **1932** A young man pressured by his family marries a rich girl instead of the woman he loves, who in turn marries a man she does not love. Routine melodrama. 81m/B VHS. Jack Oakie, Shirley Grey, Leon Ames, Shirley Grey, George Cooper, Raymond Hatton; **D:** Victor Schertzinger.

Uptown Saturday Night 🦴🦴½ **1974 (PG)** Two working men attempt to recover a stolen lottery ticket from the black underworld after being ripped off at an illegal gambling place. Good fun, with nice performances from both leads and from Belafonte doing a black "Godfather" parody of Brando. Followed by "Let's Do It Again." 104m/C VHS, DVD. Sidney Poitier, Bill Cosby, Harry Belafonte, Flip Wilson, Richard Pryor, Calvin Lockhart; **D:** Sidney Poitier; **W:** Richard Wesley; **C:** Fred W. Koenekamp.

The Uranium Conspiracy 🦴½ **1974 (PG)** A secret agent and a mercenary soldier try to stop a shipment of uranium out of Zaire from falling into enemy hands. It won't be easy. German with subtitles. 100m/C VHS, DVD. *GE IS IT* Fabio Testi, Janet Agren, Assaf Dayan, Siegfried Rauch, Herbert (Fuchs) Fux; **D:** Gianfranco Baldanello, Menahem Golan; **W:** David Paulsen, August Rieger; **C:** Adam Greenberg; **M:** Coriolano Gori, Dov Seltzer.

Uranus 🦴🦴🦴 **1991 (R)** After WWII a French provincial town has been liberated from Nazi invaders—but not its own suspicions, as citizens try to rebuild knowing some of them collaborated with the enemy. An important subject is heavily talked over in static fashion, with a robust Depardieu either a standout or a ham as the earthy saloon-keeper. Based on a novel by Marcel Ayme, himself accused of pro-Vichy leanings during the era. In French with English subtitles. 100m/C VHS. *FR* Gerard Depardieu, Michel Blanc, Jean-Pierre Marielle, Philippe Noiret, Gerard Desarthe, Michel Galabru, Fabrice Luchini, Daniel Prevost; **D:** Claude Berri; **W:** Claude Berri; **M:** Jean-Claude Petit.

Urban Cowboy 🦴🦴½ **1980 (PG)** A young Texas farmer comes to Houston to work in a refinery. After work he hangs out at Gilley's, a roadhouse bar, where he and his friends drink, fight, and prove their manhood by riding a mechanical bull. Film made Winger a star, was an up in Travolta's roller coaster career, and began the craze for country western apparel and dance and them there mechanical bulls. Ride 'em, cowboy! 135m/C VHS, DVD. John Travolta, Debra Winger, Scott Glenn, Madolyn Smith, Barry Corbin; **D:** James Bridges; **W:** James Bridges, Aaron Latham; **C:** Reynaldo Villalobos; **M:** Ralph Burns.

Urban Crossfire 🦴🦴½ **1994 (PG-13)** Two veteran white Brooklyn detectives investigating gang violence are aided by a young black patrolman whose partner was killed by a gang leader. Solid cast, fast paced action. 95m/C VHS, DVD. Mario Van Peebles, Ray Sharkey, Peter Boyle, Michael Boatman; **D:** Dick Lowry.

Urban Ghost Story 🦴🦴 **1998 (R)** Saddled with guilt after surviving a car wreck that killed her friend, 12-year-old Lizzie suspects that her near-death experience released a nasty ghost that's purposely tormenting her. When no one believes her, her mom enlists the aid of a journalist to prove Lizzie's claims—which only makes life worse as a gaggle of scientists and voyeurs swarm their grungy Glasgow home. 82m/C VHS, DVD. Jason Connery, Stephanie Buttle, Heather Ann Foster, Nicola Stapleton, James Cosmo, Elizabeth Berrington, Siri Neal, Andreas Wisniewski, Kenneth Bryans, Carolyn Bonnyman, Alan Owen, Stephen MacDonnell, Julie Austin, Nicola Greene, Nick Von Schlippe, David Haddow, Richard Syms, Andy McEwan, Aaron White, Joss Castell-Gydesen; **D:** Genevieve Jolliffe; **W:** Genevieve Jolliffe, Chris Jones; **C:** Jon Walker; **M:** Rupert Gregson-Williams. VIDEO

Urban Justice 🦴 **2007 (R)** If you're looking for a brainless, violent flick, then here it is because nothing else is offered. When the police department doesn't pursue the criminals who killed a cop in a drive-by shooting, his dad (Seagal) decides to take on the 'hood and blow the bad guys away himself. 92m/C DVD. Steven Seagal, Eddie Griffin, Danny Trejo, Kirk B.R. Woller, Carmen Serano, Cory Hart; **D:** Don E. Fauntleroy; **W:** Gilmar Fortis II; **C:** Don E. Fauntleroy; **M:** Peter Meisner. VIDEO

Urban Legend 🦴🦴 **1998 (R)** Another in the nudge-and-wink genre of horror movies. Screen scream alumni litter the screen in this ode to modern tall tales that may have actually happened to the friend of a cousin of a friend of yours. Natalie (Watt) is the standard good girl who doesn't know why her friends are getting knocked off, even though her folklore prof (Englund) is the guy who played Freddy Krueger, and the voice of Chucky the evil doll is now coming out of her gas station attendant (Dourf). The killer uses urban legends as the theme of his crimes, but he never makes anyone eat Pop Rocks then drink Pepsi. Characters are so irritating you'll cheer when they die. 100m/C VHS, DVD. Alicia Witt, Jared Leto, Rebecca Gayheart, Loretta Devine, Joshua Jackson, Tara Reid, John Neville, Robert Englund, Brad Dourif, Natasha Gregson Wagner, Danielle Harris, Michael Rosenbaum; **D:** Jamie Blanks; **W:** Silvio Horta; **C:** James Chressanthis; **M:** Christopher Young.

Urban Legends 2: Final Cut 🦴½ **2000 (R)** This entry in the current trend of tongue-in-cheek slasher flicks proves that the genre is like its crazed killer characters. It refuses to die and is getting really ugly. Nearly abandoning the urban legend aspect of the original, the "movie within a movie" schtick is stolen from the "Scream" series as film students compete for the career-starting Hitchcock award at a prestigious film school. Amy (Morrison) decides to base her movie on urban legends after a chat with Reese (Devine), the only returning cast member of the original. Soon, fellow students and their projects get killed in development. Composer and film editor Ottman, making his directorial debut, seems more intent on giving movie cliches a slight twist and making film industry inside jokes than actually delivering a coherent plot. 94m/C VHS, DVD. Jenny (Jennifer) Morrison, Anthony Anderson, Joseph Lawrence, Matthew Davis, Hart Bochner, Loretta Devine, Marco Hofschneider, Eva Mendes, Michael Bacall, Anson Mount, Jessica Cauffiel, Chas Lawther; **D:** John Ottman; **W:** Paul Harris Boardman, Scott Derrickson; **C:** Brian Pearson; **M:** John Ottman.

Urban Legends: Bloody Mary 🦴½ **2005 (R)** Mary (Fields) dies during prom night because of a jock prank gone wrong. Years later, some slumber party babes giggle and do the "Bloody Mary" chant, causing her to start playing her own bloody tricks on another group of equally thoughtless jocks. 83m/C DVD. Kate Mara, Tina Lifford, Ed Marinaro, Lillith Fields, Robert Vito, Haley McCormick, Olesya Rulin; **D:** Mary Lambert; **W:** Michael Dougherty, Dan Harris; **C:** Ian Fox; **M:** Jeff Rona. VIDEO

Urban Menace 🦴 **1999 (R)** Another "the future sucks" urban nightmare. A quarantined wasteland known as "The Downs" is the killing ground for a serial maniac. Two men, Harper and Crow, try to stop the mayhem and discover their murderer isn't even human. Features a hardcore rap and hip-hop soundtrack. 73m/C VHS, DVD. Snoop Dogg, Big Pun, Ice-T, Fat Joe, T.J. Storm, Vincent Klyn, Romany Malco, Tahitia, Karen Dyer, Ernie Hudson; **D:** Albert Pyun; **W:** Tim Story; **C:** Philip Alan Waters. VIDEO

Urban Warriors 🦴 **1975** Savage barbarians roam and pillage a post-nuclear war Earth, but one invincible warrior ushers them out. 90m/C VHS. Bruno Bilotta, Alex Vitale, Deborah Keith; **D:** Joseph Warren.

Urbania 🐾🐾 2000 (R) Urban legends turned in this disturbing film that finds Charlie (Futterman) restlessly wandering the streets of New York in search o' the handsome homophobic stranger (Ball) who turns out to be responsible for the death of Charlie's boyfriend Chris (Keeslar). Directorial debut of Shear, based on Daniel Reitz's play "Urban Folk Tales." 104m/C VHS, DVD. Dan Futterman, Matt Keeslar, Josh Hamilton, Samuel Ball, William Sage, Megan Dodds, Alan Cumming, Lothaire Bluteau, Barbara Sukowa, Paige Turco, Gabriel Olds; D: Jon Shear; W: Daniel Reitz; C: Shane Kelly; M: Marc Anthony Thompson. **TV**

Urge to Kill 🐾 1984 (PG) A man returning from a mental hospital after pleading temporary insanity to the murder of his girlfriend returns to her town, and the girlfriend returns to her town, with the help of her younger sister. 96m/C VHS. Karl Malden, Holly Hunter, William Devane, Alex McArthur; D: Mike Roee. **TV**

Ursus in the Valley of the Lions 🐾½ The Mighty Ursus Ursus 1962 Ursus attempts to rescue his love from druids but is dismayed to find that she has taken up homicide in her tree time. 92m/C VHS. IT SP Ed Fury, Luis Prendes, Moira Orfei, Cristina Gajoni, Maria Luisa Merlo; D: Carlo Campogalliani.

Used Cars 🐾🐾🐾 1980 (R) A car dealer is desperate to put his jalopy shop competitors out of business. The owners go to great lengths to stay afloat. Sometimes too obnoxious, but often funny. 113m/C VHS, DVD. Kurt Russell, Jack Warden, Deborah Harmon, Gerrit Graham, Joe Flaherty, Michael McKean, David Lander, Al Lewis, Wendie Jo Sperber, Dick Miller, Rita Taggart; D: Robert Zemeckis; W: Robert Zemeckis, Bob Gale; C: Donald M. Morgan; M: Patrick Williams.

Used People 🐾🐾½ 1992 (PG-13) A study in ethnicity and characterization, three Oscar-winning actresses lead a talented cast playing a Jewish family living in Queens in 1969. When the father dies, Joe (Mastroianni), an old friend with an old torch for the widow, Pearl (MacLaine), shows up at the funeral and manages to charm her into a date for coffee. Pearl's new relationship with her Italian suitor affects each of the somewhat off-balance family members and washes the whole clan with a sense of hope and renewal. Adapted from screenwriter Graff's play "The Grandma Plays" that was based on memories of his grandmother. Director Kidron's American debut. 116m/C VHS. Shirley MacLaine, Marcello Mastroianni, Kathy Bates, Marcia Gay Harden, Jessica Tandy, Sylvia Sidney, Bob (Robert) Dishy, Joe Pantoliano, Matthew Branton, Louis Guff, Charles Cioffi, Doris Roberts, Helen Hanft; D: Beeban Kidron; W: Todd Graff; M: Rachel Portman.

Users 🐾🐾 1978 Small-town girl who worked as a prostitute meets a faded film star and becomes involved in the movie business. Ode to decadent Hollywood. Based on the Joyce Haber novel. 125m/C VHS. Jaclyn Smith, Tony Curtis, John Forsythe, Red Buttons, George Hamilton; D: Joseph Hardy; M: Maurice Jarre. **TV**

The Usual Suspects 🐾🐾🐾½ 1995 (R) Twisted noir-ish film about some crooks, a $91 million heist, and mysterious crime lord Keyser Soze. Customs agent Kujan (Palminteri) tries to get a straight story out of small-time con man "Verbal" "Kint (Spacey) about a burning tanker in the San Pedro harbor, 27 dead bodies, and the other four temperamental criminals involved: ex-cop-turned thief Keaton (Byrne), explosives expert Hockney (Pollak), and hot-headed partners McManus (Baldwin) and Fenster (Del Toro). Nothing is as it seems, and the ending keeps everyone guessing, right up to the final credits. Terrific performances from all complement the intelligent, humorous script. And yes, the title does 'come from the famous line in "Casablanca." 105m/C VHS, DVD, Blu-ray Disc. Louis Lombardi, Kevin Spacey, Gabriel Byrne, Chazz Palminteri, Kevin Pollak, Stephen Baldwin, Benicio Del Toro, Giancarlo Esposito, Pete Postlethwaite, Dan Hedaya, Suzy Amis, Paul Bartel, Peter Greene; D: Bryan Singer; W: Christopher McQuarrie; C: Newton Thomas (Tom) Sigel;

M: John Ottman. Oscars '95: Orig. Screenplay, Support. Actor (Spacey); British Acad. '95; Orig. Screenplay, Support. Actor (Spacey); Ind. Spirit '96: Screenplay, Support. Actor (Del Toro); Natl. Bd. of Review '95: Support. Actor (Spacey); N.Y. Film Critics '95: Support. Actor (Spacey); Broadcast Film Critics '95: Support. Actor (Spacey).

Utah 🐾🐾 1945 A musical comedy star who inherits a ranch wishes to sell it to finance one of her shows. She is persuaded not to by Rogers, the ranch foreman. 54m/B VHS, DVD. Roy Rogers, Dale Evans, George "Gabby" Hayes; D: John English.

Utah Trail 🐾 1938 Lawman Ritter is hired to stop a gang of cattle rustlers. Cheapie oater made for Grand National, which went bankrupt soon after. 57m/B VHS, DVD. Tex Ritter; D: Albert Herman.

Utamaro and His Five Women 🐾🐾½ Getting Even 1983 (PG) A frustrated social worker enlists the help of his friends in his efforts to impress an attractive policewoman by taking on a large corporate utility. 94m/C VHS. C4 Robert Hays, Brooke Adams, John Matley, Ben Gordon, Helen Burns, Helene Winston; D: Harvey Hart.

Maro; Utamaro O Meguru Gonin No Onna 1946 Utamaro is a legendary 19th-century Edo artist who gained inspiration from Tokyo's "floating world" of courtesans, brothels, drinking parties, and violent passions. His gorgeous portraits worship women but he dislikes the complications that flesh-and-blood females bring. Heavily stylized look at the artistic impulse. In Japanese with English subtitles. 89m/B VHS. JP Minnosuke Bando, Kinuyo Tanaka, Kotaro Bando, Hisato Osawa, Tameyo Mochizuki, Hiroko Kawasaki; D: Kenji Mizoguchi; W: Yoshikata Yoda; C: Shigeto Miki; M: Hisato Osawa, Tameyo Mochizuki.

Utilities 🐾🐾½ Getting Even 1983 (PG) A frustrated social worker enlists the help of his friends in his efforts to impress an attractive policewoman by taking on a large corporate utility.

Utopia 🐾🐾 Atoll K. Robinson Crusoeland; Escapade 1951 Laurel and Hardy inherit a paradisiacal island, but their peace is disturbed when uranium is discovered. Final screen appearance of the team is diminished by poor direction and script. 82m/B VHS, DVD. FR Stan Laurel, Oliver Hardy, Suzy Delair, Max Elloy; D: Leo Joannon; W: Rene Wheeler, Piero Tellini, Monte (Monty) Collins Jr.; C: Louis Nee, Armand Thirard; M: Paul Misraki.

Utu 🐾🐾 1983 (R) A Maori tribesman serving with the colonizing British army in 1870 explodes into ritual revenge when his home village is slaughtered. Filmed in New Zealand. 122m/C VHS, DVD. NZ Anzac Wallace, Kelly Johnson, Tim Elliot, Bruno Lawrence; D: Geoff Murphy; W: Geoff Murphy, Keith Aberdein; C: Graeme Cowley; M: John Charles.

Utz 🐾🐾 1993 The Baron von Utz (Mueller-Stahl) collects both women and priceless porcelain figures. When his friend, art dealer Marius Fischer (Riegert), travels to Prague for a visit he finds that both Utz's housekeeper (Fricker), who has suffered from unrequited love, and the porcelain have disappeared. So Marius teams up with the Baron's old friend Dr. Orlick (Scofield) to find out what's going on. Based on the novel by Bruce Chatwin. 95m/C VHS, GB GE IT Armin Mueller-Stahl, Peter Riegert, Brenda Fricker, Paul Scofield; D: George Sluizer.

U2: Rattle and Hum 🐾🐾½ 1988 (PG-13) Very-well-done concert/documentary, focusing on the Irish band U2 and their 1988 U.S. tour. Filmed in black-and-white and color. 90m/C VHS, DVD. D: Phil Joanou; C: Robert Brinkmann, Jordan Cronenweth.

V 🐾🐾🐾 1983 Very creepy sci-fi miniseries that spawned a short-lived TV show. Advanced aliens, known as the Visitors, come to Earth on a seemingly friendly quest. But their human-like appearance is a facade—as is their mission. Fake skin masks a reptilian hide and what they want is complete planetary control. Naturally, some earthlings don't fall for their smooth talk and a resistance movement is born. Followed by miniseries conclusion "V: The Final Battle." 190m/C VHS, DVD. Marc Singer, Jane Badler, Faye Grant, Robert Englund, Michael Durrell, Peter Nelson, Neva Patterson, Andrew Prine, Richard Herd, Rafael Campos; D: Kenneth Johnson; W: Kenneth Johnson.

V 🐾½ 2007 (R) Standard slasher flick finds bickering estranged couple David (Wilson) and Amy (Beckinsale) stuck in a fleabag motel after having car trouble along a deserted backroad. Their in-room entertainment consists of dusty videotapes of torture snuff flicks they soon realize happened in the 'very room they're in. Then they figure out they're being watched. Wilson and Beckinsale give their characters a little more depth than the pic probably deserves. 80m/C DVD, Blu-ray Disc. US Luke Wilson, Kate Beckinsale, Frank Whaley, Ethan (Randal) Embry; D: Nimrod Antal; W: Mark Smith; C: Andrzej Sekula; M: Paul Haslinger.

Vacancy 🐾½ 2007 (R) Standard slasher flick finds bickering estranged couple David (Wilson) and Amy (Beckinsale) stuck in a fleabag motel.

The Vacations of Poppy Carew 🐾🐾½ 1994 Free-spirited Poppy is just trying to make funeral arrangements for her father when she becomes involved in a series of unexpected and complicated romances. Based on a novel by Mary Wesley. 109m/C VHS, GB Tara Fitzgerald, Sian Phillips, Charlotte Coleman, Samuel West, Edward Atterton, Joseph Fiennes, Daniel Massey; D: James Cellan Jones; W: William Humble; C: David Feig; M: Richard Holmes. **TV**

Vacas 🐾🐾 Cows 1991 The political and social climate of the Basque region of Spain is frequently dangerous but the region's cows (the "vacas" of the title) placidly continue as always despite what happens to the humans around them. Covering more than 50 years, from 1875 through the Spanish Civil War, the lives of two families are interwined in emotional conflict through three generations. Spanish with subtitles. 96m/C VHS, DVD. SP Carmelo Gomez, Ana Torrent, Emma Suarez, Pilar Bardem, Kandido Uranga; D: Julio Medem; M: Julio Medem, Michel Gazzambie; C: Carlos Gusi; M: Alberto Iglesias.

Va Savoir 🐾🐾½ Who Knows? 2001 Romantic farce involving theatre folk. French actress Camille (Balibar) returns to Paris as the star of an Italian theatrical company. She's involved with company director Ugo (Castellitto) but sees her ex, Pierre (Bonaffe) who has a new girlfriend, Sonia (Basler). Meanwhile, Ugo is searching for a lost play by 18th-century writer Goldoni, aided by grad student Do (de Fougerolles) who gets a crush on him, despite her half-brother Arthur's (Todeschini) dislike of the situation. That everyone will interact in each other's lives is a given. French with subtitles. 154m/C VHS, DVD. FR IT GE Jeanne Balibar, Sergio Castellitto, Jacques Bonnaffe, Marianne Basler, Helene de Fougerolles, Bruno Todeschini, Catherine Rouvel, Claude Berri; D: Jacques Rivette; W: Jacques Rivette, Christine Laurent, Pascal Bonitzer; C: William Lubtchansky.

V: The Final Battle 🐾🐾 1984 It's four-months since the Visitors appeared on earth, proclaiming their false friendship. But a resistance movement knows these reptiles, who hide behind a human appearance, are only interested as a new food source. Continuator of the TV miniseries "V." 235m/C VHS, DVD. Marc Singer, Robert Englund, Michael Ironside; D: Richard T. Heffron.

Valdez Is Coming 🐾🐾½ 1971 (PG-13) Though not a world-class western, this filmed-in-Spain saga does present a probing script (based on an Elmore Leonard novel) on the nature of race relations. A series of murders has this wimp yuppie wondering how to get rid of his unwelcome intruder. 91m/C VHS. Bill Paxton, Michael Ironside, Marshall Bell, Stuart Pankin; D: Chris Walas.

The Vagrant 🐾 1992 (R) Run-of-the-mill creeper with a mind-game playing derelict inhabiting the home of a young exec. 91m/C VHS. Bill Paxton, Michael Ironside, Marshall Bell, Stuart Pankin; D: Chris Walas.

Valentin 🐾🐾🐾½ 2002 (PG-13) Valentin is the overly adorable, 9-year-old, horn-rimmed glasses wearing 'hero of Agresti's semi-autobiographical drama set in 1960s Buenos Aires. Valentin (Noya) lives with his kooky grandmother (Maura) after being abandoned by his mother and playboy father, (director Agresti) who have long separated. Valentin attempts to rebuild his family by playing Cupid with his dad's current girlfriend, the beautiful and attentive Leticia (Cardinal) while simultaneously charming and inspiring various local, hard-ened grown-ups. The precocious boy is also an aspiring astronaut, a fact which allows him to dress up in a far-less-than-

Vacuuming Completely Nude in Paradise 🐾🐾½ 2001 Not only is Pete's (Begley) girlfriend tired of stripping to support them but she won't put out until he gets a real job. Off he goes to the local door-to-door vacuum sales office and is placed under the dubious tutelage of top seller Tommy (Spall)—a frantic, moralistically bankrupt, yet very experienced anc successful salesman. The jocularity is plentiful in this BBC-TV production as the contest for the 'Golden "Hoover" pits all the sales folks against Tommy. Spall excels in his role as Tommy the digital video format captures the essence of office life is plentiful for Boyle's use of the digital video format captures the essence of office life is plentiful. 75m/C VHS, DVD. Timothy Spall, Michael Begley, Katy Cavanagh, Caroline Ashley; D: Danny Boyle; W: Jim Cartwright; C: Anthony Dod Mantle; M: John Murphy. **TV**

Vagabond 🐾🐾🐾🐾 Sans Toit Ni Loi 1985 Bleak, emotionally shattering, powerful and compelling, this film traces the peripatetic life of an amoral and selfish young French woman who has no regard for social rules and tremendous fear of responsibility in her drifting yet inexorable journey into death. Told via flashbacks from the moment when she is found dead, alone, and unaccounted for by the roadside, this dreams of an aspiring saxophone player. 105m/C VHS, DVD. FR Sandrine Bonnaire, Macha Meril, Stephane Freiss, Elaine Cortadellas, Martha Jarnias, Yolande Moreau; D: Agnes Varda; W: Agnes Varda; C: Patrick Blossier; M: Joanne Bruzdowicz, Cesar '86. Actress (Bonnaire); L.A. Film Critics '86. Actress (Bonnaire); Foreign Film.

Vagabond Lover 🐾🐾½ 1929 The amusing tale of the loves, hopes, and dreams of an aspiring saxophone player. Rudy croons through his megaphone in his movie debut. Appealing, if dated. 'If you Were the Only Girl in the World; 'A Little Kiss Each Morning; Heigh Ho Everybody; Piccolo Pete; I Love You; I'll Be Reminded of You; I'm Just a Vagabond Lover. 66m/B VHS, DVD. Rudy Vallee, Sally Blane, Marie Dressler, Charles Sellon, Eddie Nugent; D: Marshall Neilan; W: James A. Creelman; C: Leo Tover.

The Vagabond 🐾🐾🐾 1916 The Little Tramp is a pathetic fiddler making a scant living who 'rescues a damsel in distress. Silent with musical soundtrack added. 20m/B VHS, DVD. Charlie Chaplin, Edna Purviance, Eric Campbell, Albert Austin; D: Charlie Chaplin. **TV**

homemade looking get-up and look cute, which he does for far too much of this sometimes saccharine heart-tugger. Does boast some genuinely touching moments. **86m/C DVD. AR NL** Carmen Maura, Rodrigo Noya, Alejandro Agresti, Jean Pierre Noher, Mex Urtizberea, Julieta Cardinali; **D:** Alejandro Agresti; **W:** Alejandro Agresti; **C:** Jose Luis Cajaraville; **M:** Luis Salinas, Paul M. van Brugge.

Valentine 🦴 2001 (R) Slasher film with a former nerd of a killer in a Cupid mask wreaking revenge upon the snooty girls who dissed him in junior high. After one victim's funeral, the remaining Valentines, which they, of course, promptly ignore. Boreanaz is among the doomed babes' boyfriends and a prime suspect. After yet another of the girls falls victim to the demented deity-wannabe, the remaining three grieve by throwing a bash at a swanky mansion with rambling vacant rooms that just scream, well, you get it. Eye-candy cast with mild suspense mix with dubious scripting. The only real victim here is your precious time. **96m/C VHS, DVD. US** David Boreanaz, Denise Richards, Marley Shelton, Jessica Capshaw, Katherine Heigl, Johnny Whitworth, Hedy Burress, Jessica Cauffiel, Fulvio Cecere, Daniel Cosgrove; **D:** Jamie Blanks; **W:** Donna Powers, Wayne Powers, Gretchen J. Berg, Aaron Harberts; **C:** Rick Bota; **M:** Don Davis.

Valentino 🦴🦴 1977 (R) Another one of director Russell's flamboyantly excessive screen biographies, this time of silent screen idol Rudolph Valentino (Nureyev). The details hardly matter but the movie is told in flashback from Valentino's funeral to his beginnings as a dance instructor and his eventual success as a screen lover. Nureyev is noticeably stiff in his screen debut but at least he possesses some charisma. **127m/C VHS. GB** Rudolf Nureyev, Leslie Caron, Michelle Phillips, Carol Kane, Felicity Kendal, Seymour Cassel, Peter Vaughan, William Hootkins, Huntz Hall, David de Keyser, Alfred Marks, Anton Diffring; **D:** Ken Russell; **W:** Mardik Martin, Ken Russell, John Byrum; **C:** Peter Suschitzky; **M:** Ferde Grofe Jr.

Valentino Returns 🦴🦴 1988 (R) A kid in 1955 California buys a pink Cadillac he nicknames "Valentino Returns," thinking it will help him meet girls, as his parents undergo a stormy divorce. Weak script fades fast from thin premise, good start. Nice period feel. **97m/C VHS.** Frederic Forrest, Veronica Cartwright, Jenny Wright, Barry Tubb; **D:** Peter Hoffman.

The Valet 🦴🦴½ 2006 (PG-13) La Doublure Venal tycoon Pierre Levasseur (Auteuil) is in big trouble when a paparazzo takes a photo of him and supermodel mistress Elena (Taglioni). Seems Pierre's wife Christine (Scott Thomas) owns the majority share of company stock and he can't afford a divorce. Ah, but valet Francois (Elmaleh) was also in the picture, so Pierre pays him (and Elena) to pretend that they are a couple. Francois wants the money to help out true (if oblivious) love Emilie (Ledoyen) but the complications increase in Veber's amusing bedroom farce. French with subtitles. **85m/C DVD. FR** Daniel Auteuil, Kristin Scott Thomas, Virginie Ledoyen, Gad Elmaleh, Alice Taglioni, Dany Boon; **D:** Francis Veber; **W:** Francis Veber; **C:** Robert Fraisse; **M:** Alexandre Desplat.

Valiant 🦴🦴½ 2005 (G) Feature-length film based on the WWII homing pigeons used by the British Armed Forces is cute and short, which should please the kids but the plot development never really gets off the ground. Classic "misfit gets his chance and saves the day" story focuses on Valiant (McGregor), who has not been allowed to join the Royal Homing Pigeon Service until they discover how to turn his short-falling into an asset. Plenty of jokes spoofing war movies of days-gone-by. **80m/C DVD. GB US D:** Gary Chapman; **W:** Jordan Katz, George Webster, George Melrod; **V:** Ewan McGregor, George Fenton; **M:** George Fenton; Jim Broadbent, Hugh Laurie, Daniel Roberts, John Cleese, John Hurt, Pip Torrens, Ricky Gervais, Brian Lonsdale, Olivia Williams, Rik Mayall, Sharon Horgan.

Valley Girl 🦴🦴½ 1983 (R) Slight but surprisingly likeable teen romantic-comedy inspired by Frank Zappa novelty tune. Title stereotype falls for a leather-jacketed rebel. Really. It may look like a "music video," via Southern California. Helped launch Cage's career. Music by Men at Work, Culture Club, and others. **95m/C VHS, DVD.** Nicolas Cage, Deborah Foreman, Colleen Camp, Frederic Forrest, Lee Purcell, Elizabeth (E.G. Dailey) Daily, Michael Bowen, Cameron Dye, Heidi Holicker, Michelle Meyrink; **D:** Martha Coolidge; **W:** Wayne Crawford, Andrew Lane; **C:** Frederick Elmes; **M:** Marc Levinthal, Scott Wilk.

The Valley Obscured by the Clouds 🦴🦴 1970 La Vallee A group of dropouts and seekers search for the valley of the gods in the wilds of New Guinea, and experience a sexual and spiritual metamorphosis. In French with English subtitles. **106m/C VHS, DVD. FR** Bulle Ogier, Michael Gothard, Jean-Pierre Kalfon, Jerome Beauvarlet, Monique Giraudy; **D:** Barbet Schroeder; **W:** Barbet Schroeder; **C:** Nestor Almendros; **M:** Pink Floyd.

The Valley of Decision 🦴🦴🦴 1945 Entertaining poor-girl-meets-rich-boy story with Peck as a wealthy mill owner who falls in love with beautiful housemaid Garson (the Queen of MGM at the time). Set in 1870 Pittsburgh; based on Marcia Davenport's novel. **111m/B VHS.** Gregory Peck, Greer Garson, Donald Crisp, Lionel Barrymore, Preston Foster, Gladys Cooper, Marsha Hunt, Reginald Owen, Dan Duryea, Jessica Tandy, Barbara Everest; **D:** Tay Garnett; **W:** John Meehan, Sonya Levien; **C:** Joseph Ruttenberg.

Valley of Fire 🦴🦴 1951 Autry is from a boom town that suffers from a lack of women. He decides to import a caravan of brides for the men in town but villains attempt to kidnap the women. **63m/B VHS, DVD.** Gene Autry, Gail Davis, Pat Buttram; **D:** John English.

The Valley of Gwangi 🦴🦴🦴 1969 (G) One of the best prehistoric-monster-westerns out there. Cowboys discover a lost valley of dinosaurs and try to capture a vicious, carnivorous allosaurus. Bad move, kemosabe! The creatures move via the stop-motion model animation by f/x maestro Ray Harryhausen, here at his finest. **95m/C VHS, DVD.** James Franciscus, Gila Golan, Richard Carlson, Laurence Naismith, Freda Jackson, Gustavo Rojo, Dennis Kilbane, Mario De Barros, Curtis Arden, Jose Burgos; **D:** James O'Connolly; **W:** William Bast, Julian More; **C:** Erwin Hillier; **M:** Jerome Moross.

Valley of Terror 🦴🦴½ 1938 Maynard is framed for cattle rustling. Can he prove his innocence? **59m/B VHS.** Kermit Maynard, Harley Wood, John Merton, Jack Ingram, Dick Curtis, Roger Williams; **D:** Albert) Herman.

Valley of the Dolls 🦴🦴 1967 (PG) Camp/trash classic was rated as a bomb by many critics but is really of the so-bad-it's-good variety. Three beauties, Jennifer (Tate), Neely (Duke), and Anne (Parkins), dream of Hollywood stardom but fall victim to Hollywood excess, including drug dependency (the "dolls" of the title). There's unhappy love affairs, porno parts, health risks, and hysterics of various kinds—all designed to have you dropping your jaw in disbelief. The bathroom scene between Duke and Hayward involving a wig is not to be missed. Based on the novel by Jacqueline Susann who has a bit part as a reporter. Remade for TV as "Jacqueline Susann's Valley of the Dolls" in 1981. **123m/C VHS, DVD.** Barbara Parkins, Patty Duke, Sharon Tate, Paul Burke, Tony Scotti, Martin Milner, Susan Hayward, Charles Drake, Lee Grant, Alex Davion, Robert H. Harris, Robert Viharo, Joey Bishop, George Jessel, Richard Dreyfuss; **D:** Mark Robson; **W:** Dorothy Kingsley, Helen Deutsch, Jacqueline Susann; **C:** William H. Daniels; **M:** John Williams.

Valley of the Eagles 🦴🦴½ 1951 When his wife and partner take off into the Lapland wilderness with his new invention, a scientist leads the police across the tundra in pursuit. Setting is at least a plus. **83m/B VHS. GB** Jack Warner, Nadia Gray, John McCallum, Martin Boddey, Christopher Lee; **D:** Terence Young; **M:** Nino Rota.

Valley of the Kings 🦴🦴½ 1954 Corny big dig movie that does have some nice Egyptian scenery. Archeologist Mark Brandon (Taylor) is searching for the treasure of pharoah Ra-Hotep in 1900s Egypt. Ann (Parker) would like to prove that several Bible stories are, in fact, true while her husband Philip (Thompson) is supposed to be helping Mark but is only out for himself. Although he does seem a little upset when Mark and Ann begin making goo-goo eyes at each other. **86m/C VHS.** Robert Taylor, Eleanor Parker, Kurt Kasznar, Carlos Thompson, Victor Jory, Leon Askin, Aldo Silvani; **D:** Robert Pirosh; **W:** Robert Pirosh, Karl Tunberg; **C:** Robert L. Surtees; **M:** Miklos Rozsa.

Valley of the Lawless 🦴 1936 A cowboy rides into trouble aplenty while out searching for treasure. A routine western for Brown fans only. **59m/B VHS.** Johnny Mack Brown; **D:** Robert North Bradbury; **W:** Robert North Bradbury.

Valley of the Sun 🦴🦴🦴 1942 A government agent tracks a crooked Indian liaison to prevent an Indian uprising in Arizona. Ball, well before her "Lucy" days, plays the restaurant owner both men romance. Better than average, with good cast, some laughs, and lots of excitement. **84m/B VHS.** Lucille Ball, James Craig, Cedric Hardwicke, Dean Jagger, Peter Whitney, Billy Gilbert, Tom Tyler, Antonio Moreno, George Cleveland, Hank Bell; **D:** George Marshall.

Valley of Wanted Men 🦴🦴½ 1935 Three cons escape during a jailbreak and one uses his wits and nerve to prove another was framed. **56m/B VHS, DVD.** Leroy Mason, Russell Hopton, Grant Withers, Paul Fix, Drue Layton, Frankie Darro; **D:** Alan James; **W:** Barry Barrington, Forrest Barnes; **C:** Arthur Reed.

Valmont 🦴🦴🦴 1989 (R) Another adaptation of the Choderlos de Laclos novel "Les Liaisons Dangereuses." Various members of the French aristocracy in 1782 mercilessly play each other for fools in a complex game of lust and deception. Firth and Bening are at first playfully sensual, then the stakes get too high. They share an interesting bathtub scene. Well-acted, the 1988 Frears version, "Dangerous Liaisons," is edgier. Seeing the two films together makes for interesting comparisons of characters and styles. **137m/C VHS, DVD.** Colin Firth, Meg Tilly, Annette Bening, Fairuza Balk, Sian Phillips, Jeffrey Jones, Fabia Drake, Henry Thomas, Vincent Schiavelli, T.P. McKenna, Ian McNeice; **D:** Milos Forman; **W:** Jean-Claude Carriere; **M:** Christopher Palmer. Cesar 90. Art Dir./Set Dec., Costume Des.

The Vals 🦴½ 1985 (R) The glibly hip lethargy which is characteristic of four southern California teenaged girls turns to socially conscious resolve when a local orphanage is threatened. Like, for sure. **100m/C VHS.** Jill Carroll, Elana Stratheros, Gina Calabrese, Michelle Laurita, Chuck Connors, Sonny Bono, John Carradine, Michael Leon; **D:** James Polakof.

Vamp 🦴½ 1986 (R) Two college freshmen encounter a slew of weird, semi-vampiric people in a seamy red-light district nightclub. Starts cute but goes kinky. Jones is great as the stripping vampire. **93m/C VHS, DVD.** Grace Jones, Chris Makepeace, Robert Rusler, Gedde Watanabe, Sandy Baron, Dedee Pfeiffer, Billy Drago, Lisa Lyons; **D:** Richard Wenk; **W:** Richard Wenk; **C:** Elliot Davis; **M:** Jonathan Elias.

Vamping 🦴🦴 1984 (PG) Struggling musician plans to burglarize a wealthy widow's home. Once inside, he finds himself attracted to his proposed victim. Tedious going. **110m/C VHS.** Patrick Duffy, Catherine Hyland, Rod Arrants, Fred A. Keller; **D:** Frederick King Keller.

The Vampire 🦴🦴 1957 Pale man with big teeth attempts to swindle a beautiful babe out of fortune. Followed by "The Vampire's Coffin." **95m/ B VHS, DVD. MX** Abel Salazar, Ariadne Welter, German Robles, Carmen Montejo, Jose Luis Jimenez; **D:** Fernando Mendez.

Vampire Assassin 🦴 2005 (PG-13) Martial artist Hall is a would-be triple threat in this dull vampire story in which he stars as Derek Washington, an ambitious cop who has a phobia about blood. Which is bad news when Derek realizes that bad guy

Slovak (Novak) is a blood-sucker. Derek teams up with vampire hunter Master Kao (Okamura) but soon figures out he may have to become what he hates in order to fight this evil. **87m/C VHS, DVD.** Ron Hall, Mel Novak, Rudy Ray Moore, Gerald Okamura, Anthony Chow, Merry Everest; **D:** Ron Hall; **W:** Ron Hall; **C:** Ed Tillman. VIDEO

Vampire at Midnight 🦴½ 1988 Fairly stupid homicide detective stalks a rampaging vampire in Los Angeles. Occasional moments of gratuitous sex thrown in for good measure. **93m/C VHS.** Jason Williams, Gustav Vintas, Jeanie Moore, Christina Whitaker, Leslie Milne; **D:** Gregory McClatchy.

The Vampire Bat 🦴🦴 1932 A mad scientist and a vampire bat and its supernatural demands set the stage for murders in a small town. Sets and actors borrowed from Universal Studios in this low-budget flick that looks and plays better than it should. Weird and very explotative for 1932, now seems dated. **69m/B VHS, DVD.** Lionel Atwill, Fay Wray, Melvyn Douglas, Dwight Frye, Maude Eburne, George E. Stone; **D:** Frank Strayer; **W:** Edward T. Lowe; **C:** Ira Morgan.

Vampire Centerfolds 🦴🦴 Cheer-pire Conspiracy 1998 Innocent college cheerleader (Williamson) seeks to try out her thespian skills when she's cast in a cult film about vampiric bloodlust. Then she discovers that the models and actresses involved are a secret coven of sex obsessed vamps! **125m/C VHS.** Elaine Juliette Williamson, Jasmine Jaen, Tonya Qualls, Joan A. Teeter; **D:** Geoffrey De Vallois. VIDEO

Vampire Circus 🦴🦴½ 1971 (R) A circus appears in an isolated Serbian village in the 19th century but instead of bringing joy and happiness, this circus brings only death, mutilation and misery. It seems all the members are vampires who have the unique ability to transform themselves into animals. They intend to take revenge on the small town, whose inhabitants killed their evil ancestor 100 years previously. Excellent Hammer production. **84m/C GB** Adrienne Corri, Laurence Payne, Thorley Walters, John Moulder-Brown, Lynne Frederick, Elizabeth Seal, Anthony (Corlan) Higgins, Richard Owens, Domini Blythe, David Prowse; **D:** Robert W. Young; **W:** Judson Kinberg; **C:** Moray Grant.

Vampire Cop 🦴🦴 1990 (R) A vampire cop (not to be confused with zombie, maniac, midnight, psycho, future or Robo) teams up with a beautiful reporter to collar a drug kingpin. **89m/C VHS.** Melissa Moore, Ed Cannon, Terence Jenkins; **D:** Donald Farmer.

Vampire Effect 🦴🦴½ 2003 (R) The Twins Effect; Chin gei bin 2003 (R) The evil Duke Dekotes (Hardt) wants to take over the world (and who wouldn't?) but he needs to snuff out Prince Kazaf (Chen)—the last offshoot of European vampire royalty—and round up his blood to do so. When Kazaf attempts to elude the Duke by going to Hong Kong, he unexpectedly falls for Helen (Chen)—who, of course, just happens to be the sister of butt-kicking vampire-killer, Reeve (Cheng). There's more! Helen's friend, Gypsy (Chung) wants to get in on the action and so all three band together in an effort to foil the Duke's dastardly plot. Jackie Chan cameos in this supernatural romp. Cantonese, with English subtitles. **88m/C VHS, DVD. HK** Ekin Cheng, Anthony Wong, Jackie Chan, Josie Ho, Charlene (Cheuk-Yin) Choi, Gillian (Yan-Tung) Chung, Edison Chen, Mickey Hardt, Karen Mok; **D:** Dante Lam; **W:** Jack Ng; **C:** Man Po Cheung; **M:** Kwong Wing Chan, Robert Duncan. VIDEO

The Vampire Happening 🦴½ 1971 (R) An actress travels to Transylvania to sell her family castle and discovers to her chagrin that her ancestors were vampires after she unknowingly villagers them to party hearty on the local villagers. **101m/ C VHS, DVD. GE** Ferdinand "Ferdy" Mayne, Pia Degermark, Thomas Hunter, Yvor Murillo, Ingrid van Bergen, Raoul Retzer; **D:** Freddie Francis; **W:** Karl Heinz Hummel, August Rieger; **C:** Gerard Vandenburg; **M:** Jerry Van Rooyen.

The Vampire Hookers 🦴 Cemetery Girls; Sensuous Vampires; Night of the Bloodsuckers; Twice Bitten 1978 (R) Man in makeup recruits bevy of beautiful bloodsuckers to lure warm blooded victims to his castle. High ham performance by Carradine. **82m/C VHS, PH** John Carradine, Karen Stride, Lenka Novak, Katie Dolan, Lex Winter; **D:** Cirio 1. Santiago.

Vampire in Brooklyn 1995 (R) Murphy switches gears to play a Caribbean vampire traveling to New York in search of his vampiric lady love—who turns out to be "tail-vamp-half-cop" Bassett. As in "Coming to America," Murphy plays multiple characters, but that's three times the disappointment. State humor and cheap horror effects do little to break the zombie curse plaguing Murphy's career. These days in filming, a stunt double for Bassett was killed after doing a routine jump on the set, providing a bad omen. Murphy should have heeded. **103m/C VHS, DVD,** Eddie Murphy, Angela Basset, Kadeem Hardison, Allen Payne, Zakes Mokae, John Witherspoon, Jsu Garcia; **D:** Wes Craven; **W:** Charles Murphy, Christopher Parker, Michael Lucker; **C:** Mark Irwin; **M:** J. Peter Robinson.

Vampire Journals 1996 (R) Revenge-minded Zachary (Gunn) vows to destroy Ash (Morris), the ancient vampire who created him centuries before, especially when they both become interested in the same mortal woman, Sofia (Cerre). Shot on location in Transylvania. **82m/C VHS, DVD,** David Gunn, Jonathan Morris, Kirsten Cerre Star Andreeff; **D:** Ted Nicolaou; **C:** Adolf Bartoli; **M:** Richard Kosinski.

The Vampire Lovers 1970 (R) An angry father goes after a lesbian vampire who has ravished his daughter and other young girls in a peaceful European village. Innovative story was soon used in countless other vampire vehicles. Hammer Studio's first horror film with nudity, another addiction to the genre which spread rapidly. Based on the story "Carmilla" by Sheridan Le Fanu. Followed by "Lust for a Vampire." **91m/C VHS, DVD, GB** Ingrid Pitt, Pippa Steele, Madeleine Smith, Peter Cushing, George Cole, Dawn Addams, Kate O'Mara, Ferdinand "Ferdy" Mayne, Douglas Wilmer, Harvey Hall, Charles Farrell; **D:** Roy Ward Baker; **W:** Tudor Gates; **C:** Moray Grant.

Vampire Night WOOF! 2000 Pretty Peggy (Metcalfe) runs off to Hollywood with stars in her eyes and winds up with an agent. Vezrech (Ryan), whose main talent is supplying fresh blood to his stable of vampire babes. Peggy's brother, Carl (Jerman), gets worried and comes to the big, bad city to find his sis. How can a movie with vampire babes be so dull? **76m/C VHS, DVD,** Jimmy Jerman, Heather Metcalfe, Robert Michael Ryen, Pat Downey, Eden Rae; **D:** John Robert Stephens; **W:** John Robert Stephens; **C:** Dennis Devine; **M:** Joshua Price.

The Vampire People Blood Drinkers 1966 (PG) A dwarf-assisted vampire attempts to save the life of his true love by transplanting her sister's heart. Typical Filipino vampire movie, in color and sepia-tone. **79m/C VHS, DVD, PH** Ronald Remy, Amalia Fuentes, Eddie Fernandez, Eva Montez; **D:** Gerardo (Gerry) De Leon.

Vampire Raiders—Ninja Queen WOOF! 1989 The white ninjas versus the black ninjas. The evil black ninjas are plotting to infiltrate the hotel industry. The white ninjas come to the rescue. **90m/C VHS,** Agnes Chen, Chris Petersen; **D:** Godfrey Ho.

Vampire Time Travelers WOOF! 1999 Four college gals try to pledge a strange sorority and wind up battling vampires and other supernatural creepies. It's hard to tell if it a comedy is accidental or deliberate. Low-budget amateur night. **80m/C VHS,** Micky Levy, J.J. Rodgers, Jimmy Jerman, Robert Ginty, Kaz Facchino, Lori Morrissey, Jillien Weisz; **D:** Les Sekely; **W:** Les Sekely; **C:** Dennis Devine; **M:** Jack Wheaton.

Vampire Vixens from Venus 1994 Three hideous drug smuggling aliens transform themselves into bodacious babes on earth so they can get what they came for. Seems their drug fix is derived from the life essence of men and they plan to drain every last drop they can. **90m/C VHS, DVD,** J.J. North, Leslie Glass, Michelle (McClellan) Bauer, Leon Head, Charlie

Vampyr Vampyr, Ou l'Etrange Aventure de David Gray; Vampyr, Der Traum des David Gray; Not against the Flesh; Castle of Doom; The Strange Adventure of David Gray; The Vampire 1931 Dreyer's classic portrays a hazy, dreamlike world full of chilling visions from the point of view of a young man who believes himself surrounded by vampires and who dreams of his own burial in a most disturbing way. Evil lurks around every corner as camera angles, light and shadow sometimes overwhelm plot. A high point in horror films based on a collection of horror stories by Sheridan Le Fanu. In German with English subtitles. **75m/B VHS, DVD, GE FR** Julian West, Sybille Schmitz, Henriette Gerard, Maurice Schütz, Rena Mandel, Jan Hieronimko, Albert Bras; **D:** Carl Theodor Dreyer; **W:** Carl Theodor Dreyer, Christen Jul; **C:** Rudolph Maté, Louis Née; **M:** Wolfgang Zeller.

The Vampyr 1992 Uncut version of the BBC musical production about a lustful vampire. Text sets present-day lyrics to the 1827 opera by Heinrich Marschner. Vampire Ripley (Ebrahim) has just been set free in London after having been trapped in an underground tomb for 200 years. Unless he puts the bite on three

Vampires of Sorority Row: Kickboxers From Hell 1999 Trailer-trash princess Cindy (Glass) goes to college and pledges a sorority, only to find domineering pledge mistress Denise (Lydon) and a gaggle of vampires causing a commotion. T&A competes with kickboxing action and self-mocking humor (that really works!) for viewers' attention spans. You could do worse on a Saturday night when "Gandhi" is rented and you need a laugh. **80m/C VHS, DVD,** Christine Lydon, Rich Ward, Kathryn Glass, Rita Fiora, Erika Gardener, Christian Catlin, Angelica Hayden; **D:** Dennis Devine; **W:** Dennis Devine; **M:** Jonathan Price.

Vampirella 1996 (R) Inhabitants of the planet Drakulon use a synthetic concoction to quench their thirst for blood. When Vampirella's (Soto) stepfather is murdered by rebels, led by Vlad Tepes (Daltrey), she must pursue them to earth to get justice. There she finds two opposing forces—the vampires led by Adam Van Helsing (Paul), who's out to cleanse the planet of the interlopers. But it's Vampirella who wants a final confrontation with Tepes (in Las Vegas, no less). **90m/C VHS, DVD,** Talisa Soto, Roger Daltrey, Richard Joseph Paul, Angus Scrimm, Tom Deters, Cinna Harney, Brian Bloom; **D:** Jim Wynorski; **W:** Gary Gerani; **C:** Andrea V. Rossotto; **M:** Joel Goldsmith. CABLE

The Vampire's Coffin El Ataud Del Vampiro; El Ataúd Del Coffin 1958 Count Lavud is relieved when faithful servant removes stake implanted in his heart. **86m/B VHS, MX** Abel Salazar, Ariadne Welter, German Robles; **D:** Fernando Mendez.

The Vampire's Ghost 1945 A 400-hundred-year-old vampire/zombie, doomed to walk the earth forever, hosts the African underworld. He can't be killed and can save unsuspecting souls. His future's so bright, he wears sunglasses. His future's so bright he's just gotta wear shades. **59m/B VHS,** John Abbott, Peggy Stewart; **D:** Lesley Selander.

Vampire's Kiss 1988 (R) Cage makes the cinema worthwhile; his twisted transformation from pretentious postural dude to psychotic yuppie from hell is inspired. If his demented torment of his secretary (Alonso) doesn't give you the creeps, his scene with the cockroach will. Cage fans will enjoy his facial acrobatics; Beals fans will appreciate her extensive sucking scenes (she's the vamp of his dreams). More for psych majors than horror buffs. **103m/C VHS, DVD,** Jessica Lundy, Debbie Rochon, Nicolas Cage, Elizabeth Ashley, Jennifer Beals, Maria Conchita Alonso, Kasi Lemmons, Bob Lujan, David Hyde Pierce; **D:** Robert Bierman; **W:** Joe Minion; **C:** Stefan Czapsky; **M:** Colin Towns.

Callas, Theresa Lynn; **D:** Tewd A. Bonus; **W:** Tewd A. Bonus; **C:** Curtis Mattikow; **M:** Ariel Shalit.

Vampyres Vampyres, Daughters of Dracula; Blood Hunger; Satan's Daughters of Dracula; Vampire Orgy 1974 (R) Alluring female vampires coerce unsuspecting motorists to their castle for a good time, which ends in death. Anulka was the centerfold girl in "Playboy"'s May 1973 issue. **90m/C VHS, DVD, GB** Marianne Morris, Anulka, Murray Brown, Brian Deacon, Sally Faulkner, Michael Byrne, Karl Lanchbury, Bessie Love, Elliott Sullivan; **D:** Joseph (Joss Ramon) Larraz; **W:** Diane Daubeney; **C:** Harry Waxman; **M:** James Clark.

The Van 1977 (R) A recent high school graduate passes on the college scene so he can spend more time picking up girls in his van. A lame sex (and sexist) comedy. **92m/C VHS, DVD,** Stuart Getz, Deborah White, Danny DeVito, Harry Moses, Maurice Barkin; **D:** Sam Grossman; **W:** Robert J. Rosenthal, Celia Susan Cotelo; **C:** Irv Goodnoff; **M:** Steve Eaton.

Van Gogh 1992 (R) "One doesn't produce 100 masterpieces in a state of depression—Van Gogh died from heaving had a glimpse of happiness." This is the way director Pialat sums up his approach to the last 67 days in the life of Vincent Van Gogh. Dutronc is skillful in portraying Van Gogh as a man with no excuses, and even a sense of humor. Not a psychological portrait and offers no answers—it's simply one artist's view of another. In French with English subtitles. **155m/C VHS, DVD, FR** Jacques Dutronc, Alexandra London, Gerard Sety, Bernard Le Coq, Corinne Bourdon; **D:** Maurice Pialat; **W:** Maurice Pialat; **C:** Giles Henry, Emmanuel Machuel; **M:** Edith Vesperini. '92: Actor (Dutronc).

Van Helsing 2004 (PG-13) Bram Stoker's title character takes on Frankenstein's monster, the Wolf Man and Count Dracula. Hollywood's macho "Indiana Jones meets James Bond" Van Helsing (Jackman) is a high-tech bow and arrow-slinging, creature-slaying hero who travels with sidekick Carl (Wenham), to Transylvania to kill the head vampire himself (Roxburgh). Sexy gypsy Anna (Beckinsale) turns up seeking to vanquish Dracula and lift a curse her family has suffered for centuries. With chase scenes, a masked ball, nonstop adventure, monsters galore, and a script that doesn't take itself too seriously, this f/x extravaganza will find something to appeal to everyone. **132m/C DVD, UMD, HD DVD, US CZ** Hugh Jackman, Kate Beckinsale, Richard Roxburgh, David Wenham, Shuler Hensley, Elena Anaya, Will(am) Kemp, Kevin J. O'Connor, Alun Armstrong, Thomas (Tom) Fisher, Samuel West, Robbie Coltrane, Silvia Colloca, Josie Maran, Stephen H. Fisher; **D:** Stephen Sommers; **W:** Stephen Sommers; **C:** Allen Daviau; **M:** Alan Silvestri.

Van Nuys Blvd. 1979 (R) The popular boulevard is the scene where the cool southern California guys converge for cruising and girl watching, so naturally it's where a country hick comes to test his drag racing skills and check out the action. **93m/C VHS, DVD,** Bill Adler, Cynthia Wood, Dennis Bower, Melissa Prophet; **D:** William Sachs.

lovely ladies within three days he will be condemned to eternal damnation. Everyone gets to sing in the nude. Surreally amusing. **115m/C VHS, G3** Omar Ebrahim, Willem Van Gent, Fiona O'Neill Sally-Ann Shepherson; **D:** Nigel Finch; **C:** Chris Seeger.

The Vanishing 1988 (PG) When his wife suddenly disappears, a young husband finds himself becoming increasingly obsessed with finding her. Three years down the road, his world has become one big, mad nightmare. Then, just as suddenly, the answer confronts him, but the reality of it may be too horrible to face. Well-made dark thriller based on French and Dutch with English subtitles. Remade by Sluizer in 1992. **107m/C VHS, DVD, NL FR** Bernard Pierre Donnadieu, Johanna Ter Steege, Gene Bervoets, Gwen Eckhaus, Bernadette Le Sache, Tania Latarjet, Lucille Glenn, Roger Souza; **D:** George Sluizer; **W:** George Sluizer, Tim Krabbé; **C:** Toni Kuhn; **M:** Henry Vrienten.

The Vanishing 1993 (R) Director Sluizer remakes his own 1988 Dutch film "Spoorloos" to lesser effect. Tense thriller about the disappearance of a woman (Bullock) at a highway rest stop. Her boyfriend (Sutherland) becomes obsessed with locating her, searching for memory. Unlike the Dutch original, the remake resorts to a clumsy ending designed for feel-good appeal. Based on the novel "The Golden Egg" by Tim Krabbé. **110m/C VHS, DVD,** Jeff Bridges, Kiefer Sutherland, Nancy Travis, Sandra Bullock, Park Overall Lisa Eichhorn, George Hearn, Maggie Linderman, Lynn Hamilton; **D:** George Sluizer; **W:** Todd Graff; **M:** Jerry Goldsmith.

Vanishing Act 1988 (R) While on his honeymoon, Harry Kenyon reports his wife missing to the local police. Within a short period of time his wife is found, but Harry says the woman is an impostor. This thriller follows Harry's desperate attempt to get to the truth. **94m/C VHS,** Mike Farrell, Margot Kidder, Elliott Gould, Fred Gwynne, Graham Jarvis; **D:** David Greene; **W:** Richard Levinson, William Link; **C:** Laszlo George; **M:** Kenneth Wannberg. TV

The Vanishing American 1925 The mistreatment of the American Indian is depicted in this sweeping Western epic that stars Dix as Nava o chieftain Nophale. Nophale must reconcile the heritage of his people with the 20th century

Vanilla Sky 2001 (R) Director Crowe goes existential in this puzzling surreal thriller, a remake of Alejandro Amenábar's 1997 Spanish film, "Abre los Ojos." Cruise plays David Aames, a publishing magnate and playboy who's got it all except for real love. Just when he thinks he's found it in the form of aspiring dancer Sofía (Cruz, reprising her role from the original), a bitter ex-lover (Diaz) changes the game by inadvertently changing David's pretty face. Fairly straightforward allegory becomes science fiction, where David (and the audience) can't tell dream from reality. Thought-provoking, even deliberately confusing plot may frustrate some. But for those who like rewarding, whether you like the explain-it-all ending or not. Decent acting, dreamy cinematography, and an engaging soundtrack will provide entertainment at the very least. **135m/C VHS, DVD, US** Tom Cruise, Penélope Cruz, Cameron Diaz, Jason Lee, Kurt Russell, Noah Taylor Timothy Spall, Tilda Swinton, Alicia Witt, Johnny Galecki, Michael Shannon; **D:** Cameron Crowe; **C:** John Toll; **M:** Nancy Wilson.

Vanina Vanini 1961 An acc-aimed Rossellini historical drama about the daughter of an Italian aristocrat in 1824 who nurses and falls in love with a wounded patriot hiding in her house. Based on a Stendhal short story. In Italian with English subtitles. **113m/B VHS, IT** Sandra Milo, Laurent Terzieff; **D:** Roberto Rossellini.

Vanished Spoorloos; Danielle Steel's Vanished 1995 (PG) Marielle and Charles are happily married in 1920 Paris until the tragic death of their son breaks them up. Marielle remarries and has another child who gets kidnapped and her estranged husband is arrested for the crime. **120m/C DVD,** George Hamilton, Lisa Rinna, Robert Hays, Maurice Godin, Alex D. Linz; **D:** George Kaczender; **W:** Kathleen Rowell; **C:** Pierre Mignot; **M:** Francois Dompierre. CABLE and deal with a crooked government agent. Filmed in Monument Valley and the Betatkin Cliff Dwellings of Arizona. Based on the novel by Zane Grey. **109m/B VHS, DVD.** Richard Dix, Noah Beery Sr., Lois Wilson; **D:** C. Harry Perry, Charles E. Schoenbaum.

Vanishing Legion 🐾🐾 1931 Western serial with outdoor action and gunplay. Twelve chapters. 13 minutes each. **156m/B VHS.** Frankie Darro, Harry Carey Sr.; **D:** B. Reeves Eason.

Vanishing Point 🐾🐾 1971 (R) An ex-racer makes a bet to deliver a souped-up car from Denver to San Francisco in 15 hours. Taking pep pills along the way, he eludes police, meets up with a number of characters, and finally crashes into a road-block. Rock score helps attract this film's cult following. **98m/C VHS, DVD.** Barry Newman, Cleavon Little, Gilda Texter, Dean Jagger, Paul Koslo, Robert Donner, Severn Darden, Victoria Medlin; **D:** Richard Sarafian; **W:** Guillermo Cain; **C:** John A. Alonzo; **M:** Jim Bowen, Peter Carpenter.

The Vanishing Westerner 🐾🐾 1950 A cowboy, falsely accused of murder, works to vindicate himself and uncovers a series of robberies. This one has enough plot twists to take it out of the routine. **60m/B VHS.** Monte Hale, Arthur Space, Aline Towne, Paul Hurst, Roy Barcroft, Richard Anderson, William Phipps; **D:** Philip Ford.

Vanity Fair 🐾🐾 1932 Loy stars in this tale of a wily and manipulative woman looking for the perfect marriage. This was the 58th film for the 27-year-old Loy, but even she couldn't save it. Of course, none of the three films based on the story by Thackeray have done it justice. **67m/B VHS, DVD.** Myrna Loy, Conway Tearle, Barbara Kent, Walter Byron, Anthony Bushell, Billy Bevan, Montagu Love, Mary Forbes; **D:** Chester M. Franklin.

Vanity Fair 🐾🐾½ 1967 BBC TV adaptation of William Makepeace Thackeray's novel about human folly in 19th-century England. Orphaned Becky Sharp (Little) is beautiful, clever and, despite her poverty, determined to get ahead in society so she can enjoy the same privileges as her posh childhood friend, Amelia Sedley (Grey). And she's not too particular about how she stakes her claim. Based on the novel by William Makepeace Thackeray, this Brit miniseries loses the author's acerbic voice which makes for a bland, though typically lavish, production. **300m/C VHS, DVD.** Natasha Little, Frances Grey, Nathaniel Parker, Philip Glenister, Jeremy Swift, Roger Ashton-Griffiths, Eleanor Bron, Anton Lesser, Miriam Margolyes, Michele Dotrice, David Bradley, David Ross; **D:** Marc Munden; **W:** Andrew Davies; **C:** Oliver Curtis. **TV**

Vanity Fair 🐾🐾½ 2004 (PG-13) In William Makepeace Thackeray's novel "Vanity Fair," Becky Sharp is an unrepentant social climber. But with Witherspoon tackling Becky in director Nair's version, such calculation just wouldn't do. Becky still aspires to climb the slippery social ladder in early 19th century Britain, but she has a heart. Becky first flirts with the wealthy, foppish brother (Maudsley) of her sweet-but-dim friend Amelia (Garai) but cannot bring him to marriage. She then rolls the dice with dashing gambler/soldier Rawdon Crawley (Purefoy). However, things never quite turn out for greedy Becky. Nair's hard-pressed to cover the novel's 30 years and multiple subplots so the film has a rushed feeling. Witherspoon is plucky but the supporting cast of British stalwarts (Hoskins, Atkins, Broadbent, etc.) gives the endeavor its panache. **137m/C VHS, DVD. US GB** Reese Witherspoon, Eileen Atkins, Jim Broadbent, Gabriel Byrne, Romola Garai, Bob Hoskins, Rhys Ifans, Geraldine McEwan, James Purefoy, Jonathan Rhys Meyers, Douglas Hodge, Natasha Little, Tony Maudsley; **D:** Mira Nair; **W:** Matthew Faulk, Mark Skeet, Julian Fellowes; **C:** Declan Quinn; **M:** Mychael Danna.

Vantage Point 🐾🐾½ 2008 (PG-13) Do they celebrate Groundhog day in Spain? U.S. President Ashton (Hurt) has just arrived in Spain to give the opening speech at a global "War on Terror" conference when he's shot. Sheer chaos ensues as eight different versions of the event unfold from eigh points of view. American tourist Howard Lewis (Whitaker) with his videocam; Secret Service agents Thomas Barnes (Quaid) and Kent Taylor (Fox); news producer Rex Brooks (Weaver) and others all saw the event, but in different ways. Is it terrorists or a conspiracy? Sure, each version adds another piece of the puzzle, but by the time it all actually comes together, the audience may be too confused or bored to care. **90m/C DVD. US** Dennis Quaid, Matthew Fox, Forest Whitaker, William Hurt, Sigourney Weaver, Bruce McGill, Edgar Ramirez, Said Taghmaoui, Ayelet Zurer, Zoe Saldana, Eduardo Noriega, Leonardo Nam, James LeGros; **D:** Stuart Baird, Pete Travis; **W:** Barry L. Levy; **C:** Amir M. Mokri; **M:** Atli Orvarsson.

Vanya on 42nd Street 🐾🐾🐾½ 1994 (PG) Group of actors in street clothes rehearse a workshop production of Chekhov's play, "Uncle Vanya," in New York's dilapidated New Amsterdam Theater. Theatrical director Gregory first gets his group together in 1989, with Mamet's contemporary adaptation, and they continue to work in private until Malle films their production some four years later before a small, select audience. Shawn, best known for "My Dinner with Andre" portrays Vanya with depth and complexity. The other actors shine as well, often against type, in this complex Russian drama of desperation. **119m/C VHS, DVD.** Wallace Shawn, Julianne Moore, Brooke Smith, Larry Pine, George Gaynes, Lynn Cohen, Madhur Jaffrey, Phoebe Brand, Jerry Mayer, Andre Gregory; **D:** Louis Malle; **W:** Andre Gregory, David Mamet; **C:** Declan Quinn; **M:** Joshua Redman.

Varan the Unbelievable 🐾 *Daikaiju Baran; The Monster Baran* 1961 A chemical experiment near a small island in the Japanese archipelago disturbs a prehistoric monster beneath the water. The awakened monster spreads terror on the island. Most difficult part of this movie is deciding what the rubber monster model is supposed to represent. **70m/C VHS, DVD. JP** Myron Healey, Tsuruko Kobayashi; **D:** Inoshiro Honda.

Varian's War 🐾🐾½ 2001 Based on the true story of American Varian Fry (Hurt), who is the editor of a foreign affairs publication when he witnesses the Nazi rise in Berlin and decides he must help Europe's Jews despite American neutrality. He heads off to Marseilles where a number of artists and intellectuals wait to escape Vichy France and establishes an underground rescue organization. **120m/C VHS, DVD.** William Hurt, Julia Ormond, Matt Craven, Maury Chaykin, Alan Arkin, Lynn Redgrave, Remy Girard, Chris Heyerdahl, Vlasta Vrana, Gloria Carlin, John Dunn-Hill; **D:** Lionel Chetwynd; **W:** Lionel Chetwynd; **C:** Daniel Jobin; **M:** Neil Smolar. **CABLE**

Variety 🐾🐾 *Vaudeville; Variete* 1925 Simple and tragic tale of a scheming young girl and the two men of whom she takes advantage. The European circus in all its beautiful sadness is the setting. Extraordinary cast and superb cinematography. Silent. **104m/B VHS, DVD. GE** Emil Jannings, Lya de Putti, Warwick Ward, Werner Krauss; **D:** E.A. Dupont; **W:** E.A. Dupont; **C:** Karl Freund.

Variety 🐾½ 1983 Christine (McLeod) gets a job selling tickets at a porno theatre near Times Square and starts getting curious about the milieu. Her relationships begin to change as her interest in pornography becomes all-consuming. **97m/C VHS.** Sandy McLeod, Will Patton, Richard Davidson; **B:** Bette Gordon; **W:** Kathy Acker; **C:** Tom DiCillo; **M:** John Lurie.

Variety Girl 🐾🐾½ 1947 More than 55 Paramount stars appear in this salute to the Variety Club charitable organization, so the plot is the least important element. Catherine (Hatcher) and Amber (San Juan) have both made their way to Hollywood with stars in their eyes and

eventually find themselves on the studio lot. Your basic extravaganza-type show, benefitting the charity, concludes the picture. **93m/B VHS.** Mary Hatcher, Olga San Juan, DeForest Kelley; **D:** George Marshall; **W:** Edmund Hartman, Frank Tashlin, Monte Brice, Robert L. Welch; **C:** Lionel Lindon, Stuart Thompson.

Variety Lights 🐾🐾🐾½ *Luci del Varieta; Lights of Variety* 1951 Fellini's first (albeit joint) directorial effort, wherein a young girl runs away with a travelling vaudeville troupe and soon becomes its main attraction as a dancer. Filled with Fellini's now-familiar delight in the bizarre and sawdust/tinsel entertainment. In Italian with English subtitles. **93m/B VHS, DVD.** IT Giulietta Masina, Peppino de Filippo, Carla Del Poggio, Folco Lulli; **D:** Federico Fellini, Alberto Lattuada; **W:** Federico Fellini, Alberto Lattuada, Tullio Pinelli, Ennio Flaiano; **C:** Otello Martelli; **M:** Felice Lattuada.

Varsity Blues 🐾🐾½ 1998 (R) After star quarterback Lance (Walker) goes down with an injury, backup Mox (Van Der Beek) learns the perks of stardom in a small Texas town obsessed with high school football. It's not all free six-packs and groupies in whipped cream bikinis, however. He butts heads with blood-and-guts Coach Kilmer (Voight), whose win-at-all-costs philosophy is injuring his players. Mox leads the players in a rebellion against the usual doubts about the inevitable "big game." The young cast does an admirable job lifting the material above the average jock flick, but it lurches into the gutter a little too often for some tastes. **103m/C VHS, DVD.** James Van Der Beek, Jon Voight, Paul Walker, Ron Lester, Scott Caan, Richard Lineback, Amy Smart, Thomas F. Duffy, Tony Perenski, Tiffany C. Love, Eliel Swinton, Jill Parker Jones, Joe Pichler, Ali Larter; **D:** Brian Robbins; **W:** W. Peter Iliff; **C:** Charles Cohen; **M:** Mark Isham. MTV Movie Awards '99: Breakthrough Perf. (Van Der Beek).

Vasectomy: A Delicate Matter WOOF! *Vasectomy* 1986 (PG-13) A mother of eight issues a final decree to her husband about their sex life. He must get a vasectomy or there won't be any. As good as it sounds. **92m/C VHS.** Paul Sorvino, Abe Vigoda, Cassandra Edwards, Lorne Greene, Ina Balin, June Wilkinson, William Marshall; **D:** Robert Burge; **W:** Robert Burge.

Vatel 🐾🐾 2000 (PG-13) Lavish period drama suffers from a dull screenplay and a lack of gusto. In 1671, Sun King Louis XIV (Sands) is ruling with the usual decadence when he and his court are invited to the country chateau of the Prince de Conde (Glover), who's hoping to curry favor. Conde leaves the plans for the royal visit to his steward, Francois Vatel (Depardieu). He must supply food and entertainment to keep the court amused but Vatel provokes envy as well. Depardieu is efficient but the English language cast seems to be primping more than acting. **117m/C VHS, DVD. GB FR** Gerard Depardieu, Uma Thurman, Tim Roth, Julian Glover, Julian Sands, Timothy Spall, Arielle Dombasle, Hywel Bennett, Richard Griffiths, Feodor Atkine, Phillippe LeRoy, Murray Lachlan Young; **D:** Roland Joffe; **W:** Jeanne Labrune, Tom Stoppard; **C:** Robert Fraisse; **M:** Ennio Morricone.

Vatican Conspiracy 🐾🐾 1981 The members of the Vatican's College of Cardinals do everything in their power to discredit a newly appointed radical pontiff. **90m/C VHS.** IT Fabrizio Bentivoglio, Gabriele Ferzetti, Paola Molina, Antonio Marsina, Terence Stamp; **D:** Marcello Aliprandi, Marcello Aliprandi; **W:** Marcello Aliprandi; **C:** Alejandro Ulloa; **M:** Pino Donaggio.

The Vault 🐾🐾 2000 (R) Teacher Mr. Burnett (Lyde) leads four students—Dezaray (Pride), Willy (Priester), Zipper (Walker), and Kyle (Davis) to visit an old high school, which is scheduled to be demolished. (The four kids fit the stereotypes of cheerleader, jock, nerd, and tough guy.) The school was originally a way-station for slaves and the group hopes to rescue some historical items (or something like that). Once they arrive at the school, they meet the eerie security guard Spangler (Papi), who warns them to not venture into the basement. You see, there's a very old locked door in the basement, and behind

that door is...ultimate evil. Unfortunately, the film ends just as it's beginning to get interesting. **85m/C DVD.** Ted Lyde, Shani Pride, Austin Priester, Kyle Walker, Michael Cory Davis, Leopold Papi; **D:** James Black.

Vault of Horror 🐾🐾 *Tales from the Crypt II* 1973 (R) A collection of five terrifying tales based on original stories from the E.C. comic books of the 1950s. Stories include, "Midnight Mess," "Bargain in Death," "This Trick'll Kill You," "The Neat Job," and "Drawn and Quartered." **86m/C VHS, DVD. GB** Terry-Thomas, Curt Jurgens, Glynis Johns, Dawn Addams, Daniel Massey, Tom Baker, Michael Craig, Anna Massey, Denholm Elliott; **D:** Roy Ward Baker; **W:** Milton Subotsky.

The Vector File 🐾🐾½ 2003 (R) Little Mattie got her hands on a wicked DNA code that threatens the world if not kept under wraps forcing dear old dad to fend off the terrorists in pursuit of it. Stars reallife family—Van Dien is Oxenberg's husband and India is her daughter. **92m/C VHS, DVD.** Casper Van Dien, Catherine Oxenberg, Timothy Balme, William Wallace, Katherine Kennard, India Oxenberg, Roz Turnbull, George Henare, Laurie Foel, Stephen Hall, David Stott, Chic Littlewood, Craig Hall, Paddy Wilson, Paul Norell, Roz Watrington, Chris Easley; **D:** Eliot Christopher; **W:** Iain McFadyen; **C:** Kevin Riley; **M:** Bruce Lynch. **VIDEO**

Vegas 🐾 1978 A private detective, with Las Vegas beauties as assistants and pursuers, solves the murder of a teenage runaway girl. Pilot for a TV series. Scriptwriter Mann went on to do "Miami Vice." **74m/C VHS.** Robert Urich, June Allyson, Tony Curtis, Will Sampson, Greg Morris; **D:** Richard Lang; **W:** Michael Mann. **TV**

Vegas in Space WOOF! 1994 Four male astronauts take a secret mission to the planet Clitoris, the all-female pleasure plant where men are forbidden to trod. To capture a heinous villainous, they swallow gender-reversal pills in order to infiltrate the resort as show-girls. Typical Troma trash. Boasts an all-transvestite cast. **85m/C VHS, DVD.** Doris Fish, Miss X, Ginger Quest, Ramona Fischer, Lori Naslund, Timmy Spence, Silvana Nova, Sandelle Kincaid, Tommy Pace, Arturo Galster, Jennifer Blowdryer, Freida Lay, Tippi; **D:** Phillip R. Ford; **W:** Phillip R. Ford, Doris Fish, Miss X; **C:** Robin Clark; **M:** Ramona Fischer, Timmy Spence.

The Vegas Strip Wars 🐾🐾 *Las Vegas Strip War* 1984 Rival casino owners battle it out in the land of lady luck. Unmemorable except for Jones's Don King impersonation and the fact that it was Hudson's last TV movie. **100m/C VHS, DVD.** Rock Hudson, James Earl Jones, Noriyuki "Pat" Morita, Sharon Stone, Robert Costanzo; **D:** George Englund.

Vegas Vacation 🐾 1996 (PG) It might not have come out under the "National Lampoon" banner but you'll recognize both the characters and the situations. The innocent Griswold clan head from their Chicago home to the bright lights and gambling temptations of Las Vegas. Clark (Chase) blows all their money, Ellen (D'Angelo) reveals a hidden passion for Wayne Newton, daughter Audrey (Nichols) decides to become a go-go dancer, and son Rusty (Embry) turns into a high roller who draws the attention of the mob. Oh yeah, dimwit cousin Eddie (Quaid) also tries to supply a few yucks. **98m/C VHS, DVD.** Chevy Chase, Beverly D'Angelo, Randy Quaid, Ethan (Randall) Embry, Miriam Flynn, Marisol Nichols, Shae D'Lyn, Wallace Shawn, Wayne Newton; **Cameos:** Sid Caesar, Julia Sweeney, Christie Brinkley; **D:** Stephen Kessler; **W:** Elisa Bell; **C:** William A. Fraker; **M:** Joel McNeely.

Vegas Vice 🐾½ 1994 Tweed and Jones are Vegas cops after a serial killer, who might be a hooker. Routine. **83m/C VHS, DVD.** Sam Jones, Shannon Tweed, James Gammon, Tom Fridley, Rebecca Ferratti, Branscombe Richmond; **D:** Joey Travolta; **W:** Joey Travolta; **M:** Jeff Lass.

The Velocity of Gary 🐾½ *The Velocity of Gary* (*Not His Real Name*) 1998 (R) Melodrama about love, death, and what makes a weak script, strained humor, and a screechy performance by Hayek. Gary's (Jane) a hustler in New York City who's attracted to bisexual porn star Valentino (D'Onofrio).

Valentino has a possessive waitress girlfriend, Mary Carren (Hayek), and she... to put aside their differences. **98m/C VHS, DVD.** Vincent D'Onofrio, Salma Hayek, Thomas Jane, Olivia D'Abo; **D:** Dan Ireland; **W:** James Still; **C:** Claudio Rocha.

Velocity Trap 1999 (R) In 2150, electronic crime and piracy run rampant throughout the galaxy. Cop Raymond Stokes (Gruner) is assigned to escort a federal banking ship through a section of space, known as the Velocity Run, that's equivalent to the Bermuda Triangle. Along with ship's navigator, Beth Shatfield (Coppola), Stokes must prevent thieves from grabbing the ship's loot and an asteroid from destroying the ship itself. **90m/C VHS, DVD.** Olivier Gruner, Alicia Coppola, Ken Olandt, Bruce Weitz, Craig Wasson; **D:** Phillip J. Roth; **W:** Phillip J. Roth. VIDEO

Velvet Goldmine 1998 (R) Director Haynes takes on the excesses of the '70s British glam-rock era. In 1994, journalist Arthur Stuart (Bale) is assigned to write a "Whatever Happened to" article on the 10-year disappearance of vanished superstar Brian Slade (Rhys Meyers as a cross between T-Rex's Marc Bolan and a Ziggy Stardust-era David Bowie). This leads fan Arthur to Slade's viperish ex-wife Mandy (Collette) and his ex-manager Jerry Divine (Izzard). But Arthur discovers the most important relationship in Brian's life was to self-destructive cult idol Curt Wild (MacGregor, channelling Iggy Pop). The flamboyant duo had an equally flamboyant affair that eventual lead to a downward spiral for them both. The story might be average but the visuals are spectacular and MacGregor, especially, is mesmerizing. **120m/C VHS, DVD.** Jonathan Rhys Meyers, Christian Bale, Toni Collette, Eddie Izzard, Emily Woof, Michael Feast; **D:** Todd Haynes; **W:** Todd Haynes; **M:** Carter Burwell; British Acad. '98: Costume Des.; Ind. Spirit '99: Cinematog.

Velvet Smooth 1976 (R) A protection agency's sultry boss, Velvet Smooth, gets involved solving the problems of a numbers racket. **85m/C VHS, DVD.** Johnnie Hill; **D:** Janece Fink.

Velvet Touch 1948 Well-engineered thriller about an actress who craftily murders her producer. A theatre-loving police detective winds up accusing the wrong woman—sending the over-wrought murderess into a moral tailspin. Things don't work out as you may expect. Fine acting. **97m/B VHS.** Rosalind Russell, Leo Genn, Claire Trevor, Sydney Greenstreet, Leon Ames, Frank McHugh, Walter Kingsford, Dan Tobin, Lex Barker, Nydia Westman; **D:** John Gage; **W:** Leo Rosten.

The Velvet Vampire 1971 (R) Yarnall is a sexy, sun-loving, dune buggy-riding vampiress who seduces a young, sexy, swinging, California couple in her desert home. Lots of atmosphere to go along with the blood and nudity. **97m/B VHS.** Michael Blodgett, Sherry Miles, Celeste Yarnall, Gene Shane, Jerry Daniels, Sandy Ward, Paul Prokop, Chris Woodley, Robert Tessier; **D:** Stephanie Rothman, Maurice Jules, Charles Swartz; **C:** Daniel Lacambre.

Vendetta 1985 A woman gets herself arrested and sent to the penitentiary in order to exact revenge there for her sister's death. Acting and pacing make this better than the average sexploitation flick. **89m/C VHS.** Karen Chase, Sandy Martin, Durga McBroom, Kin Shriner, Eugene Robert Glazer; **D:** Bruce Logan; **M:** David Newman.

Vendetta 1999 (R) Based on a true story. New Orleans politicians and businessman seek to wrest away control of the docks from the Italian family that controls it. An unleashed angry mob leads to the largest lynching in American history. Adapted from the book by Richard Gambino. **117m/C VHS, DVD.** Christopher Walken, Clancy Brown, Bruce Davison, Joaquim de Almeida, Edward Herrmann, Kenneth Welsh; **D:** Nicholas Meyer; **W:** Tim Prager; **C:** David Franco; **M:** John Altman. CABLE

Vendetta for the Saint 1968 A feature-length episode of the TV series "The Saint," in which Simon Templar pursues a Sicilian mobster on a personal vendetta. He attempts to redeem himself by working on his own to infiltrate the same gang. **98m/C VHS.** Roger Moore; **D:** James O'Connolly; **W:** Harry Junkin, John Kruse; **C:** Brendan Stafford; **M:** Edwin Astley. TV

Vengeance 1937 A police officer resigns in shame after failing to thwart a holdup. He attempts to redeem himself by working on his own to infiltrate the same gang. **61m/B VHS.** Lyle Talbot, Wendy Barrie, Wally Albright, Marc Lawrence; **D:** Del Lord.

Vengeance 1980 Four burglars take hostages after their robbery is bungled, but they won't get away—especially after the hostages die. **92m/C VHS.** Sally Lockett, Nicholas Jacquez, Bob Elliott; **D:** Bob Blizz.

Vengeance Is Mine 1974 (R) A bereaved young man strikes out against the injustice of his parents' murder. His revenge against the killers takes him several steps beyond the law, and he's not so sure it was the right idea. **90m/C VHS.** Brad Davis, Roxanne Hart, Brad Dourif, William Conrad; **D:** Marc Daniels. TV

Vengeance Is Mine WOOF! 1974 Fukusho Surawa Ware Ni Ari 1979 Told in flashbacks, the film focuses on the life of a habitual criminal whose life of deprivation leads to murder. Contains violence and nudity. Based on a true story. In Japanese with English subtitles. **125m/C VHS, JP** Ken Ogata, Rentaro Mikuni, Mitsuko Baisho, Chocho Miyako, Mayumi Ogawa, Nijiko Kiyokawa; **D:** Shohei Imamura; **W:** Masuru Baba; **C:** Shinsaku Himeda.

The Vengeance of She 1968 The reincarnation of 2,000-year-old queen, Ayesha, by her immortal lover, King Killikrates (Richardson). The king promises high priest Man Hari (Godfrey) immortality if he can restore Ayesha's soul. But Carol's shrink boyfriend (Judd) isn't crazy about the idea and tries to convince the king otherwise. **101m/C VHS, DVD.** GB Derek Godfrey, Edward Judd, Colin Blakely; **D:** Cliff Owen; **W:** Peter O'Donnell; **C:** Peter Suschitzky; **M:** Mario Nascimbene.

Vengeance of the Dead 2001 This homegrown horror flick never manages to live up to the big ideas which it introduces. Eric (Galvin) journeys to the town of Harvest, to visit his Grandpa (Volmers). (Although we're never told where he's been or given an idea of how long he's going to stay.) Once he's settled in, Eric has strange nightmares concerning a little girl, an act of violence, and a burning house. These dreams lead him to sleepwalk through the town and commit strange acts of vengeance. The dreams and Eric's behaviors are linked to a crime from many years ago, and a ghostly presence is seeking revenge on those responsible. Despite an interesting premise, but the film is slow, boring, and hard to follow at times. Kudos to filmmakers Adams and Picardi for squeezing as much as possible out of their limited budget, but this movie can't overcome its amateur roots. **85m/C DVD.** Michael Galvin, Mark Volmers; **D:** Don Adams, Harry James Picardi.

Vengeance of the Zombies 1972 A madman seeks revenge by setting an army of walking corpses to stalk the streets of London. **90m/C VHS, DVD.** SP Paul Naschy; **D:** Leon Klimovsky.

Vengeance Valley 1951 Lancaster and Walker are foster brothers with Walker being an envious weasel who always expects Lancaster to get him out of scrapes. Lancaster is even accused of a crime committed by Walker and must work to clear himself. Good cast is let down by uneven direction. **83m/C VHS, DVD.** Burt Lancaster, Joanne Dru, Robert Walker, Sally Forrest, John Ireland, Hugh O'Brian; **D:** Richard Thorpe; **W:** Irving Ravetch; **C:** George J. Folsey; **M:** Rudolph Kopp.

Venice, Venice 1992 (R) Alternately earnest and satirical, Jaglom pokes fun at himself and movie-making in a movie about, well, himself and movie-making. Consciously straddling the genre fence, he uses real people and events but adopts a pseudonym, Dean, in Venice, Italy, young filmmaker Alard decides to make a film about Dean/Jaglom, a plot which creates the effect of two mirrors reflecting each other into infinity. Dean/Jaglom and Alard return to Venice, California, where he conducts auditions for a movie in which he will star and direct. Art imitating life or life imitating art? More importantly, does it really matter? **108m/C VHS, DVD.** Nelly Alard, Henry Jaglom, Suzanne Bertish, Melissa Leo, Daphna Kastner, David Duchovny, Diane Salinger, Zack Norman, Marshall Barer, John Landis, Pierre Cottrell, Edna Fainaru; **D:** Henry Jaglom; **W:** Henry Jaglom; **C:** Frannia Baer.

Venom WOOF! 1982 (R) Deadly black mamba is loose in an elegant townhouse, terrorizing big-name cast. The snake continually terrorizes an evil kidnapper, his accomplices and his kidnapped victim. Participants walk through tired cliches with that far-away look in their eyes—like they wish they were anywhere else. Original director Tobe Hooper was replaced. **92m/C VHS, DVD.** Sterling Hayden, Klaus Kinski, Sarah Miles, Nicol Williamson, Cornelia Sharpe, Susan George, Michael Gough, Oliver Reed; **D:** Piers Haggard; **W:** Robert B. Carrington; **M:** Michael Kamen.

Venom 2005 (R) Swamp-set slasher flick offers redneck Ray (Cramer) getting bitten by a suitcase full of snakes that happened to belong to a voodoo priestess. Ray gets resurrected and goes after all the pretty teens (male and female) who annoyed Ray when he was alive. Hits all the genre highlights, so if voodoo and zombies and gore, oh my, are what you're searching for, look no further. **87m/C DVD.** US Agnes Bruckner, Joshua Jackson, Rick Cramer, Meagan Good, Bijou Phillips, Method Man, Laura Ramsey, Pawel Szajda, Stacey Travis, James Pickens Jr., Davetta Sherwood, D.J. Cotrona; **D:** Jim Gillespie; **W:** Flint Dille, Brandon Boyce; **C:** Steve Mason; **M:** James L. Venable.

Venomous 2001 (PG-13) Genetically altered poisonous snakes make their presence felt in a small town by spreading a deadly virus among the human population. To cover up the source of the disease, the military (the snakes are a product of their experiments gone wrong) plans to blow up the town. **97m/C VHS, DVD.** Treat Williams, Mary Page Keller, Brian Poth, J.B. Gaynor, Hannes Jaenicke, Geoffrey Pierson, Catherine Dent; **D:** Fred Olen Ray; **W:** Dan Golden, Sean McGinley; **C:** Andrea V. Rossotto; **M:** Neal Acree. VIDEO

Venus 2006 (R) The ever-charismatic, though now frail, O'Toole plays a mildly famous charmer of an actor who still takes an interest in a pretty girl, even if the flesh is weak. Maurice's best friend is his grumpy (and equally aged) fellow thespian Ian (Phillips). Ian's grand-niece Jessie (Whittaker) has ostensibly arrived to help him out but the sullen, lower-class teen is more concerned with her own interests. This doesn't prevent Maurice from becoming interested in her, though it might be more a nod to his rogue past than to Jessie herself. Funny and poignant without mawkishness; also notable is the appearance of Redgrave as Maurice's estranged ex-wife. **94m/C DVD.** GB Peter O'Toole, Leslie Phillips, Richard Griffiths, Jodie Whittaker, Vanessa Redgrave; **D:** Roger Michell; **W:** Hanif Kureishi; **C:** Hans Zambarloukos; **M:** David Arnold, Corinne Bailey Rae.

Venus Against the Son of Hercules Marte, Dio Della Guerra 1962 Our hero must use all his genetically procured musculature in his battle against the lovely but deadly Venus. **77m/C VHS, 77** Jack Le Lane, Roger Browne, Massimo Serato, Linda Sini, Dante DiPaolo; **D:** Marcello Baldi; **W:** Ernesto Gastaldi.

Venus Beauty Institute 1998 (R) Forsyth Angele (Baye) works at a Paris beauty salon along with proprietor Nadine (Ogier) and younger colleagues Samantha (Seigner) and Marie (Tautou). Angele refuses to fall in love and picks up men strictly for sex—until she's pursued by Antoine (Le Bihan), a young sculptor who insists she fall in love with her at first sight. (He basically stalks her but Angele is intrigued rather than repulsed by his devotion.) The Institute also has a parade of frequently neurotic customers in romantic dilemmas. French with subtitles. **105m/C VHS, DVD.** FR Nathalie Baye, Bulle Ogier, Samuel Le Bihan, Jacques Bonnaffe, Mathilde Seigner, Robert Hossein, Claire Nebout, Audrey Tautou; **D:** Tonie Marshall; **W:** Tonie Marshall; **C:** Gérard de Battista; **M:** Khalil Chahine, Cesar '00: Director

Venus in Furs 1995 (R) Paroxismus; Puo Una Morta Rivivere Per Amore?; Venus in Furs 1970 (R) Jazz musician working in Rio de Janeiro becomes obsessed with a mysterious woman; she resembles a murder victim whose body he discovered months earlier. Weird mix of horror, sadism, black magic, and soft porn. **70m/C VHS, DVD, GB IT GE** James Darren, Klaus Kinski, Barbara McNair, Dennis Price, Maria Rohm, Margaret Lee, Jess (Jesus) Franco; **D:** Jess (Jesus) Franco; **W:** Milo G. Cuccia, Malvin Wald, ess (Jesus) Franco; **C:** Angelo Lotti.

Venus Rising 1995 (R) In the year 2000, Eve and August manage to escape from the island prison on which they were raised. They discover that the mainland world features emotions that are controlled by drugs and love is only a game on the virtual reality network. Huned, the fugitives try to fit in and figure out what's real and what's fantasy. Be forewarned—Fairchild's role is very small. **91m/C VHS, DVD.** Audie England, Costas Mandylor, Billy Wirth, Morgan Fairchild; **D:** Leora Barish.

Vera Cruz 1953 Two soldiers of fortune become involved in the Mexican Revolution of 1866, a stolen shipment of gold, divided loyalties, and gun battles. Less than innovative plot is made into an exciting action flick. **94m/C VHS, DVD.** Gary Cooper, Burt Lancaster, Denise Darcel, Cesar Romero, George Macready, Ernest Borgnine, Charles Bronson, Jack Elam; **D:** Robert Aldrich; **W:** Roland Kibbee, James R. Webb; **C:** Ernest Laszlo.

Vera Drake 2004 (R) Compassionate, complex drama with a stellar performance by Staunton in the title role. Set in the drab postwar London of 1950, Vera is a cozy, middle-aged married house cleaner who is relentlessly cheery and helpful to all those around her. This includes the poor young women who find themselves "in trouble." Vera, as it happens, is the local abortionist—something her family discovers only when the police descend on them after one of Vera's procedures goes wrong. Her subsequent trial highlights the hypocrisy of the proceedings (matched against Vera's bewildered decency) without becoming overbearing. **125m/C DVD.** Imelda Staunton, Philip Davis, Peter Wight, Adrien Scarborough, Heather Craney, Alex Kelly, Daniel Mays, Eddie Marsan, Sally Hawkins, Ruth Sheen, Helen Coker, Sandra Voe, Allan Corduner; **D:** Mike Leigh; **W:** Mike Leigh; **C:** Dick Pope; **M:** Andrew Dickson; British Acad. '04: Actress (Staunton), Costume Des., Director (Leigh)

Verboten! 1959 In post-war occupied Berlin, an American G.I. falls in love with a German girl. Good direction maintains a steady pace. **93m/B VHS.** James Best, Susan Cummings, Tom Pittman, Paul Dubov; **D:** Samuel Fuller; **W:** Samuel Fuller; **C:** Joseph Biroc.

Verdi ✓✓ *The Life and Music of Giuseppe Verdi* 1953 The story of the Italian operatic composer and the loves of his life. Italian with subtitles. 80m/C VHS. *IT* Pierre Cressoy, Gaby Andre; **D:** Raffaello Matarazzo; **W:** Leonardo Benvenuti; **C:** Tino Santoni.

The Verdict ✓✓✓ 1982 (R) Frank Galvin (Newman) is an alcoholic failed attorney reduced to ambulance chasing. A friend gives him a supposedly easy malpractice case that pits Frank against a powerful establishment Catholic hospital in Boston in what turns out to be a last chance at redeeming himself and his career. Adapted from the novel by Barry Reed. One of Newman's finest performances. 122m/C VHS, DVD. Paul Newman, James Mason, Charlotte Rampling, Jack Warden, Milo O'Shea, Lindsay Crouse, Edward Binns, Roxanne Hart, James Handy, Wesley Addy, Joe Seneca, Julie Bovasso; **D:** Sidney Lumet; **W:** David Mamet; **C:** Andrzej Bartkowiak; **M:** Johnny Mandel. Natl. Bd. of Review '82: Director (Lumet).

Verdict in Blood ✓✓ 2002 (R) When the judge she covered is murdered, reporter Joanne Kilbourne's hunt for the culprit exposes scandalous family secrets. Based on Gail Bowen's serial novel. 90m/C VHS, DVD. Wendy Crewson, Shawn Doyle, Zachary Bennett, Neil Crone, Robert Davi, Richard Fitzpatrick, Ken James, Sally Kellerman, Kristen Lehman, Reagan Pasternak, Elizabeth Shepherd, Walter Alza, Alex Campbell, Diego Chambers, Pablo Coffey, Callahan Connor, Angela Gei, Kristen Gutoskie, Natasha La Force, Shawn Laurence, Lila Yee, Jean Yoon, Gail Bowen, Janet Maclean, Andrew Wreggitt; **D:** Stephen Williams; **W:** Jeremy Hole; **C:** David Herrington; **M:** Robert Carli. TV

Verdict on Auschwitz: The Frankfurt Auschwitz Trial 1963—1965 ✓✓✓ *Strafsache 4 Ks 2/63: Auschwitz Vor Dem Frankfurter Schwurgericht* 1993 Originally made for German TV, where it was shown as a 3-part documentary. (It was also released in 2005 in a 60-minute version.) This re-release is a loosely structured examination of the 1963-65 trial of 22 Auschwitz SS officers, based on 430 hours of audiotapes. Directors Bickel and Wagner divide this chilling recounting into the investigation, the trial (which included testimony by more than 200 survivors), and the verdict. Testimony is illustrated with footage and photographs as well as archival material. English, German, Polish, and Russian with subtitles. 180m/C DVD. **GE D:** Rolf Bickel, Dietrich Wagner; **W:** Rolf Bickel, Dietrich Wagner; **C:** Armin Alker, Dominik Schunk; **Nar:** Edgar M. Boehke.

Vermont Is for Lovers ✓✓½ 1992 Pre-wedding jitters consume stressed-out Manhattanites Marya (Cohn) and George (Thrush) when they travel to bucolic Tunbridge, Vermont to get married on Marya's Aunt Ann's farm. After continuously arguing, they decide to spend the day before the wedding apart and George wanders around the community asking marriage advice from various old-timers. The Yuppie leads aren't terribly compelling and neither is the improvised dialogue. 86m/C VHS. George Thrush, Marya Cohn, Ann O'Brien; **D:** John O'Brien; **C:** John O'Brien; **M:** Tony Silbert.

Verne Miller ✓✓ 1988 (R) A film of the true story of Verne Miller, Al Capone's hit man. After rescuing a friend from the Feds, Miller is hunted down by both the cops and the mob. 95m/C VHS. Scott Glenn, Barbara Stock, Thomas G. Waites, Lucinda Jenney, Sonny Carl Davis; **D:** Rod Hewitt.

Vernie ✓✓ 2004 Sean and Kristi were once best friends and they reunite when Sean is diagnosed with an inoperable brain tumor. When Sean asks Kristi to have his child, she surprises herself by agreeing. But the ensuing months prove to be more difficult than either of them imagined. A tearjerker with humor, combo. 86m/C DVD. Amy Colon, John Riedlinger, Patrick Coyle, Allyson Kearns, Adam Whisner, Heidi Jo Langseth; **D:** David Tufford; **W:** Kevin Ross; **C:** David Doyle; **M:** Todd Syring.

The Vernonia Incident ✓½ 1989 Urban guerillas invade a small town, killing the police chief. The townspeople gather up their shotguns and fight back. That's entertainment. 95m/C VHS. David Jackson, Shawn Stevens, Floyd Ragner, Ed Justice, Robert Louis Jakson; **D:** Ray Etheridge; **W:** Ray Etheridge.

Veronica Guerin ✓✓½ 2003 (R) A less than inspired script is nonetheless brought to life by the brilliant acting of Blanchett in the title role of the real-life Irish reporter, who took on a Dublin drug lord in the 1990s. Despite threats and extreme violence, the plucky wife and mother was relentless in her pursuit of the truth. While Guerin pays for her anti-drug crusade with her life, gunned down at a red light in 1996 by a suspected drug-world henchman, pic tones down the martyr factor by presenting a well-rounded character. Hinds effectively plays a sympathetic Guerin informant who tries to warn her of her impending doom. 98m/C VHS, DVD. *US* Cate Blanchett, Gerard McSorley, Ciaran Hinds, Brenda Fricker, Barry Barnes, David Murray, Joe Hanley, David Herlihy, Gerry O'Brien, Don Wycherley, Colin Farrell, Alan Devine; **D:** Joel Schumacher; **W:** Carol Doyle, Mary Agnes Donoghue; **C:** Brendan Galvin; **M:** Harry Gregson-Williams.

Veronico Cruz ✓✓½ *La Dueda Interna; The Debt* 1987 Despite its sincerity, Pereira's feature debut offers muddled response to the human waste incurred by the Falklands War. Set in a tiny remote village in the Argentinean mountains, the film's narrative is derived from the growing friendship between a shepherd boy and a teacher from the city. Well-meaning anti-war movie. In Spanish with English subtitles. 96m/C VHS, DVD. *AR GB* Juan Jose Camero, Gonzalo Morales, Rene Olaguivel, Guillermo Delgado; **D:** Miguel Pereira; **W:** Miguel Pereira, Eduardo Leiva Muller; **C:** Gerry Feeny; **M:** David Eppel, Jaime Torres.

Veronika Voss ✓✓✓ *Die Sehns Ucht Der Veronika Voss* 1982 (R) Highlights the real life of fallen film star Sybille Schmitz who finally took her own life out of despair. Played by Zech, Voss is exploited by her physician to turn over all of her personal belongings for morphine. A lover discovers the corruption and reveals it to the authorities. Highly metaphorical and experimental in its treatment of its subject. In German with English subtitles. 105m/C VHS, DVD. *GE* Rosel Zech, Hilmar Thate, Conny Froboess, Anna Marie Duringer, Volker Spengler; **D:** Rainer Werner Fassbinder; **W:** Pea Frolich, Peter Marthesheimer; **C:** Xaver Schwarzenberger; **M:** Peer Raben.

Vertical Limit ✓✓ 2000 (PG-13) Photographer O'Donnell joins a team of mountain climbers in order to rescue his sister Tunney, who is part of a group trapped on K2. Plot serves mainly as connective tissue for the numerous heart-stopping (and well-done) action sequences. Mountain-fodder cast has few standouts, except maybe Glenn in the crazy-but-wise-old-coot role. 126m/C VHS, DVD, Blu-ray Disc. Chris O'Donnell, Robin Tunney, Bill Paxton, Scott Glenn, Izabela Scorupco, Temuera Morrison, Stuart Wilson, Nicholas Lea, David Hayman, Ben Mendelson, Steve Le Marquand; **D:** Martin Campbell; **W:** Robert King, Terry Hayes; **C:** David Tattersall; **M:** James Newton Howard.

The Vertical Ray of the Sun ✓✓½ 2000 (PG-13) Slow-moving visual treat set in Hanoi. Three sisters plan a commemorative meal in honor of their mother's death. The two eldest sisters have marital problems and the youngest is so close to their brother that many believe the twosome are sexually involved. Over the course of a month (which ends with the anniversary of their father's death), the women deal with their emotional entanglements. Vietnamese with subtitles. 112m/C VHS, DVD. *VT FR* Tran Nu Yen-Khe, Nguyen Nhu Quynh, Le Khanh, Tran Manh Cuong, Chu Ngoc Hung, Ngo Quang Hai; **D:** Tran Anh Hung; **W:** Tran Anh Hung; **C:** Mark Lee Ping-Bin; **M:** Ton That Tiet.

Vertigo ✓✓✓✓ 1958 (PG) Hitchcock's romantic story of obsession, manipulation and fear. Stewart plays a detective forced to retire after his fear of heights causes the death of a fellow policeman and, perhaps, the death of a woman he'd been hired to follow. The appearance of her double (Novak), whom he compulsively transforms into the dead girl's image, leads to a mesmerizing cycle of madness and lies. Features Herrmann's haunting music. 126m/C VHS, DVD. James Stewart, Kim Novak, Barbara Bel Geddes, Tom Helmore, Ellen Corby, Henry Jones, Raymond Bailey, Lee Patrick; **D:** Alfred Hitchcock; **W:** Samuel A. Taylor; **C:** Robert Burks; **M:** Bernard Herrmann. AFI '98: Top 100, Natl. Film Reg. '89.

Very Annie Mary ✓✓½ 2000 Sentimental comedy set in a small Welsh village filled with eccentrics. That would include singing baker Jack (Pryce), a tyrannical widower who dominates his gauche, 30-ish daughter Annie-Mary (Griffiths). She's saving up to buy a house of her own when her father is felled by a severe stoke and she must take over running the family bakery (for which she has no talent). What Annie-Mary can do is sing and she decides to enter a talent contest in Cardiff in order to fund a trip to Disneyland for her dying friend Bethan (Page). Very twee. 105m/C VHS, DVD. *GB FR* Rachel Griffiths, Jonathan Pryce, Ioan Gruffudd, Matthew Rhys, Kenneth Griffiths, Ruth Madoc, Joanna Page, Radcliffe Gratton; **D:** Sara Sugarman; **W:** Sara Sugarman; **C:** Barry Ackroyd; **M:** Stephen Warbeck.

Very Bad Things ✓✓ 1998 (R) What begins as a not-so-innocent prenuptial bachelor party in Vegas quickly disintegrates into a murderous blood bath. Kyle (Favreau), the groom-to-be, escapes the clutches of his control-freak fiance Laura (Diaz) with some pals, including unscrupulous yuppie Boyd (Slater). When the hired "entertainment" is killed in a freak accident involving a towel hook, Boyd comes up with the idea of burying her body in the desert and going on with the wedding. A pitch-dark comedy of errors ensues. Peter Berg's first stab at writing and directing has some funny moments, mostly the kind you realize afterwards you shouldn't find funny, but relies too heavily on gratuitous gore and shock value. 100m/C VHS, DVD. Jon Favreau, Christian Slater, Cameron Diaz, Jeremy Piven, Daniel Stern, Leland Orser, Jeanne Tripplehorn, Joey Zimmerman; **D:** Peter Berg; **W:** Peter Berg; **C:** David Hennings; **M:** Stewart Copeland.

A Very Brady Christmas ✓✓ 1988 Many of the original Bradys returned for this yuletide special. After Mike and Carol's vacation plans go awry, they decide to invite the whole bunch home for a family reunion. This was the highest rated TV movie in 1989. Spawned yet another unsuccessful "Brady" series sequel. 94m/C VHS. Florence Henderson, Robert Reed, Ann B. Davis, Maureen McCormick, Eve Plumb, Jennifer Runyon, Barry Williams, Jerry Houser, Caryn Richman, (Mike) Lookinland, Jerry Houser, Caryn Richman; **D:** Peter Baldwin. TV

A Very Brady Sequel ✓✓½ 1996 (PG-13) They're back! The cast from the surprise hit "The Brady Bunch Movie" returns and Brady mom Carol (Long) is shocked when her presumed dead first husband Roy Martin (Matheson) suddenly appears on their doorstep. The Bradys must travel to Hawaii to attempt to save the family (based on a three-part episode from the original TV series). The stuck-in-the-'70s gang is still too far-out for the '90s, but in Hawaii it's always a sunshine day. Not as good as the first, but still worth a few laughs. 90m/C VHS, DVD. Shelley Long, Gary Cole, Tim Matheson, Christopher Daniel Barnes, Christine Taylor, Paul Sutera, Jennifer Elise Cox, Henriette Mantel, Olivia Hack, Jesse Lee, RuPaul Charles, Whip Hubley, John Hillerman, RuPaul Balzer, David Spade, Barbara Eden; **Cameos:** Zsa Zsa Gabor, Rosie O'Donnell; **D:** Arlene Sanford; **W:** Harry Elfont, Deborah Kaplan, Stan Zimmerman, James Berg; **C:** Mac Ahlberg; **M:** Guy Moon.

A Very British Coup ✓✓✓ 1988 McAnally plays Harry Perkins, a former steelworker who gets involved in British politics. Although a left-wing radical, the charismatic Perkins is actually elected Prime Minister. However, his radical policies cause the entrenched government officials to conspire to bring him down. And you thought American politics were dirty! 180m/C VHS, DVD. *GB* Ray McAnally, Alan MacNaughton, Keith Allen, Geoffrey Beevers, Jim Carter, Philip Madoc, Tim (McInnery) McInnery; **D:** Mick Jackson; **W:** Alan Plater; **C:** Ernest Vincze; **M:** John Keane. TV

Very Close Quarters ✓ 1984 Thirty people face many trials and tribulations as they share an apartment in Moscow. Interesting cast is wasted in this mostly un-funny flick. 97m/C VHS. Shelley Winters, Paul Sorvino, Theodore Bikel, Farley Granger; **D:** Vladmir Rif.

A Very Curious Girl ✓✓½ *La Fiancee du Pirate; Dirty Mary; Pirate's Fiancee* 1969 (R) A peasant girl realizes she is being used by the male population of her village, and decides to charge them for sex, creating havoc. In French with English subtitles. 105m/C VHS. *FR* Bernadette Lafont, Georges Geret, Michel Constantin, Julien Guiomar, Claire Maurier; **D:** Nelly Kaplan; **W:** Nelly Kaplan, Claude Makovski; **C:** Jean Badal; **M:** Georges Moustaki.

The Very Edge ✓✓½ 1963 A pregnant woman suffers a miscarriage after being brutally attacked. The repercussions nearly destroy her marriage until her attacker is caught. A disturbing psychodrama. 90m/B VHS. *GB* Anne Heywood, Richard Todd, Jeremy Brett, Jack Hedley, Barbara Mullen, Maurice Denham, William Lucas, Gwen Watford, Patrick Magee; **D:** Cyril Frankel; **W:** Elizabeth Jane Howard; **C:** Robert Huke.

The Very Long Engagement ✓✓½ *Un long dimanche de fiancailles* 2004 (R) Jeunet reteams with "Amelie" star Tautou in a bittersweet WWI-era weepie about a young woman who refuses to believe her fiance has died on the battlefield. In 1917, Manech (Ulliel) is the youngest of five soldiers court-martialed and condemned to certain death in a frontline trench. Two years later, Mathilde (Tautou) is equally certain that Manech is still alive, especially when she receives a letter from one of Manech's fellow soldiers. She hires detective Pire (Holgado) to help her investigate, in a parallel story, Tina (Cotillard), the girlfriend of another soldier, is also looking for answers, although for a much-deadlier purpose. French with subtitles; based on the 1991 novel by Sebastien Japrisot. 133m/C DVD. *FR* Audrey Tautou, Gaspard Ulliel, Jean Becker, Clovis Cornillac, Marion Cotillard, Jodie Foster, Jean-Claude Dreyfus, Albert Dupontel, Andre Dussollier, Ticky Holgado, Tcheky Karyo, Denis Lavant, Francois Levantal, Chantal Neuwirth, Dominique Pinon, Dominique Bettenfeld, Jean-Pierre Daroussin, Jerome Kircher, Jean-Paul Rouve, Rodolphe Pauly; **D:** Jean-Pierre Jeunet; **C:** Bruno Delbonnel; **M:** Angelo Badalamenti.

A Very Natural Thing ✓✓✓ 1973 Twenty-six-year-old Jason leaves the priesthood to pursue a gay lifestyle in New York. He becomes a gay director, meets ad exec David, and finds love. Considered to be the first film to explore homosexuality in a realistic manner, made by a gay director, and given national, commercial distribution. 85m/C VHS, DVD. Robert Joel, Curt Gareth, Bo White; **D:** Christopher Larkin; **W:** Christopher Larkin, Joseph Coencas; **C:** C.H. Douglass; **M:** Gordon Gottlieb, Bert Lucarelli.

A Very Old Man with Enormous Wings ✓✓ *Un Senor Muy Viejo Con Unas Alas Enormes* 1988 An angel, battered during a hurricane, seeks refuge on a tiny Caribbean island. There, two men keep him and charge an increasingly curious world admission to view the creature. A colorful, musical expose of human failings based on a story by Gabriel Garcia Marquez. In Spanish with English subtitles. 90m/C VHS. *SP IT* Daisy Granados, Asdrubal Melendez, Luis Alberto Ramirez, Fernando Biri; **D:** Fernando Biri.

A Very Private Affair ♂♂½ *Vie Privée; Vita Privata* 1962 A movie star finds that she has no privacy from the hordes of fans and paparazzi who flock to her side. The glare of publicity helps to destroy her relationship with a married director, and to fuel her desire for privacy. An appealing, better-than-average Bardot vehicle, it is nonetheless below-average (early) Malle. In French with English subtitles. **95m/C VHS, FR** Marcello Mastroianni, Brigitte Bardot; **D:** Louis Malle.

A Very Serious Person ♂♂ 2006 Precocious, orphaned 13-year-old Gil (Verhoest) lives with his grandma, Mrs. A (Bergen), and loves their beachside summers. She accepts his budding sexuality (a queen in the making), although he can't accept the fact that she is dying. Mrs. A needs professional nursing that companion Betty (Ivey) can't handle, so she hires prim Danish male nurse Jan (Busch—mostly out of drag). Jan and Gil become friends, but Jan is also overprotective. Knowing that the boy will soon be living with distant relatives, he urges Gil to say something quite different. Sixties hooker for mystery man. **96m/C DVD.** Charles Busch, Polly Bergen, Dana Ivey, Julie Halston, P.J. Verhoest, Carl Andress; **C:** Joseph Partagecco; **M:** Ed Shearmur.

The Very Thought of You ♂½ *Martha, Meet Frank, Daniel and Laurence* 1998 (PG-13) Limp romantic comedy finds a trio of longtime London friends clashing over their interest in the same woman. Actor Frank (Sewell), music executive Daniel (Hollander), and painter Laurence (Fiennes) all separately encounter Martha (Potter) and pick her up—without anyone realizing that a government agent (Sheedy) investigating MI6 is trailing the pair. **89m/C DVD.** Michael Ironside, Bobby Hosea, Ally Sheedy, Kenneth Johnson, Colin Glazer; **D:** Sidney J. Furie; **W:** J. Stephan Maunder. **VIDEO**

V.I. Warshawski ♂♂ 1991 (R) The filmmakers seem to think they can slum with the oldest cliches in detective shows just as long as the tough gumshoe is a woman. They're wrong. Turner is terrific as the leggy shamus of the title (from a popular series of books by Sara Paretsky), but the plot is nothing special, featuring stock characters in the killing of a pro athlete and a real-estate deal. **89m/C VHS, DVD.** Stephen (Steve) Root, Kathleen Turner, Jay O. Sanders, Angela Goethals, Charles Durning; **D:** Jeff Kanew; **W:** Nick Thiel, David Aaron Cohen; **M:** Randy Edelman.

Via Appia ♂♂ 1992 Fictional documentary about Frank, a German airline steward who brings a film crew with him when he travels back to Rio de Janeiro in search of the street hustler who gave him AIDS. Grim guided tour of the city's gay subculture along the "Via Appia," the Rio district where the male prostitutes hang out. Film is firmly unapologetic for its sexual explicitness and lack of moralizing, in German and Portuguese with English subtitles. **90m/C VHS. GE BP** Peter Senner, Guilherme de Padua, Yves Jansen, Margarita Schmidt, Luiz Kieber; **D:** Jochen Hick.

Vibes ♂½ 1988 (PG) Two screwball psychics are sent on a wild goose chase through the Ecuadorean Andes in search of cosmic power and, of course, fall in love. Flat offering from the usually successful team of writers, Lowell Ganz and Babaloo Mandel ("Splash" and "Night Shift"). Lauper's first starring role (and so far, her last). **99m/C VHS, DVD.** Cyndi Lauper, Julian Sands, Googy Gress, Peter Falk, Elizabeth Peña; **D:** Ken Kwapis; **W:** Babaloo Mandel, Lowell Ganz; **C:** John Bailey; **M:** James Horner.

Vibration ♂♂ *Lejonsommar* 1968 Writer Mauritz (Taube) travels to an island off the Swedish coast to enjoy some fun in the sun and immediately becomes involved with the tempting Barbro (Sjödin). But she can't compete with sex kitten Eliza (Persson), a film star who says she wants to be alone—although her actions say something quite different. Swedish erotica. **84m/B VHS, DVD, SW** Sven-Bertil Taube, Essy Persson, Margareta Sjödin; **D:** Torbjörn Axelman; **W:** Torbjörn Axelman; **C:** Hans Dittmer; **M:** Ulf Björlin.

Vibrations ♂♂½ 1994 (R) Anamrika (Applegate), a dance club manager, befriends T.J. (Marshall), a homeless, alcoholic, once-promising musician who lost his hands in a brutal attack. The duo find romance as Anamrika encourages T.J. to try again. **104m/C VHS, DVD.** James Marshall, Christina Applegate, Faye Grant, Paige Turco, Bruce Altman, David Burke, Scott Cohen, Shane Butterworth; **D:** Michael Paseornek; **W:** Michael Paseornek; **M:** Bob Christianson.

Vice Academy ♂♂ 1988 (R) Two females join the Hollywood vice squad. Allen was a former porn queen. **90m/C VHS, DVD.** Linnea Quigley, Ginger Lynn Allen, Karen Russell, Jayne Hamil, Ken Abraham, Stephen Steward, Jeannie Carol; **D:** Rick Sloane.

Vice Academy 2 ♂½ 1990 (R) The worst of the series, and not just because cult actress Linnea Quigley is absent. Wit, pacing and even sets are nonexistent as the girl's battle a toxic villainess called Malathion. **88m/C VHS, DVD.** Linnea Quigley, Ginger Lynn Allen, Jayne Hamil, Scott Layne, Jay Richardson, Joe Brewer, Marina Benverga, Teagan Clive; **D:** Rick Sloane.

Vice Academy 3 WOOF! 1991 (R) The worst of the series, and not just because cult actress Linnea Quigley is absent. **90m/C VHS, DVD.** Linnea Quigley, Ginger Lynn Allen, Julia Parton, Jay Richardson, Johanna Grika, Steve Mateo; **D:** Rick Sloane; **W:** Rick Sloane.

Vice Girls ♂½ 1996 (R) Three undercover female cops (all babes naturally) use their brains and bodies to capture a serial killer who gets his jollies by filming his victims before he kills them. Sexy fun. **85m/C VHS, DVD.** Lana Clarkson, Liat Goodson, Kimberly Roberts, A. Michael Baldwin, Richard Gabai, Caroline Keenan, Hoke Howell; **D:** Richard Gabai; **W:** A. Michael Baldwin; **C:** Gary Graver.

Vice Squad ♂♂ 1931 Lukas is forced to turn police informer to save his own neck, which almost runs him. Just when he thinks he's free of the cops they come back threatening the woman he loves unless he plays stoolie again. Rather flat, but the different cop/criminal angle makes for some unusual twists. **80m/B VHS.** Paul Lukas, Kay Francis, Helen Johnson, William B. Davidson, Esther Howard; **D:** John Cromwell; **C:** Charles Bòyant; Lang Jr.

Vice Squad WOOF! 1982 (R) Violent and twisted killer-pimp goes on a murderous rampage, and a hooker helps a vice squad plainclothesman trap him. Sleazy and disturbing, with little to recommend it. **97m/C VHS, DVD.** Wings Hauser, Season Hubley, Gary Swanson, Cheryl "Rainbeaux" Smith; **D:** Gary Sherman; **W:** Robert Vincent O'Neil.

Vice Versa ♂♂ 1988 (PG) Another '80s comedy about a workaholic father and his 11-year-old son who switch bodies, with predictable slapstick results. Reinhold and Savage carry this, appearing to have a great time in spite of overdone story. **97m/C VHS, DVD.** Judge Reinhold, Fred Savage, Swoosie Kurtz, David Proval, Corinne Bohrer, Jane Kaczmarek, William Prince, Gloria Gifford; **D:** Brian Gilbert; **W:** Dick Clement, Ian La Frenais; **M:** David Shire.

Vicious ♂ 1988 A bored young woman falls in with people your mother warned an falls in with people your mother warned you about and soon their high school hijinks turn into murder. Graphic violence.

Victim of Beauty ♂♂ 1991 A small-town girl comes to the big city and becomes a successful model. However, she then becomes the victim of a fatal attraction killer as all her would-be suitors get killed off one by one. **90m/C VHS, DVD.** Jennifer Rubin, Sally Kellerman, Stephen Shellen, Peter Outerbridge. **Cameos:** Michael Ironside; **D:** Paul Lynch. **CABLE**

Victim of Desire ♂½ 1994 (R) Mysterious death of an embezzler is investigated, only the investigator falls for the sexy widow and begins to doubt her innocence. Also available in an unrated version. **85m/C VHS.** Marc Singer, Wings Hauser, Johnny Williams, Jay Richardson, Shannon Tweed, Julie Strain; **D:** Jim Wynorski; **M:** Ross Wright.

Victim of Love ♂♂ 1991 (PG-13) A therapist doesn't know whom to believe when she finds out she and one of her more neurotic patients are sharing the same boyfriend. Only the patient claims the man murdered his wife to be with his lover. Who will be the next victim? **92m/C VHS, DVD.** Pierce Brosnan, JoBeth Williams, Virginia Madsen, Georgia Brown; **D:** Jerry Lordan, James Desmarais; **C:** Billy Dickson; **M:** Richard Hartley. **TV**

Victimless Crimes 1990 (R) The seemingly victimless crime of robbing art galleries turns deadly when betrayal and murder enter the picture. **85m/C VHS.** Debra Sandlund, Craig Blebko, Larry Brandenburg, Peggy Dunne, Richard Redin, Cheryl Lynn Bruce; **D:** Peter Hawley.

Victor/Victoria ♂♂♂ 1982 (PG) Victoria (Andrews), an unsuccessful actress in Depression-era Paris, impersonates a man impersonating a woman and becomes a star. Luscious music and sets. Warren as confused showgirl Norma and Preston as Andrews' gay-mentor Toddy are right on target; Garner is charming as gangster King Marchan, who falls for the woman he thinks she is, with Karras amusing as his bodyguard who plays a secret. **133m/C VHS, DVD.** Julie Andrews, James Garner, Robert Preston, Lesley Ann Warren, Alex Karras, John Rhys-Davies; **W:** Blake Edwards; **C:** Dick Bush; **M:** Henry Mancini. Oscars '82: Orig. Song Score or Adapt.; Cesar '83: Foreign Film; Golden Globes '83: Actress—Mus./Comedy; Natl. Bd.

Vicious Circles ♂♂½ 1997 (R) Detectives caught in the thick of Dylan Dog (Hipp) getting arrested for drug possession in Paris. So his half-sister and lover and girlfriend (Lowery) decides to help raise the money for his release by working as a ex-lover. When the blackmailers, who are responsible for his lover's suicide, are caught, Bogarde decides to prosecute them himself, even though it means revealing his hidden past. One of the first films to deal straightforwardly with homosexuality. Fine performances. **100m/B VHS, DVD. GB** Dirk Bogarde, Sylvia Syms, Dennis Price, Peter McEnery, Nigel Stock, Donald Churchill, Anthony Nicholls, Hilton Edwards, Norman Bird, Derren Nesbitt, Alan MacNaughton, Noel F-cwlett, Charles Lloyd-Pack, John Barrie, John Bennett; **D:** Basil Dearden; **W:** John McCormick, Janet Green; **C:** Otto Heller; **M:** Philip Green.

The Vicious Circle ♂♂½ *The Circle* 1957 A prominent London physician becomes involved in murder and an international crime ring when he agrees to perform an errand for a friend. Good performances and tight pacing. **84m/B VHS. GB** John Mills, Wilfrid Hyde-White, Rene Ray, Lionel Jefferies, Noelle Middleton; **D:** Gerald Thomas.

Victim ♂♂½ 1961 A successful married English barrister (Bogarde) with a hidden history of homosexuality is threatened by blackmail after the death of his

Victoria & Albert ♂♂½ 2001 In this BBC production, fabulous sets and costumes frame the story of Victoria, the girl who would be Queen, and Albert, the husband she weds by arrangement. This is a romantic tale of two people who are put together through politics but come to depend on and love each other through trust and mutual respect. The story is historically accurate, but little things pertaining to the personal relationship and family life are painted a little too rosy. Literary license aside, this is a great, romantic, period drama that makes historical figures from a distant land accessible and friendly while teaching you a little about potentially dry English history. **200m/C VHS, DVD.** Victoria Hamilton, Jonathan Firth, David Suchet, Diana Rigg, Patrick Malahide, Penelope Wilton, Peter Ustinov, Nigel Hawthorne, Pamela Brown, Basil Rathbone; **D:** George Schaefer. **TV**

Victoria Regina ♂♂ 1961 In a succession of vignettes, the life of Queen Victoria is viewed, from her ascension to the throne of England in 1837 through the celebration of her Diamond Jubilee. A presentation from "George Schaefer's Showcase Theatre." **76m/C VHS.** Julie Harris, James Donald, Felix Aylmer, Pamela Brown, Basil Rathbone; **D:** George Schaefer. **TV**

The Victors ♂♂½ 1963 Anti-war drama follows Allied soldiers in Europe in the waning days of the war. The men's romantic endeavors with European women are intercut with images of the common brutality and chaos of war. The young ensemble cast, most of whom went on to stardom, do an excellent job, but the material gets a little heavy-handed at times. **156m/B** George Peppard, George Hamilton, Eli Wallach, Vince Edwards, Jim Mitchum, Peter Fonda, Romy Schneider, Rosanna Schiaffino, Jeanne Moreau, Albert Finney, Elke Sommer, Michael Callan, Melvyn Jones, Melina Mercouri, Vanda Godsell, Patrick Jordan, Alf Kjellin, Albert Lieven, Peter Vaughan, Senta Berger, James Chase, Maurice Ronet; **C:** Christopher Challis; **M:** Sol Kaplan.

The Victory ♂♂ 1981 (PG) Soccer match between a WWII American prisoners of war and a German team is set up so that the players can escape through the sewer tunnels of Paris. Of course they want to finish the game first. Not particularly believable as either a soccer flick (even with Pele and other soccer stars) or a great escape, but watchable. **116m/C VHS, DVD.** Sylvester Stallone, Michael Caine, Max von Sydow, Pele, Carole Laure, Bobby Moore, Daniel Massey; **D:** John Huston; **W:** Jeff Maguire, Djordje Milicevic; **C:** Gerry Fisher; **M:** Bill Conti.

The Victory ♂♂½ 1995 (R) In 1913, Axel Heyst (Dafoe) is living on a remote island in the Dutch East Indies. He makes a trip to the port town of Surabaya and becomes enamored of Alma (Jacob), a violinist who plays in the hotel's orchestra. Alma is being coerced by hotel owner Schomberg (Yanne) into becoming his mistress and Axel decides to take her with him back to his island. Schomberg then sends a couple of thieves (Neill, Sewell) and becomes falsely saying that Axel has amassed a fortune. No happy endings; based on the novel by Joseph Conrad. **99m/C VHS, DVD.** Willem Dafoe, Irene Jacob, Sam Neill, Rufus Sewell, Jean Yanne, Simon Callow; **D:** Mark Peploe; **C:** Bruno de Keyzer; **M:** Richard Hartley.

Victory at Entebbe ♂♂½ 1976 An all-star cast in a made-for-TV movie that aired worldwide not long after July 4, 1976, incident in which the actual hijacked an Air France flight with a number of Israeli and Jewish passengers aboard. Israeli leaders Yitzhak Rabin and Shimon Perez go into action to put a military res-

of Review '82; Support. Actor (Preston); Writers Guild '82: Adapt. Screenplay (Preston); Writers Guild '82: Adapt. Screenplay cue team together while the plane sits on the tarmac at the Entebbe airport in Uganda, which is under the control of bombastic dictator Idi Amin. 119m/C VHS. Helmut Berger, Theodore Bikel, Linda Blair, Kirk Douglas, Richard Dreyfuss, Stefan Gierasch, David Groh, Julius W. Harris, Helen Hayes, Anthony Hopkins, Burt Lancaster, Christian Marquand, Elizabeth Taylor, Jessica Walter, Harris Yulin; **D:** Marvin J. Chomsky; **W:** Ernest Kinoy; **C:** Jim Kilgore; **M:** Charles Fox. TV

The Video Dead WOOF! 1987 (R) Gore-farce in which murderous zombies emerge from a possessed TV and wreak havoc. 90m/C VHS. Roxanna Augesen, Rocky Duvall, Michael St. Michaels; **D:** Robert Scott.

Video Murders ✗ 1987 A police detective tracks down a rapist/murderer who tapes all his own crimes. 90m/C VHS. Eric Brown, Virginia Loridans, John Ferita; **D:** Jim McCullough Sr.; **W:** Jim McCullough Sr.; **C:** Joseph M. Wilcots; **M:** Robert Sprayberry.

Video Violence ✗ 1987 A gory spoof about a video store owner who discovers that his customers have grown bored with the usual Hollywood horror movies and decide to shoot some flicks of their own. 90m/C VHS. Art Neill, Jackie Neill, William Toddie, Bart Sumner; **D:** Gary P. Cohen.

Video Violence Part 2... The Exploitation! ✗ 1987 Two sickos named Howard and Eli run a cable TV network where talk show guests are spindled and mutilated. 90m/C VHS. Uke, Bart Sumner, Lee Miller; **D:** Gary P. Cohen.

Video Voyeur: The Susan Wilson Story ✗✗½ 2002 Based on the true story of Louisiana wife and mother Susan Wilson (Harmon), whose husband Gary (Midkiff), and their kids move into her dream house. Next-door neighbor Steve Glover (Sheridan) is an old friend but Susan becomes concerned about his overly helpful nature. Then she discovers that Steve installed video surveillance equipment prior to the Wilson's moving in a home and has been spying on them every since. This prompts Wilson to lobby for a state law (which passed in 1999) making video voyeurism a felony. 91m/C VHS, DVD. Angie Harmon, Jamey Sheridan, Dale Midkiff, Tegan Moss, Garry Chalk, Teryl Rothery; **D:** Tim Hunter; **W:** Kathleen Rowell; **C:** Peter Wooste; **M:** Daniel Licht. VIDEO

Video Wars WOOF! 1984 Video games explode randomly. A wicked computer whiz is behind it all in a blackmail scheme. 90m/C VHS. George Diamond.

Videodrome ✗✗ 1983 Woods is a cable TV programmer with a secret yen for sex and violence, which he satisfies by watching a pirated TV show. "Videodrome" appears to be more worldly. Next-door neighbor Steve Glover (Sheridan) is an old friend but Susan becomes concerned about his overly helpful nature. Then she discovers that Steve installed video surveillance equipment prior to the Wilson's murder, and also seems to control the thoughts of its viewers—turning them into human VCRs. Cronenberg's usual sick fantasies are definitely love 'em or leave 'em. Special effects by Rick Baker. 87m/C VHS, DVD. CA James Woods, Deborah Harry, Sonja Smits, Peter Dvorsky; **D:** David Cronenberg; **W:** David Cronenberg; **C:** Mark Irwin; **M:** Howard Shore. Genie '84: Director (Cronenberg).

Vietnam, Texas ✗ 1990 (R) Vietnam vet leaves his past to become a priest. But he returns to violence when he discovers his Vietnamese daughter is in the hands of Houston's most relentless gangster. 101m/C VHS. Robert Ginty, Haing S. Ngor, Tamlyn Tomita, Tim Thomerson; **D:** Robert Ginty; **C:** Courtney Joyner, Tom Badal.

View from the Top ✗ 2003 (PG-13) Does for "stewardess-in-training" films what "Feds" did for the buddy-cop genre. Don't remember that one? Exactly. The problem isn't that it's a bad film, it's that it doesn't know what kind of a bad film to be (romance, comedy, or fish-out-of-water success story). Paltrow is small-town girl Donna, who aspires to a more worldly life (as a stewardess). After leaving for the big blue, Donna falls in love with Ted (Ruffalo) then loses him. She finds him again only to lose him for a shot at the big time. Other tedious stew school hijinks are involved. "Showgirls" showed more depth and logic. Only Mike Myers's lampooning saves it from being completely dreadful. 87m/C VHS, DVD. US Gwyneth Paltrow, Christina

Applegate, Mark Ruffalo, Candice Bergen, Kelly Preston, Rob Lowe, Joshua Malina, Mike Myers; **D:** Bruno Barreto; **W:** Eric Wald; **C:** Alfonso Beato; **M:** Theodore Shapiro.

A View to a Kill ✗✗ 1985 (PG) This James Bond mission takes him to the United States, where he must stop the evil Max Zorin from destroying California's Silicon Valley. Feeble and unexciting plot with unscary villain. Duran Duran performs the catchy title tune. Moore's last appearance as 007. 131m/C VHS, DVD. GB Roger Moore, Christopher Walken, Tanya Roberts, Grace Jones, Patrick Macnee, Lois Maxwell, Dolph Lundgren, Desmond Llewelyn, Robert Brown; **D:** John Glen; **W:** Michael G. Wilson; **C:** Alan Hume; **M:** John Barry.

Vigil ✗✗✗ 1984 A stark, dreamy parable about a young girl, living on a primitive farm in a remote New Zealand valley, who watches her family collapse after a stranger enters their territory. Visually ravishing and grim; Ward's first American import. Predecessor to "The Navigator." 90m/C VHS. NZ Penelope Stewart, Bill Kerr, Fiona Kay, Gordon Shields, Frank Whitten; **D:** Vincent Ward; **W:** Vincent Ward.

Vigilante WOOF! *Street Gang* 1983 (R) Frustrated ex-cop, tired of seeing criminals returned to the street, joins a vigilante squad dedicated to law and order. Often ridiculous and heavy handed. 91m/C VHS, DVD. Robert Forster, Fred Williamson, Carol Lynley, Rutanya Alda, Richard Bright, Woody Strode, Donald Blakely, Joseph Carberry, Joe Spinell, Frank Pesce; **D:** William Lustig; **W:** Richard Vetere; **C:** James (Momel) Lemmo; **M:** Jay Chattaway.

The Vigilantes Are Coming ✗✗ 1936 "The Eagle" sets out to avenge his family and upsets a would-be dictator's plot to establish an empire in California. In 12 chapters; the first is 32 minutes, and additional chapters are 18 minutes each. 230m/B VHS, DVD. Robert "Bob" Livingston, Kay Hughes, Guinn "Big Boy" Williams, Raymond Hatton, William Farnum; **D:** Mack V. Wright, Ray Taylor.

Vigilantes of Boom Town ✗½ 1946 A championship prize fight is the cover for a bank robbery which must be foiled by Red Ryder. 54m/B VHS, DVD. Allan "Rocky" Lane, Robert (Bobby) Blake, Peggy Stewart, Martha Wentworth, Roscoe Karns, Roy Barcroft, George Turner, John Dehner; **D:** R.G. Springsteen; **Nar:** Leroy Mason.

The Viking Queen ✗✗ 1967 Babe and swordplay saga. After her father dies, Salina (Carita) becomes queen and must protect her father's execution, defend his people, and fight for his country's survival against evil oppressors. At least there's a beautiful queen. When Salina escapes, she joins the fighting. 91m/C VHS, DVD. GB Carita, Don Murray, Andrew Keir, Donald Houston, Adrienne Corri, Niall MacGinnis, Nicola Pagett, Patrick Troughton; **D:** Don Chaffey; **W:** Clarke Reynolds; **C:** Stephen Dade; **M:** Gary Hughes.

The Viking Sagas ✗ 1995 (R) Kjartan (Moeller) is the warrior who must avenge his father's execution, defend his people, and fight for his country's survival against evil oppressors. At least there's a beautiful queen. When Salina escapes, she joins the fighting. Great location footage of both Norway and Brittany. Basic costume epic with good action scenes. Narrated by Welles. 116m/C VHS, DVD. Kirk Douglas, Ernest Borgnine, Janet Leigh, Tony Curtis, James Donald, Alexander Knox; **D:** Richard Fleischer; **W:** Calder Willingham; **C:** Jack Cardiff; **M:** Mario Nascimbene, Gerard Schumann; **Nar:** Orson Welles.

The Vikings ✗✗½ 1958 A Viking king and his son kidnap a Welsh princess and hold her for ransom. Depicts the Vikings' invasion of England. Great location footage of both Norway and Brittany. Basic costume epic with good action scenes. Narrated by Welles. 116m/C VHS, DVD. Kirk Douglas, Ernest Borgnine, Janet Leigh, Tony Curtis, James Donald, Alexander Knox; **D:** Richard Fleischer; **W:** Calder Willingham; **C:** Jack Cardiff; **M:** Mario Nascimbene, Gerard Schumann; **Nar:** Orson Welles.

Vile 21 ✗½ 1999 Let's see, a drug developed by Dr. Walter Hall on government orders turns an unsuspecting derelict into a part man/part reptile/part alien

monster (the title character) that goes on a rampage. And now Hall must come up with a way to destroy the creature. 80m/C VHS. Daniel Skinner, Ronnie Sortor, Steve Kelly, Byron Blakey, Brian Southwick, Tammi Strain; **D:** Mike Strain Jr.; **W:** Mike Strain Jr. VIDEO

Villa Rides ✗✗ 1968 A flying gunrunner aids Francisco "Pancho" Villa's revolutionary Mexican campaign. Considering the talent involved, this one is a disappointment. Check out Brynner's hair. 125m/C VHS. Yul Brynner, Robert Mitchum, Charles Bronson, Herbert Lom, Jill Ireland, Robert Towne; **D:** Buzz Kulik; **W:** Sam Peckinpah, Robert Towne; **C:** Jack Hildyard; **M:** Maurice Jarre.

The Village ✗✗ 2004 (PG-13) So is Shyamalan a one-trick director or are we just anticipating a trick in every film he directs? This solemn supernatural thriller is set in a 19th Century village whose insular, fearful inhabitants have formed an uneasy, unspoken truce with the monsters that live in the woods that surround it. The village elders forbid anyone to go beyond the perimeter but Lucius (Phoenix) becomes determined to defy them. Lucius is in love with blind Ivy (Howard), who is also loved by the village idiot Noah (Brody in an unfortunate role). Except that it's Ivy who finally enters the woods and is soon hearing scary noises coming in her direction. The payoff doesn't measure up to the portentousness. Maybe it's time Shyamalan does a comedy. 120m/C VHS, DVD. Joaquin Rafael (Leaf) Phoenix, William Hurt, Sigourney Weaver, Adrien Brody, Bryce Dallas Howard, Judy Greer, Jayne Atkinson, Frank Collison, Brendan Gleeson, Cherry Jones, Liz Stauber, Celia Weston, Michael Pitt, Fran Kranz; **D:** M. Night Shyamalan; **W:** M. Night Shyamalan; **C:** Roger Deakins; **M:** James Newton Howard.

A Village Affair ✗✗½ 1995 Ward is a young wife and mother, living what appears to be a perfect life in a quiet English village, when she meets a neighbor's daughter (Fox) who's just returned from America. Fox makes her interests clear and soon the two women are having an affair that shatters the peacefulness around them. Based on a novel by Joanna Trollope. 108m/C VHS. GB Sophie Ward, Kerry Fox, Nathaniel Parker, Claire Bloom, Michael Gough, Barbara Jefford, Jeremy Northam, Rosalie Crutchley; **C:** Moira Armstrong; **M:** Alma Cullen; **C:** John Else. TV

Village of Dreams ✗✗✗ 1997 Middle-aged identical twin brothers recall the sweetness of their childhood in a rural Japanese village in 1948. As mischievous eight-year-olds, the duo spend their time playing pranks, spying on their neighbors, and entertaining themselves in the woods and streams. Based on the memoir "The Village of My Paintings" by Seizo Tashima. Japanese with subtitles. 112m/C VHS, DVD. JP Keigo Matsuyama, Shogo Matsuyama; **W:** Takehiro Nakajima, Yoichi Higashi; **C:** Yoshio Shimizu.

Village of the Damned ✗✗✗ 1960 A group of unusual children are born in a small English village. They avoid their fathers and other men, except for the one who is their teacher. He discovers they are the vanguard of an alien invasion and leads the counter-attack. Exciting and bone-chilling low-budget thriller. From the novel, "The Midwich Cuckoos," by John Wyndham. 78m/B VHS, DVD. GB George Sanders, Barbara Shelley, Martin Stephens, Laurence Naismith, Michael Gwynn, John Phillips, Richard Vernon, Jenny Laird, Richard Warner, Thomas Heathcote, Charlotte Mitchell, John Stuart, Bernard Archard; **D:** Wolf Rilla; **W:** Wolf Rilla, Stirling Silliphant, George Harley; **C:** Geoffrey Faithfull; **M:** Ronald Goodwin.

Village of the Damned ✗✗½ 1995 (R) The quiet town of Midwich, California, has been enveloped by a strange force that seems to have impregnated the local women. The albino children born of this incident have disturbing telepathic powers that they display through their bright orange and red eyes—supposedly precipitating a plot to take control. A pale remake of the 1960 British horror classic, which was based on John Wyndham's novel "The Midwich Cuckoos." Fails to capture the eeriness of it's predecessor and is bogged down with awkward cast-

ing, absurd dialogue, and a brood of children with glowing eyes that make them less like a threat and more like Nintendo addicts. 98m/C VHS, DVD. Christopher Reeve, Kirstie Alley, Linda Kozlowski, Mark Hamill, Meredith Salenger, Michael Pare, Peter Jason, Constance Forslund, Karen Kahn; **D:** John Carpenter; **W:** John Carpenter, David Himmelstein; **C:** Gary B. Kibbe; **M:** John Carpenter, Dave Davies.

Village of the Giants ✗ 1965 A group of beer-guzzling teenagers become giants after eating a mysterious substance invented by a 12-year-old genius. Fun to pick out all the soon-to-be stars. Totally silly premise with bad special effects and minimal plot follow-through. Based on an H.G. Wells story. 82m/C VHS, DVD. Ron Howard, Johnny Crawford, Tommy Kirk, Beau Bridges, Freddy Cannon, Toni Basil, Tisha Sterling, Tim Rooney, Charla Doherty, Joe Turkel; **D:** Bert I. Gordon; **W:** Alan Caillou; **C:** Paul Vogel; **M:** Jack Nitzche.

Village Tale ✗ 1935 Relentlessly nasty drama about the harm gossip can do. Small town know-nothings gather at the general store to spread lies about their neighbors, leading to suicide and attempted murder. Adapted from the Philip Strong novel. 80m/B VHS. Randolph Scott, Kay Johnson, Dorothy Burgess, Donald Meek, Andy Clyde, Guinn "Big Boy" Williams, Arthur Hohl, Robert Barrat, Janet Beecher, Edward Ellis; **D:** John Cromwell; **C:** Nicholas Musuraca.

The Villain ✗✗½ *Cactus Jack* 1979 (PG) An unfunny spoof of "B" westerns that is almost like a live-action "Roadrunner" cartoon. Douglas plays Cactus Jack, a highwayman who keeps trying to kidnap fair damsel Ann-Margret. Hero Schwarzenegger keeps rescuing her. Lynde is amusing as the uptight Indian chief Nervous Elk. 89m/C VHS, DVD. Kirk Douglas, Ann-Margret, Arnold Schwarzenegger, Paul Lynde, Foster Brooks, Ruth Buzzi, Jack Elam, Strother Martin, Robert Tessier, Mel Tillis; **D:** Hal Needham; **W:** Robert G. Kane; **C:** Bobby Byrne; **M:** Bill Justis.

The Villain Still Pursued Her ✗✗ 1941 A poor hero and rich villain vie for the sweet heroine in this satire of old-fashioned temperance melodrama. Keaton manages to shine as the hero's sidekick. 67m/B VHS, DVD. Anita Louise, Alan Mowbray, Buster Keaton, Hugh Herbert; **D:** Edward F. (Eddie) Cline.

Vince Vaughn's Wild West Comedy Show ✗✗ 2006 (R) *Wild West Comedy Show* Part comedy concert film, part backstage documentary follows comedy tour mastermind Vaughn and four up-and-coming comics on a tour across the southern U.S. in 2005. Outside of a visit to a camp of people who had just been displaced by Hurricane Katrina, the film doesn't break out of its basic concept, focusing on the backgrounds of comedians Caparule, Ernst, Maniscalco, and Ahmed and their time on the road, which seems to involve very little partying or getting into trouble. The result is a tour that's not particularly wild. For stand-up fans. 100m/C DVD. US Cameos: Vince Vaughn, Ahmed Ahmed, John Caparulo, Bret Ernst, Sebastian Mansicalco; **D:** Ari Sandel; **M:** John O'Brien.

Vincent & Theo ✗✗✗ ½ 1990 (PG-13) The story of Impressionist painter Vincent van Gogh (Roth), and his brother Theo (Rhys), a gallery owner who loved his brother's work, yet could not get the public to buy it. Increasing despair and mental illness traps both men, as each struggles to create beauty in a world where it has no value. Altman has created a stunning portrait of "the artist" and his needs. The exquisite cinematography will make you feel as if you stepped into van Gogh's work. 138m/C VHS, DVD. Tim Roth, Paul Rhys, Johanna Ter Steege, Wladimir Yordanoff; **D:** Robert Altman; **W:** Julian Mitchell; **C:** Jean Lepine.

Vincent, François, Paul and the Others ✗✗✗ 1976 *Vincent, François, Paul et les Autres* Three middle-aged Frenchmen rely on their friendships to endure a host of mid-life crises. In French with English subtitles. 113m/C VHS. FR Yves Montand, Gerard Depardieu, Michel Piccoli, Stephane Audran, Serge Reggiani, Marie DuBois; **D:** Claude Sautet; **W:** Claude Sautet, Jean-Loup Da-

Vincent: The Life and Death of Vincent van Gogh ♂♂♂ '87 Van Gogh's work and creativity is examined in a documentary manner through his life and letters. Thoughtful and intriguing production. Narrated by John Hurt as van Gogh. 99m/C VHS, DVD. **D:** Paul Cox. **W:** Paul Cox; **M:** Norman Kaye; **V:** John Hurt.

The Vindicator ♂♂ '85 (R) A scientist killed in a lab accident is transformed into a cyborg who runs amok and murders indiscriminately. A modernized Frankenstein, with interesting special effects and well drawn characters. 92m/C VHS. **C:** Teri Austin, Richard Cox, David McIlwraith, Pam Grier; **D:** Jean-Claude Lord.

The Vineyard ♂ '89 (R) Hapless victims are lured to a Japanese madman's island, where he drinks their blood and maintains a questionable immortality. 95m/C VHS, DVD. **D:** James Hong, Bill Rice.

Vintage Model ♂♂ *Modelo Antiguo* 1992 Carmen hosts a radio program giving romantic advice, though she's lonely and lives on her memories of the past. When she learns she only has a short time to live, Carmen hires a chauffeur to drive her around Mexico City so she can remember. Spanish with subtitles. 97m/C VHS. **C:** Silvia Pinal, Alonso Echanove; **D:** Raul Araiza; **W:** Consuelo Garrido, Alejandro Pelayo; **C:** Rosalio Solano; **M:** Osni Cessab.

Violated ♂ '53 Pathetic production about New York police attempting to track down a sex-maniac murderer who slays his victims and then gives them a haircut. Unbelievably bad. 78m/B VHS. **C:** Ian Roberts, Lili Dawn, Mitchell Kowal, Vicki Carlson, William Martell; **D:** Walter Strate.

Violated woof! 1984 A detective endeavors to implicate a local businessman in the rapes of two beautiful women. Exploitative trash and creamy. 88m/C VHS. **C:** J.C. Quinn, April Daisy White, Samantha Fox. **D:** Richard Cannistraro.

Violence at Noon ♂♂ 1966 Highly disturbing film in which two women protect a brutal sex murderer from the law. Living among a quiet community of intellectuals, this conspiracy ends in a shocking finale in Oshima's stylized masterpiece. In Japanese with English subtitles. 99m/B VHS. **C:** Saeda Kawaguchi, Akiko Koyama; **D:** Nagisa Oshima.

Violent Breed ♂ 1983 A CIA operative is sent on a mission to put a black marketeer out of business. 91m/C VHS. **C:** Henry Silva, Harrison Muller, Woody Strode; **D:** Fernando Di Leo.

Violent Cop ♂♂ *Sono Otoko, Kyobo ni Tsuki* 1989 Think "Dirty Harry" to the nth power and you'll have some idea of the kind of cop Detective Azuma (Kitano) is. However, he also gets results, so the boss is willing to overlook the violent way Azuma does his job. His latest case involves a drug-related murder, a sadistic killer, a corrupt friend, and the kidnapping of Azuma's own mentally unstable sister. Not for the squeamish. Japanese with subtitles. 103m/C VHS, DVD, JP Takeshi "Beat" Kitano, Shiro Sano, Maiko Kawakami, Makoto Ashikawa, Shigeru Hiirazumi, Mikiko Otorashii; **D:** Takeshi "Beat" Kitano; **W:** Hisahi Nozawa; **C:** Yasushi Sasakibara; **M:** Daisaku Kune.

The Violent Men ♂♂½ *Rough Company* 1955 Big-time land baron Robinson is trying to push out all other landowners in the valley, including Ford. At first Ford refuses to fight back, but after one of his hired hands, he starts an all-out war against Robinson to save his land. Stanwyck as Robinson's wife and Keith as his brother are wicked as the two urging him on and having an affair behind his back. Based on the novel "Rough Company" by Donald Hamilton. 96m/C VHS, DVD. **C:** Glenn Ford, Barbara Stanwyck, Edward G. Robinson, Dianne Foster, Brian Keith, May Wynn; **D:** Rudolph Mate; **C:** Burnett G. Guffey.

Violette ♂♂♂ *Violette Noziere* 1978 (R) Fascinating true-life account of a 19-year-old French girl in the 1930s who, bored with her life and wanting to be with her lover, decides to poison her parents so she can receive her inheritance. Her mother survives but her father dies, and the girl is sent to prison for murder. Extraordinary performance by Huppert and the film is visually stunning. 122m/C VHS, DVD. FR Isabelle Huppert, Stephane Audran, Jean Carmet, Jean-Francoise Garreaud, Bernadette Lafont; **D:** Claude Chabrol; **W:** Odile Barski, Frederic Grendel; **C:** Jean Rabier; **M:** Pierre Jansen. Cannes '78: Actress (Huppert); Cesar '79: Support. Actress (Audran).

Viper ♂♂ 1988 A woman battles a cryptic anti-terrorist band to avenge the murder of her husband. 96m/C VHS. **D:** Peter Maris.

The V.I.P.'s ♂♂ 1963 Slick, sophisticated drama set in a British airport. Trapped by fog, several of the passengers get acquainted and are forced to face their problems as they spend the night in the airport lounge. Taylor stars as Frances Andros, a wealthy young woman leaving her husband (Burton) for life in the U.S. with her lover, Jourdan. A movie tycoon, an Australian entrepreneur, his secretary, and a duchess are among the other passengers grounded by the fog. Both Rutherford and Smith give excellent performances and it was a toss-up as to which actress would be nominated for the Oscar. 119m/C VHS, DVD, GB Elizabeth Taylor, Richard Burton, Louis Jourdan, Elsa Martinelli, Margaret Rutherford, Maggie Smith, Rod Taylor, Orson Welles, Linda Christian, Dennis Price; **D:** Anthony Asquith; **W:** Terence Rattigan; **M:** Miklos Rozsa. Oscars '63:

VIP, My Brother Superman ♂♂ 1990 The Vips are modern-day descendants of superbeings about to become legends in their own times. SuperVip is broad of chest and pure in spirit while his brother MiniVip possesses only limited powers. From the creator of "Allegro Non Troppo" comes this enticing, amusing piece of animation. 90m/C VHS. IT **D:** Bruno Bozzetto; **W:** Bruno Bozzetto; **C:** Luciano Marzetti; **M:** Franco Godi.

Violent Professionals ♂½ *La Polizia vuole Giustizia* 1973 Suspended cop runs into resistance inside and outside the force when he infiltrates the mob to get the goods on a crime boss. 100m/C VHS, DVD. IT Richard Conte, Luc Merenda; **D:** Sergio Martino.

Violent Women ♂ 1959 Five female convicts escape and embark on a bloody journey through the countryside, pursued by the authorities. Shows women can be just as brutal as any man. 61m/C VHS. **C:** Jennifer Slater, Jo Ann Kelly, Sandy Lyn; **D:** Barry Mahon.

Violent Zone ♂ 1989 Mercenaries go on a supposed rescue mission in the wilderness. 92m/C VHS, DVD. **C:** John Douglas, Chard Hayward, Christopher Weeks; **D:** John Garwood; **W:** David Prichard, John Bushelman.

The Violent Years woof! 1956 Spoiled high-school debutantes form a vicious all-girl gang and embark on a spree that includes murder, robbery, and male rape. Justice wins out in the end. Exploitive trash written by Wood, who directed the infamous "Plan 9 from Outer Space." 60m/B VHS, DVD. **C:** Jean Moorehead, Barbara Weeks, Glenn Corbett, Theresa Hancock, I. Stanford Jolley, Arthur Millan; **D:** Edward D. Wood Jr., Franz Eichhorn, William M. Morgan; **W:** Edward D. Wood Jr.; **C:** William C. Thompson.

Violets Are Blue ♂♂½ 1986 (PG-13) Two high-school sweethearts are reunited in their hometown years later and try to rekindle their romance—even though she is married. 86m/C VHS. **C:** Sissy Spacek, Bonnie Bedelia, John Kellogg, Augusta Dabney, Jim Standford; **D:** Jack Fisk; **W:** Naomi Foner; **C:** Ralf Bode; **M:** Patrick Williams.

Violent Ones woof! 1968 Three men who are suspected of raping a young girl are threatened with lynching by an angry mob of townspeople. Badly acted, poorly directed, uneven and feeble. 96m/C VHS. **C:** Fernando Lamas, David Carradine; **D:** Fernando Lamas.

Virgil Bliss ♂♂ 2001 Virgil (Jordan) is a mild-mannered career thief from Mississippi who's been paroled to a Brooklyn halfway house after 12 years in the joint. So, what's the first thing he does? Well, he listens to his new roomie Manny (Gorman) who maybe wants Virgil to do another job for her and then introduces him to tough junkie Ruby (Russell). Naturally, Virgil falls for her, there's more trouble a-coming. 94m/C VHS, DVD. **C:** Clint Jordan, Kirsten Russell, Anthony Gorman; **D:** Joe Maggio; **W:** Joe Maggio; **C:** Harlan Bosmajian.

Virgin ♂ 2003 (R) Fundamentalist's rebellious daughter becomes pregnant after being drugged and date-raped. Not remembering the assault, she declares herself Virgin Mother to the Second Coming, and it's not surprising she's attacked by her family and community. Odd feminist parable seems unsure whether to take itself seriously or not. Intense and unforgettable central performance by Moss does little to rid film of its contrived weirdness. 114m/C DVD. Robin Wright Penn, Elisabeth (Elisabeth) Moss, Daphne Rubin-Vega, Dr. Charles Socarides, Socorc Santiago, Peter Gerety, Stephanie Gatchel; **D:** Deborah Kampmeier; **W:** Deborah Kampmeier; **C:** Ben Wolf.

The Virgin and the Gypsy ♂♂½ 1970 (R) An English girl brought up in a repressive household in 1920s England falls in love with a gypsy. Based on the novel by D.H. Lawrence. Directorial debut of Miles. 92m/C VHS, GB Joanna Shimkus, Franco Nero, Honor Blackman, Mark Burns; **D:** Christopher Miles; **W:** Alan Plater.

Virgin High ♂ 1990 (R) Three young men sneak into an all-girls Catholic boarding school with hilarious consequences. 90m/C VHS. Burt Ward, Linnea Quigley, Tracy Dali, Richard Gabai, Catherine McGuinness, Chris Dempsey; **D:** Richard Gabai; **W:** Richard Gabai, Jeff Neal.

Virgin among the Living Dead ♂ 1971 (R) Young woman travels to remote castle when she hears of relative's death. Once there, she finds the residents a tad weird and has bad dreams in which zombies chase her. Bizarre even for Franco, who seems to have been going through a "Pasolini" phase while making this one. 90m/C VHS, DVD, SF Christina von Blanc, Britt Nichols, Howard Vernon, Anne Libert, Rose Kiekens, Paul Muller; **D:** Jess (Jesus) Franco.

Virgin Machine ♂♂ *Jungfrauenmaschine* 1988 Lesbian journalist Dorothy Muller (Blum) is unhappy in her native Hamburg and decides to move to California to pursue her idea of romantic love. English and German with English subtitles. 91m/B VHS, DVD. GE Ina Blum, Susie Bright, Shelley Mars, Dominique Gaspar; **D:** Monika Treut; **W:** Monika Treut; **C:** Elfi Mikesch.

The Virgin of Nuremberg ♂½ *Horror Castle; Terror Castle; Castle of Terror; La Vergine de Norimberga* 1965 A young woman enters her new husband's ancestral castle and is stalked by the specter of a legendary sadist. 82m/C VHS, DVD. IT Rossana Podesta, George Riviere, Christopher Lee, Jim Dolen; **D:** Anthony M. Dawson

The Virgin Queen ♂♂♂ 1955 Davis stars in this historical drama, which focuses on the stormy relationship between the aging Queen and Sir Walter Raleigh. Collins is the lady-in-waiting who is the secret object of Raleigh's true affections. Previously, Davis played Queen Elizabeth I in "Elizabeth and Essex." Davis holds things together. 92m/C VHS. Bette Davis, Richard Todd, Joan Collins, Herbert Marshall, Dan O'Herlihy, Jay Robinson, Romney Brent; **D:** Henry Koster.

Virgin Queen of St. Francis High ♂ 1988 (PG) Two high school foes make a bet that one of them can take the "virgin" title away from rod. Christensen by summer's end. She has to fight off their advances, but grows to like Stratace. 89m/C VHS. **C:** Joseph R. Straface, Stacy Christensen, J.T. Wotton; **D:** Francesco Lucente.

Virgin Sacrifice ♂ 1959 A great white hunter looking for zoo-bound jaguars confronts the virgin-sacrificing, Tiger God-revering natives of Guatemala. 67m/C VHS, DVD. David Dalie, Antonio Gutierrez, Angelica Morales Fernando Wagner.

The Virgin Soldiers ♂♂½ 1969 (R) A British comedy about greenhorn military recruits stationed in Singapore, increment of women as well as battle, and their struggles to overcome both situations. A good cast raises this above the usual low-brow sex farce. Based on the novel by Leslie Thomas. Followed by "Stand Up Virgin Soldiers." 96m/C VHS, GB Hywel Bennett, Nigel Davenport, Lynn Redgrave, Nigel Patrick, Rachel Kempson, Jack Shepherd, Tsai Chin; **D:** John Dexter; **W:** John Hopkins.

The Virgin Spring ♂♂♂♂ *Jungfrukallan* 1959 Based on a medieval ballad and set in 14th-century Sweden. The rape and murder of a young innocent Karin (Pettersson) spurs her father Tore (Van Sydow) to vengeance and the kills her attackers. Over the girl's dead body, the family questions how God could have let any of it happen, but he comes to find solace and forgiveness when a spring bursts forth from the spot. Stunning Bergman compositions. In Swedish with English subtitles; also available in dubbed version. 88m/B VHS, DVD, SW Max von Sydow, Birgitta Valberg, Gunnel Lincblom, Brigitte Pettersson, Axel Duborg; **D:** Ingmar Bergman; **W:** Ulla Isaaksson; **C:** Sven Nykvist; **M:** Erik Nordgren. Oscars '60: Foreign Film; Golden Globes '61: Foreign Film.

The Virgin Suicides ♂♂ 1999 (R) The five teenaged Lisbon sisters are lad and set in suburban life. Mom (Turner) is a rigid, religious harridan while Dad (Woods) is a wimpy math teacher. After 13-year-old Cecilia (Hall) tries to off herself, her parents romantic air to the who-e production (Coppola's directorial debut), which is based on the novel by Jeffrey Eugenides. 97m/C VHS, DVD. Kirsten Dunst, Kathleen Turner, James Woods, Josh Hartnett, Hanna Hall, Chelse Swain, A.J. Cook, Leslie Hayman, Danny DeVito, Scott Glenn, Jonathan Tucker, Anthony DeSimone; **D:** Sofia Coppola; **W:** Sofia Coppola; **C:** Edward Lachman; **Nar:** Giovanni Ribisi.

Virgin Witch ♂½ 1970 Lesbian Twins 1970 (R) Two beautiful sisters are sent to modeling job in the British countryside, ostensibly for a modeling job. They soon find themselves in the midst of a witches' coven however, and discover one of them is to be sacrificed. The Michelles were "Playboy" magazine's first sister centerfolds. 89m/C VHS, DVD. GB Anne Michelle, Vicki Michelle, Patricia Haines, Keith Buckley, James Chase, Neil Hallett; **D:** Ray Austin.

Virginia City ♂♂♂ 1940 Action-packed western drama set during the Civil War. Flynn is a Union soldier who escapes from a Confederate prison run by Scott, after learning of a gold shipment being sent by Southern sympathizers to aid the Confederacy. He ends up in Virginia City (where the gold-laden wagon train is to leave from) and falls for a dance-hall girl (Hopkins) who turns out to be a half-breed outlaw who aids Scott but wants the gold for himself. Considered a follow-up to "Dodge City." 121m/C VHS. Errol Flynn, Miriam Hopkins, Randolph Scott, Humphrey Bogart, Frank McHugh, Alan Hale, Guinn "Big Boy" Williams, Douglass Dumbrille, Charles Halton; **D:** Michael Curtiz; **M:** Max Steiner.

The Virginia Hill Story ♂♂ 1976 Fictionalized biography of mobster Bugsy Siegel's girlfriend who, in the mid-50s, was subpoenaed to appear before the Kefauver investigation on crime in the

U.S. As the examining lawyer presents questions regarding her background and connections with the underworld, we see the story of her life. **90m/C VHS, DVD.** Dyan Cannon, Harvey Keitel, Robby Benson, Allen (Goorwiz), Garfield, John Vernon; **D:** Joel Schumacher. **TV**

The Virginian ♂♂½ *1923.* The second silent version of Owen Wister's classic western novel, inferior to both the 1914 Cecil B. DeMille silent and the 1929 Victor Fleming talkie. Harlan plays the title role as the cowpoke who leads a posse against cattle rustlers and falls in love with a schoolteacher. **79m/B VHS.** Kenneth Harlan, Florence Vidor, Russel Simpson, Pat O'Malley, Raymond Hatton; **D:** Tom Forman.

The Virginian ♂♂½ *1929.* A classic early-talkie western about a ranch-hand defeating the local bad guys. One line of dialogue has become, with modification, a standard western cliche: "If you want to call me that, smile." Based on the novel by Owen Wister. With this starring role, Cooper broke away from the juvenile lovers he had been playing to the laconic, rugged male leads he would be known for. Huston is perfectly cast as the outlaw leader. **95m/B VHS.** Gary Cooper, Walter Huston, Richard Arlen, Chester Conklin, Eugene Pallette; **D:** Victor Fleming.

The Virginian ♂♂♂½ *1946.* Cowboy good guy, known as the Virginian (McCrea), and his best pal Steve (Tufts) both fall for Molly (Britton), the Eastern-bred schoolmarm who's come to their Wyoming town. Steve wants to make some quick money and joins up with leader Trampas' (Donlevy) cattle rustling gang. So the Virginian is forced to choose between friendship and the code of the west and Molly wonders if she can accepts the country's harsh ways. Based on Owen Wister's 1902 novel. **87m/C VHS.** Joel McCrea, Sonny Tufts, Barbara Britton, Brian Donlevy, Fay Bainter, Tom Tully, Henry O'Neill, William Frawley; **D:** Stuart Gilmore; **W:** Frances Goodrich, Albert Hackett; **C:** Harry Hallenberger; **M:** Daniele Amfitheatrof.

The Virginian ♂♂♂½ *1999.* Yet another remake (this one unremarkable but watchable) of Owen Wister's 1902 novel. Pullman (who also directed) is the cowboy of the title, who is out for a brutal brand of justice against an unscrupulous rancher. But his methods upset his schoolmarm sweetie (Lane). **95m/C VHS.** Bill Pullman, Diane Lane, John Savage, Dennis Weaver; **D:** Bill Pullman; **W:** Larry Gross. **CABLE**

Viridiana ♂♂♂♂ *1961.* Innocent Viridiana (Pinal), with strong ideas about goodness, visits her worldly uncle, Don Jaime's (Rey), home before she takes her vows as a nun. He has developed a sick obsession for her, but after drugging Viridiana, Don Jaimefinds he cannot violate her purity. He tells her, however, she is no longer chaste so she will not join the church. After her uncle's suicide, Viridiana learns she and his illegitimate son Jorge (Rabal) have inherited her uncle's run-down estate. Viridiana opens the house to all sorts of beggars, who take shameless advantage, while Jorge works slowly to restore the estate and improve the lives of those around him. Considered to be one of Buñuel's masterpieces and a bitter allegory of Spanish idealism versus pragmatism and of the state of the world. Spanish with subtitles. **90m/B VHS, DVD. SP MX** Silvia Pinal, Francesco Rabal, Fernando Rey, Margarita Lozano, Victoria Zinny; **D:** Luis Buñuel; **W:** Luis Buñuel, Julio Alejandro; **C:** Jose F. Aguayo. Cannes '61: Film.

Virtual Assassin ♂♂ *Cyberjack 1995 (R)* 21st century sci-fi actioner finds the crooked Zef (James) leading his band of thugs into a research lab to steal a powerful computer virus. Naturally, the janitor (Dudikoff) just happens to be an ex-cop with a score to settle with Zef. Predictable with decent special effects. **99m/C VHS, DVD. CA JP** Michael Dudikoff, Brion James, Jon Cuthbert, Suki Kaiser, James Thom; **D:** Robert Lee; **W:** Eric Poppen.

Virtual Combat ♂♂ *1995 (R)* Ex-cop Quarry (Wilson) teams up with some cyber-girls to stop a madman who's able to manipulate virtual reality programs into living beings and releases a killer who wants to lead a destructive virtual army. **97m/C VHS, DVD.** Don "The Dragon" Wilson, Athena Massey, Loren Avedon, Kenneth McLeod, Turhan Bey, Stella Stevens, Michael Bernardo; **D:** Andrew Stevens; **W:** William Marteli; **C:** Claude Gaudette.

Virtual Desire ♂♂½ *1995 (R)* Brad Collins is bored with his marriage and finds some excitement via sexual games on the Internet. But someone is taking a very close interest in Brad's virtual amours and when his wife is murdered, Brad becomes the prime suspect. **92m/C VHS, DVD.** Michael Meyer, Julie Strain, Gail Harris; **D:** Noble Henri.

Virtual Encounters ♂♂♂½ *1996 (R)* Top-drawer soft-core fluff follows busy executive Amy (Elizabeth Kaitan), whose birthday present is a session of virtual wish fulfillment at a high-tech fantasyland. The fantasies involve masks, leather, desks, broccoli...well, O.K., the broccoli is an exaggeration. This is sexy and kinky, not sick. The action is slickly staged and well photographed by director Richards. Also available in an unrated version at 84 minutes. **80m/C VHS, DVD.** Elizabeth Kaitan, Taylore St. Claire, Rob Lee; **D:** Cybil (Sybil) Richards; **C:** Cybil (Sybil) Richards. **VIDEO**

Virtual Girl ♂♂ *2000 (R)* Computer programmer John Lewis (Dixon) is working on an erotic virtual reality program that features a cyber-slut (Curtis). When said vixen gets rejected by her creator, she gets very, very angry. Erotica that makes the best use of its low-budget and Curtis' assets. **84m/C VHS, DVD.** Richard Gabai, Charlie Curtis, Max Dixon; **D:** Richard Gabai. **VIDEO**

Virtual Seduction ♂♂ *1996 (R)* Liam's (Fahey) taken a job testing a virtual reality pod that can interpret what the user wants—and Liam wants to see his dead girlfriend Paris (Genzel). Only he spends so much time with the virtual Paris, that his real-life gal Laura (Dolenz) is worried about his health and sanity—too bad project developer Grant (Novak) isn't so concerned. **84m/C VHS.** Jeff Fahey, Ami Dolenz, Carrie Genzel, Frank Novak, Meshach Taylor; **D:** Paul Ziller.

Virtual Sexuality ♂♂ *1999 (R)* Teen comedy, set in London, that has an amusing virtual reality plot. Cute 17-year-old Justine (Fraser) decides school stud Alex (O'Brien) is the perfect guy to lose her virginity to. But he's only interested in school vamp, "Hoover" (Bell). So Justine enters a virtual reality makeover machine at a technology fair in order to create an electronic facsimile of her perfect man. But a malfunction causes Justine to split in two—herself (with amnesia) and her perfect man, the bewildered male creation Jake (Penry-Jones). Based on the novel by Chloe Rayban. **92m/C VHS, DVD. GB** Laura Fraser, Rupert Penry-Jones, Kieran O'Brien, Luke De Lacey, Natasha Bell, Steve John Shepherd, Laura Macaulay, Marcelle Duprey; **D:** Nick Hurran; **W:** Nick Fisher; **C:** Brian Tufano; **M:** Rupert Gregson-Williams.

Virtue's Revolt ♂½ *1924.* A small-town girl is corrupted by the sleazy world of showbiz. Silent. **51m/B VHS.** Florence Lee, Eddie (Edward) Phillips, Betty Morrissey, Charles Cruz, Edith Thornton, Crauford Kent; **D:** James Chapin; **W:** Frederick Chapin; **C:** Ernest Miller.

Virtuosity ♂♂½ *1995 (R)* Ex-cop-with-a-tragic-past Parker Barnes (Washington) is sprung from prison to help capture computer-generated killer Sid 6.7 (Crowe), who escapes from cyberspace and goes on a rampage in 1997 Los Angeles. Seems this virtual reality bad guy has a personality composed of some 200 serial killers and criminal minds so Parker's got his work cut out for him. But criminal-behavior psychologist Madison Carter (Lynch) is around to lend her expert advice. Both the charismatically evil Crowe and the sufferingly noble Washington are wasted in this effects-laden thriller that sacrifices character for flash. **105m/C VHS,** DVD. Denzel Washington, Russell Crowe, Kelly Lynch, Stephen Spinella, William Forsythe, Louise Fletcher, William Fichtner, Costas Mandylor, Kevin J. O'Connor; **D:** Brett Leonard; **W:** Eric Bernt; **C:** Gale Tattersall; **M:** Christopher Young.

Virus ♂♂ *Fukkatsu no Hi 1982 (PG)* After nuclear war and plague destroy civilization, a small group of people gather in Antarctica and struggle with determination to carry on life. A look at man's genius for self-destruction and his endless hope. **102m/C VHS, DVD. JP** George Kennedy, Sonny Chiba, Glenn Ford, Robert Vaughn, Stuart Gillard, Stephanie Faulkner, Ken Ogata, Bo Svenson, Olivia Hussey, Chuck Connors, Edward James Olmos; **D:** Kinji Fukasaku.

Virus ♂½ *1996 (PG-21)* Secret Service agent Ken Fairchild (Bosworth) finds out that biological-warfare chemicals have been split in a national park that's the site for an ecological summit between the president and world leaders. It's up to Fairchild and a park ranger (Pinsent) to battle the minions of the chemical's manufacturer who wants to keep the whole thing quiet. **90m/C VHS, DVD.** Brian Bosworth, Leah K. Pinsent; **D:** Allan Goldstein.

Virus ♂♂ *1998 (R)* Curtis, Sutherland, and Baldwin are members of a tug-boat crew whose boat has been wrecked by a typhoon. They take refuge aboard a Russian research ship only to discover the whole crew has been eliminated by a strange life form. The electricity-based alien considers humanity a virus and begins making bizarre killing machines out of body parts and machinery. The plot also seems pieced together from other sci-fi horror movies that did it better. **100m/C VHS, DVD.** Jamie Lee Curtis, William Baldwin, Donald Sutherland, Joanna Pacula, Sherman Augustus, Clifford Curtis, Marshall Bell, Julio Oscar Mechoso, Yuri Chervotkin, Keith Flippen; **D:** John Bruno; **W:** Chuck Plarrer, Dennis Feldman; **C:** David Eggby; **M:** Joel McNeely.

The Vision ♂♂ *1987.* Suspenseful British production about televangelists who attempt to control their viewers' minds through worldwide satellite broadcasting. **103m/C VHS. GB** Lee Remick, Dirk Bogarde, Helena Bonham-Carter, Eileen Atkins; **D:** Norman Stone.

Vision Quest ♂♂½ *Crazy for You 1985 (R)* A high school student wants to win the Washington State wrestling championship and the affections of a beautiful older artist. He gives it his all as his "visionquest." A winning performance by Modine raises the usual teen coming-of-age movie. Madonna sings "Crazy for You" in a nightclub. Based on novel by Terry Davis. **107m/C VHS, DVD.** Matthew Modine, Linda Fiorentino, Ronny Cox, Roberts Blossom, Daphne Zuniga, Charles Hallahan, Michael Schoeffling, Forest Whitaker, Gary Kasper, James Gammon, Harold Sylvester, Raphael Sbarge; **D:** Harold Becker; **W:** Darryl Poniscan; **C:** Owen Roizman; **M:** Tangerine Dream.

Visions of Evil ♂♂ *So Sad About Gloria 1975* A young woman, recently released from a mental institution, is plagued by a series of terrifying visions when she moves into a house where a brutal axe murder took place. **85m/C VHS.** Robert Ginnaven, Lou Hoffman, Seymour Trietman, Linda Wyse, Lou Sanders, Dean Jagger; **D:** Harry Z. Thomason; **W:** Marshall Riggan; **C:** James Roberson; **M:** Jerald Reed.

Visions of Light: The Art of Cinematography ♂♂♂ *1993.* Excellent documentary on the way films look and how the art of photographing movies can contribute as much, if not more, than cast, director, and script. Scenes from 125 films, from "Birth of a Nation" to "Goodfellas" are shown, with commentary from some of cinematographers, including Gordon Willis, William A. Fraker, Conrad Hall, Ernest Dickerson, Vilmos Zsigmond, and Michael Chapman, on how they achieved certain effects and their collaborations with the director of the film. **95m/C VHS, DVD. D:** Arnold Glassman, Stuart Samuels, Todd McCarthy; **W:** Todd McCarthy; **C:** Nancy Schreiber. N.Y. Film Critics '93: Feature Doc.; Natl. Soc. Film Critics '93: Feature Doc.

Visions of Sugarplums ♂ *1999.* Amateurish and filled with stereotypes that makes for more bah-humbug than a jolly holiday. Happy gay New Yorkers Joey and Bruce are thrown into a panic by the sudden visit of Joey's conservative parents, who don't know about their son's alternative lifestyle. Bruce is temporarily kicked out of the apartment but the truth comes out anyway. **78m/C DVD.** Edward Fasulo, Mark Hardin, Mary Jean Feton, Vincent Wares; **D:** Edward Fasulo; **W:** Anthony Bruce; **C:** Chun Lee; **M:** Marty Dunayer. **VIDEO**

The Visit ♂♂♂ *2000 (R)* Harper leads an excellent cast in this story of Alex, a man imprisoned for a rape he may not have committed who only seeks the acceptance and love of his family. Through visits with his estranged, successful brother (Obatunde), his loving mother (Gibbs), and his disapproving father (Williams), as well as a prison psychiatrist (Rashad) and a childhood friend (Chong), Alex finds the peace he seeks. Yes, it sounds hokey, but the excellent performances and steady, subtle direction make it all work. The parole bed scene is a highlight. **107m/C VHS, DVD.** Hill Harper, Obba Babatunde, Billy Dee Williams, Marla Gibbs, Rae Dawn Chong, Phylicia Rashad, Talia Shire, David Clennon, Glynn Turman, Efrain Figueroa, Amy Stiller; **D:** Jordan Walker-Pearlman; **W:** Jordan Walker-Pearlman; **C:** John L. (Ndiagia) Demps Jr.; **M:** Michael Bearden.

Visitants ♂ *The Fright; Get Well Soon 1982 (R)* Psycho-killer slashes his female victims and photographs his handiwork. Grant is one of his victims who doesn't die, so the killer decides to finish the hospital and finish the job. Fairly graphic and generally unpleasant. **101m/C VHS, DVD. CA** Lee Grant, William Shatner, Linda Purl, Michael Ironside; **D:** Jean-Claude Lord; **W:** Brian Taggert; **M:** Jonathan Goldsmith.

The Visitor ♂½ *1980 (R)* Affluent handsome doctor and mate conspire with grisly devil worshippers to conceive devil child. **90m/C VHS.** Mel Ferrer, Glenn Ford, Lance Henriksen, John Huston, Shelley Winters, Joanne Nail, Sam Peckinpah; **D:** Giulio Paradisi.

The Visitor ♂♂♂ *(PG-13) 1987.* Aliens descend irreverently on a small female in the 1950s, with unexpected comedic results. **93m/C VHS.** Marcus Vaughter, Johanna Grika, Joel Hile, Nicole Rio; **D:** Rick Sloane.

The Visitor ♂♂♂ *(PG-13) 1990 (R)* A man's ability to "see" murders before they happen leads police to suspect him of committing them, and he must clear himself. **90m/C VHS.** Joe Balogh, Alice Villarreal, Tom Taylor, A.R. Newman, J.R. Pella; **D:** Stephen E. Miller.

Visitor from the Grave ♂ *1981.* When an American heiress and her boyfriend dispose of a dead man's body, his spirit comes back to haunt them. Part of the BBC's "Hammer House of Horror" TV series. **60m/C VHS, DVD. GB** Simon MacCorkindale, Kathryn Leigh Scott, Gainer "Skip" Thomas, Mia Nadasi; **D:** Peter Sasdy. **TV**

The Visitors ♂♂½ *1989 (R)* Ghosts come to stay at a young family's dream house in Sweden. Not exactly a novel treatment or a novel premise. **102m/C VHS, SW** Keith Berkeley, Lena Endre, John Force, John

Olsen, Joanna Berg, Brent Landis-garci; *D:* Joachim Back (Jack) Ersgard.

The Visitors 🐾🐾 (R) Time travel comedy features 12th-century French knight Godefroy (Reno) and his vassal Jacquasse (Clavier) crossing paths with a powerful witch (and evidently pissing her off) since she casts a spell causing Godefroy to accidentally kill his father-in-law. So Godefroy contacts a wizard to give him a time travel potion so he can go back and stop the shooting. Too bad the potion hurts knight and vassal forward into present-day France, French with subtitles. *106m/C* VHS, DVD. FR Jean Reno, Christian Clavier, Marie-Anne) Chazel, Valérie Lemercier, Christian Bujeau; *D:* Jean-Marie Poiré; *C:* Jean-Yves Le Mener; *M:* Eric Levi.

Vital Signs 🐾 1990 (R) Supernatural thriller that turns a bit silly. After six months on a solo sailing trip around the world, Georgia's (Mitchell) sloop is becalmed for several days. Not very stable to begin with (she has the requisite dark past), Georgia begins to hallucinate, only these ghostly encounters leave behind physical reminders of their presence. *88m/C* VHS, DVD. AU Radha Mitchell, Susannah York, Ray Barrett, Tottie Goldsmith; *D:* Richard Franklin; *W:* Everett de Roche; *C:* Ellery Ryan; *M:* Nerida Tyson-Chew.

Viva Knievel! WOOF! 1977 (PG) Crooks plan to sabotage Knievel's daredevil jump in Mexico and then smuggle cocaine back into the States in his coffin. Unintentionally campy. *106m/C* VHS, DVD. Evel Knievel, Gene Kelly, Lauren Hutton, Red Buttons, Leslie Nielsen, Cameron Mitchell, Marjoe Gortner, Albert Salmi, Dabney Coleman; *C:* Fred H. Jackmen Jr.; *M:* Charles Bernstein.

Viva Las Vegas 🐾🐾½ 1963 *Love in Las Vegas* 1963 Race car driver Elvis needs money to compete against rival Danova in the upcoming Las Vegas Grand Prix. He takes a job in a casino and romances fellow employee Ann-Margret, who turns out to be his rival for the grand prize in the local talent competition. Good pairing between the two leads, and the King does particularly well with the title song. "The Lady Loves Me," "I Need Somebody to Lean On; Come On, Everybody; Today; Tomorrow and Forever; If You Think I Don't Need You; Say: I Need Somebody to Lean On; Come On, Everybody; Today; Tomorrow and Forever; If You Think I Don't Need You; Appreciation; My Rival, Viva Las Vegas. *85m/C* VHS, DVD, Blu-ray Disc, HD DVD. Elvis Presley, Ann-Margret, William Demarest, Jack Carter, Cesare Danova, Nicky Blair, Larry Kent; *D:* George Sidney; *C:* Joseph Biroc.

Viva Maria! 🐾🐾½ 1965 (R) Tongue-in-cheek comedy with Bardot and Moreau as two dancers (both named Maria) in a show traveling through Mexico. The two become incensed by the poverty of the peasants and decide to turn revolutionary (especially after Moreau has an affair with revolutionary leader Hamilton, who promptly gets killed). The two French sex symbols are a fine match. *119m/C* VHS, DVD. FR IT Jeanne Moreau, Brigitte Bardot, George Hamilton, Paulette Dubost, Claudio Brook; *D:* Louis Malle; *W:* Louis Malle, Jean-Claude Carriere; *C:* Henri Decae; *M:* Georges Delerue.

Viva Max! 🐾🐾½ 1969 A blundering modern-day Mexican general and his men recapture the Alamo, and in an equally inept American force, headed by Winters, is sent to rout them out. Mostly works, with some very funny scenes. Ustinov is great. *93m/C* VHS. Peter Ustinov, Jonathan Winters, John Astin, Pamela Tiffin, Keenan Wynn; *D:* Jerry Paris.

Viva Villa! 🐾🐾🐾 1934 Exciting action biography of Mexican revolutionary Pancho Villa, well-portrayed by the exuberant Beery. The film shows the early Robin Hood-like exploits of Villa and his peasant army in overthrowing the government. But Villa's bandito instincts and ego cause problems and a power struggle ensues. Director Howard Hawks went uncredited for his work on the film, being fired by the studio after an incident while on location in Mexico. *115m/B* VHS. Wallace Beery, Fay Wray, Stuart Erwin, Leo Carrillo, Donald Cook, George E. Stone, Joseph Schildkraut, Henry B. Walthall, Katherine DeMille, David Durand, Frank Puglia; *D:* Jack Conway; *W:* Ben Hecht.

Viva Zapata! 🐾🐾🐾 1952 Chronicles the life of Mexican revolutionary Emiliano Zapata. Brando is powerful as he leads the peasant revolt in the early 1900s, only to be corrupted by power and greed. Quinn well deserved his Best Supporting Actor Oscar for his performance as Zapata's brother. Based on the novel "Zapata the Unconquered" by Edgcumb Pinchon. *112m/B* VHS, DVD. Marlon Brando, Anthony Quinn, Jean Peters, Margo, Arnold Moss, Joseph Wiseman, Mildred Dunnock; *D:* Elia Kazan; *W:* John Steinbeck; *M:* Alex North. *Oscars '52:* Actor (Quinn); *British Acad. '52:* Actor (Brando); *Cannes '52:* Actor (Brando).

Vivacious Lady 🐾🐾🐾 1938 Romantic comedy about a mild-mannered college professor who marries a chorus girl. Problems arise when he must let his conservative family and his former fiancee in on the marriage news. Good performances. Appealing. *90m/B* VHS, DVD. Ginger Rogers, James Stewart, James Ellison, Beulah Bondi, Charles Coburn, Jack Carson, Franklin Pangborn, Dorothy Moore; *D:* George Stevens.

Vive l'Amour 🐾🐾 1994 A furnished Taipei luxury apartment is the setting for three characters who make use of the space but have little connection to each other. Guimei is the real estate agent who's trying to sell the apartment and uses it for casual sex, including an encounter with street vendor Zhaorong. The third part of the triangle is young salesman Kangsheng, who's broken into the place to commit suicide but is forestalled by Zhaorong, with whom Kangsheng then becomes sexually intrigued. The trio come and go, mostly alone, so dialogue is at a minimum. Taiwanese with subtitles. *118m/C* VHS, DVD. TW Yang Guimei, Chen Zhaorong, Li Kangsheng; *D:* Tsai Ming-Liang; *W:* Tsai Ming-Liang; *C:* Pen-jung Liao, Ming-kuo Lin.

Vlad 🐾🐾½ 2003 Four grad students travel to Romania to study the vile legend of Vlad Drakul (aka Dracula) per a Bucharest professor's request. While inside his tomb (what could possibly go wrong?) they end up taking a harrowing necklace. *96m/C* VHS, DVD. Billy Zane, Brad Dourif, Francesco Quinn, John Rhys-Davies, Claudiu Bleont, Paul Popowich, Kam Heskin, Nicholas Irons, Monica Davidescu, Iva Hasperger, Emil Hostina, Guy Siner, Mircea Stoian, Andreea Macelaru, Alin Panc, Alexandra Velniciuc, Zoltan Butuc, Anca-Ioana Ardrone, Adrian Pintea, Ian Ionescu, Catalin Rotaru, Cristian Popa; *D:* Michael D. Sellers; *W:* Michael D. Sellers, Tony Shawkat; *C:* Viorel Sergovici Jr.; *M:* Christopher Field. VIDEO

Vogues of 1938 🐾🐾 *All This and Glamour Too; Vogues 1937* As a lark, a rich girl takes a job as a fashion model and incurs the displeasure of Baxter, the owner of the chic fashion house where she works. An early Technicolor fashion extravaganza. "That Old Feeling; Lovely; Turn On the Red Hot Heat (Burn the Blues Away); King of Jam. *110m/C* VHS. Warner Baxter, Helen Vinson, Mischa Auer, Hedda Hopper, Penny Singleton, Alan Campbell; *C:* Ann T. Rossetti; *M:* Irving Cummings.

Voices from a Locked Room 🐾🐾 *Voices* 1995 (R) Very loosely based on the life of British composer Peter Warlock (1894-1930) and music critic Philip Heseltine. Heseltine detests Warlock's music. Warlock threatens Heseltine, and the middle. Of course, what's really bizarre is that Warlock is Heseltine's pseudonym. Film does have a nice period look. *93m/C* VHS. GB Jeremy Northam, Tushka Bergen, Alan Corduner, Hilton McRae; *D:* Malcolm Clarke; *M:* Peter Barnes; *C:* Ann T. Rossetti; *M:* Elliot Goldenthal.

Volcano 🐾🐾 1997 (PG-13) L.A. has already had to deal with earthquakes, mudslides, raging fires, riots and the acting career of Anna Nicole Smith. Now it's completely roasted by millions of gallons of molten lava. This overblown Rescue 911 has Mike Roark (Jones), the standard take-charge guy, trying to avert total destruction while being assisted by the brainy-but-beautiful seismologist Dr. Amy Barnes (Heche). Many tongue-in-cheek jokes about the general state of chaos in from these, the dialogue is very impressive. Wilshire Blvd. was actually recreated on a 17-acre set (believed to be the biggest ever) in order to meet its fiery doom. *120m/C* VHS, DVD. Tommy Lee Jones, Anne Heche, Gaby Hoffman, Don Cheadle, Keith David, John Corbett, Michael Rispoli, John Carroll Lynch, Jacqueline Kim; *D:* Mick Jackson; *W:* Billy Ray, Jerome Armstrong; *C:* Theo van de Sande; *M:* Alan Silvestri.

Volcano: Fire on the Mountain 🐾🐾 *Fire on the Mountain* 1997 (PG) Cheesy TV disaster flick finds geologist Peter Slater (Cortese) trying to convince both his boss and the residents of Angel Falls, California that a nearby volcano is about to blow. *89m/C* VHS. Dan Cortese, Cynthia Gibb, Brian Kerwin; *D:* Graeme Campbell; *C:* Tobias Schliessler; *M:* David Michael Frank.

Volere Volare 🐾🐾½ 1992 (R) Shy sound engineer Nichetti shares a studio with his brother. The brother employs a bevy of beauties to dub sound effects onto soft-core porn films while Nichetti works on dubbing classic cartoons. He becomes so involved in his work he actually turns into a cartoon figure, which does nothing for his love life. Then he meets Martina, who's strangely attracted to this cartoon figure. Quirky comedy mixes animation and live action with too many gimmicks and not enough heart. In Italian with English subtitles. *92m/C* VHS. IT Maurizio Nichetti, Angela Finocchiaro, Mariella Valentini, Patrizio Roversi, Remo Remotti, Renato Scarpa; *D:* Maurizio Nichetti, Guido Manuli; *W:* Maurizio Nichetti, Guido Manuli. Montreal World Film Fest. '92: Director (Nichetti).

Vivacious... [continued]

Voices from Beyond 🐾🐾½ *Voci dal Profondo* 1990 After wealthy Giorgio Mainardi hemorrhages to death, his daughter Rosy (Huff) returns home from college to attend the funeral. She soon begins to have strange dreams in which her father claims that he was murdered, and begs Rosy to discover the identity of the killer. In flashbacks, we learn that Giorgio did something to enrage everyone in the household before he died, so there are many suspects. While the revelation of the murderer is a boring mess. While director Fulci is well-known for his liberal use of gore and his occasionally creepy visuals, this film has neither. The acting isn't very good, and the atrocious dubbing only makes matters worse. *91m/C* VHS, DVD. IT Duilio Del Prete, Karina Huff, Pascal Persiano, Lorenzo Flaherty, Bettina Giovannin, Demiano Azzos; *D:* Lucio Fulci; *W:* Piero Regnoli; *M:* Nicola Cipriani.

Voices of Iraq 🐾🐾🐾 2004 In April of 2004 a crew of American filmmakers distributed 150 video cameras to citizens of Iraq. Given full artistic and legal license to speak at will, the citizens participate in an unbiased experiment showing the true sentiment of the war-torn country. Surprisingly, there is little complaint of the U.S. and coalition's occupying troops and rampant hatred against their former dictator, Saddam Hussein, which leads us to believe that perhaps the cameras were given to select sects, rather that at random citizens, or likely a dictatorship in the editing room. Still, it makes for an empowering tool in the visualization of an empowering country. *79m/C* DVD. US *M:* Narciyst, Euphrates.

The Void 🐾🐾½ 2001 (R) Physicist Eva Soderstrom (Tapping) discovers that industrialist Thomas Abernathy (McDowell) is experimenting with creating an artificial black hole on Earth. This isn't a good thing so Eva hooks up with Dr. Steven Price (Paul) to stop Abernathy. So-so sci-fi. *90m/C* VHS, DVD. Amanda Tapping, Adrian Paul, Malcolm McDowell, Andrew McIlroy; *D:* Gilbert M. Shilton; *W:* Gilbert M. Shilton, Geri Guthrie; *C:* Attila Szalay; *M:* Ross Vannelli.

Volpone 🐾🐾🐾 1939 A classic adaptation of Ben Jonson's famous tale. A greedy merchant pretends he is dying, leaving a fortune behind, in order see what his family will do to become his heirs. In French with English subtitles. *95m/B* VHS. FR Harry Baur, Louis Jouvet, Fernand Ledoux; *D:* Maurice Tourneur.

Volunteers 🐾🐾 1985 (R) Ivy League playboy joins the newly formed Peace Corps to escape gambling debts and finds himself on a bridge-building mission in Thailand. Has its comedic moments, especially with Candy. *107m/C* VHS, DVD. Tom Hanks, John Candy, Rita Wilson, Tim Thomerson, Gedde Watanabe, George Plimpton, Ernest Harada; *D:* Nicholas Meyer; *W:* Ken Levine; *C:* Ric Waite; *M:* James Horner.

Volver 🐾🐾🐾🐾 2006 (R) Almodovar and the women. The writer/director tackles domestic melodrama when frustrated cleaner Raimunda (Cruz) is forced into drastic action to protect her daughter Paula (Cobo). In addition, Raimunda's hairdresser sister Sole (Duenas) is suddenly confronted by their mother Irene's (Maura) ghost, who takes up residence with Sole and helps out in her salon in order to rectify some mistakes she made with her daughters. Much sly humor and ferrale bonding and yes, Cruz is wearing a prosthetic backside to give her that sexy sway. Spanish with subtitles. *111m/C* DVD, Blu-ray Disc. SP Penelope Cruz, Lole Duenas, Carmen Maura, Chus (Maria Jesus) Lampreave, Blanca Portillo, Yohana Cobo, Maria Isabel Diaz, Antonio de la Torre, Carlos Blanco, Leonardo Rivera; *D:* Pedro Almodóvar; *W:* Pedro Almodóvar; *C:* Jose Luis Alcaine; *M:* Alberto Iglesias.

Von Ryan's Express 🐾🐾🐾 1965 An American Air Force colonel leads a group of prisoners-of-war in taking control of a freight train in order to make their exciting escape from a WWII P.O.W. camp in Italy. Strong cast. *117m/C* VHS, DVD. Frank Sinatra, Trevor Howard, Brad Dexter, Raffaella Carra, Sergio Fantoni, John Leyton, Vito Scotti, Edward Mulhare, Adolfo Celi, James Brolin, James B. Sikking, Wolfgang Preiss, John van Dreelen, Richard Bakalyan, Michael Goodliffe, Michael St. Clair, Ivan T'riesault; *D:* Mark Robson; *W:* Wendell Mayes, Joseph Landon; *C:* William H. Daniels; *M:* Jerry Goldsmith.

Voodoo 🐾🐾 1995 (R) College student Andy (Feldman) must battle a fraternity by an evil voodoo priest, when they decide to make his girlfriend their next human sacrifice. *91m/C* VHS, DVD. Corey Feldman, Sarah Douglas, Jack Nance, Joel J. Edwards; *D:* Rene Eram; *W:* Brian DiMuccio, Dino Vindeni; *C:* Dan Gillham; *M:* Keith Bilderbeck.

Voodoo Academy 🐾 2000 Imagine an episode of "Scooby Doo" crossed with a Calvin Klein ad and you'll get the idea of what video veteran Dave DeCoteau is doing in what he calls "the first horror film made for girls." A Bible college is a front for voodoo activity. The all-male students run around in their underwear trying to figure out what's going on. *100m/C* DVD. Riley Smith, Chad Burns, Debra Meyer; *D:* David DeCoteau.

Voodoo Black Exorcist 🐾 *Vudu Sangriento* 1973 Some 3000 years ago, a black prince was buried alive for messin' with another man's woman. Now he's back...and he's mad--real mad. He's prepared to kill just about everyone. Can he be stopped before all in the modern world are dead?? *88m/C* VHS. SP Aldo Sambrel, Tanyeka Stadie, Fernando (Fernand) Sancho; *D:* Manuel Cano; *W:* Santiago Moncada; *C:* Robert Ochoa; *M:* Fernando Garcia Morcillo.

Voodoo Dawn 🐾🐾 1989 (R) Two New Yorkers travel to the Deep South to visit a friend who, it turns out, is the latest victim in a series of really gross voodoo murders. A beautiful girl is written into the plot, and the New York guys have an excuse to stay in voodooville, even though bimbolina's southern accent comes and goes for no discernable reason. Filmed near Charleston, South Carolina, and co-written by Russo of "Night of the Living

Dead" fame. 83m/C VHS. Raymond St. Jacques, Theresa Merritt, Gina Gershon, Kirk Baily, Billy "Sly" Williams, J. Grant Albrecht, Tony Todd; D: Steven Fierberg; W: John A. Russo; D: Andrzej Sekula. VIDEO

Voodoo Dawn 1999 Crazy con Frank Barlow (Madsen) has learned voodoo rites in prison and is using his power to get revenge on his brother's killer. Predictable crime drama despite the occult trappings. 93m/C VHS, DVD. Michael Madsen, Rosanna Arquette, Balthazar Getty, Phillip Glasser, James Russo; D: Andrzej Sekula. VIDEO

Voodoo Moon 2005 More silly than scary. Cole (Mabius) and Heather (Carpenter) are the only survivors when a demonic presence destroyed their town. For many years, Cole has been learning how to destroy the demon and now returns with his psychic sis to put his knowledge to the test. 89m/C DVD. Eric Mabius, Charisma Carpenter, Ric Young, Jeffrey Combs, Jayne Heitmeyer, John Amos, Dee Wallace Stone; D: Kevin VanHook; W: Kevin VanHook; C: Matt Steinauer; M: Ludek Drizhal. CABLE

Voodoo Woman 1957 An innocent girl is lured into the jungle by an evil scientist who is trying to create the perfect woman to commit murders. He turns the girl into an ugly monster in an attempt to get her to obey his telepathic commands. A campy classic that's as bad as it sounds. 77m/B VHS. Maria English, Tom Conway, Mike Connors, Lance Fuller, Paul Blaisdell; D: Edward L. Cahn.

Vortex 1981 Punk/film noir style in which a female private eye becomes immersed in corporate paranoia and political corruption. 87m/C VHS. Lydia Lunch, James Russo, Bill Rice, Richard France, Ann Magnuson, Haoui Montaug, Adele Bertei, Bill Landis; D: Scott B, Beth B; W: Scott B, Beth B; C: Steven Fierberg; M: Lydia Lunch, Adele Bertei.

Voulez-Vous Danser avec Moi? Come Dance with Me; Do You Want to Dance with Me? 1959 Lighthearted comedy-mystery with a sexy Bardot starring as the newly married Virginie. After a quarrel with her husband Herve (Vidal), she follows him to a dance studio and finds him incriminated in the murder of the studio's owner. So Virginie decides to go undercover as an instructor to clear her husband's name. Based on the novel "The Blonde Died Dancing" by Kelley Roos. French with subtitles. 91m/C VHS, DVD. FR I/T Brigitte Bardot, Henri Vidal, Dawn Addams, Philippe Nicaud, Serge Gainsbourg, Dario Moreno; D: Michel Boisrond; W: Annette Wademant; C: Robert Lefebvre; M: Henri Crolla.

A Vow to Kill 1994 (PG-13) Predictable cable thriller finds the wealthy Phillips marrying the charming Grieco after a whirlwind courtship. Then, on their honeymoon, she accidentally learns that her new husband has contacted their family and is masquerading as a kidnapper—demanding a large ransom for her safe release. But maybe it's not such a masquerade after all. 91m/C VHS. Julianne Phillips, Richard Grieco, Gordon Pinsent, Peter MacNeill, Tom Cavanagh, Nicole Oliver; D: Harry S. Longstreet; W: Harry S. Longstreet, Sean Silas, Renee Longstreet; C: Francois Protat; M: John Keane. CABLE

Voyage 1993 (R) Boring rip-off of "Dead Calm" and other couple-in-peril-from-psycho-on-boat films. Hauer and Allen are having marital problems and decide to sail away from their troubles with new-found friends Roberts and Nielson. Only their guests are sociopaths. Hauer takes a breather from his psycho roles for a turn as the decent guy while Roberts could do his patented crazy act in his sleep. 88m/C VHS. Rutger Hauer, Karen Allen, Eric Roberts, Connie Nielsen; D: John MacKenzie. CABLE

Voyage en Balloon 1959 This is the delightful story of a young boy (played by the star of "The Red Balloon") who stows away on his grandfather's hot air balloon for an adventurous trip across France. 82m/C VHS. FR Pascal Lamorisse; W: Albert Lamorisse; Nar: Jack Lemmon.

Voyage en Douce 1981 Helene and Lucie have been friends since childhood. Helene wants to rent a summer house, and Lucie, fed up with her marriage, agrees to join her on a leisurely journey through the south of France. Thoughtful look at friendship among women. French with subtitles. 95m/C VHS, FR Dominique Sanda, Geraldine Chaplin; D: Michel DeVille.

Voyage in Italy Viaggio in Italia; Voyage to Italy; The Lonely Woman; Strangers 1953 Narrative of a marriage finds unhappy English couple Bergman and Sanders travelling by car to Naples. However, various crises manage to reunite them. Critically mauled upon its release, this third collaboration between Bergman and Rossellini, following "Stromboli" and "Europa '51," later became a big hit with New Wave directors. 83m/B VHS. IT Ingrid Bergman, George Sanders; D: Roberto Rossellini; W: Roberto Rossellini, Vitaliano Brancatti; C: Enzo Serafin; M: Renzo Rossellini.

Voyage of Terror: The Achille Lauro Affair 1990 Recounting of the 1985 Italian cruise-ship hijacking by four Palestinians. Lancaster is the wheelchair-bound Leon Klinghoffer and Saint is wife Marilyn. Miniseries was shot on the actual ship and route where the tragedy occurred. 120m/C VHS. Burt Lancaster, Eva Marie Saint, Robert Culp, Brian Bloom, Dominique Sanda, Rebecca Schaeffer, Joseph Nasser, Gabriele Ferzetti, Renzo Montagnani; D: Alberto Negrin. TV

Voyage of the Damned 1976 (G) The story of one of the most tragic incidents of WWII. In 1939, 1,937 German-Jewish refugees fleeing Nazi Germany are bound for Cuba aboard the Hamburg-America liner S.S. St. Louis. They are refused permission to land in Cuba (and everywhere else) and must sail back to Germany and certain death. Based on the novel by Gordon Thomas and Max Morgan-Witts. 155m/C VHS, DVD. GB Faye Dunaway, Max von Sydow, Oskar Werner, Malcolm McDowell, Orson Welles, James Mason, Lee Grant, Katharine Ross, Ben Gazzara, Lynne Frederick, Wendy Hiller, Jose Ferrer, Luther Adler, Sam Wanamaker, Denholm Elliott, Nehemiah Persoff, Julie Harris, Maria Schell, Jonathan Pryce, Janet Suzman, Helmut Griem, Michael Constantine, Victor Spinetti; D: Stuart Rosenberg; W: Steve Shagan, David Butler; C: Billy Williams; M: Lalo Schifrin. Golden Globes '77. Support. Actress (Ross).

Voyage of the Heart 1990 An aging fisherman meets up with a sexy college girl and the passion begins. 88m/C VHS. Dunja Djordjenic, Bill Ackridge, Jeremy Slate, Geoffrey Dunn, Liz Rolfe; D: Mark Schwartz; W: Geoffrey Dunn; C: Gene Evans; M: Randy Masters.

Voyage of the Rock Aliens 1987 A quasi-satiric space farce about competing alien rock stars. 97m/C VHS, DVD. Pia Zadora, Tom Nolan, Craig Sheffer, Rhett Smith, Ruth Gordon, Michael Berryman, Jermaine Jackson, Alison La Placa; D: James Fargo; W: Edward Gold, S. James Guidotti; C: Gilbert Taylor; M: Jack White.

The Voyage of the Yes 1972 (PG) Two teenagers, one white and one black, in a small sailboat hit rough weather and battle the elements while learning about themselves. Average TV movie. 100m/C VHS, DVD. Desi Arnaz Jr., Mike Evans, Beverly Garland, Skip Homeier, Della Reese, Scoey Mitchell; D: Lee H. Katzin. TV

A Voyage 'Round My Father 1989 John Mortimer's adaptation of his semi-autobiographical stage play. Olivier is the eccentric, opinionated blind barrister-father and Bates the exasperated son as both try to come to terms with their stormy family relationship. Well-acted and directed. 85m/C VHS. GB Laurence Olivier, Alan Bates, Jane Asher, Elizabeth Sellars; D: Alvin Rakoff. TV

Voyage Surprise 1946 A slapstick comedy about a crazy old man who runs a mystery tour from a dilapidated bus as he takes an unknowing mob of tourists on a cross-country escapade through a brothel, a wedding, criminals, police, terrorists and the Haute-Provence. In French with English subtitles. 108m/B VHS. FR Martine Carol, Sloel; D: Pierre Prevert; C: Jean (Yves, Georges) Bourgoin.

Voyage to the Beginning of the World Journey to the Beginning of the World; Viagem ao Principio do Mundo 1996 Autobiographical piece by 88-year-old director de Oliveira, who has been making movies since the silent film era. Mastroianni, in his last role, plays the somewhat fictionalized director named Manoel who travels to Portugal to shoot a film. Along the way he points out crumbling landmarks that he remembers from his childhood, an apt metaphor for the memories where the majority of his life now resides. Along with him is French actor Afonso (Gautier), who makes a visit to an elderly aunt (de Castro) who poignantly tells Afonso about his father and the way things used to be. Slow moving but lyrical ode to aging and the changing perspective it gives. French and Portuguese with subtitles. 93m/C VHS, DVD. PT Marcello Mastroianni, Jean-Yves Gautier, Leonor Silveira, Diogo Doria, Isabel de Castro; D: Manoel de Oliveira; W: Manoel de Oliveira; C: Renato Berta; M: Emmanuel Nunes.

Voyage to the Bottom of the Sea 1961 The crew of an atomic submarine must destroy a deadly radiation belt which has set the polar ice cap ablaze. Fun stuff, with good special effects and photography. Later became a TV series. 106m/C VHS, DVD. Walter Pidgeon, Joan Fontaine, Barbara Eden, Peter Lorre, Robert Sterling, Michael Ansara, Frankie Avalon; D: Irwin Allen; W: Charles Bennett, Irwin Allen; C: Winton C. Hoch; M: Paul Sawell, Bert Shefter.

Voyage to the Planet of Prehistoric Women WOOF! Gill Woman; Gill Women of Venus 1968 Astronauts journey to Venus, where they discover a race of gorgeous, sea-shell clad women led by Van Doren, as well as a few monsters. Incomprehensible but fun. The third film incorporating the Russian "Planeta Burg" footage. Directed (and narrated) by Bogdanovich under the pseudonym Derek Thomas. 78m/C VHS, DVD. Mamie Van Doren, Mary Mark, Paige Lee, Aldo Roman, Margot Hartman; D: Peter Bogdanovich; W: Henry Ney; Nar: Peter Bogdanovich.

Voyage to the Prehistoric Planet Voyage to a Prehistoric Planet 1965 In the year 2020, an expedition to Venus is forced to deal with dinosaurs and other perils. In the making of this movie, Roger Corman edited in special effects and additional footage from a recently acquired Russian film, "Planeta Burg," and his own "Queen of Blood." 80m/C VHS, DVD. Basil Rathbone, Faith Domergue, Marc Shannon, Christopher Brand; D: Curtis Harrington.

Voyager 1991 (PG-13) Restless, middle-aged engineer Walter Faber (Shepherd) tells his life story in a series of flashbacks. Twenty years before (the film starts in 1957) he abandons his pregnant girlfriend who promises to get an abortion. He laters hears she married, had a child, and divorced. While sailing to New York from France Walter falls in love with a young student and accompanies her to Greece to visit her mother. Only then does he realize her true identity, leading to a tragic conclusion. Shepherd's is a glum, repressed performance (in keeping with the character) while Delpy personifies youthful sweetness. Based on the novel "Homo Faber" by Max Frisch. 110m/C VHS. FR GE Sam Shepard, Julie Delpy, Barbara Sukowa, Dieter Kirchlechner, Traci Lind, Deborra-Lee Furness, August Zirner, Thomas Heinze; D: Volker Schlondorff; W: Volker Schlondorff, Rudy Wurlitzer.

The Voyeur 1994 After ten years of marriage, a couple tries to ignite those sexual fires by spending a weekend in Napa Valley and indulging in erotic sexual games. Based on Lonnie Barbach's book "Erotic Edge." 95m/C VHS. Al Sapienza, Kim (Kimberly Dawn) Dawson; D: Deborah Shames; W: Udana Power.

Vukovar 1994 Vukovar is a Croat town just across the Danube river from Serbia, in the former Yugoslavia, where different ethnic groups had managed to coexist peacefully. When Croatian Anna (Jokovic) marries her childhood sweetheart, the Serbian Toma (Isakovic), however, their celebration is marred by nationalist demonstrations. Soon Anna's pregnant, Toma has been drafted, and the town comes under siege, with Tomas' parents fleeing, Anna's family killed in a bombing, and Ann herself struggling to survive. Film was condemned by the pro-Croatian government as pro-Serbian propaganda though director Draskovic, a Serbian whose parents are Croatian and Bosnian, strove to be nonpartisan. Serbo-Croatian with subtitles. 95m/C VHS. YU Mirjana Jokovic, Boris Isakovic, Monica Romic; D: Boro Draskovic; W: Boro Draskovic, Maja Draskovic; C: Aleksandar Petkovic.

Vulcan God of Fire WOOF! Vulcan, Son of Jupiter 1962 Flash is a muscle-bound Vulcan fighting off cheesy monsters in an effort to win the hand of Venus. 76m/C VHS. IT Rob Flash, Gordon Mitchell, Bella Cortez; D: Emmimo Salvi.

Vulture 1967 In an attempt to carry out a curse on the descendants of the man who killed his forefather, a scientist tries an atomic transmutation experiment and winds up combining himself with a bird. 91m/C VHS. Robert Hutton, Akim Tamiroff, Broderick Crawford, Diane Clare, Philip Friend, Patrick Holt, Annette Carell; D: Lawrence Huntington.

Vultures 1984 A dying patriarch summons his predatory family to his home in order to straighten out the distribution of inheritance. One by one, they fall victim to a mysterious murderer. 101m/C VHS. Yvonne De Carlo, Stuart Whitman, Jim Bailey, Meredith MacRae, Aldo Ray; D: Paul Leder.

Vulture's Eye 2004 Why is it that a bunch of sexy ladies can't roam the pleasant Virginia countryside without having some creepy evil-doer Count lurking about? Thank goodness there's a stereotypical coot of a Southern doctor around to try to save the poor women's souls. That and the special strength they get from just being friends. Who knew that just having pals keeps ya from joining the undead! 100m/C DVD. Brooke Paller, Anne Flosnik, Jason King, Fred Iacovo, James Naliz, Eve Young; D: Frank Sciurba; W: Frank Sciurba. VIDEO

W 1961 I Want Her Dead 1974 (PG) A woman and her husband are terrorized and must find out why. A single letter "W" is found at the scene of the crimes. Notable only as model Twiggy's first film. 95m/C VHS, DVD. Twiggy, Dirk Benedict, John Vernon, Eugene Roche; D: Richard Quine.

Wackiest Ship in the Army 1961 A completely undisciplined warship crew must smuggle an Australian spy through Japanese waters during WWII. Odd, enjoyable mixture of action and laughs. Became a TV series. In the middle of the war effort, Nelson straps on a guitar and sings "Do You Know What It Means to Miss New Orleans." 99m/C VHS, DVD. Jack Lemmon, Ricky Nelson, Chips Rafferty, John Lund, Mike Kellin, Patricia Driscoll; D: Richard Murphy.

Wackiest Wagon Train in the West 1977 (G) Hapless wagon master is saddled with a dummy assistant as they guide a party of five characters across the West. Based on the minor TV sitcom "Dusty's Trail." Produced by the same folks who delivered the similarly premised TV series "Gilligan's Island" and "The Brady Bunch." 86m/C VHS, DVD. Ivor Francis, Lori Saunders, Bob Denver, Forrest Tucker, Jeannine Riley, William Cort; D: Elroy Schwartz; W: Sherwood Schwartz, Elroy Schwartz. TV

Wacko WOOF! 1983 (PG) Group of nymphettes and tough guys get caught up in a wild Halloween-pumpkin-lawnmower murder. This spoof of the "Halloween" series works too hard for as few laughs as it gets. 84m/C VHS. Stella Stevens, George Kennedy, Joe Don Baker, Andrew (Dice Clay) Silverstein; D: Greydon Clark.

The Wacky World of Wills & Burke 1985 Comedy based on the adventures of Wills and Burke, the two 19th-century explorers who led the first unsuccessful expedition across the outback—the Lewis and Clark of Australia, if you will. In real life they died during the adventure, a less than wacky finale. "Burke and Wills," out of the same story, was a serious treatment of the same story. **102m/C VHS, AU** Gary McDonald, Kim Gyngell, Peter Collingwood, Jonathan Hardy, Mark Little; *D:* Bob Weis.

Wag the Dog *⊘⊘½ 1997 (R)* Based on the book "American Hero" by Larry Beinhart and adapted by Hilary Henkin and David Mamet. Over-the-top Hollywood producer (Hoffman) is hired by White House officials to stage a military attack when the U.S. to divert media attention from accusations that the President fondled a Girl Scout. Show biz insiders wonder if it is one big insider's joke. Luckily, it's smart enough, and short enough, to avoid becoming tiresome. Look for cameos by Woody Harrelson and Willie Nelson. Filmed in a speedy 29 days on a $15 million budget. **96m/C VHS, DVD.** Dustin Hoffman, Robert De Niro, Anne Heche, Woody Harrelson, Denis Leary, Willie Nelson, Andrea Martin, Suzanne Cryer, John Michael Higgins, Suzy Plakson, Kirsten Dunst, William H. Macy, Michael Belson; *D:* Barry Levinson; *W:* Hilary Henkin, David Mamet; *C:* Robert Richardson; *M:* Mark Knopfler; Natl. Bd. of Review '97: Support. Actress (Heche).

Wager of Love *⊘⊘½ 1990* While vacationing on their annual pleasure cruise, four women bet on their individual power of seduction. They find themselves competing for passion as each woman's erotic adventure unravels in this exciting and sensual tale. **75m/C VHS,** Steve Landers, Shelly Johnson, Elliot Silverman, Lisa Cook; *D:* Jason Holt.

Wages of Fear *⊘⊘⊘ 1955 Le Salaire de la Peur* American oil company controls a desolate Central American town whose citizens desperately want out—so desperately that four are willing to try a suicide mission to deliver nitroglycerine to put out a well-fire raging 300 miles away. The company's cynical head has offered $2000 to each man, enough to finance escape from the hell-hole they live in. Complex, multi-dimensional cinema concentrates on character development for the first half—crucial to the film's greatness. Remade by William Friedkin as "Sorcerer" in 1977. Based on a novel by Georges Arnaud. In French with English subtitles. **138m/B VHS, DVD. FR** Yves Montand, Charles Vanel, Peter Van Eyck, Vera Clouzot, Folco Lulli, William Tubbs; *D:* Henri-Georges Clouzot; *W:* Henri-Georges Clouzot; *C:* Armand Thirard; *M:* Georges Auric; British Acad. '54; Cannes '53. Actor (Vanel), Film.

Wagner: The Complete Epic *⊘⊘ 1985* The unedited version of the epic miniseries dramatizing the life of German composer Richard Wagner. The excellent photography does justice to the subject's grandeur. Burton, a shell of his former cinematic self, is painful to watch in his last released film. Frankly, this is way too long. Also available in a edited 300-minute version, which is still too long. **540m/C VHS, DVD, GB HU** Richard Burton, Vanessa Redgrave, John Gielgud, Laurence Olivier; *D:* Tony Palmer; TV.

Wagner *⊘⊘⊘ 1985* Slightly half it's original length, the world's biggest biopic is still huge, sweeping, and long. Incoherent and over-acted. Wagner's music is conducted by Sir Georg Solti. Made for television. **300m/C VHS, GB HU** Richard Burton, Vanessa Redgrave, Ralph Richardson, John Gielgud, Laurence Olivier, Franco Nero; *D:* Tony Palmer; TV.

Wagon Master *⊘⊘⊘ 1950* Two cowboys are persuaded to guide a group of Mormons, led by Bond, in their trek across the western frontier. They run into a variety of troubles, including a band of killers who joins the wagon train to escape a posse. Sensitively directed, realistic and worthwhile. Inspired the western "Wagon Train." Also available in colorized. **85m/B VHS.** Ben Johnson, Joanne Dru, Harry Carey Jr., Ward Bond, Jane Darwell, James Arness; *D:* John Ford.

Wagon Tracks *⊘⊘ 1919* Hart searches for the man responsible for his brother's death. **64m/B VHS, DVD,** William S. Hart, Jane Novak, Robert McKim, Lloyd Bacon; *D:* Lambert Hillyer.

Wagon Trail *⊘⊘½ 1935* The sheriff's son is blackmailed into helping a gang of robbers, with terrible consequences for himself and his father (Carey), who is fired from his job after the son breaks jail. The new sheriff is secretly chief of the outlaw band. Carey rides back into town and eventually virtue triumphs. Good, tense—but not too tense—western. **59m/B VHS. DVD.** Gertrude Messinger, Edward Norris, Roger Williams, Earl Dwire, Harry Carey Sr.; *D:* Harry Fraser; *W:* Harry Fraser; *C:* Robert E. Cline.

Wagon Wheels *⊘⊘ 1934* Recycling reels in vogue in '34, when unused footage from "Fighting Caravans" (1931) with Gary Cooper was used to re-make the very same plot. The result is bio-degradable. Settlers heading to Oregon are ambushed by fur traders, Blue sics Injuns on them back home, with Lewis (out of his depth) as a neurotic ex-doctor, and McGinley stuck in the role of a gay bookseller that reeks of stereotypical mannerisms. Script is desperate for humor, which it never finds, and it's hard to watch Candy's performance knowing this mess was his last role. **54m/B VHS, DVD,** Randolph Scott, Monte Blue, Gail Patrick, Billy Lee; *D:* Charles T. Barton.

The Wagons Roll at Night *⊘⊘ 1941* The circus wagons that is. Remake of 1937's "Kid Galahad" transfers the action from the boxing arena to the circus arena. Nick Coster (Bogart) is the owner of the failing enterprise, romancing fortune teller Flo (Sidney) while trying to protect his innocent sister, Mary (Leslie) from the seedy side of life. This would have been easier if sis hadn't fallen for the new lion tamer, Matt Varney (Albert). Nick tries to break up the lovebirds with predictable results. Based on the novel by Francis Wallace. **84m/B VHS,** Humphrey Bogart, Sylvia Sidney, Eddie Albert, Joan Leslie, Sig Rumann, Cliff Clark, Charles Foy, Frank Wilcox; *D:* Ray Enright; *W:* Barry Trivers, Fred Niblo Jr.; *C:* Sid Hickox; *M:* Heinz Roemheld.

Wagon's Westward *⊘½ 1940* Good government agent Morris assumes identity of bad twin brother, who's in jail, in order to catch some outlaws. **53m/B VHS,** Chester Morris, Buck Jones, Guinn "Big Boy" Williams, Douglas Fowley, George "Gabby" Hayes, Anita Louise, Ona Munson; *D:* Lew Landers.

Wah-Wah *⊘⊘½ 2005 (R)* Grant debuts as writer/director in an autobiographical family story set in Swaziland in the late 1960s on the eve of the African nation's independence from Britain. Young Ralph (Fox) catches his mother Lauren (Richardson) committing adultery. Lauren walks out on the family, and husband/father Harry (Byrne) takes to drink, sending Ralph to boarding school. When the boy returns (now played by Hoult) he discovers his father has suddenly married a brash American. Ruby (Watson). Ruby becomes the teenager's ally, which is a good thing since the ex-pat colony is breaking apart, Harry's drinking makes him violent, and Ralph's mother suddenly decides to return. **97m/C DVD, GB FR** Gabriel Byrne, Miranda Richardson, Emily Watson, Julie Walters, Nicholas Hoult, Celia Imrie, Julian Wadham, Fenella Woolgar, Sid Mitchell, Zachary Fox, Ian Roberts; *D:* Richard E. Grant; *W:* Richard E. Grant; *C:* Pierre Aïm; *M:* Patrick Doyle.

The Wagons East! *⊘⊘ 1994 (PG-13)* Fed up with prairie hardships, pioneers decide to hitch up to a wagon train and head east. Candy (who died during filming) plays the drunken former wagonmaster hired to get them back home, with Lewis... **100m/C VHS, DVD,** Melinda Culea, John Candy, Robert Picardo, William Sanderson, Thomas F. Duffy, Russell Means, Rodney A. Grant, Michael Horse, Gailard Sartain, Lochlyn Munro, Stuart Proud Eagle Grant; *D:* Peter Markle; *W:* Matthew Carlson, Jerry Abrahamson.

Waikiki Wedding *⊘⊘ 1937* Enjoyable musical about a scheming pineapple promoter (Crosby), who meets the woman of his dreams in the contest winner Ross dislikes Hawaii and wants to go home and Crosby must keep her from going...first for business reasons and later, for love. Support cast includes Hawaiian Prince Leilani and a pig. Lots of song and dance and Hawaiian sunsets, along with Burns and Raye, the other couple destined for love on the islands. Keep the story moving, Oscar for "Sweet Leilani: Sweet is the Word for Yo... In a Little Hula Heaven; Blue Hawaii; Okolehao; Nani Ona Pua. **89m/B VHS, DVD.** Bing Crosby, Bob Burns, Martha Raye, Shirley Ross, George Barbier, Leif Erickson, Grady Sutton, Granville Bates, Anthony Quinn; *D:* Frank Tuttle; *W:* Frank Butler, Don Hartman, Walter DeLeon, Francis Martin; *C:* Karl Struss; *M:* Leo Robin, Ralph Rainger; Oscars '37: Song ("Sweet Leilani").

The Wailer *⊘⊘ La Llorona 2006* Low-budget cliched horror story based on a Mexican legend. Six vacationing American cars are offered a mountain cabin by a local. Only the one place is haunted by the ghost of a crying woman who murdered her children to be with her lover. For some reason, the ghost decides to dispense with her visitors. **85m/C DVD,** Vanessa Rice q, John Patrick Jordan, Hugo Medina, Brenda Lynn Mejia, Monique Barajas, Nicole Daniels, Rocael Leiva; *D:* Andres Navia; *W:* Raty Rivera; *C:* Curtis Petersen; *M:* Richard John Baker. **VIDEO**

Waist Deep *⊘⊘ 2006 (R)* Violent urban gangsta pic more or less delivers as expected. Parolee O2 (Gibson) is trying to live the straight and narrow when he gets carjacked with his son sleeping in the back seat. Was it a deliberate snatch and d'd his snarling mad dog rival Meat (The Game) have something to do with it? No matter—O2 is gonna get his little boy back at any cost—with some help from street-smart honey Coco (Good). **97m/C DVD, HD DVD, US** Tyrese Gibson, Meagan Good, Larenz Tate, Kimora Lee Simmons, H. Hunter Hall, The Game; *D:* Vondie Curtis-Hall; *W:* Vondie Curtis-Hall, Darin Scott; *C:* Shane Hurlbut; *M:* Terence Blanchard.

Wait Till Your Mother Gets Home *⊘⊘ 1983* "Mr. Mom"-like zaniness abounds as a football coach cares for the kids and does chores while his wife takes her first job in 15 years. Almost too darn cute, but well written. **97m/C VHS,** Paul Michael Glaser, Dee Wallace Stone, Peggy McCay, David Doyle, Raymond Buktenica, James Gregory, Joey Lawrence, Lynne Moody; *D:* Bill Persky; TV.

Wait until Dark *⊘⊘⊘ 1967* A photographer unwittingly smuggles a drug-filled doll into New York, and his blind wife, alone in their apartment, is terrorized by murderous crooks in search of it. A compelling thriller based on the Broadway hit by Frederick Knott, who also wrote "Dial M for Murder." The individual actors' performances were universally acclaimed in this spinetingler. **105m/C VHS, DVD,** Audrey Hepburn, Alan Arkin, Richard Crenna, Efrem Zimbalist Jr., Jack Weston; *D:* Terence Young; *W:* Robert E. Carrington; *C:* Charles B(ryan) Lang Jr.; *M:* Henry Mancini.

Wait until Spring, Bandini *⊘⊘½ 1990 (PG-13)* A flavorful immigrant tale about a transplanted Italian family weathering the winter in 1925 Colorado, as seen through the eyes of a young son. Alternately funny and moving, with one of Dunaway's scenery-chewing performances as a local temptation to the father. Based on the autobiographical novel by John Fante, co-produced by Francis Ford Coppola. **104m/C VHS,** Joe Mantegna, Faye Dunaway, Burt Young, Ornella Muti, Alex Vincent, Renata Vanni, Michael Bacall, Daniel Wilson; *D:* Dominique Deruddere; *W:* Dominique Deruddere; *M:* Angelo Badalamenti.

Waikiki *⊘⊘ 1980* Two private eyes set out to prove that their friend is not the "cane field murderer" who is terrorizing the Hawaiian island of Oahu. Harmless but pointless TV pilot. **96m/C VHS,** Dack Rambo, Steve Marachuk, Donna Mills, Cal Bellini, Darren McGavin; *D:* Ron Satlof; TV.

The Waiting Game *⊘⊘ 1999* Group of actor wannabes are working in a New York restaurant while waiting for their proverbial big break. They fall in and out of lust and love and suffer audition humiliation and other trials. **88m/C VHS, DVD,** Michael Raynor, Will Arnett, Terumi Matthews, Dan Riordan, Debbon Ayer; *D:* Ken Liotti; *W:* Ken Liotti.

The Waiting Time *⊘⊘½ 1999* Post-Cold War thriller based on the novel by Gerald Seymour. Tracy Barnes (Turner) is a corporal in the British Intelligence Corps who makes a seemingly unprovoked attack on German politician Dieter Krause (Becker). Befriended by solicitor's clerk Joshua Mantle (Thaw), the duo travel to Berlin to make sense of things but Joshua finds himself involved in the decade-old murder of Tracy's German lover and with the dreaded East German secret police. **150m/C VHS, DVD, GB** John Thaw, Zara Turner, Hartmut Becker, Mark Pegg, Struan Rodger, Colin Baker, Christien Anholt; *D:* Stuart Orme; *W:* Patrick Harbinson; *C:* Peter Middleton; *M:* Colin Towns; TV.

Waiting for Guffman *⊘⊘⊘ 1996 (R)* The eccentric citizens of Blaine, Missouri, plan an original musical ("Red, White, and Blaine") to celebrate the town's 150th anniversary, with the aid of former New Yorker and semi-hysteric Corky St. Claire (Guest) as their director. Everyone's very game—and almost completely talentless. The Guffman of the title is the Broadway producer Corky knows, and whom he's invited to see their disaster-in-the-making. A little too deliberately quirky for its own good, but... **84m/C VHS, DVD,** Christopher Guest, Eugene Levy, Fred Willard, Catherine O'Hara, Parker Posey, Lewis Arquette, Matt Keeslar, Paul Dooley, Paul Benedict, Bob Balaban, Larry Miller, Brian Doyle-Murray; *D:* Christopher Guest; *W:* Christopher Guest, Eugene Levy; *C:* Roberto Schaefer; *M:* Michael McKean, Harry Shearer, Christopher Guest.

Waiting for the Light *⊘⊘½ 1990 (PG)* When a woman takes over a small-town diner, she gets the surprise of her life. Seems an angel has made his home there and now the townsfolk are flocking to see him. MacLaine is wonderful and Garr is fetching and likeable. Set during the Cuban missile crisis. Enjoyable, lame comedy. **94m/C VHS, DVD,** Shirley MacLaine, Teri Garr, Vincent Schiavelli, John Bedford Lloyd; *D:* Christopher Monger; *W:* Christopher Monger.

Waiting for the Moon *⊘⊘ 1987 (PG)* Hunt as Alice B. Toklas is a relative treat in this ponderous, frustrating biopic about Toklas and Gertrude Stein, her lover. Made for "American Playhouse" on PBS. **88m/C VHS, DVD,** Linda Hunt, Linda Bassett, Andrew McCarthy, Bruce McGill, Jacques Boudet, Bernadette LaFont; *D:* Jill Godmilow; *W:* Mark Magill; *C:* Andre Neau; Sundance '87: Jury Prize; TV.

Waiting *⊘⊘ woof!* Any laughs that might have been squeezed from this comedy set at Shenanigans—an eatery more mallgeneric than a blend of Bennigan's and Applebee's—have been derailed by the genuinely pathetic lives of the staff and their patrons. Solid cast, led by Reynolds, is given table scraps in the form of predictable food pranks and self-loathing gags. **93m/C DVD, Blu-ray Disc, US** Ryan Reynolds, Anna Faris, Justin Long, David Koechner, Luis Guzman, Chi McBride, Alanna Ubach, Vanessa Lengies, Max Kasch, Dane Cook, Jordan Ladd, Emmanuelle Chriqui, Wendie Malick, John Francis Daley, Kaitlin Doubleday, Robert Patrick Benedict, Andy Milonakis; *D:* Rob McKittrick; *W:* Rob McKittrick; *C:* Matthew Irving; *M:* Adam Gorgoni.

Waiting *⊘⊘ 2000* Actor wannabe/slacker/waiter Sean (Keenan) is told by his dad that he has 30 days to find a job, his life. And dad doesn't mean that Sean should continue to wait tables at a South Philly mob-run Italian eatery and maybe find a nice girl as well. **80m/C VHS, DVD, UMD,** Will Keenan, Hannah Dalton, Kerri Kenney, Harry Philabosian, Lloyd Kaufman, Ron Jeremy; *D:* Patrick Hasson; *W:* Patrick Hasson; *C:* Michael Pearlman.

Waiting to Exhale ♂♂♂ 1995 (R) Adaptation of Terry McMillan's novel about four African-American women hoping to reach the point in their love lives when they can relax and stop waiting for the right man. After the string of dogs and users they choose, you want to tell them not to hold their breath. The women are supposed to be close friends, but all of their stories are broken up into vignettes. This erodes the ensemble feeling of the movie, but performances are strong all around. Retaining the book's feel of just-between-friends girl talk, it may be a little harsh for those who are, shall we say, estrogen-challenged. A lush R&B soundtrack is the perfect backdrop for the ladies' soulful yearning for real love. 120m/C VHS, DVD. Whitney Houston, Angela Bassett, Loretta Devine, Lela Rochon, Gregory Hines, Dennis Haysbert, Mykelti Williamson, Michael Beach, Leon, Wendell Pierce, Donald Adeosun Faison, Jeffrey D. Sams, Lamont Johnson; *Cameos:* Wesley Snipes; *D:* Forest Whitaker; *W:* Ronald Bass; *C:* Toyomichi Kurita; *M:* Kenneth "Babyface" Edmonds. MTV Movie Awards '96: Song ("Sittin' Up in My Room").

Waitress WOOF! *Soup to Nuts* 1981 (R) Three beautiful girls are waitresses in a crazy restaurant where the chef gets drunk, the kitchen explodes, and the customers riot. Awful premise, worse production. 85m/C VHS, DVD. Jim Harris, Carol Drake, Carol Bever; *D:* Lloyd Kaufman; *W:* Charles Kaufman; *C:* Lloyd Kaufman.

Waitress ♂♂♂ 2007 (PG-13) Sweet as, well, pie. Waitress Jenna (the equally appealing Russell) is a pie-baking phenom in her southern community. She's also fixing to leave her abusive jerk husband Earl (Sisto) when she discovers she's pregnant. Jenna looks for support from her diner co-workers while baking up outrageous concoctions ("I Hate My Husband Pie") that reflect her changing moods. She also decides to have a fling with her sweetly flustered OB-GYN (Fillion), and then decides to have a fling with her sweetly flustered OB-GYN (Fillion), and then decides to have a fling, the tale is uneven but cute nonetheless. Writer/director/actress Shelly (who plays Dawn) was murdered in November 2006 just after completing the film. 107m/C DVD. *US* Keri Russell, Nathan Fillion, Cheryl Hines, Lew Temple, Jeremy Sisto, Edward Jemison, Andy Griffith, Darby Stanchfield, Adrienne Shelly; *D:* Adrienne Shelly; *W:* Adrienne Shelly; *C:* Matthew Irving; *M:* Andrew Hollander.

Wake Island ♂♂♂ 1942 After Pearl Harbor, a small group of Marines face the onslaught of the Japanese fleet on a small Pacific Island. Although doomed, they hold their ground for 16 days. Exciting, realistic, and moving. The first film to capitalize on early "last stands" of WWII; also among the most popular war movies. Shown to soldiers in training camps with great morale-raising success. 88m/B VHS, DVD. Robert Preston, Brian Donlevy, William Bendix, MacDonald Carey, Albert Dekker, Walter Abel, Rod Cameron, Barbara Britton, Mikhail Rasumny, Bill Goodwin, Damian O'Flynn, Frank Albertson, Hugh Beaumont, Hillary Brooke, James Brown, Don Castle, Frank Faylen, Mary Field, Phillip Van Zandt, Phillip Terry; *D:* John Farrow; *W:* W.R. Burnett, Frank Butler; *C:* William Mellor, Theodor Sparkuhl; *M:* David Buttolph. N.Y. Film Critics '42: Director (Farrow).

Waking Life ♂♂♂ 2001 (R) Linklater's innovative and visually groundbreaking look at dreams, life, and philosophy doesn't really seem to have a plot. What it does have is several vignettes of people mostly just talking about the subjects above with a group of artists digitally "paint" over the footage, assigning different artists different scenes or actors so as to have a variety of styles. The result is a trippy experiment that might not appeal to many people except philosophy majors, computer geeks, or chemically altered college students. Film buffs looking for something new would do well to check it out. 99m/C VHS, DVD. *US* Richard Linklater, Glover Gill, Julie Delpy, Wiley Wiggins, Ethan Hawke, Adam Goldberg, Nicky Katt, Steven Soderbergh; *D:* Richard Linklater; *W:* Richard Linklater; *C:* Richard Linklater, Tommy Pallotta; *M:* Glover Gill. N.Y. Film Critics '01: Animated Film.

Waking Ned Devine ♂♂♂ 1998 (PG) Old Ned Devine has the winning ticket for the Irish National Lottery—unfortunately, the shock has killed him. Jackie O'Shea (Bannen) and the other 50 still-living residents of Tulaigh Morh conspire to fool a bored lottery official (Dempsey) into thinking that Michael O'Sullivan (Kelly) is Devine, so that they can share the wealth. As each obstacle to the payoff is overcome, a larger hurdle appears, and the comedy becomes more and more screwball until it reaches its darkly comic conclusion. Warm and full of blarney, but never becomes too sappy, or contrived. Filmed on the beautiful Isle of Man and accented with a fine score full of Celtic melodies. Veteran cast carries off even the most improbable gags (including Kelly's buck-naked motorcycle ride). 91m/C VHS, DVD. Ian Bannen, David Kelly, Fionnula Flanagan, Susan Lynch, James Nesbitt, Maura O'Malley, Robert Hickey, Paddy Ward, James Ryland, Fintan McKeown, Matthew Devitt, Eileen Dromey, Dermot Kerrigan, Brendan F. Dempsey; *D:* Kirk Jones; *W:* Kirk Jones; *C:* Henry Braham; *M:* Shaun Davey.

Waking the Dead ♂♂½ 2000 (R) Director Gordon's uneven but earnest adaptation of the Scott Spencer novel features Crudup as Fielding Pierce, an aspiring politician haunted by the death ten years earlier of his activist girlfriend Sarah (Connelly) in a car bombing. As Fielding begins a run at the Senate, he starts to see Sarah in crowds, doubting his sanity. The love story angle gets a lot of play, yet manages to be unconvincing, and the frequent jumps back and forth in time are jarring. Crudup and Connelly seem in over their heads at times. 105m/C VHS, DVD. Billy Crudup, Jennifer Connelly, Molly Parker, Janet McTeer, Paul Hipp, Sandra Oh, Hal Holbrook, Lawrence Dane; *D:* Keith Gordon; *W:* Robert Dillon; *C:* Tom Richmond; *M:* Tomandandy.

eryday people, from its own workers to competing business owners in rural areas to the consumer in general. Gives voice to the views of those opposed to the practices of the company. 98m/C DVD. *US D:* Robert Greenwald; *C:* Kristy Tully; *M:* John (Gianni) Frizzell.

Walk, Don't Run ♂♂½ 1966 Romantic comedy involving a British businessman (Grant) unable to find a hotel room in Tokyo due to the crowds staying for the 1964 summer Olympic Games. He winds up renting a room from an Embassy secretary (Eggar) and then meets and invites Hutton, a member of the U.S. Olympic walking team, also without a place to stay, to share it with him. Grant then proceeds to play matchmaker, despite the fact that Eggar has a fiance. Grant's last film. Innocuous, unnecessary remake of "The More the Merrier." 114m/C VHS, DVD. Cary Grant, Samantha Eggar, Jim Hutton, John Standing, Miiko Taka; *D:* Charles Walters; *M:* Quincy Jones.

Walk Hard: The Dewey Cox Story ♂♂½ 2007 (R) Yet another double entendre smut-fest from screenwriter Apatow (and director/writer Kasdan), who mock every music bio cliche they can twang a guitar at. Reilly goes silly for his title role as a white boy singer (with a family) tragedy that haunts him) who gets that devil rock 'n' roll in his soul and finds it leads to drugs and debauchery, if not the love of a woman (Fischer) too good for him. Much like a novelty record it's clever for a moment but repeated exposure may cause brain damage. 96m/C DVD. *US* John C. Reilly, Jenna Fischer, Raymond J. Barry, Kristen Wiig, Tim Meadows, Harold Ramis, Margo Martindale, Chris Parnell, Matt Besser, David Krumholtz, Frankie Muniz, Jack White, Justin Long, Paul Rudd, Jason Schwartzman; *D:* Jake Kasdan; *W:* Jake Kasdan, Judd Apatow; *C:* Uta Briesewitz; *M:* Michael Andrews.

A Walk in the Clouds ♂♂♂½ 1995 (PG-13) Gorgeously photographed, if sappy, romantic fantasy finds WWII vet Paul Sutton (Reeves), returning to his unhappy marriage and salesman job. So when the good-hearted Paul meets beautiful Victoria (Sanchez-Gijon), the pregnant and unmarried daughter of a possessive Napa vineyard owner (Giannini), he's more than happy to help by posing as her husband. Naturally, dad is livid at their "marriage" and Paul falls in love with his sham bride. Quinn gets to do his part as wise family patriarch and yes, there's even a grape harvest (and some grape stomping) to put everyone in the proper romantic mood. Based on the 1942 Italian film "Four Steps in the Clouds." 103m/C VHS, DVD. Keanu Reeves, Aitana Sanchez-Gijon, Giancarlo Giannini, Anthony Quinn, Angelica Aragon, Evangelina Elizondo, Freddy Rodriguez, Debra Messing; *D:* Alfonso Arau; *W:* Robert Mark Kamen; *C:* Emmanuel Lubezki; *M:* Leo Brouwer. Golden Globes '96: Score.

A Walk in the Spring Rain ♂♂½ 1970 (PG) The bored wife of a college professor follows him to rural Tennessee when he goes on sabbatical, where she meets the married Quinn and the two begin an affair. When Quinn's disturbed son learns of the affair, he attacks the woman, who then tragic results. Fine cast should have had better effect on low-key script. 98m/C VHS. Ingrid Bergman, Anthony Quinn, Fritz Weaver, Katherine Crawford, Tom Fielding, Virginia Gregg; *D:* Guy Green; *W:* Stirling Silliphant; *C:* Charles B(ryant) Lang Jr.; *M:* Elmer Bernstein.

A Walk in the Sun ♂♂♂½ 2005 *Salerno Beachhead* 1946 The trials of a group of American soldiers in WWII from the time they land in Italy to the time they capture their objective, a farmhouse occupied by the Germans. Excellent ensemble acting shows well the variety of civilians who make up any fighting force and explores their fears, motivations, and weaknesses. Producer and director Milestone also made "All Quiet on the Western Front" and the Korean War masterpiece "Pork Chop Hill." Released in the final days of the war, almost concurrently with two other WWII films of the first echelon, "The

Waking Up in Reno ♂½ 2002 (R) Redneck road pic where romance goes awry for two couples on the way to a monster truck show in Nevada. Ringleader is Little Rock car dealer Lonnie Earl (Thornton), who fools around on his wife Darlene (Richardson) with the aptly named Candy (Theron) under the nose of his best friend and Candy's husband Roy (Swayze). Candy, who desperately wants to get pregnant, is always fooling around in the back seat with Roy while Lonnie enters a steak eating contest. Cruz appears as a hooker Roy meets in a sleazy hotel bar. Flimsy setup gives way to the disappointing payoff, and you soon realize its all over but the shouting. 100m/C VHS, DVD. *US* Billy Bob Thornton, Charlize Theron, Patrick Swayze, Natasha Richardson, Holmes Osborne, Chelcie Ross, Brent Briscoe, Wayne Federman, Penelope Cruz, Mark Fauser; *Cameos:* Tony Orlando; *D:* Jordan Brady; *W:* Brent Briscoe, Mark Fauser; *C:* William A. Fraker; *M:* Marty Stuart.

Waking Up Wally ♂♂½ 2005 Innocuously-told true story based on hockey dad Walter Gretzky (McCamus), whose debilitating brain aneurysm made him forget, among other things, his famous son Wayne's (Holden-Reid) sports achievements. The family struggles through rehabilitation as Walter's lack of short-term memory leads to frustration before he (and they) can accept "Walter Gretzky: On Family, Hockey and Healing." *m/C DVD. *CA* Tom McCamus, Kris Holden-Reid, Victoria Snow, Tara Spencer-Nairn, Carey Feehan; *D:* Dean Bennett; *W:* Carol Hay; *C:* Roger Vernon; *M:* Christopher Dedrick. TV

Wal-Mart: The High Cost of Low Price ♂♂♂½ 2005 Greenwald's latest documentary investigates the economic impact of the retail giant on ev-

Story of G.I. Joe," and "They Were Expendable." 117m/B VHS, DVD. Dana Andrews, Richard Conte, John Ireland, Lloyd Bridges, Sterling Holloway, George Tyne, Norman Lloyd, Herbert Rudley, Richard Benedict, Huntz Hall, James B. Cardwell, George Offerman Jr., Steve Brodie, Matt Willis, Alvin Hammer, Victor Cutler, Jay Norris; *D:* Lewis Milestone; *W:* Robert Rossen, Harry Brown; *C:* Russell Harlan; *M:* Freddie Rich, Earl Robinson.

Walk into Hell ♂♂ 1957 A mining engineer and his assistant searching for oil meet the primitive natives of New Guinea. Tedious at times and dated, but pleasant enough. 91m/C VHS. *AU* Chips Rafferty, Francoise Christophe, Reg Lye; *D:* Lee Robinson.

Walk Like a Man ♂♂½ 1987 (PG) In a take-off of Tarzan movies, Mandel plays a man raised by wolves. Comic problems arise when he is found by his mother and the family attempts to civilize him. Juvenile script wastes fine cast. 86m/ C VHS, DVD. Howie Mandel, Christopher Lloyd, Cloris Leachman, Colleen Camp, Amy Steel, George DiCenzo; *D:* Melvin Frank.

A Walk on the Moon ♂♂♂ 1999 (R) Goldwyn's promising directorial debut has 30-ish, vaguely restless Jewish housewife Pearl (Lane) vacationing in the Catskills in the summer of 1969 with her family: teenage daughter Alison (Paquin), son Daniel (Boriello), and intrusive mother-in-law Lillian (Feldshuh). Hubby Marty (Schreiber) is working in the city and visits on the weekends. When sensitive hippie blouse peddler Walker (Mortensen) catches her eye, she decides it's time to catch up on the '60s and her lost teenage years. When she takes off for Woodstock and happens upon her daughter, the family drama is intensified. Pearl's turmoil and motivations are handled well by Lane and the screenwriter Gray, and neither of the men vying for her are cardboard stereotypes, but the abruptly feel-good ending may not work for some. 107m/C VHS, DVD. Diane Lane, Liev Schreiber, Viggo Mortensen, Anna Paquin, Tovah Feldshuh, Bobby Boriello, Lisa Bronwyn Moore; *D:* Tony Goldwyn; *W:* Pamela Gray; *C:* Anthony B. Richmond; *M:* Mason Daring.

Walk on the Wild Side ♂♂ 1962 In 1930s New Orleans, a man searches for his long-lost love, finds her working in a whorehouse and fights to save her from the lesbian madame Stanwyck. Melodrama, based only loosely on the Nelson Algren novel and adapted by cult novelist John Fante, with Edmund Morris. Much-troubled on the set, and it shows. 114m/B VHS, DVD. Jane Fonda, Laurence Harvey, Barbara Stanwyck, Capucine, Anne Baxter; *D:* Edward Dmytryk; *W:* Edmund Morris, John Fante, Ben Hecht; *C:* Joe MacDonald; *M:* Elmer Bernstein.

Walk Softly, Stranger ♂♂ 1950 Two-bit crook is reformed by the love of an innocent peasant girl. If you can stand the cliche masquerading as a plot, the performances are good. 81m/B VHS. Alida Valli, Joseph Cotten, Spring Byington, Paul Stewart, Jack Paar, Jeff Donnell, John McIntire; *D:* Robert Stevenson.

Walk the Line ♂♂♂½ 2005 (PG-13) Phoenix embodies The Man in Black, warts and all in this excellent biopic showing Johnny Cash's family strife, rise as an early 50s rock star, through his battle with drugs, and his long courtship of June Carter (an equally brilliant Witherspoon). Script and actors never shy away from the more disturbing aspects of Cash's personality and life, which makes film a powerful, if not always comfortable, film. Phoenix and Witherspoon did all their own singing, and they do it well enough to make you wonder if it's the real thing. 135m/C DVD. *US* Joaquin Rafael (Leaf) Phoenix, Reese Witherspoon, Ginnifer Goodwin, Robert Patrick, Dallas Roberts, Larry Bagby, Dan John Miller, Shelby Lynne, Tyler Hilton, Waylon Malloy Payne, Shooter Jennings; *D:* James Mangold; *W:* James Mangold, Gill Dennis; *C:* Phedon Papamichael; *M:* T-Bone Burnett. Oscars '05: Actress (Witherspoon); British Acad. '05: Actor—Mus./Comedy (Phoenix); Golden Globes '06: Actor—Mus./Comedy (Phoenix), Actress—Mus./Comedy (Witherspoon); Film—Mus./Comedy; N.Y. Film Critics '05: Actress (Witherspoon); Natl. Soc. Film Critics

'05. Actress (Witherspoon); Screen Actors Guild '05. Actress (Witherspoon).

Walk the Proud Land 🎬🎬½
1956 Story of Indian agent John Clum (Murphy), who fights for the rights of Apache in 1870s Arizona and who convinces their leader Geronimo (Silverheels) to surrender to the authorities. Adapted from the biography "Apache Agent" by Woodworth Clum. **88m/C VHS.** Audie Murphy, Jay Silverheels, Anne Bancroft, Patricia Crowley, Charles Drake; **D:** Jesse Hibbs; **W:** Jack Sher, Gil Doud; **C:** Harold Lipstein.

A Walk to Remember 🎬🎬
2002 (PG) 101m/C VHS, DVD, US Mandy Moore, Nicole Holofcener; **C:** Michael Spiller; **M:** Billy Bragg.

Walkabout 🎬🎬🎬½ **1971 (PG)**
Beautifully told and filmed story (by Roeg in his debut) about a nameless young brother (John, Roeg's six-year-old son) and sister (Agutter), who are abandoned in the Australian outback when their father kills himself. The children wander, with little chance of survival, until a young aborigine (Gumpilil) finds them. He interrupts his own "walkabout," a rite of passage, to teach them to survive, leading to betrayal and tragedy. Based on a novel by James Vance Marshall. A bitter, revisionist farce never for a moment attempting to be accurate. Matlin's unfortunate, though fortunately brief, follow-up to her Oscar-winning performance. **95m/C VHS.** Jenny Agutter, Lucien John, David Gumpilil, John Meillon; **D:** Nicolas Roeg; **W:** Edward Bond; **C:** Nicolas Roeg; **M:** John Barry.

The Walker 🎬🎬 **1987 (R)**
tongue-in-cheek historical pastiche about the real-life American William Walker (played previously in "Burn!" by Marlon Brando), and how he led a revolution in Nicaragua in 1855 and became its self-declared president. A bitter, revisionist farce never for a moment attempting to be accurate. Matlin's unfortunate, though fortunately brief, follow-up to her Oscar-winning performance. **95m/C VHS.** Ed Harris, Richard Masur, Peter Boyle, Rene Auberjonois, Marlee Matlin, Miguel Sandoval; **D:** Alex Cox; **W:** Rudy Wurlitzer; **M:** Joe Strummer.

The Walker 🎬🎬 **2007 (R)** Slapdash, tongue-in-cheek political comedy. Carter (Harrelson), an extravagantly gay DC insider who spends most of his time escorting rich married women to public events, ends up in the middle of the investigation of the murder of a powerful Beltway lobbyist who was having an affair with Carter's married friend Lynn (Scott Thomas). In order to protect her and clear his own name, Carter tries to find the real killer himself while his carefully cultivated status in DC society collapses. Harrelson's performance stands out, but otherwise this is a run-of-the-mill crime drama that flirts awkwardly with political commentary. **107m/C DVD.** GB US Woody Harrelson, Kristin Scott Thomas, Lauren Bacall, Lily Tomlin, Moritz Bleibtreu, Ned Beatty, Willem Dafoe, Geff Francis, Steven Hartley, Mary Beth Hurt; **D:** Paul Schrader; **W:** Paul Schrader; **C:** Chris Seager; **M:** Anne Dudley.

Walker: Texas Ranger: One Riot, One Ranger 🎬🎬 **1993**
(PG-13) Norris sticks with this TV action-adventure mode with this TV pilot movie goes by Chris Vaughn (The Rock) who's single and lives in Washington. Luckily, he's still carrying the big stick and taking care of business (although, oddly enough, director Bray contemplated swapping it out for an aluminum bat—c'mon, is nothing sacred?) And he does just that with the Rock, whose presence is commanding yet surprisingly subtle (something he could not have learned from the wrestling days) allowing him to rise above the mediocre script and sub-par character development. Johnny Knoxville effectively serves as the comic-relief/sidekick guy while Neal McDonough sleepwalks through what could have been a fun villain role. **86m/C VHS, DVD, US** Dwayne "The Rock" Johnson, Johnny Knoxville, Neal McDonough, Kristen Wilson, Khleo Thomas, John Beasley, Barbara Tarbuck, Michael Bowen, Ashley Scott; **D:** Kevin Bray; **W:** David Klass, Channing Gibson, David Levien, Brian Koppelman; **D:** Glen MacPherson; **M:** Graeme Revell.

Walking Tall: Lone Justice 🎬
2007 (R) Low-grade actioner that has nothing to do with the original franchise. Sheriff Nick Prescott (Sorbo) has retired but it doesn't last long when he's caught up in a federal case against a drug lord and his

Walking Back 🎬🎬 **1926** Troubled teens go for joyride and bash mirthmobile to smithereens. The body shop agrees to give them a different car, but they find plant belonging to the father of one of a heist at a different car, but they find plant belonging to the father of one of a heist at a boys. **53m/B VHS.** Sue Carol, Richard Walling, Ivan Lebedeff, Robert Edeson, Florence Turner, Arthur (L.) Rankin; **D:** Rupert Julian.

The Walking Dead 🎬🎬 **1994 (R)**
Depicts the Vietnam War from the perspectives of four black and one white Marine assigned to rescue POWs from a North Vietnam camp in 1972. Fairly routine story with stock characters (by-the-book sergeant, family man, naive youngster, cynical hustler) and flashbacks to depict their back home struggles. Cast tries but is defeated by a one-dimensional script. **89m/C VHS.** Joe Morton, Eddie Griffin, Allen Payne, Vonte Sweet, Roger Floyd; **D:** Preston A. Whitmore II; **W:** Preston A. Whitmore II; **C:** John L. (Nidaga) Demps Jr; **M:** Gary Chang.

Walking on Air 🎬🎬 **1987** Ray Bradbury's story comes to life as a handicapped boy dreams of completing a real space walk. Originally aired on PBS as part of the "Wonderworks" series. **60m/C VHS.** Lynn Redgrave, Jordan Marder, James Treuer, Katheryn Trainor; **D:** Ed Kaplan.

Walking on Water 🎬🎬 **2002**
Gavin (Bonney) has been suffering from leukemia for a long time and has asked his friends and housemates—Charlie (Cotosimo), Anna (Theodorakis), and Frank (Bishop)—to help him die with dignity at home. In the end, the time with dignity at quietly assist Gavin's suicide, which leaves him haunted by grief and guilt. He's not the only one unable to cope as Gavin's friends and family all struggle in their separate ways. **90m/C VHS, DVD, AU** Vince Colosimo, Maria Theodorakis, Nicholas Bishop, Nathaniel Dean, Judi Farr, David Bonney, Anne Lise Phillips, Daniel Roberts; **D:** Tony Ayres; **W:** Roger Monk; **C:** Robert Humphreys. Australian Film. Inst. '02: Actor (Dean), Actress (Theodorakis). Screenplay, Support. Actress (Farr).

Walking Tall 🎬🎬½ **1973 (R)** A Tennessee sheriff takes a stand against syndicate-run gambling and his wife is murdered in response. Ultra-violent crime saga wowed the movie going public and spawned several sequels and a TV series. Based on the true story of folk-hero Buford Pusser, admirably rendered by Baker. **125m/C VHS, DVD.** Joe Don Baker, Elizabeth Hartman, Noah Beery Jr., Gene Evans, Rosemary Murphy, Felton Perry; **D:** Phil Karlson; **W:** Mort Briskin; **C:** Jack Marta; **M:** Walter Scharf.

Walking Tall 🎬🎬½ **2004 (PG-13)**
Changes abound in this ho hum retelling of the 1973 version as the good guy now goes by Chris Vaughn (The Rock) who's single and lives in Washington. Luckily, he's still carrying the big stick and taking care of business (although, oddly enough, director Bray contemplated swapping it out for an aluminum bat—c'mon, is nothing sacred?) And he does just that with the Rock, whose presence is commanding yet surprisingly subtle (something he could not have learned from the wrestling days) allowing him to rise above the mediocre script and sub-par character development. Johnny Knoxville effectively serves as the comic-relief/sidekick guy while Neal McDonough sleepwalks through what could have been a fun villain role. **86m/C VHS, DVD, US** Dwayne "The Rock" Johnson, Johnny Knoxville, Neal McDonough, Kristen Wilson, Khleo Thomas, John Beasley, Barbara Tarbuck, Michael Bowen, Ashley Scott; **D:** Kevin Bray; **W:** David Klass, Channing Gibson, David Levien, Brian Koppelman; **D:** Glen MacPherson; **M:** Graeme Revell.

The Wall 🎬🎬🎬 **1999** Three stories that focus on the Vietnam Veterans Memorial and some of the objects left there. "The Pencil Holder" finds young Ben Holst (Biumas) living with his stiff-necked Army colonel father (Olmos) in Saigon in 1969 where he's mistaken by a dying soldier (Chevolleau) for his own son. "The Badge" that black soldier Bracey Mitchell (Glover) clings to as he hides from the Viet Cong and dreams of home. "The Player" is conniving wheeler-dealer Bishop (Whaley), who runs a base nightclub and gets his comeuppance from self-sacrificing schoolteacher Luis (DeLorenzo), who's a guitar-playing whiz. **94m/C VHS, DVD.** Edward James Olmos, Richard Chevolleau, Trevor Biumas, Dean McDermott, Savion Glover, Ruby Dee, Martin Roach, Linette Robinson, Frank Whaley, Michael Delorenzo, Ron White, Matthew Ferguson; **D:** Joseph Sargent; **W:** Scott Abbott, Charles Fuller, Patrick Sheane Duncan; **C:** Donald M. Morgan; **M:** Larry Brown. CABLE.

Wall 🎬🎬½ **Mar 2004** Documentary from veteran filmmaker Simone Bitton. This time she takes on the security fence being erected to divide Israel from the West Bank. Use of the term "wall" gives a hint of the filmmaker's opinion of the security fence. Israeli officials resist the use of any term apart from "fence." The strength

Walking Through the Fire 🎬🎬 **1983 (R)**
A widow hires a taxi driver to help her seek vengeance against the men who killed her husband and her son. Pusser does what he can with the lousy story and to come: a TV flick and series. **112m/C VHS, DVD.** Bo Svenson, Forrest Tucker, Leif Garret, Morgan Woodward; **D:** Jack Starrett; **C:** Robert E. Hauser.

Walking Thunder 🎬🎬½ **1994**
(PG) The McKay family are stranded in the real-life struggle with Hodgkin's disease. Rocky Mountains in 1850 when their wagon is destroyed by a grizzly bear. But they're rescued by a mountain man (Read) and a Sioux medicine man (Thin Elk), who introduce young Jacob to a number of adventures. It's wholesome, old-fashioned kid entertainment. **95m/C VHS, DVD.** John Denver, James Read, David Tom, Chief Ted Thin Elk; **D:** Craig Clyde; **W:** Craig Clyde; **M:** John Scott; **Narr:** Brian Keith.

Walking the Edge 🎬🎬 **1983 (R)**
A young woman's real-life struggle with Hodgkin's disease. Her fight for her own and her unborn baby's survival is a stirring testament to the power of faith. Absorbing drama. **143m/C VHS, DVD.** Bess Armstrong, Tom Mason, Bonnie Bedelia, Richard Masur, Swoosie Kurtz, J.D. Cannon, Jane Lockhart; **D:** Robert Day; TV.

Walking Tall: The Final Chapter 🎬🎬 **1977 (PG)** The final months in the life of Tennessee sheriff Buford Pusser, this time played less memorably by Svenson, attempts to find the man who killed his wife. Even more violent than the original. **109m/C VHS, DVD.** Bo Svenson, Noah Beery Jr, Angel Tompkins, Richard Jaeckel; **D:** Earl Bellamy.

Walking Tall: Part 2 🎬🎬 **1975**
(PG) Club-wielding Tennessee sheriff Buford Pusser, this time played less memorably by Svenson, attempts to find the man who killed his wife. Even more violent than the original. **109m/C VHS, DVD.** Bo Svenson, Noah Beery Jr, Angel Tompkins, Richard Jaeckel; **D:** Earl Bellamy.

gang who are determined to wipe out all witnesses. **94m/C DVD.** Kevin Sorbo, Haley Ramm, Laurent Martin, Rodrigo De La Rosa, Jennifer Sipes; **D:** Tripp Reed; **W:** Joc Halpin, Ben Strassmann; **C:** Jas Shelton; **M:** Eric Wurst, David Wurst. VIDEO

Schreiber, Todd Field, Kevin Corrigan, Randall Batinkoff, Joseph Siravo, Vincent Pastore, Lynn Cohen, Andrew Holofcener, Daryl Hannah, Lauren Nicole Holofcener; **C:** Michael Spiller; **M:** Billy Bragg.

Walking the Edge continued...

Wall Street 🎬🎬🎬 **1987 (R)** Stone's energetic, high-minded big business treatise in which naive, neophyte stockbroker Bud Fox (Charlie Sheen) is seduced into insider trading by sleek entrepreneur Gordon Gekko (Douglas), much to his blue-collar father's (Martin Sheen) chagrin. A fast-moving drama of '80s-style material-ism with a mesmerizing, award-winning performance by Douglas as greed personified. Expert direction by Stone, who co-wrote the not-very-subtle script. His father, to whom this film is dedicated, was a broker. Look for Stone in a cameo. **126m/C VHS, DVD, Blu-ray Disc.** Paul Guilfoyle, Michael Douglas, Charlie Sheen, Martin Sheen, Daryl Hannah, Sean Young, James Spader, Hal Holbrook, Terence Stamp, Richard Dysart, John C. McGinley, Saul Rubinek, James Karen, Josh Mostel, Millie Perkins, Cecilia Peck, Grant Shaud, Franklin Cover, Oliver Stone; **D:** Oliver Stone; **W:** Stanley Weiser, Oliver Stone; **C:** Robert Richardson; **M:** Stewart Copeland. Oscars '87: Actor (Douglas); Golden Globes '88: Actor—Drama (Douglas); Natl. Bd. of Review '87: Actor (Douglas); Golden Raspberries '87: Worst Support. Actress (Hannah).

Wall Street Cowboy 🎬 **1939**
When his land is threatened, a cowboy fights big business in the big city. **54m/B VHS.** George "Gabby" Hayes, Raymond Hatton, Pierre Watkin, Ann Baldwin, Roy Rogers; **D:** Joseph Kane; **W:** Gerald Geraghty, Norman S. Hall; **C:** Jack Marta.

Wallaby Jim of the Islands 🎬🎬 **1937** The singing captain of a pearl fishing boat must protect his treasure from marauding pirates. Pleasant enough musical adventure. **61m/B VHS.** George Houston, Douglas Walton; **D:** Charles Lamont.

Wallace & Gromit: The Curse of the Were-Rabbit 🎬🎬🎬½
2005 (G) Will appeal to adult audiences more than as a stop-action animation film would at first seem to warrant. But don't worry, there's still plenty for the kiddies. The dynamic duo is faced with the responsibility of guarding the gardens for miles around in preparation for the annual Giant Vegetable Fete. But rabbits are eating all of the vegetables! Enter Wallace's newly invented Bunny Vacuum. That the characters manage to be expressive, and hilarious, is sheer brilliance. **85m/C DVD.** GB D: Nick Park, Steve Box; **C:** Tristan Oliver, Dave Alex-Riddett; **M:** Julian Nott, Hans Zimmer; **V:** Peter Sallis, Ralph Fiennes, Helena Bonham-Carter, Nicholas C. Smith, Liz Smith, Peter Kay. Oscars '05: Animated Film; L.A. Film Critics '05; Animated Film; Broadcast Film Critics '05; Animated Film.

The Walloping Kid 🎬🎬 **1926** A B-western with photography done in Monument Valley. Silent with original organ music. **67m/B VHS.** Kit Carson, Pauline Curley;

Walls of Glass 🎬🎬½ **1985 (R)** An aging New York cabby tries to make it as an actor. Effective performances by all override the thin plot. Slow and uneven, but involving. **85m/C VHS, DVD.** Flanagan

of this documentary is in its balanced view. While showing the wall from many locations it is never clear what side of the wall is being viewed. Ultimately the wall reveals itself as a divider of people and land that neither Israelis nor Palestinians emb ace. **99m/C DVD, D:** Simone Bitton; **C:** Jacques Bouquin.

WALL-E 🎬🎬🎬🎬 **2008** Pixar animated adventure about a lonely robot named WALL-E (Waste Allocation Load Lifter Earth-Class) who has been cleaning up the planet for 700 years (it's 2805) after it was abandoned by those destructive, messy humans. Mankind has evacuated to space-ships that orbit the planet and sleek droid EVE comes to see if it's okay for humans to return. When she leaves, a smitten WALL-E chases after, which results in all sorts of space fun. Not yet reviewed. **?m/C D:** Andrew Stanton; **W:** Andrew Stanton; **V:** Fred Willard, Jeff Garlin, Ben Burtt, Sigourney Weaver, Kathy Najimy, John Ratzenberger.

Geraldine Page, Philip Bosco, William Hickey, Olympia Dukakis, Brian Bloom, Linda Thorson; **D:** Scott Goldstein.

The Walls of Hell 🦴🦴 *Intramuros* 1964 Lt. Jim Sorenson (Mahoney) leads guerilla fighters into the city of Manila, aided by freedom fighter Nardo (Poe), to defeat desperate Japanese troops hold up in the city. 88m/B VHS, DVD. **PH** Jock Mahoney, Fernando Poe Jr., Mike Parsons; **D:** Gerardo (Gerry) De Leon, Eddie Romero; **W:** Eddie Romero, Cesar Amigo, Ferde Grofe Jr.; **C:** Felipe Sacdalan; **M:** Tito Arevalo.

The Walls of Malapaga 🦴🦴 *Au-Dela des Grilles; Le Mura di Malapaga* 1949 Frenchman Gabin, who's killed his mistress, stows away aboard a ship to Italy. He arrives in Genoa only to have all his money and papers stolen. An meets Miranda, a lonely waitress with a young daughter, and the two fall in love. But it's only temporary as the authorities come closing in. French with subtitles. 91m/C VHS. *FR IT:* Jean Gabin, Isa Miranda, Vera Talchi, Andrea Checchi, Robert Dalban; **D:** Rene Clement; **W:** Jean Aurenche, Pierre Bost; **M:** Roman Vlad. Oscars '50: Foreign Film.

Walpurgis Night 🦴🦴 *Valborgsmassoafton* 1941 Soapy Swedish drama about abortion was racy for its time. Office gal Bergman secretly loves her boss (Hanson). His wife refuses to have children and goes through an abortion. An unscrupulous fellow blackmails her with this knowledge. Stay tuned... Interesting document on the mores of another time. In Swedish with English subtitles. 82m/B VHS. *SW* Lars Hanson, Karin Carlsson, Victor Sjostrom, Ingrid Bergman, Erik "Bullen" Berglund, Sture Lagerwall, Georg Rydeberg, Georg Blickingberg; **D:** Gustaf Edgren.

Walter and Henry 🦴🦴 2001 Walter (Larroquette) and his 12-year-old son Henry (Braun) live in a trailer in Brooklyn and (barely) make ends meet as street musicians in the city. However, after Walter has a psychotic breakdown and is institutionalized, Henry is forced to live with his rigid grandfather (Coburn) from whom Walter has been estranged for years. And slowly, his new life. 90m/C VHS, DVD. John Larroquette, James Coburn, Kate Nelligan, Nicholas Braun; **D:** Daniel Petrie; **W:** Geoffrey Sharp; **C:** Michael Storey; **M:** Christopher Dedrick. CABLE

The Waltons: The Christmas Carol 🦴🦴 1980 The winter solstice brings no special joy to Walton's mountain; WWII has taken many men, with short wave reports indicating the Nazi terror spreading across Europe. But huddled in the glow of Walton's barn, the children rediscover the true meaning of Christmas. 94m/C VHS, DVD. Judy Norton-Taylor, Jon Walmsley, Mary (Elizabeth) McDonough, Eric Scott, Kami Cotler, Joe Conley, Ronnie Clare, Leslie Winston, Peggy Rea; **D:** Lawrence (Larry) Dobkin. TV

Waltz across Texas 🦴🦴½ 1983 Young oil man Jastrow and good-lookin' rock scientist Archer at first don't take to each other, but there's something in the air, and romance blossoms. Jastrow and Archer cowrote and coproduced, and cohabitated as spouses in real-life. 100m/C VHS, DVD. Terry Jastrow, Anne Archer, Mary Kay Place, Richard Farnsworth; **D:** Ernest Day; **C:** Robert Elswit.

Waltz King 🦴🦴 1963 Typically hokey Disney biography of the young composer Johann Strauss during his Old Viennese heyday. Fine music, pretty German locations. Well-made family fare. 94m/C VHS. Kerwin Mathews, Senta Berger, Brian Aherne; **D:** Steve Previn.

Waltz of the Toreadors 🦴🦴🦴 *The Amorous General* 1962 Retired general Sellers doesn't care to re-kindle a 17-year-old romance with a French woman. It doesn't work out (seems his illegitimate son also has a soft spot for the lady), but the general decides to keep his eyes open for other possibilities. Interestingly cast adaptation of Jean Anouilh's play. Sellers is hilarious, as usual. 105m/C VHS, DVD. *GB* Peter Sellers, Dany Robin, Margaret Leighton, Cyril Cusack; **D:** John Guillermin; **W:** Wolf Mankowitz; **M:** Richard Addinsell.

A Waltz Through the Hills 🦴🦴 1988 Two orphans head into the Australian outback and experience many adventures en route to the coast where they can set sail for England and their grandparents. Aired on PBS as part of the "Wonderworks" series. 116m/C VHS, DVD. Tina Kemp, Andre Jansen, Ernie Dingo, Dan O'Herlihy; **D:** Frank Arnold.

Wanda Nevada 🦴🦴 1979 (PG) Gambler Fonda wins nubile young Shields in a poker game, then plays her with him to the Grand Canyon to look for gold. Director/star Fonda sure picked a lemon for his only screen appearance with dad Henry (a grizzled old varmint appearing briefly). Shields is in her usual form—stellar for a shampoo commercial. 105m/C VHS. Peter Fonda, Brooke Shields, Henry Fonda, Fiona Lewis, Luke Askew, Ted Markland, Severn Darden, Paul Fix; **D:** Peter Fonda.

Wanda, the Sadistic Hypnotist 🦴 1967 A comely vixen hypnotizes an innocent pedestrian, ties him up and whips him to indulge her whims. Despite the "victim's" protests, she unleashes a gang of sexually playful women on him, and he is subjected to a multitude of "tortures." 70m/C VHS, DVD. Katharine Shubeck, Janice Sweet, Dick Dangerfield, Daryl Cobinot; **D:** Gregory Corarito.

The Wanderer 🦴🦴 *Le Grand Meaulnes* 1967 Two friends fall in love—Frantz with Valentine and his friend Augustin with Frantz's sister, Yvonne. When the two women disappear on Frantz's wedding day, the two men begin a search to find both the women and the reasons for their disappearance. In French with English subtitles. 108m/C VHS. *FR* Brigitte Fossey, Jean Blaise, Alain Noury, Juliette Villard; **D:** Jean-Gabriel Albicocco.

Wanderers 🦴🦴🦴½ 1979 (R) Richard Price's acclaimed novel about youth gangs coming of age in the Bronx in 1963. The "Wanderers," named after the Dion song, are a gang of Italian-American teenagers about to graduate high school, who prowl the Bronx with the feeling that something is slipping away from them. Fascinating, funny and touching. Manz is unforgettable as a scrappy gal. A wonderful 60s soundtrack (Dion, the Four Seasons) colors this "coming of age the hard way" film. 113m/C VHS, DVD. Ken Wahl, John Friedrich, Karen Allen, Linda Manz, Richard Price, Toni Kalem, Tony Ganios, Alan Rosenberg, Jim Youngs, Val Avery, Dolph Sweet, Olympia Dukakis; **D:** Philip Kaufman; **W:** Philip Kaufman, Rose Kaufman; **C:** Michael Chapman.

Wandering Jew 🦴🦴½ 1920 An excellent print of this rare Austrian film version of the classic legend, one of at least three silent versions. A Jew is condemned to wander the earth for eternity. 65m/B VHS. *AT* Ernst Bath, Else Osterheim, Josef Schreiber, Rudolf Schildkraut, Joseph Schildkraut; **D:** Otto Kreisler; **W:** Heinrich Glucksmann.

Wannabes 🦴🦴 2001 Angelo (DeMeo) and his younger brother Paulie (Dubin) are waiters in a New York neighborhood joint where the local mob boss is Santo (Vitrelli). Tired of being abused, particularly by Santo's spoiled son Vinny (D'Onofrio), Angelo, Paulie and a couple of their buds become successful bookies and go into loansharking and other criminal activities. Santo likes Angelo's gumption and makes him his protege, much to Vinny's anger. Familiar stereotypes abound. 110m/C VHS, DVD. Joe (Johnny) Viterelli, Joseph (Joe) D'Onofrio, William DeMeo, Conor Dubin, Raymond Serra; **D:** William DeMeo, Charles A. Addessi; **W:** William DeMeo.

The Wannsee Conference 🦴🦴🦴½ *Wannseekonferenz* 1984 A startling, important film depicting, in real time, the conference held at the Wannsee on January 20, 1942, during which 14 members of the Nazi hierarchy decided in 85 minutes the means and logistics of effecting the Final Solution. Recreated from the original secretary's notes. Horrifying and chilling. Along with "Shoah," a must-see for understanding the Holocaust and the psychology of genocide. In German with English subtitles. 87m/C VHS, DVD. *GE* Dietrich Mattausch, Gerd Brockmann, Friedrich Beckhaus, Robert Atzorn, Jochen Busse, Hans-Werner Bussinger, Harald Dietl, Peter Fitz, Reinhard Glemnitz, Dieter Groest, Martin Luttge, Anita Mally, Gerd Riegauer; **D:** Heinz Schirk; **W:** Paul Mommertz; **C:** Horst Schier.

Wanted 🦴🦴½ 1998 (R) Jimmy Scrico (Sutton) has accidentally shot a mob boss. Naturally, this means he's on the run from the vengeful wiseguys and he finds sanctuary in a Catholic school where Jimmy's befriended by Father Donnelly (Busfield). Then the bad guys catch up with him. 90m/C VHS, DVD. Michael Sutton, Timothy Busfield, Robert Culp, Tracey Gold, James Quattrochi; **D:** Terence M. O'Keefe; **W:** Terence M. O'Keefe, Mark Evan Schwartz; **C:** Richard A. Jones.

Wanted 2008 Wes (McAvoy) is a midtwenties corporate worker drone who learns that the father he never knew was an assassin who belonged to a very secret society called the Fraternity, which is headed by Sloan (Freeman). Sexy, dangerous Fox (Jolie), part "Lara Croft", part "Mr. & Mrs. Smith")'s sent to recruit Wes to join the organization and learn how to unlock his dormant killing instincts. But the more Wes learns about the Fraternity, the more he suspects that being "the weapons of fate" may not be what he thinks. Russian Belmambetov is the directed the "Night Watch" series. Not yet reviewed. ?m/C James McAvoy, Angelina Jolie, Morgan Freeman, Terence Stamp, David O'Hara, Kristi Hager; **D:** Timur Bekmambetov; **W:** Michael Brandt, Derek Haas, Chris Morgan; **C:** Mitchell Amundsen; **M:** Danny Elfman.

Wanted: Babysitter WOOF! 1975 A young student accidentally becomes involved by her roommate in a plot to kidnap the child she is babysitting. Schneider is truly awful; Italian comic Pazzetto is at sea in a bad role as her boyfriend. Also released as "The Babysitter." 90m/C VHS. Robert Vaughn, Vic Morrow, Maria Schneider, Renato Pozzetto, Nadja Tiller, Carl Mohner, Sydne Rome; **D:** Rene Clement.

Wanted Dead or Alive 🦴🦴½ 1986 (R) Ex-CIA agent Hauer is now a high-tech bounty hunter assigned to bring in an international terrorist. When the terrorist kills Hauer's friend and girlfriend, he forgets the $50,000 bonus for bringing him in alive. Official "sequel" to the Steve McQueen TV series with Hauer as the McQueen character's great-grandson. The link is meaningless, and the plot is a thin excuse for much violence and anti-terrorist flag-waving. 104m/C VHS, DVD. Rutger Hauer, Gene Simmons, Robert Guillaume, William Russ, Jerry Hardin, Mel Harris; **D:** Gary Sherman; **W:** Brian Taggert; **C:** Alex Nepomniaschy; **M:** Joe Renzetti.

Wanted: The Perfect Guy 🦴🦴½ 1986 Danny and Melanie try to find Mister Right for their divorced Mom (Kahn). An Emmy Award winner about single parents and their children. 45m/C VHS. Ben Affleck, Pam Potillo, Keith Szarabajka, Madeline Kahn, Melanie Mayron; **D:** Caitlin Adams; **W:** Mary P. Willis; **C:** Tom Hurwitz; **M:** Jonathan Sheffer.

The War 🦴🦴½ 1994 (PG-13) Post-Vietnam war drama, set in 1970 Mississippi, centers on a children's battle over a treehouse but becomes a sermon on love, death, family values, pacifism, and the physical and spiritual wounds of war. After helping son Stu (Wood) and daughter Lidia (Randall) build their treehouse, troubled Vietnam vet Stephen Simmons (Costner) tries to coax Stu to make peace with the bullies trying to take it over. However cliched, director Avnet allows a talented cast of kids to thoughtfully express a child's view of the world but gosh-darn-it the preachy tone can get down-right annoying. 126m/C VHS, DVD, HD DVD. Elijah Wood, Kevin Costner, Lexi (Faith) Randall, Mare Winningham, Christine Baranski, Bruce A. Young, Gary Basaraba, Raynor Scheine, Nick Searcy, Lucas Black; **D:** Jon Avnet; **W:** Kathy McWorter; **C:** Geoffrey Simpson; **M:** Thomas Newman.

War 🦴🦴½ 2007 (R) Yet another of Jet Li's urban action/martial arts flicks, this time featuring British action import Statham. Rogue (Li) is an assassin manipulating two crime families into a bloody gang war. Crawford (Statham) is the FBI agent chasing him. Did Rogue kill Crawford's partner? Why is Rogue starting a gang war? Does it matter? The movie is mostly about explosions and gunfire, at the expense of the charisma and action skills of Statham and Li. What plot exists owes much to "Yojimbo" and "A Fistful of Dollars," minus the depth and the appeal of either. 103m/C DVD, Blu-ray Disc. *US* Jet Li, Jason Statham, John Lone, Devon Aoki, Luis Guzman, Saul Rubinek, Ryo Ishibashi, Sung Kang, Matthew St. Patrick, Nadine Velazquez; **D:** Philip G. Atwell; **W:** Lee Anthony Smith, Gregory J. Bradley; **C:** Pierre Morel; **M:** Brian Tyler.

War & Love 🦴🦴 1984 (PG-13) Two Jewish teenagers in Warsaw are torn apart by WWII and Nazi persecution. After the war they search for each other. Sincere, but not adequately developed, drama based on the book "The Survivors" by film's producer Jack Eisner. 112m/C VHS. Sebastian Keneas, Kyra Sedgwick; **D:** Moshe Mizrahi.

War and Peace 🦴🦴 1956 Lengthy adaptation of Tolstoy's great (and likewise lengthy) novel about three families caught up in Russia's Napoleonic Wars from 1805 to 1812; filmed in Rome. Bad casting and confused script (by six writers) are somewhat overcome by awesome battle scenes and Hepburn. Remade in 1968. 208m/C VHS, DVD. Audrey Hepburn, Mel Ferrer, Henry Fonda, Anita Ekberg, Vittorio Gassman, John Mills, Oscar Homolka, Herbert Lom, Helmut Dantine, Tullio Carminati, Barry Jones, Milly Vitale, Maria Ferrero, Wilfred Lawson, May Britt, Jeremy Brett, Lea Seidl, Patrick Crean, Sean Barrett, Richard Dawson; **D:** King Vidor; **W:** King Vidor, Bridget Boland, Mario Camerini, Ennio de Concini, Ivo Perilli, Irwin Shaw, Robert Westerby; **C:** Jack Cardiff. Oscars '69: Foreign Film; Golden Globes '57: Foreign Film.

War and Peace 🦴🦴🦴 1968 The massive Russian production of Leo Tolstoy's masterpiece, adapting the classic tome practically scene by scene. All of the production took place in the Soviet Union. So painstaking that it took more than five years to finish, no other adaptation can touch it. Hugely expensive ($100 million, claimed the Russians), wildly uneven production. Great scenes of battle and aristocratic life. Though this version is far from perfect, one asks: Is it humanly possible to do screen justice to such a novel? In Russian with English subtitles. On four tapes. (Beware the two-part, poorly dubbed version that was also released.) 373m/C VHS, DVD. *RU* Lyudmila Savelyeva, Sergei Bondarchuk, Vyacheslav Tihonor, Hira Ivanov-Golarko, Irina Gubanova, Antonina Shuranova; **D:** Sergei Bondarchuk; **C:** Jack Cardiff. Oscars '68: Foreign Film; N.Y. Film Critics '68: Foreign Film.

War and Peace 🦴🦴🦴 1973 The lengthy BBC production of the lengthy Tolstoy masterpiece that follows the trials and triumphs of two Russian families whose lives intersect against a backdrop of the Napoleonic Wars. On 6 cassettes. 750m/C VHS, DVD. *GB* Anthony Hopkins, Alan Dobie, Faith Brook, Morag Hood, Colin Baker, Neil Stacey; **D:** John (Howard) Davies; **W:** Jack Pulman.

War & Remembrance 🦴🦴½ 1988 Tedious sequel to the epic TV miniseries "The Winds of War." Herman Wouk's sweeping saga, following "The Winds of War" is created around the events of WWII, including Nazi persecution and naval battles in the Pacific. Followed by "War and Remembrance: The Final Chapter." On seven cassettes. 840m/C VHS, DVD. Charles Lane, Robert Mitchum, Jane Seymour, Hart Bochner, Victoria Tennant, Barry Bostwick, Polly Bergen, David Dukes, Michael Woods, Sharon Stone, Robert Morley, Sami Frey, Chaim Topol, John Rhys-Davies, Ian McShane, William Schallert, Jeremy Kemp, Steven Berkoff, Robert Hardy, Ralph Bellamy, John Gielgud; **D:** Dan Curtis. TV

War & Remembrance: The Final Chapter 🦴🦴½ 1989 The final episodes of Herman Wouk's sweeping saga, following "The Winds of War" and "War and Remembrance" deal with the rope. Natalie and her son, Louis, are trapped in a ghetto under the reign of a vicious Nazi, who considers a tribe for the sake of the mother and son. On five cassettes. **600m/C VHS.** Robert Mitchum, Jane Seymour, Hart Bochner, Michael Woods, Sharon Eargen, David Dukes, Sharon Stone, Robert Morley, Sami Frey, Chaim Topol, Ian McShane, William Schallert, Jeremy Kemp, Steven Berkoff, Robert Hardy, Ralph Bellamy, John Gielgud. **D:** Dan Curtis. **TV**

War Arrow 🦴🦴 1953 Army Major Howell Brady (Chandler) is sent by Washington to end the Kiowa uprisings in Texas in this cavalry vs. Indians western. Along the way, he tries to win the heart of O'Hara. **79m/C VHS, DVD.** Maureen O'Hara, Jeff Chandler, Suzan Ball, John McIntire, Noah Beery Jr., Henry (Kleinbach) Brandon, Dennis Weaver, Jay Silverheels. **D:** George Sherman. **TV**

The War at Home 🦴🦴½ 1996 (R) In 1972 Vietnam vet Jeremy Collier (Estevez) has been home in the Dallas suburbs for a year but the war and its effects still linger. Mom Maureen (Bates) is a conservative control freak and dad Bob (Sheen) just can't connect, while 'teenaged sis Karen (Williams) is going through her own rebellion. The tense situation comes to a bitter head over a Thanksgiving weekend. Based on the 1984 play "Home Front" by James Duff. **124m/C VHS, DVD.** Kathy Bates, Martin Sheen, Emilio Estevez, Kimberly Williams, Carla Gugino, Geoffrey Blake, Corin "Corky" Nemec, Ann Hearn; **D:** Emilio Estevez; **W:** James Duff. **C:** Peter Levy. **M:** Basil Poledouris.

War Between the Tates 🦴🦴 1976 A college professor's affair with a female student is the basis for a tension filled stand-off with his wife. Mediocre adaptation of the Allison Lurie novel, somewhat redeemed by Ashley's performance. **90m/C VHS.** Mina (Badiyi) Badie, Ann Wedgeworth, Annette O'Toole, Colin Fox, Harvey Atkin, Michael J. Reynolds, Richard Crenna, Elizabeth Ashley, Granville Van Dusen; **D:** Lee Philips; **W:** Barbara Turner. **M:** John Barry. **TV**

The War Boy 🦴🦴½ 1985 (R) Difficulties encountered by a young Canadian boy as he grows up in Central Europe during WWII. Not to be compared with "Empire of the Sun" or "Hope and Glory," both of which were released later; successful in its modest ambitions. Beautiful performance from 12-year-old star Hopely. **86m/C VHS. CA** Helen Shaver, Kenneth Welsh, Jason Hopely; **D:** Allan Eastman.

The War Bride 🦴🦴 2001 Slow and sometimes tedious homefront drama but Friel's a firecracker. Cockney Lily (Friel) makes a whirlwind wartime marriage to Canadian soldier Charlie (Young) and is eventually granted citizenship and shipped off to her husband's home country. Lily's in for a rude shock when she sees that she'll be living on a small hardscrabble ranch in rural Alberta with her unwelcoming in-laws—Charlie's mother Betty (Fricker) and polio-stricken sister Sylvia (Parker). But th's city sparrow is determined to make the best of things, although it's not going to be easy. **96m/C DVD. GB CA** Anna Friel, Brenda Fricker, Molly Parker, Aden Young, Loren Dean, Julia Cox; **D:** Lyndon Chubbuck. **C:** Ronald Crieux; **M:** John Sereda.

War Brides 🦴🦴 1980 Civil War brides confront life after the war. Low-budget drama. **100m/C VHS. CA** Elizabeth Richardson, Sharry Fleet, Sonja Smits; **D:** Martin Lavut. **TV**

War Bus Commando 🦴 1989 A fully loaded bus is the only way out when soldiers are caught behind enemy lines in Afghanistan. A case of the spoof coming first: The plot is almost exactly the same as "Stripes"—only this one isn't funny. In Hi-Fi. **90m/C VHS.** IT Savina Gersak, Mark Gregory, John Vernon; **D:** Frank (Fleitig Ciriaci) Valentini.

War in Space 🦴 Battle of the Stars; Anno Zero - Guerra Nello Spazio; Year Zero - War in Sace 1977 Powerful U.N. Space Bureau Starships and UFOs band together to battle alien invaders among the volcanoes and deserts of Venus. **91m/C VHS, DVD.** /T JP John Richardson, Jaetaro Baiestrieri, Yanti Somer; **D:** Alfonso Brescia; **W:** Alfonso Brescia. **C:** Silvio Fraschetti; **M:** Marcelo Giomini.

The War Lord 🦴🦴🦴 1965 Set in the 11th century, Heston stars as Chrysagon, a Norman knight and war lord who commands a peasant village. While battling his enemies, he becomes enamored of a peasant girl named Bronwyn (Forsyth), who is unfortunately engaged to someone else. Pulling rank, Chrysagon uses an ancient law that allows noblemen the first night with a bride and the two fall in love. The two vow to never part, but that sets the stage for even more bloody battles. Fine acting and great production values make this a well-adapted version of the play "The Lovers" by Leslie Stevens. **121m/C VHS, DVD.** Charlton Heston, Richard Boone, Rosemary Forsyth, Guy Stockwell, Niall MacGinnis, Henry Wilcoxon, James Farentino, Maurice Evans, Michael Conrad; **D:** Franklin J. Schaffner; **W:** John Collier, Millard Kaufman; **C:** Russell Metty.

War Lover 🦴🦴½ 1962 An American can daredevil flying captain and his co-pilot find themselves vying for the affections of a woman during WWII in England. Seeks human frailty beneath surface heroism. McQueen is impressive, no thanks to mediocre script. Excellent aerial photography, and featuring one of only a very few serviceable WWII B-17s then remaining. Based on John Hersey's novel. **105m/B B VHS, DVD. GB** Steve McQueen, Robert Wagner, Shirley Anne Field, Bill Edwards, Gary Cockrell; **D:** Philip Leacock; **W:** Howard Koch.

War of the Buttons 🦴🦴½ 1995 (PG) Two sleepy Irish fishing villages provide childish battle grounds for two groups of local lads. The Ballys (Bally-aid), and the Carricks (Carrickdowse), with leader Geronimo (Coffey), have an intense rivalry and capture by the other gang leads to the removal of every clothing button for the unfortunate captive. When Fergus becomes a Carrick victim, he organizes a retaliatory strike, and emotions threaten to overwhelm all concerned. Based on the French novel "La Guerre des Boutons" by Louis Pergaud. Filmed on location in West Cork, Ireland. **94m/C VHS.** Gregg Fitzgerald, John Coffey, Liam Cunningham, Paul Batt, Eveanna Ryan, Colm Meaney, Johnny Murphy; **D:** John Roberts; **W:** Colin Welland. **C:** Bruno de Keyzer; **M:** Rachel Portman.

The War of the Colossal Beast 🦴½ The Terror Strikes 1958 This sequel to "The Amazing Colossal Man" finds the 70-foot Colonel Manning even angrier at the attempts to kill him than he was in the first film. So he wreaks more havoc until scolded by his sister into committing suicide for being such a trouble maker. Cheesy special effects but good for a laugh. **68m/B VHS, DVD.** Dean Parkin, Sally Fraser, Russ Bender, Roger Pace, Charles Stewart; **D:** Bert I. Gordon.

War of the Gargantuas 🦴 Duel of the Gargantuas; Frankenstein Monsters; Sanda vs. Gairath; Furankenshutain No Kaiju: Sanda tai Gailah; Sanda tai Gailah 1970 (G) Tokyo is once again the boxing ring for giant monsters. This time it's a good gargantua (half human, half monster) against a bad gargantua. This is a strange one. **92m/C VHS. JP** Russ Tamblyn, Kumi Mizuno, Kenji Sahara, Jun Tazaki, Kipp Hamilton, Haruo Nakajima, Nobuo Nakamura, Ikio Sawamura, Yoshifumi Tajima; **D:** Inoshiro Honda; **W:** Inoshiro Honda, Takeshi Kimura; **C:** Hajime Koizumi; **M:** Akira Ifukube.

The War of the Roses 🦴🦴🦴 1989 (R) Acidic black comedy about a well-to-do suburban couple who can't agree on a property settlement in their divorce so they wage unreserved and ever-escalating combat on each other, using their palatial home as a battleground. Expertly and lovingly (if that's the word) directed by DeVito, who plays the lawyer. Turner and Douglas are splendid. Adapted from the novel by Warren Adler. **116m/C VHS, DVD.** Michael Douglas, Kathleen Turner, Danny DeVito, Marianne Saegebrecht, Sean Astin, G.D. Spradlin, Peter Donat, Heather Fairfield, Dan Castellaneta, Danitra Vance, Tony Crane; **D:** Danny DeVito; **W:** Michael Leeson; **C:** Stephen Burum; **M:** David Newman.

The War Room 🦴🦴🦴 1993 (PG) Eye opening, sometimes disturbing documentary presents a behind the scenes peek at what really goes on during a Presidential campaign. When filming began in June '92 Bill Clinton was an unknown political quantity and advisors George Stephanopoulous and James Carville were masterminding his campaign. The "War Room" refers to the building in Little Rock where they struggle to organize a small army of volunteers into a winning team. Highlights include the Democratic National Convention, the North Carolina leg of Clinton's campaign bus tour, three Presidential debates, and the week leading up to election night. **93m/C VHS, DVD. D:** Chris Hegedus, D.A. Pennebaker; **C:** D.A. Pennebaker, Kevin Rafferty, Nat'l Bd. of Review '93: Feature Doc.

War of the Wildcats 🦴🦴½ In Old Oklahoma 1943 Fast-moving western with Wayne as a tough cowboy battling a powerful land baron. They fight over land, oil and a woman. Unusual because Wayne's character acts on behalf of the Indians to drill and transport oil. **102m/B C VHS, DVD.** John Wayne, Martha Scott, Albert Dekker, George "Gabby" Hayes, Sidney Blackmer; **D:** Richard Caan; **W:** F. Kenneth Lin; **C:** Sidney Blackmer.

War of the Wizards 🦴🦴 Phoenix 1983 (PG) Low-budget sci-fi thriller about an alien woman with supernatural powers who comes to take over the Earth. But, lucky for all earthlings, she's challenged by a hero-type just in the nick of time. **90m/C VHS.** Charles Lang, Betty Noonan, Richard Kiel; **D:** Albert Rogell.

War of the Worlds 🦴🦴🦴½ 1953 H.G. Wells's classic novel of the invasion of Earth by Martians, updated to 1950s California, with spectacular special effects of destruction caused by the Martian war machines. Pretty scary and tense; based more on Orson Welles's radio broadcast than on the book. Still very popular, hit the top 20 in sales when released on video. Classic thriller later made into a TV series. Produced by George Pal, who brought the world much sci-fi, including "The Time Machine," "Destination Moon," and "When Worlds Collide," and who appears here as a street person. **85m/C VHS, DVD.** Gene Barry, Ann (Robin) Robinson, Les Tremayne, Lewis Martin, Robert Cornthwaite, Sandro Giglio, George Pal, Jack Kruschen, Carolyn Jones; **D:** Byron Haskin; **W:** Barre Lyndon; **C:** George Barnes; **M:** Leith Stevens; **V:** Cedric Hardwicke.

War of the Worlds 🦴🦴🦴 2005 (PG-13) Spielberg and Cruise re-team in th'rs modern sci-fi remake in the H.G. Wells classic 1898 novel (George Pal produced the 1953 film version) though the M-word (Martians, that is) is never actually uttered here. Dockworker Ray Ferrier (Cruise) is a distant dad forced together wth his teenage son Robbie (Chatwin) and 10-year-old daughter Rachel (Fanning) for the weekend. That dysfunctional scene is cut short by powerful lightning strikes that activate massive underground three-legged alien machines bent on destroying every human in sight, which puts Ray and his brood on the run. Typical breathtaking Spielberg special effects around; Cruise shows why he's an A-lister. **118m/C DVD.** US Tom Cruise, Dakota Fanning, Miranda Otto, Tim Robbins, Justin Chatwin, Rick Gonzalez, David Alan Basche, Yul Vazquez, Lenny Venito, Lisa Ann Walter, Ann (Robin) Robinson, Gene Barry; **D:** Steven Spielberg; **W:** David Koepp, Josh Friedman; **C:** Janusz Kaminski; **M:** John Williams; **Nar:** Morgan Freeman.

War Party 🦴🦴 1989 (R) During a 100-year commemoration of an Indian massacre in the Midwest, a murder occurs and a lynch mob chases a pack of young Blackfeet into the mountains before the inevitable showdown. A feeble attempt at portraying the unfair treatment of Native Americans. Un-subtle, Hollywood style, this time in favor of the Indians, and therefore un-serious. Too bad; the premise had potential. **99m/C VHS.** Kevin Dillon, Billy Wirth, Tim Sampson, M. Emmet Walsh; **D:** Franc Roddam; **C:** Brian Tufano.

The War Wagon 🦴🦴🦴 1967 The Duke plans revenge on Cabot, the greedy mine owner who stole his gold claim and framed him for murder for which he spent years in prison. He assembles a gang to aid h'm, including a wise-cracking Indian (Keel) and the man sent by Cabot to kill him (Douglas). Wayne's is to steal the gold being shipped in Cabot's armor-plated stagecoach, the "war wagon." Well-written, good performances, lots of action. Based on the book "Badman" by Clair Huffaker. **101m/C VHS, DVD.** John Wayne, Kirk Douglas, Howard Keel, Robert Walker Jr., Keenan Wynn, Bruce Cabot, Bruce Dern, Joanna Barnes; **D:** Burt Kennedy; **W:** Clair Huffaker; **C:** William Clothier; **M:** Dimitri Tiomkin.

The War Within 🦴🦴🦴 2005 (R) Pakistani student Hassan (Akhtar) is kidnapped from his Paris home and tortured for five years in a detention center during whic' time he becomes a radicalized Jihadist. After being released he is smuggled into New York where he is to play a key role in a plot to bomb targets in the city. Hassan's friend Sayeed (Bamji) allows him to stay in his home in New Jersey while Hassan is working within a sleeper cell. This sets up a sharp contrast between the western lifestyle of Sayeed's family and the extremist activities of Hassan and his cell. The chilling plausibility of the storyline makes up for any weakness in execution. **90m/C DVD.** US Ayad Akhtar, Nandana Sen, Firdous Bamji, Sarita Choudhury, Charles Daniel Sandoval, Varun Sriram, Anjell John Ventimiglia, Mike McGlone, Chapman, Aay Naidu, Aasif Mandvi; **D:** Joseph Castelo; **W:** Joseph Castelo, Ayad Akhtar, Tom Glynn; **C:** Lisa Rinzler; **M:** David Holmes.

War Six 🦴 Pavilion 6 1978 An insane asylum is the setting for various analogies regarding the perception of reality as defined by societal values. When it is felt that the residing physician is no more sane than his patients, he is placed among them, in Ward Six. Adapted from a story by Anton Chekhov. In Serbian with English subtitles. **83m/C VHS.** YU Ljuba Tadic, Slobodan 'Perovic, Zoran Radmilovic, Slavko Simic; **D:** Lucian Pintilie; **W:** Lucian Pintilie. **C:** Milorad Jaksic-Fandjo.

Warbus 🦴🦴 1985 (R) Marines lead a school bus load of Americans through war-torn Vietnam to safety. Decent action and surprisingly enjoyable characters. Otherwise mediocre. **90m/C VHS.** Daniel Stephen, Romano Kristoff, Urs Althaus; **D:** Ted Kaplan.

WarCat 🦴 Angel of Vengeance 1988 The daughter of a green beret fights for her life against a blood-thirsty gang. **72m/C VHS.** Jannina Poyriter, David O'Hara, Carl Erwin; **D:** Ted V. Mikels.

Warbirds 🦴🦴 1988 (R) American pilots are off to quell a revolution in a Middle East country. Too little action fails to support mediocre plot and characters. **88m/C VHS.** Jim Eldert, Cully Holland, Bill Brinsfield; **D:** Ulli Lommel. **W:** Ulli Lommel.

The War Zone 🦴🦴🦴 1998 (R) Harrowing and uncompromising look at a working class British family torn apart by incest and abuse. Dad (Winstone) has just moved the family to a small Devon town—a move resented by his children, 18-year-old Jessie (Belmont) and 15-year-old Tom (Cunliffe). Mum (Swinton) is too busy with a new baby to see what's going on but lonely Tom gradually (and later graphically) becomes aware that something not right is happening between Jessie and their father. Roth's disquieting directing debut; based on Stuart's novel. **98m/C VHS, DVD. GB** Ray Winstone, Tilda Swinton, Lara Belmont, Freddie Cunliffe, Aisling O'Sullivan, Colin Farrell, Annabelle Apsion, Kate Ashfield; **D:** Tim Roth; **W:** Alexander Stuart; **C:** Seamus McGarvey; **M:** Simon Boswell.

Warden of Red Rock 🦴🦴½ 2001 (PG-13) Ex-criminal John Flinders (Caan) has been an upstanding citizen in a long time. In fact, he's now the warden of the Red Rock prison in Arizona, where his old partner, Mike Sullivan (Carradine), has just been sent to serve a life sentence. Instead, though, Sullivan engineers a b'oody jail break and Flinders must set out with a posse to hunt them down. (And as expected, there's a final showdown between the two.) **89m/C VHS.** James Caan, David Carradine, Rachel Ticotin, Brian Dennehy; **C:** Stephen Gyllenhaal; **W:** James Lee Barrett; **C:** Henner Hofmann; **M:** Michel Colombier. **CABLE**

Wardogs ♂⅟₂ *The Assassination Team* 1987 A man tries to rescue his brother from becoming one of an elite, brainwashed group of ex-Vietnam vets trained by the government as professional assassins. Might not have been quite so bad; promising inversion of many 'Nam cliches wrecked by unnecessary violence and bad acting. **95m/C** SW Tim Earle, Bill Redvers; **D:** Daniel Hubenbecker.

WarGames ♂♂⅟₂ 1983 (PG) A young computer whiz, thinking that he's sneaking an advance look at a new line of video games, breaks into the country's NORAD missile-defense system and challenges it to a game of Global Thermonuclear Warfare. The game might just turn out to be the real thing. Slick look at the possibilities of an accidental start to WWII. Entertaining and engrossing, but with a B-grade ending. **110m/C VHS, DVD.** Matthew Broderick, Dabney Coleman, John Wood, Ally Sheedy; **D:** John Badham; **W:** Walter F. Parkes, Lawrence Lasker; **C:** William A. Fraker; **M:** Arthur B. Rubinstein.

Warhead ♂⅟₂ 1996 (R) Special Forces Ranger Tannen (Zagarino) has to stop a renegade military group, led by his former compatriot Craft (Lara), that has stolen a nuclear warhead and are threatening Washington. **97m/C VHS, DVD.** Frank Zagarino, Joe Lara, Elizabeth Giordano; **D:** Mark Roper; **W:** Jeff Albert; **C:** Rod Stewart; **M:** Robert O. Ragland.

Warkill ♂♂⅟₂ 1965 WWII action set in the jungles of the Philippines. Journalist who idolizes violent, hard-edged colonel, loses his illusions, but gains a more genuine respect for his men. Not-bad war flick. **99m/C VHS.** George Montgomery, Tom Drake, Eddie Infante; **D:** Ferde Grofe Jr.; **W:** Ferde Grofe Jr.

Warlock ♂♂♂ 1959 Claustrophic, resonant town-bound tale of a marshal (Fonda) and his adoring sidekick (Quinn) who clean up a town which then turns against him. Unusual story, fine performances carry this well beyond the run-of-the-mill cow flick. Fonda re-established himself at the box office as a western star, after "Stage Struck" and "Twelve Angry Men." From the novel by Oakley Hall. Look for "Bones" McCoy from "Star Trek" in a bit part. **122m/C VHS, DVD.** Henry Fonda, Anthony Quinn, Richard Widmark, Dorothy Malone, Wallace Ford, Richard Arlen, Regis Toomey, DeForest Kelley; **D:** Edward Dmytryk; **W:** Robert Alan Aurthur.

Warlock ♂♂⅟₂ 1991 (R) It's 1691 and the most powerful warlock (Sands) in the New World is only hours away from execution. Luckily, his pal, Satan, whisks him (and witchhunter Grant, by mistake) three hundred years in the future to present-day Los Angeles, where he crashlands in Singer's house. Surprisingly witty dialogue and neat plot twists outshine occasionally cheesy special effects. **103m/C VHS, DVD.** Richard E. Grant, Julian Sands, Lori Singer, Mary Woronov, Richard Kuss, Kevin O'Brien, Anna Levine, Allan Miller, David Carpenter; **D:** Steve Miner; **W:** David N. Twohy; **C:** David Eggby; **M:** Jerry Goldsmith.

Warlock 3: The End of Innocence ♂♂ 1998 (R) Kris (Laurence) decides to spend a weekend in the abandoned 16th-century family manor that she has inherited. Disturbed by visions, she comes to realize that her family has a legacy of witchcraft and now she is the sacrificial target of a warlock (Payne). Predictable, although Payne is sufficiently chilling. **94m/C VHS, DVD.** Bruce Payne, Ashley Laurence, Angel Boris, Boti Ann Bliss, Paul Francis, Rick Hearst, Jan Schweiterman; **D:** Eric Freiser, Bruce David Eisen. **VIDEO**

Warlock Moon ♂⅟₂ 1973 Young woman is lured to a secluded spa and falls prey to a coven of witches. **75m/C VHS, DVD. MX** Laurie Walters, Joe Spano, Edna Macat-

ee, Ray Goman, Steve Solinsky, Charles Raino; **D:** Bill Herbert.

Warlock: The Armageddon ♂♂⅟₂ 1993 (R) Sequel finds Sands back again as the sinister Warlock. This time he's out to gather six Druidic rune stones which have the power to summon Satan's emissary (in the wrong hands) or to stop his nefarious activities (in the right ones). A sect in a small California town serves as the keeper of the stones, only their designated champions are two unprepared teenagers. Sands has all the fun, gleefully dispatching his would-be opponents with some good special effects. **93m/C VHS, DVD.** Julian Sands, Chris Young, Paula Marshall, Steve Kahan, Charles Hallahan, R.G. Armstrong, Bruce Glover, Zach Galligan, Dawn Ann Billings, Joanna Pacula; **D:** Anthony Hickox; **W:** Kevin Rock, Sam Bernard; **C:** Gerry Lively; **M:** Mark McKenzie.

Warlords ♂⅟₂ 1988 (R) Lone soldier Carradine battles mutant hordes in a post-apocalyptic desert. Amateurish futuristic drivel. **87m/C VHS.** David Carradine, Sid Haig, Ross Hagen, Fox Harris, Robert Quarry, Victoria Sellers, Brinke Stevens, Dawn Wildsmith; **D:** Fred Olen Ray.

Warlords from Hell WOOF! 1987 (R) Two young men motorcycling through Mexico are captured by a bloodthirsty gang and forced to do hard labor in the marijuana fields. We can only hope that they just learn to say no. **76m/C VHS.** Brad Henson, Jeffray Rice; **D:** Clark Henderson.

Warlords of the 21st Century ♂⅟₂ *Battletruck* 1982 Bandit gang speed around the galaxy in an indestructible battle cruiser. Then the boys are challenged by a space lawman. Gratuitously violent action pic lacking real action. Filmed on planet New Zealand. **91m/C VHS.** Michael Beck, Annie McEnroe, James Wainwright; **D:** Harley Cokliss; **W:** Harley Cokliss, Irving Austin, John Beech; **C:** Chris Menges.

Warlords 3000 ♂⅟₂ 1993 (R) In the future, Earth is a barren wasteland ravaged by raging electrical storms. Deadly cancers are rampant and the few people who have survived take their comfort in a temporary pleasure and a permanent madness. Drug lords control the planet but one man is out to eliminate the scum and save the future. **92m/C VHS.** Jay Roberts Jr., Denise Marie Duff, Steve Blanchard, Wayne Duvall; **D:** Faruque Ahmed; **W:** Ron Herbst, Faruque Ahmed.

Warm Blooded Killers ♂♂ 2001 (R) Quirky, likeable comedy has brother/sister hitmen (hitpersons?) John and Vicky doing well for themselves until she meets a stranger who has a deadly masquerade of his own. Interestingly different, much sex, as you can imagine. Australian-made. **90m/C.** AU Wendy Hughes, Colin Friels, Norman Kaye, John Clayton, Peter Whitford; **D:** Bob Ellis; **W:** Bob Ellis, Denny Lawrence; **C:** Yuri Sokol.

Warm Nights on a Slow-Moving Train ♂⅟₂ 1987 (R) A hot-blooded schoolteacher turns tricks for cash to support her brother on the Sunday-night train to Melbourne, until she meets a stranger who has a deadly masquerade of his own. Lust, self-doubt and longing for something to hold onto draw them together as the days pass. Thoroughly self-indulgent romantic comedy that's oddly self-pitying and poorly directed. **85m/C VHS, DVD.** Kelly Lynch, Barry Tubb; **D:** Joe Gayton.

The Warning ♂ 1980 A pair of proverbial honest cops investigate ties between the mob and the police department. Hard to follow. **101m/C VHS.** IT Martin Balsam,

Giuliano Gemma, Giancarlo Zanetti; **D:** Damiano Damiani.

Warning from Space ♂⅟₂ *The Mysterious Satellite; The Cosmic Man Appears in Tokyo; Space Men Appear in Tokyo; Unknown Satellite Over Tokyo; Uchujin Tokyo Ni Arawaru* 1956 Aliens visit Earth to warn of impending cosmic doom. When it becomes apparent that the one-eyed starfish look is off-putting, they assume human form. Japanese sci fi. **87m/B VHS, DVD.** JP Toyomi Karita, Keizo Kawasaki, Isao Yamagata, Shozo Nanbu, Buntaro Miake, Mieko Nagai, Kyoko Hirai; **D:** Koji Shima.

Warning Shadows ♂♂♂ 1923 Classic example of interior German Expressionism. Brilliantly portrays a jealous husband's emotions and obsessions through shadows. Innocent events seem to reek of sin. A seldom-seen study of the oft-precarious distinction between love and quality. Silent with German and English titles. **93m/B VHS, DVD.** GE Ruth Weyher, Alexander Granach, Rudolf Klein-Rogge, Max Gulstorff, Fritz Kortner; **D:** Arthur Robison; **W:** Arthur Robison; **C:** Fritz Arno Wagner.

Warning Sign ♂⅟₂ 1985 (R) A high-tech thriller in which a small town is terrorized by the accidental release of an experimental virus at a research facility. Shades of "The Andromeda Strain" and "The China Syndrome," though less originality and quality. **99m/C VHS, DVD.** Sam Waterston, Kathleen Quinlan, Yaphet Kotto, Richard Dysart, Rick Rossovich; **D:** Hal Barwood; **W:** Hal Barwood, Matthew Robbins; **C:** Dean Cundey.

The Warrior ♂♂ 2001 (R) If you've ever watched a samurai movie, this effort will seem familiar (although less violent). Warrior Lafcadia (Khan) is an indentured enforcer in the northwest Indian state of Rajasthan. During his latest pillage with his men, Lafcadia has a mystical vision and decides to lay down his sword, which enrages his master who sends other warriors after him. Seeking redemption, Lafcadia follows his vision into the Himalayas accompanied by a young thief (Mani) and a blind woman (Marfatia) on a pilgrimage. Hindi with subtitles; there is also an English-language version. **86m/C VHS, DVD.** Irfan Khan, Puru Chibber, Damayanti Marfatia, Sunita Sharma, Noor Mani, Damayanti Mafatia, Firoz Khan, Anupam Shyam; **D:** Asif Kapadia; **W:** Tim Miller, Asif Kapadia; **C:** Roman Osin; **M:** Dario Marianelli.

The Warrior & the Sorceress ♂⅟₂ 1984 (R) Mercenary Carradine offers his services to rival factions fighting for control of a water well in an impoverished desert village located on a planet with two suns. He attempts to aggravate the conflicts between the factions, playing the shifty go-between. "A Fistful of Dollars" goes to outer space. Inoffensive, except that better judgment is expected of Carradine. **81m/C VHS, DVD.** David Carradine, Luke Askew, Maria Socas, Harry Townes; **D:** John Broderick; **W:** John Broderick.

Warrior of Justice ♂ 1996 Karate instructor has one of his students disappear after competing in a secret tournament. He then uncovers a black market ring specializing in selling human organs that's run by a former opponent. **90m/C VHS, DVD.** Richard Lynch, Jeff Langton, Nick (Nicholas, Niko) Hill, Ian Jacklin, Jorgo Ognenovski; **D:** Jorgo Ognenovski, Mike Tristano.

Warrior of the Lost World WOOF! 1984 A warrior must destroy the evil Omega Force who tyrannically rules the world in the distant future. In the best tradition of all prem-C VHS. **DVD.** Robert Ginty, Persis Khambatta, Donald Pleasence; **D:** David Worth.

Warrior Queen ♂ 1987 (R) Long ago in ancient Rome, overly histrionic mayor Pleasence married porn queen with a wandering eye Fox, and much gratuitous sex and erupting volcanoes resulted. Even the score blows. Also available in an "Unrated" version. Brit pop star Fox is

billed as Stasia Micula. **69m/C VHS.** Sybil Danning, Donald Pleasence, Richard (Rick) Hill, Josephine Jacqueline Jones, Tally Chanel, Samantha Fox; **D:** Chuck Vincent; **W:** Rick Marx; **C:** Gianlorenzo Battaglia; **M:** Ian Shaw.

Warrior Queen ♂♂⅟₂ 2003 Boudica (Kingston) is the leader of her tribe in first-century Briton, which is under Roman rule. Sickened by the increasing demands of the Emperor Nero and his occupying troops, Boudica unites the fractious Celt tribes to lead an onslaught on the Roman camps. But the Romans did not conquer the world by giving in. **90m/C VHS, DVD.** GB Alex Kingston, Steven Waddington, Hugo Speer, Gary Lewis, Emily Blunt, Leanne Rowe, Ben Faulks; **D:** Bill Anderson; **W:** Andrew Davies; **C:** Tudor Lucaciu; **M:** Nina Humphreys. **TV**

Warrior Spirit ♂♂⅟₂ 1994 (PG-13) After getting kicked out of their prep school, two boys decide to head for the Yukon and search for gold. **94m/C VHS.** Lukas Haas, Jimmy Herman, Allan Musy; **D:** Rene Manzor.

The Warriors ♂♂⅟₂ 1955 Swashbuckling adventure about Prince Edward's valiant rescue of Lady Joan and her children from the clutches of the evil Count De Ville. Flynn looks old and pudgy, but buckles his way gallantly through intrepid adventure. Also the last Flynn to see: fun, but more or less completely derivative and familiar. Filmed in England. **85m/C VHS.** GB Errol Flynn, Peter Finch, Joanne Dru, Yvonne Furneaux, Noel Willman, Michael Hordern; **D:** Henry Levin.

The Warriors ♂♂♂⅟₂ 1979 (R) Action story about a turf battle between NYC street gangs that rages from Coney Island to the Bronx. Silly plot works because of fine performances and direction, excellent use of action and color, and nonstop pace. Fight scenes are very carefully, even obviously, choreographed. **94m/C VHS, DVD. Blu-ray Disc, HD DVD.** Michael Beck, James Remar, Deborah Van Valkenburgh, Thomas G. Waites, David Patrick Kelly, Mercedes Ruehl, Dorsey Wright, David Harris, Brian Tyler, Tom McKitterick; **D:** Walter Hill; **W:** Walter Hill, David Shaber; **C:** Andrew Laszlo; **M:** Barry DeVorzon.

Warriors ♂♂ 1994 (R) Col. Frank Vail (Busey) is the leader of a top secret government anti-terrorist hit squad, considered so deadly that its members are confined behind the walls of a military prison. But when Vail escapes, it's up to his lethal protege Colin Newl (Pare) to hunt him down. **100m/C VHS.** Gary Busey, Michael Pare; **D:** Shimon Dotan.

Warriors ♂♂⅟₂ *Guerreros* 2002 Spanish troops are sent by NATO to Kosovo as non-combatants in the midst of the Serbian–Albanian war in 1999. Their job is to restore electricity to a local village. Not getting involved in the bloodshed proves futile and they face a life-and-death struggle to bail out and return to their base. In Spanish, with subtitles. **96m/C VHS, DVD. UMD.** Eloy Azorin, Eduardo Noriega, Ruben Ochandiano; **C:** Daniel Calparsoro; **W:** Daniel Calparsoro; **C:** Josep Civit; **M:** Najwa Nimri, Carlos Jean. **VIDEO**

Warriors from Hell ♂⅟₂ 1990 (R) Western forces in a small African country battle rebel fighters who threaten the hapless native villagers. **90m/C VHS.** Deon Stewardson, Shayne Leith, Adrienne Pierce, Glen Gabela, Hector Manthanda, Ivan Dean, Connie Chume; **D:** Ronnie Isaacs; **W:** Ronnie Isaacs.

Warriors of Heaven and Earth ♂♂⅟₂ *Tian di ying xiong* 2003 (R) Grand epic Chinese western has two men of honor face off against one another in frontier Asia circa 700 A.D., but soon join forces to protect an ancient relic and its bearer from marauding bandits. Beautifully filmed and rousing adventure that is frequently confusing and corny, but always a terrific ride. Particularly fun is Wang Xueqi as a flamboyant villain who looks strangely like Harvey Keitel's Sport in "Taxi Driver." **114m/C DVD, Blu-ray Disc.** CH Jiang Wen, Kiichi Nakai, Wang Xueqi, Harrison Liu, Zhao Wei, Hasi Bagen, He Tao, Zhou Yun, Zhou Yun; **D:** He Ping; **W:** He Ping, Zhang Rui; **C:** Fei Zhao; **M:** A.R. Rahman.

Warriors of the Apocalypse WOOF! *Searchers of the Voodoo Mountain; Time Raiders* 1935 (R) After a nuclear holocaust, heavily sworded and loin-clothed men search for the secret of eternal life and instead find an Amazon realm in search of scenery. A terrific waste of post-apocalyptic life. **96m/C VHS.** Michael James, Deborah Moore, Ken Metcalfe, Franco Guerrero; **D:** Bobby Suarez.

Warriors of the Wasteland WOOF! *The New Barbarians; I Nuovi Barbari* 1983 (R) It's the year 2019, and the world has been devastated by a nuclear war. The few survivors try to reach a distant land which emits radio signals indicating the presence of human life. They are hindered by attacks from the fierce homosexual Templars, led by a self-proclaimed priest called Cne. Mindless rip-off of "Road Warrior" and obviously made on the proverbial shoestring budget. **Dubbed. 92m/C VHS, DVD.** *IT* Fred Williamson, Giancarlo Prete, Anne Kanakis; **D:** Enzo G. Castellari.

Warriors of Virtue �☆☆½ 1997 **(PG)** Teenaged Ryan Jelers (Yedidia) is transported to the land of Tao where he learns five virtues (righteousness, benevolence, integrity, wisdom, and loyalty) from the kangaroo-like Warmbloods warriors, who live in harmony with humans. Then he must use his knowledge to fight the evil Komodo (MacFadyen), who wishes to steal the energy from Tao to make himself immortal. Nice message for the kids, with enough action to keep them interested, but the Warmbloods are dorky-looking. **101m/C VHS, DVD.** Mario Yedidia, Angus MacFadyen, Marley Shelton, Chao-Li Chi; **C:** Peter Pau; **M:** Don Davis.

Wasabi ☆☆½ 2001 **(R)** This is one Japanese dip you probably won't care to sample. Hubert (Reno) is a hard-assed, violence-prone French cop, who is forced to take a vacation. He winds up in Tokyo at the funeral of a woman he's loved years before. He also discovers he's been left a screechy punk daughter, Yumi (Hirosue), he didn't know about, a mysterious key, and 200 million (in dollars) in the bank. And then the yakuza get involved. High-concept and fast-paced but not particularly entertaining French and Japanese with subtitles. **94m/C VHS, DVD.** *FR* Jean Reno, Ryoko Hirosue; **D:** Gerard Krawczyk; **W:** Luc Besson; **C:** Gerard Sterin; **M:** Eric Serra.

The Wash ☆☆☆ 1988 Quiet domestic drama about a couple who drift apart after 40 years of marriage. Set interestingly among Japanese-Americans in California; treats social and cultural factors with intelligence. Superb cast takes it a notch higher. **94m/C VHS.** Mako, Nobu McCarthy, Sab Shimono; **D:** Michael Toshiyuki Uno; **W:** Philip Kan Kotanda; **C:** Walt Lloyd.

The Wash ☆☆ 2001 **(R)** Sean (Dre) loses his job and has his car booted, so pal Dee Loc (Snoop Dogg) helps him out with some news about an opening at the car wash where he works. Soon Sean is assistant manager under crusty owner Mr. Washington (Wallace). Between dealing with the resentment of Loc, and the kidnapping of the boss, along with the usual supply of quirky characters and subplots, Sean has his hands full in this very laidback, low-key tribute to 1977's "Car Wash." Appealing performances, mostly of inspired comedy, and plenty of cameos to watch for make this a pleasant way to kill some time. **95m/C VHS, DVD.** Snoop Dogg, Dr. Dre, DJ Pooh, George Wallace, Tommy (Tiny) Lister, Alex Thomas, Arif S. Kinchen, Demetrius Navarro, Thomas Chong, Pauly Shore, Lamont Bentley, Bruce Bruce, Shari Watson, Shawn Fontano, Angell Conwell; **D:** DJ Pooh; **W:** DJ Pooh; **C:** Keith L. Smith.

Washington Affair ☆☆ 1977 **(PG)** A tale of intrigue in the nation's capital. Sullivan is a businessman who uses women and blackmail to capture government contracts. Selleck is the hapless bureaucrat he preys on. Remake of Stoloff's own "Intimacy" was not released until "Magnum P.I." became a hit. **90m/C VHS.** Tom

---

Selleck, Carol Lynley, Barry Sullivan; **D:** Victor Stoloff.

Washington Heights ☆☆ 2002 **(R)** Washington Heights is an upper west side Manhattan neighborhood largely populated by immigrants from the Dominican Republic. Widower Eddie Ramirez (Millan) provides for his family by running a bodega and would like his twenty-something son Carlos (Perez) to take over the business. But Carlos is a cartoonist with dreams of his own, who wants to move out of the 'hood, although his girlfriend Maggie (Navedo) is reluctant. Then Eddie is shot and Carlos is forced to mind the store, which makes the son feel even more trapped by circumstance. An effective portrayal (warts-and-all) that has something of a pat ending. **85m/C VHS, DVD.** Manny Perez, Tomas Millan, Danny Hoch, Andrea Navedo, Jude Ciccolella, Bobby Cannavale, Judy Reyes, Callie (Calliope) Thorne, David Zayas; **D:** Alfredo de Villa; **W:** Alfredo de Villa, Junot Diaz; **C:** Claudio Chea; **M:** Leigh Roberts.

Washington Mistress ☆☆½ 1981 Eminently ordinary made-for-TV grist about Capitol Hill aide Amaz, politician Jordan, and their affair. Listless performances. **96m/C VHS.** Lucie Arnaz, Richard Jordan, Tony Bill; **D:** Peter Levin.

Washington Square ☆☆☆ 1997 **(PG)** Adaptation of Henry James' novel, which was previously filmed as "The Heiress." Set in 19th-century New York City (filmed in Baltimore), wealthy spinster Catherine Sloper (Leigh), against the will of her overbearing father (Finney), is pursued by a handsome fortune hunter (Chaplin). Director Holland tends to bluntly simplify James' complex undertones and Leigh's facial ticks can't equal "The Heiress'" Olivia de Havilland's painful plainness; nonetheless, definitely worth seeing. **115m/C VHS, DVD.** Jennifer Jason Leigh, Ben Chaplin, Albert Finney, Maggie Smith, Judith Ivey, Betsy Brantley, Jennifer Garner, Peter Maloney, Robert Stanton, Scott Jaeck; **D:** Agnieszka Holland; **W:** Carol Doyle; **C:** Jerzy Zielinski; **M:** Jan A.P. Kaczmarek.

The Wasp Woman ☆☆ 1959 In her quest for eternal beauty, a woman uses a potion made from royal wasp enzymes. Naturally, she turns into a wasp monster at night. Good fun, courtesy of Corman. **84m/B VHS, DVD.** Susan Cabot, Anthony Eisley, Barboura Morris, Michael Marks, William Roerick, Frank Gerstle, Bruno VeSota, Frank Wolff, Lynn Cartwright, Roy Gordon; **D:** Roger Corman; **W:** Leo Gordon; **C:** Harry Neumann; **M:** Fred Katz.

The Wasp Woman ☆☆ 1996 **(R)** Equally campy cable remake of the 1959 flick finds ex-supermodel-turned-cosmetics company exec Janice Starlin (Rubin) discovering that her fading beauty is causing problems both with her company and her love life. So she turns to a mysterious doctor for help and injects herself with his untested serum, an experimental wasp hormone. She's hoping to discover a fountain of youth and is instead transformed into a nasty-tempered giant insect. Cool, disgusting makeup/costuming. **81m/C VHS.** Jennifer Rubin, Daniel J. Travanti, Maria Ford, Doug Wert; **D:** Jim Wynorski; **W:** Daniella Purcell; **M:** Terry Plumeri. **CABLE.**

Wassup Rockers ☆☆ 2006 **(R)** A group of South Central Salvadoran teens hang out, skateboarding, working their punk-rock band, chasing girls—two of whom happen to be rich, so the boys travel to Beverly Hills and get into trouble and then scamper back to the 'hood. The teens are first-time actors basically playing themselves and, for Clark, the film's most surprisingly sweet. **99m/C VHS, DVD.** *US* Carlos Ramirez, Jonathan Velasquez, Francisco Pedrasa, Milton Velasquez, Usvaldo Panameno, Eddie Velasquez, Luis Rojas Salgado, Iris Zelaya, Rosalia, Laura Cellner, Jessica Steinbaum; **D:** Larry Clark; **C:** Steve Gainer; **M:** Harry Cody.

Watch It ☆☆☆ 1993 **(R)** Four self-absorbed 20-something guys share a house in Chicago for the summer. They pursue a post-adolescent game, consisting of increasingly complicated practical jokes, where the unsuspecting victim is set up for a "watch it" gag. The rivalry

---

escalates, and turns increasingly unpleasant, when cousins John and Michael vie for the affections of Anne, who's wary of involvement because of male selfishness. A first-rate cast with recognizable situations and emotions. **102m/C VHS.** Jon Tenney, Peter Gallagher, Suzy Amis, John C. McGinley, Tom Sizemore, Lili Taylor, Cynthia Stevenson, Terri Hawkes, Jordana Capra; **D:** Tom Flynn; **W:** Tom Flynn; **M:** Stanley Clarke.

Watch Me ☆ 1995 **(R)** Photog Paul (Medford) is inspired by new neighbor babe Elise (Burns) and secretly snaps her peeking in on Paul's would-be gal Samantha (Burton) who's having sex with his best bud Alex (Sherwin). Paul of course wants to get more personally involved with Elise (especially after he finds out about Samantha). Lots of nudity—no heat. **90m/C VHS, DVD.** Robert Medford, Kelly Burns, Jennifer Burton, Steven Sherwin; **D:** Lizy Ching; **W:** Ben Salmon; **C:** Andreas Kossak; **M:** Yoav Goren.

Watch Me When I Kill ☆☆ *II Gatto Dagli Occhi di Giada; The Cat With the Jade Eyes* 1977 **(R)** We'd rather not. A young nightclub dancer stops by a drugstore seconds after the owner was killed. She doesn't see the killer's face, but his raspy voice remains to torment her and the viewer. Dubbed. **95m/C VHS, DVD.** *IT* Corrado Pani, Paola Tedesco, Franco Citti, Fernando Cerulli, Paolo Malco; **D:** Antonio Bido; **M:** Mario Vulpiani.

Watch on the Rhine ☆☆☆½ 1943 Couple involved with the anti-Nazi underground has escaped the country, but are pursued and harassed by Nazi agents. Adapted by Hammett and Hellman from her play. Performed on stage before the U.S. entered the war, it was the first American play about "fascism as an ideology, as opposed to the more odious evil of its practical side. The Production Code at the time required that a killer always go the punished, but Hellman said move to portray the ugliness of fascism and move to punish the murderer (whose screen motives had been noble) refused to film the offending scene, which explains the tacked-on ending. Superb drama from a pair of highly gifted writers and a great cast. Shumlin also directed the play. **114m/B VHS.** Bette Davis, Paul Lukas, Donald Woods, Beulah Bondi, Geraldine Fitzgerald, George Coulouris, Henry Daniell, Helmut Dantine, Donald Buka, Anthony Caruso, Clyde Fillmore, Howard Hickman, Creighton Hale, Kurt Katch, Clarence Muse, Alan Hale Jr., Frank Reicher, Mary (Marsten) Young; **D:** Herman Shumlin; **W:** Lillian Hellman, Dashiell Hammett; **C:** Hal Mohr, Merritt B. Gerstad; **M:** Max Steiner; *Oscars '43:* Actor (Lukas); *Golden Globes '44:* Actor—Drama (Lukas); *N.Y. Film Critics '43:* Actor (Lukas), Film.

Watch the Birdie ☆☆½ 1950 It's Skelton three times over as cameraman, father, and grandfather! First, he accidentally films a scam that would send the lovely Miss Dahl filing for bankruptcy. Later a crazy chase scene unfolds, that will have viewers rolling, as Skelton the cameraman nabs the bad guys and turns them over to the cops. Light fun that will charm Skelton fans. **70m/B VHS.** Red Skelton, Arlene Dahl, Ann Miller, Leon Ames; **D:** Jack Donohue.

The Watcher ☆☆ 1973 A former U.S. attorney, gone underground, has a nervous breakdown and kills the narcotics agent who has him under surveillance. Self-important, too serious social/political conspiracy drama of the Watergate era. Keach and Yulin are good, but not good enough to save it. **95m/C VHS.** Stacy Keach, Harris Yulin, Bridgit Polk; **D:** John Parsons.

The Watcher ☆☆ 2000 **(R)** Serial killer Reeves leaves clues for burned-out FBI agent Spader as to who his next victim will be so Spader will get back in the game. Start with a direct-to-video feel, add a plot cribbed from better serial killer thrillers, throw in a bunch of showy visual effects, and you've got a night of talking back to the TV, MST3K-style. It's ridiculous, but that's half the fun. **97m/C VHS, DVD.** Keanu Reeves, James Spader, Marisa Tomei, Ernie Hudson, Chris Ellis, Robert Cicchini, Jenny (Jennifer) McShane, Yvonne Niami, Gina Alexander, Joe Sikora, Rebekah Louise Smith; **D:**

W: Joe Charbanic, David Elliot, Clay Ayers; **C:** Michael Chapman; **M:** Marco Beltrami.

The Watcher in the Woods ☆☆ 1981 **(PG)** When an American family rents an English country house, the children are haunted by the spirit of a long-missing young girl. A very bland attempt at a ghost story. **83m/C VHS, DVD.** Bette Davis, Carroll Baker, David MacCallum, Ian Bannen, Lynn-Holly Johnson, Kyle Richards, Frances Cuka, Richard Pasco; **D:** John Hough; **W:** Brian Clemens; **C:** Alan Hume; **M:** Stanley Myers.

Watchers ☆☆ 1988 **(R)** From the suspense novel by Dean R. Koontz, a secret experiment goes wrong, creating half-human monsters. A boy and his extremely intelligent dog are soon pursued. Low-budget Corman-influenced production is tacky but effective. **99m/C VHS, DVD.** Barbara Williams, Michael Ironside, Corey Haim, Duncan Fraser, Blu Mankuma, Dale Wilson, Colleen Winton; **D:** Jon Hess; **W:** Bill Freed; **C:** Richard Leiterman; **M:** Joel Goldsmith.

Watchers 2 ☆☆ 1990 **(R)** Sequel to "Watchers" follows the further adventures of a super-intelligent golden retriever who leads a Marine to an animal psychologist and then attempts to warn them both of a mutant killer. The dog says woof, but this movie doesn't quite. Fun for lovers of hounds or horror flicks. **101m/C VHS, DVD.** Marc Singer, Tracy Scoggins; **D:** Thierry Notz; **M:** Rick Conrad.

Watchers 3 ☆☆½ 1994 **(R)** A secret military outpost in the South American jungles is attacked by a carnivorous predator. Ex-military convicts are sent to rescue the remaining survivors and to make certain the government experiment that started the terror never comes to light. **85m/C VHS, DVD.** Wings Hauser, Gregory Scott Cummins, Daryl Roach, John K. Linton, Lolita Ronalds, Frank Novak; **D:** Jeremy Stanford.

Watchers Reborn ☆☆ 1998 **(R)** Genetically engineered mutants stalk the innocent with only a hyper-intelligent golden retriever (of course!) able to stop them. Based on the novel "Watchers" by Dean R. Koontz. **83m/C VHS, DVD.** Mark Hamill, Lisa Wilcox, Stephen Macht, Lou Rawls, Floyd Levine, Brenda Vaccaro, Leonard Rossiter, Valerie Perrine, Jimmie Walker; *Cameos:* Eric Clapton, George Harrison, Fred Gwynne, Ringo Starr; **D:** Dick Clement; **W:** Dick Clement, Ian La Frenais, Bill Persky.

Water ☆ 1985 **(PG-13)** The resident governor of a Caribbean British colony juggles various predatory interests when a valuable mineral water resource is found. The good cast is wasted in this a l-hoo-silly effort. **89m/C VHS, DVD.** *GB* Michael Caine, Gary Collins, Kane Hodder; **D:** Dick Clement; **W:** Sean Dash; **M:** Terry Plumeri.

Water ☆☆☆ 2005 **(PG-13)** Following Hindu custom in 1938 India, when child bride Chuyia's (Sarala) aged husband dies, her family sends her to live in exile with a ashram but falls in love with Narayan (Abraham), whose progressive views are inspired by Gandhi. However, their involvement leads to both tragedy and freedom. The last of Mehta's trilogy following "Fire" and "Earth." Hindi with subtitles. **117m/C DVD.** *CA* Seema Biswas, Lisa Ray, Rahul Khan, Sarala, Manorama, Vidula Javalgekar, Vinay Pathak, Seema Biswas, Gerson Da Cunha, Mohan Jhaaijani; **D:** Deepa Mehta; **C:** Giles Nuttgens; **M:** Michael Danna, A.R. Rahman.

Water Babies ☆☆ *Slip Slide Adventures* 1979 **(G)** When a chimney sweep's 12-year-old apprentice is wrongly accused of stealing silver, the boy and his dog fall into a pond and eventually rescue some of the characters they find there. Combination of live-action and animated fairy-tale story set in 19th-century London. Boring, unless you're a young child with equivalent standards. Based on the book by Charles Kingsley. **93m/C VHS, DVD.** *GB* James Mason, Billie Whitelaw, David Tomlinson, Paul Luty, Samantha Coates; **D:** Lionel Jeffries.

Water Drops on Burning Rocks

🐾🐾 ½ *Gouttes d'Eau sur Pierres Brulantes* 1999 Director Francois Ozon pays tribute to late German director Rainer Werner Fassbinder by resurrecting his unproduced play. In the '70s, 50-year-old businessman Leopold (Giraudeau) picks up 19-year-old Franz (Zidi), who winds up moving in, though the mismatched duo fight constantly. When Franz's former girlfriend, Anna (Sagnier), shows up, Leopold even begins seducing her. Then transexual Vera (Thomson), Leopold's ex-girlfriend, also comes back. And it's a very messy foursome, indeed. French with subtitles. **82m/C VHS, DVD.** *FR* Bernard Giraudeau, Anna Thomson, Malik Zidi, Ludivine Sagnier; *D:* Francois Ozon; *W:* Francois Ozon; *C:* Jeanne Lapoirie.

The Water Engine

🐾🐾 ½ 1992 Charles Lang (Macy) is a luckless machinist struggling to survive in Depression-era Chicago. Lang invents a remarkable engine, that runs on water, and holds the promise of limitless, cheap power. To protect his invention he finds a seedy patent attorney (Mahoney), which leads to the sinister Oberman (Mantegna), a mysterious and powerful figure who wants Lang's invention—at any cost. Based on the play by David Mamet. **110m/C VHS.** Charles Durning, Patti LuPone, William H. Macy, John Mahoney, Joe Mantegna, Joanna Miles, Mike Nussbaum, Treat Williams, Andrea Marcovicci, Peter Michael Goetz, David Mamet; *D:* Steven Schachter; *W:* David Mamet; *C:* Bryan England. CABLE

The Water Horse: Legend of the Deep

🐾🐾 ½ 2007 (PG) The water horse turns out to be the Loch Ness Monster and this charming family film explains how it got into that Scottish loch. Lonely young Angus (Etel) is living with his stern housekeeper mum (Watson) and sister Kirstie (Xi) on a Scottish estate while dad is off fighting in WWII. Angus finds an egg on the beach that hatches into a cute, mischievous critter. Angus names Crusoe that soon grows to mammoth size. So he must secretly be transported to the loch under the noses of snooty British soldiers stationed on the property. Visual effects are good. Based on the novel by Dick King-Smith. **111m/C DVD.** *GB US* Alexander Nathan) Etel, Emily Watson, Ben Chaplin, David Morrissey, Priyanka Xi, Brian Cox; *D:* Jay Russell; *W:* Robert Nelson Jacobs; *C:* Oliver Stapleton; *M:* James Newton Howard.

The Waterboy

🐾🐾 1998 (PG-13) Another in a continuing line of deliberately stupid comedies finds Sandler a not-too-bright, constantly picked-on waterboy for a lousy Louisiana college football team. After a player taunts him once too often, he tackles the big guy, and is suddenly promoted to player—much to the dismay of his over-protective mother, Bates. Loser player turns loser team into winners after some contrived obstacles; you've seen it before, but Sandler cultists will love it anyway. **90m/C VHS, DVD.** Adam Sandler, Kathy Bates, Henry Winkler, Fairuza Balk, Jerry Reed, Larry (Lawrence) Gilliard Jr., Blake Clark, Rob Schneider; *C:* Clint Howard, Allen Whiting, Robert Kokol; *D:* Frank Coraci; *W:* Tim Herlihy, Adam Sandler; *C:* Steven Bernstein; *M:* Alan Pasqua.

The Waterdance

🐾🐾🐾 1991 (R) Autobiographical film based on the experiences of writer/co-director Jimenez. When writer Joel Garcia (Stoltz) is paralyzed in a hiking accident he finds himself dealing with not only the rehab process itself but his feelings, the feelings of his married lover, and those of his fellow patients. Deals unsentimentally, with all the physical adjustments, including the sexual ones. Resolution may be predictable but the performances rise above any script weaknesses. The title refers to Hill's dream of drown-

ing if he stops. **106m/C VHS, DVD.** Eric Stoltz, Wesley Snipes, William Forsythe, Helen Hunt, Elizabeth Pena, Grace Zabriskie; *D:* Neal Jimenez, Michael Steinberg; *W:* Neal Jimenez; *C:* Mark Plummer; *M:* Michael Convertino. Ind. Spirit '93: First Feature, Screenplay; Sundance '92: Screenplay, Aud. Award.

Waterfront

🐾🐾 ½ 1939 Dreary dockside melodrama, with drinking and brawling longshoreman Jim (Morgan) avenging his brother's death. Based on the play "Blindspot" by Kenyon Nicholson. **59m/B VHS.** Dennis Morgan, Gloria Dickson, Marie Wilson, Larry Williams, Sheila (Manors) Mannors, Ward Bond, Frank Faylen; *D:* Terry Morse; *W:* Arthur Ripley, Lee Katz.

Waterfront

🐾🐾 1944 Nazis coerce German-Americans into helping them in WWII-era San Francisco. Credibility defying spy doings, but that's okay. Fairly entertaining wartime drama about paranoia on the home front. **68m/B VHS, DVD.** John Carradine, J. Carrol Naish, Terry Frost, Maris Wrixon, Edwin Maxwell; *D:* Steve Sekely.

Waterfront

🐾🐾 ½ 1983 Effective romantic drama set in Melbourne, Australia. Australian workers strike after taking forced pay cuts. As a result, Italian immigrants are hired as scabs to keep the docks going. Despite the tension, an Italian woman and an Australian man fall deeply in love, only to find that they must struggle to keep that love alive. **294m/C VHS.** *AU* Jack Thompson, Greta Scacchi, Frank Gallacher, Tony Rickards, Mark Little, Jay Mannering, Ray Barrett, Chris Haywood, Warren Mitchell, Noni Hazlehurst, John Karlsen, Elin Jenkins; *D:* Chris Thomson.

Waterhole Number 3

🐾🐾 ½ 1967 (PG) Three Confederate army buddies steal a fortune in gold bullion from the Union Army and hide it in a waterhole in the desert. One of the funnier entries in the Western comedy genre. **95m/C VHS, DVD.** James Coburn, Carroll O'Connor, Margaret Blye, Claude Akins, Bruce Dern, Joan Blondell, James Whitmore; *D:* William A. Graham; *C:* Robert Burks; *M:* Dave Grusin.

Waterland

🐾🐾 1992 (R) Meandering drama about a history teacher who tries to solve a personal crisis by using his class as a sounding board to describe his troubled past in England. Dark secrets abound, including incest, madness, murder, and the terrifying love between the teacher and his childhood bride. Melancholy, overwrought but partially redeemed by the lead performances of Irons and his (real-life and cinematic) wife, Cusack. The film's setting has been unfortunately moved from London to Pittsburgh, destroying story links. Based on the novel by Graham Swift. **95m/C VHS, DVD.** Jeremy Irons, Ethan Hawke, Sinead Cusack, John Heard, Grant Warnock, Lena Headey, Pete Postlethwaite, Cara Buono; *D:* Stephen Gyllenhaal; *W:* Peter Prince; *C:* Robert Elswit; *M:* Carter Burwell.

Waterloo

🐾🐾 1971 (G) Massive chronicle of Napoleon's European conquests and eventual defeat at the hands of Wellington. Filmed on location in Italy and the Ukraine, it bombed due largely to Steiger's bizarre rendition of Napoleon. **122m/C VHS.** *IT RU* Rod Steiger, Orson Welles, Virginia McKenna, Michael Wilding, Donal Donnelly, Christopher Plummer, Jack Hawkins, Dan O'Herlihy, Terence Alexander, Rupert Davies, Ivo Garrani, Gianni "John" Garko, Ian Ogilvy, Andrea Checchi, Jean Louis, Willoughby Gray, John Savident, Adrian Brine, Jeffrey Wickham, Sergei Zakariadze, Richard Heffer, Aldo Cecconi, Peter Davies, Eugene Samoilov; *D:* Sergei Bondarchuk; *W:* Sergei Bondarchuk, H.A.L. Craig, Vittorio Bonicelli; *C:* Armando Nannuzzi; *M:* Nino Rota.

Waterloo Bridge

🐾🐾🐾 1940 In London during WWI, Capt. Roy Cronin (Taylor), a soldier from an aristocratic family, begins a tragic romance with ballet dancer Myra Lester (Leigh) when they meet by chance on the foggy Waterloo Bridge. She loses her job and when Roy is listed as dead, Myra's despair turns her to prostitution. But when Roy returns from POW camp, they once again meet by accident on Waterloo Bridge, and their romance resumes, with Myra struggling to conceal her shameful secret. Four-hanky drama with fine performances by Leigh (her first after "Gone with the Wind") and

Taylor. Based on the play by Robert E. Sherwood. **109m/B VHS, DVD.** Vivien Leigh, Robert Taylor, Lucile Watson, Sir C. Aubrey Smith, Maria Ouspenskaya, Virginia Field; *D:* Mervyn LeRoy; *W:* S.N. Behrman, George Froeschel, Hans Rameau; *C:* Joseph Ruttenberg; *M:* Herbert Stothart.

Watermelon Man

🐾🐾 1970 (R) The tables are turned for a bigoted white guy when he wakes up one morning to discover he has become a black man. Broad comedy with not much place to go is still engaging. Cambridge takes on both roles, appearing in unconvincing white makeup. **97m/C VHS, DVD.** Godfrey Cambridge, Erin Moran, Estelle Parsons, Howard Caine, D'Urville Martin, Kay Kimberly, Paul Williams; *D:* Melvin Van Peebles; *W:* Herman Raucher; *C:* Herman Raucher; *M:* Melvin Van Peebles.

The Watermelon Woman

🐾🐾 1997 Cheryl (Dunye) is a young, black, lesbian video store clerk who wants to be a documentary filmmaker. She becomes obsessed with a black actress seen in some 1930s black films, who was known only as the "Watermelon Woman." Doing research, Cheryl discovers the woman's name was Fae Richards (Bronson) and that she was a lesbian who had an affair with her white director. While deciding to film a documentary about Fae, Cheryl's personal life begins to parallel Fae's when she briefly falls for white customer, Diana (Turner). **85m/C VHS, DVD.** Cheryl Dunye, Valerie Walker, Guinevere Turner, Lisa Marie Bronson; *D:* Cheryl Dunye; *W:* Cheryl Dunye; *C:* Michelle Crenshaw; *M:* Paul Shapiro.

Waterproof

🐾🐾🐾 1999 (PG-13) Reynolds is oddly cast but very effective as Eli, a Jewish shopkeeper who is shot by a young would-be robber, Thaniel (Dye). To protect him from prosecution, Thaniel's mother, Tyree (Grace), whisks her son and Eli to her childhood home in Waterproof, Louisiana. She's been away for 15 years and finds a great deal of tension with her family, but they are willing to take Tyree and Thaniel in to assist them. The film examines the struggles that exist between family members and individuals from differing ethnic backgrounds. Delivers positive message while being entertaining. Special kudos to Jones, who overcomes his comic reputation by portraying a man with severe brain damage. **94m/C DVD.** Burt Reynolds, April Grace, Cordereau Dye, Whitman Mayo, Anthony Lee, Orlando Jones, Ja'net DuBois; *D:* Barry Berman.

Water's Edge

🐾🐾 ½ 2003 (R) Tense little thriller finds New Yorkers Robert (Fillion) and Molly (West) relocating to a small town and the rustic lakeside cabin that Robert inherited from his father. But this friendly town hides some dirty secrets, including blackmail and murder. **7m/C VHS, DVD.** Nathan Fillion, Chandra West, Emmanuelle Vaugier, Daniel Baldwin, Andrew Moxham; *D:* Harvey Kahn; *W:* Craig Brewer. VIDEO

Watership Down

🐾🐾 ½ 1978 (PG) Wonderfully animated story based on Richard Adams's allegorical novel about how a group of rabbits escape fear and overcome oppression while searching for a new and better home. It's really an adult theme with sufficient violence to the poor wittle wabbits to scare the kiddies. **92m/C VHS, DVD.** *GB D:* Martin Rosen; *W:* Martin Rosen; *V:* Richard Briers, Ralph Richardson, Zero Mostel, John Hurt, Denholm Elliott, Harry Andrews, Michael Hordern, Joss Ackland.

Waterworld

🐾🐾 1995 (PG-13) "The Man From Atlantis" meets "Mad Max." Industry knives sharpened with glee before release, with some insiders calling this luck-impaired project "Fishtar" and "Kevin's Gate." Most of the estimated $150 million budget seems to have ended up on screen, which makes for a visually striking, and at times daunting, film. Costner, who did just about everything but can-can the meals, stars as Mariner, a mutant man-fish who reluctantly helps human survivors search for the mythical Dryland since the polar ice caps melted, flooding the earth. The bad guys are the Smokers, led by the evil Hopper, who can play these roles in his sleep. Entertaining, but not riv-

eting, as the budget and PR hype leads one to expect. The floating set was anchored (not very well, apparently) off the Hawaiian coast and was lost once during a tropical storm. Costner bet the boat on this one and lost more than just money. **135m/C VHS, DVD, HD DVD.** Jack Kehler, Zakes Mokae, Sab Shimono, Jack Black, Kim Coates, John Toles-Bey, Ari Barak, Sean M. Whalen, Robert LaSardo, Lee Arenberg, Kevin Costner, Dennis Hopper, Jeanne Tripplehorn, Tina Majorino, Michael Jeter, R.D. Call, Robert Joy; *D:* Kevin Reynolds; *W:* Peter Rader, Marc Norman, David N. Twohy; *C:* Dean Semler; *M:* James Newton Howard. Golden Raspberries '95: Worst Support. Actor (Hopper).

Wavelength

🐾🐾 ½ 1983 (PG) A rock star living in the Hollywood Hills with his girlfriend stumbles on an ultra-secret government project involving friendly aliens from outer space recovered from a recent UFO crash site. Fun, enthusiastically unoriginal cheap sci-fi. Soundtrack by Tangerine Dream. **87m/C VHS.** Bobby DiCicco, Robert Carradine, Cherie Currie, Keenan Wynn; *D:* Mike Gray; *W:* Mike Gray; *M:* Tangerine Dream.

Wavelength

🐾🐾 ½ 1996 (R) Physicist and Oxford professor Paul Higgins (Piven) has a few problems—a wife, Claire (Williams), a girlfriend, Lucy (Walker), Lucy's father who just happens to be the head of the physics department, and a mysterious presence (Attenborough) who's trying to help Paul with his research on nuclear fission. Piven's character is so selfish you'll wonder why either woman wants him and the happy ending feels contrived. **94m/C VHS.** *GB* Jeremy Piven, Kelli Williams, Liza Walker, James Villiers, James Faulkner, Richard Attenborough, Byrne Piven, Nicholas Marco, Dominic West; *D:* Benjamin Fry; *W:* Benjamin Fry; *C:* Chris Middleton; *M:* Michael Storey.

Wax Mask

🐾🐾 ½ *M.D.C. Maschera di Cera* 1997 Liner notes state that this loose remake of "House of Wax" was to have been directed by Lucio Fulci ("Zombie," "The Black Cat") who died before he could begin work. It was produced in part by Dario Argento, but the important thing for horror fans to know is that this one owes just as much to Stuart Gordon's "Re-Animator." It takes the same gleeful approach to outrageous medical horror and sex, though overall, it is a much more polished looking film with expensive production values, an attractive (if unknown in America) young cast, and a sharply focused image. The setting is Paris and Rome in the early 20th century. Sonia (Mondello) witnessed the brutal murder of her parents as a child. Years later, she goes to work for Boris Volkoff (Hossein), whose macabre wax museum hides terrible secrets. Director Sergio Stivaletti came to the job through special effects expertise and his work here (in both capacities) is very good. This is a man to watch. The plot goes much too far for the film ever to find a large mainstream audience, and that's the point of Grand Guignol horror. **98m/C VHS.** Gabriella Giorgelli; *IT FR* Robert Hossein, Romina Mondello, Ricardo Serventi Longhi; *D:* Sergio Stivaletti; *W:* Lucio Fulci; *C:* Sergio Salvati. VIDEO

Wax, or the Discovery of Television among the Bees

🐾🐾 ½ 1993 Intricate and eccentric fable dealing with alternate realities and perceptions. Jacob Maker (Blair) keeps a hive of very unusual bees, a family legacy passed down from his grandfather. Jacob begins experiencing a eerie communication with his bees and suffering mysterious blackouts, which cause him to perceive the world through blurred bee vision. New Mexico desert setting provides a surreal and desolate landscape. **85m/C VHS.** David Blair, Meg Savlov, Florence Ormezzano, William S. Burroughs; *D:* David Blair; *W:* David Blair; *M:* Beo Morales, Brooks Williams.

Waxwork

🐾🐾 ½ 1988 (R) A wax museum opens up, and it is soon evident that the dummies are not what they seem. Garbled nonthriller. Available in a 100-minute unrated version. **97m/C VHS, DVD.** Zach Galligan, Deborah Foreman, Michelle Johnson, Dana Ashbrook, Miles O'Keeffe, Patrick McNee, David Warner, John Rhys-Davies; *D:* Anthony

Hickox; **W:** Anthony Hickox; **C:** Gerry Lively; **M:** Roger Bellon.

Waxwork 2: Lost in Time ♂♂½ *Lost in Time* 1991 (R) A young couple (Galligan and Schnarre) barely escape with their lives when the in-famous waxworks museum burns down. A severed hand also gets loose and follows Schnarre home and murders her stepfa-ther, leaving her to take the blame. In or-der to prove her innocence, the couple must travel through a bizarre time ma-chine. Extraordinary special effects, strange plot twists, and recreations of scenes from past horror movies make this a highly entertaining sequel. 104m/C VHS, DVD. Zach Galligan, Alexander Godunov, Bruce Campbell, Michael Des Barres, Monica Schnarre, Martin Kemp, Sophie Ward, Marina Sirtis, Juliet Mills, John Ireland, Patrick Macnee, David Carra-dine, Drew Barrymore; **D:** Anthony Hickox; **W:** Henrik Galeen.

Way Back Home ♂♂ *Old Greatheart; Other People's Business* 1932 Man wants to adopt a boy to release him from the clutches of his cruel guardian. Minor role for the then unknown Davis. 81m/B VHS, DVD. Frank Albertson, Bette Davis; **D:** William A. Seiter; **M:** Max Steiner.

Way Down East ♂♂♂ 1920 Me-lodramatic silent drama of a country girl who is tricked into a fake marriage by a scheming playboy. The famous final scene of Gish adrift on the ice floes is in color. One of Griffith's last critical and pop-ular successes. This tape includes the original Griffith-approved musical score. Remade in 1935 with Henry Fonda. 107m/B VHS, DVD. Lillian Gish, Richard Barthelmess, Lowell Sherman, Creighton Hale, Burr McIntosh, Kate Bruce, Florence Short; **D:** D.W. Griffith; **W:** D.W. Griffith, Joseph R. Grismer; **C:** Billy (G.W.) Bitzer, Hendrik Sartov.

Way Down South ♂½ 1939 The orphan son of a plantation owner tries to take over his father's estate, only to find out that the place has been run into the ground by a corrupt lawyer and a cruel slave driver. Black poet Hughes and actor Muse collaborated on the screenplay. German-born director Vorhaus was in his second year in Hollywood, after making his mark in Britain directing talkies. ♫ Good Ground; Louisiana; Nobody Know De Trouble I See; Sometimes I Feel Like a Motherless Child; Lord I You Can't Come Send One Angel Down. 62m/B VHS, DVD. Bobby Breen, Alan Mowbray, Ralph Morgan, Clar-ence Muse, Steffi Duna, Sally Bane, Edwin Max-well, Matthew "Stymie" Beard, Lillian Yarbo, Charles Middleton; **D:** Bernard Vorhaus; **W:** Clar-ence Muse, Langston Hughes.

Way He Was ♂♂ 1976 (PG) A satir-ical re-enactment of the events that led up to the Watergate burglary and the coverup that followed. 87m/C VHS, Steve Friedman, Al Lewis, Merrie Lynn Ross, Doodles Weaver; **D:** Mark L. Lester.

The Way Home ♂♂♂ 2001 (PG) Because his mother has lost her job, a seven-year-old boy (Yoo) is forced to leave the city of Seoul to stay with his wiz-ened mute grandmother (Kim) in her ran-shackle rural hut. The spoiled kid can't be-lieve he has to do without fast food, let alone indoor plumbing and other modern conveniences. But what the boy eventual-ly comes to realize is that his grandmother loves him unconditionally. Korean with subtitles. 85m/C VHS, DVD. KN Seung-Ho Yoo, Eul-Boon Kim, Hyo-Hee Dong; **D:** Jeong-Hyang Lee; **W:** Jeong-Hyang Lee; **C:** Hong-Shik Yoon; **M:** Dae-Hong Kim, Yan-Hee Kim.

A Way of Life ♂½ 2004 One of those unrelentingly bleak British kitchen-sink dramas with a completely unsympath-etic lead. Leigh-Anne is a young, trouble-prone, unemployed single mum who hangs out with a bunch of racist losers to the concern of her granny, who wants cus-tody of Leigh-Ann's baby daughter. When she takes the baby to the hospital after a minor accident, suspicious doctors insist on keeping the child and paranoid Leigh-Anne blames her immigrant neighbor for her problems, resulting in more tragedy. 91m/C DVD. Brenda Blethyn, Nathan Jones, Ste-phanie James, Gary Sheppeard, Dean Wong, Sara Gregory, Oliver Haden; **D:** Amma Asante; **W:** Amma Asante; **C:** Ian Wilson; **M:** David Gray.

Way of the Black Dragon ♂ 1981 When slave-trading drug traffickers threaten the moral fiber of our nation, two commandoes join forces to halt their oper-ation. 88m/C VHS, DVD. Ron Van Cliet, Carter Wang, Charles Bonet; **D:** Chan Wui Ngai.

Way of the Gun ♂♂½ 2000 (R) Two unsuccessful career criminals (Phil-lippe and Del Toro) take up kidnapping and hold a surrogate mother (Lewis) for ransom. Only the parents-to-be are mobbed up and send two thugs (Diggs and Katt) and a philosophical enforcer (Caan) to get her back unharmed. McQuarrie shows that he still has the knack for twisty plots, surprise revelations, and cool dialogue, but he lets the pro-ceedings drag on a little longer than they need to. He's also not shy about heaping on the violence and crude language (which isn't necessarily bad, just consider yourself forewarned). 118m/C VHS, DVD. Ryan Phillippe, Benicio Del Toro, Juliette Lewis, James Caan, Taye Diggs, Nicky Katt, Scott Wilson, Kristen Lehman, Geoffrey Lewis, Dylan Kussman; **D:** Christopher McQuarrie; **W:** Christopher McQuarrie; **C:** Dick Pope; **M:** Joe Kraemer.

Way of the West ♂½ 1935 Them durn pesky sheepherders are up to it again! Okay, so the cow/sheep thing is a classic western plot, but here it's offered perfunctorily. 52m/B VHS, Wally Wales, William Desmond, Art Mix, Jim Sheridan, Bobby Nelson; **D:** Robert Emmett Tansey.

The Way Out ♂♂ *Dial 999* 1956 Av-erage crime drama starring Nelson as a fugitive accused of killing a bookie. 90m/C VHS. GB Gene Nelson, Mona Freeman, John Bentley, Michael Goodliffe, Sydney Tafler; **D:** Montgomery Tully.

Way Out West ♂♂♂ 1937 The classic twosome journey way out west to deliver the deed to a gold mine to the daughter of their late prospector pal. He'll be laughing so hard you won't notice. One of Stan and Ollie's best. Score includes the song "Trail of the Lonesome Pine." Also included on this tape is a 1932 Todd and Pitts short, "Red Noses." Available colorized. 86m/B VHS, DVD. Stan Laurel, Oliver Hardy, Rosina Lawrence, James Finlayson, Shar-on Lynne, Zasu Pitts, William Haines; **D:** James W. Horne.

Way Past Cool ♂ 2000 (R) Two gangs, both made up of pre-teens, are pit-ted against each other by a drug dealer, with all the gang staples, in-cluding turf battles, shootouts, drinking (and we're not talking juice boxes), and swearing. Sorry, can't think of a single re-deeming thing about it. 96m/C VHS, DVD. Kareem Woods, Wes Charles Jr., Jonathan Roger Neal, Luchaina Evans, D'andre Jenkins, Desmond Jenkins, Partap Khalsa; **D:** Adam Davidson; **W:** Yule Caise, Jess Mowry; **C:** Amy Vincent; **M:** Zen Amen. VIDEO

The Way We Live Now ♂♂½ 2002 Based on the 1875 novel by Anthony Trollope, this adaptation centers around shady financier Augustus Melmotte (Su-chel). An economic boom is sweeping through Europe in the 1870s and Mel-motte arrives in London with a scheme to buy himself a place in Victorian society. Melmotte is even willing to sacrifice his daughter Marie (Henderson) who has de-veloped an infatuation for debt-ridden but aristocratic Sir Felix Carbury (Macfadyen). The question for all this greedy bunch is who will get the better of whom? 300m/C VHS, DVD. GB David Suchet, Shirley Henderson, Matthew MacFadyen, Cheryl Campbell, Paloma Baeza, Douglas Hodge, Miranda Otto, Cillian Mur-phy, Michael Riley, Allan Cordurier, David Bradley, Jim Carter, Oliver Ford Davies, Joanna Davies; **D:** David Yates; **W:** Andrew Davies; **C:** Chris Seager; **M:** Nicholas Hooper. TV

The Way We Were ♂♂♂ 1973 (PG) Big boxoffice hit follows a love story between opposites from the 1930s to the 1950s. Streisand is a Jewish political radi-cal who meets the handsome WASP Red-ford at college. They're immediately at-tracted to one another, but it takes years before they act on it and eventually marry. They move to Hollywood where Redford is a screenwriter and left-wing Streisand be-comes involved in the Red scare and the blacklist, much to Redford's dismay. Though always in love, their differences are too great to keep them together. An old-fashioned and sweet romance, with much gloss. Hit title song sung by Strei-sand. Adapted by Arthur Laurents from his novel. ♫ The Way We Were. 118m/C VHS, DVD. Barbra Streisand, Robert Redford, Bradford Dillman, Viveca Lindfors, Herb Edelman, Murray Hamilton, Patrick O'Neal, James Woods, Sally Kirkland, Lois Chiles, Susan Blakely, Allyn Ann McLerie, Marcia Mae Jones, Diana Ewing, George Gaynes; **D:** Sydney Pollack; **W:** Arthur Laurents; **C:** Harry Stradling Jr.; **M:** Marvin Hamlisch. Oscars '73: Song ("The Way We Were"), Orig. Dramatic Score; Golden Globes '74: Song ("The Way We Were").

The Way West ♂♂½ 1967 A wag-on train heads to Oregon. A poor and muddled attempt at recreating the style of a John Ford western. What really galls is that it's based on the Pulitzer-winning nov-el by A.B. Guthrie Jr. Eoy; is the book bet-ter than the movie. Field's first film. 122m/C VHS, Kirk Douglas, Robert Mitchum, Richard Wid-mark, Lola Albright, Michael Witney, Stubby Kaye, Sally Field, Jack Elam; **D:** Andrew V. McLaglen; **C:** William Clothier.

Wayne Murder Case ♂♂♂ A *Strange Adventure* 1932 A fast-moving, clev-erly constructed murder mystery. A rich but cranky old man asks a new will. Though no one was standing near him a knife is found stuck in his back. 61m/B VHS, DVD. June Clyde, Regis Too-mey, Jason Robards Sr., Lucille LaVerne; **D:** Hampton Del Ruth, Philip H. (Phil. P.H.) Whitman; **W:** Arthur Hoerl; **C:** Leon Shamroy.

Wayne's World ♂♂♂ 1992 (PG-13) Destined to become one of the top movies of all time—Not! This "Saturday Night Live" skit proved to be so popular that it got its own movie, not unlike the plot, which has slimy producer Benjamin Oliver (Lowe) take the public access "Wayne's World" into the world of com-mercial television. The zany duo of Wayne (Myers) and Garth (Carvey) are as much fun on the big screen as they were on SNL and there are many funny moments, sev-eral of which are destined to become com-edy classics. A huge boxoffice hit that spawned a sequel. It also spawned Lorne Michael's desperate attempts to match its success with other non-bigscreen wor-thy skits from the show. 93m/C VHS, DVD. Mike Myers, Dana Carvey, Rob Lowe, Tia Carrere, Brian Doyle-Murray, Lara Flynn Boyle, Kurt Fuller, Colleen Camp, Donna Dixon, Ed O'Neill, Alice Cooper, Meat Loaf Aday; **D:** Penelope Spheeris; **W:** Mike Myers, Bonnie Turner, Terry Turner; **C:** Theo van den Ende; **M:** J. Peter Robinson. MTV Movie Awards '92: On-Screen Duo (Mike Myers/Dana Carvey).

Wayne's World 2 ♂♂ 1993 (PG-13) Good-natured rerun of the original has plenty of sophomoric gags, but feels tired. Wayne and Garth are on their own, planning a major concert, Waynestock. "If you book them they will come," "Jim Morri-son says in a dream. Meanwhile, Wayne's girlfriend (Carrere) is falling for slimeball record promoter Walken. Offers a few bril-liant funny segments. If you liked the origi-nal, get ready for the Village People here. Heston has a funny cameo, and Walken and Basinger push the limits without going over the top. Feature film debut for direc-tor Surjik. 94m/C VHS, DVD. Mike Myers, Dana Carvey, Tia Carrere, Christopher Walken, Ralph Brown, Kim Basinger, James Hong, Chris Farley, Ed O'Neil, Olivia D'Abo, Kevin Pollak, Drew Barry-more, Charlton Heston, Rip Taylor, Bob Odenkirk, Michael A. (M.A.) Nickles; **D:** Stephen Surjik; **W:** Bonnie Turner, Terry Turner, Mike Myers; **C:** Fran-cis Kenny; **M:** Carter Burwell.

The Wayward Wife ♂♂ *La Pro-vinciale* 1952 Young woman, married to a university professor, is blackmailed over her less-than-respectable past. Based on the novel by Alberto Moravia. Italian with subtitles. 92m/B VHS. IT Gina Lollobrigida, Ga-briele Ferzetti, Franco Interlenghi, Renato Baldini; **D:** Mario Soldati.

We All Loved Each Other So Much ♂♂♂½ 1977 Sensitive come-dy follows three friends over 30 years, be-ginning at the end of WWII. All three have loved the same woman, an actress. Hom-age to friendship and to postwar Italian cinema. Includes a full-scale re-creation of the fountain scene in "La Dolce Vita." In Italian with English subtitles. 124m/C VHS. IT Vittorio Gassman, Nino Manfredi, Stefano Satta Flores, Stefania Sandrelli, Marcello Mastroi-anni, Federico Fellini, Anita Ekberg, Vittorio De Sica; **D:** Ettore Scola.

We Are Marshall ♂♂♂ 2006 (PG) The tight-knit community of Hunting-ton, West Virginia, grieves after the real-life tragedy of a plane crash that killed 75 coaches, staff, and boosters in 1970. The school's president decides to continue the program until the student body gathers to-gether with its "We are Marshall" pep-ral-ly chant (repeated often throughout). En-ter coach Jack Lengyel (a spirited McCo-naughey) to lead the piecing together of the team and win over the doubters. Oc-casional goosebumpy moments give way to a dull script and oddly enough entirely too much on-field action. 131m/C DVD, Blu-ray Disc, HD DVD. US Matthew McConaughey, Ian McShane, Kate Mara, January Jones, Kimberly Williams; **D:** McG; **W:** Jamie Linden; **C:** Shane Hurlbut; **M:** Christophe Beck.

We Are the Children ♂♂ 1987 Cynical reporter covering the famine in Ethiopia meets an idealistic nurse who's been living there for years. Romance blos-soms among the starving in made-for-TV drama, co-produced by Danson. 92m/C VHS. Ally Sheedy, Ted Danson, Judith Ivey, Zia Mohyeddin; **D:** Robert M. Young.

We Dive at Dawn ♂♂♂ 1943 Interesting, tense British submarine dra-ma. The "Sea Tiger" attempts to sink the German battleship "Brandenburg" off Denmark. Good cast. Mills prepared for the role by riding in an actual submarine, turning "a pale shade of pea-green" when it crash-dived. 98m/B VHS, DVD. G3 Eric Port-man, John Mills; **D:** Anthony Asquith; **W:** Val Val-entine; **C:** Jack Cox.

We Don't Live Here Anymore ♂♂♂ 2004 (R) A quartet of 30-somethings discover adultery and be-trayal have repercussions in this adapta-tion of two novellas by Andre Dubus. His friends Jack (Ruffalo) and Hank (Krause) teach at a small college; Jack's married to Terry (Dern), Hank to Edith (Watts). Both couples have children; neither marriage is happy. Jack and Edith are in lust and en-joy woodland trysts while waiting to get caught. Serial womanizer Hank is seem-ingly unconcerned when he finds out but Terry is driven by fury to punish Jack by screwing Hank and then telling her hus-band—who doesn't react as expected. They're whiny, indecisive, self-involved, angry, weak, occasionally passionate, but not a group you'd want to spend a lot of time with (despite the capable perfor-mances from all four actors). 101m/C DVD. US Mark Ruffalo, Laura Dern, Peter Krause, Nao-mi Watts, Jennifer Bishop, Sam Charles, Haili Page; **D:** John Curran; **W:** Larry Gross; **C:** Maryse Alberti; **M:** Lesley Barber, Laurie Parker.

We of the Never Never ♂♂♂ 1982 (G) In turn-of-the-century Australia a city-bred woman marries a cattle rancher and moves from civilized Melbourne to the barren outback of the Northern Territory. Based on the autobiographical story writ-ten by Jeannie Gunn, the first white wom-an to travel in the aboriginal wilderness. She finds herself fighting for her own rights as well as for those of the abori-gines in this sincere, well-done film. 136m/

We

C VHS, DVD. AU Angela Punch McGregor, Arthur Dignam, Tony Barry; D: Igor Auzins.

We Own the Night 🎬🎬 2007 (R) Nightclub manager Bobby (Phoenix) has distanced himself from his cop father Bert (Duvall) and brother Joseph (Wahlberg) to work for Russian mobster Marat (Moshonov). After a raid, Vadim attacks Joseph, and Bobby nervously agrees to become an informant. The performances are okay (everyone's done better work) but Mendes is inarguably hot as Bobby's personal party girl. Set in late 1980s Brooklyn, this stark crime story superficially harkens back to the police dramas of the 70s. 117m/C DVD, Blu-ray Disc. US Joaquin Rafael (Leaf) Phoenix, Mark Wahlberg, Robert Duvall, Eva Mendes, Moni Moshonov, Alex Veadov, Danny Hoch, Tony Musante, Antoni Corone; D: James Gray; W: James Gray; C: Joaquin Baca-Asay; M: Wojciech Kilar.

We the Living 🎬🎬½ 1942 The torpid long-lost and restored Italian version of Ayn Rand's unique political tome. Deals with a young Soviet woman in revolutionary Petrograd who is slowly ruined by the system and her affair with a romantic counter-revolutionary. Made under the Fascists' nose during WWII. A fascinating dialectic between utopian melodrama and Rand dogma. In Italian with subtitles. 174m/B VHS. IT Alida Valli, Rossano Brazzi, Fosco Giachetti; D: Goffredo Alessandrini.

We Think the World of You 🎬🎬 1988 (PG) When bisexual Oldman goes to prison, his lover Bates, whose feelings are unresolved and complex, finds friendship with Oldman's dog. Odd, oft-bitter comedy-drama of love and loyalty characterized by excellent acting and respectful, gentle direction. From the novel by Joseph R. Ackerly. 94m/C VHS. GB Alan Bates, Gary Oldman, Frances Barber, Liz Smith, Max Wall, Kerry Wise; D: Colin Gregg.

We Were Soldiers 🎬🎬🎬½ 2002 (R) Writer-director Wallace once again tackles the fact-based military epic, with outstanding results. Recounting the battle of the Ia Drang Valley in 1965, the first major land battle for U.S. troops in Vietnam, the story focuses on Lt. Col. Hal Moore (Gibson) and his leadership of the 7th Air Cavalry at LZ X-Ray. Moore's combination of experience, leadership, instinct, knowledge, and genuine concern for his men make him seem too good to be true, but Gibson's portrayal, and the fact that Moore is real, help to erase disbelief. Inevitable comparisons with "Black Hawk Down" are justified, as both pics deal with chaotic battlefields and the heroism of the soldiers who must fight their way out of situations they were trained, but not quite prepared, for. But this movie goes beyond the battle to show the impact to families back home, as well as giving a nod of respect to the enemy. Elliot stands out as Moore's right-hand man, as does Pepper as reporter Galloway, while Stein, Russell, and Kinnear do well playing against type. Based on the book "We Were Soldiers Once...and Young" by Lt. Gen. Harold G. Moore (Ret.) and Joseph L. Galloway. 137m/C VHS, DVD, Blu-ray Disc, HD DVD. US Mel Gibson, Madeleine Stowe, Greg Kinnear, Sam Elliott, Chris Klein, Keri Russell, Barry Pepper, Don Duong, Ryan Hurst, Marc Blucas, Jsu Garcia, Clark Gregg, Desmond Harrington, Blake Heron, Dylan Walsh, Robert Bagnell, Josh Daugherty, Jon Hamm, Erik MacArthur, Simbi Khali, Mark McCracken, Taylor Momsen, Daniel Roebuck, Keith Szarabajka, Sloane Momsen, Matthew Lang, Edwin Morrow, Bellinger C. Tran; D: Randall Wallace; W: Randall Wallace; C: Dean Semler; M: Nick Glennie-Smith.

We Will Not Enter the Forest 🎬🎬🎬 1979 Moral dilemmas afflict a group of French Resistance fighters during WWII when they must decide what to do with four German deserters they've captured. In French with subtitles. 88m/C VHS. FR Richard Leduc, Siegfried Rauch, Jacques Higelin, Georges Claisse, Sylvain Joubert, Marie-France Pisier; D: Georges Dumoulin; W: Catherine Varlin; C: Alain Derobe; M: Michel Sendrez.

The Weaker Sex 🎬🎬½ 1949 Typical patriotic British weepie finds a British widow and her daughters trying to hold on to hope as D-Day approaches. 89m/B VHS. GB Ursula Jeans, Cecil Parker, Joan Hopkins, Derek Bond, Lana Morris; D: Roy Ward Baker.

Weapons of Mass Distraction 🎬🎬 1997 (R) Two megalomaniacal multimedia tycoons set out to destroy each other in this black comedy. Lionel Powers (Byrne) wants to buy pro football's Tucson Titans and so does his arch-rival Julian Messenger (Kingsley). So there's bribery and blackmail and airing of dirty family laundry all over the place. No heroes here but occasionally some sharp satire. 105m/C VHS, DVD. Gabriel Byrne, Ben Kingsley, Mimi Rogers, Jeffrey Tambor, Illeana Douglas, Paul Mazursky, Kathy Baker, Chris Mulkey, R. Lee Ermey, Caroline Aaron, Jason Lee, Christina Pickles; D: Stephen Surjik; W: Larry Gelbart; C: Alar Kivilo; M: Don Davis. CABLE

Weather in the Streets 🎬🎬½ 1984 (PG) A young woman enters into an ill-fated love affair after spending a few moments with an aristocratic married man. Cliched drama set in England features two world wars. 108m/C VHS, DVD. Michael York, Joanna Lumley, Lisa Eichhorn, Isabel Dean, Norman Pitt; M: Carl Davis.

The Weather Man 🎬🎬½ 2005 (R) David Spitz (Cage) is a weatherman in Chicago. Not really much of a movie in that fact alone. What makes this story move is that, as his Pulitzer Prize-winning father Robert (Caine) points out, he isn't a particularly good one. Dave's life seems to consistently point out to him the fact that he's not actually good at much at all. To illustrate the point, strangers on the street thank him for his rotten forecast with fast food showers. Just as Dave's life sinks to a new low, he is offered a prestigious position on a morning show in New York. Cage and Caine are excellent. 102m/C DVD. US Nicolas Cage, Michael Caine, Hope Davis, Gemmenne de la Pena, Nicholas Hoult, Michael Rispoli, Gil Bellows, Judith McConnell, Anne Marie Howard; D: Gore Verbinski; W: Steve Conrad; C: Phedon Papamichael; M: Hans Zimmer.

Web of Deceit 🎬🎬½ 1990 (PG-13) Defense lawyer Purl returns to her Southern hometown to defend an unjustly accused teenager. She falls in love with the prosecutor, but could he be the killer? Shades of "Jagged Edge." Good, suspenseful made-for-TV movie. 93m/C VHS. Linda Purl, James Read, Paul DeSouza, Larry Black, Len Birman, Barbara Rush; D: Sandor Stern; W: Sandor Stern.

Web of Deception 🎬 1971 (R) A jewel thief disappears with $5 million worth of jewels. When the case turns to murder, a private detective becomes the prime suspect. 90m/C VHS. SP Thomas Hunter, Aelina Nathaniel, Gabriele Tinti, Marilia Branco; D: Massimo Castellani; W: Italo Gasperini, Armando Merandi; C: Giorgio Tonti; M: Daniele Patucchi.

Web of the Spider 🎬🎬 Nella Stretta M Orsa Del Ragno; In the Grip of the Spider; Dracula in the Castle of Blood; And Comes the Dawn...But Colored Red 1970 Kinski as Poe is really the only good thing about this run-of-the-mill horror outing. A man stays the night in a spooky house to prove it's not haunted. Remake of "Castle of Blood." 94m/C VHS, DVD. GE FR IT Anthony (Tony) Franciosa, Klaus Kinski, Michele Mercier, Peter Carsten, Karin (Karen) Field; D: Anthony M. Dawson.

Webmaster 🎬 Skyggen; The Shadow 1998 (R) The futureworld Technotropolis is run by tyrant industrialist Stoiss. Hacker JB is forced to work surveillance for Stoiss and when a thief breaks into Stoiss' cyber empire, JB is given a mechanical heart that will stop in 35 hours unless he finds the intruder first. Dubbed from Danish. 102m/C VHS, DVD. DK Jorgen Kiil, Lars Bom, Puk Scharbau; D: Thomas Borch Nielsen; C: Lars Beyer.

A Wedding 🎬🎬½ 1978 (PG) The occasion of a wedding leads to complications galore for the relatives and guests on the happy day. Silent film legend Gish's 100th screen role. Miserable, self-indulgent outing for Altman, who went through quite a dry spell after "Nashville." 125m/C VHS, DVD. Tim Thomerson, Allan Nichols, Pam Dawber, Dennis Franz, Bert Remsen, Gavan O'Herlihy, Mia Farrow, Carol Burnett, Lillian Gish, Lauren Hutton, Viveca Lindfors, Geraldine Chaplin, Paul Dooley, Howard Duff, Dennis Christopher, Peggy Ann Garner, John Considine, Nina Van Pallandt, Dina Merrill, Pat McCormick, Vittorio Gassman, Desi Arnaz Jr.; D: Robert Altman; W: Robert Altman, Allan Nichols, Patricia Resnick, John Considine.

Wedding Band 🎬🎬 1989 Episodic comedy about a rock 'n' roll band that plays all sorts of weddings. Thin and lame but inoffensive. 95m/C VHS. William Katt, Joyce Hyser, Tino Insana, Fran Drescher, David Rasche, Joe Flaherty, Tim Kazurinsky, James Belushi; D: Daniel Raskov.

The Wedding Banquet 🎬🎬🎬 Xiyan; Hsi Yen 1993 (R) Charming story about a clash of customs and secrets. Naturalized American Wai Tung (Chao, in his film debut) lives comfortably with his lover Simon (Lichtenstein) while hiding the fact that he's gay from his Chinese parents. To appease his parents and get his "wife" (Chin) a green card, he marries for convenience and watches as the deception snowballs. Comedy of errors was shot on a small budget ($750,000) and examines small details with as much care as the larger ones. A fine effort from director Lee that's solidly humorous, but also poignant. In English and Chinese with subtitles. 111m/C VHS, DVD. TW Winston Chao, May Chin, Mitchel Lichtenstein, Sihung Lung, Ah-Leh Gua, Michael Gaston, Jeffrey Howard; D: Ang Lee; W: Ang Lee, Neil Peng, James Schamus; C: Jong Lin.

Wedding Bell Blues 🎬🎬 1996 (R) Three 30ish single friends/roommates cope with a variety of crises. Pregnant Tanya (Porikova) learns that her boyfriend Tom (Edson) has no intention of marrying her, Micki's (Warner) fiance has just called off their wedding, and Jasmine's (Douglas) conservative parents are upset by their promiscuous daughter's approach to life. Stressed, the women decide to seek their fortunes in Vegas—preferably through some quickie marriages and even quicker divorces. Looks like it was shot on a shoestring budget and the lighting could be better, but the dialogue rings true and the actors do a decent job. Look for Seinfeld's TV mom as Micki's overbearing mother and Jackson as a disgruntled shopper. Reynolds plays herself. 100m/C VHS, DVD. Illeana Douglas, Paulina Porizkova, Julie Warner, John Corbett, Jonathan Penner, Richard Edson, Charles Martin Smith, Stephanie Beacham, Carla Gugino, Leo Rossi, John Capodice, Victoria Jackson, Jeff Seymour; Cameos: Debbie Reynolds; D: Dana Lustig; M: Paul Christian Gordon, Tal Bergman.

Wedding Crashers 🎬🎬🎬 2005 (R) Womanizing buds John (Wilson) and Jeremy (Vaughn) are divorce mediators who crash weddings in order to pick up Ms. Right Now. Only John really falls for engaged Claire (McAdams), who's the daughter of eccentric politician William Cleary (Walken), and the duo find themselves spending the weekend at the family's waterfront estate. Harkens back to the "Animal House/Blues Brothers/Caddyshack" glory days of R-rated comedy, earning the rating and plenty of laughs. Vaughn and Wilson do what they do best, and have great chemistry. Walken, though underused, is effective. Stumbles a little toward the end, but not enough to spoil the festivities. 119m/C DVD, UMD. US Owen Wilson, Vince Vaughn, Rachel McAdams, Christopher Walken, Jane Seymour, Will Ferrell, Ellen A. Dow, Isla Fisher, Bradley Cooper, Ron Canada, Henry Gibson, Keir O'Donnell, Dwight Yoakam, Rebecca De Mornay, David Conrad, Larry Joe Campbell, Jennifer (Jenny) Alden, Geoff Stults; D: David Dobkin; W: Bob Fisher, Steve Faber; C: Julio Macat; M: Rolfe Kent.

The Wedding Date 🎬½ 2005 (PG-13) Complete waste of two attractive, amusing leads. High-strung New Yorker Kat (Messing) must fly to London for her self-absorbed half-sister Amy's (Adams) wedding. To her horror, the best man is her ex-fiance Jeff (Sheffield), who dumped her. Refusing to appear alone and needy, especially to her critical mother Bunny (Taylor), Kat decides to hire handsome escort Nick (Mulroney) to accompany her as her new beau. Nick is intelligent and somewhat mysterious; Kat is confused. There are various pre-wedding complications as sub-plots. Predictability rules. 90m/C DVD, HD DVD. US Debra Messing, Dermot Mulroney, Amy Adams, Jack Davenport, Jeremy Sheffield, Peter Egan, Holland Taylor, Sarah Parish, Jolyon James, C. Gerod Harris, Martin Barrett, Jay Simon, Stephen Lobo; D: Clare Kilner; W: Dana Fox; C: Oliver Curtis.

Wedding Daze 🎬½ The Pleasure of Your Company 2006 (R) Muddled and somewhat vulgar rom com that tries too hard for yuks. Anderson's (Biggs) been in a funk since his fiancee died of an embarrassing incident. Best pal Ted (Weston) thinks Anderson should get back in the dating game but, instead, he proposes to the next woman he meets, who happens to be quirky coffee shop waitress Katie (Fisher). And she accepts. 90m/C DVD. Jason Biggs, Isla Fisher, Joe Pantoliano, Joanna Gleason, Edward Herrmann, Mark Consuelos, Rob Corddry, Margo Martindale, Chris Diamantopoulos, Matt Malloy, Jay O. Sanders, Heather Goldenhersch; D: Michael Ian Black; W: Michael Ian Black; C: Dan Stoloff; M: Peter Nashel.

The Wedding Gift 🎬🎬🎬 Wide-Eyed and Legless 1993 (PG-13) Offbeat charm and humor go a long way to overcome the inherent tragedy in this true story made for British TV. Longtime happily marrieds Diana (Walters) and Deric (Broadbent) Longden are struggling to cope with Diana's mysterious and increasingly debilitating illness, which causes blackouts, pain, and the inability to use her limbs. Diana comes to accept the fact that she's going to die and decides to find her hubby a new wife, aided by Deric's friendship with a blind novelist (Thomas). Terrific performances temper the mawkishness at bay. Based on Deric Longden's books "Diana's Story" and "Lost for Words." 87m/C VHS, DVD. GB Julie Walters, Jim Broadbent, Sian Thomas, Thora Hird, Andrew Lancel, Anastasia Mulrooney; D: Richard Loncraine; W: Jack Rosenthal; C: Remi Adefarasin. TV

Wedding in Blood 🎬🎬 1974 (PG) Two French lovers plot to kill their respective spouses, and proceed to do so amid calamity and much table-turning. Sharp social satire and suspenseful mystery. Based on a true story. In French with English subtitles. 98m/C VHS, DVD. FR IT Claude Pieplu, Stephane Audran, Michel Piccoli; D: Claude Chabrol; W: Claude Chabrol; C: Jean Rabier.

A Wedding in Galilee 🎬🎬🎬 Noce In Galilee 1987 The elder of a Palestinian village is given permission to have a traditional wedding ceremony for his son if Israeli military officers can attend as the guests of honor. As the event approaches, conflicts arise among the villagers, the family, and the Israelis. Long but fascinating treatment of traditional culture in the modern world amidst political tension. In Arabic and Hebrew, with English subtitles. 113m/C VHS, DVD. BE FR Ali M. El Akili, Nazih Akleh, Anna Achdian; D: Michel Khleifi.

Wedding in White 🎬🎬 1972 (R) A rape and out-of-wedlock pregnancy trouble a poor British clan living in Canada during WWII. Sad, glum way to spend an evening. Kane is good in a non-comic role. Her screen father cares more for her honor than he does for her. 103m/C VHS, DVD. CA Donald Pleasence, Carol Kane, Leo Phillips; D: William Fruet.

The Wedding March 🎬🎬🎬 1928 Von Stroheim's famous silent film about romantic couplings in pre-WWI Vienna. The director also stars as a prince preparing to marry for money, who falls in love with a beautiful, but poor woman. Romance and irony, with a memorable finale. Like many of his other great films, it was taken from him and re-edited. Initially the first of two halves; the second, "The Honeymoon," has been lost. Next to "Greed," his most successful film. 113m/B VHS. Erich von Stroheim, Fay Wray, Zasu Pitts, George Fawcett, Maud(e) (Ford) George, Matthew Betz, George Nicholls, Cesare Gravina; D: Erich von Stroheim; *D:* Hal Mohr. *M:* Gaylord Carter. Natl. Film Reg. '03.

The Wedding Party 🐾🐾½ 1969 Apprehensive groom is overwhelmed by his too-eager bride and her inquisitive relatives in a prenuptial celebration. Hokey, would-be comedy. First screen appearances of both Clayburgh and De Niro (spelled DeNero in the credits). *50m/C VHS, DVD.* Jill Clayburgh, Robert De Nir, William Finley; *W:* Brian De Palma, Cynthia Munroe, Willard Leach; *W:* Brian De Palma.

The Wedding Planner 🐾🐾½ 2001 (PG-13) A film that's a bridesmaid instead of a bride. Mary Fiore (Lopez) is a workaholic wedding planner in San Francisco who has no love life of her own. The driven Mary meets cute with aw-shucks doctor Steve Edison (McConaughey) who, naturally, turns out to be the fiance of Mary's latest client, heiress Fran (Wilson). Not that the attractive duo can stay away from each other despite the good intentions. The leads nearly carry the film on charm alone before the script finally lets them down. *105m/C VHS, DVD. US* Jennifer Lopez, Matthew McConaughey, Bridgette Wilson-Sampras, Justin Chambers, Alex Rocco, Judy Greer, Kevin Pollak, Joanna Gleason, Charles Kimbrough, Fred Willard, Kathy Najimy; *D:* Adam Shankman; *W:* Michael Ellis, Pamela Falk; *C:* Julio Macat; *M:* Mervyn Warren.

Wedding Present 🐾🐾½ 1936 After "Big Brown Eyes," Grant and Bennett were re-teamed for this screwy—but not very funny—screwball comedy. Rusty (Bennett) and Charlie (Gran) are a newspaper reporters. When Charlie gets a promotion to editor, he becomes insufferable and Rusty quits. She decides to marry boring writer Dodacker (Nagel) and Charlie goes out of his way to foul her the perfect wedding present, which turns out to be himself. Grant's last contract film for Paramount. *81m/B DVD.* Cary Grant, Joan Bennett, Conrad Nagel, Gene Lockhart, William Demarest, Inez Courtney; *D:* Richard Wallace; *W:* Joseph Anthony; *C:* Leon Shamroy.

Wedding Rehearsal 🐾🐾½ 1932 A young nobleman thwarts his grandmother's plans to marry him off by finding suitors for all the young ladies offered to him until he finally succumbs to the charms of his mother's secretary. Enjoyable, fun comedy. First featured roles for actresses Oberon, Barrie, and Gardner. *84m/B VHS.* Merle Oberon, Roland Young, John Loder, Wendy Barrie, Maurice Evans, Joan Gardner; *D:* Alexander Korda.

The Wedding Singer 🐾🐾½ 1997 (PG-13) Despite almost nonexistent pacing and a script full of holes, "Singer" is an enjoyably goofy look at the mid '80s. Surprisingly toned-down and appealing Sandler is Robbie Hart, wedding singer, ultimate nice guy, and rock-star wannabe, who's jilted at the altar. Waitress Barrymore is engaged to a skirt-chasing stockbroker. It's immediately clear that they belong together, and the rest of the movie is spent on them chasing each other through various ending obstacles, to the obvious ending. Features great cameos by punk-rocker Billy Idol, Jon Lovitz (as a rival wedding singer), and Steve Buscemi (excellent as the groom's jealous "dad although liked you best" brother). Musical highlight is Sandler's heartfelt rendition of the J. Geils Band's "Love Stinks." Isn't it a little scary that we're already spoofing the '80s? *96m/C VHS, DVD.* Adam Sandler, Drew Barrymore, Christine Taylor, Allen Covert, Matthew Glave, Ellen A. Dow, Angela Featherstone, Alexis Arquette, Christine Pickles, Jon Lovitz, Steve Buscemi, Kevin Nealon; *Cameos:* Billy Idol; *D:* Frank Coraci; *W:* Tim Herlihy; *C:* Tim Suhrstedt; *M:* Teddy Castellucci. MTV Movie Awards '98: Kiss (Adam Sandler/Drew Barrymore).

Wedding Wars 🐾🐾½ 2006 Fluff comedy with a serious message. Shel (Stamos) is a gay wedding planner who's in charge of brother Ben's (Dane) nuptials to Maggie (Somerville), the daughter of the governor of Maine. When Shel learns that Ben's boss, Governor Welling (Brolin), opposes gay marriage, he picks up a picket sign and goes on strike. Soon, gays across the country are leaving their jobs to join in. Shel's protest, and the wedding, which has been turned over to the tacky Mrs. Fairfield (Kash), is a disaster waiting to happen. *87m/C DVD.* John Stamos, Eric Dane, Bonnie Somerville, James Brolin, Sean Maher, Linda Kash, Rosemary Dunsmore, Jayne Eastwood, Sean McCann; *D:* Jim Fall; *W:* Stephen Mazur; *C:* Ron Stannett. **CABLE**

Wee Willie Winkie 🐾🐾🐾 1937 (PG) A precocious little girl is taken in by a British regiment in India. Sugar-coated, if you're a cinematic diabetic, be warned. If you're a Temple fan, you've probably already seen it. If not, you're in for a treat. Inspired by the Rudyard Kipling story. *99m/B VHS.* Shirley Temple, Victor McLaglen, Cesar Romero, Constance Collier; *D:* John Ford; *C:* Arthur C. Miller.

Weeds 🐾🐾🐾 1987 (R) A highly fictionalized account of the career of Rick Cluchey, who, as a lifer in San Quentin federal prison, wrote a play. He was eventually paroled and went on to form a theatre group made up of ex-cons. Original and often enjoyable with a tight ensemble performance. Filmed on location at Stateville Correctional Center in Illinois, with inmates serving as extras. *115m/C VHS.* Nick Nolte, Rita Taggart, William Forsythe, Lane Smith, Joe Mantegna, Ernie Hudson, John Toles-Bey, Mark Rolston, Anne Ramsey, Charlie Rich; *D:* John Hancock; *W:* John Hancock, Dorothy Tristan; *M:* Angelo Badalamenti.

Week-End in Havana 🐾🐾½ 1941 Set in pre-revolution Cuba, this frothy musical finds salesgirl Faye on a long-awaited cruise when her ship gets stranded in Havana. She's escorted around town by shipping-official Payne and catches the eye of gambler-lothario Romero, who has a jealous girlfriend in Miranda. Fun fluff. 🎵Romance and Rhumba; Tropical Magic; The Nango; A Week-End in Havana; When I Love, I Love; Maria Inez; Rebola a Bola. *80m/C VHS, DVD.* Alice Faye, John Payne, Cesar Romero, Carmen Miranda, Cobina Wright Jr., George Barbier, Sheldon Leonard, Billy Gilbert; *D:* Walter Lang; *M:* Karl Tunberg; *M:* Alfred Newman.

Weekend 🐾🐾🐾 1967 A Parisian couple embark on a drive to the country. On the way they witness and are involved in horrifying highway wrecks. Leaving the road they find a different, equally grotesque kind of carnage. Godard's brilliant, surreal, hyper-paranoiac view of modern life was greatly influenced by the fact that his mother was killed in an auto accident in 1954 (he himself suffered a serious motorcycle mishap in 1975). In French with English subtitles. *105m/C VHS, DVD. FR IT* Mireille Darc, Jean Yanne, Jean-Pierre Leaud, Yves Beneyton, Jean-Pierre Kalfon, Valerie Lagrange, Jean-Pierre Leaud; *D:* Jean-Luc Godard; *M:* Antoine Duhamel.

The Weekend 🐾🐾½ 2000 Marian (Unger) and John (Harris) Kerr are hosting a weekend for family and friends at their upstate New York home to remember John's half-brother Tony (Sweeney) who died of AIDS a year before. Gathered are Tony's lover Lyle (Conrad) and his new boyfriend Robert (Duval) as well as neighbors Laura (Rowlands) and her daughter Nina (Shields). Turns out that mostly everybody was enamored of Tony and some unpleasant truths come out after too much wine. Good cast in a very gabby drama. Based on the novel by Peter Cameron. *97m/C VHS, DVD. GB US* Deborah Kara Unger, Jared Harris, Gena Rowlands, D.B. Sweeney, Brooke Shields, David Conrad, James Duval, Gary Cole.

Weekend of Shadows 🐾🐾🐾 1977 Confident, moralistic murder drama about a posse after an innocent immigrant they believe has killed a woman. Police sergeant Roberts is interested only in his reputation, not in justice. Posse member Waters begins to sympathize with the hunted man and defends his innocence. Intelligent, well-conceived, and professionally directed. *94m/C VHS.* John Waters, Melissa Jaffer, Graeme Blundell, Wyn Roberts, Barbara West, Graham Rouse; *D:* Tom Jeffrey.

Weekend Pass 🐾 1984 (R) Moronic rookie sailors who have just completed basic training are out on a weekend pass, determined to forget everything they have learned. They find this surprisingly easy to do. *92m/C VHS, DVD.* D.W. Brown, Peter Ellenstein, Phil Hartman, Patrick Hauser, Chip McAllister; *D:* Lawrence Bassoff; *W:* Lawrence Bassoff; *C:* Bryan England.

Weekend War 🐾🐾½ 1988 (PG-13) A group of National Guardsmen are sent to the Honduras for their annual tour of duty. But when a guerilla war between Honduras and Nicaragua breaks out, the Guardsmen are forced to fight for their lives. The "Bridge on the River Kwai" finale features the dilemma of a bridge linking the two countries. *96m/C VHS* Daniel Stern, Stephen Collins, Charles Haid, Evan Mirand, Michael Beach, Scott Paulin, James Tolkan; *D:* Steven Hilliard Stern; *M:* Brad Fiedel. TV

Weekend Warriors 🐾🐾½ 1986 (R) Young film-studio employees evade the draft in 1961 by enlisting for National Guard weekend duty. Grade "C" dumb comedy from professional celebrity and first-time director Convy. *88m/C VHS, DVD.* Chris Lemmon, Lloyd Bridges, Daniel Greene, Tom Villard, Vic Tayback; *D:* Bart Convy; *W:* Bruce Belland; *M:* Perry Botkin.

Weekend at Bernie's 🐾🐾½ 1989 (PG-13) Two computer nerds discover embazzlement at their workplace after being invited to their boss's beach house for a weekend party. They find their host murdered. They endeavor to keep up appearances by (you guessed it) dressing and strategically positioning the corpse during the party. Kiser as the dead man is memorable, and the two losers gamely keep the silliness flowing. Lots of fun. *101m/C VHS, DVD.* Andrew McCarthy, Jonathan Silverman, Catherine Mary Stewart, Terry Kiser, Don Calfa, Louis Giambalvo; *D:* Ted Kotcheff; *W:* Robert Klane; *C:* Francois Protat; *M:* Andy Summers.

Weekend at Bernie's 2 🐾🐾½ 1993 (PG) Unlikely but routine sequel to the original's cavorting cadaver slapstick, except now McCarthy and Silverman are frantically hunting for Bernie's (Kiser) cash stash, a quest that takes them and poor dead Bernie to the Carribean. See Bernie get stuffed in a suitcase, see Bernie hang glide, see Bernie tango, see Bernie attract the opposite sex. Thin script with one-joke premise done to death just for those in the mood 'or the postmortem antics of a comedic stiff. Plenty of well-executed gags involving the well-preserved corpse (particularly one that's been dead for two films now) should lure back fans of the 1989 original. *89m/C VHS, DVD.* Andrew McCarthy, Jonathan Silverman, Terry Kiser, Steve James, Troy Byer, Barry Bostwick; *D:* Robert Klane; *W:* Robert Klane; *M:* Peter Wolf.

Weekend at the Waldorf 🐾🐾½ 1945 Glossy, americanized remake of "Grand Hotel" set at the famous Park Avenue hotel, the Waldorf-Astoria, in New York City. Turner and Rogers star in the roles originated by Joan Crawford and Greta Garbo. Johnson and Pidgeon play their love interests. Combining drawing room comedy with slapstick and a touch of romance proved to be a hit as this film was one of the top grossers of 1945 and was just what war-weary moviegoers wanted to see. Based on the play "Grand Hotel" by Vicki Baum. *130m/B VHS.* Ginger Rogers, Walter Pidgeon, Van Johnson, Lana Turner, Robert Benchley, Edward Arnold, Leon Ames, Warner Anderson, Phyllis Thaxter, Keenan Wynn, Porter Hall, Samuel S. Hinds; *D:* Robert Z. Leonard; *W:* Samuel Spewack, Bella Spewack, Guy Bolton.

A Weekend in the Country 🐾🐾½ 1996 (R) Ensemble comedy finds a varied group of couples and would-be couples traveling to California's wine country for a weekend of relaxation at a bed and breakfast inn. Nothing quite works out as planned but Cupid's arrow does strike. Filmed on location in Temecula, CA. *94m/C VHS, DVD.* Rita Rudner, Faith Ford, Christine Lahti, Jack Lemmon, Richard Lewis, Dudley Moore, Betty White, Dan Cortese, Jennifer Elise Cox; *D:* Martin Bergman; *W:* Rita Rudner, Martin Bergman; *M:* Patrick Williams. **CABLE**

Weeping Meadow 🐾🐾🐾 *Trilogia: To Livadi pou dakryzei; Trilogy: The Weeping Meadow; Eleni; La Sorgente del fiume; La Terre qui pleure.* 2004 Greek tragedy? Part one of the Theo Angelopoulos' historical trilogy starts with a family fleeing Russia's Bolshevik Revolution in Russia and landing in Greece. Eleni (Aidini) and Alexis (Pousas-dinis) are stepsiblings who fall in love and struggle to forge and remain their romantic relationship, through the fates are continually against them. Eleni bears twin she is forced to give up for adoption. Story weaves through time as the sons grow and tragedy after tragedy besets all involved. *168m/C DVD.* Alexandra Aidini, Nikos Poursanidis, Yorgos Armenis, Vassilis Kolovos, Eva Kotamanidou, Toula Stathopoulou, Mihalis Yiannatos, Thalia Argyriou, Grigoris Evangelatos; *W:* Tonino Guerra, Petros Markaris, Giorgio Silvagni; *C:* Andreas Sinanos; *M:* Eleni Karaindrou.

Weep No More My Lady 🐾🐾 1993 (PG-13). Suspense-filled whodunit about a wealthy businessman who comes to his sister's house and babysits everyone but the tortoir's house and babysits everyone but the kids, running into a deadly game of murder. Based on the best-selling book by Mary Higgins Clark. *92m/C VHS.* Daniel J. Travanti, Shelley Winters, Kristin Scott Thomas; *D:* Michel Andrieu; *W:* Renan Polles; *M:* Rene Marc Bini.

The Weight of Water 🐾🐾 2000 (R) Photographer Jean (McCormack) arrives at Smuttynose Island, off the coast of New Hampshire, to research an infamous 1873 ax-murder case involving two Norwegian immigrant women (Cartlidge, Shaw) a local man (Hinds), and an unreliable witness (Polley). You see their story in flashback as Jean struggles with her own domestic dilemmas—her drunken poet husband Thomas (Penn), his brother Rich (Lucas), and Rich's sexy girlfriend Adaline (Hurley). Jealousy, lies, and betrayal abound in both stories. Based on the novel by Anita Shreve. *105m/C VHS, DVD. US* Catherine McCormack, Sarah Polley, Sean Penn, Josh(ua) Lucas, Elizabeth Hurley, Ciaran Hinds, Ulrich Thomsen, Anders W. Berthelsen, Katrin Cartlidge, Vinessa Shaw; *D:* Kathryn Bigelow; *W:* Alice Arlen, Christopher Kyle; *C:* Adrian Biddle; *M:* David Hirschfelder.

Weird Science 🐾🐾 1985 (PG-13) Hall is appealing, and Hughes can write dialogue for teens with the best of them. However, many of the jokes are in poor taste, and the movie seems to go on forever. Hall and his nerdy cohort Mitchell-Smith use a very special kind of software to create the ideal woman who wreaks zany havoc in their lives from the outset. *94m/C VHS, DVD.* Kelly Le Brock, Anthony Michael Hall, Ilan Mitchell-Smith, Robert Downey Jr., Bill Paxton; *D:* John Hughes; *W:* John Hughes; *C:* Matthew F. Leonetti; *M:* Ira Newborn.

Weird World of LSD 🐾🐾½ 1967 Cheap exploitation film featuring the evil effects of LSD. *75m/B VHS.* Terry Tessem, Ann Lindsay, Yolanda Morino; *D:* Robert Ground.

Weekend with the Babysitter WOOF! *Weekend Babysitter.* 1970 (R) Sordid teen drama about a weekend babysitter who goes to a film director's house and gets a flirt director. *93m/C VHS, DVD.* Susan (Suzan) Roman, George E. Carey, James Almanzar, Luanne Roberts; *D:* Don Henderson.

The Weirdo ♂ 1989 "The Jerk" meets Freddie Krueger. This film is absolutely wretched, even by horror movie standards. 91m/C VHS. D: Steve Burington. Jessica Straus; D: Andy Milligan.

Weirdsville ♂1/2 2007 (R) Heroin addict pals Dexter (Speedman) and Royce (Bentley) live in tiny Weedsville in Northern Ontario. They owe their dealer Omar (Bhaneja) and agree to deal drugs for him to settle their account. Royce's girlfriend and sometimes-hooker Matilda (Manning) seemingly overdoses on Omar's goods, and the brilliant pair decide to get rid of her by burying her in the boiler room of a drive-in theatre where Dexter briefly worked. But they run into complications. 1) She's still alive, and 2) they figure this out only after they've accidentally stumbled upon some Satanists in the middle of a human sacrifice. Pursued by the Satanists, they've still got to figure out how to pay Omar. Some would doubt the humor in heroin addiction, and this pic will definitely reinforce that doubt. 90m/C DVD. CA Scott Speedman, Wes Bentley, Taryn Manning, Matt Frewer, Greg Bryk, Maggie Castle, Raoul Bhaneja, Joe Dinicol, Jordan Prentice, Dac Ravina; D: Allan Moyle; W: Willem Wennekers; C: Adam Swica; M: Michael Doherty, John Rowley.

Welcome Back Mr. Fox 1983 An award-winning science fiction short wherein an obnoxious movie producer cheats death by being cryogenically frozen, and then wakes up years later no wiser for the experience. Suitably, he receives his comeuppance. 21m/C VHS. E.D. Phillips, Gustav Vintas; D: Walter W. Pitt III.

Welcome Home ♂♂ 1989 (R) A missing-in-action Vietnam vet (Kristofferson) leaves his wife and children in Cambodia to return to America more than 15 years after he was reported dead. He finds his first wife remarried and discovers a teenaged son he unknowingly fathered. This plotless, sporadically moving film was Schaffner's last. 92m/C VHS. Kris Kristofferson, JoBeth Williams, Sam Waterston, Brian Keith, Trey Wilson, Thomas Wilson Brown; D: Franklin J. Schaffner; C: Fred W. Koenekamp; M: Henry Mancini. CABLE

Welcome Home Roscoe Jenkins ♂1/2 2008 (PG-13) Cultures clash and cliches abound when hotshot Hollywood talk-show host Roscoe Jenkins (Lawrence) returns home to small-town Georgia with his dim fiancee (Bryant) and young son for his parents' 50th wedding anniversary. His unimpressed family-including horndog sister Betty (Mo'Nique), studly brother Otis (Duncan), slick cousin Reggie (Epps), and nemesis Clyde (Cedric the Entertainer)-doesn't exactly roll out the red carpet. In no time, old rivalries make for put-downs, pot-shots, and sight gags that alternate between amusing and embarrassing, until a not-unexpected but somewhat ironic dose of schmaltz finally ends the tedium. 113m/C DVD. US Martin Lawrence, Margaret Avery, James Earl Jones, Joy Bryant, Michael Clarke Duncan, Cedric the Entertainer, Mike Epps, Mo'Nique, Louis C.K., Nicole Ari Parker, Damani Roberts; D: Malcolm Lee; W: Malcolm Lee; C: Greg Gardiner; M: David Newman.

Welcome Home, Roxy Carmichael ♂♂ 1990 (PG-13) Ryder, as a young misfit, is the bright spot in this deadpan, would-be satire. Hollywood star Roxy Charmichael returns to her small Ohio hometown and begins fantasizing that she is really her mother. It is obvious why this deadpan, hard-to-follow movie was a boxoffice flop. 98m/C VHS, DVD. Winona Ryder, Jeff Daniels, Laila Robins, Dinah Manoff, Ava Fabian, Robbie Kiger, Sachi (MacLaine) Parker; D: Jim Abrahams; C: Paul Elliott.

Welcome Says the Angel ♂♂ 2001 Drifter Joshua (Jacobs) winds up at a seedy bar in Hollywood where he's picked up by Ana (Hauer) and the two go off to her loft. In the morning, Josh finds himself handcuffed, his wallet and Ana gone. She returns after getting her heroin fix but refuses to let Josh go. They begin to bond (must be the Stockholm Syndrome) and Josh vows to get her off drugs when he finally gets free. Maybe he wants to handcuff her instead. No-budgeter but the leads work well together. 90m/C VHS, DVD. Jon Jacobs, Aysha Hauer; D: Philippe Dib; W: Jon Jacobs, Philippe Dib; C: Gabor Satanyi; M: Nels Cline, George Lockwood.

Welcome Stranger ♂♂1/2 1947 New doctor's ideas clash with the old doctor's ways in a small town until the younger saves the live of the elder. Crosby and Fitzgerald star as the two clashing medics in this reunion of the cast of "Going My Way." He wins the heart of the town and the heart of local teacher Caulfield in the meantime. Sheekman's script calls for Marx Brothers'-like comedy and director Nugent appears in a cameo as another doctor. 107m/B VHS. Bing Crosby, Barry Fitzgerald, Joan Caulfield, Wanda Hendrix, Frank Faylen, Elizabeth Patterson, Robert Shayne, Don Beddoe, Percy Kilbride, Larry Young; Cameos: Elliott Nugent; D: Elliott Nugent; W: Arthur Sheekman; C: Lionel Lindon; M: Johnny Burke, James Van Heusen.

Welcome to Blood City ♂1/2 1977 An anonymous totalitarian organization kidnaps a man and transports him electronically to a fantasy western town where the person who murders the most people becomes the town's "kill master." Amateurish and low-budget. 96m/C VHS. Jack Palance, Keir Dullea, Samantha Eggar, Barry Morse; D: Peter Sasdy; W: Stephen Schneck, Michael Winder; C: Reginald Morris; M: Roy Budd.

Welcome to Collinwood ♂♂ 2002 (R) Ensemble comedy by the brothers Russo is a remake of the 1958 Italian classic, "Big Deal on Madonna Street." Collinwood is home to a group of hopelessly inept, dim wanna-be criminals. The dubious crew consists of single father Riley (Macy), Leon (Washington), Toto (Jetter), Pero (Rockwell) and Basil (Davoli). Broad character bits are highlighted by the always brilliant Macy and an amusing Rockwell. Producer Clooney provides a highlight as a wheelchair-bound safe cracker. A little too over-the-top, but accurately cops original's hilarious comic climax as the boys break down a wall to get at the safe. 86m/C VHS, DVD. US Luis Guzman, Michael Jeter, Patricia Clarkson, Andrew Davoli, Isaiah Washington IV, William H. Macy, Sam Rockwell, Gabrielle Union, Jennifer Esposito, George Clooney; D: Anthony Russo, Joe Russo; W: Anthony Russo, Joe Russo; C: Lisa Rinzler, Charles Minsky; M: Mark Mothersbaugh.

Welcome to 18 ♂ 1987 (PG-13) Three girls, just out of high school, take summer jobs at a dude ranch, work a local casino, flirt, tease and get in trouble. The movie isn't funny in the least, and is filled with utter nonsense. Hargitay is the daughter of actress Jayne Mansfield. 91m/C VHS. Courtney Thorne-Smith, Mariska Hargitay, Jo Ann Willette, Christine Kaufmann; D: Terry Carr.

Welcome to Hollywood ♂♂ 2000 Filmmaker Rifkin plays himself in this mockumentary that follows the career of actor Nick Decker (Markes) from wannabe to superstar, which includes his romance with married actress Everhart (playing herself). 89m/C VHS, DVD. Adam Rifkin, Tony Markes, Angie Everhart; D: Adam Rifkin, Tony Markes.

Welcome to L.A. ♂♂♂ 1977 (R) Rudolph's ambitious directorial debut focuses on the sexual escapades of a group of Southern Californians. Based on the music suite "City of the One Night Stands" by Baskin, which also (unfortunately) serves as the soundtrack. Rudolph improved greatly after this initial effort. 106m/C VHS. Allan Nicholls, Sissy Spacek, Sally Kellerman, John Considine, Keith Carradine, Geraldine Chaplin, Lauren Hutton, Viveca Lindfors, Harvey Keitel, John Considine; D: Alan Rudolph; W: Alan Rudolph; M: Richard Baskin.

Welcome to Mooseport ♂♂ 2004 (PG-13) Romano's big-screen debut is a weak-scripted mess that has him running for mayor of his small-town quirky small town against former president Hackman. Romano plays average schlub (Everybody Loves) Handy Harrison, who gets into politics when ex-President Monroe "Eagle" Cole (Hackman) hits on his long-time, waiting-for-commitment girlfriend (Tierney). A golf match for the town and her heart ensues. Hackman turns in a dependable performance but Romano shuffles through, depending too much on the audience's familiarity with his TV character while Tierney taps her foot impatiently. Riddled with stereotypical characters, the movie never moves past utterly predictable, and the laughs are few and far between. Director Petrie obviously wants to conjure the charm of old Frank Capra movies, but only manages to reach the level of a bad sitcom pilot that drags on for far too long. 110m/C DVD. US Ray Romano, Gene Hackman, Marcia Gay Harden, Maura Tierney, Christine Baranski, Fred Savage, Rip Torn, June Squibb, Wayne Robson, John Rothman, Karl Pruner; D: Donald Petrie; W: Tom Schulman, Doug Richardson; C: Victor Hammer; M: John Debney.

Welcome to Paradise ♂♂ 2007 (PG) Uplifting family drama has single mom and controversial preacher Debbie Laramie (Bernard) transferred from her pressed town of Paradise, Texas. She meets a lot of resistance from her parishioners and her church's charter is in danger of being revoked. But when the church burns down, everyone finds a reason to work together. 105m/C DVD, Crystal Bernard, Brian Dennehy, Bobby Edner, Nick Searcy, Brad Stine, Beth Grant, Ken Jenkins, William Shockley; D: Brent Huff; W: William Shockley, Brent Huff; C: Robert Hayes; M: Steve Pierson.

Welcome to Sarajevo ♂♂♂1/2 1997 (R) Fresh, unusual take on the siege of Sarajevo in 1992. A group of news correspondents, including British reporter Michael Henderson (Dillane), find themselves in the middle of the siege, and become disillusioned when the conflict is largely ignored by the rest of the world. Film sheds perspective when a particularly bloody massacre takes a backseat to the marital troubles of the royal family. Henderson becomes personally involved when his daily coverage of an orphanage sparks him to become a hero to the orphaned Emily (Sarajevan actress Nusevic). Intermingling actual news footage, Winterbottom shows the violence on a personal level. Solid supporting characters include Harrelson as the wonderfully egotistic American celeb journalist. Strong emotional content is tempered by the smart and savvy gallows humor, which keeps melodrama miles away. Loosely based on a true story by ITN reporter, Michael Nicholson. 102m/C VHS, DVD. Stephen (Dillon) Dillane, Woody Harrelson, Marisa Tomei, Kerry Fox, Emily Lloyd, Goran Visnjic, Juliet Aubrey, Gordana Gadzic, Drazen Sivak, Vesna Orel; D: Michael Winterbottom; W: Frank Cottrell-Boyce; C: Daf Hobson; M: Adrian Johnston.

Welcome to the Dollhouse ♂♂1/2 1995 (R) Eleven-year-old, glasses-wearing Dawn Wiener (Matarazzo) is the middle child of a middle-class family in an average New Jersey town. It's her first year in junior high and Dawn's bewildered-by school, by family, by life in general, and where she fits in. Puberty sucks. 87m/C VHS, DVD. Heather Matarazzo, Brendan Sexton III, Daria Kalinina, Matthew Faber, Angela Pietropinto, Eric Mabius; D: Todd Solondz; W: Todd Solondz; C: Randy Drummond; M: Jill Wisoff. Ind. Spirit '97: Debut Perf. (Matarazzo); Sundance '96: Grand Jury Prize.

Welcome to Spring Break ♂1/2 Nightmare Beach 1988 (R) College co-eds are stalked by a killer on the beaches of Florida. 92m/C VHS, DVD. Nicolas De Toth, Sarah Buxton, Lance LeGault, Rawley Valverde, John Saxon, Michael Parks; D: Umberto Lenzi; W: Umberto Lenzi; M: Claudio Simonetti.

Welcome to the Terrordome ♂1/2 1995 (R) Yet another future apocalypse. Terrordome is a city collapsing under pollution, filled with corrupt police, where blacks are confined to ghettos with rampant gang violence and drugs. Spike's young nephew is killed in a police shoot-out and his sister goes on a shooting spree, which draws more rage and has Spike being forced to choose between his homies and his preggers white girlfriend. 98m/C VHS, DVD. GB Saffron Burrows, Valentine Nonyela, Suzette Llewellyn, Felix Joseph; D: Ngozi Onwurah; W: Ngozi Onwurah.

Welcome to Woop Woop ♂1/2 1997 (R) Hit-or-miss (mostly miss) comedy about a con man meeting his match in a small Australian town of redneck eccentrics. On the lam, Teddy (Schaech) nevertheless offers a ride to buxom blonde Angie (Porter), whom he meets at a gas station. The next thing he knows (having been drugged), Teddy wakes up in the nightmarish community of Woop Woop, where Angie announces they've gotten married. And Angie's violent father, Daddy-O (Taylor), makes it clear his new son-in-law has no chance of making it out alive. Based on the book "The Dead Heart" by Douglas Kennedy. 97m/C VHS. AU Johnathon Schaech, Rod Taylor, Susie Porter, Dee Smart, Richard Moir, Rachel Griffiths, Barry Humphries; D: Stephan Elliott; W: Michael Thomas; C: Mike Molloy; M: Stewart Copeland.

The Well ♂♂♂ 1951 A young black girl disappears and a white man (Morgan) is accused of kidnapping her. When it is discovered that the girl is trapped in a deep well, Morgan's expertise is needed to help free her. 85m/B VHS, DVD. Richard Rober, Harry (Henry) Morgan, Barry Kelley, Christine Larson; D: Leo Popkin, Russell Rouse; C: Ernest Laszlo.

The Well ♂♂ 1997 Repression, isolation, and tragedy set in barren rural Australia. Drab, middleaged Hester (Rabe) hires spirited teenager Katherine (Otto) to help out on her bleak farm. Hester soon becomes emotional dependent on Katherine, who eventually convinces her to sell the property so they can travel to Europe. (Yes, "The Servant" will come to mind.) But a car accident (caused by Katherine) claims the life of a mystery man and Hester decides to hide the body in an unused well. Then they discover all their money has been stolen, probably by their dead friend, and just who's going down the well to retrieve it? Based on a novel by Elizabeth Jolley. 101m/C VHS, DVD. AU Pamela Rabe, Miranda Otto, Paul Chubb; D: Samantha Lang; W: Laura Jones; C: Mandy Walker; M: Stephen Rae. Australian Film Inst. '97: Actress (Rabe), Adapt. Screenplay, Art Dir./Set Dec.

Well-Digger's Daughter ♂♂♂ 1982 La Fille Du Puisatier 1946 As her lover goes off to war, a well-digger's daughter discovers that she is pregnant causing both sets of parents to feud over who's to blame. This is the first film made in France after the end of WWII and marks the return of the French film industry. In French with English subtitles. 142m/B VHS. FR Raimu, Josette Day, Fernandel, Charpin; D: Marcel Pagnol.

We'll Meet Again ♂1/2 1982 Cliched but touching miniseries set in a quiet English town in 1943. At least the town was quiet until the arrival of a bomber group from the U.S. Army Eighth Air Force. Soon the Yanks are chasing the local girls and getting into trouble while their commander (Shannon) finds himself falling for a married doctor (York). 690m/C VHS, DVD. GB Michael J. Shannon, Susannah York, Ronald Hines, Ed Devereaux, Christopher Malcolm, Patrick O'Connell, Joris Stuyck; D: Christopher Hodson. TV

We'll Meet Again ♂♂ 2002 (PG-13) Having been unjustly thrown in the slammer for six years for her husband's slaying makes the strong-willed Molly intent on hunting down the real killer with the aide of reporter pal Fran. But, as often is the case in these Mary Higgins Clark adaptations, the truth could have deadly results for the women. 100m/C VHS, DVD. Laura Leighton, Brandy Ledford, Michael Eklund, Eva DeViveiros, Patti Allan, Sam MacMillan, Taayla Markell; D: Michael Storey; W: Michael Thoma, John Benjamin Martin; C: Henry Lebo; M: Claude Foisy. TV

Wend Kuuni ♂♂ God's Gift 1982 A fable for modern times set in Burkina Faso before the coming of Islam or Christianity. A mute, memoryless child is found by a peddler and adopted by the peddler's village. One day the boy finds a body hanging from a tree. Shocked, he recovers his speech and tells the story of his tragic past, when he and his mother were cast out of their own village. When his mother dies, the boy is bereft of family and tradition. Without these ties to his history he loses both speech and memory. In **More** with English subtitles. **70m/C VHS.** Serge Yanogo; Rosine Yanogo; Joseph Nikiema; Colette Kabore; **D:** Gaston Kabore.

The Wendell Baker Story 🐾½ **2005** (PG-13) Con man Wendell (Luke Wilson) bumbles from a fake-ID scam to prison to working at a seedy retirement hotel where the nurses (Griffin and Owen Wilson) are scamming Medicare, stealing medicine, and forcing the residents to work for food. Wendell takes the side of the residents (Cassel, Stanton, and Kristofferson) and lazy hijinks ensue. Or something. All three Wilsons (including director Andrew) try hard to make a lazy '70s stoner comedy, but mostly coast on their proven talent while rehashing themes done better elsewhere. **95m/C DVD.** **US** Luke Wilson, Owen Wilson, Seymour Cassel, Eddie Griffin, Kris Kristofferson, Eva Menzes, Harry Dean Stanton, Jacob Vargas, Spencer Scott, Buck Taylor, Jo Harvey Allen, Azura Skye, Paul M. Wright, Mathew Greer, Will Ferrell; **D:** Luke Wilson; Andrew Wilson; **W:** Luke Wilson; **C:** Steve Mason; **M:** Aaron Zigman.

Wendigo 🐾🐾½ **2001** (R) Manhattanites George (Weber), Kim (Clarkson), and their eight-year-old son Miles (Sullivan) are heading out of the city for a weekend at a friend's farmhouse in upstate New York. Distracted George hits a deer, which enrages backwoods hunter Otis (Speredakos) who was trailing the buck. Quiet Miles notices the tension between his parents but weird things really begin to happen when a mysterious man gives Miles a Wendigo figure, a creature in Native American mythology that has destructive powers, which Miles now seems to command. **91m/C VHS, DVD, US** Patricia Clarkson, Jake Weber, Erik Per Sullivan, John Speredakos, Christopher Wynkoop; **D:** Larry Fessenden; **W:** Larry Fessenden; **C:** Terry Stacey; **M:** Michelle DiBucci.

Went to Coney Island on a Mission from God... Be Back by Five 🐾🐾 **1998** (R) Daniel (Cryer), Stan (Stear), and Richie (Baez) were all best neighborhood friends while growing up in Brooklyn. Now it's years later and Stan and Danie have lost touch with Richie, whom they hear is a mentally ill vagrant living under the boardwalk at Coney Island. So they decide to ditch their boring lives and track him down. Flashbacks to earlier incidents get confusing if not tedious. **94m/C VHS, DVD, Blu-ray, Disc.** Jon Cryer, Rick Stear, Rafael Baez, Ione Skye, Frank Whaley, Peter Gerety, Akili Prince, Aesha Waks, Dominic Chianese; **D:** Richard Schenckman; **W:** Richard Schenckman, Jon Cryer; **C:** Azam Beekman; **M:** Midge Ure.

We're Back! A Dinosaur's Story 🐾🐾½ **1993** (G) Animated adventures of a pack of revived dinosaurs who return to their old stomping grounds—which are now modern-day New York City. Smart-mouth human boy Louie and his girlfriend Cecilia take the dinos under their wing (so to speak), wise them up to modern life, and try to prevent their capture by the evil Professor Screweyes. Slow-moving with some violence. Adapted from the book by Hudson Talbott. **78m/C VHS. D:** Dick Zondag, Ralph Zondag, Phil Nibelink, Simon Wells; **W:** John Patrick Shanley; **V:** John Goodman, Felicity Kendal, Walter Cronkite, Joey Shea, Jay Leno, Julia Child, Kenneth Mars, Martin Short, Rhea Perlman, Rene LeVant, Blaze Berdahl, Charles Fleischer, Yeardley Smith.

We're in the Legion Now 🐾½ **1937** Denny and Barnett star as a couple of American gangsters who join the French Foreign Legion to escape rival hoods from back home. **55m/B VHS.** Eleanor Hunt, Claudia Dell, Robert Fazer, Rudolph Anders, Reginald Denny, Vince Barnett, Esther Ralston; **D:** Crane Wilbur; **W:** Roger Whately.

We're in the Navy Now 1927 The famed comedy duo's back again with another armed forces farce. A mild successor to "Behind the Front." **60m/B VHS.**

We're No Angels 🐾🐾½ **1955** Three escapees from Devil's Island hide out with the family of a kindly French storekeeper on Christmas Eve. Planning to rob the family, they end up helping them with various financial, romantic, and familial problems. Somewhat stagey, but great dialogue and excellent cast make for enjoyable holiday fare. One of Bogart's few comedies. From the French stage play of the same name, later remade with De Niro and Penn. **103m/C VHS, DVD.** Humphrey Bogart, Aldo Ray, Joan Bennett, Peter Ustinov, Basil Rathbone, Leo G. Carroll, Lea Penman, John Smith, Gloria Talbott, John Baer; **D:** Michael Curtiz; **W:** Ranald MacDougall; **C:** Loyal Griggs; **M:** Frederick "Friedrich" Hollander.

We're No Angels 🐾🐾½ **1989** (R) Two escaped cons disguise themselves as priests and get in the appropriate series of jams. De Niro and Penn play off each other well, turning in fine comic performances. Distantly related to the 1955 film of the same name and the David Mamet play. **110m/C VHS, DVD.** Robert De Niro, Sean Penn, Demi Moore, Hoyt Axton, Bruno Kirby, James Russo, John C. Reilly, Ray McAnally, Wallace Shawn; **D:** Neil Jordan; **W:** David Mamet; **C:** Philippe Rousselot; **M:** George Fenton.

We're Not Dressing 🐾🐾½ **1934** Loose musical adaptation of J.M. Barrie's "The Admirable Crichton" with the butler transformed into singing sailor Crosby. Fabulously wealthy heiress Lombard invites her pals for a South Seas yachting adventure. Only the ship gets wrecked and everyone winds up on a small island where the practical Crosby whips everyone into shape (and romances Lombard). Burns and Allen supply additional comedy as a pair of botanists who just happen to be studying the local fauna. ♫Good Night Lovely Little Lady; I'll Sing About the Birds and the Bees; It's Just a New Spanish Custom; Let's Play House; Love Thy Neighbor; May I?; Once in a Blue Moon; She Reminds Me of You. **74m/B VHS, DVD.** Bing Crosby, Carole Lombard, George Burns, Gracie Allen, Ethel Merman, Leon Errol, Ray Milland; **D:** Norman Taurog; **W:** Horace Jackson, Francis Martin; **M:** Harry Revel, Mack Gordon.

We're Not Married 🐾🐾🐾 **1952** Five couples learn that they are not legally married when a judge realizes his license expired before he performed the ceremonies. The story revolves around this quintet of couples who now must cope with whether or not they really do want to be married. Although the episodes vary in quality, the Allen-Rogers sequence is excellent. Overall, the cast performs well in this lightweight comedy. **85m/B VHS, DVD.** Ginger Rogers, Fred Allen, Victor Moore, Marilyn Monroe, Paul Douglas, David Wayne, Eve Arden, Louis Calhern, Zsa Zsa Gabor, James Gleason, Jane Darwell, Eddie Bracken, Mitzi Gaynor, Selmer Jackson, Lee Marvin; **D:** Edmund Goulding; **C:** Leo Tover; **M:** Cyril Mockridge.

We're Talkin' Serious Money 🐾½ **1992** (PG-13) Sal and Charlie are a couple of loser scam-artists who always owe the elusive big score. They get-rich-quick scheme and wind up over their heads with both the mob and the FBI out to get them. **92m/C VHS.** Dennis Farina, Leo Rossi, Fran Drescher, John Lamotta; **D:** James (Momel) Lemmo; **W:** Leo Rossi, James (Momel) Lemmo; **M:** Scott Grusin.

Werewolf 🐾 **1995** (R) A remote desert town is stricken by an ancient curse that turns its occupants into werewolves at the full moon. This doesn't help the tourism industry. **99m/C VHS, DVD.** Jorge (George) Fivero, Fred Cavalli, Adrianna Miles, Richard Lynch, Joe Estevez, R(ichard) C(arlos) Bates, Heidi Bjorn, Randall Oliver, Nena Belini, Tony Zarindast; **D:** Tony Zarindast; **W:** Tony Zarindast; **C:** Robert Hayes, Dan Gilman.

Werewolf in a Girl's Dormitory 🐾 *Lycanthropus; The Ghoul in School* 1961 Girls' school headmaster undergoes dental transformation at night. Atrocious dubbing, with equally atrocious

---

theme song "The Ghoul in School." **82m/B VHS, DVD.** "Barbara Lass, Carl Schell, Curt Lowens, Maurice Marsac; **D:** Richard Benson.

Werewolf of London 🐾🐾½ **1935** A scientist searching for a rare Tibetan flower is attacked by a werewolf. He scoffs at the legend, but once he's back in London, he goes on a murderous rampage every time the moon is full. Dated but worth watching as the first werewolf movie made. **75m/B VHS, DVD.** Henry Hull, Warner Oland, Valerie Hobson, Lester Matthews, Spring Byington, Lawrence Grant, Zeffie Tilbury; **D:** Stuart Walker; **W:** Robert H. Harris, John Colton; **C:** Charles Stumar.

Werewolf of Washington 🐾🐾 **1973** (PG) Stockwell is a White House press secretary with a problem—he turns into a werewolf. And bites the President, among others. Sub-plot involves a short mad scientist who operates a secret mansion-making lab in a White House basement. Occasionally engaging horror spoof, room. Occasionally engaging horror spoof, and political satire made during Watergate era. **90m/C VHS, DVD.** Dean Stockwell, Biff McGuire, Clifton James, Jane House, Beeson Carroll, Michael Dunn, Nancy Andrews, Stephen Cheng, Barbara Siegel; **D:** Milton Moses Ginsberg; **W:** Milton Moses Ginsberg; **C:** Robert M. "Bob" Baldwin Jr.; **M:** Arnold Freed.

The Werewolf vs. the Vampire Woman 🐾½ *Shadow of the Werewolf; Blood Moon; Night of Walpurgis; La Noche de Walpurgis* 1970 (R) Hirsute Spanish wolfman teams with two female students in search of witch's tomb. One is possessed by the witch, and eponymous title results. **82m/C VHS, DVD. S?** GF Paul Naschy, Gaby Fuchs, Barbara Capell, Patty (Patti) Shepard, Valenta Samarine, Julio Pena, Andres Resino. **D:** Leon Klimovsky; **W:** Paul Naschy; **C:** Leopoldo Villasenor; **M:** Anton Abril.

Werewolves on Wheels woof! 1971 (R) A group of bikers are turned into werewolves due to a Satanic spell. A serious attempt at a biker/werewolf movie, however, too violent and grim, not at all funny, and painful to sit through. McGuire had a hit with "Eve of Destruction." **85m/C VHS, DVD.** Stephen Oliver, Severn Darden, D.J. Anderson, Duece Barry, Billy Gray, Barry McGuire; **D:** Michel Levesque.

Wes Craven Presents Mind Ripper 🐾🐾 *Mind Ripper* 1995 (R) A top secret government experiment, intended to produce a superhuman, goes wrong and traps the scientists in a remote desert outpost with their deadly, pissed-off creation. **90m/C VHS.** Lance Henriksen, John Diehl, Natasha Gregson Wagner, Dan Blom, Claire Stansfield; **D:** Joe Gaytor; **W:** Jonathan Craven, Phil Mittleman; **C:** Fernando Arguelles; **M:** J. Peter Robinson.

Wes Craven Presents: They 🐾½ *They* 2002 (PG-13) Maybe Wes should stop presenting this stuff and start writing and directing it again. It might turn out better. Derivative horror flick has psych grad student Julia (Regan) visited by childhood friend and fellow nightmare sufferer Billy, who tells her that something's after them. She doesn't believe him until her old nightmares return and bring things start happening. Starts off genuinely creepy and appropriately scary, but loses itself in cliches and other plot devices you've seen done better elsewhere. Regan gives a good debut performance, though. **100m/C VHS, DVD. US** Laura Regan, Marc Blucas, Ethan (Randall) Embry, Dagmara Dominczyk, Jon Abrahams, Jay Brazeau, Alexander Gould; **D:** Robert Harmon; **W:** Brendan William Hood; **C:** Rene Ohashi; **M:** Elia Cmiral.

Wes Craven's New Nightmare 🐾🐾 *Nightmare on Elm Street 7* 1994 (R) Seems the six previous conjurings of Freddy's tortured but fictional soul have inadvertently created a real supernatural force bent on tormenting the lives of retired scream queen Langenkamp, her son (Hughes), writer-director Craven, and surprisingly mild alter-ego England. Craven's solution is to write a script that reunites series principals for a final showdown with the slashmaster in Hell. Clever and original in a genre known for neither trait, this movie-in-a-movie-about-a-movie is equal parts playful gim-

---

mick and inspired terror that will give even the most seasoned Kruegerphile the heebie-jeebies. **112m/C VHS, DVD.** Robert England, Heather Langenkamp, Miko Hughes, David Newsom, Tracy Middendorf, Fran Bennett, John Saxon, Wes Craven, Robert Shaye, Sara Risher, Marianne Maddalena; **D:** Wes Craven; **W:** Wes Craven; **C:** Mark Irwin; **M:** J. Peter Robinson.

West Beirut 🐾🐾 *West Beyrouth* 1998 Muslim teenagers Tarek (Doueiri, the director's younger brother) and Omar (Chamas) and their new friend, the Christian May (Al Amin), live in an apartment complex in Muslim-controlled West Beirut in 1975. The date is significant since Muslim and Christian militias start fighting for control of the Lebanese city and, since their school is closed, the teens have little better to do than to explore the forbidden, Arabic with subtitles. **105m/C VHS, DVD, FR** Rami Doueiri, Mohamed Chamas, Rola Al Amin, Leila Karam; **D:** Ziad Doueiri; **W:** Ziad Doueiri; **C:** Ricardo Jacques Gale. **M:** Stewart Copeland.

West-Bound Limited 🐾🐾½ **1923** A Romantic adventurer rescues a girl from certain death as a train is about to hit her, and the two fall in love. Lucky for him, she happens to be the boss' daughter. This film is a good example of classic silent melodrama with music score. **70m/B VHS.** John Harron, Ella Hall, Claire McDowell; **D:** Emory Johnson.

West is West 🐾🐾 **1987** Vikram arrives in San Francisco from Bombay to attend university and discovers the sponsor has returned to India. With little money, he gets a room in a seedy hotel run by an Indian immigrant, who also gives Vikram a menial job. As he begins to explore the city, Vikram needs to convince Sue to a green card marriage. INS ready to deport him, Vikram meets arty punk Sue, but with his visa running out and the INS ready to deport him, Vikram needs to convince Sue to a green card marriage. **80m/C VHS.** Ashutosh Gowariker, Heidi Carpenter, Pearl Padamsee; **D:** David Rathod **W:** David Rathod. **C:** Christopher Tufty.

West New York 🐾🐾 **1996** (R) Excop Tom Coletti (Vincent) has a job in Jersey, disposing of old bank bonds. He comes up with a scheme to skim some of the bonds but the news leaks to the local mob boss, Carmine (Pastore). He's unhappy he's not being cut in and decides to put out a hit to show his displeasure, so Coletti has to get to him first. **99m/C VHS.** Frank Vincent, Vincent Pastore, Victor Colicchio, Brian Burke, Gian DiDonna, Gloria Darpino, Brian McCormick; **D:** Phil Gallo.

West of Nevada 🐾🐾 **1936** A rare film, featuring the former Lieutenant Governor of Nevada (and Clara Bow's husband) in a fast-moving adventure about a band of Indians who must protect their gold from thieves. Bell is the good guy who aids the Indians. **59m/B VHS, DVD.** Georga O'Dell, Forrest Taylor, Rex Bal, Jean Barclay, Al "Fuzzy" St. John, Steve Clare; **D:** Robert F. "Bob" Hill; **W:** Robert F. "Bob" Hill; **C:** Edward Cline.

West of Pinto Basin 🐾🐾 **1940** The Range Busters are riding around checking the territory for badmen in this tale of the old West. The music score includes "That Little Prairie Gal of Mine," "Rhythm of the Saddle," and "Ridin' the Trail Tonight." **60m/B VHS.** Ray Corrigan, Max Terhune, John "Dusty" King, Gwen Gaze, Tristram Coffin, George Cheseboro, Bud Osborne, Jack Perrin; **D:** S. Roy Luby; **W:** Earle Snell; **C:** Edward Linden.

West of the Divide 🐾🐾½ **1933** A young cowboy (Wayne) impersonates an outlaw in order to hunt down his father's killer and find his missing younger brother. He saves a proud rancher and his feisty daughter along the way. A remake Wayne oater. **53m/B VHS, DVD.** John Wayne, George "Gabby" Hayes, Lloyd Whitlock, Yakima Canutt; **D:** Robert North Bradbury; **W:** Robert North Bradbury; **C:** Archie Stout.

West of the Law 🐾🐾 **1942** A group of ranchers turn to lawmen for protection from a band of outlaws. Part of the Rough Riders series. **60m/B VHS.** Buck Jones, Tim McCoy, Raymond Hatton; **D:** Howard Bretherton.

Chester Conklin, Tom Kennedy, Donald Keith, Lorraine Eason, Wallace Beery, Raymond Hatton; **D:** Edward Sutherland; **W:** Monte Brice; **C:** Charles P. Boyle.

We're No Angels 🐾🐾½ **1955** A scientist searching for a rare Tibetan flower is attacked by a werewolf. He

West of the Pecos ♪♪½ 1945 A society gal on her way to the family ranch in Texas. She's disguised as a boy for safety, which turns out to be a smart idea when outlaws attack the stagecoach. Fortunately, Pecos Smith (Mitchum) is also around to lend a hand. Based on the novel by Zane Grey; first filmed in 1935. 66m/B VHS, DVD. Robert Mitchum, Barbara Hale, Richard Martin, Thurston Hall, Rita (Paula) Corday, Russell Hopton, Harry Woods; D: Edward Killy; C: Russell Metty.

West of Zanzibar ♪♪½ 1928 Chaney plays an ivory trader, ruling a jungle kingdom, who lives for revenge on the man who left him a cripple. He decides to ruin the man's daughter and turn her into a prostitute but his plan backfires. Chaney and director Browning offer a steamy atmosphere amidst a number of script flaws. 63m/B VHS. Lon Chaney Sr., Lionel Barrymore, Warner Baxter, Mary Nolan; D: Tod Browning.

The West Point Story ♪♪½ Fine and Dandy 1950 Cagney stars as an on-the-skids Broadway director offered a job staging a show at West Point. Seems cadet MacRae has written a musical and his uncle happens to be a producer. Cagney, with girlfriend Mayo, finds all the rules and regulations getting the better of his temper, so much so that he's told unless he can conform to academy standards the show won't go on! Day is the showgirl MacRae falls for. Cagney's energy and charm carry the too-long film but it's not one of his better musical efforts. ♪♪ Ten Thousand Sheep; You Love Me; By the Kissing Rock; Long Before I Knew You; Brooklyn; It Could Only Happen in Brooklyn; Military Polka. 107m/B VHS, DVD. James Cagney, Virginia Mayo, Gordon MacRae, Doris Day, Roland Winters, Gene Nelson, Alan Hale Jr., Wilton Graff, Jerome Cowan; D: Roy Del Ruth; W: John Monks Jr., Charles Hoffman, Irving Wallace; M: Sammy Cahn, Jule Styne.

West Side Story ♪♪♪½ 1961 Gang rivalry and ethnic tension on New York's West Side erupts in a groundbreaking musical. Loosely based on Shakespeare's "Romeo and Juliet," the story follows the Jets and the Sharks as they fight for their turf while Tony and Maria fight for love. Features frenetic and brilliant choreography by co-director Robbins, who also directed the original Broadway show, and a high-caliber score by Bernstein and Sondheim. Wood's voice was dubbed by Marni Nixon and Jimmy Bryant dubbed Beymer's. ♪♪ Prologue; Jet Song; Something's Coming; Dance at the Gym; Maria; America; Tonight; One Hand, One Heart; Gee, Officer Krupke. 151m/C VHS, DVD. Yvonne Wilder, Natalie Wood, Richard Beymer, Russ Tamblyn, Rita Moreno, George Chakiris, Simon Oakland, Ned Glass; D: Robert Wise, Jerome Robbins; W: Ernest Lehman; C: Daniel F. Fapp; M: Leonard Bernstein, Stephen Sondheim. Oscars '61: Art Dir/Set Dec., Color, Color Cinematog., Costume Des. (C), Director (Wise), Film Editing, Picture, Sound, Support. Actor (Chakiris), Support. Actress (Moreno), Scoring/Musical; AFI '98: Top 100; Directors Guild '61: Director (Wise), Golden Globes '62: Film—Mus./Comedy; Support. Actor (Chakiris), Support. Actress (Moreno), Natl. Film Reg.

West to Glory ♪½ 1947 Glory isn't necessarily exciting, as the hero helps a Mexican rancher save his gold and jewels from evildoers in this slow-paced oater. 61m/B VHS. Eddie Dean, Roscoe Ates, Dolores Castle, Gregg Barton, Alex Montoya, Harry Vejar; D: Ray Taylor.

The West Wittering Affair ♪♪ 2005 Kathy (Sutcliffe) borrows a weekend retreat and invites her friends Jaime (Scheinmann) and Natasha (Cardinale), whose boyfriend Greg (Anneh) is also supposed to come. But Natasha suspects him of cheating and shows up alone, leading to an evening of too much booze and confessions and Jaime having sex with both women (separately). And this misbegotten experience still resounds with problems three years later. Ensemble comedy/drama that was frequently improvised. 90m/C DVD. GB Danny Scheinmann, Sarah Sutcliffe, Rebecca Cardinale, David Anneh; D: David Scheinmann; W: Danny Scheinmann, Sarah Sutcliffe; C: David Scheinmann; M: Marc Tschantz.

Western ♪♪ 1996 Spaniard Paco (Lopez), a traveling rep for a shoe manufacturer in France, picks up hitchhiking Russian emigre Nino (Bourdo) and soon finds himself minus a car, shoe samples, and luggage. He's rescued by local beauty Marinette (Vitali) and, since he's been fired, decides to hang around the town where she lives. But when Paco spots Nino again, he promptly beats him up, sending the Russian to the hospital. Oddly, this serves as a bond for the two men and they decide to do a little traveling through Brittany together, with Paco trying to teach the naive Nino how to pick up pretty girls. Funny, if extended, French road trip. French with subtitles. 136m/C VHS. FR Sergi Lopez, Sacha Bourdo, Elisabeth Vitali, Marie Matheron, Basile Siekoua; D: Manuel Poirier; W: Jean-Francois Goyet, Manuel Poirier; C: Nara Keo Kosal; M: Bernardo Sandoval. Cannes '97: Special Jury Prize.

Western Frontier ♪♪ 1935 Ordinary cowpoke Maynard is called on to lead the fight against a band of outlaws led by the Indian-raised sister he never knew he had. Action-packed, fast, and fun. Maynard's first outing for Columbia. 56m/B VHS. Ken Maynard, Lucille Browne, Nora Lane, Robert "Buzzy" Henry, Frank Yaconelli; D: Albert Herman.

Western Gold ♪♪ 1937 Western set during the Civil War in which Smith Ballew is sent west to stop thieves who are stealing gold from the Union. 57m/C VHS. Smith Ballew, Heather Angel, Leroy Mason, Howard Hickman, Ben Alexander, Frank McGlynn, Otis Harlan, Tom London, Bud Osborne; D: Howard Bretherton.

Western Justice ♪♪ 1935 Good Guy Steele brings western-style justice to a lawless town. Ordinary oater with horses, etc., and a few chuckles on the side. 56m/B VHS. Rene Borden, Julian Rivero, Arthur Loft, Lafe (Lafayette) McKee, Bob Steele; D: Robert North Bradbury; W: Robert North Bradbury; C: William (Bill) Hyer.

Western Mail ♪♪ 1942 Yet another western in which the hero goes undercover so he can bring the bad guys to justice. Yaconelli plays a guitar tune, accompanied by his monkey. 54m/B VHS. Tom Keene, Frank Yaconelli, Leroy Mason, Jean Trent, Fred Kohler Jr.; D: Robert Emmett Tansey.

Western Pacific Agent ♪♪ 1951 A Western Pacific agent chases an outlaw who has committed robbery and murder. The agent falls in love with the victim's sister and, of course, prevails. Rather violent. 62m/B VHS. Kent Taylor, Sheila Ryan, Mickey Knox, Robert Lowery; D: Sam Newfield; Nar: Jason Robards Sr.

Western Trails ♪ 1938 Forgettable western about the clean-up of a Wild West town terrorized by outlaws. Thin script, bad acting, and a little singin' and funnin' around. 59m/B VHS. Bob Baker, Marjorie Reynolds, Robert Burns; D: George Waggner.

Western Union ♪♪½ 1941 A lavish, vintage epic romantically detailing the political machinations, Indian warfare, and frontier adventure that accompanied the construction of the Western Union telegraph line from Omaha, Nebraska, to Salt Lake City, Utah, during the Civil War. A thoroughly entertaining film in rich Technicolor. This was Lang's second western, following his personal favorite, "The Return of Frank James." Writer Carson utilized the title, but not the storyline, of a Zane Grey book. The German Lang showed himself a master of the more American of genres, yet made only one more western, "Rancho Notorious" (1952), another masterpiece. 94m/C VHS. Randolph Scott, Robert Young, Dean Jagger, Slim Summerville, Virginia Gilmore, John Carradine, Chill Wills, Barton MacLane, Minor Watson, Charles Middleton, Irving Bacon; D: Fritz Lang.

The Westerner ♪♪♪½ 1940 Cooper stars as Cole Hardin, a sly, soft-spoken drifter who champions Texas border homesteaders in a land war with the legendary Judge Roy Bean (Brennan). Known as "The Law West of the Pecos," Bean sentences Hardin hang as a horse thief, but he breaks out of jail. Hardin then falls for damsel Jane-Ellen (Davenport) and stays in the area, advocating the rights of homesteaders, and has to have a final confrontation with the judge. Brennan's Bean is unforgettable and steals the show from Cooper. Film debuts of actors Tucker and Andrews. Amazing cinematography; Brennan's Oscar was his third, making him the first performer to pull a hat trick. 100m/B VHS, DVD. Gary Cooper, Walter Brennan, Doris Davenport, Fred Stone, Chill Wills, Dana Andrews, Forrest Tucker, Charles Halton, Lupita Tovar, Tom Tyler, Lillian Bond; D: William Wyler; W: Jo Swerling, Niven Busch; C: Gregg Toland; M: Dimitri Tiomkin. Oscars '40: Support. Actor (Brennan).

Westfront 1918 ♪♪♪ 1930 A dogmatic anti-war film by the German master (his first talkie), about German and French soldiers on the fields of WWI, dying together without victory. Stunning in its portrayal of war's futility, with excellent photography that achieves a palpable realism. In German with English subtitles. 90m/B VHS. GE Gustav Diessl, Fritz Kampers, Claus Clausen, Hans Joachim Moebis; D: G.W. Pabst.

Westler: East of the Wall ♪♪ 1985 West Berliner Felix takes a day trip to East Berlin and falls in love with Thomas. Their time together is frustrating since Felix must return before the midnight curfew and the border guards become suspicious of his frequent trips. Eventually, Felix and Thomas decide that Thomas must escape to the west. German with subtitles. 94m/C VHS. GE Sigurd Rachman, Rainer Strecker, Sasha Kogo, Andy Lucas; D: Wieland Speck; W: Wieland Speck; C: Klemens Becker; M: Engelbert Rehm.

Westward Ho ♪♪ 1935 Wayne is determined to bring to justice his parents' slayer. Haven't we seen this one before? Seems the bad guys have corrupted his brother. Wayne's group of vigilantes is called "The Singing Riders," so naturally he sings—or is made to appear to. He looks and sounds ridiculous. 55m/B VHS, DVD. John Wayne, Sheila (Manons) Mannors; D: Robert North Bradbury.

Westward Ho, the Wagons! ♪♪½ 1956 The promised land lies in the west, but to get there these pioneers must pass unfriendly savages, thieves, villains, and scoundrels galore. Suitable for family viewing, but why bother? Well, the cast does include four Mouseketeers. 94m/B VHS. Fess Parker, Kathleen Crowley, Jeff York, Sebastian Cabot, George Reeves; D: William Beaudine; M: George Bruns.

Westward the Women ♪♪♪ 1951 Buck Wyatt (Taylor) is a scout hired to wagon-train 150 mail-order brides from Chicago to California. When his lustful hired hands turn out to be all hands, Buck and the ladies must fight off attacking Indians on their own. Notable film allowing women to be as tough as men is not your typical western. Based on the Frank Capra story. 116m/C VHS. Robert Taylor, Denise Darcel, Hope Emerson, John McIntire, Beverly Dennis, Lenore Lonergan, Marilyn Erskine, Julie Bishop, Renata Vanni, Frankie Darro, George Chandler; D: William A. Wellman; W: Charles Schnee; C: William Mellor; M: Jeff Alexander.

Westworld ♪♪♪ 1973 (PG) Crichton wrote and directed this story of an adult vacation resort of the future which offers the opportunity to live in various fantasy worlds serviced by lifelike robots. Brolin and Benjamin are businessmen who choose a western fantasy world. When an electrical malfunction occurs, the robots begin to go berserk. Brynner is perfect as a western gunslinging robot whose skills are all too real. 90m/C VHS, DVD. Yul Brynner, Richard Benjamin, James Brolin, Dick Van Patten, Majel Barrett; D: Michael Crichton; W: Michael Crichton; C: Gene Polito; M: Fred Karlin.

Wet and Wild Summer woof! 1992 (R) Topless beach resort is the playground for stud lifeguards and sexy resort owners. 95m/C VHS. Christopher Atkins, Elliott Gould, Julian McMahon, Rebecca Cross; D: Maurice Murphy.

Wet Gold ♪♪ 1984 A beautiful young woman and three men journey to retrieve a sunken treasure. Nice scenery. Proves that it is possible to make "The Treasure of the Sierra Madre" without making a classic. John Huston, where are you? 90m/C VHS. Brooke Shields, Brian Kerwin, Burgess Meredith, Tom Byrd; D: Dick Lowry. TV

Wet Hot American Summer ♪♪♪ 2001 (R) Send-up of late 70s/early 80s camp flicks like "Meatballs" and "Little Darlings" focuses on the counselors trying to get laid and/or stoned on the last weekend of a Maine summer camp in 1981 while the youngsters in their charge are thrown around like chew toys. Beth (Garofalo) is the camp director with the hots for an astrophysicist (Pierce) who finds that the camp is in danger of being crushed by Skylab. The plot also involves many other cast members trying to sleep with many other cast members, but to detail more of the story would take crucial print space away from the genius that is the Vietnam vet camp cook (Meloni), whose spiritual advisor is a can of mixed vegetables. Take that whatever way you want, but trust us, you really have to see it to believe it. 97m/C VHS, DVD. US Janeane Garofalo, David Hyde Pierce, Michael Showalter, Marguerite Moreau, Paul Rudd, Zak Orth, Christopher Meloni, A.D. Miles, Molly Shannon, Bradley Cooper, Michael Ian Black, Amy Poehler, Marisa Ryan, Elizabeth Banks, Kevin Sussman, Gideon Jacobs; D: David Wain; W: Michael Showalter, David Wain; C: Ben Weinstein; M: Theodore Shapiro, Craig (Shudder to Think) Wedren.

Wetbacks ♪♪ 1956 Fishing boat skipper Jim Benson (Bridges) agrees to help the U.S. Immigration Department nab smugglers who want to use Benson's vessel to carry illegal immigrants from Mexico into the U.S. 89m/C VHS. Lloyd Bridges, Nancy Gates, Barton MacLane, John Hoyt, Harold (Hal) Peary, Nacho Galindo; D: Hank McCune; W: Pete LaRoche; C: Brydon Baker; M: Les Baxter.

Wetherby ♪♪ 1985 (R) Playwright David Hare's first directorial effort, which he also wrote, about a Yorkshire schoolteacher whose life is shattered when a young, brooding stranger comes uninvited to a dinner party, and then shoots himself in her living room. Compelling but oh, so dark. Richardson, who plays a young Redgrave, is actually Redgrave's daughter. 97m/C VHS, DVD. GB Vanessa Redgrave, Ian Holm, Judi Dench, Joely Richardson, Tim (McInnerny) McInnery, Suzanna Hamilton; D: David Hare; W: David Hare; M: Nick Bicat. Berlin Intl. Film Fest. '85: Golden Berlin Bear; Natl. Soc. Film Critics '85: Actress (Redgrave).

Whacked! ♪♪ 2002 (R) Adopted brothers Mark and Tony go from the rough streets of Brooklyn to jobs as professional killers; one for the Mob, the other for the CIA. The discovery of a plot to steal millions from the government reunites them to protect a witness and bring down the scheme. Standard actioner has some good stunt work going for it. 91m/C DVD. Paul Sampson, Patrick Muldoon, Carmen Electra, Judge Reinhold, Michael (Mike) Papajohn; D: James Bruce; W: Paul Sampson, Matthew Goodman; C: Dan Heigh.

Whale for the Killing ♪♪½ 1981 An ecologist stranded in a remote Alaskan fishing village battles to save a beached humpback whale from a malicious Russian fisherman. Platitudinous and self-congratulatory, if well-meaning. From a book by Farley Mowat. 145m/C VHS. Richard Widmark, Peter Strauss, Dee Wallace Stone, Bruce McGill, Kathryn Walker; D: Richard T. Heffron; M: Basil Poledouris. TV

Whale Music ♪♪ 1994 Off-beat saga of a burned-out rock star and the runaway who invades his life. Desmond Howl (Chaykin) has retreated to a tumbledown estate in the Pacific Northwest, tired of the music grind, and wanting to devote himself to his masterwork—a symphony for whales. Runaway Claire (Preston) provides a surprisingly welcome presence in contrast to Howl's other visitors—ex-wife Fay (Dale), who wants to sell the estate, rapacious recording exec Kenneth (Welsh), and Howl's brother, singer Daniel (Gross), who happens to be dead and haunting his sibling. Haphazard direction helps dissipate powerful lead performances. Adapted from the novel by Paul Gallico. 100m/C VHS. *C:* Maury Chaykin, Cynthia (Cyndi, Cindy) Preston, Jennifer Dale, Kenneth Welsh, Paul Gross. *D:* Richard J. Lewis. *W:* Paul Quarrington, Richard J. Lewis; *C:* Vic Sarin. *M:* George Blondheim. Genie '94: Actor (Chaykin), Song ("Clare"), Sound.

Whale of a Tale ♂ 1976 (G) A young boy trains a killer whale to perform in the big show in the main tank at "Marineland." 90m/C VHS. *C:* William S'rathner, Marty Allen, Abby Dalton, Andy Devine, Nancy O'Conner. *D:* Ewing Miles Brown.

Whale Rider ♂♂♂½ 2002 (PG-13) Pai (Castle-Hughes, wonderful in her film debut) is a very determined 12-year-old Maori girl whose very traditional grandfather Koro (Paratene) is the tribal chief. Pai's father (Curtis) should be the next in line but after the death of his wife and Pai's infant twin brother, he's left the family. Although the stubborn Koro loves Pai, he refuses to see his granddaughter as a possible successor and won't train her in the customs and won't train her in the boys. So Pai observes and learns on her own—ready to show everyone that she has what it takes. Title refers to the legend that their ancestor arrived in their land on the back of a whale. Adapted from the 1986 novel by Witi Ihimaera. 105m/C VHS, DVD. *NZ GE* Keisha Castle-Hughes, Rawiri Paratene, Vicky Haughton, Cliff Curtis; *D:* Niki Caro; *W:* Niki Caro; *C:* Leon Narbey; *M:* Lisa Gerrard. Ird. Spirit '04: Foreign Film.

The Whales of August ♂♂♂½ 1987 Based on the David Berry play, the story of two elderly sisters—one caring, the other cantankerous—in their Maine home. Gish appears on the cover of a popular magazine. With the aid of a talent agent (Boyer), Antonietta becomes a famous fashion model. Only our photographer gets jealous when she ignores him for the debonair agent. 95m/B VHS. *IT* Sophia Loren, Marcello Mastroianni, Charles Boyer, Elisa Cegani, Nino Besozzi; *D:* Alessandro Blasetti; *W:* Ernio Flaiano, Suso Cecchi D'Amico, Alessandro Continenza; *C:* Otello Martelli.

Wham-Bam, Thank You Spaceman ♂½ 1975 (R) Very silly stuff about aliens with fiberglass heads and balloon ears that infiltrate when they become excited. They transport themselves to Earth in a tiny set decorated with trivial where most of the action takes place. Their mission: to impregnate Earth women to save their race. Though the female nudity is abundant, the sexual action is pretty tame by today's standards. 79m/C DVD. Jay Rasumny, Samuel Mann, Dyanne Thorne, Maria Arnold, Valda Hansen, Sandy Carey; *D:* John Ireland Jr.; *D:* William A. Lavey; *W:* Shlomo D. Weinstein; *C:* David Platnik; *M:* Miles Goodman, David White.

The Wharf Rat ♂♂ 1995 (R) Waterfront con man Petey Martin (Phillips) teams up with journalist Dexter Ireland (Tincotti) to avenge the murder of his policeman brother by a crazy Doc (Reinhold). 88m/C VHS. Lou Diamond Phillips, Rachel Ticotin, Judge Reinhold, Rita Moreno, Scott Cohen; *D:* Jimmy Huston; *W:* Jimmy Warren. CABLE

What a Carve-Up! ♂♂ *See* No Place Like Homicide 1962

What a Girl Wants ♂♂½ 2003 (PG) Another movie intended for the tweenie girl set alla "The Princess Diaries." Spunky Daphne Reynolds (Bynes) lives in Manhattan with her single bohemian mom Libby (Preston). Daphne has never met her Dad, a once-adventurous English lord, Sir Henry Dashwood (Firth), who has gone all staid and stuffy. So Daph takes off for London to introduce herself. Henry's got a political career to think about so

the arrival of this brash American teen is getting used to the "rules" when he learns that his wife has committed suicide, damning used to the happy occasion, especially to Glynnis (Chacellor) and her snobby daughter Clarissa (Cole). But you just know that Daphne will get everything she wants (including this really cute English boy)... Adapted from a play and previously filmed as 1958's "The Reluctant Debutante" with Sandra Dee. Very loosely adapted from eyes of Sciorra. Very loosely adapted from a 20-year-old Richard Matheson novel. 113m/C VHS, DVD. HD DVD, Rosalind Chao, Robir Williams, Annabella Sciorra, Cuba Gooding Jr., Max von Sydow, Jessica Brooks Grant, Josh Paddock; *D:* Vincent Ward; *W:* Ronald Bass; *C:* Eduardo Serra; *M:* Michael Kamen. Oscars '98: Visual FX.

What a Woman! ♂♂½ *La Fortuna di Essere Donna. Lucky to Be a Woman* 1956 Shop girl Antonietta (Loren) becomes a star thanks to a sensational photo of her taken by a paparazzo (Mastroianni) that appears on the cover of a popular magazine. 90m/C VHS. *C:* Andrew Dunn; *M:* Rupert Gregson-Williams.

What a Way to Die ♂½ 1970 (R) An evil assassin plots dispatching with a difference. 87m/C VHS. William Berger, Anthony Baker, Helga Anders, Georgia Moll; *D:* Helmut Foernbacher.

What about Bob? ♂♂♂ 1991 (PG) Bob, a ridiculously neurotic patient, follows his psychiatrist on vacation, turning his life upside down. The psychiatrist's family find Bob entertaining and endearing. Murray is overly excitable characterization occasionally wears thin. 99m/C VHS, DVD, Richard Dreyfuss, Bill Murray, Julie Hagerty, Charlie Korsmo, Tom Aldredge, Roger Bowen, Fran Brill, Kathryn Erbe, Doris Belack, Susan Willis; *D:* Frank Oz; *W:* Tom Schulman, Alvin Sargent; *C:* Michael Ballhaus; *M:* Miles Goodman.

What About Your Friends: Weekend Getaway ♂♂½ 2002 Heartfelt adventures of three bright African-American high school friends as they seek out college scholarships at a weekend retreat and begin to realize the power—and retreat and begin to realize the power—full life changes that await them—including the possibility that they'll be heading in different directions. 88m/C VHS, DVD. Keisha Knight Pulliam, Angell Conwell, Monica McSwain, Alexis Fields, Louis Gossett Jr., Denise Dowse, Ella Joyce, Troy Winbush; *D:* Niva Dorell; *W:* Kim Watson; *C:* Jurgen Baum; *M:* Andre Mayon. TV

What Comes Around ♂♂ 1985 (PG) A good-ole-boy drama about a doped-up country singer who is kidnapped by his brother for his own good. The singer's evil manager sends his stooges out to find him. Might have been funny, but isn't. But is it meant to be? Good Reed songs; mildly interesting plot. 92m/C VHS, DVD. Jerry Reed, Bo Hopkins, Arte Johnson, Barry Corbin. *D:* Jerry Reed.

What Did You Do in the War, Daddy? ♂♂½ 1966 Unfunny comedy set in WWII about a group of weary American soldiers trying to get a small town in Sicily to surrender. Things don't go smoothly thanks to a combination soccer game/wine festival; not to mention the Germans deciding to attack. Director Edwards comedic verve deserted him. 119m/C VHS. Dick Shawn, James Coburn, Sergio Fantoni, Giovanna Ralli, Aldo Ray, Harry (Henry) Morgan, Carroll O'Connor, Jay Novello, Vito Scotti; *D:* Blake Edwards; *W:* William Peter Blatty, Blake Edwards; *M:* Henry Mancini.

What Dreams May Come ♂♂ 1998 (PG-13) Romantic idea and tushily colorful computer imagery combine with sappy dialogue to turn surreal fantasy into very average digital hocus-pocus. Dr. Chris Nielsen (Williams) and his artist-wife Annie (Sciorra) lose their two children to a traffic accident. Four years later the doctor himself is killed in a freak accident. He finds that his heaven is much like a painting done by his wife (or Monet or Van Gogh) of their dream cottage. Chris is just

What Happened to Rosa? ♂♂♂ 1921 This early Goldwyn release, a whimsical Cinderella story, casts Normand as an endearing shop girl duped by a gypsy's bogus predictions. Believing herself to be the reincarnation of a Castilian noblewoman she dons a fancy gown, attends a fancy ship-board ball and captures the heart of the fancy doctor of her dreams. But fearing his rejection of her true identity she slips away during the chaos of a brawl, leading the good doctor to believe that she is dead. A comedy of errors unfolds before they meet again and live happily ever after. No doubt it jerked a few tears in its day. 42m/B VHS. Mabel Normand, Hugh Thompson, Doris Pawn, Victr Scherzinger.

What Happened Was... ♂♂♂ 1994 (R) Two-character study, about a weirdly nightmarish first date. Law secretary Jackie (Sillas) has been eyeing bookish paralegal Michael (Noonan) and finally invites him for dinner at her loft. The two struggle to relax and make small talk that turns into some unexpected soul baring. Emotionally distant Michael is unexpectedly hostile about his job and claims to be writing an expose of their law firm while overly friendly Jackie is writing a children's book, which turns out to be jarringly violent and apparently autobiographical. Provides an idiosyncratic, if limited, appeal thanks to a compelling performance by Sillas. 92m/C VHS. Tom Noonan, Karen Sillas; *D:* Tom Noonan; *W:* Tom Noonan; *C:* Joe DeSalvo. Sundance '94: Screenplay. Grand Jury Prize.

What Happens in Vegas 2008 (PG-13) Two jokes, no waiting! Stranding's feature film debut tries to be a comment on how differently men and women view sex and relationships, but it spends most of its time with a humming penis. Shandling is an alien sent from a planet of test tube people to impregnate an earth woman, once he's given the proper equipment (which has the previously mentioned unfortunate feature). He disguises himself as Harold, a bank executive, and gets dating tips from a philandering co-worker (Kinnea) who recommends AA meetings as a great pick-up place. H's direct approach ("You smell nice") somehow attracts a recovering alcoholic (Bering) who's on the biological clock. The other joke (and better of the two) involves a hen-pecked FAA inspector who's suspicious of Harold's origins. Shandling's limited range is exposed, and the juvenile script doesn't do him any favors. 107m/C VHS, DVD. Garry Shandling, Annette Bening, Greg Kinnear, Ben Kingsley, Linda Fiorentino, John Goodman, Richard Jenkins, Caroline Aaron, Judy Greer, Nora Dunn, Ann Cusack, Camryn Manheim, Janeane Garofalo, Stacey Travis, Willie Garson, Sarah Silverman; *D:* Mike Nichols; *W:* Garry Shandling, Michael Leeson, Edward Solomon, Peter Tolan; *C:* Michael Ballhaus; *M:*

What Ever Happened To... ♂♂½ *What Ever Happened to Baby Jane* 1993 Sisters play sisters as the Redgraves (in their first film together) tackle this remake of "What Ever Happened to Baby Jane" in all its demented glory. Former actress Blanche (Vanessa) and former child star "Baby Jane" (Lynn) are living in a decaying mansion, which Blanche, confined to a wheelchair, is talking about selling. "Baby" snaps (not that she was ever stable) and proceeds to torment her sis (more than usual). 94m/C VHS, DVD. Vanessa Redgrave, Lynn Redgrave, Bruce A. Young, Amy Steel, John Glover; *D:* David Greene; *W:* Brian Taggert.

What Ever Happened to Baby Jane? ♂♂♂½ 1962 Davis and Crawford portray aging sisters and former child stars living together in a decaying mansion. When the demented Jane (Davis) learns of her now-crippled sister's (Crawford) plan to institutionalize her, she tortures and plans her to the hilt, unafraid of Aldrich's unsympathetic camera, and the viciousness of her character. She received her 10th Oscar nomination for the role. 132m/B VHS, DVD. Bette Davis, Joan Crawford, Victr Buono, Anna Lee, B.C. Merrill, Maidie Norman; *D:* Robert Aldrich; *W:* Lukas Heller; *C:* Ernest Haller; *M:* Frank DeVol.

What Lies Beneath ♂♂ 2000 (PG-13) Empty-nester Pfeiffer wanders around a seemingly haunted house suspecting neighbors of murder and finding herself in some Black, black comedy, perverse and funny as only Almodovar can be. In Spanish with subtitles. Nudity and profanity. 100m/C VHS, DVD. Carmen Maura, Chus (Maria Jesus) Lampreave. *D:* Pedro Almodovar; *W:* Pedro Almodovar.

What Love Is ♂½ 2007 (R) Trouble, that's what it is, especially in this talky production. Nice guy Tom (Gooding) has his live-in girlfriend (Pratt) leave him on Valentine's Day just as he was about to propose. His buds come over (followed by their gals) to offer relationship advice despite being equally clueless. 93m/C DVD. Cuba Gooding Jr., Matthew Lillard, Anne Heche, Gina Gershon, Sean Astin, Tamala Jones, Judy Tylor, Shiri Appleby, Mars Callahan, Victora Pratt, Andrew Daily; *D:* Mars Callahan; *W:* Mars Callahan; *C:* David G. Stumz; *M:* Erik Godal

What! No Beer? ♂♂ 1933 Two dim-bulb friends decide to put their money into a defunct brewery hoping for the end of Prohibition. They start up operations too soon and wind up attracting the unwelcome attentions of gangster bootleggers and the cops. Mediocre comedy and Keaton's last starring role as his own problems with alcohol affected his work. 66mB VHS. Buster Keaton, Jimmy Durante, Phyllis Barry, Roscoe Ates, John Miljan, Henry Armetta, Edward Brophy. *D:* Edward Sedgwick.

What Planet Are You From? ♂♂ 2000 (R)

What Have I Done to Deserve This? ♂½ *Que He Hecho Yo Para Merecer Esto!* 1985 A savage parody on Spanish mores, about a speed-addicted housewife who ends up selling her son and killing her husband with a ham bone. Black, black comedy, perverse and funny as only Almodovar can be. In Spanish with subtitles. Nudity and profanity. 100m/C VHS, DVD. Carmen Maura, Chus (Maria Jesus) Lampreave. *D:* Pedro Almodovar; *W:* Pedro Almodovar.

bie, that's what it is, especially in this talky production. The "surprise" ending, telegraphed by the film's marketing campaign, has nothing to do with the film's first hour, which has everything to do with atmosphere and setting up distractions. 130m/C VHS, DVD. Harrison Ford, Michelle Pfeiffer, Diana Scarwid, Joe Morton, James Remar, Miranda Otto, Amber Valletta, Katharine Towne, Victoria Birdwell; *D:* Robert Zemeckis; *W:* Clark Gregg; *C:* Don Burgess. *M:* Alan Silvestri.

uses to give them an annulment or make any decisions about their money until they've proven they've worked on their marriage (with the help of counselor Queen Latifah) for six months. So naturally the duo try to drive each other crazy. Not yet reviewed. 7m/C Cameron Diaz, Ashton Kutcher, Lake Bell, Rob Corddry, Queen Latifah, Treat Williams, Dennis Miller, Dennis Farina, Zach Galifianakis, Jason Sudeikis, Michelle Krusiec, Krysten Ritter; *D:* Tom Vaughan; *W:* Dana Fox; *C:* Matthew F. Leonetti.

What Price Glory? ♂♂♂ 1952 Remake of the 1926 silent classic about a pair of comradely rivals for the affections of women in WWI France. Strange to have Ford directing an offbeat comedy, but it works; masterful direction, good acting. Demarest broke both legs in a motorcycle accident during shooting. 111m/C VHS, DVD. James Cagney, Dan Dailey, Corinne Calvet, William James Gleason, Robert Wagner, Max (Casey Adams) Showalter, Craig Hill, Marisa Pavan; **D:** John Ford.

What Price Hollywood? ♂♂♂ 1932 Aspiring young starlet decides to crash film world by using an alcoholic director as her stepping stone. Bennett is lovely; Sherman is superb as an aging, dissolute man who watches his potential slip away. From a story by Adela Rogers St. Johns. Remade three times as "A Star is Born." 88m/B VHS. Constance Bennett, Lowell Sherman, Neil Hamilton; **D:** George Cukor; **W:** Robert Presnell Sr., Gene Fowler Sr., Jane Murfin, Ben Markson, Allen Rivkin, Rowland Brown; **C:** Charles Rosher; **M:** Max Steiner.

What the #$*! Do We Know? ♂1/2 2004 Excruciatingly upbeat New Agers' guide to the perplexed. Follows a confused woman (Maitlin) through the troubles of daily life with annoying animation and talking heads helping her search for meaning. Supposed exploration of quantum theory and its impact is a queasy mishmash of pop- and pseudo-science, with some mysticism made to please the starry-eyed and vacant. 108m/C VHS, DVD. US Marlee Matlin, Elaine Hendrix, John Ross Bowie, Robert Bailey Jr., Barry Newman, Larry Brandenburg; **D:** Mark Vicente, William Arntz, Betsy Chasse; **W:** William Arntz, Betsy Chasse, Matthew Hoffman; **C:** David Bridges; **M:** Christopher Franke.

What the Deaf Man Heard ♂♂♂ 1998 Sly comedy starts off in the '40s with 10-year-old Sammy (Muniz) winding up alone in the small town of Barrington, Georgia after his single mother (Peters) vanishes. Since she told him to keep silent, Sammy continues to obey her—even when he's taken in by kindly bus station manager Norm (Skerritt). Soon everyone believes Sammy is deaf and mute and this doesn't change as Sammy grows to adulthood (Modine) as the local handyman. In fact, everyone is happy to confide in Sammy so he knows everyone's secrets—not always a happy situation. Based on "What the Deaf-Mute Heard" by G.D. Gearino. 107m/ C VHS, DVD. Matthew Modine, Tom Skerritt, Judith Ivey, Claire Bloom, James Earl Jones, Jerry O'Connell, Anne Bobby, Stephen Spinella, Jake Weber, Bernadette Peters, Frankie Muniz; **D:** John Kent Harrison; **W:** Frank Howson; **C:** David Connell; **M:** John Capek. **TV**

What the Peeper Saw ♂♂ 1990 When a young boy is confronted by a less than friendly theatre owner, he uses favorite scenes from "Sinbad" to deal with the aggressor. 86m/C VHS. AU Max Phipps, Danielle Spencer, Andrew Shepherd, Kim Gyngell, Gary Sweet, Robyn Gibbes, Pat Evison; **D:** Pino Amenta; **W:** Frank Howson; **C:** David Connell; **M:** Stelvio Cipriani.

What Time Is It There? ♂♂ 2001 Hsiao Kang (Lee) earns a living on the streets of Taipei by selling cheap wristwatches. Shiang-Chyi (Chen) wants to buy the watch Hsiao is wearing because it displays two time zones and she's flying to Paris. After she leaves, Hsiao suddenly decides to change all the watches on display to Paris time—and then all the watches and clocks he can find all around the city, even a gigantic clock on a building—in order to keep a connection with her. French and Chinese with subtitles. 116m/C VHS, DVD. TW Kang-sheng Lee, Shiang-chyi Chen, Tien Miao, Yi-ching Lu; **Cameos:** Cecilia Yip, Jean-Pierre Leaud; **D:** Ming-liang Tsai; **W:** Ming-liang Tsai, Pi-ying Yang; **C:** Benoit Delhomme.

What to Do in Case of Fire ♂♂1/2 Was Tun, Wenn's Brennt? 2002 (R) In 1987, six friends, part of an anarchist group in Berlin, make a bomb and place it in an empty building. It sits there until it's inadvertently detonated 15 years later. Although no one is injured, there is no statute of limitations on their crime. Veteran police detective Manowsky (Lowitsch) knows just who to look for and goes after the group's two remaining holdouts Tim (Schweiger) and Hotte (Feifel). The cops find incriminating materials and the buddies must now seek out their four former members in order to get them all off the hook. German with subtitles. 101m/C VHS, DVD. GE Til Schweiger, Sebastian Blomberg, Nadja Uhl, Martin Feifel, Matthias Matschke, Doris Schretzmayer; **D:** Gregor Schnitzer; **W:** Stefan Dahnert, Anne Wild; **C:** Andreas Berger; **M:** Stephan Zacharias, Stephan Gade.

What Waits Below ♂♂1/2 1983 (PG) A scientific expedition encounters a lost race living in caves in South America. Good cast, bad acting, and lousy script. Might have been much better. 88m/C VHS. Dick Curtis, Timothy Bottoms, Robert Powell, Lisa Blount; **D:** Don Sharp.

What Women Want ♂♂1/2 2000 (PG-13) Male-chauvinist Gibson gets electrocuted in his bathroom and suddenly has the power to hear women's thoughts, which aren't very complimentary towards him. Gibson, obviously enjoying himself, shines in this intermittently funny, lightweight but enjoyable romantic comedy. Subtlety and restraint are in short supply, but Gibson's performance, especially when he's doing his neo-Rat Pack act, makes up for the overindulgences. 123m/C VHS, DVD. Mel Gibson, Helen Hunt, Marisa Tomei, Lauren Holly, Bette Midler, Mark Feuerstein, Ashley Johnson, Judy Greer, Alan Alda, Delta Burke, Valerie Perrine, Lisa Edelstein, Sarah Paulson, Ana Gasteyer, Loretta Devine, Eric Balfour, Logan Lerman; **D:** Nancy Meyers; **W:** Josh Goldsmith, Cathy Yuspa; **C:** Dean Cundey; **M:** Alan Silvestri.

What Your Eyes Don't See ♂♂ Ojos Que No Ven 1999 Abelardo Sachis is the owner/editor of a political magazine. He's murdered in his home by a masked gunman. As the police start investigating, everyone in Sachis's life has their own theory on whether the killing was political or personal. Spanish with subtitles. 90m/C VHS, DVD. AR Mauricio Dayub, Luis Luque, Malena Solda, Gaston Pauls, Alejandra Flechner; **D:** Beda Docampo Feijoo; **W:** Beda Docampo Feijoo, Enrique Cortes; **C:** Ricardo Rodriguez; **M:** Ivan Wyszogrod.

Whatever ♂♂ 1998 (R) Straightforward teenage coming of age story set in a small New Jersey town in the early 80s. Focuses on the friendship of two high school seniors, aspiring artist Anna (Weil) and party animal Brenda (Morgan). Anna copes with her bitter single mom (Rosseter) and bratty little brother and hopes to escape to a prestigious art school in New York, but is in danger of being dragged down by Brenda. The two girls numb their mostly grim home lives with drugs, alcohol and casual sex at joyless parties. The revelation that Brenda is being sexually abused at home moves the plot into the TV movie realm. 112m/C VHS. Liza Weil, Chad Morgan, Kathryn Rossetter, Frederic Forrest; **D:** Susan Skoog; **W:** Susan Skoog; **C:** Michael Barrow, Mike Mayers.

Whatever It Takes ♂♂1/2 2000 (PG-13) Dopey teen romancer, with the usual attractive cast, that tries to be a modern version of "Cyrano de Bergerac." Ya got cutie boy-next-door-type Ryan (West) and his sensitive best pal Maggie (Sokoloff), who is, of course, his unknown soulmate. But Ryan pines for snobby hottie Ashley (O'Keefe). Meanwhile, Maggie has won the eye of jock Chris (Franco). So Chris and Ryan team up so that each can get their dream girl before the prom. You know how everything turns out. 94m/C VHS, DVD. Maria Sokoloff, Jodi Lyn O'Keefe, Shane West, James Franco, Julia Sweeney, Richard Schiff, Aaron Paul, Colin Hanks; **D:** David Raynr; **W:** Mark Schwahn; **C:** Tim Suhrstedt; **M:** Ed Shearmur.

What's Cooking? ♂♂♂ 2000 (PG-13) Follows the Thanksgiving tradition of feasting amid household tension through the stories of four American families: one Jewish, one Latino, one Vietnamese, and one African American. Culture clashes, generation gaps, sexual identities, divorce, and other family flash points get addressed with sincere writing and delicate acting by all involved. Written by India-born English director Chadha and her Japanese-American husband Berges—you can't more all-American than that. 109m/C VHS, DVD. Alfre Woodard, Joan Chen, Julianna Margulies, Mercedes Ruehl, Kyra Sedgwick, Lainie Kazan, Dennis Haysbert, Victor Rivers, Douglas Spain, A. Martinez, Maury Chaykin, Estelle Harris, Will Yun Lee, Kristy Wu; **D:** Gurinder Chadha; **W:** Gurinder Chadha, Paul Mayeda Berges; **C:** Jong Lin; **M:** Craig Pruess.

What's Eating Gilbert Grape? ♂♂♂ Gilbert Grape 1993 (PG-13) Offbeat is mildly descriptive. Depp stars as Gilbert Grape, the titular head of a very dysfunctional family living in a big house in a small Iowa town. His Momma (Cates) weighs more than 500 pounds and hasn't left the house in seven years, he has two squabbling teenage sisters, and 17-year-old brother Arnie (DiCaprio) is mentally retarded and requires constant supervision. What's a good-hearted grocery clerk to do? Well, when free-spirited Becky (Lewis) is momentarily marooned in town, Gilbert may have found a true soulmate. Performances, especially DiCaprio's, save this from the oddball/cute factor although flick would have benefited from streamlining, particularly the scenes involving Depp and bad-haircut Lewis. Based on the novel by Hedges. 118m/C VHS, DVD. Johnny Depp, Leonardo DiCaprio, Juliette Lewis, Mary Steenburgen, Darlene Cates, Laura Harrington, Mary Kate Schellhardt, Kevin Tighe, John C. Reilly, Crispin Glover, Penelope Branning; **D:** Lasse Hallstrom; **W:** Peter Hedges; **C:** Sven Nykvist; **M:** Alan Parker, Bjorn Isfalt. Natl. Bd. of Review '93: Support. Actor (DiCaprio).

What's Good for the Goose ♂♂1/2 1969 Stuffy, married financial institution executive's lifestyle receives a major overhaul when he attends a banking conference and meets a beautiful and free-spirited young woman whom he takes as a lover. Unfortunately, he perpetually finds her in bed with other men, and then his wife gets in on the act, too. Classic British humor. 104m/C VHS, DVD. GB Norman Wisdom, Sarah Atkinson, Sally Bazely, Sally Geeson, Derek Francis, Terence Alexander; **D:** Menahem Golan; **W:** Norman Wisdom, Menahem Golan; **C:** William Brayne; **M:** Reg Tisley.

What's Love Got to Do with It? ♂♂1/2 1993 (R) Energetic biopic of Classic British legend Tina Turner. Short sequences cover her early life before moving into her abusive relationship with Ike and solo comeback success. Bassett may not look like Tina, but her exceptionally strong performance leaves no question as to who she's supposed to be, even during on-stage Tina sequences. Some credibility is lost when Turner is shown in the final concert sequence—Gibson would have been wise to let Bassett finish what she started. Fishburne is a sympathetic but still chilling Ike, rising to the challenge of showing both Ike's initial charm and longtime cruelty. Based on "I, Tina" by Turner and Kurt Loder. 118m/C VHS, DVD. Angela Bassett, Laurence Fishburne, Vanessa Bell Calloway, Jenifer Lewis, Phyllis Stickney, Khandi Alexander, Pamela Tyson, Penny Johnson, Rae'ven (Alyia Larrymore) Kelly, Robert Miranda, Chi McBride, Damon Hines; **D:** Brian Gibson; **W:** Kate Lanier; **C:** Jamie Anderson; **M:** Stanley Clarke. Golden Globes '94: Actress—Mus./Comedy (Bassett); Blockbuster '95: Female Newcomer, V. (Bassett).

What's New Pussycat? ♂♂♂ Quoi! De Neuf, Pussycat? 1965 A young engaged man, reluctant to give up the girls who love him, seeks the aid of a married psychiatrist who turns out to have problems of his own. Allen's first feature as both actor and screenwriter. Oscar-nominated title song sung by Tom Jones. 108m/ C VHS, DVD. Peter Sellers, Peter O'Toole, Romy Schneider, Paula Prentiss, Woody Allen, Ursula Andress, Capucine; **D:** Clive Donner; **W:** Woody Allen; **M:** Burt Bacharach, Hal David.

What's the Matter with Helen? ♂♂1/2 1971 (PG) Two women, the mothers of murderous sons, move to Hollywood to escape their past and start a new life. They open a school for talented children, and seem to be adjusting to their new lives until strange things start happening. It is soon revealed that one of the mothers is a psychotic killer, and the other mother becomes part of an eerie finale. A fine starring vehicle for two aging actresses. Great score. 101m/C VHS, DVD. Debbie Reynolds, Shelley Winters, Dennis Weaver, Agnes Moorehead, Michael MacLammoir; **D:** Curtis Harrington.

What's the Worst That Could Happen? ♂♂ 2001 (PG-13) Billionaire DeVito catches thief Lawrence robbing his mansion and, in retaliation, takes the man's lucky charm ring. Since Lawrence just received the ring from new girlfriend Ejogo, he'll do anything to get it back. It becomes an escalating, and ultimately tiresome, war of revenge and humiliation. The large and talented cast are given neither the script or the room to really shine, but some of the supporters fare well. Leguizamo, Fichtner, and Headly stand out, but Lawrence and DeVito should've been reined in a bit. 95m/C VHS, DVD. US Martin Lawrence, Danny DeVito, Nora Dunn, William Fichtner, Glenne Headly, John Leguizamo, Bernie Mac, Carmen Ejogo, Larry Miller, Richard Schiff, Ana Gasteyer, Sascha Knopf, Siobhan Fallon, GQ, Lenny Clarke; **D:** Sam Weisman; **M:** Tyler Bates.

What's Up, Doc? ♂♂♂ 1972 (G) A shy musicologist from Iowa (Ryan) travels to San Francisco with his fiance (Kahn) for a convention. He meets the eccentric Streisand at his hotel and becomes involved in a chase to recover four identical flight bags containing top secret documents, a wealthy woman's jewels, the professor's musical rocks, and Streisand's clothing. Bogdanovich's homage to the screwball comedies of the '30s. Kahn's feature film debut. 94m/C VHS, DVD. Barbra Streisand, Ryan O'Neal, Kenneth Mars, Austin Pendleton, Randy Quaid, Madeline Kahn; **D:** Peter Bogdanovich; **W:** David Newman, Buck Henry, Robert Benton; **M:** Artie Butler. Writers Guild '72: Orig. Screenplay.

What's Up Front ♂♂1/2 The Fall Guy; A Fourth for Marriage 1963 Occasionally funny '60s gag-fest about an ogle-eyed bra salesman who decides to sell door-to-door in order to save a failing brassiere company. Filmed in "Girl-O-Rama" by the young Vilmos Zsigmond. Dated and weird, with camp value. No nudity. Costumes were done by Frederick's of Hollywood. 90m/C VHS. Tommy Holden, Marilyn Manning, Carolyn Walker, William Watters; **D:** Bob Wehling.

What's Up, Tiger Lily? ♂♂♂ 1966 This legitimate Japanese spy movie—"Kagi No Kag" (Key of Keys), a 1964 Bond imitation—was re-edited by Woody Allen, who added a new dialogue track, with hysterical results. Characters Terri and Suki Yaki are involved in an international plot to secure egg salad recipe; Allen's brand of Hollywood parody and clever wit sustain the joke. Music by the Lovin' Spoonful, who make a brief appearance. 90m/C VHS, DVD. JP Tatsuya Mihashi, Mie Hama, Akiko Wakabayashi, China Lee, Eisei Amamoto, Kumi Mizuno, Tadao Nakamura, The Lovin'

Spoonful; *Nar:* Woody Allen.

The Wheeler Dealers *Separate Beds* 1963 Garner plays a supposedly penniless investor (actually a Texas millionaire) who comes to New York stock analyst Remick fo' investment advice. Her shyster boss (Backus) tells Far to sell the aw-shucks cowboy worthless stock which turns out to be wo th a fortune. Zany spoof of Wall Street ethics. **100m/C VHS, DVD** Garner, Lee Remick, Jim Backus, Phil Harris, Shelley Berman, Chill Wills, John Astin, Louis Nye; *D:* Arthur Hiller.

Wheels of Fire *Vindicator* 1984 (R) The earth is a wasteland controlled by sadistic highway hoodlums. When they kidnap the hero's sister, he fights back in a flame-throwing car. Horrible "Road Warrior" rip-off. **81m/C VHS.** Gary Watkins, Lynda Wiesmeier; *D:* Cirio H. Santiago.

Wheels of Terror 1990 (R) Possessed black car stalks children in isolated village. Bus driver Cassidy gets behind the wheel of V-8 super-charged school bus to initiate most interminable chase scene in screen history. **86m/C VHS.** Joanna Cassidy, Marcie Leeds, Carlos Cervantes, Arlen Dean Snyder; *D:* Christopher Cain; *C:* Rick Bota; *M:* Jay Gruska.

When a Man Falls in the Forest *Desires of a Housewife* 2007 (R) Three former high school classmates meet middle age. Architect Gary (Hutton) is disillusioned by his job and estranged family, with a loving husband (Garcia), two little girls, and a satisfying career. She's also a closet alcoholic. Less about a long-ago accident; and Bill (Baker), a janitor at Gary's office, listens to an instructional tape on lucid dreaming, imagining a life he wil never live. It's all low-key and bleak. **86m/C DVD.** Timothy Hutton, Dylan Baker, Pruitt Taylor Vince, Sharon Stone, Nicolas Elia; *D:* Ryan Eslinger; *W:* Ryan Eslinger; *C:* Lawrence Sher; *M:* Billy Corgan.

When a Man Loves a Woman *To Have and to Hold; Significant Other* 1994 (R) Time to get suspicious when song titles become film titles. Alice Green (Ryan) is the mother in a perfect little family, with a loving husband (Garcia). She's also a satisfying career. Her alcoholism than the effect on her family and her hubby in particular, shown as a '90s sort of guy who allows Alice to keep her secret. Ryan's detox treatments and struggle back to sobriety are fertile ground for psycho-babble and 12-step clichés, but solid performances save this picture from drying out. **125m/C VHS, DVD.** Meg Ryan, Andy Garcia, Lauren Tom, Philip Seymour Hoffman, Tina Majorino, Mae Whitman, Ellen Burstyn, Eugene Roche, LaTanya Richardson, Jackson; *C:* Lajos Koltai; *M:* Zbigniew Preisner. *Blockbuster '95. Drama. Actress: V. (Ryan).*

When a Man Rides Alone 1933 Tyler relieves trains burse swindled investors. Lovely Lacey frowns on his initiative, so he kidnaps her to keep her quiet. The two fall in love, and the man who rides alone works beside his beloved. **60m/B VHS.** Tom Tyler, Adele Lacey, Alan Bridge, Robert Burns, Frank Ball, Alma Chester, Bud Osborne; *D:* J.P. (John) McGowan.

When a Man Sees Red 1934 Jones is a ranch foreman whose new boss is Campbell (she inherited the property). The two argue constantly but then come to realize all the fighting is just nidding true love. **60m/B VHS.** Buck Jones, Peggy Campbell, Dorothy Revier, Syd Saylor, Leroy Mason, Charles French, Robert F. (Bob) Kortman; *D:* Alan James.

When a Stranger Calls 1979 (R) Babysitter is terrorized by threatening phone calls and soon realizes that the calls are coming from within the house. Story was expanded from director Walton's short film "The Sitter." Distasteful and unlikely, though the first half or so is tight and terrifying. **97m/C VHS, DVD.** Carol Kane, Charles Durning, Colleen Dewhurst, Rachel Roberts, Rutanya Alda, Carmen Argenziano, Kirsten Larkin, Ron O'Neal, Tony Beckley; *D:* Fred Walton; *W:* Fred Walton, Steve Feke; *C:* Don Peterman.

When a Stranger Calls 2006 (PG-13) The call is still coming from (gasp) inside the house in this remake of the 1979 nail-biter, except the house is now a modern high-tech glass palace (strangely without caller ID though)—in the middle of nowhere, of course (because that's where most palaces are). The violence that marked the original is toned cown to make it more teen-friendly. Unfortunately, so is the suspense. **100m/C DVD, UMD, US** Camilla Belle, Tommy Flanagan, Tessa Thompson, Brian Geraghty, Clark Gregg, Derek de Lint, David Denman, Madeleine Carroll, Kate Jennings Grant, Arthur Young, Steve Eastin, Katie Cassidy; *D:* Simon West; *W:* Jake Wade Wall; *C:* Peter Menzies Jr.; *M:* James Dooley; *V:* Lance Henriksen.

When a Stranger Calls Back 1993 (R) Sequel to "When a Stranger Calls" finds college student Julia Jenz (Schoelen) still trying to put her life together five years after a terrifying ordeal with a stalker. She turns to her advisor Jill (Kane), who went through a similar fate, but once Jill becomes involved she once again becomes the pawn of a psychopath. It's up to retired detective John Clifford (Durning), who saved Jill before, to do his heroics once again. Scary opening sequence but suspense peters out toward the end. **94m/C VHS, DVD.** Carol Kane, Charles Durning, Jill Schoelen, Gene Lythgow, Karen Austin; *D:* Fred Walton; *W:* Fred Walton; *C:* David Geddes; *M:* Dana Kaproff. CABLE

When a Woman Ascends the Stairs *Onna Ga Kaidan O Agaru Toki* 1960 A young widow with an elderly mother and a useless brother supports them all by working as a Ginza bar hostess. As she approaches the perilous professional age of 30, Keiko must decide whether to open her own bar or marry once again. In Japanese with English subtitles. **110m/B VHS, DVD, JP** Hideko Takamine, Tatsuya Nakadai, Masayuki Mori; *D:* Mikio Naruse.

When Angels Fly 1982 In this emotional tale of love and murder, a young woman sets out to find the exact circumstances surrounding the mysterious death of her sister. **96m/C VHS. CA** Patricia Collins, David Gardner, Robert Hawkins, Joan Fowler, Jennifer Dale, Robin Ward; *D:* Jack Nixon-Browne; *M:* Mary Stuart; *M:* Brian Koonin. TV

When Angels Fly 1984 (R) The uncut original version of director Leone's saga of five young men growing up in Brooklyn during the '20s who become powerful mob figures. Also available in a 143-minute version. Told from the perspective of De Niro's Noodles as an old man looking back at 50 years of crime, love, and death, told with a sweeping and violent elegance. **225m/C VHS.** Robert De Niro, James Woods, Elizabeth McGovern, Treat Williams, Tuesday Weld, Burt Young, Joe Pesci, Danny Aiello, Darlanne Fluegel, Jennifer Connelly, Pataki; *D:* Sergio Leone; *C:* Tonino Delli Colli; *M:* Ennio Morricone.

When Brendan Met Trudy 2000 Irish romantic comedy by the writers of such standout novels as "The Commitments" and "The Snapper." Brendan (McDonald) is somewhat of a pansy-boy who attracts his polar opposite Trudy (Montgomery), a street-smart sort of girl and falls in love. Brendan, a straitlaced schoolteacher, soon learns that Trudy moonlights as a thief, and after the initial shock wears off, joins his outlaw honey in some good old-fashioned felonious fun. The true fun of the film, though, is its constant classic film references, such as when a misadventure lands Brendan in the gutter, he is reminded of William Holden in "Sunset Boulevard." Even if you're not a film buff, though, you'll still enjoy this offbeat comic romp. **95m/C VHS, DVD, IR GB** Peter McDonald, Flora Montgomery, Marie Mullen, Don Wycherley, Maynard Eziashi; *D:* Kieron J. Walsh; *W:* Roddy Doyle; *C:* Ashley Rowe; *M:* Richard Hartley.

When Danger Follows You Home 1997 (PG-13) Ann Werden (Williams), a psychologist at a county mental health facility, becomes interested in the case of a disturbed patient who calls himself Gogel, a computer genius with an FBI file. When Gogel mysteriously dies in Anne's home, she finds herself accused of manslaughter—and then her son is kidnapped. Anne's got a lot to figure out if she wants her life to go back to normal. **92m/C VHS.** JoBeth Williams, William Russ, Michael Manassen, Vanessa King, Susan Hogan, Duncan Fraser, Nicolas Surovy; *D:* David Peckinpah; *W:* Sharon Elizabeth Doyle; *C:* Robert Hudececk; *M:* Charles Bernstein. CABLE

When Dinosaurs Ruled the Earth 1970 (G) When "One Million Years B.C." ruled the boxoffice the Brits cranked out a few more lively prehistoric fantasies. A sexy cavegirl, exiled because of her blond hair, acquires a cave-beau and a dinosaur guardian. Stop-motion animation from Jim Danforth, story by J.G. Ballard. Under the name Angela Dorian, Vetri was Playmate of the Year in 1968 (A.D.). **96m/C VHS. GB** Victoria Vetri, Robin Hawdon, Patrick Allen, Drewe Henley, Sean Caffrey, Magda Konopka, Imogen Hassall, Patrick Holt, Jan Rossini; *D:* Val Guest; *W:* Val Guest; *C:* Dick Bush.

When Do We Eat? 2005 (R) Stereotypical dysfunctional family comedy. The Stuckman family's Passover Seder doesn't go smoothly since no one seems to get along. Although patriarch Ira (Lerner) is feeling no pain after stoner son Zeke (Feldman) doses him with ecstasy. **96m/C DVD. US** Michael Lerner, Lesley Ann Warren, Ben Feldman, Jack Klugman, Shiri Appleby, Mili Avital, Meredith Scott Lynn, Adam Lamberg, Max Greenfield, Cynda Williams; *D:* Salvador Litvak; *W:* Salvador Litvak, Nina Davidovich; *C:* M. David Mullen; *M:* Mark Adler.

When Eight Bells Toll 1971 MacLean adapted his own adventure novel in which naval secret service agent Philip Calvert (Hopkins) discovers that millions in gold bullion is being stolen. He and agent Hunslett (Redgrave) travel to Scotland, posing as marine biologists; there they encounter hostile Scottish locals and a suspicious Greek tycoon, Skouras (Hawkins), who has a very attractive companion (Delon). Hawkins had lost his voice to throat cancer so his lines were dubbed by actor Charles Gray. **94m/C VHS, DVD, GB** Anthony Hopkins, Corin Redgrave, Jack Hawkins, Nathalie Delon, Robert Morley, Derek Bond, Ferdinand "Ferdy" Mayne, Maurice Reeves; *D:* Etienne Perier; *W:* Alistair MacLean; *C:* Arthur Ibbetson; *M:* Angela Morley.

When Every Day Was the Fourth of July 1978 A nine-year-old girl asks her father, a lawyer, to defend a mute handyman accused of murder, knowing this will bring on the contempt of the community. Well handled, but see "To Kill a Mockingbird" first. Based on producer/director Curtis's childhood. Sequel: "The Long Days of Summer." **100m/C VHS,** Katy Kurtzman, Dean Jones, Louise Sorel, Harris Yulin, Chris Petersen, Geoffrey Lewis, Scott Brady, Henry Wilcoxon, Michael Pataki; *D:* Dan Curtis. TV

When Evil Calls 2006 (R) Well, don't answer! In this horror parody, a sleazy narrator (Pertwee) informs the audience of the consequences of a deadly text message circulating among high school students. The message grants the recipient's wish—to be popular, thin, beautiful, etc.—as long as the text gets passed on to two more students. Of course the wish is "granted" in the most gory (and often naked) way possible. Originally a 20-episode series made to be downloaded to a cell phone and then re-edited. **76m/C DVD. GB** Jennifer Lim, Dominique Pinon, Sean Pertwee, Sean Brosnan, Chris (Christopher Barrie, Rick Warden, Chris Barrie, Rick Warden; *D:* Johannes Roberts; *C:* John Raggett; *M:* Alex Taylor. VIDEO

When Father Was Away on Business *Otac na Sluzbenom Putu* 1985 (R) Set in 1950s Yugoslavia. A family must take care of itself when the father is sent to jail for philandering and is denounced by a Communist Party official. The moving story of the family's day-to-day survival is seen largely through the eyes of the father's six-year-old son, who believes dad is "away on business." In Yugoslavian with English subtitles. **144m/C VHS, DVD. YU** Moreno D'E Bartolli, Miki (Predrag) Manojlovic, Mirjana Karanovic; *D:* Emir Kusturica; *W:* Abdulah Sidran; *C:* Vilko Filac; *M:* Zoran Simjanovic. *Cannes '85: Film.*

When Gangland Strikes 1956 A country lawyer, blackmailed by the mob, tries to protect his family without caving in. Unexceptional remake o' "Main Street Lawyer." **70m/B VHS.** Raymond Greenleaf, Marjie Millar, Anthony Caruso, Jack Perrin, John Hudson; *D:* R.G. Springsteen; *M:* Van Alexander.

When Good Ghouls Go Bad 2001 (PG) Twelve-year-old Danny has just moved to a new town where he discovers that because of a town curse no one is allowed to celebrate Halloween. So Danny teams up with his recently departed Uncle Fred (Lloyd) to drive away the prankster ghouls who have been causing all the mischief. Based on a story by F.L. Stine. **93m/C VHS, DVD,** Christopher Lloyd, Tom Amandes, Joe Pichler; *D:* Patrick Read Johnson; *C:* Brian J. Breheny; *M:* Christopher Gordon. TV

When Harry Met Sally... 1989 (R) Romantic comedy follows the long relationship between two adults who try throughout the changes in their lives (and their mates) to remain platonic friends—and what happens when they don't. Wry and enjoyable script is enhanced by wonderful performances. Another directorial direct hit for "Meathead" Reiner, and a tour de force of comic screenwriting for Ephron, with improvisational help from Crystal. Great songs by Sinatra sound-alike Connick. **96m/C VHS, DVD.** Billy Crystal, Meg Ryan, Carrie Fisher, Bruno Kirby, Steven Ford, Lisa Jane Persky, Michelle Nicastro, Harley Jane Kozak, Tracy Reiner; *D:* Rob Reiner; *W:* Nora Ephron; *C:* Barry Sonnenfeld; *M:* Harry Connick Jr., Marc Shaiman. *British Acad. '89. Orig. Screenplay.*

When Hell Broke Loose 1958 Routine WWII actioner about a small-time crook (Bronson) who joins the Army, changes his ways because of the love of a good woman, and gets a chance to be a hero when he stumbles upon a Nazi assassination plot against General Eisenhower. **78m/B VHS.** Charles Bronson, Violet Rensing, Richard Jaeckel, Arvid Nelson, Robert Easton; *D:* Kenneth Crane; *W:* Oscar Brodney.

When Hell Was in Session 1982 In more than seven years as a prisoner of the Viet Cong, Holbrook is subjected to torture, starvation, and psychological warfare to break his will. Based on the true story of Navy Commander Jeremiah Denton. Painful and violent. **98m/C VHS,** Mako, Sab Shimono, Paul Mantee, Ronny Cox; *D:* Paul Krasny. TV

When He's Not a Stranger 1989 Lyr is a college freshman who goes to a campus party hosted by the football team. When Ron, the star quarterback, invites Lyn to his dorm room, the situation gets out of hand. Only Lyn calls it rape and Ron calls her a liar. Intense performances get a highlight of this well-done story. **100m/C VHS, DVD.** Annabeth Gish, John Terlesky, Kevin Dillon, Paul Dooley, Kim Meyers; *D:* John Gray. TV

When I Close My Eyes *Ko Zaxrem Oci* 1993 First independent film from Slovenia is a thriller in which rural postal employee Ana uses the cover another. When a motorcyclist robs the post office while Ana is working, she uses this crime to steal some money for ...

herself. But then Ana becomes obsessed with the thief and decides to track him down. Slovenian with subtitles. **94m/C VHS, DVD.** Petra Govc, Mario Selih, Mira Sardo; **D:** Franci Slak; **W:** Franci Slak, Silvan Furlan; **C:** Sven Pepeonik.

When I Close My Eyes ♪♪

Love Letter 1995 (PG-13) After attending a memorial service for her fiance, Hiroko (Nakayama) discovers his high school yearbook and an old address. She impulsively writes a letter to the address and is shocked to receive a reply from a young woman, Itsuki (also played by Nakayama), who bears the same name as her dead lover and even went to high school with him. The two women begin to correspond, as Hiroko asks what Itsuki remembers about the young man (Kashiwabara), and the mock resentment/friendship the two maintained in school. Eventually, Hiroko decides to meet Itsuki in person, hoping that she can get over the past that haunts her. Japanese with subtitles. **116m/C VHS.** *JP* Miho Nakayama, Takashi Kashiwabara, Etsushi Toyokawa; **D:** Shunji Iwai; **W:** Shunji Iwai; **C:** Noboru Shinoda.

When Justice Fails ♪♪

1998 (R) Vigilante goes after rapists. **90m/C VHS, DVD.** Jeff Fahey, Marlee Matlin, Monique Mercure, Carl Marotte; **D:** Allan Goldstein; **W:** Tony Kayden; **C:** Barry Gravelle.

When Knights Were Bold ♪♪½

1936 An English nobleman living in India inherits a castle in his native land. Returning home, he is knocked unconscious by a falling suit of armor while trying to impress a young lady and dreams himself back to medieval days. Enjoyable comedy about that ubiquitous British class hierarchy. **55m/B VHS.** Fay Wray, Jack Buchanan, Martita Hunt; **C:** Frederick A. (Freddie) Young.

When Ladies Meet ♪♪½

Strange Skirts 1941 Entertaining story of a love quadrangle that features several of MGM's top stars of the '40s. In this remake of the 1933 film, Crawford plays a novelist and an early proponent of the women's liberation movement. She falls in love with her publisher (Marshall), who just happens to be married to Garson. Meanwhile, Taylor, who is in love with Crawford, attempts to show her that the lisa more suitable match for her than Marshall, but Crawford has yet to catch on. The lengthy dialogue on women's rights is badly dated, but the real-life rivalry between Crawford and Garson adds a certain bite to their witty exchanges. **105m/B VHS.** Joan Crawford, Robert Taylor, Greer Garson, Herbert Marshall, Spring Byington; **D:** Robert Z. Leonard; **W:** Anita Loos, S.K. Lauren.

When Lightning Strikes woof!

1934 Lightning the Wonder Dog prevents the owner of a rival lumber company from stealing his master's land. He gets to use his talents of running, swimming, barking, and smoking cigars. Proves that real woofers were made way back when, even though in 1934 they didn't feature scantily clad babes. Part of Video Yesteryear's Golden Turkey series. **51m/B VHS.** Francis X. Bushman, Alice Dahl, William Desmond, (John) P(aterson) McGowan; **D:** Burton King, Harry Revier.

When Love Comes ♪♪

1998 Katie Keen (Owen) is a 40ish one-hit pop singer who decides to return home to New Zealand to rethink her fading career and life with her manager/lover Eddie (Westaway). Her best pal is still Stephen (Prast) who is involved with the younger Mark (O'Gorman), a songwriter. Mark's friends Fig (Brunning) and Sally (Hawthorne) have a band and ask Katie to sing on a recording. Everyone eventually winds up at Katie's seaside home trying to make potentially life-altering decisions. **94m/C DVD.** *NZ* Rena Owen, Dean O'Gorman, Simon Prast, Nancy Brunning, Simon Westaway, Sally Hawthorne; **D:** Garth Maxwell; **W:** Garth Maxwell, Peter Wells, Rex Pilgrim; **C:** Daryl Ward; **M:** Chris Anderson.

When Nature Calls woof!

1985 (R) A city family "gets back to nature" in this collection of mostly ineffective gags and poor satirical ideas. Probably your first and last chance to see Liddy and Mays on screen together. **76m/C VHS, DVD.** Davie Orange, Barbara Marineau, Nicky Beim, Tina Marie Staiano, Willie Mays, G. Gordon Liddy; **D:** Charles Kaufman.

When Night Is Falling ♪♪♪

1995 (R) Camille (Bussieres) is a professor of mythology at a Calvinist college in Toronto and engaged to theologian Martin (Czerny). Vaguely unsatisfied, Camille meets Petra (Crawford), a trapeze artist in a traveling circus, gets drawn into her world, falls in love, and must decide what she wants from her life. Lots of yearning, romance, and fantasy. Lesbian lovemaking scenes caused a ratings problem (the MPAA originally deemed them worthy of NC-17). **96m/C VHS.** *CA* Pascale Bussieres, Rachael Crawford, Henry Czerny, David Fox, Don McKellar, Tracy Wright; **D:** Patricia Rozema; **W:** Patricia Rozema; **C:** Douglas Koch; **M:** Lesley Barber.

When Pigs Fly ♪♪

1993 A story with two ghosts, a rocking chair, and a lonely, struggling musician. Lilly (Faithfull) and young Ruthie (Bella) are the ghosts, who both happen to have died in the same rocking chair a century apart. The chair is now in the possession of down-and-out jazz musician Marty (Molina), who doesn't know how to react to his unworldly visitors. Whimsical but not cloying. **94m/C VHS.** Marianne Faithfull, Alfred Molina, Seymour Cassel, Rachael Bella; **D:** Sara Driver; **W:** Ray Dobbins; **C:** Robby Muller; **M:** Joe Strummer.

When Saturday Comes ♪♪½

1995 Feel-good working-class drama follows Sheffield-born Jimmy Muir (Bean), whose life revolves around a job in a brewery, the local pub, chasing girls, and playing football (soccer) on the weekends. He gets involved with co-worker Annie (Lloyd), whose Uncle Ken (Postlethwaite) coaches the local semi-pro team and who offers Jimmy a chance to play. His success leads to a trial with the pros, Sheffield United, which Jimmy blows by getting drunk. After losing his job, his girl, and having his brother die in an accident, Jimmy struggles to pull himself together, and maybe get a second chance. **97m/C VHS.** *GB* Sean Bean, Emily Lloyd, Pete Postlethwaite, John McEnery, Ann Bell, Craig Kelly; **D:** Maria Giese; **W:** Maria Giese; **C:** Gerry Fisher; **M:** Anne Dudley.

When Taekwondo Strikes ♪

1983 (R) One brave Taekwondo master leads the Korean freedom fighters against the occupying army of WWII Japan. **95m/C VHS, DVD.** Jhoon Rhee, Ann Winton, Angela (Mao Ying) Mao, Huang Ing Sik; **D:** Raymond Chow.

When the Bough Breaks ♪♪

1986 A psychologist helps the police with the case of a murder-suicide witnessed by a child. He finds one sick secret society at work in this unkinder, ungentler TV thriller, based on the novel by Jonathan Kellerman. Danson co-produced. **100m/C VHS, DVD.** Ted Danson, Richard Masur, Rachel Ticotin, David Huddleston, James Noble, Kim Miyori, Merritt Butrick; **D:** Waris Hussein.

When the Bough Breaks ♪♪

1993 (R) A Texas police chief (Sheen) discovers seven severed hands and turns to a forensic expert (Walker) for help. But then the specialist discovers a psychic link between a mentally disturbed child and the serial killer. **103m/C VHS, DVD.** Ally Walker, Martin Sheen, Ron Perlman; **D:** Michael Cohn; **W:** Michael Cohn; **C:** Michael Bonvillain.

When the Bullet Hits the Bone ♪

1996 (R) Particularly nasty vigilante flick as EMS doc Jack Davies (Wincott) decides to take on a drug cartel, after being seriously wounded while trying to help drug-addicted hooker Lisa (Johnson) get away from her vicious pimp. **82m/C VHS, DVD.** Jeff Wincott, Michelle Johnson, Doug O'Keefe, Richard Fitzpatrick; **D:** Damian Lee; **W:** Damian Lee.

When the Cat's Away ♪♪♪

Chacun Cherche Son Chat 1996 Touching Gallic frolic finds introverted Parisian make-up artist face-to-face with adventure while searching for her lost cat. Chloe (Clavel) eventually comes out of her shell, as the search for little Gris-Gris brings her into contact with a wide variety of characters, some lonely, like herself, played by real people and real cats. Best non-actor kudos to Renee Le Calm as Madame Renee, the kooky neighborhood cat lady, with her network of cat fanciers acting as the reconnaissance party for the runaway feline. Director Klapisch's comedy also tackles weightier topics along the way, including loneliness, homelessness, racism, and the modernization of a city steeped with history. Stylishly spare with adept photography, seems almost semi-documentary. **91m/C VHS.** *FR* Garance Clavel, Zinedine Soualem, Olivier Py, Renee Le Calm, Romain Duris; **D:** Cedric Klapisch; **W:** Cedric Klapisch; **C:** Benoit Delhomme.

When the Clouds Roll By ♪♪½

1919 Psycho-satire pits demented doctor against Fairbanks in experiment to make him suicidal basket case. Fairbanks seems to contract ferocious nightmares, passionate superstitions, a spurning lover, and a warrant for his arrest, none of which suppresses his penchant for acrobatics. **77m/B VHS.** Douglas Fairbanks Sr., Herbert Grimwood, Kathleen Clifford, Frank Campeau, Ralph Lewis, Daisy Robinson, Albert MacQuarrie; **D:** Victor Fleming.

When the Dark Man Calls ♪♪

1995 (R) Shock ending and a strong lead performance by Van Ark enhance this cable mystery. Call-in radio shrink Julianne Kaiser (Van Ark) is stalked by ex-con Parmenter (Lewis). Twenty-five years ago she testified that he murdered her parents although the bitter man's always proclaimed his innocence. Now Kaiser is having grisly flashbacks to her childhood but can she figure out the truth before Parmenter kills her? Based on a novel by Stuart M. Kaminsky. **89m/C VHS.** Joan Van Ark, Geoffrey Lewis, Chris Sarandon, James Read, Frances Hyland, Janet-Laine Green; **D:** Nathaniel Gutman; **W:** Pablo F. Fenjves. **CABLE**

When the Greeks ♪♪

Ton Kero Ton Hellinon 1981 At the turn of the century, a rich young landowner is kidnapped by a group of nationalist bandits who demand a hefty ransom. But soon the young man realizes he's seeing his true Greek heritage for the first time and begins to identify with his captors. Greek with subtitles. **100m/C VHS.** *GR* Alexis Damianos, Kostas Arzoglou, George Sampanis, Stavros Mermighis; **D:** George Papadakis.

When the Legends Die ♪♪

1972 (PG) A Ute Indian strives to preserve his heritage in an often harsh modern world. Recorded in hi-fi. **105m/C VHS.** Richard Widmark, Frederic Forrest; **D:** Stuart Millar.

When the Line Goes Through ♪

1973 A drifter arrives in a small West Virginia town and changes the lives of two pretty sisters. **90m/C VHS.** Martin Sheen, Davey Davison, Beverly Washburn; **D:** Clyde Ware; **W:** Clyde Ware; **C:** Jackson Deerson; **M:** Lyle Ritz.

When the North Wind Blows ♪♪

1974 (G) An old, lone trapper hunts for and later befriends the majestic snow tiger of Siberia in the Alaskan wilderness. A good family film. **113m/C VHS.** Henry (Kleinbach) Brandon, Herbert Nelson, Dan Haggerty; **D:** Stewart Raffill.

When the Party's Over ♪♪½

1991 (R) Twenty-somethings share a southern California house and a hip—but ultimately edgy—lifestyle. **114m/C VHS, DVD.** Rae Dawn Chong, Fisher Stevens, Elizabeth Berridge, Sandra Bullock, Brian McNamara, Kris Kamm; **D:** Matthew Irmas.

When the Screaming Stops ♪

1973 (R) A hunter is hired to find out who has been cutting into the hearts out of young women who reside in a small village near the Rhine River. Turns out it's a she-monster who rules a kingdom beneath the river. Bad effects; gory gore; outlandish plot. All the ingredients, in other words, of a classic dog. **86m/C VHS.** *SP* Tony Kendall, Helga Line, Silvia Tortosa; **D:** Armando de Ossorio.

When the Sky Falls ♪♪

1999 Gritty bio loosely focuses on the last years of crusading Dublin journalist Veronica Guerin, who was murdered in 1996. Sinead Hamilton (Allen) has angered Dublin politicians, the IRA, police, and crime bosses with her investigation into the city's drug scene. She ticks off bad guy Dave Hackett (Flynn) and even tough detective Mackey (Bergin) tries to warn her but threats only make Hamilton more determined to do her expose. **107m/C VHS, DVD.** *IR* Joan Allen, Patrick Bergin, Liam Cunningham, Gerard Flynn, Kevin McNally, Jimmy Smallhorne, Jason Barry, Pete Postlethwaite, Des McAleer, Ruaidhri Conroy; **D:** John MacKenzie; **W:** Michael J. Sheridan, Ronan Gallagher, Colum McCann; **C:** Seamus Deasy; **M:** Pol Brennan.

When the Time Comes ♪♪

1991 (PG-13) A woman dying of cancer wants to take her own life, but when her husband refuses, she seeks the help of a male friend. Excellent acting doesn't provide the needed depth. Less a disease-of-the-week TV movie, more of an ethical-dilemma-of-the-week, and just as trivial. **94m/C VHS.** Bonnie Bedelia, Brad Davis, Terry O'Quinn, Karen Austin, Donald Moffat, Wendy Schaal; **D:** John Erman; **M:** Marvin Hamlisch.

When the West Was Young ♪½

Wild Horse Mesa 1932 An outdoor adventure about rounding up horses in the Old West. Based on a novel by Zane Grey. **58m/B VHS, DVD.** Randolph Scott, Sally Blane, Guinn "Big Boy" Williams; **D:** Henry Hathaway.

When the Whales Came ♪♪♪

1989 (PG) A conservationist fable about two children and a grizzled old codger living on a remote British isle during WWI. They try to avert British as mysterious narwhal whales descend on the island. Moralistic and uninvolving; poorly acted; slumber-inducing. Adapted from the novel by Morpurgo. **100m/C VHS.** *GB* Paul Scofield, Helen Mirren, David Threlfall, David Suchet, Jeremy Kemp, Max Rennie, Helen Pearce, Barbara Jefford; **D:** Clive Rees; **W:** Michael Morpugo; **M:** Christopher Gunning, Ruth Rennie.

When the Wind Blows ♪♪♪

1986 An animated feature about a retired British couple when their peaceful—and naive—life in the country is destroyed by nuclear war. Poignant, sad, and thought-provoking, and just a little scary. Features the voices of Ashcroft and Mills; Roger Waters, David Bowie, Squeeze, Genesis, Hugh Cornell, and Paul Hardcastle all contribute to the soundtrack. Based on the novel by Raymond Briggs. **80m/C VHS.** *GB* Jimmy T. Murakami; **V:** Peggy Ashcroft, John Mills.

When Thief Meets Thief ♪♪½

1937 A cat burglar finds his world turned upside down when he begins to fall in love with one of his victims. Not much happening except a few nice stunts by Fairbanks. **85m/B VHS.** *GB* Douglas Fairbanks Jr., Valerie Hobson, Alan Hale, Jack Melford, Leo Genn, Ian Fleming; **D:** Raoul Walsh.

When Time Expires ♪♪

1997 (PG-13) Extraterrestrial scientist Travis Beck (Grieco) time travels from the future to present-day earth to stop the planet's destruction by evil forces. **93m/C VHS.** Richard Grieco, Cynthia Geary, Mark Hamill, Tim Thomerson, Chad Everett; **D:** David Bourla; **W:** David Bourla; **C:** Dean Lent; **M:** Todd Hayen. **CABLE**

When Time Ran Out ♪

1980 (PG) A volcano erupts on a remote Polynesian island covered with expensive hotels and tourists with no way to escape. Contains scenes not seen in the theatrically released print of the film. A very good cast is wasted in this compilation of disaster film cliches. **144m/C VHS.** Paul Newman, Jacqueline Bisset, William Holden, Ernest Borgnine, Edward Albert, Barbara Carrera, Valentina Cortese, Burgess Meredith, Noriyuki "Pat" Morita, Red Buttons; **D:** James Goldstone; **W:** Stirling Silliphant; **C:** Fred W. Koenekamp; **M:** Lalo Schifrin. **CABLE**

When Trumpets Fade ♪♪

1998 (R) Private Manning (Eldard) is the only survivor of his platoon, which is caught in the Battle of the Hurtgen Forest along the Belgian-German border in 1944. Manning is interested in nothing more than his own survival but his skills attract the attention of an officer (Donovan) who promptly promotes him to sgt. (and soon, lieutenant) and gives him his own platoon

When We Were Kings ☆☆☆ 1996 (PG) Chronicles the 1974 heavyweight championship fight, held in Zaire, between underdog Muhammad Ali and George Foreman. Gast uses original footage of the prefight hype as well as current interviews from George Plimpton and Norman Mailer (who covered the fight at the time) and later adds commentary from Spike Lee. 94m/C VHS, DVD. D: Leon Gast. Cam-ture Doc.: Broadcast Film Critics '96; Feature Doc.; CABLE

When Will I Be Loved ☆☆½ 2004 (R) Cynical, chilly love-ate thriller stars Campbell as wealthy dilettante Vera Barrie who's involved with a shady, sometimes violent street hustler named Ford (Wellen). Needing money, Ford sells Vera's favors to a visiting Italian media mogul (Chianese), but manipulative Vera turns the tables by working out her own devious deal. Despite its brief length, film's rambling and semi-improvised dialogue and structure does the story no favors, although the city of New York is nicely displayed. 81m/C DVD. US Neve Campbell, Dominic Chianese, Frederick Weller, Karen Allen, Barry Primus, Abdullah Ibrahim, James Toback; W: James Toback; D: James Toback. C: Lawrence McConkey, M: Oli "Power" Grant.

When Willie Comes Marching Home ☆☆☆ 1950 An insightful (and funny) satire from Ford with equally well-done dramatic moments. William Kluggs (Dailey) wants to become a hero when he enlists, but instead he's assigned to be the gunnery instructor in his own hometown. A town joke, Bill finally gets his chance as a B-17 gunner but winds up being rescued after aiding them, he does become a hero but is sworn to secrecy by his superiors. Bill then has to endure more abuse from the folks at home until everything is revealed. 90m/C DVD. Dan Dailey, William Demerest, Bill Calvert, Lloyd Corrigan, Colleen Townsend, James Lydon, Evelyn Varden; D: John Ford; W: Mary Loos, Richard Sale; C: Leo Tover; M: Alfred Newman.

When Wolves Cry ☆½ The Christmas Tree 1969 (G) Tearjerker about an estranged father and young son reunited on a Corsican vacation. Their newfound joy sours when the lad is diagnosed with a fatal illness. Hardly one of Holden's best films. 108m/C VHS. William Holden, Virna Lisi, Brook Fuller, Andre Bourvil; D: Terence Young.

When Women Had Tails ☆½ Quando le Donne Avevano la Coda 1970 (R) A primitive comedy about prehistoric man's discovery of sex. And boy, did they ever discover it. Harmless (more or less), though not exactly cerebral. Followed by "When Women Lost Their Tails." 99m/C VHS. IT Senta Berger, Frank Wolff; D: Pasquale Festa Campanile; M: Ennio Morricone.

When Women Lost Their Tails ☆ 1975 (R) Ostensible sequel to "When Women Had Tails" about prehistoric cavemen and their sexual habits. 94m/C VHS, DVD. IT Senta Berger; D: Pasquale Festa Campanile; M: Ennio Morricone.

When Worlds Collide ☆☆☆ 1951 (G) Another planet is found to be rushing inevitably towards earth, but a select group of people attempt to escape in a spaceship; others try to maneuver their way on board. Oscar-quality special effects and plot make up for cheesy acting and bad writing. 81m/C VHS, DVD. Richard Derr, Barbara Rush, Larry Keating, Peter Hansen; D: Rudolph Maté; W: Sydney (Sidney) Boehm; C: William Howard Greene; M: Leith Stevens.

When Your Lover Leaves ☆ 1983 Alleged comedy about a woman, dumped by her married boyfriend, who gets involved in a short-lived relationship with a neighbor. When that also doesn't work out, she decides she must first do something to please herself. Here endeth the lesson. Produced by Fonzie and Richie of "Happy Days." 100m/C VHS. Valerie Perrine, Betty Thomas, David Ackroyd, Ed O'Neill, Dwight Schultz, Shannon Wilcox; D: Jeff Bleckner; M: Randy Edelman. TV

When's Your Birthday? ☆☆½ 1937 Brown stars in this comedy about a prize-fighter who is working his way through astrology school with his fighting skills. The stars, in turn, tell him when to fight. Lame zaniness (what other kind is there?) meant as a vehicle for Brown, though Kennedy is funnier. The opening sequence, an animated cartoon showing the influence of the moon over the planets, was filmed in Technicolor. 77m/B VHS. Joe E. Brown, Marian Marsh, Edgar Kennedy; D: Harry Beaumont.

Where ☆☆ 1990 Young man living in Budapest begins a psycho-sexual relationship with a young woman that explores the nature of domination and submission. After moving to Los Angeles, he subjects himself to the whims of a student. In English and Hungarian with subtitles. 7m/C VHS. HU Miklos Acs, Dennis Cornall; D: Gabor Szabo; D: Nyika Jancso.

Where Angels Fear to Tread ☆☆ 1991 (PG) Another turn-of-the-century tale of the English in Italy from the pen of E.M. Forster. Widowed, 40ish Lilia (Mirren) is urged by her stuffy in-laws to spend some time in Italy. Much to everyone's dismay she impulsively marries a 21-year-old Italian—with disastrous consequences. Based on Forster's first novel, the characters are more stereotypical and the story less defined than his later works and the movies made from them. Impressive performances and beautiful settings make up for a somewhat lackluster direction that isn't up to the standards set by the team of Merchant-Ivory, responsible for the Forster films "A Room with a View" and "Howard's End." 112m/C VHS, DVD. GB Rupert Graves, Helena Bonham-Carter, Judy Davis, Helen Mirren, Giovanni Guidelli, Barbara Jefford, Thomas Wheatley, Sophie Kullman; D: Charles Sturridge; W: Charles Sturridge, Tim Sullivan, Derek Granger; C: Michael Coulter; M: Rachel Portman.

Where Angels Go, Trouble Follows ☆½ 1968 Follow-up to "The Trouble with Angels," with Russell reprising her role as the wise Mother Superior challenged by her mischief loving students. Younger, modern nun Stevens tries to convince Russell to update her old-fashioned ways and persuades her to take the convent students on a bus trip to a California peace rally. A very young Saint James is one of the convent's irrepressible troublemakers. Very dated but still mildly amusing. 94m/C VHS, DVD. Rosalind Russell, Stella Stevens, Binnie Barnes, Mary Wickes, Susan St. James, Dolores Sutton, Alice Rawlings; Cameos: Milton Berle, Arthur Godfrey, Van Johnson, Robert Taylor; D: James Neilson; M: Blanche Hanalis.

Where Are the Children? ☆½ 1985 (R) Based on Mary Higgins Clark's bestseller. A woman who was cleared of murdering her children from her first marriage remarries. Then the children from her second marriage are kidnapped. Suspense completely, until it falls apart. 92m/C VHS, DVD. Jill Clayburgh, Max Gail, Barnard Hughes, Clifton James, Harley Cross, Elisabeth Harrold, Elizabeth Wilson, Frederic Forrest; D: Bruce Malmuth.

Where Danger Lives ☆☆ 1950 Tough guy Mitchum plays a patsy. Young Dr. Jeff Cameron is intrigued when he treats beautiful Margo (Domergue), who attempted suicide. After Jeff gets all hot and bothered, he learns that the older man (a sneering Rains) he thought was her father, is actually her husband. During a boozy confrontation, the cuckold husband winds up dead, the doc gets a concussion, and Margo insists they have to make a run for the border. The French Domergue was a sultry, but not particularly talented, protege of Howard Hughes. While doing research for this novel on their Easter vacation. Features the film debuts of Francis, who had a hit single with the film's title song, and Prentiss. Heed the shoulders above the ludicrous '84 remake. 99m/C VHS, DVD George Hamilton, Jim Hutton, Yvette Mimieux, Connie Francis, Paula Prentiss, Dolores Hart, Frank Gorshin, Barbara Nichols, Rory Harrity, Chill Wills, Jack Kruschen; D: Henry Levin; M: George Wells; C: Robert J. Bronner; M: Pete Rugolo, George Stoll.

Where East Is East ☆☆ 1929 In Indochina a badly scarred trapper (Chaney) lives with his daughter (Velez) and sells wild animals to circuses. Velez falls in love with a circus owner's son but finds out her own mother, seeking revenge on her ex-husband, trying to seduce the young man. A gorilla figures in the plot as well. Chaney's makeup, which contributed to his "Man of a Thousand Faces" nickname, highlights a contrived movie. 140m/C B VHS. Lon Chaney Sr., Lupe Velez, Estelle Taylor, Lloyd Hughes; D: Tod Browning.

Where Have All the People Gone? ☆☆ 1974 Solar explosion turns most of Earth's inhabitants to dust. While the Anders family vacations in a cave, the family tries to return home amid the devastation. Bad timing, bad acting. 74m/C VHS, DVD. Peter Graves, Kathleen Quinlan, Michael James Wixted, George O'Hanlon Jr., Verna Bloom; D: John Llewellyn Moxey. TV

Where Is My Child? ☆☆½ 1937 Immigration to the New World brings only misfortune and betrayal in this tale of Jews in Eastern Europe between 1911 and 1937, as many experience the loss of family ties and religion. In Yiddish with English subtitles. 92m/B VHS, Celia Adler, Anna Lillian, Morris Strassberg; D: Abraham Lef, Harry Lynn.

Where Is My Friend's House? ☆☆ Where is the Friend's Home? / Khaneh-ie Doost Kojast? 1987 At the village school, Mohamad is told by his teacher that he'll be expelled if he doesn't do his homework in the required exercise book. But that evening schoolmate Ahmed realizes he's taken Mohamad's book by mistake so he sets off to find his friend's house in a neighboring village. However, Ahmed gets lost and none of the adults he meets will help him. Farsi with subtitles. Followed by "Life and Nothing More..." and "Through the Olive Trees." 90m/C VHS, DVD. /A Babak Ahmed Poor, Ahmed Ahmed Poor, Khoda Bareh Defai; D: Abbas Kiarostami; W: Abbas Kiarostami; C: Farhad Saba.

Where Love Has Gone ☆☆½ 1964 A soaper about a teenage daughter who kills her nympho mother's current boyfriend. Her divorced parents end up dragging the ordeal out in a murder trial custody battle and a lot of family skeletons come out of their closets. Davis is the manipulative grand dame grandmother. Based on the novel by Harold Robbins. 114m/C VHS. Bette Davis, Susan Hayward, Joey Heatherton, Jane Greer, George Macready; D: Edward Dmytryk; W: John Michael Hayes.

Where Sleeping Dogs Lie ☆☆½ 1991 (R) A struggling writer moves into an abandoned California home five years after a wealthy family was murdered there. While doing research for his novel on their brutal killings, he revives their ghosts as well as the very real presence of their killer. 92m/C VHS, DVD. Dylan McDermott, Tom Sizemore, Sharon Stone; D: Charles Finch.

Where the Boys Are ☆☆ 1960 Four college girls go to Fort Lauderdale to have fun and meet boys during their Easter vacation. Features the film debuts of Francis, who had a hit single with the film's title song, and Prentiss. Heed the shoulders above the ludicrous '84 remake. 99m/C VHS, DVD George Hamilton, Jim Hutton, Yvette Mimieux, Connie Francis, Paula Prentiss, Dolores Hart, Frank Gorshin, Barbara Nichols, Rory Harrity, Chill Wills, Jack Kruschen; D: Henry Levin; M: George Wells; C: Robert J. Bronner; M: Pete Rugolo, George Stoll.

Where Eagles Dare ☆☆☆ 1968 (PG) During WWII, a small group of Allied commandos must rescue an American general held by the Nazis in a castle in the Bavarian Alps. Relentless plot twists and action keep you breathless. Well-made suspense/adventure. Alistair MacLean adapted his original screenplay into a successful novel. 158m/C VHS, DVD. GB Clint Eastwood, Richard Burton, Mary Ure, Michael Hordern, Anton Diffring, Ingrid Pitt, Patrick Wymark, Robert Beatty, Donald Houston, Derren Nesbitt, Ferdinand "Ferdy" Mayne, Peter Barkworth, William Squire, Neil McCarthy, Brook Williams, Vincent Ball; D: Brian G. Hutton; W: Alistair MacLean; C: Arthur Ibbetson; M: Ronald Goodwin.

Where the Buffalo Roam ☆½ 1980 (R) Early starring role for Murray as the legendary "gonzo" journalist Hunter S. Thompson. Meandering satire based on Thompson's books "Fear and Loathing in Las Vegas" and "Fear and Loathing on the Campaign Trail '72." Either confusing or offensively sloppy, depending on whether you've read Thompson. Music by Neil Young, thank goodness, or this might be a dud. 99m/C VHS, DVD. Danny DeVito, Bill Murray, Peter Boyle, Susan Keller, Leonard Frey, Bill Murray, Rene Auberjonois, R.G. Armstrong, Rafael Campos, Craig T. Nelson; D: Art Linson; W: John Kaye; C: Tak Fujimoto; M: Neil Young.

Where the Bullets Fly ☆½ 1966 Fast-paced Bond spoof. A British spy takes on the intelligence forces of several governments in his search for a new fuel elixir. Fun, if not scintillating. 88m/C VHS. GB Tom Adams, Dawn Addams, Michael Ripper, Tim Barrett; D: John Gilling.

Where the Day Takes You ☆☆½ 1992 (R) Runaways on Hollywood Boulevard are depicted in an unfortunately heavy-handed drama. King (Mulroney) is the slightly older leader of a group of street kids who tries to discourage his friends from getting involved in the violence and drugs they see all around them. He falls in love with new runaway Heather (Boyle) but their love is doubted by the relentless bleakness of their lives. Among the other members of King's "family" are Astin, also a young druggie in thrall to his older dealer (MacLachlan) and Getty, as a young hustler drawn to violence. The story's predictability undercuts some convincing acting. 105m/C VHS, DVD. Dermot Mulroney, Lara Flynn Boyle, Balthazar Getty, Sean Astin, James LeGros, Ricki Lake, Kyle MacLachlan, Rober Knepper, Peter Dobson, Stephen Tobolowsky, Will Smith, Adam Baldwin, Christian Slater, Nancy McKeon, Alyssa Milano, David Arquette, Leo Rossi, Rachel Ticotin; D: Marc Rocco; W: Michael Hitchcock, Kurt Voss, Marc Rocco; M: Mark Morgan; V: Laura San Giacomo.

Where the Eagle Files ☆☆ Pickup on 101 1972 (PG) Ersatz '60s rock 'n' roll road movie shuffles together free spirited college coed, hobo with heart of gold, and rock and roller who's making a lane change out of the fast track. 93m/C VHS. Jack Albertson, Lesley Ann Warren, Marti Sheen, Michael Ontkean; D: John Florea.

Where the Green Ants Dream ☆☆½ Wo Die Grunen Ameisen Traumen 1984 A mining excavator in the Outback is halted by Aborigines who declare ownership of the sacred place where the mythical green ants are buried. A minor entry in the Herzog vision of modern-versus-primal civilization. Too obvious and somehow unsure of itself artistically. 99m/C VHS, DVD. GE Bruce Spence, Wandjuk Marika, Roy Marika, Ray Barrett, Norman Kaye, Colleen Clifford; D: Werner Herzog.

Where the Heart Is ☆☆ 2000 (PG-13) Pregnant 17-year-old Novalee Nation (Portman) is on her way to California with her no-good boyfriend Willy Jack (Bruno), who abandons her at an Oklahoma WalMart. With-out friends or funds, Novalee hides out in

Where the Boys Are '84 ♦ 1984 (R) Horrible remake of the 1960 comedy still features girls searching for boys during spring break in Fort Lauderdale. Telling about its era; charm gives way to prurience. 95m/C VHS. Lisa Hartman, Black, Wendy Schaal, Lorna Luft, Lynn-Holly Johnson, Christopher McDonald; D: Hy Averback; W: Jeff Burkhart; C: James A. Crabe; M: Sylvester Levay, Golden Raspberries '84: Worst Support Actress (Johnson).

the store until she gives birth there. Suddenly a local celeb, Novalee finds shelter with eccentric Sister Husband (Channing) and becomes best pals with fecund single mom, Lexi (Judd). Novalee also gets a potential romance with shy librarian Forney (Frain). Superficially one-note sap and Portman seems miscast. Based on the novel by Billie Letts. 115m/C VHS, DVD. Natalie Portman, Ashley Judd, Stockard Channing, James Frain, Dylan Bruno, Joan Cusack, Keith David, Richard Jones, Sally Field; D: Matt Williams; W: Lowell Ganz, Babaloo Mandel; C: Richard Greatrex; M: Mason Daring.

Where the Hot Wind Blows 𝒹𝒹

1959 Marietta (Lollobrigida) is a poor girl in a Sicilian fishing village who's in love with Enrico (Mastroianni), an equally impoverished engineer. But she comes up with a unique way to earn money for her dowry even as she's pursued by every male in town. Meanwhile, local mobster Brigante (Montand) wants to make sure than his son Francisco (Mattioli) doesn't get too involved with the unsuitable Lucrezia (Mercouri). Italian with subtitles. 120m/B VHS, DVD. FR IT Gina Lollobrigida, Marcello Mastroianni, Yves Montand, Melina Mercouri, Raf Mattioli, Pierre Brasseur, Paolo Stoppa; D: Jules Dassin; W: Jules Dassin, Francoise Giroud; C: Otello Martelli; M: Roman Vlad.

Where the Lilies Bloom 𝒹𝒹𝒹

1974 (G) The touching story of four backwoods children who are left orphans when their father dies. They don't report his death to authorities, because they are afraid the family will be separated and sent to an orphanage. Stanton is great as the crusty landlord the children gradually accept as a friend. Based on the book by Vera and Bill Cleaver. 96m/C VHS. Julie Gholson, Jan Smithers, Matthew Burrill, Helen Harmon, Harry Dean Stanton, Rance Howard, Sudie Bond, Tom Spratley, Helen Bragdon, Alice Beardsley; D: William A. Graham.

Where the Money Is 𝒹𝒹½

2000 (PG-13) Famed bank robber Henry (Newman) fakes a stroke so he can get transferred from prison to a nursing home. Carol (Fiorentino) is the bored former prom queen nurse who knows he's taking and enlists his help in pulling one more job. She also brings along dull but devoted hubby Wayne (Mulroney). The characters, and the superb actors playing them, are the main reasons to see this one. Newman is still more charismatic than 90% of the leading men around, while Fiorentino seem inspired just by being on the same set with him. The lightweight script depends heavily on the audience's knowledge of Newman's filmography and the standard caper comedy conventions, but still manages to entertain. 90m/C VHS, DVD. Paul Newman, Linda Fiorentino, Dermot Mulroney, Susan Barnes, Bruce MacVittie, Dorothy Gordon, Anne Pitoniak, Irma St. Paule; D: Marek Kanievska; C: Thomas Burstyn; M: Mark Isham.

Where the North Begins 𝒹

1947 A Mountie ransacks the Canadian countryside in search of crime. 41m/B VHS. Russell Hayden, Jennifer Holt, Tristram Coffin, Denver Pyle, Steve Barclay; D: Howard Bretherton; M: Betty Burbridge.

Where the Red Fern Grows 𝒹𝒹½

1974 (G) A young boy in Dust Bowl-era Oklahoma learns maturity from his love and responsibility for two Redbone hounds. Well produced, but tends to be hokey; good family fare. Followed by a sequel nearly 20 years later. 97m/C VHS, DVD. James Whitmore, Beverly Garland, Jack Ging, Lonny (Lonnie) Chapman, Stewart Petersen; D: Norman Tokar; W: Douglas Day Stewart, Eleanor Lamb; C: Dean Cundey; M: Lex de Azevedo.

Where the Red Fern Grows: Part 2 𝒹𝒹½

1992 (G) Sequel to one of the most popular family movies of all time starring Brimley as Grandpa Coleman. Set deep in the Louisiana woods, this magical coming of age tale will touch the hearts of young and old viewers alike. 105m/C VHS, DVD. Wilford Brimley, Doug McKeon, Lisa Whelchel, Chad McQueen; D: Jim McCullough; W: Samuel Bradford; C: Joseph M. Wilcots; M: Robert Sprayberry.

Where's the River Runs Black 𝒹𝒹

1986 (PG) An orphaned Indian child is raised in the Brazilian jungles by river dolphins. He is eventually befriended by a kindly priest who brings him into the modern world of violence and corruption. Slow pace okay until the boy arrives at the orphanage, at which point the dolphin premise sadly falls by the wayside. 96m/C VHS, Charles Durning, Peter Horton, Ajay Naidu, Conchata Ferrell, Alessandro Rabelo, Castulo Guerra; D: Christopher Cain; C: Juan Ruiz-Anchia; M: James Horner.

Where the Rivers Flow North 𝒹𝒹½

1994 (PG-13) Vermont logger Noel Lord (Tom) has lived on the land all his life and doesn't want to sell out to the power company. His blunt-talking Indian housekeeper/lover Bangor (Cardinal) knows it's best to take the money and move on. Set in 1927 and adapted from the novella by Howard Frank Mosher. Flat storytelling with a good performance by Cardinal. 104m/C VHS, DVD. Rip Torn, Tantoo Cardinal, Bill Raymond, Amy Wright, Dennis Mientka, Jusef Bulos, Michael J. Fox, Treat Williams; D: Jay Craven; W: Jay Craven, Don Bredes; C: Paul Ryan.

Where the Spirit Lives 𝒹𝒹½

1989 (PG) Native children kidnapped by Canadian government agents are forced to live in dreadful boarding schools where they are abused emotionally and physically. St. John is a new arrival who refuses to put up with it and tries to escape. Engrossing and moving. 97m/C VHS. CA Kim Fox, Marianne Jones, Gus Chief Moon, Clayton Julian, Michelle St. John; D: Bruce Pittman; W: Keith Ross Leckie; C: Rene Ohashi; M: Buffy Sainte-Marie.

Where the Truth Lies 𝒹𝒹½

1999 Dana Sue Lacey (Matlin) is the deaf campaign manager for a candidate who has just been murdered. When she becomes the prime suspect and goes to trial, attorney Lillian Rose Martin (King) has her work cut out for her since Dana refuses to cooperate. But the past and its secrets cannot stay hidden any longer. 92m/C VHS, DVD. Marlee Matlin, Regina King, Philip Lester, Robert Blanche, Linden Ashby, Brian McNamara, Susan Walters; D: Nelson McCormick; W: Marshall Goldberg; C: Bill Roe; M: Peter Manning Robinson. CABLE

Where the Truth Lies 𝒹𝒹 2005

Lanny (Bacon) and Vince (Firth) were a successful '50s showbiz duo (think Martin & Lewis) whose act broke up in 1957 over a sensational scandal involving a dead blonde (Blanchard) in a bathtub. Fifteen years later, ambitious and nubile blonde journalist Karen (a miscast Lohman) is trying to write Vince's bio and wants to know what really happened. Except truth is a subjective idea at best and the men still prefer their secrets to remain that way. A menage a trois scene upset the MPAA so director Egoyan released his voyeuristic noir drama unrated. Adapted from the novel by Rupert Holmes. 107m/C DVD. US CA GB Kevin Bacon, Colin Firth, Alison Lohman, Rachel Blanchard, David Hayman, Maury Chaykin, Kristin Adams, Sonja Bennett, Deborah Grover, Beau Starr; D: Atom Egoyan; W: Atom Egoyan; C: Paul Sarossy; M: Mychael Danna.

Where There's Life 𝒹𝒹½ 1947

Wisecracking Hope is a New York DJ about to be married to Marshe when he discovers he's the heir to the kingdom of Borovia (whose last king was assassinated). Hasso works her feminine wiles as the general who's guarding Hope when the assassins come after him. Oh, and Marshe and her cop brother Bendix are tracking him down to go through with the wedding ceremony. Frantic antics. 75m/B VHS, DVD. Bob Hope, Signe Hasso, William Bendix, Vera Marshe, George Coulouris, George Zucco, Denis Hoey, John Alexander; D: Sidney Lanfield; W: Melville Shavelson, Allen Boretz.

Where Time Began 𝒹 1977 (G)

The discovery of a strange manuscript of a scientist's journey to the center of the earth leads to the decision to re-create the dangerous mission. Based on Jules Verne's classic novel "Journey to the Center of the Earth," but not anywhere near as fun or stirring. 87m/C VHS, DVD. Kenneth More, Pep Munne, Jack Taylor; D: J(uan) Piquer Simon.

Where Trails Divide 𝒹½ 1937

Keene is a U.S. Marshal who poses as a lawyer to bring a gang of thieves to justice. Lacks action. 54m/B VHS, DVD. Tom Keene, Eleanor Stewart, Warner Richmond, David Sharpe, Charles French, Hal Price, Bud Osborne; D: Robert N. Bradbury.

Where Trails End 𝒹 1942

Novel sci-fi western set during WWII with just about everything, including phosphorescent-clothed good guys, Nazis, scoundrels, literate horses, and Gallic sidekicks. Interestingly different. 54m/B VHS. Tom Keene, Joan Curtis, Charles "Blackie" King; D: Robert Emmett Tansey.

Where Truth Lies 𝒹𝒹 1996 (R)

After a severe breakdown, troubled psychiatrist Ian Lazare (Savage) is sent to a clinic run by the sinister Dr. Renquist (McDowell). Lazare's given an experimental drug that causes him to have visions of executed serial killer Jonas Keller (Forrest) and also to develop ESP. The plot doesn't make much sense in any case. 92m/C VHS, DVD. John Savage, Kim Cattrall, Malcolm McDowell, Sam Jones, Eric Pierpoint, Candice Daly, Dennis Forrest; D: William H. Molina; W: William H. Molina; M: David Wurst, Eric Wurst.

Where Were You When the Lights Went Out? 𝒹𝒹 1968 (PG)

A complicated, unsuccessful farce about a retiring Broadway actress, her jealous, possibly philandering husband, her greedy agent, an embezzler, and a citywide blackout. Film was actually not based on the 1965 New York City blackout but on a French play, "Monsieur Masure" by Claude Magnier, which was written nine years before. 94m/C VHS. Doris Day, Patrick O'Neal, Robert Morse, Terry-Thomas, Lola Albright, Steve Allen, Jim Backus, Ben Blue, Pat Paulsen; D: Hy Averback.

Where's Marlowe? 𝒹𝒹 1998 (R)

Sendup of both indie filmmaking and the private eye genre in a b&w and color combo. NYU film school grads Crawley (Def) and Edison (Livingston) decide to make a documentary about private investigators and choose nearly bankrupt L.A. detectives Boone (Ferrer) and Murphy (Slattery) as their subjects. The dicks latest case seems to involve a wife, a mistress, and, soon, Murphy's demise and the two film students decide to lend a more active hand in solving the case. 99m/C VHS, DVD. Miguel Ferrer, John Slattery, John Livingston, Mos Def, Allison Dean, Clayton Rohner, Barbara Howard, Elizabeth Schofield; D: Daniel Pyne; W: Daniel Pyne, John Mankiewicz; C: Greg Gardiner; M: Michael Convertino.

Where's Piccone? 𝒹𝒹𝒹 1984

A woman attempts, with the assistance of a two-bit hustler, to locate her missing husband, only to discover that he has led a double life in the Neapolitan underworld. Giannini as the sleazy hubby is perfectly cast. On-target social and political satire. In Italian with English subtitles. 110m/C VHS. IT Giancarlo Giannini, Lina Sastri, Aldo Giuffre, Clelia Rondinelli; D: Nanni Loy.

Where's Poppa? 𝒹𝒹𝒹 1970

A Jewish lawyer's senile mother constantly ruins his love life, and he considers various means of getting rid of her, including dressing up as an ape to scare her to death. Filled with outlandish and often tasteless humor, befitting its reign as a black comedy cult classic. Adapted by Robert Klane from his novel. 84m/C VHS, DVD. George Segal, Ruth Gordon, Trish Van Devere, Ron Leibman, Rae Allen, Vincent Gardenia, Barnard Hughes, Paul Sorvino, Rob Reiner, Garrett Morris; D: Carl Reiner; W: Robert Klane; C: Jack Priestley; M: Jack Elliott.

Where's the Money, Noreen? 𝒹𝒹½ 1995 (PG-13)

Noreen's (Phillips) out on parole and trailed by the police who believe she knows the whereabouts of the $3 million she helped to steal 12 years before. 93m/C VHS. Julianne Phillips, A. Martinez, Nigel Bennett, Colm Feore; D: Artie Mandelberg; W: Carla Jean Wagner; C: Brenton Spencer; M: Richard Bellis. CABLE

Where's Willie? 1977 (G)

Willie is a very bright boy; perhaps a little too bright. When he reveals his latest invention to the folks in his small town, everyone is out to get him. 91m/C VHS. Guy Madison, Henry Darrow, Kate Woodville, Marc Gilpin; D: John Florea.

Which Way Home 𝒹𝒹 1990

A Red Cross nurse attempts to flee Cambodia with four young orphans. An Australian smuggler befriends and helps her. Way too long and wandering, though like many a TV movie, it means well. 141m/C VHS. Cybill Shepherd, John Waters, Peta Toppano, John Ewart, Ruben Santiago-Hudson, Marc Gray; D: Carl Schultz; W: Michael Lawrence.

Which Way Is Up? 𝒹𝒹½ 1977 (R)

Pryor plays three roles in this story of an orange picker who accidentally becomes a union hero. He leaves his wife and family at home while he seeks work in Los Angeles. There he finds himself a new woman, starts a new family, and sells out to the capitalists. American version of the Italian comedy "The Seduction of Mimi." Pryor as a dirty old man is the high point. 94m/C VHS, DVD. Richard Pryor, Lonette McKee, Margaret Avery, Morgan Woodward, Marilyn Coleman; D: Michael A. Schultz; W: Carl Gottlieb; C: John A. Alonzo.

Which Way to the Front? 𝒹½ 1970 (G)

Assorted Army rejects form a guerilla band and wage their own small-scale war during WWII. 96m/C VHS. Jerry Lewis, Jan Murray, George L. Baxt, Steve Franken; D: Jerry Lewis; W: Dee Caruso.

Whiffs 𝒹 1975 (PG)

A gullible man plays guinea pig in an Army experiment on germ warfare which leaves him with the intellect of a chimpanzee. Naturally, he then devises a plan to use the volatile gas in a chain of bank robberies. The title is appropriate—this movie is a stinker. 91m/C VHS. Elliott Gould, Eddie Albert, Harry Guardino, Godfrey Cambridge, Jennifer O'Neill, Alan Manson; D: Ted Post; M: Malcolm Marmorstein.

While I Live 𝒹½ 1947

Woman meets female pianist with uncanny resemblance to sister who's been dead 25 years and rethinks her position on reincarnation. 85m/B VHS. GB Tom Walls, Clifford Evans, Carole Raye, Patricia Burke, Sonia Dresdel, John Warwick; D: John Harlow; C: Frederick A. (Freddie) Young.

While the City Sleeps 𝒹𝒹𝒹 1956

Three newspaper reporters vie to crack the case of a sex murderer known as "The Lipstick Killer" with the editorship of their paper the prize. Good thriller-plus with the emphasis on the reporters' ruthless methods of gaining information rather than on the killer's motivations. Lang's last big success. Based on "The Bloody Spur" by Charles Einstein. 100m/B VHS. Dana Andrews, Rhonda Fleming, George Sanders, Howard Duff, Thomas Mitchell, Ida Lupino, Vincent Price, Mae Marsh; D: Fritz Lang; C: Ernest Laszlo.

While You Were Sleeping 𝒹𝒹𝒹 1995 (PG)

Feel-good romantic comedy finds lonely Lucy Moderatz (Bullock) collecting tokens for the Chicago train system and admiring Yuppie lawyer Peter Callaghan (Gallagher) as he commutes to and fro. Fate conspires to throw them together when Lucy rescues Peter after a mugging. Trouble is, he's not conscious so Lucy goes to the hospital with him, where she's mistaken for his fiancee. She continues the charade and is warmly welcomed by the Callaghan family, with the exception of Peter's brother, Jack (Pullman), who smells a rat even as he falls under the token collector's spell. Meanwhile, Peter remains in a coma, allowing Jack and Lucy to supply romantic comedy. Gallagher brings a serenity to his role as the unconscious Peter, while Bullock and Pullman take the predictable plot and deliver performances that earn them another notch on the climb to stardom. 103m/C VHS, DVD. Sandra Bullock, Bill Pullman, Peter Gallagher, Jack Warden, Peter Boyle, Glynis Johns, Micole Mercurio, Jason Bernard, Michael Rispoli, Ally Walker, Monica Keena; D: Jon Turteltaub; W: Fred Lebow, Daniel G. Sullivan; C: Phedon Papamichael; M: Randy Edelman. Blockbuster

The Whip and the Body 🎬🎬½ 1963 Mario Bava's 19th-century ghost/love/revenge story makes a belated arrival on home video. Nevena (Lavi) is about to be married when her ex-lover Kurt (Lee), soon to be her brother-in-law, shows up. The rest of the action is almost pure Gothic with a moody castle for setting, secret passages, ladies wandering the hallways late at night in their diaphanous gowns. Though the story doesn't quite live up to the title, it is very sexually charged for its time and Lee turns in an aggressive performance. 88m/C DVD, IT Christopher Lee, Daliah Lavi, Tony Kendall, Harriet Medin, Isli Oberon, Lawrence Bayne, Silvio Oliviero; D: Robert Bergman; W: Robert Bergman, Gerard Ciccoritti, Gleras; W: Leslie Daron.

Whipped 🎬 2000 (R) It's probably aiming for sophisticated, adult romantic comedy but all it achieves is smut. Sexpot Mia (Peet) is forced to deal with the arresting development of three Manhattan yuppies (Van Holt, Domke, Abrahams) who have prehistoric attitudes towards women. They all discover they are dating her but none wants to give Mia up and they become rivals for her questionable affections. Very unlikeable characters; very unpleasant. 82m/C VHS, DVD, Amanda Peet, Brian Van Holt, Judah Domke, Zorie Barber, Jonathan Abrahams, Callie (Calliope) Thorne; D: Peter M. Cohen; W: Peter M. Cohen, Bill Grimstad; M: Michael Montes.

Whirlwind Horseman 🎬 1938 Substandard horse opera. Maynard's search for a gold prospector friend leads him to a rancher and his pretty daughter. He beats up some bad guys, etcetera. Based on a true story. 60m/B VHS, Ken Maynard, Joan Barclay, Bill Griffith; D: Robert F. "Bob" Hill.

Whirlygirl 🎬🎬½ 2004 (R). Naive prep school student James (Morris) follows an exotic dancer known as Whirlygirl (Mazur) to New York, ditching school to learn about life. Based on a true story. 95m/C DVD, Monet Mazur, Julian Morris, Fran Kranz, Daniel Franzee; D: Jim Wilson; W: Pete McCormack. C: Christo Jakaloo; M: Deborah Lurie. VIDEO

Whiskers 🎬🎬 1996 (G) Mischievous Jed and his cat Whiskers can't seem to stay out of trouble and Jed thinks his parents may force him to get rid of his furry friend. So he makes a plea to an Egyptian goddess (they worshiped cats, you know) and Whiskers is suddenly turned into a human being. 94m/C VHS, CA Michael Caloz, Brent Carver, Steve Adams, Mark Bromilow; D: Jim Kaufman; W: Wendy Biller, Christopher Hawthorne; C: Francois Protat; M: Daniel Lavoie.

Whiskey Galore 🎬🎬½ Tight Little Island 1948 During WWII, a whiskey-less Scottish island gets a lift when a ship, carrying 50,000 cases of spirits, wrecks off the coast. A full-scale rescue operation and the evasion of both local and British government authorities ensue. The classic Ealing studio comedy is based on the actual wreck of a cargo ship off the Isle of Eriskay in 1941. 81m/B VHS, DVD, GB Basil Radford, Joan Greenwood, Gordon Jackson, James Robertson Justice; D: Alexander Mackendrick.

Whiskey Mountain 🎬 1977 (PG) Two couples go on a treasure hunt to Whiskey Mountain but instead find terror. 95m/C VHS, Christopher George, Preston Pierce, Linda Borgeson, Robena Collins, Robert Leslie; D: William Grefe.

Whisper 🎬½ 2007 (R) Kidnappers (Holloway, Cailles, Edgerton, Rooker) abduct the 10-year-old adoptive son (Woodruff) of a wealthy socialite only to find out that the boy is one of those demon spawn kiddies with his own agenda. Woodruff is a lot scarier than the kid they got for "The Omen" remake so it's routine horror show has something going for it. 95m/C DVD, Josh Holloway, Sarah Wayne Cailles, Blake Woodruff, Joel Edgerton, Michael Rooker, Dulé Hill, Teryl Rothery; D: Stewart Hendler; W: Christopher Borrelli; C: Dean Cundey; M: Jeff Rona. VIDEO

'96: Comedy Actress, Y. (Bullock), Comedy Actress; T: (Bullock).

A Whisper to a Scream 🎬🎬 1988 (R) An actress in researching a film part, takes a job at a telephone sex service, creating different personas as she talks to keep herself interested. Soon, women resembling the personas are being murdered. Great premise fails to deliver fully, though there is some suspense. 95m/C VHS, CA Nadia Capone, Yaphet Kotto, Silvio Oliviero; D: Robert Bergman.

The Whispering 🎬🎬 1994 (R) Scary little low-budget tale about an insurance investigator who's checking out several suicides and meets up with the Grim Reaper (who just happens to be female), pensent, thanks to competent scripting and directing. 89m/B VHS, DVD, CA Gregory Dantine, Mary Anderson, Paul Lucas; D: Fedor Ozep.

Whispering City 🎬🎬 1947 A female reporter receives an inside tip incriminating a prominent attorney in a murder. She tries to get the evidence she needs before she becomes his latest victim. Highly suspenseful. Highly. 88m/C VHS, Leif Garrett, Leslie Daron, Tom Patton, Maxwell Rutherford, Mette Holt; D: Gregory Gielas; W: Leslie Daron.

Whispers 🎬🎬 1989 (R) Psycho Le Clerc repeatedly bothers writer Tennant even though she seems to have killed him. This dismays police guy Sarandon. Based on the novel by Dean R. Koontz. 96m/C VHS, Victoria Tennant, Chris Sarandon, Jean LeClerc; D: Douglas Jackson; W: Anita Doohan, Don Carmody.

Whispering Shadow 🎬🎬 1933 Serial starring the master criminal known as the "faceless whisperer." Twelve chapters, 13 minutes each. 156m/B VHS, DVD, Bela Lugosi, Robert Warwick; D: A(lbert) Herman; C: Robert Clark.

Whispers: An Elephant's Tale 🎬🎬½ 2000 (G) Odd anthropomorphic film made up entirely of nature footage is similar in some respects to "The Adventures of Milo & Otis." As with that film, here we have animals photographed in the wilds of Africa, with various actors supplying voices for the animals. The film opens with the birth of Whispers (Derry-berry), an elephant. While his herd is roaming, he gets lost and can't find his mother Gentle Heart (Archer). Wandering through the bush, he meets another elephant named Groove (Bassett). Groove isn't very fond of Whispers at first, but she ultimately decides to help him find his mom. Along the way, they meet a variety of interesting animals and encounter some evil poachers. An entertaining film, but it also feels very artificial. The end result is a film with some amazing photography, but a story which comes across as hollow. 72m/C VHS, DVD; D: Dereck Joubert; W: Dereck Joubert, Jordan Moffet, Holly Goldberg Sloan; C: Dereck Joubert; M: Trevor Rabin; V: Debi Derryberry, Anne Archer, Angela Bassett, Joanna Lumley, Kevin M. Richardson, Alice Ghostley, Betty White, Kathryn Cressida, Joan Rivers.

Whispers in the Dark 🎬🎬 1992 (R) A psychiatrist counsels two odd patients—one is an ex-con turned painter with a violent streak, the other is a woman who reveals her kinky sexual experiences with a mystery man. Things get interesting when the doctor finds out her new lover is her patient's mystery man, and the patient turns up murdered. Confusing thriller seems forced but the premise is worth watching. 103m/C VHS, DVD, Annabella Sciorra, Jamey Sheridan, Anthony LaPaglia, Jill Clayburgh, John Leguizamo, Deborah Kara Unger, Alan Alda, Anthony Heald; D: Christopher Crowe; W: Christopher Crowe; M: Thomas Newman.

Whispers of White 🎬½ 1993 (R) Bridgetown's mayor has been trying for years to put a stop to the drug dealing going on in his fair community. Finally, his new Chief of Police decides to deploy a special task force to clean-up the streets—using whatever methods are necessary (and they're all violent). 98m/C VHS, Nicholette Goulet, Anthony De Sando, Tony Craig, April Bransome, Ron Gorton Sr.; D: Ron Gorton Sr.; W: Ron Gorton Sr.

The Whistle Blower 🎬🎬🎬 1987 A young government worker in England with a high-security position mysteriously dies. His father, a former intelligence agent, begins investigating his son's death agent, and discovers sinister Soviet-related connivances. A lucid, complex British espionage thriller. Adapted from the John Hale novel by Julian Bond. 98m/C VHS, DVD, GB Michael Caine, Nigel Havers, John Gielgud, James Fox, Felicity Dean, Gordon Jackson, Barry Foster; D: Simon Langton; W: Julian Bond.

Whistle down the Wind 🎬🎬🎬½ 1961 Three children of strict religious upbringing find a murderer hiding in their family's barn and believe him to be Jesus Christ. A well done and hardly grim or dull allegory of childhood innocence based on a novel by Mills's mother, Mary Hayley Bell. For a film relying heavily on child characters, it's important to portray childhood well and realistically. That is done here, as in "To Kill a Mockingbird." Mills is perfect. The film is Forbes's directorial debut and Richard Attenborough's second production. 99m/B VHS, GB Hayley Mills, Bernard Lee, Alan Bates, Norman Bird, Elsie Wagstaff, Diane Holgate, Alan Barnes, Roy Holder, Barry Dean, Diane Clare, Patrice Heneghan; D: Bryan Forbes; W: Keith Waterhouse, Willis Hall; C: Arthur Ibbetson; M: Malcolm Arnold.

Whistle Stop 🎬🎬 1946 A small-town girl divides her attentions between low-life gambler Raft, and villainous nightclub owner McLaglen, who plans a robbery-murder to rid of any rivals. A forgettable gangster drama. 65m/B VHS, DVD, George Raft, Ava Gardner, Victor McLaglen; D: Leonide Moguy; W: Philip Yordan.

Whistlin' Dan 🎬🎬 1932 Yet another lead cowpoke sets out to avenge the murder of a close relative. Maynard whistles while he walks (and rides) woodenly through this one. 60m/B VHS, DVD, Ken Maynard, Joyzelle Joyner, Lew Meehan, Georges Regnavent, Dan Terry, Harlan E. Knight, Bud McClure, Hank Bell, Iron Eyes Cody, Frank Ellis; D: Phil Rosen.

Whistling Bullets 🎬🎬½ 1936 Action galore in the story of an undercover Texas Ranger infiltrating a gang of thieves. The low budget doesn't detract from an exciting script and tight direction. 58m/B VHS, DVD, Kermit Maynard, Jack Ingram; D: John English.

Whistling in Brooklyn 🎬🎬½ 1943 Skelton again plays radio crime-solver Wally Benton in this third and last entry following "Whistling in the Dark" and "Whistling in Dixie." A cop-killer and the Brooklyn Dodgers baseball team figure in the crimes. 87m/B VHS, Red Skelton, Ann Rutherford, Jean Rogers, Rags Ragland, Ray Collins, Henry O'Neill, William Frawley, Sam Levene; D: S. Sylvan Simon; M: George Bassman.

Whistling in Dixie 🎬🎬½ 1942 The second appearance of Skelton as radio sleuth Wally "The Fox" Benton (following "Whistling in the Dark") finds him traveling to Georgia with girlfriend Carol (Rutherford). She's worried about an exsorority sister who knows the secret of a hidden Civil War treasure. When Wally gets involved, humorous trouble follows. Followed by "Whistling in Brooklyn." 73m/ B VHS, Red Skelton, Ann Rutherford, George Bancroft, Guy Kibbee, Diana Lewis, Peter Whitney, Rags Ragland; D: S. Sylvan Simon; W: Nat Perrin, Wilkie Mahoney; C: Clyde De Vinna.

Whistling in the Dark 🎬🎬🎬 1941 Skelton plays Wally Benton, a radio sleuth nicknamed "The Fox," in the first of a three-film series. Veidt (an always excellent villain) is the leader of a phony religious cult, after the money of one of his followers. He decides to kidnap Skelton and have him come up with a plan for the perfect murder but of course there are all sorts of comic complications. Skelton's first starring role is a clever comic mystery and a remake of the 1933 film. Followed by "Whistling in Dixie" and "Whistling in Brooklyn." 78m/B VHS, Red Skelton, Ann Rutherford, Conrad Veidt, Virginia Grey, Rags Ragland.

The Whistle Blower 🎬🎬 1987
Backwoods Sheol 1995 Beautifully told story from the viewpoint of determined seven-year-old Tehranian Razieh (Mohammad-khani), who wants to properly celebrate the Islamic New Year by buying a particularly plump goldfish (a symbol of harmony) from the pet shop. She manages to beg the money from her mother and sets off, but, distracted by the street sights, Razieh loses the money. Various characters seek to help her but in Reziah's resourceful brother Ali (Kafili) who gets a balloon seller to finally retrieve the money. Farsi with subtitles. 85m/C VHS, DVD, IA Aida Mohammadkhani, Mohsen Kalifi, Fereshteh Saret Orfani, Anna Bourtowska, Mohammad Shahani, Mohammad Bakhtiari; D: Jafar Panahi; W: Abbas Kiarostami; C: Farzad Jowdat; N.Y. Film Critics '96; Foreign Film.

The White Balloon 🎬🎬🎬½
White Boyz 🎬🎬 Whiteboys 1999 (R) Flip (Hoch) and his friends long to be gangsta rappers, despite being white and from Iowa. He fantasizes about duets with his idol Snoop Doggy Dogg while dealing backing soda passed off as cocaine to dimwit yuppie disco patrons. He befriends recent Chicago transplant Khalid (Bird) and persuades him to take Flip and his posse posse to the Cabrini Green projects, where Flip discovers his gangsta fantasy pales in comparison to the real thing. Uneven performances and a rather phat-free script weter down an undeniably good premise. 92m/C VHS, DVD, Danny Hoch, Dash Mihok, Eugene Bird, Mark Webber, Piper Perabo, Bonz Malone; D: Marc Levin; W: Danny Hoch, Marc Levin, Richard Stratton, Garth Belcon; C: Mark Benjamin.

The White Buffalo 🎬🎬 Hunt to Kill 1977 (PG) A strange, semi-surreal western parable about the last days of Wild Bill Hickok (Bronson) and his obsession with mythical white buffalo that represents his fear of mortality. Something of a "Moby Dick" theme set in the Wild West. Clumsy but intriguing. 97m/C VHS, Charles Bronson, Jack Warden, Will Sampson, Kim Novak, Clint Walker, Stuart Whitman, John Carradine, Slim Pickens, Cara Williams, Douglas Fowley; D: J. Lee Thompson; W: Richard Sale.

White Badge 🎬🎬 1992. Opening with the 1979 assassination of South Korean President Park Chung Hee, film depicts the trauma and struggle of the more than 300,000 Korean soldiers sent to Vietnam to fight alongside the American's. Reminiscences of a decorated White Horse Division, who fought alongside American troops in Vietnam. Now a writer, and having long suffered from post-traumatic stress, Han decides to revisit the experiences for his latest work. Flashbacks showcase a reconnaissance mission beginning. Adapted from the novel by Jung Hyo Ahn. 125m/C VHS, DVD, Sung-Ki Ahn, Kyung-Young Lee, Hye-jin Shim; D: Ji-Yong Chung.

White Badge 🎬🎬 1997 Kiu Han (Ahn) was a youthful infantry soldier in the South Korean Army's decorated White Horse Division, which takes on unexpected personal conflicts as he encounters traumatized war buddy Pyon (Lee) and tries to deal with his own repressed memories of the war. Adapted from the novel by Jung Hyo Ahn. 125m/C VHS, DVD, KH Sung-Ki Ahn, Kyung-Young Lee, Hye-jin Shim, Junho Hun, Sejun Kim, Yongjae Tokko; D: Ji-Yong Chung; W: Ji-Yong Chung.

White Cargo 🎬🎬½ 1942 Lamar

Whitcomb's War 🎬🎬 1987 Small town becomes a battleground among a host of comic characters who are unaware who really is in charge. 67m/C VHS, Patrick Pankhurst, Leon Charles, Bill Morey, Robert Denison, Garnett Smith; D: Russell S. Doughten Jr.

White Badge 🎬🎬 1992 Opening Eve Arden, Dor Douglas, Don Costello, Paul Stanton, William Tanner, Reed Hadley; D: S. Sylvan Simon; W: Harry Clork, Albert Mannheimer, Robert MacGunigle; C: Sidney Wagner.

rubber planter who advises new assistant Carlson against Lamarr's sarong-clad charms. But hormones speak louder than warnings and Pidgeon has to take some strong action to save Carlson from this femme fatale. Based on the novel "Hell's Playground" by Ida Vera Simonton and adapted for both stage and screen by Gordon. **90m/B VHS.** Hedy Lamarr, Walter Pidgeon, Richard Carlson, Frank Morgan, Reginald Owen, Bramwell Fletcher, Henry O'Neill, Clyde Cook, Richard Ainley; **D:** Richard Thorpe; **W:** Leon Gordon; **M:** Bronislau Kaper.

White Cargo 1996 Detective Joe Hargatay is investigating a series of fashion model murders that lead him to Chinatown gangsters, corrupt cops, and the crazy world of model agencies. **92m/C VHS.** Dave Bradley, Shannon Tweed, Lydie Denier, Tommy (Tiny) Lister, David Groh; **D:** Daniel Reardon.

White Chicks 2004 (PG-13) Two African-American FBI agents (Shawn and Marlon Wayans) are assigned to protect two wealthy white heiresses from a kidnapping plot. When the sisters are bruised and refuse to be seen in public, the guys disguise themselves as the heiresses to uncover the kidnappers. Hilarity allegedly ensues. Crazy premise could've been mined for class, culture and gender clash material, but instead lunges down the easy path of junior high humor. Too bad, since the Wayans brothers can be very funny when they play it smart. Disconcerting layers of latex and makeup make them look more like bizarre androgynous aliens than debutantes. **108m/C DVD, UMD.** US Marlon Wayans, Shawn Wayans, Brittany Daniel, Jaime (James) King, Jessica Cauffiel, Busy Philipps, Frankie Faison, John Heard, Lochlyn Munro, Maitland Ward, Anne Dudek, Terry Crews, Eddie Aytes, Jennifer Carpenter, Drew Sidora, Casey Lee, Suzy Joachim; **D:** Keenen Ivory Wayans; **W:** Marlon Wayans, Shawn Wayans, Keenen Ivory Wayans, Michael Anthony Snowden, Andrew McElfresh, Xavier Cook; **C:** Steven Bernstein; **M:** Teddy Castellucci.

White Christmas 1954 Two ex-army buddies become a popular comedy team and play at a financially unstable Vermont inn at Christmas for charity's sake. Many swell Irving Berlin songs rendered with zest. Paramount's first Vista Vision film. ♫The Best Things Happen While You're Dancing; Love, You Didn't Do Right By Me; Choreography; Count Your Blessings Instead of Sheep; What Can You Do With a General; Mandy; The Minstrel Show; Sisters; Heat Wave. **120m/C VHS, DVD.** Bing Crosby, Danny Kaye, Rosemary Clooney, Vera-Ellen, Dean Jagger; **D:** Michael Curtiz; **W:** Norman Panama; **C:** Loyal Griggs.

The White Cliffs of Dover 1944 Prime example of a successful 40s "women's weepie." American Dunne goes to England in 1914, falls in love, and marries the British Marshal. He joins the WWI troops and is killed, without knowing he had a son. Dunne raises the boy in England as a new threat looms with the rise of Hitler. Now grown, he goes off to do his duty and she joins the Red Cross, where she sees him again among the wounded, another victim of the ravages of war. Dunne is fine in her noble, sacrificing role. McDowall is the young son with Taylor (with whom he'd already worked in "Lassie Come Home") as a childhood friend. Based on the poem by Alice Duer Miller. Bring the hankies. **126m/B VHS.** Irene Dunne, Alan Marshal, Frank Morgan, Peter Lawford, Gladys Cooper, May Whitty, Sir C. Aubrey Smith, Roddy McDowall, Van Johnson, Elizabeth Taylor, June Lockhart, John Warburton, Jill Esmond, Norma Varden, Tom Drake, Arthur Shields, Brenda Forbes, Edmund Breon, Clyde Cook, Isobel Elsom, Lumsden Hare, Miles Mander, Ian Wolfe; **D:** Clarence Brown; **W:** George Froeschel, Jan Lustig, Claudine West; **C:** George J. Folsey; **M:** Herbert Stothart.

White Coats 2004 Low-brow comedy about the misadventures (medical and personal) of the interns at chaotic St. Albert's Hospital. Many gross-out jokes and 'familiar comedy names, but not much else to recommend it. **98m/C DVD.** CA Dave Thomas, Patrick Kelly, Viv Leacock, Dave Foley, Peter Oldring, Ingrid Kavelaars, Dan Aykroyd, Maury Chaykin, Carly Pope, Matt Frewer, Saul Rubinek; **C:** John Spooner.

White Comanche 1967 Half-breed twins battle themselves and each other to a rugged climax. **90m/C VHS, DVD.** William Shatner, Joseph Cotten, Perla Cristal, Rossana Yanni; **D:** Gilbert Kay.

The White Countess 2005 (PG-13) As you might expect from a Merchant Ivory production, the period styling is gorgeous even if the story is a little finicky. Set on the eve of Japan's WWII invasion of China in 1936, the film follows Sofia (Richardson) who lives in Shanghai, where she supports her family of exiled Russian aristocrats by scratching out a living as an exotic dancer and prostitute. She meets expatriate American Todd Jackson (Fiennes), who recognizes Sofia as the ideal hostess for his new nightclub, The White Countess. Richardson and Fiennes truly make the viewer care about their wounded characters, even as their business and personal relationships spirals downwards thanks to the chaos of war. **138m/C DVD.** US CA GB GE Ralph Fiennes, Natasha Richardson, Vanessa Redgrave, Hiroyuki (Henry) Sanada, Lynn Redgrave, Allan Corduner, Madeleine Daly, Dan Herzberg, Pierre Seznec, Luoyong Wang; **D:** James Ivory; **W:** Kazuo Ishiguro; **C:** Christopher Doyle; **M:** Richard Robbins.

White Fang 1991 (PG) Boy befriends canine with big teeth and both struggle to survive in third celluloid rendition of Alaska during the Gold Rush. Beautiful cinematography. Fun for the entire family based on Jack London's book. Followed by "White Fang 2: The Myth of the White Wolf." **109m/C VHS, DVD.** Klaus Maria Brandauer, Ethan Hawke, Seymour Cassel, James Remar, Susan Hogan; **D:** Randal Kleiser; **W:** Jeanne Rosenberg, Nick Thiel, David Fallon; **C:** Tony Pierce-Roberts; **M:** Basil Poledouris.

White Fang 2: The Myth of the White Wolf 1994 (PG) White boy and his wolf-dog lead starving Native American tribe to caribou during the Alaskan Gold Rush. Simplistic story with obvious heroes and villains, yes, but this is also wholesome (and politically correct) family fare compliments of Disney. Focuses less on the wolf, a flaw, and more on Bairstow and his love interest Craig, a Haida Indian princess, while exploring Native American mythology and dreams in sequences that tend to stop the action cold. Still, kids will love it, and there are plenty of puppies to achieve required awwww factor. Beautiful scenery filmed on location in Colorado and British Columbia. **106m/C VHS, DVD.** Scott Bairstow, Alfred Molina, Geoffrey Lewis, Charmaine Craig, Victoria Racimo, Paul Coeur, Anthony Michael Ruivivar, Al Harrington; *Cameos:* Ethan Hawke; **D:** Ken Olin; **W:** David Fallon; **M:** John Debney.

White Fang and the Hunter 1985 (G) The adventures of a boy and his dog who survive an attack from wild wolves and then help to solve a murder mystery. Loosely based on the novel by Jack London. **87m/C VHS, DVD.** Pedro Sanchez, Robert Woods; **D:** Al (Alfonso Brescia) Bradley.

White Fire 1984 Two jewel thieves will stop at nothing to own White Fire, a two hundred-carat diamond. **90m/C VHS, DVD.** Robert Ginty, Fred Williamson, Belinda Mayne, Jess Hahn; **D:** Jean Marie Pallardy; **W:** Edward John Francis; **C:** Roger Fellous; **M:** Vicky Brown.

White Fire 1995 Confusing sci-fi adventure finds edgy Manhattan internist' Driscoll Rampart (McDonough) serving his residency on Rusta, a war-torn planet located in a white-dwarf star system. The planet is divided into two hemispheres, one in perpetual darkness and the other in constant light. Rampart learns the ropes from mystical doc Akada (Winfield), who's also involved in a peace accord between Rusta's warring leaders. Visually striking but overly ambiguous—probably because it was intended as the pilot for a weekly series. **91m/C VHS.** Paul Winfield, Neal McDonough, CCH Pounder, Ele Keats, Michael McGrady, Katy Boyer; **D:** Peter Markle; **W:** Bruce Wagner; **M:** Stewart Copeland. TV

The White Dawn 1975 (PG) Three whalers are stranded in the Arctic in the 1890s and are taken in by an Eskimo village. They teach the villagers about booze, gambling, and other modern amenities. Resentment grows until a clash ensues. All three leads are excellent, especially Oates. Much of the dialogue is in an Eskimo language, subtitled in English, as in "Dances with Wolves." **110m/C VHS, DVD.** Warren Oates, Timothy Bottoms, Louis Gossett Jr., Simonie Kopapik, Joanasie Salomonie; **D:** Philip Kaufman; **C:** Michael Chapman; **M:** Henry Mancini.

The White Diamond 2004 Herzog's documentary (which he also narrates) begins with a brief history of flight and then moves on to the eccentricities of British aeronautical engineer Graham Dorrington, who designs a two-person airship meant to be used for scientific research in the Amazon rain forest. Herzog records their expedition to Guyana as they try to get Dorrington's aircraft to fly. Dorrington's crew is supported by local Guyanese diamond miners, including Mark Anthony Yhap, whose christening of the airship gives the film its title. **90m/C DVD. GE GB JP** **D:** Werner Herzog; **C:** Henning Brummer, Klaus Scheurich; **M:** Ernst Reijseger, Eric Spitzer-Marlyn.

White Eagle 1932 A white man who believes himself to be an Indian gets a job as a Pony Express rider and gets mixed up with horse rustlers. When he finds out who he really is, he is free to marry the white woman he's had his eye on. Interesting plot twist caused by the narrow-mindedness of the Hays Office. **64m/B VHS.** Buck Jones, Barbara Weeks, Robert Ellis, Jason Robards Sr., Robert Elliott, Jim Thorpe, Ward Bond; **D:** Lambert Hillyer.

White Ghost 1988 (R) An intelligence Officer who disappeared in the jungles of Asia 18 years ago is ready to come back to the United States, but not everyone wants to see him again. **89m/C VHS.** William Katt, Rosalind Chao, Martin Hewitt, Wayne Crawford, Reb Brown; **D:** B.J. Davis.

White Gold 1928 Shepherd's son weds Mexican woman and his disgruntled father contrives apparent rendezvous between the wife and a ranch-hand, who's found dead in her bedroom. Seems no one believes the wife's story. Unprecedented, dark, silent drama. **73m/B VHS.** Jetta Goudal, Kenneth Thomson, George Bancroft, George Nichols Jr., Clyde Cook; **D:** William K. Howard.

White Heat 1949 A classic gangster film with one of Cagney's best roles as a psychopathic robber/killer with a mother complex. The famous finale—perhaps Cagney's best-known scene—has Cagney trapped on top of a burning oil tank shouting "Made it, Ma! Top of the world!" before the tank explodes. Cagney's character is allegedly based on Arthur "Doc" Barker and his "Ma," and his portrayal is breathtaking. Also available colorized. **114m/B VHS, DVD.** James Cagney, Virginia Mayo, Edmond O'Brien, Margaret Wycherly, Steve Cochran, John Archer, Wally Cassell; **D:** Raoul Walsh; **W:** Ivan Goff, Ben Roberts; **C:** Sid Hickox; **M:** Max Steiner. Natl. Film Reg. '03.

White Hot 1988 (R) A young businessman loses his prestigious Wall Street job, and in order to live the good life, he resorts to selling drugs. Benson stars and directs. **95m/C VHS.** Robby Benson, Tawny Kitaen, Danny Aiello, Sally Kirkland, Judy Tenuta; **D:** Robby Benson.

White Hot: The Mysterious Murder of Thelma Todd 1991 Thelma Todd was a Hollywood starlet found dead under strange circumstances in 1935. Buffs have sought a solution to the maybe-murder ever since; this treatment (based on the book "Hot Toddy" by Andy Edmunds) leaves too many loose ends for purists and isn't sufficiently gripping for the uninitiated. **95m/C VHS, DVD.** Loni Anderson, Robert Davi, Paul Dooley, Lawrence Pressman; **D:** Paul Wendkos.

White Hunter, Black Heart 1990 (PG) Eastwood casts himself against type as Hustonesque director who is more interested in hunting large tusked creatures than shooting the film he came to Africa to produce. Based on Peter Viertel's 1953 account of his experiences working on James Agee's script for Huston's "African Queen." Eastwood's Huston impression is a highlight, though the story occasionally wanders off with the elephants. **112m/C VHS, DVD.** Clint Eastwood, Marisa Berenson, George Dzundza, Jeff Fahey, Timothy Spall, Charlotte Cornwell, Mel Martin, Alun Armstrong, Richard Vanstone; **D:** Clint Eastwood; **W:** Peter Viertel, James Bridges, Burt Kennedy; **C:** Jack N. Green; **M:** Lennie Niehaus.

White Huntress *Golden Ivory* 1957 Two brothers venturing into the jungle encounter a beautiful young woman, the daughter of a settlement leader. Meanwhile, a killer is on the loose. **86m/C VHS, DVD.** GB Robert Urquhart, John Bentley, Susan Stephen; **D:** George Breakston.

The White Legion 1936 Workers and engineers push their way through steaming jungles and raging swamps while building the Panama Canal. Many fall victim to yellow fever. Physician Keith does some medical sleuthing and saves the day. Plodding, predictable drama. **81m/B VHS.** Ian Keith, Tala Birell, Snub Pollard; **D:** Karl Brown.

White Lie 1991 (PG-13) Len Madison Jr. (Hines), a press secretary for the mayor of New York, receives an old photo of a lynched black man who he learns is his father, hung for raping a white woman. Madison returns to his Southern hometown to find out the truth behind his father's death, assisted by a white doctor (O'Toole) whose mother was a rape victim. They fall in love, adding to an already complicated situation, and incur the wrath of locals who are trying to keep the truth hidden. Based on the novel "Louisiana Black" by Samuel Charters. **93m/C VHS.** Gregory Hines, Annette O'Toole, Bill Nunn; **D:** Bill Condon.

White Lies 1998 (R) Catherine (Polley), a freshman college student at a liberal university, feels alienated from her peers and finds solace in an online chat room. She becomes increasingly involved with the shadowy National Identity Movement and becomes their spokesperson before understanding what they really represent and that they're a group of neo-Nazis. **92m/C VHS, DVD.** CA Sarah Polley, Tanya Allen, Jonathan Scarfe, Lynn Redgrave, Joseph Kell, Allison Hossack, Martha Henry, Heidi von Palleske, James Purcell, Bruce Boa; **D:** Al Waxman.

White Light 1990 (R) "Flatliners" with a flatfoot; after a near-death experience a cop returns with memories of a beautiful woman. He tries to find out who she is/was in plodding fashion. The voyage to the afterlife is represented by a jog through a storm sewer. **96m/C VHS.** Martin Kove, Allison Hossack, Martha Henry, Heidi von Palleske, James Purcell, Bruce Boa; **D:** Al Waxman.

White Lightning *McKlusky* 1973 (PG) Good ol' boy Reynolds plays a moonshiner going after the crooked sheriff who murdered his brother. Good stunt-driving chases enliven the formula. The inferior sequel is "Gator." **101m/C VHS, DVD.** Burt Reynolds, Ned Beatty, Bo Hopkins, Jen-

The White Lioness 🐾🐾 Den Vita Lejoninnan 1996 A young woman is found murdered in the Swedish countryside and the small town cop investigating realizes it's a more complicated case than he can handle. Especially when the crime leads him to Russia and South Africa and an international terrorist organization. Based on the novel by Henning Mankell. Swedish with subtitles. 104m/C VHS, SW Rolf Lassgard, Basil Apollis, Jesper Christensen, Nelson Mandela; *D:* Pe (Pelle) Berglund. *M:* Lars Bjorkman. *C:* Tony Forsberg. *M:* Thomas Lindahl.

White Line Fever 🐾🐾½ 1975 (PG) A young trucker's search for a happy life with his childhood sweetheart is complicated by a corrupt group in control of the long-haul trucking business. Well-done action film of good triumphing over evil. 89m/C VHS, Jan-Michael Vincent, Kay Lenz, Slim Pickens, L.Q. Jones, John David Garfield; *D:* Jonathan Kaplan. *W:* Jonathan Kaplan, Ken Friedman. *C:* Fred W. Koenekamp.

White Mama 🐾🐾 1980 A poor widow (Davis, in a splendid role) takes in a street-wise black kid (Harder) in return for protection from the neighborhood's dangers, and they discover friendship. Poignant drama, capably directed by Cooper, featuring sterling performances all around. Made-for-TV drama at its best. 96m/C VHS, Bette Davis, Ernest Harden Jr., Eileen Heckart, Virginia Capers, Lurene Tuttle, Anne Ramsey; *D:* Jackie Cooper.

White Man's Burden 🐾🐾 1995 (R) In a world where blacks have all the wealth and power, and whites comprise the struggling underclasses, Caucasian factory worker Louis Pinnock (John Travolta) is fired by his bigoted black CEO (Belafonte) due to a misunderstanding. Driven by poverty-level financial strain, Louis kidnaps his wealthy boss to show him how the other half lives. Gimmicky premise is full of reversed stereotypes such as black cops beating a white guy and skinheads taking over as inner-city gangsters. Treads too lightly, and rehashes too many familiar stories, to make any real impact. Travolta had to be talked into this role by "Pulp Fiction" producer Lawrence Bender. 89m/C VHS, DVD, John Travolta, Harry Belafonte, Kelly Lynch, Margaret Avery, Tom Bower, Carrie Snodgress, Sheryl Lee Ralph; *D:* Desmond Nakano. *M:* Howard Shore.

White Mane 🐾🐾🐾 1952 The poignant, poetic story of a proud and fierce white stallion that continually eludes attempts by ranchers to capture it. In French with English subtitles. 38m/B VHS, Alain Emery, Frank Silvera; at its best 96m/C VHS, '52. Film.

White Men Can't Jump 🐾🐾 1992 (R) Sometimes they can't act either. Small-time con man Harrelson stands around looking like a big nerd until something dares him to play basketball and he proves to be more adept than he looks. After he beats Snipes they become friends and start hustling together. Harrelson lays to rest the rumor that he can't act; here, he proves it. Fast-paced, obscenity-laced dialogue does not cover up for the fact that the story hovers between dull and dismal, redeemed only by the surreal "Jeopardy" game show sequence and the convincing b-ball action. Snipes manages to rise above the material as well as the rim, while Perez, as wooden Woody's spitfire Hispanic girlfriend, is appropriately energetic. 115m/C VHS, DVD, Wesley Snipes, Woody Harrelson, Rosie Perez, Tyra Ferrell, Cylk Cozart, Kadeem Hardison, Ernest Harden Jr., John Jones; *D:* Ron Shelton; *W:* Ron Shelton. *M:* Bennie Wallace.

White Mile 🐾🐾 1994 (R) Abusive L.A. advertising exec Dan Cutler (Alda) invites his top execs and important clients on a white-water rafting expedition along the Chilko River in the Canadian Rockies (filmed at Northern California's Russian River). But competition and arrogance causes the deaths of several participants and the widow of one sues the agency for damages. Alda excels in arrogant, self-serving nastiness. Fact-based TV movie based on court transcripts. 97m/C VHS, DVD, Alan Alda, Peter Gallagher, Robert Loggia, Fionnula Flanagan, Dakin Matthews, Bruce Altman, Robert Picardo, Max Wright, Jack Gilpin, Ken Jenkins; *D:* Robert Butler. *W:* Michael Butler.

White Mischief 🐾🐾🐾 1988 (R) An alternately ghastly and hilarious indictment of the English upper class between the World Wars, and the decadence the British colonists perpetrated in Kenya, which came to world attention with the murder of the philandering Earl of Erroll in 1941. Exquisitely directed and photographed. Acclaimed and grandly acted, especially by Scacchi. Howard's last appearance. 108m/C VHS, Greta Scacchi, Charles Dance, Joss Ackland, Sarah Miles, John Hurt, Hugh Grant, Geraldine Chaplin, Trevor Howard, Murray Head, Susan Fleetwood, Alan Dobie, Jacqueline Pearce; *D:* Michael Radford. *M:* George Fenton.

White Nights 🐾🐾🐾 1957 Based on a love story by Dostoyevski. A young woman pines for the return of her sailor while a mild-mannered clerk is smitten by her. Both of their romantic fantasies are explored in this dance-hall cadence is mixed with dreamy, fantastic flashbacks, in Italian with English subtitles. Equally good Soviet version made in 1959. 107m/C VHS, DVD, IT FR Maria Schell, Jean Marais, Marcello Mastroianni, Clara Calamai, Giorgio Listuzzi; *D:* Luchino Visconti. *W:* Luchino Visconti, Suso Cecchi D'Amico. *C:* Giuseppe Rotunno. *M:* Nino Rota.

White Nights 🐾🐾½ 1985 (PG-13) A Russian ballet dancer who defected to the U.S. (Baryshnikov) is a passenger on a jet that crashes in the Soviet Union. With the aid of a disillusioned expatriate tap dancer (Hines), he plots to escape again. The excellent dance sequences elevate the rather lame story. ♪ "Say You, Say Me." 135m/C VHS, DVD, Mikhail Baryshnikov, Gregory Hines, Isabella Rossellini, Helen Mirren, Jerzy Skolimowski, Geraldine Page; *D:* Taylor Hackford. *C:* David Watkin. *M:* Michel Colombier. Oscars '85: Song ("Say You, Say Me"); Golden Globes '86: Song ("Say You, Say Me").

White Noise 🐾 2005 (PG-13) Despite an eerily effective marketing campaign—touting the science behind Electronic Voice Phenomenon (EVP), in which ghosts use electric static to contact the living—this cheap Michael Keaton vehicle should have gone straight to video. After architect Jonathan Rivers (Keaton) loses his wife Anna (West) in a suspicious accident, he retreats into despair. That is, until a stranger (McNeice) convinces Rivers that Anna is sending him messages from beyond the grave via EVP. Rivers becomes obsessed with the transmissions, which awakens a malevolent force unamused with his meddling. The last hour plays like a low budget "Final Destination" retread. 101m/C VHS, DVD, HD DVD, US Michael Keaton, Chandra West, Deborah Kara Unger, Ian McNeice, Sarah Strange, Nicholas Elia, Mike Dopud; *D:* Geoffrey Sax. *W:* Niall Johnson; *C:* Chris Seager. *M:* Claude Foisy.

White Noise 2: The Light 🐾½ 2007 (PG-13) After Abe Dale's (Fillion, playing it straight and dull) family is killed and he is saved from an attempted suicide, Abe comes back from his near-death experience seeing white auras around people who are about to die. But in preventing their deaths, Abe learns there's an unexpected price to pay, since those he saves turn into demons after 72 hours—unless they die again. 99m/C DVD, HD DVD, Nathan Fillion, Katee Sackhoff, Craig Fairbrass, Teryl Rothery, Adrian Holmes, William Macdonald; *D:* Patrick Lussier; *W:* Matt Venne; *C:* Brian Pearson; *M:* Normand Corbeil.

White of the Eye 🐾🐾 1988 (R) A murdering lunatic is on the loose in Arizona, and an innocent man must find him before he saves turn into demons after '72 effective thriller; dazzling technique recalls the experimental films of the 1960s. 111m/C VHS, David Keith, Cathy Moriarty, Art Evans, Alan Rosenberg, Michael Greene, Alberta Watson, Marc Hayashi; *D:* Donald Cammell; *W:* China Kong, Donald Cammell. *M:* Nick Mason, Rick Fenn, George Fenton.

White Oleander 🐾🐾🐾 2002 (PG-13) Pfeiffer plays against type as an ice cold mother who controls her daughter's (Lonman) life from the prison where she's serving a life sentence for murder. Astrid is forced into an odyssey through the foster care system, where she is taken in by a string of damaged foster moms, including a born-again ex-stripper (Wright Penn), a needy ex-actress (Zellweger) and a greedy Russian ragpicker (Efremova). Astrid changes her looks as well as her psyche for each of these faux-mothers, but finally learns to break away and become her own person with some help from fellow foster child Paul (Fugit). The performances are good across the board, but director Kosminsky seems more interested in making the all-star cast look good then giving them an interesting story to tell. 110m/C VHS, DVD, US Alison Lonman, Michelle Pfeiffer, Robin Wright Penn, Renee Zellweger, Patrick Fugit, Billy Connolly, Cole Hauser, Noah Wyle, Amy Aquino, Svetlana Efremova; *D:* Peter Kosminsky. *W:* Mary Agnes Donoghue. *C:* Elliot Davis; *M:* Thomas Newman.

The White Orchid 🐾🐾 1954 Romantic triangle ventures into the wilds of Mexico in search of Toltec ruins. Exceptional sets. 81m/C VHS, DVD William Lundigan, Peggy Castle, Armando Silvestre, Rosenda Monteros; *D:* Reginald LeBorg.

White Palace 🐾🐾½ 1990 (R) Successful widowed Jewish lawyer Spader is attracted to older, less educated hamburger waitress Sarandon, and ethnic/cultural strife ensues, as does hot sex. Adapted from the Glenn Savan novel, it starts out with promise but fizzles toward the end. 103m/C VHS, DVD, Susan Sarandon, James Spader, Jason Alexander, Eileen Brennan, Griffin Dunne, Kathy Bates, Steven Hill, Rachel Levin, Corey Parker, Spiros Focas, Renee Taylor, Kim Myers; *D:* Luis Mandoki; *W:* Alvin Sargent, Ted Tally; *C:* Lajos Koltai; *M:* George Fenton.

White Phantom: Enemy of Darkness 🐾 1987 Ninja warriors in modern day society battling against other evil ninjas. 89m/C VHS, Page Leong, Jay Roberts Jr., Bo Svenson; *D:* Dusty Nelson; *W:* David Hamilton, Chris Gallagher.

White Pongo WOOF! 1945 A police-man goes undercover with a group of British biologists to capture a mythic white gorilla believed to be the missing link. A camp jungle classic with silly, cheap special effects. 73m/B VHS, DVD, Richard Fraser, Maris Wrixon, Lionel Royce, Al Eben, Gordon Richards, Michael Dyne, George Lloyd; *D:* Sam Newfield; *W:* Raymond L Schrock; *C:* Jack Greenhalgh.

The White Raven 🐾🐾 1998 (R) Nazi war criminal Markus Straud (Rubes) agrees to be interviewed by Chicago journalist Tully Windsor (Silvers). During the war, Straud hid a priceless diamond and various factions think he's finally going to reveal where the stone is. But Straud only offers a series of cryptic clues that lead Windsor back home, with bad guys in pursuit. 92m/C VHS, DVD, Ron Silver, Jan Rubes, Joanna Pacula, Roy Scheider; *D:* Andrew Stevens; *W:* Michael Bigelow; *C:* Michael Slovis.

White River 🐾 The White River Kid 1999 (R) Embarrassingly bad "would-be comedy based on the book "The Little Brothers of St. Mortimer" by John Fergus Ryan. Broth Edgar (Hoskins) is a fake monk, teamed up with illegal immigrant Morales Pittman (Banderas), in a scam involving selling cheap "socks for God". Traveling through Arkansas they meet up with serial killer "The White River Kid" (Bentley), his girlfriend Apple Lisa Weed (Dickens) and her eccentric family, a blind prostitute (Barkin), and a singing, corrupt sheriff (Travis). Not that you'll be interested in any of them. 90m/C VHS, DVD, Bob Hoskins, Antonio Banderas, Wes Bentley, Kim Dickens, Ellen Barkin, Randy Travis, Beau Bridges, Swoosie Kurtz; *D:* Arne Glimcher; *W:* David Leland; *C:* Michael Chapman; *M:* John (Gianni) Frizzell.

The White Rose 🐾🐾 1923 An aspiring minister travels to see the world he intends to save, and winds up falling from grace. Complicated menage a trois is finally sorted out at the end. Silent. 120m/B VHS, Mae Marsh, Carol Dempster, Ivor Novello, Neil Hamilton, Lucille LeVerne; *D:* D.W. Griffith.

The White Rose 🐾🐾🐾 Die Weisse Rose 1983 The true story of a group of dissident students in Munich in 1942, who put their lives in danger by distributing leaflets telling the truth of what was going on in the concentration camps. Hans Scholl was an Army officer who discovered the truth and told the others. In the end, most of the students were captured by the Gestapo and executed. "The White Rose" was the name of the group, but none surprisingly, Verhoeven's film telling is engrossing and compelling, with excellent acting from the young cast. In German with English subtitles. 108m/C VHS, GE Lena Stolze, Wulf Kessler, Oliver Siebler, Ulrich Tukur, Werner Stocker, Martin Benrath, Anja Kruse, Ulf-Jurgen Wagner, Mechthild Reinders, Peter Kortenbach, Gerhard Friedrich, Sabine Kretzschmar, Heinz Keller, Susanne Seufert, Christina Schwartz; *D:* Michael Verhoeven, Mario Krebs; *C:* Axel de Roche; *M:* Konstantin Wecker.

White Sands 🐾🐾½ 1992 (R) When a dead man's body is found at a remote Indian reservation clutching a gun and a briefcase filled with $500,000, the local sheriff (Dafoe) takes his identity to see where the money leads. Using a phone number found on a piece of paper in the dead man's stomach, the sheriff follows clues into the world of mixed up with a rich woman (Mastrantonio) who sels black market weapons and uses the money to support "worthy" causes, and an FBI man (Jackson) who uses him as bait to lure a CIA turncoat/arms dealer (Rourke). Sound confusing? It is, and despite the strong cast and vivid scenery of the southwest United States, this film just doesn't cut it. 101m/C VHS, DVD, Jack Keller, Willem Dafoe, Mary Elizabeth Mastrantonio, Mickey Rourke, Mimi Rogers, Samuel L. Jackson, M. Emmet Walsh, James Rebhorn, Maura Tierney, Beth Grant, Miguel (Michael) Sandoval, John Lafayette. Cameos: Fred Dalton Thompson, John P. Ryan; *D:* Roger Donaldson; *W:* Daniel Pyne; *C:* Peter Merzies Jr.; *M:* Patrick O'Hearn.

White Shadows in the South Seas 🐾🐾½ 1929 Alcohol, drugs, and prostitution take their toll on the native population of Tahiti in this early talkie. Bue plays a western doctor who marries the daughter of a native chief. However, he finds greed for the island's pearl treasures drawing other unscrupulous westerners to destroy the unspoiled paradise. 88m/B VHS, Monte Blue, Robert Anderson, Raquel Torres; *D:* Woodbridge S. Van Dyke; *C:* Clyde De Vinna. Oscars '29: Cinematog.

The White Sheik 🐾🐾 Lo Sceicco Bianco 1952 Fellini's first solo effort. A newly wed bride meets her idol from the comic pages (made with photos, not cartoons; called fumetti) and runs off with him. She soon finds he's as ordinary as her husband. Brilliant satire in charming garb. Remade as "The World's Greatest Lover." Woody Allen's "The Purple Rose of Cairo" is in a similar spirit. In Italian with subtitles. 86m/B VHS, DVD, IT Alberto Sordi, Giulietta Masina, Brunella Bovo, Leopoldo Trieste; *D:* Federico Fellini; *W:* Federico Fellini, Tullio Pinelli, Ennio Flaiano; *C:* Arturo Galea; *M:* Nino Rota.

The White Sin 🐾🐾 1924 An innocent country girl hires on as maid of a rich woman and is seduced and abandoned by the woman's profligate son, but everything turns out all right by the end of the third handkerchief. Silent with original organ music. 93m/B VHS, Madge Bellamy, John Bowers, Billy Bevan; *D:* William A. Seiter.

The White Sister 🐾🐾 1923 Gish is an Italian aristocrat driven from her home by a conniving sister. When her true love (Colman) is reported killed she decides to become a nun and enters a convent. When her lover does return he tricks her into leaving the convent but before he can persuade her to renounce her vows Vesuvius erupts and he goes off to warn the villagers, dying for his efforts. Gish then re-dedicates herself to her faith. Colman's first leading role, which made him a romantic star. Filmed on location in Italy. **108m/B VHS.** Lillian Gish, Ronald Colman, Gail Kane, J. Barney Sherry, Charles Lane; **D:** Henry King.

White Slave ♂ *Amazonia: The Catherine Miles Story* **1986 (R)** An Englishwoman is captured by bloodthirsty cannibals and, rather than being eaten, is tormented and made a slave. **90m/C VHS, DVD.** Elvire Avoray, Will Gonzales, Andrew Louis Coppola; **D:** Mario Gariazzo.

White Squall ♂♂½ **1996 (PG-13)** Based on the 1960 true story of 13 young men who become students at Ocean Academy, a year-long adventure spent aboard the brigantine Albatross. Bridges plays the ship's agonize over their various crises, making the first half of the movie into a veritable "Dead Poets Yachting Society." However, a sudden storm overtakes the ship in the Caribbean and several crew members are killed. There's a shift to a "Caine Mutiny" type trial in which Bridges must prove the tragedy was not his fault while the survivors rally to his defense. Director Scott excels at showing the fury of nature in the prolonged storm scene, but takes his time getting there. **128m/C VHS, DVD.** Jeff Bridges, Scott Wolf, Caroline Goodall, Balthazar Getty, John Savage, Jeremy Sisto, Jason Marsden, David Selby, Zeljko Ivanek, Ryan Phillippe, David Lascher, Eric Michael Cole, Julio Oscar Mechoso, Ethan (Randall) Embry; **D:** Ridley Scott; **W:** Todd Robinson; **C:** Hugh Johnson; **M:** Jeff Rona.

White Tiger ♂♂½ **1923** Three crooks pull off a major heist and hide out in a mountain cabin where their mistrust of each other grows. **81m/B VHS.** Priscilla Dean, Matt Moore, Raymond Griffith, Wallace Beery; **D:** Tod Browning.

White Tiger ♂½ **1995 (R)** DEA agent Mike Ryan (Daniels) decides to take the law into his own fists when his partner Grogan (Craven) is murdered by Chinese gang/drug leader Victor Chow (Tagawa). **93m/C VHS, DVD.** Gary Daniels, Matt Craven, Cary-Hiroyuki Tagawa, Julia Nickson-Soul; **D:** Richard Martin; **W:** Gordon Melbourne; **C:** Gregory Middleton; **M:** Graeme Coleman.

The White Tower ♂♂♂ **1950** Five men and a woman set out to scale the infamous White Tower in the Alps. Each person's true nature is revealed as he or she scales the peak, which has defied all previous attempts. Slightly overwrought, but exciting. Filmed in Technicolor on location in the Swiss Alps. **98m/C VHS.** Glenn Ford, Claude Rains, Cedric Hardwicke, Oscar Homolka, Lloyd Bridges; **D:** Ted Tetzlaff; **M:** Paul Jarrico.

White Water Summer ♂½ *Rites of Summer* **1987 (PG)** A group of young adventurers trek into the Sierras, and find themselves struggling against nature and each other to survive. Bacon is the rugged outdoorsman (yeah, sure) who shows them what's what. Chances are it was never at a theatre near you, and good reason. **90m/C VHS, DVD.** Kevin Bacon, Sean Astin, Jonathan Ward, Matt Adler, K.C. Martel; **D:** Jeff Bleckner; **M:** Michael Boddicker.

White Wolves 2: Legend of the Wild ♂♂½ **1994 (PG)** Troubled teens are on a school assignment involving a conservation foundation's rescue of a pair of young wolves. They must overcome lots of obstacles, including the fact that they can't stand each other. Average teens-in-the-woods adventure. **95m/C VHS, DVD.** Corin "Corky" Nemec, Justin Whalin, Jeremy London, Elizabeth Berkley, Ernie Reyes Jr., Elie Keats; **D:** Terence H. Winkless; **C:** John Aronson.

White Wolves 3: Cry of the White Wolf ♂♂½ **1998 (PG)** A plane crash strands three teens in the wilderness where they must depend on themselves, and the mystical white wolf, for survival. **82m/C VHS, DVD.** Rodney A. Grant, Mercedes McNab, Robin Clarke, Tracy Brooks Swope, Mick Cain, Margaret Howell; **D:** Victoria Muspratt.

The White Zombie ♂♂♂ **1932** Lugosi followed his success in "Dracula" with the title role in this low-budget horror classic about the leader of a band of zombies who wants to steal a beautiful young woman from her new husband. Set in Haiti; the first zombie movie. Rich and dark, though ludicrous. Based on the novel "The Magic Island" by William Seabrook. **73m/B VHS.** Bela Lugosi, Madge Bellamy, John Harron, Joseph Cawthorn, Robert Frazer, Brandon Hurst, George Burr Macaman, John Peters, Dan Crimmins, Clarence Muse; **D:** Victor Halperin; **W:** Garnett Weston; **C:** Arthur Martinelli; **M:** Xavier Cugat.

WhiteForce ♂ **1988 (R)** A secret agent tracks an enemy. His government tracks him. He runs around with a big machine gun and a couple of hand grenades. He fires the gun and throws the grenades. **90m/C VHS, DVD.** Sam Jones, Kimberly Pistone; **D:** Eddie Romero.

Whitewash: The Clarence Brandley Story ♂♂♂½ **2002 (R)** Black farmer Dan Brandley is shot to death in broad daylight on the main street of Conroe, Texas, in 1940. No one is ever brought to trial, even though his white killer is known. Forty years later, grandson Clarence Brandley discovers the murdered body of a white teenaged girl and learns that racism and corruption still hold sway. Clarence is tried, convicted, and sentenced to death. Now, his lawyer must prevent an innocent man's execution. **108m/C VHS.** Courtney B. Vance, Gil Bellows, Eamonn Walker, Chuck Shamata, Richard Eden, Joseph Ziegler; **D:** Tony Bill; **W:** Abby Mann; **C:** Jean Lepine. **CABLE**

Whitewater Sam ♂♂½ **1978 (G)** Whitewater Sam and his Siberian Husky, Sybar, embark on an exciting trip through the uncharted wilds of the Great Northwest. The likeable, intelligent hound steals the show. Good family adventure. **87m/C VHS.** Keith Larsen; **D:** Keith Larsen; **W:** Keith Larsen.

Whity ♂♂ **1970** Whity (Kaufman) is the illegitimate mulatto son of the wealthy white man for whom he works. An equally exploited barmaid (Schygulla) convinces Whity his one chance for freedom is to murder his masters. Kaufman was one of Fassbinder's boyfriends and the personal tensions and obsessions of their relationship spilled onto the screen. German with subtitles. **102m/C DVD.** GE Rainer Werner Fassbinder, Gunther Kaufman, Hanna Schygulla, Ulli Lommel, Harry Baer; **D:** Rainer Werner Fassbinder; **W:** Rainer Werner Fassbinder; **C:** Michael Ballhaus; **M:** Peer Raben.

Who Am I This Time? ♂♂♂ **1982** Two shy people can express their love for each other only through their roles in a local theatre production of "A Streetcar Named Desire." Good cast responds well to competent direction from Demme; poignant, touching, and memorable. Based on a story by Kurt Vonnegut Jr. **60m/C VHS, DVD.** Susan Sarandon, Christopher Walken, Robert Ridgely, Mike Bacarella, Aaron Freeman, Caitlin Hart; **D:** Jonathan Demme; **M:** John Cale. **TV**

Who Done It? ♂♂ **1942** Average Abbott and Costello comedy about two would-be radio mystery writers, working as soda-jerks, who play detective after the radio station's president is murdered. **77m/B VHS, DVD.** Bud Abbott, Lou Costello, William Gargan, Patric Knowles, Louise Allbritton, Don Porter, Jerome Cowan, William Bendix, Mary Wickes; **D:** Erle C. Kenton.

Who Done It? ♂♂½ **1956** Film debut of the rakish Hill as ice-rink sweeper, Hugo Dill. When Dill comes into some money and a dog, he launches a private investigating firm. A woman enters the picture and Hugo discovers his sleuthing has gotten him in over his head. Lots of typical gags and car chases. **85m/B VHS, DVD.** GB Benny Hill, Belinda Lee, David Kossoff, Ernest Thesiger, Garry Marsh, George Margo, Denis Shaw, Fred Schiller, Jeremy Hawk, Thorley Walters, Philip Stainton, Stratford Johns; **D:** Basil Dearden; **W:** T.E.B. Clarke; **C:** Otto Heller; **M:** Philip Green.

Who Framed Roger Rabbit ♂♂♂ **1988 (PG)** Technically marvelous, cinematically hilarious, eye-popping combination of cartoon and live action create a Hollywood of the 1940s where cartoon characters are real and a repressed minority working in films. A 'toon-hating detective is hired to uncover the unfaithful wife of 2-D star Roger, and instead uncovers a conspiracy to wipe out all 'toons. Special appearances by many cartoon characters from the past. Coproduced by Touchstone (Disney) and Amblin (Spielberg). Adapted from "Who Censored Roger Rabbit?" by Gary K. Wolf. **104m/C VHS, DVD.** Bob Hoskins, Christopher Lloyd, Joanna Cassidy, Alan Tilvern, Stubby Kaye; **D:** Robert Zemeckis; **W:** Jeffrey Price, Peter S. Seaman; **C:** Dean Cundey; **M:** Alan Silvestri; **V:** Charles Fleischer, Mae Questel, Kathleen Turner, Amy Irving, Mel Blanc, June Foray, Frank Sinatra. Oscars '88: Film Editing, Visual FX.

Who Gets to Call It Art? ♂♂♂½ **2005** Jumbled documentary about the unlikely career of Metropolitan Museum of Art curator Henry Geldzahler, who died in 1994, and his 1969 landmark 408-piece exhibition entitled "New York Painting and Sculpture: 1940-1970" that showcased works from 43 artists, including Jackson Pollock, Jasper Johns, Willem de Kooning, Andy Warhol, and David Hockney. **80m/C DVD.** US

Who Has Seen the Wind? ♂♂½ **1977** Two boys grow up in Saskatchewan during the Depression. So family viewing drama. Ferrer as a bootlegger steals the otherwise small-paced show. **102m/C VHS.** CA GB Brian Painchaud, Patricia Hamilton, Gordon Pinsent, Chapelle Jaffe, Helen Shaver, Cedric Smith, Jose Ferrer; **D:** Allan King; **W:** Patricia Watson; **C:** Richard Leiterman; **M:** Eldon Rathburn.

Who is Cletis Tout? ♂♂½ **2002 (R)** This nostalgic spoof of/homage to classic movies revolves around the efforts of cornered, man Trevor (Slater) to convince a film-loving hitman that he is not Cletis Tout, a reporter that the mob wants dead. Critical Jim (Allen) is a button man with time on his hands, so he has Trevor tell him the story like he was pitching a movie idea to a studio executive. The tale contains many obvious Hollywood plot machinations and references including a prison break, a pretty girl, elaborate con jobs and true love. Trevor is also not above taking cues from Jim, changing the story when his captor is displeased by part of it. Good premise tends to get too cute with the material, but all in all a fun ride. **92m/C VHS, DVD.** Tim Allen, Christian Slater, Portia de Rossi, Richard Dreyfuss, Billy Connolly, Peter MacNeill, Richard Chevolleau, RuPaul Charles; **D:** Christopher Ver Wiel; **W:** Christopher Ver Wiel; **C:** Jerzy Zielinski; **M:** Randy Edelman.

Who Is Harry Kellerman and Why is He Saying Those Terrible Things About Me? ♂♂½ **1971 (R)** Hoffman stars as a successful composer/singer who finds money didn't bring him happiness. **108m/C VHS.** Dustin Hoffman, Barbara Harris, Jack Warden, Dom DeLuise; **D:** Ulu Grosbard.

Who Is Killing the Great Chefs of Europe? ♂♂½ *Too Many Chefs; Someone is Killing the Great Chefs of Europe* **1978 (PG)** A fast-paced, lightly handled black comedy. When a gourmand, well-played by Morley, learns he must lose weight to live, a number of Europe's best chefs are murdered according to their cooking specialty. A witty, crisp, international mystery based on Ivan and Nan Lyon's novel. **112m/C VHS.** George Segal, Jacqueline Bisset, Robert Morley, Jean-Pierre Cassel, Philippe Noiret, Jean Rochefort, Joss Ackland, Nigel Havers; **D:** Ted Kotcheff; **M:** Henry Mancini. L.A. Film Critics '78: Support. Actor (Morley).

Who Is the Black Dahlia? ♂♂♂ **1975** In L.A. in 1947, a detective tries to find out who murdered a star-struck 22-year-old woman nicknamed "The Black Dahlia" (Arnaz). Based on a famous unsolved murder case which was later the basis for "True Confessions." Made for TV. **96m/C VHS.** Efrem Zimbalist Jr., Lucie Arnaz, Ronny Cox, MacDonald

---

Carey, Linden Chiles; **D:** Joseph Pevney; **W:** Robert W. Lenski. **TV**

Who Killed Baby Azaria? ♂♂ **1983** Parents are arrested for infanticide after they claim their baby was stolen by a wild dog while vacationing on a supposedly haunted Australian mountain, or was it an aboriginal spirit that absconded with the tyke? Less compelling than the American remake, "A Cry in the Dark." Made for Australian TV. **96m/C VHS.** AU Elaine Hudson, Peter Hamblin, Peter Carroll; **D:** Judy Rymer. **TV**

Who Killed Bambi? ♂♂½ *Qui a tu Bambi?* **2003** Proving that hospitals are creepy in any language, this French thriller uses the hygienic facade of the medical profession as its backdrop for terror. Isabelle (Quinton) is a nursing student, beginning her first residency at a large, isolated hospital. After she faints on the job, her cousin Veronique (Jacob) nicknames her "Bambi," due to her inability to stay on her feet. When the stoic, handsome Dr. Philipp (Lucas) believes that Isabelle's fainting spells might be cured by an operation, she goes under his care, only to discover that Philipp has a penchant for molesting female patients while they're unconscious. Thus begins a protracted cat-and-mouse struggle between doctor and nurse, which reaches increasingly improbable heights. **121m/C DVD.** Laurent Lucas, Catherine Jacob, Sophie Quinton, Doc Mateo; **D:** Gilles Marchand; **C:** Pierre Milon; **M:** Alexandre Beaupain, Lily Margot, Francois Eudes.

Who Killed Doc Robbin? ♂ *Sinister House; Curley and His Gang in the Haunted Mansion* **1948** A group of youngsters try to clear their friend, Dan, the town handyman, when the sinister Dr. Robbin is murdered. The follow-up to "The Adventures of Curly and His Gang," intended as part of a Roach kid-comedy series in the manner of "Our Gang." Fast pace and lots of slapstick give a first impression of spirited juvenile hijinks, but not much is genuinely funny. And the names of the two black kids—"Dis" and "Dat"—aren't funny either. **50m/C VHS, DVD.** Peter Miles, George Zucco, Paul Hurst, Larry Olsen, Don Castle, Eilene Janssen, Virginia Grey; **D:** Bernard Carr; **W:** Dorothy Davenport Reid, Maurice Geraghty; **C:** John Boyle; **M:** Marvin Hatley.

Who Killed Mary What's 'Er Name? ♂♂♂ **1971 (PG)** *Death of a Hooker* A diabetic ex-fighter tracks a prostitute's killer through Greenwich Village. Illogical, incredible and disjointed attempt at comedy/mystery. Odd, unsatisfying ending, with the boxer going into a coma. Good supporting cast. **90m/C VHS.** Red Buttons, Sylvia Miles, Conrad Bain, Ron Carey, David Doyle, Sam Waterston; **D:** Ernest Pintoff.

Who Killed the Electric Car? ♂♂½ **2006 (PG)** Advocate Paine looks at the history of the EV1, the first mass-produced electric automobile, introduced by General Motors in California in 1996 after the state passed legislation requiring automakers to make a portion of their vehicles with zero-emission engines. Despite protests, GM pulled the cars (which were only available by lease) in 2000, citing lack of consumer interest among other reasons. Paine uncovers the EV1's ultimate fate—crushed at GM's Nevada desert proving ground. **92m/C DVD.** US **D:** Charles Paine; **W:** Charles Paine; **C:** Thaddeus Wadleigh; **M:** Michael Brook.

Who Made the Potatoe Salad? ♂♂½ **2005 (R)** Vulgar comedy that wastes a lot of potential. Bumbling San Diego cop Michael (Fréderique) proposes to his girlfriend Ashley (Fréderique) and insists that they travel to L.A. for Thanksgiving to inform her family. Ashley has been keeping everyone in the dark—Michael knows nothing about them and they know nothing about him, so let the trouble begin. It seems Ashley's dad (Powell) is a former Black Panther who doesn't want a pig for a son-in-law, her brother June Bug (Davis) is a hip-hop slinging thug, and her ex (Griffin) is a con. **90m/C DVD.** Jaleel White, Clifton Powell, DeRay Davis, Eddie Griffin, Jenna Frederique, Ella Joyce, Tommy (Tiny) Lister; **D:** Damon "Coke" Daniels; **C:** Geary McLeod; **M:** Geoff Levin. **VIDEO**

Who Saw Her Die? 🐾🐾 *Chi/Ha*

Vista Morte 1972 Sculptor Franco (Lazenby)'s visited by his preteen daughter Roberta (Elmi) at his Venice home. Roberta goes missing and is found dead in a canal. When Franco and his estranged wife Elizabeth (Strindberg) investigate, they learn that there has been a cover-up concerning the murders of several other children. Italian with subtitles. 90m/C DVD. *IT* George Lazenby, Anita Strindberg, Violoetta Elmi, Adolfo Celi, Peter Chatel; *D:* Aldo Lado; *W:* Aldo Lado; Francesco Barilli; *M:* Ennio Morricone.

Who Shot Pat? 🐾🐾 *Who Shot Patatango?; Brooklyn Love Story* 1992 (R) Funny, nostalgic, coming of age story set in '50s Brooklyn. Knight stars as Bic Bickham, the leader of a clear-living "gang" of seniors at a Brooklyn vocational school. Memorable vintage soundtrack features hits by legendary artists Chuck Berry and Bo Diddly. 102m/C VHS, DVD. David Edwin Knight, Sandra Bullock, Kevin Otto, Aaron Ingram, Brad Randall; *D:* Robert Brooks; *W:* Robert Brooks, Halle Brooks; *C:* Robert Brooks.

Who Wants to Kill Jessie? 🐾🐾 1965 Lunatic Czech comedy about a jealous wife and a comic strip babe. A scientist has invented a device that makes dreams visible and she decides to see what goes on in her meek hubby's subconscious. He's dreaming about another inventor—Jessie, an imperiled va-va-voom comic strip character. When wifey interferes, the side effect is that the dreams show up in reality and chasing her. Lots of sight gags. Czech with subtitles. 79m/B DVD, CZ Jana Mednicka, Jiri Sovak, Olga Shoderova, Karel Effa, Juraj Visny; *D:* Vaclav Vorlicek; *W:* Vaclav Vorlicek, Milos Macourek; *C:* Jan Nemecek; *M:* Svatopluk Havelka.

Whodunit 🐾 1982 (R) The bad horror flicks always seem to have (usually young) characters murdered one at a time, often on a remote island. This loser is no exception. 82m/C VHS. Rick Bean, Gary Phillips; *D:* Bill Naud; *W:* Anthony Shafter.

Whole New Thing 🐾🐾 2005 Precocious 13-year-old Emerson (Webber in his feature debut) has been home-schooled by his hippie parents Kaya (Jenkins) and Rog (Joy). Worried about his social skills, Kaya decides and rognous Emerson should now attend public school, where he's promptly beaten up, which Emerson takes with remarkable poise. He's not so self-possessed about his gay middle-aged English teacher, Don (McIvor), on whom Emerson develops a major crush. Don fends off Emerson's inappropriate advances while suffering through a midlife crisis—or are shared by Emerson's parents, who are having marital problems. 92m/C DVD, CA Rebecca Jenkins, Robert Joy, Callum Keith Rennie, Daniel McIvor, Aaron Webber; *D:* Amnon Buchbinder; *W:* Daniel McIvor, Amnon Buchbinder; *C:* Christophe Bal; *M:* David Buchbinder.

The Whole Nine Yards 🐾🐾½ 2000 (PG-13) Wimpy dentist Oz (Perry) has his life turned to chaos when former hit man Jimmy (Willis) moves in next door, inspiring his wife Sophie (Arquette), who's bored and wants Oz dead for the insurance money, and Jill, Oz's receptionist, who aspires to be a hit woman herself. Sophie nags Oz into a plot to alert Jimmy's former employers of his whereabouts, which brings in a whole bunch of new over-the-top characters, all of whom want somebody dead. While it's true that most of the plot elements are not only ridiculous, but cribbed from other hit man movies, this one works because the actors all do fine jobs (except maybe Arquette).

Who Slew Auntie Roo? 🐾🐾½ *Whoever Slew Auntie Roo?; Gingerbread House* 1971 (PG) An updated twist on the Hansel and Gretel fairy tale. Winters as an odd, reclusive widow mistaken for the fairy tale's children-eating witch by one of the orphans at her annual Christmas party—with dire consequences. 90m/C VHS, DVD. Shelley Winters, Ralph Richardson, Mark Lester, Lionel Jeffries, Hugh Griffith Chiarington; *M:* Robert Bees.

The Whole Shebang 🐾🐾 2001 Low-key, sentimental romantic comedy. After the heir to the Barzini fireworks company dies, his son Giovanni (Tucci, who also directs) becomes the replacement. Giovanni has been suicidally lovesick over a heartless beauty (Champa) but his luck may change when he meets his cousin's not-so-brokenhearted widow, Val (Fonda). Val is being wooed by Joey Zito (DeSando), whose family is eager to earn Pop's pyrotechnica secrets. A big fireworks competition (which was filmed in Naples) adds some oomph. 97m/C DVD. *US* CA Stanley Tucci, Bridget Fonda, Giancarlo Giannini, Talia Shire, Anthony DeSando, Anna Maria Alberghetti, Jo Champa, Alexander Milani; *D:* George Zaloom; *W:* Jeff Rothberg, George Zaloom; *C:* Jacek Laskus; *M:* Evan Lurie.

The Whole Ten Yards 🐾½ 2004 (PG-13) Apparently, this is one yard too many. Stretching the premise of the original into a better-left-undone mess, ex-hitman Jimmy the Tulip (Willis) with his still-aspiring hit woman wife Jill (Peet), who are trying to live on the down-low in Mexico. Jill is still trying (and failing) to become an assassin while Jimmy's attempts at blending in consist of pretending to be a house-husband to terrifically bad comic effect. Oz, meanwhile is living in L.A. with wife Cynthia (Henstridge). Shred of a plot centers around the revenge scheme of Lazlo Gogolak (Pollack), whose son Janni (also Pollack) was whacked by Oz and Jimmy in the not great but infinitely better original. Joyless performances by all underscored by a spectacularly bad Pollack. 99m/C DVD. *US* Bruce Willis, Matthew Perry, Amanda Peet, Kevin Pollak, Natasha Henstridge, Frank Collison, Johnny Messner, Silas Weir Mitchell, Tasha Smith; *D:* Howard Deutch; *W:* George Gallo; *C:* Neil Roach; *M:* John Debney.

The Whole Shootin' Match 🐾½ 1979 Two 30-something Texas nobodies chase the American Dream via a sure-fire invention called the Kitchen Wizard, after failing in the small-animal biz and polyurethane. Offbeat, very low-budget independent feature shot interestingly in sepia tones. Sympathetic and human. 108m/C VHS. Lou Perryman, Sonny Carl Davis, Doris Hargrave; *D:* Eagle Pennell.

The Whole Town's Talking 🐾🐾🐾 1935 Meek clerk Arthur Jones (Robinson) usually leads an uneventful life, until the police arrest him, thinking he's escaped monster Killer Mannion (Robinson again). Arthur manages to prove his identity and is issued an ID card to settle the confusion, but the mix-up has hit the papers and when Mannion finds out about his double, he steals the card and kidnaps Arthur's Aunt Agatha (Ellsler) and coworker Wilhelmina (Arthur) to ensure his cooperation. Mann-figure a way out of his double trouble. Based on a novel by William R. Burnett. 95m/B VHS. Edward G. Robinson, Jean Arthur, Arthur Hohl, Wallace Ford, Arthur Byron, Donald Meek, Paul Harvey, Effie Ellsler; *D:* John Ford; *W:* Jo Swerling, Robert Riskin; *C:* Joseph August.

The Whole Wide World 🐾🐾🐾 1996 (PG) Adaptation of Novalyne Price Ellis's memoirs about her friendship with "Conan the Barbarian" pulp writer Robert E. Howard (in full, Wallace Ford). Set in Cross Plains, Texas schoolteacher (and aspiring writer) Price (Zellweger) arranges an introduction to local eccentric Howard (D'Onofrio), who lives with his overprotective, dying mother (Wedgeworth) and respected doctor father (Fresnell) while churning out his bloody tales. Howard has few, if any, social skills but his unpredicta...

Whoops Apocalypse 🐾🐾½ 1983 T.V. series that offers a satiric account of events leading up to WWIII. Invasion in South America leads British prime minister to suggest nuclear retaliation. Uneven, lacking in the Strangelovian element, but funny in spots. 137m/C VHS, GB John Cleese, John Barron, Richard Griffiths, Peter Jones, Bruce Montague, Barry Morse, Rik Mayall, Ian Richardson, Alexei Sayle, Herbert Lom, Joanne Pearce; *D:* John Reardon; *W:* Andrew Marshall, David Renwick.

The Whoopee Boys 🐾 1986 (R) A New York lowlife in Palm Beach tries to reform himself by saving a school for needy children so his rich girlfriend will marry him. Full of unfunny jokes and very bad taste, with no redeeming qualities whatever. 89m/C VHS. Michael O'Keefe, Paul Rodriguez; *D:* John Byrum; *W:* Jeff Buhai; *C:* Ralf Bode; *M:* Jack Nitzsche.

Whoopee! 🐾🐾 1930 Cantor stars in his first sound picture as a rich hypochondriac sent out west for his health. He encounters rugged cowboys and Indians. Filmed in two-color Technicolor and based on Ziegfeld's 1928 Broadway production with the same cast. Dances supervised by Busby Berkeley. ♫The Song of the Setting Sun; Mission Number; Makin' Whoopee; A Girlfriend of a Boyfriend of Mine; My Baby Just Cares for Me; I'll Still Belong to You; Stetson. 93m/C VHS. Eddie Cantor, Ethel Shutta, Paul Gregory, Eleanor Hunt, Betty Grable; *D:* Thornton Freeland.

---

bility appeals to the sensible Price and the two have a turbulent emotional relationship that never blooms into a full romance. Howard committed suicide in 1936 at the age of 30. 111m/C VHS, DVD. Renee Zellweger, Vincent D'Onofrio, Ann Wedgeworth, Harve Presnell, Helen Cates, Benjamin Mouton, Michael Corbett, Marion Eaton, Leslie Berger, Chris Shearer, Sandy Walper, Dell Aldrich, Libby Villari, Antonia Bogaanovich, Elizabeth D'Onofrio, Stephen Marshall; *D:* Dan Ireland; *W:* Michael Scott Myers, Novalyne Price Ellis; *C:* Claudio Rocha; *M:* Hans Zimmer, Harry Gregson-Williams.

Who'll Save Our Children? 🐾🐾 1982 Two children are abandoned and left on the doorstep of a middle-aged, childless couple. Years later the natural parents, now reformed, attempt to reclaim their children. Well cast and topical. 96m/C VHS, Shirley Jones, Len Cariou, Conchata Ferrell, Frances Sternhagen, Cassie Yates, David Hayward; *D:* George Schaefer. TV

Who'll Stop the Rain? 🐾🐾🐾½ *Dog Soldiers* 1978 (R) A temperamental Vietnam vet (Nolte) is enlisted in a smuggling scheme to transport a large amount of heroin into California. An excellent blend of drama, comedy, action, suspense, and tragedy. Based on Robert Stone's novel "Dog Soldiers." Outstanding period soundtrack by Creedence Clearwater Revival, including title song. Violent and compelling tale of late-'60s disillusionment. 126m/C VHS, DVD. Nick Nolte, Tuesday Weld, Michael Moriarty, Anthony Zerbe, Ray Sharkey, David Opatoshu, Richard Masur, Gail Strickland; *D:* Karel Reisz; *W:* Judith Rascoe; *C:* Richard H. Kline; *M:* Laurence Rosenthal.

Wholly Moses! WOOF! 1980 (PG) Set in biblical times, this alleged comedy concerns a phony religious prophet who begins to believe that his mission is to lead the chosen. Horrible ripoff of "Life of Brian," released the previous year. What a cast—what a waste! 125m/C VHS, DVD. Dudley Moore, Laraine Newman, James Coco, Paul Sand, Dom DeLuise, Jack Gilford, John Houseman, Madeline Kahn, Richard Pryor, John Ritter; *D:* Gary Wes.

Whore 🐾🐾 *If You Can't Say It, Just See It* 1991 (R) Ken Russell's gritty night in the life of cynical prostitute Theresa Russell is strong medicine, a powerful antidote to the sappy Hollywood films that glorify street-walking. Also available in the 92-minute original uncut version, an 85-minute NC-17 version, and an alternate R-Rated version. 80m/C VHS. Theresa Russell, Antonio Vargas; *D:* Ken Russell; *W:* Ken Russell.

Who's Minding the Store? 🐾🐾½ 1963 Well, it's certainly not Lewis, who plays poodle sitter Raymond Phiffer who is in love with rich girl Barbara (St. John). Barbara's imperious mother (Moorehead) is determined to break up the duo and hires Raymond to work at the family department store (hoping he'll be a disaster), instead he becomes a success in his own slapstick way. Flighty, wrongly convicted parolee kidnaps her uptight lawyer and they have wacky adventures as she goes in search of the crumb that landed her in the pokey. Plenty you're not laughing. Kind of a remake of "Bringing Up Baby" (1938). 90m/C VHS. Jerry Lewis, Jill St. John, Agnes Moorehead, John McGiver, Ray Walston, Nancy Kulp; *D:* Frank Tashlin; *W:* Frank Tashlin, Harry Tugend; *C:* Wallace Keller; *M:* Joseph J. Lilley.

Who's That Girl? 🐾 1987 (PG) A flighty, wrongly convicted parolee kidnaps her uptight lawyer and they have wacky adventures as she goes in search of the crumb that landed her in the pokey. Plenty they briefly keep you from wondering why you're not laughing. Kind of a remake of a bad one's of "Bringing Up Baby" (1938). 94m/C VHS, DVD. Madonna, Griffin Dunne, John Mills, Haviland, Griffin Dunne, John McGiver; *D:* James Foley; *C:* Jan De Bont; Golden Raspberries '87. Worst Actress (Madonna).

Whore 2 🐾½ *Bad Girls* 1994 (R) Jack is a middle-aged writer who moves into Hell's kitchen in order to do research for a book about prostitutes. Then Jack gets involved with two of the girls—the tough, jealous Lori and childlike Mary Lou. 35m/C VHS, Amos Kollek, Maria Sucratza, Marl Nelson; *D:* Amos Kollek; *W:* Amos Kollek.

Who's Afraid of Virginia Woolf? 🐾🐾🐾🐾 1966 (R) Nichols debuts as a director in this biting Edward Albee play. A teacher and his wife (Burton and Taylor), The guests get more than dinner, as the evening deteriorates into brutal verbal battles between the hosts. Taylor and Dennis won Oscars; Burton's Oscar-nominated portrait of the tortured husband is magnificent. Richard and Liz's best film together. 127m/B VHS, DVD. Richard Burton, Elizabeth Taylor, George Segal, Sandy Dennis; *D:* Mike Nichols; *W:* Ernest Lehman; *C:* Haskell Wexler; *M:* Alex North. Oscars '66: Actress (Taylor), Art Dir/Set Dec., B&W; Support. Actress (Dennis); Costume Des. (B&W), Cinematog. (B&W); British Acad. '66: Actor (Taylor), Film; Natl. Bd. of Review '66: Actress (Taylor) N.Y. Film Critics '66: Actress (Taylor).

Who's Got the Action? 🐾🐾½ 1963 Martin and Turner are a husband and wife divided by his love of playing the ponies. In order to keep his gambling under control Turner schemes to become his new bookie. But when Martin suddenly goes on a winning streak, the new bookie is in trouble with her former competition, who just happen to be the Mob. Strained, flat comedy with Turner especially miscast. 93m/C VHS. Lana Turner, Dean Martin, Walter Matthau, Eddie Albert, Nita Talbot, Margo, Paul Ford, John McGiver, Jack Albertson; *D:* Daniel Mann; *W:* Jack Rose.

Who's Harry Crumb? 🐾½ 1989 (PG-13) Bumbling detective Candy can't even investigate a routine kidnapping! His incompetence is catching—the viewer can't relate to a single genuinely funny moment. Candy is the only likeable thing in this all-around bad, mindless farce. 95m/C VHS, DVD. John Candy, Jeffrey Jones, Annie Potts, Tim Thomerson, Barry Corbin, Shawnee Smith, Valri Bromfield, Renee Coleman, Joe Flaherty, Lyle Alzado, James Belushi, Stephen Young; *D:* Paul Flaherty; *W:* Robert Conte; *M:* Michel Colombier.

Who's Minding the Mint? 🐾🐾 1967 A money checker at the U.S. Mint must replace $50,000 he accidentally destroyed. He enlists a retired money printer and an inept gang to infiltrate the mint and replace the lost cash, with predictable chaos resulting. Non-stop zaniness in this wonderful comedy that never got its cue when released. Thieves who befriend Hutton include Denver of "Gilligan's Island" and Farr, later of "M*A*S*H." 97m/C VHS. Jim Hutton, Dorothy Provine, Milton Berle, Joey Bishop, Boo Denver, Walter Brennan, Jamie Farr; *D:* Howard Morris; *C:* Joseph Biroc.

Who's That Knocking at My Door? ✰✰ *J.R.; I Call First* 1968 Interesting debut for Scorsese, in which he exercises many of the themes and techniques that he polished for later films. An autobiographical drama about an Italian-American youth growing up in NYC, focusing on street life, Catholicism and adolescent bonding. Begun as a student film called "I Call First"; later developed into a feature. Keitel's film debut. **90m/B VHS, DVD.** Harvey Keitel, Zena Bethune; **D:** Martin Scorsese.

Who's the Man? ✰✰ 1993 (R) Two clowning companions who work in a barbershop in Harlem get recruited onto the police force to investigate a murder. Doctor Dre and Ed Lover (themselves) make use of their hip-hop music connections and full-throttle slapstick humor to enliven the search. Salt of "Salt 'n' Pepa," is the female lead and Ice-T plays a gangster. First-time director Demme works his star duo for both foolish and vulgar humor. Filming done mostly on location in Harlem. Includes a lengthy list of cameo appearances by several hip-hop performers. For fans; based on a story by Dre, Lover, and Seth Greenland. **124m/C VHS, DVD.** Ed Lover, Cheryl "Salt" James, Ice-T, Jim Moody, Colin Quinn, Kim Chan, Rozwill Young, Badja (Medu) Djola, Richard Bright, Denis Leary, Andre B. Blake, Bill Bellamy, Louis Freese; **D:** Ted (Edward) Demme; **W:** Seth Greenland; **M:** Michael Wolff.

Who's Who ✰✰ 1978 In a satire on climbing the British social ladder, workers in a London brokerage firm struggle with class issues and find the higher you climb, the more you find greed, pettiness, and stupidity. **75m/C VHS, DVD.** *GB* Bridget Kane, Simon Chandler, Adam Norton, Philip Davis, Joolia Cappleman; **D:** Mike Leigh; **W:** Mike Leigh. **TV**

Who's Your Caddy? ✰1/2 2007 (PG-13) Rap mogul C-Note (Patton) tries to become a member at the conservative Carolina Pines country club, where he's opposed by snobby club president Cummings (Jones). But C-Note blackmails his way in, causing predictable havoc. Vulgarity and stereotypes abound. **93m/C DVD.** Antwan Andre Patton, Jeffrey Jones, Sherri Shepherd, Faizon Love, Jenifer Lewis, Tamala Jones, Andy Milonakis, Chase Tatum; **D:** Don Michael Paul; **W:** Don Michael Paul, Bradley Allenstein, Robert Henny; **C:** Thomas Callaway; **M:** Jon Lee.

Whose Child Am I? ✰ 1975 (R) A woman so desperately wants a child of her own that she doesn't mind who the father is. Ludicrous and vulgar. **90m/C VHS.** Kate O'Mara, Paul Freeman, Edward Judd, Felicity Devonshire; **D:** Lawrence Britten.

Whose Life Is It Anyway? ✰✰✰1/2 1981 (R) Black humor abounds. Sculptor Dreyfuss is paralyzed from the neck down in an auto accident. What follows is his struggle to persuade the hospital authorities to let him die. Excellent cast headed impressively by Dreyfuss; Lahti as his doctor and hospital head Cassavetes also are superb. From Brian Clark's successful Broadway play. **118m/C VHS, DVD.** Richard Dreyfuss, John Cassavetes, Christine Lahti, Bob Balaban, Kenneth McMillan, Kaki Hunter, Thomas Carter; **D:** John Badham; **W:** Reginald Rose, Brian Clark.

Why Change Your Wife? ✰✰✰1/2 1920 A rare, recently rediscovered silent comedy. Swanson and Meighan play married couple Beth and Robert who find themselves drifting apart after ten years of marriage. Robert becomes involved with someone else and Beth demands a divorce. After Robert remarries, Beth decides she wants him back and the real fun begins as she tries every trick in the book to regain her ex-husband. Piano scored. **100m/B VHS, DVD.** Gloria Swanson, Thomas Meighan, Bebe Daniels; **D:** Cecil B. DeMille.

Why Do Fools Fall in Love? ✰✰1/2 1998 (R) Frankie Lymon was a teen do-wop singing sensation in the mid-'50s but a career slide led to heroin addiction and an OD death at the age of 25 in 1968. The other thing Frankie liked to do was marry—without bothering to get divorced. So there are three would-be widows battling for what's left of Lymon's estate: R&B singer Zola Taylor (Berry), goodtime girl and single mom Elizabeth Waters (Fox), and churchgoing schoolteacher Emira Eagle (Rochon). (The ladies pull out of the stops but Lymon remains a mystery. **115m/C VHS, DVD.** Larenz Tate, Halle Berry, Lela Rochon, Vivica A. Fox, Paul Mazursky, Pamela Reed, Little Richard, Ben Vereen, Lane Smith, Alexis Cruz; **D:** Gregory Nava; **W:** Tina Andrews; **C:** Edward Lachman; **M:** Stephen James Taylor.

Why Do They Call It Love When They Mean Sex? ✰✰ *Por Que Lo Llaman Amor Cuando Quieren Decir Sexo?* 1992 Gloria (Forqué) works in a live-sex act but is forced to change partners and work with inexperienced Manu (Sanz), who needs some quick cash because of gambling debts. But everything goes well until Gloria and think the duo are just a nice conventional couple. **115m/C VHS, DVD.** *SP* Jorge Sanz, Veronica Forque, Fernando Colomo, Rosa Maria Sarda, Alejandra Grepi, Elisa Matilla, Isabel Ordaz; **D:** Manuel Gomez Pereira; **W:** Manuel Gomez Pereira; **C:** Hans Burman; **M:** Manuel Wolff.

Why Does Herr R. Run Amok? ✰✰ *Warum Lauft Herr R Amok?* 1969 Notorious Fassbinder black comedy about a middle-class man, unable to cope with the increasing problems of modern life, who suddenly murders his family. The characters are called by the actors' names to heighten the sense of reality. Film is based on a case history. In German with English subtitles. **88m/C VHS, DVD.** *GE* Kurt Raab, Lilith Ungerer, Amadeus Fengler, Hanna Schygulla, Franz Maron; **D:** Rainer Werner Fassbinder, Michael Fengler; **W:** Rainer Werner Fassbinder, Michael Fengler.

Why Has Bodhi-Darma Left for the East? ✰✰ 1989 Set in a remote monastery in the Korean mountains, film follows an old master, close to death, who must lead his disciples in their search for spiritual freedom. The film's title is a Zen koan—an unanswerable riddle that serves as an aid on the path to enlightenment. Korean with subtitles. **135m/C VHS, DVD.** *KN* Hae-Jin Huang, Su-Myong Ko, Yi Pan-Yong, Sin Won-Sop; **D:** Bae Young-kyun; **W:** Bae Young-kyun; **C:** Bae Young-kyun.

Why Me? ✰✰ 1990 (R) Two jewel thieves unknowingly steal an enormously valuable ruby ring and are in over their heads trying to evade the cops and everyone else. In the same vein as the much-funnier "Nuns on the Run," this caper is done in by bad acting and too much ill-conceived slapstick. Adapted by Donald E. Westlake from his own novel. **96m/C VHS.** Christopher Lambert, Christopher Lloyd, Kim Greist, J.T. Walsh, Michael J. Pollard, Tony Plana, John Hancock, Lawrence Tierney; **D:** Gene Quintano; **W:** Donald E. Westlake.

Why Shoot the Teacher ✰✰✰ 1979 A young teacher sent to a one-room schoolhouse in a small prairie town in Saskatchewan during the Depression gets a cold reception on the cold prairie. One of the more popular films at the Canadian box office. Cort was Harold in "Harold and Maude." Based on the novel by Max Braithwaite. **101m/C VHS.** *CA* Bud Cort, Samantha Eggar, Chris Wiggins; **D:** Silvio Narizzano; **W:** James DeFelice.

The Wicked ✰ 1998 (R) *Outback Vampires* 1989 Though packaged as serious horror, this is a cheap, tacky spoof with folks stranded at the country residence of a vampire family. Sole point of interest: these Transylvanian cliches take place in the Australian outback. Kids might actually like this (gore isn't severe), if they can surmount the thick Down Under accents. **87m/C VHS, DVD.** Brett Cumo, Richard Morgan, Angela Kennedy, Maggie Blinco, John (Roy Slaven) Doyle; **D:** Colin Eggleston.

Wicked ✰✰ 1998 (R) Fourteen-year-old Ellie (Stiles) has a big Electra complex—she's desperate to get Daddy Ben's (Moses) attention (he's too busy boffing their au pair) and get rid of Mom Karen (Field). Then Karen is murdered and Detective Boland (Parks) first suspects their sleazy neighbor, Lawson (Muldoon), with whom Karen had been carrying on. But Inger, Ellie's younger sister, notices that things aren't, well, normal between her sibling and their pop. But the twists aren't done yet. **87m/C VHS, DVD.** Julia Stiles, William R. Moses, Chelsea Field, Patrick Muldoon, Michael Parks, Vanessa Zima; **D:** Michael Steinberg; **W:** Eric Weiss; **C:** Bernd Heinl; **M:** Eric Martinez.

Wicked City ✰✰✰ 1989 Wild and woolly anime is similar in tone to a James Bond movie in fact, the whole production has a mid-'60s look. A young man named Taki is picked up by a sexy woman in a bar and regrets his decision when she does one of those really icky transformations. Seems she's a visitor from the parallel Black World of monsters. He's an agent of the Black Guard, a secret intelligence organization that protects the Earth from these supernatural bad guys. The story revolves around Guiseppi Mayart, a strange little character who looks (and acts) like an oversexed E.T., and is the key to a treaty between the two worlds. Taki and his reluctant female partner Makea are assigned to guard the debauched diplomat. **82m/C DVD.** *JP* **D:** Yoshiaki Kawajiri; **V:** Kisei Choo; **C:** Kinichi Ishikawa; **V:** Greg Snegoff, Michael J. Reynolds, Alexandra Kenworthy.

Wicked City ✰✰ 1992 Humans uneasily coexisting with Reptoids (creatures that can assume human shape) in this sci-fi tale based on a Japanese comic strip. Then Hong Kong police discover a plot by the Reptoids to destroy mankind and rule the world (what else is new). Nifty special effects. Available dubbed or in Cantonese with subtitles. **88m/C VHS, DVD.** *HK* Tatsuya Nakadai, Yuen Woo Ping, Roy Cheung, Jacky Cheung, Leon Lai, Michelle Li; **D:** Peter Mak; **W:** Tsui Hark, Roy Szeto; **C:** Wai Keung (Andrew) Lau, Joe Chan; **M:** Richard Yuen.

The Wicked Lady ✰✰ 1945 Posh but lame costume drama about a bored 17th century noblewoman who takes to highway robbery to spice up her life. Credulity-stretcher extraordinaire. Based on "The Life and Death of Wicked Lady Skelton" by Magdalen King-Hall. Manson is cheeky as a fellow highwayman. Remade in 1983 with Faye Dunaway. **103m/B VHS.** *GB* James Mason, Margaret Lockwood, Patricia Roc, Michael Rennie, Felix Aylmer, Enid Stamp-Taylor, Griffith Jones; **D:** Leslie Arliss.

The Wicked Lady ✰1/2 1983 (R) Remake of the 1945 costumer about a 17th-century noblewoman trying her hand at highway robbery. More noted for its low-cut costumes and racy humor than any talent (including director Winner's). **99m/C VHS.** *GB* Faye Dunaway, John Gielgud, Denholm Elliott, Alan Bates, Glynis Barber, Oliver Tobias, Prunella Scales; **D:** Michael Winner; **W:** Michael Winner; **C:** Jack Cardiff; **M:** Tony Banks.

Wicked Stepmother ✰ 1989 (PG-13) A family discovers that an aged stepmother is actually a witch. Davis walked off the film shortly before she died, and was replaced by Carrera. Davis's move was wise; the result is dismal, and would have been had she stayed. As it is the viewer wonders: How come the stepmother isn't Davis anymore? Davis's unfortunate last role. **90m/C VHS.** Bette Davis, Barbara Carrera, Colleen Camp, Lionel Stander, David Rasche, Tom Bodsley, Seymour Cassel, Evelyn Keyes, Richard Moll, Laurene Landon, James Dixon; **D:** Larry Cohen; **W:** Larry Cohen; **C:** Bryan England; **M:** Robert Folk.

Wicked Ways ✰ *A Table for One* 1999 (R) Matt Draper (Rooker) is a bigamist. And when wife Ruth (De Mornay) discovers his other life, she becomes determined to make the vow "till death do us part" a reality. Watchable cast in a familiar storyline. **110m/C VHS, DVD.** Rebecca De Mornay, Michael Rooker, Lisa Zane, Mark Rolston, Peter Dobson; **D:** Ron Senkowski; **W:** Ron Senkowski; **C:** Chris Walling; **M:** Evan Evans. **VIDEO**

The Wicked, Wicked West ✰✰ *Painted Angels* 1997 (R) Follows the desolate lives of several prostitutes and their pragmatic madam Annie Ryan (Fricker) in a prairie town bordello in the 1870s. **108m/C VHS, DVD.** Brenda Fricker, Kelly McGillis, Bronagh Gallagher, Meret Becker, Lisa Jakub; **D:** Jon Sanders; **W:** Jon Sanders; **C:** Gerald Packer.

The Wicker Man ✰✰✰1/2 1975 The disappearance of a young girl leads a devoutly religious Scottish policeman to an island whose denizens practice bizarre pagan sexual rituals. An example of occult horror that achieves its mounting terror without gratuitous gore. The first original screenplay by playwright Shaffer. Beware shortened versions that may still lurk out there; the 103-minute restored director's cut is definitive. **103m/C VHS, DVD.** *GB* Edward Woodward, Christopher Lee, Britt Ekland, Diane Cilento, Ingrid Pitt, Lindsay Kemp, Irene Sunters, Walter Carr, Geraldine Cowper, Lesley Mackie; **D:** Robin Hardy; **W:** Anthony Shaffer; **C:** Harry Waxman; **M:** Paul Giovanni.

The Wicker Man woof! 2006 (PG-13) What was originally creepily foreboding (with a shocker ending) has turned into a laughable muddle in this remake of the 1973 Brit horror pic. An overwrought Cage stars as troubled cop Edward Malus, who looks into the disappearance of ex-fiance Willow's (Beahan) young daughter. This involves traveling to an isolated island community off the Washington coast, where Malus discovers a matriarchal community of beekeepers led by Sister Summerisle (Burstyn) practicing pagan goddess rites. Why LaBute wanted to do this story in the first place is a bigger mystery than why it turned out so badly. **97m/C DVD.** *US* Nicolas Cage, Ellen Burstyn, Kate Beahan, Frances Conroy, Molly Parker, Leelee Sobieski, Diane Delano; **D:** Neil LaBute; **W:** Neil LaBute; **C:** Paul Sarossy; **M:** Angelo Badalamenti.

Wicker Park ✰✰ 2004 (PG-13) A sluggish homage to the 1996 French thriller "L'Appartement." Chicago advertising exec Matthew (Hartnett) is engaged to Rebecca (Pare), his boss' sister, when he thinks he sees his one true love, Lisa (Kruger), who disappeared from his life two years before. Matt cancels a business trip and tells no one except best bud Luke (Lillard) as he hunts for the dame. This leads him to an apartment rented by the mysterious Alex (Byrne), who was Lisa's neighbor. Romantic obsession, stalking, and many confusing flashbacks ensue and everyone, except for the goofy Lillard, seems quite glum. **115m/C DVD.** *US* Josh Hartnett, Rose Byrne, Matthew Lillard, Diane Kruger, Christopher Cousins, Jessica Pare; **D:** Paul McGuigan; **W:** Brandon Boyce; **C:** Peter Sova; **M:** Cliff Martinez, Liza Richardson.

Wide Awake ✰✰1/2 1997 (PG) After the death of his beloved grandfather (Loggia), a young Catholic school boy (Cross) begins a mission to find God in order to find out if his grandpa is O.K. He asks difficult questions of his parents (Leary and Delaney) and teachers, including O'Donnell as a sports obsessed nun who compares Jesus and his disciples to a baseball team. He explores Judaism, Islam and Buddhism as well as Christianity. Finally he has an encounter with an angel that restores his faith. While Cross comes across well, the fellow youngsters in the movie have a stagy stiffness to their lines and expressions that lend the movie a hokey feel. **88m/C VHS, DVD.** Joseph Cross, Dana Delany, Rosie O'Donnell, Denis Leary, Robert Loggia, Dan Lauria, Timothy Reifsnyder, Camryn Manheim; **D:** M. Night Shyamalan; **W:** M. Night Shyamalan; **C:** Adam Holender; **M:** Edmund Choi.

The Wide Blue Road ✰✰ *La Grande Strada Azzurra* 1957 Neo-realist melodrama stars Montand as stubborn fisherman Squarcio, who lives with his family in a small village off the Adriatic Sea. Determined to support his family by any means, he scorns the nets used by his fellow fisherman and instead goes illegal dynamite fishing. Successful at first, this practice leads to tragedy for Squarcio and his family. Italian with subtitles. **99m/C VHS, DVD.** *IT* Yves Montand, Alida Valli, Francesco Rabal, Federica Ranchi, Ronaldo Bonacchi; **D:** Gillo Pontecorvo; **W:** Gillo Pontecorvo, Franco Solinas; **C:** Mario Montuori; **M:** Carlo Franci.

Wide Open Faces ✰✰ 1938 Every crook in town is looking for some missing stolen loot. Soda jerk Brown outwits them all in his own inimitable way. The story may be predictable, but Brown's

Wide Sargasso Sea 🐾🐾 1992
(NC-17) Jamaica in the 1840s is a seething, mysterious paradise—a former British slave colony with a mix of powerful voodoo culture, beauty, and eroticism providing a very potent brew, a perfect setting for this soaper. Based on the novel by Jean Rhys, which is something of a prequel to Charlotte Bronte's "Jane Eyre." Properly English Edward Rochester meets and marries the tragic Antoinette—the same mad wife locked in the attic in the Bronte novel. Explicit nudity and sex earn the NC-17, but the film is tragic without being sensationalized. Also available in an edited R-rated and unrated versions. **80m/C VHS.** *AU* Karina Lombard, Nathaniel Parker, Rachel Ward, Michael York, Martine Beswick, Claudia Robinson, Rowena King, Huw Christie Williams; **D:** John Duigan; **C:** Geoff Burton; **M:** Stewart Copeland.

The Widow 🐾🐾 1976 A story about a woman slowly learning to deal with her own grief, her children's traumas, and monetary worries after the death of her husband. Straightforward, passable domestic drama based on Lynn Caine's best-selling novel. **99m/C VHS.** Michael Learned, Farley Granger, Bradford Dillman, Robert Lansing; **D:** J. Lee Thompson. **TV.**

Widow Couderc 🐾🐾🐾 1974 A provincial widow unknowingly includes an escaped murderer among her liaisons. Based on a novel by Georges Simenon. In French with English subtitles. **92m/C VHS.** *FR* Simone Signoret, Alain Delon; **D:** Pierre Granier-Deferre.

The Widow of Saint-Pierre 🐾🐾🐾 2002 (PG-13) *La Veuve de Saint-Pierre* is a remote French-run island off the coast of Newfoundland. In 1849, drunken sailor Neel Auguste (Kusturica) is involved in a murder and condemned to death via guillotine—known as the "widow." But the island doesn't have one and it must be sent from another French colony. In the meantime, Auguste has become a part of the community, the more the townspeople become uneasy about the rightness of his fate. French with subtitles. **112m/C VHS, DVD.** *FR* Juliette Binoche, Daniel Auteuil, Emir Kusturica, Michel Duchaussoy, Sylvia Moreau, Sarah McKenna, Reynald Bouchard, Philippe Magnan; **D:** Patrice Leconte; **C:** Eduardo Serra; **M:** Pascal Estève.

Widows 🐾🐾 1994 (R) Sean Sager (Astin) is suspicious when his wealthy dad Justin (Davison) dies in the arms of sexy, widowed Vivian (D'Angelo). So he hires detective Eddie Costello (Haysbert), who learns that the widow has left a number of dead husbands behind. But Sean's in desperate trouble when he discovers Vivian gets dad's fortune if Sean should die. Rather dull cable drama wastes its talented cast. **103m/C VHS.** Mackenzie Astin, Beverly D'Angelo, Bruce Davison, Dennis Haysbert, Michael Des Barres, Claudette Nevins; **D:** Peter Foldy; **W:** Peter Foldy, Mark Donnelly; **C:** Doyle Smith; **M:** Robert Sprayberry. **CABLE.**

Widow's Kiss 🐾🐾 1994 (R) Sean Sager (Astin) is suspicious when his wealthy dad Justin (Davison) dies in the arms of sexy, widowed Vivian. [continued]

Widow's Nest 🐾🐾 1977 Three widowed sisters live in a bizarre fantasy world when they lock themselves in a dingy mansion in Cuba of the 1930s. Filmed in Spain. **90m/C VHS.** Patricia Neal, Susan Oliver, Lila Kedrova, Valentina Cortese; **D:** Tony Navarro.

Widow's Peak 🐾🐾½ 1994 (PG) 1920s Irish community is run by a dictatorship of well-to-do widows with Mrs. Doyle-Counihan (Plowright) at the helm. Mrs. Doyle-Counihan and daughter-in-law Dina (Richardson), who attracts the town non-widow (Farrow) upon the arrival of recently widowed Broome (Richardson), who always seems torn between a script that succeeds is possible after the Wood-man and dark drama. **102m/C VHS, DVD, GB** Mia Farrow, Joan Plowright, Natasha Richardson, Adrian Dunbar, Jim Broadbent, John Kavanagh, Gemma Craven, Anne Kent, Rynagh O'Grady; **D:** John Irvin; **W:** Hugh Leonard; **C:** Ashley Rowe; **M:** Carl Davis.

The Wife 🐾🐾 1995 (R) The routine of married psychotherapists Jack (Noonan) and Rita (Hagerty), who live in an isolated Vermont farmhouse, is disrupted by the unexpected (and unwelcome) appearance of Jack's patient Cosmo (Young), who's in crisis, and his wife Arlie (Shawn), who's got secrets and marital dilemmas that come spilling out over too much wine. A variation on "Who's Afraid of Virginia Woolf?" **101m/C VHS, DVD.** Tom Noonan, Julie Hagerty, Karen Young, Wallace Shawn; **D:** Tom Noonan; **W:** Tom Noonan; **C:** Joe DeSalvo; **M:** Tom Noonan.

Wife Versus Secretary 🐾🐾½ 1936 Excellent acting against type creates a near-perfect picture of romantic relationships. Harlow and Gable play a secretary and her boss who have a wonderful professional relationship, but Loy worries something else is afoot. Could have been a heavy-handed soap opera, but the witty dialogue and Brown's fine pacing make it much more. Stewart later claimed that he purposely messed up his romantic scenes with Harlow in order to spend more time in her arms. **89m/B VHS, DVD.** Clark Gable, Jean Harlow, Myrna Loy, May Robson, Hobart Cavanaugh, James Stewart, George Barbier, Gilbert Emery, Gloria Holden; **D:** Clarence Brown; **W:** John Lee Mehin, Norman Krasna, Alice Duer Miller; **C:** Ray June; **M:** Herbert Stothart, Edward Ward.

Wifemistress 🐾🐾½ 1979 *Mogliamante*. In the early 1900s, an invalid wife resents her neglectful husband. When he goes into hiding because of a murder he didn't commit, she begins to drift into a world of sexual fantasies. Fine performances. Italian dialogue with English subtitles. **101m/C VHS.** *IT* Marcello Mastroianni, Laura Antonelli; **D:** Marco Vicario.

Wigstock: The Movie 🐾🐾½ 1995 (R) Documentary of the eponymous annual Labor Day event in Manhattan, billed as the Super Bowl of drag. Shills intercuts stage numbers with interviews from a variety of the talented, witty festival performers, such as Lypsinka, Mistress Formika, and RuPaul. One of the best numbers is performed by the Dueling Bankheads (as in Tallulah) singing "Born to Be Wild." Like the event itself, documentary is more a celebration than a probe, psychological look at drag. Won't appeal to everyone, but a lot of fun for those who can appreciate high hair and high fashion. **82m/C VHS, DVD.** RuPaul Charles, John (Lypsinka) Epperson, Alexis Arquette; **D:** Barry Shils; **C:** Wolfgang Held, Michael Barrow; **M:** Peter Fish, Robert Reale.

Wilbur Wants to Kill Himself 🐾🐾🐾 2002 (R) Indeed, Wilbur (Sives) does want to die as the opening sequence shows him eager to swallow some pills in one of his many, varied attempts to join his deceased parents. When he becomes homeless his responsible, easy-going brother, Harbour (Rawlins), who lives above their father's old dingy bookstore, provides refuge even after Harbour's new wife and her nine-year-old daughter move in. With this unconventional family unit, Danish director Scherfig's first English offering exquisitely spans the spectrum of human emotion as it shuffles between humor as dark and dreary as its backdrop (Glasgow) and the morbidity inherent in such a tale. **106m/C DVD, SW GB DK FR** Adrian Rawlins, Shirley Henderson, Jamie Sives, Lisa McKinlay, Mads Mikkelsen, Susan Vidler, Julia Davis; **D:** Lone Scherfig; **W:** Lone Scherfig, Anders Thomas Jensen; **C:** Jørgen Johansson; **M:** Joachim Holbek.

The Wilby Conspiracy 🐾🐾🐾 1975 (PG) A political activist and an Englishman on the wrong side of the law team up to escape the clutches of a prejudiced cop in apartheid Africa. The focus of the film is on the chase, around it. Well-done in taking place performances through-chase film until the end. **106m/C VHS, DVD.** Sidney Poitier, Michael Caine, Nicol Williamson, Prunella Gee, Persis Khambatta, Saeed Jaffrey, Rutger Hauer, Helmut Dantine; **D:** Ralph Nelson; **W:** Rod Amateau.

The Wild 🐾🐾½ 2006 (G) No, it's not "Madagascar 2" although you'd be forgiven for thinking so. Here young lion cub Ryan (Cipes) decides he needs to get out from under his dad Samson's (Sutherland) roar, so he escapes from a New York zoo and stows away on an Africa-bound ship. Dad follows along with opinionated giraffe Bridget (Garofalo) and her bossy squirrel acmirer, Benny (Belushi); dopey anaconda Larry (Kind); and snooty, campy koala, Nigel (a very enjoyable Izzard.) When they get to Africa, Nigel gets mistaken for a god by a herd of wildebeests, led by the sinister Kazar (Shatner), who challenges Samson for supremacy. **85m/C DVD, Blu-ray Disc.** *US* **D:** Steve "Spaz" Williams; **W:** Edward Decter, John J. Strauss, Mark Gibson, Philip Halprin; **V:** Kiefer Sutherland, James Belushi, Eddie Izzard, Janeane Garofalo, Greg Cipes, Richard Kind, William Shatner, Colin Hay, Don Cherry, Lenny Venito, Patrick Warburton, Kevin M. Richardson.

Wild America 🐾🐾🐾 1997 (G) Warner Bros. invades Disney's well-marked territory of family-friendly real-life adventure with this bio of famed nature documentarians Mark, Marty, and Marshall Stouffer. Pic focuses on the origins of the boys' fascination with animals, which started when their parents gave them a used 16mm camera to mess around with. After getting some footage of backyard wildlife, they're hooked, and hit the road to find more dangerous (and endangered) beasts to shoot (in the good way.) As you would expect, the scenery and camera work are splendid, and any expected wild animal gore and violence has been toned way down. There's plenty to hold the interest of adults as well as children, with a big assist going to the clever script. Title is taken from Marty Stouffer's long-running PBS nature series. **105m/C VHS, DVD.** Jonathan Taylor Thomas, Devon Sawa, Scott Bairstow, Jamey Sheridan, Frances Fisher, Tracey Walter, Don Stroud; **D:** William Dear; **M:** David Michael Wieger; **C:** David Burr.

The Wild and the Free 🐾🐾 1980 Light-hearted comedy about research chimps. The lab-raised bunch become the instruments for radioactive experimenting. Scheming scientists return the chimps to their home to save them from their demise. Made for TV. **100m/C VHS.** Granville Van Dusen, Linda Gray, Bill Gribble; **D:** James Hill. **TV.**

The Wild Angels 🐾🐾½ 1966 **(PG)** Excessively violent film but B-movie classic about an outlaw biker gang and the local townspeople. Typical Corman fodder was one of AIP's most successful productions. **124m/C VHS, DVD.** Peter Fonda, Nancy Sinatra, Bruce Dern, Diane Ladd, Michael J. Pollard; **D:** Roger Corman; **W:** Charles B. Griffith.

Wild & Wooly 🐾½ 1978 In 1903, a tough cowgirl and her friends must prevent the assassination of the President. Typical cowgirl biker gang and outlaw romp. **120m/C VHS.** Chris DeLisle, Susan Bigelow, Elyssa Davalos, Jessica Walter, Doug McClure, David Doyle, Ross Martin, Vic Morrow, Charles Seibert, Sherry Bain, Paul Burke; **D:** Philip Leacock; **M:** Charles Bernstein. **TV.**

Wild at Heart 🐾🐾🐾½ 1990 (R) Dern and Cage are on the lam, going across country to escape her mother, his parole officer, and life. Humorous and frightening; sensual and evocative as only Lynch can be. Sweet love story of Sailor and Lula is juxtaposed with the violent and bizarre, obsessive brand of love of the people they encounter. Unmistakable Wizard of Oz imagery sprinkled throughout, as are some scenes of graphic violence. Ladd is unnerving as Dern's on-screen mother (she also has the role off-screen.) **125m/C VHS, DVD.** Nicolas Cage, Laura Dern, Diane Ladd, Willem Dafoe, Isabella Rossellini, Harry Dean Stanton, Crispin Glover, Grace Zabriskie, J.E. Freeman, Freddie Jones, Sherilyn Fenn, Sheryl Lee, Albert "Poppy" Pegwell, Jack Nance, Charlie Spradling, William Morgan Sheppard; **D:** David Lynch; **C:** Frederick Elmes; **M:** Angelo Badalamenti. Cannes '90: Film; Ind. Spirit '91: Cinematog.

The Wild Beasts WOOf! Savage *Beasts* 1985 Children and animals clash violently after drinking water tainted with PCP. Disgusting premise; unredeemably violent. **92m/C VHS.** John Aldrich, Lorraine (De Sette) De Selle; **D:** Franco Prosperi.

Wild Bill 🐾🐾½ 1995 (R) Realistic, un-heroic portrait of Wild Bill Hickok (Bridges), seen mostly in flashback. From trapper and lawman to his last days in Deadwood, South Dakota, focus is on events haunting the glaucoma-stricken, opium-addicted legend in his later years, such as twice deserting his true love (Lane.) Action packed first 20 minutes mellows along with the aging Hickok and the rest gets a bit talky for a Western, albeit an airy one. Bridges's Hickok is brilliant, but Barkin is given a somewhat tedious Calamity Jane. Based on the novel "Deadwood" by Pete Dexter and the play "Fathers and Sons" by Thomas Babe. **97m/C VHS, DVD, Blu-ray Disc.** Jeff Bridges, Ellen Barkin, John Hurt, Diane Lane, Keith Carradine, Christina Applegate, Bruce Dern, James Gammon, David Arquette, Marjoe Gortner; **D:** Walter Hill; **W:** Walter Hill; **C:** Lloyd Ahern II; **M:** Van Dyke Parks.

The Wild Bunch 🐾🐾🐾½ 1969 **(R)** Acclaimed western about a group of aging outlaws on their final rampage, realizing time is passing them by. Highly influential in dialogue, editing style, and lyrical slow-motion photography of violence; Peckinpah's main claim to posterity. Holden and Ryan create especially memorable characters. Arguably the greatest western and one of the greatest American films of all times. Beware of shortened versions; after a pre-release showing to the East Coast critics, producer Feldman cut key scenes without Peckinpah's knowledge or consent. **145m/C VHS, DVD, Blu-ray Disc, HD DVD.** William Holden, Ernest Borgnine, Robert Ryan, Warren Oates, Strother Martin, L.Q. Jones, Albert Dekker, Bo Hopkins, Edmond O'Brien, Ben Johnson, Jaime Sanchez, Emilio Fernandez, Dub Taylor; **D:** Sam Peckinpah; **W:** Walon Green, Sam Peckinpah; **C:** Lucien Ballard; **M:** Jerry Fielding. AFI '98: Top 100, Natl. Film Reg. '99; Natl. Soc. Film Critics '69: Cinematog.

The Wild Card 🐾🐾½ 2003 Four crooks take on a new task by kidnapping a trophy wife—who's been fooling around with a gangster—but these luck runs out once the typical backstabbing seeps in. **90m/C VHS, DVD.** Ron Dean, Mik Scriba, Hillary Tuck, Barbara Alyn Woods, John J. Dalesandro, Zelda Rubinstein; **D:** Tom Whitus; **W:** Tom Whitus; **C:** Richard Siegel; **M:** Trebor Murray, Terry Quiel, Sugar Free Allstars, Deon Vozov. **VIDEO**

The Wild Cactus 🐾🐾 1992 **(R)** Philip and Alexandria Marcus decide to take a romantic vacation at a desert resort where they meet up with a homicidal ex-con and his seductive girlfriend. The two couples find themselves entangled in some violent and kinky games. An unrated version is also available. **92m/C VHS.** David Naughton, India Allen, Gary Hudson, Michelle Moffett, Kathy Shower, Robert Z'Dar, Paul Gleason, Anna Karin, David Wells; **D:** ag Mundhra; **W:** Carl Austin.

The Wild Child 🦴🦴🦴½ 1970 (G) *L'Enfant Sauvage* 1970 (G) The brilliant film based on the journal of a 19th century physician who attempts to educate and civilize a young boy who has been found living in the wilderness, without any comprehension of human life. Tenderly told coming of age tale, with surprising sensitivity for its subject. In French with English subtitles. **85m/B VHS, DVD.** *FR* Jean-Pierre Cargol, Francois Truffaut, Jean Daste, Francoise Seigner, Paul Ville; *D:* Francois Truffaut; *C:* Nestor Almendros; *M:* Antoine Duhamel. Natl. Bd. of Review '70: Director (Truffaut); Natl. Soc. Film Critics '70: Cinematog.

Wild Country 2008 (PG-13) Bratty, 16-year-old pampered L.A. princess Poppy's (Roberts) latest prank has caused her dad (Quinn) to finally go over the edge. He sends her off to a British boarding school with strict rules, a stricter headmistress (Richardon), and a clique of wealthy British misses who look down their noses at the crass American. Poppy is determined to get herself expelled until she discovers that the mother she doesn't know once attended the school and that she has been given a chance to remake herself (oh yeah, there's also a cute boy involved). Not yet reviewed. **?m/C** Emma Roberts, Natasha Richardson, Aidan Quinn, Nick Frost, Alex Pettyfer, Shirley Henderson, Juno Temple, Johnny Pacar, Hallie Kate Eisenberg; *D:* Nick Moore; *W:* Lucy Dahl; *C:* Chris Seager; *M:* Michael Price.

Wild Country 🦴🦴 1947 Tame western. A U.S. Marshal races to stop the bad guy from killing the late sheriff's daughter and snatching her ranch. **57m/B VHS.** Eddie Dean, Roscoe Ates, Peggy Wynn, Douglas Fowley, I. Stanford Jolley, William "Bill" Fawcett; *D:* Ray Taylor; *C:* Robert E. Cline.

The Wild Country 🦴🦴½ 1971 *The Newcomers* 1971 (G) Children's fare detailing the trials and tribulations of a Pittsburgh family moving into an inhospitable Wyoming ranch in the 1880s. Based on the novel "Little Britches" by Ralph Moody. **92m/C VHS.** Steve Forrest, Ron Howard, Clint Howard, Vera Miles, Jack Elam, Frank de Kova; *D:* Robert Totten; *M:* Robert F. Brunner.

Wild Frontier 🦴🦴½ 1947 A rugged old lawman and his sons team up to rid a town of outlaws. Lane, playing a character with his own name for first time, takes over from his murdered father and roots out the evildoer (Holt). Decent, enjoyable, good-guys-win western. **59m/B VHS.** Allan "Rocky" Lane, Jack Holt, Eddy (Eddie, Ed) Waller, Pierre Watkin, Roy Barcroft; *D:* Philip Ford; *W:* Albert DeMond; *C:* Alfred S. Keller.

The Wild Duck 🦴🦴 1984 (PG) A father discovers that his beloved daughter is illegitimate and turns against her. To regain his love, she plans to sacrifice her most prized possession. Irons overacts; Ullmann almost disappears into the woodwork. Child star Jones is insufferable, and the whole family squeaks with "literary" pomposity. A horrid adaptation of the classic Ibsen play. **96m/C VHS.** *AU* Jeremy Irons, Liv Ullmann, Lucinda Jones, Arthur Dignam; *D:* Henri Safran.

Wild Geese 2 🦴🦴 1985 (R) Lame sequel to the flamed and overlong "Wild Geese," which depended on its name stars. More of the same, this time sans Burton, Harris and Moore. Sure, it's got **124m/C VHS.** *GB* Laurence Olivier, Edward Fox, Scott Glenn, Barbara Carrera, Robert Webber; *D:* Peter Hunt; *W:* Reginald Rose.

The Wild Geese 🦴🦴🦴 1978 (R) The adventure begins when a veteran band of mercenaries land deep inside Africa to rescue the imprisoned leader of an emerging African nation, in the interest of protecting British commercial interest. Their mission meets an unexpected turn when they are betrayed by their financial backers. Too much training in the early part; too long; too much dialogue. Where's the action? **132m/C VHS, DVD.** *GB* Richard Burton, Roger Moore, Richard Harris, Hardy Kruger, Stewart Granger, Frank Finlay, Jeff Corey; *D:* Andrew V. McLaglen; *W:* Reginald Rose.

Wild Grizzly 🦴🦴½ 1999 (PG) A grizzly escapes from a mountain community and rampages through the small town of Pine Lake. Teenaged newcomer John Harding, Ranger Frank Bradford, wildlife tracker Jack Buck, and land developer Harlan Adams are all on a bear hunt for their own reasons. **100m/C VHS, DVD.** Daniel Baldwin, Fred (John F.) Dryer, Michele Greene, Steve Reevis, Brendan O'Brien, John Hurley, Courtney Peldon, Riley Smith; *D:* Sean McNamara. VIDEO

Wild Guitar woof! 1962 A swinging youth cycles into Hollywood and, improbably, becomes an instant teenidol. Considered by some to be a top contender for "Worst Picture of All Time" honors. **92m/B VHS, DVD.** Arch Hall Jr., Ray Dennis Steckler, Ray Dennis Steckler, Carolyn Brandt, Bob Crumb, Nancy Czar, Marie Denn, Arch (Archie) Hall Sr.; *D:* Ray Dennis Steckler; *W:* Joe Thomas, Bob Wehling, Arch (Archie) Hall Sr.; *C:* Joseph Mascelli; *M:* Alan O'Day.

Wild Gypsies 🦴 1969 A band of gypsies seek revenge against a renegade member who returned to rape and pillage. Without merit except for the good photography of Steven Burum, who has become respected doing cinematographically intriguing films like "Rumblefish." **85m/C VHS.** Todd Grange, Gayle Clark, Laurel Welcome, Wayne Lundy; *D:* Marc B. Ray; *W:* Marc B. Ray; *C:* Stephen Burum; *M:* Richard LaSalle.

Wild Hearts Can't Be Broken 🦴🦴🦴 1991 (G) Depicts the true-life story of Sonora Webster, a small town Georgia girl who runs away from a foster home to join a carnival in the early 1930s, hoping to become a stunt rider. She becomes a horse-diver (a Depression-era sideshow phenomena) and is blinded in a diving accident, but returns to find romance and ride again. Storyline has little screen tension, but it doesn't detract from this fresh family film with a feisty heroine, a sweet romance, and horses. Nice U.S. screen debut for British actress Anwar. **88m/C VHS, DVD.** Gabrielle Anwar, Cliff Robertson, Dylan Kussman, Michael Schoeffling, Kathleen York, Frank Renzulli; *D:* Steve Miner; *W:* Oley Sassone; *M:* Mason Daring.

Wild Hogs 🦴🦴 2007 (PG-13) Four middle-aged buddies in Cincinnati get together on the weekends to indulge their mild sides by putting on their leather jackets and riding their hogs around town. Then Woody (Travolta) gets the bright idea to go on a road trip. Their first blunder is enraging a true outlaw biker gang, led by Jack (Liotta). Their second is to get stuck in a desert nowheres-ville, which at least allows shy Dudley (Macy) to go gaga over waitress Maggie (Tomei). And yes, there's a showdown between the biker boys. You'll laugh, but you'll probably wonder why in the morning. **99m/C DVD, Blu-ray Disc.** *US* John Travolta, Tim Allen, Martin Lawrence, William H. Macy, Ray Liotta, Marisa Tomei, Kevin Durand, M.C. Gainey, Jill(ian) Hennessey, Tichina Arnold, Stephen Tobolowsky, John C. McGinley; *D:* Walt Becker; *W:* Brad Copeland; *C:* Robbie Greenberg; *M:* Teddy Castellucci.

Wild Horse 🦴🦴½ 1931 *Silver Devil* 1931 Gibson is the lead (in his favorite talking role), but his magnificent mount Mut commands most of the attention. Interesting historically as an example of stars' (Gibson's in this case) difficulty adjusting to talking pictures. **66m/B VHS, DVD.** Hoot Gibson, Stepin Fetchit, Edmund Cobb, Alberta Vaughn; *D:* Richard Thorpe; *M:* Sidney Algier.

Wild Horse Canyon 🦴🦴 1925 Yakima Canutt, the man credited with creating the profession of stunt man, stars in this tale about a lady rancher who requires saving from her evil foreman. The climactic stampede scene gives Yakima a chance to demonstrate a high dive off a cliff and a somersault onto his horse. Silent, with musical score. **68m/B VHS.** Yakima Canutt, Edward Cecil, Helene Rosson, Jay Talbet; *D:* Ben F. Wilson.

Wild Horse Canyon 🦴½ 1939 One of those westerns designed to run as half of a double-feature, this one's shorter than most, but hardly notable. The hero goes after a rustler who shot his brother. **57m/B VHS.** Addison "Jack" Randall, Dorothy Short, Frank Yaconelli, Dennis Moore, Warner Richmond, Charles "Blackie" King, Sherry Tansey; *D:* Robert F. "Bob" Hill.

Wild Horse Hank 🦴🦴 1979 A young woman risks everything to save a herd of wild mustangs from being slaughtered for use as dog food. Creena is good; otherwise, it's sentimental family fare. Based on the novel "The Wild Horse Killers" by Mel Ellis. **94m/C VHS.** *CA* Linda Blair, Richard Crenna, Michael Wincott, Al Waxman; *D:* Eric Till.

Wild Horse Phantom 🦴🦴 1944 A Wild West banker plans to fake a robbery in a diabolical deception to part honest ranchers from their lands. Surely this man's not a member of the F.D.I.C. Okay sagebrush saga. **56m/B VHS, DVD.** Buster Crabbe, Al "Fuzzy" St. John, Charles "Blackie" King, John Merton, Lane Chandler, Edward Cassidy, Bud Osborne; *D:* Sam Newfield.

Wild Horse Rodeo 🦴½ 1937 When a gunman appears at a rodeo, trouble starts. Part of "The Three Mesquiteers" series. Ordinary action-packed western, the good guys win. Actor Dick Weston, who sings, later gained fame as singing cowboy Roy Rogers. **53m/B VHS.** Robert "Bob" Livingston, Ray Corrigan, Max Terhune, June Martel, Walter Miller, Edmund Cobb, William (Bill) Gould, Jack Ingram, Roy Rogers; *D:* George Sherman; *W:* Betty Burbridge; *C:* William Nobles.

Wild Horses 🦴🦴 1982 A man attempts to make a living by capturing and selling wild horses. Adventure fans will love this film which deals with the common theme of man against nature. **88m/C VHS, DVD.** *NZ* Keith Aberdein, John Bach, Robyn Gibbes; *D:* Derek Morton.

Wild Horses 🦴🦴 1984 Ex-rodeo champ Rogers is hankering to relive his dull life. He joins a roundup of wild horses and with Dawber's help exposes a bureaucrat's scheme for them. Rogers is likable and sings, but the supporting cast carries this one. Made for TV. **90m/C VHS, DVD.** Kenny Rogers, Pam Dawber, Ben Johnson, Richard Masur, David Andrews, Karen Carlson; *D:* Dick Lowry. TV

Wild Horses 🦴🦴 1995 *Caballos Salvajes* 1995 Elderly loser (Alterio) resorts to bank robbery to recover his $15,000 nest egg. Young employee Pedro (Sbaraglia) gives him $500,000 and offers to be the old man's hostage. The unlikely duo hit the road for Patagonia and send the press messages detailing the money's suspects origins and their own good intentions. Spanish with subtitles. **122m/C VHS, DVD.** *AR* Hector Alterio, Leonardo Sbaraglia, Cecilia Dopazo; *D:* Marcelo Pineyro; *W:* Marcelo Pineyro, Aida Bortnik; *C:* Alfredo Mayo; *M:* Andres Calamaro.

Wild in the Country 🦴🦴½ 1961 Backwoods delinquent Presley is aided in his literary aspirations by woman psychiatrist Lange. Okay, so that's fairly novel. Strange plot lines but in general Elvis is going to college and reading and writing and singing and playing his guitar. Meanwhile Weld wanders around seductively to provide that hint of Tennessee Williams ambience as interpreted by Odet but hey, who cares? Interesting if convoluted Elvis dramatic turn. ♪Wild in the Country; In My Way; I Slipped, I Stumbled, I Fell; Lonely Man. **114m/C VHS, DVD.** Elvis Presley, Hope Lange, Tuesday Weld, Millie Perkins, John Ireland, Gary Lockwood, Alan Napier; *D:* Philip Dunne; *W:* Clifford Odets; *C:* William Mellor.

Wild in the Streets 🦴🦴½ 1968 Satire set in the future, where a malcontent rock star becomes president after the voting age is lowered to 14. Adults over 30 are imprisoned and fed a daily comeuppance when challenged by even younger youths. Very groovy, very funny, very political in its own way, very funny. **97m/C VHS, DVD.** Christopher Jones, Shelley Winters, Hal Holbrook, Richard Pryor, Diane Varsi, Millie Perkins, Ed Begley Sr., Bert Freed, Kevin Coughlin; *C:* Barry Shear; *W:* Robert Thom; *C:* Richard Moore; *M:* Les Baxter.

Wild Iris 🦴🦴🦴½ 2001 (R) After Iris Bravard's (Linney) husband commits suicide, she and her young son are forced to move back in with her overbearing yet charming mother Min (Rowlands) and work in the family bridal shop. Eight years later, Iris is an alcoholic shrew who blames her mother for everything bad in her life. Meanwhile, Iris's now-teenaged son Lonnie (Hirsch) is tired of being a referee and walking through the family minefield. **93m/C VHS.** Laura Linney, Gena Rowlands, Emile Hirsch, Lee Tergesen, Miguel (Michael) Sandoval, Fred Ward; *D:* Daniel Petrie; *W:* Kent Broadhurst; *C:* Rene Ohashi; *M:* Laurence Rosenthal. CABLE

The Wild Life 🦴 1984 (R) A recent high school graduate takes on a wild and crazy wrestler as his roommate in a swinging singles apartment complex. The same writer and producer as "Fast Times at Ridgemont High" but lacks that film's commercial success. Just as adolescent, though. **96m/C VHS.** Christopher Penn, Randy Quaid, Rick Moranis, Hart Bochner, Eric Stoltz, Jenny Wright, Lea Thompson, Sherilyn Fenn, Lee Ving, Ashley St. John, Francesca "Kitten" Natividad; *D:* Art Linson; *W:* Cameron Crowe.

Wild Man 🦴 1989 A Las Vegas gambling magnate with supernatural powers decides to avenge the murder of his friend and sets out on an adventure to find the killer. Crummy acting in yet another "ex-agent called back for one more mission" yarn. **106m/C VHS.** Ginger Lynn Allen, Michelle (McClellan) Bauer, Don Scribner, Kathleen Middleton; *D:* Fred J. Lincoln.

Wild Mustang 🦴🦴½ 1935 Sheriff's son (Gordon) joins some outlaws to spring a trap. The plan is sidetracked, and Gordon is captured and nearly branded by the baddies. Don't worry, though; everything turns out all right. Good western. **62m/B VHS.** Harry Carey Sr., Robert F. (Bob) Kortman, George Chesebro, Del Gordon; *D:* Harry Fraser.

The Wild One 🦴🦴🦴½ 1954 The original biker flick: two motorcycle gangs descend upon a quiet midwestern town and each other. Brando is the leader of one (Marvin leads the other), struggling against social prejudices and his own gang's lawlessness to find love and a normal life. The classic tribute to 1950s rebelliousness. Based vaguely on a real incident in California. Quaint after nearly 40 years, but still the touchstone for much that has come since, and still a central role in Brando's now-long career. Brando himself believes it failed to explore motivations for youth gangs and violence, only depicting them. Banned in Britain until 1967. **79m/B VHS, DVD.** Marlon Brando, Lee Marvin, Mary Murphy, Robert Keith, Jerry Paris, Alvy Moore, Jay C. Flippen, Peggy Maley, Bruno VeSota; *D:* Laszlo Benedek; *W:* John Paxton; *C:* Hal Mohr; *M:* Leith Stevens.

Wild Ones on Wheels woof! *Drivers to Hell* 1962 A gang of teenage hot-rod punks meet an ex-con in the Mojave desert who is searching for the $1 million bucks he buried there years earlier. Before they find out where the money is, they kill him. In an attempt to find the stash, they kidnap the dead con's wife, hoping she'll sing like a bird. Plenty of unintended laughter. **92m/B VHS.** Francine York, Edmund Tontini, Robert Blair, Ray Dennis Steckler; *D:* Rudolph Cusumano; *W:* Eugene Pollack; *C:* Ray Dennis Steckler.

Wild Orchid 🦴 1990 (R) One of the most controversial theatrical releases of 1990. Rourke is a mystery millionaire involved with two beautiful women in lovely Rio de Janeiro. Bisset is strange as an international real estate developer with unusual sexual mores. Very explicit sex scenes, but otherwise mostly boring and unbelievable. Rourke allegedly took his method-acting technique to the limit in the last love scene with Otis. Available in an unrated version as well. From the producers of "9 1/2 Weeks." Followed by an unrelated sequel. **107m/C VHS, DVD.** Mickey Rourke, Jacqueline Bisset, Carre Otis, Assumpta Serna, Bruce Greenwood; *D:* Zalman King; *W:* Zalman King; *M:* Simon Goldenberg, Geoff MacCormack.

Wild Orchid 2: Two Shades of Blue woof! 1992 (R) Blue's jazz-musician, heroin-addict dad dies after a bad fix and she's sold into prostitution, until she runs away to find her true love and live a "normal" life. Effort from soft-core expert King has nothing to do with the first "Wild Orchid" and is almost laughably bad. Siemaszko is whiny, the plot is unbelievable, and the dialogue is unintentional-ly funny. Yes, you get sex, lots of it, but rather than passionate, it merely looks staged. At 111 minutes. Also available in an unrated version at 107 minutes. 105m/C VHS, DVD. Nina Siemaszko, Wendy Hughes, Brent Fraser, Robert Davi, Tom Skerritt, Joe Dallesandro, Christopher McDonald, Liane (Alexandra) Curtis; D: Zalman King. W: Zalman King.

Wild Orchids ♂♂½ 1928 A husband suspects his wife of infidelity while they take a business cruise to Java. One of Garbo's earliest silent films. Garbo is lushly surrounded with great scenery, costumes and sets, making the best of her assets. Also available in a cheesy tale. 119m/ B VHS. Greta Garbo, Lewis Stone, Nils Asther; D: Sidney Franklin. C: William H. Daniels.

The Wild Pair ♂♂½ 1928 A hollow Point, Two cops track down a cocaine smuggling ring and uncover a private army planning to conquer the United States. Lloyd Bridges is memorable as a rabid right-winger and the mild pairing of Bubba and Beau inspires head-scratching. Otherwise, what we have here is a typical action pic, complete with car chases. Beau Bridges' inauspicious feature directing debut. 89m/C VHS. Beau Bridges, Bubba Smith, Lloyd Bridges, Gary Lockwood, Raymond St. Jacques; D: Beau Bridges; M: John Debney.

Wild Palms ♂♂ 1993 In 2007 Los Angeles, Harry (Belushi) takes a job at a TV station that offers virtual reality programming to viewers, only this isn't benign technology. Delay is stuck in a thankless role as his former lover, but Dickinson has the most fun as Harry's power-mad mother-in-law who's also a sadistic co-conspirator of a nasty senator (Loggia). Lesson in weird style over substance really doesn't make much sense, but unlike "Twin Peaks" (to which this TV miniseries was heavily compared) it at least has a cameo which concerns the JFK conspiracy. Based on the comic strip by Wagner. In two parts. 300m/C VHS, DVD. James Belushi, Robert Loggia, Dana Delany, Kim Cattrall, Angie Dickinson, Ernie Hudson, Bebe Neuwirth, Nick Mancuso, Charles Hallahan, Robert Morse, David Warner, Ben Savage, Bob Gunton, Brad Dourif, Charles Rocket; Cameos: Olive Stone; D: Phil Joanou, Kathryn Bigelow, Keith Gordon, Peter Hewitt; W: Bruce Wagner; C: Phedon Papamichael; M: Ryuichi Sakamoto.

The Wild Parrots of Telegraph Hill ♂♂♂ 2003 (G) This cute little documentary is for the birds. But the birds are cool, man. Free-spirit Mark Bittner moved to San Francisco during the dawn of the hippie age with dreams of becoming a professional musician. Instead of flocking fans, he acquired a flock of parrots. Over the next 25 years these escaped tropical pets often roosted on his front porch, finding the climate nice and the owner quite hospitable. Soon enough they began following him everywhere, even when he was forced to move. Bittner grows to be a local icon and tourist attraction, kind of like the Birdman of San Francisco. A tender little character study about the bohemian nature of a flock. 83m/C DVD. US D: Judy Irving; C: Judy Irving.

Wild Party ♂♂½ 1974 (R) It's 1929, a year of much frivolity in Hollywood. Drinking, dancing, maneuvering and almost every sort of romance are the rule of the night at silent film comic Jolly Grimm's sumptuous, star-studded party that climaxes with, among other things, a murder. Well performed but somehow hollow; ambitious ivory effort unfortunately falls short. Based on Joseph Moncure March's poem, and loosely on the Fatty Arbuckle scandal. 90m/C VHS, DVD. Raquel Welch, James Coco, Perry King, David Dukes.

Wild Pony ♂ 1983 A young boy spurns his new stepfather, preferring to live with his pony instead. Reversal of the evil-stepmother-and-girl-loves-horse theme. 87m/C VHS, DVD. Marilyn Lightstone, Art Hindle, Josh Byrne; D: Kevin Sullivan; M: Hagood Hardy.

Wild Rebels ♂ 1971 (R) A two-faced member of a ruthless motorcycle gang informs the police of the gang's plans to rob a bank. Lots of biker-flick, star Pastrano was a former boxing champ in real life. 90m/C VHS. Steve Alaimo, Willie Pastrano, John Vella, Bobbie Byers; D: William Grefe.

Wild Reeds ♂♂♂ Les Roseaux Sauvages 1994 Emotional coming of age tale in Algeria) (at the end of the French war in 1962 (at the end of the French war and focusing on three classmates at a French boarding school. Sensitive Francois (Morel) is just coming to the realization that he likes boys, particularly working-class Serge (Rideau) who's attracted to Francois's confidante Maite (Bouchez). Also enjoys his battles with class-born Henri (Gomy), a bitter political militant who teachers alike. Politics and youthful passions are forced into crises. French historical/political context may prove a barrier. French with subtitles. 110m/C VHS, DVD. FR Gael Morel, Stephane Rideau, Elodie Bouchez, Frederic Gomy, Michele Moretti; D: Andre Techine; W: Gilles Taurand, Olivier Massart, Andre Techine; C: Jeanne Laporte; M: Chubby Checker, Caesar '95; Director (Techine), Film Writing; L.A. Film Critics '95; Foreign Film; Natl. Soc. Film Critics '95; Foreign Film.

The Wild Ride ♂ Velocity 1960 Nicholson, in an early starring role, portrays a rebellious punk of the Beat generation who hotrods his way into trouble and tragedy. He kidnaps now-straight ex-buddy Bean's squeeze (Carter); kills a few cops; then is killed. Interesting only if you're interested in Nicholson. 59m/B VHS, DVD. Jack Nicholson, Georgianna Carter, Robert Bean; D: Harvey Berman; W: Marion Rothman.

Wild Riders ♂ Angels for Kicks 1971 (R) Two ruthless, amoral bikers molest, kidnap, rape, and beat two beautiful, naive young society ladies. Despicable story, with deplorable acting, but the ending, in which a husband slays a biker with a cello, surely is unique. 91m/C VHS. Alex Rocco, Elizabeth Knowles, Sherry Bain, Arell Blanton; D: Richard Kanter.

Wild Rovers ♂♂ 1971 (PG) An aging cowboy and his younger colleague turn to bank robbing and are pursued by a posse in a wacky comedy-adventure from director Edwards. Uneven script and too much referential baggage (faint shades of "Butch Cassidy") doom this valiant effort, with the two stars hanging tight in there all the way. 138m/C VHS. William Holden, Ryan O'Neal, Karl Malden, Lynn Carlin, Tom Skerritt, Joe Don Baker, Rachel Roberts, Moses Gunn; D: Blake Edwards; W: Blake Edwards; M: Jerry Goldsmith.

Wild Side ♂♂ 1995 (R) Bank employee Alex (Heche) moonlights as a hooker and gets caught in a federal sting operation. Forced to inform on one of her clients, Bruno (Walken) who's involved in a money-laundering scheme, Alex complicates matters by falling in love with Bruno's mistress, Victoria (Chen). The unrated version is 96 minutes. Original director Cammell (who retained his screenwriter's credit) removed his name from the film after disagreeing with cuts made by the production company. 90m/C VHS, DVD. Anne Heche, Christopher Walken, Joan Chen, Steven Bauer; D: Franklyn Brauner; W: Donald Cammell, China Cammell.

Wild Strawberries ♂♂♂ Smultronstället 1957 Bergman's landmark film of fantasy, dreams and nightmares. An aging professor, on the road to accept an award, must come to terms with his anxieties and guilt. Brilliant performance by Sjostrom, Sweden's first film director and star. Excellent use of flashbacks and emotional masterpiece. An intellectual and emotional masterpiece. In Swedish with English subtitles. 90m/B Royal Dano, Tiffany Bolling; D: James Ivory; C: Walter Lassally.

... Max von Sydow, Ingrid Thulin, Gunnar Bjornstrand, Folke Sundquist, Bjorn Bjelvenstam; D: Ingmar Bergman; W: Ingmar Bergman; C: Gunnar Fischer; M: Erik Nordgren, Golden Globes '60: Foreign Film.

Wild Style ♂♂ 1983 Zoro, a mild-mannered Bronx teenager, spends his evenings spray-painting subway cars. Intended as a depiction of urban street life, including graffiti, breakdancing and rap music. Mildly interesting social comment, with too little vision. 82m/C VHS, DVD. Lee George Quinones, Fredric Brathwaite, "Lady Pink"; C: Charlie Ahearn; M: Fred Brathwaite.

Wild Thing ♂♂ 1987 (PG-13) A modern variation on the Wild Child/Tarzan myth, as a feral kid stalks a crime-ridden ghetto. Sayles, a usually imaginative writer and director, really takes a dive here. And of course, the Troggs overplayed title hit is abused as the theme. 92m/C VHS. Kathleen Quinlan, Robert Davi, Betty Buckley, Maury Chaykin; D: Max Reid; W: John Sayles; M: George S. Clinton.

Wild Things ♂♂ 1998 (R) Titillating pulp friction can't decide between modern noir and swampy spoof. Miami guidance counselor and high school heartthrob teacher Sam Lombardo (Dillon) lectures on sex crimes and gets accused of rape by two school girls; snotty rich Kelly (Richards) and trailer trash Suzie (Campbell). The seemingly upright investigator (Bacon) thinks there's more to the story than it first appears; as does the cop) tries to figure out who's telling the truth. Murray pops up doing his best Bill Murray, but his hilarious presence doesn't help next to the oh-so-serious Dillon and gang. Even more out of place is Wagner's wooden cameo as Kelly's lawyer. Speaking of wooden, the normally fine Russell is reduced to similar stereotype as Kelly's vampy, conniving mother. Endless exercise in audience manipulation has plot twists and turns relentlessly continue through the credits for no apparent reason. 108m/C VHS, DVD, Blu-ray Disc. Matt Dillon, Neve Campbell, Kevin Bacon, Denise Richards, Theresa Russell, Daphne Rubin-Vega, Bill Murray, Robert Wagner, Carrie Snodgress, Jeffrey Perry, Marc Macaulay; D: John McNaughton; W: Stephen Peters; C: Jeffrey L. Kimball; M: George S. Clinton. L.A. Film Critics '98: Support. Actor (Murray).

Wild Things 2 ♂♂ 2004 (R) Bad-girl classmates Brittney (Ward) and Maya (Arcieri) try to get their hands on an inheritance and insurance money by using their looks and other talents to doublecross each other or anyone else who might be after the same thing. Basically the same scenario as the original, only not as well plotted or acted. Seems like the only reason it got made was to get a new pair of girls to make out in a pool. Not that there's anything wrong with that. 95m/C DVD. Susan Ward, Leila Arcieri, Katie Stuart, Anthony John (Tony) Denison, Linden Ashby, Joe Michael Burke, Isaiah Washington IV, Dylan Kussman, Ron Dean, Kathy Neff; D: Jack Perez; W: Ross Helford, Andy Hurst; M: Andrew Feltenstein, John Nau.

VIDEO

The Wild Thornberrys Movie ♂♂½ 2002 (PG) Big-screen adaptation of the popular Nickelodeon toon provides all the action, sly wit, and fully-realized characters that fans would expect. Newcomers will be entertained as well, no matter what age. The Thornberrys are nature documentary filmmakers, led by dad Nigel (Curry) and mom Marianne (Carlisle). Their intrepid brood includes angsty teen Debbie and half-feral Donnie, but the real star is daughter Eliza (Chabert), who can communicate with the animals and has a sarcastic monkey pal, Darwin (Kane). When Eliza's new playmate, a cheetah cub, is taken by poachers (Everett and Tomei), she has to escape a stuffy boarding school, where she was sent by her proper English grandmum, to save him and her family. African setting and rollicking action translate well to the big screen, but shouldn't lose anything when it returns to your TV for the numerous video viewings. Some scenes involving poachers may be a little scary for younger viewings. Some scenes involving poachers may be a little scary for younger viewings. 81m/C VHS, DVD. Tim Curry, Lynn Redgrave, Danielle Harris, Flea, Josh Carlisle, Rupert Everett, Marisa Tomei, Kevin M. Richardson, Obba Babatunde, Alfre Woodard, Melissa Greenspan, Brock Peters, Brenda Blethyn.

Wild West ♂♂ 1993 Three Pakistani brothers, living in London, decide to form an American-style country and western band they call the Honky Tonk Cowboys and dream of making it big in Nashville. A little romance, lots of energy, but too many gags leave the film unfocused. 83m/C VHS. GB Naveen Andrews, Santa Choudhury, Ronny Jhutti, Ravi Kapoor, Bhaster; D: David Attwood; W: Harwant Bains; C: Nicholas D. Knowland.

Wild Wheels woof! 1969 (PG) A group of dune-buggy enthusiasts seek revenge against a gang of motorcyclists who have ravaged a small California beach town. 81m/C VHS. Casey Kasem, Dovie Beams, Terry Stafford, Robert Dix; D: Ken Osborne; M: Ken Osborne; C: Ralph Waldo; M: Harvey Hatcher.

Wild, Wild Planet ♂½ 1965 Alien beings from a distant planet are miniaturizing Earth's leaders in a bid to destroy our planet, and a dubbed, wooden hero comes to the rescue. A rarely seen Italian SF entry, great fun to genre fans. A must for "robot" girls in skin tight leather outfits completists. 93m/C VHS, IT Tony Russell, Lisa Gastoni, Massimo Serato, Franco Nero; D: Anthony M. Dawson.

Wild, Wild West ♂ 1999 (PG-13) A wild, wild waste of time, money, and star power that saw director Sonnenfeld and star Smith re-team (after "Men in Black") for this western spy spoof based on the 60s TV series. Government agents James T. West (Smith) and master-of-disguise Artemus Gordon (Kline) are sent to stop diabolical wheelchair-bound scientist, Dr. Arliss Loveless (Branagh), from assassinating President Ulysses S. Grant in 1867. The budget was $103 million but the elaborate sets and effects are more hokey than cool and some money should have been spent on the script. And a black James West just doesn't work, no matter Smith's charm. 105m/C VHS, DVD. Will Smith, Kevin Kline, Kenneth Branagh, Salma Hayek, M. Emmet Walsh, Ted Levine, Musetta Vander, Bai Ling, Rodney A. Grant, Frederique van der Wal, Garcelle Beauvais, Sofia Eng; D: Barry Sonnenfeld; W: Brent Maddock, S.S. Wilson, Jeffrey Price, Peter S. Seaman; C: Michael Ballhaus; M: Elmer Bernstein. Golden Raspberries '99: Worst Picture, Worst Director (Sonnenfeld), Worst Song ("Wild Wild West"), Worst Screenplay.

Wild Tigers I Have Known ♂♂½ 2006 Experimental and abstract debut feature by Archer, 13-year-old Logan (Stumpf) and his best friend, science nerd Joey (Paradise), seem to be classmates, much to Joey's dismay. Logan, however, is emotionally maturing and discovering that he likes boys, especially rugged ninth-grader Rodeo (White), whose own feelings towards his precocious worshipper are ambiguous. Original wild, it was later trimmed and released under its alternate title, but here you're getting the original. 73m/C VHS, Eddie Dean, Roscoe Aces, Lash LaRue, Robert "Buzzy" Henne, Patrick Louise Currie, Warner Richmond, Chief Yowlachie, Bud Osborne; D: Robert Emmett Tansey; W: Frances Kavanaugh; C: Fred H. Jackman Jr.

Wild Times ♂♂ 1979 Too long but pleasant rendition of the life of High Cardill, early Wild West showman. Based on the novel by Brian Garfield. Made for TV, originally in two parts. 200m/C VHS. Sam Elliott, Trish Stewart, Ben Johnson, Dennis Hopper, Pat Hingle; D: Richard Compton. TV.

Wild West ♂♂ Prairie Outlaws 1946 The hero and loyal companions (with names like the Skinny, Stormy, and Soapy) form a band they call the Honky Tonk tackle desperadoes trying to stop telegraph line construction. More mild than wild. 58m/C VHS. Eddie Dean, Roscoe Ates, Lash LaRue; D: Robert Emmett Tansey; W: Frances Kavanaugh; C: Fred H. Jackman Jr.

kids. 88m/C VHS, DVD. US D: Jeff McGrath, Cathy Malkasian; W: Kate Boutilier; M: Drew Neumann; V: Lacey Chabert, Tom Kane, Tim Curry, Lynn Redgrave, Danielle Harris, Flea, Josh Carlisle, Rupert Everett, Marisa Tomei, Kevin M. Richardson, Obba Babatunde, Alfre Woodard, Melissa Greenspan, Brock Peters, Brenda Blethyn.

Wild, Wild West Revisited 🦴🦴½ 1979 A feature-length reprise of the tongue-in-cheek western TV series. Irreverent and fun, in the spirit of its admirable predecessor—though it's probably just as well the proposed new series didn't see fruition. 95m/C VHS. Robert Conrad, Ross Martin, Harry (Henry) Morgan, Rene Auberjonois; **D:** Burt Kennedy. TV

Wild Women 🦴 1953 Extremely hilarious schlocker about a safari of white women captured by a savage tribe of jungle women. Total camp. 62m/B VHS. Lewis Wilson, Frances Dubay, Dana Wilson; **D:** Norman Dawn.

Wild Women of Wongo 🦴½ 1959 The denizens of a primitive isle, essentially beautiful women and ugly men, meet the natives of a neighboring island, handsome men and ugly women. Not quite bad enough to be true camp fun, but stupidly silly in a low-budget way. 73m/C VHS, DVD. Pat Crowley, Ed Fury, Adrienne Bourbeau, Jean Hawkshaw, Johnny Walsh; **D:** James L. Wolcott; **W:** Cedric Rutherford; **C:** Harry Walsh.

The Wild World of Batwoman 🦴🦴 *She Was a Hippy Vampire* 1966 A campy cult film in which Batwoman and a bevy of Bat Girls are pitted against an evil doctor in order to find the prototype of an atomic hearing aid/nuclear bomb. 70m/C VHS. Katherine Victor, George Andre, Steve Brodie, Richard Banks, Lloyd Nelson, Steve Conte, Mel Oshins, Bruno VeSota, Bob Arbogast, Lucki Winn, Suzanne Lodge, Pam Garry, Sylvia Holiday; **D:** Jerry Warren; **W:** Jerry Warren; **C:** William G. Troiano; **M:** Erich Bromberg.

Wild Zone 🦴 1989 (R) An American ex-soldier combats mercenaries in Africa in order to rescue his kidnapped father. 100m/C VHS. Edward Albert, Philip Brown, Carla Herd; **D:** Percival Rubens.

The Wildcat 🦴🦴 1926 Manager takes his fighter to an isolated ranch in order to recover from his boozing but the boxer winds up getting involved with a pretty girl and a robbery. 52m/B VHS. Gordon Clifford, Charlotte Pierce, Frank Bond, Hooper Phillips, Ervin Renard, Arthur Millett; **D:** Harry Fraser.

Wildcat 🦴🦴 1942 Crabbe, famous as the serials' Flash Gordon, is a villain in this petrochemical adventure. The hero overextends his credit when he buys an oil well and must produce a gusher or else. 73m/B VHS. Richard Arlen, Arline Judge, Buster Crabbe, William Frawley, Arthur Hunnicutt, Elisha Cook Jr., William Benedict; **D:** Frank McDonald; **W:** Maxwell Shane; **C:** Fred H. Jackman Jr.

Wildcats 🦴🦴 1986 (R) A naive female phys-ed teacher (Hawn) is saddled with the job of coach for a completely undisciplined, inner city, high school football team. Formulaic, connect-the-dots comedy; moderately funny, and of course Hawn triumphs in adversity, but at nearly two hours a very long sitcom episode. 106m/C VHS, DVD. Goldie Hawn, James Keach, Swoosie Kurtz, Bruce McGill, M. Emmet Walsh, Woody Harrelson, Wesley Snipes, Tab Thacker, Jsu Garcia; **D:** Michael Ritchie; **M:** James Newton Howard.

Wilde 🦴🦴 1997 (R) The witty Wilde is making something of a resurgence in film, plays, and books. The Irish author/playwright (portrayed by look-alike Fry) is enjoying the London limelight and his family life with wife Constance (Ehle) and their two sons, while privately acknowledging his attraction to men. Unfortunately, this leads Oscar into a mad passion for sulky, neurotic pretty boy Bosie Douglas (Law), whose aristocratic father, the Marquess of Queensbury (Wilkinson), wants moral revenge on Wilde. His affair with Bosie leads to a celebrated trial for Oscar and a tragic outcome. Adapted from the biography by Richard Ellman. 115m/C VHS, DVD. **GB** Stephen Fry, Jude Law, Vanessa Redgrave, Jennifer Ehle, Michael Sheen, Zoe Wanamaker, Tom Wilkinson, Gemma Jones, Judy Parfitt; **D:** Brian Gilbert; **W:** Julian Mitchell; **C:** Martin Fuhrer; **M:** Debbie Wiseman.

Wilder 🦴🦴 2000 (R) Maverick cop Della Wilder (Grier) and her partner Harlan Lee (Orzari) are assigned to investigate the murder of the ex-lover of Dr. Sam Charney (Hauer). He seems the most likely suspect but the detectives find out that this is one in a series of deaths and it's not the usual sort of serial killer. In fact, the crimes are tied into a giant pharmaceutical company and Della decides to use Charney's medical expertise to prove it—if they can survive the investigation. 92m/C VHS, DVD. **CA** Pam Grier, Eugene Clark, Romano Orzari, John Dunn-Hill, Eugene Lipinski, Serge Houde; **D:** Rodney Gibbons; **W:** Terry Abrahamson; **C:** Bert Tougas; **M:** Michael Corriveau, Robert Marchaud. VIDEO

Wilder Napalm 🦴🦴½ 1993 (PG-13) Lame comedy about two at-odds brothers, the woman they both love, and their dangerous pyrokinetic abilities. Wilder (Howard) and Wallace (Quaid) Foudroyant have been feuding for years—and not just over the fact that Wallace is in love with Wilder's wife Vida (Winger). Wallace wants to use their "family" "gift" to become rich and famous but Wilder doesn't want them to exploit their fiery powers. They finally decide on an incendiary showdown to settle the score once and for all. Good actors lost in witless characters and a incoherent plot. 109m/C VHS, DVD. Dennis Quaid, Arliss Howard, Debra Winger, M. Emmet Walsh, Jim Varney, Mimi Lieber, Marvin J. McIntyre; **D:** Glenn Gordon Caron; **W:** Vince Gilligan; **M:** Michael Kamen.

Wilderness 🦴🦴½ 1996 (R) Quiet British librarian Alice White (Ooms) is keeping quite a secret. It seems when there's a full moon, she gets a little furry. She tries to cope with her affliction by seeing a shrink (Kitchen) but the weasel just wants to exploit her. And just try explaining you're a werewolf to the new guy (Teale) in your life. Think gothic romance more than straight horror. Made for British TV. 90m/C VHS, DVD. **GB** Amanda Ooms, Michael Kitchen, Owen Teale, Gemma Jones; **D:** Ben Bolt; **W:** Andrew Davies, Bernadette Davis. TV

Wildest Dreams 🦴½ 1990 *Bikini Genie* 1990 (R) Released from its bottle by a lovely nebbish, a genie puts a love spell on one beautiful girl after another in order to find him the right one, resulting in a bevy of women clamoring for our hero's attention. 84m/C VHS. James Davies, Heidi Paine, Deborah Blaisdell, Ruth (Coreen) Collins, Jane (Veronica Hart) Hamilton; **D:** Chuck Vincent.

Wildfire 🦴½ 1945 Two horse traders come to the aid of innocent people beset by horse thieves. Early color outing for Steele. Harmless, ordinary oater. 60m/C VHS. Bob Steele, Sterling Holloway, John Miljan, William Farnum, Eddie Dean, Sarah Padden, Frank Ellis; **D:** Robert Emmett Tansey.

Wildfire 🦴🦴 1988 (PG) As teenagers, Frank and Kay run away to get married but Frank is sent to prison for robbing a bank and Kay winds up making a new life for herself. Released from prison after eight years, Frank discovers Kay is married with two children and doesn't want anything further to do with him. But when Frank violates his parole, Kay discovers she can't leave him again and the two go on the run together. 98m/C VHS. Steven Bauer, Linda Fiorentino, Will Patton, Marshall Bell; **D:** Zalman King; **W:** Zalman King, Matthew Bright; **C:** Bill Butler; **M:** Maurice Jarre.

Wildflower 🦴🦴 1991 Set in the Depression-era South, Alice is a 17 year-old partially deaf girl who also suffers from epilepsy. Her stepfather believes she's possessed and confines her to a shed. Growing up ignorant and abused Alice is befriended by a neighboring brother and sister who decide to rescue her. A three-hankie family picture with moving performances and inspirational themes. Based on the novel "Alice" by Sara Flanigan. 94m/C VHS, DVD. Patricia Arquette, Beau Bridges, Susan Blakely, William McNamara, Reese Witherspoon, Collin Wilcox-Paxton, Norman (Max) Maxwell, Heather Lynch, Allison Smith, Richard Olsen, Mary Page; **D:** Diane Keaton; **W:** Sara Flanigan; **C:** Janusz Kaminski; **M:** Jon Gilutin, Ken Edwards. CABLE

Wildflowers 🦴🦴½ 1999 (R) Cathy (DuVall) is a 17-year-old tomboy who lives on a houseboat with her single dad (Arana). Longing for a female role model, Cally stumbles across hippie artist Sabine (Hannah) and gets involved in her life and a past that has some secrets Cally may not want to uncover. Especially fine performance by DuVall. 98m/C VHS, DVD. Clea DuVall, Daryl Hannah, Tomas Arana, Eric Roberts, Irene Bedard, James Gandolfini, John Doe; **D:** Melissa Painter; **W:** Melissa Painter; **C:** Paul Ryan.

Wilding 🦴½ 1990 A pair of cops are on the trail of a gang of kids who go "wilding," which involves sprees of killing, rapping and looting. Exploitive fare based on horrible, recent events in New York. The filmmakers skirt controversy by making the criminals rich suburban kids. 92m/C VHS. Wings Hauser, Joey Travolta, Karen Russell, Steven Cooke; **D:** Eric Louzil.

Wildrose 🦴🦴🦴 1985 Eichhorn is memorable as a recent divorcee who must assert herself among her otherwise all-male co-workers at a Minnesota strip mine. She finds a new love, and tries to put her life back together. Filmed on location. 96m/C VHS. Lisa Eichhorn, Tom Bower, James Cada; **D:** John Hanson; **W:** John Hanson, Eugene Corr.

Will: G. Gordon Liddy 🦴🦴½ 1982 The life of the Watergate conspirator, based on his autobiography. Made for TV. Producer/star Conrad reportedly objected strongly to cuts from the original three-hour length, apparently with cause: the first half is superficial pap. The portrayal of Liddy's time in prison, though, is fascinating, and Conrad is excellent. 100m/C VHS. Robert Conrad, Katherine (Kathy) Cannon, Gary Bayer, Peter Ratray, James Rebhorn, Red West, Maurice Woods, Danny Lloyd; **D:** Robert Lieberman. TV

Will It Snow for Christmas? 🦴🦴 *Y'aura t'il de la Niege a Noel?* 1996 A single mother and her seven children live in a drafty farmhouse in rural southern France. Their father is married, has another family, and uses his mistress and the children as cheap farm labor. He treats them all badly and their mother begins to sink into despair as the seasons pass. Finally, on Christmas Eve, everything comes to an unexpected conclusion. French with subtitles. 90m/C VHS, DVD. **FR** Dominique Reymond, Daniel Duval; **D:** Sandrine Veysset; **W:** Sandrine Veysset; **C:** Helene Louvart.

Will Penny 🦴🦴🦴½ 1967 Just back from a cattle drive, a range-wandering loner looks for work in the wrong place and offends a family of outlaws who come after him. His escape from them leads to another kind of trap—one set by a love-hungry woman (Hackett, in a strong performance). Heston considers this film his personal best, and he's probably right. Superbly directed western, with excellent cinematography and professional, realistic portrayals, flopped in theatres, moviegoers preferring simultaneous Heston outing "Planet of the Apes." 109m/C VHS, DVD. Charlton Heston, Joan Hackett, Donald Pleasence, Lee Majors, Bruce Dern, Anthony Zerbe, Ben Johnson, Clifton James, Jon(athan) Gries; **D:** Tom Gries; **W:** Tom Gries; **C:** Lucien Ballard; **M:** Elmer Bernstein.

Will Success Spoil Rock Hunter? 🦴🦴½ 1957 Dated advertising satire finds ad man Hunter (Randall) hoping to get the key to the executive washroom but he may instead find himself on the unemployment line unless he can convince the profitable Stay-Put lipstick account not to change agencies. One day Rock sees movie star Rita Marlowe (Mansfield), and her kissable lips, on TV and tries to convince her to endorse the product. But she'll only agree if he'll pose as her new boyfriend to make ex-beau Bobo (Mansfield's real-life hubby Hargitay) jealous. Naturally, the lipstick ads take off bigtime but success does indeed spoil Rock (at least temporarily). Very slightly based on the play by George Axelrod. 94m/C VHS, DVD. Tony Randall, Jayne Mansfield, Betsy Drake, Mickey Hargitay, John Williams, Henry Jones, Joan Blondell; **Cameos:** Groucho Marx; **D:** Frank Tashlin; **W:** Frank Tashlin; **C:** Joe MacDonald; **M:** Cyril Mockridge. Natl. Film Reg. '00.

Willa 🦴🦴 1979 Raffin, a hash-joint waitress with two kids and one in the pipeline, is deserted by her husband and determines to get ahead by becoming a trucker. Okay made-for-TV drama. 95m/C VHS. Cloris Leachman, Deborah Raffin, Clu Gulager, John Amos, Diane Ladd; **D:** Claudio Guzman, Joan Darling; **M:** John Barry.

Willard 🦴🦴 1971 (PG) Willard is a lonely, psychotic youngster who trains a group of rats, his only friends, to attack his enemies. Not as disgusting as it might have been (rated PG), but pretty weird and not redeemed by any sense of style or humor. Popular at the boxoffice; followed by inferior "Ben." Based on Stephen Gilbert's novel "Ratman's Notebooks." 95m/C VHS. Bruce Davison, Ernest Borgnine, Elsa Lanchester, Sondra Locke, Michael Dante, J. Pat O'Malley, Jody Gilbert, William Hansen; **D:** Daniel Mann; **W:** Gilbert Ralston; **C:** Robert B. Hauser; **M:** Alex North.

Willard 🦴🦴 2003 (PG-13) Willard is back (in the form of Glover) and he brought the rats with him. He's the beaten-down son to a hateful, domineering mom, and the punching bag for his brutish boss (Ermey). The twist in this one is that he communicates with fuzzy, white Socrates, instead of the apparently steroid-fueled giant rat Ben, which causes a vermin power struggle. Sometimes clever (the original Willard, Bruce Davison, is seen in a painting as this Willard's deceased father), but mostly soulless remake does have the advantage of Glover's presence in a role that seems made for him. He goes all-out and over-the-top to portray Willard's swirling psychosis and ever-escalating delusions of grandeur. 95m/C VHS, DVD. **US** Crispin Glover, R. Lee Ermey, Laura Elena Harring, Jackie Burroughs, David Parker; **D:** Glen Morgan; **W:** Glen Morgan; **C:** Robert McLachlan; **M:** Shirley Walker.

William Faulkner's Old Man 🦴🦴½ *Old Man* 1997 (PG) TV adaptation of a part of Faulkner's 1939 novel "The Wild Palms" that is set in the '20s. "The Old Man" in question is the mighty Mississippi, which has flooded leaving a pregnant Addie (Tripplehorn), abandoned and about to give birth. But prison-farm inmate J.J. Taylor (Howard) is sent by the warden to row to her rescue, becoming a surrogate father when the baby is born, and traveling the river to New Orleans to get mother and child to safety. 98m/C VHS. Jeanne Tripplehorn, Arliss Howard, Leo Burmester; **D:** John Kent Harrison; **W:** Horton Foote; **C:** Kees Van Oostrum; **M:** Lawrence Shragge. TV

William Shakespeare's A Midsummer Night's Dream 🦴🦴½ *A Midsummer Night's Dream* 1999 (PG-13) Shakespeare's fantasy/romance/comedy is transported to turn-of-the-century Tuscany where Oberon (Everett), King of the Fairies, is fighting with his queen, Titania (Pfeiffer). Their spats lead to trouble for a variety of humans, including with the hapless Bottom (Kline), who winds up with a donkey's head replacing his own. Kline is the most at ease with his role (Everett and Pfeiffer, primarily, have to look beautiful, which they do), while the younger foursome of would-be lovers (Flockhart, Bale, Friel, and West) prove to be less than memorable, as does the entire production. 115m/C VHS, DVD. Rupert Everett, Michelle Pfeiffer, Kevin Kline, Stanley Tucci, Calista Flockhart, Dominic West, Christian Bale, David Strathairn, Sophie Marceau, John Sessions, Anna Friel, Roger Rees, Max Wright, Gregory Jbara, Bill Irwin, Sam Rockwell, Bernard Hill; **D:** Michael Hoffman; **W:** Michael Hoffman; **C:** Oliver Stapleton; **M:** Simon Boswell.

William Shakespeare's Romeo and Juliet 🐾🐾🐾 **1996** (PG-13) Bright, loud update of Shakespeare's tragedy of feuding families and first love. Contemporary fantasy setting, Verona Beach, and attitude (the Montagues and the Capulets are business rivals), with the 16th-century Elizabethan language intact, although Luhrmann's said to have cut half the text. Hot-blooded Romeo (DiCaprio) takes one look at angelic Juliet (Danes) and falls immediately in love/lust. This doesn't please Juliet's family, including quick-tempered cousin Tybalt (Leguizamo) who goes after Romeo with far-reaching consequences. DiCaprio's remarkable and the young duo look wonderful together. A big hit with teens. Filmed in Mexico City. 120m/C VHS, DVD. Leonardo DiCaprio, Claire Danes, John Leguizamo, Paul Sorvino, Brian Dennehy, Diane Venora, Pete Postlethwaite, Paul Rudd, Harold Perrineau Jr., Jesse Bradford, Miriam Margolyes, Vondie Curtis-Hall, Christina Pickles, M. Emmet Walsh; **D:** Baz Luhrmann; **W:** Baz Luhrmann, Craig Pearce; **C:** Donald McAlpine; **M:** Nellee Hooper. British Acad. '97: Adapt. Screenplay, Art Dir./Set Dec., Director (Luhrmann), Score; MTV Movie Awards '97: Female Perf. (Danes).

Willie & Phil 🐾🐾½ **1980** (R) At the start of the '70s, two buddies (Ontkean and Sharkey) fall for the same girl (Kidder). They become a threesome and are entangled in each other's lives for the rest of the decade. Insightful comedy-drama. 111m/C VHS. Michael Ontkean, Margot Kidder, Ray Sharkey, Jan Miner, Julie Bovasso, Natalie Wood, Laurence Fishburne, Louis Guss, Kaki Hunter, Kristine DeBell; **D:** Paul Mazursky; **W:** Paul Mazursky; **C:** Sven Nykvist; **M:** Claude Bolling.

The Willies 🐾 **1990** (PG-13) Three youngsters gross each other out with juvenile tales of horror and scariness while camping out in the backyard. Pointless but not without a few yuks (in both senses of the term). 120m/C VHS. James Karen, Sean Astin, Kathleen Freeman, Jeremy Miller; **D:** Brian Peck.

Willow 🐾🐾 **1988** (PG) Blockbuster fantasy epic combines the story of Moses with "Snow White," dwarves and all. Willow is the little Nelwyn who finds the lost baby Daikini and is assigned the task of returning her safely to her people. Willow discovers that the girl is actually a sacred infant who is destined to overthrow the evil queen Baymorda and rule the land. As you might expect from executive producer George Lucas, there is much action and plenty of clever high-quality special effects. But the "Star Wars"-esque story (by Lucas) is strangely predicable, and a bit too action-packed. Not really for children. 118m/C VHS, DVD. Warwick Davis, Val Kilmer, Jean Marsh, Joanne Whalley, Billy Barty, Pat Roach, Ruth Greenfield, Patricia Hayes, Gavan O'Herlihy, Kevin Pollak; **D:** Ron Howard; **W:** Bob Dolman; **C:** Adrian Biddle; **M:** James Horner.

Willy Wonka & the Chocolate Factory 🐾🐾½ **1971** (G) When the last of five coveted "golden tickets" falls into the hands of sweet but very poor Charlie, he and his Grandpa Joe get a tour of the most wonderfully strange chocolate factory in the world. The owner is the most curious hermit ever to hit the big screen. He leads the five young "winners" on a thrilling and often dangerous tour of his fabulous factory. Adapted from Roald Dahl's "Charlie and the Chocolate Factory." Without a doubt one o' the best "kid's" movies ever made; a family classic worth watching again and again. ♪The Candy Man; Cheer Up, Charlie; I've Got a Golden Ticket; Pure Imagination; Oompa Loompa; I Want It Now. 100m/C VHS, DVD, HD DVD. Gene Wilder, Jack Albertson, Denise Nickerson, Peter Ostrum, Roy Kinnear, Aubrey Woods, Michael Bollner, Ursula Reit, Leonard Stone, Dodo Denney, Julie Dawn Cole, Gunter Meisner; **D:** Mel Stuart; **W:** Roald Dahl; **C:** Arthur Ibbetson; **M:** Leslie Bricusse, Anthony Newley, Walter Scharf.

Wilma 🐾🐾 **1977** Based on the true story of Wilma Rudolph, a young black woman who overcame childhood illness to win three gold medals at the 1960 Olympics. Plodding made-for-TV biography suffers from sub-par script and acting. 100m/C

Wilson 🐾🐾 **1944** Biography of Woodrow Wilson from his days as the head of Princeton University, to the governorship of New Jersey, and as U.S. President during WWI. After the war, Wilson conceives of the League of Nations but is unable to sell it to a U.S. still bent on isolationism. This lavish film won critical plaudits but was a major money-loser. 154m/C VHS. Alexander Knox, Charles Coburn, Geraldine Fitzgerald, Thomas Mitchell, Ruth Nelson, Cedric Hardwicke, Vincent Price, William Eythe, Mary Anderson, Sidney Blackmer, Stanley Ridges, Eddie Foy Jr., Charles Halton; **D:** Henry King; **W:** Lamar Trotti; **C:** Leon Shamroy; **M:** Alfred Newman. Oscars '44: Color Cinematog., Film Editing, Orig. Screenplay, Sound; Golden Globes '45: Actor—Drama (Knox).

Wimbledon 🐾🐾½ **2004** (PG-13) Harmlessly predictable romantic comedy set in the tennis world, where weary 30-something British Brit Peter Colt (Bettany) is coming to the end of his career with his final Wimbledon tournament. He meets cute with aggressive American superplayer Lizzie Bradbury (Dunst), who's having second thoughts when love interferes with her concentration. After all, love in tennis is a big zero. Bettany is all self-deprecating charm while Dunst manages to be both smug and vulnerable. (Neill) Lizzie's up for a little serve-and-volley and Peter suddenly finds his game (not to mention his love life) reinvigorated. Suddenly, he's a contender! But Lizzie is super cute with aggressive. 99m/C DVD. US Kirsten Dunst, Paul Bettany, Sam Neill, Jon Favreau, Bernard Hill, Eleanor Bron, Nikolaj Coster-Waldau, Austin Nichols, Robert Lindsay, James McAvoy; **D:** Richard Loncraine; **W:** Adam Brooks, Jennifer Flackett, Marc Levin; **C:** Darius Khondji; **M:** Ed Shearmur.

Wimps 🐾 **1987** (R) A collegiate wimp is subjected to a brutal fraternity initiation, but eventually gets the girl. Cheap ripoff of Cyrano de Bergerac, turned into a teen sex flick. 94m/C VHS. Louie Bonanno, Jim Abele, Deborah Blaisdell; **D:** Chuck Vincent.

Win a Date with Tad Hamilton! 🐾🐾 **2004** (PG-13) Typical young-love romance has small-town girl Rosalee (Bosworth) fall for actor-outsider Tad (Duhamel) while boy-next-door Pete (Grace) pines away in silence for her. Tad's agent (Lane) and manager (Hayes)—both oh so cleverly sharing the same name, Richard Levy—concoct the "win a date" contest to fix the bad boy image that's made him tabloid fodder. Rosalee is chosen and, to no one's surprise, Tad becomes intrigued. He pursues her much to Pete's dismay, and the usual dance ensues. Bosworth's down-to-earth appeal saves the formulaic concept but one wonders what prompted Broadway success Lane to take the bit role. 96m/C VHS, DVD. US Kate (Catherine) Bosworth, Topher Grace, Ginnifer Goodwin, Josh Duhamel, Nathan Lane, Sean P. Hayes, Gary Cole, Kathryn Hahn, Stephen Tobolowsky, Amy Smart, Octavia L. Spencer; **D:** Robert Luketic; **W:** Victor Levin; **C:** Peter Lyons Collister; **M:** Ed Shearmur.

Win, Place, or Steal 🐾½ **1972** The Big Payoff, Three For the Money, Just Another Day at the Races **1972** (PG) Lame comedy set at the racetrack about three grown men and their adolescent schemes to win big. Better you should scratch. 88m/C VHS. McLean Stevenson, Alex Karras, Dean Stockwell; **D:** Richard Bailey.

Winchell 🐾🐾½ **1998** (R) Flamboyant biopic of powerful journalist/radio personality Walter Winchell (Tucci), whose career stretched from the 1930s into the '50s. Winchell blurred the line between hard news and tabloid gossip and used his influence politically to re-elect President Roosevelt and get the U.S. involved in WWII. But he was also arrogant and mean-spirited and his grandiosity eventually proved to be his downfall. Based on the 1976 book "Walter Winchell: His Life and Times" by Neal Gabler. 105m/C VHS, DVD. Stanley Tucci, Paul Giamatti, Glenne Headly, Christopher Plummer, Xander Berkeley, Kevin Tighe, Jason Bernard, Denzel Washington, Larry B. Scott, Norman Matlock; **D:** Paul Greengrass; **C:** Arthur Ornitz; **M:** Irwin Bazelon. TV.

Winchester '73 🐾🐾🐾½ **1950** Superb acting and photography characterize this classic, landmark western. Simple plot—cowboy Stewart pursues his stolen state-of-the-art rifle as it changes hands—and carries the viewer with it, ending with an engrossing and unforgettable shoot-out. Almost singlehandedly breathed new life into the whole genre. Laser videodisc version contains a special narration track provided by Stewart. 92m/C VHS, DVD. James Stewart, Shelley Winters, Stephen McNally, Dan Duryea, Millard Mitchell, John McIntire, Will Geer, Jay C. Flippen, Rock Hudson, Tony Curtis, Charles Drake; **D:** Anthony Mann; **C:** William H. Daniels.

The Wind 🐾🐾🐾 **1928** One of the last great silents still stands as a magnificent entertainment. Gish, in an innocent Easterner who finds herself married to a rough cowpoke and raped by a married man in a bleak frontier town. Director Sjostrom has a splendid feel for landscape, and the drama—climaxing with a tumultuous desert storm—is intense yet fully believable. Based on the novel by Dorothy Scarborough. 74m/B VHS. Lillian Gish, Lars Hanson; **D:** Victor Sjostrom; **W:** Frances Marion. Natl. Film Reg. '93.

The Wind 🐾 **1987** Foster is terrorized by Hauser while attempting to write her next thriller in Greece. Let's hope her book is more exciting than this movie. Shot on location in Greece. 92m/C VHS, DVD. Meg Foster, Wings Hauser, Steve Railsback, David McCallum, Robert Morley; **D:** Nico Mastorakis; **W:** Nico Mastorakis, Fred C. Perry; **C:** Andreas Bellis; **M:** Stanley Myers, Hans Zimmer.

Wind 🐾🐾½ **1992** (PG-13) Sailor Will Parker (Modine) chooses the opportunity to be on the America's Cup team over girlfriend Grey and then has the dubious honor of making a technical error that causes their loss. Undaunted, he locates Grey and her new engineer boyfriend (Skarsgard) and convinces them to design the ultimate boat for the next set of races. ESPN carried extensive coverage of the America's Cup races for the first time in the summer of '92 and viewers discovered that a little too long a way. The same holds true for "Wind," which has stunning race footage, but little else. The script lacks substance and was written as filming progressed, and it shows. 123m/C VHS, DVD. Matthew Modine, Jennifer Grey, Cliff Robertson, Jack Thompson, Stellan Skarsgard, Rebecca Miller, Ned Vaughn; **D:** Carroll Ballard; **W:** Rudy Wurlitzer, Mac Gudgeon; **C:** John Toll; **M:** Basil Poledouris.

The Wind and the Lion 🐾🐾🐾 **1975** (PG) In turn-of-the-century Morocco, a sheik (Connery) kidnaps a feisty American woman (Bergen) and her children and holds her as a political hostage. President Teddy Roosevelt (Keith) sends in the Marines to free the captives, who are eventually released by their captor. Directed with venue and style by Milius. Highly entertaining, if heavily fictionalized. Based very loosely on a historical incident. 120m/C VHS, DVD. Sean Connery, Candice Bergen, Brian Keith, John Huston, Geoffrey Lewis, Steve Kanaly, Vladek Sheybal, Nadim Sewalha, Roy Jenson, Larry Cross, Simon Harrison, Polly Gottesmann, Marc Zuber; **D:** John Milius; **W:** John Milius; **C:** Billy Williams; **M:** Jerry Goldsmith.

Wind Chill 🐾🐾 **2007** (R) Two college students are heading home for Christmas break. Driving in whiteout conditions, they get stuck in a snowbank on a deserted road without heat or a phone signal. But staying alive through the night may not be just a matter of the weather as it seems the ghosts of those who died on that road would like some more company. 91m/C DVD. US Emily Blunt, Ashton Holmes, Martin Donovan, Ned Bellamy; **D:** Gregory Jacobs; **W:** Steven Katz, Joeseph Gangemi; **C:** Dan Laustsen; **M:** Clint Mansell.

A Wind from Wyoming 🐾½ **1994** (R) Lea's boyfriend leaves her for her mother. Her father is determined to win back his wife by means of a hypnotist. Her chubby sister is obsessed with a celebrated author who somehow falls for Lea. When the hypnotist decides he wants Lea he turns the author into a woman-hater. Humorous look at dysfunctional families that is a bit hard to follow. Subtitled. 99m/C VHS, DVD. CA FR Frances Cluzet, France Castel, Michel Cote, Marc Messier, Sarah-Jeanne Salvy, Celine Bonnier, Donald Pilon, Patrice Arcoin, Jacques Mercotte, Andre Forcier; **D:** Andre Forcier; **W:** Jacques Marcotte, Andre Forcier; **C:** Georges Dufaux; **M:** Christian Gaubert.

A Wind Named Amnesia 🐾🐾 **1993** A strange amnesia wind sweeps away all of mankind's knowledge and human civilization vanishes. Then a mysterious young man is miraculously re-educated and searches for those who destroyed man's memories. In Japanese with English subtitles. 80m/C VHS, DVD. JP D. Kazuo Yamazaki; **W:** Hideyuki Kikuchi; **M:** Hidenobu Takimoto, Kazuhiko Toyama; **V:** Susan Baker, Denica Fairman, Adam Henderson, Peter Marinker, Lee Tyler.

Wind River 🐾🐾½ **1998** (PG-13) In 1855 Utah, there's trouble between the settlers and the Shoshone tribe. The wife of Chief Weshakie (Mears) dreams that a wolf threatens the tribe and a young blond warrior saves them. So the chief sends his young man, Moragoni (Martinez) to find the boy. Moragoni meets 15-year-old settler Nicolas Wilson (Heron) and believes him to be the dream warrior and Nicolas agrees to live with the Shoshone and learn their ways. But eventually, Nicolas must choose between his real and adopted families. Based on "The White Indian Boy" by Elijah Nicolas, who was inspired by actual events. 97m/C VHS, DVD, Blake Heron, A. Martinez, Russell Means, Wes Studi, Karen Allen, Patricia Van Ingen, Joe Wardell; **D:** Tom Shell; **W:** Tom Shell, Elizabeth Hansen; **C:** Lawrence Schweich; **M:** Jeff Marsh. VIDEO

The Wind That Shakes the Barley 🐾🐾🐾 **2006** Loach's take on the Irish fight for independence from Great Britain, which resulted in the partitioning of the country, in 1920. Damien O'Donovan (Murphy) is expecting to study medicine in London, but repeated run-ins with British soldiers find him joining his activist brother, Teddy (Delaney), in the IRA. However, following the Anglo-Irish Peace Agreement, the brothers find themselves on opposite sides—Teddy is willing to support an Irish Free State while the zealous Damien continues pursuing the dream of a unified, fully independent country. Loach is unafraid to show the bitterness and tragedy that still lingers. 127m/C DVD. SP IT GE FR GB Cillian Murphy, Liam Cunningham, Mary Murphy, Padraic Delaney, Orla Fitzgerald, Mary Riordan, Laurence Barry; **D:** Ken Loach; **W:** Paul Laverty; **C:** Barry Ackroyd; **M:** George Fenton.

Windhorse 🐾🐾 **1998** In a Tibetan village in 1979, Dolkar and her brother Dorjee watch as two Chinese soldiers execute their grandfather for espousing Tibetan freedom. Eighteen years later, Dolkar has become a popular singing star by cooperating with the Chinese while her brother has become a sullen, cynical drunk. But as the Chinese initiate further crackdowns, the Tibetans decide to protest. Title refers to the prayers, written on bits of paper, that the Tibetans throw to the winds. Tibetan and Chinese with subtitles. 97m/C VHS, DVD. Dadon, Jampa Kelsang, Richard Chang; **D:** Paul Wagner; **W:** Paul Wagner, Thupten Tsering, Julia Elliott; **C:** Steven Schecter; **M:** Tommy Hayes.

Windjammer 🐾🐾 **1937** Western star O'Brien took a break from the lone prairie to make this seafaring rescue drama. He is a deputy state's attorney who signs up for a yacht 'ace in order to serve a subpoena. Bad guys arrive on the scene, and the initially moody yacht denizens rely on our trusty hero to save them. Decent adventure. 75m/B VHS, DVD. George O'Brien, Constance Worth; **D:** Sam Newfield.

Windmills of the Gods 🐾🐾½ 1988 *Sidney Sheldon's Windmills of the Gods* 1988 Glamor, romance, intrigue, and politics all mixed together in eastern Europe. Smith is named ambassador to Romania, finds she becomes the target of assassins. Based on the novel by Sidney Sheldon. **95m/C VHS.** Jaclyn Smith, Robert Wagner, Franco Nero, Christopher Cazenove, David Ackroyd, Jean-Pierre Aumont, Ruby Dee, Jeffrey DeMunn, Michael Moriarty, Ian McKellen, Susan Tyrrell; **D:** Lee Philips; **W:** John Gay; **M:** Perry Botkin. **TV**

Windom's Way 🐾🐾🐾 1957 Finch, in a strong role in this intriguing political drama, is an idealistic doctor in a remote village in Malaysia. He juggles a failing marriage and a budding romance, then finds himself caught in a local labor dispute. He works for a peaceful solution, but is captured by an insurgent army. Disillusioned, he plans to leave the country, but his wife persuades him to stay and tend the wounded. Based on a novel by James Ramsey Ullman. **90m/B VHS. GB** Peter Finch, Mary Ure; **D:** Ronald Neame.

The Window 🐾🐾🐾½ 1949 A little boy (Disney star Driscoll, intriguingly cast by director, Tetzlaff) has a reputation for telling lies, so no one believes him when he says he witnessed a murder...except the killers. Almost unbearably tense, claustrophobic thriller about the helplessness of childhood. Tetzlaff clearly learned more than a thing or two from the master, Hitchcock, for whom he photographed "Notorious." Based on the novella "The Boy Who Cried Murder" by Cornell Woolrich. Driscoll was awarded a special miniature Oscar as Outstanding Juvenile for his performance. **73m/B VHS.** Bobby Driscoll, Barbara Hale, Arthur Kennedy, Ruth Roman; **D:** Ted Tetzlaff.

Window Shopping 🐾🐾½ 1986 Multiple, confusing romances occur at the "Toison d' Or" shopping mall in Paris. A modern, French homage to the classic Hollywood musical. In French with English subtitles. **96m/C VHS. FR** Delphine Seyrig, Charles Denner, Fanny Cottencon, Miriam Boyer, Lio, Pascale Salkin, Jean-Francois Balmer; **D:** Chantal Akerman; **W:** Chantal Akerman.

Window Theory 🐾 2004 **(R)** Aimless Ethan (Large) returns to his hometown to stop the wedding of his high school honey Stephanie (O'Dell) to his ex-best friend Jeff (Flynn). Ethan wants her back but he's sure an immature jerk--especially the window that opens onto a Paris rooftop. Loony adventures ensue as Dontsov and his friends escape their dreary existence to exploit the bounties of Western capitalism in this sharp satire of Russian social ills. Relentless humor based on cross-cultural stereotypes wears thin; (the Russians are cantankerous drunks; the Parisians, self-important snobs), but it keeps a sunny cast upon what could have been a scathing commentary. Russian and French with subtitles. **92m/C VHS. RU FR** Serguej Dontsov, Agnes Soral, Viktor Michailov, Nina Oussatova; **D:** Yuri Mamin; **W:** Arkadi Tigai, Yuri Mamin; **M:** Aleksei Zalivalov, Yuri Mamin.

Windows 🐾 1980 **(R)** A lonely lesbian (Ashley) becomes obsessed with her quiet neighbor (Shire) and concocts a plot to get close to her. Director Willis is known for his unbeatable cinematography, most notably for Woody Allen in "Manhattan." His debut in the chair is a miserable, offensive flop. **93m/C VHS.** Talia Shire, Joe Cortese, Elizabeth Ashley, Kay Medford, Linda Gillin; **D:** Gordon Willis; **C:** Gordon Willis; **M:** Ennio Morricone.

Windrider 🐾½ 1986 Simple love story made in Australia. A wind surfer and a rock star become lovers. Self-indulgent overwrought garbage with rare moments of promise. **83m/C VHS. AU** Tom Burlinson, Nicole Kidman, Charles "Bud" Tingwell, Jill Perryman, Simon Chilvers; **D:** Vincent Monton.

Windrunner 🐾🐾½ 1994 **(PG)** Angry at his football-star dad and rejected by the local high school team, Greg Cima (Wiles) finds an unlikely ally in the spirit of Native American Olympic hero Jim Thorpe (Means). Seems Thorpe needs some aid to "ing" Cima, he'll also get the help he needs. Believable performances and an exploration of the power of Native American mysticism help the unlikely premise along. **110m/C VHS. DVD.** Russell Means, Jason Wiles, Amanda Peterson, Margot Kidder, Jake Busey, Max Casella, Bruce Weitz; **D:** William Clark; **W:** Mitch Davis; **M:** Arthur Kempel.

The Winds of Jarrah 🐾½ 1983 English woman runs from broken heart to Australia to become nanny for misogynist, and Harlequin code prevails. Based on a Harlequin romance novel. **78m/C VHS. AU** Terence Donovan, Susan Lyons; **D:** Mark Egerton; **M:** Bruce Smeaton.

The Winds of Kitty Hawk 🐾🐾 1978 Visually interesting but talky account of the Wright brothers attempt to beat their rival Glenn Curtiss and his backer, phone man Alexander Graham Bell. Rule of thumb: Fast-forward through the parts when they are on the ground, or see Stacy Keach's public-TV version instead. **96m/C VHS.** Michael Moriarty, David Huffman, Kathryn Walker, Eugene Roche, John Randolph, Scott Hylands; **D:** E.W. Swackhamer; **M:** Charles Bernstein.

Winds of Terror 🐾🐾 2001 FBI special agent Larry Sullivan (Hutton) is called in to investigate the sudden and mysterious deaths of a number of passengers aboard a cruise ship. It turns out to be biological terrorism and Sullivan must find out who's behind the act before they strike again. **100m/C VHS. DVD.** Timothy Hutton, Terry O'Quinn, Lane Smith, Martin Hinkle, Michael Constantine, Vanessa (Lynne) Williams; **D:** Robert Mandel; **W:** Daniel Taplitz; **C:** Claudio Chea. **TV**

Winds of the Wasteland 🐾🐾½ 1936 Would-be Pony Express contractors, Wayne and Chandler, race rivals to land government work. Competent western that put Wayne on the Hollywood map. **54m/B VHS. DVD.** John Wayne, Phyllis Fraser, Lane Chandler, Yakima Canutt; **D:** Mack V. Wright; **W:** Joseph Poland; **C:** William Nobles.

The Winds of War 🐾🐾 1983 Excruciatingly long and dull miniseries based on Herman Wouk's bestseller about WWII. The book was much better; Mitchum appears to be fighting sleep unsuccessfully for much of the show. Two follow-ups were produced: "War and Remembrance: The Final Chapter." **900m/C VHS. DVD.** Charles Lane, Robert Mitchum, Ali MacGraw, Ralph Bellamy, Polly Bergen, Jan-Michael Vincent, David Dukes, John Houseman, Victoria Tennant, Peter Graves, Chaim Topol, Ben Murphy, Jeremy Kemp, Anton Diffring, Lawrence Pressman, Andrew Duggan, Barbara Steele; **D:** Dan Curtis. **TV**

Windtalkers 🐾🐾 2002 **(R)** Woo's WW II drama squanders a promising premise and turns it into a by-the-book war flick. The plot is inspired by the true story of Navajo Native Americans recruited by the Marines in order to use their language as an unbreakable code. Sgt. Enders (Cage) is a Marine assigned to protect one of these men, Pvt. Yahzee (Beach), but he also has orders to kill him if capture is imminent to protect the secrets of the code. The stage is then set for some of Woo's favorite themes: betrayal, duty and explosive bloody violence. Unfortunately, the characters are trite and the violence a bit overwhelming. **134m/C VHS. DVD. Blu-ray Disc.** US Nicolas Cage, Adam Beach, Christian Slater, Noah Emmerich, Mark Ruffalo, Peter Stormare, Brian Van Holt, Frances O'Connor, Jason Isaacs, Martin Henderson, Roger Willie; **D:** John Woo; **W:** John Rice, Joe Batteer; **C:** Jeffrey L. Kimball; **M:** James Horner.

Windwalker 🐾🐾🐾 1981 Howard, the only cast member who is not a Native American, is an aged chief who shares the memories of his life with his grandchildren. Filmed in the Crow and Cheyenne Indian languages and subtitled in English throughout. A beautifully photographed, intelligent independent project. **108m/C VHS. DVD.** Trevor Howard, James Remar, Dusty Iron Wing McCrea; **D:** Keith Merrill.

Windy City 🐾🐾 1984 **(R)** A group of seven childhood friends must come to terms with the harsh realities of their failed ambitions when they meet for a weekend in Chicago. Told from the point of view of one of the group, recounting the sorts of memories we all prefer to forget. Typical and overwrought '80s yuppie reunion/regret drama. Aren't these people too young to be unhappy? **103m/C VHS.** John Shea, Kate Capshaw, Josh Mostel, Jeffrey DeMunn, Lewis J. Stadlen, James Sutorius; **D:** Armyan Bernstein; **W:** Armyan Bernstein; **M:** Jack Nitzsche.

Wine, Women and Horses 🐾🐾½ 1937 Well cast and powerfully presented remake of "Dark Hazard" follows a gambling man (MacLane) as he tries to leave 'the life' behind and be obedient to his self-righteous wife's wishes by taking a respectable $20-a-week job. **64m/B VHS.** Barton MacLane, Ann Sheridan, Dick Purcell, Peggy Bates; **D:** Louis King; **W:** Roy Chanslor. **VIDEO**

A Wing and a Prayer 🐾🐾🐾 1944 Better-than-average WWII Air Force action flick. Battles rage throughout the Pacific theater and the men aboard the aircraft carrier struggle to do their part to save the world for freedom. Fine cast receives Hathaway's excellent unsentimental direction. **97m/B VHS. DVD.** Don Ameche, Dana Andrews, William Eythe, Charles Bickford, Cedric Hardwicke, Kevin O'Shea, Richard Jaeckel, Harry (Henry) Morgan; **D:** Henry Hathaway; **M:** Jerome Cady; **C:** Glen MacWilliams; **M:** Hugo Friedhofer.

Wing Chun 🐾🐾 1994 Wing Chun (Yeoh) battles horse stealing bandits and the male chauvinists around her that don't think a woman can be strong and independent (as well as a fighting expert). Chinese with subtitles or dubbed. **93m/C VHS. DVD. HK** Michelle Yeoh, Donnie Yen, Waise Lee; **D:** Yuen Woo Ping.

Wing Commander woof! 1999 **(PG-13)** Unintentionally amusing sci-fi action flick combines elements from old WWII pilot movies, "Top Gun," and "Star Trek." Hot-shot space pilots (Prinz Jr. and Lillard) battle an evil race of aliens that resembles a heavily armed version of the cast of "Cats." Their real battle is with the heinous dialogue and techno-babble they are forced to regurgitate. Adapted from a video game. **105m/C VHS. DVD.** Freddie Prinze Jr., Matthew Lillard, Saffron Burrows, Tchéky Karyo, Jurgen Prochnow, David Suchet, David Warner; **D:** Chris Roberts; **W:** Kevin Droney; **C:** Thierry Arbogast; **M:** Kevin Kiner.

Winged Migration 🐾🐾🐾½ 2001 **(G)** *Le Peuple Migrateur; Traveling Birds* 2001 **(G)** Exhilarating documentary that follows the migratory patterns of birds. Shot from 1998 to 2001 by some 15 cinematographers throughout 40 countries, using a variety of gliders, balloons, and long-lensed cameras to get close enough to record the working muscles on a crane's back, among other sights. Terns float on arctic ice, rockhopper penguins waddle, gannets feed, sand grouse perform their mating dance, and flocks fly. The minimal narration identifies the birds and their journeys. English and French with subtitles. **89m/C VHS. DVD. Blu-ray Disc. FR GE SP IT SI D:** Jacques Perrin; **D:** Jacques Cluzaud, Michel Debats; **W:** Stephane Durand; **C:** Bernard Lutic, Thierry Machado, Olli Barbe, Michel Benjamin, Sylvie Carcedo, Laurent Charbonnier, Luc Drion, Laurent Fleutot, Philippe Garguil, Dominique Gentil, Stephane Martin, Fabrice Moindrot, Ernst Sasse, Michel Terasse, Thierry Thomas; **M:** Bruno Coulais; **Nar:** Jacques Perrin.

Wings 🐾🐾🐾½ 1927 The silent classic that won its award to Rogers and Arlen, who ask their rivalry for the hand of a woman. Contains actual footage of combat flying from the Great War. Won the very first Best Picture Oscar. Too-thin plot hangs on (barely) to the stirring, intrepid dogfight scenes. **139m/B VHS. DVD.** Clara Bow, Charles "Buddy" Rogers, Richard Arlen, Gary Cooper, Jobyna Ralston, El Brendel, Richard Tucker, Henry B. Walthall, Roscoe Karns, Gunboat Smith, Julia Swayne Gordon, Arlette Marchal, Carl von Haartman. **W:** Hope Loring, John Monk Saunders, Louis D. Lighton; **C:** Harry Perry; **M:** J.S. Zamecnik. Oscars '28: Picture, Natl. Film Reg. '97.

Wings in the Dark 🐾🐾½ 1935 The first (of three) pairings for Grant and Loy. Pilot Ken Gordon (Grant) is working on expanding airplane safety equipment when he meets stunt aviatrix Sheila Mason (Loy). Ken is blinded in an explosion and, unbeknownst to him, Sheila begins helping him financially. When she gets into trouble while flying in heavy fog, Ken is able to come to her rescue using his new safety instruments. Good flying sequences. **75m/B DVD.** Cary Grant, Myrna Loy, Roscoe Karns, Hobart Cavanaugh, Dean Jagger, Bert Hanlon; **D:** James Flood; **W:** Dale Van Every, Jack Kirkland, Frank Partos, E. H. Robinson; **C:** Dewey Wrigley, William Mellor.

Wings of Danger 🐾 1952 *Dead on Course* 1952 A pilot tries to save his friend from blackmailing gold smugglers. **72m/B VHS. DVD. GB** Zachary Scott, Kay Kendall, Robert Beatty, Naomi Chance; **M:** Malcolm Arnold.

Wings of Desire 🐾🐾🐾🐾 1988 **(PG-13)** *Der Himmel Über Berlin* 1988 **(PG-13)** An ethereal, haunting modern fable about angels Damiel (Ganz) and Cassiel (Sander), who observe human life in and above the broken existence of Berlin. Their attention is particularly focused on Homer (Bois), an elderly poet, American actor Peter Falk (playing himself), and a lovely French trapeze performer named marion (Dommartin). But the more Damiel observes, the more he longs to experience desire--emotional and physical--as humans do. A moving, unequivocable masterpiece, with as many beautiful things to say about spiritual need as about the schizophrenic emptiness of contemporary Germany; Wenders' magnum opus. German with subtitles, and with black-and-white sequences. **130m/C VHS. DVD. GE** Bruno Ganz, Peter Falk, Solveig Dommartin, Otto Sander, Curt Bois; **D:** Wim Wenders; **W:** Wim Wenders, Peter Handke; **C:** Henri Alekan; **M:** Jurgen Knieper. Ind. Spirit '89: Foreign Film; L.A. Film Critics '88: Foreign Film; N.Y. Film Critics '88: Cinematog.; Natl. Soc. Film Critics '88: Cinematog.

Wings of Eagles 🐾🐾½ 1957 Hollywood biography of Frank 'Spig' Wead, a famous WWI aviation pioneer turned screenwriter. Veers wildly from comedy to stolid drama, though Bond's lampoon of Ford as "John Dodge" is justly famous. **110m/C VHS. DVD.** John Wayne, Ward Bond, Maureen O'Hara, Dan Dailey, Edmund Lowe, Ken Curtis, Kenneth Tobey, Sig Rumann, Veda Ann Borg; **D:** John Ford; **C:** Paul Vogel.

Wings of Fame 🐾🐾🐾½ 1993 **(R)** Comic afterlife fantasy skewering celebrity status. Recently departed celebs check into a posh hotel, but as their fame on earth declines so do their afterlife accommodations, until they reach the state of oblivion. The latest hotel arrivals are a renowned, arrogant actor (O'Toole) and the frustrated writer (Firth) whose claim to fame has come from murdering him. **109m/C VHS.** Peter O'Toole, Colin Firth; **D:** Otakar Votocek; **W:** Herman Koch, Otakar Votocek.

The Wings of the Dove 🐾🐾🐾½ 1997 **(R)** Beautifully acted and filmed romance "inspired by" Henry James's 1902 novel. Updated to 1910, this triangular tale focuses on well-bred- but-penniless Kate Croy (Bonham Carter), who's been taken in by her imperious Aunt Maude (Rampling) with the expectation that she marry well. And this doesn't mean Kate's present beau, poor journalist Milton Densher (Roache). But when Kate meets gentle American heiress Millie Theale (Elliott), learns she's dying, and that she's also intrigued by Merton, the wheels begin to turn. A trip to Venice sets Kate's plan in motion but leads to unexpected developments for all concerned. **101m/C VHS. DVD.** GB Helena Bonham-Carter, Linus Roache, Alison Elliott, Elizabeth

McGovern, Charlotte Rampling, Michael Gambon; **D:** Iain Softley; **W:** Hossein Amini; **C:** Eduardo Serra; **M:** Gabriel Yared; British Acad. '97: Cinematog, Makeup; L.A. Film Critics '97: Actress (Bonham-Carter); Natl. Bd. of Review '97: Actress (Bonham-Carter); Broadcast Film Critics '97: Actress (Bonham-Carter).

Wings of the Morning 1937 Maria (Annabella), a descendant of Spanish gypsies, comes to Ireland with her grandmother (Vanbrugh) who's entering a horse in the race but is discovered by Canadian horse-trainer Kerry (Fonda), who promptly falls in love with her. Legendary tenor John McCormack sings several songs. The first British movie to be filmed in Technicolor. 89m/C VHS, DVD, GB **C:** Annabella, Henry Fonda, Edward Underdown, Irene Vanbrugh, Leslie Banks, Stewart Rome; **D:** Harold Schuster; **W:** Tom Geraghty; **M:** Arthur Benjamin; Henry Imus, Ray Rennahan; **Cin:** Arthur Benjamin.

Wings over the Pacific 1943 Love and his daughter Cooper are living quietly on a Pacific island when a pair of pilots, American Norris and the Nazi Gutman, crash-land after a dogfight. The island is strategic because of its oil supply but Norris manages to prevent the Nazis from taking control and wins Cooper's love in the process. Veteran actor Love died shortly before the film's release. 60m/B VHS, DVD, Montagu Love, Inez Cooper, Edward Norris, Henry Gutman, Robert Armstrong, Ernie Adams; **D:** Phil Rosen; **W:** George Wallace Sayre.

The Winner 1996 (R) Philip (D'Onofrio) is on a winning streak at the Vegas Pair-A-Dice casino and the target of estranged brother Wolf (Madsen), tempermental lounge singer Louise (DeMornay), and various other con artists and thugs, all of whom want to separate him from his winnings. Lots of good actors but this Vegas story is nothing new. Based on the play "A Darker Purpose" by Riss. 90m/C VHS, Vincent D'Onofrio, Michael Madsen, Rebecca De Mornay, Delroy Lindo, Frank Whaley, Billy Bob Thornton, Richard Edson; **D:** Alex Cox; **W:** Wendy Riss; **C:** Denis Maloney; **M:** Daniel Licht.

A Winner Never Quits 1986 (PG) A true story based on the life of 1940s baseball player Pete Gray. As a boy Gray lost his right arm above the elbow in an accident. He's determined to prove himself as a baseball player and during WWII is given a tryout, although his teammates consider him a sideshow freak. A Memphis sportswriter takes an interest in Pete's career and Gray's success on the field leads to a career with the St. Louis Browns. Along the way he becomes the inspiration to a young fan, who's also lost an arm. 96m/C VHS, Keith Carradine, Mare Winningham, Huckleberry Fox, Dennis Weaver, Dana Delany, G.W. Bailey, Charles Hallahan, Fionnula Flanagan, Jack Kehoe; **D:** Mel Damski; **W:** Burt Prelutsky; TV

Winner Takes All 1998 (R) The Boy Who Had Everything 1984 story. A young college student during the Vietnam War comes to grips with maturity and growing pains. 94m/C VHS, DVD, A.C. Lewis-TizGerald, Ian Gilmour, Laura Williams, Jason Connery, Diane Cilento; **D:** Stephen Wallace; **W:** Stephen Wallace; **C:** Geoff Burton; **M:** Ralph Schneider.

Winners of the West 1940 A landowner schemes to prevent a railroad from running through his property. The railroad's chief engineer leads the good guys in an attempt to prevent sabotage. A fun serial in 13 chapters, full of blown-up bridges, locomotives, gunfire, etc., and of course the requisite damsel in distress. 250m/B VHS, DVD, Anne Nagel, Dick Foran, James Craig, Harry Woods; **D:** Ray Taylor, Ford Beebe.

Winning 1969 (PG) A race car driver (Newman) will let nothing, including his new wife (Woodward), keep him from winning the Indianapolis 500. Newman does his own driving. Thomas' film debut. 123m/C VHS, DVD, Paul Newman, Joanne Woodward, Robert Wagner, Richard Thomas, Clu Gulager; **D:** James Goldstone; **W:** Howard Rodman; **C:** Richard Moore; **M:** Dave Grusin.

Winners Take All 1987 Supercross races. Spirited but thoroughly cliche sports flick. 103m/C VHS, DVD, Don Michael Paul, Kathleen York, Robert Krantz; **D:** Fritz Kiersch.

Winning Girls Through Psychic Mind Control 2002 Highly convoluted and slightly comedic story of a drummer in a lounge act who becomes possessed by four wise entities after listening to an audiotape on psychic mind control. This new 'power' works its way into the act wherein he mind-reads audience members revealing where items are lost, if they have hidden tattoos. The two-guys-talking effect wears out early and the comedy, although clever, is not enough to make up for the exceedingly thin plot line. 93m/C US Bronson Pinchot, Ruben Santiago-Hudson, Amy Carlson, Christopher Murney; **D:** Barry Alexander Brown; **W:** Dan Harnden; **C:** Scott Maher; **M:** Griffin Richardson, Adam Asarnow, Bill Simms Jr.

The Winning of Barbara Worth 1926 Orphaned Barbara (Banky) has been raised by rancher Jefferson Worth (Lane), whose dream is to irrigate the desert. She's in love with foreman Abe Lee (young and gorgeous Cooper) until Willard Holmes (Colman) comes to town. Holmes is an engineer who has been hired by a land speculator to dam the local river but the speculator cheats the ranchers and uses cheap materials on the dam, setting up a spectacular disaster when laws Holmes and Lee joining forces. King filmed on location in Nevada. Based on the novel by Harold Bell Wright. 89m/B DVD, Vilma Banky, Ronald Colman, Gary Cooper, Charles Lane, E.J. Ratcliffe; **D:** Henry King; **W:** Frances Marion; **C:** Gregg Toland; Georges Barens; **M:** Ted Henkel.

Winning of the West 1953 Yodelin' ranger Autry vows to protect a crusading publisher from unscrupulous crooks, including his own dog-gone brothers. The brothers see the light, and the two corral the varmints. Autry tunes include "Cowboy Blues," "Cowpoke Poking Along," and "Find Me My .45." 57m/B VHS, Gene Autry, Smiley Burnette, Gail Davis, Richard Crane; **D:** George Archainbaud.

The Winning Team 1952 Reagan stars in this biography of baseball legend Grover Cleveland Alexander and Day plays his dedicated wife. Some controversial issues were glossed over in the film, such as Alexander's real-life drinking problem and the fact that he had epilepsy. Although this was one of Reagan's favorite roles, he was upset by the studio's avoidance of all-too-human problems. Nonetheless, it's an entertaining enough movie about a very talented ballplayer. 98m/B VHS, DVD, Doris Day, Ronald Reagan, Frank Lovejoy, Eve Miller, James Millican, Russ Tamblyn; **D:** Lewis Seiler.

The Winslow Boy 1948 A cadet at the Royal Naval College is wrongly accused of theft and expelled. Donat as the boy's lawyer leads a splendid cast. Despite consequences for his family, the boy's father (Hardwicke) sues the government and fights his son's battle. The case makes the papers and he approaches bankruptcy. Plot wraps up in far-fetched if it weren't based on fact. Absorbing. Based on a play by Rattigan, who co-wrote the script. 112m/B VHS, GB Robert Donat, Cedric Hardwicke, Margaret Leighton, Frank Lawton, Kathleen Harrison, Basil Radford; **D:** Anthony Asquith; **W:** Terence Rattigan; **C:** Frederick A. (Freddie) Young.

The Winslow Boy 1998 (G) Mamet successfully treads on unfamiliar ground with this English period piece in which young Ronnie Winslow (Edwards) is accused of stealing and expelled from military school. His father (Hawthorne) becomes determined to clear his name at whatever cost. And the cost is to be high, for his family, his health, and his moderate fortune. He hires renowned lawyer Sir Robert Morton (Northam), who with consequences for family and bank balance. Although based on a real case, the story largely ignores the main events of the scandal, focusing on its affects on the various family members. Strong performances are led by Northam and Hawthorne. Based on Terence Rattigan's play. 104m/C VHS, DVD, Nigel Hawthorne, Jeremy Northam, Rebecca Pidgeon, Gemma Jones, Guy Edwards, Matthew Pidgeon, Colin Stinton, Aden Gillett, Perry Fenwick, Sarah Flind, Sara Stewart, Alan Polanski, Neil North; **D:** David Mamet; **W:** David Mamet; **C:** Benoit Delhomme; **M:** Alaric Jans.

Winter Break Sheer Bliss 2002 Cheesy-but-amusing comedy for those who liked "American Pie." College grad Matt (Ventimiglia) is wondering what to do about getting a job when his best bud, Peter (Thomas), persuades him to join their friends in Aspen for the winter. They're basically out to enjoy themselves—until Matt finds romance with Michelle (Lawson). 98m/C VHS, DVD, Milo Ventimiglia, Eddie Kaye Thomas, Maggie Lawson, Justin Urich, Eddie Mills, George Lazenby, Rachel Wilson; **D:** Mami Barack; **W:** Mark Botwinick; **C:** George Mooradian; **M:** Hope Echtvinick. VIDEO

Winter Flight 1984 A small, gentle British drama about an RAF recruit and a barmaid who quickly become lovers, and then are confronted with her pregnancy. 105m/C VHS, GB Reece Dinstala, Nicola Cowper, Gary Olsen; **D:** Roy Battersby.

The Winter Guest 1997 (R) Rickman's directorial debut looks at the lives of eight people living in a remote and icy Scottish village, focusing on the fictional relationship between real-life mother and daughter Law and Thompson. Introspective and somewhat stagey, but fine performances and excellent use of the desolate landscape make this a worthwhile debut effort. Based on the play by Sharman Macdonald, which he and Rickman adapted for the screen. 106m/C VHS, Emma Thompson, Phyllida Law, Sheila Reid, Sandra Voe, Gary Hollywood, Arlene Cockburn, Douglas Murphy, Sean Biggerstaff, Tom Watson; **D:** Alan Rickman; **W:** Alan Rickman, Sharman MacDonald; **C:** Seamus McGarvey; **M:** Michael Kamen.

Winter Kills 1979 (R) Distinctive political black comedy suffers a hilariously paranoid version of American public life. Nick Kegan (Bridges) has been drifting through life ever since his older brother, a U.S. president, was assassinated 15 years earlier. In his eccentric father (Huston) wants to draw Nick back into the family by claiming a conspiracy, but as Nick begins to dig into the past, he does uncover political machinations. Uneven, but well worth seeing; flopped at the boxoffice, but was re-edited (with the original ending restored) and re-released in 1983. Elizabeth Taylor (as Lola Comante) went uncredited. Based on the novel by Richard Condon. 97m/C VHS, DVD, Jeff Bridges, John Huston, Anthony Perkins, Richard Boone, Sterling Hayden, Eli Wallach, Ralph Meeker, Belinda Bauer, Dorothy Malone, Toshiro Mifune, Elizabeth Taylor, Donald Moffat, Tisa Farrow, Brad Dexter, Joe Spinell; **D:** William Richert; **W:** William Richert; **C:** Vilmos Zsigmond; **M:** Maurice Jarre.

The Winter Light Nattvardsgasterna 1962 The second film in Bergman's famous trilogy on the silence of God, preceded by "Through a Glass Darkly" and followed by "The Silence. Bleak and disturbing view of a tortured priest who searches for the faith and guidance he is unable to give his congregation. Hard to swallow for neophyte Bergmanites but challenging, deeply serious and rewarding for those accustomed to the Swede's angst. Polished and personal. In Swedish with English subtitles. 80m/B VHS, DVD, SW Gunnar Bjornstrand, Ingrid Thulin, Max von Sydow; **D:** Ingmar Bergman; **W:** Ingmar Bergman; **C:** Sven Nykvist.

Winter People 1989 (PG-13) A clock-making widower and a woman living alone with her illegitimate son experience tough times together with feuding families in a Depression-era Appalachian community. Silly, rehashed premise doesn't deter McGillis, who gamely gives a fine performance. Based on the novel by John Ehle. 109m/C VHS, DVD, Kurt Russell, Kelly McGillis, Lloyd Bridges, Mitchell Ryan, Jeffrey Meek, Eileen Ryan, Amelia Burnette; **D:** Ted Kotcheff; **W:** Carol Sobieski; **M:** John Scott.

Winter Lily 1998 Disturbing shocker. Photographer Peter (Gilmore) checks into a remote B&E where the only inhabitants are owner Agatha (Berryman) and her 14-year-old daughter Lily (Laferriere) who is confined to her bedroom by illness. When Peter finds Lily's diary, he discovers that she is dying because her parents are refusing her medical aid is this as a punishment for her affair with a much-older man? And just where is Lily's violent absent father (Bergeron) anyway? 90m/C VHS, DVD, CA Dorothee Berryman, Danny Gilmore, Jean-Pierre Bergeron, Kimberley Laferriere; **D:** Roshel Bissett; **W:** Roshel Bissett.

Winter Meeting 1948 Over-wrought drama with Bette Davis starring as a spinster poetess who falls in love with a war-hero who wants to be a priest. Very talky script of interest only as the sole romantic lead for James Davis, whose claim to fame was westerns and the TV series "Dallas." 104m/B VHS, Bette Davis, Janis Paige, James Davis, John Hoyt, Florence Bates, Walter Baldwin, Ransom Sherman; **D:** Bretaigne Windust; **M:** Max Steiner.

Winter Passing 2005 (R) Reese (Deschanel) is a disillusioned actress living an empty life in New York, trying not to acknowledge the fact that her mother has recently died and her father, a reclusive, alcoholic, once-famous novelist, in years. Motivated by an editor's (Madigan) offer of big money for potential love letters written by her parents long ago, Reese reluctantly returns to Michigan to reconnect with her mislaid father. Upon her arrival she's greeted by Corbit (Ferrell), her father's spaced-out caretaker, and Shelly (Warner), who handles her father's business matters. Dancing between humor and affection, the characters all carefully paint a portrait of loneliness and awakening. However, that dance is often a little too slow. Inspired performances, especially in Ferrell's wise 'restraint. 98m/C VHS, DVD, US Zooey Deschanel, Ed Harris, Will Ferrell, Amelia Warner, Amy Madigan, Dallas Roberts, Deirdre O'Connell, Robert Beitzel; **D:** Adam Rapp; **W:** Adam Rapp; **C:** Terry Stacey; **M:** John Kimbrough.

The Winter of Our Dreams 1982 Down Under slice of seamy life as a heroin-addicted prostitute becomes involved with an unhappy bookshop owner. Davis shines in otherwise slow and confusing drama. 89m/C VHS, AU Judy Davis, Bryan Brown, Cathy Downes, Baz Luhrmann, Peter Mochrie, Mervyn Drake, Margie McCrae, Marcie Deane-Johns; **D:** John Duigan; Australian Film Inst. '81: Actress (Davis).

Winter Sleepers Winterschlafer 1997 Angsty and slow (completely unlike the director's breakthrough "Run Lola Run") Rebecca (Daniel) is waiting at a mountain chalet for her boyfriend Marco (Ferch) to show up. When Marco leaves his keys in his car, Rene (Matthes) takes it for a joy ride and gets into an accident, eventually meeting Laura (Sellem) the nurse, who owns the chalet. The foursome wind-up together but nothing much matters. Based on the novel "Expense of the Spirit" by Pyszora, who co-wrote the screenplay. German with subtitles. 124m/C VHS, DVD, GE Heino Ferch, Floriane Daniel, Ulrich Matthes, Marie-Lou Sellem, Josef Bierbichler; **D:** Tom Tykwer; **W:** Tom Tykwer, Anne-Francois Pyszora; **C:** Frank Griebe; **M:** Tom Tykwer, Johnny Klimek, Reinhold Hall.

Winter Solstice ✗✗✗ 2004 (R)
Such a sad, sad gut-wrencher. But it's so good at being sad gut-wrenching that it almost makes you glad you felt the pain. Jim Winters (LaPaglia) is the struggling father of a motherless family still trying to get by without her, five years after a tragic car accident. Jim's two sons, Gabe and Peter, don't want to grab hold when he reaches out to them. They're mad at the life they live. Thankfully, writer/director Josh Sternfeld doesn't bother with much plot, something that normally distracts from emotion and character examination in these types of films. These people live and suffer, and let us watch—we wonder what'll happen to them when the movie ends. Its effect lingers long after the credits. **90m/C DVD.** *US* Anthony LaPaglia, Aaron Stanford, Mark Webber, Allison Janney, Michelle Monaghan, Ron Livingston, Brandon Sexton III, Eben Moss-Bachrach; *D:* Josh Sternfeld; *C:* Harlan Bosmajian; *M:* John Leventhal.

A Winter Tan ✗✗½ 1988 True story of New Yorker Maryse Holder (Burroughs), who's an alcoholic, drug-addicted, promiscuous one-time teacher who has decided to lose herself in the degradations Acapulco has to offer. Holder's eventually murdered by a pimp and her letters to a friend are posthumously published as "Give Sorrow Words." Self-destruction as its worst. **90m/C VHS.** *CA* Jackie Burroughs; *D:* Jackie Burroughs, John Frizzell, John Walker, Louise Clark; *W:* Jackie Burroughs; *C:* John Walker, Louise Clark. Genie '89: Actress (Burroughs).

The Winter War ✗✗✗ *Talvisota* 1989 One of Finnish films ever tells the story of the Russian war on Finland and the Finnish defense in 1939-41. **195m/C VHS.** Esko Nikkari, Tomi Salmela, Vesa Vierikko, Samuli Edelmann, Teemu Koskinen, Esko Kovero, Eero Maenpaa, Konsta Makela, Taneli Makela, Heikki Paavilainen, Antti Raivio, Miitta Sorvali, Martti Suosalo, Timo Torikka; *D:* Pekka Parikka; *W:* Pekka Parikka; *C:* Kari Sohlberg; *M:* Jukka Haavisto, Juha Tikka.

Winterbeast ✗ 1992 Winter resort community dwellers begin mysteriously disappearing until somebody remembers that the resort was built over a sacred Indian burial ground. Sgt. Bill Whitman, the valiant park ranger and his Barney Fife-like assistant Stillman, question the town's wise old sage, Sheldon, who's sitting on a secret that could threaten the entire community. **77m/C VHS.** Bob Harlow, Charles Majka, Dori May Kelly, Tim R. Morgan, Mike Magri; *D:* Christopher Thies; *W:* Christopher Thies; *M:* Michael Perlstein.

Winterhawk ✗✗½ 1976 (PG) A Black-foot Indian seeks smallpox serum from a nearby trapper camp for his stricken tribe. When he's attacked for his efforts, he takes revenge by kidnapping two of the settlement's children. Exceptional cinematography of the breathtaking scenery can't hide the cliched, melodramatic story and waste of a fine cast. This was Hunnicutt's last screen appearance. **98m/C VHS.** Leif Erickson, Woody Strode, Denver Pyle, L.Q. Jones, Elisha Cook Jr., Arthur Hunnicutt, Dennis Fimple, Dawn Wells, Jimmy Clem, Michael Dante, Charles B. Pierce, Seamon Glass; *D:* Charles B. Pierce; *W:* Charles B. Pierce, Earl E. Smith; *C:* Jim Roberson; *M:* Lee Holdridge.

Winterset ✗✗½ 1936 A son seeks to clear his father's name of a falsely accused crime 15 years after his electrocution. Powerful at the time, though time has lessened its impact. Exceptional scenery can't hide the cliched, melodramatic story and waste of a fine cast. Based loosely on the trial of Sacco and Vanzetti and adapted from Maxwell Anderson's Broadway play, with stars in the same roles. Meredith's film debut. **85m/B VHS, DVD.** Burgess Meredith, Margo, John Carradine; *D:* Alfred Santell.

Wintertime ✗✗½ 1943 Forgettable and mindless Henie musical. Plot revolves around Henie travelling in Canada with her wealthy uncle, and saving an old, run-down hotel. An appearance by Woody Herman and his Orchestra give the film a much-needed boost. **90m/B VHS.** Sonja Henie, Jack Oakie, Cesar Romero, Carole Landis, S.Z. Sakall, Cornel Wilde, Woody Herman; *D:* John Brahm; *W:* E. Edwin Moran, Jack Jevne, Lynn Starling.

Wired ✗ 1989 (R) A justly lambasted, unintentionally hilarious biography of comic genius and overdose victim John Belushi, very loosely based on Bob Woodward's bestselling muckraking book. The chronicle of addiction and tragedy is tried here as a weird sort of comedy; was it meant as a tribute to its off-kilter subject? If so, it misses by a mile. And, we're sorry, but Chiklis doesn't cut it as Belushi—who would?! **112m/C VHS.** Michael Chiklis, Ray Sharkey, Patti D'Arbanville, J.T. Walsh, Gary Groomes, Lucinda Jenney, Alex Rocco, Jere Burns, Billy Preston; *D:* Larry Peerce; *W:* Earl MacRauch; *C:* Tony Imi; *M:* Basil Poledouris.

Wired to Kill WOOF! 1986 (R) In a futuristic world, two teenagers seek justice for their parents' murder by building a remote-controlled erector set programmed for revenge. Laughably porous plot drops any pretence of credibility. Dizzyingly bad. **96m/C VHS.** Merritt Butrick, Emily Longstreth, Devin Hoelscher, Frank Collison; *D:* Francis Schaeffer.

Wirey Spindell ✗ 1999 Self-indulgent clap-trap about a self-satisfied creep. The title character (Schaeffer) is engaged to beautiful Tabatha (Thorne) but has become suddenly impotent due to extreme premarital jitters. This little dilemma leads Wirey to explore his childhood and druggie high school/college years (when the character is played by Mabius), his first love, and his falling for Tabatha. Problem is Wirey isn't a very interesting character. **101m/C VHS, DVD.** Eric Schaeffer, Callie (Callie) Thorne, Eric Mabius, Samantha Buck; *D:* Eric Schaeffer; *W:* Eric Schaeffer; *C:* Kramer Morgenthau; *M:* Amanda Kravat.

Wisdom ✗✗½ 1987 (R) Unemployed young guy (Estevez) becomes a bank robber with Robin Hood aspirations, coming to the aid of American farmers by destroying mortgage records. Estevez became the youngest person to star in, write, and direct a major motion picture. And, my goodness, it shows. **109m/C VHS.** Emilio Estevez, Demi Moore, Tom Skerritt, Veronica Cartwright; *D:* Emilio Estevez; *M:* Danny Elfman.

Wise Blood ✗✗✗½ 1979 (PG) Gothic drama about a drifter who searches for sin and becomes a preacher for a new religion, The Church Without Christ. Excellent cast in achingly realistic portrayal of ersatz religion, southern style. Many laughs are more painful than funny. Superb, very dark comedy from Huston. Adapted from the Flannery O'Connor novel. **106m/C VHS.** Brad Dourif, John Huston, Ned Beatty, Amy Wright, Harry Dean Stanton; *D:* John Huston; *M:* Alex North.

Wise Guys ✗✗½ 1986 (R) Two small-time hoods decide to rip off the mob. When their boss figures out their plan he decides to set them up instead. Lame black comedy that has too few moments. **100m/C VHS, DVD.** Joe Piscopo, Danny DeVito, Ray Sharkey, Captain Lou Albano, Dan Hedaya, Julie Bovasso, Patti LuPone; *D:* Brian De Palma; *M:* Ira Newborn.

Wisecracks ✗✗✗ 1993 Women comics perform and talk about their work in this documentary directed by Gail Singer. The comics featured have, in some cases, little more in common than their work, but all share interesting perspectives on what they do. Interesting mix of performance clips and interviews sometimes includes banal comments about the nature of comedy, but is more often insightful, especially remarks by seasoned vet Phyllis Diller. Although there exists here the potential for an angry feminist diatribe on gender-based humor, the focus is more towards talented women who are just plain funny. **93m/C VHS, DVD.** *D:* Gail Singer.

Wisegirls ✗✗½ *Wise Girls* 2002 Estrogen-injected mob flick follows Meg (Sorvino), a med school grad who moves back to New York and takes a job waitressing in a mob-infested restaurant. Trying to divorce herself from a disastrous past, Meg gets wise to just which family owns this family-owned establishment. She's less than thrilled but the worst she has to deal with is reluctantly accepting money from their boss (Nascarelli), who admires her medical skills, and fending off advances from his odious son (Maelen), until she witnesses a murder and finds herself on the wrong side of the law. Plot contains interesting twists right down to the satisfying end. Sorvino performs ably while Walters is a standout and Carey proves she has stuff to make it on the big screen. Tired premise, however, takes some of the fun out this gangster chick flick. **96m/C VHS, DVD.** Mira Sorvino, Mariah Carey, Melora Walters, Arthur J. Nascarelli, Christian Maelen, Joseph Siravo; *D:* David Anspaugh; *W:* John Meadows; *C:* Johnny E. Jensen; *M:* Keith Forsey.

Wish Me Luck ✗½ 1995 A babe genie (Avalon) has a dilemma—unless she can make a man of a geek college student (Gesner) in 48 hours, she'll become the property of an evil sorcerer out for revenge. She gets three equally bodacious college cheerleaders to help her out: Also available in an edited version that cuts six minutes worth of fleshy fantasies. **91m/C VHS.** Avalon Anders, Zen Gesner; *D:* Philip Jones.

Wish upon a Star ✗✗½ 1996 (PG) Battling teenage sisters Alexia (Heigl) and Haley (Harris) wind up switching identities when bookish Haley wishes on a falling star to be like popular Alexia. Naturally, this confuses everyone but the sisters get to see how their other sibling feels. **90m/C VHS, DVD.** Scott Wilkinson, Mary Parker Williams, Don Jeffcoat, Lois Chiles, Katherine Heigl, Danielle Harris; *D:* Blair Treu; *W:* Jessica Barondes; *C:* Brian Sullivan; *M:* Ray Colcord.

Wish You Were Dead ✗✗½ 2000 (R) Schnook insurance adjuster MacBeth (Elwes) naively signs over his million dollar life insurance policy to slutty "girlfriend" Sally (Steenburgen), who promptly hires hit woman Jupiter (Hendrix) to get rid of the excess baggage. Only Jupiter can't get over what a nice guy MacBeth is and falls in love with him instead—which doesn't mean Sally is giving up. **89m/C VHS, DVD.** Cary Elwes, Mary Steenburgen, Elaine Hendrix, Christopher Lloyd, Billy Ray Cyrus, Robin Englund, Sally Kirkland, Gene Simmons, Shannon Tweed; *D:* Valerie McCaffrey; *W:* Scott Firestone; *C:* David Klein. **VIDEO**

Wish You Were Here ✗✗✗ 1987 Poignant yet funny slice of British postwar life roughly based on the childhood memoirs of famous madame, Cynthia Payne. A troubled and freedom-loving teenager expresses her rebellion in sexual experimentation. Mum is dead and Dad just doesn't understand, so what's a girl to do, but get the boys excited? Lloyd in her first film, plays the main character with exceptional strength and feistiness. Payne's later life was dramatized in the Leland-scripted "Personal Services." **92m/C VHS, DVD.** *GB* Emily Lloyd, Tom Bell, Clare Clifford, Barbara Durkin, Geoffrey Hutchings, Charlotte Barker, Chloe Leland, Trudy Cavanagh, Jesse Birdsall, Geoffrey Durham, Pat Heywood; *D:* David Leland; *W:* David Leland; *C:* Ian Wilson; *M:* Stanley Myers. British Acad. '87: Orig. Screenplay; Natl. Soc. Film Critics '87: Actress (Lloyd).

Wishful Thinking ✗✗ 1992 A lovelorn screenwriter rescues a peculiar man from mysterious assassins and receives a magical writing pad for his efforts. It seems that whatever Michael writes on the paper will come true, so he decides to write himself into the life of the luscious Diane. **94m/C VHS, DVD.** Murray Langston, Michelle Johnson, Ruth Buzzi, Billy Barty, Johnny Dark, Ray "Boom Boom" Mancini, Vic Dunlop, Kip Addotta; *D:* Murray Langston.

Wishful Thinking ✗✗½ 1996 (R) Elizabeth (Beals) and Max (Le Gros) have been living together for four years. When Max doesn't want to get married, Elizabeth becomes withdrawn but Max decides she's having an affair. As he becomes more and more jealous, a third party enters the picture. Lena (Barrymore) decides she wants Max herself and devises a plan to get him at any cost. **89m/C VHS, DVD.** Drew Barrymore, Jennifer Beals, James LeGros, Mel Gorham, Eric Thal, Jon Stewart; *D:* Adam Park.

The Wishing Ring ✗✗½ 1914 Light and charming romance, beautifully filmed by Tourneur, based on Owen Davis' play. The son of an earl in Old England is expelled from college and told by his father he must earn half a crown on his own before the family will take him back. With the help of a minister's daughter, he sets things right. **50m/B VHS, DVD.** Vivian Martin, Alec B. Francis, Chester Barnett, Simeon Wiltsie, Walter Morton; *D:* Maurice Tourneur; *W:* Maurice Tourneur.

Wishman ✗✗½ 1993 Hollywood hustler Basie Banks (Le Mat) meets Hitch (Lewis), a two million-year-old genie whose magic bottle has been stolen. In exchange for Banks' help in recovering his home, Hitch agrees to help Banks get the girl of his dreams. **89m/C VHS.** Paul LeMat, Geoffrey Lewis, Paul Gleason, Quin Kessler, Nancy Parsons, Gaillard Sartain, Brion James; *D:* Mike Marvin; *W:* Mike Marvin.

Wishmaster ✗ *Wes Craven Presents Wishmaster* 1997 (R) An evil genie grants wishes to those who stumble upon him, but he also gets his kicks by destroying the lives of those naive enough to play along. Anemic horror tale that's as thin on plot as it is on scares. Standard-issue exploding chest cavities and flying heads can't easily erase the boredom. Make-up artist turned director Kurtzman should have wished for some directorial skills, because he hasn't got a clue. Don't be misled by Wes Craven's name, his association with this dud is meant to lure the least discriminating of horror fans. **90m/C VHS, DVD.** Tammy Lauren, Andrew Divoff, Robert Englund, Chris Lemmon, Tony Crane, Wendy Benson, Jenny O'Hara, Tony Todd, Kane Hodder; *D:* Robert Kurtzman; *W:* Peter Atkins; *C:* Jacques Haitkin; *M:* Harry Manfredini.

Wishmaster 2: Evil Never Dies ✗✗ 1998 (R) The Djinn is awakened by thief Morgana during a botched robbery and, in order to gain the souls he needs, the Djinn allows himself to be put in prison where he can offer wishes to the prisoners. But Morgana, aided by a priest, tries to stop him before the Djinn can destroy humanity. **96m/C VHS, DVD.** Andrew Divoff, Paul Johansson, Holly Fields, Bokeem Woodbine, Tommy (Tiny) Lister; *D:* Jack Sholder; *W:* Jack Sholder; *C:* Carlos Gonzalez; *M:* David Williams. **VIDEO**

Wishmaster 3: Beyond the Gates of Hell ✗ 2001 (R) Baxter College history prof Joel Barash (Connery) has a crush on student Diana (Cook) who has been helping him out. Unfortunately, her help includes releasing the demonic Djinn from its puzzle box. The Djinn then possesses Barash and goes after Diana to grant her three wishes. Diana knows there's a trick but her fellow students aren't so smart and their wishes have nasty results. Diana can wish to spare her friends but the only thing that will really destroy the evil is the magical Sword of Justice. **92m/C VHS, DVD.** A.J. Cook, Jason Connery; Tobias Mehler, Aaron Smolinski, Louisette Geiss, John Novak; *D:* Chris Angel; *W:* Alexander Wright. **VIDEO**

Wishmaster 4: The Prophecy Fulfilled ✗ 2002 (R) Same old, same old. The Djinn (Novak) gets released by Lisa (Spencer-Nairn) whose boyfriend Steven (Trucco) has been paralyzed in an accident. She gets the usual three wishes that don't come out the way she intended. This time if Lisa does her third wish, the Djinn—or something like that. Usual gore and Spencer-Nairn takes her clothes off and has a gratuitous sex scene. **92m/C VHS, DVD.** John Novak, Tara Spencer-Nairn, Michael Trucco, Victor Webster, John Benjamin Martin; *D:* Chris Angel; *W:* John Benjamin Martin; *M:* Daryl Bennett, Jim Guttridge. **VIDEO**

The Wistful Widow of Wagon Gap ✗✗ 1947 Lou, a traveling salesman, accidentally kills a man, and according to the law of the west he has to take care of the dead man's widow and children—all seven of them. Because the family is so unsavory, Lou knows that no other man will kill him, so he allows himself to be appointed sheriff and

...clears the town of lowlifes. Usual Abbott & Costello fare is highlighted with their zany antics. **78m/B VHS, DVD.** Bud Abbott, Lou Costello, Marjorie Main, George Cleveland, Gordon Jones, William Ching, Peter Thompson, Glenn Strange, Olin Howlin; **D:** Charles T. Barton.

Wit 2001 A tough topic buoyed by Thompson's fierce performance and Nichols' expert direction. Middleaged scholar Vivian Bearing (Thompson) has dedicated her work to studying the holy sonnets of John Donne. The poet's life-and-death issues take on new meaning when Vivian learns she has stage-four ovarian cancer and she agrees to undergo the most aggressive treatment available. She puts herself in the care of veteran researcher Dr. Kelekian (Lloyd) and his internist Dr. Posner (Woodward), a former student of Vivian's. Their insensitivity sparks her bitter wit as Vivian realizes the inevitable truth. Based on the 1997 Pulitzer Prize-winning play by Margaret Edson. **98m/C VHS, DVD.** Emma Thompson, Christopher Lloyd, Audra McDonald, Jonathan M. Woodward, Eileen Atkins, Harold Pinter; **D:** Mike Nichols; **W:** Emma Thompson, Mike Nichols; **C:** Seamus McGarvey. CABLE

The Witch 1994 (R) *La Strega in Amore. Aura* 1966 Historians tend to assemble the late father's works falls in love with beautiful daughter. Seems she's two angel. **103m/B VHS, DVD.** Rosanna Schiaffino, Richard Johnson, Sarah Ferati, Gian Maria Volonte, Margherita Guzzinati; **D:** Damiano Damiani.

Witch Hunt 1994 (R) Mock fantasy/mystery set in 1953 Hollywood. Private eye H. Phillip Lovecraft (Hopper) is hired by actress Kim Hudson (Miller) to shadow her philandering studio hubby Gottlieb (Rosenberg), who dies in an untimely fashion. The kicker's that witchcraft is commonplace, with the studio hiring witches and warlocks to cast spells. Also, a blowhard senator (Bogosian) is heading a McCarthy-like campaign to ban magic and Lovecraft fears his sorceress friend (Ralph) is going to be the scapegoat for Gottlieb's murder. Great special effects, fuzzy plot. **101m/C VHS,** Dennis Hopper, Penelope Ann Miller, Eric Bogosian, Sheryl Lee Ralph, Julian Sands, Alta I. Rosenberg, Valerie Mahaffey, Debi Mazar; **D:** Paul Schrader; **W:** Joseph Dougherty; **M:** Angelo Badalamenti.

Witch Who Came from the Sea 1976 (R) Witch terrorizes all the ships at sea, but doesn't exactly haunt the viewer. **88m/C VHS, DVD.** Millie Perkins, Lonny (Lonnie) Chapman, Vanessa Brown, Peggy Feury, Rick Jason; **D:** Matt Cimber.

A Witch Without a Broom 1967 *Una Bruja Sin Escoba* 1968 Shoestring time travel fantasy. When an American professor catches the eye of a 15th century apprentice witch, the trip begins. Since the witch is only learning a number of periods other than their own before the professor gets home. **78m/C VHS, SP** Jeffrey Hunter, Maria Perschy, Perla Cristal, Gustavo Rojo; **D:** Joe Lacy.

Witchboard 1987 (R) During a college party, a group of friends bring out the Ouija board and play with it for laughs. One of the girls discovers she can use the board to communicate with a small boy who died years before. In her effort to talk with him she unwittingly releases the evil spirit of an ax murderer who haunts and murders members of the group. An entertaining, relatively inoffensive member of its genre that displays some attention to characterization and plot. **98m/C VHS, DVD.** Todd Allen, Tawny Kitaen, Stephen Nichols, Kathleen Wilhoite, Burke Byrnes, Rose Marie, J.P. Luebsen, Susan Nickerson; **D:** Kevin S. Tenney; **W:** Kevin S. Tenney; **C:** Roy Wagner; **M:** Dennis Michael Tenney.

Witchboard 2: The Doorway 1993 (R) There seem to be a lot of doorways to hell because someone is always finding a new one (and making a movie about it). This time it's the innocent Paige Benedict (Dolenz), who moves into an artist's loft and finds an old Ouija board in a closet.

Through the board, Paige is contacted by a former tenant who claims to be a murder victim. Soon her fellow tenants are dying in violent and mysterious ways and Paige's dreams are haunted by evil. What could keep a bad sextant in 1692 but if you there'd be no move. So when Simon's spirit is accidentally awakened by the Dunaways (Grober and Korf) in their Salem home, they seek the help of exorcist McArthur (Overmyer). **90m/C VHS,** Lee Grober, Kim Kopf, Tom Overmyer, Jack Van Landingham, David Wells, Anthon Stuart; **D:** Joseph John Barmettler Jr.; **W:** Joseph John Barmettler Jr.; **C:** Denis Maloney.

Witchboard 3: The Possession 1995 (R) A Ouija board opens the gates to hell (yet again or we wouldn't have a movie) and in board's spirit steals Brian's soul and takes control of his body—much to the bewilderment of his girlfriend Julie, who's... **98m/C VHS.** Ami Dolenz, Laraine Newman, Timothy Gibbs, John Gatins, Julie Michaels, Marvin Kaplan, David Neerman, Locky Lambert, Cedric Smith, Donna Sarrasin; **D:** Peter Svatek; **W:** Kevin S. Tenney, Jon Ezrine; **C:** Barry Gravelle; **M:** Dennis Michael Tenney.

Witchcraft woof! 1988 (R) A young mother meets a couple killed three centuries ago for performing witchcraft. They want her baby, of course, to use as the son of the devil. "Rosemary's Baby" rip-off, that is thoroughly predictable, but does have a fair share of sex and violence. **90m/C VHS, DVD.** Anat "Topol" Barzilai, Gary Sloan, Mary Shelley, Deborah Scott, Alexander Kirkwood, Lee Kisman, Edward Ross Newton; **D:** Robert Spera; **W:** Jody Savin. **C:** Jens Sturup; **M:** Randy Miller.

Witchcraft 2: The Temptress 1990 (R) A sensuous woman seduces an innocent young man into the rituals of witchcraft and the occult. Sequel to "Witchcraft" but does have a fair share of sex and violence. **83m/C VHS, DVD.** Charles Solomon, Mia Ruiz, Delia Sheppard; **D:** Mark Woods; **W:** Jim Hanson, Sal Manna. **C:** Jens Sturup; **M:** Miriam Cutler.

Witchcraft 3: The Kiss of Death 1990 (R) Once a master of the occult, William Spanner now seeks only to live a normal life. His plans are changed, however, when a sensual creature from Hell is sent to seduce him. More sex and violence, with an emphasis on sex. The best of the "Witchcraft" trio, for those trying to plan a festive evening. **85m/C VHS, DVD.** Charles Solomon, Julie Strain, Clive Pearson, Jason O'Gulihar, Lisa Jay Harrington, William L. Baker, Lena Halt; **D:** R.L. Tillmanns.

Witchcraft 4: Virgin Heart 1992 (R) Supernatural horror continues as attorney Will Spanner sinks even deeper into his enemy's satanic trap in this shocking sequel to the popular series. His only hope is to use his own black magic powers and to enlist the help of a seductive stripper (Penthouse Pet Strain). **92m/C VHS, DVD.** Charles Solomon, Julie Strain, Clive Pearson, Barbara Dow; **D:** James Merendino.

Witchcraft 5: Dance with the Devil 1992 (R) This undistinguished horror series continues with several successful people finding the unpleasant loopholes in their satanic contracts. A demon named Cain is behind all the trouble. The horror special effects are cheap but there are several soft-core sex scenes (pointless to the plot) which provide a minimal interest. An unrated version is also available. **94m/C VHS,** Marklen Kennedy, Carolyn Taye-Loren, Nicole Sassaman, Aysha Hauer; **D:** Talun Hsu.

Witchcraft 6: The Devil's Mistress 1994 (R) Police detectives Lutz and Garner's new case involves young women turning up naked and dead. Turns out satanic disciple Savanti is expected to impress the boss with a virgin sacrifice during an impending eclipse. But since virgins are scarce, he's having a real tough time. Practically no gore but lots of skin, along with hit-or-miss humor. **89m/C VHS, DVD.** Kurt Alan, John E. Holiday, Bryan Nutter, Jerry Spicer, Shannon Lead; **D:** Julie Davis; **W:** Julie Davis.

Witchcraft 7: Judgement Hour 1995 Modern-day warlock must sacrifice his earthly existence to kill an evil vampire. **91m/C VHS, DVD.** David Bynes, April Breneman, Alisa Christensen, John Cragen, Loren Schmalle; **D:** Michael Paul Girard; **W:** Peter Fleming; **C:** Denis Maloney; **M:** Julie Davis.

Witchcraft 8: Salem's Ghost *Salem's Ghost* 1995 (R) Warlock Simon Wintrough (Van Landingham) was burned at the stake in 1692 but if you there'd be no move. So when Simon's spirit is accidentally awakened by the Dunaways (Grober and Korf) in their Salem home, they seek the help of exorcist McArthur (Overmyer). **90m/C VHS,** Lee Grober, Kim Kopf, Tom Overmyer, Jack Van Landingham, David Wells, Anthon Stuart; **D:** Joseph John Barmettler Jr.; **W:** Joseph John Barmettler Jr.; **C:** Denis Maloney.

Witchcraft 9: Bitter Flesh 1996 (R) Yet another sequel to the endless erotic horror series finds the LAPD investigating a series of murders. They get a tip from a strange call girl who claims to be channeling the spirit of a warlock, who's about to open the gates to hell. **90m/C VHS, DVD.** Landon Hall, David Bynes, Stephanie Beaton, Mikul Robins; **D:** Michael Paul Girard; **W:** Stephen J. Downing; **C:** Jeff Gazeman; **M:** Michael Paul Girard.

Witchcraft 10: Mistress of the Craft 1998 Witch Celeste Sheridan has been hunting Raven and her band of vampires outside London. Meanwhile, LAPD detective Lucy Lutz arrives in London with an extradition order for Satanic serial killer, Hyde. But Raven and her hunt down Raven and Hyde before they can finish their demonic work. **90m/C VHS, DVD.** Wendy Cooper, Eileen Daly, Stephanie Beaton, Kerry Knowlton, Sean Harry, Frank Scantori, Emily Bouffante, Lynn Michelle; **D:** Elisar Cabrera; **W:** Elisar Cabrera. VIDEO

Witchcraft 11: Sisters in Blood 2000 A college production of "Macbeth" resurrects three long-dead witches. Full of fuzzy occult logic and semi-undressed girls in peril. **m/C VHS, DVD.** Stephanie Beaton, Mikul Robins, James Servais, Miranda Odell, Laura Ian Richards, Kathleen St. Lawrence; **D:** Ron Ford; **W:** Ron Ford. **C:** Scott Spears. VIDEO

Witchery woof! 1988 (R) *Witchcraft* 1988 A photographer and his girlfriend vacation at a New England hotel where they discover a horrifying, satanic secret. One by one (as always, in this kind of bad flick, in the interest of "suspense"), people are killed and then reappear. Forget room service and bar the door. Laurenti used the pseudonym Martin Newlin. **96m/C VHS, DVD.** David Hasselhoff, Linda Blair, Catherine Hickland, Hildegarde Knef, Leslie Cumming, Bob Champagne, Richard Farnsworth, Michael Manches; **D:** Fabrizio Laurenti. VIDEO

Witchfire 1986 (R) After their psychiatrist dies in an automobile accident, three maniacal women escape from an asylum and hide out in the woods. Winters then holds seances to contact the dead doctor, but instead captures a young, very much alive hunter. For dedicated fans of Winters. **92m/C VHS,** Shelley Winters, Gary Swanson, David Mendenhall, Corinna Chateau; **D:** Vincent J. Privitera; **W:** Vincent J. Privitera.

The Witches 1966 Gwen Mayfield (Fontaine) accepts a teaching position at Haddaby School. She wants to put terrifying memories of her work in Africa behind her, but finds that the bucolic English country town is just as dangerous. The sense of menace isn't as strong as it is in the similar "Wicker Man," and the film isn't one of the strongest entries from the Hammer Studio, but it is up to their high standards in terms of production values and acting. **90m/C VHS, DVD.** Joan Fontaine, Kay Walsh, Alec McCowen, Ann Bell, John Collin, Michele Dotrice, Gwen Ffrangcon Davies, Ingrid Brett; **D:** Cyril Frankel; **W:** Nigel Kneale; **C:** Arthur Grant; **M:** Richard Rodney Bennett.

The Witches 1990 (PG) *The Devil's Own* 1966 Nine-year-old boy on vacation finds himself in the midst of a witch convention, and grand high witch Huston plans to turn all children into fury, little creatures. The boy, with the help of his good witch grandmother, attempts to prevent the mass transmutation of children into mice. Top-notch fantasy probably too spooky for the training wheel set. Wonderful special effects; the final project of executive producer Jim Henson. Based on Roald Dahl's story. **92m/C VHS, DVD.** Anjelica Huston, Mai Zetterling, Jasen Fisher, Rowan Atkinson, Charlie Potter, Bill Paterson, Brenda Blethyn, Jane Horrocks; **D:** Nicolas Roeg; **W:** Alan Scott; **C:** Harvey Harrison; **M:** Stanley Myers. L.A. Film Critics '90; Actress (Huston); Natl. Soc. Film Critics '90; Actress (Huston).

The Witching of Ben Wagner 1995 (G) Strange occurrences have Ben believing his friend Regina and her grandmother may be witches. But, if so, they're friendly ones as they help Ben adjust to a new home and neighborhood. **96m/C VHS, DVD.** Justin Gocke, Harriet Hall, Sam Bottoms; **D:** Paul Annett.

Witchfire (cont.)

Witching Time 1984 Elvira presents this film, in which a young composer is visited by a horny 17th-century witch while his wife is away from home. When the wife returns, both women fight to possess him. **60m/C VHS, DVD,** Jon Finch, Prunella Gee, Patricia Quinn, Ian McCulloch; **D:** Don Leaver.

The Witchmaker 1969 Remote, crocodile-infested bayou in Louisiana is the scene of a witchcraft and the occult as young girls are murdered in order for a group of witches to become youthful again. **101m/C VHS.** John Lodge, Alvy Moore, Thordis Brandt, Anthony Eisley, Shelby Grant, Robyn Millan, Helene...

The Witches of the Caribbean 2005 (R) Troubled teen Angela (Cavazos) is plagued by nightmares of a witch being burned at the stake. She heads to a Caribbean retreat to participate in a program organized by psychotherapist Professor Avebury (Cassidy) but evil things happen when her fellow patients start to disappear. In this standard witch tale. **82m/C DVD.** Joenna Cassidy, Nicole Cavazos, Nicole Marie Monica, Kelly Gidcish, Michael King, Nina Taparin, Kyle Jordan; **D:** David DeCoteau; **W:** Jana K. Arnold; **C:** Robert Hayes.

Witches' Mountain 1971 A troubled couple is captured by a coven of witches in the Pyrenees. Dull and pointless. **98m/C VHS, MX** Patty (Patti) Shepard, John Caffari, Monica Randall; **D:** Raul Artigot.

The Witches of Eastwick 1987 (R) "Mad" director Miller meets Hollywood in John Updike's novel about three lonely small-town New England women and their sexual liberation. A strange, rich, over-sexed stranger comes to town with devilish charm and makes their deepest desires come true with decadent excess. Raunchy fun, with Nicholson over-acting wildly as the Mephisto lends a bombastic violent edge to the effort, sometimes at the expense of the story. Filmed on location in Cohasset, Massachusetts. **118m/C VHS, DVD.** Jack Nicholson, Cher, Susan Sarandon, Michele Pfeiffer, Veronica Cartwright, Richard Jenkins, Keith Joakum, Carel Struycken; **D:** George Miller; **W:** Michael Cristofer; **C:** Vilmos Zsigmond; **M:** John Williams. L.A. Film Critics '87; Actor (Nicholson); N.Y. Film Critics '87; Actor (Nicholson).

Witches' Brew 1979 (PG) Three young women try to use their undeveloped skills in witchcraft and black magic to help Garr's husband get a prestigious position at a university, with calamitous results. Off-funny spoof is silly and unpredictable. Turner's role is small as an older, experienced witch. **98m/C VHS,** Teri Garr, Richard Benjamin, Lana Turner, Kathryn Leigh Scott; **D:** Richard Shorr, Herbert L. Strock.

Winston; **D:** William O. Brown; **W:** William O. Brown.

Witchhouse 🦴🦴 **1999 (R)** Elizabeth (McKinney), a modern-day witch, invites some fellow college students to an off-campus party at her creepy mansion. But it turns out they are all descendants of witch-hunters who burned Elizabeth's ancestor at the stake. And now it's time for revenge. **90m/C VHS, DVD.** David Oren Ward, Ashley McKinney, Matt Raftery, Monica Serene Garnich, Brooke Mueller, Ariauna Albright, Marissa Tait, Dane Northcutt, Kimberly Pullis; **D:** Jack Reed; **W:** Matthew Jason Walsh; **C:** Viorel Sergovici Jr. **VIDEO**

Witchhouse 2: Blood Coven 🦴🦴½ **2000 (R)** Four unmarked graves are discovered by a strange house that is about to be torn down. The graves may be related to a witch burned to death in the area. When a professor and her students come to investigate they find the locals aren't very friendly—especially after people start dying. Has Lilith return to take revenge? **82m/C VHS, DVD.** Ariauna Albright, Andrew Prine, Nicholas Lanier, Elizabeth Hopgood; **D:** J.R. Bookwalter. **VIDEO**

Witchhouse 3: Demon Fire 🦴🦴 **2001 (R)** Stevie (Rochon) and Rose (Krause) are filming a documentary on witchcraft, when their old friend Annie (Dempsey) comes to visit. Annie is seeking refuge from her abusive boyfriend and her buddies are glad to oblige. As part of the documentary, the three women conduct a mock seance, and inadvertently raise the spirit of the evil witch Lilith (Stevens). Soon, strange things happen and the corpses start piling up. Is Lilith real, or has one of the girls gone insane? As with the other films in this series, director Bookwalter is able to put every nickel up on-screen and create an interesting movie. This one isn't simply a horror film that offers cheap thrills, attractive ladies, and a brief escape from reality. **77m/C DVD.** Debbie Rochon, Tanya Dempsey, Tina Krause, Brinke Stevens; **D:** J.R. Bookwalter.

The WitchTrap 🦴🦴 **1989 (R)** "A mansion's new owner hires psychics to exorcise the disturbed ghost of his predecessor. **87m/C VHS.** James W. Quinn, Kathleen Bailey, Linnea Quigley; **D:** Kevin S. Tenney.

With a Friend Like Harry 🦴🦴🦴 *Harry, He's Here to Help; Harry, un Ami Qui Vous Veut du Bien; Harry, A Friend Who Wishes You Well* **2000 (R)** Twisted, surprisingly funny black comedy about a sociopath. Michel (Lucas), wife Claire (Seigner), and their three young daughters have embarked on the vacation from hell as they head to their summer home. At a rest stop, Michel happens to meet Harry (Lopez), a high school acquaintance who remembers Michel very well. Before they know it, Claire and Michel are sharing their farmhouse with Harry and his sexy girlfriend, the aptly named Plum (Guillemin). Harry's a very, very generous (if off-kilter) guy—in fact, he'll do anything to make Michel's life better, even kill French with subtitles. **117m/C VHS, DVD. FR** Sergi Lopez, Laurent Lucas, Mathilde Seigner, Sophie Guillemin; **D:** Dominik Moll; **W:** Dominik Moll, Gilles Marchand; **C:** Mathieu Poirot-Delpech; **M:** David Whitaker. Cesar '01: Actor (Lopez), Director (Moll).

With a Song in My Heart 🦴🦴🦴 **1952** Showbiz drama based on the life of singer Jane Froman, with a stellar performance by Hayward. Told in flashback, Jane (Hayward) gets her first big break in radio and decides to marry mentor Don (Wayne), who becomes increasingly jealous of her success. During a WWII troop tour, Jane's plane crashes near Lisbon and she's rescued by pilot John Burn (Calhoun), who falls in love as Jane slowly recuperates. Aided by faithful nurse Clancy (Ritter), Jane is eventually strong enough to try for a comeback and Don finally realizes that their marriage is over. Froman herself dubbed the singing for Hayward. **117m/C DVD.** Susan Hayward, Thelma Ritter, Rory Calhoun, David Wayne, Robert Wagner, Helen Westcott, Una Merkel, Leif Erickson; **D:** Walter Lang; **W:** Lamar Trotti; **C:** Leon Shamroy; **M:** Alfred Newman. Oscars '53: Orig. Score.

With Friends Like These 🦴🦴🦴 **1998 (R)** Johnny DeMartino (Constanzo) is a small time character actor in Hollywood. He, along with his three other actor buddies, makes a living playing small bit roles of Mafia henchmen, when one day he is approached with an opportunity to audition for Martin Scorsese to play the role of a lifetime, Al Capone (Scorsese wants an unknown actor). Although he was sworn to secrecy about the audition, Johnny can't help spread the good news to his friends. Faster than you can say "sleeps with the fishes," every character actor in town is trying to wrangle their own audition and practicing their best mobster impressions. Clever and funny look inside the non-glamorous side of the movie industry, with all its faults and insecurities attached. **105m/C VHS.** Adam Arkin, Robert Costanzo, Beverly D'Angelo, Elle Macpherson, Amy Madigan, David Strathairn, Jon Tenney, Lauren Tom, Carmine Costanzo, Garry Marshall, Michael McKean, Ashley Peldon, Jon Polito, Heather Stephens, Bill Murray, Martin Scorsese, Laura San Giacomo, Tom La Grua, Armando Pucci, Andrew Schafler; **D:** Philip Messina; **W:** Philip Messina; **C:** Brian Reynolds.

With Honors 🦴🦴½ **1994 (PG-13)** Pesci is a bum who finds desperate Harvard student Fraser's Honors thesis, and, like any quick-witted bum with a yen for literature, holds it for ransom. Desperate to salvage his future gold card, Fraser and his roommates agree to fix Joe's homeless state. Self-involved students learn something about love and life while Madonna drones in the background. Fraser is believable as the ambitious student about to endure Pesci's enlightenment. Pesci is doing his best to overcome numerous script difficulties. **100m/C VHS, DVD.** Joe Pesci, Brendan Fraser, Moira Kelly, Patrick Dempsey, Josh Hamilton, Gore Vidal; **D:** Alek Keshishian; **W:** William Mastrosimone; **C:** Sven Nykvist; **M:** Patrick Leonard.

With Kit Carson over the Great Divide 🦴🦴½ **1925** A large-scale silent western about a doctor's family gone asunder and then reunited during the Fremont expeditions out of St. Louis in the 1840s. Snow's final screen appearance. Recently refound. Fun cinematic history (in two senses of the phrase). Beautiful landscape. **72m/B VHS.** Roy Stewart, Henry B. Walthall, Marguerite Snow, Sheldon Lewis, Earl Metcalfe; **D:** Frank S. Mattison.

With Six You Get Eggroll 🦴🦴 *A Man in Mommy's Bed* **1968 (G)** A widow with three sons and a widower with a daughter elope and then must deal with the antagonism of their children and even their dogs. Brady Bunch-esque family comedy means well, but doesn't cut it. Hershey's debut. Jamie Farr, William Christopher, and Vic Tayback have small parts. To date, Day's last big-screen appearance. **95m/C VHS, DVD.** Doris Day, Brian Keith, Pat Carroll, Alice Ghostley, Vic Tayback, Jamie Farr, William (Bill) Christopher, Barbara Hershey; **D:** Howard Morris; **C:** Harry Stradling Jr.

Within the Rock 🦴🦴 **1996 (R)** Space crew must shift a wandering moon before it collides with earth but beyond that problem they've got an alien predator that's escaped. **91m/C VHS, DVD.** Xander Berkeley, Bradford Tatum, Brian Krause, Caroline Barclay, Calvin Levels, Earl Boen, Dale Dye; **D:** Gary J. Tunnicliffe; **W:** Gary J. Tunnicliffe; **C:** Adam Kane; **M:** Tony Fennell, Rod Gammons.

Withnail and I 🦴🦴🦴½ **1987 (R)** A biting and original black comedy about a pair of unemployed, nearly starving English actors during the late 1960s. They decide to retreat to a country house owned by Withnail's uncle, for a vacation and are beset by comic misadventures, particularly when the uncle, who is gay, starts to hit on his nephew's friend. Robinson, who scripted "The Killing Fields," makes his successful directorial debut, in addition to drafting the screenplay from his own novel. Co-produced by George Harrison and Richard Starkey (Ringo Starr). **108m/C VHS, DVD. GB** Richard E. Grant, Paul McGann, Richard Griffiths, Ralph Brown, Michael Elphick; **D:** Bruce Robinson; **W:** Bruce Robinson; **C:** Peter Hannan; **M:** David Dundas.

Without a Clue 🦴🦴½ **1988 (PG)** Spoof of the Sherlock Holmes legend, in which Holmes is actually portrayed by a bumbling, skirt-chasing actor, and Watson is the sole crime-solving mastermind, hiring the actor to impersonate the character made famous by the doctor's published exploits. The leads have some fun and so do we; but laughs are widely spaced. **107m/C VHS, DVD. GB** Michael Caine, Ben Kingsley, Jeffrey Jones, Lysette Anthony, Paul Freeman, Nigel Davenport, Peter Cook, Pat Keen; **D:** Thom Eberhardt; **W:** Gary Murphy, Larry Strawther; **M:** Henry Mancini.

Without a Paddle 🦴🦴½ **2004 (PG-13)** A harmlessly stupid buddy flick finds three lifelong friends—phobic Dan (Green), surfer dude Jerry (Lillard), and loudmouth Tom (Shepard)—mourning the unexpected death of pal Billy. Uneasily pushing 30, these faux grown-ups decide to pursue a childhood fantasy by heading into the Oregon woods to search for the lost treasure of '70s crime legend, D.B. Cooper. Now the real fun begins as they deal with growling bears, canoeing the rapids, redneck pot farmers, tree-huggers, and, briefly, a charismatically grizzled Burt Reynolds. There's a lot of standard scatological and slapstick humor as well as many nostalgic '70s and '80s references that may be lost on a younger crowd. **99m/C VHS, DVD, UMD. US** Seth Green, Matthew Lillard, Dax Shepard, Ethan Suplee, Abraham Benrubi, Rachel Blanchard, Burt Reynolds, Christina Moore, Bonnie Somerville, Ray Baker; **D:** Steven Brill; **W:** Jay Leggett, Mitch Rouse, Fred Wolf, Harris Goldberg, Tom Nursall; **D:** Jonathan Brown; **M:** Christophe Beck.

Without a Trace 🦴🦴 **1983 (PG)** One morning, a six-year-old boy is sent off to school by his loving mother, never to return. The story of the mother's relentless search for her son. Cardboard characters, wildly unrealistic ending that is different from the real-life incident on which it's based. Scripted by Gutcheon from her book "Still Missing." Jaffe's directorial debut. **119m/C VHS, DVD.** Kate Nelligan, Judd Hirsch, Stockard Channing, David Dukes; **D:** Stanley R. Jaffe; **C:** John Bailey; **M:** Jack Nitzsche.

Without Anesthesia 🦴🦴 *Rough Treatment; Bez Znieczulenia* **1978** Journalist Jerzy returns from a trip abroad to discover his wife has left him for an obnoxious young writer. Against advice, Jerzy fights the divorce and searches for an explanation. Meanwhile, he has mysteriously fallen out of political favor and finds his career falling apart as well. Polish with English subtitles. **111m/C VHS, DVD. PL** Zbigniew Zapasiewicz, Ewa Dalkowska, Krystyna Janda, Andrzej Seweryn; **D:** Andrzej Wajda; **W:** Agnieszka Holland, Andrzej Wajda.

Without Evidence 🦴🦴 **1996** When Oregon correctional director Michael Francke (Garrett) is visiting younger brother Kevin (Plank) in Florida, he mentions his suspicions about an operation within his department involving drugs in prison. Then the next phone call Kevin gets is to head to Oregon, Kevin seems to be getting the official runaround and becomes increasingly suspicious about a coverup. A tension-building true story that remains unsolved. **90m/C VHS, DVD.** Scott Plank, Anna Gunn, Andrew Prine, Angelina Jolie, Paul Perri, Allen Nause, Ernie Garrett; **D:** Gill Dennis; **W:** Gill Dennis, Phil Stanford; **C:** Victor Nunez; **M:** Franco Piersanti.

Without Honors 🦴🦴🦴 **1932** A man seeks to restore the reputation of his dead brother, accused of murder and theft. He joins the Texas Rangers and brings the real criminals to justice. Excellent location shooting lifts ordinary early western. **62m/B VHS.** Harry Carey Sr., Mae Busch, Gibson Gowland, George "Gabby" Hayes; **D:** William Nigh.

Without Limits 🦴🦴🦴 *Pre* **1997 (PG-13)** Second biopic about '70s long-distance runner Steve Prefontaine (after 1996's "Prefontaine") focuses mainly on Prefontaine's (Crudup) relationship with his University of Oregon coach Bill Bowerman (Sutherland), who later was a co-founder of Nike. Also explores the heart-break of the 1972 Olympics. Crudup does a fine job exploring the runner's playful arrogance, fearlessness, and iconoclasm (especially when dealing with the corrupt AAU). Sutherland, playing a three-dimensional character for the first time in a while, gives a fine performance. Kenny Moore, a close friend and fellow '72 Olympian, wrote the script with director Towne, with the full cooperation of Bowerman and Prefontaine's girlfriend. Terrific supporting cast keeps this minimally plotted outing afloat. **117m/C VHS, DVD.** Billy Crudup, Donald Sutherland, Monica Potter, Jeremy Sisto, Matthew Lillard, Billy Burke, Dean Norris, Gabriel Olds, Judith Ivey; **D:** Robert Towne; **W:** Robert Towne, Kenny Moore; **C:** Conrad L. Hall; **M:** Randy Miller.

Without Love 🦴🦴½ **1945** Tracy is a scientist, Hepburn, a woman with an empty basement for his laboratory. Since the neighbors woud be scandalized by the idea of unmarried people living together, however platonically, they decide to get married, although each has sworn off romance. Snappy dialogue, expertly rendered by the Tracy/Hepburn team. Terrific supporting cast keeps this minimally plotted outing afloat. Adapted from the play of the same name by Philip Barry. **113m/B VHS, DVD.** Spencer Tracy, Katharine Hepburn, Lucille Ball, Keenan Wynn, Carl Esmond, Patricia Morison, Felix Bressart; **D:** Harold Bucquet; **W:** Donald Ogden Stewart; **C:** Karl Freund.

Without Love 🦴🦴 **1980** Ambitious young journalist experiences resentment from her peers because of her aggressive methods, and they decide to teach her a lesson by drawing her into a situation destined for disaster. In Polish with English subtitles. **104m/C VHS, DVD. PL** Malgorzata Zajaczkowska, Dorota Stalinska, Wladyslaw Kowalski; **D:** Barbara Sass; **W:** Barbara Sass; **C:** Wieslaw Zdort; **M:** Seweryn Krajewski.

Without Mercy 🦴½ **1995 (R)** Marine platoon is shafted by the government when they're left to die while on a U.N. peacekeeping mission in Africa. POW training soldier John Carter (Zagarino) then winds up in Asia and gets set up by ex-soldier and general bad guy Larsen (Kove), who he must constantly battle in order to survive. **88m/C VHS.** Frank Zagarino, Martin Kove, Ayu Azhari, Frans Tumbuan; **D:** Robert Anthony; **W:** Robert Anthony.

Without Orders 🦴🦴 **1936** Playboy pilot Len (Haworth) vies with dull good guy pilot Wad (Armstrong) for the affections of stewardess Kay (Eilers). But when Len cowardly parachutes out of a crippled airplane, Kay must take over the controls, guided by Wad from the control tower. And no, this isn't played for laughs. **64m/B VHS.** Sally Eilers, Robert Armstrong, Vinton (Hayworth) Haworth, Charley Grapewin, Ward Bond, Frances Sage; **D:** Lew Landers; **W:** J. Robert Bren, Edmund L. Hartman; **C:** J. Roy Hunt.

Without Reservations 🦴🦴½ **1946** Hollywood-bound novelist Colbert encounters Marine flyer Wayne and his pal (DeFore) aboard a train. She decides he would be perfect for her newest movie. They both dislike her famous book and don't realize they're traveling with the renowned author. Misadventures and misunderstandings abound as this trio make their way to Tinseltown. Of course, Colbert and Wayne fall in love. Boxoffice success with a tired script and too few real laughs. The Duke is interesting, but miscast. Based on the novel "Thanks, God, I'll Take It From Here" by Jane Allen. **101m/B VHS.** Claudette Colbert, John Wayne, Don DeFore, Phil Brown, Frank Puglia; Cameos: Louella

Persons Cary Grant, Jack Benny. *D:* Mervyn LeRoy. *C:* Milton Krasner.

Without Warning 🎬🎬½ *The Story Without A Name* 1952 Inexperienced director and actors pull out a minor success in this fairly ordinary murder mystery, about a serial killer of beautiful blondes. 75m/C VHS, DVD, FR Maurice Ronet, Adam Williams, Gloria Franklin, Edward Binns; *D:* Arnold Laven.

Without Warning: The James Brady Story 🎬🎬 1991 (R) White House Press Secretary Brady took a bullet in the brain during the 1981 shooting of President Reagan, and made a slow, grueling recovery. This fine cable film spares none of it, concentrating on the stricken man and his family, and opting out of disease-of-the-week cliches (though the pic's politics won't please the gun-adorers). Based on Mollie Dickinson's biography "Thumbs Up." 120m/C VHS, Beau Bridges, Joan Allen, David Strathairn, Christopher Bell, Gary Grubbs, Bryan Clark, Steve Flynn, Christine Healy, Susan Brown; *D:* Michael Toshiyuki Uno; *W:* Robert Bolt. CABLE

Witness Protection WOOF! 2008 (PG-13) Another unsuccessful, unnecessary, and unfunny vehicle for Larry the Cable Guy. This time around Larry plays a cinwitted cop who kidnaps a woman in witness protection because re thinks the FBI agents at her side are ruthless drug dealers. Genius screenplay! take about 90 minutes for him to realize his mistake, allowing plenty of time to insert lame fart jokes and zingers about Araes along the way. Larry needs to start making like a real cable guy anc keep us waiting a long time before we s3e the likes of him on screen again. 97m/C DVD, US Larry the Cable Guy, Ivana Milicevic, Yaphet Kotto, Peter Stormare, Jenny McCarthy, Eric Roberts, Joe Manteigna; *D:* Charles Robert Carner; *W:* Charles Robert Carner. *C:* Michael Goi; *M:* Eric Allaman.

Witness 🎬🎬🎬 1985 (R) A young Amish boy, Samuel Lapp (Haas), traveling from his father's funeral witnesses a murder in a Philadelphia bus station. Investigating the true story of Sammy, "The Wall" Gravano (Turturro), who turned counter of alien worlds, win a poignant love story. McGillis, in her first major role, is luminous as the Amish mother, while Ford is believable as both a cop and a sensitive man. An artfully crafted drama, richly focusing or the often misunderstood Amish lifestyle. 112m/C VHS, DVD, John Head, Susan Amgren, Patrick Thomas, Chris Heyerdahl; *D:* Geoffrey Edwards; *W:* Richard Gourdrinau. *C:* Georges Archainbault; *M:* Jerry Devillers. VIDEO

The Witness 🎬½ *Fish Out of Water* 1999 (PG) Teen discovers an arsonist's plot to burn down a historic museum. Cheesy Canadian 'action' flick fails to deliver any thrills, spills, or, well, action. 95m/C VHS, DVD. John Heard, Susan Almgren, Patrick

The Witness Files 🎬🎬 2000 (R) Sandy (Butler) has been imprisoned for the murder of her abusive husband. Corrupt politician Frank Sutto (Flatman) arranges for her release so he can use her special talents (she does makeup special effects) for his own nefarious ends. But Sandy hooks up with a detective (Nerman) to doublecross Sutton. Watch "F/X" instead unless you're a particular fan of Butler. 97m/C VHS, DVD. Yancy Butler, David Nerman, Barry Flatman, Matthew Harbour; *D:* Douglas Jackson. VIDEO

Witness for the Prosecution 🎬🎬½ 1957 An unemployed man is accused of murdering a wealthy widow whom he befriended. Ailing defense attorney Laughton can't resist taking an intriguing murder case, and a straightforward court case becomes increasingly complicated in this energetic adaptation of an Agatha Christie story and stage play. Outstanding performances by real-life wife, Lanchester, as his patient nurse, Power, as the alleged killer, and Dietrich as a tragic woman are top-notch. 116m/B VHS, DVD, Charles Laughton, Tyrone Power, Marlene Dietrich, Elsa Lanchester, John Williams, Henry Daniell, Una O'Connor; *D:* Billy Wilder; *W:* Billy Wilder, Harry Kurnitz; *C:* Russell Harlan; *M:* Matty Malneck. Golden Globes '58: Support. Actress (Lanchester).

Witness Protection 🎬🎬🎬 1999 Highly watchable performances raise this cable movie about mobsters above the average. Boston goodfella Bobby Batton (Sizemore) turns state's evidence after he's betrayed by his cronies. He and his family are placed in the witness protection program under the eye of a U.S. marshal (Whitaker) but living as a regular mook proves difficult. Bobby's wife (Mastrantonio) is bitter, his kids are angry and confused, and there are no easy endings. Based on a 1996 New York Times Magazine article by Robert Sabbag. 105m/C VHS, DVD, Tom Sizemore, Forest Whitaker, Mary Elizabeth Mastrantonio, Shawn Hatosy, Richard Portnow; *D:* Richard Pearce; *W:* Daniel Theriault. CABLE

Witness to the Execution 🎬🎬 1994 (PG-13) It's 1999 and Tycom Entertainment, a pay-per-view network, its looking for some hot entertainment. Top exec Jessica (Young) decides to televise the electric chair execution of convicted criminal Dennis Casterfine (Daly). But Casterline claims to be innocent and as the execution date nears Jessica is unsettled by new evidence that may supports his claim. The cutthroat TV execs provide amusement but this TV movie fare quickly becomes muddled. 92m/C VHS, Sean Young, Timothy Daly, Len Cariou, George Newbern; *D:* Tommy Lee Wallace; *W:* Thomas Baum.

Witness to the Mob 🎬½ 1998 (R) Originally an NBC miniseries, this mob saga tells the true story of Sammy, "The Bull" Gravano (Turturro), who turned state's evidence against his boss, John Gotti. Manages to mix every cliche and stereotype along the way. 172m/C VHS, Nicholas Turturro, Tom Sizemore, Debi Mazar, Frankie Valli, Abe Vigoda, Philip Baker Hall, Frank Vincent, Michael Imperioli, Lenny Venito, Vincent Pastore, Kirk Acevedo, Richard Bright; *D:* Thaddeus O'Sullivan; *W:* Stanley Weiser; *C:* Frank Prinzi; *M:* Stephen Endelman. TV

Wittgenstein 🎬🎬 1993 Complicated experimental portrait of Viennese-born philosopher Ludwig Wittgenstein (Johnson), executed as a series of blackout sketches (that feature a green Martian dwarf and such friends as Bertrand Russell and Ottoline Morrell). Assumes a familiarity with the eccentric Wittgenstein's ideas but does manage to convey some emotion and wit. 75m/C VHS, GB Karl Johnson, Michael Gough, Tilda Swinton, John Quentin, Nabil Shaban; *D:* Derek Jarman; *W:* Derek Jarman; Terry Eagleton; Ken Butler.

Wives and Daughters 🎬🎬½ 2001 Charming adaptation of Elizabeth Gaskell's 1864 chronicle of family ties, romance, and scandal set in an 1820s English country town. Our heroine is modest Molly Gibson (Waddell), whose widower doctor father (Paterson) marries ambitious Hyacinth (Annis), who has a beautiful daughter, Cynthia (Hawes), who's Molly's age. Then there's the local gentry, Squire Hamley (Gambon), and his two sons, the poetic Osborne (Hollander) and the scientific Roger (Howell). Molly becomes everyone's confidante, but also has her own secrets. 300m/C VHS, DVD, GB Justine Waddell, Keeley Hawes, Francesca Annis, Bill Paterson, Michael Gambon, Penelope Wilton, Tom Hollander, Anthony Howell, Ian Carmichael, Ian Glen, Barbara Leigh-Hunt, Tonia Chauvet, Shaughan Seymour, Barbara Flynn, Deborah Findlay; *D:* Nicholas Renton; *W:* Andrew Davies. TV

Wives under Suspicion 🎬🎬½ 1938 While prosecuting a man who murdered his wife out of jealousy, a district attorney finds his own home life filled with similar tension. Director Whale's unnecessary remake of his own earlier film. "The Kiss Before the Mirror." He is best known for "Frankenstein." 75m/B VHS, DVD Warren William, Gail Patrick, Constance Moore, William Lundigan; *D:* James Whale.

The Wiz 🎬🎬 1973 (G) Black version of the long-time favorite "The Wizard of Oz," based on the Broadway musical. Ross plays a Harlem schoolteacher who is whisked away to a fantasy version of NYC in a search for her identity. Some good character performances and musical numbers, but generally an overblown and garish effort with Ross too old for her role. Pryor is poorly cast, but Jackson is memorable as the Scarecrow. 'High-budget' ($24 million) production with a ton of name stars, lost $11 million, and cooled studios on black films. Home's number as the Wicked Witch is the best reason to sit through this one. 🎵The Feeling That We Have; Can I Go On Not Knowing; Glinda's Theme; You Can't Win; Ease on Down the Road; What Would I Do If I Could Feel?; Slide Some Oil to Me. 133m/C VHS, DVD, Diana Ross, Michael Jackson, Nipsey Russell, Ted Ross, Mabel King, Thelma Carpenter, Richard Pryor, Lena Horne; *D:* Sidney Lumet; *W:* Joel Schumacher; *C:* Oswald Morris; *M:* Quincy Jones.

The Wizard 🎬½ 1989 (PG) Facing the dissolution of his dysfunctional family, a youngster decides to take his autistic, video game-playing little brother across the country to a national video competition. Way too much plot in a pretentious, blatantly commercial feature-length Nintendo ad, featuring the kid from "The Wonder Years." For teen video addicts only. 99m/C VHS, DVD, Fred Savage, Beau Bridges, Christian Slater, Luke Edwards, Jenny Lewis; *D:* Todd Holland; *W:* David Chisholm.

The Wizard of Gore 🎬 1970 (R) The prototypical Lewis splatter party, about a magician whose on-stage mutilations turn out to be messily real. High camp and barrels of bright movie blood. 96m/C VHS, DVD, Ray Sager, Judy Cler, Wayne Ratay, Phil Laurenson, Jim Rau, Don Alexander, Monika Blackwell, Corinne Kirkin, John Elliott; *D:* Herschell Gordon Lewis; *W:* Allen Kahn; *C:* Alex Ameri, Daniel Krogh; *M:* Larry Wellington.

The Wizard of Loneliness 🎬🎬½ 1988 (PG-13) A disturbed young boy goes to live with his grandparents during WWII, and slowly discovers family secrets centering on his aunt. Excellent performances barely save an aimless plot with an overdone denouement. Based on the novel by John Nichols. 110m/C VHS, Lukas Haas, Lea Thompson, John Randolph, Lance Guest, Anne Pitoniak, Jeremiah Warner, Dylan Baker; *D:* Jenny (H. Anne Riley) Bowen; *W:* Nancy Larson; *C:* Richard Bowen; *M:* Michel Colombier.

The Wizard of Oz 🎬🎬½ 1925 An early silent version of the L. Frank Baum fantasy, with notable plot departures from the book and later 1939 adaptation, starring long-forgotten comedian Semon as the Scarecrow supported by a pre-Laurel Hardy as the Tin Woodman. With music score. 96m/B VHS, DVD, Larry Semon, Dorothy Dwan, Bryan Washburn, Charles Murray, Oliver Hardy, Josef Swickard, Virginia Pearson; *D:* Larry Semon; *W:* L. Frank Baum Jr., Larry Semon; *C:* Leonard Smith, Frank B. Good, Hans Koenekamp.

The Wizard of Oz 🎬🎬🎬 1939 From the book by L. Frank Baum. Fantasy about a Kansas farm girl (Garland, in her immortal role) who rides a tornado to a brightly colored world over the rainbow, full of talking scarecrows and munchkins and a wizard who bears a strange resemblance to a Kansas fortune-teller. She must outwit the Wicked Witch if she is ever to go home. Delightful performances from Lahr, Bolger, and Hamilton; King Vidor is uncredited as co-director. Director Fleming originally wanted Deanna Durbin or Shirley Temple for the role of Dorothy, but settled for Garland who made the song "Over the Rainbow" her own. She received a special Academy Award for her performance. For the 50th anniversary of its release, "The Wizard of Oz" was restored and includes rare film clips of Bolger's "Scarecrow Dance" and the cut "Jitterbug" number, and shots by Buddy Ebsen as the Tin Man before he became ill and left the production. Another special release of the film, "The Ultimate Oz," contains a documentary on the making of the film, a reproduction of the original script, still photos, and liner notes. 🎵Munchkinland: Ding Dong the Witch is Dead; Follow the Yellow Brick Road; If I Only Had a Brain/a Heart/the Nerve; If I Were the King of the Forest; The Merry Old Land of Oz; Threatening Witch; Into the Forest of the Wild 'Beast; The City Gates are Open. 101m/C VHS, DVD, Judy Garland, Margaret Hamilton, Ray Bolger, Jack Haley, Bert Lahr, Frank Morgan, Charley Grapewin, Clara Blandick, Mitchell Lewis, Billie Burke; *D:* Victor Fleming; *W:* Noel Langley; *C:* Harold Rosson; *M:* Herbert Stothart. Oscars '39: Song ("Over the Rainbow"), Orig. Score; AFI '98: Top 100, Natl. Film Reg. '89.

The Wizard of Speed and Time 🎬🎬½ 1988 (PG) A special-effects wizard gets the break of his life when he's hired by a movie studio, but there's more to this particular studio than he realizes. Jittlov, a real special-effects expert, plays himself in this personally financed production. Although brimming with inside jokes and references, this self-indulgence succeeds with its enthusiasm and ambition, despite being rather obviously self-produced. Unique special effects make it Protane, crude, & typically Bakshi an fantasy with great graphics. Animated. 81m/C VHS, DVD, *D:* Ralph Bakshi; *W:* Ralph Bakshi; *M:* Andrew Belling; *V:* Bob Holt, Jesse Wells, Richard Romanus, David Proval.

Wizards 🎬🎬½ 1977 (PG) A good, bumbling sorcerer battles for the sake of a magic kingdom and its princess against his evil brother who uses Nazi propaganda films to inspire his army of mutants. Kaye Page Moore, David Conrad, Steve Brodie, John Massari, Frank Leiogatia, Philip Michael Thomas, Angelique Pettyjohn, Amelia Walker, Paulette Breen, Forest J Ackerman; *D:* Mike Jittlov; *W:* Deven Chierighino, Mike Jittlov, Richard Kaye; *C:* Russell Carpenter; *M:* John Massari.

Wizards of the Demon Sword 🎬🎬 1994 (R) Group of warriors battle over a sword with the power to control the world. 90m/C VHS, DVD Lawrence Tierney, Michael Berryman, Russ Tamblyn, Lyle Waggoner, Blake Bahner, Heidi Paine, Dan Speaker, Jay Richardson, Dawn Wildsmith; *D:* Fred Olen Ray; *W:* Can Golden, Ernest Farino, Hector Olivera.

Wizards of the Lost Kingdom 🎬🎬 1985 (PG) A boy magician, aided by various ogres and sword-ster Svenson battles an all-powerful wizard for control of his kingdom. Family fare a bit too clean and harmless. 76m/C VHS, Bo Svenson, Vidal Peterson, Thom Christopher; *D:* Hector Olivera.

Wizards of the Lost Kingdom 2 🎬 1989 (PG) A boy wizard is charged with vanquishing the evil tyrants from three kingdoms. Barely a sequel: no plot continuation or cast from earlier kiddie sword epic. 80m/C VHS, David Carradine, Bobby Jacoby, Lana Clarkson, Mel Welles, Susan Lee Hoffman, Sid Haig; *D:* Charles B. Griffith.

Wolf 🎬🎬½ 1994 (R) Harrison's original script is massaged by Nichols into an upscale new age men's movement horror spectacle lacking a suitable climax. Stressed out Manhattan book editor Will Randall's (Nicholson) car hits a wolf on a country road and he's bitten when he tries to help the animal. Normally a wishywashy guy, he notices some distinctly hairy changes to both his body and personality, leading him to make some drastic changes at work by knocking off his firm's greedy honchos and taking over. Talk about being ruthless in business. Boss' changes new animal magnetism, but is just about, it between Michelle Pfeiffer takes a shine to herself visual candy. Walks a fine line between black comedy, camp, romance, and horror, and shots by Buddy Ebsen as the Tin Man before he became ill.

Wolf 🎬 1936 To everyone's lasting regret, an ex-Vietnam POW strives to rescue an American ambassador kidnapped by Central American rebels. 95m/C VHS. J. Antonio Carreon, Ron Marchini; *D:* Charlie Ordonez.

ror, though Jack baying at the moon seems sort of campy. **125m/C VHS, DVD. Oz** (Osgood) Perkins II, Jennifer Nicholson, Jack Nelliolson, Michelle Pfeiffer, James Spader, Kate Nelligan, Christopher Plummer, Richard Jenkins, Om Puri, Eileen Atkins, David Hyde Pierce, Ron Rifkin, Prunella Scales; *D:* Mike Nichols; *W:* Wesley Strick, Jim Harrison; *M:* Giuseppe Rotunno; *M:* Ennio Morricone.

The Wolf at the Door 🐾🐾½
1987 (R) A well-appointed, sincere biography of impressionist Paul Gauguin in the middle period of life, during his transition from the petty demands of his Parisian life to the freedom of Tahiti. Not definitive or compelling, but serves the purpose of a biography—arousing interest in the subject's life and art. **90m/C VHS. DK FR** Donald Sutherland, Jean Yanne, Sofie Grabol, Ghita Norby, Max von Sydow, Merete Voldstedlund, Fanny Bastien, Valerie Morea; *D:* Henning Carlsen; *W:* Christopher Hampton; *M:* Roger Bourland.

Wolf Blood 🐾🐾½
1925 When Dick (Chesebro) is hurt in an accident, Dr. Horton uses wolf's blood for a transfusion. Soon there are unexplained deaths and Dick fears he's becoming a man-beast. Early precursor to the wolfman films. **68m/B VHS.** George Chesebro, Marguerite Clayton, Ray Hanford, Roy Watson, Milburn (Milt) Morante; *D:* George Chesebro, George Mitchell.

Wolf Call 🐾½
1939 Carroll plays the son of a miner who travels with his devoted hound to see his father's old mine and start it working again. Gangsters and a beautiful Indian maiden get in his way. Master and pooch both find romance, and both sing. From the Jack London novel. **62m/B VHS.** John Carroll, Movita, Wheeler Oakman, Peter George Lynn; *D:* George Waggner; *C:* Fred H. Jackman Jr.; *M:* Edward Kay.

Wolf Creek 🐾
2005 (R) In the Australian Outback, three young adults, Ben (Phillips), Liz (Magrath) and Kristy (Morassi) are on a cross-country car trip. Having purchased a cheap junker for the trek, the threesome find they've been stranded in the bush when the car fails to start. In an unlikely stroke of luck, a tow truck-driving bushman named Mick (Jarratt) appears and assures them he can repair the car but must tow them back to his compound. So begins the unrelenting stream of torturous (to them and the audience) horrors. More than a wee bit over the top. **95m/C DVD, HD DVD.** John Jarratt, Kestie Morassi, Nathan Phillips, Cassandra Magrath; *D:* Greg Mclean; *W:* Greg Mclean; *C:* William Gibson; *M:* Francois Tetaz.

Wolf Dog 🐾🐾
1933 A boy and his dog. Outdoor action and adventure. Twelve chapters, 13 minutes each. **156m/B VHS.** Frankie Darro, Patricia "Boots" Mallory; *D:* Harry Fraser, Colbert Clark.

The Wolf Man 🐾🐾🐾½
1941 Fun, absorbing classic horror with Chaney as a man bitten by werewolf Lugosi. His dad thinks he's gone nuts, his screaming gal pal just doesn't understand, and plants on the Universal lot have no roots. Ousspenskaya's finest hour as the prophetic gypsy woman. Ow-oool Chilling and thrilling. **70m/B VHS, DVD.** Lon Chaney Jr., Claude Rains, Maria Ouspenskaya, Ralph Bellamy, Bela Lugosi, Warren William, Patric Knowles, Evelyn Ankers, Forrester Harvey, Fay Helm; *D:* George Waggner; *W:* Curt Siodmak; *C:* Joseph Valentine; *M:* Charles Previn, Hans J. Salter, Frank Skinner.

Wolf Trap 🐾🐾
Vlci Jama 1957 Trapped indeed—small town veterinarian is suffocating in a marriage to an older, domineering and needy wife. The two adopt an orphaned teenager, which turns out to be a big mistake as the unhappy husband gradually falls in love with the girl. Czech with subtitles. **95m/C VHS. CZ** Jiriinaova Stajinova, Jana Brejchova, Miroslav Dolezal, Jaroslav Pucha; *D:* Jiri Weiss; *W:* Jiri Weiss; *C:* Vaclav Hanus.

Wolfen 🐾🐾🐾
1981 (R) Surrealistic menace darkens this original and underrated tale of super-intelligent wolf creatures terrorizing NYC. Police detective Finney tries to track down the beasts before they kill again. Notable special effects in this thriller, which covers environmental and Native American concerns while maintaining the tension. Feature film debuts of Hines and Venora. Based on the novel by Whitley Strieber. **115m/C VHS, DVD.** Albert Finney, Gregory Hines, Tom Noonan, Diane Venora, Edward James Olmos, Dick O'Neill, Dehl Berti, Peter Michael Goetz, Sam Gray, Ralph Bell; *D:* Michael Wadleigh; *W:* Michael Wadleigh, David Eyre; *C:* Gerry Fisher; *M:* James Horner.

Wolfheart's Revenge 🐾
1925 An honest cowboy, helped by Wolfheart the Wonder Dog, steps in when a sheep rancher is murdered. Silent film with original organ score. **64m/B VHS.** S.J. Bingham, Kathleen Collins, Larry Fisher, Helen Walton, Guinn "Big Boy" Williams; *D:* Charles Seeling.

The Wolfman 🐾
1982 Colin Glasgow is summoned back to his family manor to attend the funeral of his father. Unbeknownst to Colin, his father was actually murdered by his children who are in thrall to a Satanist priest. The family stalls Colin, hoping their father's "curse" will be passed on to him at the next full moon. It does, and Colin turns into a werewolf and begins a small rural rampage. Extremely amateurish "Dark Shadows" vein. The sets and models look flimsy and the acting is like that of a bad stage-play. **102m/C VHS, DVD.** Earl Owensby, Kristina Reynolds, Sid Rancker, Julian Morton; *D:* Worth Keeter; *W:* Worth Keeter; *C:* Darrell Cathcart; *M:* David Floyd, Arthur Smith.

Wolverine 🐾🐾
Code Name: Wolverine **1996 (R)** Former Navy SEAL Harry Gordini (Sabato Jr.) and his family are vacationing in Italy where he becomes an unwitting drug smuggler. After the drug cartel kidnaps his wife and son, Harry uses his training to attempt a rescue before the authorities intervene. Based on the book by Frederick Forsyth. Supplies the required action quotient. **91m/C VHS, DVD.** Antonio Sabato Jr., Richard Brooks, Traci Lind, Daniel Quinn; *D:* David S. Jackson; *W:* Robert T. Megginson; *C:* Denis Maloney; *M:* Christopher Franke. **TV**

The Wolves 🐾🐾🐾
1971 Gosha shows the world of the yakuza (gangster) during the 1920s. Reminiscent of the samurai, the movie combines ancient Japanese culture with the rapidly changing world of 20th century Japan. In Japanese with English subtitles. **131m/C VHS. JP** Tatsuya Nakadai, Noboru Ando, Komake Kurihara, Kyoko Enami, Isao Natsuyagi; *D:* Hideo Gosha; *W:* Hideo Gosha; *C:* Masaru Sato.

The Wolves 🐾🐾
1995 (PG-13) Blackie (Dalton) and his sister Barbara (Hocking) have inherit some land in the Alaskan wilderness wants to use as a toxic waste dump. But when Blackie befriends native guide Chilkoot (Cardinal) and rescues an injured wolf, he decides to fight King and his henchmen. **87m/C VHS.** Darren Dalton, Kristen Dalton, Raymond Harmstorf, Ben Cardinal, John Furey; *D:* Steve Carver; *W:* Stephen Peters, Art Bernd; *C:* Eugene Shlugleit.

The Wolves of Kromer 🐾🐾
1998 A modern-day fairytale set in the rural English town of Kromer. The hypocritical townspeople are mean-spirited gossips who look down upon the local wolf population (in this case very attractive young human/beasts in fur coats and long tails). Seth (Williams) has just "come out" as a wolf and fallen for promiscuous Gabriel (Layton). Meanwhile, two servants plot to point accusing their cruel mistress and plan to point accusing their cruel mistress and plan to poison the human populace the excuse they need for violence. Based on the play by Lambert, who wrote the screenplay. **77m/C VHS, DVD.** GB Lee Williams, James Layton, Rita Davies, Margaret Towner, Rosemary Dunham, Angharad Rees, Kevin Moore, Leila Lloyd-Evelyn, Matthew Dean, David Prescott; *D:* Will Gould; *W:* Charles Lambert, Matthew Read; *C:* Laura Remacha; *M:* Basil Moore-Asfouri; *Nar:* Boy George.

A Woman and a Woman 🐾🐾🐾
1980 Covers a ten-year period in the friendship of Barbara and Irena and how it survives their professional and personal conflicts. In Polish with English subtitles. **99m/C VHS.** PL Halina Labonarska, Anna Romantowska; *D:* Richard Bugajski.

A Woman at Her Window 🐾🐾🐾
Une Femme a sa Fentre **1977** Aristocratic, jaded Margot (Schneider), the wife of dissolute nobleman Rico (Orsini), is pursued by capitalistic businessman Raoul (Noiret). But Margot herself is taken by idealistic Michel (Lanoux), a communist evading the secret police in 1936 Greece, and has a daughter from their brief and ultimately tragic union. Years later, Margot's now-grown daughter returns to Greece to learn more about her parents. Adapted from the novel by Pierre Drieu La Rochelle. French with subtitles. **110m/C VHS. FR** Romy Schneider, Philippe Noiret, Victor Lanoux, Umberto Orsini, Delia Boccardo, Gastone Moschin, Carl Mohner; *D:* Pierre Granier-Deferre; *W:* Pierre Granier-Deferre, Jorge Semprun.

A Woman at War 🐾🐾
(PG-13) True-story of a young woman's heroic fight against the Nazis. Nineteen-year-old Helene Moskiewicz (Plimpton) has had her parents arrested by the Gestapo in occupied Brussels, Belgium. She joins the resistance and falls for Franz Boehler (Stoltz), a young businessman who is not above lining his pockets with Nazi profits. When persecution of the Jews intensifies, Helene risks infiltrating Gestapo headquarters in order to save lives. **115m/C VHS.** Martha Plimpton, Eric Stoltz; *D:* Edward Bennett; *W:* Edward Bennett.

A Woman Called Golda 🐾🐾🐾
1982 Political drama following the life and career of Golda Meir, the Israeli Prime Minister and one of the most powerful political figures of the 20th century. Davis portrays the young Golda, Bergman taking over as she ages. Superior TV bio-epic. **192m/C VHS.** Ingrid Bergman, Leonard Nimoy, Anne Jackson, Ned Beatty, Robert Loggia, Judy Davis; *D:* Alan Gibson; *W:* Steven Gethers, Harold Gast. **TV**

A Woman Called Moses 🐾🐾½
1978 The story of Harriet Ross Tubman, who bought her freedom from slavery, founded the underground railroad, and helped lead hundreds of slaves to freedom before the Civil War. Wonderful performance by Tyson but the telefilm is bogged down by a so-so script. Based on the novel by Marcy Heldish. **200m/C VHS, DVD.** Cicely Tyson, Dick Anthony Williams, Will Geer, Robert Hooks, Hari Rhodes, James Wainwright; *D:* Paul Wendkos; *W:* Lonnie Elder III; *M:* Coleridge-Taylor Perkinson. **TV**

Woman Condemned 🐾🐾
1933 A reporter's attempt to clear a woman of murder leads to a mysterious mental hospital run by a mad scientist. Not much to recommend this low-level melodrama, unless you like to see shameless mugging and overacting. **58m/B VHS, DVD.** Mischa Auer, Lola Lane, Claudia Dell, Richard Hemingway, Jason Robards Sr., Louise Beavers, Paul Ellis; *D:* Dorothy Davenport Reid; *W:* Dorothy Davenport Reid, Willis Kent; *C:* James Diamond; *M:* Lee Zahler.

Woman Hater 🐾🐾
1949 Delightful farce about the belief in the single life. Confirmed bachelor plays games with a single woman. They eventually disregard their solitary vows in favor of romance. **101m/B VHS.** Stewart Granger, Edwige Feuillere, Ronald Squire, Mary Jerrold; *D:* Terence Young.

The Woman He Loved 🐾🐾½
1988 The infamous romance of Edward VIII, who gave up the throne of England for American divorcee, Wallis Warfield Simpson. Seymour and Andrews are fine in their roles but the drama is slow-going. **100m/C VHS.** Anthony Andrews, Jane Seymour, Olivia de Havilland, Lucy Gutteridge, Julie Harris, Robert Hardy, Phyllis Calvert; *D:* Charles Jarrott.

A Woman, Her Men and Her Futon 🐾🐾
1992 A beautiful woman tries to find her identity by having a number of lovers but none can satisfy her every need. **90m/C VHS, DVD.** Jennifer Rubin, Lance Edwards, Grant Show, Michael Cerveris, Delaune Michel, Robert Lipton; *D:* Mussef Sibay; *W:* Mussef Sibay; *C:* Michael J. Davis; *M:* Joel Goldsmith.

Woman Hunt 🐾
WOOF! *The Highest Bidder* **1972 (R)** Men kidnap women, then hunt them in the jungle for fun. So deeply offensive, we would give it negative bones if we could. "Hee Haw" bimbo Todd plays a sadistic lesbian. **81m/C VHS.** John Ashley, Lisa Todd, Eddie Garcia, Laurie Rose; *D:* Eddie Romero.

A Woman Hunted 🐾½
2003 (PG-13) Lainie Wheeler's (Paul) car breaks down in the middle of nowhere and she's happy when good samaritan Harry (Higgins) stops and offers her a ride. She shouldn't be. **94m/C DVD.** CA Alexandra Paul, Linden Ashby, Michele Greene, Jonathan Higgins, Maxim Roy; *D:* Morrie Ruvinsky; *W:* Morrie Ruvinsky; *C:* Bruno Philip; *M:* Richard Bowers. **VIDEO**

The Woman Hunter 🐾½
1972 A wealthy woman recovering from a traffic accident in Mexico believes someone is after her for her jewels and possibly her life. Eden dressed well, if nothing else; suspense builds ploddingly to a "Yeah, sure" climax. **73m/C VHS, DVD.** Barbara Eden, Robert Vaughn, Stuart Whitman, Sydney Chaplin, Larry Storch, Enrique Lucero; *D:* Bernard L. Kowalski. **TV**

Woman in Black 🐾🐾🐾
1989 Chilling ghost story set in 1925 and adapted from the novel by Susan Hill. Solicitor Arthur Kidd is sent to a remote house to settle the estate of a client. He's haunted by the mysterious figure of a woman in black, who according to the locals, has put a curse on the village. Arthur's driven close to the edge of sanity by the ghostly figure and the tragedy that haunts the village's past. **100m/C VHS, DVD.** GB Adrian Rawlins, Bernard Hepton, David Daker, Pauline Moran; *D:* Herbert Wise; *W:* Nigel Kneale. **TV**

Woman in Brown 🐾🐾½
The Vicious Circle; The Circle **1948** It's Hungary, 1882, and five Jewish men are on trial for the murder of a man who actually committed suicide. Despite the prejudice and hatred from the locals, their lawyer believes in and fights for their innocence. **77m/B VHS.** Conrad Nagel, Fritz Kortner, Reinhold Schunzel, Philip Van Zandt, Eddie LeRoy, Edwin Maxwell; *D:* W. Lee Wilder.

A Woman in Flames 🐾🐾½
Die Flambierte Frau **1984 (R)** A bored middle-class housewife leaves her overbearing husband and becomes a high-priced prostitute. She has a passionless affair with an aging bisexual gigolo. Dark and dreary tale of human relationships and the role of sex in people's lives. Interesting but depressing. **106m/C VHS.** GE Gudrun Landgrebe, Robert Van Ackeren, Mathieu Carriere, Gabriele Lafari, Hanns Zischler; *D:* Robert Van Ackeren.

The Woman in Green 🐾🐾🐾
Sherlock Holmes and the Woman in Green **1945** Murder victims are found with missing index fingers, and it's up to Holmes and Watson to try to solve this apparently motiveless crime. Available colorized. **68m/B VHS, DVD.** Basil Rathbone, Nigel Bruce, Hillary Brooke, Henry Daniell, Paul Cavanagh, Frederick Worlock, Mary Gordon, Billy Bevan; *D:* Roy William Neill; *W:* Bertram Millhauser; *C:* Virgil Miller.

A Woman in Grey 🐾🐾
1920 A man and a woman battle wits when they attempt to locate and unravel the Army Code while staying one step ahead of J. Haviland Hunter, a suave villain after the same fortune. Silent. **205m/B VHS.** Arline Pretty, Henry Sell, Fred C. Jones, John Heenan, Margaret Fielding, Ann Brody; *D:* James Vincent; *W:* Walter R. Hall.

The Woman in Question 🐾🐾½
1950 When carnival fortune teller Astra (Kent) is murdered, Police Inspector Lodge (MacRae) finds that all her acquaintances have differing views about her character, making his investigation even more difficult. **82m/B VHS.** GB Jean Kent, Dirk Bogarde, Susan Shaw, Duncan MacRae, John McCallum, Hermione Baddeley, Charles Victor, Lana Morris, Vida Hope, Joe Linnane, Duncan Lamont, Bobbie Scroggins, Anthony

The Woman in Red ✶✶½
1984 (PG-13) Executive Wilder's life unravels when he falls hard for stunning Le Brock. Interior Hollywood-ized remake of a French film "Pardon Mon Affaire." Somehow the French ssem to do the sexual farce thing with more verve, but this one has its moments, and Wilder is likeable. Say I Love You: Don't Drive Drunk; It's More Than You; It's You; Love Light in Flight; Moments Aren't Moments; Weakness; Woman in Red. **87m/C VHS, DVD.** Gene Wilder, Charles Grodin, Kelly Le Brock, Gilda Radner, Judith Ivey, Joseph Bologna; **D:** Gene Wilder. **W:** Gene Wilder. **M:** John Morris. Oscars '84: Song ("I Just Called to Say I Love You"); Golden Globes '85: Song ("I Just Called to Say I Love You")

Woman in the Dunes ✶✶✶
Suna No Onna; Woman of the Dunes **1964** Splendid, resonant allegorical drama. A scientist studying insects in the Japanese sand dunes finds himself trapped with a woman in a hut at the bottom of a pit. Superbly directed and photographed (by Hiroshi Segawa). Scripted by Kobo Abe from his acclaimed novel in Japanese with English subtitles. **123m/B VHS, DVD. JP** Eiji Okada, Kyoko Kishida, Koji Mitsui, Hiroko Ito, Sen Yano; **D:** Hiroshi Teshigahara; **W:** Kobe Abe; **C:** Hiroshi Segawa; **M:** Toru Takemitsu. Cannes '64: Grand Jury Prize.

Woman in the Moon ✶✶½ *By Rocket to the Moon; Girl in the Moon* **1929** Assorted people embark on a trip to the moon and discover water, and an atmosphere, as well as gold. Lang's last silent outing is nothing next to "Metropolis," with a rather lame plot (greedy trip dashers seek gold), but interesting as a vision of the future. Lang's prediction is about space travel often hit the mark. Silent with music. **115m/B VHS, DVD. GE** Klaus Pohl, Willy Fritsch, Gustav von Wagenheim, Gerca Maurus; **D:** Fritz Lang.

Woman in the Shadows ✶✶
1934 A ex-con retreats to the woods for serenity and peace, but is assaulted by mysterious women, jealous lovers, and gun-slinging drunks, until he explodes. A man can only take so much. From a Dashiell Hammett story. **70m/B VHS.** Fay Wray, Ralph Bellamy, Melvyn Douglas, Roscoe Ates, Joe King; **D:** Phil Rosen; **C:** Joseph Ruttenberg.

Woman in the Window ✶✶✶
1944 Psycho-melodrama finds staid college professor Richard Wanley straying off the straight and narrow into a world of trouble—thanks to beautiful model Alice (Bennett). She invites him over but when her jealous boyfriend Claude (Loft) arrives unexpectedly, he attacks then both and Richard kills Claude in self-defense. Thinking no one will believe them, and afraid of scandal, the inept duo bury the body in the woods. Too bad Richard's best friend Frank (Massey) is the D.A. Or is there a blackmailer around. Or is there? Surprise ending. Based on the novel "Once Off G.ard" by J.H. Wallis. **99m/B VHS.** Edward G. Robinson, Joan Bennett, Raymond Massey, Arthur Loft, Dan Duryea, Edmund Breon, Dorothy Peterson, Robert (Bobby) Blake. **D:** Fritz Lang; **W:** Nunnally Johnson; **C:** Milton Krasner. **M:** Arthur Lange.

The Woman in White ✶✶½
1997 The happy hours half-sisters, outgoing Marian (Fitzgerald) and shy Laura (Waddell), spend with their eccentric Uncle Fairlie (Fichardson) soon turn sinister when Laura is married off to the seemingly charming Sir Percival Glyde (Wilby). Sir Percival quickly appears to be conspiring with the suspicious Count Fosco (Callow) to take control of Laura's money. When Marian visits her sister, she's alarmed by Laura's decine and equally unnerved by the mysterious woman in white, Anne (Vidler), who seems to know Glyde and tries to warn the sisters of impending danger. Based on the novel "The Moonstone," also wrote "The Moonstone." **120m/C VHS, DVD. GB** Tara Fitzgerald, Justine Waddell, James Dawson, John Boxer, Julian D'Albie, Josephine Middleton, Everley Gregg, Albert Chevalier, Richard Pearson; **D:** Anthony Asquith. **W:** Desmond Dickinson; **M:** John Wooldridge.

Woman Inside ✶✶½ **1983 (R)** Low-budget gender-bender depicts the troubled life of a Vietnam veteran who decides on a sex-change operation to satisfy his inner yearnings. Blondell's unfortunate last role as his/her aunt. Cheesy like Limburger, almost too weird and boring even for camp buffs. **94m/C VHS.** Gloria Manon, Dave Clark, Joan Blondell; **D:** Joseph Van Winkle; **W:** Steve(n) Fisher.

A Woman Is a Woman ✶✶✶
Une Femme Est une Femme; La Donna E Donna **1960** Godard's affectionate sendup of Hollywood musicals is a hilarious comedy about a nightclub dancer (Karina) who desperately wants a baby. When boyfriend Belmondo balks, she asks his best friend Brialy. Much ado is had, with the three leads all splendid. Godard's first film shot in color and cinemascope with great music. In French with English subtitles. **88m/C VHS, DVD. FR** Jean-Claude Brialy, Jean-Paul Belmondo, Anna Karina, Marie DuBois; **D:** Jean-Luc Godard; **W:** Jean-Luc Godard; **C:** Raoul Coutard; **M:** Michel Legrand.

Woman Is the Future of Man ✶✶✶ *Yeojaneun namjaui miraeda* **2004** While meeting for lunch, two old Korean friends Mun-ho (Ji-tae) and Hyeon-gon (Tae-woo) reminisce over too much rice wine about a girl they both dated years before, Seon-hwa (Hyeon-a), and how each regrets mistreating her. Even though the men have moved on with their lives—Mun-ho is a married college art lecturer while Hyeon-gon is a hopeful filmmaker—they decide to visit Seon-hwa but find that life has not gone quite as well for her. In Korean, with English subtitles. **88m/ C DVD.** Yoo Jitae, Kim Taewoo, Sung Hyunah; **D:** Hong Sang-soo; **W:** Hong Seng-soo; **C:** Kim Hyungkoo; **M:** Chong Yongjin.

A Woman Named Jackie ✶✶½ **1991 (PG)** Three-part TV miniseries covering the life of Jacqueline Bouvier Kennedy Onassis. Downey offers a pretty picture as the enigmatic and beleaguered heroine but this version is simplistic at best. Based on the book by C. David Heymann. On three cassettes. **246m/C VHS.** Roma Downey, Stephen Collins, William Devane, Joss Ackland, Rosemary Murphy, Wendy Hughes, Josef Sommer; **D:** Larry Peerce; **W:** Roger O. Hirson. **TV**

The Woman Next Door ✶✶✶
La Femme d'a Cote **1981 (R)** One of Truffaut's last films before his sudden death in 1984. The domestic drama involves a suburban husband who resumes an affair with a tempestuous now-married woman after she moves next door, with domestic complications all around. An insightful, humanistic paean to passion and fidelity by the great artist, though one of his lesser works. Supported by strong outings from the two leads. In French with English subtitles. **106m/C VHS.** FR Gerard Depardieu, Fanny Ardant, Michele Baumgartner, Veronique Silver, Roger Van Hool; **D:** Francois Truffaut; **W:** Suzanne Schiffman; **C:** William Lubtchansky; **M:** Georges Delerue.

A Woman Obsessed ✶ **1988 (R)** Pathetic, over-cooked drama about a woman obsessed with her long-lost son. She finds out husband's true profession, he kills himself and Gilbert comes back, in order to preclude happy ending, she decides the affair wasn't meant to be and expires. Tragically. Silent. **90m/B VHS.** Greta Garbo, John Gilbert, Lewis Stone, Johnny Mack Brown, Douglas Fairbanks Jr., Hobart Bosworth, Dorothy Sebastian; **D:** Clarence Brown.

A Woman of Affairs ✶✶ **1928** Garbo, who can't have the guy she really loves (Gilbert), marries scoundrel. When she finds out husband's true profession, he kills himself and Gilbert comes back, in order to preclude happy ending, she decides the affair wasn't meant to be and expires. Tragically. Silent. **90m/B VHS.** Greta Garbo, John Gilbert, Lewis Stone, Johnny Mack Brown, Douglas Fairbanks Jr., Hobart Bosworth, Dorothy Sebastian; **D:** Clarence Brown.

Woman of Desire ✶ **1993 (R)** First classic Tracy/Hepburn pairing concerns the rocky marriage of a renowned political columnist and a lowly sportswriter. Baseball scene with Hepburn

A femme fatale (Christina Ford (Derek)) is a femme fatale who is yachting with rich boyfriend Ted when there is a terrible storm. Christina,

Willy, Simon Callow, Ian Richardson, Andrew Lincoln, Susan Vidler, John Standing, Conn Redgrave; **D:** Tim Fywell; **W:** David Pirie; **M:** David Ferguson. **TV**

The Woman Inside ✶✶½ **1983 (R)** Low-budget gender-bender depicts the troubled life of a Vietnam veteran who decides on a sex-change operation to satisfy his inner yearnings. Blondell's unfortunate last role as his/her aunt. Cheesy like Limburger, almost too weird and boring even for camp buffs. **94m/C VHS.** Gloria Manon, Dave Clark, Joan Blondell; **D:** Joseph Van Winkle; **W:** Steve(n) Fisher.

A Woman of Distinction ✶✶½ **1950** Slapstick comedy with potential to be ordinary is taken over the top by a good, vivacious cast. Russell, the stuffy Dean of a women's college, is driven to distraction by a reporter linking her romantically with Milland, a visiting professor. **85m/C VHS.** Ray Milland, Rosalind Russell, Edmund Gwenn, Francis Lederer; Cameos: Lucille Ball; **D:** Edward Buzzell.

A Woman of Independent Means ✶✶✶ **1994 (PG)** Leisurely family mini-series, based on the 1979 novel by Elizabeth Forsythe Hailey. Fields stars as the title character, Bess Steed Garner (based on the author's maternal grandmother), a well-off Texas belle who marries childhood sweetheart Robert Steed (Goldwyn) in 1907 and settles down as Beth bears children, Robert tries to make a go of his insurance business, their families interfere, and tragedy strikes. **315m/C VHS.** Sally Field, Tony Goldwyn, Brenda Fricker, Charles Durning, Ron Silver, Sheila McCarthy, Ann Hearn; **D:** Robert Greenwald.

A Woman of Rome ✶✶½ **1964** *La Romana* **1965** Standard Italian star vehicle with Lollobrigida portraying a successful prostitute in Rome who's decided to change her life. Dubbed. **93m/B VHS. IT** Gina Lollobrigida, Daniel Gelin, Franco Fabrizi, Raymond Pellegrin; **D:** Luigi Zampa.

Woman of Straw ✶✶½ **1964** Connery plays off his Bond role with a villainous twist. He's Anthony Richmond, the nephew of dying tycoon Charles Richmond (Richardson), who won't write him into the will. Uncle is very fond of his nurse Anthony. He convinces her to marry the old coot and get him into the will, but Charles dies, leaving her a murder suspect. Compelling thriller does well, despite plot holes, on the strength of performances by Richardson and Connery, portraying members of a family no one would want to see at a reunion. **115m/C VHS.** Sean Connery, Gina Lollobrigida, Ralph Richardson, Alexander Knox, Johnny Sekka, Peter Madden; **D:** Basil Dearden; **W:** Stanley Mann, Michael Relph. **C:** Otto Heller.

A Woman of Substance ✶✶½ **1984** The woman of the title, Emma Harte, rises from poverty to wealth and power through self-discipline, enduring various romantic disappointments and tragedies along the way. Based on the novel by "Hold the Dream." Bradford. Followed by "Barbara Taylor Bradford. Followed by "Hold the Dream." **300m/C VHS, DVD.** Jenny Seagrove, Barry Bostwick, Deborah Kerr, Liam Neeson, Diane Baker, George Baker, Peter Chelsom, Peter Egan, Christopher Gable, Christopher Guard, Gayle Hunnicutt, John Mills, Nicola Pagett, Saskia Reeves, Miranda Richardson; **D:** Don Sharp; **W:** Lee Langley; **C:** Ernest Vincze; **M:** Nigel Hess. **TV**

The Woman of the Town ✶✶½ **1944** Frontier marshal and newspaperman Bat Masterson is portrayed convincingly by Dekker as a very human hero who seeks justice when the woman he loves, a dance hall girl who works in the town for social causes, is killed by an unscrupulous rancher. Fictionalized but realistic western shows "heroes" as good, ordinary people. **90m/B VHS.** Claire Trevor, Albert Dekker, Barry Sullivan, Henry Hull, Porter Hall, Percy Kilbride, George Archainbaud; **M:** Nigel Hess. **TV**

Woman of the Year ✶✶✶

Ted and yacht captain Jack are washed overboard and Jack is found washed ashore with no memory. When Christina Jack gets a lawyer, Walter J. Hill (played by the redoubtable Mitchum) but is he wily enough to discredit the deceitful Christina? Bo's body is once again on display. Also available in an unrated version. **97m/C VHS, DVD.** Bo Derek, Jeff Fahey, Steven Bauer, Robert Mitchum; **D:** Robert Ginty; **W:** Robert Ginty; **C:** Hano Mohr; **M:** Rene Veldsman.

Woman on Top ✶✶½ **2000 (R)** Mildly amusing romantic comedy that's held together by the charm of its lead. Beautiful Brazilian Isabella (Cruz) suffers from extreme motion sickness, which means she must always be in control. She's a whiz in the kitchen and her talents make her husband's (Eenício) restaurant a big success. But Izzie takes off for San Francisco when she discovers Toninho with another gal. Thanks to her culinary skills (and some magical realism), Isabella soon has her own cable cooking show and men (literally) falling at her feet. First there's "Like Water for Chocolate," then "Woman" completes the trifecta of food overwhelming the emotions. **93m/C VHS, DVD.** Penélope Cruz, Harold Perrineau Jr., Mark Feuerstein, Murilo Benício, John de Lancie; **D:** Fina Torres; **W:** Vera Blasi; **C:** Thierry Arbogast; **M:** Luis Bacalov.

A Woman Rebels ✶✶½ **1936** A young Victorian woman challenges Victorian society by fighting for women's rights. Excellent performance from Hepburn lifts what might have been a forgettable drama. Screen debut of Van Heflin. Based on the novel "Portrait of a Rebel." **88m/B VHS.** Katharine Hepburn, Herbert Marshall, Elizabeth Allan, Donald Crisp, Van Heflin; **D:** Mark Sandrich.

Woman, Thou Art Loosed ✶✶½ **2004 (R)** Critics may have been divided on this pic's merits but female audiences gave it strong word-of-mouth support. Based on the self-help novel by charismatic Bishop T.D. Jakes (who plays himself), "Woman" follows the lifelong misfortunes of Michele (a ferocious Elise), a young black victim of poverty, rape, drug addiction, and eventual imprisonment for murder. The flashback structure of the story (Jakes offers a compassionate ear as Michele tells her story) is somewhat distracting, but Foster's script offers multi-dimensional characters even if it's a little self-conscious. **99m/C DVD. Kimberly Elise, Loretta Devine, Debbi (Deborah) Morgan, Michael Boatman, Clifton Powell, Sean Blakemore, Ricky Harris; **D:** Michael A. Schultz; **C:** Reinhart Peschke.

Woman Times Seven ✶✶½ **1967 (PG)** Seven sketches. *Sept Fois Femme; Sette Volte Donna* Italian sexual comedy: seven sketches, each starring MacLaine with a different leading man. Stellar cast and good direction for should have delivered more, but what they have provided has its comedic moments. **99m/C VHS. IT FR** Shirley MacLaine, Peter Sellers, Rossano Brazzi, Vittorio Gassman, Lex Barker, Elsa Martinelli, Robert Morey, Alan Arkin, Michael Caine, Patrick Wymark, Anita Ekberg, Philippe Noiret, Elspeth March; **D:** Vittorio De Sica.

A Woman under the Influence ✶✶✶ **1974 (R)** Strong performances highlight this overlong drama about a family's disintegration. Rowlands is the lonely, middle-aged housewife who's having a breakdown and can't handle what's going on. Falk is her blue-collar husband who can't handle what have provided has its comedic moments. **147m/C VHS, DVD.** Gena Rowlands, Peter Falk, Matthew Cassel, Matthew Laborteaux, Christina Grisanti; **D:** John Cassavetes. Golden Globes '75: Actress (Rowlands); Natl Bd. of Review '74: Actress (Rowlands); Natl Film Reg. '90.

at her first game is delightful. Hilarious, rich entertainment that tries to answer the question "What really matters in life?" Tracy and Hepburn began a close friendship that paralleled their quarter-century celluloid partnership. Hepburn shepherded Kanin and Lardner's Oscar-winning script past studio chief Louis B. Mayer, wearing four-inch heels to press her demands. Mayer caved in, Tracy was freed from making "The Yearling," and the rest is history. **114m/B VHS, DVD.** Spencer Tracy, Katharine Hepburn, Fay Bainter, Dan Tobin, Reginald Owen, Roscoe Karns, William Bendix, Minor Watson; **D:** George Stevens; **W:** Ring Lardner Jr., Michael Kanin; **C:** Joseph Ruttenberg; **M:** Franz Waxman. Oscars '42: Orig. Screenplay, Natl. Film Reg. '99.

Woman Undone 🦴🦴½ 1995 (R) *Joshua Tree* Husband Allen Hansen (Quaid) and wife Terri (McDonnell) are involved in a car crash on a lonely stretch of desert highway. He dies, she's thrown clear, but an autopsy reveals he was actually shot in the head before the accident. Then attorney Ross Bishop (Elliott) gets involved and in a California courtroom Terri must prove that her unhappy marriage wasn't ended by murder. **91m/C VHS.** Mary McDonnell, Randy Quaid, Sam Elliott, Benjamin Bratt; *D:* Evelyn Purcell; *W:* William Mickelberry; *C:* Toyomichi Kurita; *M:* Daniel Licht.

Woman Wanted 🦴🦴 1998 (R) Vivacious Emma Riley (Hunter) is hired by as a live-in housekeeper by widowed professor Richard Goddard (Moriarty) and his troubled son Wendell (Sutherland). Both men fall in love with her and Emma, who loves Richard, nevertheless has a one-nighter with Wendell. Then she winds up pregnant. Rather yakky but these are actors who are worth watching. Based on the novel by Glass, who also wrote the screenplay. **110m/C VHS, DVD.** Holly Hunter, Michael Moriarty, Kiefer Sutherland, Jeanne Gail; *D:* Kiefer Sutherland; *W:* Joanna McClelland Glass. **CABLE**

The Woman Who Came Back 🦴🦴 1945 A young woman who believes she suffers from a witch's curse returns to her small hometown with unhappy results. Good cast; bad script. Indifference inducing. **69m/B VHS, DVD.** Nancy Kelly, Otto Kruger, John Loder, Ruth Ford, Jeanne Gail; *D:* Walter Colmes; *W:* Dennis J. Cooper, Lee Willis; *C:* Henry Sharp; *M:* Edward Plumb.

The Woman Who Loved Elvis 🦴1½ 1993 (PG-13) TV movie about an obsessive fan who converts her home into an Elvis shrine. **7m/C VHS, DVD.** Roseanne, Tom Arnold, Cynthia Gibb, Sally Kirkland, Danielle Harris, Joe Guzaldo; *D:* Bill Bixby. **TV**

The Woman Who Willed a Miracle 🦴🦴 1983 TV drama has a devoted mother encouraging her mentally retarded son to pursue his interest in the piano. **72m/C VHS.** Cloris Leachman, James Noble; *D:* Sharron Miller. **TV**

Woman with a Past 🦴🦴½ 1992 (PG-13) Reed gets out of an abusive marriage only to have her ex kidnap their kids. Since the law's no help she hires a bounty hunter to find them—committing armed robbery to pay the fees. Caught and imprisoned, Reed escapes, changes her identity, remarries, and even is reunited with her sons. Then she's suddenly arrested when her fugitive status comes to light 10 years later. Based on a true story, made for TV melodrama. **95m/C VHS.** Pamela Reed, Dwight Schultz, Paul LeMat, Carrie Snodgress, Richard Lineback; *D:* Mimi Leder. **TV**

A Woman Without Love 🦴🦴 1951 A rarely seen film from Buñuel's Mexican period based on a classic Guy de Maupassant tale about a forbidden romance. Family tragedy results later when the husband "misbequeaths" his fortune. Minor but fascinating bug-the-bourgeoisie Buñuel. In Spanish with English subtitles. **91m/C VHS.** MX Rosario Granados, Julio Villareal, Tito Junco; *D:* Luis Buñuel.

A Woman's a Helluva Thing 🦴🦴 2001 (R) Lewd men's magazine publisher Houston loses his macho swagger when he heads home for his mother's funeral and learns that not only did she have a lesbian lover but that it's his ex-girlfriend, and that she stands to inherit the entire estate. **94m/C VHS, DVD.** Angus MacFadyen, Penelope Ann Miller, Ann-Margret, Kathryn Harrold, Mary Kay Place, Barry Del Sherman, Paul Dooley, Jonas Chernick, John Robinson; *D:* Karen Leigh Hopkins; *W:* Karen Leigh Hopkins; *C:* Barry Parrell; *M:* Louis Febre, Thomas Kilzer. **VIDEO**

A Woman's Face 🦴🦴🦴 1938 *En Kvinnas Ansikte* An unpleasant, bitter woman with a hideous scar on her face blackmails illicit lovers as a form of revenge for a happiness she doesn't know. She even plots to murder a child for his inheritance. But after plastic surgery, she becomes a nicer person and doubts her plan. Lean, tight suspense with a bang-up finale. In Swedish with English subtitles. Remade in Hollywood in 1941. **100m/B VHS.** SW Ingrid Bergman, Anders Henrikson, Karin Carlsson, Georg Rydeberg, Goran Bernhard, Tore Svennberg; *D:* Gustaf Molander.

A Woman's Face 🦴🦴🦴 1941 A physically and emotionally scarred woman becomes part of a blackmail ring. Plastic surgery restores her looks and her attitude. Begins with a murder trial and told in flashbacks; tight, suspenseful remake of the 1938 Swedish Ingrid Bergman vehicle. Climax will knock you out of your chair. **107m/B VHS, DVD.** Joan Crawford, Conrad Veidt, Melvyn Douglas, Osa Massen, Reginald Owen, Albert Bassermann, Marjorie Main, Donald Meek, Charles Quigley, Henry Daniell, George Zucco, Robert Warwick; *D:* George Cukor; *W:* Donald Ogden Stewart, Elliot Paul; *C:* Robert Planck; *M:* Bronislau Kaper.

A Woman's Guide to Adultery 🦴🦴½ 1993 Four female friends, living and working in London, find their lives turned upside down by their passions for unavailable men. Political advisor Jo (Donohoe) is involved with married politician Martin (McElhinney) while art tutor Jennifer (Gillies) wants her student David (Morrissey), despite his having a live-in girlfriend. Ad execs Helen (Lacey) and Michael (Dunbar) find their marriage in tatters when Helen admits to an affair with their boss and photographer Rose (Russell) breaks her own rule about adultery by getting involved with married university instructor Paul (Bean). Based on the novel by Carol Clewlow. Made for TV. **145m/C VHS, DVD.** GB Theresa Russell, Amanda Donohoe, Sean Bean, Adrian Dunbar, Ingrid Lacey, Fiona Gillies, Neil Morrissey, Danny (Daniel) Webb, Ian McElhinney, Julie Peasgood, Caroline Lee-Johnson; *D:* David Hayman; *W:* Frank Cottrell-Boyce; *M:* Daemion Barry. **TV**

A Woman's Secret 🦴🦴 1949 O'Hara admits to murder she didn't commit. Why? It's as indiscernible as why the plot should be muddled by flashbacks. RKO lost big bucks on this one. **85m/B VHS.** Maureen O'Hara, Melvyn Douglas, Gloria Grahame, Bill Williams, Victor Jory, Jay C. Flippen; *D:* Nicholas Ray; *W:* Herman J. Mankiewicz.

A Woman's Tale 🦴🦴🦴 1992 (PG-13) The superlative performance of Florence highlights this look at aging and death. Martha, 78, has been diagnosed with terminal lung cancer. She is looked after by a much-younger nurse and in turn looks after the older friends who share her apartment house. This gentle story quietly depicts the feisty, joyous Martha's last days and the simple pleasures she derives from her remaining time. Florence herself died from cancer not long after completing the film. **94m/C VHS.** AU Sheila Florance, Gosia Dobrowolska, Norman Kaye, Chris Haywood, Myrtle Woods, Ernest Gray, Monica Maughan, Bruce Myles, Alex Menglet; *D:* Paul Cox; *W:* Paul Cox. Australian Film Inst. '91: Actress (Florance).

A Woman's World 🦴🦴🦴 1954 Slick, sophisticated look at big business in the '50s, with Webb as the boss who chooses his next general manager based on the suitability of the executive's wives. Beautiful costumes, witty dialogue, and good acting make this worthwhile viewing. Plus, film offers a nostalgic look at Fifth Avenue, Macy's, Park Avenue, and the long-gone Stork Club. Based on a story by Mona Williams. **94m/C VHS.** Clifton Webb, June Allyson, Van Heflin, Lauren Bacall, Fred MacMurray, Arlene Dahl, Cornel Wilde, Elliott Reid, Margalo Gillmore, Alan Reed, David Hoffman, George Melford; *D:* Jean Negulesco; *W:* Claude Binyon, Richard Sale, Mary Loos, Howard Lindsay, Russel Crouse; *C:* Joe MacDonald; *M:* Cyril Mockridge.

Wombling Free 🦴🦴🦴 1977 An English girl makes friends with a race of tiny, litter-hating furry creatures called Wombles. The creatures are visible only to the little girl because she is the only one who believes. Together they try to clean up a dirty world. British society is less cutting-edge about social roles, etc. than our enlightened one; be prepared for retrograde characterizations. Fun scene with Kelly-Astaire-style dance number. **86m/C VHS.** GB Bonnie Langford, David Tomlinson; *D:* Lionel Jeffries; *M:* George Bassman.

The Women 🦴🦴🦴½ 1939 A brilliant adaptation of the Clare Boothe Luce stage comedy about a group of women who destroy their best friends' reputations at various social gatherings. Crawford's portrayal of the nasty husband-stealer is classic, and the fashion-show scene in Technicolor is one not to miss. Hilarious bitchiness all around. Remade semi-musically as "The Opposite Sex." Another in that long list of stellar 1939 pics. **133m/B VHS, DVD.** Norma Shearer, Joan Crawford, Rosalind Russell, Joan Fontaine, Mary Boland, Lucile Watson, Margaret Dumont, Paulette Goddard, Ruth Hussey, Marjorie Main; *D:* George Cukor; *W:* Anita Loos; *C:* Joseph Ruttenberg. Natl. Film Reg. '07.

The Women 🦴🦴½ 1969 *Les Femmes; The Vixen* 1968 Plodding romantic comedy about a blocked writer and his muse. Dizzy Clara (Bardot) is secretary to middle-aged womanizer Jerome (Ronet), who is attempting to work on his memoirs. Inspired by her beauty, Jerome sets out to seduce Clara, which also reinvigorates his writing. But he's thinking fling and she's thinking something more permanent. French with subtitles. **86m/C VHS, DVD.** FR IT Brigitte Bardot, Maurice Ronet, Anny (Annie Legras) Duperey, Jean-Pierre Marielle, Christina Holme; *D:* Jean Aurel; *W:* Jean Aurel, Cecil Saint-Laurent; *C:* Claude Lecomte; *M:* Luis Fuentes Jr.

Women & Men: In Love There Are No Rules 🦴🦴½ 1991 (R) Extravaganza chronicling the relationships of three couples, each adapted from the short story of a renowned author. Irwin Shaw's "Return to Kansas City" tells of a young boxer who is prematurely pushed into a match by his ambitious wife. In Carson McCullers' "A Domestic Dilemma," a marriage begins to crumble thanks to an alcoholic wife. Finally, Henry Miller's "Mara" has an aging man and a young Parisian prostitute spending a revealing evening together. **90m/C VHS.** Matt Dillon, Kyra Sedgwick, Ray Liotta, Juliette Binoche, Jerry Stiller; *D:* Kristi Zea, Walter Bernstein, Mike Figgis. **CABLE**

Women & Men 2: Stories of Seduction 🦴🦴½ 1990 Three famous short stories are brought to the screen in this made-for-TV collection. Mary McCarthy's "Hills Like White Elephants" between them cover every aspect of male-female relationships. Since there are three casts and three directors, there is little to join the stories in style, calling attention to some flaws in pacing and acting ability; still, Dorothy Parker's "Dusk Before Fireworks," and Hemingway's "Hills Like White Elephants" between... **90m/C VHS, DVD.** James Woods, Melanie Griffith, Peter Weller, Elizabeth McGovern, Beau Bridges, Molly Ringwald; *D:* Ken Russell, Tony Richardson, Frederic Raphael.

Women from the Lake of Scented Souls 🦴🦴 1994 Mournful film, set in a rural Chinese village, focuses on matriarchal businesswoman Xiang (Gaowa), who runs the local sesame oil making factory that has just attracted the attention of Japanese investors. Seems the water of the nearby lotus-covered lake, scene of local tragedies, is Xiang's special ingredient. With her new-found wealth, Xiang is able to purchase a very reluctant bride, Huanhuan (Yujuan), for her mentally retarded son—a disaster in the making. Rich detail and nuanced performances; Chinese with subtitles. **105m/C VHS, DVD.** CH Siqin Gaowa, Wu Yujuan, Lei Luosheng, Chen Baoguo; *D:* Xie Fei; *W:* Xie Fei; *C:* Bao Xianran; *M:* Wang Liping.

Women in Cell Block 7 WOOF! *Diario Segreto Di Un Carcere Femminele* 1977 (R) Exploitative skinfest about women in prison suffering abuse from their jailers and each other. Seems that one of the prisoners knows the location of massive heroin stash. Badly dubbed. **100m/C VHS, DVD.** IT BR Suzanne Carvalho, Gloria Cristal, Zeni Pereira, Leonardo Jose; *D:* Michele Massimo Tarantini; *W:* Michele Massimo Tarantini; *C:* Edson Batista; *M:* Remo Usai.

Women in Fury WOOF! 1984 A woman is sentenced to imprisonment in a mostly lesbian Brazilian jail, and subsequently leads a breakout. **94m/C VHS, DVD.** IT BR...

Women in Love 🦴🦴🦴 1970 (R) Atmospheric drama of two steamy affairs, based on D.H. Lawrence's classic novel. Forward-thinking artist Gudrun (Jackson) and her teacher sister Ursula (Linden) are introduced to Gerald (Reed) and Rupert (Bates). The more conventional Ursual and Rupert marry while Gudrun and Gerald have an affair that ends violently when Gudrun takes up with another man. Deservedly Oscar-winning performance by Jackson; controversial nude wrestling scene with Bates and Reed is hard to forget. Followed nearly two decades later (1989) by a "prequel," "The Rainbow," also from Lawrence, also directed by Russell and featuring Jackson. **129m/C VHS, DVD.** GB Glenda Jackson, Jennie Linden, Alan Bates, Oliver Reed, Michael Gough, Eleanor Bron, Vladek Sheybal; *D:* Ken Russell; *W:* Larry Kramer; *C:* Billy Williams; *M:* Georges Delerue. Oscars '70: Actress (Jackson); Golden Globes '71: Foreign Film; Natl. Bd. of Review '70: Actress (Jackson); N.Y. Film Critics '70: Actress (Jackson); Natl. Soc. Film Critics '70: Actress (Jackson).

Women in Prison 🦴🦴 1970 (R) *Women without Names* 1949 A pseudo-documentary style expose of the hardships endured by women in Italian detention camps following WWII. Controversial for its examination of such themes as human rights, abortion, lesbianism, and sexuality. English, French, Italian, with English subtitles. **72m/B VHS.** IT Simone Simon; *D:* Geza Radvanyi; *W:* Geza Radvanyi.

Women of All Nations 🦴🦴 1931 Buddies in the Marines, Quirt and Flagg (McLaglen and Lowe) fought together in WWI and Panama and are post-war buddies stateside in New York, but now they find themselves fighting for the love of the beautiful Else, whom they meet in Sweden. But first they go to Nicaragua to help earthquake victims. After that, strangely, they're off to Egypt where Else's somehow gotten herself a spot in Prince Hassan's (Lugosi) harem. Apparently Humphrey Bogart was in this film, but all his scenes were cut. **72m/B VHS.** Victor McLaglen, Edmund Lowe, Greta Nissen, El Brendel; *D:* Raoul Walsh; *W:* Maxwell Anderson.

The Women of Brewster Place 🦴🦴 1989 Seven black women living in a tenement fight to gain control of their lives. (Men in general don't come out too well.) Excellent, complex script gives each actress in a fine ensemble headed by Winfrey (in her TV dramatic debut) time in the limelight. Pilot for the series "Brewster Place." Based on the novel by Gloria Naylor. Winfrey was executive producer. **180m/C VHS, DVD.** Oprah Winfrey,

Women of the Prehistoric Planet woof! 1966 On a strange planet, the members of a space rescue mission face deadly perils. Typical bad sci-fi of its era, not of the planet in question. See if you can last long enough to catch the amazing plot twist at the end. 87m/C VHS. John Agar, Wendell Ccrey, Irene Tsu, Adam Roarke, Merry Anders; **D:** Arthur C. Pierce.

Women of Valor 𝒹𝒹½ 1986 During WWII, a band of American nurses stationed in the Philippines are captured by the Japanese and struggle to survive in a brutal POW camp. TV feature was made 43 years too late, adding up to a surreal experience. 95m/C VHS. **D:** DVD. Susan Sarandon, Kristy McNichol, Alberta Watson, Valerie Mahaffey, Suzanne Lederer, Pat Eistrop, Terry O'Quinn, Neva Patterson; **D:** Buzz Kulik; **C:** Mike Fash; **M:** Georges Delerue. TV

The Women on the Roof 𝒹𝒹 1989 Kvinnorna på Taket 1989. Nava Linnea (Doms) rents an artic apartment in Stockholm, just before the start of WWI. Her neighbor is a anna (Bergstrom), an artist working on a tableau that soon involves Linnea, as the women become friends and then lovers. The reappearance of Anna's former boyfriend Willy (Skarsgard) leads to a menage a trois until an accident compels Anna to reveal secrets that alter their lives. Swedish with subtitles. 86m/C VHS. Helena Bergstrom, Amanda Doms, Stellan Skarsgard; **D:** Carl-Gustaf Nykvist; **W:** Carl-Gustaf Nykvist, Lasse Summanen; **C:** Jorgen Persson, Ulf Brantas.

Women on the Verge of a Nervous Breakdown 𝒹𝒹𝒹½ 1988 Mujeres al Borde de un Ataque de Nervios 1988 (R) Surreal and hilarious rom3 through the lives of film dubber Maura, ner ex-lover, his crazed wife, his new lover, his son, and his son's girlfriend. There's also Maura's friend Barranco, who inadvertantly gets Almodovar to American audiences. Introduced Almodovar to American audiences. In Spanish with English subtitles. 88m/C VHS. DVD. SP Carmen Maura, Fernando Guillen, Julieta Serrano, Maria Barranco, Rossy de Palma, Antonio Banderas; **C:** Jose Luis Alcaine; **M:** Bernardo Bonezzi. N.Y. Film Critics '88. Foreign Film.

Women Unchained woof! 1972 (R) Five women escape from a maximum security prison and make a run for the Mexican border, shunning civilized behavior along the way. Much less-than-honorable entry in desperate women genre. 82m/C VHS. Carolyn Judd, Teri Guzman, Darlene Mattingly, Angel Colbert, Bonita Kaem; **D:** Kent Osborne; **W:** Kent Osborne.

Women vs. Men 𝒹𝒹 2002 (R) Michael (Mantegna) is a typical married guy bewildered when Dana (Laht), his wife of 20 years, begins behaving out of character. (She's basically fed up with her hubby and their boring marriage.) His best bud Bruce (Reiser) decides they should go to a strip club and commiserate but doesn't know that Dana is following them. Furious, Dana reports the guys' sleazy night out to Bruce's wife, Brita (Headley). Equally peeved, they kick their husbands out, leaving Michael and Bruce to get advice from their swinger divorcec buddy Nick (Pastorelli). Basic battle-of-the-sexes flick. 88m/C VHS. DVD. Joe Mantegna. Christine Laht, Paul Reiser, Glenne Heady, Jennifer Coolidge. Robert Pastorelli, Marshall Herskovitz, Jon Pollto; **D:** Chazz Palmteri. **W:** David J. Burke. CABLE.

Women's Club 𝒹½ 1987 (R) Tabie-turning sex comedy about a wealthy matron who patronizes a talented (?) young movie writer, but really wants—you know what. She begins lending his services to friends—and does he ever get worn out! This excuse may be intended to be uproarious, but it's hard to tell. And all that sex gets very perfunctory after awhile. 89m/C VHS. Michael Pare, Maud Adams, Eddie Velez; **D:** Sandra Weintraub; **M:** Paul Antonelli.

Women's Prison 𝒹𝒹𝒹 1985 Four male convicts temporarily detained at a women's prison (why?) violently take hostages and generally make trouble for the author-ties and the women. Horribly dubbed. 89m/C VHS. DVD. Henry Genser, Lorraine (De Settel, De Selle, Francis Perrol, Ursula Flores, Gabriele Tinti; **D:** Gilbert Roussel.

Women's Prison Escape 𝒹½ Cell Block Girls; Thunder County 1974 Four tough broads blow the pen and are forced to high-tail it through the Everglades. They can't decide which is worse, the snakes and gators, or the corrupt and sleazy life they left behind. Only cinematic pairing of Rooney and Lurch. 90m/C VHS. DVD. Ted Cassidy, Chris Robinson, Mickey Rooney; **D:** Chris Robinson.

Wonder Boys 𝒹𝒹𝒹 2000 (R) Curtis Hanson's excellent follow up to "L.A. Confidential" pits professor and former literary star Grady (Douglas in hs finest performance in years) against a strange case of writer's block, his flamboyant New York editor (Downey), an approaching mid-life crises. His wife's just left, he's having an affair with the school chancellor (McDormand), who's the wife of his boss, and has just informed him that she's pregnant, and his prize pupil is a death-obsessed compulsive liar (Maguire) who shoots his boss's dog and steals a valuable piece of memorabilia. On paper it seems chaotic, but the screwball comedy manages to be subtle and understated. Based on Michael Chambon's novel. 112m/C VHS. DVD. Michael Douglas, Tobey Maguire, Frances McDormand, Katie Holmes, Robert Downey Jr., Richard Thomas, Rip Torn, Philip Bosco, Jane Adams; **D:** Curtis Hanson; **W:** Steven Kloves; **C:** Dante Spinotti; **M:** Christopher Young. Oscars '00: Song ("Things Have Changed"); Golden Globes '01: Song ("Things Have Changed").

Wonder Man 𝒹𝒹½ 1945 When a brash nightclub entertainer (Kaye) is killed by gangsters, his mild-mannered twin brother (Kaye) takes his place to smoke out the killers. One of Kaye's better early films. The film debuts of Vera-Ellen and Virginia Mayo. 98m/C VHS. DVD. Danny Kaye, Virginia Mayo, Vera-Ellen, Steve Cochran, S.Z. Sakall, Otto Kruger, Natalie Schafer; **D:** H. Bruce Humberstone; **W:** Jack Jevne, Eddie Moran, Don Hartman, Melville Shavelson, Philip Rapp; **C:** Victor Milner; **M:** Ray Heindorf.

The Wonderful Ice Cream Suit 𝒹½ 1998 (PG) Slapstick hokum based on Bradbury's 1957 story "The Magic White Suit" Cash-poor barrio sharpster Gomez (Mantegna) would like to buy a flashy white suit he sees in a shop window and manages to convince four more men of roughly the same size to pony up some money and have shares in the suit. Each take a turn wearing the garment and find their various dreams coming true. 77m/C VHS. Joe Mantegna, Esai Morales, Edward James Olmos, Clifton (Gonzalez) Collins Jr., Gregory Sierra, Liz Torres, Sid Caesar, Howard Morris, Lisa Vidal, Mike Moroff; **D:** Stuart Gordon; **W:** Ray Bradbury; **C:** Mac Ahlberg.

The Wonderful World of the Brothers Grimm 𝒹𝒹½ 1962 Big-budget fantasy based very loosely on the Grimm Brothers' lives and three of their stories: "The Dancing Princesses," "The Cobbler and the Elves," and "The Singing Bone." Good, fun Puppetoon scenes, but leaves much else to be desired. A mega-watt cast and the ubiquitous hand of producer-director Pal are not enough to cover the flaws. The biographical parts are ho-

Wonderland 𝒹𝒹 1999 Slice of London pic covers four November days in the lives of sisters Debbie (Henderson), Nadia (McKee), and Molly (Parker) and their daily struggles—single, pregnant, and—dates, pregnancy, separation, unemployment, and their equally frustrated parents. Yet the film is about the ability to survive rather than about succumbing to despair, loring the relationship between Sharon and Dawn, who became life-long friends. The anatomically gifted Holmes is adequately portrayed by Kilmer. Told in confused, back and forward chronology, events and motivations muddle an interesting story much better articulated in director Anderson's fictitious but far superior odb to the porn industry, "Boogie Nights" 99m/C VHS. DVD. US Val Kilmer, Kate (Catherine) Bosworth, Lisa Kudrow, Dylan McDermott, Eric Bogosian, Josh(ua) Lucas, Christina Applegate, Tim Blake Nelson, Ted Levine, Natasha Gregson Wagner, Janeane Garofalo, Franky G., M.C. Gainey, Carrie Fisher, Faizon Love; **D:** James Cox; **W:** James Cox, Captain Mauzner, Todd Samovitz, D. Loriston Scott; **C:** Michael Grady; **M:** Michael A. Levine.

Wonderland Cove 𝒹 1975 Seafaring adventurer adopts five orphan children and embarks on journeys to exotic locales. 78m/C Clu Gulager, Sean Marshall, Randi Kiger, Lori Walsh; **D:** Jerry Thorpe.

The Wonders of Aladdin 𝒹½ Les Mille Et Une Nuits; Le Meraviglie Di Alaaino 1961 Slapstick comedy based on the ancient rubbed-lamp-and-genie chestnut. Kids'll love it; adults will yawn. 93m/C VHS. DVD. Donald O'Connor, Vittorio De Sica; **D:** Henry Levin, Mario Bava.

Wonderwall: The Movie 𝒹 1969 Bizarre characters trip over themselves in love while groovy music plays in background. 82m/C VHS. DVD. GB Jack MacGowran, Jane Birkin, Irene Handl; **D:** Joe Massot; **C:** Henry Waxman; **M:** George Harrison, Eric Clapton, Ravi Shankar.

Wondrous Oblivion 𝒹𝒹𝒹 2006 (PG) Though 11-year-old David (Smith) loves the sport of cricket, he lacks the skills, so when a cricket-loving Jamaican family moves in next door he's overjoyed. The family's patriarch, Dennis Samuels (Lindo) offers to teach him. While the young Jewish boy at first has no qualms about befriending the Samuels, the rest of their South London neighbors aren't so

key, and the tales used are the wrong ones. Disappointing but historically interesting. The second-ever story film done in Cinerama. ♫The Theme From the Wonderful World of the Brothers Grimm; Gypsy Rhapsody; Christmas Land; Ah-Oom; Above the Stars; Dee-Are-A-Gee-O-En (Dragon). 134m/C VHS. Laurence Harvey, Karlheinz Boehm, Claire Bloom, Buddy Hackett, Terry-Thomas, Russ Tamblyn, Yvette Mimieux, Oscar Homolka, Walter Slezak, Beulah Bondi, Martita Hunt, Otto Kruger, Barbara Eden, Jim Backus, Arnold Stang; **D:** Henry Levin, George Pal; **W:** William Roberts; **C:** Paul Vogel. Oscars '62: Costume Des. (C).

Wonderland 𝒹𝒹𝒹 1996 Campy thriller follows two young gay boys in England, inadvertent witnesses to a murder, who find themselves on the run. Fast paced, dreamy atmosphere makes up for the sometimes confusing plot. Often overlooked British import. 103m/C VHS. GB Emile Charles, Tony Forsyth, Robert Stephens, Clare Higgins, Bruce Payne, Ritchie Coltrane, Philip Saville; **W:** Frank Carke; **C:** Dick Pope; **M:** Hans Zimmer.

Wonderland 𝒹𝒹 2003 (R) Inferior true-crime drama about down-on-his-luck, druggie porn star John C. Holmes (Kilmer) who got mixed up in a 1981 quadruple homicide at 8763 Wonderland Avenue, where Holmes partied and bought his drugs. Kudrow, in a standout performance, plays his long-suffering wife Sharon and Bosworth his much-younger girlfriend Dawn. While emphasis is on the crime and what role Holmes played in it, pic may have benefited from further exploration in the relationship between Sharon and Dawn, who became life-long friends. The anatomically gifted Holmes is adequately portrayed by Kilmer. Told in confused, back and forward chronology, events and motivations muddle an interesting story much better articulated in director Anderson's fictitious but far superior odb to the porn industry, "Boogie Nights" 99m/C VHS. DVD. US Val Kilmer, Kate (Catherine) Bosworth, Lisa Kudrow, Dylan McDermott, Eric Bogosian, Josh(ua) Lucas, Christina Applegate, Tim Blake Nelson, Ted Levine, Natasha Gregson Wagner, Janeane Garofalo, Franky G., M.C. Gainey, Carrie Fisher, Faizon Love; **D:** James Cox; **W:** James Cox, Captain Mauzner, Todd Samovitz, D. Loriston Scott; **C:** Michael Grady; **M:** Michael A. Levine.

Wonderland 𝒹𝒹 1996 The Fruit Machine Emile Charles, Tony Forsyth, Robert Stephens, Clare Higgins, Bruce Payne, Ritchie Coltrane; **D:** Philip Saville; **W:** Frank Carke; **C:** Dick Pope; **M:** Hans Zimmer.

Wonsan Operation 𝒹 1978 U.N. soldiers plunge into the muddy depths of enemy territory in search of secret information that would end the Korean War. Dubbed. 100m/C VHS. Lew Montania, Frederick Hill; **D:** Terrence Sul.

Woo 𝒹𝒹 1997 (R) Knock-out party girl Darlene "Woo" Bates (Pinkett Smith) agrees to a blind date with nice-guy law student Tim (Davidson) on the advice of her cross-dressing psychic. Tim wants to do the right thing and be honorable, but Woo seduces, endangers, and humiliates him at every turn. When Tim finally stands up for himself, she has a change of heart and appreciates his better qualities. Somewhat mean-spirited comedy trods familiar urban cliches and blind-date disasters. Through the use of flashbacks, their lives are traced from junior high to the imminent wedding day of one of the trio. Mike (Epps) and Slim (Jones) are also forced to track down reluctant groom Roland (Diggs), sober him up and get him to the church on time. Newcomer Famuyiwa based the script on his own life. Good cast is left with little interesting to do in this likable, but bland, nostalgia-fest. 107m/C VHS. DVD. Omar Epps, Sean Nelson, Richard T. Jones, Taye Diggs, Trent Cameron, Malinda Williams, Duane Finley, Sanaa Lathan, De'Aundre Bonds, LisaRaye, Cynthia Martells, Tamala Jones, Elayne J. Taylor; **D:** Rick Famuywa; **W:** Rick Famuywa; **C:** Steven Bernstein; **M:** Robert Hurst.

The Wood 𝒹𝒹½ 1999 (R) Follows the friendship of three young black men growing up together during the 80s in Inglewood, California. Through the use of flashbacks, their lives are traced from junior high to the imminent wedding day of one of the trio. Mike (Epps) and Slim (Jones) are also forced to track down reluctant groom Roland (Diggs), sober him up and get him to the church on time. Newcomer Famuyiwa based the script on his own life. Good cast is left with little interesting to do in this likable, but bland, nostalgia-fest. 107m/C VHS. DVD. Omar Epps, Sean Nelson, Richard T. Jones, Taye Diggs, Trent Cameron, Malinda Williams, Duane Finley, Sanaa Lathan, De'Aundre Bonds, LisaRaye, Cynthia Martells, Tamala Jones, Elayne J. Taylor; **D:** Rick Famuywa; **W:** Rick Famuywa; **C:** Steven Bernstein; **M:** Robert Hurst.

The Wooden Gun 𝒹𝒹½ Roveh Huliot 1979 Conflicts arise between two teenage factions in 1950s Tel Aviv: native Israelis, and the children of Jews arrived from Europe since WWII. In Hebrew with English subtitles. 91m/C VHS. DVD. IS Nadav Brenner, Nissim Eliaz, Michael Kafir, Arik Rosen, Louis Rosenberg; **D:** Ilan Moshenson; **C:** Gadi Danzig; **M:** Yossi Mar-Haim.

Wooden Horse 𝒹𝒹𝒹 1950 Lean thriller of British POWs escaping a Nazi camp through a tunnel beneath their exercise horse. Based on a true incident in 1943 and on "The Tunnel Escape" by Eric Williams; set the tone for all British prison-camp movies to follow: stiff upper lip and all that, and adolescent-style trickery reminiscent of English boarding schools. 98m/C VHS. Anthony Steel, Leo Genn, David Tomlinson, Bryan Forbes, Peter Finch; **D:** Jack Lee.

The Wooden Man's Bride 𝒹𝒹 1994 The inhabitants of this austere 1920s, northwest Chinese community live in stone fortresses, fearful of being attacked by roving armed bandits. Which is what happens to the bridal party of Young Mistress (Lan) who's kidnapped by bandit leader Tang (Mingjun). She's released unharmed when her servant Kui (Shih) presses Tang with his bravery but their bridegroom has been killed in a freak accident and formidable Madame Liu (Yu-

Woodchipper Massacre woof! 1989 Aunt Tess is frozen in the freezer, waiting to be turned into whatever free, fleshy equivalent of woodchips is by her three unloving relations, and her totally evil son has just broken out of prison looking to retrieve his inheritance. You think you have problems? You'll have one less if you leave this one on the shelf. 90m/C VHS. DVD. Jon McBride, Patricia McBride; **D:** Jon McBride.

accepting, it being the racially-charged 1960s and all, and eventually David finds himself in an awkward situation. Avoids being sappy, and Lindo really rules as the father. 106m/C DVD. Sam Smith, Jo Stone-Fewings, Emily Woof, Leagh Conwell, Dominic Barklem, Delroy Lindo, Carol MacReady, Yasmin Paige, Stanley Townsend; **D:** Paul Morrison; **W:** Paul Morrison; **C:** Nina Kellgren; **M:** Ilona Sekacz. VIDEO mel), who runs the fortress, forces her to marry a wooden likeness of the deceased. Despairing Young Mistress begins an affair with Kui, which can only end badly. Mandarin with subtitles. **114m/C VHS, DVD.** *CH* Wang Lan, Chang Shih, Wang Yu-mei, Kao Mingjun; *D:* Huang Jianxin; *W:* Yang Zhenguang; *C:* Zhang Xiaoguang; *M:* Zhang Dalong.

The Woodsman 2004 (R) Kassell's feature debut is not for the fainthearted. How do you not depict a convicted pedophile of young girls as a monster? It's a measure of Bacon's talents as Walter that if you can't sympathize with his character (and you're not asked to), you do come to some understanding of his torment. Recently paroled after a 12-year prison term, Walter finds a job in a lumberyard and an apartment opposite a grade school. As Walter struggles to keep his sexual impulses in check, he starts his first adult relationship with equally scarred co-worker Vickie (Bacon's wife Sedgwick), even as receptionist Mary-Kay (Eve) and cop Lucas (Mos Def) become suspicious of withdrawn Walter's behavior. Disturbing without becoming explicit and with a silver of hopefulness in its resolution. Co-writer Fechter adapted from his play. **87m/C DVD.** *US* Kevin Bacon, Kyra Sedgwick, Eve, Mos Def, David Alan Grier, Benjamin Bratt, Michael Shannon, Hannah Pilkes, Carlos Leon; *D:* Nicole Kassell; *W:* Nicole Kassell, Steven Fechter; *C:* Xavier Perez Grobet; *M:* Nathan Larson.

Woodstock 1970 Step into the way-back machine and return to the times of luv, peace, and understanding. Powerful chronicle of the great 1969 Woodstock rock concert celebrates the music and lifestyle of the late '60s. More than 400,000 spectators withstood lack of privacy, bathrooms, parking, and food while wallowing in the mud for four days to catch classic performers by a number of popular performers and groups. Martin Scorcese helped edit the documentary, trail-blazing in its use of split-screen montage. A director's cut is available at 225 minutes. **180m/C VHS, DVD.** *D:* Michael Wadleigh. Oscars '70: Feature Doc., Natl. Film Reg. '96.

Woodstock '94 1994 The 25th anniversary of the original festival was celebrated with a three-day music explosion (complete with mud). Includes backstage footage and interviews with some of the 30 acts, including Aerosmith, Peter Gabriel, Blind Melon, Metallica, and the Red Hot Chili Peppers. **165m/C VHS.**

The Word 1978 Intriguing premise has an archeologist finding a previously unknown text purporting to be written by the younger brother of Jesus. If authentic and publicized, it would wreak theological havoc. Janssen is off to Italy to check up; he finds murder and skullduggery. Well-acted, interesting story. **300m/C VHS.** David Janssen, James Whitmore, Florinda Bolkan, Eddie Albert, Geraldine Chaplin, Hurd Hatfield, John Huston, Kate Mulgrew, Janice Rule, Nicol Williamson; *D:* Richard Lang; *M:* Alex North.

Word Wars: Tiles and Tribulations on the Scrabble Circuit 2004 Four unconventional competitors make their way to the 2002 National Scrabble Tournament in San Diego pursuing the $25,000 grand prize. The characters are authentic oddballs, their world becomes more arcane and peculiar the longer you're in it, and the suspense approaches desperation at the end, all of which makes the film watchable in this age of reality TV. **80m/C DVD.** *D:* Eric Chaikin, Julian Petrillo; *C:* Laela Kilbourn; *M:* Thor Madsen.

Wordplay 2006 Creadon looks at the passion of crossword puzzle fans and champions by following "New York Times" crossword puzzle editor Will Shortz as he prepares for the 28th annual American Crossword Puzzle Tournament in 2005. He interviews puzzle designers, competitors, and such crossword puzzlers as John Stewart, Bill Clinton, and Ken Burns. **90m/C DVD.** *US* *D:* Patrick Creadon; *W:* Patrick Creadon, Christine O'Malley; *C:* Patrick Creadon; *M:* Peter Golub.

Words and Music 1948 Plot based on the careers of Rodgers and Hart is little more than a peg on which to hang lots of classic songs, sung by a parade of MGM stars. Also includes Kelly's dance recreation of "Slaughter on Tenth Avenue." Good advice: if no one's singing or dancing, fast forward. **122m/C VHS.** Mickey Rooney, Tom Drake, Judy Garland, Gene Kelly, Lena Horne, Mel Torme, Cyd Charisse, Marshall Thompson, Janet Leigh, Betty Garrett, June Allyson, Perry Como, Vera-Ellen, Ann Sothern; *D:* Norman Taurog; *M:* Richard Rodgers.

Words by Heart 1984 An African American family in turn of the century Missouri faces issues of discrimination and prejudice. Twelve-year-old Lena wins a speech contest and begins to question their place in the community and begins to question their place in the community and begins to pirations for a better life. Based on a book by Ouida Sebestyen. Aired by PBS as part of the "Wonderworks" family movie series. **116m/C VHS, DVD.** Charlotte Rae, Robert Hooks, Alfre Woodard; *D:* Robert Thompson.

The Worker and the Hairdresser *Metalmeccanico e Parrucchiera un Turbine di Sesso e di Politica* 1996 Married Tunin is a leftist labor organizer who falls instantly into lust with right-wing business zealot Rossella when he takes her at a political rally. The opposites may attract but Rossella is determined to put the would-be Lothario in his place. Italian with subtitles. **104m/C VHS.** /T Tullio Solenghi, Gene Gnocchi, Veronica Pivetti, Cyrielle Claire; *D:* Lina Wertmuller; *W:* Lina Wertmuller, Leonardo Benvenuti, Piero De Bernardi; *C:* Blasco Giurato.

Working Girl 1988 (R) Romantic comedy set in the Big Apple has secretary Tess McGill (Griffith) working her way to the top in spite of all manipulative boss Katherine Parker (Weaver in a powerful parody). Tess gets her chance to shine when Katherine breaks a leg and she strikes a business deal with Jack Trainer (Ford)that turns to romance. A 1980s Cinderella story that's sexy, funny, and sharply written and directed. Nice work by Ford, but this is definitely Griffith's movie. And keep an eye on Tess's gal pal Cynthia (Cusack). ♫Let the River Run. **115m/C VHS, DVD.** Melanie Griffith, Harrison Ford, Sigourney Weaver, Joan Cusack, Alec Baldwin, Philip Bosco, Ricki Lake, Nora Dunn, Olympia Dukakis, Oliver Platt, James Lally, Kevin Spacey, Robert Easton; *D:* Mike Nichols; *W:* Kevin Wade; *C:* Michael Ballhaus; *M:* Carly Simon, Rob Mounsey; Oscars '88: Song ("Let the River Run"); Golden Globes '89: Actress—Mus./Comedy (Griffith), Film—Mus./Comedy, Song ("Let the River Run"), Support. Actress (Weaver).

Working Girls 1975 (R) Three girls who share an apartment in Los Angeles are willing to do anything for money. And they do. For lack of anything else to recommend, watch for the striptease by Peterson, better known as Elvira on TV. **80m/C VHS, DVD.** Sarah Kennedy, Laurie Rose, Mark Thomas, Cassandra Peterson; *D:* Stephanie Rothman.

Working Girls 1987 An acclaimed, controversial look by independent filmmaker Borden into lives of modern brothel prostitutes over the period of one day. The sex is realistically candid and perfunctory; the docudrama centers on a prostitute who is a Yale graduate and aspiring photographer living with a female lover. Compelling, touching, and lasting, with sexually candid language and scenery. **93m/C VHS, DVD.** Amanda Goodwin, Louise Smith, Ellen McElduff, Maurisia Zach, Janne Peters, Helen Nicholas; *D:* Lizzie Borden; *W:* Sandra Kay, Lizzie Borden; *C:* Judy Irola; *M:* David Van Tiegham.

The World *Shijie* 2004 Beijing's World Park is a theme park featuring small reproductions of international landmarks such as the Eiffel Tower and the Taj Mahal. We get a behind the scenes look at the lives of some of the park's young workers, many of whom have moved from small villages to the big city to make new lives. These include dancer Tao (Zhao) and her security guard boyfriend, Taisheng (Chen), who are caught up in the dead-end artifice surrounding them. Mandarin and Shanxi dialect with subtitles. **139m/C DVD.** Zhao Tao, Chen Taisheng, Jing Jue, Jiang Zhongwei, Wang Yiqun, Hongwei Wang, Liang Jingdong, Xiang Wan, Liu Juan; *D:* Jia Zhang-ke; *W:* Jia Zhang-ke; *M:* Lim Giong.

The World According to Garp 1982 (R) Comedy turns to tragedy in this relatively faithful version of John Irving's popular (and highly symbolic) novel, adapted by Steve Tesich. Chronicles the life of T.S. Garp, a struggling everyman beset by the destructive forces of modern society. Nevertheless, Garp maintains his optimism even as his life unravels around him. At the core of the film is a subplot involving a group of extreme feminists inspired in part by Garp's mother, the author of "A Sexual Suspect." Close and Lithgow (as a giant transsexual) are spectacular, while Williams is low-key and tender as the beleaguered Garp. Ultimately pointless, perhaps, but effectively and intelligently so. **136m/C VHS, DVD.** Robin Williams, Mary Beth Hurt, John Lithgow, Glenn Close, Hume Cronyn, Jessica Tandy, Swoosie Kurtz, Amanda Plummer, Warren Berlinger, Brandon Maggart, George Roy Hill; *D:* George Roy Hill; *W:* Steve Tesich; *C:* Miroslav Ondricek; *M:* David Shire. L.A. Film Critics '82: Support. Actor (Lithgow); Support. Actress (Close); Natl. Bd. of Review '82: Support. Actress (Close); N.Y. Film Critics '82: Support. Actor (Lithgow).

The World Accuses 1935 A woman takes a job in a nursery, unaware that one child is her own, put up for adoption after her wealthy husband died. Then, her ex-lover shows up in her attic after escaping from prison and takes her hostage. Whew! Everything works out, except that the viewer is left confused and incredulous. **62m/B VHS.** Vivian Tobin, Dickie Moore, Russell Hopton, Cora Sue Collins, Mary Carr; *D:* Charles Lamont.

World and Time Enough 1988 (PG) Sculptor Mark's (Guidry) father compulsively designed Gothic cathedrals and after his death Mark decides to build his own version in a field belonging to a sympathetic cleric. Meanwhile, his equally eccentric lover, garbage-collector Joey (Giles), goes on a search for his birth parents. Lots of symbols, not much sense. **90m/C VHS, DVD.** Matt Guidry, Gregory G. Giles, Kraig Swartz, Peter Macon; *D:* Eric Mueller; *W:* Eric Mueller; *C:* Kyle Bergersen; *M:* Eugene Huddleston.

A World Apart 1988 (PG) Cinematographer Menges' first directorial effort is a blistering, insightful drama told from the point of view of a 13-year-old white girl living in South Africa, oblivious to apartheid until her crusading journalist mother is arrested under the 90-Day Detention Act, under which she might remain in prison permanently. Political morality tale is also a look at the family-vs-cause choices activists must make. Heavily lauded, with good reason; the autobiographical script is based on Slovo's parents, persecuted South African journalists Joe Slovo and Ruth First. **114m/C VHS, DVD.** *GB* Barbara Hershey, Jodhi May, Linda Mvusi, David Suchet, Jeroen Krabbe, Paul Freeman, Tim Roth, Jude Akuwidike, Albee Lesotho; *D:* Chris Menges; *W:* Shawn Slovo; *C:* Peter Biziou; *M:* Hans Zimmer. British Acad. '88: Orig. Screenplay; Cannes '88: Actress (Hershey), Actress (May, Mvusi), Grand Jury Prize; N.Y. Film Critics '88: Director (Menges).

The World Gone Mad 1933 *The Public Be Hanged; Public Be Damned* 1933 During Prohibition, a tough reporter discovers the district attorney is the intended victim of a murder plot involving crooked Wall Street types. Full circle: this interesting drama of white-collar crime is again topical, though dialogue heavy and desultory. **70m/B VHS, DVD.** Pat O'Brien, Louis Calhern, J. Carrol Naish; *D:* Christy Cabanne.

World Gone Wild 1988 (R) Action yarn about a post-apocalyptic world of the future where an evil cult leader brainwashes his disciples. Together they battle a small band of eccentrics for the world's last water source. Stale rehash (with ineffective satiric elements) of the Mad Max genre, served with Ant for campy appeal. **95m/C VHS.** Bruce Dern, Michael Pare, Adam Ant, Catherine Mary Stewart, Rick Podell; *D:* Lee H. Katzin; *C:* Don Burgess.

The World in His Arms 1952 Action and romance, circa 1850. Seal hunter Jonathan Clark (Peck) and his crew are in San Francisco when he meets beautiful Countess Marina Selanova (Blyth), who's fleeing an arranged marriage and is anxious to join her Uncle (Rumann), who happens to be the Governor General of Alaska (which is under Russian control). The twosome fall quickly in love but Marina's kidnapped by her would-be fiance, Prince Semyon (Esmond), who takes off for Alaska and Clark must go to rescue his love. Based on the book by Rex Beach. **104m/C VHS.** Gregory Peck, Ann Blyth, Anthony Quinn, Carl Esmond, Sig Rumann, John McIntire, Hans Conried, Andrea King; *D:* Raoul Walsh; *W:* Borden Chase; *C:* Russell Metty; *M:* Frank Skinner.

The World Is Full of Married Men wooff 1980 (R) A philandering ad exec gets involved with a reckless model, inspiring his fed-up wife also to look for extramarital sex. Promiscuously raunchy melodrama was written by the queen of sleaze, Jackie Collins, based on her novel. **106m/C VHS.** *GB* Anthony (Tony) Franciosa, Carroll Baker, Sherrie Croon, Gareth Hunt, Paul Nicholas; *D:* Robert W. Young; *W:* Jackie Collins.

The World Is Not Enough 1999 (PG-13) Brosnan returns in the 19th James Bond adventure in which 007 is sent to protect Elektra King (Marceau), the daughter of a murdered oil tycoon who was also an old friend of M's (Dench). The threat appears to come from terrorist Renard (Carlyle), who has a bullet in the brain courtesy of MI6 that has made him impervious to pain. Renard's playing the nuclear explosion card, which leads to this episode's Bond girl, nuclear weapons expert (!) Dr. Christmas Jones (Richards), who has minimal impact but looks fetching and (of course) falls for the dashing spy's charms. The numerous action sequences overwhelm the characters and the plot that the franchise should build on, rather than trying to top tts death-defying stunts each time. **125m/C VHS, DVD.** Pierce Brosnan, Sophie Marceau, Denise Richards, Robert Carlyle, Judi Dench, John Cleese, Desmond Llewelyn, Robbie Coltrane, Samantha Bond, Michael Kitchen, Colin Salmon, Maria Grazia Cucinotta, David Calder, Serena Scott Thomas, Ulrich Thomsen, Goldie; *D:* Michael Apted; *W:* Neal Purvis, Robert Wade, Bruce Feirstein; *C:* Adrian Biddle; *M:* David Arnold. Golden Raspberries '99: Worst Support. Actress (Richards).

The World Moves On 1934 In 1825, the Girards and the Warburtons are the most prominent families in the New Orleans cotton industry. A will unites them in business, which expands overseas to England, France, and Germany. But after some four generations, their business empire is destroyed by WWI and the stock market crash. Tone plays a Girard and Carroll a Warburton who find love over several incarnations. **104m/B DVD.** Madeleine Carroll, Franchot Tone, Lumsden Hare, Reginald Denny, Raul Roulien, Sig Rumann, Louise Dresser, Stepin Fetchit, Dudley Digges; *D:* John Ford; *W:* Reginald Berkeley; *C:* George Schneiderman; *M:* Hugo Friedhofer.

The World of Apu 1934 *Apu Sansar; Apur Sansar* 1959 Finale of director Ray's acclaimed Apu trilogy (following "Pather Panchali" and "Aparajito"). Aspiring writer Apu drops out of the university for want of money and takes up with an old chum. An odd circumstance leads him to marry his friend's cousin, whom he comes to love. She dies in childbirth (though her baby boy lives); Aziz is deeply distraught, destroys the novel he was working on, and becomes a wanderer. His friend finds him five years later and helps him begin again with his young son. Wonderfully human, hopeful story told by a world-class director. From the novel "Aparajito" by B. Bancopadhaya. In Bengali with English subtitles. **103m/B VHS, DVD, IN** Soumitra Chatterjee, Sharmila Tagore, Alok Chakravarty, Swapan Mukerji; **D:** Satyajit Ray; **M:** Ravi Shankar.

The World of Henry Orient 1964 Charming, eccentric comedy about two 15-year-old girls who, madly in love with an egotistical concert pianist, pursue him all around New York City. Sellers is hilarious. Walker and Spaeth are adorable as his teen groupies; Bosley and Lansbury are great as Walker's indulgent parents. For anyone who has ever been uncontrollably infatuated. Screenplay by this father/daughter team, Nora and Nunnally Johnson, based on Nora Johnson's novel. **106m/C VHS, DVD.** Peter Sellers, Tippy Walker, Merrie Spaeth, Tom Bosley, Angela Lansbury, Paula Prentiss, Phyllis Thaxter, Bibi Osterwald; **D:** George Roy Hill; **W:** Nunnally Johnson, Nora Johnson; **C:** Boris Kaufman; **M:** Elmer Bernstein.

A World of Strangers 1962 A harsh look at apartheid through the eyes of an Englishman who has traveled to South Africa to manage a publishing house. Filmed in strict secrecy in Johannesburg due to the film's aggressive condemnation of the practice. Based on a novel by Nadine Gordimer, based on Ivan Jackson, Zakes Mokae; **D:** Henning Carlsen.

The World of Suzie Wong 1960 Asian prostitute Kwan plays cat-and-mouse with American painter Holden. She lies to him about her profession, her family, and herself. His association with her ruins relationships in his life. Why, then, does he not get a clue? Good question, not answered by this soap opera that would be a serious drama. Offensively sanitized picture of the world of prostitution in an Asian metropolis. On the other hand, it's all nicely shot, much of it on location in Hong Kong. Based on Paul Osborn's play which was taken from Richard Mason's novel. **129m/C VHS, DVD, GB** William Holden, Nancy Kwan, Sylvia Syms, M-"Jackie" Chan; **D:** Richard Quine; **C:** Geoffrey Unsworth.

World of the Depraved do Depravados 1967 Tango: [Storm] runs an exercise club for young lovelies that are systematically robbed by the mysterious full moon sex killer. Enter police detectives Riley and Hamilton (Decker, Reed), joking types who peep on their charges through keyholes, etc. When the killer, the point of the movie has already been made clear. Silly, trivial, sophomoric humor lacking a trace of sincerity. Volume 6 of Frank Henenlotter's Sexy Shockers series. **73m/C VHS, DVD,** Tempest Storm, Johnnie Decker, Larry Reed; **D:** Herbert Jeffries.

The World Owes Me a Living 1947 Melodrama about pilot Farrar losing his memory in a plane crash and Campbell trying to spark his recollection of the past. **91m/B VHS, GB** David Farrar, Judy Campbell, Jack Livesey, John Laurie; **D:** Vernon Sewell.

World Trade Center 2006 (PG-13) Stone directs a 9/11 drama about John McLoughlin (Cage) and Will Jimeno (Pena), two Port Authority policemen trapped in the World Trade Center after they went in as part of the rescue team. Film follows their efforts at survival and escape with the fears of their families. Stone shot in chronological order to heighten the reality and tension and had the survivors and their families on the set as well. He puts aside the cynicism and paranoia for an elegantly told tale of extraordinary heroism by ordinary people. **129m/C DVD, Blu-ray Disc, HD DVD, US** Nicolas Cage, Michael Pena, Maria Bello, Maggie Gyllenhaal, Jay Hernandez, Stephen Dorff, Michael Shannon; **D:** Oliver Stone; **M:** Craig Armstrong.

World Traveler 2001 (R) One day, thirtysomething NYC architect Cal (Crudup) leaves his wife and son, gets into the family station wagon, and hits the road to drive cross country in a fine frustrating film. Although Crudup is a fine actor, the viewer never learns Cal's motives for leaving his life behind except that he's not the nicest guy around, considering the way he treats some of the people he meets on his trip, including construction worker Carl (Derricks) whose marriage Cal damages, and various female hitch-hikers. Not a lot really happens as Cal searches for himself (apparently) and the film ultimately falls flat. **104m/C VHS, DVD, US CA** Billy Crudup, Julianne Moore, Cleavant Derricks, David Keith, Mary McCormack, Diane LeGros, Karen Allen, Liane Balaban; **D:** Bart Freundlich; **W:** Bart Freundlich; **C:** Terry Stacey; **M:** Clint Mansell.

World War II: When Lions Roared 1994 The "Lions" are Franklin Delano Roosevelt, Winston Churchill and Joseph Stalin. The three Allied leaders formed an uneasy alliance to crush Hitler and Mussolini, all against much internal treachery. Uses lots of WWII newsreel footage. **186m/C VHS,** John Lithgow, Bob Hoskins, Michael Caine, Ed Begley Jr., Jan Triska; **D:** Joseph Sargent; **W:** David W. Rintels; **C:** John A. Alonzo. **TV**

World War III 1986 How's that for a title? A Russian plot is afoot to seize and destroy the Alaskan pipeline. When the plot is discovered, negotiation is needed to prevent world war. Executive branch showdown ensues between U.S. prez Hudson and Soviet chief Keith. Director Boris Sagal was killed on location, whereupon Greene took over, and shooting was moved indoors with dramatic tension lost in the transition. **188m/C VHS,** Brian Keith, David Soul, Rock Hudson, Cathy Lee Crosby, Katharine Helmond, Robert Prosky, James Hampton, Richard Yniguez, Herbert Jefferson Jr.; **D:** David Greene, Boris Sagal; **W:** Robert L. Joseph. **TV**

The Worldly Madonna 1922 Young plays two roles as Janet, a convent novitiate, and her cabaret dancer sister, Lucy. Lucy thinks she's killed a man and Janet agrees to change places with her. **47m/B VHS,** Clara Kimball Young, Richard Tucker, George Hackathorne, William P. Carleton, Jean De Limur, William Marion, Milla Davenport; **D:** Harry Garson.

The World's Fastest Indian 2005 (PG-13) Burt Munro (a refreshingly un-scary Hopkins) is the town "crazy old guy", a kooky New Zealander with a dream of setting a land-speed motorcycle record at Bonneville Flats, Utah. The Indian in the title is his bike, a 1920 Indian Scout, which, with Munro's constant tinkering, flies at a blistering 201 mph across the desert, told here by the same director of the 1971 documentary about Munro, "Offerings to the God of Speed." Mildly schmaltzy, but well-told and all heart. **127m/C DVD, US NZ** Anthony Hopkins, Diane Ladd, Aaron Murphy, Paul Rodriguez, Christopher Lawford, Annie Whittle; **D:** Roger Donaldson; **W:** Roger Donaldson; **C:** David Gribble; **M:** J. Peter Robinson.

The World's Greatest Athlete 1973 (G) Lame Disney comedy about a Tarzan-like jungle-man (Vincent) recruited by an unsuccessful American college coach (Conway) and his bumbling assistant (Conway). Fun special effects, weak script add up to mediocre family fare. Cameo by Howard Cosell as—who else?—himself. **89m/C VHS, DVD,** Jan-Michael Vincent, Tim Conway, John Amos, Roscoe Lee Browne, Dayle Haddon; **Cameos:** Howard Cosell; **D:** Robert Scheerer; **M:** Marvin Hamlisch.

The World's Greatest Lover 1977 (PG) Milwaukee baker Rudi Valentine, played oft-hilariously by Wilder, tries to make it big in 1920s Hollywood. He has a screen test as a Hollywood movie sheik, but his wife (Kane) leaves him for the real McCoy. Episodic and uneven, it's alternately uproarious, touching and downright raunchy. **89m/C VHS, DVD,** Gene Wilder, Carol Kane, Dom DeLuise, Fritz Feld, Carl Ballantine, Michael Huddleston, Matt Collins, Ronny Graham; **D:** Gene Wilder; **W:** Gene Wilder.

The World's Oldest Living Bridesmaid 1992 Hokey romantic comedy about a successful woman attorney who just can't find Mr. Right. Brenda feels even worse when she attends another friend's wedding. However, when she hires a younger, male secretary (former model Wimmer) the romance sparks fly. An appealing and attractive cast helps this TV fare. **100m/C VHS,** Donna Mills, Brian Wimmer, Beverly Garland, Winston Rekert, Art Hindle, Laura Press; **D:** Joseph L. Scanlan. **TV**

The Worm Eaters WOOF! 1977 (PG) Mean developers want to take over a reclusive worm farmer's land. He unleashes his livestock on 'em. The bad guys turn into—eeek!—"worm people." A truck runs over our hero nearly 75 minutes too late to save the viewer. **75m/C VHS, DVD,** Herb Robins, Barry Hostetler, Lindsay Armstrong Black, Joseph Sacket, Robert Garrison, Mike Garrison; **D:** Herb Robins; **W:** Herb Robins; **C:** Willis Hawkins; **M:** Theodore Stern.

The Worst Witch 1986 (G) Fantasy about a school for young witches where the educational lessons never go quite as planned. Adapted from the children's book "The Worst Witch" by Jill Murphy. **70m/C VHS, DVD,** Diana Rigg, Charlotte Rae, Tim Curry, Fairuza Balk; **D:** Robert M. Young.

Worth Winning 1989 (PG-13) A notoriously eligible Philadelphia bachelor takes a bet to become engaged to three women within three months, and finds himself in hot water. A critically dead-in-the-water chucklefest. **103m/C VHS,** Mark Harmon, Lesley Ann Warren, Madeleine Stowe, Maria Holvoe, Mark Blum, Andrea Martin, Alan Blumenfeld, Brad Hall, Tony Longo; **D:** Will MacKenzie; **W:** Sara Parriott, Josann McGibbon.

The Would-Be Gentleman 1958 The Comedie Francaise troupe performs Moliere's famous farce-comedy. Valuable as a record of the famous troupe on stage. When they're long gone, our grandkids can enjoy this. We can too (if we can't afford the trip to France), though it's less a film than a filming of a play. In French with English subtitles. **91m/C VHS, FR** Louis Seigner, Jean Meyer, Jean Piat; **D:** Jean Meyer. **CABLE**

Wounded 1997 (R) Game warden Julie Clayton (Amick) vows to get even with poacher Hanghan (Pasdar) after he murders her fiance and assaults her. The FBI tell her to stay clear but Julie is determined to track Hanghan down anywhere. **89m/C VHS,** Madchen Amick, Adrian Pasdar, Graham Greene, Richard Joseph Paul, Daniel Kash; **D:** Richard Martin; **W:** Harry S. Longstreet, Lindsay Bourne. **C:** Gregory Middleton; **M:** Ross Vannelli. **CABLE**

The Wounds Rane 1998 In 1991, 16-year-old Pinki (Pekic) and Kraut (Maric) are two relatively innocent Serbians who, by 1996, have fallen under the pernicious influence of Dickie (Bjelogrlic), a flashy black marketeer. With brutality everywhere in their war-torn country, the young men have become amoral brutes who only understand an eye-for-an-eye, even with each other. Serbo-Croatian with subtitles. **103m/C VHS, DVD,** Dragan Bjelogrlic, Dusan Pekic, Milan Maric, Branka Katic, Dragan Maksimovic; **W:** Stojan Dragojevic; **C:** Dusan Joksimovic; **M:** Aleksandar Habic.

Woyzeck 1978 Chilling portrayal of a man plunging into insanity. Mired in the ranks of the German Army, Woyzeck is harassed by his superiors and tortured in scientific experiments, gradually devolving into homicidal maniac. Based on Georg Buchner play. In German with English subtitles. **82m/C VHS, DVD, GE** Klaus Kinski, Eva Mattes, Wolfgang Reichmann, Josef Bierbichler; **D:** Werner Herzog; **W:** Werner Herzog; **C:** Jörg Schmidt-Reitwein.

Woyzeck 1994 Woyzeck (Kovács) is a flagman in a decaying train-yard—caught between his cruel employer, poverty, and his distant wife. In order to make a little extra money, he agrees to take part in a bizarre medical experiment, increasingly pushed to the edge. Woyzeck snaps when he learns his wife is having an affair. Based on the play by Georg Büchner. Hungarian with subtitles. **93m/B VHS, Hu** Lajos Kovacs, Diana Vacaru, Aleksandr Porokhovshchikov, Sandor Gaspar; **D:** Janos Szasz; **W:** Janos Szasz; **C:** Tibor Mathe.

Wozzeck 1947 The corpse of murderer Franz Wozzeck (Meisel) is being used in an anatomy lecture, while medical student Buchner (Eckard) tells the tragic story in flashbacks. A soldier, Wozzeck endures humiliation in order to barely support his wife Marie (Zulch) and their child. The beautiful Marie allows herself to be seduced by another soldier (Haussler), as Wozzeck's physical and mental health declines. And then Franz learns of her infidelity. Based on the drama by Georg Buchner. German with subtitles. **94m/B VHS,** Kurt Meisel, Helga Zulch, Richard Haussler, Max Eckard; **D:** Georg C. Klaren; **W:** Georg C. Klaren; **C:** Bruno Mondi; **M:** Herbert Trantow.

WR: Mysteries of the Organism 1971 Makavejev's breakthrough film, a surreal, essayist exploration of the conflict/union between sexuality and politics—namely, Wilhelm Reich and Stalin. A raunchy, bitterly satiric non-narrative that established the rule-breaking Yugoslav internationally. In Serbian with English subtitles. **84m/C VHS, DVD,** Milena Dravic, Jagoda Kaloper, Tuli Kupferberg, Jackie Curtis; **D:** Dusan Makavejev; **W:** Dusan Makavejev.

The Wraith 1987 (PG-13) Drag-racing Arizona teens find themselves challenged by a mysterious, otherworldly stranger. Hot cars, cool music; little else to recommend it. It's easy script; ludicrous excuse for a premise. Most of the stars here-in are related to somebody famous. **92m/C VHS, DVD,** Charlie Sheen, Nick Cassavetes, Sherilyn Fenn, Randy Quaid, Matthew Barry, Clint Howard, Griffin O'Neal; **D:** Mike Marvin; **W:** Mike Marvin.

Wrangler 1988 When an Australian rancher dies his daughter tries to hang on to the family ranch from a ruthless creditor. She also has to deal with the attentions of two men—one a businessman and the other a cattleman, both equally dashing and handsome. Beautiful scenery of the Australian Outback as well as romance and adventure. **93m/C VHS,** Jeff Fahey, Tushka Bergen, Steven Vidler, Richard Moir, Shane Briant, Drew Forsythe, Cornelia Frances, Sandy Gore, Frederick Parslow; **D:** Ian Barry; **M:** Mario Millo.

The Wrath of the Gods 1914 Boyish American sailor Tom Wilson (Borzage) is shipwrecked near a Japanese village. He soon falls in love with local beauty Toya San (Aoki). But their forbidden romance leads to divine retribution. **7m/B DVD,** Frank Borzage, Sessue Hayakawa, Tsuru Aoki, Kisaburo Kurihara; **D:** Reginald Barker; **W:** Thomas Ince.

The Wreck of the Mary Deare 1959 Slow-moving adventure drama focusing on the wreck of the freighter called the Mary Deare. He boards a seemingly empty strip one night and Cooper is the only crew member on board. Special effects are the main attraction in this interesting sea drama. Film originally was to be directed by Hitchcock, but he turned down the offer to do "North by Northwest." **105m/C VHS, DVD, GB** Gary Cooper, Charlton Heston, Michael Redgrave, Emlyn Williams, Cecil Parker, Alexander Knox, Virginia McKenna, Richard Harris; **D:** Michael Anderson Sr. **W:** Eric Ambler.

The Wrecking Crew 1968 The fourth and final of Matt Helm spy spoof series. Matt and martini babe Freya (Tate) must save the world from economic doom when evildoer Massimo (Green) steals $1 billion in gold. Tate was murdered several months after the film's release. **105m/C VHS, DVD.** Dean Martin, Sharon Tate, Nigel Green, Eike Sommer, Nancy Kwan; **D:** Phil Karlson; **W:** William McGivern; **C:** Sam Leavitt; **M:** Hugo Montenegro.

The Wrecking Crew ♂½ 1999 All-star wrestling, which is fictional anyway, gets said treatment in the appropriate way. Honest promoter (yeah, sure) bumps heads with bad-guy crooks who want in on the action. Made-for-TV opportunity for Asner to slum. **103m/C VHS, DVD.** Ed Asner, Elaine Giftos, Verne Gagne, Harold Sakata; **D:** James Westman; **W:** Eugene Gump; **C:** Gil Hubbs; **M:** William Allen Castleman.

Wrestling Ernest Hemingway ♂ 1993 (PG-13) A shy barber and a rollicking sea captain, both 75 and retired, form an unlikely companionship in a Florida retirement mecca. Duvall is the persnickety introvert who quietly follows routine and Harris is the would-be ladies' man whose endless tall tales include having tangled with Papa Hemingway in his youth. They share walks in the park, little league baseball from the bleachers, and coffee klatches that reveal the emptiness of their lives. Director Haines' focus on the principals' emotional baggage considerably dampens the proceedings. Depression in the elderly may be a topic that is not quite ready to come out of Hollywood's closet. **123m/C VHS.** Robert Duvall, Richard Harris, Piper Laurie, Shirley MacLaine, Sandra Bullock; **D:** Randa Haines; **W:** Steve Conrad; **C:** Lajos Koltai; **M:** Michael Convertino.

Wrestling with Alligators ♂½ 1998 Quiet, coming-of-ager stars Palladino as Maddy, a teenager escaping a tragic past in Florida and finding comfort in her newfound friends at an all-female boarding house on the New Jersey shore in 1959. Lulu's Look Out offers the tough teenager a place to find herself, with the help of proprietor Lulu (Bloom), an eccentric silent-screen star, and residents Mary (Shelly), an artist, and the beautiful Claire (Richardson), a French war widow. Tomboy Maddy finds herself attracted to a man for the first time when she meets carnival worker Will (Trammell). Then, when Claire becomes pregnant by the local garage owner (Sanders), Maddy finds herself growing up even more as she comes to the aid of her newfound family, which is beginning to show signs of serious strain. Unassuming portrait of four very different women is a worthy effort, with the leads displaying convincing chemistry. **95m/C VHS, DVD.** Aleksa Palladino, Joely Richardson, Claire Bloom, Adrienne Shelly, Sam Trammell, Jay O. Sanders, Tom Guiry, Sloane Shelton, Angelica Tom, Schuyler Grant; **D:** Laurie Weltz; **W:** Laurie Weltz; **C:** Richard Dallett; **M:** Andrew Hollander.

Wrestling Women vs. the Aztec Mummy Woof! *Las Luchadoras Contra la Momia; Rock and Roll Wrestling Women vs. the Aztec Mummy* 1959 Women, broad of shoulder, wrestle an ancient Aztec wrestler who comes to life. Furnished with a new rock soundtrack. **88m/C VHS, DVD. MX** Lorena Lalazquez, Armando Silvestre, Elizabeth Campbell, Maria Eugenia San Martin, Ramon Bugarini, Victor Velaquez, Chabela Romero; **D:** Rene Cardona Sr.; **W:** Alfredo Salazar, Guillermo Calderon; **C:** Ezequiel Carrasco.

Wristcutters: A Love Story ♂♂ 2006 (R) What could be worse than a miserable life? A miserable afterlife, that's what. Croatian director Gordan Dukic takes a stark and quirky peek at the limbo that exists between the two. Zia (Fugit) is dumped by girlfriend Desiree (Bibb) and decides to end it all, hoping for relief from his misery. But he finds himself

stuck in an afterlife that is marginally like the one he just left, only duller, and with worse jobs. A cast of kooky characters who have also offed themselves shares the limbo world, two of which are wild Russian rocker Eugene (Whigham) and derelict clown Kneller (an aptly-cast Waits). Zia cheers up just a bit when he finds out that Desiree followed his lead and he goes on a roadtrip to find her, but ends up falling for Mikal (Sossamon), who swears she's there by mistake and is trying to get home. **88m/C VHS, DVD.** US Patrick Fugit, Shannyn Sossamon, Shea Whigham, Leslie Bibb, Tom Waits, Mark Boone Jr., Mary Pat Gleason, Abraham Benrubi, Will Arnett, Clayne Crawford, John Hawkes, Jake Busey, Sarah Roemer, Azura Skye, Eddie Steeples, Nick Offerman; **D:** Goran Dukic; **W:** Goran Dukic; **M:** Bobby Johnston.

Write to Kill ♂½ 1991 (R) A young mystery writer seeks revenge when his brother is murdered by a ring of counterfeiters. **120m/C VHS.** Scott Valentine, Chris Mulkey, Joan Severance, G.W. Bailey, Ray Wise; **D:** Ruben Preuss.

Writer's Block ♂♂ 1991 (R) Fairchild is a successful thriller writer whose latest books feature a serial killer. She decides to kill the character off and is soon stalked by a psycho who is using her plots for some copy-cat killings. Tepid cable movie with San Diego locations the only highlight. **90m/C VHS.** Morgan Fairchild, Joe Regalbuto, Michael Praed, Cheryl Anderson, Mary Ann Pascal, Douglas Rowe, Ned Bellamy; **D:** Charles Correll; **W:** Elisa Bell. **CABLE**

Written on the Wind ♂♂♂½ 1956 Sirk's frenzied, melodrama-as-high-art dissection of both the American Dream and American movies follows a Texas oil family's self-destruction through wealth, greed and unbridled lust. Exaggerated depiction of and comment on American ambition and pretension, adapted from Robert Wilder's novel. **99m/C VHS, DVD.** Lauren Bacall, Rock Hudson, Dorothy Malone, Robert Stack, Robert Keith, Grant Williams, Edward Platt, Harry Shannon; **C:** Russell Metty. Oscars '56: Support. Actress (Malone).

The Wrong Arm of the Law ♂♂♂ 1963 Loopy gangster yarn about a trio of Aussie gangsters who arrive in London and upset the local crime balance when they dress up as cops and confiscate loot from apprehended robbers. General confusion erupts among the police, the local crooks, and the imposters. Riotous and hilarious, with Sellers leading a host of familiar faces. **94m/B VHS, DVD.** GB Peter Sellers, Lionel Jeffries, Nanette Newman, Bernard Cribbins, Dennis Price; **D:** Cliff Owen; **M:** Richard Rodney Bennett.

The Wrong Box ♂♂♂ 1966 Two elderly Victorian brothers try to kill each other so that one of them may collect the large inheritance left to them. Based on a Robert Louis Stevenson novel. Well-cast black comedy replete with sight gags, many of which flop. **105m/C VHS, DVD.** GB Peter Sellers, Dudley Moore, Peter Cook, Michael Caine, Ralph Richardson, John Mills; **D:** Bryan Forbes; **W:** Larry Gelbart; **M:** John Barry.

The Wrong Guy ♂♂ 1996 (PG-13) Hit-and-miss spoof of "man on the run" movies. Nerdy exec Nelson Hibbert (Foley) threatens his boss in front of a bunch of people and is later seen running from the man's office, screaming, covered in blood, and holding a knife. Although the police quickly figure out Nelson is not the killer, Nelson doesn't know this and he keeps ending up in the wrong place at the wrong time. **87m/C VHS, DVD.** CA Dave Foley, David Anthony Higgens, Jennifer Tilly, Joe Flaherty, Alan Scarfe, Kenneth Welsh, Enrico Colantoni, Colm Feore; **D:** David Steinberg; **W:** Dave Foley, David Anthony Higgens, Jay Kogen; **C:** David Makin; **M:** Lawrence Shragge.

The Wrong Guys ♂ 1988 (PG) Five giants of stand-up comedy star as a group of men who reunite their old boy scout pack and go camping. A crazed convict mistakes them for FBI agents. It's supposed to get zany after that, but succeeds only in being clumsy and embarassing. **86m/C VHS, DVD.** Richard Lewis, Richard Belzer, Louie Anderson, Tim Thomerson, Franklin Ajaye, John Goodman, Ernie Hudson,

Timothy Van Patten; **D:** Danny Bilson; **W:** Danny Bilson, Paul DeMeo.

Wrong Is Right ♂♂ *The Man With The Deadly Lens* 1982 (R) A black action comedy about international terrorism, news reporting and the CIA. Connery is terrific, as usual, as a TV reporter in a head-scratching attempt at satire of our TV-influenced society. **117m/C VHS, DVD.** Sean Connery, Katharine Ross, Robert Conrad, George Grizzard, Henry Silva, G.D. Spradlin, John Saxon, Leslie Nielsen, Robert Webber, Rosalind Cash, Hardy Kruger, Dean Stockwell, Ron Moody, Jennifer Jason Leigh; **D:** Richard Brooks; **W:** Richard Brooks; **C:** Fred W. Koenekamp.

The Wrong Man ♂♂♂½ 1956 Nightclub musician Fonda is falsely accused of a robbery and his life is destroyed. Taken almost entirely from the real-life case of mild-mannered bass player "Manny" Balestrero; probes his anguish at being wrongly accused; and showcases Miles (later to appear in "Psycho") and her character's agony. Harrowing, especially following more lighthearted Hitchcock fare such as "The Trouble with Harry." Part of the "A Night at the Movies" series, this tape simulates a 1956 movie evening with a color Bugs Bunny cartoon, "A Star Is Bored," a newsreel and coming attractions for "Toward the Unknown." **126m/B VHS, DVD.** Henry Fonda, Vera Miles, Anthony Quayle, Nehemiah Persoff; **D:** Alfred Hitchcock; **C:** Robert Burks.

The Wrong Man ♂♂ 1993 (R) American sailor Alex Walker (Anderson) is framed for the murder of a Mexican smuggler. He eludes the police and winds up hitching a ride from wacko couple Phillip (Lithgow) and Missy Mills (Arquette). Missy does topless table dancing and is very interested in their fugitive passenger. Alex may be better off with the police. **98m/C VHS, DVD.** GE Nastassja Kinski, Hanna Schygulla, Ruediger Vogler, Hans-Christian Blech; **D:** Wim Wenders.

The Wrong Move ♂♂½ 1978 A loose adaptation of Goethe's "Sorrows of Young Werther" by screenwriter Peter Handke. Justly acclaimed and engrossing, though slow. Kinski's first film. A young poet, searching for life's meaning, wanders aimlessly through Germany. In German with English subtitles. **103m/C VHS, DVD.** GE Nastassja Kinski, Hanna Schygulla, Ruediger Vogler, Hans-Christian Blech; **D:** Wim Wenders. **CABLE**

The Wrong Road ♂½ 1937 A young couple embark on a robbery spree, and subsequently end up in prison. On their release, they search for the loot they had previously hidden, but find the man who was holding it for them has died. Will they ever recover their ill-gotten stash? **62m/B VHS, DVD.** Richard Cromwell, Helen Mack, Lionel Atwill, Horace McMahon, Russ Powell, Billy Bevan, Marjorie Main, Rex Evans; **D:** James Cruze.

Wrong Turn ♂½ 2003 (R) Six friends are involved in a car crash that strands them in the West Virginia mountains where they are hunted by disfigured, inbred, cannibalistic mountain men. Typical victim-by-number horror flick offers no twists on the genre and only slight wit by its doomed cast. Don't expect to see this one on the West Virginia Tourist Board's recommended list. **85m/C VHS, DVD.** US Eliza Dushku, Jeremy Sisto, Emmanuelle Chriqui, Desmond Harrington, Lindy Booth, Kevin Zegers, Julian Richings, Garry Robbins, Ted Clark, Yvonne Gaudry, David Huband, Joel Harris, Wayne Robson, James Downing; **D:** Rob Schmidt; **W:** Alan B. McElroy; **C:** John Bartley; **M:** Elia Cmiral.

Wrong Turn 2: Dead End ♂ 2007 (R) Retired special forces officer Dale Murphy (Rollins) is the host of a reality TV show where contestants must survive in a remote West Virginia wilderness. But they don't expect to find themselves being hunted by an inbred family of cannibals. Just as sleazy and gross as it sounds. **93m/C DVD.** Henry Rollins, Erica Leerhsen, Daniella Alonso, Steve Braun, Kimberly Caldwell, Aleksa Palladino, Texas Battle, Crystal Lowe, Aleksa Palladino, Steve Braun, Kimberly Caldwell; **D:** Joe Lynch; **W:** Turi Meyer, Al Septien; **C:** Robin Loewen; **M:** Bear McCreary. **VIDEO**

The Wrong Woman ♂♂½ 1995 (PG-13) When Melanie Brooke's (McKeon) boss is murdered, she's framed to take by rap by the company's sleazy comptroller (Field). Melanie begins a desperate hunt for the real culprit with the killer and the cops both after her. **90m/C VHS.** Michelle Scarabelli, Gary Hudson, Stephen Shellen, Nancy McKeon, Chelsea Field; **D:** Douglas Jackson; **W:** Douglas Soesbe; **C:** Peter Benison; **M:** Marty Simon.

Wrongfully Accused ♂½ 1998 (PG-13) Yet another Nielsen spoof, with "The Fugitive" (along with several other movies) the target this time around. He's violinist Ryan Harrison who has a tryst with socialite Lauren Goodhue (Le Brock) and then gets convicted of her husband Hibbing's (York) murder. Harrison escapes, determined to find the actual killer—the one-armed, one-legged, and one-eyed man—while being hunted by Marshal Fergus Falls (Crenna). This is one genre that will probably enjoy this one with more clunkers than chuckles. **85m/C VHS, DVD.** Leslie Nielsen, Richard Crenna, Kelly Le Brock, Melinda McGraw, Michael York, Sandra Bernhard; **D:** Pat Proft; **W:** Pat Proft; **C:** Glen MacPherson; **M:** Bill Conti.

Wuthering Heights ♂♂♂ 1939 The first screen adaptation of Emily Bronte's romantic novel about the doomed love between Heathcliff and Cathy on the Yorkshire moors. Dynamically captures the madness and ferocity of the classic novel, remaining possibly the greatest romance ever filmed. Excellent performances from Wyler's sure direction, particularly Olivier's, which made him a star, and Oberon in her finest hour as the exquisite but selfish Cathy. Remade twice, in 1953 (by Luis Bunuel) and in 1970. **104m/B VHS, DVD.** Laurence Olivier, Merle Oberon, David Niven, Geraldine Fitzgerald, Flora Robson, Donald Crisp, Cecil Kellaway, Leo G. Carroll, Miles Mander, Hugh Williams; **D:** William Wyler; **W:** Ben Hecht, Charles MacArthur; **C:** Gregg Toland; **M:** Alfred Newman. Oscars '39: B&W Cinematog; AFI '98: Top 100, Natl. Film Reg. '07'; N.Y. Film Critics '39: Film.

Wuthering Heights ♂♂½ *Abismos de Pasion; Cumbres Borrascosas* 1953 Bunuel tackles the Bronte classic during his Mexican period, and comes up with a film containing little passion, but much of the customary Bunuel manic cynicism. The 1939 version is far superior, but fans of Bunuel will probably enjoy this one. Loosely adapted; in Spanish with English subtitles. Remade in another English-language version in 1970. **90m/B VHS. MX** Irasema Dilian, Jorge Mistral, Lilia Prado, Ernesto Alonso; **D:** Luis Bunuel.

Wuthering Heights ♂♂½ 1970 (G) The third screening of the classic Emily Bronte romance about two doomed lovers. Fuest's version features excellent photography, and Calder-Marshall's and Dalton's performances are effective, but fail even to approach the intensity and pathos of the 1939 film original (or of the book). Filmed on location in Yorkshire, England. **105m/C VHS, DVD.** GB Anna Calder-Marshall, Timothy Dalton, Harry Andrews, Pamela Brown, Judy Cornwell, James Cossins, Rosalie Crutchley, Hilary Dwyer, Hugh Griffith, Ian Ogilvy; **D:** Robert Fuest; **W:** Patrick Tilley; **C:** John Coquillon; **M:** Michel Legrand.

Wuthering Heights ♂♂½ 1998 Yet another adaptation of Emily Bronte's 1847 gothic romance. Cavanah plays the embittered Heathcliff while Brady is the wilfull Cathy, whose desire for a life of ease places them both on a tragic path that haunts them even after death. **120m/C VHS.** GB Robert Cavanah, Orla Brady, Crispin Bonham Carter, Peter Davison; **W:** David Skynner; **M:** Warren Bennett, Neil McKay. **TV**

Wyatt Earp ♂♂½ 1994 (PG-13) Revisionist epic suffers from bad timing as it follows "Tombstone" in telling the story of tarnished badge Earp (Costner), his brothers, and tubercular friend Doc Holliday (Quaid). Costner is barely believable as a 20-something lad, but fares better as he ages. Forty pounds lighter and likely delusional from lack of food, Quaid is unrecognizable but terrific, hacking his way to sup-

The X-Files: I Want to Believe 2008 is the truth still out there? The Hound *wants* to believe it in 1998 and the series ended in 2002 so it'd be interesting to see if creator Carter can draw an audience beyond committed X-philes (unless that's enough to make the pic a boxoffice success). Seems a muc something that feeds on radiation bursts out of the Earth's surface every 50 years or so and kills. Now, it's expanding its territory. 78m/B VHS. DVD. Dean Jagger, Leo McKern, Edward Chapman, John Harvey, William Lucas, Anthony Newley; *D*: Leslie Norman; *W*: Jimmy Sangster; *C*: Gerald Gibbs; *M*: Malcolm Arnold.

Wyatt Earp: Return to Tombstone 1994 O'Brian, who starred in TV's "The Life and Legend of Wyatt Earp" from 1955 to 1961, returns to Tombstone in 1914. Colorized clips from the series are used for flashbacks. Filmed on location in Tombstone, Arizona. 94m/C VHS. Hugh O'Brian, Bruce Boxleitner, Paul Brinegar, Harry Carey Jr., Bo Hopkins, Martin Kove, Don Meredith, Alex Hyde-White, Jay Underwood; *D*: Frank McDonald; *W*: Daniel Ullman; *C*: James Roberson; *M*: Dana Waden. TV.

The Wyvern Mystery 2000 Confusing and stodgy Gothic mystery based on an actual incident: the story revolves around a small-town man who kills an outlaw. Barry, in the role that made him a western star, is forced into crime after a corrupt politician extorts money from him in exchange for a job. Lincoln, the screen's first Tarzan, appears in a supporting role. 62m/B VHS. John Wayne, Ray Corrigan, Raymond Hatton, Donald (Don "Red") Barry, Pamela Blake, Jack Ingram, Yakima Canutt, Curley Dresden; *D*: George Sherman.

Wyoming Outlaw 1939 Based on an actual incident: the story revolves around a small-town man who kills an outlaw. Barry, in the role that made him a western star... 118m/C VHS, DVD, GB Naomi Watts, Derek Jacobi, Iain Glen, Jack Davenport, Aisling O'Sullivan, Ellie Haddington; *D*: Alex Pilla; *W*: David Pirie, *C*: Simon Maggs; *M*: Philip Appleby. TV.

The X-Files: Fight the Future 1998 (PG-13) *The X-Files: Fight the Future* 1998 (PG-13) The TV series fifth-season cliffhanger continues in the big screen adaptation, which supposedly has a plot clear enough so viewers unfamiliar with the series can still "figure out what's going on. Creator Chris Carter uses the show's "mythology" episodes to have FBI agents Mulder (Duchovny) and Scully (Anderson) battling a global conspiracy involving the Cigarette-Smoking Man (Davis) and an international syndicate, colonizing aliens, and related paranormal perplexities. The big budget allows for some big action sequences and special effects and the two leads have a comfortable partnership. 120m/C VHS, DVD. David Duchovny, Gillian Anderson, Martin Landau, William B. Davis, John Neville, Armin Mueller-Stahl, Blythe Danner, Mitch Pileggi, Terry O'Quinn, Jeffrey DeMunn, Lucas Black, Glenne Headly; *D*: Rob Bowman; *W*: Chris Carter, Frank Spotnitz; *C*: Ward Russell; *M*: Mark Snow.

X-Men: The Last Stand 2006 (PG-13) Last stand? More like "can't stand." Hack-alicious director Brett Ratner tarnishes the legacy of Bryan Singer's above-average superhero series with this lazy, unimaginative tome. Forget all the subtlety and coolness from the first two X-Men movies, because Ratner's replaced them with cheap-looking FX, incoherent storytelling, and barely disguised misogyny. Professor X's merry mutants have to contend with a resurrected Jean Grey (reborn as the all powerful Phoenix) and a new "cure" that threatens to wipe out mutantkind forever. Sounds intriguing, but you won't believe how often your eyes die stupidly, plot holes run rampant, and Wolverine cries like a wuss every ten minutes. 104m/C VHS, DVD, Blu-Ray Disc. US Patrick Stewart, Ian McKellen, Hugh Jackman, Famke Janssen, Halle Berry, Anna Paquin, Rebecca Romijn, Kelsey Grammer, Ben Foster, James Marsden, Shawn Ashmore, Ben Foster, James Marsden, Aaron Stanford, Vinnie Jones, Dania Ramirez, Olivia Williams, Shohreh Aghdashloo, Cameron Bright, Michael Murphy, Bill Duke, Eric Dane, Haley Ramm, Josef Sommer, Connor Widdows, Shauna Kain, Ken Leung, Kea Wong, Anthony Heald, Makenzie Vega; *D*: Brett Ratner; *W*: Zak Penn, Simon Kinberg; *C*: Dante Spinotti; *M*: John Powell.

X-Men 2000 (PG-13) The Marvel Comics characters, who were born with genetic mutations that give them superpowers, get their shot at the big screen. Wheelchair-bound telepath Charles Xavier (Stewart), AKA Professor X, runs a school to help others learn to use their mutant powers. The good guys, who seek to work with humans, fight against the Magneto (McKellen)-led Brotherhood, who feel mankind is expendable. The story is simple enough for newbies to follow and takes itself seriously (no camp allowed) but doesn't have a lot of surprises and, except for Wolverine (Jackman), the characters aren't very involving. The setup calls for a sequel, which may flesh things out. 104m/C VHS, DVD, UMD. Patrick Stewart, Ian McKellen, Famke Janssen, Hugh Jackman, James Marsden, Halle Berry, Rebecca Romijn, Ray Park, Tyler Mane, Anna Paquin, Bruce Davison, Shawn Ashmore; *D*: Bryan Singer; *W*: David Hayter; *C*: Newton Thomas (Tom) Sigel; *M*: Michael Kamen.

X: The Man with X-Ray Eyes 1963 First-rate Corman has Milland gain power to see through solid materials. Predates Little Caesars campaign. 79m/C VHS, DVD. Ray Milland, Diana Van Der Vlis, Harold J. Stone, John Hoyt, Don Rickles, Dick Miller, Jonathan Haze, Morris Ankrum, Barbara Morris; *D*: Roger Corman; *W*: Ray Russell, Robert Dillon; *C*: Floyd Crosby; *M*: Les Baxter.

X from Outer Space 1967 A space voyage to Mars brings back a giant rampaging creature. Badly dubbed. 85m/C VHS. JP Eiji Okada, Peggy Neal, Toshiya Wazaki, Itoko Harada, Shinichi Yanagisawa, Franz Gruber, Keisuke Sonoi, Mike Daning, Torahiko Hamada; *D*: Kazui Nihonmatsu.

X Marks the Spot 1942 When a police sergeant is killed, his detective son investigates his murder. He's drawn into a crime ring which smuggles rubber (a scarce commodity during WWII). Quick pacing enlivens standard cliches. 55m/B VHS, DVD. Damian O'Flynn, Helen Parrish, Dick Purcell, Jack La Rue, Neil Hamilton, Robert E. Homans, Anne Jeffreys, Dick Wessel, Vince Barnett. *D*: George Sherman.

Xchange 2000 (R) In the near future, bio-technology advances allow people to transfer their minds into the bodies of others. The process called "floating" lets anyone "travel" by having his or her consciousness transmitted anywhere in the world. When anti-corporate terrorists assassinate a powerful CEO, Baldwin is called in to investigate the murder. He is transported to San Francisco, where he ends up occupying the body of the lead terrorist (MacLachlan). Then he must fight to reclaim his body. The concept is more than compelling, and the action sequences generally overcome the relative low budget of the production. 110m/C VHS, DVD. CA Stephen Baldwin, Kyle MacLachlan, Kim Coates, Pascale Bussieres; *D*: Allan Moyle. VIDEO

Xica 1976 A diamond rush in 18th century Brazil transformed that country's interior into a place of undreamed wealth and excess. Black slave Xica uses her sexual allure to rise out of poverty and capture the attentions of Joao, the governor of the diamond-mining town. She gleefully wields her increasing wealth and power, becoming the unofficial Empress of Brazil. Reportedly based on a real-life character. In Portuguese with English subtitles. 109m/C VHS, ER Zeze Motta, Walmor Chages, Altair Lima, Jose Wilker, Marcus Vinicius, Elke Maravilhe; *D*: Carlos Diegues; *W*: Joao Felicio.

Xanadu 1980 (PG) Dorky star-vehicle remake of 1947's "Down to Earth") eminently of its era, which is now better forgotten. Newton-John is a muse who descends to Earth to help two friends open a roller disco. In the process she proves that as an actor, she's a singer. Kelly attempts to soft shoe some grace into the proceedings, though he seems mystified as anyone as to why he's in the movie. Don Bluth adds an animated sequence. All Over the World; Xanadu; Magic; Suddenly; Dancing; Suspended in Time. 96m/C VHS, DVD. Olivia Newton-John, Michael Beck, Gene Kelly, Sandahl Bergman; *D*: Robert Greenwald; *W*: Richard Danus; *C*: Victor Kemper; Worst Director (Greenwald).

X, Y & Zee 1972 (R) A trashy, harsh version of the menage a trois theme, wherein the vicious wife (Taylor) of a philanderer (Caine) decides to avenge herself by seducing his mistress. An embarrassment for everyone involved. 110m/C VHS. Elizabeth Taylor, Michael Caine, Susannah York, Margaret Leighton; *D*: Brian G. Hutton; *W*: Edna O'Brien; *C*: Billy Williams.

X The Unknown 1956 Geologist Adam Royston (Jagger) is sent to investigate a radioactive spot where a mysterious and deadly fissure has appeared. Seems a muc something that feeds on radiation bursts out of the Earth's surface every 50 years or so and kills. Now, it's expanding its territory. 78m/B VHS. DVD. Dean Jagger, Leo McKern, Edward Chapman, John Harvey, William Lucas, Anthony Newley; *D*: Leslie Norman; *W*: Jimmy Sangster; *C*: Gerald Gibbs; *M*: Malcolm Arnold.

X2: X-Men United 2003 (PG-13) The mutants are back as Prof. Xavier's X-Men must join forces with Magneto's mutants to battle a greater evil: a power-mad, mutant-hating general (Cox) is great as the general, full of self-righteousness and silky menace, properly denying his character the small moments of sympathy allowed to McKellan's Magneto. The story is better than in the original, even though it jams as much, if not more exposition into the plot and lingers too long on the teen romance between Rogue and Iceman. Script provides a well-executed and exciting central plot, while leaving plenty of threads and new characters that audiences will be anxious to follow in "X-Men 3." Special effects are fantastic, but they don't overshadow the story. 134m/C VHS, DVD, UMD. US Patrick Stewart, Ian McKellen, Famke Janssen, Hugh Jackman, James Marsden, Halle Berry, Rebecca Romijn, Anna Paquin, Shawn Ashmore, Brian Cox, Alan Cumming, Kelly Hu, Bruce Davison, Aaron Stanford, Katie Stuart, Cotter Smith, Daniel Cudmore, Peter Wingfield, Michael Reid MacKay, Kaely Purvis, Jill Teed, Alf Humphreys, Daniel P. "Dan" Harris; *C*: Newton Thomas (Tom) Sigel; *M*: John Ottman.

Xtro 1983 (R) An Englishman, abducted by aliens three years before, returns to his family with a deadly, transforming disease. Slime-bucket splatter flick notable for the scene where a woman gives birth to a full-grown man, and various sex slashings. 90m/C VHS, DVD, GB Philip Sayer, Bernice Stegers, Danny Brainin, Simon Nash, Maryam D'Abo, David Cardy, Anna Wing, Peter Mandell, Robert Fyfe; *D*: Harry Bromley-Davenport; *W*: Robert Smith, Iain Cassie; *C*: John Metcalfe; *M*: Harry Bromley-Davenport.

Xtro 2: The Second Encounter 1991 (R) Research facility conducts an experiment to transfer people to a parallel dimension. A sequel to "Xtro" in name only. Turns out three researchers sent to the other side, only one returns, unconscious. Turns out that he is playing host to a biohazardous creature brought over from the other dimension who escapes into the air shafts and threatens to kill everyone in the building. One more problem: if the creature isn't killed, the computer system will fill the building with radiation. Sound familiar? It should, because this is a low-budget remake of "Alien." Good photography, adequate acting, but Vincent just isn't credible as a brilliant scientist. A sequel to "Xtro" in name only. 92m/C VHS, DVD, CA Jan-Michael Vincent, Paul Koslo, Tara Buckman, aro Francsen, Nicholas Lea; *D*: Harry Bromley-Davenport. Nic Amorosa, Tracy Westerholm; *D*: Harry Bromley-Davenport.

Xtro 3: Watch the Skies 1995 (R) Military unit arrives at a remote island where the government has covered up a UFO landing. However, the island is now inhabited by a pissed-off alien whose mate has been killed. 90m/C VHS, DVD, Sal Landi, Jim Hanks, Robert Culp, Andrew Divoff, Karen Moncrieff; *D*: Harry Bromley-Davenport; *W*: Daryl Haney.

XXX 2002 (PG-13) Director Rob Cohen attempts to update the secret agent flick for the X Games crowd with this stunt-riddled explosion fest. Xander "XXX" Cage (Diesel) is a former extreme athlete recruited by NSA agent Gibbons (Jackson) after he's busted stealing a senator's car. Xander is given a choice between jail time or becoming a special ops agent. He then spends the rest of the movie jumping off, sliding down and blowing up plot devices. If you're looking for an action flick, you could do worse. 124m/C VHS, DVD. Vin Diesel, Samuel L. Jackson, Asia Argento, Marton Csokas, Michael Roof, Leila Arcieri, Eve, Danny Trejo; *D*: Rob Cohen; *W*: Rich Wilkes; *C*: Dean Semler; *M*: Randy Edelman.

XX/XY 2002 (R) In 1993, Coles Burroughs (Ruffalo) is studying film at Sarah Lawrence, meets fellow students Sam (Stange) and Thea (Robertson), and tries a menage a trois until pairing off with Sam for awhile. Ten years later, Coles is an ad exec living with longtime girlfriend Claire (Wright). Thea runs a restaurant with husband Milles (Thornton), and Sam has just returned from London after breaking her engagement. Sam and Coles meet accidentally and they're soon rekindling their long-ago flame. The sexual intrigue comes to a head during a weekend in the Hamptons. 91m/C VHS, DVD. US Mark Ruffalo, Maya Stange, Kathleen Robertson, Petra Wright, David Thornton, Kel O'Neill, Joshua Spafford, Zach Shaffer; *D*: Austin Chick; *W*: Austin Chick; *C*: Uta Briesewitz.

Xiu Xiu: The Sent Down Girl 1997 (R) To foil Chinese censors, first-time director Chen was forced into guerilla filmmaking (shooting without official permission) to get this moving effort set during the Cultural Revolution. In 1975, teenaged city girl Xiu-Xiu (Lu Lu) is sent down to a remote corner of Tibet to learn horse training from peasant Lao Jin (Lopsang). She expects only to be gone six-months but is instead stuck, forgotten, on the plains. In desperation, Xiu-Xiu begins to trade sexual favors in exchange for the chance to return home. Based on the novel "Tian Yu" (Heavenly Bath) by co-writer Geling, Manda'in with subtitles. 99m/C VHS, DVD. Lu Lu, Lopsang; *D*: Joan Chen; *W*: Joan Chen, Yan Geling; *C*: Lu Yue; *M*: Johnny Chen.

introspective drama about feelings, move along. If you're looking to watch things go "Boom!" while a thick-necked mumbling guy acts like a jackass, then put it in and get some popcorn. Cohen and Diesel previously teamed up on "The Fast and the Furious," so the bets on the duo remaking "Steel Magnolias" as their next project have officially been taken off the board. **111m/C VHS, DVD, Blu-ray Disc, UMD.** US Vin Diesel, Samuel L. Jackson, Asia Argento, Marton Csokas, Danny Trejo, Michael Roof, Tom Everett, Richy Muller, Werner Daehn; *D:* Rob Cohen; *W:* Rich Wilkes; *C:* Dean Semler; *M:* Randy Edelman.

XXX: State of the Union ♦♦ **2005 (PG-13)** Ice Cube replaces Vin Diesel (whose character, Xander Cage, is pointedly and dismissively pronounced dead about 20 minutes in) as Darius Stone, a former Navy SEAL in Gibbons' (Jackson) old unit jailed nine years ago for leading a mutiny against a general. When members of that old SEAL unit begin disappearing and Gibbons' XXX HQ is attacked, the two team up to find out why. What they find is an attempted military coup by the Secretary of Defense (Dafoe). To no one's surprise, there's plenty of explosions, gunplay, car chases, and mayhem, and none of it makes a damn bit of sense. But for those who enjoy that sort of thing, it is a wild ride. Don't expect anything resembling believability, though. **94m/C DVD, Blu-ray Disc, UMD.** US Ice Cube, Samuel L. Jackson, Willem Dafoe, Scott Speedman, Peter Strauss, Nona Gaye, Michael Roof, Sunny Mabrey, Xzibit, John G. Connolly; *D:* Lee Tamahori; *W:* Simon Kinberg; *C:* David Tattersall; *M:* Marco Beltrami.

Y Tu Mama Tambien ♦♦♦½ *And Your Mother Too* 2001 Mexican teenagers Julio (Bernal) and Tenoch (Luna) envision a guilt-free, sex-filled summer when their girlfriends go to Europe on vacation. At a wedding, they meet Luisa (Verdu), the wife of Tenoch's cousin, and begin a flirtation, telling her of their planned trip to a secluded (and non-existent) beach. When Luisa discovers her husband's infidelity, she decides to join the boys on their trip, and their adolescent sexual fantasies turn to emotional upheaval when she seduces them separately. Believe it or not, this is a comedy (and a funny one), with "American Pie" type jokes and shenanigans sprinkled throughout. But since this movie has a brain, and something of a soul, the consequences aren't always slapstick-funny. Spanish with subtitles. **105m/C VHS, DVD. MX** Gael Garcia Bernal, Diego Luna, Maribel Verdu; *D:* Alfonso Cuaron; *W:* Alfonso Cuaron, Carlos Cuaron; *C:* Emmanuel Lubezki. Ind. Spirit '03: Foreign Film; L.A. Film Critics '02: Foreign Film; N.Y. Film Critics '02: Foreign Film; Natl. Soc. Film Critics '02: Foreign Film.

Y2K ♦♦½ **1999 (R)** The gimmick of the Y2K bug is what this tame actioner hangs its plot on. A secret U.S. nuclear facility, established by the CIA in the Colombian jungle 30 years ago, is becoming destabilized because its computer thinks it's 1969 and that the U.S. is under nuclear attack. A Y2K expert (Woolvett), a crazy general (McDowell), a CIA officer (O'Ross), and the facility's designer (Gossett), among others, all try to head off disaster. **103m/C VHS.** Jaimz Woolvett, Louis Gossett Jr., Ed O'Ross, Malcolm McDowell, Sarah Chalke, Ismael Carlo; *D:* Richard Pepin; *W:* Terry Cunningham, Mick Dalrymple; *C:* Ronald Orieux; *M:* John Sponsler.

Yaaba ♦♦½ 1989 *Grandmother* Young Nopoko and her cousin Bila chance to meet an old woman named Sana, who was outcast from their village as a witch years before. When Nopoko falls seriously ill, Bila wants Sana to help save her but the villagers refuse to let the old woman near. So Sana journeys to find a doctor in hopes that he can provide a cure the suspicious villagers will accept. **90m/C VHS, with subtitles.** Assita Ouedraogo, Rasmane Ouedraogo, Fatimata Sanga, Noufou Ouedraogo, Roukietou Barry, Adama Ouedraogo, Amade Toure, Sibidou Ouedraogo, Adame Sidibe, Ismael Carlo; *D:* Idrissa Ouedraogo; *W:* Idrissa Ouedraogo; *C:* Matthias Kalin; *M:* Francis Bebey.

The Yakuza ♦♦♦½ *Brotherhood of the Yakuza* 1975 (R) An ex G.I. (Mitchum) returns to Japan to help an old army buddy find his kidnapped daughter. He learns the daughter has been kidnapped by the Japanese version of the Mafia (the Yakuza) and he must call on old acquaintances to help free her. A westernized oriental gangster drama with a nice blend of buddy moments, action, ancient ritual, and modern Japanese locations. **112m/C VHS, DVD.** Robert Mitchum, Richard Jordan, Ken Takakura, Brian Keith, Herb Edelman; *D:* Sydney Pollack; *W:* Paul Schrader, Leonard Schrader, Robert Towne; *M:* Dave Grusin.

Yanco ♦♦ 1964 A young Mexican boy makes visits to an island where he plays his homemade violin. Unfortunately, no one can understand or tolerate his love for music, save for an elderly violinist, who gives him lessons on an instrument known as "Yanco," but not exactly riveting, but sensitively played. Spanish with subtitles. **95m/B VHS. MX** Ricardo Ancona, Jesus Medina, Maria Bustamante; *D:* Servando Gonzalez; *W:* Servando Gonzalez; *C:* Alex Phillips Jr.; *M:* Gustavo Cesar Carrion.

A Yank in Australia ♦♦ 1943 Australian farce/war mystery/romance/documentary tells the story of two WWII newspaper reporters whose ship gets torpedoed, stranding them in the Australian outback, where they manage to foil a Japanese invasion. **56m/B VHS. AU** Al Thomas, Hartney Arthur, Kitty Bluett, Jane Connolly, Graham Wicker; *D:* Alfred Goulding; *W:* Alfred Goulding; *C:* George Malcolm.

Yank in Libya ♦½ 1942 No, not the American bombing raid of Khadafy, rather a low-budget WWII adventure pitting an American man and an English girl against Libyan Arabs and Nazis. **65m/B VHS, DVD.** Walter Woolf King, Joan Woodbury, H.B. Warner, Parkyakarkus (Harry Einstein); *D:* Albert Herman; *W:* Arthur St. Claire, Sherman Lowe; *C:* Edward Linden.

A Yank in the R.A.F. ♦♦½ 1941 Power's enthusiastic performance as a brash American pilot boosts this dated WWII adventure. He and his British allies seem more concerned over who gets showgirl Betty Grable than in the Nazis, but climactic air attacks retain excitement. Produced by Darryl F. Zanuck to drum up American support for embattled Britain and France. **98m/B VHS, DVD.** Tyrone Power, Betty Grable, John Sutton, Reginald Gardiner; *D:* Henry King.

Yankee Buccaneer ♦♦ 1952 With the arrival of impulsive Lt. David Farragut (Brady), Naval Captain David Porter's (Chandler) frigate is given a new assignment. The crew and ship are to sail to the Caribbean, disguised as pirates, and stop the criminals who have been preying on America's merchant fleet. Portuguese countess Donna (Ball) comes aboard since the pirates are threatening to overthrow her government, but when she and Farragut are captured, it's the noble Porter to their rescue. **86m/C VHS, DVD.** Jeff Chandler, Scott Brady, Suzan Ball, Joseph Calleia, George Mathews, Rodolfo Acosta, David Janssen; *D:* Fred de Cordova; *W:* Charles K. Peck Jr.; *C:* Russell Metty; *M:* Milton Rosen.

Yankee Clipper ♦♦½ 1927 Deceit, treachery, and romance are combined in this depiction of a fierce race from China to New England between the American ship Yankee Clipper, and the English ship Lord of the Isles. Silent. **68m/B VHS.** William Boyd, Elinor Fair, Frank "Junior" Coghlan, John Miljan; *D:* Rupert Julian.

Yankee Doodle Dandy ♦♦♦♦ 1942 Nostalgic view of the Golden Era of show business and the man who made it glitter—George M. Cohan. His early days, triumphs, songs, musicals and romances are brought to life by the inexhaustible Cagney in a rare and wonderful song-and-dance performance. Told in flashback, covering the Irishman's struggling days as a young song writer and performer to his salad days as the toast of Broadway. Cagney, never more charismatic, dances up a storm, reportedly inventing most of the steps on the spot. ♫Give My Regards to Broadway; Yankee Doodle Dandy; You're a Grand Old Flag; Over There; I Was Born in Virginia; Off the Record; You're a Wonderful Girl; Blue Skies. Grey Skies; Oh You Wonderful Girl. **126m/B VHS, DVD.** James Cagney, Joan Leslie, Walter Huston, Richard Whorf, Irene Manning, Rosemary DeCamp, Jeanne Cagney, S.Z. Sakall, Walter Catlett, Frances Langford, Eddie Foy Jr., George Tobias, Michael Curtiz; *D:* Michael Curtiz; *W:* Robert Buckner, *C:* James Wong Howe. Oscars '42: Actor (Cagney), Sound, Score/Musical; AFI '98: Top 100, Natl. Film Reg. '93'; N.Y. Film Critics '42: Actor (Cagney).

Yankee Doodle in Berlin ♦♦½ 1919 A spoof of WWI dramas, with the hero dressing up as a woman and seducing the Kaiser into giving up his war plans. Typical Sennett slapstick with a music and effects score added to the silent film. **60m/B VHS.** Ford Sterling, Ben Turpin, Marie Prevost, Bothwell Browne; *D:* F. Richard Jones; *W:* Mack Sennett; *C:* Fred W. Jackman.

Yankee Zulu ♦♦ 1995 (PG) A young black boy, Zulu, and a young white boy, Rhino, begin a friendship in their South African homeland that is torn apart by apartheid. Twenty-five years later, they are reunited by chance and forced into race-reversal roles that lead to a number of comedic disasters and a renewal of their boyhood friendship. **88m/C VHS. SA** Leon Schuster, John Matshikiza, Wilson Dunster, Terri Treas; *D:* Gray Hofmeyr; *W:* Leon Schuster, Gray Hofmeyr.

Yanks ♦♦ 1979 An epic-scale but uneventful drama depicts the legions of American soldiers billeted in England during WWII, and their impact—mostly sexual—on the staid Britons. No big story, no big deal, despite a meticulous recreation of the era. **139m/C VHS, DVD.** Richard Gere, Vanessa Redgrave, William Devane, Lisa Eichhorn, Rachel Roberts, Chick Vennera, Arlen Dean Snyder, Annie Ross; *D:* John Schlesinger; *W:* Colin Welland, Walter Bernstein; *C:* Dick Bush; *M:* Richard Rodney Bennett. British Acad. '79: Support. Actress (Roberts); Natl. Bd. of Review '79; Director (Schlesinger).

The Yards ♦♦½ 2000 (R) Director James Gray presents a gloomy, tragic New York story once again in his follow-up to "Little Odessa." Just out of the joint, Leo (Wahlberg) returns home to find that his mother Val (Burstyn) is suffering from a heart condition and his girl Erica (Theron) has taken up with his best friend Willie (Phoenix). Deciding to do right by mom, Leo decides to get a job with his Uncle Frank (Caan), whose company makes and repairs New York City trains. He discovers that his uncle isn't as squeaky clean as he thought when he joins Willie's crew, running highly illegal errands for Frank. On a sabotage mission to a competing company, Willie murders a security guard and tries to pin the crime on Leo. Leo is now chased by the cops and Uncle Frank's "family." Gray's writing is superb and the cast turns in good performances as well, although Theron's Noo Yawk accent tends to grate. **115m/C VHS, DVD.** Mark Wahlberg, James Caan, Charlize Theron, Joaquin Rafael (Leaf) Phoenix, Ellen Burstyn, Faye Dunaway, Tony Musante, Steve Lawrence, Victor Argo, Tomas Milian, Victor Arnold, Chad Aaron, Andrew Davoli, Robert Montano; *D:* James Gray; *W:* James Gray, Matt Reeves; *C:* Harris Savides; *M:* Howard Shore. Natl. Bd. of Review '00: Support. Actor (Phoenix).

The Yarn Princess ♦♦½ 1994 With her family threatened by separation, mentally retarded Marjorie Thomas (Smart) must prove to state authorities that she has the ability to take care of her six sons when husband Jake (Pastorelli) falls victim to severe schizophrenia. Boutsikaris plays Smart's defense lawyer. Average made for TV movie about a handicapped woman beating the odds. **92m/C VHS, DVD.** Jean Smart, Robert Pastorelli, Dennis Boutsikaris, Peter Crook; *D:* Tom McLoughlin; *W:* Dalene Young. TV

A Year in Provence ♦♦½ 1989 Retired London executive Peter Mayle and his wife Annie decide to leave England to live in the south of France. They buy a 200-year-old farmhouse and experience all the trials and amusements of forging a new life in a different country, complete with different language and customs. They hoped for tranquility and what they got were eccentric neighbors, endless renovations, lots of company, and a taste for good food and drink. Based on Mayle's autobiographical novels "A Year in Provence" and "Toujours Provence" and filmed on location. **360m/C VHS, DVD. GB** John Thaw, Lindsay Duncan, Bernard Spiegel, Jean-Pierre Delage, Maryse Kuster, Louis Lyonnet; *D:* David Tucker; *W:* Michael Sadler. TV

The Year My Voice Broke ♦♦♦ 1987 (PG-13) Above-average adolescent drama: a girl breaks a boy's heart by getting pregnant by a tougher, older boy, then leaves town. Blues-inducing, explicit, and not pleasant, but good acting from newcomers carries the day. Followed by "Flirting." **103m/C VHS, DVD. AU** Noah Taylor, Leone Carmen, Ben Mendelsohn, Graeme Blundell, Lynette Curran, Malcolm Robertson, Judi Farr, Bruce Spence; *D:* John Duigan; *W:* John Duigan; *C:* Geoff Burton; *M:* Christine Woodruff. Australian Film Inst. '87: Film.

The Year of Living Dangerously ♦♦♦½ 1982 (PG) Political thriller features Gibson as immature, impulsive Australian journalist Guy Hamilton, who's covering a political story in Indonesia, circa 1965. During the coup against President Sukarno, he becomes involved with British attache Jill Bryant (Weaver) at the height of the bloody fighting and rioting in Jakarta. Hunt is excellent as male photographer Billy Swan, central to the action as the moral center. Rumored to be based on the activities of CNN's Peter Arnett, although the original source is a novel by C.J. Koch, who reportedly collaborated/battled with Weir on the screenplay. Fascinating, suspenseful film, set up brilliantly by Weir, with great romantic chemistry between Gibson and Weaver. Shot on location in the Philippines (then moved to Sydney after cast and crew were threatened). First Australian movie financed by a U.S. studio. **114m/C VHS, DVD. AU** Mel Gibson, Sigourney Weaver, Linda Hunt, Michael Murphy, Noel Ferrier, Bill Kerr; *D:* Peter Weir; *W:* Peter Weir, David Williamson; *C:* Russell Boyd; *M:* Maurice Jarre. Oscars '83: Support. Actress (Hunt); L.A. Film Critics '83: Support. Actress (Hunt); Natl. Bd. of Review '83: Support. Actress (Hunt); N.Y. Film Critics '83: Support. Actress (Hunt).

Year of the Comet ♦♦♦ 1992 (PG-13) Amusing adventure/romantic comedy throws straightlaced Maggie (Miller) together with carefree Oliver (Daly) in a quest for a rare bottle of wine. Fine wine is Maggie's passion, and snagging this particular bottle will boost her status in the family business. Oliver is a pretzels and beer kind of guy, but his boss wants this bottle and will pay a lot to get it. Wants to be another "Romancing the Stone," but plot and characters are too thin. Nice chemistry between Miller and Daly sort of saves this one despite a disappointing script. Beautiful location shots of Scotland. **135m/C VHS.** Penelope Ann Miller, Timothy Daly, Louis Jourdan, Art Malik, Ian Richardson, Ian McNeice, Timothy Bentinck, Jacques Mathou; *D:* Peter Yates; *W:* William Goldman; *M:* Hummie Mann.

Year of the Dog ♦♦♦ 2007 (PG-13) Peggy (Shannon) is your basic single, middle-aged office drone whose one true love is her beagle, Pencil. When Pencil suddenly dies, Peggy goes off the deep end in her grief. Looking for a sense of purpose, Peggy takes up the cause of animal rights, with the encouragement of fellow activist Newt (Sarsgaard), and also adopts every stray she sees. Shannon plays her character absolutely straight: Peggy might be nuts, she might be unsympathetic sometimes, but she's completely sincere and those animals are lucky to have her. Screenwriter (and actor) White makes his directorial debut. **98m/C DVD. US** Molly Shannon, Peter Sarsgaard, Laura Dern, Thomas (Tom) McCarthy, Regina King, John C. Reilly, Josh Pais; *D:* Mike White; *W:* Mike White; *C:* Tim Orr; *M:* Christophe Beck.

Year of the Dragon ✗✗½ **1985 (R)** Polish-police Captain Stanley White of the NYPD vows to neutralize the crime lords running New York's China-town. Brilliant cinematography, well-done action scenes win maximum violence, a racist hero you don't want to root for, murky script, and semi-effective direction are the highlights of this tour through the black market's underbelly and tics. Based on Robert Daley's novel. **136m/C VHS, DVD.** Jack Kehler, Mickey Rourke, John Lone, Ariane, Leonard Termo, Raymond J. Barry; **D:** Oliver Stone, Michael Cimino; **W:** Oliver Stone, Michael Cimino.

Year of the Gun ✗✗½ **1991 (R)** McCarthy is an American journalist in Rome who begins a novel based on the political instability around him, using the names of real people in his first draft. Soon, ambitious photojournalist Stone wants to collaborate with him, and the Red Brigade terrorist group wants to "remove" anyone associated with the book. Although failing on occasion to balance the thin line it establishes between reality and perception, "Gun" aspires to powerful dra-ma, offering a realistic look at the lives and priorities of political terrorists. Love scenes between Stone and McCarthy are torrid. **111m/C VHS, DVD.** Andrew McCarthy, Sharon Stone, Valeria Golino, John Pankow, Mattia Sbra-gia, George Murcell; **D:** John Frankenheimer; **W:** David Ambrose, Jay Presson Allen; **M:** Bill Conti.

Year of the Horse ✗✗ **1997 (R)** Jarmusch's documentary on the nearly 30-year rock phenomenon of Neil Young & Crazy Horse. Looking as gritty as some of Horse's riffs sound, pic intercuts foot-age of the band's performances in '76, '86, and the latest '96 European and U.S. tours shot on Super-8, High Fi-8 video, and 16 mm. Jarmusch wisely lets songs run full-length with complete perfor-mances intact, though lesser fans of the band may not be as thrilled about that. Falls short in capturing the spirit and es-sence of the band and their drive to stay together after all these years, but does show some cool behind-the-scenes mo-ments that make it worthwhile to rock fans. **107m/C VHS, DVD.** **D:** Jim Jarmusch.

Year of the Quiet Sun ✗✗✗½ **1984 (FE)** A poignant, acclaimed love story about a Polish widow and an American soldier who find each other in the war-torn landscape of 1945 Europe. Beautifully rendered, with a confi-dent sense of time and place, making this much more than a simple love story. In Polish with English subtitles. **106m/C VHS, DVD.** **PL:** GE Scott Wilson, Maja Komorowska; **D:** Krzysztof Zanussi. Venice Fl'r. Fest. '84: Film.

A Year Without Love ✗✗ ½ **2005** *Un Ano Sin Amor* Patro (Minujín) is a young Argentinian writer living with AIDS who is boldly facing the physical effects of the disease while seeking a cure. As a clock sound ticks off his minutes of his fading life, Pablo still hopefully pursues a new love while partaking in the painful pleasure of S&M at various gay clubs in Buenos Aires. Taken from the real-life di-aries of Pablo Perez. **95m/C DVD.** Juan Minu-jín, Mimi Ardú, Javier Van de Couter, Carlos Eche-varria, Barbara Lombardo, Osmar Nunez, Carlos Bonelli; **W:** Anahí Barneri, Fabio Pérez; **C:** Lucio Bonelli; **M:** Lec Garcia, Martin Bauer.

The Yearling ✗✗✗½ **1946** This family classic is a tear-jerking adaptation of the Marjorie Kinnan Rawlings novel about a young boy's love for a yearling fawn during the post Civil-War era. His fa-ther's encouragement and his mother's bitterness play against the story of unqua-lified love amid poverty and the boy's com-

---

ing of age. Wonderful footage of Florida. Jarman was awarded a special Oscar as outstanding child actor. **128m/C VHS, DVD.** Gregory Peck, Jane Wyman, Claude Jarman Jr., Chill Wills, Henry Travers, Jeff York, Forrest Tuck-er, June Lockhart, Margaret Wycherly; **D:** Clarence Brown; **C:** Charles Rosher. Oscars '46: Color Cine-matog.; Golden Globes '47: Actor--Drama (Peck).

The Yearling ✗✗½ **1994** TV re-make of the classic Marjorie Kinnan Rawl-ings novel about a boy and his orphaned fawn. The Baxters are struggling in '30s Florida: Pa Penny (Strauss) is a hard-scrabble farmer and severe Ma, Ora (Smart) has lost three of her four children. Surviving son, 12-year-old Jody (Hornett), gets more than his share of life's hard les-sons—with even his adored pet causing problems. On the cloying side, the 1946 big-screen version is still the one to watch. Filmed in South Carolina. **96m/C VHS.** Peter Strauss, Jean Smart, Wil Horneff, Brad Green-quist, Jared Blanchard, Philip Seymour Hoffman, Nancy Moore Atchison; **D:** Rod Hardy; **W:** Joe Wiesenfeld; **M:** Lee Holdridge.

Yellow ✗✗ **1998** Eight Korean-Ameri-can 'teens have big plans for their gradua-tion night in L.A. but they didn't originally include Jin Lee (Chung) re-cover the large sum of his dad's dough that he lost. They get into more trouble trying to round up the cash and Sin reacts to their friendly efforts by running away and making things worse for himself. **90m/ C VHS, DVD.** Soon-Teck Oh, Amy Hill, Michael Chung, Burt Bulos, Angie Suh, Mia Suh, Jason J. Tobin, Lela Lee, Mary Chen, John Cho; **D:** Chris Chan Lee; **W:** Chris Chan Lee; **C:** Ted Cohen; **M:** John Oh.

Yellow ✗✗ **2006 (R)** Clichéd though energetic follow-your-dreams pic. Classi-cally trained dancer Amaryllis (very sultry Sanchez) moves from San Juan to New York hoping to dance on Broadway. Need-ing a job while she auditions, Amaryllis works as a stripper (whose nom de pole is "Yellow") and soon has a favorite client, depressed doctor Christian (Sweeney), who wants to sweep Amaryllis away from all the sleaze. **90m/C DVD.** Roselyn Sanchez, D.B. Sweeney, Bill Duke, Manny Perez, Jamie Ti-rell, Erika Michaels; **D:** Alfredo de Villa; **W:** Rose-lyn Sanchez, Naccima Whodery; **C:** Claudio Chea; **M:** Andre Abujamra.

Yellow Asphalt ✗✗ ½ *Asphalt Zahov* **2001** Writer-director Verete presents a col-lection of three fictional stories that high-light real-world cultural differences be-tween Arabic Bedouin tribes and the Jew-ish community in Israel: the accidental death of a child by at the hands of two callous Israelis, a German woman at-tempting to flee her stifling Bedouin mar-riage with her daughters, and a Bedouin maid caught having a 'forbidden affair. Grand view of the Middle East's desert. In Hebrew and Arabic, with English subtitles. **87m/C VHS, DVD.** Sami Samir, Tatiana Blacher, Raida Aden, Moshe Ivgy, Zavk Raz, Abed Zuabi, Motti Katz; **D:** Dan Verete; **W:** Dan Verete; **C:** Yo-ram Milio; **M:** Yves Touati. VIDEO

The Yellow Cab Man ✗✗½ **1950** Skelton plays a cab driver who is also an inventor of safety gadgets. When he invents unbreakable elastic glass he finds various crooks after him for the for-mula. Skelton's wacky inventions are amusing but the movie culminates in a breakneck chase through a home show exposition. **85m/B VHS.** Red Skelton, Gloria De Haven, Walter Slezak, Edward Arnold, James Gleason, Jay C. Flippen, Paul Harvey; **D:** Jack Do-nohue.

Yellow Cargo ✗✗ **1936** Ingenious "B" movie about a pair of undercover agents who blow the lid of a smuggling scam. It seems that the smugglers have been masquerading as a movie crew, and use disguised Chinese "extras" to trans-port their goods. The agents pose as an Al You Need is Love: Hey, Bulldog; When alleged comedy with a great cast who wan-tors to infiltrate the gang. The agents and nal Nagel, Eleanor Hunt, Vince Barnett, Jack La Rue, Claudia Dell; **D:** Crane Wilbur; **W:** Crane Wil-bur.

Yellow Dust ✗✗½ **1936** Dull story of a gold miner (Dix) who hits a big strike but before he can make good on it he's ac-cused of a series of stagecoach robberies.

So he goes undercover to clear his name. Based on the play "Mother Lode" by Dan Totheroh and George O'Neil. **68m/B VHS.** Richard Dix, Leila Hyams, Andy Clyde, Onslow Stevens, Moroni Olsen, Jessie Ralph; **D:** Wallace Fox.

Yellow Earth ✗✗✗ **1984** *Huang Tudi* **1989** In 1939 a soldier arrives in a small Chinese village to research folk songs. He becomes involved in the lives of a local peasant family, including a 14-year-old girl who wishes to escape from a pre-ar-ranged marriage. Mixture of poetry, dance, music and drama set against the barren landscape of the title. In Mandarin Chinese with English subtitles. **89m/C VHS.** **Ch:** Xue Bai, Wang Xueqi, Tan Tuo; Liu Qiang; **D:** Chen Kaige; **W:** Zhang Ziliang.

The Yellow Fountain ✗✗ *La Fuente Amarilla* **1999** Following the mysteri-ous suicide of her boyfriend, Lola (Abas-cal) heads for Madrid to research the Chi-nese side of her family, and to get clues into the ruthless Triads. Director Santesmases allows the film to unfold at a deliberate pace, as another piece of the puzzle is revealed every few minutes. The problem is that most of the story seems to be quiet Sergio (Noriega), a ner-vous government employee whose hobby is collecting data on Chinese immigrants. Together, they uncover an illegal immi-grant smuggling ring, and Lola decides to take on the ruthless Triads. **94m/C VHS.** **SP** Silvia Abascal, Eduardo Noriega, Carlos Wu, Chen Lam; **D:** Miguel Santesmases; **W:** Miguel Santes-mases; **C:** Javier Aguirresarobe.

Yellow Hair & the Fortress of Gold ✗✗½ **1984** *Yellow Hair and the Pecos Kid* Princess who's part Indian and her sidekick fight bad guys and seek gold. Well-meaning, self-conscious parody. **55m/B VHS, DVD.** Roy Rogers, Dale Evans, Grant Withers, Harry Shannon; **D:** Joseph Kane.

Yellow Submarine ✗✗✗½ **1968 (G)** The acclaimed animated fantasy based on a plethora of mid-career Beatles songs, sees the Fab Four battle the Blue Meanies for the sake of Sgt. Pepper, the Nowhere Man, Strawberry Fields, and Pepperland. The first full-length British animated feature in 14 years features a host of talented cartoonists. Fascinating LSD-esque animation and imagery. Speaking voices provided by John Clive (John), Geoff Hughes (Paul), Peter Batten (George), and Paul Angelis (Ringo). The Beatles themselves do appear in a short scene at the end of the film. Martin fills in as music director, and Segal of "Love Sto-ry" fame co-scripts. **J:** Yellow Submarine; I'm Sixty Four; Nowhere Man; Lucy in the Sky With Diamonds; Sgt. Pepper's Lonely Hearts Club Band; A Day in the Life; All Together Now. **87m/C VHS, DVD.** **GB** **D:** Georg Dunning, Dick Emery; **W:** Erich Segal, Al Brodax, Jack Mendelsohn, Lee Minoff; **M:** George Martin, George Harrison, John Lennon, Paul McCartney, Ringo Starr; **V:** John Clive, Geoff Hughes, Peter Batten, Paul Angelis, Dick Emery, Lance Percival, George Harrison, John Lennon, Paul McCartney, Ringo Starr.

Yellowbeard ✗✗ **1983 (PG)** An al-leged comedy with a great cast who wan-der about with little direction. Follows the efforts of an infamous pirate (Chapman) to locate a buried treasure using the map lat-tooed on the back of his son's head. Final role for Feldman, who died during produc-tion. **97m/C VHS, DVD.** Graham Chapman, Peter Boyle, Richard "Cheech" Marin, Thomas Chong, Peter Cook, Mary Feldman, Martin Hewitt, Michael

---

Hordern, Eric Idle, Madeline Kahn, James Mason, John Cleese, Susanah York, David Bowie, Monte Landis, Kenneth Mars, Ferdinand "Ferdy" Mayne, Beryl Reid; **D:** Mel Damski; **W:** Bernard McKenna, Graham Chapman, Peter Cook; **C:** Gerry Fisher; **M:** John Morris.

Yellowneck ✗✗ **1955** A handful of Confederate Army soldiers desert, hoping to cross the Florida Everglades and even-tually reach Cuba. The swamp takes its toll, however, and one by one men fall by the wayside. A sole survivor reaches the coast. Will the raw escape be waiting for him? **83m/C VHS, DVD.** Lin McCarthy, Steph-en Courtleigh, Berry Kroeger, Harold Gordon, Bill Mason; **D:** R. John Hugh.

Yellowstone ✗✗ **1936** An ex-con is murdered at Yellowstone National Park, at the site of a hidden cache of money, of which assorted folks are in search. Un-complicated, well-meaning mystery. **65m/B VHS, DVD.** Andy Devine, Ralph Morgan, Judith Barrett; **D:** Arthur Lubin.

Yentl ✗✗½ **1983 (PG)** The famous Barbra adaptation of Isaac Bashevis Sing-er's story set in 1900s Eastern Europe about a Jewish girl who masquerades as a boy in order to study the Talmud, and who becomes enmeshed in romantic mis-cues. Lushly photographed, with a repeti-tive score that nevertheless won an Os-car. Singer was reportedly appalled by the results of Streisand's hyper-controlled project. **J:** A Piece of Sky; No Matter What Happens; This Is One of Those Moments; Tomorrow Night; Where Is It Written; No Wonder; The Way He Makes Me Feel; Ever Look at Me That Way?; Will I ? **134m/C VHS, DVD.** Barbra Streisand, Mandy Patinkin, Amy Irving, Nehemiah Persoff, Steven Hill, Allan Corduner, Ruth Goring, David de Keyser, Bernard Spear; **D:** Barbra Streisand; **C:** David Watkin; **M:** Michel Leg-rand, Alan Bergman, Marilyn Bergman. Oscars '83: Orig. Song Score and/or Adapt.; Golden Globes '84: Director (Streisand), Film--Mus./Comedy.

Yerma ✗✗ **1999** Yerma (Sanchez-Gi-jon) desperately wants a child but is un-able to conceive. The village wise woman (Papas) puts the blame on her husband Juan (Diego). As her obsession grows so does Yerma's hatred of her hus-band and she is tempted to seduce shep-herd Victor (Cabrano) to fulfill her longings, which are now driving her to the edge of insanity. Based on a drama by Federico Garcia Lorca. Spanish with subtitles. **118m/ C VHS, DVD.** **SP** Aitana Sanchez-Gijon, Irene Papas, Juan Diego, Jesus Cabrero; **D:** Pilar Tavo-ra; **W:** Pilar Tavora; **C:** Acacio De Almeida; **M:** Vincente Sanchez.

Yes ✗✗½ **2004 (R)** When She (Allen) and He (Abkarian) cross paths in London, some serious sexual fireworks go off in-sanity. At first, they ignore their cultural differ-ences—She's an Irish-American scientist trapped in a dead-end marriage to a rich politician and He's a Lebanese refugee and surgeon-turned-chef. All good things must come to an end, though, as He des-pises Western culture while she questions Islamic values. Tries too hard to push its post-9/11 political message, as if awk-wardly uses poetic meter for dialogue. **99m/C DVD.** **US** Joan Allen, Simon Abkarian, Sam Neill, Shirley Henderson, Sheila Hancock, Saman-tha Bond, Gary Lewis, Raymond Waring, Stepha-nie Leonidas, Wil Johnson; **D:** Sally Potter; **C:** Alexei Rodionov; **M:** Sally Potter.

Yes, Giorgio ✗✗ **1982 (PG)** Opera singer Pavarotti in his big-screen debut. He has an advantage over other non-ac-tors trapped in similar situations (e.g., Hulk Hogan): He can sing (but of course, not wrestle). Lame plot (famous opera star falls for lady doctor) is the merest excuse for the maestro to belt out "If We Were in Love," "I Left My Heart in San Francisco," and arias by Verdi, Donizetti, and Puccini. **111m/C VHS.** Luciano Pavarotti, Kathryn Harrold, Eddie Albert, James Hong; **D:** Franklin J. Schaff-ner; **W:** Norman Steinberg; **M:** John Williams.

The Yes Men ✗✗ **2003 (R)** Docu-mentary follows a couple of anti-govern-ment pranksters, Andy Bichlbaum and Mike Bonanno, who travel around imper-sonating representatives of the World Trade Organization. They disrupt various economic conferences, give fake interviews and speeches, and generally behave like nitwits. They also seem to be the only ones getting the supposed joke. Fighting the man has never been so bland. **80m/C DVD.** *D:* Chris Smith, Dan Ollman, Sarah Price; *C:* Chris Smith, Dan Ollman, Sarah Price.

Yes Nurse! No Nurse! 🦴🦴½ *Zuster Nee Zuster* 2002 Residents at Nurse Klivia's Rest Home use a series of musical production numbers and a very slight storyline to fight the efforts of a nasty landlord who wants them evicted. **97m/C DVD.** NL Loes Luca, Paul Kooij, Tjitske Reidinga, Waldemar Torenstra, Paul de Leeuw, Edo Brunner, Lennart Vader, Frits Lambrechts; *D:* Pieter Kramer; *W:* Harry Bannink, Frank Houtappels; *C:* Piotr Kukla; *M:* Raymund van Santen, Ferdinand Boland.

Yes, Sir, Mr. Bones 🦴🦴½ 1951 Entertaining but dated musical about a boy who wanders into a rest home and inspires the old folks there to reminisce about their days as riverboat minstrels. 🎵 Want to Be a Minstrel Man; Stay Out of the Kitchen; Is Your Rent Paid Up in Heaven?; Flying Saucers; Memphis Bill; Southland. **60m/B VHS.** Pete Daily, Jimmy O'Brien, Sally Angtim, Cotton Watts, Chick Watts, Chet Davis, F.E. (Flourney) Miller, Scatman Crothers; *D:* Ron Ormond; *W:* Ron Ormond.

The Yesterday Machine woof! 1963 Camp sci-fi: A mad doctor tries to bring back Hitler. Don't worry, though: the good guys win. Predictable, dumb drivel. **85m/B VHS, DVD.** Tim Holt, James Britton, Jack 'Herman; *D:* Russ Marker.

Yesterday, Today and Tomorrow 🦴🦴🦴½ *Ieri, Oggi E Domani; She Got What She Asked For* 1964 Trilogy of comic sexual vignettes featuring Loren and her many charms. She plays a black marketeer, a wealthy matron, and a prostitute. Funny, and still rather racy. Loren at her best, in all senses; includes her famous striptease for Mastroianni. **119m/C VHS, DVD.** IT FR Sophia Loren, Marcello Mastroianni, Tony Pica, Giovanni Ridolfi; *D:* Vittorio De Sica (Mastroianni). '64. Foreign Film; British Acad. '64. Actor (Mastroianni).

Yesterday's Hero 🦴½ 1979 A fading soccer star finds his career and love-life on the upswing. Poor production with equally lame pop music score. **95m/C VHS.** GB Ian McShane, Suzanne Somers, Adam Faith, Paul Nicholas, Glynis Barber, Sandy Ratcliff; *D:* Neil Leifer; *W:* Jackie Collins.

Yesterday's Target 🦴🦴 1996 (R) Paul (Baldwin), Jessica (Haiduk), and Carter (Carter) all possess special psychic powers in their future society, which is on the verge of destruction. They're sent back in time to rescue a young boy who may hold the key to saving their world but a glitch leaves them with collective amnesia and ruthless hunter Holden (McDowell) on their trail. **80m/C VHS, DVD.** Daniel Baldwin, Stacy Haiduk, T.K. Carter, LeVar Burton, Malcolm McDowell, Trevor Goddard; *D:* Barry Samson.

Yi Yi 🦴🦴🦴 *A One and a Two* 2000 N.J. Jian is a middle-aged partner in a Taipei computer firm that needs to innovate if the business is to stay profitable. NJ thinks about teaming up with Japanese games designer, Ota, but a number of family difficulties begin to distract him and things unravel even more while NJ is on a business trip to Japan. Japanese and Mandarin with subtitles. **173m/C VHS, DVD.** JP TW Elaine Jin, Nianzhen Wu, Kelly Lee, Jonathan Chang, Issey Ogata, Suyun Ke; *D:* Edward Yang; *W:* Edward Yang; *C:* Weihan Yang; *M:* Kai-li Peng. Cannes '00: Director (Yang); L.A. Film Critics '00: Foreign Film; N.Y. Film Critics '00: Foreign Film; Natl. Soc. Film Critics '00: Film.

Yidl Mitn Fidl 🦴🦴 *Yiddle with a Fiddle; Castle in the Sky* 1936 Disguised as a man, a young woman travels about the countryside with a group of musicians, revealing her female identity only after falling for a man. One of Picon's finest roles and Green's biggest successes. Vaudevillian fare in Yiddish with English subtitles. 🎵 Yiddle With His Fiddle; Arye With His Bass. **92m/B VHS.** PL Molly Picon, Simche Fostel, Max Bozyk, Leon Liebgold; *D:* Joseph Green.

Yin & Yang of Mr. Go 🦴 1971 (R) A CIA operative must retrieve the stolen plans of an awesome weapons system. Set in Hong Kong, features a strong cast in a tangled tale of no particular merit. Unworthy spoof of Oriental intrigue flicks. **89m/C VHS, DVD.** Jeff Bridges, James Mason, Broderick Crawford, Burgess Meredith; *D:* Burgess Meredith; *W:* Burgess Meredith.

Yodelin' Kid from Pine Ridge 🦴½ *The Hero of Pine Ridge* 1937 Autry tries to stop a war between cattlemen and woodsmen in Georgia. Standard horse opera notable for its location. **59m/B VHS, DVD.** Gene Autry, Smiley Burnette, Betty Bronson, Charles Middleton, Art Mix; *D:* Joseph Kane.

Yog, Monster from Space 🦴 *Kessen Nankai No Daikaiju; Nankai No Daikaiju: The Space Amoeba* 1971 (G) When a spaceship crashes somewhere near Japan, the aliens in it create monsters out of ordinary critters in order to destroy all the cities. A promoter gets a gleam in his eye and sees the potential for a vacation spot featuring the viscious creatures. Standard Japanese monster flick utilizing the usual out-of-synch dub machine. Dubbed. **105m/C VHS, DVD.** JP Akira Kubo, Yoshio Tsuchiya, Kenji Sahara, Atsuko Takahashi, Yukiko Kobayashi, Yu Fujiki, Noritake Saito; *D:* Inoshiro Honda; *W:* Ei Ogawa; *C:* Taichi Kankura; *M:* Akira Ifukube.

Yojimbo 🦴🦴🦴🦴 1961 Two clans vying for political power bid on the services of a laconic masterless samurai Sanjuro (Mifune), who comes to their small town in 1860. The samurai sells his services to both parties, with devastating results for all. Japanese with subtitles or dubbed. Re-made by Sergio Leone as the 1964 western "A Fist Full of Dollars." **110m/B VHS, DVD.** JP Toshiro Mifune, Eijiro Tono, Isuzu Yamada, Seizaburo Kawazu, Kamatari (Keita) Fujiwara, Takashi Shimura, Tatsuya Nakadai, Daisuke Kato, Susumu Fujita, Hiroshi Tachikawa, Kyu Sazanka, Ko Nishimura, Ikio Sawamura, Yoko Tsukasa; *D:* Akira Kurosawa; *W:* Akira Kurosawa, Hideo Oguni, Ryuzo Kikushima; *C:* Kazuo Miyagawa; *M:* Masaru Sato.

Yol 🦴🦴🦴½ *The Way* 1982 (PG) Five Turkish prisoners are granted temporary leave to visit their families. An acclaimed, heartfelt film, written by Guney while he himself was in prison. A potent protest against totalitarianism. In Turkish with English subtitles. **126m/C VHS.** TU Tarik Akan, Serif Sezer; *D:* Yilmaz Guney, Serif Goren; *W:* Yilmaz Guney; *M:* Sebastian Argol. Cannes '82: Film.

Yolanda and the Thief 🦴🦴½ 1945 A charming, forgotten effort from the Arthur Freed unit about a con man who convinces a virginal South American heiress that he is her guardian angel. Songs include a lengthy Dali-esque ballet built around "Will You Marry Me?" 🎵This is the Day for Love; Angel; Yolanda; Coffee Time; Will You Marry Me. **109m/C VHS.** Fred Astaire, Lucille Bremer, Leon Ames, Mildred Natwick; *D:* Vincente Minnelli; *C:* Charles Rosher; *M:* Arthur Freed, Harry Warren.

Yongkari Monster of the Deep 🦴🦴 *Dai Koesu Yongkari; Monster Yongkari; Great Monster Yongkari* 1967 (PG) A giant burrowing creature is causing earthquakes and generally ruining scores of Japanese models. Dubbed. **79m/C VHS, DVD.** KN Oh Young Il, Nam Chung-Im; *D:* Kim Kidak.

Yor, the Hunter from the Future 🦴🦴 *Il Mondo Di Yor; The World of Yor* 1983 (PG) Lost in a time warp where the past and the future mysteriously collide, Yor sets out on a search for his real identity, with his only clue a golden medallion around his neck. **88m/C VHS.** IT Reb Brown, Corinne Cleny, John Steiner; *D:* Anthony M. Dawson; *W:* Anthony M. Dawson, Robert Bailey.

Yossi & Jagger 🦴🦴 2002 Lior (Levi) and Yossi (Knoller) are soldiers stationed at a remote and snowy Army base on the Israeli-Lebanese border. They also happen to be lovers. They're discreet—Yossi is a career military officer—but Lior, who's nicknamed "Jagger" because of his charisma, is ready to leave the service and come out of the closet so they can live together. Tensions are heightened when two female soldiers, Goldie (Furstenberg) and Yaeli (Koren), arrive and Yaeli immediately makes a play for Jagger. Just as the truth about Yossi and Jagger seems certain to come out, the unit is sent on a dangerous night mission. Restraint is the word for director Fox, which only makes the situation more intense. Hebrew with subtitles. **71m/C DVD.** IS Ohad Knoller, Yehuda Levi, Hani Furstenberg, Aya Koren, Assi Cohen, Sharon Reginiano, Erez Kahana; *D:* Eytan Fox; *W:* Avner Bernheimer; *C:* Yaron Sharf; *M:* Ivri Lider.

You and Me 🦴🦴½ 1938 Joe Dennis (Raft) is an ex-con now employed at the same department store as Helen (Sidney). They fall in love and marry without Helen admitting she's on parole herself and the rules forbid her to wed. When Joe realizes his marriage is illegal and his wife's a liar), he picks up with his old gang and plans a robbery. Schizophrenic film is an uneasy mixture of comedy, pathos, romance, crime, and even some songs by Lang's associate Kurt Weill. **90m/B VHS.** George Raft, Sylvia Sidney, Harry Carey Sr., Robert Cummings, Barton MacLane, Warren Hymer, Roscoe Karns, George E. Stone; *D:* Fritz Lang; *W:* Virginia Van Upp; *C:* Charles B(ryam) Lang Jr.; *M:* Boris Morros.

You Are Here * 🦴 2000 (R) You are a big loser. (Well, maybe not you personally but you get the idea.) Your job sucks, your love life sucks, life sucks in general. So you decide to quit your job and do what you've always wanted to do. And then your boss comes along and offers you a promotion. Now what? This indie feature gives you some possibilities. **86m/C VHS, DVD.** Todd Peters, Randall Jaynes, Heather Burns; *D:* Jeff Winner; *W:* Jeff Winner; *C:* Bryan Pryzpek; *M:* Byron Estep.

You Are Not Alone 🦴🦴 *Du Er Ikke Alene* 1978 Two boarding school boys find their friendship turning into first love. But the film doesn't completely dwell on this—when a fellow student is about to be expelled for a prank, the classmates organize a strike against the stern headmaster. Danish with subtitles. **90m/C DVD.** CZ Ove Sprogoe, Anders Agenso, Peter Bjerg; *D:* Ernst Johansen, Lasse Nielsen; *W:* Lasse Nielsen, Bent Petersen; *C:* Henrik Herbert.

You Can Count On Me 🦴🦴 1999 (R) Sammy (Linney) is a single mom who works at the local bank in her small hometown. Orphaned at an early age, she has grown apart from her younger brother Terry (Ruffalo), who's become a self-destructive wanderer. When Terry comes for a visit, the love they still share as siblings conflicts with their unease over their adult selves and what they now expect from each other. Great performances and no pat resolutions. **109m/C VHS, DVD.** Laura Linney, Mark Ruffalo, Matthew Broderick, Jon Tenney, Rory Culkin; *Cameos:* Kenneth Lonergan; *C:* Kenneth Lonergan; *W:* Kenneth Lonergan; Stephen Kazmierski; *M:* Lesley Barber. Ind. Spirit '01: First Feature, Screenplay; L.A. Film Critics '00: Screenplay; N.Y. Film Critics '00: Actress (Linney), Screenplay; Sundance '00: Screenplay, Grand Jury Prize; Writers Guild '00: Orig. Screenplay.

You Can't Cheat an Honest Man 🦴🦴 1939 The owner of a misfit circus suffers a variety of headaches including the wisecracks of Charlie McCarthy. Contains Field's classic ping-pong battle and some of his other best work. **79m/B VHS, DVD.** W.C. Fields, Edgar Bergen, Constance Moore, Eddie Anderson, Mary Forbes, Thurston Hall; *D:* George Marshall; *C:* Milton Krasner.

You Can't Fool Your Wife 🦴🦴 1940 Ball in two roles gives zip to this otherwise ordinary marital comedy. Previously blah better half wins him back with glamour. **69m/C VHS.** Lucille Ball, James Ellison, Robert Coote, Emma Dunn, Nita Naldi; *D:* Ray McCarey.

You Can't Hurry Love 🦴 1988 (R) A jilted-at-the-altar Ohio bachelor moves to Los Angeles and flounders in the city's fast-moving fast lane. A dull film with Fonda, daughter of "Easy Rider" Peter, playing a minor role. **92m/C VHS, DVD.** David Leisure, Scott McGinnis, Sally Kellerman, Kristy McNichol, Charles Grodin, Anthony Geary, Bridget Fonda, David Packer, Frank Bonner; *D:* Richard Martini; *C:* Peter Lyons Collister.

You Can't Take It with You 🦴🦴🦴½ 1938 The Capra version of the Kaufman-Hart play about an eccentric New York family and their non-conformist houseguests. Alice Sycamore (Arthur), the stable family member of an off-beat clan of free spirits, falls for Tony Kirby (Stewart), the down-to-earth son of a snooty, wealthy and not always quite honest family. Amidst the confusion over this love affair, the two families rediscover the simple joys of life. **127m/B VHS, DVD.** James Stewart, Jean Arthur, Lionel Barrymore, Spring Byington, Edward Arnold, Mischa Auer, Donald Meek, Samuel S. Hinds, Ann Miller, H.B. Warner, Halliwell Hobbes, Dub Taylor, Mary Forbes, Eddie Anderson, Harry Davenport, Lillian Yarbo; *D:* Frank Capra; *W:* Robert Riskin. Oscars '38: Director (Capra), Picture.

You Can't Take It with You 🦴🦴🦴 1984 Taped performance of the Kaufman and Hart comedy about the strange pastimes of the Sycamore family who must behave themselves to impress their daughter's boyfriend's stuffy family. **116m/C VHS.** Colleen Dewhurst, James Coco, Jason Robards Jr., Elizabeth Wilson, George Rose; *D:* Ellis Rabb.

You Don't Mess with the Zohan 🦴 2008 The title sucks but at least Sandler is taking a break from that crabby man-child shtick. Instead he plays number one Israeli commando Zohan, who's tired of being a killing machine. His dream is to be a hairstylist in New York so he fakes his death and makes his move into a new life until his past is exposed. Chriqui plays Zohan's Palestinian boss (and love interest) at the hair salon. (And the Arab-Israeli conflict is apparently played for laughs.) Oy vey. Not yet reviewed. **7m/C** Adam Sandler, John Turturro, Emmanuelle Chriqui, Nick Swardson, Rob Schneider, Barry Livingston, Shelley Berman, Omid Abtahi; *Cameos:* Mariah Carey; *D:* Dennis Dugan; *W:* Adam Sandler, Robert Smigel, Judd Apatow; *C:* Michael Barrett; *M:* Rupert Gregson-Williams.

You Got Served 🦴🦴 2004 (PG-13) Friends David (Granberry) and Elgin (Houston)—both from real-life hip hop groups, B2K and IMx, respectively—have a falling out before the big street-dance contest that could earn them $50,000. David is a bit of a tomcat and wants to date Elgin's cute sister, Liyah (Freeman). There's also the issue of the busted drug run. This is about as complex as the story gets. Rookie writer-director Stokes—also responsible of B2K with music-video directing credits—puts all the dancers' energy and talent out there but chops up the segments, thus diminishing the overall effect. Oh and, just to be clear, "you got served" means "I beat you...and BAD." So there. **94m/C DVD, UMD.** US Marques Houston, Michael "Bear" Taliferro, Omari (Omarion) Granderry, Jarell (J-Boog) Houston, DeMario (Raz B) Thornton, Dreux (Lil' Fizz) Frederic, Jennifer Freeman, Christopher Jones, Meagan Good, Steve Harvey, Jackee; *Cameos:* Kimberly (Lil' Kim) Jones; *D:* Christopher B. Stokes; *W:* Christopher B. Stokes; *C:* David Hennings; *M:* Tyler Bates.

You Gotta Stay Happy 🦴🦴½ 1948 Heiress Dee Dee Dillwood (Fontaine) marries the man (Parker) her family approves of and realizes her mistake on their wedding night honeymoon in New York. Distraught, she manages to hide out in the room of failing airplane cargo company owner Marvin Payne (Stewart). He takes her with him on a California-bound cargo flight that winds up crashlanding in a field. By this time Dee Dee and Marvin are in love but then he finds out the truth about his would-be fiancee. **101m/B VHS, DVD.** James Stewart, Joan Fontaine, Eddie Albert, Willard Parker, Roland Young, Halliwell Hobbes, Stanley Prager, Mary Forbes, Percy Kilbride, William "Billy" Bakewell, Arthur Walsh; *D:* H.C. Potter; *W:* Karl Tunberg; *C:* Russell Metty; *M:* Daniele Amfitheatrof.

You Kill Me 🦴🦴½ 2007 (R) Hit man in love. Frank (Kingsley) is a killer for his Polish mob family in New Jersey. Only his drinking problem wrecks havoc and he screws up eliminating rival Irish mob boss

O'Leary (Farina). So Frank's Uncle Roman (Hall) sends him to San Francisco for meetings up. Frank begins attending AA meetings (which are hilarious given Frank's profession) and gets a job at a funeral home. He also finds a grown-up romance with tough sales exec Laurel (a breezy Leoni), who doesn't faze easily. Still, Frank's family, back home is being squeezed. Kingsley), who's done a lot of crap lately, proves again wiry the Brits bothered to knight him. **92m/C DVD, US** Een Kingsley, Tea Leoni, Dennis Farina, Philip Baker Hall, Bill Pullman, Luke Wilson, Jayne East-wood, Jon Dahl, Marcus Thomas, Alison Sealy-Smith; **W:** Christopher Markus, Stephen McFeely; **C:** Jeffrey Jur; **M:** Marcelo Zarvos.

You Know My Name *&&&*
1999 Elliott is perfectly cast in this true story of legendary lawman-turned-moviemaker Bill Tilghman. Tilghman was connected to the Earp Brothers and then segued into early filmmaking, trying to produce authentic silent westerns in what turned out to be an ill-fated venture. In 1924, toward the end of his life, Tilghman is called upon by the law-abiding citizens of oil-rich boomtown Cromwell, Oklahoma to clean up its dens of iniquity. But Tilghman finds himself unexpectedly opposed by corrupt federal agent Wiley (Howard). **94m/C** VHS, DVD. Sam Elliott, Arliss Howard, Carolyn McCormick, James Gammon, R. Lee Ermey, Sheila McCarthy, Jonathan Young, Natalia Rey, James Parks; **D:** John Kent Harrison; **W:** John Kent Harrison. ♪ *You Light Up My Life.* **91m/C** VHS, DVD. Didi Conn, Michael Zaslow, Melanie Mayron, Joe Silver, Stephen Nathan; **D:** Joseph Brooks; **W:** Joseph Brooks; **C:** Eric Saarinen; **M:** Joseph Brooks. Oscars '77: Song ("You Light Up My Life"); Golden Globes '78: Song ("You Light Up My Life").

You Light Up My Life *woof*
1977 **(PG)** Sappy, sentimental story of a young singer trying to break into the music business. Debbie Boone's version of the title song was a radio smash, the constant playing of which drove many people over the edge. ♪ *You Light Up My Life.*

You, Me and Dupree *&&*
2006 **(PG-13)** Call it "The Marriage Crasher." Having recently lost his job, home, and car, down-and-out Dupree (Wilson) becomes the houseguest from hell of his best friend Carl (Dillon) and Carl's reluctant new bride, Molly (Hudson). Dupree strings together rude and crude antics while his hosts react with predictable dismay and lack of confrontation skills; a mugging Douglas adds further strain as a menacing father-in-law who stirs the pot. But Dupree's sleazy charm contrasts with Carl's uptight angst, giving Molly plenty of opportunities to offer curd and soulful looks. Too bad they couldn't be funnier in the process. **108m/C DVD, HD DVD, US** Owen Wilson, Matt Dillon, Kate Hudson, Michael Douglas, Amanda Detmer, Seth Rogen, Todd Stashwick, Harry Dean Stanton; **D:** A-thony Russo, Joe Russo; Peter Ellis; **W:** Michael LeSieur; **C:** Charles Minsky; **M:** Rolfe Kent.

You Move You Die *&½*
2007 Micro-budget Kiwi crime comedy, filmed in real time, that actually improves as it rolls along. Despite being a professional criminal, Mike (Sterling) gets mugged and robbed of the engagement ring he's just bought. He anc psycho pal Rob (Harrison) have no problem resorting to violence as they career through various Auckland neighborhoods in an effort to retrieve his property. **92m/C DVD, NZ** B-ce Hopkins, Ketzal Sterling, Julian Hansson, Patrick Clarke; **D:** Ketzal Sterling. **W:** Ketzal Sterling. **C:** Ketzal Sterling.

You Must Remember This 1992 When Uncle Buddy (Guillaume) receives a mysterious trunk, Ella's curiosity gets the best of her. She opens the trunk to discover a number of old movies made by W.B. Jackson—Uncle Buddy. Ella takes the films to a movie archive to find out about her uncle's past as an independent black filmmaker. After researching the history of black cinema, Ella convinces her uncle to be proud of his contribution to the film world. Includes a viewer's guide. Part of the "Wonderworks" series. 110m/C VHS. **M:** Rolfe Kent.

You Tell Me *&&*
2006 Three twentysomething slacker buddies on New York's Lower East Side continue to screw up their romantic lives by listening to each other's bad advice. Flint (Fenkart) has been dumped and is crashing at Jeff's (Ledoux) apartment. Jeff has just discovered that both his girlfriend and his mother (who's left his dad) have been cheating, and floundering Gray's (Cary) talented girlfriend is about to break big in the art world, leaving him even more insecure. When the body of a young woman washes up and is fished out by the barge-dwellers it sets off various reactions in all three. Joe seduces Ella under the nose of the emotionally repressed Les and a series of flashbacks reveal more about Joe's past and his relationship with Cathie (Mortimer), a young woman who reminds him of the deceased. Moody, noirish and visually engaging with stellar portrayals by all. Based on a novel by Alexander Trocchi. **98m/C DVD, FR GB** Evan McGregor, Tilda Swinton, Peter Mullan, Emily Mortimer, Alan Cooke, Jack McElhone; **D:** David Mackenzie; **W:** David Mackenzie; **C:** Giles Nuttgens. **M:** David Byrne.

You Talkin' to Me? *&*
1987 **(R)** Fledgling actor who idolizes De Niro moves to the West Coast for his big break. He fails, so he dyes his hair blond and digs the California lifestyle. Embarrassingly bad. **97m/C VHS.** Chris Winkler, Jim Youngs, Faith Ford; **D:** Charles Winkler; **W:** Charles Winkler.

You Were Never Lovelier *&&&½*
1942 Charming tale of a father who creates a phony Romeo to try to interest his daughter in marriage. Astaire appears and woos Hayworth in the flesh. The dancing, of course, is superb, and Hayworth is stunning. ♪ *Dearly Beloved; I'm Old Fashioned; Shorty George; Wedding in the Spring; You Were Never Lovelier.* 98m/B VHS, DVD. Fred Astaire, Rita Hayworth, Leslie Brooks, Xavier Cugat, Adolphe Menjou, Larry Parks; **D:** William A. Seiter; **M:** Jerome Kern, Johnny Mercer.

The Young Americans *&&*
1993 **(R)** Tough New York cop John Harris (Keitel) is sent to London to aid the police with their investigations into a series of killings related to a drug smuggling operation working out of the club scene. Harris gets to know everything to the sleazeball gangster Carl Frazer (Mortensen) that he's been trailing. Slick formula with hard-working cast. Debut for 25-year-old director Cannon. 108m/C VHS, DVD, GB Harvey Keitel, Viggo Mortensen, Iain Glen, John Wood, Keith

---

DVD, Robert Guillaume, Tim Reid, Daphne Maxwell Reid, Vonetta McGee.

You Only Live Once *&&½*
1937 Ex-con Fonda wants to mend his ways and tries to cross into Canada with his girlfriend in tow. Impressively scripted, but a glum and dated Depression-era tale. **86m/B VHS, DVD.** Henry Fonda, Sylvia Sidney, Ward Bond, William Gargan, Barton MacLane, Margaret Hamilton, Jean Dixon, Warren Hymer, Charles "Chic" Sale, Guinn "Big Boy" Williams, Jerome Cowan, John Wray, Jonathan Hale, Ben Hall, Jean Stoddard, Wade Boteler, Henry Taylor, Walter DePalma; **D:** Fritz Lang; **W:** C. Graham Baker, Gene Towne; **C:** Leon Shamroy.

You Only Live Twice *&&½*
1967 **(PG)** 007 travels to Japan to take on arch-nemesis Blofeld, who has been capturing Russian and American spacecraft in an attempt to start WWIII. Great location photography; theme sung by Nancy Sinatra. Implausible plot, however is a handicap, even though this is Bond. **125m/C VHS, DVD, GB** Sean Connery, Mie Hama, Akiko Wakabayashi, Tetsuro Tamba, Karin Dor, Charles Gray, Donald Pleasence, Tsai Chin, Bernard Lee, Lois Maxwell, Desmond Llewelyn; **D:** Lewis Gilbert; **W:** Roald Dahl; **C:** Frederick A. (Freddie) Young; **M:** John Barry.

You So Crazy *&½*
You So Crazy 1994 Scandalous star of TV show "Martin" and host of HBO's "Def Comedy Jam" follows in the footsteps of raunchy humorists Richard Pryor and Eddie Murphy. Threatened with an NC-17 rating, Lawrence refused to edit and Miramax, the original distributor, dropped it. It was picked up by Samuel Goldwyn, who released the unrated version, uncut and appropriate. Filmed live at the Brooklyn Academy of Music, Lawrence displays too much of his considerable talent, and too much vulgarity and poor taste. 85m/C VHS, DVD. Martin Lawrence; **D:** Thomas Schlamme; **W:** Martin Lawrence; **C:** Arthur Albert.

You Stupid Man *&½*
2002 Actually, "you stupid movie" would be more appropriate. First-timer Burns (brother of Ed) does his own NY romantic-comedy to mixed effect. Geeky writer Owen (Krumholz) loses hot blonde girlfriend Chloe (Richards) to L.A.'s bright lights and TV fame. So he goes on a blind date and meets brunette babe Nadine (Jovovich) and they eventually give cozy. Then Chloe's TV show gets cancelled and she comes home to the Big Apple and wants Owen back. Is this a Woody Allen fantasy or what? **95m/C DVD.** David Krumholz, Denise Richards, Milla Jovovich, Nadine Velazquez, William Baldwin, Dan Montgomery Jr.; **D:** Brian Burns; **W:** Brian Burns; **C:** David Herrington; **M:** David Schwartz.

Young Adam *&&&½*
2003 **(NC-17)** Writer/director Mackenzie uses the grim backdrop of 1950s Scotland for the richly dark character drama of his second feature. McGregor is Joe, a sexually charged but emotionally and morally devoid transient who finds work, room, and board on a barge owned by Les (Mullan) and his wife Ella (Swinton) who share a loveless marriage. When the body of a young woman washes up and is fished out by the barge-dwellers it sets off various reactions in all three.

You'll Like My Mother *&&½*
1972 **(PG)** Surprisingly tense thriller finds preggers Francesca (Duke) traveling to Minnesota to meet the family of her recently deceased husband. Mrs. Kinsolving (Murphy) refuses to acknowledge her but Fran is forced to stay the night because of a snowstorm. She meets the rest of the clan, including mentally retarded Kenny (Thomas), and homicidal Kathleen (Allen). When she learns the truth about these various relations, all the strain pushes Fran into labor and no one's about to let her go to the hospital. Adapted from the novel by Naomi A. Hintze. **92m/C VHS** Patty Duke, Rosemary Murphy, Richard Thomas, Sian Barbara Allen; **D:** Lamont Johnson; **W:** Jo Heims; **C:** Jack Marta; **M:** Gil Melle.

You'll Never Get Rich *&&&*
1941 A Broadway dance director is drafted into the Army, where his romantic troubles cause him to wind up in the guardhouse more than once. Of course gets the girl. Exquisitely funny. ♪ *Since I Kissed My Baby Goodbye; The A-stairable Rag; Shootin' the Works for Uncle Sam; Wedding Cake Walk; Dream Dancing; Boogie Barcarolle; So Near and So Far.* **88m/B VHS, DVD.** Fred Astaire, Rita Hayworth, Robert Benchley; **D:** Sidney Lanfield.

You'll Find Out *&&*
1940 A comic mix of music and mystery as Kay Kyser and his Band, along with a debutante in distress, are terrorized by Lugosi, Karloff, and Lorre. ♪ *The Bad Horror; I'd Know You Anywhere; You've Got Me This Way; Like the Fella Once Said; I've Got a One-Track Mind; Don't Think it Ain't Been Charming.* **97m/B VHS.** Peter Lorre, Kay Kyser, Boris Karloff, Bela Lugosi, Dennis O'Keefe, Helen Parrish; **D:** David Butler.

You'll Get Over It *&&* A *Cause d'un Garçon* 2002 Seventeen-year-old high schooler Vincent (Baumgartner) is the star of the swim team; has a pretty girlfriend, Noémie (Maraval); and a best pal, Stephane (Comar). But Vincent is also seeing the older Bruno (Chlund) and struggling with maintaining his secret. Then, new student Benjamin (Elkaïm) obviously pursues Vincent and he's outed before the whole school—resulting in feelings of betrayal on all fronts. Soon, Vincent is discovering who his friends really are. French with subtitles. **90m/C DVD, FR** Julien Baumgartner, François Comar, Julie Maraval, Nils Ohlund, Jérémie Elkaïm; **D:** Fabrice Cazeneuve; **W:** Vincent Molina; **C:** Stephan Massis; **M:** Michel Portal. **TV**

Young and Innocent *&&&* The *Girl Was Young* 1937 Somewhat uneven thriller about a police constable's daughter who helps a fugitive prove he didn't strangle a film star. **80m/B VHS, DVD, GB** Derrick DeMarney, Nova Pilbeam, Percy Marmont, Edward Rigby, Mary Clare, John Longden, George Curzon, Basil Radford, Pamela Carme, George Merritt, J.H. Roberts, Jerry Verno, H.F. Maltby, Beatrice Varley, Syd Crossley, Frank Atkinson, Torin Thatcher; **D:** Alfred Hitchcock; **W:** Charles Bennett, Alma Reville, Gerald Savory, Antony Armstrong, Edwin Greenwood; **C:** Bernard Knowles; **M:** Louis Levy.

Young & Free *&½*
1978 Follow-ing the death of his parents, a young man must learn to face the perils of an uncharted wilderness alone. Ultimately he must choose between nature's call for him to remain in the wild, his beloved wife and life in civilization. **87m/C VHS.** Eric Larsen; **D:** Keith Larsen.

The Young and the Guilty *&&*
1958 Two star-crossed teenagers are frustrated in their romance when their parents find one of their love letters and hit the ceiling. Told not to see each other again, the two take to sneaking around, which adds an edge to their relationship. Moving performances by the two young leads. **66m/B VHS.** Phyllis Calvert, Andrew Ray, Edward Chapman, Janet Munro, Campbell Singer; **D:** Peter Cotes.

Young and Willing *&&½* Out of the *Frying Pan* 1942 A group of struggling actors gets hold of a terrific play and tries various schemes to get it produced. Based on the Broadway Play "Out of the Frying Pan" by Francis Swann. Unexceptional but enjoyable comedy. **83m/B VHS.** William Holden, Susan Hayward, Eddie Bracken, Robert Benchley, Martha O'Driscoll, Barbara Britton; **D:** Edward H. Griffith; **W:** Virginia Van Upp; **C:** Leo Tover; **M:** Victor Young.

Young Aphrodites *&&½* 1963 Two young teenagers of a primitive Greek tribe discover sexuality. An acclaimed film retelling the myth of Daphnis and Chloe. Narrated in English. **87m/B VHS, DVD, GR** Takis Emmanouel, Kleopatra Rota, Vangelis Ioannidis, Eleni Prokopiou; **D:** Nikos Koundouros; **W:** Kostas Sfikas, Vassilis Vassilikos, Giovanni Varriano; **M:** Giannis Markopoulos. Berlin Intl. Film Fest. '63: Director (Koundouros).

Young Bess *&&&½* 1953 Simmons and real-life husband Granger star in this splashy costume drama about 16th century England's young Queen. Features outstanding performances by Simmons as most famous role) as Henry VIII. Based on the novel by Margaret Irwin. **112m/C VHS.** Jean Simmons, Stewart Granger, Deborah Kerr, Charles Laughton, Kay Walsh, Guy Rolfe, Kathleen Byron, Cecil Kellaway, Rex Thompson; **D:** George Sidney; **W:** Jan Lustig, Arthur Wimperis; **C:** Charles Rosher; **M:** Miklos Rozsa.

Young Bill Hickok *&&* 1940 A Rogers vehicle in the form of a very fictionalized biography of the famous gunfighter. **54m/B VHS, DVD.** Roy Rogers, George "Gabby" Hayes, Julie Bishop, John Miliian, Sally Payne, Monte Blue, Archie Twitchell; **D:** Joseph Kane; **W:** Olive Cooper, Norton S. Parker; **C:** William Nobles.

Young Blood *&&* 1935 A cowboy robs from the rich to help the poor. He's also interested in a foreign actress having trouble bonding with the townfolk. Lots of old fashioned western violence. 61m/B

VHS, DVD. Bob Steele, Charles "Blackie" King, Helen Foster; **D:** Phil Rosen.

The Young Bruce Lee 🐾🐾
1980 A young boy named Bruce Lee and his friend both learn the martial arts in order to defend themselves from bullies. As they grow up Lee sets his sights on becoming a movie star while his friend performs in acrobatic stage shows. Though Lee achieves stardom, he finds himself hounded by martial artists that want to challenge him. This unauthorized biopic follows the major events in Bruce Lee's life but most of it is cliched fabrication. The film is cheap and poorly crafted, but Lung (AKA Bruce Li) does a fairly successful job of mimicking Lee and he's helped by an accurate hairdo and wardrobe. As far as Bruce Lee wannabe films, you could do a lot worse. Despite the packaging, there is no Lee footage in the film—only a new sphoto of his body. **80m/C VHS, DVD, HK** Bruce Li, Bolo Yeung, Bruce Le, Lily Hua; **D:** Bruce Le; **C:** Alardar Kline.

Young Buffalo Bill 🐾🐾 **1940** Buffalo Bill battles the Spanish land-grant patrons. **54m/B VHS, DVD.** Roy Rogers, George "Gabby" Hayes, Pauline Moore; **D:** Joseph Kane.

Young Caruso 🐾🐾 *Enrico Caruso: Legenda di Una Voce* **1951** Dramatic biography of legendary tenor Enrico Caruso, following his rise from childhood poverty in Naples to the beginning of his rise to fame. Dubbed in English. **78m/B VHS, DVD.** *IT* Gina Lollobrigida, Ermanno Randi, Gino Saltamerenda, Maria V. Tasnady; **D:** Giacomo Gentilomo; **W:** Giacomo Gentilomo; **C:** Tino Santoni; **M:** Carlo Franci.

Young Catherine 🐾🐾🐾 **1991** Made-for-TV account of Russia's strongest female ruler, the girl who would be Catherine the Great. Star-studded cast and excellent production values. Script and strong cast make Ormond look like a lightweight. Filmed in Leningrad. Also available in 186-minute version. **150m/C VHS.** Vanessa Redgrave, Christopher Plummer, Marthe Keller, Franco Nero, Julia Ormond, Maximilian Schell, Reece Dinsdale, Mark Frankel; **D:** Michael Anderson Sr.; **W:** Chris Bryant.

Young Charlie Chaplin 🐾🐾 **1988** A British-made TV biography of the legendary silent screen comic. **160m/C VHS.** Ian McShane, Twiggy; **M:** Rachel Portman.

A Young Connecticut Yankee in King Arthur's Court 🐾½ **1995** A modern-day teenager timetravels back to the court of King Arthur and Camelot. Based on the book by Mark Twain. **93m/C VHS.** Michael York, Theresa Russell, Nick Mancuso, Philippe Ross, Jack Langediik, Polly Shannon, Paul Hopkins; **D:** Ralph L. (R.L.) Thomas; **W:** Ralph L. (R.L.) Thomas, Frank Encarnacao; **C:** John Berrie; **M:** Alan Reeves.

Young Doctors in Love 🐾🐾 **1982 (R)** Spoof of medical soap operas features a chaotic scenario at City Hospital, where the young men and women on the staff have better things to do than attend to their patients. Good cast keeps this one alive, though many laughs are forced. Includes cameos by real soap star, including then-General Hospital star Moore. **95m/C VHS, DVD.** Dabney Coleman, Sean Young, Michael McKean, Harry Dean Stanton, Hector Elizondo, Patrick Macnee, Pamela Reed, Saul Rubinek; **Cameos:** Demi Moore, Janine Turner; **D:** Garry Marshall; **W:** Michael Elias, Rich Eustis; **M:** Maurice Jarre.

Young Einstein 🐾🐾 **1989 (PG)** A goofy, irreverent Australian farce starring, directed, co-scripted and co-produced by Serious, depicting Einstein as a young Outback clod who splits beer atoms and invents rock and roll. Winner of several Aussie awards. Fun for the kids. **91m/C VHS, DVD.** *AU* Yahoo Serious, Odile Le Clezio, John Howard, Pee Wee Wilson, Su Cruickshank, Lulu Pinkus, Kaarin Fairfax, Jonathan Coleman; **D:** Yahoo Serious; **W:** David Roach, Yahoo Serious; **C:** Jeff Darling; **M:** Martin Armiger, William Motzing, Tommy Tycho.

Young Frankenstein 🐾🐾🐾 **1974 (PG)** Young Dr. Frankenstein (Wilder), a brain surgeon, inherits the family castle back in Transylvania. He's skittish about the family business, but when he learns his grandfather's secrets, he be- comes obsessed with making his own monster. Wilder and monster Boyle make a memorable song-and-dance team to Irving Berlin's "Puttin' on the Ritz," and Hackman's cameo as a blind man is inspired. Garr ("What knockers!" "Oh, sank you!") is adorable as a fraulein, and Leachman ("He's vass my—boyfriend!") is wonderfully scary. Wilder saves the creature with a switcheroo, in which the doctor ends up with a certain monster-sized body part. Hilarious parody. **108m/B VHS, DVD.** Peter Boyle, Gene Wilder, Marty Feldman, Madeline Kahn, Cloris Leachman, Teri Garr, Kenneth Mars, Richard Haydn, Gene Hackman, Liam Dunn, Monte Landis; **D:** Mel Brooks; **W:** Mel Brooks, Gene Wilder; **C:** Gerald Hirschfeld; **M:** John Morris. Natl. Film Reg. '03.

The Young Girl and the Monsoon 🐾🐾½ **1999** Successful photojournalist and divorced dad Hank (Kinney) agrees to take care of 13-year old daughter Constance (Muth) while her mother, with whom she usually lives, is out of town. Constance is a mass of teenage contradictions—constantly testing her boundaries (and Hank's sanity and patience). Hank has kept his work and life, including the fact that his girlfriend is a twentysomething model named Erin (Avital), from Constance but there's an explosion in every conversation. **93m/C VHS, DVD.** Terry Kinney, Ellen Muth, Mili Avital, Diane Venora, Tim Guinee, Domenick Lombardozzi; **D:** James Ryan; **W:** James Ryan; **C:** Ben Wolf; **M:** David Carbonara.

The Young Girls of Rochefort 🐾🐾½ *Les Demoiselles de Rochefort* **1968** Twins sisters Delphine and Solange (played by sisters Deneuve and Dorleac) dream of romance, which first appears in the forms of salesmen Etienne (Chakiris) and Bill (Dale), who are minor distractions for the real thing—artistic sailor Maxence (Perrin) and concert pianist Andy (Kelly). Demy's followup to the more compelling "The Umbrellas of Cherbourg" is still an equally candy-colored musical fantasy. Rochefort (like Cherbourg) is an actual town that Demy took over for filming. **125m/C VHS, DVD.** *FR* Catherine Deneuve, Francoise Dorleac, George Chakiris, Grover Dale, Gene Kelly, Jacques Perrin, Danielle Darrieux, Michel Piccoli, Pamela Hart, Jacques Riberolles, Leslie North; **D:** Jacques Demy; **W:** Jacques Demy; **C:** Ghislan Cloquet; **M:** Michel Legrand.

The Young Graduates 🐾 **1971 (PG)** Hormonally imbalanced teens come of age in spite of meandering plot. Features "Breaking Away" star Christopher in big screen debut. **99m/C VHS.** Patricia Wymer, Steven Stewart, Gary Rist, Bruce Kirby, Jennifer Ritt, Dennis Christopher; **D:** Robert Anderson.

Young Guns 🐾🐾½ **1988 (R)** A sophomoric Wild Bunch look-alike that grows up resembling a western version of the Bowery Boys. Provides a portrait of Billy the Kid and his gang as they move from prairie trash to demi-legends. Features several fine performances by a popular group of today's young stars. **107m/C VHS, DVD, Blu-ray Disc, UMD.** Emilio Estevez, Kiefer Sutherland, Lou Diamond Phillips, Charlie Sheen, Casey Siemaszko, Dermot Mulroney, Terence Stamp, Terry O'Quinn, Jack Palance, Brian Keith, Patrick Wayne, Sharon Thomas; **D:** Christopher Cain; **W:** John Fusco; **C:** Dean Semler; **M:** Anthony Marinelli, Brian Backus, Brian Banks.

Young Guns 2 🐾🐾 **1990 (PG-13)** Brat Pack vehicle neo-Western sequel about Billy the Kid (Estevez) and his gang. Told as an account by Brushy Bill Roberts who, in 1950, claims to be the real Billy the Kid and recounts his continuing adventures with Doc (Sutherland), Chavez (Phillips) and Pat Garrett (Petersen). Not bad for a sequel, thanks mostly to Petersen. **105m/C VHS, DVD.** Emilio Estevez, Kiefer Sutherland, Lou Diamond Phillips, Christian Slater, William L. Petersen, Alan Ruck, R.D. Call, James Coburn, Balthazar Getty, Jack Kehoe, Robert Knepper, Jenny Wright, Tracey Walter, Ginger Lynn Allen, Jon Bon Jovi, Viggo Mortensen, Leon Rippy, Bradley Whitford, Scott Wilson, John Hammil; **D:** Geoff Murphy; **W:** John Fusco; **C:** Dean Semler; **M:** Alan Silvestri. Golden Globes '91: Song ("Blaze of Glory").

Young Hercules 🐾🐾½ **1997 (PG-13)** Seventeen-year-old Herc (Bohen) is a confused teen, torn between his mortal and immortal sides. So concerned mom Alcmene sends the kid to Cherion's academy where Herc can learn to be a warrior and where he'll meet friends and rivals Iolus (O'Gorman), Prince Jason (Conrad), and the beautiful Yvenna (Stewart). Oh yes, war god Ares (Smith) also shows up, trying to prevent half-brother Herc and his friends from obtaining the golden fleece for Jason's dying father. **93m/C VHS, DVD.** Ian Bohen, Dean O'Gorman, Johna Stewart, Chris Conrad, Kevin Smith; **D:** T.J. Scott; **W:** Robert Tapert, Andrew Dettmann, Daniel Truly; **C:** John Mahaffie; **M:** Joseph LoDuca. VIDEO

The Young in Heart 🐾🐾🐾 **1938** A lonely, old woman allows a family of con-artists into her life for companionship. Impressed by her sweet nature, the parasitic brood reforms. The cute comedy was a real crowd-pleaser in its day, especially after the bittersweet ending was replaced with a happier variety. Based on the novel "The Gay Banditti" by I.A.R. Wylie. **90m/C VHS, DVD.** Janet Gaynor, Douglas Fairbanks Jr., Paulette Goddard, Roland Young, Billie Burke, Minnie Dupree, Richard Carlson, Charles Halton; **D:** Richard Wallace; **W:** Charles Bennett, Paul Osborn.

Young Ivanhoe 🐾🐾½ **1995** Ivanhoe learns how to be a warrior, with some help from Robin Hood and the Black Knight, inspiring others to follow him into battle to save their land from seizure by the Norman invaders. **96m/C VHS, DVD.** Stacy Keach, Nick Mancuso, Margot Kidder, Kris Holden-Ried, Rachel Blanchard, Matthew Daniels; **D:** Ralph L. (R.L.) Thomas; **W:** Ralph L. (R.L.) Thomas, Frank Encarnacao; **C:** John Berrie; **M:** Alan Reeves.

Young Lady Chatterly 2 🐾½ **1985** A poor sequel to the popular MacBride film, with only the name of the Lawrence classic. Chatterly inherits the family mansion and fools around with the servants and many any one else who comes along. Unrated version with 13 minutes of deleted footage is also available. **87m/C VHS, DVD.** Sybil Danning, Adam West, Harlee MacBride; **D:**

The Young Land 🐾½ **1959** Less-than-inspiring western does feature a good performance by Hopper as malcontent bully Hatfield Carnes. Carnes kills a respected Mexican in a barroom gunfight in 1848 California and sheriff Jim Ellison (Wayne) is quick to call territorial judge Isham (O'Herlihy) to ensure a fair trial—with the rest of the Spanish-speaking town looking on in skepticism. Based on the story "Frontier Frenzy" by John Reese. **88m/C VHS, DVD.** Dennis Hopper, Patrick Wayne, Dan O'Herlihy, Yvonne Craig, Ken Curtis, Pedro Gonzalez-Gonzalez; **D:** Ted Tetzlaff; **W:** Norman S. Hall; **C:** Winton C. Hoch, Henry Sharp; **M:** Dimitri Tiomkin.

The Young Lions 🐾🐾🐾 **1958** A cynical WWII epic following the experiences of a young American officer and a disillusioned Nazi in the war's last days. Martin does his first dramatic role. As the Nazi, Brando sensitively considers the belief that Hitler would save Germany. A realistic anti-war film. **167m/B VHS, DVD.** Marlon Brando, Montgomery Clift, Dean Martin, Hope Lange, Barbara Rush, Lee Van Cleef, Maximilian Schell, May Britt, Dora Doll, Liliane Montevecchi, Parley Baer, Arthur Franz, Hal Baylor, Richard Gardner, Herbert Rudley, L.Q. Jones; **D:** Edward Dmytryk; **W:** Edward Anhalt; **C:** Joe MacDonald; **M:** Hugo Friedhofer.

Young Love, First Love 🐾½ **1979** TV movie about a young woman who must decide whether to have sex with her boyfriend. Sound familiar? Pretty blah, earnest story, though well cast. **100m/C VHS.** Valerie Bertinelli, Leslie Ackerman, Timothy Hutton, Arlen Dean Snyder, Fionnula Flanagan; **D:** Steven Hilliard Stern. TV

Young Love—Lemon Popsicle 7 🐾 **1987 (R)** Three hunks stalk the beaches in search of babes. **91m/C VHS.** Yftach Katzur, Zachi Noy, Jonathan Sagalle, Sonja Martin; **D:** Walter Bannert.

Young Man with a Horn 🐾🐾🐾 **1950** Dorothy Baker's novel, which was loosely based on the life of jazz immortal Bix Beiderbecke, was even more loosely adapted for this film, featuring Kirk as an angst-ridden trumpeter who can't seem to hit that mystical "high note." ♪The Very Thought of You; I May be Wrong; The Man I Love; Too Marvelous for Words; With a Song in My Heart; Pretty Baby; I Only Have Eyes for You; Limehouse Blues; Melancholy Rhapsody. **112m/B VHS, DVD.** Kirk Douglas, Doris Day, Lauren Bacall, Hoagy Carmichael; **D:** Michael Curtiz.

Young Master 🐾🐾 **1980** Chan, searching for his missing brother, is mistaken for a fugitive and has to save himself from bounty hunters and police. Oh, and get the real bad guys so he can clear his name. Chinese with subtitles or dubbed. **90m/C VHS, DVD. HK** Jackie Chan, Pai Wei, Ing-Sik Whang, Ken Shih; **D:** Jackie Chan; **W:** Jackie Chan; **M:** Akira Inoue.

Young Mr. Lincoln 🐾🐾🐾½ **1939** A classy Hollywood biography of Lincoln in his younger years from log-cabin country boy to idealistic Springfield lawyer. A splendid drama, and one endlessly explicated as an American masterpiece by the French auteur critics in "Cahiers du Cinema." **100m/B VHS, DVD.** Henry Fonda, Alice Brady, Marjorie Weaver, Arleen Whelan, Eddie Collins, Ward Bond, Donald Meek, Richard Cromwell, Eddie Quillan, Charles Halton; **D:** John Ford; **W:** Lamar Trotti. Natl. Film Reg. '03.

The Young Nurses 🐾🐾 *Nightingale; Young L.A. Nurses 3* **1973 (R)** The fourth entry in the Roger Corman produced "nurses" series. Three sexy nurses uncover a drug ring run from their hospital, headed by none other than director Fuller. Also present is Moreland, in his last role. Preceded by "The Student Nurses," "Private Duty Nurses," "Night Call Nurses," followed by "Candy Stripe Nurses." Also on video as "Young L.A. Nurses 3." **77m/C VHS, DVD.** Jean Manson, Ashley Porter, Angela Gibbs, Zack Taylor, Dick Miller, Jack La Rue, William Joyce, Sally Kirkland, Allan Arbus, Mary Doyle, Don Keefer, Nan Martin, Mantan Moreland, Samuel Fuller; **D:** Clinton Kimbrough; **W:** Howard R. Cohen; **M:** Greg Prestopino.

Young Nurses in Love 🐾 **1989 (R)** Low-budget sex farce in which a foreign spy poses as a nurse to steal sperm from a sperm bank donated by world leaders, celebrities and geniuses. **82m/C VHS.** Jeanne Marie, Alan Fisher, Barbra Robb, James Davies; **D:** Chuck Vincent.

The Young One 🐾🐾½ *La Joven; Island of Shame* **1961** Traver (Hamilton) is a black jazz musician who escapes from his southern town when he's wrongly accused of raping a white woman. He hides out on a small island which is used as a private hunting ground for rich sportsmen, overseen by Miller (Scott), the game keeper. Hamilton gets work as the new handyman and becomes close to the young Evalyn (Meersman). When Miller rapes Evalyn, it's Traver who's once again accused until things can be put right. Racist elements are heavy-handed; one of Bunuel's lesser efforts. Based on the story "Travelin' Man" by Peter Matthiessen. **94m/B VHS. MX** Bernie Hamilton, Zachary Scott, Kay Meersman, Claudio Brook, Graham Denton; **D:** Luis Bunuel; **W:** Hugo Butler, Luis Bunuel.

Young People 🐾🐾🐾 **1940 (G)** Temple's 12 in this lesser vehicle and almost-adolescence doesn't serve her well with this tired plot. She's an orphan adopted by showbiz team Oakie and Greenwood who've decided to retire to rural life. They even get to put on a show to prove to the small-minded small-towners what a swell trio they are. Temple's last film for 20th-Century Fox does include nostalgic clips from earlier Shirley hits, including "Stand Up and Cheer" and "Curly Top," to explain her character's background. ♪Tra-La-La; Fifth Avenue; I Wouldn't Take a Million; The Mason-Dixon Line; Young People. **78m/B VHS.** Shirley Temple, Jack Oakie, Charlotte Greenwood, Arleen Whelan, George Montgomery, Kathleen Howard; **D:** Allan Dwan; **W:** Edwin Blum, Don Ettinger.

The Young Philadelphians ♂♂♂ *The City Jungle* 1959 Ambitious young lawyer Newman works hard at making an impression on the snobbish Philadelphia upper crust. As he schemes and scrambles, he woos debutante Rush and defends buddy Vaughn on a murder charge. Long, but worth it. Part of the "A Night at the Movies" series, running with a Bugs Bunny cartoon, "People Are Bunny," a newsreel and coming attractions for "The Nun's Story" and "The Hanging Tree." **136m/B** VHS, DVD, Paul Newman, Barbara Rush, Alexis Smith, Brian Keith; *M:* Vincent Sherman; *C:* Harry Stradling Sr.; *M:* Ernest Gold.

Young Tom Edison ♂♂½ 1940 Two teenaged years in the life of Thomas Alva Edison, as he drives his family crazy with his endless experiments on his way to becoming the famed inventor. Rooney

Young Tiger WOOF! *Police Woman; Rumble in Hong Kong* 1974 (R) A really cheesy Chan movie where he plays a bad guy, followed by a 12-minute documentary featuring Jackie Chan, kung-fu sensation, demonstrating his skills. **102m/C** VHS, DVD, HK Jackie Chan, Qui Yuen, Ken Jeong, Gam Woo; *D:* Hideng Tsu.

Young Sherlock Holmes ♂♂ 1985 (PG-13) Holmes and Watson meet as schoolboys. They work together on their first case, solving a series of bizarre murders gripping London. Watch through the credits for an interesting plot twist. Promising "what if" sleuth tale crashes and burns, becoming a typical high-tech Spielberg film. Second half fares too strong a resemblance to "Indiana Jones and the Temple of Doom." **109m/C** VHS, DVD, Nicholas (Nick) Rowe, Alan Cox, Sophie Ward, Freddie Jones, Michael Hordern; *D:* Barry Levinson; *W:* Chris Columbus; *M:* Bruce Broughton.

The Young Savages ♂♂ 1961 Gang warfare in New York's East Harlem. Three Italian teenagers are accused of murdering another teen—a blind Puerto Rican boy. Assistant DA Hank Bell (Lancaster), who grew up on the same mean streets, doesn't think the case is as cutand-dry as presented and determines that the deceased was not the innocent victim he's portrayed to be. Routine juvenile delinquent drama based on the novel "A Matter of Conviction" by Evan Hunter. **103m/B** VHS, Burt Lancaster, Dina Merrill, Edward Andrews, Shelley Winters, Vivian Nathan, Larry Gates, Telly Savalas, John Davis Chandler, Neil Nephew, Stanley Kristien; *D:* John Frankenheimer; *W:* Edward Anhalt, J.P. Miller; *C:* Lionel Lindon; *M:* David Amram.

The Young Pioneers ♂♂½ 1976 Teenaged newlyweds David and Molly Beaton head for the Dakota Territory in the 1870s to secure a homestead. They're faced with a blizzard, an army of grasshoppers that destroy their crop, and Molly's pregnancy and find their survival harder than expected. Pilot TV movie for the brief 1978 series. **96m/C** VHS, Linda Purl, Robert Hays; *D:* Michael O'Herlihy. TV

The Young Poisoner's Handbook ♂♂♂ 1994 (R) Based on the true story of London teenager Graham (O'Conor) who's obsessed with chemistry and at odds with his stepmother. So, he poisons her chocolates and she dies. Sent to Broadmoor prison for the criminally insane, Graham spends his time writing a poisoner's handbook for Dr. Ziegler. Be warned that the sufferings of the poisoned victims are gruesome. **99m/C** VHS, DVD, GB Hugh O'Conor, Anthony Sher, Ruth Sheen, Charlotte Coleman, Roger Lloyd-Pack, Paul Stacey, Samantha Edmonds, Charlie Creed-Miles; *D:* Benjamin Ross; *W:* Benjamin Ross, Jeff Rawle; *C:* Hubert Taczanowski; *M:* Robert (Rob) Lane, Frank Strobel.

Youngblood ♂♂ 1986 (R) An underdog beats the seemingly insurmountable odds and becomes a hockey champion. Some enjoyable hockey scenes although the success storyline is predictable. **111m/C** VHS, DVD, Rob Lowe, Patrick Swayze, Cynthia Gibb, Ed Lauter, George Finn, Fionnula Flanagan, Keanu Reeves; *D:* Peter Markle.

Younger & Younger ♂♂½ 1994 (R) Jonathan Younger (Sutherland) is forced to run the family storage business on his long-suffering wife Penny (Davidovich) dies. The business starts to fall, even after Jonathan's son (Fraser) arrives to help out, and the widower begins having visions of the woman he mistreated. And each time he sees her she looks younger and more beautiful than ever. **97m/C** VHS, DVD, Donald Sutherland, Brendan Fraser, Lolita (David) Davidovich, Sally Kellerman, Julie Delpy, Linda Hunt; *D:* Percy Adlon; *W:* Percy Adlon, Felix Action; *C:* Bernd Heinl; *M:* Hans Zimmer.

Your Friends & Neighbors ♂♂♂ 1998 (R) If these are your friends and neighbors, you should reconsider your decisions and address. Six yuppies lie, cheat and deceive their way around the block in La Bute's tale of modern suburban immorality. Weasel Jerry (Stiller) sleeps with Mary (Brennerman) the supposedly happy wife of his old friend Barry (Eckhart). Meanwhile, his live-in girlfriend (Keener) is having a lesbian affair with art gallery employee Cheri (Kinski), and chilly misogynist Cary (Patric) seduces and discards a string of women. Excellent performances by the entire cast bring this nasty group to life and La Bute provides riveting if unsettling material for them. **99m/C** VHS, DVD, Jason Patric, Nastassja Kinski, Ben Stiller, Catherine Keener, Aaron Eckhart, Amy Brennerman; *D:* Neil LaBute; *W:* Neil LaBute; *C:* Nancy Schreiber.

Your Place or Mine ♂ 1983 Self-indulgent yuppie pap about middleaged singles trying to find the right mate. **100m/C** VHS, Bonnie Franklin, Robert Klein, Peter Bonerz, Tyne Daly, Penny Fuller; *D:* Robert Day; *M:* Gerald Alters. TV

Your Ticket Is No Longer Valid ♂ 1984 (R) Prurient excuse for a serious drama. Impotent failed businessman has disturbing erotic dreams about his girlfriend. Adapted from a novel by Romain Gary. **96m/C** VHS, CA Richard Harris, George Peppard, Jeanne Moreau; *D:* George Kaczender.

Youth of the Beast ♂♂ *Seishun* 1963 A cop in disgrace plots to avenge the murder of a friend by infiltrating two rival yakuza gangs and having them destroy each other. Flamboyant visuals and filled with Suzuki's soon-to-be trademarked sex and violence. Japanese with subtitles. **91m/C** VHS, JP Joe Shishido, Shoji Kobayashi, Ichiro Kijima, Misako Suzuki; *D:* Seijun Suzuki.

Young Warriors ♂♂½ 1983 (R) Frat boys turn vigilante to avenge a street gang murder. Weird mix of teens sex comedy, insufferable self-righteous preachiness, and violence. **104m/C** VHS, Ernest Borgnine, James Van Patten, Richard Roundtree, Lynda Day George, Dick Shawn, Anne Bancroft, John Mills, Jack Hawkins, Ian Holm, Anthony Hopkins, Patrick Magee, Edward Woodward, Jane Seymour; *D:* Richard Attenborough. Golden Globes '73: Foreign Film.

Young Winston ♂♂♂ 1972 (PG) Based on Sir Winston Churchill's autobiography, "My Early Life: A Roving Commission." Follows him through his school days, journalistic career, and his election to Parliament at the age of 26. Ward is tremendous as the prime minister-to-be. **145m/C** VHS, GB Simon Ward, Robert Shaw, Anne Bancroft, John Mills, Jack Hawkins, Ian Holm, Anthony Hopkins, Patrick Magee, Edward Woodward, Jane Seymour; *D:* Richard Attenborough. Golden Globes '73: Foreign Film.

You're a Big Boy Now ♂♂♂ 1966 Kastner, a virginal young man working in the New York Public Library, is told by his father to move out of his house and grow up. On his own, he soon becomes involved with man-hating actress Hartman and a discotheque dancer. A wild and weird comedy, Coppola's commercial directorial debut. **96m/C** VHS, Elizabeth Hartman, Geraldine Page, Peter Kastner, Julie Harris, Rip Torn, Michael Dunn, Tony Bill, Karen Black; *D:* Francis Ford Coppola; *W:* Francis Ford Coppola.

You're Jinxed, Friend, You've Met Sacramento ♂♂ 1970 The tongue-in-cheek adventures of a coolheaded cowboy as he passes from town to colorful town. Great title, too. **99m/C** VHS, IT Ty Hardin, Christian Hay, Jenny Atkins; *D:* George Cristallini.

Yours, Mine & Ours ♂♂ 1968 Bigger, better, big screen version of "The Brady Bunch." It's the story of a lovely lady (Ball) with eight kids who marries a a widower (Fonda) who has ten. Imagine the zany shenanigans! Family comedy manages to be both wholesome and a true story. **114m/C** VHS, Lucille Ball, Henry Fonda, Van Johnson, Tim Matheson, Tom Bosley, Tracy Nelson, Morgan Brittany; *D:* Melville Shavelson; *W:* Melville Shavelson; *C:* Charles F. Wheeler; *M:* Fred Karlin.

Yours, Mine & Ours ♂♂ 2005 (PG) Over-the-top slapstick, remake of the 1968 Lucille Ball/Henry Fonda farce about blending a large family. Helen (Russo) and Frank (Quaid) shared a brief high school romance. Now it's 30 years (and 18 kids) later, they're both single, and the romance rekindles at a reunion. Conflict between the kids, their jobs, and their differing child-raising philosophies ensues, as do sporadic bits of humor. Fun and safe enough family viewing. **90m/C** VHS, DVD, US Dennis Quaid, Rene Russo, Rip Torn, Linda Hunt, Jerry O'Connell, David Koechner, Sean Faris, Katija Pevec, Tyler Patrick Jones, Danielle Panabaker, Drake Bell, Miranda Cosgrove, Dean Collins, Haley Ramm, Brecken Palmer, Bridger Palmer, Ty Panitz, Miki Ishikawa, Slade Pearce, Little JJ, Andrew Vo, Jennifer Habib, Jessica Habib, Nicholas Roget-King; *D:* Raja Gosnell; *W:* Ron Burch, David Kidd; *C:* Theo van de Sande; *M:* Christophe Beck.

Youth Aflame WOOF! *Hoodlum Girls* 1944 Trash film that tells the tale of two sisters—one good, one bad. Poor dialogue and weak performances do, however, make for some great camp. Based on a story by Helen Kiedy. **61m/B** VHS, Joy Reese, Warren Burr, Kay Morley, Michael Owen, Rod Rogers; *D:* Elmer Clifton; *W:* Elmer Clifton.

Young Warlord ♂♂ 1975 Arthur roams western England in 500 AD, leading a band of guerilla cavalrymen. When the Saxons invade, Arthur unites the tribe, holds off the attack and becomes king. **97m/C** VHS, Oliver Tobias, Michael Gothard, Jack Watson, Brian Blessed; *D:* Peter Sasdy.

Your Vice is a Closed Room and Only I Have the Key ♂♂♂ *Il tuo vizie e una stanza chiusa e solo io ne ho la chiave; Excite Me; Eye of the Black Cat; Gently Before She Dies* 1972 Italian writer Oliviero (Pistilli) enjoys tormenting and belittling women, especially his wife. When one of his mistresses is brutally murdered, followed by similar crimes, he becomes a suspect. His behavior toward his wife worsens and is witnessed by his scheming niece and the family's cat. Satisfying giallo heavily influenced by Poe. **96m/C** DVD, IT Luigi Pistilli, Anita Strindberg, Edwige Fenech, Ivan Rassimov; *D:* Sergio Martino, Ernesto Gastaldi, Luciano Martino, Sauro Scavolini; *C:* Giancarlo Ferrando; *M:* Bruno Nicolai.

Your Turn Darling ♂♂ *A Toi de Faire, Mignonne; L'Agente Federale Lemmy Caution; Ladies Man* 1963 French espionage thriller with Constantine once again playing Lemmy Caution, a U.S. secret agent involved with a gang of spies. **83m/B** VHS, FR Eddie Constantine, Gaia Germani, Elga Andersen; *D:* Bernard Borderie; *W:* Bernard Borderie; *C:* Henri Persin; *M:* Paul Misraki.

You've Got Mail ♂♂½ 1998 (PG) Third remake of "The Shop Around the Corner" ("In the Good Old Summertime" was number 2) finds independent bookstore owner Ryan battling Hanks's bookstore conglomerate to stay in business. How does this qualify as a romantic comedy? Because they're flirting with each other anonymously by e-mail. Third teaming of Ryan and Hanks relies, almost too much, on their considerable chemistry. Soundtrack music was chosen for maximum on-screen and record store effect. Must-see for hopeless romantics and fans of Hanks and/or Ryan. Others must decide based on tolerance for meet-cute situations and lightweight romantic comedy. **119m/C** VHS, DVD, Meg Ryan, Tom Hanks, Parker Posey, Greg Kinnear, Jean Stapleton, Steve Zahn, Dave Chappelle, Dabney Coleman, John Randolph Michael Badalucco, Heather Burns, Hallee Hirsh; *D:* Nora Ephron; *W:* Nora Ephron; *C:* John Lindley; *M:* George Fenton.

You've Ruined Me, Eddie ♂ *La Moglie Vergine; The Virgin Wife* 1977 (R) A young bride groom's life gets complicated after he does not sexually satisfy his bride on their wedding night. **98m/C** VHS, IT Carroll Baker, Edwige Fenech, Ray Lovelock, Renzo Montagnani; *D:* Marino Girolami; *W:* Marino Girolami.

You've Got to Have Heart ♂ *The Touch of Flesh* 1958 A spoiled rich girl gets knocked up and her boyfriend will never know peace again. Meanwhile, their once quiet town is outraged. **76m/B** VHS, DVD, Charles Martin, Robert Cannon, Ted Marshall, Jeanne Rainer, Sue Ellis, Josie Hascall; *D:* R. John Hugh; *C:* Charles T. O'Rork.

Yu-Gi-Oh! The Movie: Pyramid of Light ♂♂ 2004 (PG) Yu-Gi-Oh hits the big screen with the television cartoon's storyline (picking up at the end of the series' third season) and gameplay in tow, meaning only fans (and their suffering parents) need to see it. Yu-Gi-Oh, whose bo cy hosts an Egyptian spirit, plays a combat monster game, apparently for the future of humanity and occasionally for the players' souls. The Pyramid of Light, in question is the most powerful card, and controls the destiny of the play ers. If your kids aren't fans, count yourself lucky, if they are, keep in mind that game cards were given out as inticement to get people into the theater. **89m/C** VHS, DVD, JP Dan Green, Amy Birnbaum; *W:* Norman Grossfeld, Matthew Drdek, Lloyd Goldfine; *C:* Hiroaki Edamitsu; *M:* Elik Alvarez; *V:* Eric Stuart, Dan Green, Maddie (Medeleine) Blaustein, Wayne Grayson, Scottie Ray, Tara Jayne, Frank Frankson.

Yukon Flight ♂♂ 1940 A Renfrew of the Mounties adventure. The hero finds illegal gold mining operations and murder in the Yukon. **57m/B** VHS, DVD, James Newill, Dave O'Brien, Louise Stanley, Warren Hull, Karl Hackett, Roy Barcroft; *D:* Ralph Staub; *W:* Edward Halperin; *C:* Mack Stiengler.

Youth on Parole ♂½ 1937 Same old story: Boy gets paroled. Girl gets paroled. Parolee meets parolette and romance blossoms as they beat a further rap. **60m/B** VHS, Miles Marder, Margaret Dumont, Milburn Stone, Marian Marsh, Gordon Oliver; *D:* Phil Rosen; *W:* Hershal Rebuas; *C:* Edward Snyder.

Youth Without Youth ♂♂ 2007 (R) A disappointing return to directing for Francis Ford Coppola after a ten-year hiatus. Dominic (Roth) is a 70-year-old Romanian linguist who fears he'll die a failure and, on the eve of World War II, decides to kill himself. But his suicide plans are interrupted when he's struck by lightning and somehow begins to grow younger. Scientists of the Third Reich snatch him up for observation and soon he meets Veronica (Lara), a sexy German spy who is coincidentally also struck by lightning, but begins to age rapidly. A muddled and tiring story that "would've" been better suited as a "Twilight Zone" episode. **124m/C** DVD, US Tim Roth, Alexandra Maria Lara, Bruno Ganz, Andre Hennicke, Alexandra Pirici; *D:* Francis Ford Coppola; *W:* Francis Ford Coppola; *C:* Mihai Malaimare Jr.; *M:* Osvaldo Golijov.

The Yum-Yum Girls 🐾🐾½ 1978 (R) Pair of innocent girls arrive in NYC to pursue their dreams. Gives an inside look at the fashion industry. Not as funny or as cute as it wants to be. **89m/C VHS, DVD.** Judy Landers, Tanya Roberts, Barbara Tully, Michelle Daw; **D:** Barry Rosen.

Yuma 🐾🐾 1970 An old-style Western about a sheriff (Walker) who rides into town, cleans it up, and saves his own reputation from a plot to discredit him. Dull in places, but action-packed ending saves the day. **73m/C VHS, DVD.** Clint Walker, Barry Sullivan, Edgar Buchanan; **D:** Ted Post; **M:** George Duning. **TV**

Yuri Nosenko, KGB 🐾🐾 1986 Fact-based account of a KGB defector and the CIA agent who must determine if he's on the up-and-up. **85m/C VHS, DVD. GB** Tommy Lee Jones, Oleg Rudnik, Josef Sommer, Ed Lauter, George Morfogen, Stephen D. Newman; **D:** Mick Jackson. **TV**

Z 🐾🐾🐾🐾 1969 The assassination of a Greek nationalist in the 1960s and its aftermath are portrayed by the notorious political director as a gripping detective thriller. Excellent performances, adequate cinematic techniques, and important politics in this highly acclaimed film. **128m/C VHS, DVD. FR** Yves Montand, Jean-Louis Trintignant, Irene Papas, Charles Denner, Georges Geret, Jacques Perrin, Francois Perier, Marcel Bozzuffi; **D:** Constantin Costa-Gavras; **W:** Constantin Costa-Gavras; **M:** Mikis Theodorakis. Oscars '69: Film Editing, Foreign Film; Cannes '69: Special Jury Prize, Actor (Trintignant); Golden Globes '70: Foreign Film; N.Y. Film Critics '69: Director (Costa-Gavras), Film; Natl. Soc. Film Critics '69: Film.

Zabriskie Point 🐾🐾🐾 1970 (R) Antonioni's first U.S. feature. A desultory, surreal examination of the American way of life. Worthy but difficult. Climaxes with a stylized orgy in Death Valley. **112m/C VHS.** Mark Frechette, Daria Halprin, Paul Fix, Rod Taylor, Harrison Ford, G.D. Spradlin; **D:** Michelangelo Antonioni; **M:** Michelangelo Antonioni, Sam Shepard, Fred Gardner, Tonino Guerra, Clare Peploe.

Zachariah 🐾🐾½ 1970 (PG) A semispoof '60s rock western, wherein two gunfighters given to pursuing wealth-laden bands of outlaws separate and experience quixotic journeys through the cliched landscape. Scripted by members of The Firesign Theater and featuring appearances by Country Joe and The Fish, The New York Rock Ensemble, and The James Gang. **93m/C VHS, DVD.** Don Johnson, John Rubinstein, Pat Quinn, Dick Van Patten, William Challee, Country Joe McDonald, Elvin Jones, Doug Kershaw, Lawrence Kubik, Hank Worden; **D:** George Englund; **W:** Peter Bergman, Joe Massot, Philip Proctor, Philip Austin, David Ossman; **C:** Jorge Stahl Jr.; **M:** Jimmie Haskell.

Zack & Reba 🐾🐾 1998 (R) When Reba (Murphy) calls off her wedding a week before the ceremony, her fiance commits suicide. Guilt-ridden, Reba returns to her hometown of Spooner and its eccentric residents, which include shotgun-toting grandma, Beulah (Reynolds), and her grief-stricken grandson Zack (Flanery), who can't seem to get over the death of his wife. Naturally, Beulah thinks Zack and Reba are just made for each other. **91m/C VHS, DVD.** Sean Patrick Flanery, Brittany Murphy, Debbie Reynolds, Kathy Najimy, Martin Mull, Michael Jeter; **D:** Nicole Bettauer; **W:** Jay Stapleton; **C:** Mark Irwin; **M:** Joel McNeely.

Zafarinas 🐾🐾 *Morriras en Chafarinas* 1994 (R) Zafarinas is an ancient walled city on the island of Melilla that houses a military barracks. Two suspicious deaths force Commander Contreras (Ladoire) to release zealous corporal Jaime (Sanz) and Corporal Cidraque (Albala) from the stockades to investigate. Then there's a third death and things just aren't what they seem. Spanish with subtitles. **85m/C VHS. SP** Jorge Sanz, Javier Albala, Oscar Ladoire, Maria Barranco; **D:** Pedro Olea; **W:** Pedro Olea, Fernando Lalana; **C:** Paco Femenia.

Zalmen or the Madness of God 🐾🐾½ 1975 Elie Wiesel's mystical story about a rabbi's struggle against religious persecution in post-Stalin Russia. **120m/C VHS, DVD.** Joseph Wiseman, Dianne Wiest; **W:** Elie Wiesel. **TV**

Zandalee WOOF! 1991 (R) The sexual adventures of a bored sexy young woman who has a fling with her husband's friend. Bad script, graphic sex. Also available in an unrated version. **100m/C VHS, DVD.** Nicolas Cage, Judge Reinhold, Erika Anderson, Viveca Lindfors, Aaron Neville, Joe Pantoliano, Ian Abercrombie, Marisa Tomei, Zach Galligan; **D:** Sam Pillsbury; **M:** Mari Kornhauser.

Zandy's Bride 🐾½ 1974 (PG) Basic story about a rancher who sends for a mail-order bride. She's shocked by his ill-treatment of her and stands up to his bullying, thus winning his respect and love. Beautiful scenery, courtesy of Big Sur, California, but predictable all-around and essentially a waste of an experienced cast. Based on the novel "The Stranger" by Lillian Bos Ross. **97m/C VHS.** Gene Hackman, Liv Ullmann, Eileen Heckart, Harry Dean Stanton, Joe Santos, Sam Bottoms, Susan Tyrrell, Frank Cady; **D:** Jan Troell; **W:** Marc Norman; **C:** Jordan Cronenweth; **M:** Michael Franks.

The Zany Adventures of Robin Hood 🐾🐾 1984 Hackneyed spoof of the Robin Hood legend. Medieval man robs from the rich to help the poor. Not nearly as funny as Mel Brooks' TV series that spoofed "Robin Hood." **95m/C VHS.** George Segal, Morgan Fairchild, Roddy McDowall, Roy Kinnear, Janet Suzman, Tom Baker; **D:** Ray Austin.

Zapped! 🐾 1982 (R) Teen genius discovers he possesses telekinetic powers. He does the natural thing, using his talent to remove clothing from nearby females. A teen boy's dream come true. **98m/C VHS, DVD.** Scott Baio, Willie Aames, Robert Mandan, Felice Schachter, Scatman Crothers, Roger Bowen, Marya Small, Greg Bradford, Hilary Beane, Sue Ane Langdon, Heather Thomas, Merritt Butrick, LaWanda Page, Rosanne Katon; **D:** Robert J. Rosenthal; **M:** Charles Fox.

Zapped Again 🐾 1989 (R) The lame-brained sequel to 1982's "Zapped" about a high schooler who has telekinetic powers and lust on his mind. **93m/C VHS, DVD.** Todd Eric Andrews, Kelli Williams, Reed Rudy, Linda Blair, Karen Black, Lyle Alzado, Rossie (Ross) Harris; **D:** Doug Campbell.

Zardoz 🐾🐾 1973 A surreal parable of the far future (2293), when Earth society is broken into strict classes: a society of intellectuals known as the Eternals, a society of savages called the Brutals, and an elite unit of killers, naturally named the Exterminators, who keep the order. The Exterminators worship a stone god named Zardoz, but killer Zed (Connery) discovers that it's merely a futuristic version of "The Wizard of Oz" and that the Eternals have been manipulating the social order. His presence causes chaos and destruction (but he does get all the babes). Visually interesting but pretentious. **105m/C VHS, DVD. GB** Sean Connery, Charlotte Rampling, John Alderton, Sara Kestelman, Sally Anne Newton, Niall Buggy, Christopher Casson, Bosco Hogan, Jessica Swift; **D:** John Boorman; **W:** John Boorman; **C:** Geoffrey Unsworth; **M:** David Munrow.

Zarkorr! The Invader 🐾 1996 (PG) Aliens studying earth decide humans need a challenge (like we don't have enough problems of our own) so they send a 185-foot tall, laser-eyed monster to crush (American) cities and cause general terror in the population. And who's our hero? A postal worker—aided by a five-inch tall alien girl. Low-budget spoof has its moments, but eventually wears thin. **80m/C VHS, DVD.** Rhys Pugh, Deprise Grossman, Mark Hamilton, Charles Schneider, Eileen Wesson; **D:** Aaron Osborne; **W:** Benjamin Carr; **C:** Joe C. Maxwell; **M:** Richard Band.

Zathura 🐾🐾🐾 2005 (PG) Ten year old Walter (Hutcherson) and six year old Danny (Bobo) both fight for overstressed dad's (Robbins) attention, but he's too busy. Older sister Lisa (Stewart) is charged with babysitting the two, but she could care less. Until they all find themselves trapped in the bizarre space-world of Zathura, a game which comes to life as they play. Sort-of sequel to "Jumanji," also done by Chris Van Allsburg. Fabulous special effects and a fantastical plot is exciting stuff for both children and adults. **113m/C VHS, DVD, UMD. US** Jonah Bobo, Josh Hutcherson, Dax Shepard, Kristen Stewart, Tim Robbins; **D:** Jon Favreau; **W:** David Koepp, John Kamps; **C:** Guillermo Navarro; **M:** John Debney; **V:** Frank Oz.

Zatoichi 🐾🐾🐾½ 2003 (R) *The Blind Swordsman: Zatoichi* Versatile and popular filmmaker Kitano (who also takes on the lead role here as his actor's pseudonym) kicks butt as a legendary 19th-century samurai (an iconic figure in Japanese film and TV). The blind masseur/gambler hides his sword in his walking stick and the plot, such as it is, involves toner Zatoichi helping out geisha Okino (Daike) and her cross-dressing brother Osei (Tachibana) in their quest for revenge on the Ginzo gang, who slaughtered their family and who are now threatening the local peasants. Which makes a good excuse for Zatoichi to challenge the gang and their own formidable samurai Hattori (Asano). Lots of stylized violence and some slapstick gags; Japanese with subtitles. **115m/C DVD.** *JP* Tadanobu Asano, Takeshi "Beat" Kitano, Michiyo Ogusu, Guadalcanal Taka, Daigoro Tachibana, Yuko Daike, Ittoku Kishibe, Saburo Ishikura; **D:** Takeshi "Beat" Kitano; **W:** Takeshi "Beat" Kitano; **C:** Katsumi Yanagijima; **M:** Keiichi Suzuki.

Zatoichi: Master Ichi and a Chest of Gold 🐾🐾 1964 A violent thriller about a blind gambler and former samurai who tries to clear his name after being framed for a gold robbery. Adapted from a novel by Kazuo Miyagawa. In Japanese with English subtitles. **83m/C VHS, DVD.** *JP* Shintaro Katsu, Tomisaburo Wakayama; **D:** Kazuo Ikehiro; **W:** Shozaburo Asai; **C:** Kazuo Miyagawa; **M:** Ichiro Saito.

Zatoichi: The Blind Swordsman and the Chess Expert 🐾🐾 1965 Zatoichi, the blind gambler and former samurai, befriends a master chess player and gets involved with Japanese gangsters. In Japanese with English subtitles. **87m/C VHS, DVD.** *JP* Shintaro Katsu, Mikio Narita, Chizu Hayashi, Kaneko Iwasaki, Gaku Yamamoto; **D:** Kenji Misumi; **W:** Daisuke Ito; **C:** Chishi Makiura; **M:** Akira Ifukube.

Zatoichi: The Blind Swordsman and the Fugitives 🐾🐾 1968 This time Zatoichi, the blind masseur and master swordsman, is pitted against a band of outlaws. When the local bandits brutalize the countryside Zatoichi steps in to defend the weak and faces a showdown with outlaw leader Genpachiro. In Japanese with English subtitles. **83m/C VHS, DVD.** *JP* Shintaro Katsu, Yumiko Nogawa, Kayo Mikimoto, Kyosuke Machida; **D:** Kimiyoshi Yasuda.

Zatoichi: The Blind Swordsman's Vengeance 🐾🐾 1966 *Zatoichi's Vengeance* Zatoichi defends a dying man against a group of gangsters who have taken over an isolated village. In Japanese with English subtitles. **83m/C VHS, DVD.** *JP* Shintaro Katsu, Shigeru Amachi, Kei Sato, Mayumi Ogawa; **D:** Tokuzo Tanaka.

Zatoichi: The Life and Opinion of Masseur Ichi 🐾🐾 *The Tale of Zatoichi* 1962 The first film in the action series about the Zen-like blind masseur, gambler, and swordsman. Zatoichi is drawn into a revenge match between two ruthless gangs. When one gang tries to hire him the other hires a savage killer. This sets in motion a war between the yakuza gangs and mercenary samurai. In Japanese with English subtitles. **96m/C VHS, DVD.** *JP* Shintaro Katsu, Masayo Mari, Ryuzo Shimada, Gen Mitamura, Shigeru Amachi; **D:** Kenji Misumi.

Zatoichi vs. Yojimbo 🐾🐾½ *Zatoichi Meets Yojimbo; Zato Ichi To Yojimbo* 1970 The legendary blind warrior-samurai, Zatoichi, wants to retire, but his village is being held captive by outlaws. He is forced to fight Yojimbo, the crude wandering samurai without a master, and the sparks really fly! This was a comic send-up of Akiro Kurosawa's "Yojimbo" with Mifune recreating his role here and playing it for laughs. Subtitled. **90m/C VHS, DVD.** *JP* Toshiro Mifune, Shintaro Katsu, Osamu Takizawa; **D:** Kihachi Okamoto.

Zazie dans le Metro 🐾🐾½ 1964 *Zazie in the Underground; Zazie in the Subway* 1961 One of Malle's early movies, this is one of the best of the French New Wave comedies. A young girl, wise beyond her years, visits her drag queen uncle in Paris. She wants to ride the subway, but the ensuing hilarious adventures keep her from her goal. In French with English subtitles. **92m/C VHS.** *FR* Catherine Demongeot, Philippe Noiret, Carla Marlier; **D:** Louis Malle.

Zebra Force 🐾 1976 (R) Group of battle against organized crime, using their military training with deadly precision. Non-distinguished substandard action-adventure. **81m/C VHS.** Mike Lane, Richard X. Slattery, Rockne Tarkington, Glenn Wilder, Anthony Caruso; **D:** Joe Tornatore.

Zebra in the Kitchen 🐾🐾½ 1965 A 12-year-old boy living in a small town is upset when he sees the run-down condition of the local zoo. So he decides to set all the animals free, which causes pandemonium in the town. Pleasant family fare. **92m/C VHS, DVD.** Jay North, Martin Milner, Andy Devine, Joyce Meadows, Jim Davis; **D:** Ivan Tors.

Zebra Lounge 🐾🐾 2001 Wendy (Swanson) and Alan (Baldwin) Barnet feel their marriage has gotten dull, so they place an ad in a swingers' magazine that leads them to the Zebra Lounge. There they meet the more experienced Jack (Daddo) and Louise (Ledford) Bauer who take them on a new sexual trip. But the Barnets soon discover that their new partners are not the emotionally stable people to get involved with. **92m/C VHS, DVD. CA** Stephen Baldwin, Kristy Swanson, Cameron Daddo, Brandy Ledford; **D:** Keri Skogland; **W:** Claire Montgomery, Monte Montgomery; **C:** Barry Parrell. **VIDEO**

Zebrahead 🐾🐾🐾 1992 (R) Zack and Nikki are two high schoolers in love—which would be okay except Zack's white and Nikki's black. Writer/director Drazan's expressive debut features one of last appearances by Sharkey as Zack's dad. Outstanding performances by the young and largely unknown cast, particularly Rapaport and Wright, and a great musical score enrich the action. Filmed on location in Detroit, with plenty of authentic Motown scenery to chew on, including Cody High School and a shootout at the eastside Skateland. Developed with assistance by the Sundance Institute. **102m/C VHS, DVD.** Michael Rapaport, N'Bushe Wright, Ray Sharkey, DeShonn Castle, Ron Johnson, Marsha Florence, Paul Butler, Abdul Hassan Sharif, Dan Ziskie, Candy Ann Brown, Helen Shaver, Luke Reilly, Martin Priest, Kevin Corrigan; **D:** Tony Drazan; **W:** Tony Drazan; **C:** Maryse Alberti; **M:** Taj Mahal. Sundance '92: Filmmakers Trophy.

A Zed & Two Noughts 🐾🐾🐾 1988 A serio-comic essay by the acclaimed British filmmaker. Twin zoologists, after their wives are killed in an accident, explore their notions of death by, among other things, filming the decay of animal bodies absconded from the zoo. Heavily textured and experimental; Greenaway's second feature film. **115m/C VHS, DVD. GB** Eric Deacon, Brian Deacon, Joss Ackland, Andrea Ferreol, Frances Barber; **D:** Peter Greenaway; **W:** Peter Greenaway; **C:** Sacha Vierny; **M:** Michael Nyman.

Zeder 🐾🐾½ *Revenge of the Dead; Zeder: Voices from Beyond* 1983 A young novelist (Lavia) discovers fragments of curious documents on the ribbon of a used typewriter bought by his wife (Canovas). He comes to think that they suggest research into immortality. The rest of the film combines elements of suspense with horror in a fairly slow-moving, serious plot with references to Val Lewton's "Cat People."

Zelary 🐾🐾🐾 2003 (R)
98m/C VHS, DVD. /T Gabriele Lavia, Anne Canovas; *D:* Pupi Avati; *W:* Pupi Avati; Antonio Avati;
Maurizio Costanzo.

Zelly & Me 🐾🐾🐾½ 1988 (PG)
*A strange little drama about a young or-
phan living with her maniacally possessive
grandmother, who forces the child into her
own interior life through humiliation and
isolation from anyone she cares for. Well-
acted and interesting film in that suffers from
an overly introspective plot and confusing
gaps in the narrative. Look for director
Lynch on the other side of the camera.*
87m/C VHS. Isabella Rossellini, Alexandra
Jones, David Lynch, Pt. Roman Polanski, Janusz
Joe Morton; *D:* Tina Rathborne; *W:* Tina Rathborne; *C:* Mikael Salomon; *M:* Pino Donaggio.

Zemsta 🐾🐾 *The Revenge* 2002
*In the 17th century, two feuding noblemen occu-
py different parts of the same crumbling
castle because of their declining fortunes.
They live to make each other miserable
and marry money. Papkin (Polanski), a
boastful popinjay, is enlisted by Czesnik to
help him woo a supposedly wealthy widow
in return for the chance at romancing
Czesnik's pretty niece, who has her own
romantic plans. Adapted from the play by
Aleksander Fredro. Polish with subtitles.*
100m/C VHS, DVD, Pt. Roman Polanski, Janusz
Gajos, Andrzej Seweryn, Kasia (Kazarzyna) Figura,
Agata Buzek, Rafal Krolikowski; *D:* Andrzej Wajda;
W: Andrzej Wajda; *C:* Pawel Edelman; *M:* Wojciech Kilar.

Zentropa 🐾🐾
Europa 1992 (R) *Clever
cinematic allusions and visuals aside, this
is essentially a conventional thriller. German-American pacifist Leopold travels to
Germany in 1945 to help in the postwar
rebuilding. He finds work as a sleeping-car
conductor for a giant railway system called
Zentropa and finds himself romancing the
mysterious Katharina, who draws the hapless Leopold into an intrigue involving
Nazi sympathizers. Director von Trier uses
the voice of Von Sydow as an omniscient
narrator to address the audience and
move the story along. Filmed primarily in
black-and-white with bursts of color denoting dramatic moments. In English and
German with English subtitles.* 112m/C
VHS, DVD, GE Jean-Marc Barr Barbara Sukowa,
Udo Kier, Eddie Constantine; *D:* Lars von Trier; *W:*
Niels Vorsel, Lars von Trier; *Nar:* Max von Sydow.

Zeppelin 🐾🐾½ 1971 (G) *During
WWI, the British enlist the aid of York as a
double agent. H's mission is to steal Germany's plans for a super-airship. Accompanying the Germans on the craft's maid-
en voyage, York discovers they are actually on a mission to steal British treasures.
Although the script is poor, the battle
scenes and the airship itself are very impressive.* 102m/C VHS, GB Michael York, Elke
Sommer, Peter Carsten, Marius Goring, Anton

Zemsta ...

Zeram 🐾🐾 *Zeiram; Zeiramu* 1991 *Zeram
is a giant renegade space alien lured to
earth by a female bounty hunter. How
does she expect to capture it? Why with a
warp machine, space bazooka, electric
shield, and a computer named Bob, of
course. Dubbed.* 92m/C VHS, DVD, JP Yuko
Moriyama, Yukihiro Hotaru, Kunihiko Ida; *D:* Keita
Amemiya; *M:* Hirohazu Ohta.

Zeram 2 🐾🐾 *Zeram 2; Zeiramu* 1994
*Moriyama returns to play Investigator Iria,
an intergalactic bounty hunter, who is assisted by a new android as a trainee, but it
mixes amazing action scenes, 'gross'
monsters, and slapstick comedy.*
100m/C DVD, JP Yukihiro Hotaru, Kunihiko Iida,
Yuko Moriyama; *D:* Keito Amemiya.

Zero 1984 *WWII story about the building
of the zero fighter that was used to devastating effect in the invasion of Pearl Harbor.* 128m/C VHS; *D:* Toshio Masuda.

Zero Boys Woof! 1986 (R) *Teenage
survivalists in the Californian wilderness
are stalked by a murderous lunatic. Ex-
ploitative and mean-spirited.* 89m/C VHS,
DVD, Daniel Hirsch, Kelli Maroney, Nicole Rio, Joe
Estevez; *D:* Nico Mastorakis; *W:* Nico Mastorakis;
Fred C. Perry; *C:* Steve (Steven) Shaw; *M:* Stanley
Myers, Hans Zimmer.

Zero Degrees Kelvin 🐾🐾½
Kjaerlighetens Kjotere 1995 *Brrr!
Get the ice scraper ready, because you
may have to clear off your TV screen in
this chilly tale of trappers in 1920s Greenland. Henrik Larsen (Eidsvold), a poet living in Oslo, decides to join the band of
trappers after his girlfriend Gertrude (Martens) spurns his marriage proposal. On his
arrival in the stark and frozen landscape,
he is forced to share a cabin with the stoic,
silent Holm (Sundquist) and the lewd, violent Randbaek (Skarsgard). Randbaek
holds the newcomer and his city-boy ways
in disdain, creating an air of tension and
menace that inevitably results in a clash
between the two. Instead of dwelling on
the action aspect, director Moland uses
the minimalist landscape to echo the psychological battles the men must face with
the frigid terrain and between themselves.
Norwegian with subtitles.* 113m/C VHS, DVD,
NO Gard B. Eidsvold, Stellan Skarsgard, Bjorn
Sundquist, Camilla Martens; *D:* Hans Petter Moland; *W:* Hans Petter Moland, Lars Bill Lundhelm;
C: Philip Ogaard; *M:* Terje Rypdal.

Zero Effect 🐾🐾½ 1997 (R) *A cross
between Howard Hughes and Sherlock
Holmes, brilliant, eccentric detective Daryl
Zero (Pullman), who, along with his harried helper Steve Arlo (Stiller), takes on
the case of a blackmailed timber tycoon
(O'Neal) in this comedic whodunit. The
normally reclusive sleuth bites the bullet
and agrees to trek to Oregon to personally
investigate the particularly intriguing case,
which also involves an attractive paramedic (Dickens). Pullman pulls off another
quirky leading man performance with flair.
Stiller is stellar as the exasperated assistant. Fresh idea and hip humor mark this
debut for 22-year-old writer/director Kasdan, son of director Lawrence Kasdan.*
150m/C VHS, DVD, Bill Pullman, Ben Stiller, Ryan
O'Neal, Kim Dickens, Angela Featherstone; *D:*
Jake Kasdan; *W:* Jake Kasdan; *C:* Bill Pope.

Zero for Conduct 🐾🐾🐾 *Zero
de Conduit* 1933 Vigo's classic French fantasy about an outrageous rebellion of schoolboys against bureaucratic adults. More
of a visual poem than a drama, it inspired
Lindsay Anderson's "If...." One of only
four films created by Vigo before his early

Zero 🐾🐾 1957 *Passen-
gers and crew aboard an airliner become
sick from food poisoning and the only way
to avoid disaster is to find someone on
board who can fly the plane—and hasn't
had fish for dinner! Yep, it's the film that
inspired the classic spoof "Airplane!" And
for that, it deserves an extra half bone.*
81m/B DVD, Dana Andrews, Linda Darnell, Sterling Hayden, Geoffrey Toone, Jerry Paris, Peggy
King, Charles Quinlivan, Patricia Tiernan, Elroy
"Crazylegs" Hirsch, Willis Bouchey, Robert Stevenson; *D:* Hall Bartlett; *W:* Hall Bartlett,
John C. Champion, Arthur Hailey; *C:* John
F. Warren; *Nar:* William Conrad.

Zero Hour! 🐾🐾½ ...

Zero Patience 🐾🐾 1994 *Yes, it's
an audacious film musical about AIDS
myths and ghosts and Victorian explorers—among other things. Infamous Patient Zero (Fauteux) is the Canadian flight
attendant reputed to have carried the virus
to North America. Ghostly Zero pleads for
someone to tell his story and his cause is
taken up by Victorian explorer Sir Richard
Francis Burton (Robinson), who happens
to have achieved eternal life after an encounter with the Fountain of Youth, and
who is also preparing an exhibit on contagious diseases. Sharp mix of politics, humor, and fantasy.* 100m/C VHS, DVD, CA John
Robinson, Normand Fauteux, Dianne Heathering-
ton, Ricardo Keens-Douglas; *D:* John Greyson; *W:*
John Greyson; *M:* Glenn Schellenberg.

Zero Population Growth 🐾½
Z.P.G 1972 *In the 21st century the government has decreed that no babies may be
born for a 30-year span in order to contro
the population. But Chaplin and Reed secretly have a child and when they are discovered are sent to be executed. Can they
escape? Maudlin and simplistic.* 95m/C
VHS, Oliver Reed, Geraldine Chaplin, Diane Clen-
nin, Don Gordon; *D:* Michael Campus; *W:* Frank Di
Felitta, Max Ehrlich.

Zero to Sixty 🐾 1978 (PG) *Newly
divorced man finds his car has been repossessed for nonpayment. Seeking out
the manager of the finance company, he
gets a job as a repo man with a sassy 16-
year-old girl as his assistant. Repartee develops, stuff happens, and the movie
ends.* 96m/C VHS, Darren McGavin, Sylvia Miles,
Denise Nickerson, Joan Collins; *D:* Don Weis; *M:*
John Beal.

Zero Tolerance 🐾 1993 (R)
*FBI agent Jeff Douglas (Patrick) is as-
signed to escort a drug kingpin to Mexico,
but the cartel intervenes and pick up a
drug-runner who works for the White Hand
cartel, whose latest product is liquid heroin. When they are ambushed Douglas is
forced to carry a shipment of drugs across
the border—the lives of his wife and chic
hang in the balance. But after the dirty
deed is done, Douglas finds his family has
been murdered anyway. So he sets out to
execute the cartel drug lords.* 92m/C VHS,
DVD, Robert Patrick, Mies O'Keefe, Mick Fleetwood, Titus Welliver, Jeffrey Anderson-Gunter,
Gustav Vintas, Michael Gregory, Maurice Lamont;
D: Joseph Merhi; *W:* Jacobsen Hart.

Zeta One 🐾 *Alien Women; The Love Factor* 1969 *A soft-core British science fiction
yarn about scantily clad alien babes and
toy solves a diamond caper and proves
his mother's innocence.* 50m/C VHS, Adam
Rich, David Groh, Jane Elliot; *D:* Paul Asselin; *W:*
David Hoffman, Leslie Zerg; *C:* Erik Daerstad.

Zertigo Diamond Caper 🐾 1982
*Utilizing his heightened senses, a blind
boy solves a diamond caper and proves
his mother's innocence.* 50m/C VHS, Adam
Rich, David Groh, Jane Elliot; *D:* Paul Asselin; *W:*
David Hoffman, Leslie Zerg; *C:* Erik Daerstad.

Zeram ...

Zeram 2 ...

Zero, Rupert Davies, Alexandra
Stewart; *D:* Etienne Perier.

Zeram 🐾🐾 *Zeiram; Zeiramu* 1991
Dittring, Andrew Keir, Rupert Davies, Alexandra
Stewart; *D:* Etienne Perier.

death. Banned across Europe at release.
In French with English subtitles.
VHS, FR Jean Daste, Robert Le Flon, Louis
LeFevra, Constantin Kelber, Gerard de Bedariaux;
D: Jean Vigo; *W:* Jean Vigo; *C:* Boris Kaufman.

Ziegfeld Girl 🐾🐾🐾 1941 *Three
star-struck girls are chosen for the Zieg-
feld follies and move on to success and
heartbreak. Lavish costumes and produc-
tion numbers in the MGM style. You
Stepped Out of a Dream; I'm Always
Chasing Rainbows; Minnie from Trinidad;
You Never Looked So Beautiful.* 131m/B VHS, DVD,
James Stewart, Judy Garland, Hedy Lamarr, Lana
Turner, Tony Martin, Jackie Cooper, Ian Hunter,
Charles Winninger, Al Shean, Edward Everett Hor-
ton, Philip Dorn, Paul Kelly, Eve Arden, Dan Dai-
ley, Fay Holden, Felix Bressart, Mae Busch, Reed
Hadley; *D:* Robert Z. Leonard.

Ziegfeld Follies 🐾🐾½ 1946 *A
lavish revue of musical numbers and comedy sketches featuring many MGM stars
of the WWII era. Highlights include Astaire
and Kelly's only duet and a Astaire-Brem-
er ballet number. Bring on Those Wonderful Men; Bring on Those Beautiful Girls;
The Drinking Song; La Traviata; This
Heart is Mine; Love; When Television
Comes; There's Beauty Everywhere; The
Babbitt and the Bromide.* 115m/C VHS, DVD,
Fred Astaire, Judy Garland, Gene Kelly, Red Skelton, Fanny Brice, William Powell, Jimmy Durante,
Edward Arnold, Lucille Bremer, Hume Cronyn, Victor Moore, Lena Horne, Lucille Ball, Esther Williams; *D:* Vincente Minnelli; *C:* Charles Rosher.

ZigZag 🐾🐾½ 2002 (R) *Louis "Zig-
Zag" Fletcher (Jones) is an autistic 15-
year-old who lives in fear of his dad
Fletcher (Sniper), an abusive drug addict.
ZigZag works after school as a dishwasher for the foul-mouthed Toad (Platt) and
his one caring friend is his volunteer Big
Brother, Dean (Leguizamo), who has cancer. As if things are bad enough, after a
confrontation with Fletcher, ZigZag steals
$9,000 from Toad to give to his dad and
Dean goes to a loan shark (Goss) to get
the money to return to Toad's safe before
he realizes it's missing. Based on the novel by Landon J. Napoleon; Goyer's directorial debut. The sort of story that can easily descend into sap but doesn't thanks to
some fearless performances and Goyer's
tight control.* 101m/C VHS, DVD, Sam Jones III,

Zhou Yu's Train 🐾🐾½ *Zhou Yu
de Huoche* 2002 (PG-13) *Gong Li stars in this
slick romantic drama as porcelain painter,
Zhou Yu, who's in love with teacher/poet
Chen Ching (Leung Ka-fai). Because he
lives in a distant village, Zhou takes the
train twice a week so they can be together. Chen begins to feel overwhelmed and
transfers to an even farther away town,
meanwhile, Zhou becomes friendly with
another train passenger, Zhang (Honglei).
Gong also plays another character, Xiu,
who's involved with Chen and learns
about his time with Zhou. Except
director's Sun's theme is that love is how
you want it to appear (or something like
that). Based on the novella "Zhou Yu's
Cry" by Bei Cun. Mandarian with subtitles.*
97m/C DVD, Honglei Sun, Gong Li, Tony Leung
Kar-fai, Li Zhixiong, Shi Chunling, Liu Wei, Gao
Jingwen, Dai Ke, Pan Weiyan, Huang Mxc; *D:* Sun
Zhou; *W:* Sun Zhou, Bei Cun, Zhang Mei; *C:* Wang
Yu; *M:* Shingeru Umebayashi.

Zeus and Roxanne 🐾🐾 1996
*(PG) Hey, I know! Let's combine "Flipper"
and "Benji" with "The Parent Trap!" You
know, "or the kids! Marine biologist and
single mom Mary Beth (Quinlan) meets
her unconventional (and conveniently widowed) new neighbor Terry (Guttenberg)
and his dog Zeus. Cuteness ensues. Mary
Beth's daughters and Terry's young son
go about getting the two adults together.
Meanwhile, Zeus and Roxanne, Mary
Beth's dolphin, strike up a unique friendship of their own. Showing up to provide
drama is evil guy Claude (Vosloo), who is
vying for the same grant as Mary Beth.
Unlikely animal couple steals the show
and the story would have benefited from
focusing on the entertaining bond between those two and less on the human
romance. Not much appeal for anyone
over the age of nine.* 98m/C VHS, DVD, Kathleen Quinlan, Steve Guttenberg, Arnold Vosloo,
Miko Hughes, Dawn McMillan, Majandra Delfino;
D: George Miller; *W:* Tom Benedek; *C:* David Connell; *M:* Bruce Rowland.

John Leguizamo, Wesley Snipes, Oliver Platt, Natasha Lyonne, Sherman Augustus, Luke Goss, Michael Greyeyes, Elizabeth Peña; **D:** David S. Goyer. **W:** David S. Goyer; **C:** James L. Carter; **M:** Grant Lee Phillips.

Zipperface 1992 A Palm Beach serial killer is making mincemeat of the local prostitutes. In order to capture the scum, the prerequisite beautiful police detective goes undercover only to find herself the killer's biggest thrill. **90m/C VHS.** Dona Adams, Jonathan Mandell, David Clover, Trisha Melynkov, Richard Vidan, Harold Cannon, Bruce Brown, Rikki Brando, Timothy D. Lechner, John Dagnen; **D:** Mansour Pourmand; **W:** Barbara Bishop; **C:** F. Smith Martin; **M:** Jim Halfpenny.

Zis Boom Bah 1941 Musical-comedy star buys a cafe for her college son. He and his friends transform the place into a restaurant-theatre with predictable results. ♪Annabella; It Makes No Difference When You're in the Army; Put Your Trust in the Moon; Zis Boom Bah; Good News Tomorrow; I've Learned to Smile Again. **61m/B VHS, DVD.** Richard "Skeets" Gallagher, Jan Wiley, Peter Lind Hayes, Mary Healy, Grace Hayes, Huntz Hall, Benny Rubin; **D:** William Nigh; **W:** Harvey Gates, Jack Henley; **C:** Marcel Le Picard.

The Zodiac 2005 (R) Under-realized account of the notorious Zodiac Killer, who infamously terrorized the San Francisco area in the late '60s and has eluded the police to this day. Depressingly bland and straight-forward, unintentionally looking like an episode of "Columbo." The killer is seen in shadow and cops are bogged down in exposition and melodrama. Do not confuse this clunker with the masterful David Fincher-helmed "Zodiac" (although they probably hope you will). **92m/C DVD.** US Justin Chambers, Robin Tunney, Rory Culkin, William Mapother, Brad William Henke, Rex Linn, Philip Baker Hall, Ian Scott Mcgregor, Marty Lindsey, Shelby Alexis Irey, Natasia Costa, Kris Palm, Nate Dushku, Katelin Chesna, Jodi Feder, Kathryn Howell, George Maguire, Carolyne Smith, Munda Razooki; **D:** Alexander Bulkley; **W:** Kelly Bulkley; **C:** Denis Maloney; **M:** Michael Suby.

Zodiac 2007 (R) Drawn-out and detailed examination (with strong performances) of the still-unsolved Bay Area serial killings from the 1970s. The self-named Zodiac sends cryptic messages to the San Francisco Chronicle, where dissolute reporter Paul Avery (Downey Jr.) is on the crime beat. The paper's editorial cartoonist, Robert Graysmith (Gyllenhaal), figures out the killer's cipher and becomes obsessed with helping out. Then, SFPD detectives Dave Toschi (Ruffalo) and William Armstrong (Edwards) are assigned to the case, which eventually goes cold. Graysmith later wrote about the killings and drew his own conclusions as to the Zodiac's identity. **156m/C DVD, HD DVD.** US Mark Ruffalo, Jake Gyllenhaal, Robert Downey Jr., Brian Cox, Chloe Sevigny, John Carroll Lynch, Charles Fleischer, Zach Grenier, Philip Baker Hall, Elias Koteas, Donal Logue, Dermot Mulroney, John Terry, John Getz, Adam Goldberg, Candy Clark, John Lacy, James Le Gros; **D:** David Fincher; **W:** James Vanderbilt; **C:** Harris Savides; **M:** David Shire.

The Zodiac Killer 1971 (R) Based on a true story, this tells the violent tale of the San Francisco murders that occurred in the late 1960s. Doesn't have the suspense it should. **87m/C VHS, DVD.** Tom Pittman, Hal Reed, Bob Jones, Ray Lynch; **D:** Tom Hanson.

Zoe 2001 Teenager Zoe (Zima) longs to escape her abusive homelife and explore her Native American heritage through a Cherokee spirit guide. So she and two girlfriends (who want to go to Hollywood) run away from home and start their journey, eventually crossing paths with middle-aged Englishwoman Cecilia (Seagrove) whose mother's last request was to have her ashes scattered in the mountains of New Mexico. Recognizing a kindred spirit, Zoe leaves her friends to follow Cecilia and find her spirit guide. **92m/C VHS, DVD.** Vanessa Zima, Jenny Seagrove, Stephi Lineburg, Victoria Davis, Gordon Tootoosis, Kim Greist; **D:** Deborah Attoinese; **W:** Deborah Attoinese, Amy Dawes; **C:** Samuel Ameen; **M:** Dan Pinnella.

Zoltan... Hound of Dracula 1978 The vampire and his bloodthirsty dog go to Los Angeles to find the last of Count Dracula's living descendants. Campy and just original enough to make it almost worth watching. **85m/C VHS, DVD.** Michael Pataki, Reggie Nalder, Jose Ferrer, Jan Shutan, Libbie Chase, John Levin, Cleo Harrington, Simmy Bow, JoJo D'Amore; **D:** Albert Band; **W:** Frank Ray Perilli; **C:** Bruce Logan; **M:** Andrew Belling.

Zombie 1980 *Zombie Flesh-Eaters; Island of the Living Dead; Zombi 2* Italian-made white-men-in-the-Caribbean-with-flesh-eating-zombies cheapie. **91m/C VHS, DVD.** IT Tisa Farrow, Ian McCulloch, Richard Johnson, Al Cliver, Auretta Gay, Olga Karlatos, Stefania D'Amario, Lucio Fulci, Ugo Bologna, Monica Zanchi; **D:** Lucio Fulci; **W:** Elisa Briganti, Dardano Sacchetti; **C:** Sergio Salvati; **M:** Fabio Frizzi, Giorgio Tucci.

Zombie and the Ghost Train 1991 *Zombie ja Kummitusjuna* Absurdist punk comedy about the vicissitudes of a down-and-out bass player. Finnish with subtitles. **88m/C VHS.** FI Silu Seppala, Matti Pellonpaa, Marjo Leinonen, Vieno Saaristo; **D:** Mika Kaurismaki; **W:** Mika Kaurismaki; **C:** Olli Varja; **M:** Mauri Sumen.

The Zombie Army 1993 Tough drill sergeant tries to whip a bunch of raw female recruits up to muster for a special mission. Toward that end, the government has conveniently bought a defunct lunatic asylum as a training ground. Only problem is that a few of the former inmates have been left behind and are able to menace the troops with their penchant for psychotic weirdness. **80m/C VHS.** Steve Roberts, John Kalinowski, Jody Amato, Eileen Saddow; **D:** Betty Stapleford; **W:** Roger Scearce.

Zombie High 1987 (R) *My Brain* Students at a secluded academy are being lobotomized by the school president. Mindless, in two senses of the word. **91m/C VHS.** Virginia Madsen, Sherilyn Fenn, Paul Williams, Scott Coffey, Clare Carey, Walter Addison; **D:** Ron Link; **W:** Aziz Ghazal, Tim Doyle, Elizabeth Passerelli; **C:** Brian Coyne, David Lux; **M:** Daniel May.

Zombie Honeymoon 2004 Generally successful mix of pathos, comedy, and horror. Denise (Coogan) and Danny (Sibley) are on their honeymoon when Danny is attacked by a zombie. Denise is inconsolable until Danny returns—a changed man. Neither his increasing bloodlust or physical disintegration can drive Denise away. Is that true love or what? **83m/C DVD.** US Neal Jones, Tracy Coogan, Graham Sibley, Tonya Cornelisse, David Wallace, Phil Catalano; **D:** Dave Gebroe; **W:** Dave Gebroe; **C:** Ken Seng; **M:** Michael Tremante.

Zombie Island Massacre 1984 (R) In this trying film, tourists travel to see a voodoo ritual, and then are systematically butchered by the rite-inspired zombies. Featuring former congressional wife and "Playboy" magazine model Jenrette. **89m/C VHS, DVD.** Rita Jenrette, David Broadnax; **D:** John N. Carter.

Zombie Lake 1980 *El Lago de los Muertos Vivientes; The Lake of the Living Dead* Killed in an ambush by villagers during WWII, a group of Nazi soldiers turned zombies reside in the town's lake, preying on unsuspecting swimmers, especially dog paddling nude young women. Laughable FX, almost bad enough to be good. From the team that produced "Oasis of the Zombies." **90m/C VHS, DVD. FR SP** Howard Vernon, Pierre Escourrou, Anouchka, Antonio (Jose J. Antonio, J.A.) Mayans, Nadine Pascale, Jean Rollin; **D:** J.A. Laser, Jean Rollin; **W:** Jess (Jesus) Franco, Julian Esteban.

Zombie Nightmare 1986 woof! (R) A murdered teenager is revived by a voodoo queen and slaughters his punk-teen assailants. Cheap and stupid just about sums this one up. Music by Motorhead, Death Mask, Girlschool, and Thor. **89m/C VHS.** Adam West, Jon Miki Thor, Tia Carrere, Frank Dietz, Linda Singer, Manon E. Turbide, Hamish McEwen; **D:** John Bravman.

Zombies of Moratau woof! 1957 A diver and his girlfriend seek to retrieve an undersea treasure of diamonds protected by zombies. So boring you'll want to die. **70m/B VHS.** Gregg (Hunter) Palmer, Allison Hayes, Autumn Russel, Joel Ashley; **D:** Edward L. Cahn.

Zombies of the Stratosphere 1952 *Satan's Satellites* A serial in 12 chapters in which a cosmic policeman fights Zombies attempting to blow the Earth out of orbit. Also available in a 93-minute, colorized version. **152m/B VHS.** Judd Holdren, Aline Towne, Leonard Nimoy, John Crawford, Ray Boyle, Craig G. Kelly; **D:** Fred Brannon.

Zombies on Broadway 1944 *Loonies on Broadway* Two press agents travel to the Caribbean in search of new talent, but find Lugosi performing experiments on people and turning them into sequel material. RKO hoped this would be equally successful follow-up to "I Walked with a Zombie." **68m/B VHS.** Wally Brown, Alan Carney, Bela Lugosi, Anne Jeffreys, Sheldon Leonard, Frank Jenks, Russell Hopton, Joseph (Joe) Vitale, Ian Wolfe, Louis Jean Heydt, Darby Jones, Sir Lancelot; **D:** Gordon Douglas; **W:** Robert E. Kent, Lawrence Kimble; **C:** Jack MacKenzie; **M:** Roy Webb.

Zone of the Dead 1978 A mortician is using his morgue for other than embalming—and it isn't pretty! **81m/C VHS.** John Ericson, Ivor Francis, Charles Aidman, Bernard Fox.

Zone 39 1996 Sci-fi thriller vibrates with impending doom. A 40-year war results in an uneasy peace between two rival factions. Guard Leo (Phelps) has gone a little loopy after the death of his wife and is assigned to patrol the remote outpost of Zone 39, where a severe contamination is spreading. Thanks to the illegal drug Novan that Leo keeps taking, he's also experiencing flashbacks of his wife and its tragedies. The spectacularly desolate setting is a dry salt lake located in Woomera, Australia. **93m/C VHS, DVD. AU** Peter Phelps, William Zappa, Caroline Beck, Brad Byquar, Alex Menglet, Jeff Kovski; **D:** John Tatoulis; **W:** Deborah Parsons; **C:** Peter Zakhavor; **M:** Burkhard Dallwitz.

Zone Troopers 1984 (PG) Five American G.I.'s in WWII-ravaged Europe stumble upon a wrecked alien spacecraft and enlist the extraterrestrial's help in fending off the Nazis. **86m/C VHS.** Timothy Van Patten, Tim Thomerson, Art LaFleur, Biff Manard; **D:** Danny Bilson; **W:** Danny Bilson, Paul De Meo; **C:** Mac Ahlberg; **M:** Richard Band.

Zontar, the Thing from Venus 1966 Scientist is taken over by alien batlike thing from Venus, and attempts to take over the Earth. A parody of itself. **68m/C VHS, DVD.** John Agar, Anthony Huston, Susan Bjorman, Pat Delaney, Warren Hammack, Neil Fletcher; **D:** Larry Buchanan; **W:** Larry Buchanan, Hillman Taylor; **C:** Robert Alcott. TV

The Zoo Gang 1985 (PG-13) A group of teens want to open a nightclub. Will they bring their dream to fruition, or will the mean rival gang foil their plans? **96m/C VHS, DVD.** Jason Gedrick, Eric Gurry; **D:** John Watson, Pen Densham; **W:** John Watson, Pen Densham; **M:** Patrick Gleeson.

Zoolander 2001 (PG-13) Stiller plays Derek Zoolander, an absurdly vacuous and successful male model who's brainwashed into becoming an assassin by over-the-top designer Mugatu (Ferrell). It seems that a foreign prime minister is committed to cutting off the supply of cheap third world labor for the fashion industry, and Zoolander is the only model stupid enough to have his noggin scrubbed clean. He develops a friendship with arch-rival model Hansel (Wilson), and the dim duo try to stop the nefarious plot. Packed to the gills with celebrity cameos, including Heidi Klum, Donald Trump and, yes, Fabio. Ran into unexpected controversy because the intended target is the prime minister of Malaysia (and the Malaysians naturally objected). **89m/C VHS, DVD.** US Ben Stiller, Owen Wilson, Christine Taylor, Will Ferrell, Milla Jovovich, Jerry Stiller, Jon Voight, David Duchovny; **D:** Ben Stiller; **W:** Ben Stiller, Drake Sather; **C:** Barry Peterson; **M:** David Arnold.

Zoom 2006 (PG) Superhero Captain Zoom (Allen) has retired and gotten soft. But he's called back into action when he's needed to turn a group of misfit kids into the next generation of superheroes so that the world can be saved once again. Based on the graphic novel by Jason Lethcoe. Definitely the weak link in the "kids dealing with superpowers" genre. **88m/C DVD.** US Tim Allen, Courteney Cox, Spencer Breslin, Chevy Chase, Kate Mara, Rip Torn, Kevin Zegers, Ryan Newman, Michael Cassidy, Thomas F. Wilson, Willie Garson; **D:** Peter Hewitt; **W:** Adam Rifkin, David Berenbaum; **C:** David Tattersall; **M:** Christophe Beck.

Zooman 1995 (R) Hard-hitting message on violence and responsibility. Gang member Zooman (Kain) spots members of a rival gang in a Brooklyn neighborhood, whips out his gun, and begins firing. When the shooting stops, a little girl sitting on her stoop is dead—what's even worse for her estranged parents is the fact that obvious witnesses refuse to identify the gunman for fear of their own safety. So father Reuben (Gossett Jr.) puts up a sign that attracts lots of media attention, and neighborhood hostility. Based on Fuller's 1978 play "Zooman and the Sign." **95m/C VHS.** Louis Gossett Jr., Charles S. Dutton, Khalil Kain, Cynthia Martells, CCH Pounder, Vondie Curtis-Hall, Hill Harper; **D:** Leon ichaso; **W:** Charles Fuller. **CABLE**

Zoot Suit 1981 (R) Based on Luis Valdez' play, this murder mystery/musical is rooted in the historical Sleepy Lagoon murder in the 1940s. Valdez plays a Mexican-American accused of the crime. His friends (and defense lawyers) rally around him to fight this travesty of justice. Lots o'music and dancing. **104m/C VHS, DVD.** Edward James Olmos, Daniel Valdez, Tyne Daly, Charles Aidman, John Anderson; **D:** Luis Valdez; **W:** Luis Valdez.

Zora Is My Name! 1990 *My Name is Zora* The funny, moving story of Zora Neal Hurston, a Black writer known for her stories and folklore of the rural South of the '30s and '40s. From PBS's American Playhouse. **90m/C VHS, DVD.** Roger E. Mosley, Flip Wilson, Ruby Dee, Louis Gossett Jr.; **D:** Neema Barnette; **W:** Ann Wallace; **M:** Olu Dara.

Zorba the Greek 1964 A young British writer (Bates) comes to Crete to find himself by working his father's mine. He meets Zorba, an itinerant Greek laborer (Quinn), and they take lodgings together with an aging courtesan, who Zorba soon romances. The writer, on the other hand, is attracted to a lovely young widow. When she responds to him, the townsmen jealously attack her. Zorba teaches the young man the necessary response to life and its tragedies. Based on a novel by Nikos Kazantzakis. Masterpiece performance from Quinn. Beautifully photographed, somewhat overlong. Film later written for stage production. **142m/B VHS, DVD.** Anthony Quinn, Alan Bates, Irene Papas, Lila Kedrova; **D:** Michael Cacoyannis; **C:** Walter Lassally. Oscars '64: Art Dir./Set Dec., B&W Cinematog., Support. Actress (Kedrova); Natl. Bd. of Review '64: Actor (Quinn).

Zorro 1974 *El Zorro la belva del Colorado; El Zorro* 1974 Italian take on the Zorro legend is a light romp, with Delon as the masked one careful not to take the proceedings too seriously. Recently arrived California governor Diego runs afoul of corrupt officials and dons the famous cape and mask to help the peasants. Mostly aims to please the kids but should keep adults interested, too. **120m/C VHS. IT FR** Alain Delon, Stanley Baker, Adriana Asti, Marino (Martin) Mase, Giacomo "Jack" Rossi-Stuart, Moustache, Ottavia Piccolo, Giampiero Albertini, Enzo Cerusico; **D:** Duccio Tessari; **W:** Giorgio Arlorio; **C:** Giulio Albonico; **M:** Guido de Angelis, Maurizio de Angelis.

Zorro Rides Again 1937 Zorro risks his life to outwit gangsters endeavoring to secure ancestor's property. In 12 chapters; the first runs 30 minutes, the rest 17. **217m/B VHS, DVD.** John Carroll, Helen Christian, Noah Beery Sr., Duncan Renaldo; **D:** William Witney, John English.

Zorro, the Gay Blade 🐾🐾½ **1981 (PG)** Tongue-in-cheek sword play with Hamilton portraying the swashbuck-ling crusader and his long-lost brother, Bunny Wigglesworth, in this spoof of the Zorro legend. The fashion-conscious hero looks his best in plum. Leibman is fun to watch. **96m/C VHS, DVD.** George Hamilton, Lauren Hutton, Brenda Vaccaro, Ron Leibman, Donovan Scott, James Booth, Helen Burns, Clive Revill; **D:** Peter Medak; **W:** Greg Alt; **C:** John A. Alonzo; **M:** Ian Fraser.

Zorro's Black Whip 🐾🐾 **1944** A young girl dons the mask of her murdered brother (Zorro) to "fight outlaws in the old West. Serial in 12 episodes. **182m/B VHS, DVD.** George Lewis, Linda Stirling, Lucien Littlefield, Francis McDonald, Tom London; **D:** Spencer Gordon Bennet; **W:** Wallace Grissell.

Zorro's Fighting Legion 🐾🐾 **1939** Zorro forms a legion to help the president of Mexico fight a band of outlaws endeavoring to steal gold shipments. A serial in 12 chapters. **215m/B VHS, DVD.** Edmund Cobb, John Merton, C. Montague Shaw, Budd Buster, Carleton Young, Reed Hadley, Sheila Darcy; **D:** William Witney, John English; **W:** Barney A. Sarecky, Frank (Franklyn) Adreon, Morgan Cox; **C:** Reggie Lanning; **M:** William Lava.

Zotz! 🐾🐾 **1962** The holder of a magic coin can will people dead by uttering "zotz"; spies pursue the mild-mannered professor who possesses the talisman. Adapted from a Walter Karig novel. Typical William Castle fare, his gimic in the theatrical release of the movie was to distribute plastic "zotz" coins to the theatre patrons. **87m/B VHS.** Tom Poston, Julia Meade, Jim Backus, Fred Clark, Cecil Kellaway, Margaret Dumont, Jimmy Hawkins; **D:** Rey Russell, William Castle; **W:** Rey Russell; **C:** Gordon Avil; **M:** Bernard Green.

Zou Zou 🐾🐾½ **1934** Lavish backstage musical/drama of a laundress who fills in for the leading lady or opening night and becomes a hit. Baker's talking picture debut. In French with English subtitles. **92m/B VHS, DVD.** FR Josephine Baker, Jean Gabin; **D:** Marc Allegret.

Zu: Warriors from the Magic Mountain 🐾🐾 *Shu Shan* **1983** The forces of evil are plotting to take over the world and a warrior endures the perils of the Zu Mountains in order to find the Twin Swords, the only weapons capable of defeating the demons. Cantonese with subtitles or dubbed. **98m/C VHS, DVD.** HK Adam Cheng, Yuen Biao, Brigitte Lin, Sammo Hung, Moon Lee; **D:** Tsui Hark; **C:** Bill Wong.

Zulu 🐾🐾½ **1964** In 1879, a small group of British soldiers try to defend their African outpost from attack by thousands of Zulu warriors. Amazingly, the British win. Dated colonial epic based on an actual incident; battle scenes are magnificent. Prequel "Zulu Dawn" (1979) depicts British mishandling of the situation that led to the battle. **139m/C VHS, DVD.** Michael Caine, Jack Hawkins, Stanley Baker, Nigel Green, Ulla Jacobsson, James Booth, Paul Daneman, Neil McCarthy, Gary Bond, Patrick Magee, Dickie Owen, Larry Taylor, Dennis Folbigge, Ivor Emmanuel, Glynn Edwards, David Kernan; **D:** Cy Endfield; **W:** Cy Endfield, John Prebble; **C:** Stephen Dade; **M:** John Barry; **Nar:** Richard Burton.

Zulu Dawn 🐾🐾 **1979 (PG)** An historical epic about British troops fighting the Zulus at Ulandi in 1873. Shows the increasing tensions between the British colonial government and the Zulus. Stunning landscapes unfortunately don't translate to the small screen. Good but unoriginal colonial-style battle drama. **117m/C VHS, DVD.** Burt Lancaster, Peter O'Toole, Denholm Elliott, Nigel Davenport, John Mills, Simon Ward, Bob Hoskins, Freddie Jones; **D:** Douglas Hickox; **M:** Elmer Bernstein.

Zus & Zo 🐾🐾 *This and That; Hotel Paraiso* **2001** Sisters Michelle (Poortia), Wanda (Blok), and Sonja (Handrickx) are dismayed to learn that their gay younger brother Nino (Derwig) is going to marry Bo (Reijn) in order to collect on an inheritance. Thanks to a clause in their parents' will, he will become the sole owner of the family's waterfront hotel in Portugal, which each sister thinks she'd come to her, and which each believes that Nino will soon sell. So they scheme to break up the couple while avoiding their own domestic crises. Dutch with subtitles. **100m/C VHS, DVD.** NL Sylvia Poorta, Anneke Blok, Monic Hendrickx, Jacob Derwig, Halina Reijn, Theu Boermans, Jaap Spijkers, Pieter Embrechts, Annet Nieuwenhuyzen; **D:** Paula van der Oest; **W:** Paula van der Oest; **C:** Bert Pot; **M:** Fons Merkies.

Zvenigora 🐾🐾🐾 **1928** Dovzhenko's first major film, and a lyrical revelation in the face of Soviet formality; a passionate, funny fantasy tableaux of 1,000 years of Ukrainian history, encompassing wild folk myths, poetic drama, propaganda and social satire. Silent. **73m/B VHS.** RU Nikolai Nademsky; **D:** Alexander Dovzhenko, Semyon Svashenko; **D:** Alexander Dovzhenko.

Category List

The **Category Index** contains genre, sub-genre, thematic, or significant scene classifications, ranging from the very general terms (Western, Sports, Comedies) to the fairly particular (Heists: Casinos, Ninjas, Grandparents). The terms are defined (more or less) below. We've done our best to provide serious subject references while also including fun categories and lists to make your video viewing experience a little more enjoyable. No one list is all-inclusive. We are continuously reclassifying, adding, and subtracting movies. Many of the categories in this list are new, and therefore represent only a beginning. We're also trying to pare down some of the bigger categories, like **Cops**, by creating more focused subject categories, such as **Alien Cops** or **FBI**. VideoHound invites readers to participate in this pastime by sending in suggestions for new categories and adding movies to existing ones. **An asterisk (*) denotes a new category for this edition.**

Action-Drama: Things go Boom!, but in a dramatic way

Action-Thriller: Things go Boom!, but in a suspenseful way

Adoption & Orphans: Cute kids lacking permanent authority figures, ranging from *Annie* to *Wild Hearts Can't Be Broken*

Adultery: Gettin' a little on the side; usually ends badly

Adventure Drama: Action with more attention to dramatic content—*Apocalypse Now* to *Robin Hood, Prince of Thieves*

Advertising: Corporate shenanigans at the agency—*How to Get Ahead in Advertising* to *The Horse in the Gray Flannel Suit*

Africa: *Out of Africa* to *Zulu Dawn*

African America: Dominant African themes

AIDS: Someone usually dies; *An Early Frost* to *Longtime Companion*

Air Disasters: Contraptions up in the sky, but not for long

Airborne: Contraptions up in the sky

Alaska: The 49th state, home of the Iditarod and site of many manly Jack London adventures

Alcatraz: Prison island off San Francisco, aka *The Rock*

Alien Babes: Women who possess otherworldly beauty (and appetites)

Alien Beings—Benign: Friendly space visitors, including *Howard the Duck* and little buddy *E.T.*

Alien Beings—Vicious: Not-so-friendly space visitors, notably the multi-jawed *Alien* continually harassing Sigourney Weaver

Alien Cops: The long arm (tentacle?) of the outer space law

Aliens Are People, Too: Space visitors pretend to be human, or just take over the bodies—*Invasion of the Body Snatchers* kinda stuff

Amateur Sleuths: ...and I, woulda gotten away with it, too, if it weren't for those meddling kids!

American South: Theatrics amid much brow mopping and drawling; *A Streetcar Named Desire* rattling down *Flamingo Road*

Amnesia: Phone call for *Amnesia*

Amsterdam: City in the Netherlands where many vices are legal—just ask Vincent Vega

Amusement Parks: Cotton candy, ferris wheels, Coney Island, Godzilla on Monster Island, *Rollercoaster*

Angels: Benevolent winged visitors from above; *Wings of Desire*

Animated Musicals: Boys, girls, dogs, ducks, birds, mice, and monkeys croon; many of Disney vintage, including *Aladdin* and *Sleeping Beauty*

Animated Sci-Fi: To boldly go where no cartoon has gone before!

Animation & Cartoons: Antics o' Daffy, Donald, Bugs, Mickey, Chip, Dale, Tom, Jerry, Fred, Wilma, Charlie, and the rest of the gang

Anime: Animated cartoons from Japan with cult following

Anthology: More than one story to a package

Anti-Heroes: From *Billy Jack* to *Dirty Harry* to *Thelma & Louise*

Anti-War War Movies: Recognizes that war really is hell—from *All Quiet on the Western Front* to *Paths of Glory*

Apartheid: Afrikaans term for racial segregation in South Africa

Apartments & Apartment Buildings: Why do they call 'em apartments when they're all together? The building or an apartment becomes important to the plot

Architects & Architecture: People designing buildings for other people to build

Army Training, Sir: Tales of basic training, or boot camp, if you prefer. Are those *Stripes* on your *Full Metal Jacket*?

*Autism: Tales of families dealing with the mysterious condition

Art & Artists: They paint, pause, and propagate with equal passion

Asia: *China White, Red Dust, Sand Pebbles*

Asian America: Asian experience in the US—*The Joy Luck Club, Come See the Paradise*

Assassinations: Lincoln, JFK, *La Femme Nikita, Times of Harvey Milk,* and more

Astronauts: Houston, we have a problem.

At the Drive-In: Scenes in which people watch movies...at the drive-in.

At the Movies: The movie within a movie, or movies about watching the movies, from *The Purple Rose of Cairo* to *Last Action Hero* to *Matinee*

At the Video Store: Scenes from a video store, *Clerks, Remote Control*

Atlanta: Home of the Braves, Ted Turner, CNN, and that annoying Tomahawk Chop. Sherman dropped in a while back with some rowdy friends.

Atlantic City: Gambling mecca of the East Coast, aka Trumptown

Auditions: Trying to get that part that'll be the Big Break

Aunts & Uncles, Nieces & Nephews: Extended family members you usually spend Thanksgiving with. In the movies, they're usually causing trouble

Babysitting: Supervision of small-fry pranksters not your own; *Uncle Buck* to *The Hand that Rocks the Cradle*

Bachelor Party: The groom's last foray into debauchery before the big day; all hell generally breaks loose

Bad Bosses: When he says he wants that report by 5:00 or heads will roll...it may not be a figure of speech

Bad Dads: Daddy-Os with unpredictable mean streak; *The Shining, Kiss Daddy Goodbye*

Ballet: On your toes—*The Turning Point*

Ballooning: Up, up and away, or *Around the World in 80 Days*

Baltimore: Take a look at the Maryland city, hometown of director Barry Levinson and favorite of John Waters

Bar & Grill: Most, if not all, of the action takes place in a drinking establishment.

Barcelona: Second largest city in Spain, the capital of Catalonia; setting for recent Olympics, and some cool movies.

Baseball: Action on the diamond, ranging from *Bull Durham* to *A League of Their Own* to *Rookie of the Year*

Basketball: Roundball thrillers, including the memorable *The Fish that Saved Pittsburgh* and *White Men Can't Jump*

Bats: Flying rodents that fly into your hair and sometimes turn into centuries-old Eastern European aristocrats with strange eating habits

Beach Blanket Bingo: Annette, Frankie, sand, surf, bikinis

Bears: Most of 'em are looking for more than just pic-i-nic baskets

Beatniks: Jazz beards, bongos, poetry that doesn't rhyme, berets

Beauty Pageants: From the heartless to the hilarious, beauty is a big business—Smile girls!

Beer: Mmmmm, beer. The cause and solution to all of Homer's problems. The cities of St. Louis and Milwaukee are fueled by it...so is your brother-in-law

*Bees: Flying insects that whore around with every flower they can get their hairy little legs on, and then make delicious honey. Sometimes they get mad and go on mass stinging sprees

Behind the Scenes: Peek behind show business curtain, from *A Chorus Line* to *Truth or Dare*

Belfast: Northern Ireland city, Van Morrison's hometown (but that's not what it's famous for)

Berlin: City in Germany divided after WWII, now it's one big happy city again

Betrayal: Somebody done somebody wrong. Could be a spouse or a partner, could be the intelligence agency that used to employ you that now wants you dead

Beverly Hills: Fancy-pants area of L.A., home of Cops, Troops, Vamps, and 30-year-old teenagers

Bicycling: Two wheels, no motor, much leg action and sweating

Big Battles: Big-budget (or at least illusion of such) clash of large, opposing military forces, from Cromwell to Ran

Big Budget Bombs: Millions spent for no apparent reason

Big Cats: Lions and Tigers and Panthers and Jaguars and other large felines that sports teams get named after.

Big Digs: Anthropology and archaeology, from Indiana Jones to various mummy on-the-loose stories

Big Ideas: Philosophy, ideology and other semi-mental pursuits somehow translated to film

Big Rigs: Smokey and the Bandit speed down Thieves' Highway in a Convoy

Bigfoot/Yeti: Large, hairy, seldom-seen beast with really big feet

Bikers: Usually with a mean streak and traveling in leather-clad packs

Biopics—Artists: True stories of artists' lives. Find out if they were really starving or not

Biopics—Cops & Robbers: True stories of real life criminals and the real life cops who arrested 'em

Biopics—Military: True stories of the men and women who fought this (and other) country's wars

Biopics—Musicians: From European composers to punk rock icons, they usually end up being tales of over-indulgence and others ripping them off

Biopics—Politics: True stories of the politicians who lead countries, states, and municipalities

Biopics—Religious: Life stories of church leaders, reformers, saints, and the occasional deity

Biopics—Royalty: Life stories of kings, queens, czars. They ran things before politicians were invented

Biopics—Science/Medical: Life stories of the people who invented the medicine and products that make modern life...modern

Biopics—Showbiz: Life stories of those who entertain us. It ain't always all glamour and happy endings

Biopics—Sports: Life stories of those we admire for their athletic prowess

Biopics—Writers: Life stories of those who put thoughts, stories, or manifestos to paper and became famous for it

Birds: Beaks, feathers, talons, bird #%!; The Birds, Beaks, The Movie, Howard the Duck

Birthdays: Congratulations on making it through another year!

Bisexuality: Going both ways—Basic Instinct, Three of Hearts

Black Comedy: Funny in a biting or despairing sort of way, from The Addams Family to The Hospital

Black Gold: Oil, that is; aka Oklahoma Crude

Blackmail: I'm gonna tell, unless... The Last Seduction, Letter to My Killer

Blackout: Boom Boom, Out go the lights! In the whole city, usually

Blaxploitation: '70s remakes of horror classics, as well as B-movies made with the black audience in mind

Blind Date: Usually set up by friends or family members with the best of intentions, they rarely result in the best of relationships

Blindness: Can't see or sight impaired; Afraid of the Dark

Blizzards: Big snow storms, usually overblown by over-excited local weather people.

Bloody Messages: Cryptic warnings to the living written in the blood of the poor slob who was just killed—Redrum

Bodyguards: Costner looks after Whitney's personal business

Books and Bookstores: Literary works (such as this) and the places where they can be found, as a major plot device; La Lectrice to Crossing Delancy

Boom!: Really big explosions, bombs, and other noisy or fiery messes popular in big budget action flicks

Boomer Reunions: thirtysomethings gather and reminisce; The Big Chill

Bosnia: Has played host to Olympics and ethnic strife

Boston: Beantown, where everybody knows your name.

Bounty Hunters: Bring 'em back dead or alive—for a price

Bowling: Heavy round ball is thrown down waxed alley toward club-like pins; all fall down

Boxing: Yo, Adrian!

*Brains!: Disturbing scenes of brains being extracted, forcibly, from the brainpan

Brainwashed: Minds get scrubbed clean of what they used to know so someone can put in whatever they want; generally orders to do bad things

Break-Ups: They usually happen in the second act of romantic comedies, before the happy ending. Although sometimes they are the plot

Bridges: For crossing, or if you're in a war movie, defending and/or blowing up

Bringing Up Baby: Look Who's Talking to Raising Arizona, plus infants with that little something different—Alien 3, Basket Case 3: The Progeny

Brothers & Sisters: Siblings getting along and sometimes not

Buddhism: Eastern religion with bald guys

Buddies: Butch and Sundance, Bill and Ted, Rubin and Ed, Thelma and Louise

Buddy Cops: Couple of police hanging together, usually practicing limited repartee at a donut shop; Lethal Weapon, Tango and Cash

Bulfighters & Bullfighting: "Sport" pitting Spaniards with red capes and swords vs. future Big Macs with horns

Burglars: Thievery by stealth, usually at night, and using cool equipment, like in Entrapment

Buried Alive: I'm not quite dead, yet! Hello, Mr. grave digger person, hello!

Buses: Large truck-like passenger vehicles—Speed, The Big Bus, The Trip to Bountiful

Cabbies: Where to, Mac?

Calcutta: Big, overpopulated city in India

Camelot (New): The exploits of JFK, Jackie, and various relatives and hangers-on

Camelot (Old): The exploits of King Arthur and his Knights of the Round Table

Cambodia: Small country in Southeast Asia bordering Vietnam. Haven't had much luck with politics in the last few decades

Campus Capers: What really goes on at college—Assault of the Party Nerds

Canada: Renfrew of the Mounties plus lots of wilderness and the occasional hockey puck

Canadian Mounties: The Great White North version of cops. They always get their man

Cannibalism: People who eat people are the luckiest people; Alive, Rabid Grannies, Cannibal Women in the Avocado Jungle of Death, The Cook, the Thief, His Wife & Her Lover

Capitol Capers: Hollywood versions of hijinks in Washington, D.C.—Dave, Mr. Smith Goes to Washington, All the President's Men

Carnivals & Circuses: Big top, little top, domes: Shakes the Clown to Rollercoaster, plus Big Top Pee Wee, State Fair, and metaphoric circuses: Brewster McCloud, La Strada

Catholic School: Educational arm of the church of Rome, usually run by ruler-wielding nuns

Cats: Lesser vertebrate nonetheless much beloved by Hollywood

Cattle Drive: Git along little doggies!

Cave People: From the most primitive (The Clan of the Cave Bear) to the fairly modernized (The Flintstones)

Caves: Holes in the ground where monsters, bats, and Flintstones live

Checkered Flag: Eat My Dust; racing in the street or on the track; The Last American Hero

Cheerleaders: Give me an A! The Positively True Adventures of the Alleged Texas Cheerleader-Murdering Mom meets Revenge of the Cheerleaders

*Chefs: The fancy-schmancy preparers of fancy-schmancy foods at fancy-schmancy eateries. They have cool hats that make them seem a lot taller

Chess: Game that involves much strategy and forward thinking...as well as a lot of staring, sitting, and generally looking unconscious. Not a really good spectator sport

Chicago: City in Illinois, right at the bottom of Lake Michigan

Child Abuse: Not very funny at all—Mommie Dearest, Fallen Angel

Childhood Buddies: The pals we hang around with before puberty hits

Childhood Visions: Stories dominated by the kid point of view, or by an adult flashbacking to childhood; Au Revoir Les Enfants, Home Alone

China: The Last Emperor to Red Sorghum to The World of Suzie Wong

Christmas: Reindeer, Santa, children make appearance amid much sentimentality

Church Choirs: Big groups of singers in robes who sing in...church (Duh!). Can I get an Amen?

CIA/NSA: Men and women of the Agency. You know, the good spies...uh, usually

Cinderella Stories: Gal down on her luck meets fairy godmother (or father) and finds true love—Pretty Woman, Flashdance, Cinderella

Civil Rights: Fighting for equality—The Autobiography of Miss Jane Pittman, Mississippi Burning

Civil War: The Yankees against the Confederates; aka The Blue and the Gray

*Civil War (non-U.S.): People in the same (foreign) country fighting and killing over religion, politics, tribal affiliation, or anything else that makes people kill their own countrymen

Classic Horror: Boris Karloff, Vincent Price, piercing screams

Clergymen: Non-Catholic (they're covered elsewhere) men and women of the cloth

Cloning Around: Makin' copies—of people or animals; Multiplicity to Jurassic Park

Clowns: Big red noses, huge feet, painted smiles frighten many

Coast Guard: They, well, guard the coast, and help boaters, and bust smugglers, as well as other cool maritime duties

Cockroaches: Creepy crawlies signifying the work of the supernatural, or a lack of housekeeping skills

Cold Spots: Set in a frostbitten locale with lots of shivering; Ice Station Zebra, Never Cry Wolf, Quest for Fire

Cold War Spies: Spy vs. Spy pitting various U.S. and British alphabet soup agencies against the Commies

Coma: Some sort of head trauma usually leads to extended nap time

Comedy Anthologies: More than one yuk fest on a cassette

Comedy Drama: Drama with a comedic touch or comedy underwired with drama—Avalon, The Big Chill, Fried Green Tomatoes, One Flew Over the Cuckoo's Nest, Tootsie

Comedy Mystery: Wacky whodunits like Murder by Death, Clue

Comedy Sci-Fi: Laughs in space! Spaceballs

Comic Adventure: Adventurous romps liberally laced with humor; Romancing the Stone to Bird on a Wire to Crocodile Dundee

Comic Books: Colorful tales of superheroes and adventure play a big part in the plot, unless your mom threw 'em out

Comic Cops: Police officers that catch laughs as they catch the bad guys. Think Axel Foley or those cut-ups from the Police Academy series

Coming of Age: Hard-fought adolescent battle for adulthood, led by American Graffiti, The Apprenticeship of Duddy Kravitz, The Karate Kid

Communists & Communism: 'Way left-wingers politically. They used to run Eastern Europe, but now they just rant in coffeehouses. The ones in Asia are still around, though

Computers: Bits and bytes play major role

Concentration/Internment Camps: Nazis used them for their "final solution" while the U.S. used them to imprison Japanese-Americans

Concert Films: Rock or comedy concerts—from Woodstock to Divine Madness to Eddie Murphy: Raw

Contemporary Musicals: Thematically modern and made during last 20 years; All That Jazz

Contemporary Noir: Dark and moody or tributes to dark and moody that pay homage to the original Film Noir genre—Blue Velvet, 9½ Weeks, sex, lies, and videotape, Wild Orchid

Cops: Police and pseudo-police work, including Action Jackson, Blue Steel, The Choirboys, RoboCop, Lethal Weapon, National Lampoon's Loaded Weapon 1

Corporate Shenanigans: Big Business runs amuck—Barbarians at the Gate, Wall Street

Cousins: Progeny of your parents' sibs.

Creepy Houses: Scary dwellings—Amityville Horror 1 through 33

Crime Doesn't Pay: When the perfect crime...isn't.

Crime Drama: Gangster family dysfunction, heists gone awry, packin' pathos with your piece. The Godfather, Goodfellas, Reservoir Dogs.

Crime Sprees: Bad guy, gal or couple goes on a crime binge and other tales of obsessive criminal activity, including Bonnie & Clyde, The Boys Next Door

Crimedy: formerly So I Amuse You? Wisenheimer Guys—funny felons, amusing miscreants, if you will

Crimes of Passion: Love, sex, and death

Criminally Insane: They don't really care if crime pays, they're just following orders from the voices.

The Crusades: "Holy" wars between Christians and Muslims in the middle ages.

Cults: Something like a gang but more intense and usually governed by a state of mind similar to irrationality—Helter Skelter

Culture Clash: Hilarity ensues (or sometimes not) as people from vastly different backgrounds try to interact. Deliverance, Witness, George of the Jungle

Custody Battles: People, mostly divorced couples, fight over who keeps the kids. Kramer vs. Kramer, Losing Isaiah

Cuttin' Heads: Barber shops and Beauty salons are the scenes of all or most of the "action"

Cyberpunk: Dark, moody, futuristic flicks—Blade Runner, Freejack, Tank Girl

Dads: Fathers play a major role

Dallas: Big city in Texas. Home of the Cowboys, J.R., and scandal among the rich

Dance Fever: Whole lotta foot-tapping going on, including An American in Paris, Daddy Long Legs, and Dirty Dancing

Dates from Hell: Fun evening for two singles turns into a nightmare for one of them—Bye Bye Love, Singles, Something Wild

* = new to this edition

* = new to this edition

Day Care/Nursery School: Babysitting warehouse where parents drop off their kids while they make money to pay for daycare

DEA: G-men on the front lines of America's War on Drugs

A Day In The Life: All the action takes place within a 24-hour period

Deadly Implants: Where is that ticking coming from?

Deafness: Can't hear or hearing impaired; Bridge to Silence, The Miracle Worker

Death & The Afterlife: Could be ghosts, could be voices from the beyond, could be any number of post-dead things—Beetlejuice, Carnival of Souls, Flatliners, Poltergeist, Weekend at Bern e's

Death Row: Waitin' for a call from the Governor; Dead Man Walking, Angels with Dirty Faces

Dedicated Teachers: From The Dead Poet's Society to The Blackboard Jungle to Dangerous Minds

Deep Blue: The sea around us, including Flukes and Splash

Demons & Wizards: Swords, sorcery and wrinkled old men with wands—The Alchemist, & The Hobbit, The Sword & the Screrer

Dental Mayhem: Tooth-pickin' uproars; Marathon Man, The Dentist

Desert War/Foreign Legion: Big battles among the dunes

Deserts: Endless beach minus the water—Ishtar, Lawrence of Arabia

Detective Spoof's: Putting together clues in humorous fashion—The Adventures of Sherlock Holmes', Smarter Brother, The Naked Gun

Detroit: The Motor City, home of Motown, lots of cars, and...V deofround

Devil's Island: French island prison in the South Atlantic

Devils: Some may meet or Judgment Day

Diner: Most of the story, or at least important parts of it, occur in the smallish, very informal eating establishment

Dinosaurs: Jurassic Park thundering lizards

Disaster Flicks: Natural and man-made, including 4*, Airport sequels

Disco Musicals: '70s tackiness reigns supreme, from Saturday Night Fever to Xanadu

Disease of the Week: Bulimia, anorexia, polio, cancer, and so on

Disorganized Crime: Stupid crime, including Amos and Andrew, Dog Day Afternoon, Home Alone, Quick Change

Divorce: Breaking up is hard to do; Accidental Tourist, Heartburn, Kramer vs. Kramer

Doctors & Nurses: Men and women n scrubs concerned about health of complete strangers for profit, often to the dismay of the patient—Autopsy, Candy Stripe Nurses, Dead Ringers

Docudrama: The Thin Blue Line between documentaries and drama

Documentary: Real life manipulated on film—A Brief History of Time, The Last Waltz, Paris Is Burning, Roger and Me

Dogs In Peril: Manipulative plot device, usually in disaster flicks, where things blow up just as Fido high-tails it out of there.

Domestic Abuse: This Boy's Life, The Burning Bed, What's Love Got to Do With It?

Down Under: Australian, New Zealand settings—The Rescuers Down Under, Gallipoli, The Man from Snowy River, The Thorn Birds

Dragons: Legendary medieval lizards, usually with fiery dispositions; Dragonheart, Pete's Dragon

Dream Girls: Product of male mid-life crisis; Batting Amazons, Cycle Vixens, The Doll Squad, Woman in Red

Drug Abuse: Life with a drugstore cowboy; consumption of drugs, mostly illegal or in extra-large dosages

Dublin: Irish capitol city, home to The Commitments

Dying for a Promotion: ...or killing for one. Guess those business ethics seminars were a waste of money

Earsi: Bloody detachment and general maiming of....

Earthquakes: The Earth moved! Common occurrence in California

Easter: Holiday in the early spring celebrated with giant rabbits, eggs, chocolate bonnets...and gruesome movies depicting the crucifixion

Eastern Europe: Basically everything east of Germany and west of Asia

Eat Me: Characters end up as food; Jurassic Park, Soylent Green, Alive

Eco-Vengeance!: Nature wreaks havoc on man—watch out for Alligators, Frogs and Piranhas

Edibles: Something's cooking—Babette's Feast, Like Water for Chocolate

Edinburgh: Scottish capital city. They pronounce it "Golf" instead of "Golf" according to Judge Straulis.

Egypt—Ancient: Mummies, Pharaohs, Pyramids, when they were b'and new

Elephants: Pachyderms play a BIG part in the plot—Dumbo, Larger Than Life

Elevators: Sometimes the oddest things happen in th'em...

Emerging Viruses: Deadly virus spreads like wildfire as frantic medical personnel search for a cure; think ebola

The Empire State Building: King Kong liked to hang there.

Erotic Thrillers: Hot sex and murder, including Basic Instinct, Body of Evidence

Errant Educators: Teachers, coaches, or principals who eat at out of food, and pretend they have interests in mind, maybe because they're aliens or just mean (Teaching Mrs. Tingle)

Eskimos: Native North Americans who reside in particularly frosty climates

Escaped Cons: They busted outta the joint; now they're makin' a run for it. Con Air, We're No Angels, Papillon, Flyed

Ethics & Morals: Examination of values (or lack thereof)—Crimes & Misdemeanors, Judgment at Nuremberg

Etiquette: Usually comedy of manners; Educating Rita, My Fair Lady

Evil Doctors: Don't go to these guys for a checkup—Malice, Dead Ringers, and Doctor X

Ex-Cons: Former guests of state or federal penal institutions

Ex-Cops: Former members of the law enforcement community

Executing Revenge: Bad guys come back from being executed to cause more trouble. Fallen, Shocker

Exorcism & Exorcists: Priests try to evict evil spirits from pea-soup-spewing, head-twirling victims of possession.

Exploitation: Rigged to take advantage of viewer, including historic treats like Reefer Madness and more recent ventures such as Sleazemania

Explorers: Going boldly where no man or woman has regularly gone before

Extraordinary Pairings: Jesse James meets Frankenstein's Daughter

Eyeballs: Unnerving scenes involving pupils, irises, lids, and occasionally, lashes

Family Reunions: Vacations or picnics where extended family members get together to reintroduce themselves to each other, eat a lot of food, and pretend they have something in common besides surnames.

Family Ties: Blood runs deep—Back to the Future, Five Easy Pieces, The Godfather, Homeward Bound, Lorenzo's Oil, The River

Family Drama: Families struggling through tragedy, daily life, difficult circumstances, or too few bathrooms; teardrops and recriminations are usually involved

Family Comedy: Families find themselves in amusing situations; hilarity may or may not ensue

Family Adventure: Families find themselves in perilous or thrilling predicaments; ingenuity and derring-do usually ensues

Fairs & Expositions: Short term amusement parks; State Fair

Fantasy: Tales of the imagination, including Alice, The Faculty, E.T., Ladyhawke, My Stepmother Is an Alien

Farm Livin': Down on the farm; Bitter Harvest, Pelle the Conqueror, Jean de Florette, The River

Fatsuit Acting: Actors get big parts, and lots of padding to go with 'em

FBI: The Bureau. Federal cops with an internal focus and a dress code

Female Bonding: Women get together, usually to the men's dismay; Waiting to Exhale

Female Spies: The fairer sex uses its feminine assets and wiles to get the other side's secrets

Femme Fatale: She done him and him and wrong

Fencing: En garde, duce

Film History: America at the Movies; includes movies important to film history

Film Noir: Dark and moody or tributes to dark and moody—Farewell, My Lovely, The Postman Always Rings Twice, The Third Man, Who Framed Roger Rabbit?

Filmmaking: The making of a film within a film: The Player

Firemen: Backdraft, Frequency; and other tales of brave people with hoses

Fires: Frankenstein, Quest for Fire, Pyrates

The First Time: Y'know, the first time you had...when you broke your...when you made...when you first...uh, did it...with another person

Flashback: Why, I remember like it was yesterday. It all started when....The Usual Suspects, Casablanca

Flatulence: Embarrassing gaseous emissions

Floods: Water, water everywhere

Florida: Beaches, retirement communities, swamps, Spring Training, Disney World.

Florence: Not Alice's girls-kissing pal, but the city in Italy.

Folklore & Legend: Age-old adult tales covering Atlantis, little people, faeries, Paul Bunyan, and the like

Football: Everything from terrorist attacks on the Superbowl (Black Sunday) to prison competition (The Longest Yard) plus Diner

*Foreign Cops: The long arm of the law on other countries, or visiting law enforcement representatives helping catch international baddies here in the good ole U.S. of A.

Foreign Intrigue: Overseas mystery, with emphasis on accent and location

Frame-ups: Someone's set up to take the rap; My Cousin Vinny to Consenting Adults

France: From Dirty Rotten Scoundrels to The Moderns to Gigi to The Last Metro to Killer Tomatoes Eat France

Fraternities & Sororities: Those fun-lovin' campus cut-ups who're always pulling pranks or getting offed in bad slasher flicks

Front Page: Citizen Kane, All the President's Men, The Philadelphia Story, and other journalistic stories

Fugitives: Running from the law; Breathless, Nowhere to Hide, The Fugitive

Funny Money: Counterfeiting, and all the action movie stuff 'hat goes with it

Funerals: The final good-bye—Four Weddings and a Funeral, Gardens of Stone, The Big Chill

Future Cop: The future of law enforcement

Future Shock: Someone from our past comes to our present, or someone from our present goes to our future; Sleeper, Just Visiting

Gambling: Aces and Eights, The Color of Money, Eight Men Out, Honeymoon in Vegas

Game Shows: The Running Man and Queen for a Day

Gangs: Criminally enterprising teens and adults running in packs; State of Grace, Miller's Crossing, Public Enemy, The Wanderers

Gays: Gay themes—Kiss of the Spider Woman, The Wanderers

Gender Bending: The Crying Game, La Cage aux Folles, Her Life as a Man and other instances of boys becoming girls and vice versa

Generation X: Slacking in the '90s—Reality Bites, Singles

Genetics: Fooling with the double helix—The Fly

Genies: Aladdin finds magic lamp filled with compressed Robin Williams

*Genocide/Ethnic Cleansing: One ethnic group thinks it is so superior to another that the other group must be completely destroyed. Words cannot describe the stupidity of this view

Genre Spoofs: Wacky takes on serious films, starting with the granddaddy of them all: Airplane!

Germany: The Blue Angel, Wings of Desire

Ghosts, Ghouls, & Goblins: Ghostbusters, Topper, Poltergeist

Giants: The Amazing Colossal Man visits Village of the Giants

Gifted Children: Kids show amazing talents that astound adults, from Rookie of the Year to Little Man Tate

Glasgow: Scottish city, not the capital of Scotland.

Go Fish: Casting a line in the river that runs through it; Man of Aran, A Fish Called Wanda, Captains Courageous

Going Native: Outsiders try to blend in; Dances with Wolves, The Swiss Family Robinson

Going Postal: Neither rain, snow, sleet, nor dead of night...Hello, Newman

Golf: Slow boring game best experienced on screen ('Be tha ball, Danny)

Gospel Music: Inspirational music usually sung by people in church or who really like church

Grand Hotel: Checkout time is noon; Blame It on the Bellboy

Grand Theft Auto: Boosting cars for fun and/or profit. Just like on Cops; chases usually ensue

Grandparents: Your parents' parents; the ones who spoil you and drive your folks crazy

Great Britain: Thwarted royals (Charles & Diana: A Royal Love Story), vanished empires (Cromwell, A Man for All Seasons), criminals (The Krays, The Long Good Friday) plus multiple stiff upper lips, the Brontes, and Dickens

Great Death Scenes: Signing off with style or elaboration; Barry the Vampire Killer, Bonnie and Clyde, Breaker Morant

Great Depression: The era, not the state of mind—Bound for Glory, Of Mice and Men, The Grapes of Wrath, Rambling Rose

Great Escapes: Seizing the day for freedom—The Big Doll House, Escape from Alcatraz, Papillon

Greece—Ancient: In the immortal words of Socrates, "I drank what?"

Greece—Modern: They don't walk around in sheets and philosophize anymore, at least not in public

Grim Reaper: Time's up when the pale bald guy wearing a hood and carrying garden implements comes looking for you.

Growing Older: On Golden Pond, *batteries not included, Cocoon, Driving Miss Daisy, The View

Gunslingers: Old West killers for hire. Sometimes they killed the bad guys, sometimes they were the bad guys

Gymnastics: Human pretzels like Nadia

Gypsies: Fortune tellers with scarves around their heads and vaguely—European accents, or modern day con men are the two basic movie types

Hackers: Computer whiz kids cause havoc—or just change their grades

Halloween!: Trick or Treat!

Handyman Specials: Houses that need a little work to be livable...unless you're a ghost, serial killer, or otherwise disinclined to hire an inspector

Hard Knock Life: Poverty and bad luck; City of Joy, The Match Factory Girl

Harlem: Part of New York City you don't see in the tourism brochures

Hawaii: The 50th state, fun in the sun, if the volcanoes are behaving

*Heads!: Disturbing (or fun) scenes of heads being forcibly removed from the bodies they formerly controlled

Hearts!: Unnerving scenes involving human hearts, generally seen by the audience and almost always still pumping

Heaven Sent: Visits or returns from the place where good souls and all dogs go—Field of Dreams to Made in Heaven to Oh God!

Heists: The big lift

Heists—Armored Car: Crooks plan and carry out jobs on armored cars

Heists—Art: Crooks plan and carry out jobs to steal works of art, The Thomas Crown Affair

Heists—Bank: Crooks plan and carry out early withdrawals, sometimes incurring substantial penalties

Heists—Gold/Precious Metals: Elaborate plans to go for the gold, or silver, or platinum. Bronze isn't that valuable in this game

Heists—Jewels: Ya gotta be cool to get the ice, just ask the Reservoir Dogs

Heists—Casinos: Crooks plan to steal from the one-armed bandits; Ocean's Eleven and 3000 Miles From Graceland

Heists—Trains: Not the whole train, just the good stuff inside it. Butch Cassidy and the Sundance Kid liked the choo-choos

Hell: Not a place you wanna end up. The forecast calls for continued hot, with a 0% chance of freezing over.

Hell High School: Place where adolescents gather against their will; also known as Rock 'n' Roll High School

The Help—Female: Maids, nannies, governesses, cooks, housekeepers

The Help—Male: Butlers, chauffeurs, manservants, valets

Hide the Dead Guy: What to do with those pesky bodies after the killing's done?

High School: This is for those few movies where high school isn't treated like the hellish experience we all seem to remember it being

High School Reunions: Adults gather to impress other adults they didn't like as adolescents

Hijacked!: Terrorists take over various modes of transportation, causing much action-movie heroics

Hispanic America: Dominant Hispanic American themes (Salsa, Mi Vida Loca)

Historical Detectives: It's elementary! Sherlock, meet Elliot Ness.

Historical Drama: Usually at least loosely based on a real incident or personality

Historical Romance: Smooches, longing looks, and other activities exchanged between historical personages

Hit Men/Women: Boys and girls armed with silencers; Prizzi's Honor, Romeo is Bleeding

Hockey: Slap Shot and other icy tales of passing the puck

Holidays: Easter, Thanksgiving, New Year's, Halloween, but generally not Christmas

Holocaust: Playing for Time, Schindler's List

Home Alone: Kids find themselves without adult supervision—Adventures in Babysitting to Young Sherlock Holmes

The Homefront—England: Air raids, stiff upper lips, they were a lot closer to the action, and were just as worried about their sons and husbands.

The Homefront—U.S./Canada: The war at home during WWII—looking for spies, rationing, waiting for word about 'the boys.'

Homeless: Street people with no homes

Homicide: Murder most foul! It's what usually gets those wacky buddy-cop movies started

Honeymoon: Where the bride and groom go after the wedding's over to...get acquainted

Hong Kong: Land of the really cool action flick; Chow Yun-Fat and Jackie Chan became stars there. Great Britain gave it back to the Chinese

Horrible Holidays: Holidays with a ghoulish twist—Bloody New Year, Halloween, My Bloody Valentine, Silent Night, Bloody Night

Horror: Modern cut 'em up scare theater

Horror Anthologies: More than one scarefest per package

Horror Comedy: Tongue-in-bloody cheek—The Fearless Vampire Killers, Piranha, Sorority Babes in the Slimeball Bowl-A-Rama

Horses: Can you say Black Beauty?

Hospitals & Medicine: Dysfunctional institutional health care—Article 99, The Hospital, One Flew Over the Cuckoo's Nest, Young Doctors in Love

Hostage!: People held against their will for bargaining purposes

Housesitting: Watching a friend's house while he's gone. You know, in case it gets the idea to run away or something

Houston: That big city in Texas where J.R. didn't live, but Roger Clemens does.

Hunted!: Humans tracking humans for trophy purposes

Hunting: Where's dat wascally wabbit? Caddyshack, The Bear, White Hunter, Black Heart

Hurling: What goes down sometimes comes back up—The Exorcist, Parenthood

I'm Not Dead, Yet! Reports of their demise have been greatly exaggerated

Immigration: Melting pot stories—Avalon, Far and Away, Living on Tokyo Time

Immortality: I wanna live forever

Impending Retirement: Gold watch, a party, some tearful goodbyes...but there's always those darn loose ends to tie up first

In-Laws: The family you marry into; usually a source of conflict and punchlines

India: On the road to Bombay

*The Inquisition, What a Show!: The Spanish Inquisition, that is. No one expects it. Spanish Catholic Church officials got a little, um, enthusiastic, in their recruiting efforts in the late 1400s

Insomnia: Can't sleep at night

Insurance: Usually the cure for the above category, unless someone's killing, scamming, or frauding for the money it pays

Internet Borne: It's not just for naughty pics or fantasy sports anymore. You can find either love or death on the World Wide Web.

Interpol: International police force that fights crime and terrorism when it crosses many borders

Interracial Affairs: Couple from different racial backgrounds cause trauma for family and friends—Mississippi Masala, Jungle Fever

Interviews: When asked questions, people talk

Inventors & Inventions: Those wacky folks and their newfangled machines; Chitty Chitty Bang Bang

Invisibility: Now you see 'em, now you don't

*Iraq: Maybe you've heard of it...oil-rich country in the Middle East? We've been poking around there for a while now?

Ireland: Aye, make that a pint for take away; The Field, Cal, The Playboys

Islam: Religious themes, concentrating on Muslims

Island Fare: Thin, isolated stretch of land surrounded by water; notorious for encouraging natural appetites in men and women

Israel: Cast a Giant Shadow, Exodus

Istanbul, not Constantinople: Former seat of the Eastern Roman Empire, now the Turks run things.

Italy: Passion, vino, lust, vino, Sophia Loren

It's a Conspiracy, Man!: Just because you're paranoid doesn't mean they're not out to get you

Japan: Land of the Rising Sun, Godzilla, Hiroshima, Mon Amour

Jazz & Blues: Uniquely American music form performed mostly by tragic figures...in the movies, anyway.

Jerusalem: Much-fought-over Holy City, it's ground zero for much of the world's religious population.

Jockeying for Position: Horse racing flicks like Seabiscuit

*Joke and Dagger: Spies Like Us can be funny, even when the mission is Top Secret!

Judaism: Fiddler on the Roof meets Funny Girl

Jungle Stories: Tarzan, tribes, trees, treasure, temperature, temptresses, tigers

Junior Jocks: Kids got out onto the field, court, pitch, or rink to emulate their sports heroes, or just for fun, or to please their vicariously-thrilled parents.

Justice Prevails?: The verdict's in, but is it fair? And Justice for All, In the Name of the Father, Presumed Innocent

Karaoke: This Japanese import usually runs best on alcohol

*KGB: Not the crazy Russian poker player from Rounders but the former Soviet Union's spy organization

Kiddie Viddy: Stuff aimed at kids that's actually suitable for the little nippers to watch

Kidnapped!: Held for ransom or just for the heck of it—A Perfect World, Raising Arizona

Killer Apes and Monkeys: King Kong lives on The Planet of the Apes

Killer Appliances: Defrosted refrigerator goes on killing binge

Killer Beasts: Cloned dinosaurs run amuck in backyard, destroying patio

Killer Brains: Literally has a mind of its own, i.e., The Brain That Wouldn't Die

Killer Bugs: Giant and/or miserably mean spiders, ants, bees, worms, flies, slugs, tarantulas, wasps, and other creepy things

Killer Cars: You should have changed Christine's oil

Killer Clowns: Confirming what everybody knows: clowns are evil

Killer Dogs: Fido takes a walk on the wild side—Cujo, baby

Killer Dreams: More like nightmares on elm street

Killer Kats: Kitties with a killer instinct

Killer Pigs: Evil swine

Killer Plants: Too much fertilizer produces killer tomatoes (stewed)

Killer Reptiles: Godzilla and pals, not rampaging lawyers

Killer Rodents: Nasty mice, rats, bats, and shrews

Killer Sea Critters: Just when you thought it was safe to go back in the water; formerly Sea Critter Attack

Killer Spouses: Watch their eyes very closely when you get to the "...until death do you part" portion of the vows

Killer Toys: Demented play things develop homicidal urges; why hello, Chucky

*Killing Sprees: A person, or sometimes a couple, decides that a bunch of people need killin' in a short amount of time

Kindness of Strangers: Baffling altruistic behavior

King of Beasts (Dogs): Need we say more?

Korean War: M*A*S*H and friends

L.A.: Smoggy city in California also known as Los Angeles or the City of Angels; includes Hollywood & Beverly Hills

Labor & Unions: Hoffa and other working stiffs

Late Bloomin' Love: Better late than not blooming at all

Law & Lawyers: Tom Cruise joins The Firm and other realistic legal adventures

Leprechauns: The wee mischievous people of Irish lore who carry around pots o' gold

Lesbians: Lesbian themes—Lianna, Bar Girls

Libraries & Librarians: Important things happen where you can't talk—sometimes people even read!

Lifeguards: Rescuers of the swimming-challenged

Little People: Dwarves, munchkins, leprechauns, oompa-loompas and the like

London: City in merry old England, home to many generations of the most famous royals

Loner Cops: Dirty Harry Syndrome

Look Ma! I'm on TV!: TV becomes real life, i.e., The Truman Show, live from Pleasantville

Lost Worlds: From Brigadoon to The People That Time Forgot

Lottery Winners: Ordinary schmoes get rich quick. Be careful what you wish for...

Louisiana: Southern state on the bayou; the Mississippi ends and the party begins (at Mardi Gras time)

Lovable Loonies: Crazy, but not Norman Bates crazy; Crazy People, Benny & Joon

Lovers on the Lam: Couples commit crimes and find themselves on the run—Badlands, Natural Born Killers, True Romance

Mad Scientists: The Brain That Wouldn't Die spends an evening with Frankenhooker

Madrid: Capital of Spain, it has museums, great nightlife, and a pretty famous soccer team

Magic: Hocus pocus, often with evil intent

Magic Carpet Rides: Aladdin joins Sinbad the Sailor for The Golden Voyage of Sinbad

Mail-Order Brides: Shipping is okay, but I've got a problem with this handling charge!

Making Friends: Using spare parts to create semi-articulate, reasonable facsimiles of people. Young Frankenstein meets Frankenhooker

Marriage: Wedding bells, honeymoons, affairs, divorce, and growing old together, as well as the occasional unfortunate marital union with a blood-sucking vampire or knife-wielding Satanist

Marriage Hell: Divorce is the preferred exit strategy, but an uncooperative spouse usually has other ideas

Marriages of Convenience: Will you marry me so I can inherit boatloads of cash or not get deported? Oh, how romantic!

Mars: The Red Planet, which gave us (supposedly) little green men and the Illudium-Q Explosive Space Modulator

Martial Arts: Fists of Aluminum Foil; much head-kicking, rib-crunching, chop-socky action

Martyred Pop Icons: For us, they gave their all; Buddy Holly, Elvis, Marilyn, James Dean, Stardust Memories

Mass Media: From Network to Broadcast News to My Favorite Year

Masseurs: People who knead people...

Mathemagicians: Smarties with a good head for figures, but sometimes balancing the fine edge of sanity

May-December Romance: Older people meet younger people and the romantic sparks fly; Harold and Maude visit Atlantic City.

The Meaning of Life: The search for the elusive answer—My Life, The Remains of the Day, Shadowlands

* = new to this edition

Medieval Romps: Dirty peasants, deodorized and glorified kings and queens, splendid knights in shining armor, and one for all and all for one

Meltdown: Or how I learned to stop worrying and love the bomb; also bad wiring at local nuclear plants

Memphis: The other city in Tennessee; Elvis' home

Men in Prison: Working on a chain gang; what we have here is a failure to communicate

Men: What is man? Is he neither fish nor fowl? Or perhaps linoleum?

Mental Hospitals: Storage area for those not on speaking terms with Mr. Reality

Mental Retardation: Bill, Charly, Dominick, Lenny, Raymond (definitely)

Mercenaries: Dogs of War who like the killin, if they get paid enough

Mermaids: Half woman, half fish, alright! The Little Mermaid makes a big Splash

Mexico: South of Santa Fe and Against All Odds

Miami: Extremely warm coastal city in southern Florida

Middle East: Desert fare and camel close-ups ranging from Ishtar to Lawrence of Arabia to The Jewel of the Nile

Midlife Crisis: The point in a man's life when he trades in his car and wife for a newer, faster model. Neither decision ends well, usually

Military: Foreign: Armed forces of other nations are the focus

Military: Army: GIs, Grunts, Dogfaces

Military Comedy: Marching to a different drummer, including Stripes, M*A*S*H, and No Time for Sergeants

Military Crimes & Trials: Courtroom drama in the Armed Forces; A Few Good Men didn't follow the Rules of Engagement on their Paths to Glory

Military: Air Force: Flyboys fight America's aerial battles

Military: Navy: Fighting on the high seas and in the air

Military School: Kids get sent there to learn discipline, the art of war, and how to march in a straight line. Sometimes they learn too well and take over (Taps)

Military: Marines: Jarheads. The first ones in and the last ones out.

Military Westerns: Here comes the cavalry! Occasionally, They Died with Their Boots On

*Milwaukee: Wisconsin home of beer, brats, the Brewers, Bucks, and lots of snow

Metamorphosis: Ch-ch-ch-changes—From The Fly to Wolf

Miners & Mining: Helmets with the little flashlights are nifty; Matewan and McCabe & Mrs. Miller

Minnesota: Northern state that makes Michigan seem like the tropics. Home of the Twin cities and Prince, eh?

Missing Persons: People who disappear for a variety of reasons, sometimes because other people have taken them away

Missionaries: On a mission from God to save native populations

Mistaken Identity: You mean to say you're not the King of France?

Mockumentary: Movies in which actors pretend to be real people being followed around by fake documentary crews that are actually real filmmaking crews; This is Spinal Tap's genre, and they're still Best in Show at it.

Model Behavior: Fashion and models are the center of attention—but isn't that the point? Looker, Gia, Unzipped, Ready to Wear

Modern Cowboys: Fun-lovin' rascals adept at riding horses through busy city streets or with a yen to experience mid-life crisis by doing a rodeo

Moms: Maternal figures have a prominent role

Monkeyshines: Critters from the jungle, sometimes cute and fluffy, often wreaking havoc—Congo, Monkey Trouble, Outbreak

Monks: Of the Catholic-Friar-Tuck, Tibetan-Buddhist and Bulletproof varieties

Monster Moms: Loving on the outside, evil on the inside—Mommie Dearest, Serial Mom

Monster Yuks: Monster movies where the creatures are more funny, or cuddly, than scary

Montana: Northern plains state, home to wide-open spaces and the occasional wide-eyed loon living on a "compound"

*Monte Carlo/Monaco: European playgrounds of the rich, famous, and occasional suave secret agent

Montreal: Cosmopolitan city of francophones currently in Canada

Mormons: Religious sect headquartered in Utah; they're big on knocking on strangers' doors, polygamy, and Reservoir Dogs wardrobes

Moscow: City in Russia (the country formerly known as USSR) that has the Kremlin and Lenin's corpse

Moscow Mafia: The Russian Mob

Motor Vehicle Dept.: Chitty Chitty Bang Bang at the Car Wash, plus Tucker, Herbie, and the Repo Man

Mountaineering: Cliffhangers

Mummies: Dead guys with leather-like skin, often wrapped in sheets

Murderous Children: "Children of the Corn hang out on the outskirts of the Village of the Damned...isn't that near the 7-Eleven of Doom?

Museums: Big buildings that contain old paintings, sculptures, treasures, and the occasional ancient man-eating beastie

Musical Comedy: Laughter, singing, and dancing

Musical Drama: Singing and dancing, less laughter, more tension

Musical Fantasy: Singing and dancing in a figment of someone's imagination

Musicals: High-energy singing and dancing, often for no particular reason

Mutiny: Gang of disgruntled sailors takes over the ship

Mystery & Suspense: Edge-of-the-couch thrillers and whodunits

Nannies & Governesses: Musically-inclined women raise kids for rich people too busy to do it themselves

Nashville: Tennessee city that country music and Robert Altman made famous

Nashville Narratives: Honkytonk Man elopes with the Coal Miner's Daughter

'National Guard: Branch of the military that goes where they're needed most. Sometimes it's natural disasters in their own back yard, sometimes it's a tense social situation where order is needed, sometimes it's a patch of desert thousands of miles away

Native America: Dancing with the wolves on Pow Wow Highway

Nazis & Other Paramilitary Slugs: The Boys from Brazil and The Dirty Dozen plus SS she-wolf Ilsa and modern David Duke adaptations

Near-Death Experiences: Brushes with the Reaper, usually resulting in some extra powers upon the victim's return

Negative Utopia: Things seemed so perfect until...

Netherlands: Not to be confused with the nether regions, which are often prominently displayed in some areas of Amsterdam

New Black Cinema: Spike is Godfather

New Jersey: Butt of too many New Yorkers' jokes; home of The Chairman, The Boss, The Trump, and Jay & Silent Bob

New Orleans: City in Louisiana that boasts the Mardi Gras and cajun cookin'

New Year's Eve: Stay up late, count down with Dick Clark, drink too much, greet the New Year feeling like...

New York, New York: It's a hell of a town...

Newlyweds: Ah, the first year of marriage; the honeymoon, settling into your new life together, hanging out with Bob Eubanks...

News at 11: Broadcast "journalism" in which some local hairdo spends most of the half-hour telling you what he's gonna tell you, and the "rest of the time scaring the oejeezus outta ya

Niagara Falls: Little upstate New York border town where honeymooners and barrel riders gather. Oh yeah, they have some water thing there, too...

Nice Mice: Cute anthropomorphic or cartoon rodents, rather than the disease-carrying vermin variety

Nightclubs: Casablanca, of course

9/11: Films dealing with the events and aftermath of that day

Ninjas: Stealthy martial arts assassins in pajamas

No-Exit Motel: Sleazy motels with extremely lenient late-checkout policies

Not-So-True Identity: People pass themselves off as something else; Soul Man, Gentleman's Agreement

Nuns & Priests: Collars and habits; Agnes of God, The Cardinal, Going My Way, Nuns on the Run, Sis-ter Act

Nuns With Guns: Sister Mary Margaret has traded up from the ol' yardstick. Better practice that penmanship.

Nursploitation: Night Call Nurses offer Tender Loving Care in The Hospital of Terror.

Obsessive Lover: You like me. You really, really, really like me.

Occult: Witches, warlocks, devil worshippers, spell makers, haunted houses, and so on

Office Surprise!: Office supplies used as weapons

Oldest Profession: It's not accounting

The Olympics: Chariots of Fire and other tales of athletic discipline

On the Rocks: Alcoholism, moonshining, Prohibition—Arthur, Days of Wine and Roses, Papa's Delicate Condition, My Favorite Year

One Last Job: Crooks just wanna retire to a warm climate and enjoy their ill-gotten booty, but someone is always pullin' 'em back in!

Only the Lonely: 50 ways to play solitaire—The Cemetery Club, The Heart Is a Lonely Hunter, Sleepless in Seattle

Opera: Shouting in a melodic way while in costume

Order in the Court: Courtroom tales, including The Accused, And Justice for All, A Few Good Men, Witness for the Prosecution

Organ Transplants: Taking parts from one body that doesn't need 'em anymore and putting 'em into a body that does.

Organized Crime: Gangsters with Franklin Planners

Otherwise Engaged: Couple gets ready to march down the aisle, sometimes with a new fiancee—Moonstruck, Only You, Sleepless in Seattle

Out of Order: Movies in which the director's vision was not chronologically 20/20. Think Memento or any Quentin Tarantino movie

Out of This World Sex: Doin' the intergalactic nasty, usually with unfortunate results for earthlings

Pacific Islands: Hawaii, Tahiti, Philippines, etc.

Paperboys: Kids who toss papers everywhere but your front porch

Parades & Festivals: Animal House and Ferris Bueller's Day Off

Paradise Gone Awry: You'd think it'd be perfect, but there...

Parallel Universes: There's a whole other world out there—Cool World, Who Framed Roger Rabbit?

Parenthood: Moms, dads, substitutes—Dutch, Ma, Barker's Killer Brood, Father of the Bride, Three Men and a Baby, Yours, Mine and Ours, Raising Arizona

Paris: Ze city in France with nude occupants and ze Eiffel Tower

Paramedics: Part doctor, part fireman, part delivery driver. Cool!

Party Hell: Psycho Girls have fun at a sleepover until Monsters Crash the Pajama Party and it becomes The Slumber Party Massacre

Patriotism & Paranoia: Run the flag up the pole and salute it—Rambo, Patton, Norris, etc.

Peace: Friendly Persuasion, Gandhi

Pen Pals: Strangers correspond through the mail (or cyberspace) and become friends...or sometimes more

Penguins: Cute waddling flightless birds from Antarctica in tuxedos

Period Piece: Costume epics or evocative of a certain time and place; now divided into eras for your time traveling pleasure

15th Century—Braveheart and other tales of the end of the Middle Ages

16th Century—The Renaissance; rebirth of culture, art, science

17th Century—The Enlightenment, or Age of Reason

18th Century—The Revolutions all over the place

19th Century—more war, plus the Industrial Revolution

20th Century—Epics that span more than one decade

1900s—the decade that began the now-completed 20th century

Persian Gulf War: Smart bombs away

Philadelphia: Famous Pennsylvania city that's home to Rocky, the Liberty Bell, cheesesteaks, and M. Night Shyamalan films

Phobias!: Eeeeeeeeeeeeeek!

Phone Sex: Is it really the next best thing to being there?

Phone Terror: Don't Answer the Phone

Physical Problems: My Left Foot, Coming Home, The Elephant Man, The Other Side of the Mountain, Untamed Heart, The Waterdance

Pigs: Loveable swine—Gordy, Babe the Gallant Pig

Pirates: Avast, ye scurvy dogs! Captain Blood drops in on Treasure Island

Pittsburgh: City in western Pennsylvania, home of sports teams 'ond of the colors black and yellow.

Plastic Surgery: Using surgery to give you what nature didn't, or to take away some of the unwanted stuff with which nature was overly generous

Poetry: Not exactly a booming category, but think of Poetic Justice

Poisons: Arsenic and Old Lace and D.O.A.

Poker: Card game where fortunes, property, wives, etc. can be won or lost in a myriad of ways; Texas 'Hold 'em; Stud, Draw (particularly in the Old West)

Police Detectives: They get paid to bust open the big cases amid wild car chases and gunplay.

Politics: Bob Roberts, Mandela, Whoops Apocalypse

Pool: The Hustler

Pornography: Hardcore, Body Double

*Portland (Oregon, not Maine): Northwestern city, land lots of trees and rain, beautiful scenery, and the Trailblazers

Post Apocalypse: No more convenience stores

1910s—stories not involving World War I

1920s—Roaring '20s, Age of Jazz, Prohibition, Babe Ruth

1930s—stories not involving the Depression

1940s—stories not involving World War II

1950s—Rock 'n' Roll, Elvis, Eisenhower, McCarthyism, Civil Rights movement begins

1960s—assassinations, hippies, Vietnam, along with more mundane concerns

1970s—bad clothes, Watergate, disco, Elvis dies...let's just forget this decade happened

1980s—Reagan, Iran-Contra, John Hughes angst-fests, big hair, and greed

Postwar: After effects of war, generally WWI or WWII but sometimes the Civil War, the War of 1812, the Revolutionary War, and the Ohio Automobile Dealers War

POW/MIA: Captured by the enemy

Pregnant Men: Ahh-nuld fails the Rabbit Test

Pregnant Pauses: Humorous takes on pregnancy and birth—*Nine Months, She's Having a Baby*

Prep School: Where the children of the elite meet to learn how to be upper-crusty

Presidency: Mr. Lincoln, JFK, LBJ, FDR, and, of course, *Dave*

Price of Fame: What goes up...

Private Eyes: There's no such thing as a simple little case...

Prom: A night you'll always remember...which isn't necessarily a good thing. Right, *Carrie?*

Propaganda: Deliberately stretching the truth in order to persuade

Protests: Hell no, we won't go (to bad movies)! Make popcorn, not war!

Psychic Abilities: I see dead people! Or the future, or read minds, or have telekinesis...

Psycho-Thriller: It's all in your mind—*Bad Influence, House of Games, The Silence of the Lambs*

Psychotics/Sociopaths: *Killer Inside Me, Reservoir Dogs, The Stepfather*

Publicists: People who suck up to the press so celebrities don't have to

Punk Rock: Anarchic semi-musical revolution of the late 70s, where the message (if you could decipher it) was more important that the melody. Way, way more important.

Puppets: Usually with strings, but also muppets

Pure Ego Vehicles: Big stars doing their big star thing—*Hudson Hawk, Harlem Nights, Yes, Giorgio*

Rabbis: Jewish clergy

Rabbits: *Harvey* has a *Fatal Attraction* for the *Nasty Rabbit*

Race Against Time: Tick, tock, tock—*China Syndrome, Lorenzo's Oil*

Radio: Over the airwaves—*Easy Rider, Choose Me, Radio Days, Sleepless in Seattle*

Rags to Riches: Grit, determination, and hustling (or just pure dumb luck) lead to fortune—*Trading Places, Working Girls*

Rape: Victims and often their revenge

Real Estate: Everyone's gotta live somewhere, and most want to live on land they own. That's where agents, scams, and deals come in

REALLY Bad TV: When TV sucks...you into another dimension. How can another be anything good on when your TV is possessed?

Rebel With a Cause: Bucking the establishment for a reason

Rebel Without a Cause: Bucking the establishment just because it's the establishment

The Red Cross: Organization that helps those in need of blood, disaster relief, and war relief; also monitors treatment of POWs

Red Scare: Cold War and Communism—*The Commies Are Coming, The Commies Are Coming, Reds*

Reefer Madness: Tales of the demon weed.

Rehab: Drying out, sobering up...walking around in bathrobes.

Reincarnation: Why is everyone somebody famous in a past life?

*****Romantic Mystery:** Like there's a bigger mystery than the opposite sex??

Religion: *Witness, The Last Temptation of Christ*

Religious Epics: Charlton Heston parts the Red Sea—religion on a really big scale

Renegade Body Parts: Hands, fingers, eyes, brains with a life of their own

Repressed Men: Often British (*see* Anthony Hopkins or Hugh Grant), always with plenty of stiffness in upper lip and little elsewhere

Rescue Missions: I'll save you—*The Searcher, Free Willy*

Rescue Missions Involving Time Travel: I'll save you in another dimension—*Back to the Future*

The Resistance: WWII rebels with an anti-Nazi cause

Reunited: Usually after a long absence caused by extreme circumstances

Revenge: A key motivation—*Death and the Maiden, Death Wish*

Revolutionary War: Fought over tea

Rio: As in de Janeiro—that swingin' South American party town.

A River Runs Through the Plot: Long, sometimes winding and narrow body of water the main characters may have to get over, around, through or travel down, or fish in to get to the end of the story

Road Trip: Escapism courtesy of two- and four-wheel vehicles—*Easy Rider, Coupe de Ville, Pee Wee's Big Adventure, Wild at Heart*

Robots/Androids: Mechanical and fascinating, like the one Tom replaced Katie with; *Blade Runner* and *The Terminator*

Rock Flicks: Movies about real or made up rockers, starring rock stars, or featuring bands in concert; or rock stars who can they act? Prince (Symbol), Sting, Elvis, Lennon, The Monkees, Whitney, and so on

Rodeos: Rope tricks with steers

Rogue Cops: Corruption in the PD, cops on the take, etc. Usually, *Internal Affairs* gets involved

Role Reversal: Vice versa; empathy test—*Freaky Friday, My Fair Lady, Switch, Soul Man*

Romantic Adventures: Love among the chases and explosions—*The African Queen, Romancing the Stone*

Romantic Comedy: Falling in love has its hilarious moments—*French Kiss, Crossing Delancey, Modern Romance, Much Ado About Nothing*

Romantic Drama: Love thing leads to tension and anxiety—*Cyrano de Bergerac, Far and Away, Sommersby, Tender Mercies*

Romantic Triangles: Three where there's only room for two—*The Age of Innocence, Casablanca, Three of Hearts*

Rome—Ancient Emperors ran the show, feeding Christians to the lions, using V for U, having orgies, and throwing up on purpose...those were the days!

Rome—Modern: Capital city of Italy. The Pope has a little place there

Roommates from Hell: Sometimes they won't do the dishes, sometimes they're homicidal—*Single White Female*

Royalty: Emperors, kings, queens, princes, princesses, crowns, scepters

Royalty, British: Emperors, kings, queens, etc in Merry Olde England

Royalty, French: Kings and queens who ran France when they didn't surrender to any foreigner who happened by

Royalty, Russian: Emperors, czars, and czarinas who ran things in Moscow till those mean old Bolsheviks showed up

*****Rwanda:** Troubled country in Africa being torn apart by war, poverty, and disease

Running: Jogging, panting, collapsing

Russia/USSR: Back in what used to be the USSR

Russian Revolution: 1917, when the Bolsheviks kicked out the Czar, set up the Soviet Union, and got Russia out of WWI

San Diego: Sunny (is there any other kind?) Southern California city close to Mexico

San Francisco: Set in the Northern California city known for hills and sourdough bread

Sanity Check: Inmates running the asylum; also deviant mental states

Satanism: *Speak of the Devil*

Satire & Parody: Biting social commentary or genre spoofs, including *Being There, Airplane!, Down and Out in Beverly Hills, I'm Gonna Git You Sucka, Monty Python's The Meaning of Life, The Player*

Savannah: the city in Georgia, with the southern belles and the big social events

Savants: Half-minded geniuses; *Rain Man, Forrest Gump*

Scams, Stings & Cons: The hustle—*The Billionaire Boys Club, The Color of Money, A Fish Called Wanda, The Grifters, The Sting*

Scared 'Chuteless: Jumping out of airplanes without the proper equipment. Good candidates for a bad case of cement poisoning

School Daze: Education, school, and teachers, generally grammar school days—*Lean on Me, Dead Poet's Society, To Sir, with Love, Teachers*

Sci Fi: Imagination fueled by science and a vision of the future

Sci-Fi Westerns: You ain't from around heah, is ya?

Science & Scientists: *Altered States, Darkman, Them, They, Son of Flubber, The Story of Louis Pasteur*

Scotland: Lush hills, thick brogues, baths, bagpipes, and *Whiskey Galore*

Screwball Comedy: Snappy repartee between a man and a woman dealing with an impossibly silly situation

Scuba: Wet suits, including *The Abyss, Navy SEALS*

Sculptors: Artists who like to work with clay, rock, hammers, and chisels

Sea Disasters: We've sprung a leak—*The Poseidon Adventure*

Seattle: Showcases the city in Washington state where it rains a lot, the home of grunge rock

Second Chance: Another opportunity to set things right, fix mistakes, redeem yourself, or all of the above

Secret Service: Bodyguards to the First Family, they also investigate counterfeiting

Serial Killers: They just won't stop—*Henry: Portrait of a Serial Killer, The Rosary Murders*

Serials: Segmented adventures: Heyday was in the 1930s—*The Adventures of Red Ryder, The Little Rascals, Flash Gordon*

Sex & Sexuality: Focus is on lust, for better or worse—*Alfie, Barbarella, Emmanuelle, Looking for Mr. Goodbar, Rambling Rose, She's Gotta Have It*

Sex on the Beach: Flashing the fish and getting sand in the darnedest places; the most famous couple was in *From Here to Eternity* and *Airplane!* lost no time making fun of them

Sexcapades: The wilder edge of the whole sex thing

Sexploitation: Softcore epics usually lacking in plot but not skin—*The Erotic Adventures of Pinocchio*

Sexual Abuse: Victims and their stories—*Twin Peaks, Fire Walk with Me*

Sexual Harassment: When I say no, I mean it!

Shipwrecked: Stranded on an island when your boat sinks

Shops & Shopping: When commerce at the mall is a major plot point.

Showbiz Comedies: Laughter behind the scenes in Hollywood or on Broadway

Showbiz Dramas: Tension behind the scenes in Hollywood or on Broadway

Showbiz Musicals: Singing and dancing behind the scenes in Hollywood or on Broadway

Showbiz Thrillers: Screaming behind the scenes in Hollywood or on Broadway

Shrinkage: People become very, very small. *Honey, I Shrunk Rick Moranis's Career*

Shrinks: Psychiatry or equivalent, with *The Prince of Tides, One Flew Over the Cuckoo's Nest*

Shutterbugs: Photographers and their pictures—*The Public Eye, The Eyes of Laura Mars, Peeping Tom*

Sibling Rivalry: Brothers and sisters fighting over...well, anything, but usually romance or parental affection or wealth.

Silent Films: No small talk/no big talk/no talk talk

Silent Horror/Fantasy Classics: Silent screams, expressions of terror.

Single Parents: Divorced or widowed, they're doing the work of two—and they're back in the dating scene, usually assisted by match-making kids

Singles: Not always swinging but still solidly single—*About Last Night, Singles, When Harry Met Sally*

Skateboarding: Teens on wheels—*Gleaming the Cube*

Skating: Roller and ice, including *The Cutting Edge, Xanadu*

Skiing: Slap on a couple of waxed boards and off you go—*Downhill Racer, Swinging Ski Girls*

Skinheads: Nazi wannabes wreak havoc and cause trouble

Skydiving: Jumping from a plane with a polyester slip

Slapstick Comedy: Humor of the physical sort, including Abbott and Costello, the Marx Brothers, sports comedies, Ernest, Pink Panther, Home Alone, the Three Stooges

Slasher Flicks: Horror movies in which unsuspecting and promiscuous teens get sliced, diced, and julienned by knife, machete, drill, chainsaw, and/or farm implement-wielding maniacs

Slavery: *Roots, Spartacus*

Slob Comedy: Happily dumb comedies that provide plenty of laughs and quotes for adolescent boys of all ages. *Animal House, Stripes, Caddyshack* are the Holy Trinity

Small-Town Sheriffs: Think Sly in *Cop Land*, or Buford Pusser of *Walking Tall* fame

Smuggler's Blues: Making, transporting, and selling the drugs. Don't Blow your cool in the *Traffic*.

Snakes: Slithering creatures who frighten many—*Raiders of the Lost Ark*

Sniper: Military (and sometimes not) sharpshooters who can kill from a distance

Snowboarding: Kinda like skiing, except it's one big board attached to your feet, instead of two skinny ones. Oh, and no poles

Soccer: Known as football outside of the USA—*Victory, Ladybugs*

South America: Right below North America—*Aguirre, the Wrath of God, The Mission*

Southern Belles: Southern gals ooze charm—*Blaze, Driving Miss Daisy, Steel Magnolias*

Space Operas: Going where no spam has gone before—*Alien, Star Trek, 2001: A Space Odyssey, Apollo 13*

Spaghetti Western: Clint with a squint, *A Fistful of Dollars, My Name is Nobody, Once Upon a Time in the West*

Spain: *Siesta*

Spanish Civil War: Franco and the Fascists vs. the defenders of the newly-elected Socialist government. A preview of how WWII would be fought

Spiders: Eight-legged creepy crawlies spinning their webs, sometimes in the service of cartoon pigs

Spies & Espionage: Trench coats, dark glasses, Bond, *North by Northwest*

Sports Comedies: Humorous athletic tales, generally not based on a true story

Sports Documentaries: Non-fiction examinations of athletes and the games they play

Sports Dramas: Intense athletic tales, often based on a true story

* = new to this edition

Spring Break: Colleges and high schools empty their kids into the streets of Florida, Mexico and other exotic locales, where they search for beer and sex...if we remember correctly.

Spy Kids: Agents with a safe house on Sesame Street.

Stagestruck: Stories of the theatre, *Broadway Melody* sung at the *Stage Door* by *The Dolly Sisters*.

Stalked: No, I do not want to switch to MCI.

Star Gazing: Not Hollywood stars, astrology/astronomy type stars.

Stay-at-Home Dads: *Mr. Mom* takes care of the kids while Mom goes to the office...or just goes.

Stepparents: New spouse hiding either alien origins or sociopathic tendencies greets existing clan.

Stewardesses: *Three Guys Named Mike* go to *Stewardess School* and meet *Blazing Stewardesses*.

Stolen from Asia: American remakes of Asian classics—usually Kurosawa's; *Seven Samurai* becomes *The Magnificent Seven*.

Stolen from Europe: American remakes of European fare; *A Walk in the Clouds*, *The Vanishing*, *Scent of a Woman*.

Stolen From France: Hollywood goes to its favorite remake well; *Diabolique*, *Cousins*, *Nine Months*, *Three Men and a Baby*.

Storytelling: *Amazing Stories*, *Grim Prairie Tales*

Strained Suburbia: Neighborhood is not what it seems—*Dennis the Menace*, *Neighbors*, *Edward Scissorhands*

Strippers: Take it off, take it all off

Struggling Artists: It's hard not to struggle when your work only becomes valuable after you're dead

Struggling Musicians: Talented, but still reaching for the top

Stuntmen: Guys (and gals) paid to take the fall (and punch, and crash) for the stars

Stupid Is...: Stupidity on purpose—*Billy Madison*, *Dumb and Dumber*, or dumbness as a plot device—*Being There*, *Forrest Gump*

Submarines: Deep sea diving; *Das Boot*, *Up Periscope*, *Run Silent, Run Deep*, *Hunt for Red October*

Subways: A train for shorter trips—*Speed*, *The Taking of Pelham One Two Three*

Suicide: Self-inflicted premature ends—*The Big Chill*, *Scent of a Woman*, *Romeo and Juliet*

Summer Camp: Where children go to misbehave, including *Meatballs* and *Sleepaway Camp*

Super Heroes: Men and women of extraordinary strength and abilities wearing silly-looking costumes

Supernatural Comedies: *Beetlejuice* marries *She-Devil* and they take *The Ghost Train* to their *Haunted Honeymoon*

Supernatural Horror: Forces from beyond terrorize those who are here

Supernatural Martial Arts: *Kung Fu From Beyond the Grave*

Supernatural Westerns: Forces from beyond considered comedy premise

Surfing: Awesome wave, dude! *Mad Wax*, *The Surf Movie*, *Surf Nazis Must Die*, *Endless Summer*

Survival: *Alive*, *The Bridge over the River Kwai*, *Testament*

Suspended Animation: Frozen in time—*Coma*, *Late for Dinner*

Swashbucklers: Crossed swords and rope swinging, including *Robin Hood*, *Zorro*, various Musketeers, *Captain Blood*, *The Three Amigos*

Swimming: Ranging from *Swimmer* to *Jaws* to *The Swimmer* to *Cocoon*

Swingers: *Bob & Carol & Ted & Alice* try Group Marriage and Carol and Alice become Swinging Wives

Sword & Sandal: See Arnold Schwarzenegger's early career

Sydney: Big Aussie city, recent site of Olympic glory

Tale of the Tape: Videocassettes or audiocassettes are important plot devices...so remember to rewind

Talking Animals: *Dr. Doolittle* treats *Babe*

Tattoos: *The Illustrated Man* visits *Cape Fear* to do battle with *Cyber Bandits*

Taxing Situations: The IRS comes looking for the gummint's cut of the action. Go! dang revenooers!

Team Efforts: Working together pays off—*Hoosiers*, *Memphis Belle*, *Renaissance Man*

Tearjerkers: Crying fests—*Love Story*, *Steel Magnolias*, *Old Yeller*

Technology—Rampant: Machines that wreak havoc—*Metropolis*, *Death Ray 2000*, *Blade Runner*

Teen Angst: Adolescent anxieties, including *Baby It's You* and almost everything produced or directed by John Hughes

Teen Comedy: Teenagers yuk it up in school or out. Usually has a lot to do with sex, bodily functions, and defying authority (preferably all three at once)

Teen Drama: Kinda redundant. Teenagers deal with VERY IMPORTANT issues, or stuff that seems that way at the time, anyway.

Teen Horror: Horror flicks where the body count is skewered toward the 15-19 demographic (isn't that pretty much all of 'em?)

*****Teen Musicals:** Teens sing and dance, probably while texting their BFF. OMG!

Teen Romance: Teenagers falling in love, or lust

Tennis: Anyone?

Terminal Contusion: Luggage gets mixed up at the airport, bus station, etc. Trouble usually follows

Terminal Illness: Someone's gonna die a tragic death from a horrible disease, but probably not before falling in love or doing something inspirational. Usually will not be considered comedy premise

Terror in Tall Buildings: And there's no escape—*Dead Calm*, *Misery*, *The Shining*

Terror in the Aisles: From the *Hard* to *Speed* to *The Towering Inferno*

Terrorism: Love affairs with hidden bombs

Texas: Southern state that once was a country...and they never let anyone forget it. Apparently everything is bigger there.

Thanksgiving: Huge dinner, turkey coma, Christmas shopping may now commence

The Third Degree: Where were you on the night of...

This is My Life: Autobiographies starring the subject—Muhammad Ali in *The Greatest*, Audie Murphy goes *To Hell and Back*

This is Your Life: Biography and autobiography including *The Babe Ruth Story*, *Amazing Howard Hughes*, *Amadeus*

Thumbs Up: Hitchin' a ride—*Even Cowgirls Get the Blues*, *The Hitcher*

Tibet: So I says "Hey, Lama, how's about a little somethin' for the effort..."

Tijuana: City in Mexico that holds a special allure for Americans looking for various flavors of debauchery

Time Travel: Fast forward or reverse with Bill and Ted, Dr. Who, *Back to the Future*, and *Peggy Sue Got Married*

Time Warped: You wake up in an era not your own. Austin Powers, the Bradys and the Cleavers coping with the '90s

Titanic: The unsinkable ship that hit an iceberg its first time out...and sunk. It was in all the papers

3-D Flicks: Bring your special glasses

To the Moon!: *Apollo 13*, *From the Earth to the Moon*

Tokyo: Crowded city in Japan terrorized by Godzilla

Torrid Love Scenes: Steamy and/or sticky—*Angel Heart*, *Bull Durham*, *From Here to Eternity*, *Risky Business*, *The Unbearable Lightness of Being*

Toys: *Babes in Toyland*, *The Toys*, *Toys*

Tragedy: The fate of humankind.

Trains: Rhythm of the clackity clack—*Romance on the Orient Express*, *Throw Momma from the Train*, *Running Scared*, *The Silver Streak*

Trapped in a Killer!: And there's no escape—*Dead Calm*, *Misery*, *The Shining*

Treasure Hunt: *Klondike Fever*, *Klondike*, *Mr. Sycamore* and *The Wizard of Oz*

Trees & Forests: Can't see one for the other, that wilderness paradox—includes *Mr. Sycamore* and *The Wizard of Oz*

Triads: Chinese organized crime outfit. Chow Yun Fat is always shooting it out with 'em in John Woo flicks

True Crime: Based on fact, including *The Boston Strangler*, *The Executioner's Song*, *Helter Skelter*

True Stories: Approximations of real-life events often significantly fictionalized for the screen, including *All the President's Men*, *Chariots of Fire*, *Cry Freedom*, *Heart Like a Wheel*, *The Killing Fields*, *Silkwood*

TV Pilot Movies: Some became series; some did not

TV Series: Collections, anthologies, and individual episodes of memorable shows—*I Love Lucy*, *Star Trek*, *The Fugitive*

Twins: *Double Trouble*, *Double Vision*, *Mirror Images*

Twisted!: The big wind not caused by Mexican food that jacks up heavy things (houses, cows, trucks) and deposits them elsewhere

Under My Skin: People (or cartoon characters) get inside a guy's pelt, and crawl around for a little while

Undercover Cops: Cops pretend they're bad guys to catch more bad guys, but sometimes they get in *Too Deep*

Unexplained Phenomena: No apparent reason for an event

Unhappy Meals: Dining experience is marred by familial angst, unfortunate incidents, or people keeling over dead

Up All Night: Movie takes place mostly after the sun goes down and *Before Sunrise*

U.S. Marshals: Law enforcement branch that transports prisoners, hunts down fugitives, and in the Old West, handled the showdown duties

Urban Comedy: Taking the *Soul Plane* to the *Car Wash*, and then to the *Barbershop*. Then maybe need to *The Cookout*. Are We There Yet?

Urban Drama: *American Me* to *Boyz N the Hood* to *Grand Canyon* to *Zebrahead*

Urban Gangstas: Gangs fight it out for their piece of the mean streets of the inner city; *Colors*, *New Jack City*

The USO: Entertained the troops through two world wars and a variety of police actions—with Bob Hope usually leading the way

Vacation Hell: When the annual two-week respite from work goes horribly wrong. Usually starts with someone asking the skeevy gas station attendant for directions

Vacations: Getting away from it all, yet bringing the family.

Vampire Babes: Blood sucking dames—*The Brides of Dracula*

Vampire Spoof: Comedic blood suckers, including *Buffy*, *Andy Warhol's Dracula*, *Dracula Sucks*

Vampires: More serious vein of blood suckers, including *Dracula* in his many manifestations

Venice: Italian city of gondolas

Veterans: Retired fighting men (and women)—*Alamo Bay* to *Who'll Stop the Rain*

Veterinarians: Animal doctors, *Plasmal Dog Plasmal*

Vietnam War: *Platoon*, *Apocalypse Now*, *Good Morning, Vietnam*

Vigilantes: Individuals take the law into their own hands—*Death Wish*, *The Outlaw Josey Wales*

*****Videogames:** Interactive digital games that long ago replaced human interaction and eye contact as the preferred method of home entertainment for kids and geeks all over the world

Virtual Reality: High-tech video game that seems real...to computer geeks

Vikings: Rowdy guys with horns on their hats who like boat trips...Not those guys from Scandinavia!

Viva Las Vegas!: Celebrating America's tackiest city—*Honeymoon in Vegas*, *Sister Act*

Volcanoes: Mountain blowing off steam, including *Joe Versus the Volcano*

Volleyball: *Side Out* used to be the only one till we remembered the bare-chested boys from *Top Gun*

Voodoo: From *Angel Heart* to *How to Stuff a Wild Bikini* to *Weekend at Bernie's 2*

Vote for Me!: Political campaigns for various offices, from student council (*Election*) to U.S. President (*The Candidate*)

Wagon Train: Westward, Ho! Prairie Schooners play a big part in Westerns...such as getting people to the West

Waitresses: *Alice Doesn't Live Here Anymore*, she live to *Atlantic City* to get some *Mystic Pizza*

War, General: Generally any conflict that defies other classification—*The Alamo*, *Gunga Din*, *The Last of the Mohicans*

War Between the Sexes: Men and women battle for supremacy—*It Happened One Night*, *The King and I*, *He Said, She Said*, *Romancing the Stone*, *When Harry Met Sally*, *War of the Roses*, *Thelma & Louise*

Weathermen: Guys on the news who stand in front of a map and "predict" whether or not it will rain. Isn't there always a 50% chance of rain? Either it'll rain or it won't

Wedding Bells: Memorable weddings; *Father of the Bride*, *Four Weddings and a Funeral*, *Sixteen Candles*, *The Wedding*

Wedding Hell: Horror-filled or anxiety-ridden weddings; *The Blood Spattered Bride*, *The Brides Wore Blood*, *The Graduate*, *Wedding Banquet*

Werewolves: Full moon wonders, like *Wolf*

Westerns: Cowboys, cowgirls, horses and jingle jangling spurs on the frontier

Western Comedy: Gags and horses—*Ballad of Cable Hogue*, *Blazing Saddles*, *Rancho Deluxe*, *Support Your Local Sheriff*

Westrogens: The Old West through women's eyes

Whales: Really big sea-faring mammals. It's best to just stay out of their way...Just ask Pinocchio

Whitewater Rafting: Wild ride down a raging river, often in the company of a psycho

Wild Kingdom: Animals on their own anc interacting with confused humans, including *The Bear*, *Dumbo*, *Born Free*, *Free Willy*, *Never Cry Wolf*

Wilderness: More trees than a forest, plus wild critters—*The Life and Times of Grizzly Adams*

Wine & Vinyards: Spirits from the grape, and the places the grapes came from

Wisconsin: Chilly northern state, makers of beer and dairy products, land of Cheeseheads

Witchcraft: From *Hocus Pocus* to *Three Sovereigns for Sarah* to *The Wizard of Oz*

Witness Protection Program: Rat out your "associates," get a new identity

Women: Impressive women, less than impressive women, and issues concerning women—*Crimes of the Heart*, *My Brilliant Career*, *Passion Fish*, *Working Girls*

Women Cops: Female officers of the law

Women in Prison: The things that go on in the big doll house

Women in War: Nurses, WACs, WAVES, USO performers, sometimes prisoners—they also served...

Wonder Women: *Attack of the 50-Foot Woman, Ripley, La Femme Nikita, Supergirl*

Words Come to Life: Characters literally jump off the page

Workin' for a Livin': Focuses on working stiffs and their jobs

World War I: The First Big One, including *African Queen, Gallipoli, Grand Illusion*

World War I Spies: Espionage in the Great War. Think *Mata Hari*

World War II: The Last Big One, including *A Bridge Too Far, Guadalcanal Diary, The Guns of Navarone, Hope and Glory, Memphis Belle, Tora! Tora! Tora!*

World War II Spies: British and American agents who used stealth and deception to fight the Nazis

Wrestling: Choreographed sport involving men and women—*No Holds Barred, All the Marbles, Wrestling Women vs. the Aztec Ape*

Writers: Tortured souls who put pen to paper when they're not putting bottle to lips. Does not include the ink-stained wretches of the journalistic trade

The Wrong Man: ...has been accused or convicted. *The Fugitive* is in a *Frenzy* because *Jack's Back.*

Wrong Side of the Tracks: Often involves relationship with someone on the right side—*Cannery Row, The Flamingo Kid, Pretty in Pink, White Palace*

Yakuza: Japanese version of the Mafia, very organized crime

Yoga: Exercise you do sitting in one place that makes you all bendy

You Are Getting Sleepy!: Hypnosis, its practitioners, and effects, including glazed looks and strange behavior...Right, Katie, er, Kate?

You Big Dummy!: Ventriloquists have wooden dolls do their talking (or killing) for them

You Lose, You Die: Sports goes nuts—only the winner survives; *Arena, Rollerball, Tron*

Yuppie Nightmares: Young adults find best-laid plans for attaining wealth and privilege going astray—*Baby Boom, Desperately Seeking Susan, The Mighty Ducks, Pacific Heights, Something Wild, Wall Street*

Zombie Soldiers: Recently undead in the army—*They Saved Hitler's Brain*

Zombies: Recently undead everywhere—*I Walked with a Zombie, Night of the Living Dead*

footer: 1070 *VideoHound's Golden Movie Retriever*   * = new to this edition

Category Index

The Category Index includes subject terms ranging from straight genre descriptions (Crime Drama, Romantic Comedy, etc.) to more off-the-wall themes (Nuns with Guns, Eyeballs!). These terms can help you identify unifying themes (Baseball, Heists), settings (Miami, Period Piece; 1950s), events (The Great Depression, World War II), occupations (Clowns, Police Detectives, Doctors & Nurses), or suddenly animate objects (Killer Appliances, Killer Cars). Category definitions and cross-references precede the index; category terms are listed alphabetically. Release year is now included in this index. **A tipped triangle indicates a video rated three bones or higher.**

Abortion
Balzac and the Little Chinese Seamstress '02
The Choice '81
Choices '86
The Cider House Rules '99 ▲
Citizen Ruth '96
The Crime of Father Amaro '02 ▲
Critical Choices '97
Daddy's Gone A-Hunting '69 ▲
Dogma '99
Eye of God '97 ▲
Family Life '71
Fast Times at Ridgemont High '82 ▲
Flanders '06
4 Months, 3 Weeks, 2 Days '07 ▲
Goldstein '64
Happy Endings '05
If These Walls Could Talk '96
Listen to Me '89
Maria's Child '93
Palindromes '04 ▲
Panic in Needle Park '71 ▲
A Private Matter '92 ▲
Rain Without Thunder '93
Roe vs. Wade '89 ▲
Rude '96
Signs & Wonders '00
Silent Victim '92
The Story of Women '88 ▲
Things You Can Tell Just by Looking at Her '00 ▲
Vera Drake '04 ▲
Walpurgis Night '41 ▲

Action-Adventure
see also Action-Comedy; Action-Drama; Action-Thriller; Adventure Drama; Boom!; Comic Adventure; Disaster Flicks; Martial Arts; Romantic Adventures; Swashbucklers

Action-Comedy
see also Action-Adventure; Comedy
The Accidental Spy '01
After the Sunset '04
Agent Cody Banks 2: Destination London '04
Around the World in 80 Days '04
Bait '00
Bounty Hunters 2: Hardball '97
Camouflage '00
Charlie's Angels '00
Charlie's Angels: Full Throttle '03
Chill Factor '99
D.E.B.S. '04
Double Agent 73 '80
Double Take '01
Gorgeous '99
Hot Fuzz '07 ▲
Hot Rod '07
Hot Tamale '06
I Spy '02
The Incredibles '04 ▲
Kelly's Heroes '70
Kiss Kiss Bang Bang '05 ▲
Kung Fu Hustle '04 ▲
The Man '05
Man of the House '05
The Medallion '03
Meltdown '95
Miracles '89
Miss Congeniality 2: Armed and Fabulous '05
My Super Ex-Girlfriend '06
New York Minute '04
Nim's Island '08
Ocean's Twelve '04
The Pacifier '05
Partners '99
Pineapple Express '08
Pirates of the Caribbean: At World's End '07 ▲
Project A '33
Project A: Part 2 '87
The Rundown '03 ▲
Rush Hour '98
Rush Hour 3 '07
Sahara '05
Scooby-Doo 2: Monsters Unleashed '04
Shaolin Soccer '01 ▲
South Sea Woman '53
Spider-Man 2 '04 ▲
Starsky & Hutch '04
Taxi '04
Thunderbirds '04
Tropix '02
The Tuxedo '02
Underclassman '05
Underdog '07
Warm Blooded Killers '01
White Chicks '04
The Whole Ten Yards '04

Action-Drama
Assault on Precinct 13 '05
Blast '04
Bound by Lies '05
The Celestine Prophecy '06
Constantine '05
Domino '05
Doom '05
Elektra '05
Flight of the Phoenix '04
Flyboys '06
The Great Raid '05
Green Street Hooligans '05 ▲
Hostage '05
Illegal Tender '07
Into the Blue '05
It's All About Love '03
Jarhead '05
King Kong '05 ▲
The Last Legion '07
Lethal '04
Letters from Iwo Jima '06 ▲
Lord of War '05 ▲
The Memory of a Killer '03
Miami Vice '06
Mountain Patrol: Kekexili '04
National Treasure '04
Never Back Down '08
New Police Story '04
Oldboy '03 ▲
Ong-Bak '03 ▲
Pathfinder '07
The Promise '05
The Proposition '05
Purple Butterfly '03 ▲
Rebel Run '94
Rocky Balboa '06
The Sentinel '06
Serenity '05 ▲
Sin City '05
16 Blocks '06 ▲
Soldiers of Change '06
A Sound of Thunder '05
State Property 2 '05
Steamboy '05
Stryker '04
Submerged '05
Supercross: The Movie '05
Superman Returns '06
The Three Burials of Melquiades Estrada '05 ▲
Transporter 2 '05
Typhoon '05
The Veteran '06
Waist Deep '06
World Trade Center '06 ▲

Action-Thriller
Aeon Flux '05
Alone in the Dark '05
Archangel '05
Blade: Trinity '04
Blood Diamond '06 ▲
Cleaner '07
Conspiracy of Fear '96
Crimson Rivers 2: Angels of the Apocalypse '05
The Deal '05
Death Sentence '07
Deja Vu '06
The Detonator '06
District B13 '04
Domino '05
88 Minutes '08
The Fast and the Furious: Tokyo Drift '06
Firewall '06
Flightplan '05
The Flock '07
Ghost Rider '07
Hard As Nails '01
Hitman '07
Honor '06
The Hunt for Eagle One: Crash Point '06
Indiana Jones and the Kingdom of the Crystal Skull '08
Jumper '08
King Kong '05 ▲
The Kingdom '07
Kiss Kiss Bang Bang '05 ▲
Layer Cake '05 ▲
Live Free or Die Hard '07
Lost '05
The Memory of a Killer '03
Mexican Blow '02
Mirror Wars: Reflection One '05
Munich '05 ▲
National Treasure '04
National Treasure: Book of Secrets '07
The Net 2.0 '06
Next '07
Oldboy '03 ▲
Red Eye '05 ▲
Running Scared '06
The Secret Invasion '64
Serenity '05 ▲
Shoot 'Em Up '07
Shooter '07
Sin City '05
Sky Captain and the World of Tomorrow '04
Syriana '05 ▲
Total Force '98
Trade '07
Typhoon '06
Ultraviolet '06
Underworld: Evolution '05
Vantage Point '08
The Veteran '06
Waist Deep '06
War '07
Wanted '08
When Eight Bells Toll '71
The Witness '99
XXX: State of the Union '05

Adolescence
see also Coming of Age; Hell High School; Summer Camp; Teen Angst; Teen Comedy; Teen Drama; Teen Horror; Teen Musicals; Teen Romance

Adoption & Orphans
see also Custody Battles; Hard Knock Life; Only the Lonely
A la Mode '94
Across the Great Divide '76
Adoption '75 ▲
The Affair of the Necklace '01
After the Wedding '06 ▲
Aladdin '92
All Mine to Give '56
Aliens '86 ▲
Alex Rider: Operation Stormbreaker '06
Alone in the Dark '05
The Amazing Mrs. Holiday '43
Anastasia '97
Andre '94

▲ = *rated three bones or higher*

Adoption

Angel in a Taxi '59
Anne of Green Gables '34▶
Anne of Green Gables '85▶
Annie '82
Annie '99▶
August Rush '07
Babes on Broadway '41
Bachelor Mother '39▶
Back to the Secret Garden '01
Bambi '42▶
Batman Begins '05▶
Batman Forever '95▶
Battle Hymn '57
The Beniker Gang '83
Beshkempir the Adopted Son '98
Big Daddy '99
Big Red '62
Blossoms in the Dust '41
Blues Brothers 2000 '98
Bobbie's Girl '02
Bogus '96
Born Free '66▶
Born in America '90
The Boy with the Green Hair '48▶
Brand Upon the Brain! '06▶
The Breaks '99
Bright Eyes '34
Brute '97
Casa de los Babys '03▶
Catfish in Black Bean Sauce '00
The Chateau '01
The Children of An Lac '80
Children of the Corn 3: Urban Harvest '95
Christmas Eve '47
Christmas Lilies of the Field '84
Chronicle of a Boy Alone '64
The Cider House Rules '99▶
City Boy '93▶
The Country Bears '02
A Cry from the Streets '57
Crystalstone '68
Daddy Long Legs '19
Daddy Long Legs '55▶
Dangerous Orphans '86
D.A.R.Y.L. '85
David Copperfield '35▶
David Copperfield '70
David Copperfield '99
Deadly Sanctuary '68
Dear Wendy '05
December Boys '07
Defiant '70
The Devil's Backbone '01
Dick Tracy '90▶
Don't Cry, It's Only Thunder '82
Eagle's Shadow '84
Earthling '80
The Education of Little Tree '97
Emile '03
Escape to Witch Mountain '75▶
The Family Holiday '07
Family Jewels '65
The Father Clements Story '87
Fighting Father Dunne '48
First Love '39
The Flamingo Rising '01
Flirting with Disaster '95▶
Four Brothers '05
Free Willy '93
The Geisha Boy '58
Glass House: The Good Mother '06
Gloria '98
Great Expectations '34
Great Expectations '46▶
Great Expectations '81
Great Expectations '89▶
Great Expectations '99
Great Expectations: The Untold Story '87
The Great Water '04
Happy Endings '05
Heaven on Earth '31
Home at Last '88
A Home of Our Own '75
Hoodoo Ann '16

I Am David '04
Immediate Family '89
Intimate Relations '95
The Italian '05
The Jack Knife Man '20▶
James and the Giant Peach '96▶
Jane Eyre '34
Jane Eyre '44▶
Jane Eyre '83▶
Jane Eyre '96▶
Jane Eyre '97
Juno '07▶
The Kid '21▶
The Kid Who Loved Christmas '90
Kidnapped '05▶
King, Queen, Knave '72▶
Kings and Queen '04▶
Korczak '90▶
La Passante '83▶
Lady from Yesterday '85
The Lady Is Willing '42
The Land Before Time '88▶
Lemony Snicket's A Series of Unfortunate Events '04
Like Mike '02
Lilo & Stitch '02▶
The Little Kidnappers '90
Little Men '98
Little Orphan Annie '18
Little Orphan Annie '32
The Little Princess '87
Little Secrets '02
Loggerheads '05▶
A Long Way Home '81
Losing Isaiah '94▶
The Lost Child '00
Love Come Down '00
Lovely & Amazing '02▶
The Loves of Edgar Allen Poe '42
Love's Unending Legacy '07
Mad Max: Beyond Thunderdome '85
Madeline '98
Major Payne '95
Man, Woman & Child '83
Manny's Orphans '78
Marion Bridge '02
Martian Child '07
Meet the Robinsons '07
Mercury Rising '98
Mighty Aphrodite '95▶
Mighty Joe Young '49
Mighty Joe Young '98
Milwaukee, Minnesota '03
Min & Bill '30▶
The Mistress of Spices '05
Moll Flanders '96
Mon Amie Max '94
Mondo '96
Monsieur Ibrahim '03▶
Mostly Martha '01▶
My Blue Heaven '50
My Dog Shep '46
My Little Girl '87
My Name is Modesty: A Modesty Blaise Adventure '04
Mystery of the Million Dollar Hockey Puck '75
Nacho Libre '06
Napoleon and Samantha '72▶
Nice Girl Like Me '69
No Reservations '07
Norbit '07
Nothing But the Night '72
The Odyssey of the Pacific '82
Off Season '01
The Official Story '85▶
Oliver! '68▶
Oliver & Company '88
Oliver Twist '22▶
Oliver Twist '33
Oliver Twist '48▶
Oliver Twist '82
Oliver Twist '85
Oliver Twist '97
Oliver Twist '00▶
Oliver Twist '05▶
On the Right Track '81
One Good Cop '91
The Orphan '79
Orphan Train '79▶

The Orphanage '07▶
Orphans '87▶
Orphans of the Storm '21▶
Our Very Own '50
The Outsiders '83
Paper Moon '73▶
Peck's Bad Boy '34
Pennies from Heaven '36
Penny Serenade '41▶
Perfume: The Story of a Murderer '06
Phantasm '79
Pictures of Hollis Woods '07
Pixote '81▶
A Place for Annie '94
Pollyanna '20
Pollyanna '60▶
The Poor Little Rich Girl '36
The Prince of Central Park '77▶
Prison for Children '93
Problem Child '90
Queen Kelly '29▶
The Quest '96
The Quiet '05
Rags to Riches '87
Raising Heroes '97
Rebecca of Sunnybrook Farm '17
Record of a Tenement Gentleman '47
Red Cherry '95
Redwood Curtain '95
Relative Strangers '06
Rent-A-Kid '95
The Rescuers '77▶
The Revolt of Job '84▶
Rikisha-Man '58▶
The Road Home '95
The Road to Life '31
Rose Hill '97
The Royal Tenenbaums '01▶
Sally of the Sawdust '25
Samantha '92
Santa with Muscles '96
Scout's Honor '80
The Sea Serpent '85
Second Best '94▶
The Secret Garden '49▶
The Secret Garden '84
The Secret Garden '87▶
The Secret Garden '93▶
Secrets and Lies '95▶
Shep Comes Home '49
Shooting Fish '98
Sidewalks of London '38▶
A Simple Twist of Fate '94
Sioux City '94
The Sleepy Time Gal '01
Snow Dogs '02
Snow White and the Seven Dwarfs '37▶
Sois Belle et Tais-Toi '58
A Soldier's Daughter Never Cries '98
Spin '04
Station Jim '01
The Story of an African Farm '04
Strange Relations '02
The Stranger Who Looks Like Me '74
Streetwise '84
Stuart Little '99
Sugar Cane Alley '83▶
The Sugarland Express '74▶
Sundays & Cybele '62▶
Superman: The Movie '78▶
Susannah of the Mounties '39
Tarzan Finds a Son '39▶
They Still Call Me Bruce '86
The Thief Lord '06
Three Secrets '50
The Tie That Binds '95
To Each His Own '46▶
Tom Jones '98▶
The Tunnel of Love '58
Twisted '96
Two Alone '34
Up/Down/Fragile '95
Vanity Fair '04
A Very Serious Person '06
Way Back Home '32
Weeping Meadow '04
Welcome to Sarajevo '97▶
Whacked! '02

Where the River Runs Black '86
Which Way Home '90
Who'll Save Our Children? '82▶
Wild Hearts Can't Be Broken '91
The World Accuses '35
Young & Free '78
Young People '40
Yours, Mine & Ours '05

Adultery

A Coeur Joie '67
Angela '05
Asylum '05
Back Street '41
Battle in Heaven '05
Bed and Board '70▶
Before the Devil Knows You're Dead '07▶
Bloom '03
Bread and Tulips '01▶
The Bridges of Madison County '95▶
Brothers '05▶
Chicago '02▶
Closer '04▶
Coastlines '02
Cool and the Crazy '94
Counsellor-at-Law '33▶
Cover '08
Curse of the Golden Flower '06
Dangerous Liaisons '03
Darkness Falls '98
Dead Gorgeous '02
The Decalogue '88▶
Derailed '05
The Devil Wears Prada '06
Diary of a Mad Black Woman '05
Die Mommie Die! '03
Doctor Zhivago '65▶
Doctor Zhivago '03
The Door in the Floor '04▶
Dot the I '03
The Dying Gaul '05▶
Faithless '00▶
Fatal Attraction '87▶
Fracture '07
From the Terrace '60
The Golden Bowl '00
The Good Girl '02▶
Happily Ever After '04
Haunted Highway '05
Head On '04
The Healer '99
Heart '99
The Heart of Me '02
Heart of Stone '01
Heights '04
Hitched '01
Hollywoodland '06
I Think I Love My Wife '07
The Ice Storm '97▶
In My Country '04
In the Mood for Love '00
Jarhead '05
The Killer Must Kill Again '75
La Femme Infidele '69▶
La Mujer de Mi Hermano '06
Lady Chatterley '06▶
Lansdown '01
Lantana '01▶
Le Divorce '03
Leo '02
Lies & Alibis '06
Little Children '06▶
Lord of War '05▶
Loving '70
The Man Who Wasn't There '01▶
Match Point '05▶
Melinda and Melinda '05
Melo '86
The Monkey's Mask '00
Motives '03
My Life Without Me '03
Nathalie '03
Night Life in Reno '31
Nina Takes a Lover '94
No Money Down '97
No Other Woman '33
One Hour Photo '02▶

100 Mile Rule '02
The Other Side of the Bed '03
Out of Time '03
The Painted Veil '06
Petulia '68▶
Pleasure '31
Possession '02
Rain '01
The Reckoning '03▶
Reconstruction '03
Romance & Cigarettes '05
Romulus, My Father '07▶
Say Nothing '01
The Scarlet Letter '34
The Scarlet Letter '73▶
The Scarlet Letter '95
Second Skin '99
The Sentinel '06
The Shooting Party '85▶
Sidewalks of New York '01
Signs & Wonders '00
Six Days, Six Nights '94
Sleep Easy, Hutch Rimes '00
Sleuth '07
Smart Woman '31
Snow Angels '07▶
Someone Behind the Door '71
Sordid Lives '00
Steam: A Turkish Bath '96▶
Suckerfish '99
A Summer Place '59
Sylvia '03
The Taste of Others '00▶
Tempted '01
Therese Raquin '80
3-Way '04
Tick Tock '00▶
Time Regained '99
Town and Country '01
Tristan & Isolde '06
The Two Jakes '90
Undertow '30
Unfaithful '02▶
Unfaithfully Yours '48▶
Unfaithfully Yours '84
The Unfaithfuls '60
The Valet '06
Wah-Wah '05
Waitress '07▶
Waking Up in Reno '02
The Walker '07
We Don't Live Here Anymore '04
Y Tu Mama Tambien '01
Yes '04
Young Adam '03▶

Adventure Drama

see also Action-Adventure; Boom!; Drama

Abandon Ship '57
Ace of Aces '33
Act of Piracy '89
Action in the North Atlantic '43
The Admirable Crichton '57
The Adventures of Frontier Fremont '75
The Adventures of Huck Finn '93▶
The Adventures of Huckleberry Finn '39▶
The Adventures of Huckleberry Finn '78
The Adventures of Milo & Otis '89▶
The Adventures of the Wilderness Family '76
The Adventures of Tom Sawyer '38▶
Air Force '43▶
Air Force One '97▶
Alaska '96
Alexander Nevsky '38▶
Ali Baba and the Forty Thieves '43
All the Rivers Run '84
Allan Quatermain and the Lost City of Gold '86
Alligator Alley '72
Aloha, Bobby and Rose '74

The Amazing Panda Adventure '95
Amazon '90
The Amazons '84
America '24
American Empire '42
American Roulette '88
The American Scream '80s
The American Tiger '89
And I Alone Survived '78
Angels of the City '89
Anzacs: The War Down Under '85▶
Apocalypse Now '79▶
Apocalypto '06▶
Apollo 13 '95▶
Appointment with Crime '45
The Arab Conspiracy '76
Archer's Adventure '85
Arctic Blue '93
Arizona Heat '87
Around the World in 80 Days '56▶
Around the World in 80 Days '89
The Ascent '94
Assassination '87
The Aviator '85
Back in the USSR '92
Backdraft '91
Backlash '86
Bang Rajan '00▶
Barbary Coast '35▶
The Baron '88
Bataan '43
Battle Hell '56
The Battle of El Alamein '68
Battle of the Eagles '79
The Battle of the Japan Sea '70
Battleforce '78
Bear Island '80
Beau Geste '39▶
The Beautiful Country '04
The Beloved Rogue '27▶
Beneath the 12-Mile Reef '53
Benji: Off the Leash! '04
Benji the Hunted '87▶
Beowulf '07▶
Beowulf & Grendel '06
The Berlin Conspiracy '91
Between Heaven and Hell '56▶
Beyond Rangoon '95
Big Bad Mama '74
The Big Push '75
The Big Scam '79
The Big Turnaround '88
Bigfoot: The Unforgettable Encounter '94
Billy Budd '62▶
Black Arrow '48▶
The Black Arrow '84
Black Bikers from Hell '70
Black Moon Rising '86
Blackout '78
Blood and Sand '41▶
Blood Debts '83
Blood Diamond '06
Bloom '03
Blowing Wild '54
Blown Away '94
The Blue and the Gray '82
Blue Fin '78
The Blue Lamp '49▶
Blue Thunder '83
The Bodyguard from Beijing '94
Bomb at 10:10 '67
Bombardier '43
Border Blues '03
Born Wild '95
Botany Bay '53
The Bounty '84
The Bourne Supremacy '04▶
Breakdown '96▶
The Breed '01
Brighty of the Grand Canyon '67
Brotherhood of Death '76
A Bullet Is Waiting '54
Burke & Wills '85
The Butterfly '02▶
By Way of the Stars '92
Cadence '89
California Gold Rush '81

▶ = rated three bones or higher.

Call of the Wild '72
Camel Boy '84
Casablanca Express '89
The Castilian '63
Casualties of War '89
The Cat '66
Catwoman '04
Cellular '04
Chain Reaction '80
Chains of Gold '92
Chain Reaction '96
The Challenge '82
Challenge of a Lifetime '85
The Charge of the Light Brigade '36
The Charge of the Light Brigade '38
Children of the Wild '37
China Gate '57
Chrome Soldiers '92
Clarence, the Cross-eyed Lion '65
Claws '77
Clear and Present Danger '94
The Climb '87
The Coast Patrol '25
Code Name: Emerald '85
Cold Heat '90
Cold Justice '89
Commando Decision '48
Commando Attack '67
Con Air '97
Conspiracy Theory '97
Contagious '96
Coogan's Bluff '68
The Cop & the Girl '86
Cop-Out '91
The Corruptor '99
Corsair '31
The Count of Monte Cristo '12
The Count of Monte Cristo '34
The Count of Monte Cristo '74
The Count of Monte Cristo '99
The Count of Monte Cristo '02
Courage Mountain '89
Courage of Black Beauty '57
Courage of Rin Tin Tin '83
Crimebusters '79
Crimson Romance '34
Crimson Tide '95
Dam Busters '55
Danger Beneath the Sea '02
Dangerous Ground '96
Dangerous Moonlight '41
Dangerous Passage '44
Daring Game '68
Dark Before Dawn '89
Dark Mountain '44
Dark Tide '93
The Darkside '87
The Dawson Patrol '78
The Day Will Dawn '42
Days of Thunder '90
Deadlock '91
Deadlock 2 '94
Deadly Sanctuary '68
Death in the Garden '56
Death in the Night '85
The Death Merchant '91
Death Stalk '74
The Deceivers '88
Deliverance '72
Destination Tokyo '43
Desert Warrior '88
The Destructors '68
Dick Tracy '90
Dick Turpin '25
Die Hard '88
Die Hard 2: Die Harder '90
Die Hard: With a Vengeance '95
A Different Loyalty '04
Dinosaur Island '93
Diplomatic Immunity '91
Dive Bomber '41
Doomsdayer '99
Down to the Sea in Ships '22
Dragon Storm '04
Dragonfly Squadron '54
Duma '05
Dust '85
Each Dawn I Die '39
The Eagle Has Landed '77
East of Borneo '31
Edge of Honor '91

Eight Below '06
84 Charlie MoPic '89
The Elusive Pimpernel '50
The Emerald Forest '85
Enchanted Island '58
Enemy Below '57
Enemy of the State '98
The Enforcer '51
Eraser '96
Escape to Witch Mountain '75
Evel Knievel '72
Executive Decision '96
The Expendables '89
Eye of the Wolf '95
Fangs of the Wild '54
Fantastic Seven '79
Far from Home: The Adventures of Yellow Dog '94
A Far Off Place '93
Farewell to the King '89
The Fencing Master '92
Ferry to Hong Kong '59
55 Days at Peking '63
The Fighting Prince of Donegal '66
Fire Alarm '32
Fire in the Night '85
Firepower '79
Flame of Araby '51
Flame Over India '60
The Flash '90
Flight of the Grey Wolf '76
Flipper '63
Flying Leathernecks '51
Flying Tigers '42
Follow Me '69
For Whom the Bell Tolls '43
Fort Saganne '84
Fortunes of War '94
Forty Thousand Horsemen '41
The Four Feathers '39
F.P. 1 '33
F.P. 1 Doesn't Answer '33
The Four Feathers '78
Free Grass '69
Free Willy '93
Free Willy 2: The Adventure Home '95
Free Willy 3: The Rescue '97
Freelance '71
The Fugitive '93
Fugitive Champion '99
Full Eclipse '93
Fury to Freedom: The Life Story of Raul Ries '85
Future Zone '90
Game for Vultures '86
The Gaucho '27
The Ghost and the Darkness '96
Glory & Honor '98
God's Country '46
The Golden Compass '07
Goldrush: A Real Life Alaskan Adventure '98
Goliath Awaits '81
Gone in 60 Seconds '74
Great Adventure '75
The Great Elephant Escape '95
The Great Escape '63
The Great Escape 2: The Untold Story '88
The Great Locomotive Chase '56
The Great Train Robbery '79
The Green Glove '52
Greystoke: The Legend of Tarzan, Lord of the Apes '84
Grizzly Mountain '97
Guadalcanal Diary '43
The Guardian '00
Gun Cargo '49
Gunblast '74
Gunga Din '39
The Gunrunner '84
Hackers '95
The Halls of Montezuma '50
Hamlet '90
Hangfire '91
Hard Knocks '80

Harley '90
Harry Potter and the Goblet of Fire '05
Harry Potter and the Prisoner of Azkaban '04
Hawk and Castile '67
The Heartbreak Kid '07
Heel to the Pacific '69
Hell River '75
Hell Squad '58
Hell Squad '85
Hell to Eternity '60
Hellcats of the Navy '57
Hellfighters '68
Hell's Angels '30
Hell's Brigade: The Final Assault '80
Here Come the Littles: The Movie '85
The Heroes of Desert Storm '91
Heroes Three '84
Hidalgo '04
Himalaya '99
Himatsuri '85
Hired to Kill '73
Hiroshima: Out of the Ashes '90
Hitt '73
Homeward Bound: The Incredible Journey '93
Horatio Hornblower '99
Horatio Hornblower: The Adventure Continues '01
Hostile Waters '97
Huck and the King of Hearts '93
The Hunt for Red October '90
Hurricane Smith '92
Hustler Squad '76
Immortal Sergeant '43
In Enemy Hands '04
In Harm's Way '65
In Love and War '91
In Search of a Golden Sky '84
In Which We Serve '43
The Indian Tomb '59
Indiana Jones and the Kingdom of the Crystal Skull '08
Indiana Jones and the Last Crusade '89
Indiana Jones and the Temple of Doom '84
Inferno in Paradise '88
Into Thin Air: Death on Everest '97
The Intruder '04
The Iron Mask '29
Iron Will '93
Island at the Top of the World '74
Island Trader '71
Islands '87
Isle of Forgotten Sins '43
Istanbul '90
It Rained All Night the Day I Left '97
Jack London's The Call of the Wild '97
JAG '95
Jaguar '56
Jamaica Inn '39
Jamaica Inn '82
Jason and the Argonauts '00
Jaws of Justice '33
Jenny's War '85
Jet Pilot '57
Joey '98
Johnny Mnemonic '95
The Journey of Natty Gann '85
Journey to the Center of the Earth '88
Joy Ride to Nowhere '78
Jungle '52
Jungle Goddess '49
Juggernaut '74
Jungle Master '93
Jurassic Park '93
Jurassic Park 3 '01
Kamikaze '89 '83
The Karate Kid '84
The Karate Kid: Part 2 '86

The Karate Kid: Part 3 '89
Kashmir Run '69
Kavik the Wolf Dog '80
The Keeper: The Legend of Omar Khayyam '05
Keeping Track '86
Kid Colter '85
Kidnapped '60
Kidnapped '05
Killer Elite '75
The Killer '89
Killer Instinct '92
King Arthur '04
King of New York '90
King of the Avenger '65
King Solomon's Mines '50
King Solomon's Mines '85
King Solomon's Treasure '76
Kingfisher Caper '76
Kings of the Sun '63
Kiss and Kill '68
Klondike Fever '79
Knives of the Avenger '65
Kojiro '67
K2: The Ultimate High '92
La Guerre Est Finie '66
Lady Avenger '89
Lady Cocoa '75
Landslide '92
Lassie '94
Lassie: Adventures of Neeka '68
Lassie, Come Home '43
Lassie: Well of Love '70
Lassie '84
The Last Hunter '80
Last Man Standing '96
The Last of the Finest '90
The Last of the Mohicans '32
The Last of the Mohicans '36
The Last of the Mohicans '92
The Last Place on Earth '85
The Last Riders '90
The Last Season '87
The Legend of Billie Jean '85
The Legend of Cryin' Ryan '98
The Legend of Johnny Lingo '03
Legend of Lobo '62
The Legend of Sea Wolf '75
The Legend of the Sea Wolf '58
Lethal Pursuit '88
Lethal Weapon 2 '89
Liana, Jungle Goddess '56
Life & Times of Grizzly Adams '74
The Lion Man '36
Lion of the Desert '81
The Live Wire '34
Loaded Guns '75
Lockdown '90
Lost '83
Lost '86
The Lost World: Jurassic Park 2 '97
Lost Zeppelin '29
Macao '52
The Mad Bomber '72
Made for Love '26
Magnificent Adventurer '63
The Man from Beyond '22
The Man in the Iron Mask '39
The Man in the Iron Mask '77
The Man in the Iron Mask '97
The Man of Legend '71
Manhunt for Claude Dallas '86
The Mask of Zorro '98
Massacre in Dinosaur Valley '85
The Master of Ballantrae '53
The McConnell Story '55
Memphis Belle '90
Men in War '57
Men of Steel '88
Men of the Sword '85
Merlin and the Sword '85
Miami Vice '84
Midnight Crossing '87
Midway '76
Milo & Otis '89
MirrorMask '05
Ms. 45 '81

Mission Phantom '79
Mr. Kingstreet's War '71
Moby Dick '56
Moby Dick '98
Money Movers '78
Money Train '95
The Moon-Spinners '64
Moran of the Lady Letty '22
Mountain Family Robinson '79
Mountain of the Cannibal God '79
Moving Target '88
Murder Without Motive '92
The Mutiny of the Elsinore Game '81
Mutiny on the Blackhawk '39
My Dog Shep '46
Naked Jungle '54
The Navy Comes Through '42
Ned Kelly '03
The Negotiator '98
Night Crossing '81
The Night Train to Kathmandu '88
Nightstick '87
No Greater Love '43
No More Women '34
No Time to Die '84
Noon Sunday '75
Norseman '78
The North Star '43
Northern Pursuit '43
Northwest Passage '40
Number One with a Bullet '87
Objective, Burma! '45
Obsessed '88
Oceans of Fire '86
The Odyssey '97
Omega Syndrome '87
On Wings of Eagles '86
One Armed Executioner '80
One Man Force '89
One Minute to Zero '52
One of Our Aircraft Is Missing '41
One That Got Away '57
Operation Cross Eagles '69
Operation Hayitt '50
Operation Julie '85
Operation 'Nam '85
Operation Thunderbolt '77
Operation Warzone '89
Opposing Force '87
Oubliette '14
Outbreak '94
Outlaw Blues '77
Outlaw Force '87
The Package '89
Paco '75
Palais Royale '88
Palindromes '04
Papillon '73
Passenger 57 '92
Passion '82
The Patriot '86
Patriot Games '92
Pathfinder '07
Payoff '91
The Peacemaker '97
Penitentiary '79
Penitentiary 2 '82
Penitentiary 3 '87
The Perils of Gwendoline '84
Permission To Kill '75
The Phantom '96
Pharaoh '66
Pirates of the High Seas '50
Place in Hell '69
Platoon '86
Platoon Leader '87
Plunder Road '57
Plunge Into Darkness '77
Policewomen '73
Pork Chop Hill '59
Portrait of a Hitman '77
Pray for the Wildcats '74
The Presidio '88
Prime Target '91

Prince Brat and the Whipping Boy '95
Private Investigations '87
PT 109 '63
Pursuit of the Graf Spee '57
Queen's Messenger II '01
Radio Patrol '37
Raid on Entebbe '77
Raid on Rommel '71
Raiders of the Lost Ark '81
Rainbow Warrior '94
Ran '85
Raw Courage '84
The Real Glory '39
Reap the Wild Wind '42
Red Barry '38
Red Flag: The Ultimate Game '81
Remedy '05
Renegades '89
The Replacement Killers '98
Report to the Commissioner '74
The Rescue '88
Retreat, Hell! '52
Revelation '00
Revenge '90
Riot in Cell Block 11 '54
The River Pirates '88
The River Wild '94
Robbery '67
Robbery '85
Robin Hood: Prince of Thieves '91
RoboCop '87
Ronin '98
Rudyard Kipling's The Jungle Book '42
Runaway Train '85
Running Free '00
Running out of Time '99
The Saint '97
St. Valentine's Day Massacre '67
San Demetrio, London '47
Sands of Iwo Jima '49
The Sand Pebbles '66
Sardinia Kidnapped '75
Savage Hunger '84
Savage Justice '88
Savage Sam '63
Savage Streets '83
Scaramouche '52
The Scarlet Car '17
Scarlet Spear '54
Scorchy '76
Scott of the Antarctic '48
Sea Chase '55
Sea Devils '31
Sea Devils '53
Sea Gypsies '78
The Sea Hawk '40
The Sea Shall Not Have Them '55
Sea Wolves '81
Search and Destroy '81
Secret of Stamboul '36
Secret Weapon '90
Self-Defense '83
Sell Out '76
Sergeant York '41
Seven Alone '75
Sex Crimes '92
Shadow Force '92
The Shadow '92
Shame '87
Shame '92
Shark! '68
She '35
She Came to the Valley '77
Shell Shock '63
Shogun Assassin '80
Shooting Stars '85
Shout at the Devil '76
The Siege '98
The Siege of Firebase Gloria '89
The Silent Enemy '58
Silent Raiders '54
Silk '86
The Silver Stallion: King of the Wild Zombies '93
Sinai Commandos '68
The Sinister Urge '60
Sink the Bismarck '60
Sins of Rome '54
Six Pack '82

▶ = rated three bones or higher

Adventure

Sky Riders '76
Slow Moves '84
Smugglers '75
The Sniper '78
Sniper '92
Sniper 2 '02
Sniper 3 '04
Sno-Line '85
The Snow Walker '03
Sodom and Gomorrah '62
Soldier of Fortune '55
Sonny Boy '87
Sorcerer '77
Soul Vengeance '75
Souls at Sea '37
South of Hell Mountain '70
Spawn of the North '38
Special Forces '68
The Specialist '94
Speed '94
Spider-Man 2 '04
Spin '04
Spirit of the Eagle '90
The Spring '89
Squanto: A Warrior's Tale '94
Stanley and Livingstone '39
Star Trek: Insurrection '98
The Starfighters '63
Steamboy '05
The Steel Claw '61
The Steel Helmet '51
Steele Justice '87
Steele's Law '91
The Sting '73
The Stone Killer '73
Strange Days '95
Street Crimes '92
Street War '76
Streets of Fire '84
Strike Force '75
Striker '88
Striker's Mountain '87
Sub Down '97
Submarine Seahawk '59
Sudden Death '95
Sundown '41
Sunset Grill '92
Sunset Heat '92
Surabaya Conspiracy '75
Surfacing '84
Survival Run '80
The Swiss Family Robinson '60
Switchback '97
The Taking of Pelham One Two Three '74
Tank '83
Taps '81
Target of Opportunity '04
The Ten Million Dollar Getaway '91
Terminal Error '02
Thelma & Louise '91
They Were Expendable '45
Thirty-Six Hours of Hell '77
Those Calloways '65
The 317th Platoon '16
The Three Musketeers '16
The Three Musketeers '21
Three the Hard Way '74
Throw Down '00
Thunderbirds '04
Thunderground '89
Tides of War '90
Tiger Fangs '43
A Tiger Walks '64
Tim Tyler's Luck '37
Top Gun '86
Tour of Duty '87
Toy Soldiers '91
The Transporter '02
Tribulation '00
Triple Cross '67
Trouble in Paradise '88
True Blood '89
True Heart '97
Truth or Die '86
Turnaround '87
Twisted Justice '89
Two Brothers '04
Two Years before the Mast '46
Unconquered '47
Underworld '27
U.S. Marshals '98

U.S. Seals '98
Up Periscope '59
Valley of Wanted Men '35
The Vector File '98
Violent Breed '83
Von Ryan's Express '65
Wake Island '42
A Walk in the Sun '46
Walking Back '26
A Waltz Through the Hills '88
The War Boy '85
Warkill '65
The Warrior '01
Warriors '02
Warriors of Heaven and Earth '03
We Dive at Dawn '43
Weekend War '88
What a Way to Die '70
Wheel of Fortune '41
Where the Spirit Lives '89
White Fire '53
White Fury '90
White Hot '88
White Squall '96
The White Tower '50
White Wolves 2: Legend of the Wild '94
The Wicked Lady '83
The Wild Pair '87
Wild Riders '71
Wild Thing '87
Winning '69
Wooden Horse '50
The World in His Arms '52
World War III '86
The Year of Living Dangerously '82
Yellowneck '55
Young & Free '78
A Young Connecticut Yankee in King Arthur's Court '95
Young Warlord '75
Young Warriors '83
Zafarinas '94
Zulu '64
Zulu Dawn '79

Advertising

see also Front Page; Mass Media

Advertising Rules! '01
The Agency '81
Beauty School '93
Beer '85
Bliss '85
Bounce '00
C.O.D. '83
Crazy People '90
Derailed '05
DROP Squad '94
Eros '04
A Fool and His Money '88
The Girl Can't Help It '56
Giving It Up '99
Her Husband's Affairs '47
The Horse in the Gray Flannel Suit '68
How to Get Ahead in Advertising '89
How to Lose a Guy in 10 Days '03
The Hucksters '47
I Married a Woman '56
Image of Passion '86
In Good Company '04
Kids in the Hall: Brain Candy '96
Kramer vs. Kramer '79
Lost in America '85
Lover Come Back '61
Loving '70
The Man in the Gray Flannel Suit '56
Mr. Blandings Builds His Dream House '48
Mr. Mom '83
Mr. Write '92
No Marriage Ties '33
Nothing in Common '86
Nothing to Lose '96
One Night Stand '97
Perfect Stranger '07

Picture Perfect '96
Pray for the Wildcats '74
Pursuit of Happiness '01
Putney Swope '69
Renaissance Man '94
Revolution 9 '01
Santa Claus: The Movie '85
Son of the Mask '05
Surviving Christmas '04
Sweet November '01
Ten Speed '76
Thanks for Everything '38
Think Dirty '70
The Thrill of It All! '63
Thunder in the City '37
Transformers: The Movie '86
Waikiki Wedding '37
What Women Want '00
White Mile '94
Will Success Spoil Rock Hunter? '57

Africa

see also Apartheid

Abdulla the Great '56
Ace Ventura: When Nature Calls '95
The Adventurers '51
Africa Screams '49
An African Dream '90
African Journey '89
The African Queen '51
African Rage '78
The Air Up There '94
Albino '76
Algiers '38
Allan Quatermain and the Lost City of Gold '86
Amin: The Rise and Fall '82
Amistad '97
And Now Ladies and Gentlemen '02
The Ascent '94
Babel '06
Bamako '06
Beyond Borders '03
Black Force '75
Black Hawk Down '01
Black Jesus '68
Black Terrorist '85
Blood Diamond '06
Boesman & Lena '00
Bophal '93
Born Wild '95
The Boys of Baraka '05
The Bride & the Beast '58
The Bushbaby '70
Call Me Bwana '63
Cape of Good Hope '04
Changing Times '04
Cheetah '89
Chocolat '88
City of Blood '88
The Claw '27
Cobra Verde '88
The Color of Freedom '07
Coming to America '88
Congo '95
The Constant Gardener '05
Curious George '06
Curse 3: Blood Sacrifice '90
Dangerous Ground '97
Darfur Now '07
Dark of the Sun '68
Darkest Africa '36
Darwin's Nightmare '04
The Desert Fox '51
Dingaka '65
The Dogs of War '81
Dominion: Prequel to the Exorcist '05
A Dry White Season '89
Duma '05
East of Kilimanjaro '57
The Egyptian '54
An Elephant Called Slowly '69
Ernest Goes to Africa '97
Eyes of a Witness '94
Faces of Women '85
A Far Off Place '93
The Fighting Rats of Tobruk '44
Firefall '94
Five Weeks in a Balloon '62

The Flame Trees of Thika '81
Fort Saganne '84
The Four Feathers '02
Friends '95
Ganja and Hess '73
The Garden of Allah '36
George of the Jungle '97
The Ghost and the Darkness '96
God Grew Tired of Us '06
The Gods Must Be Crazy '84
The Gods Must Be Crazy 2 '89
The Golden Salamander '51
A Good Man in Africa '94
Gorillas in the Mist '88
The Great Elephant Escape '95
Greystoke: The Legend of Tarzan, Lord of the Apes '84
Guns at Batasi '64
Half-Caste '04
Hatari! '62
Heat of the Sun '99
Hideous Kinky '99
Hollow City '04
Hotel Rwanda '04
I Dreamed of Africa '00
In Desert and Wilderness '73
In My Country '04
In the Army Now '94
In the Shadow of Kilimanjaro '86
Inside '96
It Rained All Night the Day I Left '78
Ivory Hunters '90
Jaguar '56
Jericho '38
Jit '94
The Jewel of the Nile '85
Jungle Drums of Africa '53
Jungle Master '56
The Key to Rebecca '85
Killers '88
King Kong '33
King Solomon's Mines '37
King Solomon's Mines '50
King Solomon's Mines '85
The Kitchen Toto '87
La Vie Est Belle '87
The Last Adventure '67
The Last King of Scotland '06
The Last Safari '67
The League of Extraordinary Gentlemen '03
The Leopard Son '96
The Light in the Jungle '91
The Lion King 1 1/2 '04
The Lion King: Simba's Pride '98
The Lion of Africa '87
The Lost Patrol '34
The Lost World '92
Lumumba '01
Made for Love '26
Mama Africa '02
Mandela '87
Mandela and de Klerk '97
Manhattan Baby '82
Manhunt in the African Jungles '43
March or Die '77
The Mark of the Hawk '57
Master Harold and the Boys '84
Men of Two Worlds '46
Mercenary Fighters '88
Mighty Joe Young '49
Mighty Joe Young '98
Mines of Kilimanjaro '87
Mister Johnson '91
Mogambo '53
Monster from Green Hell '58
Moolaade '04
Mountains of the Moon '90
My African Adventure '88
Nairobi Affair '88

The Naked Prey '66
Night of the Sorcerers '70
Nine Men '43
Nowhere in Africa '02
Oddball Hall '91
One Step to Hell '67
Operation: Delta Force '97
Options '88
Out of Africa '85
Over Indulgence '87
Overseas: Three Women with Man Trouble '90
The Passenger '75
Pepe Le Moko '37
Place of Weeping '86
Primeval '07
Quartier Mozart '92
Red Scorpion '89
Return to Africa '89
Rhodes '36
Rhodes '97
Running Wild '99
Sahara '05
Sanders of the River '35
Sarafina! '92
Satan's Harvest '65
Secret Obsession '88
Shaft in Africa '73
Shaka Zulu '83
Shake Hands With the Devil: The Journey of Roméo Dallaire '04
The Sheltering Sky '90
Shooting Dogs '05
Simba '55
Skeleton Coast '89
The Snows of Kilimanjaro '52
So This Is Africa '33
Something of Value '57
Song of Freedom '36
Stander '03
The Story of an African Farm '04
Sundown '41
Tarzan '04
Tarzan 99
Tarzan and the Lost City '98
Tears of the Sun '03
Tilai '90
Time to Kill '89
To Walk with Lions '99
Tobruk '66
Touki Bouki '73
Trader Horn '31
The Treasure of Bengal '53
Tsotsi '05
Tuxedo Warrior '82
Wah-Wah '05
Warriors from Hell '90
We Are the Children '87
Wend Kuuni '82
When We Were Kings '96
White Cargo '42
White Hunter, Black Heart '90
White Mischief '88
The Wild '06
Wild Geese '78
The Wild Thornberrys Movie '02
A World Apart '88
Yaaba '89
Yankee Zulu '95
Zulu '64
Zulu Dawn '79

African America

see also New Black Cinema

Aaron Loves Angela '75
Above the Rim '94
The Affair '95
Akeelah and the Bee '06
Ali '01
All About the Benjamins '02
All About You '01
Always Outnumbered '98
American Gangster '07
American's Dream '95
And Then Came Love '07
The Angel Levine '70
Anne Rice's The Feast of All Saints '01
Antwone Fisher '02
Ashes and Embers '82

Assault at West Point: The Court-Martial of Johnson Whittaker '94
The Autobiography of Miss Jane Pittman '74
Baadasssss! '03
Baby Boy '01
Bamboozled '00
B.A.P.'s '97
Barbershop '02
Barbershop 2: Back in Business '04
Beauty Shop '05
Bebe's Kids '92
Beloved '98
The Best Man '99
Better Dayz '02
Beware '46
The Big Dis '89
Biker Boyz '03
Bird '88
Black and White '99
Black Brigade '69
Black Godfather '74
The Black King '32
Black Knight '01
Black Like Me '64
Black Sister's Revenge '76
Blade '98
Blind Faith '98
Blood Brothers '97
Blue Collar '78
Boardinghouse Blues '48
Body and Soul '24
Boesman & Lena '00
Boycott '02
The Boys of Baraka '05
Boyz N the Hood '91
The Breaks '01
Bringing Down the House '03
Broken Strings '40
Bronze Buckaroo '39
The Brother from Another Planet '84
Brother John '70
Brother to Brother '04
The Brothers '01
Brown Sugar '02
Bucktown '75
Buffalo Soldiers '97
Bulworth '98
Cabin in the Sky '43
Carmen: A Hip Hopera '01
Carmen Jones '54
Catfish in Black Bean Sauce '00
Caught Up '98
CB4: The Movie '93
Charlotte Forten's Mission: Experiment in Freedom '85
The Chateau '01
The Cherokee Kid '96
Christmas at Water's Edge '04
Chuck Berry: Hail! Hail! Rock 'n' Roll '87
Civil Brand '02
Class Act '91
Clockers '95
Code Name: The Cleaner '07
The Color of Courage '98
Color of Justice '97
The Color Purple '85
Coming to America '88
Conrack '74
Conviction '02
Cooley High '75
Cora Unashamed '00
The Corner '07
Corrupt '99
Cosmic Slop '94
Cotton Comes to Harlem '70
The Courage to Love '00
The Court Martial of Jackie Robinson '90
Cover '08
Crooklyn '94
Crossover '06
Crown Heights '02
Daddy's Little Girls '07
Dancing in September '00

♪ = rated three bones or higher

Dangerous Evidence: The Lori Jackson Story '99▶
Darktown Strutters '74
Daughters of the Dust '91▶
Dave Chappelle's Block Party '06▶
Dead Heist '07
Dead Presidents '95
The Defiant Ones '58
Deliver Us from Eva '03
Devil in a Blue Dress '95▶
The Devil's Daughter '39
Diary of a Mad Black Woman '05
Dirty Gertie from Harlem U.S.A. '46
Dirty Laundry '07
Disappearing Acts '00
Disorderlies '87
Divided We Stand '00
Do the Right Thing '89▶
Don't Be a Menace to South Central While Drinking Your Juice in the Hood '95
Don't Look Back: The Story of Leroy "Satchel" Paige '81
Double Deal '39
Double Take '01
Down to Earth '01
A Dream for Christmas '73▶
Dreamgirls '06▶
DROP Squad '94
Drumline '02▶
Drums O'Voodoo '34
Dutchman '67▶
Dynamite Chicken '71
The Ernest Green Story '93
Eubie! '82▶
Eve's Bayou '97▶
A Family Thing '96▶
Far from Heaven '02▶
Fat Albert '04
Father of Lies '07
Fear of a Black Hat '94
Final Comedown '72
Final Exam '08
Finding Buck McHenry '00
Firehouse '87
The Five Heartbeats '91▶
Fly by Night '93
Foolish '99
For Real '02
For Us, the Living '88▶
48 Hrs. '82▶
Foxy Brown '74
Free of Eden '98
Freedom Song '00▶
Fresh '94
Friday '95
Friday After Next '02▶
G '02
Gang in Blue '96
Get on the Bus '96▶
Get Rich or Die Tryin' '05
Ghetto Dawg '02
Ghetto Dawg 2: Out of the Pits '05
Ghosts of Mississippi '96▶
Girl from Chicago '32
Glory '89▶
Glory & Honor '98
Glory Road '06
Go Down Death '41
Go Tell It on the Mountain '84
The Golden Child '86
A Good Day to Die '95
Good Fences '03
The Gospel '05▶
Graffiti Bridge '90
The Great Debaters '07▶
Greased Lightning '77
The Great White Hope '70
The Greatest '77
The Green Mile '99
Green Pastures '36▶
Guess Who's Coming to Dinner '67▶
Guilty by Association '03
The Guy from Harlem '77
Half Nelson '06▶
Half Slave, Half Free '85
Hallelujah! '29▶

Hangin' with the Homeboys '91▶
Hank Aaron: Chasing the Dream '95▶
Hard Lessons '86
Harlem Nights '89
Harlem on the Prairie '38
Hav Plenty '97▶
Having Our Say: The Delany Sisters' First 100 Years '99
He Got Game '98
Heavens Fall '06
Hendrix '00
A Hero Ain't Nothin' but a Sandwich '78
Hi-De-Ho '35
Higher Learning '94
The Hit '06
Hollywood Shuffle '87
Home of the Brave '49▶
Honeydripper '07
Hoop Dreams '94▶
A House Divided '00
House Party '90▶
House Party 2: The Pajama Jam '91
House Party 3 '94
How High '01
How I Spent My Summer Vacation '97
How Stella Got Her Groove Back '98
How to Eat Your Watermelon in White Company (and Enjoy It) '05▶
How U Like Me Now? '92▶
The Hurricane '99▶
Hustle & Flow '05▶
I Accidentally Domed Your Son '04
I Got the Hook-Up '98
I Know Why the Caged Bird Sings '79▶
The Inkwell '94
Introducing Dorothy Dandridge '99▶
Intruder in the Dust '49▶
The Jackie Robinson Story '50▶
I'm Gonna Git You Sucka '88▶
Imitation of Life '34▶
Imitation of Life '59▶
In His Father's Shoes '97
In the Heat of the Night '67▶
I Think I Love My Wife '07
Identity Crisis '90
Idlewild '06
Jason's Lyric '94
Jasper, Texas '03
J.D.'s Revenge '76
The Jesse Owens Story '84
Jo Jo Dancer, Your Life Is Calling '86
Joe and Max '02▶
The Joe Louis Story '53
Joe's Bed-Stuy Barbershop: We Cut Heads '83
Joey Breaker '93▶
Johnny B. '00
The Josephine Baker Story '90▶
Juice '92
Juke Joint '47
Jump In! '07
Junior's Groove '97
Just Another Girl on the I.R.T. '93
Kansas City '95▶
Keep Punching '39
The Keeper '96
Killer Diller '48
Killer of Sheep '77▶
Killing Floor '85
King '78▶
Kingdom Come '01
The Klansman '74
Krush Groove '85
Lady Sings the Blues '72
The Last Dragon '85
Last Holiday '06▶
Laurel Avenue '93

Lean on Me '89▶
The Learning Tree '69
A Lesson Before Dying '99▶
Let's Do It Again '75
Liberty Heights '99
Life '99▶
Life Support '07▶
Lift '01
Lilies of the Field '63▶
Lily in Winter '94
Little John '02
Little Richard '00
Livin' for Love: The Natalie Cole Story '00
The Long Walk Home '89▶
Look Out Sister! '48▶
The Loretta Claiborne Story '00
Losing Isaiah '94▶
Lost Boundaries '49
The Lost Man '69
Lotto Land '95
Love Beat the Hell Outta Me '00
ove Don't Cost a Thing '03
Love Goggles '99
Love Jones '96▶
Love Song '00
Love Songs '99
Love Your Mama '89
A Low Down Dirty Shame '94
Lying Lips '39
Machine Gun Blues '95
Mahogany '75
Malcolm X '92▶
Mama, There's a Man in Your Bed '89▶
A Man Called Adam '66
Man in the Mirror: The Michael Jackson Story '04
Mandela and de Klerk '97
Manderlay '05
Mandela's Family Reunion '06
Mama Flora's Family '98
Menace II Society '93▶
Miracle in Harlem '48
Miss Evers' Boys '97
Mississippi Masala '92▶
Mississippi Burning '88▶
Mixing Nia '98
Mo' Better Blues '90
Mo' Money '92
Monster's Ball '01▶
Moon over Harlem '39
Murda Muzik '03
The Murder of Stephen Lawrence '99▶
Murder on Lenox Avenue '41
Ms. Scrooge '97
Mr. & Mrs. Loving '96▶
Mister Johnson '91▶
Mutiny '99
My Brother '06
My Brother '04
Native Son '51
Native Son '86
New Jersey Drive '95
New Jack City '91
Next Friday '00
Nightjohn '96▶
No Time for Romance '48
No Way Back '74
No Way Out '50
Nora's Hair Salon '04
Nora's Hair Salon 2: A Cut Above '08
Norbit '07
Nothing but a Man '64
The Old Settler '01
Once Upon a Time... When We Were Colored '95▶
One False Move '91▶
Original Gangstas '96
Othello '01▶
The Other Brother '02
Our Song '01▶
Out of Sync '95
Paid in Full '02
Panther '95▶
Parallel Sons '95
Paris Is Burning '91▶
Passing Glory '99
Pastime '91▶
A Patch of Blue '65▶
Paul Robeson '79
Penitentiary '79

The Perfect Holiday '07
Perfume '91
Personals '00
Phat Beach '96
Phat Girlz '06
The Piano Lesson '94▶
Pinky '49▶
Poetic Justice '93
Pootie Tang '01
The Preacher's Wife '96
Preaching to the Choir '05
Pride '07
The Proud Family Movie '05
Purlie Victorious '63
Purp e Rain '84
The Pursuit of Happyness '06▶
Putney Swope '69▶
Quarter Mozart '92
Quiet Fire '91
Race '99
Race to Freedom: The Story of the Underground Railroad '94▶
Radio '03
A Rage in Harlem '91▶
A Raisin in the Sun '61▶
A Raisin in the Sun '08
Raising the Heights '97
Rappin' '85
The Reading Room '05
Rebound: The Legend of Earl "The Goat" Manigault '96
The Red Sneakers '01
Return of Superfly '90
Rhapsody '01
Ricochet '91▶
Ride '98
The River Niger '76
Rockwell: A Legend of the Wild West '93
Roll Bounce '05▶
Roll of Thunder, Hear My Cry '78
Romeo Must Die '00
Roots '77▶
Roots: The Gift '88
Roots: The Next Generation '79▶
The Rosa Parks Story '02
Rosewood '96▶
Ruby Bridges '98
Rude '96
The Salon '05
Scar of Shame '27
School Daze '88▶
Selma, Lord, Selma '99
Separate but Equal '91▶
Sepia Cinderella '47
Sergeant Rutledge '60▶
Set It Off '96
Seventeen Again '00
The '70s '00
Shadows '60▶
Shaft '71▶
Shaft '00▶
Shaft's Big Score '72
Shanty Tramp '67
She Hate Me '04
Sheba, Baby '75
She's Gotta Have It '86▶
The Show '95
The Simple Life of Noah Dearborn '99
A Simple Promise '07
Six Degrees of Separation '93
The '60s '99
Slam '98
Small Time '91
Snow Dogs '02
A Soldier's Story '84▶
Something New '06
Song of Freedom '36
Sophisticated Gents '81
Soul Food '97▶
Soul of the Game '96▶
Soul Plane '04
Soul Survivor '75
Soul Vengeance '75
Sounder '72▶
South Central '92
Sparkle '76
Spark '98
Sprung '96
Stomp the Yard '07
Straight out of Brooklyn '91

Strange Fruit '04
Strange Justice: The Clarence Thomas and Anita Hill Story '99
A Stranger in the Kingdom '98
Strapped '93
Sudie & Simpson '90▶
Sugar Hill '94
Summer's End '99
Sun Ra & His Intergalactic Solar Arkestra: Space Is the Place '74
Superfly '72▶
Superfly T.N.T. '73
Sweet Love, Bitter '67
Sweet Sweetback's Baadasssss Song '71▶
Tales from the Hood '95
Talk to Me '07
Tap '89
Tar '96
The Temptations '98
The Tenants '05
They Call Me Sir '00
Thicker than Water '99
A Thin Line Between Love and Hate '96
30 Years to Life '01
This Christmas '07▶
Three Strikes '00
The Tiger Woods Story '98
A Time to Kill '96▶
To Sir, with Love '67▶
To Sleep with Anger '90▶
Tougher Than Leather '88
Trippin' '99
Truck Turner '74
Turn It Up '00
The Tuskegee Airmen '95▶
Two Can Play That Game '01
Tyler Perry's Meet the Browns '08
Tyler Perry's Why Did I Get Married? '07
Tyson '95
Uncle Tom's Cabin '14
Uncle Tom's Cabin '69
Uncle Tom's Cabin '87
Undercover Brother '02
Undisputed '02
The Untold Story of Emmett Louis Till '05▶
Up Against the Eight Ball '04
Uptown Angel '90
Waist Deep '06
Waiting to Exhale '95▶
The Walking Dead '94
The Wash '01
Watermelon Man '70▶
The Watermelon Woman '97
Way Down South '39
Welcome Home Roscoe Jenkins '08
What About Your Friends: Weekend Getaway '02
What's Love Got to Do with It? '93
When We Were Kings '96▶
White Chicks '04
White Man's Burden '95
White Men Can't Jump '92▶
Whitewash: The Clarence Brandley Story '02
Who Made the Potato Salad? '05
Who's Your Caddy? '07
The Wiz '78
Woman, Thou Art Loosed '04
The Women of Brewster Place '89▶
The Wood '99
Words by Heart '84
You Got Served '04
You Must Remember This '92
You So Crazy '94
Zebrahead '92
Zooman '95
Zora Is My Name! '90

AIDS
see also *Disease of the Week*
Alive and Kicking '96
All About My Mother '99▶
Amazing Grace '92
Angels in America '03▶
As Is '85
Because of You '95
Before Night Falls '00▶
Behind the Red Door '02
Blue '93
Boys on the Side '94
Close My Eyes '91
Conspiracy of Silence '03
The Constant Gardener '05▶
The Cure '95
Darwin's Nightmare '04
An Early Frost '85▶
The Event '03
Forrest Gump '94▶
Gia '98
Green Plaid Shirt '96
Heaven's a Drag '94
It's My Party '95
Jeanne and the Perfect Guy '98
Jeffrey '95
Joey Breaker '93▶
Kids '95
Les Nuits Fauves '92▶
Life '95
Life Support '07▶
Loggerheads '05▶
Longtime Companion '90▶
Love! Valour! Compassion! '97▶
The Man I Love '97
Men in Love '90
A Mother's Prayer '95
My Own Country '98
No One Sleeps '71
One Night Stand '97▶
Our Sons '91
Parting Glances '86▶
The Perfect Son '00
Peter's Friends '92
Philadelphia '93▶
A Place for Annie '94
Playing by Heart '98
Postcards from America '95
Remembering the Cosmos Flower '99
Rent '05▶
A River Made to Drown In '97
Sweet Jane '98
This Girl's Life '03
The Trip '02
The 24th Day '04
The Velocity of Gary '98
Via Appia '92
The Visit '00▶
A Year Without Love '05
Zero Patience '94

Air Disasters
see also Airborne; Disaster Flicks; Sea Disasters
Air Force One '97▶
Airport '70▶
Airport '75 '75
Airport '77 '77
The Assassination of Richard Nixon '05
Bounce '00
Broken Arrow '95
The Buddy Holly Story '78▶
Cast Away '00▶
Con Air '97▶
The Concorde: Airport '79 '79
The Crash of Flight 401 '78

▶ = rated three bones or higher

Air

Crocodile 2: Death Swamp '01
Die Hard 2: Die Harder '90▲
Escape from Wildcat Canyon '99
Executive Decision '96
Extreme Limits '01
Fearless '93▲
Fire and Rain '89
Flight of the Living Dead: Outbreak on a Plane '07
Flight of the Phoenix '04
Flight to Fury '66
The Forgotten '04
Get Shorty '95▲
The Great Plane Robbery '40
Ground Control '98
Heaven's Prisoners '95
Hero '92▲
The High and the Mighty '54▲
The Hindenburg '75
Into the Fire '05
Island in the Sky '53▲
Jet Over the Atlantic '59
Jurassic Park 3 '01
Killing Moon '00
Madam '30
Mercy Mission '93
Nowhere to Land '00
Operation Intercept '95
Ordeal in the Arctic '93
Panic in the Skies '96
The Pilot's Wife '01
Restless Spirits '99
Snakes on a Plane '06
Sole Survivor '84
Soul Plane '04
Submerged '00
Subterfuge '98
Survivor '80
Tailspin: Behind the Korean Airline Tragedy '89
A Thousand Heroes '92
The Ticket '97
Tragedy of Flight 103: The Inside Story '91▲
Turbulence '96
Turbulence 2: Fear of Flying '99
Turbulence 3: Heavy Metal '00
United 93 '06▲
U.S. Marshals '98
We Are Marshall '06
With a Song in My Heart '52▲
Zero Hour! '57

Airborne

see also Air Disasters
Above and Beyond '53▲
Ace Drummond '36
Ace of Aces '33
Aces: Iron Eagle 3 '92
Active Stealth '99
Adventures of Smilin' Jack '43
Afterburn '92▲
Air America '90
Air Force '43▲
Air Force One '97▲
Air Hawk '84
Air Rage '01
Airborne '98
Airboss '97
Airplane! '80▲
Airplane 2: The Sequel '82
Airport '70▲
Airport '75 '75
Airport '77 '77
Always '89
Amelia Earhart: The Final Flight '94
And I Alone Survived '78
Angels One Five '54
Attack Squadron '63
The Aviator '85
Bail Out at 43,000 '57
Battle of Britain '69
Battle of the Eagles '79
Beyond the Time Barrier '60
Biggles '85
Birds of Prey '72
Black Box Affair '66
Black Thunder '98

The Blue Max '66
Blue Thunder '83
Blue Tornado '90
Boeing Boeing '65
Bombardier '43
Brewster McCloud '70▲
Bulldog Drummond at Bay '37
Bulletproof '96
Bush Pilot '47
By Dawn's Early Light '89
Captains of the Clouds '42
Ceiling Zero '35▲
Chain Lightning '50
Christopher Strong '33
Con Air '97▲
The Concorde: Airport '79 '79
The Crash of Flight 401 '78
Crimson Romance '34
Danger in the Skies '79
Dangerous Moonlight '41▲
Dark Blue World '01
Dawn Patrol '38▲
Deadly Encounter '72▲
Delta Force '86
Desert Thunder '99
Devil Dogs of the Air '35
Die Hard 2: Die Harder '90▲
Disney's The Kid '00
Dive Bomber '41▲
Dr. Strangelove, or: How I Learned to Stop Worrying and Love the Bomb '64▲
The Dogfighters '95
The Doomsday Flight '66
Dragonfly Squadron '54
Drop Zone '94
Dumbo '41▲
The Eagle and the Hawk '33▲
Enola Gay: The Men, the Mission, the Atomic Bomb '80
Executive Decision '96
Family Jewels '65
Fighter Attack '53
Fighting Pilot '35
Final Approach '91
Final Destination '00
Final Mission '93
Fire Birds '90
Firefox '82
Five Came Back '39
Five Weeks in a Balloon '62
Flaming Signal '33
Flat Top '52
Flight from Glory '37
Flight from Singapore '62
Flight of Black Angel '91
Flight of the Intruder '90
Flight of the Phoenix '65▲
Flight to Fury '66
Flightplan '05
Fly Away Home '96▲
Fly Boy '99
Flyboys '06
Flying Blind '41
The Flying Deuces '39▲
Flying Down to Rio '33
The Flying Irishman '39
Flying Leathernecks '51▲
Flying Tigers '42
For the Moment '94
Forget Paris '95
Freedom Strike '98
French Kiss '95
The Geisha Boy '58
God Is My Co-Pilot '45
The Great Skycopter Rescue '82
The Great Waldo Pepper '75▲
A Guy Named Joe '44
Gypsy Angels '94
Hell's Angels '30▲
High Road to China '83
Hostage '87
Hot Shots! '91▲
The Hunters '58
Independence Day '96▲
Interceptor '92
Into the Sun '92
Iron Eagle '86
Iron Eagle 2 '88
Iron Eagle 4 '95

The Island at the Top of the World '74
It Happened at the World's Fair '63
Jet Over the Atlantic '59
Jet Pilot '57
Keep 'Em Flying '41
La Bamba '87▲
La Grande Vadrouille '66▲
Lafayette Escadrille '58
L'Annee Sainte '76
The Left Hand of God '55▲
The Lion Has Wings '40
Look Who's Talking Now '93
Lost Squadron '32
Love Affair '94
Mach 2 '00
Malta Story '53
The Man with the Golden Gun '74
The McConnell Story '55
Memphis Belle '90▲
Men of Steel '88
Men of the Fighting Lady '54▲
Mercy Mission '93
Millennium '89
Mirror Wars: Reflection One '05
Moon Pilot '62
Murder on Flight 502 '75
Mystery Squadron '33
Night Flight '33
1941 '79
No Highway in the Sky '51▲
October Sky '99▲
One of Our Aircraft Is Missing '41▲
Only Angels Have Wings '39▲
Operation Dumbo Drop '95
Out of Control '85
Pancho Barnes '88
Paradise, Hawaiian Style '66
Party Plane '90
Passenger 57 '92
Pearl Harbor '01
The Phantom '96
Phantom of the Air '33
Phone Call from a Stranger '52
Piece of Cake '88
The Pursuit of D.B. Cooper '81
Pushing Tin '99▲
Reach for the Sky '56
Red Eye '05▲
Red Flag: The Ultimate Game '81
Return to Earth '76
Revenge of the Red Baron '93
The Right Stuff '83▲
Robot Pilot '41
Sabre Jet '53
Saint-Ex: The Story of the Storyteller '95
Savage Hunger '84
Shadow of the Eagle '32
Shadow on the Sun '88
Six Days, Seven Nights '98
633 Squadron '64
Sky Heist '75
Sky Liner '49
Sky Parade '36
Sky Riders '76
Snakes on a Plane '06
Spirit of St. Louis '57▲
Spitfire '39
The Starfighters '63
Starflight One '83
Steal the Sky '88
Stealth '05
Stealth Fighter '99
Stephen King's The Langoliers '95
Stephen King's The Night Flier '96
Strategic Air Command '55
Stuart Little 2 '02▲
Stunt Pilot '39
Survivor '80
Tactical Assault '99
Tailspin: Behind the Korean Airline Tragedy '89

The Taking of Flight 847: The Uli Derickson Story '88▲
Tarnished Angels '57▲
Task Force '49
Terminal Velocity '94
Test Pilot '38▲
Texas Buddies '32
Those Endearing Young Charms '45
Those Magnificent Men in Their Flying Machines '65▲
Thunder Birds '42
Today We Live '33
Top Gun '86
Tragedy of Flight 103: The Inside Story '91▲
Turbulence '96
The Tuskegee Airmen '95▲
Twelve o'Clock High '49▲
View from the Top '03
War Lover '62
Warbirds '88
The Wedding Singer '97
We'll Meet Again '82
The White Diamond '04▲
Who Is Harry Kellerman and Why Is He Saying Those Terrible Things About Me? '71
The Winds of Kitty Hawk '78
A Wing and a Prayer '44▲
Wings '27
Wings in the Dark '35
Wings of Danger '52
Wings of Eagles '57
Without Orders '36
The World Owes Me a Living '41▲
You Gotta Stay Happy '48
Zeppelin '71
Zero '84

Airplanes

see Air Disasters;
Airborne

Alaska

see also Cold Spots
Alaska '96
Avalanche '99
Balto '95
The Big White '05
Call of the Wild '72
Call of the Wild '93
Cry Vengeance '54
Dead Ahead: The Exxon Valdez Disaster '92▲
The Edge '97▲
Extreme Limits '01
Eye of the Beholder '99
First Descent '05
The Gold Rush '25▲
Goldrush: A Real Life Alaskan Adventure '98
Grizzly Man '05▲
Insomnia '02▲
Into the Wild '07▲
Jack London's The Call of the Wild '97
Klondike Annie '36
Klondike Fever '79
Limbo '99
Mystery, Alaska '99
Never Cry Wolf '83▲
North to Alaska '60▲
On Deadly Ground '94
The Road to Utopia '46▲
Runaway Train '85▲
The Simpsons Movie '07▲
Snow Buddies '08
Spawn of the North '38
The Spoilers '14
The Spoilers '42▲
30 Days of Night '07

Alcatraz

see also Great Escapes;
Men in Prison
Birdman of Alcatraz '62▲
Dark Passage '47
Escape from Alcatraz '79▲
Half Past Dead '02
King of Alcatraz '38
Murder in the First '95

Point Blank '67
The Rock '96▲
X-Men: The Last Stand '06

Alcoholism

see On the Rocks

Alien Babes

see also Alien Beings—Benign; Alien Beings—Vicious; Aliens Are People, Too
Alien Visitor '95
Beach Babes 2: Cave Girl Island '95
Beach Babes from Beyond '93
Cat Women of the Moon '53
Cocoon '85▲
Dude, Where's My Car? '00
Last Exit to Earth '96
Leprechaun 4: In Space '96
Mars Attacks! '96
Men in Black 2 '02
My Stepmother Is an Alien '88
Planet of Blood '66
Queen of Outer Space '58
The Sender '98
Species '95
Species 2 '98
Species 4: The Awakening '07
Star Portal '97
Star Trek: First Contact '96▲
Starlight '97
Vampire Vixens from Venus '94
Vampirella '96

Alien Beings—Benign

see also Alien Babes; Alien Beings—Vicious; Alien Cops; Aliens Are People, Too; Out of This World; Sex; Space Operas
The Abyss '89▲
Aftershock '88
Alien Nation '88
Alien Nation: Body and Soul '95
Alien Nation: Dark Horizon '94
Alien Nation: Millennium '96
Alien Nation: The Enemy Within '96
Alien Private Eye '87
Amanda and the Alien '95
Aqua Teen Hunger Force Colon Movie Film for Theaters '07
The Aurora Encounter '85
*batteries not included '87
The Big Empty '04
Big Meat Eater '85
The Brother from Another Planet '84▲
Can of Worms '00
The Cat from Outer Space '78
Chicken Little '05
Close Encounters of the Third Kind '77▲
Cocoon '85▲
Cocoon: The Return '88
Communion '89
Coneheads '93
The Cosmic Eye '71▲
The Cosmic Man '59
Dark City '97
The Day the Earth Stood Still '51▲
Doctor Who '96
Doin' Time on Planet Earth '88
Earth Girls Are Easy '89
Earth vs. the Flying Saucers '56
The Empire Strikes Back '80▲

E.T.: The Extra-Terrestrial '82▲
The Ewok Adventure '84
The Ewoks: Battle for Endor '85
Explorers '85
Femalien '96
Fire in the Sky '93
Flight of the Navigator '86
Galaxy Quest '99
Gremlins '84▲
Gremlins 2: The New Batch '90▲
The Hidden '87▲
The Hitchhiker's Guide to the Galaxy '05▲
Howard the Duck '86
Hyper-Sapien: People from Another Star '86
Intruders '92
It Came from Outer Space '53▲
Josh Kirby... Time Warrior: Chapter 5, Journey to the Magic Cavern '96
Labyrinth '86▲
The Last Mimzy '07
The Last Starfighter '84
Lilo & Stitch '02▲
Lilo & Stitch 2: Stitch Has a Glitch '05
Mac and Me '88
Man Facing Southeast '86▲
The Man from Atlantis '77
The Man Who Fell to Earth '76▲
Martians Go Home! '90
Masters of Venus '62
The Mating Habits of the Earthbound Human '99
Men in Black '97▲
Missile to the Moon '59
Moon Pilot '62
Morons from Outer Space '85
Munchie '92
Muppets from Space '99
My Favorite Martian '98
My Stepmother Is an Alien '88
My Uncle: The Alien '96
Mysterious Two '82
Nukie '93
Official Denial '93
Pajama Party '64
Pet Shop '94
The Phantom Planet '61
Project: Genesis '93
Purple People Eater '88
Real Men '87
Repo Man '83▲
Return of the Jedi '83▲
Search for the Gods '75
Simon '80
Spaced Invaders '90
Star Knight '85
Star Trek 3: The Search for Spock '84
Star Trek 4: The Voyage Home '86▲
Star Trek: First Contact '96▲
Star Wars '77▲
Star Wars: Episode 1—The Phantom Menace '99▲
Stardust Memories '80
Starlight '97
Starman '84▲
Starship Invasions '77
Stranded '87
Suburban Commando '91
Super Mario Bros. '93
Supergirl '84
Superman: The Movie '78▲
Superman 2 '80▲
Superman 3 '83
Superman 4: The Quest for Peace '87
Teenage Mutant Ninja Turtles 2: The Secret of the Ooze '91
The Terrornauts '67
The 27th Day '57
UFO: Target Earth '74
Voyage of the Rock Aliens '87
Warning from Space '56
Wavelength '83

▲ = rated three bones or higher

What Planet Are You From?
'00
When Time Expires '97
Zarkorr! The Invader '96
Zera One '69

Alien Beings—Vicious

see also Alien Babes;
Alien Beings—Benign;
Alien Cops; Aliens Are
People, Too; Out of This
World Sex; Space
Operas
The Adventures of
Buckaroo Banzai Across
the Eighth Dimension '84 ▶
Alien Agent '07
Alien '79 ▶
Alien 3 '92
The Alien Agenda:
Endangered Species '97
Alien Agenda: Out of
the Darkness '96
The Alien Agenda: Under
the Skin '97
Alien Cargo '99
Alien Contamination '81
Alien Dead '79
The Alien Factor '78
Alien Fury: Countdown to
Invasion '00
Alien Massacre '67
Alien Nation: Dark Horizon
'94
Alien Predators '80
Alien Prey '83
Alien: Resurrection '97 ▶
Alien Seed '89
Alien Siege '05
Alien Space Avenger '91
Alien Terminator '95
Alien 3000 '04
Alien vs. Predator '04
Alien vs. Predator 2 '06
The Arrival '96
The Arrival 2 '96
The Astounding She-
Monster '58
The Astro-Zombies '67
Atomic Submarine '59
Attack from Mars '88
Backlash: Oblivon 2 '95
Bad Channels '92
Bad Taste '88 ▶
Battle Beyond the Stars '80
Battlefield Earth '00
Battlestar Galactica '78
Beware! The Blob '72
Bio Hazard '85
The Blob '58
The Blob '88 ▶
Bloodsuckers from Outer
Space '83
Blue Flame '93
Blue Monkey '87
Body Snatchers '93
The Borrower '89
The Brain '88
The Brain Eaters '58
The Brain from Planet Arous
'57
Breeders '86
Breeders '97
Cat Women of the Moon '53
Class of Nuke 'Em High 3:
The Good, the Bad and
the Subhumanoid '94
Cold and Dark '05
The Colony '98
The Cosmic Monsters '58
Creature '85
Creeping Terror '64
The Cremators '72
Critters '86
Critters 2: The Main Course
'88
Critters 3 '91
Critters 4 '91

Crosswords '96
The Curse '87
D-Day on Mars '45
Dark Breed '96
The Dark '79
Dark Star '74 ▶
Dr. Alien '88
Day the World Ended '55
The Day the World Ended
'01
Dead Space '90
Dead Weekend '95
Deep Red '94
Deep Space '87
Deceit '89
Dark Universe '93
Invasion! '65
Day Time Ended '80
Doctor Who '96
Dollman '90
Dracula vs. Frankenstein
'69
Dragon Storm '04
Dreamcatcher '03
Earth vs. the Flying Saucers
'56
Eat and Run '86
The Empire Strikes Back
'80 ▶
Encounter at Raven's Gate
'88
End of the World '76
Endangered Species '02
Epoch: Evolution '03
Escape from Galaxy Three
'81
Escapes '86
Evils of the Night '85
Evolution '01
The Eye Creatures '65
Eyes Behind the Stars '72
The Faculty '98
Fantastic Four: Rise of the
Silver Surfer '07
The Fear Chamber '68
Feeders '96
The Fifth Element '97
Final Fantasy: The Spirits
Within '01
First Man into Space '59
Flight to Mars '52
Forbidden World '82
Forbidden Zone: Alien
Abduction '96
Frankenstein Meets the
Space Monster '65
From Beyond '86 ▶
From Other Worlds '04
Gamera vs. Guiron '69
Gamera vs. Zigra '71
Ghidrah the Three Headed
Monster '65
The Giant Claw '57
The Giant Spider Invasion
'75
God Told Me To '76
Godzilla vs. the Cosmic
Monster '74
Godzilla vs. King Ghidora
'91
Grand Tour: Disaster in
Time '92
The Green Slime '68
Gremlins '84 ▶
Gremlins 2: The New Batch
'90 ▶
The Guyver '91
Guyver 2: Dark Hero '94
Hands of Steel '86
The Hidden '87 ▶
The Hidden 2 '94
The High Crusade '92
High Desert Kill '90
The Hitchhiker's Guide to
the Galaxy '05 ▶
Horror of the Blood
Monsters '70
The Human Duplicators
'64
Hybrid '97
I Come in Peace '90
I Married a Monster from
Outer Space '58
Impostor '02
Independence Day '96 ▶

Inseminoid '80
Interceptor Force '99
Invader '91
The Invaders '95
Invaders from Mars '53
Invaders from Mars '86
Invasion '65
Invasion of the Animal
People '62
Invasion of the Bee Girls
'73 ▶
The Invasion '07
Invasion! '07
Invasion of the Body
Snatchers '56 ▶
Invasion of the Body
Snatchers '78 ▶
Invasion of the Body
Stealers '69
Invasion of the Girl
Snatchers '73
Invasion of the Saucer Men
'57
Invasion of the Space
Preachers '90
Invisible Adversaries '77
Invisible Invaders '59
Island of the Burning
Doomed '67
It Came from Outer Space
'53 ▶
It Came from Outer Space 2
'95
It Conquered the World '56
It! The Terror from Beyond
Space '58
J-Men Forever! '79 ▶
Jimmy Neutron: Boy Genius
'01
John Carpenter's Ghosts of
Mars '01
Killer Klowns from Outer
Space '88
Killer Tongue '96
Killings at Outpost Zeta
'54
Kronos '57
Laboratory '80
Laserhawk '99
Leviathan '89
Lifeform '96
Liquid Sky '83 ▶
Lords of the Deep '89
Lost in Space '98 ▶
Mars Attacks! '96 ▶
Mars Needs Women '66
The Martian Chronicles:
Part 3 '79
Masters of Venus '62
Men in Black '97 ▶
Men in Black 2 '02
Metallica '35
Mindwarp '91
Mission Mars '67
Mom and Dad Save the
World '92
Monolith '93
The Monolith Monsters '57
Monster '78
Monster a Go-Go! '65
Monster High '89
Moontrap '89
Munchies '87
The Mysterians '58
Night Beast '83
Night Caller from Outer
Space '66
Night of the Blood Beast '58
Night of the Creeps '86
No Survivors, Please '63
Not of This Earth '88
Not of This Earth '96
Oblivion '94
The Outer Limits: Sandkings
'95 ▶
The P.A.C.K. '96
Peacemaker '90
Pet Shop '94
Phantom from Space '53
The Phantom Planet '61
The Pink Chiquitas '86
Pitch Black '00 ▶
Plan 9 from Outer Space
'56
Plan 10 from Outer Space
'95

Planet of Blood '66
Planets Against Us '61
Predator '87 ▶
Predator 2 '90
Progeny '98
The Puppet Masters '94
Quatermass 2 '57 ▶
Quatermass and the Pit '58
The Quatermass
Experiment '56 ▶
Rada: Men from the Moon
'52
Reactor '85
Remote Control '88
Reptilian '99
The Return '30
Return of the Aliens: The
Deadly Spawn '83 ▶
Revenge of the Teenage
Vixens from Outer Space
'86
Robin Cook's Invasion '97
Robot Monster '53 ▶
Rock 'n' Roll Nightmare '85
Scared to Death '80
Sci-Fighters '96
Signs '02 ▶
The Silencers '95
The Sinister Invasion '68
Slapstick of Another Kind
'84
Slaughterhouse Five '72
Space Jam '96 ▶
Species '95
Species 2 '98
Specimen '97
Spider-Man 3 '07
Split Second '92
Star Crystal '85
Star Hunter '95
Stargate '94 ▶
Starship Invasions '77
Stephen King's The
Langoliers '95
Stephen King's The
Tommyknockers '93
Strange Invaders '83 ▶
The Stranger from Venus
'54
Super Mario Bros. '93
Superman 2 '80 ▶
Supernova '99
A Taste for Flesh and Blood
'90
Teen Alien '78
Teenagers from Outer
Space '59
Terror of Mechagodzilla '78
They Came from Beyond
Space '67
They Live '88 ▶
They '77
The Thing '51 ▶
The Thing '82
This Island Earth '55
Thrill Seekers '99
Time Runner '92
Time Walker '82
Transformers '07
Tripods: The White
Mountains '84
20 Million Miles to Earth '57
2001: A Space Travesty '00
Undead '05
Unearthed '07
The Unearthly Stranger '64
Unknown Origin '95
Unseen Evil '99
V '83 ▶
V: The Final Battle '84
Vampire Vixens from Venus
'94
Village of the Damned '60 ▶
Village of the Damned '95
Virus '98
War in Space '77
War of the Wizards '83

The War of the Worlds '53 ▶
War of the Worlds '05 ▶
When Time Expires '97
Wicked City '92
Wild, Wild Planet '65
Within the Rock '96
Women of the Prehistoric
Planet '66
The X-Files '98 ▶
X from Outer Space '67
Xtro '83
Xtro 2: The Second
Encounter '91
Xtro 3: Watch the Skies '95
Zathura '05 ▶
Zarkorr! The Invader '96
Zeram '91
Zeram 2 '94 ▶
Zombies of the Stratosphere
'52
Zontar, the Thing from
Venus '66

Alien Cops

see also Alien Babes;
Alien Beings—Benign;
Alien Beings—Vicious;
Aliens Are People, Too;
Extraordinary Pairings;
Sci Fi; Space Operas
Alien '79 ▶
Alien 3 '92
The Alien Agenda: Under
the Skin '97
Alien Avengers '96
Alien: Resurrection '97 ▶
Aliens '86 ▶
The Arrival '96
The Astronaut's Wife '99
Body Snatchers '93
The Chronicles of Riddick
'04
Earth Girls Are Easy '89 ▶
The Faculty '98
The Hidden '87 ▶
The Hidden 2 '94
Invaders from Mars '53
Invaders from Mars '86
Invasion of the Body
Snatchers '56 ▶
I Married a Monster from
Outer Space '58
Impostor '02
The Invader '96
Men in Black '97 ▶
Men in Black 2 '02
Men in Black '97 ▶
Meet Dave '08
Mars Attacks! '96 ▶
K-PAX '01
Predator Island '05
Planet of the Vampires '65
Not Like Us '96
'89
My Stepmother is an Alien
'88
My Favorite Martian '99
Men in Black 2 '02
Specimen '97
Species 2 '98
Species '95
Starlight '97
Star Portal '97
Starman '84 ▶
Superman Returns '06
Taken '02
The Thing '51 ▶
The Thing '82
Thrill Seekers '99
13th Guest '32
Tomorrow at Seven '33
Unconditional Love '03
Voulez-Vous Danser avec
Moi? '59
Whistling in Brooklyn '43
Whistling in Dixie '42
Whistling in the Dark '41 ▶

Aliens Are People, Too

see also Alien Babes;
Alien Beings—Benign;
Alien Beings—Vicious;
Alien Cops;
Extraordinary Pairings;
Sci Fi; Space Operas
The Adventures of
Buckaroo Banzai Across
the Eighth Dimension '84 ▶
Alien '79 ▶
Alien 3 '92
The Alien Agenda: Under
the Skin '97
Alien Avengers '96
Alien: Resurrection '97 ▶
Aliens '86 ▶
The Arrival '96
The Astronaut's Wife '99
Body Snatchers '93
The Chronicles of Riddick
'04
Earth Girls Are Easy '89 ▶
The Faculty '98
The Hidden '87 ▶
The Hidden 2 '94
Invaders from Mars '53
Invaders from Mars '86
Invasion of the Body
Snatchers '56 ▶
I Married a Monster from
Outer Space '58
Impostor '02
The Invader '96
Men in Black '97 ▶
Men in Black 2 '02
The Puppet Masters '94
Species 2 '98
Species '95
Not Like Us '96
The Hitchhiker's Guide to
the Galaxy '05 ▶

American Indians

see also Native America.

American South

see also Atlanta;
Memphis; Miami;
Nashville; New Orleans;
Savannah; Southern
Belles

Amateur Sleuths

After the Thin Man '36 ▶
Agatha Christie's A
Caribbean Mystery '83
Agatha Christie's Murder
with Mirrors '85
Agatha Christie's Murder is
Easy '82
The Body in the Library '84
Clubhouse Detectives '96
Deathmask '69
The Detective '54 ▶
Dirkham Detective Agency
'83
Emil and the Detectives '64
Ex-Mrs. Bradford '36 ▶
Fletch '85
Fletch Lives '89
Footsteps in the Dark '41 ▶
Frog and Wombat '98
Get a Clue '02
The Glass Key '42 ▶
Gumshoe '72
Hard-Boiled Mahoney '47
Having Wonderful Crime '45
Irish Luck '39
Killing 'Em Softly '85
The Lady in Question '99
Lying Lips '39
Man from Cairo '54
The Mandarin Mystery '37
Manhattan Murder Mystery
'93 ▶
Messenger of Death '88
Mr. Arkadin '55 ▶
Murder Ahoy '64
Murder at the Gallop '63 ▶
Murder by the Book '87
Murder in a Small Town '99
A Murder is Announced '87
Murder Most Foul '65 ▶
Murder She Purred: A Mrs.
Murphy Mystery '98
Murder She Said '62
Mystery Kids '99
Mystery Liner '34
Nancy Drew '02
Nancy Drew, Reporter '39
Ruby in the Smoke '06
Shadow of the Thin Man
'41 ▶
Shooting Stars '85
A Shot in the Dark '33
A Shot in the Dark '35
The Silent Passenger '35
Song of the Thin Man '47
Speedy Death '35
Star of Midnight '35
They Might Be Giants '71 ▶
The Thin Man '34 ▶
The Thin Man Goes Home
'44
The Thin Man

American Indians

see also Native America.

V '83 ▶
V: The Final Battle '84

▶ = rated three bones or higher

American

The Autobiography of Miss Jane Pittman '74▶
The Baby Dance '98▶
Baby Doll '56▶
Bad Georgia Road '77
The Ballad of the Sad Cafe '91
Bandwagon '95
Bastard out of Carolina '96
The Beguiled '70▶
Belizaire the Cajun '86▶
Between Heaven and Hell '56▶
Beulah Land '80
Big Bad Love '02
The Big Easy '87▶
Big Fish '03▶
Big Momma's House '00
Black Like Me '64
Black Snake Moan '07
Blind Vengeance '90
Blue Ridge Fall '99
Boxcar Bertha '72
Boycott '02▶
Bucktown '75
Camilla '94
Cape Fear '61▶
Cat on a Hot Tin Roof '58▶
Cat on a Hot Tin Roof '84
The Chamber '96
Charms for the Easy Life '02
Chiefs '83
Children On Their Birthdays '02
Christy '94
Cold Mountain '03▶
Colonel Effingham's Raid '45
The Color Purple '85▶
Come Early Morning '06
The Con '98
Cookie's Fortune '99▶
Cool Hand Luke '67▶
Crazy in Alabama '99
Crazy Like a Fox '04
Cries of Silence '97
Crossroads '86
CSA: The Confederate States of America '04
Cypress Edge '99
Daddy & Them '99
Daltry Calhoun '05
Dancer, Texas—Pop. 81 '98▶
Dead Birds '04
Dead Right '68
The Delta '97
Delta Heat '92
Dirty Laundry '07
Divine Secrets of the Ya-Ya Sisterhood '02
Dixiana '30
Down in the Delta '98▶
Driving Miss Daisy '89▶
The Drowning Pool '75
Drum '76
Due East '02
The Dukes of Hazzard '05
Elizabethtown '05
Eve's Bayou '97
A Family Thing '96▶
The Fighting Temptations '03
Final Cut '88
Fire in the Night '85
Fireball 500 '66
First Love, Last Rites '98
Flamingo Road '49▶
Fled '96
Fletch Lives '89
Follow That Car '80
For Real '02
Forrest Gump '94▶
Foxfire '87▶
Frailty '02▶
Freedom Song '00▶
Fried Green Tomatoes '91▶
The Fugitive Kind '60
The General's Daughter '99
George Wallace '97▶
Gettysburg '93▶
Ghosts of Mississippi '96
The Gift '00
The Gingerbread Man '97▶
The Girl from Tobacco Row '66
The Glass Menagerie '87▶
Gods and Generals '03
God's Little Acre '58▶
Gone with the Wind '39▶
A Good Baby '99
The Grass Harp '95
Great Balls of Fire '89
The Grave '95
The Great Santini '80▶
Great World of Sound '07
The Green Mile '99▶
Hard Drivin' '60
Harlan County War '00
The Heart Is Deceitful Above All Things '04
The Heart of Dixie '89
Heavens Fall '06
Heroes of the Heart '94
Home from the Hill '60▶
Hometown Legend '02
Honeydripper '07
Hooch '76
Hootch Country Boys '75
Hope '97
Hot Spell '58
A House Divided '00
The Hunley '99
Hunter's Blood '87
Hunter's Moon '97
Hush, Hush, Sweet Charlotte '65▶
I Know Why the Caged Bird Sings '79▶
I Walk the Line '70
I'd Climb the Highest Mountain '51▶
In a Shallow Grave '88
In Old Kentucky '35
In the Flesh '97
In the Heat of the Night '67▶
Inherit the Wind '99
Intruder in the Dust '49▶
Invitation to a Gunfighter '64
Jezebel '38▶
John Grisham's The Rainmaker '97
The Journey of August King '95
Judge Horton and the Scottsboro Boys '76
Judge Priest '34▶
Kentucky Kernels '34
Kiss of Fire '98
The Klansman '74
Lady for a Night '42
Lady from Louisiana '42
The Ladykillers '04
The Last Confederate: The Story of Robert Adams '05
Last Dance '96
The Legend of Gator Face '96
A Lesson Before Dying '99▶
Life '99
The Life and Assassination of the Kingfish '76
Lily in Winter '94
A Lion in the Streets '53▶
The Little Colonel '35▶
Little Richard '00
Lone Star State of Mind '02
The Lords of Discipline '83
Louisiana '87
Louisiana Story '48▶
Macon County Line '74
Madea's Family Reunion '06
Mandingo '75
Manderlay '05
Meeting Daddy '98
The Member of the Wedding '97
Midnight in the Garden of Good and Evil '97
Miss Evers' Boys '97
Miss Firecracker '89▶
Mississippi '35
Mississippi Burning '88▶
Mississippi Masala '92▶
Mr. & Mrs. Loving '96
Monster's Ball '01▶
Moonshine Highway '96
Moonshine Mountain '64
Morgan's Ferry '99
Morning Glory '93
The Mothman Prophecies '02
Murder in Coweta County '83
The Murder of Mary Phagan '87▶
Murder on the Bayou '91▶
Murder She Purred: A Mrs. Murphy Mystery '98
My Cousin Vinny '92▶
My Dog Skip '99▶
My Louisiana Sky '02
My Own Country '98
My Sweet Charlie '70
Mystery of the Riverboat '44
The Neon Bible '95
Netherworld '90
No Mercy '86
Norma Rae '79▶
North and South Book 1 '85▶
North and South Book 2 '86▶
The Notebook '04
Nothing but a Man '64
O Brother Where Art Thou? '00
An Occasional Hell '96
Ode to Billy Joe '76
On the Run '73
On Valentine's Day '86
Once Upon a Time ... When We Were Colored '95▶
One False Move '91▶
100 Proof '96
The Only Thrill '97
Orpheus Descending '91
Other Voices, Other Rooms '95
Outside Chance '78
Paradise '91▶
Paris Trout '91
Passion Fish '92▶
The Patriot '00
Perfect Harmony '91
Plain Dirty '04
The Ponder Heart '01
Poor Pretty Eddie '73
Poor White Trash '57
Poor White Trash 2 '75
Primary Colors '98
The Prince of Tides '91▶
Psycho from Texas '81
Purlie Victorious '63
Queen Bee '55
Radio '03▶
Rambling Rose '91▶
A Real American Hero '78
The Reaping '07
Red Dirt '99
Reflections in a Golden Eye '67
The Relic '96
Return to Mayberry '85
Return to Two Moon Junction '93
Rich in Love '93
Ride the Wild Fields '00
Ride with the Devil '99
Ripe '97
The Rising Place '02
Riverbend '89
Road to Nashville '67
Roll of Thunder, Hear My Cry '78
Rooster: Spurs of Death! '83
Roots '77▶
Roots: The Next Generation '79▶
The Rosa Parks Story '02
The Rose Tattoo '55▶
Rosewood '96▶
Ruby Gentry '52
Ruby's Bucket of Blood '01
The Runaway '00
Running Mates '86▶
Rustin '01
The St. Francisville Experiment '00
Saratoga Trunk '45
Scarlett '94
Scorchers '92
Selma, Lord, Selma '99
Shadrach '98
Shag: The Movie '89▶
Shanty Tramp '67
Sherman's March '86▶
Shy People '87▶
The Simple Life of Noah Dearborn '99
Sins of the Father '01▶
Sister, Sister '87
Sixteen '72
A Slipping Down Life '99
Sling Blade '96▶
Smokey Bites the Dust '81
Snuffy Smith, Yard Bird '42
Soldier's Girl '03▶
Something for the Boys '44
Something to Talk About '95
Sonny '02
Sounder '72▶
Southern Comfort '81▶
The Southerner '45▶
Sparrows '26▶
Storm Warning '51
Stormswept '95
Storyville '92
Strange Fruit '04
A Streetcar Named Desire '51▶
A Streetcar Named Desire '84▶
A Streetcar Named Desire '95
Summer and Smoke '61
The Summer of Ben Tyler '96
Summer's End '99
The Supernaturals '86
Swamp Fire '46
Sweet Bird of Youth '62▶
Sweet Bird of Youth '89
Sweet Country Road '83
Sweet Home Alabama '02▶
Swimming '00
Tammy and the Bachelor '57
Tammy and the Doctor '63
Tank '83
The Tempest '99
Texasville '90
They Won't Forget '37▶
This Stuff'll Ya! '71
Tigerland '00▶
A Tiger's Tale '87
A Time to Kill '96▶
To Kill a Mockingbird '62▶
The Trail of the Lonesome Pine '36▶
The Trip to Bountiful '85▶
Tune in Tomorrow '90
Two Moon Junction '88
2000 Maniacs '64
Tyler Perry's Meet the Browns '08
Uncle Tom's Cabin '14
Uncle Tom's Cabin '69
Undertow '04
The Untold Story of Emmett Louis Till '05▶
Uphill All the Way '85
Video Voyeur: The Susan Wilson Story '02
Voodoo Dawn '89
Vulture's Eye '04
Waitress '07▶
Walk in the Spring Rain '70
A Walk to Remember '02
Walking Tall '73
Walking Tall: Part 2 '75
Walking Tall: The Final Chapter '77
The War '94
The Waterboy '98
We Are Marshall '06
Welcome Home Roscoe Jenkins '08
What Comes Around '85
Where the Lilies Bloom '74▶
White Lie '91
The White Rose '23▶
Wild Things '98
Wildflower '91▶
William Faulkner's Old Man '97
Wise Blood '79▶
A Woman Called Moses '78
Wrong Turn '03

Amnesia

The Addams Family '91▶
Amateur '94▶
Amnesia '96
Anastasia '56▶
Anastasia: The Mystery of Anna '86
Armistead Maupin's More Tales of the City '97
As You Desire Me '32▶
Battle Shock '56
Black Out '96
Blackout '85
Blind Horizon '04
The Blonde '92
The Blue Gardenia '53▶
The Bourne Identity '88▶
The Bourne Identity '02▶
The Bourne Supremacy '04▶
The Bourne Ultimatum '07▶
The Bumblebee Flies Anyway '99
Clean Slate '94
Code Name: The Cleaner '07
Crack-Up '46
Dead Again '91▶
Desperately Seeking Susan '85
Diabolically Yours '67
Eternal Sunshine of the Spotless Mind '04▶
Facing Windows '03
Fall Guy '47
50 First Dates '04
Final Approach '91
Forger of London '61
The Forgotten '04
The Great Dictator '40▶
Gypsy Angels '94
Hellhole '85
High Stakes '93
Hysteria '64
I Love a Bandleader '45
I Love You Again '40▶
Identity Unknown '45
The Immoral One '80
Inferno '99
Istanbul '57
The Jacket '05
Jackie Chan's Who Am I '98
Jane Doe '83
Jericho '01
The Killing Jar '96
Landslide '92
Last Rites '98
The Lazarus Man '96
The Long Kiss Goodnight '96
Lost Honeymoon '47
Love Letters '45
The Majestic '01
The Man Without a Past '02▶
Memories of Murder '90
The Memory of a Killer '03
Men in Black '97▶
Men in Black 2 '02▶
Mirage '66▶
Mission of Death '97
Moment to Moment '66
Mulholland Drive '01▶
The Muppets Take Manhattan '84▶
Murder by Night '89
Overboard '87
Palombella Rossa '89
Paycheck '03
The Perfect Daughter '96
A Pure Formality '94
Random Harvest '42▶
The Red Squirrel '93
Regarding Henry '91▶
Return of the Soldier '82▶
The Road to Hong Kong '62
The Saddest Music in the World '03
Santa with Muscles '96
The Second Woman '51
The Sender '82
Shattered '91▶
Shock '79
Siesta '87
Singapore '47
Someone Behind the Door '71
Southland Tales '06
Spellbound '45▶
Strange Awakening '58
The Stranger '87▶
Summer's Children '79
Sundays & Cybele '62▶
36 Hours '64▶
The Three Lives of Karen '97
Till Human Voices Wake Us '02
Time Lapse '01
Total Recall '90▶
Twice a Judas '69
Undesirable '92
Unholy Four '54
The Unknown Soldier '98
Unknown White Male '05▶
Virtual Sexuality '99
While I Live '47
A Wind Named Amnesia '93

Amsterdam

The Amsterdam Connection '78
The Amsterdam Kill '78
Amsterdamned '88
The Attic: The Hiding of Anne Frank '88
The Bourne Supremacy '04▶
Broken Mirrors '85
Business is Business '71
Deuce Bigalow: European Gigolo '05
The Diary of Anne Frank '59▶
Hostel '06
Katie Tippel '75
Ocean's Twelve '04
Operation Amsterdam '60
Puppet on a Chain '72
Snapshots '02

Amusement Parks

see also Carnivals & Circuses; Fairs & Expositions

The Beast from 20,000 Fathoms '53
Bebe's Kids '92
Beverly Hills Cop 3 '94
Big '88▶
Carnival of Blood '71
Carnival of Souls '62▶
The Crying Game '92▶
Curse of the Headless Horseman '72
Dr. Giggles '92
Dragonworld '94
Fatal Attraction '87▶
Final Destination 3 '06
Funland '89
Gangster World '98
Getting Even with Dad '94
Godzilla on Monster Island '72
Jimmy Neutron: Boy Genius '01
KISS Meets the Phantom of the Park '78
The Lady from Shanghai '48▶
Luv '67
Mighty Joe Young '98
My Life '93
National Lampoon's Vacation '83▶
1941 '79
Omega Doom '96
Rollercoaster '77
Rugrats in Paris: The Movie '00▶
Scooby-Doo '02
A Slipping Down Life '99
Strangers on a Train '51▶
Strike Me Pink '36
The Third Man '49▶
3 Ninjas: High Noon at Mega Mountain '97
Tremors 3: Back to Perfection '01
The World '04

Angels

see also Heaven Sent

Always '89▶
Angel-A '05
The Angel Levine '70
Angels in America '03▶
Angels in the Endzone '98
Angels in the Infield '00
Angels in the Outfield '51▶

▶ = *rated three bones or higher*

Angels

Angels in the Outfield '94
The Bishop's Wife '47 ►
Cabin in the Sky '43 ►
Christmas at Water's Edge '04
The Christmas Box '95
Circus Angel '65 ►
City of Angels '98
Clarence '91
Click '06
The Contractor '07
Cowboys and Angels '00
Creation of Adam '53
Date with an Angel '87
Defending Your Life '91 ►
Dogma '99 ►
Down to Earth '01
Faraway, So Close! '93 ►
Fallen '97
Fear No Evil '80
Field of Dreams '89 ►
For Heaven's Sake '56
Forever Darling '56
Gabriel Over the White House '33 ►
Green Pastures '36 ►
A Guy Named Joe '44
Heart and Souls '93
Heaven Can Wait '78 ►
The Heavenly Kid '85
Here Comes Mr. Jordan '41 ►
The Horn Blows at Midnight '45 ►
I Married an Angel '42
It Came Upon a Midnight Clear '84
It's a Wonderful Life '46 ►
The Kid with the Broken Halo '82
Kindergarten Ninja '94
La Merveilleuse Visite '74
A Life Less Ordinary '97
The Littlest Angel '69
Lover's Knot '96
Made in Heaven '87
Michael '96 ►
Miracle in Milan '51 ►
Neil Gaiman's NeverWhere '96
No News from God '01
Northfork '03
One Magic Christmas '85
A Perfect Day '06
The Perfect Holiday '07
The Preacher's Wife '96
The Prophecy '95
The Prophecy 2: Ashtown '97
The Prophecy 3: The Ascent '99
Raging Angels '95
A Season for Miracles '99
Slam Dunk Ernest '95
Soultaker '90
Stairway to Heaven '46 ►
The Twelve Days of Christmas Eve '04
Two of a Kind '83
Unlikely Angel '97
Waiting for the Light '90
Wide Awake '97
Wings of Desire '88 ►

Animals

see also Bears; Birds; Cats; Horses; King of Beasts (Dogs); Penguins; Wild Kingdom

Animated Musicals

see also Animation & Cartoons; Musicals
Adam Sandler's 8 Crazy Nights '02
Aladdin '92 ►
All Dogs Go to Heaven '89
All Dogs Go to Heaven 2 '95
American Pop '81
An American Tail '86 ►
An American Tail: Fievel Goes West '91 ►
Anastasia '97 ►
Beauty and the Beast '91 ►
Cats Don't Dance '97 ►
Charlotte's Web '73 ►
Cinderella '50 ►
Fantasia/2000 '00 ►
Gay Pur-ee '62
Happy Feet '06 ►
Hercules '97 ►
Home on the Range '04
Hoodwinked '05 ►
The Hunchback of Notre Dame '96 ►
The Jungle Book '67 ►
The King and I '99
Lady and the Tramp '55 ►
The Lion King '94 ►
The Little Mermaid '89 ►
The Magic Voyage '93
Melody Time '48 ►
Mulan '98 ►
The Nightmare before Christmas '93 ►
The Pebble and the Penguin '94
Pink Floyd: The Wall '82
Pinocchio '40 ►
Pocahontas '95 ►
Prince of Egypt '98 ►
Quest for Camelot '98
The Return of Jafar '94
The Road to El Dorado '00
Robin Hood '73 ►
Rock-a-Doodle '92
Shinbone Alley '70
Sleeping Beauty '59 ►
Snow White and the Seven Dwarfs '37 ►
South Park: Bigger, Longer and Uncut '99 ►
The Swan Princess '94
The Swan Princess 2: Escape from Castle Mountain '97
Thumbelina '94
Tim Burton's Corpse Bride '05 ►
The Trumpet of the Swan '01
The Tune '92
Water Babies '79
Yellow Submarine '68 ►

Animation & Cartoons

see also Animated Musicals
The Adventures of Ichabod and Mr. Toad '49 ►
The Adventures of Mark Twain '85 ►
Aladdin and the King of Thieves '96
Alice in Wonderland '50
Alice in Wonderland '51 ►
Allegro Non Troppo '76 ►
Animal Farm '55 ►
The Ant Bully '06
Antz '98 ►
Aqua Teen Hunger Force Colon Movie Film for Theaters '07
The Aristocats '70 ►
Atlantis: The Lost Empire '01
Babar: The Movie '88
Balto '95
Bambi '42 ►
Barnyard '06
Batman: Mask of the Phantasm '93 ►
Beavis and Butt-Head Do America '96
Bebe's Kids '92
Bee Movie '07
Beowulf '07 ►
The Black Cauldron '85
A Bug's Life '98 ►
Butterfly Ball '76
Cars '06 ►
Chicago 10 '07 ►
Chicken Little '05
Chicken Run '00 ►
Clifford's Really Big Movie '04
Cool World '92
The Cosmic Eye '71 ►
Curious George '06
The Dagger of Kamui '85 ►
Dinosaur '00 ►
Disney's Teacher's Pet '04 ►
Dr. Seuss' Horton Hears a Who! '08
Doogal '06
Doug's 1st Movie '99 ►
DuckTales the Movie: Treasure of the Lost Lamp '90
Dumbo '41 ►
Everyone's Hero '06
Evil Toons '90
Fantasia '40 ►
Fantastic Planet '73 ►
Felix the Cat: The Movie '91
Ferngully: The Last Rain Forest '92
Fire and Ice '83 ►
Flight of Dragons '82
Flushed Away '06 ►
The Fox and the Hound '81 ►
Freddie the Frog '92
Fritz the Cat '72 ►
Garfield: A Tail of Two Kitties '06
Garfield: The Movie '04
Gargoyles, The Movie: The Heroes Awaken '94
The Good, the Bad, and Huckleberry Hound '88
A Goofy Movie '94
The Great Mouse Detective '86 ►
Grendel, Grendel, Grendel '82
Gulliver's Travels '39 ►
Gulliver's Travels '77
Gumby: The Movie '95
Happily N'Ever After '07
Happily Ever After '93
Heavy Traffic '73 ►
Here Come the Littles: The Movie '85
Hey Arnold! The Movie '02
Hey Good Lookin' '82
Hey There, It's Yogi Bear '64
The Hobbit '78 ►
Home on the Range '04
Hoodwinked '05 ►
Hoppity Goes to Town '41
Hugo the Hippo '76
Huckleberry Finn '81
Ice Age '02 ►
Ice Age: The Meltdown '06
The Incredibles '04 ►
The Jetsons: The Movie '90
Journey Back to Oz '71
Keena: The Prophecy '03
The Land Before Time '88 ►
The Land Before Time 2: The Great Valley Adventure '94
The Land Before Time 3: The Time of the Great Giving '95
The Land Before Time 4: Journey Through the Mists '96
The Land Before Time 5: The Mysterious Island '97
The Land Before Time 6: The Secret of Saurus Rock '98
The Land Before Time 7: The Stone of Cold Fire '00
The Last Unicorn '82 ►
The Legend of Sleepy Hollow '49
Lensman '84
Light Years '88
Lilo & Stitch '02 ►
Lilo & Stitch 2: Stitch Has a Glitch '05
The Lion King '94 ►
The Lion King 1 1/2 '04 ►
The Little Mermaid '89 ►
Little Nemo: Adventures in Slumberland '92
Looney Looney Looney Bugs Bunny Movie '81 ►
Madagascar '05 ►
Mad Monster Party '68
The Many Adventures of Winnie the Pooh '77 ►
Man from Button Willow '65 ►
Marco Polo, Jr. '72
Marquis '89 ►
The Miracle Maker: The Story of Jesus '00
Monster House '06 ►
Monsters, Inc. '01 ►
Mouse and His Child '77
Nine Lives of Fritz the Cat '74
The Nutcracker Prince '91
Oliver & Company '88 ►
Once Upon a Forest '93
101 Dalmatians '61 ►
1001 Arabian Nights '59
Open Season '06 ►
Over the Hedge '06 ►
Persepolis '07 ►
Peter Pan '53 ►
The Phantom Tollbooth '69 ►
Phantom 2040 Movie: The Ghost Who Walks '03
Piglet's Big Movie '03
The Pirates Who Don't Do Anything: A VeggieTales Movie '08
The Plague Dogs '82 ►
The Point '71 ►
The Polar Express '04 ►
Pooh's Heffalump Movie '05
Popeye's Voyage: The Quest for Pappy '04
Pound Puppies and the Legend of Big Paw '88
The Powerpuff Girls Movie '02 ►
The Princess and the Goblin '94
The Proud Family Movie '05
The Puppetoon Movie '87 ►
Queer Duck: The Movie '06
Race for Your Life, Charlie Brown '77 ►
Ratatouille '07 ►
The Rescuers '77 ►
The Rescuers Down Under '90
Return to Never Land '02 ►
Robots '05 ►
Rover Dangerfield '91
Rock & Rule '83 ►
Rugrats Go Wild! '03
Rugrats in Paris: The Movie '00 ►
The Rugrats Movie '98 ►
The Secret of NIMH '82 ►
Shark Tale '04 ►
The Simpsons Movie '07 ►
Sinbad and the Eye of the Tiger '77
Sinbad: Legend of the Seven Seas '03
The Singing Princess '49
Spirit: Stallion of the Cimarron '02 ►
Spirited Away '01 ►
The SpongeBob SquarePants Movie '04 ►
Starchaser: The Legend of Orin '85
Steamboy '05
Streetfight '75
Surf's Up '07 ►
Tarzan '99 ►
The Three Caballeros '45 ►
Tiny Toon Adventures: How I Spent My Vacation '91 ►
TMNT (Teenage Mutant Ninja Turtles) '07
Todd McFarlane's Spawn '97 ►
Tom and Jerry: The Movie '93
Tom Thumb '58 ►
Toy Story '95 ►
Toy Story 2 '99 ►
A Troll in Central Park '94
The Triplets of Belleville '02 ►
Valiant '05
VIP, My Brother Superman '90
Waking Life '01 ►
Wallace & Gromit: The Curse of the Were-Rabbit '05 ►
Watership Down '78 ►
We're Back! A Dinosaur's Story '93
When the Wind Blows '86 ►
The Wild Thornberrys Movie '02 ►
Wizards '77 ►
Yu-Gi-Oh! The Movie: Pyramid of Light '04

Animated Sci-Fi

see also Anime
Final Fantasy: The Spirits Within '01 ►
Ghost in the Shell '95 ►
Heavy Metal '81 ►
Heavy Metal 2000 '00
The Incredibles '04 ►
Meet the Robinsons '07 ►
Pokemon 3: The Movie '01
Renaissance '06 ►
Space Chimps '08
Steamboy '05
Titan A.E. '00 ►
Transformers: The Movie '86 ►
WALL-E '08 ►
Yu-Gi-Oh! The Movie: Pyramid of Light '04

Anime

see also Animation & Cartoons
Akira '89 ►
The Dagger of Cagliostro '80 ►
The Dagger of Kamui '85 ►
Grave of the Fireflies '88 ►
Howl's Moving Castle '04 ►
Lensman '84
My Neighbor Totoro '88 ►
Otaku No Video '91 ►
Paprika '06 ►
Pokemon: The First Movie '99 ►
Pokemon the Movie 2000: The Power of One '00
Princess Mononoke '98 ►
Steamboy '05
Toward the Terra '80
Twilight of the Cockroaches '90
Wicked City '89 ►
A Wind Named Amnesia '93

Anthology

see also Comedy Anthologies; Horror Anthologies; Serials
The Acid House '99
Actors and Sin '52
The Air I Breathe '07 ►
America at the Movies '76
America's Dream '96 ►
Amore '48 ►
Beyond the Clouds '95
Black Sabbath '64 ►
Boys in Love '97
Boys Life '94
Boys Life 2 '97
Boys Life 3 '00
The Chaplin Revue '58 ►
Charade '53 ►
Coffee and Cigarettes '03 ►
Common Ground '00
Cosmic Slop '94
Crash '05 ►
Dark Eyes '87 ►
Deadtime Stories '86
The Decameron '70 ►
Decameron Nights '53
The Discovery Program '89
Dolls '02 ►
Eroica '94
Escapes '86
Eros '04 ►
Fallen Angels 1 '93
Fallen Angels 2 '93
Fantasia/2000 '00 ►
Four Rooms '95
From Beyond the Grave '73 ►
A Girl Thing '01 ►
The Great New Wonderful '06
Halfmoon '95
Hotel Room '93
If These Walls Could Talk '96 ►
If These Walls Could Talk 2 '00
Kaos '85 ►
Kisses in the Dark '97
Kurt Vonnegut's Monkey House '91
Kwaidan '64 ►
Le Plaisir '52 ►
Letters from My Windmill '54 ►
The Little Theatre of Jean Renoir '71 ►
Loggerheads '05 ►
Love in the City '53 ►
Love Songs '99
Marra Africa '02
Melody Time '48 ►
Mickey the Great '39
Mystery Train '89 ►
More American Graffiti '79
Night Gallery '69 ►
Night on Earth '91 ►
Nightmares '83
Nine Lives '05
Noel '04 ►
Once Upon a Midnight Scary '90
Paisan '46 ►
Paris, je t'aime '06 ►
Personal Velocity: Three Portraits '02 ►
Picture Windows '95
Prison Stories: Women on the Inside '91 ►
Pulp Fiction '94 ►
Red Shoe Diaries: Swimming Naked '00
Rendezvous in Paris '95 ►
Renoir Shorts '27 ►
Red Shoe Diaries 3: Night of Abandon '96
RoGoPaG '62
Red Shoe Diaries 2: Double Dare '92
Red Shoe Diaries: Strip Poker '96
Red Shoe Diaries 5: Weekend Pass '95
Red Shoe Diaries 6: How I Met My Husband '94
Red Shoe Diaries 7: Burning Up '96
Red Shoe Diaries 4: Auto Erotica '93
Red Shoe Diaries: Luscious Lola '00
Seven Deadly Sins '53 ►
Short Cuts '93 ►
The Silent Mr. Sherlock Holmes '12
Sin City '05 ►
Six in Paris '68
Slacker '91 ►
Strictly G.I. '44
Subway Stories '97
Tales from the Crypt '89 ►
Tales of Erotica '43
Tales of Manhattan '42 ►
Tales of the Unexpected '91
Tales That Witness Madness '73 ►
The Ten '07 ►
Terrorgram '90
That's Dancing! '85 ►
That's Entertainment '74 ►
That's Entertainment, Part 2 '76 ►
That's Entertainment, Part 3 '93
Things 2 '97
Three Cases of Murder '55 ►
Three Days of Rain '02 ►
Three Times '05 ►
Twice-Told Tales '63 ►

Anthology

Twilight Zone: The Movie '83
Twisted '96
Two Days in the Valley '96
The Unapproachable '82
The Uncanny '78
Vanishing Legion '31
The Wall '99
Women & Men: In Love There Are No Rules '91
Women & Men: Stories of Seduction '90

Anti-Heroes

see also Rebel With a Cause

Aeon Flux '05
Belly '98
Big Bad Love '02
Billy Jack '71
Blade '98
Bonnie & Clyde '67
Born Losers '67
Butch Cassidy and the Sundance Kid '69
Casino '95
A Civil Action '98
The Dead Pool '88
Dirty Harry '71
Easy Rider '69
The Enforcer '76
Gang Related '96
H '90
Hero '92
Hulk '03
Hustle '04
In a Lonely Place '50
Last Man Standing '96
Lock, Stock and 2 Smoking Barrels '98
Magnum Force '73
Niagara, Niagara '97
The Night Watchman '02
Palookaville '95
Playing God '96
The Punisher '04
Rebel without a Cause '55
Robin Hood: Prince of Thieves '91
The Secret Agent '96
Set It Off '96
Shaun of the Dead '04
16 Blocks '06
Street Kings '08
Steal This Movie! '00
Sudden Impact '83
Surviving Picasso '96
Ten Benny '98
Thelma & Louise '91
Things to Do in Denver When You're Dead '95
To Wong Foo, Thanks for Everything, Julie Newmar '95
Traveller '96
The Trial of Billy Jack '74
Trojan Eddie '96
True Crime '99
12 Monkeys '95
Twin Town '97
U-Turn '97
Ultraviolet '06
V for Vendetta '06
The Weather Man '05
Wisdom '87
Yojimbo '61

Anti-War War Movies

see also Satire & Parody

The Adventures of Werner Holt '65
All Quiet on the Western Front '30
All Quiet on the Western Front '79
Amazing Grace & Chuck '87
Apocalypse Now '79
Beaufort '07
The Big Parade '25
Born on the Fourth of July '89
The Bridge '59
The Bridges at Toko-Ri '55
The Burmese Harp '56
Castle Keep '69
Catch-22 '70
The Charge of the Light Brigade '68
Civilization '16
Come and See '85
Coming Home '78
The Cuckoo '02
Cup Final '92
Dr. Strangelove, or: How I Learned to Stop Worrying and Love the Bomb '64
The Eagle and the Hawk '33
Fahrenheit 9/11 '04
Field of Honor '87
Fiesta '95
Fires on the Plain '59
Forbidden Games '52
The Four Horsemen of the Apocalypse '21
The Four Horsemen of the Apocalypse '62
Gallipoli '81
Glory '89
Grand Illusion '37
Hamburger Hill '87
Hell in the Pacific '69
Henry V '89
Hombres Armados '97
J'Accuse '37
Jarhead '05
Joyeux Noel '05
Jud '71
King and Country '64
The King of Hearts '66
La Guerre Est Finie '66
The Last Bridge '54
Latino '85
Les Carabiniers '63
The Line '80
M*A*S*H '70
M*A*S*H: Goodbye, Farewell & Amen '83
Master of the World '61
A Midnight Clear '92
Mission to Death '66
No Man's Land '01
Nurse Edith Cavell '39
Oh! What a Lovely War '69
Paths of Glory '57
Platoon '86
Pretty Village, Pretty Flame '96
Prisoner of the Mountains '96
The Red Badge of Courage '51
Revolution '85
San Demetrio, London '47
She Goes to War '29
The Steel Helmet '51
Straight into Darkness '04
The Tiger and the Snow '05
A Time to Love & a Time to Die '58
The Tin Drum '79
Too Late the Hero '70
Twilight's Last Gleaming '77
Veronico Cruz '87
The Victors '63
Vukovar '94
Wackiest Ship in the Army '61
Westfront 1918 '30
What Price Glory? '52
The Young Lions '58

Apartheid

see also Africa; Civil Rights

An African Dream '90
After the Rain '99
Boesman & Lena '00
Bophal '93
Catch a Fire '06
City of Blood '88
The Color of Freedom '07
Cry Freedom '87
Cry, the Beloved Country '51
Cry, the Beloved Country '95
Dangerous Ground '96
A Dry White Season '89
Funeral for an Assassin '77
In My Country '04
Inside '96
Mandela '87
Mandela and de Klerk '97
Master Harold and the Boys '84
Place of Weeping '86
The Power of One '92
The Quarry '98
Sarafina! '92
The Wilby Conspiracy '75
A World Apart '88
A World of Strangers '62
Yankee Zulu '95

Apartments & Apartment Buildings

Among Brothers '05
The Apartment '60
Apartment 12 '06
Apartment Complex '98
Apartment Zero '88
As Good As It Gets '97
Baby Mama '08
Barefoot in the Park '67
Breakfast at Tiffany's '61
The Bubble '06
A Couch in New York '95
Dark Water '05
Designing Woman '57
Down With Love '03
The Dreamers '03
The Fifth Horseman Is Fear '64
Flight of the Red Balloon '08
Four and a Half Women '05
Ghostbusters '84
Inside Paris '06
Joe's Apartment '96
Kettle of Fish '06
Kill the Poor '06
The Killing Floor '06
Lady in the Water '06
Last Tango in Paris '73
L'Auberge Espagnole '02
Laura '44
The Odd Couple '68
A Perfect Murder '98
Pieces of April '03
Rear Window '54
Repulsion '65
Rope '48
Rosemary's Baby '68
Shallow Grave '87
Single White Female '92
Someone Like You '01
The Tenant '76
The Visitor '07
Unfaithful '02
Wait until Dark '67
What Love Is '07

Archaeology

see Big Digs

Architects & Architecture

The Architect '06
At First Sight '98
The Belly of an Architect '91
The Brady Bunch Movie '95
The Cocoanuts '29
The Courtyard '95
Dead End '37
Dead of Night '45
Death Wish '74
Dr. Terror's House of Horrors '65
Electric Dreams '84
Fear '96
The Fountainhead '49
Heaven '99
Housesitter '92
Indecent Proposal '93
Journey to the Lost City '58
Just Around the Corner '38
Just Looking '99
Land of the Pharaohs '55
Life as a House '01
Living in Peril '97
Lost Honeymoon '47
Midnight Lace '60
My Architect: A Son's Journey '03
Mystic Pizza '88
A Name for Evil '70
One Fine Day '96
The Palm Beach Story '42
Poor White Trash '57
Rear Window '98
The Serpent's Kiss '97
Shattered '91
A Smile Like Yours '96
Strangers When We Meet '60
The Tempest '82
Three Men and a Baby '87
Three to Tango '99
Thursday '98
Til There Was You '96
The Towering Inferno '74
Town and Country '01
A Very Brady Sequel '96
White Noise '05

Army Training, Sir!

Band of Brothers '01
Biloxi Blues '88
The Boys in Company C '77
Buck Privates '41
D.I. '57
Full Metal Jacket '87
In the Army Now '94
Stripes '81
Thunder Birds '42
Tigerland '00

Art & Artists

see also Biopics: Artists; Biopics: Musicians; Sculptors; Struggling Artists; Struggling Musicians; This Is Your Life; Writers

The Adventures of Picasso '80
Advertising Rules! '01
The Agony and the Ecstasy '65
All the Vermeers in New York '91
An American in Paris '51
Andrei Rublev '66
Art School Confidential '06
Artemisia '97
Artists and Models '55
As Good As It Gets '97
Back in the USSR '92
Basquiat '96
Battle Shock '56
Bean '97
The Belly of an Architect '91
Big Eden '00
Black Magic Woman '91
The Blue Light '32
Bluebeard '44
Body Strokes '95
Boricua's Bond '00
Bride of the Wind '01
Brush with Fate '03
A Bucket of Blood '59
Camille Claudel '89
Canvas: The Fine Art of Crime '92
Caravaggio '86
Carrington '95
Cashback '06
Castle Keep '69
Cauldron of Blood '67
Changing Habits '96
Chasing Amy '97
Circle of Two '80
Color Me Blood Red '64
The Color of Evening '95
Color of Night '94
The Competition '80
Crucible of Terror '72
Crumb '94
The Da Vinci Code '06
Dante's Inferno: Life of Dante Gabriel Rossetti '69
Dark Side of Genius '94
The Death Artist '95
Death in Venice '71
Dedication '07
The Designated Mourner '97
Detonator 2: Night Watch '95
Dirty Pictures '00
Dishonored Lady '47
A Dog of Flanders '99
The Dragon Painter '19
Driller Killer '79
Ebony Tower '86
Echoes '83
Edie in Ciao! Manhattan '72
Edvard Munch '74
Empty Canvas '64
Entre-Nous '83
Escapade in Florence '62
Evil Has a Face '96
Fakers '04
Fear and Loathing in Las Vegas '98
Femme Fatale '90
Fleshtone '94
Framed '90
Frida '84
Frida '02
From the Mixed-Up Files of Mrs. Basil E. Frankweiler '95
Frozen '98
Frozen in Fear '00
Girl with a Pearl Earring '03
Gothic '87
Goya in Bordeaux '99
Goya's Ghosts '06
Great Expectations '97
Green Dragon '01
Headless Eyes '83
The Hideaways '73
Hip Hip Hurrah! '87
The Horse's Mouth '58
Horsey '93
Hot Touch '82
Hour of the Wolf '68
Hour of D '04
House of Horrors '46
How to Steal a Million '66
Hullabaloo over Georgie & Bonnie's Pictures '78
Hunger '66
The Hypothesis of the Stolen Painting '78
I Shot Andy Warhol '96
If Lucy Fell '95
In America '02
Incognito '97
The Iris Effect '04
It Seemed Like a Good Idea at the Time '75
I've Heard the Mermaids Singing '87
Jimmy Zip '00
Junebug '05
A Kink in the Picasso '90
La Belle Noiseuse '90
La Mujer de Mi Hermano '06
La Vie de Boheme '93
Leaving Metropolis '02
The Life of Emile Zola '37
Little Noises '91
Look Both Ways '05
Love & Sex '00
Love Is the Devil '98
Love Play '60
The Low Down '00
Lucky Partners '40
Luscious '97
Lust and Revenge '95
Lust for Life '56
Max '02
Men... '85
Men Cry Bullets '00
Mirror, Mirror 3: The Voyeur '96
Missing Pieces '00
Mistral's Daughter '84
The Moderns '88
Modigliani '58
Moll Flanders '96
The Moon and Sixpence '43
Morgan: A Suitable Case for Treatment '66
Moulin Rouge '52
Murder by Numbers '89
My Best Friend '06
My Left Foot '89
My Mother's Smile '02
The Naked Maja '59
Never Met Picasso '96
New York Stories '89
The Next Big Thing '02
The Object of Beauty '91
Out of the Shadows '88
Paint It Black '89
The Painted Lady '97
A Perfect Murder '98
Picture Windows '95
Pictures of Hollis Woods '07
Pollock '00
Portrait in Terror '66
Portrait of Jennie '48
Postcards from America '95
Prick Up Your Ears '87
Primal Secrets '94
Pucker Up and Bark Like a Dog '89
A Question of Attribution '91
Rembrandt '36
Rembrandt—1669 '77
The Rendering '02
Rendezvous in Paris '95
Retribution '88
A River Made to Drown In '97
Salut l'Artiste '74
The Sandpiper '65
Savage Messiah '72
Scenario du Film Passion '82
The Science of Sleep '06
Scream, Baby, Scream '69
The Seventh Veil '46
Sheer Madness '84
Shifting Sands '18
The Silver Chalice '54
Sirens '94
Six Days, Six Nights '94
Slaves of New York '89
Speak '04
Spiral '07
Starry Night '99
Stars and Bars '88
Stay '05
Stealing Beauty '96
Still Breathing '97
Still Life '92
The Still Life '07
A Sunday in the Country '84
Sunday in the Park with George '86
Superstar: The Life and Times of Andy Warhol '90
Surviving Picasso '96
Sweet Thing '00
Tainted Image '91
The Tenant of Wildfell Hall '96
The Testament of Orpheus '59
The Thomas Crown Affair '99
Titanic '97
Track of the Vampire '66
Trespasser '81
Trust Me '89
200 Cigarettes '98
Two If by Sea '95
The Two Mrs. Carrolls '47
Two Much '96
Uncovered '94
Utamaro and His Five Women '46
Utz '93
Van Gogh '92
Victimless Crimes '90
Vincent: The Life and Death of Vincent van Gogh '87
Vincent & Theo '90
Washington Heights '02
What Dreams May Come '98
White Oleander '02
Who Gets to Call It Art? '05
The Wolf at the Door '87
The Women on the Roof '89
World and Time Enough '95
The World of Suzie Wong '60
Wrestling with Alligators '98
The Yes Men '03

▲ = rated three bones or higher

Asia
see also China; Japan

Anna and the King '99
Bang Rajan '00▶
Bangkok Dangerous '08
The Beautiful Country '04
Beyond Borders '03
Beyond Rangoon '95
Bloodsport 2: The Next Kumite '95
Brokedown Palace '99
A Bullet in the Head '90▶
Burma Convoy '41
Catfish in Black Bean Sauce '00
Chaos Factor '00
Chasing Freedom '04
China White '91
City of Ghosts '03
Eat Drink Man Woman '94▶
Emmanuelle, the Joys of a Woman '76
Entrapment '99
Escape to Burma '55
Far East '85
Flight from Singapore '62
Flower Drum Song '61
Fortunes of War '94
The Great Challenge '04
Indochine '92▶
Inn of Temptation '73
The Intended '02
The Intruder '04▶
Jackie Chan's First Strike '96▶
Jakarta '88
The Kill '73
The Killing Beach '92
The Killing Fields '84▶
K2: The Ultimate High '92
Lara Croft: Tomb Raider '01
Little Buddha '93
Lost Horizon '37▶
Malaya '49
The Man with the Golden Gun '74
Memories of Murder '03
Mr. Moto Takes a Chance '38
The Mongols '60
Natural Causes '94
Oldboy '03
Ong-Bak '03▶
Purple Butterfly '03▶
The Quest '96
The Quiet American '02▶
Rambo '08
Red Dust '32▶
Rogue Trader '98
S21: The Khmer Rouge Killing Machine '03▶
The Sand Pebbles '66▶
The Scent of Green Papaya '93▶
Shanghai Surprise '86
Singapore '47
The Story of the Weeping Camel '03▶
A Tale of Two Sisters '03▶
That's the Way I Like It '99
The 13th Mission '91
Three ... Extremes '04
Three Seasons '98
Three Times '05
Tigershark '87
Two Brothers '04
The Two Great Cavaliers '73
Typhoon '06
The Ugly American '63
Untold Scandal '03
The Vertical Ray of the Sun '00
Wake Island '42▶
White Ghost '88
Woman Is the Future of Man '04▶

Asian America

Better Luck Tomorrow '02▶
Chan Is Missing '82▶
Charlotte Sometimes '02
Color of a Brisk and Leaping Day '95
Combination Platter '93
Come See the Paradise '90▶
Dim Sum: A Little Bit of Heart '85▶
Double Happiness '94▶
Eat a Bowl of Tea '89▶

Assassination
see also Camelot (New); Foreign Intrigue; Hit Men/Women; Spies & Espionage

Abraham Lincoln '30
Ace of Hearts '85
Act of Vengeance '86
An Affair in Mind '89
African Rage '78
All the King's Men '49▶
The American Friend '77▶
The American Soldier '70
Antonio Das Mortes '68
The Arab Conspiracy '76
Ashes and Diamonds '58▶
Assassination '87
The Assassination Bureau '69▶
The Assassination File '96
The Assassination Game '92
The Assassination of Jesse James by the Coward Robert Ford '07▶
The Assassination of Richard Nixon '05
The Assassination of Trotsky '72
The Assignment '97▶
Beautiful Beast '95
Beautiful Hunter '94
Belfast Assassin '84
Black Sunday '77
Blind Horizon '04
Blood for Blood '95
Blow Out '81▶
Bobby '06
The Bourne Identity '02▶
The Bourne Supremacy '04▶
The Bourne Ultimatum '07▶
Brass Target '78
The Break '97
Brother Orchid '40▶
The Brotherhood of the Rose '89
The Burning Season '94▶
Cal '84▶
Caracara '00
Center of the Web '92
The Clockmaker '73▶
Cleopatra '99
Cold Front '89
Coming Out Alive '84
Counterstrike '03
The Criminal Mind '93
Dagger Eyes '83
The Dallas Connection '94
Dangerous Pursuit '89
The Day of the Dolphin '73
The Day of the Jackal '73▶
The Day That Shook the World '78
Dead Zone '83▶
Deadly Exposure '93
Death Force '78
Death to Smoochy '02
The Destructors '74
Diamond Run '90
The Dirty Dozen: The Next Mission '85
Disappearance '81
The Domino Principle '77
The Eagle Has Landed '77▶
The Eagle Has Two Heads '48▶
Elizabeth '98▶
Emmanuelle, the Queen '79
The Emperor and the Assassin '99
End Game '06
Enigma '82
Equalizer 2000 '86
The Evil That Men Do '84
Excellent Cadavers '99
Excessive Force 2: Force on Force '95
Executive Action '73
Expert Weapon '93
F/X '86▶
Fatal Justice '93
Flashpoint '84
Flirting with Fate '16▶
Foul Play '78▶
Friday Foster '75
From Russia with Love '63▶
Funeral for an Assassin '77
Gandhi '82▶
Ghosts of Mississippi '96
Hangmen Also Die '42▶
Harum Scarum '65
Hard Way '80
Hero '03▶
Hidden Assassin '94
Hit Lady '74
The Hunted '03
The Hunted '94
I Spit on Your Corpse '74
In the Line of Fire '93▶
The Informant '97▶
The Interpreter '05▶
Interview with the Assassin '02
Invitation to a Gunfighter '64
Jack Higgins' On Dangerous Ground '95
Jack Higgins: Midnight Man '96
The Jackal '97
JFK '91▶
Judgment Night '93
Kill Castro '80
The Killer Elite '75
Killer Likes Candy '78
The Killing Device '92
Kingfish: A Story of Huey P. Long '95
La Femme Nikita '91▶
La Passante '83▶
La Scorta '93▶
The Last Boy Scout '91
The Last Kiss Goodnight '96
Love and Anarchy '73▶
Love Kills '91
Love & Times of Scaramouche '76
Lumumba '01▶
Malcolm X '92▶
The Man Who Knew Too Much '34▶
The Man Who Knew Too Much '56▶
The Man with the Golden Gun '74
The Manchurian Candidate '62▶
Maniac '77
Mark of the Beast '87
The Mercenaries '80
Mercury Rising '98
Michael Collins '96▶
Most Wanted '97
Munich '05▶
My Little Assassin '99
Nashville '75▶
Nick of Time '95
A Night of Love '87
Night of the Assassin '77
Ninja Death Squad '87
November Conspiracy '96
The November Men '93
Nowhere to Hide '83
The Odd Job '78
Omar Khayyam '57
One Man Out '89
On the Run '83
Operation C.I.A. '65
The Ordeal of Dr. Mudd '80▶
The Parallax View '74▶
Paris Belongs to Us '60
Point of No Return '93
Programmed to Kill '86
PT 109 '63
Puerto Vallarta Squeeze '04
Queen's Messenger II '01
Quicker Than the Eye '88
Quiet Thunder '87
Red Eye '05▶
Red King, White Knight '89▶
Red Scorpion '89
Revenge of the Pink Panther '78▶
RFK '02
Rogue Male '76
Ruby '92
Running Against Time '90
Russian Roulette '75
Sabotage '96
Scorpio '73
Seven Days in May '64▶
Shooter '07▶
Silent Trigger '97
Snake Eyes '98
Soul Assassin '01
Spenser: The Judas Goat '94
Stalking Danger '86
State of Siege '73▶
Steele's Law '91
Stopover Tokyo '57
Suddenly '54▶
Supreme Sanction '99
Target: Favorite Son '87
Taxi Driver '76▶
The Terminator '84▶
The Terrorist '98
This Gun for Hire '90
Times of Harvey Milk '85▶
Two-Minute Warning '76
Veronica Guerin '03
Vantage Point '08
What a Way to Die '70
When Hell Broke Loose '58
Where There's Life '47
Windmills of the Gods '88
Without Warning: The James Brady Story '91▶
Xchange '00▶
XXX: State of the Union '05
Yojimbo '61▶
Z '69▶
Zoolander '01

Astronauts
see also Space Operas

Apollo 13 '95▶
Armageddon '98
The Astronaut Farmer '07
The Astronaut's Wife '99
Beneath the Planet of the Apes '70
Capricorn One '78▶
Countdown '68
Deep Impact '98
Escape from Mars '99
Fantastic Four '05
From the Earth to the Moon '98▶
Gattaca '97▶
In the Shadow of the Moon '07▶
Marooned '69
Mission to Mars '00
Planet of the Apes '68▶
Planet of the Apes '01▶
Red Planet '00
The Reluctant Astronaut '67
The Right Stuff '83▶
RocketMan '97
Solaris '02
Solaris '72▶
Space Cowboys '00▶
Species 2 '98
2001: A Space Odyssey '68▶
2010: The Year We Make Contact '84▶

Astronomy & Astrology
see also Star Gazing

Contact '97▶

At the Drive-In
see also At the Movies; At the Video Store

Dead End Drive-In '86
Drive-In '76
Drive-In Massacre '74
The Flamingo Rising '01
Grease '78▶
Lone Star '95▶
The Outsiders '83▶
Pee-wee's Big Adventure '85▶
Targets '68▶
Twister '96

At the Movies
see also Behind the Scenes

Anguish '88
Apartment Zero '88▶
Attack from Mars '88
The Aviator '04▶
Bonnie & Clyde '67▶
Boogie Nights '97▶
Cinema Paradiso '88▶
Come See the Paradise '90▶
Coming Up Roses '87
CQ '01
Day for Night '73▶
Demons '86
Desperately Seeking Susan '85▶
The Dying Gaul '05▶
Entropy '99
For Ever Mozart '96
Foul Play '78▶
Full Frontal '02
Get Shorty '95▶
Goodbye, Dragon Inn '03
Gremlins '84▶
Gremlins 2: The New Batch '90▶
The Hard Way '91▶
I Love Your Work '03
In and Out '97▶
The Inner Circle '91▶
Into the West '92▶
Invasion Earth: The Aliens Are Here! '87
Johnny Dangerously '84
The Kid and I '05
Last Action Hero '93▶
The Last Picture Show '71▶
The Last Shot '04
The Long Day Closes '92▶
Love and Death on Long Island '97▶
Matinee '92▶
Merton of the Movies '47
Mr. Bean's Holiday '07
The Movie House Massacre '78
A Nightmare on Elm Street 4: Dream Master '88
One Summer Love '76
Passion '82
Polyester '81
Popcorn '89
The Projectionist '71▶
The Purple Rose of Cairo '85▶
The Real Blonde '97▶
Reel Paradise '05▶
The Replacement Killers '98
Rerret '98
Sabotage '36▶
Scenes from a Mall '91
Scream '96▶
Scream 2 '97▶
Scream 3 '00▶
Shadow of the Vampire '00▶
Sherlock, Jr. '24▶
Simone '02
Slipstream '07
Something Short of Paradise '79
South Park: Bigger, Longer and Uncut '99▶
Tampopo '86▶
Things to Do in Denver When You're Dead '95▶
Trailer, the Movie '95
Tristram Shandy: A Cock and Bull Story '05▶
Two Bits '95
Variety '83
Venice, Venice '92
Wes Craven's New Nightmare '94▶
What the Moon Saw '90
White Heat '49▶
Who Framed Roger Rabbit '88▶
With Friends Like These '98▶

At the Video Store
see also At the Movies; At the Drive-In

Be Kind Rewind '08
Blast '96
Cafe Ole '00
Clerks '94▶
EDtv '99
Film Geek '06
The Fisher King '91▶
Jersey Girl '04
Little Fish '05
Love and Death on Long Island '97▶
Remote Control '88
Scream '95▶
Tainted '98
Video Violence '87
The Watermelon Woman '97

Atlanta
see also American South

Beauty Shop '05▶
Cyborg '89
Daddy's Little Girls '07
Diary of a Mad Black Woman '05▶
Driving Miss Daisy '89▶
The Dukes of Hazzard '05
Echo of Murder '00
Gone with the Wind '39▶
The Gospel '05▶
In the Flesh '97
Let's Do It Again '75▶
Midnight Blue '96
The Murder of Mary Phagan '87▶
Run for the Dream: The Gail Devers Story '96
Scarlett '94▶
Sharky's Machine '81▶
Sherman's March '86▶
Stomp the Yard '07

Atlantic City

Atlantic City '81▶
Beaches '88▶
Duane Hopwood '05▶
Gunshy '98▶
The King of Marvin Gardens '72▶
The Lemon Sisters '90
Owning Mahowny '03▶
Snake Eyes '98
Sour Grapes '98
Where the Truth Lies '05▶

Auditions

Audition '99▶
Billy Elliot '00▶
Chain of Souls '00
Dickie Roberts: Former Child Star '03
The Dolly Sisters '46
Fame '80▶
Fashion '83
Girls Just Want to Have Fun '85▶
Great World of Sound '07
The Guru '02
Hairspray '88▶
Hollywood Homicide '03
I Want Someone to Eat Cheese With '06
Inside Daisy Clover '65▶
Kiss Kiss Bang Bang '05▶
Pipe Dream '02
Shakespeare in Love '98▶
Showgirls '95
Smiley Face '07
The Thing Called Love '93
True Romance '93▶
Weeds '05
Yellow '06
You Light Up My Life '77

Aunts & Uncles, Nieces & Nephews
see also Brothers & Sisters; Family Ties

The Addams Family '91▶
Addams Family Values '93▶

▶ = rated three bones or higher

Aunts

- Airborne '93
- Alex Rider: Operation Stormbreaker '06
- All in a Night's Work '61
- American Movie '99
- Arsenic and Old Lace '44
- ATL '06
- Audrey's Rain '03
- August '95
- Auntie '73
- Auntie Mame '58
- The Ballad of the Sad Cafe '91
- Banjo Hackett '76
- Beethoven's 5th '03
- Betsy's Wedding '90
- The Beverly Hillbillies '93
- Blind Faith '98
- Blood Ties '92
- Bottoms Up '06
- Brewster's Millions '45
- Brewster's Millions '85
- Bright Eyes '34
- Brighton Beach Memoirs '86
- Broken Trail '06
- Broken Trust '93
- Bye-Bye '96
- The Camomile Lawn '92
- Casino Royale '67
- Casper '95
- Cassandra's Dream '07
- Charley's Aunt '25
- Charley's Aunt '41
- Christmas Eve '47
- City on Fire '87
- Clifford '92
- Come Undone '00
- Cookie's Fortune '99
- Country Life '95
- Cousin Bette '97
- Crazy in Alabama '99
- Cutthroat Island '95
- Damien: Omen 2 '78
- A Dangerous Woman '93
- Dark Blue '03
- Daughter of Keltoum '01
- The Dead '87
- Deadfall '93
- Deadtime Stories '86
- Desert Bloom '86
- Dogma '99
- The Dolly Sisters '46
- Don't Bother to Knock '52
- Double Trouble '67
- Down in the Delta '98
- The Dream Catcher '99
- The Dukes of Hazzard '05
- East Side Story '07
- The Embezzled Heaven '58
- Emile '03
- The Escape Artist '82
- Family Jewels '65
- Fast Girl '07
- The Fighting Temptations '03
- First Love '39
- Flipper '96
- For Real '02
- Frankenstein Reborn '98
- Galipoli '81
- Gigi '58
- Ginger and Cinnamon '03
- The Glass House '01
- The Godfather, Part 3 '90
- The Golden Compass '07
- The Good Son '93
- A Good Year '06
- The Grass Harp '95
- Great Expectations '34
- Great Expectations '46
- Great Expectations '81
- Great Expectations '89
- Great Expectations '97
- Great Expectations '99
- The Great Gildersleeve '43
- The Great Outdoors '88
- Greedy '94
- Green Dragon '01
- The Gypsy Moths '69
- Hamlet '48
- Hamlet '69
- Hamlet '90
- Hamlet '96
- Hamlet '00
- Hamlet '01
- Hannibal Rising '07
- Hard Rain '97
- Harry Potter and the Sorcerer's Stone '01
- Harry's War '84
- The Hearse '80
- Heart of Midnight '89
- Hellraiser '87
- Here Come the Littles: The Movie '85
- Hidalgo '04
- Hidden Enemy '40
- High School Confidential '58
- Honkytonk Man '82
- House Party 3 '94
- Housekeeping '87
- I Remember Mama '48
- In Country '89
- The Intended '02
- International Velvet '78
- I.Q. '94
- Jamaica Inn '39
- James and the Giant Peach '96
- Jason and the Argonauts '00
- Journey to the Center of the Earth 3D '08
- Kidnapped '05
- King, Queen, Knave '72
- Kingdom Come '01
- Kiss the Girls '97
- Land of Plenty '04
- Le Divorce '03
- Lemony Snicket's A Series of Unfortunate Events '04
- Les Destinees '00
- The Life and Adventures of Nicholas Nickleby '81
- A Light in the Darkness '02
- The Lion King '94
- The Lion King 1 1/2 '04
- The Longshots '08
- Lord of the Rings: The Fellowship of the Rings '01
- The Loved One '65
- Mame '74
- Man of the World '31
- Mansfield Park '07
- Martin '77
- Mean Streets '73
- Medea '70
- Mr. Jingles '06
- Mon Oncle '58
- Mon Oncle Antoine '71
- Mon Oncle d'Amerique '80
- Moon Over Miami '41
- More Dogs Than Bones '00
- Mostly Martha '01
- My Baby's Daddy '04
- My Beautiful Laundrette '85
- My Favorite Martian '98
- My Girl 2 '94
- My House in Umbria '03
- Nadja '95
- National Lampoon's Last Resort '94
- The Neon Bible '95
- The Nephew '97
- Never Give a Sucker an Even Break '41
- Next Friday '00
- Nicholas Nickleby '46
- Nicholas Nickleby '02
- No Reservations '07
- Off Limits '53
- Oriana '85
- The Perfect Man '05
- Pete's Meteor '98
- The Pink Panther '64
- Plunkett & Macleane '98
- Poltergeist 3 '88
- Poolhall Junkies '03
- Practical Magic '98
- The Price of Milk '00
- The Princess Diaries 2: Royal Engagement '04
- Quinceanera '06
- Raising Helen '04
- Rebecca of Sunnybrook Farm '38
- Return of the Fly '59
- Revenge of the Nerds 3: The Next Generation '92
- The Ring '02
- The Ringer '05
- Road House 2: Last Call '06
- Roger Dodger '02
- The Rugrats Movie '98
- Saving Sarah Cain '07
- The Searchers '56
- Secondhand Lions '03
- The Secret Garden '49
- The Secret Garden '84
- The Secret Garden '87
- The Secret Garden '93
- The Secret of My Success '87
- Secret of the Cave '06
- Service De Luxe '38
- Shadow of a Doubt '43
- Shaft '00
- The Sky Is Falling '00
- Sleepwalking '08
- Slums of Beverly Hills '98
- Smart People '08
- Smilin' Through '41
- Something for the Boys '44
- Spider-Man '02
- Spider-Man 3 '07
- Star Wars '77
- Stealing Harvard '02
- Steamboat Round the Bend '35
- Stiff Upper Lips '96
- Striking Distance '93
- Tatie Danielle '91
- Tea for Two '50
- 13 Ghosts '01
- 13th Guest '32
- Thr3e '07
- Time Regained '99
- Tom and Huck '95
- Travels with My Aunt '72
- The Twelve Dogs of Christmas '05
- Twins of Evil '71
- Twitches '05
- Twitches Too '07
- UHF '89
- Uncle Buck '89
- Uncle Nino '03
- Under Siege 2: Dark Territory '95
- Unstrung Heroes '95
- Urban Cowboy '80
- Venus '06
- Volver '06
- Waiting for the Light '90
- The Wings of the Dove '97
- The Wizard of Loneliness '88
- The Wizard of Oz '39
- Woman of Straw '64
- The Yards '00
- Your Vice is a Closed Room and Only I Have the Key '72
- Zatoichi '03

Australia

see Down Under

Autism

- The Boy Who Could Fly '86
- Family Pictures '93
- Guarding Eddy '04
- The Hawk Is Dying '06
- House of Cards '92
- Killer Diller '04
- Malcolm '86
- Mercury Rising '98
- Milwaukee, Minnesota '03
- Molly '99
- Mozart and the Whale '05
- Rain Man '88
- Silent Fall '94
- Snow Cake '06
- When the Bough Breaks '93

Automobiles

see Checkered Flags; Motor Vehicle Dept.

Babysitting

see also Bringing Up Baby; Parenthood

- Adventures in Babysitting '87
- Angel Blue '97
- Are You in the House Alone? '78
- Babel '06
- The Baby-Sitters' Club '95
- The Babysitter '80
- The Babysitter '95
- Battling for Baby '92
- Bebe's Kids '92
- Catch That Kid '04
- The Crazysitter '94
- Dr. Seuss' The Cat in the Hat '03
- Don't Bother to Knock '52
- Don't Tell Mom the Babysitter's Dead '91
- Flourish '06
- Four Rooms '95
- Fright '71
- A Global Affair '63
- The Guardian '90
- Halloween '78
- Implicated '98
- Laurel & Hardy: Brats '30
- Look Who's Talking '89
- Meet the Fockers '04
- The Pacifier '05
- Rita, Sue & Bob Too '87
- Rock-A-Bye Baby '57
- See Spot Run '01
- Sitting Pretty '48
- Superbabies: Baby Geniuses 2 '04
- Three's Trouble '85
- Trick or Treats '82
- Uncle Buck '89
- Unhook the Stars '96
- Wanted: Babysitter '75
- Weekend with the Babysitter '70
- When a Stranger Calls '79
- When a Stranger Calls '06
- When a Stranger Calls Back '93

Bachelor Party

see also Up All Night

- American Wedding '03
- Bachelor Party '84
- Bachelor Party 2: The Last Temptation '08
- Bachelor Party Vegas '05
- The Best Man '99
- Failure to Launch '06
- A Guy Thing '03
- House Party 3 '94
- In and Out '97
- Intimate Betrayal '96
- Laurel & Hardy: Be Big '31
- Now You Know '02
- Psycho Cop 2 '94
- Sideways '04
- Stag '97
- Very Bad Things '98

Bad Bosses

see also Corporate Shenanigans; Dying for a Promotion; Office Surprise

- Antitrust '00
- City of Ghosts '03
- Click '06
- Clockwatchers '97
- The Devil Wears Prada '06
- In Good Company '04
- Joe Somebody '01
- Kate & Leopold '01
- 9 to 5 '80
- Office Space '98
- Secretary '02
- Swimming with Sharks '94
- Willard '03
- Working Girl '88

Bad Dads

see also Dads; Monster Moms; Parenthood

- Aberdeen '00
- Affliction '97
- Aladdin and the King of Thieves '96
- Alice & Martin '98
- American Beauty '99
- American Virgin '98
- At Close Range '86
- The Attic '80
- The Audrey Hepburn Story '00
- Basil '98
- Bastard out of Carolina '96
- Beach Hotel '92
- The Beat My Heart Skipped '05
- Beatrice '88
- Behind the Mask '99
- Benefit of the Doubt '93
- Black Cloud '04
- Black Peter '63
- Blade 2 '02
- The Break '95
- Broken English '96
- The Brothers Karamazov '58
- Buddy's Song '91
- Buffalo 66 '97
- The Butcher Boy '97
- Cameron's Closet '89
- Catch Me If You Can '02
- The Celebration '98
- Character '97
- City by the Sea '02
- The Claim '00
- Click '06
- Club Land '01
- Conseil de Famille '86
- Crime and Punishment in Suburbia '00
- Croupier '97
- Dad Savage '97
- Daddy's Boys '87
- Damage '92
- Dangerous Relations '93
- Dead Pet '01
- Deconstructing Harry '97
- The Devil's Advocate '97
- Die Screaming, Marianne '73
- Dolores Claiborne '94
- Don't Come Knocking '05
- Don't Tell '05
- Dracula and Son '76
- Duane Hopwood '05
- East of Eden '54
- East of Eden '80
- Edwin '84
- El Bola '00
- Elf '03
- Elisa '94
- The Empire Strikes Back '80
- Farmer & Chase '96
- Father Hood '93
- Fear Strikes Out '57
- Finish Line '89
- First Born '84
- Flesh and Bone '93
- Forty Shades of Blue '05
- Four Days '99
- Frailty '02
- Freddy Got Fingered '01
- Friday Night Lights '04
- The General's Daughter '99
- Getting Even with Dad '94
- Goldengirl '79
- Grave of the Vampire '72
- The Great Santini '80
- Hand Gun '93
- Hanging Up '99
- Harry Potter and the Chamber of Secrets '02
- Haven '04
- He Got Game '98
- Heart of the Stag '84
- The Heiress '49
- Hoodlum & Son '03
- The Horror Chamber of Dr. Faustus '59
- How I Killed My Father '03
- Hulk '03
- Hunter's Moon '97
- I Capture the Castle '02
- Imaginary Heroes '05
- The Incredible Mrs. Ritchie '03
- Joe the King '99
- Julien Donkey-boy '99
- Keeping Up with the Steins '06
- Kicking & Screaming '05
- Kiss Daddy Goodbye '81
- Kiss Daddy Goodnight '87
- La Promesse '99
- Last Time Out '94
- L.I.E. '01
- Life as a House '01
- Like Father Like Son '05
- Lilian's Story '95
- Little Boy Blue '97
- Look at Me '04
- Love and Basketball '00
- Love Come Down '00
- A Loving Father '02
- Lucky You '07
- Luckytown '00
- MacArthur Park '01
- Magnolia '99
- Manito '03
- Martin (Hache) '97
- The Mighty '98
- The Missing '03
- Monster's Ball '01
- My Architect: A Son's Journey '03
- The Myth of Fingerprints '97
- Natural Born Killers '94
- The Neon Bible '95
- Niagara, Niagara '97
- No Looking Back '98
- The Notorious Bettie Page '06
- One True Thing '98
- Opposite Corners '96
- The Other Side of the Law '95
- Panic '00
- Parents '89
- Popeye's Voyage: The Quest for Pappy '04
- Poster Boy '04
- Price of Glory '00
- Red River '48
- Rick '03
- Riding in Cars with Boys '01
- Rites of Frankenstein '72
- Rites of Passage '99
- The River is Red '48
- Romeo Must Die '00
- The Rookie '02
- The Royal Tenenbaums '01
- Sarah, Plain and Tall: Winter's End '99
- The Savages '07
- Say Anything '89
- Shine '95
- The Shining '80
- The Simpsons Movie '07
- Sins of the Father '01
- The Spanish Gardener '57
- Spare Me '92
- Spider-Man '02
- Stakeout '62
- Star Maps '97
- Steel City '06
- The Stepfather '87
- Stepfather 2: Make Room for Daddy '89
- Stepfather 3: Father's Day '92
- Swimming Upstream '03
- Talladega Nights: The Ballad of Ricky Bobby '06
- This Boy's Life '93
- A Thousand Acres '97
- Thumbsucker '05
- Toll of the Desert '35
- Transfixed '01
- Turn It Up '00
- U-Turn '97
- Underworld: Evolution '05
- Virgin '03
- Wannabes '01
- The War Zone '98
- Washington Square '97
- Where the Hot Wind Blows '59
- ZigZag '02

Ballet

see also Dance Fever

- Alive and Kicking '96
- An American in Paris '51
- Angel in a Taxi '59
- The Bacchantes '63
- Ballet Russes '05
- Black Tights '60
- Body Beat '88
- Brain Donors '92
- Center Stage '00
- The Children of Theatre Street '77

▲ = rated three bones or higher

The Company '03▶
The Cowboy & the Ballerina '84
Dance '90
Dance, Girl, Dance '40
The Dancer Upstairs '02
Dancers '87
George Balanchine's The Nutcracker '93
Grand Hotel '32▶
Invitation to the Dance '56
Limelight '52▶
Little Ballerina '47
Meet Me in Las Vegas '56
Mirrors '85
Never Let Me Go '53
Nijinsky '80
Nine Months '95
Nutcracker Sweet '84
Nutcracker: The Motion Picture '86
The Red Shoes '48▶
Shadow Dancing '88▶
Shall We Dance '37▶
Spectre of the Rose '46
Summer Interlude '50▶
Suspiria '77▶
Tales of Beatrix Potter '71▶

Ballooning
The Adventures of Baron Munchausen '89▶
Around the World in 80 Days '56▶
Around the World in 80 Days '89
Around the World in 80 Days '04
Charlie and the Great Balloon Chase '82
Cloud Waltzing '87
Danny Deckchair '03
Enduring Love '04
Fantastic Balloon Voyage '76
Five Weeks in a Balloon '62
Flight of the Eagle '82
Frankenstein Island '81
The Great Race '65▶
Lost Zeppelin '29
Men Don't Leave '89
Mysterious Island '61▶
Night Crossing '81
Octopussy '83
Olly Olly Oxen Free '78
Police Academy 4: Citizens on Patrol '87
Queen of the Jungle '35
The Red Balloon '56▶
Those Magnificent Men in Their Flying Machines '65▶
Voyage en Balloon '59
The Wizard of Oz '39▶

Baltimore
And Justice for All '79
Avalon '90
The Boys of Baraka '05
Breathing Lessons '94
Cause of Death '00
The Climb '97
Diner '82▶
A Dirty Shame '04
First Sunday '08
Hairspray '07▶
Hairspray '88▶
He Said, She Said '91
He's Just Not That Into You '08
The Hit '01
Homicide: The Movie '00
Ladder 49 '04
Liberty Heights '99
Pecker '98
Polyester '81
The Salon '05
Sleepless in Seattle '93▶
The Sum of All Fears '02
Tin Men '87▶

Baseball
Air Bud 4: Seventh Inning Fetch '02
Alibi Ike '35
Amazing Grace & Chuck '87
Angels in the Infield '00
Angels in the Outfield '51▶
Angels in the Outfield '94▶
The Babe '92
The Babe Ruth Story '48
The Bad News Bears '76▶

Bar & Grill
see also Nightclubs
Albino Alligator '96
Americano '05
Ash Wednesday '02
Bar Girls '95
Bar Hopping '00
Barfly '87▶
Bedazzled '68▶
Before Sunrise '94▶
Bottoms Up '06
The Bowery '33▶
The Broken Hearts Club '00▶
Bucktown '75
Bunzy's Last Call '95
Cocktail '88
Coyote Ugly '00
Crocodile Dundee '86▶
Death in Brunswick '90
Death Proof '07▶
Dinner Rush '00▶
Feast '06
Flickering Lights '01
The Florentine '98
From Dusk Till Dawn '95
From Dusk Till Dawn 2: Texas Blood Money '98
From Dusk Till Dawn 3: The Hangman's Daughter '99
Headless Body in Topless Bar '96
Hedwig and the Angry Inch '00▶
Hi-Life '98
Hysterical Blindness '02
The Iceman Cometh '73
Intimacy '00
John Carpenter's Vampires '97
The Last Time I Committed Suicide '96
Lemonade Joe '64
Little Boy Blue '97
Luminarias '99
Margarita Happy Hour '01
Mondays in the Sun '02
Money Kings '98
Nobody '99
One Night at McCool's '01
Overnight '03▶
Pee-wee's Big Adventure '85▶
Phenomenon '96
Rare Birds '01
Restaurant '98
Road House '89
Road House 2: Last Call '06
Roxanne '87▶
Suicide '96
The Tavern '00
The Taste of Others '00▶
Time Served '99
Tree's Lounge '96
Twice upon a Yesterday '98
Two Family House '99
Un Air de Famille '96
Urban Cowboy '80▶
Urbania '00
The White Countess '05▶

Barcelona
see also Madrid; Spain
The Bobo '67
Dark Habits '84
Food of Love '02
Gaudi Afternoon '01
Land and Freedom '95▶
L'Auberge Espagnole '02▶
Nico and Dani '00
The White Countess '05▶

Baseball
The Bad News Bears '05
The Bad News Bears Go to Japan '78
The Bad News Bears in Breaking Training '77
Ball of Wax '03
Bang the Drum Slowly '56
Barb Wire '96
Battling Orioles '24
The Benchwarmers '06
Bingo Long Traveling All-Stars & Motor Kings '76▶
Blood Games '90
Blue Skies Again '83
The Break-Up '06
Brewster's Millions '85▶
The Bronx Is Burning '07
Bull Durham '88▶
The Busher '19
The Catcher '98
Chasing Dreams '81
Chicken Little '05
Chu Chu & the Philly Flash '81
Cobb '94▶
Comeback Kid '80
The Comrades of Summer '92
Cooperstown '93
Damn Yankees '58▶
Don't Look Back: The Story of Leroy "Satchel" Paige '81
Ed '96
Eight Men Out '88▶
Everyone's Hero '06
The Fan '96
Fear Strikes Out '57▶
Fever Pitch '05
Field of Dreams '89▶
The Final Season '07
Finding Buck McHenry '00
For Love of the Game '99
Frequency '00
Game 6 '05
The Geisha Boy '58
Hank Aaron: Chasing the Dream '95▶
Hardball '01
Headin' Home '20
Hustle '04
Ironweed '87▶
It Happens Every Spring '49▶
It's Good to Be Alive '74
It's My Turn '80
The Jackie Robinson Story '50▶
Jim Thorpe: All American '51
Joe Torre: Curveballs Along the Way '97
The Kid from Left Field '79
Kill the Umpire '50
A League of Their Own '92▶
The Life and Times of Hank Greenberg '99▶
Little Big League '94
A Little Inside '01
Long Gone '87
Love Affair: The Eleanor & Lou Gehrig Story '77▶
Major League '89▶
Major League 2 '94
Major League 3: Back to the Minors '98
The Man from Left Field '93
Mean Streak '99
Mr. Baseball '92
Mr. Destiny '90
Mr. 3000 '04
The Natural '84▶
Night Game '89
One in a Million: The Ron LeFlore Story '78
Past the Bleachers '95
Pastime '91▶
Perfect Game '00
Pride of St. Louis '52
Pistol: The Birth of a Legend '90
Pleasantville '98▶
Porky's Revenge '85
Rebound '05
Rebound: The Legend of Earl "The Goat" Manigault '96
The Red Sneakers '01
The Rookie '02▶
Rookie of the Year '93
The Sandlot '93▶
The Scout '94
Semi-Pro '08
A Season on the Brink '02
The Sixth Man '97
Slam Dunk Ernest '95
Space Jam '96
Sunset Park '96
Tall Story '60
Teen Wolf '85

Soul of the Game '96▶
Squeeze Play '79
Stealing Home '88
The Stratton Story '49▶
Summer Catch '01
Take Me Out to the Ball Game '49
Taking Care of Business '90
Talent for the Game '91
Three Wishes '95
Tiger Town '83
Trading Hearts '87
Up for Grabs '05
The Upside of Anger '05▶
Wait until Spring, Bandini '90
Whistling in Brooklyn '43
Wide Awake '97
A Winner Never Quits '86
The Winning Team '52
Woman of the Year '42▶

Basketball
Above the Rim '94
The Absent-Minded Professor '61▶
Adam Sandler's 8 Crazy Nights '02
Air Bud '97
The Air Up There '94
Alien: Resurrection '97▶
Annie O '95
The Basket '99
The Basketball Diaries '95
Believe In Me '06
Big and Hairy '98
Big Mo '73
Big Shot: Confessions of a Campus Bookie '02
Black and White '99▶
Blue Chips '94
The Cable Guy '96
Campus Confessions '38
Celtic Pride '96
Coach '78
Coach Carter '05▶
The Cookout '04
Cornbread, Earl & Me '75
Crossover '06
Eddie '96
Fast Break '79
Final Exam '98
Final Shot: The Hank Gathers Story '92
Finding Forrester '00
The Fish that Saved Pittsburgh '79
Flubber '97
For Heaven's Sake '79
Forget Paris '95
Glory Road '06
Guarding Eddy '04
Harvard Man '01
He Got Game '98
The Heart of the Game '05
Heaven Is a Playground '91
Hoop Dreams '94▶
Hoosiers '86▶
Inside Moves '80
John Tucker Must Die '06
Juwanna Mann '02
King of the Jungle '01
Like Mike '02
Love and Basketball '00▶
O '01
One on One '77
Passing Glory '99▶

Bats
see also Eco-Vengeance!; Up All Night; Wild Kingdom
The Bat '59
The Bat People '74
Batman Begins '05▶
Batman Forever '95▶
Batman Returns '92
Bats '99
The Devil Bat '41
Nightwing '79
The Vampire Bat '32

Beach Blanket Bingo
see also Lifeguards; Sex on the Beach; Surfing; Swimming
Back to the Beach '87▶
Baywatch the Movie: Forbidden Paradise '95
Beach Babes from Beyond '93
Beach Blanket Bingo '65▶
Beach Girls '82
The Beach Girls and the Monster '65
Beach House '82
Beach Party '63
Bikini Beach '64
Bikini Summer '91
Bikini Summer 3: South Beach Heat '97
Blue Crush '02▶
Body Waves '92
California Dreaming '79
Computer Beach Party '88
The Fat Spy '66
Horror of Party Beach '64
How to Stuff a Wild Bikini '65
I Wanna Be a Beauty Queen '85
Love! Valour! Compassion! '96
Malibu Beach '78
Maslin Beach '97
Muscle Beach Party '64
Nico and Dani '00
Pajama Party '64
Phat Beach '96
Psycho Beach Party '00
Ride the Wild Surf '64
Seaside Swingers '65
Shag: The Movie '89▶
South Beach Academy '96
A Summer's Tale '96
Surf Party '64
A Swingin' Summer '65
Too Good to Be True '98
Wet and Wild Summer '92
Where the Boys Are '60

Bears
see also Wild Kingdom
Almost Heroes '97
The Bear '89▶
The Bears & I '74
Berserker '87
Brother Bear '03
Brother Bear 2 '06
The Capture of Grizzly Adams '82
Claws '77
The Country Bears '02
Deadtime Stories '86
Dr. Dolittle 2 '01
The Edge '97▶
Gentle Ben '67
The Gentle Giant '67
The Golden Compass '07
The Great Outdoors '88
Grizzly '76
Grizzly Adams: The Legend Continues '90
Grizzly Falls '99
Grizzly Man '05▶

The Hotel New Hampshire '84

That Championship Season '82
That Championship Season '99
Through the Fire '05
"Tyler Perry's Meet the Browns '08
Underworld Scandal '47
Unshackled '00
White Men Can't Jump '92▶

The Bat People '74
The Bat Whispers '30
Batman Begins '05▶
Batman Forever '95▶
Batman Returns '92
Bats '99
The Devil Bat '41
The Many Adventures of Winnie the Pooh '77
Ms. Bear '97
The Parent Trap '61
Pooh's Heffalump Movie '05
Rudyard Kipling's The Jungle Book '94
Second Jungle Book: Mowgli and Baloo '97
Starbird and Sweet William '73
True Heart '97
An Unfinished Life '05▶
Wild Grizzly '99
Without a Paddle '04

Beatniks
Beat Girl '60
A Bucket of Blood '59▶
Expresso Bongo '59
Funny Face '57▶
Hairspray '88▶
The Last Time I Committed Suicide '96
The Prime Time '60
The Sleazy Uncle '89
So I Married an Axe Murderer '93

Beauty Pageants
see also Dream Girls
Beautiful '00
The Case of the Lucky Legs '35
Drop Dead Gorgeous '99▶
The Duchess of Idaho '50
Happy, Texas '99▶
I Know What You Did Last Summer '97▶
Little Miss Sunshine '06▶
Miss All-American Beauty '82
Miss Cast Away '04
Miss Congeniality '00▶
Miss Congeniality 2: Armed and Fabulous '05
Miss Firecracker '89▶
No Contest '94
Shag: The Movie '89▶
Smile '75▶
Sweet Beat '59
Waikiki Wedding '37▶

Beer
see also On the Rocks
Beer '85
Beer League '06
Beerfest '06
Happy Hour '87
The Jolly Boys' Last Stand '00
Kicked in the Head '97
The Nugget '02
The Saddest Music in the World '03
Smokey and the Bandit '77▶
Strange Brew '83▶
Take This Job & Shove It '81
Young Einstein '89

Bees
see also Killer Bugs and Slugs
Bee Movie '07
The Bees '78
Candyman '92▶
Candyman 2: Farewell to the Flesh '94
Candyman 3: Day of the Dead '98
Microcosmos '96▶
The Swarm '73

▶ = rated three bones or higher

Behind

Behind Bars
see also Great Escapes; Men in Prison; Women in Prison

Behind the Scenes
see also At the Movies; Film History

Abuse '82
Actors and Sin '52
Adaptation '02►
The Affairs of Annabel '38
An Alan Smithee Film: Burn, Hollywood, Burn '97
Alexandria Again and Forever '90
American Virgin '98
America's Sweethearts '01►
Anaconda '96
...And God Spoke '94
The Audrey Hepburn Story '00
Augustin '95
Auto Focus '02►
The Bad and the Beautiful '52►
Beaumarchais the Scoundrel '96
Best Friends '82
Beware of a Holy Whore '70
Bewitched '05
Big Fat Liar '02
The Big Knife '55►
The Big Picture '89
Big Shot's Funeral '01
Big Show '37
Bloodbath '98
Body Chemistry 3: Point of Seduction '93
The Bodyguard '92
Bombay Talkie '70
Borat: Cultural Learnings of America for Make Benefit Glorious Nation of Kazakhstan '06►
Boy Meets Girl '38►
Break a Leg '03
Broadway Rhythm '44
Bullets over Broadway '94►
Cannes Man '96
Cats Don't Dance '97
Cecil B. Demented '00
Celebrity '98►
Chaplin '92►
The Chaplin Revue '58
A Chorus Line '85
A Chorus of Disapproval '89
Chuck Berry: Hail! Hail! Rock 'n' Roll '87►
Come as You Are '05
The Confessional '95►
Contempt '64►
CQ '01
Crimetime '96
Crocodile Dundee in Los Angeles '01
Crossover Dreams '85
Cut '00
Dames '34►
Dance of Life '29
Dancing in September '00
Dancing Lady '33
Dangerous Game '93
Danny Roane: First Time Director '06
Darlings of the Gods '90
Day at the Beach '98
Day for Night '73►
The Death Kiss '33
Delirious '91
The Disappearance of Kevin Johnson '95
Don't Let Your Meat Loaf '95
Double Threat '92
The Dresser '83►
Ed Wood '94►
The End of Violence '97
Entropy '99
Everything for Sale '68
Evil Ed '96
Expresso Bongo '59
Face the Music '92
Factory Girl '06
Fall Guy '82
Festival at Cannes '82
5 Dark Souls '96
Flickers '80
The Fluffer '01
Footlight Parade '33►
For Ever Mozart '96
For Your Consideration '06►
Free and Easy '30
Free Enterprise '98
The Freeway Maniac '88
French Exit '97
The French Lieutenant's Woman '81►
Full Frontal '02
Full Tilt Boogie '97
Get Shorty '95►
The Ghost Walks '34
Give a Girl a Break '53
Glam '97
Gods and Monsters '98►
Going Hollywood '33►
The Goldwyn Follies '38
Good Times '67
Goodbye, Norma Jean '75
Goodnight, Sweet Marilyn '89
The Grace Kelly Story '83
Grief '94
Grunt! The Wrestling Movie '85
The Hard Way '91►
He Said, She Said '91
The Hearst and Davies Affair '85
Hearts of Darkness: A Filmmaker's Apocalypse '91►
Help! '65►
Hijacking Hollywood '97
Hindsight '97
Hollywood Boulevard '76
Hollywood Confidential '97
Hollywood Ending '02►
Hollywood Man '76
Hollywood Mystery '34
Hollywood North '03
Hollywood Shuffle '87
Hollywoodland '06
Hooper '78
Hughes & Harlow: Angels in Hell '77
I Could Never Be Your Woman '06
The Ice Rink '99
Identification of a Woman '82
I'll Do Anything '93
I'm Going Home '00►
In a Moment of Passion '93
In the Shadows '01
In the Soup '92
The Independent '00
Inland Empire '06
Inside Daisy Clover '65
Into the Sun '92
Introducing Dorothy Dandridge '99►
Irma Vep '96
James Dean '01
The Jayne Mansfield Story '80
Joey Breaker '93►
The Killing of Sister George '69
L.A. Confidential '97►
La Dolce Vita '60►
L.A. Goddess '92
The Last Don 2 '98
The Last Shot '04
The Last Word '95
Le Polygraphe '96
Le Schpountz '38
The Leading Man '96
Legs '83
Lies '83
Lisbon Story '94
Living in Oblivion '94►
Lobster Man from Mars '89
The Lonely Lady '83
Lucky Devils '33
Make a Wish '37
A Man in Love '87►
Man of a Thousand Faces '57►
Matinee '92
Meet the Feebles '89
A Midwinter's Tale '95
Miss All-American Beauty '82
Mistress '91
Modern Romance '81►
The Moguls '05
Movie Maker '86
Movies Money Murder '96
The Mozart Brothers '86►
Mulholland Drive '01►
The Muppets Take Manhattan '84►
The Muse '99
My Life's in Turnaround '94
My Wife is an Actress '01
Naked in New York '93
New Faces of 1952 '54
A Night for Crime '42
Night of the Living Dead, 25th Anniversary Documentary '93
The Nines '07►
Nixon '95►
Noises Off '92
Notting Hill '99
The November Men '93
On an Island with You '48
Open Season '95
Opening Night '77
The Oscar '66
Paradise, Texas '05
Paris When It Sizzles '64
Passion '82
Pastime '91►
People I Know '02
The Perils of Pauline '47
The Phantom Lover '95
Pick a Star '37
The Pickle '93
The Player '92►
Portraits Chinois '96
Postcards from the Edge '90►
Quicksand '01
Rave Review '95
Ready to Wear '94
Rented Lips '88
Return to Cabin by the Lake '01
Rhythm on the River '40
Ringmaster '98
RKO 281 '99►
Roadie '80
Rorret '87►
Scream 3 '00
Search and Destroy '94
Searching for Bobby D '05
Secret Motive '85►
Sex Is Crazy '79
Shadow of the Vampire '00►
Shoot or Be Shot '02
The Shot '96
The Show '95
Silent Motive '91
Simone '02
Sioux City Sue '46
Slaves of Hollywood '99
Slings & Arrows: Season 2 '05►
Slipstream '07
S.O.B. '81
Somewhere in Time '80
Son of Gascogne '95
Spice World: The Movie '97
Stage Door '37►
Stand-Ins '97
Stand-Ins '85
The Star Maker '95
Star Spangled Rhythm '42►
State and Main '00
State of Things '82►
The Stranger: Kablooink '95
The Stunt Man '80►
Stunts '77
The Suburbans '99
Sugar Sweet '02
Sugar Town '99
Sullivan's Travels '41►
Summer Stock '50►
Sunset '88
Sunset Boulevard '50►
Sweet Liberty '86
Sweet Perfection '90
Swimming with Sharks '94►
Tango '98
Teenager '74
10 Items or Less '06
That Thing You Do! '96►
These Old Broads '01
They Bite '95
Through the Olive Trees '94►
Tie Me Up! Tie Me Down! '90
Time Code '00
Tootsie '82►
The Travelling Players '75
Tropic Thunder '08
The TV Set '06
Ulysses' Gaze '95
Under the Rainbow '81
Users '78
Valley of the Dolls '67
Velvet Touch '48►
Venice, Venice '92
A Very Private Affair '62
Wag the Dog '97
Waiting for Guffman '96
The Waiting Game '99
The Watermelon Woman '97
Welcome to Hollywood '00
Wes Craven's New Nightmare '94►
The West Point Story '50
What Price Hollywood? '32►
Where's Marlowe? '99
White Hunter, Black Heart '90►
Whodunit '82
Wild Party '74
Witch Hunt '94
Zou Zou '34

Belfast
see also Dublin; Ireland

Belfast Assassin '84
Cal '84►
Circle of Deceit '94
The Devil's Own '96►
An Everlasting Piece '00
Four Days in July '85
Hennessy '75
In the Name of the Father '93►
The Informant '97►
Mad About Mambo '00
Nothing Personal '95►
Quiet Day in Belfast '74►
Resurrection Man '97
This is the Sea '96

Berlin
see also Germany

Aimee & Jaguar '98
The Alley Cats '65
Anita, Dances of Vice '87
The Apple '80
The Assignment '97
Before the Fall '04
Bent '97
Berlin Alexanderplatz '80►
The Berlin Conspiracy '91
Berlin Tunnel 21 '81
The Blue Hour '91
Born in '45 '65
The Bourne Supremacy '04►
Cabaret '72►
The Captain from Koepenick '56
Charlie Chan at the Olympics '37
Chinese Boxes '84
Club Extinction '89
Cold Room '84
The Company '07
David '79►
Dead Pigeon on Beethoven Street '72
Demons '86
Downfall '04►
The Edukators '04
Eurotrip '04
Faraway, So Close! '93
Fatherland '94
Flightplan '05
Forbidden '85
A Foreign Affair '48►
Funeral in Berlin '66►
Go for Zucker '05
Good Bye, Lenin! '03►
Gotcha! '85
The Good German '05
The Hard Word '02
Heart '01►
Heist '01►
Hitman '07
In the Mood for Love '00►
The Kite Runner '07►
Lady Jayne Killer '03
The League of Extraordinary Gentlemen '03►
Lord of War '05►
Love in the Time of Cholera '07
Mad Love '01
Medea '88
The Messenger: The Story of Joan of Arc '99
Mindstorm '01
Munich '05►
Once Upon a Time in America '84►
Pack of Lies '87
Philby, Burgess and MacLean: Spy Scandal of the Century '84
Ripley's Game '02►
Road House '48
Signs & Wonders '00
Smiley's People '82
Indiana Jones and the Last Crusade '89►
The Innocent '93
Invincible '01
Judgment in Berlin '88
Kamikaze '89 '83►
King of Thieves '04
The Legend of Rita '99
The Lives of Others '06►
Lola and Billy the Kid '98
The Looking Glass War '69
Mother Night '96►
The Murderers Are Among Us '46
Obsession '97
The Oppermann Family '82
The Promise '94
Run Lola Run '98►
Salmonberries '91
The Search '48►
The Serpent's Egg '78
Shining Through '92
Solo Sunny '80
The Song of Songs '33
Summer Palace '06►
Taking Sides '01►
The Third Sex '57
The Tigress '93
Timecop 2: The Berlin Decision '03
The Truce '96►
The Tunnel '01►
Verboten! '59
The Waiting Time '99
What to Do in Case of Fire '02
Wings of Desire '88►

Betrayal

Amores Perros '00►
Assault on Precinct 13 '05
Benedict Arnold: A Question of Honor '03
Blade 2 '02►
Blue Car '03►
Book of Love '04
Breach '07►
The Business of Fancydancing '02
The Business of Strangers '01
Chill Factor '99
The Count of Monte Cristo '02►
Cruel Intentions 3 '04
Cypher '02►
Dangerous Liaisons '03
The Departed '06►
The Devil's Backbone '01►
Die Another Day '02►
Enigma '01
Esther Kahn '00
Extremely Dangerous '99
Far from Heaven '02►
The Fast Runner '01►
The Good Shepherd '06►
The Great Water '04
Hangover Square '45►
Star Wars: Episode 2 — Attack of the Clones '02►
Star Wars: Episode 3 — Revenge of the Sith '05►
This Gun for Hire '42►
Tick Tock '00
Tinker, Tailor, Soldier, Spy '80►
Tropix '02
25th Hour '02
The Weight of Water '00
Wicker Park '04

Beverly Hills

Allie & Me '97
Anywhere But Here '99
B.A.P.'s '97
Beverly Hills Cop '84
Beverly Hills Cop 2 '87
Beverly Hills Cop 3 '94
Beverly Hills Madam '86
Clueless '95►
Down and Out in Beverly Hills '86
The Hollywood Knights '80
Housewife '72
Just Married '03
Legally Blonde '01
Pretty Woman '90►
The Return of the Beverly Hillbillies '81
Scenes from the Class Struggle in Beverly Hills '89
Slums of Beverly Hills '98►
Troop Beverly Hills '89
Wassup Rockers '06

Bicycling

American Flyers '85
And Soon the Darkness '70
Beijing Bicycle '01
The Bicycle Thief '48►
Blood Trails '06
BMX Bandits '83
Breaking Away '79►
Butch Cassidy and the Sundance Kid '69►
E.T.: The Extra-Terrestrial '82►
The Flying Scotsman '06
Go Further '03
Isn't Life Wonderful '24►
Off the Mark '87
Pee-wee's Big Adventure '85►
Quicksilver '86
Rad '86
Rush It '77
Ten Speed '76
The Triplets of Belleville '02►
2 Seconds '98

Big Battles
see also Civil War; Korean War; Korean War; Persian Gulf/Iraq War; Revolutionary War; Vietnam War; World War I; World War II

The Alamo '60►
The Alamo '04
Alexander '04
Alexander Nevsky '38►
Alexander the Great '55
Aliens '86►
Anzio '68
Apocalypse Now '79►
The Arena '73
Arena '89
Attila '01
Back to Bataan '45
Barry Lyndon '75►
Battle Beyond the Sun '63
Battle of Britain '69
The Battle of El Alamein '68
The Battle of the Bulge '65
The Battle of the Japan Sea '70
Battle of the Worlds '61
Battleground '49►
The Battleship Potemkin '25►
Ben-Hur '26►
Beowulf '07►
Beowulf & Grendel '06

► = rated three bones or higher

The Big Parade '25 ▶
The Big Red One '80 ▶
The Birth of a Nation '15 ▶
Braveheart '95 ▶
A Bridge Too Far '77 ▶
The Bruce '96
Cage 2: The Arena of Death '94
Captain Caution '40
The Castilian '63
Chasing the Deer '94
The Chronicles of Narnia: Prince Caspian '08
Cold Mountain '03 ▶
Crazy Horse '96
Cromwell '70
Cross of Iron '76
The Crossing '00
The Crusades '35
Das Boot '81 ▶
Days of Glory '06
Diamonds Are Forever '71 ▶
Dragonheart '96
Dragonslayer '81 ▶
Druids '01
El Cid '61 ▶
Elizabeth: The Golden Age '07
The Emperor and the Assassin '99
The Empire Strikes Back '80 ▶
Enemy Below '57 ▶
Eragon '06
Excalibur '81 ▶
The Fall of the Roman Empire '64
The Fighting Sullivans '42 ▶
First Knight '95
Flags of Our Fathers '06 ▶
The Four Feathers '02
Gallipoli '81 ▶
Gettysburg '93 ▶
The Giant of Marathon '60
Giants of Rome '63
Gladiator '00 ▶
Gladiators 7 '62
Glory '89 ▶
Godzilla vs. the Smog Monster '72
Goldfinger '64 ▶
The Guns of Navarone '61 ▶
Heaven & Earth '90 ▶
Helen of Troy '03
Henry V '44 ▶
Henry V '89 ▶
Hercules vs. the Sons of the Sun '64
Highlander '86 ▶
I Bombed Pearl Harbor '60
In the Name of the King: A Dungeon Siege Tale '08
Independence Day '96 ▶
Jeanne la Pucelle '94
Joan of Arc '99
John Paul Jones '59
Joyeux Noel '05 ▶
The King of the Kickboxers
Kings of the Sun '63
The Last Command '55
The Last Samurai '03 ▶
Letters from Iwo Jima '06 ▶
The Lighthorsemen '87 ▶
The Long Riders '80 ▶
The Longest Day '62 ▶
Lord of the Rings: The Fellowship o' the Rings '01 ▶
Lord of the Rings: The Two Towers '02 ▶
Lord of the Rings: The Return of the King '03 ▶
The Magical Legend of the Leprechauns '99
The Man Who Would Be King '75 ▶
Mars Attacks! '96
Master and Commander: The Far Side of the World '03 ▶
The Messenger: The Story of Joan of Arc '99
Midway '76
Mists of Avalon '01
The Mongols '60

Monty Python and the Holy Grail '75 ▶
Moonraker '79
Motel Hell '80
Mulan '98
The Mummy Returns '01
Napoleon '03 ▶
Night Watch '04
A Nightmare on Elm Street '84 ▶
The Odyssey '97
One from the Heart '82
The Patriot '00
Patton '70 ▶
Pearl '78
Pirates of the Caribbean: At World's End '07
Raiders of the Lost Ark '81 ▶
Ran '85 ▶
Rawhide '50 ▶
Red Dawn '84
Return of the Jedi '83 ▶
Revolution '85
Ring of Fire '91
Rob Roy '95 ▶
Robot Jox '90
Robot Warriors '96
Samson and His Mighty Challenge '64
The Sand Pebbles '66 ▶
Sands of Iwo Jima '49 ▶
Saving Private Ryan '98 ▶
The Siege of Firebase Gloria '89
The Silk Road '92
Soldier '98
Son of the Morning Star '91 ▶
Stalingrad '94
Star Crash '78
Star Trek: Nemesis '02
Star Wars '77 ▶
Star Wars: Episode 1—The Phantom Menace '99 ▶
Star Wars: Episode 2—Attack of the Clones '02 ▶
Star Wars: Episode 3—Revenge of the Sith '05 ▶
Street Hunter '90
Tales from a Parallel Universe: I Worship His Shadow '97
Ten Days That Shook the World '27 ▶
They Died with Their Boots On '41 ▶
The 13th Warrior '99
300 '07
The 300 Spartans '62
Thunderball '65 ▶
To Hell and Back '55
Total Total '70
Transformers '07
The Trench '99
The Trojan Horse '62
Troy '04
Twelve o'Clock High '49 ▶
Two for Texas '97
The Viking Queen '67
War and Peace '56
War and Peace '68 ▶
War and Peace '73
The War Lord '65
Warrior Queen '03
The Wild Bunch '69 ▶
Zulu '64 ▶
Zulu Dawn '79 ▶

Big-Budget Bombs
see also *Pure Ego; Vehicles*
The Adventurers '70
Alexander '04
Alexander the Great '55
American Anthem '86
Annie '82
The Bonfire of the Vanities '90
Boom! '68
Christopher Columbus: The Discovery '92
Cleopatra '63 ▶
The Conqueror '56
The Cotton Club '84 ▶
Dune '84
Harlem Nights '89
Heaven's Gate '81
Howard the Duck '86
Hudson Hawk '91

I'll Do Anything '93
Ishtar '87
Last Action Hero '93
The Long Ships '64
The Lovers on the Bridge

Midway '76
Money Train '95
Moon in the Gutter '83
1941 '79
Santa Claus: The Movie '85
The Scarlet Letter '95
The Shoes of the Fisherman '68
The Silver Chalice '54
Sphere '97
Summer Holiday '48
Supergirl '84
Toral Toral Toral '70 ▶
Toys '92
Two Minute Warning '76
Two of a Kind '83
Waterloo '71

Big Cats
see also *Jungle Stories; Wild Kingdom*
Across the Moon '94
The Adventures of Tarzan '21
Androcles and the Lion '52
The Big Cat '49
Bringing Up Baby '38 ▶
Cat People '42 ▶
Cheetah '89
Doctor Dolittle '67
The Ghost and the Darkness '96
The Gladiator '38
I Dreamed of Africa '00
Ice Age '02 ▶
Island of Lost Souls '32 ▶
Jungle Hell '56
The Leopard Man '43 ▶
The Lion '55
The Lost Jungle '34
Passion in the Desert '97
Rugrats Go Wild! '03
So This is Africa '33
A Tiger Walks '64
The Wild '06

Big Digs
Ancient Evil: Scream of the Mummy '00
Ancient Relic '04
Around the Bend '04
Blood from the Mummy's Tomb '71
The Body '01
Charlie Chan in Egypt '35
The Curse of King Tut's Tomb '80
Dead Are Alive '72
Deadly Intent '88
Dominion: Prequel to the Exorcist '05
Exorcist: The Beginning '04
The Golden Salamander '51
Indiana Jones and the Last Crusade '89 ▶
Indiana Jones and the Temple of Doom '84 ▶
King of the Forest Rangers '46
Legend of the Lost Tomb '97
March or Die '77
The Mask '61
The Mummy '32 ▶
The Mummy '99
The Mummy's Hand '40
The Mummy's Shroud '67
National Treasure: Book of Secrets '07
Pimpernel Smith '42
Raiders of the Lost Ark '81 ▶
The Ruins '08
Russell Mulcahy's Tale of the Mummy '99

Search for the Gods '75
Secret of the Andes '98
Sound of Horror '64
Specters '87
Stargate '94
Tomb '86
Unseen Evil '99
Valley of the Kings '54
The Word '78

Big Ideas
see also *Ethics & Morals*
The Addiction '95
The Air I Breathe '07
Amazing Grace '06 ▶
Barefoot in Athens '66
Being Human '94
Bickford Shmeckler's Cool Ideas '06
The Big Kahuna '00 ▶
Blaise Pascal '71 ▶
Blue '93
A Brief History of Time '92 ▶
The Buddha of Suburbia '78

Contact '97 ▶
Cortázar '97
Dead Man '95
The Designated Mourner '97
Destiny '97
Diary of a Seducer '95
Faraway, So Close! '93
Final Destination '00
First Snow '07
The Fountain '06
Four Days in September '97
Harvard Man '01
Hoy Man '99
The Incredible Shrinking Man '57 ▶
I.Q. '94
Jonathan Livingston Seagull '73

Judgment at Nuremberg '61 ▶
Kicking and Screaming '95
Life is a Bed of Roses '83
Meetings with Remarkable Men '79
Melvin Goes to Dinner '03
The Messiah '75
Metropolitan '90 ▶
Mindwalk: A Film for Passionate Thinkers '91 ▶
Mission to Mars '00
Mr. North '88
My Dinner with Andre '81 ▶
1900 '76 ▶
Nostradamus '93
The Passion of Ayn Rand '99
The Quarrel '93 ▶
The Razor's Edge '46 ▶
The Razor's Edge '84
Return to Eden '83
Samurai 3: Duel at Ganryu Island '56
Sans Soleil '82
The Seventh Seal '56 ▶
Sliding Doors '97 ▶
Sorceress '97
Sunshine '07
That Championship Season '82
Time of the Wolf '03 ▶
The Triumph of Love '01
Up to a Certain Point: '83
Waking Life '01
What Dreams May Come '98
What the $*!% Do We Know? '04
What to Do in Case of Fire '02
Wittgenstein '93
The Wrong Move '79
Zabriskie Point '70

Big Rigs
see also *Motor Vehicle Dept.; Road Trip*
Black Dog '98
Breakdown '96 ▶
Breaker! Breaker! '77
C.C. & Company '70
Citizens Band '77
Convoy '78
Desperate '47
Driving Force '88
Duel '71 ▶
Every Which Way But Loose '78
F.I.S.T. '78
Flatbed Annie and Sweetiepie: Lady Truckers '79
Great Smokey Roadblock '76
Hi-Jacked '50
High Ballin' '78
Joy Ride '01 ▶
Larger Than Life '96
The Long Haul '57
Maximum Overdrive '86
The Other Side of the Mountain, Part 2 '78
Pee-wee's Big Adventure '85 ▶
Road Games '81 ▶
Road Rage '01
Rolling Vengeance '87
Smokey and the Bandit '77 ▶
Smokey and the Bandit 2 '80
Smokey and the Bandit Part 3 '83
Sorcerer '77
Steel Cowboy '78
The Sure Thing '85 ▶
They Drive by Night '40 ▶
Think Big '90
Trucks '97
Wages of Fear '55 ▶
White Line Fever '75
Willa '79

Bigfoot/Yeti
The Abominable Snowman '57
Big and Hairy '98
Big Foot '72
Bigfoot: The Unforgettable Encounter '94
The Capture of Bigfoot '79
Clawed: The Legend of Sasquatch '05
Frostbite: Wrath of the Wendigo '94
Half Human '58
Harry and the Hendersons '87 ▶
Legend of Boggy Creek '75
Little Bigfoot '96
Man Beast '55
Night of the Demon '80
Night of the Howling Beast '75
Return to Boggy Creek '77
Sasquatch '02
Tha Sasquatch Gang '06
Shriek of the Mutilated '74
The Snow Creature '54
Snowbeast '77
Strange Wilderness '08
To Catch a Yeti '95

Bikers
The Acid Eaters '67
Adventures Beyond Belief '87
Angel Unchained '70
Angels Die Hard '84
Angels from Hell '68
Angels Hard As They Come '71
Angels' Wild Women '72
Any Which Way You Can '80
Beach Party '63 ▶
Beyond the Law '92
Biker Boyz '03
Black Bikers from Hell '70
Blonde in Black Leather '77
Born Losers '67
Born to Ride '91
Breaking Loose '88
The Brown Bunny '03
Bury Me an Angel '71

California Straight Ahead '25
Chopper Chicks in Zombietown '91
Chrome and Hot Leather '71
Chrome Soldiers '92
City Limits '85
Cleopatra Jones '73
Club Life '86
Crossing the Line '90
Cycle Psycho '72
Cycle Vixens '79
Cyclone '87
Danger Zone '87
Danger Zone 2 '89
Danger Zone 3: Steel Horse War '90
Dark Rider '91
Darktown Strutters '74
Deadly Reactor '89
Death Sport '78
Devil's Angels '67
Dirt Bike Kid '86
Dirt Gang '71
Easy Rider '69 ▶
Easy Wheels '89
Eat the Peach '86
Electra Glide in Blue '73 ▶
Eve Knievel '72
Every Which Way But Loose '78
Eye of the Tiger '86
The Final Alliance '89
Fugitive Champion '99
The Girl on a Motorcycle '68
The Glory Stompers '67
The Great Escape '63 ▶
Great Ride '78
The Great Skyscraper
Greedy Terror '82
Harley Davidson and the Marlboro Man '91
The Hard Ride '71
Harley '90
Hellbock 13 '97
Hellcats '68
Hellriders '84
Hell's Angels '30
Hell's Angels Forever '83
Hell's Angels on Wheels '67
Hell's Angels '69 '69
Hell's Belles '69
Hog Wild '80
Hollywood Chaos '89
In Your Face '77
Iron Horsemen '71
The Jesus Trip '71
Knightriders '81
Lone Hero '02
Loners '72
The Losers '70
Loveless '83
Mad Max '80 ▶
Mask '85 ▶
Masters of Menace '90
Master's Revenge '71
Me & Will '99
Motor Psycho '65
Motorcycle Gang '57
The Naked Angels '69
Nam Angels '88
Nomad Riders '81
Northville Cemetery Massacre '76
The Only Way Home '72
The Outlaw Bikers—Gang Wars '70
Outlaw Riders '72
Peacekillers '71
Pee-wee's Big Adventure '85 ▶
Planet Terror '07
Pray for the Wildcats '74
Psychomania '73
Punk Vacation '90
Race for Glory '89
Raising Arizona '87 ▶
Raw Courage '84
Rebel Rousers '69
Rebel Run '94
Return of the Rebels '81
Riding High '78
The Road '00
Roadside Prophets '92
Run, Angel, Run! '69
Running Cool '93
Satan's Sadists '69
Savage Dawn '84

▶ = rated three bones or higher

Bikers

The Savage Seven '68
Savages from Hell '68
Shame '87
She-Devils on Wheels '68
The Shrieking '73
Sidewinder One '77
Silver Dream Racer '83
Sinner's Blood '70
Space Riders '83
Spetters '80
Stone Cold '91
Streets of Fire '84
Supercross: The Movie '05
Survival Zone '84
Timerider '83
Torque '04
Viva Knievel '77
Warlords from Hell '87
Werewolves on Wheels '71
The Wild Angels '66
Wild Guitar '62
The Wild One '54▲
Wild Rebels '71
Wild Riders '71
Wild Wheels '69
Winners Take All '87
The World's Fastest Indian '05▲

Biography

see also Biopics: Artists; Biopics: Cops & Robbers; Biopics: Military; Biopics: Musicians; Biopics: Politics; Biopics: Religious; Biopics: Religious/Medical; Biopics: Showbiz; Biopics: Sports; Biopics: Writers; This Is My Life; This Is Your Life

Biopics: Artists

see also Art & Artists
Ballet Russes '05▲
Basquiat '96▲
Camille Claudel '89▲
Caravaggio '86▲
Carrington '95
Crumb '94▲
Dante's Inferno: Life of Dante Gabriel Rossetti '69
Edvard Munch '74
Frida '84
Frida '02
Fur: An Imaginary Portrait of Diane Arbus '06
Girl with a Pearl Earring '03▲
Goya in Bordeaux '99
Henri Langlois: The Phantom of the Cinematheque '04▲
Klimt '06
Love Is the Devil '98▲
Lust for Life '56▲
Magnificent Adventurer '63
Modigliani '58
Modigliani '04
Moulin Rouge '52▲
The Naked Maja '59
Pollock '00▲
Postcards from America '95
Rembrandt '36▲
Rembrandt—1669 '77
Savage Messiah '72
Surviving Picasso '96
Tell Them Who You Are '05
Van Gogh '92▲
Vincent & Theo '90▲
Vincent: The Life and Death of Vincent van Gogh '87▲
The Wolf at the Door '87

Biopics: Cops & Robbers

see also Crime Drama; True Crime
Aileen: Life and Death of a Serial Killer '03▲
Al Capone '59▲
Bandit Queen '94
Bonanno: A Godfather's Story '99
Bonnie & Clyde '67▲
The Buccaneer '58
Bugsy '91▲
Butch Cassidy and the Sundance Kid '69▲
Chopper '00▲
Dick Turpin '25
Dillinger '45▲
Dillinger '73
Dillinger '91
Domino '05
The Elegant Criminal '92
The General '98▲
Goodfellas '90▲
Gore Vidal's Billy the Kid '89
Gotti '96
Great Missouri Raid '51
The Grey Fox '83▲
The Hillside Strangler '04
I Am a Fugitive from a Chain Gang '32▲
I Shot Billy the Kid '50
I Shot Jesse James '49▲
J. Edgar Hoover '87
The King of the Roaring '20s: The Story of Arnold Rothstein '61
Lansky '99
Last Days of Frank & Jesse James '86
The Left-Handed Gun '58▲
Lepke '75
Lucky Luciano '74
Madame Sata '02
Mafia Princess '86
McVicar '80
Melvin Purvis: G-Man '74
Monster '03▲
Ned Kelly '70
Ned Kelly '03
The Outlaw '43
The Private Files of J. Edgar Hoover '77
A Real American Hero '78
The Rise and Fall of Legs Diamond '60
Stander '03
Sugartime '95
Walking Tall '73
Walking Tall: Part 2 '75
Walking Tall: The Final Chapter '77
Weeds '87▲
Wild Bill '95
Wyatt Earp '94▲
You Know My Name '99▲

Biopics: Military

see also Civil War; Korean War; Military; Air Force; Military: Army; Military: Foreign; Military: Marines; Military: Navy; True Stories; Vietnam War; World War I; World War II
Alexander '04
Alexander the Great '55
And Starring Pancho Villa as Himself '03▲
Antwone Fisher '02▲
Attila '01
Battle Hymn '57
Benedict Arnold: A Question of Honor '03
The Big Red One '80▲
Breaking the Code '95
A Bright Shining Lie '98
Carve Her Name with Pride '58
Cast a Giant Shadow '66
Chapayev '34▲
Churchill and the Generals '81
The Court Martial of Jackie Robinson '90
Cromwell '70
The Desert Fox '51▲
Francis Gary Powers: The True Story of the U-2 Spy '76
The Gallant Hours '60▲
George Washington '84
Geronimo '93
God Is My Co-Pilot '45
Ike '79
Ike: Countdown to D-Day '04
The Iron Duke '34
John Paul Jones '59
The Last Days of Patton '86
Lawrence of Arabia '62▲
The Long Gray Line '55▲
MacArthur '77
Men of Honor '00
Monsieur N. '03▲
Napoleon '27▲
Napoleon '55
Orde Wingate '76
Patton '70▲
PT 109 '63
Spitfire '42▲
To Hell and Back '55
We Were Soldiers '02▲

Biopics: Musicians

see also Nashville Narratives
Amadeus '84▲
Backbeat '94▲
Bandwagon '95
Beethoven '36
Beethoven Lives Upstairs '92
The Benny Goodman Story '55
Beyond the Sea '04
Bird '88▲
Bix '91
Bound for Glory '76▲
Bride of the Wind '01
The Buddy Holly Story '78▲
Callas Forever '02
Coal Miner's Daughter '80▲
Control '07
De-Lovely '04
The Devil and Daniel Johnston '05▲
DiG! '04▲
The Doors '91
The Eddy Duchin Story '56
Edith & Marcel '83
8 Mile '02▲
El Cantante '06
Elvis and Me '88
Elvis: The Movie '79
End of the Century: The Story of the Ramones '03▲
The Eternal Waltz '54
Eubie! '82▲
The Fabulous Dorseys '47
Fade to Black '04▲
Farinelli '94
The Five Pennies '59
For Love or Country: The Arturo Sandoval Story '00
The Gene Krupa Story '54
The Glenn Miller Story '54▲
Great Balls of Fire '89
The Great Caruso '51
The Great Waltz '38▲
The Harmonists '99
Harmony Lane '35
Hendrix '00
The Hours and Times '92
Hilary and Jackie '98▲
I Dream of Jeannie '52
I'll See You in My Dreams '51
I'm Not There '07▲
Immortal Beloved '94▲
Impromptu '90▲
In His Life: The John Lennon Story '00
Interrupted Melody '55▲
The Invisibles '99
The Jacksons: An American Dream '92
John & Yoko: A Love Story '85
La Bamba '87▲
Lady Sings the Blues '72
Let's Get Lost '88
The Life and Loves of Mozart '59
Life of Verdi '82
Lisztomania '75
Little Richard '00
Living Proof: The Hank Williams Jr. Story '83
Love Me or Leave Me '55▲
Madonna: Innocence Lost '95
The Magic Bow '47
Mahler '74▲
Man in the Mirror: The Michael Jackson Story '04
Mayor of the Sunset Strip '03▲
Meat Loaf: To Hell and Back '00
Melody Master '41
Metallica: Some Kind of Monster '04▲
Mo' Better Blues '90
Mozart: A Childhood Chronicle '76▲
The Mozart Story '48
The Music Lovers '71
New York Doll '05▲
Nico Icon '95▲
Night and Day '46
The Night We Called It a Day '03
Passion '99
Piaf '81
The Pianist '02▲
Protecting the King '07
The Rat Pack '98
Ray '04▲
Rhapsody in Blue '45▲
Rhapsody of Spring '98
Selena '96
Shine '95▲
Sid & Nancy '86▲
Song of Love '47▲
Song of Norway '70
Song of Scheherazade '47
A Song to Remember '45▲
Song Without End '60
Spring Symphony '86
Stoned '05
The Strauss Family '73
Sweet and Lowdown '99
Sweet Dreams '85
Sweet Love, Bitter '67
Take Me Home: The John Denver Story '00
Taking Sides '01
Tchaikovsky '71
The Temptations '98
32 Short Films about Glenn Gould '93▲
This Is Elvis '81
Three Little Words '50
Till the Clouds Roll By '46
Tous les Matins du Monde '92▲
Two of Us '00
The U.S. vs. John Lennon '06
Verdi '53
Voices from a Locked Room '95
Wagner: The Complete Epic '85
Walk Hard: The Dewey Cox Story '07
Walk the Line '05▲
Waltz King '63
Whale Music '94
What's Love Got to Do with It? '93
Why Do Fools Fall in Love? '98
Words and Music '48
Young Caruso '51

Biopics: Politics

see also Capital Capers; Politics; True Stories; Vote for Me!
Abe Lincoln in Illinois '40▲
Abraham Lincoln '30
Amazing Grace '06
Amin: The Rise and Fall '82
Balzac and the Little Chinese Seamstress '02
Barefoot in Athens '66
Blaze '89
Blind Ambition '79
Bobby '06
The Burning Season '94▲
Cesare Borgia '23
Churchill and the Generals '81
Citizen Cohn '92▲
The Courageous Mr. Penn '41
A Dangerous Man: Lawrence after Arabia '91▲
The Death of Adolf Hitler '84
Disraeli '30▲
Disraeli '79▲
Downfall '04▲
Eleanor & Franklin '76▲
Eleanor: First Lady of the World '82
Enemy of Women '44
Gandhi '82▲
The Gathering Storm '74
The Gathering Storm '02▲
George Washington: The Forging of a Nation '86
Giuliani Time '05
Give 'Em Hell, Harry! '75▲
Going Upriver: The Long War of John Kerry '04
Gore Vidal's Lincoln '88
Hitler '62
Hitler: The Rise of Evil '03
Imperial Venus '71
Inside the Third Reich '82
Invincible Mr. Disraeli '63
Jackie, Ethel, Joan: The Kennedy Women '01
Jefferson in Paris '94
The Jesse Ventura Story '99
JFK: Reckless Youth '93
John Adams '08
Johnny We Hardly Knew Ye '77
Juarez '39▲
The Kennedys of Massachusetts '95
Kingfish: A Story of Huey P. Long '95
Kissinger and Nixon '96
Kundun '97▲
The Last Emperor '87▲
Last Four Days '77
LBJ: The Early Years '88▲
The Life and Assassination of the Kingfish '76
Lumumba '01▲
Magnificent Doll '46
The Magnificent Yankee '50▲
Mandela '87▲
Michael Collins '96▲
Monsieur N. '03▲
Mosley '98
The Motorcycle Diaries '04▲
Mussolini & I '85
Napoleon '03
Nixon '95▲
Path to War '02
Pinochet's Last Stand '06
Prince Jack '83
The Reagans '04
RFK '02
Robert Kennedy and His Times '90
Rudy: The Rudy Giuliani Story '03
Sadat '83
Sakharov '84▲
Secret Honor '85▲
The Sicilian '87
Simon Bolivar '69
Stalin '92▲
Sunrise at Campobello '60▲
Truman '95▲
Viva Zapata! '52▲
Will: G. Gordon Liddy '82
Wilson '44▲
Without Warning: The James Brady Story '91▲
A Woman Called Golda '82▲
Young Mr. Lincoln '39▲

Biopics: Religious

see also Islam; Judaism; Religion
Augustine of Hippo '72▲
Bernadette '90▲
Brother Sun, Sister Moon '73
The Courageous Mr. Penn '41
The Flowers of St. Francis '50▲
From a Far Country: Pope John Paul '81
Have No Fear: The Life of Pope John Paul II '05
The Hoodlum Priest '61▲
Jesus of Nazareth '77▲
Joan of Arc '48
Joan of Arc '99
Kundun '97▲
Luther '03
The Messenger: The Story of Joan of Arc '99
Passion of Joan of Arc '28▲
The Passion of the Christ '04▲
Saint Joan '57
St. Patrick: The Irish Legend '00
The Scarlet & the Black '83
Sebastiane '79▲
The Song of Bernadette '43▲
Therese '86▲
Therese: The Story of Saint Therese of Lisieux '04
A Time for Miracles '80

Biopics: Royalty

see also Politics; Royalty; Royalty, British; Russian; True Stories
Bonnie Prince Charlie '48
Catherine the Great '34
Catherine the Great '95
Charlemagne '95
Diana: Her True Story '93
Edward and Mrs. Simpson '80
Elizabeth '98▲
Elizabeth R '72▲
Elizabeth I '05▲
Elizabeth: The Golden Age '07
The Last Emperor '87▲
Lady Jane '85▲
Ludwig '72
Mad Love '01
Marie Antoinette '38
Mary of Scotland '36▲
Nicholas and Alexandra '71
Peter the Great '86▲
The Queen's Sister '05
The Rise of Louis XIV '66▲
Six Wives of Henry VIII '71▲
Victoria Regina '61
The Virgin Queen '55▲
Warrior Queen '03
The Woman He Loved '88

Biopics: Science/Medical

see also This Is My Life; This Is Your Life
A Beautiful Mind '01▲
Bethune '77
Breaking the Code '95
The Doctor '91
Dr. Bethune '90▲
The Elephant Man '80▲
The Five of Me '81
The Great Moment '44
Holy Terror '65
Infinity '96
Kinsey '04▲
Korczak '90▲
Lamp at Midnight '66
Long Journey Back '78
Madame Curie '43▲
A Matter of Life and Death '81
The Miracle Worker '62▲
The Miracle Worker '79▲
The Miracle Worker '00
Nurse Edith Cavell '39▲
The Prisoner of Shark Island '36▲
Sakharov '84▲
The Secret Diary of Sigmund Freud '84
The Sound and the Silence '93

▲ = rated three bones or higher

The Story of Alexander Graham Bell '39 ▶
The Story of Dr. Wassell '44
The Story of Louis Pasteur '36 ▶
Theremin: An Electronic Odyssey '95 ▶
The Ann-Jillian Story '88
The Audrey Hepburn Story '00

Biopics: Showbiz
see also Price of Fame
Actor: The Paul Muni Story '78
Alex in Wonderland '70
All That Jazz '79 ▶
The Amazing Howard Hughes '77
Auto Focus '02 ▶
The Aviator '04 ▶
Baadasssss! '03 ▶
Beyond the Sea '04 ▶
Blonde '01
The Bodyguard '92
Bogie: The Last Hero '80
Bojangles '01
Bruce Lee: Curse of the Dragon '93 ▶
Bud and Lou '78
Can You Hear the Laughter? The Story of Freddie Prinze '79
The Cat's Meow '01 ▶
Cecil B. Demented '00 ▶
Chaplin '92 ▶
Confessions of a Dangerous Mind '02 ▶
Darlings of the Gods '90
Dear Brigitte '65
The Dolly Sisters '46
Dragon: The Bruce Lee Story '93 ▶
Ed Wood '94 ▶
Enter Laughing '67
Ernie Kovacs: Between the Laughter '84
F. Scott Fitzgerald in Hollywood '76
Factory Girl '06
Flynn '96
Frances '82 ▶
From the Journals of Jean Seberg '95
Funny Girl '68 ▶
Funny Lady '75 ▶
Go West, Young Man '36
The Goddess '58 ▶
Goodbye, Norma Jean '75
Goodnight, Sweet Marilyn '89
The Grace Kelly Story '83
The Great Ziegfeld '36 ▶
Gypsy '62 ▶
Gypsy '93 ▶
Harlow '65
Henri Langlois: The Phantom of the Cinematheque '04 ▶
How to Eat Your Watermelon in White Company (and Enjoy It) '05
Hughes & Harlow: Angels in Hell '77
In Person '35
The Incredible Sarah '76
Introducing Dorothy Dandridge '99 ▶
Isadora '68
James Dean '76
James Dean: Live Fast, Die Young '01
The Jayne Mansfield Story '80
Jolson Sings Again '49
The Jolson Story '46 ▶
The Josephine Baker Story '90 ▶
La Vie en Rose '07 ▶
Legend of Valentino '75
Lenny '74 ▶
Life with Judy Garland—Me and My Shadows '01 ▶

Lillian Russell '40
Lillie '79
Livin' for Love: The Natalie Cole Story '00
Look for the Silver Lining '49
The Love Goddesses '65
Lucy and Desi: Before the Laughter '91
Madame Sata '02
Mae West '84
Man in the Mirror: The Michael Jackson Story '04
Man of a Thousand Faces '57 ▶
Man on the Moon '99 ▶
Marilyn & Bobby: Her Final Affair '94
Marilyn: The Untold Story '80
Mayor of the Sunset Strip '06
Merton of the Movies '47 ▶
Mommie Dearest '81 ▶
My Favorite Year '82 ▶
My Wicked, Wicked Ways '84
Nijinsky '80
Norma Jean and Marilyn '95
The Notorious Bettie Page '06 ▶
Paul Robeson '77
The Perils of Pauline '47
Permanent Midnight '98
Prisoner of Paradise '02 ▶
Queenie '87
Quiet Days in Hollywood '97
Rainbow '78
The Reagans '03
Rita Hayworth: The Love Goddess '83
RKO 281 '99 ▶
Rock Hudson's Home Movies '92
Roseanne: An Unauthorized Biography '94
Rosie: The Rosemary Clooney Story '82
The Seven Little Foys '55 ▶
Sinatra '92
Sophia Loren: Her Own Story '80
Star! '68
The Story of Vernon and Irene Castle '39 ▶
Superstar: The Life and Times of Andy Warhol '90 ▶
Talk to Me '07
Taxi zum Klo '81
Tell Them Who You Are '05 ▶
That's Entertainment, Part 3 '93
This is Elvis '81 ▶
Thursday's Child '43
Topsy Turvy '99 ▶
Up Close and Personal '96
Valentino '77
Veronika Voss '82 ▶
What Ever Happened to Baby Jane? '62 ▶
White Hot: The Mysterious Murder of Thelma Todd '91
White Hunter, Black Heart '90 ▶
Wired '89
Yankee Doodle Dandy '42 ▶
Young Charlie Chaplin '88

Biopics: Sports
see also Baseball; Basketball; Football; Hockey; The Olympics; Running; Soccer; Sports Dramas; Team Efforts
Ali '01 ▶
Babe! '75
The Babe '92
Babe Ruth Story '48
Big Mo '73
Bobby Jones: Stroke of Genius '04
Boy in Blue '86
Breaking the Surface: The Greg Louganis Story '96
Brian's Song '71 ▶
Brian's Song '01
Champions '84
Chariots of Fire '81 ▶
Cobb '94 ▶
Coach Carter '05 ▶
Dempsey '83
Don King: Only in America '97
Fallen Champ: The Untold Story of Mike Tyson '93
Fast Company '79
Final Shot: The Hank Gathers Story '92
The Flying Scotsman '06
Follow the Sun '51
Gentleman Jim '42 ▶
Going for the Gold: The Bill Johnson Story '85
Grambling's White Tiger '81
The Great White Hope '70 ▶
The Greatest '77
Harmon of Michigan '41
Headin' Home '20
Heart Like a Wheel '83 ▶
Heart of a Champion: The Ray Mancini Story '85
Hustle '04
It's Good to Be Alive '74
The Jackie Robinson Story '50 ▶
The Jesse Owens Story '84
Jim Thorpe: All American '51
Joe and Max '02 ▶
The Joe Louis Story '53
Joe Torre: Curveballs Along the Way '97
Knute Rockne: All American '40 ▶
The Last American Hero '73
The Loneliest Runner '76
Marciano '79
Meteor & Shadow '85
Miracle '04 ▶
One in a Million: The Ron LeFlore Story '78
Pistol: The Birth of a Legend '90
Prefontaine '96
Pride '07
Pride of St. Louis '52
The Pride of the Yankees '42 ▶
Raging Bull '80 ▶
Rebound: The Legend of Earl "The Goat" Manigault '96
Richard Petty Story '72
The Rocket '05 ▶
Rocky Marciano '99
The Rookie '02 ▶
Run for the Dream: The Gail Devers Story '96
A Season on the Brink '02
61* '01 ▶
Somebody Up There Likes Me '56 ▶
Through the Fire '05
The Tiger Woods Story '98
Tyson '95
Wilma '77
A Winner Never Quits '86
The Winning Team '52
Without Limits '97 ▶

Biopics: Writers
The Adventures of Mark Twain '44 ▶
Agatha '79
Agatha Christie: A Life in Pictures '04
Almost Famous '00 ▶
An Angel at My Table '90 ▶
Balzac: A Life of Passion '99 ▶

Breaking the Surface: The Greg Louganis Story '96
Brian's Song '71
Becoming Colette '92
Before Night Falls '00 ▶
Borstal Boy '00
Byron '03
Capote '05 ▶
Children of the Century '99
Coming Through '85
Cross Creek '83
Dash and Lilly '99
The Disappearance of Garcia Lorca '96
Fallen Champ: The Untold Story of Mike Tyson '93
Finding Neverland '04 ▶
Forbidden Passion: The Oscar Wilde Movie '85
Goldeneye: The Secret Life of Ian Fleming '89
Gothic '87
Hammett '82 ▶
Hans Christian Andersen '52 ▶
Haunted Summer '88
Heart Beat '80
Henry & June '90 ▶
I Shot Andy Warhol '96 ▶
Infamous '06
Iris '01 ▶
Isn't She Great '00
Jack London '44
James Joyce's Women '85
The Keeper: The Legend of Omar Khayyam '05
Last Call: The Final Chapter of F. Scott Fitzgerald '02
The Lost Boys '78 ▶
The Loves of Edgar Allen Poe '42
Meshina: A Life in Four Chapters '85
Miss Austen Regrets '07
Miss Potter '06 ▶
Mrs. Parker and the Vicious Circle '94 ▶
My Apprenticeship '39
My Childhood '38 ▶
My Left Foot '89 ▶
My Universities '40 ▶
Nero Wolfe '79
Nora '00
The Passion of Ayn Rand '99 ▶
Pinero '01
Postcards from America '95
The Road from Coorain '02
Saint-Ex: The Story of Edgar Allen Poe '73
Shadowlands '85
Shadowlands '93 ▶
Seabiscuit '03 ▶
The Secret Life of Mrs. Beeton '06
Stevie '78
Swann '96
Sylvia '03 ▶
Tom & Viv '95
Total Eclipse '95
The Trials of Oscar Wilde '60 ▶
Un Air de Famille '96 ▶
Veronica Guerin '03
Wilde '97 ▶
The Wonderful World of the Brothers Grimm '62
Zora Is My Name! '90

Birds
Babe '95 ▶
Batman Returns '92 ▶
Beaks: The Movie '87
Birdman of Alcatraz '62 ▶
The Birds '63 ▶
The Birds 2: Land's End '94
Blood Freak '72
The Blue Bird '40 ▶
A Breed Apart '84
Brewster McCloud '70 ▶
Chicken Run '00 ▶

The Barretts of Wimpole Street '34 ▶
Breaking the Surface: The Greg Louganis Story '96
Brian's Song '71
Becoming Colette '92
Before Night Falls '00
Cry of the Penguins '71
Fly Away Home '96 ▶
The Giant Claw '57
The Golden Child '86
The Goodbye Bird '93
The Hawk is Dying '06
High Anxiety '77 ▶
Hoot '06
Howard the Duck '86
Ladyhawke '85 ▶
Magic in the Mirror: Fowl Play '96
Mating Season '81
Million Dollar Duck '71
No Fear, No Die '90
Paulie '98
The Pebble and the Penguin '94
Queer Duck: The Movie '06
The Rage '07
Rare Birds '01
The Real Macaw '01
The Rescuers '77 ▶
The Rescuers Down Under '90
Rooster: Spurs of Death! '83
Sesame Street Presents: Follow That Bird '85
Spirit of the Eagle '90
Stuart Little 2 '02 ▶
The Trumpet of the Swan '01
Valiant '05
Vulture '67
The Wild Parrots of Telegraph Hill '03 ▶
Winged Migration '01 ▶

Bisexuality
see also Gays; Lesbians
April's Shower '03
Basic Instinct '92 ▶
Bedrooms and Hallways '98
California Suite '78 ▶
Change of Heart '98
Confusion of Genders '00
Criminal Lovers '99 ▶

Birthdays
Alpha Male '06
Because I Said So '07
Bloody Birthday '80
The Boys in the Band '70 ▶
Cat on a Hot Tin Roof '58 ▶
Cat on a Hot Tin Roof '84 ▶
The Celebration '98 ▶
Child's Play '88 ▶
City Slickers '91 ▶
Creatures from the Pink Lagoon '07
Damien: Omen 2 '78
Duck Season '04 ▶
4 Months, 3 Weeks, 2 Days '07 ▶
Friends and Family '01
The Game '97 ▶
Happy Birthday, Gemini '80
Happy Birthday to Me '81
The Jerk '79 ▶
Meet Joe Black '98
Mrs. Doubtfire '93 ▶
Mob Queen '98
On Golden Pond '81 ▶
Pizza '05
Quinceañera '05 ▶
Rabid Grannies '89
The Sisters '05
Sitcom '97
Sixteen Candles '84 ▶
Skinwalkers '07
That's Life! '86
13 Going on 30 '04
30 Years to Life '01
To Gillian on Her 37th Birthday '96
What's Eating Gilbert Grape '93 ▶
Working Girl '88 ▶

Black Comedy
see also Comedy; Comedy, Drama; Satire & Parody
Abigail's Party '77
The Acid House '98
Adam's Apples '05
After Hours '85 ▶
Age Isn't Everything '91
The Alarmist '98
Alberto Express '92
Alice '88 ▶
Alone in the T-Shirt Zone '86
American Strays '96
The Americanization of Emily '64 ▶
America's Deadliest Home Video '91
Angels Over Broadway '40 ▶
The Anniversary '68
The Ape '05
The Applegates '89
Ariel '89 ▶
Army Brats '84
Arnold '73
Arrivederci, Baby! '66
Arsenic and Old Lace '44 ▶
Art School Confidential '06
The Assassination Bureau '69
Assault of the Killer Bimbos '88
At Home with the Webbers '88
The Atomic Kid '54
Baby Face Morgan '42
Baby Love '69
Bad Boy Bubby '93
Bad Charleston Charlie '73
Banjo '30
Barton Fink '91 ▶
Beat the Devil '53 ▶
Beautiful People '99 ▶
Being John Malkovich '99 ▶
Berlinguer I Love You '77
Bizarre Bizarre '39 ▶
Bliss '85 ▶
Brazil '85 ▶
Bread and Chocolate '73 ▶
Break a Leg '03
The Bride of Frank '96
Bringing Out the Dead '99 ▶
Buddy Buddy '81
Buffalo '66 ▶
Buffet Froid '79 ▶
Cabaret Balkan '98
The Cable Guy '96
Canadian Bacon '94
Careful '92

Black
see also Comedy, Black
The Crying Game '92 ▶
Dog Day Afternoon '75 ▶
Dona Herlinda & Her Son '86

Chronicle of the Raven '04
Clash of the Titans '81 ▶
Cockfighter '74
Continental Divide '81 ▶
The Crow '93 ▶
The Crow 2: City of Angels '96
Dry Cleaning '97
Eros '04
Female Perversions '96
Happily Ever After '86
Harry and Max '04
Laurel Canyon '02 ▶
Les Biches '68 ▶
Liquid Sky '83
Mary, Mary, Bloody Mary '76
One to Another '06
Pas Tres Catholique '93
Puccini for Beginners '06
The Rules of Attraction '02 ▶
The Scorpion Woman '89
Showgirls '95
Sunday, Bloody Sunday '71 ▶
Those Who Love Me Can Take the Train '99
Three of Hearts '93
Three Times '05 ▶
Threesome '94
The Trio '97
The 24th Day '04
The Velocity of Gary '98
Velvet Goldmine '98 ▶
A Woman in Flames '84

Black (continued)

The Cars That Ate Paris '74▲
Catch-22 '70▲
Celine and Julie Go Boating '74
Chalk '06
Checking Out '89
Choice of Weapons '76
The Choirboys '77
City Unplugged '95
Clay Pigeons '98
Clerks '94▲
Coldblooded '94
The Comic '69▲
Consuming Passions '88
The Cook, the Thief, His Wife & Her Lover '90▲
Coup de Torchon '81▲
Crimes of the Heart '86
The Criminal Life of Archibaldo de la Cruz '55▲
Critical Care '97
Crocodile Tears '98
Crocodiles in Amsterdam '89
Curdled '95
The Curve '97
The Dark Backward '91
Day at the Beach '98
A Day in the Death of Joe Egg '71▲
Dead Husbands '98
Dead Silence '98
Deadly Advice '93
Death Becomes Her '92▲
Death in Brunswick '90
Death to Smoochy '02
Delicatessen '92▲
Delivered '98
Divine '90
Dr. Strangelove, or: How I Learned to Stop Worrying and Love the Bomb '64▲
A Dog's Breakfast '07
Don's Party '76▲
The Doom Generation '95▲
The Dress '96
Drop Dead Gorgeous '99
Duplex '03
Eat the Rich '87
Eating Raoul '82▲
8 Heads in a Duffel Bag '96
El '52
Elle '84
Elvis Has Left the Building '04
The End '78▲
Enid is Sleeping '90
Entertaining Mr. Sloane '70
Envy '04
Eternal Sunshine of the Spotless Mind '04▲
Eulogy '04
The Ex '07
eXistenZ '99
Exquisite Corpses '88
The Exterminating Angel '62▲
Fargo '96▲
Female Trouble '74
A Fine Madness '66▲
A Fish Called Wanda '88▲
The Fireman's Ball '68▲
Four Bags Full '56
Four Rooms '95
Freaked '93
Frogs for Snakes '98
Fun with Dick and Jane '05
The Funeral '84▲
Funny Bones '94▲
The Garden of Delights '70▲
Gas-s-s-s! '70
The Gazebo '59▲
Genghis Cohn '93
Getting Away With Murder '96
Ghost Chase '88
Go for Zucker '05
Goldstein '64
Goodbye Cruel World '82
Goodbye, Dragon Inn '03
Grand Theft Parsons '03
Grave Indiscretions '96
Gravesend '97
The Great Madcap '49
The Green Butchers '03
Greetings '68▲
Gridlock'd '97
Grosse Pointe Blank '97▲
Guilty as Charged '92
Happiness '98▲
Harold and Maude '71▲
Hawks '89
Head Above Water '96
Headless Body in Topless Bar '96
Heart Condition '90
Heathers '89▲
Henry Fool '98▲
Hexed '93
Hi, Mom! '70▲
High Heels '72
High Heels '91▲
Highway 61 '91
Hold Me, Thrill Me, Kiss Me '93
A Hole in One '04
Hombres Complicados '97
Home Sweet Home '82
Homebodies '74
The Honey Pot '67
The Hot Rock '71▲
The House of Yes '97
How Harry Became a Tree '01
How Tasty Was My Little Frenchman '71
How to Get Ahead in Advertising '89▲
The Hudsucker Proxy '93▲
The Hunting Party '07
Husbands, Wives, Money, and Murder '86
I Love You to Death '90
I Ought to Be in Pictures '82
The Ice Harvest '05
In Bruges '08
In the Company of Men '96▲
The Infernal Trio '74
Intimate Relations '95
Into the Night '85
Jawbreaker '98
Junk Mail '97
Keeping Mum '05
Kill the Poor '06
Killing Grandpa '91
The Killing of Sister George '69
Kind Hearts and Coronets '49▲
King of Comedy '82▲
King, Queen, Knave '72▲
Kiss & Tell '99
Kiss Kiss Bang Bang '05▲
Kiss of Death '77
The Ladykillers '55▲
The Ladykillers '04
The Laserman '90
The Last Dance '93
The Last Supper '96
Lemony Snicket's A Series of Unfortunate Events '04
Leolo '92▲
Life is Sweet '90▲
Like It Never Was Before '95
Little Murders '71▲
Loot... Give Me Money, Honey! '70
Love and Action in Chicago '99
The Loved One '65▲
A Loving Father '02
Lucky Stiff '88
L'Udienza '71
Mad Dog and Glory '93▲
Mafioso '62
Man Bites Dog '91
Mango Yellow '02
Matador '86
A Matter of WHO '62
Max, Mon Amour '86
The Medicine Show '01
Meet the Feebles '89
Miracle Mile '89▲
Mixed Blood '84
Mojave Moon '96
Mondo Balordo '64
Monsieur Verdoux '47▲
Montenegro '81▲
Mortuary Academy '91
Mother, Jugs and Speed '76
Movies Money Murder '96
Murder Czech Style '66
Muriel's Wedding '94▲
Murphy's Fault '88
My New Gun '92
My Sweet Suicide '98
Mystery Train '89▲
The Natural History of Parking Lots '90
Never Been Thawed '05
No Problem '75
No Surrender '86▲
Noi '03
Novocaine '01
Nurse Betty '00▲
Nuts in May '76
O Lucky Man! '73▲
The Oak '89
The Odd Job '78
Of Freaks and Men '98
Office Killer '97
Oh Dad, Poor Dad (Momma's Hung You in the Closet & I'm Feeling So Sad) '67
100 Mile Rule '02
The Operator '01
The Opposite of Sex '98
Orphans '97
Our Man in Havana '59▲
Out Cold '89
Pain in the A—— '77▲
Panic '00
Parents '89▲
Parting Shots '98
Passed Away '92
Paul Bartel's The Secret Cinema '69
Penn and Teller Get Killed '90
Permanent Midnight '98
The Pornographers '66▲
Pretty Persuasion '05
Pretty Poison '68▲
Private Parts '72
The Producers '05
Raising Arizona '87▲
Ravenous '99
Reckless '95
Red '91▲
Red Earth '82
The Red Inn '51
The Ref '93▲
Repo Man '83▲
Reuben, Reuben '83▲
Rick '03
Riff Raff '92▲
Rubin & Ed '92
St. Patrick's Day '99
Salvation! '87
The Scent of a Woman '75
School for Scoundrels '06
Schtonk! '66
Seed of Chucky '04
Serial Killing 101 '04
Serial Mom '94▲
Seven Beauties '76▲
Shadey '87
Shallow Grave '94▲
She-Devil '89
Shoot Loud, Louder, I Don't Understand! '66
Siblings '04
A Sinful Life '89
Sleeping Dogs Lie '06
Smokin' Aces '07
So I Married an Axe Murderer '93
Some Girls '88
Something for Everyone '70
Something Wild '86▲
Soundman '99
Spanking the Monkey '94▲
Stars and Bars '88
The Steagle '71
Stealing Sinatra '04
Sticky Fingers '88
The Story of an African Farm '04
The Story of Fausta '88
Stuart Bliss '98
Sudden Manhattan '96
Suicide Kings '97
Sweet Revenge '98
Sweethearts '97
Swimming with Sharks '94▲
Tatie Danielle '91▲
Testosterone '03
A Texas Funeral '99
That Obscure Object of Desire '77▲
There Was a Crooked Man '70▲
Throw Momma from the Train '87▲
Tie Me Up! Tie Me Down! '90
To Be or Not to Be '42▲
To Die For '95▲
Toto le Heros '91▲
Touch '97
Trainspotting '95▲
Transylvania Twist '89
Trigger Happy '96
Triggermen '02
Trois Couleurs: Blanc '94▲
Twin Town '97
Two Days '03
Two Days in the Valley '96▲
Two Hands '98▲
The Unbelievable Truth '90
Underground '95▲
Unexplained Laughter '89
Unnatural Pursuits '91
Vacuuming Completely Nude in Paradise '01
Vampire's Kiss '88▲
Very Bad Things '98
The War of the Roses '89▲
Weapons of Mass Distraction '97
Weirdsville '07
What Have I Done to Deserve This? '85▲
Where's Picasso '84▲
Who's Poppa? '70▲
Who's Killing the Great Chefs of Europe? '78▲
The Whole Nine Yards '00
Why Does Herr R. Run Amok? '69
Wilbur Wants to Kill Himself '02▲
Wilder Napalm '93
Wise Guys '86
Wish You Were Dead '00
The Witches of Eastwick '87▲
With a Friend Like Harry '00▲
Withnail and I '87▲
Women on the Verge of a Nervous Breakdown '88▲
World of the Depraved '67
Wristcutters: A Love Story '06
The Wrong Box '66▲
Zombie and the Ghost Train '91

Black Gold

The Abyss '89
The Beverly Hillbillies '93
Black Gold '36
Blowing Wild '54
Boom Town '40
Breaking the Waves '95▲
Chain of Command '95
Comes a Horseman '78
Country Gentlemen '36
Crossfire Trail '01▲
The Crude Oasis '95
Dead Ahead: The Exxon Valdez Disaster '92▲
Devil's Crude '71
The Dive '89
Double Deal '50
Fighting Texans '33
Five Easy Pieces '70▲
The Formula '80
Gas Pump Girls '79
Giant '56▲
The Guns and the Fury '83
Hellfighters '68
Intruder Within '81
Legend of Frenchie King '71
Lie Down with Lions '94
Local Hero '83▲
Louisiana Story '48▲
The Madwoman of Chaillot '69
Mission in Morocco '59
Naked Gun 2 1/2: The Smell of Fear '91
'Neath the Arizona Skies '34
Oceans of Fire '86
Oklahoma Crude '73
On Deadly Ground '94
Red Rock West '93▲
Roughnecks '80
The Stars Fell on Henrietta '94
There Will Be Blood '07▲
Thunder Bay '53▲
Tulsa '49▲
Waltz across Texas '83
War of the Wildcats '43
Wildcat '42
The World Is Not Enough '99
Written on the Wind '56▲

Blackmail

see also Corporate Shenanigans; Crime & Criminals; Disorganized Crime; Organized Crime

The Art of Murder '99
Barocco '76
The Big Brass Ring '99
Big Nothing '06
Black Angel '46▲
Blackmale '99
Bon Voyage '03▲
Captives '94
Charlie Chan at Treasure Island '39▲
Choke '00
Clue '85
Dead Pigeon on Beethoven Street '72
Death at a Funeral '07▲
The Deep End '01▲
Derailed '05
Devil in the Flesh '98
Dogville '03
El Crimen Perfecto '04▲
Feeling Minnesota '96
First Degree '98
The First Wives Club '96
A Gentleman After Dark '42
The Golden Spiders: A Nero Wolfe Mystery '00
Goodbye, Lover '99
The Guilty '99
Happy Endings '05
Hard Evidence '94
High Heels and Low Lifes '01
Hoffman '70
An Ideal Husband '99▲
The Immoral One '80
The Informant '97▲
It Seemed Like a Good Idea at the Time '75
Johnny Skidmarks '97
Keys to Tulsa '96
The Killer Must Kill Again '75
Kiss Tomorrow Goodbye '00
Legal Deceit '95
Letter to My Killer '95
Little Sweetheart '90
Love Walked In '97
Lucky Numbers '00
Man of the World '31
Mrs. Winterbourne '96
Mulholland Falls '95
Mysterious Mr. Moto '38
Mystery Street '50
100 Mile Rule '02
The Opposite of Sex '98
Paparazzi '04
Parallel Corpse '83
Perfect Lies '97
A Perfect Murder '98
The Player '92▲
Portrait in Black '60
Pretty Persuasion '05
Punch-Drunk Love '02▲
The Sentinel '06
The Silent Partner '78▲
Slackers '02
A Slight Case of Murder '99
Tick Tock '00▲
Twilight '98▲
Undercurrent '99
Up the River '30
Victim '61▲
Water's Edge '03
Zero Effect '97▲

Blackout

City Unplugged '95
Fear of the Dark '02
Love at First Bite '79
Mirage '66▲
100 Girls '00
Where Were You When the Lights Went Out? '68

Blaxploitation

see also African America; New Black Cinema

Across 110th Street '72
Avenging Disco Godfather '76
Baadasssss! '03▲
Big Score '83
Black Belt Jones '74
Black Caesar '73▲
Black Gestapo '75
Black Godfather '74
Blackenstein '73
Blacula '73▲
Bones '01
Bucktown '75
Cleopatra Jones '73▲
Cleopatra Jones & the Casino of Gold '75
Coffy '73▲
Cotton Comes to Harlem '70▲
Detroit 9000 '73
Dr. Black, Mr. Hyde '76
Dolemite '75
Dolemite 2: Human Tornado '76
Foxy Brown '74▲
Friday Foster '75
Ganja and Hess '73
The Guy from Harlem '77
Hell Up in Harlem '73▲
Hot Potato '76
J.D.'s Revenge '76
Let's Do It Again '75
The Mack '73
Mean Johnny Barrows '75
Miracle in Harlem '48
Monkey Hustle '77
Moon over Harlem '39
No Way Back '74
One Down, Two to Go! '82
Return of Superfly '90
Savage! '73
Scream Blacula Scream '73
Shaft '71▲
Shaft in Africa '73
Shaft's Big Score '72
Sheba, Baby '75
Slaughter '72
Slaughter's Big Ripoff '73
Soul Vengeance '75
Superfly '72▲
Superfly T.N.T. '73
Sweet Sweetback's Baadasssss Song '71▲
That Man Bolt '73
Three the Hard Way '74
Top of the Heap '72
Truck Turner '74▲
Undercover Brother '02▲

Blind Date

Betrayal of the Dove '92
Blind Date '87
Blind Dating '06
Coffee Date '06
Dirty Love '05
Friends with Money '06
I'll Take You There '99
I'm with Lucy '02
Must Love Dogs '05
The Perfect Man '05
Return to Me '00
Something New '06
You Stupid Man '02

Blindness

see also Physical Problems

Afraid of the Dark '92
Alligator Eyes '90
Amazing Grace '06▲

▲ = rated three bones or higher

(Blindness, continued)

Amy '81
At First Sight '98
Aurora '84
Ballad in Blue '66
Balls of Fury '07
Blacklight '98
Blackout '50
Blind Date '84
Blind Dating '06
Blind Fear '89
Blind Fury '90
Blind Justice '94
Blind Man's Bluff '91
Blind Witness '89
Blink '93
Breaking Free '95
Butterflies Are Free '72
Cactus '86
Can You Feel Me Dancing? '85
City for Conquest '40
City Lights '31
Color of Paradise '99
Connor's War '06
Crazy Love '07
Crimes & Misdemeanors '89
Dancer in the Dark '99
Daredevil '03
The Dark Angel '35
Don't Look Now '73
Eight Witnesses '54
Elmer '76
The Eye '02
The Eye '08
Eye on the Sparrow '91
A Family Thing '96
Good Luck '96
Happy Times '00
Hollywood Ending '02
The Human Monster '39
Ice Castles '79
If You Could See What I Hear '82
Incanato '03
Jennifer 8 '92
The Killer '90
La Symphonie Pastorale '46
Last Game '80
Life on a String '90
The Lookout '07
Lost for Words '99
Love at First Sight '76
Love Leads the Way '84
Mask '85
Minnesota Clay '65
The Miracle Worker '62
The Miracle Worker '79
The Miracle Worker '00
Mr. Magoo '97
Night Gallery '69
Night Is My Future '47
Nowhere in Sight '01
Octavia '82
On Dangerous Ground '51
Once Upon a Time in Mexico '03
Ordinary Heroes '85
A Patch of Blue '65
People Who Own the Dark '75
Places in the Heart '84
Possessed '05
Proof '91
Ray '04
Red Dragon '02
Return of the Evil Dead '75
The Scent of a Woman '92
Schlock '73
Second Sight '99
See No Evil '71
See No Evil, Hear No Evil '89
Sketch Artist 2: Hands That See '94
Sneakers '92
Someone Else's America '96
They Watch '93
Things You Can Tell Just by Looking at Her '00
To Race the Wind '80
The Toxic Avenger '86
Undertow '30
Unleashed '05
Until the End of the World '91
The Village '04
A Voyage 'Round My Father '89
Wait until Dark '67
The Whales of August '87
The White Countess '05
Wild Hearts Can't Be Broken '91
Wings in the Dark '35
Year Zero '04
Young Frankenstein '74
Zatoichi '03
Zatoichi: The Blind Swordsman '89
Zatoichi the Blind Swordsman and the Chess Expert '65
Zatoichi: The Blind Swordsman's Vengeance '66
Zentigo Diamond Caper '82

Blizzards
see also Cold Spots
Babes in Toyland '86
Cold Comfort '90
The Day of the Outlaw '59
Donner Pass: The Road to Survival '84
8 Women '02
The Last Stop '99
One Special Night '99
Operation Haylift '50
Ravenous '99
The Shining '80
Snow Day '00
Snowbound: The Jim and Jennifer Stolpa Story '94
Stephen King's The Storm of the Century '99
Trapped in Paradise '94
You'll Like My Mother '72

Bloody Messages
Die Hard '88
Fatal Vision '84
The Hades Factor '06
Harold and Maude '71
Helter Skelter '76
The Jagged Edge '85
Seven '95
The Shining '80
Stephen King's The Night Flier '96
The Untouchables '87

Boating
see Sail Away

Bodyguards
Absolute Power '97
Assassination '87
Avenging Angelo '02
Be Cool '05
Black Belt '92
Blackjack '97
The Bodyguard '92
The Bodyguard from Beijing '94
The Chase '46
Drillbit Taylor '08
Eastern Promises '07
Fatal Beauty '87
Fatal Past '94
Final Voyage '99
First Kid '96
Genuine Risk '89
Get Shorty '95
Guarding Tess '94
Half a Loaf of Kung Fu '78
Heat '87
His Bodyguard '98
In the Line of Fire '93
In the Mix '05
La Scorta '94
Man on Fire '87
Man on Fire '04
Mr. Nanny '93
My Bodyguard '80
Night Eyes 4: Fatal Passion '95
On Guard! '03
The Princess Diaries 2: Royal Engagement '04
Protecting the King '07

Boom!
see also Action-Adventure; Fires
The Adventures of Ford Fairlane '90
Airport '70
Arlington Road '99
Armageddon '98
Atomic Train '99
Bad Company '02
Ballistic: Ecks vs. Sever '02
Black Dog '98
Blown Away '94
Bridge of Dragons '99
Broken Arrow '96
Casino '95
Catch a Fire '06
Chain Reaction '96
Chill Factor '99
Clear and Present Danger '94
Collateral Damage '02
Con Air '97
The Core '03
Crackerjack 2 '97
Cutthroat Island '95
Dante's Peak '97
The Day After '83
Daylight '96
Dead in a Heartbeat '02
Deep Rising '98
Deja Vu '06
Detention '03
Die Another Day '02
Die Hard '88
Die Hard 2: Die Harder '90
Die Hard: With a Vengeance '95
District B13 '04
Dr. Strangelove, or: How I Learned to Stop Worrying and Love the Bomb '64
Earthquake '74
Enemy of the State '98
The English Patient '96
Eraser '96
Extreme Limits '01
Face/Off '97
The Fifth Element '97
Fight Club '99
The Final Cut '96
Fire Down Below '97
Firestorm '97
From Dusk Till Dawn '95
The Fugitive '93
Goldeneye '95
Gone Fishin' '97
Greenmail '01
Grosse Pointe Blank '97
Hiroshima: Out of the Ashes '90
Hoodlum '96
Human Bomb '97
Independence Day '96
The Inspectors '98
Jackass: The Movie '02
John Carpenter's Vampires '97
The Kingdom '07
Lethal Weapon 3 '92
Lethal Weapon 4 '98
Live Free or Die Hard '07
Live Wire: Human Timebomb '95
The Marine '06
Mission: Impossible '96
My House in Umbria '03
Nowhere to Land '00
Path to Paradise '97
The Peacemaker '97
Pearl Harbor '01
Pushed to the Limit '92
Riot '96
The Rock '96
Sabotage '96
Sea of Sand '58
The Secret Agent '96
Second Chance '53
Second Window '04
Serial Bomber '96
Shakedown '02
The Siege '98
Simon Sez '99
Social Error '35
The Specialist '94
Speed '94
Spider-Man '02
The State Within '06
Stealth '05
Steel '97
Sudden Death '95
The Sum of All Fears '02
Sweepers '99
Swordfish '01
The Taste of Others '00
The Terminator '84
Testament '83
Thirty Seconds Over Tokyo '44
Thr3e '07
Ticker '01
Time and Tide '00
Total Recall '90
Transformers '07
The Transporter '02
The Transporter 2 '05
The Tsar's Bride '66
True Lies '94
The Usual Suspects '95
U.S. Navy SEALS: Dead or Alive '02
V for Vendetta '06
Vantage Point '08
What to Do in Case of Fire '02
The Whole Shebang '01
The X-Files '98
XXX '02
XXX: State of the Union '05

Boomer Reunions
see also Period Piece: 1960s
The Big Chill '83
The Brutal Truth '99
Come as You Are '05
Everything Relative '96
Far Harbor '96
I Think I Do '97
Indian Summer '93
Lifeguard '76
A Mighty Wind '03
Old Joy '06
Parallel Lives '94
Peter's Friends '92
Return of the Secaucus 7 '80
Spin the Bottle '00
Standing Still '05
That Championship Season '82
That Championship Season '99
Tuesdays with Morrie '99

Books & Bookstores
see also Storytelling
84 Charing Cross Road '88
Bickford Shmeckler's Cool Ideas '06
Burglar '87
Capote '05
Crossing Delancey '88
Fahrenheit 451 '66
Falling in Love '84
Funny Face '57
The Hitchhiker's Guide to the Galaxy '05
The Hoax '07
Hocus Pocus '93
I, Madman '89
In the Mouth of Madness '95
The Jane Austen Book Club '07
La Lectrice '88
The Love Letter '99
The NeverEnding Story '84
A Night to Remember '42
The Ninth Gate '99
Notting Hill '99
The Pagemaster '94
The Paper Chase '73
Phenomenon '96
Priest of Love '81
Providence '77
QB VII '74
The Russia House '90
The Seven Year Itch '55
Snapshots '02
The Spiderwick Chronicles '08
Stone Reader '02
Suburban Girl '07
Tristram Shandy: A Cock and Bull Story '05
Warlock '91
Wilbur Wants to Kill Himself '02
You've Got Mail '98

Bosnia
Beautiful People '99
Behind Enemy Lines '01
Grbavica: The Land of My Dreams '06
Harrison's Flowers '02
No Man's Land '01
Pretty Village, Pretty Flame '96
Savior '98
Shot Through the Heart '98
Sniper 2 '02
Ulysses' Gaze '95
Underground '95
Vukovar '94
Welcome to Sarajevo '97
The Wounds '98

Boston
Adrenalin: Fear the Rush '96
Alex & Emma '03
Athena '54
Bad Manners '98
A Beautiful Mind '01
Before and After '95
Behind the Red Door '02
Black Irish '07
Blown Away '94
Body Count '87
Boondock Saints '99
The Boston Strangler '68
Breeders '97
A Case of Deadly Force '86
Celtic Pride '96
Coma '78
Criminal Law '89
The Departed '06
Fear Strikes Out '57
Fever Pitch '05
The Forbidden Kingdom '08
Fuzz '72
Game 6 '05
Gentleman Bandit '81
Gone Baby Gone '07
Good Will Hunting '97
The Great Moment '44
Jill the Ripper '00
Johnny, We Hardly Knew Ye '77
Legally Blonde '01
Lemony Snicket's A Series of Unfortunate Events '04
Little Men '98
Little Shots of Happiness '97
Love Story '70
The Matchmaker '97
Money Kings '93
Monument Ave. '98
Mystic River '02
Never Met Picasso '96
Next Stop, Wonderland '98
Small Vices: A Spenser Mystery '99
Southie '98
Spenser: Ceremony '93
Spenser: Pale Kings & Princes '94
Spenser: The Judas Goat '94
Two Years before the Mast '46
21 '08
The Verdict '82
What's the Worst That Could Happen? '01
Witness Protection '99

Bounty Hunters
All About the Benjamins '02
American Streetfighter 2: The Full Impact '97
Banjo Hackett '77
The Bounty Man '72
Bounty Tracker '93
Cold Harvest '98
Constantine '05
Critters '86
Critters 2: The Main Course '88
Domino '05
The Empire Strikes Back '80
A Fistful of Dollars '64
For a Few Dollars More '65
Ghost Rider '07
The Glove '78
The Good, the Bad and the Ugly '67
Home for Christmas '93
The Hunter '80
Kidnapped '05
The Last of the Dogmen '95
Lethal '04
Midnight Run '88
Most Wanted '97
Moving Target '96
No Country for Old Men '07
Past Perfect '98
Return of the Jedi '83
The Rundown '03
Slipstream '89
Snowdown at Boot Hill '58
Star Wars '77
Star Wars: Episode 2—Attack of the Clones '02
Subhuman '04
Terminal Impact '95
The Tracker '88
True Vengeance '97
Wanted Dead or Alive '86

Bowling
Alley Cats Strike '00
The Big Lebowski '97
Dream with the Fishes '97
Dreamer '79
The Flintstones '94
Fright Night 2 '98
Greedy '94
Kingpin '96
League of Ordinary Gentlemen '04
Mr. Wonderful '93
Pleasantville '98
Spare Me '92
Uncle Buck '89

Boxing
Abbott and Costello Meet the Invisible Man '51
Against the Ropes '04
Ali '01
Animal 2 '07
Annapolis '06
Any Which Way You Can '80
Arena '89
Back Roads '81
Battling Bunyon '24

▶ = rated three bones or higher

Boxing

Battling Butler '26
Be Yourself '30
Before the Fall '04
Belle of the Nineties '34
Best of the Best '89
The Big Man: Crossing the Line '91
Black Cloud '04
Blade Boxer '97
Body and Soul '47
Body & Soul '81
Body and Soul '98
Bowery Blitzkrieg '41
Boxcar Blues '90
The Boxer '97
The Boxer and Death '63
Breakdown '53
Brutal Glory '89
The Cage '89
The Champ '32
The Champ '79
Champion '49
Cinderella Man '05
Circle Man '87
City for Conquest '40
Cock & Bull Story '03
Confessions of Tom Harris '72
Counter Punch '71
Dempsey '83
Diggstown '92
Don King: Only in America '97
Dynamite Dan '24
Fallen Champ: The Untold Story of Mike Tyson '93
Far and Away '92
Fat City '72
Fight Club: '99
Fight for the Title '57
The Fighter '52
Fighting Champ '33
Firepower '93
Fist Fighter '88
Gentleman Jim '42
Girlfight '99
Gladiator '92
Golden Boy '39
Great Guy '36
The Great White Hope '70
The Great White Hype '96
The Greatest '77
The Hammer '07
The Hurricane '99
Hard Times '75
The Harder They Fall '56
Heart '87
Heart of a Champion: The Ray Mancini Story '85
Hell's Kitchen NYC '97
Here Comes Mr. Jordan '41
The Hitter '79
Hollywood Stadium Mystery '38
Homeboy '75
Homeboy '88
Honeyboy '82
I Spy '02
Joe and Max '02
The Joe Louis Story '53
Jump In! '07
Keep Punching '39
Kelly the Second '36
The Kid '97
Kid Dynamite '43
Kid from Brooklyn '46
Kid Galahad '37
Kid Galahad '62
Kid Monk Baroni '52
Killer's Kiss '55
The Last Fight '82
Last Man Standing '87
Les Miserables '95
Like It Is '98
Love Come Down '00
Love Songs '99
Made '01
The Main Event '79
Marciano '78
Matilda '78
Meatballs 2 '84
Milky Way '36
Million Dollar Baby '04
Miracle Kid '42
Mr. Moto's Gamble '38
Movie, Movie '78
Navy Way '44

Night and the City '92
No News from God '01
Ocean's Eleven '01
Off Limits '53
On the Waterfront '54
One-Punch O'Day '26
The Opponent '00
The Opponent '01
Opposite Corners '96
Palooka '34
Penitentiary '79
Penitentiary 2 '82
Penitentiary 3 '87
Percy & Thunder '93
Play It to the Bone '99
Poor Man's Game '06
The Power of One '92
Price of Glory '00
Pride of the Bowery '41
Prison Shadows '36
Prize Fighter '79
The Prizefighter and the Lady '33
Pulp Fiction '94
The Quest '96
The Quiet Man '52
Raging Bull '80
Requiem for a Heavyweight '56
Requiem for a Heavyweight '62
Resurrecting the Champ '07
Ricky 1 '88
The Ring '27
The Ring '52
Ringside '49
Rip Roarin' Buckaroo '36
Roaring City '51
Rocky '76
Rocky 2 '79
Rocky 3 '82
Rocky 4 '85
Rocky 5 '90
Rocky Balboa '06
Rocky Marciano '99
Rude '96
Schizo '04
The Set-Up '49
Shiner '00
Snake Eyes '98
Snatch '00
Somebody Up There Likes Me '56
Spike of Bensonhurst '88
The Spirit of Youth '37
Split Decisions '88
The Sting 2 '83
Street Crimes '92
Streets of Gold '86
Teen Wolf Too '87
They Made Me a Criminal '39
They Never Come Back '32
Thunderground '89
Title Shot '81
Tough Enough '83
Tough Kid '39
Triumph of the Spirit '89
Trouble Chasers 45
24-7 '97
Tyson '95
Undefeated '03
Undisputed '02
Undisputed II: Last Man Standing '06
Vigilantes of Boom Town 46
When We Were Kings '96
When's Your Birthday? '37
The Wildcat '26
A Wind from Wyoming 94

Brainwashed

Angel Dust '96
Awakening of Candra '81
Becky Sharp '35
Brainwashed '60
Circle of Power '83
A Clockwork Orange '71
Cypher '02
Disturbing Behavior '98
DROP Squad '94
In Like Flint '67
The Ipcress File '65
Killzone '85
The Manchurian Candidate '62
The Manchurian Candidate '04
Mind Snatchers '72
1984 '56
No Dead Heroes '87
On Her Majesty's Secret Service '69
Patty Hearst '88
Simon '80
Split Image '82
Timebomb '91
Unholy '07
Zoolander '01

Break-Ups

see also Divorce; Romantic Comedy
Annie Hall '77
The Break-Up '06
The Breakup Artist '04
The Broken Hearts Club '00
Casablanca '42
Cashback '06
The Devil Wears Prada '06
Flannel Pajamas '06
Forgetting Sarah Marshall '08
Gone with the Wind '39
The Hottest State '06
Inside Paris '06
The Jane Austen Book Club '07
Jour de Fete '48
Le Divorce '03
My Blueberry Nights '07
Postcards from the Edge '90
Prime '05
Puccini for Beginners '06
Room at the Top '59
St. Elmo's Fire '85
Sweet November '68
2 Days in Paris '07
Under the Tuscan Sun '03
The Way We Were '73
What Love Is '07

Bridges

Bataan '43
The Bridge '59
The Bridge at Remagen '69
The Bridge of San Luis Rey '44
The Bridge of San Luis Rey '05
The Bridge on the River Kwai '57
Bridge to Hell '87
A Bridge Too Far '77
The Bridges at Toko-Ri '55
The Bridges of Madison County '95
Carnival of Souls '62
Crossing the Bridge '92
Dream with the Fishes '97
For Whom the Bell Tolls '43
George of the Jungle '97
The Ghost and the Darkness '96
Graffiti Bridge '90
The Girl on the Bridge '99
It's a Wonderful Life '46
The Longest Day '62

Night of the Living Dead '68
Return of the Living Dead: Rave to the Grave '05

The Lovers on the Bridge '91
Ode to Billy Joe '76
Saturday Night Fever '77
Saving Private Ryan '98
Tarzan's New York Adventure '42
The Truman Show '98
Volunteers '85
Waterloo Bridge '40

Bringing Up Baby

see also Parenthood; Pregnant Men; Pregnant Pauses
Addams Family Values '93
And Baby Makes Six 79
Angie '94
Baby '00
The Baby and the Battleship '56
Baby Boom '87
Baby Boy '01
Baby Geniuses '98
Babyfever '94
Baby's Day Out '94
Bachelor Mother '39
Basket Case 3: The Progeny '92
Being Two Isn't Easy '62
Blondie Brings Up Baby '39
Brink of Life '57
The Brood '79
Bundle of Joy '56
By Design '82
The Child '05
Cotton Mary '99
Court Jester '56
Dad on the Run '00
East Side of Heaven '39
Eastern Promises '07
The Ex '07
Eye on the Sparrow '91
The Family Man 79
Fanny '61
Fear of Fear '75
For Keeps '88
Four and a Half Women '05
Four Days in July '85
Fran '85
From Here to Maternity '85
Ghost Son '06
The Girls of Huntington House '73
A Good Baby '99
Grave of the Vampire '72
The Great Lie '41
A Hole in the Head '59
I Don't Want to Be Born '75
In Search of a Golden Sky '84
It's Alive '74
It's Alive 2: It Lives Again '78
It's Alive 3: Island of the Alive '87
Jack and Sarah '95
The Lightning Incident '91
Little Man '06
Little Man Tate '91
Look Who's Talking '89
Look Who's Talking, Too '90
Mamele '38
Meet the Fockers '04
Monika 52
Night Cries 78
Nobody's Baby '01
Not of This World '99
Novel Romance '06
The Omen '06
Paternity 81
Penny Serenade '41
Problem Child 2 '91
Psycho 4: The Beginning '90
Raising Arizona '87
Robin-B-Hood '06
Robot Stories '03
Rock-A-Bye Baby '57
Rosemary's Baby '68
The Rugrats Movie '98
Rumpelstiltskin '86
Sacred Ground '83
The Saga of the Draculas '72
Sarah's Child '96
Scarred '84
Secrets '94

Sex and Lucia '01
She's So Lovely '97
Shoot 'Em Up '07
The Snapper '93
Son of Godzilla '66
A Stranger in Town '95
The Sugarland Express '74
Superbabies: Baby Geniuses 2 '04
Table for Five '83
The Tender Years '47
The Terminator '84
Test Tube Babies '48
That's My Baby! '88
The 13th Floor '88
Thomas Graal's First Child '18
Three Men and a Baby '87
Three Men and a Cradle '85
Three Men and a Little Lady '90
Tomorrow's Child '82
Tomorrow's Children '34
Tsotsi '05
The 24 Hour Woman 99
The Unborn 2 '94
Unnatural '52
Up and Down '04
A Way of Life '04
The War Zone '98
Willa 79
Willow '88
A Woman Is a Woman '60

Brothers & Sisters

see also Family Adventure; Family Comedy; Family Drama; Sibling Rivalry; Twins
About Adam '00
Above Suspicion '88
The Accidental Tourist '88
Across the Plains '39
Adam Had Four Sons '41
The Addams Family '91
Agnes and His Brothers '04
Alaska '96
All About You '01
All Fall Down 62
All My Sons '86
All the Brothers Were Valiant '53
Alpine Fire '89
American Flyers 85
American History X '98
American Outlaws '01
American Samurai '92
American Streetfighter '96
American Wedding '03
America's Sweethearts '01
Amores Perros '00
And You Thought Your Parents Were Weird! '91
Angela '94
Angels in the Endzone '98
Anne Rice's The Feast of All Saints '01
The Anniversary '68
Arabian Flyers 42
Arabian Nights '00
The Aristocrats '99
Ash Wednesday 02
Ask Any Girl 59
At Any Cost '00
At Close Range '86
ATL '06
Atonement '07
Audrey's Rain '03
Autumn Sonata '78
The Avenging '92
Backdraft '91
Bad Blood '94
Bad Boys 2 '03
Bare Knees '28
Barjo '93
Based on an Untrue Story '93
The Basket '99
Basket Case '82
Basket Case 2 '90
Beau Geste '39
Because I Said So '07
Bee Season '05
Beerfest '06
Before the Devil Knows You're Dead '07

Behind the Red Door '02
Behind the Sun '01
Belle Epoque '92
Benny & Joon '03
Best of Youth '03
Betsy's Wedding '90
Better Daz '02
Better Than Chocolate 99
Big Brother Trouble '00
Big Business '88
Big Night '95
The Big White '05
Black Cadillac '03
Black Irish '07
The Black Room '35
Black Sheep '96
Black Sheep '06
Blind Dating '06
Blinded by the Light '82
Blood Angels '05
Blood River '95
Bobbie's Girl '02
The Bodyguard '92
The Book of Stars '99
Boondock Saints '99
Born to Run '93
The Boys and Girl From County Clare '03
Brand Upon the Brain! '06
Bread and Roses '00
The Bread, My Sweet '01
Breathing Fire '91
The Bridesmaid '04
Brilliant Lies 96
Bring It On '00
Broadway Melody 29
Broken Trust '93
The Brontes of Haworth '73
Brother '97
Brother Bear '03
Brotherhood of the Wolf 01
Brothers '05
The Brothers Grimm '05
The Brothers Karamazov '58
Brothers Three '07
Brother's Keeper '92
Brother's Keeper '02
A Brother's Kiss '97
The Brothers McMullen '94
Brothers of the Head '06
The Brothers Solomon '07
Bush Pilot '47
Bye-Bye '96
Cadillac Ranch '96
Carolina Skeletons '05
Carrie's War '04
Carry Me Back '82
Cassandra's Dream '07
Cat People '42
Cat People '82
Catacombs '00
Catherine Cookson's The Dwelling Place '94
Catherine Cookson's The Fifteen Streets '90
Catherine Cookson's The Wingless Bird '97
Cavalcade of the West '36
Cavalry Charge '51
Cellblock Sisters: Banished Behind Bars '95
The Cement Garden '93
Chain of Souls '00
Chameleon 3: Dark Angel '00
The Chateau '01
Cheaper by the Dozen '03
Cheetah '89
Children of Heaven '98
Children of the Corn 3: Urban Harvest '95
Christmas Comes to Willow Creek '87
The Chronicles of Narnia: Prince Caspian '08

The Chronicles of Narnia: The Lion, the Witch and the Wardrobe '05
Chutney Popcorn '99
City of Industry '96
Close My Eyes '91
Code Unknown '00
Come Undone '00
The Confession 20
The Confessional '95
The Conrad Boys '06
Cookie's Fortune '99
Corky Romano '01
Counterstrike '03
Coupe de Ville '90
Cowboy Up '00
Cracker: Brotherly Love '95
Cria Cuervos '76
Cries and Whispers '72
Crimes of the Heart '86
Criminal '04
The Criminal Mind '93
Cruel and Unusual '01
Curly Top '35
Cursed '04
Cyclo '95
Daddy's Little Girls '07
Dancing at Lughnasa '98
Dangerous Ground '96
A Dangerous Place '94
Daniel '83
Danielle Steel's Kaleidoscope '90
The Darjeeling Limited '07
Dark Mirror '46
Dark Odyssey '57
Dead in the Water '06
Dead Man's Shoes '04
Death at a Funeral '07
Death of a Salesman '51
Deathfight '93
December Bride '91
Delightfully Dangerous '45
Deliver Us from Eva '03
Demons in the Garden '82
Desperate Remedies '93
Deuces Wild '02
Devil's Daughter '39
The Devil's Knight '03
The Devil's Web '74
Diamonds '72
Dick Tracy '37
Die Sister, Die! '74
Dinotopia '02
Dirty Dancing: Havana Nights '04
Dixie Dynamite '76
Dr. Seuss' The Cat in the Hat '03
A Dog's Breakfast '07
Dominick & Eugene '88
Don't Tell '05
Double Dragon '94
Down in the Valley '05
Dream Street 21
The Dreamers '03
Driven '01
Drop Zone '94
Dust '01
Duel '01
Duel in the Sun '46
East of Eden '54
East of Eden '80
East Side Kids '40
EDtv '99
El Norte '83
Elizabethtown '05
Emile '03
Empire Falls '05
Endplay '75
Enid is Sleeping '90
Entertaining Mr. Sloane '70
Erskinville Kings '99
Eurotrip '04
Evening '07
Experiment in Terror '62
Eye of the Storm '91
Eyes of a Stranger '81
The Fabulous Baker Boys '89
The Fabulous Dorseys '47
Face/Off '97
Faceless '88
The Fall of the House of Usher '49
The Fall of the House of Usher '60

The Fall of the House of Usher '80
The Family Stone '05
Fanny and Alexander '83
Fantastic Four '05
Far Side of the Moon '03
Farinelli '94
The Fast Runner '01
Fatal Passion '94
The Favorite Son '94
Fear of the Dark '02
Feeling Minnesota '96
Female Perversions '96
Ferris Bueller's Day Off '86
A Few Days in September '06
Fiddler on the Roof '71
50 First Dates '04
The Fighting Sullivans '42
Final Analysis '92
Final Appeal '93
The Finger Man '55
The Florentine '98
Flowers in the Attic '87
The Flying Fool '29
Fool for Love '86
For Better or Worse '95
Force of Evil '49
Forty Guns '57
40 Days and 40 Nights '02
Four Brothers '05
Four Daughters '38
Four Men and a Prayer '38
Four Sheets to the Wind '07
Four Sons 28
Frailty '02
Frank and Jesse '94
Fred Claus '07
Freddy Got Fingered '01
Freud Leaving Home '91
From Dusk Till Dawn '95
The Game '97
Gas Food Lodging '92
Georgia '95
Get Over It! '01
Ginger Snaps '01
Ginger Snaps: Unleashed '04
The Girl with a Suitcase '60
Give Me a Sailor '38
Gladiator '00
The Glass House '01
Glass House: The Good Mother '06
God Said "Ha!" '99
The Godfather, Part 2 '74
Gone in 60 Seconds '00
Goodbye, Lover '99
The Good Old Boys '95
Good Morning, Babylon '87
Gracie's Choice '04
Grave of the Fireflies '88
Gray Matters '06
Green Dolphin Street '47
Grind '96
The Grudge 2 '06
Gun Play 36
The Hard Word '02
Halloween '07
Halloween: H20 '98
Hanging Up '99
Hannah and Her Sisters '86
Hannibal Rising '07
Hard Luck '01
The Hard Word '02
Harry and Max '04
Having Our Say: The Delany Sisters' First 100 Years '99
Head of State '03
Head of the Family '96
Heart of Dragon '85
The Heart of Me '02
Hell on Wheels '67
Her First Romance '40
Her Majesty '01
The Hiding Place 75
High School Musical '06
Hilary and Jackie '98
Hit Me '96
The Holiday '06
Hombres Complicados '97
A Home at the End of the World '04
Hooded Angels '00

The Hoodlum '51
Horizons West '52
Hot Lead & Cold Feet '78
The House of Eliott '92
The House of Strangers '49
Look Who's Talking, Too '90
Looking for Miracles '97
The House of the Seven Gables '40
The House of Usher '88
How I Killed My Father '03
How to Eat Fried Worms '06
Howard's End '92
The Human Shield '92
I Capture the Castle '03
I Love You, Alice B. Toklas! '68
I Sent a Letter to My Love '81
Ice Men '04
Igby Goes Down '02
In Celebration '75
In Dark Places '97
In Her Shoes '05
In Search of the Castaways '62
In the Cut '03
In the Flesh '97
In the Time of the Butterflies '01
The Incredible Mrs. Ritchie '03
The Indian Runner '91
Innocents '00
Inside Paris '06
Institute Benjamenta or This Dream People Call Human Life '95
Interiors '78
Invasion! '78
Inventing the Abbotts '97
Invisible Circus '00
It Could Happen to You '37
Jack Be Nimble '94
Jacob Have I Loved '88
Jason's Lyric '94
Jeepers Creepers '01
Joe Torre: Curveballs Along the Way '97
Johnson County War '02
Johnson Family Vacation '04
Josh and S.A.M. '93
Joy Ride '01
Julien Donkey-boy '99
Jumpin' at the Boneyard '92
Junebug '05
The Juniper Tree '87
Kate & Leopold '01
K'd Sister '45
Kidnapped in Paradise '98
Kill Bill Vol. 2 '04
Kill by Inches '99
Kill or Be Killed '93
Killing Me Softly '01
The King of Marvin Gardens '72
King of Texas '02
King of Thieves '04
Knocked Up '07
La Bamba '87
La Buche '00
La Chute de la Maison Usher '28
Lars and the Real Girl '07
Landscape in the Mist '88
The Last Days of Chez Nous '92
The Last Five Days '82
The Last Mimzy '07
Law of Desire '87
Le Divorce '03
Legends of the Fall '94
Lemony Snicket's A Series of Unfortunate Events '04
Les Enfants Terrible '50
Les Voleurs '96
Light of Day '87
Like a Puppet Out of Strings '05
Lilo & Stitch '02
Limbo '99
The Lion King '94
Little Giants '94
Little Nicky '00
Local Boys '02
Loco Love '03

Lola and Billy the Kid '98
The Long Riders '80
A Long Way Home '81
The Long Weekend '05
Look Who's Talking, Too '90
Looking for Miracles '97
The Lost City '05
The Lost Capone '90
Love Come Down '00
Love Ludlow '05
Love Songs '07
Love & Amazing '02
Luminarias '99
Lush '01
Ma Saison Preferee '93
Mac '93
Mad at the Moon '92
Maids of Wilko '79
The Makioka Sisters '83
A Man About the House '47
The Man in the Moon '91
Man to Man '05
Many & Lo '96
Margot at the Wedding '07
Marianne and Juliane '82
Marion Bridge '02
Martial Outlaw '93
Material Girls '07
Me & Veronica '93
Me Without You '01
Mean Creek '04
Meantime '81
The Messengers '07
Mexico City '00
Midnight Dancers '94
Midnight Warning '32
Mifune '99
Miles from Home '88
The Mill on the Floss '37
The Mill on the Floss '97
Mill ons '05
Mimic 3: Sentinel '03
Mind Lies '00
Mirror, Mirror 2: Raven Dance '94
Miss Rose White '92
Mr. Saturday Night '92
Molly '99
Montana Sky '07
Moondance '95
Mouse Hunt '97
Murder One '88
Must Love Dogs '05
My Brother '06
My Brother's War '97
My Mother Likes Women '02
My Outlaw Brother '51
My Sister, My Love '78
My Sister Eileen '55
My Sister's Keeper '02
My Summer of Love '05
My Wife is an Actress '01
Myrt and Marge '33
The Myth of Fingerprints '97

National Lampoon's Gold Diggers '04
Nenette and Boni '96
Never Been Kissed '99
New Blood '99
New York Minute '04
The Newton Boys '97
A Night at the Roxbury '98
Night Passage '57
Nightstalker '87
Nine Queens '00
No Alibi '00
No Way Home '96
Nobody Knows '04
Nobody's Baby '01
The Object of My Affection '98
The Old Settler '01
On the Waterfront '54
Once in the Life '00
Once to Another '09
One Way Out '95
The Opposite of Sex '98
Orange County '02
Orphans '87
Orphans '97
Orphans of the Storm '21
The Other Boleyn Girl '03
The Other Boleyn Girl '08
The Other Brother '02
Out of the Black '01
Outing Riley '04
The Outsiders '83
Over the Wire '95
Pandaemonium '00
Paradise Alley '78
Paranoiac '62
Parenthood '89
Pauline and Paulette '01
Peppermint Soda '77
P.D. James: The Murder Room '04
The Perfect Son '00
Persons Unknown '96
Peter Pan '03
Phantasm '79
Phantasm 4: Oblivion '98
Phantasm Brother '88
Phantom Brother '88
The Pianist '02
The Pit and the Pendulum '91
The Pit & the Pendulum '61
Pleasantville '98
Pleasure '31
Plucking the Daisy '56
Pola X '99
Power of Attorney '94
Practical Magic '98
Price of Glory '00
Pride and Prejudice '05
The Proposition '05
Psycho Girls '86
Punch-Drunk Love '02
The Quiet Man '52
Radio Inside '94
Rain Man '88
Raising Helen '04
Rated X '00
The Real Thing '97
Real Women Have Curves '02
Recipe for Disaster '03
Relative Values '99
Return of the Jedi '83
Return of Wildfire '48
Rich Man, Poor Man '76
The Right Hand Man '87
Rikky and Pete '88
Rio Bravo '59
Risk '94
The River is Red '46
A River Runs Through It '92
The Road Home '95
Rocco and His Brothers '60
Romeo Must Die '00
Rooms for Tourists '04
Row Your Boat '98
The Royal Tenenbaums '01
Rude '96
The Rugrats Movie '98
Rumble Fish '83
Sabrina '54
Sabrina '95

The Sackets '79
San Quentin '37
Satan's Little Helper '04
The Savages '07
Say It Isn't So '01
The Secret Rapture '94
Seducing Maarya '99
Sense and Sensibility '95
Sense & Sensibility '07
Sensuous Summer '91
Seven Beauties '76
Seven Brides for Seven Brothers '54
Seventeen Again '00
Seven Alone '75
75 Degrees '00
The Shadow Riders '82
Shadows '60
Shanghai Knights '03
Shark River '53
The Sheep Has Five Legs '54
Sherrybaby '06
She's the Man '06
She's the One '96
The Shining Hour '38
Shot '01
Shot in the Heart '01
Shower '00
The Sibling '07
Sibling Rivalry '90
The Sicilian Connection '85
Sidewalks of New York '31
Signs '02
The Silence '63
Silver Bullet '85
Silver City '84
Simple Men '92
A Simple Plan '98
Sin '22
Sirens '02
Sister My Sister '94
The Sisters '38
Sisters '73
Sisters '97
Sisters '05
The Sisters '05
Sisters, Or the Balance of Happiness '79
Six Days, Six Nights '94
The Sixth Man '97
Skins '02
Slap Shot 2: Breaking the Ice '02
Slums of Beverly Hills '98
Smiling Fish & Goat on Fire '99
Soft Fruit '99
A Soldier's Daughter Never Cries '98
Sons of the Shark '93
Sons of Katie Elder '65
Sophie Scholl: The Final Days '05
Sorrento Beach '95
Soul Food '97
South of Hell Mountain '70
The Spiderwick Chronicles '08
Splinter '06
Spy Kids '01
Spy Kids 2: The Island of Lost Dreams '02
State of Grace '90
Stealing Harvard '02
The Stolen Children '92
Storm Warning '51
The Story of Jacob & Joseph '74
Strapless '90
Street Hitz '92
Stuck On You '03
Sugar Hill '94
Sunday in New York '63
Sunstorm '01
Supercross: The Movie '05
Surface to Air '98
Surfing Bastards '90
Suspended Animation '02
Suture '93
Sweet Sixteen '02
Sweet Smell of Success '57
Sweetie '89
Swimming '00
Tae Guk Gi: The Brotherhood of War '04
A Tale of Two Sisters '03
The Tall Men '55
The Tempest '99
Tex '82
Texas Jack '35
That Was Then... This Is Now '85
The Thief Lord '06
Things You Can Tell Just by Looking at Her '00
Thirteen Days '00
A Thousand Acres '97
Three Brothers '80
3 Ninjas '92
3 Ninjas Kick Back '94
The Three Sisters '65
The Three Sisters '36
The Three Weird Sisters '48
Three Smart Girls Grow Up '39
Three Violent People '57
Thunder Trail '37
Thrillkill '84
Tideland '05
Till Marriage Do Us Part '74

▶ = rated three bones or higher

Till There Was You '91
Time Stands Still '82
Times Have Been Better '06
Tiptoes '03
'Tis a Pity She's a Whore '73
TMNT (Teenage Mutant Ninja Turtles) '07
To All My Friends on Shore '71 ►
Tombstone '93
Tortilla Soup '01
Trade '07
Trail of the Mounties '47
Trained to Kill '88
Trapped in Paradise '94
The Triumph of Love '01
Troublemakers '94
True Blood '89
True Confessions '81 ►
True West '86 ►
Trust the Man '06
Tully '00 ►
Twelfth Night '96
12 and Holding '05 ►
27 Dresses '08
28 Days '00
The Twilight of the Ice Nymphs '97
Twins '88
2 Brothers & a Bride '03
Two Much '96
The Two Sisters '37
Two Weeks '06
Uncle Buck '89
Under Hellgate Bridge '99
Under the Hula Moon '95
Under the Skin '97
Under the Volcano '84 ►
Undercurrent '46
Underground '41
Undertow '04
Underworld: Evolution '05
An Unremarkable Life '89
Until They Sail '57
Vampire Night '00
Vengeance Valley '51
Vertical Limit '00
The Vertical Ray of the Sun '00
Vincent & Theo '90 ►
Violent Cop '89
The Virgin Suicides '99
The Visit '00 ►
Volver '06 ►
Voodoo Moon '05
The Wagons Roll at Night '41
Walkabout '71 ►
The War Zone '98
Warm Blooded Killers '01
We Own the Night '07
The Wedding Date '05
Wedding Wars '06
Weep No More My Lady '93
The Weight of Water '00
Whacked! '02
Whale Music '94
The Whales of August '87 ►
What Ever Happened To... '88
What Ever Happened to Baby Jane? '62 ►
What's Eating Gilbert Grape '93 ►
When Angels Fly '82
When Brendan Met Trudy '00 ►
Where the Lilies Bloom '74 ►
The Wolves '95
The Woman in White '97
Wild America '97
Wild West '86
Wilder Napalm '93
The Wind That Shakes the Barley '06 ►
Windhorse '98
Wish upon a Star '96
Without Evidence '96
The Wizard '89
The Wolves '95
The Woman in White '97
Wonderland '99
Wyatt Earp '94
You Can Count On Me '99 ►
You Got Served '04
The Young Girls of Rochefort '68
Zathura '05 ►
Zatoichi '03 ►

Zus & Zo '01

Buddhism ►

The Covenant '06
The Cup '99
Green Snake '93
The Judgement '04
Kundun '97 ►
Little Buddha '93
Omaha (the movie) '95
Raw Force '81
Seven Years in Tibet '97
Siddhartha '72
Spring, Summer, Fall, Winter... and Spring '03 ►
Temptation of a Monk '94
Why Has Bodhi-Darma Left for the East '89 ►
Windhorse '98

Buddies ►

see also Buddy Cops
Abbott and Costello Meet Frankenstein '48 ►
Adios Amigo '75
The Adventures of Huck Finn '93 ►
The Adventures of Huckleberry Finn '78
The Adventures of Milo & Otis '89 ►
The Adventures of Rusty '45
Against the Wall '04
Ain't No Way Back '89
The Alamo '60 ►
All Saint's Day '98
All the Real Girls '03 ►
American Pie '99 ►
An American Story '92
Amongst Friends '93
Andre '94
Another 48 Hrs. '90
Another Day '01
Anzacs: The War Down Under '85 ►
At First Sight '95
ATL '06
The Baby-Sitters Club '95
Babyfever '94
Bachelor Party '84
Bachelor Party Vegas '05
Backbeat '94 ►
Bad Company '72 ►
Bad Girls '94
Band of Brothers '01 ►
BASEketball '98
The Basketball Diaries '95
The Battle of Blood Island '60
The Bear '89 ►
Beautiful Girls '96 ►
Beavis and Butt-Head Do America '96
Beer League '06
Belly '98
Benji: Off the Leash! '04
A Better Tomorrow, Part 1 '86 ►
A Better Tomorrow, Part 2 '88
Between Heaven and Hell '56 ►
The Big Chill '83 ►
Big Deadly Game '54
Big Eden '00
Big Mo '73
Big Shots '87
The Big Slice '90
Bigfoot: The Unforgettable Encounter '94
Bill & Ted's Bogus Journey '91
Birdy '84 ►
Black Beauty '46
Black Cadillac '03
Black Fox: The Price of Peace '94
Blackrock '97
Blonde in Black Leather '77
Blowin' Smoke '99
Blue Juice '95
Blue Ridge Fall '99
Blue Skies '46 ►
Body Shots '99
Bogus '96

Bookies '03
Boot Hill '69
Boots Malone '52
Born to Be Wild '38
Born to Be Wild '95
Boston Kickout '95
The Bowery '33 ►
A Boy and His Dog '75
The Boy Who Could Fly '86 ►
The Boys in the Band '70
The Boys Next Door '96
Branded Men '31
Breaking the Rules '92
Breakout '98
Brian's Song '01
Bride of Killer Nerd '91
Broadway Melody of 1940 '40 ►
Brooklyn Rules '07
The Brothers '01 ►
The Bucket List '07
The Buddy System '83
A Bullet in the Head '90 ►
Bulletproof '96
The Bumblebee Flies Anyway '99
Bundle of Joy '56
The Business of Fancydancing '02
The Butterfly '02 ►
The Cable Guy '96
The Caddy '53
Calendar Girl '93
Cambridge Spies '03
The Campus Corpse '77
Campus Man '87
Capitaine Conan '96 ►
Captive Hearts '87
The Cat '66
Catch and Release '07
Celtic Pride '96
Charlie's Ghost: The Secret of Coronado '94
Chasing Amy '97 ►
Cheap Shots '91
Chill Factor '99
Circle of Two '80
The Cisco Kid '94
City of Men '07 ►
City Slickers '91 ►
City Slickers 2: The Legend of Curly's Gold '94
Class Act '91
Class of '61 '92
Clay Pigeons '98
Clayton County Line '78
Clerks '94 ►
Clerks 2 '06 ►
Clown Murders '83
Cock & Bull Story '03
Colombian Love '04
The Color Purple '85 ►
Colorado Serenade '46
Company Business '91
The Concrete Cowboys '79
Convict Cowboy '95
Cops and Robbers '73
Corleone '79
Country Gentlemen '36
Courage of Black Beauty '57
Crack Up '97
Crime Busters '78
Crime Lords '91
Crime Spree '03
Crossfire '03
Crossing the Bridge '92
Crossover '06
Cry Freedom '87 ►
The Cure '95 ►
Curtis's Charm '95
Cycle Vixens '79
Dancer, Texas—Pop. 81 '98 ►
Dark Blue World '01 ►
Day Zero '07
Dead Presidents '95
Dead Reckoning '47 ►
Deadlock '91
Deadly Surveillance '91
December '91
The Deer Hunter '78 ►
Defenseless '91
The Defiant Ones '58 ►
Delta Farce '07
Detroit Rock City '99
Die Hard: With a Vengeance '95 ►
Digger '94

Diggers '06
Diner '82 ►
Dirty Work '97
Dish Dogs '98
Dogfight '91 ►
Donnie Brasco '96 ►
Donovan's Reef '63 ►
Don't Look Back '96 ►
Dopamine '03
Double Down '01
Double Team '97
Down Under '86
Downtown '89
Dragonheart '96 ►
Dragonworld '94
Dream a Little Dream 2 '94
The Dream Catcher '99
Dream with the Fishes '97
Dreamcatcher '03 ►
The Dresser '83 ►
Driving Miss Daisy '89 ►
Drop Dead Fred '91
Drums in the Deep South '51
Dude, Where's My Car? '00
Dumb & Dumber '94
Dumb and Dumberer: When Harry Met Lloyd '03
The Eagle and the Hawk '33 ►
Easy Rider '69 ►
Eat the Peach '86
Ed's Next Move '96
The Eighth Day '95
El Dorado '67 ►
Elling '01
Elmer '76
The Emperor's New Groove '00 ►
Enemy Mine '85
Enemy of the State '98
Entre-Nous '83 ►
Eurotrip '04
Every Which Way But Loose '78
Extreme Prejudice '87
Extremedays '01
F/X 2: The Deadly Art of Illusion '91
The Falcon and the Snowman '85 ►
Far from Home: The Adventures of Yellow Dog '94
Father's Day '96
Federal Hill '94
Ferris Bueller's Day Off '86 ►
Fight Club '99 ►
Finder's Fee '01
First Kid '96
The Five Heartbeats '91 ►
Fled '96
Flickering Lights '01
The Flintstones '94
The Flintstones in Viva Rock Vegas '00
Floating '97
Flyboys '06
For the Moment '94
Forgive and Forget '99
Forsaking All Others '35
Fortunes '05
The 40 Year Old Virgin '05 ►
The Four Feathers '02
Francis in the Navy '55
Free Enterprise '98
Free Willy '93
Free Willy 2: The Adventure Home '95
Free Willy 3: The Rescue '97
Freeze-Die-Come to Life '90 ►
The Frisco Kid '79
Frontier Fugitives '45
Full Count '06
The Full Monty '96 ►
Funny Valentine '05
Galaxies Are Colliding '92
Gallipoli '81 ►
Garden State '04 ►
Gerry '02
Get Over It! '01
Getting Even '92
A Girl, 3 Guys and a Gun '01
A Girl in Every Port '28
Glory Daze '96

Going All the Way '97
Going Back '83
Going Greek '01
Gold Diggers: The Secret of Bear Mountain '95
Gone Fishin' '97
The Good Humor Man '05
Good Luck '96
Good Will Hunting '97 ►
Goodfellas '90 ►
Gordy '95
Gossip '99
Grand Illusion '37 ►
Gridlock'd '96 ►
Grilled '06
Grind '03
The Groomsmen '06
Grumpier Old Men '95
Grumpy Old Men '93 ►
Guarding Tess '94
A Guide to Recognizing Your Saints '06 ►
Gunga Din '39 ►
Gunmen '93
Hangin' with the Homeboys '91 ►
Hard Core Logo '96
Hard Eight '96 ►
Hard Luck '01
Harley Davidson and the Marlboro Man '91
Harold and Kumar Go to White Castle '04
Harriet the Spy '96
Harsh Times '05
The Hasty Heart '86 ►
Hate '95 ►
Hats Off '37
Hawaii Calls '38
He Died With a Felafel in His Hand '01
Heartaches '82 ►
Heartbreakers '84 ►
Heavenly Creatures '94 ►
Henry & Verlin '94
Hercules '97 ►
The Hi-Lo Country '98 ►
The Highest Honor '84
Highway '01
Hired Hand '71
Hollywood or Bust '56
Home Free All '84
Homeward Bound 2: Lost in San Francisco '96
Hong Kong Nights '35
Hong Kong 1941 '84 ►
Honor '06
Hoot '06
Huck and the King of Hearts '93
The Hunters '58
Hurlyburly '98
Hurricane Streets '96 ►
Husbands '70
I Got Five on It '05
I Now Pronounce You Chuck and Larry '07
I Shot a Man in Vegas '96
I Spy '02
I Went Down '97 ►
Ice Age: The Meltdown '06
Ice Men '04
If I Had My Way '40
If Lucy Fell '95
I'll Remember April '99
I'm Not Rappaport '96
In the Army Now '94
The In-Laws '79 ►
In the Navy '41
Indian Summer '93
Inn of Temptation '73
Intimate Lighting '65 ►
Iron Giant '99 ►
Ishtar '87
Ivan and Abraham '94 ►
Jackass Number Two '06
Jay and Silent Bob Strike Back '01 ►
Jimmy Hollywood '94
Jindabyne '06 ►
Johnny Come Lately '43
Johnny Holiday '49
The Jolly Boys' Last Stand '00
Joy Ride to Nowhere '78
Joyride '92
Judgment Night '93
Juice '92 ►
Jules and Jim '62 ►

Junior Army '42
Just a Little Harmless Sex '99
Just Between Friends '86
K-9000 '89
The Kansas Terrors '39
The Karate Kid '84 ►
The Karate Kid: Part 2 '86 ►
The Karate Kid: Part 3 '89 ►
Kazaam '96
Keeping the Faith '00 ►
Killer Bud '00
Killer Pad '06
The Killing Fields '84 ►
King of the Mountain '81
Kingpin '96 ►
Kings of the Road—In the Course of Time '76 ►
Knock Off '98
Knockaround Guys '01
Knocked Up '07 ►
K2: The Ultimate High '92
Ladies on the Rocks '83
The Land Before Time 5: The Mysterious Island '97
Lansky '99 ►
Larry McMurtry's Dead Man's Walk '96
Last American Virgin '82
The Last Boy Scout '91 ►
The Last Kiss '06 ►
Last Orders '01 ►
Last Summer '69
The Last Time I Committed Suicide '96
Late Last Night '99
Lawn Dogs '98 ►
Le Beau Serge '58 ►
Le Doulos '61 ►
Leaving Normal '92
Les Apprentis '95
Les Comperes '83 ►
The Lesser Evil '97
Let 'er Go Gallegher '28
Let's Do It Again '75 ►
Liar's Poker '99
L.I.E. '01 ►
Life '99 ►
The Life of Jesus '96 ►
The Lion King 1 1/2 '04 ►
Little City '97
The Littlest Outlaw '54
The Lives of a Bengal Lancer '35 ►
The Long Voyage Home '40 ►
Looking for Miracles '90
Lords of Dogtown '05 ►
The Lords of Flatbush '74 ►
Lost in the Barrens '91
Love Goggles '45
Love Letters '45
Love Thy Neighbor '02
Love! Valour! Compassion! '96 ►
Lovelife '97
Love's Labour's Lost '00 ►
The Low Down '00
Macaroni '85
Mad Dog and Glory '93 ►
Made '01 ►
Made of Honor '08
Mallrats '95 ►
The Man on the Train '02 ►
The Man Who Would Be King '75 ►
Managua '97
Manhattan Melodrama '34 ►
March or Die '77
Master and Commander: The Far Side of the World '03 ►
McHale's Navy '97
Me and Him '89
Mean Frank and Crazy Tony '75
Meet Danny Wilson '52
Men Men Men '95
The Men's Club '86
Metroland '97
Midnight Cowboy '69 ►
Midnight Run '88 ►
The Mighty '98 ►
The Mighty Quinn '89 ►
Mikey & Nicky '76 ►
Mina Tannenbaum '93 ►
Misunderstood '87
Molly and Gina '94

► = rated *three bones* or *higher*

Mondays in the Sun '22
Money Talks '97
Money to Burn '94
Monster Man '03
Monsters, Inc. '01▶
Monsters Ave. '98
Moon over Miami '41▶
Moonlight and Valentino '95
Mortal Thoughts '91
The Mosaic Project '35
The Motorcycle Diaries '04▶
MXP: Most Xtreme Primate '03
My Beautiful Laundrette '85▶
My Best Friend's Girl '84
My Best Friend's Wedding '97
My Dinner with Andre '81▶
My First Mister '01
My Giant '98
My Girl '91
My Name Is Joe '98
Mystic Pizza '88▶
Mystic River '03▶
Naked Youth '59
The Naughty Nineties '45
Neil Simon's The Odd Couple 2 '98
Night Beat '48
Nightforce '86
The Nightingale '85▶
1915 '82
No Money Down '97
No Sleep Til Madison '02
Nothing to Lose '96
Now and Then '95
The Nugget '02
Ocean's 11 '60
Ocean's Eleven '01▶
Ocean's Thirteen '07▶
The Odd Couple '68▶
Old Explorers '90
Old Joy '06
Oliver & Company '88
On the Fiddle '61
On the Line '01
The Opposite Sex and How to Live With Them '93
Ordinary Sinner '02
Out to Sea '97
Palookaville '95▶

Pals '87
Papillon '73▶
Parallel Lives '94
Past the Bleachers '95
Peck's Bad Boy with the Circus '38
The Penitent '88
Perfectly Normal '91
Peter's Friends '92
Petits Freres '00
The Phantom of 42nd Street '45
Phat Beach '96
Piece of Cake '83
Pigs '07
P.K. and the Kid '85
Plan B '97
Platoon '86▶
Play It to the Bone '99
Playmates '72
A Pleasure Doing Business '79
Plunder Road '57
The Pompatus of Love '95
Portrait of a Showgirl '82
Psycho Cop 2 '94
P.U.N.K.S. '98
P.U.S.H. '06
Push '06
Racing with the Moon '84▶
Rafferty & the Gold Dust Twins '75
Rape '76
The Rat Pack '98
Ready to Rumble '00
Red Balloon '56▶
Red Meat '98
Reign Over Me '07
The Reivers '69▶
Relax... It's Just Sex! '98
Reno and the Doc '84

Requiem for Domino '91▶
The Return of Grey Wolf '22
The Return '06
Return of the Musketeers 7
Return of the Secaucus 7 '80▶
Revenge of the Nerds '84
Revenge of the Nerds 2: Nerds in Paradise '87
Rich and Famous '81
Ride the High Country '62▶
Ride with the Devil '99
Rio Conchos '64▶
The Road to El Dorado '00
The Road to Hong Kong '62
The Road to Morocco '42▶
Road Trip '00▶
Roadside Prophets '92
Robby '68
Robert et Robert '78▶
Romy and Michele's High School Reunion '97
Roommates '95
Rory O'Shea Was Here '04
Rubin & Ed '92
Rules of Engagement '00
The Run of the Country '95▶
The Rundown '03▶
Running Scared '86
Russkies '87
Rusty's Birthday '49
St. Elmo's Fire '85
The Saint of Fort Washington '93
Saints and Sinners '55
Salut l'Artiste '74▶
Same River Twice '97
The Sandlot '93▶
Saving Silverman '01
The Search for One-Eyed Jimmy '96

Searching for Bobby D '05
Searching For Wooden Watermelons '01
A Separate Peace '04
Seven Days Ashore '44
The Seventh Seal '46▶
Shag: The Movie '89▶
Shaking the Tree '92
Shanghai Knights '03
Shaun of the Dead '04▶
She Gods of Shark Reef '56
The Shot '96
Shot Through the Heart '98▶
Showdown in Little Tokyo '91
Shrek the Third '07
Shut Up and Kiss Me '05
Sideways '04▶
Silence Like Glass '90
Slackers '02
Slappy and the Stinkers '97
The Slaughter Rule '01
Sleepers '96▶
Sling Blade '96▶
Snow White and the Seven Dwarfs '33▶
So This is Washington '43
Some Like It Hot '59▶
Someone Else's America '96▶
Something of Value '57
Son of Rusty '47
Songwriter '84
Sophisticated Gents '81
The Souler Opposite '97
Souls at Sea '37
Sparkler '99
Spawn of the North '38
Spies Like Us '85
Spittin' Image '83
Spotlight Scandals '43
Spring Forward '99
Sprung '06
Stag '97
Stand by Me '86▶
Star Trek 4: The Voyage Home '86▶
Starbird and Sweet William '73
State of Grace '90▶
The Station Agent '03▶
Stealing Home '88
Steaming '86
The Steel Helmet '51▶
Stickman '03
Sticks and Stones '96

Stir Crazy '80▶
Stolen Summer '02
The Stoned Age '94
Stop-Loss '08▶
Strange Bedfellows '05
Stranger than Fiction '99
Strawberry and Chocolate '93▶
Stricken '98
Stuckey's Last Stand '80
The Substitute 3: Winner Takes All '99
suburbia '96
Sudden Death '50
Summer City '77
Summer School '87▶
Sunny Skies '30
The Sunshine Boys '75▶
Superbad '07▶
The Sweetest Thing '02
Swingers '96▶
T Bone N Weasel '92
Tadpole '02▶
Talladega Nights: The Ballad of Ricky Bobby '06▶
Tape '01▶
Target of Opportunity '04
The Tavern '00
Ten Benny '98
Ten Who Dared '60
Tenacious D in the Pick of Destiny '06
Tequila Sunrise '88▶
Terminal Bliss '91
That Championship Season '99
That Sinking Feeling '79▶
Thelma & Louise '91▶
Things to Do '06
Think Tank '06
Three Amigos '86▶
Three Legionnaires '37
Three Men and a Baby '87▶
Three Men and a Cradle '85▶
The Three Musketeers '33
The Three Musketeers '35
The Three Musketeers '48
The Three Musketeers '74▶
The Three Musketeers '93
Thunder in the Pines '49
Thursday's Game '74▶
Tin Cup '96▶
To Forget Venice '79
To Wong Foo, Thanks for Everything, Julie Newmar '95
Tombstone '93▶
Tomcats '01
Top Dog '95
Top Gun '86▶
Tough Guys '86
Tour of Duty '87
Toy Story '95▶
Toy Story 2 '99▶
Trainspotting '95▶
Tree's Lounge '96
The Triangle '01
Trippin' '99
True Colors '91
True Friends '98
The Turning Point '77
12 and Holding '05▶
25th Hour '02
Twin Warriors '93
2 Fast 2 Furious '03
Two Weeks to Live '43
2B Perfectly Honest '04
Ugetsu '53▶
Under the Lighthouse Dancing '97
Under the Sun '98
Underworld '27▶
Unholy Four '54
The Van '95▶
Veronico Cruz '87
Very Bad Things '98
The Very Thought of You '98
Vincent, Francois, Paul and the Others '76▶
The Virginian '46
The Virginian '99
Walking and Talking '96
Walking on Water '02
Warrior Spirit '94
Wayne's World '92
Wayne's World 2 '93
Wedding Crashers '05▶
Weirdsville '07

Went to Coney Island on a Mission from God...Be Back by Five '98
We're in the Legion Now '37
Western '96
What Price Glory? '52▶
When Angels Fly '84▶
When Harry Met Sally... '89▶
Where is My Friend's House? '87
Where the River Runs Black '86
Whipped '00
White Badge '92
White Christmas '54▶
White Mama '80▶
White Men Can't Jump '92▶
White Nights '85▶
Who's the Man? '93
Why Me? '90
Why Not? '77▶
Wild Hogs '07
The Wild Life '84
Wild Rovers '71
Windy City '34
Winners Take All '87
Winter Break '03
With Friends Like These '00▶
Witnall and I '87▶
The Wood '99
The Wrong Guys '88
The Wrong Road '37
Y Tu Mama Tambien '01▶
The Yakuza '75
Yankee Zulu '95
You Are Here ... '00
You, Me and Dupree '06
You Tell Me '06
Young Hercules '97
Zorro the Greek '64▶

Buddy Cops
see also Cops; Women Cops
Another 48 Hrs. '90
Arizona Heat '87
Bad Boys '95
Bad Boys 2 '03
The Black Dahlia '06
Blue Streak '99
Car 54, Where Are You? '94
City Heat '84
Collision Course '89
Cop Land '97▶
The Corruptor '99▶
Dirty '05
Exit to Eden '94
48 Hrs. '82▶
The Glimmer Man '96
The Hard Way '91▶
Hollywood Homicide '03
Hot Fuzz '07▶
Internal Affairs '90
La Chevra '81▶
Lethal Weapon '87▶
Lethal Weapon 2 '89▶
Lethal Weapon 3 '92
Lethal Weapon 4 '98
Liberty & Bash '90
The Man '05
A Man Apart '03
Men in Black '97▶
Metro '96
Miami Vice '06
Money Train '95
Mulholland Falls '95
National Lampoon's Loaded Weapon 1 '93
Night Children '89
Nighthawks '81
The Presidio '88
Red Heat '88
Renegades '89
The Rookie '90
Rush Hour '98
Rush Hour 2 '01
Rush Hour 3 '07
Shakedown '88
Shoot to Kill '88▶
Simon Sez '99
Speed '94▶
Stakeout '87
Starsky & Hutch '04
Tango and Cash '89
Taxi '04
White Chicks '04

Bullfighters & Bullfighting
see also Spain
Around the World in 80 Days '56▶
Blood and Sand '22
Blood and Sand '41▶
Blood and Sand '89
The Bobo '67
Bolero '84
Bullfighter & the Lady '50
Bullfighter '87
Carnage '02
El Matador '03
Jamon, Jamon '93
The Magnificent Matador '55
The Matador '06
Pandora and the Flying Dutchman '51
Sand and Blood '87
Talk to Her '02▶
Torero '56

Burglars
see also Crime Doesn't Pay; Crime Drama; Disorganized Crime; Heists
Absolute Power '97
After Hours '85▶
Allie & Me '97
Breaking and Entering '06
Bullet '94
Burglar '87
Canvas: The Fine Art of Crime '92
Circus Angel '65▶
Criss Cross '48▶
The Doll '62
The Educators '04
Entrapment '99
Family Business '89
Federal Hill '94
Floating '97
Following '99
Gambit '66
The General '98
Home Alone '90
The Hot Rock '70▶
Hudson Hawk '91
I Hate Blondes '83
Kid Safe '45
Laurel & Hardy: Night Owls '30
Let Him Have It '91▶
Little Sweetheart '90
Millions '05▶
Murph the Surf '75
The Night They Robbed Big Bertha's '75
Picture Windows '95
Ping! '99
The Pink Panther '64▶
Poor White Trash '00
P.S. Your Cat is Dead! '02
Raffles '30▶
Row Your Boat '98
The Set Up '95
The Spree '98
Sworn to Justice '97
Thrillkill '84
Vamping '84
Vengeance '80
When Thief Meets Thief '37

Buried Alive
Buried Alive '90
Buried Alive 2 '97
The Fifth Element '97▶
For Hire '98
The Glass Jungle '88
The Love Trap '29
Mexico City '00
My Best Friend '06▶
My Son the Fanatic '97▶
La Chute de la Maison Usher '28▶
The Fall of the House of Usher '49
The Fall of the House of Usher '60▶
The Fall of the House of Usher '80
The House of Usher '88
Kill Bill Vol. 2 '04▶
The Oblong Box '69
Oxygen '99
Premature Burial '62
Usher '04

Buses
The Adventures of Priscilla, Queen of the Desert '94▶
All God's Children '87
Almost Famous '00▶
Beavis and Butt-Head Do America '96
The Big Bus '76
Boycott '02▶
Bull Durham '88▶
Bus Stop '56▶
Bustin' Loose '81▶
Dirty Harry '71▶
Ferris Bueller's Day Off '86▶
Forrest Gump '94▶
The Fugitive '93▶
The Gauntlet '77
Get On the Bus '96▶
Heart and Souls '93
Incident at Deception Ridge '94
The Interpreter '05▶
Jeepers Creepers 2 '03
Keane '04▶
The King Is Alive '00
Lady on the Bus '78
The Laughing Policeman '74
A League of Their Own '92▶
Love Field '91▶
Love Journey Back '78
Magical Mystery Tour '67
A Man of No Importance '94▶
Mexican Bus Ride '51
National Lampoon's Senior Trip '95
Pardon My Sarong '42▶
Planes, Trains and Automobiles '87▶
Ride '98
The Runaway Bus '54
Selena '96
The Siege '98
Siam Sunset '99
Sixteen Candles '84▶
Speed '94▶
Spice World: The Movie '97
Still Crazy '98▶
Sunday in New York '63
The Sweet Hereafter '96▶
Swordfish '01
The Trip to Bountiful '85▶
Vince Vaughn's Wild West Comedy Show '06
Wassup Rockers '06
Wheels of Terror '90
Where Angels Go, Trouble Follows '68

Cabbies
All or Nothing '02
Better Than Sex '00
The Bishop's Wife '47▶
Blood & Donuts '95
Born Romantic '00
Chicago Cab '98
Claire Dolan '97
Collateral '04▶
Conspiracy Theory '97
Crocodile Dundee '86▶
Crossing Delancey '88▶
Daylight '96
D.C. Cab '83
Doc Hollywood '91
Drowning on Dry Land '00
Escape from New York '81
Extremely Dangerous '99
Fall '97
Family Jewels '65

Cabbies

Nick and Jane '96
Night on Earth '91◆
Pulp Fiction '94◆
Scrooged '88
She's the One '96
Sorry, Haters '05
Stir Crazy '80
Taxi '04
Taxi Blues '90◆
Taxi Driver '76◆
The Taxi Mystery '26
They Met in a Taxi '36
3 A.M. '01◆
Three Days of Rain '02
Too Bad She's Bad '54
Total Recall '90◆
The Town Is Quiet '00
200 Cigarettes '98
Vintage Model '92
The Yellow Cab Man '50

Calcutta

see also India

Baraka '93◆
Born Into Brothels: Calcutta's Red Light Kids '04
City of Joy '92
Days and Nights in the Forest '70
The Quest '96

Cambodia

see also Asia; Vietnam War

Apocalypse Now '79◆
City of Ghosts '03
The Expendables '89
Fortunes of War '94
The Girl Who Spelled Freedom '86◆
The Killing Fields '84◆
No Retreat, No Surrender 2 '89
S21: The Khmer Rouge Killing Machine '03◆
Swimming to Cambodia '87◆

Camelot (New)

see also Assassination; Presidency

Jackie, Ethel, Joan: The Kennedy Women '01
Jacqueline Bouvier Kennedy '81
JFK '91◆
The JFK Conspiracy '91
JFK: Reckless Youth '93
Kennedy '83
Prince Jack '83
PT 109 '63
Robert Kennedy and His Times '90
Ruby '92
Thirteen Days '00◆

Camelot (Old)

see also Medieval Romps; Swashbucklers

Arthur's Quest '99
A Connecticut Yankee '31◆
A Connecticut Yankee in King Arthur's Court '49
Excalibur '81◆
First Knight '95
A Kid in King Arthur's Court '95
Kids of the Round Table '96
King Arthur '04
King Arthur, the Young Warlord '75
A Knight in Camelot '98
Knights of the Round Table '53
Merlin '98◆
Merlin and the Sword '85
Merlin's Apprentice '06
Mists of Avalon '01◆
Monty Python and the Holy Grail '75◆
Prince Valiant '54
Prince Valiant '97
Quest for Camelot '98
The Sword in the Stone '63◆
Sword of Lancelot '63
Sword of the Valiant '83
A Young Connecticut Yankee in King Arthur's Court '95

Campus Capers

see also Fraternities & Sororities; Hell High School; School Daze

Abandon '02
The Absent-Minded Professor '61◆
Accepted '06
Accident '67
The Affairs of Dobie Gillis '53
All-American Murder '91
American Pie Presents: The Naked Mile '06
American Psycho 2: All American Girl '02
American Tiger '89
Animal Behavior '89
Assault of the Party Nerds '89
Baby Love '83
Bachelor of Hearts '58
Back to School '86◆
Beta House '83
Beware '46
Beyond Dream's Door '88
Bickford Shmeckler's Cool Ideas '06
Big Man on Campus '89
Big Shot: Confessions of a Campus Bookie '02
Black Christmas '75
Black Tower '50
Blondie Goes to College '42
Blood Cult '85
Blood Sisters '86
Blue Chips '94
Boys and Girls '00
Breeders '97
Bride of Killer Nerd '91
Bring It On Again '03
Campus Confessions '38
The Campus Corpse '77
Campus Knights '29
Campus Man '87
Carnal Knowledge '71◆
Charley's Aunt '41◆
The Cheerleaders '72
Cheers for Miss Bishop '41
A Chump at Oxford '40
Circle of Friends '94
College '27◆
College Humor '33
College Swing '38
The Computer Beach Party '88
The Computer Wore Tennis Shoes '69
Confessions of Sorority Girls '94
The Cousins '59◆
The Crimson Rivers '01◆
Cruel Intentions 3 '04
Cult '07
The Curve '97
Dead Man on Campus '97
Deadly Lessons '94
Deadly Obsession '88
Deadly Possession '88
Death Screams '83
Defying Gravity '97
Devil in the Flesh 2 '00
Didn't You Hear? '83
Divided We Stand '00
Doctor in the House '53◆
Dorm That Dripped Blood '82
Down to You '00
Drumline '02◆
The Duke of West Point '38
Ernest Rides Again '93
Escapade in Florence '62
Father Was a Fullback '49
Final Exam '81
First Affair '83
First Love '77
First Time '82
Flubber '97
Foreign Student '94
Francis Goes to West Point '52
Fraternity Vacation '85
The Freshman '25◆
The Freshman '90
Fright Night 2 '88
Getting Away With Murder '96
Getting In '94
Ghoulies 3: Ghoulies Go to College '91
Girl Crazy '43◆
Girls Night Out '83
The Gladiator '38◆
Glory Daze '96
Going Greek '01
Good News '47
Good Will Hunting '97◆
Gossip '99
Gotcha! '85
The Great Debaters '07◆
Gross Anatomy '89
Gross Misconduct '93
Hamburger... The Motion Picture '86
Happy Hell Night '92
Harmon of Michigan '41
Harold and Kumar Go to White Castle '04
Harrad Experiment '73
Harrad Summer '74
Harvard Man '01
HauntedWeen '91
The Heart of Dixie '89
Heart of Stone '01
Hell Night '81
Higher Education '88
Higher Learning '94
Horse Feathers '32◆
H.O.T.S. '79
House of the Dead 2: Dead Aim '05
The House on Sorority Row '83
House Party 2: The Pajama Jam '91
How High '01
How I Got into College '89
How I Spent My Summer Vacation '97
The Human Stain '03
I Don't Buy Kisses Anymore '92
I'll Be Home for Christmas '98
The Initiation '84
Initiation of Sarah '78
I.Q. '94
Iris '01◆
Is There Life Out There? '94
Jock Petersen '74
The Junction Boys '02
A Killer in Every Corner '74
Killer Me '01
Killer Party '86
A Killing Spring '02
Knock Outs '92
Lady Killer '97
Legally Blonde '01
Let's Go Collegiate '41
Life 101 '95
Little Sister '92
A Little Stiff '91
Loser '00
Love and Basketball '00◆
Love and Other Catastrophes '95
Lover's Knot '96
Lucky Jim '58
Maker of Men '31
The Male Animal '42
Malice '93
Man of the House '05
A Matter of Degrees '90
Mazes and Monsters '82
Me Without You '01
Midnight Madness '80
The Mirror Has Two Faces '96◆
The Misadventures of Merlin Jones '63
Mona Lisa Smile '03
The Monkey's Mask '00
Monkey's Uncle '65
Monster on the Campus '59
Mortuary Academy '91
Mugsy's Girls '85
Murder on the Campus '52
My Lucky Star '38◆
My Sex Life... Or How I Got into an Argument '96
National Lampoon's Adam & Eve '05
National Lampoon's Animal House '78◆
National Lampoon's Van Wilder '02
National Lampoon's Van Wilder 2: The Rise of Taj '06
Navy Blue and Gold '37
Necessary Roughness '91
New Best Friend '02
A Night in the Life of Jimmy Reardon '88
Night of the Creeps '86◆
Nightwish '89
Now You See Him, Now You Don't '72
The Nutty Professor '63◆
The Nutty Professor '96◆
The Nutty Professor 2: The Klumps '00
An Occasional Hell '96
Odd Jobs '85
Old School '85
Oleanna '94
100 Girls '00
Ordinary Sinner '02
The Paper Chase '73◆
Parallel Lives '94
Party Animal '83
P.C.U. '94
Pieces '83
Pigskin Parade '36
The Plastic Age '25
Pledge Night '90
Poster Boy '04
Preppies '82
The Prince & Me '04
The Prodigy '98
The Program '93
Prozac Nation '01
Pumpkin '02
Real Genius '85◆
A Reason to Believe '95
Red Letters '00
Return Engagement '78
Revenge of the Nerds '84
Revenge of the Nerds 2: Nerds in Paradise '87
Revenge of the Nerds 3: The Next Generation '92
Ring of Terror '62
Ripper: Letter from Hell '01
Roommate '84
Roommates '95
Rosalie '38
R.P.M.* (* Revolutions Per Minute) '70
Rudy '93◆
The Rules of Attraction '02
Rush Week '88
Scent of a Woman '92◆
School Daze '88◆
School Spirit '85
Scream 2 '97◆
The Secret Life of Girls '99
The Seniors '78
Senseless '98
Sensation '94
Shallow Grave '87
Silent Madness '84
Silent Scream '80
The Sixth Man '97
The Skulls '00
The Skulls 2 '02
Sky High '84
Slackers '02
Slipping into Darkness '88
A Small Circle of Friends '80
Smart People '08
Sniper '75◆
Social Error '35
Sorority Babes in the Slimeball Bowl-A-Rama '87
Sorority Boys '02
Sorority Girl '57
Sorority House Massacre '86
Sorority House Massacre 2: Nighty Nightmare '92
Sorority House Party '92
Sorority House Vampires '95
Soul Man '86
Soul Survivors '01
South Beach Academy '96
Spellbound '41
The Spirit of West Point '47
Splatter University '84
Splitz '84
Spring Break '83
Starter for Ten '06
The Sterile Cuckoo '69◆
Stitches '85
Stomp the Yard '07
Stonebrook '98
Storytelling '01◆
Stricken '98
The Strongest Man in the World '75
The Student Affair '97
The Substitute 3: Winner Takes All '99
Summer Palace '06◆
The Sure Thing '85◆
Surviving Desire '91◆
Sweet Young Thing '79
Sydney White '07
Sylvia '03
Tag: The Assassination Game '82
Talking Walls '85
Tall Lie '53
Tall Story '60
Teen Wolf Too '87
Thesis '96◆
Three in the Attic '68
Three in the Cellar '70
Threesome '94
Toga Party '77
21 '08
Underclassman '05
Undergrads '85◆
Unforgettable '96
The Unnamable '88
The Unnamable 2: The Statement of Randolph Carter '92
Up the Creek '84
Urban Legend '98
Urban Legends 2: Final Cut '00
Vampires of Sorority Row: Kickboxers From Hell '99
The Victory '88
Voodoo '95
Voodoo Academy '00
Waking the Dead '00
War Between the Tates '76
The Waterboy '98
Wavelength '96
We Are Marshall '06
What Lies Beneath '00
When He's Not a Stranger '89◆
The Wild Life '84
Wish Me Luck '95
Wishmaster 3: Beyond the Gates of Hell '01
Witchboard '87
Witches' Brew '79
With Honors '94
Wonder Boys '00◆
Zis Boom Bah '41

Canada

see also Cold Spots; Hockey

Abducted '86
The Adjuster '91
The Agency '81
All Hat '07
American Boyfriends '89
The Amityville Curse '90
And Then You Die '88◆
Angel Square '92
Angela '95
Anne of Avonlea '87◆
Anne of Green Gables '34◆
Anne of Green Gables '85◆
The Apprenticeship of Duddy Kravitz '74◆
Ararat '02◆
Atlantic City '81◆
The Bay Boy '85
Beautiful Dreamers '92
Big Bear '98
The Big Crimewave '86
Big Meat Eater '85
Big Red '62
Black Christmas '75
Black Robe '91◆
Blades of Courage '88
Blood Clan '91
Blood of the Hunter '94
Blood Relations '87
The Bloody Brood '59
Blue State '07
Boy in Blue '86
The Boys '97
The Boys Club '96
The Boys of St. Vincent '93◆
Brand Upon the Brain! '06◆
Breaking All the Rules '85
The Brood '79
Buffalo Jump '90◆
Bullies '86
Bush Pilot '47
Busted Up '86
By Design '82
By Way of the Stars '92
Bye Bye Blues '89
Cafe Romeo '91
Camilla '94
Canada's Sweetheart: The Saga of Hal C. Banks '85
Canadian Bacon '94
Candy Mountain '87
The Cariboo Trail '50
Cathy's Curse '77
The Changeling '80◆
Christina '74
Circle of Two '80
City on Fire '78
Class of 1984 '82◆
Clean '04
Clean, Shaven '93
Clearcut '92
Close to Home '86
Cold Comfort '90
Concrete Angels '87
The Confessional '95◆
Confidential '86
Conquest '98
Covergirl '83
Cross Country '83
A Cry in the Wild '90◆
Curtains '83
Dan Candy's Law '73
Dance Me Outside '95
Dancing in the Dark '86
Danger Ahead '40
Daughter of Death '82
The Dawson Patrol '78
Dead Ringers '88◆
Death Ship '80
Death Weekend '76
Deathdream '72
The Decline of the American Empire '86◆
Decoy '95
Deranged '74◆
The Deserters '83
Dirty Tricks '81
Disappearance '81
Disappearances '06
Distant Thunder '88
Dog Pound Shuffle '75◆
The Dog Who Stopped the War '84
A Doll's House '73◆
The Double Negative '80
Drying Up the Streets '76
Dudley Do-Right '99
Eddie and the Cruisers 2: Eddie Lives! '89
Edge of Madness '02
Emile '03
The Enemy '01
Everything's Gone Green '06
Explosion '69
Far Side of the Moon '03
The Fast Runner '01◆
Festival Express '03◆
Fighting Mad '39
The Fishing Trip '98
Fly Away Home '96◆
For the Moment '94
Ginger Snaps '01
Ginger Snaps: Unleashed '04
Going Home '86

◆ = rated three bones or higher

Grey Owl '99
Grizzly Falls '99
Hard Core Logo '96
Heaven on Earth '89
Heck's Way Home '95
Henry & Verlin '94
Hey, Happy! '01
Holy Matrimony '94
House of the Living Dead
  '73
Ice Men '04
The Incredible Journey '63
Intersection '93
Invasion! '99
Jaws of Justice '33
Karla '06
La Deroute '98
Ladies of the Lotus '87
Lassie's Great Adventure
  '62
Leaving Metropolis '02
The Little Kidnappers '90
The Lotus Eaters '93
Love and Human Remains
  '93
Love on the Side '04
Maelstrom '00
Magic in the Water '95
Margaret's Museum '95
Maria Chapdelaine '84
Men of Steel '88
Men with Brooms '36
Mrs. Mike '49
Murder on the Yukon '40
Murder in the Yukon '40
Murderball '05
My American Cousin '85
My Life Without Me '03
Mystery Trooper '32
A Name for Evil '70
Narrow Margin '90
'Neath Canadian Skies '46
New Waterford Girl '99
90 Days '86
No. '98
Nomads of the North '20
Northern Extremes '93
Now & Forever '02
Obsessed '88
The Perfect Son '00
Phantom Patrol '36
Poor Man's Game '06
Renfrew on the Royal
  Mounted '37
Renfrew on the Great White
  Trail '38
Restless Spirits '99
The Return of Grey Wolf '22
Riel '79
The Rocket '05
Rose Marie '36
Rupert's Land '98
Spenser: A Savage Place
  '94
Spirit Rider '53
Strange Brew '83
Strangers in Good
  Company '91
Stryker '04
The Sweet Hereafter '96
Tail Lights Fade '99
Taking Lives '04
Tales of the Klondike: In a
  Far Country '87
Tales of the Klondike:
  for Number One '87
Tales of the Klondike: The
  Unexpected '87
Termini Station '89
That Beautiful Somewhere
  '06
Time Lock '57
Tokyo Cowboy '94
Torso '01
Trail of the Mounties '47
Wedding in White '72
Weirdsville '07

Where the North Begins '47
Who Has Seen the Wind?
  '77
The Widow of Saint-Pierre
  '00▶
Yukon Flight '40

Canadian Mounties
see also Canada; Cops
Canadian Bacon '94
Courage of the North '35
Dan Candy's Law '73
Danger Ahead '40
Death Hunt '81
Dudley Do-Right '99
Fighting Mad '39
The Fighting Trooper '34
His Fighting Blood '35
Mrs. Mike '49
Murder on the Yukon '40
'Neath Canadian Skies '46
Northern Pursuit '43
Renfrew of the Royal
  Mounted '37
Renfrew on the Great White
  Trail '38
Rose Marie '36▶
Rose Marie '54▶
Silent Code '35
Sky Bandits '40
Susannah of the Mounties
  '39
Until They Get Me '18
Where the North Begins '18
Yukon Flight '40

Cannibalism
see also Edibles
Adrenalin: Fear the Rush,
  '96
Adventures of Eliza Fraser
  '76
The Alien Agenda: Out of
  the Darkness '96
Alien Prey '83
Alive '93
Auntie Lee's Meat Pies '92
Back from Eternity '56
Bad Taste '88▶
The Beast Must Die '75
Beast of the Yellow Night
  '70
Beware! Children at Play '95
Bleeders '97
Blood Clan '91
Blood Diner '87
Blood Feast '63
Blood Hook '86
Blood Sisters '86
Blood Tracks '86
Bloodsucking Freaks '75
Bloodsucking Pharaohs of
  Pittsburgh '90
Body Count '87
A Boy and His Dog '75
The 'Burbs '89
Buried Alive '81
Cannibal Apocalypse '80
Cannibal Campout '88
Cannibal Ferox '81
Cannibal! The Musical
  '96
Cannibal Women in the
  Avocado Jungle of Death
  '89
The Chilling '89
C.H.U.D. '84
C.H.U.D. 2: Bud the Chud
  '06
Consuming Passions '88
The Cook, the Thief, His
  Wife & Her Lover '90
The Corpse Grinders '71
Crazy Fat Ethel II '85
Criminally Insane '75
Daughters of Satan '72
Dawn of the Dead '78▶
Dawn of the Dead '04▶
Dawn of the Mummy '82
Deadly Culture '88
Delicatessen '92▶
Demon Barber of Fleet
  Street '36
Deranged '74▶
The Descent '05
Doctor X '32
Donner Pass: The Road to
  Survival '84
Doomsday '08
Eat the Rich '87
Eating Raoul '82▶

Ed Gein '01
Emerald Jungle '80
Enchanted Island '58
Feeders '96
Fiend '83
Flesh Eating Mothers '89
Freakmaker '74
The Further Adventures of
  Tennessee Buck '88
Gore-Met Zombie Chef from
  Hell '87
The Green Butchers '03
Grim Reaper '81
Gruesome Twosome '67
Hannibal '01
Hannibal Rising '07
Hell of the Living Dead '83
The Hills Have Eyes '06
The Hills Have Eyes '77
The Hills Have Eyes 2 '07
How Tasty Was My Little
  Frenchman '71
Human Beasts '80
I Drink Your Blood '71
I Eat Your Skin '64
Igor & the Lunatics '85
Incredible Melting Man '77
Jeepers Creepers '01
Jeepers Creepers 2 '03
Leatherface: The Texas
  Chainsaw Massacre 3 '89
The Mad Butcher '72
A Man Called Rage '84
Mom '89
The Monster Club '85
Motel Hell '80
Mountain of the Cannibal
  God '79
Murderer's Keep '88
Night of the Living Dead
  '68▶
Night of the Living Dead
  '90
Night of the Zombies '81
Nightstalker '81
The Offspring '87
Parents '89▶
The Perverse Countess '73
Porcile '69
Rabid Grannies '89
Raw Force '81
Ravenous '99
Redneck Zombies '88
Serenity '05▶
The Severed Arm '73
The Silence of the Lambs
  '91▶
Slaughterhouse '87
Slaughterhouse Rock '88
Slave Girls from Beyond
  Infinity '87
Society '92
Suspended Animation '02
Tales from the Darkside:
  The Movie '90
Tenderness of the Wolves
  '73
Terror at Red Wolf Inn '72
The Texas Chainsaw
  Massacre '74
The Texas Chainsaw
  Massacre '03
The Texas Chainsaw
  Massacre 2 '86
The Texas Chainsaw
  Massacre: The Beginning
  '06
The Time Machine '02
The 13th Warrior '99
Three on a Meathook '73
Tooth and Nail '07
The Undertaker and His
  Pals '57
The Untold Story '93
Warlock Moon '73
The Womaneater '59
Wrong Turn '03
Wrong Turn 2: Dead End
  '07

All the President's Men '76▶
An American Affair '99
The American President
  '95▶
The Aviator '04▶
Beavis and Butt-Head Do
  America '96
Born Yesterday '50▶
Born Yesterday '93
Breach '07
Bulworth '98▶
The Capitol Conspiracy '99
Charlie Wilson's War '07
The Company '07
The Contender '00
Cupid & Cate '00
Dave '93▶
The Day Reagan Was Shot
  '01
DC 9/11: Time of Crisis '04
Dick '99▶
The Distinguished
  Gentleman '92
End Game '06
Enemy of the State '98
Eraser '96▶
Fahrenheit 9/11 '04▶
Fatwa '06
First Kid '96
Get On the Bus '96▶
Guilty by Association '03
Head of State '03
The Hunting of the
  President '04
Irrage in the Line
  of Death '77
In the Line of Fire '93▶
Inferno '98
The Invasion '07
J. Edgar Hoover '87
JFK '91▶
Legally Blonde 2: Red White
  & Blonde '03
Lions for Lambs '07
Man of the Year '06
The Manchurian Candidate
  '62▶
The Manchurian Candidate
  '04▶
Mars Attacks! '96
Master Spy: The Robert
  Hanssen Story '02
Mastergate '92
Minority Report '02▶
Mr. Smith Goes to
  Washington '39▶
Most Wanted '97
Murder at 1600 '97
My Fellow Americans '96
National Lampoon's Senior
  Trip '95
Nixon '95▶
Open Cam '05
Path to War '02
The Pooch and the Pauper
  '99
Power and Beauty '02
The President's Analyst '67▶
Primary Colors '98▶
Protocol '84
Random Hearts '99
The Recruit '03
Return of the Living Dead:
  Rave to the Grave '05
The Seduction of Joe Tynan
  '79
1776 '72▶
The Shadow Conspiracy '96
Sherlock Holmes in
  Washington '43
The State Within '06
Talk to Me '07
Thank You for Smoking '06
Three Days of the Condor
  '75▶
Traffic '00▶
Trial by Media '00
Wag the Dog '97
The Walker '07
Washington Affair '77
Washington Mistress '81
Without Love '45
XXX: State of the Union '05

Portrait of an Assassin '49
P.T. Barnum '99
The Red Dwarf '99
Revenge of the Nerds '84
The Road to Zanzibar '41▶
The Rousters '90
Sally of the Sawdust '25
Santa Sangre '89
Sawdust & Tinsel '53▶
The Serpent's Egg '78
7 Faces of Dr. Lao '63▶
Shakes the Clown '92
She Creature '01
She-Freak '67
Side Show '84
So Dear to My Heart '49▶
Something Wicked This
  Way Comes '83
Spangles '26
State Fair '62
Strong Man '26▶
Texas Carnival '51
Three Texas Steers '39
Tillie Wakes Up '17
Toby Tyler '59▶
Trapeze '56▶
Two Moon Junction '88
The Unholy Three '25▶
The Unholy Three '30▶
The Unknown '27▶
Vampire Circus '71
Variety '25▶
Variety Lights '51▶
The Wagons Roll at Night
  '41
When Night Is Falling '95▶
Where East Is East '29
Wild Hearts Can't Be
  Broken '91▶
Wilder Napalm '93
The Woman in Question '50
You Can't Cheat an Honest
  Man '39▶

Catholic School
see also Killer Kids;
Absolution '81
Boys Town '38▶
The Craft '96
The Dangerous Lives of
  Alter Boys '02
Going My Way '44▶
The Gospel According to Vic
  '87
Heaven Help Us '85
House of D '04
Kentucky Fried Movie '77▶
Loving Annabelle '06
Sister Act 2: Back in the
  Habit '93
Stolen Summer '02
True Crime '95

Cats
see also Killer Kats
The Adventures of Milo 3
  Otis '89▶
After the Revolution '90
Alice in Wonderland '51▶
Alice in Wonderland '85▶
Alice in Wonderland '99
Alien '79▶
An American Tail '86
The Aristocats '70▶
Austin Powers: International
  Man of Mystery '97▶
Babe '95▶
Babe: Pig in the City '98
Batman Returns '92▶
The Big Cat '49
The Black Cat '34▶
The Black Cat '41
The Black Cat '81
Black Cat '66
The Cat '66
The Cat from Outer Space
  '78
Cat Girl '57
Cat People '82
Cats & Dogs '01
Cats Don't Dance '97
Cat's Eye '85
Catwoman '04
The Corpse Grinders '71
Disney's Teacher's Pet '04▶

Canadian Mounties

Candyman 2: Farewell to
  the Flesh '94
Captive Wild Woman '43
Carnival Lady '33
Carnival of Souls '62▶
Carnival of Souls '98
Carnival Story '54
Carny '80▶
Carousel '56▶
Castle of the Living Dead
  '64
Brewster McCloud '70▶
The Cabinet of Dr. Caligari
  '19▶
Cloud Dancer '80
Clowning Around '92
Clowning Around 2 '93
The Clowns '71▶
Clifford's Really Big Movie
  '04
Court Jester '56▶
Death Mask '98
Dixiana '30
Dual Alibi '47
Dumbo '41▶
Elvira Madigan '67▶
Encore '52▶
The Fantasticks '95
Fear '90
Final Destination 3 '06
Flamingo Road '49▶
Fox and His Friends '75▶
Franke nstein and Me '95
Freaked '93
Freaks '32▶
Freakshow '95
The Funhouse '81
Glass Tomb '55
Grease '78▶
The Great Wallendas '78
The Greatest Show on Earth
  '52▶
The Half Naked Truth '32
He Who Gets Slapped '24▶
Hoopla '33
Incredibly Strange
  Creatures Who Stopped
  Living and Became
  Mixed-Up Zombies '63
The Jerk '79
Julia Misbehaves '48▶
The Killer Klowns from
  Outer Space '88
La Strada '54▶
Larger Than Life '96
Lili '53▶
Lola Montes '55▶
Locking for Trouble '96
Love in Bloom '35
Luther the Geek '90
Make-Up '37
The Man Who Laughs '27▶
MirrorMask '05
Moscow on the Hudson '84▶
Multiple Maniacs '70
Nightmare Alley '47
O're Arabian Night '21▶
Outrage '93
Parade '74▶
Peck's Bad Boy with the
  Circus '38
Pennies from Heaven '36

Carnivals & Circuses
see also Amusement
Parks; Clowns; Fairs &
Expositions
All the Circus '39▶
Arizona Mahoney '36
At the Circus '39▶
Ava's Magical Adventure '94
Bad Man of Deadwood '41
Barney's Great Adventure
  '98
Barnum '86
Batman Forever '95▶
Behind the Sun '01
Bells of Rosarita '45
Berserk! '57
Betrayal from the East '44
Big Fish '03▶
Big Top Pee-wee '88
Billy Rose's Jumbo '62▶
Black Orpheus '58▶
Boca '94

Cats

Cats

Dr. Seuss' The Cat in the Hat '03
Felix the Cat: The Movie '91
Fritz the Cat '72
Garfield: A Tail of Two Kitties '06
Garfield: The Movie '04
Gay Purr-ee '62
Harry and Tonto '74
Hocus Pocus '93
Homeward Bound 2: Lost in San Francisco '96
The Incredible Journey '63
Ju-On: The Grudge '03
Kiki's Delivery Service '98
Le Chat '75
The Late Show '77
Meet the Fockers '04
Men in Black '97
Milo & Otis '89
Mouse Hunt '97
Murder She Purred: A Mrs. Murphy Mystery '98
Night of a Thousand Cats '72
Oliver & Company '88
Pet Sematary '89
Puss 'n Boots '84
Return of Chandu '34
Rubin & Ed '92
Sabrina the Teenage Witch '96
Seven Deaths in the Cat's Eye '72
Shrek 2 '04
The Stars Fell on Henrietta '94
Stuart Little '99
Stuart Little 2 '02
That Darn Cat '65
That Darn Cat '96
The Three Lives of Thomasina '63
Tom and Jerry: The Movie '93
Two Evil Eyes '90
The Uncanny '78
The Uninvited '88
Whiskers '96
The Witch's Away '96
Your Vice is a Closed Room and Only I Have the Key '72

Cattle Drive

see also Purdners; Westerns; Westrogens
Alvarez Kelly '66
Born Free '66
The Cowboys '72
Far Country '55
Hills of Oklahoma '50
Lonesome Dove '89
Overlanders '46
The Proposition '97
The Showdown '50
The Tall Men '55
Trail Drive '33

Cave People

see also Cave Girl
Beach Babes 2: Cave Girl Island '95
Being Human '94
The Cave '05
Cave Girl '85
Caveman '81
The Clan of the Cave Bear '86
Creatures the World Forgot '70
Encino Man '92
The Flintstones '94
The Flintstones in Viva Rock Vegas '00
History of the World: Part 1 '81
Iceman '84
Ironmaster '82
One Million B.C. '40
Prehistoric Women '50
Quest for Fire '82
Teenage Caveman '58
10,000 B.C. '06
When Dinosaurs Ruled the Earth '70
When Women Had Tails '70
When Women Lost Their Tails '75

Caves

Ace in the Hole '51
Afghan Knights '07
The Bat People '80
The Cavern '05
The Descent '05
Fixed Bayonets! '51
The Hills Have Eyes 2 '07
Turistas '06

Central America

see also Mexico; South America
Apocalypto '06
Appointment in Honduras '53
Carla's Song '97
Cyclone Cavalier '25
Delta Force Commando '87
Devil Wears White '86
El Norte '83
The Evil That Men Do '84
Exiled in America '90
The Firing Line '91
Hombres Armados '97
Last Plane Out '83
Latino '85
Marie Galante '34
The Mosquito Coast '86
No Turning Back '01
Noriega: God's Favorite '00
Panama Menace '41
Panama Patrol '39
Romero '89
Salvador '86
The Silence of Neto '94
Solo '96
The Tailor of Panama '00
Torrid Zone '40
Toy Soldiers '84
Under Fire '83
Virgin Sacrifice '59
Wages of Fear '55

Checkered Flag

see also Motor Vehicle Dept.
American Graffiti '73
Baffled '72
Banzai Runner '86
The Big Wheel '49
Bobby Deerfield '77
Born to Race '88
Born to Run '93
Brewster McCloud '70
Bullitt '68
Cannonball '76
Cannonball Run '81
Cannonball Run 2 '84
Car Crash '80
Cars '06
Catch Me... If You Can '89
The Checkered Flag '63
Daddy-O '59
Days of Thunder '90
Death Driver '78
Death Race 2000 '75
Desert Steel '94
The Devil on Wheels '47
Diamonds Are Forever '71
Dirty Mary Crazy Larry '74
Dragstrip Girl '57
Dragstrip Girl '94
Driven '01
The Dukes of Hazzard '05
Dust to Glory '05
Eat My Dust '76
The Fast and the Furious '54
The Fast and the Furious: Tokyo Drift '06
Fast Company '78
Fast Girl '07
Faster, Pussycat! Kill! Kill! '65
Fireball 500 '66
Fury on Wheels '71
Genevieve '53
Goldfinger '64
Grand Prix '66
Grandview U.S.A. '84
Grease '78
Greased Lightning '77
The Great Race '65
Gumball Rally '76
Hard Drivin' '60
Heart Like a Wheel '83
The Heavenly Kid '85
Hell on Wheels '67
Herbie: Fully Loaded '05
Herbie Goes Bananas '80
Herbie Goes to Monte Carlo '77
High Gear '33
Hot Rod '79
Hot Rod Girl '56
King of the Mountain '81
The Last American Hero '73
Last Chase '81
Le Mans '71
The Love Bug '97
A Man and a Woman: 20 Years Later '86
Private Road: No Trespassing '87
Race for Life '55
Race the Sun '96
The Racers '55
Rebel without a Cause '55
Red Line '96
Red Line 7000 '65
Redline '07
Return to Macon County '75
Richard Petty Story '72
Road Racers '59
Roaring Roads '35
Safari 3000 '82
Sahara '83
Shaker Run '85
Six Pack '82
Smash Palace '82
Smokey and the Bandit '77
Speed Racer '08
Speed Zone '88
Speedway '68
Spinout '66
Stroker Ace '83
Talladega Nights: The Ballad of Ricky Bobby '06
Those Daring Young Men in Their Jaunty Jalopies '69
Thunder Alley '67
To Please a Lady '50
2 Fast 2 Furious '03
Van Nuys Blvd. '79
Vanishing Point '71
Viva Las Vegas '63
Winning '69
The Wraith '87

Cheerleaders

see also Campus Capers; Hell High School
American Beauty '99
BASEketball '98
Bring It On '00
Bring It On Again '03
Bring It On: All or Nothing '06
Bring It On: In It to Win It '07
Buffy the Vampire Slayer '92
But I'm a Cheerleader '99
Cheering Section '73
Cheerleader Camp '88
The Cheerleaders '72
Cheerleaders' Wild Weekend '85
Death Proof '07
Flesh Gordon 2: Flesh Gordon Meets the Cosmic Cheerleaders '90
Gimme an F '85
Grease '78
Jeepers Creepers 2 '03
John Tucker Must Die '06
Kids in America '05
Lucas '86
The Majorettes '87
Man of the House '05
National Lampoon's Animal House '78
The New Guy '02
Pandemonium '82
Pep Squad '98
Pom Pom Girls '76
The Positively True Adventures of the Alleged Texas Cheerleader-Murdering Mom '93
Raising Genius '04
The Replacements '00
Revenge of the Cheerleaders '76
Satan's Cheerleaders '77
Starsky & Hutch '04
Sugar & Spice '01
The Swinging Cheerleaders '74
Varsity Blues '98

Chefs

see also Edibles
Angels Fall '07
April's Shower '03
Autumn in New York '00
Big Night '95
Felicia's Journey '99
A Fine Mess '86
Funny About Love '90
Last Holiday '50
Mostly Martha '01
No Reservations '07
Oldboy '03
Ratatouille '07
South Park: Bigger, Longer and Uncut '99
Tampopo '86
301, 302 '94
Tortilla Soup '01
Who Is Killing the Great Chefs of Europe? '78

Chess

Alice Through the Looking Glass '66
Black and White As Day and Night '78
Brainwashed '60
The Chess Player '27
The Chinese Cat '44
Dangerous Moves '84
Fresh '94
The Invisible Boy '57
Knight Moves '93
Knights of the South Bronx '05
The Luzhin Defence '00
The Mighty Pawns '87
Searching for Bobby Fischer '93
The Seventh Seal '56
Stalag 17 '53
Swept from the Sea '97
The Thomas Crown Affair '68
Treasure of Fear '45
Zatoichi: The Blind Swordsman and the Chess Expert '65

Chicago

Above the Law '88
Adventures in Babysitting '87
The Alien Agenda: Under the Skin '97
Angel Eyes '01
The Architect '06
Baby Face Nelson '97
Bad City '06
Barbershop '02
Beauty Shop '05
Big Town '87
The Blues Brothers '80
Blues Brothers 2000 '98
Bomb Squad '97
Bordertown '06
The Break-Up '06
Call Northside 777 '48
Candyman '92
Category 6: Day of Destruction '04
Chain Reaction '96
Chasing Papi '03
Chicago '02
Chicago Cab '98
Chicago 10 '07
Christmas With the Kranks '04
City That Never Sleeps '53
Code of Silence '85
The Company '03
Crime Spree '03
Deadline '05
Derailed '05
Down in the Delta '98
Dragonfly '02
Everyone's Hero '06
A Family Thing '96
Ferris Bueller's Day Off '86
First Time Felon '97
The Fixer '97
For Hire '97
The Front Page '74
The Fugitive '93
Goldstein '64
Hardball '01
Heaven Is a Playground '91
High Fidelity '00
Holiday Heart '00
Home Alone '90
Home Alone 3 '97
Hoopla '33
I, Robot '04
I Want Someone to Eat Cheese With '06
Jerry and Tom '98
John Q '02
Just Visiting '01
Keeper of the City '92
Kissing a Fool '98
The Lake House '06
Let No Man Write My Epitaph '60
Lethal Tender '96
Love and Action in Chicago '99
Love Jones '96
Mad Dog and Glory '93
Mercury Rising '98
Mickey One '65
My Best Friend's Wedding '97
My Big Fat Greek Wedding '02
My Reputation '46
The Negotiator '98
Never Been Kissed '99
The Newton Boys '97
Next of Kin '89
On the Line '01
Outing Riley '04
Primal Fear '96
Proof '05
A Raisin in the Sun '08
The Relic '96
Resurrection '99
Return to Me '00
Risky Business '83
Robin and the 7 Hoods '64
Roll Bounce '05
Running Scared '86
Save the Last Dance '01
Shall We Dance? '04
Shattered '07
The Song of the Lark '01
Stir of Echoes '99
Stir of Echoes 2: The Homecoming '07
Stolen Summer '02
Straight Talk '92
Stranger Than Fiction '06
Studs Lonigan '60
Surviving Christmas '04
Taking Care of Business '90
The Third Miracle '99
Three to Tango '99
Uncle Buck '89
Uncle Nino '03
Unconditional Love '03
U.S. Marshals '98
The Watcher '00
The Water Engine '92
The Weather Man '05
While You Were Sleeping '95
The White Raven '98
The Whole Nine Yards '00
Wicker Park '04
Witless Protection '08

Child Abuse

Abuse '82
Alias Betty '01
Antwone Fisher '02
Any Place But Home '97
Bad Education '04
Bastard out of Carolina '96
Blind Fools '40
Born Into Brothels: Calcutta's Red Light Kids '04
The Boys of St. Vincent '93
A Brother's Kiss '97
Brute '97
The Butterfly Effect '04
Capturing the Friedmans '03
Close to Home '86
Cries of Silence '97
Cronicas '04
Darkness '02
Dear Frankie '04
Dolores Claiborne '94
Dominick & Eugene '88
Don't Tell '05
El Bola '00
Ellen Foster '97
Evil '03
Evil Has a Face '96
Fallen Angel '81
Fatal Confinement '64
Father Hood '93
The Final Cut '04
The Great Water '04
The Hanging Garden '97
The Heart Is Deceitful Above All Things '04
Hollow Reed '95
Impulse '74
Indictment: The McMartin Trial '95
Joe the King '99
Johnny Belinda '82
Judgment '90
Killer Me '01
Lamb '85
The Lost Son '98
Love's Unending Legacy '07
Mockingbird Don't Sing '01
Mommie Dearest '81
Monsoon Wedding '01
Monster's Ball '01
The Mudge Boy '03
Mysterious Skin '04
The Offence '73
Oliver Twist '05
Osama '03
Postcards from America '95
Psychopath '73
A Question of Guilt '78
Radio Flyer '92
Raising Cain '92
Ripe '97
The River is Red '48
Running Scared '06
Seeing Red '99
Short Eyes '79
Shot in the Heart '01
Sleepers '96
Sleepwalking '08
South Bronx Heroes '85
The Stolen Children '92
Stolen Childhoods '05
The Stepdaughter '00
This Boy's Life '93
Threat of Exposure '02
Transamerica '05
2 by 4 '98
Where the Spirit Lives '89
Who Killed Baby Azaria? '83
Wildflower '91
The Woodsman '04
ZigZag '02

Childhood Buddies

see also Childhood Visions
Because of Winn-Dixie '05
Bloodhounds of Broadway '52
Bridge to Terabithia '07
Children On Their Birthdays '02
Cross My Heart '91
Dreamcatcher '03
El Bola '00
I'm Not Scared '03
The Jungle Book 2 '03
Keeping the Faith '00
The Kite Runner '07
Lilo & Stitch '02
Mysterious Skin '04

▲ = *rated three bones or higher*

Now and Then '95
Once Upon a Time in America '84▸
Paradise '05
The Robin Hood Gang '98
Stand by Me '86▸
A Time for Dancing '00
What About Your Friends: Weekend Getaway '02
Without a Paddle '04

Childhood Visions

see also Home Alone

A.I.: Artificial Intelligence '01
The Adventures of Sharkboy and Lavagirl in 3-D '05
Afraid of the Dark '92
Akeelah and the Bee '06
Alice in Wonderland '99
All I Want for Christmas '91
Alone in the Woods '95
Alsino and the Condor '82▸
The Amazing Mrs. Holiday '43
American Heart '92
Amy '98
And Now Miguel '66
Andre '94
Angela '94
Angela's Ashes '99
Angels in the Outfield '94
The Ant Bully '06
Army Brats '84
Arthur and the Invisibles '06
Au Revoir les Enfants '87▸
August Rush '07
Back to the Secret Garden '01
The Bad News Bears '05
Balloon Farm '97
Bastard out of Carolina '96
Beethoven Lives Upstairs '92
The Beniker Gang '83
Beyond Silence '96
Big '88▸
Big Bully '95
Big Daddy '99
Big Fella '37
Billy Elliot '00▸
The Black Stallion '79▸
Black Beauty '94▸
Blame It on Fidel '06
Blank Check '93
Bless the Child '00
The Blue Bird '40▸
The Blue Butterfly '04
Bogus '96
The Borrowers '97
Boys Will Be Boys '97
Brand Upon the Brain! '06▸
Breakout '98
Bridge to Terabithia '07
Brighton Beach Memoirs '86
Broken Harvest '94
But Where Is Daniel Wax? '74
The Butcher Boy '97▸
Butterfly '00
Cameron's Closet '89
Camp Nowhere '94
Canvas '06
Captain January '36
Careful, He Might Hear You '84▸
Carnie's War '04
Casey's Shadow '73
Casper '95▸
The Cat '66
Catherine Cookson's The Rag Nymph '96
Cathy's Curse '77
Celia: Child of Terror '89
The Cellar '90
Central Station '98▸
Charlie and the Chocolate Factory '05▸
Charlotte's Web '06▸
Child in the Night '90
Child Star: The Shirley Temple Story '01

The Children Are Watching Us '44▸
Children of Divorce '80
Children of Heaven '98▸
Child's Play '88
China, My Sorrow '89
Chocolat '88▸
Chronicle of a Boy Alone '64
The Chronicles of Narnia: Prince Caspian '08
Cider with Rosie '99
Cinema Paradiso '88▸
The Clay Bird '02
The Client '94
Clifford '92
Close to Leo '02
Clubhouse Detectives '96
The Color of Paradise '99▸
Comedy of Innocence '00
Cria '76▸
Cria Cuervos '76▸
Crooklyn '94▸
Cross My Heart and Hope to Die '94
Crows '94
Cuban Blood '03
Curly Sue '91
Curly Top '35
D.A.R.Y.L. '85
David Copperfield '35▸
David Copperfield '70
David Copperfield '99
The Day the World Ended '01
Days of Heaven '78▸
Dead Silent '99
Deadly Game '98
A Death in the Family '02
Demons in the Garden '82▸
Dennis the Menace '93
A Dennis the Menace Christmas '07
Dennis the Menace Strikes Again '98
Desert Bloom '86▸
Deutschland im Jahre Null '47▸
The Devil's Backbone '01▸
The Diary of Anne Frank '59▸
Digger '94
Digging to China '93
Disney's The Kid '00
Diva '82▸
D3: The Mighty Ducks '96
Dodson's Journey '01
Domestic Disturbance '01
Don't Tell Mom the Babysitter's Dead '91
The Dress Code '00
Earth '98
The Education of Little Tree '97▸
The Elementary School '91
Ellen Foster '97
Eloise at the Plaza '03
Emma's Shadow '88▸
Empire of the Sun '87▸
Escapade '55▸
E.T.: The Extra-Terrestrial '82▸
Eternity and a Day '97
Eve's Bayou '97▸
Eye Witness '70
FairyTale: A True Story '97
The Fallen Idol '49▸
Family Jewels '65
Family Tree '00
Fanny and Alexander '83▸
Far Away and Long Ago '74
Father '67▸
Fido '06
Finding Buck McHenry '00
Firehouse Dog '07
The Flame Trees of Thika '81▸
Flight of the Grey Wolf '76
Flight of the Innocent '93
Flight of the Red Balloon '08
Flowers in the Attic '87▸
Fly Away Home '96▸
For a Lost Soldier '93
Forbidden Games '52▸

Forever Together '00
48 Angels '06
Freedom Song '00▸
Fresh '94
Girl from Hunan '86▸
A Girl of the Limberlost '90
The Golden Compass '07
The Golden Seal '83
Goodnight, Mr. Tom '99
The Goonies '85▸
The Green House '96
Grizzly Falls '99
Grizzly Mountain '97
Gypsy Colt '54
Happiness '98▸
Hardball '01
Harriet the Spy '96
Heart of America '03
Hearts in Atlantis '01
Heavyweights '94
Heidi '37
Heidi '52
Heidi '65▸
Heidi '67
Heidi '93▸
Hidden '05
Holes '03▸
Home Alone '90▸
Home Alone 2: Lost in New York '92
Home Alone 3 '97
Home for Christmas '90
Home of Angels '94
A Home of Our Own '93
Homecoming '96
Honey, I Shrunk the Kids '89▸
Hook '91
Hope '97
Hope and Glory '87▸
House Arrest '96
House of Cards '93
How Green Was My Valley '41▸
How to Kill Your Neighbor's Dog '01
Huck and the King of Hearts '93
Hue and Cry '47▸
I Was Born But... '32▸
I'll Remember April '99
The Indian in the Cupboard '95
In America '02▸
In Desert and Wilderness '01
Into the West '92▸
Invaders from Mars '53
Invaders from Mars '86
Iron Giant '99▸
The Island on Bird Street '97
The Italian '05▸
Jack '96
Jack Be Nimble '94
Jacob Two Two Meets the Hooded Fang '99
Jacquot '91
James and the Giant Peach '96▸
Jimmy the Kid '82
Joey '98
John and Julie '55
John and S.A.M. '00
Josh and S.A.M. '93
Journey for Margaret '42▸
Jurassic Park '93▸
Kazaam '96
A Kid for Two Farthings '55
The Kid from Left Field '79
The Kid with the Broken Halo '82
Kids of the Round Table '96
The Kid with the X-Ray Eyes '99
The King of Masks '99▸
King of the Hill '93▸
The Kitchen Toto '87▸
Kikujiro '99▸
Kolya '96▸
Lamb '85
The Lady in White '88▸
Landscape in the Mist '88▸
Lassie's Great Adventure '62
The Last Mimzy '07
The Last Action Hero '93
The Last Winter '89
Lawn Dogs '96

Lawnmower Man 2: Beyond Cyberspace '95
Lazarillo '59
Le Grand Chemin '87▸
Leave It to Beaver '97
Leolo '92▸
Les Visions du Bal '74
Lies My Father Told Me '75▸
Life According to Muriel '97
Life is a Bed of Roses '83
Life-Size '00
Little Big League '94
Little Buddha '93▸
Little Fugitive '53▸
Little Lord Fauntleroy '95
Little Man Tate '91▸
Little Manhattan '05
Little Monsters '89
A Little Princess '95▸
The Little Princess '39▸
The Little Rascals '94▸
The Littlest Horse Thieves '76
Lloyd '00
Locked in Silence '99
The Longshots '08
Look Who's Talking '89▸
Look Who's Talking, Too '90
Lord of the Flies '63▸
Lord of the Flies '90
Lost in Yonkers '93▸
Louisiana Story '48▸
Love Film '70
Luminous Motion '00
Ma Vie en Rose '97▸
Madeline '98▸
Magic in the Mirror: Fowl Play '96
Magic in the Water '95
Magic of Lassie '78
Man of the House '95
Margot at the Wedding '07
Martian Child '07
Matilda '96▸
The Member of the Wedding '52
Mendel '98
Mermaid '00
The Messengers '07
The Mighty '98▸
Miracle in Lane Two '00
The Miracle Maker: The Story of Jesus '00
The Miracle of Marcelino '55
The Mirror '75▸
Misty '61
Mom, Can I Keep Her? '98
Mommie Dearest '81▸
Mondo '96
Monster House '06▸
Mosby's Marauders '66
Mother of Mine '05▸
Mr. Rice's Secret '00
Mr. Magorium's Wonder Emporium '07
Mrs. Doubtfire '93▸
Ms. Bear '97
My Childhood '38▸
My Dog Skip '00
My Friend Flicka '43▸
My Life '93
My Life As a Dog '85▸
My Life So Far '98
My Louisiana Sky '02
My Mother's Castle '91▸
My Name is Ivan '62▸
My Teacher Ate My Homework '98
Mystery Kids '99
National Velvet '44▸
The Neon Bible '95
New York Stories '89▸
The Night of the Shooting Stars '82▸
Nim's Island '08
North '94
Northfork '03
Not One Less '99
Nothing Personal '95
Now and Then '95
Off Season '01
Old Swimmin' Hole 40
Oliver '68▸
Oliver Twist '97
Oliver Twist '00▸
One Christmas '95
One Little Indian '73
One Small Hero '99

An Orphan Boy of Vienna '37
The Orphanage '07▸
The Orphans '77▸
Osama '03▸
The Other '72▸
Other Voices, Other Rooms '95
The Others '01▸
The Pagemaster '94
Pan's Labyrinth '06▸
Paradise '91
The Parent Trap '98
Parents '89▸
Paulie '98
Pay It Forward '00
Peck's Bad Boy '21
Pelle the Conqueror '88▸
Perfect Game '00
Peter Pan '24
Peter Pan '03
Pete's Meteor '98
Pete's Dragon '77▸
Pictures of Hollis Woods '07
The Pillow Book '95▸
Pixote '81▸
Pokemon 3: The Movie '01
Pollyanna '60▸
Pollyanna '82▸
Ponette '96▸
The Poor Little Rich Girl '17▸
A Poor Little Rich Girl '36
Poltergeist '82▸
Poltergeist 2: The Other Side '86
Poltergeist: The Legacy '96
Possessed '00
Powder '95
Prancer Returns '01
Prince of Central Park '00
Psycho 4: The Beginning '90
Pure '02▸
The Quest '96
The Quiet Room '96▸
Rabbit-Proof Fence '02▸
Radio Flyer '92
Rails & Ties '07
The Railway Children '70▸
The Railway Children '00▸
Ratcatcher '99▸
The Real Howard Spitz '98
Return to Never Land '02
Richie Rich '94
Ride the Wild Fields '00
Rock-a-Doodle '91
Roll of Thunder, Hear My Cry '78
Romulus, My Father '07▸
Ruby Bridges '98
Running Free '94
Safety Patrol '98
Salaam Bombay! '88▸
Savage Sam '63
Saving Sarah Cain '07
Searching for Bobby Fischer '93▸
Second Chances '98
The Secret Garden '49▸
The Secret Garden '84
The Secret Garden '87▸
The Secret Garden '93▸
The Seven Little Foys '55
Selma, Lord, Selma '99
Shiloh '97▸
Shiloh Season '99
Sidekicks '93
The Silence of Neto '94
The Silences of the Palace '94▸

Simon Birch '98
The Sixth Sense '99▸
The Skateboard Kid '90
The Skateboard Kid 2 '94
Slappy and the Stinkers '97
Sling Blade '96▸
The Slingshot '93▸
Small Change '76▸
Snap Decision '01
Snow Day '00
Snow in August '01
Sounds of Silence '91
South Park: Bigger, Longer and Uncut '99▸
Sparrows '26▸
Spirit of the Beehive '73▸
Spirited Away '01▸
Spy Kids '01▸
Square Shoulders '29
Star Kid '97▸
Star Wars: Episode 1—The Phantom Menace '99▸
Stealing Home '88
Stephen King's It '90
Stir '98
Stir of Echoes '99
Stolen Summer '02
Sudie & Simpson '90▸
The Summer of Ava '88
A Summer to Remember '85
Sunday Daughters '80▸
Sunday's Children '94▸
Taps '81▸
Tea with Mussolini '99▸
Three Wishes '95
Tideland '05▸
Tito and Me '92▸
To Kill a Mockingbird '62▸
The Tooth Fairy '06
Toothless '97
Toto le Heros '91▸
Toy Story '95▸
Train to Hollywood '86▸
Treasure Island '34▸
Treasure Island '50▸
Treasure Island '99
Treehouse Hostage '99
The Trial of Old Drum '00
Turf Boy '42
The Turn of the Screw '74
The Turn of the Screw '92
The Turn of the Screw '99
The Twelve Dogs of Christmas '05
12 Monkeys '95▸
Twisted '05
Under the Same Moon '07▸
Undercover Angel '99
An Unexpected Family '96
Village of Dreams '97▸
Wait until Spring, Bandini '90
Walkabout '71▸
Walking Thunder '94
The War '94
The War Boy '85
Water '07▸
The Water Horse: Legend of the Deep '07▸
The Way Home '07
Welcome to Sarajevo '97▸
Welcome to the Dollhouse '95▸
Wendigo '01
What the Moon Saw '90
When Father Was Away on Business '85▸
Where's Willie? '77
Whistle down the Wind '61▸
White Fang '91▸
Wide Awake '97
The Wild Country '71
Will It Snow for Christmas? '96▸
Willy Wonka & the Chocolate Factory '71▸
The Witching of Ben Wagner '95
The Wizard of Loneliness '88
Wombling Free '77
A World Apart '88▸
Yaaba '89▸
The Yearling '46▸
Yes, Sir, Mr. Bones '51
Zazie dans le Metro '61▸
Zero for Conduct '33▸
Zeus and Roxanne '96

China

see also Asia

Adventures of Smilin' Jack '43

Children

see also Animated Musicals; Animation & Cartoons; Childhood Visions; Kiddie Viddy; Storytelling

▸ = rated three bones or higher

China

The Amazing Panda Adventure '95▶
Balzac and the Little Chinese Seamstress '02▶
Beijing Bicycle '01▶
Bethune '77
Beyond the Next Mountain '87
The Bitter Tea of General Yen '33▶
Black Mask '96
The Blue Kite '93▶
Blush '95
Charlie Chan in Shanghai '35
China 43
China Cry '91
China, My Sorrow '89
Chinese Box '97
Crows and Sparrows '49▶
Curse of the Golden Flower '06
The Day the Sun Turned Cold '94▶
Deadly Target '94
Dragon Seed '44
East Palace, West Palace '96
The Emperor and the Assassin '99
Empire of the Sun '87▶
Ermo '94
Farewell My Concubine '93▶
Fleeing by Night '00
Flowers of Shanghai '98
The Forbidden Kingdom '08
Formula 17 '04
The General Died at Dawn '36▶
Girl from Hunan '86▶
The Good Earth '37▶
Goodbye, Dragon Inn '03
A Great Wall '86▶
Happy Times '00
Hero '03▶
The Horse Thief '87▶
House of Flying Daggers '04▶
The Inn of the Sixth Happiness '58▶
Iron & Silk '91
Jet Li's Fearless '06
The Joy Luck Club '93▶
Ju Dou '90▶
Kashmir Run '69
The Keys of the Kingdom '44▶
Kill Bill Vol. 2 '04▶
The Killer '90▶
The King of Masks '99▶
Kung Fu Hustle '04▶
Kung Fu Panda '08
Lan Yu '01
The Last Emperor '87▶
The Leathernck '28
The Lost Empire '01
Lust, Caution '07
M. Butterfly '93
Marco Polo '07
Mission: Impossible 3 '06▶
The Mountain Road '60
Mulan '98
The Mummy: Tomb of the Dragon Emperor '08
Not One Less '99
Once Upon a Time in China '91▶
Once Upon a Time in China III '93▶
The Painted Veil '06
Pavilion of Women '01
Princess Yang Kwei Fei '55▶
The Promise '05
Purple Butterfly '03▶
Raise the Red Lantern '91▶
Red Corner '97
Red Firecracker, Green Firecracker '93▶
Red Sorghum '87▶
The Red Violin '98
The Reincarnation of Golden Lotus '89▶
Rhapsody of Spring '98
Riding Alone for Thousands of Miles '05
The Road Home '01▶
The Sand Pebbles '66▶
Shadow Magic '00
Shadows over Shanghai '38
Shadows of the Orient '37
Shanghai Express '32▶
Shanghai Triad '95▶
The Silk Road '92
Smile '05
Soldier of Fortune '55
Song of the Exile '90
Spy Game '01
The Story of Qiu Ju '91▶
The Story of Xinghua '93
Summer Palace '06▶
Tai-Pan '86
Temptation of a Monk '94
Temptress Moon '96
Thank you, Mr. Moto '37
Think Fast, Mr. Moto '37
To Live '94▶
Together '02
2046 '04
Typhoon '06
Warriors of Heaven and Earth '03
The White Countess '05▶
Windhorse '98
Women from the Lake of Scented Souls '94
The Wooden Man's Bride '94
The World '04
The World of Suzie Wong '60
Xiu Xiu: The Sent Down Girl '97▶
Zhou Yu's Train '02

Christmas

see also Holidays;
Horrible Holidays

ABC Stage 67: Truman Capote's A Christmas Memory '66
All I Want for Christmas '91
Alvin and the Chipmunks '07
An American Christmas Carol '79
American Gun '02▶
Babes in Toyland '61
Babes in Toyland '86
Bad Santa '03
Batman Returns '92
Bernard and the Genie '91
The Bishop's Wife '47▶
Black Christmas '75
Black Christmas '06
Blast of Silence '61
Bloodbeat '85
Breathing Room '96
Call Me Claus '01
Cast Away '00▶
Chasing Christmas '05
Christmas at Water's Edge '04
The Christmas Blessing '05
The Christmas Box '95
The Christmas Card '06
A Christmas Carol '38▶
A Christmas Carol '51▶
A Christmas Carol '54
A Christmas Carol '84▶
A Christmas Carol '99
Christmas Comes to Willow Creek '87
Christmas Do-Over '06
Christmas Eve '47
Christmas Evil '80
Christmas in Connecticut '45▶
Christmas in Connecticut '92
Christmas in July '40▶
Christmas in the Clouds '01
The Christmas Kid '68
Christmas Lilies of the Field '84
The Christmas Miracle of Jonathan Toomey '07
A Christmas Reunion '93
A Christmas Shoes '02
A Christmas Story '83▶
The Christmas That Almost Wasn't '66
A Christmas to Remember '78
The Christmas Wife '88
Christmas With the Kranks '04
A Christmas Without Snow '80
The Crossing '00
The Day of the Beast '95
The Dead '87▶
Deck the Halls '06
A Dennis the Menace Christmas '07
Die Hard '88▶
Diner '82▶
Dr. Seuss' How the Grinch Stole Christmas '00
Don't Open Till Christmas '84
Dorm That Dripped Blood '82
A Dream for Christmas '73▶
Ebenezer '97
Elf '03▶
Elves '89
Ernest Saves Christmas '88
The Family Holiday '07
The Family Stone '05
Felicidades '00
Fred Claus '07
Friday After Next '02
Friends & Lovers '99
Funny Farm '88
The Gathering '77
The Gathering: Part 2 '79
George Balanchine's The Nutcracker '93
The Gift of Love '90
Go '99▶
Gremlins '84▶
Heidi '37
Heidi '52
Heidi '65▶
Heidi '67
Heidi '93▶
Here Comes Santa Claus '84
Hi-Life '98
Hobo's Christmas '87
The Holiday '06
Holiday Affair '49
Holiday Affair '96
Holiday Inn '42▶
Home Alone '90▶
Home Alone 2: Lost in New York '92
Home Alone 3 '97
Home for Christmas '90
Home of Angels '94
Homecoming: A Christmas Story '71
A House without a Christmas Tree '72
The Ice Harvest '05
I'll Be Home for Christmas '98
It Came Upon a Midnight Clear '84
It's a Wonderful Life '46▶
Jack Frost '98
Jingle All the Way '96
Joyeux Noel '05▶
Just Friends '05
The Kid Who Loved Christmas '90
Kramer vs. Kramer '79▶
La Buche '00
Lady on a Train '45▶
The Lemon Drop Kid '51
Lethal Weapon '87▶
Lily in Winter '94
The Lion in Winter '68▶
The Lion in Winter '03▶
The Little Drummer Girl '84▶
The Little Match Girl '84
The Little Match Girl '87
Little Women '94▶
The Long Kiss Goodnight '96
Look Who's Talking Now '93
Love Actually '03▶
Ma Saison Preferee '93▶
The Man in the Santa Claus Suit '79
The Man Upstairs '93
March of the Wooden Soldiers '34▶
A Matter of Principle '83
Merry Christmas, Mr. Lawrence '83▶
A Midnight Clear '92▶
Midnight Clear '06
A Midwinter's Tale '95
Miracle at Sage Creek '05
Miracle Down Under '87
Miracle in the Wilderness '91
Miracle on 34th Street '47▶
Miracle on 34th Street '94
Mrs. Santa Claus '96
Ms. Scrooge '97
Mr. Corbett's Ghost '90
Mr. St. Nick '02
Mixed Nuts '94
The Muppet Christmas Carol '92
Must Be Santa '99
My Uncle '96
The Mystery of Edwin Drood '93
Naked City: A Killer Christmas '98
National Lampoon's Christmas Vacation '89
National Lampoon's Christmas Vacation 2: Cousin Eddie's Big Island Adventure '03
Nativity '78
The Night of the Hunter '55▶
The Night They Saved Christmas '87
The Nightmare before Christmas '93▶
Noel '04
The Nutcracker Prince '91
Nutcracker: The Motion Picture '86
Off Season '01
One Christmas '95
One Magic Christmas '85▶
P2 '07
Papa's Angels '00
Parental Guidance '98
A Perfect Day '06
The Perfect Holiday '07
The Polar Express '04
Prancer '89
Prancer Returns '01
The Preacher's Wife '96
The Railway Children '70▶
'R Xmas '01
Reckless '95
The Ref '93▶
Reindeer Games '00
Remember the Night '40▶
Riot '96
The Robe '53
Roots: The Gift '88
Santa Baby '06
Santa Claus '59
Santa Claus Conquers the Martians '64
Santa Claus: The Movie '85
The Santa Clause '94▶
The Santa Clause 2 '02
The Santa Clause 3: The Escape Clause '06
The Santa Trap '02
Santa with Muscles '96
Scrooge '35▶
Scrooge '70
Scrooged '88
A Season for Miracles '99
Sheitan '06
Silent Night, Deadly Night '84
Silent Night, Deadly Night 2 '87
Silent Night, Deadly Night 3: Better Watch Out '89
Silent Night, Deadly Night 5: The Toymaker '91
Silent Night, Lonely Night '69
Sleepless in Seattle '93▶
A Smoky Mountain Christmas '86
Stalag 17 '53▶
The Sum of Us '94▶
Surviving Christmas '04
Susan Slept Here '54
A Tale of Winter '92
Thirteenth Day of Christmas '85
This Christmas '07
Three Godfathers '48▶
A Time to Remember '87
To All a Goodnight '80
To Grandmother's House We Go '94
Trading Places '83▶
Trail of Robin Hood '50
Trapped in Paradise '94
Turbulence '96
The Twelve Days of Christmas Eve '04
The Twelve Dogs of Christmas '05
24 Nights '99
Unaccompanied Minors '06
Untamed Heart '93
A Very Brady Christmas '88
The Victors '63
Visions of Sugarplums '99
The Waltons: The Christmas Carol '80
While You Were Sleeping '95▶
White Christmas '54▶
Who Slew Auntie Roo? '71
Will It Snow for Christmas? '96

Church Choirs

see also Gospel Music;
Nuns & Priests

The Chorus '03
A Christmas Without Snow '80
The Fighting Temptations '03
First Sunday '08
The Gospel '05▶
The Preacher's Wife '96
Preaching to the Choir '05
Sister Act '92
Sister Act 2: Back in the Habit '93

CIA/NSA

see also Foreign Intrigue;
Spies & Espionage

Acts of Betrayal '98
Agent Cody Banks '03
Agent on Ice '86
Aldrich Ames: Traitor Within '98
The Amateur '82
Assassin '89
The Assassination Game '92
The Assignment '97
Avalanche Express '79
Avenging Force '86
Bad Company '02
Ballistic: Ecks vs. Sever '02
A Beautiful Mind '01▶
The Berlin Conspiracy '91
Blink of an Eye '92
Bloodfist 8: Hard Way Out '96
Bomb Squad '97
The Bourne Supremacy '04▶
The Bourne Ultimatum '07▶
Call Me Bwana '63
The Capitol Conspiracy '99
Chain Reaction '96
Charlie Wilson's War '07
Chu Chu & the Philly Flash '81
C.I.A.: Code Name Alexa '92
C.I.A. 2: Target Alexa '94
Class of 1999 2: The Substitute '93
Clear and Present Danger '94▶
Code Name Alpha '67
The Company '07
Company Business '91
Confessions of a Dangerous Mind '02
Connor's War '06
Conspiracy of Fear '96
Conspiracy Theory '97▶
Crackerjack 3 '00
Crash & Byrnes '99
The Crocodile Hunter: Collision Course '02
Crossfire '98
Deadly Spygames '89
The Detonator '06
Diplomatic Siege '99
Divided by Hate '96
Double Tap '97
Double Team '97
D.R.E.A.M. Team '99
The Eiger Sanction '75
Erik '90
Escape from the KGB '87
Exiled in America '90
Exterminator '80
Extreme Limits '01
Eye See You '01
Fay Grim '06
Felony '95
Femme Fontaine: Killer Babe for the C.I.A. '95
A Few Days in September '06
The Fourth Angel '01
Francis Gary Powers: The True Story of the U-2 Spy '76
The Glimmer Man '96
The Good Shepherd '06
Harold & Kumar Escape from Guantanamo Bay '08
Hudson Hawk '91
The Hunt for Red October '90▶
The In-Laws '03
Kill Castro '80
Killer Likes Candy '78
Knock Off '98
The Listening '06
The Long Kiss Goodnight '96
Lumumba '01▶
Man on Fire '04
Mankillers '87
Memoirs of an Invisible Man '92
Militia '99
Mission: Impossible '96▶
Mission: Impossible 2 '00▶
Most Wanted '97
My Brother's War '97
My Little Assassin '99
Nixon '95▶
No Safe Haven '87
Once Upon a Time in Mexico '03▶
Operation C.I.A. '65
The P.A.C.K. '96
Patriot Games '92▶
The Peacemaker '97
President's Target '93
Puerto Vallarta Squeeze '04
The Quiet American '02▶
The Recruit '03▶
Rendition '07
Rosebud '75
Royce '93
Sahara '05
S.A.S. San Salvador '84
The Shadow Conspiracy '96
Shadow Man '06
The Siege '98
Silent Partner '05
The Situation '06
Sky High '84
Sniper 3 '04
The Spanish Prisoner '97▶
Spartan '04▶
Spies Like Us '85
The Spook Who Sat by the Door '73
Spy Games '99
Sticks '98
Street Justice '89
Subterfuge '98
The Sum of All Fears '02
Sunstorm '01
Swordfish '01
Syriana '05▶
Taken Alive '95
Target '85
Target of Opportunity '04
357 Magnum '79
Time Lapse '01
To the Limit '95
Violent Breed '83
White Ghost '88
White Sands '92
XXX '02
XXX: State of the Union '05
Yuri Nosenko, KGB '86

▶ = *rated three bones or higher*

Cinderella Stories

see also Cinderella

Angus '95
Arthur '81 ▶
B.A.P.'s '97
Boogie Nights '97 ▶
Born Yesterday '50 ▶
Born Yesterday '93
Ce-estial Clockwork '94
Cinderella '50 ▶
Cinderella '60
A Cinderella Story '04 ▶
Cinderella Man '05 ▶
Dreamer: Inspired by a True Story '05 ▶
Ella Enchanted '04 ▶
Ever After: A Cinderella Story '98 ▶
Evita '96
First Love '39
Flashdance '83
For Real '02
Heaven or Vegas '95
Haro '92 ▶
Just Friends '05
The Little Mermaid '89 ▶
The Love Trap 29
Maid in Manhattan '02
Maid to Order '87
Milk Money '94
The Mirror Has Two Faces '96
Mrs. Winterbourne '96
My Fair Lady '64 ▶
Once Around '91
Pretty Woman '90 ▶
The Prince & Me '04
The Princess Diaries '01
The Princess Diaries 2: Royal Engagement '04
Pygmalion '38 ▶
Saint Ralph '04
She's All That '99
The Slipper and the Rose '76
Splash '84
A Star Is Born '37 ▶
Stroke of Midnight '90
Up Close and Personal '96 ▶
Working Girl '88 ▶
The World of Suzie Wong '60

Circuses

see Carnivals & Circuses; Clowns

Civil Rights

see also Apartheid; Slavery

An African Dream '90
Ali '01
As Summers Die '86
The Autobiography of Miss Jane Pittman '74 ▶
Bloody Sunday '01 ▶
Boycott '02 ▶
Bucktown '75
The Color of Courage '98
The Color Purple '85 ▶
The Conversation '74 ▶
Crazy in Alabama '99
Crisis at Central High '80 ▶
Dangerous Evidence: The Lori Jackson Story '99
Driving Miss Daisy '89 ▶
A Dry White Season '89 ▶
Dutchman '67 ▶
The Ernest Green Story '93
Final Comedown '72
For Us, the Living '88 ▶
Free, White, and 21 '62
Freedom Road '79
Freedom Song '00 ▶
The Fringe Dwellers '86
Gang in Blue '96
Game for Vultures '86
George Wallace '97 ▶
Get On the Bus '96 ▶
Ghosts of Mississippi '96 ▶
The Great Debaters '07 ▶
The Heart of Dixie '89 ▶
Hairspray '07 ▶
Hairspray 90
Half Slave, Half Free '85
Hank Aaron: Chasing the Dream '95 ▶
Hawmps! '76
Hidden Agenda '90
Home of the Brave '49 ▶
The Killing Yard '01
King '78 ▶
The Kitchen Toto '87 ▶
Long Shadows '86
The Long Walk Home '89 ▶
Love Me Tender '56
Love's Savage Fury '79
Malcolm X: Make It Plain '95 ▶
The McMasters '70
Mean Streak '99
Mississippi Burning '88 ▶
Mr. & Mrs. Loving '96 ▶
A Nation Aflame '37
Panther '95
The Red Fury '84
The Ring '52
The Rising Place '02
The Rosa Parks Story '02
Rosewood '96 ▶
Ruby Bridges '98
Selma, Lord, Selma '99
A Soldier's Story '84 ▶
The Two of Us '68 ▶
The Untold Story of Emmett Louis Till '05 ▶
We of the Never Never '82 ▶

Civil War

see also American South; Southern Belles

Abraham Lincoln '30
Alvarez Kelly '66
Andersonville '95 ▶
The Andersonville Trial '70 ▶
Bad Company '72 ▶
Band of Angels '57
The Beguiled '70 ▶
The Birth of a Nation '15 ▶
Blood at Sundown '88
Bloody Trail '72
The Blue and the Gray '82
The Bushwackers '52
Cavalry '36
Cavalry Charge '51
Charlotte Forten's Mission: Experiment in Freedom '85
Civil War Diary '90 ▶
Class of '61 '92
Cold Mountain '03 ▶
Colorado '40
Copper Canyon '50
CSA: The Confederate States of America '04 ▶
Dark Command '40 ▶
Dead Birds '04
Drums in the Deep South '51
Escape from Fort Bravo '53
Finger on the Trigger '65
The Fool Killer '65
Friendly Persuasion '56 ▶
Frontier Pony Express '39
Frontier Scout '38
The General '26 ▶
The Ghost Brigade '93
Gettysburg '93 ▶
General Spanky '36
Glory '89 ▶
Gods and Generals '03 ▶
Gone with the Wind '39 ▶
The Good, the Bad and the Ugly '67 ▶
Gore Vidal's Lincoln '88
Great Day in the Morning '56
Hangman's Knot '52
Hellbenders '67
The Horse Soldiers '59
How the West Was Won '63 ▶
The Hunley '99
Innocent Voices '04
Ironclads '90
It Happened in New Orleans '36
Johnny Shiloh '63
Kansas Pacific '53
The Last Confederate: The Story of Robert Adams '05
Last Stand at Saber River '96
Little Women '33 ▶
Little Women '49 ▶
Little Women '78
Little Women '94 ▶
The Littlest Rebel '35
Louisiana '87
The Love Letter '98
Macho Callahan '70
Menace on the Mountain '70
Mosby's Marauders '66
Mysterious Island '61 ▶
No Drums, No Bugles '71
North and South Book 1 '85 ▶
North and South Book 2 '86 ▶
Of Human Hearts '38
The Old Maid '39 ▶
Oldest Confederate Widow Tells All '95 ▶
The Ordeal of Dr. Mudd '80 ▶
The Outlaw Josey Wales '76 ▶
Pharoah's Army '95
The Private History of a Campaign That Failed '81 ▶
Queen '93 ▶
Raiders of Ghost City '44
Raintree County '57
Rebel Love '85
Rebel Vixens '69
The Red Badge of Courage '51 ▶
Ride with the Devil '99 ▶
The Rose and the Jackal '90
Run of the Arrow '56
The Sacketts '79
Sahara '05
Shadow of Chikara '77
The Shadow Riders '82
Shenandoah '65 ▶
Sommersby '93 ▶
South of St. Louis '48
A Southern Yankee '48
The Supernaturals '86
The Tempest '82 ▶
True Women '97
The Undefeated '69
Virginia City '40 ▶
War Brides '80
Way Down South '39
Western Gold '37
Yellowneck '55

Civil War (non U.S.)

see also Genocide/Ethnic Cleansing; Spanish Civil War; War, General

Darfur Now '07
Rambo '08

Classic Horror

see also Horror; Anthologies

The Abominable Dr. Phibes '71 ▶
An American Haunting '05
And Now the Screaming Starts '73
The Ape '40
The Ape Man '43
The Appointment '82
Asylum '72
Asylum of Satan '72
Atom Age Vampire '61
Attack of the Beast Creatures '85
Attack of the Mayan Mummy '63
Attack of the Swamp Creature '75
Avenging Conscience '14
The Awakening '80
Barn of the Naked Dead '73
The Bat '26
The Bat '59
The Bat People '74
The Beast from Haunted Cave '60
The Beast Must Die '75
Bedlam '45 ▶
Before I Hang '40 ▶
The Birds '63 ▶
The Black Cat '34 ▶
The Black Cat '41
The Black Room '35 ▶
Black Sabbath '64 ▶
The Black Scorpion '57
Black Sunday '60 ▶
Blood and Roses '61
Blood Beast Terror '67
Blood Island '68
The Body Snatcher '45 ▶
Bride of the Gorilla '51
Bride of the Monster '55
The Brute Man '46
Burn Witch, Burn! '62 ▶
The Cabinet of Dr. Caligari '19 ▶
Carnival of Souls '62 ▶
Castle of Blood '64
Castle of Evil '66
Cat Girl '57
Cat in the Cage '68
Cat People '42 ▶
Cat People '82 ▶
Cauldron of Blood '67
Cave of the Living Dead '65
Chamber of Horrors '40
The Changeling '80 ▶
Circus of Fear '67
Condemned to Live '35
The Conqueror Worm '68 ▶
Corridors of Blood '58
Count Dracula '71
Count Yorga, Vampire '70
The Crawling Eye '58
Creature from the Black Lagoon '54 ▶
The Creature Walks among Us '56
Creature with the Blue Hand '70
The Creeper '48
The Creeping Flesh '72
Creeping Terror '64
Creepshow '82 ▶
Creepshow 2 '87
Crimes at the Dark House '39 ▶
The Crimes of Dr. Mabuse '32 ▶
The Crimes of Stephen Hawke '36
The Crimson Cult '68
Crucible of Horror '69
Cry of the Banshee '70
Cry of the Werewolf '44
Crypt of the Living Dead '73
The Curse of Frankenstein '57
Curse of Nostradamus '60
Curse of the Devil '73
Curse of the Swamp Creature '66
Cyclops '56
Daughters of Darkness '71 ▶
Darkness '02
Dementia 13 '63 ▶
Demon Barber of Fleet Street '36
Demons of the Mind '72
The Devil Bat '41 ▶
The Devil Bat's Daughter '46
Devil Doll '36 ▶
Devil's Kiss '75
Dr. Death, Seeker o' Souls '73
Dr. Jekyll and Mr. Hyde '20 ▶
Dr. Jekyll and Mr. Hyde '32 ▶
Dr. Jekyll and Mr. Hyde '41 ▶
Dr. Jekyll and Mr. Hyde '68
Dr. Jekyll and Mr. Hyde '73
Doctor X '32
Dolly Dearest '92
Dorian Gray '70
Dracula (Spanish Version) '31
Dracula '31 ▶
Dracula '73
Dracula '79
Dracula A.D. 1972 '72
Dracula 2000 '00 ▶
Dracula '57
Dracula's Castle '69
Dracula vs. Frankenstein '71
Dracula's Daughter '36 ▶
Dracula's Great Love '72
Dracula's Last Rites '79 ▶
La Chute de la Maison Usher '28 ▶
Lady Frankenstein '72
The Lair of the White Worm '88 ▶
The Legend of Blood Castle '72
Legend of the Werewolf '75
The Legend of the Wolf '77
The Living Coffin '58
Lemora, Lady Dracula '73
The Mad Monster '42
Mark of the Vampire '35 ▶
Martin '77 ▶
Mary Shelley's Frankenstein '94
Masque of the Red Death '64 ▶
Masque of the Red Death '89
Maniac '77
The Man They Could Not Hang '39 ▶
The Manson Family '04
The Fall of the House of Usher '60 ▶
The Fall of the House of Usher '49 ▶
Eyes of the Panther '90 ▶
Fangs of the Living Dead '68
The Fear Chamber '68
Fear No Evil '80
The Fog '78 ▶
The Gorgon '64 ▶
Gothic '87 ▶
Grave of the Vampire '72
Graveyard Shift '90
The Greed of William Hart '48
The Ghoul '34
Guardian of the Abyss '82
Halloween Night '90
The Hanging Woman '72
The Haunted Strangler '59 ▶
Haunted Summer '88
The Head '59
The Horror of Dracula '58 ▶
House of Dark Shadows '70 ▶
The House of Usher '88
House of Dracula '45 ▶
House of Frankenstein '44 ▶
The Haunting '63 ▶
The Haunting '99
Haunting Fear '91
The Haunting of Morella '91
Haxan: Witchcraft through the Ages '22 ▶
The House of the Black Death '65
House of Wax '53 ▶
House on Haunted Hill '58 ▶
The House that Dripped Blood '71 ▶
How to Make a Monster '58
The Hunger '83 ▶
The Hunchback of Notre Dame 23 ▶
I Walked with a Zombie '43 ▶
I Was a Teenage Werewolf '57
Invasion of the Vampires '61
The Invisible Dr. Mabuse '62 ▶
The Invisible Man '33 ▶
The Exorcist '73 ▶
Exorcist: The Beginning '04
The Evil of Frankenstein '64 ▶
Eyes of Fire '84
Eyes of the Demon '87
Frankenstein '31 ▶
Frankenstein '73
Frankenstein '82
Frankenstein and the Monster from Hell '74
Frankenstein Created Woman '66 ▶
Frankenstein '80 '79
Frankenstein Island '81
Frankenstein's Daughter '58
Frankenstein Unbound '90 ▶
Frankenstein Meets the Wolfman '42 ▶
Frankenstein Must Be Destroyed '69
The Fury '78
The Fury of the Wolfman '70
Genie of Darkness '62
George A. Romero's Land of the Dead '05 ▶
The Ghost of Frankenstein '42 ▶
Fright Night '85 ▶
Fright Night 2 '88
The Invisible Ray '36
The Island of Dr. Moreau '77
Isle of the Dead '45 ▶
Jaws '75 ▶
Jaws 2 '78
Jaws 3 '83
Jaws: The Revenge '87
King of the Zombies '41 ▶
Miami Horror '87
Mirrors '32 ▶
The Mummy '59 ▶
Murders in the Rue Morgue '32
Mystery of the Wax Museum '33 ▶
The Neighbor No. Thirteen '05 ▶
Night of Dark Shadows '71 ▶
Nosferatu '22 ▶
Once Upon a Midnight Scary '90
Pandora's Box '28 ▶
The Phantom of the Opera '43 ▶
The Phantom of the Opera '25 ▶
The Phantom of the Opera '89
Picture of Dorian Gray '45 ▶
The Pit and the Pendulum '91
The Pit & the Pendulum '61 ▶
Psycho '60 ▶
The Raven '35 ▶
Return of the Vampire '43 ▶
Revenge of the Creature '55
Revenge of the Zombies '43
Scared to Death '46
The Snow Creature '54
Son of Dracula '43 ▶
Son of Frankenstein '39 ▶
Teenage Frankenstein '58
Three... Extremes '04
Undead '05
Vampyr '31 ▶
Van Helsing '04 ▶
The Undying Monster '42
The Vampire '57
The Vampire Bat '32
The Vampire People '66
The Vampire's Coffin '58
The Vampire's Ghost '45
Vampire Woman '70
When a Stranger Calls '06
Werewolf of London '35 ▶
The Werewolf '56
The White Zombie '32 ▶
The Wolf Man '41 ▶
The Mummy '32 ▶
The Mummy '78
The Mummy's Curse '44
The Mummy's Ghost '44
The Mummy's Hand '40 ▶
The Mummy's Tomb '42
Malevolence '04

Clergymen

see also Nuns & Priests; Religion; Religious Epics

Angel Baby '61

Clergymen

Angels and Insects '95
The Apostle '97
Bear Ye One Another's Burden... '88
Because of Winn-Dixie '05
The Bishop's Wife '47
The Bridge of San Luis Rey '05
Cold Turkey '71
The Disappearance of Aimee '76
Dragnet '87
Elmer Gantry '60
The Europeans '79
First Sunday '08
Footloose '84
The Gospel '05
Hallelujah! '29
Little Church Around the Corner '23
Little Minister '34
A Man Called Peter '55
Miss Sadie Thompson '53
The Night of the Hunter '55
The Preacher's Wife '96
Purlie Victorious '63
The Quick and the Dead '95
Rain '32
The Rector's Wife '94
The Scarlet Letter '34
The Scarlet Letter '73
The Scarlet Letter '79
The Scarlet Letter '95
The Second Chance '06
Signs '02
Sirens '94
A Walk to Remember '02
Wise Blood '79
Woman, Thou Art Loosed '04

Cloning Around

Alien: Resurrection '97
Attack of the Sabretooth '05
The Boys from Brazil '78
The Clones '73
The Clonus Horror '79
Godsend '04
The Island '05
Jurassic Park '93
The Last Sentinel '07
The Lost World: Jurassic Park 2 '97
Multiplicity '96
Repli-Kate '01
Replicant '01
Resident Evil: Extinction '07
Resurrection of Zachary Wheeler '71
The 6th Day '00
Species '95
Species 2 '98
Species 4: The Awakening '07
Spy Kids '01
Star Trek: Nemesis '02
Star Wars: Episode 2 — Attack of the Clones '02
2001: A Space Travesty '00

Clowns

see also Carnivals & Circuses; Killer Clowns
Carnival of Souls '98
Clown House '88
Clown Murders '83
Clowning Around '92
Clowning Around 2 '93
The Clowns '71
Court Jester '56
Family Jewels '65
The Funhouse '81
Funland '89
He Who Gets Slapped '24
House of 1000 Corpses '03
Killer Klowns from Outer Space '88
Make-Up '37
The Man Who Laughs '27
Mr. Jingles '06
Painted Hero '95
Pee-wee's Big Adventure '85
Poltergeist '82
Quick Change '90
Rize '05
Shakes the Clown '92

The Ice Runner '93
Ice Spiders '07
Ice Station Zebra '68
L'Iceberg '05
Into Thin Air: Death on Everest '97
Intruder Within '81
Iron Will '93
Island in the Sky '53
Jack Frost '98
Jack Frost 2: Revenge of the Mutant Killer Snowman '00
Jack London's The Call of the Wild '97
The Juniper Tree '87
Kavik the Wolf Dog '80
Klondike Annie '36
The Last Place on Earth '85
The Last Stop '99
Lost in Alaska '52
Lost Zeppelin '29
Lovers of the Arctic Circle '99
Map of the Human Heart '93
Meltdown '06
MXP: Most Xtreme Primate '03
Mystery, Alaska '99
Never Cry Wolf '83
North Star '96
North to Alaska '60
Operation Haylift '50
Ordeal in the Arctic '93
Out Cold '01
Pathfinder '87
The Pebble and the Penguin '94
Pipe Dreams '76
Quest for Fire '82
Reindeer Games '00
Salmonberries '91
The Santa Clause 2 '02
The Santa Clause 3: The Escape Clause '06
Shackleton '02
Shadow of the Wolf '92
She '35
The Shining '80
Silent Hunter '94
A Simple Plan '98
Smilla's Sense of Snow '96
Snow Angels '07
Snow Day '00
Snow Dogs '02
The Snow Queen '02
The Snow Walker '03
Snowboard Academy '96
Snowbound: The Jim and Jennifer Stolpa Story '94
Sometimes They Come Back... For More '99
Spawn of the North '38
The Spoilers '42
Spy Games '99
The Stranger: Kabloonak '95
Sub Down '97
Suspended Animation '02
Tentacles of the North '26
The Thing '51
The Thing '82
30 Days of Night '07
Unaccompanied Minors '06
Vertical Limit '00
The Viking Sagas '95
Virus '82
The White Dawn '75
White Fang 2: The Myth of the White Wolf '94
White Wolves 3: Cry of the White Wolf '98
Wind Chill '07
Winter Break '02
Winter Passing '05
Winter People '89
Winter Sleepers '97
The Winter War '89
The X-Files: I Want to Believe '08
X2: X-Men United '03
Yossi & Jagger '02
You'll Like My Mother '72
Zero Degrees Kelvin '95

Coast Guard

see also Military: Navy; Sail Away
Don Winslow of the Coast Guard '43
The Guardian '06
Sea Devils '37
Waking the Dead '00
Wetbacks '56
Yours, Mine & Ours '05

Cockroaches

see also Killer Bugs and Slugs
Addicted to Love '96
The Applegates '89
Bird on a Wire '90
The Craft '96
Creepshow '82
Honey, We Shrunk Ourselves '97
Joe's Apartment '96
Just Married '03
Men in Black '97
Mimic '97
The Nest '88
Pacific Heights '90
Shinbone Alley '70
Team America: World Police '04
Twilight of the Cockroaches '90
Vampire's Kiss '88

Cold Spots

The Abominable Snowman '57
Adam Sandler's 8 Crazy Nights '02
Alaska '96
Alien vs. Predator '04
Antarctica '84
Arctic Blue '93
Arctic Tale '07
Atomic Submarine '59
Avalanche '99
Balto '95
The Big Push '75
Black Cadillac '03
Boa '02
Bog '84
Call of the Wild '93
Cold Fever '95
Cool Runnings '93
Courage Mountain '89
Crackerjack '94
The Crimson Rivers '01
Cry of the Penguins '71
The Day the Earth Froze '59
Dead Ahead: The Exxon Valdez Disaster '92
Dead of Winter '87
Devil's Island '96
Die Another Day '02
Doctor Zhivago '65
Downhill Willie '96
The Empire Strikes Back '80
Extreme Ops '02
Fallen Angel '03
The Fast Runner '01
Firefox '82
Fixed Bayonets! '51
The Forbidden Quest '93
Fred Claus '07
Friends & Lovers '99
Glory & Honor '98
The Golden Compass '07
Happy Feet '06
Heart of Light '97
The Heroes of Telemark '65
Ice Age '02
Ice Men '04
Ice Palace '60

S.I.C.K. Serial Insane Clown Killer '03
Spawn '97
Stephen King's It '90
13 Moons '02
To Catch a Killer '92

Cold War

see also Cold War Spies; Communists & Communism; Red Scare

Cold War Spies

see also Communists & Communism; Red Scare
Act of War '96
Alamut Ambush '86
Aldrich Ames: Traitor Within '98
Avalanche Express '79
The Berlin Conspiracy '91
Big Jim McLain '52
Black Box Affair '66
Bullet to Beijing '95
Call Me Bwana '63
Caravan to Vaccares '74
Charlie Muffin '79
Code Name: Alpha '67
Code Name: Dancer '87
Codename Kyril '91
Cold War Killers '86
The Company '07
Company Business '91
Company Man '00
Conspirator '49
Dead Aim '87
Deadly Recruits '86
Death Rides the Range '40
Defense Play '88
A Different Loyalty '04
Diplomatic Courier '52
The Eiger Sanction '75
Emissary '72
The Endless Game '89
The English Patient '96
An Englishman Abroad '83
Enigma '82
The Experts '89
The Falcon and the Snowman '85
Final Assignment '80
Firefox '82
Firehead '90
First Yank into Tokyo '45
Flight from Vienna '56
For Your Eyes Only '81
The Fourth Protocol '87
Francis Gary Powers: The True Story of the U-2 Spy '76
From Russia with Love '63
Funeral in Berlin '66
Girl Hunters '63
The Good Shepherd '06
Gotcha! '85
The Great Armored Car Swindle '64
The Hot Line '69
The House on Carroll Street '88
The Human Factor '79
The Hunt for Red October '90
The Ice Runner '93
Ice Station Zebra '68
In-Laws '79
In the Company of Spies '99
The Innocent '93
The Inside Man '84
Intrigue '90
The Ipcress File '65
Jet Pilot '57
The Jigsaw Man '84
Jumpin' Jack Flash '86
The KGB: The Secret War '86
Kill Castro '80
Laser Mission '90
Lisbon '56
The Living Daylights '87
The Looking Glass War '69
M. Butterfly '93
Mackintosh Man '73
The Man Who Knew Too Little '97
The Manchurian Candidate '62
The Mercenaries '80
Mission Phantom '79
Nasty Rabbit '64
Night Flight from Moscow '73
No Dead Heroes '87

No Way Out '87
Octopussy '83
Operation C.I.A. '65
The Osterman Weekend '83
Our Man in Havana '59
The Package '68
The Peking Blond '68
A Perfect Spy '88
Philby, Burgess and MacLean: Spy Scandal of the Century '84
Pickup on South Street '53
The Prize '63
Provocateur '96
Pueblo Affair '73
A Question of Attribution '91
Ravishing Idiot '64
Roboman '75
The Russia House '90
Russian Roulette '75
The Rutanga Tapes '90
Scorpio '73
Sebastian '68
Second Best Secret Agent in the Whole Wide World '65
Secret Weapons '85
Sell Out '76
Shack Out on 101 '55
Sky High '51
Sky High '84
Sky Liner '49
Spies Like Us '85
Spy Games '99
The Spy Who Came in from the Cold '65
S*P*Y*S '74
Steal the Sky '88
Stopover Tokyo '57
The Tamarind Seed '74
Telefon '77
The Thief '52
Topaz '69
Tom Curtain '66
The Trouble with Spies '87
The Ultimate Imposter '79
The Whistle Blower '87
White Nights '85
Wonsan Operation '78
Yuri Nosenko, KGB '86

Coma

see also Disease of the Week; Doctors & Nurses; Hospitals & Medicine
Anaconda '96
Awakenings '90
Bad Dreams '88
Brainwaves '82
The Brothers Solomon '07
Buried Alive 2 '97
The Cell '00
Children of the Corn 666: Isaac's Return '99
The Clay Pigeon '49
Coma '78
The Dead Zone '02
Devil Doll '64
Eden '98
18 Again! '88
Face/Off '97
Forever Young '92
Ghost Dad '90
Good Bye, Lenin! '03
Halloween 4: The Return of Michael Myers '88
Halloween 5: The Revenge of Michael Myers '89
Hard to Kill '89
The Invisible '07
Just like Heaven '05
Kickin' It Old Skool '07
Kids in the Hall: Brain Candy '96
Kill Bill Vol. 1 '03
Monkeybone '01
New Best Friend '02
Patrick '78
Rocky 2 '79
The Safety of Objects '01
Saint Ralph '04
Seven Hours to Judgment '88
Shock! '46
3 Women '77

28 Days Later '02
Unleashed '05
While You Were Sleeping '95

Comedy

see also Black Comedy; Comedy Anthologies; Comedy Drama; Comedy Mystery; Comedy Sci-Fi; Comic Adventure; Crimedy; Detective Spoofs; Genre Spoofs; Horror Comedy; Military Comedy; Musical Comedy; Romantic Comedy; Satire & Parody; Screwball Comedies; Showbiz Comedies; Slapstick Comedy; Sports Comedies; Stupid Is...; Western Comedy

Comedy Anthologies

see also Comedy
Amazon Women on the Moon '87
And Now for Something Completely Different '72
Boccaccio '70 '62
Everything You Always Wanted to Know about Sex (But Were Afraid to Ask) '72
Foreplay '75
The Groove Tube '72
Hollywood Boulevard '76
Kentucky Fried Movie '77
Kid 'n' Hollywood and Polly Tix in Washington '33
Laurel & Hardy and the Family '33
Laurel & Hardy: At Work '32
Laurel & Hardy On the Lam '30
Laurel & Hardy Spooktacular '34
Laurel & Hardy: Stan "Helps" Ollie '33
Looney Looney Looney Bugs Bunny Movie '81
The Lost Stooges '33
Love Notes '88
Mack & Carole '28
The Marx Brothers in a Nutshell '90
Monty Python's The Meaning of Life '83
National Lampoon Goes to the Movies '81
National Lampoon's Favorite Deadly Sins '95
New York Stories '89
No Sleep 'Til Madison '02
Nora's Hair Salon '04
Oldest Profession '67
Parade '74
Plaza Suite '71
Queen for a Day '51
Really Weird Tales '86
Sex and Buttered Popcorn '91
SuperGuy: Behind the Cape '02
Tigers in Lipstick '80
Tunnelvision '76
Woman Times Seven '67
Yours, Mine & Ours '68

Comedy Drama

see also Black Comedy; Comedy
Adventure '45
Alfie '04
Alice Doesn't Live Here Anymore '74
Alice's Restaurant '69
All I Want for Christmas '91
All My Good Countrymen '68
All Screwed Up '74
An Almost Perfect Affair '79
Aloha Summer '88
Always '85

Amarcord '74 ▶
The Amazing Mrs. Holiday '43
American Boyfriends '89
American Graffiti '73 ▶
Amy '98
Androcles and the Lion '52
Andy Hardy Gets Spring Fever '39
Andy Hardy's Double Life '42
Andy Hardy's Private Secretary '41
Angie '94
Angel in a Taxi '59
The Anniversary Party '01 ▶
Antonia's Line '95 ▶
The Apprenticeship of Duddy Kravitz '74 ▶
Arabian Nights '74 ▶
Arizona Dream '94
Armistead Maupin's More Tales of the City '97
Armistead Maupin's Tales of the City '93
Art School Confidential '06
Article 99 '92
Author! Author! '82
Autumn Marathon '79
Avalon '90 ▶
Avenue Montaigne '06
Awakenings '90 ▶
Ay, Carmela! '90 ▶
Baby, Take a Bow '34
Baby It's You '82 ▶
The Baby-Sitters Club '95
Babette's Feast '87 ▶
The Baker's Wife '33 ▶
Balloon Chase '82
Band of Outsiders '64 ▶
The Band's Visit '07 ▶
Barcelona '94 ▶
Bartleby '70
Baxter '89
The Baxter '05
Beautiful Girls '96
Beautiful Thing '95 ▶
Because of Winn-Dixie '05
Bed and Board '70
Being Human '94
Being Two Isn't Easy '62
The Bells of St. Mary's '45 ▶
Benji '74 ▶
Best Men '98
The Best Way '76
Bhaji on the Beach '94 ▶
Big '88 ▶
The Big Chill '83 ▶
The Bishop's Wife '47 ▶
The Black King '32
Bleak Moments '71
Blueberry Hill '88
Blume in Love '73
Bogus '96
Bon Voyage '03 ▶
Bongwater '98
Bonjour Monsieur Shlomi '03 ▶
Boogie Nights '97 ▶
Born to Win '71
Borsalino '70 ▶
Bought and Sold '03
Box of Moonlight '96
The Boys Next Door '96
The Breakfast Club '85 ▶
Breaking Away '79 ▶
Breaking the Rules '92
Breaking Up Is Hard to Do '79
The Bretts '68
Bright Eyes '34
Bright Young Things '03 ▶
Brighton Beach Memoirs '86 ▶
Broadcast News '87 ▶
Broken Flowers '05 ▶
The Bucket List '07
Bud and Lou '78

The Buddha of Suburbia '92
Buddy's Song '91
A Bunny's Tale '85
Bureau of Missing Persons '33
Butterflies Are Free '72 ▶
Cadillac Ranch '96
Caesar and Cleopatra '46 ▶
Cafe Express '83
Calendar Girl '93
Candy Mountain '87
Cannery Row '82
Captain Newman, M.D. '63 ▶
Caramel '05
Carbon Copy '81
Carnal Knowledge '71 ▶
Carnival in Flanders '35
Caro Diario '93 ▶
Carried Away '95
Casey's Shadow '78
Caterina in the Big City '03 ▶
Celestial Clockwork '94
Cesar '36 ▶
Cesar & Rosalie '72
The Challengers '89
Charles et Lucie '79
Charlie and the Great Balloon Chase '82
Charlie McCarthy, Detective '39
Charlie Wilson's War '07 ▶
Cheaper to Keep Her '80
A Chef in Love '96
Chicago Cab '98
Children of the Revolution '95
Chimes at Midnight '67 ▶
China, My Sorrow '89
Chloe in the Afternoon '72 ▶
Choose Me '84 ▶
A Chorus of Disapproval '89
The Christmas Wife '88
The Chumscrubber '05
Chungking Express '95 ▶
City Lights '31 ▶
City of Women '81
Claire's Knee '71 ▶
Clara's Heart '88
Class Reunion '72
Cleo from 5 to 7 '61 ▶
Clipped Wings '53
Coast to Coast '80
Coast to Coast '04 ▶
Cocoon: The Return '88
Combination Platter '93 ▶
Comment Ca Va? '76
Commandments '96
Conspiracy of Terror '75
Cookie's Fortune '99 ▶
Cooperstown '93 ▶
Corvette Summer '78
Country Life '95
The Courtship of Eddie's Father '62
Cousin, Cousine '76 ▶
Cousins '89
Crazy from the Heart '91 ▶
Crimes & Misdemeanors '89 ▶
Criminal '04
Crooklyn '94 ▶
Cruel Intentions '98
Danny Boy '46
The Darjeeling Limited '07 ▶
David Holzman's Diary '67
The Decameron '70
The Decline of the American Empire '86 ▶
Deconstructing Harry '97 ▶
Deep in the Heart (of Texas) '98
Der Purimshpiler '37
Destiny Turns on the Radio '95
Details of a Duel: A Question of Honor '89
Detour to Danger '45
The Devil & Daniel Webster '41 ▶
Devil on Horseback '54
The Devil's Eye '60
The Devil Wears Prada '06 ▶

Diary of a Chambermaid '46 ▶
Diary of a Mad Black Woman '05
Diary of a Mad Housewife '70 ▶
Diary of a Young Comic '79
Diary of Forbidden Dreams '73
Different for Girls '96
Digger '94
Dim Sum: A Little Bit of Heart '85 ▶
The Dining Room '86
Dinner at Eight '33 ▶
Dinner at Eight '89
The Discovery Program '89
Dixie Lanes '88
Doctor at Sea '56
Don Quixote '57
Don Quixote '00
Don't Drink the Water '69
Double Happiness '94 ▶
Down by Law '86 ▶
Dr. Christian Meets the Women '40
Dream with the Fishes '97
The Dream Team '89
Dream Chasers '82
Duane Hopwood '05
Duets '99
Earthly Possessions '99
Eat a Bowl of Tea '89 ▶
Eat Drink Man Woman '94 ▶
Eat My Dust '76
Eat the Peach '86
Eating '90
Eddie Presley '92
Educating Rita '83 ▶
El Cochecito '60
The Elementary School '91 ▶
Eli Eli '40
Elizabeth of Ladymead '48
Elizabethtown '05
Elmore Leonard's Gold Coast '97
Emanon '83
End of the Line '88
Enemies, a Love Story '89 ▶
Enormous Changes '83
Even Cowgirls Get the Blues '94
The Evening Star '96
Everybody Says I'm Fine! '06
Everything is Illuminated '05 ▶
Extra Girl '23
Eyes Right! '26
The Fabulous Baker Boys '89 ▶
Faithful '95
Family Business '89
The Family Stone '05
Fandango '85
Far North '88
Fast Talking '86
Fatso '80
Feeling Minnesota '96
The Fifth Monkey '90
First Name: Carmen '83
The Fisher King '91 ▶
Five Corners '88 ▶
The Five Heartbeats '91 ▶
The Flamingo Kid '84 ▶
Flesh '68
Flickers '80
Flirting '89 ▶
Floundering '94
Flourish '06
FM '78
Follow the Leader '44
Foolish '99
For Keeps '88
For the Love of Benji '77
A Foreign Field '93
Forrest Gump '94 ▶
Four Adventures of Reinette and Mirabelle '89 ▶

Four and a Half Women '05
Four Days in July '85
Four Deuces '75
Four Friends '81 ▶
The Four Musketeers '75 ▶
The Four Seasons '81 ▶
Freud Leaving Home '91
Fried Green Tomatoes '91 ▶
From the Hip '86
From the Mixed-Up Files of Mrs. Basil E. Frankweiler '95
Full Moon in Blue Water '88
Fuzz '72
Game 6 '05
Garbo Talks '84
Generation '69
George! '66
Georgy Girl '66 ▶
Get Shorty '95 ▶
Getting Over '81
Getting Straight '70
Ghost Chasers '51
The Gig '85 ▶
Gin Game '85
Ginger & Fred '86 ▶
The Girl in the Cafe '05 ▶
Girl Play '04
The Girl with the Hat Box '27
Girlfriends '78 ▶
A Girl's Folly '17
Go '99 ▶
Go Now '96
The Gold of Naples '54
Gone Are the Days '63
Good Bye, Lenin! '03 ▶
Good Luck '96
A Good Man in Africa '94
Good Morning, Vietnam '87 ▶
Good Sam '48
A Good Year '06
The Goodbye Bird '93
Goodbye Columbus '69 ▶
The Goodbye People '83
Goodnight, Michelangelo '89
The Gospel According to Vic '87
The Graduate '67 ▶
The Grand Role '04
Grandview U.S.A. '84
The Great Man Votes '38 ▶
The Great McGinty '40 ▶
The Great New Wonderful '06
The Great Wall '86
The Great War '59 ▶
Gregory's Girl '80 ▶
Grief '94 ▶
The Groomsmen '06
Gross Anatomy '89
Grown Ups '80
Grumpy Old Men '93 ▶
Guess What We Learned in School Today? '70
Guess Who's Coming to Dinner '67 ▶
Half a Sixpence '67
Hangin' with the Homeboys '91 ▶
Hannah and Her Sisters '86 ▶
Happily Ever After '86
Happily Ever After '04
Happy Endings '05
Happy Since I Met You '89
Hard Promises '92
Harlem Nights '89
The Hard Way '89
Harry and Max '04
The Hawks & the Sparrows '67

Head Winds '25
The Heartbreak Kid '72 ▶
Heartbeat '86
Here Come the Marines '52
Hero '92 ▶
Hero of the Year '85
Hey, Babu Riba '88
The Hideaways '73
Hideous Kinky '99
Highball '97
His Double Life '33
His First Command '29
Hold Your Man '33

A Hole in the Head '59
Hollywood Heartbreak '89
Hollywood Vice Squad '86
Holy Man '98
Home for the Holidays '95 ▶
Home Free All '84
Homegrown '97
Homer and Eddie '89
Horsemasters '61
The Hot Line '69
The Hotel New Hampshire '84
House of Angels '92 ▶
Household Saints '93 ▶
The Householder '63 ▶
Housekeeping '87 ▶
I Live My Life '35
I Live with Me Dad '86
I Vitelloni '53 ▶
The Ice Flood '26
If You Could See What I Hear '82
Il Sorpasso '63 ▶
I'll Never Forget What's 'Isname '67
Illuminata '98
I'm Not Rappaport '96
Imaginary Heroes '05
Immediate Family '89
Impure Thoughts '86
In Her Shoes '05 ▶
In Praise of Older Women '78
In the Mood '87
In the Soup '92 ▶
Indian Summer '93
Inside Monkey Zetterland '93
Insignificance '85
International Lady '41
Irish Jam '05
It Couldn't Happen Here '88
It Started in Naples '60
It's a Wonderful Life '46 ▶
It's All Gone, Pete Tong '04 ▶
Jack and Sarah '95
Jailbird's Vacation '65
Jamon, Jamon '93
The January Man '89
Jazzman '84
Jimmy Hollywood '94
Jo Jo Dancer, Your Life is Calling '86
Joe '70
Joe's Bed-Stuy Barbershop: We Cut Heads '83
Johnny Suede '92
The Jolly Paupers '38
Joshua Then and Now '85
Judge Priest '34
Judy Berlin '99 ▶
Juno '07 ▶
Just Another Pretty Face '58
Kicking and Screaming '95 ▶
The Kid '21 ▶
Kid Dynamite '43
The Kid from Left Field '79
Kids in America '05
The Killing Game '67
A King in New York '57
King of California '07
King of the Corner '04
Kingdom Come '01
Kisses in the Dark '97
Kitchen Stories '03 ▶
Knights & Emeralds '87
Knots '05
Kolya '96 ▶
Kostas '79
Kotch '71
La Discrete '90 ▶
La Dolce Vita '60 ▶
La Ronde '51 ▶
Lady by Choice '34
Lady for a Day '33 ▶
The Lady Says No '51
Larks on a String '68
Lars and the Real Girl '07 ▶
The Last Days of Chez Nous '92 ▶
The Last Detail '73 ▶
Last Holiday '50 ▶
Last Night '98
The Last of Mrs. Cheyney '37
Last Summer in the Hamptons '96 ▶
Law and Disorder '74 ▶

Le Beau Serge '58 ▶
Le Petit Amour '87
A League of Their Own '92 ▶
Leap of Faith '92
Leave 'Em Laughing '81
The Lemon Sisters '90
Let's Talk About Sex '98
Letters from My Windmill '54 ▶
Letting Go '85
Life '99 ▶
Life 101 '95
Like Water for Chocolate '93 ▶
Lily in Love '85
Little Annie Rooney '25 ▶
Little Miss Sunshine '06 ▶
Little Red Schoolhouse '36
A Little Sex '82
The Little Theatre of Jean Renoir '71 ▶
The Little Thief '89 ▶
Little Vegas '90
Little Voice '98 ▶
Living Out Loud '98
Local Hero '83 ▶
Loch Ness '95
Lonesome Jim '06
Long Shot Kids '81
Look at Me '04 ▶
Loose Connections '87
The Lovable Cheat '49
Love and Human Remains '93
Love Finds Andy Hardy '38 ▶
Love in the City '53 ▶
Love Me If You Dare '03 ▶
Lover Girl '97
Lovers and Other Strangers '70
Love! Valour! Compassion! '96
Loving '70
The Low Life '95
Lucas '86 ▶
Ma Vie en Rose '97 ▶
Mac and Me '88
Madame Sousatzka '88 ▶
Made for Each Other '39 ▶
Made in USA '88
Madea's Family Reunion '06
Magic Town '47
Make Room for Tomorrow '81
Mame Turns a Hundred '06
The Man Upstairs '58 ▶
Manny's Orphans '78
Mantrap '26
Marathon '80
Maria's Child '93
Marie '93
Marilyn Hotchkiss' Ballroom Dancing & Charm School '06 ▶
Marius '31 ▶
The Marriage of Maria Braun '79 ▶
Marry Me, Marry Me '69
The Marrying Kind '52
Masala '91
The Matador '06 ▶
Mauvaise Graine '33
Max Dugan Returns '83
May Fools '90 ▶
Maybe Baby '99
Me and You and Everyone We Know '05 ▶
Me Myself I '99
Mediterraneo '91 ▶
Meantime '81
Melinda and Melinda '05
Men at Work '90
Men Don't Leave '89 ▶
M*A*S*H '70 ▶
M*A*S*H: Goodbye, Farewell & Amen '83 ▶
Memories of Me '88
Mermaids '90 ▶
Metropolitan '90 ▶
Mexican Bus Ride '51
Middle Age Crazy '80
Midnight Auto Supply '78
Mifune '99 ▶
The Mighty Ducks '92

▶ = rated three bones or higher

Comedy

The Mighty Quinn '89
The Milagro Beanfield War '88
Million Dollar Kid '44
Millions '05
Min & Bill '30
Miracle on 34th Street '94
Mischief '85
The Misfit Brigade '87
Miss Annie Rooney '42
Miss Pettigrew Lives for a Day '08
Mrs. 'Arris Goes to Paris '92
Mrs. Henderson Presents '05
Mrs. Palfrey at the Claremont '05
Mrs. Wiggs of the Cabbage Patch '34
Mr. Deeds Goes to Town '36
Mr. Mom '83
Mr. North '88
Mr. Saturday Night '92
Mr. Winkle Goes to War '44
M'Lady's Court '73
Mom, the Wolfman and Me '80
Money for Nothing '93
The Moneytree '93
Moon over Parador '88
Moonlighting '85
More American Graffiti '79
Morgan Stewart's Coming Home '87
Moscow on the Hudson '84
Mother '96
The Mozart Brothers '86
Murmur of the Heart '71
My Beautiful Laundrette '85
My Blue Heaven '50
My Bodyguard '80
My Dinner with Andre '81
My Girl '91
My Life As a Dog '85
My Other Husband '85
My Therapist '84
My Twentieth Century '90
My Wonderful Life '90
Mystic Pizza '88
Nadine '87
The Nanny Diaries '07
The Nasty Girl '90
'Nea '78
'Neath Brooklyn Bridge '42
Never Let Go '60
The New Age '94
A New Life '88
New Year's Day '89
Next Stop, Greenwich Village '76
Next Summer '84
Night on Earth '91
1969 '89
1999 '98
90 Days '86
The Ninth Configuration '79
No Man of Her Own '32
No Money '97
No Small Affair '84
Nobody's Fool '94
Noi '03
Norman, Is That You? '76
North '94
North Dallas Forty '79
Nothing in Common '86
Nueba Yol '95
Nurse on Call '88
The Object of Beauty '91
The Object of My Affection '98
Oblomov '81
Off Your Rocker '80
Oh, Alfie '75
Oh, What a Night '92
Olly Olly Oxen Free '78
Omaha (the movie) '95
Once Around '91
One Arabian Night '21
One Flew Over the Cuckoo's Nest '75
One Last Thing '05
Only One Night '42
Only When I Laugh '81
Orphans '87
Other People's Money '91

Our Little Girl '35
Out '88
Outrageous! '77
Outside Chance of Maximillian Glick '83
Over the Brooklyn Bridge '83
Paddy '70
Padre Nuestro '85
Palm Springs Weekend '63
Palooka '34
The Paper '94
The Paper Chase '73
Parental Guidance '98
Parenthood '89
Paris, je t'aime '06
Parting Shots '98
Patch Adams '98
Patti Rocks '86
The Pentagon Wars '98
People Will Talk '51
Peppermint Soda '77
Perfect Timing '85
Perfumed Nightmare '89
Period of Adjustment '62
Pete 'n' Tillie '72
Peter's Friends '92
The Philadelphia Story '40
The Pickle '93
Pictures '80s
Ping Pong '87
Pink Cadillac '89
Pink Nights '87
P.K. and the Kid '85
Playboy of the Western World '62
The Players Club '98
Pocketful of Miracles '61
The Pointsman '86
Pollyanna '20
Pollyanna '60
Pontiac Moon '94
Popi '69
Portnoy's Complaint '72
Post Concussion '99
Power '28
Powwow Highway '89
A Prairie Home Companion '06
The Preacher's Wife '96
Pretty in Pink '86
Pretty Persuasion '05
Pride of the Bowery '41
Primrose Path '40
Prisoner of Second Avenue '74
Prisoners of Inertia '89
The Private History of a Campaign That Failed '81
Prizzi's Honor '85
Problem Child '90
Promised Land '88
Pronto '97
Provincial Actors '79
Punchline '88
Purple People Eater '88
Pushing Hands '92
Pushing Tin '99
Queen of Hearts '89
The Rachel Papers '89
Racquet '79
Rafferty & the Gold Dust Twins '75
Rags to Riches '87
Raining Stones '93
Raising Helen '04
The Rascals '81
Ratboy '86
The Reception '05
Reckless '97
Reckless: The Sequel '98
The Red Light Sting '84
Remedy for Riches '40
Reno and the Doc '84
Return of the Secaucus 7 '80
Rich and Famous '81
Ride the Wild Surf '64
Robert et Robert '78
Robert Gibralter '88
Rocket Science '07
Roll Bounce '05
Romance of a Horsethief '71
Roommate '84
Roommates '95
The Rules of the Game '39
The Runnin' Kind '89
Rupert's Land '89

Russian Dolls '05
The Saddest Music in the World '03
Sadie McKee '34
Saved! '04
Saving Grace '86
Saving Grace '00
Say Anything '89
Scenes from a Mall '91
School of Life '06
Schultze Gets the Blues '03
Searching For Wooden Watermelons '01
Second Best '05
Second Thoughts '83
Secrets of Women '52
Seduced and Abandoned '64
The Seducer '69
A Self-Made Hero '95
The Seven-Per-Cent Solution '76
Seven Thieves '60
Shadows and Fog '92
Shag: The Movie '89
She Hate Me '04
She Must Be Seeing Things '87
Shirley Valentine '89
A Shock to the System '90
Shooters '89
Shopgirl '05
Short Cuts '93
Side Out '90
Sideways '04
Signs of Life '89
Simon Birch '98
Simon, King of the Witches '71
A Simple Twist of Fate '94
Single Bars, Single Women '84
Sisterhood of the Traveling Pants '05
Six in Paris '68
Six Weeks '82
Sizzle Beach U.S.A. '74
Skin Game '71
Slap Shot '77
Slaves of New York '89
SLC Punk! '99
Sliding Doors '97
Slightly Honorable '40
The Slingshot '93
The Slugger's Wife '85
Smart Alecks '42
Smart People '08
Smoke Signals '98
Smugglers' Cove '48
The Snapper '93
Soldier in the Rain '63
Some Kind of Hero '82
Some Kind of Wonderful '87
Someone Else's America '96
Something in Common '86
Something Special '86
Something to Talk About '95
Song of the Thin Man '47
Soul Food '97
Soul Man '86
Southern Belles '05
Spencer's Mountain '63
Spike of Bensonhurst '88
Spitfire '34
Spoiled Children '77
Spook Busters '48
Spy Games '99
The Squid and the Whale '05
Stage Door '37
Star Maps '97
Star of Midnight '35
Star Spangled Girl '71
Stardust Memories '80
Starlight Hotel '90
The Stars Fell on Henrietta '94
Starting Over '79
Staying Together '89
Stealing Hearts '96
Steamboat Bill, Jr. '28
The Stepford Wives '04
Stoogemania '85
Storm in a Teacup '37
The Story of Seabiscuit '49
Stranger than Paradise '84

Strawberry Blonde '41
Street Music '81
Striptease '96
Strong Man '26
Stroszek '77
Stuck on You '84
Student Confidential '87
Sueno '05
Sugarbaby '85
The Sugarland Express '74
Summer Fantasy '84
Summer Snow '94
The Sunshine Boys '75
Suppose They Gave a War and Nobody Came? '70
Swedenhielms '35
Sweet Adeline '26
Sweet Hearts Dance '88
Sweet Lorraine '87
Sweet William '79
Sweetie '89
Swept Away... '75
Swing Shift '84
Sylvia Scarlett '35
T Bone N Weasel '92
Table Settings '84
Take Down '79
Take This Job & Shove It '81
Take Your Best Shot '82
A Tale of Springtime '89
The Talent Given Us '04
Tales of Manhattan '42
Talk '94
Talking Walls '85
The Taste of Others '00
Taxi Blues '90
A Taxing Woman '87
Teachers '84
Teacher's Pet '58
Teddy at the Throttle '16
Ten Things I Hate about You '99
Teresa Venerdi '41
Texasville '90
That Thing You Do! '96
That's Life! '86
That's My Baby! '88
There Goes My Baby '92
They Might Be Giants '71
The Thin Man Goes Home '44
Things Change '88
Things I Never Told You '96
13 Moons '02
This Is My Life '92
Those Lips, Those Eyes '80
A Thousand Clowns '65
Three for the Road '87
Three in the Attic '68
Three Men and a Baby '87
Three Men and a Cradle '85
Three Men and a Little Lady '90
Thunder in the City '37
Thursday's Child '43
Thursday's Game '74
A Tiger's Tale '87
The Time of Your Life '48
Tin Men '87
The Tip-Off '31
Tito and Me '92
To Please a Lady '50
To Sleep with Anger '90
Toby Tyler '59
Tom Brown's School Days '40
Tom Brown's School Days '51
Tom Sawyer '30
Tony Draws a Horse '51
Too Bad She's Bad '54
Too Pretty to Be Honest '72
Tootsie '82
Topaze '33
Topaze '51
Torch Song Trilogy '88
Toys '92
Trading Hearts '87
The Tragedy of a Ridiculous Man '81
Train to Hollywood '86
Traveller '96
Travels with My Aunt '72
Trouble along the Way '53
Trouble in the Glen '54

True Love '89
Truly, Madly, Deeply '91
The Truman Show '98
Trust '91
Truth about Women '58
Turk 182! '85
Turkish Delight '73
Twenty Bucks '93
Twenty-One '91
The 24 Hour Woman '99
29th Street '91
Twister '89
Two for the Road '67
Two for the Seesaw '62
2B Perfectly Honest '04
Twogether '94
Ugetsu '53
Under the Biltmore Clock '85
Under the Boardwalk '89
Underworld '96
The Unfaithfuls '60
An Unfinished Piece for a Player Piano '77
Up and Down '04
Up the Down Staircase '67
Up the Sandbox '72
Used People '92
Vacuuming Completely Nude in Paradise '01
The Vals '85
The Van '95
Varsity Blues '98
Venice, Venice '92
Very Close Quarters '84
The Virgin Soldiers '69
Volpone '39
Wait until Spring, Bandini '90
Waitress '07
Walls of Glass '85
Wassup Rockers '06
We Think the World of You '88
The Weather Man '05
Weekend at the Waldorf '45
Welcome Home, Roxy Carmichael '90
Went to Coney Island on a Mission from God... Be Back by Five '98
We're No Angels '55
West Is West '87
The West Wittering Affair '05
What the $*! Do We Know? '04
What's Cooking? '00
When Your Lover Leaves '83
Where the Heart Is '90
Whitcomb's War '87
The Whole Shootin' Match '79
The Whole Town's Talking '35
Who's Who '78
Whose Life Is It Anyway? '81
Widow's Peak '94
The Wife '95
Wild in the Streets '68
Willie & Phil '80
A Wind from Wyoming '94
Wings of Eagles '57
Winter Kills '79
Wired '89
Wise Guys '86
Wish upon a Star '96
Wish You Were Here '87
With Honors '94
The Wizard '89
The Women '39
Women of All Nations '31
The World According to Garp '82
The World of Henry Orient '64
WR: Mysteries of the Organism '71
The Wrong Arm of the Law '63
A Yank in Australia '43
A Year in Provence '93
The Year My Voice Broke '87
Year of the Dog '07

Yesterday, Today and Tomorrow '64
You and Me '38
You Are Here * '00
The Young in Heart '38
You're a Big Boy Now '66
A Zed & Two Noughts '88
Zombie Honeymoon '04

Comedy Mystery

see also Black Comedy; Comedy; Comedy Drama; Genre Spoofs; Horror Comedy; Satire & Parody

Charade '63
Clubhouse Detectives '96
Clue '85
Curse of the Pink Panther '83
Deathtrap '82
Get a Clue! '98
Goodbye, Lover '99
The Gracie Allen Murder Case '39
Hard-Boiled Mahoney '47
High Anxiety '77
Hoodwinked '05
Kiss Kiss Bang Bang '05
Lady on a Train '45
Murder by Death '76
Mystery Kids '99
Off and Running '90
The Pink Panther '64
The Pink Panther '06
The Pink Panther Strikes Again '76
The Princess Comes Across '36
Return of the Pink Panther '74
Revenge of the Pink Panther '78
Safe House '99
Scoop '06
A Shot in the Dark '64
Trail of the Pink Panther '82
Trixie '00
Voulez-Vous Danser avec Moi? '59
Whistling in Brooklyn '43
Whistling in Dixie '42
Whistling in the Dark '41
Zero Effect '97

Comedy Performance

see Concert Films

Comedy Sci-Fi

see also Comedy; Comic Adventure; Genre Spoofs; Satire & Parody; Sci Fi

The Absent-Minded Professor '61
Alien Avengers '96
Beach Babes 2: Cave Girl Island '95
Beach Babes from Beyond '93
Bug Buster '99
Can of Worms '00
Class of Nuke 'Em High '86
Class of Nuke 'Em High 2: Subhumanoid Meltdown '91
Clockstoppers '02
Coneheads '93
The Creature Wasn't Nice '81
Dinosaur Valley Girls '96
Doin' Time on Planet Earth '88
Earth Girls Are Easy '89
Evolution '01
From Other Worlds '04
Galaxy Quest '99
Hell Comes to Frogtown '88
Hellboy '04
The Hitchhiker's Guide to the Galaxy '05
Honey, I Blew Up the Kid '92

Howard the Duck '86
Ice Pirates '84
The Incredibles '04▶
Invasion of the Saucer Men '57
Cartouche '62▶
Captain Swagger '25
Chasers '94
Cheaper by the Dozen '03▶
Chu Chu & the Philly Flash '81
Dirt Bike Kid '86
Danny Deckchair '03
Doctor Detroit '83
Dog Pound Shuffle '75▶
Dolemite 2: Human Tornado '76
Meet Dave '08
Man in Black 2 '02
Man in Black '97▶
My Favorite Martian '98
My Uncle: The Alien '96
Out There '95
Robots '05
The Sex Machine '75
Sleeper '73▶
Son of Flubber '63
Spaceballs '87
Star Kid '97
Theodore Rex '95
Wham-Bam, Thank You Spaceman '75
Zoom '06

Comic Adventure
see also Action-Adventure; Comedy

Adventures Beyond Belief '87
Adventures in Babysitting '87▶
Adventures in Spying '92
Adventures of a Taxi Driver '76
Adventures of a Private Eye '77
The Adventures of Bullwhip Griffin '66
Agent Cody Banks '03▶
Air America '90
Alien from L.A. '87
All the Lovin' Kinfolk '70
All the Way, Boys '73
The Amazing Dobermans '76
The Americano '17
The Ambushers '67
Andy and the Airwave Rangers '89
Angel of H.E.A.T. '82
Angels Hard As They Come '71
The Ant Bully '06
Another 48 Hrs. '90
Avenging Disco Godfather '76
Baby on Board '92
Back Roads '81
Back to the Future '85▶
Back to the Future, Part 2 '89
Back to the Future, Part 3 '90▶
Bad Guys '86
Bagdad Cafe '83▶
The Baltimore Bullet '80
Bananas Boat '78
Behind the Fort '26
Beverly Hills Ccp '84▶
Beverly Hills Ccp 2 '87
Beverly Hills Ccp 3 '94
The Big Lebowski '97▶
The Big Slice '90
The Big White '05
Big Zapper '73
Bingo '91
Bird on a Wire '90
Bloodstone '88
Blue Iguana '88
Body Trouble '92
Bon Voyage '03▶
Boris and Natasha: The Movie '92
Bridget Jones: The Edge of Reason '04
Brink's Job '76▶
Brothers O'Toole '73
Burglar '87
Butler's Dilemma '43
California Straight Ahead '25
Campus Knights '29
Cannibal Women in the Avocado Jungle of Death '89
Cannonball Run 2 '84
Cannonball Run '81
The Captain from Koepenick '56
City Heat '84
Club Med '83
Collision Course '89
The Concrete Cowboys '79
Crocodile Dundee '86▶
Crocodile Dundee 2 '88
Doogal '05
Double Crossbones '51
The Double O Kid '92
Down to Earth '17▶
Drop Dead Sexy '05
Every Girl Should Have One '78
Explosion '69
Fast Getaway '91
Feds '88
The Fifth Musketeer '79
The Fighting American '24
Flatfoot '78
Flipper '96▶
Flirting with Fate '16▶
Forever Young '92
48 Hrs. '82▶
Foul Play '78▶
Free Ride '86
The Further Adventures of Tennessee Buck '88
Garfield: The Movie '04
Ghostbusters '84▶
Ghostbusters 2 '89
Go for It '83
The Golden Child '86
Gozu '03
The Gumshoe Kid '89
Gunmen '93
Hambone & Hillie '84
Harriet the Spy '96
Hawthorne of the USA '19
Hellboy '04▶
Here We Go Again! '42
High Road to China '83
High Voltage '29
Highpoint '80
How to Eat Fried Worms '06
Hudson Hawk '91
In 'n Out '36
In Like Flint '67
It's in the Bag '45▶
Jackie Chan's Who Am I '98
Jake Speed '86
Jane & the Lost City '87
The Jewel of the Nile '85
Just Tell Me You Love Me '80
Kazaam '96
Kindergarten Cop '90
King Kung Fu '87
Kiss My Grits '82
Kuffs '92
Landlord Blues '87
Last Action Hero '93
Last Holiday '06▶
Leonard Part 6 '87
Lemony Snicket's A Series of Unfortunate Events '04
The Life Aquatic with Steve Zissou '04
Looking for Trouble '96
A Low Down Dirty Shame '94
Lucky Devil '25
Lunch Wagon '81
Lust in the Dust '85▶
Mad About Money '37
Madigan's Millions '67
Magic Island '95
Magic Kid '92
A Man Called Sarge '90
The Man in the Raincoat '57
The Man Who Wasn't There '83
The Man with One Red Shoe '85
Master Mind '73
The Masters of Menace '90
Memoirs of an Invisible Man '92
Miami Supercops '85
Midnight Madness '80
Midnight Run '88▶
Miracles '86
Mr. Billion '77
Mr. Nanny '93
Mr. Nice Guy '98
Mr. Robinson Crusoe '32
Mr. Superinvisible '73
Mitchell '75
Mo' Money '92
Mob Story '90
Mom and Dad Save the World '92
The Money '75
Money Talks '97
Monkey Hustle '77
Monkey's Uncle '65
Monsters in Paradise '84
Muppet Treasure Island '96
My African Adventure '87
My Dog, the Thief '69
My Science Project '85
The Naked Sword of Zorro '69
No Deposit, No Return '76
O Brother, Where Art Thou? '00▶
Oddball Hall '91
Odds and Evens '78
Off the Lip '04
Operation Condor 2: The Armour of the Gods '86
Operation Dumbo Drop '95
Our Man Flint '66▶
Over the Hill '93
Paiookaville '95▶
Pippi Goes on Board '69
Pippi in the South Seas '70
Pippi Longstocking '69
Pippi on the Run '70
Pirates '86
Pirates of the Caribbean: Dead Man's Chest '06
Pizza '05
Pootie Tang '01
Prehysteria '93
The Prince of Thieves '48
Red Lion '69
Reggie Mixes In '16▶
The Reivers '69
Rescue Me '93
The Return of the Musketeers '89
The Return of the Rebels '81
Riff-Raff '47▶
Romancing the Stone '84▶
Round Trip to Heaven '92
Royal Flash '75▶
Rumble in the Bronx '96
Running Scared '86
Russkies '87
Seven '79
She's Back '88
Sherlock: Undercover Dog '94
Shoot '92
Short Time '90
Shredder Orpheus '89
Shrek 2 '04▶
Silver Streak '76▶
Ski Patrol '89
Sky High '04
Slither '70
Smokey and the Bandit '77
Smokey and the Bandit 2 '80
Smokey and the Bandit, Part 3 '83
Smokey and the Judge '80
Smokey Bites the Dust '81
Spaghetti House '82
Special Delivery '76
Special Zone '88
Speed Zone '89
Speedy '28▶
Spies, Lies and Naked Thighs '91
Spy Trap '92
Spy with a Cold Nose '66
S*P*Y*S '74
The Squeeze '87
Stakeout '87
Stand-In '85
Steelyard Blues '73
Stepmonster '92
The Stick-Up '77
The Sting 2 '83
Stingray '78
Stop! or My Mom Will Shoot '92
Stop That Cab '51
Stuntwoman '81
Suburban Commando '91
Suffering Bastards '90
The Suitors '88
Summer Night with Greek Profile, Almond Eyes & Scent of Basil '87
Sunburn '79
Super Fuzz '81
Surf Nazis Must Die '87
Surf Ninjas '93
Survivors '83
Swashbuckler '76
The Tall Blond Man with One Black Shoe '72▶
A Taxing Woman's Return '88▶
Teenage Mutant Ninja Turtles: The Movie '90▶
Teenage Mutant Ninja Turtles 2: The Secret of the Ooze '91
Teenage Mutant Ninja Turtles 3 '93
Terminal Exposure '89
That Man from Rio '64▶
That Sinking Feeling '79▶
They Met in Bombay '41
The Thief Who Came to Dinner '73
Think Big '90
This Time I'll Make You Rich '75
Those Daring Young Men in Their Jaunty Jalopies '69
Those Fantastic Flying Fools '67
Those Magnificent Men in Their Flying Machines '65▶
Three Amigos '86
Three Fugitives '89
Three Kinds of Heat '87
The Three Musketeers '74▶
3 Ninjas '92
3 Ninjas Kick Back '94
3 Ninjas Knuckle Up '95
Thunder and Lightning '77
Thunder in the Pines '49
Thursday '98
Title Shot '81
Toga Party '77
Tom and Huck '95▶
Too Hot to Handle '38▶
Top Dog '95
Topkapi '64▶
Tough Guys '86
Treasure of the Moon Goddess '88
Trenchcoat '83
TripleCross '66
TripleCross '83
Trouble in Store '53
The Trouble with Spies '87
True Lies '94▶
12 Plus 1 '70▶
Twin Dragons '92
Twins '88▶
Ultrachrist! '03
Under the Hula Moon '95
Under the Rainbow '81
Up the Creek '84
Uphill All the Way '85
Uptown Saturday Night '74
Vampire Effect '03
Van Nuys Blvd. '79
Vice Academy '88
Vice Academy 2 '90
Vice Academy 3 '91
Viva Maria! '65▶
Wackiest Ship in the Army '61
Wallace & Gromit: The Curse of the Were-Rabbit '05▶
We're No Angels '89
When the Clouds Roll By '19▶
Who Killed Mary What's 'Er Name? '71
The Wild and the Free '80
Wishman '93
Without a Paddle '04
Women of All Nations '31
World Gone Wild '88
Wrong Is Right '82
Year of the Comet '92
The Yum-Yum Girls '78

Comic Cops
see also Crime

The Animal '01
Big Trouble '02
Dragnet '87▶
Feds '88
Find the Lady '76
Freebie & the Bean '74▶
Inspector Clouseau '68
It Seemed Like a Good Idea at the Time '75
K-9 '89
Me, Myself and Irene '00▶
The Naked Gun: From the Files of Police Squad '88▶
Naked Gun 2 1/2: The Smell of Fear '91
Naked Gun 33 1/3: The Final Insult '94
National Lampoon's Loaded Weapon 1 '93
Police Academy '84
Police Academy 2: Their First Assignment '85
Police Academy 3: Back in Training '86
Police Academy 4: Citizens on Patrol '87
Police Academy 5: Assignment Miami Beach '88
Police Academy 6: City under Siege '89
Police Academy 7: Mission to Moscow '94
Reno 911!: Miami '07
Rush Hour '98
Rush Hour 2 '01
Rush Hour 3 '07
Stakeout '87
Super Troopers '01
Superbad '07▶
Taxi '04
Turner and Hooch '89

Comic Books
see also Disorganized

American Splendor '03▶
Artists and Models '55
Chasing Amy '97▶
Comic Book: The Movie '04
The Dangerous Lives of Altar Boys '02▶
Dark Justice '00
I Want to Go Home '89▶
Jay and Silent Bob Strike Back '01
Mallrats '95
Son of the Mask '05

Coming of Age
see also Teen Angst

Across the Great Divide '76
Ah, Wilderness! '35▶
A la Mode '94
Alan & Naomi '92
Alexandria...Why? '78
All Fall Down '62▶
All I Want '02
All I Wanna Do '98
All Over Me '96
All the Right Moves '83
All Things Fair '95
Aloha Summer '88
Alpine Fire '89▶
Amarcord '74▶
American Boyfriends '89
American Graffiti '73▶
An American Rhapsody '01▶
An American Summer '90
Americano '05
Among the Cinders '83
... And the Earth Did Not Swallow Him '94
Angela '34
Angelo My Love '83▶
Anne of Green Gables '85▶
Anthony Adverse '36
Anywhere But Here '99▶
Aparajito '58▶
The Apprenticeship of Duddy Kravitz '74▶
Au Revoir les Enfants '87▶
An Awfully Big Adventure '94
A Nos Amours '84▶
Babe '95▶
Baby Boy '01
Baby It's You '82▶
Back Door to Heaven '39▶
Barnyard '06
Batman Begins '05▶
The Battle of Shaker Heights '03
Battling Bunyon '24
Beautiful Thing '95▶
Beshkempir the Adopted Son '98
Big '88▶
The Big Bet '85
The Big Red One '80▶
Billy Bathgate '91
Black Cloud '04
Black Peter '63
Blue Car '03▶
Blue Fin '78
Blue Jeans '78
The Blue Kite '93▶
The Blue Lagoon '80
Blue River '95
Blue Velvet '86▶
Bonjour Monsieur Shlomi '03▶
Borstal Boy '00
Boss' Son '78
The Boys in Company C '77▶
The Boys in the 2nd Street Park '03
Boys Life '94
Brave New Girl '04
Breaking Away '79▶
Breaking Home Ties '87
Bridge to Terabithia '07▶
Brighton Beach Memoirs '86▶
A Bronx Tale '93▶
Brother to Brother '04
The Buddha of Suburbia '92▶
Buddy's Song '91
Buffalo Boy '04
Butterfly '99▶
By Way of the Stars '92
Calendar Girl '93
Can You Feel Me Dancing? '85
Can't Buy Me Love '87
Carnal Knowledge '71▶
Carry Me Home '04
Catherine Cookson's The Cinder Path '94
Catherine Cookson's The Dwelling Place '94
Catherine Cookson's The Glass Virgin '95
The Chicken Chronicles '77
China, My Sorrow '89
The Chorus '04▶
Christy '94
The Cider House Rules '99▶
Circle of Friends '94▶
City Boy '93
Civil War Diary '90▶
Class '83
Class of '44 '73
The Claw '27
Closely Watched Trains '66▶
Clowning Around 2 '93
Cocktail '88
Cold Sassy Tree '89▶
The Color of Money '86▶
Come and See '85▶
Come Undone '00
Coming Home '98
Coming Soon '99
Courage Mountain '89
Courtship '87▶

▶ = rated three bones or higher

Coming

Cowboys & Angels '04▶
Crazy Moon '87
Cria '76▶
The Crossing '92
Crossing the Bridge '92
Crutch '04▶
A Cry in the Wild '90▶
Cry of Battle '63
Culpepper Cattle Co. '72
Dakota '88
Dallas 362 '03
Damien: Omen 2 '78
Dancer, Texas—Pop. 81 '98▶
The Dangerous Lives of Altar Boys '02▶
The Dark Side of the Sun '88
David Copperfield '70▶
David Copperfield '99
David Holzman's Diary '67▶
Dead Beat '94
Dead Poets Society '89▶
December '91
The Deer Hunter '78▶
Desert Bloom '86▶
The Devil's Playground '76▶
Diner '82▶
Dirty Dancing '87▶
The Doe Boy '01
Dogfight '91▶
Dragstrip Girl '57
Dreamland '06▶
Driving Lessons '06▶
D3: The Mighty Ducks '96
Dutch Girls '87
Eat Drink Man Woman '94▶
Edge of Seventeen '99
The Education of Little Tree '97▶
Edward Scissorhands '90▶
Ellen Foster '97
Emanon '86
Eragon '06
Ernesto '79
Experience Preferred... But Not Essential '83
The Eyes of Youth '19
Eyes Right! '26
Family Prayers '91
Fandango '85
Fast Times at Ridgemont High '82▶
Father '67
Feelin' Screwy '90
Fellini Satyricon '69▶
Fierce People '05
Fiesta '95
The Fire in the Stone '85
First Affair '83
First Love '77
First Time '69
The Flamingo Kid '84▶
For a Lost Soldier '93
For Love Alone '86
Forever '78
Forever Young '85
Four and a Half Women '05
The 400 Blows '59▶
Foxes '80
Freedom Is Paradise '89▶
Freud Leaving Home '91
Friends Forever '86▶
A Friendship in Vienna '88
Gas Food Lodging '92▶
A Generation '54▶
A Gentleman's Game '01
Get Real '99
The Getting of Wisdom '77
Gidget '59
Ginger Snaps '01
Girl '98
A Girlfight '99▶
Girls Can't Swim '99
Go Tell It on the Mountain '84
Going All the Way '97
The Gold & Glory '88
The Good Humor Man '05
Goodbye Columbus '69▶
Goodbye, Miss 4th of July '88
Goodbye, My Lady '56
The Graduate '67▶
The Grass Harp '95

The Great Outdoors '88
The Great Santini '80▶
The Great Water '04▶
Gregory's Girl '80▶
Grown Ups '80
A Guide to Recognizing Your Saints '06
Hairspray '88▶
Hammers over the Anvil '91
Hangin' with the Homeboys '91▶
Happy Birthday, Gemini '80
Hard Choices '84▶
Harry Potter and the Order of the Phoenix '07 ▶
Hearts in Atlantis '01▶
Heathers '89▶
Heaven Help Us '85
A Hero Ain't Nothin' but a Sandwich '78
Higher Education '88
Hole in the Sky '95
Holy Girl '04▶
Holy Matrimony '94
Homeboy '82
Homework '82
The Horse '82▶
The Horsemen '70
Hot Moves '84
The Hour of the Star '85▶
House of D '04
How I Learned to Love Women '66
Huck and the King of Hearts '93
The Human Comedy '43▶
Hurricane Streets '96
I Capture the Castle '02
I Don't Want to Talk About It '94
I Know Why the Caged Bird Sings '79▶
I Love You, I Love You Not '97
Il Vitelloni '53▶
If Looks Could Kill '91
Il Sorpasso '63
I'm Not Scared '03
In Her Shoes '05▶
In Praise of Older Women '78
In the Custody of Strangers '82▶
The Incredible Mrs. Ritchie '03
Indian Paint '64
The Inheritors '82
Introducing the Dwights '07
Inventing the Abbotts '97
Invisible Circus '00
The Islander '88
Jacob Have I Loved '88
Jerry Maguire '96▶
JFK: Reckless Youth '93
Joe the King '99
Joey '85
Johnny Be Good '88
Jory '72
The Journey of Jared Price '00
The Journey of Natty Gann '85▶
Just Looking '99
The Karate Kid '84▶
The Karate Kid: Part 2 '86
The Karate Kid: Part 3 '89
Keeping Up with the Steins '06
Kicking and Screaming '95▶
King of the Gypsies '78
King of the Hill '93▶
Kings Row '41▶
Kipperbang '82
The Kitchen Toto '87▶
La Boum '81
La Symphonie Pastorale '46▶
Labyrinth '86▶
The Last Prostitute '91
Late Summer Blues '87
The Lawrenceville Stories '88
Le Grand Chemin '87▶
Le Sexe des Etoiles '93
The Learning Tree '69
The Legend of Johnny Lingo '03

L'Homme Blesse '83▶
Liam '00
L.I.E. '01
Life 101 '95
Like A Bride '94▶
The Lion King '94▶
Little Ballerina '47
A Little Romance '79▶
Little Women '49▶
Little Women '78
The Littlest Viking '94
The Lords of Flatbush '74
The Long Day Closes '92▶
Lost Legacy: A Girl Called Hatter Fox '77
A Lost Year '93
Love Film '70
Lover Girl '97
Lucas '86▶
Maid to Order '87
Malena '00
The Man from Snowy River '82
The Man in the Moon '91▶
A Man of Passion '88
The Man Without a Face '93
The Mango Tree '77
Martha '91▶
Matinee '92
Mean Creek '04▶
Mean Streets '73▶
The Member of the Wedding '52▶
The Member of the Wedding '97
Memoirs of a Geisha '05
Men of Ireland '38
Metropolitan '90▶
Mickey '48
A Midnight Clear '92▶
Milk Money '94
Mirrors '85
Mischief '85
Monika '52
Monsieur Ibrahim '03▶
More American Graffiti '79
Mosby's Marauders '66
The Mudge Boy '03
Murmur of the Heart '71▶
My American Cousin '85▶
My Apprenticeship '39▶
My Bodyguard '80▶
My Brilliant Career '79▶
My Girl '91
My Girl 2 '94
My Life As a Dog '85▶
My Life on Ice '02
My Tutor '82
My Universities '40▶
Mystic Pizza '88▶
New Waterford Girl '99
Next Stop, Greenwich Village '76▶
Nicholas Nickleby '46▶
Nicholas Nickleby '02▶
Nico and Dani '00
A Night in the Life of Jimmy Reardon '88
1969 '88▶
No Regrets for Our Youth '46▶
No Secrets '91
No Time for Sergeants '58▶
Norman Loves Rose '82
The Nostradamus Kid '92
Now and Then '95
Nowhere in Africa '02▶
Odd Birds '85
Oddballs '84
Ode to Billy Joe '76
Oh, What a Night '92
Old Enough '84
One on One '77
Only the Brave '94
Oranges Are Not the Only Fruit '89
The Other Side of Sunday '96
Other Voices, Other Rooms '95
Out of the Blue '80▶
Outside Providence '99
The Outsiders '83▶
Over the Edge '79▶
Over the Summer '85
A Painted House '03
The Pallbearer '95

Palm Beach '79
Palookaville '95▶
The Paper Chase '73▶
Paradise '82
The Passing of Evil '70
Pather Panchali '54▶
Pauline at the Beach '83▶
P.C.U. '94
Peck's Bad Boy '34
Peppermint Soda '77▶
Persepolis '07▶
Peter Lundy and the Medicine Hat Stallion '77
A Place in the World '92▶
Platoon '86▶
Portrait of a Lady '67
Portrait of a Lady '96▶
The Power of One '92
The Prodigal '83
Promised Land '88▶
Prozac Nation '01
Purgatory House '04
Quadrophenia '79▶
Quinceanera '06▶
Racing with the Moon '84▶
Rain '01
Raise Your Voice '04
Rambling Rose '91▶
Ramparts of Clay '68▶
The Rascals '81
The Razor's Edge '46▶
The Razor's Edge '84
Real Women Have Curves '02▶
A Real Young Girl '75
Red Dirt '99
The Red Fury '84
Red Kiss '85
Red Nights '87
The Reivers '69▶
Restless Spirits '99
Reunion '88▶
Ricochet River '98
Ride with the Devil '99
Risky Business '83▶
A River Runs Through It '92▶
The Road from Coorain '02
Roger Dodger '02▶
A Room with a View '86▶
Rudyard Kipling's The Jungle Book '94
Rumble Fish '83▶
A Rumor of Angels '00
The Run of the Country '95▶
Running with Scissors '06
Rushmore '98▶
St. Elmo's Fire '85
Samurai 1: Musashi Miyamoto '55▶
The Sandlot '93▶
Sands of Iwo Jima '49▶
Sarafina! '92▶
Savage Is Loose '74
Say Anything '89▶
Scent of a Woman '92▶
The Scent of Green Papaya '93▶
Schizo '04
Season of Change '94
Secondhand Lions '03▶
A Secret Space '88
Secrets '82
A Separate Peace '73
A Separate Peace '04
Set Me Free '99
Seven Minutes in Heaven '86
Shaking the Tree '92
Sharma & Beyond '84
She's Out of Control '89
Shipwrecked '90
Shout '91
Showgirls '95
Side Show '81
The Silence of Neto '94
The Silences of the Palace '94▶
Simon Birch '98
Sisterhood of the Traveling Pants '05
Sixteen '72
Skipped Parts '00
The Slingshot '93▶
Slums of Beverly Hills '98▶
Small Faces '95▶
Smile '05

Smooth Talk '85▶
Snow: The Movie '03
Soldier of Orange '78▶
A Soldier's Daughter Never Cries '98
Soldiers of Change '06
Some Kind of Wonderful '87
Somersault '04
Sons of Steel '35
Sounder '72▶
Sous Sol '96
SpaceCamp '86
Spanking the Monkey '94▶
Spring, Summer, Fall, Winter... and Spring '03▶
Spy of Napoleon '36
Square Dance '87
The Squid and the Whale '05▶
Stacking '87
Star Wars '77▶
Star Wars: Episode 1—The Phantom Menace '99▶
Starlight Hotel '90
The Stripper '63
Stuckey's Last Stand '80
Studs Lonigan '60
Summer Affair '79
Summer Fantasy '84
Summer Holiday '48
Summer Interlude '50▶
Summer of '42 '71▶
Summer Vacation: 1999 '88
Summer's End '99
Sunnyside '79
Sweet 15 '90
Swimming '00
Swing Kids '93
The Sword in the Stone '63▶
Teenage Mutant Ninja Turtles 2: The Secret of the Ooze '91
Telling Lies in America '96
Tex '82
That Brennan Girl '46
That Naughty Girl '58
That Night '93
That Was Then... This Is Now '85
There Goes My Baby '92
36 Fillete '88▶
This Boy's Life '93▶
This Is England '06
Those Glory, Glory Days '83
Thumbsucker '05▶
Thunder Alley '85
A Tiger's Tale '87
Time of the Gypsies '90▶
Time Stands Still '82▶
A Time to Remember '87
Toby Tyler '59▶
The Tollbooth '04
Tomboy & the Champ '58
Tonio Kroger '65
Top Gun '86
Totally F***'ed Up '94
A Tree Grows in Brooklyn '45▶
Tumbleweeds '98
Twenty-One '91
Twist & Shout '84▶
Two Bits '96
Two Daughters '61▶
Undertow '04
Unstrung Heroes '95
Vision Quest '85
Wah-Wah '05
Walking and Talking '96
Wanderers '79▶
West Beirut '98
Whale Rider '02▶
What About Your Friends: Weekend Getaway '02
Whatever '98
What's Eating Gilbert Grape '93▶
Where the Red Fern Grows: Part 2 '92
White Oleander '02
Who Has Seen the Wind? '77
Who Shot Pat? '92
Whole New Thing '05
Why Shoot the Teacher '79▶
Wide Awake '97
Wild America '97▶

The Wild Child '70▶
Wild Reeds '94▶
Wild Tigers I Have Known '06
Winner Takes All '84
The Wishing Ring '14▶
With Honors '94
Wonder Boys '00▶
Wrestling with Alligators '98
Y Tu Mama Tambien '01
The Year My Voice Broke '87▶
The Yearling '46▶
The Yearling '94
The Young and the Guilty '58
The Young Graduates '71
Young Guns 2 '90
Young Love, First Love '79
Young Sherlock Holmes '85
Youngblood '86
You're a Big Boy Now '66▶
Zapped! '82
Zoe '01

Communists & Communism

see also Cold War Spies; Red Scare; Russia/USSR

Balzac and the Little Chinese Seamstress '02
Black Peter '63
Cambridge Spies '03
Dark Blue World '01
Frida '02
Good Bye, Lenin! '03▶
The Great Water '04
Indiana Jones and the Kingdom of the Crystal Skull '08
Innocent Voices '04
Land and Freedom '95▶
The Lost City '05
Reds '81▶
S21: The Khmer Rouge Killing Machine '03▶
The Seventh Dawn '64
Stalin '92
The Tunnel '01▶

Computers

see also Robots & Androids; Technology—Rampant

Agatha Christie's Murder is Easy '82
Alchemy '05
Alien '79▶
Antitrust '00
Big Momma's House 2 '06
Blast '04
The Computer Wore Tennis Shoes '69
Conceiving Ada '97
Copycat '95
Cyberstalker '96
Dangerous Game '90
Dean Koontz's Black River '01
Dee Snider's Strangeland '98
Demon Seed '77▶
Desk Set '57▶
Dopamine '03
The Double O Kid '92
The Dying Gaul '05▶
Electric Dreams '84
Entrapment '99
Every Mother's Worst Fear '98
Evilspeak '82
Fair Game '95
The First $20 Million is Always the Hardest '02
Hackers '95
Hard Drive '94
Homewrecker '92
The Honeymoon Machine '61
Hostile Intent '97
How to Make a Monster '01
The Human Factor '75
Interface '84
Johnny Mnemonic '95
Jumpin' Jack Flash '86

▶ = rated three bones or higher

Jurassic Park '93▶
The Lawnmower Man '92▶
Lawnmower Man 2: Beyond Cyberspace '96
The Matrix '99▶
Live Free or Die Hard '07▶
The Matrix Reloaded '03
Menno's Mind '96
Mission: Impossible '96▶
Mission: Impossible 2 '00▶
The Net '95▶
The Net 2.0 '06
New Games '03
New World Disorder '99
Nirvana '97
Office Space '98
Pi '98▶
The Pirates of Silicon Valley '99
Prime Risk '84
Pulse '01
Resident Evil '02
Revenge of the Nerds '84
The Scorpio Factor '90
Silicon Towers '99
Sneakers '92
Stealing Candy '04
Superman '83
Superman 3 '83
Terminal Error '02
This Thing of Ours '03
Thomas in Love '01
Tin Man '83
Tom Clancy's Netforce '98
Twilight Man '96
Virtual Assassin '95
Virtual Desire '95
WarGames '83
Weird Science '85
Y2K '99
You've Got Mail '98

Concentration/Interment Camps

see also Nazis & Other Paramilitary Slugs; POW/MIA;

Army of Shadows '69▶
Bent '97
The Boxer and Death '63▶
Come See the Paradise '90▶
The Counterfeiters '07▶
The Devil's Arithmetic '99
Fateless '05▶
Forced March '90
The Girl of Your Dreams '99
The Great Raid '05
The Great Water '04
Green Dragon '01
The Grey Zone '01
The Hiding Place '75
Holocaust '78▶
I Am David '04
I Love You, I Love You Not '97
Landscape After Battle '70
The Last Butterfly '92
Life is Beautiful '98▶
Merry Christmas, Mr. Lawrence '83▶
The Ninth Day '04
One Day in the Life of Ivan Denisovich '71
Paradise Road '97
Playing for Time '80
Red Dawn '84
The Road to Guantanamo '06
S21: The Khmer Rouge Killing Machine '03
Schindler's List '93▶
Seven Beauties '76▶
The Siege '98
Snow Falling on Cedars '99
Sophie's Choice '82
A Town Like Alice '85
Triumph of the Spirit '89
The Truce '96
The Verdict on Auschwitz: The Frankfurt Auschwitz Trial 1963–1965 '93▶

Lighting in a Bottle '04
Lenny '74
Magic '05
Mr. Mike's Mondo Video '79
Monster in a Box '92
Monterey Pop '68▶
National Lampoon's Class of '86 '86
Neil Young: Heart of Gold '06
Punchline '88
Queens of Comedy '01
Sarah Silverman: Jesus is Magic '05
Search for S'gns of Intelligent Life in the Universe '91
The Secret Policeman's Other Ball '82
The Secret Policeman's Private Parts '81
Sex, Drugs, Rock & Roll: Eric Bogosian '91
Spalding Gray: Terrors of Pleasure '88
Stop Making Sense '84▶
U2: Rattle and Hum '88
Vince Vaughn's Wild West Comedy Show '06
Wisecracks '93
Woodstock '70▶
Woodstock '94 '94
Year of the Horse '97
You Can't Take it with You '84
You So Crazy '94

Concert Films

see also Rock Stars on Film

The Aristocrats '05▶
Awesome! I F***in' Shot That! '06
Buena Vista Social Club '99▶
Calling '86
Cherry Crush '07
Dave Chappelle's Block Party '06▶
Fade to Black '04▶
Festival Express '03▶
Gimme Shelter '70▶
The Jimmy Show '01
JoJo Dancer, Your Life is Calling '86
John Cleese on How to Irritate People '68
The Last Waltz '78▶

Contemporary Musicals

see also Musicals

Absolute Beginners '86
All That Jazz '79▶
The Apple '80
Blame it on the Night '84
Body Beat '88
Breakin' '84
Breakin' 2: Electric Boogaloo '84
Breakin' Through '84
Breaking Glass '80
A Chorus Line '85
Fame '80
The Josephine Baker Story '90
One from the Heart '82
A Prairie Home Companion '06
Rent '05
State Property 2 '05
Susno '05

Contemporary Noir

see also Film Noir

After Dark, My Sweet '90
After Hours '85▶
Against All Odds '84
The American Friend '77
Blade Runner '82▶
Blood Simple '85▶
Blue Velvet '86▶
Bodies, Rest & Motion '93
Body Double '84
Body Heat '81▶
Brick '06▶
Bring Me the Head of Alfredo Garcia '74▶
Bringing Out the Dead '99
Bulletproof Heart '95▶
Cape Fear '91
Chinatown '74▶
Choose Me '84▶
City of Industry '96
Croupier '97▶
The Crude Oasis '95
Curter's Way '81
Dance with a Stranger '85▶
Dark City '97▶
Deceiver '97
Deepwater '05
Devil in a Blue Dress '95▶
D.O.A. '88
Dogwatch '97
Dressed to Kill '80
The Driver '78
The Embalmer '03
Eyes of Laura Mars '78
Experiment in Terror '62
Fatal Attraction '87
52 Pick-Up '86
First Degree '95
Flypaper '97
Forever Mine '99
Following '99
The Girl in a Swing '89
Goodbye, Lover '99
The Grifters '90▶
Guncrazy '92
Hammett '82
Hard Eight '96▶
The Hi-Lo Country '98
Hit Me '96
Hollywoodland '06
The Horseplayer '91
The Hot Spot '90
Husbands and Lovers '91
The Hustle '75
I Want You '98
Inevitable Grace '94
Jigsaw '99
Kill Me Again '89
The Kill-Off '90
Killing Zoe '94
Kiss Tomorrow Goodbye '00
L.A. Confidential '97▶
The Last Seduction '94▶
Le Cercle Rouge '70▶
Le Samourai '67▶
Let the Devil Wear Black '99
Lights in the Dusk '06
The Limey '99▶
Live Flesh '97
The Locusts '97
The Long Goodbye '73▶
The Lookout '07▶
Love Walked In '97
The Manchurian Candidate '62▶
Marlowe '69
Manhunter '86
The Million Dollar Hotel '99
Mirage '94
Mulholland Falls '95
The Music of Chance '93
Narrow Margin '90
Night Moves '75
9 1/2 Weeks '86
No Good Deed '02
No Way Out '87
Novocaine '01
One False Move '91
Palmetto '98
Payback '98
Performance '70
Place Vendome '98
Promised Land '88
The Public Eye '92
Pulp Fiction '94▶
Purple Noon '60
Red Rock West '93▶
Reservoir Dogs '92▶
The Rich Man's Wife '96
River of Grass '94
Romeo is Bleeding '93
The Salton Sea '02
sex, lies and videotape '89▶
Shattered '91
The Silence of the Lambs '91▶
Simpatico '99
Sin City '05▶
A Slight Case of Murder '99
So Close to Paradise '98
Something Wild '86
The Spanish Prisoner '97▶
Spare Me '92
Stormy Monday '88
Sticks '98
Taxi Driver '76▶
Tequila Sunrise '88
Things to Do in Denver When You're Dead '95
This World, Then the Fireworks '97
To Live & Die in L.A. '85▶
Track 29 '88
Trouble in Mind '86
True Believer '89
True Confessions '81
Twilight '98
Two Days in the Valley '96
The Two Jakes '90
U-Turn '97
The Underneath '95
Union City '81
The Usual Suspects '95▶
The Walker '07
Where the Truth Lies '05
Where Will I Be Loved '04
Who'll Stop the Rain? '78▶
Wild at Heart '90▶
Wild Orchid '90
Wild Orchid 2: Two Shades of Blue '92
Wild Things '98
You Kill Me '07

Cooking

see also Chefs; Edibles

Cops

see also Alien Cops; Biopics: Cops & Law Enforcers; Buddy Cops; Comic Cops; DEA; FBI; Future Cops; Historical Detectives; Loner Cops; Police Detectives; Private Eyes; Rogue Cops; Small-Town Sheriffs; Undercover Cops; Women Cops;

Abraxas: Guardian of the Universe '90
Absence of the Good '99
Across 110th Street '72
Across the Line '00
Adrenalin: Fear the Rush '96
The Adventures of a Gnome Named Gnorm '93
Affliction '97▶
Against the Law '98
Alien Nation '88
Alone in the Neon Jungle '87
American Cop '94
American Gangster '07▶
American Justice '86
The Amsterdam Kill '78
Angel Eyes '01
Animal Instincts '92
Antibodies '05
Apartment Complex '98
Assault on Precinct 13 '76▶
At Gunpoint '90
Back in Action '94
Backlash '99
Backstreet Justice '93
Badge 373 '73
Ballbuster '89
Band of the Hand '86
Bandits '99
Bang '95
Before Morning '33
Belfast Assassin '84
Bellamy '80
Beretta's Island '92
Best Kept Secrets '88
Best Seller '87
Beverly Hills Cop '84▶
Beverly Hills Cop 2 '87
Beverly Hills Cop 3 '94
Beyond Forgiveness '94
Big Chase '54
Big Combo '55▶
The Big Easy '87▶
Big Score '83
Bitter Sweet '98
Blade '72
Blade Boxer '97
Blind Faith '98
Blood for Blood '95
Blood on the Badge '92
Blood Relatives '77
Bodily Harm '95
Blue Flame '93
Blue Lamp '49
Blue Thunder '83▶
Blown Away '94
Blowback '99
Bloodfist 7: Manhunt '95
Bloodhounds '96
Bloodlines '05
Bophal '93
Border Blues '03
Border Patrol '01
The Boston Strangler '68▶
Brainscan '94
Brannigan '75
Brass '85
Breach of Trust '95
Breaking Point '94
Broken Badge '85
Bullet Down Under '94
Bulletproof '96
Bunco '77
Busting '74
Cafe Society '97
Captive '97
Carmen, Baby '66
Caroline at Midnight '93
The Carpathian Eagle '81
Carpool '96
A Case of Deadly Force '86
The Caveman's Valentine '96
Cement '99
The Chase '66
The Chase '91
Chiefs '83
Children of Hannibal '98
China Moon '91
The Chinatown Murders: Man against the Mob '89
Chinatown Connection '90
The Choirboys '77
Chungking Express '95▶
City Hall '95
City That Never Sleeps '53
Clayton County Line '78
Clockers '95
Cobra '86
Cold Blooded '00
Cold Front '89
Cold Light of Day '95
Cold Steel '87
Coldfire '90
Colors '88▶
Confessions of a Police Captain '72
Conflict of Interest '92
Coogan's Bluff '68▶
Cop '88
Cop and a Half '93
Cop-Out '91
Cops and Robbersons '94
Cornbread, Earl & Me '75
Cotton Comes to Harlem '70▶
Cover Me '95
Cover Up '84
Cracker: Best Boys '95
Cracker: Brotherly Love '95
Cracker: Men Should Weep '94
Cracker: To Be a Somebody '94
Cracker: True Romance '95
Crime Busters '78
Crime Story '86▶
The Crimson Rivers '71
The Crow '93▶
The Custodian '94
Danger Ahead '40
The Dark '94
Dark Before Dawn '89
Dark City '97
Dead Badge '94
Dead End '98
Dead Heat '88
Dead Heat '96
Dead to Rights '93
Deadly Conspiracy '9?
Deadly Diamonds '91
Deadly Hero '76
Deadly Sins '95
Deadly Surveillance '91
Death Shot '73
The Death Squad '73
Deceiver '97
Deceptions '90
Deep Cover '92▶
Deep Space '87
The Delicate Delinquent '56
Delta Heat '92
Demolition Man '93
The Designated Mourner '97
Detroit 9000 '73
Devil in a Blue Dress '95
The Devil's Angels '67
The Devil's Own '96
The Devil's Undead '75
Devlin '92
Dirty Mind of Young Sally '72
Distant Justice '92
Diva '82▶
Dog Bite Dog '06
Dolman '90
Dollman vs Demonic Toys '93
Double Cover '9?
Double Edge '97
Double Take '97
Double Trouble '91
Drowning Mona '00
Drying Up the Streets '76
Dying Gaze '94
East Palace, West Palace '96
Edison Force '05
Electra Glide in Blue '73▶
Evil Has a Face '96
Ex-Cop '93
Exorcist 3: Legion '90
Extreme Justice '93
Extreme Prejudice '87
Extreme Vengeance '90
An Eye for an Eye '81
Eyes of Laura Mars '78
Eyewitness '81
Eyewitness to Murder '93
Faith '01
Fallen '97
Family of Cops '95
Family of Cops 2: Breach of Faith '97
Family of Cops 3 '98
The Fast and the Furious '01
Fatal Chase '77
Fatal Chase '82
Fatal Error '83
Fatal Instinct '92
Felony '95
The Female Jungle '56
Fever '88
Fever '99
Final Combination '93
Final Embrace '92
Final Equinox '95
Firepower '93
Fireworks '97

Cops

First Degree '95
Flashpoint '84
Flatfoot '78
Flipping '96
The Formula '80
Fort Apache, the Bronx '81♦
Fortune Dane '86
44 Minutes: The North Hollywood Shootout '03
Foul Play '76
Frame by Frame '95
Frame Up '91
The French Connection '71♦
French Connection 2 '75♦
French Quarter Undercover '85
French Silk '94
Frequency '00
From Dusk Till Dawn 2: Texas Blood Money '98
Full Count '06
Full Eclipse '93
Full Exposure: The Sex Tape Scandals '89
Future Cop '76
Future Force '89
Fuzz '72
Gang in Blue '96
Gen-X Cops '99
Get On the Bus '96♦
The Glass Shield '95
The Glitter Dome '84
Glitz '88
Go '99♦
Go for It '83
Gone Are the Days '84
The Good Thief '03♦
Goodbye, Lover '99
Gorky Park '83♦
Guilty by Association '03
Hands of a Stranger '87
The Happy Face Murders '99
Hard Justice '95
The Hard Truth '94
Hard Vice '94
Hardcase and Fist '89
Hate '95♦
Hawkeye '88
He Walked by Night '48♦
Hear No Evil '93
Heart of Dragon '85
Hellbound '94
Heroes in Blue '39
High & Low '62♦
High Crime '73
Highway Patrolman '91
Hollywood Vice Sqaud '86
Hologram Man '95
Homicide '91♦
Homicide: The Movie '00
The Hot Rock '70♦
Humanity '99
The Hunted Lady '77
I Take This Oath '40
The Ice House '97♦
Illegal in Blue '95
Illtown '96
In the Kingdom of the Blind the Man with One Eye Is King '94
Indecent Behavior '93
The Indian Runner '91
Indiscreet '98
The Informant '97♦
Innocent Blood '92
The Innocent Sleep '95
Inside Information '34
Interpol Connection '92
It Could Happen to You '94
It's the Rage '99
Jackie Brown '97♦
Jailbait '93
The January Man '89
Jennifer 8 '92
Jigsaw '71
John Carpenter's Ghosts of Mars '01
Johnny Skidmarks '97
Jumanji '95
Jungleground '95
Just Cause '94
K-911 '99
K-9000 '89
Kamikaze 89 '83♦
Karate Cop '91
Keaton's Cop '90
Keeper of the City '92
Kidnapped '87
The Kill Reflex '89
Killer Condom '95
The Killer's Edge '90
The Killing Mind '90
The Killing Time '87
Killing Time '99
Kiss and Tell '96
Kiss & Tell '99
Kiss of Death '47♦
Kiss or Kill '97
The Klansman '74
Knife in the Head '78
Kuffs '92
L.627 '92♦
L.A. Bounty '89
L.A. Heat '88
L.A. Vice '89
L.A. Wars '94
Ladykiller '92
Laguna Heat '87
Laser Moon '92
Last Man Standing '95
The Last Marshal '99
The Last of the Finest '90
The Last Stop '99
The Laughing Policeman '74
Law and Disorder '74♦
Legacy of Lies '92
Les Miserables '95
Les Miserables '97♦
Les Voleurs '96♦
Lethal Obsession '87
Lethal Seduction '97
Lightblast '85
Like a Puppet Out of Strings '05
The Limbic Region '96
The Lives of Others '06♦
Lockdown '90
Lone Star Law Men '42
Love '05
Love on the Run '85
Love the Hard Way '01
Mad Dog and Glory '93♦
Mad Max '80♦
Madigan '68♦
Magic Hunter '96
Magnolia '99♦
Malarek '89
Man from Mallorca '84
A Man in Uniform '93
The Man Inside '76
Man on a String '71
The Man on the Roof '76
Mardi Gras for the Devil '93
Martial Law '90
Martial Law 2: Undercover '91
Mask of Death '97
Matter of Trust '98
Maximum Force '92
The Memory of a Killer '03
Miami Beach Cops '93
Miami Blues '90
Miami Cops '89
Miami Vice '84
Midnight Ride '92
Midnight Witness '93
Mimic 2 '01
A Mind to Kill '95
Mind Twister '93
Mission of Justice '92
Mr. Inside, Mr. Outside '74
Mr. Reliable: A True Story '95
Mistrial '96
Mitchell '75
Model by Day '94
Money to Burn '94
Monolith '93
Moonshine Highway '96
Mortal Challenge '97
Mosquitoman '05
Moving Violations '85
The Murder of Stephen Lawrence '99♦
Murder Without Motive '92
Murdered Innocence '94
My Husband's Secret Life '98
Mystery Date '91
Nails '92
The Naked City '48♦
The Narrow Margin '52♦
The New Centurions '72
New Jack City '91
New Police Story '04
New York Cop '94
New York Ripper '82
Next of Kin '89
Night Game '89
Night of the Cyclone '90
Night Partners '83
The Night Patrol '26
Night Patrol '85
Night Vision '97
Nightmare '91
Nightstalker '02
Ninja Vengeance '93
No Code of Conduct '98
No Escape, No Return '93
No Good Deed '02
No Place to Hide '93
Octopus 2: River of Fear '02
Off the Wall '82
The Offence '73♦
One Man Force '89
One Man Jury '78
One Tough Cop '98
Organized Crime & Triad Bureau '93
Othello '01♦
Out in Fifty '99
Outside the Law '95
The Painted Lady '97♦
Pair of Aces '90
Paper Bullets '99
Past Perfect '98
Past Tense '94
Pendulum '69
Phoenix '98
P.I. Private Investigations '87
Picture Snatcher '33
Piece of the Action '77
Point of Impact '93
Police '85
Portraits of a Killer '95
Post Mortem '99
Prime Target '91
Prince of the City '81♦
Private Investigations '87
Probable Cause '95
Profile for Murder '96
Pronto '97
The Prophecy '95
The Proposal '00
Provoked '89
Prowler '51
Puppet on a Chain '72
A Pure Formality '94♦
Q & A '90
The Quarry '98
Question of Honor '80
Rage and Honor 2: Hostile Takeover '93
Rainbow Drive '90
Random Hearts '99
Rapid Fire '92
Raw Nerve '99
Raw Target '95
The Razor: Sword of Justice '72
Reach the Rock '98
Recruits '86
Red Sun Rising '94
Regular Guys '96
Renaissance '06
Renfrew of the Royal Mounted '37
The Replacement Killers '98
Replicant '01
Return to Macon County '75
Return to Mayberry '85
The Right to Remain Silent '95
Riot in the Streets '96
Rising Sun '93♦
The Road '00
Rock House '88
Rogue Force '99
Roots of Evil '91
Route 9 '98
Rumble in the Streets '96
Runaway '84
The Runaway '00
Running Scared '86
The Rutherford County Line '87
Sands of Sacrifice '21
Santa Fe '97
The Satan Killer '93
Saw 4 '07
Sawbones '95
Scanner Cop '94
Scanner Cop 2: Volkin's Revenge '94
Scanners: The Showdown '94
Scarred City '98
Sci-Fighters '96
Scream 3 '00
Season for Assassins '71
Self-Defense '83
Sgt. Kabukiman N.Y.P.D. '91
Serial Killer '95
Seven Seconds '05
Shadow Force '92
Shadow of a Scream '97
Shadowhunter '93
Shameless '94
Sharon's Secret '95
Shoot It Black, Shoot It Blue '74
Shoot to Kill '90
Shootfighter 2: Kill or Be Killed! '96
Short Time '90♦
The Shot '96
Sirens '02
Sirens '94
Siringo '94
Sketch Artist '92
Sketch Artist 2: Hands That See '94
Skins '02
Skull: A Night of Terror '88
Slipstream '89
Slow Burn '00
A Small Killing '81
Smokey & the Judge '80
Snake Eyes '98
Snapdragon '93
Soggy Bottom U.S.A. '84
Solar Force '94
Son of the Pink Panther '93
Soul Patrol '80
Speed 2: Cruise Control '97
Speedtrap '78
Stamp of a Killer '87
Steele's Law '91
The Stendahl Syndrome '95
Stephano Quantestorie '93
The Stone Killer '73
Stonewall '75
Stop! or My Mom Will Shoot '92
Strange Days '95♦
Stranger by Night '94
Street Asylum '90
Street Crimes '92
Street Kings '08
Street War '76
Strike Force '75
Strip Search '97
Super Fuzz '81
Supercop '92
Supercop 2 '93
Supervixens '75
Suspicious Agenda '94
S.W.A.T. '03
Sweet Trash '70
Sword of Honor '94
T-Force '94
The Take '90
Taking the Heat '93
Tar '97
The Taxman '60♦
Terminal Justice: Cybertech P.D. '95
Terror Stalks the Class Reunion '93
Theodore Rex '95
They Crawl '01
They Only Kill Their Masters '72
Three Blind Mice '02
Three Strikes '00
Tightrope '84
Till Death Do Us Part '92
A Time to Die '91
Timecop '94
Timecop 2: The Berlin Decision '03
To Protect and Serve '92
Too Fast, Too Young '96
Top of the Heap '72
Total Recall 2070: Machine Dreams '99
Traces of Red '92
Trancers '84
Trancers 2: The Return of Jack Deth '91
Trancers 3: Deth Lives '92
Trancers 4: Jack of Swords '93
Trancers 5: Sudden Deth '94
Truth or Consequences, N.M. '97
Tunnel Vision '95
Twin Sisters '91
Twisted Justice '89
Two Days in the Valley '96♦
Two Small Bodies '93
Ultraviolet '98
Under Investigation '93
Under Oath '97
Undercover '87
Undercover '94
Undercover Cop '94
The Underground '97
Underground Terror '88
Unforgettable '96
Union Station '50
The Untold Story '93
Urban Crossfire '94
Vampire Cop '90
Vampire in Brooklyn '95
Vegas Vice '94
Vengeance '37
Vice Academy '88
Vice Academy 2 '90
Vice Academy 3 '91
Virtuosity '95
Walker: Texas Ranger: One Riot, One Ranger '93
The Warning '80
We Own the Night '07
The Wharf Rat '95
When Danger Follows You Home '97
Where's the Money, Noreen? '95
Whispers of White '93
White Cargo '96
The White Lioness '96
The Wicker Man '06
The Wild Pair '87
Witchcraft 6: The Devil's Mistress '94
The Young Americans '93
Youth of the Beast '63
Zipperface '92

Corporate Shenanigans

see also Advertising; Dying for a Promotion; Salespeople; Workin' for a Livin'

The Abduction of Allison Tate '97
Ablaze '00
Acceptable Risks '86
The Alarmist '99
The Alchemists '99
All in a Night's Work '61
All My Sons '48♦
All My Sons '86♦
And Nothing But the Truth '82
Antitrust '00
Any Wednesday '66
The Apartment '60♦
April Fools '69
As Young As You Feel '51♦
Ask Any Girl '59
The Associate '96
The Associate '79
Avalanche '99
Baby Geniuses '98
Bad Company '94
The Bad Sleep Well '60♦
The Bank '01
Barbarians at the Gate '93♦
Barbershop 2: Back in Business '04♦
BASEketball '98
The Battle of the Sexes '60♦
Beggars in Ermine '34
The Best of Everything '59♦
The Bible and Gun Club '96
Big Business '88
Big Business Girl '31
The Big One '98
Big Trees '52♦
The Bikini Car Wash Company '90
The Bikini Car Wash Company 2 '92
Blonde Ambition '07
Blood Red '88
Body & Soul '93♦
Body Language '92
Boiler Room '00♦
Bombshell '97
Boom Town '40
Boomerang '92
The Boss of It All '06
Boys Will Be Boys '97
Burning Daylight '28
The Business of Strangers '01
Buy & Cell '89
The Capture of Bigfoot '79
The Carpetbaggers '64
Cash McCall '60
Catherine & Co. '76
Catwoman '04
Chairman of the Board '97
Changing Lanes '02♦
The China Syndrome '79♦
China White '91
C.H.O.M.P.S. '79
Circle of Power '83
A Civil Action '98
Class of Nuke 'Em High 2: Subhumanoid Meltdown '91
Clockwatchers '97
The Closet '00
The Coca-Cola Kid '84♦
Cold Turkey '71♦
The Colombian Connection '91
The Colony '95
Comedy of Power '06
Comic Book: The Movie '04♦
Consuming Passions '88
Corporate Affairs '90
Corporate Affairs '07
The Corporate Ladder '97
The Corporation '96
Crime of Honor '85
The Crime of Monsieur Lange '36♦
Cyborg 2 '93
Cypher '02♦
Dark River: A Father's Revenge '90
The Daydreamer '75
Deadlier Than the Male '67
Deadly Business '86♦
Deadly Conspiracy '91
Dealers '89
Death Chase '87
Death Collector '89
Death Machine '95
Demonlover '02
The Devil & Miss Jones '41♦
The Devil's Advocate '97
Devil's Crude '71
Disclosure '94
Dr. Dolittle '98
Dodsworth '36♦
Double Play '96
Dragonfight '90
Dutch Treat '86
Ebbtide '94
The Efficiency Expert '92
Empire '02
Empire Records '95
Fast Food Nation '06♦
Fatal Confinement '64
Fatal Skies '90
Feel the Motion '86
Fierce Creatures '96
Fire Down Below '97
Firetrap '01
First Degree '98
The First $20 Million is Always the Hardest '02
The Flintstones '94

♦ = rated three bones or higher

FM '78
For Love or Money '93
Ford: The Man & the Machine '87
Forest Warrior '95
Freaked '93
Frozen Assets '92
Gas '81
Gas Pump Girls '79
Glengarry Glen Ross '92 ▶
Good Burger '97
Good Neighbor Sam '64 ▶
Goodfellas '90 ▶
Gorgeous '99
Gremlins 2: The New Batch '90 ▶
Gung Ho '85
Hackers '95
Haiku Tunnel '00
Hamlet '00 ▶
Happy Hour '87
The Harder They Come '72 ▶
Head Office '86
Her Husband's Affairs '47
Herbie Rides Again '74
Hey Arnold! The Movie '02
His Girl Friday '40 ▶
Hold the Dream '86
Home Town Story '51
Hot '06
Hot Chocolate '92
How the West Was Fun '95
How to Get Ahead in Advertising '89 ▶
How to Succeed in Business without Really Trying '67 ▶
The Hucksters '47 ▶
The Hudsucker Proxy '93 ▶
I Love Huckabees '04 ▶
Heart Candy '96
A Kiss Before Dying '91
La Truite '83 ▶
Ladies Who Do '63
Land of Promise '74
Let the Devil Wear Black '99
Letter to My Killer '95
Life Stinks '91
Limit Up '89
The Listening '06
Little Bigfoot '96
Little Giant '46
Lloyds of London '35 ▶
Local Hero '83 ▶
The Loved One '65 ▶
Ma and Pa Kettle at Waikiki '55
Major League '89
Mama, There's a Man in Your Bed '89 ▶
The Man in the Gray Flannel Suit '56
The Man in the White Suit '51 ▶
The Man Inside '90

I Witness '03
Ivory Tower '97
Johnny Mnemonic '95
Journey to Spirit Island '92
Jack and the Beanstalk: The Real Story '01
Janice Beard '99
Joe Somebody '01
John Grisham's The Rainmaker '97
The Lavender Hill Mob '51 ▶
Lawnmower Man 2: Beyond Cyberspace '95
Le Bonheur Est Dans le Pre '95
Legal Deceit '95
Les Destinees '00
If I Were Rich '33
In Good Company '04 ▶
In the Company o' Men '96
Indio 2: The Revolt '92
The Inheritance '03
I Love Trouble '94
Meet Joe Black '98
Megaville '91
Memron '04
Michael Clayton '07 ▶
Millions '04 ▶
Miss Grant Takes Richmond '49
Missionary Man '07
Mr. Accident '99
Mr. Destiny '90
Mo' Money '92
Monkey Hustle '77
Monsters, Inc. '01 ▶
Moon 44 '90
Morals for Women '31
Naked Gun 2 1/2: The Smell of Fear '91
Network '76 ▶
Never 2 Big '98
New Rose Hotel '98
Night of January 16th '41
Nine to Five '80
No Marriage Ties '33
No Room to Run '78
No Time to Die '84
Noble House '88
Nowhere to Run '93
Office Killer '97
Office Space '98
Oktober '98
One, Two, Three '61 ▶
Open Season '95
The Other Side of Midnight '77
Out Cold '01
Outfoxed: Rupert Murdoch's War on Journalism '04 ▶
Outland '81
Other People's Money '91
Overdrawn at the Memory Bank '83
The Pajama Game '57 ▶
The Paper '94 ▶
Parrish '61
Patterns '55
Paycheck '03
Perfume '01
The Pirates of Silicon Valley '99
Playback '95
The Player '92 ▶
Pootie Tang '01
Power '86
Primal Scream '87
The Prime Gig '00
The Prince '96
Private Parts '96
Private Wars '93
A Public Affair '62
P.U.N.K.S. '98
Purpose '02
Putney Swope '69 ▶
The Queen of Mean '90
Quicksand '01
Quicksand: No Escape '91
Race the Sun '96
Rancid Aluminium '00
Ravenhawk '95
The Reluctant Agent '95
Return Fire '91
Richie Rich '94
Rick '03
Rising Sun '93 ▶
RoboCop '87 ▶
RoboCop 2 '90
RoboCop 3 '91
Robots '05
Roger & Me '89 ▶
Rogue Trader '98
Rollover '81
Sabrina '95
Sahara '95
Santa with Muscles '96
Scrooged '88
The Secret of My Success '87
The Secretary '94 ▶
Secretary '02 ▶
The Manchurian Candidate '04 ▶
Married to It '53
Material Girls '06
A Matter of WHO '62
Maxed Out: Hard Times, Easy Credit, and the Era of Predatory Lenders '06

Sensations of 1945 '44
Shadow of China '91 ▶
The Shawshank Redemption '94 ▶
She Hate Me '04
Shining Star '75
A Shock to the System '90 ▶
Side Effects '05
Silicon Towers '99
The Silver Horse '30
The Simple Life of Noah Dearborn '99
Sing Me a Love Song '37
Sins '85
The 6th Day '00
Ski Bum '75
Skyscraper Souls '32 ▶
Smilla's Sense of Snow '96
Solid Gold Cadillac '56 ▶
Soul Assassin '01
The Spanish Prisoner '97 ▶
Stand-in '37 ▶
The State Within '06
Stormy Monday '88
The Story of O, Part 2 '87
Strange Bedfellows '65
Strange Brew '83
Strange Confession '45 ▶
The Strongest Man in the World '75
Sunshine State '02 ▶
Switching Channels '88
Switching with Sharks '94 ▶
Synapse '95
Taffin '88
Take This Job & Shove It '81
A Taxing Woman '87 ▶
The Temp '93
There Will Be Blood '07 ▶
They All Kissed the Bride '42
They Drive by Night '40 ▶
3 Ninjas Knuckle Up '95
Tiger Heart '96
Tin Men '87
Tommy Boy '95
Topaze '33 ▶
Topaze '51 ▶
The Toxic Avenger, Part 3: The Last Temptation of Toxie '89
Toys '92
Trading Places '83 ▶
Tucker: The Man and His Dream '88 ▶
The TV Set '06
Two Weeks Notice '02
Undercurrent '46
The Uppercrust '81
Utilities '83
Vendetta '99
Virus '96
The Void '01
Vortex '81
Wal-Mart: The High Cost of Low Price '05 ▶
Wall Street '87 ▶
Wall Street Cowboy '39
Washington Affair '77
The Way We Live Now '02
Weapons of Mass Distraction '97
Weekend at Bernie's '89
Weekend at Bernie's 2 '93
The Wheeler Dealers '63 ▶
Which Way Is Up? '77
White Mile '94
Who Killed the Electric Car? '06
Who's Who '78
Wilder '00
Wolf '94
A Woman's World '54 ▶
Working Girl '88 ▶
The World Gone Mad '33
The World Moves On '34
The Wrong Woman '95
You've Got Mail '98

Courtroom Drama

see also Aunts & Uncles;
Brothers & Nephews;
Family Ties

see Law & Lawyers;
Order in the Court

Cousins

Niece's & Nephews;

ABC Stage 67: Truman Capote's A Christmas Memory '66
The Addams Family '91
The Age of Innocence '93 ▶
Airborne '93
Almost Strangers '01 ▶
American Cousins '02
American Pie Presents: Beta House '07
Arsenic and Old Lace '44 ▶
Barbershop 2: Back in Business '04 ▶
Barcelona '94 ▶
Black Magic '92
Blanche Fury '48
Blood & Chocolate '07
Body Count '87
Born to Be Bad '50 ▶
Brighton Beach Memoirs '86
Bye-Bye '96
Cafe Romeo '91
The Camomile Lawn '92
Catherine Cookson's The Black Candle '92 ▶
Coffee and Cigarettes '03 ▶
Cousin, Cousine '76 ▶
The Cousins '89 ▶
Cousins '89 ▶
Desperate Motives '92
Doctor Zhivago '03
Dreaming About You '92
The Dukes of Hazzard '05
First Love '39
The Four Horsemen of the Apocalypse '21 ▶
The Four Horsemen of the Apocalypse '62
Friday After Next '02
Go for Zucker '05
The Godfather, Part 3 '90 ▶
Going Greek '01
The Good Son '93
Gothic '87 ▶
The Great Outdoors '88
The Groomsmen '06
The Guru '02
A Guy Thing '03
The Heartbreak Kid '07
The Hellfire Club '61
The Hillside Strangler '04
The Hillside Strangler '89
The Importance of Being Earnest '52 ▶
The Importance of Being Earnest '02 ▶
The Interded '02
Jude '96 ▶
Jude the Obscure '71
Kiss of Death '94
Kissin' Cousins '64
Madhouse '90
Mansfield Park '99
Mansfield Park '07
Marvin '00
Men Cry Bullets '00
Miss Firecracker '89 ▶
My American Cousin '85 ▶
My Baby's Daddy '04
My Cousin Vinny '92 ▶
National Lampoon's Christmas Vacation '89 ▶
National Lampoon's Vacation '83 ▶
Next Friday '00 ▶
Nora's Hair Salon 2: A Cut Above '08
On Guard! '03 ▶
One Night at McCool's '01
Phat Girlz '06
The Players Club '98 ▶
The Pope of Greenwich Village '84 ▶
Portrait of a Lady '67
Portrait of a Lady '96 ▶
Prisoner of Zenda '37 ▶

Creepy Houses

The Abandoned '06
An American Werewolf in Paris '97
The Amityville Horror '79
Amityville 2: The Possession '82
Amityville 3: The Demon '83 ▶
Amityville 4: The Evil Escapes '89
The Amityville Curse '90
Amityville Horror '05
Amityville 1992: It's About Time '92 ▶
Anger of the Night '98
The Attic '06
The Bat Whispers '30 ▶
Believe '99
Beneath '07
Beyond Darkness '92
Beyond Evil '80
Black Cat '80
The Black Cat '41
The Black Castle '52
The Black Widow '05
Blondie Has Trouble '40
Blood Island '68
Blood Legacy '73
Blue Blood '73
Bones '01
Burnt Offerings '76
Candles at Nine '44
Carnage '84
Casper '95 ▶
Castle Freak '95
Castle in the Desert '42
Castle of Blood '64
Castle of the Living Dead '64
The Cat and the Canary '79
Celine and Julie Go Boating '74 ▶
The Cellar Dweller '87
The Changeling '80 ▶
Chasing Sleep '00
Chronicle of the Raven '04
Cold Creek Manor '03
The Coicny '95
Contagion '87
The Craft '96 ▶
Crazed '82
Cthulhu Mansion '91
Dark Water '05
Dead Birds '04
A Dead Calling '06
Dead Silence '07
Demon Seed '77 ▶
Demon Wind '90
The Diary of Ellen Rimbauer '03
Die Sister, Die! '74
Dolls '87 ▶
Don't Be Afraid of the Dark '73
The Doorway '00
Dream Demon '88
Dream House '96
Endless Night '71
The Evictors '79
The Evil '78
Evil Laugh '86
Evil Toons '90
The Exorcist '73 ▶
The Fall of the House of Usher '49
The Fall of the House of Usher '60 ▶
Fatally Yours '95
Fear in the Night '47 ▶

Creepy

Rabbit-Proof Fence '02 ▶
Ratas, Ratones, Rateros '99
The Rugrats Movie '98 ▶
The Secret Garden '49 ▶
The Secret Garden '84
The Secret Garden '87 ▶
The Secret Garden '93 ▶
Slums of Beverly Hills '98 ▶
Sour Grapes '98
Stranger than Paradise '84 ▶
Striking Distance '93
Summer of Fear '78
Traveller '96 ▶
Under Capricorn '82 ▶
Vegas Vacation '96
We're No Angels '55
The Yards '00

Flowers in the Attic '87
Forever: A Ghost of a Love Story '92
Francis in the Haunted House '56
Fright House '89
Fright Night '85
Funnyman '94
The Ghastly Ones '68
The Ghost and Mr. Chicken '66 ▶
The Ghost Breakers '40 ▶
Girls School Screamers '86
The Glass House '01
Goblin '93
Great Expectations '97
The Grudge '04
The Grudge 2 '06
Halloween: Resurrection '02
Haunted '95
Home '91
House 4: Home Deadly Home '91
House '86 ▶
House 2: The Second Story '87
The Haunted Mansion '03
The Haunting '63 ▶
The Haunting '99 ▶
The Haunting of Hell House '99
The Heirloom '05
House of Mystery '34
House of 9 '05
House of the Long Shadows '82
House of the Rising Sun '87
House of the Seven Gables '40
The House of the Devil '08
The House of Usher '06
House on Haunted Hill '58
House on Haunted Hill '99
The House on Tombstone Hill '92
The House that Bled to Death '81
The House that Dripped Blood '71
The House that Vanished '73
House Where Evil Dwells '82
The Innocents '61 ▶
Killer Pad '08
Knocking on Death's Door '99
La Chute de la Maison Usher '28 ▶
The Legend of Hell House '73 ▶
Malice '93
The Mephisto Waltz '71 ▶
The Messengers '07
Monster House '06 ▶
Monsters Crash the Pajama Party '65
Mother's Day '80
Mouse Hunt '97 ▶
Munster, Go Home! '66
Murder by Death '76 ▶
Murder Mansion '70
The Nesting '80
Next of Kin '82
Night Nurse '77
Night of the Demons '88
Night of the Demons 2 '94
Office Killer '97
The Old Dark House '32 ▶
The Orphanage '07 ▶
The Others '01 ▶
Panic Room '02 ▶
Paperhouse '89 ▶
Paranoiac '62
The People under the Stairs '91
The Perverse Countess '73
The Phantom '31
Psycho '60 ▶
Psycho '98
Psycho 2 '83
Psycho 3 '86
Psycho 4: The Beginning '90
Rest in Pieces '87

▶ = rated three bones or higher

Creepy

Return to House on Haunted Hill '07
Revenge in the House of Usher '82
The Rocky Horror Picture Show '75
Rooms for Tourists '04
The St. Francisville Experiment '00
Salem's Lot '79
Scary Movie 2 '01
The Screaming Skull '58
Secret Window '04
Seven Days to Live '01
Shock '79
Silent Scream '80
Sister, Sister '87
The Skeleton Key '05
Smart House '00
Spectre '96
Spirit Lost '96
Spookies '85
Stephen King's Rose Red '02
Stormswept '95
A Strange and Deadly Occurrence '74
Superstition '82
Tangled Destinies '32
Teenage Exorcist '93
Terror House '97
Terror in the Haunted House '58
Terror Tract '00
Things 2 '97
13 Ghosts '60
13 Ghosts '01
Three Cases of Murder '55
Treasure of Fear '45
The Uninvited '44
Visions of Evil '75
Warlock 3: The End of Innocence '98
Web of the Spider '70
What a Carve-Up! '62
Who Killed Doc Robbin? '48
Witchouse '99
Witchouse 2: Blood Coven '00
The Wyvern Mystery '00

Crime & Criminals

see Biopics; Cops & Robbers; Crime Drama; Crime Sprees; Crimes of Passion; Disorganized Crime; Frame-Ups; Fugitives; Gangs; Grand Theft Auto; Heists; Hit Men/Women; Juvenile Delinquents; Killer Spouses; Organized Crime; Scams, Stings & Cons; Serial Killers; Smuggler's Blues; True Crime; Urban Drama; Vigilantes

Crime Doesn't Pay

see also Crime Drama; Crimedy; Disorganized Crime; Heists
Alpha Dog '06
The Bank Job '08
Bookies '03
Burnt Money '00
City on Fire '87
Crime Wave '54
Double Indemnity '44
Federal Hill '94
Fool's Gold: The Story of the Brink's-Mat Robbery '92
44 Minutes: The North Hollywood Shootout '03
The Front Line '06
Hero Wanted '08
The Killing '56
Klepto '03
The Ladykillers '04
Lansdown '01
Lift '01
Living & Dying '07
The Lookout '07
Love Is Colder Than Death '69

Macbeth '06
Ocean's 11 '60
The Postman Always Rings Twice '46
The Postman Always Rings Twice '81
A Slight Case of Murder '38
T Bone N Weasel '92
Two Tough Guys '03
Vengeance '80

Crime Drama

see also Drama
The Abduction of Allison Tate '92
The Abduction of Kari Swenson '87
Against the Law '98
The Air I Breathe '07
Al Capone '59
Albino Alligator '96
Alibi '29
American Gangster '07
American Me '92
Angel-A '05
Angels with Dirty Faces '38
Another Day in Paradise '98
Another Man's Poison '52
Assault on Precinct 13 '76
Assault on Precinct 13 '05
At Close Range '86
Baby Face Nelson '97
Backlash '99
Bad Boys '83
Bad City '06
Bad Lieutenant '92
Bait '02
Bandits '86
The Bank Job '08
Basic Instinct 2 '06
Battle in Heaven '05
Before the Devil Knows You're Dead '07
Belly '98
Best Laid Plans '99
A Better Way to Die '00
The Big Turnaround '88
Billionaire Boys Club '87
Billy Bathgate '91
Bitter Sweet '98
The Black Legion '37
Black Rain '89
Blackrock '97
Blast of Silence '61
Blink '93
Blood & Wine '96
Blood, Guts, Bullets and Octane '99
Blood In ... Blood Out: Bound by Honor '93
Blood Money '98
Blood Vows: The Story of a Mafia Wife '87
Blue Ridge Fall '99
Body Count '97
Bodywork '99
Boiling Point '93
Bonanno: A Godfather's Story '99
Bonnie's Kids '73
Border Incident '49
Bordertown '06
Born to Run '93
Borough of Kings '98
Bought and Sold '03
The Box '03
The Brave One '07
A Bronx Tale '93
A Brooklyn State of Mind '97
Brother '97
Brother '00
The Bubble '06
Bugsy '91
B.U.S.T.E.D. '99
Butterfly Collectors '99
Bye-Bye '96
Capone '89
Carbon Copy '69
Casino '95
Cassandra's Dream '07
Catherine Cookson's The Black Candle '92
Cement '99
Charlie '04
Chasing Ghosts '05
Children of Fury '94
Choice of Arms '83

City of Men '07
Close Your Eyes '02
Coastlines '02
Collateral '04
Confidence '03
The Contract '07
Cop Land '97
Crash '05
Crime and Punishment in Suburbia '00
Crime Wave '54
Crimebroker '93
Criminal '04
Crimson Gold '03
Cronicas '04
Dad Savage '97
The Damned Don't Cry '50
Dead Bodies '03
Dead Presidents '95
Death Sentence '07
The Debt '03
Decoy '46
The Deliberate Stranger '86
The Departed '06
Derailed '05
Detour '99
Dilemma '97
Dillinger '45
Dillinger '73
Dillinger '91
Dillinger and Capone '95
Dirty '05
Doctor Chance '97
Dogville '03
Donnie Brasco '96
Dostoevsky's Crime and Punishment '97
Double Edge '97
Eastern Promises '07
The Edukators '04
88 Minutes '08
Element of Doubt '96
Endgame '01
Entrapment '99
Essex Boys '99
Fallen Angels '95
Family of Cops 2: Breach of Faith '97
Family of Cops 3 '98
15 Minutes '01
Final Appeal '93
The Finger Man '55
Fingers '78
Firewall '06
Five Days '07
Flawless '07
Flypaper '97
For Whom He Stands '98
Force of Evil '49
Foreign Land '95
.45 '06
Four Days '99
Freedomland '06
The Front Line '06
"G" Men '35
Gang Busters '55
Gang Related '96
Genealogies of a Crime '97
The General '98
A Gentleman After Dark '42
Get Carter '71
Get Carter '00
Get Rich or Die Tryin' '05
Ghost Dog: The Way of the Samurai '99
Gloria '80
Gloria '98
Gozu '03
Gunshy '98
Hate Crime '05
Haven '04
Heat '95
Hero Wanted '08
Hidden '05
High & Low '62
The Highway Man '99
A History of Violence '05
Honor Thy Father '73

Honor Thy Father and Mother: The True Story of the Menendez Brothers '94
The Hoodlum '51
Hoodlum '96
Hostage '05
House of Bamboo '55
I Went a Murderer '39
I Went Down '97
I'll Sleep When I'm Dead '03
Illtown '96
In Cold Blood '67
In Cold Blood '96
In the Line of Duty: A Cop for the Killing '90
In the Line of Duty: Ambush in Waco '93
In the Line of Duty: The FBI Murders '88
In the Middle of Nowhere '93
In the Valley of Elah '07
In Too Deep '99
Incognito '97
Infernal Affairs '02
Inferno '99
The Innocent Sleep '95
Inside Man '06
Internal Affairs '90
Into the Blue '05
The Intruder '04
Jackie Brown '97
Jesse Stone: Death in Paradise '06
Jesse Stone: Night Passage '06
Jesse Stone: Stone Cold '05
Jindabyne '06
Judas Kiss '98
Juice '92
Kalifornia '93
Kansas City '95
Key Largo '48
Kidnap Syndicate '76
The Killers '46
The Killing of a Chinese Bookie '76
Killing Zoe '94
King of the Ants '03
King of the Roaring '20s: The Story of Arnold Rothstein '61
Kiss or Kill '97
Kiss the Girls '97
Klepto '03
Kontroll '03
The Krays '90
Lansky '99
The Last Don '97
The Last Don 2 '98
Last Man Standing '96
Layer Cake '05
Le Samourai '67
Liar's Poker '99
The Life Before This '99
Life Tastes Good '99
Lights in the Dusk '06
The Limey '99
Little Caesar '30
Little Odessa '94
Lonely Hearts '06
The Long Good Friday '80
The Lookout '07
Lord of War '05
The Lost Angel '04
The Lost Capone '90
The Lost Man '69
Love Is Colder Than Death '69
Love to Kill '97
Lucky Luciano '74
Lucky Number Slevin '06
M '31
Macbeth '06
Mafia Princess '86
Malevolence '95
The Maltese Falcon '31
The Maltese Falcon '41
Mam'zelle Pigalle '58
Man from Mallorca '84
Man on Fire '04
Manhunt '05
Match Point '05
Mean Streets '73
Melissa '97
Memento '00

Memories of Murder '03
Men of America '32
Men of Means '99
Men of Respect '91
Menace II Society '93
Miami Vice '06
Michael Clayton '07
Midnight Murders '91
Miller's Crossing '90
Millions '05
Mr. Brooks '07
Mobsters '91
Money Kings '98
Montana '97
Monument Ave. '98
Munich '05
Murder in New Hampshire: The Pamela Smart Story '91
Naked City: Justice with a Bullet '98
Narc '02
Natural Born Killers '94
Ned Kelly '03
Never Die Alone '04
New Blood '99
New Jack City '91
Night Falls on Manhattan '96
The Night Heaven Fell '57
Nightwaves '03
No Alibi '00
No Country for Old Men '07
No Tomorrow '99
Normal Life '96
Once Upon a Time in America '84
One False Move '91
One of Her Own '97
One Tough Cop '98
Optic Fiber '97
Out of Sight '98
The Outfit '93
Outside Ozona '98
The Painted Lady '97
Pale Saints '97
The Palermo Connection '91
Palmetto '98
Paper Bullets '99
Parisian Love '25
Party Girl '58
Payback '98
Persons Unknown '96
Petty Crimes '02
Phantom Lady '44
Phoenix '98
Pigalle '95
Played '06
Playing God '96
The Pope of Greenwich Village '84
Post Mortem '99
The Prince '07
Prince of Poisoners: The Life and Crimes of William Palmer '98
The Proposition '05
Public Enemy '31
Pulp Fiction '94
Purple Noon '60
Pusher '96
Q & A '90
Railroaded '47
Ratas, Ratones, Rateros '99
Raven's Ridge '97
Read My Lips '01
The Real Thing '97
Real Time: Siege at Lucas Street Market '00
Redacted '07
Reindeer Games '00
Reservoir Dogs '92
Revolver '05
The River King '05
Road Ends '97
The Roaring Twenties '39
Romeo Must Die '00
The Rook '07
Row Your Boat '98
Rude Boy: The Jamaican Don '03
Running Scared '06
Savage Island '03
A Scandal in Paris '46
Scarface '31
Scarface '83
Scarface Mob '62

Score '95
The Score '01
The Second Track '62
Seven '95
Sexy Beast '00
Shade '03
Shadowboxer '06
Shoot to Kill '88
Showdown '94
The Sicilian Connection '85
Side Street '50
A Simple Plan '98
Sirens '02
Six Ways to Sunday '99
16 Blocks '06
Slow Burn '05
Smalltime '96
Soft Deceit '94
Sonatine '96
Spanish Judges '99
The Spree '96
Stakeout '62
Stander '03
State of Grace '90
State Property 2 '05
Straight out of Compton '99
Strange Fruit '04
Stray Bullet '98
Street Gun '96
Street Kings '08
Suspect Zero '04
Suspicion '03
Sweet Sixteen '02
Sworn Enemies '96
Take Me '01
Taking Lives '04
Tension '50
10th & Wolf '06
The Tesseract '03
They Call It Murder '71
They Made Me a Fugitive '47
Thick as Thieves '99
Things to Do in Denver When You're Dead '95
Third World Cop '99
This Is Not a Love Song '02
This Thing of Ours '03
The Thomas Crown Affair '68
The 3 Marias '03
Thumbsucker '05
Tight Spot '55
Tom Clancy's Netforce '98
Trojan Eddie '96
True Friends '98
Tsotsi '05
Turn It Up '00
Under Hellgate Bridge '99
Undermind '03
The Underneath '95
United States of Leland '03
Uno '04
The Untouchables '87
Waist Deep '06
The Walker '07
Way of the Gun '00
We Own the Night '07
West New York '96
Wetbacks '56
Whacked! '02
When Angels Fly '84
When the Sky Falls '99
Without Evidence '96
Witness to the Mob '98
The Wounds '98
Wozzeck '47
The Yards '00
Young Adam '03
The Young Americans '93
Zodiac '07

Crime Sprees

see also Fugitives; Lovers on the Lam
America's Deadliest Home Video '91
Baise Moi '00
The Big Bounce '69
Bonnie & Clyde '67
Border Radio '88
The Boys Next Door '85
Butterfly Kiss '94
The Chant of Jimmie Blacksmith '78
Cop Killers '73
Cracker: Best Boys '95

➤ = rated three bones or higher

Crackers '84
Enemy Gold '93
Explosion '69
Fatal Bond '91
15 Minutes '01
Flash & Firecat '75
Fun With Dick and Jane '05
Heat '95
High Rolling in a Hot Corvette '77
Idiot Box '97
In Cold Blood '96
Jessi's Girls '75
Lewis and Clark and George '97
Love and a .45 '94
Love is Colder Than Death '69
Marshal Law '96
Messidor '77
Murder One '88
Naked Youth '59
Natural Born Killers '94
Normal Life '96
On the Run '73
One Way Out '95
Public Enemies '96
Rampage '87
Road Kill USA '93
Saw '04
Saw II '05
Set It Off '96
She Came on the Bus '69
Shopping '93
Stander '03
Steelyard Blues '73
Sworn Enemies '93
That Sinking Feeling '79
Thieves Like Us '74
Too Fast, Too Young '96
Twin Town '97
Virtuosity '95
Waist Deep '06
When Brendan Met Trudy '00
The Whole Town's Talking '35
Why Does Herr R. Run Amok? '69
The Wrong Road '37

Crimedy
see also **Comic Cops; Disorganized Crime**
Analyze That '02
Analyze This '98
Avenging Angelo '02
Betsy's Wedding '90
Big Nothing '06
Big Trouble '02
Blonde and Blonder '07
Chaos & Cadavers '03
Corky Romano '01
The Crew '00
Dead Fish '04
Dead Lenny '06
8 Heads in a Duffel Bag '96
Fakers '04
First Sunday '08
Forget About It '06
Friends and Family '01
Get Shorty '95
Gigli '03
Hoodlum & Son '03
The Jerky Boys '95
Kangaroo Jack '02
Knockaround Guys '01
Lies & Alibis '06
Mad Dog and Glory '93
Mad Money '08
Married to the Mob '88
Mafia! '98
The Mexican '01
A New Wave '07
Ocean's Thirteen '07
Oscar '91
Pineapple Express '08
Pizzi's Honor '85
Robin-B-Hood '06
Strictly Sinatra '01
Table One '00
They Met in a Taxi '36
The Wendell Baker Story '05
You Move You Die '07

Crimes of Passion
Backfire '88
Bad Boy Bubby '93
Being at Home with Claude '92
The Big Clock '48
Bizarre '87
Blood Vows: The Story of a Mafia Wife '87
Born to Kill '47
Casque d'Or '52
China Moon '91
Concealed Weapon '94
Cracker: True Romance '95
Crime of Passion '57
The Crucible '96
A Dark Adapted Eye '93
Deadbolt '92
Deception '45
Dupont Lajoie '74
Fatal Attraction '87
For Your Love Only '79
The Gingerbread Man '97
The Girl '86
Homicidal Impulse '92
I Love You to Death '90
Intimate Relations '95
Jade '95
Knots '05
The Last Dance '93
Lethal Lolita—Amy Fisher: My Story '92
Love and Hate: A Marriage Made in Hell '90
The Love Flower '20
Make Haste to Live '54
The Man in the Attic '94
The Mask of Dijon '46
Men Are Not Gods '37
Murder in New Hampshire: The Pamela Smart Story '91
Murder Rap '87
Niagara '52
Passion '82
The People vs. Jean Harris '81
The Prepple Murder '89
Roadhouse Girl '53
Secret Beyond the Door '48
Sex Crimes '92
Sharon's Secret '95
The Shooting Party '77
Single White Female '92
This World, Then the Fireworks '97
To Die For '95
Tomorrow Never Comes '77
Victim of Beauty '91
The Walls of Malapaga '49
Woman in the Window '44
The Worldly Madonna '22
Wozzeck '47

Criminally Insane
see also **Crime Sprees; Sanity Check; Torn in Two (or More)**
Criminally Insane '75
The Dark Knight '08
High Tension '03
Ricochet '91
Unbreakable '00

The Crusades
The Adventures of Robin Hood '38
King Richard and the Crusaders '54
Kingdom of Heaven '05
Lionheart '90
Robin and Marian '76
Robin Hood: Prince of Thieves '91
The Night God Screamed '71

Cults
see also **Occult; Satanism**
Alien Nation: Millennium '96
Bad Dreams '88
Batman Begins '05
Because the Cats '74
The Believers '07
Believers '87
Beware! Children at Play '95
Blinded by the Light '82
Blood Clan '90
Bloodbath '76
Burial of the Rats '95
Chain of Souls '00
Children of the Corn 2: The Final Sacrifice '92
Cobra Woman '44
Cut of the Cobra '95
The Dark Secret of Harvest Home '78
Deadly Blessing '81
Death of an Angel '86
The Deceivers '88
The Devil's Prey '01
Divided by Hate '96
Down in the Delta '98
The Dreamers '03
East is East '99
Fatal Passion '94
Force: Five '81
Forever Evil '87
The Guyana Tragedy: The Story of Jim Jones '80
Hellraiser: Deader '05
Helter Skelter '76
Helter Skelter Murders '71
Holy Smoke '99
The House on Todville Road '95
In the Line of Duty: Ambush in Waco '93
Isaac Asimov's Nightfall '00
The Lightning Incident '91
Lord of Illusions '95
The Loved One '65
The Manson Family '04
The Mephisto Waltz '71
Mind, Body & Soul '92
Mindstorm '01
Next One '84
Night of the Death Cult '75
Putney Swope '69
The Pyx '73
Raging Angels '95
The Reincarnate '71
Rest in Pieces '87
Revenge '86
Sabata '55
Safe '95
Savage Messiah '02
Servants of Twilight '91
Shock 'Em Dead '90
The Snake Hunter Stranger '66
The Snake People '68
Soul's Midnight '06
The Spellbinder '88
Split Image '82
Steps from Hell '92
They Crawl '01
Thou Shalt Not Kill...Except '87
Ticket to Heaven '81
Treasure of the Four Crowns '82
Ultrachrist '03
Withnail and I '87

Cuba
see also **Red Scare**
Assault of the Rebel Girls '59
Before Night Falls '00
The Company '07
Company Man '00
Cuba '79
Cuban Blood '03
Dance with Me '98
Dirty Dancing: Havana Nights '04
A Few Good Men '92
Fidel '02
For Love or Country: The Arturo Sandoval Story '00
The Godfather, Part 2 '74
Guantanamera '95
Havana '90
Key Largo '48
Lansky '99
The Last Supper '76
Letters from the Park '88
The Lost City '05
Memories of Underdevelopment '68
The Motorcycle Diaries '04
The Old Man and the Sea '58
The Old Man and the Sea '90
Original Sin '01
Our Man in Havana '59
A Paradise Under the Stars '99
The Perez Family '94
Plato's Run '96
Rough Riders '96
Ruby '92
Scarface '83
Sicko '07
Strawberry and Chocolate '93
Tamango '59
Thirteen Days '00
Up to a Certain Point '83

Culture Clash
American Adobo '02
An American Rhapsody '01
At Play in the Fields of the Lord '91
Babe: Pig in the City '98
Babel '06
The Baby Dance '98
The Beautiful Country '04
The Beverly Hillbillies '93
Black Robe '91
Borat: Cultural Learnings of America for Make Benefit Glorious Nation of Kazakhstan '06
Breaking and Entering '06
Bride & Prejudice '04
Bringing Down the House '03
The Brother from Another Planet '84
Brothers in Trouble '95
Cabaret '72
Carla's Song '97
Caterina in the Big City '03
Catfish in Black Bean Sauce '00
The Chateau '01
Chutney Popcorn '99
City of Ghosts '03
City of Joy '92
The Comfort of Strangers '91
Coneheads '93
Conrack '74
The Cookout '04
C'ash '05
crazy/beautiful '01
Crocodile Dundee '86
Crocodile Dundee in Los Angeles '01
Dead Heat '96
Deliverance '72
Down in the Delta '98
The Dreamers '03
East is East '99
The Emerald Forest '85
Encino Man '92
The Europeans '79
Everything is Illuminated '05
The Family Stone '05
The Fast and the Furious: Tokyo Drift '06
For Richer or Poorer '97
G '02
George of the Jungle '97
Georgia Rule '07
Gorillas in the Mist '88
The Great New Wonderful '06
Green Dragon '01
Greystoke: The Legend of Tarzan, Lord of the Apes '84
The Guru '02
Heart of Light '97
Heat and Dust '82
Heat and Dust '98
Holy Man '98
Hotel Colonial '88
House of Angels '92
I Want to Go Home '89
Just Visiting '01
The Last Samurai '03
Late Marriage '01
Lawrence of Arabia '62
Le Divorce '03
Leningrad Cowboys Go America '89
Like A Bride '94
Lila Says '04
The Lost Child '00
Malibu's Most Wanted '03
Maryam '00
Meet the Fockers '04
Meet the Parents '00
The Mission '86
Mississippi Masala '92
Mister Johnson '91
Mixing Nia '98
Moonlighting '82
Moscow on the Hudson '84
The Namesake '06
The Nephew '95
A Passage to India '84
Pathfinder '07
Pizzicata '96
Quigley Down Under '90
Red Doors '05
Rescue from Gilligan's Island '78
Rock My World '02
Rodgers & Hammerstein's South Pacific '01
Rush Hour '98
Saving Face '04
The Science of Sleep '06
Shadow Magic '00
Shanghai Knights '03
Shanghai Noon '00
The Sheltering Sky '90
Shogun '80
Snow Dogs '02
The Snow Walker '03
Someone Else's America '96
Songcatcher '99
South Pacific '58
Spanglish '04
Splash '84
Starman '84
Strangers with Candy '06
Swept from the Sea '97
Thunderheart '92
Tokyo Cowboy '94
2 Brothers & a Bride '03
Uncle Nino '03
Wasabi '01
Wassup Rockers '05
West is West '87
Witness '85
Wondrous Oblivion '06
Yes '04
Zorba the Greek '64

Custody Battles
see also **Divorce; Order in the Court; Single Parents**
Big Daddy '99
Careful, He Might Hear You '84
Changing Lanes '02
Daddy's Little Girls '07
Dark Water '05
Evelyn '02
Faithless '00
Gaudi Afternoon '01
The Good Mother '88
I Am Sam '01
Irreconcilable Differences '84
Kramer vs. Kramer '79
Losing Isaiah '94
Mrs. Doubtfire '93
Rain Man '88

Cuttin' Heads
Abbott and Costello in Hollywood '45
Allie & Me '97
The Barber Shop '33
Barbershop '02
Barbershop 2: Back in Business '04
The Beautician and the Beast '97
The Big Tease '99
Black Shampoo '76
Blow Dry '00
Born to Win '71
Caramel '07
Chain of Fools '00
Claire Dolan '97
Coming to America '88
The Crying Game '92
Demon Barber of Fleet Street '36
Earth Girls Are Easy '89
Educating Rita '83
An Everlasting Piece '00
The French Touch '54
Frolics in the '39
The Hairdresser's Husband '92
Hairspray '88
Honey '03
Joe's Bed-Stuy Barbershop: We Cut Heads '83
The Man Who Wasn't There '01
Mississippi Burning '88
Nore's Hair Salon 2: A Cut Above '08
Nutty Professor 2: The Klumps '00
Poetic Justice '93
Runaway Bride '99
The Salon '05
Shampoo '75
Spotlight Scandals '43
Steel Magnolias '89
Stigmata '99
Sweeney Todd '07
Sweeney Todd: The Demon Barber of Fleet Street '84
Sweeney Todd: The Demon Barber of Fleet Street '07
Venus Beauty Institute '98
You Don't Mess with the Zohan '08

Cyberpunk
Arcade '93
Blade Runner '82
The Crow 2: City of Angels '96
Cyborg '89
Cyborg 2 '93
Cyborg Cop '93
Cyborg Soldier '94
Demolition Man '93
Escape from New York '81
The Fifth Element '97
Freejack '92
Hackers '95
Johnny Mnemonic '95
The Lawnmower Man '92
The Lawnmower Man 2: Beyond Cyberspace '95
Mad Max '80
Mad Max: Beyond Thunderdome '85
Megaville '91
Nemesis '93
Overdrawn at the Memory Bank '83
RoboCop '87
RoboCop 2 '90
RoboCop 3 '91
Stealing Candy '04
Tank Girl '94
TekWar '94
The Terminator '84
Terminator 2: Judgment Day '91
Tetsuo: The Iron Man '92
Tetsuo 2: Body Hammer '97
Total Recall '90
Tron '82
Universal Soldier '92
Universal Soldier 2: Brothers in Arms '98
Universal Soldier 3: Unfinished Business '98
Universal Combat '95
The Return '99
Virtuosity '95
Webmaster '98

▶ = rated three bones or higher

Dads

see also Bad Dads; Moms; Monster Moms; Parenthood

About Schmidt '02▸
Address Unknown '96
The Adventures of Pinocchio '96
After the Deluge '03▸
Alice et Martin '98
All My Sons '48▸
American Gun '02▸
American Heart '92▸
Animal '05
April Fool '26
Armageddon '98
Artemisia '97
Austin Powers In Goldmember '02
Author! Author! '82
Autumn Marathon '79
Back to School '86
The Ballad of Jack and Rose '05▸
Ballistic '94
Bandits '86
Barnyard '06
The Baron and the Kid '84
Beat Girl '60
The Bed You Sleep In '93
Behind Prison Walls '43
Betsy's Wedding '90
Between Men '35
Beyond Obsession '82
Big Daddy '99
Big Fish '03▸
A Bill of Divorcement '32
Billy Elliot '00▸
Billy Galvin '86
Billy Madison '94
The Birdcage '95▸
Black Eyes '39
Blood Diamond '06
Bloodfist 4: Die Trying '92
Bloodfist 8: Hard Way Out '96
Bloodlines '05
Blue Fin '78
Boiler Room '00▸
Bonjour Tristesse '57▸
Boomerang '76
Bophal '93▸
Boss' Son '78▸
The Brady Bunch Movie '95▸
Breaking Away '79▸
Bringing Down the House '03
Broken Angel '88
A Bronx Tale '93▸
The Buddha of Suburbia '92▸
Butterfly '82
Bye Bye, Love '94
Cal '84▸
Call of the Forest '49
The Capture of Grizzly Adams '82
Carbon Copy '81
Carousel '56▸
Casanova Brown '44
Casper '95▸
Caterina in the Big City '03
Catherine Cookson's The Glass Virgin '95
Celine and Julie Go Boating '74
The Champ '32▸
The Champ '79
Chasing Destiny '00
Chasing the Deer '94
Chicken Little '05
City of Men '07▸
Class Action '91▸
Click '06
The Climb '97
Clown '53
Cody '77
Cold Comfort '90
The Color of Paradise '99
Come and Get It! '36▸
Common Ground '00
Complex World '92
Cookie '89
A Cool, Dry Place '98
The Cooler '03▸
Cop-Out '67

Corky Romano '01
The Courtship of Eddie's Father '62▸
crazy/beautiful '01
Crush '93
A Cry from the Mountain '85
Cry, the Beloved Country '51▸
The Dance Goes On '92
The Dancer Upstairs '02
Dancing in Twilight '05
Daredevil '03
The Dark Side of the Sun '88
Daughter of Don Q '46
David '97
Dead to Rights '93
Deadlocked '00
Death of a Salesman '51▸
The Death of Richie '76
Definitely, Maybe '08▸
Demonstrator '71
Desert Blue '98
Desperate Measures '98
Diamonds '99
Dinner Rush '00
Distant Thunder '88
Django Strikes Again '87
Dodson's Journey '01
Domestic Disturbance '01
Donkey Skin '70▸
Donovan's Reef '63▸
The Dream Catcher '99
A Dream of Kings '69▸
Dreamer: Inspired by a True Story '05
Dreaming of Rita '94
Drifting Weeds '59▸
Duets '00
East and West '24▸
Eat Drink Man Woman '94▸
Eden Valley '94▸
11:14 '03
Elisa, Vida Mia '77
The Emerald Forest '85▸
Empire Falls '05
The Enemy '01
Escape from Atlantis '97
Evelyn '02
Everybody's Famous! '00
Everybody's Fine '90
Eyes of a Witness '95
Eyes of an Angel '91
Faceless '88
Family Business '89
Family Tree '00
Fast Getaway 2 '94
Fatal Justice '93
Father '90
Father and Scout '94
Father and Son '03
Father Figure '80
Father of the Bride '50▸
Father Was a Fullback '49
Fathers and Sons '92
Father's Day '96
A Father's Revenge '88
The Favorite Son '94▸
Fear '96
Fingers '78▸
Finding Nemo '03▸
Firehouse Dog '07
Five Easy Pieces '70▸
Floating '97
For Richer, for Poorer '97
Force on Thunder Mountain '77
Forty Shades of Blue '05
Fourth Wish '75
Free Willy 3: The Rescue '97
Freedom Is Paradise '89▸
Freedom Song '00▸
Frequency '00▸
Friday After Next '02
Friends & Lovers '07
The Game Plan '07

Gepetto '00
Ghost Dad '90
The Golden Bowl '72▸
The Golden Bowl '00
A Goofy Movie '94
The Gospel '05▸
Grace Is Gone '07▸
Green Eyes '76▸
The Green Promise '49
Grizzly Falls '99
Gunman's Walk '58
Gunslinger's Revenge '98
Harry & Son '84
Heaven Tonight '93
Hidden Guns '56▸
Hidden in America '96
High & Low '62▸
High Command '37
His Greatest Gamble '34
Hobson's Choice '53▸
Hobson's Choice '83
A Hole in the Head '60▸
Holiday in Mexico '46
Home from the Hill '60▸
Home Is Where the Hart Is '88
Honey, We Shrunk Ourselves '97
The Horse '82▸
The Horse in the Gray Flannel Suit '68
The Horsemen '70
House Arrest '96
A House Divided '00
A House without a Christmas Tree '72
Hud '63▸
I Am Sam '01
I Live with Me Dad '86
I Ought to Be in Pictures '82
I Was Born But... '32▸
Il Grido '57
I'll Be There '03
I'll Do Anything '93
I'm Not Rappaport '96
Imaginary Crimes '94▸
In Good Company '04▸
In His Father's Shoes '97
In the Gloaming '97▸
In the Name of the Father '93▸
In the Valley of Elah '07▸
The Incredibles '04▸
The Independent '00
Indiana Jones and the Last Crusade '89▸
Invisible Dad '97
It's a Date '40
Jack Frost '98
Jack the Bear '93
Jersey Girl '04
Jet Li's The Enforcer '95
Jingle All the Way '96
Joe Somebody '01
Joey '85
John Q '02
Johnny's Girl '95
The Judgement '04
Jumanji '95
Jungle 2 Jungle '96
Just Like Dad '96
Just Write '97
Keeping Up with the Steins '06
Kicking & Screaming '05
The Kid and I '05
King of California '07
King of Texas '02▸
King of the Corner '04▸
Kings and Queen '04▸
Knockaround Guys '01
Kolya '96▸
Kramer vs. Kramer '79▸
La Deroute '98
The Lady Eve '41▸
The Lady Refuses '31
Lamb '85
Lara Croft: Tomb Raider '01
The Last Hard Men '76
The Last Hit '93
Late Spring '49▸
Laughing at Life '33
Le Sexe des Etoiles '93
The Legend of Zorro '05
Leon the Pig Farmer '93
Les Comperes '83▸
Les Destinees '00
Letter of Introduction '38

Liar Liar '97
Life Is Beautiful '98▸
Life with Father '47▸
Like Father, Like Son '87
The Limey '99▸
The Lion King '94▸
Little Dorrit, Film 1: Nobody's Fault '88▸
Little Dorrit, Film 2: Little Dorrit's Story '88▸
Little Indian, Big City '95
Little John '02
A Little Princess '95▸
The Lives of a Bengal Lancer '35▸
Lone Star '96▸
Looking for an Echo '99
Luna Park '91
Lust and Revenge '95
Magic in the Water '95
Maker of Men '31
Malibu's Most Wanted '03
Mamma Mia! '08
Marci X '03
The Marshal's Daughter '53
The Mask of Zorro '98▸
Matchstick Men '03▸
Meet the Fockers '04
Meet the Parents '00▸
Meeting Daddy '98
Memories of Me '88
Men with Brooms '02
Missing Pieces '00
Mr. Mom '83▸
Mr. St. Nick '02
Misunderstood '84
Misunderstood '87
Mom and Dad Save the World '92
Mulan '98
Must Be Santa '99
Mutual Respect '77
My Date with the President's Daughter '98
My Father Is Coming '91
My Father the Hero '93
My Old Man '79
My Son the Fanatic '97▸
My Stepmother Is an Alien '88
National Lampoon's Dad's Week Off '97
Never Down '06
Nick of Time '95
Night at the Museum '06
Night Falls on Manhattan '96▸
Night Zoo '87
No Turning Back '01
No Way Back '96
Noah '98
Nobody's Fool '94▸
Nothing in Common '86
Oldest Living Graduate '80▸
On a Clear Day '05
On the Edge '86
On the Third Day '83
One Christmas '95
Our Vines Have Tender Grapes '45▸
Over the Top '86
The Patriot '00
The Pillow Book '95
Platinum High School '60
Pokemon 3: The Movie '01
Ponette '95▸
Pontiac Moon '94
Pop Always Pays '40
Popi '69▸
Princess of Thieves '01
Proof '05▸
The Pursuit of Happyness '06
Race to Space '01
Raining Stones '93
Raising Flagg '06
Reservation Road '07
Return to Lonesome Dove '93
Revenge of the Musketeers '94
Revolution '85
Riding Alone for Thousands of Miles '05
Rio Grande '50▸
The River Rat '84

A River Runs Through It '92▸
Road to Perdition '02▸
Rocky Balboa '06
Romulus, My Father '07▸
Rugrats in Paris: The Movie '00▸
The Run of the Country '95▸
The Santa Clause '94
The Santa Clause 2 '02
Sci-Fighter '04
Sea Devils '37
Second Best '94▸
Secre of the Andes '98
The Secret Agent Club '96
The Secret Passion of Robert Clayton '92
The Sender '98
Severance '88
Shadow Man '06
Shattered '21▸
The Shepherd of the Hills '41▸
She's the One '96
Shiner '00
Shower '00
Signs '02▸
A Simple Wish '97
Skeletons in the Closet '00
Slaughter of the Innocents '93
Sleepless in Seattle '93▸
Slums of Beverly Hills '98▸
Snow Dogs '02
So I Married an Axe Murderer '93
A Soldier's Daughter Never Cries '98
Spanglish '04
Special Olympics '78
Speed of Life '99
The Spring '00
Spring Forward '99
Star Spangled Rhythm '42▸
Stolen Summer '02
The Stupids '95
The Sum of Us '94▸
Superdad '73
Swing Vote '08▸
Tank '83
The Tempest '63
The Tempest '82▸
The Tempest '99
The 10th Kingdom '00
Texas Lightning '81
The Thing About My Folks '05
13 Moons '02
The Three Lives of Thomasina '63▸
Three Men and a Cradle '85▸
Three Men and a Little Lady '90
The Tiger Woods Story '98
A Time to Kill '96▸
Time Without Pity '57
To Gillian on Her 37th Birthday '96
Together '02
The Tomorrow Man '01
Tortilla Soup '01
The Tracker '88
Tully '00▸
25th Hour '02▸
Two Kinds of Love '85
Undercover Angel '99
A Very Brady Sequel '96
A Voyage 'Round My Father '89▸
Wait Till Your Mother Gets Home '83
Walter and Henry '01▸
The War '94
The War at Home '96
War of the Worlds '05▸
Wasabi '01
Washington Heights '02
The Weather Man '05
What a Girl Wants '03
Winter Solstice '04
Woman Wanted '98
The Young Girl and the Monsoon '99

Dallas

see also Black Gold; Houston; Texas

Asteroid '97
Big Show '37
A Cool, Dry Place '98
Dr. T & the Women '00▸
Free, White, and 21 '62
JFK '91▸
Love Field '91
North Dallas Forty '79▸
Pioneer Marshal '49
Ruby '92
Steele's Law '91
Suspect Zero '04
Talk Radio '88▸
The Thin Blue Line '88▸
A Woman of Independent Means '94▸
The X-Files '98

Dance Fever

see also Ballet; Disco; Musicals

Alive and Kicking '96
All That Jazz '79▸
An American in Paris '51▸
Anchors Aweigh '45▸
April in Paris '52
Assassination Tango '03▸
Babes in Arms '39
The Bacchantes '63
The Band Wagon '53▸
The Barefoot Contessa '54▸
The Barkleys of Broadway '49▸
Beat Street '84
Because of You '95
The Belle of New York '52
Bert Rigby, You're a Fool '89
Billy Elliot '00▸
Billy Rose's Jumbo '62▸
Black Orpheus '58▸
Blood Wedding '81▸
Body Moves '90
Body Rock '84
Bojangles '01
Boogie Nights '97▸
Bootmen '00
Born to Dance '36
Breakin' '84
Breakin' 2: Electric Boogaloo '84
Breakin' Through '84
Broadway Melody of 1940 '40
Cabin in the Sky '43▸
Can-Can '60
Captain January '36
Carefree '38▸
Carmen '83▸
Center Stage '00
Charleston '26▸
A Chorus Line '85
Cover Girl '44▸
Curdled '95
Daddy Long Legs '55▸
Dames '34▸
Dance or Die '87
Dance with Me '98
Dancing Lady '33
Danzon '91▸
Deadly Dancer '90
Delightfully Dangerous '45
Delivery Boys '84
Dirty Dancing '87▸
Dirty Dancing: Havana Nights '04
The Discovery Program '89
Doll Face '46
The Eighties '83
El Amor Brujo '86▸
Everybody's Dancin' '50
Everyone Says I Love You '96▸
Faith '90
Fame '80▸
Fass Black '77
Fast Forward '84
Faster, Pussycat! Kill! Kill! '65▸
Femmes de Paris '53
Flashdance '83
Flower Drum Song '61

▸ = rated three bones or higher

Flying Down to Rio '33
Follies Girl '43
Follow the Fleet '36▸
Footlight Parade '33▸
Footloose '84
The Forbidden Dance '90
42nd Street '33▸
French Can-Can '55▸
From Dusk Till Dawn '95
The Gay Divorcee '34▸
The Full Monty '96▸
Ginger & Fred '86▸
Girl in Gold Boots '69
Girls Just Want to Have Fun '85
Give a Girl a Break '53
The Glass Slipper '55
Gold Diggers of 1933 '33▸
Gold Diggers of 1935 '35▸
Grease 2 '82
Grease '78▸
Groove '00▸
Hair '79▸
Hairspray '88▸
Hairspray '07▸
Happy Feet '06▸
The Harvey Girls '46▸
Heavenly Bodies '84
Hit the Deck '55
Hocus Pocus '93
Holiday in Havana '49
Honey '03
How She Move '08
Human Traffic '99
Idiot's Delight '39▸
The In Crowd '88
Isadora '68▸
It Started in Naples '60▸
Kickin' It Old Skool '07
Kiss Me Kate '53▸
Lambada '89
The Last Dance '91
The Last Days of Disco '98▸
Le Bal '82▸
Legs '83
Les Girls '57
Let's Dance '50
Lilo & Stitch 2: Stitch Has a Glitch '05
Liquid Dreams '92
Little Ballerina '47
Look Who's Talking '89▸
Mad About Mambo '00
Mad Hot Ballroom '05▸
Mad Youth '40
Manhattan Merengue! '95
Mantis in Lace '68
Marilyn Hotchkiss' Ballroom Dancing & Charm School '06
Meet Me in Las Vegas '56
Michael '96
Midnight Dancer '87
Music in My Heart '40
Neurotic Cabaret '90
The Next Step '55
No Time for Romance '48
Nutcracker: The Motion Picture '86
Orgy of the Dead '65
Out to Sea '97
Paris is Burning '91▸
Party Girl '58▸
Pennies from Heaven '81▸
The Pirate '48▸
Pizzicata '96
Portrait of a Showgirl '82
Portrait of a Stripper '79
Pulp Fiction '94▸
Queen of the Stardust Ballroom '75▸
Reality Bites '94
Rhythm Romance '39
Rize '05▸
Roberta '35▸
Romance in Manhattan '34
Romy and Michele's High School Reunion '97
Rooftops '89
Roseland '77▸
Salome, Where She Danced '45
Salsa '88
Satin Rouge '02
Saturday Night Fever '77
Save the Last Dance '01▸
Scent of a Woman '92▸
Seamless '00
Second Chorus '40
Seven Brides for Seven Brothers '54▸
Shag: The Movie '89▸
Shall We Dance '37▸
Shall We Dance? '96▸
Shall We Dance? '04▸
Showgirls '95
Silk Stockings '57▸
Singin' in the Rain '52▸
Siren of the Tropics '27
Sixdance '89
So This Is Paris '26▸
Staying Alive '83
Step Up '06▸
Stepping Out '91
Stomp the Yard '07
The Story of Vernon and Irene Castle '39▸
Strictly Ballroom '92▸
Stripped to Kill II: Live Girls '89
Summer Stock '50▸
Sunset Strip '91
Sweet Charity '69▸
Swing Kids '33
Swing Time '36▸
Take the Lead '06
Take Me Out to the Ball Game '49
Tango '36
Tango '98
Tango Bar '88
The Tango Lesson '97
Tap '89
Taxi Dancers '93
Teen Wolf '85
Thank God It's Friday '78
That's Dancing! '85▸
That's Entertainment, Part 2 '76
That's Entertainment, Part 3 '93
That's the Way I Like It '99
They Shoot Horses, Don't They? '69▸
Those Lips, Those Eyes '80
A Time for Dancing '00
Top Hat '35▸
The Turning Point '77▸
Urban Cowboy '80
Voulez-Vous Danser avec Mo.? '76
West Side Story '61▸
What's the Matter with Helen? '71
Words and Music '48
Yankee Doodle Dandy '42▸
Yellow '06
You Got Served '04
You Were Never Lovelier '42▸
You'll Never Get Rich '41▸
Zatoichi '03▸
Ziegfeld Follies '46
Ziegfeld Girl '41▸
Zou Zou '34

Day Care/Nursery School
see also Babysitting
Daddy Day Camp '07
Daddy Day Care '03
Indictment: The McMartin Trial '95▸
Superbabies: Baby Geniuses 2 '04

Dates from Hell
see also Singles
After Hours '85▸
Blind Date '87
Body Shots '99
Bride of Chucky '98
Bye Bye, Love '94
Ed's Next Move '96
The 40 Year Old Virgin '05▸
Harold and Maude '71▸
Mr. Woodcock '07
Night of the Creeps '86
Perfect Strangers '03
The Personals '99
Reality Bites '94
Singles '92▸
Something Wild '86
The Third Wheel '02
20 Dates '99
Walking and Talking '96
What Happened Was... '94
Woo '97

DEA
see also Buddy Cops; FBI; Smuggler's Blues; Undercover Cops
Basic '03
Cash Crop '01
Codename: Wildgeese '84
Crash & Byrnes '99
Drug Wars: The Camarena Story '90▸
Gang Related '96
Hollow Point '96
Love Lies Bleeding '07
A Low Down Dirty Shame '94
A Man Apart '03
Marked for Death '90
Ninja: American Warrior '90
Road House 2: Last Call '06
Traffic '00▸
White Tiger '95
Winner Takes All '98

Death & the Afterlife
see also Angels; Funerals; Ghosts, Ghouls, & Goblins; Great Death Scenes; Heaven Sent; Hell; Immortality; Occult; Reincarnation; Suicide; Terminal Illness

A Day in the Life...
see also Up All Night
American Graffiti '73▸
Barbershop '02▸
Before Sunrise '94
Before Sunset '04▸
The Best Man '97
Bobby '06
Bomb Squad '97
The Boys '98▸
The Breakfast Club '85▸
Conversations with Other Women '05
Crank '06
The Daytrippers '96
Deadlocked '00
Falling '06
Ferris Bueller's Day Off '86▸
Flypaper '97
For One More Day '07
Full Frontal '02
Groundhog Day '93▸
Head On '98▸
Heights '04
Interceptor Force '99
Judy Berlin '99
Killing Time '97
Last Night '98▸
The Life Before This '99
Little Athens '05
Love and Other Catastrophes '95
Magnolia '99▸
Midaq Alley '95
Miss Pettigrew Lives for a Day '08▸
Mrs. Dalloway '97
My Mother's Courage '95
North Shore Fish '97
Nothing Personal '95▸
Nowhere '96
One Fine Day '96
100 Proof '96
12:01 '93
25th Hour '02▸
24 Hours in London '00
Ulysses '67
Working Girls '87▸

Deafness
see also Physical Problems
Amy '81
Babel '06▸
Beyond Silence '96
Bridge to Silence '89
Children of a Lesser God '86▸
Cop Land '97▸
Crazy Moon '87
Crossfire '98
Dead Frankie '04
Dead Silence '96
The Family Stone '05▸
For the First Time '59
Four Weddings and a Funeral '94▸
Goya in Bordeaux '99
Hear No Evil '93
The Heart is a Lonely Hunter '68▸
His Bodyguard '98
Immortal Beloved '94
In the Company of Men '96
It's All Gone, Pete Tong '04
Johnny Belinda '48▸
Johnny Belinda '82
Mandy '53▸
The Miracle Worker '62▸
The Miracle Worker '75▸
The Miracle Worker '00
Mr. Holland's Opus '95▸
Murderer's Keep '88
Music Within '07
Psych-Out '68
The Quiet '05
Read My Lips '01▸
Secret of Yolanda '82
See No Evil, Hear No Evil '89
Silent Victory: The Kitty O'Neil Story '79▸
Sincerely Yours '56
The Sound and the Silence '93
Sound of Love '78
The Sphinx '33
The Story of Alexander Graham Bell '39▸
A Summer to Remember '84
Suspect '87
Tin Man '83
Two Shades of Blue '98
Where the Truth Lies '99

Deadly Implants
Alien: Resurrection '97▸
Bombshell '97
Drive '96
Escape from L.A. '96
Escape from New York '81▸
Fortress '92
Fortress 2 '99
King of Kong Island '78
Live Wire: Human Timebomb '95
The Mosaic Project '95
Star Trek: First Contact '96▸
Street Asylum '90
Synapse '96
Terminal Impact '95
The Terminal Man '74
Total Recall '90▸

After Life '98
The Alchemist '81
Alive and Kicking '06
All About My Mother '99▸
All of Me '84
All That Jazz '79▸
Always '89
The Amityville Horror '79
Amityville 2: The Possession '82
Amityville 3: The Demon '83
Amityville 4: The Evil Escapes '89
The Amityville Curse '90
Amityville 1992: It's About Time '92
Angel Eyes '01
Angel on My Shoulder '46▸
Angel on My Shoulder '80
Another Chance '88
The Asphyx '72▸
Audrey Rose '77
Avanti! '72
Baby Girl Scott '87
Backwoods '87
Beetlejuice '88▸
Beyond Tomorrow '40
Bill & Ted's Bogus Journey '91
Black Force 2 '78
Black Magic '92
Blithe Spirit '45▸
Blood of the Vampire '58
Bloody New Year '87
The Bone Yard '90
Bowery at Midnight '42
Boys on the Side '94▸
The Bramble Bush '60
Breaking the Rules '92
Bulletproof Heart '95
Burnt Offerings '76▸
The Canterville Ghost '44▸
Carnival of Souls '62▸
Carousel '56▸
Carry Me Back '82
Castle of the Creeping Flesh '68
The Cat and the Canary '27▸
The Chair '87
The Changeling '80▸
Chances Are '89▸
A Christmas Carol '38▸
A Christmas Carol '51▸
A Christmas Carol '84▸
A Christmas Carol '99
City of Angels '98
Cold Heaven '92
Courage Under Fire '96▸
The Crow '94▸
The Crow 2: City of Angels '96
The Crow: Wicked Prayer '05
Curse of the Cat People '44▸
Curse of the Living Corpse '64
Da '88
Daddy's Dyin'... Who's Got the Will? '90
Dark of the Night '85
Dark Tower '87
Dark Victory '39▸
Daughter of Horror '55
The Day It Came to Earth '77
Dead Heat '88
Dead Leaves '98
Dead Mate '88
The Death Curse of Tartu '66
Death Becomes Her '92▸
Death Be Not Proud '75▸
Death Row Diner '88
Death Takes a Holiday '34▸
Defending Your Life '91▸
Deja Vu '84
The Devil & Max Devlin '81
Devil's Kiss '75
The Diabolical Dr. Z '65
Diary of the Dead '80
Digging Up Business '91
D.O.A. '49▸
D.O.A. '88
Dr. Death, Seeker of Souls '73
Dr. Hackenstein '88
Doctor Phibes Rises Again '72
Dominique Is Dead '79
Dona Flor and Her Two Husbands '78▸
Donkey Skin '70▸
Donovan's Brain '53▸
Don't Go in the House '80
Don't Let Me Die on a Sunday '98
Doomed Love '83
Dragonfly '02
The Duellists '77▸
Early Days '81
Earthling '80
Eleni '85
Emerald of Artama '67
Encounter with the Unknown '75
The End '78▸
The English Patient '96▸
Enrapture '90
The Entertainer '60▸
Estate of Insanity '70
Eternity and a Day '97
Evil Spirits '91
Executive Suite '54▸
The Eye '08
The Eyes, the Mouth '83
Fearless '93▸
The Fig Tree '87
Flatliners '90▸
Fluke '95
For Roseanna '96
The Forgotten One '89
Frida '02▸
Friendly Fire '79▸
Frightmare '81
The Frighteners '96▸
Frisk '95
From the Dead of Night '89▸
The Funeral '84▸
Funeral Home '80
Garbo Talks '84
Gates of Hell '80
The Ghost '63
Ghost '90▸
The Ghost and Mrs. Muir '47▸
Ghost Writer '89
Ghosts Can Do It '87
Ghosts Can't Do It '90
Ghosts of Berkeley Square '47
Go Down Death '41
Gotham '88
The Granny '94
Grave Secrets '89
The Green Room '78
Griffin and Phoenix: A Love Story '76
Hawks '89
Heart and Souls '93▸
Heart Condition '90
Heaven '87
Heaven Can Wait '43▸
Heaven Can Wait '78▸
The Heavenly Kid '85
Heaven's a Drag '94
Hello Again '87
Hercules and the Legendary Journeys, Vol. 4: In the Underworld '94
Here Comes Mr. Jordan '41▸
Hideaway '94
High Plains Drifter '73▸
High Spirits '88▸
Highlander: Endgame '00
Highway 61 '91
Hocus Pocus '93
Hold That Ghost '41▸
Hollow Gate '88
Homeward Bound '80
The Hours '02▸
Human Nature '02
I Bury the Living '58▸
I Married a Witch '42▸
I Walked with a Zombie '43▸
I'm Losing You '98
Impure Thoughts '86
in an Old Manor House '84
In Between '92
In the Gloaming '97▸
The Indestructible Man '56
Infinity '96
Into the West '92▸
Intruso '93
The Invisible '07
It Came Upon a Midnight Clear '84
It Could Happen to You '39

▸ = rated three bones or higher

It's a Wonderful Life '46▶
It's My Party '95
Jacob's Ladder '90
Judge & Jury '96
Just like Heaven '05
The Kid with the Broken Halo '82
Killing Grandpa '91
Kiss Me Goodbye '82
Kiss of Death '77
Kissed '96
La Vie Continue '82
The Lady in White '88▶
The Last Best Year '90
Last Light '93
Left in Darkness '06
The Legend of Hell House '73▶
Liliom '35▶
Living Doll '90
Look Both Ways '05
Look... Give Me Money, Honey! '70
Love Letters '99▶
Love One Death '84
The Loved One '65
Macbeth '48▶
Macbeth '71▶
Macbeth '88
Made in Heaven '87
Magnolia '99▶
The Man from Elysian Fields '01▶
The Man with Two Lives '42
Mannequin '87
Marvin's Room '96
Mausoleum '83
Maxie '85
Meet Joe Black '98
Mermaid '00
The Midnight Hour '86
The Miracle of the Bells '48
Mr. Corbett's Ghost '90
Monkeybone '01
Monty Python's The Meaning of Life '83▶
Moonlight and Valentino '95
Moonlight Mile '02▶
Mortuary Academy '91
Mother and Son '97
A Mother's Prayer '95
My Life '93
Necropolis '87
The Newlydeads '87
Night of the Death Cult '75
Night of the Demons '88
Night of the Demons 2 '94
Night of the Living Dead '68▶
Night of the Living Dead '90
The Nightcomers '72
Nightmare Castle '65
Oh Dad, Poor Dad (Momma's Hung You in the Closet & I'm Feeling So Sad) '67
Oh, Heavenly Dog! '80
On Borrowed Time '39▶
The Oracle '85
Our Sons '91
Out of the Rain '90
Over Her Dead Body '08
Papa's Angels '00
Passed Away '92
The Peanut Butter Solution '85
Pet Sematary '89
Phantasm '79
Phantasm 2 '88
Phantasm 3: Lord of the Dead '94
The Phantom Chariot '20
Phantom of the Ritz '88
The Plague '92
Playroom '90
Poltergeist '82▶
Poltergeist 2: The Other Side '86
Poltergeist 3 '88
Ponette '95
Portrait of Jennie '48▶
The Possessed '77
Premonition '71
The Premonition '75
Prison '88
Promises in the Dark '79
The Prophecy '95
P.S. I Love You '07

The Psychic '78
Psychomania '73
Purgatory House '04
The Reincarnation of Peter Proud '75
Resurrection of Zachary Wheeler '71
Retribution '88
Return '88
Revenge of the Dead '84
Riders to the Sea '88
Riding the Bullet '04
Rimfire '49
A River Made to Drown In '97
Robot Stories '03
The Rue Morgue Massacres '73
Savage Hearts '95
Saved by the Light '95
Scared Stiff '53▶
School Spirit '85
Scrooge '35▶
Scrooge '70
Scrooged '88
Seven Days to Live '01
The Seventh Seal '56▶
Shadow Play '86
She Waits '71
Shock Waves '77
Sibling Rivalry '90
Silence Like Glass '90
The Sixth Man '97
The Sixth Sense '99▶
Sole Survivor '84
Sometimes They Come Back '91
Somewhere Tomorrow '85
Soultaker '90
South Park: Bigger, Longer and Uncut '99
Spawn '97▶
Stand by Me '86▶
Star Trek 3: The Search for Spock '84
Stones of Death '88
Strangers of the Evening '32
The Substitute Wife '94
Supernatural '33
Tell Me a Riddle '80
Tequila Body Shots '99
Terror Eyes '87
They Came Back '04
They Watch '93
Things to Do in Denver When You're Dead '95▶
13 Ghosts '60
13 Moons '02
Tim Burton's Corpse Bride '05▶
To Dance with the White Dog '93▶
To Forget Venice '79
To Gillian on Her 37th Birthday '96
Tomb of Torture '65
Topper '37▶
Topper Returns '41▶
Topper Takes a Trip '39▶
Trick or Treat '86
Truly, Madly, Deeply '91▶
Truth or Dare? '86
12 and Holding '05▶
Twice Dead '88
Two Days '03
Two of a Kind '83
The Unnamable '88
Unnatural '52
Unstrung Heroes '95
The Vacillations of Poppy Carew '94
The Vampire's Ghost '45
Vengeance '89
Visitor from the Grave '81
The Visitors '89
Vulture's Eye '04
Weekend at Bernie's '89
Weekend at Bernie's 2 '93
Welcome Back Mr. Fox '83
What Dreams May Come '98
Where the Lilies Bloom '74▶

Whispers '89
White Light '90
White Noise 2: The Light '07
The Widow '94
Wings of Fame '93
A Woman's Tale '92▶
Wristcutters: A Love Story '06
A Zed & Two Noughts '88▶
Zone of the Dead '78

Death Row
see also Executing Revenge; Men in Prison; Women in Prison
Angels with Dirty Faces '38▶
Beyond the Call '96
Black Angel '46▶
The Chamber '96
The Condemned '07
Convicted '04
Crime of the Century '96
Daniel '83
A Dark Adapted Eye '93▶
Dead Man Out '89▶
Dead Man Walking '95▶
Decoy '46
Desperate Measures '98
The Detective '68▶
88 Minutes '08
The Executioner's Song '82
The Green Mile '99▶
Hellblock 13 '97
I Want to Live! '58▶
Identity '03
In Cold Blood '67▶
In Cold Blood '96
Killer: A Journal of Murder '95
Last Dance '96
Last Rites '98
A Lesson Before Dying '99▶
Let Him Have It '91▶
Letters from a Killer '98
The Life of David Gale '03
Live! From Death Row '92
Lost Highway '96
Mommy 2: Mommy's Day '96
Monster's Ball '01▶
Pennies from Heaven '36
A Place in the Sun '51▶
The Seventh Sign '88
Shot in the Heart '01▶
The State Within '06
The Thin Blue Line '88▶
True Crime '99
Under Suspicion '92
Whitewash: The Clarence Brandley Story '02
The Widow of Saint-Pierre '00▶

Dedicated Teachers
see also Hell High School; School Daze
Akeelah and the Bee '06
Amy '81
Anna and the King '99
Balance of Power '96
Blackboard Jungle '55▶
Born Yesterday '50
Born Yesterday '93
Bossa Nova '99
Burn Witch, Burn! '62▶
Butterfly '99▶
Carried Away '95
Chalk '06
Cheaters '00
Cheers for Miss Bishop '41
A Child Is Waiting '63▶
Children of a Lesser God '86▶
The Chorus '04▶
Christy '94
Ciao, Professore! '94
Coach Carter '05▶
Comic Book: The Movie '04▶
Coming Out '89
Conrack '74▶
The Corn Is Green '45▶
The Corn Is Green '79▶
Dangerous Minds '95

Dead Poets Society '89▶
Detention '03
Disney's Teacher's Pet '04▶
Eden '98
Educating Rita '83▶
Election '99▶
The Elementary School '91
The Emperor's Club '02
Fever Pitch '05
Forever Mary '89▶
Freedom Writers '07
Friday Night Lights '04▶
Goodbye, Mr. Chips '39▶
Goodbye, Mr. Chips '02
The Great Debaters '07▶
Half Nelson '06▶
Heart of America '03
High School High '96
The History Boys '06
Homework '82
How You Look to Me '05
If Lucy Fell '95
The Incredible Mrs. Ritchie '03
Inherit the Wind '60▶
Inherit the Wind '99
Institue Benjamenta or This Dream People Call Human Life '95
Johnny Tiger '66
Kindergarten Cop '90
Knights of the South Bronx '05
Lean on Me '89▶
L'Eleve '95
A Lesson Before Dying '99▶
Life Is a Bed of Roses '83
Like Father Like Son '05
Lovey: A Circle of Children 2 '82
Luna e L'Altra '05
Mad Hot Ballroom '05▶
Madame Sousatzka '88▶
The Male Animal '42
Matilda '96▶
Miracle '04▶
The Miracle Worker '62▶
The Miracle Worker '79▶
The Miracle Worker '00
Mr. Holland's Opus '95▶
Mona Lisa Smile '03
Music of the Heart '99
Necessary Roughness '91
The Next Karate Kid '94
Night Visitor '89
Not One Less '99
October Sky '99▶
Oktober '98
187 '97
The Paper Chase '73▶
Paper Clips '04▶
Passion for Life '48
The Piano Teacher '01
Powder '95
The Prime of Miss Jean Brodie '69▶
The Principal '87
Race the Sun '96
Rachel, Rachel '68▶
Rachida '05▶
Rebound '05
Renaissance Man '94
The Road Home '01▶
The Rookie '02▶
School of Life '06
School of Rock '03▶
Shooting Dogs '05
Stand and Deliver '88▶
The Substitute '96
Summer School '87
Sunset Park '96
Take the Lead '06
Teachers '84
To Sir, with Love '67▶
Twenty-Four Eyes '54▶
Up the Down Staircase '67▶
Wildcats '86

Deep Blue
see also Go Fish; Sail Away; Shipwrecked; Submarines
The Abyss '89▶
Andre '94
Assault on a Queen '66

Baywatch the Movie: Forbidden Paradise '95
The Beast '96
The Big Blue '88
Crimson Tide '95▶
Danger Beneath the Sea '02
Deep Blue '03▶
Deep Blue Sea '99
ffolkes '80
Flipper '96▶
1492: Conquest of Paradise '92
Free Willy '93
Free Willy 2: The Adventure Home '95
Free Willy 3: The Rescue '97
Happy Feet '06▶
Hello Down There '69
Lords of the Deep '89
Men of Honor '00
Mission of the Shark '91▶
Moby Dick '98
Namu, the Killer Whale '66
Pirates '86
Shipwrecked '90
The Silent Enemy '58
Splash '84
The Spy Who Loved Me '77
Waterworld '95
Whale of a Tale '76
Wind '92

Demons & Wizards
see also Occult
The Alchemist '81
Archer: The Fugitive from the Empire '81
Army of Darkness '92▶
Arthur's Quest '99
Beyond Darkness '92
Bloodlust: Subspecies 3 '93
Bloodstone: Subspecies 2 '92
Blue Blood '73
Born of Fire '87
Bram Stoker's Shadowbuilder '98
The Church '98▶
Conan the Barbarian '82▶
Conan the Destroyer '84
Constantine '05▶
The Convent '00
Cthulhu Mansion '91
Curse of the Ultimate Sacrifice '90
Dead Waters '94
Deathstalker '83
Deathstalker 3 '89
Deathstalker 4: Match of Titans '92
Demon Rage '82
Demon Wind '90
Demonoid, Messenger of Death '81
The Demons '74
Demons '86
Demons of Ludlow '75
Demonstone '89
Demonwarp '87
Devil Woman '76
The Devil's Web '74
El Barbaro '84
Eragon '06
Ernest Scared Stupid '91
Evil Dead '83
Evil Dead 2: Dead by Dawn '87
Evil Toons '90
Excalibur '81▶
Fantasia '40▶
Fire and Ice '83
Funnyman '94
The Gate '87
Gate 2 '92
Ghost Son '06
Ghosts That Still Walk '77
The Giants of Thessaly '60
Gor '88
The Guardian '00
Guardian '01
Harry Potter and the Goblet of Fire '05▶
Harry Potter and the Order of the Phoenix '07

Harry Potter and the Prisoner of Azkaban '04
The Hazing '04
Hellboy '04▶
Hellraiser '87
Hellraiser 4: Bloodline '95
Hellraiser: Deader '05
The Heroic Trio '93
The Hobbit '78▶
Howl's Moving Castle '04▶
The Immortal '01
In the Name of the King: A Dungeon Siege Tale '08
Jack-O '95
Just Visiting '01
The King and I '99
Krull '83
Ladyhawke '85
The Legacy '79
Lord of the Rings: The Fellowship of the Rings '01▶
Lord of the Rings: The Two Towers '02▶
Lord of the Rings: The Return of the King '03▶
The Mephisto Waltz '71▶
Merlin's Apprentice '06
The Minion '98
Mirror, Mirror '90
Natas... The Reflection '83
Night of the Demons 3 '97
Outlaw of Gor '87
Possessed '00
Pumpkinhead '88
Pumpkinhead 2: Blood Wings '94
Pumpkinhead 3: Ashes to Ashes '06
Pumpkinhead 4: Blood Feud '07
Quest for the Mighty Sword '90
The Raven '63▶
Rawhead Rex '87
Red Sonja '85
The Return of the King '80
Rock & Rule '83
Savage Harvest 2: October Blood '06
Seizure '74
Silent Night, Deadly Night 4: Initiation '90
Sinthia: The Devil's Doll '70
Sorceress '82
Spellcaster '91
Stay Awake '87
Supergirl '84
Survival Island '02
Sword & the Sorcerer '82
The Sword in the Stone '63▶
Tales from the Crypt Presents Demon Knight '94
Talisman '98
Terror Eyes '87
Trancers 4: Jack of Swords '93
Troll '86
Troll 2 '92
The Unholy '88
The Unnamable 2: The Statement of Randolph Carter '92
Voodoo Moon '05
Warlock '91
Warlock: The Armageddon '93
Willow '88▶
Witchcraft 5: Dance with the Devil '92
The Witchmaker '69
Wizards of the Lost Kingdom '85
Wizards of the Lost Kingdom 2 '89
Zu: Warriors from the Magic Mountain '83

Dental Mayhem
see also Doctors & Nurses; Evil Doctors
Almost Heroes '97
Brazil '85▶
Captives '94
Charlie and the Chocolate Factory '05▶

▶ = *rated three bones or higher*

Compromising Positions '85
The Dentist '32▶
The Dentist '96
The Dentist 2: Brace Yourself '98
Dentist in the Chair '60
Diabolique '55▶
Don't Raise the Bridge, Lower the River '68
Eversmile New Jersey '89
Finding Nemo '03▶
Houseguest '94
The In-Laws '79▶
Little Shop of Horrors '60▶
Little Shop of Horrors '86▶
Marathon Man '76▶
Novocaine '01
The Paleface '48▶
Poltergeist 2: The Other Side '86
Reign Over Me '07
Reuben, Reuben '63▶
The Secret Lives of Dentists '02▶
Serial Mom '94▶
The Shakiest Gun in the West '68
Snow Dogs '02
Strawberry Blonde '41▶
Toothless '97
12 Monkeys '95▶
The Whole Nine Yards '00
The Whole Ten Yards '04

Desert War/Foreign Legion
see also *Deserts; Persian Gulf/Iraq War*
Abbott and Costello in the Foreign Legion '50
The Adventures of Priscilla, Queen of the Desert '94▶
Beau Geste '39▶
Beau Travail '98
Delta Force 3: The Killing Game '87
The Flying Deuces '39▶
Follow That Camel '67
Gunga Din '39▶
Jarhead '05
The Last Remake of Beau Geste '77
Lionheart '87
Man of Legend '71
March or Die '77
Morocco '30▶
Nine Men '43
Occupation: Dreamland '05▶
Outpost in Morocco '49
Sahara '43▶
Secondhand Lions '03
Legionnaire '98
Lost '05
Operation Condor '91
The Passenger '75▶
Passion in the Desert '97
Patriot Games '92▶
Picking Up the Pieces '99
The Road to Morocco '42▶
Sahara '43▶
Sahara '05
Samson and Delilah '96
Scorpion Spring '96
Sea of Sand '58
The Sheik '21▶
Shoot or Be Shot '02
Slow Burn '00
Son of the Sheik '26▶
Star Wars '77▶
Stargate '94
The Story of the Weeping Camel '03▶
Strawberry Fields '97
The Three Burials of Melquiades Estrada '05▶
Tremors '89
Tremors 2: Aftershocks '96
Twentynine Palms '03
White Sands '92
Yellow Asphalt '01

Deserts
see also *Desert War; Foreign Legion*
The Adventures of Priscilla, Queen of the Desert '94▶
American Strays '96
Back of Beyond '04
Baja '95
Beavis and Butt-Head Do America '96
The Big Empty '04
Broken Arrow '95
Children of Dune '03
Desert Blue '98
The Desert Fox '51▶
Desert Gold '36
Desert Hearts '86▶
Desert Heat '99
The Desert Rats '53▶
The Desert Song '53
Desert Winds '95
Drowning on Dry Land '00
Duma '05▶
Dune '84
Dune '00
Dune Warriors '91
Dust to Glory '05
The English Patient '96▶
Evolution '01
A Far Off Place '93
Faster, Pussycat! Kill! Kill! '65
Feast '06
Five Graves to Cairo '43▶
Flame of Araby '51
Flight of the Phoenix '04
The Forsaken '01
The Four Feathers '02
Frankenstein and Me '96
Grand Theft Parsons '03
Hidalgo '04

Detective Spoofs
see also *Detectives; Historical Detectives; Police Detectives; Private Eyes*
Ace Ventura: Pet Detective '93
Ace Ventura: When Nature Calls '95
The Adventures of Sherlock Holmes' Smarter Brother '78▶
Assault of the Party Nerds 2: Heavy Petting Detective '95
Blondes Have More Guns '95
Camouflage '00
Carry On Dick '75
Carry On Screaming '66
The Cheap Detective '78▶
Clean Slate '94
Clue '85
The Crooked Circle '32
Cry Uncle '71
The Curse of the Jade Scorpion '01
Curse of the Pink Panther '83
Dead Men Don't Wear Plaid '82
Detective School Dropouts '85
Dragnet '87
Fatal Instinct '93
Gumshoe '72
The Hollywood Detective '89
Hollywood Harry '86
Hoodwinked '05▶
How to Kill 400 Duponts '68
The Hound of the Baskervilles '77
Inspector Gadget '99
Inspector Gadget 2 '02
Love Happy '50
The Man with Bogart's Face '80
Master Mind '73
Murder by Death '76
My Favorite Brunette '47
The Naked Gun: From the Files of Police Squad '88▶
The Naked Gun 2 1/2: The Smell of Fear '91
Naked Gun 33 1/3: The Final Insult '94
Night Patrol '85
Oh, Heavenly Dog! '80
One Body Too Many '44
The Pink Chiquitas '86
The Pink Panther '64▶
The Pink Panther Strikes Again '76▶
The Private Eyes '80
Pure Luck '91
Rentadick '72
Return of the Pink Panther '74
Revenge of the Pink Panther '78
Ryder P.I. '86
The Shot '42
Second Sight '89
Secret Agent 00-Soul '89
Sherlock, Jr. '24▶
A Shot in the Dark '64▶
The Strange Case of the End of Civilization As We Know It '93
Terror 2000 '92
Trail of the Pink Panther '82
Who Done It? '42
Who Done It? '56
Who's Harry Crumb? '89
Without a Clue '88
Zero Effect '97

Detectives
see also *Amateur Sleuths; CIA/NSA; Cops; Detective Spoofs; FBI; Historical Detectives; Police Detectives; Private Eyes*

Detroit
see also *Checkered Flag: Motor Vehicle Dept.*
Aspen Extreme '93
Assault on Precinct 13 '05
Beverly Hills Cop '84
Beverly Hills Cop 2 '87
Beverly Hills Cop 3 '94
Bird on a Wire '90
Chameleon Street '89▶
Collision Course '89
The Color of Courage '98
Coupe de Ville '90
Crimewave '85
Crossover '06
Crossing the Bridge '92
Detroit 9000 '73
Detroit Rock City '99
The Dollmaker '84
Dreamgirls '06▶
8 Mile '02▶
Exit Wounds '01
Four Brothers '05
Gridlock'd '96▶
Grosse Pointe Blank '97▶
Hoffa '92▶
Indian Summer '93
Let's Kill All the Lawyers '93
The Life and Times of Hank Greenberg '99▶
The Man '05
Mirrors '08
Mr. Mom '83▶

Devil's Island
see also *Great Escapes; Men in Prison*
Condemned '29
The Life of Emile Zola '37▶
Mysterious Mr. Moto '38
Papillon '73▶
Passage to Marseilles '44▶
Strange Cargo '40
We're No Angels '55

Devils
Beauty and the Devil '50
Bedazzled '68
Bedazzled '00
Constantine '05
The Craft '93
Crazy as Hell '02
Crocodile Tears '98
Damn Yankees '58▶
Dark Angel: The Ascent '94
Deal of a Lifetime '99
The Devil & Max Devlin '81
The Devils '71▶
The Devil's Advocate '97▶
End of Days '99▶
The Exorcism of Emily Rose '05▶
Exorcist: The Beginning '04
Faust '26▶
Gates of Hell 2: Dead Awakening '96
Ghost Rider '07
Guardian of the Abyss '82
Haunted Symphony '94
Hell's Belles '95
High Strung '91
Highway to Hell '92
Hocus Pocus '93
Judgment Day '88
Legend '86▶
Les Visiteurs du Soir '42▶
Little Nicky '00
Lost Souls '00
Magic Hunter '96
The Mangler '94
Mr. Frost '89
Needful Things '93
The Ninth Gate '99
No News from God '01
The Omen '06
The Prophecy '95
Second Time Lucky '84
The Sorrows of Satan '25▶
South Park: Bigger, Longer and Uncut '99
Stephen King's The Stand '94
Tales from the Hood '95
The Witches of Eastwick '87▶

Diner
see also *Bar & Grill; Eateries; Waiters & Waitresses*
Alice Doesn't Live Here Anymore '74

Dinosaurs
see also *Killer Beasts*
Adventures in Dinosaur City '92
Anonymous Rex '04
At the Earth's Core '76
Baby... Secret of the Lost Legend '85
Barney's Great Adventure '98
Carnosaur '93
Carnosaur 2 '94
Carnosaur 3: Primal Species '96
Caveman '81▶
Clifford '92
The Crater Lake Monster '77
Dennis the Menace: Dinosaur Hunter '93
Dinosaur '00
Dinosaur Island '93
Dinosaur Valley Girls '96
Dinotopia '02
Genjasaurus Rex '87
Jurassic Park '93▶
Jurassic Park 3 '01
King Kong '05▶
The Land Before Time '88▶
The Land Before Time 2: The Great Valley Adventure '94
The Land Before Time 3: The Time of the Great Giving '95
The Land Before Time 4: Journey Through the Mists '96
The Land Before Time 5: The Mysterious Island '97
The Land Before Time 6: The Secret of Saurus Rock '98
The Land Before Time 7: The Stone of Cold Fire '00
The Land That Time Forgot '75
The Land Unknown '57
The Lost Continent '51
The Lost World '25
The Lost World '92
The Lost World '60
The Lost World: Jurassic Park 2 '97
Massacre in Dinosaur Valley '85
Meet the Robinsons '07
My Science Project '85
A Nymphoid Barbarian in Dinosaur Hell '94
One Million B.C. '40
One Million Years B.C. '66
One of Our Dinosaurs Is Missing '75
Pee-wee's Big Adventure '85▶
The People That Time Forgot '77
Planet of the Dinosaurs '80
Prehistoria '93
Prehistoria 2 '94
Prehistoria 3 '95
Pterodactyl Woman from Beverly Hills '97
Return to the Lost World '93
Sir Arthur Conan Doyle's The Lost World '98
Sound of Horror '64
Super Mario Bros. '93
Tammy and the T-Rex '94
Teenage Caveman '58
Theodore Rex '95
Toy Story '95▶
Toy Story 2 '99▶
Two Lost Worlds '50
Unknown Island '48
The Valley of Gwangi '69▶
We're Back! A Dinosaur's Story '93
When Dinosaurs Ruled the Earth '70

Disaster Flicks
see also *Action-Adventure; Air Disasters; Meltdown; Sea Disasters*
Accident '08
After the Shock '90
Aftershock: Earthquake in New York '99
Airport '70▶
Airport 75 '75
Airport '77 '77
Alive '93
Armageddon '98
Assignment Outer Space '61
Asteroid '97
Atomic Train '99
Avalanche '78
Avalanche '99
Avalanche Express '79
Beyond the Poseidon Adventure '79
The Big Bus '76
Brittanic '99
The Cassandra Crossing '76
Category 6: Day of Destruction '04
Category 7: The End of the World '05
The China Syndrome '79▶
The Christmas Coal Mine Miracle '77
City on Fire '79
The Concorde: Airport '79
The Crash of Flight 401 '78
Dante's Peak '97
The Day After Tomorrow '04
The Day the Sky Exploded '57
Daybreak '01
Daylight '96
Dead Ahead: The Exxon Valdez Disaster '92▶
Deep Core '00
Deep Impact '98
The Doomsday Flight '66
Earthquake '74
Earthstorm '05
Falling Fire '97

American Strays '96
Blood Diner '87
The Box '03
Coffee and Cigarettes '03▶
Deterrence '00
Diner '82▶
The Lost Bus '02
Narc '02▶
One in a Million: The Ron LeFlore Story '78
Out of Sight '98▶
Paper Lion '68
Presumed Innocent '90▶
Private Parts '96
R.I.C.O. '02
Renaissance Man '94
RoboCop '87▶
RoboCop 2 '90
RoboCop 3 '91
Roger & Me '89▶
The Rosary Murders '87
Scarecrow '73
Standing in the Shadows of Motown '02▶
Tainted '98
Tiger Town '83
True Romance '93▶
Tucker: The Man and His Dream '88▶
The Upside of Anger '05▶
The Wrecking Crew '69
Empire Falls '05
Exiled in America '90
Eye of the Storm '91
Five Easy Pieces '70▶
Frankie and Johnny '91▶
Gloomy Sunday '02▶
Heavy '94▶
Here on Earth '00
Into the Fire '88
It Could Happen to You '94
Kisses in the Dark '97
Leo '02
Loveless '83
The Maldonado Miracle '03
Monster's Ball '01▶
My Blueberry Nights '07
Nickel Mountain '85
Parallel Sons '95
Payback '94
Pennies from Heaven '36
Petrified Forest '36▶
Pulp Fiction '94▶
Queen of Hearts '89▶
Recipe for Disaster '03
A Season for Miracles '99
Sliding Doors '97
Swimming '00
Trouble in Mind '86▶
The Undertaker and His Pals '67
Waiting for the Light '90
Waitress '07▶
When Harry Met Sally... '89▶
The Life and Times of Hank Greenberg '99▶
The Man '05
Mirrors '08
Mr. Mom '83▶
The Forsaken '01
Greenberg '99▶
The Man '05
Mirrors '08
Mr. Mom '83▶

Disaster

Fallout '01
Fatal Contact: Bird Flu in America '06
Final Warning '90
Fire '77
Fire and Rain '89
Firestorm '97
Firestorm: 72 Hours in Oakland '93
Firetrap '01
Flood! '76
Flood: A River's Rampage '97
Gale Force '01
Gray Lady Down '77
Hard Rain '97
The High and the Mighty '54▶
The Hindenburg '75
The Hurricane '37▶
Hurricane '74
Hurricane '79
In Old Chicago '37▶
Independence Day '96▶
Inferno '98
Judgment Day '99
Last Days of Pompeii '35
The Last Voyage '60
The Last Warrior '99
The Last Woman on Earth '61
The Lost Missile '58
Magma: Volcanic Disaster '06
Meltdown '06
Meteor '79
Morning Departure '50
A Night to Remember '58▶
Pandemic '07
Panic in the Skies '96
The Perfect Storm '00
Planet on the Prowl '65
Poseidon '06
The Poseidon Adventure '72
Power Play '02
The Rains Came '39
Raise the Titanic '80
Red Alert '77
Red Planet '00
Right at Your Door '06
St. Helen's, Killer Volcano '82
Scorcher '02
Snowblind '78
Snowbound: The Jim and Jennifer Stolpa Story '94
S.O.S. Titanic '79
Space: 1999—Alien Attack '79▶
The Survivalist '87
Survivor '87
Tailspin: Behind the Korean Airline Tragedy '89
Terror on the 40th Floor '74
Tidal Wave '75
Titanic '97▶
The Towering Inferno '74
Tragedy of Flight 103: The Inside Story '91▶
Twister '96
Two Minute Warning '76
Tycus '98
Velocity Trap '99
Volcano '97
Volcano: Fire on the Mountain '97
When Time Ran Out '80
White Squall '96
Y2K '99
Zero Hour! '57

Disco Musicals

see also Musicals
Can't Stop the Music '80
Car Wash '76
KISS Meets the Phantom of the Park '78
Pirate Movie '82
The Rocky Horror Picture Show '75▶
Roll Bounce '05▶
Saturday Night Fever '77
Thank God It's Friday '78
The Wiz '78
Xanadu '80

Disease of the Week

see also AIDS; Emerging Viruses
The Affair '73▶
And Now Ladies and Gentlemen '02
The Ann Jillian Story '88
As Good As It Gets '97▶
Away From Her '06▶
Bang the Drum Slowly '56
Batman and Robin '97
Beaches '88▶
Bear Ye One Another's Burden... '88
The Best Little Girl in the World '81▶
Between Two Women '86
The Blue Butterfly '04
Bobby Deerfield '77
The Book of Stars '99
The Boy in the Plastic Bubble '76
Brian's Song '71▶
Brian's Song '01
Bubble Boy '01
Camille '36▶
The Carrier '87
The Cassandra Crossing '76
Champions '84
Checking Out '89
Children of the Corn 4: The Gathering '96
Chinese Box '97
C.H.U.D. '84
Cleo from 5 to 7 '61▶
Cold Harvest '98
Contagious '07
The Contaminated Man '01
Crash Course '00
Cries and Whispers '72▶
Crystal Heart '87
The Curse '87
Damien: The Leper Priest '80
Daybreak '93
Dead Man Walking '88
Dead Space '90
Dick Barton, Special Agent '48
The Doctor '91
Dr. Akagi '98
Doctor Bull '33
Down in the Delta '98▶
A Dream of Kings '69
Duet for One '86
Dying Young '91
An Early Frost '85▶
East of Kilimanjaro '57
The End '78▶
Eric '75▶
Erin Brockovich '00▶
The First Deadly Sin '80
First Do No Harm '97
Fourth Wish '75
Gaby: A True Story '87▶
Germicide '74
Girls' Night '97
Glory Enough for All: The Discovery of Insulin '92
Go Now '96▶
Griffin and Phoenix: A Love Story '76
Hangman's Curse '03
Here on Earth '00
Hilary and Jackie '98▶
Incredible Melting Man '77
Interrupted Melody '55▶
Intimate Contact '87▶
Iris '01▶
Isle of the Dead '45
Isn't She Great '00
Jack '96
Jericho Fever '93
John Grisham's The Rainmaker '97
Killer on Board '77
L.A. Bad '85
The Last Best Year '90
Last Breath '96
The Last Man on Earth '64
Look Both Ways '05
Lorenzo's Oil '92▶
Love Affair: The Eleanor & Lou Gehrig Story '77▶
Love Story '70▶
Love Under Pressure '78

Mad Death '83
Marvin's Room '96
A Matter of WHO '62
Miles to Go '86
Miss Evers' Boys '97
Molokai: The Story of Father Damien '99
A Mother's Prayer '95
My Father's House '75
My Life '93
Nasty Rabbit '64
Niagara, Niagara '97
On Her Majesty's Secret Service '69▶
One True Thing '98▶
Osmosis Jones '01
The Painted Veil '06
Panic in Echo Park '77
Parting Glances '86▶
Philadelphia '93▶
Pictures of Hollis Woods '07
Pilgrim, Farewell '82
The Plague '92
The Plague Dogs '82
The Pride of the Yankees '42▶
Princes in Exile '90
Project: Alien '89
Promises in the Dark '79
The Proud Ones '53
Quarantine '89
Question of Faith '93
A Quiet Duel '49
Rabid '77
Rasputin: Dark Servant of Destiny '96▶
Reborn '81
Right of Way '84
The Road to Galveston '96
The Road to Wellville '94
Safe House '99
The Shadow Box '80▶
Shadowlands '93▶
A Shining Season '79▶
Silence Like Glass '90
The Silver Streak '34
Simon Birch '98
Six Weeks '82
A Song for Martin '01
Steel Magnolias '89▶
Stepmom '98▶
Stigma '73
Strange Relations '02
Sunchaser '96
Terms of Endearment '83▶
Terror Creatures from the Grave '66
That Russell Girl '08
The Theory of Flight '98
The Tic Code '99
A Time to Live '85
A Time to Remember '03
Venomous '01
Waking Up Wally '05
Walking Through the Fire '80
The Wedding Gift '93▶
When the Time Comes '91
When Wolves Cry '69
The White Legion '36
Xtro '83
ZigZag '02▶

Disorganized Crime

see also Comic Cops; Crime Doesn't Pay; Comedy; Organized Crime
The Adventures of Pluto Nash '02
The Adventures of Rocky & Bullwinkle '00
Airheads '94
Albino Alligator '96
All About the Benjamins '02
All Saint's Day '98
Allie & Me '97
Amos and Andrew '93
The Apple Dumpling Gang '75
The Apple Dumpling Gang Rides Again '79
Armed and Dangerous '86
Baby on Board '07
Baby's Day Out '94
Bait '00

Bandits '01
Beautiful Creatures '00
Before the Devil Knows You're Dead '07▶
Big Nothing '06
Big Trouble '02
Born Bad '97
Bottle Rocket '95
Buffalo 66 '97▶
Children of Hannibal '98
Cop and a Half '93
Crackers '84
Crime Spree '03
Disorganized Crime '89
Dr. Otto & the Riddle of the Gloom Beam '86
Drowning Mona '00
Dying to Get Rich '98
8 Heads in a Duffel Bag '96
Ernest Goes to Jail '90
Everybody's Famous! '00
Face '97
Fargo '96▶
Find Me Guilty '06▶
Finders Keepers '84
A Fine Mess '86
Fish in a Barrel '01
Get Shorty '95▶
Glitch! '88
Goodbye South, Goodbye '96
Gravesend '97
Gridlock'd '96▶
The Gun in Betty Lou's Handbag '92
Gun Shy '00
Happy New Year '87
Headless Body in Topless Bar '96
Held Up '00
Her Alibi '89
Herbie Goes Bananas '80
High Heels and Low Lifes '01
Hit Me '96
Home Alone '90▶
Home Alone 2: Lost in New York '92
Hoods '98
I Wonder Who's Killing Her Now? '76
Idiot Box '97
In Bruges '07
In the Country Where Nothing Happens '99
Inside the Law '42
The Italian Job '69
The Jerky Boys '95
Keys to Tulsa '96
Kicked in the Head '97
Kill Me Later '01
Killing Zoe '94
Knockaround Guys '01
The League of Gentlemen '60▶
Leather Jackets '90
L.I.E. '01
Lock, Stock and 2 Smoking Barrels '98▶
Love, Honour & Obey '00
Lucky Numbers '00
Lunch Wagon '81
A Man, a Woman, and a Bank '79
Man of the House '95
Menage '86▶
Mexican Hayride '48
Milo Milo '79
Miss Grant Takes Richmond '49
Mixed Nuts '94
More Dogs Than Bones '00
Mutant on the Bounty '89
A New Wave '07
The Night They Robbed Big Bertha's '75
Ocean's 11 '60
Once in the Life '00
Once Upon a Crime '92
101 Dalmatians '96
102 Dalmatians '00
Out on a Limb '92
Palookaville '95
Partners '99
The Perfect Score '04
Perpetrators of the Crime '98
Picking Up the Pieces '99

Ping! '99
Poor White Trash '00
Pouvoir Intime '87
Quick Change '90
Ransom Money '88
Reservoir Dogs '92▶
The River's Red '48
Round Trip to Heaven '92
Ruthless People '86▶
Safe Men '98
St. Benny the Dip '51
Scorched '02
See No Evil, Hear No Evil '89
See Spot Run '01
Shake Hands with Murder '44
Shark Tale '04
The Shot '96
Silver Bears '78
Sister Act '92
Sitting Ducks '80▶
A Slight Case of Murder '99
Small Time Crooks '00
Snatch '00▶
Stealing Harvard '02
Stop! or My Mom Will Shoot '92
The Super '91
Survivors '83
Tall, Tan and Terrific '46
The Thief Who Came to Dinner '73
Things to Do in Denver When You're Dead '95▶
Three Kinds of Heat '87
Thrilled to Death '88
Too Many Crooks '59
Trapped in Paradise '94
Triggermen '02
Trouble Chasers '45
Truth or Consequences, N.M. '97
Two If by Sea '95
Two Tough Guys '03
Warm Blooded Killers '01
Welcome to Collinwood '02
We're Talkin' Serious Money '92
What's the Worst That Could Happen? '01
With Friends Like These '98▶
The Wrong Arm of the Law '63▶
The Young in Heart '38▶
Zoolander '01

Divorce

see also Marriage; Single Parents; Singles; Stepparents
The Accidental Tourist '88▶
All I Want for Christmas '91
Alpha Beta '73
Angels in America '03▶
The Assassination of Richard Nixon '05
The Awful Truth '37▶
Between Friends '83
A Bill of Divorcement '32
Blue Car '03▶
Breaking Up '78
Breaking Up Is Hard to Do '79
Bringing Down the House '03
Bye Bye, Love '94
California Suite '78▶
Can She Bake a Cherry Pie? '83
Catch Me If You Can '02▶
Celebrity '98
Cheaper to Keep Her '80
Children of Divorce '80
City by the Sea '02
Clara's Heart '88
Cold Heat '90
A Conspiracy of Love '87
A Cooler Climate '99
Cross My Heart '88
Definitely, Maybe '08▶
Desert Hearts '86▶
Diary of a Mad Black Woman '05

Divorce American Style '67
Divorce His, Divorce Hers '72
Divorce—Italian Style '62▶
The Divorcee '30
Dr. T & the Women '00▶
Dodson's Journey '01
Duane Hopwood '05▶
Duck Season '04▶
Dying to Get Rich '98
Early Frost '84
Edie & Pen '95
Empire Falls '05▶
Escapade '55▶
E.T.: The Extra-Terrestrial '82▶
Every Other Weekend '91▶
The Ex '96
Expectations '97
Face the Music '92
Faces '68▶
Faithless '00▶
Falling Down '93
Family Pictures '93▶
Father Figure '80
Fergie & Andrew: Behind Palace Doors '93
A Fight for Jenny '90
The First Wives Club '96
5x2 '04
Fool's Gold '08
For Richer or Poorer '97
Found Alive '34
The Full Monty '96▶
The Fury Within '98
The Good Father '87▶
The Good Mother '88
Goodbye Love '34
Hard Promises '92
The Healer '02
Heartbreakers '01
Heartburn '86▶
High Society '56▶
History Is Made at Night '37▶
Hollow Reed '95▶
Hope Floats '98
House Arrest '96
How to Break Up a Happy Divorce '76
How to Commit Marriage '69
Husbands and Wives '92▶
Interiors '78▶
Intolerable Cruelty '03▶
Irreconcilable Differences '84
The Kiss You Gave Me '00
Kramer vs. Kramer '79▶
Late Marriage '01
Laws of Attraction '04
Le Divorce '03
Les Destinees '00
Let's Make It Legal '51
Liar Liar '97▶
The Liberation of L.B. Jones '70
Living Out Loud '98
Love '05
Love and Hate: A Marriage Made in Hell '90
Love Matters '93
Marie '85▶
Marriage on the Rocks '65
The Marrying Kind '52
Me & Mrs. Jones '02
Me and You and Everyone We Know '05▶
Melanie '82
Misbehaving Husbands '41
The Misfits '61▶
Mrs. Doubtfire '93
Mr. Skeffington '44▶
Mr. Wonderful '93
Mother '96
Must Love Dogs '05
My Foolish Heart '49
Nadine '87
Naked Paradise '78
Necessary Parties '88
Never Say Goodbye '46
A New Life '88
Night Life in Reno '31
Nothing in Common '86
Now and Then '95
Ocean's Eleven '01▶
The Odd Couple '68▶
The Odd Job '78

▶ = rated three bones or higher

Old School '03
Ora Cooks, the Other
Doesn't '83
The Parent Trap '61
The Parent Trap '98
Petti Rocks '88▶
Peggy Sue Got Married '86
The Personals '83
Petulia '68▶
Pilgrim, Farewell '82
Play It Again, Sam '72▶
The Prize Pulitzer '89
Reckless '97▶
Rich Kids '79
Riptide '34▶
The Santa Clause '94
Sarabrand '03▶
Scenes from a Marriage '73▶
Sex and the Single Parent '82
Shattered Silence '71
Signs & Wonders '00
The Solitary Man '82
Something's Gotta Give '03▶
The Squid and the Whale '05▶
The Starter Wife '07
Staring Over '79▶
Stepmom '98▶
Strange Bedfellows '65
Sweet Revenge '90
Table for Five '83
Tattle Tale '92
Tell It to the Judge '49
Tell Me That You Love Me '84
Tenth Month '79
Thank You for Smoking '06
That Old Feeling '96
Till Murder Do Us Part '92
Town and Country '01
Twister '96
Under the Tuscan Sun '03
The Upside of Anger '05▶
Valentino Returns '88
Wah-Wah '05
Wanted: The Perfect Guy '86
The War of the Roses '89▶
The Weather Man '05
Welcome to Mooseport '04
Without Anesthesia '78

Doctors & Nurses
see also AIDS; Dental
Mayhem; Disease of the
Week; Emerging Viruses;
& Medicine; Hospitals
Evil Doctors; Hospitals
Nursploitation; Sanity
Check; Shrinks

All Creatures Great and
Small '74▶
Alone in the Dark '82
And the Band Played On
'93▶
The Android Affair '95
Anne of Green Gables: The
Continuing Story '99
Any Given Sunday '99▶
Arachnophobia '90
Armistead Maupin's More
Tales of the City '97
Arrowsmith '32
Article 99 '92
Ashanti, Land of No Mercy
'79
The Asphyx '72▶
At First Sight '58
Atonement '07▶
Awake '07
Awakenings '90▶
Baby Girl Scott '87
Bad Medicine '85
Battle Circus '53
Beautiful People '99
Behind the Mask '99
Bethune '77
Between Wars '74

Beyond Borders '03
Beyond Re-Animator '03
Bikini House Calls '96
Bikini Med School '98
Doctor in the House '53▶
Black Friday '40
The Black Dragons '42
Blade '98
Bless the Child '00
Blind Justice '94
Bliss '96
Blood Work '02
Blood Mania '70
Body Parts '91
Bone Daddy '97
Botany Bay '53
Brain Dead '89▶
The Bramble Bush '60
Breast Men '97
Broken Glass '96
Brute Force '47▶
The Bumblebee Flies
Anyway '98
Calling Paul Temple '48
Candy Stripe Nurses '74
Carry On Doctor '68▶
Castle of the Creeping Flesh
'68
Caught '49▶
Century '94
Charlie Bravo '80
Children of Rage '75
Children of the Corn 4: The
Gathering '96
China Beach '88▶
The Cider House Rules '99▶
The Citadel '60
Circus of Horrors '60
City of Angels '98
City of Joy '92
Club Havana '46
Coastlines '02
Coma '78▶
Contagious '96
Corregidor '43
Corridors of Blood '58
Courageous Dr. Christian
'40
Cries of Silence '97
Crimes & Misdemeanors
'89▶
Critical Care '97
Critical Choices '97
Crossover '82
Dark City '97
Dead in a Heartbeat '02
Dead Ringers '88▶
Dead Sleep '91
Death Becomes Her '92▶
Death by Prescription '86
Death Nurse '87
The Death of Mr. Lazarescu
'05

Decoy '46
Deep Crimson '96
The Devil's Web '74
Dirty Pretty Things '03▶
Doc Hollywood '91
The Doctor '91
Dr. Akagi '98
Dr. Alien '88
The Doctor and the Devils
'85
Doctor at Large '57
Doctor at Sea '56
Dr. Bell and Mr. Doyle: The
Dark Beginnings of
Sherlock Holmes '00
Dr. Bethune '90▶
Dr. Black, Mr. Hyde '76
Doctor Blood's Coffin '62
Doctor Bull '33
Doctor Butcher M.D. '80
Dr. Caligari '89
Dr. Christian Meets the
Women '40
Dr. Cyclops '40
Dr. Death, Seeker of Souls
'73
Dr. Detroit '83
Doctor Dolittle '67
Dr. Dolittle '98
Doctor Dolittle 2 '01
Dr. Faustus '68

Dr. Frankenstein's Castle of
Freaks '74
Dr. Hackyl and Mr. Hype '80
Doctor in Distress '63
Dr. Jekyll and Mr. Hyde '32
Dr. Jekyll & Mr. Hyde '73
Johnny Belinda '48▶
Dr. Jekyll & Mr. Hyde '99
Dr. Kildare's Strange Case
'40
Dr. Mabuse, The Gambler
'22▶
Dr. Mabuse vs. Scotland
Yard '64
Dr. Petiot '90
Dr. T & the Women '00▶
Doctor Satan's Robot '40
Doctor Takes a Wife '40▶
Dr. Tarr's Torture Dungeon
'75
Dr. Terror's House of
Horrors '65
Doctor Who '96
Doctor X '32
Doctor Zhivago '65▶
Doctor Zhivago '02
Doctors and Nurses '03
Doctor's Wives '70
Dominick & Eugene '88▶
Don't Cry, It's Only Thunder
'82
Don't Look in the Basement
'78
Dragonfly '02
Drunken Angel '48▶
East of Borneo '31
The Egyptian '54
The Elephant Man '80▶
Emmanuelle in the Country
The English Patient '96▶
Extreme Measures '96
Eyes Wide Shut '99
False Faces '32
Fantastic Voyage '66▶
Fatal Error '99
The Fifth Horseman Is Fear
'64
First Do No Harm '97
Flatliners '90
The Flesh and the Fiends
'60
Flesh Feast '69
Foreign Body '86
The Fortune Cookie '66▶
The Fugitive '93▶
Girl, Interrupted '99
Glory Enough for All: The
Discovery of Insulin '90
The Great Moment '44
Gross Anatomy '89
Guess Who's in the House '44
Gun Shy '00
Halloween 2: The
Nightmare Isn't Over! '81
Hands Up '81▶
Hard to Kill '89
Harold and Kumar Go to
White Castle '04
He Loves Me ... He Loves
Me Not '02

Healer '36
High Heels '72
A Hole in One '04
Holy Girl '04▶
Holy Terror '65
Hombres Armados '97▶
The Home Front '02
Honor Among Thieves '68
The Horrible Dr. Hichcock
'62
The Horror Chamber of Dr.
Faustus '59▶
Horror Hospital '73
The Hospital '71▶
Hospital of Terror '78
House Calls '78▶
How I Killed My Father '03▶
I Love My... Wife '70
I Never Promised You a
Rose Garden '77▶
In Dreams '98
The In-Laws '79▶
In Love and War '96
The Incredible Journey of
Dr. Meg Laurel '79▶
An Indecent Obsession '85

Internes Can't Take Money
'37
The Interns '62▶
Invasion '65
Jesse '88
Dr. Jekyll and Mr. Hyde '53▶
Johnny Belinda '48▶
Junior '94
Just like Heaven '05
Kidnapping of Baby John
Doe '88
Killing Moon '00
Kiss and Make Up '34
Korczak '90▶
La Sentinelle '92
Larceny On the Air '37
The Last Angry Man '59▶
The Last Bridge '54
The Last King of Scotland
'06▶
Laurel Canyon '02
The Lazarus Syndrome '79
Les Cas da Dr. Laurent '57▶
Les Patterson Saves the
World '90
Let's Get Married '60
Lie Down with Lions '94
Life is a Long Quiet River
'83▶
The Light in the Jungle '91
Like Father, Like Son '87
Looking for an Echo '99
Love '05
Love for Rent '05
Love in the Time of Cholera
'07
Love Is a Many-Splendored
Thing '55
Lover's Knot '96
Mad Love '35▶
The Mad Monster '42
The Madness of King
George '94▶
Make-Up '37
Making Love '82
Malice '93
Maniac Nurses Find
Ecstasy '94
Marvin's Room '96
M*A*S*H '70▶
M*A*S*H: Goodbye,
Farewell & Amen '83▶
The Mask of Fu Manchu '32
Mester and Commander:
The Far Side of the World
'03▶
A Matter of Life and Death
'81
Matter of Trust '98
Maze '59
The Medicine Show '01
Meet Dr. Christian '39
Memories of Me '88
Men of Ireland '38
Mesmer '94
Metamorphosis: The Alien
Factor '93
The Millionairess '60
Miss Evers' Boys '97
Mr. North '88
Mockingbird Don't Sing '01
Molly '99
Monty Python's The
Meaning of Life '83▶
Murder in Texas '81▶
Murder or Mercy '74
Murder Once Removed '71
My Own Country '98
Nell '94
Night Call Nurses '72
Night Monster '42
Night Nurse '31▶
Nightbreaker '89▶
Nine Months '95
No One Man '32
No Way Out '50
Noel '04
Nomads '86
Not a Stranger '55
Not of This Earth '96
Nurse '80
Nurse Betty '00▶
Nurse Edith Cavell '39▶
Nurse Marjorie '20
Nurse on Call '88
Old Swimmin' Hole '40

One Flew Over the
Cuckoo's Nest '75▶
Only Love '98
The Ordeal of Dr. Mudd '80▶
Outbreak '94▶
The Painted Veil '06
Pandemic '07
Panic in Echo Park '77
Panic in the Streets '50▶
Paper Mask '91
Patch Adams '98
Pathology '08
The Patriot '99
Pearl Harbor '01
People Will Talk '51▶
Perfect Assassins '98
Persona '65▶
Petulia '68▶
Phenomenon '96▶
A Place for Annie '94
The Plague '92
Planet Terror '07
Playing God '96
Praying Mantis '83
The Princess and the
Warrior '00▶
Private Duty Nurses '71
Promises in the Dark '79
Purple Hearts '84
A Quiet Duel '49▶
Race Against Time '00
The Raven '35▶
The Real Glory '39▶
Reckless '97▶
Reckless Disregard '84
Reckless: The Sequel '98▶
Red Beard '65▶
Restoration '94▶
Riot Squad '41
The Road to Wellville '94
Robin Cook's Terminal '96
Rodgers & Hammerstein's
South Pacific '01
Roommates '95
Salem's Lot '04
Saw '04
Saw III '06
Sawbones '95
Say Goodbye, Maggie Cole
'72
Scalpel '76
The Secret of Dr. Kildare '39
Seducing Doctor Lewis '03
Series 7: The Contenders
'01
Serving in Silence: The
Margarethe
Cammemeyer Story '95
The Singing Detective '03
Sister Kenny '46▶
Sister Dora '77
Skeeze '82
The Skeleton Key '05
Slaughter Hotel '71
Smart People '08
So Proudly We Hail '43▶
Someone Behind the Door
'71
Something's Gotta Give
'03▶
Sour Grapes '98
South Pacific '58▶
Sprague '84
The Spring '00
State of Emergency '94
Stigma '73
Stitches '85
A Stolen Face '52
The Story of Dr. Wassell
'44
Strange Confession '45▶
The Student Nurses '70
Sublime '07
Sunchaser '96
The Surgeon '94
Talk to Her '02▶
Teenage Frankenstein '58
Tender Loving Care '73
Testament of Youth '79
Things You Can Tell Just by
Looking at Her '00
30 Years to Life '01
Torture Ship '39
Touched '05
Trial by Media '00
Tundra '36

The Twelve Days of
Christmas Eve '04
The Twilight of the Ice
Nymph '97
The Unbearable Lightness
of Being '88▶
The Unknown Soldier '98
A Very Serious Person '06
The Vicious Circle '57
Vital Signs '90
Vulture's Eye '04
Waitress '07▶
We Are the Children '87
Welcome Stranger '47
What Dreams May Come
'98
When the Bullet Hits the
Bone '95
Where Danger Lives '50
Where the Money Is '00
White Coats '04
White Dwarf '95
Who Killed Bambi? '03
Wit '01▶
Woman of Straw '64
Women of Valor '86
Woman '07▶
The Young Doctors in Love '82
The Young Nurses '73
Zelary '03▶
Zerc Hour! '57

Docudrama
see also Documentary

Above Us the Waves '56▶
Adam '83▶
After the Shock '90
Al Capone '59▶
Alexandria Again and
Forever '90
Blind Ambition '79
The Boston Strangler '68
Bound for Glory '76▶
Boycott '02▶
Baadasssss! '03▶
Babyfever '94
The Battle of Algiers '66▶
The Battle of the Rails '45▶
Beefcake '99
Call Me: The Rise and Fall
of Heidi Fleiss '04
Casualties of Love: The
"Long Island Lolita" Story
'93
Chasing Freedom '04
Christian the Lion '76
Close to Home '06
Cocaine: One Man's
Seduction '83
Conspiracy: The Trial of the
Chicago Eight '87▶
The Cool World '63
Countdown '68
The Courtesans of Bombay
'85▶
Crown Heights '02
The Cruel Sea '53▶
A Cry in the Dark '88▶
DC 9/11: Time of Crisis '04
Edge of the World '37▶
8A '92
The Flaming Teen-Age '56
Free, White, and 21 '62
The General Line '29▶
H '90
Helter Skelter Murders '71
Henry: Portrait of a Serial
Killer '90▶
Hiroshima '95▶
Hostages '93
Immortal Battalion '44▶
Inside the Third Reich '82
Iron & Silk '91
James Dean '76
The Jayne Mansfield Story
'80
Journey Through Rosebud
'72
Kamikaze Hearts '91

▶ = 'rated three bones or higher

Docudrama

Kids '95
King '78
Lethal Lolita—Amy Fisher: My Story '92
The Lion Has Wings '40
Looking for Richard '96
Mandela and de Klerk '97
The Manson Family '04
Miss Evers' Boys '97
Moolaade '04
Murder in Texas '81
The Naked City '48
No Turning Back '01
Our Music '04
Panther '95
Pickpocket '59
The Poppy Is Also a Flower '66
Prince of the City '81
Qui Etes Vous, Mr. Sorge? '61
Real Life '79
The Red Menace '49
The Road to Guantanamo '06
Shaka Zulu '83
S.O.S. Titanic '79
Special Bulletin '83
The Spy Who Came in from the Cold '65
Stealing Sinatra '04
Tailspin: Behind the Korean Airline Tragedy '89
Take the Money and Run '69
Tamation '03
Teenage Devil Dolls '53
Ten Days That Shook the World '27
That's Adequate '90
The Thin Blue Line '88
32 Short Films about Glenn Gould '93
This Revolution '05
Times of Harvey Milk '83
Touching the Void '03
Uprising '01
What the $*! Do We Know? '04
Women in Prison '49
Working Girls '87

Documentary

see also Docudrama

After Innocence '05
Aileen: Life and Death of a Serial Killer '03
Air Guitar Nation '06
American Fabulous '92
American Movie '99
America's Heart and Soul '04
Anna '93
Arctic Tale '07
The Aristocrats '05
Assassination of Trotsky '72
The Atomic Cafe '82
Awesome! I F*** in' Shot That! '06
Ballet Russes '05
The Big One '98
Born Into Brothels: Calcutta's Red Light Kids '04
Born to Boogie '72
Bowling for Columbine '02
The Boys of Baraka '05
The Boys of 2nd Street Park '03
A Brief History of Time '92
Brother's Keeper '92
Bruce Lee: Curse of the Dragon '93
Buena Vista Social Club '99
Burden of Dreams '82
Bush's Brain '04
Capturing the Friedmans '03
The Celluloid Closet '95
Chicago 10 '07
The Children of Theatre Street '77
Chuck Berry: Hail! Hail! Rock 'n' Roll '87
Ciao Federico! Fellini Directs Satyricon '69
The Clowns '71
Control Room '04
Crazy Love '07
Crumb '94
Dance Hall Racket '58
Darfur Now '07
Darwin's Nightmare '04
Dave Chappelle's Block Party '06
A Decade Under the Influence '02
December 7th: The Movie '91
Decline of Western Civilization 1 '81
Decline of Western Civilization 2: The Metal Years '88
Deep Blue '03
Derby '71
The Devil and Daniel Johnston '05
DIGI '04
Dust to Glory '05
Ebony Dreams '80
The 11th Hour '07
Elvis in Hollywood '93
Encounter with the Unknown '75
End of the Century: The Story of the Ramones '03
The Endless Summer '66
The Endless Summer 2 '94
Enron: The Smartest Guys in the Room '05
Fade to Black '04
Fahrenheit 9/11 '04
Fallen Champ: The Untold Story of Mike Tyson '93
Fast, Cheap & Out of Control '97
Fellini: I'm a Born Liar '03
Festival Express '03
The Filth and the Fury '99
First Descent '05
The Fog of War: Eleven Lessons from the Life of Robert S. McNamara '03
Full Tilt Boogie '97
Germany in Autumn '78
Giuliani Time '05
Go Further '03
God Grew Tired of Us '06
The Goebbels Experiment '05
Going Upriver: The Long War of John Kerry '04
Gray's Anatomy '96
Grizzly Man '05
The Ground Truth '06
Guilty of Treason '50
Gunner Palace '04
Hank Aaron: Chasing the Dream '95
Harlan County, U.S.A. '76
Haxan: Witchcraft through the Ages '22
The Heart of the Game '05
Hearts of Darkness: A Filmmaker's Apocalypse '91
Heavy Petting '89
Hell's Angels Forever '83
The Hellstrom Chronicle '71
Henri Langlois: The Phantom of the Cinematheque '04
Hide and Seek '80
Hijacking Catastrophe: 9/11, Fear and the Selling of America '04
Hoop Dreams '94
How to Eat Your Watermelon in White Company (and Enjoy It) '05
Hugh Hefner: Once Upon a Time '92
The Hunting of the President '04
I Wanna Be a Beauty Queen '85
In the Pit '06
In the Shadow of the Moon '07
Incident at Oglala: The Leonard Peltier Story '92
An Inconvenient Truth '06
Inside Deep Throat '05
The Ister '04
It Happened in the Park '56
It's All True '93
The JFK Conspiracy '91
Journeys with George '02
The Kid Stays in the Picture '02
Kidco '83
The King of Kong: A Fistful of Quarters '07
The Last Waltz '78
LBJ: A Biography '91
Le Joli Mai '62
League of Ordinary Gentlemen '04
The Leopard Son '96
Let It Be '70
Let's Get Lost '88
The Life and Times of Hank Greenberg '99
Lighting in a Bottle '04
Long Shadows '86
Lost in La Mancha '03
Louisiana Story '48
Love Meetings '64
The Love Goddesses '65
Mad Hot Ballroom '05
Malcolm X: Make It Plain '95
Man in the Silk Hat '83
Man of Aran '34
The Man with the Movie Camera '29
Many Faces of Sherlock Holmes '86
March of the Penguins '05
Marjoe '72
Mayor of the Sunset Strip '03
Metallica: Some Kind of Monster '04
Microcosmos '96
Moana, a Romance of the Golden Age '26
Mondo Cane '63
Mondo Cane 2 '64
Mondovino '04
Moon over Broadway '98
Murderball '05
My Architect: A Son's Journey '03
My Date With Drew '05
Neil Young: Heart of Gold '06
New York Doll '05
Nico Icon '95
Night of the Living Dead, 25th Anniversary Documentary '93
No End in Sight '07
Occupation: Dreamland '05
Only the Strong Survive '03
Orwell Rolls in His Grave '03
Our Brand Is Crisis '05
Outfoxed: Rupert Murdoch's War on Journalism '04
Overnight '03
Paper Clips '04
Paris Is Burning '91
Peace, Propaganda & the Promised Land '04
Prelude to War '42
Prisoner of Paradise '02
Protocols of Zion '05
The Real Dirt on Farmer John '05
Reel Paradise '05
Riding Giants '04
Rize '05
Rock Hudson's Home Movies '92
Rock School '05
Roger & Me '89
S21: The Khmer Rouge Killing Machine '03
Sasquatch '76
Sex and Buttered Popcorn '91
Shake Hands With the Devil: The Journey of Romeo Dallaire '04
Sherman's March '86
The Show '95
Sicko '07
Soft and Hard '85
The Sorrow and the Pity '71
Spellbound '02
Standing in the Shadows of Motown '02
Step Into Liquid '03
Stolen Childhoods '05
Stone Reader '02
The Story of the Weeping Camel '03
Streetwise '84
Stripper '86
Super Size Me '04
Superstar: The Life and Times of Andy Warhol '90
Swimming to Cambodia '87
Tarnation '03
Taxi to the Dark Side '07
Tell Them Who You Are '05
Thank You & Good Night '91
Theremin: An Electronic Odyssey '95
The Thin Blue Line '88
39 Pounds of Love '05
This Film Is Not Yet Rated '06
Through the Fire '05
Tokyo-Ga '85
Tokyo Olympiad '66
Touching the Void '03
Triumph of the Will '34
The Troubles We've Seen '94
Truth or Dare '91
20 Dates '99
Uncovered: The War on Iraq '04
The U.S. Vs. John Lennon '06
Unknown White Male '05
An Unreasonable Man '06
The Untold Story of Emmett Louis Till '05
Unzipped '94
Up for Grabs '05
Verdict on Auschwitz: The Frankfurt Auschwitz Trial 1963—1965 '93
Vince Vaughn's Wild West Comedy Show '06
Visions of Light: The Art of Cinematography '93
Voices of Iraq '04
Wal-Mart: The High Cost of Low Price '05
Wall '04
The War Room '93
When We Were Kings '96
The White Diamond '04
Who Gets to Call It Art? '05
Who Killed the Electric Car? '06
The Wild Parrots of Telegraph Hill '03
Winged Migration '01
Wisecracks '93
Word Wars: Tiles and Tribulations on the Scrabble Circuit '04
Wordplay '06
The Yes Men '03

Dolls That Kill

see Killer Toys

Domestic Abuse

see also Sexual Abuse

The Abduction '96
Angel Eyes '01
The Break Up '98
The Burning Bed '85
Cafe Ole '00
Casualties '97
Dangerous Child '01
Dangerous Game '93
Dear Frankie '04
Edge of Madness '02
Enough '02
Evil '03
Fallen Angel '99
Falling Down '93
Far Cry from Home '81
45 '06
The Gift '00
Honey & Ashes '96
The House Next Door '01
The Human Stain '03
The Ice House '97
In the Bedroom '01
Independence Day '83
Instinct to Kill '01
Intimate Strangers '77
John John in the Sky '00
Lea '96
Lift '01
Love Come Down '00
Love Letters '45
Mesmerized '84
Mortal Thoughts '91
Nil by Mouth '96
Olivia '83
The Opponent '01
Our Mother's Murder '97
Perfect Crime '97
Personal Velocity: Three Portraits '02
Plain Dirty '04
Remember Me '85
Ryna '05
Shattered Dreams '90
Sleep Easy, Hutch Rimes '00
Sleeping with the Enemy '91
Solas '99
Take My Eyes '03
The Tenant of Wildfell Hall '96
This Boy's Life '93
An Unfinished Life '05
Waitress '07
What's Love Got to Do with It? '93
Woman Undone '95
Woman with a Past '92
Your Vice is a Closed Room and Only I Have the Key '72

Doofus Dads

see also Bad Dads; Dads; Single Parents; Slapstick Comedy; Stepparents

Caddyshack 2 '88
Cheaper by the Dozen '03
Cheaper by the Dozen 2 '05
Daddy Day Camp '07
Father of the Bride '91
Father of the Bride Part 2 '95
Honey, I Shrunk the Kids '89
Kicking & Screaming '05
Little Miss Sunshine '06
National Lampoon's Christmas Vacation '89
National Lampoon's European Vacation '85
National Lampoon's Vacation '83
Parenthood '89
RV '06
Three Men and a Baby '87
Vegas Vacation '96
What about Bob? '91

Doublecross!

see also Crime Drama; Heists; Revenge; Scams, Stings & Cons

Casino Royale '06
Circus '00
The Contractor '07
Criss Cross '48
Cypher '02
Decoy '46
Diamond Run '00
Dot the I '03
The Family '70
Four Days '99
The Hades Factor '06
Heist '01
The Italian Job '03
Killer '73
Lucky Number Slevin '06
National Lampoon's Gold Diggers '04
Niagara '52
No Good Deed '02
Partners '99
Payback '98
Score '95
The Sentinel '06
The Set Up '95
Sniper 3 '04
Swindled '04
Thicker than Water '99
Tick Tock '00
The Ultimate Weapon '97
Wild Things '98
Wild Things 2 '04

Down Under

The Adventures of Priscilla, Queen of the Desert '94
The Alice '04
Alien Visitor '95
Alvin Purple '73
Anzacs: The War Down Under '85
Around the World in 80 Ways '86
Back of Beyond '95
Barry McKenzie Holds His Own '74
Battle Cry '55
Between Wars '74
Black Water '07
Blackrock '97
Blackwater Trail '95
Blood Surf '00
The Blue Lightning '86
Bootmen '00
Botany Bay '53
Boulevard of Broken Dreams '88
The Boys '98
Brides of Christ '91
Broken English '96
Burke & Wills '85
Caddie '76
Candy '06
The Cars That Ate Paris '74
Cass '78
The Castle '97
The Chant of Jimmie Blacksmith '78
Children of the Revolution '95
Chopper '00
Country Life '95
Crocodile Dundee '86
Crocodile Dundee 2 '88
Crocodile Dundee in Los Angeles '01
The Crocodile Hunter: Collision Course '02
A Cry in the Dark '88
The Custodian '94
Danny Deckchair '03
Dark Age '88
Dead Alive '93
Dead Easy '82
Dead Heart '96
Death of a Soldier '85
December Boys '07
The Desert Rats '53
Dingo '90
The Dish '00
Do or Die '01
Down Under '86
The Dunera Boys '85
Dusty '85
The Echo of Thunder '98
Erskinville Kings '99
Eureka Stockade '49
Fair Game '85
Fast Talking '86
Fierce Creatures '96
15 Amore '98
Finding Nemo '03
Forty Thousand Horsemen '41
Freedom '82
The Fringe Dwellers '86
Gallagher's Travels '87
Gallipoli '81
Garage Days '03
The Getting of Wisdom '77
The Good Wife '86
Great Gold Swindle '84
Ground Zero '88
Hammers over the Anvil '91

The Hard Word '02
Head On '98▶
Heaven's Burning '97
Holy Smoke '99
Howling 3: The Marsupials '87
Hurricane Smith '92
The Incredible Journey of Mary Bryant '05
The Irishman '78
Jackie Chan's First Strike '96
Japanese Story '05▶
Jindabyne '06
Kangaroo Jack '02
Kings in Grass Castles '97
Kitty and the Bagman '82
Lantana '01▶
The Lighthorsemen '87▶
A Little Bit of Soul '97
Little Boy Lost '78
Love Serenade '96
Mad Dog Morgan '76
The Man from Snowy River '82
Maslin Beach '97
Miracle Down Under '87
Mission: Impossible 2 '00▶
Mr. Nice Guy '98
Mr. Reliable: A True Story '95
Money Movers '78
Monkey Grip '82▶
Moving Out '83
Muriel's Wedding '94▶
My Brilliant Career '79▶
The Naked Country '85
Ned Kelly '70
Ned Kelly '03
Nevil Shute's The Far Country '85
The Night We Called it a Day '03
The Nugget '02
On the Beach '59▶
On the Beach '00
Once Were Warriors '94▶
One Crazy Night '93
Only the Brave '94
Oscar and Lucinda '97
Overlanders '46▶
Palm Beach '79
Passion '99
Perfect Strangers '03
Phar Lap '84
Praise '98▶
Prince and the Great Race '83
Prisoners of the Sun '91▶
The Quest '86
Quigley Down Under '90
Rabbit-Proof Fence '02▶
Race the Sun '96
Rebel '85
Reckless Kelly '93
The Rescuers Down Under '90
Return to Snowy River '88▶
Ride a Wild Pony '75▶
The Right Hand Man '87
The Road from Coorain '02
Robbery under Arms '57
Romulus, My Father '07▶
Run, Rebecca, Run '81
Sara Dane '81
Savage Attraction '83
Shine '95◄
The Shrimp on the Barbie '90
Silver City '84
The Silver Stallion: King of the Wild Brumbies '93
Sirens '94
Sister Kenny '45▶
Soft Fruit '99
Sorrento Beach '95
Squizzy Taylor '84
Stones of Death '88
Strange Bedfellows '04
Strange Fits of Passion '99
Strictly Ballroom '92▶
Summer City '77
The Sundowners '60▶
Sweet Talker '91
Talk '94
The Thorn Birds '83▶

Tim '79
Two Hands '98▶
Undead '05
Under Capricorn '49
Under Capricorn '82
Under the Lighthouse Dancing '97
Waterfront '83
We of the Never Never '82▶
The Wacky World of Wills & Burke '85
A Waltz Through the Hills '88
Walkabout '71▶
Welcome to Woop Woop '97
Where the Green Ants Dream '84
The Winds of Jarrah '83
The Winter of Our Dreams '82
Wolf Creek '05
Wrangler '88

Dragons
see also Medieval Romps
Beowulf '07◄
Captain Sinbad '63
Dragon Storm '04
Dragonheart '96
Dragonheart: A New Beginning '00
Dragonslayer '81◄
Dragonworld '94
Dungeons and Dragons '00
Eragon '06
Erik the Viking '89
Ghidrah the Three Headed Monster '65
Goliath and the Dragon '61
Harry Potter and the Goblet of Fire '05◄
Jabberwocky '77
Jack the Giant Killer '62◄
Jason and the Argonauts '63▶
The Magic Sword '62
Mulan '98◄
The NeverEnding Story '84◄
Pete's Dragon '77
Puffnstuf '77
Quest for Camelot '98
Reign of Fire '02
The Seventh Voyage of Sinbad '58▶
Shrek '01◄
Sleeping Beauty '59▶
Sword & the Dragon '56
The Wonderful World of the Brothers Grimm '62

Drama
see Adventure Drama; Comedy Drama; Coming of Ages; Crime Drama; Docudrama; Historical Drama; Musical Drama; Romantic Drama; Showbiz Dreams; Sports Dreams; Tearjerkers; Tragedy; Urban Drama

Dream Girls
see also Beauty Pageants
A la Mode '94
American Graffiti '73▶
Angus '95
The Arena '73
Barb Wire '96
The Barbarians '87
Baywatch the Movie: Forbidden Paradise '95
Beauties of the Night '52
Beautiful Girls '96▶
Beauty School '93
Bikini Bistro '94
The Bikini Car Wash Company '90
The Bikini Car Wash Company 2 '92
Bikini Drive-In '94
Bikini Island '91
Bikini Summer '91
Bikini Summer 3: South Beach Heat '97

Blondes Have More Guns '95
Bluebeard '72
Bolero '84
Burial of the Rats '95
California Girls '84
Cannonball Run '81
Cannonball Run 2 '84
Cheerleader Camp '88
The Chosen One: Legend of the Raven '98
City of Women '81
Cover Me '95
Creatures the World Forgot '70
Cupid '96
Cycle Vixens '79
Daddy-O '59
Day of the Warrior '96
Deadly Weapons '70
Def Jam's How to Be a Player '97
Desperate Cargo '41
Desperate Moves '86
Devil Girl from Mars '54
The Devil's Hand '61
Diamonds Are Forever '71▶
Dinosaur Valley Girls '96
Divine Nymph '71
Do or Die '91
Dr. Alien '88
Dr. Goldfoot and the Bikini Machine '65
Dr. No '62▶
The Doll '62
The Doll Squad '73
The Dolls '83
Domino '88
Dracula: Dead and Loving It '95
Dream Trap '90
Dreaming of Rita '94
Dumb & Dumber '94
Emmanuelle '74
Emmanuelle 4 '84
Emmanuelle & Joanna '78
Emmanuelle in the Country '78
Emmanuelle on Taboo Island '76
Emmanuelle, the Queen '79
Emmanuelle, the Joys of a Woman '76
Emmanuelle's Daughter '79
Enchanted '07
Enchanted Island '58
Evil Toons '90
Exotica '94
Fair Game '82
Fate '90
Femme Fontaine: Killer Babe for the C.I.A. '95
Fire Maidens from Outer Space '56
Fireballs '90
Forbidden Games '95
Forbidden Planet '56▶
Forbidden Zone: Alien Abduction '96
Gamera vs. Guiron '69
Gator Bait '73
Ghosts Can't Do It '90
Girl Shy '24▶
Gold of the Amazon Women '79
Goldeneye '95▶
Good Luck Chuck '07
The Good Night '07
The Grace Kelly Story '83
Great Bikini Off-Road Adventure '94
Guns '90
Hard Hunted '92
Helen of Troy '56
Hell's Belles '95
Hercules and the Princess of Troy '65
Hired to Kill '91
Hollywood Boulevard '76
Hollywood Boulevard 2 '89
Hollywood or Bust '56
How I Learned to Love Women '66
How to Succeed with Girls '64
I, a Woman '66

I Married a Centerfold '84
I Posed for Playboy '91
Interstate 60 '02
It Takes a Thief '59
Junk Mail '97
Just Looking '99
Kiss and Kill '68
Kiss and Make Up '34
La Collectionneuse '67
Last Dance '91
Les Girls '57
Les Mistons '57▶
The Lion of Thebes '64▶
Lost and Found '99
The Loves of Hercules '60
Maeina '00
A Man with a Maid '73
Masseuse '95
The Mermaids of Tiburon '62
Mirror Images '91
Mirror Images 2 '93
Mirror, Mirror 3: The Voyeur '96
Missile to the Moon '59
Mysterious Island of Beautiful Women '79
Mystery Date '91
Naked Souls '95
National Lampoon's Vacation '83▶
Never Say Never Again '83
Nine Ages of Nakedness '69
The Notorious Bettie Page '06
A Nymphoid Barbarian in Dinosaur Hell '91
Oxford Blues '84
Panther Squad '84
Party Incorporated '89
Phat Beach '96
Pin-Up Girl '44
Posed for Murder '89
Priceless Beauty '90
Princess Daisy '83
Private Affairs '89
Queen of Outer Space '58
Queen of the Jungle '35
The Reckless Way '36
Return to Savage Beach '97
Revenge of the Cheerleaders '76
Round Trip to Heaven '92
Savage Beach '89
Seduce Me: Pamela Principle 2 '94
The Seven Year Itch '55▶
She Gods of Shark Reef '56
She's Dressed to Kill '79
Sidekicks '93
Silk 'n' Sabotage '94
Sizzle Beach U.S.A. '74
Ski School 2 '94
Slumber Party Massacre '82
Some Like It Hot '59▶
Sorceress '82
Soup for One '82
South Beach Academy '96
Spinout '66
The Spring '89
Star Crash '78
The Story of a Love Story '73
Strawberry Blonde '41▶
The Sure Thing '85◄
Swimsuit '89
The Swinging Cheerleaders '74
Tammy and the Doctor '63
Tanya's Island '81
Tarzan, the Ape Man '81
Thieves of Fortune '89
Thunder & Mud '89
To the Limit '95
Tomorrow Never Dies '97
Too Shy to Try '82
Total Exposure '91
Trojan War '97
Undercover '94
Underground Aces '80
Vampire Vixens from Venus '94

Vampire's Kiss '88▶
Vice Academy 3 '91
Voyage to the Planet of Prehistoric Women '68
Wayne's World '92▶
Wayne's World 2 '93
Weird Science '85
Wet and Wild Summer '92
When Dinosaurs Ruled the Earth '70
Who Wants to Kill Jessie? '65
Will Success Spoil Rock Hunter? '57▶
Wish Me Luck '95
Wishful Thinking '92
The Woman in Red '84
Woo '97
You Only Live Twice '67
Young Nurses in Love '89
Zeta One '69

Drug Use & Abuse
see also On the Rocks; Reefer Madness; Rehab
Above the Law '88
Aces: Iron Eagle 3 '92
The Acid Eaters '67
Across the Tracks '69
Acts of Worship '01
Adventures in Spying '92
Air America '90
Alien Nation '88
All That Jazz '79▶
Alphabet City '84
Altered States '80▶
American Fabulous '92
Amongst Friends '93
The Amsterdam Connection '78
The Amsterdam Kill '78
And Then You Die '88▶
Angel's Brigade '79
The Anniversary Party '01▶
Another Day in Paradise '98
Armistead Maupin's Tales of the City '93
Around the Fire '98
Assassin of Youth '35
At Any Cost '00
Autopsy: A Love Story '02
Avenging Disco Godfather '79
Awakenings of the Beast '68
B. Monkey '97
Back in Action '94
Bad Boys '95
Bad Lieutenant '92▶
Bad Medicine '85
Baja '95
The Basketball Diaries '95
Basquiat '96▶
The Beach '00
Beat '00
Belly '98
Beretta's Island '92
Best Revenge '83
The Big Lebowski '97▶
Bird '88▶
Black Circle Boys '97
Black Snow '89
Black Starlet '74
Blast-Off Girls '67
Blind Spot '93
Blindside '88
Blood & Concrete: A Love Story '90
Blood Freak '72
Blood in ... Blood Out: Bound by Honor '93
The Bloody Brood '59
Blow '01
Blowin' Smoke '99
Blue Sunshine '78
Bongwater '97
Boogie Boy '98
Boogie Nights '97▶
The Boost '88
Bordertown '50
Born to Lose '99
Born to Win '71

Drug
The Boys of 2nd Street Park '03▶
Bright Lights, Big City '88
Bringing Out the Dead '99
Broken Vessels '98▶
Brotherhood of Justice '86
A Brother's Kiss '97
Bully '01
Burnt Money '00
Busting '74
Bye-Bye '96
Candy '06
Capital Punishment '96
Captain Blackjack '51
Captive Heart '88
Carlito's Way '93▶
Carlito's Way: Rise to Power '05
Caroline at Midnight '93
Casino '95
Casual Sex '86
Catch the Heat '87
Caught '96
Cause of Death '96
Cement '99
Chained 2 '92
Chains of Gold '92
Cheech and Chong: Still Smokin' '83
Cheech and Chong's Next Movie '80
Chelsea Walls '01
The Children of Times Square '86
China White '91
Chinatown Connection '90
Christiane F. '82▶
Chrome Soldiers '92
The Chumscrubber '05
Chungking Express '95▶
The Cider House Rules '99▶
Circuit '02
City by the Sea '02
City of Ghosts '03
Class of 1984 '82
Clean '04
Clean and Sober '88▶
Clockers '95▶
Club Life '80
Cocaine Cowboys '79
Cocaine Fiends '36
Cocaine: One Man's Seduction '83
Cocaine Wars '86
Coffy '73
Coldfire '90
The Colombian Connection '91
Commando Squad '87
Comrades in Arms '91
Confessions of a Vice Baron '42
The Connection '61▶
Contraband '86
The Cool World '63
The Corner '00
Corridors of Blood '58
Countryman '83
Courage '86
Covert Action '88
Crack House '89
crazy/beautiful '01
The Crow 2: City of Angels '96
Cruel Intentions '98
Crutch '04
A Cry for Love '80
The Curfew Breakers '57
Curtis's Charm '96
Cut and Run '85
Dance or Die '87
Dangerous Game '93
Dangerous Heart '93
Darkman 3: Die Darkman Die '95
Day of Atonement '93
Day of the Cobra '84
Dazed and Confused '93▶
Dead Aim '87
Dead Presidents '95
Dead Ringers '88▶
Deadly Surveillance '91
Death Drug '83
The Death of Richie '76
Death Shot '73

▶ = rated three bones or higher

Drug

Death Wish 4: The Crackdown '87
Deep Cover '92
Delta Heat '92
Desert Snow '89
Desperado '95
Desperate Lives '82
The Destructors '74
The Devil's Sleep '51
Dick '99
Dirty Laundry '87
Distant Justice '92
Dr. Jekyll and Mr. Hyde '20 ◄
Dr. Jekyll and Mr. Hyde '32 ◄
Dr. Jekyll and Mr. Hyde '41 ◄
Dr. Jekyll and Mr. Hyde '68
Dr. Jekyll and Mr. Hyde '73
Dogs in Space '87
Don't Look Back '96 ◄
The Doom Generation '95 ◄
Dot.Kill '05
Double-Crossed '91
Down & Dirty '76 ◄
Down in the Delta '98 ◄
Down to the Bone '04
Dream with the Fishes '97
Drug Wars 2: The Cocaine Cartel '92
Drugstore Cowboy '89 ◄
Drunks '96
Drying Up the Streets '76
Easy Kill '89
Easy Rider '69
Ed Wood '94 ◄
Edge of Sanity '89
Edie in Ciao! Manhattan '72
8 Million Ways to Die '85
El Cantante '06
The End of Innocence '90
Enter the Dragon '73
Equilibrium '02
Exposure '91
Extreme Prejudice '87
Factory Girl '06
Fall from Innocence '88
Fall Guy '47
Fast Money '83
Fatal Beauty '87
Fatal Fix '80
Fear and Loathing in Las Vegas '98
Federal Hill '94
Feelin' Screwy '90
Fever '88
Fierce People '05
The Fifth Floor '80
54 '98
The Finger Man '55
Fiona '98
Fire Birds '90
First Born '84
The Five Heartbeats '91 ◄
The Fix '84
The Flaming Teen-Age '56
Flashback '89 ◄
Flatfoot '78
Flesh '68 ◄
Fletch '85
Four Friends '81 ◄
Foxes '80
Frances '82 ◄
The French Connection '71 ◄
French Connection 2 '75 ◄
French Intrigue '70
Fresh '94 ◄
Fresh Kill '87
The Fury of the Wolfman '70
Ganjasaurus Rex '87
Garage Days '03
The Gene Krupa Story '59
Georgia '95 ◄
Gia '98
Ginger Snaps: Unleashed '04
Go '99 ◄
Godmoney '97
Gone Dark '03
The Good Thief '03 ◄
Goodfellas '90 ◄
Gordon's War '73
Gothic '87
Gracie's Choice '04
Gridlock'd '96 ◄
Gunmen '93
H '90
Hair '79
Half-Baked '97
Half Nelson '06 ◄

Hallucination '67
Hangman's Curse '03
Hard Evidence '94
Hardcore '04
Harsh Times '05
Harvard Man '01
Haunted Summer '88
The Heart Is Deceitful Above All Things '04
Heart of America '03
Heat '72
Heaven's Prisoners '95
Hell's Kitchen NYC '97
Help Wanted Female '68
Hendrix '00
A Hero Ain't Nothin' but a Sandwich '78
Heroes for Sale '33 ◄
High Art '98
High Crime '73
High Risk '81
Hit! '73
Holiday Heart '00
A Home at the End of the World '04
Homegrown '97
The Hooked Generation '69
Horsey '99
How Come Nobody's On Our Side? '73
Hugo Pool '97
Human Traffic '99
Hussy '80
I Come in Peace '90
I Drink Your Blood '71
I Got Five on It '05
Idle Hands '99
Igby Goes Down '02 ◄
Illtown '96
I'm Dancing as Fast as I Can '82
The Impostor '84
In Hot Pursuit '77
In the Line of Duty: A Cop for the Killing '90
Inside Edge '92
The Invisibles '99
Iron Horsemen '71
Island Monster '53
Jaguar Lives '79
Jane Doe '96
Jekyll and Hyde '90
Jekyll & Hyde... Together Again '82
Jesus' Son '99 ◄
Jo Jo Dancer, Your Life Is Calling '86
Jumpin' at the Boneyard '92
Kamikaze Hearts '91
Kandyland '87
Kemek '70
Keys to Tulsa '96
Kickboxer the Champion '91
Kicked in the Head '97
Kids '95 ◄
Kids in the Hall: Brain Candy '96
Kill or Be Killed '93
Killing Zoe '94
The Killing Zone '90
L.627 '92 ◄
La Bamba '87 ◄
La Vie en Rose '07 ◄
L.A. Wars '94
Lady Sings the Blues '72
Last Flight to Hell '91
The Last of the Finest '90
Lenny '74 ◄
Less Than Zero '87
Let No Man Write My Epitaph '60
Let's Get Harry '87
Let's Get Lost '88
License to Kill '89
Life Support '07
Light Sleeper '92 ◄
Little Fish '05 ◄
Live and Let Die '73
Livin' for Love: The Natalie Cole Story '00
Loaded '94
Loaded '08
Loaded Guns '75
London '05
London Kills Me '91

Long Day's Journey into Night '62 ◄
Long Day's Journey into Night '88
Long Day's Journey Into Night '96
Loser '97
Lost Angels '89
Love Come Down '00
Love Liza '02 ◄
Lovely... But Deadly '82
MacArthur Park '01
Magnolia '99 ◄
Mainline Run '98
The Man with the Golden Arm '55 ◄
Marihuana '36
Marked for Death '90
Maybe I'll Be Home in the Spring '70
McBain '91 ◄
McQ '74
The Messenger '87
Miami Vendetta '87
Midnight Cop '88
Midnight Express '78 ◄
Mike's Murder '84
Mindfield '89
Mission Manila '87
Mrs. Parker and the Vicious Circle '94
Mixed Blood '84
Mob War '88
The Mod Squad '99
The Moneytree '93
Monkey Grip '82 ◄
More '69
My Life and Times with Antonin Artaud '93 ◄
The Mystery of Edwin Drood '35
Naked Lunch '91 ◄
Narc '02 ◄
The Narcotics Story '58
National Lampoon's Senior Trip '95
Never Die Alone '04
New Best Friend '02
New Jack City '91 ◄
New York Doll '05 ◄
Newman's Law '74
Nico Icon '95 ◄
Night Friend '87
The Night of the Iguana '64 ◄
Night Zoo '87
Nil by Mouth '96 ◄
Ninja in the U.S.A. '88
No Escape, No Return '93
No Vacancy '99
Not My Kid '85
Nowhere '96
Olga's Girls '64
On the Edge: The Survival of Dana '79
On the Outs '05
One False Move '91 ◄
100 Proof '96
One Man's Justice '95
The Organization '71
Out of Sync '95
Out of the Rain '90
Over the Edge '79 ◄
Pace That Kills '28
The Palermo Connection '91
Pandaemonium '00
Panic in Needle Park '71 ◄
Party Monster '03
Passion for Power '85
People I Know '02
The People Next Door '70
The People vs. Larry Flynt '96 ◄
The Perfect Daughter '96
Performance '70 ◄
Permanent Midnight '98
Pete's Meteor '98
Pharmacist '32
Pigalle '95
Pinero '01
Platoon of the Warriors '88
Point of No Return '93
Police '85
The Poppy Is Also a Flower '66
Postcards from the Edge '90 ◄

Pot, Parents, and Police '71
Praise '98 ◄
Premonition '71
Pretty Smart '87
Prey for Rock and Roll '03
Prime Cut '72
Private Investigations '87
Protector '85
Prozac Nation '01
Psych-Out '68
Pulp Fiction '94 ◄
Puppet on a Chain '72
Pure '02
Purgatory House '04
Pusher '96
Question of Honor '80
Quiet Cool '86
Rage and Honor '92
Rapid Fire '92
Rated X '00
Raw Target '95
Ray '04 ◄
Rebound: The Legend of Earl "The Goat" Manigault '96
Reckless Disregard '84
Red Blooded American Girl '90
Red Heat '88
Red Surf '90
Remedy '05
Rent '05
Requiem for a Dream '00 ◄
Resurrection Man '97
Retribution '98
Return of the Tiger '78
Return to Paradise '98 ◄
Revenge of the Ninja '83
Revenge of the Stepford Wives '80
Ricochet '91
Riding in Cars with Boys '01
Rip-Off '77
River's Edge '87 ◄
Rock House '88
Rodrigo D: No Future '91
The Rose '79 ◄
The Royal Tenenbaums '01 ◄
Rude '96
Running Out of Time '94
Running Scared '86
Running with Scissors '06
Rush '91
Saigon Commandos '88
Saints and Sinners '95
The Salton Sea '02
Satan's Instinct '65
Savage Instinct '89
A Scanner Darkly '06
Scarface '83 ◄
Schnelles Geld '84
Scorchy '76
Scorpion Spring '96
Secret Agent Super Dragon '66
The Seducers '70
The Seven-Per-Cent Solution '76 ◄
The '70s '00
Severance '88
Shameless '94
She Shoulda Said No '49
The Show '95
Showdown in Little Tokyo '91
Sicilian Connection '72
Sid & Nancy '86 ◄
Silk '06
The 60s '99
SLC Punk! '99
The Slender Thread '65
The Snake People '68
SnakeEater 2: The Drug Buster '90
Sno-Line '85
Sorry, Wrong Number '89
Sorted '04
Speed of Life '99
Spenser: Pale Kings & Princes '94
Spun '02
Stand Alone '85
Stella Does Tricks '96
Still Crazy '98
Stoned '05
The Stoned Age '94
Straight Up '90

Strange Days '95 ◄
Street Girls '75
Street Wars '91
Streetwalkin' '85
Strike Force '75
The Substitute '96
The Substitute 3: Winner Takes All '99
Suicide Kings '97
Sunset Heat '92
Sunset Strip '85
Super Bitch '73
Superfly '72
Surrender Dorothy '98
The Sweet Hereafter '96 ◄
Sweet Jane '98
Sweet Nothing '96 ◄
The Take '90
Talons of the Eagle '92
Target Eagle '84
Tchao Pantin '84 ◄
Teenage Devil Dolls '53
TekWar '94
The Temptations '98
Temptress Moon '96
Tequila Sunrise '88
The Tesseract '03
Things We Lost in the Fire '07
The Third Man '49 ◄
This Time I'll Make You Rich '75
Thunder Alley '85
Tideland '05
The Tingler '59 ◄
To Die Standing '91
Tombstone '93 ◄
The Tong Man '19
Tongs: An American Nightmare '88
Too Young to Die '90
Torchlight '85
Tough and Deadly '94
Toughlove '85
The Town Is Quiet '00
Traffic '00 ◄
Traffik '91 ◄
Trainspotting '95 ◄
Transmutations '85
Trash '70
Trespass '92
The Trip '67
Tropical Snow '88
Trouble in Paradise '88
Tweek City '05
Twenty-One '91
21 Grams '03 ◄
24 Hour Party People '01 ◄
24-7 '97
Twin Peaks: Fire Walk with Me '92
Twin Town '97
Twisted '96
Ulee's Gold '97 ◄
Under Hellgate Bridge '99
Undercover '87
Valley of the Dolls '67
Vanishing Point '71 ◄
Velvet Goldmine '98
Vicious Circles '97
Virgil Bliss '01
Wait until Dark '67 ◄
Walk Hard: The Dewey Cox Story '07
Walk the Line '05 ◄
Wanda, the Sadistic Hypnotist '67
Warlords from Hell '87
Warlords 3000 '93
Watched '73
Weekend with the Babysitter '70
Weird World of LSD '67
Weirdsville '07
Welcome Says the Angel '01
What Have I Done to Deserve This? '85 ◄
Whispers of White '93
Who'll Stop the Rain? '78 ◄
Why Do Fools Fall in Love? '98
Wild Bill '95
Wild in the Streets '68
The Winter of Our Dreams '82
A Winter Tan '88

Wired '89
Withnail and I '87 ◄
Woman, Thou Art Loosed '04
Women on the Verge of a Nervous Breakdown '88 ◄
Wonder Boys '00 ◄
Wonderland '03
Woodstock '70 ◄
The Young Americans '93
Zero Tolerance '93
ZigZag '02
Zone 39 '96

Drugs
see Drug Use & Abuse

Dublin
see also Ireland
About Adam '00
Agnes Browne '99
Circle of Friends '94 ◄
The Commitments '91 ◄
The Dead '87 ◄
Disco Pigs '01
Echoes '88
Evelyn '02 ◄
Frankie Starlight '95
The Front Line '06
The General '98 ◄
Girl with Green Eyes '64
In Bruges '08
The Informer '35 ◄
Into the West '92 ◄
The Lonely Passion of Judith Hearne '87 ◄
A Man of No Importance '94 ◄
Michael Collins '96 ◄
My Left Foot '89 ◄
Nora '00
Ordinary Decent Criminal '99
Pete's Meteor '98
Rory O'Shea Was Here '04
Shake Hands with the Devil '59
The Snapper '93 ◄
The Van '95 ◄
Veronica Guerin '03
When Brendan Met Trudy '00 ◄
When the Sky Falls '99

Dying for a Promotion
see also Bad Bosses; Corporate Shenanigans; Office Surprise
El Crimen Perfecto '04
He Was a Quiet Man '07
Office Killer '97
Severance '06
A Shock to the System '90 ◄
The Temp '93

Ears!
see also Eyeballs!; Renegade Body Parts
Blue Velvet '86 ◄
Django '68
Feeling Minnesota '96
High Plains Drifter '73
I, Madman '89
Lust for Life '56 ◄
Reservoir Dogs '92 ◄
Say It Isn't So '01
Van Gogh '92 ◄
Vincent & Theo '90 ◄
White Mischief '88

Earthquakes
see also Disaster Flicks; L.A.; San Francisco
Aftershock: Earthquake in New York '99
Black Scorpion 2: Ground Zero '01
Daybreak '01
Earthquake '74
Escape from L.A. '96

◄ = rated three bones or higher

The Great Los Angeles Earthquake '91
Earthquake '91 ▶
The Last Warrior '99
Life and Nothing More... '92
Marshall Law '96
Prenomenon '96
Power Play '02
Quake '92
The Rains Came '39
San Francisco '36 ▶
The Seventh Sign '89
Shakedown '02

Easter
see also Holidays; Religion; Religious Epics
Angel of Death '02
Easter Parade '48 ▶
Fourth Wise Man '85
Jesus '00 ▶
Jesus Christ, Superstar '73 ▶
Jesus of Montreal '89 ▶
Jesus of Nazareth '28
Jesus of Nazareth '77 ▶
The Long Good Friday '80 ▶
Mary, Mother of Jesus '99
The Passion of the Christ '04 ▶
Resurrection '99
The Robe '53 ▶

Eastern Europe
4 Months, 3 Weeks, 2 Days '07 ▶
Black Peter '63
Blood & Chocolate '07
Brute '97
Dark Blue World '01 ▶
The Death of Mr. Lazarescu '05 ▶
Divided We Fall '00 ▶
Dracula: The Dark Prince '01
Dust '01
Everything is Illuminated '05 ▶
Gloomy Sunday '22 ▶
The Good Fairy '35 ▶
The Great Water '04
Hostel '06
I Am David '04 ▶
Invincible '01
The Ister '04 ▶
Kontroll '03 ▶
Last Holiday '06
Love '05
The Pianist '02 ▶
Second in Command '06
The Secret Invasion '64
Severance '06
The Troubles We've Seen '94

Eco-Vengeance!
see also Cannibalism; Killer Beasts; Killer Bugs and Slugs; Killer Plants
Alligator '80 ▶
Anaconda '96
Ants '77
The Applegates '89
Arachnophobia '90 ▶
Ben '72
Body Snatchers '93 ▶
The Core '03
The Crawlers '93
Day of the Animals '77
Deadly Harvest '72
Falling Fire '97
Fangs '75
Ferngully: The Last Rain Forest '92 ▶
The Fire Next Time '93
Food of the Gods '76
Frogs '72 ▶
Grizzly '76
Habitat '97
The Happening '08
The Host '06 ▶
Idaho Transfer '73
Jaws '75 ▶
Jaws 2 '78
Jaws 3 '83
Jaws: The Revenge '87
Jurassic Park '93 ▶
Kingdom of the Spiders '77 ▶
Last Days of Planet Earth '74
Magic in the Water '95
On Deadly Ground '94
Phantom 2040 Movie: The Ghost Who Walks '95
Piranha '78 ▶
Piranha 2: The Spawning '82
Prophecy '79
The Ruins '08
Savage Capitalism '93
The Simpsons Movie '07 ▶
Squirm '76
The Swarm '78
Thunder Bay '53 ▶
Ticks '93
The Toxic Avenger '86 ▶
Virus '96
Willard '71

Eating
see also Cannibalism; Chefs; Edibles
The Age of Innocence '93 ▶
American Adobo '02
Aqua Teen Hunger Force Colon Movie Film for Theaters '07
Babette's Feast '87 ▶
Bar-B-Q '00
Big Eden '00 ▶
The Big Hit '98
Big Night '95 ▶
Bikini Bistro '94
The Bread, My Sweet '01
A Bug's Life '98 ▶
Charlie and the Chocolate Factory '05 ▶
A Chef in Love '96
Chocolat '00 ▶
Chronically Unfeasible '00
Combination Platter '93
Coneheads '93
Consuming Passions '88
The Cook, the Thief, His Wife & Her Lover '90 ▶
Cool Hand Luke '67 ▶
Dick '99 ▶
Dim Sum: A Little Bit of Heart '85 ▶
The Dinner Game '98 ▶
Dinner Rush '00 ▶
The Duchess of Duke Street '78 ▶
Eat a Bowl of Tea '89 ▶
Eat Drink Man Woman '94 ▶
Eat the Rich '87
Eat Your Heart Out '96
Facing Windows '03
Far Harbor '96
Feed '05
Felicia's Journey '99 ▶
Friday '95 ▶
Friends and Family '01
Gabriela '84
Goodfellas '90 ▶
Grave Indiscretions '96
Hamburger... The Motion Picture '86
Harold and Kumar Go to White Castle '04 ▶
Home for the Holidays '95
Home Fries '98
Hot Chocolate '92
How to Go Out on a Date in Queens '06
I Really Hate My Job '07
Ice Cream Man '95
Just Your Luck '96
La Grande Bouffe '73
Larry the Cable Guy: Health Inspector '05
Lawless Heart '01
Life is Sweet '90 ▶
Like Water for Chocolate '93 ▶
Love is All There is '96
Mambo Cafe '00
Meatballs '79
Men '97
Michael '96 ▶
Monty Python's The Meaning of Life '83 ▶
Mostly Martha '01 ▶
My Big Fat Greek Wedding '02
My Blueberry Nights '07
National Lampoon's Animal House '78 ▶
9 1/2 Weeks '86
The Nutty Professor '96 ▶
The Nutty Professor 2: The Klumps '00
Palmy Days '31
The Pirates Who Don't Do Anything: A Veggie Tales Movie '08
Pretty Woman '90 ▶
Ratatouille '07 ▶
Revenge of the Nerds '84
Scary Movie 2 '01
Scotland, PA '02
Shallow Hal '01
Simply Irresistible '99
Small Time Crooks '00
Soul Food '97
The Spitfire Grill '95
Splash '84 ▶
Stand by Me '86 ▶
The Story of Boys & Girls '91
Super Size Me '04 ▶
Sweeney Todd: The Demon Barber of Fleet Street '07 ▶
A Tale of Two Pizzas '03
Tales from a Parallel Universe: Eating Pattern '97
Tampopo '86 ▶
301, 302 '94
Tom Jones '63 ▶
Tortilla Soup '01
The Untold Story '93
The Van '95 ▶
The Waiting Game '99
Waitress '07 ▶
What's Cooking? '00 ▶
Who Is Killing the Great Chefs of Europe? '78 ▶
Willy Wonka & the Chocolate Factory '71 ▶
Woman on Top '00
Yours, Mine & Ours '68

Eat Me
see Eating

Edibles
see also Cannibalism

Edinburgh
see Scotland
The Body Snatcher '45 ▶
The Love Guru '08

Egypt—Ancient
see also Terror by Night
Cleopatra '34 ▶
Cleopatra '63 ▶
Cleopatra '99
The Godfather '72 ▶
The Godfather, Part 3 '90 ▶
Land of the Pharaohs '55
The Mummy '32 ▶
The Mummy '59 ▶
The Mummy '99 ▶
The Mummy Returns '01
Prince of Egypt '98 ▶
The Scorpion King '02
Two Nights with Cleopatra '54
Yu-Gi-Oh! The Movie: Pyramid of Light '04

Elementary School/Junior High
see also School Daze
Akeelah and the Bee '06 ▶
Anna and the King of Siam '45 ▶
Bee Season '05 ▶
Big Bully '95
Billy Madison '94
The Boys of Baraka '05 ▶
Catina in the Big City '03 ▶
Chicken Little '05
Children of a Lesser God '86 ▶
The Children's Hour '61 ▶
The Chorus '04 ▶
Eden '98
The Elementary School '91 ▶
Frog and Wombat '98
Goodbye, Mr. Chips '39 ▶
Goodbye, Mr. Chips '69
The Guinea Pig '48
Half Nelson '06 ▶
Hoot '06
How to Eat Fried Worms '06
Jack '96
Kindergarten Cop '90
Knights of the South Bronx '05
Little Men '98
The Little Princess '39 ▶
The Little Princess '95 ▶
Lloyd '00
Mad Hot Ballroom '05 ▶
Masterminds '96
Matilda '96 ▶
Max Keeble's Big Move '01
Mean Creek '04 ▶
Music of the Heart '99
Paper Clips '04
Rebound '05
Saint Ralph '04
School of Rock '03 ▶
Shooting Dogs '05
The Sixth Sense '99 ▶
Sleepover '04
Star Kid '97
Treehouse Hostage '99
12 and Holding '05
Whole New Thing '05
Wild Tigers I Have Known '06

Elephants
see also Carnivals & Circuses; Wild Kingdom
Babar: The Movie '88
Billy Rose's Jumbo '62
Dr. Seuss' Horton Hears a Who! '08
Dumbo '41 ▶
Ele, My Friend '93
Elephant Boy '37 ▶
An Elephant Called Slowly '69
Elephant Walk '54
Fantasia '40 ▶
Freddy Got Fingered '01
George of the Jungle '97
Jupiter's Darling '55
Larger Than Life '96
Maya '66
Operation Dumbo Drop '95
Whispers: An Elephant's Tale '00
White Hunter, Black Heart '90 ▶

Elevators
see also Terror in Tall Buildings
Basic Instinct '92 ▶
Blast from the Past '98
The Client '94 ▶
Cursed '04
Deceived '91
Deep Rising '98
Die Hard '88 ▶
El Crimen Perfecto '04
Fatal Attraction '87 ▶
In the Line of Fire '93 ▶
Just My Luck '06
The Lift '85
Mallrats '95 ▶
The Man with Two Brains '83 ▶
Mission: Impossible '96 ▶
Mixed Nuts '94
Nick of Time '95
The Omen '06
Poltergeist 3 '88
Pretty Woman '90 ▶
The Secret of My Success '87
The Shaft '01
The Shaggy Dog '06
The Silence of the Lambs '91 ▶
Sleepless in Seattle '93 ▶
Speed '94 ▶
Terminator 2: Judgment Day '91 ▶
Thoroughly Modern Millie '67 ▶
The Towering Inferno '74 ▶
Toy Story 2 '99 ▶
True Lies '94 ▶
The Untouchables '87 ▶
What about Bob? '91 ▶
Willy Wonka & the Chocolate Factory '71 ▶

Emerging Viruses
see also Disease of the Week
Adrenalin: Fear the Rush '96
And the Band Played On '93 ▶
The Andromeda Strain '71 ▶
Body Armor '96
Cabin Fever '03
Dead Cold '95
Dead On '93
Derailed '02
Doomsday '08
Escape from L.A. '96
Fatal Contact: Bird Flu in America '06
Fatal Error '99
Feardotcom '02
Future Fear '97
The Hades Factor '06
I Am Legend '07 ▶
The Invasion '07
Jericho Fever '93
Killing Moon '00
Les Patterson Saves the World '90
Mimic '97
Mission: Impossible 2 '00
Outbreak '94 ▶
Pandemic '07
Panic in the Streets '50 ▶
The Patriot '99
The Rage '07
Resident Evil '02
Resident Evil: Apocalypse '04
Resident Evil: Extinction '07
Robin Cook's Invasion '97
Sahara '05
Sci-Fighters '96
Shakedown '02
Stephen King's The Stand '94

Elevators — (Egypt / other)
Greyfriars Bobby '61
The Prime of Miss Jean Brodie '69 ▶
Pooh's Heffalump Movie '05
Smokey and the Bandit 2 '80
Terror by Night '46 ▶
Trainspotting '95 ▶

Erotic Thrillers
see also Sex & Sexuality
An Affair to Remember '57 ▶
Animal Instincts 2 '94
Animal Instincts 3: The Seductress '95
Basic Instinct '92 ▶
Baton Rouge '88
Beyond Desire '94
Bitter Harvest '93
Blindfold: Acts of Obsession '94
Blown Away '93
Body Chemistry '90
Body Chemistry 3: Point of Seduction '93
Body Chemistry 4: Full Exposure '95
Body of Evidence '92
Body of Influence '93
Body of Influence 2 '96
Body Shot '93
Body Strokes '95
Broken Trust '93
Business for Pleasure '96
Caroline at Midnight '93
Chain of Desire '93
Color of Night '94
Cod Sweat '93
Cover Story '93
The Crush '93
The Dangerous '95
The Dangerous Indiscretion '94
Dangerous Touch '94
The Dark Dancer '95
Dark Secrets '95
Dark Tide '93
Dead Cold '95
Dead On '93
Deadly Past '95
Deadly Sexy '01
Death and Desire '97
Deceptions 2: Edge of Deception '94
Deception '94
Desire '95
Die Watching '93
Disclosure '93 ▶
Discretion Assured '93
Dot the I '03
Double Cross '94
Double Threat '92
Ebbtide '94
Embrace of the Vampire '95
Entangled '93
The Escort '97
Eternal '04
Every Breath '93
Evil Obsession '96
Exit '95
Extramarital '96
Fascination '04
Fatal Instinct '92
Fatal Past '94
Final Analysis '92 ▶
Final Judgment '92
The Girl Next Door '98
Hard Drive '94
Hourglass '95
I Like to Play Games '95
Illegal in Blue '95
Illicit Behavior '91
Illicit Dreams '94
Improper Conduct '94
Impulse '08
In a Moment of Passion '93
In Dark Places '97

The Empire State Building
see also New York, New York
An Affair to Remember '57 ▶
Enchanted '07 ▶
King Kong '33 ▶
King Kong '76
Love Affair '39 ▶
Love Affair '94
On the Town '49 ▶
The Shadow '94
Sleepless in Seattle '93 ▶

Terminal Virus '95
12 Monkeys '95 ▶
28 Days Later '02 ▶
28 Weeks Later '07 ▶
Ultraviolet '06
Zero Patience '94

▶ = rated three bones or higher

In the Heat of Passion 2: Unfaithful '94
Indecent Behavior '93
Indecent Behavior 2 '94
Indecent Behavior 3 '95
Inner Sanctum 2 '94
Invasion of Privacy '92
Kept '01
Killer Looks '94
Killing for Love '95
Lady in Waiting '94
The Last Seduction '94
The Last Seduction 2 '98
Lethal Seduction '97
Lipstick Camera '93
Listen '96
The Little Death '95
Lonely Hearts '91
Love Is a Gun '94
The Man in the Attic '94
Maniac Nurses Find Ecstasy '94
Match Point '05
Mercy '00
Midnight Blue '96
Midnight Confessions '95
Midnight Tease '94
Midnight Tease 2 '95
Mind Twister '93
Mirror Images '91
Mirror Images 2 '93
Motel Blue '98
Night Eyes '90
Night Eyes 2 '91
Night Eyes 3 '93
Night Eyes 4: Fatal Passion '95
Night Fire '94
The Nightman '93
Object of Obsession '95
Outside the Law '95
Over the Wire '95
Payback '94
A Place Called Truth '98
Playback '95
Playmaker '94
Poison '01
Poison Ivy 2: Lily '95
Poison Ivy 3: The New Seduction '97
Possessed by the Night '93
Private Obsession '94
Rubdown '93
Running Wild '94
Saturday Night Special '92
Save Me '93
Scorned '94
Scorned 2 '96
Secret Games '92
Secret Games 2: The Escort '93
Secret Games 3 '94
The Seductress '00
Sexual Malice '93
Sexual Roulette '96
Shadow Dancer '96
Shame, Shame, Shame '98
The Showgirl Murders '95
Sinful Intrigue '95
Sins of Desire '92
Sins of the Night '93
Silver '93
Snapdragon '93
Spirit Lost '96
Stolen Hearts '95
Stormswept '95
Stormy Nights '97
Strike a Pose '93
Suite 16 '94
Sunset Grill '92
Sweet Evil '96
Sweet Killing '93
Temptation '94
Temptress '95
Terrified '94
3-Way '04
Trade Off '95
Tryst '94
Turn of the Blade '97
Two Shades of Blue '98
Under Investigation '93
Undercover '94
Vicious Circles '97
Victim of Desire '95
Virtual Desire '95
Virtual Girl '00
Vulture's Eye '04
When Will I Be Loved '04
Wild Cactus '92

Young Adam '03

Errant Educators

see also Dedicated Teachers; Hell High School

Blue Car '03
Disturbing Behavior '98
Dumb and Dumberer: When Harry Met Lloyd '03
The Faculty '98
Loving Annabelle '06
Notes on a Scandal '06
Teaching Mrs. Tingle '99
When Brendan Met Trudy '00
Wild Things '98

Escaped Cons

see also Fugitives; Great Escapes; Men in Prison

Another Man's Poison '52
Axe '06
Bandits '01
Big Momma's House '00
The Big Sweat '90
Black Cat Run '98
Chasers '94
Choice of Arms '83
Con Air '97
Cool Hand Luke '67
Crime Wave '54
Dark Passage '47
Dead of Night '99
Deadlock '91
Deadlock 2 '94
The Defiant Ones '58
Destiny Turns on the Radio '95
Do or Die '01
Double Jeopardy '99
Duets '00
The Escape '95
Escape from Alcatraz '79
Face/Off '97
The Falcon Takes Over '42
Firestorm '97
Fled '96
48 Hrs. '82
From Dusk Till Dawn '95
The Fugitive '93
Gang Busters '55
A Gentleman After Dark '42
The Goonies '85
Great Expectations '34
Great Expectations '46
Great Expectations '89
Great Expectations '97
Great Expectations '99
Great Expectations: The Untold Story '87
Happy, Texas '99
Harold & Kumar Escape from Guantanamo Bay '08
His Greatest Gamble '34
I Am a Fugitive from a Chain Gang '32
Identity '03
The Incredible Journey of Mary Bryant '05
Instinct to Kill '01
Jailbreakers '94
Jailbreakin' '72
Jeopardy '53
Johnny Was '05
King of Alcatraz '38
The Last Hard Men '76
The Last Marshal '99
Le Cercle Rouge '70
Lewis and Clark and George '97
Lonely Are the Brave '62
The Man Who Broke 1,000 Chains '87
The Mighty '98
Moonbase '97
Morgan's Ferry '99
Next Friday '00
Night Screams '87
Nobody's Baby '01
O Brother Where Art Thou? '00
One Way Passage '32
Out of Sight '98
Papillon '73
Parallel Sons '95
Passage to Marseilles '44
Passenger 57 '92
A Perfect World '93
Point Blank '98
Prison on Fire 2 '91
Proximity '01
Raising Arizona '87
Red Letters '00
Rites of Passage '99
Runaway Train '85
San Quentin '37
A Scandal in Paris '46
School's Out '99
Slow Burn '00
Soft Deceit '94
Spider-Man 3 '07
Spoiler '98
Stakeout '87
The Stunt Man '80
T Bone N Weasel '92
Two for Texas '97
Up the River '30
Warden of Red Rock '01
We're No Angels '55
We're No Angels '89
Where the Money Is '00
The Wrong Guys '88
Wrongfully Accused '98

Eskimos/Inuit

Map of the Human Heart '93
On Deadly Ground '94
Shadow of the Wolf '92
Smilla's Sense of Snow '96
The White Dawn '75

Ethics & Morals

see also Big Ideas

All the King's Men '49
And Justice for All '79
Any Man's Death '90
The Assault '86
Barbarians at the Gate '93
The Best Man '64
Blame It on Rio '84
Blue Chips '94
Boiler Room '00
The Border '82
The Boy with the Green Hair '48
The Bridge on the River Kwai '57
Casualties of War '89
Changing Lanes '02
Chinese Roulette '86
Chloe in the Afternoon '72
Circle of Power '83
The Citadel '38
City Hall '95
City of Ghosts '03
A Civil Action '98
Commandments '96
The Contender '00
The Conversation '74
The Corruptor '99
Crime and Punishment in Suburbia '00
Crimes & Misdemeanors '89
Cruel Intentions '98
Cutter's Way '81
A Dangerous Woman '93
The Deep End '01
Deep Six '58
The Defiant Ones '58
The Doctor '91
Double Identity '89
The Dreamlife of Angels '98
Election '99
The Elephant Man '80
Elmer Gantry '60
Extreme Measures '96
Fifth Day of Peace '72
The Fifth Seal '76
Force of Evil '49
Fortunes of War '94
The Funeral '84
Fury '36
Getting Away With Murder '96
Gossip '99
Harriet the Spy '96
The Ice Storm '97
The Image '89
It Could Happen to You '94
Jerry Maguire '96
Jezebel '38
The Judge and the Assassin '75
Judgment at Nuremberg '61
Keys to Tulsa '96
Kings Row '41
Knocks at My Door '93
La Truite '83
La Ronde '51
L'Avventura '60
The Last of England '87
The Lazarus Syndrome '79
License to Kill '84
Love with the Proper Stranger '63
The Magdalene Sisters '02
Malicious '74
The Man Inside '76
The Man Who Shot Liberty Valance '62
Manhattan Melodrama '34
Marihuana '36
A Matter of Dignity '57
Midnight '34
The Millionairess '60
Mindwalk: A Film for Passionate Thinkers '91
Mr. Smith Goes to Washington '39
Mom & Dad '47
Muriel '63
Network '76
News at Eleven '86
The Next Voice You Hear '50
Nixon '95
No Man's Land '87
Oedipus Rex '67
One Flew Over the Cuckoo's Nest '75
Other People's Money '91
Overture to Glory '40
The Ox-Bow Incident '43
Paris Trout '91
Penalty Phase '86
A Place in the Sun '51
Platoon '86
Playing God '96
The Ploughman's Lunch '83
Prime Suspect '82
Private Hell 36 '54
The Proposition '97
Quiz Show '94
Rabbit-Proof Fence '02
Ran '85
Reckless Disregard '84
Return to Paradise '98
Riel '79
The Sacrifice '86
Scandal Man '67
The Scarlet Letter '34
The Scarlet Letter '73
Shampoo '75
The Shootist '76
Silent Witness '85
Soul Man '86
S*P*Y*S '74
SS Girls '77
The Star Chamber '83
The Story of Women '88
Strangers When We Meet '60
Sweet Smell of Success '57
Test Tube Babies '48
The Things of Life '70
To Live & Die in L.A. '85
A Touch of Class '73
The Toy '82
Tulsa '49
Twelve Angry Men '57
Twelve Angry Men '97
Twenty-One '91
Tycoon '47
Under Fire '83
Viridiana '61
Wall Street '87
The Wheeler Dealers '63
With Honors '94
Zabriskie Point '70
Zero Degrees Kelvin '95

Etiquette

Born Yesterday '50
Educating Rita '83
My Fair Lady '64
Papa's Delicate Condition '63
Phantom of Liberty '74
Pleasure '31
Pygmalion '38
The Ruling Class '72
True Love '89

Evil Doctors

see also Doctors & Nurses; Mad Scientists

The Abominable Dr. Phibes '71
Anatomy '00
The Awful Dr. Orloff '62
Baby Geniuses '99
Batman Begins '05
Blackmale '99
Body Melt '93
The Curious Dr. Humpp '70
Curse of the Puppet Master: The Human Experiment '98
Dead Ringers '88
Death and the Maiden '94
The Dentist '96
Dr. Alien '88
The Doctor and the Devils '85
Dr. Black, Mr. Hyde '76
Doctor Blood's Coffin '62
Doctor Butcher M.D. '80
Dr. Caligari '89
Dr. Cyclops '40
Dr. Death, Seeker of Souls '73
Dr. Frankenstein's Castle of Freaks '74
Dr. Giggles '92
Dr. Goldfoot and the Bikini Machine '66
Dr. Hackenstein '88
Dr. Jekyll and Mr. Hyde '20
Dr. Jekyll and Mr. Hyde '41
Dr. Jekyll and Mr. Hyde '68
Dr. Jekyll and Mr. Hyde '73
Dr. Jekyll and Sister Hyde '71
Dr. Jekyll and the Wolfman '71
Dr. Jekyll's Dungeon of Death '82
Dr. Mabuse, The Gambler '22
Dr. Mabuse vs. Scotland Yard '64
Dr. No '62
Dr. Orloff and the Invisible Man '72
Dr. Otto & the Riddle of the Gloom Beam '86
Doctor Phibes Rises Again '72
Doctor Satan's Robot '40
Dr. Tarr's Torture Dungeon '75
Dr. Terror's House of Horrors '65
Doctor X '32
Extreme Measures '96
Feast for the Devil '71
Jekyll and Hyde '90
Mad Doctor of Blood Island '68
Malice '93
Night of the Bloody Apes '68
Night of the Bloody Transplant '86
Prince of Poisoners: The Life and Crimes of William Palmer '98
Slaughter Hotel '71
Strange World of Coffin Joe '68
Subject Two '06
Tuntista '06
The Two Faces of Dr. Jekyll '60
Who Killed Bambi? '03

Ex-Cons

see also Crime Drama; Escaped Cons; Men in Prison; Revenge; Women in Prison

A Nous la Liberte '31
All Hat '07
Always Outnumbered, Always Outgunned '98
American Heart '92
American Madness '32
And Now My Love '74
The Anderson Tapes '71
Animal '05
Any Number Can Win '63
Appointment with Crime '45
Baby Boy '01
Ballistic '01
Barbershop '02
Barbershop 2: Back in Business '04
Benefit of the Doubt '93
Beyond Desire '94
Beyond Suspicion '00
The Big Scam '79
Black Dog '98
Blastfighter '85
Bloody Mama '70
Bound '96
The Box '03
Bug '06
Bustin' Loose '81
Carlito's Way '93
Caught Up '98
The Chase '91
Coastlines '02
Cold Creek Manor '03
Crime Wave '54
Dead Heat '01
Dead Heat on a Merry-Go-Round '66
Deadly Past '95
Department Store '35
Disorganized Crime '89
Dolemite '75
The Dream Catcher '99
Drop Zone '94
Emma's Shadow '88
Enforcer from Death Row '78
Eye of God '97
Eye of the Tiger '86
Fallen Angels '95
Family Business '89
Farewell, My Lovely '75
Feeling Minnesota '96
Fever '91
The Finger Man '55
Force Five '75
Frankie and Johnny '91
Getting Out '94
The Glove '78
Going Places '74
Graveyard of Honor '02
Guncrazy '92
Hard Frame '70
Hard Knocks '80
The Hard Word '02
Headless Body in Topless Bar '96
The Heist '89
Hell's Kitchen NYC '97
Henry: Portrait of a Serial Killer '90
Hi-Jacked '50
High Country '81
Hitler: Dead or Alive '43
Home Team '98
The Hoodlum Priest '61
Hot Money '79
A House in the Hills '93
The Impostor '84
In Cold Blood '67
In Cold Blood '96
Jail Party '47
Jailbird's Vacation '65
Jon Jost's Frameup '93
Judge Dredd '95
Kansas City Confidential '52
Keeping Mum '05
Killer '02
The Killing '56
Kiss of Death '47
Kiss of Death '94
Klepto '03
Le Cercle Rouge '70
Le Doulos '61
Leo '02
Levity '03
The Limey '99
Little Children '06
Loan Shark '52
Luck of the Draw '00

▲ = rated three bones or higher

Manito '03
Masked and Anonymous '03
Max Dugan Returns '83
The Mighty '98▶
Morning Glory '93
Murder at Devil's Glen '99
Murder, My Sweet '44▶
My Baby's Daddy '04
My Summer of Love '05
Mystic River '03▶
Nasty Hero '89
Never Down '06
New Pastures '62
Ocean's Eleven '01▶
Oceans of Fire '86
Odds Against Tomorrow '59▶
On the Run '73
One More Chance '90
The Onion Field '79▶
Outlaw Blues '77
Palmetto '98
The Passion of Anra '70▶
Payback '94
Pennies from Heaven '36
Pier 23 '51
Pinero '01
Played '06
Poor Man's Game '06
Q (The Winged Serpent) '82▶
Raising Arizona '87▶
Rappin' '85
Ratas, Ratones, Rateros '99
The Ravagers '65
Read My Lips '01
The Real Thing '97
Red Road '06
Red Water '01
Renegade Trail '39
Revolver '05
Riff Raff '92▶
The River Rat '84
Row Your Boat '98
Rude '96
Scarecrow '73
The Set Up '95
Sex, Love and Cold Hard Cash '93
Sherrybaby '06
Shooters '00
Sins of the Night '93
Slaughterday '77
A Small Town in Texas '76
Spring Forward '99
Stakeout '87▶
Stand Off '93
Stealing Candy '03
Stick '85
Straight Time '78▶
Strangers with Candy '06
Street Law '95
The Swap '71
Switchblade Sisters '75
Swordfish '01
Sympathy for the Underdog '71
Temptation '94
This Is Not a Love Song '02
Three Fugitives '89
3000 Miles to Graceland '01
Till the End of the Night '94
Tough Guys '86
2 Fast 2 Furious '03
The Unbelievable Truth '90
Under Capricorn '49
Waist Deep '06
Weeds '87▶
The Wendell Baker Story '05
When the Dark Man Calls '95
Whispers in the Dark '92
Wild Cactus '92
Wild Ones on Wheels '62
Woman in the Shadows '34
Wonderland '03
Yellowstone '36
You and Me '38
You Only Live Once '37

Ex-Cops
see also Private Eyes; Rent-a-Cop
Albino '76
American Streetfighter 2: The Full Impact '97
Back to Back '96
A Better Way to Die '00
Black Scorpion '95
Bodily Harm '95
Body Chemistry 2: Voice of a Stranger '91
Breaking Point '94
Brown's Requiem '98
Choice of Weapons '76
Day of the Cobra '84
Dead Evidence '00
Dead Heat '87
Deadly Force '83
The Death Squad '73
8 Million Ways to Die '85
End of Days '99
Face Down '97
Final Payback '99
Gang Boys '97
Girls Night Out '83
The Glove '78
The Heist '96
Hope Ranch '02
Hostage Hotel '00
Identity '03
Into the Homeland '87
The Invader '96
The Isle '01
It Had to Be You '00
Jill the Ripper '00
Kansas City Confidential '52
Le Cercle Rouge '70▶
Little Children '06▶
Mad Max '80▶
The Man on the Roof '76
Midnight Run '88▶
The Morning After '85
Night of the Juggler '80
An Occasional Hell '96
Odds Against Tomorrow '59▶
Once a Thief '96▶
One Shoe Makes It Murder '82
The Onion Field '79▶
Payoff '91
Persons Unknown '96
Physical Evidence '89
Piece of the Action '77
Prime Time Murder '92
Q & A '90
Question of Honor '80
Raising Arizona '87▶
Raw Justice '93
Raw Nerve '99
Ripper Man '94
Romeo Must Die '00
Saw '04
Separate Lives '94
Sin '02
Street Corner Justice '96
Street Knight '93
Tchao Pantin '84▶
36 Hours to Die '99
Till Death Do Us Part '92
Traxx '87
Trouble in Mind '86▶
True Romance '93
Twilight '98▶
Undercurrent '99
Underdog '07
The Usual Suspects '95▶
Vigilante '83
Virtual Assassin '95
Virtual Combat '95
Virtuosity '95
West New York '96

Executing Revenge
see also Afterlife; Death Row; Men in Prison; Revenge
Before I Hang '40▶
Blowback '99
Destroyer '88
Exorcist 3: Legion '90
Fallen '97
The First Power '89
The Horror Show '89
I Know What You Did Last Summer '97▶
The Indestructible Man '56
Judge & Jury '96
Kidnapped '87
Kinjite: Forbidden Subjects '89
Lethal Dose '03
The Man They Could Not Hang '39
Munch '05▶
Prison '88
Shocker '89
Soldier '98
The 3 Marias '03

Existentialism
see The Meaning of Life

Exorcism & Exorcists
see also Nuns & Priests; Supernatural Horror:
The Amityville Horror '05
Dominion: Prequel to the Exorcist '05
The Exorcism of Emily Rose '05▶
London Voodoo '04
Lost Souls '00
Night of Evil '62
The Possessed '77
Possessed '00
Repossessed '90
Scary Movie 2 '01
Teenage Exorcist '93

Exploitation
see also Sexploitation
Abduction '75
Agony of Love '66
American Nightmare '81
Angel of the City '89
Angels of H.E.A.T. '82
Armed Response '86
Assassin of Youth '35
Bad Girls from Mars '90
Bam of the Naked Dead '73
Basic Training '86
Beatrice '88▶
Betrayal '78
Beyond the Valley of the Dolls '70
Black Shampoo '76
Blackenstein '73
Blood Games '90
The Bloody Brood '59
Blue Movies '88
Boss '74
The Cage '89
Caged Terror '72
Certain Sacrifice '80
Chained for Life '51
Common Law Wife '63
Confessions of a Vice Baron '42
Cover Girl Models '75
The Curfew Breakers '57
The Cut Throats '69
Cycle Psycho '72
Cycle Vixens '79
Dance Hall Racket '58
Dangerous Obsession '88
The Dark Side of Love '79
Deadly Sanctuary '68
Def Jam's How to Be a Player '97
Devil's Wedding Night '73
Escape from Safehaven '88
Exterminator 2 '84
Five Minutes to Love '63
The Flaming Teen-Age '56
For Ladies Only '81
Fox and His Friends '75▶
Foxy Brown '74
Ghoulies 3: Ghoulies Go to College '91
Girl on a Chain Gang '65
Gun Girls '56
Heat of the Flame '76
High School Caesar '60
Hitler's Children '43▶
Hollywood after Dark '65
Hollywood Dreams '94
The Hollywood Strangler Meets the Skid Row Slasher '79
House of Whipcord '75
In Trouble '67
Island of Lost Girls '68
Jock Petersen '74
L.A. Heat '88
L.A. Vice '89
Last Call '90
Little Girl, Big Tease '75
Little Miss Innocence '73
The Lonely Sex '59
Love Camp '81
The Mack '73
Malibu Express '85
Mancinga '77
M'Lady's Court '73
My Wonderful Life '90
The Naked Flame '68
Naked in the Night '58
Naked Vengeance '85
The Narcotics Story '58
Night Friend '87
Nomugi Pass '79
One Down, Two to Go '82
One Night Only '84
One Plus One '61
One Too Many '51
Overexposed '90
Paradise Motel '84
Party Incorporated '89
Pin Down Girls '51
Policewoman Centerfold '83
Poor Pretty Eddie '73
Reefer Madness '38
Ringmaster '98
The Road to Ruin '28
S.O.B. '81
Satan's Cheerleaders '77
Savages from Hell '68
Screaming Dead '03
Secrets of Sweet Sixteen '74
Sensual Partners '87
Sex Adventures of the Three Musketeers '71
She Shoulda Said No '49
Sin You Sinners '63
Single Room Furnished '66
Slaughter '72
Slaughter's Big Ripoff '73
Slaves in Bondage '37
Something Weird '68
SS Girls '77
Star 80 '83
Street of Forgotten Women '25
Student Confidential '87
Suite 16 '94
Summer School Teachers '75
Sunset Strip '91
Sunstorm '01
Swamp Women '55
Sweet Spirits '80s
Taxi Dancers '93
The Teacher '74
Teenage Doll '57
Test Tube Babies '48
They're Playing with Fire '84
Three in the Attic '68
Thunder & Mud '89
Tomorrow's Children '34
Violated '53
Warrior Queen '87
Weekend with the Babysitter '70
Weird World of LSD '57
Women's Club '87
Women Hunt '72
Yesterday's Hero '79
Young Lady Chatterly 2 '85
Youth Aflame '44

Explorers
The Adventures of Marco Polo '38
Almost Heroes '97
Apollo 13 '95▶
Atlantis: The Lost Empire '01
Cabeza de Vaca '90▶
Call Me Bwana '63
The Cavern '05
Christopher Columbus '49
Christopher Columbus '85
Christopher Columbus: The Discovery '92
Congo '95
The Conqueror & the Empress '64
The Far Horizons '55
The Forbidden Quest '93
Forgotten City '98
1492: Conquest of Paradise '92
Glory & Honor '98
How Tasty Was My Little Frenchman '71
King Solomon's Mines '50▶
King Solomon's Mines '85
The Last Place on Earth '85
The Live Wire '34
The Lost World '98
The Lost World '92
The Lost World '25▶
Marco Polo '07
Mountains of the Moon '90▶
The New World '05▶
Shackleton '02▶
She '35
Sir Arthur Conan Doyle's The Lost World '98
The Sky Above, the Mud Below '61
The Valley Obscured by the Clouds '70
The Wacky World of Wills & Burke '85
Wagon Wheels '34
Wake of the Red Witch '49▶

Eyeballs!
see also Hearts!
Anguish '88
Austin Powers: International Man of Mystery '97▶
The Birds '63▶
A Clockwork Orange '71▶
The Crawling Eye '58
Damien: Omen 2 '78
Demolition Man '93
Die Hard 2: Die Harder '90▶
Evil Dead 2: Dead by Dawn '87▶
The Eye '08
The Eye Creatures '65
Eyeball '75
Eyes '08
Eyes of Laura Mars '78
Friday the 13th, Part 3 '82
The Fury '78
The Godfather '72▶
Halloween '78▶
Headless Eyes '83
Idle Hands '99
Minority Report '02▶
Nightmare '96
Nightmare Eyes '83
The Nightmare Isn't Over! '81
Peeping Tom '60▶
The Phantom '96
Pitch Black '00▶
Rocky '76▶
Scanners '81▶
See No Evil '06
Silver Bullet '85
Sleepy Hollow '99▶
Strange Behavior '81
Summer School '87
The Terminator '84▶
True Lies '94▶
Un Chien Andalou '28▶
Wild Palms '93
X: The Man with X-Ray Eyes '63▶
Zombie '80

Extraordinary Pairings
Abbott and Costello Meet Frankenstein '48▶
All About the Benjamins '02
Alien vs. Predator '04
Almost Heroes '97
Bela Lugosi Meets a Brooklyn Gorilla '52
Billy the Kid Versus Dracula '66
The Breed '01
Bulletproof Monk '03
Dr. Jekyll and the Wolfman '71
Doctor of Doom '62
Dracula vs. Frankenstein '71
Frankenstein Meets the Space Monster '65
Frankenstein Meets the Wolfman '42▶
Freddy vs. Jason '03
The Hollywood Strangler Meets the Skid Row Slasher '79
Jesse James Meets Frankenstein's Daughter '65
King Kong vs. Godzilla '63
Living Out Loud '98
My Giant '98
Nim's Island '08
Rolling Family '04
The River Wild '94▶
Rush Hour '98▶
Santa Claus Conquers the Martians '64
Speed Racer '08
The Spiderwick Chronicles '08
The Swiss Family Robinson '60▶
Those Calloways '65
The Wild Thornberrys Movie '02▶
Zeus and Roxanne '96

Fairs & Expositions
see also Amusement Parks; Carnivals & Circuses
Babe '95▶
Charlotte's Web '73▶
Howling 6: The Freaks '90
It Happened at the World's Fair '63
Ma and Pa Kettle at the Fair '52
Megasnake '07
My Girl '91
Shag: The Movie '89▶
State Fair '45▶
Swap Meet '79

Family Adventure
see also The Adventures of the Wilderness Family
Alaska '96
All Mine to Give '56
Cal of the Forest '49
Chang: A Drama of the Wilderness '27▶
The Chisholms '79
Disappearances '06
Escape from Wildcat Canyon '99
Far from Home: The Adventures of Yellow Dog '94
Force on Thunder Mountain '77
Further Adventures of the Wilderness Family, Part 2 '77
The Happening '08
Little House on the Prairie '74▶
The Mummy: Tomb of the Dragon Emperor '08
Nancy Drew '07
Nim's Island '08
Outlaw Trail '06

Family Comedy
see also Aunts & Uncles; Nieces & Nephews; Bad Dads; Brothers & Sisters; Cousins; Dads; Family Drama; Family Reunions; Moms; Monster Moms:
About Adam '00
The Addams Family '91▶
The Addams Family Values '93
Air Bud 5: Buddy Spikes
Alberto Express '92
Alvin and the Chipmunks '07
And Baby Makes Six '79
And You Thought Your Parents Were Weird! '91
Are Parents People? '25
Are We Done Yet? '07
Are We There Yet? '05

▶ = rated three bones or higher

♦ = rated three bones or higher

Family

At Home with the Webbers '94
Baby of the Bride '91
Beethoven's 4th '01
Belles on Their Toes '52
Bend It Like Beckham '02
Betsy's Wedding '90
The Beverly Hillbillies '93
Beverly Hills Family Robinson '97
Big and Hairy '98
Big Bully '95
The Big Day '99
Bon Voyage! '62
The Brady Bunch Movie '95
California Dreaming '07
Cars '06
Cheaper by the Dozen '50
Cheaper by the Dozen '03
Cheaper by the Dozen 2 '05
Christmas Do-Over '06
A Christmas Story '83
Christmas With the Kranks '04
Chutney Popcorn '99
Click '06
Coffee Date '06
Cold Comfort Farm '71
Cold Comfort Farm '94
Collier & Co.: Hot Pursuit '06
Coneheads '93
Cote d'Azur '05
Daddy & Them '99
Daddy Day Camp '07
Daddy's Dyin'... Who's Got the Will? '90
Dan in Real Life '07
The Daytrippers '96
Death at a Funeral '07
Dennis the Menace '93
A Dennis the Menace Christmas '07
Dirty Laundry '07
Dr. Dolittle '98
Dr. Dolittle 2 '01
Doogal '05
East is East '99
East Side of Heaven '39
Eat a Bowl of Tea '89
El Carro '04
The Family Holiday '07
The Family Plan '05
The Family Stone '05
Father of the Bride '50
Father of the Bride '91
Father of the Bride Part 2 '95
Father Was a Fullback '49
Father's Little Dividend '51
Firehouse Dog '07
First Kid '96
Folks! '92
Freaky Friday '76
Freaky Friday '03
Freaky Friday '07
The Game Plan '07
Garfield: A Tail of Two Kitties '06
Getting Even with Dad '94
The Girl Next Door '53
Go for Zucker '05
Good Morning '59
The Great Outdoors '88
Guess Who '05
Harry and the Hendersons '87
Hello Down There '69
Honey, I Blew Up the Kid '92
Honey, I Shrunk the Kids '89
Honey, We Shrunk Ourselves '97
Hoot '06
Houseboat '58
How Sweet It Is! '68
Ice Age: The Meltdown '06
The Incredibles '04
Introducing the Dwights '07
Johnson Family Vacation '04
Jungle 2 Jungle '96
Juno '07
Keeping Up with the Steins '06
Krippendorf's Tribe '98
Leave It to Beaver '97
Little Indian, Big City '95
A Little Romance '79
The Little Vampire '00
Look Who's Talking '89
Look Who's Talking Now '93
Look Who's Talking, Too '90
Madea's Family Reunion '06
Manna from Heaven '02
Meet the Fockers '04
Meet the Robinsons '07
Mr. Blandings Builds His Dream House '48
Mr. Mom '83
Monster-in-Law '05
My Mother Likes Women '02
My Summer Story '94
Nanny McPhee '06
National Lampoon's Christmas Vacation '89
National Lampoon's European Vacation '85
National Lampoon's Vacation '83
No Dessert Dad, 'Til You Mow the Lawn '94
Our Italian Husband '04
The Pacifier '05
The Parent Trap '61
The Parent Trap '98
Parenthood '89
Please Don't Eat the Daisies '60
The Prince and the Pauper '07
The Proud Family Movie '05
Racing Stripes '05
Raising Flagg '06
Ratatouille '07
Recipe for Disaster '03
Red Doors '05
Robots '05
Rumor Has It... '05
RV '06
Santa Baby '06
The Santa Trap '02
Saving Face '04
Secondhand Lions '03
Serial Mom '94
The Shaggy Dog '06
The Simpsons Movie '07
Sordid Lives '00
Spanglish '04
Step Brothers '08
Stuart Saves His Family '94
The Stupids '95
Surviving Christmas '04
A Tale of Two Pizzas '03
The Thing About My Folks '05
This Christmas '07
The Tollbooth '04
Too Busy to Work '32
Trading Mom '94
Tyler Perry's Meet the Browns '08
Uncle Buck '89
Uncle Nino '03
Up and Down '04
Valiant '05
Vegas Vacation '96
A Very Brady Sequel '96
Wait Till Your Mother Gets Home '83
Wallace & Gromit: The Curse of the Were-Rabbit '05
Welcome Home Roscoe Jenkins '08
What about Bob? '91
When Do We Eat? '05
Who Made the Potatoe Salad? '05
Yours, Mine & Ours '68
Yours, Mine & Ours '05

Family Drama

see also Aunts & Uncles, Nieces & Nephews; Bad Dads; Brothers & Sisters; Cousins; Dads; Family Comedy; Family Reunions; Grandparents; Moms; Monster Moms

The Accidental Tourist '88
Adam Had Four Sons '41
The Adventures of Sebastian Cole '99
Affliction '97
After the Promise '87
Agnes Browne '99
Alice et Martin '98
All Fall Down '62
All I Desire '53
All Mine to Give '56
All My Sons '48
All My Sons '86
All or Nothing '02
Alpha Male '06
American Beauty '99
An American Haunting '05
American Heart '92
American History X '98
... And the Earth Did Not Swallow Him '94
Angela '94
Angela's Ashes '99
Angelo My Love '83
Animal '05
The Anniversary '68
Antonia's Line '95
Anywhere But Here '99
Around the Bend '04
Astoria '00
The Astronaut Farmer '07
At Close Range '86
Atonement '07
August '95
August Rush '07
Aurora Borealis '06
Avalon '90
The Ballad of Jack and Rose '05
The Barbarian Invasions '03
The Battle of Shaker Heights '03
Because of Winn-Dixie '05
Becoming Jane '07
Bee Season '05
Behind the Sun '01
Beshkempir the Adopted Son '98
Best of Youth '03
The Betsy '78
Billy Elliot '00
Black Irish '07
Blame It on Fidel '06
Blessing '94
Blind Spot '93
Bridge to Terabithia '07
Broken Wings '02
The Brontes of Haworth '73
Brooklyn Lobster '05
Brothers '05
The Brothers Karamazov '58
Buffalo Boy '04
The Butcher Boy '97
Canvas '06
Caterina in the Big City '03
Catherine Cookson's Colour Blind '98
Catherine Cookson's The Black Velvet Gown '02
Catherine Cookson's The Cinder Path '94
Catherine Cookson's The Fifteen Streets '90
Catherine Cookson's The Man Who Cried '93
Catherine Cookson's The Wingless Bird '97
The Celebration '98
Charms for the Easy Life '02
The Children Are Watching Us '44
The Christmas Blessing '05
The Christmas Box '95
The Christmas Shoes '02
The Chronicles of Narnia: The Lion, the Witch and the Wardrobe '05
Cider with Rosie '98
Cinderella Man '05
Close to Leo '02
Cookie's Fortune '99
The Crow Road '96
Daddy's Little Girls '07
Damage '92
Dancing at Lughnasa '98
Dark Blue Almost Black '06
Daughters of the Dust '91
Dear Frankie '04
The Derby Stallion '05
Desire Under the Elms '58
Distant Voices, Still Lives '88
Doing Time on Maple Drive '92
Don't Come Knocking '05
Don't Tell '05
Down in the Delta '98
Down to the Bone '04
Dreamer: Inspired by a True Story '05
Duma '05
Eat Drink Man Woman '94
Eighteen '04
Elizabethtown '05
Emile '03
Empire Falls '05
Evelyn '02
The Evening Star '96
Eve's Bayou '97
Eye of the Dolphin '06
The Family '87
Family Pictures '93
Family Prayers '91
Fanny and Alexander '83
The Favorite Son '94
Feast of July '95
Fierce People '05
Finding Home '03
Fiorile '93
Flambards '78
The Flame Trees of Thika '81
Flicka '06
Flight of the Red Balloon '08
Floating Life '95
Follow the Stars Home '01
A Fond Kiss '04
For One More Day '07
Forbidden Choices '94
Four Men and a Prayer '38
Four Sheets to the Wind '07
Frailty '02
Gas Food Lodging '92
Georgia Rule '07
Giant '56
Gideon's Daughter '05
God's Sandbox '02
Gracie '07
Gracie's Choice '04
Happiness '98
Henry & Verlin '94
Hidden Places '06
A History of Violence '05
Home for the Holidays '72
Home for the Holidays '95
A Home of Our Own '93
Homecoming '96
House of D '04
The House of the Spirits '93
The House of Yes '97
Household Saints '93
Hush Little Baby '93
I Remember Mama '48
The Ice Storm '97
Illegal Tender '07
Imaginary Heroes '05
In America '02
In Her Shoes '05
In the Gloaming '97
In the Land of Women '06
The Inheritance '03
Inside Paris '06
The Intended '02
Into the West '92
Inventing the Abbotts '97
JFK: Reckless Youth '93
Joshua '07
Julien Donkey-boy '99
Junebug '05
Kill the Poor '06
Killer of Sheep '77
King of the Corner '04
Kingdom Come '01
Kings and Queen '04
The Last Hard Men '76
The Last Mimzy '07
Last Summer in the Hamptons '96
Legends of the Fall '94
Leolo '92
Liam '00
Life as a House '01
Life Is Sweet '90
Life Support '07
Like Father Like Son '05
Limbo '99
Little Boy Blue '97
Little Miss Sunshine '06
Lonesome Jim '06
The Long Day Closes '92
Look at Me '04
Lorenzo's Oil '92
The Lost City '05
Lost Embrace '04
The Lost Language of Cranes '92
Love Comes Softly '03
Love Your Mama '89
Loverboy '05
Love's Enduring Promise '04
Love's Long Journey '05
Love's Unending Legacy '06
Ma Saison Preferee '93
The Magnificent Ambersons '42
The Magnificent Ambersons '02
Manito '03
Margot at the Wedding '07
Martian Child '07
Martin (Hache) '97
Miss Austen Regrets '07
Moondance Alexander '07
My Boy Jack '07
My Brother '06
My Family '94
My Life So Far '98
My Mother's Smile '02
The Myth of Fingerprints '97
Nearing Grace '05
New Blood '99
Night Moves '75
Nil by Mouth '96
No Reservations '07
Nobody Knows '04
O Pioneers! '91
Of Human Hearts '38
Off the Map '03
Once Were Warriors '94
Ordinary People '80
Other Voices, Other Rooms '95
A Painted House '03
Paradise, Texas '05
The Piano Lesson '94
Pieces of April '03
Poor Man's Game '06
Private Property '06
The Prize Winner of Defiance, Ohio '05
Proof '05
Protecting the King '07
The Pursuit of Happyness '06
The Quiet Room '96
Rails & Ties '07
The Railway Children '70
The Railway Children '00
Rain '06
A Raisin in the Sun '08
Ratcatcher '99
Real Women Have Curves '02
Redwood Curtain '95
Reservation Road '07
Riding in Cars with Boys '01
A River Runs Through It '92
Rocket Gibraltar '88
Romulus, My Father '07
The Royal Tenenbaums '01
Running on Empty '88
Running with Scissors '06
Ryna '05
Safe Passage '94
The Savages '07
Saraband '03
Sarah, Plain and Tall '91
Sarah, Plain and Tall: Skylark '93
Sarah, Plain and Tall: Winter's End '99
Saving Shiloh '06
The Secret of Roan Inish '94
Set Me Free '99
The Shipping News '01
Since Otar Left... '03
The Sisters '05
Sleepwalking '08
Smart People '08
The Son's Room '00
Spencer's Mountain '63
Steamboy '05
Steel City '06
Stolen Summer '02
The Story of Boys & Girls '91
The Sundowners '60
Swimming Upstream '03
The Syrian Bride '04
The Talent Given Us '04
10th & Wolf '06
That Russell Girl '08
Things We Lost in the Fire '07
Though None Go With Me '06
Through a Glass Darkly '61
Time of the Wolf '03
Time to Leave '05
To Live '94
Tortilla Soup '01
Transamerica '05
12 and Holding '05
21 Grams '03
The Twilight of the Golds '97
Two Weeks '06
Typhoon '06
Un Air de Famille '96
Uncle Nino '03
Under the Same Moon '07
Undertow '04
Up and Down '04
The Upside of Anger '05
Volver '06
Waking Up Wally '05
The War '94
The War Bride '01
The War Zone '98
Washington Heights '02
The Water Horse: Legend of the Deep '07
We Own the Night '07
Weeping Meadow '04
Welcome to Paradise '07
Welcome to the Dollhouse '95
What's Cooking? '00
What's Eating Gilbert Grape '93
When Father Was Away on Business '85
Wild Iris '01
Winter Passing '05
Winter Solstice '04
A Woman of Independent Means '94
Wondrous Oblivion '06
The World Moves On '34

Family Reunions

see also Aunts & Uncles; Nieces & Nephews; Brothers & Sisters; Cousins; Dads; Family Comedy; Family Drama; Grandparents; Moms; Vacations

Aberdeen '00
Alias Betty '01
Almost Strangers '01
American Heart '92
Around the Bend '04
August Rush '07
Autumn Sonata '78
Back Home '90
Behind the Red Door '02
Blue River '95
Brothers '05
Carnegie Hall '47
Catfish in Black Bean Sauce '00
The Claim '00
The Confessional '95
Daddy Nostalgia '90
Dan in Real Life '07
The Dance Goes On '92
Dangerous Relations '93
The Darjeeling Limited '07
Death at a Funeral '07
The Deep End of the Ocean '98
Don't Tell '05
Elf '03
The Emerald Forest '85
Family Life '71
Family Reunion '88
A Family Thing '96

Fred Claus '07
The Gathering '77
The Gathering, Part 2 '79
A Guide to Recognizing Your Saints '06
Halloween '07
The Heartbreak Kid '07
Housekeeping '87▸
How I Killed My Father '03▸
Jeremy's Family Reunion '04
Jumpin' at the Boneyard '92
Junebug '05▸
Leon the Pig Farmer '93
The Lost Child '00
Madea's Family Reunion '06
Magnolia '99▸
Margot at the Wedding '07
Marion Bridge '02
The Mayor of Casterbridge '03
Me & Veronica '93
Montana Sky '07
My Heroes Have Always Been Cowboys '91
My Twentieth Century '90▸
The Nephew '97
Nobody's Fool '94▸
Olivier, Olivier '92▸
On Golden Pond '81▸
Paris, Texas '83▸
Passed Away '92
The Princess Diaries '01
Pushing Hands '92
The Reception '05
The River's Red '48
The River Rat '84
Rupert's Land '98
The Searchers '56▸
Secrets and Lies '95
75 Degrees '00
Soft Fruit '99
Sorrento Beach '95
That Talent Given Us '04▸
This Christmas '07
Those Who Love Me Can Take the Train '98
A Time to Remember '03
Two Weeks '06
Tyler Perry's Meet the Browns '08
Under the Same Moon '08
An Unexpected Family '96
Welcome Home Roscoe Jenkins '08
What a Girl Wants '03
When Wolves Cry '69
Winter Passing '05▸
You Can Count On Me '99▸

Family Ties
see also *Aunts & Uncles; Brothers & Sisters; Cousins; Dads; Grandparents; In-Laws; Moms; Parenthood; Stepparents; Twins*

A.I.: Artificial Intelligence '01
Abraham '94
The Adventures of Felix '99
The Adventures of the Wilderness Family '76
After Julius '78
After the Deluge '03▸
Agent Cody Banks 2: Destination London '04
Air Force One '97▸
Alice '90▸
Alien Nation: Millennium '96
Alien Nation: The Enemy Within '96
All I Want for Christmas '91
All the Kind Strangers '74
An American Christmas Carol '79
American Dream '81▸
American Gothic '88
American Pop '81▸
American Rhapsody '01▸
An American Wedding '03
Amityville Dollhouse '96
Andy Hardy Gets Spring Fever '39

Andy Hardy Meets Debutante '40
Andy Hardy's Double Life '42
Andy Hardy's Private Secretary '41
Angel Eyes '01
Angela '77
Angela '01
Angels and Insects '95▸
Angie '94
Angus '95
Animal 2 '07
Anne of Green Gables '34▸
The Apprenticeship of Duddy Kravitz '74▸
Army Brats '84
The Arrangement '69
Avanti! '72
Baba '73▸
Baby, Love '69
Baby, the Rain Must Fall '64
Back to School '86
Back to the Future '85▸
Bastard out of Carolina '96
Batting for Baby '92
Beach Hotel '92
Beast in the Cellar '70
The Beast Within '82
Bed & Breakfast '92
Beethoven '92
Beethoven's 2nd '93
Beethoven's 3rd '00
Before and After '95
Being Human '94
Bella Mafia '97
A Better Tomorrow, Part 3 '89
Beulah Land '80
Beverly Hills Brats '89
Beyond Darkness '92
Big Girls Don't Cry... They Get Even '92
Big Trouble '02
Billboard Dad '98
Billy Liar '63▸
The Birch Interval '78
Black Orchid '59
The Blackheath Poisonings '92
Blondie Brings Up Baby '39
Blondie Goes Latin '42
Blondie Goes to College '42
Blondie Has Trouble '40
Blondie Meets the Boss '39
Blondie On a Budget '40
Blondie Plays Cupid '40
Blondie Takes a Vacation '39
Blondie's Blessed Event '42
Blood & Wine '96
Blood Brothers '97
Blood for Blood '95
Blood Money '99
Blood Red '88
Blood Ties '87
Blood Ties '92
Bloodbrothers '78
Bloodknot '95
The Blot '21
Blue Collar '78▸
The Blue Kite '93▸
The Blue Yonder '86
Body & Soul '93▸
Body Count '87
Bolero '82
Bonanza: The Return '93
Bonjour Monsieur Shlomi '03▸
Border Vengeance '35
The Borrowers '93▸
Bouquet of Barbed Wire '76
The Boxer '97▸
The Boys '98▸
Boyz N the Hood '91▸
Bread and Tulips '01▸
Breakfast of Champions '98
Breaking Home Ties '87
Breakout '98
The Breaks '99
The Bretts '88▸
Bridge to Terabithia '07
Bright Angel '91
Broadway Bound '91
Broken Harvest '94
Buffalo 66 '97▸
Burnt by the Sun '94▸

B.U.S.T.E.D. '99
Butterfly Wings '91
Cahill: United States Marshal '73
Call to Glory '84
Calm at Sunset '96
Candles at Nine '44
Candles on '03
Captain Ron '92
Capturing the Friedmans '03▸
Careful, He Might Hear You '84▸
Caresses '97
Caroline? '90▸
The Case of the Frightened Lady '39
Castle Freak '95
Cat on a Hot Tin Roof '58
Cat on a Hot Tin Roof '84
Caught '96
Cavalcade '33▸
Cavalry '36
Centennial '78▸
The Chamber '96
Chances Are '89▸
A Chef in Love '96
Cheatin' Hearts '93
Charley and the Angel '73
The Chisholms '79
Children of Dune '03▸
Children of Sanchez '79
A Christmas Reunion '93
A Christmas to Remember '51
Choices '86
Cimarron '31
Cimarron '60
Clean, Shaven '93
Clifford '92
Clockstoppers '02
Close to Eden '90
The Closer '00
Cold Creek Manor '03
Cold Heat '90
Comin' 'Round the Mountain '51
Coming Out Alive '84
Communion '89
Confessions of a Hit Man '94
Consenting Adult '85
A Conspiracy of Love '87
Coquette '29
The Corner '00
Countdown '68
Country '84▸
The Country Bears '02
Country Life '95
Cousin Bette '97▸
Cracker: True Romance '95
Crazy in Love '92
The Crazy Stranger '98
Crooked Hearts '91
Crooklyn '94▸
Crossing Delancey '88▸
Crumb '94▸
Cupid & Cate '00
Curse of the Starving Class '94
Cypress Edge '99
Daddy's Girl '96
Dalva '95
Daniel Deronda '02
A Dark Adapted Eye '93▸
The Dark Angel '91▸
A Day for Thanks on Walton's Mountain '82
The Day the Sun Turned Cold '94▸
Dead End '96
Dead Silent '99
Deadfall '93
Deadly Sunday '82
Dear Dead Delilah '72
Dear Wife '49
Death Be Not Proud '75▸
Death of a Salesman '86▸
Death of a Stranger '76
The Defenders: Payback '97
Demons of the Mind '72
Deranged '02
Desert Bloom '86▸
Desperate Living '77

Devi '60▸
Devil Dog: The Hound of Hell '78
The Devil's Own '96▸
The Devil's Rejects '05▸
Devil's Island '96
Diamond Head '62
Die Mommie Die! '03
Digger '94
Dimples '36
Disappearance '02
Discontent '16
Distortions '87
Divided by Hate '96
Dixie Lanes '88
Dr. Dolittle '98
Donnie Darko '01▸
Don't Drink the Water '69
Don't Go to Sleep '82
Double Happiness '94▸
Double Play '96
Down & Dirty '76▸
Down in the Valley '05
The Dress Code '99
Dummy '02
Dune '00
An Early Frost '85▸
Early Summer '51▸
The Echo of Thunder '98
Eight on the Lam '67
8 Women '02▸
18 Again! '88
The Eighteenth Angel '97
Electra '95
Eli Eli '40
Elizabeth of Ladymead '46▸
Ellen Foster '97
Embassy '85
The Emigrants '72▸
Emma '97▸
Encore '52▸
Endless Love '81
The Entertainer '60▸
Equinox Flower '58
Erendira '83
Ermo '94▸
Escape from Wildcat Canyon '99
Escape Velocity '99
The Eternal '99
Eternal Return '43
Eulogy '04
The Europeans '79▸
The Everlasting Secret Family '88
Every Mother's Worst Fear '98
Everyone Says I Love You '96▸
Everything That Rises '98
Excess Baggage '96
The Executioner '78
Exotica '94▸
Expectations '97
Eye of the Storm '91
The Eyes of the Amaryllis '82
The Eyes, the Mouth '83
Face to Face '76▸
Faces of Women '85
Faith '97
Fallen Angel '03
Falling from Grace '92
The Family '87▸
Family '94▸
Family Jewels '65
Family of Cops '95
Family of Cops 2: Breach of Faith '97
Family of Cops 3 '98
Family Reunion '79
Family Secrets '84
Family Sins '87
Family Viewing '87▸
Fangs of the Living Dead '68
Far North '88
Fast Talking '86
The Feud '90
Fiddler on the Roof '71▸
Field of Dreams '89▸
Fight for Your Life '77
Final Approach '04
Final Verdict '91
The Fire Next Time '93
First Do No Harm '97

The Fishing Trip '98
Five Days One Summer '82
The Fixer '97
Flash '98
The Flintstones '94
Flirting with Disaster '95▸
Fly Boy '99
Follow That Dream '61
Footlight Glamour '43
For Love or Money '63
For Which He Stands '98
Forbidden Planet '56▸
Forever and a Day '43▸
Forever Love '98
Forever Together '00
The Four Horsemen of the Apocalypse '21▸
The Four Horsemen of the Apocalypse '62
Freaky Friday '76
Freaky Friday '03▸
Friend of the Family '95
Friendly Persuasion '56▸
Friends and Family '01
Friendly Fire '79▸
From the Terrace '60
The Fringe Dwellers '86
Fulfillment '89
The Funeral '84▸
The Funeral '96
Funny Bones '94▸
Funnyman '94
Further Adventures of the Wilderness Family, Part 2 '77
The Fury '78
Fuzz '72▸
Gabbeh '96▸
The Game Is Over '66
Gang Boys '97
The Garden of Delights '70▸
The Garden of the Finzi-Continis '71▸
Garden State '04▸
Gaudi Afternoon '01
Generation '69
Gervaise '56▸
A Girl on Her Own '76
Girly '70
The Go-Masters '82▸
The Godfather '72▸
The Godfather 1902-1959: The Complete Epic '81▸
The Godfather, Part 2 '74▸
The Godson '98
Golden Earth '93
Good Bye, Lenin! '03▸
The Good Earth '37▸
Good Fences '03
Goodbye, Miss 4th of July '88
Goodnight, Michelangelo '89
Gostford Park '01▸
Grand Avenue '96
The Grandfather '98
The Granny '94
The Grapes of Wrath '40▸
The Grass is Always Greener Over the Septic Tank '78
Grave Indiscretions '96
Great Day '45
The Great Man Votes '38▸
The Great Madcap '49
A Great Wall '86▸
The Great Wallendas '78
Greedy '94
Green Horizon '80
The Green House '96
The Green Wall '70▸
Grown Ups '80
Grown Ups '86
Guess Who's Coming to Dinner '67▸
Gulliver's Travels '95
The Habitation of Dragons '92
Habitat '97
Halloween with the Addams Family '79
Hamlet '90
Hamlet '96
Hamlet '00
Hamlet '01
The Hand that Rocks the Cradle '92

The Hanging Garden '97▸
Happiness '98▸
Hard Target '93▸
Harriet the Spy '96
Harvest '98
The Hatfields & the McCoys '75
The Haunted Mansion '03
Head of the Family '71
Heart of a Nation '43▸
Heat '95▸
Height of the Sky '99
Heimat '84▸
Heimat 2 '92
Henry Fool '98▸
Here Come the Nelsons '52
Here Comes Cookie '35
Hi Diddle Diddle '43
Hidden in Plain Sight '80▸
Hideaway '94
The Hit List '88
High Heels '91▸
Hobo's Christmas '87
Hold the Dream '86
Hollow Reed '96
Hollywood Safari '96
The Holy Innocents '84▸
Holy Matrimony '94
Holy Smoke '99
Home Alone '90▸
A Home at the End of the World '04▸
Home of Angels '94
Home to Stay '79
Homecoming: A Christmas Story '71▸
Honor Thy Father '73
Honor Thy Father and Mother: The True Story of the Menendez Brothers '94
Hook '91▸
Hope '97
Hope and Glory '87▸
A Horse for Danny '95
The Horse Whisperer '97▸
Horton Foote's Alone '97
Hot Spell '58
House Arrest '96
House of Dreams '64
The House of Sand and Fog '03▸
The House on Chelouche Street '73
The House that Bled to Death '81
Houseguest '94
How Green Was My Valley '41▸
How the West Was Won '63▸
How to Commit Marriage '69
How to Deal '03
The Howards of Virginia '40
Hugo Pool '97
Hurricane Streets '96
I Want You '51
The Ice Flood '26
I'd Give My Life '36
If Things Were Different '79
I Live in Fear '55▸
I Love You, I Love You Not '97
I Love You to Death '90▸
I Never Sang for My Father '70▸
In Cold Blood '96
In His Father's Shoes '97
In Search of a Golden Sky '84
Immediate Family '89
The Imported Bridegroom '89
In the Custody of Strangers '82▸
In the Heat of Passion 2: Unfaithful '94
In the Presence of Mine Enemies '97
In This Our Life '42▸

▸ = rated three bones or higher

The Incredibles '04 ▲
Independence Day '83 ▲
The Inkwell '94 ▲
Innocence Unprotected '68
Innocent Lies '95
Inside Monkey Zetterland '93
Inspector Lynley Mysteries: A Great Deliverance '01 ▲
Internes Can't Take Money '37
Intimate Relations '95
Invisible Child '99
Iphigenia '77 ▲
The Irishman '78
Is There Life Out There? '94 ▲
The Island '61 ▲
Islands in the Stream '77
It Came from the Sky '98
It Runs in the Family '03
It's a Great Life '43
It's a Wonderful Life '46 ▲
It's My Party '95
Ivan and Abraham '94
Jack '96
The Jacksons: An American Dream '92
Jacob '94
Jalsaghar '58
Jamon, Jamon '93
Jason Goes to Hell: The Final Friday '93
The Jazz Singer '27
The Jazz Singer '80
Jeremy's Family Reunion '04
John and the Missus '87
Joseph '95
Journey '95
Journey of Hope '90 ▲
Junebug '05 ▲
Juno and the Paycock '30
Just for You '52
K-PAX '01
Karmina '96
Kazaam '96
Keep the Change '92
The Kennedys of Massachusetts '95
The Kettles in the Ozarks '56
The Kid Who Loved Christmas '90
Kidnapping of Baby John Doe '88
Killing Grandpa '91
Killing of Randy Webster '81
Kind Hearts and Coronets '49 ▲
The King and Four Queens '56
King Lear '71 ▲
King Lear '98 ▲
King of the Gypsies '78
King of the Hill '93 ▲
Kingfisher Caper '76
Kings in Grass Castles '97
The Kiss '88
The Kissing Place '90
Kotch '71 ▲
Kristin Lavransdatter '95
Kuffs '92
Kuni Lemel in Tel Aviv '77
La Boum '81
La Ceremonie '95 ▲
La Chartreuse de Parme '48
La Rupture '70
La Silence de la Mer '47
A Symphonie Pastorale '46 ▲
La Terra Trema '48 ▲
Lady Audley's Secret '00
Lady Mobster '88
Lantern Hill '90
The Last Assassins '96
The Last Don '97
The Last Don 2 '98
The Last of the High Kings '96
Last Resort '86
The Last September '99
Last Stand at Saber River '96
The Last Winter '89
Late Marriage '01

Laurel Avenue '93 ▲
The Lawless Breed '52 ▲
Lawn Dogs '96
Leapin' Leprechauns '95
Left Luggage '98
Legacy of Lies '92
The Legend of Black Thunder Mountain '79
L'Eleve '95
Les Violons du Bal '74
Let the Devil Wear Black '99
Lethal Weapon '87 ▲
Lethal Weapon 4 '98 ▲
Let's Dance '50
Letting the Birds Go Free '86
Liar Liar '97
Liar's Edge '92
Liar's Moon '82
Liberty Heights '99
License to Kill '84
The Lickerish Quartet '70
Lies My Father Told Me '75 ▲
Life and Nothing More ... '92
Life Is a Long Quiet River '88 ▲
Lift '01
Like Father, Like Son '87
Like Water for Chocolate '93 ▲
Lily Dale '96
Lily in Winter '94
The Lion in Winter '68 ▲
The Lion King '94 ▲
The Lion King: Simba's Pride '98
The List of Adrian Messenger '63 ▲
Little Bigfoot '96
Little Buddha '93
The Little Death '95
Little House on the Prairie '74 ▲
The Little Kidnappers '90
Little Lord Fauntleroy '95
Little Nellie Kelly '40
Little Nicky '00
Little Odessa '94
Little Richard '00
Little Women '33
Little Women '49
Little Women '94 ▲
The Littlest Viking '94
Locked in Silence '99
Lone Star '95 ▲
Long Day's Journey into Night '62 ▲
Long Day's Journey into Night '88 ▲
Long Day's Journey Into Night '96 ▲
The Long, Hot Summer '58 ▲
The Long, Hot Summer '86 ▲
The Long Kiss Goodnight '96
Lorna Doone '34
Lorna Doone '90
Lost Boundaries '49
The Lost Boys '87
Lost Honeymoon '47
Lost in Space '98
Lost in Yonkers '93
Lots of Luck '85
Lotto Land '95
The Lotus Eaters '93
Louder than Bombs '01
Love Finds Andy Hardy '38 ▲
Love, Honour & Obey '00
Love Kills '98
Love Laughs at Andy Hardy '46
Love Me Tender '56
Love on the Dole '41
Lover Girl '97
Lovers and Other Strangers '70
A Loving Father '02
The Low Life '95
Lucky Stiff '88
Ma and Pa Kettle '49
Ma and Pa Kettle at Home '54
Ma and Pa Kettle at the Fair '52

Ma and Pa Kettle at Waikiki '55
Ma and Pa Kettle Back On the Farm '51
Ma and Pa Kettle Go to Town '50
Ma and Pa Kettle on Vacation '53
Ma Barker's Killer Brood '60
Ma Vie en Rose '97 ▲
Mad Max '80 ▲
M.A.D.D.: Mothers Against Drunk Driving '83
Made in America '93
The Madness of King George '94 ▲
Mafia! '98
Mafia Princess '86
Magenta '96
Magic Kid '92
The Magnificent Ambersons '42 ▲
Make Room for Tomorrow '81
The Maker '98
Mama Turns a Hundred '79 ▲
Mambo Italiano '03
Mame '74
Man & Boy '71
The Man from Laramie '55 ▲
The Man in the Gray Flannel Suit '56
The Man in the Santa Claus Suit '79
A Man of Passion '88
Man of the House '95
Man, Woman & Child '83
Mandy '53 ▲
Maniac '63
Mansfield Park '85 ▲
Mansfield Park '99 ▲
Margaret's Museum '95 ▲
Maria's Day '84
Marooned in Iraq '02
Martha and I '91
Martin Chuzzlewit '94
Marvin's Room '96
Masala '91
Masterminds '96
The Mating Game '59 ▲
A Matter of Principle '83
Maverick '94 ▲
May Fools '90 ▲
Maybe I'll Be Home in the Spring '70
Me and the Mob '94
Meet Me in St. Louis '44 ▲
Meet the Hollowheads '89
Meet the Parents '91
Meet the Parents '00 ▲
The Member of the Wedding '52 ▲
The Member of the Wedding '83
Memory of Us '74
Menace on the Mountain '70
Merlin '92
Miami Rhapsody '95
Midnight '34 ▲
The Migrants '74 ▲
Milk Money '94
The Million Dollar Kid '99
Min & Bill '30 ▲
Mind Games '89
The Miniver Story '50
Miracle at Midnight '98
Miracle Down Under '87
Miracle on 34th Street '47 ▲
Miracle on 34th Street '94 ▲
The Mirror Has Two Faces '96
Missing Brendan '03
Mississippi Masala '92 ▲
Missouri Traveler '58 ▲
Mrs. Doubtfire '93 ▲
Mrs. Miniver '42 ▲
Mr. & Mrs. Bridge '90 ▲
Mr. Hobbs Takes a Vacation '62
Mr. Skitch '33
Mob Boss '90
Model Behavior '00
Mom, Can I Keep Her? '98
Mom and Dad '47
Mon Oncle '58 ▲
A Mongolian Tale '94

Monkey Trouble '94
Monsieur Verdoux '47 ▲
Monsoon Wedding '01 ▲
Moonlight Mile '02 ▲
Moonstruck '87 ▲
The Mortal Storm '40 ▲
The Mosquito Coast '86
Mother '26 ▲
Mother '52 ▲
Mother '94 ▲
Mother '96 ▲
Mother & Daughter: A Loving War '80
Mother and Son '31
Mother Wore Tights '47 ▲
Mother's Boys '94
Mouchette '67 ▲
Moving '88
Multiplicity '96
The Mummy Returns '01
Murder, He Says '45
Murders in the Doll House '79
Music from Another Room '97
My Architect: A Son's Journey '03 ▲
My Best Girl '27 ▲
My Big Fat Greek Wedding '02 ▲
My Daughter's Keeper '93
My Father, My Mother, My Brothers and My Sisters '99
My Father's Glory '91 ▲
My Friend Walter '93
My Grandpa Is a Vampire '92
My Life '93
My Mother's Castle '91 ▲
My Other Husband '85
My Son, My Son '40 ▲
My Uncle Silas '01 ▲
Mystic River '03 ▲
Nadja '95
Naked Paradise '78
National Lampoon's The Don's Analyst '97
National Treasure '04
Natural Enemies '79
The Natural History of Parking Lots '90
The New Land '73 ▲
New Waterford Girl '99
New York Stories '89 ▲
Next of Kin '89
Next Stop, Greenwich Village '76 ▲
Next Summer '84 ▲
Nice Girl? '41
Nicholas Nickleby '46 ▲
Nicholas Nickleby '02 ▲
Night Crossing '81
Night Must Fall '37 ▲
Night of Terror '08
The Night of the Hunter '55 ▲
Night of the Twisters '95
Nights and Days '76
Nine Months '95
1900 '76
No End '84
No Laughing Matter '97
No Place to Hide '81
No Place to Run '72
Noah's Ark '99
Noon Wine '84 ▲
The Norman Conquests, Part 1: Table Manners '78 ▲
The Norman Conquests, Part 2: Living Together '78 ▲
The Norman Conquests, Part 3: Round and Round the Garden '78 ▲
North '94
Not in This Town '97
Not My Kid '85
Not Quite Human '87
Not Quite Human 2 '89
Now and Forever '34
Nowhere in Africa '02 ▲
Numero Deux '75
The Nutty Professor '96 ▲
Nutty Professor 2: The Klumps '00
The Object of My Affection '98

Off Season '01
Oh Dad, Poor Dad (Momma's Hung You in the Closet & I'm Feeling So Sad) '67
O'Hara's Wife '82
The Old Curiosity Shop '94
The Old Dark House '32 ▲
Old Yeller '57 ▲
Ollie Hopnoodle's Haven of Bliss '88
Olly Olly Oxen Free '78
On Moonlight Bay '51
On Valentine's Day '86 ▲
Once Around '91
Once Upon a Time in the Midlands '02
Once Upon a Time ... When We Were Colored '95 ▲
The One and Only, Genuine, Original Family Band '68
One Cooks, the Other Doesn't '83
One Good Cop '91
One More Chance '90
The Only Thrill '97
Only You '94
Orange County '02
Ordet '55 ▲
Our Mother's Murder '97
Our Mutual Friend '98 ▲
Our Town '40 ▲
Our Town '77 ▲
Our Very Own '50
Out of the Blue '80 ▲
Out of Time '00
Out on a Limb '92
Outcasts of the Trail '49
Outside Chance of Maximilian Glick '88
Overboard '87
Overture to Glory '40
The Ox '91 ▲
Paco '75
Padre Nuestro '85 ▲
Padre Padrone '77 ▲
The Painted Lady '97 ▲
Panic in the Year Zero! '62
Papa's Angels '00
Paradise '91
A Paradise Under the Stars '99
Parental Guidance '98
Parrish '61
Passion '92
Pecker '98
Peg o' My Heart '22
Peggy Sue Got Married '86 ▲
The Perez Family '94
The Perfect Daughter '96
Perfect Family '92
A Perfect Little Murder '90
Personal Exemptions '88
Persuasion '71
Persuasion '95 ▲
Pet Sematary '89
Phaedra '62 ▲
Phedre '68
Philadelphia '93 ▲
Ping Pong '87
Pinocchio's Revenge '96
Pitfall '48 ▲
A Place in the World '92 ▲
Poil de Carotte '31
Poison Ivy '92
Poldark '75 ▲
Poldark '96 ▲
Poldark 2 '75 ▲
Polish Wedding '97
Pollyanna '60 ▲
Poltergeist '82 ▲
Poltergeist 2: The Other Side '86
Poltergeist: The Legacy '96
Popeye's Voyage: The Quest for Pappy '04
The Portrait '93 ▲
Prehistoria '93
Prehysteria 3 '95
Pretty in Pink '86 ▲
Pride and Prejudice '40 ▲
Pride and Prejudice '85 ▲
Pride and Prejudice '95 ▲
Prince of Pennsylvania '88
The Prince of Tides '91 ▲

Prizzi's Honor '85 ▲
The Prodigal '55
The Prodigal '83
Promised a Miracle '88
The Proposition '96
Psycho Sisters '98
Queen Margot '94 ▲
Queen of Hearts '89 ▲
The Quickie '01
Quiz Show '94 ▲
Radiance '98
Radio Flyer '92
Rage of Angels: The Story Continues '86
Raging Bull '80 ▲
Rainbow's End '35
A Raisin in the Sun '61 ▲
A Raisin in the Sun '89 ▲
Ran '85 ▲
Ransom '96 ▲
The Real Charlotte '91
Red Dirt '99
Red Firecracker, Green Firecracker '93
The Red Pony '49 ▲
The Red Pony '76 ▲
The Ref '93 ▲
Regarding Henry '91 ▲
Regina '83
Relative Fear '95
Remember the Night '40 ▲
Respiro '02
Return '88
The Return of the Borrowers '96 ▲
Return to Africa '89
Return to Me '00 ▲
Rhapsody in August '91 ▲
Rich, Young and Pretty '51
Richie Rich '94
Riders of the Purple Sage '25
Riot in the Streets '96
Rivals '72
The River Niger '76 ▲
The River Wild '94 ▲
Road Racers '59
Road to Salina '68 ▲
Robert Kennedy and His Times '90
The Rocking Horse Winner '49 ▲
Roger Dodger '02 ▲
RoGoPaG '62
Roll of Thunder, Hear My Cry '78 ▲
Rolling Home '48
Romeo and Juliet '54
Romeo and Juliet '68 ▲
Romola '25
Ronnie and Julie '97
Roommates '95
Roosters '95
The Royal Bed '31
Royal Deceit '94
Ruby Bridges '98 ▲
A Rumor of Angels '00
Runaway Father '91
Running Mates '86 ▲
Running Wild '94
Saint Maybe '98 ▲
St. Patrick's Day '99
A Saintly Switch '99
Sallah '63 ▲
Samantha '92
Same Old Song '97 ▲
Sand '00
Sandra of a Thousand Delights '65
The Saphead '21
Sardinia Kidnapped '75
Satan in High Heels '61
Savage Is Loose '74
Savage Island '03
Saving Shiloh '06
Scarlett '94
Scent of a Woman '92 ▲
Scott Turow's The Burden of Proof '92
Scream for Help '86
The Sculptress '97 ▲
The Sea '02 ▲
The Search '48 ▲
Searching for Bobby Fischer '93 ▲
Searching For Wooden Watermelons '01

▲ = rated three bones or higher

A Season for Miracles '99
Season of Change '94
Season of Fear '89
The Secret '93
Secrets '94
Seduced and Abandoned '64
The Seducers '70
See You in the Morning '89
The Seekers '79
Selena '96
Separate Vacations '86
7 Faces of Dr. Lao '63
Shadow of a Doubt '43
Shameless '94
The Shanghai Gesture '42
The Shell Seekers '89
Shenandoah '65
The Shepherd of the Hills '41
She's So Lovely '97
Shiloh '97
Shock '79
Shoot the Moon '82
Shoot Through the Heart '98
Showdown '94
Shy People '87
Siberiade '79
Siblings '04
Silence '73
The Silence of Neto '94
The Silences of the Palace '94
Silent Rebellion '82
Silent Tongue '92
The Silver Stallion: King of the Wild Brumbies '93
Simple Justice '89
A Simple Plan '98
Since You Went Away '44
Sinners '89
Sins of the Mind '97
Sioux City '94
Sitcom '97
Six in Paris '68
Sixteen Candles '84
The '60s '99
Skag '79
Skeletons '96
Skin Game '31
The Sleazy Uncle '89
Sleeping Dogs Lie '06
The Slingshot '93
Smart House '00
Smilin' Through '33
Smoke '70
Smoke Signals '98
The Snapper '93
Snow Day '00
Snowbound: The Jim and Jennifer Stolpa Story '94
Sofie '92
The Solitary Man '82
Something in the Wind '47
Something to Talk About '95
Sometimes a Great Notion '71

Sometimes They Come Back... Again '96
Son-in-Law '93
Son of Flubber '63
Son of Frankenstein '39
The Son of the Bride '01
Son of Fury '42
Song of the Exile '90
Song of the Islands '42
The Song of Songs '33
Sons '89
Sorceress '94
Sorrows of Gin '79
The Sound of Music '65
Sous Sol '96
South Central '92
South Riding '37
The Southerner '45
Souvenir '88
Spectre '96
Spider '02
Spider Baby '64
Spirit Rider '93
Splendor '35
Split Decisions '88
Split Image '82
Splitting Heirs '93
Sprague '84

Spy Kids '01
Spy Kids 3-D: Game Over '03
Star Maps '97
State Fair '45
State Fair '62
Stealing Beauty '96
Steal This Movie! '00
Stella Dallas '37
Stepmonster '93
Stepsisters '74
Still Not Quite Human '92
Stir of Echoes '99
The Stone Boy '84
The Storm Within '48
Storyteller '01
Storyville '92
The Strange Door '51
Strange Interlude '32
Strange Relations '02
The Stranger '92
Strangers in the City '62
Strangers: The Story of a Mother and Daughter '79
The Strauss Family '73
Street Girls '75
Street Hero '84
Street Justice '89
Struggle '31
Stuart Little '99
Stuck on You '84
The Subject Was Roses '68
The Substance of Fire '96
The Substitute Wife '94
Such a Long Journey '98
Suddenly, Last Summer '59
Sugar Cane Alley '83
Summer Holiday '48
Summer Magic '63
The Summer of Aviya '88
Summer of Fear '78
Summer of the Monkeys '98
A Sunday in the Country '84
Sunday's Children '94
Sunshine '99
Sure Fire '90
Susan and God '40
Susana '51
Suzanne '80
Swedenhielms '35
The Sweeper '95
The Sweet Hereafter '96
Sweet Home Alabama '02
Sweet Nothing '96
Sweet Thing '00
The Swiss Family Robinson '60
Switched at Birth '91
Table Settings '84
Teenage Exorcist '93
Temptress Moon '96
Ten Days Wonder '72
The Tenant of Wildfell Hall '96
Teorema '68
Terminator 2: Judgment Day '91
Terminal Station '89
Terranova '91
Testament '83
Tex '82
Teyve '39
A Texas Funeral '99
Thank You & Good Night '91
That Eye, the Sky '94
There's No Business Like Show Business '54
They Call Me Sir '00
They Watch '93
The Thief '97
The Third Sex '57
Things in Their Season '74
This Boy's Life '93
This Happy Breed '47
This Is My Father '99
This Is My Life '92
This Is the Sea '96

This Property is Condemned '66
A Thousand Clowns '65
Threads '85
Three Daring Daughters '48
The Three Lives of Karen '97
Three Wishes '95
Three's Trouble '85
Thunderbirds '04
Thursday's Child '43
The Ticket '97
Ticket to Heaven '81
The Tie That Binds '95
Tieta of Agreste '96
Tiger Warsaw '87
Time Indefinite '93
Time Out '01
A Time to Live '85
A Time to Live and a Time to Die '85
Timemaster '95
Tito and Me '92
T.N.T. '98
To Dance with the White Dog '93
To Die For 2: Son of Darkness '91
To Gillian on Her 37th Birthday '96
To Paris with Love '55
To Sleep with Anger '90
Toby McTeague '87
Tokyo Cowboy '94
Tokyo Story '53
Tollbooth '94
Tommy Boy '95
Toughlove '85
Tourist Trap '98
The Town Is Quiet '00
Toys '92
Toys in the Attic '63
Track 29 '88
Trade Secrets '86
Traffic Jam '91
The Trail of the Lonesome Pine '36
Tramp at the Door '87
Traps '93
Traveller '96
Treasure of the Sierra Madre '48
The Tree of Wooden Clogs '78
Trois Couleurs: Blanc '94
Trois Couleurs: Bleu '93
Tromeo & Juliet '95
True Love '89
True Women '97
Trusting Beatrice '92
Tuck Everlasting '02
The Turning '92
The Tuttles of Tahiti '42
29th Street '91
Twice in a Lifetime '85
Twister '89
Two Small Bodies '93
2 by 4 '98
Ulee's Gold '97
Uncle Moses '32
Uncle Nino '03
Uncommon Valor '83
Uncorked '98
Under the Boardwalk '89
Undergrads '85
Uneasy Terms '48
An Unexpected Life '97
The Unforgiven '60
The Unsaid '01
Up/Down/Fragile '95
Up the Sandbox '72
The Uprising '81
Used People '92
Vacas '91
Vera Drake '04
A Very Brady Christmas '88
A Very Brady Sequel '96
Vigil '84
Village of Dreams '97
Violette '78
Viridiana '61
The Visit '00
Voyage en Ballon '59
Voyager '91
Vultures '84
A Walk in the Clouds '95

Walk in the Spring Rain '70
Walking on Water '02
Walking Thunder '94
The Wall '99
The Waltons: The Christmas Carol '80
The War at Home '96
War & Remembrance: The Final Chapter '88
Waterproof '99
The Way We Live Now '02
The Wedding Banquet '93
Wedding Bell Blues '96
Wedding Crashers '05
Wedding in White '72
The Weekend '00
Welcome Home '89
Wendigo '01
What the Peeper Saw '72
When Nature Calls '85
When Saturday Comes '95
Where East Is East '29
Where Have All the People Gone? '74
Where Love Has Gone '64
Where the Heart Is '90
While You Were Sleeping '95
The White Balloon '95
The White Cliffs of Dover '44
Whity '70
Why Do They Call It Love When They Mean Sex? '92
Why Does Herr R. Run Amok? '69
Wicked '98
Wicked Stepmother '89
Wide Awake '97
The Wide Blue Road '57
Widow's Kiss '94
The Wild Country '71
The Wild Duck '84
Wild Pony '83
The Wild Thornberrys Movie '02
Wild Zone '89
Wildflower '91
William Shakespeare's Romeo and Juliet '96
The Winds of War '83
The Winner '96
The Winslow Boy '98
Winter Guest '97
Winter Kills '79
Winter People '89
The Wistful Widow of Wagon Gap '47
With Six You Get Eggroll '68
Witness Protection '99
Wives and Daughters '01
The Wizard of Oz '39
A Woman under the Influence '74
Women on the Verge of a Nervous Breakdown '88
Woodchipper Massacre '89
The Word '78
The World Accuses '35
World and Time Enough '95
A World Apart '88
The World of Apu '55
The Yam Princess '94
The Yearling '94
Yellow Earth '89
Yi Yi '00
You Can't Take It with You '38
You'll Like My Mother '72
Younger & Younger '94
Zack & Reba '98
Zertigo Diamond Caper '82
Zooman '95

▶ = rated three bones or higher

Fantasy

see also Animation & Cartoons; Musical Fantasy

A Nous la Liberte '31
The Acid Eaters '67
Adventures in Dinosaur City '92
The Adventures of a Gnome Named Gnorm '93
The Adventures of Baron Munchausen '89
The Adventures of Mark Twain '85
The Adventures of Pinocchio '96
The Adventures of Sharkboy and Lavagirl in 3-D '05
Aladdin and His Wonderful Lamp '84
Aladdin '86
Alice '88
Alice in Wonderland '85
Alice in Wonderland '99
Alice Through the Looking Glass '98
Alien from L.A. '87
Almost '90
Alone Against Rome '62
Amazing Mr. Blunden '72
The Amazing Spider-Man '77
Amazing Stories '85
Amazons '86
America 3000 '86
The Amphibian Man '51
Angel-A '05
Angel on My Shoulder '46
Angel on My Shoulder '80
Aquamarine '06
Arthur and the Invisibles '06
Ashik Kerib '88
Atlantis, the Lost Continent '61
Atlantis: The Lost Empire '01
Atlas '60
Atlas in the Land of the Cyclops '61
Ator the Fighting Eagle '83
Babe '95
Babe: Pig in the City '98
Baby... Secret of the Lost Legend '85
Barbarella '68
Barbarian Queen '85
Baron Munchausen '43
Batman '89
Batman and Robin '97
Batman Forever '95
Batman Returns '92
*batteries not included '87
Beastmaster '82
Beastmaster 2: Through the Portal of Time '91
Beastmaster 3: The Eye of Braxus '95
Beauties of the Night '52
Beauty and the Devil '50
Beowulf & Grendel '06
Bernard & the Genie '91
Between Heaven and Earth '93
Beyond Atlantis '73
Beyond Tomorrow '40
Big '88
Big Top Pee-wee '88
Biggles '85
Bill & Ted's Excellent Adventure '89
The Bishop's Wife '47
The Black Cauldron '85
Blade: Trinity '04
The Blood of a Poet '30
BloodRayne '06
Blue Monkey '87
The Borrowers '93
The Boy Who Could Fly '86
The Boy Who Loved Trolls '84
Bridge to Terabithia '07
The Brothers Grimm '05
Brothers Lionheart '77
Cabin Boy '94
The Canterville Ghost '44
The Canterville Ghost '96
Cars '06
The Cat from Outer Space '78
Celine and Julie Go Boating '74
The Challenge '26
Charleston '82
Charley and the Angel '73

Charlie and the Chocolate Factory '05
The Children of Noisy Village '86
The Christmas That Almost Wasn't '66
The Chronicles of Narnia '89
The Chronicles of Narnia: Prince Caspian '08
The Chronicles of Narnia: The Lion, the Witch and the Wardrobe '05
Cinderella 2000 '78
Cinderella '65
Circus Angel '65
The City of Lost Children '95
The Clan of the Cave Bear '86
Clarence '91
Clash of the Titans '81
Click '06
Cocoon '85
Cocoon: The Return '88
The Company of Wolves '85
Conan the Barbarian '82
Conan the Destroyer '84
A Connecticut Yankee '31
A Connecticut Yankee in King Arthur's Court '89
Conquest '83
Conquest of Mycene '63
Constantine '05
Corrina, Corrina '94
Cor-Ciel... '05
The Crazy Ray '22
Crossworlds '96
The Crow '93
The Crow 2: City of Angels '96
Curse of the Cat People '44
Darby O'Gill & the Little People '59
The Dark Crystal '82
The Day the Earth Froze '59
Death Takes a Holiday '34
Deathstalker '83
Deathstalker 2: Duel of the Titans '87
Deathstalker 3 '89
Deathstalker 4: Match of Titans '92
Desperate Living '77
The Devil & Max Devlin '81
The Devil and the Son of Hercules '62
Diary of Forbidden Dreams '73
Digby, the Biggest Dog in the World '73
Dinotolia '02
Donkey Skin '70
Dragonheart '96
Dragonheart: A New Beginning '00
Drago-Islayer '81
Drago-world '94
Dream a Little Dream '89
Dream a Little Dream 2 '94
Dreamchild '85
Dreamscape '84
Drop Dead Fred '91
Dungeonmaster '83
Dungeons and Dragons '00
Edward Scissorhands '90
Elektra '05
Ella Enchanted '04
Elmer Gantry...
Emmanuelle 4 '84
Enchanted '07
The Enchanted Cottage '45
The Enchantress '85
Endgame '85
Epoch: Evolution '03
Eragon '06
Eraserhead '78
Eroti: Escape '72
Erotic Touch of Hot Skin '65
Escapes '86
Escape from Atlantis '97
E.T.: The Extra-Terrestrial '82
Eternal Return '43
Everybody Says I'm Fine! '06
The Ewok Adventure '84
The Ewoks: Battle for Endor '85

Fantasy

Excalibur '81▸
Explorers '85
The Fantastic Night '42▸
Fantasy Island '76
Faraway, So Close! '93
Field of Dreams '89▸
The Final Programme '73
Fire and Ice '83
Flight of Dragons '82
Flight of the Navigator '86
Fluke '95
The Forbidden Kingdom '08
Francis Goes to the Races '51
Francis the Talking Mule '49▸
Frankenstein and Me '96
Freddie the Frog '92
French Quarter '78
From the Earth to the Moon '58
Galgameth '96
George's Island '91▸
The Ghost and Mrs. Muir '47▸
Ghost Chase '88
Ghost Writer '89
Ghosts Can't Do It '90
Ghostwarrior '86
The Giants of Thessaly '60
Gladiators 7 '62
The Glass Slipper '55
The Gnome-Mobile '67
The Golden Compass '07
Golden Voyage of Sinbad '73
The Golem 20▸
Goliath Against the Giants '63
Goliath and the Barbarians '60
Goliath and the Dragon '61
Goliath and the Sins of Babylon '64
The Good Night '07
Gor '88
The Great Land of Small '86
Grendel, Grendel, Grendel '82
Gryphon '88
Gulliver's Travels '39
Gulliver's Travels '77
Gulliver's Travels '95
A Gun, a Car, a Blonde '97
A Guy Named Joe '44
The Hanged Man '74
Harvey '50▸
Hawk the Slayer '81
Heartbreak Hotel '88
Hearts & Armour '83
Heaven Can Wait '43▸
Heaven Can Wait '78▸
Heavy Metal '81▸
Helen of Troy '56
Hellboy 2: The Golden Army '08
Herbie Rides Again '74
Hercules '58
Hercules Unchained '59
Here Come the Littles: The Movie '85
Here Comes Mr. Jordan '41▸
Hey There, It's Yogi Bear '64
Highlander 2: The Quickening '91
Highlander: Endgame '00
Highlander: The Final Dimension '94

The Hobbit '78▸
Hobgoblins '87
The Holes '72
Hook '91
Hoppity Goes to Town '41
Horrors of the Red Planet '64
Howl's Moving Castle '04
A Hungarian Fairy Tale '87▸
Hyper-Sapien: People from Another Star '86
I Married a Witch '42▸
The Immortal '01
In the Name of the King: A Dungeon Siege Tale '08
The Incredible Hulk '08
The Incredible Mr. Limpet '64
Incubus '65
The Indian in the Cupboard '95
Indiana Jones and the Last Crusade '89▸
Inhibition '76
The Invasion of Carol Enders '74
The Invincible Gladiator '63
Invisible Agent '42
The Invisible Kid '88
Invisible: The Chronicles of Benjamin Knight '93
Irish Cinderella 22
The Iron Crown '41
Iron Warrior '87
It Happened Tomorrow '44
It's a Wonderful Life '46▸
Jack the Giant Killer '62▸
Jacob Two Two Meets the Hooded Fang '99
James and the Giant Peach '96▸
Jason and the Argonauts '63▸
Jason and the Argonauts '00
Jimmy, the Boy Wonder 66
Jonathan Livingston Seagull '73
Josh Kirby... Time Warrior: Chapter 1, Planet of the Dino-Knights '95
Josh Kirby... Time Warrior: Chapter 2, The Human Pets '95
Josh Kirby... Time Warrior: Chapter 3, Trapped on Toyworld '95
Josh Kirby... Time Warrior: Chapter 4, Eggs from 70 Million B.C. '95
Josh Kirby... Time Warrior: Chapter 5, Journey to the Magic Cavern '96
Journey Beneath the Desert '61
Journey to the Center of the Earth '59▸
Journey to the Center of the Earth '99
Journey to the Lost City '58
Julia and Julia '87
Julia Has Two Lovers '91
Jumanji '95
The Jungle Book '42
Jungle Boy '96
Jungle Hell '55
Just like Heaven '05
Just My Luck '06
Kaena: The Prophecy '03
Kazaam '96
A Kid in Aladdin's Palace '97
Kids of the Round Table '96
King Kong '33▸
King Kong '76
King Kong '05▸
Kiss Me Goodbye '82
Kriemhilde's Revenge '24▸
Krull '83
Kull the Conqueror '97
La Merveilleuse Visite '74
L.A. Story '91▸
Labyrinth '86▸
Lady in the Water '06
Ladyhawke '85
The Lake House '06
Land of Doom '84

The Land of Faraway '87
The Last Days of Pompeii '60
The Last Mimzy '07
The Last Unicorn '82
Le Magnifique '76
Leapin' Leprechauns '95
Legend '86
The Legend of Cryin' Ryan '98
The Legend of Suram Fortress '85
Legion of Iron '90
Lemony Snicket's A Series of Unfortunate Events '04
Leprechaun 2 '94
Les Visiteurs du Soir '42▸
The Lickerish Quartet '70
Like Father, Like Son '87
The Lion of Thebes '64▸
The Little Mermaid '75
Little Monsters '89
Little Nemo: Adventures in Slumberland '92
Little Red Riding Hood '83▸
Logan's Run '76
The Lord of the Rings '78
Lord of the Rings: The Fellowship of the Rings '01▸
Lord of the Rings: The Two Towers '02▸
Lord of the Rings: The Return of the King '03▸
Lords of Magick '88
The Lost Continent '51
The Lost Empire '01
Love Notes '88
The Loves of Hercules '60
Maciste in Hell '60
Made in Heaven '87
The Magic Fountain '61
Magic Hunter '96
Magic in the Mirror: Fowl Play '96
Magic in the Water '95
Magic Island '95
Magic Serpent '66▸
The Magic Voyage of Sinbad '52
The Magical Legend of the Leprechauns '99
The Magician '58▸
The Man in the Santa Claus Suit '79
The Man Who Could Work Miracles '37▸
The Man Who Wagged His Tail '57
Mannequin 2: On the Move '91
Marco Polo, Jr. '72
The Martian Chronicles: Part 1 '79
The Martian Chronicles: Part 2 '79
The Martian Chronicles: Part 3 '79
Master of the World '61
Masters of the Universe '87
Maxie '85
Mazes and Monsters '82
Medusa Against the Son of Hercules '62
Meet Joe Black '98
Merlin '92
Merlin '98▸
Merlin and the Sword '85
Merlin's Apprentice '06
Messalina vs. the Son of Hercules '64
Michael '96
A Midsummer Night's Dream '35▸
Mighty Joe Young '49
Mighty Joe Young '98
Mighty Morphin Power Rangers: The Movie '95
Million Dollar Duck '71
Miracle Beach '92
Miracle in Milan '51▸
MirrorMask '05
Mr. Destiny '90
Mr. Magorium's Wonder Emporium '07
Mr. Rice's Secret '00
Mr. Sycamore '74

The Mistress of Spices '05
Mists of Avalon '01▸
Mole Men Against the Son of Hercules '61
Momentum '03
Monkeybone '01
Moon over Tao '97▸
The Moon Stallion '85
More about the Children of Noisy Village '87
Mortal Kombat 1: The Movie '95
Mortal Kombat 2: Annihilation '97
Mouse and His Child '77
Munchie '92
The Muppets' Wizard of Oz '05
My Friend Walter '93
My Neighbor Totoro '88
My Science Project '85
My Stepmother Is an Alien '88
The Mysterious Stranger '82
Mystery Island '81
Nanny McPhee '06
Natas... The Reflection '83
The Navigator '88▸
Neil Gaiman's NeverWhere '96
Neutron vs. the Amazing Dr. Caronte '61
Neutron vs. the Death Robots '62
Neutron vs. the Maniac '62
The NeverEnding Story '84▸
NeverEnding Story 2: The Next Chapter '91
The NeverEnding Story 3: Escape from Fantasia '94
Night Tide '63
Night Watch '04
The Nightmare before Christmas '93▸
Nine Lives of Fritz the Cat '74
November '05▸
Nutcracker: The Motion Picture '86
The Ogre '96
Once a Hero '88
One Magic Christmas '85
1001 Arabian Nights '59
One Wish Too Many '55
The Original Fabulous Adventures of Baron Munchausen '61
Orpheus '49
Outlaw of Gor '87
The Pagemaster '94
Painted Skin '93
Pandora and the Flying Dutchman '51
Pan's Labyrinth '06▸
Paperhouse '89▸
Parasite '03
Patchwork Girl of Oz '14
The Peanut Butter Solution '85
Peau D'Ane '71▸
Penelope '06
Peter Pan '24
Peter Pan '53▸
Peter Pan '03
Pete's Dragon '77
The Phantom Chariot '20
Phantom Tollbooth '69▸
The Phoenix and the Magic Carpet '95
Piano Tuner of Earthquakes '05
The Plague Dogs '82
Pleasantville '98▸
The Point '71
The Polar Bear King '94
Powder '95
Prancer '89
Prehistoric Bimbos in Armageddon City '93
Prehistoric Women '50
Prehysteria '93
Prehysteria 2 '94
Prehysteria 3 '95
Prelude to a Kiss '92
The Price of Milk '00
Private Passions '85
The Promise '05
Pufnstuf '70

The Puppetoon Movie '87
Quest for the Mighty Sword '90
Quest of the Delta Knights '93
Radio Flyer '92
Ratboy '86
Real Men '87
Reckless '95
The Red Balloon '56▸
Red Sonja '85
Renoir Shorts '27▸
The Rescuers Down Under '90
Restless Spirits '99
Return from Witch Mountain '78
The Return of Jafar '94
The Return of Peter Grimm '35
The Return of the Borrowers '96▸
Return of the Fly '59
The Return of the King '80
Return to Fantasy Island '77
Return to Never Land '02
Return to Oz '85
Return to the Lost World '93
Revolt of the Barbarians '64
The Rise & Rise of Daniel Rocket '86
Robots '05
Rock & Rule '83
Roland the Mighty '56
The Rook '99
Rookie of the Year '93
Salome's Last Dance '88
Samson '61
Samson Against the Sheik '62
Samson and His Mighty Challenge '64
Samson and the 7 Miracles of the World '62
Santa Claus '59
Santa Claus Conquers the Martians '64
Santa Claus: The Movie '85
The Saragossa Manuscript '65
The Scalawag Bunch '75
The Science of Sleep '06
Sea of Dreams '90
Sea People '00
The Sea Serpent '85
The Seventh Voyage of Sinbad '58▸
The Shaggy Dog '59
The Shaggy Dog '06
She '25
She '83
Shredder Orpheus '89
Shrek '01▸
Shrek 2 '04
Siegfried '24▸
A Simple Wish '97
Simply Irresistible '99
Sinbad and the Eye of the Tiger '77
Sinbad of the Seven Seas '89
Slave Girls from Beyond Infinity '87
Sleepwalk '88
Snow White: A Tale of Terror '97
Snow White: The Fairest of Them All '02
Solarbabies '86
Something Wicked This Way Comes '83
Son of Hercules in the Land of Darkness '63
Son of Kong '33
Son of Samson '62
Son of Sinbad '55

Song Spinner '95
Sorceress '82
A Sound of Thunder '05
Southland Tales '06
Space Raiders '83
Space Soldiers Conquer the Universe '40
Spellbreaker: Secret of the Leprechauns '95
The Spiderwick Chronicles '08▸
Splash '84
The Spring '89
Stairway to Heaven '46▸
Stalker '79▸
Stand Up and Cheer '34
Stardust '07▸
Starry Night '99
The Steagle '71
Steel Dawn '87
Story of a Cowboy Angel '81
Storybook '95
Student of Prague '13▸
Super Mario Bros. '93
Supergirl '84
Superman: The Movie '78▸
Superman 2 '80▸
Superman 3 '83
Superman 4: The Quest for Peace '87
Superman & the Mole Men '51
Superman Returns '06
Sword & the Dragon '56
Sword & the Sorcerer '82
The Sword in the Stone '63▸
Sword of the Valiant '83
Sylvia and the Phantom '45▸
Tales of Beatrix Potter '71▸
Tall Tale: The Unbelievable Adventures of Pecos Bill '95
Tammy and the T-Rex '94
Tank Girl '94
Tanya's Island '81
Teenage Mutant Ninja Turtles: The Movie '90
The Tempest '63
The 10th Kingdom '00
Terror of Rome Against the Son of Hercules '64
Terror of the Steppes '64
Test Tube Teens from the Year 2000 '93
The Testament of Dr. Cordelier '59▸
The Testament of Orpheus '59▸
They Came Back '04
The Thief and the Cobbler '96▸
The Thief Lord '06
The Thief of Bagdad '40▸
The Thief of Bagdad '24▸
Thief of Baghdad '61
The Thief of Baghdad '78
Thor and the Amazon Women '60
A Thousand and One Nights '45
Three Wishes '95
The Three Worlds of Gulliver '59
Thumbelina '82▸
Thumbelina '04
Thunderbirds '04
Tideland '05▸
Tim Burton's Corpse Bride '05▸
Time Bandits '81
The Time of Their Lives '46▸
Timestalkers '87
Tin Man '07
Tobor the Great '54
Tom Thumb '58▸
Toy Story '95▸
Toy Story 2 '99▸
Trading Mom '94
Train to Hollywood '86▸
Transformers: The Movie '86
The Trip '67
A Troll in Central Park '94
Tropical Malady '04
Trouble in Mind '86▸
The Tune '92

▸ = rated three bones or higher

Turbo: A Power Rangers Movie '96
20,000 Leagues under the Sea '54►
20,000 Leagues Under the Sea '97
The Twilight of the Ice Nymphs '97
Twisted '96
Twisted '05
Twitches Too '07
The Two Worlds of...enny Logan '79
Undersea Kingdom '36
Unidentified Flying Oddball '79
Ursus in the Valley of the Lions '62
The Valley of Gwangi '69►
Venus Against the Son of Hercules '62
A Very Old Man with Enormous Wings '88
Vibes '88
Vice Versa '88►
Vulcan God of Fire '62
Walking on Air '87
The Warrior & the Sorceress '84
'Warrior Queen '87
Warriors of Virtue '97
The Water Horse: ...legend of the Deep '07
Watership Down '78
Wax, or the Discovery of Television among the Bees '93
Waxworks '24►
What Dreams May Come '98
The White Sheik '52►
Wild Women of Wongo '59
Wildest Dreams '90
William Shakespeare's A Midsummer Night's Dream '99
Willow '88
Window to Paris '95
Wings of Desire '98►
Wings of Fame '93
Witch Hunt '94
A Witch Without a Broom '68
Wizards '77
The Witching of Ben Wagner '95
The Wizard of Oz '25
The Wizard of Speed and Time '88
The Wolves of Kromer '98
Wombling Free '77
The Wonderful World of the Brothers Grimm '62
The Worst Witch '86
Yor, the Hunter from the Future '83
Youth Without Youth '07
Yu-Gi-Oh! The Movie: Pyramid of Light '04
Zapped! '82
Zardoz '73
Zathura '05►
Zero for Conduct '33►
Zone Troopers '84
Zu: Warriors from the Magic Mountain '83

Farm Livin'

...And the Earth Did Not Swallow Him '94
Animal Farm '99
Balloon Farm '97
Barnyard '06
Bitter Harvest '81►
Blessing '94
Bloodsuckers from Outer Space '83
Boy Takes Girl '83
The Bridges of Madison County '95►
Broken Harvest '94
Buffalo Jump '90►
The Cabin in the Cotton '32
Cash Crop '07
The Castaway Cowboy '74
Charlotte's Web '73
Charlotte's Web '06►
Chicken Run '00►
The Cider House Rules '99►
Country '84►
Country Life '95
The Curse '87
Curse of the Starving Class '94
Dark Before Dawn '89
Days of Heaven '78►
Deadly Stranger '88
December Bride '91
Demon Wind '90
Desire Under the Elms '58
The Devil & Daniel Webster '41►
Doc Hollywood '91
Dog Day '83
The Dukes of Hazzard '05
Earth '30►
Earthwork Tractors '36
The Echo of Thunder '98
Egg and I '47►
Eli Eli '40
Far from the Madding Crowd '67►
The Farmer's Other Daughter '65
The Field '90►
15 Amore '98
The General Line '29►
Giant '56►
The Girl from Paris '02►
God's Little Acre '58►
The Good Old Boys '95
The Grapes of Wrath '40►
The Green Promise '49
Harvest '37►
Harvest '98
Harvest of Fire '95
Home on the Range '04
Horton Foote's Alone '97
In the Winter Dark '98
The Inheritors '98
Jean de Florette '87►
The Kettles in the Ozarks '54
Kings in Grass Castles '97
The Land Girls '98
Little John '02►
Ma and Pa Kettle at Home '54
The Mating Game '59►
Mifune '99►
The Milagro Beanfield War '88►
Missouri Traveler '58►
Morning Glory '93
My Antonia '94
Northern Lights '79►
Nowhere in Africa '02
Nowhere to Run '93
Oklahoma Bound '81
Our Daily Bread '34►
The Outsider '02
A Painted House '03
Pelle the Conqueror '88►
Places in the Heart '84►
The Price of Milk '00
The Proposition '96
The Purchase Price '32
Rachel and the Stranger '48►
Rage '72
Ride the Wild Fields '00
The River '84
The Road from Coorain '02
Rock-a-Doodle '92
Romulus, My Father '07►
Ruggles of Red Gap '35►
Sarah, Plain and Tall '91
Sarah, Plain and Tall: Skylark '93
Sarah, Plain and Tall: Winter's End '99►
Secondhand Lions '03
Signs '02►
Sommersby '93
Son-in-Law '93
Sounder '72►
The Southerner '45►
Stacking '87►
The Stars Fell on Henrietta '94
Steal Big, Steal Little '95
The Stone Boy '84►
The Story of Xinghua '93
Summer of the Monkeys '98
Sunday Too Far Away '74►
The Sundowners '60►
Sunrise '27►
This Is My Father '99
A Thousand Acres '97
Tomboy & the Champ '58
The Tree of Wooden Clogs '78►
Tully '00►
2 Brothers & a Bride '03
Under the Sun '98
Vacas '91
The Well '97
Will It Snow for Christmas? '96
Wisdom '87
The Yearling '94
The Young Pioneers '76

Farming

see Farm Livin'

Fashion

A la Mode '94►
The Bitter Tears of Petra von Kant '72
Bratz '07
Chanel Solitaire '81
The Devil Wears Prada '06►
Don't Tell Mom the Babysitter's Dead '91
The Dress '96
Fashions of 1934 '34
Fernandel the Dressmaker '57
Hourglass '95
The House of Eliott '92
I'm Dangerous Tonight '90
Intern '00
Kill by Inches '99
Kinky Boots '06
A Life of Her Own '50
Lovely to Look At '52►
Maytime in Mayfair '49
Mrs. 'Arris Goes to Paris '92
My Lucky Star '38
102 Dalmatians '00
Perfume '01
Phat Girlz '06
Portraits Chinois '96
Princess Daisy '83
Ready to Wear '94
Romy and Michele's High School Reunion '97
Scruples '80
Selena '96
Sins '85
Stroke of Midnight '90
Tales of Manhattan '42►
27 Dresses '08
Unzipped '94►
Vogues of 1938 '37
Yours, Mine & Ours '05

Fatsuit Acting

America's Sweethearts '01
Austin Powers 2: The Spy Who Shagged Me '99►
Austin Powers in Goldmember '02
Big Momma's House '00
Big Momma's House 2 '06
Death Becomes Her '92►
Hairspray '07►
Just Friends '05
Monty Python's The Meaning of Life '83►
Norbit '07
The Nutty Professor '96►
The Nutty Professor 2: The Klumps '00
The Santa Clause '94►
The Santa Clause 2 '02
The Santa Clause 3: The Escape Clause '06
Shallow Hal '01►
Stephen King's Thinner '95
Tropic Thunder '08

FBI

see also CIA/NSA; Crime; Drama

Acts of Betrayal '98
After the Sunset '04
Airboss '97
Along Came a Spider '01
American Yakuza '94
Analyze That '02►
Analyze This '98►
The Art of War '00
The Assassination File '96
The Astronaut Farmer '07
Bait '00
Ballistic: Ecks vs. Sever '02
Beavis and Butt-Head Do America '96►
Best Men '98
Betrayed '88►
A Better Way to Die '00
Big Momma's House '00
Big Momma's House 2 '06
Big Trouble '02►
Bird on a Wire '90
Black Dog '98
Black Moon Rising '86
Black Sunday '77►
Black Widow '87►
Blade: Trinity '04
Blast '04
Bless the Child '00
Blood, Guts, Bullets and Octane '99
Blood Work '02
Bloodfist 5: Human Target '93
Boondock Saints '99
Boss of Bosses '99
Breach '07
The Breed '01
Broken Trust '95
Caracara '00►
Catch Me If You Can '02►
The Cell '00
Chain Reaction '96
Chasing Papi '03
Children of Fury '94
City of Ghosts '03
Civic Duty '06
Clay Pigeons '98
The Clearing '04►
The Client '94►
Cloak & Jagger '84
Club Fed '90
Code Name Alpha '67
Corky Romano '01
Crime Killer '85
Crime Spree '03
The Crimson Code '99
Daughter of the Tong '39
Dead Aim '87
Dead Bang '89
Dead Silence '96
Death Rides the Range '40
Deja Vu '06
Desperate Hours '90
Die Hard '88►
Dillinger '73
Dillinger and Capone '95
Domino '05
Donnie Brasco '96►
88 Minutes '08
Double Take '01
Double Vision '02
F/X '86►
Face/Off '97►
Fast Getaway '91
The FBI Girl '52
The FBI Story '59►
Federal Agents vs. Underworld, Inc. '49
Feds '88
Felony '95
Final Destination '00►
The Firm '93►
The Fix '84
The Flashback '89►
Flight to Nowhere '46
The Flock '07
Follow That Car '80
Frailty '01►
Full Disclosure '00
"G" Men '35►
G-Men Never Forget '48
The Glass Jungle '88
Golden Gate '93
Government Agents vs. Phantom Legion '51
Grosse Pointe Blank '97►
Gun Girl '36
Half Past Dead '02
Hannibal '01
Hard Cash '01
Harvard Man '01
Hellboy '04►
Hellboy 2: The Golden Army '08
Hit Woman: The Double Edge '93
Hollow Point '95
Honor and Glory '92
House on 92nd Street '45►
The Hunted '03
The House on Carroll Street '88
I'll Get You '53
In the Line of Duty: The FBI Murders '88►
The Interpreter '05►
J. Edgar Hoover '87
The Jackal '97►
Johnnie Gibson F.B.I. '87
Judas Kiss '98
Kill Me Later '01
The Kingdom '07
The Last Shot '04
Let 'Em Have It '35
Lethal '04
Little Nikita '88
Live Wire '88
Live Wire: Human Timebomb '95
Lure of the Islands '42
Man of the House '05
Manhunter '86►
Married to the Mob '88►
Master Spy: The Robert Hanssen Story '02
Maximum Risk '96►
Me and the Mob '94
Mean Streak '99
Medium Cool '69►
Melvin Purvis: G-Man '74
Mercury Rising '98
Mickey Blue Eyes '99
Midnight Murders '91
Midnight Run '88►
Mindhunters '05
Mindstorm '01
Miss Congeniality '00►
Miss Congeniality 2: Armed and Fabulous '05
Mississippi Burning '88►
Momentum '03
Most Wanted '97
My Blue Heaven '90
Naked Lies '98
Next '07
No Way Back '96
Nowhere Land '98
The Outfit '93
Pandemic '07
Panther '95
Paradise Canyon '35
Partners in Crime '99
Path to Paradise '97
Perfect Assassins '98
Perfect Lies '97
The Private Files of J. Edgar Hoover '77
Plughead Rewired: Circuitry Man 2 '94
Pups '99
The Punisher '04►
The Rage '99
Ransom '96►
Raw Deal '86
Red Dragon '02
The Reluctant Agent '02
The Return of Eliot Ness '91
Revolver '92
Road Ends '98
Robin of Locksley '95
The Rock '96►
Rollercoaster '77
Rush-Hour '98
Sabotage '96
Saw 4 '07
Scam '93
See Spot Run '01
Serial Bomber '96
Shattered Image '93
Shoot to Kill '88►
Shooter '07
The Siege '98►
Silence of the Hams '93
The Silence of the Lambs '91►
The Silencer '99
Silk Degrees '94
Sky Liner '49
Slaughter of the Innocents '93
Sleeper Cell '05
Smashing the Rackets '38
Smokin' Aces '07
Snakes on a Plane '06►
Spartan '04►
Special Investigator '36
Standoff '97
Stone Cold '91
Sugartime '95
Sunstorm '01
Suspect Zero '04
Switchback '97
Taking Lives '04
10th & Wolf '06
That Darn Cat '65
That Darn Cat '96
3 Ninjas '92
Thunderheart '92►
Tom Clancy's Netforce '99
Torque '04
Trail of a Serial Killer '98
Triplecross '95
Turbulence 3: Heavy Metal '00
Twin Peaks: Fire Walk with Me '92►
Undercover Blues '93
U.S. Marshals '98►
The Untouchables '87►
The Usual Suspects '95►
War '07
The Watcher '00
White Chicks '04
White Sands '92
Wild Side '95
Winds of Terror '01
Witless Protection '08
Wounded '97
The X-Files '98
The X-Files: I Want to Believe '08
Zero Tolerance '93

Female Bonding

see also Women; Wonder Women

Across the Moon '94
All I Wanna Do '98
Allie & Me '97
Antonia's Line '95
Aquamarine '06
Autumn Tale '99
Baby Mama '08
Bandits '99
The Banger Sisters '02
B.A.P.'s '97
Beaches '88►
Beautiful Creatures '00
Berkeley Square '98
Between Strangers '02
The Big Bad Swim '06
Blonde and Blonder '07
Blue Crush '02►
Bonneville '06
Boys on the Side '94►
The Business of Strangers '01
Cadillac Ranch '96
Calendar Girls '03
Camilla '94►
Caramel '07►

► = rated three bones or higher

Female

Casa de los Babys '03
The Cemetery Club '93
Chaos '01
Charms for the Easy Life '02
Chasing Papi '03
Clockwatchers '97
Cold Mountain '03
Collected Stories '98
The Color of Courage '98
Coming Soon '99
Confessions of a Teenage Drama Queen '04
Connie and Carla '04
A Cooler Climate '99
The Craft '96
Crossroads '02
Crush '02
Dancing at the Blue Iguana '00
Daughters of the Dust '91
Dead Gorgeous '02
Desert Hearts '86
Divine Secrets of the Ya-Ya Sisterhood '02
Don't Tell '05
Dreamgirls '06
Dreamland '06
The Dreamlife of Angels '98
8 Women '02
Emma '96
Emma '97
Evening '07
Everything Relative '96
Falling '06
The First Wives Club '96
4 Months, 3 Weeks, 2 Days '07
Foxfire '96
Freeway 2: Confessions of a Trickbaby '99
Fried Green Tomatoes '91
Friends with Money '06
Georgia Rule '07
Getting Played '05
Girl, Interrupted '99
A Girl Thing '01
Girls Can't Swim '99
Girls' Night '97
Girls Town '96
Grace & Glorie '98
The Heidi Chronicles '95
High Heels and Low Lifes '01
Hilary and Jackie '98
Home Room '02
How to Make an American Quilt '95
Hysterical Blindness '02
The Ice House '97
It's My Turn, Laura Cadieux '98
Jackie, Ethel, Joan: The Kennedy Women '01
The Jane Austen Book Club '07
John Tucker Must Die '06
The Joy Luck Club '93
Just a Little Harmless Sex '99
The Killing Club '01
The Land Girls '98
The Last of the Blonde Bombshells '00
The Lemon Sisters '90
Let's Talk About Sex '98
Little Witches '96
Live-In Maid '04
Living Out Loud '98
Losing Chase '96
A Lost Year '93
Love and Other Catastrophes '95
Lover Girl '97
Luminarias '99
Mad Money '08
The Magdalene Sisters '02
Manny & Lo '96
Margarita Happy Hour '01
Me & Will '99
Me Without You '01
Miss Congeniality 2: Armed and Fabulous '05
Miss Pettigrew Lives for a Day '08
Mists of Avalon '01
Mona Lisa Smile '03

Moonlight and Valentino '95
Morvern Callar '02
My Very Best Friend '96
Nevada '97
9 to 5 '80
Nora's Hair Salon '04
Notes on a Scandal '06
Now and Then '95
One True Thing '98
Our Song '01
Passion Fish '92
Phat Girlz '06
Prey for Rock and Roll '03
Private Benjamin '80
P.S. I Love You '07
Radiance '98
Rip It Off '02
The Road to Galveston '96
Romy and Michele's High School Reunion '97
Secret Society '00
Set It Off '96
Sex and the City: The Movie '08
Sisterhood of the Traveling Pants '05
Sisterhood of the Traveling Pants 2 '08
The Smokers '00
Some Mother's Son '96
Some Prefer Cake '97
Stand-Ins '97
The Starter Wife '07
Steel Magnolias '89
Stepmom '98
Sugar & Spice '01
The Sweetest Thing '02
Talk '94
Tea with Mussolini '99
Terranova '91
Thelma & Louise '91
These Girls '05
These Old Broads '01
Things You Can Tell Just by Looking at Her '00
Thirteen '03
Two Can Play That Game '01
Two Friends '86
Under the Tuscan Sun '03
Unhook the Stars '96
Up Against the Eight Ball '04
Uptown Girls '03
Vulture's Eye '04
Waiting to Exhale '95
Waitress '07
Walking and Talking '96
Water '05
Wedding Bell Blues '96
The Well '97
Where the Heart Is '00
Widows '02
Wildflowers '99
Wisegirls '02
A Woman's Guide to Adultery '93
Women '97
Zoe '01

Feminism

see also Women; Wonder Women

Female Spies

see also Spy Kids; World War I Spies; World War II Spies
The Abductors '72
Call Me Bwana '63
Call Out the Marines '42
Caprice '67
C.I.A.: Code Name Alexa '92
Court Jester '56
D.E.B.S. '04
Harriet the Spy '96
Head in the Clouds '04
Mata Hari '32
Mr. & Mrs. Smith '05
Monte Carlo '86
My Favorite Blonde '42
Notorious '46
Secret of Stamboul '36
Shining Through '92
Spy Kids '01
Spy Kids 2: The Island of Lost Dreams '02
Spy Kids 3-D: Game Over '03
The World Is Not Enough '99

Femme Fatale

see also Wonder Women
The Accused '48
Addams Family Values '93
Algiers '38
All About Eve '50
The Amy Fisher Story '93
Armored Command '61
Auntie Lee's Meat Pies '92
Austin Powers: International Man of Mystery '97
Austin Powers 2: The Spy Who Shagged Me '99
Backstab '90
Basic Instinct '92
Basic Instinct 2 '06
Batman and Robin '97
Beautiful Beast '95
Beautiful Hunter '94
Bedelia '46
The Beneficiary '97
Beverly Hills Ninja '96
Beverly Hills Vamp '88
The Big Bounce '69
Big Town '87
Bitter Harvest '93
The Black Dahlia '06
Black Magic Woman '91
Black Widow '87
Blood of Dracula '57
The Blood Spattered Bride '72
Blown Away '93
The Blue Angel '30
Body Heat '81
Body of Evidence '92
Body Trouble '92
Bound '96
The Bridesmaid '04
The Brothers Grimm '05
Brute Force '47
Buddy Boy '99
Bulletproof Heart '95
The Cabin in the Cotton '32
Caesar and Cleopatra '46
Carmen: A Hip Hopera '01
Carried Away '95
Casque d'Or '52
Casualties of Love: The "Long Island Lolita" Story '93
Champagne for Caesar '50
Clash by Night '52
Clean Slate '94
Cleopatra '34
Cleopatra '63
Cleopatra '99
Crime of Passion '57
Criss Cross '48
Cruel Intentions '98
Crush '93
The Crush '93
The Dallas Connection '94
The Damned Don't Cry '50
Dance Hall '41
Dangerous Ground '96
Dangerous Liaisons '88
Dangerous Liaisons '03
Daughter of the Tong '39
Dead Reckoning '47
Deadly Past '95
Death in Deep Water '74
Deception '08
Deceptions '90
Decoy '46
Detour '46
Detour '92
The Devil's Daughter '91
Diamond Run '00
Disclosure '94
Dishonored Lady '47
Dr. Caligari '89
Dr. Jekyll and Sister Hyde '71
Double Indemnity '44
Double Jeopardy '92
Dream Lover '93
Drowning by Numbers '87
Emmanuelle, the Queen '79
Eve of Destruction '90
Eye of the Beholder '99
The Fall '98
Fallen Angel '97

Fangs of the Living Dead '68
Far from the Madding Crowd '67
Faster, Pussycat! Kill! Kill! '65
Federal Agents vs. Underworld, Inc. '49
Femme Fatale '92
Final Analysis '92
First Name: Carmen '83
Flame of the Islands '55
The Flesh and the Devil '27
A Fool There Was '14
A Foreign Affair '48
Frankenhooker '90
The Gingerbread Man '97
The Girl from Tobacco Row '66
Girl Hunters '63
Girl in His Pocket '57
A Girl to Kill For '90
Girlfriend from Hell '89
Great Flamarion '45
Grievous Bodily Harm '89
The Grifters '90
The Hard Word '02
Heat Wave '54
Hedda '75
Hellgate '89
Hit Me '96
Hoopla '33
Hostel '06
Human Desire '54
I Spit on Your Corpse '74
I Want You '98
Illusions '91
Impact '49
Impulse '55
Inner Sanctum '91
International Lady '41
Intersection '93
Into the Fire '88
Invasion of the Bee Girls '73
Irresistible Impulse '95
Jay and Silent Bob Strike Back '01
The Jayne Mansfield Story '80
Jezebel '38
Kill Bill Vol. 1 '03
Kill Bill Vol. 2 '04
Kill Cruise '90
The Killers '46
L'Addition '85
Lady and the Tramp '55
Lady for a Night '42
Lady Frankenstein '72
The Lady from Shanghai '48
The Lair of the White Worm '88
The Last Seduction '94
The Last Seduction 2 '98
Le Samourai '67
Leave Her to Heaven '45
The Legend of the Wolf Woman '77
Lemora, Lady Dracula '73
The Leopard Woman '20
Les Vampires '15
Lethal Lolita—Amy Fisher: My Story '92
Lethal Seduction '97
The Lifetaker '89
Lights in the Dusk '06
Like a Fish Out of Water '99
Linda '93
The Little Death '95
Lonely Hearts '06
Love Is a Gun '94
Love Walked In '97
Mado '76
The Malibu Beach Vampires '91
Malice '93
Malicious '95
Mantis in Lace '68
Married to the Mob '88
Mata Hari '32
Mata Hari '85
Medusa Against the Son of Hercules '62
Mesa of Lost Women '52
Mirage '94
Ms. 45 '81

Mountaintop Motel Massacre '86
Mutual Needs '97
Nana '55
Nana '82
The Natural '84
Net Games '03
Night Angel '90
The Night Evelyn Came Out of the Grave '71
Night of the Cobra Woman '72
Night Tide '63
The Ninth Gate '99
No Good Deed '02
No Way Out '87
Novocaine '01
An Occasional Hell '96
Of Human Bondage '34
Of Human Bondage '64
On Her Majesty's Secret Service '69
One Night at McCool's '01
The Opposite of Sex '98
Out Cold '89
Out of the Past '47
Palmetto '98
The Pamela Principle '91
Party Girls '29
Pepe Le Moko '37
Perfect Alibi '94
Planet of Blood '66
Playing Murder for Me '91
Playing God '96
Point of No Return '93
Poison Ivy '92
Poison Ivy 2: Lily '95
Possession: Until Death Do You Part '90
The Postman Always Rings Twice '46
Praying Mantis '93
Pretty Poison '68
Prey of the Chameleon '91
Queen Bee '55
The Quick and the Dead '95
The Rage: Carrie 2 '99
A Rage in Harlem '91
Ran '85
Range Renegades '48
Reckless '35
Ring of Steel '94
Roadhouse Girl '53
Salome '53
Salome '85
Samson and Delilah '50
Samson and Delilah '84
Samson and Delilah '96
Sand Trap '97
Satanik '69
Scandal '89
Scarlet Street '45
Schemes '95
Scorned '93
Sea of Love '89
Second Skin '00
Secret Weapons '85
The Secretary '94
Serpent's Lair '95
Seven Sinners '40
Sexpot '88
Shadows in the Storm '88
The Showgirl Murders '95
Sins of Jezebel '54
Sleep of Death '79
Sleepy Eyes of Death: The Chinese Jade '63
Snow White and the Seven Dwarfs '37
Some Came Running '58
Something Wild '86
The Specialist '75
Species '95
Stormy Nights '97
The Strange Woman '46
Sunrise '27
Sunset Boulevard '50
Suspicious Minds '96
The Temp '93
The Temptress '49
A Thin Line Between Love and Hate '96
Third Degree Burn '89
Tomb '86
Too Late for Tears '49
Torso '01
Trading Favors '97
Truth or Dare '05

U-Turn '97
Under Suspicion '92
The Untamable '23
Valmont '89
Vanity Fair '32
The Velvet Vampire '71
Venus Against the Son of Hercules '62
Venus in Furs '70
Victim of Desire '94
The Wasp Woman '59
When Will I Be Loved '04
White Cargo '42
Who Framed Roger Rabbit '88
Wicked Ways '99
Widow's Kiss '94
Witchcraft 3: The Kiss of Death '90
Woman of Desire '93
Wrongfully Accused '98
XXX: State of the Union '05

Fencing

see also Swashbucklers
By the Sword '93
Court Jester '56
Dangerous Beauty '98
The Fencing Master '92
The Last Musketeer '00
Ring of Steel '94
Rob Roy '95
Sunshine '99

Fifties

see Period Piece: 1950s

Film History

America at the Movies '76
Burden of Dreams '82
The Cat's Meow '01
The Celluloid Closet '95
A Decade Under the Influence '02
Forgotten Silver '96
Many Faces of Sherlock Holmes '86
Heavy Petting '89
Intervista '87
The Kid Stays in the Picture '02
A Kiss for Mary Pickford '27
The Little Theatre of Jean Renoir '71
Lost Squadron '32
The Love Goddesses '65
That's Entertainment '74
That's Entertainment, Part 2 '76
That's Entertainment, Part 3 '93
This Film Is Not Yet Rated '06
Visions of Light: The Art of Cinematography '93

Film Noir

see also Contemporary Noir
The Accused '48
Act of Violence '48
Al Capone '59
Amateur '94
Angel Face '52
The Asphalt Jungle '50
Beware, My Lovely '52
Beyond a Reasonable Doubt '56
The Big Clock '48
Big Combo '55
The Big Heat '53
The Big Sleep '46
Black Angel '46
Black Lizard '68
Black Widow '54
Blast of Silence '61
The Blue Dahlia '46
The Blue Gardenia '53

◆ = rated three bones or higher

Bob le Flambeur '55 ►
Boomerang '47 ►
Born to Kill '47 ►
Brute Force '47 ►
Caged '50 ►
Cornered '45 ►
Crack-Up '46 ►
Crime Wave '54 ►
Criss Cross '48 ►
Crossfire '47 ►
Dangerous Crossing '53 ►
Dark Corner '46 ►
Dark Mirror '46 ►
Dark Passage '47 ►
Dead Again '91 ►
Dead Silence '90
Deadline at Dawn '46
Decoy '46
Delusion '91
Desperate '47
Detour '46 ►
The Devil Thumbs a Ride '47 ►
D.O.A. '49 ►
Don't Bother to Knock '52
Double Indemnity '44 ►
The Element of Crime '84
The Enforcer '51
Fallen Angels 1 '93
Fallen Angels 2 '33 ►
Farewell, My Lovely '75 ►
Fear in the Night '47 ►
Force of Evil '49 ►
Frantic '58
Gilda '46 ►
The Glass Key '42 ►
Gotham '88 ►
Gun Crazy '49 ►
He Walked by Night '48 ►
High & Low '62 ►
High Sierra '41 ►
The Hitch-Hiker '53 ►
House of Bamboo '55
Human Desire '54
In a Lonely Place '50 ►
Jigsaw '49 ►
Johnny Angel '45 ►
Key Largo '48 ►
The Killers '46 ►
Killer's Kiss '55 ►
The Killing '56 ►
King Creole '58
Kiss Me Deadly '55 ►
Kiss of Death '47 ►
The Lady from Shanghai '48 ►
Lady in the Death House '44
Lady in the Lake '46 ►
The Las Vegas Story '52 ►
Laura '44 ►
Le Doulos '61 ►
Leave Her to Heaven '45 ►
The Long Night '47 ►
Macao '52 ►
The Maltese Falcon '41 ►
The Mask of Dimitrios '44 ►
Mikey & Nicky '76
Mildred Pierce '45 ►
Ministry of Fear '44 ►
Murder, My Sweet '44 ►
Mystery Street '50 ►
The Naked City '48 ►
Naked Kiss '64
The Narrow Margin '52 ►
Niagara '52 ►
Night and the City '50 ►
Nightfall '56 ►
Nightmare Alley '47 ►
Nocturne '46
Odds Against Tomorrow '59 ►
On Dangerous Ground '51 ►
Our Man in Havana '59 ►
Out of the Past '47 ►
Panic in the Streets '50 ►
Phantom Lady '44 ►
Pickup on South Street '53 ►
Pitfall '48 ►
Portrait o' an Assassin '49
The Postman Always Rings Twice '46 ►
The Postman Always Rings Twice '81 ►
Prowler '51
Railroaded '47 ►
Raw Deal '48 ►
The Rec House '48 ►

Rendez-vous '85 ►
Road House '48 ►
Rope '48 ►
The Scar '48 ►
Scarlet Street '45 ►
The Set-Up '49 ►
Shoot to Kill '47 ►
Side Street '50 ►
Signal 7 '83 ►
Slow Moves '84
Sorry, Wrong Number '48 ►
Station '81
Story of a Love Affair '50 ►
Strange Impersonation '46
The Strange Love of Martha Ivers '46 ►
Sudden Fear '52 ►
Sunset Boulevard '50 ►
Sweet Smell of Success '57 ►
T-Men '47 ►
Tchao Pantin '84 ►
Tension '50 ►
They Live by Night '49 ►
The Third Man '49 ►
This Gun for Hire '42 ►
3-Way '04
Too Late for Tears '49 ►
Touch of Evil '58 ►
Undercurrent '46 ►
Vortex '82
Where Danger Lives '50 ►
While the City Sleeps '56 ►
White Heat '49 ►
The Window '49 ►
A Woman's Secret '49 ►
The Wrong Man '56 ►

Filmmaking
see also At the Movies;
Behind the Scenes;
Abbott and Costello Meet
the Keystone Kops '54
The Adjuster '91
An Alan Smithee Film: Burn,
Hollywood, Burn '97
Alexandra Again and
Forever '90
All the Wrong Places '00
An Almost Perfect Affair '79
American Movie '99 ►
...And God Spoke '94
And Starring Pancho Villa
as Himself '03 ►
Ararat '02
Art House '98
Baadasssss! '03 ►
Barton Fink '91 ►
Ee Kind Rewind '08
Beyond the Clouds '95
Big Show '37
Black Cat '37
The Blair Witch Project '99
Bloodbath in Psycho Town '89
Body Chemistry 3: Point of
Seduction '93
Bombay Talkie '70
Bowfinger '99 ►
Cannes Man '96
Cass '78
Children Shouldn't Play with
Dead Things '72
Ciao Federico! Fellini
Directs Satyricon '69
Comment Ca Va? '76
Contempt '64 ►
The Cool Surface '92
CQ '01
Dangerous Game '93
Danny Roane: First Time
Director '06
David Holzman's Diary '67 ►
The Dead Hate the Living '99
Dead Silence '90
A Decade Under the
Influence '02 ►
Deep in the Heart (of Texas)
'98
Drifting '82
DuBeat-E-O '84
Ec Wood '94 ►
84 Charlie MoPic '89 ►
Elsa, Elsa '85
Elvis in Hollywood '93

F/X 2: The Deadly Art of
Illusion '91
Fellini '91
Festival at Cannes '02
Film Geek '06
Final Cut '88
Flickers '80
Full Tilt Boogie '97
Get Shorty '95 ►
Good Morning, Babylon '87 ►
Gosford Park '01 ►
Hearts of Darkness: A
Filmmaker's Apocalypse
'91 ►
Hi, Mom! '70 ►
Hit and Runway '01
Hollywood Chaos '89
Hollywood Mystery '34
Hotel '01
The House of Seven
Corpses '73
How to Eat Your
Watermelon in White
Company (and Enjoy It)
'05 ►
How to Make a Monster '58
Identification of a Woman
'82
I'll Do Anything '93
In a Moment of Passion '93
Intervista '87 ►
Iron Cowboy '68
Invasion Force '90
Island of Blood '82
It's All True '93 ►
Jacquot '91 ►
Kamikaze Hearts '91
The Kid Stays in the Picture
'02 ►
The King of the Kickboxers
'91
Kisses in the Dark '97
La Petite Lili '03
The Last Broadcast '98 ►
The Last Porno Flick '74
Les Violons du Bal '74 ►
Living in Oblivion '94 ►
Loaded '94
Lost in La Mancha '03 ►
A Man Like Eva '83 ►
The Mirror Crack'd '80
Mistress '92
Money, Money, Murder '96
Mute Witness '95
My Dream Is Yours '49
My Life's in Turnaround '94
Nightmare in Wax '69
Nightmare in Blood '75
Nudity Required '90
On an Island with You '48 ►
Once in Paris... '79
One Hundred and One
Nights '95
Overnight '03 ►
Passion '82
The Pickle '93
Pictures '80s
Pipe Dream '02
The Player '92 ►
The Pornographer '00
The Red Raven Kiss-Off '90
RKO 231 '99 ►
Secret File of Hollywood '62
Sex is Comedy '04
She Must Be Seeing Things
'87
Shoot or Be Shot '02
Silent Motive '91
Skin Deep '94
Slaves of Hollywood '99
A Slave of Love '78 ►
Spenser: A Savage Place
'94
Stand-In '85
Storytelling '01 ►
The Stunt Man '80 ►
Sullivan's Travels '41 ►
The Swap '71
Sweet Liberty '86
Swimming with Sharks '94 ►
The Tango Lesson '97
Tristram Shandy: A Cock
and Bull Story '05 ►
Two Weeks in Another
Town '62 ►
Ulysses' Gaze '95

Understudy: The Graveyard
Shift 2 '88
Venice, Venice '92
Visions of Light: The Art of
Cinematography '93 ►
Voyage to the Beginning of
the World '96
Wes Craven's New
Nightmare '94 ►
Where's Marlowe? '98
White Hunter, Black Heart
'90 ►
The Wizard of Speed and
Time '88
You Know My Name '99
You Must Remember This
'92

Firemen
see also Fires
Ablaze '00
The Accidental Husband '08
Always '89 ►
Backdraft '91 ►
Blast '04
Club Paradise '86
Collateral Damage '02
Evolution '01
Fahrenheit 451 '66 ►
15 Minutes '01
Fire Alarm '32
Fire Serpent '07
Fireballs '90
Firefight '03
Firehouse '72
Firehouse Dog '07
The Fireman '16
The Firemen's Ball '68 ►
Firestorm '97
Frequency '00 ►
The Guys '02
Hellfighters '68
I Heart Huckabees '04
Now Pronounce You
Chuck and Larry '07
Inferno in Paradise '88
Just One Time '00
Ladder 49 '04
Point of Origin '02
Reign of Fire '02
Roxanne '87 ►
Trespass '92
Turk 182! '85
World Trade Center '06 ►

Fires
see also Boom!; Disaster
Flicks; Firemen
Ablaze '00
Always '89 ►
Backdraft '91 ►
Blue Smoke '07
The Burning Bed '85 ►
Burning Rage '84
Carrie '76 ►
City on Fire '78
The Claim '00
The Crematons '72
Dinosaurus! '60
Don't Go in the House '80
Endless Love '3'
Erendira '83
Fire '77
Fire Alarm '32
Fire Serpent '07
Firehead '90
The Fireman '16
Firestarter '84
Firestarter 2: Rekindled '02
Firestorm '97
Firestorm: 72 Hours in
Oakland '93
Firetrap '01
The Flaming U'ge '53
Flashfire '94
Frankenstein '31 ►
Ghost Rider '07
In Old Chicago '37 ►
Inferno '01
Interview with the Vampire
'94 ►
Island of the Burning
Doomed '67
Ladder 49 '04

The Lion King '94 ►
Little Men '98
Look Who's Talking, Too '90
Meet the Parents '00 ►
The Michigan Kid '28
Mighty Joe Young '49
Nice Girls Don't Explode '87
Oil '78
The Outsiders '83
Point of Origin '02
Pretty Poison '68 ►
Pyrates '91
Quest for Fire '82 ►
Rosewood '96 ►
Save the Tiger '73 ►
Sounds of Silence '91
Specimen '97
Speeding Up Time '71
Spontaneous Combustion
'89
SuperFire '02
Terror on the 40th Floor '74
Ticks '93
The Towering Inferno '74 ►
The Triangle Factory Fire
Scandal '79
12 and Holding '05
Twin Town '97
Volcano '97
Wilder Napalm '93
The Witness '99

The First Time
see also Sex & Sexuality;
Teen Angst
American Pie '99 ►
Biloxi Blues '88 ►
The Crime of Father Amaro
'02 ►
December Boys '07
Dreaming About You '92
Driving Lessons '06
Earth & Water '99
Fast Times at Ridgemont
High '82 ►
Food of Love '02
Getting It '06
Ginger and Cinnamon '33
Juno '07 ►
Little Darlings '80
Losin' It '82
Marie Antoinette '06 ►
My Tutor '82
National Lampoon's Adam
& Eve '05
Nico and Dani '00 ►
Porky's '82
Pretty Baby '78 ►
Risky Business '83 ►
The Rules of Attraction '02
Running with Scissors '06
Saved! '00
Skipped Parts '00
Tadpole '02
Teeth '07
The Ten '07

All In '06
All Over the Guy '01
Alpha Male '06
At the King's Men '06
Amazing Grace '06 ►
American Beauty '99 ►
Amores Perros '00 ►
Anne Rice's The Feast of All
Saints '01
Antonia's Line '95 ►
Antwone Fisher '02 ►
Ararat '02
Back of Beyond '95
Bandits '01
Batman Forever '95
Beau Geste '39
Beau Travail '98 ►
Behind the Red Door '02
Being at Home with Claude
'92
Belles on Their Toes '52
Beloved '98
Best Laid Plans '59
Betrayal '83 ►
Beyond Borders '03
Big Fish '03 ►
Black Book '06 ►

Flashback
Black Christmas '06
Blind Faith '98
Bonanno: A Godfather's
Story '99
Boondock Saints '95
Boss of Bosses '99
Boys '95 ►
Brand Upon the Brain! '06 ►
Breaking Up '97
Broken Harvest '94
Brothers Three '07
The Brutal Truth '99
The Business of
Fancydancing '02
The Camomile Lawn '92
Can't Hardly Wait '98
Carried Away '95
Casablanca '42 ►
Casanova '05
Catch Me If You Can '02 ►
Catfish in Black Bean Sauce
'00
Cello '05
Cement '99
Chaos Theory '08
Character '97 ►
Charming Billy '98
The Chorus '04 ►
Citizen Kane '41 ►
Come Undone '00
Company Man '00
The Confessional '95 ►
The Constant Gardener '05 ►
Courage Under Fire '96 ►
Cover '08
Criminal Lovers '99
Dad Savage '97
Danny Roane: First Time
Director '06
Dark Blue World '01
December Boys '07
Decoy '46
Deeply '00
Definitely, Maybe '08 ►
The Devil Is a Woman '35 ►
The Disappearance of
Garcia Lorca '96
The Diving Bell and the
Butterfly '07 ►
Dogfight '91 ►
Dolores Claiborne '94 ►
Don Juan (Or If Don Juan
Were a Woman) '73
Don't Tell '05
Drowning Mona '00
Dust '01
Eddie and the Cruisers '83
Edward Scissorhands '90 ►
Eighteen '04
El Cantante '06
Emile '03
The Emperor's Club '02
Eternity and a Day '97
Event Horizon '97
Eve's Bayou '97 ►
Exotica '94 ►
Eye of God '97
Facing Windows '03
Faithless '00
Fallen Angel '03
A Family Thing '96 ►
Far Side of the Moon '03
Fear and Loathing in Las
Vegas '98
Fever Pitch '96 ►
Fight Club: '99 ►
Final '01
Finding Home '03
Flags of Our Fathers '06
The Forgotten '04
The Forbidden Quest '93
Frankie Starlight '95
Frailty '02 ►
Frozen '05
Fur: An Imaginary Portrait of
Diane Arbus '06
Gangster No. 1 '00
Genealogies of a Crime '97
The General '26 ►
The General's Daughter '99
Gloomy Sunday '02 ►

Flashback

God is My Co-Pilot '45
The Godfather, Part 2 '74 ▶
Godmoney '98
Gods and Monsters '98 ▶
God's Sandbox '06
The Good Shepherd '06
A Good Year '06
The Great Water '04
Grey Owl '99
Grizzly Falls '99
A Guide to Recognizing Your Saints '06
The Hanging Garden '97
Headspace '02
Heart '99
The Heart of Me '02
Hearts in Atlantis '01
Hedwig and the Angry Inch '00 ▶
Helas pour Moi '94
Hellraiser 4: Bloodline '95
Hero '03 ▶
Hero Wanted '08
The Hi-Lo Country '98
Hidden '05 ▶
High Fidelity '00 ▶
Highlander: Endgame '00 ▶
Hiroshima, Mon Amour '59 ▶
Hitman '07
The Hole '01
Holes '03 ▶
Hollywoodland '06
A Home at the End of the World '04
Horatio Hornblower: The Adventure Continues '01 ▶
Houdini '98 ▶
A House Divided '00
How I Killed My Father '03 ▶
The Human Stain '03
The Hunted '03
I Shot a Man in Vegas '96
In His Life: The John Lennon Story '00
Inferno '99
Instinct '99
Into the Wild '07 ▶
Jackie's Back '99
Jacob's Ladder '90 ▶
Jerry and Tom '98
Jet Li's Fearless '06 ▶
John John in the Sky '00
Johnny Dangerously '84
Jungle Woman '44
Just Married '03
Karla '06
Keillers Park '05
Kicking and Screaming '95 ▶
Ladder 49 '04
Lansky '99
The Last Letter '04
Last Orders '01 ▶
The Lawless Breed '52 ▶
Leave Her to Heaven '45 ▶
The Legend of Bagger Vance '00
The Legend of 1900 '98
Les Voleurs '96
The Lesser Evil '97
Liebestraum '91
Life '99
The Life Before This '99
The Life of David Gale '03
Life Tastes Good '99
Lone Star '95 ▶
The Long Night '47
The Loss of Sexual Innocence '98
Love Come Down '00
Love Letters '99 ▶
Lumumba '01 ▶
Mad Love '01
Marilyn Hotchkiss' Ballroom Dancing & Charm School '06
The Marrying Kind '52
Memento '00 ▶
Mrs. Dalloway '97 ▶
Mrs. Harris '05
Mr. Woodcock '07
Monsieur N. '03 ▶
Mother Night '96 ▶
Mother of Mine '05 ▶
Murder at Devil's Glen '99
Murder in Greenwich '02
Murder in Mind '97
Murderous Intent '06 ▶

My Brother '06
My Foolish Heart '49
My Name is Modesty: A Modesty Blaise Adventure '04
The Neon Bible '95
Never Been Kissed '99
New Blood '99
Nina Takes a Lover '94
The Ninth Configuration '79 ▶
Notes on a Scandal '06 ▶
Now and Then '95
On the Air '95
Once Upon a Time in America '84 ▶
Once Upon a Time in Mexico '03 ▶
One Kill '00
Only Love '98
Oriana '85
Oscar and Lucinda '97
Paid in Full '02
Passage to Marseilles '44 ▶
Passenger '61
Perfect Crime '97
Perfume: The Story of a Murderer '06
Permanent Midnight '98 ▶
Post Mortem '99
Premonition '07
Pretty Village, Pretty Flame '96 ▶
The Proposition '97
P.S. I Love You '07 ▶
A Rather English Marriage '98
The Razor's Edge '46 ▶
The Razor's Edge '84
Red Meat '98
The Red Violin '98 ▶
Reservoir Dogs '92 ▶
The Return '06
The Rising Place '02
The Road Home '01 ▶
Romy and Michele's High School Reunion '97
Rosie '99
The Rules of Attraction '02
The Safety of Objects '01
Saint-Ex: The Story of the Storyteller '95
Salem's Lot '04
The Salton Sea '02
Saw 4 '07
Saw III '06
Sea Wife '57
Secondhand Lions '03 ▶
Sergeant Rutledge '60 ▶
Sex and Lucia '01
Shattered '91
Shining Through '92
Short Night of Glass Dolls '71
Shot in the Heart '01
The Silences of the Palace '94
Simon Birch '98
Simpatico '99
SLC Punk! '99
Slow Burn '05
Smoke Signals '98 ▶
Snapshots '02
Snow Angels '07 ▶
Snow Falling on Cedars '99
Solaris '02
A Soldier's Sweetheart '98
South Sea Woman '53
Spider '02 ▶
Spy Game '01
Steal This Movie! '00
Stealing Home '88
Stella Does Tricks '96
Stephanie Daley '06
Stephen King's It '90
Stoned '05
Straight into Darkness '04
The Stranger: Kabloonak '95
Stricken '98
Sweet and Lowdown '99 ▶
Sweet Nothing '96 ▶
Sweetwater: A True Rock Story '99
Swept from the Sea '97
Swindled '04
T-Men '47 ▶
Tangled '01

The Tenant of Wildfell Hall '96
A Texas Funeral '99
There's Something about Mary '98 ▶
Things We Lost in the Fire '07
This Is My Father '99
Though None Go With Me '06
The Three Lives of Karen '97
301, 302 '94 ▶
Till Human Voices Wake Us '02
To Each His Own '46 ▶
Total Eclipse '95
Tuck Everlasting '02 ▶
28 Days '00
Two for the Road '67 ▶
Two Friends '86
The Ugly '96
Unbreakable '00 ▶
Under Heavy Fire '01
The Underneath '95 ▶
Urbania '00
The Usual Suspects '95 ▶
Valentino '77
Velvet Goldmine '98
Walkabout '71 ▶
The Wedding Party '97
The Weekend '00
The Weight of Water '00
Weirdsville '07
Welcome to Collinwood '02
Went to Coney Island on a Mission from God... Be Back by Five '98
What Dreams May Come '98
When I Close My Eyes '95
When the Dark Man Calls '95
White Badge '97
Who is Cletis Tout? '02
Why Do Fools Fall in Love? '98
The Wicker Man '06
Wicker Park '04
Wild Bill '95
The Wild Bunch '69 ▶
With a Song in My Heart '52
The Wood '99
Wozzeck '47
Zone 39 '96

Flatulence

Austin Powers: International Man of Mystery '97 ▶
Austin Powers in Goldmember '02
Beavis and Butt-Head Do America '96
Bio-Dome '96
Blazing Saddles '74 ▶
Dr. Dolittle '98
Dr. Dolittle 2 '01
Dumb & Dumber '94
Ed '96
Friday After Next '02
Grumpier Old Men '95
Jay and Silent Bob Strike Back '01
A Knight's Tale '01
Larry the Cable Guy: Health Inspector '06
The Lion King '94 ▶
Lost and Found '99
Major Payne '95
Mystery Men '99
National Lampoon's Senior Trip '95
The Nutty Professor '96 ▶
Nutty Professor 2: The Klumps '00
Osmosis Jones '01
Rain Man '88 ▶
The Road to Wellville '94
RocketMan '97
The Santa Clause '94
Sugar & Spice '01

Flight

see Airborne

Flood

see also Disaster Flicks
The Day After Tomorrow '04
Flood! '76
Flood: A River's Rampage '97
Hard Rain '97
Heroes of the Heart '94
The Last Wave '77 ▶
Noah's Ark '99
The Rains Came '39 ▶
The River '84
Waterworld '95
William Faulkner's Old Man '97
The Winning of Barbara Worth '26

Florence

see also Italy
Obsession '76
Romola '25
A Room with a View '86 ▶
Tea with Mussolini '99
Up at the Villa '00

Florida

see also American South; Miami
Adaptation '02 ▶
The Alien Agenda: Endangered Species '97
Aquamarine '06
Because of Winn-Dixie '05
Blue Car '03 ▶
Blue City '86
Body Heat '81 ▶
The Boynton Beach Club '05
Bully '01
Canvas '06
Coastlines '02
The Devil's Advocate '97
Elmore Leonard's Gold Coast '97
Fascination '04
The Flamingo Rising '01
A Flash of Green '85
Follow That Dream '61
Gal Young 'Un '79 ▶
Grace is Gone '07
Great Expectations '97
The Hawk is Dying '06
Heartbreakers '01
Hello Down There '69
House of Wax '05
Illtown '96
In Her Shoes '05 ▶
Just Cause '94
Larry the Cable Guy: Health Inspector '06
Last Rites '98
Meet the Fockers '04
Miami Blues '90
Monster '03 ▶
Never Back Down '08
Off Season '01
Out of Time '03
Palmetto '98
Porky's '82
Porky's 2: The Next Day '83
Porky's Revenge '85
Race to Space '01
River of Grass '94
Rosewood '96 ▶
Ruby in Paradise '93 ▶
The Sleepy Time Gal '01
Sunshine State '02 ▶
The Sweetest Gift '98
Things Behind the Sun '01
Tollbooth '94
Trading Hearts '87
Ulee's Gold '97 ▶
Wild Things '98
Wild Things 2 '04
Wrestling with Alligators '98
The Yearling '46 ▶
The Yearling '94

Flying Saucers

see Alien Babes; Alien Beings—Benign; Alien Beings—Vicious; Alien Cops; Aliens Are People, Too; Out of This World Sex; Space Operas

Folklore & Legends

see also Storytelling
Antonio Das Mortes '68
Atlas in the Land of the Cyclops '61
Beauty and the Devil '50
Beowulf & Grendel '06
Black Cat, White Cat '98 ▶
Black Orpheus '58 ▶
The Blair Witch Project '99
Brotherhood of the Wolf '01 ▶
The Brothers Grimm '05
Candyman '92 ▶
Candyman 2: Farewell to the Flesh '95
Chunhyang '00
Coyote Waits '03
Crossroads '86
Darby O'Gill & the Little People '59 ▶
Donkey Skin '70 ▶
Down to Earth '47
Erik the Viking '89
The Fast Runner '01 ▶
Faust '26 ▶
The Fool Killer '65
Force on Thunder Mountain '77
Gabbeh '96 ▶
The Giant of Marathon '60
The Giant of Metropolis '61
The Giants of Thessaly '60
Golden Voyage of Sinbad '73
Goliath Against the Giants '63
Goliath and the Barbarians '60
Goliath and the Dragon '61
Goliath and the Sins of Babylon '64
Grendel, Grendel, Grendel '82
Heart of Glass '74 ▶
Helen of Troy '56
Hercules 2 '85
Hercules the Legendary Journeys, Vol. 1: The Lost Kingdom '94
Hercules the Legendary Journeys, Vol. 2: The Amazon Women '94
Hercules the Legendary Journeys, Vol. 3: The Circle of Fire '94
Hercules the Legendary Journeys, Vol. 4: In the Underworld '94
If They Tell You I Fell '89
Into the West '92 ▶
Invincible Gladiators '64
Invitation to the Dance '56
Iphigenia '77 ▶
Jason and the Argonauts '63 ▶
Johnny Appleseed '86
King Arthur '04
Kismet '20
Kriemhilde's Revenge '24 ▶
Leapin' Leprechauns '95
The Legend of Gator Face '96
The Legend of Sleepy Hollow '86
The Legend of Suram Fortress '85
Leprechaun 2 '94
Life on a String '90
The Lost Empire '01
Magic in the Water '95
Merlin and the Sword '85
Messalina vs. the Son of Hercules '64
A Midsummer Night's Dream '68
A Midsummer Night's Dream '96

Monty Python and the Holy Grail '75 ▶
Mulan '98
Ned Kelly '03
The Odyssey '97
Out of Time '00
Pancho Villa Returns '50
Pandora and the Flying Dutchman '51
Pathfinder '87
Pecos Bill '86
Phedre '68
Phoenix '78
The Phoenix and the Magic Carpet '95
The Relic '96
The Secret of Navajo Cave '76
The Secret of Roan Inish '94 ▶
The Secret of the Loch '34
The Seventh Stream '01
Siegfried '24 ▶
Skinwalker '02
Son of Samson '62
Tall Tale: The Unbelievable Adventures of Pecos Bill '95
Thor and the Amazon Women '60
Tristan & Isolde '06
Tropical Malady '04
Ulysses '55
Urban Legend '98
Urban Legends: Bloody Mary '05
Ursus in the Valley of the Lions '62
Vulcan God of Fire '62
Walking Tall '04
Wend Kuuni '82
Wendigo '01
Whale Rider '02 ▶
The Wonderful World of the Brothers Grimm '62
Zvenigora '28 ▶

Food

see Edibles

Football

Ace Ventura: Pet Detective '93
Air Bud 2: Golden Receiver '98
All the Right Moves '83
Angels in the Endzone '98
Any Given Sunday '99
Backfield in Motion '91
The Best of Times '86
Black Sunday '77
Blue Ridge Fall '99
Brian's Song '71 ▶
Brian's Song '01
Buffalo 66 '97 ▶
Cheaper by the Dozen '03
Cheering Section '73
Cheerleaders' Wild Weekend '85
College Humor '33
The Comebacks '07
Diner '82 ▶
The Dropkick '27
Easy Living '49
Everybody's All American '88
Father Was a Fullback '49
First & Ten: The Team Scores Again '85
The Fortune Cookie '66 ▶
The Freshman '25 ▶
Friday Night Lights '04 ▶
The Galloping Ghost '31
The Game Plan '07
The Garbage-Picking, Field Goal-Kicking Philadelphia Phenomenon '98
Good Luck '96
Good News '47
Grambling's White Tiger '81
Gridiron Gang '06
Gus '76
The Halfback of Notre Dame '96
Harmon of Michigan '41
Heaven Can Wait '78 ▶
Hold 'Em Jail '32

▶ = *rated three bones or higher*

Hometown Legend '02
Horse Feathers '32▶
Invincible '06▶
Jerry Maguire '96▶
Jim Thorpe: All American '51
Johnny Be Good '88
Knute Rockne: All American '40▶
Leatherheads '08
Last Game '80
Last Time Out '94
Little Giants '94
The Longest Yard '74▶
The Longest Yard '05
The Longshots '08
Lucas '86▶
Maker of Men '31
Man of the House '05
Midnight Heat '95
Monday Night Mayhem '02
Navy Blue and Gold '37
Necessary Roughness '91
North Dallas Forty '79▶
The O.J. Simpson Story '94
One Night Only '84
Paper Lion '68
Pigskin Parade '35
Players '99
Possums '99
The Program '93
Quarterback Princess '85
Radio '03
Remember the Titans '00▶
The Replacements '00
Roberta '35▶
Romeo Must Die '00
Rudy '93
Rustin '01
A Saintly Switch '99
School Ties '92▶
Semi-Tough '77
The Slaughter Rule '01
The Spirit of West Point '47
They Call Me Sir '20
Trouble along the Way '53
Two Minute Warning '76
Varsity Blues '98
The Waterboy '98
We Are Marshall '06
Wildcats '86
Windrunner '94

Foreign Cops
see also Foreign Intrigue; Interpol; Police Detectives

The Bourne Supremacy '04▶
Collision Course '89
Coup de Torchon '81▶
Cradle 2 the Grave '03
Dudley Do-Right '99
Framed '93▶
Hard-Boiled '92
Hot Fuzz '07▶
Infernal Affairs '02▶
Inspector Clouseau '63
Jet Li's The Enforcer '95
The King of the Kickboxers '91
La Balance '82▶
La Scorta '94▶
The Medallion '03
The Pink Panther '64▶
The Pink Panther '06
Police Story '85
Prime Suspect '92▶
Red Heat '88
The Return of Dr. Mabuse '61
Return of the Pink Panther '74
Revenge of the Pink Panther '78

Foreign Intrigue
see also Spies & Espionage

Above Suspicion '43▶
Ambassador Bill '31
American Roulette '88
Anne of Green Gables: The Continuing Story '99
Austin Powers: International Man of Mystery '97▶
Battle Beneath the Earth '68
Bulldog Drummond at Bay '37
Call Him Mr. Shatter '74
Catch Me a Spy '71
Chinese Boxes '84
Chinese Wet '78
Cover-Up '91
Crimson Tide '95▶
Deadly Alliance '78
The Destructors '74
Devil Wears White '85
Diamonds Are Forever '71▶
Diplomatic Courier '52▶
Dr. No '62▶
The Dogs of War '81
Don't Drink the Water '69
The Eiger Sanction '75
An Englishman Abroad '83▶
Enigma '82
Erik '90
Escapade in Florence '62
Escape from the KGB '87
Escape to Love '82
Escape to the Sun '72
The Executioner '70
The Experts '89
Exposed '83
Exposure '91
Federal Agent '36
Foreign Correspondent '40▶
The Fourth Protocol '87▶
Frederick Forsyth's Icon '05
The Glimmer Man '96
A Global Affair '63
Gunpowder '87
Half Moon Street '86
Hamlet '96▶
The Human Factor '75
The Hunt for Red October '90▶
In the Company of Spies '99
The Interpreter '05▶
Jaguar Lives '79
Jumpin' Jack Flash '86
The Key to Rebecca '85
La Passante '83▶
License to Kill '89▶
The Little Drummer Girl '84▶
Man from Headquarters '28
The Man Who Knew Too Little '97
The Man Who Knew Too Much '34▶
The Man Who Knew Too Much '56
Marathon Man '76▶
The Mask of Dimitrios '44▶
Natural Causes '94
The Odessa File '74
Overthrow '82
Panama Hattie '42
Postmark for Danger '56
Puzzle '78
Reilly: Ace of Spies '87▶
Return of the Man from U.N.C.L.E. '83
Return of the Tall Blond Man with One Black Shoe '74
Rollover '81
The Russia House '90
Saigon: Year of the Cat '87
Sebastian '68
The Secret Agent '96
The Spy Who Came in from the Cold '65▶
Strangers '91
Sweet Country '87
They Met in Bombay '41
The Third Man '49▶
Tokyo Joe '49
Too Bad She's Bad '54
Topaz '69▶
Torn Curtain '66
Undeclared War '91
The White Countess '05▶
The Wind and the Lion '75▶
Windmills of the Gods '88

Foreign Legion
see also Desert Warfare; Foreign Intrigue

The Life & Times of the Chocolate Killer '88

Frame-Ups

Abbott and Costello Meet the Invisible Man '51▶
Agatha Christie's The Pale Horse '96
Animal 2 '07
Another Pair of Aces: Three of a Kind '91▶
The Art of War '00
Backfire '22
Bedroom Eyes '86
Best Revenge '83
Below the Deadline '29
Big Score '83
The Big Sweat '90
Bitter Vengeance '94
The Black Sleep '56
Blackout '54
Blade: Trinity '04
Blind Man's Bluff '91
The Blum Affair '48
The Bourne Supremacy '04▶
Breakdown '53
Buried Alive '39
Caged Fear '92
Candyman 3: Day of the Dead '98
Capital Punishment '96
Caught in the Act '93
Chain Reaction '96
A Challenge for Robin Hood '68
City Hall '95▶
Class of Fear '91
The Clay Pigeon '49
Consenting Adults '92
Cop-Out '91
Covered Wagon Days '40
Crime and Punishment in Suburbia '00
Cry Vengeance '54
Dancing Man '33
Dark Corner '46▶
Deadline at Dawn '46
Death Sentence '74
The Desperadoes '43
Deuce Bigalow: European Gigolo '05
The Disappearance of Christina '93
Double Take '01
Each Dawn I Die '39
Escape from DS-3 '81
Exit in Red '97
Extremely Dangerous '99
F/X '86▶
A Face to Kill For '99
Family of Cops '95
Fast Getaway 2 '94
The Fighting Rookie '34
Final Payback '99
Fingerprints Don't Lie '51
Firestone '94
Framed by Frame '95
Framed '75
Framed '93▶
Free to Love '25
The Fugitive '93▶
Gang Related '96
Get Rita '75
The Ghost Camera '33
The Gilded Cage '54
The Glimmer Man '96
Girls in Prison '56
Hi-Jacked '50
How to Frame a Figg '71
The Inner Circle '46
An Innocent Man '89
Judge Dredd '95
Judicial Consent '94
Kentucky Blue Streak '35
Killing 'Em Softly '85
The Killing Yard '01
Kiss of the Dragon '01
The Lady Confesses '45
Lady in the Death House '44
Left for Dead '78
Legacy of Rage '86
Les Miserables '95
Let's Go to Prison '06
Letters from a Killer '98
A Lizard in a Woman's Skin '71
Linda '93
Louisiana Purchase '41▶
Lucky Cisco Kid '40
Macon County Line '74
Malevolence '95
The Manhunt '86
The Mighty Quinn '89
Mr. Wise Guy '42
Most Wanted '97
Motel Blue '98
Moving Target '96
Moving Target '00
Murder '30▶
Murphy's Law '86
My Cousin Vinny '92▶
My Favorite Americans '96
Nasty Hero '89
The Net 2.0 '06
The Net '95▶
Never 2 Big '98
Nightmare in Badham County '76
Nightwatch '96
No Escape, No Return '93
North by Northwest '59▶
Now and Forever '82
The Obsessed '51
Off the Wall '82
Old Mother Riley's New Venture '49
Out of Time '03
Palmetto '98
Phantom Lady '44▶
Plato's Run '96
Powder Burn '96
Presumed Innocent '90▶
Prime Suspect '88
Prison Break '38
Prison for Fire '87
Red Corner '97
The Rich Man's Wife '96
Ricochet '91
Road House '48▶
Rubdown '93
Saboteur '42▶
Sabotage '96
The Sentinel '06
The Shadow Conspiracy '96
Shakes the Clown '92
Shelter '98
Shooter '07
The Sphinx '33
Stir Crazy '80▶
Storm Catcher '99
Street Kings '06
Sunset Heat '92
Suspended Alibi '56
The Take '07
Tank '83
TekWar '94
Thick as Thieves '99
Today I Hang '42
Torque '04
Undisputed II: Last Man Standing '06
U.S. Marshals '98▶
White Fire '53
Wild Things '98▶
Woman Condemned '33
The Wrong Man '93
The Wrong Woman '95
The Yards '00

France
see also Paris

A la Mode '94
The Accompanist '93▶
The Adventures of Felix '99
The Affair of the Necklace '01
Alice et Martin '98
The Ambassador's Daughter '56
An American in Paris '51▶
An American Werewolf in Paris '97
Anatomy of Hell '04
And Soon the Darkness '70
Apres-Vous '03
Arch of Triumph '48▶
Army of Shadows '69
Before Sunset '04▶
Bedtime Story '63
Becoming Colette '92
Big Fella '37
Bluebeard's Eighth Wife '38
Bon Voyage '03▶
Borsalino '70▶
Breathless '59▶
Brotherhood of the Wolf '01
Buffet Froid '79▶
The Butterfly '02▶
Can-Can '60
Cannes Man '96
Captain Scarlett '53
Carnage '02
Carnival in Flanders '35▶
Carve Her Name with Pride '58
Catch Me If You Can '02
Catherine & Co. '76
Cesar '36▶
Charade '63▶
Charlotte Gray '01
Chasing Butterflies '94
The Chateau '01
The Chorus '04▶
Chocolat '00▶
Cloud Waltzing '87
Come Undone '00
The Count of Monte Cristo '02▶
Criminal Lovers '99
Danton '82▶
Days of Glory '06
Desiree '54
Diane '55
Dirty Rotten Scoundrels '88▶
Dr. Petiot '90
The Dreamlife of Angels '98▶
Dubarry '30
The Duellists '77▶
Dupont Lajoie '74
8 Women '02▶
The Elusive Corporal '62▶
Ever After: A Cinderella Story '98▶
Fanfan la Tulipe '51▶
The Fatal Image '90
Festival at Cannes '02
5x2 '04
Flyboys '06
The Foreman Went to France '42
Forget Paris '95
The 4 Musketeers '05
Frantic '88▶
French Connection 2 '75▶
French Intrigue '70
French Kiss '95
The French Lesson '86
French Postcards '79
The French Woman '79
Full Speed '96
Games of Love and Chance '03
The Gendarme of Saint-Tropez '64
Gigi '58▶
Girls Can't Swim '99
The Good Thief '03▶
A Good Year '06
Goya in Bordeaux '99
Happily Ever After '04
Harvest '37▶
Hate '95▶
He Loves Me... He Loves Me Not '02
Heart of a Nation '43▶
Hellraiser 4: Bloodline '95
Henri Langlois: The Phantom of the Cinematheque '04▶
Hidden '05▶
The Horseman on the Roof '95
How to Steal a Million '66▶
I Stand Alone '98
If Looks Could Kill '86
Impromptu '90▶
The Intruder '04▶
Is Paris Burning? '66▶
Jeanne la Pucelle '94
Jefferson in Paris '95
Joan of Arc '48
Joan of Arc '99
Joan of Paris '42
The Josephine Baker Story '90▶
Just Visiting '01
Killer Tomatoes Eat France '91
Killing Zoe '94
Kings and Queen '05▶
Kings Go Forth '58
A Knight's Tale '01
La Ceremonie '95▶
La Collectionneuse '67
La Marseillaise '37▶
La Passante '83▶
La Petite Lili '03
La Silence de la Mer '47
La Vie de Boheme '93▶
La Vie Promise '02
The Lacemaker '77▶
Lafayette Escadrille '58
The Last Metro '80▶
Last Tango in Paris '73▶
The Last Time I Saw Paris '54
The Last Train '74
Le Bal '82▶
Le Complot '73▶
Le Corbeau '43▶
Le Joli Mai '62▶
Le Million '31▶
Lemming '05
Les Destinees '00
Les Grandes Manoeuvres '55▶
Les Miserables '35▶
Les Miserables '57▶
Les Miserables '78▶
Les Miserables '95
Les Miserables '97▶
The Life of Emile Zola '37▶
Lila Says '04
The Longest Day '62▶
Love Me If You Dare '03▶
Lovely to Look At '52▶
Loves & Times of Scaramouche '76
Lucie Aubrac '98
Ma and Pa Kettle on Vacation '53
Macame Bovary '91▶
Madame Bovary '00
Mademoiselle Fifi '44
Maniac '50
Maniac '63
The Man in tha Iron Mask '39
The Man in tha Iron Mask '77▶
The Man in the Iron Mask '98▶
The Man of My Life '06
Man on the Eiffel Tower '48▶
Marie Antoinette '38
Marie Antoinette '06▶
Marie Baie des Anges '97
Marius '31▶
Maximum Risk '96
May Fools '90▶
Me and the Colonel '58
Mr. Bean's Holiday '07
The Moderns '88▶
Modigliani '04
Moliere '07
Mondo '96
Mondovino '04
Moment to Moment '66
Monkeys, Go Home! '66
Monsieur Beaucaire '24
Monsieur Beaucaire '46▶
Monsieur N. '03▶
Monsieur Verdoux '47▶
The Moon and Sixpence '43▶
The Moonraker '58

France

Moulin Rouge '52▲
The Mountain '56
My Father's Glory '91▲
My Life on Ice '02
Napoleon 27▲
Napoleon 55
A New Kind of Love '63
New World '95
The Night and the Moment '94
The Old Lady Who Walked in the Sea '91
O.S.S. '46▲
Passion '19
Passion '82
Passion of Joan of Arc '28▲
Passion of Mind '00
Paths of Glory '57▲
Plaf '81
Prisoner of Honor '91▲
The Proprietor '96
Quality Street '37
Quatorze Juliet '32
Queen Margot '94▲
Read My Lips '01
Ready to Wear '94
The Red Inn '51
Reign of Terror 49
Reunion in France '42
Revenge of the Musketeers '94
Ridicule '96▲
Round Midnight '86▲
The Rover '67
The Rules of the Game '39▲
Sade '00
Saint Joan '57
The Scarlet Pimpernel '34▲
The Scarlet Pimpernel '82▲
The Scarlet Pimpernel '99
The Scarlet Pimpernel 2: Mademoiselle Guillotine '99
The Scarlet Pimpernel 3: The Kidnapped King '99
Sex is Comedy '02
Silk Stockings '57▲
Sister My Sister '94
A Soldier's Daughter Never Cries '98
Spy of Napoleon '36
The Statement 03
Straight into Darkness '04
Strayed '03
Suite 16 '94
A Summer's Tale '96
Surviving Picasso '96
Sweet Ecstasy 62
Swimming Pool '03▲
A Tale of Two Cities '36▲
A Tale of Two Cities '58▲
A Tale of Two Cities '80
A Tale of Winter '92
The Taste of Others '00▲
Theatre of Death '67
Therese Raquin '80
Therese: The Story of Saint Therese of Lisieux '04
This Land Is Mine '43▲
Those Magnificent Men in Their Flying Machines '65▲
Timeline '03
To Catch a Thief '55▲
Tous les Matins du Monde '92▲
The Town Is Quiet '00
The Transporter '02▲
The Trench '99
Tropic of Cancer '70▲
True Colors '87
Uncertain Glory '44
Until September '84
Uranus '91▲
Valmont '89▲
Varian's War '01
Vatel '00
A Very Long Engagement '04▲
The Victors '63
Waterloo '71
Western '96▲
What Price Glory? '52▲
Who Killed Bambi? '03
Will It Snow for Christmas? '96
Window to Paris '95
With a Friend Like Harry '00▲
A Year in Provence '89▲

Fraternities & Sororities

see also Campus Capers

American Pie Presents: Beta House '07
Among Brothers '05
Black Christmas 75
Black Christmas '06
Bright Lights, Big City 88
Broadway Melody of 1936 '35▲
The Campus Corpse '77
Confessions of Sorority Girls '94
Dead Man on Campus '97
Defying Gravity '99
Funny About Love '90
Going Greek '01
Happy Hell Night '92
Hell Night '81
H.O.T.S. '79
The Initiation '84
Initiation of Sarah '78
Insecticidal '05
Little Sister '92
Midnight Madness '80
Monsters Crash the Pajama Party 65
National Lampoon's Adam & Eve '05
National Lampoon's Animal House 78▲
National Lampoon's Van Wilder '02
National Lampoon's Van Wilder 2: The Rise of Taj '06
Old School '03
Pumpkin '02
Revenge of the Nerds 84
Ring of Terror '62
Scream 2 '97▲
Senseless '98
The Skulls 2 02
Sorority Babes in the Slimeball Bowl-A-Rama '87
Sorority Boys '02
Sorority Girl '57
Sorority House Massacre '86
Sorority House Massacre 2: Nighty Nightmare '92
Sorority House Party '92
Sorority House Vampires '95
Stomp the Yard '07
Sydney White '07
Urban Legend '98
Vampire Time Travelers '98
Wimps '87

Friendship

see also Buddies; Buddy Cops; Childhood Buddies; Female Bonding; Pardners

Front Page

see also Mass Media; Paperboys; Shutterbugs

Absence of Malice '81
Ace in the Hole '51▲
Act of Passion: The Lost Honor of Kathryn Beck '83
Action in Arabia '44
The Adventures of Nellie Bly '81
Against the Ropes '04
Alice in the Cities '74▲
All the President's Men '76▲
American Autobahn 84
America's Sweethearts '01
AngKor: Cambodia Express '81
Anima '98
Another Time, Another Place 58
Anzio '68
The Average Woman '24
The Barcelona Kill 77
The Beniker Gang '83
Between the Lines '77▲
Beyond Re-Animator '03
Big Brown Eyes 36
The Big Hurt '87
Big News '29
Big Town '47
Big Town After Dark 47
Blessed Event '32▲
Bloody Proof '99▲
The Blue Gardenia '53▲
Boca '94
Boeing Boeing '65
Bordertown '06
Brenda Starr '86
Bright Lights, Big City 88
Broadway Melody of 1936 '35▲
Brown Sugar '02
Bruce Almighty '03
Bulldog Edition '36
A Bunny's Tale '85
The Business of Fancydancing '02
Call Northside 777 '48▲
Caroline at Midnight '93
The Case of the Scorpion's Tail 71
Chinese Box '97
Circumstantial Evidence '35
Citizen Kane '41▲
City in Fear '80▲
Close to Home '86
Cobb '94▲
Cold Blooded '00
Concrete Beat '84
Continental Divide '81
Control Room '04▲
Cover Story '93
Criminal Act '88
Crocodile Dundee '86▲
Crocodile Dundee in Los Angeles '01
Cry Freedom '87
Cut and Run '85
Dark Secrets '95
Dark Side of Genius '94
Dead Air '94
Dead Connection '94
Deadline '81
Deadline '87
Deadline '00
Deadly Exposure 93
Deep Impact '98
Defense of the Realm '85▲
Diamond Trail '33
Diary of a Serial Killer '97
The Disappearance of Garcia Lorca '96
Don't Look Back '98
Don't Torture a Duckling '72
Double Cross '92
Double Edge '92
Double Exposure 82
Down Came a Blackbird '94
Each Dawn I Die '39▲
Easy to Wed '46
Echo of Murder '00
Eight Men Out '88▲
Everything Happens at Night '39▲
Extramarital '98
Eyes Behind the Stars 72
Eyes of a Stranger '81
A Face in the Fog '36
Far East '85
Fast Money '96
Father Hood '93
Fatherland '94
The Feminine Touch '95
Fever Pitch 85
Final Assignment '80
Finnegan Begin Again '84
Fit for a King '37
A Flash of Green '85
Fletch '85
Fletch Lives '89
Footsteps '98
The Forbidden Quest '93
Foreign Correspondent '40▲
Francis Covers the Big Town '53
Freeze Frame '92
The Front Page '31▲
The Front Page 74
Full Disclosure '00
Full Frontal '02
Gentleman's Agreement '47▲
Get a Clue '02
The Ghost and Mr. Chicken '66▲
G.I. War Brides '46
Good Advice '01
The Great Muppet Caper '81▲
Grown Ups '86
Gunshy '98▲
The Guys '02▲
Harrison's Flowers '02
Headline Woman '35
Heads '93
Heartaches '47
Heat Wave '90▲
Hellraiser: Deader '05
Her Life as a Man '83
Hero 92▲
His Girl Friday '40▲
Hit the Ice '44
Hour of Decision 57
How to Lose a Guy in 10 Days '03
The Hudsucker Proxy '93▲
Hue and Cry 47▲
Hustling '75▲
I Cover the Waterfront '33
I Love Trouble '94
The Image 89
Imagining Argentina '04
Impolite '92
In and Out '97▲
In My Country '04
An Inconvenient Woman '91
The Infiltrator '95
The Innocent Sleep '95
The Insider '99▲
Invasion of Privacy '92
Istanbul '90
It Happened Tomorrow '44
Joe Gould's Secret '00
Johnny Come Lately 43
Journey for Margaret 42▲
The Jury's Secret '38
Just One of the Guys '85
Keeper of the City '92
Keeper of the Flame '42
Kid from Not-So-Big '78
Kill Slade 89
The Killing Beach '92
The Killing Device '92
The Killing Fields '84▲
A Killing Spring '02
Killing Stone 78
L.A. Confidential '97▲
La Dolce Vita '60▲
Lana in Love '92
The Last Debate '00
The Last Word '95
Late Extra '35
Leatherheads '08
Legalese '98
Let 'er Go Gallegher '28
Lethal Charm '90
Libeled Lady '36▲
Life Begins at Forty 35
The Life of David Gale '03
Lip Service '88▲
L'Odeur des Fauves '66
Lonelyhearts '58
Love Is a Many-Splendored Thing '55
The Love Machine 71
Malarek '89
The Man Inside '90
Man of Iron '81▲
The Mask '94▲
Me & Mrs. Jones '02
Mean Season '85
Message in a Bottle '98
Michael '96
Midnight Edition '93
Midnight in the Garden of Good and Evil '97
Midnight Warrior 89
Mr. Deeds '02
Mr. Deeds Goes to Town '36▲
Money Talks '97
The Mothman Prophecies '02
Murder on the Campus 52
Murrow '86
My Wife is an Actress '01
Mystic Circle Murder 39
Natas... The Reflection '83
The Natural '84▲
Never Been Kissed '99
News at Eleven '86
Newsbreak '00
Newsfront 78▲
Newsies '92
Night Hunter '95
The Night Stalker '71
The Night Strangler '72
The Nightmare Years '89
Nina Takes a Lover '94
No Man's Land '01
No Time to Die '84
Not for Publication '84
Nothing Sacred '37▲
Notting Hill '99▲
Novel Desires 92
November Conspiracy '96
The Odessa File '74▲
Off the Lip '04
On Our Merry Way 48
One Fine Day 96
One Man Out '89
One True Thing '98▲
Optic Fiber '97
Orwell Rolls in His Grave '03
The Other Woman '92
Our Music '04
Outfoxed: Rupert Murdoch's War on Journalism '04▲
The Outlaws Is Coming! '65
The Paper '94▲
Paper Lion '68
The Payoff '43
The Pelican Brief '93
Perfect '85
The Philadelphia Story '40▲
Platinum Blonde '31▲
The Ploughman's Lunch '83▲
Power Play '02
Premonition '98
Primary Motive '92
Private Investigations 87
Profile '54
Qui Etes Vous, Mr. Sorge? '61
The Quiet American '02▲
Reckless Disregard '84
Reed: Insurgent Mexico 73
Resurrecting the Champ '07
Resurrection Man '97
Resurrection of Zachary Wheeler '71
Retribution '98
Revenge of the Radioactive Reporter '91
Riding on Air '37
The Ring '02
Roman Holiday '53▲
Roxie Hart '42
The Rumor Mill '86
Runaway Bride '99▲
Safari 3000 '82
Salome, Where She Danced '45
Salvador '86▲
Savage Capitalism '93
Saving Sarah Cain '07
Scandal '50
Scandal Sheet '85
Scream 2 '97▲
The Secrets of Wu Sin 32
Seeds of Doubt '96
Sex & Mrs. X '00
Sex and the Single Girl '64
Sex Through a Window '72
The Shadow Conspiracy '96
The Shaft '01
Shattered Glass '03▲
The Shipping News '01
Short Corridor '63▲
Short Fuse '88
Shriek in the Night '33
Shy People '87▲
Silver City '04
The Sixth Man '97
Skeletons '96
Sky Captain and the World of Tomorrow '04
Snake Eyes '98
Snow Falling on Cedars 99
Somewhere I'll Find You '42▲
Soul Patrol '80
Special Bulletin '83▲
Speed Reporter '36
Spice World: The Movie '97
Star Reporter '39
State of Play '03▲
Stavisky '74▲
Stay Tuned for Murder '88
Stephen King's The Night Flier '96
The Story of G.I. Joe '45▲
Straight Talk '92
The Strange Love of Molly Louvain '32
Stranger on the Third Floor '40▲
Street Smart '87
Sucker Money '34
Superman: The Movie '78▲
Sweet Rosie O'Grady 43
Sweet Smell of Success '57▲
Sweetwater: A True Rock Story '99
Switching Channels '88
Tainted Blood '93
Tarnished Angels '57▲
Teacher's Pet '58▲
Texas Lady '56
That Certain Age '38
That Lucky Touch 75
The Theory of the Leisure Class '01
They All Kissed the Bride '42
They Got Me Covered '43
The Thin Blue Lie '00
Things Behind the Sun '01
The Thirteenth Man '37
Thirteenth Reunion '81
Those Glory, Glory Days '83
Three Kings '99▲
Three o'Clock High '87
Tomorrow at Seven '33
Too Hot to Handle '38▲
Tough Assignment '49
Tower of Terror '97
Trahir '93▲
Transylvania 6-5000 '85
Traps '93
True Crime 99
27 Dresses '08
Under Fire '83▲
Under Heavy Fire '01
Underworld Scandal '47
The Underworld Story '50
Unexplained Laughter '89
Universal Soldier 2: Brothers in Arms '98
Universal Soldier 3: Unfinished Business '98
Up in Central Park '48
Up to a Certain Point '83
Up Your Alley '89
Velvet Goldmine '98
Veronica Guerin '03
Virgin Machine 88
Wedding Present '36
Welcome to Sarajevo '97▲
The Wharf Rat '95
Where the Sky Falls '99
Where the Buffalo Roam '80
While the City Sleeps '56▲
Whispering City '47▲
White Badge '92
The White Raven '98
Winchell '98
Without Love '80
Woman Condemned '33
Woman of the Year '42▲
A World Apart '88▲
The World Gone Mad '33
The Year of Living Dangerously '82▲

Fugitives

see also Escaped Cons; *Lovers on the Lam*

Agent on Ice '86
Bad Girls '94
Bail Jumper '89
Ball of Fire '41▲
Ballad of Gregorio Cortez '83▲
Bandits of Orgosolo '61
Bed & Breakfast '92
The Big Fix 78▲
Bloodfist 7: Manhunt '95

▲ = *rated three bones or higher*

(continued)

Bobbie Jo and the Outlaw '76
The Boldest Job in the West '71
A Boy Called Hate '95
Boys on the Side '94
Brannigan '75
Breathless '83
Bushwhacked '95
Butch and Sundance: The Early Days '79
Butch Cassidy and the Sundance Kid '69▶
Cadillac Ranch '96
Captured in Chinatown '35
The Chase '91
Chain Reaction '96
Clyde '93
Connie and Carla '04
Cyber-Tracker 2 '95
Danger: Diabolik '68
Dead Easy '82
The Deserters '83
Desperate '47
Desperate Measures '98
The Desperate Trail '94
Dogville '03
Eddie Macon's Run '83
Eight on the Lam '67
The Escape '95
Escape 2000 '81
Father Hood '93
Fled '96
Frank and Jesse '94
Free Grass '69
The Fugitive '93▶
Fugitive Among Us '92
Good Girls Don't '95
The Great Texas Dynamite Chase '76
Gridlock'd '96▶
Hard Knocks '80
Hiding Out '87
Hold Me, Thrill Me, Kiss Me '93
Hollow Point '95
I Died a Thousand Times '55
I Met a Murderer '39
In the Middle o' Nowhere '93
The Jesus Trip '71
Jungle Inferno '72
Keeping Track '86
Kiss of Death '47▶
Klondike Annie '36
La Vie Promise '02
Le Doulos '61▶
Leather Jackets '90
Liberators '65
Loners '72
Long Pants '27
The Love Flower '20
The Man Upstairs '93
Marked Man '96
Miami Cops '89
Miles from Home '88
Minority Report '02
Moving Target '89
Moving Violation '76
North by Northwest '59▶
Northwest Trail '46
Nowhere to Hide '83
On the Run '73
One Away '76
The Outlaw and His Wife '17
Outlaw Riders '72
Paris Express '53
A Perfect World '93▶
Posse '93▶
The Pursuit of D.B. Cooper '81
The Quarry '98
The Red Half-Breed '70
Rider on the Rain '70▶
Rough Cut '80
The Savage Woman '91
Scorpion Spring '96
Sea Devils '37
The Second Awakening of Christa Klages '75
The Secret Agent '96
Shallow Grave '87
Shoot to Kill '88▶
Simple Men '92
The Simpsons Movie '07▶
Slate, Wyn & Me '87
Sonny and Jed '73
The Spy Within '94
The Statement '03
Storm Catcher '99
Stray Dog '49▶
Strike Back '80
Suspect Device '95
Teenage Bonnie & Klepto Clyde '93
Three Days of the Condor '75▶
Three Fugitives '89
Three Strikes '00
Thunder County '74
Truth or Consequences, N.M. '97
Twilight Man '96
U.S. Marshals '98
The Walls of Malapaga '49
The Way Out '56
Woman with a Past '92
The Wrong Guy '96
The Wrong Man '93
Wrongfully Accused '98

Funerals
see also Death & the Afterlife

About Schmidt '02▶
The Addams Family '91
The Adventures of Ford Fairlane '90
Big Chill '83▶
Big Eden '00
Big Shot's Funeral '01
Blackwater Trail '95
Bonneville '06
The Business of Fancydancing '02
The Camomile Lawn '92
Catch and Release '07
City Hall '95▶
Crazy Eights '06
The Crow: Road '96
Cruel Intentions '99
A Death in the Family '07
Death at a Funeral '07
Dangerous Ground '96
Elizabethtown '05
Erskinville Kings '99
Eulogy '04
The Evening Star '96
Falling '06
Final Cut '98
First Knight '95
The Flamingo Rising '01
Four Brothers '05
Four Sheets to the Wind '07
Four Weddings and a Funeral '94▶
Full Count '06
Funeral Home '82
Gardens of Stone '87
Go for Zucker '05
Grand Theft Parsons '03
Guantanamera '95▶
The Guys '02▶
Harold and Maude '71▶
Hearts in Atlantis '01
Heathers '89▶
High Fidelity '00▶
Himalaya '99▶
Hope Floats '98
The House of Usher '06
I Love You, Alice B. Toklas! '68
I'll Bury You Tomorrow '02
Infested: Invasion of the Killer Bugs '02
Jack and Sarah '95
Kingdom Come '01
Kissed '96
La Buche '00
Last Orders '01▶
Lawless Heart '01
Louder than Bombs '01
The Loved One '65
Malicious Intent '99
Men with Brooms '02▶
Mr. Saturday Night '92
Moonlight Mile '02▶
My Girl '91
My Girl 2 '94
One Night Stand '97▶
Only the Lonely '91
Orphans '97
The Pallbearer '95
Premonition '07
The Queen '06▶
Red, White & Busted '75
Reservation Road '07
The Road Home '01▶
Roommates '95
Rupert's Land '98
Saving Sarah Cain '07
Simon Birch '98
Sleepless in Seattle '93▶
Snow Cake '06
Sordid Lives '00
Steel Magnolias '89▶
Terms of Endearment '83▶
A Texas Funeral '99
Things We Lost in the Fire '07
Those Who Love Me Can Take the Train '98
The Three Burials of Melquiades Estrada '05▶
Till Human Voices Wake Us '02
Tom and Huck '95▶
24-7 '97
Tyler Perry's Meet the Browns '08
Under Hellgate Bridge '99
Walking on Water '02
Wes Craven Presents: They '02
What's Eating Gilbert Grape '93▶
The Wings of the Dove '97▶
The Winter Guest '97▶

Funny Money
see also Crime Drama; Disorganized Crime; Organized Crime

Bad Men of the Border '45
Beverly Hills Cop 3 '94
The Castle of Cagliostro '80
The Clay Pigeon '49
The Counterfeiters '07▶
Fighting Caballero '35
Honeymoon Academy '90
The In-Laws '79▶
Kounterfeit '96
Lethal Weapon 4 '98
Luck of the Draw '00
The Magician '93
Murder on the Yukon '40
Naked Lies '98
Paradise Canyon '35
Phantom Ranger '38
Playing God '96
Renfrew of the Royal Mounted '37
Rush Hour '01
Spy Smasher '42
T-Men '47▶
To Live & Die in L.A. '85▶
Wolfen '81▶

Future Cop
see also Cops

Apprentice to Murder '88
The Believers '87
Demolition Man '93
The Dying Truth '91
The Fifth Element '97
The First Power '89
God Told Me To '76
I, Robot '04
The Last Sentinel '07
Maniac Cop '88
Maniac Cop 2 '90
Maniac Cop 3: Badge of Silence '93
Minority Report '02▶
RoboCop '87▶
RoboCop 2 '90
RoboCop 3 '93
Rush Hour 2 '01
Split Second '92
Timecop '94▶

Future Shock
see also Post-Apocalypse; Time Travel; Time

A.I.: Artificial Intelligence '01▶
Aeon Flux '05
Austin Powers: International Man of Mystery '97▶
Back to the Future, Part 2 '89
Bicentennial Man '99
Bill & Ted's Excellent Adventure '89▶
Children of Men '06▶
The Deal '05
Doomsday '08
Forever Young '92
The Fountain '06
Ghostwarrior '86
Idiocracy '06
Immortal '04
Just Visiting '01
Late for Dinner '91
Minority Report '02▶
Planet of the Apes '68▶
The Postman '97
Renaissance '06
A Sound of Thunder '05
Sleeper '73▶
Ultraviolet '06
The Visitors '95

Gambling
see also Viva Las Vegas!

Action for Slander '38
Alex & Emma '03
Alibi Ike '35
All in '06
All or Nothing at All '63
Any Number Can Play '49
Any Number Can Win '63
Atlantic City '81▶
Barry Lyndon '75▶
Big Shot: Confessions of a Campus Bookie '02
Big Town '87
A Billion for Boris '90
Birds & the Bees '56
Bitter Sweet '33
Bitter Sweet '40
Bob le Flambeur '55▶
Bookies '03
The Boys '97
Buffalo 66 '97▶
Bugsy '91▶
Caddyshack '80▶
Canyon Passage '46▶
Casino '80
Casino '80
Casino Royale '06▶
Cassandra's Dream '07
Catch Me... If You Can '89
Catherine Cookson's The Gambling Man '98
Charlie Chan at Monte Carlo '37
Charlie Chan at the Race Track '36
The Cheaters '76
Circus '00
Cockfighter '74▶
The Color of Money '86▶
The Cooler '03▶
Cro-upier '97▶
The Dark Dealer '95
Dead Heat '01
Deadly Impact '84
The Debt '98
The Devil '97
Diamonds Are Forever '71▶
Diggstown '92
Dinner Rush '00▶
Dona Flor and Her Two Husbands '78▶
Double Down '01
Double Dynamite '51
Draw! '81
The Duchess and the Dirtwater Fox '76
Easy Money '83
Eight Men Out '88▶
Even Money '06
Eyes of an Angel '91
Family Prayers '91
Fever Pitch '85
A Fine Mess '86
Firepower '93
Five Card Stud '68
Flame of the Barbary Coast '45
Flame of the Islands '55
The Flamingo Kid '84▶
Force of Evil '49▶
Four Rooms '95
Frankie and Johnny '65
The Gamble '88
Gamble on Love '86
The Gambler '74▶
The Gambler '97
The Gambler & the Lady '52
Gambling Ship '33
Get Shorty '95▶
Gilda '46▶
Glory Years '87
Golden Rendezvous '77
The Good Thief '03▶
The Great Mike '44
The Great Sinner '49
Gun Crazy '69
Guys and Dolls '55▶
Half a Lifetime '86
Hard Eight '96▶
Hardball '01
The Harder They Fall '56▶
Heat '95▶
Heaven '99
Hell's Angels '69
Here Come the Marines '52
Hi-Life '98
Hoodlum '96
Household Saints '93▶
Huck and the King of Hearts '93
Hustle '04
The Hustler '61▶
In Like Flint '67
Indecent Proposal '93
Inn of Temptation '73
Inside Out '91
Intacto '01▶
Jinxed '82
Lady 'o' a Night '42
Lady from Louisiana '42
Las Vegas Hillbillys '66
Las Vegas Lady '76
The Las Vegas Story '52
Las Vegas Weekend '85
Le Million '31▶
The Lemon Drop Kid '51
Let It Ride '89
Let's Do It Again '75
Let's Make It Legal '51
Liberty Heights '99
Little Miss Marker '34▶
Little Miss Marker '80
Little Vegas '90
Living to Die '91
Lock, Stock and 2 Smoking Barrels '98▶
Lookin' to Get Out '82
Lost in America '85▶
Lucky You '07
Luckytown '00
Manhattan Melodrama '34▶
The Marrying Man '91
Maverick '94▶
McCabe & Mrs. Miller '71▶
McHale's Navy '64
Mean Machine '01
Meet Me in Las Vegas '56
Michael Clayton '07▶
Michael Shayne: Private Detective '40
Mickey One '65
Money Kings '98
Money Train '95
Monte Carlo '30
Mother and Son '31
Mr. Lucky '43▶
Mr. Muggs Rides Again '45
Murderers' Row '66
My Blueberry Nights '07
My Darling Clementine '46▶
My Little Chickadee '40▶
Ninja, the Violent Sorcerer '86
No Man of Her Own '32
Ocean's Eleven '01▶
Ocean's Thirteen '07▶
Oklahoma Kid '39▶
One Last Ride '03
One Tough Cop '98
Order to Kill '73
Oscar and Lucinda '97
Our Man Flint '66
Out to Sea '97
Owning Mahowny '03
Paradise Island '30
Phoenix '98
Pink Cadillac '89
Players '03
Pleasure Palace '80
Poker Alice '87
Poolhall Junkies '02▶
The Queen of Spades '49▶
Quintet '79
Rain Man '88▶
Rat Race '01
Riders of the Range '50
Rimfire '49
The Ringer '05
Roaring City '51
The Roaring Twenties '39▶
Robbery '85
Robin-B-Hood '06
The Rocking Horse Winner '49
Ruggles of Red Gap '35▶
The Runner '99
Say Yes! '86
Sgt. Bilko '96
Shade '03
The Shanghai Gesture '42
The Shadow Man '53
Shoot '76
Showgirls '95
Silver Queen '42
Sno-Line '85
Song of the Thin Man '47
Sorrowful Jones '49
Sour Grapes '98
Spent '00
The Squeeze '87
Stacy's Knights '83
Stickmen '01
The Sting '73▶
Strike It Rich '90
Support Your Local Sheriff '69▶
Swing Time '36▶
The Tailor of Panama '00▶
Tall Story '60
Talons of the Eagle '92
Tax Season '90
Taxi Dancers '93
Ten Benny '96
Tennessee's Partner '55
Thief '71
Things Change '88▶
This Is a Hijack '73
Thoroughbreds Don't Cry '37
Three Men on a Horse '36▶
3000 Miles to Graceland '01
Tomcats '01
Trading Places '83▶
21 '08
Two for the Money '05
29th Street '91
The Underneath '95
Uphill All the Way '85
Uptown Saturday Night '74
The Vegas Strip Wars '84
Vegas Vacation '96
Walking Tall '73▶
Welcome to 18 '87
The Westerner '40▶
Wheel of Fortune '41
Who's Got the Action? '63
The Winner '96
Wise Guys '86

Game Shows

Champagne for Caesar '50▶
The Computer Wore Tennis Shoes '69
Confessions of a Dangerous Mind '02
Deathrow Gameshow '88
Everything You Always Wanted to Know about Sex (But Were Afraid to Ask) '72

▶ = rated three bones or higher

Game

For Love or Money '84
Groundhog Day '93▶
The Low Down '00
Mallrats '95
National Lampoon's European Vacation '85
Prize of Peril '84
Queen for a Day '51
Quiz Show '94▶
Reckless '95
The Running Man '87
Shock Treatment '81
Starter for Ten '06
White Men Can't Jump '92

Gangs

see also Juvenile Delinquents; Moscow Mafia; Organized Crime; Urban Gangstas

Abduction of St. Anne '75
Alien Private Eye '87
All Dogs Go to Heaven '89
Alley Cat '84
Alvin Rides Again '74
American Me '92▶
Angel Town '89
Angels Die Hard '84
Apache Woman '55
Assault on Precinct 13 '76▶
Baby Face Morgan '42
Bad Guys '79
Ballbuster '89
Behave Yourself! '52
Bells of Death '90
Belly '98
A Better Tomorrow, Part 1 '86
A Better Tomorrow, Part 2 '88
Beyond the Law '92
Big Bad Mama '74
Big Bad Mama 2 '87
The Big Brawl '80
Black Bikers from Hell '70
Black Caesar '73
The Black Cobra '87
Black Gestapo '75
Blood In ... Blood Out: Bound by Honor '93
Bloody Mama '70
Blue '68
Blues Busters '50
Bonnie & Clyde '67▶
Borderline '50
Boricua's Bond '00
Borsalino '70▶
Boss of Big Town '43
Boulevard Nights '79
Bowery Blitzkrieg '41
Boyz N the Hood '91▶
Breaking Loose '90
Bring Me the Head of Alfredo Garcia '74
Broadway Danny Rose '84▶
The Bronx War '90
Brother Orchid '40▶
Buckeye and Blue '87
Buddy Buddy '81
Bulldog Drummond's Bride '39
Bulldog Edition '36
Bulldog Jack '35▶
Bullet '94
Bullets or Ballots '38▶
Cartouche '62▶
C.C. & Company '70
Chains '89
Chains of Gold '92
The Chase '46
China '87
China O'Brien '88
Chrome and Hot Leather '71
City of God '02
City of Men '07▶
Class of 1984 '82
Class of 1999 '90
Class of 1999 2: The Substitute '93
Clipped Wings '53
Coach Carter '05▶
Code of Silence '85
Commando Squad '87
The Concentratin' Kid '30

Confidential '35
Contraband '86
Cookie '89
The Cool World '63
Cop in Blue Jeans '78
Corruption '70
Cosh Boy '61
The Cross & the Switchblade '72
The Crow: Wicked Prayer '05
Cruisin' High '75
Cry-Baby '90▶
Cry of a Prostitute: Love Kills '72
Cry Terror '76
Danger Zone '87
Danger Zone 2 '89
Dangerous Ground '96
Dangerous Mission '54
Dark Rider '91
Darktown Strutters '74
The Day It Came to Earth '77
Dead End City '88
Deadly Encounter '72▶
Deadly Revenge '83
Dear Wendy '05
Death Sentence '07
Defiance '79
Defiant '70
Delta Fox '77
Designing Woman '57▶
Deuces Wild '02
Devil's Angels '67
Dick Tracy vs. Cueball '46
Dillinger '45▶
Dillinger '73
Dirt Gang '71
Dirty '05
Dirty Laundry '87
Disorganized Crime '89
Diva '82▶
The Divine Enforcer '91
Dixie Jamboree '44
The Doberman Gang '72
The Dog Who Stopped the War '84
The Don Is Dead '73
Each Dawn I Die '39
East L.A. Warriors '89
East Side Kids '40
The Education of Sonny Carson '74
Emil and the Detectives '64
Enemy Territory '87
The Enforcer '51
The Enforcer '76
Escape from L.A. '96
Escape from the Bronx '85
Every Which Way But Loose '78
Exterminator '80
Eye of the Tiger '86
Fear in the City '81
Fight Club: '99▶
The Final Alliance '89
Foolish '99
Forced Vengeance '82
Forever, Lulu '87
Four Jacks and a Jill '41
Foxy Brown '74
Full Eclipse '93
"G" Men '35▶
The Gambler & the Lady '52
Gambler's Choice '44
Game of Death '79
Gang Boys '97
Gang Busters '38
Gang Bullets '42
Gang Justice '94
Gang Wars '75
Gangs of New York '02▶
The Gangster '47
Gangster Wars '81
Gangway '37
Ghetto Blaster '89
The Ghost and the Guest '43
Ghost Chasers '51
Gimme Shelter '70
The Glory Stompers '67
Golden Lady '79
Gone Are the Days '84
Goodfellas '90▶
The Great Mike '44

The Great Skycopter Rescue '82
Green Street Hooligans '05▶
The Grissom Gang '71▶
The Gumshoe Kid '89
Gun Girls '56
The Gunrunner '84
Guns Don't Argue '57
Hard As Nails '07
Hard-Boiled Mahoney '47
Hard Lessons '86
Harley '90
Hawk's Vengeance '96
Heartbreaker '83
Heat Street '87
Hell on Frisco Bay '55
Hellcats '68
High Ballin' '78
High Sierra '41▶
Hitz '89
Homeboy '75
Homeboys '92
Hoodlum Empire '52
I Died a Thousand Times '55
I, Mobster '58
I'd Give My Life '36
Illtown '96
Impulse '55
Inside the Law '42
Jinxed '82
Johnny Apollo '40
Johnny Dangerously '84
Jungleground '95
Just William's Luck '47
Key Largo '48▶
Killer Dill '47
Knights of the City '85
Kung Fu Hustle '04▶
L.A. Bad '85
La Balance '82▶
L.A. Gangs Rising '89
Lady from Nowhere '36
Lady in a Cage '64▶
Lady in Red '79
Last Fight to Hell '91
Last Man Standing '96
The Last Ride of the Dalton Gang '79
The Last Riders '90
Latin Dragon '03
Law of the Underworld '38
Leather Jackets '90
Lepke '75
Lethal Games '90
Lethal Obsession '87
Like a Puppet Out of Strings '05
Little Dragons '80
Little Laura & Big John '73
The Lost Capone '90▶
Love Me or Leave Me '55▶
Lucky Luciano '74
Ma Barker's Killer Brood '60
Machine Gun Kelly '58
Manhattan Merry-Go-Round '37
Marie Baie des Anges '97
Marked Woman '37▶
Marshal Law '96
The Masters of Menace '90
Master's Revenge '71
The Maverick Queen '55
Meet the Mob '42
Men of Respect '91
Menace II Society '93▶
The Meteor Man '93
Mi Vida Loca '94
Midnight '34
Million Dollar Kid '44
Miracle in Harlem '48
Mr. Majestyk '74
Mob Boss '90
Mob Story '90
Mob War '88
Motorcycle Squad '41
Murda Muzik '03
My Samurai '92
Mystery Date '91
The Naked Angels '69
Nashville Beat '89
'Neath Brooklyn Bridge '42
Ned Kelly '03
The Neon Empire '89
Never a Dull Moment '68
Never Let Go '60
Never Love a Stranger '58

The New Kids '85
99 & 44/100 Dead '74
Ninja Brothers of Blood '89
No Trace '50
The Noose Hangs High '48▶
Omega Man '96
One Man's Justice '95
Original Gangstas '96
The Outsiders '83
Paco '75
Paradise in Harlem '40
Parole, Inc. '49
The Payoff '43
Peacekillers '71
Performance '70▶
Petrified Forest '36▶
Pickup on South Street '53▶
Pierrot le Fou '65▶
Play Murder for Me '91
The Power of the Ninjitsu '88
Prayer of the Rollerboys '91
Prime Cut '72
The Prime Time '60
The Principal '87
Prize Fighter '79
Pulp '72
Punk Vacation '90
The Purifiers '04
Quatorze Juillet '32
The Racket '51▶
The Racketeer '29
Rapid Fire '92
The Reading Room '05
Renegades '89
Return of the Dragon '73
Return of the Rebels '81
Return of the Tiger '78
Revenge '90
Revenge of the Ninja '83
Ricochet '91▶
Riot Squad '41
The Rise and Fall of Legs Diamond '60
The Ritz '76▶
Rooftops '89
Rumble Fish '83▶
Rumble in the Bronx '96
Running Woman '98
Satan's Sadists '69
Scared Stiff '53▶
Scarface '83▶
The Sea Serpent '85
Second Chance '53
The Second Chance '06
The Set-Up '49▶
Sexton Blake and the Hooded Terror '38
Shaft '71▶
She's Back '88
Shining Star '75
Shoot the Piano Player '62▶
Showdown '73
Sidewalks of New York '31
16 Years of Alcohol '03
Slam '98
Small Faces '95▶
Smart Alecks '42
SnakeEater 3: His Law '92
Sno-Line '85
Some Like It Hot '59▶
South Central '92
Speedy '28▶
Spike of Bensonhurst '88
Splinter '06
Spook Busters '48
Star Reporter '39
Stavisky '74▶
Steel '97
Sticky Fingers '88
Stingray '78
Stone Cold '91
Straight Line '88
Street Corner Justice '96
Street Crimes '92
Street Hitz '92
The Street King '02
Street Knight '93
Street Soldiers '91
Street Warriors '87
Street Warriors, Part 2 '87
The Street with No Name '48▶
The Streets of L.A. '79
Stryker '04
The Substitute '96
Sucker Free City '05▶

Sunnyside '79
The Sun's Burial '60▶
Switchblade Sisters '75
T-Bird Gang '59
Teenage Doll '57
Teenage Gang Debs '66
Teenage Wolfpack '57
Thicker than Water '99
This Time I'll Make You Rich '75
Three Strikes '00
Timber Queen '44
The Tin Soldier '95
The Tip-Off '31
Tongs: An American Nightmare '88
Too Late for Tears '49▶
Topaze '51▶
Torque '04
Tough Assignment '49
Tough Enough '83
Tough to Handle '37
Tropical Snow '88
True Believer '89
True Blood '89
Truck Stop Women '74
Two to Tango '88
The Underground '97
Underground Terror '88
The Underworld Story '50
Urban Crossfire '94
Vengeance '94
Verne Miller '88
Vietnam, Texas '90
Violent Professionals '73
The Violent Years '56
The Virginia Hill Story '76
Waist Deep '06
Wanderers '79▶
The Warriors '79▶
West Side Story '61▶
When Gangland Strikes '56
The Wild One '54▶
Wilding '90
Wonder Man '45▶
Wonderland '88▶
The Wrecking Crew '99
The Wrong Arm of the Law '63▶
Year of the Dragon '85
The Young Savages '61
Young Warriors '83
Zooman '95▶

Gays

see also Bisexuality; Gender Bending; Lesbians

Abuse '82
Adam & Steve '05
The Adventures of Felix '99
AKA '02
Alive and Kicking '96
All Over the Guy '01
Amazing Grace '92
American Fabulous '99▶
American Fabulous '92
Amor de Hombre '97
Anatomy of Hell '04
Angel '82
Angels in America '03▶
Another Country '84
Apart from Hugh '94
Arabian Nights '74▶
Armistead Maupin's More Tales of the City '97
Armistead Maupin's Tales of the City '93
As Good As It Gets '97▶
As Is '85
B. Monkey '97
Bad Education '04▶
Bam Bam & Celeste '05▶
Be Cool '05
Beautiful Thing '95▶
Bedrooms and Hallways '98
Before Night Falls '00▶
Behind the Red Door '02
Beloved/Friend '99
Bent '97
The Best Way '76
The Big Brass Ring '99

Big Eden '00
The Big Tease '99
Billy's Hollywood Screen Kiss '98
The Birdcage '95▶
Blast from the Past '98
Blue '93
Boat Trip '03
Boondock Saints '99
Borstal Boy '00
Boy Culture '06
Boyfriends '96
Boys in Love '95
The Boys in the Band '70
Boys Life '90
Breaking the Code '95
Breaking the Surface: The Greg Louganis Story '96
Broadway Damage '98
Brokeback Mountain '05▶
'00▶
Brother to Brother '04
The Bubble '06
Burnt Money '00
The Business of Fancydancing '02
B.U.S.T.E.D. '99
Cabaret '72▶
Cambridge Spies '03
Camp '03
Carandiru '03
Caresses '97
Carrington '95
The Celluloid Closet '95▶
Children of Hannibal '98
Chuck & Buck '00▶
Circuit '02
City in Panic '86
Close to Leo '02
The Closet '00
Coffee Date '06
Colonel Redl '84▶
Color Me Kubrick '05
Come Undone '00
Coming Out '89
Common Ground '00
The Conformist '71▶
Connie and Carla '04
The Conrad Boys '06
Consenting Adult '85
Cote d'Azur '05
Cowboys and Angels '00
Cowboys & Angels '04▶
Cracker: Best Boys '95▶
Creatures from the Pink Lagoon '07
Crocodile Tears '98
Cruel Intentions '98
Cruising '80
The Crying Game '92▶
Curse of the Queerwolf '87
David Searching '97
Days '04
De-Lovely '04
Dear Boys '80
Death in Venice '71▶
D.E.B.S. '04
The Deep End '01▶
Defying Gravity '99
The Delta '97
The Detective '68▶
Die Mommie Die! '03
Different Story '78
Dirty Laundry '07
A Dirty Shame '04
Dog Gone Love '03
Doing Time on Maple Drive '92
Dress Gray '86▶
Drift '00
Drifting '82
The Dying Gaul '05▶
An Early Frost '85▶
East Palace, West Palace '96
Eating Out '04
Eating Out 2: Sloppy Seconds '06
Eban and Charley '01
Eclipse '94
Edge of Seventeen '99
Edward II '92
El Diputado '78▶
The Embalmer '03▶
An Empty Bed '90▶
Enduring Love '04
Entertaining Mr. Sloane '70

▶ = rated three bones or higher

Ernesto '79
The Event '03
The Everlasting Secret
Family '88
Execution of Justice '99
Facing Windows '03
Far from Heaven '02
Finding North '97
First Love and Other Pains /
One of Them '99
Fleeing by Night '00
Flipping '96
Flirt '95
Floating '97
The Flutter '01
Food of Love '02
For a Lost Soldier '93
Forbidden Passion: The
Oscar Wilde Movie '85
Forgive and Forget '99
Formula 17 '04
Fortune and Men's Eyes '71
Four Weddings and a
Funeral '94▶
Fox and His Friends '75▶
Frank McKlusky, C.I. '02
Friends and Family '01
Friends & Lovers '99
Frisk '95
Full Speed '96
Fun Down There '88
The Garden '90
The Gay Deceivers '69
Get Real '99
Go Fish '94▶
Go West '05
Gods and Monsters '99▶
Goodbye, Dragon Inn '03
Gorgeous '99
The Graffiti Artist '04
Green Plaid Shirt '95
Grief '94
Guys and Balls '04
The Hanging Garden '97
Happy, Texas '99▶
Happy Endings '05
Happy Together '96
Hard Pill '05
Harry and Max '04
Hate Crime '05
Head On '98▶
Hearing Voices '90
Heaven's a Drag '94
Heights '04
Her and She and Him '69
His Secret Life '01▶
The History Boys '06
Hit and Runway '01
Hollow Reed '95▶
A Home at the End of the
World '04
Home for the Holidays '95
The Hours '02▶
The Hours and Times '92▶
Hustler White '96
I Can't Sleep '93
I Love You Baby '01
I Now Pronounce You
Chuck and Larry '07
I Think I Do '97
Ice Men '04
If You Only Knew '00
Illuminata '98
In and Out '97▶
In the Flesh '97
Infamous '06
It's My Party '95
It's the Rage '99
Jeffrey '95
Joey Breaker '93▶
The Journey of Jared Price
'00
Just One Time '70
Killers Park '05
Killer Condom '95
Kiss Me, Guido '97
Kiss Kiss Bang Bang '05▶
Kiss of the Spicer Woman
'85▶
Km. 0 '00
La Cage aux Folles '78▶
La Cage aux Folles 2 '81
La Cage aux Folles 3: The
Wedding '86
Lan Yu '01
The Laramie Project '02▶

Last Days '05
Latter Days '04
Lawless Heart '01
The Leather Boys '63
Leather Jacket Love Story
'98
Leaving Metropolis '02
Les Nuits Fauves '92▶
L'Escorte '96
L'Homme Blesse '83▶
L.I.E. '01
Lie Down with Dogs '95
Like a Brother '05
Like It Is '98▶
Like It Never Was Before
'95
Lilies '96
The Line of Beauty '06
Lisa Picard Is Famous '01
Little Miss Sunshine '06▶
The Living End '92
Loggerheads '05▶
Lola and Billy the Kid '98
Long-Term Relationship '06
Longtime Companion '90▶
The Lost Language of
Cranes '92▶
Love and Death on Long
Island '97
Love and Human Remains
'93▶
Love Is the Devil '98▶
Love Kills '98
Lovel Valour! Compassion!
'96
Ludwig '72
Luminarias '99
Luster '02
Madagascar Skin '95
Madame Sata '02
Making Love '82
Mambo Italiano '03
The Man I Love '97
The Man of My Life '06
A Man of No Importance
'94▶
Maurice '87▶
Maybe... Maybe Not '94▶
Men in Love '90
Men Men Men '95
Menage '86▶
Merci Docteur Rey '04▶
Meteor & Shadow '85
The Mexican '01
Midnight Cowboy '69▶
Midnight Dancers '94
Midnight in the Garden of
Good and Evil '97
Mouth to Mouth '95
The Mudge Boy '03
The Music Lovers '71
My Beautiful Laundrette
'86▶
My Best Friend's Wedding
'97
My Father Is Coming '91
My Own Private Idaho '91▶
Mysterious Skin '04▶
The Naked Civil Servant
'75▶
Naked Lunch '91▶
Nerolo '96
Never Met Picasso '96
The Next Best Thing '00
Next Year in Jerusalem '98
Nico and Dani '01
The Night Listener '06
Nighthawks '78
Nijinsky '80
No One Sleeps '01
Norman, Is That You? '76
Nowhere '96
Nowhere in Sight '00
O Fantasma '00
The Object of My Affection
'98
Okoge '93
Open Cam '05
The Opposite of Sex '98
Ordinary Sinner '02
Other Voices, Other Rooms
'95
Our Lady of the Assassins
'01
Our Sons '91
Outing Riley '04
The Painted Lady '97▶
Parallel Sons '95
Paris Is Burning '91▶

Parting Glances '86▶
Partners '82
Pedale Douce '96
Perfume '01
The Perfect Son '00
Philadelphia '93▶
The Pillow Book '95
Possible Loves '00▶
Postcards from America '95
Prick Up Your Ears '87▶
Priest '94
P.S. Your Cat is Dead! '02
Queer Duck: The Movie '06
Querelle '83
Quinceanera '06▶
Quiet Days in Hollywood '97
Raising Heroes '97
Ready to Wear '94
The Reception '05
Red Dirt '99
Reflections in a Golden Eye
'67
Regular Guys '96
Relax... It's Just Sex! '98
Rent '05
Rites of Passage '99
The Ritz '76▶
A River Made to Drown In
'97
Rock Haven '07
Rock Hudson's Home
Movies '92
The Rocky Horror Picture
Show '75▶
Rope '48▶
Rude '96
Sand and Blood '87
Satan's Brew '76
Saved! '04
Say Uncle '05
The Sculptress '97
Second Best '05
Second Skin '99
Sebastian '76
Seducing Maarya '02
Sergeant Matlovich vs. the
U.S. Air Force '78
Shock to the System '06
Sitcom '97
Smoke '93
Sordid Lives '00
Speedway Junky '99
Spent '00
Spring Forward '99
The Sprinter '84
The State Within '06
Steam: A Turkish Bath '96▶
Stonewall '95▶
Straight for the Heart '88
Strange Bedfellows '04
Strange Fits of Passion '99
Strange Fruit '04
Strawberry and Chocolate
'93▶
The Sum of Us '94▶
Sunday, Bloody Sunday
'71▶
Surveillance 24/7 '07
Sweet November '01
Swoon '91▶
Taboo '99
The Talented Mr. Ripley '99
Tarnation '03
Taxi zum Klo '81▶
Testosterone '03
These Foolish Things '06
Third Man Out: A Donald
Strachey Mystery '05
This Special Friendship '67
Three to Tango '99
Threesome '94
Tidy Endings '88
Time to Leave '05▶
Times Have Been Better '05
Times of Harvey Milk '83▶
To Forget Venice '79
To Play or to Die '91
The Toilers and the
Wayfarers '97
Tomcats '01

Transamerica '05▶
Trick '99▶
The Trio '97
The Trip '02
Tropical Malady '04
The 24th Day '04
29th & Gay '05
24 Nights '99
The Twilight of the Golds '97
Twist '03▶
Twisted '96
Unconditional Love '03
Under One Roof '02
Urbania '00
Very Annie Mary '00
A Very Natural Thing '73
A Very Serious Person '06
Victim '61▶
Via Appia '92
Victor/Victoria '82▶
Visions of Sugarplums '99
Viva l'Amour '94
The Walker '07
Walking on Water '02
Water Drops on Burning
Rocks '99
We Think the World of You
'88▶
Wedding Wars '06
The Weekend '00
Wester, East of the Wall '85
When Love Comes '98
Whole New Thing '05
Wild Reeds '94▶
Wild Tigers I Have Known
'06
Wilde '97
Withnail and I '87▶
Wittgenstein '93
The Wolves of Kromer '98
Wonderland '98
World and Time Enough '95
A Year Without Love '05
Yossi & Jagger '02
You'll Get Over It '02
Zero Patience '94
Zus & Zo '01

Gender Bending
see also Gays; Lesbians;
Role Reversal
Abroad with Two Yanks '44
The Adventures of Priscilla,
Queen of the Desert '94▶
The Adventures of
Sebastian Cole '99
All About My Mother '99▶
All the Queen's Men '02
Angel '82
Anything for Love '93
At War with the Army '50
Auntie '73
The Badge '02
The Ballad of Little Jo '93
Better Than Chocolate '99
Blue Murder at St. Trinian's
'56▶
Boy! What a Girl '45
Connie and Carla '04
The Crying Game '92▶
The Damned '69
Desperate Living '77
Different for Girls '96▶
Divine '90
Dr. Jekyll and Ms. Hyde '95
Dressed to Kill '80
Ed Wood '94▶
First a Girl '35
Flawless '99
Forever Mary '89▶
Gaudi Afternoon '01
Glen or Glenda? '53
Go West '05
Hairspray '88▶
Happily Ever After '86
Hedwig and the Angry Inch
'00▶
Her Life as a Man '83
He's My Girl '87
Holiday Heart '00
I Like It Like That '94▶
I Shot Andy Warhol '96▶
I Wanna Be a Beauty
Queen '65
I Want What I Want '72
I Was a Male War Bride '49▶

In a Year of 13 Moons '78
It's Pat: The Movie '94
Just Like a Woman '95
Just One of the Girls '93
Just One of the Guys '85
Kill Your Darlings '06
Kinky Boots '06
La Cage aux Folles '78▶
La Cage aux Folles 2 '81
La Cage aux Folles 3: The
Wedding '86
Law of Desire '86▶
Le Sexe des Etoiles '93
Lilies '96
Lola and Billy the Kid '98
Lust in the Dust '85▶
Ma Vie en Rose '97▶
Madame Sata '02
Mascara '87
The Merchant of Venice
'04▶
Mrs. Doubtfire '93
Mr. Headmistress '98
The Newlydeads '87
Nobody's Perfect '90
Normal '03
Nowhere '96
Nuns on the Run '90
Old Mother Riley's Ghosts
'41
Outrageous! '77
Paris Is Burning '91▶
Pink Flamingos '72
Polyester '81
Psycho '60▶
The Rocky Horror Picture
Show '75▶
Shadey '87
She's the Man '05
The Silence of the Lambs
'91▶
Skin Deep '94
So This Is Africa '33
Soldier's Girl '03▶
Some Like It Hot '59▶
Sonny Boy '87
Sorority Boys '02
Stonewall '95▶
Surrender Dorothy '98
Switch '91▶
Those Who Love Me Can
Take the Train '98
Tipping the Velvet '02
To Wong Foo, Thanks for
Everything, Julie Newmar
'95
Tootsie '82▶
Torch Song Trilogy '88
Transamerica '05▶
Transfixed '01
Trash '70
Twelfth Night '96
Twisted '96
Unveiled '05
Vegas in Space '94
Velvet Goldmine '98
Victor/Victoria '82▶
Water Drops on Burning
Rocks '99
The Wedding Singer '97
White Chicks '04
Wigstock: The Movie '95
The Woman Inside '83
Woman on Top '00
The World According to
Garp '82▶
The Year of Living
Dangerously '82▶
Yentl '83
Zatoichi '03▶
Zazie dans le Metro '61▶

Generation X
All the Wrong Places '00
Bandwagon '95
The Beach '00
Beautiful Girls '96▶
Before Sunrise '94
Blade '98
Bodies, Rest & Motion '93

Bottle Rocket '95
Charlie White '04
Chasing Amy '97▶
Clerks '94▶
Don't Do It '94
Dream for an Insomniac '96
Ed's Next Move '96
Empire Records '95
Flounding '94
Gen-X Cops '99
Glory Daze '96
Half-Baked '97
Home '05
Into the Wild '07▶
Keys to Tulsa '96
Kicked in the Head '97
Kicking and Screaming '95▶
Knocked Up '07
A Little Stiff '91
Little Athens '05
Live Bait '04
Loaded '94
Love and Other
Catastrophes '95
The Low Life '95
Mallrats '95
Mi Butterfly '93
M. Butterfly '93
Metropolitan '90▶
Nadja '95
Nowhere '96
Omaha (the movie) '95
101 Ways (The Things a
Girl Will Do to Keep Her
Volvo) '00
Party Girl '95
Reality Bites '94▶
S.F.W. '94
Singles '92▶
Slacker '91▶
Sleep with Me '94
Something More '99
Strange Fits of Passion '99
subUrbia '96
When the Party's Over '91

Genetics
see also Mad Scientists;
Metamorphosis
Alien Nation: Body and Soul
'95
Biohazard: The Alien Force
'95
The Boys from Brazil '78
Corn '02
Ed's Next Move '96
The Fly '58▶
The Fly '86▶
The Fly 2 '89
Forbidden World '82
Gattaca '97▶
Godsend '04
The Island of Dr. Moreau '96
Metamorphosis: The Alien
Factor '93
Mimic '97
Rats '83
Sabretooth '01
The Sender '98
Species 2 '99
Species '93
Tomcat: Dangerous Desires
'93
The Twilight of the Golds '97
Wes Craven Presents Mind
Ripper '95
X-Men: The Last Stand '06

Genies
see also Magic Carpet
Rides
Aladdin '92▶
Aladdin and His Wonderful
Lamp '84
Aladdin and the King of
Thieves '96
Arabian Nights '00
Bernard and the Genie '91
The Brass Bottle '63
Kazaam '96
A Kid in Aladdin's Palace
'97

▶ = rated three bones or higher

Genies

A Thousand and One Nights '45
Three Wishes '95
Wildest Dreams '90
Wish Me Luck '95
Wishman '93
Wishmaster '97
Wishmaster 4: The Prophecy Fulfilled '02
The Wonders of Aladdin '61

Genocide/Ethnic Cleansing

see also *Civil War (non U.S.)*; *The Holocaust*
Ararat '02▲
Beyond Borders '03
Blood Diamond '06
Darfur Now '07
Hotel Rwanda '04
The Killing Fields '84▲
The Last King of Scotland '06▲
S21: The Khmer Rouge Killing Machine '03▲
Shooting Dogs '05
Sometimes in April '05▲
Swimming to Cambodia '87▲
Tears of the Sun '03

Genre Spoofs

see also *Comedy*; *Sci-Fi*; *Detective Spoofs*; *Satire & Parody*; *Vampire Spoof*; *Western Comedy*
Airplane! '80▲
Airplane 2: The Sequel '82
All Through the Night '42▲
April Fool's Day '86
Austin Powers: International Man of Mystery '97▲
Austin Powers 2: The Spy Who Shagged Me '99▲
Based on an Untrue Story '93
Beverly Hills Ninja '96
The Big Bus '76
The Big Crimewave '86
Blazing Saddles '74▲
Blondes Have More Guns '95
Bloodbath at the House of Death '85
Bordello '79
Bugsy Malone '76
Cairo '42
Cannibal! The Musical '96
Casino Royale '67
Code Name: Chaos '90
Code Name: The Cleaner '07
The Comebacks '07
Corky Romano '01
Creature from the Haunted Sea '60
The Creature Wasn't Nice '81
Creatures from the Pink Lagoon '07
Date Movie '06
Don't Be a Menace to South Central While Drinking Your Juice in the Hood '95
Drive-In '76
18 Fingers of Death '05
Epic Movie '07
Fatal Instinct '93
Fathom '67
Fay Grim '06
Ferocious Female Freedom Fighters '88
Flesh Gordon '72
Frankenstein General Hospital '88
Frankenstein's Great Aunt Tillie '83
Galactic Gigolo '87
Galaxina '80
Ganjasaurus Rex '87
Get Crazy '83
Ghoul School '90
The Godson '98
Happily N'Ever After '07
Hell Comes to Frogtown '88

Hercules '97▲
High Anxiety '77
The Hollywood Detective '89
Hollywood Harry '86
Hot Fuzz '07▲
Hot Shots! '91▲
Hot Shots! Part Deux '93
The Hound of the Baskervilles '77
Hysterical '83
I'm Gonna Git You Sucka '88▲
Invasion! '99
J-Men Forever! '79▲
Jake Speed '86
Jet Benny Show '86
Johnny English '03
Kentucky Fried Movie '77▲
Kung Fu Hustle '04
Last Action Hero '93
Lemonade Joe '64
Lust in the Dust '85▲
Mafia! '98
The Man Who Knew Too Little '97
The Man with Two Brains '83▲
Mars Attacks! '96
Meet the Spartans '08
Mob Boss '90
Modesty Blaise '66
Monster in the Closet '86
Monty Python and the Holy Grail '75▲
Mosquitoman '05
Murder by Death '76
Mutant on the Bounty '89
The Naked Gun: From the Files of Police Squad '88▲
National Lampoon's Loaded Weapon 1 '93
99 & 44/100 Dead '74
Not Another Teen Movie '01
Once Bitten '85
Orgazmo '98
Pandemonium '82
A Perfect Little Murder '90
Phantom of the Paradise '74
The Pink Chiquitas '86
Plan 10 from Outer Space '95
Plump Fiction '97
Pros & Cons '99
Psycho Beach Party '00
Repossessed '90
Return of Captain Invincible '83
Ricky 1 '88
Robin Hood: Men in Tights '93
Robin of Locksley '95
Rustler's Rhapsody '85
Saturday the 14th '81
Saturday the 14th Strikes Back '88
Scary Movie 2 '01
Scary Movie 3 '03
Scary Movie 4 '06
Scream '96▲
Silence of the Hams '93
The Silencers '66
A Slight Case of Murder '38
A Slight Case of Murder '99
So This Is Africa '33
Soapdish '91▲
Space Truckers '97
Spaceballs '87
Spaceship '81
The Specials '00▲
Spy Hard '96
Strange Invaders '83▲
SuperGuy: Behind the Cape '02
Superhero Movie '08
Supersonic Man '78
Support Your Local Gunfighter '71▲
Support Your Local Sheriff '69▲
Surf Ninjas '93
Team America: World Police '04▲
Teenage Exorcist '93
Terror Eyes '87
That Man from Rio '64

They Call Me Bruce? '82▲
They Call Me Trinity '72
They Live '88▲
They Still Call Me Bruce '86
Three Amigos '86
Too Many Crooks '59
Top Secret! '84▲
Transylvania 6-5000 '85
Trinity Is Still My Name '75
Tromeo & Juliet '95
The Trouble with Spies '87
2069: A Sex Odyssey '78
UHF '89
Undercover Brother '02▲
Union City '81
Unmasked Part 25 '88
Vegas in Space '94
The Video Dead '87
Video Violence '87
Video Violence Part 2... The Exploitation! '87
The Villain '79
Voyage of the Rock Aliens '87
Wacko '83
Werewolf of Washington '73
Wet Hot American Summer '01▲
Who Framed Roger Rabbit '88▲
The Wrecking Crew '68
The Wow Guy '96
Wrongfully Accused '98
The Zany Adventures of Robin Hood '84
Zarkorr! The Invader '96

Germany

see also *Berlin*
Ali: Fear Eats the Soul '74▲
Alice in the Cities '74▲
All the Queen's Men '01
Backbeat '94▲
Beerfest '06
Berlin Alexanderplatz '80▲
The Blue Angel '30▲
The Bridge '59
The Brothers Grimm '05
Buffalo Soldiers '01▲
Carnival Story '54
The Damned '69
The Desert Fox '51▲
Die Grosse Freiheit Nr. 7 '45
The Dirty Girls '64
Dr. Mabuse, The Gambler '22▲
Downfall '04▲
Dresden '06
The Edukators '04
The Empty Mirror '99
Faraway, So Close! '93
Flightplan '05
Flirt '95
Geheimakte WB1 '42
Germany, Pale Mother '80
G.I. Blues '60
The Girl of Your Dreams '99
Go for Zucker '05
The Goebbels Experiment '05
Good Bye, Lenin! '03▲
The Hamburg Cell '04
The Harmonists '99
Hart's War '02
Head On '04▲
Hitler: The Last Ten Days '73
Hitler: The Rise of Evil '03
Human Bomb '97
I Was Nineteen '68
The Infiltrator '95
Isn't Life Wonderful '24▲
The Ister '04▲
Jew-Boy Levi '99
Jud Suess '40▲
Kapo '59▲
Kaspar Hauser '93
Knife in the Head '78
Landscape After Battle '70
The Legend of Paul and Paula '73
Luther '03
Marianne and Juliane '81▲
The Marriage of Maria Braun '79▲
Max '02

Mephisto '81▲
The Merchant of Four Seasons '71▲
Mr. Emmanuel '44
Mostly Martha '01▲
Mother Night '96▲
Munich '05▲
Nico Icon '95▲
The Ninth Day '04▲
Nuremberg '00
The Odessa File '74
The Ogre '96
Once Upon a Honeymoon '42
Porcile '69
Prelude to War '42
Prince Brat and the Whipping Boy '95▲
Prisoner of Paradise '02▲
The Promise '94
Regular Guys '96
Schtonk '92
Schultze Gets the Blues '03
Something for Everyone '70
Sophie Scholl: The Final Days '05▲
The Sound of Music '65▲
SS Girls '77
The Stationmaster's Wife '77
Swing Kids '93
Tenderness of the Wolves '73
Terror 2000 '92
They Were So Young '55
Three Comrades '38▲
Tiefland '44
Town without Pity '61
Triumph of the Will '34▲
The Tunnel '96▲
Underground 41
Unveiled '05
Verdict on Auschwitz: The Frankfurt Auschwitz Trial 1963-1965 '93▲
Water Drops on Burning Rocks '99
When Trumpets Fade '98
Wings of Desire '88▲
Woyzeck '78▲

Ghosts, Ghouls, & Goblins

see also *Death & the Afterlife*; *Demons & Wizards*; *Occult*
Afghan Knights '07
All Souls Day '05
Amazing Mr. Blunden '72
An American Affair '99
An American Haunting '05
An American Werewolf in Paris '97
Beetlejuice '88▲
Believe '99
Beloved '98
Below '02
Beyond Tomorrow '40
The Black Gate '95
Blithe Spirit '45▲
Blondie Has Trouble '40
Blood Gnome '02
Bones '01
Boo! '05
Boogeyman '05
The Brothers Grimm '05
The Canterville Ghost '91
The Canterville Ghost '96
Carved '07
Casper '95▲
Cello '05
The Changeling '80▲
Charlie's Ghost: The Secret of Coronado '94
Children Shouldn't Play with Dead Things '72
A Christmas Carol '84▲
A Christmas Carol '99
The Club '94
Cold Sweat '93
Crazy Eights '06
The Crying Child '96
Curse of the Blue Lights '88
Curtain Call '97
Dark Remains '05
Darkness Falls '03

A Dead Calling '06
Deadly Advice '93
Death Dreams '92
Death Magic '92
Death Tunnel '05
Dedication '07
The Devil's Backbone '01▲
The Diary of Ellen Rimbauer '03
Dona Flor and Her Two Husbands '78▲
Dragonfly '02
Ebenezer '97
El Crimen Perfecto '04▲
The Empire of Passion '76▲
Encounter with the Unknown '75
The Eye '02
The Eye '08
Fatally Yours '95
The Fog '78
The Fog '05
For One More Day '07
Forest Warrior '95
Forever: A Ghost of a Love Story '92
The Forgotten One '89
1408 '07▲
The Frighteners '96▲
The Fury Within '98
The Gate '87▲
Genghis Cohn '93
Ghost '90▲
The Ghost and Mr. Chicken '66
The Ghost and Mrs. Muir '47▲
The Ghost Breakers '40▲
The Ghost Brigade '93
Ghost Dad '90
The Ghost Goes West '36▲
Ghost Rider '35
Ghost Rider '43
Ghost Ship '53
Ghost Ship '02
Ghost Story '81
Ghostbusters '84▲
Ghostbusters 2 '89
Ghosts of Berkeley Square '47
GhostWatcher '02
The Ghoul '34
The Green Man '91▲
The Grudge '04
The Grudge 2 '06
Hangman's Curse '03
Haunted '95
Haunted '98
Haunted Highway '05
Haunted Honeymoon '86
The Haunted Mansion '03
The Haunting '99
Heart and Souls '93
Heaven's a Drag '94
High Spirits '88
Hollywood's New Blood '88
The House of Dies Drear '88
House Where Evil Dwells '82
The Innocents '61▲
The Invisible '07
Ju-On: The Grudge '03
Just like Heaven '05
The Kingdom '95▲
The Kingdom 2 '97▲
Kiss Me Goodbye '82
Knocking on Death's Door '99
Kwaidan '64▲
The Legend of Cryin' Ryan '98
The Legend of Lucy Keyes '06
Life in the Fast Lane '00
Little Orphan Annie '18
Lurking Fear '94
Madhouse '04
The Messengers '07
The Midnight Phantom '35
Mr. Barrington '03
Mr. Vampire '86
The Mummy's Ghost '44
My Friend Walter '93
Mystic Circle Murder '39

Night of the Scarecrow '95
No End '84
O'Hara's Wife '82
Old Mother Riley's Jungle Treasure '51
One Missed Call '08
The Orphanage '07▲
The Others '01▲
Our Town '03
Over Her Dead Body '08
Phantasm 3: Lord of the Dead '94
The Phantom '31
Phantoms '97
Pirates of the Caribbean: Dead Man's Chest '06▲
Poltergeist '82▲
Poltergeist 2: The Other Side '86
Poltergeist 3 '88
Poltergeist: The Legacy '96
The Princess and the Goblin '94
Purgatory '99
Red Riding Hood '03
Restless Spirits '99
Revenge of the Red Baron '93
Riding the Bullet '04
The Ring 2 '05
The St. Francisville Experiment '00
Scary Movie 2 '01
Scoop '06
Screaming Dead '03
Seance '06
Seven Keys to Baldpate '17
Seven Keys to Baldpate '29
Shadow Dancing '88▲
Shutter '08
Silent Hill '06
Silent Tongue '92
The Simian Line '99
The Sixth Sense '99▲
Sleepy Hollow '99▲
Slings & Arrows: Season 2 '05▲
Soft for Digging '01
Sometimes They Come Back... Again '96
Somewhere Tomorrow '85
Soultaker '90
Spectre '96
The Speed Spook '24
The Spiderwick Chronicles '08▲
Spirit Lost '96
Spirited Away '01
Stir of Echoes '99
Stir of Echoes 2: The Homecoming '07
Stormswept '95
The Supernaturals '86
Sylvia and the Phantom '45▲
A Tale of Two Sisters '03▲
Things '93
13 Ghosts '60
13 Ghosts '01
The Time of Their Lives '46
To Gillian on Her 37th Birthday '96
Topper '37▲
Topper Returns '41▲
Topper Takes a Trip '39▲
The Turn of the Screw '74
The Turn of the Screw '92
The Turn of the Screw '99
Twice Dead '88
Ugetsu '53▲
Under the Sand '00▲
The Uninvited '44▲
Urban Ghost Story '98
Visitor from the Grave '81
The Visitors '89
Visitors '03
Volver '06▲
The Wailer '06
The Watcher in the Woods '81
Whale Music '94
What Lies Beneath '00▲
When Good Ghouls Go Bad '01
When Pigs Fly '93
White Noise '05
Wind Chill '07

▶ = rated three bones or higher

Wir/dunner '94
Woman in Black '89
Wuthering Heights '98
Younger & Younger '94
Zero Patience '94

Giants
see also *Monsters, General*

The Amazing Colossal Man '57
Attack of the 50 Foot Woman '58
Attack of the 50 Ft. Woman '93
Attack of the 60-Foot Centerfold '95
Beanstalk '94
Beavis and Butt-Head Do America '96
Big Fish '03▶
Boggy Creek II '83
Bride of the Monster '55
Cyclops '56
The Deadly Mantis '57
Digby, the Biggest Dog in the World '73
Dr. Cyclops '40
Ella Enchanted '04▶
Giant from the Unknown '58
Godzilla vs. Mega on '76
Honey, I Blew Up the Kid '92
Humongous '82
Iron Giant '99▶
Josh Kirby... Time Warrior: Chapter 2, The Human Pets '95
Kronos '57
Mighty Joe Young '49
Mighty Joe Young '98
My Giant '98
The Mysterians '58
The Nutty Professor '61
The Phantom Planet '61
The Princess Bride '87▶
The Spy Who Loved Me '77
Starship Troopers '97▶
Tarantula '55▶
Teenage Mutant Ninja Turtles: The Movie '90
Teenage Mutant Ninja Turtles 2: The Secret of the Ooze '91
Them! '54▶
Tremors '89
Tremors 2: Aftershocks '96
Village of the Giants '65
The War of the Colossal Beast '58
Zarkorr! The Invader '96

Gifted Children
see also *Childhood; Visions*

And You Thought Your Parents Were Weird! '91
Bee Season '05▶
Dangerous Holiday '37
Dear Brigitte '65
Escape to Witch Mountain '75▶
Joshua '07▶
Lemony Snicket's A Series of Unfortunate Events '04
Little Man Tate '91▶
Loverboy '05
Matilda '96▶
On the Right Track '81
Powder '95
Real Genius '85▶
Rookie of the Year '93
Searching for Bobby Fischer '93▶

Glasgow
see also *Scotland*

American Cousins '02
Beautiful Creatures '00
The Big Tease '99
Carla's Song '97
Comfort and Joy '84▶
Doomsday '08
A Fond Kiss '04
My Name Is Joe '98
On a Clear Day '05
Orphans '97
The Purifiers '04
Red Road '06
Small Faces '95▶
Wilbur Wants to Kill Himself '02▶

Go Fish
see also *Deep Blue; Killer Sea Critters*

Alamo Bay '85
Around the World Under the Sea '65
Big Fish '03▶
Black Water '94
Bright Future '04
Cabin at Sunset '96
Captains Courageous '37▶
Captains Courageous '95
Darwin's Nightmare '04▶
The Day of the Dolphin '73
Detour to Danger '45
Dodson's Journey '01
Doomwatch '72
Finding Nemo '03▶
A Fish Called Wanda '88▶
Flipper '96▶
Forrest Gump '94▶
Frankenfish '04
Free Willy '93
Gone Fishin' '97
Grumpier Old Men '95
Grumpy Old Men '93▶
The Incredible Mr. Limpet '64
The Islander '88
The Isle '01
It Came from Beneath the Sea '55▶
The Inspectors '98
The Inspectors 2: A Shred of Evidence '00
Johnny Frenchman '46
Junk Mail '97
Killer Fish '79
La Terra Trema '43▶
A Letter to Three Wives '49▶
Letters from a Killer '98
The Life Aquatic with Steve Zissou '04
Like a Fish Out of Water '99
Limbo '99
Love Serenade '96
Maelstrom '00
Man of Aran '34▶
Man's Favorite Sport? '63
Megalocon '03
Milwaukee, Minnesota '03
Mr. Peabody & the Mermaid '48
Moby Dick '56▶
Moby Dick '98
My Summer Story '94
Northern Extremes '93
The Old Man and the Sea '58▶
The Old Man and the Sea '90
On Golden Pond '81▶
Orca '77
Red Water '01
Respiro '02
Riff Raff '35
A River Runs Through It '92▶
Scorpion with Two Tails '82
The Sea '02
Seducing Doctor Lewis '03
The Seventh Stream '01
Shark Hunter '79
Shark Tale '04
Sixteen Fathoms Deep '34
Spawn of the North '38
The SpongeBob SquarePants Movie '04
Thunder Bay '53▶
The Treasure of Jamaica Reef '74
Up from the Depths '79
Wallaby Jim of the Islands '37
Whale for the Killing '81
Where the Hot Wind Blows '59
The Wide Blue Road '57▶

Golf
Bobby Jones: Stroke of Genius '04
The Caddy '53
Caddyshack '80▶
Caddyshack 2 '88
Carefree '38▶
Dead Solid Perfect '88
Enter the Dragon '73▶
Follow the Sun '51
The Foursome '06
A Gentleman's Game '01
Goldfinger '64▶
Goof Balls '87
The Greatest Game Ever Played '05
Happy Gilmore '96▶
Homeguest '94
In Like Flint '67
The Legend of Bagger Vance '00
The Man with the Perfect Swing '95
My Favorite Brunette '47
National Lampoon's Golf Punks '99
Pat and Mike '52▶
The Price of Milk '00
Second Best '05
Shelter Island '03
Space Jam '96
The Sweetest Thing '02
There's Something about Mary '98▶
The Tiger Woods Story '98
Tin Cup '96▶
Who's Your Caddy? '07

Going Postal
Dead Letter Office '98
84 Charing Cross Road '86▶
Going Postal '98
He Was a Quiet Man '07
The Inspectors '98
The Inspectors 2: A Shred of Evidence '00
Letter from an Unknown Woman '48▶
A Letter to Three Wives '49▶
The Minus Man '99
Overnight Delivery '96
Postal Inspector '36
The Postman '94▶
The Postman '97
See Spot Run '01
The Shop Around the Corner '40▶
Side Street '50
You've Got Mail '98

Going Native
Apocalypse Now '79▶
The Blue Lagoon '80
The Bounty '84
Congo '95
Dances with Wolves '90▶
The Emerald Forest '85▶
Farewell to the King '89
George of the Jungle '97▶
Grizzly Adams: The Legend Continues '90
Jeremiah Johnson '72▶
Jungle 2 Jungle '96
Krippendorf's Tribe '98
Little Indian, Big City '95
Lord of the Flies '63▶
Lord of the Flies '90
A Man Called Horse '70▶
The Mosquito Coast '86
Mutiny on the Bounty '35▶
Mutiny on the Bounty '62
Pagan Island '60
Paradise '82
The Return of a Man Called Horse '76
Robinson Crusoe '36
A Stranger Among Us '92
The Swiss Family Robinson '60▶
Up to His Neck '54
Zeus and Roxanne '96

Gospel Music
America's Heart and Soul '04
The Fighting Temptations '03
The Gospel '05▶
Preaching to the Choir '05
Ray '04▶
Sister Act '92
Sister Act 2: Back in the Habit '93

Governesses
see also *The Help: Female; Nannies & Governesses*

Grand Hotel
see also *No-Exit Motel*

An Affair of Love '99
Agent of Death '99
Almost Strangers '01
And Now Ladies and Gentleman '02
Ants '77
Appetite '98
Argentine Nights '40
The Avenging Hand '36
Beach Hotel '92
Billy Madison '00
Blame It on the Bellboy '92
Blonde Takes a Vacation '39
Bloody Wednesday '87
Blue Crush '02▶
Bobby '06
Brewster's Millions '45
Brewster's Millions '85
The Business of Strangers '01
Chaos & Cadavers '03
Chelsea Walls '01
City of Ghosts '03
Come September '61
Conversations with Other Woman '05
Crawlspace '86
Crocodile Dundee '86▶
Detective '85
Dirty Dancing '87▶
Dirty Pretty Things '03▶
The Duchess of Duke Street '78
Dunston Checks In '95
Eden '93
Eden 2 '93
Eden 3 '93
Eden 4 '93
Eloise at the Plaza '03
The Fifth Element '97▶
Five Graves to Cairo '43▶
For Love or Money '93
Forgetting Sarah Marshall '08▶
Four Rooms '95
French Kiss '95
The Girl with the Hungry Eyes '94
Grand Hotel '32▶
The Green Man '91▶
Hit Me '96
Holiday Inn '42▶
Holiday Hotel '77
Home Alone 2: Lost in New York '92▶
Hostage '05
Hostel '05
Hotel '67
Hotel de Love '96
Hotel du Lac '86
Hotel Imperial '27
Hotel Reserve '44▶
Hotel Room '93
Hotel Rwanda '04▶
It Happened at Nightmare Inn '70
Italian for Beginners '01
Jet Lag '02
Juny Duty '06
The Last Stop '99
Lost in Translation '03▶
Meltdown '95
The Million Dollar Hotel '99
Mistaken Identity '36
Mrs. Palfrey at the Claremont '05
My Bodyguard '80▶
Mystery Train '89▶
New Rose Hotel '98
Nick of Time '95
Night at the Golden Eagle '02
A Night in Casablanca '46▶
The Night Porter '74▶
The Night We Called it a Day '03
Nightmare on the 13th Floor '90
Off Season '01
Old Mother Riley's New Venture '49
One Crazy Night '93
The Out-of-Towners '99
Plaza Suite '71▶
Pretty Woman '90▶
Priceless '06
Prom Night '08
Psycho '60▶
Psycho '83
Psycho 3 '86
The Queen of Mean '90
The Red Inn '51
Roadside Prophets '92
Room Service '38
Rosebud Beach Hotel '85
Secret of the Black Trunk
See No Evil '06
Separate Tables '58▶
Separate Tables '83
The Shining '80▶
A Single Girl '96
Sleeping with Strangers
Smokin' Aces '07
The Snow Queen '02
Snowball Express '72
Somewhere in Time '80▶
Spare Parts '79
Stir '93
Suite 16 '94
Superman 2 '80▶
Sweet Lorraine '87▶
The Terror '38▶
Terror at Red Wolf Inn '72
This Property is Condemned '66▶
Three Strikes '00
3:10 to Yuma '57▶
Tower of Terror '97
2046 '04▶
Twin Falls Idaho '99▶
Weekend at the Waldorf '45▶
A Weekend in the Country '96
Witchery '88

Grand Theft Auto
B.A.D. Cats '80
Black Moon Rising '85
Corvette Summer '78
Eat My Dust '76
The Fast and the Furious '01
Gone in 60 Seconds '74
Gone in 60 Seconds '00
Grand Theft Auto '77▶
Kiss of Death '94
Motor Patrol '50
Nasty Hero '89
New Jersey Drive '95
No Man's Land '87
Rat Race '01▶
The Rookie '90
T Bone N Weasel '92
Tsotsi '05▶
Twin Town '97

Grandparents
All I Want for Christmas '91
American Gun '02
An American Rhapsody '01
American Wedding '03
Anastasia '97▶
Arthur and the Invisibles '06
Aurora Borealis '06
Beerfest '06
Big Eden '00
Bulletproof Monk '03
Carolina '03
Charlie and the Chocolate Factory '05▶
Chronicle of the Raven '04
Clean '04
The Company of Wolves '85▶
Cuban Blood '03
Death Valley: The Revenge of Bloody Bill '04
Diary of a Mad Black Woman '05
A Dog of Flanders '99
The Education of Little Tree '97▶
18 Again! '88
800 Bullets '02
East Side Story '07
Evergreen '04
Everything is Illuminated '05▶
Family Business '89
Father's Little Dividend '51▶
Flowers in the Attic '87
Georgia Rule '07
Gracie's Choice '04
Grandma's Boy '06
Happenstance '00
The Heart is Deceitful Above All Things '04
Heidi '37
Heidi '52
Heidi '55▶
Heidi '93
Hey Arnold! The Movie '02
Hoodwinked '05▶
How to Deal '03
I'll Take You There '99
I'm Going Home '00▶
In Her Shoes '05▶
In the Land of Women '06
Jersey Girl '04
Keeping Up with the Steins '06
Life Support '07▶
The Little Colonel '35▶
Little Miss Sunshine '06▶
Master of Disguise '02
Mrs. Palfrey at the Claremont '05
The Mother '03▶
My Louisiana Sky '02
The Night of the Iguana '64▶
On a Clear Day '05
On Borrowed Time '39▶
Pennies from Heaven '36
Persepolis '07▶
Pete's Meteor '98
Pinky '49▶
Powder '95
The Princess Bride '87▶
The Princess Diaries '01▶
The Princess Diaries 2: Royal Engagement '04
Pure '02▶
Rain '06
Raising Victor Vargas '03
The Red Stallion '47
Restless Spirits '99
Rumor Has It... '05
Saraband '03▶
Sci-Fighter '04
The Secret of Roan Inish '94▶
Sixteen Candles '84▶
Sleepwalking '08
Spy Kids 2: The Island of Lost Dreams '01
Spy Kids 3-D: Game Over '03
Tammy and the Bachelor '57
Tell Me a Riddle '80
Time to Leave '05▶

Grandparents

The Triplets of Belleville '02▸
Two Bits '96
The Ultimate Gift '06
A Very Serious Person '06
Walter and Henry '01▸
The Way Home '01
Wee Willie Winkie '37▸
Whale Rider '02▸
Where the Red Fern Grows: Part 2 '92
Willy Wonka & the Chocolate Factory '71▸
The Wizard of Loneliness '88
Zelly & Me '88▸

Great Britain

see also Ireland; London; Scotland

The Affair '95
Alien Prey '83
Amazing Mr. Blunden '72▸
American Friends '91
Among Giants '98
And a Nightingale Sang '91
Angels and Insects '95▸
Angels One Five '54
Anne of the Thousand Days '69▸
Asylum '05
August '95
An Awfully Big Adventure '94
Back Home '90
Back to the Secret Garden '01
Band of Gold '95▸
Barry Lyndon '75▸
Basil '98
Bean '97▸
Beau Brummel '54▸
Becoming Jane '07
Bhaji on the Beach '94
The Big Scam '79
Billy Elliot '02▸
Birthday Girl '02
Black Panther '77
The Black Windmill '74
Blue Jeans '78
Bonnie Prince Charlie '48
The Borrowers '97
Borstal Boy '00
Boston Kickout '95
Brassed Off '96
Brighton Rock '47▸
The Brontes of Haworth '73
Brothers of the Head '06
The Browning Version '94
The Buccaneers '95▸
Bullshot '83
Calendar Girls '03
Cambridge Spies '03
Camelot '67
The Canterville Ghost '96
Carrington '95
Catherine Cookson's Colour Blind '98
Catherine Cookson's The Black Velvet Gown '92
Catherine Cookson's The Cinder Path '94
Catherine Cookson's The Dwelling Place '94
Catherine Cookson's The Fifteen Streets '90
Catherine Cookson's The Round Tower '98
Catherine Cookson's Tilly Trotter '99
The Charge of the Light Brigade '68
Charles & Diana: A Palace Divided '93
Chicago Joe & the Showgirl '90
Chicken Run '00▸
Children of Men '06▸
The Choir '95▸
A Chump at Oxford '40
Cider with Rosie '99
Circus '00
Cold Comfort Farm '71
Cold Comfort Farm '94▸
Cold Light of Day '95
Coming Home '98
The Constant Gardener '05▸
Control '07
The Corn Is Green '45▸
The Corn Is Green '79▸
The Courtney Affair '47
Cromwell '70
Crush '02
A Cry from the Streets '57
CSA: The Confederate States of America '04
Dad Savage '97
A Dance to the Music of Time '97
Danger UXB '81
Dark Blue World '01
Deathwatch '02
Deja Vu '98
Devices and Desires '91▸
Devotion '31
Diana: Her True Story '93
Dick Turpin '25
Disraeli '30▸
Distant Voices, Still Lives '88▸
Doogal '05
The Duke '99
The Eagle Has Landed '77▸
Eden Valley '94▸
Edge of the World '37▸
Edward and Mrs. Simpson '80
Elizabeth of Ladymead '48▸
Elizabeth R '72▸
Elizabeth: The Golden Age '07
Elizabeth, the Queen '68
Emma '96▸
Emma '97▸
Enduring Love '04
The Englishman Who Went up a Hill But Came down a Mountain '95▸
Enigma '01
Everybody Wins '90
Excalibur '81▸
FairyTale: A True Story '97
Fame Is the Spur '47
Far from the Madding Crowd '97▸
Feast of July '95
Fergie & Andrew: Behind Palace Doors '93
The Final Cut '95▸
Finding Neverland '04▸
Firelight '97
Flambards '78
Flickers '80
Foreign Affairs '93▸
Forever and a Day '43▸
Formula 51 '01
The Four Feathers '02
Four Weddings and a Funeral '94▸
Framed '93▸
Frenchman's Creek '44
Frenchman's Creek '98
Funny Bones '94▸
Gallowglass '95▸
Garfield: A Tail of Two Kitties '06
The Gathering '02
Go Now '96▸
Goal! The Dream Begins '06
Goodbye, Mr. Chips '69▸
Goodbye, Mr. Chips '02
Goodnight, Mr. Tom '99
Gosford Park '01▸
Grave Indiscretions '96
Great Expectations: The Untold Story '87
The Great Muppet Caper '81▸
Greenfingers '00
Gulliver's Travels '95
Harnessing Peacocks '92
Harry Potter and the Goblet of Fire '05▸
Haunted '95
The Hellfire Club '61
High Hopes '88▸
The History Boys '06
The History of Mr. Polly '07
The Holiday '06
Hot Fuzz '07▸
The Hours '02▸
House of Cards '90▸
House of Eliott '92▸
The House of Secrets '37
How Green Was My Valley '41▸
I Capture the Castle '02
I'll Be There '03
Imagine Me & You '06
The Importance of Being Earnest '02
In His Life: The John Lennon Story '00
The Innocents '61▸
Inspector Clouseau '68
Intimate Relations '95
Invincible Mr. Disraeli '63
Iris '01▸
The Iron Duke '34
Jack Higgins' On Dangerous Ground '95
Jamaica Inn '82
Jane Eyre '96▸
Jane Eyre '97
Johnny English '03
Jude '96▸
Killing Time '97
The King's Thief '55
Ladies in Lavender '04▸
Lady Chatterley '06▸
Lady Jane '85▸
The Lady's Not for Burning '87
The Land Girls '98
Lara Croft: Tomb Raider '01
The Last of England '87▸
Lawless Heart '01
The Libertine '05
Lillie '78▸
The Lion in Winter '68▸
Lipstick on Your Collar '94
Lloyds of London '36▸
Lock, Stock and 2 Smoking Barrels '98▸
The Long Day Closes '92▸
The Long Good Friday '80▸
Looking for Richard '96▸
Lorna Doone '34
Lorna Doone '90
Lorna Doone '01▸
Love for Lydia '79▸
Lucky Break '01
Madagascar Skin '95
Made in Heaven '52
The Madness of King George '94▸
A Man for All Seasons '66▸
A Man for All Seasons '88▸
The Man from the Pru '89
The Man in Grey '45▸
The Man Who Knew Too Little '97
Mapp & Lucia '85▸
Mary of Scotland '36▸
Merlin '98▸
A Midwinter's Tale '95▸
The Mill on the Floss '37
The Mill on the Floss '97
Millions '05▸
A Mind to Murder '96
Miss Potter '06▸
Mrs. Brown '97▸
Mrs. Miniver '42▸
Mrs. Palfrey at the Claremont '05▸
Mister Drake's Duck '50
Mr. Toad's Wild Ride '96
The Moonraker '58
Mosley '98
The Mother '03▸
Munster, Go Home! '66
Murder Elite '86
My Brother Tom '86
My Summer of Love '05▸
My Uncle Silas '01▸
The Naked Civil Servant '75▸
Nanny McPhee '06▸
National Lampoon's Van Wilder 2: The Rise of Taj '06
The New World '05▸
Night Must Fall '37▸
Nine Days a Queen '36▸
No Surrender '86▸
None But the Lonely Heart '44▸
Oh! What a Lovely War '69
Oliver Twist '05▸
The Omen '06
Once Upon a Time in the Midlands '02
Pack of Lies '87
Pandaemonium '00
Passport to Pimlico '49
Persuasion '95▸
Pictures '80s
Pink String and Sealing Wax '45
Plenty '85
Poldark '75▸
Portrait of a Lady '96▸
Pride and Prejudice '95▸
Pride and Prejudice '05▸
Prince of Poisoners: The Life and Crimes of William Palmer '98
Princess Caraboo '94
The Proposition '96
Pure '02▸
The Queen's Sister '05
A Question of Attribution '91▸
Raffles '30▸
The Railway Children '70▸
The Railway Children '00▸
Reckless '97▸
Reckless: The Sequel '98▸
The Reckoning '03▸
The Red Violin '98▸
A Respectable Trade '98
The Return of the Native '94
Rhodes '97
Richard III '12▸
Richard III '95▸
The Riddle of the Sands '79
Riders '88
Riff Raff '92▸
Robbery '67
Room to Let '49
A Royal Scandal '96
Royal Wedding '51▸
The Ruling Class '72▸
The Saint '97
Say Hello to Yesterday '71
Scandal '89▸
The Scarlet Tunic '97
Scoop '06
The Secret Garden '49▸
Secret of the Black Trunk '62
The Seeker: The Dark Is Rising '07
Sense and Sensibility '95▸
The Serpent's Kiss '97
The Servant '63▸
Shadowlands '03
Shanghai Knights '03
Shaun of the Dead '04▸
Shopping '93
Silver Dream Racer '83
Six Wives of Henry VIII '71▸
Soldier in Love '67
South Riding '37
Speedy Death '99▸
Split Second '92
Starter for Ten '06
Station Jim '01
The Stick-Up '77
Stiff Upper Lips '96
Still Crazy '98▸
Strange Relations '02
Sweet Revenge '98
Swept from the Sea '97
Sylvia '03
Testament of Youth '79
That Sinking Feeling '79▸
This England '42
Those Magnificent Men in Their Flying Machines '65▸
To Play the King '93▸
Tom Jones '63▸
A Touch of Class '73▸
Tristan & Isolde '06
Tristram Shandy: A Cock and Bull Story '05▸
Tunes of Glory '60▸
24 Hour Party People '01
Under the Skin '97
Vacuuming Completely Nude in Paradise '01
Valiant '05
Vanity Fair '04
Velvet Goldmine '98▸
A Very British Coup '88▸
Victoria Regina '61
A Village Affair '95
The Virgin Queen '55▸
Wallace & Gromit: The Curse of the Were-Rabbit '05▸
Warrior Queen '03
We Think the World of You '88▸
We'll Meet Again '82
When Saturday Comes '95
Whiskey Galore '48▸
The Whistle Blower '87▸
The White Cliffs of Dover '44▸
Wild Child '08
Wives and Daughters '01▸
The Wolves of Kromer '98
The Woman He Loved '88▸
Woman in Black '89
A Woman of Substance '84
Wondrous Oblivion '06▸
Wuthering Heights '39▸
Yanks '79
Year of the Comet '92
The Young Americans '93
Young Bess '53▸
Young Winston '72▸

Great Death Scenes

see also Death & the Afterlife; Funerals

Bonnie & Clyde '67▸
Breaker Morant '80▸
Bring Me the Head of Alfredo Garcia '74
Buffy the Vampire Slayer '92▸
Butch Cassidy and the Sundance Kid '69▸
Camille '36▸
The Champ '79
Coquette '29
Dangerous Liaisons '88▸
Dark Victory '39▸
Demolition Man '93
Die Hard: With a Vengeance '95
Evita '96
Face/Off '97▸
From Dusk Till Dawn '95
Gallipoli '81▸
Gettysburg '93▸
Glory '89▸
The Godfather '72▸
The Green Mile '99
Highlander '86▸
Highlander: The Gathering '92
Jeanne la Pucelle '94
Joan of Arc '99
John Carpenter's Vampires '97
Johnny Mnemonic '95
Jude '96▸
Julius Caesar '53▸
Jurassic Park '93▸
The Last Temptation of Christ '88▸
The Lost World: Jurassic Park 2 '97
Mimi '35
Monty Python and the Holy Grail '75▸
The Omen '76▸
The Omen '06
The Passion of the Christ '04▸
Pat Garrett & Billy the Kid '73▸
Psycho '60▸
Public Enemy '31▸
Scream '96▸
Shadowlands '93▸
A Song to Remember '45▸
Starship Troopers '97▸
Strangers on a Train '51▸
Things to Do in Denver When You're Dead '95▸
Valmont '89▸
The Wizard of Oz '39▸

Great Depression

see also Hard Knock Life; Homeless

After the Promise '87
All the King's Men '49▸
American Madness '32▸
Angela's Ashes '99▸
Annie '99▸
Ask the Dust '06
The Assistant '97
Baby Face Nelson '57
The Ballad of the Sad Cafe '91
Big Bad Mama '74
Big Bad Mama 2 '87
Billy Bathgate '91
Bloody Mama '70
Bonnie & Clyde '67▸
Bound for Glory '76▸
Boxcar Bertha '72
Catherine Cookson's The Man Who Cried '93
Charley and the Angel '73
Chinatown '74▸
A Christmas to Remember '78
Cinderella Man '05▸
The Cradle Will Rock '99
Dance Fools Dance '31▸
Dillinger '45▸
Dillinger '73
Dillinger '91
Dillinger and Capone '95
Dogville '03
Dream Chasers '82
Eleanor & Franklin '76▸
Emperor of the North Pole '73▸
Falling for a Dancer '98
Fatty Finn '84
Four Deuces '75
Fresh Horses '88
The Grapes of Wrath '40▸
The Green Mile '99
The Group '66
Hallelujah, I'm a Bum '33
Hard Times '75▸
Hard Traveling '85
Henry & Verlin '94
Hidden Places '06
Hit the Dutchman '92
Homecoming: A Christmas Story '71
Honkytonk Man '82
Hoodlum '96
Hunter's Moon '97
In a Savage Land '99
The Inheritors '98
Inside Daisy Clover '65▸
Ironweed '87▸
It Happened One Night '34▸
The Journey of Natty Gann '85▸
Just Around the Corner '38
Kansas City '95▸
King Kong '05▸
The King of Masks '99▸
King of the Hill '93▸
Kingfish: A Story of Huey P. Long '95
The Lady in Question '99
Last Man Standing '96
Laurel & Hardy: Below Zero '30
Life '99
The Life and Times of Hank Greenberg '99▸
Long Road Home '91
Love on the Dole '41▸
Melvin Purvis: G-Man '74
Mrs. Henderson Presents '05▸
Modern Times '36▸
Morning Glory '93
O Brother Where Art Thou? '00▸
Of Mice and Men '39▸
Of Mice and Men '81▸
Of Mice and Men '92▸
Oscar '91
Our Daily Bread '34▸
The Outfit '93
Paper Moon '73▸
Pennies from Heaven '81▸
The Piano Lesson '94▸
Places in the Heart '84▸
Possessed '31
The Postman Always Rings Twice '46▸
The Postman Always Rings Twice '81
Public Enemies '96
Rambling Rose '91▸

▸ = rated three bones or higher

The Road Home '95
The Saddest Music in the World '03
Seabiscuit '03
Shadrach '98
Sir Arthur Conan Doyle's The Lost World '98
Sounder '72
The Stars Fell on Henrietta '94
Street Scene '31
Sullivan's Travels '41
Sweet Land '05
The Tale of Ruby Rose '87
They Shoot Horses, Don't They? '69
Thieves Like Us '74
The Twelve Dogs of Christmas '05
Two Bits '96
Victor/Victoria '82
Voices from a Locked Room '95
The Water Engine '92
White Hot: The Mysterious Murder of Thelma Todd '91
Who Has Seen the Wind? '77
Why Shoot the Teacher '79
Wild Hearts Can't Be Broken '91
Wildflower '91
William Faulkner's Old Man '97
Winter People '89
The Yearling '94
You Only Live Once '37

Great Escapes

see also Men in Prison; POW/MIA; War, General; Women in Prison:

Alias, La Gringa '91
The Ascent '94
Assassination '87
Austin Powers: International Man of Mystery '97
Bandits '99
Before Night Falls '00
Berlin Tunnel 21 '81
The Big Doll House '71
Blood on the Mountain '88
Born to Be Wild '95
Brady's Escape '84
The Break '97
Breakout '75
Brute Force '47
Butch Cassidy and the Sundance Kid '69
Caged Fear '92
The Chase '66
Chasers '94
Chicken Run '00
The Colditz Story '55
Con Air '97
Condition Red '95
Crashout '55
A Day in October '92
Deadlock 2 '94
The Deer Hunter '78
Desperate Measures '98
Deadly Target '94
Diamonds of the Night '64
Die Hard '88
Die Hard: With a Vengeance '95
Dirty Heroes '71
Double Team '97
Down by Law '86
Era Notte a Roma '50
Escape '90
The Escape Artist '82
Escape from Atlantis '97
Escape from Cell Block 3 '74
Escape from Death Row '73
Escape from El Diablo '83
Escape from Fort Bravo '53
Escape from Galaxy Three '81
Escape from Hell '79
Escape from L.A. '96
Escape from Mars '99
Escape from New York '81
Escape from Safehaven '88
Escape from Sobibor '87
Escape from the KGB '87
Escape: Human Cargo '98
Escape to Love '82
Escape to Witch Mountain '75
Escapist '83
Extremely Dangerous '99
Face/Off '97
Fantastic Voyage '66
Fast Walking '82
The Fast Runner '01
Feeling Minnesota '96
Flame Over India '60
Fled '96
Flight from Vienna '56
Follow the River '95
Fortress '93
Fortress 2: Re-Entry '99
The Four Feathers '02
Frenchman's Creek '44
Frenchman's Creek '98
Gang Busters '55
Girls in Prison '56
The Grave '95
The Great Escape '63
The Great Escape 2: The Untold Story '88
The Great Train Robbery '79
Hangfire '91
Harold & Kumar Escape from Guantanamo Bay '08
Hart's War '02
Heaven '01
Hellraiser 5: Inferno '00
The Horseman on the Roof '95
Hostile Intentions '94
Houdini '53
Houdini '99
I Am David '04
In Hot Pursuit '77
The Ice Runner '93
Inside Out '75
Iron Eagle '86
The Island '05
Jailbreakin' '72
Kidnapped '72
La Nuit de Varennes '82
Ladyhawke '85
The Last Confederate: The Story of Robert Adams '05
The Last Samurai '90
Le Trou '59
Leaving Normal '92
Les Miserables '35
Les Miserables '57
Les Miserables '78
Les Violons du Bal '74
Lonely Are the Brave '62
The Long Riders '80
Lucky Break '01
Macho Callahan '70
Madagascar '05
A Man Escaped '57
The Man Who Broke 1,000 Chains '87
The Manhunt '86
McKenzie Break '70
McVicar '80
Midnight Edition '93
Midnight Express '78
Missing in Action '84
Mrs. Soffel '84
The Mole People '56
Murder One '88
Murder in the First '95
The Muthers '76
Mysterious Island '61
Naked Youth '59
Night Crossing '81
No Escape '94
North by Northwest '59
Not Without My Daughter '90
On Wings of Eagles '86
One That Got Away '57
Operation Thunderbolt '77
Pacific Inferno '85
Papillon '73
Passage to Marseilles '44
A Perfect World '93
Poseidon '06
Prison Break '38
The Prize '63
The Promise '94
Raiders of the Lost Ark '81
Raising Arizona '87
Raw Deal '48
Rescue Dawn '06
Ricochet '91
Rob Roy '95
The Rock '96
Romancing the Stone '84
Romeo Must Die '00
Run '91
Runaway Train '85
The Saint '97
St. Ives '98
Samar '62
The Secret War of Harry Frigg '68
The Seventh Cross '44
The Seventh Floor '93
The Shawshank Redemption '94
The Shining '80
Skin Game '71
The Sound of Music '65
The Spy Who Came in from the Cold '65
Stalag 17 '53
Stalag Luft '93
Strange Cargo '40
Strike Back '80
The Sugarland Express '74
Sweet Poison '91
Tequila Sunrise '88
Teresa's Tattoo '94
Texas Payback '95
Three Days of the Condor '75
Thunder County '74
To Catch a Thief '55
Torn Curtain '66
Toy Story '95
Toy Story 2 '99
Train of Life '98
The Truman Show '98
UKM: The Ultimate Killing Machine '06
Venus Rising '95
Victory '81
Violent Women '59
Von Ryan's Express '65
Warbus '85
Welcome to Woop Woop '97
We're No Angels '55
White Nights '85
The Wild '06
Women Unchained '72
Wooden Horse '50
XXX: State of the Union '05
Zebra in the Kitchen '65

Greece—Ancient

Alexander '04
Alexander the Great '55
Atlantis, the Lost Continent '61
Barefoot in Athens '66
Clash of the Titans '81
Conquest of Mycene '63
Helen of Troy '56
Helen of Troy '03
Iphigenia '77
Jason and the Argonauts '63
Jason and the Argonauts '00
The Lion of Thebes '64
The Loves of Hercules '60
Medea '88
Medusa Against the Son of Hercules '62
Meet the Spartans '08
The Odyssey '97
300 '07
The 300 Spartans '62
The Triumph of Hercules '66
The Trojan Horse '62
Trojan Women '71
Troy '04

Greece—Modern

Captain Corelli's Mandolin '01
The Case of the Scorpion's Tail '71
Children of Nature '91
Chimes at Midnight '67
Eleni '85
Forty Carats '73
I Live My Life '35
Jupiter's Thigh '79
Mamma Mia! '08
The Mediterranean in Flames '72
Murderball '05
Shirley Valentine '89
Signs & Wonders '00
Sisterhood of the Traveling Pants '05
Sisterhood of the Traveling Pants 2 '08
Weeping Meadow '04
Z '69

Grim Reaper

see also Death &...; Afterlife:

Death Takes a Holiday '34
El Crimen Perfecto '04
The Exorcist '73
Exorcist 2: The Heretic '77
Exorcist 3: Legion '90
Exorcist: The Beginning '04
Final Destination '00
Final Destination 2 '03
Final Destination 3 '06
The Frighteners '96
Last Action Hero '93
Meet Joe Black '98
Monty Python's The Meaning of Life '83
The Order '03
Riding the Bullet '04
The Seventh Seal '56
Soul Survivors '01

Growing Older

see also Death & the...; Afterlife; Grandparents; Impending Retirement; Late Bloomin' Love:

About Schmidt '02
After the Rehearsal '84
Age Isn't Everything '91
Age Old Friends '89
Amos '85
The Angel Levine '70
Anna '87
Another Lonely Hitman '95
Any Number Can Win '63
Around the Bend '04
Around the World in 80 Ways '86
As Young As You Feel '51
Atlantic City '81
Aurora Borealis '06
Autumn Leaves '56
Away From Her '06
The Ballad of Narayama '83
The Banger Sisters '02
*batteries not included '87
Belle Toujours '06
The Best of Times '86
Better Late Than Never '79
Blue Moon '00
The Boynton Beach Club '05
Breathing Lessons '94
Bubba Ho-Tep '03
The Bucket List '07
Buena Vista Social Club '99
Bullet to Beijing '95
Camilla '94
Casanova '05
The Cemetery Club '93
Central Station '99
Changing Times '04
Charlie: Dead or Alive '69
Chasing Butterflies '94
The Cheyenne Social Club '70
Choices '86
The Christmas Box '95
Citizen Kane '41
City Slickers '91
Cobb '94
Cocoon '85
Cocoon: The Return '88
Collected Stories '02
The Color of Evening '95
Come Along with Me '84
The Conductor '80
Cooperstown '93
Dad '89
Daddy Nostalgia '90
Death Becomes Her '92
Death of a Salesman '86
The Death of Mr. Lazarescu '05
Diamonds '99
Don't Come Knocking '05
Dorian Gray '70
Drawl! '81
Dream a Little Dream '89
Dream Chasers '82
Dreaming of Rita '94
Driving Miss Daisy '89
Duplex '03
Early Days '81
Easy Living '49
Ebony Tower '86
An Empty Bed '90
The Enchanted Forest '45
Enemies of Laughter '00
The Evening Star '96
Facing Windows '03
Family Upside Down '78
Fantasy Man '84
Father of the Bride Part 2 '95
The Final Hit '30
The Fireman's Ball '68
Fly Boy '99
Folks! '92
For Love of the Game '99
A Foreign Field '93
Forever Young '92
Forget About It '06
Forty Carats '73
Forty Shades of Blue '05
Foxfire '87
The Gathering Storm '02
Getting Up and Going Home '92
Gideon '99
Gin Game '84
Ginger & Fred '86
The Girl from Paris '01
The Godfather, Part 3 '90
Gods and Monsters '98
Going in Style '79
The Good Guys and the Bad Guys '69
The Good Old Boys '95
The Good Thief '03
The Goodbye People '83
Goodnight, Mr. Tom '99
Grace & Glorie '98
Grace Quigley '84
The Grandfather '98
Great Smokey Roadblock '76
Greedy '94
Grumpier Old Men '95
Grumpy Old Men '93
Hamsun '96
Hanging Up '99
Harakiri '62
Hard Labour '73
Hardbodies '84
Harry and Tonto '74
Heading South '05
Home Free All '84
Home Is Where the Heart Is '87
Homebodies '74
Home to Stay '78
Horton Foote's Alone '97
The Hunger '83
Hurry Up or I'll Be Thirty '73
Husbands '70
Hush, Hush, Sweet Charlotte '65
I Can't Sleep '93
I'm Going Home '00
I'm Not Rappaport '96
In Custody '94
The Incredible Mrs. Ritchie '03
Iris '01
Iron Horsemen '71
Judy Berlin '99
Killing Grandpa '91
The King of Masks '99
Kotch '71
Larry McMurtry's Streets of Laredo '95
The Last Days of Frankie the Fly '96
The Last Good Time '94
The Last Laugh '24
The Last Lieutenant '94
Late Chrysanthemums '54
The Leech Woman '59
Lifeguard '76
Light Sleeper '92
Lightning Jack '94
Lilian's Story '95
The Limey '99
Lip Service '88
The Locket '02
Lost for Words '99
Love Among the Ruins '75
Ma Saison Preferee '93
Mafia! '98
Marathon '80
Martin Chuzzlewit '94
Meet Joe Black '98
The Memory of a Killer '03
Middle Age Crazy '80
Mind the Gap '04
Miss Firecracker '89
Mrs. Dalloway '97
Mrs. Palfrey at the Claremont '05
Mr. Saturday Night '92
Money to Burn '83
Monte Walsh '70
Monte Walsh '03
My Heroes Have Always Been Cowboys '91
Neil Simon's The Odd Couple 2 '98
Never Again '01
Next of Kin '82
The Next Step '95
Nobody's Fool '94
The Notebook '04
No Sleep 'Til Madison '02
Off Your Rocker '80
The Old Explorers '90
The Old Lady Who Walked in the Sea '91
The Old Man and the Sea '58
The Old Man and the Sea '90
Oldest Living Graduate '80
On Golden Pond '81
One Hundred and One Nights '95
Our Lady of the Assassins '01
The Out-of-Towners '99
Over the Hill '93
Pals '87
Pauline and Paulette '01
Pelle the Conqueror '88
A Piano for Mrs. Cimino '82
The Pickle '93
Picture of Dorian Gray '45
Picture of Dorian Gray '74
The Portrait '93
The Private Life of Henry VIII '33
Pushing Hands '92
Queens Logic '91
The Quiet American '02
Rabid Grannies '89
Ran '85
A Rather English Marriage '98
The Rejuvenator '88
Return of the Rebels '81
Rhapsody in August '91
The Road to Galveston '96

Growing

Rocket Gibraltar '88
Rocky Balboa '06
Roommates '95
Rooster Cogburn '75
Roses Bloom Twice '77
The Rounders '65
Ruby Jean and Joe '96
Safe House '99
Satanik '69
The Savages '07
Sea People '00
The Set-Up '49
Seven Thieves '60
The Shell Seekers '89
Shirley Valentine '89
A Shock to the System '90
The Shootist '76
Side by Side '88
The Silent Touch '94
The Simple Life of Noah Dearborn '99
Soft for Digging '01
The Son of the Bride '01
A Song for Martin '01
Space Cowboys '00
Standing in the Shadows of Motown '02
Star Trek: Insurrection '98
Starting Out in the Evening '07
Stephen King's Golden Years '91
The Straight Story '99
Strangers in Good Company '91
Street Music '81
Summer Snow '94
Summer Solstice '81
Summer Wishes, Winter Dreams '73
Tell Me a Riddle '80
Texas Guns '90
That's Life! '86
These Old Broads '01
Things Change '88
30 is a Dangerous Age, Cynthia '68
Three Strange Loves '49
To Dance with the White Dog '93
To Forget Venice '79
Tokyo Story '53
Toto le Heros '91
Tough Guys '86
Traveling Companion '96
Tuesdays with Morrie '99
Twilight '98
Two for the Road '67
Two of a Kind '82
2 Seconds '98
Two Weeks in Another Town '62
Umberto D '55
Unforgiven '92
Unhook the Stars '96
Venus '06
Voyage of the Heart '90
Voyage to the Beginning of the World '96
The Wasp Woman '59
The Wendell Baker Story '05
The Whales of August '87
When a Woman Ascends the Stairs '60
Where the Money Is '00
The Wild Bunch '69
Wild Horses '95
Wild Strawberries '57
A Woman's Tale '92
The World's Fastest Indian '05
Wrestling Ernest Hemingway '93
Yes Nurse! No Nurse! '02

Gunslingers

see also Pardners;
Second Chance; Western
Comedy; Western
Westerns;
Westrogens

Adios, Sabata '71
The Alamo '04
The Assassination of Jesse James by the Coward Robert Ford '07
Blind Justice '07
Cat Ballou '65
Dear Wendy '05
Death of a Gunfighter '69
The Desperadoes '43
Dust '01
El Dorado '67
A Fistful of Dollars '64
For a Few Dollars More '65
Forty Guns '57
From Noon Till Three '76
A Gunfight '71
Gunfight at the O.K. Corral '57
The Gunfighter '50
Gunfighter '98
Gunfighter's Moon '96
Gunslinger '70
High Noon '52
High Noon '00
The Legend of Butch & Sundance '04
The Long Ride Home '01
The Magnificent Seven '60
The Man Who Shot Liberty Valance '62
More Dead Than Alive '68
My Darling Clementine '46
Once Upon a Time in the West '68
The Outsider '02
The Quick and the Dead '87
The Quick and the Dead '95
Return of Sabata '71
Rio Bravo '59
Sabata '69
Shane '53
Shanghai Noon '00
The Shootist '76
Support Your Local Gunfighter '71
3:10 to Yuma '07
3:10 to Yuma '57
Ticket to Tomahawk '50
Tombstone '93
Unforgiven '92
Westward '73
Wyatt Earp '94

Gymnastics

American Anthem '86
Breaking Free '95
Dream to Believe '85
The Gymnast '06
I Was a Teenage Werewolf '57
Nadia '84
Peaceful Warrior '06
Stick It '06

Gypsies

The Advocate '93
Angelo My Love '83
Babes in Toyland '61
Black Cat, White Cat '98
Carmen '83
Chocolat '00
The Hunchback of Notre Dame '23
The Hunchback of Notre Dame '39
The Hunchback of Notre Dame '57
The Hunchback of Notre Dame '82
The Hunchback of Notre Dame '96
The Hunchback of Notre Dame '97
Incredibly Strange Creatures Who Stopped Living and Became Mixed-Up Zombies '63
Into the West '92
Le Gitan '75
Little Minister '34
Love Potion #9 '92
The Man Who Cried '00
The Raggedy Rawney '90
Snatch '00
Stephen King's Thinner '96
Time of the Gypsies '90
Triumph of the Spirit '89
The Wolf Man '41

Hackers

see also Computers

Category 6: Day of Destruction '04
Confess '05
The Core '03
Demolition Man '93
Die Hard '88
Double Play '96
Ferris Bueller's Day Off '86
Hackers '95
Hellraiser: Hellworld '05
Jumpin' Jack Flash '86
The Lather Effect '06
Live Free or Die Hard '07
Mission: Impossible '96
The Net '95
Real Genius '85
Sneakers '92
Superman 3 '83
Swordfish '01
Twilight Man '96
WarGames '83
Weird Science '85

Halloween

American Nightmare '00
Boo! '05
Casper '95
Clown Murders '83
Double Double Toil and Trouble '94
E.T.: The Extra-Terrestrial '82
The Fear: Halloween Night '99
Frankenstein and Me '96
Frankenstein Sings... The Movie '95
Halloween '78
Halloween '07
Halloween 2: The Nightmare Isn't Over! '81
Halloween 3: Season of the Witch '82
Halloween 4: The Return of Michael Myers '88
Halloween 5: The Revenge of Michael Myers '89
Halloween 6: The Curse of Michael Myers '95
Halloween: H20 '98
Hocus Pocus '93
The Hollywood Knights '80
House of 1000 Corpses '03
Idle Hands '99
I've Been Waiting for You '98
Jack-O '95
KISS Meets the Phantom of the Park '78
The Legend of Sleepy Hollow '86
The Midnight Hour '85
Mozart and the Whale '05
Night of the Demons '88
Night of the Demons 2 '94
Night of the Demons 3 '97
The Nightmare before Christmas '93
Return of the Living Dead: Rave to the Grave '05
Revenge of the Living Zombies '88
Satan's Little Helper '04
Spaced Invaders '90
Teen Alien '78
Trick or Treat '86
Trick or Treats '82
Twin Falls Idaho '99
Wacko '83
When Good Ghouls Go Bad '01

Hallucinations/ Illusions

A Beautiful Mind '01
Bug '06
Buried Alive '90
The Caveman's Valentine '01
The Craft '96
Cria Cuervos '76
Dark Water '05
Double Vision '02
Evil Eyes '04
The Eye '08
The Fever '04
Final '01
Ghost of the Needle '03
Ghost Ship '02
The Good Night '07
Gothika '03
Hellraiser: Hellseeker '02
Images '72
Impostor '02
Invisible Child '99
Killer Me '01
Klimt '06
Last Call: The Final Chapter of F. Scott Fitzgerald '02
A Light in the Darkness '02
Memory '06
Mirrors '78
Monkeybone '01
The Mothman Prophecies '02
Naked Lunch '91
Nightwish '89
The Nines '07
Operation Sandman: Warriors in Hell '00
Paranoia 1.0 '04
Pi '98
Rapturious '07
Repulsion '65
The Return '06
The Singing Detective '03
Soho Square '00
Solaris '03
Stir of Echoes 2: The Homecoming '07
Visitors '03
Waking Life '01
Who Wants to Kill Jessie? '65

Handyman Specials

see also Real Estate

Are We Done Yet? '07
Cold Creek Manor '03
The Evictors '79
House of Sand and Fog '03
Life as a House '01
Mr. Blandings Builds His Dream House '48
The Money Pit '86
Pacific Heights '90
Please Don't Eat the Daisies '60
The Tooth Fairy '06
Under the Tuscan Sun '03

Hard Knock Life

see also Great
Depression; Homeless

Agnes Browne '99
All or Nothing '02
Always Outnumbered Always Outgunned '98
American Buffalo '95
Angel '82
Angela's Ashes '99
The Assistant '97
The Baby Dance '98
Beggars in Ermine '34
Beijing Bicycle '01
Black Tower '50
Blessing '94
Boesman & Lena '00
A Brivele der Mamen '38
Broken Blossoms '19
Cafe Express '83
Captain Scarlett '53
Carrie '52
Catherine Cookson's The Rag Nymph '96
Charlie and the Chocolate Factory '05
The Child '05
Children of Heaven '98
City of Joy '92
Clockers '95
Code Unknown '00
The Cow '93
Crisscross '92
Crows and Sparrows '49
The Damned Don't Cry '50
Dancing at Lughnasa '98
Daughters of the Sun '00
David Copperfield '70
David Copperfield '99
Devil's Island '96
A Dog of Flanders '99
Dolores Claiborne '94
The Dreamlife of Angels '98
8 Mile '02
Elena and Her Men '56
The Entertaining Dorothy Day Story '96
Erin Brockovich '00
Extreme Measures '96
Eye of God '97
Foolish '99
Forbidden Choices '94
The Full Monty '97
The Good Earth '37
Grbavica: The Land of My Dreams '06
The Grim Reaper '62
Here Comes Cookie '35
Heroes of the Heart '94
Hidden in America '96
Hideous Kinky '99
Hollow City '04
A Home of Our Own '93
I Capture the Castle '02
In America '02
The Inheritors '98
The Italian '15
Joe Dirt '01
Jude '96
Jude the Obscure '71
Juno and the Paycock '30
Killer of Sheep '77
The King of Masks '99
La Vie en Rose '07
Lamerica '95
Laughing Sinners '31
Le Gitan '75
Les Miserables '35
Les Miserables '57
Les Miserables '78
Les Miserables '97
Liam '00
Lies My Father Told Me '75
Little Dorrit, Film 1: Nobody's Fault '88
Little Dorrit, Film 2: Little Dorrit's Story '88
Little Heroes '91
Little Women '94
Live-In Maid '04
Lolo '92
Madame Sata '02
Mama Africa '02
Mama Flora's Family '98
Marius and Jeannette '97
The Match Factory Girl '90
Me You Them '00
Meantime '81
Mrs. Wiggs of the Cabbage Patch '34
Moll Flanders '96
Monster's Ball '01
Monument Ave. '98
Mother Teresa: In the Name of God's Poor '97
My Name is Joe '98
Nicholas Nickleby '02
None But the Lonely Heart '44
Not One Less '99
The Old Curiosity Shop '94
Oliver Twist '97
Oliver Twist '00
100 Proof '96
One Third of a Nation '39
Paid in Full '02
Pay It Forward '00
Pettis Freres '00
Pocketful of Miracles '61
The Pope of Greenwich Village '84
The Pursuit of Happyness '06
Ratas, Ratones, Rateros '99
Ratcatcher '99
Restoration '94
The Road Home '01
Rosetta '99
Salaam Bombay! '88
Scrooged '88
Set It Off '96
Shadrach '98
Small Faces '95
Sparrows '26
Spider '02
Stakeout '62
Steel City '06
The Story of Fausta '88
Street Scene '31
The Super '91
The Sweetest Gift '98
Tess '79
Tess of the D'Urbervilles '98
Tess of the Storm Country '22
They Call Me Sirr '00
This Is My Father '99
Under the Moonlight '01
Vagabond '85
A Way of Life '04
Where the Hot Wind Blows '59
White Man's Burden '95
The Wide Blue Road '57
Will It Snow for Christmas? '96
Willy Wonka & the Chocolate Factory '71
Woyzeck '94
Year Zero '04
Yellow Earth '89

Harlem

see also New York, New York

American Gangster '07
Brother to Brother '04
A Brother's Kiss '97
The Cotton Club '84
Hoodlum '96
Machine Gun Blues '95
Never Die Alone '04
The Old Settler '01
Paid in Full '02
Preaching to the Choir '05
A Rage in Harlem '91
Ride '98

Hawaii

see also Island Fare

Acapulco Gold '78
The Big Bounce '04
The Black Camel '31
Blue Crush '02
Blue Hawaii '62
Charlie Chan in Honolulu '38
50 First Dates '04
Forgetting Sarah Marshall '08
Hawaii '66
Hercules '83
In God's Hands '98
Lilo & Stitch '02
Lilo & Stitch 2: Stitch Has a Glitch '05
Magnum P.I.: Don't Eat the Snow in Hawaii '80
Paradise, Hawaiian Style '66
Pearl '78
Pearl Harbor '01
Picture Bride '94
Punch-Drunk Love '02
Race the Sun '96
Riding Giants '04
Sailor Beware '52
Silk 2 '89
A Very Brady Sequel '96
Waikiki '80
Waikiki Wedding '37

Heads!

see also Brains!; Ears!;
Eyeballs!; Renegade
Body Parts

Botched '07
The Brain that Wouldn't Die '63
Braveheart '95
8 Heads in a Duffel Bag '96
Highlander '86
Highlander 2: The Quickening '91
Highlander: The Final Dimension '94
The Hitchhiker's Guide to the Galaxy '81

The Incredible Two-Headed Transplant '71
The Man with Two Brains '83▶
Mystery Men '99
Seven '79

Hearts!

see also Eyeballs!

An American Werewolf in Paris '97
Angel Heart '87
Apocalypto '06▶
Article 99 '92
Awake '07
Blood Work '02
Brainstorm '83
City of Angels '98
Dead in a Heartbeat '02
Dumb & Dumber '94
From Dusk Till Dawn '95
Heart '99
Indiana Jones and the Temple of Doom '84▶
The Intruder '04▶
John Q '02
The Last of the Mohicans '92▶
Legends of the Fall '94
Mary Shelley's Frankenstein '94
My Bloody Valentine '81
The Prophecy '95
The Prophecy 2: Ashtown '97
Pulp Fiction '94▶
Return to Me '00
Split Second '92
Tales from the Crypt Presents Bordello of Blood '96
The Terminator '84▶

Heaven Sent

see also Angels

All Dogs Go to Heaven '89
All Dogs Go to Heaven 2 '95
All of Me '84
Almost an Angel '90
Always '89
Angel on My Shoulder '46▶
Angel on My Shoulder '80
The Bishop's Wife '47▶
Brewster McCloud '70▶
Brother John '70▶
Bruce Almighty '03
Carousel '56▶
Chances Are '89▶
Charley and the Angel '73
Clarence '91
Constantine '05
Date with an Angel '87
Defending Your Life '91▶
Dogma '99
Down to Earth '01
The Family Man '79
Field of Dreams '89▶
Forever Darling '56
Ghost '90▶
Ghost Dad '90
A Guy Named Joe '44
He Sees You When You're Sleeping '02
Heading for Heaven '47
Heart Condition '90
Heaven '87
Heaven Can Wait '43▶
Heaven Can Wait '78▶
The Heavenly Kid '85
Hello Again '87
Here Comes Mr. Jordan '41▶
The Horn Blows at Midnight '41▶
I Married an Angel '42
It Came Upon a Midnight Clear '84
It's a Wonderful Life '46▶
Kiss Me Goodbye '82
Liliom '35▶
The Littlest Angel '69
Made in Milan '51▶
Mr. Destiny '90
The Next Voice You Hear '50
No News from God '01
Noah '98
Oh, God! '77
Oh, God! Book 2 '80
Oh, God! You Devil '84
One Magic Christmas '85
The Preacher's Wife '96
The Return of Peter Grimm '35
Stairway to Heaven '46▶
Static '87
The Three Lives of Thomasina '63▶
To Gillian on Her 37th Birthday '96
Toothless '97
Truly, Madly, Deeply '91▶
Two of a Kind '83
What Dreams May Come '98
White Light '90
Wide Awake '97
Xanadu '80

Heists

see also Scams, Stings & Cons

Aladdin and the King of Thieves '96
Almost Partners '87
The Amazing Transparent Man '60
The Anderson Tapes '71▶
The Apple Dumpling Gang '75
Army of One '93
The Asphalt Jungle '50▶
Assault at the Rebel Girls '59
At Gunpoint '55
Back in the USSR '92
Bad Boys '95
Bad Santa '03
The Badlanders '58▶
Bandits '86
Bank Robber '93
Bellman and True '88
Bells of Coronado '50
Belly '98
Best Men '98
Beyond Fear '75
The Bicycle Thief '48▶
Big Chase '54
Big Deal on Madonna Street '58▶
Bitter Vengeance '94
The Black Lash '52
Blind Justice '94
Blood & Wine '96
The Boatniks '70
Bonnie & Clyde '67▶
Born Bad '97
Bottle Rocket '95
Bound '96
The Brain '69
Breathing Fire '91
Butch and Sundance: The Early Days '79
Captain Blackjack '51
Casino '95▶
The Catamount Killing '74
C.I.A. 2: Target Alexa '94
City Unplugged '95
The Cobra Strikes '48
Cold Around the Heart '97
Crack Up '97
Crackerjack '94
Crime Broker '94
Crime Spree '03
Crooks & Coronets '69
Croupier '97▶
The Curse of Inferno '96
The Curse of the Jade Scorpion '01
Danger: Diabolik '68
Daring Dobermans '73
Dead Heat on a Merry-Go-Round '66▶
Dead Presidents '95
Deadly Diamonds '91
Death Tide '58
The Deputy Drummer '35
Desperate Cargo '41
The Desperate Trail '94
Destiny Turns on the Radio '95
Dog Eat Dog '64
Dollars '71▶
Double Deal '84
Double Trouble '91
Dunston Checks In '95
11 Harrowhouse '74▶
Extreme Honor '01
Face '97
Fast Money '96
Firetrap '01
Five Golden Dragons '67
The Florida Connection '74
Four Ways Out '57
Free Ride '86
French Kiss '95
The Getaway '72
The Getaway '93
Getting Even with Dad '94
Going in Style '79▶
Grand Larceny '92
Great Bank Hoax '78
Great Gold Swindle '84
The Green Glove '52
Grisbi '53
Gun Crazy '49▶
Gun Girls '56
Guns Don't Argue '57
Gypsy '75
Hard Gun '93
Happy New Year '87
Happy, Texas '99▶
Hard Cash '01
Hard Hunted '92
The Hard Truth '94
The Hard Word '02
Harley Davidson and the Marlboro Man '91
The Hoodlum '51
The Horse Without a Head '63
Hot Target '85
Hot Touch '82
How to Steal a Million '66▶
I Died a Thousand Times '55
Ice '93
The Immortals '95
Incident at Deception Ridge '94
Inside Information '34
Interceptor '92
Jet Ride to Nowhere '78
Kelly's Heroes '70
Killer Force '75
The Killing '56▶
Killing Zoe '94
Killing in the Sun '73
King's Ransom '91
Lassiter '84
The Last of Mrs. Cheyney '37
Late Extra '35
The Lavender Hill Mob '51▶
The League of Gentlemen '60▶
Letting the Birds Go Free '86
A Life Less Ordinary '97
Lightning Jack '94
Like a Fish Out of Water '99
The Lion's Share '79
Look, Stock and 2 Smoking Barrels '98▶
Loophole '83
Mad Money '08
A Man, a Woman, and a Bank '79
Man Trouble '92
Marbella '85
Marked Money '28
Master Touch '74
Midnight Limited '40
Mission Batangas '69
Money Movers '78
Money to Burn '83
Motorama '91
My Dog, the Thief '69
Normal Life '96
Diamond Fleece '92
Diamond Trail '33
The Diamond Trap '91
Die Hard '88▶
Die Hard: With a Vengeance '95
On the Border '98
Once a Thief '96▶
Operation Condor 2: The Armour of the Gods '86
Out of Sight '98▶
Palookaville '95
Pardon My Sarong '42
Passionate Thief '60
The Perfect Score '04▶
Persons Unknown '96
Point Break '91
Queen of Diamonds '70
The Real McCoy '93
The Real Thing '97
The Rebel Set '59
Reindeer Games '00
The Return of Boston Blackie '27
Rififi '54▶
The Rip Off '78
Robbery '67
Robbery '85
Rough Cut '80
R.P.M. '97
Scarlet Street '45▶
The Score '01
Set It Off '95
Sexy Beast '00▶
Shadow Man '75
Slaughterday '77
Sneakers '92▶
Spider's Web '01
The Spree '96
The Squeeze '87
Stranger in the House '97
Styx '00
They Met in Bombay '41
Thick as Thieves '99
Thief '81▶
The Thief Who Came to Dinner '73
Three Kings '99▶
To Catch a Thief '55▶
Too Many Crooks '59
Topkapi '64▶
Trapped in Paradise '94
Truth or Consequences, N.M. '97
Two by Four '95
Two-Way Stretch '60
The Underneath '95▶
The Usual Suspects '95▶
Velocity Trap '99
When I Close My Eyes '93
Where the Money is '00
White Fire '84
White Tiger '23
Who'll Stop the Rain? '78▶
The Wrong Arm of the Law '63▶
The Wrong Road '37
X Marks the Spot '42

Heists: Armored Car

Armored Car Robbery '50
Burnt Money '00
Criss Cross '48▶
Firefight '03
Hard Rain '97
Kansas City Confidential '52▶
Raven's Ridge '97
Seven Seconds '05
The Take '07

Heists: Art

Art Heist '05
Body Count '97
Canvas: The Fine Art of Crime '92
Entrapment '99
Four Dogs Playing Poker '00
Gambit '66
The Good Thief '03▶
Milo Milo '79
Once a Thief '90
Ordinary Decent Criminal '99

Heists: Gold/Precious Metals

Adios, Sabata '71
B.A.D. Cats '80
Exiled '06
Fool's Gold: The Story of the Brink's-Mat Robbery '92
Ocean's 11 '60
Ocean's Eleven '01
Ocean's Thirteen '07▶
Rip It Off '02
Seven Thieves '60▶
3000 Miles to Graceland '01
Plunder Road '57
Raiders of Ghost City '44
Red Desert '50
Sam Whiskey '63
South Park: Bigger, Longer and Uncut '99
Spawn '97▶
Western Gold '37
What Dreams May Come '98
When Eight Bells Toll '71
Witchery '88

Heists: Banks

American Madness '32
Bandits '01
The Bank Dick '40▶
The Bank Job '08▶
Bank Shot '74▶
The Big Scam '79
City of Industry '96
City on Fire '87
Crime Wave '54
Crimson Gold '03
Fish in a Barrel '01
Flawless '07
44 Minutes: The North Hollywood Shootout '03
The Front Line '06
Fun With Dick and Jane '05
The Great St. Louis Bank Robbery '59
Heat '95▶
Heaven's Burning '97
Hero Wanted '08
Hot Money '79
Inside Man '06▶
Inspector Gadget 2 '02
Kill Me Later '01
Killer '73
Lights in the Dusk '06
Living & Dying '07
The Lookout '07▶
Lost '05
Love is Colder Than Death '69
Malevolence '04
A New Wave '07
No Good Deed '02
Odds Against Tomorrow '59▶
Pups '99
The Robin Hood Geng '98
Robin's Hood '03
Scorched '02
The Set Up '95
Shakedown '02
Small Time Crooks '00
Stander '03
Stark Raving Mad '02
The Stickup '01
Sugar & Spice '01
Swindle '02
Taxi '04
Thunderbirds '04

Heists: Casinos

Any Number Can Win '63
The Aura '05▶
Bob le Flambeur '55▶
Ghost of a Chance '01
The Good Thief '03▶
The Hollywood Sign '01
The Ladykillers '04
My Name is Modesty: A Modesty Blaise Adventure '04

Heists: Trains

Alberto Express '92
Butch Cassidy and the Sundance Kid '69▶
The Great Train Robbery '79▶
The Gray Fox '85▶
House of Bamboo '55
Money Train '95
Night Passage '57
Tough Guys '86

Heists: Jewels

After the Sunset '04
All About the Benjamins '02
And Now Ladies and Gentlemen '02
Before the Devil Knows You're Dead '07▶
Big Brown Eyes '36
Bliss '35▶
Bloodstone '88
Botched '07
Cradle 2 the Grave '03
Diamond Run '00
Every Girl Should Have One '78
Fathom '67
Femme Fatale '02
The Hot Rock '70▶
The Hot Tamale '06
I Hate Blondes '06
Le Cercle Rouge '70▶
Lift '01
Little Man '06
Mad Mission 3 '84
Modesty Blaise '66
The Moonstone '72
Mr. Takes a Vacation '39
Murph the Surf '75
Ocean's Twelve '04
Operation Amsterdam '60
Picture Claire '01
The Pink Panther '64▶
Place Vendome '98▶
Resevoir Dogs '92▶
Score '95
Snatch '00▶
The Squeeze '80
They Met in a Taxi '36
Triplecross '95
Welcome to Collinwood '02
The Old Lady Who Walked in the Sea '91
Old Mother Riley's New Venture '49
The Thomas Crown Affair '68▶
The Thomas Crown Affair '99▶
The Wrecking Crew '68
Widows '02

Hell

see also Death & the Afterlife; Devils; Religion: Satanism

Bill & Ted's Bogus Journey '91
Constantine '05
Dark Angel: The Ascent '94
The Doorway '00
Faust: Love of the Damned '00
Freddy vs. Jason '03
Hellbound: Hellraiser 2 '88
Hellboy '04
Hellboy 2: The Golden Army '08
Hellraiser '87
Hellraiser 3: Hell on Earth '92
Hellraiser 4: Bloodline '95
Hellraiser 5: Inferno '00
Highway to Hell '92
Little Nicky '00
Rapturous '07

Hell High School

see also Cheerleaders; High School; Dedicated Teachers; Errant Educators; High School Reunions; Prom; School Daze; Teen Angst

Angus '95
Animal Room '95
Anything for Love '93
Bad Reputation '05
The Beat '88
Big Bully '95
Bill & Ted's Excellent Adventure '89
Billy Madison '94
Black Circle Boys '97
Blackboard Jungle '55
Blood of Dracula '57
Bloodmoon '90
Boltneck '98
Born Innocent '74
Boy's Reformatory '39
The Brady Bunch Movie '95
Brutal Fury '92
Buffy the Vampire Slayer '92
Carrie '76
Carrie '02
Catch Me... If You Can '89
Cemetery High '89
Cheaters '00
Cheering Section '73
Cherry Hill High '76
The Chicken Chronicles '77
A Cinderella Story '04
Class '83
Class Act '91
Class of Fear '91
Class of '44 '73
The Class of Miss MacMichael '78
Class of 1984 '82
Class of 1999 '90
Class of 1999 2: The Substitute '93
Class of Nuke 'Em High '86
Class of Nuke 'Em High 2: Subhumanoid Meltdown '91
Class of Nuke 'Em High 3: The Good, the Bad and the Subhumanoid '94
Class Reunion Massacre '77
The Club '94
Clueless '95
Coach '78
Coneheads '93
Cooley High '75
The Craft '96
Creepers '85
Crisis at Central High '80
Cruel Intentions 2 '99
Cry-Baby '90
Cutting Class '89
Dangerously Close '86
Dazed and Confused '93
Deadly Fieldtrip '74
Deal of a Lifetime '99
Death Goes to School '53
Demolition High '95
Detention '03
Disturbing Behavior '98
Echoes in the Darkness '87
Elephant '03
Ernest Goes to School '94
The Ernest Green Story '93
Evil '03
The Faculty '98
Fast Times at Ridgemont High '82
Fear '96
Ferris Bueller's Day Off '86
Finishing School '33
5 Dark Souls '96
Ginger Snaps '01
Graduation Day '81
Grease 2 '82
The Great St. Trinian's Train Robbery '66
Hadley's Rebellion '84

Halloween: H20 '98
Hangman's Curse '03
Hard Knox '83
Hard Lessons '86
Heart of America '03
Heathers '89
Hell High '86
Hide and Go Shriek '87
Hiding Out '87
High School Caesar '60
High School Confidential '58
High School High '96
High School USA '84
Hollywood High '77
Home Room '02
Homework '82
Hoosiers '86
Hostage High '97
I Was a Teenage Werewolf '57
I Was a Teenage Zombie '87
If... '69
The Impostor '84
The Invisible Kid '88
The Invisible Maniac '90
Joy of Sex '84
Just One of the Girls '93
Kids in America '05
Killing Mr. Griffin '97
The Lawrenceville Stories '88
Light It Up '99
Little Witches '96
Lone Wolf '88
Loose Screws '85
Lust for a Vampire '71
Major Payne '95
The Majorettes '87
Making the Grade '84
Massacre at Central High '76
Maya '82
Mean Girls '04
Mirror, Mirror '90
Mr. Woodcock '07
Monster High '89
My Bodyguard '80
Napoleon Dynamite '04
National Lampoon's Senior Trip '95
Night Visitor '89
Nowhere to Run '88
On the Edge: The Survival of Dana '79
187 '97
One Night Only '84
Only the Strong '93
Pandemonium '82
Peggy Sue Got Married '86
Pep Squad '98
Plain Clothes '88
Platinum High School '60
Porky's '82
Porky's 2: The Next Day '83
The Positively True Adventures of the Alleged Texas Cheerleader-Murdering Mom '93
Pretty Persuasion '05
Princess Academy '87
Prison for Children '93
Prom Night '80
Prom Night 4: Deliver Us from Evil '91
Pump Up the Volume '90
The Quiet '05
The Rage: Carrie 2 '99
Rebel High '88
Return to Horror High '87
Rock 'n' Roll High School Forever '91
Rock, Pretty Baby '56
Satan's Cheerleaders '77
Satan's School for Girls '73
School Ties '92
School's Out '99
Screwballs '83
Senior Trip '81
Serial Killing 101 '04
Show Me Love '99
Showdown '93

Shriek If You Know What I Did Last Friday the 13th '00
Sidekicks '93
Sister Act 2: Back in the Habit '93
Sixteen Candles '84
Slaughter High '86
Some Kind of Wonderful '87
Speak '04
Spliced '03
Stay Awake '87
Strangers with Candy '06
Student Affairs '88
Student Bodies '81
The Substitute '93
The Substitute '96
Summer School '87
Sunset Park '96
Superstar '99
Teaching Mrs. Tingle '99
Teenage Strangler '64
Terror Squad '87
3:15—The Moment of Truth '86
Three o'Clock High '87
Tom Brown's School Days '51
Trick or Treat '86
Twisted Brain '74
Undercover '87
Valentine '01
Wanderers '79
Werewolf in a Girl's Dormitory '61
When Evil Calls '06
White Squall '96
Zero for Conduct '33
Zombie High '87

The Help: Female

Adelheid '69
Alex Rider: Operation Stormbreaker '06
Au Pair Girls '72
Backstairs at the White House '79
The Beautician and the Beast '97
Blue Crush '02
Boeing Boeing '65
The Brady Bunch Movie '95
The Chase '01
Cora Unashamed '00
Cotton Mary '99
Cries and Whispers '72
Diary of a Chambermaid '46
Diary of a Chambermaid '64
Die Mommie Die! '03
Dreaming About You '92
8 Women '02
Elvira's Haunted Hills '02
End of Desire '62
Eternal '04
The Farmer's Daughter '47
For Love of Ivy '68
For Real '02
Friends with Money '06
Girl with a Pearl Earring '03
Gone with the Wind '39
Gosford Park '01
Grave Indiscretions '96
His Butler's Sister '44
Houseboat '58
The Housekeeper '86
I Can't Sleep '93
Imitation of Life '34
Imitation of Life '59
In the White City '83
Jane Eyre '06
Kama Sutra: A Tale of Love '96
Keeping Mum '05
The King and I '99
La Ceremonie '95
The Long Walk Home '89
Love Actually '03
Loyalties '86
Made in Heaven '52
The Maid '90
Maid in Manhattan '02
Maid to Order '87
Maid's Night Out '38

A Matter of Time '76
The Member of the Wedding '97
Miss Pettigrew Lives for a Day '08
Mrs. Parkington '44
Murder by Death '76
My Chauffeur '86
The Omen '06
The Others '01
Personal Maid '31
Plain Jane '01
Poison '01
Private Lessons '75
Rebecca '40
Rebecca '97
The Remains of the Day '93
The Rules of the Game '39
The Silences of the Palace '94
Sister My Sister '94
The Skeleton Key '05
Spanglish '04
That Funny Feeling '65
That Obscure Object of Desire '77
Traveling Companion '96
Under the Same Moon '07
Under the Sun '98
Uptown Girls '03
A Very Brady Sequel '96
The Well '97
A Woman of Substance '84
Woman Wanted '98

The Help: Male

The Admirable Crichton '57
Arthur '81
Arthur 2: On the Rocks '88
Backstairs at the White House '79
B.A.P.'s '97
Batman '89
Batman and Robin '97
Batman Begins '05
Batman Forever '95
Batman Returns '92
Bernard and Doris '08
The Black Widow '05
Blue Blood '73
Bob the Butler '05
Candleshoe '78
Casanova '05
Catherine Cookson's The Moth '96
The Cowboys '72
The Dark Knight '08
Driving Miss Daisy '89
The Duke '99
The Empty Acre '07
The Fallen Idol '49
Family Jewels '50
Far from Heaven '02
Fido '06
Gosford Park '01
Grave Indiscretions '96
Heaven Can Wait '78
Institue Benjamenta or This Dream People Call Human Life '95
The Kite Runner '07
The Ladies' Man '61
Lady Chatterley's Lover '55
Lady Chatterley's Lover '81
Lara Croft: Tomb Raider '01
Maurice '87
Miss Julie '99
Mrs. Brown '97
Murder by Death '76
My Man Godfrey '36
My Man Godfrey '57
Nothing But Trouble '44
On the Run '83
The Princess Diaries 2: Royal Engagement '04
Private Lessons '75
The Remains of the Day '93
Richie Rich '94
Ruggles of Red Gap '35
Screwed '00
The Servant '63

Sheitan '06
Sitting Pretty '48
Stiff Upper Lips '96
Trading Places '83
The Water Horse: Legend of the Deep '07

Hide the Dead Guy

Arsenic and Old Lace '44
Black Cat, White Cat '98
Blue Ridge Fall '99
Dead Bodies '03
Drop Dead Sexy '05
El Crimen Perfecto '04
Enid is Sleeping '90
Grand Theft Parsons '03
Head Above Water '96
I'll Bury You Tomorrow '02
Jawbreaker '98
Jindabyne '06
The Last Supper '96
Little Miss Sunshine '06
Living Doll '90
Lost Junction '03
Pulp Fiction '94
Shallow Grave '94
Siblings '04
Silver City '04
A Slight Case of Murder '38
The Three Burials of Melquiades Estrada '05
The Trouble with Harry '55
Up at the Villa '00
Very Bad Things '98
Volver '06
Waking Ned Devine '98

High School

see also Hell High School; Teen Angst

American Gun '05
American Pie '99
Angel Rodriguez '05
Apt Pupil '97
Believe in Me '06
Better Luck Tomorrow '02
Blackboard Jungle '55
Blue Car '03
The Boys of Baraka '05
Bratz '07
The Breakfast Club '85
Brick '06
Can't Buy Me Love '87
Can't Hardly Wait '98
Chalk '06
Charlie Bartlett '07
A Cinderella Story '04
Coach Carter '05
Confessions of a Teenage Drama Queen '04
The Craft '96
Dangerous Minds '95
Drillbit Taylor '08
Dumb and Dumberer: When Harry Met Lloyd '03
Election '99
Encino Man '92
Evergreen '04
The Fast and the Furious '01
Ferris Bueller's Day Off '86
The Final Season '07
Freedom Writers '07
Friday Night Lights '04
Full of It '07
Games of Love and Chance '03
Get a Clue '02
Get Over It! '01
The Girl Next Door '04
Gracie '07
Grease '78
Hairspray '07
The Heart of the Game '05
High School High '96
High School Musical '06
High School USA '84
Hometown Legend '02
Hoosiers '86
The Hot Chick '02
How to Deal '03
Ice Princess '05
Jawbreaker '98
John Tucker Must Die '06
Juno '07
Just Friends '05
Kids in America '05

Lean on Me '89
Lord Love a Duck '66
Love Don't Cost a Thing '03
Maryam '00
Mean Girls '04
Mr. Holland's Opus '95
Murder in New Hampshire: The Pamela Smart Story '91
Napoleon Dynamite '04
Never Back Down '08
Never Been Kissed '99
The New Guy '02
Noi '03
Not Another Teen Movie '01
O '01
187 '97
Orange County '02
The Perfect Score '04
Platinum High School '60
Players '03
Porky's '82
Porky's 2: The Next Day '83
Porky's Revenge '85
Possums '99
Pretty in Pink '86
The Principal '87
Radio '03
The Red Sneakers '01
Rock 'n' Roll High School '79
Rock 'n' Roll High School Forever '91
Rocket Science '07
The Rookie '02
Rushmore '98
Rustin '01
Save the Last Dance '01
Saved! '04
Seventeen Again '00
She's All That '99
Sixteen Candles '84
Sky High '05
Some Kind of Wonderful '87
Stand and Deliver '88
Step Up '06
Sugar & Spice '01
Summer School '87
Swimfan '02
Take the Lead '06
Teachers '84
Ten Things I Hate about You '99
There Goes My Baby '92
They Call Me Sirr '00
Through the Fire '05
A Time for Dancing '00
Underclassman '05
Varsity Blues '98
Virgin '03

High School Reunions

see also School Daze

Archie: Return to Riverdale '90
Beautiful Girls '96
Class Reunion '72
Class Reunion Massacre '77
Grosse Pointe Blank '97
Just Friends '05
Mutual Needs '97
National Lampoon's Class Reunion '82
Peggy Sue Got Married '86
Romy and Michele's High School Reunion '97
Since You've Been Gone '97
Something Wild '86
Terror Stalks the Class Reunion '93

Hijacked!

Agent Red '00
Air Force One '97
Airport '77 '77
The Annihilators '85
Appointment in Honduras '53
Cotton Comes to Harlem '70
Delta Force '86
Die Hard 2: Die Harder '90

▶ = rated three bones or higher

Drop Zone '94
Final Approach '04
The Fourth Angel '01
The Hamburg Cell '04
Hi-Jacked '50
Hostage '87
Maniac '77
Overland Stage Raiders '38
Passenger 57 '92
The Pursuit of D.B. Cooper '81
Star Trek 5: The Final Frontier '89
The Taking of Pelham One Two Three '74
Under Siege 2: Dark Territory '95
United 93 '06
Victory at Entebbe '76

Hinduism

Earth '98
Fire '96
Gandhi '82
The Guru '02
The Mystic Masseur '01
Water '05

Hip-Hop/Rap

Be Cool '05
Brown Sugar '02
Bulworth '98
Bunny Whipped '06
Carmen: A Hip Hopera '01
CB4: The Movie '93
Cool As Ice '91
Da Hip Hop Witch '00
Dave Chappelle's Block Party '06
8 Mile '02
Fade to Black '04
Fear of a Black Hat '94
Feel the Noise '07
Fly by Night '93
Friday '95
G '02
Get Rich or Die Tryin' '05
The Gospel '05
Hip Hop 4 Life '02
The Hit '06
Hollywood Homicide '03
Honey '03
House Party '90
House Party 2: The Pajama Jam '91
House Party 3 '94
Hustle & Flow '05
In the Mix '05
Irish Jam '05
Kickin' It Old Skool '07
Krush Groove '85
Leprechaun 5: In the Hood '99
Makin' Baby '02
Malibu's Most Wanted '03
Marci X '03
Murda Muzik '03
New Jersey Drive '95
The Perfect Holiday '07
Rapturous '07
Rude Boy: The Jamaican Don '03
The Show '95
Snipes '01
State Property 2 '05
Tougher Than Leather '88
The Underground '97
Who's the Man? '93
You Got Served '04

Hispanic America

Barrio Wars '02
Chasing Papi '03
crazy/beautiful '01
The Dead One '07
Dragstrip Girl '94
East Side Story '07
Fools Rush In '97
Gabriela '01
Hitz '89
I Like It Like That '94
Illegal Tender '07
Lone Star '95
Lotto Land '95
Luminarias '59
Maid in Manhattan '02
The Maldonado Miracle '03
Mambo Cafe '00
Mambo '03
Maricela '88
Mi Vida Loca '94
Miami Rhapsody '95
My Family '94
Our Song '01
Pinero '01
Quinceanera '06
Race '99
Raising Victor Vargas '03
Real Women Have Curves '02
The Ring '52
Roosters '95
Salsa '88
Selena '96
Spin '04
Stand and Deliver '88
Steal Big, Steal Little '95
The Street King '02
Sueno '05
Sweet 15 '90
Tortilla Soup '01
Wassup Rockers '06
The Wind That Shakes the Barley '06
Zoot Suit '81

Historical Detectives

The Adventures of Sherlock Holmes '39
The Alphabet Murders '65
Appointment with Death '88
The Barbary Coast '74
The Crucifer of Blood '91
Death on the Nile '78
Dressed to Kill '46
Evil under the Sun '82
Great K & A Train Robbery '26
The Great Mouse Detective '86
Hands of a Murderer '90
Heat of the Sun '99
The Hound of the Baskervilles '39
The Hound of the Baskervilles '59
The Hound of the Baskervilles '77
The Hound of the Baskervilles '83
The Hound of the Baskervilles '00
The Hound of the Baskervilles '02
House of Fear '45
Masks at the Baskervilles '37
Murder at the Baskervilles '37
Murder by Decree '79
Murder on Approval '56
Murder on the Orient Express '74
The Name of the Rose '86
The Pearl of Death '44
The Private Life of Sherlock Holmes '70
Pursuit to Algiers '45
The Ripper '97
The Rose and the Jackal '90
Scarlet Claw '44
The Seven-Per-Cent Solution '76
Sherlock Holmes and the Deadly Necklace '62
Sherlock Holmes and the Incident at Victoria Falls '91
Sherlock Holmes and the Secret Weapon '42
Sherlock Holmes Faces Death '43
Sherlock Holmes in Washington '43
Sherlock Holmes: The Voice of Terror '42
The Sign of Four '83
The Sign of Four '01
The Silent Mr. Sherlock Holmes '12
The Speckled Band '31
Spider Woman '44
A Study in Scarlet '33
A Study in Terror '66
Terror by Night '46
The Triumph of Sherlock Holmes '35
The Woman in Green '45
Young Sherlock Holmes '85

Historical Drama

see also Medieval Romps; Period Piece

Abe Lincoln in Illinois '40
Across the Wide Missouri '51
A.D. '85
The Adventures of Tom Sawyer '73
The Affair of the Necklace '01
The Agony and the Ecstasy '65
The Alamo '60
The Alamo '04
The Alamo: Thirteen Days to Glory '87
Alexander '04
Alexander the Great '55
Almost Peaceful '02
Alone Against Rome '62
Amadeus '84
Amazing Grace '06
Anastasia '56
Anastasia: The Mystery of Anna '86
Andrei Rublev '66
Anne of the Thousand Days '69
Antony and Cleopatra '73
Apocalypto '06
Army of Shadows '69
Artemisia '97
Assassination of Trotsky '72
The Attic: The Hiding of Anne Frank '88
Attila '01
Augustine of Hippo '72
The Autobiography of Miss Jane Pittman '74
Backstairs at the White House '79
The Ballad of Narayama '83
Bang Rajan '00
Barabbas '62
Barefoot in Athens '66
The Bastard '78
The Battle of Algiers '66
Battle of Britain '69
Battle of the Bulge '65
Battle of Valiant '63
The Battleship Potemkin '25
Beau Brummel '54
Becket '64
Beethoven's Nephew '88
Ben-Hur '26
Ben-Hur '59
Beowulf '07
Beowulf & Grendel '06
Bhowani Junction '56
The Big Red One '80
The Birth of a Nation '15
Black Robe '91
Blaise Pascal '71
The Blue Yonder '86
Bonnie Prince Charlie '48
The Bounty '84
Braveheart '95
A Bridge Too Far '77
Brigham Young: Frontiersman '40
Brother Sun, Sister Moon '73
The Bruce '96
The Bushido Blade '80
Cabeza de Vaca '90
Cabiria '14
Caesar and Cleopatra '46
Captain from Castile '47
Captain Caution '40
Carthage in Flames '60
Catherine Cookson's The Rag Nymph '96
Catherine the Great '34
Catherine the Great '95
Centennial '78
A Connecticut Yankee '31
Conquest '37
The Court Martial of Billy Mitchell '55
Crazy Horse '96
Cris at Central High '80
Cromwell '70
The Crossing '00
The Crucible '96
The Crusades '35
Curse of the Golden Flower '06
Dances with Wolves '90
A Dangerous Man: Lawrence after Arabia '91
Danton '82
David and Bathsheba '51
David Copperfield '35
David Copperfield '70
David Copperfield '99
The Day That Shook the World '78
DC 9/11: Time of Crisis '04
De Mayerling a Sarajevo '40
Demetrius and the Gladiators '54
Desiree '54
The Devils '71
The Devil's Disciple '59
Diane '55
Doctor Zhivago '65
Doctor Zhivago '03
Downfall '04
Druids '01
Drums in the Deep South '51
Dynasty '76
Edward II '92
Eight Men Out '88
El Cid '61
Eleanor & Franklin '76
Eleanor: First Lady of the World '82
Elizabeth '98
Elizabeth R '72
Elizabeth: The Golden Age '07
Elizabeth, the Queen '68
The Emperor and the Assassin '99
The Emperor's Shadow '96
Erik, the Viking '89
The Eternal Waltz '54
Eureka Stockade '49
Extramuros '85
Fabiola '48
FairyTale: A True Story '97
The Fall of the Roman Empire '64
The Far Horizons '55
Fellini Satyricon '69
Fiesta '35
Fire Over England '37
The First Olympics: Athens 1896 '84
Flyboys '06
Forever and a Day '43
Forty Days of Musa Dagh '85
47 Ronin, Part 1 '42
47 Ronin, Part 2 '42
1492: Conquest of Paradise '92
Freedom Road '79
Gallipoli '81
Gangs of New York '02
Gate of Hell '54
The Gathering Storm '74
Geheimakte WB1 '42
Geronimo: An American Legend '93
Gettysburg '93
Giants of Rome '63
The Girl of Your Dreams '99
Gladiator of Rome '63
Glory '89
Gods and Generals '03
Gonza the Spearman '86
Good Night, and Good Luck '05
The Gospel of John '03
Goya's Ghosts '06
The Great Commandment '41
The Greatest Game Ever Played '05
The Greatest Story Ever Told '65
Guilty by Suspicion '91
Harem '85
Hawaii '66
The Hellfire Club '61
Henry V '44
Henry V '89
Hero '03
Hiroshima '95
Hitler '62
The Horseman on the Roof '95
Hotel Rwanda '04
The Howards of Virginia '40
Hunter in the Dark '80
I Shot Andy Warhol '96
If They Tell You I Fell '89
Ike: Countdown to D-Day '04
Imperial Venus '71
In Old Chicago '37
Innocent Voices '04
The Invaders '63
The Iron Crown '41
The Iron Duke '34
Ironclads '90
Ivan the Terrible, Part 1 '44
Ivan the Terrible, Part 2 '46
Ivanhoe '52
Ivanhoe '82
Ivanhoe '97
Jakob the Liar '99
Jeanne la Pucelle '94
Jefferson in Paris '94
Jesus of Nazareth '77
The Jew '96
The Jewel in the Crown '84
JFK '91
Joan of Arc '48
Joan of Arc '99
John Adams '08
Johnny Tremain & the Sons of Liberty '58
Joyeux Noel '05
Judith of Bethulia '14
Julius Caesar '53
Justin Morgan Had a Horse '81
Kama Sutra: A Tale of Love '96
Kaspar Hauser '93
Khartoum '66
King David '85
King Richard and the Crusaders '54
Kingdom of Heaven '05
Kolberg '45
Kundun '97
La Marseillaise '37
La Nuit de Varennes '82
The Lady and the Highwayman '89
Lady Godiva '55
Lady Jane '85
Last Days of Pompeii '35
The Last Emperor '87
Last Four Days '77
The Last Legion '07
The Last of the Mohicans '85

The Charge of the Light Brigade '36
The Charge of the Light Brigade '68
Chasing the Deer '94
Children of Paradise '44
Christopher Columbus '49
Christopher Columbus: The Discovery '92
Cleopatra '34
Cleopatra '63
Condemned to Live '35

The Last Valley '71
Lawrence of Arabia '62
Le Complot '73
The Libertine '05
The Lighthorsemen '87
The Lindbergh Kidnapping Case '76
The Lion in Winter '68
The Lion in Winter '03
The Lion of Thebes '64
Lionheart '87
Little House on the Prairie '74
Lloyds of London '36
Long Shadows '86
The Lost City '05
Ludwig '72
Luther '74
The Magician of Lublin '79
The Mahabharata '89
A Man for All Seasons '66
A Man for All Seasons '88
Mandela '87
Mandela '96
Marie Antoinette '38
Marie Antoinette '06
The Marquise of O '76
Martin Luther '53
Mary of Scotland '36
Mary, Queen of Scots '71
Masada '81
Mata Hari '85
Mayerling '68
Mayflower: The Pilgrims' Adventure '79
The Messenger: The Story of Joan of Arc '99
Michael Collins '96
Missiles of October '74
The Motorcycle Diaries '04
Mountain Man '77
Mountbatten: The Last Viceroy '86
Mrs. Brown '97
Munich '05
Mutiny on the Bounty '35
Mutiny on the Bounty '62
The Nativity Story '06
Nefertiti, Queen of the Nile '64
The New World '05
Nicholas and Alexandra '71
Nightjohn '96
Nine Days a Queen '36
The Ninth Day '04
Nixon '95
Norseman '78
Omar Khayyam '57
The Ordeal of Dr. Mudd '80
Orphan Train '79
Orphans of the Storm '21
Overlanders '46
Passion of Joan of Arc '28
The Passover Plot '75
Pathfinder '07
The Pathfinder '94
The Patriot '00
Peter and Paul '81
Peter the First: Part 1 '37
Peter the First: Part 2 '38
Peter the Great '85
Pharoah's Army '95
Portrait of a Lady '96
Portrait of a Rebel: Margaret Sanger '82
The Power of One '92
Pride and Prejudice '40
The Private Life of Henry VIII '33
The Private Lives of Elizabeth & Essex '39
Queen Christina '33
Queen Margot '94
Quo Vadis '12
Quo Vadis '51
Quo Vadis '85
Ragtime '81
Raintree County '57
Rasputin '96
Rasputin '85
Rasputin and the Empress '33
Rasputin: Dark Servant of Destiny '96
The Rebels '79
The Red and the Black '57
Reign of Terror '49
A Respectable Trade '98

▶ = *rated three bones or higher*

Restoration '94▲
Revolution '85
Richard III '55▲
The Right Stuff '83▲
Rikyu '90▲
The Rise of Louis XIV '66▲
Roanoak '86
Rob Roy—The Highland Rogue '53
The Robe '53
Robin and Marian '76
Roots '77▲
Roots: The Gift '88
Roots: The Next Generation '79▲
Rosewood '96▲
Royal Deceit '94
A Royal Scandal '96
Saint Joan '57
St. Michael Had a Rooster '72
St. Patrick: The Irish Legend '00
Salome '53
Samson and Delilah '96
Samurai Banners '69
Samurai Reincarnation '81
Scarlet Empress '34▲
The Scarlet Letter '95
The Scarlet Pimpernel '34▲
The Scarlet Pimpernel '82▲
The Scarlet Pimpernel '99
The Scarlet Pimpernel 2: Mademoiselle Guillotine '99
The Scarlet Pimpernel 3: The Kidnapped King '99
The Scarlet Tunic '97
Sebastiane '79▲
The Seekers '79
Senso '54▲
Separate but Equal '91▲
September Dawn '07
Shaka Zulu '83▲
Shenandoah '65▲
Shin Heike Monogatari '55▲
The Sicilian '87
The Sign of the Cross '33
The Silk Road '92
Sins of Rome '54
Six Wives of Henry VIII '71▲
Soldier in Love '67
Soldier of Orange '78▲
Song of Love '47▲
Sophie Scholl: The Final Days '05▲
Soul of the Game '96▲
Spartacus '60▲
Spy of Napoleon '36
Sunrise at Campobello '60▲
Surviving Picasso '96
The Sword of El Cid '62
Tai-Pan '86
A Tale of Two Cities '89▲
Tamango '59
The Ten Commandments '23
The Ten Commandments '56▲
Ten Days That Shook the World '27▲
Ten Who Dared '60
Tharus Son of Attila '87
That Hamilton Woman '41▲
There Will Be Blood '07▲
Therese '86▲
They Died with Their Boots On '41▲
Thirteen Days '00▲
'38: Vienna before the Fall '88
This England '42
The Thorn Birds '83▲
300 '07
Three Sovereigns for Sarah '85
To End All Wars '01
The Tower of London '39
The Tower of London '62
Tower of Screaming Virgins '68
The Triangle Factory Fire Scandal '79
The Truce '96▲
True Women '97
The Tunnel '01▲
Uncle Tom's Cabin '14
Uncle Tom's Cabin '69

Untold Scandal '03
Uranus '91▲
Vanina Vanini '61▲
Victoria Regina '61
The Virgin Queen '55▲
Viva Zapata! '52▲
The War Lord '65▲
Warrior Queen '87
The Warriors '55
Waterloo '71
Weeping Meadow '04
The White Rose '83▲
Who Has Seen the Wind? '77
The Winds of Kitty Hawk '78
The Winter War '89▲
A Woman Called Golda '82▲
A Woman Called Moses '78
Young Bess '53▲
Young Catherine '91▲
Young Mr. Lincoln '39▲

Historical Romance

see also Historical Drama
The Affair of the Necklace '01
The Agony and the Ecstasy '65
Alexander '04
Anne of the Thousand Days '69▲
Becoming Jane '07
Braveheart '95▲
Caesar and Cleopatra '46
Casanova '05
Catherine the Great '34
Catherine the Great '95
Clarissa '91▲
Cleopatra '34
Cleopatra '63
Cleopatra '99
David and Bathsheba '51▲
Doctor Zhivago '65▲
Doctor Zhivago '03
Eleanor & Franklin '76▲
The Hunchback of Notre Dame '57
The Hunchback of Notre Dame '82▲
The Hunchback of Notre Dame '96▲
Ivanhoe '52▲
Ivanhoe '82
Ivanhoe '97▲
Jefferson in Paris '94
Kama Sutra: A Tale of Love '96
The Last of the Mohicans '85
Mrs. Brown '97▲
The New World '05▲
Nicholas and Alexandra '71
The Other Boleyn Girl '08
Portrait of a Lady '67
Portrait of a Lady '96▲
Pride and Prejudice '40▲
The Private Life of Henry VIII '33▲
The Private Lives of Elizabeth & Essex '39▲
Ragtime '81▲
Silk '07

Hit Men/Women

see also Assassination; Organized Crime
African Rage '78
Amateur '94▲
Amores Perros '00▲
Angel's Dance '99
Assassins '95
Assassination Tango '03▲
Back to Back '96
Baja '95
Ballistic: Ecks vs. Sever '02
Bangkok Dangerous '08
Big City Blues '99
The Big Hit '98
Big Trouble '02
Blackjack '97
Blast of Silence '61
Blonde and Blonder '07
Body Count '95
The Bodyguard '92
The Bourne Identity '02▲
Breakaway '95
Brother '97
Bulletproof Heart '95▲
Bulworth '98▲
Chain of Fools '00
Chameleon '98
Codename: Jaguar '00
Cold Sweat '93
Collateral '04▲
The Collectors '99
Confessions of a Dangerous Mind '02
Confessions of a Hit Man '94
The Contract '98
The Contract '07
The Contractor '07
Crossfire '98
Cybercity '99
Daredevil '03▲
DaVinci's War '92
Dead Fish '04
Deadlier Than the Male '67
Decay '98
Deja Vu '89
Deliberate Intent '01
Desert Saints '01
Desperado '95▲
Destination Vegas '95
Devils on the Doorstep '00
Diary of a Hitman '91
Dinner Rush '00▲
Direct Hit '93
Dog Bite Dog '06
Dumb & Dumber '94
8 Heads in a Duffel Bag '96
El Mariachi '93▲
Elmore Leonard's Gold Coast '97
Escape Clause '96
Exiled '06
Faithful '95
Fallen Angels '95
The Family '70
Fatal Chase '77
Fatal Justice '93
The Feminine Touch '95
A Few Days in September '06
Final Mission '84
Firepower '79
Fish in a Barrel '01
Formula 51 '01
Full Disclosure '00
The Funeral '96▲
Ghost Dog: The Way of the Samurai '99
Gigli '03
Goodbye, Lover '99
Grosse Pointe Blank '97▲
Hard-Boiled '92
Her Name Is Cat '99
Hidden Agenda '01
The Hit '84▲
The Hit List '93
Hit Men '73
Hit Woman: The Double Edge '93
Hitman '07
Hitman's Journal '99
Hitman's Run '99
Hollow Point '95
Honor and Glory '92
Hotel '01
I Accidentally Domed Your Son '04
In Bruges '08▲
In the Shadows '01
Intolerable Cruelty '03▲
The Jackal '97
Jerry and Tom '98
The Job '03
Joyride '97
Kill Bill Vol. 1 '03▲
Kill Bill Vol. 2 '04▲
The Killer '90▲
The Killers '46▲
Killing Emmett Young '02
Killing Time '97
King of the Ants '03
La Femme Nikita '91▲
Lady Jayne Killer '03
Lansdown '01
The Last Hit '93
Le Samourai '67▲
Lethal Panther '90
Life Tastes Good '99
Life Without Dick '01
Little Odessa '94
Love '05
Love and Action in Chicago '99
Lucky Number Slevin '06
Made Men '99
The Man Who Knew Too Little '97
Man with a Gun '95
The Manchurian Candidate '62▲
The Matador '06▲
Mean Johnny Barrows '75
The Mechanic '72
The Memory of a Killer '03
The Mexican '01
Mr. & Mrs. Smith '05▲
Mr. Nice Guy '86
Montana '97
Murda Muzik '03
Mysterious Mr. Moto '38
The Naked City '48▲
Nemesis 4: Cry of Angels '97
Night of the Running Man '94
No Witness '04
Nurse Betty '00▲
On the Run '83
Once Upon a Time in Mexico '03▲
One Night at McCool's '01
Our Lady of the Assassins '01
The Outside Man '73
Over the Wire '95
The Pact '99
Paid to Kill '54
Panic '00
Perfect Assassins '98
Perfect Killer '77
Pistol Whipped '08
The Pleasure Drivers '05
Point of No Return '93
Portrait of a Hitman '77
The Positively True Adventures of the Alleged Texas Cheerleader-Murdering Mom '93▲
Prisoner of Love '99
Pizzi's Honor '85▲
The Professional '94
Project: Kill! '77
Puerto Vallarta Squeeze '04
Pulp Fiction '94▲
Quick '93
Raising Heroes '97
Razor Blade Smile '98
Red King, White Knight '89
Red Rock West '93▲
The Replacement Killers '98
R.I.C.C.O. '02
Rick '03
Ripley's Game '02▲
Road to Perdition '02▲
Sabotage '98
Sanctuary '98
Savage Hearts '95
Season for Assassins '75
The Shadow Conspiracy '96
Shadowboxer '06
Shattered Image '98
Shoot 'Em Up '07
The Silencer '99
Sin City '05
Six Ways to Sunday '99
Sleepers '96
Smokin' Aces '07
The Specialist '75
The Specialist '94
Stiletto '69
Strangers on a Train '51▲
Suddenly '54▲
Suicide Ride '97
Ten 'Til Noon '06
The Tesseract '03
Things to Do in Denver When You're Dead '95
This Gun for Hire '42▲
Thrill Seekers '99
Too Hot to Handle '76
Triggermen '02
Two Days in the Valley '96▲
Two Tough Guys '03
U-Turn '97
Wanted '08
War '07
Warm Blooded Killers '01
Whacked! '02
Who is Cletis Tout? '02
The Whole Nine Yards '00
The Whole Ten Yards '04
Wish You Were Dead '00
The Wrecking Crew '99
You Kill Me '07▲

Hitchhikers

see Thumbs Up

Hockey

see also Skating
Accident '83
The Boys '97
The Cutting Edge '92
D3: The Mighty Ducks '96
D2: The Mighty Ducks '94
The Duke of West Point '38
Dutch Girls '87
Happy Gilmore '96
Hockey Night '84
The Ice Rink '99
Jack Frost '98
Lethal Weapon 3 '92
The Love Guru '08
Love Story '70▲
The Mighty Ducks '92
Miracle '04▲
Miracle on Ice '81
MVP (Most Valuable Primate) '00
Mystery, Alaska '99
Mystery of the Million Dollar Hockey Puck '75
No Sleep 'Til Madison '02
Paperback Hero '73
The Rocket '05▲
Slap Shot '77▲
Slap Shot 2: Breaking the Ice '02
Strange Brew '83
Sudden Death '95
Touch and Go '86
Waking Up Wally '05
Youngblood '86

Holidays

see also Christmas; Halloween; Horrible Holidays; New Year's Eve; Thanksgiving
Adam Sandler's 8 Crazy Nights '02
Carry On Behind '75
Easter Parade '48▲
Groundhog Day '93▲
Jack Frost '97
Plan B '97
Strange Days '95▲
Turumba '84▲
Two Weeks with Love '50
The White Balloon '95▲

The Holocaust

see also Germany; Nazis & Other Paramilitary Slugs; Judaism; World War II
Alan & Naomi '92
Almost Peaceful '02▲
Amen '02▲
The Assault '86
The Assisi Underground '84
The Attic: The Hiding of Anne Frank '88
Au Revoir les Enfants '87▲
The Boxer and Death '63▲
A Call to Remember '97
Charlie Grant's War '80
Christabel '89
Cold Days '66
Conspiracy '01
The Counterfeiters '07▲
David '79
A Day in October '92
The Devil's Arithmetic '99
Diamonds of the Night '64▲
The Diary of Anne Frank '59▲
Dominion: Prequel to the Exorcist '05
Enemies, a Love Story '89▲
Era Notte a Roma '60▲
Europa, Europa '91▲
Everything Is Illuminated '05
The Execution '85
Facing Windows '03
Fateless '05▲
Forced March '90
The Garden of the Finzi-Continis '71▲
Genghis Cohn '93
Getting Away With Murder '96
The Girl of Your Dreams '99
The Goebbels Experiment '05
Good Evening, Mr. Wallenberg '93
The Grey Zone '01
Hanna's War '88
The Hiding Place '75
Hitler '62
The Holcroft Covenant '85
Holocaust '78▲
Holocaust Survivors... Remembrance of Love '83
I Love You, I Love You Not '97
In a Glass Cage '86
In the Presence of Mine Enemies '97
Jacob the Liar '74
Jakob the Liar '99▲
Kanal '56▲
Kapo '59▲
Korczak '90▲
The Last Butterfly '92
The Last Metro '80▲
Les Miserables '95
Les Violons du Bal '74
Max and Helen '90
Mendel '98▲
Murderers Among Us: The Simon Wiesenthal Story '89▲
The Murderers Are Among Us '46
Never Forget '91
The Ninth Day '04▲
Paper Clips '04▲
Passenger '61▲
The Pawnbroker '65▲
The Pianist '02▲
Playing for Time '80▲
Prisoner of Paradise '02▲
Rescuers: Stories of Courage—Two Couples '98
Reunion '88▲
The Revolt of Job '83
The Rose Garden '89
Rosenstrasse '03▲
Schindler's List '93▲
The Serpent's Egg '78
The Shop on Main Street '65▲
Sophie's Choice '82▲
Speak Up! It's So Dark '93
The Substance of Fire '96
Sunshine '99
Transport from Paradise '65
Triumph of the Spirit '89▲
The Truce '96▲
Uprising '01▲
Verdict on Auschwitz: The Frankfurt Auschwitz Trial 1963–1965 '93▲
The Wannsee Conference '84▲
War & Love '84
The White Rose '83▲

Home Alone

see also Childhood Visions
Adventures in Babysitting '87
And You Thought Your Parents Were Weird! '91
Anything for a Thrill '37
The Apple Dumpling Gang '75
Baby's Day Out '94
Blank Check '93

The Homefront: U.S./Canada

Bless the Beasts and Children '71
The Blue Lagoon '80
Boys Will Be Boys '97
Camp Nowhere '94
Christina's House '99
Cloak & Dagger '84
Cohen and Tate '88
Courage Mountain '89
Cross My Heart '91
Dakota Detective Agency '83
Dirt Bike Kid '86
Don't Tell Mom the Babysitter's Dead '91
Duck Season '04
Explorers '85
Famous Five Get Into Trouble '87
Fatal Skies '90
Fear of the Dark '02
Four Rooms '95
Gleaming the Cube '89
The Goonies '85
He Is My Brother '75
Home Alone '90
Home Alone 2: Lost in New York '92
Home Alone 3 '97
Honey, I Shrunk the Kids '89
Honey, We Shrunk Ourselves '97
Hook '91
The Horse Without a Head '63
House Arrest '96
Invaders from Mars '53
Invaders from Mars '86
Island Trader '71
Just William's Luck '47
Legend of Billie Jean '85
The Littlest Horse Thieves '76
Lord of the Flies '63
Lord of the Flies '90
Mr. Wise Guy '42
Monkey Trouble '94
The Monster Squad '87
Nightwaves '03
Nobody Knows '04
Paradise '82
Playing Dangerous '95
The Rescue '88
Return to the Blue Lagoon '91
Scream '96
Shipwrecked '90
Snow Treasure '67
3 Ninjas Kick Back '94
3 Ninjas '92
Tideland '05
2 Brothers & a Bride '03
A Waltz Through the Hills '88
The Window '49
Young Sherlock Holmes '85

see also *World War II*
Air Raid Wardens '43
Blondie for Victory '42
Bye Bye Blues '89
Come See the Paradise '90
Flags of Our Fathers '06 ▶
For the Moment '94
The Home Front '02
The Human Comedy '43
I'll Remember April '99
In Love and War '87
In the Mood '87
A League of Their Own '92
1941 '79
Racing with the Moon '84
Raggedy Man '81
Ride the Wild Fields '00
Salaam Bombay! '88
Samaritan: The Mitch Snyder Story '86
Scarecrow '73
Show Me '04
Silas Marner '85
Since You Went Away '44 ▶
Soldier '98
Stop-Loss '08 ▶
The Stray '00
Streetwise '84
Sullivan's Travels '41
Summer Magic '63
Swing Shift '84
They Shall Have Music '39
The Third Wheel '02
Times Square '80
Up Your Alley '89
The Vagrant '92
Where the Day Takes You '92

The Homefront: England

see also *World War II*
The Affair '95
And a Nightingale Sang '91
Carrie's War '04
Hope and Glory '87 ▶
The Land Girls '98
The Last of the Blonde Bombshells '00
Mrs. Henderson Presents '05
Mrs. Miniver '42 ▶
Salute John Citizen '42 ▶
The Water Horse: Legend of the Deep '07
The Weaker Sex '49
The White Cliffs of Dover '44 ▶

Homeless

see also *Great Depression; Hard Knock Life; Yuppie Nightmares*
Accatone! '61 ▶
All Mine to Give '56
Amores Perros '00 ▶
August Rush '07
The Billion Dollar Hobo '78
Billy: Portrait of a Street Kid '77
Brother to Brother '04
Bums '93
Caught '96
The Child '05
Children of Sanchez '79
City Lights '31 ▶
Curly Sue '91
Distant Thunder '73
Dodes 'ka-den '70 ▶
Down, Out and Dangerous '95
Drillbit Taylor '08
Eddie Presley '92
Emanon '86
Emperor of the North Pole '73 ▶
First, Last and Deposit '00
The Fisher King '91 ▶
God Bless the Child '88 ▶
The Grapes of Wrath '40 ▶
Guarding Eddy '04
Heater '99
Home for Christmas '90
Home of Angels '94
Homecoming '96
The Innocent Sleep '95
Into the West '92
Joe Gould's Secret '00
Kanal '56
The Kid '21 ▶
Land of Plenty '04
Le Petit Lieutenant '05
Life Stinks '91
Los Olvidados '50 ▶
The Lovers on the Bridge '91
The Lower Depths '36 ▶
The Lower Depths '57 ▶
The Man from Left Field '93
The Man Without a Past '02 ▶
Michael Shayne: Private Detective '40
Midnight Cowboy '69 ▶
Mon Homme '96
Mondo '96
Noel '04
None But the Lonely Heart '44 ▶
Oliver! '44 ▶
Oliver Twist '33 ▶
Oliver! '68 ▶
Oliver '22
Oliver Twist '97
Oliver Twist '85
Oliver Twist '48 ▶
Oliver Twist '82
Oliver Twist '00
Oliver Twist '05
Original Intent '91
An Orphan Boy of Vienna '37
Pardon My Trunk '52
Pinero '01
The Prince of Central Park '77
The Pursuit of Happyness '06
Resurrecting the Champ '07
The Saint of Fort Washington '93

Homicide

Abandon '02
Absolute Power '97 ▶
Agatha Christie's Murder is Easy '82
Alpha Dog '06
American Gun '05
The Amityville Horror '05
Among Brothers '05
The Badge '02
Basic '03
Beast '00
Behind the Sun '01
Between Your Legs '99
Big Brown Eyes '36
The Black Camel '31
The Black Dahlia '06
The Black Doll '38
The Blackheath Poisonings '92
The Bloodstained Shadow '78
The Blue Gardenia '53
Bon Voyage '03 ▶
Borderline '06
Bordertown '06
The Bridesmaid '04
Bright Future '03
Bubble '06
Bunny Whipped '06
The Case of the Bloody Iris '72
The Case of the Scorpion's Tail '71
Cassandra's Dream '07
The Cat's Meow '01
Cause of Death '00
The Caveman's Valentine '01
Charlie Chan at Monte Carlo '37
Charlie Chan at the Circus '36
Charlie Chan in City of Darkness '39
Charlie Chan in Honolulu '38
Charlie Chan in Shanghai '35
Charlie Chan on Broadway '37
Chicago '02 ▶
City by the Sea '02
Close Your Eyes '02
Crash '05 ▶
Criminal Lovers '99
Day of Wrath '06
Dead Girl '06
A Dead Calling '06
Dead Broke '99
Dead Gorgeous '02
Dead Ringer '64
Dead Silence '07
Die Mommie Die! '03
Dr. Bell and Mr. Doyle: The Dark Beginnings of Sherlock Holmes '00
A Dog's Breakfast '07
8 Women '02
Elephant '03 ▶
11:14 '03
Eye of the Storm '98
Fascination '04
The Fast Runner '01 ▶
Fear X '03
Gangs of New York '02 ▶
The Good German '06
Gosford Park '01 ▶
Gothika '03
Hangover Square '45
Hate Crime '05
Heart of Crime '01
The Hole '01
Hollywood Homicide '03
Hollywoodland '06
Identity '03
I'm Not Scared '03
In the Bedroom '01 ▶
In the Cut '03
In the Valley of Elah '07 ▶
Insomnia '02 ▶
Inspector Lynley Mysteries: A Great Deliverance '01
Irreversible '01
The Jacket '05
Jesse Stone: Death in Paradise '06
Jesse Stone: Night Passage '06
Jesse Stone: Stone Cold '05
Jimmy Glick in LaLa Wood '05
Jindabyne '06
Ju-On: The Grudge '03
Keeping Mum '05
Keilers Park '05
The Killer Must Kill Again '75
The Killing Club '01
The Killing of John Lennon '07
A Killing Spring '02
La Femme Infidele '69 ▶
La Vie Promise '02
Le Petit Lieutenant '05
Like Father Like Son '05
Loaded '08
Lola and Billy the Kid '98
Lonely Hearts '06
Love '05
Macbeth '06
Malicious Intent '99
The Man Who Wasn't There '01
The Man in the House '99
The Manson Family '04
Melissa '97
Memento '00 ▶
Merci pour le Chocolat '00 ▶
A Mighty Heart '07 ▶
Miami Vice '06
Motives '03
Murder at Devil's Glen '99
Murder by Numbers '02
Murder in Greenwich '02
Murder in Greenwich Village '37
The Murder of Stephen Lawrence '99
Murderous Intent '06
Mystery Street '50
Mystic River '03 ▶
Night Train Murders '75
Nightwaves '03
November '05
The Number 23 '07
The Omen '06
One Kill '00
100 Mile Rule '02
One to Another '06
One Way Out '02
Our Lady of the Assassins '01
Out of Time '03
Pathology '08
P.D. James: Death in Holy Orders '03
P.D. James: The Murder Room '04
Perfect Murder, Perfect Town '00
Perfect Stranger '07
Perfume: The Story of a Murderer '06 ▶
The Pink Panther '06
Posers '02
Protector '97
Quicksand '03
The Reckoning '03 ▶
R.S.V.P. '02
Running Scared '06 ▶
Saw II '05
Series 7: The Contenders '01
Signs & Wonders '00
Sleep Easy Hutch Rimes '00
Slow Burn '05
Soldier's Girl '03 ▶
Spider '02 ▶
Sudden Manhattan '96
Taboo '02
Three Blind Mice '01
Torso '01
The Truth About Charlie '02
Tsotsi '05 ▶
Unfaithful '02 ▶
United States of Leland '03
Valentine '01
Veronica Guerin '03
The Village '04
Volver '06 ▶
The Walker '07
Water's Edge '03
The Weight of Water '00
What Your Eyes Don't See '99
White Oleander '02
With a Friend Like Harry '00 ▶
Wonderland '03
The Wrong Guy '96

Homosexuality

see also *Bisexuality; Gays; Lesbians*

Honeymoon

see also *Marriage; Newlyweds; Wedding Bells*
Above Suspicion '43
Awakening of Candra '81
The Bat People '74
Battle Shock '56
Beyond the Rocks '22
The Blood Spattered Bride '72
Bloodstone '88
The Bride & the Beast '58
Bulldog Drummond's Bride '39
Caged Fear '92
Cat Girl '57
Chaos & Cadavers '03
Dangerous Crossing '53
Devil's Pond '03
Dr. Jekyll & Mr. Hyde '99
The Ghost and the Guest '43
A Good Woman '04
Halfmoon '95
Haunted Honeymoon '86
Having Wonderful Crime '45
The Heartbreak Kid '07
Heaven's Burning '97
Honeymoon Academy '90
Honeymoon Horror '82
Honeymoon in Vegas '92 ▶
Jupiter's Thigh '81
Just Married '03
The Long, Long Trailer '54
Lucky in Heaven '40
Made in Heaven '52
The Moon's Our Home '36
Move Over, Darling '63
Murder on the Midnight Express '74
Never Say Die '39
The Newlydeads '87
Niagara '52 ▶
Out to Sea '97
The Palermo Connection '91
Photographing Fairies '97
Prelude to a Kiss '92
Private Lives '31
The Red Rope '37
Sextette '78
Shattered Image '98
The She-Beast '65
Shutter '08
Strike It Rich '90

Hong Kong

see also *Asia; China*
The Amsterdam Kill '78
The Art of War '00
Autumn Moon '92
A Better Tomorrow, Part 1 '86
Black Mask '96
Blade in Hong Kong '85
Bloodsport '88
Chinese Box '97
Chungking Express '95 ▶
Cleopatra Jones & the Casino of Gold '75
Crime Lords '07
Detonator 2: Night Watch '95
Dr. Jekyll & Mr. Hyde '99
Double Impact '91
Dream Lovers '86
Enter the Dragon '73 ▶
Eros '04
Fallen Angels '95
First Love and Other Pains / One of Them '99
Five Golden Dragons '67
Forced Vengeance '82
Gen-X Cops '99
Hong Kong 1941 '84
Hong Kong '97 '94
In the Mood for Love '00
Internal Affairs '02 ▶
Just Like Weather '86
Knock Off '98
Koroshi '67
Kung Fu Hustle '04 ▶
La Moustache '05
Love is a Many-Splendored Thing '55 ▶
The Medallion '03
New Police Story '04
Noble House '88
Once a Thief '96
Romeo Must Die '00
Rush Hour 2 '01
Shadow of China '91
Silver Hawk '04
Tai-Pan '86
That Man Bolt '73
TNT Jackson '75
To Live and Die in Hong Kong '89
2046 '04 ▶
Twin Dragons '92
Vampire Effect '03
Yin & Yang of Mr. Go '71

Horrible Holidays

see also *Christmas; Holidays; Halloween Isn't Over!; New Year's Eve; Thanksgiving; Vacation Hell*
American Gun '02
April Fool's Day '86
Bad Santa '03
Black Christmas '06
Black Christmas '75
Bloodbeat '85
Bloody New Year '87
Chasing Christmas '05
Christmas Evil '80
Don't Open Till Christmas '84
Dorm That Dripped Blood '82
Frankenstein Sings... The Movie '95
Gremlins '84 ▶
Halloween '78 ▶
Halloween '07
Halloween 2: The Nightmare Isn't Over! '81
Halloween 3: Season of the Witch '82
Halloween 4: The Return of Michael Myers '88
Halloween 5: The Revenge of Michael Myers '89
Halloween 6: The Curse of Michael Myers '95

Halloween: H20 '98▶
Halloween Night '90
Happy Birthday to Me '81
Home for the Holidays '72
Home Sweet Home '80
I Still Know What You Did
Last Summer '98
Jack-O '95
Jam '06
Mixed Nuts '94
Mother's Day '80
My Bloody Valentine '81
The Myth of Fingerprints '97
New Year's Evil '78
The Night After Halloween
'79
Night of the Demons '88
Night of the Demons 2 '94
Night of the Demons 3 '97
'R Xmas '01
Reckless '95
The Ref '93▶
Resurrection '99
Sheitan '06
Silent Night, Bloody Night
'73
Silent Night, Deadly Night
'84
Silent Night, Deadly Night 2
'87
Silent Night, Deadly Night 3:
Better Watch Out! '89
Silent Night, Deadly Night 4:
Initiation '90
Silent Night, Deadly Night 5:
The Toymaker '91
Teen Alien '78
Trick or Treats '82
Uncle Sam '96
Valentine '01
Wacko '83
What Love Is '07
When Do We Eat? '05

Horror Anthologies

Alien Massacre '67
Asylum '72
Body Bags '93
Campfire Tales '98
Creepshow '82
Creepshow 2 '87
Cremains '00▶
The Dark Dealer '95
Dead Alive '93
Dead Heat '88
Dr. Jekyll and Sister Hyde
'71
Dog Soldiers '01
Dolls '87
Doom Asylum '88
Dracula Blows His Cool '82
Dracula: Dead and Loving It
'95
Eat and Run '86
Ed and His Dead Mother '93
Elvira, Mistress of the Dark
'88
Evil Spawn '87
Face of the Screaming
Werewolf '59
The Fearless Vampire
Killers '67▶
Fido '06
Frankenhooker '90

Two Evil Eyes '90
The Uncanny '78
Vault of Horror '73
The Willies '90

Horror Comedy

Adventures of Eliza Fraser
'76
American Vampire '97
An American Werewolf in
Paris '97
Andy Warhol's Dracula '74▶
Andy Warhol's Frankenstein
'74
April Fool's Day '86
Arachnophobia '90
Army of Darkness '92▶
Atomic Dog '98
Attack of the Killer
Tomatoes '77
Attack of the Robots '66
Auntie Lee's Meat Pies '92
Autopsy: A Love Story '02
Autopsy of a Ghost '67
Bad Channels '92
Bad Taste '88▶
Beauty on the Beach '61
Beetlejuice '88▶
Bela Lugosi Meets a
Brooklyn Gorilla '52
Beverly Hills Bodysnatchers
'89
Beyond Re-Animator '03
Big Meat Eater '85
Billy the Kid Versus Dracula
'66
Biozombie '98
Black Magic '92
Black Sheep '06
Blood & Donuts '95
Blood Angels '05
Blood Beach '81
Blood Hook '86
Bloodbath at the House of
Death '85
Body Bags '93
The Bogus Witch Project '00
The Bone Yard '90
The Boogie Man Will Get
You '42
Botched '07
Bowery Boys Meet the
Monsters '54
Brain Damage '88
Bride of Chucky '98
Bride of Re-Animator '89
Bubba Ho-Tep '03▶
A Bucket of Blood '59▶
Buggedl '96
Carry On Screaming '66
C.H.U.D. '84
C.H.U.D. 2: Bud the Chud
'89
The Comedy of Terrors '64
Creature from the Haunted
Sea '60
The Creeps '97
Critters '86
Critters 2: The Main Course
'88
Critters 3 '91
Critters 4 '91
Curse of the Queerwolf '87
Cutting Class '89

Frankenstein Sings... The
Movie '95
Frankenstein's Great Aunt
Tillie '83
The Frighteners '96
From Beyond '86▶
Funnyman '94
The Ghost Breakers '40▶
Ghoulies '84
Ghoulies 2 '87
Ghoulies 3: Ghoulies Go to
College '91
Ghoulies 4 '93
Goblin '93
Gore-Met Zombie Chef from
Hell '87
The Granny '94
Gremlins '84▶
Gremlins 2: The New Batch
'90▶
Hard to Die '90
The Haunted Mansion '03
Head of the Family '96
Hellboy '04
Highway to Hell '92
Hillbillies in a Haunted
House '67
The Horror of Frankenstein
'70
House '86▶
House 2: The Second Story
'87
House of the Long Shadows
'82
Human Beasts '80
Hysterical '83
I Married a Vampire '87
I Was a Teenage Zombie
'87
Idle Hands '99
Incredibly Strange
Creatures Who Stopped
Living and Became
Mixed-Up Zombies '63
The Invisible Maniac '90
Jack Frost 2: Revenge of
the Mutant Killer
Snowman '00
Killer Condom '95
Killer Klowns from Outer
Space '88
Killer Pad '06
Killer Tomatoes Eat France
'91
Killer Tomatoes Strike Back
'90
Killer Tongue '96
The Kingdom '95▶
The Kingdom 2 '97▶
Little Shop of Horrors '60▶
Little Shop of Horrors '86▶
Mama Dracula '80
A Man with a Maid '73
The Mask '94▶
Matinee '92
Microwave Massacre '83
Mindkiller '87
Mr. Vampire '86
Mom '89
Monster in the Closet '86
Monster Man '03
Motel Hell '80
Munchies '87
My Boyfriend's Back '93
My Demon Lover '87
My Grandpa Is a Vampire
'92
My Mom's a Werewolf '89
My Son, the Vampire '52
Near Dark '87▶
Night of a Thousand Cats
'72
Night of the Creeps '86
Night of the Laughing Dead
'75
Nightlife '90
Nocturna '79
Nothing But Trouble '91
The Old Dark House '32▶
Old Mother Riley's Ghosts
'41
Once Bitten '85
Out of the Dark '88
Pep Squad '98
Phantom Brother '88
Phantom Empire '87
Piranha '78

Piranha 2: The Spawning
'82
Psycho Girls '86
Psychos in Love '87
Q (The Winged Serpent)
'82▶
Rabid Grannies '89
Re-Animator '84▶
Redneck Zombies '88
The Refrigerator '91
Return of the Killer
Tomatoes! '88
Return of the Living Dead
'85
Return of the Living Dead 2
'88
Return of the Living Dead 3
'93
Revenge of the Red Baron
'93
Roman '06
Saturday the 14th '81
Saturday the 14th Strikes
Back '88
Scary Movie 2 '01
Scary Movie 3 '03
Scary Movie 4 '06
Schlock '73
Seed of Chucky '04
Severance '06
Sheitan '06
Shrunken Heads '94
Son of Ingagi '40
Sorority Babes in the
Slimeball Bowl-A-Rama
'87
Speak of the Devil '90
Spider Baby '64
Spooks Run Wild '41
Strangers of the Evening '32
Street Trash '87
The Stuff '85
Student Bodies '81
Tainted '98
Tales from the Crypt
Presents Bordello of
Blood '96
Tales from the Crypt
Presents Demon Knight
'94
Teenage Exorcist '93
Teeth '07
Tequila Body Shots '99
Terror Tract '00
Terrorvision '86
Theatre of Blood '73▶
There's Nothing out There
'90
The Thing with Two Heads
'72
Three ... Extremes '04
The Toxic Avenger '86
The Toxic Avenger, Part 2
'89
The Toxic Avenger, Part 3:
The Last Temptation of
Toxie '89
Treasure of Fear '45
The Treat '98
Tremors '89▶
Tremors 2: Aftershocks '96
Tremors 3: Back to
Perfection '01
The Tripper '06
Undead '05
The Undertaker and His
Pals '67
Vamp '86
The Vampire Happening '71
Vampire in Brooklyn '95
Vampire Time Travelers '98
Vampire of Sorority Row:
Kickboxers From Hell '99
When Evil Calls '06
When Good Ghouls Go Bad
'01
Zombies on Broadway '44

Horse Racing

see Gambling; Horses;
Jockeying for Position

Horses

The Adventures of Gallant
Bess '48

All Hat '07
All the Pretty Horses '00
The Appaloosa '66
Banjo Hackett '76
Bells of San Angelo '47
Black Beauty '46
Black Beauty '94▶
The Black Stallion '79▶
The Black Stallion Returns
'83
Blazing Saddles '74▶
Blue Fire Lady '78
Broken Trail '06▶
By Dawn's Early Light '00
Call of the Forest '49
Casey's Shadow '78
Chino '75
City Slickers 2: The Legend
of Curly's Gold '94
Come on Tarzan '32
Courage of Black Beauty '57
Courage of the North '35
Coyote Summer '96
Danielle Steel's Palomino
'91
Danny '79
Dark Horse '92
David Harum '34
Devil Horse '32
The Dreamer: Inspired by a True
Story '05
Eagle's Wing '79
Eden Valley '94▶
The Electric Horseman '79
Envy '04
Equus '77
Far North '88
The Fighting Stallion '26▶
Flash '98
Flicka '06
The Flying Deuces '39▶
Forbidden Trails '41
Francis Goes to the Races
'51
A Girl in Every Port '52
The Golden Stallion '49
The Great Mike '44
Gypsy Colt '54
Hair '79▶
Half-Baked '97
Heart of the Rockies '51
Hell's Hinges '16
Hit the Saddle '37
The Horse in the Gray
Flannel Suit '68
The Horse Whisperer '97
Horsemasters '61
The Horsemen '70
Hot to Trot '88
In Old Kentucky '35
In Pursuit of Honor '95
Indian Paint '64
International Velvet '78
Into the West '92▶
It Ain't Hay '43
It's a Great Life '43
Justin Morgan Had a Horse
'81
King of the Sierras '38
King of the Stallions '42
King of the Wild Horses '24▶
King of the Wind '93
The Lighthorsemen '87▶
The Littlest Horse Thieves
'76
The Littlest Outlaw '54
Lotna '64
Lucky Luke '94
The Man from Snowy River
'82
Marshal of Cedar Rock '53
Meet Wally Sparks '97
Michael Shayne: Private
Detective '40
The Miracle of the White
Stallions '63
The Misfits '61▶
Misty '61
Moondance Alexander '07
My Friend Flicka '43▶
My Pal Trigger '46
National Lampoon's Animal
House '78▶
Racing Stripes '05
A Rare Breed '81

The Red Fury '84
The Red Pony '49▶
The Red Pony '76▶
Return of Wildfire '48
Return to Snowy River '88▶
Ride a Wild Pony '75▶
Ride Him, Cowboy '32▶
Riders '88
Riding High '50
Rolling Home '48
The Rounders '65
Running Free '00
Running Wild '73
Saddle Buster '32
Second Chances '98
Shooting Fish '98
Silver Stallion '41
The Silver Stallion: King of
the Wild Brumbies '93
Simpatico '99
Something to Talk About '95
Speedy '28▶
Spirit: Stallion of the
Cimarron '02
Sundown Saunders '36
Texas to Bataan '42
Toy Story 2 '99▶
Two Bits & Pepper '95
The Undefeated '69
Under the Pampas Moon
'35
When the West Was Young
'32
White Mane '52▶
Wild Hearts Can't Be
Broken '91▶
Wild Horse Hank '79
Wild Horses '82
Wild Horses '84
Wild Pony '83

Hospitals & Medicine

see also Disease of the
Week; Doctors &
Nurses; Emerging
Viruses; Sanity Check;
Shrinks
Article 99 '92
Asylum of the Damned '03
Awake '07
Awakenings '90▶
The Barbarian Invasions
'03▶
BASEketball '98
Bool '05
B.O.R.N. '88
Bringing Out the Dead '99
Britannia Hospital '82
Calendar Girls '03
Carry On Nurse '59
A Child Is Waiting '63▶
China Beach '88▶
City of Angels '98
City of Joy '92
The Clonus Horror '79
Coma '78
Come to the Stable '49▶
Crazy Eights '06
Critical Care '97
Critical Condition '86
Dead Ringers '88▶
The Death of Mr. Lazarescu
'05
Desperate Measures '98
Disorderlies '87
Disorderly Orderly '64
Doctor at Large '57
Dr. Kildare's Strange Case
'40
Doctors' Wives '70
East of Kilimanjaro '57
The Egyptian '54
Extreme Measures '96
For Roseanna '96
Frankenstein General
Hospital '88
The Fugitive '93▶
Green for Danger '47
Gross Anatomy '89
Halloween 2: The
Nightmare Isn't Over! '81
Hard-Boiled '92
Hard to Kill '89
The Hasty Heart '86
The Healer '02
Horror Hospital '73

▶ = rated three bones or higher

The Hospital '71
Hospital Massacre '81
Hospital of Terror '78
In for Treatment '82
In Love and War '96
The Interns '62
Invasion '65
Nine Months '95
Nurse '80
John Q '02
Junior '94
One Flew Over the Cuckoo's Nest '75
Open Your Eyes '97
The Kingdom '95
The Kingdom 2 '97
Lifespan '75
Like Father, Like Son '87
Miracle Dogs '03
Miss Evers' Boys '97
Naked Is Better '73
The Red Squirrel '93
The Singing Detective '03
State of Emergency '94
A Stolen Face '52
Sublime '07
The Surgeon '94
Take Down '92
Tales from the Gimli Hospital '88
Talk to Her '02
Tender Loving Care '73
Terminator 2: Judgment Day '91
13 Moons '02
Threshold '83
12 Monkeys '95
28 Days '00
The Ugly '96
Vital Signs '90
Welcome Stranger '47
Where Truth Lies '96
While You Were Sleeping '95
White Coats '04
Whose Life Is It Anyway? '81
Young Doctors in Love '82

Hostage!
see also Kidnapped!;
Missing Persons
The Abduction '96
Against the Wall '94
Air Force One '97 ▶
Air Rage '01
Airheads '94
Albino Alligator '96
Allie & Me '97
Amos and Andrew '93
Autumn Born '79
Bait '02
Bandits '01
Black Cobra 2 '89
Black Fox: Good Men and Bad '94
Blackout '78
Blast '96
Blood of the Hunter '94
Body Count '97
Born Bad '97
Botched '07
The Boys Club '96
Cadillac Man '90
Captivity '06
Carpool '96
Chameleon 2: Death Match '99
Civic Duty '06
The Clearing '04
Codename: Vengeance '87
Cold Sweat '71
Crackerjack 2 '97
Cradle 2 the Grave '03
Crime Wave '54
Cube '98
Cube 2: Hypercube '02
Cul de Sac '66
Days of Hell '64
Dead Ahead '96
Dead Silence '96
Deadlocked '00
Deadly Outbreak '96
Death and the Maiden '94
Death Stalk '74
Demolition High '95
Desperate Hours '90
Die Hard '88 ▶
Die Hard 2: Die Harder '90 ▶
Dog Day Afternoon '75 ▶
Door to Door Maniac '61
Escape from New York '81 ▶
Face the Evil '97
Fatal Mission '89
Fall Time '95
Field of Fire '92
Firestorm '97
Firewall '06
First Sunday '08
For Which He Stands '98
48 Hours to Live '60
Friends and Family '01
Funny Games '97
Funny Games '07 ▶
Gigli '03
Gone Dark '03
Half Past Dead '02
Headless Body in Topless Bar '95
Held Up '00
The Heist '96
Hostage '05
Hostage High '97
Hostage Hotel '00
Hostages '93
Housewife '72
Human Bomb '97
In the Middle of Nowhere '93
Inside '06
Inside Man '06 ▶
Iron Eagle '86
Jeopardy '53
The Jesus Trip '71
Johnny 100 Pesos '93
John Q '02
Kill Me Later '01
King of Comedy '82 ▶
The Last Samurai '90
The Legend of Wolf Mountain '92
Lethal Tender '96
Light It Up '99
Live! From Death Row '92
Living & Dying '07
Mad City '97
The Marine '06
Masterminds '96
Meltdown '95
Midnight Fear '90
Miss Congeniality 2: Armed and Fabulous '05
Mr. Reliable: A True Story '95
Mistrial '96
Morgan's Ferry '99
Munich '05 ▶
My Name is Modesty: A Modesty Blaise Adventure '04
The Negotiator '98
Nick of Time '95
No Contest '94
No Good Deed '02
Nothing to Lose '96
One Way Out '95
Open Fire '94
Operation Thunderbolt '77
P2 '07
Perfect Strangers '03
A Perfect World '93
Peril '00
Petrified Forest '36 ▶
A Prayer in the Dark '97
Provoked '89
P.S. Your Cat is Dead! '02
Pups '99
Quake '92
Quick Change '90
Raising the Heights '97
Rambo '08
Red Mercury '05
The Ref '93
Rock All Night '57
Saw 4 '07
Saw II '05
The Seventh Floor '36
Sex and the Other Man '95
S.F.W. '94
The Shot '96
16 Blocks '06
Skyscraper '95
Snatched '72
Space Marines '96
Spaghetti House '82
Speed 2: Cruise Control '97
Split Second '53
Stand Off '53
A Stranger is Watching '82
Stranglehold '94
Striptease '95
Sudden Death '95
Suddenly '54
Suspended Animation '02
Sweet Hostage '75
Take Down '92
The Taking of Pelham One Two Three '74 ▶
Terror Stalks the Class Reunion '93
This Gun for Hire '42 ▶
3 Ninjas: High Noon at Mega Mountain '97
The Trap '59
Truth or Consequences, N.M. '97
Tube '03
12 Monkeys '95 ▶
Uninvited Guest '99
Victory at Entebbe '76

Housekeepers
see The Help: Female

Houston
see also Black Gold;
Texas
Apollo 13 '95 ▶
The Bad News Bears in Breaking Training '77
Brewster McCloud '70 ▶
Charlie Wilson's War '07 ▶
Dance with Me '98
Dancing in Twilight '05
Enron: The Smartest Guys in the Room '05 ▶
The Evening Star '96
Full Fathom Five '90
Jason's Lyric '94 ▶
Last Night in the Alamo '83 ▶
Night Game '89
Reality Bites '94
The Swarm '78
Terms of Endearment '83 ▶
Thursday '98
Urban Cowboy '80 ▶
Vietnam, Texas '90

Housesitting
Deuce Bigalow: Male Gigolo '99
Hard to Kill '89
A House in the Hills '93
My Boss's Daughter '03
Opportunity Knocks '90

Hunted!
see also Survival
Apocalypto '06 ▶
Arctic Blue '93
Beyond Rangoon '95
Beyond Fear '93
Bigfoot: The Unforgettable Encounter '94
Bounty Hunter 2002 '94
The Cursed Mountain
Cyborg 2 '93
Damned River '89
Deadly Game '91
Death Hunt '81
Decoy '95
Deliverance '72 ▶
Desperate Prey '94
Diary of a Hitman '91
Dominion '94
Ex-Cop '93
Eyes of the Beholder '92
Fair Game '82
Final Round '93
5 Dark Souls '96
Fortress '85
First Blood '82 ▶
Forest of Little Bear '87
Frostbiter: Wrath of the Wendigo '94
The Ghost and the Darkness '94
Gitl '65
Harry Black and the Tiger '58
The Hunt '65 ▶
Ice Men '04
The Last Hunt '56
The Last Safari '67
Mogambo '53 ▶
Mystery '93
Night of the Grizzly '66
No Country for Old Men '07 ▶
Primeval '07
Shoot '35
Shooting '82
Those Calloways '65
To Catch a Yeti '95
White Hunter, Black Heart '90 ▶

Hunting
see also Go Fish
The Amazing Panda Adventure '95
The Bear '89 ▶
The Belstone Fox '73
The Bridge to Nowhere '86
Dan Candy's Law '73
Deadly Prey '87
The Dog Boy '01
Escanaba in da Moonlight '01
First Blood '82 ▶
Freejack '92
Fugitive X '96
The Good Guys and the Bad Guys '69
Hard Target '93
The Hunted '94
The Hunted '03
Hunter's Blood '87
Illegal Entry: Formula for Fear '93
Incident at Deception Ridge '83 ▶
Jumper '08 ▶
Jungleground '95
Killing at Hell's Gate '81
Ladykillers '88
The Last of the Dogmen '95
Last Witness '88
Little Bigfoot '96
Maximum Risk '96
Midnight Murders '91
Montana '97
The Most Dangerous Game '32
The Naked Prey '66 ▶
Nemesis 2: Nebula '94
Nightmare at Bittercreek '91
No Way Back '96
Open Season '06
Overkill '96
The Pest '56
Prey for the Hunter '92
Primeval '07
Project Shadowchaser 3000 '95
Rumble in the Streets '96
Seraphim Falls '06 ▶
Severance '06 ▶
Shadowhunter '93
Shoot to Kill '88 ▶
Skinwalkers '07
Soo '96
Southern Comfort '81 ▶
Star Hunter '95
Survival Quest '89
Surviving the Game '94
Tracked '98
Trial and Error '92
Uncivilized '94
Warriors '94
Wild Grizzly '99
Wounded '97
Wrong Turn '03
Yesterday's Target '96

I'm Not Dead, Yet!
Blackout '50
Dawn of the Dead '04 ▶
Elektra '05

Immigration
The Adventures of Felix '99
An American Rhapsody '01 ▶
An American Tail '86 ▶
Arizona '40 ▶
Avalon '90 ▶
Baran '01 ▶
The Beautiful Country '04
Blood Red '88
Border Blues '03
Border Incident '49 ▶
Borderline '80
Bread and Chocolate '73 ▶
Bread and Roses '00 ▶
Breaking and Entering '06
Brothers in Trouble '95
Buck Privates Come Home '47 ▶
Bye-Bye '96
Chasing Freedom '04
Children of Men '06 ▶
Code 46 '03
Code Unknown '00
Combination Platter '93
Coming to America '88 ▶
The Cowboy Way '94
Crossing Over '08
Dancer in the Dark '99 ▶
Dirty Pretty Things '03 ▶
Does This Mean We're Married? '90
Drachenfutter '87 ▶
Driving Me Crazy '91
East is East '99 ▶
El Super '79 ▶
The Emigrants '72 ▶
Enemies, a Love Story '89 ▶
Far and Away '92
Fast Food Nation '06 ▶
Floating Life '95
Four Sons '28
Gangs of New York '02 ▶
The Great New Wonderful '06
Green Card '90 ▶
Heaven Before I Die '96
Hester Street '75 ▶
House of Sand and Fog '03 ▶
I Can't Sleep '94
I Cover the Waterfront '33
The Immigrant '17
In America '02 ▶
The Italian '15
Journey of Hope '90 ▶
A King in New York '57 ▶
Kings in Grass Castles '97
La Promesse '96
Late Marriage '01
Letters from Alou '90
Liam '00 ▶
Living on Tokyo Time '87
The Maldonado Miracle '03
Manhattan Merengue! '95
The Marions of America '81
Maricela '88
Maryam '00
Miami Rhapsody '95
Midnight Auto Supply '78
The Mistress of Spices '05
Monkey Business '31
Moscow on the Hudson '84 ▶
My Girl Tisa '48
My Sweet Victim '85
The Namesake '06 ▶
The New Land '73 ▶
No Turning Back '01
Nueba Yol '95
O Quatrilho '95
Pelle the Conqueror '88 ▶
Petty Crimes '02
The Roundup '65
Saving Face '04 ▶
Sommersby '93
Three for the Show '55
A Very Brady Sequel '96
Hello Again '87
Incubus '05
The Lazarus Man '96
Move Over, Darling '63
My Favorite Wife '40
Skyline '84
Sky High '22
Someone Else's America '96
Spanglish '04
Sueno '05
Tarantella '95
The Terminal '04 ▶
The Three Burials of Melquiades Estrada '05 ▶
Under the Same Moon '07
The Visitor '07 ▶
Wait until Spring, Bandini '90
West is West '87
Wetbacks '56
Where Is My Child? '37

Immortality
Bram Stoker's Way of the Vampire '05
Escape from the KGB '87
Highlander '86 ▶
Highlander 2: The Quickening '91
Highlander: Endgame '00
Highlander: The Final Dimension '94
Immortal '04
The Man from Earth '07
The Medallion '03
The Seeker: The Dark Is Rising '07
She '35 ▶
Spring, '00
Spring Forward '99
Spy Game '01
Suicide Ride '97
To Live & Die in L.A. '85 ▶

Impending Retirement
see also Growing Older;
One Last Job
Assault on Precinct 13 '05
The Blue Knight '75 ▶
Cellular '04
Chasing Ghosts '05
Crackerjack 3 '00
Diamond Men '01 ▶
Fallen Angels '03
Fallen Angels '87 ▶
Falling Down '93 ▶
Firetrap '01
The First Deadly Sin '80
The Flock '07
Hitman's Journal '99
In the Secret State '85
K-9 3: P.I. '01
K-911 '99
Lethal Weapon '87 ▶
Love to Kill '93
Loving Annabelle '06
Major League 3: Back to the Minors '98
The Mask of Zorro '98 ▶
Mission: Impossible 3 '06 ▶
Must Be Santa '99
The Pledge '00 ▶
The Princess Diaries 2: Royal Engagement '04
The Quickie '01
Royal Engagement '04
Schultze Gets the Blues '03
Seven '95 ▶
She Wore a Yellow Ribbon '49 ▶
Sonatine '96 ▶

In-Laws
Affair in Trinidad '52 ▶
Ash Wednesday '02
August '95
Between Two Women '86
Bittersweet Love '76
Blacksnake! '73
Blood Relations '87
Cal '84 ▶
Commandments '96
Deadly Blessing '81
Deliver Us from Eva '03 ▶
Diary of a Mad Old Man '88

In-Laws

Diary of the Dead '80
Die! Die! My Darling! '65
The Ex '07
For Better or Worse '95
Free Money '99
Girl with a Pearl Earring '03▶
The Grandfather '98
Hush '98
I Met a Murderer '39
The In-Laws '79▶
The In-Laws '03
The Inheritance '76
Junebug '05▶
Kill the Umpire '50
The Last Days of Chez Nous '92
Lawless Heart '01
Le Divorce '03
Leila '97
Love '71▶
Love Crazy '41▶
Love Liza '02
Love Songs '99
Madame X '37
Meet the Fockers '04▶
Meet the Parents '00▶
Mirele Efros '38
Monster-in-Law '05
Move Over, Darling '63
Murder-in-Law '92
Mussolini & I '85
My Brother's Wife '89
Norman Loves Rose '82
Onibaba '64▶
Passion in Paradise '89
Portrait of a Stripper '79
Reign Over Me '07▶
Rocky Balboa '06
The Santa Clause 3: The Escape Clause '06
Secrets of Women '52▶
Shrek the Third '07
Silent Witness '85
The Sister-in-Law '95
Son-in-Law '93
Stir of Echoes '99
Storm Warning '51
Summer Snow '94
A Time of Destiny '88
The War Bride '01
The Weight of Water '00
You, Me and Dupree '06

Incest

see also Family Ties

Against the Wind '90
Alpine Fire '89
An American Haunting '05
Andy Warhol's Frankenstein '74
Angels and Insects '95▶
The Ballad of Jack and Rose '05▶
Black Christmas '06
Blood Relatives '77
Brotherhood of the Wolf '01▶
The Cement Garden '93
The Cider House Rules '99▶
Close My Eyes '91
The Fishing Trip '98
Flowers in the Attic '87
The Grifters '90▶
Harry and Max '04
The House of Yes '97
I Stand Alone '98
Innocent Lies '95
Little Boy Blue '97
Mad Cowgirl '06
My Sister, My Love '78
Natural Born Killers '94
Novocaine '01
Pola X '99
Ringmaster '98
Say It Isn't So '01
Seducing Maarya '99
Sitcom '97
Spanking the Monkey '94▶
The Sweet Hereafter '96▶
Tarnation '03
This World, Then the Fireworks '97
A Thousand Acres '97
'Tis a Pity She's a Whore
U-Turn '97
Vicious Circles '97
The War Zone '01

India

see also Calcutta

The Adversary '71
Aparajito '58▶
Autobiography of a Princess '75
Bandit Queen '94
Bhowani Junction '56
The Big City '63
The Black Devils of Kali '55
Black Narcissus '47▶
Born into Brothels: Calcutta's Red Light Kids '04
Bride & Prejudice '04▶
Charulata '64
City of Joy '92
Conduct Unbecoming '75
Cotton Mary '99
The Courtesans of Bombay '85▶
The Darjeeling Limited '07▶
The Deceivers '88
Distant Thunder '73▶
Drums '38
Earth '98
Ele, My Friend '93
The Far Pavilions '84
Fire '96
Flame Over India '60▶
Gandhi '82▶
Gunga Din '39▶
Heat and Dust '82▶
The Home and the World '84▶
Hullabaloo over Georgie & Bonnie's Pictures '78
In Custody '94
The Indian Tomb '21
Jalsaghar '58
The Jewel in the Crown '84▶
Journey to the Lost City '58
Jungle Boy '96
Jungle Hell '55
Kama Sutra: A Tale of Love '96
Kim '50▶
Kim '84
Lagaan: Once upon a Time in India '01▶
The Lives of a Bengal Lancer '35▶
Looking for Comedy in the Muslim World '06
The Mahabharata '89
The Man Who Would Be King '75▶
Masala '91
Maya '66
The Middleman '76
Mission Kashmir '00
The Mistress of Spices '05
Monsoon '97
Monsoon Wedding '01▶
Mother Teresa: In the Name of God's Poor '97
Mountbatten: The Last Viceroy '86
The Namesake '06▶
Octopussy '83
A Passage to India '84▶
Pather Panchali '54▶
The Rains Came '39
The Razor's Edge '46▶
The River '51▶
Rudyard Kipling's The Jungle Book '94
Sabaka '55
Shakespeare Wallah '65▶
Sharpe's Challenge '06
Siddhartha '72
Spices '86▶
Staying On '80
Stiff Upper Lips '96
Such a Long Journey '98▶
Tales of the Kama Sutra: The Perfumed Garden '98
Two Daughters '61▶
The Warrior '01
Water '05
Waterland '92
The Weight of Water '00
Wee Willie Winkie '37▶
Wicked '69
Woman, Thou Art Loosed '04
The World of Apu '59▶

Inheritance

All in a Night's Work '61
The Aristocats '70▶
The Bachelor '99
Bailey's Billion$ '05
Billy Madison '94
Black Widow '87▶
The Black Widow '05
Bleak House '05
Brewster's Millions '45
Brewster's Millions '85
Broken Trust '93
Carry Me Back '82
Casper '95▶
Catherine Cookson's The Black Candle '92
The Chateau '01
The Cheyenne Social Club '70
Chilly Dogs '01
Christmas Eve '47
Chronicle of the Raven '04
Cutthroat Island '95
Daddy's Dyin'... Who's Got the Will? '90
Dangerous Passage '44
Dawg '02
Die Mommie Die! '03
Double or Nothing '37
Easy Money '83
Elvira, Mistress of the Dark '88
The Fighting Temptations '03
Finding Home '03
Fletch Lives '89
Freaks '32▶
Gaslight '44▶
The Glass House '01
Go for Zucker '05
Gold Diggers: The Secret of Bear Mountain '95
A Good Year '06▶
Greedy '94
The Hearse '80
Heart of Midnight '89
The Hellfire Club '61
Hot to Trot '88
I Capture the Castle '02
In the Heat of Passion 2: Unfaithful '94
The Inheritance '03
Kidnapped '05▶
King of Texas '02▶
La Cage aux Folles 3: The Wedding '86
Larger Than Life '96
Lemony Snicket's A Series of Unfortunate Events '04
Little Big League '94
Lord of the Rings: The Fellowship of the Rings '01▶
Love Kills '98
Milwaukee, Minnesota '03
Mr. Deeds '02
Mr. Deeds Goes to Town '36▶
Montana Sky '00
Moon over Miami '41▶
Mouse Hunt '97▶
No More Women '34
On Guard! '03▶
Oriana '85
Purlie Victorious '63
The Reception '05
Scavenger Hunt '79
The Sea '02
Seven Chances '25▶
Shanghai Kiss '07
Siblings '04
Snow Dogs '02
Splitting Heirs '93
Strangers in Love '32
13 Ghosts '01
UHF '89
The Ultimate Gift '07
Wild Things 2 '04
Woman of Straw '64
A Woman's a Helluva Thing '01
Zus & Zo '01

The Inquisition, What a Show!

see also Period Piece; 15th Century

Captain from Castile '47▶
Christopher Columbus: The Discovery '92
Fire Over England '37▶
Goya's Ghosts '06
History of the World: Part 1 '81
Jesse Stone: Death in Paradise '06
Jesse Stone: Night Passage '06
Jesse Stone: Stone Cold '05
Man of La Mancha '72
Nostradamus '93
Paid to Kill '54
Pas Tres Catholique '93
Pitfall '48▶
The Pit and the Pendulum '61▶
The Tempter '74

Insomnia

see also Up All Night

Bringing Out the Dead '99
Dream for an Insomniac '96
Fight Club: '99▶
The Haunting '99
I Can't Sleep '93
The Machinist '04
Taxi Driver '76▶
The Tempter '74

Insurance

About Schmidt '02▶
The Adjuster '91
Alias Jesse James '59
Along Came Polly '04
Amnesia '96
The Apartment '60▶
Baby Face Morgan '42
Bedelia '46▶
Beyond Suspicion '00
The Big Squeeze '96
Big Trouble '86
Burning Down the House '01
The Case of the Scorpion's Tail '71
Cause of Death '00
Changing Lanes '02▶
City of Ghosts '03
Code 46 '03
The Connection '73
Counter Attack '84
Critical Care '97
The Crocodile Hunter: Collision Course '02
The Curse of the Jade Scorpion '01
Dangerous Summer '82
The Darwin Awards '06
Dead Cold '96
Dead Eyes of London '61
Deadlier Than the Male '67
Deadly Desire '91
Death Benefit '96
Death Collector '89
Dillinger and Capone '95
Double Indemnity '44▶
Dying to Get Rich '98
The Electronic Monster '57
Enchanted Island '58
Entrapment '99
Escape Clause '96
The Favorite Son '94▶
Firestarter 2: Rekindled '02
First Do No Harm '97
Flawless '07
Folks! '92
Four Dogs Playing Poker '00
Frank McKlusky, C.I. '02
Frauds '93
Gold Raiders '51
Gone in 60 Seconds '74
Goodbye, Lenin! '99
The Great Plane Robbery '40
High Strung '91
Hook, Line and Sinker '30
The Hunted '98
I Now Pronounce You Chuck and Larry '07
I Wonder Who's Killing Her Now? '76
In the Mouth of Madness '95
John Grisham's The Rainmaker '97
Kafka '91
The Killers '46▶
Lady Ice '73
The Last Adventure '67
Linda '93
Lloyds of London '36▶
Love, Lies and Murder '91
Lush '01
The Man from the Pru '89
Master Touch '74
Murder, He Says '45
National Lampoon's Gold Diggers '04
The Odd Job '78
One Body Too Many '44
One Night in the Tropics '40
Paid to Kill '54
Pas Tres Catholique '93
Pitfall '48▶
The Prince of Poisoners: The Life and Crimes of William Palmer '98
Quick '93
Risk '00
Save the Tiger '73▶
Schemes '95
The Settlement '99
Sicko '07
Sins of the Night '93
Sleep Easy, Hutch Rimes '00
Sleuth '72▶
Stranger in the House '97
Sunburn '79
Sweet Lies '88
They Call It Murder '71
Things Happen at Night '48
The Thomas Crown Affair '68▶
The Thomas Crown Affair '99▶
Till Death Do Us Part '92
A Touch of Class '73▶
Tropical Heat '93
The Truman Show '98▶
The Whispering '94
The Whole Nine Yards '00
Wish You Were Dead '00
A Woman of Independent Means '94▶
The Yellow Rose of Texas '44

Internet Borne

see also Computers; Hackers

The Blair Witch Project '99
Confess '05
Dee Snider's Strangeland '98
Devour '05
Dot.Kill '05
Every Mother's Worst Fear '98
Feardotcom '02
Feed '05
GhostWatcher '02
Halloween: Resurrection '02
Hard Candy '06
Hellraiser: Hellworld '05
Jay and Silent Bob Strike Back '01
Mail to the Chief '00
Must Love Dogs '05
The Net '95
Open Cam '05
Pulse '01
Pulse '06
Southland Tales '06
Suspicion '03
Tom Clancy's Netforce '98
Turbulence 3: Heavy Metal '00
Untraceable '08
You've Got Mail '98

Interpol

Assassins '95
Black Cobra 2 '89
The Case of the Scorpion's Tail '71
The Castle of Fu Manchu '68▶
Cave of the Living Dead '65
Feed '05
Framed '90
Hitman '07
The King of the Kickboxers '91
Lord of War '05▶
The Medallion '03
Nighthawks '81
The Return of Dr. Mabuse '61
Soul Assassin '01
Terror of Mechagodzilla '78

Interracial Affairs

After the Rain '99
Ali: Fear Eats the Soul '74▶
Barbershop 2: Back in Business '04▶
Beauty Shop '05▶
Bleeding Hearts '94
The Bodyguard '92
Broken Blossoms '19▶
Bulworth '98▶
Cafe au Lait '94▶
Cake '05
Cape of Good Hope '04
Chaos '05
Chinese Box '97
Colorz of Rage '97
Come See the Paradise '90▶
Corrina, Corrina '94
Crash '05▶
Dark Blue '03▶
Dear Wendy '05
The Delta '97
Driving Miss Daisy '89▶
The Family Stone '05
A Fight for Jenny '90
A Fond Kiss '04
Freedomland '06
Glory Road '06
Guess Who '05
Guess Who's Coming to Dinner '67▶
Hairspray '07▶
Heaven and Earth '93
The Human Stain '03▶
Hustle & Flow '05▶
In My Country '04
In the Mix '05
Japanese Story '03▶
Jungle Fever '91▶
The Liberation of L.B. Jones '70
Love Field '91▶
Love Is a Many-Splendored Thing '55
Love Song '03
Machine Gun Blues '95
Made in America '93
Manderlay '05
Marci X '03
Melinda and Melinda '05▶
Miami Rhapsody '95
Mississippi Masala '92▶
Mr. & Mrs. Loving '96▶
Monster's Ball '01▶
My Baby's Daddy '04
My Beautiful Laundrette '85▶
The Nephew '97
Never Die Alone '04
The New World '05▶
Norman, Is That You? '76
November '05▶
Now & Forever '02
One Night Stand '97▶
Othello '22
Othello '52▶
Othello '65▶
Othello '95▶
Parallel Sons '95
A Patch of Blue '65▶
The Pianist '91
Pieces of April '03▶
Pinky '49▶
Pocahontas '95▶
Relax... It's Just Sex! '98
A Respectable Trade '98
Restaurant '98
Romeo Must Die '00
The Royal Tenenbaums '01▶
Ruby's Bucket of Blood '01
Save the Last Dance '01▶

The Second Chance '06
Shadowboxer '06
Shadows '60
Snow Falling on Cedars '99
Soldiers of Change '06
Something New '06
The Story of a Three Day Pass '68
Storytelling '01
Taxi Blues '90
The Tenants '06
The Tic Code '99
Walking Tall '04
Wassup Rockers '06
The Watermelon Woman '97
The Wedding Banquet '93
Welcome II the Terrordome '95
The Wrath of the Gods '14
Yes '04
Zebrahead '92

Interviews
see also This Is Your Life
An American Haunting '05
America's Heart and Soul '04
Catch a Fire '06
Chuck Berry: Hail Hail! Rock 'n' Roll '87
Crazy Love '07
A Decade Under the Influence '02
Dirty Pictures '00
Fellini: I'm a Born Liar '03
The Filth and the Fury '99
The Fog of War: Eleven Lessons from the Life of Robert S. McNamara '03
Having Our Say: The Delany Sisters' First 100 Years '99
Hearts of Darkness: A Filmmaker's Apocalypse '91
In the Shadow of the Moon '07
Interview '07
Interview with the Assassin '02
The JFK Conspiracy '91
La Salamandre '71
The Laramie Project '02
The Life of David Gale '03
No End in Sight '07
Only the Strong Survive '03
Roger & Me '89
Sicko '07
Standing in the Shadows of Motown '02
Stone Reader '02
Stripper '86
Surf's Up '07
Taxi to the Dark Side '07
The Thin Blue Line '88
When We Were Kings '96
Wisecracks '93

Inventors & Inventions
see also Mad Scientists; Science & Scientists
The Absent-Minded Professor '61
Back to the Future '85
A Bug's Life '98
Chairman of the Board '97
Chitty Chitty Bang Bang '68
C.H.O.M.P.S. '79
The Demi-Paradise '43
Edison the Man '40
Envy '04
Flubber '97
The Great Moment '44
Gremlins '84
Hello Down There '69
Hidden Enemy '40
Homewrecker '92
Honey, I Blew Up the Kid '92
Honey, I Shrunk the Kids '89
Honey, We Shrunk Ourselves '97
Invisible Mom '96
Iron Man '08
The Jerk '79
The Last Word '80
Longitude '00
The Machine '96
The Man in the White Suit '51
The Man Who Fell to Earth '76
Mom's Outta Sight '01
The Mosquito Coast '86
Mystery Plane '39
Not Quite Human '87
Not Quite Human 2 '89
The Nut '21
Orgazmo '98
Primer '04
P.U.N.K.S. '98
Roaring Speedboats '37
Rogue's Gallery '44
Service De Luxe '38
So This Is Washington '43
Son of Flubber '63
The Sound and the Silence '93
The Spanish Prisoner '97
Spitfire '42
Steamboy '05
Still Not Quite Human '92
The Story of Alexander Graham Bell '39
Strange Impersonation '46
Theremin: An Electronic Odyssey '95
Time After Time '79
Time Chasers '95
Under the Hula Moon '95
Village of the Giants '65
The Water Engine '92
Where's Willie? '77
The Whole Shootin' Match '79
The Yellow Cab Man '50
Young Tom Edison '40

Invisibility
see also Ghosts
Abbott and Costello Meet the Invisible Man '51
The Amazing Transparent Man '60
Clash of the Titans '81
The Dancing Princesses '84
Dick Tracy vs. Crime Inc. '41
Doctor Faustus '68
Dr. Orloff and the Invisible Man '72
Forbidden Planet '56
Golden Voyage of Sinbad '73
Hollow Man '00
Hollow Man 2 '06
Invisible Agent '42
Invisible Avenger '58
The Invisible Dr. Matuse '62
Invisible Invaders '59
Invisible Kid '88
The Invisible Man '33
The Invisible Man Returns '40
The Invisible Maniac '90
The Invisible Man's Revenge '44
Invisible Mom '96
Invisible Mom 2 '99
The Invisible Monster '50
The Invisible Strangler '76
The Invisible Terror '63
Invisible: The Chronicles of Benjamin Knight '93
The Invisible Woman '40
The League of Extraordinary Gentlemen '03
Leapin' Leprechauns '95
Mad Monster Party '68
The Man Who Wasn't There '83
Memoirs of an Invisible Man '92
Mr. Superinvisible '73
Mom's Outta Sight '01
My Magic Dog '97
Mystery Men '99
My Brother's War '97
The Nephew '97
The New Invisible Man '58
Now You See Him, Now You Don't '72
Orloff and the Invisible Man '70
Panama Menace '41
The Phantom Creeps '39
Phantom from Space '53
Phantom 2040 Movie: The Ghost Who Walks '95
Predator '87
The Quiet Man '52
Return of Chandu '34
Riding with Death '76
Sound of Horror '64

Iraq
see also Civil War (non U.S.); Genocide/Ethnic Cleansing; Middle East; Persian Gulf/Iraq War
The Ground Truth '06
Manticore '05
No End in Sight '07
Redacted '07
Stop-Loss '08

Ireland
see also Belfast; Dublin
American Women '00
Angela's Ashes '99
Beloved Enemy '36
Bloody Sunday '01
Brown Away '94
Bobbie's Girl '02
The Boxer '97
The Boys and Girl From County Clare '03
The Break '97
The Brylcreem Boys '96
The Butcher Boy '97
Captain Boycott '47
Children in the Crossfire '84
Conspiracy of Silence '03
Cowboys & Angels '04
The Crying Game '92
Dancing at Lughnasa '98
Danny Boy '82
Darby O'Gill & the Little People '59
The Dawning '88
December Bride '91
Durango '99
Echoes '88
The Eternal '99
Falling for a Dancer '98
Far and Away '92
The Field '90
The Fighting Prince of Donega '66
Fools of Fortune '90
48 Angels '06
Hangman's House '28
Hear My Song '91
The Honeymooners '03
How Harry Became a Tree '01
I See a Dark Stranger '46
I Went Down '97
Images '72
The Informer '29
Irish Cinderella '22
Irish Jam '06
James Joyce: A Portrait of the Artist as a Young Man '77
Johnny Nobody '61
Lamb '85
The Last September '99
Laws of Attraction '04
Leprechaun '93
A Love Divided '01
The Magdalene Sisters '02
The Magical Legend of the Leprechauns '99
The Manions of America '81
The Matchmaker '01
Men of Ireland '38
Moondance '95
My Brother's War '97
The Nephew '97
Odd Man Out '47
Oh, Mr. Porter '37
Ordinary Decent Criminal '99
The Playboys '92
Poltergeist: The Legacy '96
Prayer for the Dying '87
P.S. I Love You '07
The Purple Taxi '77
The Real Charlotte '91
Rory O'Shea Was Here '04
The Run of the Country '95
Ryan's Daughter '70
St. Patrick: The Irish Legend '00
Scarlett '94
The Secret of Roan Irish '94
Secret of the Cave '06
The Seventh Stream '01
She Creature '01
Some Mother's Son '96
Song o' My Heart '29
Spectre '96
Spellbreaker: Secret of the Leprechauns '96
Taffin '88
This Is My Father '99
Trojan Eddie '96
Troubles '88
Waking Ned Devine '98
War of the Buttons '95
Widow's Peak '94
The Wind That Shakes the Barley '06
Wings of the Morning '37

Islam
see also Middle East
The Clay Bird '02
God's Sandbox '02
Hamsin '83
Honey & Ashes '96
The Keeper: The Legend of Omar Khayyam '05
Leila '97
Looking for Comedy in the Muslim World '06
Malcolm X: Make It Plain '95
The Message '77
Monsieur Ibrahim '03
My Son the Fanatic '97
Osama '03
Paradise Now '05
Persepolis '07
Red Mercury '05
The Road to Guantanamo '06
Silent Waters '03
Sorry, Haters '05
The Suitors '88

Island
Cabin Boy '94
Captain Corelli's Mandolin '01
Captain Ron '92
Cast Away '00
The Castaway Cowboy '74
Chandu on the Magic Island '34
Club Dread '04
Club Paradise '86
The Condemned '07
The Conqueror & the Empress '64
The Cover Girl Murders '93
Crusoe '89
Cutthroat Island '95
Dark Harbor '98
Dead of Night '99
Dead Waters '94
Deadly Currents '93
Deeply '99
Dinatopia '02
Dinosaur Island '93
DOA: Dead or Alive '06
Doomsdayer '99
Dungeon of Harrow '64
The Ebb-Tide '37
Echoes of Paradise '86
Emmanuelle on Taboo Island '76
Escape from Atlantis '97
Exit to Eden '94
Eye of the Dolphin '06
The Fat Spy '66
Father Goose '64
Finding Home '03
Flipper '96
Four Last Songs '06
F.P. 1 '33
Gale Force '01
Gargantua '98
Ginger and Cinnamon '03
Girl in Black '56
Hack! '07
Haven '04
Hawk of the Wilderness '38
Head Above Water '96
Heading South '05
Heaven Knows, Mr. Allison '57
Horrors of Spider Island '59
House of the Dead '03
Hurricane '79
Ibiza Dream '02
The Idol Dancer '20
In a Savage Land '99
The Invitation '03
The Island '80
Island of Dr. Moreau '77
Island of Lost Souls '32
Island of the Blue Dolphins '64
Island of the Dead '00
Island of the Lost '68
Jack Frost 2: Revenge of the Mutant Killer Snowman '00
Jacob Two Two Meets the Hooded Fang '99
Joe Versus the Volcano '90
Jurassic Park '93
Jurassic Park 3 '01
Kidnapped in Paradise '98
Klima, Queen of the Amazons '75
King Kong '05
King of the Damned '36
The Kovak Box '06
L'Enfant d'Eau '95
The Lost World: Jurassic Park 2 '97
The Lunatic '92
Ma and Pa Kettle at Waikiki '55
Madagascar '05
Magic on Love Island '80
A Man of Passion '88
Mararia '98
McHale's Navy '97
Mediterraneo '91
Melody in Love '78
Men of War '94
Mindhunters '05
Mr. Moto in Danger Island '39
Molokai: The Story o' Father Damien '99
Mutiny on the Bounty '35
Mutiny on the Bounty '62
My Father the Hero '93
My Little Assassin '99
Mysterious Island '61
Mysterious Island of Beautiful Women '79
The Mystic Masseur '01
National Lampoon's Last Resort '94
Nim's Island '08
No Escape '94
No Man Is an Island '62
The Noah '75
Northern Extremes '93
Old Mother Riley's Jungle Treasure '51
On an Island with You '48
Once Upon a Wedding '05
One Night in the Tropics '40
The Other Side of Heaven '02
The Others '01
Pagan Island '60
Paradise '82
Passion in Paradise '89
The Passion of Ana '70
Pearl of the South Pacific '55
Perfect Strangers '03
Pippi in the South Seas '70
Pirates of the Caribbean: Dead Man's Chest '06
The Postman '94
The Prisoner of Shark Island '36
PT 109 '63
Puhtnu? '70
The Quest '96
Rapa Nui '93
The Ravagers '65
The Real Macaw '98
Reel Paradise '05
Rescue from Gilligan's Island '78
Respiro '02
Return to Paradise '53
Return to the Blue Lagoon '91
Robinson Crusoe '96
Rugrats Go Wild! '03
Savage Is Loose '74
The Sea God '30
The Seducers '70
The Seventh Dawn '64
Sex and Lucia '01
Shadow Warriors '97
Shelter Island '03
Signs of Life '68
Six Days, Seven Nights '98
The Sleeping Dictionary '02
The Snake People '68
Somewhere in Time '80
Son of Fury '42
Speed 2: Cruise Control '97
Spy Kids 2: The Island of Lost Dreams '02
Stephen King's The Storm of the Century '99
The Story of Dr. Wassell '44
Summer Affair '79
Surf's Up '07
Survival Island '02
Swept Away '02
Swept Away... '75
A Swingin' Summer '65
Tales of the Kama Sutra 2: Monsoon '98
The Tempest '82
Terror in Havana '41
Third World Cop '99
Trouble in Paradise '88
The Tuttles of Tahiti '42
Undercurrent '99
Up to His Neck '54
Utopia '51
Vibration '68
Victory '95
Waikiki Wedding '37
Week-End in Havana '41
The Weight of Water '00
We're Not Dressing '34
When Time Ran Out '80
The Wicker Man '06
Wide Sargasso Sea '92

Island Fare
see also Pacific Islands; Sex on the Beach
The Admirable Crichton '57
The Adventures of Sade '55
Affair in Trinidad '52
All the Brothers Were Valiant '53
Arachnid '01
Atlantis, the Lost Continent '61
Attack of the Sabretooth '05
Attack of the Crab Monsters '57
Bare Essentials '91
Baywatch the Movie: Forbidden Paradise '95
The Beach '00
Beverly Hills Family Robinson '97
Bikini Island '91
Bird of Paradise '32
Blacksnake! '73
Bleeders '97
The Blue Lagoon '80
Body Trouble '92
Boom! '68
The Bounty '84
Brand Upon the Brain! '06
The Breed '06

= rated three bones or higher

Island

The Widow of Saint-Pierre '00
Wings over the Pacific '43
Witches of the Caribbean
Xtro 3: Watch the Skies '95

Israel

see also The Holocaust; Judaism

Amazing Grace '92
Ancient Relic '02
The Band's Visit '07►
Bonjour Monsieur Shlomi '03►
Broken Wings '02►
The Bubble '06
Cast a Giant Shadow '66
Children of Rage '75
Colombian Love '04
Cup Final '92
Diamonds '72
Double Edge '92
Eagles Attack at Dawn '70
Exodus '60►
Free Zone '05
Hide and Seek '80
Hill 24 Doesn't Answer '55►
Intimate Story '81
James' Journey to Jerusalem '03
Kippur '00►
Land of Plenty '04
Late Marriage '01
Late Summer Blues '87
The Little Drummer Girl '84►
The Man Who Captured Eichmann '96
Mother Night '96►
Munich '05►
Operation Thunderbolt '77
Or (My Treasure) '04
Paradise Now '05►

Istanbul, not Constantinople

Climates '06►
Fay Grim '06
From Russia with Love '63►
Istanbul '57
Istanbul '85
Istanbul '90
Journey into Fear '42►
The Mask of Dimitrios '44►
The Net 2.0 '06
Steam: A Turkish Bath '96►
Topkapi '64►
The World Is Not Enough '99

Italy

see also Florence; Rome—Ancient; Rome—Modern; Venice

Accatone! '61►
Acla's Descent into Floristella '87
Acqua e Sapone '83
After Midnight '04
All Screwed Up '74►
Amarcord '74►
Angela '02
Avanti! '72
Best of Youth '03►
Beyond the Clouds '95
The Bicycle Thief '48►
A Blade in the Dark '83
Blame It on the Bellboy '79
Blood '79
Catch-22 '70►
Caterina in the Big City '03
Cemetery Man '95
The Children '90
Christ Stopped at Eboli '79►
Ciao, Professore! '94
Cinema Paradiso '88►
Cobra '25
Come September '61
The Conformist '71►
Cry of a Prostitute: Love Kills '72
Death Takes a Holiday '34►
Divorce—Italian Style '62►
Don't Torture a Duckling '72
Double Team '97
1860 '33
The Eighteenth Angel '97
Elective Affinities '97
Enchanted April '92
Eros '04
Escapade in Florence '62
Europa '51 '52
Excellent Cadavers '99
Executioner of Venice '63
A Face in the Rain '63
The Fallen '05►
Fellini's Roma '72
Fiances '63
Final Justice '84
For Roseanna '96
The Forbidden Christ '50
The 4th Tenor '02
Francesco '93
Gallowglass '95►
The Garden of Redemption '97
The Garden of the Finzi-Continis '71►
The Godfather, Part 3 '90►
A Good Woman '04
Heaven '01
His Secret Life '01►
Hornet's Nest '70
Hotel '01
I'm Not Scared '03
In Love and War '96
In Love and War '01
It Started in Naples '60►
Italian for Beginners '01►
The Italian Job '03►
Kaos '85►
La Chartreuse de Parme '48
La Dolce Vita '60►
La Scorta '94►
La Terra Trema '48►
The Leopard '63►
The Lickerish Quartet '70
Life Is Beautiful '98►
The Lizzie McGuire Movie '03
Lost Moment '47
Love and Anarchy '73►
Love in the City '53►
The Love Light '21
The Luzhin Defence '00
Macaroni '85
Mafioso '62
Malena '00
Mamma Roma '62►
A Man About the House '47
Massacre in Rome '73
A Month by the Lake '95
Mussolini & I '85
My House in Umbria '03►
My Mother's Smile '02
Night Sun '90
1900 '76►
Nora '00
Nostalghia '83
Only You '94
Open City '45►
Orchestra Rehearsal '78
The Organizer '64
Ossessione '42►
Paisan '46►
The Palermo Connection '91
Passion of Love '82►
Pizzicata '96
The Postman '94►
Prince of Foxes '49
Pronto '97
A Rare Breed '81
The Red Violin '98►
Ripley's Game '02►
The Roman Spring of Mrs. Stone '03
Rome Adventure '62
St. Michael Had a Rooster '72
The Scent of a Woman '75
Screw Loose '99
Season for Assassins '71
The Secret of Santa Vittoria '69
The Seven Hills of Rome '58
Shoeshine '47►
The Sicilian '87
The Sky Is Falling '00
The Son's Room '00►
Spice World: The Movie '97
Stealing Beauty '96
Stiff Upper Lips '96
The Stone Merchant '06
The Story of G.I. Joe '45►
Taken Alive '95
The Talented Mr. Ripley '99►
That Long Night in '43 '60
Three Coins in the Fountain '54
Too Bad She's Bad '54
The Tree of Wooden Clogs '78►
The Truce '96►
Two Women '61►
Uncle Nino '03
Under the Tuscan Sun '03
The Victors '63
Von Ryan's Express '65►
Voyage in Italy '53
The Walls of Malapaga '49
What Did You Do in the War, Daddy? '66
Where Angels Fear to Tread '91►
The Wide Blue Road '57►
William Shakespeare's A Midsummer Night's Dream '99
Wolverine '96
Women in Prison '49
Year of the Gun '91

It's a Conspiracy, Man!

see also Capitol Capers; Mystery & Suspense

Absolute Power '97
The Alchemists '99
All the President's Men '76►
Anatomy '00►
The Arrival '96
The Arrival 2 '98
The Assassination File '96
Attack Force '06
Backlash '99
The Bank Job '08►
Before I Say Goodbye '03
Blind Horizon '04
The Capitol Conspiracy '99
Chain Reaction '96
City Hall '95►
Company Business '91
Conspiracy Theory '97►
The Constant Gardener '05►
Cop Land '97►
Crimson Rivers 2: Angels of the Apocalypse '05
The Da Vinci Code '06►
Dead Bang '89
Echo of Murder '00
End Game '06
The Manchurian Candidate '62►
The Manchurian Candidate '04►
The Matrix '99►
The Matrix Reloaded '03►
The Matrix Revolutions '03►
Mulholland Falls '95
Muppets from Space '99
Murder at 1600 '97
Nixon '95►
No Way Out '87►
November Conspiracy '96
Oktober '98
The Parallax View '74►
Perfect Target '98
Pistol Whipped '08
Poodle Springs '98
Power Play '02
Rangers '00
Red Corner '97
Renaissance '06
Robin Cook's Terminal '96
Rush Hour 2 '01
Seven Days in May '64►
The Shadow Conspiracy '96
Shooter '07
16 Blocks '06►
Sneakers '92
Southland Tales '06
The Star Chamber '83
The State Within '06
Storm Catcher '99
Storm Tracker '99
Submerged '05
They Crawl '01
They Live '88
Three Days of the Condor '75►
Tom Clancy's Netforce '98
Unholy '07
Venomous '01
Wanted '08►
Winter Kills '79►
The X-Files '98

Jail

see also Alcatraz; Death Row; Great Escapes; Men in Prison; Women in Prison

Japan

see also Asia; Tokyo

Akira '89
As You Like It '06
The Ballad of Narayama '83►
Barbarian and the Geisha '58
The Battle of the Japan Sea '70
Behind the Rising Sun '43
Black Rain '88►
Black Rain '89
Blood on the Sun '45
Bright Future '03►
Cafe Lumiere '05
Captive Hearts '87
Cold Fever '95
The Cruel Story of Youth '60►
Demonlover '02
Destination Tokyo '43
Dr. Akagi '98
Dodes 'ka-den '70►
Dolls '02►
The Eel '96►
Eijanaika '81►
Enjo '58
Escapade in Japan '57
Flirt '95
Force of the Ninja '88
47 Ronin, Part 1 '42►
47 Ronin, Part 2 '42►
The Geisha Boy '58
Geisha Girl '52
Girls of the White Orchid '85
Gozu '03
The Grudge '04►
Gung Ho '85
Harakiri '62►
Heaven & Earth '90►
The Hidden Blade '04
Hiroshima '95►
Hiroshima Maiden '88
Hiroshima, Mon Amour '59►
House Where Evil Dwells '82
The Hunted '94
The Idiot '51►
The Imperial Japanese Empire '85
Journey of Honor '91
Kikujiro '99
King's Ransom '91
The Last Samurai '03►
Letters from Iwo Jima '06►
Life of Oharu '52►
Lost in Translation '03►
Love and Faith '78►
MacArthur's Children '85►
Madame Butterfly '95
A Majority of One '56
The Makioka Sisters '83►
Memoirs of a Geisha '05
The Men Who Tread on the Tiger's Tail '45
Midway '76
Minbo—Or the Gentle Art of Japanese Extortion '92
Mishima: A Life in Four Chapters '85►
Mr. Baseball '92
Mother '52►
The Neighbor No. Thirteen '05
No '98
No Regrets for Our Youth '46►
Nomugi Pass '79
Objective, Burma! '45►
Okoge '93
Osaka Elegy '36
Otaku No Video '91►
The Pillow Book '95
Prisoners of the Sun '91►
Ran '85►
Rashomon '51►
Red Beard '65►
Rikyu '91
Rising Sun '93►
Saga of the Vagabond '59
Samurai Banners '69
Samurai Cowboy '93
Samurai Rebellion '67►
Samurai Reincarnation '81
Sansho the Bailiff '54►
Sayonara '57►
Seven Samurai '54►
Shall We Dance? '96►
She and He '63
Shin Heike Monogatari '55►
Shogun '80►
Showdown in Little Tokyo '91
Silk '07
Sisters of the Gion '36
Snow Country '57
Sonatine '96►
The Sun's Burial '60►
Taboo '99
Teenage Mutant Ninja Turtles 3 '93
Thirty Seconds Over Tokyo '44►
3 Ninjas Kick Back '94
Tokyo-Ga '85►
Tokyo Pop '88
Tora! Tora! Tora! '70►
Traffic Jam '91
Twenty-Four Eyes '54►
The Twilight Samurai '02►
Ugetsu '53►
Under the Flag of the Rising Sun '72►
Utamaro and His Five Women '46
Village of Dreams '97
Walk, Don't Run '66
What's Up, Tiger Lily? '66►
When I Close My Eyes '95
The Wolves '71►
The Wrath of the Gods '14
The Yakuza '75►
You Only Live Twice '67
Zatoichi '03►
Zatoichi vs. Yojimbo '70►

Jazz & Blues

see also Price of Fame; Struggling Musicians

Almost Blue '93
American Blue Note '89
The Benny Goodman Story '55
Big Business Girl '31
Billy's Holiday '95
Bird '88►
Birth of the Blues '41
Blueberry Hill '88
The Blues Brothers '80►
The Blues Brothers 2000 '98
Cool Mikado '63
The Cotton Club '84►
Crossroads '86
Dingo '90
The Duke Is Tops '38
Eubie! '82►
The Five Pennies '59
Forty Shades of Blue '05
The Gene Krupa Story '59
G.I. Blues '60
Giant Steps '92
The Gig '85
The Glenn Miller Story '54►
Hi-De-Ho '35
The Jazz Singer '27
The Jazz Singer '80
Jazzman '84►
Kansas City '95►
Killer Diller '04
King of Jazz '30
Lady Sings the Blues '72
Let's Get Lost '88
Lighting in a Bottle '04
Lost Highway '96►
Lush Life '94►
Machine Gun Blues '95
Mo' Better Blues '90
Mystery in Swing '40
New Orleans '47
New York, New York '77►
Paris Blues '61
Pete Kelly's Blues '55
Ragtime '81►
Ray '04►
Rendez-vous de Juillet '49
Round Midnight '86►
Schultze Gets the Blues '03
Sepia Cinderella '47
Shadows '60►
Silver Hawk '04
Some Like It Hot '59►
A Song Is Born '48►
Stormy Monday '88
Sweet and Lowdown '99
Sweet Love, Bitter '67
Swing '98
Swing High, Swing Low '37
Swing It, Professor '37
The Talented Mr. Ripley '99►
Wild Orchid 2: Two Shades of Blue '92
Young Man with a Horn '50►

Jealousy

Amor da Hombre '97
Amores Perros '00►
The Break-Up '06
Cold Showers '05
Crush '02
Curse of the Golden Flower '06
Daddy & Them '99
The Devil's Backbone '01►
Dirty Love '05
Do Not Disturb '65
Enigma '01
Envy '04
The Fast Runner '01►
Fast Sofa '01
For Your Consideration '06
The Girl in the Red Velvet Swing '55
Gosford Park '01►
Heart '99
Honeymoon Lodge '43
The Last Man '00
Leaving Metropolis '02
Little Black Book '04
Lonely Hearts '06
The Male Animal '42
Me Without You '01
Merci pour le Chocolat '00►

► = rated three bones or higher

My Wife is an Actress '01
Nora '00
Othello '01
Out of Time '03
Pandaemonium '00
The Piano Teacher '01
The Prestige '06
The Price of Milk '00
Pumpkin '02
Second Best '05
Sex and Breakfast '07
Signs & Wonders '00
Sleuth '07
Sylvia '03
Taboo '99
Time '06
The Valet '06
The Weather Man '05
The Weight of Water '00
Who Wants to Kill Jessie? '65
Wife Versus Secretary '36

Three Men on a Horse '36

Jockeying for Position

Archer's Adventure '85
The Bashful Bachelor '42
Bite the Bullet '75
The Black Stallion '79
Boots Malone '52
Broadway Bill '34
Casey's Shadow '78
Champions '84
Cold Feet '89
A Day at the Races '37
Dead Heat '01
Devil on Horseback '54
The Devil's Cargo '48
Down Argentine Way '40
Dreamer: Inspired by a True Story '05
Duke of the Derby '62
Ex-Mrs. Bradford '36
Far and Away '92
A Fine Mess '86
Flame of Araby '51
Francis Goes to the Races '51
Glory '56
Great Dan Patch '49
Hidalgo '04
A Horse for Danny '95
Kentucky Blue Streak '35
Law of the Wild '34
Le Gentleman D'Epsom '62
The Lemon Drop Kid '51
Let It Ride '89
Lightning: The White Stallion '86
The Longshot '86
Ma and Pa Kettle at the Fair '52
Moon over Miami '41
My Old Man '79
National Velvet '44
Off and Running '90
On the Right Track '81
Phar Lap '84
Prince and the Great Race '83
The Quiet Man '52
Racing Luck '35
The Red Stallion '47
Riding High '50
Run for the Roses '78
Saratoga '37
Seabiscuit '03
Shooting Fish '98
Simpatico '99
The Story of Seabiscuit '49
Sylvester '85
Tennessee Stallion '78
Thoroughbreds Don't Cry '37
Trail to San Antone '47
Turf Boy '42
Win, Place, or Steal '72
Wings of the Morning '37

Jerusalem

Appointment with Death '88
Ben-Hur '59
The Body '01
The Crusades '35
Every Time We Say Goodbye '86
Kadosh '99
Kingdom of Heaven '05
The Silver Chalice '54

Joke and Dagger

see also Female Spies; Genre Spoofs; Spies & Espionage; Spy Kids
The Accidental Spy '01
The Adventures of Rocky & Bullwinkle '00
Agent Cody Banks '03
Agent Cody Banks 2: Destination London '04
Austin Powers: International Man of Mystery '97
Austin Powers 2: The Spy Who Shagged Me '99
Austin Powers in Goldmember '02
Boris and Natasha: The Movie '92
Call Me Bwana '63
Casino Royale '67
Chu Chu & the Philly Flash '81
Code Name: The Cleaner '07
Condorman '81
D.E.B.S. '04
Dead Men Don't Wear Plaid '82
Don't Raise the Bridge, Lower the River '68
The Double O Kid '92
Duck Soup '33
Get Smart '08
Get Smart, Again! '89
Hopscotch '80
Hudson Hawk '91
I Dood It '43
I Spy '02
If Looks Could Kill '86
The In-Laws '03
The In-Laws '79
In Like Flint '67
Isthar '87
Looney Tunes: Back in Action '03
The Man Who Knew Too Little '97
The Man with One Red Shoe '85
Memoirs of an Invisible Man '92
My Favorite Brunette '47
A Night in Casablanca '46
The Nude Bomb '80
Our Man Flint '66
The President's Analyst '67
Real Men '87
Secret Agent 00-Soul '89
The Shakiest Gun in the West '68
Spies Like Us '85
Spy Hard '96
S*P*Y*S '74
Top Secret! '84
True Lies '94
Undercover Brother '02
What's Up, Tiger Lily? '66
Zoolander '01

Journalism

see From Page; News at 11

Judaism

see also The Holocaust; Israel; Rabbi
Adam Sandler's 8 Crazy Nights '02
Aimee & Jaguar '98
All My Loved Ones '00
American Matchmaker '40
The Angel Levine '70
Angry Harvest '85
The Apprenticeship of Duddy Kravitz '74
The Assistant '97
Atalia '85
The Attic: The Hiding of Anne Frank '88
Au Revoir les Enfants '87
Autumn Sun '98
Bee Season '05
The Believer '01
Black Book '06
The Blum Affair '48
A Brivele der Mamen '38
Broken Glass '96
The Cantor's Son '37
Charlie Grant's War '80
The Chosen '81
Commissar '81
Conspiracy of Hearts '60
Counsellor-at-Law '33
Crossfire '47
Crossing Delancey '88
Dan On the Run '00
Daniel Deronda '02
David '97
David '79
A Day in October '92
Deconstructing Harry '97
The Devil's Arithmetic '99
The Diary of Anne Frank '59
Disraeli '79
Divided We Fall '00
Drifting '82
The Dunera Boys '85
The Dybbuk '37
East and West '24
Eli Eli '40
Enemies, a Love Story '89
Esther '98
Esther Kahn '00
Evan Almighty '07
Everything Is Illuminated '05
Exodus '60
Fateless '05
Fiddler on the Roof '71
The Fixer '68
Freud Leaving Home '91
A Friendship in Vienna '88
The Frisco Kid '79
Funny Girl '68
The Garden of the Finzi-Continis '71
Gentleman's Agreement '47
Go for Zucker '05
God, Man and Devil '49
The Golem '20
Good Evening, Mr. Wallenberg '93
Goodbye, New York '85
The Grand Role '04
Green Fields '37
The Grey Zone '01
Hamsin '83
Hanna's War '88
The Harmonists '99
Hester Street '75
H24 Doesn't Answer '55
Holocaust '78
Homicide '91
The House on Chelouche Street '73
I Love You, Alice B. Toklas! '68
I Love You, I Love You Not '97
I Love You Rosa '72
The Infiltrator '95
In the Presence of Mine Enemies '97
Invincible '01
The Island on Bird Street '97
It Runs in the Family '03
Ivan and Abraham '94
Jacob the Liar '74
James' Journey to Jerusalem '03
The Jazz Singer '27
The Jazz Singer '80
Jeremiah '98
The Jew '96
Jew-Boy Levi '99
Jud Süss '40
Kadosh '99
Keeping the Faith '00
Keeping Up with the Steins '06
King David '85
King of the Corner '04
Kissing Jessica Stein '02
Kuni Lemel in Tel Aviv '77
Lansky '99
The Last Metro '80
The Last Winter '84
Late Marriage '01
Left Luggage '98
Leon the Pig Farmer '93
Les Violons du Bal '74
Liberty Heights '99
Lies My Father Told Me '75
The Life and Times of Hank Greenberg '99
The Light Ahead '39
The Mad Adventures of Rabbi Jacob '73
Madman '79
The Man Who Captured Eichmann '96
The Man Who Cried '00
Martha and I '91
Masada '81
Max '02
Me and the Colonel '58
Mendel '98
The Merchant of Venice '04
Miracle at Midnight '98
Miracle at Moreaux '86
Miss Rose White '92
Mr. Emmanuel '44
Moses '96
The Murder of Mary Phagan '87
My Michael '75
My Mother's Courage '95
The Nativity Story '06
Next Year in Jerusalem '98
No Way to Treat a Lady '68
Noa at Seventeen '82
November Moon '85
Nowhere in Africa '02
Once Upon a Time in America '84
The Only Way '70
Outside Chance of Maximilian Glick '88
Over the Brooklyn Bridge '83
The Pawnbroker '65
The Pianist '02
Playing Mona Lisa '00
Power '34
A Price above Rubies '97
Prime '06
The Proprietor '96
Protocols of Zion '05
The Quarrel '93
Radio Days '87
Rescuers: Stories of Courage—Two Couples '98
Rescuers: Stories of Courage—Two Women '97
Rescuers: Stories of Courage: "Two Women"
The Revolt of Job '84
Safe Men '98
Salah '65
Schindler's List '93
School Ties '92
A Secret Space '88
The Serpent's Egg '78
The Shop on Main Street '65
The Sky Is Falling '00
Snow in August '01
Sofie '92
Solomon '98
Solomon and Gaenor '98
The Sorrow and the Pity '71
Steel Toes '06
Stolen Summer '02
A Stranger Among Us '92
The Substance of Fire '96
The Summer of Aviya '88
The Summer of My German Soldier '78
Sunshine '99
Table Settings '84
The Taxman '98
Tevye '39
They Were Ten '61
'38: Vienna before the Fall '88
Time of Favor '00
The Tollbooth '04
Train of Life '98
Transport from Paradise '65
The Twilight of the Golds '97
Uncle Moses '32
Under the Domim Tree '95
Under the Earth '86
Unsettled Land '88
Unstrung Heroes '95
Uprising '01
Used People '92
Voyage of the Damned '76
Wall '04
Wandering Jew '20
War & Love '84
When Do We Eat? '05
Where Is My Child? '37
Where's Poppa? '70
The Wooden Gun '79
Yellow Asphalt '01
Yentl '83
You Don't Mess with the Zohan '08
Zalmen or the Madness of God '75

Jungle Stories

see also Monkeyshines; Treasure Hunt
Ace Ventura: When Nature Calls '95
Active Stealth '99
Africa Screams '49
Aguirre, the Wrath of God '72
All the Way, Boys '73
Amazon '90
Amazon Jail '85
Anaconda '96
Anacondas '04
At Play in the Fields of the Lord '91
Baby... Secret of the Lost Legend '85
Back from Eternity '56
Bat 21 '88
Bela Lugosi Meets a Brooklyn Gorilla '52
Beyond Rangoon '95
Black Cobra 3: The Manila Connection '90
The Black Devils of 'Kali '55
Blonde Savage '47
Brenda Starr '86
The Bride & the Beast '58
Bride of the Gorilla '51
Cannibal Women in the Avocado Jungle of Death '89
Cobra Woman '44
Codename: Terminate '90
The Colombian Connection '91
Commando Invasion '87
Congo '95
Curious George '06
Death in the Garden '56
Delta Force Commando '87
The Diamond of Jeru '01
Diplomatic Immunity '91
DNA '97
Dr. Cyclops '40
Dr. Seuss' Horton Hears a Who! '08
East of Borneo '31
Elephant Boy '37
Elephant Walk '54
The Emerald Forest '85
Emerald Jungle '80
Emmanuelle 6 '88
End of the Spear '06
Enemy Unseen '91
Escape from Hell '79
Escape to Burma '55
Escape 2000 '81
Farewell to the King '89
Fatal Mission '89
Field of Fire '92
Field of Honor '86
Final Mission '84
Fire in the Amazon '93
Firehawk '92
Firewalker '86
Fitzcarraldo '82
Five Came Back '39

Jungle

Flight from Singapore '62
Found Alive '34
The Further Adventures of Tennessee Buck '88
Gold Raiders '83
Gorillas in the Mist '83
Green Fire '55
Green Inferno '72
Green Mansions '59
Greystoke: The Legend of Tarzan, Lord of the Apes '84
Harry Black and the Tiger '58
Heart of Darkness '93
Hell's Headquarters '32
How Tasty Was My Little Frenchman '71
Indio '90
Indio 2: The Revolt '92
Instinct '99
The Intended '02
Invincible Barbarian '83
Jane & the Lost City '87
Jumanji '95
Jungle '52
The Jungle Book '42
The Jungle Book '67
The Jungle Book 2 '03
Jungle Boy '98
Jungle Drums of Africa '53
Jungle Goddess '49
Jungle Heat '84
Jungle Inferno '55
Jungle Master '56
Jungle Patrol '48
Jungle Raiders '85
Jungle Siren '42
Jungle Warriors '84
Killers '88
Killing Heat '84
King of the Jungle '33
King of the Kongo '29
King Solomon's Treasure '76
Krippendorf's Tribe '98
The Land Unknown '57
Law of the Jungle '42
Liane, Jungle Goddess '56
The Lion King '94
The Lion Man '36
Lion Man '75
Lost City '34
Lost City of the Jungle '45
The Lost Continent '51
The Lost Tribe '49
Lure of the Islands '42
Managua '97
Medicine Man '92
Mercenary 2: Thick and Thin '97
Merrill's Marauders '62
Mighty Jungle '64
The Mighty Peking Man '77
Miracles '86
Missing in Action '84
M'stress of the Apes '79
Mogambo '53
The Mosquito Coast '86
The Muthers '76
Mysterious Island of Beautiful Women '79
Nabonga '44
Naked Jungle '54
The Naked Prey '66
The New Adventures of Tarzan '35
Night Creature '79
Nightforce '86
No Man Is an Island '62
Objective, Burma! '45
Omoo Omoo, the Shark God '49
Operation Dumbo Drop '95
Options '88
Overkill '96
Perils of the Darkest Jungle
The Phantom '96
The Pink Jungle '68

▶ = rated three bones or higher

Jungle

Predator '87
Prehistoric Women '67
Proof of Life '00
Queen of the Amazons 47
Queen of the Jungle '35
The Real Glory '39►
Red Dust '32
River of Death '90
River of Evil '64
The Road to Zanzibar '41►
Robbers of the Sacred Mountain '83
Romancing the Stone '84►
Rudyard Kipling's The Jungle Book '94
Rudyard Kipling's the Second Jungle Book: Mowgli and Baloo '97
The Ruins '08
The Rundown '03►
Samar '62
The Savage Girl '32
Shame of the Jungle '75
Sheena '84
Snakeman '05
Sniper '92
Solo '96
Son of Kong '33
Stormquest '87
Sweet Revenge '87
Tarzan '99►
Tarzan and His Mate '34►
Tarzan and the Green Goddess '38
Tarzan and the Lost City '98►
Tarzan and the Trappers '58
Tarzan Escapes '36►
Tarzan Finds a Son '39►
Tarzan, the Ape Man '17
Tarzan, the Ape Man '32►
Tarzan, the Ape Man '81
Tarzan the Fearless '33
Tarzan the Tiger '29
Tarzana, the Wild Girl '69
Tarzan's Revenge '38
Tarzan's Secret Treasure '41
Tears of the Sun '03
Terror in the Jungle '68
Terror of the Bloodhunters '62
The Thin Red Line '98►
The Thirsty Dead '74
Tiger Fangs '43
Trader Horn '31
Trap Them & Kill Them '77
The Treasure of the Amazon '84
Troma's War '88
Tropic Thunder '08
Tropical Heat '93
Tropical Malady '04
Turistas '06
Two Brothers '04
Typhoon Treasure '39
Virgin Sacrifice 59
Volunteers '85
Voodoo Woman '57
Wages of Fear '55►
Warkill 65
Warriors of the Apocalypse '85
Watchers 3 '94
West of Zanzibar '28
Where the River Runs Black '86
White Cargo 42
White Ghost 88
White Huntress '57
The White Legion '36
The White Orchid '54
White Pongo 45
Wild Women '53
Woman Hunt 72
The World's Greatest Athlete '73
Y2K '99
Zombie Island Massacre '84

Junior Jocks

see also Baseball; Basketball; Childhood; Football; Hockey; Sports Comedies; Team Efforts Dramas; Team Efforts

Adam Sandler's 8 Crazy Nights '02
Amazing Grace & Chuck '87►
The Bad News Bears '76►
The Bad News Bears '05
Bend It Like Beckham '02►
The Big Green '95
D2: The Mighty Ducks '94
Kicking and Screaming '95►
Ladybugs '92
Like Mike '02
Little Big League '94
Little Giants '94
Max Dugan Returns '83
The Mighty Ducks '92
Past the Bleachers '95
Rebound '05
The Sandlot '93►
Stick It '06

Justice Prevails...?

see also Order in the Court

Above Suspicion '95
Absence of Malice '81►
The Accused '88►
The Advocate '93►
After Innocence '05►
All-American Murder '91
And Justice for All '79►
Assault at West Point: The Court-Martial of Johnson Whittaker '94
The Avenging Angel '95
Bamako '06
Beau Geste 39►
Better Off Dead '94
Beyond Reasonable Doubt '80
The Burning Season '94►
A Case for Murder '93
Cause Celebre '87►
Cause of Death '00
A Certain Justice '99
The Chamber '96►
Circumstantial Evidence '35
A Civil Action '98►
Color of Justice '97
Comedy of Power '06
The Confession '98
Crash Course '00
Creature with the Blue Hand '70
Crime of the Century '96►
Cross Examination '32
The Crucible '96►
A Cry in the Dark '88►
Cyber-Tracker '93
Dangerous Evidence: The Lori Jackson Story '99
Dark Justice '91
The Day the Sun Turned Cold '94►
Dead Right 68
Deadlocked '00
Death Sentence '07
Dingaka '65
A Dry White Season '89►
Eddie Macon's Run 83
Edwin '84
8-A '92
Erin Brockovich '00►
Excellent Cadavers '99
Execution of Justice '99►
The Execution of Private Slovik '74►
An Eye for an Eye '95
False Arrest '92
Fatal Vision 84
Final Justice '98
Find Me Guilty '06►
Forgotten Prisoners '90
Fracture '07►
Ghosts of Mississippi '96►
The Good Fight 92
Guilty as Charged '92
Guilty as Sin '93
A Gun in the House '81
The Hanging Tree '59►
Heavens Fall '06
Hollow Reed '95►
Honor Thy Father and Mother: The True Story of the Menendez Brothers '94
I Am Sam '01►
In Self Defense '93
In the Name of the Father '93►
Indictment: The McMartin Trial '95►
Invasion of Privacy '96
The Jack Bull '99
The Jagged Edge 85
Jasper, Texas '03
JFK '91►
Judge Dredd '95
Judicial Consent '94
Jury Duty '95
Just Cause '94
The Killing Yard '01
Last Dance '96
Lawman '71►
Laws of Deception '97
Let Him Have It '91►
Life & Times of Judge Roy Bean 72
Losing Isaiah '94►
The Magnificent Yankee '50►
Man in the Shadow '57
Melanie Darrow '97
Mr. & Mrs. Loving '96►
Mother Night '96►
Murder in the First '95
The Murder of Mary Phagan '87►
The Murder of Stephen Lawrence '99►
Music Box '89
Mutiny '99
Night Falls on Manhattan '96►
Nuremberg '00►
Nuts '87►
One Kill '00►
The Paper '94►
Pinochet's Last Stand '06
Presumed Innocent '90►
The Prisoner of Shark Island '36
Prisoners of the Sun '91►
The Quarry '98
Reservation Road '07
Restraining Order '99
Reversal of Fortune '90►
Roe vs. Wade '89►
Rules of Engagement '00►
The Runaway '00
Runaway Jury '03►
Separate but Equal '91►
Shoot to Kill 90
The Shooting Party 77
Showdown 73
Sins of the Father '01►
Sirens '99
Skin '89
Sleepers '96
Slow Burn '05
Snap Decision '01
Storm Warning '51
The Story of Qiu Ju '91►
The Summer of Ben Tyler '96►
A Time to Kill '96►
A Town Has Turned to Dust '98
Trial & Error '62
Trial and Error '92
The Trial of Old Drum '00
The Trials of Oscar Wilde '60►
An Unforgettable Summer '94
The Verdict '82►
Weekend of Shadows '77►
White Lie '91
Whitewash: The Clarence Brandley Story '02
The Winslow Boy '98►
Woman Undone '95
The Wrong Man '56►
The Young Land 59
The Young One '61
The Young Savages '61

Juvenile Delinquents

see also Gangs; Hell High School; Teen Angst

Angels with Dirty Faces '38►
Bad Boys '83►
Blackboard Jungle 55►
Boys Town '38►
The Chorus '04►
Coach Carter '05►
The Day of the Outlaw '59►
Detention '03
Gridiron Gang '06
Holes '03►
The Hoodlum Priest '61►
Hope Ranch '02
The Mayor of Hell '33
See No Evil '06
Step Up '06
12 and Holding '05►
The Young Savages '61

Karaoke

The Astronaut's Wife '99
The Cable Guy '96
Crossroads '02
Duets '00
High School Musical '06
I Still Know What You Did Last Summer '98
Jackpot '01
Junk Mail '97
A Life Less Ordinary '97
Lost in Translation '03►
Love, Honour & Obey '00
My Best Friend's Wedding '97
Pushing Tin '99►
Rush Hour 2 '01
A Smile Like Yours '96
The Watermelon Woman '97
When Harry Met Sally... '89►

KGB

see also CIA/NSA; Cold War Spies; Russia/USSR

American Roulette '88
Cambridge Spies '03
Codename Kyril '91
The Company '07
Company Business '91
East-West '99
Enigma '82
The Experts '89
Fair Game '95
The Fourth Protocol '87►
From Russia with Love '63►
Gorky Park '83►
Indiana Jones and the Kingdom of the Crystal Skull '08
The Inner Circle '46
The Jigsaw Man '84
Lie Down with Lions '94
The Living Daylights '87►
Munich '05►
No Way Out '87►
Red Dawn '84
Red Scorpion '89
The Second Front '05
Sleepers '96
Smiley's People '82
Spy Hard '96
The Spy Who Loved Me '77►
Subterfuge '98
Telefon '77
Tinker, Tailor, Soldier, Spy '80►
Topaz 69►
White Nights '85
The World Is Not Enough '99

Kiddie Viddy

see also Animation & Cartoons

Cars '06►
Family Tree '00
Finding Nemo '03►
Inspector Gadget's Biggest Caper Ever '05
The Land Before Time 6: The Secret of Saurus Rock '98
Monsters, Inc. '01►
My Dog Skip '99►
The Pirates Who Don't Do Anything: A Veggie Tales Movie '08
Pooh's Heffalump Movie '05
Saving Shiloh '06
The SpongeBob SquarePants Movie '04

Kidnapped!

see also Hostage!; Missing Persons

Abducted '86
Abducted 2: The Reunion '94
Abduction 75
The Abduction of Allison Tate '92
The Abduction of Kari Swenson '87
Ace Ventura: Pet Detective '93►
Act of Piracy '89
Adam '83►
African Rage '78
Against a Crooked Sky '75
Agent of Death '99
Air Bud 6: Air Buddies '06
An Alan Smithee Film: Burn, Hollywood, Burn '97
Alias Betty '01
All Over Town '37
Alone in the Woods '95
Along Came a Spider '01►
Alpha Dog '06
American Kickboxer 2: To the Death '93
And Hope to Die '72►
Any Place But Home '97
The Art of War '00
Ashanti, Land of No Mercy '79
The Atomic City '52
Autumn Born 79
Baby's Day Out '94
Ballistic: Ecks vs. Sever '02
Battle in Heaven '05
Beach Blanket Bingo '65►
Beethoven's 2nd '93
Believers '07
Benji '74►
Best Revenge '83
Beverly Hills Brats '89
Beyond Fear '75
Beyond Justice '92
Big Brother Trouble '00
The Big Hit '98
The Big Lebowski '97►
Black Cat Run '98
Black Samurai '77
Blacklight '07
Bless the Child '00
Blind Heat '00
Blink of an Eye '92
Blood at Sundown '88
Blown Away '90
Bound and Gagged: A Love Story '93
Buffalo 66 '97►
Burial of the Rats '95
B.U.S.T.E.D. '99
The Butterfly '02►
Captivity '07
Cecil B. Demented '00
Cellular '04►
Celtic Pride '96
Charlie Chan at the Olympics '37
Charlie's Angels '00
The Chase '93
The Chumscrubber '05
The City of Lost Children '95►
The Clearing '04►
Clifford's Really Big Movie '04
Close Your Eyes '02
Cohen and Tate '88
Cold Blood '75
Collateral '04►
The Collector '85►
Commando '85►
The Concentratin' Kid '30
Contraband '40
The Coroner '98
Crime of the Century '96
Crime Story '93
Crimebusters 79
Crows '94
The Crying Game '92►
Dance with the Devil '97
Dead Air '94
The Deep End of the Ocean '98
Dirty Little Secret '98
Distant Justice '92
Django Strikes Again '87
Don't Say a Word '01
Door to Door Maniac '61
Double Play '96
Dumb & Dumber '94
Earthly Possessions '99
The Educators '04
Emma's Shadow '88►
The End of Violence '97
Ernest Goes to Africa '97
Ernie Kovacs: Between the Laughter '84
Everybody's Famous! '00
Excess Baggage '96
Executive Target '97
Extreme Dating '04
Eye '96
Faceless '88
Fargo '96►
Fatal Combat '96
Final Justice '98
Find the Lady 76
Fire in the Sky '93
Fireback 78
First Daughter '99
Flightplan '05►
Follow the River '95
Force of the Ninja '88
Four Days in September '97
Fugitive Champion '99
Gallowglass '95►
The Gay Desperado '36
The Gingerbread Man '97►
A Girl, 3 Guys and a Gun '01
The Golden Compass '07
The Grissom Gang '71►
Guarding Tess '94
Gun Fury 53
Hangfire '91
Harem '86
Hearts & Armour '83
Hidalgo '04
Hide and Seek '00
Hollywood Cop 87
Honeybaby 74
Hostage for a Day '94
I'm Not Scared '03►
Implicated '98
In a Stranger's Hand '92
In Desert and Wilderness '01
In Old New Mexico '45
In the Country Where Nothing Happens '99
In the Doghouse '98
In the Name of the King: A Dungeon Siege Tale '08
Incident at Deception Ridge '94
Invasion of Privacy '96
Island Monster 53
Jack and His Friends '92
Jailbait '93
Judas Kiss '98
Judgment Day '99
Kansas City '95►
Kentucky Jubilee '51
Kickboxer 3: The Art of War '92
Kid Colter '85
Kidnap Syndicate '76
Kidnapped '87
Kidnapped '95
Kidnapped '05►
Kidnapped in Paradise '98
King's Ransom '05
Lake Consequence '92
The Last Assassins '96
The Last Hard Men '76
Last Lives '98
A Life Less Ordinary '97
The Lightning Incident '91
The Lindbergh Kidnapping Case '76►
Live Free or Die Hard '07►
Lorna Doone 22
A Loving Father '02
Ma and Pa Kettle at Waikiki '55
Malibu's Most Wanted '03
Man on Fire '04►
The Man Who Captured Eichmann '96
Manipulator 71

► = *rated three bones or higher.*

Manny & Lo '96▶
Marrionier '05
Martin's Day '85
Master of Disguise '02
Memphis '91
Mercy '96
Midnight in Saint Petersburg '97
The Mighty '98▶
A Mighty Heart '07▶
Miss Congeniality 2: Armed and Fabulous '05
Mission: Impossible '03▶
Mr. Nanny '93
The Money '93
Moran of the Lady Letty '22
The Mummy Returns '01
Munich '05▶
MXP: Most Xtreme Primate '03
Mystery Men '99
Mystic River '03▶
National Lampoon's The Don's Analyst '97
Never Say Die '94
New Blood '99
Nick of Time '95
The Night of the Following Day '69
The Nightmare before Christmas '93▶
Nightstick '87
No '98
No Deposit, No Return '76
No Way Back '96
Omega Syndrome '87
101 Dalmatians '96
One Small Hero '99
The Only Way Home '72
Operation Condor 2: The Armour of the Gods '86
Operation Delta Force 2: Mayday '97
Orphans '87▶
Out of Sight '98▶
Outlaw Force '87
Paper Bullets '99
Parker '84
Pay or Die '83
Perfect Strangers '03
A Perfect World '93
Perpetrators of the Crime '08
The Pirates Who Don't Do Anything: A Veggie Tales Movie '08
The Pleasure Drivers '05
Prince of Pennsylvania '88
Private Obsession '94
Proof of Life '00
Public Enemies '96
Pulse '03
Queen's Messenger II '01
The Quest '96
'R Xmas '01
Raising Arizona '87▶
Ransom '96▶
Ransom Money '88
A Rare Breed '81
The Real McCoy '93
Red Eye '05▶
Remote Control '94
Renaissance '06
Rendition '07
Rescue Me '93
Return to Never Land '02
The Revenger '90
Riders of the Purple Sage '25
Ring of Fire 2: Blood and Steel '92
Ring of the Musketeers '93
Rio Diablo '93
Riot '96
The Road Killers '95
Robin-B-Hood '06
Rockabye '86
Rosebud '75
Rumpelstiltskin '96
Runaway Nightmare '84
Running Scared '06
Rush Hour '98

Ruthless People '86▶
Sahara '83
Savage Abduction '73
Saw '04
Screwed '00
Second Sight '89
Seven Hours to Judgment '88
Sexus '64
Shadow Man '06
Shanghai Noon '00
Sharpe's Challenge '06
Sharpe's Enemy '94
Shattered Image '93
Show Me '04
Silver Hawk '04
Singapore '47
Sky Captain and the World of Tomorrow '04
Slate, Wyn & Me '87
Sloane '84
SnakeEater '89
Snipes '01
So Close to Paradise '98
Social Error '35
Soldier Boyz '95
Soldier's Fortune '91
Son of the Pink Panther '93
Son of the Sheik '26▶
Spartan '04▶
The Squeeze '77
Stakeout '87
Starved '62
Stealing Candy '04
Stealing Sinatra '94
Street Fighter '94
Suicide Kings '97
Sunchaser '96
Sunstroke '92
Sweet Poison '91
Switchback '97
Tar '97
Tarzan's New York Adventure '42
Teaching Mrs. Tingle '99
Teresa's Tattoo '94
Terror Stalks the Class Reunion '93
Terror 2000 '93
That Darn Cat '96
That Man from Rio '64
Thin Air '00
Thou Shalt Not Kill...Except '87
The Three Burials of Melquiades Estrada '05▶
Three Days to a Kill '91
3 Ninjas '92
3 Ninjas Knuckle Up '95
3-Way '04
Tie Me Up! Tie Me Down! '90
Till the End of the Night '94
To Grandmother's House We Go '94
Toy Story 2 '99▶
Trade '07
The Transporter '02
Transporter 2 '05
The Trap '22
Trapped '02
Trapped Alive '93
The Triplets of Belleville '02▶
Tropix '02
Try and Get Me '50
Tsotsi '05▶
Tuck Everlasting '02
The 24th Day '04
Twinsitters '95
Two Bits & Pepper '95
Under the Hula Moon '95
Unlawful Passage '94
The Vanishing '93
A Vow to Kill '94
Waikiki Wedding '37
Waist Deep '06
The Warrior '01
The Wash '01
Way of the Gun '00
When Danger Follows You Home '97
When the Greeks... '97

Whistling in the Dark '41▶
The Whole Ten Yards '04
The Wild Card '03
Wild Ones on Wheels '62
The Wind and the Lion '75▶
Winterhawk '76
Wolverine '96
The World in His Arms '52

Killer Apes and Monkeys

see also Monkeyshines

The Ape '40
A*P*E* '76
The Ape Man '43
Battle for the Planet of the Apes '73
The Beast That Killed Women '65
Beneath the Planet of the Apes '70
The Bride & the Beast '58
Congo '95
Conquest of the Planet of the Apes '72
Doctor of Doom '62
Dr. Orloff and the Invisible Man '72
Gorilla '56
In the Shadow of Kilimanjaro '86
Jungle Captive '45
Jungle Woman '44
King Kong '33▶
King Kong '76
King Kong '05▶
King Kong Lives '86
King Kong vs. Godzilla '63
King Kong of Kong Island '78
Link '86
Mighty Joe Young '49
Mighty Joe Young '98
The Mighty Peking Man '77
Monkey Boy '90
Monkey Shines '88
Planet of the Apes '68▶
Primal Rage '90
Rat Pfink a Boo-Boo '66
Return of the Ape Man '44
Son of Ingagi '40
Son of Kong '33

Killer Appliances

see also Technology—Rampant

Final Destination 2 '03
Ghost in the Machine '93
The Mangler '94
Maximum Overdrive '86
Microwave Massacre '83
The Refrigerator '91

Killer Beasts

see also Killer Apes and Monkeys; Killer Dogs; Killer Kats; Killer Pigs; Killer Rodents

The Abomination '88
Attack of the Beast Creatures '85
Beaks: The Movie '87
Berserker '87
Bog '84
The Brain Eaters '58
The Cave '05
Chupacabra Terror '05
Clash of the Titans '81
Creepshow '82
Day of the Animals '77
Food of the Gods '76
Grizzly '76
Half-Caste '04
In the Shadow of Kilimanjaro '86
Island of Terror '66
Jabberwocky '77
Jason and the Argonauts '63▶
Jason and the Argonauts '00
Jaws of Satan '81
Jurassic Park '93▶
The Lost World: Jurassic Park 2 '97
Mad Death '83
The Monster Walks '32
Monty Python and the Holy Grail '75▶
Mysterious Island '61▶
Naked Jungle '54▶
Night of the Grizzly '66
The Rats Are Coming! The Werewolves Are Here! '72
Return to Boggy Creek '77
Rodan '56
Shakma '89
Sleepwalkers '92
The Slime People '63
Snowbeast '77
Subspecies '90
Swamp of the Lost Monster '65
Vulture '67
The Wild Beasts '85
Winterbeast '92

Killer Brains

see also Renegade Body Parts

Black Friday '40
Blood of Ghastly Horror '72
The Brain '62
The Brain '88
Brain Damage '88
The Brain from Planet Arous '57
Brain of Blood '71
The Brain that Wouldn't Die '63
Donovan's Brain '53▶
Fiend without a Face '58
Mindkiller '87

Killer Bugs and Slugs

Ants '77
The Applegates '89
Arachnid '01
Arachnophobia '90▶
Attack of the Giant Leeches '59
The Bees '78
Beginning of the End '57
The Black Scorpion '57
Blood Beast Terror '67
Blue Monkey '87
Bug '75
Bug Buster '99
Bugged! '96
Centipede! '05
The Cosmic Monsters '58
Creepers '85
Creepshow '82
Curse of the Black Widow '77
The Deadly Mantis '57
DNA '97
Earth vs. the Spider '58
Earth vs. the Spider '01
Eight Legged Freaks '02
Empire of the Ants '77
Evil Spawn '87
Food of the Gods '76
The Giant Spider Invasion '75
The Glass Trap '04
Godzilla vs. Megalon '76
Godzilla vs. Mothra '64
Horrors of Spider Island '59
Infested: Invasion of the Killer Bugs '02
Insecticidal '05
Island of the Dead '00
Kingdom of the Spiders '77
Kiss of the Tarantula '75
The Lair of the White Worm '88▶
Last Days of Planet Earth '74
Lord of the Rings: The Return of the King '03▶
Man of the House '95
Mansquito '05
Mimic '97▶
Mimic 2 '01
Mimic 3: Sentinel '03
The Mist '07▶
Monster from Green Hell '58
The Monster That Challenged the World '57
Monster Dog '92
Monster '03
Mosquitoman '05
Mosquito '95
Mothra '62▶
The Nest '88
Parasite '82
Phase 4 '74
Rebirth of Mothra '96
Rebirth of Mothra 2 '97
Return of the Fly '59
The Savage Bees '76
The Scorpion's Tail '74
Shriek of the Mutilated '74
Skeeter '93
Slither '06
Slugs '87
Son of Godzilla '66
Spider Woman '44▶
Spiders 2: Breeding Ground '01
Squirm '76
Starship Troopers '97▶
Subhuman '04
The Swarm '78
Tarantula '55▶
Tarantulas: The Deadly Cargo '77
Terror Out of the Sky '78
Them! '54▶
They Came from Within '75
They Crawl '01
Ticks '93
Tremors '89
Tremors 2: Aftershocks '96
Tremors 3: Back to Perfection '01
The Wasp Woman '59
The Wasp Woman '96
The Worm Eaters '77

Killer Cars

see also Motor Vehicle Dept.

Black Cadillac '03
The Cars That Ate Paris '74▶
Christine '84
Dark of the Night '85
Death Race 2000 '75
Death Sport '78
Duel '71▶
The Hearse '80
Mad Max '80▶
Maximum Overdrive '86
One Deadly Owner '74
The Road Warrior '82▶
Wheels of Terror '90

Killer Clowns

see also Carnivals & Circuses; Clowns

Carnival of Souls '98
Clown House '88
The Devil's Rejects '05
House of 1000 Corpses '03
Killer Klowns from Outer Space '88
Killjoy '81
Killjoy '03
S.I.C.K.: Serial Insane Clown Killer '03
Spawn '97▶
Stephen King's It '90
When Evil Calls '06

Killer Dogs

see also King of Beasts (Dogs)

Atomic Dog '98
The Breed '06
Cujo '83
Devil Dog: The Hound of Hell '78
Dogs of Hell '83
The Hound of the Baskervilles '39▶
The Hound of the Baskervilles '59
The Hound of the Baskervilles '00
The Hound of the Baskervilles '02▶
Man's Best Friend '93
Monster Dog '92
The Pack '77
Pet Sematary 2 '92
Play Dead '81
Resident Evil '02
Revenge '86
Zoltan... Hound of Dracula '78

Killer Dreams

Alias John Preston '56
Bad Dreams '88
Beneath '07
Blooc Rage '87
Chronicle of the Raven '04
Dario Argento's Trauma '93
Dark Corners '06
Deac of Night '45▶
Dream No Evil '75
Deadly Dreams '88
Evil Eyes '04
Freddy's Dead: The Final Nightmare '91
In Dreams '99
Jack O'Lantern '04
The Lathe of Heaven '80
The Lathe of Heaven '02
A Lizard in a Women's Skin '71
Mirrors '78
A Nightmare on Elm Street '84▶
A Nightmare on Elm Street 2: Freddy's Revenge '85
A Nightmare on Elm Street 3: Dream Warriors '87
A Nightmare on Elm Street 4: Dream Master '88
A Nightmare on Elm Street 5: Dream Child '89
NightScreams '97
Paperhouse '89▶
Paprika '06
Phantasm '79
Premonition '07
Strange Impersonation '46
Twisted Nightmare '87
Waking Life '01
Wes Craven's New Nightmare '94▶
Witches of the Caribbean '05

Killer Kats

see also Cats

Batman Returns '92
The Black Cat '81
Cat People '42▶
Cat People '82
Cat Women of the Moon '53
Claws '85
The Corpse Grinders '71
The Corpse Grinders 2 '00
The Creeper '48
Curse of the Cat People '42▶
The Leopard Man '43
Mutator '90
Night Creature '79
Night of a Thousand Cats '72
Pet Sematary '89
Seven Deaths in the Cat's Eye '72
Strays '91
Tromba, the Tiger Man '52
The Uncanny '78
The Uninvited '88

Killer Kiddies

see also Childhood Visions

Alice Sweet Alice '76
The Bad Seed '56
The Bad Seed '85
Before and After '95
The Child '76
The Children '80
Children of the Corn '84
Children of the Corn 2: The Final Sacrifice '92
Children of the Corn 3: Urban Harvest '95
Children of the Corn 5: Fields of Terror '98
Children of the Corn: Revelation '01
Children of the Damned '63
Daddy's Girl '96

▶ = rated three bones or higher

Killer

Damien: Omen 2 '78
Don't Go to Sleep '82
The Good Son '93
Gummo '97
Joshua '07
The Little Girl Who Lives down the Lane '76
Milo '98
The Omen '76
The Omen '06
The Other '72
Red Riding Hood '03
Relative Fear '95
Soft for Digging '01
Village of the Damned '60
Village of the Damned '95
Way Past Cool '00
Whisper '07

Killer Pigs

see also Pigs
The Amityville Horror '79
Evilspeak '82
Pigs '73
Razorback '84

Killer Plants

Attack of the Killer Tomatoes '77
Attack of the Mushroom People '63
Body Snatchers '93
Day of the Triffids '63
Dr. Terror's House of Horrors '65
The Freakmaker '73
Godzilla vs. Biollante '89
Invasion of the Body Snatchers '56
Invasion of the Body Snatchers '78
It Conquered the World '56
Killer Tomatoes Eat France '91
Killer Tomatoes Strike Back '90
Little Shop of Horrors '60
Little Shop of Horrors '86
Navy vs. the Night Monsters '66
Please Don't Eat My Mother '72
Return of the Killer Tomatoes! '88
The Ruins '08
Seedpeople '92
Seeds of Evil '76
The Womaneater '59
Yog, Monster from Space '71

Killer Reptiles

Alligator '80
Alligator 2: The Mutation '90
Black Water '07
Copperhead '84
Crocodile '81
Crocodile '00
Crocodile 2: Death Swamp '01
Dark Age '88
Destroy All Monsters '68
Dinosaurus! '60
Dragonslayer '81
Fangs '75
Frogs '72
Gamera, the Invincible '66
Gamera vs. Barugon '66
Gamera vs. Gaos '67
Gamera vs. Guiron '69
Gamera vs. Zigra '71
Gargantua '98
Gator King '70
The Giant Gila Monster '59
Godzilla '98
Godzilla, King of the Monsters '56
Godzilla 1985 '85
Godzilla on Monster Island '72
Godzilla Raids Again '55
Godzilla 2000 '99
Godzilla vs. Biollante '89
Godzilla vs. King Ghidora '91

Godzilla vs. Mechagodzilla II '93
Godzilla vs. Megalon '76
Godzilla vs. Monster Zero '68
Godzilla vs. Mothra '64
Godzilla vs. the Cosmic Monster '74
Godzilla vs. the Sea Monster '66
Godzilla vs. the Smog Monster '72
Godzilla's Revenge '69
Hell Comes to Frogtown '88
King Kong vs. Godzilla '63
Komodo '99
Lake Placid '99
Lake Placid 2 '07
The Mole People '56
Mothra '62
Primeval '07
Q (The Winged Serpent) '82
Rana: The Legend of Shadow Lake '75
Rattlers '76
The Relic '96
Reptilian '99
Reptilicus '62
Return to Frogtown '92
Slithis '78
Spasms '82
Stanley '72
Venom '82
Yongkari Monster of the Deep '67

Killer Rodents

see also Bats; Nice Mice
The Bat '59
The Bat People '74
Bats '99
Ben '72
Burial of the Rats '95
Deadly Eyes '82
The Devil Bat '41
Flushed Away '06
Food of the Gods '76
Food of the Gods: Part 2 '88
The Killer Shrews '59
Night of the Lepus '72
Nightwing '79
Of Unknown Origin '83
Rats '83
The Rats '01
The Rats Are Coming! The Werewolves Are Here! '72
Trilogy of Terror 2 '96
Willard '71
Willard '03

Killer Sea Critters

see also Deep Blue; Go Fish; Killer Beasts
Alligator '80
Around the World Under the Sea '65
Attack of the Giant Leeches '59
Attack of the Swamp Creature '75
Barracuda '78
The Beach Girls and the Monster '65
The Beast '96
The Beast from 20,000 Fathoms '53
Beneath Loch Ness '01
Beyond Atlantis '73
Blood Beach '81
Blood Surf '00
Bloodstalkers '76
The Cave '05
Creature from Black Lake '76
Creature from the Black Lagoon '54
Creature from the Haunted Sea '60
Creature of Destruction '67
The Creature Walks among Us '56
Creatures from the Abyss '94
Curse of the Swamp Creature '66
Deep Blue '03

Deep Blue Sea '99
Deep Rising '98
Deepstar Six '89
Demon of Paradise '87
Devil Monster '46
Devilfish '84
Fer-De-Lance '74
Finding Nemo '03
The Flesh Eaters '64
Frankenfish '04
Godzilla vs. Mothra '64
Godzilla vs. the Sea Monster '66
Gorgo '61
The Great Alligator '81
Hello Down There '69
Horror of Party Beach '64
The Host '06
Humanoids from the Deep '80
Humanoids from the Deep '96
Into the Blue '05
Island Claw '80
It Came from Beneath the Sea '55
Jason and the Argonauts '63
Jaws '75
Jaws 2 '78
Jaws 3 '83
Jaws of Death '76
Jaws: The Revenge '87
Killer Fish '79
Kraken: Tentacles of the Deep '06
The Loch Ness Horror '82
The Man from Atlantis '77
The McConnell Story '55
Mean Streets '73
Megalodon '03
Memphis Belle '90
Monster from the Ocean Floor '54
The Monster of Piedras Blancas '57
The Monster That Challenged the World '57
Mysterious Island '61
New York, New York '77
None But the Brave '65
Obsession '71
Octaman '71
Octopus '00
Octopus 2: River of Fear '02
Orca '77
Parasite '03
The Phantom from 10,000 Leagues '56
Piranha '95
Piranha '78
Piranha 2: The Spawning '82
Reap the Wild Wind '42
Red Water '03
Revenge of the Creature '55
Scorpion with Two Tails '82
Screams of a Winter Night '79
The Sea Serpent '85
Serpent Island '54
Shark! '68
Shark Attack '99
Shark Attack 2 '00
Shark Attack 3: Megalodon '02
She Creature '01
Sphere '97
Swamp Thing '82
Tentacles '77
Terror in the Swamp '85
They Bite '95
Tintorera... Tiger Shark '78
20,000 Leagues under the Sea '54
20,000 Leagues Under the Sea '97
Up from the Depths '79
War of the Gargantuas '70
What Waits Below '83

Killer Teens

Devon's Ghost: Legend of the Bloody Boy '05
Disturbing Behavior '98
Heathers '89
Little Sweetheart '87
River's Edge '87
Scream '96
Under One Roof '02
United States of Leland '03

Killer Toys

Amityville Dollhouse '96
Black Devil Doll from Hell '84
Bride of Chucky '98
Child's Play '88
Child's Play 2 '90
Child's Play 3 '91
Dance of Death '68
Dead Silence '07
Demonic Toys '90
Devil Doll '36
Devil Doll '64
Devil's Gift '84
Dollman vs Demonic Toys '93
Dolls '87
Dolly Dearest '92
Halloween 3: Season of the Witch '82
Magic '78
Marrionnier '05
Pinocchio's Revenge '96
Poltergeist '82
The Preacher's Wife '96
Puppet Master '89
Puppet Master 2 '90
Puppet Master 3: Toulon's Revenge '90
Puppet Master 4 '93
Puppet Master 5: The Final Chapter '94
Retro Puppet Master '99
Seed of Chucky '04
Silent Night, Deadly Night 5: The Toymaker '91
Small Soldiers '98
Tales from the Hood '95
Trilogy of Terror '75
Trilogy of Terror 2 '96
Wired to Kill '86

Killing Sprees

September Dawn '07

Kindness of Strangers

Amelie '01
Angels Over Broadway '40
The Big Push '75
Dear God '96
Forrest Gump '94
Good Sam '48
Lilies of the Field '63
Major Barbara '41
The Matchmaker '97
Mr. Deeds '02
Mr. Deeds Goes to Town '36
Mr. Lucky '43
Mr. Smith '88
Powder '95
The Rich Man's Wife '96
She Couldn't Say No '52
Sincerely Yours '56
The Toll Gate '20
Touch & Go '80
The Vals '85

Killer Spouses

see also Wedding Hell
Black Widow '87
Body Heat '81
Deliberate Intent '01
Diabolique '55

Diabolique '96
Double Jeopardy '99
Fracture '07
High Stakes '93
Sleeping with the Enemy '91
What Lies Beneath '00
White Oleander '02

King of Beasts (Dogs)

see also Killer Dogs
The Accidental Tourist '88
Across the Bridge '57

The Adventures of Milo & Otis '89
The Adventures of Rusty '45
After the Thin Man '36
Air Bud '97
Air Bud 2: Golden Receiver '98
Air Bud 3: World Pup '00
Air Bud 4: Seventh Inning Fetch '02
Air Bud 5: Buddy Spikes Back '03
All Dogs Go to Heaven '89
All Dogs Go to Heaven 2 '95
The Amazing Dobermans '76
Amores Perros '00
Antarctica '84
As Good As It Gets '97
Atomic Dog '98
The Awful Truth '37
Babe '95
Babe: Pig in the City '98
Bad Moon '96
Balto '95
Bark! '02
Baxter '89
Beautiful Creatures '00
Because of Winn-Dixie '05
Beethoven '92
Beethoven's 2nd '93
Beethoven's 3rd '00
Beethoven's 4th '01
Beethoven's 5th '03
Behave Yourself! '52
Benji '74
Benji: Off the Leash! '04
Benji the Hunted '87
Best in Show '00
Big Red '62
Bingo '91
Blondie Brings Up Baby '39
Blondie in Society '41
A Boy and His Dog '75
Buck and the Magic Bracelet '97
Call of the Wild '72
Call of the Wild '93
Captured in Chinatown '35
Cats & Dogs '01
Challenge To Be Free '76
Challenge to Lassie '49
Challenge to White Fang '86
Children of the Wild '37
Chilly Dogs '01
Chips, the War Dog '90
C.H.O.M.P.S. '79
Clean Slate '94
Clifford's Really Big Movie '04
Cool Hand Luke '67
Courage of Lassie '46
Courage of Rin Tin Tin '57
A Cry in the Dark '88
Cujo '83
Cybermutt '02
Danny Boy '46
Daring Dobermans '73
The Dawson Patrol '78
Dead Dog '00
Devil Dog: The Hound of Hell '78
Digby, the Biggest Dog in the World '73
Dirkham Detective Agency '83
Disney's Teacher's Pet '04
The Doberman Gang '72
Dr. Dolittle '98
Dr. Dolittle 4: Tail to the Chief '08
Dr. Seuss' How the Grinch Stole Christmas '00
A Dog of Flanders '59
A Dog of Flanders '99
Dog Park '98
Dog Pound Shuffle '75
The Dog Who Stopped the War '84
Dogs of Hell '83
Doogal '05

The Duke '99
Dumb & Dumber '94
Dusty '85
The Echo of Thunder '98

Eight Below '06
Elmer '76
Eyes of an Angel '91
Eyes of Texas '48
Fabulous Joe '47
Famous Five Get into Trouble '87
Fangs of the Wild '54
Far from Home: The Adventures of Yellow Dog '94
Flaming Signal '33
Fluke '95
For the Love of Benji '77
The Fox and the Hound '81
Frankenweenie '84
George! '70
Ghetto Dawg '02
Ghetto Dawg 2: Out of the Pits '05
Gift! '65
God's Country '46
Good Boy! '03
The Good, the Bad, and Huckleberry Hound '88
Goodbye, My Lady '56
A Goofy Movie '94
Great Adventure '75
Greyfriars Bobby '61
Hambone & Hillie '84
Heart of the Rockies '51
Heck's Way Home '95
The Hills Have Eyes '77
Hollow Gate '88
Homeward Bound 2: Lost in San Francisco '96
Homeward Bound: The Incredible Journey '93
The Hound of the Baskervilles '59
I Am Legend '07
In the Doghouse '98
The Incredible Journey '63
Inside Information '34
Iron Will '93
It's a Dog's Life '55
Jack London's The Call of the Wild '97
The Jerk '79
Jury Duty '95
K-9 '89
K-911 '99
K-9000 '89
Kavik the Wolf Dog '80
Lady and the Tramp '55
Lassie '94
Lassie: Adventures of Neeka '68
Lassie, Come Home '43
Lassie: Well of Love '70
Lassie's Great Adventure '62
Laurel & Hardy: Laughing Gravy '31
Legally Blonde '01
Legally Blonde 2: Red White & Blonde '03
Lightning Warrior '31
Little Nicky '00
The Little Rascals '94
The Lone Defender '32
Look Who's Talking Now '93
Lost and Found '99
Love Leads the Way '78
Magic of Lassie '78
Man Trouble '92
The Man Who Wagged His Tail '57
Man's Best Friend '93
The Mask '94
Meet the Fockers '04
Men in Black 2 '02
The Mexican '01
Michael '96
Milo & Otis '89
Mr. Brown, You've Got a Lovely Daughter '68
Mr. Superinvisible '73
Mom, the Wolfman and Me '80
Mongrel '83
Monster Dog '82
Monster-in-Law '05
More Dogs Than Bones '00
Murder She Purred: A Mrs. Murphy Mystery '98
Must Love Dogs '05

▶ = rated three bones or higher

My Dog Shep '46
My Dog Skip '99▶
My Magic Dog '97
Napoleon '96
The Night Cry '26
N<ki, the Wild Dog of the North '61
Nutty Professor 2: The Klumps '00
Ch. Heavenly Dog! '80
C.d Yeller '57▶
Oliver & Company '88
101 Dalmatians '61▶
101 Dalmatians '96
The Pack '77
The Painted Hills '51
Ping! '99
The Plague Dogs '82
Play Dead '81
Foco '77
The Pooch and the Pauper '99
Pound Puppies and the Legend of Big Paw '88
Quigley '03
The Return of Grey Wolf '22
Reuben, Reuben '83▶
Rin Tin Tin, Hero of the West '55
Rough Magic '95
Rover Dangerfield '91
Rugrats Go Wild! '03
Rusty's Birthday '49
The Sandlot '93▶
Savage Sam '63
Saving Shiloh '06
Scooby-Doo '02
Screwed '00
Shadow of the Th.n Man '41▶
The Shaggy D.A. '76
The Shaggy Dog '59
The Shaggy Dog '06
Shep Comes Home '49
Sherlock: Undercover Dog '94
Shiloh '97
Shiloh 2: Shiloh Season '99
Silver Stallion '41
Six of a Kind '34▶
Skeezer '82
Skull & Crown '35
Sleeping Dogs L.e '05
Smoke '70
Snow Buddies '08
Snow Dogs '02
Soccer Dog: The Movie '98
Son of Lassie '45
Son of Rusty '47
Song of the Thin Man '47
Spy with a Cold Nose '66
Sputnik '61
Station Jim '01
Storm in a Teacup '37
Summerdog '7E
Sweet November '01
Teddy at the Throttle '16
The Tender Years '47
There's Something about Mary '98▶
They Only Kill Their Masters '72
The Thin Man '34▶
The Thin Man Goes Home '44
Three Wishes '95
To Dance with the White Dog '93▶
Toby McTeague '87
Tom and Jerry: The Movie '93
Top Dog '95
Tracked '98
The Triplets of Belleville '02▶
The Truth about Cats anc Dogs '96▶
Turner and Hcoch '89
The Twelve D;gs of Christmas '05
Twin Town '97
The Ugly Dacshund '65
Umberto D '52▶
The Undercover Kid '95
The Underdog '43
Watchers '88
Watchers 2 '90

Watchers Reborn '98
We Think the World of You '88▶
When Lightning Strikes '34
Where the Red Fern Grows '74
Where the Red Fern Grows: Part 2 '92
White Fang 2: The Myth of the White Wolf '94
White Fang and the Hunter '85
Whitewater Sam '78
The Wizard of Oz '39▶
Wolf Dog '33
Wolfheart's Revenge '25
Wonder Boys '00▶
Zeus and Roxanne '96
Zoltan... Hound of Dracula '78

Kings
see Royalty; Royalty, British; Royalty, French; Royalty, Russian

Korean War
All the Young Men '60▶
American Gun '02▶
Battle Circus '53
Battle Hymn '57
Big Fish '03▶
The Bridges at Toko-Ri '55▶
Dragonfly Squadron '54
Field of Honor '86
Fixed Bayonets! '51▶
For the Boys '91
The Hunters '58
I Want You '51
Iron Angel '64
The Last Picture Show '71▶
MacArthur '77
The Manchurian Candidate '62▶
M*A*S*H '70▶
M*A*S*H: Goodbye, Farewell & Amen '83▶
Men in War '57
Men of the Fighting Lady '54
Mr. Walkie Talkie '52
One Minute to Zero '52
Operation Dames '59
Pork Chop Hill '59▶
Retreat, Hell! '52
Sabre Jet '53
Sayonara '57▶
Sergeant Ryker '68
The Steel Helmet '51▶
Tae Guk Gi: The Brotherhood of War '04▶
Torpedo Alley '53
Wonsan Operation '78

Kung Fu
see Martial Arts

L.A.
see also Earthquakes
Abbott and Costello in Hollywood '45
Act of Violence '48
Against the Law '98
Agent of Death '99
Akeelah and the Bee '06
An Alan Smithee Film: Burn, Hollywood, Burn '97
The Alarmist '98
All About You '01
All Over the Guy '01
Alvin and the Chipmunks '07
Always Outnumbered '98▶
American Rhapsody '01▶
American Virgin '09
Amy's O '02
Angel's Dance '99
The Anniversary Party '01▶
Apartment Complex '98
Ask the Dust '06
Assault on Precinct 13 '76▶
At Any Cost '00
The Aviator '04▶
Baby Boy '01▶
Daybreak '01

Bad Influence '90
Bandits '01▶
Bang '95
Bar Hopping '00
Bark! '02
Barton Fink '91▶
Be Cool '05
Bean '97▶
Beefcake '99
Bellyfruit '99
The Beverly Hillbillies '93
Beverly Hills Bodysnatchers '89
Beverly Hills Brats '89
Beverly Hills Ninja '96
Beyond Suspicion '00
Big Fat Liar '02
The Big '95
The Big Lebowski '97▶
Big Momma's House 2 '06
The Big Picture '89
The Big Tease '99
Biker Boyz '03
Billy's Hollywood Screen Kiss '98
The Black Dahlia '06
Black Scorpion 2: Ground Zero '96
Blast from the Past '98
Bloodstream '00
Blow '01
Blue Streak '99
Body Double '84▶
Border Blues '03
Born to Lose '99
Bottoms Up '06
Bowfinger '99▶
A Boy Called Hate '95
The Boys Next Door '85
Bram Stoker's Way of the Vampire '05
Bread and Roses '00
Break of Dawn '88
The Breaks '99
The Broken Hearts Club '00▶
Broken Vessels '98▶
Brown's Requiem '98
Bulletproof '96
Call Me: The Rise and Fall of Heidi Feiss '04
Candyman 3: Day of the Dead '98
Celebrity '98▶
Cement '99
Chain of Souls '00
Charlotte Sometimes '02
Chasing Papi '03
A Cinderella Story '04
Circuit '01
City of Angels '98
City of Industry '96
Cleopatra's Second Husband '00
Collateral '04▶
Collateral Damage '02
Color of a Brisk and Leaping Day '95
Come See the Paradise '90▶
Confidence '03
Constantine '05
Cool Blue '88
Cover Me '95
Cradle 2 the Grave '03
Crank '06
crazy/beautiful '01
Crimes of Passion '84▶
Criminal '04
Crocodile Dundee in Los Angeles '01
Crossing Over '08
The Crow 2: City of Angels '96
Crystal's Diary '99
Cursed '04
Dark Blue '03▶
Dark Justice '03
Darkwolf '03
The Day After Tomorrow '04
The Day of the Locust '75▶
A Day Without a Mexican '04

Dead Again '91▶
Dead Bang '89
The Dead Girl '06
Dead Lenny '06
Dead Sexy '01
Dear God '96
Death Wish 2 '82
Death Heat '92
Defying Gravity '99
Delta Heat '92
The Dentist '96
The Destiny of Marty Fine '96
Devil in a Blue Dress '95▶
Devil's Knight '03
Die Hard '86▶
Dinner and Driving '97
Dirty '05
The Disappearance of Kevin Johnson '95
Disney's Th3 Kid '00
Doc Hollywood '91▶
The Dog Problem '06
Domino '05
Don't Be a Menace to South Central While Drinking Your Juice in the Hood '95
The Doom Generation '95▶
Double Down '01
Down in the Valley '05
Drift '00
Dunston Checks In '95
East Side Story '07
Eastside '59
8mm '98
Ellie Parker '05▶
Encino Man '92
The End of Violence '97
Escape from L.A. '96
Face/Off '97▶
Falling Down '93▶
The Fast and the Furious '01
Fast Sofa '01
Fast Times at Ridgemont High '82▶
Female Perversions '96
52 Pick-Up '86
Final Combination '93
The Fluffer '01
44 Minutes: The North Hollywood Shootout '03
Four Dogs Playing Poker '00
Four Rooms '95
Fracture '07
Free Enterprise '98
Freeway '88
French Exit '95
Friends with Money '06
Frisk '95
Full Contact '93
Full Frontal '02
Gang Boys '97
Get On the Bus '96▶
Get Shorty '95▶
Glam '97
The Glass House '01
The Glimmer Man '95
Go '99▶
Goal! The Dream Begins '06
Gods and Monsters '98▶
Going Shopping '05
Goodbye, Lover '99
Grand Canyon '91▶
Grand Theft Parsons '03
Gridiron Gang '06
The Guardian '00
Guarding Eddy '04
Hair Show '04
Hancock '08
Hanging Up '99
Happy Endings '05
Hard As Nails '01
Hard Candy '06
Harsh Times '05
He Walked by Night '48▶
Heart of Stone '01
Heat '95▶
Hijacking Hollywood '97
Hindsight '07
The Hillside Stranger '04
The Holiday '06
Hollywood Homicide '03
Hollywoodland '06
Hostage '05
Hot Tamale '06

How to Kill Your Neighbor's Dog '01
How to Lose Your Lover '04
Hugo Pool '97
Hunrypool '98
Hustler White '96
I Love You, Alice B. Toklas! '68
I Love You, Don't Touch Me! '97
In God We Trust '80
Internal Affairs '90▶
Intolerable Cruelty '03
The Italian Job '03▶
It's My Party '96
Jackie Brown '97▶
Jack's Back '87▶
Jimmy Hollywood '94
johns '96
The Journey of Jared Price '00
Just Write '97
K-911 '99
Kate's Addiction '99
The Kid and I '05
Killer of Sheep '77▶
Kiss & Tell '49
Kiss Kiss Bang Bang '05▶
Kiss Tomorrow Goodbye '50
L.A. Bad '85
L.A. Bounty '89
L.A. Confidential '97▶
L.A. Crackdown '87
L.A. Crackdown 2 '88
L.A. Dicks '05
L.A. Goddess '92
L.A. Law '86▶
L.A. Rules: The Pros and Cons of Breathing '04
L.A. Story '91▶
L.A. Vice '89
Lady Jayne Killer '03
Land of Plenty '04
L.A.P.D.: To Protect and Serve '01
Last Call: The Final Chapter of F. Scott Fitzgerald '02
The Last Days of Frankie the Fly '96
Late Last Night '99
Latin Dragon '03
Laurel Canyon '04
Lawnmower Man 2: Beyond Cyberspace '95
The Learning Curve '01
Let the Devil Wear Black '99
Lethal Weapon 4 '98
Liberty Stands Still '02
Lies & Alibis '06
The Limey '99▶
Living in Peril '97
Long-Term Relationship '06
Lost Angels '89
Love Don't Cost a Thing '03
The Loved One '65
Loveless in Los Angeles '07
Lover Girl '97
The Low Life '95
Luminarias '99
Luster '02
MacArthur Park '01
The Man from Elysian Fields '01▶
Marshal Law '96
Matter of Trust '98
Mayor of the Sunset Strip '03▶
Memento '00▶
Men '97
The Mexican '01
Midnight Blue '96
Million Dollar Baby '04▶
The Mod Squad '99
Modern Vampires '98
Momrie Dearest '81
More Dogs Than Bones '00
Mortal Challenge '97
Mulholland Drive '01▶
The Muse '99
My Uncle: The Alien '95
Nails '03
Nancy Drew '07
National Security '03
Neil Simon's The Odd Couple 2 '98
Never Die Alone '04

The New Age '94
Next '07
The Next Best Thing '00
Nick of Time '95
Night at the Golden Eagle '02
A Night at the Roxbury '98
Night Hunter '95
Night on Earth '91▶
Nightstalker '02
The Nines '07▶
Nowhere '96
187 '97
1941 '79
Permanent Midnight '98
Phat Beach '96
Pie in the Sky '95
The Player '92▶
Point Blank '67
Predator 2 '90
P.S. Your Cat is Dead! '02
Pursuit of Happiness '01
Quiet Days in Hollywood '97
Quinceañera '06▶
Race '99
Raging Angels '95
Raise Your Voice '04
Rampage: The Hillside Strangler Murders '04
Rave Review '95
Real Women Have Curves '02▶
Recoil '97
Redbelt '08
Relax... It's Just Sex! '98
The Replacement Killers '93
Repo Man '83▶
Revenge Quest '96
Right at Your Door '06
Riot in the Streets '96
Rize '05▶
Rumor Has It... '05
Rumpelstiltskin '96
Running Mates '98
Running Woman '98
Rush Hour '98▶
Ruthless People '86▶
Safe House '99
Scandal Sheet '85
Scorcher '02
Scream 3 '00
Seamless '05
Seed of Chucky '04
Serpent's Lair '95
Set It Off '96
Shadow Dancer '96
Shadow of Doubt '98
Shakedown '02
Sherrybaby '06
Shopgirl '05▶
Short Cuts '93▶
The Shot '96
Showtime '02
The Singing Detective '03▶
Sink or Swim '97
Skyscraper '95
Slaves of Hollywood '99
Sleeper Cell '05
Smiley Face '07
Smiling Fish & Goat on Fire '99
Sol Goode '01
Solder's Fortune '91
Somebody to Love '94
Something New '06
The Souler Opposite '97
Southland Tales '06
Spanglish '04▶
Spanish Judges '99
Speed '94▶
Splendor '99
Splinter '06
Spun '02
Stand and Deliver '88▶
Stand-Ins '97

▶ = rated three bones or higher

Standing on Fishes '99
Standing Still '05
Star Maps '97
Starry Night '99
Steel '97
Sticks '98
Still Breathing '97
Storm Tracker '99
Strange Days '95
Street Corner Justice '96
The Street King '02
Street Kings '08
The Streets of L.A. '79
Sueno '05
Sugar Town '99
Sunset Boulevard '50
Swimming with Sharks '94
Swingers '96
Swordfish '01
The Take '07
The Talent Given Us '04
Talking about Sex '94
Telling You '98
10 Items or Less '06
Testosterone '03
They Call Me Sir '00
Thicker than Water '99
This Christmas '07
This World, Then the Fireworks '97
Three Strikes '00
Time Code '00
Tinseltown '97
To Live & Die in L.A. '85
Too Fast, Too Young '96
Tortilla Soup '01
Totally F*** Up '94
Touch '96
The Towering Inferno '74
Training Day '01
The Trigger Effect '96
The Trip '02
20 Dates '99
Twilight '98
Two Days in the Valley '96
The Two Jakes '90
Under the Same Moon '07
The Underground '97
Unlawful Entry '92
Vampire Night '00
Virtuosity '95
Volcano '97
Waist Deep '06
The Wash '01
Wassup Rockers '06
Welcome Says the Angel '01
Whatever It Takes '00
Where the Truth Lies '05
Where's Marlowe? '98
Who Made the Potatoe Salad? '05
The Whole Ten Yards '04
Witchcraft 9: Bitter Flesh '96
With Friends Like These '98
Wonderland '03
Yellow '98
You Got Served '04

Labor & Unions
see also Miners & Mining

Act of Vengeance '86
Black Fury '35
Blue Collar '78
Boxcar Bertha '72
Bread and Roses '00
Brother John '70
The Burning Season '94
Canada's Sweetheart: The Saga of Hal C. Banks '85
Daens '92
Deadly Stranger '88
The Devil & Miss Jones '41
The End of St. Petersburg '27
End of the Line '88
Fame Is the Spur '47
F.I.S.T. '78
The $5.20 an Hour Dream '80
Gung Ho '85
Harlan County, U.S.A. '76
Harlan County War '00
Hoffa '92

Roman Spring of Mrs. Stone '61
I'm All Right Jack '59
Joyride '77
Keeping On '81
Killing Floor '85
Land of Promise '74
Last Exit to Brooklyn '90
Liam '00
Long Road Home '91
Mac '93
Man of Iron '81
Man of Marble '76
Matewan '87
Molly Maguires '70
Moonlighting '82
Never Steal Anything Small '59
Newsies '92
Norma Rae '79
North Dallas Forty '79
On the Waterfront '54
The Organizer '64
The Pajama Game '57
Riff Raff '92
Salt of the Earth '54
Silkwood '83
Singleton's Pluck '84
Sons of Steel '35
Strike '24
Take This Job & Shove It '81
Teamster Boss: The Jackie Presser Story '92
The Triangle Factory Fire Scandal '79
Waterfront '83
Which Way Is Up? '77

Las Vegas
see Viva Las Vegas!

Late Bloomin' Love
see also Growing Older

Adorable Julia '62
The African Queen '51
Ali: Fear Eats the Soul '74
Atlantic City '81
Autumn Sun '98
Bed & Breakfast '92
Breakfast in Paris '81
The Bridges of Madison County '95
Brief Encounter '46
Camilla '94
Cass Timberlane '47
Charly '68
Children of Nature '91
The Christmas Wife '88
Circle of Two '80
Cold Sassy Tree '89
Crazy from the Heart '91
Devil in the Flesh '46
Digger '94
Doctor in Distress '63
End of August '82
A Fine Romance '84
Finnegan Begin Again '84
Forbidden Love '82
Foreign Affairs '93
Forty Carats '73
Gal Young 'Un '79
Gin Game '84
Grumpier Old Men '95
Grumpy Old Men '93
Harold and Maude '71
If Ever I See You Again '78
Innocence '00
La Symphonie Pastorale '46
Ladies in Lavender '04
The Last Winters '71
Lonely Hearts '82
The Lonely Passion of Judith Hearne '87
Love Among the Ruins '75
Macaroni '85
A Majority of One '56
A Man and a Woman '66
Mrs. 'Arris Goes to Paris '92
A Month by the Lake '95
The Night of the Iguana '64
One Special Night '99
Other People's Money '91
The Pamela Principle '91
Players '79
Queen of the Stardust Ballroom '75
The Rainmaker '56

The Defenders: Taking the First '98
Degree of Guilt '95
Deliberate Intent '01
Destination Vegas '95
The Devil's Advocate '97
Dirty Mary Crazy Larry '74
Disorganized Crime '89
The Divorce of Lady X '38
Dr. Dolittle 2 '01
Down the Drain '89
Dragons Forever '88
Ebbtide '94
Enemy of the State '98
The Enforcer '51
Erin Brockovich '00
Evelyn '02
Evelyn Prentice '34
The Exorcism of Emily Rose '05
Eye Witness '49
Fair Game '95
False Witness '89
Father's Day '96
Fear and Loathing in Las Vegas '98
Female Perversions '96
Fever '91
A Few Good Men '92
Final Appeal '93
Final Justice '98
Final Verdict '91
Find Me Guilty '06
The Firm '93
First Monday in October '81
The Fixer '97
For Roseanna '96
Forbidden Sins '99
Force of Evil '49
Fracture '07
The Franchise Affair '52
Frank McClusky, C.I. '02
A Free Soul '31
From the Hip '86
Genealogies of a Crime '97
Georgia '87
Getting Gotti '94
The Ghost of Spoon River '00
Ghosts of Mississippi '96
Gideon's Trumpet '80
The Glass Shield '95
The Good Fight '92
The Great American Sex Scandal '94
Guilty '99
Guilty as Sin '93
Guilty Conscience '85
The Hard Word '02
Having Wonderful Crime '45
Heaven Is a Playground '91
Heavens Fall '06
High Crimes '02
Honor Thy Father and Mother: The True Story of the Menendez Brothers '94
I Am Sam '01
I Am the Law '38
I Love You, Alice B. Toklas! '68
I Now Pronounce You Chuck and Larry '07
The Ice Harvest '05
Illegal '55
Illegal Affairs '96
I'm No Angel '33
In Pursuit '00
In the Name of the Father '93
The Incident '89
Inherit the Wind '99
Intolerable Cruelty '03
The Island of Dr. Moreau '96
It Runs in the Family '03
It's the Rage '99
JAG '95
The Jagged Edge '85
John Grisham's The Rainmaker '97
The Judge '49
Judge Dredd '95
Judge Priest '34
Judicial Consent '94
The Juror '96
Jury Duty '95
Just Cause '95
The Killing Yard '01

King and Country '64
L.A. Law '86
Lansdown '01
Last Dance '96
The Last Innocent Man '87
Laws of Attraction '04
Laws of Deception '97
Legal Deceit '95
Legal Eagles '86
Legalese '98
Legally Blonde '01
Legally Blonde 2: Red White & Blonde '03
Legend of Billie Jean '85
Let Freedom Ring '39
Let's Kill All the Lawyers '93
Liar Liar '97
Life & Times of Judge Roy Bean '72
Losing Isaiah '94
Love Among the Ruins '75
Love Crimes '92
Love Letters '99
Love Stinks '99
Loved '97
Lucky Seven '03
Luminarias '99
Madame X '66
The Magnificent Yankee '50
Man from Colorado '49
Man of the House '95
The Man Who Shot Liberty Valance '62
Manhattan Melodrama '34
Marked Woman '37
Marriage on the Rocks '65
Matter of Trust '98
Melanie Darrow '97
The Merchant of Venice '04
Michael Clayton '07
Minbo—Or the Gentle Art of Japanese Extortion '92
Misbehaving Husbands '41
Mr. & Mrs. Loving '96
Moonlight Mile '02
Move Over, Darling '63
A Murder of Crows '99
Murder in the First '95
My Cousin Vinny '92
The Narrow Margin '52
Night and the City '92
Night Falls on Manhattan '96
Nixon '95
North '94
North Country '05
Nuremberg '00
One Night at McCool's '01
Ordeal by Innocence '84
Original Intent '91
Our Mutual Friend '98
The Paper Chase '73
Party Girl '58
The Pelican Brief '93
Penthouse '33
The People vs. Larry Flynt '96
Perfect Witness '89
Perry Mason Returns '85
Philadelphia '93
Physical Evidence '89
Picture Windows '95
Pinocchio's Revenge '96
Plain Dirty '04
Poor White Trash '00
Portraits of a Killer '95
Power of Attorney '94
Presumed Innocent '90
Primal Fear '96
Promised a Miracle '88
Psychopath '73
Red Corner '97
Reet, Petite and Gone '47
Regarding Henry '91
Restraining Order '99
Return to Paradise '98
R.I.C.C.O. '02
Road Agent '26
Rounders '98
Roxie Hart '42
Runaway Father '91
Runaway Jury '03
Rustler's Valley '37
Scandal '50
Scott Turow's The Burden of Proof '92

The Sea Inside '04
Shadow of Doubt '98
The Shaggy Dog '06
Shakedown '88
Shall We Dance? '04
Sharon's Secret '95
Shoot to Kill '47
A Simple Twist of Fate '94
The Skeleton Key '05
Sleepers '96
The Sleepy Time Gal '01
Slightly Honorable '40
Split Second '99
The Star Chamber '83
State's Attorney '31
Steel Toes '06
Stephen King's Thinner '96
A Stranger in the Kingdom '98
Street Law '95
The Summer of Ben Tyler '96
The Sun Shines Bright '53
The Sweet Hereafter '96
Swoon '91
They Call It Murder '71
A Time to Kill '96
To Kill a Mockingbird '62
Too Young to Die '90
Town without Pity '61
The Trial '93
Trial & Error '62
Trial and Error '92
Trial and Error '96
Trial by Jury '94
The Trial of Old Drum '00
Trois Couleurs: Rouge '94
True Believer '89
True Colors '91
Truth or Die '86
Twelve Angry Men '57
Twelve Angry Men '97
Undermind '03
Up for Grabs '05
The Verdict '82
Victim '61
Web of Deceit '90
Where the Truth Lies '99
Whitewash: The Clarence Brandley Story '02
Wild Things '98
The Winslow Boy '48
The Winslow Boy '98
The Wistful Widow of Wagon Gap '47
Woman of Desire '93
The World's Oldest Living Bridesmaid '92
The Young Philadelphians '59

Leprechauns

Darby O'Gill & the Little People '59
Finian's Rainbow '68
Leprechaun '93
Leprechaun 2 '94
Leprechaun 3 '95
Leprechaun 4: In Space '96
Leprechaun 5: In the Hood '99
Leprechaun 6: Back 2 Tha Hood '03
The Magical Legend of the Leprechauns '99
Spellbreaker: Secret of the Leprechauns '96

Lesbians
see also Bisexuality; Gays; Gender Bending

Aimee & Jaguar '98
Alien Prey '83
All Over Me '96
The Alley Cats '65
Another Way '82
April's Shower '03
Bam Bam & Celeste '05
Bar Girls '95
The Berlin Affair '85
Better Than Chocolate '99
The Bitter Tears of Petra von Kant '72
Black Cobra '83
The Black Dahlia '06
The Blood Spattered Bride '72

▶ = rated *three bones* or *higher*

Blow Dry '00
Bobbie's Girl '02
Bound '96
Boys on the Side '94
Bug '06
But I'm a Cheerleader '99
Butterfly Kiss '94
The Celluloid Closet '95
Chasing Amy '97
The Children's Hour '61
Chuck & Buck '00
Crutney Popcorn '99
Claire of the Moon '92
Common Ground '00
Crocodiles in Amsterdam '89
Daughters of Darkness '71
D.E.B.S. '04
Desert Hearts '86
Desperate Remedies '93
Devotion '95
Different Story '78
D:I Love You? '02
Double Face '70
Entre-Nous '83
Eternal '04
Eulogy '04
Even Cowgirls Get the Blues '94
Everything Relative '96
Extramuros '85
A Family Affair '01
Fanci's Persuasion '95
Fire '96
Fish Without a Bicycle '03
The Fourth Sex '61
Foxfire '96
French Twist '95
Gaudi Afternoon '01
Gia '98
Gigli '03
The Girl '01
Girl Play '04
Gray Matters '06
The Gymnast '06
Happy Endings '05
Hardcore '04
He Died With a Felafel in His Hand '01
Head in the Clouds '04
Her and She and Him '69
High Art '98
Higher Learning '94
The Hours '02
The Hunger '83
If These Walls Could Talk 2 '00
Imagine Me & You '06
The Incredibly True Adventure of Two Girls in Love '95
It's in the Water '96
I've Heard the Mermaids Singing '87
The Jane Austen Book Club '07
Just One Time '00
Kamikaze Hearts '91
The Killing of Sister George '69
Kissing Jessica Stein '02
Late Bloomers '95
L'Auberge Espagnole '02
Law of Desire '86
Le Jupon Rouge '87
Les Voleurs '96
Lianna '83
Listen '96
Little City '97
Lost and Delirious '01
Love and Other Catastrophes '95
Love on the Side '04
Loving Annabelle '06
Maedchen in Uniform '31
May '02
The Monkey's Mask '00
My Baby's Daddy '04
My Father Is Coming '91
My Mother Likes Women '02
My Sister, My Love '78
My Summer of Love '05
Nadja '95
November Moon '85
Nowhere '96
101 Reykjavik '00
Only the Brave '94

Oranges Are Not the Only Fruit '89
Personal Best '82
Possession '02
Pretty Persuasion '05
Prey for Rock and Roll '03
A Question of Love '78
The Rainbow '89
Relax... It's Just Sex! '98
Rent '05
Robin's Hood '03
Russian Dolls '05
Saving Face '04
The Scorpion Woman '89
Seducers '77
Serving in Silence: The Margarethe Cammermeyer Story '95
Set It Off '96
Shades of Black '93
She Hate Me '04
She Must Be Seeing Things '87
Shelter Island '03
Show Me Love '99
The Silence '63
Simone Barbes '80
Skin Deep '94
Slaves to the Underground '96
Some Prefer Cake '97
The Souler Opposite '97
Standing Still '05
The Sticky Fingers of Time '97
Sugar Cookies '77
Sugar Sweet '02
Therese & Isabelle '67
These Three '36
Things You Can Tell Just by Looking at Her '00
Three of Hearts '93
Three Times '05
Tick Tock '00
Tipping the Velvet '02
Tokyo Cowboy '94
Totally F***ed Up '94
The Truth About Jane '00
The Twilight Girls '57
Under the Tuscan Sun '03
Unveiled '05
The Vampire Lovers '70
Vampyres '74
A Village Affair '95
Virgin Machine '88
Walk on the Wild Side '62
The Watermelon Woman '97
When Love Comes '98
When Night Is Falling '95
Windows '80
A Woman's a Helluva Thing '01
The Women on the Roof '89
X, Y & Zee '72

Libraries and Librarians

Adventure '45
Black Mask '96
The Breakfast Club '85
City of Angels '98
Desk Set '57
Foul Play '78
Fright Night 2 '88
Ghostbusters '84
Good News '47
Goodbye Columbus '69
The Gun in Betty Lou's Handbag '92
Hard-Boiled '92
It's a Wonderful Life '46
Kicking and Screaming '95
Last Life in the Universe '03
Mr. Sycamore '74
The Mummy '99
The Music Man '62
The Name of the Rose '86
No Man of Her Own '32
Off Beat '86
Only Two Can Play '62
The Pagemaster '94
Party Girl '94
7 Faces of Dr. Lao '63
Redemption '94
The Shawshank Redemption '94
Shooting the Past '99
Something Wicked This Way Comes '83
Where the Heart Is '00
With Honors '94

Lifeguards

see also Beach Blanket Bingo; Swimming

Baywatch the Movie: Forbidden Paradise '95
Caddyshack '80
Fun in Acapulco '63
Lifeguard '76
The Sandlot '93
That Summer of White Roses '90
Wet and Wild Summer '92

Little People

Bad Santa '03
Clean '04
Close My Eyes '91
Fred Claus '07
The Hobbit '78
In Bruges '08
Little Man '06
The Lord of the Rings '78
Lord of the Rings: The Fellowship of the Rings '01
Lord of the Rings: The Return of the King '03
Lord of the Rings: The Two Towers '02
Do:l Love You? '02
Snow White and the Seven Dwarfs '37
Snow White: The Fairest of Them All '02
Time Bandits '81
Under the Rainbow '81
Willow '88
The Wizard of Oz '25
The Wizard of Oz '39

London

see also Great Britain; Royalty

Abbott and Costello Meet Dr. Jekyll and Mr. Hyde '52
About a Boy '02
Agatha Christie's Murder is Easy '82
Agent Cody Banks 2: Destination London '04
AKA '02
Alfie '66
All or Nothing '02
Almost Strangers '01
Amazing Grace '06
American Roulette '88
An American Werewolf in London '81
Annie: A Royal Adventure '95
The Assassination Bureau '69
Atonement '07
Austin Powers: International Man of Mystery '97
Autobiography of a Princess '75
The Avengers '98
B. Monkey '97
Bad Behavior '92
The Bank Job '08
Basic Instinct 2 '06
Beat Girl '60
Beautiful People '99
Beautiful Thing '95
Bedlam '45
Bedrooms and Hallways '98
Being Julia '04
Bend It Like Beckham '02
Berkeley Square '98
Betrayal '83
Beyond Borders '03
Born Romantic '00
The Bourne Ultimatum '07
Breaking and Entering '06
Bridget Jones: The Edge of Reason '04
Bridget Jones's Diary '01
Bright Young Things '03
Broken Blossoms '19
The Buddha of Suburbia
Carpet of Horror '64
Cassandra's Dream '07
Century '94
A Certain Justice '99
Charlie '04
Charlie Chan in London '34
Charlie White '04
Chicago Joe & the Showgirl '90
The Chronicles of Narnia: The Lion, the Witch and the Wardrobe '05
Claudia '85
Colour Me Kubrick '05
Comic Act '98
Contraband '40
Croupier '97
Curse of the Yellow Snake '63
Danger UXB '81
Dead Fish '04
Dead Gorgeous '02
Deadlier Than the Male '67
Dick Barton, Special Agent '48
Die Another Day '02
Different for Girls '96
Dirty Pretty Things '03
Disraeli '29
Double Vision '92
Dracula's Daughter '36
Dream Street '21
The Duchess of Duke Street '78
Eastern Promises '07
An Egyptian Story '82
84 Charing Cross Road '86
The Elephant Man '80
11 Harrowhouse '74
Elizabeth '98
The End of the Affair '55
The End of the Affair '99
Endgame '01
Entrapment '99
Esther Kahn '00
Eurotrip '04
Espresso Bongo '59
Face '97
Faith '94
Fanny Hill: Memoirs of a Woman of Pleasure '64
Fever Pitch '96
Fierce Creatures '96
Flawless '07
Flushed Away '06
Fool's Gold: The Story of the Brink's-Mat Robbery '92
Foreign Affairs '93
Foreign Correspondent '40
Forever and a Day '43
Forgive and Forget '99
The Fourth Angel '01
Frenzy '72
Friends & Crocodiles '05
The Frightened City '61
From Hell '01
Full Moon in Paris '84
The Gambler & the Lady '52
Gangster No. 1 '00
Gaslight '40
The Gathering Storm '02
The Gay Lady '49
Gentlemen's Relish '01
Gideon's Daughter '05
The Golden Bowl '72
The Golden Bowl '00
The Great Muppet Caper '81
Great Expectations '46
Green Street Hooligans '05
Hands of a Murderer '90
Hangover Square '45
The Heart of Me '02
Heaven's a Drag '94
High Heels and Low Lifes '01
Hope and Glory '87
The Horse's Mouth '58
The House of Eliot '92
Husbands '70
I, Monster '71
I Really Hate My Job '07
An Ideal Husband '99
If Only '04
I'll Sleep When I'm Dead '03
Imagine Me & You '06
Immortality '98
In Bruges '08
In the Name of the Father '93
Incognito '97
The Innocent Sleep '96
Intimacy '00
Janice Beard '99
John and Julie '55
Johnny Was '05
Journey for Margaret '42
Just Like a Woman '95
Killing Me Softly '01
The Knack '65
The Krays '90
The L-Shaped Room '62
Lady L '65
Lamb '85
Last Orders '01
Layer Cake '05
The Leading Man '96
The League of Extraordinary Gentlemen '03
Like It Is '98
The Line of Beauty '06
The Little Princess '39
London Voodoo '04
The Long Good Friday '80
The Lost Boys '78
The Lost Language of Cranes '91
The Lost Son '98
Love Actually '03
Love Among the Ruins '75
Love and Death on Long Island '97
Love Is the Devil '98
The Low Down '00
Lured '47
The Magician '93
Man in the Attic '53
The Man Who Knew Too Little '97
The Man Who Made Husbands Jealous '98
Mary Poppins '64
Mary Reilly '96
Match Point '05
Maybe Baby '00
Me & Mrs. Jones '02
Me Without You '01
Meantime '81
A Merry War '97
Metroland '97
Midnight Lace '60
Ministry of Fear '44
Miranda '01
Miss Pettigrew Lives for a Day '08
Mission: Impossible '96
The Missionary '82
Mrs. 'Arris Goes to Paris '92
Mrs. Dalloway '97
Mrs. Henderson Presents '05
Mrs. Palfrey at the Claremont '05
Moll Flanders '96
Moonlighting '82
The Mother '03
The Mummy Returns '01
The Murder of Stephen Lawrence '99
Murder on Line One '90
My Beautiful Laundrette '85
My Friend Walter '93
My Wife is an Actress '93
The Mysterious Dr. Fu Manchu '29
The Mysterious Magician '65
Mysterious Mr. Moto '38
Naked '93
National Lampoon's European Vacation '85
Neil Gaiman's Neverwhere '96
Nicholas Nickleby '02
Night and the City '50
Nighthawks '78
Nil by Mouth '96
Notes on a Scandal '76
Notting Hill '99
The Old Curiosity Shop '94
Oliver Twist '85
Oliver Twist '97
Oliver Twist '05
101 Dalmatians '96
One Wish Too Many '55
Othello '01
Our Mutual Friend '98
The Painted Lady '97
The Parent Trap '98
P.D. James: The Murder Room '04
Penelope '06
The Phantom of the Opera '62
Phantom Fiend '35
Photographing Fairies '97
Pinochet's Last Stand '06
Plain Jane '01
Played '06
Plunkett & Macleane '98
Polcark '96
Possession '02
Preaching to the Perverted '97
Priest '94
Pure '02
Quatermass and the Pit '58
Rancid Aluminium '00
Razor Blade Smile '98
Reign of Fire '02
The Return of Dr. Fu Manchu '30
Return to Never Land '02
The Ripper '97
Robert Louis Stevenson's The Game of Death '99
Romance and Rejection '96
Rough Cut '80
Royal Wedding '51
Ruby in the Smoke '06
Run, Fat Boy, Run '07
Russian Dolls '05
Sabotage '36
The Saint in London '39
Sammy & Rosie Get Laid '87
Say Hello to Yesterday '71
Scenes of a Sexual Nature '06
The Secret Agent '96
The Secret Life of Mrs. Beeton '06
Secrets and Lies '95
Seeing Red '99
Seven Days to Noon '50
Sexy Beast '00
Shakespeare in Love '98
Shanghai Knights '03
Shaun of the Dead '04
She Wolf of London '46
Sherlock: Case of Evil '02
Shooters '00
Shooting Fish '98
Shooting the Past '99
Sliding Doors '97
Snatch '00
Soho Square '00
Solitaire for 2 '94
Sorted '00
Spice World: The Movie '97
Spider '02
Split Second '92
Stage Beauty '04
Stella Does Tricks '96
Strange Bedfellows '65
Strapless '90
Sunday, Bloody Sunday '71

▶ = rated three bones or higher

Surveillance 24/7 '07
Sweeney Todd: The Demon Barber of Fleet Street '07
Tale of a Vampire '92
The Tall Guy '89 ▲
These Foolish Things '06
They Made Me a Fugitive '47
The Three Penny Opera '62
Time After Time '79 ▲
Tinker, Tailor, Soldier, Spy '80 ▲
Tipping the Velvet '02
To Each His Own '46 ▲
To Sir, with Love '67
Topsy Turvy '99 ▲
Touch of Pink '04
Touching Evil '97 ▲
Turtle Diary '86 ▲
24 Hours in London '00
28 Days Later '02 ▲
28 Weeks Later '07 ▲
Twice upon a Yesterday '98
Ultraviolet '98
Unknown White Male '05 ▲
V for Vendetta '06 ▲
Vanity Fair '99
Venus '06 ▲
Vera Drake '04 ▲
The Very Thought of You '98
Virtual Sexuality '99
Water Babies '79
Waterloo Bridge '40 ▲
The Way We Live Now '02 ▲
The Wedding Date '05
Werewolf of London '35 ▲
What a Girl Wants '03
Wild West '93
Wilde '97 ▲
Wimbledon '04
The Wings of the Dove '97 ▲
The Winslow Boy '98 ▲
Witchcraft 10: Mistress of the Craft '98
A Woman's Guide to Adultery '93
Wonderland '99 ▲
The Young Americans '93
The Young Poisoner's Handbook '94 ▲
Young Sherlock Holmes '85 ▲

Loneliness

see Only the Lonely

Loner Cops

see also Cops
Above the Law '88
Action Jackson '88
Bad Attitude '93
Bad Lieutenant '92 ▲
The Blue Knight '75
The Breed '01
Code of Silence '85
The Cop & the Girl '86
Cop in Blue Jeans '78
Dead Bang '89
The Dead Pool '88
Deadly Dancer '90
Die Hard '88 ▲
Die Hard 2: Die Harder '90 ▲
Die Hard: With a Vengeance '95
Dirty Harry '71 ▲
The Enforcer '76
Excessive Force '93
Exit Wounds '01
Force of One '79
The Gauntlet '77
Hard-Boiled '92 ▲
Heat '87
Heat '95 ▲
In the Heat of the Night '67 ▲
Judge Dredd '95
Klute '71 ▲
Live Free or Die Hard '07 ▲
Magnum Force '73
Martial Outlaw '93
McQ '74
Minority Report '02 ▲
Mission of Death '97
Murder by Numbers '02
Navajo Blues '97
Nightstick '87
Northwest Trail '46
One Good Cop '91

One Man Jury '78
The Pledge '00 ▲
Rent-A-Cop '87
RoboCop '87 ▲
Serpico '73 ▲
Sharky's Machine '81
SnakeEater '89
SnakeEater 2: The Drug Buster '89
SnakeEater 3: His Law '92
Soho Square '00
Speed '94 ▲
Stick '85
Stone Cold '91
The Street King '02
Striking Distance '93
Sudden Impact '83
Ten to Midnight '83
Top Dog '95
Year of the Dragon '85 ▲

Look Ma! I'm on TV!

see also Mass Media
Are You Scared? '06
At Home with the Webbers '94
Auto Focus '02 ▲
The Condemned '07
Confessions of a Dangerous Mind '02 ▲
Cruel World '05
Death to Smoochy '02
Eat Your Heart Out '96
EDtv '99
15 Minutes '01
Gale Force '01
Hairspray '07 ▲
Halloween: Resurrection '02
Love or Money '01
Loveless in Los Angeles '07
Magnolia '99 ▲
Monday Night Mayhem '02
My Best Friend '06
The New Gladiators '83
The Nines '07
Paul Bartel's The Secret Cinema '69
Pleasantville '98 ▲
Series 7: The Contenders '01
Showtime '02
Sink or Swim '97
Starter for Ten '06
Stay Tuned '92
Strange Wilderness '08
Stuck On You '03
Sugar Sweet '02
The Truman Show '98 ▲
The TV Set '06
The 24 Hour Woman '99
Woman on Top '00
Wrong Turn 2: Dead End '07

Lost Worlds

see also Parallel Universe
At the Earth's Core '76
Beyond Atlantis '73
Brigadoon '54 ▲
Creatures the World Forgot '70
Gold of the Amazon Women '79
Jane & the Lost City '87
Journey to the Center of the Earth '59 ▲
Journey to the Center of the Earth '99
Jumanji '95
The Land That Time Forgot '75
The Land Unknown '57
The Lost Continent '51
Lost Horizon '37 ▲
The Lost World '25
Mysterious Island '61 ▲
Mysterious Island of Beautiful Women '79
The People That Time Forgot '77
Warriors of Virtue '97
What Waits Below '83
When Dinosaurs Ruled the Earth '70
Where Time Began '77

Lottery Winners

Antoine et Antoinette '47
Babette's Feast '87 ▲
Dual Alibi '47
Everything's Gone Green '06
Finder's Fee '01
Fox and His Friends '75 ▲
How Much Do You Love Me? '05
It Could Happen to You '94
Just Your Luck '96
Le Million '31 ▲
Loco Love '03
Lots of Luck '85
Lottery Bride '30
Lucky Numbers '00
Lucky Partners '40
The Million Dollar Kid '99
Next Friday '00
The Squeeze '87
The Ticket '97
29th Street '91
Uptown Saturday Night '74 ▲
Waking Ned Devine '98 ▲
The Wrong Box '66 ▲

Louisiana

see also American South; New Orleans; Southern Belles
All the King's Men '49 ▲
The Apostle '97 ▲
As Summers Die '86 ▲
Bayou Romance '86
Blaze '89
Divine Secrets of the Ya-Ya Sisterhood '02
The Drowning Pool '75
Eve's Bayou '97 ▲
Fletch Lives '89
Frankenfish '04
Heaven's Prisoners '95
House of Wax '05
JFK '91 ▲
Kingfish: A Story of Huey P. Long '95 ▲
Louisiana '87
Louisiana Purchase '41
Louisiana Story '48 ▲
Mammoth '06
No Mercy '86
Passion Fish '92 ▲
Road House 2: Last Call '06
The Skeleton Key '05
A Soldier's Story '84 ▲
Sounder '72 ▲
Stay Alive '06
Steel Magnolias '89 ▲
Tigerland '00 ▲
Venom '05
Way Down South '39

Lovers on the Lam

see also Fugitives
Badlands '74 ▲
Blood & Wine '96
Bobby Z '07
Bonnie & Clyde '67 ▲
Boys '95
Criminal Lovers '99
Feeling Minnesota '96
The Getaway '93
The Getaway '93
Ghost of a Chance '01
Gun Crazy '49 ▲
Guncrazy '92
Heaven's Burning '97
Helen of Troy '03
The Island '05
Jailbreakers '94
Jimmy & Judy '06
Kalifornia '93
Kill Me Later '01
Kiss or Kill '97
Love and a .45 '94
Love Lies Bleeding '07
Mad Love '95
Man Who Loved Cat Dancing '73
Natural Born Killers '94 ▲
Niagara, Niagara '97
On the Run '73
River of Grass '94 ▲
The Road '00
Rough Magic '95
The Sugarland Express '74 ▲
Trojan Eddie '96 ▲
True Romance '93 ▲
Two If by Sea '95
Underworld: Evolution '05 ▲
When Brendan Met Trudy '00 ▲
Where Danger Lives '50
Wild at Heart '90 ▲

Lovable Loonies

see also Shrinks
Bean '97
Benny & Joon '93
Best in Show '00 ▲
Beyond Therapy '86
Box of Moonlight '96
The Couch Trip '87
Crazy People '90
Crazylove '05
David and Lisa '62
The Eighth Day '95
The Fisher King '91 ▲
Ghost World '01 ▲
Gridlock'd '96
Julian Po '97
King of California '07
The King of Hearts '66 ▲
Lars and the Real Girl '07 ▲
Meet Wally Sparks '97
The Ninth Configuration '79
One Flew Over the Cuckoo's Nest '75 ▲
Patch Adams '98
The Ruling Class '72 ▲
Sing and Like It '34
Superstar '99
What about Bob? '91 ▲

Mad Scientists

see also Inventors & Inventions; Science & Scientists
Alien Terminator '95
Alone in the Dark '05
The Amazing Transparent Man '60
The Animal '01
The Ape '40
The Ape Man '43
Atom Age Vampire '61
Attack of the Puppet People '58
Attack of the 60-Foot Centerfold '95 ▲
Attack of the Swamp Creature '75
The Avengers '98
Before I Hang '40 ▲
Bela Lugosi Meets a Brooklyn Gorilla '52
Beverly Hills Bodysnatchers '89
Beyond Re-Animator '03
The Black Sleep '56
Bloodbath at the House of Death '85
Bloodlust '59
Bloodstorm: Subspecies 4 '98
Body Armor '96
The Body Shop '72
The Boogie Man Will Get You '42
Bowery Boys Meet the Monsters '54
The Brain that Wouldn't Die '63
Brenda Starr '86
Bride of Re-Animator '89 ▲
Bride of the Monster '55
Bug Buster '99
Captain America '44
Captive Wild Woman '43
The Cars That Ate Paris '74 ▲
Castle of Evil '66
Castle of the Creeping Flesh '68
The City of Lost Children '95 ▲
Clockstoppers '02
The Cobweb '55

The Corpse Vanishes '42
Creator '85
Creature of the Walking Dead '60
The Creeper '48
The Creeping Flesh '72
The Creeps '97
The Crime of Dr. Crespi '35
Crimes of Dr. Mabuse '32 ▲
The Curse of the Aztec Mummy '59
Cyborg Cop '93
Darkman '90 ▲
Darkman 2: The Return of Durant '94
Darkman 3: Die Darkman Die '95
The Dead Next Door '89
Dead Pit '89
Dead Sleep '91
Death Warmed Up '85
Deep Red '94
Devil Doll '36 ▲
Dr. Black, Mr. Hyde '76
Doctor Blood's Coffin '62
Doctor Butcher M.D. '80
Dr. Caligari '89
Dr. Cyclops '40
Dr. Death, Seeker of Souls '73
Dr. Frankenstein's Castle of Freaks '74
Dr. Goldfoot and the Bikini Machine '20 ▲
Dr. Jekyll and Mr. Hyde '20 ▲
Dr. Jekyll and Mr. Hyde '32 ▲
Dr. Jekyll and Mr. Hyde '41 ▲
Dr. Jekyll and Mr. Hyde '68
Dr. Jekyll and Mr. Hyde '73
Dr. Jekyll and Sister Hyde '71
Dr. Jekyll and the Wolfman '71
Dr. Jekyll's Dungeon of Death '82
Dr. No '62 ▲
Dr. Orloff's Monster '64
Doctor X '32 ▲
Donovan's Brain '53 ▲
The Double O Kid '92
Dracula 2: Ascension '03
Embryo '76
Evil Town '87
Faceless '88
The Fear Chamber '68
Firestarter 2: Rekindled '02
The Flesh Eaters '64
Frankenhooker '90
Frankenstein '31 ▲
Frankenstein '73
Frankenstein '82
Frankenstein '93
Frankenstein and the Monster from Hell '74
Frankenstein '80 '79
Frankenstein General Hospital '88
Frankenstein Must Be Destroyed '69
Frankenstein Reborn '98
Frankenstein Unbound '90 ▲
Frankenstein's Daughter '58
Freaked '93
The Freakmaker '73
Geisha Girl '52
The Giant Spider Invasion '75
Girl in His Pocket '57
The Glass Trap '04
Godsend '04
The Head '59
Hellmaster '92
Hideous Sun Demon '59
Hollow Man '00
House of Frankenstein '44
Hyena of London '62
I, Monster '71
The Immortalizer '89
The Incredible Two-Headed Transplant '71
The Indestructible Man '56
Invasion! '99
Invasion of the Zombies '61
The Invisible Dr. Mabuse '62
The Invisible Man '33 ▲
The Invisible Ray '36 ▲
The Invisible Terror '63

The Island of Dr. Moreau '77
The Island of Dr. Moreau '96
Island of Lost Souls '32 ▲
Jekyll and Hyde '90
Jungle Captive '45
Jungle Woman '44
Jurassic Park '93 ▲
Kids in the Hall: Brain Candy '96
The Killing Device '92
King of Kong Island '78
King of the Zombies '41
Lady Frankenstein '72
The Lawnmower Man '92
Lawnmower Man 2: Beyond Cyberspace '95
Lightblast '85
The Living Dead '33
The Lost City '34
The Mad Ghoul '43
Man Made Monster '41
The Man They Could Not Hang '39
The Man Who Lived Again '36
The Man with Two Lives '42
Mandroid '93
Maniac '34
The Manster '59
Marronnier '05
Mary Shelley's Frankenstein '94 ▲
Master Minds '49
Metamorphosis '90
Miami Horror '87
Mr. Stitch '95
Mom's Outta Sight '01
The Monster '25 ▲
The Monster Maker '44
Monsters Crash the Pajama Party '65
The Mosaic Project '95
The Munsters' Revenge '81
Murders in the Rue Morgue '32
Mystery Science Theater 3000: The Movie '96
Naked Souls '95
Nightmare Castle '65
Nightmare Weekend '86
Orloff and the Invisible Man '70
The Outer Limits: Sandkings '95 ▲
Philadelphia Experiment 2 '93
Piano Tuner of Earthquakes '05
The Pink Panther Strikes Again '76 ▲
Proteus '95
Puzzlehead '05
The Rage '07
Re-Animator '84 ▲
Red Blooded American Girl '90
Retroactive '97
Return of the Killer Tomatoes! '88
Revenge of the Zombies '43
Revolt of the Zombies '36
Rites of Frankenstein '72
The Robot vs. the Aztec Mummy '59
Sabretooth '01
Samson in the Wax Museum '63
Savage '96
Scanner Cop '94
Science Crazed '90
Screamers '80
Seven Days to Noon '50
Severed Ties '92
Shadow Creature '96
Shadow of Chinatown '36
She Demons '58
Shock Waves '77
Sky Captain and the World of Tomorrow '04 ▲
Spider-Man '02 ▲
Spider-Man 2 '04 ▲
Spy Kids 3-D: Game Over '03
Star Trek: Generations '94 ▲
Strange Behavior '81
Strange Case of Dr. Jekyll & Mr. Hyde '68
Superargo '67

▲ = *rated three bones or higher*

Supersonic Man '78
Tammy and the T-Rex '94
Teenage Zombies '53
Terror Is a Man '59
Testament of Dr. Mabuse '62
The Tingler '59
Torture Ship '39
Transmutations '85
Underdog '07
The Unearthly '57
The Vampire Bat '32
Vie 21 '99
Virtual Seduction '96
Vulture '67
The Wasp Woman '96
Werewolf of London '35
Wes Craven Presents Mind Ripper '95
Wild Wild West '99
Woman Condemned '33

Madrid
see also Barcelona; Spain
All About My Mother '99
The Barefoot Contessa '54
Km. 0 '00
Labyrinth of Passion '82
Live Flesh '97
Martin (Hache) '97
The Method '05
?epi, Luci, Bom and Other Girls on the Heep '80
What Have I Done to Deserve This? '85
Women on the Verge of a Nervous Breakdown '88

Magic
see also Genies; Magic Carpet Rides; Occult
Alabama's Ghost '72
The Alchemist '81
Arabian Nights '00
The Brothers Grimm '05
The Butcher's Wife '91
Bedknobs and Broomsticks '71
Bewitched '05
The Black Cauldron '85
Black Magic Terror '79
Bogus '96
Celine and Julie Go Boating '74
Chandu on the Magic Island '34
Chandu the Magician '32
The Chronicles of Narnia: The Lion, the Witch and the Wardrobe '05
The Craft '96
Cthulhu Mansion '91
The Day the Earth Froze '59
Death Magic '32
Deathstalker 3 '89
Doctor Mordrid: Master of the Unknown '90
Don't Torture a Duckling '72
Doogal '05
Dream a Little Dream 2 '94
Dungeons and Dragons '00
Ella Enchanted '04
Enchanted '07
Escape to Witch Mountain '75
Eternally Yours '39
FairyTale: A True Story '97
The Geisha Boy '58
Gryphon '88
Happily N'Ever After '07

The Illusionist '06
Kids of the Round Table '96
Killing Grandpa '91
Lady in Distress '39
The Linguini Incident '92
Lord of the Rings: The Fellowship of the Rings '01
Lord of the Rings: The Two Towers '02
Lord of the Rings: The Return of the King '03
Luna e L'Altra '96
Magic Moments '89
Magic Serpent '66
The Magician '56
The Magician of Lublin '79
The Man in the Santa Claus Suit '79
Mary, My Dearest '83
Merlin '92
Merlin '98
Merlin's Apprentice '06
Merlin's Magical Wonder Emporium '07
The Mistress of Spices '05
My Chauffeur '86
The Mysterious Stranger '82
Nanny McPhee '06
Next '07
Penelope '06
Penn and Teller Get Killed '90
Pick a Card '97
Practical Magic '98
The Prestige '06
Prospero's Books '91
Puffnstuf '70
Quicker Than the Eye '88
Ratz '99
Rough Magic '95
Scoop '06
The Seeker: The Dark Is Rising '07
7 Faces of Dr. Lao '63
Simon the Magician '99
A Simple Wish '97
Stardust '07
Stephen King's Thinner '96
The Swan Princess 2: Escape from Castle Mountain '97
Sword & the Sorcerer '82
Teen Witch '89
The Tempest '99
13 Going on 30 '04
Three... Extremes '04
Turnaround '87
Tut & Tuttle '82
Wedding Band '89
Willow '88
The Wizard of Gore '70
Wizards of the Demon Sword '94
Zotz! '62

Magic Carpet Rides
see also Genies
Aladdin '92
Aladdin and the King of Thieves '96
Arabian Nights '00
Golden Voyage of Sinbad '73
1001 Arabian Nights '59
The Seventh Voyage of Sinbad '58
Sinbad and the Eye of the Tiger '77
Sinbad of the Seven Seas '89
Sinbad, the Sailor '47
The Thief of Bagdad '40
The Thief of Baghdad '24
Thief of Baghdad '61
The Thief of Baghdad '78

Mail-Order Brides
see also Marriage; Wedding Bells
Birthday Girl '02
Mail Order Wife '04
Mississippi Mermaid '69
Naked Jungle '54
Naughty Marietta '35
Original Sin '01

The Purchase Price '32
Sweet Land '05
2 Brothers & a Bride '03
Zandy's Bride '74

Mafia
see Organized Crime

Making Friends
see also Mad Scientists; Renegade Body Parts
Andy Warhol's Frankenstein '74
Deadly Friend '86
Frankenhooker '90
Frankenstein '31
Frankenstein '73
Frankenstein '82
Frankenstein Created Woman '66
Frankenstein Must Be Destroyed '69
Frankenstein Reborn '98
Frankenstein Unbound '90
Frankenstein's Daughter '58
Lost in Space '98
Making Mr. Right '86
Mary Shelley's Frankenstein '94
Multiplicity '96
Repli-Kate '01
The Vindicator '85
Young Frankenstein '74

Marriage
see also Divorce; In-Laws; Killer Spouses; Marriage Hell; Marriages of Convenience; Otherwise Engaged; War Between the Sexes; Wedding Bells; Wedding Hell
Above Suspicion '00
Abraham's Valley '93
Absent Without Leave '95
The Accidental Husband '08
Accused '36
Across the Wide Missouri '51
The Adjuster '91
The Adultress '77
The Adventures of Mark Twain '44
An Affair in Mind '89
Afterglow '97
After Sex '07
The Age of Innocence '93
Alfredo, Alfredo '72
All Things Fair '95
All This and Heaven Too '40
Almost You '85
Always '85
American Beauty '99
American Matchmaker '40
America's Sweethearts '01
Amnesia '36
Angel '37
Angie '94
The Anniversary Party '01
Antoine et Antoinette '47
April's Shower '03
Arabian Nights '00
The Aristocrats '99
Arnold '73
Arrivederci, Baby! '66
As You Desire Me '32
Ash Wednesday '73
Ask Any Girl '59
Assault and Matrimony '87
The Astronaut's Wife '99
Asunder '99
Attack of the 50 Ft. Woman '93
Auto Focus '02
Autumn Leaves '56
Autumn Marathon '79
Awake '07
Away From Her '06
Baby Doll '56
The Baby Maker '70
Bachelor Party '84
Bachelor in Paradise '69
Back to the Wall '56

Backstreet Dreams '90
Bad Behavior '92
Bad Manners '98
Barfly '93
Bark! '02
The Barkleys of Broadway '49
Battle of the Sexes '28
A Beautiful Mind '01
Because of You '52
Becky Sharp '35
Bed and Board '70
Bedazzled '46
Bedroom Eyes 2 '89
Being John Malkovich '99
The Beneficiary '97
Best Enemies '86
Best Friends '82
Best Intentions '92
The Best Man '97
Betrayal '83
Betsy's Wedding '90
Beyond the Rocks '22
Big Business Girl '31
Big Fish '03
The Big Squeeze '96
A Black Veil for Lisa '68
Blanche Fury '48
Blindfold: Acts of Obsession '94
Bliss '96
The Bliss of Mrs. Blossom '68
Blonde Venus '32
Blondie '38
Blondie Hits the Jackpot '49
Blondie in Society '41
Blondie Knows Best '46
Blondie Plays Cupid '40
Blood Oranges '97
Blood Wedding '81
Bloom '03
Blue Heaven '84
Blue in the Face '95
Blue Moon '00
Blue Sky '91
Bluebeard's Eighth Wife '38
Blume in Love '73
Body Chemistry '90
Body Strokes '95
Book of Love '04
Boulevard of Broken Dreams '88
Brand New Life '72
Bread and Tulips '01
Breaking the Waves '95
Breaking Up '97
Breathing Lessons '94
Bride & Prejudice '04
The Bride & the Beast '53
Bride of the Wind '01
The Bride Walks Out '36
Broken Glass '96
Brothers '05
Brown Sugar '02
The Browning Version '94
The Buccaneers '95
Bullwhip '58
Burn Witch, Burn! '62
The Burning Bed '85
A Business Affair '93
The Butcher's Wife '91
By Love Possessed '61
By the Light of the Silvery Moon '53

Calendar '93
Captain's Paradise '53
Car Trouble '86
Casanova Brown '44
Cast a Dark Shadow '55
Catherine Cookson's The Round Tower '98
Catherine Cookson's Colour Blind '98
Catherine Cookson's The Man Who Cried '93
Caught '96
Cause for Alarm '51
Chained '34
A Change of Heart '98
A Change of Seasons '80
Changing Times '04
Chaos '01
Chaos Theory '08
Charles & Diana: A Palace Divided '93

Charulata '64
Cheaper by the Dozen 2 '05
Cheaters '84
Cheatin' Hearts '93
Child Bride of Short Creek '81
China Moon '91
Chinese Roulette '86
Chloe in the Afternoon '72
The Chocolate Soldier '41
Choices '86
Christina '74
Cinderella Man '05
Circumstances Unknown '95
Circus '00
Claire's Knee '71
Clash by Night '52
The Clearing '04
Click '06
Close My Eyes '91
Coast to Coast '80
Coast to Coast '04
Cold Heaven '92
Come Back, Little Shaba '52
The Comfort of Strangers '91
Coming to America '88
Committed '99
Common Law Wife '63
Company Man '00
Conflict '45
Consenting Adults '92
Consolation Marriage '31
Conspiracy of Terror '75
The Convent '95
Cool and the Crazy '94
Cosmic Slop '94
Cotton Mary '99
Country Girl '54
Country Girl '82
The Cowboy and the Lady '38
Crash '95
Crazy in Love '92
Creation of Adam '93
Crime & Passion '75
Critic's Choice '63
A Cry in the Night '33
The Crying Child '96
Cul de Sac '66

Damage '92
Dancing in the Dark '86
Dangerous Game '93
Dangerous Liaisons '60
Daniel Deronda '02
Danielle Steel's Changes '91
Darlings of the Gods '90
The Daytrippers '96
De-Lovely '04
De Mayerling a Sarajevo '40
The Dead '87
Dead Husbands '98
Dead in the Water '91
Dead Mate '88
Dead On '93
Death Kiss '74
Deception '92
Deep in the Heart (of Texas) '98
Deja Vu '98
Designing Woman '57
Desire and Hell at Sunset Motel '92
Desire Under the Elms '58
Desperate Characters '71
Desperate Hours '90
Desperate Remedies '93
The Devil in Silk '56
The Devil's Advocate '97
Diabolically Yours '67
Dial "M" for Murder '54
Diary of a Mad Black Woman '05
Diary of a Mad Housewife '70
Diary of Ellen Rimbauer '03
Diary of the Dead '80
Dinner with Friends '01
The Disappearance of Christina '93
The Disciple '15
Divided We Fall '00
Divorce '15
Divorce American Style '67
Divorce—Italian Style '62

The Divorce of Lady X '38
Do Not Disturb '65
Doctor Zhivago '65
Doctor's Wives '70
Dodsworth '36
Doing Time on Maple Drive '92
Dollar '38
A Doll's House '59
A Doll's House '73
A Doll's House '73
Dominique Is Dead '79
Don Juan DeMarco '94
Dona Flor and Her Two Husbands '78
Donkey Skin '70
Don't Raise the Bridge, Lower the River '68
Don't Say a Word '01
Don't Talk to Strangers '94
Doomsday '28
The Door in the Floor '04
Dot the I '03
Double Deal '84
Double Exposure '93
Double Indemnity '44
Double Standard '88
Doubting Thomas '35
Dream Lover '93
Dressmaker '56
Drifting Souls '32
Drowning by Numbers '87
Drums Along the Mohawk '39
Dry Cleaning '97
Duane Hopwood '05
Duplex '03
Easy Living '37
Easy Living '49
East Is East '99
East Side, West Side '49
Eat a Bowl of Tea '89
Ecstasy '33
Edward and Mrs. Simpson '80
Effi Briest '74
Egg and I '47
El '52
El Cantante '06
El Crimen Perfecto '04
Elective Affinities '96
Element of Doubt '96
Elizabeth of Ladymead '48
Ellie '84
Elvis and Me '88
Emmanuelle '74
Emmanuelle, the Queen '79
Encore '52
End of Desire '62
The End of the Affair '99
The End of the Road '70
The Entertainer '60
Entre-Nous '83
Enough '02
Enormous Changes '83
Ernie Kovacs: Between the Laughter '84
Erotic Images '85
Escapade '35
Escape Clause '96
Estate of Insanity '70
Eternally Yours '39
Ethan Frome '92
Eureka! '81
Evelyn Prentice '34
Every Breath '93
Every Girl Should Be Married '48
Everybody's All American '88
Everyone Says I Love You '96
Eve's Bayou '97
The Ex '96
Ex-Lady '33
Experiment Perilous '45
The Eyes of Youth '19
Eyes Wide Shut '99
Faces '68
Facing Windows '03
The Facts of Life '60
Faithful '95
Faithless '00

▶ = rated three bones or higher

Falling for a Dancer '98
Falling from Grace '92
The Family Man '79
The Family Stone '05
Family Upside Down '78▶
Far Cry from Heaven '81
Far from Heaven '02▶
The Farmer's Wife '28
Fatal Attraction '87▶
Father of the Bride '50▶
Fear of Fear '75
Fearless '93▶
Feast of Love '07
Femme Fatale '90
Fergie & Andrew: Behind Palace Doors '93
Fever '88
Fictitious Marriage '88
Fiddler on the Roof '71▶
A Fine Romance '92
Fireworks '97
First Affair '83
5x2 '04
Flannel Pajamas '06
Flint '95
The Flower of My Secret '95▶
Follow the Boys '44▶
Fools '70
Fools Rush In '97
For Keeps '88
For Love or Country: The Arturo Sandoval Story '00
For Love or Money '63
For Pete's Sake '74
Forbidden Fruit '52▶
Forever Love '98
Forget Paris '95
Fortune's Fool '21
Fortunes of War '87▶
Four Daughters '38▶
Four Days in July '85
Four Rooms '95
The Four Seasons '81
Fourth Story '90▶
Free Money '99
French Twist '95
Frida '02
Frieda '47
Friends with Money '06
From the Terrace '60
Full of Life '56
Fun with Dick and Jane '77
Fun With Dick and Jane '05
Funny About Love '90
Fur: An Imaginary Portrait of Diane Arbus '06
Gabbeh '96▶
Gabrielle '05
Games '67
Gaslight '40▶
Gaslight '44▶
A Gathering of Eagles '63
The Gathering Storm '02▶
A Gentle Woman '69
George Washington '84
George Washington: The Forging of a Nation '86
Gertrud '64▶
Get Out Your Handkerchiefs '78▶
Getting Up and Going Home '92
Ghosts Never Sleep '05
The Gift of Love '90
Girl from Hunan '86▶
Girl with a Pearl Earring '03▶
Goin' to Town '35
The Golden Bowl '72▶
The Golden Bowl '00
The Golden Girl '02▶
The Good Wife '86
Gore Vidal's Lincoln '88
Gosford Park '01▶
Grace of My Heart '96
Grand Isle '92
Grand Theft Auto '77
The Grass Is Greener '61
Greed '24▶
The Greek Tycoon '78
Grievous Bodily Harm '89
Group Marriage '72
Grown Ups '80
Grumpier Old Men '95
The Guardsman '31▶
Guess Who '05

Guess Who's Coming to Dinner '67▶
Guest Wife '45
A Guide for the Married Man '67▶
A Guide for the Married Woman '78
The Hairdresser's Husband '92
Halfmoon '95
Hammers over the Anvil '91
Hamsun '96
A Handful of Dust '88▶
Happily Ever After '04
Happiness '98▶
Hard Promises '92
The Hard Word '02
Harlan County War '00
Harriet Craig '50▶
Harrison's Flowers '02
The Hawk '93
Head Above Water '96
Head On '04
The Healer '02
The Heart of Me '02▶
Heartburn '86▶
Heaven '99
Heaven's Prisoners '95
Heist '01▶
He as pour Moi '94
Hel-Ship Morgan '36
Here We Go Again! '42
Hidden '05▶
High Crimes '02
High Heels '72
High Society '56▶
Highway Patrolman '91
Hilary and Jackie '98▶
Hindsight '97
His Secret Life '01▶
Hitched '01
Homecoming '28▶
Honeymoon Lodge '43
The Honeymooners '05
Hope Floats '98
The Horrible Dr. Hichcock '62
Hostage for a Day '94
Hot Spell '58
Hot Tip '35
Hotel Room '93
Houdini '99
The Hours '02▶
House of Mirth '00▶
The Householder '63
How to Be a Woman and Not Die in the Attempt '91
How to Break Up a Happy Divorce '76
How to Commit Marriage '69
How to Kill Your Neighbor's Dog '01
How to Make an American Quilt '95
How to Marry a Millionaire '53
How to Murder Your Wife '64▶
Howard's End '92▶
The Howards of Virginia '40
Hurry, Charlie, Hurry '41
Husbands '70
Husbands and Lovers '91
Husbands and Wives '92▶
Hush '98
I Dood It '43
I Like It Like That '94▶
I Love My... Wife '70
I Love You Again '40▶
I Love You, Goodbye '74
I Love You Rosa '72
I Love Your Work '03
I Married a Vampire '87
I Married a Woman '56
I Only Want You to Love Me '76
I Think I Love My Wife '07
I Was a Male War Bride '49▶
I Will, I Will for Now '76
I Wonder Who's Killing Her Now? '96
An Ideal Husband '99▶
Il Bell'Antonio '60
Il Grido '57
I'll See You in My Dreams '51
Illicit '31

Illusions '91
Immortal Bachelor '80
The Imported Bridegroom '89
In a Savage Land '99
In Celebration '75▶
In Name Only '39
In the Bedroom '01▶
In the Lake of the Woods '96
In the Mood for Love '00▶
Indecent Proposal '93
Inevitable Grace '94
Infinity '96
The Innocent '76▶
Innocents with Dirty Hands '76
Intersection '93
Intimacy '00
Intimate Story '81
Intimate Strangers '77
Intruso '93
The Invasion of Carol Enders '74
The Invisible Ghost '41
Ira & Abby '06
Iris '01▶
Isn't She Great '00
It Came from the Sky '98
It Runs in the Family '03
It Started with a Kiss '59
It Takes Two '88
It's the Rage '99
Jackie, Ethel, Joan: The Kennedy Women '01
Java Head '35▶
Jenny '70
The Jeweller's Shop '90
John Adams '08
Josepha '82▶
Ju Dou '90▶
Jubal '56
Jubilee Trail '54
Jude '96▶
Jude the Obscure '71
Juliet of the Spirits '65▶
Just a Little Harmless Sex '99
Just Like Weather '86▶
Kadosh '99
The Keeper '96
Keeper of the Flame '42
Keeping Mum '06
The Kettles on Old MacDonald's Farm '57
The Kill-Off '90
Killing Heat '84
Killing Me Softly '01
A Kind of Loving '62▶
King's Ransom '05
Kira's Reason—A Love Story '01
Kiss and Be Killed '91
Kuni Lemel in Tel Aviv '77
La Bete Humaine '38▶
La Chienne '31▶
La Deroute '98
La Moustache '05
La Mujer de Mi Hermano '06
La Vengeance d'une Femme '89
La Vie Continue '82
Lady Audley's Secret '00
Lady Chatterley's Lover '55
Lady Chatterley's Lover '06
Lady Godiva '55
Lady L '65
Lady Windermere's Fan '25
Lantana '01▶
Last Breath '96
The Last Dance '93
The Last Days of Chez Nous '92▶
The Last Kiss '06
The Last Married Couple in America '80
L'Atalante '34▶
Late Spring '49▶
Laurel & Hardy: Be Big '31
Lawless Heart '01
Le Beau Marriage '82▶
Le Bonheur '65
Le Bonheur Est Dans le Pre '95
Le Chat '75▶
Lea '96
The Leather Boys '63
Leaving Metropolis '02
The Legend of Zorro '05

Leila '97
L'Enfer '93▶
Leo Tolstoy's Anna Karenina '96
Les Destinees '00
Lesson in Love '54
Let's Get Married '60
Lianna '83▶
The Liars '64
Liar's Moon '82
Lie Down with Lions '94
Life of Oharu '52▶
Like It Never Was Before '95
Linda 29
Linda 93
The Lion in Winter '68▶
Listen, Darling '38
A Little Sex 82
The Long Haul '57
Lonely Wives '31
Lord Love a Duck 66
Losing Chase '96
Lost Highway '96
Lost Honeymoon '47
Lost in Translation '03▶
The Lotus Eaters '93
Loulou '80▶
Love, Cheat & Steal '93
A Love Divided '01
Love, etc. '96
Love from a Stranger '37
Love in the Time of Cholera '07
Love Matters '93
Love Thy Neighbor '02
Love Walked In '97
The Lovers '59▶
Lovers and Other Strangers '70▶
Loving Couples '80
Lucia, Lucia '03
Lucie Aubrac '98
Lucy and Desi: Before the Laughter '91
Lured Innocence '97
Lust and Revenge '95
The Luzhin Defence '00
Ma Saison Preferee '93▶
Maborosi '95▶
Mad at the Moon '92
Mad Love '01
Madame Bovary '91▶
Madame Bovary '00
Madame Butterfly '95
Magnolia '99▶
Mail Order Wife '04
Making Love '82
The Makioka Sisters '83▶
The Male Animal '42
The Man from Elysian Fields '01▶
Man from Nowhere '37
The Man of My Life '06
Man of the House '95
The Man Who Made Husbands Jealous '98
The Man Who Wasn't There '01▶
Manhattan Murder Mystery '93
A Map of the World '99
Maria Chapdelaine '34▶
Marie Antoinette '06
The Marquise of O '76
The Marriage Circle '24▶
Marriage Is Alive and Well '80
Marriage Italian Style '64▶
The Marriage of Maria Braun '79▶
Marriage on the Rocks '65
Married? '26
Married People, Single Sex 2: For Better or Worse '94
Married to It '93
Married Too Young '62
A Married Woman '65▶
The Marrying Kind '52
Martha and I '91▶
Marty '55▶
Mary, Queen of Scots '71▶
Master Spy: The Robert Hanssen Story '02
Matrimaniac '16
A Matter of Dignity '57

Max, Mon Amour '86
Maybe Baby '99
McLintock! '63▶
Me Myself I '99
Me You Them '00▶
The Member of the Wedding '83
Memories of a Marriage '90▶
Memory of Us '74
Men... '85▶
Merci pour le Chocolat '00▶
The Merry Widow '52
Metroland '97
Mexican Spitfire at Sea '42
Miami Rhapsody '95
Microwave Massacre '83
Mid-Channel '20
Midnight '39▶
Midnight Crossing '87
Mighty Aphrodite '95▶
A Mighty Heart '07▶
Milk and Honey '03
The Millionairess '60
Miracle of Morgan's Creek '44▶
The Mirror Has Two Faces '96
Misbehaving Husbands '41
Mrs. Dalloway '97
Mrs. Mike '49
Mr. & Mrs. Smith '41▶
Mr. & Mrs. Smith '05▶
Mr. Barrington '03
Mr. Love '86
Mr. Mom '83▶
Mr. Skeffington '44▶
Mr. Sycamore '74
Mr. Wonderful '93
Mistress '53▶
Modern Love '90
Moment to Moment '66
Mona Lisa Smile '03
The Money Pit '86
Montana '90
Moon over Harlem '39
Moonlight Mile '02▶
The Moon's Our Home '36
Mouth to Mouth '95
Move Over, Darling '63
Multiplicity '96
Murder at 45 R.P.M. '65
Murder Czech Style '66
Murder So Sweet '93
Murders in the Zoo '33
Muriel's Wedding '94▶
The Music Lovers '71
My Dear Secretary '49
My First Wife '84▶
My 5 Wives '00
My Foolish Heart '49
My Husband's Double Life '01
My Life So Far '98
My Life Without Me '03▶
My Little Chickadee '40▶
My Michael '75
My New Gun '92
My Other Husband '85
My Sweet Victim '85
My Wife is an Actress '01
Naked Jungle '54▶
The Namesake '06▶
Napoleon '03
Narc '02▶
Nathalie '03
The New Age '94
Night Ride Home '99
Nightkill '80
Nina Takes a Lover '94
Nora '00
Normal '03▶
Normal Life '96
Not Tonight Darling '72
Notes on a Scandal '06▶
The Notorious Lady '27
Nouvelle Vague '90
Now and Forever '82
Nowhere in Africa '02▶
Nudo di Donna '83▶
Nurse Marjorie '20
O Quatrilho '95
Odd Obsession '60
O'Hara's Wife '82
The O.J. Simpson Story '94
Oldest Confederate Widow Tells All '95▶
On Approval '44▶

On Golden Pond '81▶
On Her Majesty's Secret Service '69▶
On Valentine's Day '86
One Good Turn '85
One Hour Photo '02▶
One Hour with You '32
One Night in the Tropics '40
One of My Wives Is Missing '76
One Trick Pony '80
Only with Married Men '74
Orchestra Wives '42▶
Othello '01▶
Our Italian Husband '04
Our Town '03
Out of Order '03
The Paint Job '93
Paint Your Wagon '69
The Painted Veil '34
The Painted Veil '06
Pajama Tops '83
The Palm Beach Story '42▶
Pandaemonium '00
Panic '00▶
Paper Marriage '88
Paper Marriage '93
Paradise '91▶
Pardon Mon Affaire '76▶
Pardon Mon Affaire, Too! '77
Parenthood '89▶
Paris, France '94
Party '96
Passion in Paradise '89
The Passion of Ayn Rand '99
A Passion to Kill '94
Pavilion of Women '01
Pedale Douce '96
Peggy Sue Got Married '86
The Penitent '88
Pennies from Heaven '81▶
Perfect Alibi '94
The Perfect Bride '91
Perfect Crime '97
The Perfect Marriage '46
A Perfect Murder '98
Period of Adjustment '62▶
Persuasion '71
Pete 'n' Tillie '72
Petulia '68▶
Phaedra '61
Phffft! '54
The Philadelphia Story '40▶
The Piano '94▶
Picture Bride '94
A Piece of Pleasure '74▶
Pipe Dreams '76
Platinum Blonde '31▶
Playing Dead '15
Pollock '00▶
Portrait of a Lady '96▶
Portrait of an Assassin '49
Portrait of Teresa '79▶
The Postman Always Rings Twice '46▶
The Postman Always Rings Twice '81
Praying Mantis '93
Premonition '07
Pride and Prejudice '05▶
Primary Colors '98
The Primitive Lover '16
Prisoner of Second Avenue '74
Prisoners of Inertia '89
Private Confessions '98
Private Life '82
Private Lives '31▶
Promises! Promises! '63
Provincial Actors '79
Prowler '51
The Pumpkin Eater '64▶
The Purchase Price '32
Pushing Hands '92
Quartet '81▶
Queen Bee '55
Queen Margot '94▶
Question of Faith '93
Race for Life '55
Raging Bull '80▶
Rain '01
Raise the Red Lantern '91▶
Rally 'Round the Flag, Boys! '58
Range of Motion '00

▶ = rated three bones or higher

Rape and Marriage: The Rideout Case '80
Rebecca '40▶
Rebecca '97
Reckless '97▶
The Rector's Wife '94
Red Lights '04▶
Red Rock West '93▶
Remember Me '85
The Rendering '02
A Respectable Trade '98
Revenge of the Stepford Wives '80
Reversal of Fortune '90▶
Rich and Famous '81
The Rich Man's Wife '96
Rider from Tucson '50
Riptide '34▶
Risky Business '28
Rocky 2 '79
Romantic Englishwoman '75▶
The Roof '56
Rose of Washington Square '39
Roseanne: An Unauthorized Biography '94
A Royal Scandal '96
The Royal Tenenbaums '01▶
Rumor Has It... '05
Runaways '75
Ryan's Daughter '70
Safe Passage '94
The Safety of Objects '01
The Sandy Bottom Orchestra '99
The Santa Clause 2 '02
Santa Fe '97
Saraband '03▶
Sarah's Child '96
Satan's Black Wedding '75
Saturday Night and Sunday Morning '60▶
Savage Attraction '83
Say Nothing '01
Say Yes! '86
Scar of Shame '27
Scarlet Dawn '32
Scenes from a Mall '91
Scenes from a Marriage '73▶
Scorchers '92
Score '72
Scotland, PA '02
Season of Fear '89
Second Chance '50
Second Skin '99
Secret Beyond the Door '48
Secret Lives of Girls '99
The Secret Life of Mrs. Beeton '06
The Secret Lives of Dentists '02▶
Secrets of Women '52▶
Seeing Other People '04
Seems Like Old Times '80
Send Me No Flowers '64▶
Separate Vacations '86
Separate Ways '82
Seven Chances '25▶
The Seven Year Itch '55▶
The Seventeenth Bride '84
Seventh Heaven '99
75 Degrees '00
Sex and the Single Girl '64
The Sex Monster '99
Sexpot '88
Sexual Malice '93
Shadowlands '65▶
Shadowlands '93
The Shakiest Gun in the West '68
Shall We Dance? '04
The Shame '68▶
Shattered '72
She and He '63
She-Devil '89
She Waits '71
She's So Lovely '97
She's the One '96
Shoot the Moon '82▶
Shooting Elizabeth '92
The Show Off '26
Sibling Rivalry '90
Sidewalks of New York '01
Signs & Wonders '00

Silent Tongue '92
Silent Victim '92
Sin and Redemption '94
Sin Takes a Holiday '30
The Singing Blacksmith '38
The Single Standard '29
The Sisters '33
Sketch Artist '92
Skinner's Dress Suit '26
The Slugger's Wife '85
Small Time Crooks '00
Smart Woman '31
Smash Palace '82
Smash-Up: The Story of a Woman '47▶
The Smiling Lieutenant '31
Smoking/No Smoking '94
Smoldering Fires '25
Snow White: A Tale of Terror '97
So This Is Paris '26▶
The Soft Skin '64▶
Sofie '92
Something About Sex '98
Something to Talk About '95
The Son's Room '00▶
A Song for Martin '01
Soul Food '97
Sound of Murder '82
Splendor '35
The Stationmaster's Wife '77
Steam: A Turkish Bath '99
The Stepford Wives '75▶
The Story of Xinghua '93
Story of a Love Affair '50
The Story of Boys & Girls '91▶
The Story of Esther Costello '57
The Story of Us '99
Strange Bedfellows '65
Stromboli '50
The Student Affair '97
The Substitute Wife '94
Sudden Fear '52▶
Summer Wishes, Winter Dreams '73
Suspicion '41▶
Suspicion '03
Sweet Hearts Dance '88
Sweet Home Alabama '02
Sweet Move '61
Sweet Nothing '96
Sweet Poison '91
Sweet Revenge '90
Sweethearts '38▶
Sylvia '03
W '74
The Syrian Bride '04
The Tailor of Panama '00▶
Tarnished Angels '57▶
The Taste of Others '00▶
Tell Me a Riddle '80
Tell Me That You Love Me '84
The Tenant of Wildfell Hall '96
Tender Is the Night '55
Tess of the D'Urbervilles '98
Test Pilot '38▶
Thanks for the Memory '38
That Certain Thing '28
That Old Feeling '96
That Uncertain Feeling '41
Thicker Than Water '93
The Third '72
Third Walker '79▶
30 Is a Dangerous Age, Cynthia '68
Three Broadway Girls '32▶
Three Daring Daughters '48
Three for the Show '55
Three Husbands '50
Three Smart Girls '36▶
Thursday's Game '74▶
Till Death Do Us Part '72
Till Marriage Do Us Part '74
Till Murder Do Us Part '92
Till the End of the Night '94
Tim Burton's Corpse Bride '05▶
Tin Men '87
To Joy '50▶
Tom & Viv '94▶
Too Beautiful for You '88
Too Hot to Go '73▶
Torchlight '85
The Torture of Silence '17

Town and Country '01
Trade Off '95
Traps '93
Tricks of the Trade '88
Tristan & Isolde '06
Tropix '02▶
True Lies '94
True Love '89▶
The Truman Show '98▶
Trust the Man '06
The Tunnel '89
The Tunnel of Love '58
Turn of the Blade '97
Twice a Woman '79
Twilight '98▶
The Twilight of the Golds '97
Two Family House '99
Two for the Road '67▶
The Two Mrs. Carrolls '47
Tyler Perry's Why Did I Get Married? '07
Ulysses '67▶
The Unchastened Woman '25
Under Capricorn '49
Under Capricorn '82
Under the Lighthouse Dancing '97
Under the Sand '00▶
Under the Volcano '84▶
Une Parisienne '58
Undercover '46
Undercover Blues '93
Unfaithfully Yours '48▶
Unfaithfully Yours '84
Unholy Wife '57
The Unkissed Bride '66
Until September '84
Uptown New York '32
The Van '95
Vanishing Act '88
Vanity Fair '67
Vanity Fair '99
Vasectomy: A Delicate Matter '86
Velvet Goldmine '98
The Vertical Ray of the Sun '00
Victoria & Albert '01
A Village Affair '95
Violets Are Blue '86
The Virgin of Nuremberg '65
Vivacious Lady '38▶
A Vow to Kill '94
Voyage in Italy '53
Vukovar '94▶
Waking Up in Reno '02
A Walk in the Clouds '95
Walk in the Spring Rain '70
Walking and Talking '96▶
Waltz of the Toreadors '62▶
War Brides '80
The Wash '88▶
Waterland '92
Way Down East '20▶
The Wayward Wife '52
We Don't Live Here Anymore '04
A Wedding '78
The Wedding '98
The Wedding Gift '93▶
Wedding in Blood '74▶
A Wedding in Galilee '87
The Weight of Water '00
We're Not Married '52▶
What Lies Beneath '00
What's Good for the Goose '69
When a Man Loves a Woman '94
Where Angels Fear to Tread '91▶
Where Were You When the Lights Went Out? '68
White Gold '28▶
White Mischief '88▶
White Noise '05
Who's Afraid of Virginia Woolf? '66▶
Who's Got the Action? '63
Why Do Fools Fall in Love? '98
Wicked Ways '99
The Widow of Saint-Pierre '00▶
Widow's Kiss '94

A Touch of Class '73▶
Wife Versus Secretary '36▶
Wifemistress '79
Wilde '97▶
With a Friend Like Harry '00▶
With Six You Get Eggroll '68
Without Anesthesia '78
Wolf Trap '57
The Woman in White '97
A Woman Named Jackie '91
The Woman Next Door '81▶
A Woman's Guide to Adultery '93
A Woman's World '54▶
The Women '39▶
Women from the Lake of Scented Souls '94
Women vs. Men '02
The Wooden Man's Bride '94
The World Is Full of Married Men '80
World's Greatest Lover '77
Worth Winning '89
Woyzeck '79
X, Y & Zee '72
A Year in Provence '89▶
Yenma '99
You Can't Fool Your Wife '40
You've Got to Have Heart '77
You, Gotta Stay Happy '48
The Young Pioneers '76
Younger & Younger '94
Yours, Mine & Ours '68
Yours, Mine & Ours '05
Zandy's Bride '74
Zebra Lounge '01
Zombie Honeymoon '04

Marriage Hell
see also Divorce; Domestic Abuse; Killer Spouses; Marriages of Convenience

Abraham's Valley '93
The Adulteress '77
An Affair in Mind '89
Affairs of Anatol '21
After Sex '97
Afterglow '97
All Things Fair '95
Amelia '06
American Beauty '99▶
Amnesia '96
Angel '37
Angels in America '03▶
Arnold '73
Arrivederci, Baby! '66
Assault and Matrimony '87
Attack of the 50 Ft. Woman '93
Autumn Leaves '56
Back to the Wall '56
Bad Manners '98
Bedelia '46▶
The Best Intentions '92▶
Betrayal '83
The Big Squeeze '96
The Bigamist '53▶
A Black Veil for Lisa '68
Blanche Fury '48
Blindfold: Acts of Obsession '94
Blonde Venus '32▶
The Blood Oranges '97
Blood Wedding '81▶
Boulevard of Broken Dreams '88
The Buccaneers '95▶
The Burning Bed '85▶
Cast a Dark Shadow '55▶
Catherine Cookson's The Man Who Cried '93
Cause for Alarm '51▶
Chained '34
A Change of Seasons '80
Charles & Diana: A Palace Divided '93
Charulata '64

The Wife '95
Cheaters '84
Cheatin' Hearts '93
Child Bride of Short Creek '81
Chinese Roulette '86
Christina '74
Clash by Night '52▶
Cold Heaven '92
Come Back, Little Sheba '52▶
The Comfort of Strangers '91▶
Committed '99
Conflict '45▶
Cool and the Crazy '94
Cotton Mary '99
Country Girl '54▶
Country Girl '82
Cover '08
Crazy Love '07▶
Crime & Passion '75
A Cry in the Night '93
Cul de Sac '66▶
Damage '92▶
Dangerous Game '93
Dangerous Liaisons '50
Daniel Deronda '02
Dead Husbands '98
Dead in the Water '98
Dead Mate '88
Dead On '93
Dead Water '9?
Deadly Illusion '87
Death Kiss '74
Desire and Hell at Sunset Motel '92
Desire Under the Elms '58
The Devil in Silk '56
Dial "M" for Murder '54▶
Diary of a Mad Black Woman '05
Diary of a Mad Housewife '70▶
The Diary of Ellen Rimbauer '03
The Disappearance of Christina '93
The Divorcee '30▶
A Doll's House '59
A Doll's House '73▶
Dominique Is Dead '79
Doomsday 28
The Door in the Floor '04▶
Double Exposure '83
Double Indemnity '44▶
Double Standard '89
Dream Lover '93
Drifting Souls '32
Drowning by Numbers '87▶
Easy Living '49
Effi Briest '74▶
El '52
Element of Doubt '96
Ellie '84
Emmanuelle, the Queen '79
End of Desire '62
Enough '02
The Entertainer '60▶
Ethan Frome '92
Faithful '00
Faithless '00▶
Falling for a Dancer '98
Far Cry from Home '81
Far from Heaven '02▶
Fergie & Andrew: Behind Palace Doors '93
5x2 '04
The Flower of My Secret '95▶
Forbidden Fruit '52▶
French Twist '95
Gaslight '40▶
Gaslight '44▶
A Gentle Woman '69
The Girl in the Red Velvet Swing '55
The Golden Bowl '72
The Golden Bowl '00
The Good Wife '86
Greed '24▶
Harriet Craig '50▶
The Hawk '93
Head Above Water '96
The Heart of Me '02
Heartburn '86▶
Heaven '99
Hell-Ship Morgan '36

He's Just Not That Into You '08
Hindsight '97
Hitched '01
The Horrible Dr. Hichcock '62
Hostage for a Day '94
Husbands and Lovers '91
Husbands and Wives '92▶
Hush '98
Illicit '37
In a Savage Land '99
In Name Only '39▶
The Innocent '76▶
Innocents with Dirty Hands '76
The Jane Austen Book Club '07▶
Ju Dou '90▶
Jude the Obscure '71
The Kill-Off '90
Killing Me Softly '01
La Bete Humaine '38▶
La Chienne '31▶
Lantana '01▶
The Last Dance '93
The Last Days of Chez Nous '92▶
Le Chat '75▶
Lea '96
L'Enfer '93▶
Leo Tolstoy's Anna Karenina '96
Linda '93
Loulou '80▶
A Love Divided '01
The Love Guru '08
Love Matters '93
The Love Parade '29▶
The Lovers '59▶
Lured Innocence '97
Mad Love '01
Madame Bovary '91▶
Madame Bovary '00
Madame Butterfly '95
Mail Order Wife '04
Married People, Single Sex 2: For Better or Worse '94
A Matter of Dignity '57
Mid-Channel '20
Moon over Harlem '39
Mouth to Mouth '95
Murder Czech Style '66
Murder So Sweet '93
Murders in the Zoo '33
The Music Lovers '71
My Blueberry Nights '07
My First Wife '84
My Foolish Heart '49
My Husband's Double Life '01
The Nanny Diaries '07
Nightkill '80
Nora '00
Normal Life '96
Odd Obsession '60
One Trick Pony '80
Out of Order '84
The Painted Veil '34
The Painted Veil '06▶
A Passion to Kill '94
A Perfect Alibi '94
A Perfect Murder '98
Petulia '68▶
Portrait of a Lady '67
Portrait of an Assassin '49
Praying Mantis '93
Private Confessions '98
The Pumpkin Eater '64▶
Queen Bee '55
Rape and Marriage: The Rideout Case '80
Reversal of Fortune '90▶
The Rich Man's Wife '96
Romance & Cigarettes '05
Rose of Washington Square '39
A Royal Scandal '96
Savage Attraction '83
Scar of Shame '27
Scenes from a Mall '91
Scenes from a Marriage '73▶
Scorchers '92
Second Skin '99

▶ = rated three bones or higher

Marriage

Secret Beyond the Door '48
The Secret Life of Girls '99
Seventh Heaven '98
She-Devil '89
Shoot the Moon '82
Silent Victim '92
Sleeping with the Enemy '91
Smart Woman '31
Snow Angels '07▸
Sound of Murder '82
The Stepford Wives '75▸
The Stepford Wives '04
The Stone Merchant '06
Story of a Love Affair '50
The Story of Xinghua '93
Sudden Fear '52▸
Suspicion '41▸
Suspicion '87
Sylvia '86
Tension '50
Till Murder Do Us Part '92
Tom & Viv '94
Too Far to Go '79▸
Town and Country '01
Two for the Road '67▸
Under Capricorn '49
Under Capricorn '82
Undercurrent '46
Vacancy '07
A Vow to Kill '94
The War of the Roses '89▸
We Don't Live Here Anymore '04
What Happens in Vegas '08
Who's Afraid of Virginia Woolf? '66▸
With a Song in My Heart '52▸
Wolf Trap '57

Marriages of Convenience

Brokeback Mountain '05▸
The Crown Prince '06
De-Lovely '04
Fall Guy '82
Flickers '80
The Great McGinty '40▸
Green Card '90
Head On '04
Honeymoon '87
I Now Pronounce You Chuck and Larry '07
Kill the Poor '06
Loco Love '03
Love for Rent '05
Love or Money '01
Mail Order Wife '04
Never Say Die '39
A Paper Wedding '89▸
Rachel and the Stranger '48▸
Seducing Maarya '99
Tim Burton's Corpse Bride '05▸
2 Brothers & a Bride '03
The Wedding Banquet '93▸

Mars

see also Space Operas
Abbott and Costello Go to Mars '53
The Angry Red Planet '59
Buck Rogers in the 25th Century '79
Capricorn One '78▸
Doom '05
Escape from Mars '99
Flight to Mars '52
Frankenstein Meets the Space Monster '65
The Invader '96
It! The Terror from Beyond Space '58
John Carpenter's Ghosts of Mars '01
Mars Attacks! '96
The Martian Chronicles: Part 1 '79
The Martian Chronicles: Part 2 '79
The Martian Chronicles: Part 3 '79
Martians Go Home! '90
Mission to Mars '00
My Favorite Martian '98

Planet of Blood '66
Project Shadowchaser 3000 '95
Red Planet '00
Red Planet Mars '52
RocketMan '97
Rocketship X-M '50
Santa Claus Conquers the Martians '64
Species 2 '98
Total Recall '90▸
Zombies of the Stratosphere '52

Martial Arts

see also Ninjas; Supernatural Martial Arts
Above the Law '88
Aeon Flux '05
Alley Cat '84
Aloha Summer '88
American Chinatown '96
American Kickboxer 1 '91
American Kickboxer 2: To the Death '93
American Ninja '85
American Ninja 2: The Confrontation '87
American Ninja 3: Blood Hunt '89
American Ninja 4: The Annihilation '91
American Samurai '92
American Shaolin: King of the Kickboxers 2 '92
American Streetfighter '96
The Amsterdam Connection '78
Angel of Fury '93
Angel Town '89
Back in Action '94
Balance of Power '96
Balls of Fury '07
Bells of Death '90
Best of the Best '89
Best of the Best 2 '93
Best of the Best 3: No Turning Back '95
Best of the Best: Without Warning '98
Beverly Hills Ninja '96
The Big Brawl '80
Big Trouble in Little China '86
Black Belt '92
Black Belt Jones '74
Black Eagle '88
Black Mask '96
Black Samurai '77
Blackbelt 2: Fatal Force '93
Blind Fury '90
Blind Rage '78
Blood for Blood '95
Blood Ring '93
Blood Warriors '93
Bloodfist '89
Bloodfist 2 '90
Bloodfist 3: Forced to Fight '92
Bloodfist 4: Die Trying '92
Bloodfist 5: Human Target '93
Bloodfist 6: Ground Zero '94
Bloodfist 7: Manhunt '95
Bloodfist 8: Hard Way Out '96
Bloodmatch '91
Bloodsport '88
Bloodsport 2: The Next Kumite '95
Bloodsport 3 '97
Bloodsport 4: The Dark Kumite '98
The Bodyguard '76
Born Losers '67
Bounty Tracker '93
Braddock: Missing in Action 3 '88
Brain Smasher... A Love Story '93
Breaker! Breaker! '77
Breathing Fire '91
The Bride with White Hair '93
The Bride with White Hair 2 '93

The Bronx Executioner '86
Bruce Lee: Curse of the Dragon '93▸
Bruce Lee Fights Back from the Grave '76
Bulletproof Monk '03
The Bushido Blade '80
Cage 2: The Arena of Death '94
Capital Punishment '96
Catch the Heat '87
Challenge of the Masters '89
China O'Brien '88
China O'Brien 2 '89
China White '91
The Chinatown Kid '78
Chinese Connection '73
Chinese Connection 2 '77
Circle of Iron '78
Clash of the Ninja '86
Cleopatra Jones '73
Cleopatra Jones & the Casino of Gold '75
Clones of Bruce Lee '80
The Cobra '68
Counter Attack '84
Crack Shadow Boxers '79
Cradle 2 the Grave '03
Crime Story '93
The Crippled Masters '82
Crouching Tiger, Hidden Dragon '00▸
Curse of the Golden Flower '06
Cyber Ninja '94
A Dangerous Place '94
Day of the Panther '88
Deadly Bet '91
Deadly Target '94
Death Challenge '80
Death Machines '76
Death Match '94
Death Ring '93
Death Warrant '90
Deathfight '93
Desert Kickboxer '92
The Divine Enforcer '91
DOA: Dead or Alive '06
Dolemite '75
Double Dragon '94
Double Impact '91
Dragon Fury '95
Dragon Lord '82
Dragon: The Bruce Lee Story '93▸
Dragons Forever '88
Drunken Monkey '02
Duel of Fists '71
The Dynamite Brothers '74
Dynasty '77
Eagle's Shadow '84
18 Fingers of Death '05
Elektra '05
The Eliminators '86
Enter the Dragon '73▸
Enter the Ninja '81
Equal Impact '96
The Executioners '93
An Eye for an Eye '81
Fantasy Mission Force '84
Fatal Combat '96
Fearless '06
Ferocious Female Freedom Fighters '88
The Fighter '95
Fighting Black Kings '76
Final Impact '91
Firecracker '71
Firewall '06
Fist of Fear, Touch of Death '80
Fist of Glory '95
Fist of Legend '94
Fist of Steel '93
Fists of Blood '87
Fists of Fury '73▸
Fists of Iron '94
The Forbidden Kingdom '08
Force of One '79
Force of the Ninja '88
Forced Vengeance '82
Forgotten Warrior '86
Four Robbers '87
Full Contact '93
Full Metal Ninja '89
Futurekick '91

G2: Mortal Conquest '99
The Gambling Samurai '60
Game of Death '79
Gang Justice '94
Gang Wars '75
Ghostwarrior '86
Gladiator Cop: The Swordsman 2 '95
The Glimmer Man '96
Goldfinger '64▸
Good Guys Wear Black '78
The Great Challenge '04
Guardian Angel '94
Gymkata '85
Half a Loaf of Kung Fu '78
Hard to Kill '89
Hawk's Vengeance '96
Heart of Dragon '85
Heatseeker '95
Hero '03▸
Hero and the Terror '88
The Heroic Trio '93
Honor '06
Hot Potato '76
House of Flying Daggers '04▸
Immortal Combat '94
In Your Face '77
The Instructor '83
Invasion U.S.A. '85
Iron Monkey '93
Iron Thunder '89
Ironheart '92
Jackie Chan's First Strike '96▸
Jaguar Lives '79
Jet Li's Fearless '06
Jet Li's The Enforcer '95
Joe Somebody '01
Karate Cop '91
The Karate Kid '84▸
The Karate Kid: Part 2 '86
The Karate Kid: Part 3 '89
Karate Warrior '88
Kentucky Fried Movie '77▸
The Kick Fighter '91
Kick of Death: The Prodigal Boxer '73
Kickboxer '89
Kickboxer 2: The Road Back '90
Kickboxer 3: The Art of War '92
Kickboxer 4: The Aggressor '94
Kickboxer the Champion '91
Kill and Kill Again '81
Kill Bill Vol. 1 '03▸
Kill Bill Vol. 2 '04▸
Kill Line '91
Kill or Be Killed '80
Kill Squad '81
Kill the Golden Goose '79
Killer Elephants '76
The King of the Kickboxers '91
Kingfisher the Killer '81
Kiss of the Dragon '01
Knights '93
Knock Off '98
The Kumite '03
Kung Fu '72
Kung Fu Hustle '04▸
Kung Fu Panda '08
Kung Fu: The Movie '86
Kung Powl Enter the Fist '02
Lady Dragon '92
Lady Dragon 2 '93
The Last Dragon '85
Last Hurrah for Chivalry '78
Latin Dragon '03
Legacy of Rage '86
The Legend of Drunken Master '94▸
The Legend of the 7 Golden Vampires '73
Lethal Ninja '93
Lethal Panther '90
Lionheart '90
Little Dragons '80
Little Ninjas '92
Lone Wolf and Cub '72
Lone Wolf and Cub: Baby Cart at the River Styx '72
Mafia vs. Ninja '84
Magic Kid '92
Magic Kid 2 '94
Magnum Killers '76

Manchurian Avenger '84
Marked for Death '90
Martial Law '90
Martial Law 2: Undercover '91
Martial Outlaw '93
Master with Cracked Fingers '71
Master's Revenge '71
Maximum Risk '96
The Medallion '03
Meltdown '95
The Millionaire's Express '86
Mission of Justice '92
Mr. Nice Guy '98
Mortal Kombat 1: The Movie '95
Mortal Kombat 2: Annihilation '97
The Mosaic Project '95
Moving Target '00
My Samurai '92
Naked Killer '92
Never Back Down '08
New Fist of Fury '76
New York Cop '94
The Next Karate Kid '94
Night Hunter '95
Night Master '87
Night of the Kickfighters '91
Night of the Warrior '91
9 1/2 Ninjas '90
Nine Deaths of the Ninja '85
Ninja 3: The Domination '84
Ninja Academy '90
Ninja: American Warrior '90
Ninja Brothers of Blood '89
Ninja Champion '80
Ninja Commandments '87
Ninja Condors '87
Ninja Connection '90
Ninja Death Squad '87
Ninja Destroyer '70
Ninja Fantasy '86
Ninja Hunt '80s
Ninja in the U.S.A. '88
Ninja Masters of Death '85
Ninja Mission '84
Ninja, the Violent Sorcerer '86
Ninja Operation: Licensed to Terminate '87
Ninja Phantom Heroes '87
Ninja Powerforce '90
Ninja Showdown '90
Ninja Strike Force '88
Ninja the Battalion '91
Ninja Vengeance '93
No Retreat, No Surrender '86
No Retreat, No Surrender 2 '89
No Retreat, No Surrender 3: Blood Brothers '91
Octagon '80
Omega Cop '90
Once Upon a Time in China '91▸
Once Upon a Time in China II '92▸
Once Upon a Time in China III '93▸
The One '01
One Down, Two to Go! '82
One-Eyed Swordsman '63
One Man Army '93
Ong-Bak '03▸
Only the Strong '93
Open Fire '94
Operation Condor '91
Operation Golden Phoenix '94
Operation Orient '78
Out for Blood '93
Out for Justice '91
Overkill '86
Pay or Die '83
The Perfect Weapon '91
Pit Fighter '05
The Power of the Ninjitsu '88
The Power Within '95
Pray for Death '85
The Prisoner '90
The Prodigal Son '82

Project A '83
Project A: Part 2 '87
The Promise '05
Protector '85
The Purifiers '04
Pursuit '04
Pushed to the Limit '92
The Quest '96
Rage and Honor '92
Rage and Honor 2: Hostile Takeover '93
Rage of Honor '87
Ragin' Cajun '90
Rapid Fire '92
Raw Force '81
Raw Target '95
Red Sun Rising '94
Redbelt '08▸
Redemption: Kickboxer 5 '95
Remo Williams: The Adventure Begins '85
Retrievers '82
Return of the Dragon '73
Return of the Street Fighter '74
Return of the Tiger '78
Revenge of the Ninja '83
Ring of Fire '91
Ring of Fire 2: Blood and Steel '92
Ring of Fire 3: Lion Strike '94
Ring of Steel '94
Riot '96
Roller Blade '85
Romeo Must Die '00
Rumble in the Bronx '96
Sanshiro Sugata '43▸
Sci-Fighter '04
Scorpion '86
Shanghai Knights '03
Shaolin Soccer '01
Shogun's Ninja '83
Shootfighter: Fight to the Death '93
Shootfighter 2: Kill or Be Killed! '96
Showdown '93
Showdown in Little Tokyo '91
Sidekicks '93
Silent Assassins '88
Silver Rage '82
Silver Hawk '04
Sister Street Fighter '76
Slaughter in San Francisco '81
Sleepy Eyes of Death: The Chinese Jade '63
Sloane '84
Stickfighter '89
The Stranger and the Gunfighter '76
Stranglehold '94
The Street Fighter '74
The Street Fighter's Last Revenge '74
Street Hunter '90
Street Soldiers '91
Supercop '92
Supercop 2 '93
Surf Ninjas '93
Survival Game '87
Sword of Doom '67▸
Sword of Honor '94
Swords of Death '71
Swordsmen in Double Flag Town '91
Sworn to Justice '97
Taken Alive '95
Talons of the Eagle '92
Teenage Mutant Ninja Turtles: The Movie '90
Teenage Mutant Ninja Turtles 2: The Secret of the Ooze '91
Teenage Mutant Ninja Turtles 3 '93
They Call Me Bruce? '82
They Still Call Me Bruce '86
The Three Avengers '80
3 Ninjas '92
3 Ninjas Kick Back '94
3 Ninjas Knuckle Up '95
Throw Down '00

Tiger Claws '91
Tiger Heart '96
Tigershark '87
Tirecop '94
Tirecop 2: The Berlin
  Decision '03
TNT Jackson '75
To Be the Best '93
To the Death '93
Tokyo Warriors '00
Tongs: An American
  Nightmare '88
Too Dog '95
Tough Guy '70
Trancers 3: Deth Lives '92
Triple Impact '92
Tsui Hark's Vampire
  Hunters '02
Tube '03
24 Hours to Midnight '92
Twin Dragons '92
Twin Warriors '93
The Two Great Cavaliers
  '73
U-Violet '06
Undefeatable '94
Unleashed '05
Unmasking the Idol '86
Vampire Assassin '05
Vampire Effect '03
Vampire Raiders—Ninja
  Queen '90
Warrior of Justice '96
Warriors of Heaven and
  Earth '03
Way of the Black Dragon '81
When Taekwondo Strikes
  '83
White Phantom: Enemy of
  Darkness '87
White Tiger '95
Wing Chun '94
Without Mercy '95
The Young Bruce Lee '80
Young Tiger '74
Zatoichi: Master Ichi and a
  Chest of Gold '64
Zatoichi: The Blind
  Swordsman and the
  Chess Expert '65
Zatoichi: The Blind
  Swordsman's Vengeance
  '66
Zatoichi vs. Yojimbo '70

Martyred Pop Icons
see also Rock Stars on
  Film
Beatlemania! The Movie '81
Blue Hawaii '62
The Buddy Holly Story '78
Bus Stop '56
Club Band '78
Clambake '67
The Doors '91
Elvis and Me '88
Elvis: The Movie '79
Fun in Acapulco '63
Highway '01
I Shot Andy Warhol '96
John & Yoko: A Love Story
  '85
King Creole '58
Kissin' Cousins '64
La Bamba '87
Lenny '74
Live a Little, Love a Little '68
Love Me Tender '56
Marilyn: The Untold Story
  '80
Norma Jean and Marilyn '95
Paradise, Hawaiian Style
  '66
Rebel without a Cause '55
Roustabout '64
Sgt. Pepper's Lonely Hearts
  Club Band '78
The Seven Year Itch '55
Speedway '68
Spinout '66
Stardust Memories '80
Stay Away, Joe '68
This Is Elvis '81
Train to Hollywood '66
The Trouble with Girls (and
  How to Get into It) '69

Mass Media
see also From Page;
  Radio
Against the Law '93
America '86
American Tragedy '00
And Nothing But the Truth
  '82
At Home with the Webbers
  '94
The Barefoot Executive '71
Behind the Rising Sun '43
Bigfoot: The Unforgettable
  Encounter '94
Blankman '94
Broadcast Bombshells '95
The Cable Guy '95
A Case of Libel '83
Chill Factor '90
Color of Justice '97
Crimetime '96
A Cry in the Dark '88
Dead Men Don't Die '91
Death Watch '80
Deep Impact '98
Demonstone '89
E. Nick: A Legend in His
  Own Mind '84
Eternity '90
Exiled to Shanghai '37
The Gladiators '70
Good Night, and Good Luck
  '05
Hero '92
Holy Man '98
I Was a Teenage TV
  Terrorist '87
The Image '89
In and Out '97
Indictment: The McMartin
  Trial '95
International House '33
Interview '07
Intern '00
King of the Airwaves '94
The Last Minute '01
The Late Shift '96
Lions for Lambs '07
Lipstick Camera '93
Little Black Book '04
Live! From Death Row '92
Livin' Large '91
The Lost Honor of Katharina
  Blum '75
Love and a .45 '94
Mad City '97
Mastergate '92
Medium Cool '69
Meet Wally Sparks '97
Mrs. Doubtfire '93
Mr. Reliable: A True Story
  '95
My Favorite Year '82
Naked City: A Killer
  Christmas '98
National Lampoon's Attack
  of the 5 Ft. 2 Women '94
Natural Born Killers '94
Network '76
No Such Thing '01
Nothing Sacred '37
Orwell Rolls in His Grave
  '03
Outfoxed: Rupert Murdoch's
  War on Journalism '04
The Passenger '75
Pleasantville '98
Pray TV '80
Primary Colors '98
Prime Suspect '82
Prime Time Murder '92
Primeval '07
Private Parts '96
Quiz Show '94
Ratings Game '84
Raising the Heights '97
Ready to Wear '94
Riders of the Storm '88
RKO 281 '99
Scream '96
Scrooged '88
The Second Civil War '97
The Seduction '82
Serving in Silence: The
  Margarethe
  Cannermeyer Story '95
Sex Through a Window '72
S.F.W. '94
Showtime '02
Soft and Hard '85
Stardom '00
The Story of Esther Costello
  '57
The Stuff '85
Superstar: The Life and
  Times of Andy Warhol
  '90
Tabloid! '88
This Revolution '05
The Thrill of It All! '63
Tomorrow Never Dies '97
Tootsie '82
Trial by Media '90
The Truman Show '98
Tunnelvision '75
24 Hour Party People '01
UHF '89
Videodrome '83
Wayne's World '92
Weapons of Mass
  Distraction '97
Welcome to Sarajevo '97
Wild Horses '95
Witness to the Execution
  '94

Masseurs
At First Sight '98
Breathtaking '00
Happy Times '00
Living Out Loud '98
Love Kills '98
The Mystic Masseur '01
Never Say Never Again '83

Mathemagicians
Agatha Christie's Murder is
  Easy '82
The Bank '01
A Beautiful Mind '01
Breaking the Code '95
The Computer Wore Tennis
  Shoes '69
Conceiving Ada '97
Cube '98
Dear Brigitte '65
Enigma '01
Good Will Hunting '97
Pi '98
Proof '91
Proof '05
Rain Man '88
Raising Genius '04
Real Genius '85
Sphere '97
Stand and Deliver '88
Stand-In '37
21 '08
21 Grams '03

May-December Romance
see also Coming of Age;
  Growing Older;
  Romantic Adventures;
  Romantic Comedy;
  Romantic Drama
After Sex '07
All That Heaven Allows '55
Atlantic City '81
Autumn in New York '00
Cass Timberlane '47
The Cat's Meow '01
The Color of Evening '95
Crush '02
Fascination '04
Forty Shades of Blue '05
The Gang's All Here '43
Georgy Girl '66
Girl with Green Eyes '64
Goodbye Again '61
The Graduate '67
Guinevere '99
Harold and Maude '71
The Housekeeper '02
The Human Stain '03
I Heart Huckabees '04
Live Bait '95
Lolita '62
Lolita '97
Love in the Afternoon '57
The Love Letter '99
Lurec Innocence '97
The Mother '03
Nelly et Monsieur Arnaud
  '95
Our Lady of the Assassins
  '01
The Pallbearer '95
Paris in Spring '35
Perfect Love '96
Prime '05
P.S. '04
The Quiet American '02
Reckless: The Sequel '98
Roman Spring of Mrs. Stone
  '61
Rumor Has It... '05
Sabrina '54
Seducing Maarya '99
Shopgirl '05
Six Days, Seven Nights '98
Suburban Girl '07
That Obscure Object of
  Desire '77
Tim '79
Trojan Eddie '96
Venus '06

The Meaning of Life
The Apostle '97
At Home with the Webbers
  '94
Bad Lands '74
Being Human '94
The Blood of Others '84
Breathing Lessons '94
The Castle '68
The Designated Mourner
  '97
Enc of the Road '70
Field of Dreams '89
The French Lieutenant's
  Woman '81
Full Body Massage '95
Funny Face '95
Galaxies Are Colliding '92
Gospa '94
Heaven Can Wait '43
Heaven Can Wait '78
Here Comes Mr. Jordan
  '41
The Hitchhiker's Guide to
  the Galaxy '05
Joey Breaker '93
Julian Po '97
Land and Freedom '95
Life Upside Down '64
Love and Death '75
Monty Python's The
  Meaning of Life '83
My Life '93
My Own Private Idaho '91
Off the Lip '04
The Razor's Edge '46
The Razor's Edge '84
The Remains of the Day
  '93
Searching For Wooden
  Watermelons '01
Shadowlands '93
The Sheltering Sky '90
Tattoo, a Love Story '02
The Trial '93
Why Has Bodhi-Dharma Left
  for the East '89
Wings of Desire '88
A Woman's a Helluva Thing
  '02
Zabriskie Point '70

Medieval Romps
see also Camelot (Old);
  Historical Drama; Period
  Piece; Swashbucklers
The Adventures of Marco
  Polo '38
The Adventures of Robin
  Hood '38
Army of Darkness '92
Beatrice '88
Becket '64
Being Human '94
The Beloved Rogue '27
Black Knight '01
The Black Rose '50
Braveheart '95
Brothers Lionheart '77
Camelot '67
The Canterbury Tales '71
The Castilian '63
A Challenge for Robin Hood
  '68
Choice of Weapons '76
Chunhyang '00
The Company of Wolves
  '85
Conquest of the Normans
  '62
Deathstalker '83
Deathstalker 2: Duel of the
  Titans '87
The Decameron '70
Decameron Nights '53
Destiny '97
Diane '55
Don Quixote '00
Donkey Skin '70
Dragon Storm '04
Dragonheart '96
Dragonheart: A New
  Beginning '00
Dragonslayer '81
El Cid '61
Excalibur '81
The Fighting Prince of
  Donegal '66
Fire and Sword '82
First Knight '95
The Flame & the Arrow '50
Flesh and Blood '85
Francesco '93
Galgameth '96
Gate of Hell '54
Hamlet '90
Hawk and Castle '67
Hawk the Slayer '81
In the Name of the King: A
  Dungeon Siege Tale '08
Inquisition '76
Ivanhoe '52
Ivanhoe '82
Ivanhoe '97
Jabberwocky '77
Jack the Giant Killer '62
The Juniper Tree '87
Just Visiting '01
King Arthur, the Young
  Warlord '75
Kingdom of Heaven '05
A Knight in Camelot '98
Knights of the Round Table
  '53
A Knight's Tale '01
Kojiro '67
Kristin Lavransdatter '95
Ladyhawke '85
The Lady's Not for Burning
  '87
Lancelot of the Lake '74
Legend '86
Leonor '75
The Lion in Winter '68
The Lion in Winter '03
The Mongols '60
Monty Python and the Holy
  Grail '75
The Name of the Rose '86
Naughty Knights '71
The Navigator '88
Omar Khayyam '57
Onibaba '64
Passion of Joan of Arc '28
Perceval '78
Pippin '81
The Prince of Thieves '48
Prince Valiant '97
Princess of Thieves '01
Quest for Camelot '98
Ran '85
Rashomon '51
The Return of Martin Guerre
  '83
Richard III '55
Robin and Marian '76
Robin Hood '22
Robin Hood '73
Robin Hood '91
Robin Hood: Men in Tights
  '93
Robin Hood: Prince of
  Thieves '91
Robin Hood... The Legend:
  Herne's Son '85
Robin Hood... The Legend:
  Robin Hood and the
  Sorcerer '83
Robin Hood... The Legend:
  The Swords of Wayland
  '83
Robin Hood... The Legend:
  The Time of the Wolf '85
Ruybas '48
Sansho the Bailiff '54
The Scalawag Bunch '75
The Secret of El Zorro '57
Seven Samurai '54
The Seventh Seal '56
Skullduggery '79
Sorceress '88
Star Knight '85
Stealing Heaven '88
Sword & the Dragon '56
Sword in the Stone '63
The Sword & the Sorcerer '82
Sword of Lancelot '63
Sword of Sherwood Forest
  '60
Sword of the Valiant '83
Tales of Robin Hood '52
Temptation of a Monk '94
Tha us Son of Attila '87
The 13th Warrior '99
Throne of Blood '57
Time Bandits '81
Time Trackers '88
Timeline '03
Tor '64
Tristan & Isolde '06
The Undead '57
Unidentified Flying Oddball
  '79
The Vikings '58
Warriors of Heaven and
  Earth '03
When Knights Were Bold
  '36
Wholly Moses! '80
Wizards of the Demon
  Sword '94
Wizards of the Lost
  Kingdom '85
Young Ivanhoe '95
Young Warlord '75
The Zany Adventures of
  Robin Hood '84

Meltdown
see also Disaster Flicks
Above and Beyond '53
Access Code '84
The Amazing Grace & Chuck '87
The Atomic Cafe '82
The Atomic Kid '54
Beneath the Planet of the
  Apes '70
Black Rain '88
Bloodfist 6: Ground Zero '94
Bomb Squad '97
Bombs Away! '66
Broken Arrow '95
Chain Reaction '80
The China Syndrome '79
Cloak and Dagger '46
Control '87
Crimson Tide '95
Critical Mass '00
Cyclotrode "X" '46
Danger Beneath the Sea '02
The Day After '83
The Day the Earth Caught
  Fire '61
The Death Merchant '91
Desert Bloom '86
Dick Barton Strikes Back '48
Disaster at Silc 7 '88

► = rated three bones or higher

Meltdown

Dr. Strangelove, or: How I Learned to Stop Worrying and Love the Bomb '64▲
Doomsday '99
Doomsday+ '01
Enola Gay: The Men, the Mission, the Atomic Bomb '80
Fail-Safe '64▲
Fat Man and Little Boy '89
Final Sanction '89
First Spaceship on Venus '60▲
First Strike '85
First Yank into Tokyo '45
Flight of Black Angel '91
The Fourth Protocol '87▲
Freedom Strike '98
Full Fathom Five '90
Future Kill '85
Geisha Girl '52
Glen and Randa '71
Ground Zero '88▲
H-Man '59
Hiroshima '95▲
Hiroshima Maiden '88
Hiroshima: Out of the Ashes '90▲
I Live in Fear '55▲
Invasion U.S.A. '52
Jackie Chan's First Strike '96▲
A Man Called Rage '84
The Manhattan Project '86
Massive Retaliation '85
Miracle Mile '89▲
Modern Problems '81
Night Siege Project: Shadowchaser 2 '94
Nuclear Conspiracy '85
A Nymphoid Barbarian in Dinosaur Hell '94
Omega Man '71
On the Beach '59▲
On the Beach '00
One Night Stand '84▲
Panic in the Year Zero! '62
The Patriot '86
The Peacekeeper '98
The Peacemaker '97
Plutonium Incident '82
Prisoner in the Middle '74
Radioactive Dreams '86
Rats '83
Reactor '85
The Reflecting Skin '91
Rhapsody in August '91
Rocket Attack U.S.A. '58
The Sacrifice '86▲
Scorcher '02
The Spy Who Loved Me '77
State of Things '82▲
Superman 4: The Quest for Peace '87
TC 2000 '93
Testament '83▲
This Is Not a Test '62
Threads '85▲
True Lies '94
The 27th Day '57
U.S. Seals 2 '01
Unknown World '51
Utopia '51
Voyage to the Bottom of the Sea '61▲
WarGames '83
Warhead '96
When the Wind Blows '86▲
The World Is Not Enough '99
Young Lady Chatterly 2 '85

Memphis

see also American South; Nashville Narratives
The Client '94
Elvis and Me '88
Elvis: The Movie '79
Finding Graceland '98
The Firm '93▲
Forty Shades of Blue '05
Hustle & Flow '05▲
John Grisham's The Rainmaker '97
My Blueberry Nights '07
Mystery Train '89▲
The Silence of the Lambs '91▲
Walk the Line '05▲

Men

see also Dads; Repressed Men; War Between the Sexes
Bachelor Apartment '31
Beefcake '99
The Bible and Gun Club '96
Blades of Glory '07
Carnal Knowledge '71▲
City Hall '95▲
City Slickers '91▲
Escanaba in da Moonlight '01
The Full Monty '96▲
Good Luck '96
The Hammer '07
Hurlyburly '98
Hustler White '96
In the Company of Men '96
The Incredible Shrinking Man '57▲
The King of Kong: A Fistful of Quarters '07
La Grande Bouffe '73▲
Lakeboat '00
The Men's Club '86
Mr. Mom '83▲
90 Days '86
Patti Rocks '88▲
Planet of the Apes '68▲
Raging Bull '80▲
The Saint of Fort Washington '93
School for Scoundrels '06
Sleuth '07
Swingers '96▲
Talk to Her '02▲
Three Men and a Baby '87▲
Three Men and a Cradle '85▲
Thursday's Game '74▲
Truth or Die '86
Twelve Angry Men '97
Up to a Certain Point '83
Vince Vaughn's Wild West Comedy Show '06
Watch It '93▲
When a Man Falls in the Forest '07
Wild Hogs '07
The Wonderful Ice Cream Suit '98
The Young Poisoner's Handbook '94▲

Men in Prison

see also Fugitives; Great Escapes; POW/MIA; Women in Prison
After Innocence '05▲
Against the Wall '94▲
Alias, La Gringa '91
All the Pretty Horses '00
American History X '98
American Me '92▲
Andersonville '95▲
Angels with Dirty Faces '38▲
Animal '05
Animal 2 '07
Animal Factory '00
Appointment with Crime '45
Attica '80▲
Baba '73▲
Bad Boys '83▲
Bait '00
Band of the Hand '86
Beaumarchais the Scoundrel '96
Before Night Falls '00▲
Behind Prison Walls '43
Beyond Re-Animator '03
Beyond the Call '96
Beyond the Walls '84
Birdman of Alcatraz '62▲
Black Lemons '70
Blind Faith '89
Bloodsport 2: The Next Kumite '95
Bloodsport 4: The Dark Kumite '98
Blow '01
Blues Brothers 2000 '98
Botany Bay '53
Boy's Reformatory '39
The Break '97
Break of Dawn '88
Breaker Morant '80▲
Breakout '75
The Brig '64▲
Broken Melody '34
Brubaker '80▲
Brute Force '47▲
Buried Alive '39
Buy & Cell '89
The Cable Guy '96
Caged Heat 2: Stripped of Freedom '94
Caged in Paradiso '89
Call Northside 777 '48▲
Captives '94
Carandiru '03
Catch a Fire '06
Catch Me If You Can '02
Chain Gang Killings '80
The Chair '87
The Chamber '96
Chopper '00
City Without Men '43
Club Fed '90
Colonel Chabert '94
The Color of Freedom '07
Coming Out of the Ice '82▲
Con Air '97▲
Con Games '02
Condemned '29
Confusion of Genders '00
Convict Cowboy '95
Conviction '02
Cool Hand Luke '67▲
The Count of Monte Cristo '12
The Count of Monte Cristo '34▲
The Count of Monte Cristo '74▲
The Count of Monte Cristo '99
The Count of Monte Cristo '02
Crashout '55
Criminal Code '31
Cry Danger '51▲
Dangerous Relations '93
Dark Blue World '01
Darkdrive '98
Dead Man Out '89▲
Dead Right '68
Deadlock '91
Deadlock 2 '94
Death House '88
Death Warrant '90
Deathrow Gameshow '88
The Defiant Ones '58▲
Devil's Canyon '53
The Devil's Cargo '48
The Dirty Dozen '67▲
The Dirty Dozen: The Deadly Mission '87
The Dirty Dozen: The Fatal Mission '88
The Dirty Dozen: The Next Mission '85
Doin' Time '85
Doing Time for Patsy Cline '97
The Domino Principle '77
Double Team '97
Down by Law '86▲
Each Dawn I Die '39
Eagles Attack at Dawn '70
Embassy '72
Empire of the Sun '87▲
Ernest Goes to Jail '90
Escape from Alcatraz '79▲
Escape from Death Row '73
Escape from DS-3 '81
Escape from El Diablo '83
Escape from New York '81▲
The Executioner's Song '82
The Experiment '01
Face/Off '97▲
Fast Walking '82
The Fence '94
The Fiend Who Walked the West '58
First Time Felon '97
The Fixer '68▲
Fled '96
Fortress '93
Fortress 2: Re-Entry '99
Framed '75
Freedom Is Paradise '89▲
Gang Busters '55
Gideon's Trumpet '80▲
The Glass House '72▲
The Grave '95
The Green Mile '99▲
Greenfingers '00
Gulag '85
Half-Baked '97
Half Past Dead '02
Hangfire '91
Hard Frame '70
Hard Justice '95
The Hard Word '02
He Got Game '98▲
The Hill '65
Hold 'Em Jail '32
House Across the Bay '40
The Hurricane '99▲
I Am a Fugitive from a Chain Gang '32▲
I Killed That Man '42
In God's Hands '98
In Hell '03
In Hot Pursuit '77
In the Name of the Father '93▲
An Innocent Man '89
Inside '96▲
Instinct '99
Invasion '65
The Invisible Strangler '76
Jailbreakin' '72
Jailhouse Rock '57▲
The Jericho Mile '79
John Carpenter's Ghosts of Mars '01
Johnny Handsome '89▲
Kansas City Confidential '52▲
The Keeper '96
Killer: A Journal of Murder '95
The Killing Yard '01
King of the Damned '36
Kiss of the Spider Woman '85▲
L'Addition '85
Land of the Blind '06
The Last Castle '01
The Last Detail '73▲
Last Rites '98
Le Trou '59▲
Leo '02
Les Miserables '95
Les Miserables '97▲
A Lesson Before Dying '99▲
Let's Go to Prison '06
Life '99
Life '99
The Life of David Gale '03
The Life of Emile Zola '37▲
Lilies '96
The Line '80
Little Red Schoolhouse '36
Live Flesh '97▲
Live! From Death Row '92
Lockdown '00
Lockup '89
The Longest Yard '74▲
The Longest Yard '05
Lost Highway '96
Lucie Aubrac '98
Lucky Break '01
A Man Escaped '57▲
Man of La Mancha '72
The Man Who Broke 1,000 Chains '87
Maximum Security '87
McKenzie Break '70▲
McVicar '80
Mean Frank and Crazy Tony '75
Mean Machine '01
Memron '04
Midnight Express '78▲
Mrs. Soffel '84
Mr. Frost '89
Monster's Ball '01▲
Moon 44 '90
Most Wanted '97
Murder in the First '95
Mutiny in the Big House '39
My Boys Are Good Boys '78
My Cousin Vinny '92▲
New Crime City: Los Angeles 2020 '94
New Eden '94
The New Guy '02
The Night and the Moment '94
The Night Visitor '70
No Escape '94
Ocean's Eleven '01▲
Off the Wall '82
On the Yard '79
Out in Fifty '99
Out of Sight '98▲
Papillon '73▲
Pardon Us '31
Payback '94
Penitentiary '79
Penitentiary 2 '82
Penitentiary 3 '87
Phantom Empire '87
Pressure Point '62▲
Prison '88
Prison Break '38
Prison on Fire '87
Prison on Fire 2 '91
Prison Planet '92
Prison Train '38
The Prisoner '90
The Prisoner of Shark Island '36
Pros & Cons '99
Proximity '00
The Pursuit of Happiness '70
Real Bullets '90
Red Dragon '02
Redeemer '02
Return to Paradise '98▲
Riot '69
Riot in Cell Block 11 '54▲
The Road to Guantanamo '06
The Rock '96▲
Runaway Train '85▲
Sade '00
St. Michael Had a Rooster '72
Samar '62
San Quentin '37
Scum '79▲
A Sense of Freedom '78▲
The Shawshank Redemption '94▲
Shoeshine '47▲
Shooting Fish '98
Short Eyes '79▲
Shot in the Heart '01▲
Slam '98
Slaughterhouse Rock '88
A Slipping Down Life '99
Some Mother's Son '96▲
Soul Vengeance '75
Space Rage '86
Spy Game '01
Steel City '06
Stir Crazy '80
The Survivor '98
Taking Care of Business '90
Tank '83
Terminal Island '73
Terror of the Bloodhunters '62
Terror on Alcatraz '86
There Was a Crooked Man '70▲
There's Something about Mary '98▲
They Never Come Back '32
They Went That-a-Way & That-a-Way '78
Timelock '99
Tomb of the Undead '72
Torture Ship '39
Tracked '98
Tracks '05
Trading Places '83▲
Triumph of the Spirit '89▲
The Truce '96▲
True Crime '99
Truth or Die '86
Two-Way Stretch '60▲
Ulee's Gold '97▲
Undisputed '02
Undisputed II: Last Man Standing '06
Unshackled '00
Up the River '30
The Visit '00▲
Warden of Red Rock '01
Weeds '87▲
Who Is Cletis Tout? '02
William Faulkner's Old Man '97
Wishmaster 2: Evil Never Dies '98
Without Evidence '96
Women's Prison Massacre '85
XXX: State of the Union '05
Yol '82▲

Mental Hospitals

see also Doctors & Nurses; Sanity Check; Shrinks
Asylum '05
Beyond the Wall of Sleep '06
Boogeyman 2 '07
Crazy as Hell '02
Crazylove '05
Elling '01
Final '01
Girl, Interrupted '99
Gothika '03
Halloween: Resurrection '02
Happy Hell Night '92
House of Fools '02
The Jacket '05
Killer Instinct '00
Kings and Queen '04▲
Kisses in the Dark '97
A Light in the Darkness '02
Madhouse '04
Manic '01
Murder Without Conviction '04
On the Edge '00
Revolution 9 '01
Screaming Dead '03
Session 9 '01
Shoot or Be Shot '02
Stateside '04
A Tale of Two Sisters '03▲
Tarnation '03
When Angels Fly '82
Woman Condemned '33

Mental Retardation

see also Physical Problems; Savants
All the Little Animals '98
Behind the Mask '99
Bill '81▲
Bill: On His Own '83▲
Charly '68▲
A Child Is Waiting '63▲
A Dangerous Woman '93
Dark Night of the Scarecrow '81
A Day in the Death of Joe Egg '71▲
Digging to China '98
Dominick & Eugene '88▲
Dreamcatcher '03
The Eighth Day '95▲
Family Pictures '93▲
Gideon '99
Gigli '03
Guarding Eddy '04
Heart of Dragon '85
Hit Me '96
Homer and Eddie '89
House of D '04
I Am Sam '01
It Came from the Sky '98
The Judgement '04
King of the Jungle '01
Larry '74
L'Enfant d'Eau '95
The Lookout '07▲
Lovey: A Circle of Children 2 '82
Malcolm '86
Mifune '99
Milwaukee, Minnesota '03
Molly '99

▲ = rated three bones or higher

My Brother '06
My Louisiana Sky '02
Of Mice and Men '35▶
Of Mice and Men '81▶
Of Mice and Men '92▶
The Other Sister '98
Pauline and Paulette '01
Radio '03
Rain Man '88▶
The Rain People '69▶
Shooting Fish '98
Sling Blade '96▶
Slipping Into Darkness '88
Some Folks Call It a Sling Blade '94▶
There's Something about Mary '98▶
Sweetie '89
Square Dance '87
Tim '79
Two of a Kind '82
The Village '04
What's Eating Gilbert Grape '93▶
The Wizard '89
The Woman Who Willed a Miracle '83
The Yarn Princess '94
ZigZag '02▶

Mermaids
see also Folklore & Legends
Aquamarine '06
Beach Blanket Bingo '65▶

Night Tide '63
Sea People '00
She Creature '01
Splash '84

Mercenaries
Airboss '97.
Babylon AD '08
Barb Wire '96
Blast '04
Blood, Guts, Bullets and Octane '99
Bridge of Dragons '99
A Bullet for the General '68
The Chronicles of Riddick '04
Codename: Term nate '90
Codename: Wildceess '84
Congo '95
Counterforce '87
Crossfire '98
Dark of the Sun '68
The Dogs of War '81
The Foreigner '03
Franz '72
The General Died at Dawn '36▶
George A. Romero's Land of the Dead '05▶
Green Inferno '72
Hired to Kill '91
Honeybaby '74
Honor Among Thieves '68
Last Man Standing '96
Lethal Weapon 3 '92
The Lost World: Jurassic Park 2 '97
The Magnificent Seven '60▶
The Mercenaries '62
The Mercenaries '80
Mercenary '96
Mercenary 2: Thick and Thin '97
Mercenary Fighters '88
Mission... Kill '85
The Peacekeeper '98
Perfect Target '98
Proof of Life '00
Rambo '08
RoboCop 3 '91
Ronin '98
Skeleton Coast '89
Soldier's Fortune '91
Streets of Fire '84
The Substitute '96
The Substitute 2: School's Out '97
The Substitute 3: Winner Takes All '99
The Target '02
The Transporter '02
The Ultimate Weapon '97
Wild Geese '78
World Gone Wild '88
Yojimbo '61▶

Metamorphosis
see also Genetics;
Werewolves
An American Werewolf in London '81▶
Boogie Nights '97▶
Cat People '42▶
Cat People '82
The Curse of the Werewolf '61
Earth vs. the Spider '01
The Fly '58▶
The Fly '86▶
The Fly 2 '89
The Howling '81▶
I Was a Teenage Werewolf '57
Jack Frost '98
Jungle Captive '45
Jungle Woman '44
The Lair of the White Worm '88,
Miss Congeniality '00
Naked Lunch '91▶
The Nutty Professor '96▶
The Nutty Professor 2: The Klumps '00
Silver Bullet '85
Slither '06▶
Species '95
Stephen King's Thinner '96
Vampire in Brooklyn '95
The Wasp Woman '60▶
When the Cat's Away '96▶
Wolfen '81▶
The Wolfman '82

Meteors, Asteroids, and Comets
see also Alien Beings—
Vicious; Disaster Flicks;
Space Operas
Alien Dead '79
Armageddon '98
Black Horizon '01
The Blob '58
The Blob '88▶
Creepshow '82
The Day It Came to Earth '77
Day of the Triffids '63▶
Deep Impact '98
Die, Monster, Die! '65
Dinosaur '00
Dragon Storm '04
Falling Fire '97
Fire in the Sky '36
The Invisible Ray '36
Judgment Day '99
Lifeforce '85
Mammoth '06
Meteor '79
The Meteor Man '93
Night of the Comet '84
The Monolith Monsters '57
The Phantom Creeps '39
Return of the Aliens: The Deadly Spawn '83
Stalker '79▶
Teenage Monster '57
Trapped in Space '94
Tycus '98

Mexico
see also Central America
Adios, Sabata '71
Across the Bridge '57
Against All Odds '84
The Alamo '04
All Souls Day '05
All the Pretty Horses '00
Amores Perros '00▶
And Starring Pancho Villa as Himself '03▶
Babel '06▶
Battle in Heaven '05
Battle Shock '55
Beat '00
Big Steal '49▶
The Black Scorpion '57
Bloody Proof '99,
Borderline '80
Bordertown '06
The Border '82▶
Breakout '75
A Bullet for the General '68
Bullfighter & the Lady '50
Bullfighters '45
Captain from Castile '47▶
Catwoman '04
The Cisco Kid '94
Circus Angel '65▶
The Company of Wolves '85,
Commando Squad '87
Compañeros '70
Crazy from the Heart '91▶
The Crime of Father Amaro '02▶
Crocodile 2: Death Swamp '01
Danzon '91▶
Deep Crimson '96
Delta Farce '07
Desperado '95▶
Django '68
Double Take '01
Drug Wars: The Camarena Story '90▶
Duck Season '04▶
Dust to Glory '05▶
8 Heads in a Duffel Bag '96
El Mariachi '93▶
Escape from Cell Block 3 '74
The Falcon in Mexico '44
Five Giants from Texas '66
Found Alive '34
Frida '84
From Dusk Till Dawn '95▶
From Dusk Till Dawn 3: The Hangman's Daughter '99
Fun in Acapulco '63▶
Glory Road '06▶
Goal! The Dream Begins '06
The Heartbreak Kid '07
Highway Patrolman '91
His Kind of Woman '51▶
Holiday in Mexico '46
A Home of Our Own '75
The Hottest State '06
I Witness '03
In 'n Out '86
In Pursuit '00
In the Pit '05
Interval '73
Jeopardy '53
John Carpenter Presents Vampires: Los Muertos '02

Juarez '39
Kid from Spain '32
Kill Bill Vol. 2 '04▶
Kings of the Sun '63
La Cucaracha '99
La Mujer de Mi Hermano '06
Like A Brice '94▶
Lolo '92
Los Olvidados '50▶
Love Has Many Faces '65
Lucia, Lucia '03
The Magnificent Seven '60▶
Man on Fire '04
Marriage on the Rocks '65
The Masked Rider '41
The Matador '06▶
The Mexican '01
Mexican Hayride '48
Mexico City '00
Midaq Alley '95▶
Missing Pieces '00
My Father, My Mother, My Brothers and My Sisters '99
Nacho Libre '06
The Night of the Iguana '64▶
Octaman '71
Old Gringo '89
On the Line '83

Once Upon a Time in Mexico '03▶
One Man's Hero '98
Out to Sea '97
Outta Time '01
The Pearl '48
Perfect Assassins '98
The Professionals '66▶
The Proud Ones '53
Puerto Vallarta Squeeze '04
Pure Luck '91
Que Viva Mexico '32▶
Red Salute '35
Reed: Insurgent Mexico '73
The Road to El Dorado '00
Rough Magic '95▶
The Ruins '08
Rx '06
Sanitos '99
The Scout '94
Second Chance '53
Selena '97▶
Shark Attack 3: Megalodon '02
Sonny and Jed '73
South of Santa Fe '32
Spanglish '04
Survival Run '80
Three Amigos '86▶
The Three Burials of Melquiades Estrada '05▶
The Torch '50
Touch of Evil '58▶
Traffic '00▶
Treasure of the Sierra Madre '48▶
Two Mules for Sister Sara '70▶
Under the Volcano '84▶
Vadez Is Coming '71
Vera Cruz '53
Villa Rides '68
Vintage Model '92
Viva Knievel! '77
Viva Villa! '34▶
Viva Zapata! '52▶
The Waller '06
Warlords from Hell '87
Way of the Gun '00▶
The White Orchid '54
The Whole Ten Yards '04
Wild Rovers '71
A Winter Tan '88
Y Tu Mama Tambien '01▶

Miami
see also American South
Ace Ventura: Pet Detective '93▶
All About the Benjamins '02
Analyze This '98▶
Any Given Sunday '99▶
Bachelor Party 2: The Last Temptation '08
Bad Boys '95▶
Bad Boys 2 '03
Band of the Hand '86
Big Trouble '02▶
The Birdcage '95▶
The Blackout '97
Blood & Wine '96
Catherine's Grove '98
Chasing Papi '03▶
The Crew '00
Cronicas '04
Curdled '95
Elmore Leonard's Gold Coast '97
Fair Game '95
Fires Within '91
Forever Mine '99
Get Shorty '95▶
Illtown '96
In the Shadows '01
Instinct '99
Lansky '99
The Last Marshal '99
Laws of Deception '97
Let's Talk About Sex '98
Miami Beach Cops '93
Miami Blues '90
Miami Cops '89
Miami Horror '87
Miami Hustle '96
Miami Rhapsody '95

Miami Supercops '85
Miami Vendetta '87
Miami Vice '84
Miami Vice '06
Moon over Miami '41▶
Nasty Hero '89
Notorious '46▶
Off and Running '90
Out of Sight '98▶
The Perez Family '94
The Pest '96
The Prince and the Pauper '07
Pronto '97
Push '06
Reno 911!: Miami '07
Ride '98
Scam '93
Scarface '83▶
Stick '85
There's Something about Mary '98▶
Tony Rome '67
Transporter 2 '05
2 Fast 2 Furious '03
Wild Things '98

Middle East
see also Desert War;
Foreign Legion; Deserts;
Genies; Islam; Israel;
Persian Gulf/Iraq War;
Terrorism
Abbott and Costello Meet the Mummy '55
Action in Arabia '44
A.D. '85
Afghan Knights '07
Ali Baba and the Forty Thieves '43▶
Ali Baba and the 40 Thieves '54▶
All the King's Men '99
The Ambassador '84
The Arab Conspiracy '76
Arabian Nights '42
Arabian Nights '00
The Assignment '97
Bagdad '49
Beaufort '07▶
Black Thunder '98
Bloodstone '88
Boutique '04
Brothers '05▶
Caramel '07▶
A Casualty of War '90
Chain of Command '95
Chronicle of a Disappearance '96
Control Room '04▶
Counterforce '87
The Crusades '35
Cup Final '92
Desert Thunder '99
A Different Loyalty '04▶
Eagles Attack at Dawn '70
The Egyptian '54
Escape: Human Cargo '98▶
Exorcist: The Beginning '04
Fahrenheit 9/11 '04▶
Fictitious Marriage '88
Five Graves to Cairo '43▶
Flame of Araby '51
Flanders '06▶
The Flight of the Phoenix '65,
Gabbeh '96▶
The Glory Boys '84
The Great Armored Car Swindle '64
Gunnar Palace '04▶
The Guns and the Fury '83
Halfmoon '95
Hamsin '83▶
Hanna K. '83
Harem '99
Harum Scarum '65
Held Hostage '91
Here and Elsewhere '75
Hidalgo '04
Hijacking Catastrophe: 9/11, Fear and the Selling of America '04
Honeybaby '74,
Hostages '93▶

Ilsa, Harem Keeper of the Oil Sheiks '76
The Invincible Six '68
Iran: Days of Crisis '91
Iron Eagle '86
Iron Eagle 2 '88
Ishtar '87
Jarhead '05
The Jewel of the Nile '85
Joseph '95
Kandahar '01
The Keeper: The Legend of Omar Khayyam '05
Khartoum '66▶
Killing Streets '91
King Richard and the Crusaders '54
The Kingdom '07▶
Land of Plenty '04
Lawrence of Arabia '62▶
Legend of the Lost Tomb '97
Leila '97
Life and Nothing More... '92
The Lighthorsemen '87▶
The Lone Runner '88
Looking for Comedy in the Muslim World '06
Maroon'd in Iraq '02
A Matter of WHO '62
Mercenary '96
A Mighty Heart '07▶
Moses '96
The Nativity Story '06
Occupation: Dreamland '05,
Orde Wingate '76
Osama '03▶
Our Music '04
Paradise '82
Paradise Now '05▶
Passion in the Desert '97
The Passion of the Christ '04▶
Peace, Propaganda & the Promised Land '04
Raiders of the Lost Ark '81▶
The Road to Guantanamo '06▶
The Road to Morocco '42▶
The Roof '53
Roseburg '75
Sedat '83
The Sheik '21▶
The Silences of the Palace '94▶
Silent Waters '03
Sirocco '51
Son of Ali Baba '52
Spartan '04▶
The Spy Who Loved Me '77
Steel Sharks '97
Surface to Air '98
Syriana '05▶
Team America: World Police '04▶
Through the Olive Trees '94▶
The Tiger and the Snow '05
Tom Apart '89
Trident Force '89
Turtles Can Fly '04▶
Uncovered: The War on Iraq '04
Unveiled '94
Voices of Iraq '04▶
Wall '04
The War Within '05
Warbirds '88
A Wedding in Galilee '87▶
West Beirut '98
Yellow Asphalt '01

Midlife Crisis
see also Adultery;
Growing Older; Straitlaced Suburbia
American Beauty '99▶
Being Julia '04▶
The Black Marble '79▶
Box of Moonlight '96
Broken Flowers '05▶
City Slickers '91▶
Falling in Love Again '80
Fortunes '05
Full Moon in Blue Water '88
The Hammer '07

▶ = rated three bones or higher

I Love You, Alice B. Toklas! '68
I Think I Love My Wife '07
King of the Corner '04
L'Ennui '98
Loving '70
The Man of My Life '06
The Matador '06
Milk and Honey '03
Notre Histoire '84
On a Clear Day '05
The Savages '07
Shall We Dance? '04
Shirley Valentine '89
Sideways '04
States of Control '98
Step Brothers '08
The Tempest '82
Vincent, Francois, Paul and the Others '76
The Weather Man '05
When a Man Falls in the Forest '07
Whole New Thing '05
Wild Hogs '07

Military: Air Force
see also Airborne

Afterburn '92
Air Force '43
Battle Hymn '57
Black Thunder '98
Call to Glory '84
Desert Thunder '99
God is My Co-Pilot '45
Hot Shots! '91
Hot Shots! Part Deux '93
Mach 2 '00
McHale's Navy Joins the Air Force '65
Memphis Belle '90
Operation Haylift '50
The Pentagon Wars '98
Rally 'Round the Flag, Boys! '58
Rescue Dawn '06
Sergeant Matovich vs. the U.S. Air Force '78
Space Cowboys '00
Storm Catcher '99
Strategic Air Command '55
Tactical Assault '99
Terminator 3: Rise of the Machines '03
Terror Street '54
Valiant '05
War Lover '62

Military: Army

Active Stealth '99
After the Rain '99
American Soldiers '05
Band of Brothers '01
The Base '99
Basic '03
Battle of the Bulge '65
Battle of the Commandos '71
Behind the Lines '97
Big Bear '98
Big Red One '80
Big Steal '49
Black Hawk Down '01
Bloody Sunday '01
Buffalo Soldiers '97
Call Out the Marines '42
Casualties of War '89
Chaos '00
Combat Killers '80
Courage Under Fire '96
The Court Martial of Billy Mitchell '55
The Court Martial of Jackie Robinson '90
The Crossing '00
Dead Men Can't Dance '97
D.I. '57
The Dirty Dozen '67
The Dirty Dozen: The Deadly Mission '87
The Dirty Dozen: The Fatal Mission '88
The Dirty Dozen: The Next Mission '85
Elvira Madigan '67
Ernest in the Army '97
Evolution '01
Fatal Error '99
Fatal Vision '84
A Foreign Affair '48
Francis Joins the WACs '54
The Gay Deceivers '69
The General's Daughter '99
Geronimo: An American Legend '93
Gettysburg '93
G.I. Blues '60
Gods and Generals '03
Godzilla '98
The Good German '06
The Great Raid '05
The Green Berets '68
Hart's War '02
Home of the Brave '06
The Hunt for Eagle One: Crash Point '06
The Hunted '03
Ignition '01
In Pursuit of Honor '95
In the Valley of Elah '07
Independence Day '96
The Last Castle '01
Lost Battalion '01
MacArthur '77
The Major and the Minor '42
M*A*S*H '70
M*A*S*H: Goodbye, Farewell & Amen '83
A Midnight Clear '92
The Missing '03
Never Wave at a WAC '52
New World '95
1915 '82
1941 '79
Occupation: Dreamland '05
One Little Indian '73
One Man's Hero '98
Operation Dumbo Drop '95
Patton '70
The Peacemaker '97
The Perfect Furlough '59
Platoon '86
Platoon Leader '87
Private Benjamin '80
Rangers '00
Ravenous '99
Red Salute '35
Redacted '07
Saving Private Ryan '98
Serving in Silence: The Margarethe Cammermeyer Story '95
The Siege '98
Slayer '06
Soldier '98
Soldier's Girl '03
A Soldier's Story '84
Something for the Boys '44
Spirit: Stallion of the Cimarron '02
Starship Troopers '97
Steel '97
Stop-Loss '08
The Story of a Three Day Pass '68
The Story of G.I. Joe '45
Stripes '81
Taking Sides '01
Taxi to the Dark Side '07
The Thin Red Line '64
The Thin Red Line '98
Three Kings '99
Tigerland '00
To End All Wars '01
Tomahawk '51
The Trench '99
28 Days Later '02
28 Weeks Later '07
UKM: The Ultimate Killing Machine '06
Wackiest Ship in the Army '61
The Wall '99
We'll Meet Again '82
When Trumpets Fade '98
When Willie Comes Marching Home '50
X2: X-Men United '03
XXX: State of the Union '05
Yossi & Jagger '02

Military Comedy
see also Comedy; War, General

Abbott and Costello in the Foreign Legion '50
Abroad with Two Yanks '44
Article 99 '92
As You Were '51
At War with the Army '50
The Baby and the Battleship '56
Basic Training '86
Best Defense '84
Best Foot Forward '43
Biloxi Blues '88
Black and White in Color '76
The Captain from Koepenick '56
Carbide and Sorrel '63
Caught in the Draft '41
Chesty Anderson USN '76
Clipped Wings '53
Combat Academy '86
Delta Farce '07
Don't Go Near the Water '57
Down Periscope '96
Ensign Pulver '64
Ernest in the Army '97
The Flying Deuces '39
Follow That Camel '67
Follow the Leader '44
Francis Goes to West Point '52
Francis in the Navy '55
Francis Joins the WACs '54
The Gendarme of Saint-Tropez '64
Getting Wasted '80
G.I. Blues '60
G.I. Jane '91
Going Under '91
Here Come the Marines '52
Hillbilly Blitzkrieg '42
Hot Shots! '91
Hot Shots! Part Deux '93
In the Army Now '94
Jumping Jacks '52
Leave It to the Marines '51
Major Payne '95
A Man Called Sarge '90
M*A*S*H '70
M*A*S*H: Goodbye, Farewell & Amen '83
McHale's Navy '64
McHale's Navy Joins the Air Force '65
Miracle of Morgan's Creek '44
Mr. Walkie Talkie '52
The Mouse That Roared '59
Never Wave at a WAC '52
1941 '79
No Time for Sergeants '58
The Odd Squad '86
Off Limits '53
Operation Dames '59
The Perfect Furlough '59
Private Benjamin '80
Private Manoeuvres '83
Private Navy of Sgt. O'Farrell '68
The Private War of Major Benson '55
Privates on Parade '84
Renaissance Man '94
The Sad Sack '57
Sgt. Bilko '95
She's in the Army Now '81
Snuffy Smith, Yard Bird '42
Soldier in the Rain '63
Stripes '81
Suppose They Gave a War and Nobody Came? '70
Tanks a Million '41
Three Legionnaires '37
23 1/2 Hours Leave '37
The Virgin Soldiers '69
Viva Max '69
Weekend Pass '84
Weekend Warriors '86
We're in the Legion Now '37
We're in the Navy Now '27
The West Point Story '50

Military Crimes & Trials
see also Foreign Intrigue; Military; Air Force; Military; Army; Military Comedy; Military; Foreign; Military; Navy; Order in the Court

Buffalo Soldiers '01
The Caine Mutiny '54
The Caine Mutiny Court Martial '88
Carrington, V.C. '54
Casualties of War '89
The Clay Pigeon '49
The Court Martial of Billy Mitchell '55
The Court Martial of Jackie Robinson '90
A Few Good Men '92
A Glimpse of Hell '01
Hart's War '02
High Crimes '02
The Hill '65
Ignition '01
The Last Castle '01
One Kill '00
Paths of Glory '57
Rules of Engagement '00
A Rumor of War '80
Sergeant Matovich vs. the U.S. Air Force '78
Sergeant Rutledge '60
South Sea Woman '53
Under the Flag of the Rising Sun '72

Military: Foreign

The Adventures of Werner Holt '65
All Quiet on the Western Front '30
All Quiet on the Western Front '79
All the King's Men '99
Ambush '99
The Ascent '76
Atonement '07
Battle of Britain '69
The Beast '88
Beaufort '07
Black and White in Color '76
Breaker Morant '80
The Brylcreem Boys '96
Captain Corelli's Mandolin '01
Captains of the Clouds '42
Captive Heart '47
The Charge of the Light Brigade '36
The Charge of the Light Brigade '68
The Cuckoo '02
Cup Final '92
Das Boot '81
Days of Glory '06
The Devil is a Woman '35
Devils on the Doorstep '00
Die Another Day '02
Dog Soldiers '01
Doomsday '08
Dresden '06
The Duchess of Langeais '07
Enemy at the Gates '00
Escape from Sobibor '87
The Fighting Rats of Tobruk '44
Five Cartridges '60
Five Graves to Cairo '43
Flags of Our Fathers '06
Flanders '06
For the Moment '94
The Four Feathers '02
Gallipoli '81
Gloria '89
The Hasty Heart '86
The Hill '65
Hostile Waters '97
The Hunt for Red October '90
I Was Nineteen '68
I'll Remember April '99
In Which We Serve '42
An Indecent Obsession '85
The Indian Tomb '21
The Informant '97
King and Country '64
Kippur '00
Lagaan: Once upon a Time in India '01
The Last Lieutenant '94
The Last September '99
Letters from Iwo Jima '06
The Lighthorsemen '87
The Marquise of O '76
The Milky Way '97
Mister Drake's Duck '50
Night of the Generals '67
No Man's Land '01
100 Days Before the Command '90
The One That Got Away '96
Passion in the Desert '97
Passion of Love '82
Pretty Village, Pretty Flame '96
Prisoner of the Mountains '96
Savior '98
The Scarlet Tunic '97
Sharpe's Challenge '06
633 Squadron '64
Soldier of Orange '78
Stairway to Heaven '46
Stalingrad '94
Story of a Prostitute '65
Sword of Honour '01
The 300 Spartans '62
The 317th Platoon '65
Time of Favor '00
To End All Wars '01
Traffic '00
Troubles '88
Two Men Went to War '02
The Unknown Soldier '98
Victory at Entebbe '76
Warriors '02
The Water Horse: Legend of the Deep '07
White Badge '97
The Widow of Saint-Pierre '00
The Wind That Shakes the Barley '06
Woyzeck '78
Wozzeck '47
Zafarina '94
Zone 39 '96

Military: Marines

Annapolis '06
Back to Bataan '45
Bataan '43
Battle Cry '55
Dangerous Evidence: The Lori Jackson Story '99
Death Before Dishonor '87
Doom '05
A Few Good Men '92
Flags of Our Fathers '06
Flying Leathernecks '51
Full Metal Jacket '87
Guadalcanal Diary '43
The Halls of Montezuma '50
Heartbreak Ridge '86
High Crimes '02
Jarhead '05
Leprechaun 4: In Space '96
The Marine '06
Most Wanted '97
One Kill '00
Perfect Crime '97
Platoon '86
Pork Chop Hill '59
Quicksand '01
The Real Glory '39
The Rock '96
Rules of Engagement '00
Sands of Iwo Jima '49
Second in Command '05
The Siege of Firebase Gloria '89
Sniper 2 '02
South Sea Woman '53
Spartan '04
Stateside '04
Surface to Air '98
The Walking Dead '94
The Wind and the Lion '75
Windtalkers '02

Military: Navy
see also Sail Away

Agent Red '00
Anchors Aweigh '45
Annapolis '28
Annapolis '06
An Annapolis Story '55
Antwone Fisher '02
Behind Enemy Lines '01
The Bridges at Toko-Ri '55
The Caine Mutiny '54
Chasers '94
Common Ground '00
Crimson Tide '95
Danger Beneath the Sea '02
Dive Bomber '41
Down Periscope '96
Enemy Below '57
A Few Good Men '92
Fighting Seabees '44
The Fighting Sullivans '42
Flags of Our Fathers '06
Francis in the Navy '55
Freedom Strike '98
The Gallant Hours '60
G.I. Jane '01
A Glimpse of Hell '01
Hellcats of the Navy '57
Here Come the Waves '45
The Honeymoon Machine '61
Horatio Hornblower '99
Horatio Hornblower: The Adventure Continues '01
Hostile Waters '97
The Hunt for Red October '90
In Love and War '91
John Paul Jones '59
The Last Detail '73
The Man Without a Country '73
Master and Commander: The Far Side of the World '03
McHale's Navy '64
McHale's Navy '97
McHale's Navy Joins the Air Force '65
Men of Honor '00
Mission of the Shark '91
Mister Roberts '55
Moment to Moment '66
Mutiny '99
Navy Blue and Gold '37
The Navy Comes Through '42
Navy SEALS '90
Navy vs. the Night Monsters '66
Navy Way '44
No Man Is an Island '62
No Way Out '87
An Officer and a Gentleman '82
On the Town '49
Operation Bikini '63
Operation Petticoat '59
The Pacifier '05
Pearl '78
Pearl Harbor '01
Perfect Crime '97
Private Navy of Sgt. O'Farrell '68
PT 109 '63
Rodgers & Hammerstein's South Pacific '01
Run Silent, Run Deep '58
Sabotage '96
Sailor Beware '52
The Sand Pebbles '66
Seas Beneath '31
The Sender '98
Shadow Warriors '97
Skirts Ahoy! '52
South Pacific '58
Stateside '04
Stealth '05
Steel Sharks '97
Submerged '00
Surface to Air '98
Tears of the Sun '03
They Were Expendable '45
Top Gun '86
True Vengeance '97
U-571 '00
Under Siege '92

▲ = rated three bones or higher

Military School

Child's Play 3 '91
Damien: Omen 2 '78
Dress Gray '86▶
Evilspeak '82
Junior Army '42
Major Payne '95
The Private War of Major Benson '55
Renaissance Man '94
Taps '81
Toy Soldiers '84
Up the Academy '80
U.S. Navy SEALS: Dead or Alive '02
U.S. Seals '98
U.S. Seals 2 '01
Wolverine '96
XXX: State of the Union '05
Yankee Buccaneer '52

Military Westerns

see also Military: Army; Westerns

The Alamo '60▶
Bugles in the Afternoon '52
Cavalry Charge '51
Cavalry Command '63
Escape from Fort Bravo '53
The Glory Trail '36
Hawmps! '76
Hondo '53▶
The Horse Soldiers '59
In Pursuit of Honor '95
Pharoah's Army '95
Rio Grande '50▶
Sergeant Rutledge '60▶
She Wore a Yellow Ribbon '49▶
Shenandoah '65▶
Soldier Blue '70
They Died with Their Boots On '41▶
Virginia City '40▶

Milwaukee

see also Romantic Mystery

American Movie '99▶
BASEketball '98
Dawn of the Dead '04▶
Ed's Next Move '96
The Giant Spider Invasion '75
Mr. 3000 '04

Miners & Mining

Ace in the Hole '51▶
Act of Vengeance '86
The Adventures of Bullwhip Griffin '66
Angels Die Hard '84
Backlash: Oblivion 2 '95
Ballad of Cable Hogue '70▶
The Big Man: Crossing the Line '91▶
Billy Elliot '00▶
Black Fury '35▶
Blood Diamond '06
Brassed Off '96
Burning Rage '84
Cannibal! The Musical '96
Chained Heat 3: Hell Mountain '98
Challenge to White Fang '86
The Christmas Coal Mine Miracle '77
The Claim '00
Coal Miner's Daughter '80▶
The Corn Is Green '79▶
Dear Wendy '05
Dudley Do-Right '99
Eureka Stockade '49
Fighting Cowboy '33
Fighting Valley '43
Fire Down Below '97
Flaming Frontiers '38
Gangster's Den '45
Gangsters of the Frontier '44
Garden of Evil '54
Germinal '93▶
Ghost Town Renegades '47
Girl Rush '44
Goldrush: A Real Life Alaskan Adventure '98
Grand Canyon Trail '48
Green Fire '55
The Hallelujah Trail '65
Harlan County War '00
Harlan County, U.S.A. '76▶
Haunted Gold '32
Hills of Utah '51
How Green Was My Valley '41▶
Human Hearts '22
Jack London's The Call of the Wild '97
The Jackals '67
Kameradschaft '31▶
King Solomon's Mines '85
Little Church Around the Corner '23
Lucky Texan '34
The Men from Music Mountain '38
Margaret's Museum '95▶
Matewan '87▶
McCabe & Mrs. Miller '71▶
Molly Maguires '70
Naked Hills '56
'Neath Canadian Skies '46
No Man's Law '27
North Country '05
North Star '96
North to Alaska '60▶
The Nugget '02
October Sky '99▶
Out of the Black '01
Paint Your Wagon '69
Pale Rider '85▶
Panama Flo '32
Phantom Gold '38
Picture Windows '95
Poldark '96
Poldark 2 '75▶
Precious Find '96
The Rainbow Gang '73
Red Earth '82
Rider from Tucson '50
The Rundown '03
Salt of the Earth '54▶
Sands of Sacrifice '21
Silver: Bandit '70
Smilla's Sense of Snow '96
Solomon and Gaenor '98
The Spoilers '42▶
The Stars Look Down '39▶
The Strangeness '85
Wanda Nevada '79
The War Wagon '67▶
Way Out West '37▶
Where the Green Ants Dream '84
Wildrose '85
Within the Rock '95
Xica '76

Minnesota

Aurora Borealis '06
Beautiful Girls '96▶
D3: The Mighty Ducks '96
D2: The Mighty Ducks '94
The Emigrants '72▶
Far North '88
Fargo '96▶
Feeling Minnesota '96
The Good Son '93
Grace Is Gone '07▶
Graffiti Bridge '90
The Great Northfield Minnesota Raid '72
Grumpier Old Men '95
Grumpy Old Men '93▶
The Heartbreak Kid '72▶
Ice Castles '79
Iron Will '93
Jingle All the Way '96
Joe Somebody '01
Jungle Goddess '49
Keane '04▶
Kentucky Jubilee '51
Kidnap Syndicate '76
The Lady Vanishes '38▶
The New Land '73▶
North Country '05
Patti Rocks '88▶
The Personals '83
A Prairie Home Companion '06
A Simple Plan '98▶
Slaughterhouse Five '72
That Was Then... This Is Now '85
Untamed Heart '93
Wildrose '85

Missing Persons

see also Kidnapped!; Hostage!;

Abandon '02
Adam '83▶
Agatha '79
Agatha Christie: A Life in Pictures '04
Almost Human '79
American Nightmare '81
Anastasia '56▶
Anastasia: The Mystery of Anna '86
AngKor: Cambodia Express '81
Assassination in Rome '65
Big Jake '71▶
Bloodstream '00
Breakdown '96▶
Bureau of Missing Persons '33
Cavalcade of the West '36
Chain of Souls '00
Chasing Sleep '00
Christina '74
Coming Out Alive '84
Conspiracy '08
The Crow Road '96
Curse of the Pink Panther '83
Dangerous Crossing '53
Disappearance '81
Dying Room Only '73
The Emerald Forest '85▶
Empire State '87
The Empty Acre '07
The Empty Beach '85
Equinox '71▶
Experiment in Terror '62▶
Eye Witness '49
Final Cut '88
Five Days '07
The Flock '07
Foxtrap '85
Frantic '88▶
Freedomland '06
From Hollywood to Deadwood '89
Get a Clue '02
Girl Hunters '63
Gone Baby Gone '07▶
The Good German '06
Grayeagle '77
Green Eyes '77
Grievous Bodily Harm '89
Harem '85
Harper '66▶
Harrison's Flowers '02
Heading for Heaven '47
Hell Squad '85
Hide in Plain Sight '80▶
High Road to China '83
The Hit List '88
Hollywood Chaos '89
Home for Christmas '93
Home Is Where the Hart Is '88
Hurricane Smith '92
Imagining Argentina '04
In the Mouth of Madness '95
Into Thin Air '07
The Invisible '07
The Iris Effect '04
The Island at the Top of the World '74
Journey to the Center of the World '74
The Lady Vanishes '79
The Last Winter '84
Long Time Since '97
Looking for Kitty '04
A Low Down Dirty Shame '94
Lucky Number Slevin '06
Mexico City '00
Midnight Warning '32
Misery '90▶
Missing '82▶
The Missing '03
Missing Brendan '03
The Missing Corpse '45
Murder, My Sweet '44▶
Nickel & Dime '92
Nim's Island '08
The Norliss Tapes '73
Norseman '78
Old Gringo '89
The Orphanage '07▶
Perfect Assassins '98
Picnic at Hanging Rock '75▶
The Port of Missing Girls '38
Prisoner of Zenda '37▶
The Professionals '66▶
Psycho from Texas '81
Psych-Out '68
Pure Luck '91
Raising Arizona '87▶
Romancing the Stone '84▶
Scandalous '88
Seance on a Wet Afternoon '64▶
The Search for One-Eyed Jimmy '96
The Searchers '56▶
Short Night of Glass Dolls '71
Sin '02
Skull: A Night of Terror '88
Stark '85
Street Girls '75
Street Justice '89
Surfacing '84
Tarzan the Fearless '33
Terminal Force '88
The Theory of the Leisure Class '01
Thin Air '00
Threat of Exposure '02
Tokyo Joe '49
Vampire Night '00
The Vanishing '88▶
Wanted: Babysitter '75
Where Are the Children? '85
Where's Picone '84▶
White Fire '53
Who Saw Her Die? '72
The Wicker Man '06
The Wicker Man '75▶
Without a Trace '83

Missionaries

see also Nuns & Priests; Religion; Religious Epics

The African Queen '51▶
At Play in the Fields of the Lord '91▶
Beyond the Next Mountain '87
Black Robe '91▶
Christmas in the Clouds '01
City of Ghosts '03
The Keys of the Kingdom '44▶
The Mission '86▶
Mission to Glory '80
The Missionary '82
The Other Side of Heaven '02
Paradise Road '97
Rambo '08

Mistaken Identity

see also Amnesia; Gender Bending; Role Reversal

Across the Bridge '57
The Adventurer '17
The Adventures of Bullwhip Griffin '66
Along Came Jones '45▶
Alvin Rides Again '74
American Cop '94
Amos and Andrew '93
Another You '91
Apres-Vous '03
As Good as Dead '95
As You Desire Me '32▶
As You Like It '36
As Young As You Feel '51▶
The Assignment '97
The Associate '79
The Aura '05
Bachelor Mother '39▶
The Ballad of Little Jo '93
Baran '01
Barocco '76
The Beautician and the Beast '97
A Better Way to Die '00
Being There '79▶
Betrayed '54▶
Beyond Suspicion '00
The Big Lebowski '97▶
Big Mouth '67
Billy the Kid Returns '38
Bittersweet Love '76
Black Glove '54
Blackjack '78
Blame It on the Bellboy '92
Blind Justice '86
Blonde Knows Best '46
Bobby Z '07
Body Snatchers '93
Borderline '50
The Boss of It All '06
Boy's Reformatory '39
Breakin' All The Rules '04
Brighton Strangler '45
Broadway Limited '41
Broken Melody '34
Bullets or Ballots '38▶
Bullseye! '90
Bundle of Joy '56
Buona Sera, Mrs. Campbell '68
Bushwhacked '95
Butler's Dilemma '43
Camp Cucamonga: How I Spent My Summer Vacation '90
The Capture '50▶
Caroline? '90
Carry On Admiral '57
A Case of Deadly Force '86▶
CB4: The Movie '93
Center of the Web '92
The Challengers '89
Chameleon Street '89▶
Charade '63▶
Charley's Aunt '25
The Chase '66▶
The Closet '00
Colonel Chabert '94
Company Man '00
Convicted '86
Convicts at Large '38
Cornbread, Earl & Me '75
A Couch in New York '95
The Couch Trip '87
Counterblast '48
Court Jester '56▶
Daughters of the Sun '00
Dave '93▶
Deadwood '65
Deconstructing Sarah '94
The Desert Song '53
Dog Gone Love '03
Don Juan DeMarco '94
Don't Tell Her It's Me '90
Double Play '96
Double Take '01
Double Take '07
Double Vision '92
El Mariachi '93▶
End of the Spear '06
Ernest Goes to Jail '90
Erotic Touch of Hot Skin '65
Ethan '36
Evergreen '34
Everyman's Law '36
Execution of Raymond Graham '85
F/X 2: The Deadly Art of Illusion '91
The Family Plan '05
Family Reunion '88
Fargo Express '32
Fatal Exposure '91
Father '90
Feet First '41
Fighting Parson '30
Five Graves to Cairo '43▶
The Flame of New Orleans '41▶
Flightplan '05
Focus '01
Gangway '37
Garfield: A Tail of Two Kitties '06
The Gay Divorcee '34▶
Generale Della Rovere '60▶
Gentleman Bandit '81
Get That Man '35
The Glass Bottom Boat '66
Good Neighbor Sam '64▶
Grosse Fatigue '94▶
The Great Dictator '40▶
The Gun in Betty Lou's Handbag '92
Gunsmoke Trail '38
Happy Go Lovely '51
Hell on Frisco Bay '55
Her Life as a Man '33
Hero '92▶
High & Low '62▶
Highway 13 '48
Highway 61 '92
His Brother's Ghost '45
His Wife's Lover '31▶
Hittin' the Trail '37
Hollywood Chaos '89
Hometown Boy Makes Good '93
Honolulu '39
A House in the Hills '93
Houseguest '94
I Love You '81
I Want to Live! '58▶
I Will, I Will for Now '76
If Looks Could Kill '91
The Impostor '84
The Imposters '98
In Person '35
In Society '44
The Inspector General '49
Intimate Strangers '04▶
It Started with Eve '41▶
It Takes Two '95
It! The Terror from Beyond Space '58
Jade '95
Johnny Handsome '89▶
Johnny Stecchino '92▶
Junk Mail '97
Just Write '97
Kansas City Confidential '52▶
Keaton's Cop '90
Kid from Spain '32
Killer Dill '47
The Killing Time '87
The King of Masks '99▶
A Kiss Before Dying '91
Km. 0 '00
Lady Killer '97
Landslide '92
The Last Man '06
The Last Contract '86
The Last Winter '84
Laurel & Hardy: The Hoose-Gow '29
Law of the Underworld '38
Le Bonheur Est Dans le Pre '95
Life Is a Long Quiet River '88▶
Lisa '90
The Little Drummer Girl '84▶
Little Man '06
Little Sister '92
The Lizzie McGuire Movie '03
The Lookalike '90
Lost Highway '96
Love at Large '89▶
Lucky Cisco Kid '40
Lucky Number Slevin '06
Mad About Music '38▶
Made in America '93

▶ = rated three bones or higher

Mistaken

Maid's Night Out '38
The Majestic '01
The Man '05
The Man in the Raincoat '57
The Man on the Box '25
Man on the Run '49
The Man Who Knew Too Little '97
The Man with One Red Shoe '85
Manhandled '24
The Mark of Zorro '40
McHale's Navy Joins the Air Force '65
Meet the Deedles '98
Meet the Mob '42
Memento '00
Miami Hustle '95
Mickey Blue Eyes '99
The Misadventures of Mr. Wilt '90
Mississippi Mermaid '69
Mistaken Identity '36
Mr. Headmistress '98
Mr. Klein '76
Monsieur Beaucaire '46
Monsignor Quixote '91
The Monster '96
Monte Carlo Nights '34
My Geisha '62
My Man Godfrey '36
My Outlaw Brother '51
My Twentieth Century '90
Mystery Date '91
Naked Tango '91
Naughty Marietta '35
Never a Dull Moment '68
Next of Kin '84
Nick and Jane '96
Nightfall '56
Nobody's Perfect '90
North by Northwest '59
The Nutt House '95
The Obsessed '51
Obsession '76
Off Season '01
One Body Too Many '44
Only You '94
Opportunity Knocks '90
Oscar '91
Out of Bounds '86
Out on a Limb '92
Pale Saints '97
Palmy Days '31
Paper Mask '91
Paperback Hero '99
Pardon My Sarong '42
The Parent Trap '61
The Parent Trap '98
The Passenger '75
The Perfect Man '05
Phantom Fiend '35
Phantom Killer '42
Picture Perfect '96
Pier 23 '51
The Player '92
The Pope Must Diet '91
Prelude to a Kiss '92
Priceless '06
Prime '05
The Princess Comes Across '36
Private Life of Don Juan '34
The Private Secretary '35
Profile '54
Purple Noon '60
Ranson's Folly '26
Rattler Kid '68
Red Firecracker, Green Firecracker '93
The Red Half-Breed '70
Red Heat '85
Red Rock West '93
Reindeer Games '00
The Reluctant Agent '91
The Reluctant Astronaut '67
Return of Jesse James '50
The Return of Martin Guerre '83
Return of the Tall Blond Man with One Black Shoe '74
River Beat '54
The Road to Guantanamo '06
Romance on the High Seas '48
Running Hot '83
Ruybas '48
Safe Men '98
St. Benny the Dip '51
The Santa Clause '94
Santa with Muscles '96
Say It Isn't So '01
The Scar '48
Scream of Fear '61
Seconds '66
The Secret of My Success '87
A Self-Made Hero '95
The 7th Commandment '61
She Must Be Seeing Things '87
She's the Man '06
The Sinister Invasion '68
Sister Act '92
Sister Act 2: Back in the Habit '93
Six Gun Gospel '43
Six of a Kind '34
The Sleepy Time Gal '01
Slightly Terrific '44
Small Kill '93
Smokey and the Bandit, Part 3 '83
Social Error '35
Soldat Duroc... Ca Va Etre 'ta Fete! '75
Someone at the Door '50
Something in the Wind '47
Splitting Heirs '93
Stolen Identity '53
A Stolen Life '46
Straight Talk '92
Stray Bullet '98
The Stupids '95
The Suitors '88
Sunday '96
Supergrass '87
Support Your Local Gunfighter '71
Suture '93
Switched at Birth '91
Taken Alive '95
Tatte Tale '92
10 Rillington Place '71
The Tenth Man '88
Texas Carnival '51
Texas Cyclone '32
They Knew What They Wanted '40
The Thin Blue Line '88
Things Change '88
Things I Never Told You '96
The 39 Steps '35
Toto le Heros '91
Tombstone Terror '34
Top Hat '35
Tropic Thunder '08
True Identity '91
The Truth about Cats and Dogs '96
Twelfth Night '96
Twin Dragons '92
Two Much '96
The Unholy Three '30
The Well '51
We're No Angels '45
West of the Pecos '45
While You Were Sleeping '95
Whiskers '96
White Eagle '32
White of the Eye '88
Who's Harry Crumb? '89
Wings of the Morning '37
Withnail and I '87
The Worldly Madonna '22
The Wrong Guys '88
Young Master '80
Zertigo Diamond Caper '82

Mockumentary

see also Documentary; Genre Spoofs

Acapulco Gold '78
All You Need Is Cash '78
...And God Spoke '94
Best in Show '00
The Blair Witch Project '99
Bob Roberts '92
Borat: Cultural Learnings of America for Make Benefit Glorious Nation of Kazakhstan '06
Born to Lose '99
Brothers of the Head '06
Comic Book: The Movie '04
Confetti '06
CSA: The Confederate States of America '04
Danny Roane: First Time Director '06
A Day Without a Mexican '04
Drop Dead Gorgeous '99
Elvis Meets Nixon '98
Fear of a Black Hat '94
Flyboys '06
For Your Consideration '06
Forgotten Silver '96
Glen or Glenda? '53
Grunt! The Wrestling Movie '85
Hard Core Logo '96
Incident at Loch Ness '04
It's All Gone, Pete Tong '04
Jackie's Back '99
The Last Broadcast '98
The Last Polka '84
Lisa Picard Is Famous '01
Mail Order Wife '04
Memron '04
A Mighty Wind '03
Never Been Thawed '05
On Edge '03
Pittsburgh '06
Real Time: Siege at Lucas Street Market '00
Rescue Dawn '06
The Return of Spinal Tap '92
Stardom '00
SuperGuy: Behind the Cape '02
This Is Spinal Tap '84
Tristram Shandy: A Cock and Bull Story '05
Waiting for Guffman '96
Walk Hard: The Dewey Cox Story '07
Zelig '83

Model Citizens

Abdulla the Great '56
Blackjack '97
The Bride Is Much Too Beautiful '58
Captivity '07
The Case of the Bloody Iris '72
Cover Girl '44
Cover Girl Models '75
The Cover Girl Murders '93
Covergirl '83
Daniella by Night '61
Darling '65
Designing Woman '57
Domino '05
D.R.E.A.M. Team '99
The Eighteenth Angel '97
Eyes of Laura Mars '78
Faceless '88
Fall '97
Funny Face '57
Gia '98
Giving It Up '99
Head Over Heels '01
Human Desires '97
In and Out '97
Intimate Deception '96
The Invisibles '99
Looker '81
Mahogany '75
Model Behavior '82
Model Behavior '00
Model by Day '94
Nothing Underneath '85
Obsession: A Taste for Fear '89
One Last Thing '05
The Pink Jungle '68
Pleasure '31
Portfolio '88
Raising Helen '04
Ready to Wear '94
Screaming Dead '03

Modern Cowboys

see also Western Comedy; Westerns

All the Pretty Horses '00
Another Pair of Aces: Three of a Kind '91
Barbarosa '82
The Big Empty '04
Brokeback Mountain '05
Bronco Billy '80
By Dawn's Early Light '00
City Slickers '91
City Slickers 2: The Legend of Curly's Gold '94
Coogan's Bluff '68
Cowboy Up '00
The Cowboy Way '94
Don't Come Knocking '05
Down in the Valley '05
Dudes '87
8 Seconds '94
The Electric Horseman '79
Fool for Love '86
The Hi-Lo Country '98
Hope Ranch '02
The Horse Whisperer '97
The Last of the Dogmen '95
Lonely Are the Brave '62
My Heroes Have Always Been Cowboys '91
A Prairie Home Companion '06
Rhinestone '84
Ruby Jean and Joe '96
Samurai Cowboy '93
Sweet Creek County War '79
Toy Story '95
Toy Story 2 '99
True West '86
An Unfinished Life '05
Wild Horses '84

Moms

see also Bad Dads; Dads; Monster Moms; Parenthood

Above the Rim '94
Agnes Browne '99
Alice Doesn't Live Here Anymore '74
All About My Mother '99
All That Heaven Allows '55
Amazing Grace '74
American Marie '99
Antonia's Line '95
Anywhere But Here '99
Applause '29
Aurora '84
Autumn Sonata '78
Baby '00
Baby Boom '87
Bad Boy '39
The Bad Seed '56
The Bad Seed '85
The Banger Sisters '02
Bastard out of Carolina '96
Beautiful '00
Beautiful Thing '95
Because I Said So '07
Beloved '98
Better Than Chocolate '99
Bogus '96
The Brady Bunch Movie '95
Bridge to Silence '89
A Brivele der Mamen '38
Cadillac Girls '93
A Call to Remember '97
Carnegie Hall '47
Charms for the Easy Life '02
Children of the Revolution '95
Chocolat '00
Cider with Rosie '99
Cinderella Liberty '73
Clean '04
Come Undone '00
Comedy of Innocence '00
Crash Course '00
The Damned Don't Cry '50
Dangerous Beauty '98
Dangerous Child '01
Dark Water '05
Daughter of Keltoum '01
The Daytrippers '96
Dead Ahead '96
The Dead Girl '06
The Dead End '01
The Deep End of the Ocean '98
The Deli '97
Detective Sadie & Son '84
The Devil's Sleep '51
Digging to China '98
Dim Sum: A Little Bit of Heart '85
Do or Die '01
The Dollmaker '84
Dona Herlinda & Her Son '86
Double Jeopardy '99
Double Parked '00
Double Platinum '99
Down in the Delta '98
Driving Lessons '06
Drop Dead Gorgeous '99
Dumbo '41
Edward the King '75
Evening '07
Every Other Weekend '91
A Family Affair '01
First Born '84
First Do No Harm '97
First, Last and Deposit '00
Flight of the Red Balloon '08
Food of Love '02
For One More Day '07
Forrest Gump '94
Found Alive '34
Four Sons '28
Frank McKlusky, C.I. '02
Frankie Starlight '95
Freaky Friday '76
Freaky Friday '03
Garbo Talks '84
Gas Food Lodging '92
Georgia '87
Getting Out '94
Gia '98
The Girl '68
Good Said "Hal" '99
Good Bye, Lenin! '03
Gypsy '62
Gypsy '93
Hairspray '07
Harnessing Peacocks '92
Heartbreakers '01
Heavy '94
Held for Murder '32
High Tide '87
Holiday Affair '96
Homage '95
A Home of Our Own '93
Hope Floats '98
The Horse Whisperer '97
The Hours '02
House Arrest '96
House of Cards '92
Hysterical Blindness '02
I Don't Want to Talk About It '94
I Remember Mama '48
Illegal Tender '07
Imitation of Life '34
Imitation of Life '59
In the Gloaming '97
The Incredible Shrinking Woman '81
Indochine '92
Into Thin Air '85
Invisible Mom '96
The Iris Effect '04
Jenny's War '85
The Joy Luck Club '93
Junior's Groove '97
The Juror '96
King of the Jungle '01
Kissing Jessica Stein '02
La Cicada '83
Ladies of the Chorus '49
Lady by Choice '34
Lady Jayne Killer '03
Laurel Canyon '02
Leo '02
Let No Man Write My Epitaph '60
Lift '01
The Lion King 1 1/2 '04
Listen, Darling '38
Little Women '94
Lola and Billy the Kid '98
Lost for Words '99
Love Come Down '00
The Love Letter '99
Love Strange Love '82
Lovely & Amazing '02
Loverboy '05
Lucky Seven '03
Luminous Motion '00
Mad About Music '38
Madame X '66
Made in America '93
Mama Flora's Family '98
Mamma Roma '62
Manny & lo '96
Marius and Jeannette '97
Mary, Mother of Jesus '99
Mask '85
Meet Myself I '99
Meet the Fockers '04
Mermaids '90
The Mighty '98
Mildred Pierce '45
Mrs. Wiggs of the Cabbage Patch '34
Mrs. Winterbourne '96
Mr. Woodcock '07
The Mother '03
Mother and Son '97
Mother and Mine '05
A Mother's Prayer '95
Murmur of the Heart '71
My Family Treasure '93
My Life Without Me '03
My Mother Likes Women '02
My Mother's Secret Life '84
Nancy Goes to Rio '50
Never Met Picasso '96
'night, Mother '86
Night Ride Home '99
Nightmare '91
Nowhere to Run '93
The Old Maid '39
On My Own '92
One True Thing '98
101 Reykjavik '00
Only the Lonely '91
Only When I Laugh '81
Or (My Treasure) '04
Oranges Are Not the Only Fruit '89
Our Sons '91
Out of Sight, Out of Her Mind '89
Over the Hill '93
Panic Room '02
Pavilion of Women '01
Pay It Forward '00
The Perfect Man '05
Pilgrim, Farewell '82
Places in the Heart '84
Playing by Heart '98
Poor White Trash '00
Postcards from the Edge '90
The Prize Winner of Defiance, Ohio '05
Psycho '98
A Question of Love '78
Rachel, Rachel '68
Rain '01
The Real McCoy '93
Real Women Have Curves '02
The Reception '05
Reckless Moment '49
Relative Values '99
Requiem for a Dream '00
The River Wild '94
The Road from Coorain '02
The Road Home '01

▲ = rated *three bones* or higher

Roost Stories '03
Rockabye '86
Roses Bloom Twice '77
Rumpelstiltskin '96
Santitos '99
Satan's Little Helper '04
Say Uncle '05
Scandal in a Small Town '88
See How She Runs '78
She-Devil '89
She's Having a Baby '88
Silent Hill '06
Simon Birch '98
The Sin of Madelon Claudet '31
S;nce Otar Left... '03
A Sinful Life '89
Skipped Parts '00
Snap Decision '01
So I Married an Axe Murderer '93
Soft Fruit '99
Solas '99
Some Mother's Son '96
Something's Gotta Give '03
Star Wars: Episode 2— Attack of the Clones '02
Stella '89
Stella Dallas '37
Stop! or My Mom Will Shoot '92
The Story of Esther Costello '57
Striptease '96
Tamation '03
Terms of Endearment '83
Third Walker '79 ▶
Thirteen '03 ▶
The 24 Hour Woman '99
Two Women '61 ▶
Under One Roof '02
Under the Same Moon '07
Under the Skin '97
An Unexpected ..ife '03
Unhook the Stars '96
A Very Brady Sequel '96
The Visit '00
Volver '06 ▶
A Walk on the Moor '99
The War at Home '96
The Waterboy '98
What Time Is It There? '01
When a Man Loves a Woman '94
Where's Poppie? '77 ▶
Will It Snow for Christmas? '96
The Winter Guest '97 ▶
A Woman's a Helluva Thing '01
The Yards '00

Monkeyshines
see also Jungle Stories; Killer Apes and Monkeys; Wild Kingdom
Babe: Pig in the City '98
The Barefoot Executive '71
Bedtime for Bonzo '51
Born to Be Wild '95
The Bride & the Beast '53
Buddy '97
Congo '95
Curious George '06
Dr. Dolittle '98
Dunston Checks in '95
Ed '96
George of the Jungle '97 ▶
Instinct '99
Jay and Silent Bob Strike Back '01
Jungle Captive '45
King Kong '33 ▶
King Kong '76
Mom, Can I Keep Her? '98
Monkey Shines '88
Monkey Trouble '94
Monkeybone '01
MVP: Most Valuable Primate '00
MVP2: Most Vertical Primate '01
MXP: Most Xtreme Primate '03
Outbreak '94 ▶
Planet of the Apes '01
The Powerpuff Girls Movie '02
Race to Space '01
The Rundown '03
The Sisters '05
Space Chimps '08
Summer of the Monkeys '98
Tarzan '99 ▶
Terror Tract '00
The Wild Thornberrys Movie '02

Monks
see also Clergymen; Martial Arts
The Da Vinci Code '06 ▶
The Forbidden Kingdom '08
Hitman '07
The Judgement '04
Kundun '97 ▶
Monty Python and the Holy Grail '75 ▶
Nacho Libre '06
The Name of the Rose '86
Rasputin '85
Rasputin and the Empress '33
Rasputin: Dark Servant of Destiny '96 ▶
Van Helsing '04 ▶

Monster Moms
see also Bad Dads; Dads; Moms; Parenthood
Alias Betty '01
Almost Dead '94
The American '01
The Anniversary '68
The Baby '72
Bad Boy Bubby '93
Bellissima '51 ▶
Beowulf '07
Berlinguer I Love You '77
Beyond the Door '75
Big Bad Mama '74
Big Bad Mama 2 '87
Bloody Mama '70
Brand Upon the Brain! '06 ▶
Carrie '76 ▶
Carrie '02
Carved '07
Catfish in Black Bean Sauce '00
Chutney Popcorn '99
Cora Unashamed '00
Dead Alive '93 ▶
Deadly Advice '93
Dead Pet '01
Die Die My Darling! '65
Die Mommie Die! '03 ▶
Divine Secrets of the Ya-Ya Sisterhood '02
Dolores Claiborne '95
East of Eden '54 ▶
East of Eden '80
Ed and His Dead Mother '93
Felicia's Journey '99 ▶
Fiona '98
Flesh Eating Mothers '89
From Dusk Till Dawn 3: The Hangman's Daughter '99
A Gentleman After Dark '42
Ghosts Never Sleep '05
Glass House: The Good Mother '06
Gone Baby Gone '07 ▶
Gorgo '61
Gracie's Choice '04
The Graveyard '74
The Grifters '90 ▶
His Greatest Gamble '34
Hush '98
Hush Little Baby '93
Ice Princess '05
The Intended '02
Introducing the Dwights '07

Moms
see also Bad Dads; Dads; Monster Moms; Parenthood
A Matter of Dignity '57
Medea '70
Mommie Dearest '81
Mom '89
Mommy '95
Mommy 2: Mommy's Day '96
Monster-in-Law '05
Monster's Ball '01 ▶
Mother '94 ▶
Mother's Boys '94
Mother's Day '80
The Nightman '93
Parents '89
Passion '99
The Positively True Adventures of the Alleged Texas Cheerleader- Murdering Mom '93 ▶
Psycho '60 ▶
Psycho 2 '83
Psycho 3 '86
Public Enemies '96
Rosetta '99 ▶
Running with Scissors '06
Santa Sangre '90 ▶
Say It Isn't So '01
Serial Mom '94 ▶
Six Ways to Sunday '99
Sleepwakers '92
Sleepwalking '08
Small Sacrifices '89
Sonny '02
Spanglish '04
Spanking the Monkey '94 ▶
The Star '52
The Stepmother '71
Sybil '76 ▶
Touch of Pink '04
Trilogy of Terror 2 '96
The Ugly '96
White Oleander '02
Wild at Heart '90 ▶
Wild Iris '01
Willard '03

Monster Yuks
Abbott and Costello Meet Dr. Jekyll and Mr. Hyde '52
Abbott and Costello Meet Frankenstein '48 ▶
Abbott and Costello Meet the Killer, Boris Karloff '49
Abbott and Costello Meet the Mummy '55
The Addams Family '91 ▶
Addams Family Values '93 ▶
Drop Dead Fred '91
Little Monsters '89
Monsters, Inc. '01 ▶
Munster, Go Home! '66
Scooby-Doo 2: Monsters Unleashed '04

Monsters, General
see also Bigfoot/Yeti; Ghosts, Ghouls, & Goblins; Giants; Killer Beasts; Killer Bugs and Slugs; Killer Plants; Killer Reptiles; Killer Toys; Mad Scientists; Mummies; Robots & Androids; Vampires; Werewolves; Zombies

Monte Carlo/ Monaco
Charlie Chan at Monte Carlo '37
The Counterfeiters of Monte Carlo '27
The Garden of Eden '28
Grand Prix '66 ▶
Herbie Goes to Monte Carlo '77
Monaco Forever '83
Monte Carlo '30
Monte Carlo '86
Monte Carlo Nights '34
Priceless '06
Rebecca '40 ▶
The Red Shoes '48 ▶
Seven Thieves '60
Strike It Rich '90
Those Daring Young Men in Their Jaunty Jalopies '69

Montana
see also Big Sky
Always '89
Amazing Grace & Chuck '87
The Ballad of Little Jo '93
Big Eden '00 ▶
Bright Angel '91
Bustin' Loose '81 ▶
Cattle Queen of Montana '54
Clay Pigeons '98
Cold Feet '89
Disorganized Crime '89
Evel Knievel '72
Everything That Rises '98
Fear X '03 ▶
Forrest Gump '94 ▶
A Guy Named Joe '44
The Horse Whisperer '97
Jeremiah Johnson '72 ▶
Keep the Change '92
The Killer Inside Me '75
Legends of the Fall '94 ▶
Little Big Man '70 ▶
Lonesome Dove '89 ▶
Me & Will '99
Missouri Breaks '76
Montana '90
Montana '97 ▶
Montana Belle '52
Rancho Deluxe '75 ▶
Return to Lonesome Dove '93 ▶
The River Wild '94
Season of Change '94
The Slaughter Rule '01
Stacking '87
Stay Away, Joe '68
The Stone Boy '84 ▶
They Died with Their Boots On '41 ▶
Thunderbirds & Lightfoot '74 ▶
Under Siege 2: Dark Territory '95
War Party '89
Winterhawk '76

Montreal
see also Canada
The Apprenticeship of Duddy Kravitz '74 ▶
The Barbarian Invasions '03 ▶
Because Why? '93
Being at Home with Claude '92
Café Olé '00
Eddie and the Cruisers 2: Eddie Lives! '89
Eliza's Horoscope '70
Eternal '04
Jesus of Montreal '89 ▶
Karmina '96
L'Escorte '96
Leolo '92 ▶
Love and Human Remains '93
Malarek '89
Mambo Italiano '03
Mystery of the Million Dollar Hockey Puck '75
Night Zoo '87
The Pact '99
Pale Saints '97
The Quarrel '93 ▶
The Red Violin '98 ▶

Mormons
see also Religion
Angels in America '05 ▶
The Avenging Angel '95
Brigham City '01 ▶
Brigham Young: Frontiersman '40
Georgia Rule '07
Latter Days '04
Lies & Alibis '06
A Mormon Maid '17
Messenger of Death '88
Orgazmo '98
The Other Side of Heaven '01
September Dawn '07
Wagon Master '50 ▶

Moscow
see also Russia/USSR
American Cop '94
Back in the USSR '92
Black Eyes '39
Botched '07
The Bourne Ultimatum '07 ▶
Comrade X '40
Day Watch '06
An Englishman Abroad '83 ▶
Gorky Park '83 ▶
How I Learned to Love Women '66
Luna Park '91
Moscow Does Not Believe in Tears '80 ▶
Moscow on the Hudson '84 ▶
Moscow Parade '92
Mute Witness '95 ▶
Night Watch '04
Police Academy 7: Mission to Moscow '94
PU-239 '06
Red Heat '88 ▶
Redline '07
The Russia House '90
The Saint '97
Silent Partner '05
Taxi Blues '90 ▶
Very Close Quarters '84

Moscow Mafia
see also Organized Crime; Russia/ USSR
Birthday Girl '02
Brother '97 ▶
City Unplugged '92
Eastern Promises '07 ▶
Goldeneye '95 ▶
Rounders '98
We Own the Night '07

Motor Vehicle Dept.
see also Bikers; Cars; Checkered Flag; Killer Cars
The Adventures of Ford Fairlane '90
American Graffiti '73 ▶
Back to the Future '85 ▶
Bail Out '90
Belle Americaine '61
The Betsy '78
Black Cat Run '98
Black Moon Rising '86
Blitz '85

Blood, Guts, Bullets and Octane '99
The Blues Brothers '80 ▶
Cadillac Man '90
Captured '99
The Car '77
Car Trouble '86
Car Wash '76 ▶
Carpool '96
Chitty Chitty Bang Bang '68 ▶
Coneheads '93
Corvette Summer '79
Coupe de Ville '90
Crash '05 ▶
Cry Panic '74
Dangerous Curves '88
Dark of the Night '85
D.C. Cab '84
Deadline Auto Theft '83
Death Proof '07
Devil's Knight '03
Dream Machine '91
Drive-In '76
Drive-In Massacre '74
The Driver '78 ▶
Driving Me Crazy '91
Duel '71 ▶
The Dukes of Hazzard '05
Dumb & Dumber '94
The Fast and the Furious '01
Ferris Bueller's Day Off '86 ▶
Firebird 2015 A.D. '81
Follow That Car '80
Ford: The Man & the Machine '87
Free Ride '86
Freeway '88
Freeway '96
Freedom '82
Gone in 60 Seconds '74
Gone in 60 Seconds '00
Great American Traffic Jam '80
Gung Ho '85 ▶
The Hearse '80
Herbie Fully Loaded '05
Herbie Rides Again '74
High Rolling in a Hot Corvette '77
Highway Patrolman '91 ▶
Highwaymen '03
The Hollywood Knights '80
Hometown U.S.A. '79
Hotwire '80

Jade '95
Joyride '97
The Karate Kid '84 ▶
License to Drive '88
The Love Bug '68 ▶
The Love Bug '97
Maximum Overdrive '86
Mr. Toad's Wild Ride '96
Moonshine Highway '96
Motorama '91
Moving Violations '85
My Chauffeur '86
National Lampoon's Vacation '83
Night on Earth '91 ▶
One Deadly Owner '74
Pepper and His Wacky Taxi '72
Pie in the Sky '95
Repo Jake '90
Repo Man '83 ▶
Road to Nhil! '97
Roger & Me '89 ▶
R.P.M. '97
Silkwood '83 ▶
Smokey & the Hotwire Gang '79
Steel Arena '72
Stephen King's Thinner '96
Stingray '78
The Sucker '65
Sunset Limousine '83
Superbug Super Agent '76
Tail Lights Fade '99
Tomboy '85
Traffic '71
True Lies '94 ▶
Tucker: The Man and His Dream '88 ▶
Two Lane Blacktop '71 ▶

The Score '01 ▶
Seducing Doctor Lewis '03 ▶
Seducing Maarya '99
Set Me Free '99
Steel Toes '06
Straight for the Heart '88
2 Seconds '98
Taking Lives '04
The Victory '88
The Whole Nine Yards '00 ▶
A Wind from Wyoming '94

Invaders from Mars '53 ▶
Invaders from Mars '86
A Light in the Darkness '02
Little Voice '98 ▶
The Locusts '97
Ma Barker's Killer Brood '60
Mad Youth '40
The Manchurian Candidate '62 ▶

★ = rated three bones or higher

Uncle Buck '89▶
Used Cars '80▶
The Van '77
Vanishing Point '71
Wheels of Terror '90▶
Zero to Sixty '78

Mountaineering

The Abominable Snowman '57
Alpine Fire '89
The Ascent '94
Bushwhacked '95
The Challenge '38▶
Cliffhanger '93▶
The Climb '87
Courage Mountain '89
The Eiger Sanction '75
Extreme Ops '02
Five Days One Summer '82
God's Bloody Acre '75
Heidi '67
Into Thin Air: Death on Everest '97
K2: The Ultimate High '92
Mountain Patrol: Kekexili '04
My Side of the Mountain '69
Seven Years in Tibet '97
Storm and Sorrow '90
Third Man on the Mountain '59
Touching the Void '03▶
Vertical Limit '00▶
The White Tower '50▶

Mummies

see also Zombies
Abbott and Costello Meet the Mummy '55
All New Adventures of Laurel and Hardy: For Love or Mummy '98
Ancient Evil: Scream of the Mummy '00
Attack of the Mayan Mummy '63
The Awakening '80
Blood from the Mummy's Tomb '71
Bram Stoker's The Mummy '99
Bubba Ho-Tep '03▶
Castle of the Living Dead '64
The Creeps '97
The Curse of the Aztec Mummy '59
Dawn of the Mummy '82
The External '99
Mad Monster Party '68
The Monster Squad '87
The Mummy '32▶
The Mummy '59▶
The Mummy '99
Mummy & Curse of the Jackal '67
The Mummy Lives '93
The Mummy Returns '01
The Mummy: Tomb of the Dragon Emperor '08
The Mummy's Curse '44
The Mummy's Ghost '44
The Mummy's Hand '40
The Mummy's Revenge '73
The Mummy's Shroud '67
The Mummy's Tomb '42
The Robot vs. the Aztec Mummy '59
Russell Mulcahy's Tale of the Mummy '99
Sphinx '81
Wrestling Women vs. the Aztec Mummy '59

Museums

Abbott and Costello Meet Frankenstein '48▶
After Midnight '04
All New Adventures of Laurel and Hardy: For Love or Mummy '98
Blood Relic '05
Charlie Chan at the Wax Museum '40
Crucible of Terror '72
Curious George '06▶
The Da Vinci Code '06▶
Dirty Pictures '00
Erotic House of Wax '97
From the Mixed-Up Files of Mrs. Basil E. Frankweiler '95
Ghostbusters 2 '89
The Hideaways '73
House of Wax '53▶
House of Wax '05
Mad City '97
Mammoth '06
Manticore '05
Midnight at the Wax Museum '36
Mr. Takes a Vacation '39
The Mummy Returns '01
Mystery of the Wax Museum '33▶
Night at the Museum '06
Nightmare in Wax '69
The Outing '87
Paul Bartel's The Secret Cinema '69
P.D. James: The Murder Room '04
The Pick-Up Artist '87
The Relic '96
Scooby-Doo 2: Monsters Unleashed '04
The Shape of Things '03
Tenacious D in the Pick of Destiny '06
Terror in the Wax Museum '73
The Thomas Crown Affair '99▶
Topkapi '64▶
Vibes '88
Waxwork '88
Waxwork 2: Lost in Time '91
Waxworks '24▶
The Witness '99

Musical Comedy

see also Musicals
The Adventures of Priscilla, Queen of the Desert '94▶
The Affairs of Dobie Gillis '53
Almost Angels '62
Amateur Night '85
Andy Hardy Meets Debutante '40
April in Paris '52
Around the World '43
Artists and Models '55
Athena '54
Babes in Arms '39
Babes on Broadway '41
Bathing Beauty '44
Be Yourself '30
Beach Blanket Bingo '65▶
Beach Party '63▶
Because You're Mine '52
Bert Rigby, You're a Fool '89
Best Foot Forward '43
The Best Little Whorehouse in Texas '82
The Big Broadcast of 1938 '38
Bikini Beach '64
Billy Rose's Jumbo '62▶
Birth of the Blues '41
Blossoms on Broadway '37
The Blues Brothers '80▶
Blues Brothers 2000 '98
Boardinghouse Blues '48
The Boy Friend '71▶
Boy! What a Girl '45
The Boys and Girl From County Clare '03
Bride & Prejudice '04
Broadway Melody of 1936 '35▶
Broadway Rhythm '44
Bundle of Joy '56
Bye, Bye, Birdie '63▶
Cairo '42
Call Out the Marines '42
Cannibal! The Musical '96
Captain January '36
Carefree '38▶
The Cocoanuts '29
College Humor '33
College Swing '38
Copacabana '47
Court Jester '56▶
Cover Girl '44▶
Cry-Baby '90▶
Dames '34▶
Dance, Girl, Dance '40
Dangerous When Wet '53
Darling Lili '70
Delightfully Dangerous '45
The Devil's Brother '33
Diplomaniacs '33
Disorderlies '87
Dixiana '30
Dixie Jamboree '44
Doll Face '46
Double or Nothing '37
Du Barry Was a Lady '43
The Duchess of Idaho '50
Easy Come, Easy Go '67
Easy to Wed '46
The Eighties '83
Escape to Paradise '39
Evergreen '34
Everybody Sing '38
Everyone Says I Love You '96▶
Fashions of 1934 '34
Feel the Motion '86
Femmes de Paris '53
Finian's Rainbow '68▶
The First Nudie Musical '75
Flirtation Walk '34
Flower Drum Song '61
Follow That Dream '61
Follow That Rainbow '66
Four Jacks and a Jill '41
Frankie and Johnny '65
The French Line '54
The French Way '40
Frolics on Ice '39
Fun in Acapulco '63
Funny Face '57▶
A Funny Thing Happened on the Way to the Forum '66▶
The Gay Desperado '36
The Gay Divorcee '34▶
Gentlemen Prefer Blondes '53▶
George White's Scandals '45
G.I. Blues '60
Gigi '58▶
The Girl Can't Help It '56
Girl Crazy '43▶
Girl Happy '65
The Girl Most Likely '57
Girl of the Golden West '38
Girl Rush '44
Girls! Girls! Girls! '62
Give a Girl a Break '53
Give Me a Sailor '38
Glorifying the American Girl '30
Godspell '73
Going Hollywood '33▶
Going My Way '44▶
Gold Diggers of 1933 '33▶
Gold Diggers of 1935 '35▶
The Goldwyn Follies '38
Good News '47
Grease '78▶
Grease 2 '82
The Great American Broadcast '41▶
Guys and Dolls '55▶
Gypsy '62▶
Gypsy '93
Hairspray '88▶
Hairspray '07
Hallelujah, I'm a Bum '33
The Happiest Millionaire '67
Happy Go Lovely '51
Havana Widows '33
The Harvey Girls '46▶
Head '68▶
The Heat's On '43
Hello, Dolly! '69▶
Help! '65▶
Here Come the Girls '53
Here Come the Waves '45▶
Here Comes the Groom '51
Here is My Heart '34
High Society '56▶
Hips, Hips, Hooray '34
His Butler's Sister '44
Hit the Deck '55
Holiday in Havana '49
Holiday in Mexico '46
Holiday Inn '42▶
Hollywood Canteen '44▶
Honolulu '39
How to Stuff a Wild Bikini '65
How to Succeed in Business without Really Trying '67▶
Huckleberry Finn '74
I Dood It '43
I Dream of Jeannie '52
I Dream Too Much '35
I Love a Bandleader '45
I Love Melvin '53
I Married an Angel '42
I'll Be Yours '47
In the Good Old Summertime '49▶
In the Navy '41
International House '33▶
It Happened in Brooklyn '47
It's a Date '40
It's a Great Feeling '49
It's Love Again '36
Jive Junction '43
Juke Joint '47
Jupiter's Darling '55
Just for You '52
Keep 'Em Flying '41
Kid from Spain '32
Kid Galahad '62
Kid Millions '34
King Kelly of the U.S.A. '34
King of Jazz '30
Kiss Me Kate '53▶
Kissin' Cousins '64
Lady Be Good '41
Latin Lovers '53
Le Million '31▶
Les Girls '57
Let's Dance '50
Let's Go Collegiate '41
Life Begins for Andy Hardy '41▶
Li'l Abner '59
Lili '53▶
Lily of Killarney '34
Little Nellie Kelly '40
Little Shop of Horrors '86▶
Live a Little, Love a Little '68
Look Out Sister '48
Louisiana Purchase '41
The Love Parade '29
Lovely to Look At '52▶
Lucky Me '54
Lullaby of Broadway '51
Make a Wish '37
Mame '74
Mamele '38
A Matter of Degrees '90
Maytime in Mayfair '49
Meet Me in Las Vegas '56
Melody Cruise '32
The Merry Widow '34▶
The Merry Widow '52
Mississippi '35
Mr. Music '50
Monte Carlo '30
The Muppet Christmas Carol '92▶
The Muppet Movie '79▶
The Muppets Take Manhattan '84▶
Muscle Beach Party '64
My Blue Heaven '50
My Dream Is Yours '49
My Sister Eileen '55▶
My Song Goes Round the World '34
Nancy Goes to Rio '50
Naughty Marietta '35
Neptune's Daughter '49
Never a Dull Moment '50
New Faces of 1952 '54
Newsies '92
Nice Girl? '41
No Time for Romance '48
On a Clear Day You Can See Forever '70
On the Avenue '37▶
One from the Heart '82
One Hour with You '32
One in a Million '36▶
One Night in the Tropics '40
One Touch of Venus '48
The Opposite Sex '56
Paint Your Wagon '69
The Pajama Game '57▶
Pajama Party '64
Pal Joey '57▶
Palmy Days '31
Panama Hattie '42
The Perils of Pauline '47
The Perils of Pauline '67
Phantom of the Paradise '74▶
Pigskin Parade '36
Pin-Up Girl '44
The Pirate '48▶
The Pirates of Penzance '83
Pittsburgh '06
Popeye '80
Presenting Lily Mars '43
The Producers '05
Rebecca of Sunnybrook Farm '38
Rhythm on the Range '36
Rhythm on the River '40
Rhythm Romance '39
Riding High '50
The Road to Bali '53▶
The Road to Morocco '42▶
Road to Nashville '67
The Road to Rio '47▶
The Road to Singapore '40
The Road to Utopia '46▶
The Road to Zanzibar '41▶
Roadie '80
Roberta '35▶
Robin and the 7 Hoods '64
Rock 'n' Roll High School '79▶
Rock 'n' Roll High School Forever '91
Roman Scandals '33
Romance & Cigarettes '05
Romance on the High Seas '48▶
Royal Wedding '51▶
Running out of Luck '86
The Saddest Music in the World '03
Sarah Silverman: Jesus Is Magic '05
Second Fiddle '39
Sensations of 1945 '44
Sgt. Pepper's Lonely Hearts Club Band '78
Seven Brides for Seven Brothers '54▶
Seven Days' Leave '42
The Seven Little Foys '55▶
1776 '72▶
Sextette '78
Shake, Rattle and Rock! '57
Shake, Rattle & Rock! '94
Shall We Dance '37▶
Ship Ahoy '42
Shock Treatment '81
Show Business '44▶
Silk Stockings '57▶
Sing Me a Love Song '37
Sing Your Worries Away '42
Singin' in the Rain '52▶
Sioux City Sue '46
The Sky's the Limit '43
Small Town Girl '53
The Smiling Lieutenant '31
A Song Is Born '48▶
Song of the Islands '42
Speedway '68
Spice World: The Movie '97
Spinout '66
Spotlight Scandals '43
Springtime in the Rockies '42
Stage Struck '36
Star Spangled Rhythm '42▶
Starstruck '82
State Fair '45▶
State Fair '62
Step Lively '44
The Stooge '51
The Stork Club '45
Strike Me Pink '36
Strike Up the Band '40▶
Summer Holiday '48
Summer Stock '50▶
Sun Valley Serenade '41▶
Sunny '41
Sunny Skies '30
Sweet Rosie O'Grady '43
Sweethearts '38▶
Swing '98
Swing It, Professor '37
Swing Time '36▶
Take Me Out to the Ball Game '49
Tea for Two '50▶
Texas Carnival '51
That Certain Age '38
That Girl from Paris '36
There's No Business Like Show Business '54▶
Thin Ice '37▶
Thoroughly Modern Millie '67
Three Daring Daughters '48
Three for the Show '55
The Three Musketeers '39
Three Smart Girls '36▶
Tickle Me '65
Tokyo Pop '88
Too Many Girls '40
Top Hat '35▶
23 1/2 Hours Leave '37
Two Girls and a Sailor '44▶
Two Tickets to Broadway '51
Two Weeks with Love '50
The Unsinkable Molly Brown '64▶
Up in Arms '44
Up in Central Park '48
Vogues of 1938 '37
Waikiki Wedding '37▶
Wallaby Jim of the Islands '37
We're Not Dressing '34▶
White Christmas '54▶
Whoopee! '30
A Woman Is a Woman '60▶
Wonder Man '45
Yes, Giorgio '82
Yes Nurse! No Nurse! '02
Yidl Mitn Fidl '36
Yolanda and the Thief '45
You Were Never Lovelier '42▶
You'll Find Out '40
You'll Never Get Rich '41▶
Ziegfeld Follies '46
Zis Boom Bah '41

Musical Drama

see also Musicals
Across the Universe '07
Actor: The Paul Muni Story '78
The Band Wagon '53▶
The Barkleys of Broadway '49▶
Beatlemania! The Movie '81
The Belle of New York '52
Bells Are Ringing '60▶
Beware '46
Big Fella '37
Blonde Venus '32▶
Blue Hawaii '62
Body Moves '90
Body Rock '84
Broadway Serenade '39
The Buddy Holly Story '78▶
Cabaret '72▶
Camelot '67
Can-Can '60
Carmen: A Hip Hopera '01
Carmen Jones '54▶
Carnegie Hall '47
Carnival Rock '57
Casbah '48▶
The Cat and the Fiddle '34▶
The Chocolate Soldier '41
A Christmas Carol '54
Clambake '67
Club Havana '46
Coal Miner's Daughter '80▶
Concrete Angels '87
Congress Dances '31
Cool Mikado '63
The Cotton Club '84▶
Crossover Dreams '85
Curly Top '35
Daddy Long Legs '55▶
A Damsel in Distress '37▶
Dance Hall '41
Dance of Life '29
Dancing Lady '33
Dancing Pirate '36
A Date with Judy '48
De-Lovely '04

Deadman's Curve '78
The Deputy Drummer '35
Dimples '36
Dogs in Space '87
Don Quixote '35▶
Double Trouble '67
Down Argentine Way '40▶
Dreamgirls '06▶
The Duke Is Tops '38
Evita '96
Espresso Bongo '59
The Farmer Takes a Wife '53
Fast Forward '84
Feel the Noise '07
Fiddler on the Roof '71▶
The Firefly '37
Fisherman's Wharf '39
The Five Pennies '59
Flashdance '83▶
Follow the Boys '44▶
Footloose '84
The Forbidden Dance '90
42nd Street '33▶
Frankie and Johnny '36
Funny Girl '68▶
Funny Lady '75
Gangway '37
George Balanchine's The Nutcracker '93
The Glenn Miller Story '54▶
Go, Johnny Go! '59
Goodbye, Mr. Chips '69
Graffiti Bridge '90
Great Balls of Fire '89
The Great Caruso '51
The Great Waltz '38▶
The Great Ziegfeld '36▶
Greek Street '30
Hard to Hold '84
The Harder They Come '72
Harmony Lane '35
Harum Scarum '65
Heart's Desire '37
Hello, Frisco, Hello '43
Honeysuckle Rose '80
Honkytonk Nights '78
How She Move '08
Hustle & Flow '05▶
I Could Go on Singing '63
Idolmaker '80
If You Knew Susie '48
I'll Cry Tomorrow '55▶
I'll See You in My Dreams '51
I'm Not There '07▶
The In Crowd '88
It Happened at the World's Fair '63
It's Always Fair Weather '55
Jailhouse Rock '83▶
The Jazz Singer '27
The Jazz Singer '80
Jeanne and the Perfect Guy '98
Jesus Christ, Superstar '73▶
Jesus Christ Superstar '00
Jolson Sings Again '49
The Jolson Story '46▶
The Josephine Baker Story '90
Jungle Patrol '48
Just Around the Corner '38
The King and I '56▶
King Creole '58
Knights of the City '85
La Bamba '87▶
Ladies of the Chorus '49
Lady Sings the Blues '72
Lagaan: Once upon a Time in India '01
Lambada '89
Life of Verdi '32
Light of Day '87
Little Colonel '35▶
Little Miss Broadway '38
The Littlest Angel '69
The Littlest Rebel '35
Lottery Bride '30
Love Me or Leave Me '55▶
Love Me Tender '56
Love Songs '07
Mack the Knife '46▶
The Man I Love '46▶
Man of La Mancha '72
Marco '73

A Matter of Time '76
Meet Danny Wilson '52
Melody Master '41
Miss Sadie Thompson '53▶
MTV's Wuthering Heights '03
Murder at the Vanities '34
Murder with Music '45
The Music Lovers '71
The Music Man '62▶
Musica Proibita '43
My Fair Lady '64▶
Never Steal Anything Small '59
New Moon '40
New Orleans '47
New York, New York '77▶
Night and Day '46
No, No Nanette '40
Northwest Outpost '47
The Old Curiosity Shop '75
Oliver! '68▶
Once '06
The One and Only, Genuine, Original Family Band '68
One Night of Love '34▶
One Trick Pony '80
Opera do Malandro '87
Orchestra Wives '42▶
Orfeu '99
An Orphan Boy of Vienna '37
Paradise, Hawaiian Style '66
Paradise in Harlem '40
Paradise Island '30
Paris Blues '61
Pennies from Heaven '36
Pennies from Heaven '81▶
Pete Kelly's Blues '55
The Phantom of the Opera '06
Piaf '81
The Poor Little Rich Girl '36
A Prairie Home Companion '06
Princess Tam Tam '35▶
Purple Rain '84
Quadrophenia '79▶
Rainbow '78
Rappin' '85
Reckless '35
The Red Shoes '48▶
Rent '05
Rhapsody in Blue '45▶
Rock, Baby, Rock It '57
Rock, Rock, Rock '56
Rooftops '89
Rose Marie '36▶
Rose Marie '54▶
Rose of Washington Square '39
Roustabout '64
Sailing Along '38
Salsa '88
Same Old Song '97▶
Sarafina! '92▶
Satisfaction '88
Scrooge '70
Senora Tentacion '49
Shining Star '75
Shout '91
Show Boat '36▶
Show Boat '51
Sincerely Yours '56
Sing '89
The Singing Detective '86▶
Smilin' Through '41
Something to Sing About '36
Song of My Heart '29
Song of Freedom '36
Song of Norway '70
Song of Scheherazade '47
Song Without End '60
Songwriter '84
The Sound of Music '65▶
Sparkle '76
Stars and Stripes Forever '52▶
Start! '68
State Property 2 '05
Stay Away, Joe '68
Stepping Out '91▶
Stowaway '36▶
Sueno '05

Musicals
see also Animated
Musicals: Contemporary
Musicals: Disco
Comedy; Musical
Comedy; Musical
Drama; Musical
Fantasy

Alexander's Ragtime Band '38.

Sunday in the Park with George '86▶
Sweeney Todd: The Demon Barber of Fleet Street '07
Sweet Charity '69▶
Sweet Dreams '85
Sweetheart of the Navy '37
Tap '89
They Shall Have Music '39
This Is the Army '43
The Three Penny Opera '62
Thunder Alley '85
Tommy '75▶
Transatlantic Merry-Go-Round '34
Umbrellas of Cherbourg '64▶
Up/Down/Fragile '95
Waltz King '63
Way Down South '39
West Side Story '61▶
What's Love Got to Do with It? '93
Yankee Doodle Dandy '42▶
Yentl '83▶
Young at Heart '54
Young Caruso '51
Young Man with a Horn '50▶
Ziegfeld Girl '41▶
Zoot Suit '81▶
Zou Zou '34

Musical Fantasy
see also Musicals

Alice '86
Anything But Love '02
Babes in Toyland '61
Bedknobs and Broomsticks '71
Brigadoon '54▶
Butterfly Ball '76
Cabin in the Sky '43▶
Carousel '56▶
Cinderella '64
Cinderella '97
Chitty Chitty Bang Bang '68▶
Comic Book Kids '82
A Connecticut Yankee in King Arthur's Court '49
Damn Yankees '58▶
Dancer in the Dark '99
Doctor Dolittle '67
Down to Earth '47
8 Women '02▶
Fairy Tales '76
The 5000 Fingers of Dr. T '53▶
Gepetto '00
High School Musical '06
Kismet '55
Labyrinth '86▶
Magical Mystery Tour '67
Mary Poppins '64▶
Moulin Rouge '01▶
The New Adventures of Pippi Longstocking '88
Once Upon a Brothers Grimm '77
Peter Pan '60▶
Return to Waterloo '85
Rumpelstiltskin '86
The Singing Detective '03
Sleeping Beauty '89
The Slipper and the Rose '76
Strange Frequency 2 '01
Willy Wonka & the Chocolate Factory '71▶
The Wizard of Oz '39▶
Wonderwall: The Movie '69
Xanadu '80
Zero Patience '94

An American in Paris '51▶
Oh! What a Lovely War '69
Oklahoma! '55▶
On Moonlight Bay '51
On the Town '49▶
100 Men and a Girl '37▶

Anchors Aweigh '45▶
Annie '82
Annie '99▶
Annie Get Your Gun '50▶
Pagan Love Song '50
Pippin '81▶
Private Buckaroo '42
Rainbow over Broadway '33
Red Garters '54
Reet, Petite and Gone '47▶
Rhapsody '54
Rhythm Parade '43
Rich, Young and Pretty '51
Rodgers & Hammerstein's South Pacific '01
Rosalie '37
Second Chorus '40
Sepia Cinderella '47
The Seven Hills of Rome '58
She Shall Have Music '36
Something in the Wind '47
South Pacific '58▶
Square Dance Jubilee '51
Stage Door Canteen '43
Stormy Weather '43▶
The Story of Vernon and Irene Castle '39▶
The Student Prince '54
Sweet Adeline '35
Swing Parade of 1946 '46
Take It Big '44
Terror of Tiny Town '38
Thank Your Lucky Stars '43▶
That Midnight Kiss '49
That's Dancing! '85▶
That's Entertainment '74▶
That's Entertainment, Part 2 '76
That's Entertainment, Part 3 '93
The Threepenny Opera '31
Thrill of a Romance '45
Tin Pan Alley '40
The Toast of New Orleans '50
Tonight and Every Night '45
The Trouble with Girls (and How to Get into It) '69▶
Under the Cherry Moon '86
The Vagabond Lover '29
The Vampyr '32
Viva Las Vegas '63▶
Week-End in Havana '41
Welcome Stranger '47
Wigstock: The Movie '95
Window Shopping '86
Wintertime '43
Words and Music '48
Yes, Sir, Mr. Bones '51
The Young Girls of Rochefort '68
Young People '40

Mutiny
see also Deep Blue; Sail Away; Sea Disasters; Shipwrecked

All the Brothers Were Valiant '53
Amistad '97▶
The Bounty '84
The Caine Mutiny '54▶
The Caine Mutiny Court-Martial '88▶
Crimson Tide '95▶
The Legend of the Sea Wolf '58
Mutiny '52
The Mutiny of the Elsinore '39
Mutiny on the Blackhawk '39
Mutiny on the Bounty '35▶
Mutiny on the Bounty '62▶
Pirate Ship '49
The Sea Wolf '41▶
The Sea Wolf '93

Mystery & Suspense
see also Contemporary Noir; Crime Drama; Film Noir; Psycho-Thriller; Serial Killers; Spies & Espionage

Abduction of St. Anne '75
Above Suspicion '43▶
Above Suspicion '95
Absolution '81
Accidental Meeting '93
Accomplice '46
Accused '36
Ace Drummond '36
Ace of Hearts '85
Across the Bridge '57
Acting on Impulse '93
Address Unknown '96
Adrift '93
Adventures of a Private Eye '87
The Adventures of Sherlock Holmes '39▶
An Affair in Mind '89
African Rage '78
After Dark, My Sweet '90▶
After Pilkington '88
After the Thin Man '36▶
Agatha '79
Agatha Christie's A Caribbean Mystery '83
Agatha Christie's Sparkling Cyanide '83
Agatha Christie's The Pale Horse '96
Agatha Christie's Thirteen at Dinner '85
Alias John Preston '56
Al-American Murder '91
Alligator Eyes '90
Almost Partners '87
The Alphabet Murders '65▶
Alphaville '65▶
The Amateur '82
Amazing Mr. X '48
The Amazing Mr. Blunden '72
The Ambassador '84
The American Friend '77▶
American Gigolo '79▶
Amnesia '96
Amsterdamned '88
And Soon the Darkness '70
And Then There Were None '45▶
The Anderson Tapes '71▶
Android '82
The Andromeda Strain '71▶
Angel Dust '96
Angel Heart '87
Animal Factory '00▶
Animal Instincts 2 '94
Another Thin Man '39▶
Arizona Stagecoach '42
The Arsenal Stadium Mystery '39
The Art of Crime '75
As Good as Dead '95
Assassin '86
Assassin '89
The Assassination File '96
The Assassination Run '84
Apology '86
Appointment with Death '88
Appointment with Fear '85
Apprentice to Murder '88
Arabesque '66▶
Are You in the House Alone? '78
Any Number Can Win '63
Any Man's Death '90

Aubrey...
Autopsy '74
The Atomic City '52
The Avenging Hand '36
The Baby Doll Murders '92
The Babysitter '95
Back from Eternity '56
Back to Hannibal: The Return of Tom Sawyer and Huckleberry Finn '90

▶ = rated three bones or higher

Back to the Wall '56
Backfire '88
Backstab '90
Backstreet Justice '93
Backtrack '89▶
B.A.D. Cats '80
Bad Company '94
Bad Ronald '74▶
The Banker '89
The Barcelona Kill '77
Basic Instinct '92
The Bat Whispers '30
Battle Shock '56
Bedford Incident '65
Bedroom Eyes '86
Bedroom Eyes 2 '89
The Bedroom Window '87
Before I Say Goodbye '03
Before Morning '33
Behind Locked Doors '48
Bell from Hell '74
Bellamy '80
The Beneficiary '97
Benefit of the Doubt '93
Berlin Express '48▶
Berserk! '67
Best Seller '87▶
Betrayal of the Dove '92
Betrayed '88
Beyond a Reasonable Doubt '56
Beyond the Bermuda Triangle '75
Beyond the Silhouette '90
Big Deadly Game '54
The Big Easy '87▶
The Big Fall '96
The Big Fix '78▶
The Big Heat '53▶
The Big Hurt '87
Big News '29
The Big Sleep '46▶
The Big Sleep '78
The Big Switch '70
Big Town After Dark '47
Bikini Island '91
The Bird with the Crystal Plumage '70
Birgitt Haas Must Be Killed '83
Bitter Harvest '93
Bitter Vengeance '94
Black Abbot '63
Black Bird '75
Black Box Affair '66
The Black Camel '31
The Black Cat '81
Black Cobra '83
The Black Doll '38
The Black Gate '95
Black Glove '54
Black Gold '36
Black Ice '92
Black Limelight '38
Black Magic Woman '91
Black Panther '77
Black Rainbow '91▶
Black Raven '43
Black Sunday '77
Black Tower '50
A Black Veil for Lisa '68
Black Water '94
Black Widow '87▶
The Black Windmill '74
Blackmail '29▶
Blackmail '91▶
Blackout '54
Blackout '85
Blackwater Trail '95
Blind Date '84
Blind Fear '89
Blind Horizon '04
Blind Justice '86
Blind Man's Bluff '91
Blind Side '93
Blind Vision '91
Blind Witness '89
Blindfold: Acts of Obsession '94
Blindside '88
Blindsided '93
Blitz '85
Blonde Blackmailer '58
Blood Frenzy '87
Blood on the Sun '45
Blood Relations '87

Blood Relatives '77
Blood Simple '85▶
Bloodhounds '96
Bloody Avenger '80
Blow Out '81▶
Blown Away '93
Blue City '86
Blue Desert '91▶
Blue Ice '92
Blue Smoke '07
Blue Steel '90
Blue Tornado '90
Blue Velvet '86▶
Blue, White and Perfect '42
Bodily Harm '95
Body Chemistry '90
Body Chemistry 3: Point of Seduction '93
Body Double '84▶
The Body in the Library '84
Body Language '92
Body Language '95
Body of Influence '93
Body Parts '94
Body Shot '93
The Body Vanished '39
Boomerang '47▶
Borderline '50
B.O.R.N. '88
The Boston Strangler '68
Bounty Hunters '89
The Bourne Identity '88▶
The Boys from Brazil '78
Brass Target '96
Breakdown '96▶
Breakheart Pass '76
Breaking All the Rules '85
Brick '06▶
The Bride Wore Black '68▶
Brighton Strangler '45
Broken Vows '87
Brotherly Love '85
Bubble '06
Bulldog Drummond '29
Bulldog Drummond at Bay '37
Bulldog Drummond Comes Back '37
Bulldog Drummond's Bride '39
Bulldog Drummond's Peril '38
Bulldog Drummond's Revenge '37
Bulldog Drummond's Secret Police '39
Bullet to Beijing '95
Bulletproof Heart '95▶
Bums '93
Burndown '89
Buying Time '89
By Dawn's Early Light '89
By the Blood of Others '73▶
The Caller '87
Calendar Girl Murders '84
Calling Paul Temple '48
Candles at Nine '44
Caper of the Golden Bulls '67
Cardiac Arrest '74
Caribe '87
Carnival Lady '33
Carolina Moon '07
Caroline at Midnight '93
A Case for Murder '93
The Case of the Lucky Legs '35
Cast a Dark Shadow '55▶
Cast a Deadly Spell '91▶
Castle in the Desert '42
Cat and Mouse '78▶
The Cat and the Canary '27▶
The Cat and the Canary '79
Cat Chaser '90
The Cat o' Nine Tails '71
Catacombs '89
The Catamount Killing '74
Catch Me a Spy '71
Catherine's Grove '98
Caught in the Act '93
Cause for Alarm '51
Center of the Web '92
The Centerfold Girls '74
Chain of Desire '93

Challenge of McKenna '70
Charlie Chan and the Curse of the Dragon Queen '81
Charlie Chan at Monte Carlo '37
Charlie Chan at the Circus '36
Charlie Chan at the Olympics '37
Charlie Chan at the Opera '36▶
Charlie Chan at the Race Track '36
Charlie Chan at the Wax Museum '40
Charlie Chan in Egypt '35
Charlie Chan in London '34
Charlie Chan in Paris '35
Charlie Chan in Rio '41
Charlie Chan in Shanghai '35
Charlie Chan in the Secret Service '44
Charlie Chan on Broadway '37
Charlie Chan's Secret '35
Charlie McCarthy, Detective '39
Charlie Muffin '79
Child in the Night '90
Child of Glass '78
Chill Factor '90
The China Lake Murders '90
China Moon '91▶
Chinatown '74▶
The Chinese Cat '44
Choice of Arms '83
Christina '74
City in Panic '86
City Killer '87
City of Blood '88
City of Shadows '48
The Clay Pigeon '49
A Climate for Killing '91
Cloak and Dagger '46
The Clouded Yellow '51▶
Clouds over Europe '39▶
Clown Murders '83
The Clutching Hand '36
The Cobra Strikes '48
The Cobweb '55
Code Name Alpha '67
Code Name: Diamond Head '77
Codename: Foxfire '85
Codename: Icarus '85
Cohen and Tate '88
Cold Comfort '90
Cold Eyes of Fear '70
Cold Sweat '93
The Colony '95
Color Me Dead '69
Color of Night '94
Columbo: Murder by the Book '71
Columbo: Prescription Murder '67
Coma '78▶
Coming Out Alive '84
Compromising Positions '85
Concealed Weapon '94
Concrete Beat '84
The Confession '20
Confessions of a Hit Man '94
Confidentially Yours '83▶
Consenting Adults '92
The Constant Gardener '05▶
The Conversation '74▶
Convicted '32
Convicted '04
Corn '02
The Corpse Vanishes '42
Counter Punch '71
The Cover Girl Murders '93
Cover Me '95
Cover Story '93
Coyote Waits '03
Crack-Up '46
The Cradle Will Fall '83
Crash '05▶
Crime Broker '94
Criminal Court '46
Criminal Law '89
Criminals Within '41
Crimson Rivers 2: Angels of the Apocalypse '05

Criss Cross '48▶
Cross Country '83
Crow Hollow '52
The Crucifer of Blood '91
The Crude Oasis '95
Cruise into Terror '78
Cruise Missile '78
Cruising '80
Cry Danger '51▶
A Cry in the Night '93
The Cry of the Owl '87
Cry Panic '74
Cry Terror '76
Cry Wolf '47
The Crying Child '96
Curiosity Kills '90
Curse of the Yellow Snake '63
Cutter's Way '81
Cycle Psycho '72
The Da Vinci Code '06▶
Dagger Eyes '83
The Dain Curse '78
Damned River '89
Dance Macabre '91
Dance with Death '91
Dancing with Danger '93
Danger of Love '95
Danger on the Air '38
Danger Zone '51
The Dangerous '95
Dangerous Appointment '34
Dangerous Corner '34▶
Dangerous Game '90
Dangerous Heart '93
Dangerous Love '87
Dangerous Mission '54
Dangerous Obsession '88
Dangerous Summer '82
Danielle Steel's Kaleidoscope '90
The Dark Angel '91▶
Dark Corner '46▶
Dark Forces '83
Dark Night of the Scarecrow '81
Dark of the Night '85
Dark Passage '47▶
Dark Side of Genius '94
Dark Side of Midnight '86
The Dark Wind '91
Darker than Amber '70
Darkness '02
The Darkside '87
Daughter of Horror '55
Day of the Jackal '73▶
Day of the Maniac '77
Dead Again '91▶
Dead Air '94
Dead Certain '92
Dead Cold '96
Dead Connection '94
Dead Eyes of London '61
Dead Funny '94
Dead Heat on a Merry-Go-Round '66▶
Dead in the Water '91
Dead Lucky '60
Dead of Winter '87▶
Dead on Sight '94
Dead on the Money '91
Dead Pigeon on Beethoven Street '72
Dead Reckoning '47▶
Dead Reckoning '89
Dead Ringer '64
Dead Women in Lingerie '90
Deadfall '93
Deadline '81
Deadline at Dawn '46
Deadly Business '77
Deadly Currents '93
Deadly Dancer '90
Deadly Embrace '88
Deadly Exposure '93
Deadly Fieldtrip '74
Deadly Games '80
Deadly Illusion '87
Deadly Impact '84
Deadly Innocence '88
Deadly Passion '85
Deadly Possession '88
Deadly Rivals '92

The Deadly Secret '94
Deadly Sins '95
Deadly Spygames '89
Deadly Sting '82
Deadly Strangers '82
Deadly Surveillance '91
Dear Dead Delilah '72
Dear Detective '78
Death at Love House '75
Death by Prescription '86
Death Cruise '74
Death Dreams '92
Death from a Distance '36
Death Games '80
Death Goes to School '53
The Death Kiss '33
Death Magic '92
Death on the Nile '78▶
Death Rage '77
Death Ray 2000 '81
Death Sentence '74
Death Train '79
Death Valley '81
Death Warrant '90
Death Weekend '76
Deathmask '69
Deceived '87
December Flower '84
Deception '92
Deceptions '91
The Deep '77
Deep Cover '88
Defense of the Realm '85▶
Defenseless '91
Deja Vu '89
Delusion '84
Delusion '91
Deranged '87
Deranged '01
Descending Angel '90▶
Desire and Hell at Sunset Motel '92
Desperate '47
Desperate Hours '55▶
Desperate Hours '90
Desperate Motives '92
The Detective '54▶
The Detective '68▶
Detective '85
Devices and Desires '91▶
Devil Diamond '37
Devil in a Blue Dress '95▶
The Devil Thumbs a Ride '47▶
The Devil's Cargo '48
Devil's Party '38
The Devil's Undead '75
Devlin '92
Diabolically Yours '67
Dial Help '88
Dial "M" for Murder '54▶
Diamond Run '90
The Diamond Trap '91
Diamonds '72
Diamond's Edge '88
Dick Tracy '37
Dick Tracy, Detective '45
Dick Tracy Meets Gruesome '47
Dick Tracy Returns '38
Dick Tracy; The Spider Strikes '37
Dick Tracy vs. Crime Inc. '41
Dick Tracy's Dilemma '47
Die Die My Darling! '65
Die Screaming, Marianne '73
Die Sister, Die! '74
Die Watching '93
Dinner at the Ritz '37
Diplomatic Courier '52▶
Dirkham Detective Agency '83
Dirty Harry '71▶
Disappearance '81
The Disappearance of Christina '93
Disconnected '87
Discretion Assured '93
Dishonored Lady '47
Distortions '87
Disturbance '89
Diva '82▶
D.O.A. '49▶

D.O.A. '88
Dr. Mabuse vs. Scotland Yard '64
Dr. Tarr's Torture Dungeon '75
Dog Day '83
Dog Day Afternoon '75▶
Dominique Is Dead '79
The Domino Principle '77
Donor Unknown '95
Don't Bother to Knock '52
Don't Go in the House '80
Don't Look in the Attic '81
Don't Look Now '73▶
Don't Open the Door '74
Don't Torture a Duckling '72
Doomed to Die '40
The Doomsday Flight '66
Door with the Seven Locks '62
Double Agents '59
Double Cross '92
Double Cross '94
Double Exposure '82
Double Exposure '93
Double Face '70
Double Identity '89
Double Indemnity '44▶
Double Jeopardy '92
The Double McGuffin '79
The Double Negative '80
Double Obsession '93
Double Threat '92
Double Vision '92
The Draughtsman's Contract '82▶
Dream Lover '85
Dream Man '94
Dream No Evil '75
Dress Gray '86▶
Dressed for Death '74
Dressed to Kill '46
Dressed to Kill '80▶
Driven to Kill '90
Driver's Seat '73
The Drowning Pool '75▶
Drums of Jeopardy '31
Duel '71▶
The Dummy Talks '43
Dying Game '94
Dying Room Only '73
Dying to Remember '93
The Dying Truth '91
Dynasty of Fear '72
Early Frost '94
Ebbtide '94
Echo Murders '45
Echoes '83
Edge of Darkness '86▶
The Eiger Sanction '75
Eight Witnesses '54
11:14 '03▶
Embassy '72
Embassy '85
Emil and the Detectives '64
Emissary '89
The Empty Beach '85
Endangered Species '82
Endless Night '71
Enigma '82
Enrapture '90
Equus '77▶
Escapade in Florence '62
Escape '90
Escape Clause '96
Escapist '83
Estate of Insanity '70
Evelyn Prentice '34
Even Angels Fall '90
Everybody Wins '90
Everybody's Dancin' '50
Evidence of Blood '97
Evil under the Sun '82▶
Ex-Mrs. Bradford '36▶
Exit in Red '97
The Executioner '70
Experiment in Terror '62▶
Experiment Perilous '45▶
The Expert '95
Exposure '83
Exposure '91
Express to Terror '79
Exterminator '80
Extreme Measures '96
Eye of the Needle '81▶
Eye Witness '70
Eyes of Laura Mars '78▶

Eyewitness '81
Eyewitness to Murder '93
F/X '86▶
The Face at the Window '39
A Face in the Fog '36
Fade to Black '93
Fail-Safe '64▶
Fake Out '82▶
The Falcon and the Snowman '86▶
The Falcon in Hollywood '44
The Falcon in Mexico '44
The Falcon's Brother '42
The Fan '81
The Fantasist '89
Far from Home '89
Farewell, My Lovely '75▶
Fatal Bond '91
Fatal Charm '92
Fatal Exposure '90
Fatal Exposure '91
Fatal Games '84
The Fatal Hour '40
The Fatal Image '90
Fatal Instinct '92
Fatal Past '94
Fatherland '94
FBI Girl '52
Fear '88
Fear '90
Fear City '85
Fear in the Night '47▶
Fearless '89
Fearmaker '89
The Female Jungle '56
The Feminine Touch '95
Femme Fatale '90
Fer-De-Lance '74
Fever '88
The Fifth Floor '80
52 Pick-Up '86
The Fighting Westerner '35
Final Analysis '92
Final Assignment '80
Final Combination '93
Final Cut '88
The Final Embrace '92
Final Judgment '92
The Final Option '82
The Finishing Touch '92
First Degree '95
The Firm '93▶
First Degree '98
Five Graves to Cairo '43▶
Five Dolls for an August Moon '70
Flashfire '94
Flashpoint '84
Flatliners '90
Fleshtone '94
Flowers in the Attic '87▶
Flying from the Hawk '86
Fog Island '45
Follow Me Quietly '49▶
The Fool Killer '65
Footsteps in the Dark '41▶
For Hire '98
Forbidden Games '95
Forbidden Sun '89
The Force '94
Foreign Correspondent '40▶
Forger of London '61
Forget Mozart '85
The Forgotten One '89
The Forgotten '04
Formula for a Murder '80
The Formula '80
Fortress '85
The Fourth Protocol '87▶
Fourth Story '90▶
Frame by Frame '95
The Franchise Affair '52
Frantic '58▶
Frantic '88
Freedomland '06
French Intrigue '70
The French Detective '75▶
French Silk '94
Frenzy '46
Frenzy '72▶
Fresh Kill '87

Fright '71
From Hollywood to Deadwood '89
Frozen Alive '64
From the Dead of Night '89▶
Fugitive Among Us '92
Full Circle '77
Full Exposure: The Sex Tape Scandals '89
Full Fathom Five '90
Funeral in Berlin '66▶
The Game '89
Game of Seduction '86
Gang Busters '42
Gaslight '40▶
The Gathering '02
Georgia '87
Get That Man '35
Getting Even '86
The Ghost Camera '33
Ghost Ship '53
The Ghost Train '41
The Ghost Walks '34
Girl Hunters '63
The Girl in a Swing '89
The Girl in Lover's Lane '60
A Girl to Kill For '90
Girls Night Out '83
Glass '88
The Glass Cage '96
The Glass Key '42▶
Glass Tomb '55
Go-Ge-'Em-Haines '35
Golden Lady '79
Golden Rendezvous '77
The Golden Spiders: A Nero Wolfe Mystery '00
Gone Dark '03
Gone to Ground '76
Gorky Park '83▶
Gotham '88▶
The Grave '95
The Great Riviera Bank Robbery '79
The Great St. Louis Bank Robbery '59
Green Archer '40
Green Eyes '34
Green for Danger '47
Green Ice '81
The Green Man '91▶
Grievous Bodily Harm '89
Ground Zero '88
Guest in the House '44
Guilty as Sin '93
Guilty Conscience '85▶
Gunpowder '87
Half a Soldier '40
Hammett '82▶
Hand Gun '93
Hands of a Stranger '87
Hanky Panky '82
Happily Ever After '86
Hard Drive '94
Hard Evidence '94
The Hard Truth '94
Harper '66▶
Harry Potter and the Goblet of Fire '05▶
The Harvest '92
The Haunted Castle '21▶
The Haunted Sea '97
Haunting of Harrington House '82
The Haunting Passion '83
The Hawk '93
He Lives: The Search for the Evil One '67
He Sees You When You're Sleeping '02
Heads '93
Hear No Evil '93
Heartaches '47
The Heat of the Day '91
Heat of the Sun '99▶
Heat Wave '54
Heatwave '83▶
Heaven's Prisoners '95
The Heist '89
Hell Harbor '30
Hell's Headquarters '32
Help! '65▶
Hidden Agenda '90
Hi-Jacked '50
Hidden City '87
Hidden Fears '93

Hidden Obsession '92
The Hidden Room '49▶
Hide in Plain Sight '80▶
High Frequency '88
High Stakes '89
Highway 13 '48
The Hillside Strangler '89
The Hit List '93
The Hit List '88
The Hitman '91
Hollywood '06
Home for the Holidays '72
Homicide '91▶
Hollywoodland '06
Hollywood Confidential '97
Hollywood Stadium Mystery '38
The Holcroft Covenant '85
The Hooded Terror '38
The Horse Without a Head '63
The Horseplayer '91
Hostage '92
Hostages '80
Hot Child in the City '87
Hotel '01
Hotel Colonial '88
Hotel Reserve '44▶
Hotline '82
The Hound of London '93
The Hound of the Baskervilles '59
The Hound of the Baskervilles '39▶
The Hound of the Baskervilles '83
Hour of Decision '57
A House in the Hills '93
House of Fear '45
House of Mystery '34
The House of Secrets '37
House of the Damned '63
House of the Rising Sun '87
House on Carroll Street '88
The Housekeeper '86
Human Desires '97
Human Gorilla '48
The Human Monster '39
Hunt the Man Down '50
Hunter '76
The Hunting '92
The Hustle '75
Hysteria '64
I Am the Cheese '83
I Bury the Living '58▶
I Confess '53▶
I Killed That Man '42
I, Madman '89
I Saw a Dark Stranger '46▶
I Stand Condemned '36
I, the Jury '82
The Ice House '97▶
I'd Give My Life '36
If It's a Man, Hang Up '75
If Looks Could Kill '86
I'll Get You '53
I'll Name the Murderer '36
Illicit Behavior '91
Illicit Dreams '94
Illusions '91
I'm Not Scared '03▶
Impulse '55
Impulse '84
Impulse '90

Improper Conduct '94
Image of Death '77
For '86
I'm the One You're Looking '74
I'm the Girl He Wants to Kill '74
In a Lonely Place '50▶
In a Moment of Passion '93
In a Stranger's Hand '92
In an Old Manor House '84
In Self Defense '93
In the Cold of the Night '89
In the Deep Woods '91
In the Heat of the Night '67▶
In the Kingdom of the Blind the Man with One Eye Is King '94
In the Line of Fire '93▶
In the Secret State '85
In the Spirit '90
In the Valley of Elah '07▶
Indecency '92
Indecent Behavior '93
Indecent Behavior 2 '94
The Indian Scarf '63
Indiscreet '47
Infamous Crimes '47
The Inheritor '06
Inland Empire '06
Inheritance '47
The Innocent '93
Innocent Lies '95
Innocent Victim '90
Innocents with Dirty Hands '75
The Inquiry '87
The Inside Man '84
Insanity '76
Inspector Lynley Mysteries: A Great Deliverance '01
The Instructor '83
Interface '84
International Crime '37
Internecine Project '73
The Interpreter '05▶
Interrupted Journey '49
Intimate Stranger '91
Into the Blue '97
Into the Fire '88
Intrigue '90
Intruder '73
Invasion of Privacy '92
Investigation '79
The Invisible '07
The Invisible Avenger '58
The Invisible Killer '40
Invitation to Hell '84
The Iris Effect '04
Irish Luck '39
Island Monster '53
Istanbul '85
It Could Happen to You '39
It Happened at Nightmare Inn '70

Jack's Back '87▶
The Jade Mask '45
The Jagged Edge '85
Jane Doe '83
Jaws of Death '76
Jennifer 8 '92
Jenny Lamour '47
Jezebel's Kiss '90
Jigsaw '30
Jigsaw '90
The Jigsaw Man '84
Jigsaw Murders '89
Johnny Angel '45▶
Johnny Nobody '61
Johnny Skidmarks '97
Journey into Fear '42▶
Journey into Fear '74
Joy House '64
Judicial Consent '94
Juggernaut '74▶
Jungle Bride '33
The Junkman '82
Just Another Pretty Face '58
Just Cause '94
Kafka '91
Keane '04▶
Kemek '70
The Kennel Murder Case '33▶
Kentucky Jubilee '51
Keys to Tulsa '96
The KGB: The Secret War '86
Kid '90
The Kidnapping of the President '80
Kidnapped '87
Kill Cruise '90
Kill-Off '90
Killer Image '92
Killer Likes Candy '78
Killer in Every Corner '74
Killer Looks '94
Killer with Two Faces '74
The Killers '64▶
A Killing Affair '85
The Killing Game '87

Killing Hour '84
The Killing Jar '96
The Killing Kind '73
The Killing Mind '90
Killing Obsession '94
Killing Stone '78
The Killing Time '87
Killjoy '81
Killjoy '00
Killpoint '84
A Kiss Before Dying '91
Kiss Daddy Goodnight '87
Kiss Me, Kill Me '69
The King Murder '32
Klute '71▶
L.A. Confidential '97▶
L.A. Goddess '05
La Moustache '05
La Passante '83
The Lady Confesses '45
The Lady from Shanghai '48▶
Lady Audley's Secret '00
Lady Beware '87
Lady in a Cage '64▶
Lady in Cement '68
Lady in Question '99
Lady in the Death House '44
The Lady in White '88▶
Lady of Burlesque '43
Lady Scarface '41
The Lady Vanishes '38▶
The Lady Vanishes '79
LadyKiller '92
LadyKillers '88
Laguna Heat '87
Last Dance '91
Last Embrace '79▶
The Last of Philip Banter '87
The Last of Sheila '73▶
Last Rites '88
Last Song '80
The Last Show '80
The Laughing Policeman '74
Laura '44▶
Le Corbeau '43▶
Le Magnifique '76
Le Polygraphe '96
Left for Dead '78
Legacy of Lies '92
Legal Deceit '95
Lemming '05▶
Letter to My Killer '95
The Liars '64
Liar's Edge '92
Lie Down with Lions '94
Liebestraum '91
Lies '83
Lies Before Kisses '92
The Life of David Gale '03
Lifespan '75
The Lift '85
The Lightning Incident '91
Lights! Camera! Murder '89
Lily Was Here '89
The Limping Man '53
Linda '93
Lipstick Camera '93
Lisa '90
Lisbon '56
The List of Adrian Messenger '63▶
The Little Drummer Girl '84▶
The Little Girl Who Lives down the Lane '76
Little Nikita '88
Living to Die '91
The Lodger '26▶
Lonely Hearts '91
The Long Goodbye '73▶
Long Time Gone '86
Loose Cannons '90
The Lost Angel '04
Lost Junction '03
The Lost Jungle '34
The Lost Tribe '89
Love '05
Love and Hate: A Marriage Made in Hell '90
Love & Murder '91
Love at Large '89▶
Love Camp '81
Love Kills '91
Love from a Stranger '37
Love from a Stranger '47

Love on the Run '85
Lower Level '91
Lure of the Islands '42
Lying Lips '39
The Machinist '04
Mackintosh Man '73▶
The Mad Executioners '65
Madame Sin '71
Madeleine '50
Madigan '68▶
Magic Moments '89
Malevolence '04
Malibu Express '85
Malice '93
Malicious '95
Man on Fire '87
Man on Fire '04
Man on the Run '49
Man on the Roof '76▶
The Man Outside '88
The Man Who Haunted Himself '70
The Man Who Knew Too Much '34▶
The Man Who Knew Too Much '56▶
The Man from Headquarters '28
Man from the Pru '89
The Man Inside '90
The Man Who Wouldn't Die '42
The Manchurian Candidate '62▶
The Mandarin Mystery '37
Manfish '56
Manhunter '86▶
The Manhattan Project '86
Maniac '63
Marathon Man '76▶
Margin for Murder '81
Marie Galante '34▶
Mark of Cain '84
Mark of the Beast: '87
Mark of the Dragon '51
Marlowe '69
Marnie '64▶
Maroc 7 '67
Mascara '87
Masks of Death '86
Masquerade '88▶
Masquerade '65
Master Touch '74
Masters of Horror: Cigarette Burns '05
Masters of Horror: Deer Woman '05
Masters of Horror: Dream Cruise '07
Masters of Horror: Dreams in the Witch House '05
Masters of Horror: Fair Haired Child '06
Masters of Horror: Family '05
Masters of Horror: Homecoming '05
Masters of Horror: Imprint '05
Masters of Horror: Jenifer '05
Masters of Horror: Pelts '06
Masters of Horror: Pro-Life '06
Masters of Horror: Right to Die '07
Masters of Horror: Sick Girl '06
Masters of Horror: Sounds Like '06
Masters of Horror: The Screwfly Solution '06
Masters of Horror: The V Word '05
Masters of Horror: The Washingtonians '07
Masters of Horror: Valerie on the Stairs '06
Masters of Horror: We All Scream for Ice Cream '07
A Matter of WHO '62
The Maze '53▶
Mazes and Monsters '82
The McGuffin '85

▶ = rated three bones or higher

Medusa '74
Meeting at Midnight '44
Memories of Murder '90
Memories of Murder '03
Men at Work '90
Messenger of Death '88
Miami Blues '90
Michael Shayne: Private Detective '40
Midnight '34
Midnight at the Wax Museum '36
Midnight Faces '26
Midnight Girl '25
Midnight Heat '95
Midnight in Saint Petersburg '97
Midnight Limited '40
Midnight Warning '32
Midnight Witness '93
Mike's Murder '84
Million Dollar Mystery '87
Mind, Body & Soul '92
A Mind to Kill '95
A Mind to Murder '96
Mind Twister '93
Mindfield '89
Mirage '66▶
The Mirror Crack'd '80
Mirror Images '91
Mirror Images 2 '93
Missing Pieces '83
Mistaken Identity '41
Mr. Frost '89
Mr. Moto in Danger Island '39
Mr. Moto Takes a Chance '38
Mr. Moto's Gamble '38
Mr. Moto's Last Warning '39▶
Mr. Reeder in Room 13 '38
Mr. Scarface '77
Mr. Wong, Detective '38
Mr. Wong in Chinatown '39
Money Madness '47
Monique '76
Monsieur N. '03▶
The Monster Walks '32
Moon in Scorpio '86
Moonlighting '85
The Moonstone '97▶
The Morning After '86
Mortal Passions '90
The Most Dangerous Game '32▶
Mother's Boys '94
Mr. Takes a Vacation '39
Motor Patrol '50
Motorcycle Squad '41
Murder '30▶
Murder Ahoy '64
Murder at 45 R.P.M. '65
Murder at Midnight '31
Murder at 1600 '97
Murder at the Baskervilles '37
Murder at the Gallop '63▶
Murder by Decree '79▶
Murder by Natural Causes '79▶
Murder by Night '89
Murder by Numbers '89
Murder by Phone '82
Murder by Television '35
Murder by the Book '87
Murder in a Small Town '99
Murder in Mind '97
Murder in Space '85
Murder in the Footlights '46
A Murder is Announced '87
Murder Most Foul '65▶
Murder, My Sweet '44▶
A Murder of Crows '99
A Murder of Quality '90
Murder on Approval '56
Murder on the Campus '52
Murder on the High Seas '32
Murder on the Midnight Express '74
Murder on the Orient Express '74▶
Murder Once Removed '71
Murder 101 '91
Murder over New York '40
Murder Rap '87

Murder She Purred: A Mrs.
Murphy Mystery '98
Murder She Said '62
Murder So Sweet '93
Murder Story '89
Murder: Ultimate Grounds for Divorce '84
Murder Without Conviction '04
Murdered Innocence '94
Murderers' Row '66
Murderlust '86
Murderous Vision '91
Murders at Lynch Cross '85
Murders in the Doll House '79
Murders in the Rue Morgue '71
The Murders in the Rue Morgue '86▶
Mute Witness '95
My Man Adam '86
My Sister, My Love '78
My Sweet Victim '85
The Mysterious Magician '65
Mysterious Mr. Moto '38
Mysterious Mr. Wong '35
Mystery in Swing '40
Mystery Liner '34
The Mystery Man '35
Mystery Mansion '83
The Mystery of Edwin Drood '35
The Mystery of Edwin Drood '93
Mystery of Mr. Wong '39
The Mystery of Rampo '94▶
The Mystery of the Mary Celeste '35
Mystery of the Riverboat '44
Mystery Plane '39
Mystery Woman: Mystery Weekend '05
Mystic Circle Murder '39
The Naked Edge '61
The Naked Face '84
Naked Obsession '91
The Name of the Rose '86
Nancy Drew '07
Nancy Drew and the Hidden Staircase '39
Nancy Drew—Detective '38
Nancy Drew, Reporter '39
Nancy Drew—Trouble Shooter '39
The Narrow Margin '52▶
Narrow Margin '90
National Treasure: Book of Secrets '07
Natural Causes '94
Natural Enemy '96
Nature's Playmates '62
The Neighbor '93
Nemesis Game '03
Neutron vs. the Maniac '62
Never Say Die '90
New Year's Evil '78
New York Ripper '82
Newman's Law '74
The Next Victim '71
Next Victim '74
Niagara '52
Night and the City '50▶
Night Angel '90
Night Birds '31
Night Cries '78
Night Eyes '90
Night Eyes 2 '91
Night Eyes 3 '93
Night Fire '94
A Night for Crime '42
The Night Has Eyes '42
The Night Listener '06
The Night Stalker '72
Night Moves '75▶
Night of Terror '33
Night of the Assassin '77
Night of the Cyclone '90
Night of the Hunter '55▶
Night of the Juggler '80
Night Rhythms '92
Night School '81
Night Shadow '90
Night Stalker '87
Night Terror '76
A Night to Remember '42▶
Night Train to Munich '40▶

The Night Visitor '70
Night Watch '72
The Nightcomers '72
Nighthawks '81
Nightkill '80
The Nightman '93
Nightmare in Badham County '76
Nightwaves '03
Nightwing '79
No Mercy '86
No Place to Hide '81
No Place to Hide '93
No Problem '75
No Secrets '91
No Way Out '87▶
No Way to Treat a Lady '68▶
No Witness '04
Nocturne '46
Non-Stop New York '37
Norman Conquest '53
North by Northwest '59▶
Nothing Underneath '85
Notorious '46▶
November Conspiracy '96
Nowhere to Hide '83
Nuclear Conspiracy '85
No. 17 '32▶
The Number 23 '07
The Oblong Box '69
The Obsessed '51
Obsession '76
Obsession: A Taste for Fear '89
Obsessive Love '84
An Occasional Hell '96
Octagon '80
The October Man '48▶
The Odessa File '74
Oldboy '03▶
On Dangerous Ground '51▶
On the Run '83
One Frightened Night '35
One Night Stand '95
One of My Wives Is Missing '76
One Shoe Makes It Murder '82
Open House '86
Open Secret '48
Operation Amsterdam '60
Ordeal by Innocence '84
The Osterman Weekend '83
The Other Woman '92
Out of Annie's Past '94
Out of Bounds '86
Out of Order '84
Out of Sight, Out of Her Mind '89
Out of the Darkness '85▶
Out of the Past '47▶
Out of the Shadows '88
Out on Bail '89
The Outside Man '73
Outside the Law '95
The Oval Portrait '88
Over Indulgence '87
Overexposed '90
Paid to Kill '54
Paint It Black '89
Painted Hero '95
The Pamela Principle '91
Panic in the Streets '50▶
Panic on the 5:22 '74
Panique '47▶
The Panther's Claw '42
Paperhouse '89▶
The Parallax View '74▶
Paranoia '69
Paris Belongs to Us '60
Paris Express '53
Parker '84
Party Girls for Sale '54
Party Line '88
Passion Flower '86
Passion in Paradise '89
Past Midnight '92
Past Tense '94
The Payoff '43
The Pearl of Death '44
The Pelican Brief '93
Pendulum '69
Penthouse '33▶
The Perfect Bride '91
Perfect Crime '79
Perfect Family '92
A Perfect Murder '98

A Perfect Spy '88
Perfect Strangers '84
Perfect Victims '87
Peril '85
Perry Mason Returns '85▶
Perry Mason: The Case of the Lost Love '87
Personals '90
Peter Gunn '89
The Phantom Broadcast '33
The Phantom Creeps '39
Phantom Express '32
Phantom Fiend '35
Phantom Killer '42
The Phantom Light '35
Phantom of Chinatown '40
The Phantom of 42nd Street '45
The Phantom of Soho '64
Phobia '80
The Phone Call '89
Photographer '75
Physical Evidence '89
Picnic at Hanging Rock '75▶
Picture Mommy Dead '66
Pier 23 '51
Play Misty for Me '71▶
Play Nice '92
The Pledge '00▶
Plumber '79
A Pocketful of Rye '87
Poor Girl, a Ghost Story '74
Portrait in Black '60
Portraits of a Killer '95
Posed for Murder '89
Positive I.D. '87
Possessed '05
Power of Attorney '94
Power Play '81
The Practice of Love '84
Praying Mantis '93
President's Mistress '78
The President's Mystery '36
The Presidio '88
Presumed Innocent '90▶
Prey of the Chameleon '91
Primal Secrets '94
Prime Suspect '88
Prime Suspect '92▶
Prime Time Murder '92
Prison Shadows '36
The Private Life of Sherlock Holmes '70▶
Private Obsession '94
The Prize '63▶
Probable Cause '95
Probe '72
Project: Eliminator '91
Project X '87
Promise to Murder '56
Prowler '51
Psychic '91
Psycho '60▶
Psycho 2 '83
Psycho 3 '86
Psychomania '63
Pulp '72
Pursuit '72▶
Pursuit to Algiers '45
Puzzle '78
Quake '92
Quicker Than the Eye '88
Quicksand: No Escape '91
The Quiller Memorandum '66▶
Radioland Murders '94
Rage '72
The Rain Killer '90
Raw Nerve '54▶
Rear Window '54▶
Rebecca '40▶
Rebecca '97▶
Reckless Moment '49▶
The Reckoning '03▶
Red Corner '97
Red Eye '05▶
The Red House '47▶
Red King, White Knight '89
Red Lights Ahead '36
Red Raven Kiss-Off '90
Red Rock West '93▶
Red Wind '91
Rednecks '73
Reflections of Murder '74
Regina '83
Rehearsal for Murder '82
Reilly: Ace of Spies '87▶

The Reincarnation of Peter Proud '75
Relentless 3 '93
Relentless 4 '94
Remember Me '85
Rendition '07
Return '88
The Return of Boston Blackie '27
Return of Chandu '34
The Return of Dr. Mabuse '61
Return of Frank Cannon '80
Revenge '71
Revenge of the Stepford Wives '80
Rich and Strange '32
The Rich Man's Wife '96
Rider on the Rain '70▶
Riders to the Sea '88
Rififi '54▶
Rising Sun '93
Road Games '81
Road to Salina '68▶
Roaring City '51
Rogue's Gallery '44
Rogue's Tavern '36
Rogue's Yarn '56
Romeo Is Bleeding '93
The Rook '99
Room 43 '58
Roots of Evil '91
Rope '48▶
The Rosary Murders '87▶
R.S.V.P. '84
Ruby in the Smoke '06
Rude Awakening '81
Rule 3 '93
Run If You Can '87
Runaways '75
Russian Roulette '75
Russian Roulette '93
Saboteur '42▶
The Saint '68
The Saint in London '39
The Saint in New York '38
The Saint Strikes Back '39
The Saint Strikes Back: Criminal Court '46
The Saint Takes Over '40
The Saint's Double Trouble '40
The Salamander '82
The Salzburg Connection '72
Sanctuary of Fear '79
Sanders of the River '35▶
Satan's Little Helper '04
Savage Hearts '95
Savages '75
Save Me '93
Scalp Merchant '77
Scam '93
Scandal Man '67
Scandalous '88
Scarlet Claw '44▶
The Scarlet Clue '45
Scarlet Street '45▶
Scavengers '87
Scene of the Crime '85
Scene of the Crime '87▶
Scenes from a Murder '72
Schemes '95
Schnelles Geld '84
Scissors '91
Scorned '93
Scorpio '73
The Scorpio Factor '90
Scotland Yard Inspector '52
Scream '83
Scream Bloody Murder '72
Scream for Help '86
Screamer '74
The Sculptress '97
Sea of Love '89▶
Seance on a Wet Afternoon '64▶
Season of Fear '89
The Second Woman '51
Secret Agent 00 '67
Secret of the Black Trunk '62
The Secret Passion of Robert Clayton '92
The Set Up '95
Seven Doors to Death '44

Seven Hours to Judgment '88
The Seven-Per-Cent Solution '76▶
The Seventh Sign '88
Sexpot '88
Sexton Blake and the Hooded Terror '38
Sexual Intent '94
Sexual Malice '93
Sexual Response '92
Shades of Fear '93
The Shadow '36
The Shadow Conspiracy '96
Shadow Dancing '88▶
The Shadow Man '53
Shadow of a Doubt '43▶
Shadow of a Scream '97
Shadow of Doubt '98
Shadow of the Thin Man '41▶
Shadow Play '86
The Shadow Strikes '37
Shadows on the Stairs '41
Shaft '71▶
Shallow Grave '87
The Shanghai Cobra '45
Shattered '91
Shattered Image '93
Shattered Silence '71
She Waits '71
Sherlock Holmes and the Secret Weapon '42▶
Sherlock Holmes Faces Death '43▶
Sherlock Holmes and the Deadly Necklace '62
Sherlock Holmes and the Incident at Victoria Falls '91
Sherlock Holmes in Washington '43
Sherlock Holmes: The Voice of Terror '42
She's Dressed to Kill '79
Shock! '46
Shock to the System '06
Shoot to Kill '88
A Shot in the Dark '33
A Shot in the Dark '35
The Shout '78▶
A Show of Force '90
Show Them No Mercy '35▶
Shriek in the Night '33
Side Show '84
Sidney Sheldon's Bloodline '79
The Sign of Four '83
The Silencer '92
Silent Assassins '88
Silent Fall '94
The Silent Mr. Sherlock Holmes '12
Silent Motive '91
The Silent Partner '78▶
The Silent Passenger '35
Silhouette '91
Silver City '04
Sins of Desire '92
Sins of the Night '93
Sioux City '94
The Sister-in-Law '74
Sister, Sister '87
Sisters of Death '76
Skeletons '96
Sketch Artist '92
Sketch Artist 2: Hands That See '94
Sketches of a Strangler '78
Skinwalker '02
Sky Liner '49
Slamdance '87
The Slasher '72
Slaughter of the Innocents '93
Slayground '84
Sleepers West '41
Sleeping Car to Trieste '45
Sleepwalk '88
Sleuth '72▶
Sleuth '07
Slightly Honorable '40
Slipping into Darkness '88
Silver '93
Slow Burn '86
Small Kill '93

▶ = rated three bones or higher

Smile, Jenny, You're Dead '74
Smilla's Sense of Snow '96
Smooth Talker '90
Snatched '72
Sneakers '92
Snow Kill '90
Snowblind '78
Scis Belle et Tais-Toi '58
Soldier of the Night '84
Somebody Has to Shoot the Picture '90
Someone to Watch Over Me '87
Song of the Thin Man '47
Sorted '04
Sound of Murder '82
Spaceways '53
Speedy Death '99
Spellbound '45
The Spaniard's Curse '58
Spare Parts '79
Spenser: A Savage Place '94
Spenser: Ceremony '93
Spenser: Pale Kings & Princes '94
Spenser: The Judas Goat '94
Special Police '85
The Speckled Band '31
Spectre of the Rose '46
Spider Woman '44
The Spider and the Fly '94
The Spider's Stratagem '70
Spiders '18
Sphinx '81
The Sphinx '33
The Spy Who Came in from the Cold '65
The Spy Within '94
The Squeaker '37
The Squeaker '65
The Squeeze '77
The Squeeze '80
Stacey '73
Stage Fright '50
Stamp of a Killer '87
Stormy Monday '88
The Strange Affair of Uncle Harry '45
A Stolen Face '52
Stone Cold Dead '80
Star of Midnight '35
Star Time '92
State Department File 649 '49

State of Things '82
Station '81
Stay '05
Stay Tuned for Murder '88
The Stepmother '71
The Stepsister '97
Stick '85
Still Life '92
Still of the Night '82
Stir '98
Stranger of the Swamp '46
Strangler of Blackmoor Castle '63
The Strangler '64
Strangers on a Train '51
Strangers '91
The Stranger Within '74
Strange Shadows in an Empty Room '76
The Stranger '46
A Stranger Among Us '92
A Stranger in the House '97
Stranger in Town '57
A Stranger Is Watching '82
Strange Confession '45
The Strange Countess '61
Stranger on the Third Floor '40
Stray Dog '49
Strike Force '81
Stripped to Kill '87
Stripped to Kill II: Live Girls '89
A Study in Scarlet '33
A Study in Terror '66
The Substitute '93
Subterfuge '68
Sucker Money '34

Sudden Fear '52
Suddenly '54
Summer Heat '87
Sunstroke '92
Surrogate '88
Suspect '87
Suspicion '41
Svengali '55
Swiss Conspiracy '77
Sweet Murder '93
Tag: The Assassination Game '82
Tagget '90
Tainted Blood '93
Take Two '87
Taking the Heat '93
Tale of a Vampire '92
Tales of the Unexpected '91
The Tall Blond Man with One Black Shoe '72
Tangiers '83
Tangled Destinies '32
Target '85
The Tattered Web '71
The Taxi Mystery '26
The Teacher '74
Teleton '77
Temptation '94
Ten Days Wonder '72
Ten Little Indians '75
Ten Little Indian's '89
10 Rillington Place '71
Tequila Sunrise '88
Tereza '61
Terminal Choice '85
Terminal Entry '87
The Terror '38
Terror at London Bridge '85
Terror by Night '46
Terror Stalks the Class Reunion '93
Terror Street '54
Terrorists '88
Thank you, Mr. Moto '37
There Goes Kelly '45
They Call Me Mr. Tibbs! '70
They Meet Again '41
They Only Kill Their Masters '72
They Watch '93
They Won't Believe Me '47
They're Playing with Fire '84

3 Women '77
Thrilled to Death '88
ThrillKill '84
Through Naked Eyes '87
Thundersquad '85
Tiara Tahti '62
The Ticker '97
Tiger Bay '59
Tightrope '84
Till Death '92
Till Death Do Us Part '72
Till There Was You '91
Time for Revenge '82
A Time to Die '91
Time Without Pity '57
Times to Come '81
To Catch a King '84

The Thin Man '34
The Thin Man Goes Home '44
Think Fast, Mr. Moto '37
Third Degree Burn '89
The Third Key '57
The Third Man '49
Third Man Out: A Donald Strachey Mystery '05
13th Guest '32
The 39 Steps '35
The Thirteenth Man '37
The Thirty-Nine Steps '79
This Is a Hijack '73
This Lightning Always Strikes Twice '77
This Man Must Die '70
This Sweet Sickness '77
Threat '49
Three by Hitchcock '22
Three Cases of Murder '55
Three Days of the Condor '75
A Thief of Time '04
A Thief of Hearts '84
Thief '71
Thief '81

To Catch a Thief '55
To Kill a Clown '72
To Kill a Stranger '84
The Todd Killings '71
Tomorrow at Seven '33
Tony Rome '67
Too Scared to Scream '85
Topaz '69
Torment '85
Torn Curtain '66
Total Exposure '91
Touch Me Not '74
Touch of Evil '58
Touching Evil '97
Tough Assignment '49
Tough Guys Don't Dance '87
Tour of Terror '97
Tourist Trap '79
Town That Dreaded Sundown '76
Traces of Red '92
Track 16 '02
Track 29 '88
Trade Secrets '86
The Trap '59
The Trap Killer '83
Trapped '89
Trauma '62
Treacherous Crossing '92
The Trouble with Harry '55
The Triumph of Sherlock Holmes '35
Tropical Heat '93
Tropix '02
True Believer '89
True Crime '95
Trial and Error '92
Trial by Jury '94
Twenty Dollar Star '91

Twilight '98
Twilight Mar '96
Twin Sisters '91
Twisted Obsession '90
Two by Forsyth '86
Two Fathers' Justice '85
The Two Jakes '90
Ultimate Desires '91
The Ultimate Imposter '79
The Ultimate Thrill '74
Ultraviolet '91
Uncovered '94
Under Capricorn '49
Under Capricorn '82
Under Investigation '93
Under Suspicion '92
Undercover '94
Uneasy Terms '48
Unholy Four '54
Unholy Wife '57
Union City '81
Union Station '50
Unsane '82
Unsuitable Job for a Woman '82
Unveiled '94
Up in the Air '40
Urge to Kill '84

Utz '93
The Usual Suspects '95
The Vagrant '92
Vamping '84
The Vanishing '88
The Vanishing '93
Vanishing Act '88
Vatican Conspiracy '81
The Vector File '03
Vegas '78
Velvet Touch '48
Verdict in Blood '02
Vertigo '58
The Very Edge '63
Vicious '88
The Vicious Circle '57
Victim of Beauty '91
Victim of Desire '94
Victim of Love '91
Video Murders '87
The Village '04
Violette '78
The Vision '87
Visions '90
Visiting Hours '82
A Vow to Kill '94
Vultures '84
W '74
Waikiki '80

Wanted: Babysitter '75
Warm Nights on a Slow-Moving Train '87
Warning Sign '85
Watched '73
The Way Out '56
Wayne Murder Case '32
We'll Meet Again '93
Weep No More My Lady '93
Whatever Happened to Aunt Alice? '69
When a Stranger Calls '79
When a Stranger Calls Back '93
When I Close My Eyes '93
Where's the Money, Noreen? '95
Where Are the Children? '85
Where Sleeping Dogs Lie '91
Where the Truth Lies '05
When the Bough Breaks '86
A Whisper to a Scream '88
Whispering City '47
Whispering Shadow '33
Whispers in the Dark '92
The Whistle Blower '87
White Cactus '92
White Fire '84
White Hot: The Mysterious Murder of Thelma Todd '91
White Mischief '88
White Noise '05
White of the Eye '88
The White Raven '98
White Sands '92
Who Is the Black Dahlia? '75
Who Killed Baby Azaria? '83
Who Killed Bambi? '03
Who Killed Mary What's 'Er Name? '71
Whodunit '87
The Window '49
The Wind '87
Witchfire '86
Without Warning '52
Witness for the Prosecution '57
The Woman in White '97
The Woman in Question '50
The Woman in Green '45
The Woman in Black '89
The Woman Hunter '72
Woman Hunt '72
Woman Condemned '33
The Woman Who Came Back '45
A Woman's Face '33
A Woman's Face '41
Woman of Desire '93
Woman Undone '95
The Woman in Question '50
Witchcraft '86
Wild West '46
Wild Things '98
Widow's Kiss '94
W-dow Couderc '74
The Word '78
Wonderland '88
Writer's Block '91
The Wrong Man '56
The Wrong Man '93
The Wrong Woman '95
Yellowstone '36
Young and Innocent '37
Young Sherlock Holmes '85
Vegas '78
Z '69
Zentropa '92
Zero Boys '86
Zerfigo Diamond Caper '71
The Zodiac Killer '71

Mythology

see also Folklore & Legends
Atlantis, the Lost Continent '61
Beowulf '07
Chupacabra Terror '05
Clash of the Titans '81
Colossus and the Amazon Queen '64
Conquest of Mycene '63
The Fury of Hercules '61
The Gorgon '64
Helen of Troy '03
Hercules '58
Hercules '83
Hercules '97
Hercules against the Moon Men '64
Hercules and the Captive Women '53
Hercules and the Princess of Troy '65
Hercules in New York '70
Hercules in the Haunted World '64
Hercules, Prisoner of Evil '64
Hercules Unchained '59
Hercules vs. the Sons of the Sun '64
The Loves of Hercules '60
Medusa Against the Son of Hercules '62
Sinbad '71
Sinbad and the Eye of the Tiger '77
Sinbad: Legend of the Seven Seas '03
Sinbad of the Seven Seas '89
Son of Hercules in the Land of Darkness '63
Terror of Rome Against the Son of Hercules '66
The Triumph of Hercules '66
Troy '04
Young Aphrodites '63
Jason and the Argonauts '00

Nannies & Governesses

see also Babysitting;
Bringing Up Baby; The
Help: Female;
Parenthood
Adam Had Four Sons '41
Addams Family Values '93
All This and Heaven Too '40
Anna and the King of Siam '46
Baby Monitor: Sound of Fear '97
Becky Sharp '35
Berkeley Square '33
Big Mcmma's House 2 '06
Blanche Fury '48
Blue Blood '73
The Chalk Garden '64
Corrina, Corrina '94
Cousin Bette '97
The Devil's Own '96
Eloise at the Plaza '03
The Family Holiday '07
Flame Over India '60
Flight of the Red Balloon '08
Friend of the Family 2 '96
The Governess '98
The Hand that Rocks the Cradle '92
The Haunting of Morella '91
Heidi '37
The Innocents '61
Invisible Child '99
Jack and Sarah '95
Jane Eyre '34
Jane Eyre '44
Jane Eyre '83
Jane Eyre '96
Jane Eyre '97
Jane Eyre '06
The King and I '56
The King and I '99
Lady Audley's Secret '00
Left Luggage '98
Lily in Winter '94
Mary Poppins '64
Midnight's Child '93
Miss Mary '86
Mrs. Doubtfire '93
Mr. Nanny '93
My Daughter's Keeper '91
The Nanny '65
The Nanny Diaries '07
Nanny McPhee '06
The Nightcomers '72
Perfect Family '92
The Perfect Nanny '00
Peter Pan '53
Peter Pan '60
Provocateur '96
Rescuers: Stories of Courage "Two Women" '97
The Sound of Music '65
The Turn of the Screw '74
The Turn of the Screw '89
The Turn of the Screw '92
The Turn of the Screw '99
Undesirable '92
Uptown Girls '03
Vanity Fair '67
Vanity Fair '99

Nashville

see also American South;
Biopics: Musicians;
Southern Belles
Baja Oklahoma '87
Cessie '83
The City '76
CoalMiner's Daughter '80
The Concrete Cowboys '79
Doing Time for Patsy Cline '97
Falling from Grace '92
Hard Part Begins '73
Honeysuckle Rose '80
Honkytonk Man '82
Nashville '75
Nashville Beat '89
Nashville Girl '76
The Night the Lights Went Out in Georgia '81
Neil Young: Heart of Gold '06
The Night the Lights Went Out in Georgia '81
Payday '73
Pure Country '92
Rhinestone '84
Rikky and Pete '88
Road to Nashville '67
Saturday Night Special '92
A Smoky Mountain Christmas '86
Songwriter '84
Sweet Dreams '85
Tender Mercies '83
The Thing Called Love '93
Sweet Country Road '83

Nashville Narratives

see also Nashville

National Guard

see also Military: Army;
Persian Gulf/Iraq War
Attack! '56
Between Heaven and Hell '56
Delta Farce '07
First Blood '82
The Ground Truth '06
The Hills Have Eyes 2 '07
Kent State '81
Night of the Lepus '72
Southern Comfort '81
Viva Max '69

Native America

see also Military: Allison
The Abduction of Allison Tate '92
Across the Wide Missouri '51
Angry Joe Bass '76

♦ = rated three bones or higher

Apache Blood '75
Apache Chief '50
Apache Woman '55
The Avenging '92
Bad Lands '39
The Bears & I '74
Big Bear '98
Big Eden '00
Billy Jack '71
Billy Two Hats '74
Black Cloud '04
Black Fox: Blood Horse '94
Black Fox: The Price of Peace '94
Black Robe '91▲
Born Losers '67
Braveheart '25
Broken Arrow '50
Broken Chain '93
Brother Bear '03
Brother Bear 2 '06
Brotherhood of the Wolf '01▲
Buck and the Magic Bracelet '97
Buffalo Bill Rides Again '47
Buffalo Soldiers '97▲
Bugles in the Afternoon '52
Bury My Heart at Wounded Knee '07
The Business of Fancydancing '02
Canyon Passage '46▲
Captain Apache '71
The Captive: The Longest Drive 2 '76
Cavalier of the West '31
Cavalry Charge '51
Centennial '78▲
Chato's Land '71
Cheyenne Autumn '64
Cheyenne Warrior '94
Christmas in the Clouds '01▲
Chuka '67
Circle of Death '36
Clearcut '92
Comanche Moon '08
The Comancheros '61▲
Conquest of Cochise '53
Cotter '72
Coyote Waits '03
Crazy Horse '96▲
Crazy Horse and Custer: "The Untold Story" '90
Crypt of Dark Secrets '76
Custer's Last Fight '12
Dakota Incident '56
Dalva '95
Dan Candy's Law '73
Dance Me Outside '95
Dances with Wolves '90▲
The Dark Wind '91
Dead Man '95
Diplomaniacs '33
The Doe Boy '01
The Education of Little Tree '97
Escape from Fort Bravo '53
Eyes of Fire '84
The Far Horizons '55
Fish Hawk '79
Flags of Our Fathers '06▲
Flaming Star '60▲
Fleshburn '84
Follow the River '95
Four Sheets to the Wind '07
The Gatling Gun '72
Geronimo '62
Geronimo '93
Geronimo: An American Legend '93
Ghost Dance '83
The Glory Trail '36
A Good Day to Die '95
Grand Avenue '96
Gunman's Walk '58
Hondo '53▲
I Heard the Owl Call My Name '73
I Will Fight No More Forever '75▲
Incident at Oglala: The Leonard Peltier Story '92▲
The Indian Fighter '55▲
The Indian in the Cupboard '95
Island of the Blue Dolphins '64

Jim Thorpe: All American '51
Joe Panther '76
Johnny Firecloud '75
Johnny Tiger '66
Journey Through Rosebud '72
Journey to Spirit Island '92
Lakota Woman: Siege at Wounded Knee '94
The Last of His Tribe '92
The Last of the Dogmen '95
The Last of the Mohicans '20▲
The Last of the Mohicans '32
The Last of the Mohicans '36
The Last of the Mohicans '85
The Last of the Mohicans '92▲
The Last of the Redmen '47
Legend of Walks Far Woman '82
The Legend of Wolf Mountain '92
The Light in the Forest '58
Little Big Man '70▲
The Lost Child '00
Lost Legacy: A Girl Called Hatter Fox '77
The Magic Stone '95
The Magnificent Seven '98
A Man Called Horse '70▲
Man of the House '95
The Manitou '78
Map of the Human Heart '93
Massacre '34
Miracle at Sage Creek '05
The Missing '03▲
Mission to Glory '80
A Mormon Maid '17
Natas... The Reflection '83
Navajo Blues '97
The New World '05▲
Northern Passage '95
On Top of the Whale '82
One Little Indian '73
The Pathfinder '94
Pathfinder '07
Pocahontas '95▲
Pocahontas: The Legend '96
Poltergeist 2: The Other Side '86
Powwow Highway '89▲
The Prophecy '95
Ravenhawk '95
Rebel Run '94
The Red Fury '84
The Red Half-Breed '70
Renegades '89
Requiem for a Heavyweight '56▲
Requiem for a Heavyweight '62▲
Ricochet River '98
Roanoak '86
Running Brave '83
Savage Sam '63
The Savage Seven '68
Savage Wilderness '55
The Secret of Navajo Cave '76
Shadowhunter '93
Silent Tongue '92
Sioux City '94
Sitting Bull '54
Skins '02
Skinwalker '02
Skipped Parts '00
Smith! '69
Smoke Signals '98▲
Spirit Rider '93▲
Spirit: Stallion of the Cimarron '02▲
Squanto: A Warrior's Tale '94▲
Sunchaser '96
Tecumseh: The Last Warrior '95
Tell Them Willie Boy Is Here '69▲
Terror in the Jungle '68
Texas John Slaughter: Geronimo's Revenge '60

A Thief of Time '04
3 Ninjas Knuckle Up '95
Three Warriors '77
Thunder Warrior '85
Thunder Warrior 2 '85
Thunderheart '92▲
Tomahawk '51
Tonka '58
Track of the Moonbeast '76
True Heart '97
True Women '97
Unconquered '47
Undead or Alive '07
Uninvited '93
The Vanishing American '25
The Villain '79
Wagon Wheels '34
Walk the Proud Land '56
War Party '89
Where the Spirit Lives '89
White Fang 2: The Myth of the White Wolf '94
Wind River '98
Windrunner '94
Windtalkers '02
Windwalker '81▲
Winterhawk '76
Zoe '01

Nazis & Other Paramilitary Slugs

see also Germany; The Holocaust; Judaism; World War II

All the Queen's Men '02
All Through the Night '42▲
Amen '02▲
Angel of Death '86
Angel with the Trumpet '50
Angry Harvest '85▲
Anima '98
Any Man's Death '90
Apt Pupil '97
Ark of the Sun God '82
Army of Shadows '69▲
The Assisi Underground '84
Background to Danger '43▲
Bedknobs and Broomsticks '71
The Berlin Affair '85
Berlin Express '48▲
Betrayed '54▲
Black Book '06▲
The Black Klansman '66
The Blues Brothers '80▲
Bon Voyage '03▲
The Boxer and Death '63
The Boys from Brazil '78
Brady's Escape '84
Brainwashed '60
Broken Glass '96
Bulletproof Monk '03
Cabaret '72▲
Cabo Blanco '81
Casablanca '42▲
Casablanca Express '89
Charlie Grant's War '80
Clipped Wings '53
Closet Land '90
Cold Days '66
Commandos Strike at Dawn '43
The Conformist '71▲
Conspiracy '01▲
Contraband '40
Cottage to Let '41
Counterblast '48
The Counterfeit Traitor '62▲
The Counterfeiters '07▲
The Coward '62
The Cut Throats '69
Dam Busters '55▲
Dawn Express '42
A Day in October '92
Dead Bang '89
Death is Called Engelchen '63▲
The Death of Adolf Hitler '84
Descending Angel '90▲
Desert Commandos '67
The Desert Fox '51▲
Despair '78▲
The Devil's Brigade '68
The Diary of Anne Frank '59▲
The Dirty Dozen '67▲

The Dirty Dozen: The Deadly Mission '87
The Dirty Dozen: The Fatal Mission '88
The Dirty Dozen: The Next Mission '85
Dirty Heroes '71
Divided We Fall '00▲
Dominion: Prequel to the Exorcist '05
Downfall '04▲
Edge of Darkness '43▲
Elves '89
The Empty Mirror '99
Enemy at the Gates '00
Enemy of Women '44
Enigma Secret '79
Equalizer 2000 '86
Escape from Sobibor '87▲
Europa, Europa '91▲
The Execution '85
Eye of the Needle '81▲
A Face in the Rain '63
The Fallen '05▲
The Fallen Sparrow '43▲
Fateless '05▲
Father '90
Fatherland '94
The Fifth Horseman Is Fear '64
Firewalker '86
Five Fingers '52▲
Five Graves to Cairo '43▲
The Flesh Eaters '64
Flesh Feast '69
Forbidden '85
Force 10 from Navarone '78
Foreign Correspondent '40▲
The Forty-Ninth Parallel '41▲
Four Bags Full '56
The Four Horsemen of the Apocalypse '62
A Friendship in Vienna '88
Genghis Cohn '93
Getting Away With Murder '96
Ghost on the Loose '43
The Girl of Your Dreams '99
The Gleiwitz Case '61
The Goebbels Experiment '05
Goldengirl '79
Good Evening, Mr. Wallenberg '93
The Great Dictator '40▲
The Great Escape '63▲
The Grey Zone '01▲
Hamsun '96
Hangmen Also Die '42▲
Hanna's War '88
Hanussen '88▲
The Harmonists '99
Hart's War '02
He Lives: The Search for the Evil One '67
Head in the Clouds '04
Hell Commandos '69
Hell Hunters '87
Hell River '75
Hell Squad '58
Hellboy '04▲
Heroes in Hell '73
The Heroes of Telemark '65
The Hiding Place '75▲
Higher Learning '94
Hitler '62
Hitler: Dead or Alive '43
Hitler: The Rise of Evil '03
Hitler's Children '43▲
Hitler's Daughter '90
Holocaust '78▲
The Home Front '02
Hornet's Nest '70
Hotel Reserve '44▲
The House on Carroll Street '88
The House on Garibaldi Street '79
House on 92nd Street '45▲
Ilsa, Harem Keeper of the Oil Sheiks '76
Ilsa, She-Wolf of the SS '74
In a Glass Cage '86
In the Presence of Mine Enemies '97
The Incredible Mr. Limpet '64

Indiana Jones and the Last Crusade '89▲
Indiana Jones and the Temple of Doom '84▲
The Infiltrator '95
Inside Out '75
Inside the Third Reich '82
Into the Homeland '87
Invincible '01
Invisible Agent '42
The Island on Bird Street '97
Jack Higgins' The Windsor Protocol '97
Jacob the Liar '74
Jakob the Liar '99▲
Jenny's War '85
Jew-Boy Levi '99
Joe and Max '02▲
Judgment at Nuremberg '61▲
Julia '77▲
Jungle Siren '42
Kanal '56▲
Kapo '59▲
The Keep '83
The Key to Rebecca '85
The Klansman '74
Kojak: The Belarus File '85
Korczak '90▲
La Passante '83▲
Lassiter '84
The Last Butterfly '92
The Last Drop '05
The Last Five Days '82
The Last Metro '80▲
The Last Train '74
Law of the Jungle '42
Les Miserables '95
Les Violons du Bal '74
Life is Beautiful '98▲
Lifeboat '44▲
The Longest Day '62▲
Lucie Aubrac '98
The Lucifer Complex '78
Madame Rosa '77▲
A Man Escaped '57▲
The Man in the Glass Booth '75▲
The Man Who Captured Eichmann '96
Marathon Man '76▲
Martha and I '91▲
Massacre in Rome '73
Master Key '44
Master Race '44
Me and the Colonel '58
The Mediterranean in Flames '72
Mephisto '81▲
Ministry of Fear '44▲
Miracle at Midnight '98
Miracle at Moreaux '86
Mr. Klein '76▲
The Mortal Storm '40▲
Mosley '98
Mother Night '96▲
Music Box '89▲
My Mother's Courage '95
The Nasty Girl '90▲
A Night in Casablanca '46▲
Night of the Fox '90
Night of the Generals '67▲
The Night Porter '74
Night Train to Munich '40▲
Night Train to Venice '93
The Ninth Day '04▲
No Dead Heroes '87
The North Star '43▲
Northern Pursuit '43
Notorious '46▲
Novemberg '00
Nuremberg '00
Oasis of the Zombies '82
The Odessa File '74
The Ogre '96▲
Old Gun '76▲
Once Upon a Honeymoon '42
One of Our Aircraft Is Missing '41▲
The Only Way '70
Open City '45▲
O.S.S. '46▲
Passage to Marseilles '44▲
The Pedestrian '73▲
The Pianist '02▲
Pimpernel Smith '42▲

Porcile '69
A Prayer for Katarina Horovitzova '69
Prayer of the Rollerboys '91
Pressure Point '62▲
Prisoner of Paradise '02▲
Puppet Master 3: Toulon's Revenge '90
The Quiller Memorandum '66▲
Raid on Rommel '71
Raiders of the Lost Ark '81▲
Rescuers: Stories of Courage "Two Women" '97▲
Reunion in France '42
The Revolt of Job '84▲
Richard III '95▲
Rio Rita '42
River of Death '90
River of Diamonds '90
The Rocketeer '91▲
The Rose Garden '89
Rosenstrasse '03▲
The Salzburg Connection '72
Savage Attraction '83
The Scarlet & the Black '83▲
Schindler's List '93▲
Schtonk '92
Scream and Scream Again '70
Sea of Sand '58
The Secret Code '42
Secret Mission '42
The Secret War of Harry Frigg '68
The Seventh Cross '44▲
Severed Ties '92
She Demons '58
Shining Through '92
Shock Waves '77
Silent Scream '84
633 Squadron '64
Skinheads: The Second Coming of Hate '88
Snow Treasure '67
So Ends Our Night '41▲
Soldier of Orange '78▲
A Soldier's Tale '88
Son of Lassie '45
Sophie Scholl: The Final Days '05▲
The Sorrow and the Pity '71▲
The Sound of Music '65▲
Stalag 17 '53▲
Stalag Luft '93
The Statement '03▲
The Stranger '46▲
Strangers in Paradise '84
Strayed '03▲
Sundown '41
Surf Nazis Must Die '87
Sweet Light in a Dark Room '60▲
Swing Kids '93
A Taxing Woman's Return '88▲
That Summer of White Roses '90
They Saved Hitler's Brain '64
13 Rue Madeleine '46▲
'38: Vienna Before the Fall '88
This Land Is Mine '43▲
Tiger Fangs '43
Tigershark '87
To Be or Not to Be '42▲
To Be or Not to Be '83
To Catch a King '84
Tomorrow the World '44
Top Dog '95
Top Secret! '84▲
The Tormentors '71
Train of Life '98▲
Transport from Paradise '65
Triumph of the Spirit '89▲
Triumph of the Will '34▲
True Colors '87
U-Boat Prisoner '44
Underground '41
Uprising '01▲
Uranus '91▲
War & Love '84
War & Remembrance '88

▲ = rated three bones or higher

War & Remembrance: The Final Chapter '89
Watch on the Rhine '43 ▶
Waterfront '44
Where Eagles Dare '68 ▶
Where Trails End '42
Wild Geese 2 '85
The Winds of War '83
Wings over the Pacific '43
W zards '77
A Woman at War '94
Wooden Horse '50 ▶
Yank in Libya '42
The Yesterday Machine '63
Zeiary '03 ▶
Zentropa '92
Zombie Lake '80
Zone Troopers '84

Near-Death Experiences
see also *Death & the Afterlife*
Dead Zone '83 ▶
Fearless '93 ▶
Flatliners '90
The Princess and the Warrior '00 ▶
Urban Ghost Story '98

Negative Utopia
see also *Paradise Gone Awry; Post-Apocalypse; Technology—Rampant*
Alphaville '65 ▶
Animal Farm '55 ▶
Brazil '85 ▶
Code 46 '03
El Norte '83 ▶
Futureworld '76
Gattaca '97
The Island '05
Metropolis '26 ▶
Moonraker '79
The Mosquito Coast '86
1984 '56 ▶
1984 '84 ▶
Rollerball '75
Soylent Green '73
10th Victim '65 ▶
THX 1138 '71 ▶
V for Vendetta '06
Whodunit '82
Zardoz '73

Netherlands
see also *Amsterdam*
Antonia's Line '95
The Audrey Hepburn Story '00
Black Book '06 ▶
A Bridge Too Far '77
Dutch Girls '87
For a Lost Soldier '93
The Hiding Place '75
The Last Drop '05
Moonlight '82
Spetters '80
Turkish Delight '73

New Black Cinema
see also *African American; Blaxploitation*
Bamboozled '00
Belly '98
Boyz N the Hood '91 ▶
Clockers '95 ▶
Crooklyn '94 ▶
Do the Right Thing '89 ▶
The Five Heartbeats '91 ▶
Get On the Bus '96 ▶
Girl 6 '96
Hangin' with the Homeboys '91 ▶
Hollywood Shuffle '87
I'm Gonna Git You Sucka '88 ▶
Joe's Bed-Sty Barbershop: We Cut Heads '63
Jungle Fever '91 ▶
Just Another Girl on the I.R.T. '93 ▶
Livin' Large '91
Menace II Society '93 ▶
The Meteor Man '93 ▶
Mo' Better Blues '90
The Players Club '98 ▶
Poetic Justice '93
Posse '93 ▶
A Rage in Harlem '91 ▶
School Daze '88 ▶
Set It Off '96
She's Gotta Have It '86 ▶
Soul Plane '04
Straight out of Brooklyn '91 ▶
To Sleep with Anger '90 ▶

New Jersey
see also *New York, New York*
Atlantic City '81 ▶
Baby It's You '82 ▶
Be Kind Rewind '08 ▶
Beer League '06
Bogus '96
Bought and Sold '03
Chasing Amy '97 ▶
Cheaper by the Dozen '50 ▶
Cinderella Man '05 ▶
Cleaner '07
Clerks '94 ▶
Clerks 2 '06 ▶
Cold Hearts '99
Confessions of a Teenage Drama Queen '04 ▶
The Cookout '04
Cop Land '97 ▶
Coyote Ugly '00 ▶
Dogma '99 ▶
Eddie and the Cruisers '83
Eversmile New Jersey '89
Family Man '00 ▶
Freedomland '06
Garden State '04 ▶
Harold and Kumar Go to White Castle '04
Hysterical Blindness '02
In the Mix '05
Jersey Girl '92
Jersey Girl '04
Just Friends '05
The Last Broadcast '98 ▶
Lean on Me '89 ▶
Mallrats '95 ▶
Moving '88
Nearing Grace '05
New Jersey Drive '95 ▶
Now You Know '02
On the Outs '05
Palindromes '04 ▶
The Purple Rose of Cairo '85 ▶
Return of the Secaucus 7 '80 ▶
Rocket Science '07 ▶
Second Best '05
The Station Agent '03 ▶
This Thing of Ours '03
The Toxic Avenger '86
Tracks '05
Trade '07
War of the Worlds '05 ▶
The Whole Shebang '01
Winter Solstice '04 ▶
Zombie Honeymoon '04

New Orleans
see also *American South; Holidays: Mardi Gras*
The Dangerous '95
The Dark Side of Love '79
Dead Man Walking '95 ▶
French Quarter '78
French Quarter Undercover '85
French Silk '94
The Glass Cage '96
Hard Target '93
Heaven's Prisoners '95
Hotel '67
The Invisible Avenger '58
It Happened in New Orleans '36
J.D.'s Revenge '76
Judas Kiss '98
King Creole '58 ▶
Last Holiday '06
A Love Song for Bobby Long '04
Mardi Gras for the Devil '93
Mardi Gras Massacre '78
Mirrors '78
My Forbidden Past '51
New Orleans '47
New Orleans After Dark '58
Night of the Strangler '73
One Christmas '95
Panic in the Streets '50 ▶
Pretty Baby '78 ▶
Ruby Bridges '98
Runaway Jury '03 ▶
A Saintly Switch '99
Saratoga Trunk '45
The Savage Bees '76
Sonny '02
Storyville '74
Storyville '92
Suddenly, Last Summer '59 ▶
A Streetcar Named Desire '51 ▶
A Streetcar Named Desire '84 ▶
Thunderground '89
Tightrope '84 ▶
Toys in the Attic '63
Tune in Tomorrow '90
Undercover Blues '93
The Unholy '88
Vendetta '99
Walk on the Wild Side '62
The World Moves On '34

New Year's Eve
see also *Christmas; Holidays: Horrible Holidays*
About Last Night... '86 ▶
Are We There Yet? '05
The Art of War '00
The Art of War 2 '08
Assault on Precinct 13 '05
The Best Man '97 ▶
Bloodhounds of Broadway '89
Bloody New Year '87
Century '94
Dirty Dancing: Havana Nights '04
Doctor Who '96
End of Days '99
The Enforcer '76
Entrapment '99 ▶
Four Rooms '95
Gridlock'd '96 ▶
Happy New Year '73 ▶
A Happy New Year '87
Hay Plenty '97
Holiday Affair '96
The Hudsucker Proxy '93 ▶
The January Man '89
Long Time Since '97
More about the Children of Noisy Village '87
New Year's Day '89 ▶
New Year's Evil '78
1999 '98
Ocean's Eleven '01 ▶
Peter's Friends '92
Plan B '97
Poseidon '06
The Poseidon Adventure '72 ▶
P.S. Your Cat's Dead! '02
The Quickie '01
The Real Thing '97
Strange Days '95 ▶
Strange Planet '99
The Sum of Us '94 ▶
Taboo '02
Trading Places '83 ▶
200 Cigarettes '98 ▶
Virtual Seduction '96
Waiting to Exhale '95 ▶
When Harry Met Sally... '89 ▶

New York, New York
see *The Empire State Building*
A Lot Like Love '05
The Accidental Husband '08
Across 110th Street '72
Across the Universe '07 ▶
Adam & Steve '05
Addicted to Love '96
Addicted to Murder 2: Tainted Blood '97
Addicted to Murder 3: Bloodlust '99
The Addiction '95
Adrift in Manhattan '07
An Affair to Remember '57 ▶
After Hours '85 ▶
Aftershock: Earthquake in New York '99
Alfie '04
Alice '90 ▶
All About Eve '50 ▶
All Over Me '96 ▶
All That Jazz '79 ▶
All the Vermeers in New York '91 ▶
Alphabet City '84
Amarilly of Clothesline Alley '18
American Psycho '99 ▶
Analyze That '02 ▶
Analyze This '98 ▶
The Anderson Tapes '71 ▶
Angel Rodriguez '05
Angels My Love '83
Angels with Dirty Faces '38 ▶
Anne of Green Gables: The Continuing Story '99
Annie '82 ▶
Annie '99 ▶
Annie Hall '77 ▶
Another Woman '88 ▶
Anything But Love '02
Anything Else '03 ▶
The Apartment '60 ▶
Armageddon '98 ▶
Arthur '81 ▶
Arthur 2: On the Rocks '88
As Good As It Gets '97 ▶
Ash Wednesday '02
The Astronaut's Wife '99
August Rush '07
Autumn in New York '00
Awake '07
Awakenings '90 ▶
Bad Lieutenant '92 ▶
Bam Bam & Celeste '05
Barefoot in the Park '67 ▶
The Basketball Diaries '95 ▶
Basquiat '96 ▶
The Beautician and the Beast '97
The Beautiful, the Bloody, and the Bare '64
Because of Him '45
Because of You '95
Bed of Roses '95
Before Night Falls '00 ▶
Being John Malkovich '99 ▶
The Believer '01 ▶
Big '88 ▶
The Big Bus '76
Big Business '88
Big Daddy '99 ▶
Big Night '95 ▶
Birth '04 ▶
Blackboard Jungle '55 ▶
The Blackout '97
Blade '72 ▶
Blast of Silence '61
Bless the Child '00
Blink '93
Blonde Ambition '07
Bloodhounds of Broadway '52
Bloodmoon '97
Blue in the Face '95 ▶
Blue Skies '46 ▶
Blue Steel '90 ▶
Boiler Room '00 ▶
Bomb the System '05
Bonanno: A Godfather's Story '99
The Bone Collector '99 ▶
The Bonfire of the Vanities '90
Booty Call '96
Boricua's Bond '00
Born to Win '77
Boss of Bosses '99
The Bostonians '84 ▶
The Bourne Supremacy '04 ▶
The Bourne Ultimatum '07 ▶
The Bowery '33 ▶
The Brave One '07 ▶
The Break '97
Breakfast at Tiffany's '61 ▶
Breathing Room '96
Breeders '86
Bright Lights, Big City '88
Brighton Beach Memoirs '86
Bringing Out the Dead '99 ▶
Broadway Bound '92
Broadway Damage '98
Broadway Danny Rose '84 ▶
The Broadway Drifter '27
Broadway Limited '41
Broadway Melody '29
Broadway Melody of 1936 '35 ▶
Broadway Melody of 1938 '37
Broadway Melody of 1940 '40
Broadway Rhythm '44
Broadway Serenade '39
Broken English '07
The Bronx Executioner '86
The Bronx Is Burning '07
A Bronx Tale '90 ▶
Brooklyn Lobster '05
Brooklyn Rules '07
The Brother from Another Planet '84 ▶
A Brother's Kiss '97
Brown Sugar '02 ▶
Bullet '94
Bulletproof Monk '03
Bullets over Broadway '94 ▶
Burny's Last Call '95
Cafe Society '97
Capote '05 ▶
Carlito's Way '93 ▶
Carlito's Way: Rise to Power '05
Carnal Knowledge '71 ▶
Carnegie Hall '47
Cat People '82 ▶
The Caveman's Valentine '01 ▶
Center Stage '00
Chain of Desire '93
Changing Lanes '02 ▶
Charlie Chan on Broadway '37
Chasing Papi '03
Chelsea Walls '01
A Chorus Line '85 ▶
Chutney Popcorn '99
City by the Sea '02
City Hall '95 ▶
City of Ghosts '03
City Slickers '91 ▶
Claire Dolan '97
Clockers '95 ▶
Cloverfield '08 ▶
Cocktail '88
The Cocoanuts '29 ▶
Codename: Jaguar '00
Collected Stories '02 ▶
The Collectors '99
Color of Justice '97
Coming to America '88 ▶
Coming Soon '99
Compromising Positions '85
Conspiracy Theory '97 ▶
Conversations with Other Women '05
Coogan's Bluff '68 ▶
The Corruptor '99 ▶
Corrupt '99
The Cotton Club '84 ▶
A Couch in New York '95
Counsellor-at-Law '33 ▶
The Cowboy Way '94
Coyote Ugly '00 ▶
Cracked Nuts '41
The Cradle Will Rock '99 ▶
Crazy Love '07 ▶
Crimes & Misdemeanors '89 ▶
Critic's Choice '63
Crocodile Dundee '86 ▶
Crocodile Dundee 2 '88
Crooklyn '94 ▶
Crossfire '98
Crossing Delancey '88 ▶
Crossroads '86
Cruel Intentions '98 ▶
Cruising '80 ▶
Curious George '06 ▶
The Curse of the Jade Scorpion '01 ▶
Daredevil '03 ▶
Dark Odyssey '57
Dave Chappelle's Block Party '06 ▶
David Searching '97
The Day After Tomorrow '04 ▶
Day at the Beach '98
Day Night Day Night '06 ▶
Day Zero '07
Daylight '96 ▶
The Daytrippers '96
DC 9/11: Time of Crisis '04
Dead Dog '00
Dead Funny '94
Dead Presidents '95 ▶
The Deal '05
Death to Smoochy '02 ▶
Deception '08
Dedication '07
Definitely, Maybe '08 ▶
The Deli '97
Desolation Angels '95
Desperate Characters '71 ▶
Desperately Seeking Susan '85 ▶
Detective Story '51 ▶
The Devil Wears Prada '06 ▶
The Devil's Advocate '97 ▶
The Devil's Own '96 ▶
Diamond Run '00
Die Hard: With a Vengeance '95 ▶
Dinner Rush '00 ▶
Disappearing Acts '00
Do the Right Thing '89 ▶
Dog Day Afternoon '75 ▶
Donnie Brasco '96 ▶
Don't Say a Word '01 ▶
The Doorbell Rang: A Nero Wolfe Mystery '01
Double Edge '97
Down to Earth '01 ▶
Down to You '00
Down With Love '03 ▶
The Dream Team '89

▶ = rated three bones or higher

Dressed to Kill '80
Drunks '96
Duplex '03
Dust '01
Easy Living '37▲
Eddie '96
Ed's Next Move '96
84 Charing Cross Road '86▲
El Cantante '06
Elf '03▲
Empire '02
Enchanted '07
End of Days '99
Entertaining Angels: The Dorothy Day Story '96
Escape from New York '81
The Event '03
Everyone Says I Love You '96▲
Everyone's Hero '06
Eyes of Laura Mars '78
Eyes Wide Shut '99
Eyewitness '81
F/X '86▲
Face Down '97
Factory Girl '06
The Falcon Takes Over '42
Fall '97
Falling in Love '84
Fame '80▲
Fantastic Four '05
Fatal Attraction '87▲
Fear, Anxiety and Depression '89
Feardotcom '02
Feel the Noise '07
Fever '99
15 Minutes '01
The Fifth Element '97
54 '98
Finder's Fee '01
Finding Forrester '00
A Fine Madness '66▲
Fingers '78▲
Fiona '98
First Love '39
The First Wives Club '96
The Fisher King '91▲
Flannel Pajamas '06
Flawless '99
Fleshpot on 42nd Street '71
Flirt '95
Focus '01
Food of Love '02
For Love or Money '93
The Foreigner '78
Fort Apache, the Bronx '81▲
42nd Street '33▲
.45 '06
Four and a Half Women '05
Frankie and Johnny '91▲
The French Connection '71▲
Frequency '00
The Freshman '90
Friends and Family '01
Frogs for Snakes '98
The Funeral '96▲
Funny Girl '68▲
Fur: An Imaginary Portrait of Diane Arbus '06
G '02
Game 6 '05
Games '67
Gangs of New York '02▲
Get a Clue '02
Get Rich or Die Tryin' '05
Get Well Soon '01
Ghost '90▲
Ghostbusters '84▲
Ghostbusters 2 '89
Gildersleeve on Broadway '43
The Girl in the Red Velvet Swing '55
Giuliani Time '05
Giving It Up '99
Glitter '01
Gloria '98
The Godfather '72▲
The Godfather, Part 2 '74▲
The Godfather, Part 3 '90▲
Godspell '73
Godzilla '98
The Golden Spiders: A Nero Wolfe Mystery '00
The Good Night '07
The Goodbye Girl '77▲

Goodbye, New York '85
Goodfellas '90▲
Gossip '99
Gotti '96
Grace of My Heart '96
Gravesend '97
Gray Matters '06
Great Expectations '97
The Great Gatsby '49
The Great Gatsby '74
The Great New Wonderful '06
Green Card '90
The Greenwich Village '44
Greetings '68▲
The Guardian '84
The Guys '02▲
Gypsy 83 '01
Habit '97
Hair '79▲
The Half Naked Truth '32
Half Nelson '06▲
Hamlet '00▲
Hangin' with the Homeboys '91▲
Hanging Up '99
Hannah and Her Sisters '86▲
Happy Accidents '00
Happy Hour '03
Harlem Nights '89
Harry and Tonto '74▲
Hav Plenty '97▲
Head Over Heels '01
Headless Body in Topless Bar '96
Heartburn '86▲
Heartstrings '93
Heaven Help Us '85
Heights '04
Hello Again '87
Henry Fool '98▲
Hester Street '75▲
Hi-Life '98
Hi, Mom! '70▲
Hide and Seek '05
High Art '98
Highlander '86▲
Highlander: Endgame '00
His Butler's Sister '44
His Girl Friday '40▲
Hit and Runway '01
Hitch '05
The Hoax '06
Home Alone 2: Lost in New York '92
A Home at the End of the World '04
Honey '03
Hoodlum '96
The Hottest State '06
The Hours '02▲
House of D '04
House of Mirth '00▲
How to Lose a Guy in 10 Days '03
The Hunger '83
Hurricane Streets '96
Husbands and Wives '92▲
I Am Legend '07▲
I Think I Love My Wife '07
The Iceman Cometh '73
If I Had My Way '40
If You Only Knew '00
Igby Goes Down '02▲
I'll Be Yours '47
I'll Take You There '99
Illuminata '98
Immortal '04
In America '02▲
In Good Company '04
In the Cut '03
In the Mix '05
Inside Man '06▲
Intern '00
The Interpreter '05▲
Interview '07▲
Into the Fire '05
Ira & Abby '06
It Could Happen to You '94
It Had to Be You '00
It Happened in Brooklyn '47
It Runs in the Family '03
It Should Happen to You '54▲

It's All About Love '03
It's My Turn '80
Jane Doe '96
The January Man '89
Jeffrey '95
Joe '70
Joe Gould's Secret '00
Joe's Apartment '96
Joe's Bed-Stuy Barbershop: We Cut Heads '83
Johnny Suede '92
Joshua '07▲
Juice '92
Jumpin' Jack Flash '86
Jungle Fever '91▲
Jungle 2 Jungle '96
Just a Kiss '02
Just My Luck '06
Just One Time '00
Just the Ticket '98
K-PAX '01
Kate & Leopold '01
Keane '04▲
Keeping the Faith '00
Key Exchange '85
Kicked in the Head '97
Kids '95
Kill by Inches '99
Kill the Poor '06
Killer Condom '95
The Killing of John Lennon '07
King Kong '33▲
King Kong '05▲
King of Comedy '82▲
King of New York '90▲
King of the Gypsies '78
King of the Jungle '00
Kiss Me, Guido '97
Kissing Jessica Stein '02
Klute '71▲
Knights of the South Bronx '05
Kramer vs. Kramer '79▲
Lady on a Train '45▲
The Last Days of Disco '98▲
Last Exit to Brooklyn '90▲
The Last Seduction '94▲
The Last Time '06
Laws of Gravity '92▲
Legal Eagles '86
Let It Snow '99
The Life and Times of Hank Greenberg '99▲
A Life of Her Own '50
Life Support '07▲
Light Sleeper '92
Liquid Sky '83▲
Lisa Picard Is Famous '01
Little Manhattan '05
Little Miss Marker '34▲
Little Nicky '00
Living in Oblivion '94▲
Living Out Loud '98
London '05
Lonely Hearts '06
Long Time Since '97
Look Who's Talking, Too '90
Looking for Kitty '04
Looking for Richard '96▲
Lord of War '05
The Lords of Flatbush '74
Loser '00
Lost in Yonkers '93
Lotto Land '95
Love '05
Love Affair '94
Love at First Bite '79
Love in the Time of Money '02
Love Is Better Than Ever '52
Love Story '70▲
Love the Hard Way '01
The Love Trap '29
Loving '70
Lucky Number Slevin '06
Lullaby of Broadway '51
Lulu on the Bridge '98
Ma and Pa Kettle Go to Town '50
Mad Hot Ballroom '05▲
Made '01
Maid in Manhattan '02
Mail Order Wife '04
Malcolm X '92▲
Mambo Cafe '00
Man of the Century '99

The Manchurian Candidate '62▲
Manhattan '79▲
Manhattan Melodrama '34▲
Manhattan Merengue! '95
Manhattan Merry-Go-Round '37
Manhattan Murder Mystery '93▲
Manito '03▲
Marathon Man '76▲
Margarita Happy Hour '01
Maria Full of Grace '04▲
Marty '55▲
Maximum Risk '96
Maze '01
Mean Streets '73▲
Meet Dave '08
Melinda and Melinda '05
Melvin Goes to Dinner '03
Men in Black '97▲
Men in Black 2 '02▲
Mercy '96
Metropolitan '90▲
Michael Clayton '07▲
Mickey Blue Eyes '99
Midnight Cowboy '69▲
Mighty Aphrodite '95
Milk and Honey '03
Mimic '97
Mimic 2 '01
Mind the Gap '04
The Minion '98
Minnie and Moskowitz '71
Miracle on 34th Street '47▲
Miracle on 34th Street '94
The Mirror Has Two Faces '96
Mirrors '85
Misery '90▲
Mo' Better Blues '90
Money Train '95
Moon over Broadway '98▲
Morning Glory '33
Mortal Thoughts '91
Moscow on the Hudson '84▲
Mr. Takes a Vacation '39
The Muppets Take Manhattan '84▲
Murda Muzik '07
Music & Lyrics '07
Music of the Heart '99
My Blueberry Nights '07
My Favorite Year '82▲
My Little Assassin '99
My Man Godfrey '36▲
My Sister Eileen '55▲
My Super Ex-Girlfriend '06
Mysterious Skin '04▲
Nadja '95▲
The Naked City '48▲
Naked City: A Killer Christmas '98
Naked City: Justice with a Bullet '98
Naked in New York '93
The Namesake '06▲
The Nanny Diaries '07
National Treasure '04
The Natural '84▲
Network '76▲
Never Again '01
New Jack City '91
New York Cop '94
New York Minute '04
New York, New York '77▲
New York Nights '84
New York Ripper '82
New York Stories '89▲
New York's Finest '87
News from Home '76
The Next Big Thing '02
Next Stop, Greenwich Village '76▲
Next Time We Love '36
Next Year in Jerusalem '98
Nick and Jane '96
Nico Icon '95▲
Night and the City '92▲
Night at the Museum '06

Night Falls on Manhattan '96▲
Night on Earth '91▲
Night Shift '82
The Night They Raided Minsky's '69▲
The Night We Never Met '93
9 1/2 Weeks '86
1931: Once Upon a Time in New York '72
The Ninth Gate '99
No Reservations '07
No Such Thing '01
Noel '04
Nueba Yol '95
The Object of My Affection '98
Octopus 2: River of Fear '02
The Odd Couple '68▲
Off Beat '86
Olga's Gifts '64
Oliver & Company '88
On the Town '49▲
On the Waterfront '54▲
Once in the Life '00
One Fine Day '96
One Last Thing '05
One Tough Cop '98
Online '01
Only When I Laugh '81▲
Our Italian Husband '04
Our Song '01▲
The Out-of-Towners '70▲
The Out-of-Towners '99
Outrageous! '77▲
The Painted Lady '97▲
The Palermo Connection '91
Panic in Needle Park '71▲
Panic Room '02
Paradise Alley '78
Paris Is Burning '91▲
The Park Is Mine '85
Party Girl '94
Party Monster '03
Passion of Mind '00
Path to Paradise '97
The Peacemaker '97
People I Know '02
A Perfect Murder '98
Perfect Stranger '07
Permanent Vacation '84
Personal Maid '31
Personals '00
Petty Crimes '02
The Phantom '96
Phone Booth '02
Pi '98
The Pick-Up Artist '87
Pieces of April '03
Pillow Talk '59▲
Pinero '00
Pipe Dream '02
Plaza Suite '71▲
Pollock '00▲
The Pompatus of Love '95
The Pope of Greenwich Village '84
Portrait of Jennie '48▲
Postcards from America '95
A Price above Rubies '97
The Prince of Central Park '77▲
Prince of Central Park '00
Prince of the City '81▲
The Prince of Tides '91▲
The Princess & the Call Girl '84
Prisoner of Second Avenue '74
Private Parts '96
The Producers '05
Protocols of Zion '05▲
P.S. I Love You '07
The Public Eye '92▲
Puccini for Beginners '06
Pushing Tin '99▲
The Quest '96
Quick Change '90
'R Xmas '01
Radio Days '87▲
A Rage in Harlem '91▲
Rage of the Werewolf '99
Raging Bull '80▲
Ragtime '81▲

A Raisin in the Sun '61▲
A Raisin in the Sun '89▲
Raising Helen '04
Raising Victor Vargas '03
Ransom '96▲
The Rat Race '60▲
The Rats '01
A Rat's Tale '98
Ready to Wear '94
The Real Blonde '97
Rear Window '54▲
Reign Over Me '07
Remedy '05
Rent '05
Return to Paradise '98▲
Revolution 9 '01
Ride '98
Rift '96
Risk '94▲
The Roaring Twenties '39▲
Rockabye '86
Roger Dodger '02
Romance & Cigarettes '05
Rosemary's Baby '68▲
Rounders '98
The Royal Tenenbaums '01▲
Rudy: The Rudy Giuliani Story '03
Rumble in the Bronx '96
Runaway Bride '99▲
The Saint in New York '38
Saturday Night Fever '77▲
Saving Face '04
Scent of a Woman '92▲
School for Scoundrels '06
Scrooged '88
Searching for Bobby Fischer '93▲
Searching for Paradise '02
Serendipity '01
Serpico '73▲
Service De Luxe '38
Seven '95▲
The Seven-Ups '73
The Seven Year Itch '55▲
Sex and the City: The Movie '08
Shadows and Fog '92
ShadowZone: The Undead Express '96
Shaft '00▲
She-Devil '89
Shattered Glass '03▲
Shelter Island '03
She's Gotta Have It '86▲
She's the One '96
Shining Star '75
Sidewalks of New York '01
The Siege '98
Single White Female '92
The Sisters '05
Six Days, Six Nights '94
Six Degrees of Separation '93
16 Blocks '06▲
61* '01▲
Sky Captain and the World of Tomorrow '04
Slaves of New York '89
Sleepers '96▲
Silver '93
Small Time Crooks '00
Smithereens '82
Someone Else's America '96▲
Someone Like You '01
Something Short of Paradise '79
Something Wild '86▲
Somewhere in the City '97
Sophie's Choice '82▲
Sorry, Haters '05
The Spanish Prisoner '97▲
Speedy '28▲
Spider-Man '02▲
Spider-Man 2 '04▲
Spider-Man 3 '07▲
Splash '84▲
The Squid and the Whale '05▲
Stage Door '37▲
Starting Out in the Evening '07
State of Grace '90▲
Stay '05
Staying Alive '83
Step Lively '44

▲ = rated three bones or higher

Stepmom '98
Stepping Out '91 ▶
The Sticky Fingers of Time '97
Still of the Night '82
Stir Crazy '80
Stonewall '95 ▶
Straight out of Brooklyn '91
Stranger than Paradise '84 ▶
Street Scene '31 ▶
Street Smart '87
Street Trash '87
Stuart Little 2 '02 ▶
The Substitute of Fire '96
The Substitute 2: School's Out '97
Suburban Girl '07
Subway Stories '97
Sudden Manhattan '96
Sugar Hill '94
Summer of Sam '99
Sunday '96
Sunday in New York '63
Sunset Park '96
The Super '91
Superfly '72
Sweet Charity '69 ▶
Sweet Home Alabama '02
Sweet Nothing '96
Sweet Smell of Success '57
Swindle '02
Table One '00
Tadpole '02
Take the Lead '06
The Talent Given Us '04 ▶
A Tale of Two Pizzas '03
Talk to Me '84
Tart '01
Tarzan's New York Adventure '42
Taxi '04
Taxi Driver '76 ▶
The Tenants '06
The Tender Trap '55
The 10th Kingdom '00
They Call It Sin '32
The Thing About My Folks '05
Thirteen Conversations About One Thing '01 ▶
Thirty Day Princess '34
30 Years to Life '01
This Revolution '05
The Thomas Crown Affair '99 ▶
3 A.M. '01 ▶
Three Days of the Condor '75 ▶
Three Men and a Baby '87 ▶
Through the Eyes of a Killer '92
Through the Fire '05 ▶
The Tic Code '99
Timeless '96
Times Square '80
TMNT (Teenage Mutant Ninja Turtles) '07
To Catch a Yeti '95
The Tollbooth '04
Tootsie '82 ▶
Torch Song Trilogy '88
Town and Country '01
Transamerica '05 ▶
Trash '70
The Treatment '05
A Tree Grows in Brooklyn '45 ▶
Trick '99 ▶
A Troll in Central Park '94
True Blue '01
Trust the Man '06
25th Hour '02 ▶
The 24 Hour Woman '99
29th Street '91
Twisted '96
2 by 4 '98
Two for the Money '05
Two Girls and a Guy '98 ▶
200 Cigarettes '98
Two Ninas '00
Two of Us '00
Two Weeks Notice '02
Ultrachrist '03
Under Hellgate Bridge '99

Underground U.S.A. '84
Unfaithful '02 ▶
Unknown White Male '05 ▶
An Unmarried Woman '78 ▶
Untamed Heart '93
Unzipped '94 ▶
Up in Central Park '48
Uptown Girls '03
Uptown New York '32
Urbania '00
Vampire in Brooklyn '95
Vanilla Sky '01 ▶
Vanya on 42nd Street '94 ▶
Variety '83
The Velocity of Gary '98
A Very Natural Thing '73
Visions of Sugarplums '99
The Visitor '07 ▶
Voulez-Vous Danser avec Moi? '59
The Waiting Game '99
Walking and Talking '96
Wall Street '87 ▶
Walls of Glass '85
Wannabes '01
The War Within '05
Washington Heights '02
Washington Square '97 ▶
The Way We Were '73 ▶
The Wedding Party '69
We're Back! A Dinosaur's Story '93
West Side Story '61 ▶
What Happens in Vegas '08
When Angels Fly '84 ▶
When Harry Met Sally... '89 ▶
When Will I Be Loved '04
Where Were You When the Lights Went Out? '68
Whipped '00
Whirlygirl '04
Who Gets to Call It Art? '05
Who's That Knocking at My Door? '68 ▶
The Wild '06
Wild Style '83
Winter Passing '05
Wirey Spindell '99
Wise Guys '85
Wisegirls '02
Witness to the Mob '98
Wolf '94
Wolfen '81 ▶
Working Girl '88 ▶
World Trade Center '06 ▶
X-Men '00 ▶
XXXV '02
The Yards '00 ▶
Year of the Dragon '85
Yellow '06
You Don't Mess with the Zohan '08
You Stupid Man '02
You Tell Me '06
The Young Girl and the Monsoon '99
The Young Savages '61 ▶
You've Got Mail '98

New Zealand
see Down Under

Newlyweds
see also Wedding Bells
Absent Without Leave '95
Are We Done Yet? '07
Barefoot in the Park '67 ▶
Bittersweet Love '76
The Blood Spattered Bride '72
Born in '45 '65
Churn Yang '00
Devil's Pond '03
A Good Woman '04
The Heartbreak Kid '72 ▶
Highball '97 ▶
Honeymoon Academy '90
Honeymoon Horror '82
I Married a Monster from Outer Space '58 ▶
Identity '03
Just Married '03
The Long, Long Trailer '54 ▶
Love Actually '03
Love from a Stranger '47
Made for Each Other '39 ▶

Made in Heaven '52
Mail Order Bride '04
Mannequin '37
Mexican Spitfire '40
Mr. & Mrs. Loving '96 ▶
Mister Drake's Duck '50
National Lampoon's Gold Diggers '04
The Ponder Heart '01
Prelude to a Kiss '92
The Reception '05
She's Having a Baby '88
Shrek 2 '04 ▶
So I Married an Axe Murderer '93

News at 11
see also Front Page;
Look Ma! I'm on TV!;
Mass Media
Anchorman: The Legend of Ron Burgundy '04
Broadcast News '87 ▶
Bruce Almighty '03
The China Syndrome '79 ▶
Control Room '04 ▶
Eyewitness '91
A Face in the Crowd '57 ▶
15 Minutes '01
Good Night, and Good Luck '05 ▶
The Hunting Party '07
The Insider '99 ▶
Life or Something Like It '02
Live from Baghdad '03 ▶
Natural Born Killers '94
Network '76 ▶
News at Eleven '86
The Night We Called It a Day '03
Outfoxed: Rupert Murdoch's War on Journalism '04 ▶
Switching Channels '88
This Revolution '05
To Die For '95 ▶
Up Close and Personal '96
Vantage Point '08
Weapons of Mass Distraction '97 ▶

Newspapers
see Front Page

Niagara Falls
Niagara '52
Niagara Motel '06
Niagara, Niagara '97
Superman 2 '80 ▶

Nice Mice
see also Killer Rodents
An American Tail '86 ▶
An American Tail: Fievel Goes West '91
Babe '95 ▶
Babe: Pig in the City '98 ▶
Dr. Seuss' Horton Hears a Who! '08
Escape from Alcatraz '79 ▶
Flushed Away '06 ▶
The Great Mouse Detective '86
The Green Mile '99 ▶
The Hitchhiker's Guide to the Galaxy '05
The Island of Dr. Moreau '77 ▶
Mouse Hunt '97 ▶
Ratatouille '07 ▶
A Rat's Tale '98

Ratz '99
The Rescuers '77 ▶
The Rescuers Down Under '90
Road Trip '00
The Secret of NIMH '82 ▶
Sitcom '97
Stuart Little '99 ▶
Stuart Little 2 '02 ▶

Nightclubs
The Adventures of Pluto Nash '02
Amateur Night '85
Animal Instincts '92
Anything But Love '02
Backbeat '94 ▶
Be Yourself '30
Berlin Blues '89
Better Than Chocolate '99 ▶
Birth of the Blues '41
Black Angel '46 ▶
Black Glove '54
The Blue Angel '30 ▶
Bocy Shot '99
Born Romantic '00
The Bride Wore Red '37
A Bunny's Tale '85
Bus Stop '56 ▶
Cabaret '72 ▶
Cabaret Balkan '98
Cafe Society '97
Can-Can '50
The Cotton Club '84 ▶
Dance, Girl, Dance '40 ▶
Dance Hall Racket '58
Dancing at the Blue Iguana '00
Dark Secrets '95
Deadly Revenge '83
Decay '98
Desperate Cargo '41
Dick Tracy '90 ▶
Double or Nothing '37
Dracula Blows His Cool '82
The Dreamlife of Angels '98 ▶
The Fabulous Baker Boys '89 ▶
Fake Out '82
Femmes de Paris '53
Flaming Lead '39
Foxstyle '73
Framed '75
French Can-Can '55 ▶
The French Way '40
Fun in Acapulco '63
G.I. Blues '60
Girls! Girls! Girls! '62
Greenwich Village '44
Harlem Nights '89 ▶
Honeydripper '07 ▶
Idlewild '06
If I Had My Way '40
In the Mix '05
Invincible '02
Irreversible '02
It's All Gone, Pete Tong '04
Jive Junction '43
The Killing of a Chinese Bookie '76 ▶
King Creole '58 ▶
La Cage aux Folles '78 ▶
La Cage aux Folles 2 '81
La Cage aux Folles 3: The Wedding '86
Lady on a Train '45 ▶
Lambada '89
Last Night at the Alamo '83 ▶
Le Samourai '67 ▶
Lenny '74 ▶
Like It Is '98
Liquid Dreams '92

Little Shots of Happiness '97
The Lost City '05 ▶
Love Come Down '00
Love Goggles '99
Love Jones '96 ▶
Lullaby of Broadway '51
Lured '47 ▶
Machine Gun Blues '95
Mad Dog and Glory '93 ▶
Madame Sata '02 ▶
The Mambo Kings '92 ▶
Marked Woman '37 ▶
Martial Law 2: Undercover '91
The Mask '94 ▶
Mickey One '65
Midnight Warrior '89
Mighty Joe Young '49
Miracles '89
Miss Pettigrew Lives for a Day '08 ▶
Morocco '30 ▶
Moulin Rouge '01 ▶
New Orleans '47 ▶
Night After Night '32
A Night at the Roxbury '98
A Night in Heaven '83
The Night They Raided Minsky's '69 ▶
No Surrender '86 ▶
The Nutty Professor '63 ▶
Pandora and the Flying Dutchman '51
A Paradise Under the Stars '99
Party Girl '58 ▶
Party Girl '94
Party Monster '03
Pecker '98
Pete Kelly's Blues '55
Play Murder for Me '91
Playing by Heart '98 ▶
Preaching to the Perverted '97
The Public Eye '92 ▶
Rebel '85
Ripper Man '96
Roger Dodger '02 ▶
Ruby '92 ▶
Ruby's Dream '82
The Score '01 ▶
Sea Racketeers '37
Sex, Drugs, and Rock-n-Roll '84
Shanghai Triad '95 ▶
The Shining Hour '38
Showgirls '95
Smash-Up: The Story of a Woman '47 ▶
So Close to Paradise '98
Sorted '04
Stark Raving Mad '02
Stonewall '95 ▶
Suffering Bastards '90
Sweet Evil '98
Swingers '96 ▶
The Talented Mr. Ripley '99 ▶
That Naughty Girl '58
They Never Come Back '32
30 Is a Dangerous Age, Cynthia '68
To Catch a King '84
Treasure of the Moon Goddess '88
Trigger Happy '96
24 Hour Party People '01 ▶
200 Cigarettes '98
Undercurrent '99
Underground U.S.A. '84
Uptown Saturday Night '74
Vamp '86
We Own the Night '07 ▶
Whistle Stop '46
Winning Girls Through Psychic Mind Control '02
A Woman Is a Woman '60 ▶
Wonderland '88 ▶
Woo '97
Xanadu '80
The Zoo Gang '85

9/11
DC 9/11: Time of Crisis '04
A Few Days in September '06
Giuliani Time '05

The Great New Wonderful '06
The Hamburg Cell '04
Hijacking Catastrophe: 9/11, Fear and the Selling of America '04
Protocols of Zion '05 ▶
Reign Over Me '07 ▶
3 Ninjas Kick Back '94
United 93 '06 ▶
World Trade Center '06 ▶

Ninjas
see also Martial Arts
Batman Begins '05 ▶
Black Tight Killers '66 ▶
Elektra '05 ▶
Ninja: American Warrior '90
Ninja in the U.S.A. '88
RoboCop 3 '91
3 Ninjas Kick Back '94
TMNT (Teenage Mutant Ninja Turtles) '07

Ninjitsu
see Martial Arts.

No-Exit Motel
see also Grand Hotel
Above Suspicion '00
Axe '06
Bug '06
Cheap Shots '91
Dead Simple '01
Eaten Alive '76
Identity '03
Memento '00 ▶
Motel Hell '80
Mountaintop Motel Massacre '86
Psycho '60 ▶
Psycho '98
Psycho 2 '83
Psycho 3 '86
Psycho 4: The Beginning '90
Slaughter Hotel '71
Tape '01 ▶
Vacancy '07

Not-So-True Identity
see also Grand Hotel
AKA '02
Albino Alligator '96 ▶
The Amazing Mrs. Holiday '43
Anonymous Rex '04
Apt Pupil '97 ▶
Armistead Maupin's Tales of the City '93
The Associate '96
Autumn Sun '58
Bad Santa '03 ▶
Batman Begins '05 ▶
Beggars of Life '28
Big Momma's House '00 ▶
Big Momma's House 2 '06
The Blue Angel '30 ▶
Boet '07
Boys Don't Cry '99 ▶
The Breaks '99
Bubba Ho-Tep '03 ▶
Buccaneer's Girl '50
Catch Me If You Can '02 ▶
Charley's Aunt '41 ▶
Charlotte Gray '01
Chasing Liberty '04
The Claim '00 ▶
Clancy Street Boys '43
Code Name: The Cleaner '07
Color Me Kubrick '05
Corky Romano '01
The Cotton Club '84 ▶
The Count of Monte Cristo '02 ▶
Daniel Deronda '02
Dear Frankie '04 ▶
Deceived '91
Deception '08

Not-So-True

▶ = rated three bones or higher

Defying Gravity '99
The Departed '06▲
Devil in the Flesh 2 '00
A Different Loyalty '04▲
Easy to Wed '46▲
Elf '03▲
The Emperor's New Clothes '01
Europa, Europa '91▲
Exit Wounds '01
Face/Off '97▲
Face the Music '00
Failure to Launch '06
Femme Fatale '02
For Richer or Poorer '97
Forever Mine '99
Gattaca '97▲
Gentleman's Agreement '47▲
G.I. War Brides '46
Good Advice '01
The Good Fairy '35▲
Gosford Park '01▲
The Governess '98
Grey Owl '99
Gun Shy '00
The Guru '02
The Half Naked Truth '32
Happy, Texas '99▲
Head Over Heels '01
Hi, Good Lookin'! '44
High Crimes '02
The History of Mr. Polly '07
A History of Violence '05▲
Homegrown '97
The Human Stain '03
I Married a Dead Man '82
I Now Pronounce You Chuck and Larry '07
If You Only Knew '00
Imitation of Life '34▲
Imitation of Life '59▲
The Importance of Being Earnest '02
Impostor '02
Infernal Affairs '02▲
Just My Luck '06
Juwanna Mann '02
A Knight's Tale '01
The Lady Eve '41▲
The Legend of Rita '99
Les Miserables '97▲
Lip Service '00
Little Man '06
The Long Kiss Goodnight '96
Lost Boundaries '49
The Mad Adventures of Rabbi Jacob '73▲
Maid in Manhattan '02
The Major and the Minor '42▲
Malibu's Most Wanted '03
Mask of Death '97
The Mask of Zorro '98▲
Master of Disguise '02
Me & Mrs. Jones '02
Mrs. Palfrey at the Claremont '05
Mrs. Winterbourne '96
Mr. & Mrs. Smith '05▲
Model Behavior '00
Monte Carlo '30
Moon over Miami '41▲
Mother Night '96▲
Mulan '98
Mulholland Drive '01▲
Mumford '99▲
My First Wedding '04
Never Been Kissed '99
Nevil Shute's The Far Country '85
The Next Big Thing '02
Olivier, Olivier '92▲
Orlando '92▲
Our Man in Havana '59▲
Our Mutual Friend '98
Out to Sea '97
The Painted Lady '97▲
A Paradise Under the Stars '99
The Parent Trap '98
Perfect Stranger '07
Pinky '49▲
Pipe Dream '02
The Prince & Me '04
The Prince and the Pauper '07

The Prince and the Surfer '99
Princess of Thieves '01
The Principal Takes a Holiday '98
The Quarry '98
The Ringer '05
Rock My World '02
The Rowdy Girls '00
The Saint '97
The Scarlet Pimpernel '34▲
The Scarlet Pimpernel '82▲
The Scarlet Pimpernel '99
The Scarlet Pimpernel 2: Mademoiselle Guillotine '99
The Scarlet Pimpernel 3: The Kidnapped King '99
The Secret Invasion '64
Shadows '60▲
Shallow Hal '01
The Silencer '99
Silver Hawk '04
Sing Me a Love Song '37
Ski Party '65
Soul Man '86
Strange Bedfellows '04
Taking Care of Business '90
Taking Lives '04
The Talented Mr. Ripley '99
Tension '50
Texas Trouble '41
That Funny Feeling '65
That Night in Rio '41
The Thief '97
Thirty Day Princess '34
Three to Tango '99
Train of Life '98
Trial and Error '96
The Triumph of Love '01
True Identity '91
The Truman Show '98▲
The Truth About Charlie '02
Twin Dragons '92
Two Shades of Blue '98
Uniform '03
Unveiled '05
The Valet '06
Virtual Sexuality '99
What the Dead Man Heard '98▲
Who Is Cletis Tout? '02
The Witness Files '00
You Don't Mess with the Zohan '08

Nuclear Disaster
see Disaster Flicks; Meltdown

Nuclear Energy
The Abyss '89▲
Choke Canyon '86
The Chosen '77
Class of Nuke 'Em High '86
Class of Nuke 'Em High 2: Subhumanoid Meltdown '91
Class of Nuke 'Em High 3: The Good, the Bad and the Subhumanoid '94
Desert Warrior '88
Devices and Desires '91▲
Die, Monster, Die! '65
Dirty Games '89
Final Warning '90
Godzilla '98
Ground Zero '88
Journey to the Center of Time '67
Nightbreaker '89▲
PU-239 '06
Radar Secret Service '50
Red Alert '77
Return from Witch Mountain '78
The Return of Dr. Mabuse '61
Warning from Space '56

Nuns & Priests
see also Missionaries; Religion; Religious Epics
Absolution '81

Agnes of God '85▲
The Agony and the Ecstasy '65
All About My Mother '99▲
Amateur '94▲
Amen '02▲
The American '01
Angels with Dirty Faces '38▲
Anna '51
The Apostate '98
The Assisi Underground '84
The Atonement of Gosta Berling '24▲
Bad Education '04▲
The Barbarian Invasions '03▲
Beautiful Hunter '94
Beavis and Butt-Head Do America '96
Becket '64▲
The Bells of St. Mary's '45▲
Black Narcissus '47▲
Black Robe '91▲
The Bloodstained Shadow '78
The Blues Brothers '80▲
Blues Brothers 2000 '98
Body & Soul '93▲
The Boys of St. Vincent '93▲
Boys Town '38▲
Brides of Christ '91
The Bridge of San Luis Rey '44▲
The Bridge of San Luis Rey '05
Camila '84▲
The Cardinal '63
Change of Habit '69
Changing Habits '96
Child of Darkness, Child of Light '91
Chocolat '00▲
Cold Justice '89
Come to the Stable '49▲
The Confession '20
The Confessional '75
The Confessional '95▲
The Confessor '04
Conspiracy of Hearts '60▲
Conspiracy of Silence '03
The Crime of Father Amaro '02▲
The Cross & the Switchblade '72
Cry, the Beloved Country '95▲
Curse 4: The Ultimate Sacrifice '90
Daens '92▲
Damien: The Leper Priest '80
The Dangerous Lives of Altar Boys '02▲
Daredevil '03
The Day of the Beast '95
Dead Man Walking '95▲
Dead Waters '94
Death of an Angel '86
Demonia '90
The Detective '54▲
The Devil '71▲
The Devil's Playground '76▲
Diary of a Country Priest '50▲
The Divine Enforcer '91
Dixie: Changing Habits '85▲
Dominion: Prequel to the Exorcist '05
Dracula 2: Ascension '03
Dracula 3: Legacy '05
The Duchess of Langeais '07▲
The Eighteenth Angel '97
Elmer Gantry '60▲
End of Days '99
The End of the Affair '99▲
End of the World '76
The Exorcism of Emily Rose '05▲
The Exorcist '73▲
The Exorcist 2: The Heretic '77
Exorcist: The Beginning '04
Extramuros '85
The Father Clements Story '87
The Fifth Element '97

Fighting Father Dunne '48
First Legion '51
For Better and for Worse '87
Forever Young '85
40 Days and 40 Nights '02
The Fugitive '48▲
The Garden of Redemption '97
Gentleman Bandit '81
Going My Way '44▲
Gospa '94
Goya's Ghosts '06
Happy Hell Night '92
Heaven Knows, Mr. Allison '57▲
Hideous Kinky '99
A Home of Our Own '75
The Hoodlum Priest '61▲
Hot Under the Collar '91
I Confess '53
I Heard the Owl Call My Name '73
I, the Worst of All '90
In the Region of Ice '76▲
In This House of Brede '75▲
Jesus of Montreal '89▲
John Carpenter Presents Vampires: Los Muertos '02
Joshua '02
Joyeux Noel '05▲
Judgment '90▲
Keeping the Faith '00
Kid Monk Baroni '52
Knocks at My Door '93
Lamb '85
The Last Don 2 '98
Last Rites '88
The Left Hand of God '55▲
Leon Morin, Priest '61
Liam '00
License to Wed '07
Lilies of the Field '63▲
Los Locos Posse '97
Loving Annabelle '06
Loyola, the Soldier Saint '52
Madeline '98
The Magdalene Sisters '02▲
The Maldonado Miracle '03
Manna from Heaven '02
Mass Appeal '84
Massacre in Rome '73
Mission to Glory '80
Molokai: The Story of Father Damien '99
Monsignor '82
Mortal Sins '92
Most Wanted '76
Mother Joan of the Angels '60▲
My First Wedding '04
My Mother's Smile '02
Nacho Libre '06
Nasty Habits '77
Nazarin '58▲
Night of the Assassin '77
Night of the Demons 2 '94
Night Sun '90
The Ninth Day '04▲
Noel '04
Northfork '03▲
Not of This World '99
The Nun '66
Nuns on the Run '90
The Nun's Story '59▲
The Omen '76▲
The Order '03
Oscar and Lucinda '97▲
Pale Rider '85▲
Passing Glory '99▲
Pier 23 '51
Pope John Paul II '84
The Pope Must Diet '91
Possessed '77
Possessed '00
Prayer for the Dying '87
Priest '94▲
Primal Fear '96▲
Prince of Darkness '87
The Prisoner '55▲
The Private War of Major Benson '55
The Proposition '97
The Ravagers '65
The Reaping '07
The Reckoning '03▲

The Red Inn '51
Revenge of the Musketeers '94
Romance '30
The Rosary Murders '87
The Runner Stumbles '79
Salem's Lot '04
Sanctuary '98
Saving Grace '86
The Scarlet & the Black '83
Scary Movie 2 '01
Sea Wife '57
Second Sight '89
Secret Ingredient '92
September Gun '83
Shattered Vows '84
The Shoes of the Fisherman '68
Shooting Dogs '05
Silver Bullet '85
The Singing Nun '66
Sister Act '92
Sister Act 2: Back in the Habit '93
Sisters of Satan '75
Sleepers '96
Sorcerers '88▲
Soul Survivors '01
The Sound of Music '65▲
Spirits '90
Stigmata '99
Stolen Summer '02
Therese '86▲
Therese: The Story of Saint Therese of Lisieux '04
The Third Miracle '99
To Kill a Priest '89
Trouble along the Way '53
The Trouble with Angels '66▲
True Confessions '81▲
Under Satan's Sun '87▲
Under the Red Robe '36
The Unholy '88
Vatican Conspiracy '81
Wanted '98
We're No Angels '89
Where Angels Go, Trouble Follows '68
The White Sister '23▲
Wide Awake '97
The Winter Light '62▲
The X-Files: I Want to Believe '08

Nuns with Guns
The Enforcer '76
Girlfriend from Hell '89
Ms. 45 '81▲
Nuns on the Run '90
Two Mules for Sister Sara '70▲
We're No Angels '89

Nursploitation!
see also Doctors & Nurses; Sexploitation
Born for Hell '76
Candy Stripe Nurses '74
Emmanuelle in the Country '78
Hospital of Terror '78
Inner Sanctum '91
Night Call Nurses '72
Nurse on Call '88
Private Duty Nurses '71
The Sensuous Nurse '76
The Student Nurses '70
Tender Loving Care '73
The Young Nurses '73

Obsessive Love
Aaron Loves Angela '75
Addicted to Love '96
After Sex '97
Against All Odds '84
Alone With Her '07
Anna Karenina '35▲
Anna Karenina '48
Anna Karenina '85
Anna Karenina '97
The Aviator's Wife '80▲
The Best Man '97
Betty Blue '86▲
Beyond the Clouds '95
Borderline '02▲

The Bridesmaid '04
Brief Encounter '46▲
Can't Buy Me Love '87
Cause Celebre '87
The Center of the World '01
Changing Times '04
Chungking Express '95▲
The Climax '44
Cracker: True Romance '95▲
Crazy Love '07▲
Crazy Moon '87
The Crown Prince '06
The Crush '93
Cupid '96
Cyrano de Bergerac '25▲
Cyrano de Bergerac '50▲
Cyrano de Bergerac '85
Cyrano de Bergerac '90▲
Damage '92▲
Danger of Love '95
Death and Desire '97
Deceptions 2: Edge of Deception '94
Deep Crimson '96
Devil in the Flesh '87
Devil in the Flesh '98
Doctor Zhivago '03
The Duchess of Langeais '07▲
8 1/2 Women '99
El '52
Emily Bronte's Wuthering Heights '92
End of the Affair '55
The End of the Affair '99▲
Endless Love '81
Enduring Love '04
The English Patient '96▲
Eros '04
Eva '62
The Ex '96
Eye of God '97▲
Eye of the Beholder '99
Far from the Madding Crowd '97▲
Fatal Attraction '87▲
Fear '96
Fever Pitch '05
Film Geek '06
First Love, Last Rites '98
For Sale '98
G '02
Ghost '90▲
Going Postal '98
The Good Girl '02▲
The Good Night '07
Goodbye, Dragon Inn '03
He Loves Me ... He Loves Me Not '02
The Heartbreak Kid '72▲
Her and She and Him '69
Homage '95
Hush '98
I Want You '98
Jealousy '99
Junk Mail '97
Kama Sutra: A Tale of Love '96
Last Breath '96
L'Ennui '98
Leo Tolstoy's Anna Karenina '96
Letters from a Killer '98
Live Flesh '97▲
Lost and Delirious '01
Love and Death on Long Island '97
Love and Rage '99
Love in the Time of Cholera '07
Loved '97
Loverboy '05
Lust, Caution '07▲
Mad Love '95
Mad Love '01
Mararia '98
Midnight Blue '96
Miss Monday '98
Mr. Wrong '95▲
The Mystery of Edwin Drood '35
Notre Histoire '84
Obsession '97
One Kill '00▲
Only Love '98
Our Mutual Friend '98

▲ = *rated three bones or higher*

Perfect Strangers '03
Phantom '22
The Phantom of the Opera '25
The Phantom of the Opera '34
'43
The Phantom of the Opera '62
The Phantom of the Opera '89
The Phantom of the Opera '90
The Phantom of the Opera '98
A Place in the Sun '51
Pain Jane '01
A Place in the Sun '89
Sea of Love '89
Shades of Black '33
Show Boat '36
Show Boat '51
Skin Deep '94
A Slipping Down Life '99
Some Kind of Wonderful '87
The Sterile Cuckoo '69
Swimfan '02
Sylvia '03
Tempress Moon '96
10 '79
Testosterone '03
There's Something about Mary '98
A Thin Line Between Love and Hate '96
Time '06
To Gillian on Her 37th Birthday '96
Truly, Madly, Deeply '91
Twisted Love '95
Twisted Obsession '90
Walk the Line '05
West Side Story '61
Wicker Park '04
Wilde '97
Wuthering Heights '39
Wuthering Heights '53
Wuthering Heights '70
Wuthering Heights '98

Occult

see also Demons & Devils; Satanism; Witchcraft; Wizards

Alabama's Ghost '72
Alone in the Dark '05
The Amazing Mr. X '48
The American Scream '26s
Amityville Dollhouse '96
Apprentice to Murder '88
Army of Darkness '92
Bad Dreams '88
Barbarian Queen '85
Because of the Cats '74
The Believers '87
Beyond Dream's Door '88
Beyond Evil '80
Beyond the Door 3 '91
The Black Cat '81
Black Circle Boys '97
Black Magic Terror '79
Black Magic Woman '91
Blackbeard's Ghost '67
Bless the Child '00
Blood Diner '87
The Blood on Satan's Claw '71
Blood Orgy of the She-Devils '74
Bloodspell '87
Born of Fire '87
The Brainiac '61
Brimstone & Treacle '82
The Brotherhood 3: The Young Demons '02
Brotherhood of the Wolf '01
The Burning Court '62
Cabin in the Sky '43
Cat Girl '57
Cat in the Cage '68
The Cellar '90
Chandu on the Magic Island '34
Child of Glass '78
Children Shouldn't Play with Dead Things '72
Close Your Eyes '02
Come Along with Me '84
The Craft '96
The Craze '96
The Crow: Wicked Prayer '05
Curse of Nostradamus '60
The Curse of the Crying Woman '61
Curse of the Demon '57
Curse of the Devil '73
Damien: Omen 2 '78
Damn Yankees '58
Dance with the Devil '97
The Dark Secret of Harvest Home '78
Darkness '02
Dead Men Don't Die '91
Deathstalker 4: Match of Titans '92
Deep Red: Hatchet Murders '75
Demon Possessed '93
Demon Rage '82
Demon Wind '90
Demonoid, Messenger of Death '81
Demons 2 '87
Demons of Ludlow '75
The Devil & Daniel Webster '41
Devil Dog: The Hound of Hell '78
Devil Doll '36
Devil Doll '64
The Devils '71
The Devil's Daughter '39
The Devil's Eye '60
Devil's Gift '84
The Devil's Hand '61
Devil's Kiss '75
The Devil's Mistress '68
The Devil's Nightmare '71
Devil's Rain '75
Devil's Son-in-Law '77
Diary of a Madman '63
Dick Tracy, Detective '45
Doctor Faustus '68
Dr. Strange '78
Dominique is Dead '79
Dona Flor and Her Two Husbands '78
Don't Be Afraid of the Dark '73
Dream Man '94
Dreamscape '84
The Dunwich Horror '70
The Dybbuk '37
The Dying Truth '91
Encounter with the Unknown '75
The Entity '83
Equinox '71
Eternal Evil '87
The Evictors '79
The Evil '78
Evil Altar '89
Evil Dead '83
Evil Dead 2: Dead by Dawn '87
The Evil Mind '34
Evilspeak '82
Excalibur '81
Exorcism '74
The Exorcist '73
The Exorcist 2: The Heretic '77
Exorcist 3: Legion '90
Eye of the Demon '87
Eyes of Fire '84
Fallen '97
Feast for the Devil '71
The Final Conflict '81
The First Power '89
The Fish that Saved Pittsburgh '79
Fright House '89
Full Circle '77
Gates of Hell 2: Dead Awakening '96
Genie of Darkness '62
Ghosts That Still Walk '77
The Girl in a Swing '89
God Told Me To '76
Grave Secrets '89
The Guardian '90
Hat of Heaven '86
Haunted Symphony '94
Haxan: Witchcraft through the Ages '22
The Hearse '80
Home '78
Horror Hotel '60
House of the Yellow Carpet '84
The House on Skull Mountain '74
The House that Bled to Death '81
I Don't Want to Be Born '75
I'm Dangerous Tonight '90
Inferno '80
Inner Sanctum '48
Into the Badlands '92
Invasion of the Blood Farmers '72
The Invasion of Carol Enders '74
KISS Meets the Phantom of the Park '78
Lady Terminator '89
Land of the Minotaur '77
The Legacy '79
The Legend of Hell House '73
Leonor '75
Life-Size '00
The Living Head '59
Lost Souls '00
The Magician '58
Making Contact '86
The Mangler '94
Manos, the Hands of Fate '66
Mardi Gras for the Devil '93
Mardi Gras Massacre '78
Maxim Xul '91
Medea '70
Men of Two Worlds '46
Midnight '81
Midnight Cabaret '90
Mirror, Mirror '90
Mirror, Mirror 2: Raven Dance '94
Mirror of Death '87
Mirrors '78
Mists of Avalon '01
The Monster Demolisher '60
Mystic Circle Murder '39
Natas... The Reflection '83
Necromancer: Satan's Servant '88
Necropolis '88
The Night Stalker '71
The Night Strangler '72
Ninja, the Violent Sorcerer '86
The Occultist '89
Omoo Omoo, the Shark God '49
Only You '94
The Oracle '85
Orgy of the Dead '65
Out on a Limb '87
Phantasm '79
Phantasm 2 '88
Phantasm 3: Lord of the Dead '94
Poltergeist '82
Poltergeist 2: The Other Side '86
Poltergeist 3 '88
Possession: Until Death Do You Part '90
The Power '80
The Psychic '68
The Psychic '78
Psychic Killer '75
Psychomania '73
Puppet Master '89
Quest of the Delta Knights '93
Race with the Devil '75
The Raven '63
A Reflection of Fear '72
The Reincarnate '71
Rendez-Moi Ma Peau '81
Repossessed '90
Rest in Pieces '87
Retribution '88
Return '88
Return from Witch Mountain '78
Return of Chandu '34
Rosemary's Baby '68
Ruby '77
Run if You Can '87
The Runestone '91
Sabaka '55
Satan's Princess '90
Satan's Touch '84
Scared Stiff '87
Season of the Witch '73
Second Sight '89
Seduced by Evil '94
Seizure '74
Sensation '94
The Sentinel '76
The Seventh Sign '88
The Seventh Victim '43
The Shaman '87
Shock 'Em Dead '90
Silent Night, Deadly Night 3: Better Watch Out! '89
Sorceress '82
The Spaniard's Curse '58
Speak of the Devil '90
The Spellbinder '88
Spellbound '41
Spiritism '61
Student of Prague '13
Summer of Fear '78
Supergirl '84
Teen Witch '89
The Tempter '74
Temptress '95
Terror Beach '75
Terror Creatures from the Grave '66
That Darn Sorceress '88
Three Sovereigns for Sarah '85
To the Devil, a Daughter '76
The Torture Chamber of Dr. Sadism '69
The Touch of Satan '70
Treasure of the Four Crowns '82
The Undead '57
Unknown Powers '80
Venus in Furs '70
Vibes '88
The Visitor '80
Warlock Moon '73
Who Killed Doc Robbin? '48
The Wicker Man '75
Wild Man '89
Wishmaster '97
Wishmaster 4: The Prophecy Fulfilled '02
Witch Hunt '94
Witch Who Came from the Sea '76
Witchboard '87
Witchboard 2: The Devil's Doorway '93
Witchboard 3: The Possession '95
The Witch's Mirror '60
The Wizard of Oz '39
Wizards '77
The Woman Who Came Back '45
Zapped Again '69
The Zodiac Killer '71

Office Surprise

Casino '95
Daredevil '03
Dead Again '91
Dial "M" for Murder '54
Die Hard '88
Goldeneye '95
Grosse Pointe Blank '97
Henry: Portrait of a Serial Killer '90
La Femme Nikita '91
Misery '90
Mission: Impossible '96
9 to 5 '80
Office Killer '97
Point of No Return '93
The Temp '93

Oil

see Black Gold

Oldest Profession

see also Women in Prison

Accatone! '61
Alexander: The Other Side of Dawn '77
Alien Warrior '85
The Allnighter '87
American Gigolo '79
American Heart '92
American Justice '86
American Psycho '99
Amor Bandido '79
The Amsterdam Connection '78
Angel '32
Angel '84
Angel 3: The Final Chapter '88
Anna Christie '23
Anna Christie '30
Another Lonely Hitman '95
Armistead Maupin's More Tales of the City '97
Aroused '66
Auntie '73
Avenging Angel '85
Back Roads '81
Bad Girls '94
The Balcony '63
Band of Gold '63
Being at Home with Claude '92
Belle de Jour '67
Beloved/Friend '99
The Best Little Whorehouse in Texas '82
Beverly Hills Madam '86
Beverly Hills Vamp '88
Beyond Desire '94
Big City Blues '99
Blood Money: The Story of Clinton and Nadine '88
Blow Out '81
The Blue Hour '91
Blush '95
Boiling Point '93
The Book of Stars '99
Bordello '79
Born into Brothels: Calcutta's Red Light Kids '04
Boulevard '94
Broken Mirrors '85
Broken Trail '06
Business is Business '71
Butterfield 8 '60
Cafe Society '97
Call Me: The Rise and Fall of Heidi Fleiss '04
Candy Tangerine Man '75
Caravaggio '86
Carmen, Baby '66
Casino '95
Catherine & Co. '76
Celebrity '98

Oceans

see Deep Blue; Go Fish; Killer Sea Critters; Mutiny; Scuba; Shipwrecked; Submarines

Oldest

Chained Heat 2 '92
The Cheyenne Social Club '70
Christiane F. '82
Cinderella Liberty '73
The Claim '00
Claire Dolan '97
Class of 1984 '82
Club Life '86
The Confessional '95
Confessions of a Vice Baron '42
Corporate Affairs '07
Corvette Summer '78
The Courtesans of Bombay '85
Cracker: Brotherly Love '95
Crimes of Passion '84
Cross Country '83
Cry of a Prostitute: Love Kills '72
Cry, the Beloved Country '95
Cyclo '95
Dagger Eyes '83
Dangerous Beauty '98
The Dark Side of the Heart '92
Dead End Street '83
Deadly Sanctuary '68
Death Shot '73
Death Target '83
Deceiver '97
Deconstructing Harry '97
Dedee d'Anvers '49
Desperate Crimes '93
The Desperate Trail '94
Deuce Bigalow: European Gigolo '05
Deuce Bigalow: Male Gigolo '99
Diamond Men '01
Diamonds '99
Diary of a Lost Girl '29
The Dirty Girls '64
Diva '82
Dixie: Changing Habits '85
Doctor Detroit '83
Dr. Jekyll and Sister Hyde '71
Double Cross '92
Dressed to Kill '80
Drying Up the Streets '76
8 Million Ways to Die '85
Elmer Gantry '60
Emily '77
Emmanuelle & Joanna '78
Endgame '01
Erendira '83
Eros '04
Eva '62
Everybody Wins '90
Fall from Innocence '88
Fiona '98
Firepower '93
Flesh '68
Fleshpot on 42nd Street '71
Flowers of Shanghai '98
For Sale '98
Forbidden Fruit '52
Forever Amber '47
Foxy Brown '74
Frankenhooker '90
Frankie and Johnny '36
French Quarter '78
From Hell '01
From the Edge of the City '98
Full Exposure: The Sex Tape Scandals '89
Fyre '78
Gate of Flesh '64
George A. Romero's Land of the Dead '05
Get Rita '75
Ghetto Dawg 2: Out of the Pits '05
The Gift '82
Gigi '58
Girls of the White Orchid '85
God's Lonely Man '96
Half Moon Street '86
The Happy Hooker '75
The Happy Hooker Goes Hollywood '80
The Happy Hooker Goes to Washington '77

▶ = rated three bones or higher

Oldest

Hard As Nails '01
Hard Bounty '94
Hard Vice '94
Hardcore '04
Harnessing Peacocks '92
He Got Game '98
Heaven or Vegas '98
Help Wanted Female '68
High Stakes '89
Highway '01
Highway Patrolman '91
The Hillside Strangler '04
Hindsight '97
Hitman '07
Hollywood Chainsaw Hookers '88
Hollywood Vice Squad '86
Hot Blooded '98
Hotel '01
Hotel Room '93
How Much Do You Love Me? '05
Hurlyburly '98
The Hustle '75
Hustler Squad '76
Hustler White '96
Hustling '75▸
I Am Frigid... Why? '72
I Want to Live! '58▸
Identity '03
The Immoral One '80
Impulse '90
In the Flesh '97
Intimate Betrayal '96
Irma La Douce '63
Italian Movie '93
Jack's Back '87▸
Jade '95
Jamon, Jamon '93
John Carpenter's Vampires '97
johns '96
Just a Gigolo '79
Justine '69
Katie Tippel '75
Killing Zoe '94
Kinjite: Forbidden Subjects '89
Kiss of the Dragon '01
Kiss the Night '87
Kitty and the Bagman '82
Klute '71▸
Km. 0 '00
L.A. Confidential '97▸
L.A. Crackdown '87
L.A. Crackdown 2 '88
La Vie Promise '02
Ladies of the Lotus '87
Lady in Waiting '94
Lady of the Evening '75
Lady of the House '78
The Last Prostitute '91
The Last Temptation of Christ '88▸
Leaving Las Vegas '95▸
Les Miserables '97
Life of Oharu '52▸
A Life of Sin '92
The List '99
Little Ladies of the Night '77
Lolo Montes '55▸
Lolo '92
Love by Appointment '76
Love Strange Love '82
The Machinist '04
Madame Rosa '77▸
Magdalene '88
Malibu High '79
Mamma Roma '62▸
The Man from Elysian Fields '01▸
Man of Flowers '84
The Man Who Knew Too Little '97
Mandragora '97
Manon '50
Marriage Italian Style '64▸
Mayflower Madam '87
McCabe & Mrs. Miller '71▸
Miami Blues '90
Mid Knight Rider '79
Midnight Auto Supply '78
Midnight Cop '88
Midnight Cowboy '69▸

Midnight Dancers '94
Mifune '99
The Million Dollar Hotel '99▸
Miss Sadie Thompson '53▸
The Missionary '82
Mob Queen '98
Moll Flanders '96
Mon Homme '96
Mona Lisa '86▸
Monsieur Ibrahim '03▸
Monster '03▸
Moulin Rouge '01▸
Murderlust '86
Murphy's Law '86
My Life to Live '62▸
My Mother's Secret Life '84
My Own Private Idaho '91▸
My Pleasure Is My Business '74
My Son the Fanatic '97▸
Mysterious Skin '04▸
Naked Tango '91
Nana '55▸
Nana '82
Never on Sunday '60▸
New York's Finest '87
Night at the Golden Eagle '02
Night Friend '87
Night of the Generals '67▸
Night Shift '82
Night Slasher '69
The Night They Robbed Big Bertha's '75
Nightmare in Badham County '76
Nights of Cabiria '57▸
Nightwatch '96
No One Cries Forever '85
No Prince for My Cinderella '78
No Vacancy '99
The Nun '66
Nuts '87▸
Off Limits '87
Oldest Profession '67
Olivia '83
Once Upon a Time in America '84▸
100 Mile Rule '02
One Night Only '84
Out of the Dark '88
Padre Nuestro '85
Pandora's Box '28▸
Panic in Needle Park '71▸
Party Girls '29
The Passing of Evil '70
Pennies from Heaven '81▸
Personal Services '87
Pigalle '95
Play for Me '01
The Players Club '98▸
Poker Alice '87
Postcards from America '95
Pretty Baby '78▸
Pretty Woman '90▸
Prettykill '87
Prime Cut '72
The Princess & the Call Girl '84
Prison of Secrets '97
The Pyx '73▸
Queen Kelly '29▸
Quick, Let's Get Married '71
Quiet Days in Hollywood '97
Rain '32
Raw Justice '93
Reason to Die '90
Red Kimono '25
Rent-A-Cop '88
The Ripper '97
Risky Business '83▸
A River Made to Drown In '97
Road Movie '72
Roman Spring of Mrs. Stone '61▸
Room 43 '58
Roots of Evil '91
Running Out of Time '94
Saint Jack '79▸
Sandakan No. 8 '74▸
Sansho the Bailiff '54▸
Santitos '99
Scarred '84
Schnelles Geld '84
Scorchers '92

Secret Games '92
Secrets of a Married Man '84
Sessions '83
Sex, Love and Cold Hard Cash '93
Shadow of Angels '76
Sharky's Machine '81
The Silencer '92
Sin City '05▸
Single Room Furnished '68
Sketches of a Strangler '78
Skin Art '93
Slaves in Bondage '37
Sonny '02
Speedway Junky '99
Spenser: Ceremony '93
Spider '02▸
SS Girls '77
Star Maps '97
State's Attorney '31
Stella Does Tricks '96
Stickmen '01
Stone Cold Dead '80
Story of a Prostitute '65
Storyville '75
Street Girls '75
Street of Forgotten Women '25
Street of Shame '56▸
Street Smart '87▸
Streetwalkin' '85
The Substitute Wife '94
The Sun's Burial '60▸
Suspicious River '00
Sweet Charity '69▸
Sweet Revenge '87
Sweet Sweetback's Baadasssss Song '71▸
Sweet Trash '70
The Sword and the Cross '58
Talons of the Eagle '92
Taxi Driver '76▸
They Were So Young '55
Things to Do in Denver When You're Dead '95▸
Things '93
Thomas in Love '01
Thousand Pieces of Gold '91▸
Three Seasons '98
Tightrope '84▸
Time After Time '79▸
Tipping the Velvet '02
The Toilers and the Wayfarers '97
Tokyo Decadence '91
Too Young to Die '90
Trading Places '83▸
Traffic in Souls '13▸
Train Station Pickups '70s
The Treat '98
Tricks '97
Tricks of the Trade '88
Truck Stop Women '74
Twenty Dollar Star '91
2046 '04▸
Twin Peaks: Fire Walk with Me '92
Twin Sisters '91
Twist '03▸
Twisted '96
Two or Three Things I Know about Her '66
Ultimate Desires '91
Uncaged '91
Utamaro and His Five Women '46
The Vampire Hookers '78
Via Appia '92
Vice Squad '82
Vicious Circles '97
Virgil Bliss '01
Walk on the Wild Side '62
The Walker '07
Warm Nights on a Slow-Moving Train '87
Warrior Queen '87
Waterloo Bridge '40▸
The Wedding Date '05
Whore '91
Whore 2 '94
The Wicked, Wicked West '97
Wild Bill '95

Wild Orchid 2: Two Shades of Blue '92
Wild Side '95
The Winter of Our Dreams '82
A Woman in Flames '84▸
A Woman of Rome '56
Working Girls '75
Working Girls '87▸
The World of Suzie Wong '60

The Olympics

see also Sports Dramas

Alex '92
American Anthem '86
Best of the Best '89
Blades of Courage '88
Blades of Glory '07
Blast '96
Breaking the Surface: The Greg Louganis Story '96
Chariots of Fire '81▸
Charlie Chan at the Olympics '37
Cool Runnings '93
Crossbar '79
The Cutting Edge '92
The First Olympics: Athens 1896 84
Going for the Gold: The Bill Johnson Story '85
International Velvet '78
The Jesse Owens Story '84
The Loretta Claiborne Story '00
A Million to One '37
Miracle on Ice '81
Munich '05▸
Pentathlon '94
Personal Best '82▸
Prefontaine '96
The Ringer '05
Rowing Through '96
Run for the Dream: The Gail Devers Story '96
Running Brave '83
Special Olympics '78
Sword of Gideon '86
Tokyo Olympiad '66▸
21 Hours at Munich '76▸
Walk, Don't Run '66
Wilma '77
Without Limits '97▸

On the Rocks

see also Drug Use & Abuse

Abandon '02
Aberdeen '00
Ace in the Hole '51▸
Affliction '97▸
Angela's Ashes '99
Arthur '81▸
Arthur 2: On the Rocks '88
The Bad News Bears '05
Bad Santa '03▸
Barfly '87▸
Beat '00
Betty '92
The Big Hangover '50
The Big Lebowski '97▸
Black Angel '46▸
Black Cloud '04
Blackout '54
Blue Heaven '84
Bounce '00
Break of Hearts '35
The Butcher Boy '97▸
Can't Hardly Wait '98
Casino '95▸
Cat on a Hot Tin Roof '58▸
Cat on a Hot Tin Roof '84
The Chamber '96
Chelsea Walls '01
Clean and Sober '88▸
Cocktail '88
Come Back, Little Sheba '52▸
Come Early Morning '06
Cop-Out '67
Country Girl '54▸
Country Girl '82
Country Life '95
crazy/beautiful '01
The Crossing Guard '94▸

Crutch '04
A Cry for Love '80
Daddy & Them '99
Dance of Life '29
Dancer, Texas—Pop. 81 '98▸
Danger in the Skies '79
Dangerous '35
Dash and Lilly '99
Days of Wine and Roses '58▸
Days of Wine and Roses '62▸
Dead Heat '01
Desert Bloom '86▸
The Devil at 4 O'Clock '61
The Devil Thumbs a Ride '47▸
Divine Secrets of the Ya-Ya Sisterhood '02
Doing Time on Maple Drive '92
Dona Flor and Her Two Husbands '78▸
Drunken Angel '48▸
Drunks '96
Educating Rita '83▸
8 Heads in a Duffel Bag '96
800 Bullets '02
El Dorado '67▸
The Electric Horseman '79
The Entertainer '60▸
Evergreen '04
Eye of the Killer '99
Eye See You '01

Factotum '06▸
Fat City '72▸
The Fire Within '64▸
The First Wives Club '96
Fish Hawk '79
The Flaming Teen-Age '56
Flesh and Bone '93▸
Floating '97
For One More Day '07
The Fountainhead '49▸
Frances '82▸
A Free Soul '31
Georgia '95▸
Gervaise '56▸
The Great Man Votes '38▸
The Green Man '91▸
Hancock '08
Heaven's Prisoners '95
Honkytonk Man '82
Hot Summer in Barefoot County '74
I Live with Me Dad '86
The Iceman Cometh '73
I'll Cry Tomorrow '55▸
The Informer '35▸
Ironweed '87▸
Izzy & Moe '85
Jack and Sarah '95
Jack the Bear '93
Jesse Stone: Death in Paradise '06
Jesse Stone: Night Passage '06
Jesse Stone: Stone Cold '05
Jiminy Glick in LaLa Wood '05
Joe the King '99
Kill Cruise '90
La Cucaracha '99
The Last American Hero '73▸
Last Call: The Final Chapter of F. Scott Fitzgerald '02
Last Time Out '94
Le Beau Serge '58▸
Leaving Las Vegas '95▸
License to Kill '84
Little Boy Blue '97
Little Voice '98▸
Living Proof: The Hank Williams Jr. Story '83
Long Day's Journey into Night '62▸
Long Day's Journey into Night '88
Long Day's Journey into Night '96▸
The Lost Weekend '45▸
Love on a Pillow '62

A Love Song for Bobby Long '04
Lush '01
M.A.D.D.: Mothers Against Drunk Driving '83
Marvin & Tige '84
Matter of Trust '98
Mean Dog Blues '78
Mrs. Parker and the Vicious Circle '94
The Morning After '86
My Favorite Year '82▸
My Name Is Joe '98
National Lampoon's Animal House '78▸
Nightmare Alley '47
No Laughing Matter '97
No Marriage Ties '33
No Such Thing '01
Notre Histoire '84
Once Were Warriors '94▸
One for the Road '82
100 Proof '96
One Too Many '51
Only When I Laugh '81▸
Papa's Delicate Condition '63▸
Place Vendome '98▸
Pollock '00▸
Police Court '32
Prozac Nation '01
Pushing Tin '99
Red Lights '04▸
Reuben, Reuben '83▸
Revenge of the Nerds '84
Rio Bravo '59▸
The River Is Red '48
The Robe '53
Rosetta '99
Scandal Sheet '85
Scent of a Woman '92▸
The Secret Rapture '94
Shakes the Clown '92
She's So Lovely '97
A Shot at Glory '00
The Sin of Harold Diddlebock '47
The Singing Blacksmith '38
16 Years of Alcohol '03
Skin Deep '89
Skins '02
Sling Blade '96▸
Smash-Up: The Story of a Woman '47▸
Snow Angels '07
Somebody Is Waiting '96
Son-in-Law '93
Spent '00
The Star '52▸
A Star Is Born '54▸
A Star Is Born '76
Straight Up '90
Stranded '87
Strange Brew '83
Street Kings '08
Struggle '31
Stuart Saves His Family '94
Take Me Home: The John Denver Story '00
Tales of Ordinary Madness '83
Ten Nights in a Bar-Room '31
Ten Nights in a Barroom '13▸
The Tenant of Wildfell Hall '96
Termini Station '89
Thirteen '03▸
Tree's Lounge '96
True Crime '99
24-7 '97
28 Days '00
Twisted '31
Under Capricorn '49
Under Capricorn '82
Under the Volcano '84▸
Unearthed '07
Unnatural Pursuits '91
The Verdict '82▸
Wagons East '94
What Price Hollywood? '32▸
When a Man Loves a Woman '94
Whiskey Galore '48▸
White Lightning '73
Wild Iris '01
Willa '79
The Winning Team '52

▸ = rated three bones or higher

Winter Passing '05
A Winter Tan '88
You Kill Me '07

One Last Job
see also Crime Drama; Heists; Hit Men/Women; Organized Crime; Scams, Stings & Cons

Assassins '95
Canvas: The Fine Art of Crime '92
City of Industry '96
City on Fire '87
Crime Wave '54
The Debt '03
Dillinger and Capone '95
Entrapment '99
Exiled '06
Ghetto Dawg 2: Out of the Pits '05
Going in Style '79
Gone in 60 Seconds '00
Heat '95
The Hard Word '02
Heist '01
The Job '03
The Killer '90
The Mummy: Tomb of the Dragon Emperor '08
Once a Thief '90
Out of Sight '98
The Ref '93
The Score '01
The Squeeze '80
The Star '52
Thief '81
3-D '05
Things to Do in Denver When You're Dead '95
Tough Guys '86
Two If by Sea '95
The Usual Suspects '95

Only the Lonely

Abducted '86
The Abduction of Kari Swenson '87
Adrift in Manhattan '07
The Adventures of Sharkboy and Lavagirl in 3-D '05
After the Wedding '06
An Autumn Afternoon '62
Autumn Tale '98
Avenue Montaigne '06
Bed of Roses '95
Besieged '98
Betrayal '74
Birdman of Alcatraz '62
The Body Shop '72
Born Romantic '00
Bossa Nova '99
Bread and Tulips '01
Breakfast in Paris '81
Broken English '01
Broken Flowers '05
The Browning Version '51
Buddy Boy '99
The Business of Strangers '01
The Cemetery Club '93
The Center of the World '01
Central Station '98
Charlotte Sometimes '02
Choose Me '84
A Chorus of Disapproval '89
A Christmas Without Snow '80
Citizen Kane '41
The Closet '00
Conversations with Other Women '05
Cotter '72
Cowboys Don't Cry '88
Cyrano de Bergerac '25
Cyrano de Bergerac '50
Cyrano de Bergerac '85
Cyrano de Bergerac '90
Day Night Day Night '06
Dead Letter Office '98
Desperately Seeking Susan '85
Didn't You Hear? '83
Dirty Dishes '78
Distant Thunder '88
Docks of New York '28
Doin' Time on Planet Earth '88
The Doll '62
A Doll's House '59
A Doll's House '73
A Doll's House '73
Eagle vs. Shark '07
Eat Drink Man Woman '94
The Eclipse '56
84 Charing Cross Road '86
El Super '79
An Empty Bed '90
The Enchanted Cottage '45
Escapade in Japan '57
E.T.: The Extra-Terrestrial '82
Every Man for Himself & God Against All '75
Eye of the Needle '81
Fanatic '82
Felicia's Journey '99
Fever '99
Fiances '63
The Final Alliance '89
Fire '96
Full Moon in Blue Water '88
Full Moon in Paris '84
The Game of Love '90
Ginger Snaps '01
God's Lonely Man '96
The Gun in Betty Lou's Handbag '92
Happy Endings '05
Hard Pill '05
Harold and Maude '71
The Heart is a Lonely Hunter '68
Heavy '94
Hell Hounds of Alaska '73
High Country '81
Hiroshima, Mon Amour '59
Hoffman '70
The Human Stain '03
The Hunchback of Notre Dame '39
The Hunchback of Notre Dame '57
Husbands and Wives '92
I Don't Give a Damn '88
I Sent a Letter to My Love '81
I Want Someone to Eat Cheese With '06
In the White City '83
In the Winter Dark '98
Inside Out '11
Kaspar Hauser '93
La Petite Sirene '80
La Vie Continue '82
Lana in Love '92
Lars and the Real Girl '07
The Last Best Year '90
The Legend of 1900 '98
Les Bons Debarras '81
Les Voleurs '96
The Locket '02
The Lonely Guy '84
The Lonely Hearts '82
Lonely Hearts '06
The Lonely Passion of Judith Hearne '87
Lonelyhearts '58
Looking for Kitty '04
Looking for Mr. Goodbar '77
Lost in Translation '03
Lulu on the Bridge '98
Lunatics: A Love Story '92
Luther the Geek '90
Madagascar Skin '95
Man of Flowers '84
Marty '55
The Match Factory Girl '90
Men Don't Leave '89
Midnight Clear '06
Miles to Go Before I Sleep '74
Mind the Gap '04
Minnie and Moskowitz '71
Mrs. Palfrey at the Claremont '05
Mouchette '67
My First Mister '01
976-EVIL '88
Ninotchka '39
The Noah '75
Noel '04
None But the Lonely Heart '44
Not of This World '99
Notes from Underground '95
O Fantasma '00
Once Around '91
Only the Lonely '91
Only You '92
Our Miss Brooks '56
Pan's Labyrinth '06
Panic Station '32
The Passion of Anna '70
Persona '66
Pi '98
A Price above Rubies '97
Primal Secrets '94
The Prime of Miss Jean Brodie '69
The Prince of Central Park '77
Private Fears in Public Places '06
The Pursuit of Happiness '70
Queen of the Stardust Ballroom '75
The Rachel Papers '89
Rachel, Rachel '68
The Red Desert '64
Red Kimono 25
Restless '72
Return Engagement '78
Rhythm Thief '94
Richie Rich '94
Risk '94
Robert et Robert '78
Roman '06
Roseland '77
Samurai 2: Duel at Ichijoji Temple '55
Scene of the Crime '87
The Seagull '71
The Seagull '75
Secret Life of an American Wife '68
Seize the Day '86
Separate Tables '58
Separate Tables '83
September '88
Shadows in the Storm '88
Sherman's March '86
Single Bars, Single Women '84
Sleepless in Seattle '93
Slipstream '73
Snow Cake '06
Solas '99
The Solitary Man '82
Someone to Love '87
Somersault '04
South of Reno '87
The Spectator '04
Spider '02
The Station Agent '03
Street Heart '98
Stuart Saves His Family '94
Summer '86
Sunday '96
Sunday, Bloody Sunday '71
Tales of the Klondike: The Scorn of Women '87
Tenth Month '79
That Cold Day in the Park '69
Thomas in Love '01
Til There Was You '96
Tomorrow '72
Too Shy to Try '82
Turtle Diary '86
12 and Holding '05
Twin Falls Idaho '99
Under the Skin '97
Vagabond '85
The Visitor '07
The Walls of Malapaga '49
The War Zone '98
What Happened Was... '94
What the Cat's Away '96
When Your Lover Leaves '83
While You Were Sleeping '95
Who is Harry Kellerman and Why is He Saying Those Terrible Things About Me? '71
Wildest Dreams '90
Willard '71
Willard '03
Woman in the Shadows '34
World Traveler '01
The Young in Heart '38
Zelly & Me '88

Opera
see also Musicals

Callas Forever '02
The Climax '44
Cosi '95
Farinelli '94
Fleeing by Night '00
Four Play '78
Interrupted Melody '55
Joyeux Noel '05
Madame Butterfly '95
Tha Man Who Cried '00
Merci Docteur Rey '04
Musica Proibita '43
Naughty Marietta '35
A Night at the Opera '35
Opera '88
The Perfect Husband '92
The Phantom of the Opera '62
The Phantom of the Opera '90
The Phantom of the Opera '92
The Phantom of the Opera
Piano Tuner of Earthquakes '05
Puccini for Beginners '06
Rhapsody of Spring '98
Riding Alone for Thousands of Miles '05
Romance '30
Tonight or Never '31

Order in the Court
see also Justice Prevails...; Law & Lawyers; Military Crimes & Trials

Absence of Malice '81
The Accused '48
The Accused '88
Action for Slander '38
Adam's Rib '50
All God's Children '80
Amazing Dr. Clitterhouse '38
The Ambush Murders '82
American Tragedy '00
Anatomy of a Murder '59
...And Justice for All '79
The Andersonville Trial '70
Angel Face '52
Artemisia '97
As Summers Die '86
Assault at West Point: The Court-Martial of Johnson Whittaker '94
Bamako '06
Bee Movie '07
Beefcake '07
Before and After '95
Beyond a Reasonable Doubt '56
Big Daddy '99
The Black Legion '37
Blind Faith '98
Body Chemistry 4: Full Exposure '95
Body of Evidence '92
Boomerang '47
Bounce '00
The Bramble Bush '60
Breaker Morant '80

Broken Trust '95
The Burning Bed '85
The Caine Mutiny Court Martial '88
Carrington, V.C. '54
A Case of Libel '83
The Castle '97
Cause Celebre '87
The Chamber '96
The Chatterley Affair '06
Chicago 10 '07
A Civil Action '98
Class Action '91
Clearcut '91
The Client '94
Cold Days '66
Color of Justice '97
Comedy of Power '06
Compulsion '59
Conduct Unbecoming '75
The Confession '98
Conspiracy: The Trial of the Chicago Eight '87
Convicted '86
The Court Martial of Billy Mitchell '55
Crazy in Alabama '99
Crime Broker '94
Crime of the Century '96
Crimebroker '93
Criminal Court '46
Cross Examination '32
The Crucible '96
A Cry in the Dark '88
Dancer in the Dark '99
Dangerous Beauty '98
Dangerous Evidence: The Lori Jackson Story '99
Deacon Brodie '98
Deadlocked '00
Dear God '96
Death of a Soldier '85
Death Sentence '74
The Defenders: Payback '97
The Defenders: Taking the First '98
Degree of Guilt '95
Deliberate Intent '01
Delinquent Parents '38
The Devil & Daniel Webster '41
The Devil's Advocate '97
Dirty Pictures '00
Disclosure '94
Dishonored Lady '47
The Drake Case '29
A Dry White Season '89
8-A '92
Ernest Goes to Jail '90
Eureka! '81
Evelyn '02
Evelyn Prentice '34
Execution of Justice '99
The Exorcism of Emily Rose '05
A Few Good Men '92
Final Appeal '93
Final Justice '98
Final Verdict '91
Find Me Guilty '06
A Free Soul '31
From the Hip '86
Getting Gotti '94
Ghosts of Mississippi '96
Gideon's Trumpet '80
The Gift '00
The Girl in the Red Velvet Swing '55
The Good Father '87
The Good Fight '92
The Good Mother '88
Gospa '94
The Great American Sex Scandal '94
Guilty as Sin '93
Guilty of Innocence '87
Hard Traveling '85
Hitz '89
Honor Thy Father and Mother: The True Story of the Menendez Brothers '94
How Many Miles to Babylon? '82
The Hurricane '99
I Want to Live! '58
Illegally Yours '87
In the Name of the Father '93
Indictment: The McMartin Trial '95
Inherit the Wind '60
Inherit the Wind '99
Invasion of Privacy '96
It Could Happen to You '37
Jaded '96
The Jagged Edge '85
Jailbait: Betrayed By Innocence '86
Jasper, Texas '03
Jeanne la Pucelle '94
Joan of Arc '99
John Grisham's The Rainmaker '97
The Judge '49
The Judge and the Assassin '75
Judge Horton and the Scottsboro Boys '76
Judgment at Nuremberg '61
Judgment in Berlin '88
Judicial Consent '94
The Juror '96
Jury Duty '95
A Killing in a Small Town '90
The Killing Yard '01
King and Country '64
King of the Pecos '36
Knock on Any Door '49
Knots '05
L.A. Law '86
The Last Innocent Man '87
The Last Letter '04
The Last Wave '77
Legalese '98
Legally Blonde '01
Les Assassins de L'Ordre '71
Liar Liar '97
The List '99
Little Gloria... Happy at Last '84
The Long Dark Hall '51
The Love God? '77
Loved '97
Lucky Partners '40
Lured Innocence '97
A Map of the World '99
Madame X '37
Madame X '66
Madeleine '50
The Man in the Glass Booth '75
Martial '68
Melanie Darrow '97
The Merchant of Venice '04
Midnight '34
Midnight in the Garden of Good and Evil '97
Miracle on 34th Street '47
Miracle on 34th Street '94
Miracle in the First '95
Mistrial '96
Monsieur Beaucaire '24
Moonlight Mile '02
Move Over, Darling '63
Mr. Deeds Goes to Town '36
Mrs. R's Daughter '79
Mrs. Harris '05
Murder in the First '95
Murder '30
Murder or Mercy '74
Music Box '89
Mutiny '99
My Cousin Vinny '92
Naked Lie '89
Never Forget '91
The Next Best Thing '00
Night Falls on Manhattan '96
Nuremberg '00
Nuts '87
One of Her Own '94
Outrage! '86
The Paradine Case '47
Passion of Joan of Arc '28
Penalty Phase '86
The People vs. Larry Flynt '96
Perfect Crime '97

▶ = rated three bones or higher

Order

Perry Mason Returns '85▲
Perry Mason: The Case of the Lost Love '87
Philadelphia '93▲
The Ponder Heart '01
Presumed Innocent '90▲
Primal Fear '96
Prisoners of the Sun '91▲
Psychopath '97
Question of Silence '83▲
Rampage '87
Red Corner '97
Red Kimono '25
Remember the Night '40▲
The Respectful Prostitute '52
Return to Paradise '98▲
Reversal of Fortune '90▲
The Rite '69
The Rite '08
Riverbend '89
Roe vs. Wade '89▲
The Rose Garden '89
Roxie Hart '42
Rules of Engagement '00
Runaway Jury '03▲
Sacco & Vanzetti '71
The Runner Stumbles '79
The Scorpion Woman '89
The Secret Passion of Robert Clayton '92
Separate but Equal '91▲
Sergeant Rutledge '60▲
Sergeant Ryker '68
Shadow of Doubt '98
The Shaggy Dog '06
Silent Victim '92
A Simple Twist of Fate '94
Skullduggery '70
Sleepers '96
Small Sacrifices '89
Snow Falling on Cedars '99
Souls at Sea '37
Stairway to Heaven '46▲
The Star Chamber '83
State's Attorney '31
A Stranger in the Kingdom '98
Stuck on You '84
Suspect '87
Swoon '91▲
They Won't Believe Me '47▲
A Time to Kill '96▲
Tom and Huck '95▲
Too Young to Die '90
Town without Pity '61
The Trial '63▲
The Trial '93
Trial & Error '62
Trial and Error '96
Trial by Jury '94
The Trial of Lee Harvey Oswald '77
The Trial of Old Drum '00
Trial of the Catonsville Nine '72
The Trials of Oscar Wilde '60▲
Twelve Angry Men '57▲
Twelve Angry Men '97
Two Years before the Mast '46
The Verdict '82▲
Verdict on Auschwitz: The Frankfurt Auschwitz Trial 1963–1965 '93▲
The Weight of Water '00
When Every Day Was the Fourth of July '78
When Thief Meets Thief '37
Where Love Has Gone '64
Where the Truth Lies '99
White Mischief '88▲
White Squall '96
Why Do Fools Fall in Love? '98
Wilde '97▲
The Winslow Boy '48▲
Witness for the Prosecution '57▲
Wives under Suspicion '38
Woman in Brown '48
Woman Undone '95
A Woman's Face '38▲
A Woman's Face '41▲
The Young Philadelphians '59▲
The Young Savages '61

Organ Transplants

see also Disease of the Week; Doctors & Nurses; Hospitals & Medicine; Second Chance

The Awful Dr. Orloff '62
Black Friday '40
Blood Work '02
Bowery Boys Meet the Monsters '54
Brain of Blood '71
The Brain that Wouldn't Die '63
Brainwaves '82
The Eye '08
Heart '99
I'll Bury You Tomorrow '02
The Incredible Two-Headed Transplant '71
The Intruder '04▲
John Q '02
The Man with Two Brains '83▲
New Blood '99
Night of the Bloody Apes '68
Race Against Time '00
Return to Me '00
13 Moons '02
21 Grams '03▲
Untamed Heart '93
Young Frankenstein '74▲

Organized Crime

see also Comedy; Disorganized Crime; Gangs; Moscow Mafia; Triads; Urban Gangsters; Yakuza

Absence of Malice '81
Across 110th Street '72
Action U.S.A. '89
Acts of Betrayal '98
Agent on Ice '86
Alibi '29
The Alien Agenda: Under the Skin '97
Almost Human '79
Alphabet City '84
American Born '89
American Chinatown '96
American Cop '94
American Cousins '02
American Justice '86
The American Soldier '70
American Yakuza '94
Analyze That '02
Analyze This '98▲
Angel's Dance '99
Angels with Dirty Faces '38▲
Another Stakeout '93
Armed for Action '92
Armed Response '86
Atlantic City '81▲
Avenging Disco Godfather '76
Baby Face Nelson '97
Baby on Board '92
Back to Back '96
Backtrack '89▲
Bad Charleston Charlie '73
Bad Georgia Road '77
Ball of Fire '41▲
Ballistic '94
The Barber Shop '33▲
The Barcelona Kill '77
Batman Begins '05▲
Be Cool '05
Beautiful Hunter '94
Beautiful Joe '00
Bella Mafia '97
Best of the Best: Without Warning '98
A Better Way to Die '00
Beverly Hills Bodysnatchers '89
Beverly Hills Cop 3 '94
Big Bad Mama 2 '87
Big Boss '77
Big Combo '55▲
The Big Hit '98
Big News '29
The Big Slice '90
The Big Sweat '90
The Big Switch '70
Big Town After Dark '47
Billy Bathgate '91
Birth of the Blues '41
Bitter Sweet '98
Black Belt Jones '74
Black Caesar '73
Black Godfather '74
Black Hand '73
Black Lemons '70
Black Lizard '68
Black Shampoo '76
Black Snow '89
Blackjack '78
Blank Check '93
Blind Fury '90
Blood Brothers '74
Blood Money '98
Blood Money '99
Blood Ties '87
Blood Vows: The Story of a Mafia Wife '87
Blown Away '90
Blue Money '84
Boca '94
Body Trouble '92
Bonanno: A Godfather's Story '99
Bookies '03
Boondock Saints '99
Born to Run '93
Boss of Bosses '99
Bought and Sold '03
Bound '96
The Box '03
The Boys '97
Branded to Kill '67
Breach of Trust '95
Breakaway '95
Brighton Rock '47▲
A Bronx Tale '93▲
Brooklyn Rules '07
A Brooklyn State of Mind '97
Brother '97
The Brotherhood '68
Bugsy '91▲
Bugsy Malone '76
A Bullet for Joey '55
Bullets over Broadway '94▲
California Casanova '89
Camorra: The Naples Connection '85
Capone '89
Car Crash '80
Car 54, Where Are You? '94
Casino '95▲
Chasing Ghosts '05
The Chinatown Murders: Man against the Mob '89
Chu Chu & the Philly Flash '81
City Hall '95▲
City Unplugged '95
The Client '94
Cobra '71
Cohen and Tate '88
Cold Heat '90
Coldblooded '94
The Collectors '99
Comfort and Joy '84▲
Confessions of a Hit Man '94
Connie and Carla '04
Cookie '89
Cop in Blue Jeans '78
Cops and Robbersons '94
Corky Romano '01
Corleone '79
The Corruptor '99▲
Corruption '70
The Cotton Club '84▲
Courier of Death '84
Crazy Six '08
The Crew '00
Crime Killer '85
Crime Spree '03
The Criminal Mind '93
Crosscut '95
Dagger Eyes '83
Dangerous Charter '62
Darker than Amber '70
Darkman 3: Die Darkman Die '95
Daughter of the Tong '39
Day at the Beach '98
Dead Heat '01
Dead Lenny '06
Dead Pigeon on Beethoven Street '72
Dead Silent '99
Deadly Game '98
Deadly Rivals '92
Deadly Target '94
Deadly Vengeance '81
Deadly Weapons '70
Death Force '78
Death to Smoochy '02
Death Wish 5: The Face of Death '94
Decay '98
Deja Vu '89
Delta Fox '77
The Departed '06▲
Desperate '47
Desperate Crimes '93
The Destiny of Marty Fine '96
Detour '99
Deuces Wild '02
Dick Tracy '90▲
Dinner Rush '00▲
Dirty Deeds '02▲
Dirty Work '92
Doctor Detroit '83
The Don Is Dead '73
Donnie Brasco '96▲
Double Bang '01
Double Deal '39
Double Dragon '97
Drunken Angel '48▲
Eastside '99
Elmore Leonard's Gold Coast '97
The Embalmer '03▲
The Enforcer '51
Ernest Goes to Jail '90
Essex Boys '99
Eurekal '81
Excellent Cadavers '99
Excessive Force '93
The Executioner '78
The Executioner, Part 2: Frozen Scream '84
Exiled '06
Extreme Vengeance '90
Extremely Dangerous '99
An Eye for an Eye '81
Faith '90
Fake Out '82
The Family '71
A Family Matter '91
Family of Cops 2: Breach of Faith '97
Fass Black '77
Fast Money '96
Fatal Chase '77
Fatal Past '94
Fatally Yours '95
Fear in the City '81
Federal Protection '02
The Fighting Rookie '34
Final Justice '84
The Finger Man '55
Fingers '78▲
Fireback '78
The Firm '93▲
First Degree '95
Fist of Honor '92
The Fixer '97
Fled '96
Flipping '96
For Which He Stands '98
Force of Evil '49▲
The Freshman '90▲
The Frightened City '61
Friends and Family '01
Frogs for Snakes '98
Fugitive Rage '96
The Funeral '96▲
Gang War '40
Gangster No. 1 '00
Gangster Wars '81
Gangster's Law '86
Getting Gotti '94
Ghetto Dawg '02
Ghetto Dawg 2: Out of the Pits '05
Ghost Dog: The Way of the Samurai '99
Gigli '03
The Girl Who Had Everything '53
Gloria '80
Gloria '98
The Godfather '72▲
The Godfather 1902–1959: The Complete Epic '81▲
The Godfather, Part 2 '74▲
The Godfather, Part 3 '90▲
The Godson '98
Goodfellas '90▲
Gotti '96
Gozu '03
The Great Plane Robbery '40
Gun Shy '00
Gunblast '74
Gunshy '98▲
Hard-Boiled '92
The Harder They Fall '56▲
Harlem Nights '89
Harvard Man '01
Hawk's Vengeance '96
He Sees You When You're Sleeping '02
Heat '87
Hell on Frisco Bay '55
Hell Up in Harlem '73
Heroes in Blue '39
Hiding Out '87
High Heels and Low Lifes '01
High Stakes '89
High Voltage '98
Highway '01
Hired to Kill '73
A History of Violence '05▲
Hit Lady '74
The Hit List '88▲
Hit Men '73
Hit the Dutchman '92
Hitman's Journal '99
Hitman's Run '99
Hollywood Cop '87
Hollywood Man '76
The Hollywood Sign '01
Hong Kong Nights '35
Honor Thy Father '73
Hooch '76
Hoodlum '96
Hoodlum & Son '03
Hoods '98
The Hunted Lady '77
Hurricane Smith '92
I Accidentally Domed Your Son '04
I Died a Thousand Times '55
I, Mobster '58
I Promise to Pay '37
I Went Down '97▲
Ice '93
The Ice Harvest '05
I'll Sleep When I'm Dead '03▲
Illegal Tender '07
In Bruges '08
In the Kingdom of the Blind the Man with One Eye Is King '94
In the Mix '05
Infernal Affairs '02▲
Innocent Blood '92
Internes Can't Take Money '37
Johnny Stecchino '92
The Juror '96
Kansas City '95▲
Keaton's Cop '90
Keeper of the City '92
The Key Man '57
Kid Monk Baroni '52
Kill Me Again '89
The Kill Reflex '89
The Killer '90▲
Killer Instinct '92
The Killers '46▲
The Killers '64
Killing in the Sun '73
The Killing Man '94
The Killing of a Chinese Bookie '76
Killing Time '97
The King of the Roaring '20s: The Story of Arnold Rothstein '61
Kiss of Death '94
Kiss Toledo Goodbye '00
Kiss Tomorrow Goodbye '50
Knockaround Guys '01
The Krays '90▲
La Scorta '94
L.A. Wars '94
Ladies of the Lotus '87
Lady Jayne Killer '03
Lady Mobster '88
Lady of the Evening '75
Lady Scarface '41
Lansky '99
The Last Contract '86
The Last Days of Frankie the Fly '96
The Last Don '97
The Last Don 2 '98
Last Exit to Brooklyn '90▲
Last Rites '88
The Last Shot '04
The Last Word '95
Laws of Deception '97
Layer Cake '05▲
Legacy of Lies '92
Lepke '75
Lethal Games '90
Lethal Panther '90
Life Tastes Good '99
Little Caesar '30▲
Little Odessa '94
Little Vegas '90
Loan Shark '52
The Long Good Friday '80▲
Lost Highway '96
Love, Honour & Obey '00
Love to Kill '97
Luck of the Draw '00
Lucky Luciano '74
Lucky Number Slevin '06
Ma and Pa Kettle Go to Town '50
Macbeth '06
Machine Gun Blues '95
Mad Dog and Glory '93▲
Made '01
Madigan's Millions '67
Mafia! '98
Mafia Princess '86
Mafia vs. Ninja '84
Mafioso '62
Magic Kid '92
Making the Grade '84
Mambo Cafe '00
The Man I Love '46▲
Man on a String '72
Man with a Gun '95
Manderlay '05
The Manhandlers '73
Manhunt '73
Manhunter '83
Married to the Mob '88▲
Mauvais Sang '86
The Mayor of Hell '33
Me and the Mob '94
Mean Machine '73
Mean Streets '73▲
The Mechanic '72
Meet Danny Wilson '52
Melvin Purvis: G-Man '74
Men of Means '99
Men of Respect '91
The Messenger '87
Mickey Blue Eyes '99
Mickey One '65
Mikey & Nicky '76
Miller's Crossing '90▲
Miracles '89
The Mission '99
Mr. Majestyk '74
Mister Mean '77
Mob Queen '98
Mob Boss '90
Mobsters '91
Money Kings '98
The Monster and the Girl '41
Montana '97
Moon over Harlem '39
Movie... In Your Face '90
Moving Target '89
Moving Target '96
Mulholland Falls '95
My Blue Heaven '90
My Husband's Secret Life '98
The Narrow Margin '52▲
National Lampoon's The Don's Analyst '97
Never Steal Anything Small '59
New Blood '99
New Mafia Boss '72
Next of Kin '89

▲ = rated three bones or higher

1931: Once Upon a Time in New York '72
Nitti: The Enforcer '88
No Way Back '96
Nowhere Land '98
Odd Jobs '85
Once a Thief '96►
Once Upon a Time in America '84►
Opposite Corners '96
Organized Crime & Triad Bureau '93
Our Family Business '81
Out for Justice '91
The Outfit '93
The Outside Man '73
Overkill '96
Palais Royale '88
The Palermo Connection '91
Panic Button '62
Paper Bullets '99
Party Girl '58►
Passion for Power '85
Payoff '91
Penthouse '33►
Perfect Killer '77
Perfect Witness '89
Played '06
Players '03
The Plot Against Harry '69►
Point Blank '67
Police Academy 7: Mission to Moscow '94
The Pope Must Die '91
Port of New York '49
Power and Beauty '02
Power of Attorney '94
Pray for Death '85
Prime Target '91
Prizzi's Honor '85►
Pronto '97
The Proposal '0C
The Public Eye '92►
Pulp Fiction '94►
Quick '93
The Quickie '01
Rancid Aluminium '00
Rapid Fire '92
Raw Deal '86
Recoil '97
Red Heat '88
The Red Light Sting '84
Red Line '96
Remote Control '94
The Replacement Killers '38
The Revenger '90
Ricco '74
Ring of Fire 3: Lion Strike '94
Ring of the Musketeers '95
Ripley's Game '02►
The Rise and Fall of Legs Diamond '60
Road to Perdition '02►
The Roaring Twenties '39►
Rock, Baby, Rock It '57
Romeo Is Bleeding '93
Romeo Must Die '00
Ruby '92
Rude Boy: The Jamaican Don '03
Rulers of the City '76
Run '91
The Runner '99
Running Scared '06
Rush Hour 3 '07
Safe Men '98
Savage Hearts '95
Scarface '31►
Scarface Mob '62
Sex, Love and Cold Hard Cash '93
Shade '03
Shaft's Big Score '72
Shoot to Kill '47
Showdown '94
Sicilian Connection '72
The Sicilian Connection '85
Sitting Ducks '80►
Sizzle '81
Slaughter '72
Slaughter's Big Ripoff '73
Sleepers '96
A Slight Case of Murder '38
Sloane '84
Slow Burn '97
Smalltime '96

Smashing the Rackets '38
Smokescreen '90
Smokin' Aces '07
Snatch '00►
Sno-Line '85
Soul Survivor '95
Southie '98
Special Investigator '36
Squizzy Taylor '84
Stand-In '85
Stark Raving Mad '02
State of Grace '90►
State's Attorney '31
Stephen King's Thinner '96
Sticks '98
Stiletto '69
Stiletto Dance '01
The Stone Killer '73
Stonebrook '98
Street Gun '96
Street Hero '84
Street People '76
Street War '76
Sugartime '95
Suicide Ride '97
T-Men '47►
The Takeover '94
Taking the Heat '93
Target for Killing '66
The Taxman '98
Temptress Moon '96
Terminal Force '88
They Call Me Bruce? '82
They Paid with Bullets: Chicago 1929 '69
This Could Be the Night '57
The Threepenny Opera '31
Ticket of Leave Man '37
Tight Spot '55►
To Die For '95►
To the Limit '95
Tokyo Drifter '66
Tony Rome '67
Too Hot to Handle '76
The Trap '59
Trial by Jury '94
Trigger Happy '96
TripleCross '85
Trojan Eddie '96►
True Identity '91
True Romance '93
24 Hours in London '00
Ulterior Motives '92
Under Hellgate Bridge '99
The Undertaker's Wedding '97
Underworld 27...
Underworld '96
Underworld U.S.A. '60►
Undisputed II: Last Man Standing '06
Unleashed '05
The Untouchables '87►
Velvet Smooth '76
Vendetta for the Saint '68
Verne Miller '88
Veronica Guerin '03
Wannabes '01
Wanted '09
We're Talkin' Serious Money '92
West New York '96
Whacked! '22
What No Beer? '33
When Angels Fly '84►
Where the Hot Wind Blows '59
White Cargo '96
White Heat '49►
White Hot: The Mysterious Murder of Thelma Todd '91
Who's Got the Action? '63
The Wild Card '03
The Wild Ten Yards '04
The Whole Ten Yards '04
White Sands '92
Wise Guys '86
Wiseguts '02
With Friends Like These '98►
Witness Protection '99►
Intimate Betrayal '96

Witness to the Mob '98
The Wrestler '73
Zatoichi: Zatoichi's Flashing Sword '64
Zatoichi: The Life and Opinion of Masseur Ichi '62
Zebra Force '76
Jea ... '99

Otherwise Engaged
see also Romantic Triangles; Wedding Bells; Wedding Hell
The Accidental Husband '08
An Affair to Remember '57
The Age of Innocence '93►
Aladdin '92►
Alibi '35
Arthur '81►
The Bachelor '99
Ball & Chain '34
The Battle of Shaker Heights '03
The Baxter '05
Bell, Book and Candle '58
The Big Hit '98
The Birdcage '95►
Black Cat, White Cat '98
Blind Date '87
Blind Dating '06
The Breakup Artist '04
The Brothers '01►
Bubble Boy '01
Captain Corelli's Mandolin '01
Catherine Cookson's The Black Candle '92
Catherine Cookson's The Wingless Bird '97
Clarissa '91►
Clerks 2 '06►
Come as You Are '05
Come September '61
Coming to America '88►
Cupid & Cato '00
The Dark Angel '35
Dinner and Driving '97
Divine Secrets of the Ya-Ya Sisterhood '02
A Dog's Breakfast '07
Dot the I '03
East Side of Heaven '39
Easy to Wed '46
Emma '97►
Eva '62
Everyone Says I Love You '96►
The Family Stone '05
Fandango '85
Fantastic Four '05
The Fiance '96
Fiances '63
FireFall '94
The First to Go '97
The Florentine '99
Forces of Nature '99
The Four Feathers '02
Four Weddings and a Funeral '94►
Frankenhooker '90
French Kiss '95
Friends and Family '01
Gabriela '01
George of the Jungle '97►
Gildersleeve on Broadway '43
Gone with the Wind '39►
The Graduate '67►
Gray Matters '06
Guess Who '05
A Guy Thing '03
Happy Times '00
Heights '24
Held Up '00
Her First Romance '40
High Society '56►
His Girl Friday '40►
Hotel de Love '96
The House of Yes '97
How to Deal '03
I Capture the Castle '02
The Illusionist '06
I'm Reed Fish '06
In and Out '97►
The Intended '02

Intimate Lighting '65
I.Q. '94
It Had to Be You '00
It Takes Two '95
The Jolly Boys' Last Stand '00
Just One Night '00
Just One Time '00
The King's Guard '01
Kiss Toledo Goodbye '99
Kissing a Fool '98
Kristin Lavransdatter '95
The Last Time '06
Laurel Canyon '02
Legally Blonde '01
License to Wed '07
Lies and Whispers '98
Lorna Doone '01►
Love Affair '39►
Love Affair '94
Love and Basketball '00►
The Love Letter '98
Lucky Partners '40
Made for Each Other '71
Made of Honor '08
Man of the World '31
Match Point '05►
Miami Rhapsody '95
Minna von Barnhelm or The Soldier's Fortune '52
Miss Julie '99
Mission: Impossible 3 '06►
Mississippi '35
Monster-in-Law '05
Moonstruck '87►
Music from Another Room '97
My Best Friend's Wedding '97
My Big Fat Greek Wedding '02
Night Shift '82
No Looking Back '98
The Old Settler '01
Once Upon a Wedding '05
One Wonderful Sunday '47
Onegin '99
Only You '94
Our Mutual Friend '98
Over Her Dead Body '08
Paperback Hero '99
Paperback Romance '96
Persuasion '71
The Philadelphia Story '40►
Picture Perfect '96
Pizzicata '96
The Price of Milk '00
Pride and Prejudice '95►
The Princess & the Call Girl '84
The Princess Bride '87►
The Princess Diaries 2: Royal Engagement '04►
The Reception '05
Relative Strangers '06
Relative Values '99
Revolution 9 '01
Ride Clear of Diablo '54
River Street '95
Robin Hood: Prince of Thieves '91
Rough Magic '95
Rumor Has It... '05
Runaway Bride '99►
Running Wild '34
Sabrina '95
Saving Silverman '01
Say It Isn't So '01
The Scarlet Tunic '97
Seeing Other People '04
Serendipity '01
Shag: The Movie '89►
Shakespeare in Love '98►
Shooting Fish '98
Sideways '04►
Six Days, Seven Nights '98
Sleeping Dogs Lie '06
Sleepless in Seattle '93►
Son-in-Law '93
Speechless '94
Speedy Death '99►
Stealing Harvard '02
Sunday in New York '63
Sweet Home Alabama '02

Swordsmen in Double Flag Town '91
Tarzan and the Lost City '98
The Tender Trap '55
That Old Feeling '96
13 Going on 30 '04
Trial and Error '96
The True and the False '55
27 Dresses '08
Under the Yum-Yum Tree '63
Vermont Is for Lovers '92
A Very Long Engagement '04►
Voices from a Locked Room '95
Wedding Crashers '05►
Wedding Daze '06
The Wedding Planner '01
The Wedding Singer '97►
Welcome Home Roscoe Jenkins '08
Who Made the Potatoe Salad? '05
Window Theory '04
Wirey Spindell '99
You Gotta Stay Happy '48

Out of This World Sex
see also Alien Babes; Alien Beings—Benign; Alien Beings—Vicious; Aliens Are People, Too; Sexploitation; Space Operas
Alien Visitor '95
Beach Babes from Beyond '93
Breeders '86
Species '95
Species 2 '98
2069: A Sex Odyssey '78
Vantage Point '08

Out of Order
see also Flashback
Always Will '06
Before the Devil Knows You're Dead '07►
Betrayal '83
Big Fish '03►
Cashback '06
Deja Vu '06
Following '99
The Fountain '06
Hero '03►
Irreversible '02
Kill Bill Vol. 1 '03►
Kill Bill Vol. 2 '04►
The Killing '56►
The Lake House '06
Memento '00►
Pinero '01
Premonition '07
Pulp Fiction '94►
Reservoir Dogs '92►
Ten Til Noon '06
21 Grams '03►
Vantage Point '08

Painting
see also Art & Artists

Paperboys
The Benchwarmers '06
Better Off Dead '85►
The Brady Bunch Movie '95►
Newsies '92
The Paper Brigade '96
While You Were Sleeping '95►
Willy Wonka & the Chocolate Factory '71►

Pacific Islands
see also Island Fare
Aloha Summer '88
Balboa '82
Blue Hawaii '62
Carlton Browne of the F.O. '59
Castaway '87
Cry of Battle '63
Dangerous Life '89
Don't Go Near the Water '57
Enchanted Island '58
Ethan '71
Fighting Marines '36
Flags of Our Fathers '06►
Flaming Signal '33
Fog Island '45
Food of the Gods '76
From Hell to Borneo '64
From Here to Eternity '53►
The Great Raid '05
House '78►
Hell in the Pacific '68
Hell Raiders '69
His Majesty O'Keefe '53
Hula '28

The Island '61►
The Island of Dr. Moreau '77
The Last Flight of Noah's Ark '80
The Last Warrior '89
The Legend of Johnny Lingo '03
Letters from Iwo Jima '06►
Lt. Robin Crusoe, U.S.N. '66
Mad Doctor of Blood Island '68
The Mermaids of Tiburon '62
Miss Sadie Thompson '53►
Mission Manila '87
Mr. Robinson Crusoe '32
Moana, a Romance of the Golden Age '26►
Mysterious Island '51►
Noon Sunday '75
Operation Bikini '63
Paradise, Hawaiian Style '66
Pardon My Sarong '42
Rain '32
Reel Paradise '05►
Rodgers & Hammerstein's South Pacific '01
South Seas Woman '53
Tabu: A Story of the South Seas '31►
Till There Was You '91
Tora! Tora! Tora! '70
Wackiest Ship in the Army '61
Wake Island '42►
White Shadows in the South Seas '29
Windjammers '58►
Windtalkers '02
The Year of Living Dangerously '82►

Parades & Festivals
see also Carnivals & Circuses
Barney's Great Adventure '98
Doc Hollywood '91
Easter Parade '48►
Ferris Bueller's Day Off '86►
Festival Express '03►
The Fugitive '93►
Groundhog Day '93►
Jingle All the Way '96
The Matchmaker '97
Miracle on 34th Street '47►
Miracle on 34th Street '94
National Lampoon's Animal House...

Paradise Gone Awry
The Beach '00
Club Paradise '86
Kiss the Sky '98
The Mosquito Coast '86
Six Days, Seven Nights '98

Parallel Universe
see also Lost Worlds
Alice in Wonderland '50
Alice in Wonderland '51►
Alice in Wonderland '99

► = rated three bones or higher

Parallel

Blue Flame '93
The Butterfly Effect '04
The Chronicles of Narnia: The Lion, the Witch and the Wardrobe '05
Citizen Toxie: The Toxic Avenger 4 '01
Cool World '92
Crossworlds '96
Dark City '97
Inland Empire '06
Journey to the Center of the Earth '59▶
Journey to the Center of the Earth '88
Julia and Julia '87
Jumanji '95
Last Action Hero '93
Last Lives '98
The Little Mermaid '89▶
Logan's Run '76
Lost in the Bermuda Triangle '98
Magic in the Mirror: Fowl Play '96
Me Myself I '99
MirrorMask '05
Mortal Kombat 2: Annihilation '97
Neil Gaiman's NeverWhere '96
The One '01
Passion of Mind '00
Possible Loves '00▶
The Purple Rose of Cairo '85▶
Silent Hill '06
Splash '84
Super Mario Bros. '93
The 10th Kingdom '00
The Thirteenth Floor '99
Tin Man '07
Twisted '96
Undermind '03
Who Framed Roger Rabbit '88▶

Paramedics

Bringing Out the Dead '99
Broken Vessels '98▶
Mother, Jugs and Speed '76
Paramedics '88
There's Something about Mary '98▶

Pardners

see also Buddies;
Westerns

Butch and Sundance: The Early Days '79
Butch Cassidy and the Sundance Kid '69▶
The Cowboy Way '94
Open Range '03▶
Pardners '56
Shanghai Noon '00
Silverado '85▶
Texas Rangers '01
Tombstone '93▶
Wyatt Earp '94
Young Guns '88
Young Guns 2 '90

Parenthood

see also Adoption & Orphans; Bad Dads; Bringing Up Baby; Custody Battles; Dads; Moms; Monster Moms; Single Parents; Stepparents

Adam '83▶
Addams Family Values '93
The Adventures of Rusty 45
The Adventures of Sebastian Cole '99
Afraid of the Dark '92
Alice in the Cities '74▶
Aliens '86▶
All the Kind Strangers '74
Alpha Beta '73
Amazing Grace '74
American Heart '92▶
An Autumn Afternoon '62▶
Babel '06▶

Baby Boom '87
Baby Girl Scott '87
Bachelor Mother '39▶
Back to the Beach '87
Backfield in Motion '91
The Ballad of Narayama '83▶
The Banger Sisters '02
Basket Case 3: The Progeny '92
Battling for Baby '92
Being Two Isn't Easy '62
Between Two Women '86
Beyond Silence '96
Big Daddy '99
Big Fella '37
Big Girls Don't Cry... They Get Even '92
The Big Wheel 49
Blind Fools '40
Blondie's Blessed Event '42
Blow '01
Bobbie's Girl '02
Boys Town '38▶
Broken Wings '02▶
Bye Bye, Love 94
Cahill: United States Marshal '73
A Call to Remember '97
Careful, He Might Hear You '84▶
Casanova Brown '44
Casey's Shadow '78
Cheaper by the Dozen '50▶
Cheaper by the Dozen '03
The Child '05
The Children of Times Square '86
Cody 77
Cold River '81
Commissar '68▶
A Cool, Dry Place '98
The Courtship of Eddie's Father '62▶
Cowboys Don't Cry '88
Crisscross '92
Crooklyn '94▶
A Cry in the Dark '88▶
Da '88
Daddy Nostalgia '90▶
Danielle Steel's Daddy '91
Danielle Steel's Fine Things '90
The Day My Parents Ran Away '93
The Deep End of the Ocean '98
Distant Voices, Still Lives '88▶
Dona Herlinda & Her Son '86
Drop-Out Mother '88
Duplicates '92
Dutch '91
Eat Drink Man Woman '94▶
The Emerald Forest '85▶
Endless Love '81
Enormous Changes '83
Ernie Kovacs: Between the Laughter '84
Every Other Weekend '91▶
Family Life '71
Fatal Confinement '64
Father and Son '03
Father Figure '80
Father of the Bride '50▶
Father of the Bride Part 2 '95
A Fight for Jenny '90
Firelight '97
Flirting with Disaster '95▶
Follow That Rainbow '66
Follow the Stars Home '01
Forbidden Planet '56▶
The Forgotten '04
40 Pounds of Trouble 62
The Game Plan '07
Ghost Dad '90
A Global Affair 63
God Bless the Child '88▶
Godsend '04
The Good Father '87▶
The Good Mother '88
A Goofy Movie '94
Grace Is Gone '07▶
Guess What We Learned in School Today? '70
Gypsy 62▶

Gypsy '93
Harry & Son '84
Held for Murder '32
High Tide '87▶
A Hole in the Head '59
Holiday Heart '00
Hollow Reed '95▶
Home from the Hill '60▶
A Home of Our Own '93
Hope Floats 98
House Arrest '96
House of Sand '05▶
Houseboat '58
I Accuse My Parents '45
I Live with Me Dad '86
I Never Sang for My Father '70▶
I Ought to Be in Pictures '82
I Remember Mama '48▶
I'll Do Anything '93
I'll Take Sweden '65
Immediate Family '89
In the Bedroom '01▶
Innocent Victim '90
Irreconcilable Differences '84
Jack and Sarah '95
Jersey Girl '04
Joshua '07▶
Journey for Margaret '42▶
Judy Berlin '99
Jungle 2 Jungle '96
Jurassic Park 3 '01
Kiss Daddy Goodbye '81
The Kiss You Gave Me '00
Kolya '96▶
The Lady Is Willing '42
Ladybird, Ladybird '93▶
Les Bons Debarras '81
Liar Liar 97
Life as a House '01
Little Children '06▶
Long Time Gone '86
Losing Isaiah '94▶
Lost Angels 89
Love Is All There Is '96
Love Under Pressure '78
Ma and Pa Kettle Back On the Farm '51
Ma Barker's Killer Brood '60
Mad Youth '40
M.A.D.D.: Mothers Against Drunk Driving '83
Magic in the Water '95
Mama Flora's Family '98
Mamma Roma '62▶
Matilda '96▶
Max Dugan Returns '83
Memory of Us '74
Men Don't Leave '89
Mermaids '90▶
Miracle on 34th Street '94
Mirele Efros '38
Mrs. Doubtfire '93
Mrs. R's Daughter 79
Mr. Mom '83▶
Misunderstood '84
Mom '89
Mom & Dad 47
Monkey Grip '82▶
Mother & Daughter: A Loving War 80
Mother and Son '31
My Baby's Daddy '04
My Life '93
My Mom's a Werewolf '89
The Namesake '06▶
National Lampoon's European Vacation 85
Natural Enemies '79
The Next Best Thing '00
Next of Kin '84
Night Cries 78
No Dessert Dad, 'Til You Mow the Lawn '94
North 94
Nothing in Common '86
On Golden Pond '81▶
On the Third Day 83
One Fine Day '96
One Man's War '90
Only the Lonely 91
Only When I Laugh 81▶
The Others '01▶
The Pacifier '05
Padre Padrone 77▶
The Parent Trap '98
Parenthood '89▶

Parents '89
Paris, Texas '83▶
Penny Serenade 41▶
A Place for Annie '94
Poil de Carotte '31
Psycho 4: The Beginning '90
The Quiet Room '96
Raising Arizona '87▶
Raising Genius '04
Raising Helen '04
Red Doors '05
The Red House '47▶
Red River '48▶
Relative Strangers '06
The Reluctant Debutante '58▶
Rent-A-Kid '91
Revenge '71
The Revolt of Job '84▶
Riding in Cars with Boys '01
Rising Son '90▶
The River Rat '84
Runaway Father '91
Saint Maybe '98
The Sandy Bottom Orchestra '00
The Santa Clause '94
Sarah's Child '96
Scream for Help '86
Secret Ceremony '69
Secrets and Lies 95▶
Sex and the Single Parent '82
The Shaggy D.A. '76
She Hate Me '04
Sherrybaby '06
Silence of the Heart '84▶
Silent Witness '99
A Simple Twist of Fate '94
A Slightly Pregnant Man 79
Somebody's Waiting '96
Son of Godzilla '66
Special Olympics '78
Speeding Up Time 71
Steel Magnolias '89▶
Stella '89
Stella Dallas '37▶
The Storm Within '48▶
The Strange Love of Molly Louvain '32
Sunstroke '92
Superdad '80
Suzanne 80
Taken Away '89
Target '85
Tea with Mussolini 99▶
Teenage Bad Girl '59
Tequila Sunrise '88▶
Terminator 2: Judgment Day '91▶
Terms of Endearment '83▶
Thank You for Smoking '06▶
There Will Be Blood '07▶
This Property Is Condemned 66
Three Fugitives '89
Three Men and a Baby '87▶
Three Men and a Cradle '85▶
Throw Momma from the Train '87▶
Times Have Been Better 06
Trading Mom '94
Tumbleweeds '98▶
The Turning Point '77▶
Ulee's Gold '97▶
The Unborn 2 '94
Undercover Blues '93
An Unexpected Family '96
Unfinished Business 89
The Unstoppable Man 59
Valentin '02
Wanted: The Perfect Guy '86
When Wolves Cry '69
Where Are the Children? '85
Where's Poppa? 70▶
With Six You Get Eggroll 68
Without a Trace '83
The Woman Who Willed a Miracle 83
Yours, Mine & Ours '68
The Zodiac '05

Paris

see also France

A la Mode '94
The Accompanist '93
Accused '36
An Affair of Love '99
After Sex '97
AKA '02
Alberto Express '87▶
Alias Betty '01
Alice et Martin '98
Almost Peaceful '02▶
Alphaville '65▶
The Ambassador's Daughter '56
Amelie '01▶
The American '01
American Dreamer '84
An American in Paris '51▶
An American Werewolf in Paris '97
Angel '37
Angel-A '05
Another 9 1/2 Weeks '96
Antoine et Antoinette '47
Apres-Vous '03
April in Paris '52
Arch of Triumph '48▶
Arch of Triumph '85
The Assignment '97
Augustin '95
Avenue Montaigne '06
The Aviator's Wife '80▶
Baise Moi '00
Ballet Russes '05▶
Balzac: A Life of Passion '99▶
Beau Pere '81▶
Beaumarchais the Scoundrel '96
Bed and Board '70▶
Before Sunset '04▶
Belle Americaine '61
Belle Toujours '06▶
Beyond the Clouds '95
Blame It on Fidel '06
Boeing Boeing '65
The Bourne Identity '02▶
Boy Meets Girl '84▶
Breakfast in Paris '81
Breathless '59▶
Broken English '07
The Butterfly '02▶
The C-Man '49
Camille '36▶
Cartouche '62▶
Casque d'Or '52▶
Catacombs 07
Catherine & Co. 76
Celestial Clockwork '94
Chaos '01
Charade '63▶
Chariots of Fire '81▶
Charlie Chan in City of Darkness '39
Charlie Chan in Paris '35
Children of Paradise '44▶
Children of the Century '99
China White '91
Circle of Love 64
Circle of Passion '97
Clean '04
Cleo from 5 to 7 '61▶
Clowning Around '92
Code Unknown '00
Comedy of Innocence '00
Confusion of Genders '00
Cousin Bette '97
The Cousins '59▶
CQ '01
Crainquebille '23
The Crazy Ray '22▶
Crime Spree '03
Crimson Rivers 2: Angels of the Apocalypse '05
The Da Vinci Code '06▶
Dad On the Run '00
Dangerous Liaisons '03
A Dangerous Man: Lawrence after Arabia '91▶
Daniella by Night '61
Dear Brigitte '65
Delicatessen '92▶
Delta of Venus '95
Demonlover 02

The Destructors '74
Detective '85
The Devil, Probably '77
The Devil Wears Prada '06▶
Diary of a Seducer '95
Dingo 90
The Dirty Girls '64
The Disenchanted '90
District B13 04
Diva '82▶
Does This Mean We're Married? '90
Dracula and Son '76
The Dreamers '03
The Duchess of Langeais '07▶
Elisa '94
The Emperor's New Clothes '01
Entangled '93
Everyone Says I Love You '96▶
The Face at the Window '39
Faithless '00▶
The Fall '98
The Fantastic Night '42▶
Fashions of 1934 '34
The Fatal Image '90
The Favor, the Watch, & the Very Big Fish '92
Fay Grim '06
Femme Fatale '02
A Few Days in September '06
A Fine Romance '92
Flight of the Red Balloon '08
Forget Paris '95
The Fourth Sex '61
Frantic '88▶
French Can-Can '55▶
French Kiss '95
The French Lesson '86
French Postcards 79
The French Touch '54
The French Way '40
Friday Night '02
From Hell to Victory 79
Funny Face '57▶
Gabrielle '05
Games of Love and Chance '03
Gentlemen Prefer Blondes '53▶
Gigi '58▶
The Girl '01
A Girl on Her Own 76
The Girl on the Bridge '98▶
The Grand Role '04
The Green House '96
Half-Shot at Sunrise '30
Hannibal Rising '07
Happenstance '00
Happily Ever After '04
Head in the Clouds '04
Heartbeat 46
Henri Langlois: The Phantom of the Cinematheque '04▶
Henry & June '90▶
Her and She and Him 69
Hidden '05▶
The Holes '72
House of D '04
The Housekeeper '02
How to Steal a Million '66
The Hunchback '97
The Hunchback of Notre Dame '39▶
The Hunchback of Notre Dame '57▶
The Hunchback of Notre Dame '82▶
The Hunchback of Notre Dame '96▶
I Am Frigid... Why? 72
I Can't Sleep '93
I Want to Go Home '89
If I Were King '38▶
It Looks Could Kill '91
I'm Going Home '01
The Immoral One '80
In Praise of Love '01
Incognito 97
Innocents in Paris '53
Inside Paris '06
Interview with the Vampire '94
Intimate Strangers '04▶

▶ = rated three bones or higher

Intolerance '16
Invisible Circus '00
The Invisibles '99
Irma Vep '96
Is Paris Burning? '66 ▶
Jeanne and the Perfect Guy '98
Jefferson in Paris '94
Killing Zoe '94
Kiss of the Dragon '01
La Boum '81
La Marseillaise '37 ▶
La Moustache '05
La Sentinelle '92
La Separation '92 ▶
La Vie de Boheme '93 ▶
La Vie en Rose '07 ▶
Lady L. '65
The Last Metro '80 ▶
Last Tango in Paris '73 ▶
The Last Time I Saw Paris '54
Le Cercle Rouge '70 ▶
Le Divorce '03
Le Joli Mai '62 ▶
Le Petit Lieutenant '05
...e Samourai '67 ▶
Le Schpountz '38
Le Trou '59 ▶
Les Miserables '95 ▶
Les Miserables '97 ▶
Les Vampires '15 ▶
Like a Brothe' '05
Little Italian, Big City '95
A Little Romance '79 ▶
Look at Me '04 ▶
Love After Love '54
Love Play '60
Love Songs '07
The Lovers on the Bridge '91 ▶
Ma and Pa Kettle on Vacation '53
Ma Vie en Rose '97 ▶
The Mad Adventures of Rabbi Jacob '73 ▶
Madame X '37
Madeleine '98
The Madwoman of Chaillot '69
The Man in the Iron Mask '98
Man of the World '31
The Man Who Cried '00
Marquis de Sade '96
Mauvaise Graine '33
Max, Mon Amour '86
Melo '94
Mesmer '94
Metroland '97
Mina Tannenbaum '93
Mrs. 'Arris Goes to Paris '92
Modigliani '04
The Moderns '88 ▶
Mon Oncle d'Amerique '80 ▶
Monsieur Ibrahim '03 ▶
Monsieur N. '03
Moulin Rouge '01 ▶
Murders in the Rue Morgue '71
The Murders in the Rue Morgue '86
My Best Friend '06
My Life and Times with Antonin Artaud '93
My Sex Life... Or How I Got into an Argument '96
My Wife is an Actress '01
Napoleon '03
Neily et Monsieur Arnaud '95 ▶
The New Eve '98
A New Kind of Love '63
Night on Earth '91 ▶
Ninotchka '39 ▶
November Moon '85
Now and Forever '34
Oliver Twist '33
Once in Paris... '79
One Against the Wind '91
One Hour with You '32
Opheus '49
Panique '47 ▶
Paris Blues '61
Paris Holiday '57
Paris in Spring '35
Paris, je t'aime '06 ▶

Paris When It Sizzles '64
Parisian Love '25
Peddle Douce '96
Peppermint Soda '77 ▶
The Perfect Furlough '59
Perfume: The Story of a Murderer '06
Perfumed Nightmare '89 ▶
Petits Freres '00
The Phantom of the Opera '25 ▶
The Phantom of the Opera '43
The Phantom of the Opera '90
The Phantom of the Opera '98
The Phantom of the Opera '04
Pigalle '95
The Pink Panther '06
Place Vendome '98 ▶
Plucking the Daisy '56
Pola X '99
Portraits Chinois '96
The Private Affairs of Bel Ami '47
Private Fears in Public Places '06 ▶
Ratatouille '07 ▶
Ready to Wear '94
Red Kiss '85 ▶
Red Lights '04 ▶
Renaissance '06
Rendez-vous de Juillet '49
Rendezvous in Paris '95 ▶
Rich, Young and Pretty '51
Ridicule '96 ▶
Ronin '98 ▶
Round Midnight '86 ▶
Rugrats in Paris: The Movie '00 ▶
Rush Hour 3 '07
Russian Dolls '05
Same Old Song '97 ▶
A Scandal in Paris '46
The Science of Sleep '06
A Self-Made Hero '95 ▶
Sex & Mrs. X '00
Shoot the Piano Player '62 ▶
Simon the Magician '99
Simone Barbes '80
The Sin of Madelon Claudet '31
Since Otar Left... '03
A Single Girl '96
Siren of the Tropics '27
Six in Paris '68
Something's Gotta Give '03 ▶
Son of Gascogne '95
Sons '89
The Story of a Three Day Pass '63
The Street '23
Subway '85
Summer '86 ▶
The Tango Lesson '97
Target '85
Team America: World Police '04 ▶
The Testament of Dr. Cordelier '59
Theatre of Death '67
13 Rue Madeleine '46 ▶
Time Out for Love '61
To Paris with Love '55
Total Eclipse '95
Triple Agent '04 ▶
The Triplets of Belleville '02 ▶
Tropic of Cancer '70
The Truth About Charlie '02
2 Days in Paris '07 ▶
Two or Three Things I Know about Her '66 ▶
Under the Roofs of Paris '29 ▶
Under the Sand '00 ▶
Until September '84
Up/Down/Fragile '95
Va Savoir '01 ▶
Venus Beauty Institute '98
A Very Long Engagement '04 ▶
Vicious Circles '97

Victor/Victoria '82 ▶
Victory '81
View from the Top '03
What Time Is It There? '01
When the Cat's Away '96
Window Shopping '86
Zazie dans le Metro '61 ▶

Party Hell

The Anniversary Party '01 ▶
April Fool's Day '86
The Club '94
Happy Birthday to Me '81
Hell Night '81
Hello Mary Lou: Prom Night 2 '87
Home '05
Killer Party '86
London '05
Meet Wally Sparks '97
Monsters Crash the Pajama Party '65
Night of the Demons '88
Old School '03
Party '65
Prom Night '80
Prom Night 3: The Last Kiss '89
Prom Night 4: Deliver Us from Evil '91
Psycho Cop '89
Rabid Grannies '89
The Rage: Carrie 2 '99
Slumber Party Massacre '82
Slumber Party Massacre 2 '87
Slumber Party Massacre 3 '90
Twilight Zone: The Movie '83 ▶

Patriotism & Paranoia

see also Propaganda

Amber Waves '82
Born on the Fourth of July '89 ▶
The Chase '56
Civic Duty '06
The Commies Are Coming, the Commies Are Coming '57
The Cosmic Man '59
Day Zero '07
Death of a Bureaucrat '66
Delta Force '86
Dress Gray '86
F/X '86 ▶
Fahrenheit 9/11 '04 ▶
The Fallen '04
Fellow Traveler '89 ▶
Firefox '82
First Blood '82 ▶
Good Night, and Good Luck '05 ▶
The Good Shepherd '06 ▶
Guilty by Suspicion '91
Harry's War '84
Heroes for Sale '33 ▶
The Insurgents '06
Ivan the Terrible, Part 1 '44 ▶
Ivan the Terrible, Part 2 '46 ▶
Keeper of the Flame '42
Missing in Action '84
Murrow '86
Nixon '95 ▶
Panama Patrol '39
Paranoia 1.0 '04
Paris Belongs to Us '60
Patton '70 ▶
The Prisoner '55 ▶
Radar Patrol vs. Spy King '49
Rambo: First Blood, Part 2 '85
Rambo 3 '88
Red Dawn '84
The Red Menace '49
Rendition '07
Reunion in France '42
The Sea Hawk '40 ▶
The Secret Four '40
Shooter '07
The Siege '98

Skinheads: The Second Coming of Hate '88
Sky High '51
So Proudly We Hail '43 ▶
Sparan '04
The Spider's Stratagem '70 ▶
Strictly G.I. '44
Taps '81 ▶
Thirty Seconds Over Tokyo '44 ▶
The 27th Day '57
XXX: State of the Union '05

Peace

The Day the Earth Stood Still '51 ▶
The Deserters '83
Destry Rides Again '39 ▶
Diplomaniacs '33
Firehead '90
Friendly Persuasion '56 ▶
Gandhi '82 ▶
Joyeux Noel '05 ▶
A Midnight Clear '92 ▶
Sadat '83 ▶
Sophie Scholl: The Final Days '05 ▶
War and Peace '56 ▶
War and Peace '68 ▶

Peculiar Partners

see also Buddies; Buddy Cops; Cops

Alien Nation '88
Alien Nation: Dark Horizon '94
The Beautician and the Beast '97
Blades of Glory '07 ▶
Cop and a Half '93
Dead Heat '88
Dillman '90
Dream with the Fishes '97
The Forbidden Kingdom '08
The Glimmer Man '96
Grdlock'd '96
The Hard Way '91 ▶
The Hidden '87 ▶
The Hidden 2 '94
Judge Dredd '95
K-9 '89
K-911 '99
Stop! or My Mom Will Shoot '92
Theodore Rex '95
Top Dog '95
Turner and Hooch '89
Under Siege '92 ▶

Pen Pals

see also Going Postal

Bell, Book and Candle '58
Convicted '04
Eurotrip '04
Eye of God '97 ▶
Leo '02
Love Letters '99
Never Say Goodbye '46
Reindeer Games '00
The Shop Around the Corner '40 ▶
Strong Man '26 ▶
You've Got Mail '98 ▶

Penguins

see also Cold Sports; Wild Kingdom

Batman Returns '92 ▶
Billy Madison '94
Happy Feet '06 ▶
Madagascar '05 ▶
March of the Penguins '05 ▶
My Favorite Blonde '42 ▶
Surf's Up '07 ▶
Toy Story 2 '99 ▶
The Wild '06

Period Piece

see also Historical Drama; Medieval Romps; Royalty

Alexander '04
Curse of the Golden Flower '06 ▶
Duel to the Death '82
House of Flying Daggers '04 ▶
The Keeper: The Legend of Omar Khayyam '05
Marco Polo '07
Pathfinder '07
The Phantom of the Opera '07
The Promise '05
The Reckoning '03 ▶
Tristan & Isolde '06
Troy '04

Period Piece: 15th Century

The Advocate '93
Cesare Borgia '23
Christopher Columbus '49
Christopher Columbus '85
Dracula: The Dark Prince '01
If I Were King '38 ▶
Jeanne la Pucelle '94
Joan of Arc '48
Joan of Arc '99
Mad Love '01
The Messenger: The Story of Joan of Arc '99
The Warrior '01

Period Piece: 16th Century

Aguirre, the Wrath of God '72 ▶
Anything: A Veggie Tales Movie '07
Elizabeth, the Queen '68
The Fountain '06
Henry V '44 ▶
Henry V '89 ▶
Highlander: Endgame '00
Kagemusha '80 ▶
Kama Sutra: A Tale of Love '96
Love and Faith '78
Luther '03 ▶
Mad Love '01
A Man for All Seasons '66 ▶
A Man for All Seasons '88
Mary of Scotland '36
The Merchant of Venice '04 ▶
The Merry Wives of Windsor '50
The Other Boleyn Girl '03
The Other Boleyn Girl '08
The Prince and the Pauper '01
Prince of Foxes '49
The Private Life of Henry VIII '33 ▶
The Private Lives of Elizabeth & Essex '39 ▶
Queen Margot '94 ▶
Rikyu '90 ▶
The Road to El Dorado '00
Samurai Banners '69
The Sea Hawk '40 ▶
Seven Samurai '54 ▶
Shakespeare in Love '98 ▶
Taras Bulba '62
The Virgin Queen '55
Young Bess '53

Ever After: A Cinderella Story '98 ▶
Forever Amber '47
The Four Musketeers '75 ▶
Frenchman's Creek '44
Girl with a Pearl Earring '03 ▶
Harakiri '62 ▶
Highlander: Endgame '00
I, the Worst of All '90
The Iron Mask '29 ▶
Journey of Honor '91
Kidnapped '05
The King's Thief '55
The King's Whore '90
Lazarillo '59
The Libertine '05
Lorna Doone '22
Lorna Doone '34
Lorna Doone '90
The Man in the Iron Mask '39 ▶
The Man in the Iron Mask '77 ▶
The Man in the Iron Mask '98
Marquis de Sade '96
Mayflower: The Pilgrims' Adventure '79
Moliere '07 ▶
Monsieur Vincent '47 ▶
Mother, Joan of the Angels '60
Queen Christina '33 ▶
Rapa Nui '93
Rembrandt '36
Rembrandt—1669 '77
Restoration '94 ▶
The Return of the Musketeers '89
Revenge of the Musketeers '94
Samurai Reincarnation '81
Stage Beauty '04 ▶
The Scarlet Letter '34
The Scarlet Letter '73
The Scarlet Letter '79
The Scarlet Letter '95
The Serpent's Kiss '97
Squanto: A Warrior's Tale '94
The Three Musketeers '16
The Three Musketeers '21
The Three Musketeers '35 ▶
The Three Musketeers '39
The Three Musketeers '48 ▶
The Three Musketeers '73 ▶
The Three Musketeers '74 ▶
The Three Musketeers '93
Tous les Matins du Monde '92 ▶
Vatel '00
The Wicked Lady '45
The Wicked Lady '83
Zemsta '02

Period Piece: 17th Century

At Sword's Point '51
Black Robe '91 ▶
Carnival in Flanders '35
The Conqueror Worm '68 ▶
The Crucible '57
The Crucible '96 ▶
The Deluge '73
Delusions of Grandeur '76
The Devils '71 ▶

Period Piece: 18th Century

The Affair of the Necklace '01
Amadeus '84 ▶
Amazing Grace '06
The Amorous Adventures of Moll Flanders '65
The Aristocrats '99
As You Like It '06 ▶
Bang Rajan '00
Barry Lyndon '75 ▶
Beaumarchais, the Scoundrel '96
Becoming Jane '07 ▶
The Black Castle '52
Bleak House '05 ▶
BloodRayne '06
Botany Bay '53

▶ = rated three bones or higher

The Bounty '84
The Bridge of San Luis Rey '05
Brotherhood of the Wolf '01
Cartouche '62
Casanova '87
Casanova '05
Casanova's Big Night '54
Catherine the Great '34
Catherine the Great '95
The Chess Player '27
The Crossing '00
Dangerous Liaisons '88
Danton '82
Deacon Brodie '98
Du Barry Was a Lady '43
Fanny Hill: Memoirs of a Woman of Pleasure '64
Farinelli '94
Follow the River '95
Forget Mozart '85
George Washington '84
George Washington: The Forging of a Nation '86
Goya's Ghosts '06
Gulliver's Travels '39
Gulliver's Travels '77
Gulliver's Travels '95
Haunted Symphony '94
Highlander: Endgame '00
Immortal Beloved '94
The Incredible Journey of Mary Bryant '05
Interview with the Vampire '94
John Adams '08
Joseph Andrews '77
Kidnapped '95
La Marseillaise '37
La Nuit de Varennes '82
The Lady and the Duke '01
The Last of the Mohicans '20
The Last of the Mohicans '32
The Last of the Mohicans '36
The Last of the Mohicans '85
The Last of the Mohicans '92
The Last of the Redmen '47
The Last Supper '76
Les Miserables '35
Les Miserables '52
Les Miserables '57
Les Miserables '78
Les Miserables '97
Longitude '00
Loves & Times of Scaramouche '76
The Madness of King George '94
Marie Antoinette '38
Marie Antoinette '06
The Marquise of O '76
Mesmer '94
Minna von Barnhelm or The Soldier's Fortune '62
Moll Flanders '96
Monsieur Beaucaire '46
Mutiny on the Bounty '35
Mutiny on the Bounty '62
Napoleon '03
Night Sun '90
On Guard! '03
Orlando '92
Pandaemonium '00
Passion '19
The Patriot '00
Perfume: The Story of a Murderer '06
Plunkett & Macleane '98
Poldark '75
Poldark 2 '75
Power '34
Prince Brat and the Whipping Boy '95
Princess Yang Kwei Fei '55
Ridicule '96
The Road to Yesterday '25
Rob Roy '95
Rob Roy—The Highland Rogue '53
Sade '00
Sally Hemings: An American Scandal '00
Samurai Rebellion '67
The Scarlet Pimpernel '34
The Scarlet Pimpernel '82
The Scarlet Pimpernel '99
The Scarlet Pimpernel 2: Mademoiselle Guillotine '99
The Scarlet Pimpernel 3: The Kidnapped King '99
The Seekers '79
Seraphim Falls '06
Shogun '80
Sleepy Hollow '99
Son of Fury '42
A Tale of Two Cities '36
A Tale of Two Cities '58
A Tale of Two Cities '80
A Tale of Two Cities '89
Tom Jones '63
Tom Jones '98
The Triumph of Love '01
Untold Scandal '03
Valmont '89
Xica '76

Period Piece: 19th Century

Adios, Sabata '71
The Adventures of Mark Twain '44
The Age of Innocence '93
The Alamo '04
All the Brothers Were Valiant '53
Allonsanfan '73
The American '01
An American Haunting '05
American Outlaws '01
Angels and Insects '95
Anna and the King '99
Anna and the King of Siam '46
Anna Karenina '35
Anna Karenina '48
Anna Karenina '85
Anna Karenina '00
Anne Rice's The Feast of All Saints '01
Anthony Adverse '36
The Assassination Bureau '69
The Assassination of Jesse James by the Coward Robert Ford '07
Assault at West Point: The Court-Martial of Johnson Whittaker '94
August '95
Back to Hannibal: The Return of Tom Sawyer and Huckleberry Finn '90
The Ballad of Little Jo '93
Balzac: A Life of Passion '99
Band of Angels '57
The Barbary Coast '74
The Barretts of Wimpole Street '34
Beau Brummel '24
Beau Brummel '54
Beautiful Dreamers '92
Becky Sharp '35
Becoming Colette '92
Belizaire the Cajun '86
Belle of the Nineties '34
The Best Man '97
Beulah Land '80
Big Bear '98
The Blackheath Poisonings '92
Blacksnake! '73
Blanche Fury '48
Bleak House '85
Blood Red '88
The Bostonians '84
The Bowery '33
Boy in Blue '86
Bram Stoker's Dracula '92
Broken Trail '06
The Brontes of Haworth '73
Brother of Sleep '95
The Brothers Grimm '05
The Brothers Karamazov '58
The Buccaneers '95
Buffalo Girls '95
Bury My Heart at Wounded Knee '07
By Way of the Stars '92
Byron '03
Call of the Wild '93
Camille Claudel '89
Captain Boycott '47
Catherine Cookson's The Black Candle '91
Catherine Cookson's The Black Velvet Gown '92
Catherine Cookson's The Dwelling Place '94
Catherine Cookson's The Fifteen Streets '90
Catherine Cookson's The Glass Virgin '95
Catherine Cookson's Tilly Trotter '99
The Chant of Jimmie Blacksmith '78
The Charge of the Light Brigade '36
The Charge of the Light Brigade '68
Children of the Century '99
A Christmas Carol '38
A Christmas Carol '51
A Christmas Carol '54
A Christmas Carol '99
The Cisco Kid '94
The Claim '00
Cobra Verde '88
Colonel Chabert '94
Comanche Moon '08
Conceiving Ada '97
Conduct Unbecoming '75
Conquest '37
Conquest of Cochise '53
The Count of Monte Cristo '74
The Count of Monte Cristo '99
The Count of Monte Cristo '02
Cousin Bette '97
The Covered Wagon '23
The Crown Prince '06
Daisy Miller '74
Damn the Defiant! '62
Daniel Deronda '02
Dante's Inferno: Life of Dante Gabriel Rossetti '69
The Dark Angel '91
David Copperfield '70
David Copperfield '99
David Harum '34
Dead Man '95
The Deceivers '88
Demons of the Mind '72
Desiree '54
The Desperate Mission '60
Desperate Remedies '93
Disraeli '30
Disraeli '79
Dr. Bell and Mr. Doyle: The Dark Beginnings of Sherlock Holmes '00
A Dog of Flanders '99
A Doll's House '59
A Doll's House '73
A Doll's House '73
Dostoevsky's Crime and Punishment '99
The Duchess of Langeais '07
Duel of Hearts '92
Edge of Madness '02
Edvard Munch '74
Effi Briest '74
1860 '33
Eljanaika '81
Elective Affinities '96
The Elegant Criminal '92
The Elephant Man '80
Elvira Madigan '67
Elvira's Haunted Hills '02
The Emigrants '72
Emma '72
Emma '96
Emma '97
The Emperor's New Clothes '01
End of Summer '97
Ethan Frome '92
The Europeans '79
Every Day's a Holiday '38
Far and Away '92
Far from the Madding Crowd '67
Far from the Madding Crowd '97
The Far Pavilions '84
The Far Side of Jericho '06
The Farmer Takes a Wife '35
The Farmer Takes a Wife '53
Feast of July '95
The Fighting Kentuckian '49
Finding Neverland '04
Fiorile '93
Firelight '97
The First Olympics: Athens 1896 '84
Five Weeks in a Balloon '62
The Flame of New Orleans '41
The Flesh and the Fiends '60
Flight of the Eagle '82
Flowers of Reverie '84
The Four Feathers '39
The Four Feathers '78
The Four Feathers '02
Frankenstein '31
Frankenstein '73
Frankenstein '82
Frankenstein '93
Frankie and Johnny '65
Freedom Road '79
The French Lieutenant's Woman '81
From Hell '01
The Gambler '97
Gangs of New York '02
Gaslight '40
Gaslight '44
Germinal '93
Geronimo '62
Geronimo '93
Geronimo: An American Legend '93
Gervaise '56
The Getting of Wisdom '77
The Golden Bowl '72
Goldrush: A Real Life Alaskan Adventure '98
The Gorgeous Hussy '36
Gothic '87
The Governess '98
Goya in Bordeaux '99
Great Expectations '34
Great Expectations '46
Great Expectations '81
Great Expectations '89
Great Expectations '99
Great Expectations: The Untold Story '87
The Great Moment '44
The Great Train Robbery '79
Green Dolphin Street '47
Greyfriars Bobby '61
Hamlet '96
Hands of a Murderer '90
Harmony Lane '35
Haunted Summer '88
Hawaii '66
The Heiress '49
Hidalgo '04
The Hidden Blade '04
Hip Hip Hurrah! '87
The History of Mr. Polly '07
Hobson's Choice '53
Hobson's Choice '83
Hooded Angels '00
Horatio Hornblower '99
Horatio Hornblower: The Adventure Continues '01
The Horse Soldiers '59
The Hound of the Baskervilles '39
The Hound of the Baskervilles '59
The Hound of the Baskervilles '83
The Hound of the Baskervilles '00
The Hound of the Baskervilles '02
The House of the Seven Gables '40
Hunger '66
I Dream of Jeannie '52
I, Monster '71
Immortal Beloved '94
The Importance of Being Earnest '02
Impromptu '90
In Desert and Wilderness '01
In Old Chicago '37
Interview with the Vampire '94
The Iron Horse '24
The Jack Bull '99
Jamaica Inn '39
Jamaica Inn '82
Jane Eyre '34
Jane Eyre '44
Jane Eyre '83
Jane Eyre '96
Jane Eyre '97
Java Head '35
Jericho '01
Jezebel '38
John Adams '08
Johnson County War '02
Joshua '02
The Journey of August King '95
Journey to the Center of the Earth '99
Jude '96
Jude the Obscure '71
Kaspar Hauser '93
Kate & Leopold '01
Katie Tippel '75
Kim '50
Kim '84
The King and I '56
The King and I '99
Kings in Grass Castles '97
The Kissing Bandit '48
La Chartreuse de Parme '48
La Grande Bourgeoise '74
Lady Audley's Secret '00
Lady Caroline Lamb '73
Lady for a Night '42
Lady from Louisiana '42
The Last Samurai '03
The Lawless Breed '52
The League of Extraordinary Gentlemen '03
The Legend of Zorro '05
Leo Tolstoy's Anna Karenina '96
The Leopard '63
The Life and Adventures of Nicholas Nickleby '81
Life with Father '47
Lillian Russell '40
Lisztomania '75
The Little Colonel '35
Little Dorrit, Film 1: Nobody's Fault '88
Little Dorrit, Film 2: Little Dorrit's Story '88
Little House on the Prairie '74
Little Men '40
Little Men '98
The Little Princess '39
The Little Princess '87
Little Women '33
Little Women '49
Little Women '78
Little Women '94
The Lives of a Bengal Lancer '35
Lloyds of London '36
The Long Ride Home '01
Love and Death '75
Love and Rage '99
Love Comes Softly '03
Love in the Time of Cholera '07
Love's Enduring Promise '04
Love's Long Journey '05
Love's Unending Legacy '07
The Loves of Edgar Allen Poe '42
Madame Bovary '34
Madame Bovary '49
Madame Bovary '91
Madame Bovary '00
Mademoiselle Fifi '44
The Magician '58
Magnificent Doll '46
The Magnificent Seven '98
The Man from Snowy River '82
The Man in Grey '45
Man in the Attic '53
Mansfield Park '85
Mansfield Park '99
Mansfield Park '07
The Mark of Zorro '40
Mary Reilly '95
Master and Commander: The Far Side of the World '03
Mayerling '36
Mayerling '68
The Mayor of Casterbridge '03
Melody Master '41
Mesmerized '84
Middlemarch '93
The Mill on the Floss '37
The Mill on the Floss '97
Miracle at Sage Creek '05
Miss Austen Regrets '07
Miss Julie '99
The Missing '03
Mississippi '35
Mrs. Brown '97
Modigliani '58
Molokai: The Story of Father Damien '99
Monsieur N. '03
Monte Walsh '03
The Moonstone '72
The Moonstone '97
Moulin Rouge '01
Mutiny on the Blackhawk '39
My Antonia '94
My Apprenticeship '39
My Childhood '38
My Universities '40
The Mystery of Edwin Drood '35
The Mystery of Edwin Drood '93
Nanny McPhee '06
Napoleon '03
Ned Kelly '03
The New Land '73
Newsies '92
Nicholas Nickleby '46
Nicholas Nickleby '02
Northanger Abbey '87
Northanger Abbey '07
Oliver! '68
Oliver Twist '22
Oliver Twist '48
Oliver Twist '82
Oliver Twist '85
Oliver Twist '97
Oliver Twist '05
Once Upon a Time in China '91
One Man's Hero '98
Onegin '99
The Organizer '64
Original Sin '01
Orlando '92
Oscar and Lucinda '97
The Outsider '02
The Ox '91
Pandaemonium '00
Pelle the Conqueror '88
The Perfect Husband '92
Persuasion '71
Persuasion '95
Persuasion '07
The Phantom of the Opera '25
The Phantom of the Opera '43
The Phantom of the Opera '62
The Phantom of the Opera '90
The Phantom of the Opera '98
The Phantom of the Opera '04
The Piano '93
Pink String and Sealing Wax '45
Poldark '96

▶ = rated three bones or higher

Portrait of a Lady '67►
Portrait of a Lady '96►
The Possessed '88
Possession '02
The Prestige '06►
Pride and Prejudice '40►
Pride and Prejudice '85►
Pride and Prejudice '95►
Pride and Prejudice '05►
Prince of Poisoners: The Life and Crimes of William Palmer '98
Princess Caraboo '94
The Private Affairs of Bel Ami '47►
The Proposition '05
P.T. Barnum '99
Race to Freedom: The Story of the Underground Railroad '94
The Real Charlotte '91
Return of Sabata '71
The Return of the Native '94
The Right Hand Man '87
The Ripper '97
Robert Louis Stevenson's The Game of Death '99
The Rover '67
Rowing with the Wind '88
Ruby in the Smoke '06
Sabata '69
St. Ives '98
Saratoga Trunk '45
A Scandal in Paris '46
Scarlet '94
Sea Devils '53
The Secret Garden '49►
The Secret Garden '84►
The Secret Garden '87►
The Secret Garden '93►
The Secret Life of Mrs. Beeton '06
Sense & Sensibility '85►
Sense & Sensibility '95►
Sense & Sensibility '07
Senso '54►
September Dawn '07
Sergeant Rutledge '60►
Shanghai Knights '03
Shanghai Noon '00
Sharpe's Battle '94
Sharpe's Challenge '06
Sharpe's Company '94
Sharpe's Eagle '93
Sharpe's Enemy '94
Sharpe's Gold '94
Sharpe's Honour '94
Sharpe's Justice '97
Sharpe's Legend '97
Sharpe's Mission '96
Sharpe's Regiment '96
Sharpe's Revenge '97
Sharpe's Rifles '93
Sharpe's Siege '96
Sharpe's Sword '94
Sharpe's Waterloo '97
Sherlock: Case of Evil '02
The Sign of Four '83
The Sign of Four '01
Silas Marner '85►
Silk '07
Sister Dora '77
Sitting Bull '54
Skin Game '71►
Sofie '92
Sommersby '93
A Song to Remember '45►
Song Without End '60
Souls at Sea '37
The Sound and the Silence '93
Spirit: Stallion of the Cimarron '02
Spring Symphony '86
Station Jim '01
Steamboy '05
The Story of Alexander Graham Bell '39►
The Story of an African Farm '04
The Strauss Family '73
The Substitute Wife '94
Sweeney Todd: The Demon Barber of Fleet Street '07
Swept from the Sea '97

Taboo '99
Tai-Pan '86
Tamango '59
Tchaikovsky '71
The Tenant of Wildfell Hall '96
Tess '79►
Tess of the D'Urbervilles '98
The Texans '38
Texas Rangers '01
That Forsyte Woman '50
Therese Raquin '80
Therese: The Story of Saint Therese of Lisieux '04
The Thorn Birds: The Missing Years '96►
Tim Burton's Corpse Bride '05►
Tipping the Velvet '02
Tom and Huck '95►
Tom Sawyer '30►
Tom Sawyer '73
Topsy Turvy '99
Torrents of Spring '90
Total Eclipse '95
Twelfth Night '96
The Twilight Samurai '02►
Two Years before the Mast '46
Under Capricorn '49►
Under Capricorn '82
Under the Greenwood Tree '05
Utamaro and His Five Women '46
Vacas '91
The Valley of Decision '45►
Van Gogh '92►
Vanity Fair '32
Vanity Fair '67
Vanity Fair '99
Vanity Fair '04
Victoria & Albert '01
The Village '04
Vincent & Theo '90►
Waltz King '63
War and Peace '56
War and Peace '68►
War and Peace '73
Washington Square '97►
The Way We Live Now '02
The Weight of Water '00
Wide Sargasso Sea '92
The Widow of Saint-Pierre '00►
Wild Bill '95
Wild Wild West '99
Wilde '97►
Wind River '98
Wives and Daughters '01
The Wolf at the Door '87
A Woman Rebels '36
The World in His Arms '52
The World Moves On '34
The Wyvern Mystery '00
The Young Pioneers '76
Young Sherlock Holmes '85
Zatoichi '03►
'00►
Iris '01►
JFK: Reckless Youth '93
Lagaan: Once upon a Time in India '01
Lansky '99

Period Piece: 20th Century

America's Dream '95►
The Babe '92
Bride of the Wind '01
Carrington '95
Century '95
Cobb '94►
Coming Through '85
A Dance to the Music of Time '97
Dash and Lilly '99
Dust '01
Frida '02
Gypsy '62►
Gypsy '93
Hold the Dream '86
House of Sand '05►
Indochine '92►
Interview with the Vampire '94
It's a Dog's Life '55
Jet Li's Fearless '06
Klimt '06
Klimt '06
La Ronde '51►
Lady L '65
Land of Promise '74
Les Destinees '00
Liebelei '32
Like Water for Chocolate '93►
The Lost Boys '78►
Love Among the Ruins '75►
Madame Butterfly '95
The Magician of Lublin '79
Love in the Time of Cholera '07
Legends of the Fall '94
Lillie '79►
The Legend of 1900 '98
The Last Emperor '87►

Period Piece: 1900s

Anne of Green Gables '85►
The Bachelor '93►
Back Street '41
Berkeley Square '98
The Best Intentions '92►
Beyond the Wall of Sleep '06
Cheaper by the Dozen '50►
City Boy '93
Cold Sassy Tree '89►
Colonel Redl '84►
Daens '92
Daughters of the Dust '91►
The Dead '87►
December Bride '91
The Dolly Sisters '46
Fanny and Alexander '83►
Fiddler on the Roof '71►
55 Days at Peking '63►
Finding Neverland '04►
The Flame Is Love '79
The Forbidden Quest '93
Fulfillment '89
Gentlemen's Relish '01
Glory & Honor '98
The Go-Between '71►
The Good Old Boys '95
Grand Isle '92
The Guns and the Fury '83
Hamlet '01
Hangover Square '45
Harem '26
Heart of Darkness '93
Hester Street '75►
Home at Last '88
House of Mirth '00►
I Remember Mama '48►
Illuminata '98
The Illusionist '06►
The Imported Bridegroom '89
Institute Benjamenta or This Dream People Call Human Life '95
The Magnificent Ambersons '42►
The Magnificent Ambersons '02
Malcolm X '92►
Mama Flora's Family '98
Me Without You '01
Nanny McPhee '06►
Nicholas and Alexandra '71
O Pioneers! '91
Orlando '92►
Our Town '03
Our Town '40►
Our Town '77►
Our Town '89
Rasputin: Dark Servant of Destiny '96►
Rasputin and the Mad Monk '66
Rich Man, Poor Man '76►
The Sexual Life of the Belgians '94
The Song of the Lark '01
Start '68
Sunshine '99
There Will Be Blood '07►
Trahir '93►
Tom & Viv '94►
The Travelling Players '75
Two Brothers '04►
Winchell '98
A Woman of Substance '84
The World Moves On '34
Youth Without Youth '07

Period Piece: 1910s

The Man in the Attic '94
Man of Evil '48
Meet Me in St. Louis '44►
A Midsummer Night's Sex Comedy '82►
Miss Potter '06►
Mrs. Soffel '84►
Max '02
Michael Collins '96►
Mr. Toad's Wild Ride '96
Mrs. Santa Claus '96►
Modigliani '04
Jazzman '84►
Johnny Dangerously '84
Killer: A Journal of Murder '95
Lily Dale '96
A Little Princess '95►
The Lost World '02
The Lost Place on Earth '85
The Lawrenceville Stories '87►
My Uncle Silas '01►
My Twentieth Century '90►
Nora '00
Of Freaks and Men '98
On Valentine's Day '86
Peg o' My Heart '22
Picture Bride '94►
Plain Jane '01
Ragtime '81►
A River Runs Through It '92►
The Railway Children '70►
The Railway Children '00►
The Road to Wellville '94►
A Room with a View '86►
San Francisco '36►
Secrets '24
Shadow Magic '00
She Creature '01
A Summer Story '88►
Tales from the Gimli Hospital '88
Valley of the Kings '54
Viva Zapata! '52►
We of the Never Never '82►
When the Greeks '81
Where Angels Fear to Tread '91►
William Shakespeare's A Midsummer Night's Dream '99
Yentl '83►

Period Piece: 1920s

Abbott and Costello Meet the Keystone Kops '54
And Starring Pancho Villa as Himself '03►
Atlantis: The Lost Empire '01
The Basket '99
Britannic '99
Burial Glory '89
Catherine Cookson's Colour Blind '98
The Chambermaid on the Titanic '97►
Christy '94
Cider with Rosie '99
Country Life '95
Courage Mountain '89
A Death in the Family '02
Doctor Zhivago '65►
Eight Men Out '88►
The Englishman Who Went up a Hill But Came down a Mountain '95►
Fairy Tale: A True Story '97►
The Fixer '68►
The Flame Trees of Thika '81►
Forest of Little Bear '87
The Front Page '74
The Great Gatsby '49
The Great Gatsby '74►
The Great Gatsby '01
The Great Waldo Pepper '75►
Greenwich Village '44
The Grissom Gang '71►
The Harmonists '99
Haunted '95
Agatha Christie: A Life in Pictures '04
Al Capone '59►
The Aviator '04►
Balto '95
Bare Knees '28
Belles on Their Toes '52
Bix '90
Bobby Jones: Stroke of Genius '04
The Bretts '88►
Bright Young Things '03
Bullets over Broadway '94►
By the Light of the Silvery Moon '53
The Cat's Meow '01
Character '97
Chicago '02►
Cold Comfort Farm '71
Cold Comfort Farm '94►
The Cotton Club '84►
De-Lovely '04
Deja Vu '89
The Disappearance of Aimee '76►
Dr. Bethune '30►
Elie, My Friend '93
Enchanted April '92►
Entertaining Angels: The Dorothy Day Story '96
Flambards '78
The Flame Trees of Thika '81►
Flickers '80
From Dusk Till Dawn 3: The Hangman's Daughter '99
Gabrielle '05
The Girl in the Red Velvet Swing '55
Good Morning, Babylon '87►
Goodbye, Miss 4th of July '88
The Greatest Game Ever Played '05►
Grizzly Falls '99
Heartland '81►
Hole in the Sky '95
Howard's End '92►
The Iceman Cometh '73
Iron Will '93
Jet Li's Fearless '06
Klimt '06

The Hearst and Davies Affair '85
High Road to China '83
Hit the Dutchman '92
The House of Eliott '92►
I'll See You in My Dreams '51►
Incantato '03
Inherit the Wind '99
The Intended '02
Intimate Affairs '01
The Jazz Singer '80
The Luzhin Defence '00
The Lover '92
Longitude '00►
Legend of Valentino '75
Vance '00
Legionnaire '98
Les Destinees '00
Legend of Bagger Vance '00
The Modems '86►
The Mummy '99►
My Life So Far '98
Naked Tango '91
The Newton Boys '97
Once Upon a Time in America '84►
The Painted Veil '06
Pancho Barnes '88
Party Girl '58►
A Passage to India '84►
Pictures '80s
Private Confessions '98
The Quest '96
Red Sorghum '86
Return to Paradise '53
The Roaring Twenties '39►
Robin and the 7 Hoods '64►
Rosewood '96►
Roxie Hart '42
The St. Valentine's Day Massacre '67
Shadow of the Vampire '00►
Shake Hands with the Devil '59►
The Slingshot '93►
Speedy Death '99►
Splendor in the Grass '61►
The Stationmaster's Wife '77►
The Stranger: Kabloonak '95
Studs Lonigan '60
Sweet Land '05
Swoon '91►
Tenderness of the Wolves '73
The Theremin: An Electronic Odyssey '95
The Tigress '93
Temptess Moon '96►
Thoroughly Modern Millie '67►
Twenty-Four Eyes '54►
Under the Biltmore Clock '85
The Untouchables '87►
Underworld '27►
An Unforgettable Summer '94
Valentino '77
Weeping Meadow '04
When Angels Fly '84►
Where the Rivers Flow North '94
Wild Party '74
The Wind That Shakes the Barley '06►
The Wolves '71►
Woman in Black '89

Period Piece: 1930s

The Wooden Man's Bride '94
You Know My Name '99

Period Piece: 1930s

Acla's Descent into Floristella '87
All My Loved Ones '00
Ask the Dust '06
Atonement '07
The Aviator '04
The Bay Boy '85
Being Julia '04
Belle Epoque '92
Borstal Boy '00
Break of Dawn '88
Broken Glass '96
Burnt by the Sun '94
Butterfly '98
Cambridge Spies '03
Cause Celebre '87
The Charmer '87
Child Star: The Shirley Temple Story '01
Cora Unashamed '00
Crime of the Century '96
Dancing at Lughnasa '98
The Devil's Backbone '01
Disappearances '06
Dogville '03
Drunken Monkey '02
Durango '99
The Education of Little Tree '97
Emma's Shadow '88
Everyone's Hero '06
The Field '90
Fleeing by Night '00
The Gathering Storm '02
Go Tell It on the Mountain '84
A Good Woman '04
Gosford Park '01
The Grass Harp '95
The Great Debaters '07
The Habitation of Dragons '91
The Harmonists '99
Head in the Clouds '04
Heat of the Sun '99
Heavens Fall '06
The Hindenburg '75
Hoodlum & Son '03
I Capture the Castle '02
I Don't Want to Talk About It '94
Idlewild '06
The Imposters '98
In Pursuit of Honor '95
In the Realm of the Senses '76
The Inheritors '82
Innocent Lies '95
Invincible '01
Ivan and Abraham '94
Jew-Boy Levi '99
Joe and Max '02
The Journey to Kafiristan '01
King Kong '05
Ladies in Lavender '04
Lassie '05
Last Call: The Final Chapter of F. Scott Fitzgerald '02
Liam '00
Love's Labour's Lost '00
Madame Sata '02
The Man from the Pru '89
The Man Who Cried '00
Manderlay '05
Memoirs of a Geisha '05
A Merry War '97
Miracles '89
Miss Petigrew Lives for a Day '08
Mrs. Henderson Presents '05
The Mummy Returns '01
Murder in a Small Town '99
Nowhere in Africa '02
Out of the Cold '99
Pandora and the Flying Dutchman '51
Papa's Angels '00
Pavilion of Women '01
The Phantom Lover '95
The Prime of Miss Jean Brodie '69
The Proposition '97
Purple Butterfly '03
Rabbit-Proof Fence '02
Radioland Murders '94
Ray '04
The Remains of the Day '93
Richard III '95
Road to Perdition '02
The Rocketeer '91
The Saddest Music in the World '03
Shadow on the Sun '88
Shanghai Triad '95
Sirens '94
Sky Captain and the World of Tomorrow '04
The Sleeping Dictionary '02
The Stick-Up '77
Swing Kids '93
Tea with Mussolini '99
These Foolish Things '06
The Thirteenth Floor '99
This Is My Father '99
Triple Agent '04
Under the Volcano '84
Up at the Villa '00
Walk on the Wild Side '62
Weeping Meadow '04
The White Countess '05
The Whole Wide World '96
A Woman at Her Window '77
Yellow Earth '89

Period Piece: 1940s

Aimee & Jaguar '98
All the King's Men '06
All the Pretty Horses '00
All Things Fair '95
Almost Peaceful '02
An American Story '92
The Aviator '04
Back Home '90
Back to the Secret Garden '01
Barton Fink '91
Batman: Mask of the Phantasm '93
Before the Fall '04
The Black Dahlia '06
Bon Voyage '03
Broken Silence '01
Buffalo Boy '04
Bugsy '91
Bye Bye Blues '89
Carry Me Home '04
Catherine Cookson's The Round Tower '98
Charms for the Easy Life '02
Children On Their Birthdays '02
The Chorus '04
The Chosen '81
The Chronicles of Narnia: The Lion, the Witch and the Wardrobe '05
The Cider House Rules '99
Color of a Brisk and Leaping Day '95
The Color of Courage '98
Confessing to Laura '90
The Counterfeiters '07
The Curse of the Jade Scorpion '01
A Dark Adapted Eye '93
Dead Gorgeous '02
Deep Crimson '96
Delta of Venus '95
Devil in a Blue Dress '95
The Dollmaker '84
The Doorbell Rang: A Nero Wolfe Mystery '01
Downfall '04
Earth '98
East of Elephant Rock '76
East-West '99
Exorcist: The Beginning '04
The Fallen '05
Farewell, My Lovely '75
15 Amore '98
The Fifth Horseman Is Fear '64
Focus '01
For a Lost Soldier '93
The Forbidden Quest '93
The Franchise Affair '88
Gate of Flesh '64
The Golden Spiders: A Nero Wolfe Mystery '00
Good Evening, Mr. Wallenberg '93
The Good German '06
The Good Shepherd '06
Goodbye, Mr. Chips '69
Goodnight, Mr. Tom '99
The Grass Harp '95
The Grey Zone '01
Hannibal Rising '07
Head in the Clouds '04
The Heart of Me '02
Hong Kong 1941 '84
The Hours '02
The Human Stain '03
In the Mood '87
Joe Gould's Secret '00
Kinsey '04
Kung Fu Hustle '04
La Vie en Rose '07
The Last Time I Committed Suicide '96
A League of Their Own '92
Les Miserables '95
A Lesson Before Dying '99
Lonely Hearts '06
The Lost City '05
Lost in Yonkers '93
Malena '00
The Man Who Wasn't There '01
Mararia '98
Margaret's Museum '95
Married Life '07
The McCullochs '75
The Member of the Wedding '52
The Member of the Wedding '83
The Member of the Wedding '97
Memoirs of a Geisha '05
Miss Rose White '92
Mrs. Henderson Presents '05
Mountbatten: The Last Viceroy '86
The Mummy: Tomb of the Dragon Emperor '08
My Dog Skip '99
The Mystery of Rampo '94
The Mystic Masseur '01
The Neon Bible '95
The Ninth Day '04
The Notebook '04
Nowhere in Africa '02
Nuremberg '00
The Old Settler '01
Orde Wingate '76
Other Voices, Other Rooms '95
The Others '01
Pan's Labyrinth '06
Partition '07
Passion in Paradise '89
The Pianist '02
Pizzicata '96
Pollock '00
Possessed '00
The Power of One '92
The Public Eye '92
The Quarrel '93
Racing with the Moon '84
Ray '04
The Return of Eliot Ness '91
Ride the Wild Fields '00
The Rising Place '02
RKO 281 '99
The Road from Coorain '02
The Rocket '05
Rocky Marciano '99
Rosenstrasse '03
The Runaway '00
Salome '85
Season of Change '94
A Separate Peace '04
The Seventh Dawn '64
Snow Falling on Cedars '99
Snow in August '01
Something for Everyone '70
Sophie Scholl: The Final Days '05
Stand-Ins '97
Strayed '03
Sudie & Simpson '90
The Summer of Ben Tyler '96
Surviving Picasso '96
Swing Shift '84
Three Comrades '38
A Time to Live and a Time to Die '85
Torso '93
The Two Jakes '90
Village of Dreams '97
The Water Horse: Legend of the Deep '07
A Winner Never Quits '86
With a Song in My Heart '52
Zelary '03

Period Piece: 1950s

Absolute Beginners '86
The Affairs of Dobie Gillis '53
Alex '92
All the King's Men '06
An American Rhapsody '01
As Summers Die '86
The Audrey Hepburn Story '00
Austin Powers In Goldmember '02
Back to the Future '85
Back to the Future, Part 2 '89
Badlands '74
Bear Ye One Another's Burden... '88
A Beautiful Mind '01
Beefcake '99
Beyond the Sea '04
Big Night '95
Big Town '87
Blind Faith '98
The Blue Kite '93
Book of Love '91
Born Reckless '59
Boycott '02
The Buddy Holly Story '78
Bye, Bye, Birdie '63
Cafe Society '97
Calendar Girl '93
Capote '05
Celia: Child of Terror '89
Chicken Run '00
Child Bride of Short Creek '81
Chocolat '00
Circle of Friends '94
The Climb '97
Club Land '01
Common Ground '00
The Company '07
The Confessional '95
Cool and the Crazy '94
Corrina, Corrina '94
Cotton Mary '99
Crazy Love '07
Crazy Mama '75
Cry-Baby '90
Cuban Blood '03
Dance with a Stranger '85
Daniel Takes a Train '83
Dark Blue World '01
Dark of the Sun '68
Dead Poets Society '89
Desire and Hell at Sunset Motel '92
Deuces Wild '02
Devil's Island '96
Diner '82
Dirty Dancing '87
Dirty Dancing: Havana Nights '04
The Door in the Floor '04
Dreaming of Joseph Lees '99
Echoes '88
Elvis: The Movie '79
End of the Spear '06
The Ernest Green Story '93
Eros '04
Evelyn '02
Evening '07
Evil '03
Fall Time '94
Far from Heaven '02
Father of the Bride '50
Fellow Traveler '89
For the Boys '91
The Front '76
Fur: An Imaginary Portrait of Diane Arbus '06
The Game of Their Lives '05
Girls' Town '59
Going All the Way '97
Golden Gate '93
Good Night, and Good Luck '05
The Good Shepherd '06
Grease '78
Grease 2 '82
Ground Zero '88
Guilty by Suspicion '91
A Gun, a Car, a Blonde '97
Hannibal Rising '07
Her Majesty '01
A Hole in One '04
Hollywoodland '06
Hometown U.S.A. '79
Honeydripper '07
The Hours '02
The House on Carroll Street '88
Housekeeping '87
The Hudsucker Proxy '93
I Am David '04
In His Life: The John Lennon Story '00
Indiana Jones and the Kingdom of the Crystal Skull '08
Intimate Relations '95
Introducing Dorothy Dandridge '99
Inventing the Abbotts '97
I.Q. '94
Jailbreakers '94
James Dean '76
James Dean '01
James Dean: Live Fast, Die Young '97
Just Looking '99
A King in New York '57
Kinsey '04
Kitchen Stories '03
The Kitchen Toto '87
La Bamba '87
L.A. Confidential '97
La Vie en Rose '07
Last Exit to Brooklyn '90
The Last Picture Show '71
Liberty Heights '99
Lily in Winter '94
Little Richard '00
The Long Day Closes '92
Long Gone '87
The Long Walk Home '89
The Lords of Flatbush '74
The Lost City '05
Lost, Lonely, and Vicious '59
A Love Divided '01
Loveless '83
Mac '93
The Majestic '01
The Mambo Kings '92
The Man in the Moon '91
Mendel '98
Mischief '85
Mona Lisa Smile '03
Monaco Forever '83
Moscow Does Not Believe in Tears '80
The Motorcycle Diaries '04
Mulholland Falls '95
My American Cousin '85
My Favorite Year '82
My Louisiana Sky '02
My Michael '75
The Mystic Masseur '01
New World '95
Newsfront '78
Nightbreaker '89
Northfork '03
The Notorious Bettie Page '06
Oh, What a Night '92
Once Upon a Time ... When We Were Colored '95
One Plus One '61
Ordeal by Innocence '84
The Other Side of Heaven '02
The Other Side of Sunday '96
Our Time '74
Outlaw Trail '06
A Painted House '03
Palais Royale '88
Parents '89
The Passion of Ayn Rand '99
Peggy Sue Got Married '86
Perfect Harmony '91
Pillow Talk '59
The Playboys '92
Pollock '00
Porky's '82
The Prize Winner of Defiance, Ohio '05
The Producers '05
The Quiet American '02
Quiz Show '94
A Rage in Harlem '91
A Raisin in the Sun '89
A Raisin in the Sun '08
Ray '04
Red Hot '95
Red Kiss '85
The Reflecting Skin '91
Relative Values '99
The Road Home '01
Roadracers '94
Rock All Night '57
Rock, Baby, Rock It '57
The Rocket '05
Rocky Marciano '99
The Rosa Parks Story '02
Round Midnight '86
Saint Ralph '04
The Scent of Green Papaya '93
School Ties '92
Shadowlands '85
Shadowlands '93
Shake, Rattle and Rock! '57
Shake, Rattle & Rock! '94
Shout '91
The Silence '94
The Singing Detective '03
Snow Falling on Cedars '99
Sparkle '76
Stacking '87
The Star Maker '95
Starkweather '04
The Sticky Fingers of Time '97
Strange Invaders '83
A Stranger in the Kingdom '98
The Summer House '94
Superdad '73
Suzanne '80
Swimming Upstream '03
Sylvia '03
Tae Guk Gi: The Brotherhood of War '04
The Talented Mr. Ripley '99
Teenage Doll '57
Terranova '91
That'll Be the Day '73
The Thief '97
This Boy's Life '93
This World, Then the Fireworks '97
Though None Go With Me '06
Three Wishes '95
Tito and Me '92
Trading Hearts '87
Traps '93
The Trial of Old Drum '00
Tune in Tomorrow '90
Two Family House '99
Valentino Returns '88
Vera Drake '04
Visitants '87
Walk the Line '05
The War of the Worlds '53
The Way We Were '73
When Father Was Away on Business '85
Where the Truth Lies '05
Who Shot Pat? '92
The Wild One '54

▲ = rated *three bones* or *higher*

Witch Hunt '94
The Wooden Gun '79
Wrestling with Alligators '99
You've Ruined Me, Eddie '58

Period Piece: 1960s
see also Boomer Reunions

A la Mode '94
Across the Universe '07
Adam at 6 a.m. '70
Agatha Christie: A Life in Pictures '04
Agnes Browne '99
Ali '01
Alice's Restaurant '69
All I Wanna Do '98
American Blue Note '89
American Gangster '07
American Graffiti '73▶
Angels Hard As They Come '71
Asylum '05
Austin Powers 2: The Spy Who Shagged Me '99▶
Auto Focus '02▶
Awakenings of the Beast '68
Backbeat '94▶
Bad Education '04▶
The Beautiful, the Bloody and the Bare '64
Believe in Me '06
Best Enemies '86
Best of Youth '05▶
Best Revenge '83
Beyond the Sea '04
The Big Chill '83▶
The Big Fix '78▶
Blast-Off Girls '67
The Blue Kite '93▶
Bob & Carol & Ted & Alice '69
Bobby '06
Born on the Fourth of July '89▶
Brian's Song '01
The Bridges of Madison County '95▶
Brokeback Mountain '05▶
A Bronx Tale '93▶
Burnt Money '00
Capote '05▶
Catch Me If You Can '02
Charlie '04
Chasing Christmas '05
The Chatterley Affair '06
Chicago 10 '07▶
Children Shouldn't Play with Dead Things '72
City of God '02
The Clay Bird '02
The Company '07
Company Man '00
Confessions of a Dangerous Mind '02
Confessions of Sorority Girls '94
Conspiracy: The Trial of the Chicago Eight '87▶
CQ '01
Crazy in Alabama '99
The Crimson Cult '68
Dangerous Liaisons '05
Dead Beat '94
Dead Presidents '95
December Boys '07
Dirty Deeds '02▶
The Dish '00▶
Dogfight '91▶
The Doors '91
Down With Love '03
Dreamgirls '06▶
Dynamite Chicken '70
Easy Rider '69▶
El Cantante '06
Eros '04
Even Cowgirls Get the Blues '94

Factory Girl '06
Family Prayers '91
Fatherland '94
First Love and Other Pains / Rude Awakening '89
Five Corners '88▶
The Flamingo Rising '01
Flashback '89▶
Flawless '07
Flawless '99▶
Four Friends '81▶
Free Grass '69
Freedom Song '00▶
Fritz the Cat '72▶
From the Earth to the Moon '98▶
Gangster No. 1 '00
Ginnie Shelter '70
Girl, Interrupted '99
Glory Road '06
The Glory Stompers '67
God's Sandbox '02
Godspell '73
The Good Shepherd '06
Grace of My Heart '96
Greetings '68▶
Hair '79▶
Hairspray '07▶
Head '68▶
Hearts in Atlantis '01
Help Wanted Female '68
Hendrix '00
Hideous Kinky '99
High Hopes '83▶
The Hollywood Knights '80
Hope '97
The Hours and Times '92▶
I Drink Your Blood '71
I Love You, Alice B. Toklas! '68
I Shot Andy Warhol '96▶
If These Walls Could Talk 2 '00
Imaginary Crimes '94▶
In His Father's Shoes '97
In the Mood for Love '00
Infamous '06
Isn't She Great '00
John John in the Sky '00
K-19: The Widowmaker '02
The Krays '90▶
Like A Bride '94
The Locusts '97
Longford '06
The Lords of Discipline '83
The Lotus Eaters '93
Love Field '91
Lumumba '00
M. Butterfly '93
The Magdalene Sisters '02▶
Malevolence '95
The Manson Family '04
Mantis in Lace '68
Married to It '93
Matinee '92
Metroland '97
The Milky Way '97
Monsieur Ibrahim '03▶
More '69
More American Graffiti '79
My Little Assassin '99
Odd Birds '85
Off Limits '87
One Crazy Night '93
The Only Thrill '97
Out '88
Pack of Lies '87
Passing Glory '99▶
Path to War '02▶
Peppermint Soda '77▶
A Perfect World '93
Petit Con '84
Poodle Springs '98
Power and Beauty '02
Psych-Out '68
Psycho Beach Party '00
Race to Space '01
Rainbow Bridge '71
Ray '04▶
The Rebel Set '59
Rescue Dawn '06▶
RFK '02
Rhapsody of Spring '98
Riding in Cars with Boys '01
Riding the Bullet '04▶
Romulus, My Father '07▶

R.P.M.* (* Revolutions Per Minute) '70
Ruby Bridges '98
Ruby's Bucket of Blood '01
Saint Maybe '98▶
The Sandlot '93▶
The Sandpiper '65
Satan's Sadists '69
Sea Devils '31
Second Thoughts '83
Selma, Lord, Selma '99
Set Me Free '99
Shag: The Movie '89▶
The '60s '99
61* '01▶
'68 '87
Skipped Parts '00
Slashed Dreams '74
A Small Circle of Friends '80
The Snake People '68
Soldiers of Change '06
The Speed Lovers '68
Steal This Movie! '00
Stoned '05
The Stoned Age '94
The Strawberry Statement '70
Sugartime '95
Sweetwater: A True Rock Story '99
Swimming Upstream '03
Sylvia '03
Talk to Me '07
Telling Lies in America '96
A Texas Funeral '99
That Night '93
That Thing You Do! '96▶
There Goes My Baby '92
There's a Girl in My Soup '70
Thirteen Days '00▶
Three Times '05
Thumb Tripping '72
Tin Men '87▶
The Trip '67
The Tunnel '01▶
Used People '92
Valentin '02
Wah-Wah '05
Waiting for the Light '90
Walk Hard: The Dewey Cox Story '07
A Walk on the Moon '99
Walk the Line '05▶
Where Angels Go, Trouble Follows '68
Where the Eagle Flies '72
Who'll Stop the Rain? '78▶
Wild in the Streets '68
Wild Reeds '94▶
Wondrous Oblivion '06▶
The Woods '03
Woodstock '70▶
The World's Fastest Indian '05▶
Yellow Submarine '68▶
The Zodiac '05
Zodiac '07▶
Blow '01

Period Piece: 1970s

After the Rain '99
Ali '01
Almost Famous '00▶
American Gangster '07▶
Anchorman: The Legend of Ron Burgundy '04
Armistead Maupin's More Tales of the City '93
Armistead Maupin's Tales of the City '93
The Assassination of Richard Nixon '05
Austin Powers in Goldmember '02
Auto Focus '02▶
Baadasssss! '03▶
Bad Education '04▶
Balzac and the Little Chinese Seamstress '02
The Bank Job '08▶
Best of Youth '05▶
Blame It on Fidel '06
Bloody Sunday '01▶
Boogie Nights '97▶
The Bronx Is Burning '07
Brothers of the Head '06
Callas Forever '02
Carlito's Way: Rise to Power '05
Casino '95▶
Catch Me If You Can '02
Chopper '00▶
City of God '02▶
Common Ground '00
Confessions of a Dangerous Mind '02
Control '07
Creatures from the Pink Lagoon '07
Crooklyn '94▶
Crossing the Bridge '92
The Dangerous Lives of Altar Boys '02▶
Dazed and Confused '93▶
A Decade Under the Influence '02▶
Detroit Rock City '99
Dick '99▶
Diggers '06
Donnie Brasco '96▶
Dreamgirls '06▶
Drugstore Cowboy '89▶
East Is East '99▶
El Cantante '06
The Emperor's Club '02
Escape: Human Cargo '98▶
Execution of Justice '99
Fear and Loathing in Las Vegas '98
Forever Mine '99
Frailty '02▶
From the Earth to the Moon '98▶
Gia '98▶
Good Fences '03
The Good Humor Man '05
Gracie '07
Grand Theft Parsons '03
Green Dragon '01
Green Plaid Shirt '96
Heading South '05▶
Hedwig and the Angry Inch '00▶
Hideous Kinky '99
The Hillside Strangler '04
The Hoax '06▶
The Ice Storm '97▶
I'm Not Scared '03
Imagining Argentina '04
Invincible '06▶
Jesus' Son '99
Jill the Ripper '00
Joe the King '99
The Killing Beach '92
The Killing Yard '01
Kippur '00
The Kite Runner '07▶
The Ladies Man '00
The Last King of Scotland '06▶
The Last of the High Kings '96
Left Luggage '98
The Legend of Rita '99
The Lesser Evil '97
Long Time Since '97
Lords of Dogtown '05
A Lost Year '93
Man on the Moon '99
Maryam '00
Meat Loaf: To Hell and Back '00
Metroland '97
Miracle '04▶
Moonlight Mile '02▶
Munich '05▶
Murder in Greenwich '02
Music Within '07
Nearing Grace '05
New Waterford Girl '99
The Night We Called It a Day '03
No '98
North Country '05

Period Piece: 1980s

The Adventures of Sebastian Cole '99
American Psycho '00▶
Angela '02
Apt Pupil '97
Ash Wednesday '02
The Assignment '97
Bad Education '04▶
Beyond Borders '03
Best of Youth '05▶
Billy Elliot '00▶
Blow '01
Brooklyn Rules '07
Buffalo Soldiers '01
Capturing the Friedmans '03▶
Catch a Fire '06
Charlie Wilson's War '07
City of God '02
The Confessional '95▶
Dangerous Evidence: The Lori Jackson Story '99
The Day Reagan Was Shot '01
Donnie Darko '01▶
Drug Wars: The Camarena Story '90▶
Dumb and Dumberer: When Harry Met Lloyd '03

Nothing Personal '95▶
Of Love and Shadows '94
Off the Map '03▶
Persepolis '07▶
Pinero '01
Pride '07
Protecting the King '07
Radio '03
Rain '01
Rampage: The Hillside Strangler Murders '04
Ratcatcher '99
Resurrection Man '97
Rhapsody of Spring '98
Riding in Cars with Boys '01
Roll Bounce '05▶
The Royal Tenenbaums '01▶
Running with Scissors '06
Scotland, PA '02
Seeing Red '99
Semi-Pro '08
The '70s '00
Shot in the Heart '01▶
Silent Waters '03
Slums of Beverly Hills '98▶
Spider '02▶
Spy Game '01
Stander '03
Starsky & Hutch '04
Steal This Movie! '00
Stolen Summer '02
Strawberry and Chocolate '93▶
Such a Long Journey '98▶
Summer of Sam '99▶
Take Me Home: The John Denver Story '00
That's the Way I Like It '99
The Thin Blue Lie '00
The Third Miracle '99
Tigerland '00▶
Torremolinos 73 '03
The Trip '02
24 Hour Party People '02▶
Two of Us '00
The U.S. vs. John Lennon '06
Velvet Goldmine '98▶
The Virgin Suicides '99▶
Waking the Dead '00
Walk Hard: The Dewey Cox Story '07
The War '94
Water Drops on Burning Rocks '99
We Are Marshall '06
West Beirut '98
Where the Truth Lies '05
Without Limits '97▶
Xiu Xiu: The Sent Down Girl '97▶
Zodiac '07▶

Period Piece: 1990s

Amelie '01▶
Among Brothers '05
Behind the Red Door '02
Beyond Borders '03

Edge of Seventeen '99
An Everlasting Piece '00
Fever Pitch '96
Fierce People '05
Find Me Guilty '06
Fool's Gold: The Story of the Brink's-Mat Robbery '92
Forever Mine '99
4 Months, 3 Weeks, 2 Days '07▶
Friday Night Lights '06
Friends & Crocodiles '05
Game 6 '05
Good Bye, Lenin! '03▶
Green Plaid Shirt '96
A Guide to Recognizing Your Saints '06
The History Boys '06
Hollywood North '03
Hurlyburly '98
Hustle '04
Hysterical Blindness '02
In America '02▶
The Informant '97▶
Innocent Voices '04
The Killing of John Lennon '07
Lan Yu '01
The Last Days of Disco '98▶
The Last Shot '04
The Legend of Rita '99
The Line of Beauty '06
The Lives of Others '06▶
The Lovers on the Bridge '91
The Magician '93
Man on the Moon '99
Memories and Murder '03
Miracle '04▶
Mrs. Harris '05
Monster '03▶
Nightstalker '02
No Country for Old Men '07▶
Noriega: God's Favorite '00
Owning Mahowny '03
Paid in Full '02
Party Monster '03
The Perez Family '94
Persepolis '07▶
Pinero '01
Point of Origin '02
The Pursuit of Happyness '06▶
Rent '05
The Replacements '00
Riding in Cars with Boys '01
Rock Star '01
Safe Men '98
A Season on the Brink '02
SLC Punk! '99
Sonny '02
Spicer '02
Spy Game '01
Stander '03
Starter for Ten '06
Stateside '04
Summer Palace '06▶
Summer's End '99
This Is England '06▶
To Walk with Lions '99
The Trip '02
24-7 '97
24 Hour Party People '02▶
200 Cigarettes '98
Typhoon '06
Valentine '01
Velvet Goldmine '98▶
Waking the Dead '00
The Wedding Singer '97▶
We Own the Night '07▶
Wet Hot American Summer '01▶
Whatever '98
Wonderland '03
The Wood '99

▶ = rated three bones or higher

Period

Big Shot: Confessions of a Campus Bookie '02
Black Hawk Down '01
Bully '01
Color Me Kubrick '05
Dark Blue '03
Definitely, Maybe '08
The Diving Bell and the Butterfly '07
Exiled '06
The Final Season '07
44 Minutes: The North Hollywood Shootout '03
Freedom Writers '07
Friends & Crocodiles '05
Go West '05
Highway '01
House of Fools '02
The Human Stain '03
The Hunting Party '07
Into the Wild '07
Jasper, Texas '03
Kandahar '01
The Listening '06
Live from Baghdad '03
Man of the Century '99
Marooned in Iraq '02
Mountain Patrol: Kekexili '04
The Murder of Stephen Lawrence '99
The Navigators '01
No Man's Land '01
Party Monster '03
Pinochet's Last Stand '06
PU-239 '06
The Queen '06
'R Xmas '01
Shattered Glass '03
Shooting Dogs '05
Spy Game '01
Strange Justice: The Clarence Thomas and Anita Hill Story '99
Summer Palace '06
10th & Wolf '06
Three Kings '99
21 '08
Waking Up Wally '05

Persian Gulf/Iraq War
see also Desert War; Foreign Legion
American Soldiers '05
Courage Under Fire '96
Grace Is Gone '07
The Heroes of Desert Storm '91
Home of the Brave '06
The Human Shield '92
The Jacket '05
Jarhead '05
Lions for Lambs '07
Live from Baghdad '03
The One That Got Away '96
Redacted '07
The Situation '06
Stir of Echoes 2: The Homecoming '07
Stop-Loss '08
Tactical Assault '99
Taxi to the Dark Side '07
Three Kings '99

Philadelphia
Baby Mama '08
Birdy '84
Blow Out '81
Cover '08
Downtown '89
Fat Albert '04
The Garbage-Picking, Field Goal-Kicking Philadelphia Phenomenon '98
Happy Birthday, Gemini '80
A History of Violence '05
I Don't Buy Kisses Anymore '92
In Her Shoes '05
Invincible '06
King of the Corner '04
Kitty Foyle '40
Like Mike '02
Mannequin '87
Mannequin 2: On the Move '91
Marnie '64
Money for Nothing '93
My Baby's Daddy '04
My Little Girl '87
Nasty Habits '77
National Treasure '04
Philadelphia '93
The Philadelphia Story '40
Pride '07
Rock School '05
Rocky '76
Rocky 2 '79
Rocky 3 '82
Rocky 4 '85
Rocky 5 '90
Rocky Balboa '06
The Sixth Sense '99
Snipes '01
State Property 2 '05
Stonewall '95
The Thin Blue Lie '00
Time at the Top '99
Trading Places '83
12 Monkeys '95
Two Bits '96
Two Plus One '95
Unbreakable '00
Up Close and Personal '96
Waiting '00
The Watermelon Woman '97
Winter Kills '79
Witness '85
The Young Philadelphians '59

Philanthropy
see Kindness of Strangers

Phobias!
Arachnophobia '90
As Good As It Gets '97
Blackjack '97
Body Double '84
Copycat '95
GhostWatcher '02
High Anxiety '77
Home Remedy '88
Inside Out '91
Pontiac Moon '94
Pretty Woman '90
Vertigo '58
What about Bob? '91

Phone Sex
see also Sex & Sexuality; Sexploitation
Denise Calls Up '95
Girl 6 '96
Happiness '98
Listen '96
Love in the Time of Money '02
Mouth to Mouth '95
1-900 '94
Punch-Drunk Love '02
Short Cuts '93
The Truth about Cats and Dogs '96
Walking and Talking '96
A Whisper to a Scream '88

Phone Terror
Are You Lonesome Tonight '92
Black Christmas '06
Black Sabbath '64
Call Me '88
Cavite '05
Cellular '04
Dead Connection '94
Dial Help '88
Don't Answer the Phone '80
88 Minutes '08
The Jerky Boys '95
Lady Beware '87
Liberty Stands Still '02
Lisa '90
Listen '96
Midnight Lace '60
The Night Caller '97
976-EVIL '88
976-EVIL 2: The Astral Factor '91
One Missed Call '08
Party Line '88
Phone Booth '02
Red '91
Scream '96
Scream 2 '97
Scream 3 '00
Smooth Talker '91
Sorry, Wrong Number '48
Sorry, Wrong Number '89
Telefon '77
Thr3e '07
When a Stranger Calls '79
When a Stranger Calls '06
When a Stranger Calls Back '93

Photography
see Shutterbugs

Physical Problems
see also Blindness; Deafness; Mental Retardation; Savants
Acorn People '82
Act of Violence '48
The Affair '73
An Affair to Remember '57
Alien: Resurrection '97
Amy '81
Amy '98
The Aura '05
Autumn Sonata '78
The Big Lebowski '97
Big Street '42
Blankman '94
The Bone Collector '99
Born on the Fourth of July '89
Breaking the Waves '95
A Brief History of Time '92
Broken Strings '40
Brotherhood of the Wolf '01
The Brute Man '46
Catherine Cookson's The Wingless Bird '97
Chained for Life '51
Chinese Roulette '86
Choices '81
Closer and Closer '96
Coming Home '78
The Craft '96
Cries of Silence '97
The Crippled Masters '82
Crossbar '79
Dance Me to My Song '98
A Day in the Death of Joe Egg '71
Dead Silent '99
Deuce Bigalow: Male Gigolo '99
Diamonds '99
The Diving Bell and the Butterfly '07
Don't Say a Word '01
Double Parked '00
Dracula 2: Ascension '03
The Duchess of Langeais '07
Eden '98
El Cochecito '60
The Elephant Man '80
Endgame '85
Even Cowgirls Get the Blues '94
Event Horizon '97
Everything That Rises '98
The Ex '07
Fallen Angels '95
Fireworks '97
Flawless '99
Floating '97
Follow the Stars Home '01
Frankie Starlight '95
Freddy Got Fingered '01
The Fugitive '93
George Wallace '97
The Glass Menagerie '87
Go Now '96
Good Luck '96
Goodbye, Dragon Inn '03
Gray's Anatomy '96
A Gun, a Car, a Blonde '97
He Was a Quiet Man '07
Hearing Voices '90
High Country '81
Home of the Brave '06
Hugo Pool '97
The Hunchback '97
The Hunchback of Notre Dame '23
The Hunchback of Notre Dame '39
The Hunchback of Notre Dame '57
The Hunchback of Notre Dame '96
I Don't Want to Talk About It '94
I Know Who Killed Me '07
I Want You '98
Inside Moves '80
It Runs in the Family '03
It's Good to Be Alive '74
Joni '79
The Kid and I '05
Kingpin '96
Knife in the Head '78
Lady Chatterley '06
Lea '96
Lewis and Clark and George '97
Lightning Jack '94
Locked in Silence '99
Long Journey Back '78
Looking for Richard '96
The Loretta Claiborne Story '00
Love Affair '39
Love Affair '94
Mac and Me '88
The Man with the Golden Arm '55
The Man Without a Face '93
Mask '85
The Men '50
Million Dollar Baby '04
Miracle in Lane Two '00
The Miracle Worker '62
The Miracle Worker '79
The Miracle Worker '00
Mrs. Munck '95
Monkey Shines '88
Murderball '05
Music Within '07
Mute Witness '95
My Left Foot '89
Next Victim '74
Niagara, Niagara '97
Night Monster '42
Night Must Fall '37
Of Human Bondage '34
Off the Mark '87
Once a Thief '90
One-Eyed Swordsman '63
Orphans '97
The Other Side of the Mountain '75
The Other Side of the Mountain, Part 2 '78
Out of the Black '01
Outside Providence '99
Paperback Romance '96
Passion Fish '92
The Passion of Anna '70
The Penalty '20
Penelope '06
The People vs. Larry Flynt '96
Persons Unknown '96
The Phantom of the Opera '25
The Phantom of the Opera '43
The Pit '81
Portrait of an Assassin '49
Powder '95
Pumpkin '02
Ratboy '86
Reach for the Sky '56
Rear Window '54
Rear Window '98
The Red Dwarf '99
Regarding Henry '91
Revolver '92
Richard III '55
Ride a Wild Pony '75
The River '51
Rocket Science '07
Rory O'Shea Was Here '04
Roxanne '87
Rumble in the Bronx '96
Saved! '04
Scent of a Woman '92
The Sea Inside '04
Second Chances '98
The Secret '93
Seizure: The Story of Kathy Morris '80
The Seventh Veil '46
Shallow Hal '01
Short Night of Glass Dolls '71
Silence '73
Silence Like Glass '90
Silent Witness '99
Silver Bullet '85
Sitcom '97
Skag '79
The Sky Pilot '21
The Small Back Room '49
The Son of the Bride '01
Sound of Love '78
Speak '04
Special Olympics '78
The Spiral Staircase '46
Spiral Staircase '00
The Station Agent '03
Steel '97
The Steel Claw '61
Stella Maris '18
The Stone Merchant '06
The Story of Esther Costello '57
The Stratton Story '49
Suite 16 '94
The Sum of Us '94
Sweet and Lowdown '99
Talk to Me '84
Teeth '07
The Terry Fox Story '83
A Test of Love '84
There's Something about Mary '98
Things to Do in Denver When You're Dead '95
39 Pounds of Love '05
To All My Friends on Shore '71
Touched '05
Twin Falls Idaho '99
Untamed Heart '93
Very Annie Mary '00
Vibrations '94
Walking on Air '87
The Waterdance '91
What Ever Happened to Baby Jane? '62
What the Deaf Man Heard '98
What's Eating Gilbert Grape '93
Whose Life Is It Anyway? '81
Wild Wild West '99
A Winner Never Quits '86
A Woman's Face '38
A Woman's Face '41
X-Men '00
X2: X-Men United '03

Pigs
see also Killer Pigs
The Advocate '93
Animal Farm '99
Babe '95
Babe: Pig in the City '98
The Black Cauldron '85
Charlotte's Web '73
Charlotte's Web '06
Doc Hollywood '91
Gordy '95
Leon the Pig Farmer '93
A Private Function '84
The Simpsons Movie '07
Toy Story '95
Toy Story 2 '99
Waikiki Wedding '37

Pirates
see also Island Fare; Sail Away; Swashbucklers
Abbott and Costello Meet Captain Kidd '52
Against All Flags '52
The Black Swan '42
Blackbeard the Pirate '52
Blackbeard's Ghost '67
The Buccaneer '58
Buccaneer's Girl '50
Captain Blood '35
Captain Kidd '45
Captain Ron '92
Crimson Pirate '52
Cutthroat Island '95
Dancing Pirate '36
Double Crossbones '51
Frenchman's Creek '44
Frenchman's Creek '98
His Majesty O'Keefe '53
Hook '91
Ice Pirates '84
Long John Silver '54
The Master of Ballantrae '53
Morgan the Pirate '60
Muppet Treasure Island '96
Naughty Marietta '35
New Moon '40
Old Ironsides '26
Peter Pan '53
Peter Pan '60
Peter Pan '03
The Phantom '96
The Pirate '48
Pirate Movie '82
Pirates of Penzance '83
Pirates of the Caribbean: At World's End '07
Pirates of the Caribbean: Dead Man's Chest '06
Pirates of the Caribbean: The Curse of the Black Pearl '03
The Pirates Who Don't Do Anything: A Veggie Tales Movie '08
The Princess and the Pirate '44
The Princess Bride '87
Return to Never Land '02
The Sea Hawk '40
Shipwrecked '90
Six Days, Seven Nights '98
Son of Captain Blood '62
Space Marines '96
Space Truckers '97
The Spanish Main '45
Stardust '07
Swashbuckler '76
The Swiss Family Robinson '60
Tiger of the Seven Seas '62
Treasure Island '34
Treasure Island '50
Treasure Island '72
Treasure Island '89
Treasure Island '99
Treasure Planet '02
Yankee Buccaneer '52
Yellowbeard '83

Pittsburgh
Alone in the Neon Jungle '87
Angels in the Outfield '51
Angels in the Outfield '94
Backstreet Justice '93
Bloodsucking Pharoahs of Pittsburgh '90
Bob Roberts '92
The Bread, My Sweet '01
The Cemetery Club '93
Diabolique '96
Dominick & Eugene '88
The Fish that Saved Pittsburgh '79
Flashdance '83
Houseguest '94
Innocent Blood '92
Lady Beware '87
Mrs. Soffel '84
No Other Woman '33
The Piano Lesson '94
Pittsburgh '06
Roommates '95
Silent Witness '85
Smart People '08
Stigmata '99
Striking Distance '93
Sudden Death '95
10th & Wolf '06
The Valley of Decision '45
Wonder Boys '00

Plastic Surgery
Ash Wednesday '73
The Black Dragons '42

Breast Men '97
The Broken Mask '23
Charlie Chan at the Wax Museum '40
Circus of Horrors '60
Dark Passage '47
Death Becomes Her '92
Face/Off '97
Faceless '88
Fallen Angel '99
G-Men Never Forget '48
I Accidentally Domed Your Son '04
The Jigsaw Man '84
The Man with Bogart's Face '80
The Promise '79
Rabid '77
A Stolen Face '52
Strange Impersonation '46
30 Years to Life '01
Time '06

Poetry

The Barretts of Wimpole Street '34►
Before Night Falls '00►
Blue Car '03►
The Business of Fancydancing '02
Byron '03
The Color of Pomegranates '69►
A Fine Madness '66►
Groundhog Day '93►
Hedd Wyn '92
Henry Fool '98►
I Heart Huckabees '04►
I, the Worst of All '90
In Custody '94
The Ister '04►
Lady Caroline Lamb '73
My Life and Times with Antonin Artaud '93►
Pinero '01
Poetic Justice '93
Possession '02
The Postman '94►
Satan's Brew '76
So I Married an Axe Murderer '93
Stevie '78
Swann '96
Sylvia '03
Tales of Ordinary Madness '83
Till Human Voices Wake Us '02
Tom & Viv '94►
Total Eclipse '95

Poisons

Agatha Christie's Sparkling Cyanide '83
Arsenic and Old Lace '44►
Barracuda '78
Batman and Robin '97
Color Me Dead '69
The Crazies '73
D.O.A. '49►
D.O.A. '88
Doomwatch '72
The Emperor's New Groove '00►
The Invisible Killer '40
Juggernaut '37
Kiss and Kill '68
Safe '95►
Snow White and the Seven Dwarfs '37►
Surf 2 '84
The Young Poisoner's Handbook '94►

Poker

see also Gambling

Aces and Eights '36
Angels Over Broadway '40►
A Big Hand for the Little Lady '66
Casino Royale '06
The Cincinnati Kid '65
Cowboy '58►
Destry Rides Again '39►
Finder's Fee '01
The Gambler Returns: The Luck of the Draw '93
Half a Lifetime '86
Havana '90
Hit Me '96
Honeymoon in Vegas '92
House of Games '87►
It Happened at the World's Fair '63
Kenny Rogers as the Gambler '80
Kenny Rogers as the Gambler, Part 2: The Adventure Continues '83
Kenny Rogers as the Gambler, Part 3: The Legend Continues '87
The Killing of a Chinese Bookie '76
Knock Outs '92
Lucky You '07
Maverick '94
Mr. Mom '83►
The Music of Chance '93
Ocean's Eleven '01►
Poker Alice '87
Red Shoe Diaries: Strip Poker '96
Rounders '98►
Ruggles of Red Gap '35►
Shade '03
Sheriff of Tombstone '41
The Showdown '40
Sink or Swim '97
Smart Money '31
The Stranger from Pecos '45
Thursday's Game '74►
Warda Nevada '79
Wild Bill '95

Police Detectives

Abandon '02
Above the Law '88
Abduction of St. Anne '75
All-American Murder '91
Along Came a Spider '01
Angel of Death '02
Angels Don't Sleep Here '00
Another Stakeout '93
B.A.D. Cats '80
Batman Begins '05►
Beautiful Creatures '00
Because of the Cats '74
Below the Deadline '29
Between Your Legs '99
Big Brown Eyes '36
The Black Belly of the Tarantula '71
Black Widow '54
Blackmail '29►
Blink '93
Bloodbath '98
Bloody Avenger '80
Bloody Proof '99►
Blossoms on Broadway '37
Borderline '02►
Bound by Lies '05
The Box '07
The Brave One '07
Brother's Keeper '02
Bubble '05►
A Bullet for Joey '55
Bullitt '68►
Butterfly Collectors '99
Carrie '02
Cat and Mouse '78►
Catherine's Grove '98
Catwoman '04
Chain of Fools '00
Charlie Chan at Treasure Island '39
Charlie Chan in Honolulu '38
Columbo: Prescription Murder '67►
Columbo: Murder by the Book '71
Cookie's Fortune '99►
Cover '28
Coyote Waits '03
Crash '05►
Crime Wave '54
Criminals Within '41
Crimson Rivers 2: Angels of the Apocalypse '05
Curse of the Pink Panther '83
Cyberstalker '96
The Dancer Upstairs '02►
Darkwolf '03
Dead Connection '94
Dead in a Heartbeat '02
Dead Sexy '01
Dead Silence '01
Death from a Distance '36
The Detective '68►
Detective '85
Detective Story '51►
Diamond Run '00
Dick Tracy '37
Dick Tracy '90►
Dick Tracy, Detective '45
Dick Tracy Meets Gruesome '47
Dick Tracy Returns '38
Dick Tracy: The Spider Strikes '37►
Dick Tracy vs. Cueball '46
Dick Tracy's Dilemma '47
Dick Tracy vs. Crime Inc. '41
Dogwatch '97
Dot.Kill '05
Double Vision '02
Double Whammy '01
Dragnet '54
Dragnet '87
Edge of Darkness '86
The Element of Crime '84
The Enforcer '76
Escape Clause '96
Eternal '04
Fall Guy '47
Fallen Angel '99
Falling Down '93►
Fear X '03►
Feardotcom '02
15 Minutes '01
Final Move '06
Final Notice '89
The First Deadly Sin '80
Five Days '07
Follow Me Quietly '49►
The Force '94
Formula 51 '01
Foul Play '78►
Freedomland '06
The French Detective '75►
From Hell '01►
Fugitive Among Us '92
Gambler's Choice '44
Gone Baby Gone '07►
The Gore-Gore Girls '72
Green Eyes '34
Green for Danger '47►
The Guardian '00
Guardian Angel '94
The Gunman '03
Hard As Nails '01
Heat '95►
Hellraiser 5: Inferno '00
Hero Wanted '08
Hollywood Stadium Mystery '38
Home Room '02►
Hostage '05►
The House of Mystery '41
The House of the Arrow '53►
The Human Monster '39
The Hunt for Dr. Mabuse '61
The Hustle '75
In the Cut '03
In the Valley of Elah '07►
Infernal Affairs '02►
Innocent Lies '95
Insomnia '97►
Insomnia '02►
The Invisible Killer '40
Jill the Ripper '00
Just Another Pretty Face '58
K-9 '89
K-9:3: P.I. '01
K-911 '99
Karate Dog '04
Kept '01
A Killing Spring '02
Killing Emmett Young '02
Kiss the Girls '97
Kojak: The Belarus File '85
L.A. Confidential '97►
Lantana '01►
Laura '44►
Le Petit Lieutenant '05
Lies & Alibis '06
A Lizard in a Woman's Skin '71
Lonely Hearts '06
Loose Cannons '90
The Lost Angel '04
Love and Bullets '79
Magnum Force '73►
The Mad Bomber '72
The Magician '93
Mean Streak '99
Memories of Murder '03►
The Memory of a Killer '03►
Mercy '00
Midnight 2: Sex, Death, and Videotape '93
Mind Lies '00
A Mind to Murder '96
Mr. Brooks '07
Murder at 1600 '97
Murder at the Vanities '34
Murder by Numbers '02►
Murder in Greenwich '02
My New Partner '84
Mystic River '03
Mystery Street '50►
Naked City: A Killer Christmas '98
Naked City: Justice with a Bullet '98
New Orleans After Dark '58
Newman's Law '74
Nick Knight '89
Night School '81
Night Stalker '87
Nightwatch '96►
No Way to Treat a Lady '68►
No One Sleeps '01
Nocturne '46
November '05►
Number One with a Bullet '87
On Dangerous Ground '51►
One Good Cop '91
One Missed Call '08
One Night at McCool's '01
Open Cam '05
Operation Julie '85
The Organization '71►
Out of the Darkness '85►
Out of the Shadows '88
Out of Time '03
Partners in Crime '99
P.D. James: Death in Holy Orders '03
The Phantom Light '35
The Phantom of Soho '64
Phone Booth '02►
The Pink Panther '06
Play Nice '92
Postmark for Danger '56
Practical Magic '98
The Presidio '88
Prettykill '87
Private Hell 36 '54
The Prophet's Game '99
Relentless '89
Relentless 2: Dead On '91
Relentless 3 '93
Relentless 4 '94
The Return of Dr. Mabuse '61
Resurrection '99
Revenge Quest '96
Ricochet '91►
Ring of Death '69
The River King '05
Rough Cut '80
Rush Hour 3 '07
Sanctimony '01
Sapphire '59►
Saw II '05
Scotland, PA '02
Sea of Love '89►
Second Sight '99►
Seduced: Pretty When You Cry '01
Seeds of Doubt '96
Seven '95►
The Seven-Ups '73
Shadows of the Orient '37
Showtime '02
Silk '86
Sin City '05►
16 Blocks '05►
Skinwalker '02
Sleepless '01
Someone to Watch Over Me '87►
South Seas Massacre '74
The Spider and the Fly '49
Splinter '05
The Squeeze '77
Stakeout '87►
Station '81
Stray Dog '08
Street Kings '08
Strike a Pose '93
Suicide Club '02
Tales from the Crypt Presents Bordello of Blood '96
Tangled '01
Tension '50
That Beautiful Somewhere '06
They Call Me Mr. Tibbs! '70
The Third Key '57
Third World Cop '99
The Thomas Crown Affair '99►
Ticker '01
To Catch a Killer '92►
Touching Evil '97►
Transfixed '01
True Blue '01
True Romance '93►
Twisted '04
V for Vendetta '06►
Vampire Assassin '05
Vertigo '58►
Video Murders '87
Violated '84
Wasabi '01
What to Do in Case of Fire '02
What Your Eyes Don't See '99
When the Sky Falls '99
Who Is the Black Dahlia? '75►
Wild Things '98►
Wilder '00
Witchcraft 10: Mistress of the Craft '98
Witness '85►
World of the Depraved '67
X Marks the Spot '42
Zodiac '07►

Politics

see also Capital Capers; Presidency: Vote for Me!

Absolute Power '97►
The Act '82
All the King's Men '06►
Amazing Grace '06►
The American President '95►
An American Story '92
The Americano '17
Americathon '79
And the Band Played On '93►
Angels in America '03►
Ang Vera '78►
Animal Instincts '92
Antonio Das Mortes '68►
Archangel '05
The Art of War '00
Article 99 '92
The Assassination of Richard Nixon '05►
Attila '01
Bear Ye One Another's Burden... '88
Beggars in Ermine '34
Being There '79►
Beyond Obsession '82
Beyond Rangoon '95►
The Big Brass Ring '99
The Big Hurt '87
The Birdcage '96►
Black Jesus '68
Black Sheep '96
Blame It on Fidel '06►
Blaze '89►
Blood Money: The Story of Clinton and Nadine '88
The Blue Kite '93►
Bob Roberts '92►
Bophal '93
The Break '97
Break of Dawn '88
Bulworth '98►
Buried Alive '39
The Burning Season '94►
Burnt by the Sun '94►
Bush's Brain '04
Call Him Mr. Shatter '74
Canadian Bacon '94
The Candidate '72►
Cape of Good Hope '04
Cara's Song '97
Carry On Emmanuelle '78
Casino '95►
Caterina in the Big City '03
Chain of Command '95
Charlie Wilson's War '07
Chasing Freedom '04
Chicago 10 '07►
Children of Men '06►
Children of the Revolution '95
China Gate '57►
Citizen Cohn '92►
City Hall '96►
Clear and Present Danger '94►
Code Name: Chaos '90
The Colombian Connection '91
Colonel Effingham's Raid '45
The Comedians '67►
Complex World '92
Confessing to Laura '90
Conspiracy '89
Conspiracy: The Trial of the Chicago Eight '87►
The Contender '00►
Corporate Affairs '90
Country '84►
Country Life '95►
The Cradle Will Rock '99
crazy/beautiful '01►
CSA: The Confederate States of America '04
A Dangerous Man: Lawrence after Arabia '91►
A Day Without a Mexican '04
DC 9/11: Time of Crisis '04
Dead Center '94
The Dead Zone '02
Deadly Exposure '93
The Deal '05
Dear Wendy '05►
Death and the Maiden '94►
Death of a Bureaucrat '66►
Defense of the Realm '85►
Devil in a Blue Dress '95►
The Devils '71►
Devlin '92
The Disappearance of Garcia Lorca '96
Disraeli '29►
Disraeli '80►
The Distinguished Gentleman '92►
Don's Party '76
Double Cross '92
Double Edge '92
Down Came a Blackbird '94
Earth Entranced '66
The Edukators '04►
8-A '92
Eljianaika '81►
Elizabeth '98►
Elizabeth R '72►
Eminent Domain '91
The Emperor and the Assassin '99►
The Emperor's New Clothes '01
The Enemy Within '94
Enron: The Smartest Guys in the Room '05►
An Everlasting Piece '00►
Evita '96►

► = rated three bones or higher

Execution of Justice '99
Eye of the Stranger '93
Eyes of a Witness '94
Fahrenheit 9/11 '04▸
Faith '94
Fame Is the Spur '47
The Farmer's Daughter '47▸
Fatwa '06
Fever Mounts at El Pao 59
Fidel '02▸
The Final Cut '95▸
The Final Days '89
Fires Within '91
First Daughter '04
First Family '80
First Monday in October '81
A Flash of Green '85
The Fog of War: Eleven Lessons from the Life of Robert S. McNamara '03▸
A Foreign Affair 48▸
Foreplay '75
Four Days in September '97
The French Detective '75▸
The French Woman '79
Friday Foster '75
Friends '88
Gabriel Over the White House '33▸
Gangs of New York '02▸
George Wallace '97
Germany in Autumn '78
G.I. Jane '97
The Girl in the Cafe '05
A Girl on Her Own '76
Giuliani Time '05
Gladiator '00▸
Going Upriver: The Long War of John Kerry '04
A Good Man in Africa '94
Good Night, and Good Luck '05▸
The Gorgeous Hussy 36
The Great Man's Lady '42
The Great McGinty '40▸
The Great Water '04
Guilty by Suspicion '91
Hangar 18 '80
Hijacking Catastrophe: 9/11, Fear and the Selling of America '04
Hombres Armados '97▸
The Home and the World '84▸
Hoodlum Empire '52
Hostages '93
Hour of the Assassin '86
House of Cards '90▸
The House of the Spirits '93
How to Frame a Figg '71
The Hunting of the President '04
An Inconvenient Truth '06▸
Indochine '92▸
The Interpreter '05▸
Jack Higgins' On Dangerous Ground '95
Jack Higgins' The Windsor Protocol '97
Jackie, Ethel, Joan: The Kennedy Women '01
Jefferson in Paris '94
In the Lake of the Woods 96
In the Line of Duty: Ambush in Waco '93
In the Line of Fire '93▸
In the Name of the Father '93▸
JFK '91▸
John and the Missus '87
A Joke of Destiny, Lying in Wait Around the Corner Like a Bandit '84
Journeys with George '02
Just Like Weather '86▸
Kansas City '95▸
The Keeper: The Legend of Omar Khayyam '05
Killer Image '92
The Killing Beach '92
The Killing Device '92
Kingfish: A Story of Huey P. Long '95

Kissinger and Nixon '96
Knife in the Head '78
Knocks at My Door '93
Kundun '97▸
Kurt Vonnegut's Harrison Bergeron '95
Lamerica '95▸
Land and Freedom '95▸
Land of the Blind '06
Land of the Free 98
Larks on a String 68▸
The Last Supper '96
Laurel & Hardy: Chickens Come Home '31
Le Complot '73▸
Les Miserables '97▸
The Life and Assassination of the Kingfish 76
A Lion Is in the Streets 53▸
Lions for Lambs '07
A Little Bit of Soul '97
The Little Drummer Girl '84▸
Little Mother '71
Lone Star Kid '88
Looking for Comedy in the Muslim World '06
The Lost City '05
Louisiana Purchase '41
Love Actually '03▸
Love Letters '99▸
Lumumba '01▸
M. Butterfly '93
Magnificent Doll '46
Malevolence '95
The Man Who Shot Liberty Valance 62▸
The Manchurian Candidate '62▸
The Manchurian Candidate '04▸
Mandela '87▸
Mandela and de Klerk '97
Manderlay '05
Marianne and Juliane '82▸
Marilyn & Bobby: Her Final Affair '94
Maryam '00
Mastergate '92▸
The Matchmaker '97
The Mating Game 59▸
Max '02
Mayerling '68
Medium Cool '69▸
Meet Wally Sparks '97
Meeting Venus '91
Michael Collins '96▸
The Milky Way '69
Mission of Justice '92
Mr. Smith Goes to Washington '39▸
Mosley '92▸
Mountbatten: The Last Viceroy '86
My Brother's War '97
My Little Assassin '99
My Universities '40▸
The November Men '93
Naked Obsession '91
National Lampoon's Senior Trip 95
Nick of Time '95
Nightbreaker '89▸
Nixon '95▸
No '98
No End in Sight '07▸
No Witness '04
Noriega: God's Favorite '00
Northern Extremes '93
Nurse Marjorie '20
Of Love and Shadows '94
The Omen '06
Open Doors 89▸
Orwell Rolls in His Grave '03
Our Brand Is Crisis '05▸
Outfoxed: Rupert Murdoch's War on Journalism '04▸
Palombella Rossa 89
Paradise Now '05▸
Peace, Propaganda & the Promised Land '04
The Pelican Brief '93
People I Know '02
The Perez Family '94
Pizza Man '91
A Place in the World '92▸
Poldark '96

The Possessed '88
Presumed Innocent '90▸
Primary Colors '98
Primary Motive '92
The Promise '94
Purple Butterfly '03▸
The Queen '06▸
Quiet Fire '91
Rage of Angels: The Story Continues 86
Rain Without Thunder '93
Red Hot 95
Red Kiss '85▸
Rendition '07
Report to the Commissioner '74▸
Rhodes 97
Richard III '12
Richard III '95▸
Robert Kennedy and His Times '90
Ronnie and Julie '97
Rosa Luxemburg '86
Running Mates '86▸
Running Mates '92▸
Running Mates '00
St. Michael Had a Rooster 72▸
Salt of the Earth '54▸
Samaritan: The Mitch Snyder Story '86▸
The Sea Inside '04▸
The Second Civil War '97
The Secret '93
Seduced '85
The Seduction of Joe Tynan 79
The '70s '00
The Shadow Conspiracy '96
The Silence of Neto 94
Silver City '04
Some Mother's Son '06
Sophie Scholl: The Final Days '05▸
Spartan '04▸
Speak Up! It's So Dark '93
Special Police '85
Speechless '94
Stalin 92
Star Wars: Episode 3—Revenge of the Sith '05▸
State of Play '03▸
State of the Union '48▸
The State Within '06
Stop-Loss '08▸
Storyville '92
Strange Justice: The Clarence Thomas and Anita Hill Story '99
Strawberry and Chocolate '93▸
Striptease '96
Superfly T.N.T. '73
Supreme Sanction '99
Syriana '05▸
Tanner '88 '88▸
Tanner on Tanner '04
Taxi Blues '90▸
Temptation of a Monk 05
This Revolution '05
Three Cases of Murder '55▸
Timecop '94
Tito and Me '92▸
To Live '94▸
To Play the King '93▸
The Travelling Players '75
Trial by Media '00
Truman '95
The Tunnel '01▸
Two Deaths '94
Typhoon '06
Uncovered: The War on Iraq '04
Under Western Stars '38
An Unforgettable Summer '94
The U.S. Vs. John Lennon '06
Unnatural Causes '86▸
Up at the Villa '00
Up in Central Park '48
The Uppercrust 81
V for Vendetta '06▸
The Vector File '03
The Veteran '06
A Very British Coup '88▸
Viva Villa! '34▸
Viva Zapata! '52▸

Wag the Dog 97▸
Wall '04▸
The War Room '93▸
Washington Mistress '81
Wedding Wars '06
Welcome to Mooseport '04
Werewolf of Washington '73
Who Killed the Electric Car? '06
Wild in the Streets '68
Wild Reeds '94▸
The Wind That Shakes the Barley '06▸
Windhorse '98
A Woman Named Jackie '91
The Worker and the Hairdresser '96
World War II: When Lions Roared '94
XXX: State of the Union '05
The Yes Men '03
Zero Population Growth 72

Pool

see also Gambling

Albino Alligator '96
The American President '95▸
The Baltimore Bullet '80
The Baron and the Kid '84
The Color of Money '86▸
The Hustler '61▸
Kiss Shot '89
The Last Time I Committed Suicide '96
The Music Man '62▸
Pool Hustlers '83
Poolhall Junkies '02
Stickmen '01
Think Tank '06
Up Against the Eight Ball '04

Pornography

see also Sex & Sexuality; Sexploitation

Amateur '94▸
Auto Focus '02▸
Beyond Justice '01
Body Double '84▸
Boogie Nights '97▸
Come as You Are '05
Defenseless '91
Demonlover '02
Dirty Pictures '00
8mm '98
Every Mother's Worst Fear '98
Fallen Angel '81
The Fluffer '01
Frisk '95
Gentlemen's Relish '01
The Girl Next Door '04
The Glitter Dome '84
The Guru '02
Hardcore '79
Heavy Traffic '73▸
Hi, Mom! '70▸
Hollywood Vice Squad '86
Inserts '76
Inside Deep Throat '05▸
It's Called Murder, Baby '82
Kamikaze Hearts '91
Kidnapped '87
Knocked Up '07
The Last Porno Flick 74
The Love God? '70
The Love ... 73
M'Lady's Court 73
The Moguls '05
Of Freaks and Men '98
Orgazmo '98
The People vs. Larry Flynt '96▸

Portland (Oregon, not Maine)

Bigger Than the Sky '05
Body of Evidence '92
Brain Smasher... A Love Story '93
Drugstore Cowboy '89▸
Elephant '03▸
Feast of Love '07
The Hunted '03
Magnificent Obsession '54
Mr. Brooks '07
My Own Private Idaho '91▸
Paranoid Park '07
Saving Sarah Cain '07
Spiral '07
Untraceable '08
Zero Effect '97

Post-Apocalypse

see also Negative Utopia; Technology—Rampant

A. I.: Artificial Intelligence '01
After the Fall of New York '85
Aftermath '85
Amazon Warrior '97
Armageddon: The Final Challenge '94
Babylon AD '08
Battle for the Planet of the Apes '73
Battle Queen 2020 '99
Beneath the Planet of the Apes '70
The Blood of Heroes '89
Bounty Hunter 2002 '94
A Boy and His Dog 75
Bridge of Dragons '99
Chained Heat 3: Hell Mountain '98
Circuitry Man '90
City Limits '85
Class of 1999 '90
Cold Harvest '98
Crash and Burn '90
The Creation of the Humanoids 62
Crime Zone 88
Cyborg '89
Damnation Alley '77
Day of the Dead '85
Day the World Ended '55
Daybreak 93
Dead Man Walking '88
Deadly Reactor '89
Def-Con 4 '85
Doom Runners '97
Doomsday '08
Double Dragon '94
Dragon Fury '95
Driving Force '88
Dune Warriors '91
The Element of Crime '84
Endgame '85
Equalizer 2000 '86
Equilibrium '02
Escape from Safehaven '88
Exterminators in the Year 3000 '83
The Final Executioner '83
Final Sanction '89
Firefight '87
First Spaceship on Venus '60▸
Fortress of Amerikka '89
Future Hunters '88
Future Kill '85
Glen and Randa '71
The Handmaid's Tale '90
Hardware '90
Hell Comes to Frogtown '88
Hey, Happy! '01
Hybrid '97
I Am Legend '07▸
In the Aftermath: Angels Never Sleep '87
Interzone '88
Judge Dredd '95
Karate Cop '91
Knights '93
Land of Doom '86
The Last Man '84
The Last Man on Earth '64
The Lawless Land '88

Le Dernier Combat '84▸
Lord of the Flies 63▸
Mad Max '80▸
Mad Max: Beyond Thunderdome '85
A Man Called Rage '84
Maniac Warriors '88
The Matrix '99▸
The Matrix Reloaded '03
The Matrix Revolutions '03▸
Nautilus '99
Nemesis '93
Neon City '91
Night of the Comet '84
1990: The Bronx Warriors '83
The Noah 75
Omega Cop '90
Omega Doom '96
Omega Man '71
On the Beach 59▸
On the Beach '00
Osa '85
Panic in the Year Zerol '62
People Who Own the Dark 75
Phoenix the Warrior '88
Planet Earth '74
Planet of the Apes '68▸
Plughead Rewired: Circuitry Man 2 '94
The Postman '97
Prayer of the Rollerboys '91
Prison Planet '92
Pulse 01
The Quiet Earth '85▸
Quintet '79
Radioactive Dreams '86
Raiders of the Sun '92
Rats '83
Rebel Storm '90
Reign of Fire '02
Resistance '92
The Road Warrior '82▸
Robo Warriors '96
RoboCop '87▸
Robot Holocaust '87
RoGoPaG 62
Roller Blade '85
Rush 84
Screamers '96
The Seventh Sign '88
She 83
Shepherd '99
Silent Running '71▸
The Sisterhood '88
Six-String Samurai '98
The Slime People 63
Soldier '98
Southland Tales '06
Star Quest '94
Starlight '97
Steel Dawn '87
Steel Frontier '94
Stephen King's The Stand '94
Strange New World 75
Survival Zone '84
Survivor '87
Tank Girl 94
Teenage Caveman 58
Teenage Caveman '01
Terminator 2: Judgment Day '91▸
The Terror Within 2 '91
Testament '83▸
Things to Come '36▸
The Time Machine '02
Time of the Wolf '03▸
The Time Travelers '64
Time Troopers '89
Titan A.E. '00
Tooth and Nail '07
12 Monkeys '95▸
28 Days Later '02
28 Weeks Later '07▸
2020 Texas Gladiators '85
Ultra Warrior '92
Ultraviolet '06
Urban Warriors 75
Virus 82
WarCat 88
Warlords 88
Warlords of the 21st Century '82
Warlords 3000 '93
Warriors of the Apocalypse '85

Postwar
see also Veterans

Act of Violence '45
Adelheid '69
All My Sons '48▶
All My Sons '86▶
An American Story '92
Americana '81
An Awfully Big Adventure '94
Back Home '90
Baltic Deputy '37▶
Behold a Pale Horse '64
Berlin Express '48▶
The Best Years of Our Lives '46▶
Bitter Rice '49▶
Black Rain '88▶
Bloody Trail '72
The Blum Affair '48
Born on the Fourth of July '89▶
Buffalo Soldiers '97▶
The Burmese Harp '56▶
The Bushwackers '52
Cabo Blanco '81
Carbide and Sorrel '63
Chattahoochee '89▶
Cinema Paradiso '88▶
Courage Under Fire '96▶
The Cruel Story of Youth '60▶
A Dangerous Man: Lawrence after Arabia '91▶
Demons in the Garden '82
Deutschland im Jahre Nr.I '47▶
Distant Thunder '88
Distant Voices, Still Lives '88▶
Dixie Lanes '88
D.P. '85
Early Summer '51▶
Eat a Bowl o' Tea '89▶
Ebony Dreams '80
Europa '51 '52
Exodus '60▶
Father '67▶
The Fighting Kentuckian '49
First Blood '82
Foolish Wives '22▶
Fools of Fortune '90
Four in a Jeep '51
Frieda '47
Gate of Flesh '64
The Good German '06
Grave of the Fireflies '88▶
Grbavica: The Land of My Dreams '06
Green Eyes '75▶
Gun Fury '53
Heroes '77
The Hi-Lo Country '98▶
Hiroshima, Mon Amour '59▶
Hiroshima: Out of the Ashes '90▶
Horizons West '52
House '85▶
I Am a Fugitive from a Chain Gang '32▶
I Don't Give a Dam! '88
In a Glass Cage '86
The Indian Runner '91
The Innocent '93
Inside Out '75
Isn't Life Wonderful '24▶
It Happened in New Orleans '36
Jacob's Ladder '90
Judgment at Nuremberg '61▶
The Last Time I Saw Paris '54
Le Dernier Combat '84◀
The Left Hand of God '55▶
Les Rendez-vous D'Anna '78
Lilies of the Field '63▶
The Limping Man '53
Love Is a Many-Splendored Thing '55
Love Nest '51
MacArthur's Children '85◀
The Man in the Glass Booth '75▶
Man of Marble '76▶
The Man Who Broke 1,000 Chains '87
Manor '50
Maria's Day '84◀
Maria's Lovers '84
The Marriage of Maria Braun '79◀
Master Race '44
Max '02
Mine Own Executioner '47▶
The Miniver Story '50
Miss Rose White '92▶
Mrs. Dalloway '97
A Month in the Country '87▶
Mother '52
Mother Night '96▶
The Murderers Are Among Us '46
The Odessa File '74
Ore Wonderful Sunday '47
Panique '47
Photographing Fairies '97
Plenty '85
A Private Function '84
QB VII '74◀
Quality Street '37
Rambo: First Blood, Part 2 '85
Random Harvest '42▶
The Razor's Edge '46▶
Rendez-vous de Juillet '49
Reunion '88▶
Rich Man, Poor Man '76▶
Rio Conchos '64▶
Robin Hood of the Pecos '41
The Rose Garden '89
Savage Dawn '84
The Search '48▶
A Self-Made Hero '95▶
Seraphin Falls '06
Sergeant Ryker '68
Shoeshine '47▶
Something for Everyone '70
Sommersby '93
Sophie's Choice '82▶
Souvenir '88
Strategic Air Command '55
The Subject Was Roses '68▶
Sunshine '99▶
Taking Sides '01▶
The Teahouse of the August Moon '56
The Texans '38
They Made Me a Fugitive '47
The Third Man '49▶
Three Comrades '38▶
Till the End of Time '46
Time of Indifference '64
Torpedo Alley '53
Trained to Kill, U.S.A. '75
The Truce '96◀
Uranus '91▶
Verboten! '59
Vietnam, Texas '90
A Walk in the Clouds '95
We All Loved Each Other So Much '77◀
Who'll Stop the Rain? '78◀
Wish You Were Here '87▶
Wolf Lake '79
Women in Prison '49
The Yakuza '75
Year of the Quiet Sun '84◀
Zentropa '92

POW/MIA
see also War, General; World War II

Against the Wind '48
All My Sons '86◀
American Commandos '84
The Andersonville Trial '70◀
Andersonville '95▶
Another Time, Another Place '83▶
The Ascent '94
Au Revoir les Enfants '87▶
Ay, Carmela! '90◀
Bat 21 '88
The Beast '88
Blockhouse '73
Bomb at 10:10 '67
The Boxer and Death '63▶
Brady's Escape '84
Brainwashed '60
The Bridge on the River Kwai '57▶
The Brylcream Boys '96
Bye Bye Blues '89
Captive Heart '47▶
Captive Hearts '87
Charlie Bravo '80
The Clay Pigeon '49
Codename: Terminate '90
Come See the Paradise '90▶
Cornered '45▶
Crossfire '89
Devils on the Doorstep '00
Dirty Heroes '71
The Dunera Boys '85▶
The Elusive Corporal '62▶
Empire of the Sun '87▶
Era Notte a Roma '60▶
Escape '90
Escape from Fort Bravo '53
Escape from Sobibor '87▶
Escape to Athena '79
15 Amore '98
Fighting Mad '77
The Forgotten '89
Generale Della Rovere '50▶
Grand Illusion '37▶
The Great Escape '63▶
The Great Escape 2: The Untold Story '88
The Great Raid '05
The Hand '60
Hanoi Hilton '87
Hart's War '02
Hell to Eternity '60
Heroes in Hell '73
Homecoming '28▶
The Human Condition: A Soldier's Prayer '61◀
Hunted '88
In Enemy Hands '04
In Gold We Trust '91
In Love and War '01
The Incident '89◀
The Iron Triangle '89
Jenny's War '85
King Rat '65▶
A Love in Germany '84
McKenzie Break '70◀
Merry Christmas, Mr. Lawrence '83
Mine Own Executioner '47◀
Missing in Action '84
Nam Angels '88
Night Wars '88
Objective, Burma! '45▶
On Wings of Eagles '86
One That Got Away '57◀
Operation 'Nam '85
Operation Warzone '89
Pacific Inferno '85
Paradise Road '97
Porridge '91
The P.O.W. Escape '86
Prisoners of the Sun '91◀
The Purple Heart '44
Raiders of Leyte Gulf '63
Rescue Dawn '06
The Road to Guantanamo '06
Rolling Thunder '77
St. Ives '98
Seven Years in Tibet '97
The Seventh Cross '44▶
Some Kind of Hero '82
Stalag 17 '53▶
Stalag Luft '93
The Summer of My German Soldier '78▶
Three Came Home '50▶
Three Wishes '95
To End All Wars '01
Victory '81
Von Ryan's Express '65▶
When Hell Was in Session '82
Women of Valor '86
Wooden Horse '50▶

Pregnant Men

Enemy Mine '85
Junior '94
Rabbit Test '78
A Slightly Pregnant Man '79

Pregnant Pauses
see also Bringing Up Baby

Alien³ '92
All About My Mother '99◀
Almost Pregnant '91
Alternative '76
Angel Baby '95◀
Angel Rodriguez '05
Angie '94
Are We Done Yet? '07
Armistead Maupin's More Tales of the City '97
The Astronaut's Wife '99
Baby '00
Baby of the Bride '91
The Baby Dance '98◀
The Baby Maker '70
Baby Mama '08
Babyfever '94
Barbershop '02◀
Barbershop 2 '04
Beautiful People '99
Bed and Board '70◀
Bellyfruit '99
Beloved/Friend '99
Between Heaven and Earth '93
Billy: Portrait of a Street Kid '77
Black Irish '07
Bleeding Hearts '94
Boys on the Side '94
Brand New Life '72
Brink of Life '57
The Brothers Solomon '07
Butterfly Wings '91
Café au Lait '94◀
Café Lumiere '05
Caged '07
Cast the First Stone '89
Catherine Cookson's The Dwelling Place '94
Catherine Cookson's The Round Tower '98
Catherine Cookson's The Wingless Bird '97
Cheyenne Warrior '94
Child of Darkness, Child of Light '91
Children of Men '06◀
Choices '86
Chutney Popcorn '99
The Circle '00
Citizen Ruth '96
Cocktail '88
Coming Out '89
Conceiving Ada '97
The Confessional '95◀
Confusion of Genders '00
The Cooler '03◀
The Corner '03▶
The Crime of Father Amaro '02▶
Crossroads '02
Dancing at the Blue Iguana '00
Danielle Steel's Heartbeat '93
Dawn of the Dead '04◀
Demon Seed '77◀
Divided We Fall '00◀
Down, Out and Dangerous '95
Due East '02
Earth & Water '99
Earthly Possessions '99
Eraserhead '78◀
Escape from the Planet of the Apes '71◀
Everything Put Together '00
The Evil Within '89
Falling for a Dancer '98
False Prophets '06
Fargo '96◀
Father of the Bride Part 2 '95
Father's Little Dividend '51◀
Felicia's Journey '99◀
Flickers '80
Fools Rush In '97
Friends '71
Generation '69
The Good Girl '02▶
Good Luck Chuck '07
The Heart of Me '02
Heartburn '86▶
Hell Comes to Frogtown '88
Help Wanted: Male '82
Hide and Seek '00
Home Fries '98
How to Deal '03
Hush '98
I Married a Dead Man '96
If These Walls Could Talk '96
Immediate Family '89
Interlocked '02▶
The Invader '96
Invasion of Privacy '96
Jailbait '00
Julier Donkey-boy '99
Juno '07▶
Just Another Girl on the I.R.T. '93
Kill the Poor '06
A Kind of Loving '62▶
Knocked Up '07
The L-Shaped Room '62▶
La Buche '99
Labor Pains '09
Lars and the Real Girl '07▶
The Last Kiss '01
The Last Kiss '06
Le Cas du Dr. Laurent '57▶
Le Divorce '03
Let's Get Married '60
Lethal Weapon 4 '98
Levitation '97
Lift '01
Lily Was Here '89
Look Both Ways '05
Love Child '82◀
Love for Rent '05
Luc e Aubrac '99
Makin' Baby '02
Manny & Lo '96▶
Margot at the Wedding '07
Maria Full of Grace '04▶
The Marquise of O '76◀
The Match Factory Girl '90◀
Maternal Instincts '96
Maybe Baby '99
Maybe, Maybe Not '94
Maze '01
Me You Them '00
The Miracle '48◀
Mischegotten '98
Mists of Avalon '01▶
A Modern Affair '94
Mom & Dad '47
Morning Glory '93
My Baby's Daddy '04
My Blue Heaven '50
My Foolish Heart '49
My Life '93
My Little Assassin '99
My Wife is an Actress '01◀
The Nativity Story '06
Nenette and Boni '96◀
The New Eve '98◀
Nickel Mountain '85
Nine Lives '05◀
Nine Months '95
No Alibi '00
No Laughing Matter '97
North Shore Fish '97
Now and Then '95
The Object of My Affection '98
On the Outs '05
101 Dalmatians '96
One Last Ride '03
101 Reykjavik '00
The Opposite of Sex '98
Our Song '01▶
Our Time '74◀
Outrageous! '77▶
Palindromes '04◀
Parenthood '89◀
Paternity '81
Personal Velocity: Three Portraits '02▶
Pilgrimage '33
Polish Wedding '97
Progeny '98
Promises! Promises! '63
The Prophecy 2: Ashtown '97
Pure '02▶
Quinceanera '06▶
Rendition '07
Riding in Cars with Boys '01▶
Robin Hood: Prince of Thieves '91▶
Rosemary's Baby '68▶
Runaway Daughters '94
A Saintly Switch '99
The Santa Clause 3: The Escape Clause '06
Saturday Night and Sunday Morning '60▶
Saved! '04
Savior '98◀
Seducing Maarya '99
Seed of Chucky '04
Series 7: The Contenders '01
The Seventh Sign '88
Sex and the City: The Movie '08
Shadowboxer '06
She's Having a Baby '88
Shrek the Third '07
A Single Girl '96
Skipped Parts '00
Sliding Doors '97
A Smile Like Yours '96
Solomon and Gaenor '98
Soul's Midnight '06
Spice World: The Movie '97
Splendor '99
Star Wars: Episode 3—Revenge of the Sith '05◀
Steel Magnolias '89◀
Stephanie Daley '06
The Stranger Within '74
Sugar & Spice '01▶
Sweet Evil '95
Talk to Her '02▶
A Taste of Honey '61▶
Tenth Month '79
The Terminator '84◀
Tess of the Storm Country '22
3 Women '77▶
Time and Tide '00
Tiptoes '03
Tomorrow '72▶
Turn It Up '00
The 24 Hour Woman '99
The Twilight of the Gods '97
Two Family House '99
Twogether '94
The Unborn '91
The Unearthing '93
An Unexpected Life '97
Under the Skin '97
Under the Tuscan Sun '03
The Very Edge '63
Vernie '06
Waiting Up in Reno '02
Waitress '07▶
A Walk in the Clouds '95
The Way of the Gun '00
A Weekend in the Country '96
Wedding Bell Blues '96
What Planet Are You From? '00
Where the Heart Is '00

▶ = rated three bones or higher

William Faulkner's Old Man '97
Winter Flight '84
Woman Wanted '98
Wonder Boys '00▶
Wrestling with Alligators '98
Year Zero '04
You'll Like My Mother '72
The Young Pioneers '76
Yours, Mine & Ours '68
You've Ruined Me, Eddie '58
Zero Population Growth '72

Prep School
*see also Hell High
School; Teen Angst*
Agent Cody Banks '03
Brotherhood 2: The Young
 Warlocks '01
Chasing Holden '01
The Covenant '06
CryWolf '05
Dead Poets Society '89▶
The Emperor's Club '02
The Fraternity '01
Harry Potter and the
 Chamber of Secrets '02▶
Harry Potter and the Goblet
 of Fire '05▶
Harry Potter and the Order
 of the Phoenix '07
Harry Potter and the
 Sorcerer's Stone '01▶
The History Boys '06
If.... '69▶
Lost and Delirious '01
Making the Grade '84
Murderous Intent '06▶
Notes on a Scandal '06▶
O '01▶
Outside Providence '99
The River King '05
Scent of a Woman '92▶
School Ties '92
A Separate Peace '04
She's the Man '06
The Smokers '00
Tadpole '02
Tart '01
Underclassman '05
Whirlygirl '04
Wild Child '08
The Woods '03

Presidency
*see also Camelot (New);
Politics*
Abe Lincoln in Illinois '40▶
Absolute Power '97
Advise and Consent '62▶
Agent of Death '99
Air Force One '97▶
All the President's Men '76▶
American Dreamz '06
The American President
 '95▶
Amistad '97▶
Assassination '87
The Assassination File '96
The Assassination of
 Richard Nixon '05
Backstairs at the White
 House '79▶
The Best Man '64▶
Black Sunday '77
Chasing Liberty '04
Dave '93▶
The Day Reagan Was Shot
 '01
DC 9/11: Time of Crisis '04
Deep Impact '98
Deterrence '00
Dick '99▶
Dirty Tricks '81
Dr. Dolittle 4: Tail to the
 Chief '08
Eleanor & Franklin '76▶
Eleanor: First Lady of the
 World '82
Elvis Meets Nixon '98
The Enemy Within '94
Escape from New York '81▶
Executive Action '73
Executive Target '97
Fahrenheit 9/11 '04▶
Fail Safe '00

The Final Days '89
First Daughter '99
First Family '80
First Kid '96
For the Love of Mary '48
Foreplay '75
Forrest Gump '94▶
Gabriel Over the White
 House '33▶
Gore Vidal's Lincoln '88
Guarding Tess '94
Hail '73
Hitman '07
The Hunting of the
 President '04
Imagemaker '86
In the Line of Fire '93▶
Independence Day '96▶
Jefferson in Paris '94
JFK '91▶
The JFK Conspiracy '91
John Adams '08
Journeys with George '02
Kennedy '83
The Kennedys of
 Massachusetts '95
The Kidnapping of the
 President '80
Kisses for My President '64
Kissinger and Nixon '96
The Last Bastion '84
LBJ: A Biography '91
LBJ: The Early Years '88▶
Magnificent Doll '46
Mail to the Chief '00
Man of the Year '06▶
Mars Attacks! '96
Meteor '79
Missiles of October '74▶
Murder at 1600 '97
My Date with the President's
 Daughter '98
My Fellow Americans '96
My Uncle: The Alien '96
Nixon '95▶
Path to War '02
The Pooch and the Pauper
 '99
Power and Beauty '02
The President's Analyst '67▶
President's Mistress '78
The President's Plane Is
 Missing '71
Primary Colors '98
Prince Jack '83
The Rat Pack '98
The Reagans '04
RFK '02
Ruby '92
Sadat '83
Sally Hemings: An
 American Scandal '00
The Second Civil War '97
Secret Honor '85▶
The Sentinel '06
The Shadow Conspiracy '96
Suddenly '54▶
The Sum of All Fears '02
Sunrise at Campobello '60▶
Swing Vote '08
Thirteen Days '00▶
Truman '95▶
The Undercover Kid '95
Vantage Point '08
The War Room '93▶
Wild in the Streets '68
Wilson '44▶
Winter Kills '79▶
XXX: State of the Union '05
Young Mr. Lincoln '39▶

Price of Fame
see also Rags to Riches
Abraham Lincoln '30
All About Eve '50▶
All That Jazz '79▶
American Blue Note '89
At Any Cost '00
The Bad and the Beautiful
 '52▶
Bank Robber '93
Bert Rigby, You're a Fool
 '89
Beyond the Valley of the
 Dolls '70
The Big Knife '55▶
Black Starlet '74

The Bodyguard '92
The Buddy Holly Story '78▶
By the Sword '93
Byron '03
Call Me: The Rise and Fall
 of Heidi Fleiss '04
Cassie '83
Champion '49▶
A Chorus Line '85
Citizen Kane '41▶
Coal Miner's Daughter '80▶
Comeback '83
The Comic '69▶
The Commitments '91▶
Control '07
The Cotton Club '84▶
Country Girl '82
Covergirl '83
Crossover Dreams '85
Darling '65▶
Dead Ringers '88▶
Dreamgirls '06▶
Echo Park '86
Eddie and the Cruisers '83
Eddie and the Cruisers 2:
 Eddie Lives! '89
Edie in Ciao! Manhattan '72
EDtv '99
Elmer Gantry '60▶
Elvis and Me '88
Elvis: The Movie '79
Eureka! '81
Extra Girl '23
Factory Girl '06
Fame '80▶
The Fan '81
Feel the Noise '07
Fellow Traveler '89▶
The Five Heartbeats '91▶
Flashdance '83
Frances '82▶
Gemini Affair '74
The Gene Krupa Story '59
The Goddess '58▶
Goodbye, Norma Jean '75
Goodnight, Sweet Marilyn
 '89
Gore Vidal's Lincoln '88
Grosse Fatigue '94▶
The Gunfighter '50▶
Hail Caesar '94
A Hard Day's Night '64▶
Hard Part Begins '73
Harvest Melody '43
Hero at Large '80
Hollywood Heartbreak '89
I Ought to Be in Pictures '82
Idolmaker '80
I'll Cry Tomorrow '55▶
I'm Not There '07▶
Imitation of Life '34
Imitation of Life '59▶
Inside Daisy Clover '65
Irreconcilable Differences
 '84
It Could Happen to You '94
It Should Happen to You
 '54▶
The Jacksons: An American
 Dream '92
Jacqueline Bouvier
 Kennedy '81
James Dean '76
The Jayne Mansfield Story
 '80
The Jazz Singer '80
Jimmy Hollywood '94
Jo Jo Dancer, Your Life Is
 Calling '86
John & Yoko: A Love Story
 '85
Keep Punching '39
King of Comedy '82▶
La Bamba '87▶
La Dolce Vita '60▶
Lady Grey '82
Lady Jane '85▶
Lady Sings the Blues '72▶
The Lady Without Camelias
 '53
Lenny '74▶
Let It Rock '86
Little Caesar '30▶
The Lonely Lady '83
Lords of Dogtown '05
Love Me or Leave Me '55▶

Lucy and Desi: Before the
 Laughter '91
The Magnificent Ambersons
 '42▶
The Magnificent Ambersons
 '02
Mahogany '75
The Main Event '79
Man in the Mirror: The
 Michael Jackson Story '04
The Man Who Would Be
 King '75▶
Marilyn: The Untold Story
 '80▶
Meat Loaf: To Hell and Back
 '00
Mephisto '81▶
Miss All-American Beauty
 '82
Mistress '91
Mommie Dearest '81
Music & Lyrics '07
My Fair Lady '64▶
My Favorite Year '82▶
Naked in New York '93
Oh, God! You Devil '84
The One and Only '78
One Trick Pony '80
The Oscar '66
Payday '73
Pecker '98
A Perfect Day '06
Police Court '32
Postcards from the Edge
 '90▶
Prisoner of Rio '89
Provincial Actors '79
Pure Country '92
Purple Rain '84
The Queen of Mean '90
Raging Bull '80▶
Ransom '96▶
Rocky '76▶
Rocky 2 '79
Rocky 3 '82
Rocky 4 '85
Rocky 5 '90
The Rose '79▶
Scarlet Diva '00
The Seduction '82
Shadow of China '91
Shakes the Clown '92
Shop Angel '32
Show People '28▶
Sins '85
Small Town Boy '37
Smash-Up: The Story of a
 Woman '47▶
Smithereens '82
S.O.B. '81
Soldier in Love '67
Solo Sunny '80
Star 80 '83
A Star Is Born '37▶
A Star Is Born '54▶
Stardom '00
Stardust Memories '80▶
Stoned '05
Sunset Boulevard '50▶
Svengali '83
Sweet Dreams '85▶
Sweet Love, Bitter '67
Sweet Perfection '90
Sweethearts '38▶
The Thing Called Love '93
The Tiger Woods Story '98
True Colors '91
Tucker: The Man and His
 Dream '88▶
Twenty Dollar Star '91
Two Weeks in Another
 Town '62
Valley of the Dolls '67
Velvet Goldmine '98
A Very Private Affair '62
What Ever Happened to
 Baby Jane? '62▶
What Price Hollywood? '32▶
What's Love Got to Do with
 It? '93
While the City Sleeps '56▶
Winning '69▶
Wired '89
A Woman Named Jackie '91
You Light Up My Life '77
Ziegfeld Girl '41▶

Princes/Princesses
*see Royalty; Royalty,
British; Royalty,
French; Royalty,
Russian*

Prison
*see Alcatraz; Devil's
Island; Escaped Cons;
Great Escapes; Men in
Prison; POW/MIA;
Women in Prison*

Private Eyes
Abbott and Costello Meet
 the Invisible Man '51▶
Accomplice '46
Adventures of a Private Eye
 '87
Alone in the Dark '05
Alphaville '65▶
Angel Heart '87
Anonymous Rex '04
Are You Lonesome Tonight
 '92
Arrest Bulldog Drummond
 '38
The Art of Crime '75
Asylum '97
Backstreet Justice '93
Bad Seed '00
Bedelia '46▶
Beyond Justice '01
The Big Empty '98▶
The Big Fall '96
The Big Sleep '46▶
The Big Sleep '78
Big Store '41
Black Bird '75
The Black Camel '31
The Black Doll '38
Blackout '54
Blade in Hong Kong '85
Bloodhounds 2 '96
Blue, White and Perfect '42
Bootleg '85
Brown's Requiem '98
Bulldog Drummond '29
Bulldog Drummond at Bay
 '37
Bulldog Drummond Comes
 Back '37
Bulldog Drummond
 Escapes '37
Bulldog Drummond's Bride
 '39
Bulldog Drummond's Peril
 '38
Bulldog Drummond's
 Revenge '37
Bulldog Drummond's Secret
 Police '39
Bulldog Jack '35▶
Calling Paul Temple '48
Camouflage '00
The Case of the Lucky Legs
 '35
Cast a Deadly Spell '91▶
Castle in the Desert '42
Charlie Chan and the Curse
 of the Dragon Queen '81
Charlie Chan at Monte Carlo
 '37
Charlie Chan at the Circus
 '36
Charlie Chan at the
 Olympics '37
Charlie Chan at the Opera
 '36▶
Charlie Chan at the Race
 Track '36
Charlie Chan at the Wax
 Museum '40
Charlie Chan in Egypt '35
Charlie Chan in London '34
Charlie Chan in Paris '35
Charlie Chan in Rio '41
Charlie Chan in Shanghai
 '35
Charlie Chan in the Secret
 Service '44
Charlie Chan on Broadway
 '37
Charlie Chan's Secret '35
Chinatown '74▶

The Chinese Cat '44
Clean Slate '94
Conspiracy of Terror '75
Cry Uncle '71
The Curse of the Jade
 Scorpion '01
The Dain Curse '78
Dancing with Danger '93
Dark Corner '46▶
The Dark Hour '36
Dark Side of Midnight '86
Dead Again '91▶
Dead Evidence '00
Dead Men Don't Wear Plaid
 '82▶
Dead Pigeon on Beethoven
 Street '72
Deadly Force '83
Deadly Illusion '87
Deadly Passion '85
Deadly Sins '95
Death Train '79
Deceptions 2: Edge of
 Deception '94
Detective Sadie & Son '84
Devil in a Blue Dress '95▶
The Devil's Cargo '48
Diabolique '96
The Doorbell Rang: A Nero
 Wolfe Mystery '01
The Drowning Pool '75
8mm '98
The Empty Beach '85
The End of the Affair '99▶
Entangled '93
Everybody Wins '90
Eye of the Killer '99
Face Down '97
Faceless '88
The Falcon in Hollywood '44
The Falcon in Mexico '44
The Falcon's Brother '42
False Witness '89
Farewell, My Lovely '75▶
Fearless '77
Fiction Makers '67
For Sale '98
Forbidden Games '95
Fourth Story '90▶
From Hollywood to
 Deadwood '89
Ginger '72
Girl Hunters '63
The Golden Spiders: A Nero
 Wolfe Mystery '00
Gone Baby Gone '07▶
Gotham '88▶
The Great Plane Robbery
 '40
The Gumshoe Kid '89
A Gun, a Car, a Blonde '97
Hat Box Mystery '47
Hollywood Confidential '97
Hollywoodland '06▶
House of Mystery '34
Human Desires '97
Hustle '04
I Heart Huckabees '04
I, the Jury '82
Indiscreet '98
Infamous Crimes '47
The Inner Circle '46
Intolerable Cruelty '03
The Invisible Avenger '58
The Jade Mask '45
Last Days '05
The Late Show '77▶
The Long Goodbye '73▶
The Long Kiss Goodnight
 '96
Long Time Gone '86
Looking for Kitty '04
Lord of Illusions '95
The Lost Son '98
Love at Large '89▶
Love Walked In '97

A Low Down Dirty Shame '94
Magnum P.I.: Don't Eat the Snow in Hawaii '80
The Maltese Falcon '31 ▶
The Maltese Falcon '41 ▶
The Man Who Would Not Die '75
The Man Who Wouldn't Die '42
The Man with Bogart's Face '80
Margin for Murder '81
Marlowe '69
Meet Sexton Blake '44
Meeting at Midnight '44
Michael Shayne: Private Detective '40
Midnight Limited '40
Mindstorm '01
Mirage '94
Missing Pieces '83
Mr. Moto in Danger Island '39
Mr. Moto Takes a Chance '38
Mr. Moto's Gamble '38
Mr. Moto's Last Warning '39 ▶
Mr. Wong, Detective '38
Mr. Wong in Chinatown '39
Mr. Takes a Vacation '39
Mortal Sins '90
Moonlighting '85
Murder by Death '76
Murder, My Sweet '44 ▶
Murder over New York '40
Murderous Vision '91
Murders in the Doll House '79
Mysterious Mr. Moto '38
Mystery of Mr. Wong '39
Nature's Playmates '62
The Next Big Thing '02
Night Moves '75 ▶
One of My Wives Is Missing '76
One Shoe Makes It Murder '82
Out of the Past '47 ▶
The Panther's Claw '42
Pas Tres Catholique '93
Perfect Lies '97
Peter Gunn '89
Phantom of Chinatown '40
Pier 23 '51
Poodle Springs '98
Powder Burn '96
A Prairie Home Companion '06
Radioactive Dreams '86
The Red Raven Kiss-Off '90
The Return of Boston Blackie '27
Return of Frank Cannon '80
The Right Temptation '00
Roaring City '51
Ryder P.I. '85
Satan Met a Lady '36
Satan's Harvest '65
Scalp Merchant '77
The Scarlet Clue '45
Secret Agent 00-Soul '29
Sexton Blake and the Hooded Terror '38
Shaft '71 ▶
Shaft '00 ▶
Shaft in Africa '73
Shaft's Big Score '72
Shall We Dance? '04
Shamus '73
The Shanghai Cobra '45
Sheba, Baby '75
Shock to the System '06
Silver City '04
Sin City '05
The Singing Detective '86 ▶
The Singing Detective '03
Sleepers West '41
Slow Burn '86
Small Vices: A Spenser Mystery '99
Smile, Jenny, You're Dead '74
The Soft Kill '94
South Beach '92
Speedtrap '78
Spenser: A Savage Place '94
Spenser: Ceremony '93
Spenser: Pale Kings & Princes '94
Spenser: The Judas Goat '94
Stolen Kisses '66 ▶
Story of a Love Affair '50
Strange Shadows in an Empty Room '76
Strechey Mystery '05
Sunset Grill '92
Suspicious Minds '96
Sweet Lies '88
TekWar '94
Thank you, Mr. Moto '37
There's Something about Mary '98 ▶
They All Laughed '81
Thin Air '00
Think Fast, Mr. Moto '37
Third Degree Burn '89
Third Man Out: A Donald Strechey Mystery '05
Tick Tock '00 ▶
Tony Rome '67 ▶
Trade Secrets '86
TripleCross '85
Trixie '00
Twilight '98 ▶
The Two Jakes '90
Ulterior Motives '92
Under Suspicion '92
Uneasy Terms '48
Unsuitable Job for a Woman '82
Vegas '78
V.I. Warshawski '91
Victim of Desire '94
Vortex '81
Waikiki '80
Web of Deception '71
Where's Marlowe? '98
Who Framed Roger Rabbit '88 ▶
Witch Hunt '94
Zero Effect '97

Prohibition Gangs
see also Gangs; Organized Crime; Period Piece; 1920s
Al Capone '59 ▶
City Heat '84
Corsair '31
Defenders of the Law '31
The King of the Roaring '20s: The Story of Arnold Rothstein '61
Lady Killer '33 ▶
Miller's Crossing '90 ▶
Mobsters '91
Nitti: The Enforcer '88
Once Upon a Time in America '84 ▶
Public Enemy '31 ▶
The Roaring Twenties '39 ▶
Robin and the 7 Hoods '64
The St. Valentine's Day Massacre '67 ▶
The Untouchables '87 ▶
Zvenigora '28 ▶

Prom
see also Hell High School; School Daze
Carrie '76 ▶
Carrie '02
The Club '94
Drive Me Crazy '99
Hello Mary Lou: Prom Night 2 '87 ▶
Jawbreaker '98
Never Been Kissed '99
The Night Before '88
Peggy Sue Got Married '86
Pretty in Pink '86 ▶
Prom Night '80
Prom Night '08
Prom Night 3: The Last Kiss '89
Prom Night 4: Deliver Us from Evil '91
The Rage: Carrie 2 '99
Rock, Rock, Rock '56 ▶
Saved! '04 ▶
She's All That '99
The Texas Chainsaw Massacre 4: The Next Generation '95
Trippin' '99
Urban Legends: Bloody Mary '05
Whatever It Takes '00

Propaganda
see also Paranoia; Politics
Air Force '43 ▶
Arsenal '29 ▶
The Atomic Cafe '82 ▶
Baltic Deputy '37 ▶
Behind the Rising Sun '43
The Black King '32
Blood on the Sun '45
Born American '86
Chapayev '34 ▶
China '43
The Commies Are Coming, the Commies Are Coming '57
Corregidor '43
Dangerous Hours '19
DC 9/11: Time of Crisis '04
Desperate Journey '42 ▶
The End of St. Petersburg '27 ▶
Fighting Seabees '44 ▶
The General Line '29 ▶
The Green Berets '68
Guadalcanal Diary '43
Hangmen Also Die '42 ▶
Invasion U.S.A. '52
Jud Suess '40
Mrs. Miniver '42 ▶
A Mormon Maid '17
No Greater Love '43
Passage to Marseilles '44 ▶
Que Viva Mexico '32 ▶
The Red Menace '49
Reefer Madness '38 ▶
Reunion in France '42
Rocket Attack U.S.A. '58
Shack Out on 101 '55 ▶
Strike '24 ▶
Teenage Devil Dolls '53
Ten Days That Shook the World '27 ▶
Ten Nights in a Bar-Room '31
The Thief '52
Threads '85 ▶
To the Shores of Tripoli '42
Tomorrow's Children '34
Trapped by the Mormons '22 ▶

Prostitutes
see Oldest Profession

Protests
see also Rebel With a Cause
Born on the Fourth of July '89 ▶
Forrest Gump '94 ▶
Hairspray '88 ▶
In the Name of the Father '93 ▶
The Long Walk Home '89 ▶
Malcolm X '92 ▶
Matewan '87 ▶
Michael Collins '96 ▶
Norma Rae '79 ▶
Panther '95 ▶
Red Kiss '85 ▶
Silkwood '83 ▶

Psychiatry
see Shrinks

Psychic Abilities
see also Psycho-Thriller
After Midnight '89
The Black Camel '31 ▶
Blink of an Eye '92
Carolina Moon '07
Carrie '76 ▶
Carrie '02
Close Your Eyes '02
Dark Sanity '03
Dead Zone '83 ▶
Deadtrap '82
Don't Look Now '73 ▶
Dream Man '94
Dreamscape '84 ▶
Everybody Says I'm Fine! '05
Fear '90
Final Destination '00 ▶
Firestarter '84
Firestarter 2: Rekindled '02
First Snow '07
Forbidden Games '95
Friday the 13th, Part 7: The New Blood '88
The Frighteners '96 ▶
From Hell '01 ▶
The Gift '00 ▶
Ghost '90 ▶
The Haunting '63 ▶
Hearts in Atlantis '01 ▶
Imagining Argentina '04
L.A. Dicks '98
The Legend of Hell House '73 ▶
Life Without Dick '01
Love and Human Remains '93 ▶
Mindstorm '01
Momentum '03
The Mothman Prophecies '02
Next '07
The Orphanage '07 ▶
Over Her Dead Body '08
The Psychic '68
Scanner Cop '94
Scanner Cop 2: Volkin's Revenge '94
Scanners '81 ▶
Scanners 2: The New Order '91
Scanners 3: The Takeover '92
Seance on a Wet Afternoon '64 ▶
Second Sight '89
Serenity '05 ▶
The Shining '80 ▶
The Sixth Sense '99 ▶
Stephen King's Rose Red '02
Sworn to Justice '97
Thicker than Water '99
Trancers '84 ▶
Vibes '88
Voodoo Moon '05
What Women Want '00
Winning Girls Through Psychic Mind Control '02

Psycho-Thriller
see also Mystery & Suspense
Absolute Power '97
Afraid of the Dark '92
After Darkness '85
After Midnight '89
Alligator Eyes '90
Almanac of Fall '85
Alone With Her '07
Ambition '91
Anatomy of a Psycho '61
Apartment Complex '98
Apology '86
The Arousers '70
The Art of Dying '90
The Astronaut's Wife '99
Asunder '99
Asylum '97
Asylum '05
The Attic '80
The Aura '05 ▶
Awakening of Candra '81
Baby Monitor: Sound of Fear '97
The Babysitter '80
Bad Education '04 ▶
Bad Influence '90
The Bad Seed '56 ▶
Baffled '72
Being at Home with Claude '92
Beneath '07
The Berlin Affair '85
Betrayal '74
Beware, My Lovely '52
Beyond Erotica '79
Birth '04 ▶
Bird of Prey '95
Bitter Moon '92
Bizarre '87
Black and White As Day and Night '78
Black Cadillac '03
Black Day Blue Night '95
Blacklight '98
Blackwoods '02
Bloodknot '95
Blow-Up '66 ▶
Body Chemistry 2: Voice of a Stranger '91
Bone Daddy '97
Boogeyman '05
Born for Hell '76
Bound '96 ▶
The Boys Club '96
Breach of Conduct '94
The Break '95
Breaking Point '98
The Bridesmaid '04 ▶
Bright Future '03 ▶
Brighton Strangler '45
A Brilliant Disguise '93
Brimstone & Treacle '82 ▶
By the Blood of Others '73 ▶
Call Me '88
Cape Fear '61 ▶
Cape Fear '91 ▶
Captive '97
Captivity '07
The Case of the Frightened Lady '39
Cat's Play '74
Cause for Alarm '51
Cellular '04 ▶
Circumstances Unknown '95
Civic Duty '06
The Clearing '04 ▶
Close Your Eyes '02
Closer and Closer '96
Cold Heaven '92
Cold Light of Day '95
Cold Room '84
Collateral '04 ▶
The Collector '65 ▶
The Comfort of Strangers '91 ▶
Conflict '45
The Corporate Ladder '97
The Courtyard '95
The Crew '95
Crimetime '96
Cronicas '04 ▶
The Crush '93
Cul de Sac '66 ▶
Cupid '96
Curse of the Stone Hand '64
Cyberstalker '96
Daddy's Gone A-Hunting '69 ▶
Dangerous Pursuit '89
Dangerous Touch '94
A Dark Adapted Eye '93
Dark Mirror '46 ▶
The Dark Past '49
The Dark Ride '84
Dark Waters '44
Darkroom '90
Day of Wrath '43 ▶
The Day the Sun Turned Cold '94
Dead As a Doorman '85
Dead Calm '89 ▶
Deadbolt '92
Deadly Daphne's Revenge '93
Deadly Game '82
Deadly Hero '75 ▶
Deadly Lessons '94
Deadly Sunday '82
Death Benefit '96
Deceit '05
Deceiver '97
Deconstructing Sarah '94
Depraved '05
Deranged '87
Desperate Measures '98
Desperate Prey '94
Devil in the Flesh '98
Diabolique '55 ▶
Diabolique '96
Diary of a Serial Killer '97
Disturbance '89
Disturbia '07 ▶
Dogville '03 ▶
Dolores Claiborne '94 ▶
The Donor '94
Don't Answer the Phone '80
Don't Talk to Strangers '94
Doppelganger: The Evil Within '95
Dot.Kill '05
Down, Out and Dangerous '95
Dream Lover '85
Dream Lover '93
The Drifter '88
Dynasty of Fear '72
8mm '98 ▶
Entangled '93
Every Breath '93
Evil Has a Face '96
Evil Judgment '85
The Ex '96
The Exorcist: The Beginning '04
The Experiment '01 ▶
Eye of the Beholder '99
Eye of the Storm '91
Eyes of the Beholder '92
Fabled '02
Facade '98
Facing the Enemy '00
Fair Game '89
The Fall '98
Fallen '97 ▶
Falling Down '93 ▶
The Fan '96
Fatal Attraction '87 ▶
A Fatal Inversion '92
Fatally Yours '95
Fear '46
Fear '90
Final Approach '91
The Final Cut '04
Final Move '06
First Snow '07
The Flaming Urge '53
Flinch '94
Force of Evil '77
The Forgotten '04
The 4th Floor '99
Fracture '07 ▶
Freeway '88
Freeway '95 ▶
Freeze Frame '04
Frenchman's Farm '87
Fright '56
Funny Games '97 ▶
Funny Games '07
Gallowglass '95
The Game '97 ▶
Gaslight '44 ▶
The Gingerbread Man '97 ▶
Girl in Black Stockings '57
Girly '70
The Glass House '01
Godsend '04
Gross Misconduct '93
The Grudge '04 ▶
Half Light '05
Hallucination '67
The Hand '60
The Hand that Rocks the Cradle '92 ▶
Hard Candy '06 ▶

▶ = rated three bones or higher

Psycho-Thriller

Hate Crime '05
Haunted '95
Headspace '02
Hellbent '88
Hidden '05▶
Hide and Seek '05
High Tension '03
Highway Hitcher '98
The Hitch-Hiker '53▶
The Hitcher '07
The Hole '01
Honeymoon '87
House of Games '87▶
House of Wax '05
The House on Todville Road '95
Hush '98
Hush, Hush, Sweet Charlotte '65▶
I Know Who Killed Me '07
I Love Your Work '03
I Never Promised You a Rose Garden '77▶
Identity '03
I'll Sleep When I'm Dead '03▶
I'm Not Scared '03
In a Glass Cage '86
In Dreams '98
In the Heat of Passion '91
In the Heat of Passion 2: Unfaithful '94
In the Lake of the Woods '96
In the Winter Dark '98
The Incident '67
Inevitable Grace '94
Innocent Prey '88
Inside '06
Intimate Stranger '91
Intimate Strangers '04▶
Invasion of Privacy '96
Investigation '79
The Invisible Ghost '41
Irresistible '06
It's All About Love '03
Jack Be Nimble '94
The Jacket '05
Jacob's Ladder '90
Jade '95
Jealousy '99
Jericho Mansions '03
Joshua '07▶
Joy Ride '01▶
Joyride '97
Juggernaut '37
Julia and Julia '87
The Juror '96
Kaaterskill Falls '01
Kill by Inches '99
The Killer Inside Me '76
The Killing Floor '06
The Killing Mind '90
King of the Ants '03
A Kiss of a Killer '93
Knife in the Water '62▶
Knight Moves '93
Kontroll '03
La Moustache '05
La Rupture '70
La Vengeance d'une Femme '89
Lady in Waiting '94
Laser Moon '92
Last Breath '96
Last Life in the Universe '03
The Last of Sheila '73
The Last Seduction '94▶
Le Boucher '69▶
Leave Her to Heaven '45▶
Lemming '05
Les Bonnes Femmes '60▶
Letters from a Killer '98
The Limbic Region '96
Little Fish '05▶
Living in Peril '97
Lonely Hearts '06
Love '05
Love, Cheat & Steal '93
Love Crimes '92
Love, Lies and Murder '91
The Machine '96
The Maddening '95
Madhouse '04
Magic '78
Make Haste to Live '54
Man on Fire '04

Man on the Eiffel Tower '48▶
The Man Who Haunted Himself '70
The Manchurian Candidate '04▶
The Mark '61▶
Marnie '64▶
Match Point '05▶
Maternal Instincts '96
Mayalunta '86
The Meal '75
Mean Season '85
Memories of Murder '90
Merci pour le Chocolat '00▶
Midnight Edition '93
Midnight Lace '60
Midnight Tease '94
Mind Games '89
Mind Lies '00
Misbegotten '98
Misery '90▶
Mrs. Munck '95
Mr. Brooks '07
Mortal Sins '90
Mortal Sins '92
The Most Dangerous Game '32▶
Mother '94
Moving Targets '87
Murder by Numbers '02
Murphy's Law '86
My Brother Has Bad Dreams '72
My Very Best Friend '96
A Name for Evil '70
Nature of the Beast '94
The Net '95
Net Games '03
Never Talk to Strangers '95
The Night Caller '87
The Night of the Following Day '69
Night Train to Venice '93
The Night Walker '64
Nightmare at Bittercreek '91
Nightwatch '96
November '05▶
Number One Fan '94
The Number 23 '07
The Offence '73▶
The Omen '06
One Good Turn '95
One Night Stand '78
Open Water '03▶
Opposing Force '87
Outrage '93
Pacific Heights '90▶
The Paint Job '93
Panic Station '82
Paparazzi '04
The Paperboy '94
Paranoia '98
The Passion of Anna '70▶
A Passion to Kill '94
Peephole '93
Peeping Tom '60▶
The Penthouse '92
Perfect Alibi '94
Perfect Assassins '98
Perfect Stranger '07
Perfect Strangers '03
Perfect Tenant '99
Performance '70▶
Play Misty for Me '71▶
Playgirl Killer '66
Playmaker '94
Poison Ivy '92
Portrait in Terror '66
Posed for Murder '89
Posers '02
Possessed '05
Postmortem '98
Powder Burn '96
Power '98 '96
Praying Mantis '83
Premonition '07
Pretty Poison '68▶
Prey of the Chameleon '91
Primer '04▶
Psycho 3 '86
Psychomania '63
The Punisher '04
A Pure Formality '94
Rage '95
Raising Cain '92
Ransom '96▶

Reason to Die '90
Red Lights '04▶
Red Riding Hood '03
A Reflection of Fear '72
Relentless '89
Repulsion '65▶
Requiem for Murder '99
Ricochet '91▶
Riding the Bullet '04
The Ring 2 '05
Rituals '79
Room to Let '49
Rorret '87▶
Sabotage '36▶
Savage Abduction '73
Saw '04
Seconds '66▶
Secret Beyond the Door '48
Secret Ceremony '69
Secret Games '92
Secret Games 2: The Escort '93
Secret Games 3 '94
Secret Window '04
The Secretary '94
Secrets of Three Hungry Wives '78
Seduced '85
Seduced by Evil '94
The Seduction '82
Sensation '94
Separate Lives '94
Serial Killer '95
Seven '95▶
The Seventh Floor '93
Shadow Puppets '07
Shadows in the Storm '88
Shallow Grave '94
Sharon's Secret '95
Shattered Image '98
Siesta '87
The Silence of the Lambs '91▶
Single White Female '92
Single White Female 2: The Psycho '05
The Sister-in-Law '95
The Sixth Sense '99▶
Sleeping with the Enemy '91
Slow Burn '05
A Small Killing '81
Snapdragon '93
The Soft Kill '94
Someone Behind the Door '71
Someone to Die For '95
Sorry, Haters '05
Sorry, Wrong Number '48▶
Sorry, Wrong Number '89
Spartan '04▶
Spiral '07
The Spiral Staircase '46▶
Spiral Staircase '75
Stalked '94
Stalking Laura '93
Stardust Memories '80
Stay '05
The Stepfather '87▶
Stepfather 2: Make Room for Daddy '89
Stepfather 3: Father's Day '92
Stigmata '99
Storm '87
Strange Illusion '45
The Stranger '87▶
Stranger by Night '94
A Stranger in Town '95
Striking Distance '93
Stripteaser '95
Suspect Zero '04
Suspended Animation '02
Suture '93
Svengali '31▶
Svengali '83
Sweet Killing '93
Taboo '02
Tails You Live, Heads You're Dead '95
Taking Lives '04
Tall, Dark and Deadly '95
A Taste for Killing '92
Tattoo '81
The Temp '93
The Tenant '76▶
Terrified '94
Thesis '96
Thicker Than Water '93

36 Hours '64▶
Thr3e '07
The Three Lives of Karen '97
Through a Glass Darkly '61▶
Through the Eyes of a Killer '92
The Tie That Binds '95
Till the End of the Night '94
Timebomb '91
To Play or to Die '91
Tower of Terror '42
Trapped '89
Trapped '02
Trauma '62
Tryst '94
Tunnel Vision '95
Twisted '04
Twisted Love '95
The Two Mrs. Carrolls '47
Undertow '95
Unforgettable '96
Unlawful Entry '92
Unspeakable '02
The Vanishing '88▶
Vengeance Is Mine '79▶
Vengeance of the Dead '01
Victim of Love '91
Violated '53
Voyage '93
Wait until Dark '67▶
Web of Deceit '90
What Ever Happened To... '93
When a Stranger Calls '06
When Hell Was in Session '82▶
When the Bough Breaks '93
When the Dark Man Calls '95
Where Are the Children? '85
While I Live '47
Who Killed Bambi? '03
Wicked '98
Wicked Ways '99
Wicker Park '04
The Wind '87
A Woman Hunted '03
Woman in the Window '44▶
You'll Like My Mother '72
Young Adam '03▶
The Young Poisoner's Handbook '94▶

Psychotics/Sociopaths

see also Roommates from Hell

Accidental Meeting '93
Albino Alligator '96
Angel Face '52▶
Apartment Zero '88▶
The Assassination of Jesse James by the Coward Robert Ford '07▶
The Assassination of Richard Nixon '05
The Avenger '60
Bad Ronald '74▶
The Bad Seed '56
Badlands '74▶
Ball of Wax '03
Bellamy '80
Berserk! '67
Black Eliminator '78
Black Panther '77
Black Pit of Dr. M '47
Blind Side '93
Blind Vision '91
Blue Steel '90
Body Bags '93
Bone Daddy '97
Born for Hell '76
The Boston Strangler '68
Boxing Helena '93
The Boys '98▶
The Boys Next Door '85
Breakdown '96▶
Broken Arrow '95
The Butcher Boy '97▶
The Cable Guy '96
Cape Fear '61▶
Cape Fear '91▶
The Centerfold Girls '74
City Killer '87
Clay Pigeons '98

Cold Creek Manor '03
Cold Eyes of Fear '70
Cold Steel '87
Con Air '97▶
Consenting Adults '92
Crimes of Dr. Mabuse '32▶
The Crush '93
Damned River '89
Dario Argento's Trauma '93
The Dark Past '49▶
The Dark Ride '84
Dead As a Doorman '85
Dead Boyz Can't Fly '93
Deadbolt '92
Deadly Daphne's Revenge '93
Deadly Game '82
Death Benefit '96
Death of a Soldier '85
Death Sentence '74
Dee Snider's Strangeland '98
Demolition Man '93
Demon Hunter '88
The Dentist '96
Deranged '74▶
Deranged '87
Desperate Measures '98
Desperate Motives '92
Diary of a Teenage Hitchhiker '82
Dr. Giggles '92
Don't Answer the Phone '80
Don't Talk to Strangers '94
Doppelganger: The Evil Within '90
Dot.Kill '05
Down in the Valley '05
Down, Out and Dangerous '95
The Drifter '88
Escape Velocity '99
The Escort '97
Ex-Cop '93
Eye of God '97▶
Eye of the Beholder '92
Fade to Black '80
Fair Game '82
Falling Down '93▶
The Fan '81
The Fan '96
Fast Gun '93
Fatal Attraction '87▶
Fear '88
Fear '96
Fear City '85
Fear Inside '92
The Fiance '96
The Fiend Who Walked the West '58
The Fool Killer '65
Force of Evil '77
From Dusk Till Dawn '95
The Front Line '06
Funny Games '07▶
Gallowglass '95▶
The Gingerbread Man '97▶
Girl in Black Stockings '57
The Glimmer Man '96
Gloria '98
Guardian Angel '94
Guilty as Sin '93
Halloween: H20 '98▶
Headless Body in Topless Bar '96
Heat '95▶
Helter Skelter '76
Helter Skelter Murders '71
High Tension '03
Highway Hitcher '98
The Hitcher '07
Homage '95
Homer and Eddie '89
Honeymoon '87
The Hostage '67
Hot Potato '76
Hot Touch '82
House of Terror '72
The Housekeeper '86
Hush '98
I Know What You Did Last Summer '97▶
I Still Know What You Did Last Summer '98
In Dreams '98
In the Lake of the Woods '96
In the Line of Fire '93▶
In the Mouth of Madness '95

Invasion of Privacy '96
The Invisible Terror '63
Kalifornia '93
Keys to Tulsa '96
The Killer Inside Me '76
Killing Obsession '94
Killing Zoe '94
Killzone '85
Kiss the Girls '97
Lightning Bolt '67
The Lightship '86
The Little Girl Who Lives down the Lane '76
Live Wire '92
Lonely Hearts '06
Lunatic '91
The Machine '96
The Mad Bomber '72
The Mad Executioners '65
Mademoiselle '66
A Man in Uniform '93
Maniac Warriors '88
Maternal Instincts '96
Meet the Deedles '98
Metro '96
Midnight 2: Sex, Death, and Videotape '93
Midnight Edition '93
Midnight Fear '90
Midnight Ride '92
Misbegotten '98
Mommie Dearest '81
Mondo Balordo '64
Most Wanted '76
Mother's Boys '94
Motor Home Massacre '05
Moving Targets '87
Murder by Numbers '02
Murder Elite '86
Murderkill '86
The Naked Flame '68
Natural Enemy '96
The Neighbor '93
The Neighbor No. Thirteen '05
No Country for Old Men '07▶
Office Killer '97
One Good Turn '95
Pacific Heights '90▶
The Paperboy '94
Past Midnight '92
Perfect Family '92
Perfect Victims '87
Perfume: The Story of a Murderer '06
Play Nice '92
Playgirl Killer '66
Poison Ivy '92
Pretty Poison '68▶
Prime Time Murder '92
Prom Night '08
Psycho '60▶
Psycho 2 '83
Psycho 3 '86
Psycho 4: The Beginning '90
Psycho Girls '86
Psychos in Love '87
Pulse '03
Quake '92
The Rage '96
Rampage '87
Relentless '89
Repulsion '65▶
Reservoir Dogs '92▶
Resurrection Man '97
Retroactive '97
The Rich Man's Wife '96
Ricochet '91▶
Ripley's Game '02▶
The River Wild '94
The Road Killers '95
Roadkill '89
The Sadist '63
Sarah's Child '96
Savage Abduction '73
Saw II '05
Saw III '06
Scream '96▶
Scream 2 '97
The Sea Wolf '41▶
Secret Window '04
The Secretary '94
The Seduction '82
See No Evil '06
Seven '95▶

▶ = rated three bones or higher

Seven Hours to Judgment '88
The Seventh Floor '93
Shattered '07
The Shining '80
The Silencer '92
Single White Female '92
Single White Female 2: The Psycho '05
Skinner '93
The Sister-in-Law '95
Small Kill '93
Someone Behind the Door '71
Speed '94▶
Speed 2: Cruise Control '97
Stalked '94
Starved '97
The Stepfather '87▶
The Stepfather 2: Make Room for Daddy '89
Stepfather 3: Father's Day '92
Still Life '92
Stripped to Kill '87
Striptease '95
Suspect Zero '04
Suspicious River '00
Sweet Hostage '75
Tainted Blood '93
Taking Lives '04
The Taking of Beverly Hills '91
The Talented Mr. Ripley '99
Tall, Dark and Deadly '95
Ted & Venus '93
The Temp '93
The Tenant '76▶
Tetsuo: The Iron Man '92
A Thin Line Between Love and Hate '96
Thirteenth Day of Christmas '85
Three on the Hard Way '74
3000 Miles to Graceland '01
Through the Eyes of a Killer '92
To Die For '95
The Tripper '06
Truth or Consequences, N.M. '97
Turbulence '96
Twin Peaks: Fire Walk with Me '92
The Two Mrs. Carrolls '47
U-Turn '97
Ultraviolet '91
Unspeakable '02
Urban Legend '98
The Vanishing '93
Vice Squad '82
Violence at Noon '66▶
Voyage '93
What Ever Happened to Baby Jane? '62▶
When a Stranger Calls '06
When a Stranger Calls Back '93
Whispers '89
White Heat '49▶
With a Friend Like Harry '00▶
Wolf Creek '05
The Witness '99
Writer's Block '91
The Young Poisoner's Handbook '94▶
Zero Degrees Kelvin '95
The Zombie Army '93

Publicists
see also Behind the Scenes

Amelia Earhart: The Final Flight '94
America's Sweethearts '01
Cursed '04
For Your Consideration '06
Gideon's Daughter '05
Go West, Young Man '36
The Half Naked Truth '32
Hancock '08
The Harder They Fall '56▶
Jersey Girl '04
Jimmy Glick in LaLa Wood '05
Loving You '57
Mad About Music '38▶
The Nines '07▶
The Parent Trap '98
People I Know '02
Phone Booth '02
Sweet Smell of Success '57▶
Win a Date with Tad Hamilton! '04

Pure Ego Vehicles
see also Big-Budget Bombs; Rock Stars on Film

The Adventures of Ford Fairlane '90
Air America '90
Assault on the Rebel Girls '59
The Big One '98
Boom! '68
Charade '53
Conan the Destroyer '84
The Dead Pool '88
Dee Snider's Strangeland '99
Dirty Love '05
Fire Down Below '97
Foolish '99

Puerto Rico

The Apostate '98
Assassins '95
D.R.E.A.M. Team '99
Feel the Noise '07
Frankenstein Meets the Space Monster '65
Illegal Tender '07
Ship Ahoy '42
Sunstorm '01

Punk Rock
see also Rock Flicks

Born to Lose '99
Control '07
Decline of Western Civilization 1 '81▶
End of the Century: The Story of the Ramones '03▶
The Filth and the Fury '99
Hard Core Logo '96
Repo Man '83▶
Rock 'n' Roll High School '79▶
Rock 'n' Roll High School Forever '91
Sid & Nancy '86▶
Times Square '80
24 Hour Party People '01

Puppets
see also Killer Toys; Toys

The Adventures of Pinocchio '96
Alice in Wonderland '50
The Human Experiment '98
The Dark Crystal '82▶
Devil Doll '64
Dolls '02▶
Gepetto '00
The Great Gabbo '29
The Great Rupert '50▶
Lili '53▶
Magic '78
Meet the Feebles '89
MirrorMask '05
The Muppets' Wizard of Oz '05
Pinocchio '40▶
Pinocchio '02
Puppet Master '89
Puppet Master 2 '90
Puppet Master 4 '93
Puppet Master 5: The Final Chapter '94
A Rat's Tale '98
Retro Puppet Master '99
Saw '04
The Sound of Music '65▶
Team America: World Police '04▶

Rabbi
see also Clergymen; Judaism

Before the Rain '94▶
Bulletproof Monk '03
The Chosen '77
Enemies, a Love Story '89▶
In the Presence of Mine Enemies '97
Lucky Number Slevin '06
Outside Chance of Maximillian Glick '88
The Quarrel '93
Rasputin '85▶
Rasputin and the Empress '33▶
Stolen Summer '02
Time of Favor '00

Rabbits

Alice '88▶
Alice in Wonderland '51▶
Alice in Wonderland '99
Bambi '42▶
Bunny Whipped '06
Donnie Darko '01▶
Fatal Attraction '87▶
The Geisha Boy '58
Harvey '50▶
Hoodwinked '05▶
Inland Empire '06
The Last Mimzy '07
Mona Lisa '86▶
Monty Python and the Holy Grail '75▶
Nasty Rabbit '64
Night of the Lepus '72
Phenomenon '96
Roger & Me '89▶
Space Jam '96
Wallace & Gromit: The Curse of the Were-Rabbit '05▶
Watership Down '78
Who Framed Roger Rabbit '88▶

Queens
see also Royalty; Royalty, British; French; Royalty, Russian

Get Carter '00
Gummo '97
Harlem Nights '89
Hello, Dolly! '69
Hudson Hawk '91
I Got the Hook-Up '98
The Jazz Singer '80
Last Action Hero '93
Le Repos du Guerrier '62
Marie Antoinette '38
Modern Love '90
On Deadly Ground '94
Private Parts '96
Purple Rain '84
Rambo III '88
Richard Petty Story '72
Running out of Luck '86
The Scarlet Letter '95
Sidekicks '93
SnakeEater '89
Sophia Loren: Her Own Story '80
Staying Alive '83
Sweet Country Road '83
Tarzan, the Ape Man '81
Thank Your Lucky Stars '43▶
A Thin Line Between Love and Hate '96
Torch Song '53
200 Motels '71
Under the Cherry Moon '86
Vampire in Brooklyn '95
Waterworld '95
What Comes Around '85
Wildcats '86
The Wizard of Speed and Time '88
Yes, Giorgio '82

Race Against Time

Acceptable Risks '86
Alien Space Avenger '91
The Andromeda Strain '71
Apollo 13 '95▶
Around the World in 80 Days '04
Baltz '07
Bitter Harvest '81▶
Blown Away '94
The Borrowers '97
Broken Arrow '95
Cellular '04
Cha a Reaction '80
The China Syndrome '79▶
Collateral '04▶
Coma '78▶
Convicted '04
The Corporation '96
Daylight '96
Deja Vu '06
D.O.A. '49▶
D.O.A. '88
88 Minutes '08
Escape from L.A. '96
Fail-Safe '64▶
Free Willy 2: The Adventure Home '95
Free Willy 3: The Rescue '97
Germicide '74
Grand Tour: Disaster in Time '92
Hell Commandos '69
I'll Be Home for Christmas '98
In Pursuit of Honor '95
Independence Day '96▶
Jet Over the Atlantic '59
Killer on Board '77
Last Dance '96
Last Flight Out: A True Story '90
Lorenzo's Oil '92▶
Nick of Time '95
Octopussy '83
Once Upon a Forest '93
Outbreak '94▶
Panic in Echo Park '77
The Peacemaker '97
The Princess Diaries 2: Royal Engagement '04
Prisoner in the Middle '74
Pursuit '72
Race Against Time '00
Return to Paradise '98▶
Robot in the Family '94
Saw '04
The Silver Streak '34
Somebody Has to Shoot the Picture '90▶
Sudden Death '95
The Taking of Beverly Hills '91
Terror Street '54
Things to Do in Denver When You're Dead '95▶
Time Lock '57
Time Without Pity '57
Tramp, Tramp, Tramp '26
TripFall '00
True Crime '99
Twister '96
Tycus '98
WarGames '83

Radio
see also Mass Media

The Accidental Husband '08
The Adventures of Ford Fairlane '90
Airheads '94
American Graffiti '73▶
American Nightmare '00
Amy's O '02
Bad Channels '92
The Brave One '07
Break of Dawn '88
Breakfast in Hollywood '46
Bye Bye, Love '94
Carefree '38▶
Choose Me '84▶
Citizens Band '77▶
City in Panic '86
Comfort and Joy '84▶
The Couch Trip '87
Danger on the Air '38
The Day Silence Died '98
Dead Air '94
Dirty Mind of Young Sally '72
The Fisher King '91▶
FM '78
The Fog '78
Freeway '88
Freeway '00
Girls Night Out '83
Good Morning, Vietnam '87▶
The Great American Broadcast '41
Grosse Pointe Blank '97▶
The Hucksters '47▶
The Jackpot '50
The Key Man '57
Laser Moon '92
Look Who's Laughing '41
Love Serenade '96
The Man Who Came to Dinner '41▶
Midnight Confessions '95
Mr. Rock 'n' Roll: The Alan Freed Story '99
My Blue Heaven '90
My Dream Is Yours '49
The Next Voice You Hear '50
No Trace '50
Old Barn Dance '38
On the Air '95
On the Air Live with Captain Midnight '79
The Night Caller '97
The Night Listener '06
Night Rhythms '92
The Night Watchman '02
Once Upon a Honeymoon '42
Open House '86
Outside Ozona '98
People Are Funny '46
People's Choice '46
The Phantom Broadcast '33
Play Misty for Me '71▶
Pot o' Gold '41
Power 98 '96
A Prairie Home Companion '06▶
Private Parts '96
Psycho 4: The Beginning '90
Pump Up the Volume '90▶
Rachel River '87
Radioland Murders '94▶
Rebecca of Sunnybrook Farm '38
Requiem for Murder '99
Rude '96
Sexual Response '92
Sleepless in Seattle '93▶
The Sleepy Time Gal '01
Straight Talk '92
Strike Up the Band '40
Talk Radio '88▶
Talk to Me '07
Telling Lies in America '96
There Goes Kelly '45
The Truth about Cats and Dogs '96▶
Tune in Tomorrow '90
Up in the Air '40
The Warriors '79
When the Dark Man Calls '95
Whistling in Brooklyn '43
Who Done It? '42
Winchell '98

Rags
see also Cinderella Stories; Price of Fame; Wrong Side of the Tracks

The Abe Lincoln of Ninth Avenue '39
Aladdin '92▶
All the King's Men '49▶
The Amorous Adventures of Moll Flanders '65
Annie '82

Rags to Riches

B.A.P.'s '97
Better Late Than Never '83
The Beverly Hillbillies '93
Blank Check '93
Body Slam '87
Boogie Nights '97▶
Breaking Glass '80
Brewster's Millions '35
The Buddy Holly Story '78▶
Callie and Son '81
Can You Hear the Laughter? The Story of Freddie Prinze '79
Christmas in July '40▶
Cinderella Man '05▶
Citizen Kane '41▶
Coal Miner's Daughter '80▶
The Cookout '04
Covergirl '83
Craig's Wife '36
Daddy Long Legs '55▶
The Damned Don't Cry '50
Dangerous When Wet '53
Darling '65▶
Dodsworth '36▶
Dreamer '79
Drifting Souls '32
EDtv '99
Emperor Jones '33▶
Envy '04
Evita '96
Fifth Avenue Girl '39
Film Geek '06
Footlight Parade '33▶
For Richer, for Poorer '92
Forever Amber '47
G '02
Give a Girl a Break '53
Goal! The Dream Begins '06
Great Expectations '97
The Great Rupert '50▶
Hero '92▶
Honeyboy '82
The Hudsucker Proxy '93▶
I Love Melvin '53
It Could Happen to You '94▶
The Jerk '79
Jimmy Hollywood '94
Joseph Andrews '77
Kept Husbands '31
Kipps '41▶
La Vie Est Belle '87
Lady Grey '82
The Last American Hero '73▶
The Last Laugh '24▶
Laurel & Hardy: Below Zero '30
Lenny '74▶
Lili '53▶
Little Lord Fauntleroy '36▶
Little Lord Fauntleroy '80
Little Lord Fauntleroy '95
Livin' Large '91
Lots of Luck '85
Love Nest '51
Lucky Partners '40
The Mambo Kings '92▶
The Manions of America '81
Mannequin '37
Meet John Doe '41▶
Memoirs of a Geisha '05▶
Million Dollar Baby '04▶
A Million to Juan '94
Miss Melody Jones '73
Mrs. Harris '05
Mrs. Wintertoune '96
Money for Nothing '93
Mr. Billion '77
Mr. Deeds '02
My Fair Lady '64▶
New York's Finest '87
The Object of Beauty '91▶
One in a Million: The Ron LeFlore Story '78
Only One Night '42
Overnight '03▶
The Patsy '64
The Pearl '47
Peddlin' in Society '47
Possessed '31
Power '34
Pride of the Clan '18
The Prince and the Pauper '37▶
The Prince and the Pauper '78

▶ = rated three bones or higher

Rags

The Prince and the Pauper '01
The Prince and the Showgirl '57
Princess Tam Tam '35▶
Pygmalion '38▶
Rebecca of Sunnybrook Farm '17
The Return of the Beverly Hillbillies '81
Rocky '76▶
Scarlet Dawn '32
Scruples '80
The Secret of My Success '87
Sepia Cinderella '47
The Sin of Harold Diddlebock '47
The Sin of Madelon Claudet '31▶
Sing Your Worries Away '42
Speak Easily '32
The Stars Fell on Henrietta '94
The Stork Club '45
Straight Talk '92
Striker's Mountain '87
Sweet Adeline '26
Sweet Hearts Dance '88
The Tall Guy '89▶
Tennessee Stallion '78
There Will Be Blood '07▶
Three Coins in the Fountain '54
The Toast of New Orleans '50
Toast of New York '37▶
Trading Places '83▶
Trois Couleurs: Blanc '94◀
The Unsinkable Molly Brown '64◀
Up Close and Personal '96▶
Vanity Fair '04▶
What Price Hollywood? '32◀
Willy Wonka & the Chocolate Factory '71▶
A Woman of Substance '84
Working Girl '88▶
Ziegfeld Girl '41▲

Rape
see also Sexual Abuse
The Accused '88▶
Act of Vengeance '74
The Adventurers '70
American Commandos '84
American Gun '05
And Justice for All '79
Awakening of Candra '81
Backlash '86
Bad Lieutenant '92▲
Baise Moi '00
Bandit Queen '94
Bastard out of Carolina '96
The Beast Within '82
Because of the Cats '74
Blackrock '97
Blind Justice '86
Blue Desert '91▶
Body Shots '99
Bordertown '06
Born Innocent '74
Boys Don't Cry '99▲
Broken Badge '85▶
A Brother's Kiss '97
Bullies '86
Caged Heat 2: Stripped of Freedom '94
Caged Terror '72
Cast the First Stone '89
Casualties of War '89▶
The Center of the World '01
Certain Sacrifice '80
Chain Gang Women '72
Chaos '05
Class of 1984 '82▶
A Clockwork Orange '71▲
Code of Honor '82
Convicted '86
Coward of the County '81
Cracker: Men Should Weep '94
Cronicas '04▶
Dead Man Walking '95▲
Deadline Assault '90
Deadly Daphne's Revenge '93

Deadly Darling '85
Deadly Twins '94▲
Death and the Maiden '94◀
Death Blow '87
Death Wish '74
Deep in the Heart '83
Deliverance '72▲
Demented '80
Demon Seed '77▶
Derailed '05
Descent '07
Desolation Angels '95
The Desperados '70
Diary of a Lost Girl '29▲
Diary of a Teenage Hitchhiker '82
Divided We Stand '00
Dogville '03▲
Emmanuelle's Daughter '79
The Entity '83
Extremities '86
An Eye for an Eye '95
Final Justice '84
Flesh and Blood '85
Forbidden Sun '89
Forced Entry '75
Free, White, and 21 '62
From the Life of the Marionettes '80▶
Fugitive Among Us '92
The General's Daughter '99
Gentle Savage '73
Girls Town '95
Gossip '99
Guncrazy '92
Hands of a Stranger '87
Hannie Caulder '72
The Heart Is Deceitful Above All Things '04
Heat of the Flame '76
His Name Was King '85
Home Before Midnight '84
The Hooked Generation '69
The Hotel New Hampshire '84
I Am Frigid... Why? '72
I Spit on Your Grave '77
I'll Sleep When I'm Dead '03▶
I'm the One You're Looking For '88
In Trouble '67
Irreversible '02
It's Alive '74▶
Jackson County Jail '76
Jaded '96
Jailbait: Betrayed By Innocence '86
Judge Horton and the Scottsboro Boys '76
Kika '94
Kiss a Killer '93
The Kite Runner '07▶
The Ladies Club '86
Landscape in the Mist '88◀
Lethal Woman '88
Lipstick '76
Liquid Sky '83▶
The Marquise of O '76
Memoirs of a Geisha '05
Memories of Murder '03
Ms. 45 '81▶
Mrs. R's Daughter '79
Most Wanted '76
Motor Psycho '65
The Mudge Boy '03
Multiple Maniacs '70
Mysterious Skin '04▶
Naked Vengeance '85
Necromancer: Satan's Servant '88
Night of the Demon '80
Northville Cemetery Massacre '76
Olivier, Olivier '92▶
Once Upon a Time in America '84▲
One of Her Own '97
One Tough Cop '98
Open Doors '89▲
Outrage '93
Palindromes '04▶
A Passage to India '84▲
The Phantom of Soho '64
Positive I.D. '87
Postcards from America '95
The Principal '87
Purgatory '89

Quiet Days in Hollywood '97
Rage '80▶
Rape and Marriage: The Rideout Case '80
Rape of Love '79
Rashomon '51▲
A Reason to Believe '95
The Reckoning '03▶
Redacted '07
Rider on the Rain '70▶
Rob Roy '95▶
Sci-Fighters '96
Screamer '74
Sex Crimes '92
Shame '87
Shame '92
The Shaming '71
She Came on the Bus '69
Short Fuse '88
Showgirls '95
Silent Witness '85
Sin and Redemption '94
Sirens '02
Slashed Dreams '74
Sketch Artist 2: Hands That See '94
Speak '04▶
The Story of Esther Costello '57
A Stranger Is Watching '82
Straw Dogs '72▶
Streets '90
Studs Lonigan '60
Sudden Death '85
Sudden Impact '83
Suspicious River '00
Tainted '88
Talk to Her '02▲
Tarnation '03
Things Behind the Sun '01
Time to Kill '89
A Time to Kill '96▶
Titus '99
To Kill a Mockingbird '62▲
To Kill a Stranger '84
The Tormentors '71
Town without Pity '61
Trade '07
Trespasses '86
Violated '84
Violent Ones '68
The Violent Years '56
Virgin '03
The Virgin Spring '59▲
Vukovar '94▲
When He's Not a Stranger '89▶
When Justice Fails '98
Wild Riders '71
The Wind '28▶
Woman, Thou Art Loosed '04
The Young One '61

Real Estate
Are We Done Yet? '07
Barbershop 2: Back in Business '04▶
*batteries not included '87
Battle of the Sexes '28
The Beat My Heart Skipped '05▶
The Big Bounce '04
Boy, Did I Get a Wrong Number! '66
Boys on the Side '94
A Brooklyn State of Mind '97
Burning Daylight '28
Career Girls '97
Chasing Butterflies '94
Clean and Sober '88▶
Confidentially Yours '83▶
Contagion '87
Daughter of Don Q '46
The Deadly Secret '94
Deadly Stranger '88
Different Story '78
Duplex '03
Empire of the Ants '77
The Evictors '79
For Love or Money '88
For Love or Money '93
Glengarry Glen Ross '92▲
A Good Year '06
The Haunted Mansion '03
Hollywood Homicide '03
House 4: Home Deadly Home '91

Irresistible Impulse '95
Kill the Poor '06
Killer Instinct '00
Last Call '90
The Last Word '80
Love on the Side '04
The Low Down '00
Make Me an Offer '80
Meatballs 4 '92
Messenger of Death '88
Miranda '01
Moonlight Mile '02▶
My 5 Wives '00
Open House '86
Protection '01
Read My Lips '01
Remedy for Riches '40
River Street '95
Rubin & Ed '92
Rude Awakening '81
Rule 3 '93
Same Old Song '97▶
Shadow of Angels '76
South Riding '37
Stay Hungry '76▶
Stormy Monday '88
The Stranger from Pecos '45
Sunshine State '02▶
Teenage Exorcist '93
Terror Tract '00
To Die For '89
The Two Jakes '90
Two Weeks Notice '02
Vive l'Amour '94
Wild Orchid '90

REALLY Bad TV—
see also Technology—Rampant
Poltergeist '82▶
Remote Control '88
The Ring '02
Terrorvision '86
The Video Dead '87
Videodrome '83

Rebel With a Cause
see also Rebel Without a Cause; The Resistance
Acceptable Risks '86
The Accused '88▲
Ace High '68
Aeon Flux '05
Afterburn '97
Alice's Restaurant '69
American Tiger '89
And Starring Pancho Villa as Himself '03▶
Ann Vickers '33
The Applegates '89
Armageddon: The Final Challenge '94
As Young As You Feel '51▶
The Attic: The Hiding of Anne Frank '88
Basquiat '96▶
Billy Jack '71
The Blob '58
Blue Collar '78▶
Born Losers '67
Boyz N the Hood '91▲
Braveheart '95▲
Broken Silence '01▶
Brubaker '80▶
Burglar '87▶
The Burmese Harp '56▶
The China Syndrome '79▶
Courage '96▶
Courageous Dr. Christian '40
Crime of Honor '85
Dark Rider '91
Daybreak '93
Dead Poets Society '89▶
Deadly Business '86▶
Deadly Stranger '88
Demolition High '95
Die Hard '88▲
Die Hard 2: Die Harder '90▶
Disturbing Behavior '98
Dragon Fury '95
A Dream for Christmas '73▶
Dust '85▶
East of Eden '54▲
East of Eden '80
Easy Wheels '89

The Edukators '04
Exiled in America '90
The Fighter '52▶
The Fighter '95
The Final Alliance '89
The Firing Line '91
The $5.20 an Hour Dream '80
Flesh and the Spur '57
Flight of the Intruder '90▶
Foxfire '96
The Fugitive '48▲
The Gambling Samurai '60
Game of Survival '89
Gandhi '82▲
Go Further '03
Gorillas in the Mist '88▲
Guess Who's Coming to Dinner '67▲
Hair '79▶
Hardcore '79
Hidden City '87
In the Name of the Father '93▲
Iron Horsemen '71
Iron Thunder '89
James Dean: Live Fast, Die Young '97
Jesse 88
Joe Kidd '72
Johnny Firecloud '75
Katherine '75
Kidnapped '95
Killing of Randy Webster '81
Knights of the City '85
Kung Fu '72
La Marseillaise '37▲
The Last American Hero '73▶
Lawrence of Arabia '62▲
Legend of Billie Jean '85
Legend of Earl Durand '74
Legend of the Lone Ranger '81
Light It Up '99
Little Tough Guys '38
Lois Gibbs and the Love Canal '82
The Loneliness of the Long Distance Runner '62▶
Lust for Life '56▲
Luther '74
Man of Marble '76▲
The Manhattan Project '86
Marie '85▶
Memories of Underdevelopment '68
Michael Collins '96▲
Mr. Smith Goes to Washington '39▲
Mountain Man '77
Network '76▲
Night of Evil '62
Norma Rae '79▲
Northern Lights '79
Odd Man Out '47▶
One-Eyed Jacks '61▶
One Man's War '90
One Man's War '91
Original Intent '91
Outbreak '94▶
Overdrawn at the Memory Bank '83
Patch Adams '98
Paths of Glory '57▲
Patty Hearst '88
Plutonium Baby '87
Prefontaine '96
The Principal '87
Private Parts '96
Project X '87
Quarantine '89
A Raisin in the Sun '61▲
A Raisin in the Sun '89▶
Rob Roy '95▶
Robin Hood: Prince of Thieves '91▶
The Rock '96▶
Roe vs. Wade '89▶
Rooster: Spurs of Death! '83
Runaway Daughters '94
Sakharov '84▶
Samaritan: The Mitch Snyder Story '86▶
The Sand Pebbles '66▲
Sansho the Bailiff '54▲
Save the Lady '82
The Scarlet Pimpernel '34▲

The Scarlet Pimpernel '82▲
The Scarlet Pimpernel '99
The Scarlet Pimpernel 2: Mademoiselle Guillotine '99
The Scarlet Pimpernel 3: The Kidnapped King '99
The Secret Agent '96
Secret of Stamboul '36
Serpico '73▶
The Shock '23
Silkwood '83▶
Sins of Rome '54
Solo '96
Somebody Has to Shoot the Picture '90▶
Stay Away, Joe '68
Steel Frontier '94
The Stranger '95
The Stranger Wore a Gun '53
Sympathy for the Devil '70
Taffin '88
Tank Girl '94
The Texican '66
This Land Is Mine '43▲
The Tin Star '57▶
To Kill a Priest '89
Trial of the Catonsville Nine '72
True Believer '89
Under Western Stars '38
V: The Final Battle '84
Vengeance '86
WarGames '83
The Westerner '40▶
When a Man Rides Alone '33
Wisdom '87
Without Limits '97▶

Rebel Without a Cause
see also Rebel With a Cause
Across the Tracks '89
All Night Long '81▶
Badlands '74▶
A Boy and His Dog '75
The Boys Next Door '85
Breathless '59▶
Breathless '83
Cheech and Chong's Up in Smoke '79
A Clockwork Orange '71▲
Cool As Ice '91
The Cruel Story of Youth '60▶
Dino '57
Easy Rider '69▶
The Electric Horseman '79
The Fence '94
Ferris Bueller's Day Off '86▶
Five Easy Pieces '70▶
The Fugitive Kind '60
Fury to Freedom: The Life Story of Raul Ries '85
Girls' Town 59
Going Places '74▶
Gore Vidal's Billy the Kid '89
Great Missouri Raid '51
Guncrazy '92
Heart Beat '80
Hud '63▶
I Was a Teenage Werewolf '57
If... '69▶
Inventing the Abbotts '97
Just for the Hell of It '68
Kicked in the Head '97
Leather Jackets '90
The Little Valentino '79
Loser '97
Lost Angels '89
Niagara, Niagara '97
Noi '03
On the Edge: The Survival of Dana '79
Over the Edge '79▶
Petit Con '84
Presumed Guilty '91
Pump Up the Volume '90
Rambo: First Blood, Part 2 '85
Rambo 3 '88
Rebel High '88
Rebel Rousers '69

▲ = rated three bones or higher

Rebel Run '94
Rebel without a Cause '55 ▶
Reckless '84
Roadracers '94
Road House '89 ▶
Rocky 4 '85
September 30, 1955 '77
sex, lies and videotape '89 ▶
Shopping '93
S.L.C Punk! '99 ▶
Snow Kill '90
Suburbia '83
Summer Camp Nightmare '86
That Was Then... This is Now '85
3:15—The Moment of Truth '86

Red Cross
China Beach '88 ▶
One Against the Wind '91 ▶
So Proudly We Hail '43 ▶
The White Cliffs of Dover '44 ▶

Red Scare
see also Cold War Spies; Communists & Foreign Intrigue; Politics; Russia/ USSR
Arsenal '29 ▶
Baltic Deputy '37 ▶
The Bamboo Saucer '68
Battle Beneath the Earth '58
A Beautiful Mind '01 ▶
Big Jim McLain '52
A Bullet for Joey '55
Chapayev '34 ▶
China Cry '91
China, My Sorrow '89
Coming Out of the Ice '82 ▶
Comment Ca Va? '76
The Commies Are Coming, the Commies Are Coming '57
Commissar '68 ▶
Comrade X '40 ▶
Conspirator '49
Dash and Lilly '99 ▶
Death of a Bureaucrat '66 ▶
Earth '30 ▶
Eminent Domain '91
Fellow Traveler '89 ▶
Golden Gate '93
The Great Armored Car Swindle '64
Guilty by Suspicion '91 ▶
Guilty of Treason '50
Hands Up '81 ▶
Hawthorne of the USA '19
Indochine '92 ▶
The Inner Circle '91 ▶
The Interrogation '82 ▶
Invasion U.S.A. '52
Invasion U.S.A. '85
Jet Pilot '57
Little World of Don Camillo '51 ▶
Man of Iron '81 ▶
Man of Marble '76 ▶
The Manchurian Candidate '62 ▶
Mandela '87 ▶
Mother Kusters Goes to Heaven '76 ▶
Mother of Kings '82
Never Let Me Go '53
Nicholas and Alexandra '71 ▶
Night Crossing '81
Night Flight from Moscow '73
The Oak '93 ▶
Oh, Bloody Life! '80
Open Doors '89 ▶
Red Dawn '84
The Red Menace '49
Reds '81 ▶
Requiem for Dominic '91 ▶

Revolution! A Red Comedy '91
The She-Beast '65
Sideburns '91
Strike '24 ▶
The Theme '79 ▶
Thoughts Are Free '84 ▶
Tito and Me '92 ▶
Tobor the Great '54
Trahir '93
The Ugly American '63 ▶
Uranus '91 ▶
When Father Was Away on Business '85 ▶

Reefer Madness
see also Drug Use & Abuse; On the Rocks
Alpha Dog '06
Cash Crop '01
Cheech and Chong's Next Movie '80
Cheech and Chong's Nice Dreams '81
Cheech and Chong's Up in Smoke '79
Friday '95 ▶
The Good Girl '02 ▶
Grandma's Boy '06
Half-Baked '97
Harold and Kumar Escape from Guantanamo Bay '08
Harold and Kumar Go to White Castle '04 ▶
How High '01
I Love You, Alice B. Toklas! '68
Knocked Up '07 ▶
Pineapple Express '08 ▶
Puff, Puff, Pass '06
Reefer Madness '38
Saving Grace '00 ▶
Smiley Face '07
Strange Wilderness '08
The Wash '01

Rehab
see also Drug Use & Abuse; On the Rocks
Bounce '00
Clean '04
Clean and Sober '88 ▶
Crutch '04
Down to the Bone '04 ▶
Eye See You '01
Girdlock'd '96
Jesus' Son '99 ▶
Scandal Sheet '85
Slums of Beverly Hills '98 ▶
28 Days '00
When a Man Loves a Woman '94 ▶

Reincarnation
see also Death & the Afterlife
Angel on My Shoulder '46 ▶
Angel on My Shoulder '80
Audrey Rose '77
Birth '04 ▶
Bram Stoker's The Mummy '97
Chances Are '89 ▶
Cleo/Leo '89
Creature of Destruction '67
Dead Again '91 ▶
Devi '60 ▶
Down to Earth '01
Fluke '95
Goodbye Charlie '64
Heart and Souls '93 ▶
Heaven Can Wait '78 ▶
Here Comes Mr. Jordan '41 ▶
I Married a Witch '42 ▶
Little Buddha '93 ▶
The Mummy '99
The Mummy Lives '93
The Mummy Returns '01 ▶
Oh, Heavenly Dog! '80
On a Clear Day You Can See Forever '70
P.S. '04
Quigley '03
Rapturous '07
The Reincarnation of Peter Proud '75

The Robot vs. the Aztec Mummy '59
The Search for Bridey Murphy '56
Switch '91 ▶
Tales of the Kama Sutra 2: Monsoon '98
Tequila Body Shots '99
The Vengeance of She '68
Youth Without Youth '07

Religion
see also Buddhism; Islam; Judaism; Missionaries; Nuns & Priests; Religious Epics; Saints
Abduction of St. Anne '75
Absolution '81
Adam's Apples '05 ▶
The Addiction '95 ▶
Alice Sweet Alice '76
Amazing Grace '06 ▶
Ancient Relic '02
Androcles and the Lion '52
Angel '94
Angels in America '03 ▶
Anna '51
The Apostle '97 ▶
Augustine of Hippo '72 ▶
The Avenging Angel '95
Bad Education '04 ▶
Bear Ye One Another's Burden... '88
Before the Rain '94 ▶
Bernadette '90
The Big Squeeze '96
The Birch Interval '78
Blood of Jesus '41 ▶
The Body '01
Body and Soul '24 ▶
Breaking the Waves '95 ▶
Brides of Christ '91 ▶
Brigham City '01 ▶
Brigham Young: Frontiersman '40 ▶
Broken Vows '87
Brother Sun, Sister Moon '73
Brotherhood of the Wolf '01 ▶
Brothers in Arms '88
The Butcher Boy '97 ▶
Camila '84 ▶
Catholics '73 ▶
Chariots of Fire '81 ▶
Chocolat '00 ▶
The Choir '95 ▶
The Chronicles of Narnia: The Lion, the Witch and the Wardrobe '05 ▶
The Church '90
Citizen Ruth '96 ▶
Come to the Stable '49 ▶
Commandments '96
Conquest of Space '55
Conspiracy of Silence '03
Contact '97 ▶
The Convent '95
Cosmic Slop '94 ▶
The Courageous Mr. Penn '41
Cracker: The Big Crunch '94 ▶
Crimes of Passion '84 ▶
Critical Choices '97
The Crucible '57 ▶
A Cry from the Mountain '85
The Da Vinci Code '06 ▶
The Devil at 4 O'Clock '61 ▶
The Disappearance of Aimee '76
Divided by Hate '96
Dr. Syn '37 ▶
Dr. Syn, Alias the Scarecrow '64
Dogma '99 ▶
A Dream for Christmas '73 ▶
Earth '98 ▶
El Cid '61 ▶

Elizabeth '98 ▶
Emaron '86
The Embezzled Heaven '58
The End of the Affair '99 ▶
Enjo '58
Entertaining Angels: The Dorothy Day Story '96
An Everlasting Piece '00
The Exorcism of Emily Rose '05
Extramuros '85
Eye of God '97 ▶
False Prophets '05
Father of Lies '07
The Favor, the Watch, & the Very Big Fish '92
The Fiend '71
Final Judgment '92
The Flowers of St. Francis '50 ▶
A Fond Kiss '04 ▶
A Fool and His Money '98
Francesco '93
Friendly Persuasion '56 ▶
From a Far Country: Pope John Paul II '81
The Garden '90
The Gathering '02
The Gaucho '27 ▶
The Ghoul '75
Glory! Glory! '90 ▶
Go Down Death '41
The Godfather, Part 3 '90 ▶
God's Gun '75
Gospa '94
The Gospel '05 ▶
The Gospel '84
The Greaser's Palace '72
The Greatest Story Ever Told '65
Green Pastures '36 ▶
The Guyana Tragedy: The Story of Jim Jones '80 ▶
Hail Mary '85
Hallelujah! '29 ▶
Harvest of Fire '95
Hate Crime '05
Hazel's People '73
The Healer '02
The Heart is Deceitful Above All Things '04
Heavens Above '63 ▶
Hellas pour Moi '94
Hellfire '48
Holy Girl '04 ▶
Holy Man '98
Holy Matrimony '94
Household Saints '93 ▶
The Hunchback '97
I, the Worst of All '90
I'd Climb the Highest Mountain '51 ▶
In God We Trust '80
In the Line of Duty: Ambush in Waco '93
Inherit the Wind '60 ▶
The Inquiry '87
Invasion of the Space Preachers '90
Iron Horsemen '71
Jeanne la Pucelle '94 ▶
Jerusalem '96 ▶
Jesus '79 ▶
Jesus Christ, Superstar '73 ▶
Jesus Christ Superstar '00
Jesus of Nazareth '28
Jesus of Nazareth '77 ▶
The Jesus Trip '71
The Jew '77
Joan of Arc '48 ▶
Joan of Arc '99 ▶
Joshua '02
Joni '79
The Judas Project: The Ultimate Encounter '94
Keeping Mum '05 ▶
The Keeper: The Legend of Omar Khayyam '05

The Last Temptation of Christ '88 ▶
Latter Days '04 ▶
Laughing Sinners '31
Leap of Faith '92 ▶
Leaves from Satan's Book '19 ▶
Left Behind: The Movie '00
Les Destinees '00 ▶
Levity '03
The Light of Faith '22
Lilies '96 ▶
Little Buddha '93 ▶
Little Church Around the Corner '23
Little Richard '00
The Littlest Angel '69
Loggerheads '05 ▶
Looking for Comedy in the Muslim World '06
The Loss of Sexual Innocence '98
Love and Faith '78
A Love Divided '01 ▶
Lust and Revenge '95
Luther '03 ▶
Major Barbara '41 ▶
The Maldonado Miracle '03
A Man Called Peter '55
A Man for All Seasons '66 ▶
A Man for All Seasons '88 ▶
Marjoe '72 ▶
Martin Luther '53 ▶
Mary, Mother of Jesus '99
Mary, Queen of Scots '71 ▶
Mayflower: The Pilgrims' Adventure '79
The Message '77 ▶
The Milky Way '68 ▶
The Milky Way '97 ▶
The Miracle '48 ▶
Miracle in Rome '88
The Miracle of Marcelino '55 ▶
Miracle of Our Lady of Fatima '52
The Miracle Woman '31 ▶
Monsieur Vincent '47 ▶
Monsignor Quixota '91
Monty Python's Life of Brian '79 ▶
A Mormon Maid '17
Mother Joan of the Angels '60 ▶
Mother Teresa: In the Name of God's Poor '97
My Mother's Smile '02
The Neon Bible '95
The Next Voice You Hear '50
The Night of the Iguana '64 ▶
The Ninth Day '04 ▶
Nostalghia '83 ▶
Oh, God! '77 ▶
The Omen '06
One Man's Way '63
Oranges Are Not the Only Fruit '89 ▶
Ordet '55 ▶
Ordinary Sinner '02
The Other Side of Heaven '02
The Other Side of Sunday '96
Pacie Nuestro '85
Paradise Now '05 ▶
Partition '07
Pass the Ammo '88
The Passion of Darkly Noon '95
The Passion of Joan of Arc '28 ▶
The Passover Plot '75
P.D. James: Death in Holy Orders '03
The Penitent '88
Peter and Paul '81
Pi '98 ▶
Picking Up the Pieces '99
Pray '07
Pray TV '82
Pray TV '80
A Prayer in the Dark '97
Preacherman '83
The Preacher's Wife '96 ▶
Priest '94 ▶
Prisoner of Rio '89
The Private Secretary '35
Private Confessions '98 ▶
The Prodigal Planet '88
Promised a Miracle '88
Protocols of Zion '05 ▶
The Quarry '98 ▶
Queen Margot '94 ▶

Quo Vadis '51 ▶
Quo Vadis '85
Rain '32 ▶
The Rapture '91 ▶
The Reckoning '03 ▶
The Rector's Wife '94 ▶
Red Planet Mars '52
Resurrection '80 ▶
Resurrection '99
Return to Paradise '53 ▶
Revelation '01
Rock Haven '07
RoGoPaG '62 ▶
Romero '89 ▶
The Rook '99
Sacrilege '86
St. Benny the Dip '51
Saint Maybe '98 ▶
St. Patrick: The Irish Legend '00 ▶
Saint Ralph '04 ▶
Saints and Soldiers '03 ▶
Salome '85
Salvation! '87
Sanctuary of Fear '79
The Scarlet Letter '79
Sebastiane '79 ▶
The Second Chance '06
Shadowlands '93 ▶
The Sky Pilot '21 ▶
The Song of Bernadette '43 ▶
Stigmata '99
Stolen Summer '02
A Stranger in the Kingdom '98
Susan and God '40 ▶
Tales from the Crypt Presents Bordello of Blood '96
That Eye, the Sky '94 ▶
There Will Be Blood '07 ▶
The Third Miracle '99 ▶
This Stuff'll Kill 'Ya! '71
Through a Glass Darkly '61 ▶
The Tollbooth '04
Touch '96
Tournament '29
Trapped by the Mormons '22
Tribulation '00
21 Grams '03 ▶
Ultrachrist '03
Under the Moonlight '01 ▶
Virgin '03 ▶
A Walk to Remember '02
Wall '04 ▶
Welcome to Paradise '07
West Beirut '98 ▶
Where Angels Go, Trouble Follows '68
When Night is Falling '95 ▶
Whistle down the Wind '61 ▶
Whistling in the Dark '41 ▶
Whitcomb's War '87
The White Rose '23 ▶
Wholly Moses! '80
Why Has Bodhi-Dharma Left for the East? '89 ▶
The Wicker Man '06
Wide Awake '98 ▶
The Winter Light '62 ▶
Wise Blood '79 ▶
Witness '85 ▶
Woman, Thou Art Loosed '04
The Word '78 ▶
The Worldly Madonna '22

Religious Epics
see also Religion
Abraham '94 ▶
A.D. '85
The Agony and the Ecstasy '65
...And God Spoke '94
Barabbas '62 ▶
Ben-Hur '26 ▶
Ben-Hur '59 ▶
The Bible '66
Cleopatra '63 ▶
David '97
David and Bathsheba '51 ▶

▶ = *rated three bones or higher*

Religious

Demetrius and the Gladiators '54
The Egyptian '54
El Cid '61
From the Manger to the Cross '15
The Gospel According to St. Matthew '64
The Gospel of John '03
In the Name of the Pope-King '85
Jacob '94
Jesus '00
Jesus of Nazareth '28
Joseph '95
Judith of Bethulia '14
The King of Kings '61
Kingdom of Heaven '05
The Messiah '75
Moses '76
Moses '96
The Nativity Story '06
Noah's Ark '99
The Passion of the Christ '04
Prince of Egypt '98
The Prodigal '55
The Robe '53
Samson and Delilah '96
The Sign of the Cross '33
Sodom and Gomorrah '62
The Song of Bernadette '43
The Ten Commandments '23
The Ten Commandments '56

Renegade Body Parts

see also Killer Brains
The Addams Family '91
Addams Family Values '93
And Now the Screaming Starts '73
The Animal '01
The Beast with Five Fingers '46
Blood of Ghastly Horror '72
Body Parts '91
Body Parts '94
The Brain that Wouldn't Die '63
The Crawling Eye '58
The Crawling Hand '63
Crazy in Alabama '99
Demonoid, Messenger of Death '81
Doctor Butcher M.D. '80
Dr. Terror's House of Horrors '65
8 Heads in a Duffel Bag '96
Evil Dead 2: Dead by Dawn '87
Gravesend '97
The Hand '81
Hands of a Stranger '62
The Hands of Orlac '25
The Hands of Orlac '60
How to Get Ahead in Advertising '89
Idle Hands '99
The Incredible Two-Headed Transplant '71
Killer Tongue '96
The Kingdom '95
The Kingdom 2 '97
Machined '06
Mad Love '35
The Man with Two Brains '83
Mindkiller '87
Picking Up the Pieces '99
Planet Terror '07
Quicksilver Highway '98
Severed Ties '92
The Thing with Two Heads '72
Virus '98
Waxwork 2: Lost in Time '91

Rent-a-Cop

Above the Rim '94
Armed and Dangerous '86
The Cookout '04
Critical Mass '00
Cyber-Tracker '93
The Doll '62
Eddie Presley '92
End of Days '99
Fear X '03
Friday After Next '02
The Heist '89
Hobgoblins '87
Inspector Gadget '99
Light It Up '99
Looney Tunes: Back in Action '03
Mannequin '87
National Security '03
Night at the Museum '06
P2 '07
Rent-A-Cop '88
The Shape of Things '03
Star Spangled Rhythm '42
Tapeheads '89
Trixie '00
Unbreakable '00
Underdog '07
Urban Legend '98

Repressed Men

see also Men
The Age of Innocence '93
American Beauty '99
Beloved/Friend '99
Bitter Moon '92
Bleak Moments '71
The Bodyguard '92
Box of Moonlight '96
Changing Times '04
Creation of Adam '93
El '52
Falling Down '93
Far Side of the Moon '03
Felicia's Journey '99
Fight Club: '99
The Game '97
The Good Shepherd '06
The Hawk Is Dying '06
Howard's End '92
In and Out '97
Kiss the Sky '98
Last Life in the Universe '03
Like It Never Was Before '95
Little Children '06
The Little Kidnappers '90
Love and Death on Long Island '97
Maurice '87
My Best Friend '06
On a Clear Day '05
The Preacher's Wife '96
A Rather English Marriage '98
The Red Dwarf '99
The Remains of the Day '93
Shadowlands '93
Sirens '94
Split Second '99
Till Human Voices Wake Us '02
Yi Yi '00
Zero Degrees Kelvin '95

Rescue Missions

see also Rescue Missions Involving Time Travel
Agent of Death '99
Air Rage '01
Alaska '96
Alone in the Woods '95
The Amazing Panda Adventure '95
Any Place But Home '97
Apollo 13 '95
Balto '95
Behind Enemy Lines '96
Behind Enemy Lines '01
Berlin Tunnel 21 '81
Beyond Borders '03
Black Hawk Down '01
Blade 2 '02
Blind Heat '00
Boomerang '76
Born to Be Wild '95
Breakout '75
A Bug's Life '98
Caged Fear '92
The Chamber '90
The Children '90
The City of Lost Children '95
Comanche Station '60
Commando '85
Con Air '97
Courage Under Fire '96
Crossfire '89
Dante's Peak '97
Daredevils of the Red Circle '38
Dark Mountain '44
The Day After Tomorrow '04
Daylight '96
Dead Ahead '96
Desperate Women '78
The Diamond of Jeru '01
Die Hard '88
Die Hard 2: Die Harder '90
Die Hard: With a Vengeance '95
The Dirty Dozen: The Deadly Mission '87
Django Strikes Again '87
Dragonworld '94
Eight Below '06
Ernest Scared Stupid '91
Escape from L.A. '96
Event Horizon '97
The Ewok Adventure '84
Executioner of Venice '63
Executive Decision '96
Expect No Mercy '95
Far from Home: The Adventures of Yellow Dog '94
Fever '91
Finding Nemo '03
First Daughter '99
Force: Five '81
Free Willy '93
Free Willy 2: The Adventure Home '95
Free Willy 3: The Rescue '97
The Golden Compass '07
The Great Raid '05
Grizzly Mountain '97
The Guardian '06
Hard Ticket to Hawaii '87
The Hidden Fortress '58
High Velocity '76
The Hills Have Eyes 2 '07
Hired to Kill '91
Honeybaby '74
Hoot '06
Ice Age '02
In the Company of Spies '99
Independence Day '96
The Inn of the Sixth Happiness '58
Island in the Sky '53
Jenny's War '85
Jeopardy '53
Joey '98
Journey to the Center of the Earth '99
Jurassic Park 3 '01
Kidnapped in Paradise '98
Kids of the Round Table '96
Killing Streets '91
The Last Hard Men '76
Legend of the Lost Tomb '97
Lisbon '56
The Lone Runner '88
The Losers '70
Losing Isaiah '94
Lucie Aubrac '98
The Magnificent Seven '60
Managua '97
The Marine '06
Master of Disguise '02
The Matrix Revolutions '03
Mercenary 2: Thick and Thin '97
Mercy Mission '93
Miracle at Midnight '98
Ms. Bear '97
The Missing '03
Missing in Action '84
Missing in Action 2: The Beginning '85
Mission: Impossible 3 '06
Mission to Mars '00
Morning Departure '50
Naked Souls '95
Navy SEALS '90
Oliver & Company '88
One Small Hero '99
Operation Cross Eagles '69
Operation Delta Force 2: Mayday '97
Operation Dumbo Drop '95
Ordeal in the Arctic '93
Outbreak '94
Pirates of the Caribbean: The Curse of the Black Pearl '03
Pirates of the Caribbean: At World's End '07
Pray for Death '85
Prince Valiant '97
Raid on Entebbe '77
Rambo: First Blood, Part 2 '85
Red Planet '00
The Rescue '88
Rescue Me '93
The Rescuers '77
The Rescuers Down Under '90
Rescuers: Stories of Courage—Two Couples '98
Return of Chandu '34
Revenge of the Barbarians '60
Revenge of the Musketeers '94
Riot '96
The Rock '96
Rules of Engagement '00
Sasquatch '02
Saving Private Ryan '98
Saving Shiloh '06
The Sea Shall Not Have Them '55
The Searchers '56
The Secret Agent Club '96
The Secret Invasion '64
Seven Samurai '54
Seven Seconds '05
Shadow Warriors: Hunt for the Death Merchant '97
Shanghai Noon '00
Shrek '01
Silver Hawk '04
The Slender Thread '65
Soldier of Fortune Inc. '97
Soldier Boyz '97
Space Marines '96
Spy Game '01
Spy Kids '01
Star Trek: Insurrection '98
Steel Sharks '97
The Story of Dr. Wassell '44
Stranglehold '94
Street Fighter '94
Submarine Attack '54
Submerged '00
Sudden Death '95
Supernova '99
Surface to Air '98
The Survivor '98
The Taking of Flight 847: The Uli Derickson Story '88
Tears of the Sun '03
A Thousand Heroes '92
Three Bad Men '05
Three Days to a Kill '91
Thunder in Paradise '93
Thunder in Paradise 2 '94
Toy Story '95
Toy Story 2 '99
The Tunnel '01
Two Bits & Pepper '95
2001: A Space Travesty '00
Uncommon Valor '83
Valiant '05
Varian's War '01
Vertical Limit '00
Victory at Entebbe '76
Volcano '97
Waikiki Wedding '37
Welcome to Sarajevo '97
The Wild '06
William Faulkner's Old Man '97
Wings in the Dark '35
Wolverine '96
The World in His Arms '52
The World Is Not Enough '99
World Trade Center '06
X2: X-Men United '03
The Yakuza '75
Yankee Buccaneer '52
Zathura '05

Rescue Missions Involving Time Travel

see also Rescue Missions
Back to the Future '85
Back to the Future, Part 2 '89
Back to the Future, Part 3 '90
Bill & Ted's Excellent Adventure '89
Deja Vu '06
Disney's The Kid '00
Frequency '00
Jumanji '95
Lost in Space '98
Maximum Breakout '91
Millennium '89
The Navigator '88
Star Trek IV: The Voyage Home '86
Star Trek: First Contact '96
Superman: The Movie '78
The Terminator '84
Terminator 2: Judgment Day '91
Terminator 3: Rise of the Machines '03
Time After Time '79
Timeline '03
Timemaster '95
Trancers 2: The Return of Jack Deth '90
When Time Expires '97
Yesterday's Target '96
Zathura '05

The Resistance

see also World War II; World War II Spies
Action in the North Atlantic '43
Alien Siege '05
Army of Shadows '69
Black Book '06
Carve Her Name with Pride '58
Casablanca '42
Charlotte Gray '01
The Day and the Hour '63
A Day in October '92
Edge of Darkness '43
Equilibrium '02
A Generation '54
Hangmen Also Die '42
The Heroes of Telemark '65
Holocaust '78
Johnny Frenchman '46
Julia '77
The Last Lieutenant '94
The Last Metro '80
Les Miserables '98
Lucie Aubrac '98
Manon '50
One Against the Wind '91
Passage to Marseilles '44
Soldier of Orange '78
Sophie Scholl: The Final Days '05
That Summer of White Roses '90
This Land Is Mine '43
To Be or Not to Be '42
To Be or Not to Be '83
The Train '65
Underground '41
Victory at Entebbe '76
Watch on the Rhine '43
When Willie Comes Marching Home '50
The White Rose '83
A Woman at War '94

Reunited

see also Amnesia; I'm Not Dead, Yet!; Island Fare; Missing Persons
Before Sunset '04
Cast Away '00
The Deep End of the Ocean '98
The End of the Affair '99
Garden State '04
The Groomsmen '06
Hard to Kill '89
Hired Hand '71
Johnson Family Vacation '04
Keeping Up with the Steins '06
Love '05
Magnolia '99
Marilyn Hotchkiss' Ballroom Dancing & Charm School '06
Matchstick Men '03
Mrs. Wiggs of the Cabbage Patch '34
Move Over, Darling '63
My Favorite Wife '40
The Parent Trap '61
The Parent Trap '98
Pronto '97
Riding Alone for Thousands of Miles '05
Rude '96
A Simple Twist of Fate '94
Sons '89
Story of a Love Affair '50
The Sunshine Boys '95

Revealing Swimwear

The American Angels: Baptism of Blood '89
Beach Babes from Beyond '93
Beach Girls '82
The Bikini Car Wash Company '90
The Bikini Car Wash Company 2 '92
Bikini Island '91
Bikini Summer '91
Bikini Summer 2 '92
Blood of Dracula's Castle '69
Body Waves '92
Buford's Beach Bunnies '92
California Girls '84
The Cover Girl Murders '93
Dark Tide '93
The Dolls '83
Fit to Kill '93
Frankenstein Island '81
Fun in Acapulco '63
Girls Next Door '79
Great Bikini Off-Road Adventure '94
Hardbodies '84
Hollywood High, Part 2 '81
Hollywood Hot Tubs '84
Hollywood Hot Tubs 2: Educating Crystal '89
Horrors of Spider Island '59
Hot Resort '85
The House that Vanished '73
Island of Lost Girls '68
L'Annee des Meduses '86
Malibu Beach '78
The Malibu Beach Vampires '91
Malibu Bikini Shop '86
Malibu Express '85
Mugsy's Girls '85
Ocean Drive Weekend '85
Pauline at the Beach '83
Pin-Up Girl '44
Playgirl Killer '66
Private Lessons, Another Story '94
Slumber Party Massacre 2 '87
Sorority House Party '92
Starhops '78
Summer City '77
Summer Fantasy '84
Swimsuit '89
Tarzan, the Ape Man '81

▲ = *rated three bones or higher*

They Were So Young '55
Tintorera... Tiger Shark '78
Vice Academy 3 '91
Welcome to Spring Break '88
When Dinosaurs Ruled the Earth '70

Revenge

see also *Vigilantes*

Act of Aggression '73
Act of Passion: The Lost Honor of Kathryn Beck '83
Act of Vengeance '74
Act of Violence '48
An Actor's Revenge '63
Addicted to Love '96
Adios, Hombre '68
The Adventurers '70
The Alchemist '81
Alien Seed '89
All Dogs Go to Heaven '89
Already Dead '07
Amazon Warrior '07
Ambush '99
American Buffalo '95
American Commandos '84
American Eagle '90
American Samurai '92
Anatomy of a Psycho '61
Angel and the Badman '47
Angel of Destruction '94
Angel Square '92
Angels from Hell '68
Appointment with Crime '45
Archer: The Fugitive from the Empire '81
Arizona Terror '31
Ash Wednesday '31
Asylum '72
Attack of the 50 Ft. Woman '93
The Avenging '82
Avenging Angel '85
Avenging Angelo '02
Avenging Force '86
Back in Action '94
Back to Back '90
Bad Blood '94
Bad Reputation '05
Ballad of Cable Hogue '70
The Ballad of the Sad Cafe '91
Bandits '86
Bang '95
Banzai Runner '86
The Baron '88
Basket Case '82
Batman Begins '05
The Beast with Five Fingers '46
The Beguiled '70
Behind the Sun '01
Bell from Hell '74
Bella Mafia '97
Benefit of the Doubt '93
Beowulf & Grendel '06
Best of the Best 2 '93
Beyond Forgiveness '94
Big Bully '95
Big Jake '71
Bird of Prey '95
Bitter Sweet '98
Bitter Vengeance '94
The Black Arrow '48
The Black Arrow '84
Black Cobra '83
Black Doll '38
Black Fox: Good Men and Bad '94
The Black Hand '50
The Black Klansman '66
The Black Pirate '26
The Black Raven '43
Black Scorpion '95
The Black Six '74
The Black Sleep '56
Black Sunday '60
A Black Veil for Lisa '68
Blackbelt 2: Fatal Force '93
Blastfighter '85
Blind Vengeance '90
Blood and Guns '79
Blood Crime '02
Blood for a Silver Dollar '66
Blood on the Mountain '88
Blood Red '88

Blood Ring '95
Bloodfist '89
Bloodknot '95
Bloodmatch '91
BloodRayne '06
Bloody Birthday '80
Blue City '86
Blue Knight '75
The Blue Lamp '49
Blue Tiger '94
Body Count '95
Boiling Point '93
Bones '01
Border Rangers '50
Bounty Hunters '89
Bounty Tracker '93
Branded a Coward '35
Breakdown '96
Bride of Killer Nerd '91
Broken Harvest '94
Bronze Buckaroo '39
Brotherhood of Justice '86
The Brute Man '46
Bugles in the Afternoon '52
Buildance '88
Bulldog Courage '35
Bullet '94
Bullet for Sandoval '70
Bullies '86
Buried Alive 2 '97
The Burning '82
Bury Me an Angel '71
Cadillac Man '90
Caged Heat 2: Stripped of Freedom '94
Caged Terror '72
The Caravan Trail '46
Cape Fear '61
Cape Fear '91
Carolina Skeletons '92
Carson City Kid '40
Cartouche '62
Cellblock Sisters: Banished Behind Bars '95
Certain Sacrifice '80
Chain Gang Women '72
The Chair '87
Challenge '74
Chameleon '95
Chan Is Missing '82
Changing Lanes '02
The Chase '46
The Chosen One: Legend of the Raven '98
Chisum '70
Chrome and Hot Leather '71
Circumstances Unknown '95
Class of 1984 '82
Clayton County Line '78
Closure '07
Cobra '71
Code Name: Zebra '84
Code of Honor '82
Coffy '73
Cold Eyes of Fear '70
Cold Steel '87
Cold Sweat '71
Cole Justice '89
Collateral Damage '02
Commando Invasion '87
Conflict of Interest '92
The Conqueror & the Empress '64
The Contract '98
Cornered '45
The Coroner '98
Coroner Creek '48
The Corsican Brothers '42
Cousin Bette '97
Covert Assassin '94
The Cowboys '72

Crack House '89
The Craft '96
Crank '06
Crazed Cop '88
Creepers '85
Creepshow 2 '87
Crimebusters '79
Crimson Gold '03
The Crippled Masters '82
The Crossing Guard '94
The Crow '93
The Crow 2: City of Angels '96
The Crow: Salvation '00
The Crow: Wicked Prayer '05
The Crucible '96
Cry Danger '51
Cry of the Innocent '80
Cry of the Owl '87
Cry Vengeance '54
Curse of the Devil '73
Cybercity '99
Daddy-O '59
Daddy's Gone A-Hunting '69
Danger Zone 2 '89
Dangerous Obsession '88
Dangerous Orphans '86
Daredevil '03
Dark August '76
Dark River: A Father's Revenge '90
Darkman '90
Darkness Falls '98
Daughter of the Dragon '31
DaVinci's War '92
Dawn Rider '35
The Day the Women Got Even '80
Dead Boyz Can't Fly '93
Dead Dog '00
Dead Man's Revenge '93
Dead Man's Shoes '04
Dead on the Money '91
Dead Silence '98
Deadly Daphne's Revenge '93
Deadly Darling '85
Deadly Game '91
Deadly Lessons '94
Deadly Reactor '89
The Deadly Secret '94
Deadly Sting '82
The Deadly Trackers '73
Deadly Twins '85
Deadly Vengeance '81
Deadly Weapon '88
Death and the Maiden '94
Death Magic '92
Death Row Diner '88
Death Sentence '07
Death to Smoochy '02
Death Valley: The Revenge of Bloody Bill '04
Death Wish '74
Death Wish 2 '82
Death Wish 3 '85
Deep in the Heart '83
The Defenders: Payback '97
Demented '80
The Demons '74
Demonwarp '87
Descent '07
Desert Heat '99
Desolation Angels '95
Desperado '95
The Desperados '70
Desperate Crimes '93
Devastator '85
Devil Times Five '74
Devil Woman '76
Devil's Canyon '53
Devil's Knight '03
The Devil's Mistress '68
The Devil's Possessed '74
The Devil's Rejects '05
Devonsville Terror '83
The Diabolical Dr. Z '65
Die! Die! My Darling! '65
Die Hard: With a Vengeance '95
Dingaka '65
Dinner at the Ritz '37
Dinner Rush '00
Diplomatic Immunity '91
Dirty Harry '71

Dirty Little Secret '98
Dirty Work '97
Disclosure '94
Dixie Dynamite '76
Do or Die '91
Dr. Jekyll & Mr. Hyde '20
Dr. Syn, Alias the Scarecrow '64
Dr. Terror's House of Horrors '65
Dogville '03
Dogwatch '97
Dolemite '75
Double Exposure '93
Double Impact '91
Double Jeopardy '99
The Double Negative '80
Double Revenge '89
Driven to Kill '09
Drop Zone '94
Drums of Jeopardy '31
Dudes '87
Duel at Silver Creek '52
Dynasty '77
Eagle vs. Shark '07
Eagles Attack at Dawn '70
Easy Kill '89
Edge of Darkness '86
The Eiger Sanction '75
El Barbaro '84
Election '99
The Eliminators '86
Emmanuelle, the Queen '79
The Empire of Passion '76
Enough '02
Escape '90
The Evil That Men Do '84
Evilspeak '82
The Ex '96
Ex-Cop '93
The Executioner, Part 2: Frozen Scream '84
The Expert '95
Exterminator '80
Exterminator 2 '84
Extreme Vengeance '90
Extremities '85
An Eye for an Eye '61
An Eye for an Eye '95
Eye of the Eagle 2 '89
Eye of the Tiger '86
Face/Off '97
A Face to Kill For '99
Facing the Enemy '00
Fair Game '95
Faithful '95
The Fall of the House of Usher '49
The Fall of the House of Usher '60
The Family '70
Far Country '55
Faust: Love of the Damned '00
Felony '95
Fight for Us '89
Fight for Your Life '77
The Fighter '52
Fighting Back '82
The Fighting Legion '30
Final Impact '91
Final Mission '84
Fine Gold '88
Fiorile '93
Firecracker '71
The First Wives Club '96
Fist Fighter '89
Fist of Honor '92
Fists of Blood '87
Fists of Iron '94
Flesh and Blood '22
Flesh and Blood '85
Flesh and the Spur '57
Fleshburn '84
Flesh Feast '59
Fog Island '45
For Which He Stands '98
For Your Eyes Only '81
The Forbidden Christ '50
Forbidden Sun '89
Force of Evil '77

Forced Vengeance '82
Forgotten Warrior '86
Four Brothers '05
The Fourth Angel '01
Frame Up '91
Framed '75
Freakshow '95
Freaks '32
Freeway '88
Friend of the Family 2 '96
Frightmare '81
Frogs '72
Full Contact '92
Full Contact '93
Full Metal Jacket '87
Full Metal Ninja '89
The Funeral '96
Funland '89
Future Kill '85
"G" Men '35
Galloping Dynamite '37
The Gambling Samurai '60
Gang Boys '03
Gang of Roses '03
Gangs, Inc. '41
Gangs of New York '02
Garringo '69
Gator Bait 2: Cajun Justice '88
Genghis Cohn '93
Gentleman from Dixie '41
Get Carter '00
Get Carter '71
Getting Even '92
Ghetto Dawg 2: Out of the Pits '05
The Ghost '63
Ghost Dance '83
The Ghost of Yotsuya '58
Ghostriders '87
The Girl with the Hungry Eyes '94
Gladiator '00
The Godfather '72
The Godfather, Part 2 '74
The Godfather, Part 3 '90
The Complete Epic 1902-1959 '81
Gone with the West '72
God's Gun '75
Grave of the Vampire '72
The Graveyard '74
Green Mansions '59
Gunfighter '98
Gunplay '51
Gunsmoke: Return to Dodge '87
Halloween '78
Halloween 6: The Curse of Michael Myers '95
Hamlet '48
Hamlet '90
Hamlet '96
Hamlet '01
Hang 'Em High '67
Hannibal '01
Hannibal Rising '07
Hannie Caulder '72
Harakiri '62
Hard Bounty '94
Hard Candy '05
Hardcase and Fist '89
Harold Robbins' Body Parts '99
The Haunted Palace '63
HauntedWeen '91
Hawkeye '88
Hello Mary Lou: Prom Night 2 '87
He Who Gets Slapped '24
Headless Eyes '83
Heat Street '87
Heavy Metal 2000 '00
The Heist '89
Hell Hunters '87
Hell on Frisco Bay '55
Hellbent '88
Hell's Angels '69
Hell's Belles '69
Hell's Kitchen NYC '97
Hennessy '75
Hi-Riders '77
The Hidden Room '49
High Command '37
High Noon '00
Highlander: Endgame '00
The Highway Man '99

Highwaymen '03
Hired Hand '71
Hit! '73
Hit & Run '82
Hitched '01
Hog Wild '80
Homeboy '75
Hornet's Nest '70
Horror Rises from the Tomb '72
The Horror Show '89
Hostage Hotel '00
Hot Lead '51
Hour of the Gun '67
Hourglass '95
House Across the Bay '40
House of Horrors '46
House of Strangers '49
House of Usher '88
Housewife '72
How to Make a Monster '58
Human Beasts '80
The Human Factor '75
Hunter '76
I Drink Your Blood '71
I Married a Witch '42
I Met a Murderer '39
I Spit on Your Grave '77
If I Die Before I Wake '98
Igor & the Lunatics '85
I'll Sleep When I'm Dead '03
The Indestructible Man '56
The Indian Tomb '21
Inn of the Damned '74
Innocent Victim '90
Inquisition '76
Instant Justice '86
Instinct to Kill '01
The Invisible Man's Revenge '44
Ironheart '92
Irreversible '02
The Italian Job '03
Jack Frost 2: Revenge of the Mutant Killer Snowman '00
The Jayhawkers '59
Jenny Lamour '47
Jessi's Girls '75
The Jitters '88
Joe Somebody '01
John Tucker Must Die '06
Johnny Handsome '89
Joshua '76
Jubal '56
Kansas City Confidential '52
Karate Warrior '88
The Karate Kid: Part 2 '86
Kemek '70
Keys to Tulsa '96
Kickboxer 4: The Aggressor '94
Kickboxer 2: The Road Back '90
Kid '90
Kid Colter '85
Kid Vengeance '75
Kidnap Syndicate '76
Kill Alex Kill '76
Kill Bill Vol. 1 '03
Kill Bill Vol. 2 '04
Kill Line '91
Killcrazy '89
The Killing Kind '73
Killing Time '97
The Killing Zone '90
King of the Ants '03
King of the Kickboxers '91
King of the Pecos '36
Kingfisher the Killer '81
Kiss Daddy Goodbye '81
Kiss of Death '94

★ = rated three bones or higher

Kufts '92
L.A. Bounty '89
L.A. Crackdown '87
L.A. Heat '88
La Passante '83►
La Vengeance d'une Femme '89
L.A. Vice '89
The Ladies Club '86
The Ladies of the Bois de Bologne '44
Lady Avenger '89
Lady Dragon '92
Lady Dragon 2 '93
Lady in White '88►
Lady Mobster '88
Lady Street Fighter '86
Lady Vengeance '05
L'Annee des Meduses '86
Laserblast '78
Last Bullet '50
The Last Days of Dolwyn '49
The Last Don 2 '98
The Last Hard Men '76
The Last Hour '91
Last House on the Left '72
Last Hurrah for Chivalry '78
The Last Outlaw '93
The Last Reunion '80
The Late Show '77►
The Last Train from Gun Hill '59►
Law of the Sea '32
Legacy of Rage '86
Let's Go to Prison '06
License to Kill '89▲
The Life Aquatic with Steve Zissou '04►
The Limey '99►
Lionheart '90
The Lion's Share '79
Lip Service '00
Lipstick '76
Little Boy Blue '97
Little Moon & Jud McGraw '78
Live Flesh '97►
Living Doll '90
Lorna Doone '34
Lorna Doone '90
Lorna Doone '01►
Lovely... But Deadly '82
Lure of the Sila '49
Lust and Revenge '95
Macbeth '70►
Macbeth '88
Macho Callahan '70
Mad Dog '84
Mad Max '80►
Magdalene '88
Make a Million '35
Malicious '95
Malicious Intent '99
A Man Apart '03
The Man from Laramie '55►
The Man in the Iron Mask '39►
The Man in the Iron Mask '77
The Man in the Iron Mask '98►
Man in the Wilderness '71
The Man on Fire '04
The Man They Could Not Hang '39
The Manhandlers '73
Manhunt '73
Maniac '77
Manon of the Spring '87►
Marathon Man '76►
Mars '96
The Mask '94►
Mask of Death '97
Massacre at Central High '76
The Match Factory Girl '90
Maternal Instincts '96
McBain '91►
McQ '74
Mean Creek '04►
Mean Girls '04►
Mean Machine '73
Medea '88
Memento '00▲
Memories of Murder '90
Men... '85►
Mercenary '96

The Merchant of Venice '04►
Merchants of Death '99
Mercy '96
The Messenger '87
Metro '96
Miami Cops '89
Miami Vendetta '87
Midnite Spares '85
Millie '31
Mind Trap '91
Mindstorm '01
Missing Pieces '83
Mission Kashmir '00
Missionary Man '07
Mrs. Munck '95
Model by Day '94
Molly and Gina '94
The Monster and the Girl '41
Monte Walsh '70►
Monument Ave. '98
Mooncussers '62
Moonshine County Express '77
Motor Psycho '65
The Mummy '59►
Murder on Lenox Avenue '41
Murdered Innocence '94
The Murderers Are Among Us '46
Murphy's Law '86
Murphy's War '71
The Mysterious Dr. Fu Manchu '29
Nails '92
The Naked Angels '69
Naked Vengeance '85
Narc '02►
Nasty Hero '89
Navajo Joe '67
Necromancer: Satan's Servant '88
The Neighbor No. Thirteen '05
The Nesting '80
Nevada Smith '66
Never Pick Up a Stranger '79
Never Say Die '94
The New Frontier '35
The New Kids '85
The Newlydeads '87
Next of Kin '89
Night Creature '79
Night Hunter '95
Night Train Murders '75
The Night Visitor '70
Nightmare Castle '65
Nightmare in Wax '69
9 to 5 '80
No Name on the Bullet '59►
No Safe Haven '87
Nomad Riders '81
Nowhere to Run '88
The Nurse '97
Object of Obsession '95
Obsessed '88
Ocean's Thirteen '07►
Offerings '89
Office Killer '97
Oklahoma Kid '39►
Old Boyfriends '79
Old Gun '76►
Oldboy '03►
Olivia '83
On Dangerous Ground '51►
On Guard! '03►
Once a Thief '90
Once Upon a Time in Mexico '03►
One Arabian Night '21►
One Armed Executioner '80
One Deadly Summer '83►
One-Eyed Jacks '61►
One Man Army '93
One Man's Justice '95
One Man's War '90
One Russian Summer '73
Operation Intercept '95
The Operator '01
Orca '77
Original Gangstas '96
Othello '65►
Othello '95►
The Other Side of Midnight '77

Out for Blood '93
Out for Justice '91
Outlaw Force '87
The Outlaw Josey Wales '76►
Outrage! '93
Outrage '93
Overkill '86
The Page Turner '06
Paparazzi '04
Paper Bullets '99
Parting Shots '98
Pathfinder '87►
Pathfinder '07
The Patriot '00
Patriot Games '92►
Pay Off '89
Payback '89
Payback '90
Payback '94
Payback '98►
Payoff '91
Pecos Kid '35
The Penalty '20
Pepi, Luci, Bom and Other Girls on the Heap '80
The Perfect Bride '91
The Perfect Weapon '91
The Perfect Wife '00
The Phantom Bullet '26
The Phantom of Soho '64
Phantom of the Paradise '74
The Pit '81
Pit Fighter '05
Platoon the Warriors '88
Play Dead '81
Pledge Night '90
Plutonium Baby '87
Point Blank '67
Poison Ivy 3: The New Seduction '97
Positive I.D. '87
Posse '93►
Possession: Until Death Do You Part '90
The Power of the Ninjitsu '88
Premature Burial '62
President's Target '93
Pretty Persuasion '05
Prey of the Jaguar '96
Prison '88
The Professional '94
Prom Night '80
The Prowler '81
Psychic Killer '75
Psycho Girls '86
Psychopath '73
Pumpkinhead '88
The Punisher '90
The Punisher '04
Puppet Master 3: Toulon's Revenge '90
Pursued '47►
Pushed to the Limit '92
The Quick and the Dead '95
Quiet Cool '86
Quiet Fire '91
Rage '72
Rainbow Ranch '33
Rapid Fire '89
The Raven '35►
Raven '97
Raw Deal '48►
Raw Target '95
Recoil '97
Redline '07
Redline '07
Relentless '89
Renegades '89
The Replacement Killers '98
Reservoir Dogs '92►
The Restless Breed '58
Retribution '88
The Return of Dr. Fu Manchu '30
Return of Frank James '40►
Return of the Evil Dead '75
Return of the Magnificent Seven '66
The Return of the Musketeers '89
Return of the Vampire '43
Return to Wildfire '48
Return to Macon County '75
Revenge '86
Revenge '90

Revenge of the Barbarians '85
Revenge of the Nerds '84
Revenge of the Nerds 2: Nerds in Paradise '87
Revenge of the Radioactive Reporter '91
Revenge of the Red Baron '93
The Revenge Rider '35
Revolt of the Zombies '36
Revolver '92
Ricco '74
Ricochet '91►
Ride Clear of Diablo '54
Ride Lonesome '59
Ride to Glory '77
Ride with the Devil '99
Ringside '49
Rio Lobo '70
Rip Roarin' Buckaroo '36
Rise: Blood Hunter '07
Rites of Frankenstein '72
Road to Perdition '02►
Rock House '88
Rolling Thunder '77
Rolling Vengeance '87
Romola '25
Rose of Rio Grande '38
Rosewood '96►
Round Numbers '91
Royal Deceit '94
Ruby Gentry '52
Rulers of the City '76
Runaways '75
Rushmore '98►
Rustler's Paradise '35
Ruyblas '48
Sacrifice '00
Sacrilege '86
Samurai Reincarnation '81
The Satan Killer '90
Savage Drums '51
Savage Instinct '89
Savage Island '00
Savage Justice '88
Savage Run '70►
Savage Streets '83
Scam '93
Scanner Cop 2: Volkin's Revenge '94
Scorned '93
Scorned 2 '96
Scream Dream '89
Screamer '74
Search and Destroy '81
Second Victory '87
The Secret Four '40
Seraphim Falls '06
Serial Bomber '96
Seven Hours to Judgment '88
The Seven-Ups '73
Severed Ties '92
Sex Crimes '92
The Shadow Man '53
Shame '92
Shame '92
Sharpe's Eagle '93
The She-Beast '65
She-Devil '89
She Devils in Chains '76
She-Freak '67
Shoot Out '71
Shootfighter 2: Kill or Be Killed! '96
The Shooting '66►
Shooting Fish '98
Short Eyes '79
The Showdown '50
The Showdown '93
Silent Night, Deadly Night 2 '87
Simba '55►
Simple Justice '89
Sin '02
Sin City '05►
The Sin of Harold Diddlebock '47
Sirens '02
The Sister-in-Law '95
Sisters of Death '76
Six Shootin' Sheriff '38
Sizzle '81
Slaughter '72
Slaughter's Big Ripoff '73
Slayground '84

Sleep Easy, Hutch Rimes '00
Sleepers '96
Sleeping with the Enemy '91
Sloane '84
A Small Town in Texas '76
Smart Money '91
Smoke in the Wind '75
The Smokers '00
SnakeEater '89
SnakeEater 3: His Law '92
Soldier Blue '70
Soldier's Fortune '91
Sometimes They Come Back '91
Sons of Katie Elder '65►
Sorority Girl '57
Soul Vengeance '75
Sound of Murder '82
Sour Grapes '98
Special Investigator '36
The Specialist '94
Speed 2: Cruise Control '97
Speeding Up Time '71
Spider-Man 3 '07
Stanley '72
Star Trek 2: The Wrath of Khan '82►
Star Trek: First Contact '96►
Steel and Lace '90
Steele Justice '87
The Sting 2 '83
Straight Shooter '99
Strange Confession '45►
Strange Shadows in an Empty Room '76
Stranger in Paso Bravo '68
Strangler of the Swamp '46
Straw Dogs '72►
Street Hunter '90
Street Law '74
Street Vengeance '95
Street War '76
Street Wars '91
Striker '88
The Substitute '96
The Substitute 2: School's Out '97
Sudden Death '85
Sudden Impact '83
Super Force '90
The Supernaturals '86
Sweeney Todd: The Demon Barber of Fleet Street '07
Sweet Justice '92
Sweet Poison '91
Sweet Revenge '98
Swift Justice '88
Sword of Gideon '86
Sword of Venus '53
Swordsmen in Double Flag Town '91
Sworn Enemies '96
Tactical Assault '99
Take Two '87
Talion '66
Taste the Blood of Dracula '70
Terror Creatures from the Grave '66
Terror in a Texas Town '58
Texas Kid '43
Texas Payback '95
The Texican '66
Theatre of Blood '73►
They Made Me a Fugitive '47
Things '80s
This Gun for Hire '42►
This Man Must Die '70►
Thou Shalt Not Kill...Except '87
Threat '49
Three Husbands '50
Three in the Cellar '70
The 3 Marias '03
Thunder in the Desert '38
Thunder Warrior 3 '88
Tillie's Punctured Romance '14
A Time of Destiny '88
Time to Die '83
A Time to Kill '96►
Timecop 2: The Berlin Decision '03
Titus '99

To Be the Best '93
Today We Kill, Tomorrow We Die '71
Tombs of the Blind Dead '72
Top of the Heap '72
Tormented '60
The Tormentors '71
The Torture Chamber of Dr. Sadism '69
Toy Soldiers '84
The Trackers '71
Trained to Kill '88
Trapped '02
Trapper County War '89
Trick or Treat '86
Tricks '97
Trigger Tricks '30
Trois Couleurs: Blanc '94►
Truck Turner '74
Tube '03
Turk 182! '85
The 24th Day '04
24 Hours to Midnight '92
Twice a Judas '69
Twilight People '72
Twin Town '97
Twisted Brain '74
Twisted Nightmare '87
Two by Forsyth '88
Two Fathers' Justice '85
2000 Maniacs '64
Undefeatable '94
Under the Gun '88
Underworld '96
Underworld, U.S.A. '60►
Unfaithfully Yours '48►
Unfaithfully Yours '84
Unholy Four '54
Universal Soldier: The Return '99
The Unstoppable Man '59
Until They Get Me '18
Up River '79
Urban Justice '07
The Usual Suspects '95►
Utu '83►
V for Vendetta '06
Valentine '01
Valmont '89►
Vampire Journals '96
Vendetta '85
Vengeance '80
Vengeance of the Zombies '72
The Vernonia Incident '89
Vietnam, Texas '90
The Vigilantes Are Coming '36
Viper '88
The Virgin Spring '59►
Voodoo Black Exorcist '73
Voodoo Dawn '99
Walking Tall '73
Walking Tall: Part 2 '75
Walking the Edge '83
War '07
The War Wagon '67►
Water Rustlers '39
Waterfront '39
Weekend of Shadows '77►
The Weirdo '89
West of Zanzibar '28
The Wharf Rat '95
What's the Worst That Could Happen? '01
When Will I Be Loved '04
The White Sheik '52►
White Tiger '95
Wild Bill '95
Wild Gypsies '69
Wild Man '89
Wild Wheels '69
Wired to Kill '86
Witchouse '99
Without Honors '32
Wolf '94
Wolf Lake '79
The Women '39►
Wonder Man '45
Wounded '97
Write to Kill '91
X Marks the Spot '42
X2: X-Men United '03►
Xtro 3: Watch the Skies '95
Young Warriors '83
Youth of the Beast '63
Yuma '70
Zero Tolerance '93

▲ = rated three bones or higher.

Revolutionary War

- America '24
- Benedict Arnold: A Question of Honor '03
- The Bastard '78
- The Crossing '00
- The Devil's Disciple '59
- George Washington '84
- The Howards of Virginia '40
- John Paul Jones '53
- Johnny Tremain & the Sons of Liberty '58
- The Patriot '00
- The Rebels '79
- Revolution '85
- The Seekers '79
- 1776 '72
- Sweet Liberty '86
- The Time of Their Lives '46

(Preceding the above, at top of column:) Zombie Lake '80 / Zombie Nightmare '86

Rio

- Amor Bandido '79
- Before the Devil Knows You're Dead '07
- Black Orpheus '58
- Blame It on Rio '84
- Boca '94
- Bossa Nova '99
- Central Station '98
- City of God '02
- City of Men '07
- Exposure '91
- Flying Down to Rio '33
- Herbie Goes Bananas '80
- Kickboxer 3: The Art of War '92
- Madame Sata '02
- Notorious '46
- Orfeu '99
- Party Girls for Sale '54
- Possible Loves '00
- The Road to Rio '47
- The Story of Fausta '88
- Subway to the Stars '87
- That Night in Rio '41
- Venus in Furs '70
- Via Appia '92
- Wild Orchid '90

A River Runs Through the Plot

see also Sail Away; Whitewater Rafting

- The Adventures of Huck Finn '93
- The Adventures of Huckleberry Finn '39
- The Adventures of Huckleberry Finn '60
- The Adventures of Huckleberry Finn '78
- The Adventures of Huckleberry Finn '85
- The African Queen '51
- Anacondas: The Hunt for the Blood Orchid '04
- Apocalypse Now '79
- Bend of the River '52
- Beyond the Call of Duty '92
- The Big Sky '52
- The Bridge at Remagen '69
- The Bridge on the River Kwai '57
- Cape Fear '91
- Cold Fever '95
- Death on the Nile '78
- Delinquent Parents '38
- The Edge '97
- The Far Horizons '55
- Lord of the Rings: The Fellowship of the Rings '01
- Lord of the Rings: The Return of the King '03
- Mean Creek '04
- Missouri Breaks '76
- Mystic River '03
- The Outlaw Josey Wales '76
- The River '51
- The River '84
- River of No Return '54
- A River Runs Through It '92
- The River Wild '94
- River's Edge '87
- Rooster Cogburn '75
- Striking Distance '93
- White River '99
- Without a Paddle '04

Road Trip

see also Bikers; Checkered Flag; Motor Vehicle Dept.

- Aberdeen '00
- About Schmidt '02
- The Acid Eaters '67
- Across the Great Divide '76
- Adrenaline Drive '99
- The Adventures of Felix '99
- The Adventures of Huck Finn '93
- The Adventures of Milo & Otis '89
- The Adventures of Priscilla, Queen of the Desert '94
- Alice Doesn't Live Here Anymore '74
- Alligator Eyes '90
- Almost Famous '00
- Aloha, Bobby and Rose '74
- Along for the Ride '00
- American Autobahn '84
- American Fabulous '92
- American Gun '02
- Another Day in Paradise '98
- Are We There Yet? '05
- Ariel '89
- Armed for Action '92
- Around the Bend '04
- Around the World in 80 Days '56
- Around the World in 80 Days '89
- As Good As It Gets '97
- Ashik Kerib '88
- Babel '06
- Babylon AD '08
- Bad Company '72
- Bam Bam & Celeste '05
- Bandwagon '95
- The Beautiful Country '04
- Beautiful Joe '00
- Beavis and Butt-Head Do America '96
- Because of You '95
- Beethoven's 3rd '00
- Beggars of Life '28
- Betty '97
- Bingo '91
- Bird on a Wire '90
- Black Day Blue Night '95
- The Black Rose '50
- Blue Murder at St. Trinian's '56
- Blue State '07
- The Blues Brothers '80
- Blues Brothers 2000 '98
- Bolero '84
- Bonneville '06
- Boogie Boy '98
- Borat: Cultural Learnings of America for Make Benefit Glorious Nation of Kazakhstan '06
- Born to Be Wild '95
- Bound for Glory '76
- The Bourne Ultimatum '07
- Box of Moonlight '96
- Boxcar Blues '90
- A Boy Called Hate '95
- Boys on the Side '94
- Breaking the Rules '92
- Breathing Lessons '94
- Bright Angel '91
- Broken Flowers '05
- Bronson's Revenge '72
- The Brothers Grimm '05
- The Brown Bunny '04
- Bubble Boy '01
- Buck and the Preacher '72
- The Bucket List '07
- Bustin' Loose '81
- Butch Cassidy and the Sundance Kid '69
- Butterfly Kiss '94
- By Dawn's Early Light '00
- Bye Bye Brazil '79
- Calendar Girl '93
- California Dreaming '07
- Camilla '94
- Candy Mountain '87
- Cannonball '76
- Cannonball Run 2 '84
- Cannonball Run '81
- A Canterbury Tale '44
- Carbide and Sorrel '63
- Central Station '98
- Changes '69
- The Chase '93
- Chasers '94
- Chasing Liberty '04
- Cheech and Chong: Things Are Tough All Over '82
- Children of Hannibal '98
- Clockhopper '17
- Coast to Coast '80
- Coast to Coast '04
- Cold Around the Heart '97
- Cold Fever '95
- Cold Mountain '03
- Committed '00
- The Concrete Cowboys '79
- Cooperstown '93
- Coupe de Ville '90
- Crazy in Alabama '99
- Crazy Mama '75
- Crossroads '86
- Crossroads '02
- The Cure '95
- Cycle Vixens '79
- Daddy & Them '99
- Damnation Alley '77
- Danzon '91
- The Darjeeling Limited '07
- Daughter of Keltoum '01
- The Daytrippers '96
- The Delivery '99
- Delusion '91
- Der Purimshpiler '37
- Detour '46
- The Devil Thumbs a Ride '47
- Diamond Men '01
- Diamonds '99
- Disappearances '06
- Disney's Teacher's Pet '04
- Doctor Chance '97
- Dogma '99
- Doing Time for Patsy Cline '97
- Don't Come Knocking '05
- The Doom Generation '95
- Down by Law '86
- The Dream Catcher '99
- Dream with the Fishes '97
- Dreaming of Rita '94
- Drive '96
- Driving Lessons '06
- Drowning on Dry Land '00
- Dumb & Dumber '94
- Dutch '91
- The Easy Life '63
- Easy Rider '69
- Elvis Has Left the Building '04
- End of the Line '88
- Endplay '75
- Eternity and a Day '97
- Eurotrip '04
- Every Other Weekend '91
- Every Which Way But Loose '78
- Everything is Illuminated '05
- Extremedays '01
- Eye of the Beholder '99
- Fandango '85
- Far Out Man '89
- Fast Sofa '01
- Father Hood '93
- Fear and Loathing in Las Vegas '98
- Finders Keepers '84
- Finding Graceland '98
- Finding North '97
- Flash & Firecat '75
- Flight of the Innocent '93
- Flim-Flam Man '67
- Flirting with Disaster '95
- Forces of Nature '99
- The Forsaken '01
- Four Days '99
- Free Zone '05
- Freeway 2: Confessions of a Trickbaby '99
- From Dusk Till Dawn '95
- Get On the Bus '96
- Girl in the Cadillac '94
- Go Further '03
- Goodbye Pork Pie '81
- A Goofy Movie '94
- Grace is Gone '07
- Grand Theft Parsons '03
- The Grapes of Wrath '40
- Great Smokey Roadblock '76
- The Great Texas Dynamite Chase '76
- Greedy Terror '78
- Guantanamera '95
- Gypsy 83 '01
- The Happening '08
- Hard Core Logo '96
- Hard Luck '07
- Harold and Kumar Go to White Castle '04
- Henry and Tonto '74
- Having Wonderful Crime '45
- Heart Beat '80
- Heaven's Burning '97
- Heck's Way Home '95
- Hedwig and the Angry Inch '00
- High Rolling in a Hot Corvette '77
- Hell's Angels on Wheels '57
- Highway '01
- Highway Hitcher '08
- The Highway Man '99
- Highway 61 '91
- Highwaymen '03
- The Hitcher '86
- The Hitcher '07
- The Hitcher 2: I've Been Waiting '03
- Hitchhikers '72
- Hollywood or Bust '56
- Hombres Complicados '97
- Home of Angels '94
- Homecoming '96
- Homer and Eddie '89
- Homeward Bound 2: Lost in San Francisco '96
- Homeward Bound: The Incredible Journey '93
- Honkytonk Man '82
- Hot Blooded '98
- House of Wax '05
- Huck and the King of Hearts '93
- I Accidentally Domed Your Son '04
- I Am David '04
- I Got Five on It '05
- Ice Age: The Meltdown '06
- Il Sorpasso '63
- I'll Be Home for Christmas '98
- I'll Take You There '99
- In This World '03
- The Incredible Journey '63
- Innocents '00
- Interstate 60 '02
- Into the Night '85
- Into the West '92
- Into the Wild '07
- The Intruder '04
- It Takes Two '88
- The Italian '05
- It's a Mad, Mad, Mad, Mad World '63
- Jackpot '01
- Jam '06
- James' Journey to Jerusalem '03
- Jay and Silent Bob Strike Back '01
- Jeepers Creepers '01
- Jerome '98
- Jiminy Glick in LaLa Wood '05
- Joe Dirt '01
- Johnson Family Vacation '04
- Jon Jost's Frameup '93
- Josh and S.A.M. '93
- The Journey of Natty Gann '85
- The Journey to Kafiristan '01
- Joy Ride '01
- Joy Ride to Nowhere '78
- Joyride '77
- Kalifornia '93
- Kandahar '01
- Kikujiro '99
- Kill Your Darlings '06
- Killer Bud '00
- Kingpin '96
- Kings of the Road—In the Course of Time '76
- Kiss My Grits '82
- Kiss or Kill '97
- La Strada '54
- La Vie Promise '02
- Ladies on the Rocks '83
- Lady Jayne Killer '03
- Lamerica '95
- Landscape in the Mist '88
- Larger Than Life '96
- Lassie '05
- The Last Legion '07
- Last Orders '01
- Leaving Normal '92
- Leningrad Cowboys Go America '89
- Les Rendez-vous D'Anna '78
- Lewis and Clark and George '97
- A Life Less Ordinary '97
- The Lion of Africa '87
- Lisboa '99
- Little Miss Sunshine '06
- The Living End '92
- Lolita '97
- Loners '72
- The Long Haul '57
- The Long, Long Trailer '54
- Loose Connections '87
- Lord of the Rings: The Fellowship of the Rings '01
- Lord of the Rings: The Return of the King '03
- Lord of the Rings: The Two Towers '02
- Los Locos Posse '97
- Lost '05
- Lost in America '85
- Love and a .45 '94
- Luminous Motion '00
- Mad Love '95
- Made in USA '83
- Marooned in Iraq '02
- Me and the Kid '93
- Me & Will '99
- Me, Myself, and Irene '00
- Meet the Fockers '04
- The Mexican '01
- Michael '96
- Midnight Run '88
- Mob Story '90
- Monsieur Ibrahim '03
- Monster Man '03
- More '69
- The Motorcycle Diaries '04
- Moving McAllister '07
- The Muppet Movie '79
- The Music of Chance '93
- My Blueberry Nights '07
- My Fellow Americans '96
- My Own Private Idaho '91
- National Lampoon's Vacation '83
- Natural Born Killers '94
- Neil Simon's The Odd Couple 2 '98
- Neon City '91
- Never on Tuesday '58
- Niagara, Niagara '97
- Night on Earth '91
- No Place to Run '72
- No Sleep Til Madison '02
- Nurse Betty '00
- The Odyssey '97
- Omaha (the movie) '95
- One Way '01
- The Opposite of Sex '98
- Out '88
- Outside Ozona '98
- Over the Hill '93
- Overnight Delivery '96
- Palindromes '04
- Paper Moon '73
- The Passing of Evil '70
- Patti Rocks '88
- Paulie '98
- Pee-wee's Big Adventure '85
- Phat Beach '96
- Pieces of April '03
- Pierrot le Fou '65
- Pink Cadillac '89
- Pinocchio '02
- Planes, Trains & Automobiles '87
- Play It to the Bone '99
- The Pleasure Drivers '05
- Pontiac Moon '94
- Powwow Highway '89
- Prime Target '91
- Prison Train '38
- Pulse '03
- The Raffle '94
- Rain Man '88
- The Rain People '69
- Rainbow Bridge '71
- Rat Race '01
- Reckless '95
- Red Blooded 2 '96
- Red Lights '04
- The Reivers '69
- Rescue Me '93
- Retroactive '97
- Ride '98
- Ride in the Whirlwind '66
- Riding Alone for Thousands of Miles '05
- The Road '00
- Road Games '81
- Road Kill USA '63
- Road Killers '95
- Road Movie '72
- Roadie '80
- The Road Warrior '82
- Roadkill '89
- Roadside Prophets '92
- Rockin' Road Trip '85
- Rolling Family '04
- Rough Magic '95
- Round Trip to Heaven '92
- Rubin & Ed '92
- The Runaway Bus '54
- Runaway Daughters '94
- Running Hot '83
- Running Wild '94
- RV '06
- Rx '06
- The Saragossa Manuscript '65
- Sawdust & Tinsel '53
- Say It Isn't So '01
- Scarecrow '73
- Schultze Gets the Blues '03
- Searching for Bobby D '05
- Secret Ballot '01
- September Gun '83
- Serving Sara '02
- Sesame Street Presents: Follow That Bird '85
- A Shadow You Soon Will Be '94
- Sherman's March '86
- Shrek the Third '07
- Siddhartha '72
- Sideways '04
- Silk '07
- The Simpsons Movie '07
- Sincerely Charlotte '86
- Six of a Kind '34
- Six-String Samurai '98
- Slither '73
- Smoke Signals '98
- Something Wild '86
- Sorcerer '77
- Spare Me '92

► = rated three bones or higher

Sparkler '99
Speed Racer '08
Spies Like Us '85
Starlight Hotel '90
Starman '84
Stay As You Are '78
Stir Crazy '80
Stop-Loss '08
Strawberry Fields '97
Summer City '77
Sunchaser '96
The Sure Thing '85
The Sweetest Thing '02
The Talent Given Us '04
Tenacious D in the Pick of Destiny '06
Testosterone '03
Thelma & Louise '91
The Thing About My Folks '05
39 Pounds of Love '05
Those Magnificent Men in Their Flying Machines '65
The Three Burials of Melquiades Estrada '05
Three for the Road '87
Thumb Tripping '72
Tilt '78
Time of the Wolf '03
Time Out '01
To Wong Foo, Thanks for Everything, Julie Newmar '95
Tokyo Pop '88
Tommy Boy '95
Torque '04
Tourist Trap '98
Trading Favors '97
Transamerica '05
Traveling Man '89
Trouble Bound '92
The Truce '96
True Romance '93
Truth or Consequences, N.M. '97
Twentieth Century '34
28 Days Later '02
Twentynine Palms '03
Twins '88
Two for the Road '67
Until the End of the World '91
Vince Vaughn's Wild West Comedy Show '06
Voyage in Italy '53
Wagons East '94
Waking Up in Reno '02
The Way West '67
Wedding Bell Blues '96
Weekend '67
Western '96
Where the Eagle Flies '72
Where the Heart Is '00
White Line Fever '75
White River '99
Wild America '97
Wild at Heart '90
Wild Hogs '07
Wild Horses '95
The Wizard '89
The Wizard of Oz '39
World Traveler '01
Wristcutters: A Love Story '06
The Wrong Man '93
Y Tu Mama Tambien '01
Zoe '01

Robots & Androids

see also Technology—Rampant

A.I.: Artificial Intelligence '01
Alien '79
Alien Chaser '96
Alien: Resurrection '97
Aliens '86
American Cyborg: Steel Warrior '94
And You Thought Your Parents Were Weird! '91
Android '82
The Android Affair '95
A.P.E.X. '94

Assassin '86
The Astro-Zombies '67
Automatic '94
Bicentennial Man '99
Bill & Ted's Bogus Journey '91
The Black Hole '79
Blade Runner '82
Carver's Gate '96
The Chess Player '27
Chicken Little '05
Chopping Mall '86
Circuitry Man '90
Class of 1999 '90
Class of 1999 2: The Substitute '93
The Companion '94
The Creation of the Humanoids '62
Cyber-Tracker '93
Cyber-Tracker 2 '95
Cyberzone '95
Cyborg '89
Cyborg 2 '93
Cyborg 3: The Recycler '95
Cyborg Cop '93
Cyborg Soldier '94
Daleks—Invasion Earth 2150 A.D. '66
D.A.R.Y.L. '85
The Day the Earth Stood Still '51
Devil Girl from Mars '54
Digital Man '94
Dr. Goldfoot and the Bikini Machine '66
Doctor of Doom '62
Doctor Satan's Robot '40
Downdraft '96
Edward Scissorhands '90
The Eliminators '86
The Empire Strikes Back '80
Eve of Destruction '90
Evolver '94
The Fifth Element '97
Forbidden Planet '56
Future Cop '76
Ghost in the Shell '95
Heartbeeps '81
Heatseeker '95
The Hitchhiker's Guide to the Galaxy '81
The Hitchhiker's Guide to the Galaxy '05
How to Make a Doll '68
The Human Duplicators '64
Humanoid Defender '85
I, Robot '04
Inhumanoid '96
The Invisible Boy '57
Iron Giant '99
K-9000 '89
Knights '93
Kronos '57
Light Years '88
Lost in Space '98
Mac and Me '88
Mandroid '93
Marebito '04
Megaville '91
Metropolis '26
Mortal Challenge '97
Mystery Science Theater 3000: The Movie '96
Nemesis '93
Nemesis 2: Nebula '94
Nemesis 3: Time Lapse '96
Night Siege Project: Shadowchaser 2 '94
Not Quite Human '87
Not Quite Human 2 '89
Omega Doom '96
Piano Tuner of Earthquakes '05
Planets Against Us '61
Plughead Rewired: Circuitry Man 2 '94
Programmed to Kill '86
Project: Shadowchaser '92
Project Shadowchaser 3000 '95
Prototype '83
Prototype X29A '92
Puzzlehead '05
Return of the Jedi '83
Robo Warriors '96
RoboCop '87

RoboCop 2 '90
RoboCop 3 '91
Roboman '75
Robot Holocaust '87
Robot in the Family '94
Robot Jox '90
Robot Monster '53
Robot Stories '03
The Robot vs. the Aztec Mummy '59
Robot Wars '93
Robots '05
R.O.T.O.R. '88
Runaway '84
Running Delilah '93
Serenity '05
Shadow Warriors '95
Short Circuit '86
Short Circuit 2 '88
Silent Running '71
Sky Captain and the World of Tomorrow '04
Solo '96
Space Truckers '97
Star Crash '78
Star Trek: First Contact '96
Star Trek: Generations '94
Star Trek: Nemesis '02
Star Wars '77
Star Wars: Episode 1—The Phantom Menace '99
Star Wars: Episode 2—Attack of the Clones '02
Star Wars: Episode 3—Revenge of the Sith '05
Starship '87
Steel and Lace '90
The Stepford Wives '04
Still Not Quite Human '92
Storm Trooper '98
Suspect Device '95
T-Force '94
TC 2000 '93
The Terminator '84
The Terminator 2: Judgment Day '91
Terminator 3: Rise of the Machines '03
Terror of Mechagodzilla '78
Tobor the Great '54
Total Recall 2070: Machine Dreams '99
Transformers '07
Treasure Planet '02
Universal Soldier: The Return '99
The Vindicator '85
Virus '98
Voyage of the Rock Aliens '87
WALL-E '08
Westworld '73
Zathura '05

Rock Flicks

The Adventures of Buckaroo Banzai Across the Eighth Dimension '84
Almost Famous '00
Alvin and the Chipmunks '07
American Pop '81
At Any Cost '00
Awesome! I F***'in' Shot That! '06
Backbeat '94
Beat Street '84
Beyond the Valley of the Dolls '70
Blame It on the Night '84
The Blues Brothers '80
Blues Brothers 2000 '98
Born to Boogie '72
Brothers of the Head '06
Bummer '73
Burglar '87
Chuck Berry: Hail! Hail! Rock 'n' Roll '87
The Commitments '91
Confessions of a Teenage Drama Queen '04
The Courier '88
Cry-Baby '88
Dead Girls '90
Decline of Western Civilization '81

Decline of Western Civilization 2: The Metal Years '88
Detroit Rock City '99
DiG! '04
Disorderlies '87
The Doors '91
Double Trouble '67
Eddie and the Cruisers '83
Eddie and the Cruisers 2: Eddie Lives! '89
Elvis and Me '88
Elvis: The Movie '79
End of the Century: The Story of the Ramones '03
Face the Music '00
Festival Express '03
The Filth and the Fury '99
The Five Heartbeats '91
FM '78
Follow That Dream '61
Frankie and Johnny '65
Garage Days '03
Get Crazy '83
Gimme Shelter '70
The Girl Can't Help It '56
Give My Regards to Broad Street '84
Grace of My Heart '96
Grand Theft Parsons '03
Great Balls of Fire '89
Gypsy 83 '01
Hail Caesar '94
Hard Core Logo '96
A Hard Day's Night '64
Head '68
Heaven Tonight '93
Hedwig and the Angry Inch '00
Help! '65
Horsey '99
I'll Be There '03
In His Life: The John Lennon Story '00
Incident at Channel Q '86
It Couldn't Happen Here '88
The Jacksons: An American Dream '92
Jailhouse Rock '57
Johnny Suede '92
Josie and the Pussycats '01
The Kids Are Alright '79
KISS Meets the Phantom of the Park '78
La Bamba '87
Last Days '05
The Last Waltz '78
Laurel Canyon '02
Leningrad Cowboys Go America '89
Let It Be '70
Light of Day '87
Lip Service '00
Little Richard '00
Loving You '57
Masked and Anonymous '03
A Matter of Degrees '90
Mayor of the Sunset Strip '03
Meat Loaf: To Hell and Back '00
Monterey Pop '68
Music & Lyrics '07
Neil Young: Heart of Gold '06
Netherworld '90
Nico Icon '95
1991: The Year Punk Broke '92
Party! Party! '83
Prey for Rock and Roll '03
Quadrophenia '79
Queen of the Damned '02
Red Hot '95
The Return of Spinal Tap '92
Rock & Roll Cowboys '92
Rock & Rule '83
Rock, Baby, Rock It '57
Rock My World '02
Rock 'n' Roll High School '79
Rock 'n' Roll High School Forever '91
Rock 'n' Roll Nightmare '85

Rock, Pretty Baby '56
Rock Star '01
Rocktober Blood '85
Running out of Luck '86
Satisfaction '88
Scenes from the Goldmine '87
School of Rock '03
Shock 'Em Dead '90
Shooting Livien '05
Shout '91
Sid & Nancy '86
Six-String Samurai '98
Spellcaster '91
Spice World: The Movie '97
Still Crazy '98
Streets of Fire '84
The Suburbans '99
Sugar Town '99
Sunset Strip '85
Sweetwater: A True Rock Story '99
Tapeheads '89
Tenacious D in the Pick of Destiny '06
Terror on Tour '83
That Thing You Do! '96
Theremin: An Electronic Odyssey '95
This Is Elvis '81
This Is Spinal Tap '84
Thunder Alley '85
Thunder & Mud '89
Tokyo Pop '88
Tommy '75
Trick or Treat '86
24 Hour Party People '01
U2: Rattle and Hum '88
Velvet Goldmine '98
Vibrations '94
Voyage of the Rock Aliens '87
Walk Hard: The Dewey Cox Story '07
When Love Comes '98
Wild Guitar '62
Woodstock '70
Yellow Submarine '68
Zombie and the Ghost Train '91

Rock Stars on Film

see also Concert Films; Martyred Pop Icons; Pure Ego Vehicles

Absolute Beginners '86
All You Need Is Cash '78
Backbeat '94
Bill & Ted's Excellent Adventure '89
Black Dog '98
Blow-Up '66
Blue Hawaii '62
The Blues Brothers '80
Blues Brothers 2000 '98
The Bodyguard '92
Breaking Glass '80
The Bride '85
B.U.S.T.E.D. '99
Carny '80
Caveman '81
Charro! '69
Chuck Berry: Hail! Hail! Rock 'n' Roll '87
Cinderella '97
Clambake '67
Coal Miner's Daughter '80
The Crossing Guard '94
Crossroads '86
Detroit Rock City '99
DiG! '04
Double Trouble '67
Dune '84
Easy Come, Easy Go '67
Elvis: The Movie '79
End of the Century: The Story of the Ramones '03
End of the Line '88
Festival Express '03
Fire Down Below '97
Flaming Star '60
Follow That Dream '61
Frankie and Johnny '65
Freddy's Dead: The Final Nightmare '91
Fun in Acapulco '63

G.I. Blues '60
The Girl Can't Help It '56
Girl Happy '65
Girls! Girls! Girls! '62
Give My Regards to Broad Street '84
Go, Johnny Go! '59
Gypsy 83 '01
A Hard Day's Night '64
The Harder They Come '72
Harum Scarum '65
Head '68
Heat '95
Help! '65
How I Won the War '67
The Hunger '83
I Still Know What You Did Last Summer '98
It Happened at the World's Fair '63
Jailhouse Rock '57
Jawbreaker '98
Johnny Mnemonic '95
Kid Galahad '62
King Creole '58
KISS Meets the Phantom of the Park '78
Kissin' Cousins '64
La Bamba '87
Labyrinth '86
The Last Temptation of Christ '88
The Leading Man '96
The Legacy '79
Let It Be '70
Lisztomania '75
Live a Little, Love a Little '68
Lock, Stock and 2 Smoking Barrels '98
Love Me Tender '56
Loving You '57
The Magic Christian '69
Magical Mystery Tour '67
The Man Who Fell to Earth '76
Mayor of the Sunset Strip '03
McVicar '80
Merry Christmas, Mr. Lawrence '83
Metallica: Some Kind of Monster '04
Mrs. Brown, You've Got a Lovely Daughter '68
Monster Dog '82
Moonlight and Valentino '95
My Life '93
Neil Young: Heart of Gold '06
No Looking Back '98
Nomads '86
One Trick Pony '80
Paradise, Hawaiian Style '66
Pat Garrett & Billy the Kid '73
Performance '70
Pink Floyd: The Wall '82
The Players Club '98
Poetic Justice '93
The Postman '97
The Preacher's Wife '96
Quadrophenia '79
Return to Waterloo '85
Rock 'n' Roll High School '79
Roustabout '64
Row Your Boat '98
Runaway '84
The Running Man '87
Sgt. Pepper's Lonely Hearts Club Band '78
Sextette '78
Speedway '68
Spice World: The Movie '97
Spinout '66
Stay Away, Joe '68
That'll Be the Day '73
This Is Elvis '81
Tickle Me '65
Tommy '75
Traveller '96
The Trouble with Girls (and How to Get into It) '69
Under the Cherry Moon '86
Viva Las Vegas '63
Waiting to Exhale '95
The Wedding Singer '97

▸ = *rated three bones or higher*

Wild in the Country '61
Woodstock '70
Yellow Submarine '68

Rodeos

see also Westerns

The Adventures of Gallant Bess '48
Arizona Cowboy '49
Bells of Capistrano '42
Born Reckless '59
Convict Cowboy '95
Cowboy Up '00
The Cowboy Way '94
Desert Trail '35
8 Seconds '94
Feud of the West '35
Girl from Calgary '32
Goldenrod '77
Junior Bonner '72 ▶
Kid from Gower Gulch '50
Lady Takes a Chance '43 ▶
The Last Ride '94
Lights of Old Santa Fe '47
The Lusty Men '52
Luzia '88
Man from Utah '34
The Misfits '61 ▶
My Heroes Have Always Been Cowboys '91
Never a Dull Moment '50
Oklahoma Cyclone '30
Painted Hero '95
Pee-wee's Big Adventure '85 ▶
Rhythm on the Range '36
Rider from Tucson '50
Rodeo Girl '80
Rodeo King and the Senorita '51
Rolling Home '48
Ruby Jean and Joe '96
Saddle Buster '32
Stir Crazy '80 ▶
Trouble in Texas '37
Wild Horse '31
Wild Horse Rodeo '37

Rogue Cops

see also Crime Drama; Organized Crime

Armed and Dangerous '86
Assault on Precinct 13 '05 ▶
Back in Business '96
Bad Lieutenant '92 ▶
Badge of the Assassin '85
Big Momma's House 2 '06
Blastfighter '85
Chasing Ghosts '05
Cop Land '97 ▶
Corrupt '84
Dark Blue '03 ▶
Dirty '05
Dogwatch '97
Double Bang '01
Endgame '02
Enough '02
Eraser '96
Exit Wounds '01
Final Payback '99
Fish in a Barrel '01
Flashfire '94
Gang Related '96
The Gauntlet '77
The Glass Shield '95
Goodbye South, Goodbye '96
Hard to Kill '89
Harsh Times '05
Heaven '01
Internal Affairs '90
Kiss of the Dragon '01 ▶
L.A. Confidential '97 ▶
L.A.P.D.: To Protect and Serve '01
Last Man Standing '96
Lethal Force '00
Lethal Weapon 3 '92
Lone Star '95 ▶
Magnum Force '73
The Mod Squad '99
Narc '02 ▶
The Negotiator '98
New Jersey Drive '95
Night Falls on Manhattan '96
One of Her Own '97
One Way Out '02
Our Man in Havana '59
Payback '98 ▶
Payback '02
Pressure '02
The Professional '94
Rent-A-Cop '88
Rip It Off '02
Romeo is Bleeding '93
The Salton Sea '02
Serpico '73 ▶
Shaft '00 ▶
Shakedown '88
16 Blocks '06 ▶
Sin City '05 ▶
The Spree '96
Stander '03
The Stickup '02
Striking Distance '93
Super Troopers '01
S.W.A.T. '03
Tales from the Hood '95
The Thin Blue Lie '00
Things to Do in Denver When You're Dead '95 ▶
Touch of Evil '58 ▶
Training Day '01 ▶
2 Fast 2 Furious '03
Unlawful Entry '92
Violent Cop '89
Witness '85 ▶

Role Reversal

see also Gender Bending

Age Isn't Everything '91
All of Me '84 ▶
Anastasia '56
Anastasia: The Mystery of Anna '85
Angel '84
Angel on My Shoulder '46 ▶
Angel on My Shoulder '80
Babe '95 ▶
Bad Manners '84
The Bank Dick '40
Before Morning '33
Big '88 ▶
Biggles '85
Billy Madison '94
Blood of Dracula '57
Bloodlink '86
The Captain from Koepenick '56
Captive Heart '47 ▶
Cheech and Chong's The Corsican Brothers '84
Christmas in Connecticut '45 ▶
Cinderfella '60
Cambeke '67
Class Act '91
Cleo/Leo '89
Coming to America '88 ▶
Condorman '81
The Couch Trip '87
Courage '86
Dating the Enemy '95
Dave '93 ▶
The Deputy Drummer '35
Desperately Seeking Susan '85 ▶
Devil's Canyon '53
Dr. Black, Mr. Hyde '76
Doctor Detroit '83
Doctor Dolittle '67 ▶
Dr. Heckyl and Mr. Hype '80
Dr. Jekyll and Mr. Hyde '20 ▶
Dr. Jekyll and Mr. Hyde '32 ▶
Dr. Jekyll and Mr. Hyde '41 ▶
Dr. Jekyll and Mr. Hyde '68
Dr. Jekyll and Mr. Hyde '73
Doctors and Nurses '82
Down and Out in Beverly Hills '86
A Dream a Little Dream '89
A Dream of Passion '78
18 Again! '88
Extremities '86
The $5.20 an Hour Dream '80
For Ladies Only '81
48 Hrs. '82 ▶
Freaky Friday '76
Freaky Friday '03 ▶
Garfield: A Tail of Two Kitties '06
The Gladiator '86
The Grand Duchess and the Waiter '26
The Great Gabbo '29
Greystoke: The Legend of Tarzan, Lord of the Apes '84
Guest Wife '45
Gunfire '50
Heart Like a Wheel '83 ▶
Her Life as a Man '83
Hero '92
Hiding Out '87
The Hot Chick '02
Identity Crisis '90
The Incredible Mr. Limpet '64
Iron Maze '91
Jekyll and Hyde '90
Johnny Guitar '53 ▶
Junior '94
Just One of the Guys '85
Kagemusha '80 ▶
Kim '50
Kings and Desperate Men '83
La Femme Nikita '91 ▶
La Ronde '51 ▶
The Lady Vanishes '38 ▶
The Lady Vanishes '79
Ladybugs '92
Law and Order '42
Liane, Jungle Goddess '56
Like Father, Like Son '87
Liquid Sky '83
Lonely Wives '31
Maid to Order '87
Male and Female '19 ▶
The Man Who Haunted Himself '70
The Man Who Wagged His Tail '57
Man with Two Heads '72
Mrs. Winterbourne '96
Mr. Fix It '06
Monkey Business '52 ▶
Moon over Parador '88
My Blue Heaven '90
My Fair Lady '64 ▶
Naked Souls '95
Now, Voyager '42 ▶
Opportunity Knocks '90
Overboard '87
Panamint's Bad Man '38
Paris When It Sizzles '64
People's Choice '46
Performance '70
Persona '66 ▶
Pocketful of Miracles '61
Point of No Return '93
Posse '75
The Prince and the Pauper '37 ▶
The Prince and the Pauper '62
The Prince and the Pauper '78
Prisoner of Zenda '37 ▶
Prisoner of Zenda '52
Prisoner of Zenda '79
Psycho '60 ▶
Quicksilver '86
Rabbit Test '78
The Raggedy Rawney '90
Raid on Rommel '71
Red Lion '69
Red Rock Outlaw '47
Rendez-Moi Ma Peau '81
Rider of the Law '35
The Road to Yesterday '25
A Saintly Switch '99
Satank '69
Savages '72
Scalpel '76
The Scarlet Pimpernel '82 ▶
September Affair '50
The Shaggy D.A. '76
The Shaggy Dog '59
Showdown in Little Tokyo '91
Silent Night, Deadly Night '84
Slapstick of Another Kind '84
A Slightly Pregnant Man '73
Small Town Boy '37
Something Special '86
Sommersby '93
Song of Texas '43
A Stolen Face '52
Stogemania '85
Straight Talk '92
Summer Night with Greek Profile, Almond Eyes & Scent of Basil '87
Sweet Revenge '90
Switch '91
Sylvia Scarlett '35
Taking Care of Business '90
A Tale of Two Cities '89
The Tango Lesson '97
That's My Baby! '88
Tomboy '40
Tootsie '82 ▶
Trading Places '83 ▶
Triple Echo '77
The Two Faces of Dr. Jekyll '60
Ultimate Desires '91
Vice Versa '48 ▶
Victor/Victoria '82 ▶
Watermelon Man '70
White Man's Burden '95
White Sands '92
Wish upon a Star '96
Wonder Man '45
Yankee Zulu '95
Yenti '83
Yidl Mitn Fidl '36

Romance

see Late Bloomin' Love; Lovers on the Lam; Romantic Adventures; Romantic Comedy; Romantic Drama; Romantic Triangles; Teen Romance

Romantic Adventures

Above Suspicion '43
The African Queen '51 ▶
Antz '98
Arabian Nights '42
Arabian Nights '00
As You Like It '06
Baby... Secret of the Lost Legend '85
Bagdad '49
Brigham Young: Frontiersman '40
Caprice '67
Captain from Castile '47
Casanova '05
Casanova '05
Chasing Liberty '04
China Seas '35
Crouching Tiger, Hidden Dragon '00 ▶
Destiny Turns on the Radio '95
Down Argentine Way '40
Durango '99
Ever After: A Cinderella Story '98
Fanfan la Tulipe '51 ▶
Flame of Araby '51
Fool's Gold '08
Frenchman's Creek '44
Frenchman's Creek '98
Gun Crazy '49
Guncrazy '92
Gypsy Angels '94
If I Were King '38
The Indian Fighter '55
Invisible Agent '42
The Jewel of the Nile '85
Joe Versus the Volcano '90
A Knight's Tale '01
The Last of the Mohicans '92 ▶
Lie Down with Lions '94
The Mask of Zorro '98 ▶
Mogambo '53
Oscar and Lucinda '97
Pocahontas '95
The Proposition '95
Red Dust '32 ▶
Robot Pilot '41

Romantic Comedy

A Lot Like Love '05
Abdulla the Great '56
About Adam '00
About Last Night... '86
Acqua e Sapone '83
Adam's Rib '50 ▶
Addicted to Love '96
Adorable Julia '62
Adrenaline Drive '99
The Adventures of Sadie '55
Advertising Rules! '01
After Midnight '04
Aggie Appleby, Maker of Men '33
Alchemy '05
Alex & Emma '03
Alfredo, Alfredo '72
All I Want '07
All Night Long '81
All Over the Guy '01
All the Wrong Places '00
All Tied Up '92
The Allnighter '87
All's Fair '89
Almost '90
Almost an Angel '90
Almost Famous '00 ▶
Almost Pregnant '91
Along Came Polly '04
Amarcord '73 ▶
The Ambassador's Daughter '56
America's Sweethearts '01
American Dreamer '84
American Friends '91
American Matchmaker '40
The American President '95 ▶
American Women '00
Amor de Hombre '97
Amore! '93
The Amorous Adventures of Moll Flanders '65
Anchorman: The Legend of Ron Burgundy '04
And Then Came Love '07
And You Thought Your Parents Were Weird! '91
Animal Behavior '89
Anna Christie '30 ▶
Anna Karenina '35
Annie Hall '77 ▶
Another Chance '88
Another Thin Man '39
Antoine et Antoinette '47
Anything But... Love '02
Anything Else '03
The Apartment '60 ▶
Apartment 12 '06
Apres-Vous '03
April Fools '69
April Fool '26
April's Shower '03
Are Parents People? '25
The Arrangement '99
Arthur '81 ▶
Arthur 2: On the Rocks '88
As Good As It Gets '97 ▶
Ask Any Girl '59
Avanti! '72
The Aviator's Wife '80
Baby Boom '87
Babycakes '89
Bachelor Bait '34
Bachelor Apartment '31
Bachelor in Paradise '61
Back to the Beach '87
Bahama Passage '42
Baja Oklahoma '87
Ball & Chain '04
Ball of Fire '41 ▶
Bar Girls '95
Bare Essentials '91
Barefoot in the Park '67 ▶
Barnaby and Me '77
The Bashful Bachelor '42
Battling Butler '26
The Baxter '05
Beachcomber '38
The Beautician and the Beast '97
Beautiful Joe '00
Because I Said So '07
Bed & Breakfast '92
Bedrooms and Hallways '98
Belle Epoque '92 ▶
Bells Are Ringing '60 ▶
Benny & Joon '93
The Best Man '97
Betsy's Wedding '90
Better Than Chocolate '99
Better Than Sex '00
Beyond Tomorrow '40
The Big Day '05
Bigger Than the Sky '05
Billy's Hollywood Screen Kiss '98
Birds & the Bees '56
Birthday Girl '02
Black Peter '63
Blame It on Rio '84
Blast from the Past '98
Blind Date '87
Blind Dating '06
The Bobo '67
Blonde Crazy '31
Blue Country '77
Bluebeard's Eighth Wife '38
Bombshell '33
Boom Town '40
Boomerang '92
Born Romantic '00
Born Yesterday '50 ▶
Born Yesterday '93
Bossa Nova '99
Boyfriends '96
Boyfriends & Girlfriends '88
The Boynton Beach Club '05
Boys and Girls '00
Bread and Tulips '01 ▶
The Bread, My Sweet '01
The Break-Up '06
Breakfast at Tiffany's '61 ▶
Breakin' All the Rules '04
Breaking Up '97
The Breakup Artist '04
Breath of Scandal '60
Breathing Room '96
Bride & Prejudice '04
The Bride Came C.O.D. '41
Bridget Jones's Diary '01 ▶
Bridget Jones: The Edge of Reason '04
Broadway Damage '98
The Butcher's Wife '91
But Not for Me '59
Buying the Cow '02
Bye Bye Baby '88
Cactus Flower '69
Cafe au Lait '94
Cafe Ole '00
Cake '05
California Casanova '89
California Suite '78
Came a Hot Friday '85
The Cameraman '28 ▶
Campus Confessions '38
Can She Bake a Cherry Pie? '83
Can't Buy Me Love '87
Can't Hardly Wait '98
Caprice '67
Captain's Paradise '53
Car Trouble '86
Career Opportunities '91
Cartier Affair '84
Casanova '37
Casanova Brown '44
Casanova '05
Casanova '65
The Cemetery Club '93

Chain of Fools '00
Chances Are '89►
A Change of Seasons '80
Changing Habits '96
Chaos Theory '08
Charley's Aunt '25
Chasing Amy '97
Chasing Destiny '00
Chasing Papi '03
The Cheerful Fraud '27
Chicks, Man '99
Chilly Scenes of Winter '79
Christmas in Connecticut '45►
Christmas in Connecticut '92
Christmas in the Clouds '01
A Cinderella Story '04
Class of '44 '73
The Clock '45►
Closely Watched Trains '66►
Clueless '95►
Cold Feet '84
Colombian Love '04
Come Blow Your Horn '63►
Come September '61
Comeback Kid '80
Coming Soon '99
Coming to America '88►
Committed '99
Confessions of a Sociopathic Social Climber '05
Conquest '98
Continental Divide '81
Cool Blue '88
A Couch in New York '95
A Countess from Hong Kong '67
Court Jester '56►
The Cowboy and the Lady '38
Crazy in Love '92
Crazy Little Thing '02
Crazy Moon '87
Creator '85
Crocodile Dundee '86►
Cross My Heart '88
Crossing Delancey '88►
Curly Sue '91
The Curse of the Jade Scorpion '01
Curtain Call '97
Dan in Real Life '07
Dance with Me '98
Danny Deckchair '03
The Dark Side of the Heart '92
Date Movie '06
Date with an Angel '87
Dating the Enemy '95
David Searching '97
Dawg '02
Dead Letter Office '98
Dear Brigitte '65
Dear Detective '77
Decameron Nights '53
Dedication '07
Defending Your Life '91►
Definitely, Maybe '08►
Deliver Us from Eva '03
The Demi-Paradise '43►
Designing Woman '57►
Desk Set '57►
Desperate Moves '86
Desperately Seeking Susan '85
The Devil & Miss Jones '41►
Diary of a Seducer '95
Different Story '78
Dinner and Driving '97
Dirty Love '05
Dirty Rotten Scoundrels '88►
Dish Dogs '98
The Divorce of Lady X '38
Do Not Disturb '65
Doc Hollywood '91
Doctor in Distress '63
Dr. T & the Women '00►
Does This Mean We're Married? '90
Dog Gone Love '03
Dog Park '98
The Dog Problem '06
Dollar '38

Dona Flor and Her Two Husbands '78►
Dona Herlinda & Her Son '86
Don't Do It '94
Don't Hang Up '90
Don't Tell Her It's Me '90
Dopamine '03
Down to You '00
Down With Love '03
Dream Date '93
Dream for an Insomniac '96
Dream Trap '90
Dreaming About You '92
Dreaming of Rita '94
Dreams Come True '84
Drive Me Crazy '99
Eagle vs. Shark '07
East and West '24►
Eat Your Heart Out '96
Eating Out 2: Sloppy Seconds '06
Edie & Pen '95
Ed's Next Move '96
Eight Days a Week '97
Electric Dreams '84
Elizabethtown '05
Ella Enchanted '04►
Elsa, Elsa '85
Enchanted '07
Enemies of Laughter '00
The Englishman Who Went up a Hill But Came down a Mountain '95►
Esmeralda Comes by Night '98
Eternal Sunshine of the Spotless Mind '04►
Eversmile New Jersey '89
Every Girl Should Be Married '48
Every Which Way But Loose '78
Everybody Says I'm Fine! '06
Extreme Dating '04
Face the Music '92
Face the Music '00
The Facts of Life '60
Failure to Launch '06
Fall '97
A Family Affair '01
Family Man '00
The Family Stone '05
The Farmer's Daughter '47►
The Farmer's Other Daughter '65
Fate '90
Father Goose '64
The Favor '92
Feelin' Screwy '90
Feet First '30
Fever Pitch '96
Fever Pitch '05
Fifth Avenue Girl '39
50 First Dates '04
A Fine Romance '92
First Daughter '04
First Time '82
The First to Go '97
Fish Without a Bicycle '03
The Flame of New Orleans '41►
Flirt '95
Foolin' Around '80
Fools Rush In '97
For Better or Worse '95
For Heaven's Sake '26►
For Love of Ivy '68
For Love or Money '63
For Love or Money '84
For Love or Money '93
For Roseanna '96
For the Love of Mary '48
A Foreign Affair '48►
Forever Together '00
Forget Paris '95
Forgetting Sarah Marshall '08►
A Forgotten Tune for the Flute '88►
Formula 17 '04
Forty Carats '73
40 Days and 40 Nights '02
The 40 Year Old Virgin '05►
Four Weddings and a Funeral '94►
Framed '90

Frankie and Johnny '91►
French Exit '97
French Kiss '95
The French Lesson '86
French Twist '95
Fridays of Eternity '81
Friends & Lovers '99
Friends, Lovers & Lunatics '89
Full of Life '56
Funny About Love '90
Funny Valentine '05
Gabriela '84
Garden State '04►
The Gay Lady '49
Get Out Your Handkerchiefs '78►
Get Over It! '01
Get Well Soon '01
Getting Gertie's Garter '45
The Girl in the Picture '86
Getting It Right '89
Getting Played '05
The Ghost and the Guest '43
Gidget '59
Gidget Goes Hawaiian '61
Gidget Goes to Rome '63
Ginger and Cinnamon '03
Ginger in the Morning '73
A Girl, a Guy and a Gob '41
The Girl from Missouri '34►
The Girl from Petrovka '74
The Girl in the Picture '86
The Girl Next Door '04
Girl Shy '24►
Girl Under the Sheet '61
Giving It Up '99
The Glass Bottom Boat '66
Go Fish '94►
The Gold of Naples '54►
Good Advice '01
The Good Fairy '35►
A Good Woman '04
A Good Year '06
The Goodbye Girl '77►
Goodbye, New York '85
The Grand Duchess and the Waiter '26►
The Grass Is Greener '61
Gray Matters '06
The Great Gildersleeve '43
Green Card '90►
Groundhog Day '93►
Guess Who '05
A Guy Thing '03
The Halfback of Notre Dame '96
Hammersmith Is Out '72
Hanky Panky '82
Happy Accidents '00
Happy New Year '73►
Happy Together '89
Hardhat & Legs '80
Hav Plenty '97►
Having It All '82
Having Wonderful Crime '45
Having Wonderful Time '38
He Said, She Said '91
Head Over Heels '01
Hear My Song '91►
Heartaches '82►
Heartbeat '46
Heartbeeps '81
The Heartbreak Kid '07
Heartstrings '93
Heaven Before I Die '96
Heaven or Vegas '98
Heaven's a Drag '94
Her Alibi '88
Her First Romance '40
Herbie Goes to Monte Carlo '77
Hi Diddle Diddle '43
Hi-Life '98
High Fidelity '00►
High Spirits '88
Higher Education '88
His First Flame '26►
His Wife's Lover '31►
Hitch '05
Hobson's Choice '53►
Hobson's Choice '83
Hoffman '70
The Holiday '06
Home Fries '98
Honeymoon Academy '90
Honeymoon in Vegas '92►
Honeymoon Lodge '43

The Honeymooners '03
Hook, Line and Sinker '30
The Horizontal Lieutenant '62
Hot Chocolate '92
Hotel de Love '96
House Calls '78►
Houseboat '58
Housesitter '92
How I Spent My Summer Vacation '97
How to Lose a Guy in 10 Days '03
How to Lose Your Lover '04
How to Marry a Millionaire '53
How to Steal a Million '66►
How U Like Me Now? '92►
Hurry, Charlie, Hurry '41
Hurry Up or I'll Be Thirty '73
I Could Never Be Your Woman '06
I Don't Buy Kisses Anymore '92
I Know Where I'm Going '45►
If You Only Knew '00
Il Bell'Antonio '60
I'll Take Sweden '65
I'll Take You There '99
I'm with Lucy '02
I Love Trouble '94
I Love You, Don't Touch Me! '97
Imagine Me & You '06
The Importance of Being Earnest '02
Impostors '80
Impromptu '90►
In Good Company '04►
In Love with an Older Woman '82
In Person '35
In the Mix '05
The Incredible Mr. Limpet '64
The Incredibly True Adventure of Two Girls in Love '95
Indiscreet '31
Indiscreet '58►
Indiscreet '88
Innerspace '87
Instant Karma '90
Intolerable Cruelty '03►
Invitation to the Wedding '73
I.Q. '94
Iris Blond '98
Irma La Douce '63
It '27
It Could Happen to You '94
It Had to Be You '00
It Happened One Night '34►
It Should Happen to You '54►
It Started with a Kiss '59
It Started with Eve '41►
It Takes Two '88
Italian for Beginners '01
It's My Turn '80
I've Heard the Mermaids Singing '87►
Jeffrey '95
Jerry Maguire '96►
Jersey Girl '92
Jersey Girl '04
Jet Lag '02
Jit '94
Jock Petersen '74
Joe Versus the Volcano '90
Joey Breaker '93►
John Tucker Must Die '06
The Judge Steps Out '49
Julia Has Two Lovers '91
June Bride '48►
Jupiter's Thigh '81
Just a Kiss '02
Just a Little Harmless Sex '99
Just Friends '05

Just Like a Woman '95
Just like Heaven '05
Just Married '03
Just Me & You '78
Just My Luck '06
Just One Night '00
Just One of the Girls '93
Just One Time '00
Just Tell Me What You Want '80
Just the Ticket '98
Just the Way You Are '84
Just Write '97
Kate & Leopold '01
Keeping the Faith '00
Kettle of Fish '06
Key Exchange '85
Key to the City '50
Kill Me Later '01
The King on Main Street '25
King Ralph '91
A Kiss for Mary Pickford '27
Kiss Me Goodbye '82►
Kiss Shot '89
Kissing a Fool '98
Kissing Jessica Stein '02
Km. 0 '00
Knocked Up '07
Kuni Lemel in Tel Aviv '77
La Collectionneuse '67
La Lectrice '88
L.A. Story '91►
La Vie de Bohème '93►
Labor Pains '09
The Lady Eve '41►
The Lady Is Willing '42
Lady L '65
Lady on a Train '45►
Lady Takes a Chance '43►
The Lady's Not for Burning '87
L'Annee des Meduses '86
Lassie from Lancashire '38
The Last Fling '86
The Last Kiss '01
The Last Married Couple in America '80
The Last of the High Kings '96
Late Bloomers '95
Later for Dinner '91
Latter Days '04
L'Auberge Espagnole '02►
Laws of Attraction '04
Le Beau Mariage '82►
Le Magnifique '76
The Leading Man '96
Legal Eagles '86
Lena's Holiday '90
Les Grandes Manoeuvres '55►
Let It Snow '99
Let's Make It Legal '51
Let's Make Love '60
License to Wed '07
Lt. Robin Crusoe, U.S.N. '66
Life in the Fast Lane '00
Life or Something Like It '02
Life Without Dick '01
The Linguini Incident '92
Listen to Your Heart '83
Little Black Book '04
Little City '97
Little Manhattan '05
Little Noises '91
A Little Romance '79►
Little Sister '92
A Little Stiff '91
Little White Lies '89
Live Bait '95
Loco Love '03
The Lonely Guy '84
Lonely Hearts '82►
Lonely in America '90
Long-Term Relationship '06
Look Who's Talking '89►
Look Who's Talking, Too '90
Loose in New York '74
Lost and Found '79
Lost in Yonkers '93
Love Actually '03
The Love Affair; or, The Case of the Missing Switchboard Operator '67
Love Among the Ruins '75►
Love & Sex '00
Love at First Sight '76

Love by Appointment '76
Love Can Seriously Damage Your Health '96
Love Don't Cost a Thing '03
Love for Rent '05
Love Hurts '91
Love in the Afternoon '57
Love Is All There Is '96
Love Is Better Than Ever '52
Love Jones '96►
Love Laughs at Andy Hardy '46
Love, Ludlow '05
Love Me if You Dare '03
Love on the Run '36
Love Potion #9 '92
Love Stinks '99
The Love Trap '29
Loveless in Los Angeles '07
Lovelife '97
Lovelines '84
Lover Come Back '61
Loverboy '89
Lovers and Liars '81
Lover's Knot '96
Lovers Like Us '75
Lovers' Lovers '94
Loves & Times of Scaramouche '76
Love's Labour's Lost '00
Loving Couples '80
Loving Jezebel '99
The Low Down '00
Lucky Seven '03
Luminarias '99
The Lunatic '92
Lunatics: A Love Story '92►
Luster '02
Made in America '93
Made in Heaven '52
Made of Honor '08
Magic on Love Island '80
The Magnificent Dope 42►
The Maid '90
Maid in Manhattan '02
Maid's Night Out '38
The Main Event '79
Main Street to Broadway '53
A Majority of One '56
Making Mr. Right '86
Male and Female '19►
The Male Animal '42
Mama, There's a Man in Your Bed '89►
Mambo Italiano '03
A Man, a Woman, and a Bank '79
Man Trouble '92
The Man Who Loved Women '77►
The Man Who Loved Women '83
The Man Who Made Husbands Jealous '98
Manhattan '79►
Manhattan Merenguel '95
Mannequin '87
Marius and Jeannette '97
The Marriage of Figaro '49
Marriage Italian Style '64►
Married? '26
Married to the Mob '88►
The Marrying Man '91
The Matchmaker '58►
The Matchmaker '97
The Mating Habits of the Earthbound Human '99
Matrimaniac '16
May Wine '90
Me and You and Everyone We Know '05►
Me, Myself & I '92
Me, Myself, and Irene '00►
Meeting Daddy '98
Meeting Venus '91
Miami Rhapsody '95
Michael '96
Mickey Blue Eyes '99
Micki & Maude '84
A Midsummer Night's Dream '35►
A Midsummer Night's Dream '68
A Midsummer Night's Dream '96
The Millionairess '60
Milk Money '94
Minnie and Moskowitz '71

► = rated three bones or higher

Miracle Beach '92
The Mirror Has Two Faces '96
The Misadventures of Merlin Jones '63
Miss Right '81
Miss Winterbourne '96
Mr. Boggs Steps Out '38
Mr. Fix It '06
Mr. Jealousy '98
Mr. Love '86
Mr. Lucky '43▶
Mr. Peabody & the Mermaid '48
Mr. Wonderful '93
Mr. Write '92
A Modern Affair '94
Modern Love '90
Modern Romance '81▶
Monaco Forever '83
Money Buys Happiness '99
Monsoon Wedding '01▶
A Month by the Lake '95
The Moon Is Blue '53
Moon Pilot '62
Moonstruck '87▶
Morgan: A Suitable Case for Treatment '66
Mostly Martha '01▶
Mouth to Mouth '95
Move Over, Darling '63
Much Ado about Nothing '93,
Murphy's Romance '85▶
Music & Lyrics '07
Music from Another Room '97
Must Love Dogs '05
My Best Friend's Girl '84
My Best Friend's Wedding '97
My Boss's Daughter '03
My Brother's Wife '89
My Dear Secretary '49
My First Wedding '04
My Girl '91
My Girl 2 '94
My Love For Yours '39
My Man Godfrey '57
My Night at Maud's '69▶
My Sex Life... Or How I Got into an Argument '96
My Stepmother Is an Alien '88
My Tutor '82
Mystery Date '91
The Mystery Man '35
Naked in New York '93
Never Again '01
Never Been Kissed '99
Never Met Picasso '96
Never on Sunday '60▶
The New Eve '98▶
A New Kind of Love '63
A New Leaf '71
The Night Club '25
Night and Day '91▶
The Night We Never Met '93
Nina Takes a Lover '94
Ninotchka '39▶
No Reservations '07
Nobody's Fool '86
The Norman Conquests, Part 1: Table Manners '78▶
The Norman Conquests, Part 2: Living Together '78▶
The Norman Conquests, Part 3: Round and Round the Garden '78,
North to Alaska '60▶
Nothin' 2 Lose '00
Notting Hill '99▶
Novel Romance '06
Off Beat '86
Okoge '93
On Approval '44▶
On the Line '01
On the Sunny Side '62
Once Around '91
Once Upon a Wedding '05
One Fine Day '96
One Rainy Afternoon '36
One, Two, Three '61▶
One Wild Moment '78
Only the Lonely '91
Only with Married Men '74
Only You '92
Only You '94
The Opposite Sex and How to Live With Them '93
The Other Brother '02
The Other Side of the Bed '03
The Other Sister '98
Our Miss Brooks '56
Outrageous Fortune '87
Over Her Dead Body '08
Overboard '87
Overnight Delivery '96
The Owl and the Pussycat '70▶
The Pallbearer '95
Panama Lady '39
Pantaloons '57
Paper Marriage '88
Paper Marriage '93
Paperback Hero '99
Paperback Romance '96
A Paradise Under the Stars '99
Pardon Mon Affaire '76▶
Paris Holiday '57
Party '96
Peggy Sue Got Married '86
Penelope '06
The Perfect Gift '95
The Perfect Holiday '07
The Perfect Man '05
Perfect Match '88
Perfectly Normal '91
Personal Property '37
The Personals '83
The Personals '98
Personals '00
Phffft! '54
Pick a Card '01
The Pick-Up Artist '87
Picture Perfect '97
Pie in the Sky '95
Pillow Talk '59▶
Pizza '05
Play It Again, Sam '72▶
Playing Mona Lisa '00
Playmates '72
Please Not Now! '61
The Pompatus of Love '95
Pool Hustlers '83
Pool Sharks '15
Pop Always Pays '40
Possible Loves '00▶
Practical Magic '98
Preaching to the Perverted '97
Prelude to a Kiss '92
Pretty Woman '90
The Price of Milk '00
Priceless '06
Priceless Beauty '90
Prime '05
The Prince & Me '04
The Prince and the Showgirl '57
The Princess and the Pirate '44▶
The Princess Diaries 2: Royal Engagement '04
Prisoner of Zenda '79
Private Lives '31▶
Probation '32
Promise Her Anything '66
Promises! Promises! '63
Protocol '84
Puccini for Beginners '06
The Purple Rose of Cairo '85▶
Pursuit of Happiness '01
A Pyromaniac's Love Story '95
Quackser Fortune Has a Cousin in the Bronx '70▶
Queens Logic '91
Quick Change '90
The Quiet Man '52▶
The Raffle '94
The Rage of Paris '38▶
The Ranch '88
The Rat Race '60▶
Rattle of a Simple Man '64
Reaching for the Moon '31
Reality Bites '94
Regular Guys '96
Relative Values '99
Relax... It's Just Sex! '98
The Reluctant Debutante '58▶
Remember the Night '40▶
Rendez-vous de Juillet '49
Return to Me '00
Rich in Love '93
The Ritz '76▶
River Street '95
Road to Ruin '91
Roads to the South '78
The Roaring Road '19
Roman Holiday '53▶
Romance and Rejection '96
Romantic Comedy '83
Roses Bloom Twice '77
Round Numbers '91
Roxanne '87▶
Roxie Hart '42
Rumor Has It... '05
Run, Fat Boy, Run '07
Runaway Bride '99▶
Running Mates '92▶
Russian Dolls '05
Sabrina '54
Sabrina '95
St. Ives '98
Saratoga '37
Saving Face '04
Scorchers '92
Seaside Swingers '65
Secret Admirer '85
Secret Ingredient '92
Secret Life of an American Wife '68
The Secret of My Success '87
See You in the Morning '89
Seeing Other People '04
Seems Like Old Times '80
Send Me No Flowers '64▶
The Sensual Man '74
The Sensuous Nurse '76
Separate Vacations '86
Serendipity '01
Service De Luxe '38
Seven Days Ashore '44
Seven Girlfriends '00
Seven Minutes in Heaven '86
The Seven Year Itch '55▶
Sex and the Single Girl '64
Sex and the Single Parent '82
Sex Is Comedy '02
The Sex Monster '99
Shadow of the Thin Man '41▶
Shakespeare in Love '98▶
Shall We Dance? '04
Shallow Hal '01
Shanghai Surprise '86
She Done Him Wrong '33▶
She's All That '99
She's Gotta Have It '86▶
She's Having a Baby '88
She's the One '96
The Shop Around the Corner '40▶
Shopgirl '05
Shore Leave '25
Short Circuit '86
The Shrimp on the Barbie '90
Shut Up and Kiss Me '05
Sibling Rivalry '90
Sidewalks of New York '01
Silver Streak '76▶
Simply Irresistible '99
Singles '92▶
Sixteen Candles '84▶
Skin Deep '89
Sleepless in Seattle '93▶
A Smile Like Yours '96
Smiles of a Summer Night '55▶
Smiling Fish & Goat on Fire '99
Smokescreen '90
Snapshots '02
Snow: The Movie '83
Snowball'n '71
So This Is Paris '26▶
Soapdish '91▶
The Social Secretary '16
Sol Goode '01
Soldat Duroc... Ça Va Être Ta Fete! '75
Solitaire for 2 '94
Someone Like You '01
Something About Sex '98
Something More '05
Something Short of Paradise '79
Something's Gotta Give '03
Son of Gascogne '95
The Souler Opposite '97
Soup for One '82
Southern Belles '05
Spanglish '04
Speechless '94
Spice World '97
Splash '84▶
Splendor '99
Sprung '96
Standing on Fishes '99
Starter for Ten '06
State of the Union '48▶
The Station '92
The Sterile Cuckoo '69▶
Still Breathing '97
Stolen Kisses '68▶
The Story of Boys & Girls '91▶
The Story of Us '99
Straight Talk '92
Strange Bedfellows '65
Strange Planet '99
Strictly Ballroom '92▶
Strictly Business '91
Stroke of Midnight '90
The Student Affair '97
Suburban Girl '07
Sugar Sweet '02
A Summer's Tale '96
Summer School '77
Sunset Limousine '83
Sunshine in New York '63
Surf Party '64
Surrender '87
Surviving Desire '91▶
Suzy '36
The Swan '25
The Swan '56
Sweet Home Alabama '02
Sweet Lies '88
Sweet Talker '91
The Sweetest Thing '02
Tadpole '02
The Tall Guy '89▶
The Taming of the Shrew '29
The Taming of the Shrew '67▶
Tammy and the Bachelor '57
Tammy and the Doctor '63
The Tao of Steve '00▶
Tattoo, a Love Story '02
The Teahouse of the August Moon '56
Ted & Venus '91
The Tender Trap '55
The Terminal '04
Thanks for the Memory '38
That Certain Thing '28
That Funny Feeling '65
That Lucky Touch '75
That Old Feeling '96
That Touch of Mink '62
That Uncertain Feeling '41
Theodora Goes Wild '36▶
There's a Girl in My Soup '70
There's Something about Mary '98▶
They All Kissed the Bride '42
They All Laughed '81
They Got Me Covered '43
The Thing Called Love '93
The Things of Life '70▶
The Third Wheel '02
13 Going on 30 '04
Thirty Day Princess '34
30 Is a Dangerous Age, Cynthia '68
30 Years to Life '01
Thomas Graal's Best Film '17▶
Thomas Graal's First Child '18
Those Endearing Young Charms '45
Three Broadway Girls '32▶
Three Coins in the Fountain '54
Three for Bedroom C '52
Three Guys Named Mike '51
Three Hearts '93
Three Husbands '50
Three Smart Girls Grow Up '39▶
Three Way Weekend '81
Threesome '94
Tieta of Agreste '96
Tiger and the Pussycat '67
Til There Was You '96
Till Marriage Do Us Part '74
Tillie's Punctured Romance '14
Time of the Gypsies '90▶
Tin Cup '96▶
To Cross the Rubicon '91
To Paris with Love '55
Together '70
Tokyo Cowboy '94
Tom Jones '63▶
Tom, Dick, and Harry '41
Tomboy '40
Tomboy '85
Too Beautiful for You '88
Too Smooth '98
Topsy Turvy '84
Totally Blonde '01
A Touch of Class '73▶
Touch of Pink '04
Town and Country '01
The Treatment '06
Trick '99▶
Trippin' '99
The Triumph of Love '01
Trojan War '97
Trouble in Paradise '32▶
The Truth about Cats and Dogs '96▶
The Truth About Love '04
Tulips '81
Tune in Tomorrow '90
Twelfth Night '95
24 Nights '99
27 Dresses '08
Twice upon a Yesterday '98
2 Brothers & a Bride '03
2 Days in Paris '07▶
Two-Faced Woman '41▶
Two by the Sea '03
Two Much '96
Two Nights with Cleopatra '54
Two Ninas '00
Two of a Kind '83
Two Weeks Notice '12
Under One Roof '02
Undercover Angel '99
Underground Aces '80
The Undertaker's Wedding '97
Une Parisienne '58
The Unkissed Bride '66
Up Your Alley '89
Utilities '83
The Vacillations of Poppy Carew '94
Valley Girl '83▶
Venus Beauty Institute '98
The Very Thought of You '98
Victor/Victoria '82▶
Vivacious Lady '38▶
Waiting for the Light '90
Walk, Don't Run '66
Warm Summer Rain '89
Watch It '93▶
Wavelength '96
We All Loved Each Other So Much '77▶
The Wedding Banquet '93▶
Wedding Bell Blues '96
The Wedding Date '05
Wedding Daze '06
The Wedding Party '69
The Wedding Planner '01
The Wedding Singer '97▶
A Weekend in the Country '96
We're Not Married! '52▶
What a Woman! '56
What Happened to Rosa? '21▶
What Happens in Vegas '08
What Women Want '00
Whatever It Takes '20
What's Good for the Goose '69
What's New Pussycat? '65▶
When Brendan Met Trudy '00▶
When Harry Met Sally... '89▶
When Ladies Meet '41
While You Were Sleeping '95▶
Whipped '00
Who Am I This Time? '82▶
The Whole Shebang '01
The Whoopee Boys '86
Why Change Your Wife? '20
Wildest Dreams '90
William Shakespeare's A Midsummer Night's Dream '99
Wimbledon '04
Wimps '87
Win a Date with Tad Hamilton! '04
A Wind from Wyoming '94
Wishful Thinking '92
With Six You Get Eggroll '68
Without Love '45
Without Reservations '46
A Woman Hater '49
The Woman in Red '84
The Woman of the Year '42▶
Woman on Top '00
A Woman's a Helluva Thing '01
The Women '63▶
Working Girl '88▶
World and Time Enough '95
The World's Oldest Living Bridesmaid '92
Worth Winning '89
You Can't Fool Your Wife '40
You Gotta Stay Happy '48
You, Me and Dupree '06
You Stupid Man '02
You Tell Me '92
Younger & Younger '94
Your Place or Mine '83
You've Got Mail '98▶
You've Got to Have Heart '77
Zack & Reba '98
Zeus and Roxanne '96
Zus & Zo '01

Romantic Drama

A Coeur Joie '67
Aaron Loves Angela '75
Absent Without Leave '95
The Accidental Tourist '88▶
The Accompanist '93
Adelheid '69
The Adorable Cheat '28
An Affair '95
An Affair of Love '99
An Affair to Remember '57▶
The African Queen '51▶
After Julius '78
After Sex '07
After the Wind '33
Afterglow '97
Against All Odds '84
Against the Wind '90
The Age of Innocence '93▶
Aimee & Jaguar '98
Algiers '38▶
Ali: Fear Eats the Soul '74▶
Alice '90
Alice Adams '35

▶ = rated three bones or higher

Romantic

Alice et Martin '98
Alive and Kicking '96
All About You '01
All That Heaven Allows '55▲
All the Pretty Horses '00
All the Real Girls '03▲
All the Vermeers in New York '91▲
All This and Heaven Too '40▲
Almost Blue '93
Always '89
The American '01
Anatomy of a Seduction '79
And a Nightingale Sang '91
And Now My Love '74▲
Angel '37
Angel Baby '95▲
Angel Eyes '01
Angel Square '92
Angels and Insects '95▲
The Animal Kingdom '32▲
Ann Vickers '33
Anna '51
Anna Christie '23▲
Anna Karenina '48▲
Anna Karenina '85
Anna Karenina '00
Annapolis '28
An Annapolis Story '55
Anne of Avonlea '87▲
Another Time, Another Place '83▲
Another Way '82▲
Anthony Adverse '36
Apart from Hugh '94
Arch of Triumph '48▲
Arch of Triumph '85
As Is '85
Ask the Dust '06
Aspen Extreme '93
At First Sight '98
Atalia '85
Atonement '07▲
The Atonement of Gosta Berling '24▲
Audrey's Rain '03
Autumn Moon '92
The Average Woman '24
Back Street 41
Back Street 61
Backstreet Dreams '90
Bad Love '95
The Ballad of the Sad Cafe '91
Balzac and the Little Chinese Seamstress '02
Band of Angels '57
Barbarian and the Geisha '58
The Barretts of Wimpole Street '34▲
Basil '98
Bayou Romance '86
The Beast '75
Beau Revel 21▲
Beauty and the Beast '46▲
Because of You '52
Becoming Jane '07
Bed of Roses '95
Before Sunrise '94
Before Sunset '04▲
Before the Rain '94▲
Beloved Enemy '36▲
Beloved Infidel '59
Berlin Blues '89
Besieged '98
The Best Intentions '92▲
The Best of Everything '59▲
Betty Blue '86▲
Beware of Pity '46
Beyond Borders '03
Beyond the Clouds '95
Beyond the Rocks '22
The Big Parade '25▲
Big Street '42
The Bigamist '53
Bird of Paradise '32
Bitter Sugar '96▲
Bitter Sweet '33
The Bitter Tea of General Yen '33▲
The Bitter Tears of Petra von Kant '72
The Black Marble '79▲
Black Orchid '59
Bleeding Hearts '94

Blind Husbands '19▲
The Blonde '92
Blood and Sand '22
Blood and Sand '89
Blood Feud '79
The Blood of Others '84
Bloom '03
The Blue Hour '91
The Blue Light '32▲
Blue Smoke '07
Blush '95
Bolero '84
Bombay Talkie '70
Born to Be Bad '50
Born Under Libra '01
The Boss Is Served '76
Bounce '00
The Boxer '97
Boy Takes Girl '83
Boys '95
Breakfast in Paris '81
Breaking and Entering '06
Breathless '59▲
Bride of the Wind '01
The Bride Wore Red '37
The Bridge '00▲
The Bridges of Madison County '95▲
Brief Encounter '46▲
Broken English '07
Broken Silence '01▲
The Brylcreem Boys '96
Buffalo Jump '90▲
Bullfighter & the Lady '50
Burning Secret '89
Buster and Billie '74
By Love Possessed '61
Bye Bye Blues '89
Cabiria '14
Cabo Blanco '81
Cactus '86
Cactus in the Snow '72
Caddie '76
Calendar '93
Camila '84▲
Camille '36▲
Camille Claudel '89▲
Captive Hearts '87
Captives '94
Carla's Song '97
Carmen '83▲
Carnival Story '54
Carolina '03
Carrington '95
Casablanca '42▲
Casino '80
Cass Timberlane '47
Castaway '87
The Castaway Cowboy '74
Catch and Release '07
Catherine Cookson's The Fifteen Streets '90
Catherine Cookson's The Moth '96
Catherine Cookson's The Secret '00▲
Catherine Cookson's The Wingless Bird '97
Catherine Cookson's Tilly Trotter '99
Caught '49▲
Chain Lightning '50
Chained '34
The Chambermaid on the Titanic '97
Chanel Solitaire '81
Changing Times '04
Chapter Two '79
Charles & Diana: A Palace Divided '92
Charlotte Gray '01
Charulata '64
The Children '90
Children of a Lesser God '86▲
Children of the Century '99
The Christmas Card '06
Christopher Strong '33
Chunhyang '00
Cinderella Liberty '73▲
Circle of Friends '94
Circle of Love '64
Circle of Passion '97
Circus World 64

City for Conquest '40▲
City Girl 30
Claire of the Moon '92
Clash by Night '52▲
Climates '06▲
Close My Eyes '91
Closer '04▲
Cloud Waltzing '87
Cobra 25
Cocktail 88
Code 46 '03
Cold Sassy Tree '89▲
Collector's Item '89▲
The Color of Evening '95
Come and Get It '36▲
Come See the Paradise '90▲
Coming Home '98
The Coming of Amos '25▲
Coming Through '85
The Competition '80▲
Condemned 29
Conquest '37▲
Consolation Marriage '31
The Constant Gardener '05▲
The Cooler '03▲
Corregidor '43
Corrina, Corrina '94
The Courage to Love '00
The Cousins' 59▲
The Cowboy & the Ballerina '84
The Cranes Are Flying '57▲
crazy/beautiful '01
Crazylove '05
The Crossing '92
Crystal Heart '87
The Cutting Edge '92
The Cutting Edge: Going for the Gold '05
Cyrano de Bergerac '25▲
Cyrano de Bergerac '50▲
Daddy Long Legs 19
Daisy Kenyon 47
Dalva '95
Damage '92▲
Dance '90
Dancers '87
Dangerous Beauty '98▲
Dangerous Liaisons '88▲
Dangerous Liaisons '03
Daniel Deronda 02
Danielle Steel's Changes '91
Danielle Steel's Daddy '91
Danielle Steel's Heartbeat '93
Danielle Steel's Palomino '91
Danielle Steel's Star '93
The Dark Angel 35
Dark Eyes '87▲
Dark Journey '37▲
Dark Odyssey '57
The Dark Side of the Sun '88
Dash and Lilly '99
The Dawning '88
A Day in October '92
Daybreak 93
Days and Nights in the Forest '70
Dead Beat '94
Deadly Desire '91
Death Takes a Holiday '34▲
December Bride '91
Deception '46▲
A Dedicated Man 86
Deja Vu '84
Deja Vu '98
The Delta '97
The Deluge 73
Desert Hearts '86▲
Desert Winds '95
Desire '36▲
Desire '93
Desperate Remedies '93
Devil in the Flesh '46▲
Devil in the Flesh '87
The Devil Is a Woman '35▲
Devil's Wanton '49
Devotion '31
Devotion '95
Die Grosse Freiheit Nr. 7 '45
Disappearing Acts '00
The Divorcee '30
Doctor Zhivago '65▲
Doctor Zhivago '03

Dogfight '91▲
Dogtown '97
The Dolls 83
Dolls '02▲
The Dolphin '87
Don Juan DeMarco '94
Doomsday '28
Dot the I '03
Down in the Valley '05
A Dream of Kings '69▲
The Dreamers '03
Dreams Lost, Dreams Found '87
Dresden '06
The Dressmaker '89
Dubarry '30
The Duchess of Langeais '07▲
Duel of Hearts '92
The Dying Gaul '05▲
Dying Young '91
Dynasty '76
The Eagle Has Two Heads '48▲
Earth & Water '99
East Side, West Side 49
Echoes '88
Ecstasy '33
Edward and Mrs. Simpson '80
Effi Briest '74▲
8 Seconds '94
84 Charing Cross Road '86▲
El Diputado '78▲
Elective Affinities '96
Elena and Her Men '56▲
Elephant Walk '54
Elizabeth '05▲
Elizabethtown '05▲
Eliza's Horoscope '70
Emily Bronte's Wuthering Heights '92
Emma '72
Emma '96▲
Emma '97▲
Empty Canvas 64
Enchanted April '92▲
End of August '82
End of Summer '97
The End of the Affair '99▲
Endless Love '81
The English Patient '96▲
Entropy '99
Escape to Love '82
Eternal Sunshine of the Spotless Mind '04▲
Ethan '71
Ethan Frome '92
Evangeline 29
Every Time We Say Goodbye '86
Everybody's All American '88
Everything Happens at Night '39▲
Ex-Lady '33
The Eyes, the Mouth 83
The Fable of the Beautiful Pigeon Fancier '88
Facing Windows '03
Faithless '00▲
Falling for a Dancer '98
Falling in Love '84
The Family Man 79
Fanny '32▲
Fanny '61▲
The Fantastic Night '42▲
Far and Away '92
Far from Heaven '02▲
Far from the Madding Crowd '67▲
Far from the Madding Crowd '97
The Far Pavilions '84
A Farewell to Arms '32▲
The Farmer Takes a Wife '35
Fascination '04
Fatal Attraction '80
Feast of July '95
Feast of Love '07
Fergie & Andrew: Behind Palace Doors '93
Fiances 63
Fire '96
Fire and Ice '87
Fire and Sword 82

Fire with Fire '86
Firelight '97▲
Fires Within '91
First Affair '83
First Knight '95
First Love 70
First Love 77
First Love and Other Pains / One of Them '99
First Love, Last Rites '98
Five Days One Summer '82
5x2 '04▲
The Flame Is Love 79
Flannel Pajamas '06▲
Flor Silvestre 58
The Flying Fool 29
For Sale '98
A Fond Kiss '04▲
Food of Love '02
Fool for Love '86▲
Fools 70
For Love Alone '86
For Love or Money '88
For the Love of Angela '82
For the Moment '94
Forbidden 85
Forbidden Fruit '52▲
Foreign Affairs '93▲
Foreign Student '94
Forever 78
Forever: A Ghost of a Love Story '92
Forever Emmanuelle '75
Foxfire Light 82
Franz '72
The French Lieutenant's Woman '81▲
French Postcards 79
Fresh Cut Grass '04
Fresh Horses '88
The Fugitive Kind '60▲
Fulfillment '89
Full Moon in Paris '84▲
G '02
Gabriela '01
Gal Young 'Un 79▲
Gamble on Love '86
The Game of Love '90
A Gentle Woman '69▲
Georgia, Georgia '72
Ghost '90▲
G.I. War Brides '46
Girl in Black '56
The Girl in Blue '74
The Girl in the Cafe '05
The Girl with a Suitcase '60
The Girl with Green Eyes '64
Glitter '01
The Go-Between '71▲
Going Shopping '05
Golden Demon '53
Golden Gate '93
Gone with the Wind '39▲
The Good German '06
Goodbye Again '61
The Gorgeous Hussy '36
The Governess '98
Grand Isle '92
The Great Gatsby '01
The Great Lie '41▲
Green Dolphin Street '47
Green Fields '37
Green Fire '55
Green Mansions '59
Griffin and Phoenix: A Love Story 76
The Gymnast '06
The Hairdresser's Husband '92▲
Hammers over the Anvil '91
Hanover Street 79
Harem 85
Harem 86
Harnessing Peacocks '92
Havana '90
Head On '04
Head Over Heels '67▲
Hearing Voices '90
The Hearst and Davies Affair '85
Heart of Humanity '18
Heartbreakers '84▲
Heartwood '98
Heat and Dust '82▲
The Heiress '49▲
Henry Hill '00

Here on Earth '00
Heroes 77
He's Just Not That Into You '08
The Hidden Blade '04
Hide-Out '34
High Art '98
His Private Secretary '33
History Is Made at Night '37▲
Hold the Dream '86
Holiday Affair '49
Holiday Affair '96
Holocaust Survivors... Remembrance of Love '83
The Home and the World '84▲
Home Before Midnight '84
Home Sweet Home 14
Homecoming '48
Hong Kong 1941 '84
Honky '71
Hope Floats '98
The Horse Whisperer '97
Horsey '93
Hotel Room '93
The Hottest State '06
Humoresque '46▲
Husbands and Wives '92▲
I Can't Escape 34
I Capture the Castle '02▲
I Conquer the Sea '36
I Live in Grosvenor Square '46
I Love All of You '83
I Love N.Y. '87
I Love You '81
I Never Sang for My Father '70▲
Ice Castles 79
If Only '04
Iguana '89
Image of Passion '86
In a Shallow Grave '88
In Dangerous Company '88
In Love and War '96
In Love and War '01
In Search of Anna 79
In the Mood for Love '00▲
In the Shadows '98
In Too Deep '90
Incantato '03
An Indecent Obsession '85
Independence Day '93
Indecent Proposal '93
Indiscretion of an American Wife 54
Indochine '92▲
Innocence '00▲
Infinity '96
Interval 73
Intimate Strangers '04▲
Intrigue and Love 59
Intruso '93
Inventing the Abbotts '97
Invisible Circus '00
Iron Cowboy '68
Island of Desire 52
Isle of Secret Passion 82
Istanbul '57
It's All About Love '03
It's My Party '95
I've Always Loved You '46
Jacko & Lise '82
Jailbreakers '94
The Jane Austen Book Club '07▲
Jane Doe '96
Jane Eyre '34
Jane Eyre '44▲
Jane Eyre '83▲
Jane Eyre '96▲
Jane Eyre '06
Japanese Story '03▲
Jason's Lyric '94
Jenny '70
Jewels '92
Johnny Frenchman '46
Jon Jost's Frameup '93
Josepha '82▲
Jude '96▲
Jude the Obscure 71
Jules and Jim '62▲
Jungle Fever '91▲
Just Between Friends '86
Kept Husbands '31

The Key '58
Killing Heat '84
King Kong '05
Kings Go Forth '58
The King's Rhapsody '55
The King's Whore '90
K:pertang '82
Kiss of Fire '98
Kissed '96
Kitty Foyle '40 ▶
Knight Without Armour '37 ▶
Knights of the Round Table '53
Kristin Lavransdatter '95
The L-Shaped Room '62 ▶
La Chartreuse de Parme '48 ▶
La Grande Bourgeoise '74
La Mujer de Mi Hermano '06
La Petite Lili '03
La Petite Sirene '80
La Separation '98 ▶
La Strada '54 ▶
Lagaan: Once upon a Time in India '01 ▶
L'Amour en Herce '77
Lana in Love '92
The Land Girls '98
Landscape After Battle '70 ▶
The Last Confederate: The Story of Robert Adams '05
The Last Kiss '06
The Last Prostitute '91
The Last Ride '04
The Last Time I Saw Paris '54
The Last Train '74
The Last Winters '71
The Last of the Twins '91
Le Bonheur '65
Le Jupon Rouge '87
Le Petit Soldat '60 ▶
Le Repos du Guerrier '62
A Legacy for Leonette '85
The Legend of Paul and Paula '73
Legends of the Fall '94 ▶
Leo Tolstoy's Anna Karenina '96
Leon Morin, Priest '61 ▶
The Leopard '63 ▶
Leopard in the Snow '78
Letters from the Park '83 ▶
Lianna '83
Liebelei '32
Lies and Whispers '98
Lies of the Twins '91
The Life and Loves of Mozart '59
Life and Nothing But '80 ▶
A Life of Her Own '50
Light of My Eyes '01
Lilith '64 ▶
Limbo '99
Linda '29
Listen to Me '89
The Little American '17
Little Dorrit, Film 2: Little Dorrit's Story '88 ▶
Little Minister '34 ▶
Lola '61
Lola '69 ▶
Long Ago Tomorrow '71
The Long, Hot Summer '58 ▶
The Long, Hot Summer '86 ▶
Lorna Doone '34
Lorna Doone '90
Loma Doone '01 ▶
Louisiana '87
Loulou '80 ▶
Love Affair '39 ▶
Love Affair '94 ▶
Love Affair: The Eleanor & Lou Gehrig Story '77 ▶
Love and Basketball '00 ▶
Love and Faith '75 ▶

Love and the Frenchwoman '60
Love at the Top '86
Love Goggles '99
Love in Bloom '35
Love in Germany '84
Love in the Time of Cholera '07
Love is a Many-Splendored Thing '55
The Love Letter '98
Love Letters '45
Love Letters '83
Love Letters '99 ▶
Love Light '21
Love on a Pillow '62
Love on the Run '78 ▶
Love Play '60
Love Songs '99
Love Songs '07
Love Streams '84
Love with the Proper Stranger '63 ▶
Love Without Pity '91
The Lover '92
The Lovers '59 ▶
Lovers: A True Story '90 ▶
Lovers of the Arctic Circle '98
The Lovers on the Bridge '91
The Loves of Carmen '48
Love's Savage Fury '79
Lovespell '79
Lulu on the Bridge '98 ▶
Lust, Caution '07 ▶
The Luzhin Defence '00
Lydia '41 ▶
Machine Gun Blues '35
Mad Bull '77
Mad Love '95
Madagascar Skin '95
Madame Bovary '34 ▶
Madame Bovary '49 ▶
Madame Bovary '91
Madame Bovary '00 ▶
Maelstrom '00
Magenta '96
The Magnificent Matador '55
Maids of Wilko '79
Mambo '55
A Man and a Woman '66 ▶
The Man in Grey '45 ▶
The Man in the Moon '91 ▶
Man is Not a Bird '65
The Man Who Cried '00
The Man Who Guards the Greenhouse '88
Mannequin '37
Manon '50
Mansfield Park '99 ▶
Mansfield Park '07
Map of the Human Heart '93
Margaret's Museum '95
Maria Chapdelaine '34
Maria Chapdelaine '84 ▶
Marilyn & Bobby: Her Final Affair '94
Marjorie Morningstar '58
Martha and I '91 ▶
Marty '55 ▶
Match Point '05 ▶
A Matter of Love '78
Mayerling '36 ▶
Mayerling '68
Medicine Man '92
Melo '86
Melody '71
Memoirs of a Geisha '05 ▶
Men '97
Merry-Go-Round '23
Message in a Bottle '98
Middlemarch '93 ▶
The Mill on the Floss '37
The Mill on the Floss '97
The Million Dollar Hotel '99
Minna von Barnheim or The Soldier's Fortune '62
Mirrors '85
Mississippi Masala '92 ▶
Mississippi Mermaid '69 ▶

Mrs. Mike '49
Mrs. Soffel '84
Mr. & Mrs. Loving '96
Mr. Jones '93
The Mistress of Spices '05
Model Behavior '82
Mogambo '53 ▶
Monsoon '97
Moondance '95
Moonlight Sonata '38
Morgan's Ferry '99
Morning Glory '93
Morocco '30 ▶
The Mother '03
Mouvements du Desir '94
Mozart and the Whale '05 ▶
My Antonia '94
My Brother Tom '86
My Forbidden Past '51
My Man Adam '86
My Name is Joe '98 ▶
My Reputation '46
Mysteries '84
Nairobi Affair '88
Nais '45 ▶
Naked Tango '91
Nativity '78
Neily et Monsieur Arnaud '95 ▶
The Nest '80
Nevil Shute's The Far Country '85
New York Nights '84
Next Time '99
Next Time We Love '36
Nicole '72
The Night and the Moment '94
A Night Full of Rain '78
Night Games '80
A Night in Heaven '83
A Night is My Future '47
No Looking Back '98
No One Man '32
North Shore '87
Northanger Abbey '87
Northanger Abbey '07
The Notebook '04
Not Quite Paradise '86
Notorious '46 ▶
Nouvelle Vague '90
November Moon '85
Now and Forever '82
Now & Forever '02
O Pioneers! '91
O Quatrilho '95
Obsession '97
Of Human Bondage '34 ▶
Of Love and Shadows '94
Of Mice and Men '39 ▶
An Officer and a Gentleman '82 ▶
Old Gringo '89
Oliver's Story '78
Once in Paris... '79
One Brief Summer '70
One Summer Love '76
Only Love '98
Only Once in a Lifetime '79
Only the Thrill '97
The Other Boleyn Girl '03
The Other Boleyn Girl '08
The Other Side of the Mountain '75 ▶
The Other Side of the Mountain, Part 2 '78
Our Modern Maidens '29
Our Mutual Friend '98 ▶
Our Time '74
Out of Season '75
Outcasts of the City '58
Over the Summer '85
The Painted Veil '06 ▶
Panama Flo '32
A Paper Wedding '89 ▶
Parrish '61
Partition '07
Passion of Love '82
A Patch of Blue '65 ▶
Paul and Michelle '74
Pay It Forward '00
Pepe Le Moko '37 ▶

Persuasion '07
Petty Crimes '07
The Phantom of the Opera '90
The Pianist '91
The Piano '93 ▶
Picnic '55 ▶
Pittsburgh '42
Pizzicata '96
The Playboys '92
Playing Around '30
Playing by Heart '98
Pleasure '31
Poetic Justice '93
Poor White Trash '57
Portrait of Call '48
Portraits Chinois '96
Possessed '31 ▶
Possession '02
The Promise '79
The Promise '94
Proof of Life '00
The Proposition '96
The Proud Ones '53
P.S. '04
P.S. I Love You '07
The Public Eye '92
Pure Country '92
Purple Hearts '84
The Purple Taxi '77
Quality Street '37 ▶
Quatorze Juillet '32
Queen Bee '55 ▶
Queen Christina '33 ▶
Queen of the Stardust Ballroom '75
Rachel, Rachel '68 ▶
Rachel's Man '75
Racing with the Moon '84 ▶
Raffles '30
Rage of Angels '83
Rage of Angels: The Story Continues '86
The Railway Station Man '92
The Rainmaker '56 ▶
Raise Your Voice '04
Random Hearts '99
Reach the Rock '98
The Real Charlotte '91
Rebel '85
Rebel Love '85
Reckless '84
Reconstruction '03
Red Firecracker, Green Firecracker '94
Red Headed Woman '32
Red Kiss '85 ▶
Red Sorghum '87 ▶
The Red Squirrel '93 ▶
Regeneration '15
Rendezvous in Paris '95 ▶
Return Engagement '78
The Return of Martin Guerre '83 ▶
Return of the Native '94
Return of the Soldier '82 ▶
Return to Paradise '53
Return to the Blue Lagoon '91
Return to Two Moon Junction '93
Reunion in France '42
The Ring '27
Risk '94
The Road Home '01 ▶
The Road to Yesterday '25
Rob Roy '95 ▶
Rock Haven '07
Roman Spring of Mrs. Stone '61
Romance '30
Romance in Manhattan '34

Persuasion '95 ▶
Personal Maid '31
The Perfect Husband '92
Perfect Love '96
Persuasion '71
Persuasion '95

Romance on the Orient Express '89
Romantic Englishwoman '75 ▶
Rome Adventure '62
Romeo and Juliet '36 ▶
Romeo and Juliet '54 ▶
Romeo and Juliet '68 ▶
Romper Stomper '92
Room at the Top '59 ▶
A Room with a View '36 ▶
The Rose Tattoo '55 ▶
The Rover '67
Rowing with the Wind '88
Ruby's Bucket of Blood '01
The Run of the Country '95 ▶
Running Away '89
Running Out of Time '94
Ruyblas '48 ▶
Ryan's Daughter '70 ▶
Sadie Thompson '28 ▶
The Sailor Who Fell from Grace with the Sea '76
Sally Hemings: An American Scandal '00
Sam & Janet '02
Same Time, Next Year '78 ▶
San Francisco '36 ▶
Sand and Blood '87
The Sandpiper '65
Santa Fe '97
Sarah, Plain and Tall '91 ▶
Saratoga Trunk '45
Savage Capitalism '93
Savage Messiah '72
Saving Face '04 ▶
Say Hello to Yesterday '71
Sayonara '57 ▶
Scarlet Dawn '32
Scarlet '32
Scenes from the Goldmine '87
Scenes of a Sexual Nature '06
Sea Wife '57
Second Wind '76
Secret Obsession '88
Secret of Yolanca '82
Secret Passions '78
Sense & Sensibility '85
Sense & Sensibility '95 ▶
The Separation '07
September Affair '50 ▶
The Serpent's Kiss '97
The Seventh Stream '01
Shadow of China '91
Shadowlands '85 ▶
The Shape of Things '03
The Shining Hour '38
Shining Through '92
Shoot the Piano Player '62 ▶
Shop Angel '32
Shopworn Angel '38
A Slave of Love '78 ▶
Sleep with Me '94
The Sleeping Dictionary '02
A Slipping Down Life '99
Slipstream '73
Smilin' Through '33 ▶
Snow Country '58
The Soft Skin '64 ▶
A Soldier's Tale '91
Solomon and Gaenor '98
Somewhere I'll Find You '42 ▶
Somewhere in Time '80 ▶
Somewhere Tomorrow '85
Sommersby '93
A Song for Martin '01
A Song of Songs '33
A Song to Remember '45 ▶
Sooner or Later '78
The Sorrows of Satan '26
South Riding '37 ▶
A Special Day '77 ▶
The Spider and the Fly '49

Splendor '35
Stage Beauty '04
Stanley and Iris '90
Stateside '04
Stealing Heaven '88 ▶
Stella '55
The Stilts '84
Stolen Hours '63
Stormy Waters '41 ▶
The Story of a Three Day Pass '68 ▶
The Story of the Late Chrysanthemum '39 ▶
The Story of Xinghua '93
The Strange Love of Molly Louvain '32
Strangers Kiss '83
Strangers When We Meet '60
Strapless '90 ▶
Strayed '03
Street Scene '31 ▶
The Student Prince in Old Heidelberg '27 ▶
Sugartime '95
Summer Affair '79
Summer Lovers '82
Summer Palace '06
A Summer Story '88 ▶
Summertime '55 ▶
Suspicious River '00
Swept from the Sea '97
Sweet Bird of Youth '89
Sweet Land '05 ▶
Sweet Light in a Dark Room '60 ▶
Sweet November '68
Swimming Pool '70
Swimming Pool '03
A Tale of Two Cities '80
A Tale of Winter '92 ▶
Talk of Angels '96
Talk to Me '84
Tango '98
Tango Bar '88
Tarzan Escapes '36 ▶
Tears in the Rain '88
The Tempest '28
The Tempest '63
The Tenant of Wildfell Hall '96 ▶
Tender Mercies '83 ▶
Tess of the D'Urbervilles '98
Tess of the Storm Country '22
Test Pilot '38 ▶
That Long Night in '43 '60
That Night '93
That Summer of White Roses '90
The Theory of Flight '98
Therese Raquin '80
They Call It Sin '32
36 Fillete '86
This is My Father '99 ▶
This is the Sea '96
The Thorn Birds: The Missing Years '96
Three Comrades '38 ▶
Three Times '05 ▶
Through the Olive Trees '94 ▶
The Tiger and the Snow '05
Tilai '90 ▶
Till Human Voices Wake Us '02
Tim '79
Time Out for Love '61
A Time to Love & a Time to Die '58
Timeless '96
Tiptoes '03
To Have & Have Not '44 ▶
To Love Again '80
Today We Live '33
Together? '79
Tom & Viv '94 ▶
Tom Apart '89
Torn Between Two Lovers
Torrents of Spring '90
The Torture of Silence '17
The Touch '71
Touched '05
A Town Like Alice '85 ▶

▶ = rated three bones or higher

Trapeze '56▶
Tristan & Isolde '06
Tristana '70▶
Tropical Malady '04
Trouble in Mind '86▶
True Romance '93
True Heart Susie '19
Trust the Man '06
The Tsar's Bride '66▶
The Tunnel '89
21 Days '37
24 Hours in a Woman's Life '61
2046 '04
Twin Falls Idaho '99▶
Twist & Shout '84▶
Two Daughters '61▶
Two English Girls '72▶
Two Moon Junction '88
Two Plus One '95
Un Coeur en Hiver '93
The Unbearable Lightness of Being '88▶
Under the Greenwood Tree '05
Under the Lighthouse Dancing '97
Under the Sun '98
Undertow '30
The Unknown Soldier '98
An Unremarkable Life '89
Untamed Heart '93
Up Close and Personal '96▶
The Upside of Anger '05▶
The Valley of Decision '45▶
Vanity Fair '32
Vanity Fair '04
Verboten! '59
A Very Long Engagement '04▶
Vibrations '94
The Victory '88
The Virgin and the Gypsy '70
Virgin Machine '88▶
Vive l'Amour '94
Voyage of the Heart '90
Voyager '91▶
A Walk in the Clouds '95
A Walk on the Spring Rain '70
Walk Softly, Stranger '50
A Walk to Remember '02
The Walls of Malapaga '49
Waltz across Texas '83
The Wanderer '67
War & Love '84
War and Peace '56
War and Peace '68▶
War and Peace '73
War Lover '62
Washington Mistress '81
Waterfront '83
The Way We Were '73▶
We the Living '42
Weather in the Streets '84
Wedding in Blood '74▶
The Wedding March '28▶
Weeping Meadow '04
We'll Meet Again '82
West Side Story '61▶
What Dreams May Come '98
When I Close My Eyes '95
When Love Comes '98
When Night is Falling '95▶
When the Time Comes '91
When Thief Meets Thief '37
Where the Boys Are '60
Which Way Home '90
Whistle Stop '46
White Cargo '42
The White Countess '05▶
White Light '90
White Nights '57▶
White Palace '90
The White Sister '23▶
Wicker Park '04
Wide Sargasso Sea '92
Wife versus Secretary '36▶
Wild at Heart '90▶
Wild Hearts Can't Be Broken '91▶
Wildfire '88
William Shakespeare's Romeo and Juliet '96▶
Wind '92
The Wind and the Lion '75▶

Windmills of the Gods '88
Windrider '86
The Winds of Jarrah '83
Wings '27
Wings of Desire '88▶
The Wings of the Dove '97▶
Wings of the Morning '37
Winter Flight '84
Winter People '89
Without Orders '36
Wives and Daughters '01
A Woman at Her Window '77
A Woman at War '94
The Woman He Loved '88
Woman Is the Future of Man '04▶
The Woman Next Door '81▶
A Woman of Substance '84
A Woman Without Love '51▶
A Woman's Guide to Adultery '93
The Women on the Roof '89
The World of Suzie Wong '60
The Wrath of the Gods '14
Wuthering Heights '39▶
Wuthering Heights '53
Wuthering Heights '70
Wuthering Heights '98
Yanks '79
Year of the Quiet Sun '84▶
Yes '04
Yesterday's Hero '79
You and Me '38
You Light Up My Life '77
The Young and the Guilty '58
Young Lady Chatterly 2 '85
Youth on Parole '37
Zelary '03▶
Zhou Yu's Train '02

Romantic Mystery

see also Mystery & Suspense; Psycho-Thriller; Romantic Drama

American Dreamer '84
Angels Fall '07
The Black Widow '05
Blue Smoke '07
Carolina Moon '07
Charade '63▶
Every Woman Knows a Secret '99
Laura '44▶
Married Life '07▶
Montana Sky '07
The Moon-Spinners '64
Notorious '46▶
Rear Window '54▶
Rough Cut '80
The Thin Man '34▶
To Catch a Thief '55▶
To Have & Have Not '44▶

Romantic Triangles

see also Otherwise Engaged

A Coeur Joie '67
After Midnight '04
The Age of Innocence '93▶
Aladdin '92▶
All the Brothers Were Valiant '53
All Things Fair '95
The Alley Cats '65
Amateur '94▶
Amnesia '94
Among Giants '98
Amores Perros '00▶
Angie '94
Anna '51
Another Woman's Husband '00
Anything But Love '02
Apres-Vous '03
The Art of Murder '99
Ash Wednesday '02
Autopsy: A Love Story '02
The Aviator's Wife '80▶
Baby Monitor: Sound of Fear '97
Baja '95

Balzac and the Little Chinese Seamstress '02
Bandits '01
Baton Rouge '88
The Baxter '05
The Best Man '97
A Better Tomorrow, Part 3 '89
Beyond the Rocks '22
The Big Bounce '69
Bitter Moon '92
The Black Dahlia '06
Black Day Blue Night '95
Blue Skies '46▶
Blush '95
Body Heat '81▶
Bon Voyage '03▶
Book of Love '04
Boom Town '40
The Boys and Girl From County Clare '03
Breakin' All The Rules '04
Bride of the Wind '01
Bridget Jones: The Edge of Reason '04
Broadcast News '87▶
Brothers '05▶
The Brylcreem Boys '96
Bubble '06
Bugles in the Afternoon '52
Bull Durham '88▶
A Business Affair '93
Business for Pleasure '96
Cactus Flower '69
Cafe au Lait '94▶
Cake '05
Calendar '93▶
Call Out the Marines '42
Canyon Passage '46▶
Captain Corelli's Mandolin '01
Carnal Knowledge '71▶
Carny '80▶
Carried Away '95
Carrington '95
Casablanca '42▶
Casino '95▶
Caught '96
Celine and Julie Go Boating '74
Children of the Century '99
Circle of Passion '97
Cleopatra's Second Husband '00
Closer '04▶
Coastlines '02
The Color of Evening '95
Coming Out '89
Condition Red '95
The Cook, the Thief, His Wife & Her Lover '90▶
Country Life '95
Cowboy Up '00
Cowboys and Angels '00
The Crucible '96▶
Cruel Intentions 3 '04
The Cuckoo '02
Daisy Kenyon '47
Dalva '95
Damage '92▶
The Dangerous '95
Dangerous Indiscretion '94
Dangerous Passion '95
A Dangerous Woman '93
The Dark Angel '35
Dark Blue World '01
Dark Harbor '98
Days '02
Dead Beat '94
Dead in the Water '01
Dead Ringers '88▶
Dear Wendy '05
Death in Brunswick '90
Deceit '06
December Bride '91
The Devil Is a Woman '35▶
Devotion '95
Diabolique '96
Dinner and Driving '97
The Doom Generation '95▶
Dot the I '03
The Dreamers '03
Dreaming of Joseph Lees '99
Dreamland '06▶
Drift '00
Driven '01
Dry Cleaning '97

The Dying Gaul '05▶
East Side Story '07
The Edukators '04
Elephant Walk '54
The Embalmer '03▶
Emma '96▶
End of the Affair '55
The End of the Affair '99▶
Enduring Love '04
The English Patient '96▶
Eros '04
Ethan Frome '92
Everyone Says I Love You '96▶
The Ex '96
Facing Windows '03
Faithless '00▶
A Family Affair '01
Far from Heaven '02▶
The Favor '92
Feast of July '95
Feast of Love '07
Fever '91
First Knight '95
The First Wives Club '96
The Flame of New Orleans '41▶
Fleeing by Night '00
Flirt '95
The Fluffer '01
A Foreign Affair '48▶
Forever Mine '99
Forty Shades of Blue '05
Foxfire Light '82
French Kiss '95
French Twist '95
G '02
Garage Days '03
The Getaway '72▶
The Getaway '93
The Girl with a Suitcase '60
Gloomy Sunday '02▶
The Golden Bowl '00
The Golden Bowl '72▶
Goodbye, Lover '99
Gray Matters '06
The Great Gatsby '49
The Great Gatsby '74
Grind '96
Gunshy '98▶
Happily Ever After '04
Hard Evidence '94
The Hard Truth '94
Head in the Clouds '04
The Heart of Me '02
Henry & June '90▶
Here on Earth '00
Hero '03▶
The Hi-Lo Country '98
High Art '98
High Society '56▶
Hilary and Jackie '98▶
Hindsight '97
Hollywoodland '06
Homage '95
A Home at the End of the World '04
Hong Kong 1941 '84
I Love You Baby '01
Imagine Me & You '06
In the Shadows '98
Indecent Proposal '93
Indiscreet '98
Interlocked '98
Intersection '93
Intimate Betrayal '96
Intimate Relations '95
Intruso '93
Irreversible '02
Is Money Everything? '23
It Could Happen to You '94
Jason's Lyric '94
Jules and Jim '62▶
Kaaterskill Falls '01
The Keeper: The Legend of Omar Khayyam '05
Keeping the Faith '00▶
Kid Sister '45
Killer Looks '94
Kiss the Sky '98
Kissing a Fool '98
La Mujer de Mi Hermano '06
La Petite Lili '03
La Piscine '69
Ladies in Lavender '04▶
The Ladies of the Bois de Bologne '44
Lady Chatterley '92

The Last Days of Chez Nous '92
The Last Kiss '01
The Last Man '00
The Last of the Mohicans '92▶
The Last Time '06
Le Jupon Rouge '87
The Leading Man '96
Leaving Metropolis '02
Legends of the Fall '94
Les Voleurs '96▶
L'Escorte '96
Liebelei '32
Lloyds of London '36▶
Love Actually '03▶
Love, etc. '96
Love Play '60
Love Serenade '96
Love Songs '07
Love Thy Neighbor '02
Love Walked In '97
The Lovers '59▶
Lucky Seven '03
Lured Innocence '97
Mad of Honor '08
Magenta '96
Making Love '82
The Man I Love '97
The Man in the Attic '94
Man in the Saddle '51
Mararia '98
The Married Life '07▶
The Married Virgin '18
Match Point '05▶
Matter of Trust '98
Maybe... Maybe Not '94
Maze '77
Melinda and Melinda '05▶
Melo '86
Mildred Pierce '45▶
Miller's Crossing '90▶
Mr. Jealousy '98
Mists of Avalon '01▶
Mo' Better Blues '90
Mogambo '53▶
Mojave Moon '96
Moment to Moment '66
Money Train '95
Moondance '95
Moonshine Highway '96
The Mother '03
The Mother and the Whore '73▶
Mouth to Mouth '95
Murder Czech Style '66
My Best Friend's Wedding '97
My Favorite Wife '40▶
My Husband's Secret Life '98
Never Say Die '39
Next Time We Love '36
Nick and Jane '96
No One Man '32
No Way Home '96
Obsession '97
On the Beach '00
Once a Thief '96▶
Once Upon a Time in the Midlands '02
One Night Stand '97▶
Only You '94
The Opposite of Sex '98▶
Ordinary Sinner '02
The Other Boleyn Girl '08
Out of Africa '85▶
The Pallbearer '95
Palmetto '98
Pearl Harbor '01
Pedale Douce '96
The Perfect Gift '95
The Philadelphia Story '40▶
The Pianist '91
Plain Dirty '04
Play It to the Bone '99
Playing by Heart '98
Polish Wedding '97
Portrait in Black '60
Portraits Chinois '96
Possessed by the Night '93
Power and Beauty '02
A Price above Rubies '97
Private Confessions '98
The Promise '05
Puccini for Beginners '06
Pushing Tin '99▶

Puzzlehead '05
Queer Duck: The Movie '06
The Quiet American '02▶
Quiet Days in Hollywood '97
Radio Inside '94
Reality Bites '94
Reckless '97▶
Reckless: The Sequel '98▶
Restoration '94▶
Revenge '90
Riders '88
Rift '96
Risk '00
Road House '48
Road to Riches '01
Robin Hood: Prince of Thieves '91
A Room with a View '86▶
Rory O'Shea Was Here '04
Rumor Has It... '05
Sabrina '54▶
Sabrina '95
Samurai Banners '69
Sand and Blood '87
Saturday Night and Sunday Morning '60▶
Saturday Night Special '92
Savage Capitalism '93
Scorned 2 '96
The Second Front '05
Second Skin '99
The Separation '94
The Serpent's Kiss '97
Sex and the Other Man '95
The Sex Monster '99
She's Gotta Have It '86▶
She's So Lovely '97
Shopgirl '05▶
Silk '07
Simpatico '99
The Situation '06
Six Days, Six Nights '94
Sky Captain and the World of Tomorrow '04
Slaves to the Underground '96
Sleep with Me '94
Sleepless in Seattle '93▶
Sliding Doors '97
The Smiling Lieutenant '31
Something More '99
Something's Gotta Give '03▶
Sommersby '93
The Song of Songs '33
The Spectator '04
Splendor '99
Stella '55
Stella Maris '18▶
Stonewall '95▶
Stormy Nights '97
Story of a Prostitute '65
The Story of Xinghua '93
The Student Affair '97
Sueno '05
Summer Catch '01
Summer Lovers '82
Superman Returns '06
Sweet Home Alabama '02
A Tale of Winter '92
Talk of Angels '96
Tangled '01
Tango '01▶
Tape '01
Tempted '01
The Tenant of Wildfell Hall '96
The Tenants '06
Tequila Sunrise '88▶
Tess '79▶
Tess of the D'Urbervilles '98
There's Something about Mary '98▶
These Foolish Things '06
Three of Hearts '93
A Thin Line Between Love and Hate '96
Three to Tango '99
3-Way '04
Threesome '94
Thunder Birds '42
Tilai '90
Time of Favor '00
Tin Cup '96▶
Tollbooth '94

Torrents of Spring '90
Totally Blonde '01
Town and Country '01
Trace of Stones '66
The Trio '97
Triplecross '95
Trojan War '97
Trouble in Paradise '32
The Truth about Cats and Dogs '96
Twice upon a Yesterday '98
Twister '96
Two Girls and a Guy '98
Two Much '96
Two Ninas '00
Two Plus One '95
Two Shades of Blue '98
U-Turn '97
The Unbearable Lightness of Being '88
Under Hellgate Bridge '99
The Underneath '95
Undertow '30
Unfaithful '02
The Unknown Soldier '98
Untold Scandal '03
The Valet '06
Valley of the Kings '54
The Velocity of Gary '98
A Village Affair '95
Vive l'Amour '94
Waiting to Exhale '95
A Walk on the Moon '99
Wavelength '96
We Don't Live Here Anymore '04
The Wedding Banquet '93
The Wedding Singer '97
Welcome to Mooseport '04
The West Wittering Affair '05
What a Woman! '56
When Will I Be...oved '04
While You Were Sleeping '95
White Mischief '88
The Whole Nina Yards '00
Wild Things '98
Willie & Phil '80
A Wind from Wyoming '94
The Wings of the Dove '97
The Winning of Barbara Worth '26
Wishful Thinking '96
Without Orders '36
Wolf Trap '57
A Woman at Her Window '77
Woman Is the Future of Man '04
Woman Wanted '98
A Woman's a Helluva Thing '01
Worth '26
The Women on the Roof '89
X, Y & Zee '72
XXXY '02
Yes '04
You Gotta Say Happy '48
You Stupid Man '02
Zhou Yu's Train '02

Rome—Ancient
see also Historical Drama; Italy

A.D. '85
Alone Against Rome '62
Amazons and Gladiators '01
Attila '01
Battle of Valiant '63
Ben-Hur '26
Ben-Hur '59
Caesar and Cleopatra '46
Caligula '80
Cleopatra '34
Cleopatra '63
Cleopatra '99
Demetrius and the Gladiators '54
Druids '01
Duel of Champions '61
Fabiola '48
The Fall of the Roman Empire '64
Fellini Satyricon '69
Gladiator '00
Julius Caesar '53
Julius Caesar '70
King Arthur '04
Last Days of Pompeii '35
Last Days of Pompeii '50
The Last Legion '07
Quo Vadis '12
Quo Vadis '51
Quo Vadis '85
The Robe '53
Roman Scandals '33
Rome '78
Rome '78
The Sign of the Cross '33
Spartacus '60
Three Ages '23
Titus '99
Troy '04

Rome—Modern
see also Italy

Artemisia '97
Assassination in Rome '65
Bellissima '51
The Belly of an Architect '91
Besieged '98
Caterina in the Big City '03
Daniella by Night '61
Days '02
Don't Tell '05
Facing Windows '03
Fellini's Roma '72
The Frightened Woman '71
Ginger & Fred '86
Hudson Hawk '91
Indiscretion of an American Wife '54
La Dolce Vita '60
The Last Kiss '01
The Listening '06
My Own Private Idaho '91
National Lampoon's European Vacation '85
Night on Earth '91
Ocean's Twelve '04
The Oman '06
The Order '03
Portrait of a Lady '96
Red Riding Hood '03
Roman Holiday '53
Roman Spring of Mrs. Stone '61
The Scarlet & the Black '83
A Special Day '77
The Spectator '04
Steam: A Turkish Bath '96
The Stendahl Syndrome '95
The Talented Mr. Ripley '99
Traveling Companion '96
The Unfaithfuls '60
The White Sheik '52

Roommates from Hell
see also Psychotics/Sociopaths

Deadbolt '92
The Fear Inside '92
He Died With a Felafel in His Hand '01
The Last Supper '95
Lip Service '00
Malice '93
Man in the Attic '53
The Night We Never Met '93
Pacific Heights '90
Perfect Tenant '99
Shallow Grave '94
Single White Female '92
Single White Female 2: The Psycho '05
Sweet Murder '93
Zero Degrees Kelvin '95

Royalty
see also Historical Drama; Medieval Romps; Period Piece; Royalty, British; Royalty, Russian

Abdulla the Great '56
The Adventures of Marco Polo '38
A Funny Thing Happened on the Way to the Forum '66
Aladdin '92
Ali Baba and the Forty Thieves '43
Ali Baba and the 40 Thieves '54
Anna and the King '99
Anna and the King of Siam '46
Annie: A Royal Adventure '95
Arabian Nights '42
Arabian Nights '00
Atlantis: The Lost Empire '01
Autobiography of a Princess '75
Bagdad '49
Balalaika '39
Barbarian Queen 2: The Empress Strikes Back '89
The Beautician and the Beast '97
Beowulf '07
Beowulf & Grendel '06
The Black Cauldron '85
Bonnie Prince Charlie '48
Boots & Saddles '37
Caligula '80
Camelot '67
Carlton-Browne of the F.O. '59
Carry On Henry VIII '71
Charlemagne '94
Charles & Diana: A Palace Divided '93
Children at Midnight '67
The Chronicles of Narnia: Prince Caspian '08
Cinderella '97
Cleopatra '34
Cleopatra '63
Cleopatra '99
Cobra Woman '44
The Coming of Amos '25
A Connecticut Yankee in King Arthur's Court '89
Conquest of the Normans '62
Court Jester '56
The Crown Prince '06
The Crusades '35
Curse of the Golden Flower '06
David '97
De Mayerling a Sarajevo '40
Dr. Syn, Alias the Scarecrow '64
Donkey Skin '70
Dracula: The Dark Prince '01
Dragonheart '96
Du Barry Was a Lady '43
Dune '84
Dune '00
The Eagle Has Two Heads '48
East of Borneo '31
The Egyptian '54
Elena and Her Men '56
Ella Enchanted '04
The Emperor and the Assassin '99
Emperor Jones '33
The Emperor Waltz '48
The Emperor's New Clothes '01
The Emperor's New Groove '00
The Emperor's Shadow '96
Enchanted '07
Eragon '06
Esther '98
Ever After: A Cinderella Story '98
Excalibur '81
Fairy Tales '76
Farinelli '94
Fergie & Andrew: Behind Palace Doors '93
The Fighting Prince of Donegal '66
First Knight '95
Fit for a King '37
Flame of Araby '51
Forever Amber '47
The Fountain '06
Galgameth '96
Gladiator '00
Goya's Ghosts '06
The Grace Kelly Story '83
The Grand Duchess and the Waiter '26
Hamlet '96
Hamlet '01
Haram '99
Helen of Troy '03
Hennessy '75
Hercules the Legendary Journeys, Vol. 2: The Lost Kingdom '94
Hero '03
His Majesty, the American '19
If I Were King '38
The Illusionist '06
In the Name of the King: A Dungeon Siege Tale '08
The Indian Tomb '21
Jason and the Argonauts '00
Joseph '95
Julius Caesar '53
Julius Caesar '70
Just Suppose '25
Kama Sutra: A Tale of Love '96
Kaspar Hauser '93
A Kid in Aladdin's Palace '97
A Kid in King Arthur's Court '95
A King in New York '57
The King and I '56
The King and I '99
King Lear '71
The King on Main Street '25
King Ralph '91
The King's Guard '01
Kings of the Sun '63
The King's Rhapsody '55
The King's Thief '55
The King's Whore '90
The Lady and the Duke '01
Lancelot of the Lake '74
The Last Emperor '87
The Leopard '63
Lillie '79
Lion Man '75
Lost in a Harem '44
Love's Labour's Lost '00
Love Parade '29
Ludwig '72
Macbeth '48
Macbeth '71
Macbeth '06
Mad Love '01
The Magic Fountain '61
The Man Who Would Be King '75
Manrequin 2: On the Move '91
Marbella '85
The Master of Ballantrae '53
Mayerling '36
Mayerling '68
Medea '88
Meet the Spartans '08
A Midsummer Night's Dream '35
A Midsummer Night's Dream '96
Mom and Dad Save the World '92
Monsieur Beaucaire '24
Monsieur Beaucaire '46
Monte Carlo '30
Moses '95
Mulan '98
My Pal, the King '32
A Night of Love '87
Nostradamus '93
Options '88
Passion '19
Phoenix '78
The Pirates Who Don't Do Anything: A VeggieTales Movie '08
The Polar Bear King '94
Power '34
The Prince '78
The Prince and Me '04
The Prince and Me 2: Royal Wedding '06
The Prince and the Pauper '37
The Prince and the Pauper '62
The Prince and the Pauper '78
The Prince and the Showgirl '57
The Prince and the Surfer '99
Prince Brat and the Whipping Boy '95
The Princess and the Pea '83
The Princess Caraboo '94
The Princess Comes Across '36
The Princess Diaries '01
The Princess Diaries 2: Royal Engagement '04
Princess Tam Tam '35
Princess Yang Kwei Fei '55
Prisoner of Zenda '37
Prisoner of Zenda '52
The Promise '05
Queen Christina '33
Queen Kelly '29
Quest for Camelot '98
The Rape of the Sabines '61
Return to Oz '85
Roman Holiday '53
Royal Deceit '94
The Royal Bed '31
Ruyblas '48
The Saragossa Manuscript '65
Shanghai Noon '00
Sharpe's Challenge '06
Shin Heike Monogatari '55
Shrek '01
Shrek 2 '04
Shrek the Third '07
The Sign of the Cross '33
The Silences of the Palace '94
The Singing Princess '49
The Smiling Lieutenant '31
Snow White and the Seven Dwarfs '37
Snow White: The Fairest of Them All '02
Soldier in Love '67
Solomon '98
Solomon and Sheba '59
Son of Ali Baba '52
Song Spinner '95
Splitting Heirs '93
Star Knight '85
Stardust '07
Start the Revolution without Me '70
Storm over Asia '28
The Story of David '76
Storybook '95
Surf Ninjas '93
The Swan '25
The Swan '56
The Swan Princess 2: Escape from Castle Mountain '97
The Sword & the Rose '53
Sword of El Cid '62
The Sword of the Sorcerer '82
The Thief and the Cobbler '96
Thirty Day Princess '34
A Thousand and One Nights '45
Throne of Blood '57
Titus '99
To Play the King '93
Tower of London '39
The Tower of London '62
Tower of Screaming Virgins '68
The Triumph of Love '01
Two Nights with Cleopatra '54
Vatel '00
The War Lord '65
The Warriors '55
The Wedding March '28
Where There's Life '47
Willow '88

Royalty, British
see also Great Britain; Historical Drama; Medieval Romps; Period Piece; Royalty

Becket '64
Black Knight '01
The Black Shield of Falworth '54
Braveheart '95
The Bruce '96
Chasing the Deer '94
Diana: Her True Story '93
Edward and Mrs. Simpson '80
Edward II '92
Edward the King '75
Elizabeth '98
Elizabeth R '72
Elizabeth I '05
Elizabeth: The Golden Age '07
Henry V '44
Henry V '89
Henry IV '85
Henry VIII '03
Ivanhoe '97
Jack Higgins' Midnight Man '96
John and Julie '55
King Lear '98
King Richard and the Crusaders '54
A Knight in Camelot '98
Lady Godiva '55
Lady Jane '85
The Libertine '05
The Lion in Winter '68
The Lion in Winter '03
Looking for Richard '96
The Madness of King George '94
A Man for All Seasons '66
A Man for All Seasons '88
Mary, Queen of Scots '36
Mary, Queen of Scots '71
Merlin '98
Mists of Avalon '01
Mrs. Brown '97
Nine Days a Queen '36
Orlando '92
The Other Boleyn Girl '03
The Other Boleyn Girl '08
The Prince and the Pauper '01
Prince Valiant '97
Princess of Thieves '01
The Private Life of Henry VIII '33
The Private Lives of Elizabeth & Essex '39
The Queen '06
The Queen '09
Restoration '95
Richard III '55
Richard III '95
A Royal Scandal '45
Shakespeare in Love '98
Shanghai Knights '03
Six Wives of Henry VIII '71
Tristan & Isolde '06
Victoria & Albert '01
Victoria Regina '61
The Virgin Queen '55
The Woman He Loved '88
Young Bess '53

► = rated three bones or higher

Royalty,

Royalty, French

see also France; Paris; Royalty; Royalty, British

The Affair of the Necklace '01
At Sword's Point '51
Beaumarchais the Scoundrel '96
Brotherhood of the Wolf '01
Desiree '54
Fanfan la Tulipe '51
The Fifth Musketeer '79
The 4 Musketeers '05
The Iron Mask '29
Jeanne la Pucelle '94
Joan of Arc '48
Joan of Arc '99
La Nuit de Varennes '82
The Lion in Winter '03
The Man in the Iron Mask '39
The Man in the Iron Mask '77
The Man in the Iron Mask '97
The Man in the Iron Mask '98
Marie Antoinette '38
Marie Antoinette '06
Napoleon '03
Queen Margot '94
The Return of the Musketeers '89
Revenge of the Musketeers '94
Ridicule '96
The Rise of Louis XIV '66
Spy of Napoleon '36
The Three Musketeers '16
The Three Musketeers '21
The Three Musketeers '33
The Three Musketeers '35
The Three Musketeers '39
The Three Musketeers '48
The Three Musketeers '74
The Three Musketeers '93

Royalty, Russian

see also Historical Drama; Medieval Romps; Period Piece; Royalty; Russia/USSR

Alexander Nevsky '38
Anastasia '56
Anastasia '97
Anastasia: The Mystery of Anna '86
Catherine the Great '34
Catherine the Great '95
The Chess Player '27
I Killed Rasputin '67
Ivan the Terrible, Part 1 '44
Ivan the Terrible, Part 2 '46
Never Say Die '39
Nicholas and Alexandra '71
Peter the Great '86
Rasputin '85
Rasputin and the Empress '33
Rasputin: Dark Servant of Destiny '96
Rasputin the Mad Monk '66
Scarlet Empress '34
The White Countess '05
Young Catherine '91

Running

Across the Tracks '89
Billie '65
Chariots of Fire '81
College '27
Finish Line '89
Forrest Gump '94
The Four Minute Mile '88
Go for the Gold '84
The Gold & Glory '88
Goldengirl '79
The Jericho Mile '79
The Jesse Owens Story '84
Jim Thorpe: All American '51
The Loneliest Runner '76
The Loneliness of the Long Distance Runner '62
The Loretta Claiborne Story '00

Marathon '80
Marathon Man '76
Meatballs '79
Off the Mark '87
On the Edge '86
Prefontaine '96
Raw Courage '84
Run, Fat Boy, Run '07
Run for the Dream: The Gail Devers Story '96
Running Brave '83
Saint Ralph '04
Sam's Son '84
See How She Runs '78
A Shining Season '79
The Sprinter '84
The Terry Fox Story '83
Wildcats '86
Without Limits '97

Russia/USSR

see also Moscow; Red Scare

The Abandoned '06
American Cop '94
Anastasia '56
Anastasia '97
Anastasia: The Mystery of Anna '86
Anna '93
Archangel '05
The Ascent '76
Assassination of Trotsky '72
Back in the USSR '92
Balalaika '39
Ballet Russes '05
Baltic Deputy '37
The Battleship Potemkin '25
Beyond Borders '03
BloodRayne '06
The Bourne Supremacy '04
The Brothers Karamazov '58
Burglar '87
Burnt by the Sun '94
Children of the Revolution '95
Citizen X '95
Come and See '85
Coming Out of the Ice '82
The Commies Are Coming, the Commies Are Coming '57
Commissar '68
Comrade X '40
Creation of Adam '93
Crimson Tide '95
Days of Glory '43
The Deal '05
The Death of Mr. Lazarescu '05
Dersu Uzala '75
A Different Loyalty '04
Doctor Zhivago '65
Doctor Zhivago '03
Don't Drink the Water '69
Dostoevsky's Crime and Punishment '99
Drums of Jeopardy '31
The Eagle '25
East-West '99
The End of St. Petersburg '27
Enemy at the Gates '00
The Extraordinary Adventures of Mr. West in the Land of the Bolsheviks '24
Final Assignment '80
Final Warning '90
First Strike '85
The Fixer '68
Frederick Forsyth's Icon '05
Freeze-Die-Come to Life '90
The Gambler '97
The Girl from Petrovka '74
Goldeneye '95
Gorky Park '83
Gulag '85
Hitman '07
House of Fools '02
The Hunt for Red October '90
I Killed Rasputin '67

The Ice Runner '93
In Hell '03
The Inner Circle '91
The Ister '04
The Italian '05
Ivan the Terrible, Part 1 '44
Ivan the Terrible, Part 2 '46
The Jackal '97
K-19: The Widowmaker '02
Kindergarten '84
Laser Mission '90
Last Command '28
The Light Ahead '39
Little Vera '88
Love and Death '75
The Man with the Movie Camera '29
The Mirror '75
Moscow Does Not Believe in Tears '80
Mother '26
Mother and Son '97
Mute Witness '95
My Family Treasure '93
My Name Is Ivan '62
Never Let Me Go '53
Nicholas and Alexandra '71
Night Watch '04
Nostalghia '83
One Day in the Life of Ivan Denisovich '71
100 Days Before the Command '90
One Russian Summer '73
The Peacemaker '97
Peter the Great '86
The Possessed '88
Prisoner of the Mountains '96
Rasputin '85
Rasputin and the Empress '33
Rasputin the Mad Monk '66
The Red and the White '68
Red Cherry '95
Red Heat '88
Red Hot '95
Reds '81
The Road to Life '31
The Russia House '90
Russian Dolls '05
Russian Roulette '93
The Saint '97
Sakharov '84
Scarlet Dawn '32
Scarlet Empress '34
Schizo '04
The Seagull '71
Siberiade '79
Sideburns '91
Since Otar Left... '03
A Slave of Love '78
Solo Voyage: The Revenge '90
Stalin '92
Stalingrad '94
Taxi Blues '90
Terminal Velocity '94
Theremin: An Electronic Odyssey '95
The Thief '97
Three Legionnaires '37
The Three Sisters '65
Torrents of Spring '90
The Truce '96
2 Brothers & a Bride '03
The Ultimate Imposter '79
War and Peace '56
War and Peace '68
We the Living '42
White Nights '85
Window to Paris '95
The Winter War '89
World War III '86
Young Catherine '91

Russian Revolution

see also Red Scare; Russia/USSR; World War I

Anastasia '56
Anastasia '97
Anastasia: The Mystery of Anna '86

The Battleship Potemkin '25
Doctor Zhivago '65
Doctor Zhivago '03
Nicholas and Alexandra '71
Rasputin '85
Rasputin and the Empress '33
Rasputin the Mad Monk '66
Reds '81
Scarlet Dawn '32
Ten Days That Shook the World '27
Three Legionnaires '37

Rwanda

see also Africa

Gorillas in the Mist '88
Hotel Rwanda '04
Shake Hands With the Devil: The Journey of Romeo Dallaire '04
Shooting Dogs '05
Sometimes in April '05

Sail Away

see also Deep Blue; Go Fish; Killer Sea Critters; Mutiny; Scuba; Shipwrecked; Submarines

Abandon Ship '57
Adrift '93
Adventure Island '47
The Adventures of Huckleberry Finn '39
An Affair to Remember '57
The African Queen '51
All the Brothers Were Valiant '53
And the Ship Sails On '83
Anna Christie '30
Annapolis '28
Assault on a Queen '66
Away All Boats '56
The Baby and the Battleship '56
The Battleship Potemkin '25
Beat the Devil '53
Beyond the Poseidon Adventure '79
The Big Broadcast of 1938 '38
Billy Budd '62
Bitter Moon '92
Blast '04
Blondie Goes Latin '42
Blood Voyage '77
Blood Work '02
Blue, White and Perfect '42
Boat Trip '03
The Boatniks '70
Botany Bay '53
The Bounty '84
Boy in Blue '86
Britannic '99
Brittanic '00
Cabin Boy '94
The Caine Mutiny Court Martial '88
Captain Caution '40
Captain Horatio Hornblower '51
Captain Jack '98
Captain Ron '92
Captains Courageous '37
Captains Courageous '95
Captain's Paradise '53
The Captain's Table '60
Carry On Admiral '57
Carry On Cruising '62
The Cat's Meow '01
Charlie Chan in Honolulu '38
China Seas '35
Christopher Columbus '85
Chupacabra Terror '05
The Coast Patrol '25
Convoy '40
Counterstrike '03
A Countess from Hong Kong '67
The Crew '95
Crimson Tide '95
Cruise into Terror '78
Damn the Defiant '62
Danger Beneath the Sea '02

Dangerous Charter '62
Dangerous Crossing '53
Dangerous Passage '44
Dark Tide '93
Das Boot '81
Day of the Assassin '81
The Day Will Dawn '42
Dead Ahead: The Exxon Valdez Disaster '92
Dead Calm '89
Dead in the Water '01
Dead Reckoning '89
Dead Tides '97
Deadly Voyage '96
Death Cruise '74
Death Ship '80
Death Tide '58
The Deep '77
Deep Rising '98
Destroyer '43
Die Hard: With a Vengeance '95
Dixie Jamboree '44
Doctor at Sea '56
Don Winslow of the Coast Guard '43
The Dove '74
Down Periscope '96
Down to the Sea in Ships '22
The Ebb-Tide '97
Ensign Pulver '64
Erik, the Viking '65
Escape from Atlantis '97
Escape under Pressure '00
The Evil Below '87
Failure to Launch '06
Far from Home: The Adventures of Yellow Dog '94
Feet First '30
Ferry to Hong Kong '59
The Fighting Sullivans '42
The Final Countdown '80
Final Voyage '99
Flat Top '52
Flight of the Intruder '90
Flipper '96
Fool's Gold '08
Francis in the Navy '55
Friday the 13th, Part 8: Jason Takes Manhattan '89
Gambling Ship '33
Gangway '37
Gehelmaktie WB1 '42
The Ghost Ship '43
Ghost Ship '53
Ghost Ship '02
The Gift Horse '52
A Girl in Every Port '28
A Girl in Every Port '52
Give Me a Sailor '38
Going Overboard '89
Going Under '91
Golden Rendezvous '77
Goliath Awaits '81
Gone Fishin' '97
Gray Lady Down '77
The Great Lover '49
Gun Cargo '49
The Hairy Ape '44
Haunted Harbor '44
The Haunted Sea '97
Hawaii Calls '38
He Is My Brother '75
Hell-Ship Morgan '36
History Is Made at Night '37
Horatio Hornblower '99
Horatio Hornblower: The Adventure Continues '01
Horror of Zombies '74
The Hunt for Red October '90
I Conquer the Sea '36
The Imposters '98
In Which We Serve '43
The Incredible Mr. Limpet '64
The Incredible Petrified World '58
Ironclads '90
Isle of Forgotten Sins '43
JAG '95
Jason and the Argonauts '00
Jaws '75

Jaws 2 '78
The Jewel of the Nile '85
Johnny Angel '45
Juggernaut '74
Kill Cruise '90
Killer on Board '77
King Kelly of the U.S.A. '34
King of Alcatraz '38
Knife in the Water '62
Lakeboat '00
The Last of Sheila '73
The Last Voyage '60
Law of the Sea '32
Le Crabe Tambour '77
The Legend of Sea Wolf '75
The Legend of 1900 '98
The Legend of the Sea Wolf '58
Lifeboat '44
The Lightship '86
Live and Let Die '73
Loch Ness '95
Long John Silver '54
The Long Ships '64
The Long Voyage Home '40
Longitude '00
Lord Jim '65
Lost in the Bermuda Triangle '98
Lost Voyage '01
Love Affair '39
Madison '01
The Magic Stone '95
A Majority of One '56
Manfish '56
Master and Commander: The Far Side of the World '03
Mayflower: The Pilgrims' Adventure '79
McHale's Navy '64
Mean Creek '04
The Mermaids of Tiburon '62
Message in a Bottle '98
Mister Roberts '55
Monkey Business '31
Moon in Scorpio '86
Moran of the Lady Letty '22
Morituri '65
Muppet Treasure Island '96
Murder on the High Seas '32
Mutiny '52
The Mutiny of the Elsinore '39
The Mystery of the Mary Celeste '35
The Navigator '24
The Navy Comes Through '42
New Moon '40
A Night to Remember '58
No More Women '34
The Odyssey '97
Old Ironsides '26
One Crazy Summer '86
One Way Passage '32
Operation Petticoat '59
Out to Sea '97
Oxford Blues '84
Passenger '61
The Perfect Storm '00
Pirate Ship '49
Pirates of the Caribbean: At World's End '07
Pirates of the Caribbean: The Curse of the Black Pearl '03
The Port of Missing Girls '38
The Poseidon Adventure '72
The Princess Comes Across '36
Pueblo Affair '73
Pursuit of the Graf Spee '57
Rainbow Warrior '94
Reaching for the Moon '31
Reap the Wild Wind '42
Rich and Strange '32
Roaring Speedboats '37
Romancing the Stone '84

▲ = rated three bones or higher

see also *Religion*

Run Silent, Run Deep '58▶
The Sand Pebbles '65▶
Save the Lady '82
Sea Chase '55
Sea Devils '31
Sea Racketeers '37
The Sea Wolf '41▶
Seven Days Ashore '44
Shades of Fear '93
Sharks' Treasure '75
She Creature '01
She Shall Have Music '36
Ship Ahoy! '42
Ship of Fools '65▶
Ships in the Night '28
Shout at the Devil '76
Sinbad: Legend of the Seven Seas '03
Sinbad, the Sailor '47▶
Sink the Bismarck '60▶
South Seas Massacre '74
Speed 2: Cruise Control '97
Spiders 2: Breeding Ground '01
Steamboat Bill, Jr. '28▶
Steamboat Round the Bend '35
Submarine Seahawk '59
Swashbuckler '76
The Talented Mr. Ripley '99▶
Tamango '59
Task Force '49
Temptation '94
Tentacles of the North '26
They Were Expendable '45▶
The 13th Warrior '99
Think Fast, Mr. Moto '37
Thunder in Paradise '93▶
The Daring Daughters '45
Till There Was You '91
Titanic '53▶
Titanic '96
Titanic '97▶
To Gillian on Her 37th Birthday '96
Today We Live '33
Torpedo Run '58
Transatlantic Merry-Go-Round '34
Treacherous Crossing '92
The Treasure of Jamaica Reef '74
Treasure Planet '02
The Triangle '01
2103: Deadly Wake '97
Two Years before the Mast '46
U-Boat Prisoner '44
Under Siege '92▶
The Unsinkable Molly Brown '64▶
Up the Creek '58
Up the Creek '84
Virus '98
Visitors '03
Voyage '93
Voyage of Terror: The Achille Lauro Affair '90
Voyage of the Damned '76▶
Wake of the Red Witch '49
Waterworld '95
The Weight of Water '00
We're Not Dressing '34▶
Wetbacks '56
White Squall '96
Wild Orchids '26
Wind '92
Windjammer '37
Windrider '86
Winds of Terror '01
Witch Who Came from the Sea '76
The World in His Arms '52
The Wreck of the Mary Deare '59
Yankee Clipper '27

St. Peterburg (Russia)

see also Russia/USSR

Anastasia '97
Anna Karenina '35▶
Anna Karenina '48
Anna Karenina '85
Anna Karenina '00
Brother '97
Bullet to Beijing '95
Leo Tolstoy's Anna Karenina '96
Midnight in Saint Petersburg '97
The Music Lovers '71
Of Freaks and Men '98
Onegin '99
2 Brothers & a Bride '03
Water '05

Saints

see also Religion

Augustine of Hippo '72▶
Bernadette '90
Brother Sun, Sister Moon '73
The Flowers of St. Francis '50▶
Francesco '93
Joan of Arc '48
Millions '05▶
Miracle in Rome '88
Miracle of Our Lady of Fatima '52
My Mother's Smile '02
Passion of Joan of Arc '28▶
The Proprietor '96
Saint Joan '57
St. Patrick: The Irish Legend '00
Sebastiane '79▶
The Song of Bernadette '43▶
Therese '86
Therese: The Story of Saint Therese of Lisieux '04
A Time for Miracles '80

Salespeople

see also Corporate Shenanigans

Adventures in Babysitting '87
The Alarmist '98
The Assassination of Richard Nixon '05
The Bible and Gun Club '96
Big Fish '03▶
The Big Kahuna '00
Cadillac Man '90
Death of a Salesman '51▶
Death of a Salesman '86▶
Diamond Men '01▶
El Crimen Perfecto '04
Failure to Launch '06
The Fan '96
First Snow '07
Foul Play '78▶
Glengarry Glen Ross '92▶
A Good Baby '99
The Good Girl '02▶
Great World of Sound '07
Grilled '06
Happily Ever After '04
The Iceman Cometh '73
Jingle All the Way '96▶
Last Holiday '06
Lisboa '99
The Man '05
Me and You and Everyone We Know '05▶
Miss Rose White '92
Moscow on the Hudson '84▶
The Music Man '62▶
My First Mister '01
100 Mile Rule '02
Pennies from Heaven '81▶
Phat Girlz '06
Pretty Woman '90▶
The Rainmaker '56▶
Risk '00
Side Effects '05
Sing Me a Love Song '37
Super Sucker '03
Suckerfish '99
Tin Men '87
Torremolinos 73 '03
The Traveling Saleswoman '50
Trojan Eddie '96▶

Samurai

see also Japan

The Adventures of Buckaroo Banzai Across the Eighth Dimension '84▶
American Samurai '92
Blind Fury '90
The Bushido Blade '80
The Challenge '82
Cyber Ninja '88
47 Ronin, Part 1 '42▶
47 Ronin, Part 2 '42▶
The Gambling Samurai '60
Ghost Dog: The Way of the Samurai '99▶
Ghostwarrior '86
Gonza the Spearman '86
Harakiri '62▶
Heaven & Earth '90▶
The Hidden Blade '04
House Where Evil Dwells '82
Hunter in the Dark '80
Kill Bill Vol. 1 '03▶
The Last Samurai '03▶
Lone Wolf and Cub: Baby Cart to Hades '72
Moon over Tao '97
One-Eyed Swordsman '63
Rashomon '51▶
Red Sun '71
Samurai Banners '69
Samurai '54▶
Sanjuro '62▶
Seven Samurai '54▶
Shogun '80▶
Shogun Assassin '80
Sword of Doom '67▶
Taboo '99
Throne of Blood '57▶
The Twilight Samurai '02▶
Yojimbo '61▶
Zatoichi '03▶
Zatoichi: Master Ichi and a Chest of Gold '64
Zatoichi: The Blind Swordsman and the Chess Expert '65
Zatoichi: The Blind Swordsman's Vengeance '66
Zatoichi: The Life and Opinion of Masseur Ichi '62
Zatoichi vs. Yojimbo '70▶

San Diego

Anchorman: The Legend of Ron Burgundy '04
Antwone Fisher '02▶
The Cat's Meow '01
Devil Dogs of the Air '35
Dive Bomber '41▶
Flirting with Disaster '95▶
In the Navy '41
Life Tastes Good '99
Lightblast '85
Little City '97
Magnum Force '73▶
My Blue Heaven '90
Sideways '04▶
Top Gun '86▶
Traffic '00▶
Tumbleweeds '98
29th & Gay '05

San Francisco

see also Earthquakes

After the Shock '90
Against the Wall '04
All About You '01
All Dogs Go to Heaven 2 '95
The Amazing Mrs. Holiday '43
Armistead Maupin's More Tales of the City '97
Armistead Maupin's Tales of the City '93
The Bachelor '99
Barbary Coast '35▶
The Barbary Coast '74
Basic Instinct '92▶
Beyond the Door '75
Big Trouble in Little China '86▶
Bullitt '68▶
Cardiac Arrest '74
Chan Is Missing '82▶
Charlie Chan at Treasure Island '39
Cherish '02
Clowning Around 2 '33
Climber '05
The Conversation '74▶
Copycat '95
Days of Wine and Roses '62▶
The Dead Pool '88
Desperate Measures '98
Desperate Moves '86
Dim Sum: A Little Bit of Heart '85▶
Dirty Harry '71▶
Dr. Dolittle '98
Dr. Jekyll's Dungeon of Death '82
Doctor Who '96
Dogfight '91▶
Dogwatch '97
Dopamine '03
Dream for an Insomniac '96
Dream with the Fishes '97▶
Dying to Remember '93
The Enforcer '76▶
An Eye for an Eye '81
Execution of Justice '99
The Fan '94
Fanci's Persuasion '95
Final Analysis '92▶
Fisherman's Wharf '39
Flame of the Barbary Coast '45
Flower Drum Song '61▶
Fools '70
40 Days and 40 Nights '02▶
48 Hrs. '82▶
Foul Play '78▶
Freebie & the Bean '74
The Frisco Kid '79▶
The Game '97▶
George of the Jungle '97▶
Golden Gate '93
Groove '00
Ground Zero '88
Guinevere '99▶
Haiku Tunnel '01
Hello, Frisco, Hello '43
Homeward Bound 2: Lost in San Francisco '96▶
I Remember Mama '48▶
It Came from Beneath the Sea '55▶
Jade '95
Just like Heaven '05
Just One Night '00
Key to the City '50
Kicks '85
Kuffs '92
Lady from Louisiana '42
Lady of the House '78
The Laughing Policeman '74
The Maltese Falcon '41▶
Memoirs of an Invisible Man '92
The Men's Club '86
Metro '96
Mission '00
The Mistress of Spices '05
Monster in the Closet '86
Mysterious Mr. Wong '35
Nightmare in Blood '75
Nim's Island '08
Nina Takes a Lover '94
Nine Months '95
No One Sleeps '01
Pacific Heights '90▶
Playing Mona Lisa '00
Poltergeist: The Legacy '96
The Presidio '88▶
The Princess Diaries '01
The Pursuit of Happyness '06▶
Rated X '00
The Rock '96▶
The Saint Strikes Back '39
Salome, Where She Danced '45
San Francisco '36▶
San Franpsycho '06
Serendipity '01▶
Serial '80▶
Seven Days Ashore '44
The Shock '23
The Single Standard '29
The Sisters '38▶
So I Married an Axe Murderer '93▶
Some Prefer Cake '97
Sucker Free City '05▶
Sudden Impact '83▶
Sweet November '01
The Sweetest Thing '02▶
Time After Time '79▶
Times of Harvey Milk '83▶
True Crime '99
Tweek City '05
Twisted '04
Up for Grabs '05
Vertigo '58▶
Waterfront '44
The Wedding Planner '01▶
West Is West '87
What's Up, Doc? '72▶
The Wild Parrots of Telegraph Hill '03▶
Wild West '93
Wildflowers '99
Woman on Top '00
You Kill Me '07▶
The Zodiac '05
Zodiac '07▶
The Zodiac Killer '71

Sanity Check

see also Doctors & Nurses; Hospitals & Medicine; Shrinks

Affliction '97▶
Aguirre, the Wrath of God '72▶
All the Little Animals '98
Alone in the Dark '82
Along for the Ride '00
The Amazing Howard Hughes '77
American Eagle '90
American Psycho '99▶
American Psycho 2: All American Girl '02
Amos '85
An Angel at My Table '89▶
Angels Fall '07
Anger Management '03▶
Anguish '88
Another Time, Another Place '58
Apartment Complex '99
Appointment with Fear '85
Arabian Nights '00
Arsenic and Old Lace '44▶
The Astronaut's Wife '99
Asylum '72▶
Asylum '97
Asylum of Satan '72
Bad Dreams '88
Bark! '02
Bartleby '01
Bartleby '70
Batman Forever '95▶
Battle Shock '56
Beautiful Dreamers '92
A Beautiful Mind '01▶
Beauty on the Beach '61
Bedlam '45▶
Behind Locked Doors '48
Behind the Lines '97
Being John Malkovich '99▶
The Bell Jar '79
The Bells '26▶
Beloved '98
Beneath '07
Beyond Therapy '86
Blackwoods '02
Black Snake Moan '07
A Blade in the Dark '83
Blood Frenzy '87
Blood Salvage '90
Bloody Song '82
Bloody Wednesday '87
Body Chemistry '90
Borderline '02▶
Boxing Helena '93
The Boys Next Door '96
Brain Dead '90
Bringing Out the Dead '99▶
Bug '75
Buried Alive '89
Burnt Money '00
The Butterfly Effect '04▶
Cabaret Balkan '98
Camille Claudel '89▶
Canvas '06
Cannibal Man '71
Captain Newman, M.D. '63▶
Captive '97
The Carpenter '89
Cat in the Cage '68
Cause for Alarm '51▶
The Caveman's Valentine '01▶
Cecil B. Demented '00▶
The Cell '00▶
Cello '05
Charles: Dead or Alive '69
Charming Billy '98
Chasing Holden '01
Chattahoochee '89
Clockwise '86▶
The Cobweb '55
Cobra Verde '88▶
Close Encounters of the Third Kind '77▶
Coast to Coast '80
Come Undone '00
Comedy of Innocence '00
Committed '91
The Confession '98
Conspiracy Theory '97▶
Cotton Mary '99
The Couch Trip '87
The Cracker Factory '79
The Craft '96▶
Crazed '07
Crazy as Hell '02
Crazy Fat Ethel II '85
Crazy in Alabama '99▶
Crazy Like a Fox '04
Crazy People '90▶
Criminally Insane '75
The Crime of Dr. Crespi '35
Crime and Punishment '35
Crime and Punishment USA '70
Crow Hollow '52
Cry Wolf '47
Cutting Class '89
The Dark Knight '08
Dark Obsession '90
Dark Places '73
Dark Sanity '82
Dark Water '05
Dark Waters '44▶
Darkness Falls '03
Darkroom '90
A Day at the Races '37▶
Dead Man Out '89▶
Dead of Night '45▶
Dead Pit '89
Deadly Innocence '88
Deadly Intruder '84
Deadly Strangers '82
The Deadly Trap '71
Death Kiss '74
Death Nurse '87
Dee Snider's Strangeland '98
Dementia 13 '63▶
A Demon in My View '92
Demons of the Mind '72
Deranged '87
Despair '78▶
Desperate Living '77
Deutschland im Jahre Null '47▶
Devi '60▶
Devil Doll '36▶
The Devil Bat '41▶
The Devil Bat's Daughter '46
The Devil in Silk '56
Devil in the Flesh '87

▶ = rated three bones or higher

Sanity

Devil in the Flesh 2 '00
Devil Times Five '74
Devil Wears White '86
The Devil's Advocate '97
Devil's Pond '03
Diary of a Mad Housewife '70
Diary of a Madman '63
Diary of a Young Comic '79
Diary of Forbidden Dreams '73
Dick Barton, Special Agent '48
Die! Die! My Darling! '65
Die Screaming, Marianne '73
Disorder '06
Disturbance '89
Disturbed '90
The Doctor and the Devils '85
Doctor Blood's Coffin '62
Doctor Butcher M.D. '80
Dr. Caligari '89
Dr. Frankenstein's Castle of Freaks '74
Dr. Hackenstein '88
Dr. Jekyll and Mr. Hyde '20
Dr. Jekyll and Mr. Hyde '32
Dr. Jekyll and Mr. Hyde '41
Dr. Jekyll and Mr. Hyde '68
Dr. Jekyll and Mr. Hyde '73
Dr. Jekyll and the Wolfman '71
Dr. Matuse, The Gambler '22
Dr. Matuse vs. Scotland Yard '64
Dr. Strangelove, or: How I Learned to Stop Worrying and Love the Bomb '64
Dr. T & the Women '00
Dr. Tarr's Torture Dungeon '75
Dog Day Afternoon '75
The Doll '00
Dominique Is Dead '79
Don Quixote '00
Donnie Darko '01
Don't Go in the House '80
Don't Go in the Woods '81
Don't Look in the Basement '73
Don't Look Now '73
Don't Mess with My Sister! '85
Don't Open Till Christmas '84
Don't Say a Word '01
Doom Asylum '88
Dostoevsky's Crime and Punishment '99
A Double Life '47
Dream Lover '93
Dream No Evil '75
Easy Rider '69
Eaten Alive '76
Echoes '83
Ed Gein '01
Eddie Presley '92
Edge of Sanity '89
Elling '01
The Empty Acre '07
Evan Almighty '07
Event Horizon '97
Everything Put Together '00
Evil Eyes '04
Exorcism's Daughter '74
The Eye '02
Eye of the Beholder '99
Eye of the Storm '98
Eyeball '78
The Eyes of the Amaryllis '82
Fabled '02
Facade '98
The Fall of the House of Usher '49
The Fall of the House of Usher '60
The Fall of the House of Usher '80
False Identity '90
Family Life '71
The Fan '96
Far Harbor '96
Fat Guy Goes Nutzoid '86
Fear of Fear '75
Fear Strikes Out '57
Fever '99
The Fiend Who Walked the West '58
The Fifth Floor '80
Fight Club: '99
Final '01
The Fisher King '91
The Five of Me '81
The Flying Scotsman '06
Follow Me Quietly '49
Forced March '90
1408 '07
The 4th Man '79
Frailty '02
Frances '82
Fright '71
From Noon Till Three '76
From the Life of the Marionettes '80
Games '67
Genealogies of a Crime '97
Get Well Soon '01
The Ghost Ship '43
The Gift '00
The Girl in Room 2A '76
Girl, Interrupted '99
A Girl Thing '01
Gloria '98
The Goalie's Anxiety at the Penalty Kick '71
Going Postal '98
Gothika '03
Great Expectations '97
Gulliver's Travels '95
The Hairdresser's Husband '92
Halloween '07
Hamlet '90
Hamlet '96
Hamlet '01
Hammersmith Is Out '72
Hannibal '01
Happy Accidents '00
Hard Candy '06
Hard Luck '01
Harsh Times '05
Harvey '50
The Haunting '63
The Haunting '99
Haunting of Sarah Hardy '89
Haunts '77
He Loves Me ... He Loves Me Not '02
Heart '99
Heart of Midnight '89
Heat and Sunlight '87
Heavenly Creatures '94
Hell's Gate '01
Henry IV '85
Heroes '77
Hey, Happy! '01
Hider in the House '90
Hip Hip Hurrah! '87
The Horrible Dr. Hitchcock '62
The Horror Chamber of Dr. Faustus '59
Horror Hospital '73
Horror House on Highway 5 '86
The Hospital '71
Hotline '82
The Hours '02
House of Fools '02
House of 1000 Corpses '03
The House of Usher '88
The House of Yes '97
The Housekeeper '86
How to Get Ahead in Advertising '89
How to Make a Monster '58
Hush '98
Hush, Hush, Sweet Charlotte '65
Hysteria '64
I Am the Cheese '83
I Dismember Mama '74
I Know Who Killed Me '07
I Never Promised You a Rose Garden '77
I Stand Alone '98
Icy Breasts '75
The Idiots '99
If Things Were Different '79
I'll Take You There '99
Illusions '91
Images '72
Impulse '84
In Dreams '98
In the Mouth of Madness '95
The Incredible Two-Headed Transplant '71
Innocent Victim '90
Innocents '00
Insanity '76
Inside Paris '06
Instinct '99
Interiors '78
The Invisible Ghost '41
Irma Vep '96
It Happened at Nightmare Inn '70
It's Alive! '68
The Jacket '05
Jekyll and Hyde '90
Joe Gould's Secret '00
Juggernaut '37
Julien Donkey-boy '99
K-PAX '01
Keane '04
Keeper '84
Kill Your Darlings '06
The Killing of John Lennon '07
King Lear '98
King of California '07
The King of Hearts '66
Kira's Reason—A Love Story '01
Lassie: A Love Story '92
The Last Don 2 '98
The Last of Philip Banter '87
The Last Ride '91
The Last Seduction '94
Leave Her to Heaven '45
Lethal Weapon '87
Let's Scare Jessica to Death '71
Life Upside Down '64
A Light in the Darkness '02
Lilian's Story '95
Lilith '64
Little Boy Blue '97
Living Doll '90
The Locusts '97
The Lonely Sex '59
Los Lonely Posse '97
Lost Angels '89
Lower Level '91
Ludwig '72
Lunatics: A Love Story '92
Luther the Geek '90
Macabre '80
The Machinist '04
Mad Cowgirl '06
Mad Love '35
Mad Love '95
Mad Love '01
Man Facing Southeast '86
Manhunter '86
Manic '01
Mary, My Dearest '83
May '02
Michael Clayton '07
Midnight Warning '32
Mind Games '89
Mine Own Executioner '47
Ministry of Fear '44
Mr. Deeds Goes to Town '36
Mr. Jingles '06
Mr. Jones '93
Mixed Nuts '94
Morgan: A Suitable Case for Treatment '66
Mother Kusters Goes to Heaven '76
Murder in Mind '97
Murder in the First '95
My First Wife '84
My Sister's Keeper '02
My Very Best Friend '96
Network '76
Night of Bloody Horror '69
Night of Terror '87
The Night Visitor '70
Night Wars '88
Night Watch '72
Nijinsky '80
1941 '79
The Ninth Configuration '79
The Noah '75
Nobody's Perfekt '79
The Number 23 '07
Nurse Betty '00
Nuts '87
The October Man '48
Offerings '89
Office Killer '97
One Flew Over the Cuckoo's Nest '75
One Hour Photo '02
125 Rooms of Comfort '83
One Summer Love '76
The Onion Field '79
Open Your Eyes '97
The Order '03
The Others '01
Out of Sight, Out of Her Mind '89
Overexposed '90
Pale Blood '91
Paperback Hero '73
Passion of Mind '00
Pay Off '89
Pecker '98
Peeping Tom '60
The Perfect Nanny '00
Performance '70
Peril '00
A Piano for Mrs. Cimino '82
The Piano Teacher '01
Picture Mommy Dead '66
Pigs '73
Pink Floyd: The Wall '82
The Pink Panther Strikes Again '76
The Pit and the Pendulum '61
The Pit & the Pendulum '91
Play Misty for Me '71
Poison '91
Poison '01
The Possessed '47
Post Concussion '99
The President's Analyst '67
Premonition '07
Prettykill '87
Prime Suspect '88
Private Parts '72
Psychic Killer '75
Psycho '60
Psycho '98
Psycho 2 '83
Psycho Cop '88
Psycho Cop 2 '94
Psychos in Love '87
Question of Silence '83
Raising Cain '92
Rasputin '85
The Red Desert '64
Reign Over Me '07
The Rejuvenator '88
Remember Me '85
Rescue Dawn '06
Respiro '02
Return of the Ape Man '44
Return to Cabin by the Lake '01
Return to Waterloo '85
Revenge in the House of Usher '82
Revolt of the Zombies '36
Revolution 9 '01
Richard III '55
Romulus, My Father '07
Room to Let '49
The Ruling Class '72
Scarlet Empress '34
Scissors '91
The Scout '94
Scream Bloody Murder '72
Scream for Help '86
Screamer '74
Screw Loose '99
Seance on a Wet Afternoon '64
Secret Beyond the Door '48
Secretary '02
The Sender '82
Session 9 '01
Sessions '83
Seven Days in May '64
Seventh Heaven '98
Shades of Black '93
Shadow Play '86
Shattered '72
Shattered Image '98
Shattered Silence '71
Shattered Spirits '86
The Shining '80
Shock Corridor '63
The Silence of the Lambs '91
Silent Night, Bloody Night '73
Sisters '73
Sisters, Or the Balance of Happiness '79
Skeletons in the Closet '01
Sketches of a Strangler '78
Slaughter Hotel '71
Sledgehammer '83
Sling Blade '96
Sniper '75
Solaris '72
Solaris '02
Some Folks Call It a Sling Blade '94
Sophie's Choice '82
Sordid Lives '00
Soul Survivors '01
Soundman '99
South of Reno '87
Spectre of the Rose '46
Spellbound '45
Spider '02
Star Maps '97
States of Control '98
The Story of Adele H. '75
Strait-Jacket '64
Strange Illusion '45
Stranger Than Fiction '06
Strangers on a Train '51
Street Asylum '90
A Streetcar Named Desire '51
A Streetcar Named Desire '84
Strong Medicine '84
Stuart Bliss '98
Stuart Saves His Family '94
The Substance of Fire '96
The Survivalist '87
Suspended Animation '02
Svengali '55
Sweeney Todd: The Demon Barber of Fleet Street '07
Sweethearts '97
Sybil '76
Sylvia '03
Tainted Image '91
The Tenant '76
Teenage Frankenstein '58
The Testament of Dr. Cordelier '59
They Might Be Giants '71
The Thin Red Line '64
Thomas in Love '01
The Three Faces of Eve '57
The 300 Year Weekend '71
Three Nuts in Search of a Bolt '64
Tideland '05
Time Out '01
Titus '99
Torture Train '75
Touched '82
Tracks '76
Trapped in Silence '74
The Turn of the Screw '92
The Turn of the Screw '99
12 Monkeys '95
Twilight Man '96
Twin Peaks: Fire Walk with Me '92
Twinsanity '70
Twister '89
Two Drifters '05
The Two Faces of Dr. Jekyll '60
The Ugly '96
Under the Sand '00
Under the Skin '97
The Unsaid '01
Urge to Kill '84
Vampire's Kiss '88
Vengeance Is Mine '79
Vincent & Theo '90
Violated '53
Virtual Seduction '96
Walter and Henry '01
Ward Six '78
Watched '73
What about Bob? '91
What Ever Happened to Baby Jane? '62
What's the Matter with Helen? '71
Where Danger Lives '50
While I Live '47
White Badge '97
White Heat '49
The Wind '87
Witchfire '86
Woman in Black '89
The Woman in White '97
A Woman under the Influence '74
Woyzeck '94
Year of the Dog '07
Yerma '99

Satanism

see also Demons & Wizards; Devils; Occult

Alison's Birthday '79
Amazon Jail '85
Angel on My Shoulder '80
Asylum of Satan '72
Bad Dreams '88
Beast of the Yellow Night '70
Beyond the Door 3 '91
The Black Cat '34
Black Roses '88
Black Sunday '60
Bless the Child '00
The Blood on Satan's Claw '71
Blood Orgy of the She-Devils '74
The Bloodsuckers '70
The Brotherhood of Satan '71
Child of Darkness, Child of Light '91
The Chosen '77
The Convent '00
The Crimson Cult '68
The Crow: Wicked Prayer '05
Damien: Omen 2 '78
The Day of the Beast '95
The Demon Lover '77
Demonoid, Messenger of Death '81
The Devil & Daniel Webster '41
The Devil Rides Out '68
The Devils '71
The Devil's Daughter '91
The Devil's Eye '60
The Devil's Mistress '68
The Devil's Nightmare '71
The Devil's Partner '58
The Devil's Possessed '74
The Devil's Prey '01
Devil's Rain '75
Devil's Son-in-Law '77
The Devil's Web '74
Disciple of Death '72
Doctor Faustus '68
Dominion: Prequel to the Exorcist '05
Equinox '71
Eternal Evil '87
Evil Altar '89
Evilspeak '82
Exorcism '74
The Exorcist '73
The Exorcist 2: The Heretic '77
Eye of the Demon '87
Family Reunion '89
Fear No Evil '80
The Final Conflict '81
Ghoulies 4 '93
Guardian of the Abyss '82
Hack O'Lantem '87
Halloween Night '90
Highway to Hell '92

▶ = rated three bones or higher

House of the Black Death '65
I Don't Want to Be Born '75
I Drink Your Blood '71
Inferno '80
Invitation to Hell '84
Jaws of Satan '81
Leaves from Satan's Book '19
The Legend of Hillbilly John '73
Leonor '75
A Little Bit of Soul '97
Lost Souls '00
The Man and the Monster '65
The Mangler '94
Maxim Xul '91
The Mephisto Waltz '71 ▶
Merchants of Death '99
Midnight '81
Midnight Cabaret '50
Midnight's Child '92
Mind, Body & Soul '92
Mysterious Doctor Satan '40
Necromancer: Satan's Servant '88
Night Visitor '89
976-EVIL '88
976-EVIL 2: The Astral Factor '91
The Ninth Gate '99
The Occultist '89
Oh, God! You Devil '84
One of Them '03
The Omen '76
Other Hell '85
Prime Evil '88
Prince of Darkness '87
The Pyx '73 ▶
Race with the Devil '75
Raging Angels '95
The Relic '96
Rest in Pieces '87
Revenge '86
Rosemary's Baby '68 ▶
The Satanic Rites of Dracula '73
Satan's Black Wedding '75
Satan's Blood '77
Satan's Cheerleaders '77
Satan's Princess '90
Satan's School for Girls '73
Satan's Touch '84
Satanwar '79
The Sentinel '76
Servants of Twilight '91
The Seventh Victim '43 ▶
Sheitan '06
Shock 'Em Dead '90
Sisters of Satan '75
Speak of the Devil '90
Specters '87
The Spellbinder '88
Sugar Cookies '77
The Tempter '74
Terror Beach '75
To the Devil, a Daughter '75
Tombs of the Blind Dead '72
The Visitor '80
Warlock '91
Warlock: The Armageddon '93
Weirdsville '07
Witchcraft '88
Witchcraft 3: The Kiss of Death '90
Witchcraft 5: Dance with the Devil '92
Witchcraft 6: The Devil's Mistress '94
Witchcraft 10: Mistress of the Craft '98
Witch Trap '85

Satire & Parody
see also Black Comedy;
Comedy; Genre Spoof?
A Propos de Nice '29 ▶
Abbot and Costello Go to Mars '53
Abduction '75
The Act '82
The Adventures of Picasso '80

The Adventures of Sherlock Holmes' Smarter Brother '78 ▶
The Affairs of Annabel '38
Aftershock '88
Airplane! '80 ▶
Airplane 2: The Sequel '82
An Alan Smithee Film: Burn, Hollywood, Burn '97
Alex in Wonderland '70
All Through the Night '42 ▶
All You Need Is Cash '78 ▶
The Alphabet Murders '65
Amazing Dr. Clitterhouse
Amazon Women on the Moon '87
America 3000 '86
American Dreamz '06
American Psycho '99
American Ticker '76
America's Deadliest Home Video '91
Americathon '79
...And God Spoke '94
Andy Warhol's Dracula '74 ▶
Andy Warhol's Frankenstein '74
Animal Farm '55 ▶
Animal Farm '99
Any Wednesday '66
The Apartment '60 ▶
As Young As You Feel '51 ▶
The Associate '96
Attack of the Robots '66
Auntie Mame '58 ▶
Austin Powers: International Man of Mystery '97 ▶
Austin Powers 2: The Spy Who Shagged Me '99 ▶
Backfire! '94
Bad Manners '84
Bad Medicine '85
Bamboozled '00
Bananas '71 ▶
Bank Robber '93
Banjo '93
Barry McKenzie Holds His Own '74
Based on an Untrue Story '93
Basic Training '86
The Bawdy Adventures of Tom Jones '76
Beautiful '00
Being There '79 ▶
Best in Show '00 ▶
The Best Man '64 ▶
Beyond the Valley of the Dolls '70
Beyond Therapy '86
The Big Bus '76
Big Deal on Madonna Street '58 ▶
The Big Picture '89
The Big Tease '99
Big Trouble in Little China '86
Black and White in Color '76 ▶
Black Bird '75
Bob & Carol & Ted & Alice '69
Bob Roberts '92 ▶
The Bogus Witch Project '00
The Bonfire of the Vanities '90
Born in East L.A. '87
Boss '74
Boy Meets Girl '38 ▶
The Brady Bunch Movie '95 ▶
Bread and Chocolate '73 ▶
Breakfast of Champions '98
Bring It On '00 ▶
Britannia Hospital '82
Buffalo Soldiers '01
Bullshot '83
Bulworth '98 ▶
The 'Burbs '89
But I'm a Cheerleader '99
Camera Buff '79
Canadian Bacon '94
The Candidate '72 ▶
Candy '68
Candy '06
Carry On Cleo '65
Carry On Dick '75
Casino Royale '67

Caveman '81
CB4: The Movie '93
Cecil B. Demented '00
Champagne for Caesar '50 ▶
Chaos Theory '08
The Cheap Detective '78 ▶
Cherry Falls '00
Children of the Revolution '95
Chronically Unfeasible '00
Citizen Ruth '96
A Clockwork Orange '71 ▶
Clockwise '86
Club Dread '04
Code Name: Chaos '90
Cold Turkey '71 ▶
Contract '80 ▶
Coup de Grace '78
Crainquebille '23 ▶
Creature from the Haunted Sea '60
Crimewave '85
Curtain Up '53
Dark Habits '84
Dark Star '74 ▶
Danktown Strutters '74
Date Movie '06
Darling Lili '70
A Day Without a Mexican '04
Dead Men Don't Die '91
Dead Men Don't Wear Plaid '82
Deal of the Century '83
Death of a Bureaucrat '66 ▶
Deathrow Gameshow '88
Diary of a Chambermaid '64 ▶
Dick '99 ▶
Dirty Dishes '78 ▶
The Disappearance of Kevin Johnson '95
The Discreet Charm of the Bourgeoisie '72 ▶
Dr. Heckyl and Mr. Hype '80
Doctors and Nurses '86
Don't Be a Menace to South Central While Drinking Your Juice in the Hood '95
Down & Dirty '76 ▶
Down and Out in Beverly Hills '86
Down to Earth '47 ▶
Down Under '86
Dracula: Dead and Loving It '95
Dracula Sucks '79
Dragnet '87
Drop Dead Gorgeous '99
E. Nick: A Legend in His Own Mind '84
Easy Wheels '89
Election '99 ▶
11 Harrowhouse '74 ▶
Ella Cinders '26 ▶
Erik the Viking '89
Evil Roy Slade '71 ▶
Exposed '03
The Extraordinary Adventures of Mr. West in the Land of the Bolsheviks '24
The Family Game '83 ▶
The Fat Spy '66
Fatal Instinct '93
Fay Grim '06
Fear of a Black Hat '94 ▶
Ferocious Female Freedom Fighters '88
Fido '06
First Family '80
The Flaming Teen-Age '56
Flesh Gordon '72
Flicks '85
Floundering '94
Forgotten Silver '96 ▶
The Fortune Cookie '66 ▶
Frankenstein General Hospital '88
Frankenstein Sings... The Movie '95
Frankenweenie '84 ▶
The French Touch '54
The Freshman '90 ▶
From Here to Maternity '85

The Front '76 ▶
Funny Money '82
Fuse '03
Gabriel Over the White House '33 ▶
Galactic Gigolo '87
Galaxina '80
Ganjasaurus Rex '87
Gas '81
Geek Maggot Bingo '83
Genevieve '53 ▶
Gentlemen Prefer Blondes '53 ▶
Girls in Prison '94
Glory! Glory! '90 ▶
Go for Zucker '05
Going Berserk '83
Going Places '74 ▶
Going Postal '98
Gosford Park '01 ▶
Greaser's Palace '72
Great American Traffic Jam '80
The Great Dictator '40 ▶
The Great Madcap '49
The Great McConagall '75
The Great White Hype '96
The Groove Tube '72
Grunt! The Wrestling Movie
Gulliver's Travels '95
Gumshoe '72 ▶
Gypsy '75
Hail '73
Hail the Conquering Hero '44 ▶
Hairspray '88 ▶
Half a Sixpence '67
Happiness '32
Heaven Can Wait '43 ▶
Heavens Above '63 ▶
Hexed '93
High Anxiety '77 ▶
High Hopes '88 ▶
High School High '96
High Season '96
Hijacking Hollywood '97
History of the World: Part 1 '81 ▶
Hollywood Harry '86
Hollywood North '03
Home Movies '79
The Horror of Frankenstein '70
The Hospital '71 ▶
Hot Shots! '91 ▶
Hot Shots! Part Deux '93 ▶
The Hound of the Baskervilles '77
How I Got into College '89 ▶
I Love You, Alice B. Toklas! '68
I Married a Vampire '87
I Was a Zombie for the FBI '82
I Was Born But... '32 ▶
The Icicle Thief '89 ▶
Idiocracy '06
I'll Do Anything '93
I'm All Right Jack '59 ▶
I'm Gonna Git You Sucka '88 ▶
The Incredible Shrinking Woman '81
Incredibly Strange Creatures Who Stopped Living and Became Mixed-Up Zombies '63
The Inspector General '52
Intern '00
Invasion Earth: The Aliens Are Here! '87
Irma Vep '96 ▶
Is There Sex After Death?
It Couldn't Happen Here '88
J-Men Forever! '79 ▶
Jabberwocky '77
Jack and His Friends '92
Jail Party '04
Jailbait! '00
Jamon, Jamon '33
Jay and Silent Bob Strike Back '01
Jekyll & Hyde... Together Again '82
Jet Benny Show '86

Johnny Dangerously '84
A Joke of Destiny, Lying in Wait Around the Corner Like a Bandit '84
The Kaiser's Lackey '51
Kentucky Fried Movie '77 ▶
Kids in the Hall: Brain Candy '96
The King of Hearts '66 ▶
Kurt Vonnegut's Harrison Bergeron '95
The Ladies' Man '61
The Last Polka '84 ▶
Lawn Dogs '96
Le Schpountz '38
Legalese '98
Leon the Pig Farmer '93 ▶
Let's Kill All the Lawyers '93
Lip Service '88 ▶
Look Out Sister '48 ▶
Lord Love a Duck '66 ▶
Love and a .45 '94
Love and Death '75 ▶
Love at Stake '87
The Lovec One '65 ▶
Mad City '97
Mad Mission 3 '84
Mad Monster Party '68
Malibu's Most Wanted '03
Man Bites Dog '91 ▶
Man in the White Suit '51 ▶
The Man Who Came to Dinner '41 ▶
The Man with Bogart's Face '80
The Man with Two Brains '83 ▶
Mapp & Lucia '85
Mars Attacks! '96 ▶
Mastergate '92 ▶
Me and the Colonel '58
Men... '85 ▶
The Meteor Man '93
Mickey '17
A Mighty Wind '03 ▶
The Milky Way '03 ▶
Minbo—Or the Gentle Art of Japanese Extortion '92
Miss Cast Away '04
The Missionary '82 ▶
Mr. Write '92
Mob Boss '90
Modern Times '36 ▶
Monster in a Box '92 ▶
Monty Python and the Holy Grail '75 ▶
Monty Python's Life of Brian '79 ▶
Monty Python's The Meaning of Life '83 ▶
More Wild, Wild West '80
The Mouse on the Moon '62 ▶
The Mouse That Roared '59 ▶
Movers and Shakers '85
Movie, Movie '78
Murder by Death '76 ▶
Mutant on the Bounty '89
My Best Friend Is a Vampire '88
My Best Girl '27 ▶
Myra Breckinridge '70
Mystery Science Theater 3000: The Movie '96
The Naked Gun: From the Files of Police Squad '88 ▶
Naked in New York '93
Nasty Habits '77
National Lampoon Goes to the Movies '81
National Lampoon's Animal House '78 ▶
National Lampoon's Attack of the 5 ft. 2 Women '94
National Lampoon's Loaded Weapon 1 '93
Natural Born Killers '94 ▶
Night Patrol '85
99 & 44/100 Dead '74 ▶
Nocturna '79
Northanger Abbey '87

The Nutty Professor '63 ▶
Office Space '98 ▶
On the Avenue '37 ▶
Open Season '95
Orchestra Rehearsal '78
Oscar '91
Overdrawn at the Memory Bank '83
Padre Nuestro '85
Pajama Tops '83
Pandemonium '82
Paramedics '88
Pardners '56
Partners '82
Pass the Ammo '88
P.C.U. '94
The Pentagon Wars '98
Personal Services '87
Phantom of Liberty '74 ▶
Pictures '80s
The Pink Chiquitas '86
Pipe Dream '02
Plan 10 from Outer Space '95
The Player '92 ▶
Polyester '81 ▶
The Positively True Adventures of the Alleged Texas Cheerleader-Murdering Mom '93 ▶
Pray TV '80
The Prisoner of Rio '89
Prime Time '77
Primary Colors '98 ▶
The Princess Bride '87 ▶
A Private Function '84 ▶
Prize of Peril '84
The Producers '68 ▶
Putney Swope '69 ▶
Rat Pfink a Boo-Boo '66
Ready to Wear '94
Real Men '87
Really Weird Tales '86
Red Desert Penitentiary '83
Red Earth '82
Red Garters '54
Repentance '87 ▶
The Report on the Party and the Guests '66 ▶
Repossessed '90
Return of Captain Invincible '83
The Return of Spinal Tap '92
Revolution! A Red Comedy '92
Ricky 1 '88
Ring of the Musketeers '93
Robin Hood: Men in Tights '93 ▶
The Rocky Horror Picture Show '75 ▶
Romeo is Bleeding '93
Rosalie Goes Shopping '89 ▶
The Royal Bed '31
Rude Awakening '89
The Ruling Class '72 ▶
Running Mates '92 ▶
Running Mates '00
Sallah '63 ▶
Salvation! '87
Sammy & Rosie Get Laid '87 ▶
Saved! '04 ▶
Scary Movie '00 ▶
Scary Movie 4 '06
Scenes from the Class Struggle in Beverly Hills '89
Schizopolis '97
Scream '96 ▶
Scream 2 '97 ▶
Scream 3 '00
Scrooged '88 ▶
Search and Destroy '94
The Second Civil War '97 ▶
Second Time Lucky '84
Secret Agent 00-Soul '89
The Secret Diary of Sigmund Freud '84
Seduction of Mimi '72 ▶
The Senator Was Indiscreet '47 ▶
Serial '80 ▶
Serial Mom '94 ▶

▶ = rated three bones or higher

Satire

Series 7: The Contenders '01
A Session with The Committee '68
Sex Adventures of the Three Musketeers '71
Sex with a Smile '76
Shame of the Jungle '75
Shampoo '75
A Shock to the System '90 ▶
Shoot or Be Shot '02
Shriek If You Know What I Did Last Friday the 13th '00
Sideburns '91
Silence of the Hams '93
Silent Movie '76
Silver City '04
Simon of the Desert '66 ▶
Sink or Swim '97
Slammer Girls '87
Sleeper '73 ▶
Smile '75 ▶
S.O.B. '81
Soul Plane '04
Spaceballs '87
Spaced Out '80
Spaceship '81
Spare Me '92
The Specials '00 ▶
Spirit of '76 '91
Spy Hard '96
Starsky & Hutch '04
State of Things '82
Stay Tuned '92
Stiff Upper Lips '96
Straight to Hell '87
Strange Invaders '83 ▶
Streetfight '75
Sullivan's Travels '41 ▶
Sunset '73 ▶
SuperGuy: Behind the Cape '02
Suppose They Gave a War and Nobody Came? '70
Surf Nazis Must Die '87
Swimming with Sharks '94 ▶
Sympathy for the Devil '70
Tanner '88 '88 ▶
Tanner on Tanner '04
Tapeheads '89
A Taste for Flesh and Blood '90
Team America: World Police '04 ▶
Terror 2000 '92
Thank You for Smoking '06
That's Adequate '90
They Call Me Bruce? '82
They Live '88 ▶
They Still Call Me Bruce '86
This Is Spinal Tap '84 ▶
The Thorn '74
Three Amigos '86 ▶
The Thrill of It All! '63
To Be or Not to Be '83 ▶
Tom and Francie '05 ▶
Too Many Crooks '59
Top Secret! '84 ▶
Trailer: the Movie '99
Transylvania 6-5000 '85
Trash '70
Traxx '87
Trial & Error '62
True Stories '86 ▶
Trust Me '89
Tunnelvision '76
Turumba '84 ▶
The TV Set '06
2001: A Space Travesty '00
Uforia '81 ▶
UHF '89 ▶
Ultrachrist! '03
Undercover Brother '02 ▶
Unmasking the Idol '86
Up from the Depths '79
Up the Academy '80
Vacuuming Completely Nude in Paradise '01
Vanity Fair '67
Vanity Fair '99
A Very Brady Sequel '96
A Very Curious Girl '69
The Villain Still Pursued Her '41
Virgin High '90

Voyage of the Rock Aliens '87
Waiting for Guffman '96 ▶
Walker '87
Watermelon Man '70
Way He Was '76
Weapons of Mass Distraction '97
What to Do in Case of Fire '02
What's Up, Tiger Lily? '66 ▶
The Wheeler Dealers '63 ▶
When Nature Calls '85
When Willie Comes Marching Home '50 ▶
Where the Buffalo Roam '80
Where the Bullets Fly '66
Where's Marlowe? '98
The White Sheik '52 ▶
Wholly Moses! '80
Who's Who '78
Wild, Wild West Revisited '79
Will Success Spoil Rock Hunter? '57
Window to Paris '95
Without a Clue '88
World Gone Wild '88
The Worm Eaters '77
The Would-Be Gentleman '58
Yin & Yang of Mr. Go '71
You'll Find Out '40
Young Doctors in Love '82
Young Frankenstein '74 ▶
Young Nurses in Love '89
Zachariah '70
The Zany Adventures of Robin Hood '84
Zarkorr! The Invader '96
Zelig '83 ▶
Zeta One '69
Zoolander '01 ▶
Zorro, the Gay Blade '81

Savannah
see also American South; Crime and Punishment in Suburbia '00

Savants
see also Mental Retardation
Being There '79 ▶
Champagne for Caesar '50 ▶
Charly '68 ▶
Doctor Dolittle '67
Forrest Gump '94 ▶
King Lear '71 ▶
Malcolm '86
Mercury Rising '98
Rain Man '88 ▶
Tony Draws a Horse '51

Scams, Stings & Cons
see also Heists
Abbott and Costello Meet the Keystone Kops '54
Adios Amigo '75
After the Fox '66 ▶
Alien Fury: Countdown to Invasion '00
The Amazing Mr. X '48
American Buffalo '95 ▶
Angel-A '05
Another You '91
Anton, the Magician '78
Argentine Nights '40
Assault on a Queen '66
Backflash '01
Bad Company '02
Barnaby and Me '77
Beautiful Joe '00
Bedtime Story '63
Best Laid Plans '99
Best of the Badmen '50
Beyond a Reasonable Doubt '56

The Big Bounce '04
The Big Lebowski '97 ▶
The Big Squeeze '96
Big Trouble '86
Billionaire Boys Club '87
Birds & the Bees '56
Birthday Girl '02
Black Cat, White Cat '98 ▶
Black Oak Conspiracy '77
Blackheart '98
Blackmail '91 ▶
Blackout '54
Blonde Crazy '31
Blood on the Moon '48
Blossoms on Broadway '37
Blue Murder at St. Trinian's '56 ▶
Border Phantom '37
Border Saddlemates '52
Bottle Rocket '95
The Brothers Grimm '05
Brown's Requiem '98
Buffalo Stampede '33
Buona Sera, Mrs. Campbell '68
Burning Down the House '01
Butterfly Affair '71
Came a Hot Friday '85
Candleshoe '78
Caper of the Golden Bulls '67
Capricorn One '78 ▶
The Captain from Koepenick '56
Cartier Affair '84
Casino '95 ▶
Catch Me a Spy '71
Catch Me If You Can '02 ▶
Cause for Alarm '51
Chameleon Street '89 ▶
The Charmer '87
Cheap Shots '91
Cheech and Chong: Things Are Tough All Over '82
Children On Their Birthdays '02
Chinatown '74 ▶
Circus '00
City of Ghosts '03
Club Fed '90
Cold Justice '89
Color Me Kubrick '05
The Color of Money '86 ▶
The Con '98
The Con Artists '80
Confidence '03
Consenting Adults '92
The Conversation '74 ▶
Convicts at Large '38
Cops and Robbers '73
Cotton Comes to Harlem '70 ▶
Country Gentlemen '36
Crack-Up '46
Cracked Nuts '41
Criminal '04
Croupier '97 ▶
Curly Sue '91
The Curse of Inferno '96
Dangerous Summer '82
Dead Heat on a Merry-Go-Round '66 ▶
The Dead Pool '88 ▶
Deadfall '93
The Deal '05
Dear God '96
Deception '92
Deception '08
Deep Crimson '96
Dennis the Menace Strikes Again '98
The Desperate Trail '94
Destiny Turns on the Radio '95
Diggstown '92
Dirty Rotten Scoundrels '88 ▶
The Distinguished Gentleman '92
Dr. Christian Meets the Women '40
Dollar '38
Dudley Do-Right '99
Elmer Gantry '60 ▶
The Embezzled Heaven '58
Every Day's a Holiday '38

Everything's Gone Green '06
F/X '86 ▶
F/X 2: The Deadly Art of Illusion '91 *
Fakers '04
The Family Holiday '07
Fargo '96 ▶
Federal Agents vs. Underworld, Inc. '49
Fierce Creatures '96
A Fish Called Wanda '88 ▶
Flim-Flam Man '67
For Better or Worse '95
Forger of London '61
Formula for a Murder '85
The Fortune Cookie '66 ▶
The Fourth Protocol '87 ▶
The 4th Tenor '02
Framed '90
Frauds '93
Freelance '71
The Frighteners '96 ▶
Gang Related '96
The Gang's All Here '40
Get Shorty '95 ▶
A Girl in Every Port '52
Girl Under the Sheet '61
Glengarry Glen Ross '92 ▶
Glory! Glory! '90 ▶
Goin' to Town '44
Gone Fishin' '97
Good Neighbor Sam '64 ▶
Goodbye, Lover '99
Great Bank Hoax '78
The Great Impostor '61
The Great White Hype '96
Great World of Sound '07
Green Card '90
The Grifters '90 ▶
Gun Smoke '31
Harlem Rides the Range '39
Harry & Walter Go to New York '76
Heartbreakers '01
Hearts On '43
Hi Diddle Diddle '43
The Hoax '06
Hold Your Man '33 ▶
The Honeymoon Machine '61
Hopscotch '80 ▶
The Hot Rock '70 ▶
House of Errors '42
House of Games '87 ▶
Housesitter '92
I Got the Hook-Up '98
I Love Melvin '53
I Love You Again '40 ▶
If I Were Rich '33
Il Bidone '55
In the Soup '92
The Inspectors 2: A Shred of Evidence '00
Invasion of the Space Preachers '90
Irish Jam '05
Irresistible Impulse '95
Jackie Brown '97
Just the Ticket '98
Kid from Not-So-Big '78
Killer '73
The Killing '56 ▶
Kind Hearts and Coronets '49 ▶
The King and Four Queens '56
The King of Marvin Gardens '72
King's Ransom '05
Kiss or Kill '97
The Lady Eve '41 ▶
The Ladykillers '04
Lamerica '94
The Last Adventure '67
The Last of Mrs. Cheyney '37 ▶
The Last Seduction 2 '98
Law and Order '42
Le Gentleman D'Epsom '62
Leap of Faith '92
The Learning Curve '01
The Lemon Drop Kid '51
Let's Do It Again '75 ▶
The Liars '64
Lies '83
Life Stinks '91

Like a Fish Out of Water '99
Lock, Stock and 2 Smoking Barrels '98 ▶
Lonely Hearts '91
Lonely Hearts '06
Louisiana Hayride '44
The Lovable Cheat '49
Love Kills '98
Love the Hard Way '01
Lovers: A True Story '90 ▶
The Madwoman of Chaillot '69
The Magician of Lublin '79
Malone '87
The Man '05
Man of the World '31
Manhattan Melodrama '34 ▶
Marshal of Cedar Rock '53
The Mask of Dijon '46
Matchstick Men '03 ▶
Maverick '94
McHale's Navy '64
McHale's Navy '97
Me and the Kid '93
Medicine Man '30
Mexican Hayride '48
Mexican Spitfire at Sea '42
Miami Hustle '95
Millions '90
Milwaukee, Minnesota '03
The Miracle Woman '31
Miranda '01
Mistaken Identity '36
Mr. Boggs Steps Out '38
Mr. Lucky '43 ▶
Mo' Money '92
The Monster '96
Murder for Sale '68
Murder on Approval '56
Murder on the Yukon '40
The Music Man '62 ▶
National Lampoon's Gold Diggers '04
Never Give a Sucker an Even Break '41 ▶
Never Say Never Again '83
The Next Big Thing '02
Nickel & Dime '92
Night and the City '50 ▶
Night and the City '92 ▶
Nightmare Alley '47
Nine Queens '00
No Way Out '87 ▶
None But the Lonely Heart '44 ▶
Nothing Sacred '37 ▶
Now and Forever '34
Ocean's Thirteen '07 ▶
Office Space '98
The Old Lady Who Walked in the Sea '91
Old Spanish Custom '36
On the Fiddle '61
One Christmas '95
100 Mile Rule '02
One of My Wives Is Missing '76
One Way Passage '32
Opportunity Knocks '90
Ossessione '42 ▶
Out to Sea '97
Pale Saints '97
Palmetto '98
Panic Button '62
Paper Man '71
Paper Moon '73 ▶
The Parallax View '74 ▶
Parole, Inc. '49
Pass the Ammo '88
The Pest '96
Phantom Gold '38
Piece of the Action '77
The Pope Must Diet '91
Popi '69 ▶
Portrait of a Lady '96 ▶
The President's Plane Is Missing '71
The Prime Gig '00
Prisoner of Rio '89
The Producers '68 ▶
The Producers '05
The Promoter '52 ▶
Purlie Victorious '63
The Quest '96
Quiz Show '94 ▶
Reborn '81
The Red Light Sting '84
Remedy for Riches '40

The Ringer '05
Risk '00
Risky Business '83 ▶
The Road to El Dorado '00
The Road to Zanzibar '41
Roaring Speedboats '37
Rule 3 '93
Ruthless People '86 ▶
Sands of Sacrifice '21
Save the Tiger '73 ▶
Scam '93
Scandalous '84
Schemes '95
Schtonk '92
Sgt. Bilko '95
The Settlement '99
Sexual Intent '94
Shade '03
Shattered Image '93
Shooting Fish '98
Silk 'n' Sabotage '94
Silver Bears '78
Simpatico '99
Six Degrees of Separation '93
Skin Game '71 ▶
Sky Hei$t '75
Slackers '02
Slither '73 ▶
Small Hotel '57
Something for Everyone '70
South Riding '37
Southern Belles '05
The Spanish Prisoner '97 ▶
Spenser: A Savage Place '94
The Squeeze '80
The Squeeze '87
Stacy's Knights '83
Stagecoach to Denver '46
The Star Maker '95
Stavisky '74 ▶
Still Breathing '97
The Sting '73 ▶
The Sting 2 '83
Stolen Hearts '95
The Story of a Cheat '36 ▶
The Story of Esther Costello '57
The Stranger from Pecos '45
Sucker Money '34
Suicide Kings '97
Sunburn '79
Support Your Local Gunfighter '71 ▶
Sweet Talker '91
The Swindle '97
Swindle '04
Swindled '04
Tall in the Saddle '44
A Taste for Killing '92
Tax Season '98
The Taxman '98
The Ten Million Dollar Getaway '91
Tequila Sunrise '88 ▶
Things Change '88 ▶
Things to Do in Denver When You're Dead '95 ▶
The Third Key '57
36 Hours '64 ▶
This Is a Hijack '73
This World, Then the Fireworks '97
365 Nights in Hollywood '34
Thrilled to Death '88
Ticket of Leave Man '37
The Tigress '93
Title Shot '81
Too Bad She's Bad '54
Too Pretty to Be Honest '72
Tootsie '82 ▶
Touch '96
Train Robbers '73
Traveller '96 ▶
Tricheurs '84
Trojan Eddie '96 ▶
Trouble in Paradise '32 ▶
Trust Me '89
Two Much '96
Underworld Scandal '47
The Unholy Three '30 ▶
Walpurgis Night '41 ▶
The Warrior & the Sorceress '84
Watch the Birdie '50

- The Wendell Baker Story '05
- We're Talkin' Serious Money '92
- Whacked! '02
- The Wharf Rat '95
- When Will I Be Loved '04
- Where the Money Is '00
- White Men Can't Jump '92
- White River '99
- Why Me? '90
- Wild Things '98
- The Winner '96
- Wish You Were Dead '00
- Write to Kill '91

Scared 'Chuteless

see also Skydiving

- Con Air '97▶
- Double Team '97
- Eraser '96
- Firehouse Dog '07
- Goldeneye '95▶
- Point Break '91
- Terminal Velocity '94

School Daze

see also Campus Capers; Hell High School

- Absolution '81
- Accident '67
- The Adventures of Sebastian Cole '99
- All God's Children '80
- All I Wanna Do '98
- All Things Fair '95
- American Friends '91
- Amy '81
- Angels in the Endzone '98
- Anna and the King of Siam '46▶
- Around the Fire '98
- Art School Confidential '06
- Au Revoir les Enfants '87▶
- Back to School '86
- Backfield in Motion '91
- Before the Fall '04
- The Beguiled '70▶
- The Belles of St. Trinian's '53▶
- The Bells of St. Mary's '45▶
- Big and Hairy '98
- Big Bully '95
- Billy Madison '94
- Black Narcissus '47▶
- Blue Jeans '78
- Blue Ridge Fall '99
- Bluffing it '87
- Boarding School '83
- Boys '95
- Buried Alive '89
- Cheaters '00
- Cheers for Miss Bishop '41
- Children of a Lesser God '86▶
- The Chocolate War '88▶
- Christy '94
- Ciao, Professore! '94
- Clueless '95▶
- Common Ground '00
- The Convent '00
- The Corn Is Green '45▶
- crazy/beautiful '01
- Crazy for Love '52
- Crazy from the Heart '91▶
- Cruel Intentions '98
- The Dangerous Lives of Altar Boys '02▶
- Dead Poets Society '89▶
- Deadly Sins '95
- Death Tunnel '05
- The Devil's Backbone '01
- The Devil's Playground '76▶
- Diabolique '96
- Doctor Dolittle '67
- Dream to Believe '85
- Dress Gray '86▶
- Drive Me Crazy '99
- D3: The Mighty Ducks '96

- Eden '98
- Educating Rita '83▶
- The Elementary School '91
- The Ernest Green Story '93
- Europa, Europa '91▶
- Eyes Right! '26
- The Faculty '98
- Fame '80▶
- Fast Times at Ridgemont High '82▶
- Final Exam '98
- Finding Forrester '00
- Flirting '89▶
- Flubber '97
- Forever Mary '89▶
- Free of Eden '98
- The French Lesson '86
- French Postcards '79
- Frog and Wombat '98
- Games Girls Play '75
- Get Real '99
- Getting It On '83
- The Getting of Wisdom '77
- Getting Straight '70
- Getting Wasted '80
- The Girl, the Body and the Pill '67
- The Girl Who Spelled Freedom '86▶
- The Girls of Huntington House '73
- The Goodbye Bird '93
- Goodbye, Mr. Chips '39▶
- Goodbye, Mr. Chips '69
- The Gospel According to Vic '87
- Grown Ups '80
- Guess What We Learned in School Today? '70
- The Guinea Pig '48
- The Halfback of Notre Dame '96
- The Happiest Days of Your Life '50▶
- Hard Knox '83
- Hard Lessons '86
- Heavenly Creatures '94▶
- Here Come the Co-Eds '45
- The History Boys '06
- Homework '82
- Horsemasters '61
- How I Got into College '89
- How to Eat Fried Worms '06
- Idle Hands '99
- Impure Thoughts '86
- In a Class of His Own '99
- Iron & Silk '91
- Is There Life Out There? '94
- Jack '96
- Johnny Holiday '49
- Johnny Tiger '66
- Judy Berlin '99
- The Kid with the 200 I.Q. '83
- Kindergarten Cop '90
- Kurt Vonnegut's Harrison Bergeron '95
- Lambaca '89
- Last Time Out '94
- Lete Bloomers '95
- Leader of the Band '87
- Liberty Heights '99
- Little Man '98
- The Little Princess '39▶
- A Little Princess '95▶
- Little Red Schoolhouse '36
- Lloyd '00
- The Long Gray Line '55▶
- The Lords of Discipline '83
- Love Me if You Dare '03
- Luna e L'Altra '96
- Maedchen in Uniform '31▶
- The Major and the Minor '42▶
- Major Payne '95
- Married to It '93
- Masterminds '96
- Matilda '96▶
- Max Keeble's Big Move '01
- Mean Girls '04▶
- A Minor Miracle '83
- Mr. Headmistress '98
- A Murder of Quality '90
- Murder 101 '91
- Music of the Heart '99
- My Teacher Ate My Homework '98
- My Teacher's Wife '95

- National Lampoon's Class Reunion '82
- National Lampoon's Senior Trip '95
- The NeverEnding Story '84▶
- Nightmaws '75
- Not Quite Human 2 '89
- Old Mother Riley, Headmistress '50
- Oleanna '94
- Our Time '74
- Outside Providence '99
- Oxford Blues '84
- Passing Glory '99▶
- Passion for Life '48
- The People '71
- Perfect Harmony '91
- Porky's '82
- Powder '95
- Prep School '81
- Pride of Jesse Hallum '81
- The Prime of Miss Jean Brodie '69▶
- The Principal '87
- The Private War of Major Benson '55
- The Pure Hell of St. Trinian's '61
- Rachel, Rachel '68▶
- The Rage: Carrie 2 '99
- The Rascals '81
- Real Genius '85▶
- Rebel '70
- Renaissance Man '94
- Ricochet River '98
- Robin of Locksley '96
- Ruby Bridges '98
- Sabrina the Teenage Witch '96
- Safety Patrol '98
- The St. Tammany Miracle '94
- The Sandpiper '65
- Satan's School for Girls '73
- School of Life '05
- Secret Places '84▶
- A Separate Peace '73
- September Gun '83
- Shout '91
- Sing '89
- The Sixth Sense '99▶
- Stanley and Iris '90
- Star Kid '97▶
- The Strange One '57
- Student Confidential '87
- The Student Teachers '73
- The Substitute '93
- The Substitute 2: School's Out '97
- The Substitute 4: Failure is Not an Option '00
- Summer School Teachers '75
- Tea and Sympathy '56▶
- To Sir, with Love '67
- Tom Brown's School Days '40
- Tom Brown's School Days '51▶
- Tommy Boy '95
- Topaze '33
- Topaze '51▶
- Toy Soldiers '91
- Treehouse Hostage '99
- Trippin' '99
- The Trouble with Angels '66
- Twenty-Four Eyes '54▶
- The Twilight Girls '57
- The Underachievers '88
- Undergrads '85▶
- Up the Academy '80
- Up the Down Staircase '67▶
- Virgin Queen of St. Francis High '88
- Vital Signs '90
- Waterland '92
- Whatever It Takes '00
- Where is My Friend's House? '87
- Why Shoot the Teacher '79▶
- Wild Reeds '94▶
- The Winslow Boy '48▶
- With Honors '94
- The Worst Witch '86
- Yentl '83
- You Are Not Alone '78

Sci Fi

see also Alien Babes; Alien Beings—Benign; Alien Beings—Vicious; Alien Cops; Aliens Are People, Too; Animated Sci-Fi; Clowning Around; Comedy Sci-Fi; Fantasy; Future Cop; Future Shock; Out of This World; Sex; Sci-Fi; Westerns; Space Operas

- A.I.: Artificial Intelligence '01
- Abbott and Costello Go to Mars '53
- Abraxas: Guardian of the Universe '90
- The Abyss '89▶
- Acceptable Risk '01
- Access Code '84
- Adrenalin: Fear the Rush '96
- Aelita: Queen of Mars '24
- Aeon Flux '05
- After the Fall of New York '85
- Afterwards '88
- Akira '89
- The Alchemists '99
- Alien '79▶
- Alien 3 '92
- Alien Agenda: Out of the Darkness '96
- Alien Chaser '96
- The Alien Factor '78
- Alien from L.A. '87
- Alien Intruder '93
- Alien Nation '88
- Alien Nation: Body and Soul '95
- Alien Nation: Dark Horizon '94
- Alien Nation: Millennium '96
- Alien Nation: The Enemy Within '96
- Alien Predators '80
- Alien Private Eye '87
- Alien: Resurrection '97▶
- Alien Space Avenger '91
- Alien Terminator '95
- Alien vs. Predator '04
- Alien Warrior '85
- Alienator '89
- Aliens '86▶
- Aliens Are Coming '80
- Aliens from Spaceship Earth '77
- Aliens vs. Predator: Requiem '07
- Allegro '05
- The Alpha Incident '76
- Alphaville '65▶
- Altered States '80▶
- The Amazing Colossal Man '57
- Amazing Stories '85
- American Cyborg: Steel Warrior '94
- Android '82
- The Android Affair '95
- The Angry Red Planet '59
- Anna to the Infinite Power '84
- A.P.E.X. '94
- The Apocalypse '96
- Arcade '93
- Arena '89
- Armageddon: The Final Challenge '94
- Around the World Under the Sea '65
- The Arrival '90
- The Arrival '96
- The Arrival 2 '98
- The Asphyx '72▶
- Assassin '86
- Assignment Outer Space '61
- The Astounding She-Monster '58
- The Astro-Zombies '67

- At the Earth's Core '76
- Atom Man vs. Superman '50
- The Atomic Brain '64
- Atomic Submarine '59
- Attack from Mars '98
- Attack of the 50 Foot Woman '58
- Attack of the 50 Ft. Woman '93
- Attack of the Giant Leeches '59
- Attack of the Killer Tomatoes '77
- Attack of the Mushroom People '63
- The Aurora Encounter '85
- Automatic '94
- Babylon AD '08
- Backlash: Oblivion 2 '95
- Bad Channels '92
- Bad Girls from Mars '90
- The Bamboo Saucer '68
- Barb Wire '96
- Barbarella '68
- The Bees '78
- Beginning of the End '57
- Beneath the Bermuda Triangle '08
- Beneath the Planet of the Apes '70
- Beware! The Blob '72
- Beyond the Stars '89
- Beyond the Time Barrier '60
- Bicentennial Man '99
- Biohazard: The Alien Force '95
- The Black Hole '79
- Black Scorpion '95
- Blade Runner '82▶
- Blake of Scotland Yard '36
- The Blob '58
- The Blob '88▶
- The Blood of Heroes '89
- Blue Flame '93
- Blue Monkey '87
- Body Melt '93
- Body Snatchers '93
- Bog '84
- Bombshell '97
- Boom in the Moon '46
- Bounty Hunter 2002 '94
- A Boy and His Dog '75
- The Brain Eaters '58
- The Brain from Planet Arous '57
- Brainstorm '83
- Brainwaves '82
- Breeders '86
- The Bronx Executioner '86
- The Brother from Another Planet '84▶
- Buck Rogers Conquers the Universe '39
- Buck Rogers in the 25th Century '79
- Bug '75
- Caged Heat 3000 '95
- Capricorn One '78▶
- Captive Planet '78
- Carver's Gate '96
- The Castle of Fu Manchu '68
- Cat Women of the Moon '53
- The Cave '05
- Chameleon '95
- Chameleon 2: Death Match '99
- Chameleon 3: Dark Angel '00
- Charly '68▶
- Cherry 2000 '88
- Children of Dune '03
- Children of the Damned '63

- The Chronicles of Riddick '04
- Cinderella 2000 '78
- Circuitry Man '90
- City Limits '85
- Class of 1999 '90
- Class of 1999 2: The Substitute '93
- The Clones '73
- The Clonus Horror '79
- Close Encounters of the Third Kind '77▶
- Cloverfield '08
- Club Extinction '89
- Cocoon '85▶
- Code 46 '03
- The Colony '98
- Colossus: The Forbin Project '70▶
- Communion '89
- The Companion '94
- Conquest of Space '55
- Conquest of the Planet of the Apes '72
- Contact '97▶
- Convict 762 '98
- The Cosmic Man '59
- The Cosmic Monsters '58
- Cosmic Slop '94
- Cosmos: War of the Planets '80
- Crash and Burn '90
- The Crazies '73
- The Creation of the Humanoids '62
- Creature '85
- Creatures the World Forgot '70
- Crime Zone '88
- Cube '98
- Cube 2: Hypercube '02
- Cube Zero '04
- Cyber Bandits '94
- Cyber Ninja '94
- Cyber-Tracker '93
- Cyber-Tracker 2 '95
- Cybercity '99
- Cyberzone '95
- Cyborg '89
- Cyborg 2 '93
- Cyborg 3: The Recycler '95
- Cypher '02▶
- D-Day on Mars '45
- Dagora, the Space Monster '65
- Daleks—Invasion Earth 2150 A.D. '66
- Damnation Alley '77
- Dark Breed '96
- Dark City '97
- Dark Planet '97
- Dark Side of the Moon '90
- Dark Universe '93
- Darkdrive '98
- Darkman '90▶
- D.A.R.Y.L. '85
- Day of the Triffids '63▶
- The Day the Earth Caught Fire '61▶
- The Day the Earth Stood Still '51▶
- The Day the Sky Exploded '57
- Day Time Ended '80
- Day Watch '06▶
- Dead End Drive-In '86
- Dead Red '94
- Deep Red '94
- Deep Space '87
- Deepstar Six '89
- Def-Con 4 '85
- Deja Vu '06
- Deluge '33
- Demolition Man '93
- Demon Seed '77▶
- Destination Moon '50

▶ = rated three bones or higher

Destination Moonbase
 Alpha '75
Destination Saturn '39
Destroy All Monsters '68
Destroy All Planets '68
Devil Girl from Mars '54
Digital Man '94
Dinosaurus! '60
Doc Savage '75
Dr. Alien '88
Dr. Cyclops '40
Dr. Goldfoot and the Bikini
 Machine '66
Doctor Mordrid: Master of
 the Unknown '90
Doctor Satan's Robot '40
Doctor Who '96
Donovan's Brain '53▲
Doom Runners '97
Doomsday '08
Dragon Fury '95
Dragon Fury 2 '96
Dragon Storm '04
Dune '84
Dune '00
Dune Warriors '91
Duplicates '92
Earth vs. the Flying Saucers
 '56
Earth vs. the Spider '58
Electra '95
The Electronic Monster '57
The Element of Crime '84
The Eliminators '86
Embryo '76
Empire of the Ants '77
The Empire Strikes Back
 '80▲
Encounter at Raven's Gate
 '88
End of the World '76
Endangered Species '02
Endgame '85
Endless Descent '90
Enemy Mine '85
Epoch '00
Epoch: Evolution '03
Equalizer 2000 '86
Equilibrium '02
Escape from Galaxy Three
 '81
Escape from L.A. '96
Escape from New York '81
Eve of Destruction '90
Event Horizon '97
eXistenZ '99
Expect No Mercy '95
Exterminators in the Year
 3000 '83
Eyes Behind the Stars '72
The Faculty '98
Fahrenheit 451 '66▲
Falling Fire '97
Fangs '75
Fantastic Four: Rise of the
 Silver Surfer '07
Fantastic Planet '73▲
Fantastic Voyage '66▲
Feeders '96
Femalien '96
Fiend without a Face '58
The Fifth Element '97
The Final Cut '04
Final Encounter '00
Final Equinox '95
The Final Executioner '83
The Final Programme '73
Fire in the Sky '93
Fire Maidens from Outer
 Space '56
The Fire Next Time '93
Fire Serpent '07
Firebird 2015 A.D. '81
First Encounter '97

First Man into Space '59
First Men in the Moon '64
First Spaceship on Venus
 '60▲
Flash Gordon '80
Flash Gordon Conquers the
 Universe '40
Flash Gordon: Mars Attacks
 the World '39
Flash Gordon: Rocketship
 '40
The Flesh Eaters '64
Flesh Gordon '72
Flesh Gordon 2: Flesh
 Gordon Meets the Cosmic
 Cheerleaders '90
Flight to Mars '52
The Fly '58▲
The Fly '86▲
The Fly 2 '89
The Flying Saucer '50
Forbidden Planet '56▲
Forbidden World '82
Forbidden Zone '80
Forbidden Zone: Alien
 Abduction '96
Force on Thunder Mountain
 '77
The Forgotten '04
Fortress '93
Fortress 2: Re-Entry '99
Fortress of Amerikka '89
Four Sided Triangle '53
The 4D Man '59
Frankenfish '04
Frankenstein Meets the
 Space Monster '65
Freejack '92
Frequency '00
Futuresport '98
Futurekick '91
Futuresport '98
Futureworld '76
G2: Mortal Conquest '99
Galactic Gigolo '87
Galaxis '95
Galaxy Invader '85
Galaxy of Terror '81
Game of Survival '89
Gamera, the Invincible '66
Gamera vs. Barugon '66
Gamera vs. Gaos '67
Gamera vs. Guiron '69
Gamera vs. Zigra '71
The Gamma People '56
Gangster World '98
Gappa the Trifibian Monster
 '67
Gattaca '97▲
Geisha Girl '52
Ghidrah the Three Headed
 Monster '65
Ghost Patrol '36
The Giant Claw '57
The Giant Gila Monster '59
The Giant Spider Invasion
 '75
The Gladiators '70
Glen and Randa '71
Godzilla '98
Godzilla, King of the
 Monsters '56
Godzilla 1985 '85
Godzilla Raids Again '55
Godzilla vs. Biollante '89
Godzilla vs. King Ghidora
 '91
Godzilla vs. Megalon '76
Godzilla vs. Monster Zero
 '68
Godzilla vs. Mothra '64
Godzilla vs. the Cosmic
 Monster '74
Godzilla vs. the Sea
 Monster '66
Godzilla vs. the Smog
 Monster '72
Godzilla's Revenge '69
Gorath '62
Gorgo '61

Grand Tour: Disaster in
 Time '92
The Green Slime '68
The Groundstar Conspiracy
 '72▲
The Guyver '91
Guyver 2: Dark Hero '94
H-Man '59
Habitat '97
Half Human '58
The Handmaid's Tale '90
Hands of Steel '86
Hangar 18 '80
Hardware '90
Headspace '02
Heatseeker '95
Heavy Metal 2000 '00
The Hidden '87▲
The Hidden 2 '94
Hide and Seek '77
Hideous Sun Demon '59
The High Crusade '92
High Desert Kill '90
Highlander 2: The
 Quickening '91
The Hitchhiker's Guide to
 the Galaxy '81▲
The Hitchhiker's Guide to
 the Galaxy '05▲
Hollow Man 2 '06
Hollywood Boulevard 2 '89
Hologram Man '95
Homewrecker '92
Horrors of the Red Planet
 '64
Howl's Moving Castle '04
The Human Duplicators '64
Humanoid Defender '85
Hybrid '97
Hyper-Sapien: People from
 Another Star '86
Hyper Space '89
I Am Legend '07▲
I Come in Peace '90
I Married a Monster '98
I Married a Monster from
 Outer Space '58
I, Robot '04
Iceman '84▲
Idaho Transfer '73
The Illustrated Man '69▲
Immortal '04
In the Aftermath: Angels
 Never Sleep '87
In the Cold of the Night '89
In the Dead of Space '99
Incredible Melting Man '77
The Incredible Petrified
 World '58
The Incredible Shrinking
 Man '57▲
Independence Day '96▲
Infra-Man '76
Inhumanoid '96
Innerspace '87
Inseminoid '80
Interzone '88
Intruder Within '81
Intruders '92
Invader '91
The Invader '96
The Invaders '95
Invaders from Mars '53
Invaders from Mars '86
Invasion '65
Invasion: Earth '98
Invasion Earth: The Aliens
 Are Here! '87
Invasion of the Animal
 People '62
Invasion of the Bee Girls
 '73▲
Invasion of the Body
 Snatchers '56▲
Invasion of the Body
 Snatchers '78▲
Invasion of the Body
 Stealers '69
Invasion of the Girl
 Snatchers '73
Invasion of the Space
 Preachers '90
Invisible Adversaries '77
The Invisible Boy '57
Invisible Invaders '59
The Invisible Man Returns
 '40▲
The Invisible Terror '63

Invisible: The Chronicles of
 Benjamin Knight '93
Isaac Asimov's Nightfall '00
The Island '05
Island of Terror '66▲
Island of the Burning
 Doomed '67
Island of the Lost '68
It Came from Beneath the
 Sea '55▲
It Came from Outer Space
 '53▲
It Came from Outer Space 2
 '95
It Conquered the World '56
It! The Terror from Beyond
 Space '58
It's All About Love '03
Jason X '01
Johnny 2.0 '99
Josh Kirby... Time Warrior:
 Chapter 6, Last Battle for
 the Universe '96
Journey Beneath the Desert
 '61
Journey to the Center of the
 Earth '59▲
Journey to the Center of the
 Earth '88
Journey to the Center of
 Time '67
Journey to the Far Side of
 the Sun '69▲
Jumper '08
Kaena: The Prophecy '03
Killers from Space '54
The Killing Edge '86
Killings at Outpost Zeta '80
King Dinosaur '55
King Kong '05▲
King Kong vs. Godzilla '63
The Kirlian Witness '78
Knights '93
Kronos '57
Krull '83
Kurt Vonnegut's Harrison
 Bergeron '95
Laboratory '80
The Land That Time Forgot
 '75
The Land Unknown '57
The Lathe of Heaven '80
The Lathe of Heaven '02
The Lawless Land '88
The Lawnmower Man '92
Lawnmower Man 2: Beyond
 Cyberspace '95
Legion '98
Leprechaun 4: In Space '96
Lethal Dose '03
Leviathan '89
Lifeforce '85
Lifeform '96
Lifepod '80
Lifepod '93
Light Years '88
Liquid Sky '83▲
The Living Dead '33
Lobster Man from Mars '89
Lock 'n' Load '90
Logan's Run '76
Lolida 2000 '97
Looker '81
Lords of the Deep '89
The Lost Empire '83
Lost in Space '98
The Lost Missile '58
Lost Planet Airmen '49
The Lucifer Complex '78
Making Mr. Right '86
A Man Called Rage '84
The Man from Atlantis '77
The Man from Planet X '51
The Man Who Fell to Earth
 '76▲
Mandroid '93

Manhunt of Mystery Island
 '45
Maniac Warriors '88
The Manster '59
Marooned '69
Mars '96
Mars Attacks! '96
Mars Needs Women '66
The Martian Chronicles:
 Part 1 '79
The Martian Chronicles:
 Part 2 '79
The Martian Chronicles:
 Part 3 '79
Masters of Venus '62
The Matrix '99▲
The Matrix Reloaded '03▲
The Matrix Revolutions '03▲
Meet the Hollowheads '89
Meet the Robinsons '07
Megaforce '82
Megalodon '03
Megaville '91
Mesa of Lost Women '52
Metallica '85
Metalstorm: The Destruction
 of Jared Syn '83
Metamorphosis '90
Metropolis '26▲
Millennium '89
Mimic '97
Mind Snatchers '72
Mind Trap '91
Mind Warp '72
Mindwarp '91
Minority Report '02▲
Misfits of Science '85
Missile to the Moon '59
Mission Galactica: The
 Cylon Attack '79
Mission Mars '67
Mission Stardust '68
Mistress of the World '59
The Mole People '56
Momentum '03
Monkey Boy '90
Monolith '93
The Monolith Monsters '57
Monster a Go-Go! '65
Monster from Green Hell '58
Monster from the Ocean
 Floor '54
The Monster Maker '44
The Monster of Piedras
 Blancas '57
Monster on the Campus '59
The Monster That
 Challenged the World '57
Moon 44 '90
Moon Pilot '62
Moontrap '89
Moontrap '97
Mortal Challenge '97
Mosquito '95
Mothra '62▲
Murder by Moonlight '91
Murder in Space '85
Mutant Hunt '87
Mutant Species '95
Mutator '90
The Mysterians '58
Mysterious Island '61▲
Mysterious Two '82
Mystery Science Theater
 3000: The Movie '96
Naked Souls '95
Navy vs. the Night Monsters
 '66
Nemesis '93
Nemesis 2: Nebula '94
Nemesis 3: Time Lapse '96
Nemesis 4: Cry of Angels
 '97
Neon City '91
The Nest '88
Neutron and the Black Mask
 '61
Neutron vs. the Amazing Dr.
 Caronte '61
Neutron vs. the Death
 Robots '62
New Crime City: Los
 Angeles 2020 '94
New Eden '94
The New Gladiators '83
The New Invisible Man '58
Next One '84
Night Beast '83

Night Caller from Outer
 Space '66
Night of the Blood Beast '58
Night of the Lepus '72
Nightfall '88
Nightflyers '87
1984 '56▲
1984 '84▲
No Survivors, Please '63
Norman's Awesome
 Experience '88
Not Like Us '96
Not of This Earth '88
Not of This Earth '96
Nude on the Moon '61
Oblivion '94
Octaman '71
Official Denial '93
Omega Doom '96
Omega Man '71
On the Comet '68▲
One Million B.C. '40
The Original Fabulous
 Adventures of Baron
 Munchausen '61
The Outer Limits: Sandkings
 '95▲
Outland '81▲
The P.A.C.K. '96
Paprika '06
Parasite '82
Parasite '03
Past Perfect '97▲
Peacemaker '90
The People '71
The People That Time
 Forgot '77
People Who Own the Dark
 '75
The Phantom Empire '35
Phantom from Space '53
The Phantom from 10,000
 Leagues '56
The Phantom Planet '61
Phase 4 '74
The Philadelphia
 Experiment '84
Philadelphia Experiment 2
 '93
Phoenix '95
Pitch Black '00▲
Plan 9 from Outer Space '56
Plan 10 from Outer Space
 '95
Planet Burg '62
Planet Earth '74
Planet of Blood '66
Planet of the Apes '68▲
Planet of the Apes '01▲
Planet of the Dinosaurs '80
Planet of the Vampires '65
Planet on the Prowl '65
Planets Against Us '61
Plughead Rewired: Circuitry
 Man 2 '94
The Postman '97
The Power Within '79
Precious Find '96
Predator '87
Predator 2 '90
Prehistoric Women '50
Primal Impulse '74
Primal Scream '87
Primer '04▲
Prisoners of the Lost
 Universe '84
The Professor '58
Progeny '98
Programmed to Kill '86
Prototype '83▲
Prototype X29A '92
PSI Factor '80
The Psychotronic Man '91
Pulse '88
The Puma Man '80
The Puppet Masters '94
The Purple Monster Strikes
 '45

▲ = rated three bones or higher

Purple People Eater '88
Puzzlehead '05
Quarantine '89
Quarantine 2 '57▶
Quatermass and the Pit '58
Quatermass Conclusion '79
The Quatermass Experiment '56▶
Queen of Outer Space '58
Quest for Love '71
The Quiet Earth '85▶
Quintet '79
Race Against Time '00
Radar Men from the Moon '52
Radioactive Dreams '86
Raiders of Atlantis '33
Rats '83
Ravager '97
Razorteeth '05
Reactor '85
Rebel Storm '90
Rebirth of Mothra '96
Rebirth of Mothra 2 '97
Red Planet Mars '52
Redline '97
Remote Control '88
Replikator: Cloned to Kill '94
Reptilian '99
Reptilicus '62
Resident Evil: Apocalypse '04
Resident Evil: Extinction '07
Resistance '92
Resurrection of Zachary Wheeler '71
The Return '80
Return from Witch Mountain '78
Return of Chandu '34
The Return of Swamp Thing '89
Return of the Aliens: The Deadly Spawn '83
Return of the Fly '59
Return of the Jedi '83▶
Return to Frogtown '92
Revenge of the Teenage Vixens from Outer Space '86
Revenge Quest '96
Riding with Death '76
Robin Cook's Invasion '97
Robinson Crusoe on Mars '64
Robo-Chic '89
Robo Warriors '96
Robot Holocaust '87
Robot Jox '90
Roboman '75
Robot Monster '53
Robot Stories '03
Robots '05
Rock & Roll Cowboys '92
Rocket Attack U.S.A. '58
Rocketship '36
Rocketship X-M '50
Rocky Jones, Space Ranger: Renegade Satellite '54
Roller Blade '85
Roller Blade Warriors: Taken By Force '90
Rollerball '75
Rollerball '02
The Rook '99
R.O.T.O.R. '88
Runaway '84
Running Against Time '90
Running Delilah '93
The Running Man '87
Rush '84
Saturn 3 '80
Savage '96
Scanner Cop '94
Scanner Cop 2: Volkin's Revenge '94
A Scanner Darkly '06
Sci-Fighters '04
Scorpio One '97
Scream and Scream Again '70
Screamers '96
The Sea Serpent '86
Search and Destroy '88

The Secret of the Golden Eagle '91
The Secret of the Telegian '61
The Sender '98
Serenity '05▶
Shadow Warriors '95
Shadowzone '89
She '83
Shepherd '99
The Silencers '95
Silent Running '71▶
The Sisterhood '88
Skeeter '93
Sky Captain and the World of Tomorrow '04
Sky Pirates '87
Slaughterhouse Five '72
Slave Girls from Beyond Infinity '87
The Slime People '63
Slipstream '89
Solar Crisis '92
Solar Force '94
Solarbabies '86
Solaris '72
Solaris '02
Son of Godzilla '66
A Sound of Thunder '05
Soylent Green '73
Space Marines '96
Space Monster '64
Space Mutiny '88
Space: 1999—Alien Attack '79▶
Space Rage '86
Space Raiders '83
Space Soldiers Conquer the Universe '40
Space Truckers '97
SpaceCamp '86
Spaced Invaders '90
Spacehunter: Adventures in the Forbidden Zone '83
Spacejacked '98
Spaceship '81
Species '95
Species 2 '98
Specimen '97
Sphere '97
Split '90
Split Second '92
Spoiler '98
Sputnik '61
Stalker '79▶
Star Crash '78
Star Crystal '85
Star Knight '85
Star Portal '97
Star Quest '89
Star Quest '94
Star Slammer '87
Star Trek: The Motion Picture '79
Star Trek 2: The Wrath of Khan '82▶
Star Trek 3: The Search for Spock '84
Star Trek 4: The Voyage Home '86▶
Star Trek 5: The Final Frontier '89
Star Trek 6: The Undiscovered Country '91
Star Trek: First Contact '96▶
Star Trek: Generations '94▶
Star Trek: Insurrection '98
Star Trek: Nemesis '02
Star Wars '77▶
Star Wars: Episode 1—The Phantom Menace '99▶
Starchaser: The Legend of Orin '85
Starflight One '83
Stargate '94
Stargate: The Ark of Truth '08
Starman '84▶
Starship '97
Starship Invasions '77
Starship Troopers '97▶
Steamboy '05
Steel and Lace '90
Steel Frontier '94
The Stepford Wives '04

Stephen King's The Langoliers '95
Storm Trooper '98
Stranded '87
Strange New World '75
The Stranger from Venus '54
Strangers in Paradise '84
Stryker '83
Sun Ra & His Intergalactic Solar Arkestra: Space Is the Place '74
Sunshine '07
Super Force '90
Superman Returns '06
Survival Zone '84
The Survivor '98
Survivor '87
Suspect Device '95
Swamp Thing '82
Synapse '90
Syngenor '90
T-Force '94
Taken '02
Tales from a Parallel Universe: Eating Pattern '97
Tales from a Parallel Universe: Giga Shadow '97
Tales from a Parallel Universe: I Worship His Shadow '97
Tales from a Parallel Universe: Super Nova '97
Tarantula '55▶
A Taste for Flesh and Blood '90
Teen Alien '78
Teenage Caveman '58
Teenage Monster '57
Teenagers from Outer Space '59
TekWar '94
10th Victim '65▶
Terminal Error '02
Terminal Impact '95
Terminal Justice: Cybertech P.D. '95
The Terminal Man '74
Terminal Virus '96
The Terminator '84▶
Terminator 2: Judgment Day '91▶
Terminator 3: Rise of the Machines '03▶
Terror Beneath the Sea '66
Terror Is a Man '59
Terror of Mechagodzilla '78
The Terror Within '88
The Terror Within 2 '91
The Terronauts '67
Test Tube Teens from the Year 2000 '93
Tetsuo: The Iron Man '92
Tetsuo 2: Body Hammer '97
Them! '54▶
They '77
They Came from Beyond Space '67
The Thing '51▶
The Thing '82
Things to Come '36▶
This Is Not a Test '62
This Island Earth '55
Those Fantastic Flying Fools '67
The Three Worlds of Gulliver '59
Thunderbirds '04
THX 1138 '71▶
Ticks '93
Time After Time '79▶
Time Chasers '95
The Time Guardian '87
The Time Machine '60▶
The Time Machine '78
Time Runner '92
Time Tracers '97
Time Trackers '88
Time Travelers '64
Time Troopers '89
Time Walker '82
Timecop '94
Timecop 2: The Berlin Decision '03
Timelock '99

Timemaster '95
Timerider '83
Timestalkers '87
Tin Man '07
Tobor the Great '54
Total Recall '90
Total Recall 2070: Machine Dreams '99
Toward the Terra '80
A Town Has Turned to Dust '98
Trancers '84
Trancers 2: The Return of Jack Deth '90
Trancers 3: Deth Lives '92
Trancers 4: Jack of Swords '93
Trancers 5: Sudden Deth '94
Transatlantic Tunnel '35
Transformations '88
Trapped in Space '94
The Trial of the Incredible Hulk '89
Tripods: The White Mountains '84
Trcn '82
The Trouble with Dick '88
12 Monkeys '95▶
12:01 '93
2069: A Sex Odyssey '78
UFO: Target Earth '74
Ufoia '81
The Ultimate Warrior '75
Ultraviolet '06
Undersea Kingdom '36
The Unearthly Stranger '64
Unknown Origin '95
Unknown World '51
Unnatural '52
Until the End of the World '91▶
Urban Menace '99
V '83▶
V: The Final Battle '84
The Valley of Gwangi '69▶
Vampire Vixens from Venus '94
Vampirella '96
Vegas in Space '94
Velocity Trap '99
Venus Rising '95
Village of the Damned '60▶
Village of the Damned '95
Village of the Giants '65
Virtual Assassin '95
Virtual Combat '95
Virtual Seduction '96
Virtuosity '95
Virus '82
Virus '98
Vistants '87
The Void '01
Voyage of the Rock Aliens '87
Voyage to the Bottom of the Sea '61▶
Voyage to the Planet of Prehistoric Women '68
Voyage to the Prehistoric Planet '65
War in Space '77
The War of the Colossal Beast '58
War of the Gargantuas '70
War of the Wizards '83
The War of the Worlds '53▶
Warlords '88
Warlords of the 21st Century '82
Warning from Space '56
Warrior of the Lost World '84
Waterworld '95
Wavelength '83
Waxwork 2: Lost in Time '91
Webmaster '98
Weird Science '85▶
Welcome Back Mr. Fox '83

Wes Craven Presents Mind Ripper '95
Westworld '73▶
What Waits Below '83
When Dinosaurs Ruled the Earth '70
When Time Expires '97
When Time Began '77
When Worlds Collide '51▶
White Dwarf '95
White Palms '93
Wicked City '92
Wild, Wild Planet '65
A Wind Named Amnesia '93
Wing Commander '99
Wired to Kill '86
Within the Rock '96
Woman in the Moon '29
The Womaneater '59
Women of the Prehistoric Planet '66
World Gone Wild '88
Xtro '83
Xtro 2: The Second Encounter '91
Xtro 3: Watch the Skies '95
X from Outer Space '67
X: The Man with X-Ray Eyes '63▶
Xchange '00▶
The X-Files '98
The X-Files: I Want to Believe '08
The Yesterday Machine '63
Yesterday's Target '96
Yongkari Monster of the Deep '67
Zardoz '74
Zarkorr! The Invader '96
Zeram '91
Zeram 2 '94
Zero Population Growth '72
Zeta One '69
Zombies of the Stratosphere '52
Zone 39 '96
Zone Troopers '84
Zontar, the Thing from Venus '66

Sci-Fi Westerns
see also Sci Fi:
Supernatural Westerns;
Westerns
Back to the Future, Part 3 '90▶
Backlash: Oblivion 2 '95
Battle Beyond the Stars '80
Ghost Patrol '36
Human Gorilla '48
Neon City '91
Oblivion '94
Outland '81▶
The Phantom Empire '35
Teenage Monster '57
Welcome to Blood City '77
Westworld '73▶

Science & Scientists
see also Genetics;
Inventors & Inventions;
Mad Scientists
After Innocence '05
Agent Cody Banks '03
The Alien Agenda: Under the Skin '97
Alien Nation: Body and Soul '95
Alien: Resurrection '97▶
Alien vs. Predator '04
Altered States '80▶
Android '82
The Andromeda Strain '71
Around the World Under the Sea '65
Arrowsmith '32
Assassin '86
The Atomic City '52
The Atomic Man '56
Attack of the Robots '66
Beach Party '63
A Beautiful Mind '01▶
Bombshell '97
A Brief History of Time '92▶
Brotherhood of the Wolf '01
A Bullet for Joey '55

Caravan to Vaccares '74
Chain Reaction '96
Children of the Damned '63
Chill Factor '99
Com '02
Contact '97▶
The Core '03
Cybermutt '02
The Dallas Connection '94
Dam Busters '55▶
Darkman '90▶
Dark Star '74▶
The Darwin Conspiracy '99
The Day After Tomorrow '04
The Day of the Dolphin '73
Dead Men Don't Wear Plaid '82
The Dead Next Door '89
Deadly Friend '86
Deadly Outbreak '96
Deep Blue Sea '99
Deep Core '00
Demon Seed '77▶
Dick Barton, Special Agent '48
Die Laughing '80
Die, Monster, Die! '55
Dirty Games '89
The Dish '00▶
Doctor Dolittle '67
Dr. Alien '88
Dr. Jekyll and Ms. Hyde '95
Dragon Fury 2 '96
Eight Below '06
Electra '95
The Eliminators '86
Evolution '01
Fantastic Voyage '66▶
Fat Man and Little Boy '89
The Fly '58▶
The Fly '86▶
The Fly 2 '89
Forbidden World '82
Forever Darling '56
Four Sided Triangle '53
The 4D Man '59
From the Earth to the Moon '58
Gattaca '97▶
Geheimakte WB1 '42
Glory Enough for All: The Discovery of Insulin '92
Habitat '97
The Henderson Monster '80
How to Make a Doll '68
Hulk '03
Human Nature '02
Humanoid Defender '85
Illegal Entry: Formula for Fear '93
Illumination '73
An Inconvenient Truth '06▶
Infinity '96
International House '33
The Invisible Man Returns '40▶
I.Q. '94
The Lister '04▶
Journey to the Center of the Earth 3D '08
Jurassic Park '93▶
Jurassic Park 2: Jurassic Park 2 '97
Kate & Leopold '01
Kinsey '04▶
Kitchen Stories '03
Last Day of the War '69
Laughing at Danger '24
Lifeform '96
Link '86
A Little Bit of Soul '97
The Lost World '97
The Lost World: Jurassic Park 2 '97
Love Potion #3 '92
Magma: Volcanic Disaster '06
The Man with Two Brains '83▶
Mary Reilly '96
Medicine Man '92
Mimic '97
Miracle Mile '89▶
Mr. Superinvisible '73

Science

Monkey Boy '90
Monkey Business '52▶
Monkey's Uncle '65
Mosquitoman '05
My Science Project '85
My Stepmother Is an Alien '88
Nautilus '99
Neptune Factor '73
October Sky '99▶
Outbreak '94▶
Pete's Meteor '98
Phantom Empire '87
Project X '87
Prototype X29A '92
The Quiet Earth '85▶
Real Genius '85▶
The Reaping '07
The Relic '96
Return of Captain Invincible '83
Return of the Ape Man '44
Return of the Fly '59
The Rocky Horror Picture Show '75▶
The Saint '97
The Secret of the Telegian '61
Senseless '98
The Sex Machine '75
Shaker Run '85
Shakma '89
Simon '80
Sir Arthur Conan Doyle's The Lost World '98
Smilla's Sense of Snow '96
Son of Flubber '63
A Sound of Thunder '05
Spaceways '53
Species '95
Sphere '97
Stephen King's Golden Years '91
The Story of Louis Pasteur '36▶
The Structure of Crystals '69
Sub Down '97
Sunshine '07
Surf 2 '84
Swamp Thing '82
Tarantula '55▶
The Thing '82
Things to Come '36▶
This Island Earth '55
Threshold '83
Tidal Wave '75
Time Trackers '88
The Time Travelers '64
Timeline '03
Tomcat: Dangerous Desires '93
12:01 '93
Ultraviolet '98
Unforgettable '96
Unknown Island '48
Unknown World '51
Virus '98
The Void '01
What the $*! Do We Know? '04
Where Time Began '77
The Wild and the Free '80
Woman in the Dunes '64▶
Yes '04
The Yesterday Machine '63

Scotland

see also Edinburgh; Glasgow

Aberdeen '00
The Acid House '98
Another Time, Another Place '83▶
Behind the Lines '97
Beneath Loch Ness '01
The Big Man: Crossing the Line '91▶
Blood Clan '91
Bonnie Prince Charlie '48
Bonnie Scotland '35
Braveheart '95▶
Breaking the Waves '95▶
Brigadoon '54▶
The Bruce '96
Challenge to Lassie '49
Chasing the Deer '94
Deacon Brodie '98

Dear Frankie '04▶
Devil Girl from Mars '54
The Devil's Undead '75
Dr. Bell and Mr. Doyle: The Dark Beginnings of Sherlock Holmes '00
Dog Soldiers '01
Dragonworld '94
Dreams Lost, Dreams Found '87
Entrapment '99
Escape '90
The Flying Scotsman '06
The Gospel According to Vic '87
The Governess '98
Gregory's Girl '80▶
Greystoke: The Legend of Tarzan, Lord of the Apes '84
Happy Go Lovely '51
Highlander: Endgame '00
I Know Where I'm Going '45▶
Incident at Loch Ness '04▶
Joyeux Noel '05▶
Kidnapped '95
Kidnapped '05▶
Lady of the Lake '28
The Last Musketeer '00
Little Minister '34▶
Local Hero '83▶
Loch Ness '95
Made of Honor '08
Madeleine '50
Mary of Scotland '36▶
Mary, Queen of Scots '71
The Master of Ballantrae '53
The Match '99
Morvern Callar '02
My Life So Far '98
One More Kiss '99
The Pointsman '86
Pride of the Clan '18
Ratcatcher '99
Ring of Bright Water '69▶
Rob Roy '95▶
Rob Roy—The Highland Rogue '53
St. Ives '98
The Secret of the Loch '34
A Shot at Glory '00
Sweet Sixteen '02
This Is Not a Love Song '02
The Three Lives of Thomasina '63▶
Tragedy of Flight 103: The Inside Story '91▶
Trouble in the Glen '54
Urban Ghost Story '98
The Water Horse: Legend of the Deep '07
When Eight Bells Toll '71
Whiskey Galore '48▶
Wilbur Wants to Kill Himself '02▶
Year of the Comet '92
Young Adam '03▶

Screwball Comedy

see also Comedy; Romantic Comedy; Slapstick Comedy

All in a Night's Work '61
Amazing Adventure '37
Ambassador Bill '31
America '86
And Baby Makes Six '79
Antonio '73
Argentine Nights '40
As You Like It '36
As You Were '51
Assault at the Party Nerds '89
Attention Shoppers '99
Auntie '73
The Awful Truth '37▶
The Baby and the Battleship '56
The Bachelor and the Bobby-Soxer '47
Bachelor Mother '39▶
Bachelor of Hearts '58
Back to School '86
Bank Shot '74▶
Bedazzled '68▶
Bedtime Story '63

Beer '85
Big Brown Eyes '36
Big Business '88
Blame It on the Bellboy '92
The Bliss of Mrs. Blossom '68▶
Blue Murder at St. Trinian's '56▶
Boeing Boeing '65
The Break-Up '06
Bringing Down the House '03
Bringing Up Baby '38▶
Bullseye! '90
Buona Sera, Mrs. Campbell '68
Camp Cucamonga: How I Spent My Summer Vacation '90
Carry On Admiral '57
The Chaplin Revue '58
Charlie Chaplin: Night at the Show '15
Charlie Chaplin... Our Hero! '15▶
Christmas in the Clouds '01
The Circus '19▶
Combat Academy '86
Connie and Carla '04
The Couch Trip '87
The Count '16
Crackers '84
Days of Thrills and Laughter '61▶
Doctor in the House '53▶
Dr. Otto & the Riddle of the Gloom Beam '86
Doctor Takes a Wife '40▶
Don Juan, My Love '90
Double Wedding '37▶
Doubting Thomas '35
Down Among the Z Men '52
Down the Drain '89
Easy Living '37
Easy Money '83
Easy Street '16▶
Egg and I '47▶
El Matador '03
Everything You Always Wanted to Know about Sex (But Were Afraid to Ask) '72▶
The Family Stone '05
The Favor, the Watch, & the Very Big Fish '92
Fireballs '90
The Fireman '16
Fit for a King '37
The Floorwalker '17▶
Forces of Nature '99
Forever Darling '56
Forsaking All Others '35
The Gay Deceivers '69
The Geisha Boy '58
Get Crazy '83
Gray Matters '06
Hands Across the Table '35▶
A Hard Day's Night '64▶
Harvey '50▶
Her Husband's Affairs '47
He's My Girl '87
Holiday '38▶
How Sweet It Is! '68
I Heart Huckabees '04▶
I Love My... Wife '70
I Love You Again '40▶
Inspector Hornleigh '39
Intolerable Cruelty '03▶
Italian Straw Hat '27▶
It's the Old Army Game '26
Joy of Living '38▶
La Chevre '81▶
Labyrinth of Passion '82
The Lady Eve '41▶
The Lady Man '00
Laws of Attraction '04
Leatherheads '08
Libeled Lady '36▶
A Life Less Ordinary '97
Life Stinks '91
Lobster Man from Mars '89
The Long, Long Trailer '54▶
Lots of Luck '85
The Love Bug '68
Love Crazy '41▶
Lucky Partners '40
Lunatics & Lovers '76

Madhouse '90
The Major and the Minor '42▶
Make Mine Mink '60▶
Malibu Beach '78
Malibu Bikini Shop '86
The Marriage Circle '24▶
Marriage on the Rocks '65
The Marx Brothers in a Nutshell '90▶
The Mating Game '59▶
Me and Him '89
Meatballs 2 '84
Meet the Parents '00▶
A Midsummer Night's Sex Comedy '82▶
Miracle of Morgan's Creek '44▶
Mr. & Mrs. Smith '41▶
Modern Girls '86
The Money Pit '86
Monkey Business '52▶
Monkeys, Go Home! '66
The Moon's Our Home '36
The More the Merrier '43▶
Morons from Outer Space '85
Mugsy's Girls '85
The Munsters' Revenge '81
My American Cousin '85▶
My Chauffeur '86
My Favorite Brunette '47▶
My Favorite Wife '40▶
My Man Godfrey '36▶
My Mother Likes Women '02
Naked Is Better '73
National Lampoon's Christmas Vacation '89
National Lampoon's Christmas Vacation 2: Cousin Eddie's Big Island Adventure '03
National Lampoon's European Vacation '85▶
National Lampoon's Vacation '83▶
Nervous Ticks '93
No Vacancy '99
Noises Off '92
Not for Publication '84
Nothing Sacred '37▶
The Nude Bomb '80
Ollie Hopnoodle's Haven of Bliss '88
One Woman or Two '85
The Palm Beach Story '42▶
Pink Flamingos '72
Platinum Blonde '31▶
Police Academy 3: Back in Training '86
Polyester '81
Reaching for the Moon '17
Recruits '86
The Rink '16▶
Romance with a Double Bass '74▶
Running Wild '27
The Saddest Music in the World '03
See No Evil, Hear No Evil '89
Shoot or Be Shot '02
Simon '80
The Smallest Show on Earth '57▶
Social Intercourse '01
Some Like It Hot '59▶
Somewhere in the City '97
A Southern Yankee '48
Spaced Invaders '90
Spring Break '83
Starhops '78
Start the Revolution without Me '70▶
The Statue '71
Stewardess School '86
Still Not Quite Human '92
Stir Crazy '80
Stitches '85
Stroker Ace '83
Stuckey's Last Stand '80
Student Affairs '88
The Student Teachers '73
Summer School Teachers '75
Superdad '73
Supergrass '87
Swap Meet '79

Sweet Revenge '90
Sweet Young Thing '79
Swing It, Sailor! '37
The Swinging Cheerleaders '74
Switching Channels '88
Talk of the Town '42▶
Teen Vamp '88
Teen Witch '89
Tell It to the Judge '49
That Naughty Girl '58
They Went That-a-Way & That-a-Way '78
Three in the Cellar '70
Thunder & Mud '89
Tigers in Lipstick '80
Tricks of the Trade '88
Truck Stop
Twin Beds '42
Twist '76
Two Weeks to Live '43
The Underachievers '88
The Vagabond '16
Vibes '88
Vice Versa '88▶
Waitress '81
Waltz of the Toreadors '62▶
Watch the Birdie '50
Wedding Present '36
What's Up, Doc? '72▶
When Women Had Tails '70
When Women Lost Their Tails '75
Where Were You When the Lights Went Out? '68
Which Way Is Up? '77
Whoops Apocalypse '83
Who's That Girl? '87
Wild Women of Wongo '59
Wonder Boys '00▶
World's Greatest Lover '77
You Can't Cheat an Honest Man '39▶
You Can't Take It with You '38▶
Zotz! '62

Scuba

see also Deep Blue

The Abyss '89▶
Beneath the 12-Mile Reef '53
The Big Blue '88
The Cave '05
Daring Game '68
The Deep '77
Easy Come, Easy Go '67
The Evil Below '87
ffolkes '80
Flipper '63▶
Flipper's New Adventure '64▶
Fool's Gold '08
Full Fathom Five '90
Into the Blue '05
Isle of Forgotten Sins '43
Leviathan '89
The Life Aquatic with Steve Zissou '04
Men of Honor '00
Navy SEALS '90
Neptune Factor '73
Never Say Never Again '83
Night of the Sharks '87
Oceans of Fire '86
Open Water '03▶
The Sea Serpent '85
Thunderball '65
The Treasure Seekers '79
Underwater! '55

Sculptors

see also Art & Artists

The Agony and the Ecstasy '65
Before and After '95
A Bucket of Blood '59▶
Camille Claudel '89▶
Fly Away Home '96▶
House of Wax '53▶
The Juror '96
The Silver Chalice '54
The Song of Songs '33

Sea Disasters

see also Air Disasters; Deep Blue; Disaster Flicks; Shipwrecked

The Abyss '89▶
Airport 77 '77
Beyond the Poseidon Adventure '79
Das Boot '81▶
Deep Rising '98
Deepstar Six '89
Far from Home: The Adventures of Yellow Dog '94
The Fog '05
The Ghost Ship '43
Goliath Awaits '81
Juggernaut '74▶
K-19: The Widowmaker '02
The Last Voyage '60
Leviathan '89
Men of Honor '00
A Night to Remember '58▶
Open Water '03▶
Poseidon '06
The Poseidon Adventure '72
Raise the Titanic '80
The Seducers '70
S.O.S. Titanic '79
Souls at Sea '37
Titanic '53▶
Titanic '97▶
The Unsinkable Molly Brown '64▶
Waterworld '95

Seattle

Agent Cody Banks '03
Bombs Away! '86
Boy Culture '06
Breaking Point '94
Dead in a Heartbeat '02
The Diary of Ellen Rimbauer '03
Dream Man '94
88 Minutes '08
Georgia '95▶
Greenmail '01
A Guy Thing '03
The Heart of the Game '05
The Hitman '91
It Happened at the World's Fair '63
The Last Mimzy '07
Life or Something Like It '02
Little Buddha '93
Lucky Seven '03
My Own Private Idaho '91▶
Ray '04▶
Shattered Image '98
Singles '92▶
Slaves to the Underground '96
Sleepless in Seattle '93▶
The Slender Thread '65▶
Stakeout '87
Streetwise '84▶
Things We Lost in the Fire '07
Thr3e '07

Second Chance

Audrey's Rain '03
Before Sunset '04▶
Chances Are '89▶
Gridiron Gang '06
Hell's Kitchen NYC '97
Hope Ranch '02
Hysterical Blindness '02
If Only '04
Leo '02
Levity '03
Life as a House '01
A Little Inside '01
Lord Jim '65▶
Mr. Destiny '90
Mr. 3000 '04
Once Upon a Time in the Midlands '02
Place Vendome '98▶
The Princess and the Warrior '00▶
The Rookie '02▶
Seventeen Again '00
Snapshots '02
Solaris '02

Secret Service

see also Capitol Capers; Funny Money

Absolute Power '97
Agent of Death '99
Air Force One '97▶
Along Came a Spider '01
Assassination '87
Avenging Force '86
Boiling Point '93
Chain of Command '00
Chasing Liberty '04
Counterstrike '03
Dave '93▶
D.E.B.S. '04
End Game '06
First Daughter '99
First Daughter '04
First Kid '96
Guarding Tess '94
Hackers '95
Holt of the Secret Service '42
In the Line of Fire '93▶
The Interpreter '05▶
Kelly of the Secret Service '36
The Kidnapping of the President '80
The League of Extraordinary Gentlemen '03
Mach 2 '00
Murder at 1600 '97
Raiders of Ghost City '44
The Restless Breed '58
The Sentinel '06
The Silencers '95
Spartan '04▶
T-Men '47▶
To Live & Die in L.A. '85
Under the Rainbow '81
Vantage Point '08
They Never Come Back '32
Unshackled '00

Serial Killers

see also Crime & Criminals; Crime Sprees

Addams Family Values '93
Addicted to Murder '95
Addicted to Murder 2: Tainted Blood '97
Addicted to Murder 3: Bloodlust '99
Aileen: Life and Death of a Serial Killer '03▶
A Demon in My View '92
Along Came a Spider '01
Ambition '91
American Girl '02
American Nightmare '00
American Psycho '99
American Psycho 2: All American Girl '02
American Strays '96
American Streetfighter 2: The Full Impact '97
Amsterdamned '88
Angel Dust '96
Angel of Death '02
Antibodies '05
The Apostate '98
Aroused '66
Art School Confidential '06
Asylum '97
The Awful Dr. Orloff '62
The Baby Doll Murders '92
Band of Gold '95▶
The Banker '89
Beyond Redemption '99
Black & White '99
The Black Belly of the Tarantula '71
Blackwater Trail '95
Blondes Have More Guns '95
Blood Work '02
Bloodhounds 2 '96
Bloodmoon '97
Bloodstream '00
Bloody Proof '99▶
Blowback '00
Bluebeard '63
Body Parts '91
The Bone Collector '99
Border Patrol '01
The Boston Strangler '68
Bound by Lies '05
Breaking Point '94
Bride of Chucky '04
The Bride of Frank '96
Brigham City '01
Broken Mirrors '85
BTK Killer '06
Burns '93
Butterfly Kiss '94
Cabin by the Lake '00
Captivity '07
Carolina Moon '07
The Cell '00
Chaos '05
Cherry Falls '00
The China Lake Murders '90
Citizen X '95▶
Clay Pigeons '98
Close Your Eyes '02
Closer and Closer '96
Club Dread '04
Cold Blooded '00
Cold Front '89
Cold Light of Day '95
Con Air '97▶
Confessions of a Serial Killer '87
Cop '88
Copycat '95
The Coroner '98
Cosh Boy '61
The Crimson Code '99
Cronicas '04
Cruel and Unusual '01
Curdled '95
Cyberstalker '96
Dahmer '02
Dancing with Danger '93
Dangerous Love '87
Dark Asylum '01
Dark Corners '05
The Dark Ride '84
The Darwin Awards '06
Dead Certain '92
Dead Evidence '00
Dead Girls '90
Dead on Sight '94
Dead to Rights '93
Deadly Force '83
Deadly Games '80
Deadly Neighbor '91
Decay '98
The Deliberate Stranger '86▶
Delivered '98
Desire '95
Destroyer '88
Diary of a Serial Killer '97
Dirt Boy '01
Dirty Harry '71▶
Disturbia '07
Dot.Kill '05
Double Vision '02
Ed Gein '01
88 Minutes '08
The Element of Crime '84
Endangered Species '02
Evil Laugh '86
Evil Obsession '96
Exorcist 3: Legion '90
Eye of the Beholder '99
Eye of the Killer '99
Eye See You '01
Eyes of a Stranger '81
Eyes of Laura Mars '78
Eyes of the Beholder '92
Fallen '97
Fallen Angel '99
Fatal Charm '92
Fathers and Sons '92
The Fear: Halloween Night '99
Feardotcom '02
Felicia's Journey '99▶
Final Combination '93
Final Move '06
Final Notice '89
The First Power '89
Frailty '02▶
Freeway '95
Freeway 2: Confessions of a Trickbaby '99
The Freeway Maniac '88
Frequency '00
The Frighteners '96
Ghost in the Machine '93
The Girl Who Knew Too Much '63
The Glimmer Man '96
The Gunman '03
Hangman '00
Hannibal '01
The Hawk '93
Heartaches '47
Henry: Portrait of a Serial Killer '90▶
Henry: Portrait of a Serial Killer 2: Mask of Sanity '96
Hidden Obsession '92
Hideaway '94
Highwaymen '03
The Hills Have Eyes '06
The Hillside Strangler '89
The Hillside Strangler '04
Honeymoon Killers '70▶
The Horror Show '89
The Hunt for the Night Stalker '91
I Can't Sleep '93
I Know Who Killed Me '07
Identity '03
Impulse '74
In Dreams '98
In the Deep Woods '91
Inhumanity '00
Inn on the River '62
The Invisible Strangler '76
Jack Frost '97
Jack the Ripper '76
Jack the Ripper '88▶
Jack's Back '87▶
The January Man '89
Jason X '01
Jennifer 8 '92
Kalifornia '93
Karla '06
Killer Me '01
Kiss the Girls '97
Kontroll '03▶
L.A. Crackdown 2 '88
Lady in Waiting '94
Lady Killer '92▶
Laser Moon '92
The Last Letter '04
The Laughing Policeman '74
The Limbic Region '96
Listen '96
The Lost Angel '04
Love and Human Remains '93
Lured '47
M '31▶
Machined '06
The Mad Executioners '65
Malevolence '04
A Man Bites Dog '91
Man in the Attic '53
Maniac Cop '88
Mean Streak '99
Memories of Murder '03
Mercy '00
Mind Lies '00
A Mind to Kill '95
Mindhunters '05
The Minus Man '99
Mr. Brooks '07
Mr. Frost '89
Mixed Nuts '94
The Monster '03▶
Mortal Sins '92
Naked City: A Killer Christmas '98
Natural Born Killers '94
Nature of the Beast '94
The Neighbor No. Thirteen '05
Never Talk to Strangers '95
Night Divides the Day '01
Night Shadow '90
Night Stalker '87
Night Vision '97
Nightscare '93
Nightstalker '02
Nightwatch '96
No One Sleeps '01
No Way to Treat a Lady '68▶
Office Killer '97
Open Cam '05
Outside Ozona '98
The Paint Job '93
Pale Blood '91
The Perfect Witness '07
The Pledge '00▶
Portraits of a Killer '95
Postmortem '98
Power 98 '96
Prey of the Chameleon '91
Prime Suspect '92▶
Probable Cause '95
Profile for Murder '96
The Prophet's Game '99
Psychic '91
Psychopath '97
The Rain Killer '90
Rampage: The Hillside Strangler Murders '04
Ravenous '99
The Reaper '97
Red Dragon '02
Relentless '89
Relentless 3 '93
Relentless 4 '94
Replicant '01
Resurrection '99
Retribution '98
Return to Cabin by the Lake '01
Revenge Quest '96
Rites of Frankenstein '72
The Rosary Murders '87
Sacrifice '00
San Franpsycho '06
Sanctimony '01
The Satan Killer '93
Satan's Little Helper '04
Saw '04
Saw II '05
Saw IV '07
Scary Movie '00
Scoop '06
Scream '96
Scream 2 '97▶
Scream 3 '00
Serial Killer '95
Serial Killing 101 '04
Serial Mom '94▶
Serial Slayer '03
Seven '95▶
Shadow of a Scream '97
Shadow Ground '04
The Silence of the Lambs '91▶
Slaughter of the Innocents '93
Sleepless '01
Sleepstalker: The Sandman's Last Rites '94
Snapdragon '93
So I Married an Axe Murderer '93
Soho Square '00
Split Second '92
Stagefright '87
Stamp of a Killer '87
Star Time '92
Starkweather '04
The Stendahl Syndrome '95
Still Life '92
Strangler by Night '94
Strangler of Blackmoor Castle '63
Striking Distance '93
Summer of Sam '99
Suspect Zero '04
Sweeney Todd: The Demon Barber of Fleet Street '07
Switchback '97
Tails You Live, Heads You're Dead '95
Taking Lives '04
10 Rillington Place '71▶
Ten to Midnight '83
Tenderness of the Wolves '73
Terror at London Bridge '85
There's Something about Mary '98▶
Things 2 '97
Thr3e '07
3 A.M. '01▶
Tinseltown '97
To Catch a Killer '92▶
The Todd Killings '71
Trail of a Serial Killer '98
Transfixed '01
True Crime '95
Tunnel Vision '95
Turbulence '96
Twisted '04
The Ugly '96
Unconditional Love '03
Uncovered '94
Undetectable '94
Unspeakable '02
Untraceable '08
Urban Menace '99
Valentine '01
Vegas Vice '94
Vice Girls '96
The Watcher '00
When a Stranger Calls '06
When the Bough Breaks '93
While the City Sleeps '56▶
White River '99
Witchcraft 10: Mistress of the Craft '98
Without Warning '52
Wolf Creek '05
Writer's Block '91
Zipperface '92
The Zodiac '05
Zodiac '07

Serials

Ace Drummond '36
The Adventures of Captain Marvel '41
The Adventures of Frank and Jesse James '48
Adventures of Red Ryder '40
Adventures of Smilin' Jack '43
The Adventures of Tarzan '21
Amazing Stories '85
Atom Man vs. Superman '50
Battling with Buffalo Bill '31
The Black Widow '47
Blake of Scotland Yard '36
Captain America '44▶
Cheyenne Rides Again '38
The Clutching Hand '36
Curse of Nostradamus '60
Custer's Last Stand '36
Cyclotrode "X" '46
D-Day on Mars '45
Daredevils of the Red Circle '38
Darkest Africa '36
Daughter of Don Q '46
Destination Saturn '39
Devil Horse '32
Dick Tracy '37
Dick Tracy Returns '38
Dick Tracy vs. Crime Inc. '41
Doctor Satan's Robot '40
Don Daredevil Rides Again '51
Don Winslow of the Coast Guard '43
Don Winslow of the Navy '43
Drums of Fu Manchu '40▶
Federal Agents vs. Underworld, Inc. '49
Federal Operator 99 '45
Fighting Devil Dogs '43
Fighting Marines '36
Fighting with Kit Carson '33
Flaming Frontiers '38
Flash Gordon Conquers the Universe '40
Flash Gordon: Mars Attacks the World '39
Flash Gordon: Rocketship '36
The Galloping Ghost '31
Genie of Darkness '62
Government Agents vs. Phantom Legion '51
Green Archer '40
The Green Hornet '39
Haunted Harbor '44
Hawk of the Wilderness '38
Holt of the Secret Service '42
Hurricane Express '32
The Invisible Monster '50
The Ivory Handled Gun '35
Jesse James Rides Again '47
Jungle Drums of Africa '53
Junior G-Men '40
Junior G-Men of the Air '42
King of the Congo '52
King of the Forest Rangers '46
King of the Kongo '29
King of the Rocketmen '49
King of the Texas Rangers '41
Last Frontier '32
The Last of the Mohicans '32
Law for Tombstone '35
Law of the Wild '34
A Lawman Is Born '37▶
Les Vampires '15▶
Lightning Warrior '31
The Lone Defender '32
The Lone Ranger '38
The Lone Ranger '56
The Lost City '34
The Lost Jungle '34
Lost City of the Jungle '45
Lost Planet Airmen '49
Manhunt in the African Jungles '43
Manhunt of Mystery Island '45
The Masked Marvel '43
Master Key '44
Masters of Venus '62
The Miracle Rider '35
The Monster Demolisher '60
Mysterious Doctor Satan '40
Mystery Mountain '34
Mystery of the Riverboat '44
Mystery Squadron '33
Mystery Trooper '32
The New Adventures of Tarzan '35
Nyoka and the Tigermen '42
Overland Mail '42
The Painted Stallion '37
The Perils of Pauline '34
Perils of the Darkest Jungle '44
Phantom Empire '35
Phantom of the Air '33
The Phantom '43
The Phantom Creeps '39
The Phantom Empire '35
The Phantom of the West '31
The Phantom Rider '36
The Phantom Rider '46
Pirates of the High Seas '50
The Purple Monster Strikes '45
Queen of the Jungle '35
Radar Men from the Moon '52
Radar Patrol vs. Spy King '49
Radio Patrol '37
Raiders of Ghost City '44
Red Barry '38
Return of Chandu '34
Riders of Death Valley '41
Robinson Crusoe of Clipper Island '36
Robinson Crusoe of Mystery Island '36
Rustlers of Red Dog '35
S.O.S. Coast Guard '37
Savage Fury '35
Sea Hound '47
The Secret Code '42
Shadow of Chinatown '36
Shadow of the Eagle '32
Son of Zorro '47
Space Soldiers Conquer the Universe '40
Spy Smasher '42
Spy Smasher Returns '42
Stone Cold Dead '80
Stone of Silver Creek '35
Sunset on the Desert '42
Tailspin Tommy '34
Tarzan the Fearless '33
Tarzan the Tiger '29
Texas to Bataan '42
The Three Musketeers '33
Tim Tyler's Luck '37
Trader Tom of the China Seas '54
The Trail of the Silver Spurs '41
Trail Riders '42

▶ = rated three bones or higher

Serials

Tumbledown Ranch in Arizona '41
Undersea Kingdom '36
Vanishing Legion '31
The Vigilantes Are Coming '36
Whispering Shadow '33
Winners of the West '40
Wolf Dog '33
A Woman in Grey '20
Zombies of the Stratosphere '52
Zorro Rides Again '37
Zorro's Black Whip '44
Zorro's Fighting Legion '39

Sex & Sexuality

see also Crimes of Passion; Erotic Thrillers; Pornography; Sex on the Beach; Sexploitation

About Adam '00
Accident '67
Acting on Impulse '93
The Adjuster '91
The Adultress '77
Adventures of a Private Eye '87
Adventures of a Taxi Driver '76
The Adventures of Sadie '55
The Advocate '93
An Affair of Love '99
Affairs of Anatol '21
Afterglow '97
Alfie '66
Alfie '04
Alien Nation: Body and Soul '95
All Things Fair '95
The Alley Cats '65
The Allnighter '87
Almost Pregnant '91
Alpine Fire '89
Alvin Purple '73
Alvin Rides Again '74
The Amazing Transplant '70
American Beauty '99
American Gigolo '79
American Pie '99
American Pie 2 '01
American Virgin '98
The Amorous Adventures of Moll Flanders '65
The Amy Fisher Story '93
Anatomy of Hell '04
And God Created Woman '57
And God Created Woman '88
Angel Blue '97
Angel of H.E.A.T. '82
Angels and Insects '95
Angels in America '03
Animal Instincts '92
Animal Instincts 2 '94
Animal Instincts 3: The Seductress '95
Anne Rice's The Feast of All Saints '01
Any Wednesday '66
The Apartment '60
Arrivederci, Babyl '66
Art for Teachers of Children '95
The Arousers '70
Assault '70
Asylum '05
Baby Doll '56
The Baby Doll Murders '92
Baby Face '33
Baby Love '69
The Baby Maker '70
The Bachelor '99
Bachelor in Paradise '69
Bachelor Party '84
Bad Company '94
Bad Company '99
Bad Girls from Mars '90
The Banger Sisters '02
Bank Robber '93
Barbarella '68
Basic Instinct 2 '06

Basic Training '86
Baton Rouge '88
Battle in Heaven '05
Battle of the Sexes '28
The Bawdy Adventures of Tom Jones '76
Beach Girls '82
The Beast '75
Beau Pere '81
Becoming Colette '92
Bedroom Eyes '86
Bedroom Eyes 2 '89
Before Sunrise '94
Belle Epoque '92
Belle of the Nineties '34
Beneath the Valley of the Ultra-Vixens '79
Bent '97
The Best Little Whorehouse in Texas '82
Betrayal '78
Better Than Chocolate '99
Better Than Sex '00
Beverly Hills Madam '86
Beyond Erotica '79
Beyond the Silhouette '90
The Big Bet '85
The Big Dis '89
Bikini House Calls '96
Bikini Med School '98
Bilitis '77
The Bitch '78
Bitter Harvest '93
Bitter Rice '49
Black & White '99
Black Book '06
The Black Room '82
Black Starlet '74
Blind Vision '91
Blindfold: Acts of Obsession '94
Bliss '96
Blood and Sand '41
Body Chemistry '90
Body Chemistry 2: Voice of a Stranger '91
Body Chemistry 3: Point of Seduction '93
Body Double '84
Body Language '95
Body of Influence 2 '96
Body Shots '99
Body Waves '92
Boeing Boeing '65
Bonjour Tristesse '57
Booty Call '96
Born Romantic '00
The Boss's Wife '86
Bound by Lies '05
Boxing Helena '93
A Boy and His Dog '75
Boys' Night Out '62
The Boys of 2nd Street Park '03
Bram Stoker's Dracula '92
Breaking the Waves '95
Breathless '83
The Bride Is Much Too Beautiful '58
Brides of the Beast '68
Broken Flowers '05
Broken Trust '93
The Brown Bunny '03
Bully '01
Business As Usual '88
Business for Pleasure '96
Butterfield 8 '60
Butterfly '82
Bye Bye Baby '88
Cactus in the Snow '72
Cal '84
Camille 2000 '69
Can I Do It... Till I Need Glasses? '77

Can't Hardly Wait '98
The Canterbury Tales '71
Captives '97
Caresses '97
Carmen, Baby '66
Carnal Crimes '91
Carnal Knowledge '71
Carnival in Flanders '35
Carried Away '95
Carry On Camping '71
Carry On Emmanuelle '78
Carry On Henry VIII '71
Casanova '87
Casanova 70 '65
Casual Sex? '88
Cat on a Hot Tin Roof '58
Cat on a Hot Tin Roof '84
Cat People '82
Cave Girl '85
Cesar & Rosalie '72
Chain of Desire '93
Champagne for Breakfast '35
Chasing Amy '97
Chatterbox '76
The Chatterley Affair '06
Cheaters '84
Cheech and Chong's Up in Smoke '79
Cherry Falls '00
Cherry 2000 '88
The Chicken Chronicles '77
Chinese Roulette '86
Choose Me '84
Chuck & Buck '00
Cinderella 2000 '78
Claire's Knee '71
Class '83
Class of '63 '73
Class Reunion '72
Cleo/Leo '89
Cleopatra '99
Closely Watched Trains '66
The Cool Surface '92
Cool World '92
The Cooler '03
Corruption '70
Cock & Bull Story '03
Cold Sweat '93
Collector's Item '89
Color of Night '94
Come Early Morning '06
Come Undone '00
Coming Apart '69
Coming Soon '99
Compromising Positions '85
Conspiracy '89
Contagion '87
Conversations with Other Women '05
Crush '93
Crush '02
Crutch '04
Cry Uncle '71
Crystal's Diary '99
Damage '92
Dance with the Devil '97
Dangerous Game '93
Dangerous Indiscretion '94
Dangerous Liaisons '88
Dangerous Liaisons '03
Dangerous Touch '94
The Dark Side of Love '79
The Dark Side of the Heart '92
Dark Tide '93
Daughters of Satan '72
David Searching '97
Dead On '93
Dead Weekend '95
Dear Boys '80
Death and Desire '97
Death of a Centerfold '81
The Decameron '70
Decameron Nights '53
Deceit '89
Deceptions '90

The Decline of the American Empire '86
Deep Down '94
Def Jam's How to Be a Player '97
Denial: The Dark Side of Passion '91
Depraved '98
Desire '93
Desire and Hell at Sunset Motel '92
Desk Set '57
Devil in the Flesh '46
The Devils '71
The Devil's Eye '60
The Devil's Nightmare '71
The Devil's Playground '76
Devil's Wedding Night '73
Diary of a Chambermaid '64
Diary of a Mad Housewife '70
Diary of a Mad Old Man '88
Die Watching '93
Diner '82
The Dirty Girls '64
Dirty Love '05
A Dirty Shame '04
Discretion Assured '93
The Disenchanted '90
Divine Nymph '71
Divorce—Italian Style '62
Dr. Alien '88
Dr. Caligari '89
Dog Day Afternoon '75
Dollar '38
Doll Face '46
Domino '88
Don Juan (Or If Don Juan Were a Woman) '73
Don's Party '76
Double Cross '94
Double Suicide '69
Dracula Sucks '79
The Dreamers '03
Dreams '55
Dreams Come True '84
Driver's Seat '73
Drum '76
Dry Cleaning '97
Eating Raoul '82
Ebbtide '94
Ebony Tower '86
Echoes of Paradise '86
The Eclipse '66
Eclipse '94
Ecstasy '34
Eden '93
Eden 2 '93
Eden 3 '93
Eden 4 '93
Edge of Seventeen '99
El '52
El Crimen Perfecto '04
Electra '95
Elizabeth '98
Elmer Gantry '60
Elvira, Mistress of the Dark '88
Embrace of the Vampire '95
Emily '77
Emmanuelle '74
Emmanuelle 4 '84
Emmanuelle & Joanna '78
Emmanuelle in the Country '78
Emmanuelle, the Joys of a Woman '76
Emmanuelle, the Queen '79
Emmanuelle's Daughter '79
End of August '82
Endless Love '81
Enemies, a Love Story '89
Enormous Changes '83
Enrapture '90
Ernesto '79
Eros '04
Erotic Escape '72
Erotic Images '85
Erotic Touch of Hot Skin '65
Erotique '94
The Escape '95
Every Breath '93
Everything You Always Wanted to Know about Sex (But Were Afraid to Ask) '72

Evils of the Night '85
Expose '97
Extramarital '98
Eyes Wide Shut '99
Fairy Tales '76
Fall '97
Fanny Hill '83
Fanny Hill: Memoirs of a Woman of Pleasure '64
The Fantasist '89
Farinelli '94
Fast Food '89
Fast Times at Ridgemont High '82
Fatal Attraction '80
Fatal Attraction '87
Fatal Bond '91
Fatal Charm '92
Fatal Instinct '92
Fatal Past '94
The Favor '92
Federal Protection '02
Feelin' Screwy '90
Female Perversions '96
Female Trouble '74
Female Vampire '73
Femalien '96
Femme Fatale '02
Final Judgment '92
The Finishing Touch '92
Fire '96
First Affair '83
The First Time '69
First Time '82
Flesh '68
Flesh Gordon '72
A Flight of Rainbirds '81
Flirt '95
Forbidden Sins '99
Forbidden Zone: Alien Abduction '96
Foreign Body '86
Foreplay '75
Forever Emmanuelle '75
40 Days and 40 Nights '02
The 40 Year Old Virgin '05
The 4th Man '79
The Fourth Sex '61
Foxes '80
Frankenstein Unbound '90
Frasier the Sensuous Lion '73
Fraternity Vacation '85
French Fried Vacation '79
The French Woman '79
Frenzy '72
Friday Night '02
Friend of the Family '95
Friend of the Family 2 '96
Friends & Lovers '99
Fritz the Cat '72
The Fugitive Kind '60
Full Exposure: The Sex Tape Scandals '89
Gabriela '84
Galactic Gigolo '87
The Game Is Over '66
Games Girls Play '75
The Garden '90
Gas Pump Girls '79
Gate of Flesh '64
The General's Daughter '99
Gentlemen Prefer Blondes '53
Genuine Risk '89
Georgy Girl '66
Get Out Your Handkerchiefs '78
Get Real '99
Ghosts Can Do It '87
The Gift '82
Gilda '46
Ginger Ale Afternoon '89
The Girl '86
Girl '98
The Girl Next Door '98
The Girl on a Motorcycle '68
Girl 6 '96
Glen or Glenda? '53
Go West, Young Man '36
The Goddess '58
God's Comedy '95
Going All the Way '97
Good-bye, Emmanuelle '77
Good Luck Chuck '07
The Good Mother '88
Goodbye Charlie '64

Goodbye, Lover '99
Gorp '80
Gothic '87
The Graduate '67
Grave Indiscretions '96
The Great American Sex Scandal '94
Gross Misconduct '93
Habit '97
The Handmaid's Tale '90
Happily Ever After '86
Happily Ever After '04
Happiness '97
Hard Drive '94
Hardbodies 2 '86
Harem '99
Harrad Experiment '73
Harrad Summer '74
Head On '98
Head On '04
Heading South '05
Heart of the Stag '84
Heaven Can Wait '43
Heavy Petting '89
Hell Comes to Frogtown '88
Her and She and Him '69
Higher Education '88
Hindsight '91
Hit and Runway '01
The Hit List '93
Hold Me, Thrill Me, Kiss Me '93
Holy Girl '04
Holy Smoke '99
Homework '82
Honey '81
Hoopla '33
The Horseplayer '91
Hostel '06
Hot Child in the City '87
The Hot Spot '90
Hot Target '85
Hot Under the Collar '91
The Hotel New Hampshire '84
Hotel Paradiso '66
Hotel Room '93
Hourglass '95
How Funny Can Sex Be? '76
How to Pick Up Girls '78
How to Seduce a Woman '74
Hugh Hefner: Once Upon a Time '92
Human Nature '02
Humanity '99
Hurlyburly '98
Hustler White '96
I, a Woman '66
I Am Curious (Yellow) '67
I Like to Play Games '95
I Think I Love My Wife '07
I Want Someone to Eat Cheese With '06
I Will, I Will for Now '76
Illegal Affairs '96
Illegal in Blue '95
Illicit Dreams '94
Ilsa, Harem Keeper of the Oil Sheiks '76
I'm No Angel '33
The Immoral One '80
Impure Thoughts '86
In a Savage Land '99
In Dark Places '97
In Praise of Older Women '78
In the Heat of Passion '91
In the Heat of Passion 2: Unfaithful '94
An Inconvenient Woman '91
Indecency '92
Indecent Behavior '93
Indecent Behavior 2 '94
Indecent Behavior 3 '95
Indecent Proposal '93
Indochine '92
Inner Sanctum 2 '94
Inside Out '91
Inside Paris '06
Intimacy '00
Intimate Affairs '01
Intimate Betrayal '96
Intimate Deception '96
Invasion of Privacy '92

Invasion of the Bee Girls '73
Inventing the Abbotts '97
Irezumi '83▶
Iris '01▶
Is There Sex After Death? '71▶
Isadora '68▶
It '27
The Italian Stallion '73
It's Not the Size That Counts '74
Jailbait '93
Jailbait '00
Jamon, Jamon '93
Jeanne and the Perfect Guy '98
Jeffrey '95
Justine '69
Just Looking '99
Just a Kiss '02
Kandyland '87
Karmina '96
Kevin & Perry Go Large '00
Kids '95
Kika '94
Killer Looks '94
Killer Condom '95
Killer Workout '86
Killing for Love '95
The Killing Game '87
Killing Grandpa '91
Kinsey '04▶
A Kiss Goodnight '94
Kiss Me, Stupid! '64
Kiss of a Killer '93
The Knack '65▶
Kristin Lavransdetter '95
L'Annee des Meduses '86
Ladykillers '88
Ladylike '32
Lady Chatterley '92
Lady Chatterley's Lover '55
Lady Chatterley's Lover '81
Lady Frankenstein '72
Lady on the Bus '78
Lady Caroline Lamb '73
Labyrinth of Passion '82
La Ronde '51▶
La Collectionneuse '67
La Cicada '83
L.A. Goddess '92
Lap Dancing '95
The Laserman '90
Last Breath '96
Last Call '90
Last of the High Kings '96
Last of the Red Hot Lovers '72
Last Resort '86
Last Summer '59
Last Tango in Paris '73▶
Late August, Early September '98
Laws of Deception '97
Le Boucher '69
Le Cavaleur '78
Le Sex Shop '73▶
Leather Jacket Love Story '98
L'Ennui '98
Les Nuits Fauves '92▶
L'Escorte '96
Lethal Lolita—Amy Fisher: My Story '92
Let's Talk About Sex '98
The Libertine '69
The Lickerish Quartet '70
L.I.E. '01
Liebestraum '91
Lies Before Kisses '92
The Life of Jesus '96
A Life of Sin '92
Lifeforce '85
The Lifetaker '89
Like Water for Chocolate '93▶
Lila Says '04
Lipstick Camera '93
Liquid Sky '33▶
Little Boy Blue '97
The Little City '97
Little Darlings '80
Little Mother '77
The Little Death '95
A Little Sex '82

Live Nude Girls '95
The Locusts '97
Lolita 2000 '97
Lolita '62▶
Lolita '97
Looking for Mr. Goodbar '77
Loulou '80▶
The Love Affair, or The Case of the Missing Switchboard Operator '67▶
Love After Love '94
Love & Sex '00
Love Crimes '92
The Love Goddesses '65▶
Love in the Time of Cholera '07
Love in the Time of Money '02
Love Is a Gun '94
Love Letters '83▶
Love Matters '93
Love Meetings '64
Love Thy Neighbor '02
Loverboy '89
Lover Girl '97
Lovers '83▶
Lovers: A True Story '90▶
Lovers' Lovers '94
Loving Couples '80
The Low Down '00
Lunch Wagon '81
Luscious '97
Lust and Revenge '95
Mademoiselle '66
Madame Bovary '34▶
Magnolia '99▶
Mae West '84
Making Love '82·
Malicious '74
The Man in the Attic '94
Man Who Had Power Over Women '70
The Man Who Loved Women '77▶
The Man Who Loved Women '83
The Man Who Made Husbands Jealous '98
A Man with a Maid '73
Maria's Lovers '84
Marilyn: The Untold Story '80▶
Marquis '90
Married People, Single Sex '93
Married People, Single Sex 2: For Better or Worse '94
A Married Woman '65▶
Mars Needs Women '66
Masseuse '95
Mata Hari '85
Me and Him '89
Menage '86▶
Mercy '00
Metroland '97
Midnight Blue '96
Midnight Tease '94
A Midsummer Night's Sex Comedy '82▶
Millions '90
Mirror Images '91
Mirror Images 2 '93
Mirror, Mirror 3: The Voyeur '96
Miss Julie '50
Miss Julie '99
Miss Right '81
Miss Sadie Thompson '53▶
Mistress '87
Mo' Better Blues '90
Mon Homme '98
Mondo Trasho '69
Monsieur Hire '89▶
Monster's Ball '01▶
Montenegro '81▶
Monty Python's The Meaning of Life '83▶
The Moon Is Blue '53
Mortal Sins '90
Motel Blue '98
The Mother '03▶
The Mother and the Whore '73▶
Mouth to Mouth '95
Mouvements du Desir '94
Movers and Shakers '85

My Best Friend's Girl '84
My Chauffeur '86
My Demon Lover '87
My Life to Live '62▶
My Sex Life... Or How I Got into an Argument '96
My Teacher's Wife '95
My Wonderful Life '90
Myra Breckinridge '70
The Mystery of Alexina '86
The Naked Country '85
Naked Lie '89
Naked Obsession '91
Naked Tango '91
Naked Wishes '00
National Lampoon's Adam & Eve '05
Nea '78
Negatives '68
Nekromantik 2 '91
Nekromantik '97
Nenette and Boni '96▶
Nerolio '96
Never Talk to Strangers '95
New Rose Hotel '98
New York Nights '84
Nice Girls Don't Explode '87
Night and Day '91▶
Night Fire '94
Night Games '80
A Night of Love '87
Night of the Living Babes '87
Night Shade '97
Night Zoo '87
The Nightman '93
No Sex Please—We're British '73
No Secrets '91
No Vacancy '99
Noir et Blanc '86
Norma Jean and Marilyn '95
Norman Loves Rose '82
The Notorious Bettie Page '06
Novel Desires '92
Nudo di Donna '83▶
O Fantasma '00
Oh! Calcutta! '72
Once Is Not Enough '75
100 Girls '00
One Night Stand '95
One Night Stand '97▶
One Plus One '61
The Other Side of Midnight '77
The Other Woman '92
Over the Wire '95
Paddy '70
The Painted Lady '97▶
Paradisio '61
Paranoia '69
Pardon Mon Affaire, Too! '77
Party Animal '83
Passion '82
Passion '99
The Perils of Gwendoline '84
Peyton Place '57▶
Picnic '55▶
Pigalle '95
Pinero '01
A Place Called Truth '98
Play Time '94
Playback '95
Playgirl Killer '66
Playmaker '94
A Pleasure Doing Business '79
Point of Terror '71
Poison Ivy '92
Poison Ivy 2: Lily '95
Poison Ivy 3: The New Seduction '97
The Pornographers '66▶
Portnoy's Complaint '72

Possessed by the Night '33
The "Postman Always Rings Twice '46▶
The Postman Always Rings Twice '81
Power, Passion & Murder '83
Praise '98▶
Preacherman '83
Prep School '81
Pretty Baby '78▶
Pretty Woman '90▶
The Princess & the Call Girl '84
Private Lessons '75
Private Lessons, Another '94
Quartier Mozart '92
Quiet Days in Hollywood '97
Rain '32▶
Raising Cain '01
Rambling Rose '91▶
Rattle of a Simple Man '64
The Razor: Sword of Justice '72
A Real Young Girl '75
Reckless '97▶
Reckless: The Sequel '98▶
Red Blooded 2 '96
Red Kiss '85▶
Red Meat '97
Red Shoe Diaries '92
Red Shoe Diaries 2: Double Dare '92
Red Shoe Diaries 3: Another Woman's Lipstick '93
Red Shoe Diaries 4: Auto Erotica '93
Red Shoe Diaries 5: Weekend Pass '95
Red Shoe Diaries 6: How I Met My Husband '96
Red Shoe Diaries 7: Burning Up '96
Red Shoe Diaries 8: Night of Abandon '97
Red Shoe Diaries: Four on the Floor '96
Red Shoe Diaries: Luscious Lola '00
Red Shoe Diaries: Strip Poker '96
The Red Violin '98▶
The Reincarnation of Golden Lotus '89▶
Rendez-vous '85▶
Repo Jake '90
Repulsion '65▶
Restless '72
Return to Peyton Place '61
Riders '88
The Right Temptation '00
Ripe '97
Rita, Sue & Bob Too '87▶
Rites of Frankenstein '72
The Road to Wellville '94
The Rocky Horror Picture Show '75▶
Roger Dodger '02▶
Romance '99▶
Roseland Beach Hotel '85
The Rowdy Girls '00
R.S.V.P. '84
Rubdown '93
The Rue Morgue Massacres '73
Russian Dolls '05
The Sailor Who Fell from Grace with the Sea '76
Saints and Sinners '95
Salmonberries '91
Salome '85
Sammy & Rosie Get Laid '87▶
Save Me '93
The Scarlet Letter '79▶
Scene of the Crime '87▶
Scenes from the Class Struggle in Beverly Hills '89
Scorchy '76
Score '73
Scorned '93
Scorned 2 '96

Screwball Academy '86
Scrubbers '82
Sea of Love '89▶
Secret Games 2: The Escort '93
Secret Games 3 '94
Secret Life of an American Wife '68
Secrets '71
Secrets of Three Hungry Wives '78
Seduce Me: Pamela Principle 2 '94
The Seduction of Joe Tynan '79
Seduction: The Cruel Woman '89
Seeing Other People '04
The Seniors '78
Sensuous Summer '93
Separate Vacations '86
Serpent's Lair '95
Sex '20
Sex and Breakfast '07
Sex and Lucia '01
Sex & Mrs. X '00
Sex and the Other Man '95
Sex and Zen '93
Sex Crimes '92
Sex's Comedy '02
Sex on the Run '78
Sextette '78
Sexual Intent '94
The Sexual Life of the Belgians '94▶
Sexual Malice '93
Sexual Response '92
Sexual Roulette '96
Sexus '64
Shadow Dancer '96
Shadow of a Scream '97
Shame '68▶
Shame, Shame, Shame '98
The Shaming '71
Shampoo '75▶
Sherrybaby '06
She's Gotta Have It '86▶
Shopgirl '05▶
Showgirls '95
Sibling Rivalry '90
Siddhartha '72
Silk 'n' Sabotage '94
Silver Strand '95
Sinbad '71
Single Bars, Single Women '84
Sins of the Mind '97
Sirens '94▶
The Sister-in-Law '74
Sisters '97
Six Days, Six Nights '94
Ski School '91
Skin Deep '89
The Slap '76
Sleeping with Strangers '94
Smooth Talker '90
Snapdragon '93
Somersault '04▶
Something About Sex '98
Somewhere in the City '97
Sooner or Later '78
Sous Sol '96
Spirit Lost '96
Splendor in the Grass '61▶
Sprung '96
Star 80 '83
The Stationmaster's Wife '77
The Statue '71
Stiff Upper Lips '96
The Stilts '84
The Storm Within '48▶
Stormswept '95
Storyville '95
Strangers '91
The Strangers '98
Strike a Pose '93
Stripped to Kill '87
The Stripper '63
The Stud '78
Sugarbaby '85▶
Summer Heat '87

Summer Lovers '82
Summer School Teachers '75
Super Bitch '73
Superbad '07▶
Supervixens '75
Surfacing '84
Susan Slept Here '54
Susana '51▶
Sweet Ecstasy '62
Sweet Evil '98
Sweet Lies '88
Sweet Movie '75
Sweet Poison '91
Sweet Spirits '80s
Swimming Pool '70
Swimming Pool '03▶
Swingers '96▶
Swirl '32
Sylvia '03
Tales of Two Sisters '89
Tales of Erotica '93
Tales of the Kama Sutra: The Perfumed Garden '98
Talkin' Dirty after Dark '91
Talking Walls '85
The Taste of Others '00▶
Tattoo '81
Teach Me '97
Tea for Three '84
Tea and Sympathy '56▶
Temptation '07
Tempted '01
Temptress Moon '96
Teorema '68
Terrified '94
The Terror Within '88
Test Tube Babies '48
Texasville '90
Thérèse & Isabelle '67
Thief of Hearts '84
Things You Can Tell Just by Looking at Her '00
36 Fillete '88▶
Thirteen '03▶
This Property Is Condemned '66
This Sweet Sickness '77
Three in the Attic '68
Three in the Cellar '70
3-Way '04
The Tigress '93
Tigers in Lipstick '80
'Tis a Pity She's a Whore '73
To Sleep with a Vampire '92
Together? '79
Tom Jones '63▶
Tom Jones '98▶
Tonight for Sure '51
Too Good to Be True '88
Trash '70▶
Trojan War '97
Tropic of Cancer '70▶
Tropical Heat '33
Truth about Women '58
Tryst '94
Turkish Delight '73
Twentynine Palms '03
Twenty-One '01
Twin Peaks: Fire Walk with Me '92
Twins of Evil '71▶
Twist '76
2 by 4 '98
2 Days in Paris '07▶
Two Days in the Valley '96▶
Two Deaths '94
The Ultimate Thrill '74
The Unbearable Lightness of Being '88▶
Under Investigation '93
Under Suspicion '92
Under the Skin '97▶
Under the Yum-Yum Tree '63
The Underachievers '88
Untold Scandal '03
Vacuuming Completely Nude in Paradise '01
The Valley Obscured by the Clouds '70
Valmont '89▶
Vanilla Sky '01▶

▶ = rated three bones or higher

Sex

Variety '83
A Very Curious Girl '69
Via Appia '92
Vibration '68
Vicious Circles '97
A View to a Kill '85
Virgin Queen of St. Francis High '88
The Virgin Soldiers '69
Virtual Encounters '96
Virtual Girl '00
Virtual Sexuality '99
The Voyeur '94
Wager of Love '90
Waiting '05
Watch Me '96
Water Drops on Burning Rocks '99
We Don't Live Here Anymore '04
Wedding in Blood '74
Weekend Pass '84
Welcome to L.A. '77
What Planet Are You From? '00
What's Good for the Goose '69
What's Up Front '63
When Will I Be Loved '04
When Women Had Tails '70
Where '90
Where the Boys Are '84
Where the Hot Wind Blows '59
Where the Truth Lies '05
A Whisper to a Scream '88
Whispers in the Dark '92
Wide Sargasso Sea '92
Wild at Heart '90
Wild Things '98
Winter Sleepers '97
A Winter Tan '88
Wish Me Luck '95
Wish You Were Here '87
The Witches of Eastwick '87
A Woman, Her Men and Her Futon '92
A Woman in Flames '84
The Woman Next Door '81
Woman of Desire '93
Woman Times Seven '67
Women in Love '70
Women on the Verge of a Nervous Breakdown '88
Women's Club '87
The Worker and the Hairdresser '96
Working Girls '75
Working Girls '87
The World Is Full of Married Men '80
The Wrong Man '93
X, Y & Zee '72
Xica '76
Yanks '79
Yesterday, Today and Tomorrow '64
Young Adam '03
Young Aphrodites '63
Young Lady Chatterley 2 '85
Young Lady, First Love '79
Young Nurses in Love '89
Your Friends & Neighbors '98
Your Ticket Is No Longer Valid '84
You've Got to Have Heart '77
The Yum-Yum Girls '78
Zabriskie Point '70
Zandalee '91
Zapped! '82
Zombie Island Massacre '84

Sex on the Beach
see also Island Fare
Against All Odds '84
Airplane! '80
The Beach '00
The Blue Lagoon '80
Come Undone '00
Cote d'Azur '05
The Firm '93
From Here to Eternity '53
Heading South '05
Kiss Tomorrow Goodbye '00
Maslin Beach '97

Memoirs of an Invisible Man '92
Mixed Nuts '94
Phat Beach '96
Sweet Ecstasy '62
Swept Away... '75
Swept Away... '02
Tales of the Kama Sutra 2: Monsoon '98
Vibration '68
Young Adam '03

Sexcapades
Agnes and His Brothers '04
Alfie '04
American Pie Presents: The Naked Mile '06
American Wedding '03
Andy Warhol's Dracula '74
Andy Warhol's Frankenstein '74
Angel Heart '87
Another 9 1/2 Weeks '96
Audition '99
Auto Focus '02
Bad Lieutenant '92
Basic Instinct '92
Being at Home with Claude '92
Belle de Jour '67
Betty Blue '86
Between Your Legs '99
Bitter Moon '92
Black Snake Moan '07
The Blackout '97
Blue Velvet '86
Body of Evidence '92
Byron '03
Caligula '80
The Camomile Lawn '92
Candy '68
The Center of the World '01
Circuit '02
Cleopatra's Second Husband '00
The Comfort of Strangers '91
Confusion of Genders '00
The Cook, the Thief, His Wife & Her Lover '90
Cougar Club '07
Crash '95
Crazy Little Thing '02
Crimes of Passion '84
Cruising '80
Dark Side '02
Deception '08
Delta of Venus '95
Devil in the Flesh '87
A Dirty Shame '04
Dona Herlinda & Her Son '86
Don't Let Me Die on a Sunday '98
8 1/2 Women '99
8mm '99
El Crimen Perfecto '04
En la Cama '05
Exit to Eden '94
Exotica '94
Fellini Satyricon '69
The First 9 1/2 Weeks '98
First Turn On '83
Forbidden Homework '92
Four Times That Night '69
French Fried Vacation '79
Frida '02
The Frightened Woman '71
Frisk '95
Getting It '06
Giving It Up '99
God's Comedy '95
Harvard Man '01
Havoc 2: Normal Adolescent Behavior '07
Henry & June '90
Hey, Happy! '01
Homework '90
Husbands and Lovers '91
I Am Frigid... Why? '72
Ice Men '04
In the Cut '03
In the Realm of the Senses '76
Irreversible '02
The Isle '01

Jade '95
Jill the Ripper '00
Just One Time '00
Kama Sutra: A Tale of Love '96
Kill Me Tomorrow '99
Killing Me Softly '01
Kiss the Sky '98
Kissed '96
Lady Chatterley '06
Lake Consequence '92
Laurel Canyon '02
Little Shots of Happiness '97
The Long Weekend '05
Love and Human Remains '93
Love and Rage '99
Love Is the Devil '98
Lust, Caution '07
Mad Cowgirl '06
Maitresse '76
Mango Yellow '02
Marquis de Sade '96
Men Cry Bullets '00
Miranda '02
The Monkey's Mask '00
Naked Lunch '91
Never Again '01
The New Eve '98
The Night Porter '74
9 1/2 Weeks '86
Not Tonight Darling '72
One Night at McCool's '01
OnLine '01
The Other Side of the Bed '03
Paris, France '94
Payback '98
Peeping Tom '60
Perfect Stranger '07
The Piano Teacher '01
Pigs '07
The Pillow Book '95
Preaching to the Perverted '97
Priceless '06
Return to Two Moon Junction '93
The Rules of Attraction '02
Secretary '02
Seduced; Pretty When You Cry '01
sex, lies and videotape '89
The Sex Machine '75
Simone Barbes '80
Sitcom '97
Sleeping Dogs Lie '06
The Story of O '75
The Story of O, Part 2 '87
Suite 16 '94
The Sweetest Thing '02
Take Me '07
Teenage Caveman '01
Teeth '07
The Ten '07
These Girls '05
Tie Me Up! Tie Me Down! '90
Tokyo Decadence '91
Tomcats '01
Torremolinos 73 '03
The Trio '97
Two Moon Junction '88
Unfaithful '02
When Will I Be Loved '04
Whipped '00
White Mischief '88
Whore '91
Why Do They Call It Love When They Mean Sex? '92
Wild Orchid '90
Wild Orchid 2: Two Shades of Blue '92
Y Tu Mama Tambien '01
Zebra Lounge '01

Sexploitation
see also Erotic Thrillers; Exploitation
The Abductors '72
The Acid Eaters '67
Agony of Love '66
Amazon Jail '85
Angel 3: The Final Chapter '88
Aroused '66

Au Pair Girls '72
Baby Love '69
Bad Girls Do Cry '54
Bad Girls Go to Hell '65
Barbarian Queen 2: The Empress Strikes Back '89
The Bawdy Adventures of Tom Jones '76
Beach Babes 2: Cave Girl Island '95
Beach Babes from Beyond '93
The Beast That Killed Women '65
Bedroom Eyes '86
The Bellboy and the Playgirls '62
Beneath the Valley of the Ultra-Vixens '79
The Big Bust Out '73
The Big Doll House '71
The Bikini Car Wash Company '90
The Bikini Car Wash Company 2 '92
Black Venus '83
Blazing Stewardesses '75
Blood Gnome '02
Bolero '84
Broadcast Bombshells '95
Caged Fury '90
Candy Stripe Nurses '74
Candy Tangerine Man '75
Carnal Crimes '91
Chain Gang Women '72
Champagne for Breakfast '35
Cheering Section '73
The Cheerleaders '72
Cheerleaders' Wild Weekend '85
Cherry Hill High '76
Chesty Anderson USN '76
Class Reunion '72
Cleo/Leo '89
Corruption '70
The Curious Dr. Humpp '70
Dandelions '74
Deadly Embrace '88
Def Jam's How to Be a Player '97
Delinquent School Girls '84
Devil's Wedding Night '73
Dinosaur Island '93
Dirty Mind of Young Sally '72
Domino '88
Dracula Sucks '79
Eastern Promises '07
Ecstasy '84
Emily '77
Emmanuelle '74
Emmanuelle 4 '84
Emmanuelle 5 '87
Emmanuelle 6 '88
Emmanuelle & Joanna '78
Emmanuelle in the Country '78
Emmanuelle on Taboo Island '76
Emmanuelle, the Joys of a Woman '76
Erotic Escape '72
Erotic Touch of Hot Skin '65
Fanny Hill: Memoirs of a Woman of Pleasure '64
Fantasies '73
Feelin' Up '76
Firehouse '87
The First Nudie Musical '75
Flesh Gordon '72
Flesh Gordon 2: Flesh Gordon Meets the Cosmic Cheerleaders '90
Fleshpot on 42nd Street '71
Forever Emmanuelle '75
The French Woman '79
Ghosts Can't Do It '90
Gimme an F '85
Ginger '72
The Girl, the Body and the Pill '67
Good-bye, Emmanuelle '77
Great Bikini Off-Road Adventure '94
The Happy Hooker '75
The Happy Hooker Goes to Washington '77

Hard Ticket to Hawaii '87
Hard to Die '90
Hardbodies '84
Help Wanted Female '68
Hollywood Boulevard 2 '89
Hollywood High '77
Hollywood High, Part 2 '81
Hollywood Hot Tubs '84
Hollywood Hot Tubs 2: Educating Crystal '89
Homework '82
Honkytonk Nights '78
Hot Moves '84
Hot T-Shirts '79
H.O.T.S. '79
How to Make a Doll '68
Human Trafficking '05
Ilsa, She-Wolf of the SS '74
Ilsa, the Tigress of Siberia '79
Ilsa, the Wicked Warden '78
Inferno in Paradise '88
Inhibition '76
Invasion of the Girl Snatchers '73
The Invisible Maniac '90
Joy of Sex '84
Kandyland '87
Knock Outs '92
Lady Godiva Rides '68
Last Dance '91
Liane, Jungle Goddess '56
Lips of Blood '75
Liquid Dreams '92
Little Miss Innocence '73
The Living Dead Girl '82
Love Desperados '68
Love Notes '88
Lust for Dracula '04
Lust for Freedom '87
Mistress Pamela '74
Modern Girls '86
Mondo Balordo '64
My Pleasure Is My Business '74
My Therapist '84
Mysterious Jane '81
Naked Killer '92
The Naked Sword of Zorro '69
Naked Venus '58
Nature's Playmates '62
Naughty Knights '71
Night Call Nurses '72
The Night Evelyn Came Out of the Grave '71
Nine Ages of Nakedness '69
Nude on the Moon '61
Nurse on Call '88
Olga's Girls '64
Orgy of the Dead '65
Pagan Island '60
Paranoia '69
Party Favors '89
Party Plane '90
Perfect Timing '84
The Perverse Countess '73
Please Don't Eat My Mother '72
Prehistoric Bimbos in Armageddon City '93
Preppies '82
The Prime Time '60
Private Duty Nurses '71
Private Passions '85
Profile for Murder '96
Rebel Vixens '69
Red Shoe Diaries 2: Double Dare '92
Return to the Blue Lagoon '91
Revenge of the Cheerleaders '76
Revenge of the Virgins '62
Sacrilege '86
Screen Test '85
Scum of the Earth '63
Sea of Dreams '90
The Seducers '70
Sensual Partners '87
The Sensuous Teenager '70
Sex Adventures of the Three Musketeers '71
Sex and Buttered Popcorn '91

Sex Through a Window '72
Shanty Tramp '67
She Came on the Bus '69
She Devils in Chains '76
Slammer Girls '87
Slumber Party Massacre 3 '90
Snapshot '77
Snowballing '85
Sorority Babes in the Slimeball Bowl-A-Rama '87
Sorority House Party '92
Spaced Out '80
The Speed Lovers '68
Strange World of Coffin Joe '68
The Student Nurses '70
The Student Teachers '73
Submission '77
Suburban Roulette '67
Sugar Cookies '77
Superchick '71
Supervixens '75
Sweater Girls '78
Sweet Georgia '72
Sweet Young Thing '79
The Swinging Cheerleaders '74
Tarzana, the Wild Girl '69
Tender Flesh '97
Tender Loving Care '73
Test Tube Teens from the Year 2000 '93
The Vampire Hookers '78
Venus in Furs '70
Vice Academy '88
Vice Academy 2 '90
Vice Academy 3 '91
Wanda, the Sadistic Hypnotist '67
Wham-Bam, Thank You Spaceman '75
Witchcraft 2: The Temptress '90
Witchcraft 3: The Kiss of Death '90
Witchcraft 5: Dance with the Devil '92
World of the Depraved '67
The Young Nurses '73
The Zombie Army '93

Sexual Abuse
see also Domestic Abuse; Rape
The Accused '88
Bad Education '04
The Bed You Sleep In '93
Boxing Helena '93
The Boys of St. Vincent '93
Breathtaking '00
The Devils '71
Fall from Innocence '88
Fortune and Men's Eyes '71
Hard Candy '06
Heart of the Stag '84
Ilsa, Harem Keeper of the Oil Sheiks '76
Loved '97
Man of Ashes '86
Mesmerized '84
Mysterious Skin '04
Mystic River '03
The Night Porter '74
The Notorious Bettie Page '06
Priest '94
Romper Stomper '92
Southern Man '99
Trade '07
Twin Peaks: Fire Walk with Me '92
Whatever '98
Woman, Thou Art Loosed '04

◄ = rated three bones or higher

Sexual Harassment
Brilliant Lies '96
Disclosure '94
Foxfire '96
G.I. Jane '97
Improper Conduct '94
9 to 5 '80
North Country '05
Oleanna '94
Strange Justice: The Clarence Thomas and Anita Hill Story '99

Ships
see Deep Blue; Mutiny; Sail Away; Shipwrecked; Submarines

Shipwrecked
see also Sea Disasters
Adventures of Eliza Fraser '76
Benji the Hunted '87
The Black Pirate '26▶
The Black Stallion '79▶
The Blue Lagoon '80
Cabeza de Vaca '90▶
Dead of Night '99
Dungeon of Harrow '64
Eye of the Needle '81
Far from Home: The Adventures of Yellow Dog '94
Greystoke: The Legend of Tarzan, Lord of the Apes '84
Hawk of the Wilderness '38
He Is My Brother '75
Humongous '82
The Island of Dr. Moreau '77
Island of Lost Souls '32▶
Jungle Bride '33
Kilma, Queen of the Amazons '75
The Legend of the Sea Wolf '58
Light at the Edge of the World '71
Madagascar '05
Male and Female '19▶
The Most Dangerous Game '32▶
Mutiny on the Bounty '35▶
Mutiny on the Bounty '62
My Favorite Wife '40▶
Pardon My Sarong '42
Princess Caraboo '94
Project: Genesis '93
Rich and Strange '32
Robby '68
Robinson Crusoe '36
Robinson Crusoe '96
Robinson Crusoe & the Tiger '72
Sea Gypsies '78
The Sea Wolf '41▶
The Sea Wolf '93
She Gods of Shark Reef '56
Shogun '80▶
Summer Affair '79
Swept Away... '75▶
Swept from the Sea '97
The Swiss Family Robinson '60▶
Trader Tom of the China Seas '54
20,000 Leagues under the Sea '54▶

Shops & Shopping
Attention Shoppers '99
Bad Santa '03
Clueless '95
Dawn of the Dead '04
Department Store '35
Elf '03
The 40 Year Old Virgin '05▶
Going Shopping '05
Heater '99
Holy Man '98
Lost Embrace '04
Mr. Magorium's Wonder Emporium '07
Pretty Woman '90▶
Priceless '06
Scenes from a Mall '91
Seven Doors to Death '44
Shopgirl '05▶
Shopping '93
Low Price '05
Wal-Mart: The High Cost of Low Price '05▶
Washington Heights '02
Where the Heart Is '00
Who's Minding the Store? '63
Two Lost Worlds '50

Showbiz Comedies
Adaptation '02▶
Alex in Wonderland '70
Alvin and the Chipmunks '07
America's Sweethearts '01
American Dreamz '06
Art House '98
Bamboozled '00
Be Cool '05
Because of Him '45
Being John Malkovich '99▶
Betty '97
Bewitched '05
The Big Broadcast of 1938
Big Fat Liar '02
The Big Picture '89
Blazing Saddles '74▶
Bloodhounds of Broadway '89
Boardinghouse Blues '48
Bowfinger '99▶
The Boy Friend '71▶
Broadway Melody of 1936
Broadway Melody of 1938
Broadway Melody of 1940
Bullets over Broadway '94▶
Burning Down the House '01
Camp '03
Cannes Man '96
Cats Don't Dance '97
Celebrity '98▶
The Comic '69▶
Comic Act '98▶
Crazy House '43
Critic's Choice '63
The Dark Backward '91
The Day the Women Got Even '80
Delirious '91
Dickie Roberts: Former Child Star '03
Die Mommie Die! '03
Dog Pound Shuffle '75▶
EDtv '99
Ella Cinders '26▶
Ellie Parker '05
Enemies of Laughter '00
The Errand Boy '61
Everybody Sing '38
Everybody's Famous! '00
Exposed '03
Extra Girl '23
Fall Guy '82
The Final Hit '02
Fish Without a Bicycle '03
Forever Female '53
Free and Easy '30
Funny Bones '94▶
Galaxy Quest '99
Ganked '05
George White's Scandals '45
Get Shorty '95▶
Glam '97
Good Times '67
Goodbye Charlie '64
The Grand Role '04
Grave Secrets '89
Gypsy '62
Gypsy '93
The Hard Way '91▶
Havana Widows '33
Hear My Song '91▶
Here Comes Cookie '35
Hit and Runway '01
Hollywood Boulevard 2 '89
Hollywood Boulevard '01
Hollywood Dreams '06
Hollywood Heartbreak '89
Hollywood Mystery '34
Hollywood Chaos '89
Hollywood Ending '02▶
Hollywood in Trouble '87
Hollywood North '03
Hollywood Party '34
Hollywood Shuffle '87▶
The Hollywood Sign '01
Hooper '78
I'll Do Anything '93
In the Doghouse '98
The Independent '00
Introducing the Dwights '07
It's a Great Feeling '49
It's a Date '40
Jackie's Back '99
Jay and Silent Bob Strike Back '01
Jiminy Glick in Lala Wood '05
Josie and the Pussycats '01
Joey Breaker '93▶
Just Write '98
The Kid and I '05
Lady Killer '33▶
The Last Shot '04
Let's Make Love '60
Life with Mikey '93
Lisa Picard Is Famous '01
Looney Tunes: Back in Action '03
Louisiana Hayride '44
The Muse '99
Music & Lyrics '07
My Blue Heaven '50
My Date With Drew '05▶
My Dream Is Yours '49
My Favorite Year '82▶
Nancy Goes to Rio '50
The Night They Raided Minsky's '69▶
Notting Hill '99▶
Nudity Required '90
Panama Hattie '42
Panic Button '62
The Party '68▶
Pick a Star '37
Pipe Dream '02
Postcards from the Edge '90▶
The Prince and the Showgirl '57
The Producers '68▶
The Producers '05
Ratings Game '84
The Real Blonde '97
Rock-A-Bye Baby '57
Rubberface '81
Salut l'Artiste '74▶
Searching for Bobby D '05
Second Fiddle '39
Seed of Chucky '04
Shoot or Be Shot '02
S.O.B. '81
The Souler Opposite '97
Soundman '99
Stage Struck '36
Star Spangled Rhythm '42▶
Still Crazy '98
The Sunshine Boys '95
Swingers '96▶
Tapeheads '89
There's No Business Like Show Business '54▶
These Old Broads '01
13 Moons '02
365 Nights in Hollywood '34
Tinseltown '97
Tom and Frances '05▶
Too Smooth '98
Tropic Thunder '08
Tune in Tomorrow '90
The 24 Hour Woman '99
Wag the Dog '97▶
Waiting for Guffman '96▶
Walk Hard: The Dewey Cox Story '07
Who Framed Roger Rabbit '88▶
Win a Date with Tad Hamilton! '04
Winning Girls Through Psychic Mind Control '02
With Friends Like These '97
The Wizard of Speed and Time '88

Showbiz Dramas
Actors and Sin '52
Agatha Christie's Thirteen at Dinner '85
All About Eve '50▶
American Blue Note '89
The Anna Jillian Story '88
Anna '87▶
The Anniversary Party '01▶
The Audrey Hepburn Story '00▶
The Aviator '04▶
Baadasssss! '03▶
The Barefoot Contessa '54▶
The Beatniks '60
Being Julia '04▶
The Big Knife '55▶
Blast-Off Girls '67
Blonde '01
The Bodyguard '92
Boogie Nights '97▶
Can You Hear the Laughter? The Story of Freddie Prinze '79
Cassie '83
The Cat's Meow '01▶
Child Star: The Shirley Temple Story '01
A Chorus Line '85
Clean '04
Club Land '01
The Comic '85
Concrete Angels '87
Control '07
The Cradle Will Rock '99
Dancing in September '00
Dangerous '35▶
Day for Night '73▶
The Day of the Locust '75▶
Doll Face '46
Double Platinum '99
Dragon: The Bruce Lee Story '93▶
The Dresser '83▶
The Dying Gaul '05▶
Eddie Presley '92
El Cantante '06
Entropy '99
Ernie Kovacs: Between the Laughter '84
Everything for Sale '68
F. Scott Fitzgerald in Hollywood '76
The Fabulous Dorseys '47
Fame '80▶
Flynn '96
For Ever Mozart '96
For the Boys '91
Frances '82▶
From the Journals of Jean Seberg '95
Funny Girl '68▶
Funny Lady '75
The Girl Said No. '37
The Goddess '58▶
Gods and Monsters '98▶
Goodnight, Sweet Marilyn '89
Grace of My Heart '96▶
Happily Ever After '82
Hard Part Begins '73
Harlow '65
The Hit '06
Hollywoodland '06
Honey '03
Honeydripper '07
Hughes & Harlow: Angels in Hell '77
I'm Losing You '98▶
The Incredible Sarah '76
Introducing Dorothy Dandridge '99▶
Isn't She Great '00
The Jacksons: An American Dream '92
James Dean '01
James Dean: Live Fast, Die Young '97
King Kong '05▶
King of Comedy '82▶
La Dolce Vita '60▶
La Vie en Rose '07
Last Call: The Final Chapter of F. Scott Fitzgerald '02
The Last Metro '80▶
Last Summer in the Hamptons '96▶
The Last Tycoon '76▶
Lenny '74▶
Lillian Russell '40
Little Voice '98▶
Livin' for Love: The Natalie Cole Story '00
The Lonely Lady '83
Lucky Devils '33
Lucy and Desi: Before the Laughter '91
Madonna: Innocence Lost '94
Man in the Mirror: The Michael Jackson Story '04
A Man Called Adam '66
Man of a Thousand Faces '57▶
Man on the Moon '99▶
Marilyn: The Untold Story '80▶
Max '79
Mickey One '65
Mommie Dearest '81▶
My Wicked, Wicked Ways '84
Network '76▶
The Next Step '95
Night and Day '46
The Night of Nights '39
Norma Jean and Marilyn '95
Once in Paris... '79
Out of Order '23
Out of the Cold '99
Paparazzi '04
Payday '73▶
Permanent Midnight '98
The Player '92▶
Postcards from the Edge '90▶
Protecting the King '07
Pure Country '92
Rainbow over Broadway '33
Rhapsody in Blue '45▶
Rita Hayworth: The Love Goddess '83
RKO 281 '99▶
Sam's Son '84
Scandal Sheet '85
Searching for Paradise '02
Second Coming of Suzanne '80
Sex Is Comedy '02
Shadow of the Vampire '00▶
Shakespeare Wallah '65▶
Sidewalks of London '38▶
Simone '02
Sinatra '92
Smash-Up: The Story of a Woman '47▶
Somebody to Love '94
Something to Sing About '36
Sparkle '76▶
Stage Struck '57
Stand-Ins '37▶
The Star '52▶
Star! '68
Star 80 '83
A Star Is Born '37▶
A Star Is Born '54▶
A Star Is Born '76
The Starter Wife '07
State and Main '00▶
Stoned '05
Sugar Town '99
Sunset Boulevard '50▶
Targets '68▶
They Call It Sin '32
Time Code '00
Topsy Turvy '99▶
What's Love Got to Do with It? '93▶
Where the Truth Lies '05
Who Is Harry Kellerman and Why Is He Saying Those Terrible Things About Me? '71
Why Do Fools Fall in Love? '98
Wired '89
With a Song in My Heart '52▶
Young '97

Showbiz Musicals
see also Musical Fantasy; Musicals; Showbiz Comedies
All That Jazz '79▶
Bloodhounds of Broadway '89
Broadway Serenade '39
Bye Bye Birdie '95
Cats Don't Dance '97
Chicago '02▶
A Chorus Line '85
Glitter '01
Greenwich Village '44
Hedwig and the Angry Inch '00▶
Idlewild '06
If I'm Lucky '46
Kiss Me Kate '53▶
Kiss Tomorrow Goodbye '50
Lady of Burlesque '43
Moulin Rouge '01▶
Noises Off '92
Sing and Like It '34
Singin' in the Rain '52▶
Something for the Boys '44
Step Lively '44
The Suburbans '99
Swingin' Johnny '43
The Temptations '98
There's No Business Like Show Business '54▶
Three for the Show '55
Three Little Words '50
Til the Clouds Roll By '46
Variety Girl '47
Yankee Doodle Dandy '42▶

Showbiz Thrillers
Children Shouldn't Play with Dead Things '72
Dead of Winter '87▶
The Dead Pool '88
Destroyer '88
F/X '86▶
F/X 2: The Dead Art of Illusion '91
The House of Seven Corpses '73
I Wake Up Screaming '41▶
Kiss Me Kate '53...
Number One Fan '94
Return to Cabin by the Lake '00
Return to Horror High '87
Satan in High Heels '61
Stage Fright '83▶
Strangers Kiss '83
The Stunt Man '80▶
Up in the Air '40
What Ever Happened to Baby Jane? '62▶
What Ever Happened to... '95
The Wizard of Speed and Time '88

Shrinkage
see also Metamorphosis
The Ant Bully '06
Arthur and the Invisibles '06
Attack of the Puppet People '58
Bad Channels '92
Dr. Cyclops '40
Honey, I Shrunk the Kids '89

▶ = rated three bones or higher

Shrinkage

Honey, We Shrunk Ourselves '97
The Incredible Shrinking Man '57
The Incredible Shrinking Woman '81
Phantasm '79
The Hole '01
The Seventh Voyage of Sinbad '58

Shrinks

see also *Doctors & Nurses*

Agnes of God '85
Almost Dead '94
Analyze That '02
Analyze This '98
Angel Dust '96
Anger Management '03
Antwone Fisher '02
Assault on Precinct 13 '05
Bark! '02
Basic Instinct 2 '06
Batman Forever '95
Baton Rouge '88
Beauty on the Beach '61
Behind the Lines '97
Betrayal '78
Betty '97
Beyond Reason '77
Beyond Therapy '86
Big Jim McLain '52
Bliss '96
Blood Frenzy '87
Body Chemistry 2: Voice of a Stranger '91
Body of Influence '93
Body of Influence 2 '96
Borderline '02
The Brain '88
Breathtaking '00
A Brilliant Disguise '93
Captain Newman, M.D. '63
The Cell '00
Charlie Bartlett '07
The Cobweb '55
Color of Night '94
Coming Apart '69
Conspiracy Theory '97
A Couch in New York '95
The Couch Trip '87
Cracker: Best Boys '95
Cracker: Brotherly Love '95
Cracker: Men Should Weep '94
Cracker: The Big Crunch '94
Cracker: To Be a Somebody '94
Cracker: True Romance '95
Crazy as Hell '02
Cruel Intentions '98
Dallas 362 '03
Dark Asylum '01
Dark Mirror '46
The Day the World Ended '01
Dead Man Out '89
Deconstructing Harry '97
Disney's The Kid '00
Disturbing Behavior '98
The Dog Problem '06
Don Juan DeMarco '94
Don't Look Down '98
Don't Say a Word '01
The Dream Team '89
88 Minutes '08
Eros '04
The Evening Star '96
Exit in Red '97
The Eye '02
Face to Face '76
Faithful '95
Fear '90
The Fear '94
Female Perversions '96
Final '01
Final Analysis '92
A Fine Approach '91
A Fine Madness '66
Future Shock '93
Genealogies of a Crime '97
A Girl Thing '01
Good Will Hunting '97
Gothika '03
Grosse Pointe Blank '97
Gun Shy '00
Halloween '78
Hangman '01
Happiness '98
Heaven '99
Hell's Gate '01
High Anxiety '77
The Hole '01
Home Movies '79
Hometown Boy Makes Good '93
House of Games '87
Human Experiments '79
I Don't Buy Kisses Anymore '92
I Never Promised You a Rose Garden '77
I, Robot '04
I Was a Teenage Werewolf '57
If Lucy Fell '95
The Impossible Years '68
Indecent Behavior 2 '94
Inevitable Grace '94
Inside Out '05
Instinct '99
Intimate Strangers '04
The Invasion '07
Jade '95
K-PAX '01
Karla '06
Kill Your Darlings '06
Lantana '01
Last Rites '98
Lies and Whispers '98
A Lizard in a Woman's Skin '71
Locked in Silence '99
Lovesick '83
Lovey: A Circle of Children 2 '82
The Machine Who Loved '06
The Man Who Loved Women '83
Manic '01
Matchstick Men '03
Merci Docteur Rey '04
Mercy '00
A Mind to Murder '96
Mine Own Executioner '47
Mr. Frost '89
Mr. Jones '93
Mr. Stitch '95
Moment to Moment '66
Monkeybone '01
Mulholland Falls '95
Mumford '99
Murder in Mind '97
Murderous Intent '06
The Myth of Fingerprints '97
National Lampoon's The Don's Analyst '97
Nell '94
The Night Caller '97
Night Eyes 4: Fatal Passion '95
Nightmare Alley '47
Numb '07
On a Clear Day You Can See Forever '70
On the Edge '00
One Fine Day '96
One Flew Over the Cuckoo's Nest '75
Open Your Eyes '97
Panic '00
Passion of Mind '00
A Passion to Kill '94
Peephole '93
Portnoy's Complaint '72
The President's Analyst '67
Pressure Point '62
Primal Fear '96
Prime '05
The Prince of Tides '91
Profile for Murder '96
Progeny '98
Prozac Nation '01
Quicksand '01
Rampage: The Hillside Strangler Murders '04
Red Wind '91
Reign Over Me '07
The Royal Tenenbaums '01
Running with Scissors '06
The Scar '48
Schizoid '80
Seventh Heaven '98
Sharon's Secret '95
Shock! '46
Silent Fall '94
The Sixth Sense '99
The Sleeping Tiger '54
Solaris '02
Sometimes They Come Back... Again '96
The Son's Room '00
Speak Up! It's So Dark '93
Spellbound '45
Sphere '97
Stephanie Daley '06
Still of the Night '82
Strange Relations '02
The Stranger '87
Stranger Than Fiction '06
Stuart Saves His Family '94
The Student Affair '97
Sworn to Justice '97
Sybil '76
They Might Be Giants '71
36 Hours '64
Thomas in Love '01
The Three Faces of Eve '57
The 300 Year Weekend '71
Through a Glass Darkly '61
Till Human Voices Wake Us '02
Tin Cup '96
The Treatment '06
12 Monkeys '95
Twisted '04
The Ugly '96
Underworld '96
The Unsaid '01
Victim of Love '91
The Victor '00
The Watcher '00
Wes Craven Presents: They '02
What Lies Beneath '00
What's New Pussycat? '65
When Danger Follows You Home '97
When the Dark Man Calls '95
Where Truth Lies '96
Whispers in the Dark '92
The Wife '95
Wild in the Country '61
Wilderness '96
The Young Poisoner's Handbook '95

Shutterbugs

see also *Front Page*

Addicted to Love '96
Adrift in Manhattan '07
Adventures in Spying '92
Amelie '01
Art for Teachers of Children '95
Austin Powers: International Man of Mystery '97
Austin Powers 2: The Spy Who Shagged Me '99
Backbeat '94
The Beautiful, the Bloody and the Bare '64
Beefcake '99
Bikini Island '91
Billy's Hollywood Screen Kiss '98
Blondie Meets the Boss '39
Blood Gnome '02
Blow-Up '66
The Blue Gardenia '53
Body Shot '93
Bound by Lies '05
The Bridges of Madison County '95
Calendar '93
Camera Buff '79
The Caveman's Valentine '01
Closer '04
The Corrupt Ones '67
Dagger Eyes '83
Darkroom '90
Death and Desire '97
Dirty Love '05
Dr. Mabuse vs. Scotland Yard '64
The Dolls '83
Don't Answer the Phone '80
Don't Change My World '83
Double Exposure '82
Double Exposure: The Story of Margaret Bourke-White '89
The Double Negative '80
Down in the Delta '98
Easy Money '83
Eyes Behind the Stars '72
Eyes of Laura Mars '78
Family Jewels '89
Fatal Exposure '91
Fatal Images '89
The Favor, the Watch, & the Very Big Fish '92
Femme Fatale '02
Fire on the Amazon '93
Firefall '94
Footsteps '98
Funny Face '57
The Governess '98
Guinevere '99
Hard Candy '06
Harrison's Flowers '02
Heat and Sunlight '87
Heights '04
High Art '98
High Season '88
Hope Floats '98
I Love Melvin '53
Joe Gould's Secret '00
Johnny Skidmarks '97
Journey '95
Killer Image '92
Love & Murder '91
Love Crimes '92
Love Is a Gun '94
Machine to Kill Bad People '48
Mad Dog and Glory '93
Memento '00
Mr. Brooks '07
Model Behavior '82
Not for Publication '84
The Notorious Bettie Page '06
November '05
Of Love and Shadows '94
One Hour Photo '02
Out There '95
The Outcasts '86
Paparazzi '04
Pecker '98
Peeping Tom '60
Perfect Timing '84
Perfume '01
Photographer '75
Photographing Fairies '97
Picture Snatcher '33
The Pink Jungle '68
The Portrait '95
Portraits of a Killer '95
Pretty Baby '78
Private Lessons, Another Story '94
Proof '91
The Public Eye '92
Rear Window '54
Return to Boggy Creek '77
Screaming Dead '03
Secret File of Hollywood '62
Seduce Me: Pamela Principle 2 '94
Shadow Magic '00
Shoot '92
Shoot It Black, Shoot It Blue '74
Shooting the Past '99
Shutter '08
Smoke '95
Snap Decision '01
Snapshot '77
Somebody Has to Shoot the Picture '90
Spice World: The Movie '97
Stephen King's The Night Flier '96
Stepmom '98
Straight for the Heart '88
Sunset Strip '92
Sunset Strip '85
Temptress '95
A Time to Die '91
Time to Leave '05
The Truth about Cats and Dogs '96
The Unbearable Lightness of Being '88
Until the End of the World '91
Watch Me '96
Watch the Birdie '50
The Watcher '00
The Weight of Water '00
What a Woman! '56
Where the Heart Is '00
Wild America '97
The Winter Guest '97

Sibling Rivalry

see also *Brothers & Sisters*

Across the Tracks '89
Agnes and His Brothers '04
All the Brothers Were Valiant '53
American Flyers '85
America's Sweethearts '01
Before the Devil Knows You're Dead '07
Big Brother Trouble '00
The Boys and Girl From County Clare '03
The Brotherhood '68
A Brother's Kiss '97
The Brothers McMullen '94
Brothers of the Head '06
Cadillac Ranch '96
Dead Ringer '64
A Dog's Breakfast '07
East of Eden '54
East of Eden '80
Fred Claus '07
Georgia '95
Go for Zucker '05
Hair Show '04
Hilary and Jackie '98
King Lear '71
King Lear '98
My Sister's Keeper '02
The Perfect Son '00
Sibling Rivalry '90
Six Days, Six Nights '94
A Thousand Acres '97
Yours, Mine & Ours '05
Zus & Zo '01

Silent Films

see also *Silent Horror/Fantasy Classics*

A Propos de Nice '29
The Adorable Cheat '28
The Adventurer '17
The Adventures of Tarzan '21
Aelita: Queen of Mars '24
Amarilly of Clothesline Alley '18
American Aristocracy '17
American Pluck '25
The Americano '17
Anna Christie '23
Annapolis '28
April Fool '26
Are Parents People? '25
Arsenal '29
The Atonement of Gosta Berling '24
The Average Woman '24
Avenging Conscience '14
Backfire '22
Backstairs '21
Bare Knees '28
The Bargain '15
The Bat '26
Battle of Elderbush Gulch '13
The Battleship Potemkin '25
Battling Bunyon '24
Battling Butler '26
Beau Brummel '24
Beau Revel '21
Bed and Sofa '27
Beggars of Life '28
Behind the Front '26
The Bells '26
The Beloved Rogue '27
Below the Deadline '29
Ben-Hur '26
Beyond the Rocks '22
The Big Parade '25
Big Stakes '22
The Birth of a Nation '15
The Black Pirate '26
Blind Husbands '19
Blood and Sand '22
The Blot '21
Body and Soul '24
Brand Upon the Brain! '06
The Broadway Drifter '27
Broken Blossoms '19
Broken Hearts of Broadway '23
The Broken Mask '28
Burlesque on Carmen '16
Burning Daylight '28
The Busher '19
The Cabinet of Dr. Caligari '19
Cabiria '14
California Straight Ahead '25
Camille '21
Campus Knights '29
Captain Swagger '25
The Cat and the Canary '27
Cesare Borgia '23
Champagne '28
The Chaplin Revue '58
Charleston '26
Charley's Aunt '25
Charlie Chaplin: Night at the Show '15
Charlie Chaplin ... Our Hero! '15
The Cheat '15
The Cheerful Fraud '27
Child of the Prairie '18
The Cigarette Girl of Mosselprom '24
The Circus '19
City Girl '30
City Lights '31
Civilization '16
Clodhopper '17
Cobra '25
College '27
The Coming of Amos '25
The Confession '20
The Count '16
The Count of Monte Cristo '12
The Country Kid '23
County Fair '20
The Covered Wagon '23
Crainquebille '23
The Crazy Ray '23
Cricket on the Hearth '23
The Crowd '28
The Cure '17
Custer's Last Fight '12
Cyclone Cavalier '25
Daddy Long Legs '19
Dames Ahoy '30
Dancing Mothers '26
Dangerous Hours '19
Dante's Inferno '24
Days of Thrills and Laughter '61
Desert of the Lost '27
Destiny '21
Diary of a Lost Girl '29
The Disciple '15
Discontent '16
Docks of New York '28
Dr. Jekyll and Mr. Hyde '20
Dr. Mabuse, The Gambler '22
Dog Star Man '64
Don Juan '26
Don Q., Son of Zorro '25
Doomsday '28
Down to Earth '17
Down to the Sea in Ships '22
The Dragon Painter '19
The Drake Case '29
Dream Street '21
The Dropkick '27
Dynamite Dan '24
The Eagle '25
Earth '30
East and West '24
Easy Street '16
Easy Virtue '27
Ella Cinders '26

▲ = rated three bones or higher

The End of St. Petersburg '27▶
Evangeline 29
Extra Girl 23
The Extraordinary Adventures of Mr. West in the Land of the Bolsheviks 24
Eyes of Julia Deep 24
The Eyes of Youth '19
Eyes Right! 26
False Faces '25
Fangs of Fate '25
The Farmer's Wife '28
Faust '26▶
Feel My Pulse 28
The Fighting American 24
Fighting Blood 24
The Fighting Stallion '26▶
The Fireman '16
Flesh and Blood 22
Flirting with Fate '16▶
The Floorwalker '17▶
The Flying Scotsman 29
A Fool There Was '14
Foolish Wives 22▶
For Heaven's Sake 26▶
The Forbidden City 18
Fortune's Fool 21
The Four Horseman of the Apocalypse 21▶
Free to Love 25
The Freshman '25▶
From the Manger to the Cross '15
The Fugitive: Taking of Luke McVane '15
The Garden of Eden '28▶
The Gaucho 27▶
The General '26▶
The General Line 29▶
A Girl's Folly '17
The Girl with the Hat Box 27
Girl Shy 24▶
A Girl in Every Port 28
The Gold Rush '25▶
The Golem 20▶
The Grand Duchess and the Waiter 26▶
The Greatest Question '19
Greed 24▶
Gypsy Blood '18
The Hands of Orlac 25
Hands Up 26
Happiness '32
Hawthorne of the USA 19
Haxan: Witchcraft through the Ages 22▶
He Who Gets Slapped 24▶
Head Winds 25
Headin' Home 20
His Picture in the Papers '16
Home Sweet Home '14
Homecoming 26▶
Hoodoo Ann '16
Hotel Imperial 27
Hula 28
Human Hearts 22
The Hunchback of Notre Dame 23▶
The Ice Flood 25
The Idol Dancer 20
The Immigrant '17▶
In the Days of the Thundering Hard & the Law & the Ou'aw '14
Intolerance '16▶
Irish Cinderella 22
The Iron Mask '29
The Island '61▶
It 27
Isn't Life Wonderful '24▶
The Italian '15
It's the Old Army Game '27▶
Italian Straw Hat '27▶
The Jack Knife Man '20▶

Jesse James Under the Black Flag 21
Jesus of Nazareth '25▶
Joyless Street '25▶
Judith of Bethulia '14▶
Just Suppose 26
The Kid '21▶
The Kid Brother '27▶
King of Kings '27▶
King of the Kongo 29
King of the Rodeo 28
Kismet 20▶
The Kiss '29▶
The King on Main Street '25
Kriemhilde's Revenge '24▶
La Chute de la Maison Usher '28▶
Lady Windermere's Fan '25
The Lamb '15
Last Command '28▶
The Last Laugh 24▶
The Last of the Mohicans '20▶
The Last Outlaw '27
Laughing at Danger '24
Leap Year 24
The Leatherneck 28
Leaves from Satan's Book 19
The Leopard Woman 20
Let 'er Go Gallegher 28
Let's Go! 23
The Light of Faith '22
Linda 29
Little American '17
Little Annie Rooney 25
Little Church Around the Corner '23
The Lodger '26▶
Long Pants 26▶
The Lost World '25
Love 'Em and Leave 'Em '26▶
The Love Flower 20
The Love of Jeanne Ney 27
Lucky Devil 25
Mabel & Fatty '16
Mack & Carole 28
The Mad Whirl 25
Male and Female '19▶
The Man from Beyond 22
The Man from Painted Post '17
Man in the Silk Hat '15
Man in the Silk Hat '83▶
The Man on the Box 25
The Man Who Laughs 27▶
The Man with the Movie Camera '29▶
Manhandled 24
Manslaughter 24
The Manxman '29
Mantrap 26
Mark of Zorro 20
Marked Money 28
The Marriage Circle '24▶
Married? 26
Master of the House 25
Matrimaniac '16
Merry-Go-Round 23▶
Metropolis 26▶
The Michigan Kid 28
Mickey '17
Mid-Channel 20
Midnight Faces 26
Moana, a Romance of the Golden Age 26▶
Modern Times '36▶
The Mollycoddle 20
Monsieur Beaucaire 24
Moran of the Lady Letty 22
A Mormon Maid '17
Mother 26▶
My Best Girl 27▶
My Boy 21
My Lady of Whims 25
The Mysterious Lady 28
Napoleon 27▶
Narrow Trail '17▶
The Navigator '24▶
The Nervous Wreck 26▶
Nevada 27
The Night Club 25
The Night Cry 26
The Night Patrol '26
No Man's Law '27
Nomads of the North 20

Nosferatu '22▶
The Notorious Lady 27
Nurse Marjorie 20
The Nut 21
Old Ironsides '26▶
Oliver Twist '22▶
On the Night Stage '15
One A.M. '16
One Arabian Night 21▶
One-Punch O'Day 26
Orphans of the Storm 21▶
Othello 22
The Outlaw and His Wife '17
Outside the Law 21
Pace That Kills 28▶
Pandora's Box 28▶
Passion '19
Passion of Joan of Arc 28▶
Patchwork Girl of Oz '14
Paths to Paradise '25▶
Pawnshop '16▶
The Peacock Fan 29
Peck's Bad Boy 21
Peg o' My Heart 22
Peter Pan '24
Phantom 22
The Phantom Chariot 20
The Phantom Flyer 28
The Phantom of the Opera '25▶
The Plastic Age '25
Playing Dead '15
Pollyanna 20
The Pony Express '25▶
Pool Sharks '15
Power 28
The Prairie King 27
The Prairie Pirate 25
Pride of the Clan '18
The Primitive Lover '16
Q Ships '28
Queen Kelly 29▶
Quo Vadis '12
Ranson's Folly '26
The Raven '15
Reaching for the Moon '17▶
Rebecca of Sunnybrook Farm '17
Red Kimono 25
Red Signals 27
Regeneration '15
Reggie Mixes In '16▶
Renoir Shorts 27▶
The Return o' Boston Blackie '27
Return of Draw Egan '16▶
The Return of Grey Wolf 22
Riders of the Range 24
Riders of the Purple Sage '25
The Ring '27
The Rink '16▶
Risky Business 28
The Road to Ruin 28
The Road to Yesterday '25
The Roaring Road '19
Robin Hood '22▶
Robinson Crusoe '36
Romola 24
Rounding Up the Law '22
Running Wild '27
Sadie Thompson '28▶
Safety Last '23▶
Salambo '14
Sally of the Sawdust 25
Salome '22
Sands of Sacrifice 21
Scar of Shame '27
The Scarlet Car '17
The Sea Lion 21
Secrets of a Soul '25
Seven Chances 25▶
Seven Years Bad Luck 21▶
Sex 20
She 25
Shadows '22
Shattered '21
The Sheik '21▶
Shifting Sands '18
Ships in the Night 28
The Shock 23
Show People '28▶
Siegfried 24▶

The Silent Mr. Sherlock Holmes '12
Silent Movie '76
The Single Standard '29
Siren of the Tropics 27
Skinner's Dress Suit 26
Sky High 22
So This Is Paris 26▶
The Social Secretary '16
Son of a Gun '19
The Sorrows of Satan 26▶
Soul-Fire 25
The Spoilers 14▶
Square Shoulders 29
Stand and Deliver 28
Steamboat Bill, Jr. '28▶
Stella Maris '18▶
Storm over Asia '28▶
Straight Shootin' '17
The Street '23
Street of Forgotten Women '25
Strike '24▶
Student Prince in Old Heidelberg 27▶
The Student of Prague '13▶
Sucs '20
Sunny Side Up 28
Sunrise '27▶
The Swan '25
Sweet Adeline '26
Tabu: A Story of the South Seas '31▶
Tarzan of the Apes '17
Tarzan the Tiger 29
The Taxi Mystery 26
Teddy at the Throttle '16▶
The Tempest '28▶
The Ten Commandments 23
Ten Days That Shook the World '27▶
Ten Nights in a Barroom '13
Tentacles of the North 26
Tess of the Storm Country '22
Test of Donald Norton '26
That Certain Thing '28
The Thief '52
The Thief of Baghdad '24▶
Thomas Graal's Best Film '17
Thomas Graal's First Child '18▶
Three Ages '23▶
Three Charlies and One Phoney! '18
Three Musketeers '16
The Three Musketeers '21▶
Three Word Brand '21
Through the Breakers '28
Tillie Wakes Up '17
Tillie's Punctured Romance '14
Tol'able David '21
The Toll Gate '20
The Tomboy 24
The Tong Man '19
Too Wise Wives '21
The Torture of Silence '17
Tournament 29
Traffic in Souls '13▶
Trailin' 21
Tramp, Tramp, Tramp '26▶
The Trap '22
Trapped by the Mormons '22
Treasure of Arne '19
True Heart Susie '19
20,000 Leagues under the Sea '16▶
Two Men & a Wardrobe '58
Un Chien Andalou '28▶
The Unchastened Woman '25
Uncle Tom's Cabin '14
Uncle Tom's Cabin '27
Underworld '27▶
The Unholy Three '25▶
The Unknown '27▶
The Untamable 23

Until They Get Me '18
The Vagabond '16▶
The Vanishing American 25
Variety '25▶
The Virginian 23
Virtue's Revolt 24
Wagon Tracks '19
Walking Back 26
The Wallping Kid 26
Warning Shadows 23▶
Waxworks 24▶
Way Down East '20▶
We're in the Navy Now 27
The Wedding March '28▶
West of Zanzibar 28
West-Bound Limited '23
What Happened to Rosa? '21▶
When the Clouds Roll By '19▶
Where East Is East 29
White Gold '28▶
The White Rose '23▶
The White Sin 24
The White Sister '23▶
Why Change Your Wife? 20
Wild Horse Canyon 25
Wild Orchids 28
The Wind '28▶
Wings 27▶
The Wishing Ring '14▶
With Kit Carson over the Great Divide '25
The Wizard of Oz 25
Wolf Blood 25
Wolfheart's Revenge '25
A Woman of Affairs 28
A Woman in Grey 20
Woman in the Moon 29
The Worldly Madonna 22
The Wrath of the Gods '14
Yankee Clipper 27
Yankee Doodle in Berlin '19
Zvenigora '28▶

Silent Horror/Fantasy Classics

see also Silent Films
Aelita, Queen of Mars '24
The Cabinet of Dr. Caligari '19▶
Dante's Inferno 24▶
Dr. Jekyll and Mr. Hyde '20▶
The Golem '20▶
The Hunchback of Notre Dame 23▶
La Chute de la Maison Usher '28▶
Les Vampires '15▶
Metropolis 26▶
The Monster '25
Nosferatu '22▶
The Penalty 20
The Phantom of the Opera '25▶
The Thief of Baghdad '24▶
20,000 Leagues under the Sea '16▶
Vampyr '31▶
The Wizard of Oz '25

Single Parents

see also Bringing Up Baby; Parenthood
About a Boy '02▶
Air Bud 2: Golden Receiver '98
Akeelah and the Bee '06
Alias Betty '01
All About My Mother '99▶
American Gun '05
American History X '98
And Then Came Love '07
Anywhere But Here '99
Are We There Yet? '05
As Good As It Gets '97▶
Baby Boom '87
Beautiful '00
Because I Said So '07
Because of Winn-Dixie '05
Blue Car '03▶
Bogus '96
Boricua's Bond '00
Brave New Girl '04
Broken Wings '02▶

Bye Bye, Love '94
Cape of Good Hope '04
Casper '95▶
Catch and Release '07
Chicken Little '05
Chitty Chitty Bang Bang '68▶
Crows '94
Cybermutt '02
Daddy's Little Girls '07
Daltry Calhoun '05
Dancer in the Dark '99
Dark Water '05
Dear Frankie '04
Double Parked '00
Enchanted '07▶
Erin Brockovich '00▶
E.T.: The Extra-Terrestrial '82▶
Evelyn '02▶
Evergreen '04
Father and Son '03
Fay Grim '06
Fierce People '05
First, Last and Deposit '00
Flight of the Red Balloon '08
Flightplan '05
The Girl Next Door '53
Girlfight '99▶
The Goodbye Girl '77▶
Gravitaca: The Land of My Dreams '06
The Green Promise '49
Hears in Atlantis '01'
Hide and Seek '05
Hideous Kinky '99
House of D '04
How I Killed My Father '03▶
How Stella Got Her Groove Back '98
Hysterical Blindness '02
I Am Sam '01
I'll Be There '03
In the Valley of Elah '07▶
Introducing the Dwights '07
Jerry Maguire '96▶
Jersey Girl '04
The Karate Kid '84▶
Kramer vs. Kramer '79▶
Life According to Muriel '97
Limbo '99
A Little Inside '01
Loverboy '05
Maid in Manhattan '02
Mamma Mia! '08
Margarita Happy Hour '01
Martian Child '07
Me and You and Everyone We Know '05▶
Message in a Bottle '98
Millions '05▶
Mind the Gap '04
Mrs. Wiggs of the Cabbage Patch '34
The Mother '03▶
The Mudge Boy '03
Music of the Heart '99
Must Love Dogs '05
My Baby's Daddy '04
Nanny McPhee '06
Never Back Down '08
No Reservations '07
Novel Romance '06
One Fine Day '96▶
The Pacifier '05
Pay It Forward '00
The Perfect Holiday '07
The Perfect Man '05
The Players Club '98
The Principal '87
Private Property '06
Pure '02▶
The Ring '02▶
Row Your Boat '98
Rugrats in Paris: The Movie '00▶
Sabotage '96
Scandal Sheet '85
The Shipping News '01
The Sixth Sense '99▶
Skeletons in the Closet '00
Sleepless in Seattle '93▶
Sleepwalking '08

▶ = rated three bones or higher

Single

The Spiderwick Chronicles '08▲
The Spring '00
Sweet Sixteen '02▲
The Sweetest Gift '98
Ten Things I Hate about You '99
Things You Can Tell Just by Looking at Her '00
Thirteen '03▲
The Tic Code '99
Time to Leave '05▲
The Town Is Quiet '00
Tyler Perry's Meet the Browns '08
The Ultimate Gift '07
Undertow '04
An Unfinished Life '05
Untraceable '08▲
Waist Deep '06
A Walk to Remember '02
Welcome to Paradise '07
What a Girl Wants '03
Where the Heart Is '00
The White Countess '05▲
Wilbur Wants to Kill Himself '02▲
Wildflowers '99
Winter Solstice '04▲
You Can Count On Me '99▲
Yours, Mine & Ours '05
Zeus and Roxanne '96

Singles

see also Dates from Hell
About a Boy '02▲
At Last Night... '86▲
Bar Hopping '00
Beautiful Girls '96▲
Before Sunrise '94
Boys' Night Out '62▲
Breakfast at Tiffany's '61▲
Bridget Jones's Diary '01▲
Bye Bye, Love '94
Crossing Delancey '88▲
Ed's Next Move '96
Everyone Says I Love You '96▲
Everything Relative '96
Extreme Dating '04
Forget Paris '95
Funny Valentine '05
He Said, She Said '91
He's Just Not That Into You '08
Kicking and Screaming '95▲
Love & Sex '00
Metropolitan '90▲
Mr. Wonderful '93
Mr. Wrong '95
Mystic Pizza '88▲
The Opposite Sex and How to Live With Them '93
The Personals '98
Pillow Talk '59▲
Reality Bites '94
St. Elmo's Fire '85
Singles '92▲
Sleepless in Seattle '93▲
Sliding Doors '97
That Touch of Mink '62
The Thing Called Love '93
Trial and Error '96
Wedding Bell Blues '96
When Harry Met Sally... '89▲
When the Cat's Away '96▲
The Wild Life '84

Sixties

see also Period Piece: 1960s

Skateboarding

Above and Beyond '53▲
Back to the Future '85▲
Clueless '95▲
Gleaming the Cube '89
Grind '03
Gummo '97
Kids '95
The Last Drop '05
Lords of Dogtown '05
MVP2: Most Vertical Primate '01
Paranoid Park '07▲
Skateboard '77
The Skateboard Kid 2 '94
Wassup Rockers '06

Skating

see also Hockey
Airborne '93
ATL '06
Blades of Courage '88▲
Blades of Glory '07▲
Breaking the Ice '38
Brink '98
The Cutting Edge '92
The Cutting Edge: Going for the Gold '05
Death to Smoochy '02▲
Derby '71▲
Everything Happens at Night '39▲
Frolics on Ice '39
Hans Brinker '69
Happy Landing '38
Ice Castles '79
Ice Pawn '92
Ice Princess '05
The Ice Rink '99
Iceland '42
It's All About Love '03
My Life on Ice '02
My Lucky Star '38
On Edge '03
One in a Million '36▲
Prayer of the Rollerboys '91
Roll Bounce '05
Roller Boogie '79
Schizo '77
Sun Valley Serenade '41
Unholy Rollers '72
Wintertime '43
Xanadu '80

Skiing

Aspen Extreme '93
Avalanche '78
Better Off Dead '85
Christmas in the Clouds '01
Club Med '83
Downhill Racer '69
Downhill Willie '96
Dumb & Dumber '94
Extreme Ops '02
Fire and Ice '87
Fire, Ice and Dynamite '91
For Your Eyes Only '81▲
Going for the Gold: The Bill Johnson Story '85
Hot Dog... The Movie! '83
Iced '88
Lost and Found '79
On Her Majesty's Secret Service '69▲
One Last Run '89
The Other Side of the Mountain '75
The Other Side of the Mountain, Part 2 '78
Out Cold '01
Red Snow '91
Reno and the Doc '84
Ski Bum '75
Ski Party '65
Ski Patrol '89
Ski School '91
Ski School 2 '94
Ski Troop Attack '60
Skier's Dream '88
Snow: The Movie '83
Snowball Express '72
Snowballin' '71
Snowballing '85
Snowblind '78
Striker's Mountain '87
True Lies '94

Skinheads

see also Nazis & Other Paramilitary Slugs
Adam's Apples '05
American History X '98
An American Werewolf in Paris '97
The Believer '01
Brotherhood of Murder '99
Cracker: To Be a Somebody '94
The Infiltrator '95
Lola and Billy the Kid '98
Luna Park '91
Meantime '83
The Murder of Stephen Lawrence '99▲
Red Scorpion 2 '94
Romper Stomper '92
Skin '89
Speak Up! It's So Dark '93
Steel Toes '06
The Substitute 4: Failure is Not an Option '00
Surf Nazis Must Die '87
Terror 2000 '92
This Is England '06
The Turning '92
White Lies '98

Skydiving

Cutaway '00
Drop Zone '94
Fandango '85
The Gypsy Moths '69
Honeymoon in Vegas '92
Point Break '91
Terminal Velocity '94

Slapstick Comedy

see also Comedy; Screwball Comedy
Abbott and Costello Go to Mars '53
Abbott and Costello in Hollywood '45
Abbott and Costello in the Foreign Legion '50
Abbott and Costello Meet Captain Kidd '52
Abbott and Costello Meet Dr. Jekyll and Mr. Hyde '52
Abbott and Costello Meet Frankenstein '48▲
Abbott and Costello Meet the Invisible Man '51▲
Abbott and Costello Meet the Keystone Kops '54
Abbott and Costello Meet the Killer, Boris Karloff '49
Abbott and Costello Meet the Mummy '55
Abroad with Two Yanks '44
Ace Ventura: Pet Detective '93
Ace Ventura: When Nature Calls '95
The Adventurer '17
The Adventures of Buckaroo Banzai Across the Eighth Dimension '84▲
Africa Screams '49
After the Fox '66
Air Raid Wardens '43
All New Adventures of Laurel and Hardy: For Love or Mummy '98
All of Me '84
All Over Town '37
Alvin Purple '73
Alvin Rides Again '74
American Aristocracy '17
American Pluck '25
Amos and Andrew '93
Animal Crackers '30▲
Any Which Way You Can '80
Armed and Dangerous '86
Around the World in 80 Ways '86
Around the World in a Daze '63
Assault and Matrimony '87
At the Circus '39▲
Baby's Day Out '94
The Bad News Bears '76▲
The Bad News Bears Go to Japan '78
The Bad News Bears in Breaking Training '77
The Bank Dick '40▲
The Barber Shop '33▲
The Barefoot Executive '71
The Battle of the Sexes '60▲
Bean '97▲
Bedtime for Bonzo '51
Beethoven '92
Beethoven's 2nd '93
The Bellboy '60
Big Mouth '67
Big Store '41
Black Cat, White Cat '98▲
Block-heads '38▲
Bohemian Girl '36▲
Bonnie Scotland '35
Bowery Boys Meet the Monsters '54
Boy, Did I Get a Wrong Number! '66
Boys Will Be Boys '97
Brain Donors '92
Buck Privates '41
Buck Privates Come Home '47▲
Bullfighters '45
The Caddy '53
Candleshoe '78
Carolina Cannonball '55
Carry On at Your Convenience '71
Carry On Behind '75
Carry On Camping '71
Carry On Cruising '62
Carry On Doctor '68▲
Carry On Emmanuelle '78
Carry On England '76
Carry On Henry VIII '71
Carry On Nurse '59
Casanova's Big Night '54
Cheech and Chong: Still Smokin' '83
Cheech and Chong: Things Are Tough All Over '82
Cheech and Chong's Next Movie '80
Cheech and Chong's The Corsican Brothers '84
Cheech and Chong's Up in Smoke '79
Christmas in July '40▲
A Chump at Oxford '40▲
Cinderfella '60
Cockeyed Cavaliers '34
College '27▲
Comin' Round the Mountain '51
Corky Romano '01
Cracking Up '83
The Cure '17
Dance with Me, Henry '56
Date Movie '06
A Day at the Races '37▲
The Delicate Delinquent '56
The Dentist '32▲
Detective School Dropouts '85
Disorderly Orderly '64
Don't Raise the Bridge, Lower the River '68
Double Trouble '41
Doughboys '30
Dragons Forever '88
Duck Soup '33▲
Ernest Goes to Africa '97
Ernest Goes to Camp '87
Ernest Goes to Jail '90
Ernest Goes to School '94
Ernest Rides Again '93
Ernest Scared Stupid '91
The Errand Boy '61
Family Jewels '65
The Feud '90
Finders Keepers '84
A Fine Mess '86
Flim-Flam Man '67
Flubber '97
The Flying Deuces '39▲
Folks! '92
Follow That Camel '67
Francis Covers the Big Town '53
Francis Goes to the Races '51
Francis Goes to West Point '52
Francis in the Haunted House '56
Francis in the Navy '55
Francis Joins the WACs '54
Francis the Talking Mule '49▲
Freddy Got Fingered '01
Free and Easy '30
The Fuller Brush Girl '50
The Fuller Brush Man '48
Funny Farm '88
George Washington Slept Here '42▲
Get Smart, Again! '89
The Ghost and Mr. Chicken '66
Ghost in the Noonday Sun '74
Ghost on the Loose '43
A Girl in Every Port '52
The Gods Must Be Crazy '84▲
The Gods Must Be Crazy 2 '89
Going Bananas '88
The Gorilla '39
Great Guns '41
The Great Lover '49
The Great Race '65
A Guide for the Married Man '67▲
Gus '76
Half-Shot at Sunrise '30
Hands Up '26
Hardly Working '81
Have Rocket Will Travel '59
Here Come the Co-Eds '45
Hold That Ghost '41▲
Hollywood or Bust '56
Home Alone '90▲
Home Alone 2: Lost in New York '92
Home Alone 3 '97
The Horn Blows at Midnight '45▲
Horse Feathers '32▲
Hot Lead & Cold Feet '78
I Hate Blondes '83
The Imposters '98
In Society '44
Ishtar '87
It Seemed Like a Good Idea at the Time '75
It's a Mad, Mad, Mad, Mad World '63
Jack & the Beanstalk '52
Jackass: The Movie '02
The Jerk '79
Jingle All the Way '96
Johnson Family Vacation '04
Jour de Fete '48▲
Julia Misbehaves '48▲
Jumping Jacks '52
Kentucky Kernels '34
The Kettles in the Ozarks '56
The Kettles on Old MacDonald's Farm '57
The Klutz '73
The Last Remake of Beau Geste '77
Laurel & Hardy and the Family '33
Laurel & Hardy: Another Fine Mess '30
Laurel & Hardy: At Work '32
Laurel & Hardy: Be Big '31
Laurel & Hardy: Below Zero '30
Laurel & Hardy: Berth Marks '29
Laurel & Hardy: Blotto '30
Laurel & Hardy: Brats '30
Laurel & Hardy: Chickens Come Home '31
Laurel & Hardy: Hog Wild '30
Laurel & Hardy: Laughing Gravy '31
Laurel & Hardy: Men O'War '29
Laurel & Hardy: Night Owls '30
Laurel & Hardy On the Lam '30
Laurel & Hardy: Perfect Day '29
Laurel & Hardy Spooktacular '34
Laurel & Hardy: Stan "Helps" Ollie '33
Laurel & Hardy: The Hoose-Gow '29
Let's Go! '23
Little Giant '46
Long Pants '27▲
Lost in a Harem '44
Lost in Alaska '52
The Lost Stooges '33
Love Happy '50
Ma and Pa Kettle '49
Ma and Pa Kettle at the Fair '52
Ma and Pa Kettle at Waikiki '55
Ma and Pa Kettle Back On the Farm '51
Ma and Pa Kettle Go to Town '50
The Mad Adventures of Rabbi Jacob '73▲
Man of the House '95
Man's Favorite Sport? '63
Matilda '78
Meatballs 3 '87
Meatballs 4 '92
Menage '86▲
Mexican Hayride '48
Milky Way '36
Mr. Bean's Holiday '07
Mr. Hulot's Holiday '53▲
Mr. Magoo '97
Monkey Business '31▲
Monkey Trouble '94
The Monster '96
My Friend Irma '49
The Naughty Nineties '45
The Navigator '24▲
Never Give a Sucker an Even Break '41▲
A Night at the Opera '35▲
A Night in Casablanca '46▲
The Noose Hangs High '48▲
Norbit '07
The North Avenue Irregulars '79
Not Quite Human '87
Not Quite Human 2 '89
Nothing But Trouble '44
Nuns on the Run '90
Odd Jobs '85
Off Limits '53
Off the Wall '82
One A.M. '16
Our Relations '36▲
Out of the Blue '47
The Out-of-Towners '99
The Outlaws Is Coming! '65
Pack Up Your Troubles '32
Pardon My Sarong '42
Pardon My Trunk '52
Pardon Us '31
The Party '68▲
The Patsy '64
Pawnshop '16
Pharmacist '32
The Pink Panther '06
Playtime '67▲
Police Academy 2: Their First Assignment '85
Police Academy 4: Citizens on Patrol '87
Police Academy 5: Assignment Miami Beach '88
Police Academy 6: City under Siege '89
Police Academy 7: Mission to Moscow '94
Problem Child 2 '91
Quick, Let's Get Married '71
Railroder '65▲
Rally 'Round the Flag, Boys! '58
Reckless Kelly '93
Red Salute '35
Rescue from Gilligan's Island '78
Rio Rita '42
The Road to Hong Kong '62
Robin Hood: Men in Tights '93
RocketMan '97
Rockin' Road Trip '85
Room Service '38
Sailor Beware '52
Saps at Sea '40
Say It Isn't So '01
Seducing Doctor Lewis '03
Serving Sara '02
Seven Years Bad Luck '21▲
Show People '28▲
Sidewalks of New York '31
Slapstick of Another Kind '84

▲ = rated three bones or higher

Snow White and the Three Stooges '61
So This Is Africa '33
Son of the Pink Panther '93
Sons of the Desert '33▶
The Speed Spook '24
Strangers with Candy '06
The Strongest Man in the World '75
The Stupids '95
Superstar '99
Surviving Christmas '04
Swiss Miss '38
Take the Money and Run '69▶
Tanks a Million '41
The 30-Foot Bride of Candy Rock '59
Three Charlies and One Phoney! '18
Three Stooges in Orbit '62
The Three Stooges Meet Hercules '61
Tillie Wakes Up '17
Too Shy to Try '82
Trial and Error '96
Tramp, Tramp, Tramp '26
Two-Way Stretch '60
Up the Creek '58
Utopia '51
Voyage Surprise '46▶
Walk Like a Man '87
Weekend at Bernie's '89
Weekend at Bernie's 2 '93
What No Beer? '33
Who Done It? '42
Who Killed Doc Robbin? '48
The Whole Nine Yards '00▶
Who's Minding the Store? '63
Why Me? '90
Wide Open Faces '38
A Woman of Distinction '50▶
The Wonders of Aladdin '61
Yankee Doodle in Berlin 19
The Yellow Cab Man '50
Yellowbeard '83
Yours, Mine & Ours '05

Slasher Flicks
see also Bloody Messages; Horror; Serial Killers; Supernatural Horror; Teen Horror
The Amityville Horror '79
Amityville 2: The Possession '82
Amityville 3: The Demon '83
Amityville 4: The Evil Escapes '89
Amityville: A New Generation '93
The Amityville Curse '90
Amityville 1992: It's About Time '92
Are You Scared? '06
Bad Dreams '88
Bad Reputation '05▶
Black Christmas '06
Boogeyman 2 '07
Born for Hell '76
Chaos '05
CryWolf '05
Cult '07
Death Proof '07
The Descent '05
Devon's Ghost: Legend of the Bloody Boy '05
Evil Dead '83
Evil Dead 2: Dead by Dawn '87
Freddy vs. Jason '03
Freddy's Dead: The Final Nightmare '91
Friday the 13th '80
Friday the 13th, Part 2 '81
Friday the 13th, Part 3 '82
Friday the 13th, Part 4: The Final Chapter '84
Friday the 13th, Part 5: A New Beginning '85
Friday the 13th, Part 6: Jason Lives '86
Friday the 13th, Part 7: The New Blood '88
Friday the 13th, Part 8: Jason Takes Manhattan '89
Hack! '07
Halloween '07
Halloween '78▶
Halloween 2 '81
Halloween 3: Season of the Witch '82
Halloween 4: The Return of Michael Myers '88
Halloween 5: The Revenge of Michael Myers '89
Halloween 6: The Curse of Michael Myers '95
Halloween: Resurrection '02
Halloween: H20 '98
Hangman's Curse '03
Happy Birthday to Me '81
Happy Hell Night '92
He Knows You're Alone '80
Hello Mary Lou: Prom Night 2 '87
High Tension '03
The Hills Have Eyes '06
Hostel '06
House of Wax '05
I Know What You Did Last Summer '97▶
I Still Know What You Did Last Summer '98
Incubus '05
Jack Frost '97
Jason Goes to Hell: The Final Friday '93
Motel Hell '80
Motor Home Massacre '05
Night Screams '87
A Nightmare on Elm Street '84
A Nightmare on Elm Street 2: Freddy's Revenge '85
A Nightmare on Elm Street 3: Dream Warriors '87
A Nightmare on Elm Street 4: The Dream Master '88
A Nightmare on Elm Street 5: Dream Child '89
P2 '07
Prom Night '80
Prom Night 3: The Last Kiss '89
Prom Night 4: Deliver Us from Evil '91
Rooms for Tourists '04▶
School's Out '99
Scream '96▶
Scream 2 '97▶
Scream 3 '00
Seance '06
See No Evil '06
Shriek If You Know What I Did Last Friday the 13th '00
Slaughter High '86
Sweet Insanity '06
Terror Train '80
The Texas Chainsaw Massacre '74
The Texas Chainsaw Massacre 2 '86
Tourist Trap '79
Vacancy '07
Valentine '01
Wes Craven's New Nightmare '94▶
Wishmaster '97
Wishmaster 2: Evil Never Dies '98
Wishmaster 3: Beyond the Gates of Hell '01
Wishmaster 4: The Prophecy Fulfilled '02

Slavery
see also Civil Rights
The Abductors '72
Acla's Descent into Floristella '87
The Adventures of Huckleberry Finn '85
Amazing Grace '06▶
Amistad '97▶
The Arena '73
Band of Angels '57
Being Human '94
Beloved '98
The Big Bust Out '73
Black Fox: The Price of Peace '94
Blacksnake! '73
Brother Future '91
Buck and the Preacher '72
Burn! '70▶
Candyman 2: Farewell to the Flesh '94
Cobra Verde '88
The Colombian Connection
CSA: The Confederate States of America '04
Dragonard '88
Gladiator '00▶
Gone Are the Days '63
Half Slave, Half Free '85
A House Divided '13
The House of Dies Drear '88
The House of 1,000 Dolls '67
Intimate Power '89
Island of Lost Girls '68
Jefferson in Paris '94
Joseph '95
The Journey of August King '95
Kill the Conqueror '97
The King and I '56▶
The Last Supper '76▶
Lust for Freedom '87
The Magic Stone '95
Man Friday '75
Man from Deep River '77
Mandela '87
Mandingo '75
Moses '96
Mutiny on the Blackhawk '39
Nightjohn '96
Olga's Girls '64
Once Upon a Time in China 2 '91▶
Planet of the Apes '01▶
The Promise '05
Pudd'nhead Wilson '84
Queen '93▶
Quilombo '84
Race to Freedom: The Story of the Underground Railroad '94
A Respectable Trade '98
Ride with the Devil '99
The Road to Morocco '42▶
The Robe '53
Roots '77▶
Roots: The Gift '88
Sally Hemings: An American Scandal '00
Sansho the Bailiff '54▶
Shadrach '98
Shaft in Africa '73
The Silencer '92
Skin Game '71▶
Slavers '77
Slaves '69
Souls at Sea '37
Spartacus '60▶
Stolen Childhoods '05
Sunshine Run '79
Tamango '59
Traffic in Souls '13▶
True Women '97
Uncle Tom's Cabin '14
Uncle Tom's Cabin '27
Uncle Tom's Cabin '69
Uncle Tom's Cabin '87
Wanda the Sadistic Hypnotist '67
White Slave '86
A Woman Called Moses '78
Xica '76▶

Slob Comedy
see also Comedy; Slapstick; Comedy; Stupid Is...
Accepted '06
Airheads '94
Anger Management '03
The Animal '01
Bachelor Party '84
Beer League '06
Beerfest '06
The Benchwarmers '06
Better Off Dead '85
Beverly Hills Ninja '96
Big Daddy '99
Bill & Ted's Bogus Journey '91
Bill & Ted's Excellent Adventure '89
Billy Madison '95
Bio-Dome '96
Black Sheep '96
Blues Brothers '80▶
Blues Brothers 2000 '98
Bubble Boy '01
Caddyshack '80▶
Caddyshack 2 '88
Dead Man on Campus '98
Deuce Bigalow: Male Gigolo '99
Dirty Work '97
Dodgeball: A True Underdog Story '04
Dude, Where's My Car? '00
Dumb & Dumber '94
Employee of the Month '06
Friday '95
Friday After Next '02
Grandma's Boy '05
Grind '03
Half-Baked '97
Happy Gilmore '96
Harold and Kumar Go to White Castle '04
The Hollywood Knights '80
The Hot Chick '02
How High '01
Idiocracy '06
In the Army Now '94
Jackass: The Movie '02
Jackass Number Two '06
Joe Dirt '01
Kangaroo Jack '03
Knocked Up '07
Let's Go to Prison '06
Little Athens '05
Little Nicky '00
Making the Grade '84
Malibu's Most Wanted '03
Meatballs '79
Mr. Deeds '02
The Moguls '05
My Baby's Daddy '04
Nacho Libre '06
National Lampoon's Animal House '78▶
National Lampoon's Holiday Reunion '06
National Lampoon's Van Wilder '02
National Lampoon's Van Wilder 2: The Rise of Taj '06
The New Guy '02
Next Friday '00
Night Shift '82
The Nugget '02
Old School '03▶
One Crazy Summer '86
P.C.U. '94
Police Academy '84
Porky's '82
Porky's 2: The Next Day '83
Porky's Revenge '85
Road Trip '00
School of Rock '03▶
Screwed '00
Shakes the Clown '92
Son-in-Law '93
Sorority Boys '02
Spies Like Us '85
Strange Brew '83
Stripes '81
Super Troopers '01
Tomcats '01
Tommy Boy '95
Waiting... '05
The Waterboy '98
Wayne's World '92▶
Wayne's World 2 '93
The Wedding Singer '97
White Coats '04
Without a Paddle '04

Small-Town Sheriffs
Ace in the Hole '51▶
Angels Fall '07
The Badge '02
Best Men '98
Black Cadillac '03
Blood Crime '02
Blue Ridge Fall '99
Brigham City '01
Cash Crop '01
Cherry Falls '00
Children On Their Birthdays '02
Coastlines '02
Cop Land '97▶
Dear Wendy '05
Death of a Gunfighter '69
The Desperados '69
The Devil's Rejects '05
Down in the Valley '05
The Dukes of Hazzard '05
Eight Legged Freaks '02
El Dorado '67▶
Exiled in America '90
Eye of the Storm '98
Forty Guns '57
The Gunfight at Dodge City '59
Happy, Texas '99▶
Hard Luck '01
Hard Rain '97
A History of Violence '05▶
I Walk the Line '70
In the Heat of the Night '67▶
Jesse Stone: Death in Paradise '06
Jesse Stone: Night Passage '06
Jesse Stone: Sea Change '07
Jesse Stone: Stone Cold '05
Knockaround Guys '01
The Last Hard Men '76
Lone Star '95▶
The Mothman Prophecies '02
No Country for Old Men '07▶
Pardners '56
Planet Terror '07
A Real American Hero '78
Red Rock West '93▶
Rio Bravo '59▶
Rustin '01
Shallow Ground '04
The Sheriff of Fractured Jaw '59
Silverado '85▶
Slither '06
A Small Town in Texas '76
Strange Fruit '04
Sudden Impact '83
Switchback '97
The Texas Chainsaw Massacre '03
The Texas Chainsaw Massacre: The Beginning '06
Walking Tall '73
Walking Tall: Part 2 '75
Walking Tall: The Final Chapter '77
Walking Tall '04
Walking Tall: Lone Justice '07
We Own the Night '07

Smuggler's Blues
see also Crime & Criminals; Drug Use & Abuse
Acapulco Gold '78
American Gangster '07▶
Bad Boys 2 '03
Better Luck Tomorrow '02▶
The Big Turnaround '88
The Blonde '92
Blow '01
Blue, White and Perfect '42
Bobby Z '07
Brick '06▶
Brother '00▶
Charlie Chan in Shanghai '35
City of God '02▶
Codename: Wildgeese '84
The Corner '00
Cutaway '00
Detention '03
Deuces Wild '02
Drug Wars: The Camarena Story '90▶
Drug Wars 2: The Cocaine Cartel '92
Empire '02
Erik '90
Essex Boys '99
Exit Wounds '01
Formula 51 '01
Gone Baby Gone '07▶
The Guardian '00
Half-Baked '97
High School Confidential '58
In Too Deep '99
Jimmy Zip '00
The Last Minute '01
Lethal Weapon 2 '89▶
Loaded '08
A Man Apart '03
Maria Full of Grace '04▶
Memento '00▶
Mexican Blow '02
Miami Vice '06
Once in the Life '00
Operation Orient '73
Our Lady of the Assassins '01
Outta Time '01
Paid in Full '02
Party Monster '03
Pineapple Express '08
Rare Birds '01
Requiem for a Dream '00▶
Return of the Living Dead: Rave to the Grave '05▶
Rude Boy: The Jamaican Don '03
The Rules of Attraction '02
Shaft '00▶
Sherlock: Case of Evil '02
Spun '02
Starsky & Hutch '04
The Street Fighter's Last Revenge '74
Street Vengeance '95
Subterfuge '98
Sugar Hill '94
Sunstorm '01
Super Troopers '01
Sweet Sixteen '02▶
The Taste of Others '00▶
Time and Tide '00
Torque '04
Training Day '01▶
True Romance '93
Tweek City '05
25th Hour '02▶
Under Hellgate Bridge '99
Up and Down '04
Veronica Guerin '03
Weirdsville '07

Snakes
see also Killer Reptiles; Wild Kingdom
Anaconda '96
Anacondas: The Hunt for the Blood Orchid '04
Black Cobra '83
Boa '02
Copperhead '84
Curse 2: The Bite '88
Fer-De-Lance '74
Fools Rush In '97
Foul Play '78▶
Green Snake '93
Halfmoon '95
Harry Potter and the Chamber of Secrets '02
Indiana Jones and the Last Crusade '89▶
Indiana Jones and the Temple of Doom '84▶
Jennifer '78
Journey to the Lost City '58
Journey to the Jungle Book '67▶

▶ = rated three bones or higher

Snakes

Kill Bill Vol. 2 '04▶
King Cobra '98
Lewis and Clark and George '97
Megasnake '07
Natural Born Killers '94
Python '00
Python 2 '02
Raiders of the Lost Ark '81▶
Rattled '96
Rattlers '76
The Reptile '66
The Road Warrior '82▶
Silent Predators '99
Silver Stallion '41
The Snake People '68
Snakeman '05
Snakes on a Plane '06▶
Spasms '82
Sssssss '73
Stanley '72
Venom '05
Venomous '01
The Wild '06
Women's Prison Escape '74

Sniper

see also Crime Sprees;
Hit Men/Women;
Military; Army
Agent Cody Banks '03
Conspiracy '08
Dirty Harry '71▶
Enemy at the Gates '00
Jarhead '05
Liberty Stands Still '02
The Manchurian Candidate '04▶
The Musketeer '01
Phone Booth '01
Point Break '91
Shooter '07
Shot Through the Heart '98▶
Sniper '75▶
The Sniper '78
Sniper '92
Sniper 2 '02
Two Minute Warning '76
Winter Kills '79▶

Snowboarding

see also Skiing
Extreme Ops '02
First Descent '05
Out Cold '01

Soccer

Air Bud 3: World Pup '00
Bend It Like Beckham '02▶
Big Brother Trouble '00
The Big Green '95
Bossa Nova '99
The Club '81▶
Cracker: To Be a Somebody '94
The Cup '99
Cup Final '91
Fever Pitch '96
The Final Goal '94
The Game of Their Lives '05
Go Now '96▶
Goal! The Dream Begins '06
The Goalie's Anxiety at the Penalty Kick '71▶
Gracie '07
Green Street Hooligans '05▶
Gregory's Girl '80▶
Guys and Balls '04
The Hero '71
Home Team '98
Hot Shot '86
Hothead '78
Joyeux Noel '05▶
Kicking & Screaming '05
Ladybugs '92
Long Shot Kids '81
The Match '99
Mean Machine '01
One Fine Day '96
The Pink Panther '06
Shaolin Soccer '01
She's the Man '06
A Shot at Glory '00
Soccer Dog: The Movie '98
Stuart Little 2 '02▶
Those Glory, Glory Days '83
Victory '81
When Saturday Comes '95
Yesterday's Hero '79

South America

see also Central America
Aguirre, the Wrath of God '72▶
Amazon '90
The Americano '17
Americano '55
Anacondas: The Hunt for the Blood Orchid '04
Apartment Zero '88▶
Argentine Nights '40
Assassination Tango '03▶
At Play in the Fields of the Lord '91▶
Bananas '71▶
Behind the Sun '01
Black Orpheus '58▶
Boca '94
The Bridge of San Luis Rey '05
Burden of Dreams '82▶
The Burning Season '94▶
Burnt Money '00
Butch Cassidy and the Sundance Kid '69▶
Bye Bye Brazil '79
Carandiru '03
Casa de los Babys '03▶
Catch the Heat '87
The Celestine Prophecy '06
Chronically Unfeasible '00
Chronicle of the Raven '04
Clear and Present Danger '94
Cobra Verde '88
Collateral Damage '02
The Colombian Connection '91
Cronicas '04
The Dancer Upstairs '02
The Dark Side of the Heart '92
Death and the Maiden '94▶
Death in the Garden '56
Diplomatic Immunity '91
Doctor Chance '97
Down Argentine Way '40▶
800 Leagues Down the Amazon '93
El Carro '04
El Muerto '75
The Emerald Forest '85▶
End of the Spear '06
Evita '96
Mighty Jungle '64
Miracles '86
Miss Mary '86
The Mission '86▶
Missing '82▶
Mission... Kill '87
Moon over Parador '88
The Motorcycle Diaries '04▶
The Muthers '76
Naked Jungle '54▶
Naked Tango '91
Nancy Goes to Rio '50
Night Flight '33
Night Gallery '69▶
Nine Queens '00
Nostromo '96
O Quatrilho '95
Of Love and Shadows '94
One Man Out '89
Only Angels Have Wings '39▶
Oriana '85
Our Brand Is Crisis '05▶
Our Lady of the Assassins '01
Overkill '96
The Pink Jungle '68
A Place in the World '92▶
The Plague '92
Play for Me '01
Quilombo '84
Ratas, Ratones, Rateros '99
Rodrigo D: No Future '91
Rolling Family '04
Romancing the Stone '84▶
Secre of the Andes '98
A Shadow You Soon Will Be '94
Shoot to Kill '90
Simon Bolivar '69
Slayer '06
The Son of the Bride '01▶
The Story of Fausta '88
Sweet Country '87
Tango '98
Terranova '91
Terror in the Jungle '68
Testosterone '03
The Three Caballeros '45
To Kill a Stranger '84
Turistas '06
Under the Pampas Moon '35
Valentin '02
Veronico Cruz '87
What Your Eyes Don't See '99
The White Diamond '04▶
Wild Orchid '90
Xica '76▶
A Year Without Love '05
You Were Never Lovelier '42▶

A Streetcar Named Desire '51▶
A Streetcar Named Desire '84▶
A Streetcar Named Desire '95
The Trip to Bountiful '85▶

Space Operas

see also Alien Beings—Benign; Alien Beings—Vicious
Alien '79▶
Alien Cargo '99
The Apocalypse '96
Apollo 13 '95▶
Assignment Outer Space '61
Battle Beyond the Stars '80▶
Battle Beyond the Sun '63
Battlestar Galactica '78▶
The Black Hole '79
Black Horizon '01
Buck Rogers Conquers the Universe '39
Capricorn One '78▶
Cat Women of the Moon '53
Conquest of Space '55
Contact '97
Countdown '68
Creature '85
Dark Breed '96
Dark Side of the Moon '90
Dark Star '74▶
The Day the Sky Exploded '57
Dead Fire '98
Destination Moon '50
Destination Moonbase Alpha '75
Destination Saturn '39
The Dish '00▶
Earthstorm '06
Escape from Mars '99
Escape from Planet Earth '67
Escape Velocity '99
Event Horizon '97
Explorers '85
Fire Maidens from Outer Space '56
First Encounter '97
First Men in the Moon '64▶
First Spaceship on Venus '60▶
Flight to Mars '52
Forbidden Planet '56▶
From the Earth to the Moon '58
From the Earth to the Moon '98▶
Galaxy of Terror '81
Gattaca '97▶
The Green Slime '68
Hangar 18 '80
Have Rocket Will Travel '59
Heavens Above '63▶
Hellraiser 4: Bloodline '95
Horrors of the Red Planet '64
In the Dead of Space '99
In the Shadow of the Moon '07▶
Inseminoid '80
John Carpenter's Ghosts of Mars '01
Journey to the Far Side of the Sun '69▶
Killings at Outpost Zeta '80
Laser Mission '90
The Last Starfighter '84▶
Lifepod '80
Lifepod '93
Lost in Space '98
Marooned '69
Megaforce '82
Mission Galactica: The Cylon Attack '78
Mission Mars '67
Mission to Mars '00
Mom and Dad Save the World '92
Moon 44 '90
Moonraker '79
Moontrap '89
The Mouse on the Moon '62▶
Murder in Space '85
Mutant on the Bounty '89
Mystery Science Theater 3000: The Movie '96
Nude on the Moon '61
Outland '81
Planet Burg '62
Planet of the Apes '68▶
Planet of the Apes '01▶
Planet of the Dinosaurs '80
Planet of the Vampires '65
Precious Find '96
Project Moon Base '53
PSI Factor '80
Race to Space '01
Red Planet '00
The Reluctant Astronaut '67
Return of the Jedi '83▶
Return to Earth '76
The Right Stuff '83▶
Robinson Crusoe on Mars '64
RocketMan '97
Rocketship X-M '50
Scorpio One '97
Serenity '05▶
Silent Running '71▶
Solar Crisis '92
Solaris '72
Solaris '02
Space Chimps '08
Space Cowboys '00▶
Space Mutiny '88
Space Rage '86
Space Raiders '83
Spaceballs '87
SpaceCamp '86
Spacejacked '98
Star Crash '78
Star Slammer '87
Star Trek: The Motion Picture '79
Star Trek 2: The Wrath of Khan '82▶
Star Trek 3: The Search for Spock '84
Star Trek 4: The Voyage Home '86▶
Star Trek 5: The Final Frontier '89
Star Trek 6: The Undiscovered Country '91
Star Trek: First Contact '96▶
Star Trek: Generations '94▶
Star Trek: Insurrection '98
Star Trek: Nemesis '02
Star Wars '77▶
Star Wars: Episode 2—Attack of the Clones '02▶
Star Wars: Episode 3—Revenge of the Sith '05▶
Stargate: The Ark of Truth '08
Starship '87
Sunshine '07▶
Supernova '99
Tales from a Parallel Universe: Eating Pattern '97
Tales from a Parallel Universe: Giga Shadow '97
The Terromauts '67
Three Stooges in Orbit '62
Titan A.E. '00
Transformations '88
Trapped in Space '94
Treasure Planet '02▶
2001: A Space Odyssey '68▶
2010: A Space Travesty '00
2010: The Year We Make Contact '84▶
Vegas in Space '94
Velocity Trap '99
Voyage to the Planet of Prehistoric Women '68
Voyage to the Prehistoric Planet '65
Walking on Air '87
Warlords of the 21st Century '82
Wing Commander '99
Woman in the Moon '29
Woman of the Prehistoric Planet '66

Southern Belles

see also American South; Nashville Narratives
Blaze '89
Cat on a Hot Tin Roof '58▶
Cat on a Hot Tin Roof '84
Children On Their Birthdays '02
Crimes of the Heart '86▶
Dear Dead Delilah '72
Driving Miss Daisy '89▶
The Glass Menagerie '87▶
Gone with the Wind '39▶
Hush, Hush, Sweet Charlotte '65▶
Jezebel '38▶
Miss Firecracker '89▶
Nashville '75▶
North and South Book 1 '85▶
North and South Book 2 '86▶
The Notebook '04▶
Other Voices, Other Rooms '95
Queen Bee '55
Rich in Love '93
Scarlett '94
Scorchers '92
Southern Belles '05
Steel Magnolias '89▶

Spaghetti Western

see also Western Comedy; Westerns
Ace High '68
Adios, Hombre '68
Adios, Sabata '71
And God Said to Cain '69
Any Gun Can Play '67
Apache's Last Battle '64
Belle Starr '79
Beyond the Law '68
Blood for a Silver Dollar '66
The Boldest Job in the West '71
Boot Hill '69
Bullet for Sandoval '70
Bullet for the General '68
Chino '75
Django Shoots First '74
800 Bullets '02
Fistful of Death '71
A Fistful of Dollars '64▶
A Fistful of Dynamite '72▶
Fistful of Lead '70
Five Giants from Texas '66
For a Few Dollars More '65▶
Garringo '69
The Good, the Bad and the Ugly '67▶
The Grand Duel '73
Gunfight at Red Sands '63
Gunfire '78
Gunslinger '70
Hang 'Em High '67▶
Hellbenders '67
His Name Was King '85
The Last Tomahawk '65
Minnesota Clay '65
A Minute to Pray, a Second to Die '67
My Name Is Nobody '74
Navajo Joe '67
Once Upon a Time in the West '68▶
Red Sun '71
Return of Sabata '71
Rough Justice '87
Sabata '69
Shoot the Living, Pray for the Dead '70
Spaghetti Western '75
The Stranger and the Gunfighter '76
Stranger in Paso Bravo '68
Take a Hard Ride '75
Tramplers '66
Trinity Is Still My Name '75
Twice a Judas '69
You're Jinxed, Friend, You've Met Sacramento '70

Spain

see also Barcelona; Madrid; Spanish Civil War
Against the Wind '90
Americano '05
Angel of Death '02
Ay, Carmela! '90▶
Bad Education '04▶
Barcelona '94▶
The Barcelona Kill '77
Behold a Pale Horse '64
Belle Epoque '92▶
Blood and Sand '41▶
Broken Silence '01▶
Butterfly '98▶
Carmen, Baby '66
Carnage '02
The Castilian '63
Day of Wrath '06
Desire '36▶
Destiny '97
The Devil Is a Woman '35▶
The Devil's Backbone '01▶
The Disappearance of Garcia Lorca '96
800 Bullets '02
El Crimen Perfecto '04▶
Extramuros '85
Fiesta '95
Food of Love '02

▶ = rated three bones or higher

For Whom the Bell Tolls '43▶
Gaudí Afternoon '01
The Grandfather '98
Honeymoon Academy '90
I'm the One You're Looking For '88
Intacto '01
It's All Gone, Pete Tong '04
Kevin & Perry Go Large '00
Kim '00
Land and Freedom '95▶
The Last Seduction 2 '98
Lazarillo '59
L'Auberge Espagnola '02▶
Letters from Alou '90
Live Flesh '97▶
Love Can Seriously Damage Your Health '96
Mad Love '01
Marbella '85
Mondays in the Sun '02
Morvern Callar '02
My Mother Likes Women '02
The Naked Maja '59
Nico and Dani '00
The Orphanage '07▶
The Other Side of the Bed '03
Pandora and the Flying Dutchman '51
Pan's Labyrinth '06▶
The Pride and the Passion '57
Running Out of Time '94
Sand and Blood '87
The Sea Inside '04▶
Second Skin '99
Sexy Beast '00▶
Siesta '87
Solas '99
The Spanish Gardener '57▶
Surprise Attack '70
The Sword of El Cid '62
Take My Eyes '03
Talk of Angels '96
Talk to Her '02▶
Tierra '95
Torremolinos 73 '03
A Touch of Class '73▶
Vacas '91
Vantage Point '08
Volver '06▶
Warriors '02

Spanish Civil War
Behold a Pale Horse '64
Broken Silence '01▶
The Devil's Backbone '01
The Disappearance of Garcia Lorca '96
The Fallen Sparrow '43▶
For Whom the Bell Tolls '43▶
The Girl of Your Dreams '99
Head in the Clouds '04
If They Tell You I Fell '89
Land and Freedom '95▶
The Night Has Eyes '42
Vacas '91

Spiders
see also Killer Bugs and Slugs

The Amazing Spider-Man '77
The Angry Red Planet '59
Arachnophobia '90
Blade Master '84
Charlotte's Web '73
Charlotte's Web '06▶
The Covenant '06
Curse of the Black Widow '77
Earth vs. the Spider '58
Eight Legged Freaks '02
The Giant Spider Invasion '75
Hell Hunters '87
Ice Spiders '07
James and the Giant Peach '96▶
Kingdom of the Spiders '77
Kiss of the Tarantula '75
Lord of the Rings: The Return of the King '03▶
Lost in Space '98
Microcosmos '96▶
Tarantulas: The Deadly Cargo '77

Spies & Espionage
see also CIA/NSA; Cold War Spies; Foreign Intrigue; Joke and Dagger; Spy Kids; Terrorism; World War I Spies; World War II Spies

Above Suspicion '43▶
Access Code '84
Agent Cody Banks 2: Destination London '04
Agent Cody Banks '03
Agent on Ice '86
The Apocalypse Watch '97
Arabesque '66
The Art of War '00
Artists and Models '55
As If It Were Raining '63
Assassin '89
The Assassination Game '92
The Assassination Run '84
The Atomic Kid '54
Attack of the Robots '66
Austin Powers: International Man of Mystery '97▶
Austin Powers 2: The Spy Who Shagged Me '99▶
Austin Powers in Goldmember '02
The Avengers '98
Bad Company '94
Ballistic: Ecks vs. Sever '02
Balls of Fury '07
The Bank Job '08▶
The Black Windmill '74
Blue '92
Beaumarchais the Scoundrel '96
Behind Enemy Lines '85
Big Deadly Game '54
The Big Lift '50
Black Brigade '69
Black Eagle '88
Blue, White and Perfect '42
The Bourne Ultimatum '07▶
The Bourne Supremacy '04▶
The Bourne Identity '02▶
Breach '07▶
British Intelligence '40
Bulldog Drummond at Bay '37
Bulldog Drummond Escapes '37
Bulletproof '88
Cambridge Spies '03
Carolina Cannonball '55
Casablanca '42▶
Casino Royale '67
Casino Royale '06▶
A Casualty of War '90
Charge of the Model T's '76
Charlie Chan at the Olympics '37
Clear and Present Danger '94
Code Name: Chaos '90
Code Name: Diamond Head '77
Codename: Foxfire '85
Codename: Icarus '85
Codename: Wildgeese '84
Comrades in Arms '91
Contraband '40
Cradle 2 the Grave '03
Criminals Within '41
Dandy in Aspic '68
Daniel '83
Daniella by Night '61
Dark Journey '37▶
Deadly Spygames '89
The Deadly Trap '71
Death Ray 2000 '81
Deathcheaters '76
Delta Force Commando 2 '90
Derailed '02▶
Desperate Cargo '41
Diamonds Are Forever '71▶
Die Another Day '02▶
A Different Loyalty '04▶
Dishonored '31
Dr. No '62▶
The Doll Squad '73
Don't Drink the Water '69
Doomsday Gun '94
Double Agents '59
Double Deal '50
Down Among the Z Men '52
The Dunera Boys '85▶
Edge of Darkness '86
Elizabeth '98▶
Embassy '85
Enforcer from Death Row '78
Erik '90
Escape from Fort Bravo '53
Espionage in Tangiers '65
The Executioner '70
Extremely Dangerous '99
Eyewitness '81
The Falcon's Brother '42
False Faces '13
Fathom '67
Fay Grim '06▶
Federal Agent '36
A Few Days in September '06
The Final Option '82
Fire Over England '37▶
Firetail '98
Flight to Nowhere '46
Flying Blind '41
The Foreigner '78
The Formula '80
French Intrigue '70
The General Died at Dawn '36
Get Smart '08
Get Smart, Again! '89
Girls Are for Loving '73
The Glass Bottom Boat '66
Golden Earrings '47
Goldeneye: The Secret Life of Ian Fleming '89
Goldeneye '95▶
Goldfinger '64▶
The Groundstar Conspiracy '72
Gunpowder '87
The Hades Factor '06
Hanky Panky '82
Hard Ticket to Hawaii '87
Head Over Heels '87
Hidden Agenda '89
Hillbillies in a Haunted House '67
The Holcroft Covenant '85
The Holly Terror '85
Honeymoon Academy '90
Hostage '92
Hour of the Assassin '86
The House on Garibaldi Street '79
House on 92nd Street '45▶
The Hunt for Red October '90▶
Hunter '73
I Stand Condemned '36
The Impossible Spy '87▶
In the Secret State '85
Inside the Lines '30
Internecine Project '73
It Means That to Me '60
J-Men Forever! '79▶
Jack Higgins: The Windsor Protocol '97
Jakarta '88
Joan of Paris '42▶
Johnny English '03
Journey into Fear '43▶
Jungle Drums of Africa '53
Keep Talking Baby '61
Kill Factor '78
Kim '50▶
Koroshi '67
La Cage aux Folles 2 '81
Last Embrace '79▶
Last Run '01
Le Magnifique '76
Le Professionnel '81▶
License to Kill '64
License to Kill '89▶
Lie Down with Lions '94
Lighting Bolt '67
Lipstick Camera '93
The Little Drummer Girl '84▶
Live and Let Die '73▶
The Lives of Others '06▶
Loaded Guns '75
Lost Diamond '86
The Love Light '21
Love on the Run '36
Ma and Pa Kettle on Vacation '53
Mad Mission 3 '84
Madame Sin '71
Malone '87
Man from Headquarters '28
The Man on the Box '25
The Man Outside '68
The Man Who Wasn't There '83
The Man with the Golden Gun '74
Marie Galante '34▶
Marco 7 '67
The Mask of Dimitrios '44▶
Master Spy: The Robert Hanssen Story '02
Mata Hari '32▶
Mata Hari '85
The Medallion '03
Midnight in Saint Petersburg '96
Mind Trap '91
Mindfield '89
Mr. Majestyk '73
Modesty Blaise '66
The Monocle '64
Moonraker '79
Murder for Sale '68
Murder on the Midnight Express '74
Murderers' Row '66
The Mysterious Lady '28
Mystery Plane '39
Never Say Never Again '83
Never Too Young to Die '86
Ninja Champion '80
North by Northwest '59▶
Number 1 of the Secret Service '69▶
The Odessa File '74
Old Mother Riley's Ghosts '41
On Her Majesty's Secret Service '69▶
One Armed Executioner '80
One of Our Dinosaurs Is Missing '75
Pack of Lies '87
Panama Patrol '39
Paper Tiger '74
Paradiso '61
Pascali's Island '88▶
Patriot Games '92▶
Permission To Kill '75
Picasso Trigger '89
President's Mistress '78
Prime Risk '84
The Quiller Memorandum '66▶
Rebel Love '85
The Recruit '03
Reilly: Ace of Spies '87▶
Rescue from Gilligan's Island '78
Retrievers '82
Return of the Man from U.N.C.L.E. '83
Return to Savage Beach '97
Robinson Crusoe of Mystery Island '36
Ronin '98▶
Running Blind '78
Running Delilah '93
Running Scared '79
Sabotage '36▶
The Saint '97
S.A.S. San Salvador '84
Sea Devils '53
The Secret Agent '36▶
The Secret Agent '96
Secret Agent 00 '67
Secret Agent Super Dragon '66
Secret Weapon '90
Shadows over Shanghai '38
S*H*E '79
Sky Parade '36
The Silencers '66
Smiley's People '82
Sneakers '92▶
The Soldier '82
A Show of Force '90
A Southern Yankee '48
The Spanish Prisoner '97▶
Spartan '04▶
Spies '28▶
Spies, Lies and Naked Thighs '91
Spitfire '94
Spy '89
Spy Game '01
Spy in Black '39▶
Spy of Napoleon '36
The Spy Ring '38
The Spy Who Loved Me '77▶
Spy with a Cold Nose '66
The Spy Within '94
Spymaker: The Secret Life of Ian Fleming '90
State Department File 649 '49
Strike Commando '87
Subterfuge '68
Swordfish '01
Syriana '05▶
Tangiers '83
Target for Killing '66
Target of Opportunity '04
Terminal Entry '87
Terminal Velocity '94
Texas to Bataan '42
There Goes Barder '54
They Got Me Covered '43
The 39 Steps '35▶
The Thirty-Nine Steps '79
Three Days of the Condor '75▶
Three Kinds of Heat '87
Thunderball '65
Tiffany Jones '75
Tinker, Tailor, Soldier, Spy '80▶
To Live and Die in Hong Kong '89
Tokyo Joe '49
Tomorrow Never Dies '97▶
Trader Tom of the China Seas '54
Trenchcoat '83
Trident Force '88
Triple Agent '04
Tripwire '89
The Tuxedo '02
Undeclared War '91
Under the Rainbow '81
Undercover Blues '93
Undercover Brother '02
The Uranium Conspiracy '78
A View to a Kill '85
Viper '83
Virginia City '40▶
The Waiting Time '99
Wanted Dead or Alive '86
When Eight Bells Toll '71
Where the Bullets Fly '66
White Ghost '88
WhiteForce '88
Wild Wild West '99
The Wrecking Crew '68
XXX '02
Yin & Yang of Mr. Go '71
You Only Live Twice '67
Young Nurses in Love '89

Sports
see Baseball; Basketball; Bicycling; Boxing; Football; Golf; Hockey; The Olympics; Running; Scuba; Skating; Skiing; Skydiving; Soccer; Sports Comedies; Sports Dramas; Surfing; Swimming; Tennis; Volleyball

Sports Comedies
Air Bud '97
Air Bud 2: Golden Receiver '98
Air Bud 3: World Pup '00
Air Bud 4: Seventh Inning Fetch '02
The Air Up There '94
Alibi Ike '35
Angels in the Infield '00
Angels in the Outfield '94
The Bad News Bears '76▶
The Bad News Bears '05
The Bad News Bears Go to Japan '78
The Bad News Bears in Breaking Training '77
BASEketball '98
Beer League '06
The Benchwarmers '06
Bend It Like Beckham '02▶
The Best of Times '86
Big and Hairy '98
The Big Green '95
Billie '65
Bingo Long Traveling All-Stars & Motor Kings '76▶
Blades of Glory '07▶
Blue Juice '95
Blue Skies Again '83
Body Slam '87
Bowery Blitzkrieg '41
The Boys '97
Bull Durham '88▶
Cars '06▶
Celtic Pride '96
Comeback Kid '80
The Comebacks '07
The Comrades of Summer '92
Cool Runnings '93
The Cup '99
Day the Bookies Wept '39
Diggstown '92
Dodgeball: A True Underdog Story '04
Downhill Willie '96
D3: The Mighty Ducks '96
D2: The Mighty Ducks '94
Ed '96
Eddie '96
Fast Break '79
Fever Pitch '05
Fever Pitch '96
First & Ten: The Team Scores Again '85
The Fish that Saved Pittsburgh '79
For Heaven's Sake '79
The Freshman '25▶
The Game Plan '07
Game 6 '05
Goal! '06
Good Balls '87
The Great White Hype '96
Gus '76
Guys and Balls '04
The Hammer '07
Happy Gilmore '96
Hold 'Em Jail '32
Home Team '98
Hot Dog... The Movie! '83
Hothead '78
It Happens Every Spring '49▶
Jerry Maguire '96▶
Jocks '87
Johnny Be Good '88

Your Turn Darling '63
Zeppelin '71
Zeta One '69
Zotz! '62

▶ = rated three bones or higher

Sports

Kicking & Screaming '05
Kill the Umpire '50
Kingpin '96
Ladybugs '92
A League of Their Own '92▲
Leatherheads '08
Little Big League '94
Little Giants '94
The Longest Yard '74▲
The Longshot '86
Major League '89
Major League 2 '94
Major League 3: Back to the Minors '98
The Man with the Perfect Swing '95
The Match '99
Men with Brooms '02
The Mighty Ducks '92
Mr. Baseball '92
Mr. 3000 '04
Monty Python's The Meaning of Life '83▲
MVP (Most Valuable Primate) '00
Mystery, Alaska '99
Nacho Libre '06
National Lampoon's Golf Punks '99
Necessary Roughness '91
North Dallas Forty '79▲
Off the Mark '87
The One and Only '78
One-Punch O'Day '26
Paper Lion '68
Pat and Mike '52▲
Perfect Game '00
Possums '99
Prehysteria 3 '95
Prize Fighter '79
Rebound '05
The Replacements '00
The Ringer '05
Rookie of the Year '93
Run, Fat Boy, Run '07
The St. Tammany Miracle '94
The Sandlot '93▲
The Scout '94
Semi-Pro '08
Semi-Tough '77
Shaolin Soccer '01
The Sixth Man '97
Ski School '91
Slam Dunk Ernest '95
Slap Shot '77▲
Slap Shot 2: Breaking the Ice '02
Soccer Dog: The Movie '98
Space Jam '96
Splitz '84
Spring Fever '81
Squeeze Play '79
Stick It '06
Sunset Park '96
Swim Team '79
Tin Cup '96▲
Trading Hearts '87
The Waterboy '98
White Men Can't Jump '92
Who's Your Caddy? '07
Wildcats '86
Wimbledon '04
The World's Greatest Athlete '73

American Kickboxer 1 '91
Annapolis '06
Any Given Sunday '99▲
Babel '92
The Babe '92
Babe Ruth Story '48
Ball of Wax '03
Bang the Drum Slowly '56
Bang the Drum Slowly '73▲
Believe in Me '06
The Big Blue '88
Big Mo '73
Black Cloud '04
Blades of Courage '88
Blue Chips '94
Bobby Jones: Stroke of Genius '04
Body and Soul '47▲
Body & Soul '81
Boy in Blue '86
The Break '95
Breaking Away '79▲
Breaking Free '95
Brian's Song '71▲
The Bronx Is Burning '07
Brutal Glory '89
Challenge of a Lifetime '85
Champion '49▲
Champions '84
Chariots of Fire '81▲
Chasing Dreams '81
The Club '81▲
Coach '78
Coach Carter '05▲
Cobb '94▲
The Color of Money '86▲
Crossbar '79
Crossover '06
The Cutting Edge '92
Dawn! '83
Days of Thunder '90
Dempsey '83
Diving In '90
Don't Look Back: The Story of Leroy "Satchel" Paige '81
Downhill Racer '69
Dream to Believe '85
Dreamer '79
Dreamer: Inspired by a True Story '05
Dynamite Dan '24
Eight Men Out '88▲
8 Seconds '94
The Fan '96
Fat City '72▲
Field of Dreams '89▲
Fight for the Title '57
The Final Season '07
Final Shot: The Hank Gathers Story '92
Finish Line '89
The First Olympics: Athens 1896 '84
The Flying Scotsman '06
Follow the Sun '51
For Love of the Game '99
The Four Minute Mile '88
Friday Night Lights '04▲
Futuresport '98
The Game of Their Lives '05
Game 6 '05
Gentleman Jim '42▲
Girlfight '99▲
Gladiator '92
Glory Road '06
Go for the Gold '84
Goal! The Dream Begins '06
Going for the Gold: The Bill Johnson Story '85
The Gold & Glory '79
Goldengirl '79
Gracie '07
Grambling's White Tiger '81
The Greatest Game Ever Played '05
Green Street Hooligans '05▲
Gridiron Gang '06
Guarding Eddy '04
He Got Game '98
Heart Like a Wheel '83
Heaven Is a Playground '91
The Hero '71
Hockey Night '84
Honeyboy '82
Hoosiers '86▲
Hot Shot '86
The Hustler '61▲

Ice Castles '79
Ice Pawn '92
Ice Princess '05
International Velvet '78
Invincible '06▲
The Jericho Mile '79
The Jesse Owens Story '84
Jim Thorpe: All American '51
The Joe Louis Story '53
Joe Torre: Curveballs Along the Way '97
Kid Galahad '37▲
Kid Monk Baroni '52
Knute Rockne: All American '40▲
Lagaan: Once upon a Time in India '01
The Last American Hero '73▲
The Last Fight '82
Last Time Out '94
The Legend of Bagger Vance '00
The Loneliest Runner '76
Long Gone '87
The Longshots '08
Love and Basketball '00▲
Madison '01
Maker of Men '31
Marciano '79
A Matter of Honor '95
Miracle '04▲
Miracle on Ice '81
My Champion '81
Nadia '84
The Natural '84▲
O '01▲
On the Edge '86
One in a Million: The Ron LeFlore Story '78
One Last Run '89
One on One '77
Opposite Corners '96
Over the Top '86
Paperback Hero '73
Passing Glory '99▲
Pastime '91▲
Peaceful Warrior '06
Personal Best '82▲
Pistol: The Birth of a Legend '90
Players '79
Prefontaine '96
Price of Glory '00
Pride '07
Pride of St. Louis '52
Pride of the Yankees '42▲
The Program '93
Pulsebeat '85
Radio '03
Raging Bull '80▲
Rebound: The Legend of Earl "The Goat" Manigault '96
Red Line 7000 '65
Red Surf '90
Remember the Titans '00▲
Requiem for a Heavyweight '56▲
Requiem for a Heavyweight '62▲
Resurrecting the Champ '07
The Rocket '05▲
Rocky '76▲
Rocky 2 '79
Rocky 3 '82
Rocky 4 '85
Rocky 5 '90
Rocky Marciano '99
Rollerball '02
Rowing Through '96
Rudy '93▲
Run for the Dream: The Gail Devers Story '96
Running Brave '83
Saint Ralph '04
School Ties '92▲
A Season on the Brink '02
Shiner '00
A Shot at Glory '00
Side Out '90
61* '01▲
Skier's Dream '88
Soul of the Game '96▲
The Spirit of West Point '47
The Sprinter '84

The Spy Ring '38
The Stratton Story '49▲
Summer Catch '01
Supercross: The Movie '05
Swimming Upstream '03
Talent for the Game '91
That Championship Season '82
They Call Me Sirr '00
This Sporting Life '63▲
Tiger Town '83
The Tiger Woods Story '98
Touch and Go '86
Touchdown '31
21 Hours at Munich '76▲
Two for the Money '05
Varsity Blues '98
Victory '81
Vision Quest '85
We Are Marshall '06
When Saturday Comes '95
Wilma '77
Wind '92
A Winner Never Quits '86
The Winning Team '52
Without Limits '97▲
Wondrous Oblivion '06▲
The World's Fastest Indian '05▲
Youngblood '86

Sports Documentaries

Hank Aaron: Chasing the Dream '95▲
The Heart of the Game '05
Hoop Dreams '94▲
The Life and Times of Hank Greenberg '99▲
Murderball '05▲
Through the Fire '05▲
Up for Grabs '05
When We Were Kings '96▲

Sports Dramas

Above the Rim '94
Airborne '93
Alex '92
All the Right Moves '83
American Anthem '86
American Flyers '85

Spring Break

see also Vacations

From Justin to Kelly '03
Lauderdale '89
Palm Springs Weekend '63
Spring Break '83
Teresa's Tattoo '94
There's Nothing out There '90
Where the Boys Are '60

Spy Kids

see also Childhood Visions; Spies & Espionage; Teen Angst

Adventures in Spying '92
Agent Cody Banks '03
Agent Cody Banks 2: Destination London '04
Alex Rider: Operation Stormbreaker '06
Cloak & Dagger '84
Codename: Icarus '85
The Day Will Dawn '42▲
Defense Play '88
The Double O Kid '92
The Fantastic World of D.C. Collins '84
Hangman's Curse '03
Harriet the Spy '96
If Looks Could Kill '91
The Kid with the X-Ray Eyes '99
Kim '84
My Name Is Ivan '62▲
The Secret Agent Club '96
Spy Kids '01▲
Spy Kids 2: The Island of Lost Dreams '02▲
Spy Kids 3-D: Game Over '03
Spy Trap '92
Thunderbirds '04

Stagestruck

see also Showbiz Comedies; Showbiz Dramas; Showbiz Thrillers

All About Eve '50▲
Applause '29▲
Because of Him '45
Being Julia '04▲
Bigger Than the Sky '05
Black Widow '54
Bloodhounds of Broadway '52
Bloodhounds of Broadway '89
Broadway Damage '98
Broadway Danny Rose '84▲
Broadway Limited '41
Broadway Melody '29
Broadway Melody of 1938 '37
Broadway Rhythm '44
Bullets over Broadway '94▲
Carnegie Hall '47
The Cradle Will Rock '99
Critic's Choice '63
Dancing Lady '33
The Dolly Sisters '46
Esther Kahn '00
Fame '80▲
First a Girl '35
Fish Without a Bicycle '03
Frogs for Snakes '98
The Great Ziegfeld '36▲
Gypsy '62▲
Gypsy '93
The Half Naked Truth '32
Haunted '98
Heights '04
Illuminata '98
I'm Going Home '00▲
Interview with the Vampire '94▲
Introducing the Dwights '07
Jesus of Montreal '89▲
The King of Masks '99▲
Kiss Me, Guido '97
The Lady in Question '99
The Last Metro '80▲
The Leading Man '96
Let's Make Love '60
Lillian Russell '40
Lillie '79▲
Look for the Silver Lining '49
Lucky Break '01
A Midwinter's Tale '95
Mrs. Henderson Presents '05
Moon over Broadway '98▲
Morning Glory '33
Mother Wore Tights '47▲
Myrt and Marge '33
The Next Step '95
Next Time We Love '36
Nicholas Nickleby '02▲
No '98
The Phantom Lover '95
The Producers '05
The Reckoning '03▲
Shakespeare in Love '98▲
Slightly Terrific '44
Slings & Arrows: Season 2 '05▲
Stage Door '37▲
Stage Struck '57
Stagefright '87
Star! '68
Tea for Two '50▲
These Foolish Things '06
Tipping the Velvet '02
Topsy Turvy '99▲
Vanya on 42nd Street '94▲
William Shakespeare's A Midsummer Night's Dream '99
Witchcraft 11: Sisters in Blood '00
Yankee Doodle Dandy '42▲

Stalked!

see also Obsessive Love

Addicted to Love '96
Alone With Her '07
Backwoods '87
Blood Trails '06
The Bottom of the Sea '03▲
Breach of Conduct '94
Buddy Boy '99
The Cable Guy '96
The Case of the Bloody Iris '72
Cherish '02
Christina's House '99
Chuck & Buck '00
Copycat '95
Dying Game '94
Enduring Love '04
Evil Obsession '96
The Fan '81
The Fan '96
Fatal Attraction '87▲
The Gingerbread Man '97
Irresistible '06
The Killing Floor '06
The Killing of John Lennon '07
A Kiss Goodnight '94
Klute '71▲
Living in Peril '97
Mr. Wrong '95
Number One Fan '94
O Fantasma '00
P2 '07
Perfect Strangers '03
Prom Night '08
Red Road '06
The Rendering '02
Secret Window '04
The Seduction '82
Stalked '99
Stalker '98
Stalking Laura '93
Taxi Driver '76▲
Turn of the Blade '97
Twilight Man '96
Wicker Park '04

Star Gazing

The Arrival '96
Deep Impact '98
Eliza's Horoscope '70
The Fish that Saved Pittsburgh '79
How Come Nobody's On Our Side? '73
Lamp at Midnight '66
Local Hero '83▲
My Stepmother Is an Alien '88
Roxanne '87▲

Stay-at-Home Dads

see also Dads; Doofus Dads

The Ballad of Jack and Rose '05▲
Daddy Day Care '03
Kramer vs. Kramer '79▲
Mr. Mom '83▲
Signs '02▲

Stepparents

see also Family Ties; Parenthood

The Adventures of Rusty '45
The Adventures of Sebastian Cole '99
All the Little Animals '98
The Amityville Horror '05
Angel Face '52▲
Ararat '02▲
Are We Done Yet? '07
Beat Girl '60
Beau Pere '81▲
Benji: Off the Leash! '04
Big Girls Don't Cry... They Get Even '92
Cafe Lumiere '05
Cinderella '50▲
Cinderella '84▲
A Cinderella Story '04
Domestic Disturbance '01
Electra '95
Ellie '84
Enchanted '07
Ever After: A Cinderella Story '98▲
Everyone Says I Love You '96▲
Fascination '04
Fear '96
Georgia Rule '07
Happily N'Ever After '07
Happy Times '00
Hard Frame '70
Home for Christmas '93
Hot Rod '07
I Capture the Castle '02
The Judgement '02
Kangaroo Jack '02
Lassie '94
Look at Me '04▲
Lost '83
Love Actually '03▲
Merci pour le Chocolat '00▲
Night of the Twisters '95
The Orphan '79
Out on a Limb '92

Pan's Labyrinth '06▶
Petits Freres '00
Private Passions '85
Rivals '72
Running Scared '06
Second Sight '99▶
Shadowboxer '06
Siblings '04
Snow White: A Tale of Terror '97
Snow White: The Fairest of Them All '02
Step Brothers '08
The Stepdaughter '00
The Stepfather '87▶
Stepfather 2: Make Room for Daddy '89
Stepfather 3: Father's Day '92
Stepmom '98▶
The Stepmother '71
The Stepsister '97
A Summer to Remember '61▶
Tadpole '02
A Tale of Two Sisters '03▶
This Boy's Life '93▶
Time Regained '99
Transamerica '05▶
Unleashed '05
Wah-Wah '05
Yours, Mine & Ours '05

Stewardesses
see also Airborne

Airplane! '80▶
Black Tight Killers '66▶
Blazing Stewardesses '75
Boeing Boeing '65
Elizabethtown '05
Executive Decision '96
Jackie Brown '97▶
Passenger 57 '92
Stewardess School '86
The Terminal '04
Three Guys Named Mike '51
Turbulence '96
View from the Top '03
Zero Hour! '57

Stolen from Asia

Dark Water '05
The Departed '06▶
The Eye '08
A Fistful of Dollars '64▶
The Grudge '04
The Grudge 2 '06
Last Man Standing '96
The Magnificent Seven '60▶
One Missed Call '08
Pulse '06
Reservoir Dogs '92▶
The Ring '02
Shall We Dance? '04
Shutter '08
Speed Racer '08
Star Wars '77▶

Stolen from Europe

The Associate '96
Head Above Water '96
Insomnia '02▶
Interview '07▶
The Invisible '07
Jakob the Liar '99▶
Kiss Me Goodbye '82
Last House on the Left '72
The Last Kiss '06
Nightwatch '08
No Reservations '07
Pathfinder '07
Scent of a Woman '92▶
Solaris '02
Swept Away '02
Vanilla Sky '01
The Vanishing '93
A Walk in the Clouds '95
Welcome to Collinwood '02

Stolen from France

The Birdcage '95▶
Blame It on Rio '84
Breathless '83
Buddy Buddy '81
Cactus Flower '69
Casbah '48▶
Cousins '89▶
Diabolique '96
Down and Out in Beverly Hills '86
The Man Who Loved Women '83
Three Fugitives '89
Three Men and a Baby '87▶
The Toy '82
True Lies '94
12 Monkeys '95▶
Under Suspicion '00
Unfaithful '02▶
The Woman in Red '84

Storytelling

Babyfever '94
Big Fish '03▶
The Company of Wolves '85▶
Grim Prairie Tales '89
Lakeboat '00
Little Orphan Annie '18
Monster in a Box '92▶
My Dinner with Andre '81▶
The NeverEnding Story 3: Escape from Fantasia '94
The Osterman Weekend '83
Paper Tiger '94
The Princess Bride '87▶
Sommersby '93
Sorcerer '77
The Story Lady '93
Taxi '04

Strained Suburbia
see also Yuppie Nightmares

Adventures in Spying '92
Alpha Dog '06
American Beauty '99▶
The Amityville Horror '79
Amongst Friends '93
Amos and Andrew '93
Arlington Road '99
Beavis and Butt-Head Do America '96
Blue Velvet '86▶
The Brady Bunch Movie '95▶
The 'Burbs '89
Catch Me If You Can '02
Christmas With the Kranks '04
The Chumscrubber '05
Civic Duty '06
Clown House '88
Cold Turkey '71▶
Coneheads '93
Consenting Adults '92
The Cookout '04
Crime and Punishment in Suburbia '00
The Crude Oasis '95
Deadly Neighbor '91
Deck the Halls '06
Dennis the Menace '06
Dennis the Menace Strikes Again '98
Desperate Hours '55▶
Desperate Hours '90
Disturbia '07▶
Don't Talk to Strangers '94
Don't Tell Mom the Babysitter's Dead '91
Edward Scissorhands '90▶
11:14 '03
Elephant '03▶
Envy '04
Faithful '95
Fatal Fix '80
The Girl Next Door '04
Godmoney '97
Good Fences '03
The Graduate '67▶
Grand Canyon '91
The Grass Is Always Greener Over the Septic Tank '78
Happy New Year '87
Hidden '05▶
Hocus Pocus '93
Home Alone '90▶
Home Alone 3 '97
House '86▶
How to Beat the High Cost of Living '80
I Love My... Wife '70
I Think I Love My Wife '07
Imaginary Heroes '05
Inside Out '05
Intersection '93
Jungle 2 Jungle '96
Just Visiting '01
Krippendorf's Tribe '98
Little Children '06▶
Little Man '06
Loving '70
Madhouse '90
Marked for Death '90
The Meal '75
Men Don't Leave '89
The Mirror Has Two Faces '96
Mixed Nuts '94
Mr. Blandings Builds His Dream House '48▶
The Money Pit '86
Monster House '06
My Blue Heaven '90
My Father the Hero '93
My New Gun '92
Neighbors '81▶
Next Friday '00
Nine Months '95
1941 '79
101 Ways (The Things a Girl Will Do to Keep Her Volvo) '00
Opportunity Knocks '90
Over the Edge '79▶
Over the Hedge '06▶
Palindromes '04▶
Parents '89▶
The People Next Door '70
Please Don't Eat the Daisies '60
Point of No Return '93
Poltergeist '81
The Positively True Adventures of the Alleged Texas Cheerleader-Murdering Mom '93
Premonition '07▶
The Prize Winner of Defiance, Ohio '05▶
Pure Luck '91
Quick Change '90
Rally 'Round the Flag, Boys! '58
Red Doors '05
Return of the Living Dead 2 '88▶
Revenge of the Stepford Wives '80
Scenes from the Class Struggle in Beverly Hills '89
Serial Mom '94▶
Serial Slayer '03
Shattered Spirits '86
Short Cuts '93▶
The Stepford Wives '75▶
The Stepford Wives '04
The Stranger '46▶
The Swimmer '68▶
Terrorvision '86
Three Wishes '95
The Trigger Effect '96
Twelve and Holding '05▶
Twice in a Lifetime '85▶
The Underworld Story '50
A Very Brady Sequel '96
The Virgin Suicides '99
The War of the Roses '89▶
The Willies '90
Windwalker '81▶

Strippers

American Wedding '03
The Badge '02
Blaze '89
Blood Money '98
Body Language '95
The Box '03
Breakdown '96▶
Cadillac Ranch '96
The Center of the World '01
Closer '04▶
Club Vampire '98
Crystal's Diary '99
Dance at the Blue Iguana '00
Dancing at the Blue Iguana '00
Dangerous Ground '96
The Dark Dancer '95
Day of the Warrior '96
A Dirty Shame '04
The Dog Problem '06
Dogma '99▶
Exit '95
Exotica '94▶
The Fluffer '01
For Ladies Only '81
From Dusk Till Dawn '95
The Full Monty '96▶
The Glass Cage '96
Gypsy '62▶
Gypsy '93
Hard As Nails '01
The Heart Is Deceitful Above All Things '04
Headless Body in Topless Bar '96
Heaven '99
Hustle & Flow '05▶
I Know Who Killed Me '07
Kiss of Fire '98
Lady of Burlesque '43
Lap Dancing '95
The Last Word '95
Laws of Deception '97
Lenny '74▶
Master Spy: The Robert Hanssen Story '02
Miami Hustle '95
Midnight Tease '94
Midnight Tease 2 '95
Mrs. Henderson Presents '05
A Night in Heaven '83
Night Junkies '07
Overnight Delivery '96
Pecker '98▶
Pigalle '95
Planet Terror '07
The Players Club '98▶
Plucking the Daisy '56
Seven Thieves '60▶
Shadow Dancer '96
The Showgirl Murders '95
Showgirls '95
Sin City '05▶
Sins of the Night '93
Sparkler '99
Stag '97
Step Search '97
The Stripper '63
Stripper '86
Striptease '96
Striptease '95
Studs Lonigan '60
Sweet Evil '98
13 Moons '02
Time Served '99
Tin Cup '96▶
True Lies '94
Truly '00
Under Siege '92
Vacuuming Completely Nude in Paradise '01
Vamping '84
Vibrations '94
Whirlygirl '04
Winning Girls Through Psychic Mind Control '02
Working Girls '75

Struggling Artists
see also Art & Artists; Biopics: Artists

Apartment 12 '06
Art School Confidential '06
Basquiat '96
Before Night Falls '00▶
Brother to Brother '04
Heights '04
Love Letters '99▶
Shopgirl '05▶
A Simple Promise '07
Standing on Fishes '99
The Tollbooth '04
Vincent & Theo '90▶
Yellow '06

Struggling Musicians

The Adventures of Buckaroo Banzai Across the Eighth Dimension '84▶
All You Need Is Cash '78▶
American Blue Note '89
Backbeat '94▶
The Beat My Heart Skipped '05▶
Beyond the Valley of the Dolls '70
Bikini Summer '91
Billy's Holiday '95
Blast-Off Girls '67▶
Breaking Glass '80
Bye Bye Blues '89
Cheech and Chong's Up in Smoke '79
The Competition '80▶
Cotton Candy '82
Crossover Dreams '85
Crossroads '86▶
Dangerous Holiday '37
Dogs in Space '87▶
Doing Time for Patsy Cline '97
Eddie and the Cruisers '83
Eddie and the Cruisers 2: Eddie Lives! '89
The Eternal Waltz '54
The Fabulous Dorseys '47
Falling from Grace '92
Fear of a Black Hat '94▶
The Five Heartbeats '91▶
Ganked '05
Gridlock'd '96▶
Heaven Tonight '93
Hustle & Flow '05▶
Idiot Box '07
In God We Trust '80
The Jerk '79▶
The Jerky Boys '95
Joe Dirt '01
Kickin' It Old Skool '07
Killer Bud '00
Knights of the City '85
Let's Go to Prison '06
Light of Day '87▶
Little Nicky '00
Love Song '00
Meet the Deedles '98
Mr. Accident '99
Mr. Bean's Holiday '07
Murder Rap '87
Mo' Better Blues '90▶
Oh, God! You Devil '84
One Trick Pony '80
Orgazmo '98
Purple Rain '84▶
The Return of Spinal Tap '92
Rhinestone '84
Road Trip '00▶
Rock & Rule '83
Rock School '05
Rock Star '01
The Rose '79▶
Satisfaction '88
School of Rock '03▶
A Simple Promise '07
A Slipping Down Life '99
A Star Is Born '76
Strange Wilderness '08
Streets of Fire '84▶
Tender Mercies '83▶
This Is Spinal Tap '84▶
Vamping '84
Wayne's World '92▶

Stupid Is...

American Pie Presents Band Camp '05
Be Kind Rewind '08
Bean '97▶
Beavis and Butt-Head Do America '96
Bill & Ted's Excellent Adventure '89▶
Bill & Ted's Bogus Journey '91▶
Billy Madison '94
Bio-Dome '96
Black Sheep '96▶
Blonde and Blonder '07
Caddyshack '80▶
Chairman of the Board '97
The Curse of Inferno '96
The Dinner Game '98▶
Drowning Mona '00
Dudley Do-Right '99
Dumb and Dumber '94▶
Dumb and Dumberer: When Harry Met Lloyd '03
Employee of the Month '06
The Extreme Adventures of Super Dave '98
Fast Times at Ridgemont High '82▶
Forrest Gump '94▶
Frank McKlusky, C.I. '02
Get Smart '08
Half-Baked '98
Happy Gilmore '96▶
Hot Rod '07
Idiot Box '07
Idle Hands '99
Jackass Number Two '06
The Nutty Professor '63▶
National Lampoon's Animal House '78▶
Pee-wee's Big Adventure '85▶
Ready to Rumble '00
Road Trip '00▶
Romy and Michele's High School Reunion '97▶
The Sasquatch Gang '06
Scary Movie 4 '06
Son-in-Law '93
Stealing Harvard '02
Step Brothers '08
Strange Wilderness '08
The Stupids '95
Tommy Boy '95▶
The Waterboy '98
White Mile '93
Wayne's World '92▶
Witless Protection '08
Young Einstein '89
Zoolander '01▶

Stuntmen

Death Proof '07▶
800 Bullets '02
Fantastic Seven '79
Ghost Rider '07
Hooper '78▶
Hot Rod '07
Looney Tunes: Back in Action '03
Lucky Devils '33
Movie Stuntmen '53
The Stunt Man '80▶
Vendetta '85

Submarines
see also Deep Blue

Above Us the Waves '56▶

▶ = rated three bones or higher

Submarines

The Abyss '89▶
Action in the North Atlantic '43
Agent Red '00
Assault on a Queen '66
Atlantis: The Lost Empire '01
Atomic Submarine '59
Bear Island '80
Below '02
Beneath the Bermuda Triangle '98
Counter Measures '99
Crash Dive '43
Crash Dive '96
Crimson Tide '95▶
Danger Beneath the Sea '02
Das Boot '81▶
The Day Will Dawn '42
Destination Tokyo '43
Down Periscope '96
Enemy Below '57▶
Fer-De-Lance '74
First Strike '85
For Your Eyes Only '81▶
Full Fathom Five '90
Going Under '91
Hostile Waters '97
The Hunley '99
The Hunt for Red October '90▶
Ice Station Zebra '68
In Enemy Hands '04
The Incredible Mr. Limpet '64
The Inside Man '84
K-19: The Widowmaker '02
The League of Extraordinary Gentlemen '03
Leviathan '89
Magma: Volcanic Disaster '06
Morning Departure '50
Mysterious Island '61▶
Nautilus '99
1941 '79
Octopus '00
On the Beach '00
Operation Bikini '63
Operation Delta Force 2: Mayday '97
Operation Delta Force 3: Clear Target '98
Operation Petticoat '59▶
Q Ships '28
Raise the Titanic '80
Run Silent, Run Deep '58▶
Sailor Beware '52
The Spy Who Loved Me '77
Steel Sharks '97
Sub Down '97
U-571 '00
Up Periscope '59
Voyage to the Bottom of the Sea '61▶
Submerged '05
Torpedo Alley '53
Torpedo Attack '72
Torpedo Run '58
20,000 Leagues under the Sea 16▶
20,000 Leagues under the Sea '54▶
20,000 Leagues Under the Sea 97
We Dive at Dawn '43▶
Yellow Submarine '68▶
You Only Live Twice 67

Subways

see also Trains

Adventures in Babysitting '87
Angel Dust '96
Bulletproof Monk '03
Carlito's Way '93▶
Daybreak '01
Die Hard: With a Vengeance '95
Dutchman 67▶
Eve of Destruction '90
The French Connection '71▶
The Fugitive '93▶
Highlander 2: The Quickening '91
The Incident '67
The Italian Job '03▶
The Jackal '97
Kontroll '03▶
Lethal Weapon 3 '92
Mimic '97
Money Train '95
Next Stop, Wonderland '98
On the Line '01
Predator 2 '90
Quatermass and the Pit 58
Reconstruction '03
Risky Business '83▶
ShadowZone: The Undead Express '96
Sliding Doors '97
Speed '94▶
Subway '85
Subway Stories '97
The Taking of Pelham One Two Three '74▶
Trick '99▶
Tube '03
The Warriors '79
Zazie dans le Metro 61▶

Suicide

see also Death & the Afterlife

Absence of Malice '81
Alien 3 '92
All My Sons 48▶
American Strays '96
Angels Over Broadway '40▶
The Apartment '60▶
Apres-Vous '03
Ararat '02▶
The Arrangement 69
Asylum '97
Attack Squadron '63
Autopsy 74
Bad Girls Dormitory '84
Bedazzled '68▶
Believers '07
The Bell Jar 79
Better Off Dead '85
The Big Chill '83▶
Blacklight '98
Body & Soul '93▶
Brute Force 47▶
Buddy Buddy 81
Can You Hear the Laughter? The Story of Freddie Prinze 79
Cause Celebre '87▶
The Chumscrubber '05
Club Extinction '89
Come Undone '00
The Confessor '04
Conspiracy of Silence '03
Control 07
Cookie's Fortune '99▶
Courage Under Fire '96▶
Crimes of the Heart '86
The Crown Prince '06
The Crude Oasis '95
Crumb '94▶
The Curve '97
Dangerous Corner '34▶
Dark Remains '05
Dark Side '02
Dead Man on Campus '97
Dead Poets Society '89▶
Death Wish Club '83
Delicatessen '92▶
Delinquent Daughters '44
Der Todesking '89
Deutschland im Jahre Null 47▶
The Devil in Silk 56
Divine '90
Docks of New York '28▶
Dolls '02▶
Dominique Is Dead 79
Double Suicide '69▶
Dream with the Fishes '97
The Eagle and the Hawk '33▶
Elisa '94
Elizabethtown '05
The End '78▶
Europa '51 '52
Eva 62
The Event '03
Event Horizon '97
The Eyes, the Mouth '83
Faithful '95
Father's Day '97
The Fire Within '64▶
The First Wives Club '96
For One More Day '07
From the Journals of Jean Seberg '95
Frozen '98
Full Metal Jacket '87▶
Fuzz 72
A Gentle Woman 69
The Girl on the Bridge '98▶
Golden Gate '93
Goodbye Cruel World '82
The Guyana Tragedy: The Story of Jim Jones '80
The Hanging Garden '97
Hangman's Curse '03
Harold and Maude '71▶
Head On '04
Heading for Heaven 47
Heat '95▶
Heathers '89▶
Hide and Seek '05
Hollywoodland '06
The Hours '02▶
The Hudsucker Proxy '93▶
The Hustle '75
The Iceman Cometh '73
Imaginary Heroes '05
Iris '89
The Isle '01
It's a Wonderful Life '46▶
Julian Po '97
Junk Mail '97
Kill Me Later '01
Kill Your Darlings '06
Kings and Queen '04▶
The Kovak Box '06
Last Cry for Help 79
Last Days '05
Last Life in the Universe '03
Last Tango in Paris 73▶
The Last Time I Committed Suicide '96
Law of the Sea 32
Le Corbeau '43▶
Leaving Las Vegas '95▶
Love Liza '02
Love on a Pillow '62
Maborosi '95▶
Madame Bovary '00
Maedchen in Uniform '31▶
Marebito 04
M*A*S*H '70▶
Melo 86
Memorial Day '83
Missing Pieces '00
Mrs. Dalloway '97
Mixed Nuts '94
Monster's Ball '01▶
Mortal Danger '94
Morvern Callar '02
Mother Kusters Goes to Heaven '76▶
Mouchette '67▶
My Sweet Suicide '98
Nais '45▶
Natural Enemies 79
night, Mother '86
The Night Watchman '02
Now & Forever '02
The Odd Job 78
Ode to Billy Joe '76
On the Edge '00
One Flew Over the Cuckoo's Nest '75▶
Ordinary People '80▶
Pain in the A— '77▶
The Pallbearer '95
Paradise Now '05▶
Peeping Tom '60▶
Permanent Record '88
Possession '02
Primary Colors '98
Prozac Nation '01
Pulse '01
Pulse '06
Purgatory House '04
Remolino de Pasiones 68
Retribution 88
Return of Frank Cannon '80
Reuben, Reuben '83▶
Riding the Bullet '04
Right of Way 84
Robert Louis Stevenson's The Game of Death 99
Romeo and Juliet '36▶
Romeo and Juliet '54
Romeo and Juliet '68▶
Romulus, My Father '07
The Rules of Attraction '02
Scent of a Woman '92▶
The Sea Inside '04▶
Silence of the Heart '84▶
Sisters, Or the Balance of Happiness 79
The Slender Thread '65▶
Solo Sunny '80
Stay '05
Stealing Home '88
Stella Maris '18▶
Suicide Club '02
Sylvia '03
A Tale of Two Sisters '03▶
Talk to Her '02▶
The Taste of Cherry '96
The Tenant '76▶
Things I Never Told You '96
Two Days '03
Unholy '07
The Unknown Soldier '98
The Unsaid '01
Village Tale '35
The Virgin Suicides '99
Warm Summer Rain 89
Wetherby '85▶
Whale Music '94
What Dreams May Come '98
Where the Truth Lies '05
Whose Life Is It Anyway? '81▶
Wilbur Wants to Kill Himself '02▶
Wristcutters: A Love Story '06

Summer Camp

Addams Family Values '93
American Pie Presents Band Camp '05
Arizona Summer '03
Backwoods '87
Berserker '87
The Best Way 76
Bloody Murder '99
Bloody Murder 2 '03
The Burning '82
Bushwhacked '95
But I'm a Cheerleader '99▶
Camp 03
Camp Cucamonga: How I Spent My Summer Vacation '90
Camp Nowhere '94
Cannibal Campout '88
A Cry from the Mountain '85
Daddy Day Camp '07
Deliverance '72▶
Don't Go in the Woods '81
Ernest Goes to Camp '87
Escanaba in da Moonlight '01
Evil Dead '83
Evils of the Night '85
Father and Scout '94
The Final Terror '83
First Turn On '83
Forever Evil '87
Friday the 13th '80
Friday the 13th, Part 2 81
Friday the 13th, Part 3 82
Friday the 13th, Part 4: The Final Chapter 84
Gimme an F '85
Gorp '80
The Great Outdoors '88
Grim Prairie Tales 89
Grizzly 76
Happy Campers '01
Heavyweights '94
The Hills Have Eyes 77
Hot Resort '85
Indian Summer '93
Little Darlings '80
Man of the House '95
Meatballs '79▶
Meatballs 2 '84
Meatballs 3 '87
Meatballs 4 '92
Memorial Valley Massacre '88
Mother's Day '80

Super Heroes

The Adventures of Sharkboy and Lavagirl in 3-D '05
The Amazing Spider-Man '77
Batman 66
Batman 89▶
Batman and Robin '97
Batman Begins '05▶
Batman Forever '95▶
Batman: Mask of the Phantasm '93
Batman Returns '92
Black Mask 96
Black Scorpion '95
Blade: Trinity '04
Blankman '94
Captain America '79
Captain America '89
Captain America 2: Death Too Soon '79
Catwoman '04
Chinese Web '78
The Chosen One: Legend of the Raven '98
Cloak & Dagger '84
Comic Book: The Movie '04▶
Condorman '81
Constantine '05
Daredevil '03
Dark Justice '00
The Dark Knight '08
Death of the Incredible Hulk '90
Dr. Strange '78
Elektra '05
Fantastic Four '05
Fantastic Four: Rise of the Silver Surfer '07
The Flash '90
Flash Gordon '80
Freddie the Frog '92
Hancock '08
Howard the Duck '86
The Incredible Hulk 77
The Incredible Hulk '08
The Incredible Hulk Returns '88
The Incredibles '04▶
Infra-Man '76
Iron Man '08▶
The League of Extraordinary Gentlemen '03
The Legend of Zorro '05
The Mask '94▶
The Meteor Man '93
Mighty Morphin Power Rangers: The Movie '95
My Super Ex-Girlfriend '06
Mystery Men '99
Orgazmo 98
The Phantom '96
Phantom 2040 Movie: The Ghost Who Walks '95
Pootie Tang '01
Prey of the Jaguar '96
The Puma Man '80
The Punisher '90
The Punisher '04
Rat Pfink a Boo-Boo '66
Return of Captain Invincible '83
Sgt. Kabukiman N.Y.P.D. '94
The Shadow '94
Silver Hawk '04
Sky High '05▶
Spawn '97
The Specials '00▶
Spider-Man '02
Spider-Man 2 '04▶
Spider-Man 3 '07
Spiderman: The Deadly Dust '78
Steel 97
The Strongest Man in the World '75
Super Fuzz '81
Supergirl '84
SuperGuy: Behind the Cape '02
Superhero Movie '08
Superman: The Movie '78▶
Superman 2 '80▶
Superman 3 '83
Superman 4: The Quest for Peace '87
Superman & the Mole Men '51
Superman Returns '06
Supersonic Man 78
3 Ninjas: High Noon at Mega Mountain '97
TMNT (Teenage Mutant Ninja Turtles) '07
Todd McFarlane's Spawn '97▶
The Toxic Avenger, Part 2 '89
The Trial of the Incredible Hulk '89
Turbo: A Power Rangers Movie '96
Unbreakable '00
Underdog '07
VIP, My Brother Superman '90
The Wild World of Batwoman 66
X-Men '00▶
X-Men: The Last Stand '06
X2: X-Men United '03▶
Zoom '06
Zorro 74

Supernatural Comedies

see also Comedy

Angels in the Outfield '94
Bedazzled '00
Beetlejuice '88▶
Bell, Book and Candle '58
Bernard and the Genie '91
Blackbeard's Ghost '67
The Craft '96
Dead Heat '88
The Devil & Max Devlin '81
Fridays of Eternity '81
The Frighteners '96
Ghost Chasers '51
Ghost Dad '90
Ghost Fever '87
The Ghost Goes West '36▶
Ghost Writer 89
Ghostbusters '84▶
Ghostbusters 2 '89
Ghosts Can Do It '87
Ghosts of Berkeley Square '47
Haunted Honeymoon '86
Heart and Souls '93
High Spirits 88
Hillbillies in a Haunted House 67
Hocus Pocus '93
Just like Heaven '05

▶ = rated three bones or higher

Just My Luck '06
Limit Up '89
Love at Stake '87
The Man in the Santa Claus Suit '79
Matilda '96
Michael '96
My Best Friend Is a Vampire '88
Oh, God! '77
Oh, God! Book 2 '80
Oh, God! You Devil '84
Quigley '03
Rockula '90
Saturday the 14th '81
Saturday the 14th Strikes Back '88
She-Devil '89
The Sixth Man '97
Son of the Mask '05
Spook Busters '48
Spooks Run Wild '41
Teen Wolf '85
Teen Wolf Too '87
Topper '37
Topper Returns '41
Topper Takes a Trip '39
When Pigs Fly '93
Who Killed Doc Robbin? '48
Wicked Stepmother '89
Winning Girls Through Psychic Mind Control '02
Wishful Thinking '92
A Witch Without a Broom '68

Supernatural Horror

see also Classic Horror

The Abandoned '06
Afghan Knights '07
Alabama's Ghost '72
Alison's Birthday '79
All Souls Day '05
Alone in the Dark '05
An American Haunting '05
The Amityville Horror '79
Amityville II: The Possession '82
Amityville 3: The Demon '83
Amityville 4: The Evil Escapes '89
Amityville: A New Generation '93
The Amityville Horror '05
Amityville 1992: It's About Time '92
The Appointment '82
Asylum of the Damned '03
Attack of the Puppet People '58
Audrey Rose '77
Bad Dreams '88
The Believers '87
Beyond Evil '80
The Black Cat '81
Blade: Trinity '04
Bless the Child '00
Blood from the Mummy's Tomb '71
Blood Gnome '02
Blood Orgy of the She-Devils '74
Blood Relic '05
Bloodbeat '85
Bloodlust '59
BloodRayne '06
Bones '01
Boogeyman '05
Book of Shadows: Blair Witch 2 '00
Border Patrol '01
Born of Fire '87
The Brainiac '61
Bruiser '00
The Butterfly Effect 2 '06
Candyman '92
Carved '07
Cassandra '87
Charlie Boy '81
The Child '76
Children of the Night '92
Chupacabra Terror '05
Close Your Eyes '02
Constantine '05
The Covenant '06
Crimes of Dr. Mabuse '32
The Crow: Salvation '00
Crypt of Dark Secrets '76
Cut '07
Curse of the Black Widow '77
Curse of the Blue Lights '88
The Curse of the Crying Woman '61
Curse of the Demon '57
Curse of the Headless Horseman '72
Curse of the Living Corpse '64
Curse of the Stone Hand '64
Curse of the Werewolf '61
The Cursed Mountain Mystery '93
Daemonia '90
Damien: Omen 2 '78
Dance of Death '68
The Dark '79
Dark Places '73
Dark Remains '05
The Dark Secret of Harvest Home '78
Dark Tower '87
Dark Water '05
Darkness Falls '03
The Daughter of Dr. Jekyll '57
Daughters of Satan '72
Dawn of the Mummy '82
Day Watch '06
Dead Are Alive '72
Dead and Buried '81
The Dead Don't Die '75
Death Curse of Tartu '66
Death Mask '98
Death Ship '80
Death Tunnel '05
Death Valley: The Revenge of Bloody Bill '04
Deathdream '72
Deathhead Virgin '74
Deathwatch '02
Deep Red: Hatchet Murders '75
Def by Temptation '90
The Demon Lover '77
Demon of Paradise '87
Demon Rage '82
Demon Wind '90
Demonia '90
Demonoid, Messenger of Death '81
The Demons '74
Demons '86
Demons 2 '87
Demons of Ludlow '75
Demonstone '89
Demonwarp '87
Destroyer '88
Devil Dog: The Hound of Hell '78
Devil Doll '64
The Devil Rides Out '68
Devil Woman '76
Devil's Daughter '39
The Devil's Daughter '91
Devil's Gift '84
The Devil's Hand '61
The Devil's Nightmare '71
The Devil's Partner '58
The Devil's Possessed '74
Devil's Rain '75
The Devil's Web '74
Devil's Wedding Night '73
Devonsville Terror '83
Devour '05
The Diabolical Dr. Z '65
Diary of a Madman '63
Diary of the Dead '80
Die, Monster, Die! '65
Disciple of Death '72
The Doctor and the Devils '85
Doctor Butcher M.D. '80
Dr. Frankenstein's Castle of Freaks '74
Doctor Phibes Rises Again '72
Dr. Tarr's Torture Dungeon '72
Dr. _terror's House of Horrors '65
Dominion: Prequel to the Exorcist '05
Don't Be Afraid of the Dark '73
Don't Go to Sleep '82
The Drop '06
The Dunwich Horror '70
Dust Devil '93
Edge of Sanity '89
The Eighteenth Angel '97
Embrace of the Vampire '95
Endangered Species '02
Equinox '71
The Evil '78
Evil Altar '89
Evil Dead Trap '88
Evil Town '87
Evilspeak '82
Exorcism '74
The Exorcism of Emily Rose '05
Exorcist '73
The Exorcist 2: The Heretic '77
The Eye '08
Fallen '97
Feast for the Devil '71
Female Vampire '73
The Final Conflict '81
Firestarter '84
The First Power '89
The Fog '05
14C8 '07
From Beyond the Grave '73
From Dusk Till Dawn '95
The Fury Within '98
The Gate '87
Gate 2 '92
Gates of Hell 2: Dead Awakening '96
George A. Romero's Land of the Dead '05
The Ghastly Ones '68
The Ghost '63
The Ghost Brigade '93
Ghost Dance '83
Ghost Keeper '80
The Ghost of Yotsuya '58
Ghost Rider '07
Ghost Story '81
Ghosthouse '88
Ghostriders '87
The Ghosts of Hanley House '68
Ghosts That Still Walk '77
GhostWatcher '02
Giant from the Unknown '58
Ginger Snaps Back: The Beginning '04
Ginger Snaps Unleashed '04
God Told Me To '76
Godsend '04
Grave Secrets: The Legacy of Hilltop Drive '92
The Grudge '04
The Grudge 2 '06
Half-Caste '04
Half Light '05
Haunted Highway '05
The Haunted Palace '63
The Hazing '04
Headspace '05
The Hearse '80
Hellbound: Hellraiser 2 '88
Hellraiser '87
Hellraiser 3: Hell on Earth '92
Hellraiser 4: Bloodline '95
Hellraiser: Deader '05
Hellraiser: Hellseeker '02
Hellraiser: Hellworld '05
Hide and Seek '05
The Horrible Dr. Hichcock '62
The Horrible Dr. Bones '00
Horror Express '72
Horror Hotel '60
Horror of the Blood Monsters '70
Horror Rises from the Tomb '72
The House by the Cemetery '83
The House in Marsh Road '60
The House of Seven Corpses '73
The House of the Dead '03
House of the Yellow Carpet '82
House Where Evil Dwells '82
The Howling '81
Howling 2: Your Sister Is a Werewolf '85
Howling 3: The Marsupials '87
Howling 4: The Original Nightmare '88
Howling 5: The Rebirth '89
Howling 6: The Freaks '90
The Indestructible Man '56
Inferno '80
The Innocents '61
Inquisition '76
Invasion of the Blood Farmers '72
Invasion of the Zombies '61
The Invisible '07
Invitation to Hell '82
It's Alive! '68
Jack O'Lantern '04
Jaws of Satan '81
Jennifer '78
J.D.'s Revenge '76
Ju-On: The Grudge '03
Judgment Day '88
Kill, Baby, Kill '66
The Kiss '88
Kiss Daddy Goodbye '81
Knocking on Death's Door '99
Kwaidan '64
Land of the Minotaur '77
The Last Broadcast '98
The Last Gasp '94
The Last Man on Earth '64
Left in Darkness '06
The Legacy '79
The Legend of Hell House '73
The Legend of Lucy Keyes '06
Lethal Dose '03
Let's Scare Jessica to Death '71
Lisa and the Devil '75
Living Doll '90
The Living Head '59
Lord of Illusions '95
Lost Souls '00
Lurkers '88
Lust for a Vampire '71
The Man and the Monster '65
Manhattan Baby '82
Maniac '34
Manos, the Hands of Fate '66
Manticore '05
Mardi Gras for the Devil '93
Mardi Gras Massacre '78
Mark of the Devil '69
Mark of the Devil 2 '72
Marionnier '05
Mary, Mary, Bloody Mary '76
Maxim Xul '91
The Medusa Touch '78
Megalodon '03
The Mephisto Waltz '71
Meridian: Kiss of the Beast '90
The Messengers '07
Messiah of Evil '74
Midnight '93
Midnight's Child '93
Mirror, Mirror '90
Mirror of Death '87
The Mist '07
The Monster Demolisher '60
The Mummy's Revenge '73
The Mummy's Shroud '67
Necromancer: Satan's Servant '88
Necropolis '87
Neon Maniacs '86
The Nesting '80
Netherworld '90
The Night Evelyn Came Out of the Grave '71
Night Life '90
Night of Horror '78
Night of the Death Cult '75
Night of the Demons '88
Night of the Demons 2 '94
Night of the Ghouls '59
Night of the Sorcerers '70
Night Orchid '97
The Night Stalker '72
The Night Strangler '72
Night Visitor '89
Night Vision '89
Night Watch '04
Nightlife '89
Nightmare Castle '65
Nightmare in Blood '75
Nightmare Sisters '87
Nightmare Weekend '86
Nightstalker '81
Nightwish '89
Nomads '85
The Norliss Tapes '73
Nothing But the Night '72
The Occultist '89
Of Unknown Origin '83
Omen 4: The Awakening '91
The Omen '76
The Omen '06
The Order '03
Orgy of the Dead '65
Orgy of the Vampires '73
The Orphanage '07
The Other '72
Other Hell '85
The Others '01
Out of the Body '88
The Outing '87
Pan's Labyrinth '06
Parasite '03
Patrick '78
Pet Sematary '89
Pet Sematary 2 '92
Phantasm '79
Phantasm 2 '88
Phantom of the Ritz '88
Phantoms '97
Poltergeist '82
Poltergeist 3 '88
Poltergeist: The Legacy '96
The Possessed '77
The Possession of Joel Delaney '72
Premonition '75
The Premonition '05
The Prophecy '95
The Psychic '68
Psychomania '73
Pulse '06
Pulse '01
Pumpkinhead '88
Pumpkinhead 3: Ashes to Ashes '06
Pumpkinhead 4: Blood Feud '07
Rapturous '07
Rawhead Rex '87
The Reaping '07
The Relic '96
Return to House on Haunted Hill '07
Revolt of the Zombies '36
The Ring '02
The Ring 2 '05
Route 666 '01
Salem's Lot '04
Savage Harvest 2: October Blood '06
Scream of the Wolf '74
Seance '01
Session 9 '01
Shallow Ground '04
Shock 'Em Dead '90
Shutter '08
Signs '02
Silent Hill '06
The Skeleton Key '05
The Sleeping Car '90
Sleepstalker: The Sandman's Last Rites '94
Sorceress '94
Soul Survivors '01
Spectres '87
Spooky Encounters '80
Stephen King's Rose Red '02
Stephen King's The Storm of the Century '99
Stephen King's Thinner '96
Stir of Echoes '99
The Supernaturals '86
A Tale of Two Sisters '03
Terror Creatures from the Grave '66
They Watch '93
13 Ghosts '60
13 Ghosts '01
The Tooth Fairy '06
The Turn of the Screw '74
The Turn of the Screw '89
The Turn of the Screw '92
The Turn of the Screw '99
Unseen Evil '01
Unspeakable '00
Urban Ghost Story '98
The Vault '00
The Village '04
The Visitors '89
Vlad '03
Voices from Beyond '90
Voodoo Academy '00
Vulture's Eye '04
Wendigo '01
Wes Craven Presents: They '02
The Whip and the Body '63
White Noise '05
White Noise 2: The Light '07
Wind Chill '07
Witchcraft 4: Virgin Heart '92
Witchcraft 10: Mistress of the Craft '98
The Witches '66
The Wraith '87

Supernatural Martial Arts

The Crow '93
Hellbound '94
The Heroic Trio '93
The Legend of the 7 Golden Vampires '73
Lone Wolf and Cub: Baby Cart at the River Styx '72
Lone Wolf and Cub: Baby Cart to Hades '72
The Mummy: Tomb of the Dragon Emperor '08
Ninja, the Violent Sorcerer '86
Remo Williams: The Adventure Begins '85
Sgt. Kabukiman N.Y.P.D. '90
TMNT (Teenage Mutant Ninja Turtles) '07
Vampire Raiders—Ninja Queen '89
Zu: Warriors from the Magic Mountain '83

Supernatural Westerns

Billy the Kid Versus Dracula '66
BloodRayne 2: Deliverance '07
Curse of the Undead '59
Dead Birds '04
The Devil's Mistress '68
Ghostriders '87
Grim Prairie Tales '89
The Hitcher '86
Into the Badlands '92
Jesse James Meets Frankenstein's Daughter '65
John Carpenter's Vampires '97
Mad at the Moon '92

▶ = rated three bones or higher

Supernatural

Near Dark '87
Sundown '91
Timerider '83

Surfing

see also Beach Blanket Bingo

Aloha Summer '88
Beach Blanket Bingo '65
Beach Party '63
Big Wednesday 78
Bikini Beach '64
Blackrock '97
Blood Surf '00
Blue Crush '02
Blue Juice '95
California Dreaming 79
Chairman of the Board '97
Computer Beach Party '88
The Endless Summer '66
The Endless Summer 2 '94
Escape from L.A. '96
Fantastic Four: Rise of the Silver Surfer '07
Follow Me '69
Gidget '59
How to Stuff a Wild Bikini '65
In God's Hands '98
Lauderdale '89
Lilo & Stitch '02
Local Boys '02
Mad Wax: The Surf Movie '90
Meet the Deedles '98
Muscle Beach Party '64
North Shore '87
Off the Lip '04
Point Break '91
Psycho Beach Party '00
Puberty Blues '81
Red Surf '90
Ride the Wild Surf '64
Riding Giants '04
South Beach Academy '96
Step Into Liquid '03
Summer City '77
Surf Nazis Must Die '87
Surf Party '64
Surf 2 '84
Surf's Up '07

Survival

see also Hunted!; Negative Utopia; Post-Apocalypse

Abandon Ship '57
The Admirable Crichton '57
Adrift '93
Adventure Island '47
Adventures of Eliza Fraser 76
Alive '93
Alpine Fire '89
And I Alone Survived 78
Antarctica '84
Arctic Blue '93
Arctic Tale '07
Attack of the Beast Creatures '85
The Aviator '85
Back from Eternity '56
Bat 21 '88
Battlefield Earth '00
Beverly Hills Family Robinson '97
Black Book '06
Black Rain '88
Born Killer '89
Born Wild '95
The Bridge on the River Kwai '57
Buffalo Rider '78
A Bullet Is Waiting '54
Cage 2: The Arena of Death '94
Caged in Paradise '89
Captain January '36
A Captive in the Land '91
Cast Away '00
Challenge To Be Free 76
Cheyenne Warrior '94
Clearcut '92
Cliffhanger '93
Clown '53
Cold Mountain '03
Cold River '81

The Last Flight of Noah's Ark '80
The Last of the Dogmen '95
Le Dernier Combat '84
Legend of Alfred Packer '80
The Legend of Wolf Mountain '92
Legionnaire '98
L'Enfant d'Eau '95
The Leopard Son '96
The Life and Death of Colonel Blimp '43
Lifeboat '44
Lily Was Here '89
Limbo '99
Little Dorrit, Film 1: Nobody's Fault '88
Little Dorrit, Film 2: Little Dorrit's Story '88
Lord of the Flies '63
Lord of the Flies '90
Lost '83
Lost '86
Love on the Dole '41
Male and Female '19
Man in the Wilderness 71
Marooned in Iraq '02
Manon '50
Melody 71
Merry Christmas, Mr. Lawrence '83
Mr. Robinson Crusoe '32
Morning Departure '50
The Mosquito Coast '86
The Most Dangerous Game '32
My Side of the Mountain 69
Mysterious Island '61
The Naked Prey 66
Nightmare at Bittercreek '91
Nightmare at Noon '88
Objective, Burma! '45
On the Beach '59
On the Beach '00
Once Before I Die '65
Ordeal in the Arctic '93
Osa 85
Out of Control 85
Packin' It In '83
Pagan Island '60
Panic in the Year Zero! '62
Panic Room '02

Standoff '97
Starbird and Sweet William 73
Storm and Sorrow '90
Sub Down '97
Survival Quest '89
Survival Run '80
Sweet Sweetback's Baadasssss Song 71
Swept Away '02
The Swiss Family Robinson '60
The Terror '63
Testament '83
Thief '81
Three Came Home '50
The Ticket '97
Titanic '96
Tooth and Nail '07
Touching the Void '03
Trouble in Paradise '88
Trucks '97
True Heart '97
Tundra '36
28 Days Later '02
Two Women '61
Unsettled Land '88
Voyage 93
The Voyage of the Yes 72
Vukovar '94
Wagon Master '50
Walkabout 71
Walking Thunder '94
Warriors of the Apocalypse '85
Waterworld '95
When Trumpets Fade '98
The White Dawn 75
White Fang and the Hunter '85
White Water Summer '87
White Wolves 3: Cry of the White Wolf '98
Wild America '97
World Trade Center '06
Zarkorr! The Invader '96

Suspended Animation

Alien 3 '92
Aliens '86
Austin Powers: International Man of Mystery '97
Batman and Robin '97
Buck Rogers in the 25th Century 79
Chances Are '89
Coma 78
Demolition Man '93
Dragon Fury 2 '96
Encino Man '92
Forever Young '92
Late for Dinner '91
Planet of the Apes '68

Suspense

see also Mystery & Suspense

Almost Strangers '01
Arlington Road 99
Black Book '05
Bound by Lies '05
Breach '07
Dead Dog '00
The Devil's Advocate '97
Disturbia '07
Gone Dark '03
The Good Shepherd '06
The Gunman '03
Half Light '05
I'm Not Scared '03
Incubus '05
King of the Ants '03
Lady Killer '97
The Lookout '07
The Lost of Others '06
Man in the Attic '53
The Mapmaker '01
Marebito '04
Mr. Brooks '07
Next '07
The Night Watchman '02
Panic Room '02
Perfect Stranger '07
Pulse '03

Red Road '06
Rx '06
Savage Island '03
Shelter Island '03
Sphere '97
Ten 'Til Noon '06
The Tesseract '03
That Beautiful Somewhere '06
Trail of a Serial Killer '98
The 24th Day '04
Urban Ghost Story '98
The Well '97
The Wild Card '03
Your Vice is a Closed Room and Only I Have the Key 72
Zeder '83

Swashbucklers

see also Action-Adventure; Fencing; Medieval Romps

Abbott and Costello Meet Captain Kidd '52
Adventures of Captain Fabian '51
Adventures of Don Juan '49
The Adventures of Robin Hood '38
Against All Flags '52
Ali Baba and the Forty Thieves '43
Ali Baba and the 40 Thieves '54
Anthony Adverse '36
Arabian Nights 42
At Sword's Point '51
The Black Pirate '26
The Black Rose '50
The Black Shield of Falworth '54
The Black Swan '42
Blackbeard the Pirate '52
Blackbeard's Ghost '67
Bluebeard 72
The Bold Caballero '36
The Buccaneer '58
Buccaneer's Girl '50
Captain Blood '35
Captain Horatio Hornblower '51
Captain Kidd '45
Captain Kronos: Vampire Hunter 74
Captain Ron '92
Cartouche '62
Casanova '05
The Challenge '82
Cheech and Chong's The Corsican Brothers '84
China Seas '35
The Conqueror & the Empress '64
Corsair '31
The Corsican Brothers 42
The Count of Monte Cristo '12
The Count of Monte Cristo '34
The Count of Monte Cristo '74
The Count of Monte Cristo '99
The Count of Monte Cristo '02
Court Jester 56
Crimson Pirate '52
Cutthroat Island '95
Dancing Pirate '36
Dr. Syn '37
Dr. Syn, Alias the Scarecrow '64
Don Juan DeMarco '94
Don Q., Son of Zorro '25
Double Crossbones '51
The Elusive Pimpernel '50
Executioner of Venice 63
Fanfan la Tulipe 51
The Fencing Master '92
The Fifth Musketeer 79
Fighting Marines '36
The Fighting Prince of Donegal 66
The Flame & the Arrow '50
The Four Musketeers 75

The 4 Musketeers '05
Frenchman's Creek '44
Frenchman's Creek '98
Ghost in the Noonday Sun 74
Gypsy 75
Hawk of the Wilderness '38
Hell Ship Mutiny '57
Highlander: The Gathering '92
His Majesty O'Keefe 53
Hook '91
If I Were King '38
The Iron Mask 29
The Island '80
Island Trader 71
Kidnapped '05
The King's Guard '01
The King's Thief 55
Kojiro '67
The Lady and the Highwayman '89
The Lamb '15
The Legend of Zorro '05
The Lives of a Bengal Lancer '35
Long John Silver '54
Magic Island '95
The Man in the Iron Mask '39
The Man in the Iron Mask '77
The Man in the Iron Mask '97
The Man in the Iron Mask '98
Marauder '65
Mark of Zorro '20
The Mark of Zorro '40
The Mask of Zorro '98
The Master of Ballantrae '53
The Master of Dragonard Hill '89
Monty Python's The Meaning of Life '83
Mooncussers '62
Moonfleet 55
Moran of the Lady Letty '22
Morgan the Pirate '60
Muppet Treasure Island '96
The Musketeer '01
My Favorite Year '82
My Wicked, Wicked Ways '84
The Naked Sword of Zorro '69
Nate and Hayes '83
Naughty Marietta '35
New Moon '40
Old Ironsides '26
On Guard! '03
The Phantom '96
The Pirate '48
Pirate Movie '82
Pirate Warrior '64
Pirates '86
The Pirates of Penzance '83
Pirates of the Caribbean: At World's End '07
Pirates of the Caribbean: The Curse of the Black Pearl '03
Pirates of the Coast 61
Pirates of the Seven Seas 62
Prince of Foxes 49
The Princess and the Pirate '44
The Princess Bride '87
Princess of Thieves '01
Prisoner of Zenda '37
Prisoner of Zenda '52
Prisoner of Zenda 79
Project A '83
Project A: Part 2 '87
Quest of the Delta Knights 93
The Return of the Musketeers '89
Revenge of the Musketeers '94
Ring of the Musketeers '93
Robin Hood 73
Romola 25
Royal Flash 75
Scaramouche '34
The Scarlet Pimpernel '82
The Scarlet Pimpernel 99

The Scarlet Pimpernel 2: Mademoiselle Guillotine '99
The Scarlet Pimpernel 3: The Kidnapped King '99
Sea Hound '47
The Sea Hawk '40▶
The Secret of El Zorro '57
Shipwrecked '90
The Sign of Zorro '60
Sinbad and the Eye of the Tiger '77
Sinbad the Sailor '47▶
Son of Ali Baba '52
Son of Captain Blood '62
Son of Fury '42▶
Son of Monte Cristo '40
Son of Zorro '47
South of Pago Pago '40
South Seas Massacre '74
The Spanish Main '45
The Story of Robin Hood & His Merrie Men '52▶
Swashbuckler '76
The Swiss Family Robinson '60▶
Sword & the Sorcerer '82
Sword of Sherwood Forest '60
The Swordsman '92
Three Amigos '86
The Three Musketeers '16
The Three Musketeers '21
The Three Musketeers '33
The Three Musketeers '35
The Three Musketeers '39
The Three Musketeers '48
The Three Musketeers '74▶
The Three Musketeers '93
Tiger of the Seven Seas '62
Treasure Island '34▶
Treasure Island '50▶
Treasure Island '72
Treasure Island '89
Treasure Island '99
Treasure of the Golden Condor '53
Treasure of the Moon Goddess '86
Two Lost Worlds '50
Under the Red Robe '36
Wallaby Jim of the Islands '37
The Warriors '55
The Wicked Lady '83
Yankee Buccaneer '52
Yellowbeard '83
Zorro '74
Zorro, the Gay Blade '81

Swimming
see also Deep Blue; Go Fish; Island Fare; Killer Sea Critters; Lifeguards; Pacific Islands
Alex '92
Back to School '86
Barracuda '78
Bathing Beauty '44
The Big Bad Swim '06
The Bridges at Toko-Ri '55▶
Cocoon '85▶
Dangerous When Wet '53
Dawn! '83
Easy to Love '53
Fast Times at Ridgemont High '82▶
The Guardian '06
Gremlins '84▶
Imaginary Heroes '05
Jaws '75▶
The Man from Atlantis '77
Million Dollar Mermaid '52
Neptune's Daughter '49
Off the Mark '87
On a Clear Day '05
Pride '07
Sea People '00
Sleeping with the Enemy '91
Splash '84▶
Swim Team '79
Swimfan '02
The Swimmer '68▶
Swimming Upstream '03
Thrill of a Romance '45
The Tunnel '01▶
Unbreakable '00▶

Swingers
Bob & Carol & Ted & Alice '69
A Change of Seasons '80
Eating Raoul '82▶
Group Marriage '72
9 1/2 Weeks '86
The Other Side of the Bed '03
The Party '68▶
The Swap '71
The Swinging Cheerleaders '74
The Unfaithful '60▶
Your Friends & Neighbors '98▶

Sydney
see also Down Under
Better Than Sex '00
Cosi '95▶
Dirty Deeds '02▶
Doing Time for Patsy Cline '97
Don's Party '76▶
Floating Life '95
He Died With a Felafel in His Hand '01
Introducing the Dwights '07
Joey '98
The Last Wave '77▶
Lilian's Story '95
Little Fish '05▶
Me Myself I '99
Napoleon '96
Out of the Body '88
Over the Hill '93
Paperback Hero '99
The Road from Coorain '02
The Sum of Us '94▶
Young Einstein '89

Sword & Sandal
see also Sexcapades
Alexander '04
Ali Baba and the Forty Thieves '43
Amazons and Gladiators '01
Arabian Nights '42
The Avenger '62
Battle of Valiant '63
Colossus and the Amazon Queen '64
Colossus of the Arena '62
Coriolanus, Man without a Country '64
Duel of Champions '61
Fabiola '48▶
Fire Monsters Against the Son of Hercules '62
Giants of Rome '63
Gladiator '00▶
Gladiator of Rome '63
Gladiators 7 '62
Goliath Against the Giants '63
Goliath and the Barbarians '60
Goliath and the Dragon '61
Goliath and the Sins of Babylon '64
Gor '88
Hercules '58
Hercules against the Moon Men '64
Hercules and the Captive Women '63
Hercules and the Princess of Troy '65
Hercules in the Haunted World '64
Hercules, Prisoner of Evil '64
Hercules Unchained '59
Hercules vs. the Sons of the Sun '64
Hero of Rome '63
The Invincible Gladiator '63
The Last Days of Pompeii '60
Revenge of the Barbarians '64
Roland the Mighty '56
Samson '61
Samson Against the Sheik '62
Samson and His Mighty Challenge '64
Samson and the 7 Miracles of the World '62
Samson and the Princess
The Scorpion King '02
Sins of Rome '54
Son of Ali Baba '52
Son of Hercules in the Land of Darkness '63
Sword of Venus '53
Terror of the Steppes '64
Thor and the Amazon Women '67
The 300 Spartans '62
300 '07
Tristan & Isolde '06
The Triumph of Hercules '66
The Trojan Horse '62
Troy '04
Warriors of Heaven and Earth '03

Tale of the Tape
see also Sexcapades
Alone With Her '07
Auto Focus '02▶
Be Kind Rewind '08
Benny's Video '92
The Big Hit '98
The Blair Witch Project '99
Capturing the Friedmans '03▶
Cloverfield '08
Comedy of Innocence '00
The Darwin Awards '06
Diary of the Dead '07
Enemy of the State '98
The Fantastic World of D.C. Collins '84
Felony '95
Final Cut '98
Final Assignment '80
Forbidden Homework '92
Freeze Frame '04
Hard to Kill '89
Homework '90
I'm Reed Fish '06
Interview with the Assassin '02
Janice Beard '99
Jimmy & Judy '06
The Jolly Boys' Last Stand '00
Love or Money '01
My Life on Ice '02
100 Mile Rule '02
The Perfect Witness '07
Red Road '06
Road Trip '00
The Rutanga Tapes '90
Savage Harvest 2: October Blood '06
sex, lies and videotape '89▶
Sky High '84
Silver '93
Spy Games '99
Two Weeks '05
Vacancy '07
Video Murders '87
Video Violence '87
Warm Blooded Killers '01

Talking Animals
see also Wild Kingdom
Air Bud 6: Air Buddies '06
Air Bud '97
Animal Farm '99
The Ape '05
Babe '95▶
Babe: Pig in the City '98
Barnyard '06
Big Top Pee-wee '88
Brother Bear 2 '06
Cats & Dogs '01
Charlotte's Web '06▶
Chicken Little '05
Dinotopia '02
Dr. Dolittle '98
Dr. Dolittle 2 '01
Dr. Dolittle 3 '06
Dr. Dolittle 4: Tail to the Chief '08
Dr. Seuss' Horton Hears a Who! '08▶
Flushed Away '06▶
Francis Covers the Big Town '53
Francis Goes to the Races '51
Francis Goes to West Point '52
Francis in the Haunted House '56
Francis in the Navy '55
Francis Joins the WACs '54
Francis the Talking Mule '49
Garfield: A Tail of Two Kitties '06
George of the Jungle '97▶
The Golden Compass '07
Good Boy! '03
Home on the Range '04
Homeward Bound: The Incredible Journey '93▶
Homeward Bound 2: Lost in San Francisco '96
Hoodwinked '05▶
Inland Empire '06
Karate Dog '04
Kung Fu Panda '08
Little Nicky '00
Madagascar '03
Malibu's Most Wanted '03
Men in Black '97▶
Men in Black 2 '02
Over the Hedge '06▶
Paulie '98
Pooh's Heffalump Movie '05
Racing Stripes '05
The Real Macaw '95
Sherlock: Undercover Dog '94
Shrek the Third '07
The SpongeBob SquarePants Movie '04
Stuart Little '99
The Undercover Kid '95

Tattoos
Blue Tiger '94
Cape Fear '91▶
The Crow 2: City of Angels '96
Cyber Bandits '94
Double Take '01
Down Periscope '96
Eastern Promises '07▶
Escape from L.A. '96
Foxfire '96
Hitman '07
The Illustrated Man '69▶
In the Cut '03
Lust in the Dust '85▶
Memento '00▶
The Night of the Hunter '55▶
Prey for Rock and Roll '03▶
Skin Deep '94
Son-in-Law '93
Starship Troopers '97▶
Stir Crazy '80
Tattoo '81
Tattoo, a Love Story '02
Teresa's Tattoo '94
Waterworld '95
The Yakuza '75

Taxing Situations
The Brady Bunch Movie '95▶
Exotica '94▶
Hair Show '04
Lagaan: Once upon a Time in India '01
The Mating Game '59▶
Off the Map '03▶
Speedway '68
Strange Bedfellows '64
Stranger Than Fiction '06▶
A Taxing Woman '87▶
A Taxing Woman's Return '88▶
The Taxman '98

Team Efforts
The Alamo '60▶
The Bad News Bears '05
The Bad News Bears Go to Japan '78
The Bad News Bears in Breaking Training '77
Beerfest '06
Breaking Away '79▶
The Club '80
Coach '78
Codename: Foxfire '85
Codename: Wildgeese '84
The Comebacks '07
The Cutting Edge '92
The Dirty Dozen '67▶
The Dirty Dozen: The Deadly Mission '87
The Dirty Dozen: The Fatal Mission '88▶
The Dirty Dozen: The Next Mission '85
The Doll Squad '73
D3: The Mighty Ducks '96
D2: The Mighty Ducks '94
Eddie '96
Fantastic Four '05
The Final Season '07
Finger on the Trigger '65
Force 10 from Navarone '78
Force Five '75
The Game of Their Lives '05
The Game Plan '07
The Guns of Navarone '61▶
Hoosiers '86▶
Innocents with Dirty Hands '76
Kicking & Screaming '05
Kill and Kill Again '81
Ladybugs '92
Let's Get Harry '87
The Longest Yard '05
The Losers '70
The Magnificent Seven '60▶
Major League 3: Back to the Minors '98
Memphis Belle '90▶
The Mighty Ducks '92
Miracle '04▶
Miracle on Ice '81
The Mod Squad '99
Necessary Roughness '91
Ocean's Eleven '01▶
Ocean's Eleven '60
Ocean's Twelve '04
Pride '07
Race the Sun '96
Radio '03
Rebound '05
Recipe for Disaster '03
Remember the Titans '00▶
Renaissance Man '94
School of Rock '03▶
Seven Magnificent Gladiators '84
Seven Samurai '54▶
Silverado '85▶
The Sixth Man '97
Soldier Boyz '95
Space Jam '96
Steel '97
Sunset Park '96
S.W.A.T. '03
Team America: World Police '04▶
That Thing You Do! '96▶
Three the Hard Way '74
The Tunnel '01▶
Twister '96
Uncommon Valor '83
The Untouchables '87▶
Varsity Blues '98
Victory '81
White Squall '96
Wild Geese '78
Wild Geese 2 '85
Wind '92

Tearjerkers
Acorn People '82
An Affair to Remember '57▶
After the Promise '87
All About My Mother '99▶
All Dogs Go to Heaven '89
All Fall Down '62
All Mine to Give '56
Angels in America '03▶
Another Time, Another Place '58
Autumn in New York '00
Baby Face '33
Back Street '61
Balboa '82
Ballad in Blue '66
Bang the Drum Slowly '56
Bang the Drum Slowly '73▶
Beaches '88▶
Because of You '52
Big Bluff '55
Bittersweet Love '76
Black Eyes '39
Black Peter '63
Blind Spot '93
The Blood of Jesus '41
Blossoms in the Dust '41
Bonjour Tristesse '57▶
Bouquet of Barbed Wire '76
Breaking the Rules '92
Brian's Song '71▶
The Cabin in the Cotton '32
Camille '21
Carry On Cruising '62
Cast the First Stone '89
The Champ '32▶
The Champ '79
Change of Heart '98
Chantilly Lace '93
The Cheat '15
Chinatown After Dark '31
Choices '81
Christmas Comes to Willow Creek '87
City That Never Sleeps '53
City Without Men '43
Claudia '43
Clown '53
Coquette '29
The Country Kid '23▶
The Courtney Affair '47
Craig's Wife '36▶
Crawlspace '86
Curly Sue '91
Dance Fools Dance '31▶
Danielle Steel's Fine Things '90
Dead Wrong '83
Death Be Not Proud '75▶
Dedee d'Anvers '49
Delinquent Parents '38
A Dog of Flanders '59▶
A Dog Pound Shuffle '75▶
An Early Frost '85▶
Easy Virtue '27
The Eddy Duchin Story '56
Eric '75▶
Escape Me Never '47
The Evening Star '96
The Event '03
Fire Down Below '57
Flamingo Road '49▶
Forever Love '98
The Forbidden City '18
Fortune's Fool '21
Found Alive '34
Fulfillment '89
Gangs, Inc. '41
The Garden of Allah '36▶
The Gathering '77
The Gathering, Part 2 '79
Ghost '90▶
Gideon '99
Girl from Chicago '32
The Girl Who Had Everything '53
Goodbye, Mr. Chips '39▶
Great Day '46
The Greatest Question '19
Griffin and Phoenix: A Love Story '76
Harlow '65
The Healer '35
Hearts of Humanity '32
Heaven and Earth '93

Tearjerkers

Heaven's a Drag '94
Hell-Ship Morgan '36
Her Silent Sacrifice '18
Here on Earth '00
High Gear '33
A Home of Our Own '93
Home Room '02 ◣
Honky Tonk '41
Hot Spell '58
Human Desire '54
Human Hearts '22
I Conquer the Sea '36
I Sent a Letter to My Love '81 ◣
Ice Castles '79
If Ever I See You Again '78
Imitation of Life '34
In This Our Life '42
Inside Daisy Clover '65
Intermezzo '36
Intermezzo '39 ◣
Introducing Dorothy Dandridge '99 ◣
Jack the Bear '93
Johnny Belinda '48 ◣
Johnny Belinda '82
Johnny Eager '42 ◣
Journey for Margaret '42 ◣
Keep Punching '39
The Kid with the Broken Halo '82
La Bete Humaine '38 ◣
La Chienne '31 ◣
Lady Caroline Lamb '73
The Lady Without Camelias '53
The Last Best Year '90
Le Jour Se Leve '39 ◣
Legends of the Fall '94
Leo '02
Leopard in the Snow '78
Leper '76
Letter from an Unknown Woman '48 ◣
The Little Match Girl '84
The Little Princess '39 ◣
A Little Princess '95 ◣
Look Who's Talking Now '93
Looking for an Echo '99
Love Affair '39 ◣
Love Affair '94
Love Affair: The Eleanor & Lou Gehrig Story '77
Love Butcher '82
The Love Flower '20
The Love Has Many Faces '65
The Love Light '21
Love Songs '85
Love Story '70
Lovers of Their Time '85
Loving '84
Lure of the Sila '49
Madame Butterfly '95
Madame X '37
Magnificent Obsession '54
Man of Evil '48
The Marxman '29
Marvin's Room '96
Matters of the Heart '90
Mayerling '68 ◣
Mildred Pierce '45 ◣
Miles to Go '86
Millie '31
Mimi '35
The Miniver Story '50
Miss Julie '50
Missing Brendan '03
Mrs. Silly '85
Mr. Holland's Opus '95 ◣
Mr. Skeffington '44 ◣
Mistress '87
Moon over Harlem '39
A Mormon Maid '17 ◣
Mother and Son '31
Murder on Lenox Avenue '41
My Foolish Heart '49
My Girl '91
My Life Without Me '03 ◣
The Nest '80
The Night Cry '26
Night Life in Reno '31
Nomads of the North '20
Now, Voyager '42 ◣
Old Yeller '57 ◣
One More Kiss '99
One True Thing '98 ◣

Only Angels Have Wings '39 ◣
An Orphan Boy of Vienna '37
The Other Side of the Mountain '75
The Other Side of the Mountain, Part 2 '78
Our Sons '91
Our Time '74
Paradise Road '97
The Passing of the Third Floor Back '36
Pattes Blanches '49
Peg o' My Heart '22
Penny Serenade '41 ◣
A Place in the Sun '51 ◣
The Pride of the Yankees '42 ◣
The Promise '79
Question of Faith '93
A Question of Guilt '78
Quicksand '50
The Racket '51
Rage of Angels '83
Rain Man '88 ◣
The Rains Came '39
Random Harvest '42 ◣
Rebecca of Sunnybrook Farm '17
Red Kimono '25
Remolino de Pasiones '68
Rikisha-Man '58 ◣
The Road to Ruin '28
Romola '25
Scar of Shame '27
Secrets of a Married Man '84
Seizure: The Story of Kathy Morris '80
Sex '20
Shadowlands '93 ◣
She Goes to War '29
A Shining Season '79
The Shock '23
Shopworn Angel '38 ◣
Silent Night, Lonely Night '69
The Sin of Madelon Claudet '31
Since You Went Away '44 ◣
Six Weeks '82
Smilin' Through '33
Sommersby '93
Sooner or Later '78
Sparrows '26 ◣
Steel Magnolias '89 ◣
Stella '89
Stella Dallas '37 ◣
Stella Maris '18 ◣
Stolen Hours '63
The Story of Esther Costello '57
Strangers: The Story of a Mother and Daughter '79 ◣
Stromboli '50
Struggle '31
Suds '20
Summer and Smoke '61
A Summer Place '59
Sunny '41
Sunny Skies '30
Susan Lenox: Her Fall and Rise '31
Sweet November '68
Sweet November '01
Tango '36
Tell Me That You Love Me '84
Tender Comrade '43
Terms of Endearment '83 ◣
Test Tube Babies '48
That Certain Woman '37
They Drive by Night '40 ◣
Things in Their Season '74
This Boy's Life '93
Three Secrets '50
Thursday's Child '43
Tietland '44
A Time for Dancing '00
To Gillian on Her 37th Birthday '96
Tomorrow's Children '34
The Tong Man '19
Torch Song '53
Toute Une Nuit '82
Traffic in Souls '13

Trapped by the Mormons '22
Two Drifters '05
Under the Roofs of Paris '29 ◣
The Underdog '43
The Unholy Three '25 ◣
The Unholy Three '30 ◣
Untamed Heart '93
Uptown New York '32
Valentin '02
The Visit '00 ◣
Walk on the Wild Side '62
Walpurgis Night '41 ◣
Waterfront '39
Waterloo Bridge '40 ◣
Waterproof '99 ◣
Way Down East '20 ◣
The Weaker Sex '49
Welcome Home '89
West-Bound Limited '23
West of Zanzibar '28
When Wolves Cry '69
Where East is East '29
Where the Red Fern Grows '74 ◣
The White Rose '23 ◣
The White Cliffs of Dover '44 ◣
Wide Sargasso Sea '92
Winter Meeting '48
Without a Trace '83
A Woman of Affairs '28
The World Accuses '35
The World Is Full of Married Men '80
The World Owes Me a Living '47
Written on the Wind '56 ◣
X, Y & Zee '72
The Yarn Princess '94
The Yearling '46 ◣

Technicolor Yawn

Ace Ventura: When Nature Calls '95
Anaconda '96
BASEketball '98
Blood Simple '85 ◣
Boat Trip '03
Car Wash '76
The Crying Game '92 ◣
The Cutting Edge '92
Dogfight '91
Eating Raoul '82 ◣
The Exorcist '73 ◣
Fear and Loathing in Las Vegas '98
52 Pick-Up '86
Heathers '89 ◣
Jackass Number Two '06
Jaws '75 ◣
Kingpin '96
Larry the Cable Guy: Health Inspector '06
Monty Python's The Meaning of Life '83 ◣
My Giant '98
National Lampoon's Animal House '78 ◣
Osmosis Jones '01
Parenthood '89 ◣
Poltergeist 2: The Other Side '86
The Sandlot '93 ◣
Sirens '94
Stand by Me '86 ◣
This Is Spinal Tap '84 ◣
The Verdict '82 ◣
The Witches of Eastwick '87

Technology—Rampant

see also Computers; Killer Appliances; Robots & Androids
A Nous la Liberte '31 ◣
The Android Affair '95
Armageddon: The Final Challenge '94
Assassin '86
Attack of the Robots '66
Baby Girl Scott '87
Back to the Future '85 ◣
Batman Forever '95
Best Defense '84

Bicentennial Man '99
The Bionic Woman '75
Black Cobra 3: The Manila Connection '90
The Black Hole '79
Blade Runner '82 ◣
Blades '89
Bloodlust '59
Brainscan '94
Breakout '98
Bullet to Beijing '95
Chameleon '98
Chameleon 2: Death Match '99
Chameleon 3: Dark Angel '00
Chandu the Magician '32
Charly '68 ◣
Chopping Mall '86
Circuitry Man '90
Colossus: The Forbin Project '70
The Companion '94
Computer Beach Party '88
Computer Wizard '77
Confess '05
The Corporation '96 ◣
Crash and Burn '90
The Creation of the Humanoids '62
Cyber Bandits '94
Cyber-Tracker 2 '95
Dean Koontz's Black River '01
Dean Koontz's Mr. Murder '98
Death Ray 2000 '81
Defense Play '88
Demon Seed '77 ◣
Demonlover '02
Denise Calls Up '95
Detonator 2: Night Watch '95
Devour '05
Diamonds Are Forever '71 ◣
Digital Man '94
Dr. Goldfoot and the Bikini Machine '66
Doctor of Doom '62
Doomsdayer '99
Downdraft '96
Dungeonmaster '83
Duplicates '92
Electric Dreams '84
The Eliminators '86
Enemy of the State '98
Eve of Destruction '90
Evolver '94
Fail-Safe '64 ◣
Fair Game '95
Family Viewing '87 ◣
Fatal Error '99
Feardotcom '02
The Fifth Element '97 ◣
Final Mission '93
The Final Programme '73
The Fly '58 ◣
The Fly '86 ◣
The Fly 2 '89
Fugitive Mind '99
Future Cop '76
Futureworld '76
Geheimakte WB1 '42
Ghost in the Machine '93
Goldeneye '95 ◣
Hackers '95
Hide and Seek '77
Hologram Man '95
Hostile Intent '97
How to Make a Monster '01
I, Robot '04
Improper Channels '82
Interface '84
The Invisible Boy '57
Johnny Mnemonic '95
Johnny 2.0 '99
A Joke of Destiny, Lying in Wait Around the Corner Like a Bandit '84
Judge Dredd '95
A King in New York '57
Lawnmower Man 2: Beyond Cyberspace '95
The Lift '85
Live Free or Die Hard '07 ◣
Live Wire: Human Timebomb '95

Lost in Space '98
Lost Legacy: A Girl Called Hatter Fox '77
The Matrix '99 ◣
The Matrix Reloaded '03
The Matrix Revolutions '03 ◣
Maximum Overdrive '86
Metropolis '26 ◣
Microwave Massacre '83
Mr. Toad's Wild Ride '96
Modern Times '36 ◣
Mon Oncle '58 ◣
Moonraker '79
The Mosaic Project '95
The Munsters' Revenge '81
Murder by Phone '82
Murder by Television '35
Mutant Hunt '87
Mutant Species '95
The Net '95
New Crime City: Los Angeles 2020 '94
Night of the Kickfighters '91
Nightflyers '87
One Deadly Owner '74
OnLine '01
Out of Order '84
Panique '47 ◣
Perfect Stranger '07
The Philadelphia Experiment '84
The Pirates of Silicon Valley '99 ◣
Plughead Rewired: Circuitry Man 2 '94
The Power Within '79
Project: Eliminator '91
Project: Shadowchaser '92
Pulse '06
The Quiet Earth '85 ◣
Rage '95
Ravager '97
Redline '97
Remote '93
Repiikator: Cloned to Kill '94
Resident Evil '02
RoboCop '87 ◣
RoboCop 2 '90
RoboCop 3 '91
Robot Holocaust '87
Robot Jox '90
Rock & Roll Cowboys '92
R.O.T.O.R. '88
Runaway '84
Screamers '96
Search and Destroy '88
The Seventh Floor '93
Shadowzone '89
Shaker Run '85
Shocker '89
Short Circuit '86
Short Circuit 2 '88
Simone '02
Small Soldiers '98
Smart House '00
Sneakers '92 ◣
Soldier '98
Solo '96
Speaking Parts '89 ◣
Speed 2: Cruise Control '97
The Spy Who Loved Me '77
Stay Tuned '92
Stealth '05
Steel and Lace '90
Strange New World '75
Subliminal Seduction '96
Terminal Choice '85
Terminal Entry '87
Terminal Impact '95
The Terminal Man '74
The Terminator '84 ◣
Terminator 2: Judgment Day '91 ◣
Terminator 3: Rise of the Machines '03
Terrorvision '86
Things to Come '36 ◣
The Thirteenth Floor '99
Three Blind Mice '02
Thrillkill '84
Tom Clancy's Netforce '98
Touki Bouki '73
Tron '82
12:01 '93
2001: A Space Odyssey '68 ◣

Teen Angst

see also Coming of Age; Hell High School; Teen Comedy; Teen Drama; Teen Horror; Teen Romance
Above the Rim '94
Abuse '82
Across the Tracks '89
Address Unknown '96
Adventures in Dinosaur City '92
The Adventures of Sebastian Cole '99
The Adventures of Werner Holt '65
Age Isn't Everything '91
Ah, Wilderness! '35 ◣
Airborne '93
Alex '92
All Over Me '96 ◣
All the Real Girls '03 ◣
All Things Fair '95
Always Will '06
American Beauty '99 ◣
American Graffiti '73 ◣
American Pie '99 ◣
American Pie 2 '01
An American Rhapsody '01 ◣
An American Summer '90
American Virgin '98
Amor Bandido '79
Andy Hardy Gets Spring Fever '39
Andy Hardy Meets Debutante '40
Andy Hardy's Double Life '42
Andy Hardy's Private Secretary '41
Angel '84
Angel Rodriguez '05
Angels with Dirty Faces '38 ◣
Angus '95
Annie O '95
Anything for Love '93
Anywhere But Here '99
Apt Pupil '97
Around the Fire '98
Art for Teachers of Children '95
Arthur's Quest '99
Autumn Moon '92
Baby It's You '82 ◣
The Baby-Sitters' Club '95
The Bachelor and the Bobby-Soxer '47
Backstreet Dreams '90
Bad Boys '83 ◣
Bad Company '99
Bad Ronald '74 ◣
The Banger Sisters '02
The Basketball Diaries '95
The Battle of Shaker Heights '03
The Bay Boy '85
Beach Blanket Bingo '65 ◣
Beach House '82
Beach Party '63
The Beat '88
Beau Pere '81 ◣
Beautiful Thing '95 ◣
Beavis and Butt-Head Do America '96
Before and After '95
Beijing Bicycle '01
Bellyfruit '99
Bend It Like Beckham '02 ◣
The Beniker Gang '83
Benny's Video '92
Berserker '87

The Ultimate Imposter '79
The Unborn '91
Under Siege 2: Dark Territory '95
The Vindicator '85
Virtual Sexuality '99
Virtuosity '95
WarGames '83 ◣
Warning Sign '85
Webmaster '98
Weird Science '85 ◣
Westworld '73 ◣
Wild Palms '93
Wired to Kill '86
Zardoz '73

The Best Little Girl in the World '81 ▶
Better Luck Tomorrow '02 ▶
Beyond Innocence '97
The Big Bet '85
Big Bully '95
Big Fat Liar '02
Big Girls Don't Cry... They Get Even '92
Big Town '87
Bikini Beach '64
Bill & Ted's Excellent Adventure '89
Black Irish '07
Blackboard Jungle '55 ▶
Bleeding Hearts '94
Blue Car '03 ▶
BMX Bandits '83
Body Snatchers '93
Bonjour Monsieur Shlomi '03 ▶
Book of Love '91
Born Bad '97
Born Innocent '74
Born to Be Wild '95
Borstal Boy '00
Boston Kickout '95
A Boy Called Hate '95
Boys '95
The Boys Club '96
Boys Life '94
Boy's Reformatory '39
Boyz N the Hood '91 ▶
Brainscan '94
Bratz '07
Brave New Girl '04
The Break '95
The Breakfast Club '85 ▶
Breaking All the Rules '85
Breaking Away '79 ▶
Breaking Free '95
The Bridge '59
Brotherhood of Justice '86
Buck and the Magic Bracelet '97
Buffy the Vampire Slayer '92 ▶
Bully '01
The Bumblebee Flies Anyway '98
Burglar '87 ▶
Buster and Billie '74
But I'm a Cheerleader '99
Buying Time '89
By Dawn's Early Light '00
Bye, Bye, Birdie '33 ▶
Cadillac Girls '93
Can You Feel Me Dancing? '85
Candy '68
Can't Buy Me Love '87
Can't Hardly Wait '98
The Canterville Ghost '96
Captain Nuke and the Bomber Boys '95
Career Opportunities '91
Carrie '76 ▶
Carried Away '95
Carrie '02
Catch Me If You Can '02
Cave Girl '85
The Cement Garden '93
The Chalk Garden '64 ▶
Cherry Falls '00
The Chicken Chronicles '77
Children of the Corn 2: The Final Sacrifice '92
China, My Sorrow '89
Choices '81
The Choppers '61
The Chosen '81 ▶
Christine '84
The Class of Miss MacMichael '78
The Class of '83
Clayton County Line '78
Clockstoppers '02
The Club '94
Clueless '95 ▶
Coneheads '93
Condemned to Hell '84
Confessions of a Teenage Drama Queen '04
The Cool World '63
Cooley High '75 ▶
The Corner '00
Corvette Summer '78 ▶
Cotton Candy '82

Coyote Summer '96
The Craft '96
crazy/beautiful '01
Cries and Silence '97
Crime and Punishment in Suburbia '00
Criminal Lovers '99
Cruel Intentions '98
Cruel Intentions 2 '99
The Cruel Story of Youth '60 ▶
The Crush '93
Crutch '04
Cry-Baby '90 ▶
A Cry in the Wild '90 ▶
The Cure '95
The Curfew Breakers '57
Dance Me Outside '95
Dancer, Texas—Pop. 81 '98
A Dangerous Age '57
Dangerous Child '01
Dangerous Curves '88
The Dangerous Lives of Altar Boys '02 ▶
A Dangerous Place '94
Dangerous Minds '95
Dangerous Youth '58
Dangerously Close '86
Dario Argento's Trauma '93
Dark Horse '92
Date Bait '60
A Date with Judy '48
Daughter of Death '82
The Day My Parents Ran Away '93 ▶
Dazed and Confused '93 ▶
Dead Beat '94
Dead End '37 ▶
Dead Poets Society '89 ▶
The Deadbeat Club '04
Deadly Weapon '88
Desert Blue '98
Deal of a Lifetime '99
Death Wish Club '83
December Boys '07
The Deep End '01 ▶
The Deep End '04
The Devil on Wheels '47
The Devil's Arithmetic '99
The Devil's Sleep '51
The Diary of Anne Frank '59 ▶
Dick '99 ▶
Dino '57
Disco Pigs '01
The Disenchanted '90
Distubia '07
Diving In '90
Dogs in Space '87
Doin' Time on Planet Earth '88
Donnie Darko '01 ▶
Don't Tell Mom the Babysitter's Dead '91
The Doom Generation '95 ▶
Double Platinum '99
Double Play '96
Down in the Valley '05
Dracula A.D. 1972 '72
Dreaming About You '92
Dream Date '93
Dream Machine '91
Dream to Believe '85
Driving Lessons '06
Drive-In '76
Drive Me Crazy '99
Dudes '87
Due East '02
Dutch Girls '87
Dutch '91
East of Eden '54 ▶
East of Eden '80
East Side Kids '40
Eban and Charley '01
The Echo of Thunder '98
Eden Valley '94 ▶
Edge of Seventeen '99
The Effect of Gamma Rays on Man-in-the-Moon Marigolds '73 ▶

Eight Days a Week '97
Empire Records '95
Encino Man '92
Endless Love '81
The Ernest Green Story '93
The Escape Artist '82 ▶
E.T.: The Extra-Terrestrial '82 ▶
Every Mother's Worst Fear '98
Evils of the Night '85
Eyes of the Dolphin '06
Eyes Right! '26
Eyes of the Panther '90
Fall Time '94
Fame '80 ▶
Family Life '71
Fast Talking '86
Fast Times at Ridgemont High '82 ▶
Fat Albert '04
Father's Day '36
Fear '96 ▶
Fear No Evil '80
Fear Runs Silent '99
Fellini's Roma '72
Ferris Bueller's Day Off '86 ▶
Fighting Elegy '66
Final Destination '00
Final Exam '89
Fire with Fire '86
First Daughter '99
First, Last and Deposit '00
The First Time '69
5 Dark Souls '96
The Flamingo Kid '84 ▶
Flash '98
Flipper '96 ▶
Flirting '93 ▶
The Fly 2 '89
Footloose '84
For Keeps '88
For Real '02
The Forbidden Kingdom '08
Force of Impulse '60
Forever '78
Four Days '99
Foxes '80
Foxfire '96
The Franchise Affair '52
Frankenstein Reborn '98
Freaky Friday '03 ▶
Free of Eden '98
Freeze Frame '92
Friends '77
Friends Forever '86 ▶
A Friendship in Vienna '88
From the Edge of the City '98
Full of It '07
Fun '94
Galgameth '96
Gas Food Lodging '92 ▶
Gate 2 '92
Georgia Rule '07
Get Over It! '01
Get Real '99
Ghetto Dawg 2: Out of the Pits '05
Ghost World '01 ▶
Girl '98
Girl from Hunan '86 ▶
Girl, Interrupted '99 ▶
A Girl of the Limberlost '90
The Girl, the Body and the Pill '67
Girlfriend from Hell '89
Girls Can't Swim '99
Girls Just Want to Have Fun '85
Girls Town '95
Gleaming the Cube '89
Good Burger '97 ▶
The Goodbye Bird '93
Goodbye, Miss 4th of July '88
A Goofy Movie '94
Grand Avenue '96
Grease '78 ▶
Grease 2 '82
Gregory's Girl '80 ▶
The Guinea Pig '48
Gummo '97 ▶
Gypsy 83 '01
Hackers '95
Hadley's Rebellion '84

Hairspray '88 ▶
The Halfback of Notre Dame '96
Halloween '78 ▶
Halloween 6: The Curse of Michael Myers '95
The Hanging Garden '97 ▶
Hard Knocks '79
Hardcore '79 ▶
Harley '90
Head On '98 ▶
He Got Game '98 ▶
Heathers '89 ▶
Heavenly Creatures '94 ▶
The Heavenly Kid '85
Heavyweights '94
Here on Earth '00
Hide and Go Shriek '87
High School Caesar '60
High School Confidential '58 ▶
High School USA '84
High '82 ▶
The Hole '01
Hollywood High '77
Hollywood High, Part 2 '81
The Hollywood Knights '80
A Home of Our Own '93
Hometown U.S.A. '79
Homework '82
Hoop Dreams '94 ▶
Hoosiers '86 ▶
Hope Ranch '02
Hornet's Nest '70
The Horse Whisperer '97
Hct Bubblegum '81
Hct Summer '68
Hot Times '74
How I Got into College '89
How to Deal '03
How to Stuff a Wild Bikini '65
Hurricane Streets '96
I Accuse My Parents '45
I Am the Cheese '83
I Never Promised You a Rose Garden '77 ▶
I Wanna Hold Your Hand '78
I Was a Teenage Werewolf '57
I Was a Teenage Zombie '87
If Looks Could Kill '91
I'll Be Home for Christmas '98
Imaginary Crimes '94 ▶
Imaginary Heroes '05
The Impossible Years '68
The In Crowd '88
In His Father's Shoes '97 ▶
The Incredibly True Adventure of Two Girls in Love '95
The Inkwell '94
Iron Eagle 4 '95
It Came from the Sky '98
I've Been Waiting for You '98
Jailbait! '00
Jailbreakers '94
Jawbreaker '98
Jennifer '78
Jimmy Zip '00
Joe the King '99
Johnny 100 Pesos '93
Juno '07 ▶
Just Another Girl on the I.R.T. '93
Just for the Hell of It '68
Just Looking '99
Just One of the Girls '93
Kansas '88
Kevin & Perry Go Large '00
The Kid '97
Kid Dynamite '43
A Kid in King Arthur's Court '95
Kids '95
Kill Me Tomorrow '99
Kim '84
King Creole '58 ▶
King of California '07
Kitten with a Whip '64
Knights & Emeralds '87
La Bamba '87 ▶
La Petite Sirene '80

L'Eleve '95 ▶
Les Enfants Terrible '50 ▶
Les Enfants '57 ▶
L'Amour en Herbe '77
Last Cry for Help '79
The Last Best Sunday '98
The Last of the High Kings '96
Last Summer '69
Lauderdale '89
The Lawrenceville Stories '91
License to Drive '88
L.I.E. '01 ▶
Life as a House '01 ▶
Life Begins for Andy Hardy '41 ▶
Light It Up '99
Like Father Like Son '05
Like Mike '02
Limbo '99
Lisa '90
Liar's Edge '92
Little Darlings '80
Little Men '98
The Little Mermaid '89 ▶
A Little Romance '79 ▶
Little Secrets '02
Little Sweetheart '90
The Little Thief '89 ▶
Little Valentino '79
The Lizzie McGuire Movie '03
Loners '72
Looking for Miracles '90
The Loneliest Runner '76
The Loneliness of the Long Distance Runner '62 ▶
Loose Screws '85
Losin' It '82
Lost Angels '89
Lost and Delirious '01 ▶
The Lost Boys '87 ▶
Love Don't Cost a Thing '03
Love Laughs at Andy Hardy '46
Lovelines '84
Lover Girl '97
Lucas '86 ▶
Mad About You '90
Mad Love '95
Made in USA '88
Magenta '96
Magic '07
Major Payne '95
Making the Grade '84
Malibu Beach '78
Man from Texas '39
The Man in the Attic '94
The Man in the Moon '91 ▶
Mandragora '97
The Manhattan Project '86
Manic '01 ▶
Manny & Lo '96 ▶
Marie Baie des Anges '97
Married Too Young '62
Marvin's Room '96 ▶
Mastermind '96
Masterminds '97
Mean Creek '04 ▶
Mean Girls '04 ▶
Meatballs '79 ▶
Meatballs 2 '84
Meatballs 3 '87
Meatballs 4 '92
The Member of the Wedding '52 ▶
The Member of the Wedding '83
Mermaids '90 ▶
Metal Skin '94
Metropolitan '90 ▶
Min & Bill '30
The Miracle '91
Mirror, Mirror '90
Mischief '85
Misfits of Science '85
Miss A & Miss M '86
Miss Annie Rooney '42
Model Behavior '00
Mommy 2: Mommy's Day '96

Moondance Alexander '07
Morgan Stewart's Coming Home '87
Mortal Danger '94
Motorcycle Gang '57
Mouchette '67 ▶
The Mudge Boy '03
Murder in Greenwich '02
Murder in New Hampshire: The Pamela Smart Story '91
Muscle Beach Party '64
My American Cousin '85 ▶
My Antonia '94
My Best Friend Is a Vampire '88
My Boyfriend's Back '93
My Boys Are Good Boys '78
My Date with the President's Daughter '98
My Father, My Rival '85
My Father the Hero '33 ▶
My First Mister '01
My Girl 2 '94
My Life on Ice '02
My Own Private Idaho '91 ▶
My Science Project '85
My Teacher's Wife '95
My Uncle: The Alien '96
Mystery Date '91
Mystic Pizza '88 ▶
Naked Youth '59
Nancy Drew '07
Napoleon Dynamite '04 ▶
National Lampoon's Senior Trip '95
Nearing Grace '05
Nenette and Boni '96 ▶
The Neon Bible '95
Never Been Kissed '99
New Jersey Drive '95
New Waterford Girl '99
The Next Karate Kid '94
Nice Girls Don't Explode '87
Nickel Mountain '85
Night Life '90
Night of Evil '62
Night of the Twisters '95
Nightbreed '90
The Night Before '88
Night Friend '87
Night in the Life of Jimmy Reardon '88
A Nightmare on Elm Street '84 ▶
A Nightmare on Elm Street 2: Freddy's Revenge '85
A Nightmare on Elm Street 3: Dream Warriors '87 ▶
A Nightmare on Elm Street 4: Dream Master '88
A Nightmare on Elm Street 5: Dream Child '89
1969 '89 ▶
No Big Deal '83
No Laughing Matter '97
Nobody's Perfect '90
Noi '03
Not Another Teen Movie '01
Not My Kid '85
Now and Then '95
Nowhere '97
Nowhere to Run '88
O.C. and Stiggs '87
October Sky '99 ▶
Odd Birds '85
Ode to Billy Joe '76
On My Own '92
On the Edge '00
On the Edge: The Survival of Dana '79
One Crazy Night '93
One Dark Night '82
Only the Brave '94
Only the Strong '93
Ordinary Magic '93
The Other Side of Sunday '96
Our Song '01 ▶
Our Time '74
Our Very Own '50
Outside Providence '99
Outside Chance of Maximillian Gick '88
The Outsiders '83 ▶
Over the Edge '79 ▶
Over the Summer '85
The Pact '99
Pajama Party '64
Palindromes '04 ▶

La Promesse '96 ▶
Monika '52 ▶
Mon Oncle Antoine '71 ▶
Monkey Business '52 ▶

▶ = rated three bones or higher

Palm Springs Weekend '63
The Paper Brigade '96
Paradise Motel '84
Parenthood '89▸
Partyl Partyl '83
Pathfinder '87▸
Pecker '98
Peggy Sue Got Married '86▸
The People Next Door '70
Peppermint Soda '77▸
The Perfect Score '04
Petits Freres '00
Phantom 2040 Movie: The Ghost Who Walks '95
Phat Beach '96
A Pig's Tale '94
Pin... '88
Pippin '81▸
Platypus Cove '86
Playing for Keeps '86
Poison Ivy '85
Poison Ivy '92
Pom Pom Girls '76
Porky's '82
Porky's 2: The Next Day '83
The Positively True Adventures of the Alleged Texas Cheerleader-Murdering Mom '93▸
Pot, Parents, and Police '71
Powder '95
The Power Within '95
Prayer of the Rollerboys '91
Pretty in Pink '86▸
Pretty Smart '87
The Prime of Miss Jean Brodie '69▸
The Prince and the Surfer '99
Princes in Exile '90
The Princess Diaries '01
Prison for Children '93
Psycho Beach Party '00
Puberty Blues '81
Pump Up the Volume '90
Pups '99
Purgatory House '04
Quarterback Princess '85
Race the Sun '96
Racing with the Moon '84▸
Rad '86
The Rage: Carrie 2 '99
Rain '01
Raising Victor Vargas '03▸
Rambling Rose '91▸
Ratz '99
Real Women Have Curves '02▸
Rebel without a Cause '55▸
Reckless '84
Red Kiss '85▸
Remembering the Cosmos Flower '99
Return to Horror High '87
Return to the Blue Lagoon '91
Revenge of the Living Zombies '88
Ripe '97
River's Edge '87▸
Roadhouse 66 '84
Robin of Locksley '95
Rock 'n' Roll High School Forever '91
Rock, Rock, Rock '56
Rockula '90
Rodrigo D.: No Future '91
Roger Dodger '02▸
Romeo and Juliet '54
Romeo and Juliet '68▸
Ronnie and Julie '97
Rooftops '89
Rosetta '99
Rosie '99
Roustabout '64
Ruby Jean and Joe '96
The Run of the Country '95▸
Running Mates '86▸
Rushmore '98▸
Sabrina the Teenage Witch '96
Save the Last Dance '01
Saved! '04
Scared '84
Scary Movie '00
Schizo '04
Scream for Help '86

Screen Test '85
Screwballs '83
Seamless '00
Season of Change '94
Secret Admirer '85
The Secret Life of Girls '99
Secrets of Sweet Sixteen '74
Seizure: The Story of Kathy Morris '80
Senior Trip '81
Serial Killing 101 '04
Set Me Free '99
Seven Minutes in Heaven '86
Seventeen Again '00
The Seventh Coin '92
S.F.W. '94
ShadowZone: The Undead Express '91
Shag: The Movie '89▸
Shake, Rattle and Rock! '57
Shake, Rattle & Rock! '94
Sharma & Beyond '84
Sharon's Secret '95
She's All That '99
She's Out of Control '89
Shine '95▸
Shooting '82
Shout '91
Show Me Love '99
Shriek If You Know What I Did Last Friday the 13th '00
Silence of the Heart '84▸
The Silent One '86
Sing '89
Sixteen Candles '84▸
Skateboard '77
Skeletons in the Closet '00
Skipped Parts '00
SLC Punk! '99
Sleepers '96
Small Faces '95▸
Small Soldiers '98
Smart People '08
Smokey Bites the Dust '81
Smugglers' Cove '48▸
Snowballing '85
Social Misfits '00
Solarbabies '86
Some Kind of Wonderful '87▸
Somebody Is Waiting '96
Something Special '86
Sooner or Later '78
The Spell '77
Spetters '80
Spirit Rider '93▸
Splendor in the Grass '61▸
Spring Fever '81
Squeeze '97
Stand and Deliver '88▸
Starchaser: The Legend of Orin '85
State and Main '00▸
Stealing Beauty '96
Stella Does Tricks '96
Sticks and Stones '96
Sticky Fingers '88
Still Not Quite Human '92
Stones of Death '88
Straight out of Brooklyn '91
Straight Up '90
Strange Illusion '45
Strawberry Fields '97
Streets '90
The Stripper '63
Student Bodies '81
Suburbia '83
Sugar & Spice '01▸
Suicide Club '02
Summer Camp Nightmare '86
Summer Holiday '48
Summer of '42 '71▸
The Summer of My German Soldier '78▸
Summer School '77
Summer School '87
Sunchaser '96
Sunnyside '79
Swap Meet '79
Sweet Jane '98
Sweet 16 '81
Sweet Sixteen '02▸
Swim Team '79
Swimming Pool '03▸
Swing Kids '93

A Swingin' Summer '65
Tadpole '02
Tainted Blood '93
Take It to the Limit '00
Talisman '98
Tammy and the T-Rex '94
Tearaway '87
Teen Wolf '85
Teenage '44
Teenage Bad Girl '59
Teenage Bonnie & Klepto Clyde '93
Teenage Caveman '58
Teenage Caveman '01
Teenage Crime Wave '55
Teenage Doll '57
Teenage Mother '67
Teenage Mutant Ninja Turtles 2: The Secret of the Ooze '91
Teenage Strangler '64
Teenage Wolfpack '57
Teenager '74
Teenagers from Outer Space '59
Telling Lies in America '96
The Tender Age '84
Terminal Bliss '91
Tex '82
That Certain Age '38
That Dam Cat '96
That Night '84
That Thing You Do! '96▸
That Was Then... This Is Now '85
There Goes My Baby '92
Therese & Isabelle '67
They Made Me a Criminal '39
Thirteen '03▸
13 Going on 30 '04
36 Fillete '88▸
This Boy's Life '93▸
This Special Friendship '67
Thrashin' '86
3:15—The Moment of Truth '86
Three o'Clock High '87
Tiger Heart '96
Time at the Top '99
Time Stands Still '82▸
Timeless '96
Times Square '80
To Die For '95▸
To Gillian on Her 37th Birthday '96
To Play or to Die '91
Together '02
The Toilers and the Wayfarers '97
Tom Brown's School Days '51▸
Too Young to Die '90
Totally F***ed Up '94
12 and Holding '05▸
24-7 '97
Twirl '81
Twist & Shout '84▸
Twisted '86
Twisted Love '95
Two Friends '86
Two Hands '98▸
Uncle Buck '89▸
Under the Boardwalk '89
Under the Domim Tree '95
Unfinished Business '89
United States of Leland '03
The Unsaid '01
Unstrung Heroes '95▸
Up Against the Wall '91
Uptown Angel '90
Valley Girl '83▸
The Vals '85
The Van '77
Varsity Blues '98
A Very Brady Sequel '96
Village of the Giants '65
Virgin High '90

The Virgin Suicides '99▸
Virtual Sexuality '99
Vision Quest '85
The Voyage of the Yes '72
A Walk to Remember '02
Walking Back '26
Wanderers '79▸
The War Zone '98
Warriors of Virtue '97
Weird Science '85
Welcome Home, Roxy Carmichael '90
Welcome to 18 '87
Welcome to the Dollhouse '95▸
West Beirut '07
What a Girl Wants '03
Whatever '98
Whatever It Takes '00
Where Angels Go, Trouble Follows '68
Where the Boys Are '84 '84
Where the Day Takes You '92
White Oleander '02
White Squall '96
White Wolves 2: Legend of the Wild '94
White Wolves 3: Cry of the White Wolf '98
Wild Iris '01
The Wild Life '84
Wild Ones on Wheels '62
Wild Pony '83
Wild Things 2 '04
Wildflowers '99
William Shakespeare's Romeo and Juliet '96▸
Windrunner '94
Wish upon a Star '96
Wish You Were Here '87▸
The Wooden Gun '79
The Wounds '98
The Wraith '87
X-Men '00▸
X2: X-Men United '03▸
Xiu Xiu: The Sent Down Girl '97▸
The Year My Voice Broke '87▸
Yellow '98
You'll Get Over It '02
A Young Connecticut Yankee in King Arthur's Court '95
The Young Girl and the Monsoon '99
The Young Graduates '71
Young Guns '88
Young Hercules '97
Young Love, First Love '79
The Young Poisoner's Handbook '94▸
Youngblood '86
Youth Aflame '44
Youth on Parole '37
You've Ruined Me, Eddie '58
Zebrahead '92▸
Zero Boys '86
Zoe '01
Zombie Nightmare '86
The Zoo Gang '85

Teen Comedy

see also High School
Agent Cody Banks '03
Agent Cody Banks 2: Destination London '04
Ah, Wilderness! '35▸
American Pie '99▸
American Pie Presents: The Naked Mile '06
Aquamarine '06
The Baby-Sitters Club '95
Better Off Dead '85▸
Big Fat Liar '02
The Biggest Fan '02
Bill & Ted's Bogus Journey '91
Bill & Ted's Excellent Adventure '89
Book of Love '91
The Brady Bunch Movie '95▸
Bring It On '00
Calendar Girl '93
Camp '03
Can't Hardly Wait '98
Clueless '95▸
Confessions of a Teenage Drama Queen '04
D.E.B.S. '04
Don't Tell Mom the Babysitter's Dead '91
Drillbit Taylor '08
Duck Season '04▸
Fast Times at Ridgemont High '82▸
Fat Albert '04
Ferris Bueller's Day Off '86▸
First Daughter '04
Full of It '07
Getting It '06
The Girl Next Door '04
Happy Campers '01
Hoot '06
Hot Summer '68
House Party '90▸
John Tucker Must Die '06
Jump In! '07
Just One of the Girls '93
Kevin & Perry Go Large '00
Kids in America '05
The Lizzie McGuire Movie '03
Mean Girls '04▸
Modern Girls '86
My Father the Hero '93
New Waterford Girl '99
New York Minute '04
Not Another Teen Movie '01
One Crazy Night '93
One Crazy Summer '86
One Last Thing '05
Orange County '02
The Perfect Man '05
The Perfect Score '04
Porky's '82
Porky's 2: The Next Day '83
Porky's Revenge '85
Quarterback Princess '85
Raising Genius '04
The Red Sneakers '01
Risky Business '83▸
Rock 'n' Roll High School '79▸
Rock, Rock, Rock '56
She's All That '99
Sisterhood of the Traveling Pants '05
Sky High '05▸
Sleepover '04
Stick It '06
Sugar & Spice '01▸
Superbad '07
Sydney White '07
These Girls '05
Thumbsucker '05▸
Unaccompanied Minors '06
Wassup Rockers '06
Wild Child '08

Teen Drama

see also Hell High School; High School; Teen Horror; Teen Romance
Alex Rider: Operation Stormbreaker '06
Angel Rodriguez '05
ATL '06
Bomb the System '05
Brick '06▸
The Chumscrubber '05
800 Bullets '02
Evil '03▸
The Fast and the Furious: Tokyo Drift '06
Fly with the Hawk '85
Freedom Writers '07
Freeway '95▸
Full Count '06
The Good Humor Man '05
Gracie '07
Hard Candy '06
Hardcore '04
Havoc '05
Heart of America '03
The History Boys '06
Holy Girl '04▸
If... '69▸
Love Under Pressure '78
Murderous Intent '06▸
Never Back Down '08
On the Outs '05
One Last Thing '05
Paranoid Park '07
Pretty Persuasion '05
The Quiet '05
Quinceanera '06▸
Rocket Science '07▸
Running with Scissors '06
Ryna '05
Say Anything '89▸
Somersault '04
Stephanie Daley '06
Take the Lead '06
True Crime '95
Wah-Wah '05
Wassup Rockers '06
The Witness '99

Teen Horror

see also Hell High School; Horror Comedy; Teen Angst
Blood & Chocolate '07
The Brotherhood 3: The Young Demons '02
Centipede '05
Chaos '05
Cherry Falls '00
CryWolf '05
Cursed '04
Dead Silence '98
Devon's Ghost: Legend of the Bloody Boy '05
Devour '05
Disturbing Behavior '98
Fear of the Dark '02
Final Destination 3 '06
Freddy vs. Jason '03
Ginger Snaps '01
The Glass House '01
Hangman's Curse '03
Happy Hell Night '92
The Hitcher '07
The Hollow '04
Hostel '06
I Know What You Did Last Summer '97▸
I Still Know What You Did Last Summer '98
The Invisible '07
Killer Instinct '00
One of Them '03
Predator Island '05
Prom Night '08
Pulse '01
Red Riding Hood '03
School's Out '99
Scream '96▸
Serial Killing 101 '04
Spliced '03
Stay Alive '06
Superhero Movie '08
Sweet Insanity '06
Swimfan '02
Teeth '07
Venom '05
When a Stranger Calls '06
When Evil Calls '06
Wishmaster 3: Beyond the Gates of Hell '01
Witches of the Caribbean '05

Teen Musicals

Absolute Beginners '86
Cry-Baby '90▸
Fame '80▸
Grease '78▸
Grease 2 '82
Hairspray '88▸
High School Musical '06
High School Musical 2 '07
How She Moved '08
Josie and the Pussycats '01
Rock 'n' Roll High School '79▸
Rock 'n' Roll High School Forever '91
Rock, Pretty Baby '56

Teen Romance
see also Cinderella Stories; High School; Teen Angst; Teen Comedy

- Aaron Loves Angela '75
- Aloha Summer '88
- Aquamarine '06
- Beautiful Thing '95 ►
- The Biggest Fan '02
- The Blue Lagoon '80
- Book of Love '04
- Boys '95
- Boys and Girls '00
- Buster and Billie '74
- Can't Buy Me Love '87
- Cherry Crush '07
- Cold Showers '05
- crazy/beautiful '01
- Down in the Valley '05
- Dreaming About You '92
- Drive Me Crazy '99
- Ella Enchanted '04 ►
- Endless Love '81
- First Daughter '04
- Flirting '89 ►
- Forever '78
- Games of Love and Chance '03
- Get Over It! '01
- Gregory's Girl '80 ►
- Here on Earth '00
- High School Musical '06
- High School Musical 2 '07
- I Love You, I Love You Not '97
- The Incredibly True Adventure of Two Girls in Love '95
- Jacob Have I Loved '88
- John Tucker Must Die '06
- Kids in America '05
- Like a Brother '05
- Lila Says '04
- The Man in the Moon '91 ►
- My Summer of Love '05
- O '01 ►
- Ode to Billy Joe '76
- Pizza '05
- Pretty in Pink '86
- Raise Your Voice '04
- Romeo and Juliet '68 ►
- Romeo and Juliet '97
- Sixteen Candles '84 ►
- Snow Angels '07 ►
- Some Kind of Wonderful '87
- Step Up '06
- Ten Things I Hate about You '99 ►
- This is the Sea '96
- Valley Girl '83
- Whatever It Takes '00
- William Shakespeare's Romeo and Juliet '96 ►
- Zebrahead '92 ►

Terminal Confusion

- Beavis and Butt-Head Do America '96
- Big Trouble '02
- Dumb & Dumber '94
- 8 Heads in a Duffel Bag '96
- Home Alone 2: Lost in New York '92
- Home Alone 3 '97
- Jet Lag '02
- Knockaround Guys '01
- More Dogs Than Bones '00
- The Out-of-Towners '99 ►
- Stray Bullet '98
- Wait until Dark '67 ►
- What's Up, Doc? '72 ►

Television
see also Look Me! I'm on TV!; Mass Media; TV Pilot Movies

Tennis

- The Break '95
- Fletch '85
- Jocks '87
- Match Point '05 ►
- Nobody's Perfect '90
- Players '79
- Racquet '79
- Spring Fever '81
- The Squid and the Whale '05 ►
- Wimbledon '04
- The Witches of Eastwick '87

Terminal Illness
see also Disease of the Week

- The Barbarian Invasions '03 ►
- Beaches '88 ►
- Because of You '95
- Behind the Red Door '02
- Big Bad Love '02
- Big Fish '03 ►
- Blow Dry '03
- The Blue Butterfly '04
- Boom! '68
- The Bread, My Sweet '01
- The Bucket List '07
- The Bumblebee Flies Anyway '98
- The Christmas Shoes '02
- The Claim '00
- Crank '06
- Cria Cuervos '76 ►
- Cries and Whispers '72 ►
- The Dark Side of the Sun '88
- Death Be Not Proud '75 ►
- The Death of Mr. Lazarescu '05
- Dying Young '91 ►
- The End of the Affair '99 ►
- Evening '07
- 48 Angels '06
- The Fountain '06
- The Grand Role '04
- Girls' Night '97
- Hard Luck '01
- Here on Earth '00
- Hong Kong 1941 '84
- Igby Goes Down '02 ►
- In America '02 ►
- In the Shadows '98
- Klimt '06
- Last Holiday '06
- Late August, Early September '98
- Life as a House '01
- Magnolia '99 ►
- Marion Bridge '02
- The Medicine Show '01
- Missing Brendan '03
- Mrs. Wiggs of the Cabbage Patch '34
- Mr. Rice's Secret '00
- Moulin Rouge '01 ►
- My Brother '06
- My First Mister '01
- My Life Without Me '03
- Never Say Die '39
- Next Time We Love '36
- The Night Listener '06
- One Last Thing '05
- One More Kiss '99
- One True Thing '98 ►
- One Way Passage '32
- Parting Shots '98
- The Perfect Son '00
- Perfume '01
- Pieces of April '03
- Rails & Ties '07
- Red Meat '98
- Ripley's Game '02 ►
- The Secret of Dr. Kildare '39
- The Settlement '99
- Shadowboxer '06
- The Sleepy Time Gal '01
- Soft Fruit '99
- Speed of Life '99
- Stealing Beauty '96
- Stepmom '98 ►
- Sweet November '68
- Sweet November '01
- Terms of Endearment '83 ►
- The Theory of Flight '98
- Things You Can Tell Just by Looking at Her '00
- 13 Moons '02
- Time to Leave '05 ►
- Tuesdays with Morrie '99
- 21 Grams '03 ►
- Two Weeks '06
- The Ultimate Gift '07
- Under the Lighthouse Dancing '97
- Vernie '04
- A Very Serious Person '06
- The Visit '00 ►
- Vintage Model '92
- A Walk to Remember '02 ►
- The Wings of the Dove '97 ►
- Wit '01 ►
- With Honors '94

Terror in Tall Buildings
see also Elevators; Mystery & Suspense

- Blackout '78
- Botched '07
- Die Hard '88 ►
- Firetrap '01
- George A. Romero's Land of the Dead '05 ►
- The Glass Trap '04
- Hard to Die '90
- Poltergeist 3 '88
- Project: Shadowchaser '92
- Skyscraper '95
- Speed '94 ►
- Terror on the 40th Floor '74
- Tower of Terror '42
- The Towering Inferno '74 ►
- World Trade Center '06 ►

Terrorism
see also Crime & Criminals; Foreign Intrigue; Spies & Espionage

- Act of Passion: The Lost Honor of Kathryn Beck '83
- Act of Piracy '89
- Act of War '96
- Active Stealth '99
- Agent Red '00
- Air Force One '97 ►
- Airboss '98
- The Amateur '82
- American Dreamz '06
- Angel of Fury '93
- Antibody '02
- The Applegates '89
- Arlington Road '99 ►
- The Assassination Run '84
- The Assignment '97 ►
- Bad Company '02
- Barcelona '94 ►
- Belfast Assassin '84
- Black Cobra 2 '89
- Black Cobra 3: The Manila Connection '89
- Black Sunday '77 ►
- Black Terrorist '85
- Blast '96
- Blast '04
- Blink of an Eye '92
- Bloodfist 6: Ground Zero '94
- Blown Away '94
- Bomb Squad '97
- Bombshell '97
- Captain America 2: Death Too Soon '79
- The Cassandra Crossing '76
- Children of Men '06 ►
- Children of Rage '75
- C.I.A.: Target Alexa '94
- C.I.A. 2: Target Alexa '94
- Circle of Deceit '94
- Civic Duty '06
- Codename: Vengeance '87
- Collateral Damage '02
- Commando '85 ►
- Could It Happen Here? '77
- Counter Measures '99
- Counterstrike '03
- Cover-Up '91
- Covert Assassin '94
- Crackerjack 2 '97
- Crash and Burn '90
- Crash & Byrnes '99
- Crash Dive '96
- Critical Mass '00
- Crossfire '98 ►
- Cry of the Innocent '80 ►
- The Crying Game '92 ►
- The Dancer Upstairs '02 ►
- Dark Rider '91
- Day Night Day Night '06 ►
- DC 9/11: Time of Crisis '04
- Dead in a Heartbeat '02
- Deadline '87
- Deadly Heroes '96
- Deadly Outbreak '96
- Death Before Dishonor '87
- The Death Merchant '91
- Death of the Incredible Hulk '90
- Delta Force 2 '90
- The Delta Force '86
- Delta Force 3: The Killing Game '91
- Delta Force Commando '87
- Delta Force Commando 2 '90
- Demolition High '95
- Desert Thunder '99
- The Devil's Own '96 ►
- Dick Barton, Special Agent '48
- Die Hard '88 ►
- Die Hard 2: Die Harder '90 ►
- Die Hard: With a Vengeance '95
- Diplomatic Siege '99
- Dirty Games '89
- Dr. Otto & the Riddle of the Gloom Beam '86
- Dog Day Afternoon '75 ►
- The Dogfighters '95
- Doomsdayer '01
- Double Team '97
- D.R.E.A.M. Team '99
- The Enforcer '76
- Eraser '96
- Escape under Pressure '00
- The Evil That Men Do '84
- Executive Decision '96 ►
- Exposed '83
- Extreme Limits '01
- Extreme Ops '02
- Face/Off '97 ►
- Fahrenheit 9/11 '04 ►
- Falling Fire '97
- Fast Kill '73
- A Father's Revenge '88
- Fatwa '06
- ffolkes '80
- The Final Cut '96
- The Final Option '82
- Final Voyage '99
- Flashpoint Africa '84
- Fortress of Amerikka '89
- 48 Hours to Live '60
- The Fourth Angel '01
- Freedom Strike '98
- French Quarter Undercover '85
- Full Disclosure '00
- Full Fathom Five '90
- Futuresport '98
- Galyon '77
- Germicide '74
- The Glass Jungle '88
- The Glory Boys '84
- The Great New Wonderful '06
- Harold & Kumar Escape from Guantanamo Bay '08
- Heaven '01
- Held Hostage '91
- Hell Squad '85
- Hidden Agenda '90
- Hologram Man '95
- Hostage '87
- Human Bomb '97
- The Hunt for Eagle One: Crash Point '06
- In the Name of the Father '93 ►
- The Insurgents '06
- Invasion Force '90
- Invasion U.S.A. '85
- Invisible Circus '00
- Iran: Days of Crisis '91
- Jericho Fever '93
- Judgment in Berlin '88
- Juggernaut '74 ►
- July Group '81
- Jungle Assault '89
- Kamikaze '89 '83 ►
- Katherine '75
- The Kidnapping of the President '80
- The Kingdom '07 ►
- Kings and Desperate Men '83
- Knock Off '98
- L'Annee Sainte '76
- The Legend of Rita '99
- Lethal Target '96
- The Little Drummer Girl '84 ►
- Live Free or Die Hard '07
- Live Wire '92
- The Lost Command '66
- The Mad Bomber '72
- The Man Who Knew Too Little '97
- Marianne and Juliane '82
- McHale's Navy '97
- Memorial Day '98
- Merchants of War '90
- Michael Collins '96 ►
- Midnight in Saint Petersburg '97
- Molly Maguires '70
- Munich '05 ►
- Navy SEALS '90
- Night of the Assassin '77
- Nighthawks '81
- Nightstick '87
- Ninja Connection '90
- Ninja the Battalion '90
- No '98
- No Contest '94
- No Dead Heroes '87
- Odd Man Out '47 ►
- Omega Syndrome '87
- Once Upon a Time in China II '92
- Open Fire '94
- Operation Thunderbolt '77
- Panic in the Streets '50 ►
- Panic on the 5:22 '74
- Paradise Now '05 ►
- The Passenger '75 ►
- Passenger 57 '92
- Path to Paradise '97
- The Patriot '86
- Patriot Games '92 ►
- Patty Hearst '88
- The Peacekeeper '98
- The Peacemaker '97
- Programmed to Kill '86
- Project: Alien '89
- Protocols of Zion '05 ►
- Pursuit '72
- Python Wolf '88
- Rachida '05 ►
- Raid on Entebbe '77 ►
- The Railway Station Man '92 ►
- Rangers '00
- Rapid Assault '99
- Rebel '70
- Red Mercury '05
- Rendition '07 ►
- Riot '96
- The Rock '96 ►
- Rollercoaster '77
- Rosebud '75
- Royal Warriors '86
- Running Delilah '93
- Running Out of Time '94
- The Rutanga Tapes '90
- The Secret Agent '96 ►
- Secret Agent 00 '67
- Secret Agent Super Dragon '66
- Shakedown '02
- The Siege '98 ►
- Silk Degrees '94
- Skeleton Coast '89
- Skull: A Night of Terror '88
- Sleeper Cell '05
- Sniper 3 '04
- Special Bulletin '83 ►
- Stalking Danger '86
- The State Within '06
- The Stone Merchant '06
- Submerged '00
- Sudden Death '95
- The Sum of All Fears '02 ►
- Sweepers '99
- Swordfish '01 ►
- Syriana '05 ►
- The Taking of Flight 847: The Uli Derickson Story '88
- The Taking of Pelham One Two Three '74 ►
- Team America: World Police '04 ►
- Terminal Entry '87
- Terminal Rush '96
- Termination Man '97
- Terror in Beverly Hills '90
- Terror in Paradise '90
- Terror Squad '87
- The Terrorist '98 ►
- The Terrorists '74
- Terrorists '88
- Thunder Run '86
- Thunderball '65 ►
- Time of Favor '00
- A Town Called Hell '72
- Toy Soldiers '91 ►
- The Tragedy of a Ridiculous Man '81
- Tragedy of Flight 103: The Inside Story '90
- Trained to Kill, U.S.A. '75
- Treasure of the Lost Desert '83
- Trident Force '86
- Troma's War '88
- True Lies '94 ►
- Tube '03
- Turbulence 2: Fear of Flying '99
- Turk 182! '85
- 21 Hours at Munich '76 ►
- Typhoon '05
- Undeclared War '91
- Under Siege '92 ►
- United 93 '06 ►
- U.S. Navy SEALs: Dead or Alive '02
- V for Vendetta '06 ►
- The Vector File '03
- The Veronica Incident '89
- Victory at Entebbe '76
- Viper '88
- Voyage of Terror: The Achille Lauro Affair '90
- Wanted Dead or Alive '86
- The War Within '05
- The White Lioness '96
- Winds of Terror '01
- Women on the Verge of a Nervous Breakdown '88 ►
- The World is Not Enough '99 ►
- World Trade Center '06 ►
- Wrong Is Right '82
- Year of the Gun '91
- You Don't Mess with the Zohan '08
- You Only Live Twice '67 ►

Texas
see also American South; Dallas; Houston; Westerns

- The Alamo '60 ►
- The Alamo '04 ►
- Alamo Bay '85
- All the Pretty Horses '00 ►
- The Astronaut Farmer '07
- Blood Simple '85 ►
- Boom Town '40
- Dancer, Texas—Pop. 81 '98 ►
- Days of Heaven '78 ►
- Dazed and Confused '93 ►
- The Deadbeat Club '04
- Dr. T & the Women '00 ►
- Drop Dead Sexy '05
- Duel in the Sun '46 ►
- Friday Night Lights '04 ►
- Giant '56 ►
- Glory Road '06

► = rated three bones or higher

Texas

The Great Debaters '07
Happy, Texas '99
Hope Floats '98
The Hot Spot '90
JFK '91
Kill the Umpire '50
Larry McMurtry's Streets of Laredo '95
The Last Picture Show '71
The Life of David Gale '03
Little Boy Blue '97
Lonesome Dove '89
Man of the House '05
Nadine '87
No Country for Old Men '07
Paradise, Texas '05
Paris, Texas '83
A Perfect World '93
Places in the Heart '84
Planet Terror '07
The Positively True Adventures of the Alleged Texas Cheerleader-Murdering Mom '93
Raggedy Man '81
The Return '06
Rio Lobo '70
The Road to Galveston '96
The Searchers '56
75 Degrees '00
Sons of Katie Elder '65
Soul's Midnight '06
The Stars Fell on Henrietta '94
Stop-Loss '08
The Sugarland Express '74
Tarnation '03
Terror in a Texas Town '58
There Will Be Blood '07
39 Pounds of Love '05
The Three Burials of Melquiades Estrada '05
Three Texas Steers '39
Thunder Over Texas '34
Tin Cup '96
The Trip to Bountiful '85
True Stories '86
Varsity Blues '99
Vietnam, Texas '90
The Wendell Baker Story '05

Thanksgiving

see also Holidays
Avalon '90
Breathing Room '96
A Day for Thanks on Walton's Mountain '82
Hannah and Her Sisters '86
Home for the Holidays '95
The House of Yes '97
The Ice Storm '97
Mrs. Wiggs of the Cabbage Patch '34
The Myth of Fingerprints '97
National Lampoon's Holiday Reunion '03
Pieces of April '03
Planes, Trains & Automobiles '87
Squanto: A Warrior's Tale '94
Tadpole '02
A Time to Remember '03
The War at Home '96
What's Cooking? '00
Who Made the Potatoe Salad? '05

The 3rd Degree

Antibodies '05
Being at Home with Claude '92
The Box '07
Brainwashed '60
Cover '08
Deceiver '97
East Palace, West Palace '96
The Informant '97
The Interview '98
Murderous Intent '06
A Pure Formality '95

Seduced: Pretty When You Cry '01
Taxi to the Dark Side 07
Under Suspicion '00

This Is My Life

see also This Is Your Life
The Ann Jillian Story '88
The Flying Irishman '39
The Greatest '77
A Guide to Recognizing Your Saints '06
The Island on Bird Street '97
The Jackie Robinson Story '50
Jo Jo Dancer, Your Life Is Calling '86
The Kid Stays in the Picture '02
Livin' for Love: The Natalie Cole Story '00
Persepolis '07
Private Parts '96
Richard Petty Story '72
Running with Scissors '06
Searching For Wooden Watermelons '01
Sophia Loren: Her Own Story '80
To Hell and Back '55

This Is Your Life

see also Biopics: Artists; Biopics: Cops & Robbers; Biopics: Military; Biopics: Musicians; Biopics: Politics; Biopics: Religious; Biopics: Royalty; Biopics: Science/Medical; Biopics: Showbiz; Biopics: Sports; Biopics: Writers; Camelot (New); Nashville Narratives
Amarcord '74
American Graffiti '73
American Splendor '03
Anita, Dances of Vice '87
Annie Oakley '35
Antony and Cleopatra '73
Au Revoir les Enfants '87
The Autobiography of Miss Jane Pittman '74
Barnum '86
Beaumarchais the Scoundrel '96
Bernard and Doris '08
The Best Intentions '92
Blades of Courage '88
Blossoms in the Dust '41
Blow '01
Bluebeard '63
Born Again '78
Born on the Fourth of July '89
Borstal Boy '00
Cabeza de Vaca '90
Caddie '76
Calamity Jane '82
Canada's Sweetheart: The Saga of Hal C. Banks '85
Caro Diario '93
Casanova '87
Chain Lightning '50
Chanel Solitaire '81
A Chef in Love '96
Child Star: The Shirley Temple Story '01
Christopher Columbus '49
Christopher Columbus: The Discovery '92
The Color of Pomegranates '69
Conrack '74
Cowboy '58
Crazy Horse '96
Crime Lords '91
Damien: The Leper Priest '80
Dance with a Stranger '85
Daniel Boone '34
Dawn! '83
Destiny '97
Diary of a Rebel '68

The Diary of Anne Frank '59
The Disappearance of Aimee '76
Double Exposure: The Story of Margaret Bourke-White '89
Dracula: The Dark Prince '01
Dreamchild '85
Edie in Ciao! Manhattan '72
Edison the Man '40
The Education of Sonny Carson '74
8 Seconds '94
Eleni '85
Europa, Europa '91
Evel Knievel '72
Evita '96
Fanny and Alexander '83
Fidel '02
For Us, the Living '88
Ford: The Man & the Machine '87
The Fountainhead '49
1492: Conquest of Paradise '92
Francesco '93
Gia '98
The Gorgeous Hussy '36
Gorillas in the Mist '88
The Great Impostor '61
The Great Wallendas '78
The Greatest Story Ever Told '65
The Greek Tycoon '78
Grey Owl '99
Hamsun '96
Hank Aaron: Chasing the Dream '95
The Happy Hooker Goes Hollywood '80
Having Our Say: The Delany Sisters' First 100 Years '99
Heaven and Earth '93
Hitler: The Last Ten Days '73
Hoffa '92
Home Sweet Home '14
Hoodoo Ann '16
Houdini '53
Houdini '99
Hugh Hefner: Once Upon a Time '92
The Hunter '80
I, the Worst of All '90
I'll Cry Tomorrow '55
In Love and War '96
In Love and War '91
The Inn of the Sixth Happiness '58
Jacqueline Bouvier Kennedy '81
The Jayne Mansfield Story '80
Jeanne la Pucelle '94
Jesse James Under the Black Flag '21
Jesus '79
Jesus '00
Jesus Christ, Superstar '73
The Jew '96
Joni '79
Judith of Bethulia '14
Kennedy '83
King '78
The King of Kings '61
La Signora di Tutti '34
Lakota Woman: Siege at Wounded Knee '94
The Late Shift '96
The Learning Tree '69
Lepke '75
The Life and Times of Hank Greenberg '99
The Life of Emile Zola '37
The Light in the Jungle '91
The Lost Child '00
Love Affair: The Eleanor & Lou Gehrig Story '77
Loyola, the Soldier Saint '52
Madman '79
Malcolm X '92
Malcolm X: Make It Plain '95
A Man Called Peter '55

Marco '73
Marie '85
Marjoe '72
Martin Luther '53
Mary, Mother of Jesus '99
Mary White '77
Mesmer '94
Mr. Rock 'n Roll: The Alan Freed Story '99
Molokai: The Story of Father Damien '99
Monsieur Vincent '47
Mother Teresa: In the Name of God's Poor '97
Murderers Among Us: The Simon Wiesenthal Story '89
Murrow '86
My Father's Glory '91
Nadia '84
The Naked Civil Servant '75
Nostradamus '93
October Sky '99
Onassis '88
One Man's Way '63
Padre Padrone '77
Pancho Barnes '88
Pancho Villa '72
Papa's Delicate Condition '63
Patty Hearst '88
The People vs. Larry Flynt '96
Perfumed Nightmare '89
Personal Services '87
Peter and Paul '81
The Pirates of Silicon Valley '99
Poor Little Rich Girl: The Barbara Hutton Story '87
Pope John Paul II '84
Portrait of a Rebel: Margaret Sanger '82
Power and Beauty '02
Prick Up Your Ears '87
Priest of Love '81
Private Parts '96
P.T. Barnum '99
Queen '93
The Queen of Mean '90
Queenie '87
Rainbow '78
Rasputin '85
Rasputin: Dark Servant of Destiny '96
Rasputin the Mad Monk '66
Rated X '00
The Raven '15
Reilly: Ace of Spies '87
Return to Earth '76
Rhodes '36
Rhodes '97
Riel '79
Ring of Bright Water '69
Rodeo Girl '80
Romero '89
The Rosa Parks Story '02
Rosa Luxemburg '86
Rowing with the Wind '88
Ruby '92
Rush '91
Sade '00
Samaritan: The Mitch Snyder Story '86
A Scandal in Paris '46
Schindler's List '93
A Sense of Freedom '78
Seven Years in Tibet '97
The Sexual Life of the Belgians '94
Shadow on the Sun '88
Silent Victory: The Kitty O'Neil Story '79
Sister Kenny '46
Soldier in Love '67
Spirit of St. Louis '57
Squizzy Taylor '84
Stars and Stripes Forever '52
Steal This Movie! '00
The Story of Adele H. '75
The Stratton Story '49
Striker's Mountain '87
Sunday's Children '94
Sylvia '86
Teamster Boss: The Jackie Presser Story '92

The Ten Commandments '56
The Testament of Orpheus '59
Testament of Youth '79
That Hamilton Woman '41
This Boy's Life '93
Three Came Home '50
To Kill a Priest '89
To Race the Wind '80
To Walk with Lions '99
Tom Horn '80
24 Hour Party People '01
An Unreasonable Man '06
Veronika Voss '82
Victoria & Albert '01
The Virginia Hill Story '76
Viva Villa! '34
Wagner: The Movie '85
Wait until Spring, Bandini '90
Waiting for the Moon '87
Walk the Proud Land '56
Wild America '97
Wild Hearts Can't Be Broken '91
Winchell '98
The Winds of Kitty Hawk '78
Wings of Eagles '57
Wittgenstein '93
A Woman Called Moses '78
A Woman Named Jackie '91
Young Bill Hickok '40
The Young Bruce Lee '80
Young Buffalo Bill '40
Young Winston '72

3-D Flicks

Amityville 3: The Demon '83
Andy Warhol's Frankenstein '74
The Bellboy and the Playgirls '62
Cat Women of the Moon '53
Creature from the Black Lagoon '54
The Creature Walks among Us '56
Devil's Canyon '53
Dogs of Hell '83
Dynasty '77
Flesh and Blood Show '73
The French Line '54
Friday the 13th, Part 3 '82
Gun Fury '53
House of Wax '53
It Came from Outer Space '53
Jaws 3 '83
Kaena: The Prophecy '03
Kiss Me Kate '53
The Man Who Wasn't There '83
The Mask '61
Miss Sadie Thompson '53
Paradisio '61
Parasite '82
Revenge of the Creature '55
Robot Monster '53
Spacehunter: Adventures in the Forbidden Zone '83
Spy Kids 3-D: Game Over '03
Starchaser: The Legend of Orin '85
The Stranger Wore a Gun '53

Thumbs Up

The Adventures of Felix '99
Alligator Eyes '90
Black Day Blue Night '95
Blood Simple '85
Bonneville '06
Cold Around the Heart '97
Creepshow 2 '87
Diary of a Teenage Hitchhiker '82
Doing Time for Patsy Cline '97
The Dream Catcher '99
The Drifter '88
Easy Rider '69
Even Cowgirls Get the Blues '94
Fear and Loathing in Las Vegas '98

Finding Graceland '98
The Forsaken '01
The Hitcher '86
The Hitcher '07
The Hitcher 2: I've Been Waiting '03
Hitchhikers '72
The Hitchhiker's Guide to the Galaxy '81
The Hitchhiker's Guide to the Galaxy '05
I Love You, Alice B. Toklas! '68
Invitation au Voyage '82
Jerome '98
Josh and S.A.M. '93
Kaaterskill Falls '01
Kalifornia '93
Larger Than Life '96
Lost Junction '03
Melvin and Howard '80
Moving McAllister '07
My Own Private Idaho '91
Pee-wee's Big Adventure '85
Personal Velocity: Three Portraits '02
Pink Flamingos '72
Riding the Bullet '04
Road Games '81
Ruby Jean and Joe '96
Save the Tiger '73
Score '95
The Sure Thing '85
The Texas Chainsaw Massacre '74
Thelma & Louise '91
There's Something about Mary '98
Track 29 '88
Transamerica '05
Vagabond '85
Vanishing Point '71
Western '96
World Traveler '01

Tibet

The Cup '99
Himalaya '99
Kundun '97
Mountain Patrol: Kekexili '04
Seven Years in Tibet '97

Tijuana

see also Mexico
Kitten with a Whip '64
The Long Goodbye '73
Losin' It '82

Time Travel

see also Rescue Missions Involving Time Travel
Adventures in Dinosaur City '92
The Alien Agenda: Out of the Darkness '96
Amazing Mr. Blunden '72
Ancient Relic '02
A.P.E.X. '94
Army of Darkness '92
The Arrival '90
Arthur's Quest '99
Austin Powers In Goldmember '02
Back to the Future '85
Back to the Future, Part 2 '89
Back to the Future, Part 3 '90
Battle for the Planet of the Apes '73
Beastmaster 2: Through the Portal of Time '91
Being Human '94
Beneath the Bermuda Triangle '98
Beneath the Planet of the Apes '70
Beyond the Time Barrier '60
Biggles '85
Bill & Ted's Bogus Journey '91
Bill & Ted's Excellent Adventure '89
Blue Flame '93
The Blue Yonder '86

► = rated three bones or higher

Brother Future '91
Buck Rogers in the 25th Century '79
The Butterfly Effect '04
The Butterfly Effect 2 '06
Chasing Christmas '05
The Sticky Fingers of Time '97
A Connecticut Yankee in King Arthur's Court '49
A Connecticut Yankee in King Arthur's Court '31◄
A Connecticut Yankee '31◄
Day Time Ended '60
The Devil's Arithmetic '99
Dinosaur Valley Girls '96
Doctor Mordrid: Master of the Unknown '90
Doctor Who '96
The Eliminators '86
Escape from the Planet of the Apes '71◄
Escapes '86
The Final Countdown '80◄
The Forbidden Kingdom '08
Frankenstein Unbound '90◄
Freejack '92
Future Zone '90
Galaxis '95
Godzilla vs. King Ghidora '91
Grand Tour: Disaster in Time '92
Grizzly Mountain '97
Harry Potter and the Prisoner of Azkaban '04
Hercules in New York '70
Highlander 2: The Quickening '91
Highlander: The Final Dimension '94
Hocus Pocus '93
Idaho Transfer '73
In His Father's Shoes '97
The Indian in the Cupboard '95
The Jacket '05
Josh Kirby ... Time Warrior, Chapter 1, Planet of the Dino-Knights '95
Josh Kirby ... Time Warrior, Chapter 2, The Human Pets '95
Josh Kirby ... Time Warrior, Chapter 3, Trapped on Toyworld '95
Josh Kirby ... Time Warrior, Chapter 4, Eggs from 70 Million B.C. '55
Josh Kirby ... Time Warrior, Chapter 5, Journey to the Magic Cavern '96
Josh Kirby ... Time Warrior, Chapter 6, Last Battle for the Universe '96
Journey to the Center of Time '67
Just Visiting '01
A Kid in Aladdin's Palace '97
A Knight in Camelot '98
The Lake House '05
Lords of Magick '88
Lost in Space '98
The Love Letter '98
Mannequin 2: On the Move '91
Meet the Robinsons '07
Millennium '89
Nautilus '99
The Navigator '88◄
Next One '84
Night of Dark Shadows '71◄
Past Perfect '98
Peggy Sue Got Married '86
Phantasm 4: Oblivion '95
The Philadelphia Experiment '84
Philadelphia Experiment 2 '93
Planet of the Apes '68◄
Primer '04◄
Roman Scandals '33
Running Against Time '50
The Seeker: The Dark Is Rising '07
Somewhere in Time '80
A Sound of Thunder '05

Spirit of '76 '91
Star Trek 4: The Voyage Home '86◄
Star Trek: First Contact '96◄
Stargate '94
The Swordsman '92
Teenage Mutant Ninja Turtles 3 '93
The Terminator '84◄
Terminator 2: Judgment Day '91◄
Terminator 3: Rise of the Machines '03◄
Test Tube Teens from the Year 2000 '93
The Thirteenth Floor '99
The Three Stooges Meet Hercules '61
Thrill Seekers '99
Time After Time '79◄
Time at the Top '99
Time Bandits '81
Time Chasers '95
The Time Guardian '87
The Time Machine '60◄
The Time Machine '78
The Tomorrow Man '01
Timecop 2: The Berlin Decision '03
Timecop '94
Timerider '83
Timeline '03
Timemaster '95
Timestalkers '87
Time Machine '02
Time Runner '92
Time Tracers '97
Time Trackers '88
Timecrimes '07
Trancers 5: Sudden Deth '94
Trancers 4: Jack of Swords '93
Trancers 3: Deth Lives '92◄
Trancers 2: The Return of Jack Deth '90
Trancers '84
The Visitors '95
Vlad '03
Warlock '31
Waxwork 2: Lost in Time '91
When Time Expires '97
A Witch Without a Broom '68
Yor, the Hunter from the Future '83
A Young Connecticut Yankee in King Arthur's Court '95

Time Warped

Austin Powers: International Man of Mystery '97◄
Austin Powers 2: The Spy Who Shagged Me '99◄
Black Knight '01
Blast from the Past '98
The Brady Bunch Movie '95◄
Demolition Man '93
Disney's The Kid '00
Encino Man '92
Forever Young '92
Groundhog Day '93◄
Kate & Leopold '01
Kickin' It Old Skool '07
La Vie en Rose '07
Late for Dinner '91
Leave It to Beaver '97
Paycheck '03
Peggy Sue Got Married '86
Pleasantville '98◄
Retroactive '97
13 Going on 30 '04
The Two Worlds of Jenny Logan '79
A Very Brady Sequel '96
Zathura '05◄

Titanic

The Chambermaid on the Titanic '97
A Night to Remember '58◄
Raise the Titanic '80
S.O.S. Titanic '79
Titanic '53◄
Titanic '96
Titanic '97◄
The Unsinkable Molly Brown '64◄

Tokyo

see also *Japan*

Akira '89
Angel Dust '96
Austin Powers In Goldmember '02
An Autumn Afternoon '62◄
Babel '06◄
The Bad News Bears Go to Japan '78
Black Lizard '68
Black Rain '89
Bright Future '03◄
Cafe Lumiere '05
Dodes 'ka-den '70◄
The Dragon Painter '19
Escaped in Japan '57
The Fast and the Furious: Tokyo Drift '06
First Yank into Tokyo '45
Gamera vs. Barugon '66
Gappa the Trifibian Monster '67
Ghidrah the Three Headed Monster '65
Godzilla, King of the Monsters '56
Godzilla 2000 '99
Godzilla vs. Megalon '76
Godzilla vs. King Ghidora '91
The Grudge '04
The Grudge 2 '06
H-Man '59
House of Bamboo '55
Ju-On: The Grudge '03
Kill Bill Vol. 1 '03◄
Marebito '04
Mothra '62◄
Nobody Knows '04
Okoge '93
One Wonderful Sunday '47
Otaku No Video '91◄
Proof of the Man '77
Pulse '01
Running Brave '83
Shutter '08
Stopover Tokyo '57
Street of Shame '56◄
Suicide Club '02

To the Moon!

see also *Space Operas*

The Adventures of Baron Munchausen '89◄
The Adventures of Pluto Nash '02
Alien Fury: Countdown to Invasion '00
Apollo 13 '95◄
Beyond the Stars '89
Cat Women of the Moon '53
Countdown '68
Dark Side of the Moon '90
Destination Moon '50
Destination Moonbase Alpha '75
The Dish '00◄
First Men in the Moon '64
From the Earth to the Moon '58
From the Earth to the Moon '98◄
In the Shadow of the Moon '07◄
Missile to the Moon '59
Moon Pilot '62
The Mouse on the Moon '62◄
Project Moon Base '53
Quatermass 2 '57◄
Radar Men from the Moon '52
They Came from Beyond Space '67

Toronto

see also *Canada*

Ararat '02◄
Between Strangers '02
Exotica '94◄
Hollywood North '03
How She Move '08
Jimmy Glick in LaLa Wood '05
Last Night '98◄
The Life Before This '99
The Newton Boys '97
Owning Mahowny '03
Paris, France '94
Picture Claire '01
Rude '96
Siblings '04
Skin Deep '94
Soul Survivor '95
Spenser: A Savage Place '94
Twist '03

Torn in Two (or More)

Abbott and Costello Meet Dr. Jekyll and Mr. Hyce '52
Batman Forever '95◄
Carson Copy '69
Color of Night '94
The Dark Knight '08
Dr. Heckyl and Mr. Hype '80
Dr. Jekyll and Ms. Hyde '95
Dr. Jekyll and Mr. Hyde '20◄
Dr. Jekyll and Mr. Hyde '32◄
Dr. Jekyll and Mr. Hyde '41◄
Dr. Jekyll and Mr. Hyde '68
Dr. Jekyll and Mr. Hyde '73
Dr. Jekyll and Sister Hyde '71
Edge of Sanity '89
Exorcist 3: Legion '90
The Five of Me '81
Hulk '03
Jekyll '07
Jekyll & Hyde '90
I, Monster '71◄
The League of Extraordinary Gentlemen '03
Luna e L'Altra '96
Mary Reilly '95
Me, Myself, and Irene '00◄
Mirage '94
Multiplicity '96
Never Talk to Strangers '95
The Nutty Professor '63◄
The Nutty Professor '96◄
The Nutty Professor 2: The Klumps '00
Passion of Mind '00
Primal Fear '96
Psycho Beach Party '00
Raising Cain '92
A Scanner Darkly '06
Separate Lives '94
Shattered Image '98
Spider-Man '02◄
Sybil '76◄
The Three Faces of Eve '57
Three Lives and Only One Death '96
The Three Lives of Karen '97
Terra '95
Voices from a Locked Room '95

Torrid Love Scenes

see also *Sex & Sexuality; Sexploitation*

Against All Odds '84
Alien Prey '83
Angel Heart '87◄
Atlantic City '81◄
Basic Instinct '92
The Berlin Affair '85
Betty Blue '86◄
The Big Easy '87◄
Bitter Moon '92
Black Ice '92
Blue Velvet '86◄
Body Double '84◄
Body Heat '81◄
Body of Evidence '92
Bram Stoker's Dracula '92◄
Breathless '83
Broken English '96
Bull Durham '88◄
Cat Chaser '90
Cat on a Hot Tin Roof '58◄
Close My Eyes '91
The Cook, the Thief, His Wife & Her Lover '90◄
Crimes of Passion '84◄
Dark Obsession '90
Deadly Desire '91
The Dolphin '87
Dona Flor and Her Two Husbands '78◄
Don't Look Now '73◄
Everything Relative '96
The Executioner's Song '82
Exit to Eden '94
The Fabulous Baker Boys '89◄
Fatal Attraction '87◄
Five Easy Pieces '70◄
From Here to Eternity '53◄
Green Fire '55
The Harvest '92
Heat of Desire '84
Henry & June '90◄
The Hunting '92
In the Realm of the Senses '76◄
Jason's Lyric '94
Kiss Me a Killer '91
La Mujer de Mi Hermano '06
Lady Godiva Rides '68
Last Tango in Paris '73◄
Law of Desire '86◄
The Lawnmower Man '92
Live Flesh '97◄
The Lover '92
The Lovers '59
Lust, Caution '07
The Mambo Kings '92◄
Mad Dog and Glory '93◄
Moon in the Gutter '83
Moonstruck '87◄
Night Eyes 2 '91
Night Eyes 3 '93
9 1/2 Weeks '86
1900 '76◄
An Officer and a Gentleman '82◄
The Pamela Principle '91
The Postman Always Rings Twice '81
Prizzi's Honor '85◄
Pyrates '91
Rage of Angels '83
Revenge '90◄
Risky Business '83◄
Sea of Love '89◄
Secrets '71
Sexual Response '92
Siesta '87
Silver '93
Something Wild '86
The Story of O '75
Summer Palace '06◄
Swept Away... '75◄
Tattoo '81
Tequila Sunrise '88
Threesome '94
The Unbearable Lightness of Being '88◄
White Palace '90
Wide Sargasso Sea '92
Wild at Heart '90◄
Wild Orchid '90
Wild Orchid 2: Two Shades of Blue '92
The Woman Next Door '81◄

Toys

see also *Killer Toys*

Babes in Toyland '61
Big '88◄
Child's Play '88
Child's Play 2 '90
Dance of Death '68
Demonic Toys '90
Dolls '87
Dolly Dearest '92
Home Alone 3 '97
Jingle All the Way '96
Josh Kirby ... Time Warrior, Chapter 3, Trapped on Toyworld '95
Life-Size '00
Mr. Magorium's Wonder Emporium '07
Not Quite Human '87
Silent Night, Deadly Night 5: The Toymaker '91
The Toy '82
Toy Story '95◄
Toy Story 2 '99◄
Toys '92
Wired to Kill '86
Zathura '05◄

Tragedy

see also *Drama;*

After the Deluge '03◄
Against the Wind '90
All the King's Men '49
Anna Karenina '35◄
Argel at the King's Men '99
Babel '06◄
Baba '73◄
Battle in Heaven '05
Bitter Sweet '33
Boutique '04
Brothers '05◄
Camille '36◄
Catherine Cookson's The Fifteen Streets '90
Celebrity '85
Charly '68◄
The Crucified Lovers '54◄
Damage '92◄
Danielle Steel's Palomino '91
Dark Odyssey '57
Deadman's Curse '78
Death Sentence '07
Deep End '70◄
The Discovery Program '89
The Door in the Floor '04◄
Dream Lovers '86
Dreaming of Joseph Lees '99
Dying Young '91
East of Eden '54◄
East of Eden '80
Effi Briest '74◄
El Amor Brujo '86◄
El Bruto '52
The Embalmer '03◄
End of the Road '70
Enduring Love '04
Enemies, a Love Story '89◄
Ernie Kovacs: Between the Laughter '84
Ethan Frome '92
Evangeline '29
Everybody's All American '88
The Fighting Sullivans '42◄
First Knight '95
Flowers of Reverie '84
Forbidden Choices '94
Franz '72
The French Lieutenant's Woman '81◄
From the Journals of Jean Seberg '95
Gate of Hell '54◄
Girl in Black '56
Golden Boy '39◄
A Good Day to Die '95
Hamlet '48◄

Women & Men: In Love There Are No Rules '91
Women in Love '70◄
Year of the Gun '91
Zancalee '91

◄ = rated three bones or higher

Hamlet '69
Hamlet '96
Hamlet '01
Harmony Lane '35
Heaven '01
Henry IV '85
Hong Kong 1941 '84
House of Cards '92
House of Sand and Fog '03
Howard's End '92
The Hunchback of Notre Dame '57
I Dreamed of Africa '00
I Walk the Line '70
Il Grido '57
In Memoriam '76
In the Bedroom '01
Into the Wild '07
Intrigue and Love '59
Jalsaghar '58
Jude '96
Jude the Obscure '71
Jules and Jim '62
Julius Caesar '53
Julius Caesar '70
King Lear '71
King Lear '87
King Lear '98
Landscape After Battle '70
Leo Tolstoy's Anna Karenina '96
Love Is a Many-Splendored Thing '55
Love Story '70
Lovespell '79
Lush Life '93
Macbeth '48
Macbeth '70
Macbeth '71
Macbeth '88
Madame Bovary '49
Madame Bovary '91
Madame Butterfly '95
A Map of the World '99
Margaret's Museum '95
Maria Candelaria '46
Marilyn & Bobby: Her Final Affair '94
Martha and I '91
Mary of Scotland '36
The Merchant of Venice '73
A Mighty Heart '07
Mother '96
The Mummy '59
Mystic River '03
The Nest '80
Night Ride Home '99
Nothing Personal '95
The Notorious Lady '27
O '01
Oedipus Rex '67
Onegin '99
Othello '22
Othello '52
Othello '65
Othello '95
Our Time '74
Pennies from Heaven '81
The Perfect Storm '00
Phaedra '61
Piece of Cake '88
A Place in the Sun '51
The Prestige '06
Princess Yang Kwei Fei '55
Queen Bee '55
Ran '85
The Red Violin '98
Reign Over Me '07
Reservation Road '07
The Return of the Native '94
Romeo and Juliet '36
Romeo and Juliet '54
Romeo and Juliet '68
Savior '98
The Scarlet Tunic '97
The Secret Agent '96
Selena '96
Shadowlands '93
Shadows of Forgotten Ancestors '64
Shattered '21
The Shooting Party '77
Silent Tongue '92
16 Years of Alcohol '03
Solomon and Gaenor '98

The Son's Room '00
Stag '97
Stella '55
Stephanie Daley '06
Sure Fire '90
The Sweet Hereafter '96
Swept from the Sea '97
Tess '79
Tess of the D'Urbervilles '98
Three Comrades '38
Throne of Blood '57
Tilai '90
Titanic '53
Tragedy of Flight 103: The Inside Story '91
Trois Couleurs: Bleu '93
Trojan Women '71
Turkish Delight '73
The Unknown Soldier '98
Variety '25
A Very Private Affair '62
The Virgin Spring '59
Voyager '91
The Walls of Malapaga '49
The War Zone '98
The Wedding Gift '93
Where Angels Fear to Tread '91
The White Cliffs of Dover '44
White Mile '94
The White Sister '23
William Shakespeare's Romeo and Juliet '96
A Woman at Her Window '77
The Woman Next Door '81
The Wooden Man's Bride '94
The World According to Garp '82
Wuthering Heights '70
Wuthering Heights '98

Trains

see also Heists; Trains; Subways

Across the Bridge '57
Agatha Christie's Murder is Easy '82
Alberto Express '92
Around the World in 80 Days '04
Atomic Train '99
Avalanche Express '79
Back to the Future, Part 3 '90
Before Sunrise '94
Berlin Express '48
Blood and Steel '25
Boxcar Bertha '72
The Brain '69
Breakheart Pass '76
Broken Arrow '95
Bullet to Beijing '95
Cafe Lumiere '05
The Cassandra Crossing '76
Chattanooga Choo Choo '84
Closely Watched Trains '66
Color of a Brisk and Leaping Day '95
Courage Under Fire '96
Crackerjack 2 '97
Dakota '45
Danger Lights '30
Daniel Takes a Train '83
The Darjeeling Limited '07
Death Train '79
The Denver & Rio Grande '51
Derailed '02
Detonator '93
The Dirty Dozen: The Fatal Mission '88
Emperor of the North Pole '73
End of the Line '88
Eurotrip '04
Express to Terror '79
Finders Keepers '84
Flame Over India '60
The Flying Scotsman '29
Free Money '99

From Russia with Love '63
The Fugitive '93
Gambling Ship '33
The General '26
The Ghost and the Darkness '96
The Ghost Train '41
The Glory Trail '36
Go Kill and Come Back '68
Great K & A Train Robbery '26
The Great Locomotive Chase '56
The Great Train Robbery '79
The Greatest Show on Earth '52
The Grey Fox '83
The Harvey Girls '46
Horror Express '72
Hot Lead & Cold Feet '78
The Illusion Travels by Streetcar '53
Indiscretion of an American Wife '54
Inner Sanctum '48
Interrupted Journey '49
The Iron Horse '24
Jesse James at Bay '41
The Journey of Natty Gann '85
La Bete Humaine '38
The Lady Eve '41
Lady on a Train '45
The Lady Vanishes '38
The Lady Vanishes '79
The Legend of Zorro '05
The Major and the Minor '42
Malcolm '86
Man Who Loved Cat Dancing '73
Man Without a Star '55
Midnight Limited '40
The Millionaire's Express '86
Mission: Impossible '96
Mrs. Winterbourne '96
Mouvements du Desir '94
Murder on the Midnight Express '74
Murder on the Orient Express '74
My House in Umbria '03
My Twentieth Century '90
Mystery Mountain '34
Narrow Margin '90
The Navigators '01
The Newton Boys '97
Night Passage '57
Night Train Murders '75
Night Train to Munich '40
Night Train to Terror '84
Night Train to Venice '93
No. 17 '32
The Odyssey of the Pacific '82
Oh, Mr. Porter '37
Once Upon a Time in the West '68
The Out-of-Towners '99
Panic on the 5.22 '74
Paris Express '53
The Peacemaker '97
Phantom Express '32
Plunder Road '57
The Polar Express '04
Prison Train '38
Railrodder '65
Rails & Ties '07
Red Lights '04
Red Signals '27
The Return of Casey Jones '34
Return to Waterloo '85
Rhythm on the Range '36
The Road Home '95
The Road to Yesterday '25
Robbery '67
Romance on the Orient Express '89
Runaway Train '85
Running Scared '86
Saratoga Trunk '45
Shanghai Express '32
The Silver Streak '34
Silver Streak '76
Sleepers West '41

The Sleeping Car '90
Sleeping Car to Trieste '45
Some Like It Hot '59
Starman '84
The Station Agent '03
Station Jim '01
Strangers on a Train '51
Subway '85
Switchback '97
A Tale of Winter '92
Terror Train '80
Thomas and the Magic Railroad '00
Those Who Love Me Can Take the Train '98
Three for Bedroom C '52
3:10 to Yuma '57
Throw Momma from the Train '87
Thunder Over Texas '34
Ticket to Tomahawk '50
Torture Train '95
Tough Guys '86
Tracks '76
Trading Places '83
The Trail of the Lonesome Pine '36
The Train '65
The Train Killer '83
Train of Life '98
Train Robbers '73
Train to Tombstone '50
The Truce '96
Tube '03
Two Weeks to Live '43
Unbreakable '00
Under Siege 2: Dark Territory '95
Union Pacific '39
Von Ryan's Express '65
Warm Nights on a Slow-Moving Train '87
While You Were Sleeping '95
Without Reservations '46
Zentropa '92
Zhou Yu's Train '02

Transvestites & Transsexuals

see Gender Bending

Trapped with a Killer!

see also Psychotics/Sociopaths

Adrift '93
Air Force One '97
Alien Terminator '95
Blind Witness '89
Blink '93
Blood at Sundown '88
Blood Bride '80
Clue '85
Con Air '97
Copycat '95
Dead Calm '89
Deadbolt '92
Extremities '86
Eye of the Needle '81
Eyes of the Beholder '92
Fatal Attraction '87
Fever '91
Final Justice '94
Headless Body in Topless Bar '96
Hider in the House '90
High Tension '03
The Hills Have Eyes '06
Kalifornia '93
Kiss the Girls '97
Lifepod '93
The Maddening '95
Malevolence '04
Manhunter '86
Mindhunters '05
Misery '90
Mute Witness '95
Narrow Margin '90
No Way Back '90
Pacific Heights '90
Saw '04
See No Evil '06
Serial Slayer '80
The Shining '80

The Silence of the Lambs '91
Slaughter of the Innocents '93
Ten Little Indians '75
Ten Little Indians '89
The Terror '63
Terror Train '80
The Texas Chainsaw Massacre: The Beginning '06
Through the Eyes of a Killer '92
The Tie That Binds '95
Tracks of a Killer '95
Turbulence '96
Undertow '95
Unveiled '94
Virus '98
Voyage '93
Wait until Dark '67
What's the Matter with Helen? '71
When a Stranger Calls '79
When a Stranger Calls '06
When a Stranger Calls Back '93

Treasure Hunt

Abbott and Costello Meet the Mummy '55
Adventure of the Action Hunters '87
The Adventurers '51
After the Storm '01
All the Brothers Were Valiant '53
Arthur and the Invisibles '06
Beethoven's 5th '03
Big Mouth '67
Blue Jeans and Dynamite '76
Cabo Blanco '81
Call of the Wild '93
City Slickers 2: The Legend of Curly's Gold '94
Comin' Round the Mountain '51
Curse of the Crystal Eye '93
Cutthroat Island '95
The Diamond of Jeru '01
Diamonds '99
Double Trouble '41
Enemy Gold '93
Ernest Rides Again '93
Escape under Pressure '00
The Fat Spy '66
The Fiend Who Walked the West '58
Finger on the Trigger '65
Fool's Gold '08
Forgotten City '98
Girls in Prison '56
Gold Diggers: The Secret of Bear Mountain '95
The Goonies '85
The Grave '95
Greedy '94
Green Fire '55
The Haunted Sea '97
Hear No Evil '93
Holes '03
Hunters of the Golden Cobra '82
Inside Out '75
Into the Blue '05
It's a Mad, Mad, Mad, Mad World '63
The Jewel of the Nile '85
Jupiter's Thigh '81
Kelly's Heroes '70
The Killing Grounds '97
King of California '07
Klondike Fever '79
Kraken: Tentacles of the Deep '06
Kull the Conqueror '97
Lara Croft: Tomb Raider '01
The Last Adventure '67
Legends of the North '95
Lewis and Clark and George '97
Lust in the Dust '85
Max Is Missing '95

The Mermaids of Tiburon '62
Million Dollar Mystery '87
Missing Pieces '91
Muppet Treasure Island '96
My Family Treasure '93
Naked Hills '56
National Treasure '04
National Treasure: Book of Secrets '07
Old Mother Riley's Jungle Treasure '51
One-Eyed Soldiers '67
Operation Condor '91
Operation Golden Phoenix '94
Outlaw Trail '06
Pattern for Plunder '62
Payback '94
The Phantom of the Range '38
The Pink Jungle '68
Rat Race '01
The Ravagers '65
The Real Macaw '98
Red Water '01
Romancing the Stone '84
Rudyard Kipling's The Jungle Book '94
The Rundown '03
Russell Mulcahy's Tale of the Mummy '99
Sahara '05
The Sea God '30
Secre of the Andes '98
The Secret of the Golden Eagle '91
Secret of the Ice Cave '89
Shadow of Chikara '77
Sleepover '04
Slow Burn '00
Tarzan's Secret Treasure '41
Terror on Alcatraz '86
Thank you, Mr. Moto '37
That Man from Rio '64
There Goes the Neighborhood '92
Thieves of Fortune '89
Tom and Huck '95
Treasure Island '34
Treasure Island '50
Treasure Island '72
Treasure Island '89
Treasure Island '99
The Treasure of Jamaica Reef '74
The Treasure of Matecumbe '76
The Treasure of the Amazon '84
Treasure of the Four Crowns '82
Treasure of the Golden Condor '53
Treasure of the Sierra Madre '48
The Treasure of the Yankee Zephyr '83
Treasure Planet '02
The Treasure Seekers '79
Trespass '92
The Triangle '01
Undertow '04
Uninvited '93
Warrior Spirit '94
Whistling in Dixie '42
Wild Ones on Wheels '62
Without a Paddle '04
The Wrong Road '37

Trees & Forests

see also Wilderness

Adam's Apples '05
The Adventures of Robin Hood '38
Alien 3000 '04
As You Like It '06
Bambi II '06
Big Trees '52
Blackwoods '02
Blood Crime '02
Blood Trails '06
The Brothers Grimm '05
The Burning Season '94
The Contract '07

A Crack in the Floor '00
Criminal Lovers '99
Crosscut '95
Dead in the Water '06
Dr. Tarr's Torture Dungeon '75
Equinox '71►
Evil Dead '83
Family Tree '00
Fatal Passion '94
Fear Runs Silent '99
Fenguily: The Last Rain Forest '92
5 Dark Souls '96
Fly with the Hawk '35
Forest Warrior '95
Heartwood '98
Himatsuri '85►
Hole in the Sky '95
Hoodwinked '05►
The Hunted '03
The Ice Flood '26
Inferno '01
It Waits '05
Jailbird's Vacation '65
King of the Forest Rangers '46
Lassie: Adventures of Neeka '68
The Last Broadcast '98►
Lunatic '91
The Many Adventures of Winnie the Poon '77
Mrs. Mike '49
Motor Home Massacre '05
Murder at Devil's Glen '99
The Night Brings Charlie '90
Old Joy '06►
Open Season '06
Out of Time '00
The Passion of Darkly Noon '95
Piglet's Big Movie '03
Poltergeist 2: The Other Side '86
SuperFire '02
Soft for Digging '01
Surfacing '84
Surviving the Game '94
The Tripper '06
Vertigo '58►
The Village '04
The Watcher in the Woods '81
Where the Rivers Flow North '94
William Shakespeare's A Midsummer Night's Dream '99
The Wizard of Oz '39►
The Woods '03
Wounded '97
Wrong Turn '03

Triads
see also China; Gangs
The Art of War '00
The Corruptor '99►
Dogwatch '97
Hard-Boiled '92►
Internal Affairs '02►
The Killer '90►
Lethal Weapon 4 '98►
Robin-B-Hood '06
Rush Hour 2 '01►
Time and Tide '00
War '07

True Crime
see also Crime & Criminals; This Is Your Life; True Stories
Alien: Life and Death of a Serial Killer '03►
Alpha Dog '06
American Gangster '07►
American Tragedy '00
Among Brothers '05
Angela '02
The Assassination of Richard Nixon '04
At Close Range '86►
Awakening of Candra '81
Ballad of Gregorio Cortez '83
The Bank Job '08►
Beyond Reasonable Doubt '80
Big Shot: Confessions of a Campus Bookie '02
Billionaire Boys Club '87
The Black Dahlia '06
Black Oak Conspiracy '77
Black Panther '77
Blackrock '97
Blanche Fury '48
Bluebeard '63
Bordertown '06
Boomerang '47►
Boys Don't Cry '99►
BTK Killer '06
Bully '01
Burnt Money '00
Capote '05►
Capturing the Friedmans '03►
Catch Me If You Can '02►
Cause Celebre '87►
Chicago Joe & the Showgirl '90
Chopper '00
Citizen X '95►
City by the Sea '02
City of Goc '02
Color Me Kubrick '05
Compulsion '59►
Crazy Love '07►
Crimson Gold '03
Crime of the Century '96
Dahmer '02
Danger of Love '95
Deadly Voyage '96
Death Scream '75
Deep Crimson '96
The Deliberate Stranger '86►
Dick Turpin '25
Dillinger '73
Dr. Petiot '90
Double-Crossed '91
Drug Wars: The Camarena Story '90►
Echo of Murder '00
Echoes in the Darkness '87
Ed Gein '01
The Elegant Criminal '92
Essex Boys '99
Excellent Cadavers '99
Execution of Justice '99
The Executioner's Song '82►
The Falcon and the Snowman '85►
Final Appeal '93
Fool's Gold: The Story of the Brink's-Mat Robbery '92
44 Minutes: The North Hollywood Shootout '03
From Hell '01►
The General '98►
Getting Gotti '94
The Girl in the Red Velvet Swing '55
Gotti '96►
Great Gold Swindle '84
The Great St. Louis Bank Robbery '59
The Happy Face Murders '99
Headless Body in Topless Bar '96
Heavens Fall '06
Helter Skelter '76
Helter Skelter Murders '76
The Hillside Strangler '04
The Hillside Strangler '89
Hollywoodland '06►
Honor Thy Father and Mother: The True Story of the Menendez Brothers '94
I Can't Sleep '93
In Cold Blood '96
Jasper, Texas '03
Johnny 100 Pesos '93
Karla '06
Kellers Park '05
Killer: A Journal of Murder '95
L'Appat '94
The Laramie Project '02►
Let Him Have It '91►
The Life Before This '99
Lonely Hearts '06
Mad Dog Morgan '76
The Magician '93
The Man from the Pru '89
The Man in the Attic '94
The Manson Family '04
Master Spy: The Robert Hanssen Story '02
McVicar '80
Midnight in the Garden of Good and Evil '97
Mrs. Harris '05
Mrs. Soffel '84
Money Movers '78
Monster '03►
Murder in Coweta County '83
Murder in Greenwich '02
Murder in New Hampshire: The Pamela Smart Story '91
Murder in Texas '81►
The Murder of Stephen Lawrence '99►
Murph the Surf '75
The Newton Boys '97
Nightstalker '02
Normal Life '96
Nowhere to Run '88
The O.J. Simpson Story '94
100 Proof '96
One Kill '00
One of Her Own '94
The Onion Field '79►
Our Mother's Murder '97
Owning Mahowny '03
Party Monster '03
Path to Paradise '97
The People vs. Jean Harris '81►
Perfect Crime '97
Perfect Murder, Perfect Town '00
Point of Origin '02
The Preppie Murder '89
Prince of Poisoners: The Life and Crimes of William Palmer '38
The Pursuit of D.B. Cooper '81
Rainbow Warrior '94
Rampage '87
Rampage: The Hillside Strangler Murders '04
Rule 3 '93
Sister My Sister '94
Soldier's Girl '03►
Squizzy Taylor '84
Stalking Laura '93
Stand Off '93
Stander '03
Starkweather '04
Summer of Sam '99►
Swoon '91►
The Theory of the Leisure Class '01
Till Murder Do Us Part '92
Too Young to Die '90
Tracks '05
Triple Agent '04
Triple Cross '67►
Under the Pear Tree '73
Undercover Cop '94
The Untold Story of Emmett Louis Till '05►
Verdict on Auschwitz: The Frankfurt Auschwitz Trial 1963–1965 '93►
Verne Miller '88
Veronica Guerin '03
When the Sky Falls '99
A Winter Tan '88
Without Evidence '96
Witness to the Mob '98
Wolf Creek '05
Wonderland '03
Zodiac '07
The Zodiac Killer '71
The Zodiac '06

True Stories
see also This Is Your Life; True Crime
Alamo Bay '85
Aldrich Ames: Traitor Within '05
Alive '93
All Mine to Give '56
All My Loved Ones '00
All the King's Men '99
The Amy Fisher Story '93
And I Alone Survived '78
And the Band Played On '93►
Andersonville '95►
Andre '94
Angel '82
The Ann Jillian Story '88
Anna and the King of Siam '46►
Antwone Fisher '02►
Apollo 13 '95►
Apprentice to Murder '88
Archer's Adventure '85
The Aristocrats '99
Art for Teachers of Children '95
Artemisia '97
The Ascent '94
The Assassination of Richard Nixon '05
Assault at West Point: The Court-Martial of Johnson Whittaker '94
The Assisi Underground '84
The Attic: The Hiding of Anne Frank '88►
Attica '80►
Au Revoir les Enfants '87►
The Aviator '04►
Awakening of Candra '81
Awakenings '90►
Away All Boats '56
Baadasssss! '03►
Bad Blood '87
Badge of the Assassin '85
Badlands '74►
Ballad in Blue '65
Ballad of Gregorio Cortez '83
The Ballad of Little Jo '93
Balto '95
Bataan '43
The Basketball Diaries '95
Battle Hell '56
Battle Hymn '57
Battle of the Eagles '79
Beaufort '07►
Beautiful Dreamers '92
Behind the Mask '99
Believe in Me '06
The Believer '01►
Beloved Infidel '59
Bernard and Doris '08►
Beyond the Next Mountain '87
Beyond Reasonable Doubt '80
Big Mo '73
The Big Red One '80►
Bill '81►
Bill: On His Own '83►
Bitter Harvest '81►
Black Robe '91►
Blind Ambition '79
Blood Clan '91
Bloody Sunday '01►
Blow '01►
The Blue Butterfly '04
Bonanno: A Godfather's Story '99►
Bonnie & Clyde '67►
The Boston Strangler '68
The Bounty '84►
The Boys of St. Vincent '93►
Breach '07►
Breaker Morant '80►
Brian's Song '71►
The Bridge at Remagen '69
Brink's Job '78►
Britannic '00
Brittanic '00
The Bronx Is Burning '07
Brotherhood of Murder '99
Brutal Glory '89
Burke & Wills '85
The Burning Bed '85►
The Burning Season '94►
Cabeza de Vaca '90►
Cafe Society '97
Calendar Girls '03
Call Me: The Rise and Fall of Heidi Fleiss '04
Call Northside 777 '48►
Cambridge Spies '03
Camel Boy '84
Camila '84►
Can You Hear the Laughter? The Story of Freddie Prinze '79
The Cantor's Son '37
Carandiru '03
Carve Her Name with Pride '58
A Case of Deadly Force '86►
Cast the First Stone '89
Castaway '87
Casualties of Love: The "Long Island Lolita" Story '93
Casualties of War '89►
Catch a Fire '06
Chameleon Street '89►
Champions of Fire '81►
Chariots of Fire '81►
Charlie Grant's War '80
Charlie Wilson's War '07►
Charlotte Forten's Mission: Experiment in Freedom '85►
The Chase '91
Chattahoochee '89
Cheaper by the Dozen '50►
Cheaters '00►
Cheyenne Autumn '64
The Children of An Lac '80
Children of Fury '94
Chira Cry '91
Christabel '89
Christian the Lion '76
Christiane F. '22►
Churchill and the Generals '81
Cinderella Man '05►
Circle of Power '83
Citizen X '95►
A Civil Action '98►
The Climb '87
Coach Carter '05►
The Color of Courage '98
Coming Out of the Ice '82►
Coming Through '85
Communion '89
Confessions of a Serial Killer '87
Confessions of Tom Harris '72
Conrack '74►
Convicted '86
Conviction '02►
Cool Runnings '93
The Counterfeit Traitor '62►
The Counterfeiters '07►
Courage '86►
The Courage to Love '00
The Court Martial of Billy Mitchell '55►
The Court Martial of Jackie Robinson '90►
Cowboy '58►
The Cradle Will Rock '99
Crash Course '00
Crime of Flight 401 '78
Crimson Gold '03
The Crossing '00
The Crown Prince '06
A Cry in the Dark '88►
Dance with a Stranger '85►
Dangerous Life '89
Dangerous Minds '95►
David and Lisa '62►
Dawn! '83
Day One '89►
The Day Reagan Was Shot '01
Days of Glory '06
DC 9/11: Time of Crisis '04
Dead Ahead: The Exxon Valdez Disaster '92►
Dead Ringers '88►
Deadly Business '86►
Death of a Centerfold '81
Death of a Soldier '85
The Death of Adolf Hitler '84
The Death of Richie '76
The Deliberate Stranger '75
Delta Force '86►
Deranged '74►
The Diary of Anne Frank '59►
Dr. Bethune '90
Dr. Death '07
The Doctor '91►
Dog Day Afternoon '75►
Domino '05
Donner Pass: The Road to Survival '84
Donnie Brasco '96►
Don't Cry, It's Only Thunder '82
Doomsday Gun '94
Double-Crossed '91
Double Exposure: The Story of Margaret Bourke-White '89
The Dove '74
Dreamer: Inspired by a True Story '05
Drugstore Cowboy '89►
Drum Beat '54►
Duma '05►
East-West '95
Echoes in the Darkness '87
Eddie Macon's Run '83
Edie in Ciao! Manhattan '72
Edison the Man '40
The Education of Sonny Carson '74
Edward and Mrs. Simpson '80
Egg and I '47►
8-A '92
Eight Below '06
Eight Men Out '88►
8 Seconds '94
84 Charing Cross Road '86►
Eleni '85

► = rated three bones or higher

True

The Elephant Man '80▲
Elvira Madigan '67▲
Elvis and Me '88
Elvis Meets Nixon '98
Elvis: The Movie '79
The Emerald Forest '85▲
Eminent Domain '91
Empire of the Sun '87▲
Encounter with the Unknown '75
End of the Spear '06
Endangered Species '82
Enemy at the Gates '00
Enemy of Women '44
The Enforcer '51
An Englishman Abroad '83▲
Enigma Secret '79
Enjo '58
Enola Gay: The Men, the Mission, the Atomic Bomb '80
Enter Laughing '67
Entertaining Angels: The Dorothy Day Story '96
The Entity '83
Eric '75▲
Erin Brockovich '00▲
The Ernest Green Story '93
Escape from Sobibor '87▲
Escape: Human Cargo '98▲
Europa, Europa '91▲
Evel Knievel '72
Evelyn '02▲
Every Man for Himself & God Against All '75▲
Evil '03▲
The Execution of Private Slovik '74▲
The Execution of Raymond Graham '85
The Executioner's Song '82
Exodus '60▲
Extreme Justice '93
Eye on the Sparrow '91
The Falcon and the Snowman '85▲
False Arrest '92
Farinelli '94▲
Fast Company '78
Fat Man and Little Boy '89
Fatal Vision '84
The Father Clements Story '87
The FBI Story '59▲
Fear Strikes Out '57▲
Fifth Day of Peace '72
Fighting Father Dunne '48
The Fighting Seabees '44
The Fighting Sullivans '42▲
The Final Days '89
The Final Season '07
Final Warning '90
Find Me Guilty '06▲
Fire and Rain '89
Fire in the Sky '93
First Time Felon '97
Fitzcarraldo '82▲
The Fixer '68▲
Flight of the Eagle '82
Flyboys '06
The Flying Scotsman '06
For Love or Country: The Arturo Sandoval Story '00
The Forbidden Christ '50
Forever Love '98
Forty Days of Musa Dagh '85
Foul Play '76
Four Days in September '97
Francis Gary Powers: The True Story of the U-2 Spy '76
Frances '82▲
Freedom Writers '07▲
Friday Night Lights '04▲
Gaby: A True Story '87▲
The Game of Their Lives '05
Gentleman Bandit '81
George Wallace '97▲
Geronimo '93▲
Get Rich or Die Tryin' '05
The Ghost and the Darkness '96
Ghosts of Mississippi '96
Gia '98
Gideon's Trumpet '80
The Girl Who Spelled Freedom '86▲

Girls of the White Orchid '85
The Gleiwitz Case '61
Glory Enough for All: The Discovery of Insulin '92
Glory Road '06
Going for the Gold: The Bill Johnson Story '85
Going Home '86
Goldrush: A Real Life Alaskan Adventure '98
Good Evening, Mr. Wallenberg '93
Good Night, and Good Luck '05▲
Goodbye, Miss 4th of July '88
Goodfellas '90▲
Gospa '94
Gracie '07
Gracie's Choice '04
Grain of Sand '84▲
Grambling's White Tiger '81
Grand Theft Parsons '03
Grave Secrets: The Legacy of Hilltop Drive '92
The Great Debaters '07▲
The Great Escape '63▲
Great Gold Swindle '84
The Great Impostor '61
The Great Locomotive Chase '56
The Great Raid '05▲
The Great Riviera Bank Robbery '79
The Great Train Robbery '79▲
The Great Wallendas '78
The Greatest Game Ever Played '05
The Greek Tycoon '78
Greenfingers '00▲
The Grey Fox '83▲
Grey Owl '99
The Grey Zone '01
Gridiron Gang '06
Gross Misconduct '93
Guarding Eddy '04
Guilty of Innocence '87
The Guyana Tragedy: The Story of Jim Jones '80
The Guys '02▲
Hanna's War '88
Hard Choices '86
Hard Lessons '86
Harlan County War '00
The Harmonists '98
The Hatfields & the McCoys '75
He Walked by Night '48▲
He Who Walks Alone '78
The Heart Is Deceitful Above All Things '04
Heart Like a Wheel '83▲
Heartland '81▲
Heavenly Creatures '94▲
Hedd Wyn '92
Held Hostage '91
Hell to Eternity '60
Hellcats of the Navy '57
Helter Skelter '76
Helter Skelter Murders '71
Henry & June '90▲
Henry: Portrait of a Serial Killer '90▲
Hide in Plain Sight '80▲
The Hiding Place '75
The Highest Honor '84
Hilary and Jackie '98▲
The Hindenburg '75
The Hoax '06
Holy Terror '06
A Home of Our Own '75
A Home of Our Own '93
Honeymoon Killers '70
Honor Thy Father '73
Honor Thy Father and Mother: The True Story of the Menendez Brothers '94
Hoodlum Empire '52
The Hoodlum Priest '61▲
The Horse Soldiers '59
Hostage High '97
Hostages '93▲
Hostile Waters '97
Hotel Rwanda '04▲
A House Divided '00

The House on Garibaldi Street '79
The House on Todville Road '95
The Hunley '99
The Hunt for the Night Stalker '91
The Hunter '80
The Hurricane '99▲
I Am a Fugitive from a Chain Gang '32▲
I Dreamed of Africa '00
I Love You to Death '90
I Only Want You to Love Me '76
I Shot Andy Warhol '96▲
I, the Worst of All '90
I Will Fight No More Forever '75▲
If You Could See What I Hear '82
I'm Dancing as Fast as I Can '82
The Impossible Spy '87▲
In a Class of His Own '99
In Cold Blood '67▲
In Love and War '95
In Pursuit of Honor '95
In the Line of Duty: Ambush in Waco '93
In the Line of Duty: The FBI Murders '88▲
In the Mood '87
In the Name of the Father '93▲
In the Time of the Butterflies '01
In Which We Serve '43▲
The Incredible Journey of Mary Bryant '05
Indictment: The McMartin Trial '95▲
The Infernal Trio '74
The Infiltrator '95
Infinity '96
The Insider '99▲
Interrupted Melody '55▲
Intimate Relations '95
Into the Wild '07▲
Into Thin Air: Death on Everest '97
Invincible '01
Invincible '06▲
Iron Will '93
Ironclads '90
Island of the Blue Dolphins '64
It's Good to Be Alive '74
It's My Party '95
Izzy & Moe '85
The Jayne Mansfield Story '80
Jenny's War '85
Jerusalem '96
The Jesse Owens Story '84
The Jesse Ventura Story '99
Jesus Christ, Superstar '73▲
The Jew '91▲
JFK '91▲
Jo Jo Dancer, Your Life Is Calling '86
Joe Torre: Curveballs Along the Way '97
Johnson County War '02
Joni '79
Journey of Hope '90▲
The Journey to Kafiristan '01
Joyeux Noel '05▲
Judge Horton and the Scottsboro Boys '76
Judgment in Berlin '88
Julia '77▲
Justin Morgan Had a Horse '81
K-19: The Widowmaker '02
Kaspar Hauser '93
Kidco '83
Killer: A Journal of Murder '95
The Killing Fields '84▲

A Killing in a Small Town '90▲
The Killing Yard '01
King of the Wind '93
Kinky Boots '06▲
Knights of the South Bronx '05
Knute Rockne: All American '40▲
Korczak '90▲
The Krays '90▲
Kundun '97▲
Ladies They Talk About '33
Lady Jane '85▲
Lady of the House '78
Ladybird, Ladybird '93▲
Larry '74
The Last American Hero '73▲
Last Call: The Final Chapter of F. Scott Fitzgerald '02
The Last Days of Dolwyn '49
The Last Five Days '82
Last Flight Out: A True Story '90
The Last Place on Earth '85
The Last Shot '04
The Last Supper '76▲
The Late Shift '96
Lean on Me '89▲
The Legend of Blood Castle '72
Legend of Boggy Creek '75
Let Him Have It '91▲
Lethal Lolita—Amy Fisher: My Story '92
The Libertine '05
Life & Times of Grizzly Adams '74
Life Support '07▲
Little Boy Lost '78
Little Gloria... Happy at Last '84
Little Heroes '91
Little Laura & Big John '73
A Little Stiff '91
Live from Baghdad '03▲
Locked in Silence '99
Lone Star Kid '88
Longford '06▲
Longitude '00▲
The Longshots '08
Lords of Dogtown '05
Lorenzo's Oil '92▲
The Loretta Claiborne Story '00
Lost '86
Lost Battalion '01
Lost Boundaries '49
The Lost Boys '78▲
The Lost Child '00
The Lost One '51
Love and Rage '99
A Love Divided '01
Love Leads the Way '84
Love, Lies and Murder '91
Lovey: A Circle of Children 2 '82
Lucie Aubrac '98
Lumumba '01▲
Luna: Spirit of the Whale '07
M. Butterfly '93▲
Ma Barker's Killer Brood '60
Machine Gun Kelly '58▲
Mad Dog Morgan '76
Madeleine '50
Madison '01
Madman '79
A Man Escaped '57▲
The Man Who Captured Eichmann '96
The Man Who Never Was '55▲
Mandela and de Klerk '97
Manhunt for Claude Dallas '86
The Manson Family '04
Marciano '79
Marie '85▲
Marianne and Juliane '82▲
Mark Twain and Me '91
Marked Woman '37▲
Mary White '77

Mask '85▲
Massacre in Rome '73
Mata Hari '32▲
Matewan '87▲
A Matter of Life and Death '81
Mayerling '36▲
Mayerling '68
The McConnell Story '55
Melvin and Howard '80▲
Memphis Belle '90▲
Men of Honor '00
Michael Collins '96▲
Midnight Express '78▲
A Mighty Heart '07▲
Miracle '04▲
Miracle in Lane Two '00
Miracle of Our Lady of Fatima '52
The Miracle Worker '62▲
The Miracle Worker '79▲
The Miracle Worker '00
Miss Evers' Boys '97
Missing '82▲
Mission of the Shark '91▲
Mrs. R's Daughter '79
Mrs. Soffel '84
Mr. & Mrs. Loving '96▲
Mr. Horn '79
Mr. Reliable: A True Story '95
Mockingbird Don't Sing '01
Molly Maguires '70
Molokai: The Story of Father Damien '99
Money for Nothing '93
Money Movers '78
Mother Joan of the Angels '60▲
Mother of Mine '05▲
Mother Teresa: In the Name of God's Poor '97
A Mother's Prayer '95
The Mothman Prophecies '02
Mountain Man '77
Mountain Patrol: Kekexili '04▲
Mozart and the Whale '05
Murder in Coweta County '83
Murder in the First '95▲
Murder in the Old Red Barn '36
The Murder of Mary Phagan '87▲
Murder One '88
Murder Ordained '87
Murph the Surf '75
Music of the Heart '99▲
Music Within '07
Mutiny '99
Mutiny on the Bounty '35▲
Mutiny on the Bounty '62▲
My Darling Clementine '46▲
My Husband's Double Life '01
My Left Foot '89▲
My Mother's Courage '95
My Name is Bill W. '89▲
My Own Country '98
My Pleasure Is My Business '74
My Sister's Keeper '02
The Mystery of Alexina '86
The Mystery of the Mary Celeste '35
A Night to Remember '58▲
The Night We Called It a Day '03
Nightmare at 43 Hillcrest '74
The Ninth Day '04▲
Nitti: The Enforcer '88
No Man Is an Island '62
Norma Rae '79▲
Normal Life '96
North Country '05▲
Not in This Town '97
Not Without My Daughter '90
Nowhere to Run '88

Nuremberg '00
Nurse Edith Cavell '39▲
October Sky '99▲
Old Gringo '89
Olivier, Olivier '92
On the Outs '05
On Wings of Eagles '86
One Against the Wind '91▲
One in a Million: The Ron LeFlore Story '78
One Man's Hero '98
One That Got Away '57▲
The One That Got Away '96
The Onion Field '79▲
Operation Haylift '50
Operation Thunderbolt '77
Opposing Force '87
The Ordeal of Dr. Mudd '80▲
The Other Side of the Mountain '75
The Other Side of the Mountain, Part 2 '78
The Ox '91
Pack of Lies '87
Pancho Barnes '88
Passion in Paradise '89
Passion of Joan of Arc '28▲
Pat Garrett & Billy the Kid '73▲
Paths of Glory '57▲
Patton '70▲
Patty Hearst '88
The Pentagon Wars '98
The People vs. Larry Flynt '96▲
The Perfect Storm '00
Phar Lap '84
Philby, Burgess and MacLean: Spy Scandal of the Century '84
The Pianist '02▲
Pinochet's Last Stand '06
A Place for Annie '94
Playing for Time '80▲
Portrait of a Rebel: Margaret Sanger '82
The Positively True Adventures of the Alleged Texas Cheerleader-Murdering Mom '93▲
Possessed '00
The Prepple Murder '89
Pressure Point '62▲
Pretty Village, Pretty Flame '96▲
Prick Up Your Ears '87▲
Pride '07
Primeval '07
Prince of the City '81▲
Princess Caraboo '94
The Prisoner of Shark Island '36
A Private Matter '92▲
The Prize Pulitzer '89
The Prize Winner of Defiance, Ohio '05▲
Promised a Miracle '88
Protecting the King '07
PT 109 '63
The Pursuit of Happyness '06▲
The Queen '06▲
A Question of Attribution '91
Question of Faith '93
Question of Honor '80
Qui Etes Vous, Mr. Sorge? '61
Rated X '00
Reach for the Sky '56▲
A Real American Hero '78
Rebound: The Legend of Earl "The Goat" Manigault '96
Reckless Disregard '84
Red Cherry '95
Redacted '07
Reds '81▲
Reilly: Ace of Spies '87▲

▲ = rated three bones or higher

Rescue Dawn '06
Rescuers: Stories of Courage—Two Couples '98
Rescuers: Stories of Courage "Two Women" '97
The Return of Martin Guerre '83
Reversal of Fortune '90
Rhodes '97
Riding in Cars with Boys '01
Ring of Bright Water '69
Ring of Terror '62
Riot in Cell Block 11 '54 ►
Riot in the Streets '96
The Road to Galveston '96
River's Edge '87 ►
Rodeo Girl '80
Roe vs. Wade '89 ►
Rogue Trader '98
Roswell: The U.F.O. Cover-Up '94
Rough Riders '97 ►
A Royal Scandal '96
Ruby '92
Ruby Bridges '98
Rudy '93 ►
The Rumor Mill '86
A Rumor of War '80
Run for the Dream: The Gail Devers Story '96
Runaway Father '91
The Runner Stumbles '79 ►
Running Brave '83
Sacco & Vanzetti '71
Sadat '83
St. Helen's: Killer Volcano '82
The St. Valentine's Day Massacre '67
Sakharov '84 ►
Samaritan: The Mitch Snyder Story '86
Samurai 1: Musashi Miyamoto '55 ►
Samurai 2: Duel at Ichijoji Temple '55 ►
Samurai 3: Duel at Ganryu Island '56 ►
Savage Attraction '83
Savage Messiah '02
Saved by the Light '95
Scandal '89 ►
A Scandal in Paris '46
Schindler's List '93 ►
Sea Gypsies '78
The Sea Inside '04 ►
Sea Wolves '81
The Search for Bridey Murphy '56
Searching for Bobby Fischer '93 ►
Secret Weapon '90
Seeing Red '99 ►
Seizure: The Story of Kathy Morris '80
Selena '96
Selma, Lord, Selma '99 ►
Separate but Equal '91 ►
Sergeant Matovich vs. the U.S. Air Force '78
Sergeant York '41 ►
Serpico '73 ►
Serving in Silence: The Margarethe Cammermeyer Story '95
Seven Years in Tibet '97
Sexual Intent '94
Shackleton '02 ►
Shadow on the Sun '88
Shadowlands '93 ►
Shake Hands With the Devil: The Journey of Romeo Dallaire '04 ►
Shattered Dreams '90
Shattered Class '03
Shattered Vows '84
Shine '96 ►
A Shining Season '79
Shooting Dogs '05 ►
Shot in the Heart '01 ►
Shot Through the Heart '98 ►
The Sicilian '87
Shout at the Devil '76 ►
Sid & Nancy '86 ►

Silence of the North '81
Silent Victim '92
Silent Victory: The Kitty O'Neil Story '79
Silkwood '83 ►
The Singing Nun '66
Six Degrees of Separation '93
Sins of the Father '01 ►
Skeezer '82
Skin '89
The Slender Thread '65 ►
Small Sacrifices '89
Smile '05
Snap Decision '01
Sniper '75
Snowbound: The Jim and Jennifer Stolpa Story '94
So Proudly We Hail '43 ►
Soldier Blue '70
The Son of the Shark '93
Sophie Scholl: The Final Days '05 ►
Soul of the Game '96
The Sound of Music '65 ►
Spartacus '60 ►
The Spirit of St. Louis '57
Spirit of West Point '47
Springfield Rifle '52
Squizzy Taylor '84 ►
Stand and Deliver '88 ►
Star 80 '83 ►
Starved '06
Stealing Heaven '88
Stonewall '95
Storm and Sorrow '90
The Story of Dr. Wassell '44 ►
The Straight Story '99 ►
Strange Justice: The Clarence Thomas and Anita Hill Story '99
The Stratton Story '49 ►
Street Smart '87 ►
The Sugarland Express '74 ►
Sugartime '95
Sweetwater: A True Rock Story '99
Swimming Upstream '03
Switched at Birth '91
10 Rillington Place '71 ►
Take the Lead '06
The Taking of Flight 847: The Uli Derickson Story '88
Taking Sides '01 ►
Talk to Me '07 ►
Teamster Boss: The Jackie Presser Story '92
The Ten Million Dollar Getaway '91
Thirteen Days '00 ►
Thirty Seconds Over Tokyo '44 ►
A Thousand Heroes '92
A Thousand Pieces of Gold '91 ►
Three Came Home '50
The Three Faces of Eve '57
The 300 Spartans '62
The Tiger Woods Story '98
Till Death Do Us Part '92
Time Out '01 ►
Titanic '53
Titanic '96
Titanic '97 ►
To Catch a Killer '92
To End All Wars '01
To Heal a Nation '88
To Kill a Priest '89
Toast of New York '37
Torso '01
Touched by Love '80
Touching the Void '03 ►
Town That Dreaded Sundown '76
Tragedy of Flight 103: The Inside Story '91
The Trial of Old Drum '00
The Triangle Factory Fire Scandal '79

21 '08 ►
24 Hour Party People '01 ►
29th Street '91 ►
The Tunnel '01 ►
Tuesdays with Morrie '99
Tyson '95
Two Men Went to War '02
Under the Lighthouse Dancing '97
United 93 '06 ►
Unknown White Male '05 ►
Unshackled '00
The Untold Story of Emmett Louis Till '05 ►
Valentin '02 ►
Varian's War '01
Vendetta '99 ►
Vengeance Is Mine '79 ►
Victory at Entebbe '76
Video Voyeur: The Susan Wilson Story '02
Violette '78
Voyage of Terror: The Achille Lauro Affair '90
Voyage of the Damned '76
Waking Up Wally '05
Walk the Proud Land '56
Walking Tall '73 ►
Walking Tall: Part 2 '75
Walking Tall: The Final Chapter '77
Walking Through the Fire '80
The Wall '83 ►
The Wannsee Conference '84
We Are Marshall '06
The Wedding Gift '93
Wedding in Blood '74 ►
Weeds '87
Welcome to Sarajevo '97 ►
What's Love Got to Do with It? '93 ►
When Hell Was in Session '82
Whirlygirl '04
White Mile '94
White Mischief '88 ►
The White Rose '83
Whitewash: The Clarence Brandley Story '02
The Whole Wide World '96 ►
The Wild Child '70 ►
Wild America '97
Wild Hearts Can't Be Broken '91 ►
Will: G. Gordon Liddy '82
A Winner Never Quits '86
With a Song in My Heart '52 ►
Without a Trace '83
A Woman at War '94
A Woman Called Golda '82 ►
The Woman He Loved '88
Woman with a Past '92
Wooden Horse '50
A World Apart '88 ►
World Trade Center '06 ►
The World's Fastest Indian '05 ►
The Wrong Man '56 ►
You Know My Name '99
The Young Poisoner's Handbook '94 ►
Yours, Mine & Ours '68
Yuri Nosenko, KGB '86
Zoot Suit '81 ►
Zulu '64 ►

TV Pilot Movies

Africa Texas Style '67
The Alice '04
American Dream '81
The Art of Crime '75
Balboa '82
Battlestar Galactica '78
The Bionic Woman '75
Blade in Hong Kong '85
Blue De Ville '86
Brass '85
Buck Rogers in the 25th Century '79
Call to Glory '84
China Beach '88 ►
Christy '94
Columbo: Prescription Murder '67 ►
Conspiracy of Terror '75
Cruel Intentions 2 '99
Daring Game '68
The Dead Zone '02
Death Ray 2000 '81
Destination Moonbase Alpha '75
Dr. Strange '78
Evil Roy Slade '71
Express to Terror '79
Fantasy Island '76
The Flash '90
Force Five '75
The Gunfighters '87
Hercules and the Princess of Troy '65
Hercules and the Legendary Journeys, Vol. 1: And the Amazon Women '94
Highlander: The Gathering '92
The Hunted Lady '77
Hunter '73
The Immortal '01
The Incredible Hulk '77
JAG '95
Jigsaw '71
The Kid with the Broken Halo '82
Kung Fu '72 ►
L.A. Law '86 ►
The Lazarus Man '96
The Legend of Butch & Sundance '04
Little House on the Prairie '74
Loving '84
The Magnificent Seven '98
Magnum, P.I.: Don't Eat the Snow in Hawaii '80
Miami Vice '84
Misfits of Science '85
Moonlighting '85 ►
Nick Knight '89
Night Gallery '69
The Night Stalker '71 ►
Our Family Business '81
Out of Order '03
Poltergeist: The Legacy '96
Probe '72
Rags to Riches '87
Riding with Death '76
Sabrina the Teenage Witch '96
Sanctuary of Fear '79
Scarface Mob '62
Search for the Gods '75
She's in the Army Now '81
Skag '74
Smile, Jenny, You're Dead '74
Soldier of Fortune Inc. '97
Space: 1999—Alien Attack '75
Sprague '84
Stalk the Wild Child '76
Stark '85
Strange New World '75
The Streets of San Francisco '72 ►
Strike Force '75
Superman & the Mole Men '51
TekWar '94
Terraces '77
Thunder in Paradise '93
Tour of Duty '87
Vegas '78
Waikiki '80
Walker, Texas Ranger: One Riot, One Ranger '93
White Dwarf '95
The Women of Brewster Place '89 ►
The Young Pioneers '76

TV Series

Aeon Flux '05

Twins

see also Brothers & Sisters; Family Ties

Triple Cross '67
Triumph of the Spirit '89 ►
True Confessions '81 ►
The Truth About Jane '00
The Tuskegee Airmen '95 ►
The Abandoned '06
Adaptation '02 ►
After Darkness '85
Angels Don't Sleep Here '00
The Attic '06
Bad Company '02
Basket Case '82 ►
Basket Case 2 '90
Basket Case 3: The Progeny '92
Big Business '88
Billboard Dad '98
Bloodlink '86
The Bride with White Hair '93 ►
Brotherly Love '85
Brothers of the Head '06
Campus Knights '29
Chained for Life '51
Children of Dune '03
A Cinderella Story '04
Citizen Toxie: The Toxic Avenger 4 '01
City of Shadows '86
Class of Nuke 'Em High 3: The Good, the Bad and the Subhumanoid '94
Cobra Woman '44
Coffee and Cigarettes '03 ►
The Corsican Brothers '42
The Crazysitter '94
Dark Side '02
Dead Men Walk '43
Dead Ringer '64
Dead Ringers '88 ►
Deadly Twins '85
Decay '98
Devil's Wedding Night '73
Double Double Toil and Trouble '94
Double Impact '91
The Double Life of Veronique '91 ►
Double Trouble '92
Double Vision '92
The Dreamers '03
Dual Alibi '47
Equal Impact '96
Equinox '93
The Eyes, the Mouth '83
The Fat Spy '66
The Fifth Musketeer '79
Freaks '32 ►
The Good Thief '03 ►
Hangman's Curse '03
Here Come the Waves '45
Hotel de Love '96
House of Wax '05
How the West Was Fun '95
Into the Fire '05
Invitation au Voyage '82
It Takes Two '95
Jack's Back '87
Killer with Two Faces '74
The Krays '90 ►
Lies of the Twins '91
Looney Tunes: Back in Action '03
Lost Honeymoon '47
Love! Valour! Compassion! '96 ►
Madhouse '87
Major League 3: Back to the Minors '98

And Now for Something Completely Different '72 ►
The Man in the Iron Mask '39 ►
The Man in the Iron Mask '77
The Man in the Iron Mask '97
The Man in the Iron Mask '98 ►
Man with a Gun '95
Maximum Risk '96
Mirror Images '91
Mirror Images 2 '93
Mother Lode '82
New York Minute '04
Nuke '93
The Nutt House '92
The Other '72 ►
Out on a Limb '92
The Parent Trap '61 ►
The Parent Trap '98 ►
Preaching to the Choir '05
The Prince and the Pauper '37 ►
Private Property '06
Raising Cain '92
Rebirth of Mothra '96
Rebirth of Mothra 2 '97
The Reluctant Agent '95
Ripe '97
Schizopolis '97
Second Sight '99
Seed of Chucky '04
Sisters '73 ►
Slightly Terrific '44
The Sphinx '33
The Spiderwick Chronicles '08
Spy Smasher '42
Spy Smasher Returns '42
Start the Revolution without Me '70 ►
Steal Big, Steal Little '95
A Stolen Life '46 ►
Strangers in Love '32
Stuck On You '03 ►
Thicker Than Water '93
This World, Then the Fireworks '97
Three ... Extremes '04 ►
Thunder Heart '27
To Grandmother's House We Go '94
Trail of the Mounties '47
12 and Holding '05 ►
Twin Dragons '92
Twin Falls Idaho '99 ►
Twin Sisters '91
Twin Town '97
Twins '88
Twins of Evil '71
Twinsanity '70
Twisters '95
Twitches '05
Twitches Too '07
Urban Legends 2: Final Cut '00
Vampire Effect '03
Village of Dreams '97
Wagon's Westward '40
Woman Concerned '33
Wonder Man '45 ►
The Worldly Madonna '22
The Young Girls of Rochefort '68

Twister!

see also Disaster Flicks

Category 7: The End of the World '05
Category 6: Day of Destruction '04
The Day After Tomorrow '04 ►
Eye of the Storm '98
Night of the Twisters '95
Places in the Heart '84 ►
Storm Chasers: Revenge of the ...
Storm Tracker '99
Tornado! '95
Twister '96 ►
Where the Heart Is '00
The Wizard of Oz '25
The Wizard of Oz '39 ►

UFOs

see Alien Beings—
Benign; Alien Beings—
Vicious; Space Operas

Under My Skin

Antibody '02
Fantastic Voyage '66▶
Innerspace '87
Osmosis Jones '01

Undercover Cops

see also Crime Drama;
Organized Crime
Angel of Destruction '94
Assault on Precinct 13 '05
Bad Boys 2 '03
Ballistic '94
Beyond Suspicion '00
Beyond the Law '92
Big Momma's House '00
Big Momma's House 2 '06
Border Incident '49
Break a Leg '03
Bullets or Ballots '38▶
City on Fire '87
Con Games '02
Cruising '80
Cutaway '00
Dead Pigeon on Beethoven
Street '72
Death Rides the Range '40
The Departed '06▶
District B13 '04
Donnie Brasco '96▶
Drug Zone '94
Drug Wars: The Camarena
Story '90▶
The Finishing Touch '92
Force Five '75
Get Christie Love! '74
Hard-Boiled '92
Hellcats '68
Hot Stuff '80
House of Bamboo '55
Idiot Box '97
Impulse '90
In the Flesh '97
In the Line of Duty: A Cop
for the Killing '90
In the Shadows '01
In Too Deep '99
Infernal Affairs '02
Kindergarten Cop '90
Kiss of Death '94
The Last Shot '04
Miami Vice '06
Miss Congeniality 2: Armed
and Fabulous '05
The Mod Squad '99
Motor Patrol '50
The Naked Gun: From the
Files of Police Squad '88▶
Narc '02▶
No Man's Land '87
Plain Clothes '88
Protector '97
Raw Deal '86
Reservoir Dogs '92▶
Running Scared '06
Rush '91▶
Saints and Sinners '95
A Scanner Darkly '06
Serpico '73▶
Sharky's Machine '81
Small Kill '93
The Sweeper '95
Stiletto Dance '01
Stone Cold '91
Swindle '02
TekWar '94
Threat of Exposure '02
Traffic '00▶
Training Day '01▶
Tube '03
2 Fast 2 Furious '03
Underclassman '05
White Chicks '04
Wisegirls '02
Witness '85▶

Unexplained Phenomena

The Amityville Curse '90
Angel Baby '61
Beyond the Bermuda
Triangle '75
The Birds '63▶
Black Rainbow '91▶
Blue Tornado '90
Book of Shadows: Blair
Witch 2 '00
The Carpathian Eagle '81
The Carpenter '89
Carrie '76▶
Carrie '02
Catacombs '89
Cube '98
Cube 2: Hypercube '02
A Day Without a Mexican
'04
Dead Again '91▶
Dead Zone '83▶
Delusion '84
Destiny Turns on the Radio
'95
Die, Monster, Die! '65
Dream a Little Dream 2 '94
Dying to Remember '93
Encounter with the
Unknown '75
Endgame '85
The Entity '83
Escapes '86
E.S.P. '83
Eternal Evil '87
The Evil Mind '34
Eyes of Laura Mars '78
Fallen '97
Fire in the Sky '93
Firestarter '84
The 4D Man '59
The Fury '78
Ghost Chasers '51
Ghost Town '88
The Ghosts of Hanley
House '68
Grandma's House '88
Hangar 18 '80
The Haunting Passion '83
The House of Seven
Corpses '73
In Dreams '98
Lisa and the Devil '75
Lost Voyage '01
Lurkers '88
Maximum Overdrive '86
Michael '96
Miracle in Rome '88
Miracle of Our Lady of
Fatima '52
Mondo Balordo '64
Murphy's Fault '88
A Name for Evil '70
Nomads '86
Out There '95
Phenomenon '96
Psychic '91
The Psychotronic Man '91
The Rage: Carrie 2 '99
The Reaping '07
Retribution '88
Return from Witch Mountain
'78
Roswell: The U.F.O. Cover-
Up '94
Salem's Lot '79
Scared Stiff '53▶
Shattered Silence '71
The Sleeping Car '90
Spook Busters '48
The Stranger '73
Things Happen at Night '48
The Three Lives of
Thomasina '63▶
The Tin Drum '79▶
Truly, Madly, Deeply '91▶
The Undead '57
Visions '90
Visions of Evil '75
Waiting for the Light '90
Wavelength '96
Web of the Spider '70
The X-Files '98
X: The Man with X-Ray
Eyes '63

Unhappy Meals

see also Cannibalism;
Edibles
Alien '79▶
Better Off Dead '85
The Birdcage '95▶
Blind Date '87
The Cook, the Thief, His
Wife & Her Lover '90▶
Dinner at Eight '33▶
Dinner at Eight '89
The Invitation '03
The Last Supper '96
The Meal '75
Meet the Parents '00▶
Melinda and Melinda '05
Monty Python's The
Meaning of Life '83▶
The Myth of Fingerprints '97
Pieces of April '03
Road Trip '00
Super Size Me '04▶
Tadpole '02

U.S. Marshals

see also Loner Cops;
Westerns
Cahill: United States
Marshal '73
Con Air '97▶
Dear Wendy '05
Eraser '96
The Fugitive '93▶
Gunfight at the O.K. Corral
'57
Hang 'Em High '67
Heaven's Gate '81
High Noon '52▶
The Kansan '43
My Darling Clementine '46▶
Out of Sight '98▶
Outland '81
Renegade Trail '39
Rooster Cogburn '75
South of Heaven, West of
Hell '00
Texas Rangers '01
Tombstone '93▶
True Grit '69▶
U.S. Marshals '98
The Usual Suspects '95▶
Witness Protection '99▶
Wyatt Earp '94

Up All Night

see also Vampire Babes;
Vampires
After Hours '85▶
Albino Alligator '96
American Graffiti '73▶
The Anniversary Party '01
Assault on Precinct 13 '05
Batman '89▶
Before Sunrise '94
Big City Blues '99
The Big Kahuna '00
Black Christmas '06
Blade Runner '82▶
Border Patrol '01
Cabaret Balkan '98
Caresses '97
Cashback '06
Chicago Cab '98
Collateral '04▶
Dazed and Confused '93▶
Death Proof '07
East Palace, West Palace
'96
En la Cama '05
Escape from New York '81
Fear of the Dark '02
54 '98
Flourish '06
The French Connection '71▶
Friday Night '02
From Dusk Till Dawn '95
Funny Games '07
The Ghost Train '41
Go '99▶
Gone in 60 Seconds '00
Groove '00▶
Head On '98▶
Hocus Pocus '93
Into the Night '85

Urban Comedy

see also African America
Are We There Yet? '05
Barbershop '02
Barbershop 2: Back in
Business '04
Beauty Shop '05▶
Big Momma's House '00
Blue Collar '78▶
Booty Call '96
Buying the Cow '02
Car Wash '76
CB4: The Movie '93
Coming to America '88▶
The Cookout '04
Cowboys & Angels '04▶
Def Jam's How to Be a
Player '97
Don't Be a Menace to South
Central While Drinking
Your Juice in the Hood
'95
Fat Albert '04
Fear of a Black Hat '94
Friday '95
Friday After Next '02
Harlem Nights '89
Hollywood Shuffle '87
The Honeymooners '05
House Party '90▶
House Party 2: The Pajama
Jam '91
House Party 3 '94
I Got Five on It '05
I Got the Hook-Up '98
I'm Gonna Git You Sucka
'88▶
Jail Party '04
Jeremy's Family Reunion
'04
Johnson Family Vacation
'04
King's Ransom '05
Let's Do It Again '75
Makin' Baby '02
Malibu's Most Wanted '03
The Meteor Man '93
Mo' Money '92
Next Friday '00
Piece of the Action '77
Pootie Tang '01
Roll Bounce '05▶
She Hate Me '04
Soul Plane '04
Two Can Play That Game
'01
Up Against the Eight Ball '04
Uptown Saturday Night '74
The Wash '01

Urban America

Jet Lag '02
Judgment Night '93
Just One Night '00
The Last Days of Disco '98▶
Late Night '99
Little Nemo: Adventures in
Slumberland '92
Mannequin '87
Miracle Mile '89
Miss Julie '99
Night at the Golden Eagle
'02
Night at the Museum '06
Nightwatch '96
Panic Room '02
Pitch Black '00▶
Pizza '05
Prom Night '08
Reach the Rock '98
Rites of Passage '99
Roger Dodger '02▶
Salem's Lot '04
Simone Barbes '80
Sleepover '04
Superbad '07▶
Swingers '96▶
Tainted '98
Taxi Driver '76▶
30 Days of Night '07
Trick '99▶
25th Hour '02
200 Cigarettes '98
Unaccompanied Minors '06
Weirdsville '07
Wind Chill '07
Woo '97
Yellow '98

Urban Drama

Above the Rim '94
Acts of Worship '01
Against the Wall '04
Akeelah and the Bee '06
American Heart '92▶
American Me '92▶
Animal '05
The Architect '06
The Asphalt Jungle '50▶
ATL '06
Baby Boy '01
Back in the Day '05
Bad Attitude '93
Bad Lieutenant '92▶
Barrio Wars '02
Belly '98
Better Dayz '02
Black and White '99▶
Blood Brothers '97
Bomb the System '00
Boricua's Bond '00
Boston Kickout '95
Boyz N the Hood '91▶
The Bronx War '90
Brother to Brother '04
A Brother's Kiss '97
Bullet '94
Carlito's Way '93▶
Carlito's Way: Rise to Power
'05
Caught Up '98
Changing Lanes '02▶
City Hall '95▶
City of M '01
Colors '88▶
Cooley High '75▶
Corrupt '99
Crash '05▶
Crossing the Bridge '92
Cry, the Beloved Country
'95▶
Curtis's Charm '96
Dangerous Minds '95
Dead Boyz Can't Fly '93
Deep Trouble '01
Devil's Knight '03
Dirty '05
Do the Right Thing '89▶
Dope Case Pending '00
Empire '02
Erskinville Kings '99
The Fence '94
Final Exam '89
Fly by Night '93
Free of Eden '98
Fresh '94▶
Gang Related '96
Get Rich or Die Tryin' '05
The Graffiti Artist '04
Grand Canyon '91▶
Half Lesson '06▶
Hard Lessons '86
Harsh Times '05
Head On '98▶
Head On '04
Heaven Is a Playground '91
Hell's Kitchen NYC '97
Hip Hop 4 Life '03
Hustle & Flow '05▶
Jason's Lyric '94
Juice '92
Jungleground '95
Junior's Groove '97
Just Another Girl on the
I.R.T. '93
Kill the Poor '06
Latin Dragon '03
Levity '03
Lift '01
Light It Up '99
Loser '97
Love Your Mama '89
MacArthur Park '01
Menace II Society '93▶
Mi Vida Loca '94
Money for Nothing '93
Murda Muzik '03
Naked '93▶
New Jack City '91▶
New Jersey Drive '95
Night Falls on Manhattan
'96▶
Nora's Hair Salon '04

Urban Gangstas

see also Gangs; Urban
Drama
Animal '05
Back in the Day '05
Better Dayz '02
Carlito's Way: Rise to Power
'05
Charlie '04
Colors '88▶
Cradle 2 the Grave '03
Get Rich or Die Tryin' '05
Ghetto Dawg '02
Ghetto Dawg 2: Out of the
Pits '05
Guilty by Association '03
Honor '06
In Too Deep '99
Paid in Full '02
Rhapsody '01
R.I.C.C.O. '02
Shot '01
Snipes '01
State Property 2 '05
Stryker '04
The Substitute 2: School's
Out '97
Training Day '01
Urban Justice '07
Waist Deep '06
Wassup Rockers '06
Way Past Cool '00
Winner Takes All '98

The USO

see also World War II
China Beach '88▶
For the Boys '91
Stage Door Canteen '43

Vacation Hell

The American Scream '80s
An American Werewolf in
London '81▶
Backwoods '87
The Beach '00
The Breed '06
Brokedown Palace '99
The Comfort of Strangers
'91▶

Which Way Is Up? '77
Who's the Man? '93

(Urban Drama continued)

Once Were Warriors '94▶
Original Gangstas '96
Out of Sync '95
Paid in Full '02
Poetic Justice '93
'R Xmas '01
Raising the Heights '97
The Reading Room '05
R.I.C.C.O. '02
Roll Bounce '05▶
Rude '96
Rude Boy: The Jamaican
Don '03
Slam '98
Soul Survivor '95
South Central '92
Southie '98
Squeeze '97
State Property 2 '05
Straight out of Brooklyn '91
Strange Days '95▶
Strapped '93
Street Wars '91
Stryker '04
Sucker Free City '05▶
Sugar Hill '94
Take the Lead '06
Tar '97
Ten Benny '98
13 Moons '02
This Revolution '05
Training Day '01
Turn It Up '00
Twist '03▶
Urban Crossfire '94
Waist Deep '06
Wassup Rockers '06
What About Your Friends:
Weekend Getaway '02
White Man's Burden '95
The World '04
A Year Without Love '05
Zebrahead '92▶
Zooman '95

▶ = rated three bones or higher

(continued)

Dangerous Prey '95
Dead Cold '96
Deadly Intruder '84
Deadly in the Water '06
Death Stalk '74
Death Weekend '76
Deliverance '72▶
Devil Wears White '86
Disappearance '02
8 Heads in a Duffel Bag '96
The Fatal Image '90
A Fatal Inversion '92
Frantic '58▶
Grotesque '87
Hostel '06
Hostel: Part 2 '07
Jack Frost 2: Revenge of the Mutant Killer Snowman '00
Jeopardy! '53
Jindabyne '06
Judgment Day '88
Killing at Hell's Gate '81
The Man Who Knew Too Much '34▶
Midnight Express '78▶
Mr. Bean's Holiday '07
Nightmare at Bittercreek '91
Open Water '03▶
Overkill '86
Red Lights '04▶
Ring of Fire 3: Lion Strike '94
The River Wild '94
The Ruins '08
Russian Roulette '93
Shark Attack 3: Megalodon '02
Six Days, Seven Nights '98
Target '85
Terror at Red Wolf Inn '72
Terror at Tenkiller '86
Tracks of a Killer '95
TripFall '00
Turistas '06
Twitch of the Death Nerve '71
The Two Faces of Evil '82
Vacancy '07
The Waiter '06
Witchery '88

Vacations

The Adventures of Sharkboy and Lavagirl in 3-D '05
Agatha Christie's A Caribbean Mystery '83
American Goth c '83
American Pie 2 '01
The American Scream '80s
An American Werewolf in London '81▶
Assassination n Rome '65
Babel '06▶
Backwoods '87
Beethoven's 3rd '00
Beverly Hills Family Robinson '97
Beyond the Door 3 '91
Blame It on Rio '84
Blondie Takes a Vacation '39
Body Trouble '92
Bread and Tulips '01▶
Brokedown Palace '99
Cabin Boy '94
California Dreaming '07
California Suite '78▶
Camilla '94
Cancel My Reservation '72
Captain Ron '92
Casual Sex? '88
Charlie Chan at the Circus '36
Cheaper by the Dozen 2 '05
City Slickers '91▶
Claire's Knee '71▶
Club Dread '04
Cold Fever '95
Come September '61
The Comfort of Strangers '91▶
Cote d'Azur '05
Crackerjack '94
Dangerous Prey '95
Dead Cold '96
Deadly Intruder '84
Death Stalk '74
December Boys '07
Deliverance '72▶
Devil Wears White '86
Dirty Dancing '87▶
Dr. Dolittle 3 '06
Dodson's Journey '01
8 Heads in a Duffel Bag '96
A Fatal Inversion '92
The Fatal Image '90
Feeders '96
The First to Go '97
Forgetting Sarah Marshall '08
Frantic '88▶
Fraternity Vacation '85
French Fried Vacation '79
From Justin to Kelly '03
Funny Games '07
Far from Home '89
A Far Off Place '93
Gidget Goes Hawaiian '61
Gidget Goes to Rome '63
Ginger and Cinnamon '03
Girls Can't Swim '00
The Girl Getters '66
The Great Outdoors '88
Grotesque '87
Harry and the Hendersons '87
Head Above Water '96
Heading South '05▶
The Hills Have Eyes '06
The Hills Have Eyes '77
Home Alone '90▶
Home Alone 2: Lost in New York '92
Hot Pursuit '87
Hot Summer '68
The Hours and Times '92▶
The Housekeeper '02
How Stella Got Her Groove Back '98
The Inkwell '94
Jack Frost 2: Revenge of the Mutant Killer Snowman '00
Judgment Day '88
Just Looking '99
Kevin & Perry Go Large '00
Killing at Hell's Gate '81
The King Is Alive '00
La Collectionneuse '67
La Piscine '69
Last Holiday '06
The Last of the High Kings '96
Last Summer in the Hamptons '96
Lena's Holiday '90
Lie Down with Dogs '95
Like It Never Was Before '95
Little Bigfoot '96
The Long, Long Trailer '54
Love! Valour! Compassion! '96
The Lunatic '92
Matisse '62
Magic in the Water '95
Magic Kid '92
The Man of My Life '06
The Man Who Knew Too Much '34▶
Mr. Hulot's Holiday '53▶
Mr. Hobbs Takes a Vacation '62▶
A Month by the Lake '95
Morvern Callar '02
My Father, My Mother, My Brothers and My Sisters '99
The Men of My Life '06
National Lampoon's Christmas Vacation '89
National Lampoon's Dad's Week Off '97
National Lampoon's European Vacation '85
National Lampoon's Vacation '83▶
Nico and Dani '00
Nightmare at Bittercreek '91
Off Season '01
Ollie Hopnoodle's Haven of Bliss '88
Open Water '03▶
The Out-of-Towners '70▶
Overkill '96
Pauline at the Beach '83▶
Phat Girlz '06
Poor White Trash 2 '75
Rain '01
Raising Victor Vargas '03
Red Lights '04▶
Red Salute '35
Ring of Fire 3: Lion Strike '94
The River Wild '94
Rugrats Go Wild! '03
Russian Roulette '93
RV '06
Shark Attack 3: Megalodon '02
Six Days, Seven Nights '98
Sisterhood of the Traveling Pants '05
Sisterhood of the Traveling Pants 2 '08
Spellbreaker: Secret of the Leprechauns '96
Spring Break '83
Stealing Beauty '96
The Sucker '65
Summer Rental '85
A Summer's Tale '96
Swimming Pool '03▶
A Tale of Winter '92
Target '85
Terror at Red Wolf Inn '72
Terror at Tenkiller '86
Tourist Trap '98
Tracks of a Killer '95
TripFall '00
Twitch of the Death Nerve '71
2 Days in Paris '07
The Two Faces of Evil '82
Two for the Road '67▶
Two If by Sea '95
Tyler Perry's Why Did I Get Married? '07
Uncivilized '94
Unlawful Passage '94
Vegas Vacation '96
Vibration '68
The Waiter '06
A Walk on the Moon '99
Week-End in Havana '41
Weekend at Bernie's '89
A Weekend in the Country '96
Welcome to Spring Break '88
Where the Boys Are '60
Where the Boys Are '84, '84
Wild Cactus '92
The Wild Life '84
Witchery '88
With a Friend Like Harry '00▶

Vampire Babes

see also Up All Night; Vampires

Buffy the Vampire Slayer '92▶
Cold Hearts '99
The Craving '80
Daughters of Darkness '71▶
Demon Queen '80
Dracula's Daughter '36▶
Elvira's Haunted Hills '02
Eternal '04
Fangs of the Living Dead '69
The Fearless Vampire Killers '67▶
The Forsaken '01
Fright Night '85
The Girl with the Hungry Eyes '94
Habit '97
The Insatiable '06
Interview with the Vampire '94
John Carpenter Presents Vampires: Los Muertos '02
John Carpenter's Vampires '97
Karmina '96
The Kiss '88
The League of Extraordinary Gentlemen '03
Lemora, Lady Dracula '73
Lips of Blood '75
Lust for a Vampire '71
Mary, Mary, Bloody Mary '76
The Midnight Hour '86
Nadja '95▶
Night Junkies '07
Night Shade '97
Night of the Sorcerers '70
Nightlife '90
Once Bitten '85
Queen of the Damned '02
Razor Blade Smile '98
Rise: Blood Hunter '07
Samson vs. the Vampire Women '61
Saturday the 14th Strikes Back '88
Sergio Lapel's Drawing Blood '99
Sorority House Vampires '95
Stephen King's The Night Flier '96
Tales from the Crypt Presents Bordello of Blood '96
The Thirst '06
Twins of Evil '71
Ultraviolet '06
Underworld: Evolution '05
Vamp '86
Vampire Centerfolds '93
The Vampire Lovers '70
Vampire Night '20
Vampires From Hell '99
Vampyres '74
Van Helsing '04▶
The Velvet Vampire '71
Witchcraft 10: Mistress of the Craft '98

Vampire Spoof

see also Horror Comedy; Vampires

Andy Warhol's Dracula '74▶
Beverly Hills Vamp '88
Buffy the Vampire Slayer '92▶
Dracula: Dead and Loving It '95
Elvira's Haunted Hills '02
The Fearless Vampire Killers '67▶
Gore-Met Zombie Chef from Hell '87
I Married a Vampire '87
Karmina '96
The Little Vampire '00
Love at First Bite '79
The Malibu Beach Vampires
Mr. Vampire '86
My Best Friend Is a Vampire '88
My Grandpa Is a Vampire '92
Once Bitten '85
A Polish Vampire in Burbank '83
Rockula '90
Teen Vamp '88
Vamp '86
The Vampire Happening '71

Vampires

see also Up All Night; Vampire Babes; Vampire Spoof

The Addiction '95
Addicted to Murder '95
Addicted to Murder 2: Tainted Blood '97
Addicted to Murder 3: Bloodlust '99
Alien Massacre '67
Angel of the Night '98
Attack from Mars '68
The Bat People '74
Beast of Morocco '66
Billy the Kid Versus Dracula '66
The Black Room '82
Black Sabbath '64▶
Blacula '72
Blade '98
Blade 2 '02
Blade: Trinity '04
Blood & Donuts '95
Blood and Roses '61
Blood Freak '72
Blood of Dracula's Castle '69
Blood of the Vampire '58
The Blood Spattered Bride '72
Blood Thirst '65
Blood Ties '92
Bloodbath '98
Bloodlust '59
Bloodlust: Subspecies 3 '93
BloodRayne '06
BloodRayne 2: Deliverance '07
Bloodstone: Subspecies 2
Bloodstorm: Subspecies 4
Bloodsuckers '98
The Bloodsuckers '70
Bloodsuckers from Outer Space '83
Body Snatcher from Hell '69
Bram Stoker's Dracula '92▶
The Breed '01
The Brides of Dracula '60
Buffy the Vampire Slayer '92▶
Captain Kronos: Vampire Hunter '74▶
Cave of the Living Dead '65
Children of the Night '92
Club Vampire '98
Cold Hearts '99
Condemned to Live '35
Count Dracula '71
Count Yorga, Vampire '70
The Craving '80
Cronos '94
Crypt of the Living Dead '73
Curse of Nostradamus '60
Curse of the Undead '59
Dance of the Damned '88
Daughters of Darkness '71▶
Day Watch '06▶
Dead Men Walk '43
Demon Queen '80
The Devil Bat '41
The Devil Bat's Daughter '46
The Devil's Wedding Night '73
Dr. Terror's House of Horrors '65
Dracula '31▶
Dracula '73
Dracula '79
Dracula (Spanish Version) '31
Dracula 2000 '00
Dracula A.D. 1972 '72
Dracula's Daughter '36▶
Dracula's Great Love '72
Dracula's Last Rites '79
Dracula's Widow '88
Dracula: Dead and Loving It '95
Dracula Has Risen from the Grave '68
Dracula Rising '93
Dracula vs. Frankenstein
Elvira, Mistress of the Dark '88
Elvira's Haunted Hills '02
Embrace of the Vampire '95
Eternal '04
Evils of the Night '85
Fangs of the Living Dead '69
The Fearless Vampire Killers '67▶
Female Vampire '73
The Forsaken '01
Fright Night '85
Fright Night 2 '88
From Dusk Till Dawn '95
From Dusk Till Dawn 2: Texas Blood Money '98
From Dusk Till Dawn 3: The Hangman's Daughter '99
Ganja and Hess '73
Genie of Darkness '62
The Girl with the Hungry Eyes '94
Grave of the Vampire '72
Graveyard Shift '87
Habit '97
Heartstopper '92
The Horror of Dracula '58▶
Horror of the Blood Monsters '70
House of Dark Shadows '70▶
House of Dracula '45
House of Frankenstein '44
The House that Dripped Blood '71
Howling 6: The Freaks '90
The Hunger '83
I, Vampiri '56
I Like Bats '85
I Married a Vampire '87
Immortality '98
Innocent Blood '92
Interview with the Vampire '94
Invasion of the Vampires '61
Isle of the Dead '45
John Carpenter's Vampires '97
Karmina '96
Karmina 2 '01
The Kiss '88
The Last Man on Earth '64
The Last Platoon '89
The League of Extraordinary Gentlemen '03
Lemora, Lady Dracula '73
Les Vampires '15▶
Let's Scare Jessica to Death '71
Life Force '85
Lips of Blood '75
The Little Vampire '00
The Lost Boys '87
The Lost Platoon '89
Love at First Bite '79
Lust for a Vampire '71
The Malibu Beach Vampires
Mark of the Vampire '35▶
Martin '77▶
Mary, Mary, Bloody Mary '76
The Midnight Hour '86
Midnight Kiss '93
Modern Vampires '98
The Monster Club '85
The Monster Demolisher '60
The Monster Squad '87
Mr. Vampire '86
My Best Friend Is a Vampire '88
My Grandpa Is a Vampire '92
My Son, the Vampire '52
Nadja '95▶
Near Dark '87▶
Nick Knight '89
Night Hunter '95
Night Junkies '07
Night of Dark Shadows '71▶
Night of the Sorcerers '70
The Night Stalker '71
Night Watch '04
Nightlife '90

Vampires

Nightmare in Blood '75
Ninja, the Violent Sorcerer '86
Nocturna '79
Nosferatu '22►
Nosferatu the Vampyre '79
Not of This Earth '88
Not of This Earth '96
Once Bitten '85
Orgy of the Vampires '73
Pale Blood '91
Planet of Blood '66
Planet of the Vampires '65
Project Vampire '93
Pulse '03
Queen of the Damned '02
Rabid '77
Red Blooded American Girl '90
The Reflecting Skin '91
The Return of Count Yorga '71
Return to the Vampire '43
Return to Salem's Lot '87
Rise: Blood Hunter '07
The Saga of the Draculas '72
Salem's Lot '79
Salem's Lot '04
Samson vs. the Vampire Women '61
The Satanic Rites of Dracula '73
The Scars of Dracula '70
Scream Blacula Scream '73
Shadow of the Vampire '00►
ShadowZone: The Undead Express '96
The Slaughter of the Vampires '62
Slayer '06
Sleepwalkers '92
Son of Dracula '43►
Sorority House Vampires '95
Stephen King's The Night Flier '96
The Thirst '06
The Thirsty Dead '74
30 Days of Night '07
To Die For '89
To Die For 2: Son of Darkness '91
To Sleep with a Vampire '92
Track of the Vampire '66
Transylvania Twist '89
Tsui Hark's Vampire Hunters '02
Twins of Evil '71
Ultraviolet '98
Uncle Was a Vampire '59
Understudy: The Graveyard Shift 2 '88
Underworld '03
Underworld: Evolution '05
The Unearthing '93
Vamp '86
The Vampire '57
Vampire Assassin '05
The Vampire at Midnight '88
The Vampire Bat '32
Vampire Circus '71
Vampire Cop '90
Vampire Effect '03
The Vampire Happening '71
The Vampire Hookers '78
Vampire in Brooklyn '95
Vampire Journals '96
The Vampire Lovers '70
The Vampire People '66
Vampire Time Travelers '98
Vampirella '96
The Vampire's Coffin '58
The Vampire's Ghost '45
Vampire's Kiss '88►
Vampyr '31►

The Vampyr '92
Vampyres '74
Van Helsing '04►
The Velvet Vampire '71
Vlad '03
The Werewolf vs. the Vampire Woman '70
The Wicked '89
Witchcraft 7: Judgement Hour '95
Zoltan... Hound of Dracula '78

Venice

see also Italy
Assassination in Rome '65
Betrayal '83
Blame It on the Bellboy '92
The Bloodstained Shadow '78
Bread and Tulips '01►
Casanova '05►
Casanova '05
The Children '90
Children of the Century '99
The Comfort of Strangers '91►
Dangerous Beauty '98►
Death in Venice '71►
Don't Look Now '73►
Eternal '04
Everyone Says I Love You '96►
A Few Days in September '06
The Honeymoon Machine '61
Indiana Jones and the Last Crusade '89►
The Italian Job '03►
The League of Extraordinary Gentlemen '03
A Little Romance '79►
Marco Polo '07
The Merchant of Venice '04►
Night Train to Venice '93
Only You '94
Othello '65►
Othello '95►
Panic Button '62
Summertime '55►
The Thief Lord '06
Tonight or Never '31
Venice, Venice '92
Walk, Don't Run '66
Who Saw Her Die? '72
The Wings of the Dove '97►

Veterans

see also Postwar
Act of Violence '48
Air Force One '97►
Alamo Bay '85
Americana '81
American Eagle '90
Anatomy of Terror '74
Angels from Hell '68
The Annihilators '85
Article 99 '92
Ashes and Embers '82
Backfire '88
Bad Company '72►
The Ballad of Andy Crocker '69
The Best Years of Our Lives '46►
A Bill of Divorcement '32
Billy Jack '71
Birds of Prey '72
Birdy '84►
The Black Six '74
Born for Hell '76
Braddock: Missing in Action 3 '88
Bug '06
The Bushwackers '52
The Cage '89
Cannibal Apocalypse '80
Cease Fire '85
Chattahoochee '89
Child Bride of Short Creek '81
Chrome Soldiers '92

Colonel Effingham's Raid '45
Combat Shock '84
Conspiracy '08
Crimson Gold '03
Cry of the Innocent '80►
Dark Before Dawn '89
Distant Thunder '88
The Enchanted Cottage '45
Fear '88
Fireback '78
First Blood '82
Fleshburn '84
Forced Vengeance '82
The Forgotten '89
Ghetto Revenge '71
G.I. Executioner '71
Going Upriver: The Long War of John Kerry '04
The Great American Broadcast '41►
The Ground Truth '06
Harsh Times '05
Heated Vengeance '87
Heroes '77
Heroes for Sale '33►
Hidden Places '06
Home of the Brave '06
House '86►
The Iceman Cometh '73
Identity Unknown '45
In a Shallow Grave '88
In Country '89
The Jacket '05
Jud '71
Jungle Assault '89
Kill Alex Kill '76
Killcrazy '89
The Killer's Edge '90
Killzone '85
Land of Plenty '04
Last Mercenary '84
Lethal Weapon '87►
Liberty & Bash '90
The Line '80
The Manchurian Candidate '04►
Memorial Day '83
Mr. Majestyk '74
Moon in Scorpio '86
The Park Is Mine '85
Rambo 3 '88►
Red, White & Busted '75
Ride in a Pink Car '74
Riders of the Storm '88
Robbery '85
Rolling Thunder '77
Savage Dawn '84
Scent of a Woman '92►
Shark River '53
Shooter '07
Skin Art '93
Soldier's Revenge '84
Stand Alone '85
Stanley '72
Steele Justice '87
Tagget '90
To Heal a Nation '88
To Kill a Clown '72
Tracks '76
The War '94
The War at Home '96
Who'll Stop the Rain? '78►
The Woman Inside '83

Veterinarians

see also Cats; Doctors & Nurses; Farm Livin'; King of Beasts (Dogs)
Baby Boom '87
Bark! '02
Beethoven '92
Cape of Good Hope '04
Doctor Dolittle '67
Dr. Dolittle '98
Dr. Dolittle 2 '01
Dr. Dolittle 3 '06
Dr. Dolittle 4: Tail to the Chief '08
50 First Dates '04
Garfield: The Movie '04
The Three Lives of Thomasina '63►
Turner and Hooch '89

Videogames

Cloak & Dagger '84
Evolver '94
The 40 Year Old Virgin '05►
Grandma's Boy '06
The King of Kong: A Fistful of Quarters '07
The Last Starfighter '84
Police Academy 7: Mission to Moscow '94
Stay Alive '06
Tron '82
WarGames '83
The Wizard '89

Vietnam War

see also Postwar; POW/MIA
Air America '90
American Commandos '84
Americana '81
The Annihilators '85
Apocalypse Now '79►
Ashes and Embers '82
The Ballad of Andy Crocker '69
Bat 21 '88
The Beautiful Country '04
Beyond the Call of Duty '92
Birdy '84►
The Black Six '74
Born on the Fourth of July '89►
The Boys in Company C '77
The Boys of 2nd Street Park '03►
Braddock: Missing in Action 3 '88
A Bright Shining Lie '98
Cactus in the Snow '72
Cannibal Apocalypse '80
Casualties of War '89►
Cease Fire '85
Charlie Bravo '80
The Children of An Lac '80
China Beach '88►
China Gate '57►
Combat Shock '84
Coming Home '78►
Commando Invasion '87
Conspiracy: The Trial of the Chicago Eight '87►
Crossfire '89
Dead Presidents '95
Deathdream '72
The Deer Hunter '78►
The Deserters '83
Dogfight '91►
Don't Cry, It's Only Thunder '82
Eastern Condors '87
84 Charlie MoPic '89►
Explosion '69
Eye of the Eagle '87
Eye of the Eagle 2 '89
Eye of the Eagle 3 '91
Fatal Mission '89
Fear '88
Fighting Mad '77
Firehawk '92
First Blood '82
Fist of Glory '95
Flight of the Intruder '90
The Fog of War: Eleven Lessons from the Life of Robert S. McNamara '03►
For the Boys '91
The Forgotten '89
Forgotten Warrior '86
Forrest Gump '94►
Four Friends '81►
Friendly Fire '79►
Full Metal Jacket '87►
Gardens of Stone '87
Ghetto Revenge '71
Going Upriver: The Long War of John Kerry '04
Good Morning, Vietnam '87►
The Green Berets '68
Green Eyes '76►
Hail, Hero! '69
Hair '79►
Hamburger Hill '87
Hanoi Hilton '87
The Hard Ride '71

Heated Vengeance '87
Heaven and Earth '93
In Country '89
In Gold We Trust '91
In Love and War '91
In the Lake of the Woods '96
The Iron Triangle '89
Jacknife '89►
Jacob's Ladder '90
Jenny '70
Jud '71
Jungle Assault '89
Kent State '81
The Killing Fields '84►
Kissinger and Nixon '96
Lady from Yesterday '85
Last Flight Out: A True Story '90
The Last Hunter '80
Memorial Day '83
Missing Brendan '03
Missing in Action '84
Missing in Action 2: The Beginning '85
More American Graffiti '79
Nam Angels '88
Night Wars '88
1969 '89►
No Dead Heroes '87
The Odd Angry Shot '79
Off Limits '87
Operation C.I.A. '65
Operation Dumbo Drop '95
Operation 'Nam '85
Operation Warzone '89
Ordinary Heroes '85
Platoon '86►
Platoon Leader '87
P.O.W. Deathcamp '89
The P.O.W. Escape '86
Primary Target '89
Private War '90
Purple Hearts '84
Rambo: First Blood, Part 2 '85
Rambo 3 '88►
Red, White & Busted '75
Rescue Dawn '06►
Return of the Secaucus 7 '80►
Ride in a Pink Car '74
Rolling Thunder '77
A Rumor of War '80►
Running on Empty '88►
Saigon Commandos '88
Saigon: Year of the Cat '87
Search and Destroy '81
The Siege of Firebase Gloria '89
The '60s '99
Skin Art '93
Soldier's Change '06
Soldier's Revenge '84
A Soldier's Sweetheart '98
Some Kind of Hero '82
Streamers '83
Strike Commando '87
Summertree '71
Thou Shalt Not Kill...Except '87
The 317th Platoon '65►
Tigerland '00►
To Heal a Nation '88
To the Shores of Hell '65
Tornado '83
Tour of Duty '87
Trial of the Catonsville Nine '72
Twilight's Last Gleaming '77
Uncommon Valor '83
Under Heavy Fire '01
Unnatural Causes '86►
The Veteran '06
The Walking Dead '94
The War '94
The War '99
The War at Home '96
Warbus '85
Wardogs '87
We Were Soldiers '02►
Welcome Home '89
When Hell Was in Session '82►
Which Way Home '90
White Badge '92
White Badge '97
Winner Takes All '84

Woodstock '70►

Vigilantes

see also Revenge
After Hours '85►
American Commandos '84
The Avenging Angel '95
Best of the Best 3: No Turning Back '95
Black Fox: Blood Horse '94
Boondock Saints '99
The Brave One '07
Brutal Fury '92
Bunny Whipped '06
Combat Shock '84
Dark Angel: The Ascent '94
Dark Justice '00
Death Sentence '07
The Death Squad '73
Death Wish '74
Death Wish 2 '82
Death Wish 3 '85
Death Wish 5: The Face of Death '94
Defiance '79
The Devil's Rejects '05
Dirty Harry '71►
Double Bang '01
Double Tap '98
DROP Squad '94
Elektra '05
An Eye for an Eye '95
Falling Down '93
Force Five '75
Gang Boys '97
The Gunman '03
Hard Candy '06
Jimmy Hollywood '94
Keeper of the City '92
Land of Plenty '04
Latin Dragon '03
Mystic River '03►
One Man Jury '78
Original Gangstas '96
Out for Blood '93
Outlaw '07
The Outlaw Josey Wales '76►
Outrage '98
Paparazzi '04
Prey of the Jaguar '96
The Punisher '90
The Punisher '04
Quiet Cool '86
Ransom '96►
Raw Deal '86
Red Riding Hood '03
Rogue Force '99
Self-Defense '83
Shadows and Fog '92►
Skins '02
SnakeEater '98
SnakeEater 2: The Drug Buster '89
The Sniper '78
Soldier of the Night '84
Steele Justice '87
The Stranger Wore a Gun '53
Street Corner Justice '96
Street Hunter '90
Swordfish '01
Sworn to Justice '97
Target Eagle '84
Taxi Driver '76►
This Is Not a Love Song '02
To Protect and Serve '92
Trespasses '86
When Justice Fails '98
When the Bullet Hits the Bone '96
Zebra Force '76

Vikings

Erik, the Viking '65
The Island at the Top of the World '74
The Long Ships '64
Pathfinder '87►
Pathfinder '07
Royal Deceit '94
The 13th Warrior '99

► = *rated three bones or higher*

Virtual Reality
see also Computers;
Technology—Rampant

Arcade '93
Brainstorm '83
Caver's Gate '96
Conceiving Ada '97
Cyber Bandits '94
Cybercity '99
Darkdrive '98
eXistenZ '99
Future Shock '93
Gamebox 1.0 '04
Hologram Man '95
How to Make a Monster '01
The Lawnmower Man '92
The Lawnmower Man 2: Beyond
Cyberspace '95
Looker '81
The Matrix '99
The Matrix Reloaded '03
The Matrix Revolutions '03
Megaville '91
Subterano '01
TekWar '94
Terminal Justice: Cybertech
P.D. '95
The Thirteenth Floor '99
Thomas in Love '01
Total Recall 2070 Machine
Dreams '99
Venus Rising '95
Virtual Assassin '95
Virtual Combat '95
Virtual Desire '95
Virtual Encounters '96
Virtual Girl '00
Virtual Seduction '96
Virtual Sexuality '99
Virtuosity '95
Wild Palms '93

Viva Las Vegas!
see also Gambling

Austin Powers: International
Man of Mystery '97
Bachelor Party Vegas '05
Beautiful Joe '00
Beavis and Butt-Head Do
America '96
Beyond Desire '94
Beyond the Sea '04
The Bible and Gun Club '96
Big Shot: Confessions of a
Campus Bookie '02
Blackjack '78
Bodily Harm '95
Bogus '96
Casino '95
The Center of the World '01
Con Air '97
Cool World '92
The Cooler '03
Corvette Summer '78
Crazy in Alabama '99
Dance with Me '96
Destination Vegas '95
Destiny Turns on the Radio
'95
Diamonds Are Forever '71
Dodgeball: A True
Underdog Story '04
Elvis Has Left the Building
'04
Fear and Loathing in Las
Vegas '98
Feeling Minnesota '96
The Flintstones in Viva Rock
Vegas '00
Fools Rush In '97
For Which He Stands '58
Gamble on Love '86
Get Shorty '95
The Girl Next Door '04
Girls' Night '97
Go '99
The Great White Hype '96
Happily Ever After '82
Hard Vice '94
Heat '87
Heaven or Vegas '98
Hell Squad '85
High Stakes '93
Honey, I Blew Up the Kid '92
Honeymoon in Vegas '92
I Shot a Man in Vegas '96

Indecent Proposal '93
Jinxed '82
Jocks '87
Kingpin '96
Kiss Me, Stupid! '64
Lady Cocoa '75
Las Vegas Hillbillys '66
Las Vegas Lady '86
Las Vegas Serial Killer '76
The Las Vegas Story '52
Las Vegas Weekend '85
Leaving Las Vegas '95
Leprechaun 3 '95
Looney Tunes: Back in
Action '03
Lucky You '07
Luckytown '00
The Marrying Man '91
Meet Me in Las Vegas '56
The Mexican '01
Miss Congeniality 2: Armed
and Fabulous '05
My Blueberry Nights '07
Nature of the Beast '94
The Night Stalker '71
Ocean's 11 '60
Ocean's Eleven '01
The Offspring '87
Play It to the Bone '99
Rain Man '88▶
The Rat Pack '98
Rat Race '01
Rock-a-Doodle '92
R.S.V.P. '02
The Runner '99
Rush Hour 2 '01
The Showgirl Murders '95
Showgirls '95
Sister Act '92
Six-String Samurai '98
Sparkler '99
Speedway '68
Starman '84▶
Stripshow '95
Sugartime '95
Swingers '96▶
Sword of Honor '94
Texas Payback '95
3000 Miles to Graceland '01
Tomcats '01
Tricks '97
21 '08
Two for the Money '05
Up Against the Eight Ball '04
Vampirella '96
The Vegas Strip Wars '84
Vegas Vacation '96
Vegas Vice '94
Very Bad Things '98
Viva Las Vegas '63
Wedding Bell Blues '96
What Happens in Vegas '08
The Wild Card '03
The Winner '96

Volcanoes
see also Disaster Flicks

Dante's Peak '97
The Devil at 4 O'Clock '61
Joe Versus the Volcano '90
Last Days of Pompeii '35
The Last Days of Pompeii
'62▶
Magma: Volcanic Disaster
'06
My Date with the President's
Daughter '98
St. Helen's, Killer Volcano
'82
Volcano '97
Volcano: Fire on the
Mountain '97
Waikiki Wedding '37▶
When Time Ran Out '80

Volleyball

Air Bud 5: Buddy Spikes
Back '03
Cast Away '00▶
Meet the Parents '00▶
Side Out '90
South Beach Academy '96
Superdad '73
Top Gun '86

Vote for Me!
see also Capitol Capers

All the King's Men '06
The Big Brass Ring '99
Bobby '06
Bulworth '98▶
The Candidate '72▶
The Contract '98
Definitely, Maybe '08▶
Election '99▶
Hard to Kill '89
Head of State '03
Homicide: The Movie '00
If I'm Lucky '46
JFK: Reckless Youth '93
The Last Debate '00
Life Begins at Forty '35
Mail to the Chief '00
Man in Manhattan '02
Malibu's Most Wanted '03
The Manchurian Candidate
'62▶
Me & Mrs. Jones '02
Menno's Mind '96
My Date with the President's
Daughter '98
The Palermo Connection
'91
Poster Boy '04
Primary Colors '98
Race '99
Random Hearts '99
Running Mates '00
The Seduction of Joe Tynan
'79
Slow Burn '05
Southland Tales '06
Swing Vote '08
An Unreasonable Man '06▶
Waking the Dead '00

Voodoo
see also Occult

Angel Heart '87
Asylum '72
Black Devil Doll from Hell
'84
Black Magic Woman '91
Blues Brothers 2000 '98
Caribe '87
Curse 3: Blood Sacrifice '90
Curtis's Charm '96
The Devil's Daughter '39
Dr. Terror's House of
Horrors '65
Eve's Bayou '97▶
Headhunter '89
The House on Skull
Mountain '74
Household Saints '93▶
I Eat Your Skin '64
I Walked with a Zombie '43▶
Jungle Drums of Africa '53
Live and Let Die '73
London Voodoo '04
Macumba Love '60
Marked for Death '90
Plague of the Zombies '66
The Possession of Joel
Delaney '72
Scared Stiff '87
Scream Blacula Scream '73
The Serpent and the
Rainbow '87▶
Shrunken Heads '94
The Snake People '68
Tales from the Hood '95
Theatre of Death '67
Venom '05
Voodoo '95
Voodoo Academy '00
Voodoo Black Exorcist '73
Voodoo Dawn '89
Voodoo Dawn '99
Weekend at Bernie's 2 '93

Wagon Train
see also Military; Westerns

Across the Plains '39
Bend of the River '52▶
Big Trail '30▶
Covered Wagon Trails '40
Dawn on the Great Divide
'42
Donner Pass: The Road to
Survival '84
The Hallelujah Trail '65
The Indian Fighter '55▶
The Painted Stallion '37
Roi, Wagons, Roi '39
September Dawn '07
Silverado '85▶
Soleris '02
Thunder Trail '37
Time to Leave '05▶
Untamed Heart '93
Wagon Master '50▶
The Waiting Game '99
Wagon Wheels '34
Wagons East '94
Wagons West '35
Westward Ho '35

Waiters &
Waitresses

About Adam '00
Alice Doesn't Live Here
Anymore '74
Along Came Polly '04
Amelie '01▶
Anything But Love '02
As Good As It Gets '97▶
Arthur '81▶
Ask the Dust '06
Atlantic City '81▶
Avenue Montaigne '06
Battle Shock '56
Bikini Bistro '94
Broken English '96
Bug '06
Cafe Romeo '91
Celebrity '98▶
Code Name: The Cleaner
'07
Coffee and Cigarettes '03▶
Come Back to the Five &
Dime, Jimmy Dean, Jimmy
Dean '82▶
The Cooler '03▶
Coyote Ugly '00
Dancer, Texas—Pop. 81
'98▶
Dream for an insomniac '96
Duets '00
East Side Story '07
The Embalmer '03▶
Exiled in America '90
Eye of God '97▶
Fear and Loathing in Las
Vegas '98
Feeling Minnesota '96
Five Easy Pieces '70▶
The 4th Tenor '02
Frankie and Johnny '91▶
Gloomy Sunday '02▶
Hard Eight '96▶
Heavy '94▶
Highway Hitcher '98
Hysterical Blindness '02
It Could Happen to You '94
Joey Breaker '93▶
Jon Jost's Frameup '93
Just a Kiss '02
Love on the Side '04
The Machinist '04
Million Dollar Baby '04▶
Monster's Ball '01▶
Moon over Miami '41▶
The Muppets Take
Manhattan '84▶
My Blueberry Nights '07
Mystic Pizza '88▶
No Looking Back '98
Nurse Betty '00▶
Office Space '99
Player '97
The Postman Always Rings
Twice '46▶
The Postman Always Rings
Twice '81
Pure Danger '96

The Purple Rose of Cairo
'85▶
Quiet Days in Hollywood '97
Restaurant '98
Return to Me '00
The Runner '99
Salem's Lot '04
A Season for Miracles '99
Sex and Lucia '01
Skipped Parts '00
Sliding Doors '97
Spare Me '92
The Spitfire Grill '95
A Summer's Tale '96
Swimming '00
Thelma & Louise '91▶
Time to Leave '05▶
Untamed Heart '93
Waiting '05
Waiting '00
The Waiting Game '99
Waitress '81
Waitress '07▶
Wedding Daze '06
The Wedding Singer '97
White Palace '90
Willa '79
Wisegirls '02

War Between the
Sexes
see also Divorce;
Marriage; Singles

About Last Night... '86▶
Adam's Rib '50▶
The African Queen '51▶
All of Me '84▶
All That '92
Ali's Fair '89
Alternative '76
Always '85▶
America 3000 '86
Anchorman: The Legend of
Ron Burgundy '04
Annie Hall '77▶
Around the World Under the
Sea '65
Autumn Marathon '79
The Awful Truth '37▶
The Ballad of the Sad Cafe
'91
Bare Essentials '91
Basic Training '86
Battle of the Sexes '60
Behind Office Doors '31
The Best Intentions '92▶
Beware of Pity '46
The Bigamist '53
Blood and Sand '41▶
The Bodyguard '92
Bonnie's Kids '73
Boomerang '92
The Bride Walks Out '36
Bringing Up Baby '38▶
Buffalo Jump '90▶
Bull Durham '88▶
Cannibal Women in the
Avocado Jungle of Death
'89
Carmen '83▶
Carmen Jones '54▶
Carrington, V.C. '54▶
Carry On Nurse '59
Casablanca '42▶
Casanova's Big Night '54
Castaway '87
Casual Sex? '88
Chained '34
Cold Heat '90
Concrete Beat '84
Cruel Intentions '98
The Cry of the Owl '87
The Cutting Edge '92
Dangerous Liaisons '88▶
Dating the Enemy '95
Dear Murderer '47
Dear Wife '49
Def Jam's How to Be a
Player '97
Designing Woman '57▶
Disclosure '94
Divorce His, Divorce Hers
'72
Divorce—Italian Style '62▶
Dogfight '91▶

Don Juan, My Love '90
Easy Wheels '89
Far and Away '92
The Favor '92
The Female Bunch '69
Fever '91
The Fighting Sheriff '31
The First to Go '97
The First Wives Club '96
First Monday in October '81▶
Forever Fabulous '56
Forget Paris '95
Frankie and Johnny '91▶
A Girl in a Million '46
Gone with the Wind '39▶
The Good Father '87▶
Goodbye Love '34
Guarding Tess '94
The Happy Ending '69
Hardhat & Legs '80
Having It All '82
He Said, She Said '91
Hearing Voices '90
Heartburn '86▶
His Girl Friday '40▶
Hot Summer '68
Hotel Room '93
Housesitter '92
I Live My Life '35
I Love All of You '83
I Love My... Wife '70
I Love Trouble '94
I Love You '81
In the Good Old
Summertime '49▶
In the Line of Fire '93▶
Intimate Story '81
Irreconcilable Differences
'84
It Happened One Night '34▶
The Jewel of the Nile '85
Juliet of the Spirits '65▶
June Bride '48▶
Just Tell Me What You Want
'80
Kay Exchange '65
The King and I '56▶
Kiss Me Kate '53▶
Kramer vs. Kramer '79▶
La Discrete '90▶
The Lady Says No '51
The Last Woman on Earth
'61
Le Chat '75▶
Legion of Iron '90
Letters to an Unknown
Lover '84
Lily in Love '84
The Lion in Winter '68▶
Love Crazy '41▶
Love in the Afternoon '57
Love Nest '51
Lover Come Back '61
Loyalties '86
Lucky Partners '40
Man of Destiny '73
The Man Who Guards the
Greenhouse '88
Maria's Lovers '84
The Marriage of Maria
Braun '79▶
The Marrying Man '91
A Matter of Love '78
Maverick '94▶
McLintock! '63▶
Men... '85▶
A Midsummer Night's
Dream '35
A Midsummer Night's
Dream '99
A Midsummer Night's
Dream '96
Moonlighting '85
Moonstruck '87▶
Mortal Thoughts '91
Much Ado about Nothing
'93▶
Murphy's Law '86
My Brilliant Career '79▶
Near Misses '91
A New Leaf '71▶
9 to 5 '80▶
Nothing in Common '86
One Woman or Two '86
The Opposite Sex and How
to Live With Them '93
Pajama Tops '83
Pat and Mike '52▶

▶ = rated three bones or higher

Patti Rocks '88
Pauline at the Beach '83▲
A Piece of Pleasure '74▲
Pillow Talk '59
Places in the Heart '84▲
Portrait of Teresa '79▲
The Practice of Love '84
Private Lives '31▲
Prizzi's Honor '85▲
Public Enemy '31▲
Queen of Outer Space '58
Question of Silence '83▲
The Quiet Man '52▲
Ramrod '47
The Ref '93▲
Romancing the Stone '84▲
Rooster Cogburn '75
Running Mates '92▲
Sabrina '54▲
Sabrina '95
Scenes from a Mall '91
Seance on a Wet Afternoon '64▲
The Sensual Man '74
Sex and the College Girl '64
She-Devil '89
Shore Leave '25▲
Siberian Lady Macbeth '61▲
The Single Standard '29
The Social Secretary '16
Solitaire for 2 '94
Someone Like You '01
Sotto, Sotto '85
Speechless '94
Speedtrap '78
Spies, Lies and Naked Thighs '91
Star 80 '83
The Story of Fausta '88
Summer Night with Greek Profile, Almond Eyes & Scent of Basil '87
Swept Away '02
Switch '91
Switching Channels '88
The Taming of the Shrew '29
The Taming of the Shrew '67▲
A Taxing Woman '87▲
Teacher's Pet '58
Ted & Venus '93
That Old Feeling '96
That's My Baby! '88
Thelma & Louise '91▲
The Thing '51▲
Thor and the Amazon Women '60
Tony Draws a Horse '51
True Love '89▲
Two-Faced Woman '41
Two Weeks Notice '02
Vasectomy: A Delicate Matter '86
War Between the Tates '76
The War of the Roses '89▲
When Harry Met Sally... '89▲
When Ladies Meet '41
When Women Lost Their Tails '75
Who's Afraid of Virginia Woolf? '66▲
Wife Versus Secretary '36▲
The Witches of Eastwick '87
Without Love '45
A Woman of Distinction '50
Woman of the Year '42▲
Women & Men: In Love '91
Women & Men: Stories of Seduction '90
Women on the Verge of a Nervous Breakdown '88▲
Women vs. Men '02
The World According to Garp '82▲
Year of the Comet '92
Yesterday, Today and Tomorrow '64▲

Your Friends & Neighbors '98▲
You're a Big Boy Now '66▲

War, General

see also Anti-War War Movies; Big Battles; Civil War; Korean War; Persian Gulf/Iraq War; Postwar; POW/MIA; Revolutionary War; Terrorism; Veterans; Vietnam War; World War I; World War II

The Alamo '60▲
The Alamo: Thirteen Days to Glory '87
Alexander '04
Alexander Nevsky '38▲
Alexander the Great '55
Alone Against Rome '62
Alsino and the Condor '82▲
And Starring Pancho Villa as Himself '03
Anna Karenina '48
Atlas '61
The Avenger '62
Ay, Carmela! '90▲
Ballad of a Soldier '60▲
Bang Rajan '00▲
Barb Wire '96
Battle Hell '56
The Battle of Algiers '66▲
The Battle of Austerlitz '60
The Beast '88▲
Beau Geste '39▲
Before the Rain '94▲
Behind the Front '26
The Bitter Tea of General Yen '33▲
Blood Diamond '06▲
Braveheart '95▲
Brothers '05▲
The Buccaneer '58
A Bullet for the General '68▲
By Dawn's Early Light '89▲
Captain Caution '40
Captain Horatio Hornblower '51▲
Carthage in Flames '60
Cast a Giant Shadow '66
Cavalry Command '63
Chapayev '34▲
Civilization '16▲
Codename: Terminate '90
Colonel Chabert '94▲
Colonel Wolodyjowski '69
The Conqueror '56
Conquest of the Normans '62
Control Room '04▲
Coup de Grace '78
The Court Martial of Billy Mitchell '55▲
Cromwell '70▲
Cup Final '92▲
Danton '82▲
Days of Hell '84
Deadline '87▲
The Deluge '73
The Desert of the Tartars '76
Devil Wears White '86
Distant Drums '51
Dragon Seed '44
Eagles Attack at Dawn '70
1860 '33▲
El Cid '61▲
El Paso Stampede '53
Elizabeth of Ladymead '48
Emissary '89
The Enchanted Cottage '45
The End of St. Petersburg '27▲
The Expendables '89
Fahrenheit 9/11 '04▲
The Fall of the Roman Empire '64▲
Field of Honor '87
Fiesta '95
The Fighter '52
Fighting Marines '36
Fighting Pilot '35

The Fighting Prince of Donegal '66
The Finest Hour '91
Fire Over England '37▲
The Firing Line '91
Flor Silvestre '58
Flowers of Reverie '84
Forever and a Day '43
Fort Apache '48▲
Forty Days of Musa Dagh '85
The Four Feathers '39▲
The Four Feathers '78
F.P. 1 '33
Funny, Dirty Little War '83▲
Guerilla Brigade '39
Gunga Din '39▲
Gunner Palace '04▲
Guns at Batasi '64
Hail the Conquering Hero '44▲
Harry's War '84
Heart of a Nation '43
Heartbreak Ridge '86▲
Hearts & Armour '83
Heaven & Earth '90
Hell in the Pacific '69▲
Hell on the Battleground '88
Hell Raiders '68
Henry V '89▲
Hero Bunker '71
The Hidden Fortress '58▲
Hijacking Catastrophe: 9/11, Fear and the Selling of America '04
Hill 24 Doesn't Answer '55
Hollow City '04
The Holy Terror '37
Holy Terror '65
Hombres Armados '97▲
Homecoming '28
Hotel Rwanda '04▲
House of Fools '02
How I Won the War '67
Howl's Moving Castle '04▲
In the Name of the Pope-King '85▲
The Informer '35▲
Innocent Voices '04
The Invincible Gladiator '63
Jarhead '05▲
Johnny Got His Gun '71▲
Judith of Bethulia '14▲
Khartoum '66
Killers '88
King Arthur '04
Kingdom of Heaven '05▲
Kippur '00▲
Kolberg '45▲
La Marseillaise '37
La Nuit de Varennes '82▲
The Last Command '55
The Last of the Mohicans '20▲
The Last of the Mohicans '32
The Last of the Mohicans '36
The Last of the Mohicans '85
The Last of the Mohicans '92▲
The Last Valley '71
Late Summer Blues '87
Latino '85
Laughing at Life '33
Le Petit Soldat '60▲
Legion of Missing Men '37
The Life and Death of Colonel Blimp '43▲
Lion of the Desert '81▲
Lipstick on Your Collar '94
The Longest Day '62▲
The Lost Command '66
Mademoiselle Fifi '44
Man from the Alamo '53▲
Man with a Cross '43
Massive Retaliation '85
Megaforce '82
Mercenary Fighters '88
Mission Kashmir '00▲
Mission to Glory '80
The Mongols '60
The Moonraker '58
Mother '26▲
The Mouse That Roared '59▲
Mulan '98▲

Napoleon '27▲
No Man's Land '01▲
Occupation: Dreamland '05▲
An Occurrence at Owl Creek Bridge/Coup de Grace '62▲
Old Gringo '89
One Night Stand '84
Orphans of the Storm '21▲
Our Music '04
Peace, Propaganda & the Promised Land '04
The Phantom Planet '61
Planet of the Apes '01
Prehistoric Bimbos in Armageddon City '93
The Pride and the Passion '57
Prisoner of the Mountains '96▲
Project: Alien '89
Purple Butterfly '03▲
Rage to Kill '88
The Rape of the Sabines '61
The Real Glory '39▲
A Reason to Live, a Reason to Die '73
The Red and the Black '57▲
The Red and the White '68▲
Red Dawn '84
Reed: Insurgent Mexico '73
Reign of Terror '49
Revenge of the Barbarians '60
Rhodes '36
Richard II '12
Richard III '95▲
Ride to Glory '71
River of Unrest '36
The Road to Guantanamo '06
Rough Riders '97▲
Ryan's Daughter '70▲
Saga of the Vagabond '59
Salome, Where She Danced '45
Sanders of the River '35▲
Senso '54▲
The Seventeenth Bride '84▲
Shake Hands with the Devil '59▲
Shake Hands With the Devil: The Journey of Romeo Dallaire '04▲
The Shame '68▲
Sharpe's Battle '94▲
Sharpe's Company '94▲
Sharpe's Eagle '93▲
Sharpe's Enemy '94▲
Sharpe's Gold '94▲
Sharpe's Honour '94▲
Sharpe's Justice '97▲
Sharpe's Legend '97▲
Sharpe's Mission '96▲
Sharpe's Regiment '96▲
Sharpe's Revenge '97▲
Sharpe's Rifles '93▲
Sharpe's Siege '96▲
Sharpe's Sword '94▲
Sharpe's Waterloo '98▲
Shot Through the Heart '98▲
Simon Bolivar '69
Sinai Commandos '68
Smugglers '75
Something of Value '57▲
South Park: Bigger, Longer and Uncut '99▲
Starship Troopers '97▲
Storm over Asia '28▲
Striker '88
Taras Bulba '62▲
This England '42
This Island '55
The 317th Platoon '65▲
Tiger Joe '85
Time to Kill '89
The Torch '50
Treasure of the Lost Desert '83
Tristan & Isolde '06
The Troubles We've Seen '94
Troy '04
Turtles Can Fly '04▲
The Ugly American '63
Ulysses' Gaze '95▲

Uncovered: The War on Iraq '04
Under Fire '83▲
The Uprising '81
Vera Cruz '53
Villa Rides '68
Voices of Iraq '04▲
Walker '87
War and Peace '56
War and Peace '68▲
War and Peace '73▲
War Bus Commando '89
Warbirds '88
Warriors '02
Waterloo '71
Weekend War '88
Welcome to Sarajevo '97▲
White Dwarf '95
Wild Geese 2 '85
Wing Commander '99
The World Owes Me a Living '47
World War III '86
Yank in Libya '42
Young Winston '72▲
Zulu Dawn '79▲

Washington, DC

see Capitol Capers

Weathermen

see also News at 11

The 4th Floor '99
Groundhog Day '93▲
L.A. Story '91▲
Lucky Numbers '00
The Perfect Storm '00
Twister '96
The Weather Man '05

Wedding Bells

see also Marriage; Otherwise Engaged; Wedding Hell

About Schmidt '02▲
After the Wedding '06▲
Aladdin and the King of Thieves '96
American Wedding '03
Anne of Green Gables: The Continuing Story '99
April's Shower '03
The Arrangement '99
The Bachelor '99
The Baxter '05
Because I Said So '07
Bend It Like Beckham '02▲
The Best Man '99▲
Betsy's Wedding '90
Blind Date '87
The Bread, My Sweet '01
The Bride Came C.O.D. '41
The Bride Walks Out '36
Buying the Cow '02
Cake '05
Chaos Theory '08
Common Ground '00
Confusion of Genders '00
Conversations with Other Women '05▲
Cowboys and Angels '00
Dan in Real Life '07
Date Bait '60
The Duke '99
Easy Money '83
8 Seconds '94
Emma '96▲
Emma '97
Esmeralda Comes by Night '98
Evening '07
Everyone Says I Love You '96▲
Fanci's Persuasion '95
Fandango '85
Fantastic Four: Rise of the Silver Surfer '07
Father of the Bride '50▲
Father of the Bride '91
Fiddler on the Roof '71▲
Foolin' Around '80
For Better and for Worse '92
Forget Paris '95
Four Weddings and a Funeral '94▲
Freaky Friday '03

Full of Life '56
Give Me a Sailor '38
The Godfather '72▲
Good Luck Chuck '07
The Groomsmen '06
Hard Promises '92
Heartbreakers '01
Holy Matrimony '94
Honeymoon in Vegas '92
House Party 3 '94
Housesitter '92
I'm with Lucy '02
Imagine Me & You '06
Intolerable Cruelty '03
It Started with Eve '41▲
Jack and Sarah '95
Jerry Maguire '96▲
The Jewel of the Nile '85
Kissing a Fool '98
Love, etc. '96
Lovers and Other Strangers '70▲
Ma Vie en Rose '97▲
Mamma Mia! '08
Margot at the Wedding '07
The Marriage of Figaro '49
The Marrying Man '91
Meet the Fockers '04
The Member of the Wedding '97
Miami Rhapsody '95
Mickey Blue Eyes '99
Minnie and Moskowitz '71
The Mirror Has Two Faces '96
Mrs. Winterbourne '96
Monsoon Wedding '01▲
Moonstruck '87▲
Murders in the Rue Morgue '32
Muriel's Wedding '94▲
My Best Friend's Wedding '97▲
My Big Fat Greek Wedding '02▲
My Favorite Wife '40▲
My First Wedding '04
Nanny McPhee '06
Neil Simon's The Odd Couple 2 '98
Nine Months '95
Notting Hill '99▲
The Nutty Professor 2: The Klumps '00
Only You '94
The Philadelphia Story '40▲
Pirates of the Caribbean: Dead Man's Chest '06
Polish Wedding '97
Prelude to a Kiss '92
The Prince & Me 2: Royal Wedding '06
Reckless: The Sequel '98▲
Revenge of the Nerds 4: Nerds in Love '94
Rhythm on the Range '36
Ride with the Devil '99▲
Roommates '95
The Roundup '41
Royal Wedding '51▲
Sex and the City: The Movie '08
She's Having a Baby '88
Sixteen Candles '84▲
The Son of the Bride '01▲
The Sound of Music '65▲
Splendor '99
Standing Still '05
Star Trek: Nemesis '02
Steel Magnolias '89▲
The Summer House '94
The Tender Trap '55
That Old Feeling '96
The 30-Foot Bride of Candy Rock '59
Three Men and a Little Lady '90
Three Smart Girls Grow Up '39▲
Tim Burton's Corpse Bride '05▲
To Each His Own '46▲
27 Dresses '08
Two Moon Junction '88
Two Weeks Notice '02
Waikiki Wedding '37▲
A Wedding '78
Wedding Band '89

▲ = rated three bones or higher

Wedding Hell

see also Marriage;
Engaged; Wedding Bells

Analyze This '98▶
Arthur '81▶
The Best Man '97
Best Men '98
The Big Day '99
Blood Bride '80
The Blood Spattered Bride
'72
The Bride '85
The Bride of Frankenstein
'35▶
Bride of Killer Nerd '91
Bride of Re-Animator '89
Bride of the Gorilla '51
Bride of the Monster '55
The Bride with White Hair
'93
The Bride Wore Black '58▶
Brides of the Beast '68
Captive '97
The Catered Affair '56▶
Cheatin' Hearts '93
Confetti '06
Contract '06
Dr. T & the Women '00▶
Feeling Minnesota '96
The Flame of New Orleans
'41▶
Forces of Nature '99
Ganja and Hess '73
The Graduate '67▶
The Hanging Garden '97
Hangman's House '28
He Knows You're Alone '60
Highway to Hell '92
Honeymoon '87
Honeymoon Killers '70▶
I Married a Monster from
Outer Space '58
I Think I Do '97
In and Out '97▶
The In-Laws '03
Kill Bill Vol. 1 '03
Kill Bill Vol. 2 '04▶
Last Lives '98
Late Marriage '01
Love Stinks '99
Meet the Parents '00▶
Monster-in-Law '05▶
My New Gun '92
Niagara '53
Norbit '07
Old School '03
The Perfect Bride '91
Riding in Cars with Boys '01
River Street '55
Runaway Bride '99▶
Saving Silverman '01
The Sweetest Thing '02
That Old Feeling '97
Tim Burton's Corpse Bride
'05▶
Tomcats '01
Trojan Eddie '96▶
True Love '86▶
28 Days '00
The Undertaker's Wedding
'97
Very Bad Things '98
The Wedding Banquet '93▶
Wedding in Blood '72
Wedding in White '72
The Wedding Planner '01
The Wedding Singer '97▶

Wedding Bell Blues '96
Wedding Crashers '05▶
The Wedding Date '05
The Wedding March '28▶
The Wedding Party '69
The Wedding Party '97
Wedding Present '36
Wedding Rehearsal '32
Wedding Wars '06
West Is West '87
When Harry Met Sally...
'89▶
Where the Heart Is '00
Where There's Life '47
The Wood '99
The World's Oldest Living
Bridesmaid '92

Werewolves

see also Metamorphosis

An American Werewolf in
London '81▶
An American Werewolf in
Paris '97
Bad Moon '96
The Beast Must Die '75
Big Fish '03▶
Blood & Chocolate '07
Blood of Dracula's Castle
'69
Bride of the Gorilla '51
Children of the Full Moon
'84
The Company of Wolves
'85▶
The Craving '80
The Creeps '97
Cry of the Werewolf '44
Curse of the Devil '73
Curse of the Queerwolf '87
The Curse of the Werewolf
'61
Cursed '04
Darkwolf '03
Deathmoon '78
Dr. Jekyll and the Wolfman
'71
Dr. Terror's House of
Horrors '65
Dog Soldiers '01
Dracula vs. Frankenstein
'69
Face of the Screaming
Werewolf '59
Frankenstein Meets the
Wolfman '42▶
Full Eclipse '93
The Fury of the Wolfman '70
Ginger Snaps '01
Ginger Snaps Back: The
Beginning '04
Ginger Snaps: Unleashed
'04
Harry Potter and the
Prisoner of Azkaban '04
Hercules, Prisoner of Evil
'64
House of Dracula '45
House of Frankenstein '44
The Howling '81▶
Howling 2: Your Sister Is a
Werewolf '85
Howling 3: The Marsupials
'87
Howling 4: The Original
Nightmare '88
Howling 6: The Freaks '90
The Howling: New Moon
Rising '95
I Was a Teenage Werewolf
'57
Legend of the Werewolf '75
The Legend of the Wolf
'75
Lone Wolf '88
Mad at the Moon '92
The Mac Monster '42
Meridian: Kiss of the Beast
'90
Monster Dog '82
The Monster Squad '87
Moon of the Wolf '72
My Mom's a Werewolf '89
Night of the Howling Beast
'75
Orgy of the Dead '65
Project Metalbeast: DNA
Overload '94
Rage of the Werewolf '99
The Rats Are Coming! The
Werewolves Are Here! '72
Return of the Vampire '43
Scream of the Wolf '74
She Wolf of London '46
Silver Bullet '85
Skinwalkers '07
The Strangers '98
Teen Wolf '85
Teen Wolf Too '87
Underworld '03
Underworld: Evolution '05
The Undying Monster '42
Van Helsing '04▶
Waxwork '88
Werewolf '95

Werewolf in a Girl's
Dormitory '61
Werewolf of London '35
Werewolf of Washington '73
The Werewolf vs. the
Vampire Woman '70
Werewolves on Wheels '71
Wilderness '96
Wolf '94
Wolf Blood '25
The Wolf Man '41▶
Wolfen '81▶
The Wolfman '82
The Wolves of Kromer '98

Western Comedy

see also Comedy;
Westerns

Adios Amigo '75
Alias Jesse James '59
Along Came Jones '45▶
The Apple Dumpling Gang
'75
The Apple Dumpling Gang
Rides Again '79
Bad Man's River '72
Ballad of Cable Hogue '70▶
Bang Bang Kid '67
The Beautiful Blonde from
Bashful Bend '49
Beyond the Trail '26▶
Blazing Saddles '74▶
Bordello '77
Border Phantom '37
Boss '74
Bowery Buckaroos '47
Branded Men '31
Bronco Billy '80
Brothers O'Toole '73
Bus Stop '56▶
Carry On Cowboy '66
Catlow '71
Check & Double Check '30
The Cherokee Kid '96
The Cheyenne Social Club
'70
The Cisco Kid '94
City Slickers '91▶
City Slickers 2: The Legend
of Curly's Gold '94
Cold Feet '89
Comancheros '70
The Cowboy Way '94
Desperate Women '78
Destry Rides Again '39▶
The Duchess and the
Dirtwater Fox '76
Ebenezer '97
800 Bullets '02
El Diablo Rides '39
Evil Roy Slade '71▶
Four Eyes and Six Guns '93
Four for Texas '63
The Frisco Kid '79
From Noon Till Three '76
Go West '40
Goin' South '78▶
Gold Raiders '51
The Good Guys and the
Bad Guys '69
Greaser's Palace '72
Great Scout & Cathouse
Thursday '76
Gun Crazy '69
The Hallelujah Trail '65
Hangman's Knot '52
Hawmps! '76
Hearts of the West '75▶
Home on the Range '04
How the West Was Fun '95
I'm from Arkansas '44
The Incredible Rocky
Mountain Race '77
The Kid Brother '27▶
Lemonade Joe '64
Life & Times of Judge Roy
Bean '72
Lighting Jack '94
Local Badman '32
Lucky Luke '94
Maverick '94
McLintock! '63▶
More Wild, Wild West '80
The Nervous Wreck '26▶
Oklahoma Is Coming! '65
The Outlaws Is Coming! '65

Over the Hill Gang '69
The Paleface '48▶
Partners '56
Pocket Money '72
Rachel and the Stranger
'48▶
Rancho Deluxe '75▶
Red Garters '54
Rhythm on the Range '36
Ride 'Em Cowboy '42▶
The Rounders '65
Ruster's Rhapsody '85
Sam Whiskey '69
The Scalphunters '68
Scandalous John '71
September Gun '83
The Shakiest Gun in the
West '68
Shame, Shame on the Bixby
Boys '82
Shanghai Knights '03
Shanghai Noon '00▶
The Sheriff of Fractured Jaw
'58
Sodbusters '94
Son of Paleface '52▶
Sons of Trinity '95
Sting of the West '72
Straight to Hell '87
Sunset '88
Support Your Local
Gunfighter '71▶
Support Your Local Sheriff
'69▶
Take Me Back to Oklahoma
'40
Texas Across the River '66
There Was a Crooked Man
'70▶
They Call Me Trinity '72
Three Godfathers '48▶
Ticket to Tomahawk '50
The Traveling Saleswomen
'50
Trinity Is Still My Name '75
Troublemakers '94
Undead or Alive '07
Under Montana Skies '30
The Villain '79
Wackiest Wagon Train in
Wagons East '94
Waterhole Number 3 '67
Way Out West '37▶
Wild & Wooly '78
Wild Horse Phantom '44
Wild Rovers '71
Wild, Wild West Revisited
'79
The Wistful Widow of
Wagon Gap '47
Yellow Hair & the Fortress
of Gold '84
Zachariah '70

Westerns

see also Sci-Fi Westerns;
Spaghetti Westerns;
Supernatural Westerns;
Western Comedy;
Westexplorers

Abilene Town '46▶
Aces and Eights '36
Aces Wild '37
Across the Line '00
Across the Plains '39
The Adventures of Gallant
Bess '48
Adventures of Red Ryder
'40
Against a Crooked Sky '75
The Alamo '60▶
The Alamo '04
Alias Billy the Kid '46
Alias John Law '35
All the Pretty Horses '00
Allegheny Uprising '39
Along the Great Divide '51
Along the Navaho Trail '45
Along the Sundown Trail '42
Alvarez Kelly '66
Ambush '50▶
Ambush at Tomahawk Gap
'53
Ambush Trail '46
American Empire '42

American Outlaws '01
Americano '55
Angel and the Badman '47▶
Animal Called Man '87
Another Man, Another
Chance '77
Another Pair of Aces: Three
of a Kind '91▶
Apache '54
Apache Blood '75
Apache Chief '50
Apache Kid's Escape '30
Apache Rose '47
Apache Uprising '66
Apache Woman '55
The Appaloosa '66
Arizona '41
Arizona Bound '41
Arizona Bushwackers '67
Arizona Cowboy '49
Arizona Days '37
Arizona Gangbusters '40
Arizona Gunfighter '37
Arizona Kid '39
Arizona Mahoney '36
Arizona Raiders '65
Arizona Roundup '42
Arizona Stagecoach '42
Arizona Terror '31
Arizona Whirlwind '44
Arrowhead '53
The Assassination of Jesse
James by the Coward
Robert Ford '07▶
At Gunpoint '55
The Avenging Angel '95
The Avenging '92
Back in the Saddle '41
Backfire '22
Bad Company '72▶
Bad Day at Black Rock '54▶
Bad Guys '79
Bad Jim '89
Bad Lands '39
Bac Man of Deadwood '41
The Badlanders '58▶
Badmen's Territory '46▶
Badmen of Nevada '33
Badmen's Territory '46▶
Ballad of a Gunfighter '64
Ballad of Gregorio Cortez
'83▶
Bandit King of Texas '49
Bandit Queen '51
The Bandits '67
Bandolero! '68
Banjo Hackett '76
Barbarosa '82▶
The Bargain '15
Baron of Arizona '51▶
Battle of Elderbush Gulch
'13
Battling Marshal '48
Battling with Buffalo Bill '31
Below the Border '42
Bells of San Angelo '47
Bells of San Fernando '47
Bells of Coronado '50
Bells of Rosarita '45
Bells of San Fernando '47
Bend of the River '52▶
Best of the Badmen '50
Between Fighting Men '32
Between God, the Devil & a
Winchester '72
Between Men '35
Beyond the Rockies '32
Big Jake '71▶
Big Show '37
The Big Sky '52▶
The Big Sombrero '49
The Big Stampede '32
Big Stakes '22
Big Trail '30▶
Billy the Kid '41
Billy the Kid in Texas '40
Billy the Kid Returns '38
Billy the Kid Trapped '42
Billy Two Hats '74
Bite the Bullet '75▶

Black Fox: The Price of
Peace '94
Black Hills '48
The Black Lash '52
Black Market Rustlers '43
Blazing Across the Pecos
'48
Blazing Guns '50
Blinc Justice '94
Blood at Sundown '58
Blood on the Moon '48▶
Bloody Trail '72
Blue Canadian Rockies '52
Blue Steel '34
Boiling Point '32
Bonanza: The Return '93
Bonanza Town '51
Boot Hill Bandits '42
Booth Hill Brigade '37
Boots & Saddles '37
Boots of Destiny '37
Border Badmen '45
Border Bandits '46
Border Caballero '36
Border Devils '32
Border Feud '47
Border Law '31
The Border Legion '40
Border Patrol '43
Border Rangers '50
Border Romance '30
Border Roundup '41
Border Shootout '90
Border Vengeance '35
Border Vigilantes '41
Borderland '37
Borderdown Gunfighters '43
Born in America '90
Boss Cowboy '35
Boss of Bullion City '41
Boss of Rawhide '44
The Bounty Man '72
Brand of Fear '45
Brand of Hate '34
Brand of the Outlaws '36
The Bravados '58▶
Breakheart Pass '76
Breed of the Border '33
Broadway to Cheyenne '32
Brokeback Mountain '05▶
Broken Arrow '50▶
Broken Lance '54▶
Broken Trail '06▶
Bronson's Revenge '72
Bronze Buckaroo '39
Brothers of the West '37
Buck and the Preacher '72▶
Buckaroo and Blue '87
Buckeye '68
Buckskin Frontier '43
Bull of the West '71
Bulldog Courage '35
Bullet Code '4C
Bullwhip '58
The Burning Hills '56
Bury Me Not on the Lone
Prairie '41
The Bushwackers '52
Butch and Sundance: The
Early Days '79
Butch Cassidy and the
Sundance Kid '69▶
Buzzy Rides the Range '40
Cahill: United States
Marshal '73
Cain's Cutthroats '71
California Joe '43
Call of the Canyon '42
Call of the Forest '49
Call of the Rockies '44
Can't Help Singing '45
Canyon Passage '46▶
Captain Apache '71
The Captive: The Longest
Drive 2 '76
Black Fox: Good Men and
Bad '94

Westerns

The Caravan Trail '46
The Cariboo Trail '50
Carson City Kid '40
Cattle Queen of Montana '54
Cavalcade of the West '36
Cavalier '31
Challenge of McKenna '70
Charro! '69
Chato's Land '71
Check Your Guns '48
Cheyenne Autumn '64
Cheyenne Kid '33
Cheyenne Rides Again '38
Cheyenne Takes Over '47
Child of the Prairie '18
The Chisholms '79
Chisum '70
The Christmas Kid '68
Chuka '67
Cimarron '31
Cimarron '60
Circle Canyon '33
Circle of Death '36
The Claim '00
Clearing the Range '31
Code of the Fearless '39
Colorado '40
Colorado Serenade '46
Colorado Sundown '52
Colt Comrades '43
Comanche Moon '08
Comanche Station '60
Comanche Territory '50
The Comancheros '61▲
Come on, Cowboys '37
Come on Danger! '32
Come on Rangers '38
Come on Tarzan '32
Conagher '91
The Concentratin' Kid '30
Conquest of Cochise '53
Convict Cowboy '95
Copper Canyon '50
Cornered '32
Coroner Creek '48
Cotter '72
Courageous Avenger '35
Cow Town '50
Cowboy '58▲
Cowboy & the Bandit '35
Cowboy & the Senorita '44
Cowboy Commandos '43
Cowboy Counselor '33
Cowboy Counselor '35
Courtin' Wildcats '29
Cowboy Millionaire '35
Cowboys from Texas '39
Coyote Trails '35
Crazy Horse and Custer: "The Untold Story" '90
The Crimson Trail '35
Crooked Trail '36
Crossfire Trail '01▲
Cry Blood, Apache '70
Culpepper Cattle Co. '72
Custer's Last Fight '12
Custer's Last Stand '36
Cyclone of the Saddle '35
Dakota '45
Dakota Incident '56
Dan Candy's Law '73
Danger Trails '35
Daniel Boone '34
Daniel Boone: Trail Blazer '56
Daring Danger '32
Dark Command '40▲
Dawn Rider '35
Days of Jesse James '39
Dead for a Dollar '70
Dead Man '95
Dead Man's Revenge '93
Dead or Alive '44
Deadly Companions '61
The Deadly Trackers '73
Deadwood '65
Deadwood Pass '33
Death of a Gunfighter '69
Death Rides the Plains '43
Death Rides the Range '40
Death Valley '46
Death Valley Manhunt '43
Death Valley Rangers '44

The Deerslayer '78
Demon for Trouble '34
The Denver & Rio Grande '51
Deputy Marshal '50
Desert Gold '36
Desert Phantom '36
Desert Snow '89
Desert Trail '35
The Desperadoes '43
Desperados '69
The Desperados '70
The Desperate Mission '60▲
The Desperate Trail '94
Devil & Leroy Basset '73
Devil Horse '32
Devil Riders '44
Devil's Canyon '53
Diamond Trail '33
The Disciple '15
Distant Drums '51
Django '68
Dodge City '39▲
Don Daredevil Rides Again '51
Donner Pass: The Road to Survival '84
Don't Fence Me In '45
The Doolins of Oklahoma '49
Doomed at Sundown '37
Down Dakota Way '49
Down in the Valley '05
Down Mexico Way '41
Down Texas Way '42
Down the Wyoming Trail '39
Drawl '81
Drift Fence '36
The Drifter '32
The Driftin' Kid '41
Driftin' River '46
Drum Beat '54
Drum Taps '33
Drums Along the Mohawk '39▲
The Dude Bandit '33
Dude Ranger '34
Duel at Diablo '66▲
Duel at Silver Creek '52
Duel in the Sun '46▲
Durango Valley Raiders '38
Dynamite and Gold '88
Dynamite Canyon '41
Dynamite Pass '50
Dynamite Ranch '32
Eagle's Wing '79
El Condor '70
El Diablo '90
El Dorado '67▲
El Paso Stampede '53
The Electric Horseman '79
Enemy of the Law '45
Everyman's Law '36
Everything That Rises '98
Extreme Prejudice '87
Eyes of Texas '48
False Colors '43
Fangs of Fate '25
Far Country '55▲
Far Frontier '48
Fargo Express '32
Fast Bullets '36
Fastest Guitar Alive '68
Fastest Gun Alive '56▲
Feud Maker '38
Feud of the Trail '37
Feud of the West '35
The Fiddlin' Buckaroo '33
The Fiend Who Walked the West '58
$50,000 Reward '25
Fight for Gold '86
The Fighter '95
Fightin' Ranch '30
Fighting Caballero '35
Fighting Champ '33
Fighting Cowboy '33
Fighting Fists of Shanghai Joe '65
Fighting Fool '32
Fighting Jack '26
The Fighting Kentuckian '49
The Fighting Legion '30
The Fighting Marshal '32
Fighting Parson '35
The Fighting Redhead '50
Fighting Renegade '39
Fighting Shadows '35

The Fighting Sheriff '31
The Fighting Stallion '26▲
Fighting Texans '33
Fighting Thru '30
Fighting Valley '43
Fighting Vigilantes '47
Fighting with Kit Carson '33
Finger on the Trigger '65
Firecreek '68
Five Card Stud '68
Flame of the Barbary Coast '45
Flaming Bullets '45
Flaming Frontiers '38
Flaming Lead '39
Flaming Star '60▲
Flesh and the Spur '57
Forbidden Trails '41
Forlorn River '37
Fort Apache '48▲
Forty Guns '57
Four Faces West '48
Four Rode Out '69
Frank and Jesse '94
Frontier Days '34
Frontier Fugitives '45
Frontier Horizon '35
Frontier Justice '35
Frontier Law '43
Frontier Outlaws '44
Frontier Pony Express '39
Frontier Scout '38
Frontier Uprising '61
Frontier Vengeance '40
The Frontiersmen '38
The Fugitive: Taking of Luke McVane '15
Fugitive Valley '41
The Gallant Fool '33
Galloping Dynamite '37
Galloping Romeo '33
The Gambler Returns: The Luck of the Draw '93
The Gambling Terror '37
The Gambling Man '56
Gangster's Den '45
Gangsters of the Frontier '44
Garden of Evil '54
The Gatling Gun '72
Gaucho Serenade '40
The Gay Ranchero '42
Gentle Savage '73
The Gentleman from California '37
Gentleman from Dixie '41
Gentleman from Texas '46
The Gentleman Killer '69
Geronimo '62
Geronimo: An American Legend '93
Geronimo's Revenge '60
Get That Girl '32
Ghost City '32
Ghost Rider '35
Ghost Rider '43
Ghost Town '37
Ghost Town '88
Ghost Town Gold '36
Ghost Town Law '42
Ghost Town Renegades '47
Ghost Town Riders '38
Ghost Valley '32
Girl of the Golden West '38
Git Along Little Dogies '37
God's Country and the Man '37
God's Gun '75
The Golden Stallion '49
Gone with the West '72
Good Day for a Hanging '58
A Good Day to Die '95
The Good Old Boys '95
Gore Vidal's Billy the Kid '89
Grand Canyon Trail '48
Grayeagle '77
Great Day in the Morning '56
The Great Gundown '75
Great Jesse James Raid '49
Great Missouri Raid '51
The Great Northfield Minnesota Raid '72
Great Treasure Hunt '72
Gun Code '40
Gun Fury '53
Gun Glory '57
Gun Girl '36
Gun Law '33

Gun Lords of Stirrup Basin '37
Gun Packer '38
The Gun Ranger '34
Gun Play '36
Gun Riders '69
Gun Smoke '31
A Gunfight '71
The Gunfight at Dodge City '59
Gunfight at the O.K. Corral '57▲
The Gunfighter '50▲
Gunfighter '98
The Gunfighters '87
Gunfighter's Moon '96
Gunfire '50
Gunman from Bodie '41
Gunman's Walk '58
Gunners & Guns '34
Gunplay '51
Guns for Dollars '73
Guns in the Dark '37
Guns of Diablo '64
Guns of Fury '49
Guns of Justice '50
Guns of the Law '44
Guns of the Magnificent Seven '69
Gunslinger's Revenge '98
Gunsmoke '53
Gunsmoke: Return to Dodge '87
Gunsmoke Trail '38
The Half-Breed '51
Hands Across the Border '43
The Hanged Man '74
The Hanging Tree '59▲
Hannie Caulder '72
Hard Bounty '94
Hard Hombre '31
Harlem on the Prairie '38
Harlem Rides the Range '39
Harry Tracy '83
The Harvey Girls '46▲
Haunted Gold '32
Haunted Ranch '43
Hawaiian Buckaroo '38
The Hawk of Powder River '48
Hawken's Breed '87
Headin' for the Rio Grande '36
Heart of Texas Ryan '17
Heart of the Golden West '42
Heart of the Rio Grande '42
Heart of the Rockies '37
Heart of the Rockies '51
Heaven's Gate '81
Hell Fire Austin '32
Helldorado '46
Heller in Pink Tights '60
Hellfire '48
Hello Trouble '32
Hell's Hinges '16
Helltown '38
Heritage of the Desert '33
Heroes of the Alamo '37
Heroes of the Hills '38
Hidden Gold '33
Hidden Guns '56
Hidden Valley '32
High Lonesome '50
High Noon '52▲
High Noon '00
High Noon: Part 2 '80
High Plains Drifter '73
Hills of Oklahoma '50
Hills of Utah '51
Hired Hand '71
His Brother's Ghost '45
Hit the Saddle '37
Hittin' the Trail '37
Hole in the Sky '95
Hombre '67▲
Home in Oklahoma '47
Homesteaders of Paradise Valley '47
Honor of the Range '34
Hopalong Cassidy '35▲
Hopalong Cassidy: Borrowed Trouble '48
Hopalong Cassidy: Dangerous Venture '48
Hopalong Cassidy: False Paradise '48

Hopalong Cassidy: Hoppy's Holiday '47
Hopalong Cassidy: Renegade Trail '39
Hopalong Cassidy Returns '36
Hopalong Cassidy: Riders of the Deadline '43
Hopalong Cassidy: Silent Conflict '48
Hopalong Cassidy: Sinister Journey '48
Hopalong Cassidy: The Dead Don't Dream '48
Hopalong Cassidy: The Devil's Playground '46
Hopalong Cassidy: The Marauders '47
Hopalong Cassidy: Unexpected Guest '47
Hoppy Serves a Writ '43
Horizons West '52
Hostile Guns '67
Hot Lead '51
Hour of the Gun '67
How the West Was Won '63▲
Hurricane Express '32
I Shot Billy the Kid '50
I Shot Jesse James '49▲
I Will Fight No More Forever '75▲
Idaho '43
In Old Caliente '39
In Old California '42
In Old Cheyenne '41
In Old Colorado '41
In Old Montana '39
In Old Santa Fe '34
In the Days of the Thundering Herd & the Law & the Outlaw '14
The Indian Fighter '55▲
Indian Paint '64
Indian Uprising '51
Invitation to a Gunfighter '64
The Iron Horse '24▲
Iron Mountain Trail '53
The Ivory Handled Gun '35
The Jack Bull '99
The Jayhawkers '59
Jeepers Creepers '39
Jeremiah Johnson '72▲
Jericho '01
Jesse James '39▲
Jesse James at Bay '41
Jesse James Rides Again '47
Jesse James Under the Black Flag '21
Joe Kidd '72
Johnny Reno '66
Johnson County War '02
Jory '72
Joshua '76
Jubal '56▲
Jubilee Trail '54
Junior Bonner '72▲
Justice of the West '61
Justice Rides Again '32
The Kansan '43
Kansas Pacific '53
The Kansas Terrors '39
Keep the Change '92
Kenny Rogers as the Gambler '80
Kenny Rogers as the Gambler, Part 2: The Adventure Continues '83
Kenny Rogers as the Gambler, Part 3: The Legend Continues '87
The Kentuckian '55
Kentucky Rifle '55
Kid Courageous '35
Kid from Gower Gulch '50
Kid Ranger '36
Kid Vengeance '75
Kid's Last Ride '41
The King and Four Queens '56
King of Texas '02▲
King of the Bullwhip '51
King of the Cowboys '43
King of the Grizzlies '69
King of the Pecos '36
King of the Rodeo '28
King of the Sierras '38

King of the Stallions '42
King of the Texas Rangers '41
King of the Wild Horses '24▲
Kit Carson '40
Knights of the Range '40
The Lamb '15
Land of Hunted Men '43
Land of the Lawless '47
Laramie Kid '35
Last Raiders '69
Larry McMurtry's Dead Man's Walk '96
Larry McMurtry's Streets of Laredo '95▲
Last Bullet '50
The Last Command '55
Last Days of Frank & Jesse James '86
Last Frontier '32
Last Gun '64
The Last Hard Men '76
The Last Hunt '56
Last of the Clintons '35
Last of the Comanches '52
The Last of the Dogmen '95
Last of the Pony Riders '53
Last of the Warrens '36
Last of the Wild Horses '49
The Last Outlaw '27
Last Outlaw '36
The Last Outlaw '93
The Last Ride of the Dalton Gang '79
Last Stand at Saber River '96
Last Train from Gun Hill '59▲
The Law and Jake Wade '58
Law and Lawless '33
Law and Order '42
Law for Tombstone '35
Law of the Land '76
Law of the Lash '47
Law of the Pampas '39
Law of the Saddle '43
Law of the Texan '38
The Law Rides '36
The Law Rides Again '43
Law West of Tombstone '38
The Lawless Breed '52▲
Lawless Frontier '35
Lawless Range '35
A Lawless Street '55
Lawman '71▲
A Lawman Is Born '37▲
Lawmen '44
The Lazarus Man '96
Leather Burners '43
The Left-Handed Gun '58▲
Legend of Alfred Packer '80
The Legend of Butch & Sundance '04
Legend of Earl Durand '74
The Legend of Frank Woods '77
Legend of Frenchie King '71
The Legend of Jedediah Carver '76
Legend of the Lone Ranger '81
Legend of Tom Dooley '59
The Legend of Zorro '05
Legion of the Lawless '40
The Light of Western Stars '30
The Light of Western Stars '40
Lightnin' Carson Rides Again '38
Lightning Bill '35
Lightning Bill Crandall '37
Lightning Raiders '45
Lightning Range '33
Lightning Strikes West '40
Lightning Warrior '31
Lights of Old Santa Fe '47
Lion's Den '36
Little Big Horn '51
Little Big Man '70▲
Little Moon & Jud McGraw '78
Loaded Pistols '48
The Lone Avenger '33
Lone Bandit '33
The Lone Defender '32
Lone Justice '93
Lone Justice 2 '93

▲ = rated three bones or higher

Lone Justice 3: Showdown at Plum Creek '96
The Lone Ranger '58
Lone Ranger '56
The Lone Rider in Cheyenne '42
The Lone Rider in Frontier Fury '41
The Lone Rider in Ghost Town '41
Lone Star '52
Lone Star '95▶
Lone Star Law '95▶
The Lone Star Ranger '30
Lonely Man '57
Lonely Are the Brave '62▶
Lone Wolf McQuade '83
The Longest Drive '76
The Long Riders '80▶
The Long Ride Home '01
Lonesome Trail '55
Lonesome Dove '89▶
Lost Canyon '43
Los Locos Posse '97
Love Comes Softly '03
Love Desperados '68
Love's Enduring Promise '04
Love's Long Journey '05
Lucky Cisco Kid '40
Lucky Terror '36
Lucky Texan '34
Lust for Gold '49
The Lusty Men '52▶
Macho Callahan '70
MacKenna's Gold '69
Madron '70
The Magnificent Seven '60▶
Major Dundee '65▶
Man & Boy '71
A Man Alone '55
A Man Called '43
A Man Called Horse '70▶
A Man Called Sledge '71
Man from Cheyenne '42
Man from Colorado '49
The Man from Gun Town '36
The Man from Hell '34
Man from Hell's Edges '32
Man from Laramie '55▶
Man from Monterey '33
Man from Montana '41
Man from Music Mountain '38
The Man from Painted Post '17
The Man from Snowy River '82
Man from Texas '39
Man from the Alamo '53▶
Man from Thunder River '43
Man from Utah '34
Man in the Saddle '51
Man in the Shadow '57
Man of Action '33
Man of the Forest '33
Man of the West '58
Man or Gun '58
Man Who Loved Cat Dancing '73
The Man Who Shot Liberty Valance '62▶
Man Without a Star '55▶
Manchurian Avenger '84
The Manhunt '86
Man's Country '38
Man's Land '32
Mark of the Spur '32
Marked for Murder '45
Marked Trails '44
Marshal of Cedar Rock '53
The Marshal's Daughter '53
The Masked Rider '41
Mason of Heldorado '50
McCabe & Mrs. Miller '71▶
The McMasters '70
Melody of the Plains '37
Melody Ranch '40
Melody Trail '35
Men of America '32
Mesquite Buckaroo '39
Miracle at Sage Creek '05
Miracle in the Wilderness '91

The Miracle Rider '35
The Missing '03▶
Missouri Breaks '76
Missourians '50
Mr. Horn '79
Mohawk '56
Molly & Lawless John '72
Montana '90
Montana Belle '52
Montana Justice '30
Monte Walsh '03
Monte Walsh '70▶
More Dead Than Alive '68
Mosby's Marauders '66
Mountain Justice '30
Mountain Men '80
My Darling Clementine '46▶
My Heroes Have Always Been Cowboys '91
My Outlaw Brother '51
My Pal, the King '32
My Pal Trigger '46
Mysterious Desperado '49
The Mysterious Rider '33
The Mysterious Rider '38
The Mysterious Rider '42
Mystery Man '44
Mystery Mountain '34
Mystery of the Hooded Horseman '37
Mystery Ranch '34
Mystery Trooper '32
Naked Hills '56
Naked in the Sun '57
The Naked Spur '53▶
Narrow Trail '17▶
'Neath the Arizona Skies '34
'Neath the Rainbow's End '30
Ned Kelly '70
Nevada '27
Nevada '44
Nevada City '41
Nevada Smith '66
The Nevadan '50
The New Frontier '35
Night of the Grizzly '66
Night Passage '57
Night Rider '32
Night Riders of Montana '50
Night Stage to Galveston '52
Night Time in Nevada '48
The Nine Lives of Elfego Baca '58
No Man's Law '27
No Man's Range '35
No Name on the Bullet '59▶
North of the Great Divide '50
Northern Passage '95
Oath of Vengeance '44
Oh Susannah '38
Oklahoma Annie '51
Oklahoma Badlands '48
Oklahoma Cyclone '30
The Oklahoman '56
Old Barn Dance '38
Old Corral '36
On the Night Stage '15
On the Old Spanish Trail '47
On Top of Old Smoky '53
One-Eyed Jacks '61▶
100 Rifles '69
One Little Indian '73
Only the Valiant '50
Open Range '03▶
The Outcast '54
Outcasts of the Trail '49
The Outlaw '43
Outlaw Country '49
The Outlaw Deputy '35
Outlaw Express '38
Outlaw Fury '50
Outlaw Gang '49
Outlaw Justice '32
Outlaw Justice '98
Outlaw of the Plains '46
Outlaw Roundup '44
Outlaw Rule '36
The Outlaw Tamer '33
Outlaw Trail '44
Outlaw Women '52
Outlaws of Sonora '38
Outlaws of the Desert '41
Outlaws of the Range '36
The Outlaw Josey Wales '76▶
Outlaw's Paradise '39
The Outsider '02
Overland Mail '42

Overland Stage Raiders '38▶
The Ox-Bow Incident '43▶
Painted Desert '31
Pair of Aces '90
Pale Rider '85▶
Pals of the Range '35
Pals of the Saddle '38
Panamint's Bad Man '38
Pancho Villa '72
Pancho Villa Returns '50
Pardon My Gun '30
Paroled to Die '37
Partners of the Trail '44
Passion '54
Pat Garrett & Billy the Kid '73▶
Pecos Kid '35
Peter Lundy and the Medicine Hat Stallion '77
The Phantom Bullet '26
The Phantom of the Range '38
The Phantom Rider '36
The Phantom Rider '46
Phantom of the West '31
Phantom Patrol '36
Phantom Rancher '39
Phantom Stallion '54
Phantom Thunderbolt '33
Pinto Canyon '40
Pinto Rustlers '36
Pioneer Marshal '49
Pioneer Woman '73
Pioneers '41
Pistoleros Asesinos '87
A Place Called Glory '66
The Plainsman '37
The Prairie Pirate '25
Prairie Moon '38
The Prairie King '27
Powdersmoke Range '35
Posse '75▶
Posse '93▶
Pony Express '53▶
Pony Express Rider '76▶
Pony Post '40
The Pony Express '25
The Pocatello Kid '31
The Professionals '66▶
The Proposition '05▶
Prairie Pals '42
Prescott Kid '36
Public Cowboy No. 1 '37
Proud Rebel '58▶
Proud Men '87
Purgatory '99
Purple Vigilantes '38
Pursued '47▶
Quigley Down Under '90
Racketeers of the Range '39
Rage at Dawn '55
Raiders of Red Gap '43
Raiders of the Border '44
Rainbow over Texas '46
Rainbow Ranch '33
Rainbow's End '35
Rancho Notorious '52▶
Randy Rides Alone '34
Range Busters '40
Range Feud '31
Range Law '31
Range Law '44
Range Renegades '48
Range Riders '35
Rangeland Empire '50
Ranger and the Lady '40
Ranger's Roundup '38
The Rangers Step In '37
The Rangers Take Over '42
The Rare Breed '66
Rattler Kid '68
Rawhide '38
Rawhide '50▶
Rawhide Romance '34
A Reason to Live, a Reason to Die '73
Red Desert '50
Red Headed Stranger '87
Red River '48▶
Red River Valley '36
Red Rock Outlaw '47
The Red Rope '37

The Redhead from Wyoming '53
Redwood Forest Trail '50
Renegade Girl '46
Renegade Trail '39
The Restless Breed '58
The Return of a Man Called Horse '76
Return of Draw Egan '16
Return of Frank James '40▶
Return of Jesse James '50
The Return of Josey Wales '86
Return of the Bad Men '48
Return of the Lash '47
Return of the Magnificent Seven '66
Return to Lonesome Dove '93
Return to Snowy River '88▶
Return to Wildfire '48
The Revenge of the Virgins '52
The Revenge Rider '35
The Ride Back '57
Ride Clear of Diablo '54
Ride 'Em Cowboy '41
Ride, Ranger, Ride '36
Ride Him, Cowboy '32▶
Ride in the Whirlwind '65
Ride Lonesome '59
Ride the High Country '62▶
Ride the Man Down '53
Ride to Glory '71
Rider from Tucson '50
Rider of Death Valley '35
Rider of the Law '35
Riders of Death Valley '41
Riders of Destiny '33
Riders of Pasco Basin '40
Riders of the Desert '32
Riders of the Purple Sage '25
Riders of the Purple Sage '96
Riders of the Range '24
Riders of the Range '50
Riders of the Rockies '37
Riders of the Timberline '41
Riders of the West '42
Riders of the Whistling Pines '49
Riders of the Whistling Skull '37
Ridin' Down the Canyon '42
Ridin' on a Rainbow '41
Ridin' the Lone Trail '37
Ridin' Thru '34
The Riding Avenger '36
Riding On '37
Riding Speed '35
The Riding Tornado '32
Riding the California Trail '47
Riding the Sunset Trail '41▶
Rimfire '49
Rim of the Canyon '49
Rin Tin Tin, Hero of the West '55
Rio Bravo '59▶
Rio Conchos '64▶
Rio Diablo '92
Rio Grande '50▶
Rio Grande Raiders '46
Rio Lobo '70
Rio Rattler '35
River of No Return '54
Road Agent '26
The Roamin' Cowboy '37
Roamin' Wild '36
Roarin' Lead '37
Roaring Guns '36
Roaring Ranch '30
Roaring Six Guns '37
Robbery under Arms '57
Robin Hood of Texas '47
Robin Hood of the Pecos '41
Rock River Renegades '42
Rockwell: A Legend of the Wild West '93
Rocky Mountain Rangers '40
Rodeo Girl '80
Rodeo King and the Senorita '51
Rogue of the Range '36
Rogue of the Rio Grande '30

Roll Along Cowboy '37
Roll on Texas Moon '46
Rollin' Plains '38
Romance on the Range '42
Rooster Cogburn '75
Rootin' Tootin' Rhythm '38
Rose Hill '97
Rose of Cimarron '52
Rough Riders' Roundup '39
Rough Night in Jericho '67
Rough Riders of Cheyenne '45
Rough Ridin' Ranger '35
Rough Ridin' Rhythm '37
Round-Up Time in Texas '37
Rounding Up the Law '22
The Roundup '41
Run of the Arrow '56▶
Running Wild '73
Rustler's Hideout '44
Rustler's Paradise '35
Rustlers' Roundup '33
Rustlers of Red Dog '35
Rustlers' Valley '37
The Sacketts '79
Sacred Ground '83
Saddle Buster '32
Saddle Mountain Roundup '41
Saga of Death Valley '39
Sagebrush Law '43
Sagebrush Trail '33▶
San Antonio '45
San Fernando Valley '44
Sandflow '37
Santa Fe '51
Santa Fe Bound '37
Santa Fe Marshal '40
Santa Fe Stampede '38
Santa Fe Trail '40
Santa Fe Uprising '46
Santee '73
Savage Journey '83
Savage Land '84
Savage Wilderness '55
Scalps '83
The Searchers '56▶
September Dawn '07
Seraphim Falls '06
Seven Cities of Gold '55
Seventh Cavalry '56
The Shadow Riders '82
Shadows of Death '45
Shadows of Tombstone '53
Shalako '68
Shane '53▶
Sheriff of Tombstone '41
Shine on, Harvest Moon '38
Shoot Out '71
Shoot the Sun Down '81
The Shooter '97
The Shooting '66▶
The Shootist '76▶
Shotgun '55
The Showdown '40
The Showdown '50
Showdown '73
Showdown at Boot Hill '58
Showdown at Williams Creek '91
Silent Tongue '92
Silent Valley '35
The Silver Bandit '50
The Silver Bullet '34
Silver City '51
Silver City Bonanza '51
Silver City Kid '45
Silver Lode '54
Silver Queen '42
Silver River '48
Silver Spurs '43
Silver Stallion '41
Silver Star '55
Silverado '85▶
Sing, Cowboy, Sing '37
Singing Buckaroo '37
The Singing Cowgirl '39
Siringo '94
Sitting Bull '54
Six Gun Gospel '43
Six Gun Rhythm '39
Six Shootin' Sheriff '38
Sky High '22
Slaughter Trail '51
Smoke in the Wind '75
Smokey Smith '36

The Sombrero Kid '42
Somewhere in Sonora '33
Son of a Gun '19
Son of God's Country '48
Son of the Morning Star '91▶
Song of Arizona '46
Song of Nevada '44
Song of Old Wyoming '45
Song of Texas '43
Song of the Gringo '36
Song of the Trail '36
Songs and Bullets '38
Sonora Stagecoach '44
Sons of Katie Elder '65▶
Sons of the Pioneers '42
Sons of Heaven, West of Hell '00
South of Arizona '38
South of Monterey '47
South of St. Louis '48
South of Santa Fe '42
South of the Border '39
South of the Rio Grande '45
Southward Ho! '39
Spirit of the West '32
Springfield Rifle '52
Springtime in the Rockies '37
Springtime in the Sierras '47
Spurs '30
Square Dance Jubilee '51
Stage to Mesa City '48
Stagecoach '39▶
Stagecoach '86
Stagecoach to Denver '46
The Stalking Moon '69
Standing Tall '78
The Star Packer '34
Station West '48▶
Stone of Silver Creek '35
Storm Rider '57
Stormy Trails '36
Straight Shootin' '17
The Stranger from Pecos '45
The Stranger Wore a Gun '53
Strawberry Roan '33
Sudden Death '50
Sundance and the Kid '76
Sundown Fury '42
Sundown Kid '43
Sundown Riders '48
Sundown Saunders '36
Sunrise Trail '31
Sunset in El Dorado '45
Sunset in the West '50
Sunset on the Desert '42
Sunset Range '35
Sunset Serenade '42
Sunset Trail '32
Susana Pass '49
Sweet Georgia '72
Swifty '35
Talion '66
Tall in the Saddle '44
The Tall Men '55▶
The Tall T '57▶
Tall Tale: The Unbelievable Adventures of Pecos Bill '95
Taste of Death '58
Telegraph Trail '33
Tell Them Willie Boy Is Here '69▶
Tennessee's Partner '55
Tension at Table Rock '56
Terror in a Texas Town '58
Terror of Tiny Town '38
Terror Trail '33
Test of Donald Norton '26
Tex Rides with the Boy Scouts '37
The Texans '38
Texas '94
Texas '41
Texas, Adios '66
Texas Bad Man '32
Texas Buddies '32
Texas Cyclone '32
Texas Gunfighter '32
Texas Guns '90
Texas Jack '35
Texas John Slaughter: Geronimo's Revenge '60

▶ = rated three bones or higher

Westerns

Texas John Slaughter: Stampede at Bitter Creek '62
Texas Justice '42
Texas Kid '43
Texas Legionnaires '43
Texas Masquerade '44
Texas Pioneers '32
The Texas Rangers '36
The Texas Rangers '51
The Texas Rangers Ride Again '40
Texas Terror '35
Texas to Bataan '42
Texas Trouble '41
Texas Wildcats '39
The Texican '66
Thousand Pieces of Gold '91
Three Bad Men '05
Three Bullets for a Long Gun '73
The Three Burials of Melquiades Estrada '05
Three Desperate Men '50
Three Faces West '40
Three in the Saddle '45
Three on the Trail '36
3:10 to Yuma '57
3:10 to Yuma '07
Three Texas Steers '39
Three Violent People '57
The Throwback '21
Thunder in God's Country '51
Thunder in the Desert '38
Thunder Mountain '35
Thunder Over Texas '34
Thunder Pass '37
Thunder Pass '54
Thunder River Feud '42
Thundering Gunslingers '44
Thundering Trail '51
The Tin Star '57
The Tioga Kid '48
To the Last Man '33
Today We Kill, Tomorrow We Die '71
The Toll Gate '20
Toll of the Desert '35
Tom Horn '80
Tomahawk '51
Tombstone '93
Tombstone Canyon '32
Tombstone Terror '34
Tonto Basin Outlaws '41
The Tonto Kid '35
The Topeka Terror '45
Treasure of Pancho Villa '55
Tribute to a Bad Man '56
Trigger, Jr. '50
Trigger Men '41
Trigger Pals '39
Trigger Tricks '30
The Trigger Trio '37
Trail Beyond '34
Trail Drive '33
Trail of Robin Hood '50
Trail of Terror '35
Trail of the Hawk '37
Trail of the Mounties '47
Trail of the Silver Spurs '41
Trail Riders '42
Trail Street '42
Trail to San Antone '47
Trailin' '21
Trailing Double Trouble '40
Trailing Trouble '30
The Traitor '36
Triumphs of a Man Called Horse '83
Trouble Busters '33
Trouble in Texas '37
True Grit '69
Tumbledown Ranch in Arizona '41
Tumbleweed Trail '42
Tumbleweeds '25
Twilight in the Sierras '50
Twilight on the Rio Grande '41
Twilight on the Trail '41
Two Fisted Justice '31

Two-Fisted Justice '43
Two-Fisted Law '32
Two for Texas '97
Two Gun Man '31
Two-Gun Man from Harlem '38
Two-Gun Troubador '37
Two Mules for Sister Sara '70
Two Rode Together '61
Ulzana's Raid '72
The Undefeated '69
Under California Stars '48
Under Colorado Skies '47
Under Nevada Skies '46
Under Western Stars '38
Undercover Man '36
Underground Rustlers '41
An Unfinished Life '05
The Unforgiven '60
Unforgiven '92
Uninvited '93
Union Pacific '39
The Unknown Ranger '36
Up River '79
Utah '45
Utah Trail '38
Valdez Is Coming '71
Valley of Fire '51
Valley of Terror '38
Valley of the Lawless '36
Valley of the Sun '42
The Vanishing American '25
Vanishing Legion '31
The Vanishing Westerner '50
Vengeance Valley '51
Vigilantes of Boom Town '46
Villa Rides '68
The Violent Men '55
The Virginian '23
The Virginian '29
The Virginian '46
The Virginian '99
Wagon Tracks '19
Wagon Trail '35
Wagon's Westward '40
Walk the Proud Land '56
Walking Thunder '94
Wall Street Cowboy '39
The Walloping Kid '26
Wanda Nevada '79
War Arrow '53
War of the Wildcats '43
The War Wagon '67
Warden of Red Rock '01
Warden of the Law '42
Warlock '59
Water Rustlers '39
Way of the West '35
The Way West '67
West of Nevada '36
West of Pinto Basin '40
West of the Divide '33
West of the Law '42
West of the Pecos '45
West to Glory '47
Western Frontier '35
Western Gold '37
Western Justice '35
Western Mail '42
Western Pacific Agent '51
Western Trails '38
Western Union '41
The Westerner '40
Westward Ho, the Wagons! '56
Westward the Women '51
When a Man Rides Alone '33
When a Man Sees Red '34
When the Legends Die '72
When the West Was Young '32

Wild Horse Canyon '25
Wild Horse Canyon '39
Wild Horse Rodeo '37
Wild Mustang '35
Wild Times '79
Wild West '46
Wild Wild West '99
The Wildcat '26
Wildfire '45
Will Penny '67
Winchester '73 '50
The Wind '28
Wind River '98
Winds of the Wasteland '36
Winners of the West '40
The Winning of Barbara Worth '26
Winning of the West '53
With Kit Carson over the Great Divide '25
Without Honors '32
Wolf Call '39
Wolfheart's Revenge '25
The Woman of the Town '44
Wrangler '88
Wyatt Earp '94
Wyatt Earp: Return to Tombstone '94
Wyoming Outlaw '39
Yellow Dust '36
The Yellow Rose of Texas '44
Yodelin' Kid from Pine Ridge '37
You Know My Name '99
Young Bill Hickok '40
Young Blood '33
Young Buffalo Bill '40
Young Guns '88
Young Guns 2 '90
The Young Land '59
The Young Pioneers '76
Yuma '70
Zandy's Bride '74
Zorro Rides Again '37
Zorro's Fighting Legion '39

Westrogens

see also Westerns; Wonder Women

Angel and the Badman '47
Annie Get Your Gun '50
Annie Oakley '35
Bad Girls '94
The Ballad of Little Jo '93
The Beautiful Blonde from Bashful Bend '49
Belle Starr '79
A Big Hand for the Little Lady '66
Buffalo Girls '95
Calamity Jane '53
Calamity Jane '82
Cat Ballou '65
Comes a Horseman '78
Even Cowgirls Get the Blues '94
The Far Side of Jericho '06
Gang of Roses '03
Girl from Calgary '32
The Gunslinger '56
Hannie Caulder '72
Heartland '81
Hooded Angels '00
Johnny Guitar '53
The Maverick Queen '55
McCabe & Mrs. Miller '71
Nevada '97
Poker Alice '87
The Quick and the Dead '95
Raiders of Sunset Pass '43
Ramrod '47
Riders of the Purple Sage '96
The Rowdy Girls '00
Texas Lady '56
Tulsa '49
Two Mules for Sister Sara '70
The Wicked, Wicked West '97
Wild Women '70
Zorro's Black Whip '44

Whales

see also Deep Blue; Wild Kingdom

The Adventures of Baron Munchausen '89
The Adventures of Pinocchio '96
Deep Blue '03
Free Willy '93
Free Willy 2: The Adventure Home '95
Free Willy 3: The Rescue '97
Luna: Spirit of the Whale '07
Moby Dick '56
Moby Dick '98
Namu, the Killer Whale '66
Orca '77
Pinocchio '40
Star Trek 4: The Voyage Home '86
Whale for the Killing '81
Whale Music '94
Whale of a Tale '76
The Whales of August '87
When the Whales Came '89
The White Dawn '75

Whitewater Rafting

A Cry from the Mountain '85
Deliverance '72
Good Luck '96
Race for Your Life, Charlie Brown '77
The River Wild '94
Same River Twice '97
Scream '83
White Water Summer '87

Widows & Widowers

see also Single Parents; Stepparents

About Schmidt '02
Akeelah and the Bee '06
Alpha Male '06
Audition '99
Belles on Their Toes '52
Beyond Justice '01
Birth '04
Bonneville '06
The Boynton Beach Club '05
Cafe Ole '00
Caged '50
Calendar Girls '03
Cape of Good Hope '04
The Cemetery Club '93
Children On Their Birthdays '02
The Christmas Miracle of Jonathan Toomey '07
The Clay Pigeon '49
Dan in Real Life '07
Dancing in Twilight '05
Dead Ringer '64
Doctor Bull '33
Dragonfly '02
Dreamland '06
Due East '02
The Emperor's New Clothes '01
Fascination '04
Final Cut '98
Finding Neverland '04
First Degree '98
Fraility '02
Georgia Rule '07
The Girl Next Door '53
Good Will Hunting '97
Grace Is Gone '07
The Green Promise '49
The Gunman '03
Heaven '01
Hidden Places '06
His Secret Life '01
The Home Front '02
Hondo '53
Hoodlum & Son '03
House of D '04
House of Sand '05
The Human Stain '03
I Now Pronounce You Chuck and Larry '07
Illegal Tender '07

Innocence '00
The Intended '02
Kings and Queen '04
Lethal Weapon '87
Local Boys '02
Love and Rage '99
Love Comes Softly '03
Love Liza '02
Love's Unending Legacy '07
A Man Apart '03
Manderlay '05
Marilyn Hotchkiss' Ballroom Dancing & Charm School '06
Married Life '07
The Merchant of Venice '04
Message in a Bottle '98
A Mighty Heart '07
Mrs. Henderson Presents '05
Monster's Ball '01
The Mother '03
The Mothman Prophecies '02
Move Over, Darling '63
The Mudge Boy '03
My Reputation '46
Nanny McPhee '06
Nightmare Alley '47
Nightwaves '03
No Turning Back '01
One Last Thing '05
The Passion of Anna '70
The Pilot's Wife '01
Private Benjamin '80
P.S. I Love You '07
Pure '02
Race to Space '01
The Reading Room '05
Renegade Trail '39
Return to Me '00
Rick '03
The Road Home '01
Rocky Balboa '06
The Roman Spring of Mrs. Stone '03
Safe Harbour '07
St. Patrick's Day '99
The Salton Sea '02
Sam Whiskey '69
Satin Rouge '02
Schizo '04
7 Faces of Dr. Lao '63
The Shipping News '01
Signs '02
Silent Waters '03
Skinwalkers '07
Sleepless in Seattle '93
Smart People '08
Song of Love '47
Starman '84
Strayed '03
Things We Lost in the Fire '07
This Revolution '05
Time of the Wolf '03
To Gillian on Her 37th Birthday '96
The Treatment '06
The Trial of Old Drum '00
Trouble in Paradise '32
The Truth About Charlie '02
21 Grams '03
The Twilight Samurai '02
Under the Flag of the Rising Sun '72
Undertow '04
Used People '92
The Visitor '07
Volver '06
Water '05
We'll Meet Again '02
What Time Is It There? '01
White Noise '05
The Whole Shebang '01
Widows '02
Winter Solstice '04
Witness '85
Yours, Mine & Ours '68
Yours, Mine & Ours '05

Wild Kingdom

see also Bears; Birds; Cats; Dinosaurs; Elephants; Killer Apes and Monkeys; Killer Beasts; Killer Bugs and Slugs; Killer Dogs; Killer Kats; Killer Pigs; Killer Sea Critters; King of Beasts (Dogs); Monkeyshines; Nice Mice; Pigs; Rabbits; Talking Animals; Whales; Wilderness

Ace Ventura: When Nature Calls '95
The Adventures of Ford Fairlane '90
The Adventures of Tarzan '21
Africa Texas Style '67
Alaska '96
All Creatures Great and Small '74
All Dogs Go to Heaven 2 '95
The Amazing Panda Adventure '95
An American Tail '86
Andre '94
The Animal '01
Animal Farm '55
Arctic Tale '07
Attack of the Sabretooth '05
Ava's Magical Adventure '94
Bambi '42
Bambi II '06
The Barefoot Executive '71
The Bear '89
The Bears & I '74
The Beast That Killed Women '65
Beastmaster '82
Beastmaster 2: Through the Portal of Time '91
Beasts '83
Bedtime for Bonzo '51
The Belstone Fox '73
Black Cobra '83
Bless the Beasts and Children '71
Born Free '66
Born to Be Wild '95
Born Wild '95
The Brave One '56
A Breed Apart '84
Bringing Up Baby '38
Brother Bear 2 '06
Brotherhood of the Wolf '01
Buddy '97
Buffalo Rider '78
Call of the Wild '72
Captive Wild Woman '43
Carnage '02
Catch as Catch Can '68
Charlie, the Lonesome Cougar '67
Cheetah '89
Christian the Lion '76
The Chronicles of Narnia '89
Clarence, the Cross-eyed Lion '65
Courage of the North '35
The Crocodile Hunter: Collision Course '02
A Cry in the Dark '88
A Cry in the Wild '90
Dark Age '88
Darkest Africa '36
Day of the Animals '77
The Day of the Dolphin '73
Doctor Dolittle '67
Dr. Dolittle '98
Dr. Dolittle 2 '01
Duma '05
Dumbo '41
Dunston Checks In '95
Eaten Alive '76
Ed '96
The Edge '97
Ele, My Friend '93
The Electric Horseman '79
Elephant Boy '37
An Elephant Called Slowly '69
The Emperor's New Groove '00
Every Which Way But Loose '78

▲ = rated three bones or higher

Eyes of the Wolf '95
Eyes of the Panther '90
Far from Home: The Adventures of Yellow Dog '94
Fierce Creatures '96
The Fifth Monkey '90
50 First Dates '04
Flight of the Grey Wolf '76
Flipper '63
Flipper '96
Fly Away Home '96 ►
The Fox and the Hound '81 ►
Francis Covers the Big Town '53
Francis Goes to the Races '51
Francis Goes to West Point '52
Francis in the Haunted House '56
Francis in the Navy '55
Francis Joins the WACs '54
Francis the Talking Mule '49 ►
Frasier the Sensuous Lion '73
Futz '69
Gentle Giant '67
George of the Jungle '97 ►
The Ghost and the Darkness '96
Gladiator '00 ►
Going Ape! '81
Going Bananas '88
The Golden Seal '83
Gordy '95
Gorilla '56
Gorillas in the Mist '88 ►
The Great Adventure '53 ►
The Great Elephant Escape '95
The Great Rupert '50 ►
Grizzly Adams: The Legend Continues '90
Grizzly Man '05 ►
Groundhog Day '53 ►
Gus '76
Harry and the Hendersons '87
Hatari '62 ►
Hawmps! '76
Hollywood Safari '76
Homeward Bound 2: Lost in San Francisco '96
Hoot '06
I Dreamed of Africa '00
Ice Age '02 ►
In the Shadow of Kilimanjaro '86
The Island of Dr. Moreau '96
Island of Lost Souls '32 ►
Island of the Blue Dolphins '64
Joey '98
Jumanji '95
Jungle '52
The Jungle Book '67 ►
The Jungle Book 2 '03
Jungle Boy '96
Jungle Drums of Africa '53
King Kung Fu '87
King of the Grizzlies '69
Lassie, Come Home '43
The Last Safari '67
Legend of Lobo '62 ►
Leonard Part 6 '87
The Leopard Son '96 ►
The Lion King '94 ►
The Lion King 1 1/2 '04 ►
The Lion King: Simba's Pride '98 ►
Living Free '72
The Many Adventures of Winnie the Pooh '77 ►
March of the Penguins '05 ►
Matilda '78
Max, Mon Amour '86
The Mighty Peking Man '77
The Misadventures of Merlin Jones '63
Monkey Trouble '94
Monkeys, Go Home! '66
Monkey's Uncle '65
The Monster and the Girl '41

Mountain Family Robinson '79
Mountain Man '77
Murders in the Rue Morgue '32
My Sister, My Love '78
Napoleon '96
Napoleon and Samantha '72 ►
Never Cry Wolf '83 ►
Night of the Grizzly '66
Nikki, the Wild Dog of the North '61
Noah's Ark '99
Once Upon a Forest '93
Operation Dumbo Drop '95
Operation Haylift '50
Pardon My Trunk '52
Passion in the Desert '97
Paulie '98
Pet Sematary 2 '92
Piglet's Big Movie '03
Pippi Longstocking '69
Planet of the Apes '68 ►
Project X '87 ►
Razorback '84
Red Earth '82
The Rescuers '77 ►
The Rescuers Down Under '90
Ring of Bright Water '69 ►
Rock-a-Doodle '92
Rudyard Kipling's The Jungle Book '94
Rudyard Kipling's The Second Jungle Book: Mowgli and Baloo '97
The Runaways '75
Running Free '94
Running Wild '99
Sabretooth '01
Sammy, the Way-Out Seal '62
The Secret of NIMH '82 ►
Shakma '89
Silver Streak '76 ►
Slappy and the Stinkers '97
Soul of the Beast '23
Stalk the Wild Child '76
The Story of the Weeping Camel '03 ►
A Summer to Remember '84
Super Seal '77
The Tender Warrior '71
Those Calloways '65
Thumbelina '82
A Tiger Walks '64
To Walk with Lions '99
Tomboy & the Champ '58
Trap on Cougar Mountain '72
Two Brothers '04
Vampire Circus '71
The Wagons Roll at Night '41
Walk Like a Man '87
Watership Down '78 ►
When the North Wind Blows '74
Whispers: An Elephant's Tale '00
The White Buffalo '77
White Pongo '45
White Wolves 2: Legend of the Wild '94
The Wild '06
Wild America '97 ►
Wild Horses '82
The Wild Thornberrys Movie '02 ►
The Yearling '46 ►
The Yearling '94 ►
Zebra in the Kitchen '65
Zeus and Roxanne '96

Wilderness
see also Trees & Forests
Abducted '86
Across the Great Divide '76
The Adventures of Frontier Fremont '75
The Adventures of the Wilderness Family '76
Alaska '96
All Mine to Give '56
Almost Heroes '93
Arctic Blue '93

Backwoods '87
The Bear '89 ►
Beyond Fear '93
Black Fear '91
Black Robe '91 ►
Blood of the Hunter '94
The Bridge to Nowhere '86
Brother Bear '03
Bullies '86
Bushwhacked '95
Cannibal! The Musical '96
The Capture of Grizzly Adams '82
Claws '77
Clearcut '92
Cold River '81
Continental Divide '81
The Cowboys '72 ►
Cross Creek '83
Davy Crockett and the River Pirates '56
Davy Crockett, King of the Wild Frontier '55 ►
Dead Ahead '96
Death Hunt '81
Decoy '95
Dominion '94
Duma '05 ►
Earthling '80
The Edge '97
Edge of Honor '91
Edge of Madness '02
Endangered '94
Eyes of Fire '84
Far from Home: The Adventures of Yellow Dog '94
Father and Scout '94
Ferngully: The Last Rain Forest '92
Flight from Glory '37
Further Adventures of the Wilderness Family, Part 2 '77
Gerry '02
God's Country '46
Great Adventure '75
The Great Outdoors '88
Grizzly '76
Grizzly Adams: The Legend Continues '90
Grizzly Falls '99
Grizzly Man '05 ►
Grizzly Mountain '97
Heaven on Earth '89
Hunter's Blood '87
Ice Palace '60
Into the Wild '07 ►
Jeremiah Johnson '72 ►
Just Before Dawn '80
Kid Colter '85
The Last of the Dogmen '95
The Legend of Wolf Mountain '92
The Legend of Grizzly Adams '74
Life & Times of Grizzly Adams '74
Little Bigfoot '96
Lost '83
Lost in the Barrens '91
Man in the Wilderness '71
The Many Adventures of Winnie the Pooh '77 ►
March of the Penguins '05 ►
Mountain Charlie '80
Mountain Family Robinson '79
Mountain Man '77
Napoleon '96
Napoleon and Samantha '72 ►
Never Cry Wolf '83 ►
Northwest Passage '40 ►
Northwest Trail '46
Orphans of the North '40
The Parent Trap '61
Quest for Fire '82 ►
Shoot to Kill '88 ►
Silence '73
Silence of the North '81
Silver Wolf '98
Slashed Dreams '74
Sourdough '77
Spirit of the Eagle '90
Starbird and Sweet William '73
Strange Wilderness '08
The Tale of Ruby Rose '87 ►

Tales of the Klondike: In a Far Country '87
Tales of the Klondike: Race for Number One '87
Tales of the Klondike: The Scorn of Women '87
Tales of the Klondike: The Unexpected '87
The Ticket '97
Timber Queen '44
True Heart '97
Tundra '36
Violent Zone '89
Warrior Spirit '94
White Fang '91 ►
White Fang and the Hunter '85
The White Tower '50
White Water Summer '87
White Wolves 3: Cry of the White Wolf '98
Whitewater Sam '78
The Wolves '95
Young & Free '78
Zero Degrees Kelvin '95

Wisconsin
All Mine to Give '56
American Movie '99 ►
BASEketball '98
Citizen Cohn '92
Critical Choices '97
Deranged '74 ►
Dogma '99
Ed's Next Move '96
Fear X '03
The Giant Spider Invasion '75
Love Actually '03 ►
A Map of the World '99
Mr. 3000 '04
No Sleep 'Til Madison '02
Our Vines Have Tender Grapes '45
The Prince & Me '04
The Smokers '00
Things in Their Season '74
Wayne's World '92 ►

Wine & Vinyards
Cloud Waltzing '87
A Good Year '06
I Am David '04
May Fools '90
Mondovino '04
The Parent Trap '98
Sideways '04 ►
The Vineyard '89
A Walk in the Clouds '95

Witchcraft
see also Wizards; Occult; Demons & Witchcraft
Bell, Book and Candle '58
Bewitched '05
Beyond Darkness '92
Black Magic '92
Black Sunday '60 ►
Book of Shadows: Blair Witch 2 '00
The Bride with White Hair '93
The Bride with White Hair 2 '93
Brotherhood 2: The Young Warlocks '01
The Brothers Grimm '05
Burn Witch, Burn! '62 ►
Cast a Deadly Spell '91 ►
The Conqueror Worm '68 ►
The Covenant '06
The Craft '96
The Crucible '57
The Crucible '96 ►
Cry of the Banshee '70
The Curse of the Crying Woman '61
The Curse of the Devil '73
Daughters of Satan '72
Day of Wrath '43 ►
The Day the Earth Froze '59
The Demons '74
The Devil Rides Out '68 ►
The Devils '71 ►

Devonsville Terror '83
Dr. Strange '78
Double Double Toil and Trouble '94
The Eternal '99
Eyes of the Demon '87
Final Encounter '00
The Forbidden Kingdom '08
Four Rooms '95
Fright House '89
The Golden Compass '07
Harry Potter and the Prisoner of Azkaban '04 ►
The Haunted Palace '63 ►
The Haunting of Morella '91
Hellblock 13 '97
Hercules, Prisoner of Evil '64
Hocus Pocus '93
Horror Hotel '60
Horror Rises from the Tomb '72
The Hospital '71 ►
House of the Black Death '65
Howl's Moving Castle '04 ►
I Married a Witch '42 ►
I've Been Waiting for You '98
Inquisition '76
The Juniper Tree '87
Kiki's Delivery Service '98 ►
Kill, Baby, Kill '66
Kill Me Tomorrow '99
The Lady's Not for Burning '87
Lisa and the Devil '75
Little Witches '96
Lost Legacy: A Girl Called Hatter Fox '77
Love at Stake '87
Maciste in Hell '60
Mark of the Devil '69
Mark of the Devil 2 '72
The Muppets' Wizard of Oz '05
Nanny McPhee '06 ►
Netherworld '90
Night of the Scarecrow '95
The Polar Bear King '94
Practical Magic '98
Pufnstuf '70
Pumpkinhead 3: Ashes to Ashes '06
Pumpkinhead 4: Blood Feud '07
Quartier Mozart '92
Rendez-Moi Ma Peau '81
The Resurrected '91
Return to Oz '85
Ruddigore '82
Sabrina the Teenage Witch '95
Season of the Witch '73
The She-Beast '65
The Shrieking '73
Silent Hill '06
Sleepy Hollow '99 ►
Snow White: A Tale of Terror '97
Snow White: The Fairest of Them All '02
Something Weird '68
Sorceress '88
Sorceress '94
Spellbreaker: Secret of the Leprechauns '96
Stardust '07 ►
Summer of Fear '78
The Terror '79
Terror Beach '75
That Darn Sorceress '88
Three Sovereigns for Sarah '85
The Touch of Satan '70
Troll 2 '92
Twitches '05
Twitches Too '07
The Undead '57
The Virgin Witch '70
Warlock '89 ►
Warlock 3: The End of Innocence '98
Warlock: The Armageddon '93 ►
Warlock Moon '73

The Werewolf vs. the Vampire Woman '70
Wicked Stepmother '89
The Witch '66
A Witch Who Came from the Sea '76
A Witch Without a Broom '68
Witchboard '86
Witchcraft '88
Witchcraft 3: The Kiss of Death '90
Witchcraft 4: Virgin Heart '92
Witchcraft 7: Judgement Hour '95
Witchcraft 8: Salem's Ghost '95
Witchcraft 9: Bitter Flesh '96
Witchcraft 10: Mistress of the Craft '98
Witchcraft 11: Sisters in Blood '00
Witchery '88
The Witches '66 ►
The Witches '90 ►
Witches' Brew '79
Witches' Mountain '71
The Witches of Eastwick '87 ►
Witches of the Caribbean '05
The Witching of Ben Wagner '95
The Witchmaker '69
Witchouse '99
Witchouse 2: Blood Coven '00
Witchouse 3: Demon Fire '01
WitchTrap '89
The Wizard of Oz '39 ►
The Woman Who Came Back '45
The Woods '03
The Worst Witch '86
Yaeba '89

Witness Protection Program
see also Organized Crime; U.S. Marshals
Acts of Betrayal '97
Ballistic '94
Bird on a Wire '90
Charlie's Angels: Full Throttle '03
Drop Zone '94
Eraser '96
Federal Protection '02
Forget About It '06
The Godfather, Part 2 '74 ►
Goodfellas '90 ►
Hide in Plain Sight '80 ►
Lethal Weapon 2 '89 ►
My Blue Heaven '90
Navajo Blues '97
Nowhere Land '98
The Pact '99
Protection '01
Romeo Is Bleeding '93
See Spot Run '01
Shadowboxer '06
Sister Act '92
Sister Act 2 '93
The Whole Nine Yards '00
Witness Protection '08 ►

Women
see also Dream Girls; Femme Fatale; Moms; Westerners; Wonder Women in Prison; Women in...
Absolutely Fabulous: The Last Shout '96
Accidental Meeting '93
Acts of Worship '01
Alice Doesn't Live Here Anymore '74 ►
Amelia Earhart: The Final Flight '94
Anatomy of Hell '04
Anna '87 ►
Another Way '88
Another Woman '88 ►
Antonia and Jane '91 ►
Arizona '40

Women

Artemisia '97
The Astounding She-Monster '58
Babyfever '94
Bachelor Mother '39◀
Backstreet Justice '93
Bandit Queen '94
Bang '95
Bar Girls '95
Beaches '88◀
Beauty Shop '05◀
Becoming Jane '07
Bella Mafia '97
Betty '92
Bhaji on the Beach '94
The Big City '63
Black Day Blue Night '95
Black Scorpion '95
Blood and Sand '41◀
Blood Games '90
Blue De Ville '86
The Bostonians '84
Boulevard '94
Boys on the Side '94
Bridget Jones: The Edge of Reason '04
The Buccaneers '95◀
A Bunny's Tale '85
Business As Usual '88
Camilla '94
Cape of Good Hope '04
Come Early Morning '06
Comedy of Power '06
Commissar '68◀
Conceiving Ada '97
Challenge of a Lifetime '85
Chantilly Lace '93
The Children's Hour '61
China Beach '88◀
The Circle '00
Citizen Ruth '96
City Without Men '43
Claire of the Moon '92
The Color Purple '85◀
Come to the Five & Dime Jimmy Dean, Jimmy Dean '82◀
A Dangerous Woman '93
Darktown Strutters '74
The Day the Women Got Even '06
The Dead Girl '06
Dead Men Can't Dance '97
Deconstructing Harry '97
Defenseless '91
The Descent '05
The Desperate Trail '94
The Devil Wears Prada '06
Dirty Dishes '78◀
Dogs: The Rise and Fall of an All-Girl Bookie Joint '96
Dogville '03
A Doll's House '59
A Doll's House '73
A Doll's House '73◀
Double Obsession '93
The Dreamlife of Angels '98◀
Dreams '55
The Duchess of Duke Street '78◀
Early Summer '51◀
Easy Virtue '27
Eating '90
Ebony Dreams '80
Eddie '96
8 1/2 Women '99
Eleanor: First Lady of the World '82
Enchanted April '92
Enid Is Sleeping '90
Enormous Changes '83◀
Entertaining Angels: The Dorothy Day Story '96
Erotique '94

Even Cowgirls Get the Blues '94
Evita '96
The Execution '85
An Eye for an Eye '95
Faces of Women '85
Family Secrets '84
Feast of July '95
Feds '88
Female Perversions '96
Fire '96
Fire in the Night '85
The First Wives Club '96
Fish Without a Bicycle '03
Flatbed Annie and Sweetiepie: Lady Truckers '79
The Flower of My Secret '95◀
Follow the River '95
Fran '85
Free Zone '05
Fried Green Tomatoes '91◀
Friends '95
From the Journals of Jean Seberg '95
Fur: An Imaginary Portrait of Diane Arbus '06
Gangs, Inc. '41
A Geisha '53◀
Gentlemen Prefer Blondes '53◀
G.I. Jane '97
Girl '96
A Girl Thing '01
Girlfriends '78◀
Going Shopping '05
Good Girls Don't '95
Grace of My Heart '96
The Great Man's Lady '42
The Group '66
Guardian Angel '94
The Happy Ending '69
Hard Country '81
Harvest of Fire '95
Head of the Family '71
Heading South '05◀
Heat and Dust '82◀
Heaven and Earth '93
The Heidi Chronicles '95
Hellcats '68
The Heroic Trio '93
Hidden Assassin '94
Honey & Ashes '96
The Hours '02◀
Horror of the Zombies '74
House of Whipcord '75
Household Saints '93◀
How to Be a Woman and Not Die in the Attempt '91
How to Make an American Quilt '95
How to Marry a Millionaire '53
I Dreamed of Africa '00
I Like It Like That '94◀
I Really Hate My Job '07
If These Walls Could Talk '96
In the Land of Women '06
In This House of Brede '75◀
The Insect Woman '63◀
Introducing Dorothy Dandridge '99◀
Is There Life Out There? '94
Island of Lost Girls '68
Isn't She Great '00
Jaded '96
James Joyce's Women '85◀
Jamon, Jamon '93
Je Tu Il Elle '74
The Journey to Kafiristan '01
The Joy Luck Club '93◀
Joy Ride to Nowhere '78
Judicial Consent '94
Juliet of the Spirits '65◀
Just Another Girl on the I.R.T. '93
Kamikaze Hearts '91
Kandahar '01
Katie Tippel '75
The Ladies Club '86
Ladies on the Rocks '83
Ladybird, Ladybird '93◀
The Last Best Year '90
The Late Chrysanthemums '54
A League of Their Own '92◀

Leaving Normal '92
The Legend of Blood Castle '72
Les Bonnes Femmes '60◀
Little Mother '71
Little Women '33◀
Little Women '49◀
Little Women '78
Little Women '94◀
Live Nude Girls '95
Lola Montes '55◀
Losing Isaiah '94◀
Love After Love '94
The Love Goddesses '65◀
Lucia, Lucia '03
Lumiere '76
Madame Bovary '34◀
Madame Bovary '91◀
Madame Bovary '00
Madonna: Innocence Lost '95
Maedchen in Uniform '31◀
The Magic Bubble '93
Magnificent Doll '46
Malou '83
Mapp & Lucia '85
Marianne and Juliane '82◀
Marilyn: The Untold Story '80◀
Mars Needs Women '66
Mary, Queen of Scots '71
Memoirs of a Geisha '05
Memories of Murder '90
Messidor '77
Mil Vida Loca '94
Miles to Go '86
Mina Tannenbaum '93
Miss Firecracker '89◀
Moll Flanders '96
Monkey Grip '82◀
Monster '03◀
Mooladé '04
Moonlight and Valentino '95
Mortal Thoughts '91
Moscow Does Not Believe in Tears '80◀
Mother & Daughter: A Loving War '80
Mother Teresa: In the Name of God's Poor '97
My Brilliant Career '79◀
My Twentieth Century '90◀
Nine Lives '05◀
9 to 5 '80
Nomugi Pass '79
Nora's Hair Salon '04
Norma Jean and Marilyn '95
North Country '05
Now and Then '95
The Nun '66
One Sings, the Other Doesn't '77
One True Thing '98◀
The Opposite Sex '56
Osaka Elegy '36
Overseas: Three Women with Man Trouble '90◀
Pancho Barnes '88
Passenger '61◀
Passion Fish '92◀
Patti Rocks '88◀
Perfume '91
Persepolis '07◀
Personal Velocity: Three Portraits '02◀
The Pillow Book '95
Poetic Justice '93
Poor Little Rich Girl: The Barbara Hutton Story '87
Portrait of a Lady '96◀
Portrait of a Showgirl '82
Portrait of Teresa '79◀
Posers '02
A Price above Rubies '97
Prime Suspect '92◀
Quartier Mozart '92
Queen of Diamonds '91
The Queen's Sister '05
Question of Silence '83◀
The Rector's Wife '94
Rescuers: Stories of Courage "Two Women" '97

Rosa Luxemburg '86
The Rosa Parks Story '02
Roseanne: An Unauthorized Biography '94
Rosenstrasse '03◀
Ruby in Paradise '93◀
Run for the Dream: The Gail Devers Story '96
Running Mates '00
Salmonberries '91
Samson vs. the Vampire Women '61
Sandra of a Thousand Delights '65
The Scent of Green Papaya '93◀
Searching For Wooden Watermelons '01
Set It Off '96
The '70s '00
Sexual Intent '94
Shadow on the Sun '88
She-Devil '89
Sherman's March '86◀
The Silences of the Palace '94
A Single Girl '96
Sister Street Fighter '76
The Sisterhood '88
Sisters of the Gion '36
Sisters, Or the Balance of Happiness '79
Snapdragon '93
Soroeress '88◀
Spices '86◀
The Spitfire Grill '95
Stage Door '37◀
Star! '68
Steaming '86
Steel and Lace '90
Steel Magnolias '89◀
The Story of Qiu Ju '91◀
The Story of Women '88◀
The Stranger '95
Strangers in Good Company '91◀
Strangers: The Story of a Mother and Daughter '79◀
Street of Shame '56◀
Stripper '86
Sudden Death '85
Sunset Strip '91
Swann '96
Talk '94
Talking about Sex '94
The Tango Lesson '97
Tara '05
The Taxi Mystery '26
Tell Me Where It Hurts '74
Tender Comrade '43
The Terrorist '00
Testament of Youth '79◀
30 Years to Life '01
The 3 Marias '03
301, 302 '94
Three Secrets '50
3 Women '77◀
Tomorrow's Children '34
Trojan Women '71
True Women '97
Trumps '83
Twenty-One '91
Unhook the Stars '96
An Unmarried Woman '78◀
Unnatural '52
Untraceable '08
Up/Down/Fragile '95
Utamaro and His Five Women '46
Veronica Guerin '03
Visiting Hours '82
Viva Maria! '65
Volver '06◀
Voyage en Douce '81
Waiting to Exhale '95◀
Walpurgis Night '41◀
Warrior Queen '03
Washington Square '97◀
The Weight of Water '00
We'll Meet Again '02
Westward the Women '51◀
What's Love Got to Do with It? '93
When a Woman Ascends the Stairs '60
Whose Child Am I? '75
The Wicker Man '06
Widow's Peak '94

Wildrose '85◀
Wing Chun '94
Witchfire '86
A Woman and a Woman '80
A Woman Named Jackie '91
A Woman Rebels '36
Woman, Thou Art Loosed '04
The Women '39◀
Women from the Lake of Scented Souls '94
Women in Prison '49
The Women of Brewster Place '89◀
Women on the Verge of a Nervous Breakdown '88◀
Working Girl '88◀
Working Girls '87◀
Wrestling with Alligators '98
The Wrong Woman '95

Women Cops

see also Cops

Arizona Heat '87
Black Widow '87◀
Blue Steel '90
China O'Brien '88
Copycat '95
Corky Romano '01
Dear Detective '77
Dear Detective '78
The Deep End of the Ocean '98
Do or Die '91
The Enforcer '76
Fargo '96◀
Fatal Beauty '87
Get Christie Love! '74
Impulse '90
L.A. Crackdown '87
L.A. Crackdown 2 '88
Miss Congeniality '00
The Mod Squad '99
One of Her Own '97
Policewoman Centerfold '83
Policewomen '73
Prey of the Chameleon '91
Scorchy '76
The Silence of the Lambs '91◀
Silk 2 '89
A Stranger Among Us '92
Tereza '61◀
Twisted '04
V.I. Warshawski '91
Vice Girls '96

Women in Prison

see also Exploitation; Men in Prison; Sexploitation

Alien 3 '92
Amazon Jail '85
Bad Girls Dormitory '84
Bandits '99
Better Off Dead '94
The Big Bird Cage '72
The Big Doll House '71
Born Innocent '74
Bridget Jones: The Edge of Reason '04
Brokedown Palace '99
Caged '50◀
Caged Fear '92
Caged Fury '80
Caged Fury '90
Caged Hearts '95
Caged Heat '74
Caged Heat 2: Stripped of Freedom '94
Caged Heat 3000 '95
Caged in Paradiso '89
Caged Women '84
Cell Block Sisters: Banished Behind Bars '95
Chained Heat '83
Chained Heat 2 '92
Chasers '94
Chicago '02◀
The Circle '00
Civil Brand '02
The Concrete Jungle '82
Condemned to Hell '84
Condition Red '95
Convicted '04

Convicted: A Mother's Story '87
Deadlock '91
Deadlock 2 '94
Desperate Women '78
East-West '99
Escape from Cell Block 3 '74
Escape from Hell '79
False Arrest '92
Fugitive Rage '96
Fun '94
Getting Out '94
Girl on a Chain Gang '65
Girls in Chains '43
Girls in Prison '56
Girls in Prison '94
Girls Riot '88
Hellblock 13 '97
Hot Box '72
Human Experiments '79
I Want to Live! '58◀
Ilsa, the Wicked Warden '78
Jailbird Rock '88
Ladies They Talk About '33
Lady in the Death House '44
Last Dance '96
Longford '06
Love Child '82
Lust for Freedom '87
A Map of the World '99
Me & Veronica '93
Midnight '34
Mommy 2: Mommy's Day '96
The Muthers '76
Naked Cage '86
Nightmare in Badham County '76
99 Women '69
Off the Wall '82
Outside Chance '78
Paradise Road '97
Playing for Time '80◀
Prison of Secrets '97
Prison Stories: Women on the Inside '91◀
Purgatory '89
Red Heat '85
Red Letters '00
Reflections in the Dark '94
Reform School Girls '57
Reform School Girls '86
Savage Island '85
Scrubbers '82
Slammer Girls '87
Star Slammer '87
Sweet Sugar '72
10 Violent Women '79
Terminal Island '73
Time Served '99
V for Vendetta '06
Vendetta '85
Vera Drake '04◀
Violent Women '59
White Oleander '02
Women in Cell Block 7 '77
Women in Fury '84
Women Unchained '72
Women's Prison Escape '74
Women's Prison Massacre '85

Women in War

see also Doctors & Nurses; Korean War; Vietnam War; Women; World War I; World War II

China Beach '88◀
Courage Under Fire '96◀
The English Patient '96◀
A Farewell to Arms '32◀
G.I. Jane '97
A Guy Named Joe '44
Hanna's War '88
In Love and War '96
Nurse Edith Cavell '39◀
Paradise Road '97
Purple Hearts '84
Rodgers & Hammerstein's South Pacific '01
She Goes to War '29
So Proudly We Hail '43◀
South Pacific '58◀
A Town Like Alice '85

◀ = rated three bones or higher

Wonder Women

see also Dream Girls

The Abductors '72
Act of Vengeance '74
Against the Ropes '04
Alien '79 ▶
Alien 3 '92
Alien: Resurrection '97 ▶
Aliens '86 ▶
Alley Cat '84
Amazon Warrior '97
The Amazons '84
Amazons '86
Amazons and Gladiators '01
The American Angels: Baptism of Blood '89
Angel's Brigade '79
Angel's Dance '99
The Associate '96
Attack of the 50 Foot Woman '58
Attack of the 50 Ft. Woman '93
Attack of the 60-Foot Centerfold '95
Bad Georgia Road '77
Barbarian Queen '85
Barbarian Queen 2: The Empress Strikes Back '89
Basic Training '86
Batman and Robin '97
Batman Returns '92
Battle Queen 2020 '99
Beauty for the Asking '39
Big Bad Mama 2 '87
The Big Bust Out '73
Billie '65
Bimini Code '84
The Bionic Woman '75
Black Scorpion 2: Ground Zero '96
Blonde in Black Leather '77
Blonde Savage '47
Blue Tiger '94
Buffy the Vampire Slayer '92
Bury Me an Angel '71
Business As Usual '88
Chameleon '98
Chameleon 2: Death Match '99
Chameleon 3: Dark Angel '00
Charlie's Angels '00
Charlie's Angels: Full Throttle '03
China O'Brien 2 '89
Chopper Chicks in Zombietown '91
The Clan of the Cave Bear '86
Cleopatra '34
Cleopatra '63
Cleopatra Jones '73
Coffy '73
Colossus and the Amazon Queen '64
Crouching Tiger, Hidden Dragon '00
Cutthroat Island '95
Danger Zone '87
The Deadly and the Beautiful '73
Deadly Weapons '70
Death Proof '07
The Demolitionist '95
Do or Die '91
DOA: Dead or Alive '06
Doctor of Doom '62
Doomsday '08
Dragon Fury 2 '96
Elektra '05
Evita '96
The Executioners '93
The $5.20 an Hour Dream '80
Fugitive Rage '96
Galaxis '95
Get Christie Love! '74
G.I. Jane '97
God Said "Ha!" '99 ▶
Golden Lady '79
The Great Texas Dynamite Chase '76
Heartland '81 ▶
Heavy Metal 2000 '00
Hercules the Legendary Journeys, Vol. 1: And the Amazon Women '94
Hot Box '72
Hundra '85
Invincible Barbarian '83
Kill Bill Vol. 1 '03 ▶
Kill Bill Vol. 2 '04 ▶
Kima, Queen of the Amazons '75
Kisses for My President '64
La Femme Nikita '91 ▶
Lady Scarface '41
Lara Croft Tomb Raider '01
Lara Croft Tomb Raider: The Cradle of Life '03
Lethal Panther '90
Lethal Woman '88
The Long Kiss Goodnight '96
The Longshots '08
The Lost Empire '83
Mame '74
Mankillers '87
Marie '85 ▶
The Messenger: The Story of Joan of Arc '99
Mind Trap '91
Mission of Justice '92
Mistress of the Apes '79
Moonshine County Express '77
My Name is Modesty: A Modesty Blaise Adventure '04
My Super Ex-Girlfriend '06
Nancy Drew... Reporter '39
Night Partners '83
Not Without My Daughter '90
Nyoka and the Tigermen '42
One Million Years B.C. '66
Panther Squad '84
The Perils of Pauline '34
Phoenix the Warrior '88
Pocahontas '95 ▶
Point of No Return '93
Prehistoric Women '50
Queen of the Road '84
Ravenhawk '95
Resurrection '80 ▶
The River Wild '94
Roller Blade '85
Runaway Nightmare '84
Running Delilah '93
Sara Dane '81
Savage Beach '89
The Savage Girl '32
Savage Streets '83
See How She Runs '78 ▶
Sheena '84
She'll Be Wearing Pink Pajamas '84
She's in the Army Now '81
The Silence of the Lambs '91 ▶
Silver Hawk '04
Sister Kenny '46 ▶
Skyscraper '95
Speed 2: Cruise Control '97
Spice World: The Movie '97
Stormquest '87
Sunstorm '01
Superchick '71
Supergirl '84
Sweet Revenge '87
Switchblade Sisters '75
Terminal Velocity '94
Thor and the Amazon Women '60
Tiffany Jones '75
Trapped '89
Tulsa '49 ▶
The 24 Hour Woman '99
Uncaged '91
Velvet Smooth '76
Waiting to Exhale '95 ▶
The Wild World of Batwoman '66
The Wind and the Lion '75 ▶
A Woman Rebels '36
Women '60
The World Is Not Enough '99 ▶
Wrestling Women vs. the Aztec Mummy '59
Zorro's Black Whip '44

Words Come to Life

see also Parallel Universe; Writers

Adaptation '02 ▶
Alex & Emma '03
American Dreamer '84
Cashback '06
The Crow Road '96
Nim's Island '08
The Number 23 '07
P.S. I Love You '07
Sex and Lucia '01
Something's Gotta Give '03 ▶
Stranger Than Fiction '06

Workin' for a Livin'

All or Nothing '02 ▶
Astoria '00
Bartleby '01
Bee Movie '07
Belles on Their Toes '52
Blonde Ambition '07
Brown Sugar '02
Bubble '06
Clockwatchers '97 ▶
Close My Eyes '91
Come Early Morning '06
Diggers '06
Dirty Pretty Things '03 ▶
Employee of the Month '06
Everything's Gone Green '06
The Ex '07
Factotum '05 ▶
The Family Plan '05
Far from Heaven '02 ▶
Flawless '07
Friday After Next '02
Friends & Crocodiles '05
The Good Girl '02 ▶
Happy Times '00
High School Musical 2 '07
The Human Stain '03
I Promise to Pay '37
I Really Hate My Job '07
Janice Beard '99
Killer of Sheep '77 ▶
Kinky Boots '06
Mad Money '08
Maid in Manhattan '02
The Man Without a Past '02 ▶
Memron '04
The Method '04
Mondays in the Sun '02
My Boss's Daughter '03
The Mystic Masseur '01
The Nanny Diaries '07
The Navigators '01
9 to 5 '80
No Other Woman '33
North Country '05
Office Space '99
101 Ways (The Things a Girl Will Do to Keep Her Volvo) '00
One Hour Photo '02 ▶
The Pursuit of Happyness '06
Punch-Drunk Love '02 ▶
Read My Lips '01
Real Women Have Curves '02 ▶
Revolution 9 '01
Revolution '85
Spring Forward '99
10 Items or Less '06
Time Out '01
Traveling Companion '96
Vacuuming Completely Nude in Paradise '01
Very Annie Mary '01
Wine, Women and Horses '37
Working Girl '88 ▶
You Kill Me '07 ▶

World War I

see also Espionage; Spies & World War I

All Quiet on the Western Front '79
All Quiet on the Western Front '30 ▶
Anne of Green Gables: The Continuing Story '99
Anzacs: The War Down Under '85 ▶
Arsenal '29 ▶
Behind the Lines '97
The Big Parade '25 ▶
Biggles '85
The Blue Max '66 ▶
Capitaine Conan '96 ▶
Catherine Cookson's The Cinder Path '94
Catherine Cookson's The Wingless Bird '97
The Chaplin Revue '58
Charge of the Model T's '76
Crimson Romance '34
The Dark Angel '35
Dark Journey '37 ▶
Darling Lili '70
Dawn Patrol '38 ▶
The Day That Shook the World '78
Deathwatch '02
Devil in the Flesh '46 ▶
Dishonored '31 ▶
Dr. Mabuse, The Gambler '22 ▶
Doctor Zhivago '65 ▶
Doctor Zhivago '03
Doughboys '30
The Eagle and the Hawk '33 ▶
Elizabeth of Ladymead '48
The End of St. Petersburg '27 ▶
FairyTale: A True Story '97 ▶
False Faces '18
A Farewell to Arms '32 ▶
Fifth Day of Peace '72
The Fighting 69th '40 ▶
Flambards '78
Flyboys '06
For Me and My Gal '42 ▶
Fort Saganne '84
The Four Horsemen of the Apocalypse '21 ▶
Four Sons '28
Gallipoli '81 ▶
Gods and Monsters '98 ▶
Going Home '86
Grand Illusion '37 ▶
The Great War '59
Half-Shot at Sunrise '30
Heart of Humanity '18
Hearts of the World '18 ▶
Hell's Angels '30 ▶
Hotel Imperial '27
How Many Miles to Babylon? '22
An Indecent Obsession '85
In Love and War '96
Inside the Lines '30
The Iron Major '43
Isn't Life Wonderful '24 ▶
Jericho '38
Joyeux Noel '05 ▶
The Killing Floor '85
King and Country '64 ▶
The Land That Time Forgot '75
Lawrence of Arabia '62 ▶
The Legend of Bagger Vance '00
Legends of the Fall '94 ▶
Les Destinées '00
The Life and Death of Colonel Blimp '43 ▶
Life and Nothing But '89 ▶
The Lighthorsemen '87 ▶
The Little American '17
Lost Battalion '01
The Lost Patrol '34 ▶
The Love Light '21
Man of Legend '71
Mata Hari '32 ▶
Mata Hari '85
Memron '04
Miracle of Our Lady of Fatima '52
My Boy Jack '07 ▶
My Son, My Son '40
Nicholas and Alexandra '71 ▶
1915 '82
1918 '85
Nurse Edith Cavell '39 ▶
Oh! What a Lovely War '69 ▶
The Patriots '33 ▶
Paths of Glory '57 ▶
Photographing Fairies '97
Pilgrimage '33 ▶
Q Ships '28
Revolt of the Zombies '36
Return of the Soldier '82 ▶
She Goes to War '29
Shopworn Angel '38 ▶
Shout at the Devil '76
Spy in Black '39 ▶
Suicide Fleet '31
Suzy '36
Testament of Youth '79 ▶
Three Legionnaires '37
Tin Pan Alley '40 ▶
Today We Live '33
Tomorrow Is Forever '46
The Trench '99
The Unknown Soldier '98
A Very Long Engagement '04 ▶
Waterloo Bridge '40 ▶
Weeping Meadow '04
Westfront 1918 '30 ▶
What Price Glory? '52 ▶
When the Whales Came '89
The White Cliffs of Dover '44 ▶
Wilson '44 ▶
Wings '27 ▶
Wings of Eagles '57
Women of All Nations '31
Yankee Doodle in Berlin '19
Zeppelin '71

World War I Spies

see also Espionage; Spies & World War I

Charge of the Model T's '76
Dark Journey '37 ▶
Darling Lili '70
Dishonored '31 ▶
False Faces '18
Hotel Imperial '27
The Love Light '21
Mata Hari '32 ▶
Mata Hari '85
Seas Beneath '31
Spy in Black '39 ▶
Zeppelin '71

World War II

see also Biopic: Military; The Holocaust; The Homefront: England; The Homefront: U.S.; Canada; Nazis & Other Paramilitary Slugs; Postwar; POW/MIAs; The Resistance; World War II Spies

Abroad with Two Yanks '44
Above and Beyond '53 ▶
Above Suspicion '43 ▶
Above Us the Waves '56 ▶
Absent Without Leave '95
The Accompanist '93
Action in the North Atlantic '43 ▶
The Adventures of Smilin' Jack '43
The Adventures of Werner Holt '65
The Affair '95
After the Deluge '03 ▶
Air Force '43 ▶
Alan & Naomi '92
Alexandria... Why? '78 ▶
All the Queen's Men '02
Ambush '99 ▶
The Americanization of Emily '64 ▶
And a Nightingale Sang '91
Angels One Five '54
Angry Harvest '85 ▶
An Annapolis Story '55
Another Time, Another Place '58
Another Time, Another Place '83 ▶
Anzio '68
Arch of Triumph '48 ▶
Arch of Triumph '85
Army of Shadows '69 ▶
Around the World '43
The Ascent '76 ▶
The Ascent '94
Ashes and Diamonds '58 ▶
The Assault '86 ▶
Assault on Agathon '75
The Assisi Underground '85
Atonement '07 ▶
Attack! '56 ▶
Attack Force Z '84
Attack Squadron '63
The Attic: The Hiding of Anne Frank '88
Au Revoir les Enfants '87 ▶
The Audrey Hepburn Story '00
Away All Boats '56
Back Home '90
Band of Brothers '01 ▶
Bataan '43 ▶
Battle Cry '55 ▶
The Battle of Blood Island '60
Battle of Britain '69 ▶
The Battle of El Alamein '68
Battle of Neretva '69
Battle of the Bulge '65 ▶
Battle of the Commandos '71
Battle of the Eagles '79
The Battle of the Japan Sea '70
Battleforce '78
Battleground '49 ▶
Bedknobs and Broomsticks '71 ▶
Behind Enemy Lines '85
Below '02
The Best Years of Our Lives '46 ▶
Betrayal from the East '44
The Big Lift '50 ▶
The Big Red One '80 ▶
Black Brigade '69
Black Rain '88 ▶
Blockhouse '73
The Blood of Others '84
Blood on the Sun '45 ▶
The Boat Is Full '81 ▶
Bomb at 10:10 '67
Bombardier '43
Bon Voyage '03 ▶
The Boxer and Death '63 ▶
Brainwashed '60
Brass Target '78
The Brave Bunch '70
Breaking the Code '95 ▶
Breakthrough '78
The Bridge '59 ▶
The Bridge at Remagen '69 ▶
Bridge to Hell '87
A Bridge Too Far '77 ▶
The Bridge on the River Kwai '57 ▶
Brief Encounter '46 ▶
The Brylcreem Boys '96
Burma Convoy '41
The Burmese Harp '56 ▶
The Caine Mutiny '54 ▶
The Camomile Lawn '92
A Canterbury Tale '44 ▶
The Canterville Ghost '44 ▶
Captain Corelli's Mandolin '01 ▶
Captain Newman, M.D. '63 ▶
Captains of the Clouds '42
Captive Heart '47 ▶
Captive Hearts '87
Carrie's War '04
Carry Me Home '04
Carry On England '76
Casablanca '42 ▶
Casablanca Express '89
Castle Keep '69 ▶
Catch-22 '70 ▶
Chain Lightning '50 ▶
Charlie Grant's War '80
Charlotte Gray '01 ▶

▶ = rated three bones or higher

Chicago Joe & the Showgirl '90
China '43
China Sky '44
Chips, the War Dog '90
Christ Stopped at Eboli '79
Christabel '89
The Chronicles of Narnia: The Lion, the Witch and the Wardrobe '05
Churchill and the Generals '81
Class of '44 '73
The Clock '45
Closely Watched Trains '66
Cold Days '66
The Colditz Story '55
Combat Killers '80
Come and See '85
Come See the Paradise '90
Coming Home '98
Command Decision '48
Commando Attack '67
Commando Squad '76
Commandos '73
Commandos Strike at Dawn '43
Conspiracy '01
Conspiracy of Hearts '60
Contraband '40
Convoy '40
Cornered '45
Corregidor '43
Cottage to Let '41
The Coward '62
The Cranes Are Flying '57
Crash Dive '43
Cross of Iron '76
The Cruel Sea '53
Cry of Battle '63
The Cuckoo '02
D-Day, the Sixth of June '56
Dam Busters '55
Danger UXB '81
Dangerous Moonlight '41
Darby's Rangers '58
Dark Blue World '01
Das Boot '81
David '79
The Day and the Hour '63
A Day in October '92
Day One '89
Days of Glory '43
Days of Glory '06
Deadly Mission '78
Death Is Called Engelchen '63
Death of a Soldier '85
The Death of Adolf Hitler '84
December '91
Desert Commandos '67
The Desert Fox '51
The Desert Rats '53
Despair '78
Desperate Journey '42
Destination Tokyo '43
Destroyer '43
The Devil's Brigade '68
Devils on the Doorstep '00
Diamonds of the Night '64
The Diary of Anne Frank '59
The Dirty Dozen '67
The Dirty Dozen: The Deadly Mission '87
The Dirty Dozen: The Fatal Mission '88
The Dirty Dozen: The Next Mission '85
Dirty Heroes '71
Distant Thunder '73
Distant Voices, Still Lives '88
Dive Bomber '41
Divided We Fall '00
Dr. Akagi '98
Dr. Petiot '90
Dominion: Prequel to the Exorcist '05
Downfall '04
Dresden '06
The Dresser '83

The Dressmaker '89
The Dunera Boys '85
The Eagle Has Landed '77
Ebony Dreams '80
Edge of Darkness '43
Eighteen '04
Elizabeth of Ladymead '48
The Elusive Corporal '62
Empire of the Sun '87
The Empty Mirror '99
End of the Affair '55
End of the Affair '99
Enemy at the Gates '00
Enemy Below '57
Enemy of Women '44
The English Patient '96
Enigma '01
Enigma Secret '79
Enola Gay: The Men, the Mission, the Atomic Bomb '80
Ensign Pulver '64
Era Notte a Roma '60
Escape from Sobibor '87
Escape to Athena '79
Europa, Europa '91
Every Time We Say Goodbye '86
Everything is Illuminated '05
The Execution '85
The Execution of Private Slovik '74
A Face in the Rain '63
Fall from Grace '94
The Fallen '05
Farewell to the King '89
Fat Man and Little Boy '89
Fateless '05
Father '67
Father Goose '64
The Fifth Seal '76
Fighter Attack '53
The Fighting Rats of Tobruk '44
Fighting Seabees '44
The Fighting Sullivans '42
Fireball Forward '72
Fires on the Plain '59
First Yank into Tokyo '45
Fist of Legend '94
Five Fingers '52
Flags of Our Fathers '06
Flame to the Phoenix '85
Flat Top '52
Flying Leathernecks '51
Flying Tigers '42
Follow the Boys '44
For the Boys '91
For the Moment '94
Forbidden Games '52
Force 10 from Navarone '78
Foreign Correspondent '40
A Foreign Field '93
The Foreman Went to France '42
Fortunes of War '87
The Forty-Ninth Parallel '41
Forty Thousand Horsemen '41
Four Bags Full '56
The Four Horsemen of the Apocalypse '62
Four in a Jeep '51
Foxtrot '76
Frieda '47
From Hell to Victory '79
From Here to Eternity '53
From Here to Eternity '79
G-Men vs. the Black Dragon '43
The Gallant Hours '60
The Gang's All Here '43
The Garden of Redemption '97
The Garden of the Finzi-Continis '71
Geheimakte WB1 '42
Generale Della Rovere '60
A Generation '54
Germany, Pale Mother '80
The Gift Horse '52

The Girl of Your Dreams '99
The Gleiwitz Case '61
Gloomy Sunday '02
Go for Broke! '51
God is My Co-Pilot '45
The Goebbels Experiment '05
Golden Earrings '47
Great Day '46
The Great Escape '63
The Great Escape 2: The Untold Story '88
The Great Raid '05
The Great Water '04
Green for Danger '47
The Green Glove '52
The Green House '96
Greta '86
Guadalcanal Diary '43
Gung Ho! '43
The Guns of Navarone '61
A Guy Named Joe '44
The Gypsy Warriors '78
The Halls of Montezuma '50
Hamsun '96
The Hand '60
Hanna's War '88
Hanover Street '79
Hart's War '02
The Hasty Heart '86
Head in the Clouds '04
The Heat of the Day '91
Heaven Knows, Mr. Allison '57
Hell Commandos '69
Hell Is for Heroes '62
Hell River '75
Hell Squad '58
Hell to Eternity '60
Hellcats of the Navy '57
Hell's Brigade: The Final Assault '80
Heroes Die Young '60
The Heroes of Telemark '65
The Hiding Place '75
The Highest Honor '84
The Hill '65
Hillbilly Blitzkrieg '42
Hiroshima '95
Hiroshima Maiden '88
Hiroshima: Out of the Ashes '90
Hitler '62
Hitler: The Last Ten Days '73
Hitler's Children '43
Hitler's Prayer '61
Hollywood Canteen '44
Holocaust '78
The Home Front '02
Home of the Brave '49
Homecoming '48
Hope and Glory '87
The Horizontal Lieutenant '62
Hornet's Nest '70
The Human Comedy '43
The Human Condition: A Soldier's Prayer '61
The Human Condition: No Greater Love '58
The Human Condition: Road to Eternity '59
Hunted '88
Hunters of the Golden Cobra '82
Hustler Squad '76
I Bombed Pearl Harbor '60
I Was a Male War Bride '49
I'll Remember April '99
Immortal Battalion '44
Immortal Sergeant '43
The Imperial Japanese Empire '85
In a Shallow Grave '88
In Enemy Hands '04
In Harm's Way '65
In Love and War '01
In Which We Serve '43
The Incident '89
The Incredible Mr. Limpet '64
Infinity '96
The Inheritors '82

Inside the Third Reich '82
Is Paris Burning? '66
The Island on Bird Street '97
Jacob the Liar '74
Jenny's War '85
Jive Junction '43
Joan of Paris '42
Johnny Frenchman '46
Journey for Margaret '42
Judgment at Nuremberg '61
Julia '77
Jungle Patrol '48
Kanal '56
Kapo '59
Kelly's Heroes '70
The Key '58
The Key to Rebecca '85
Kindergarten '84
King Rat '65
Kings Go Forth '58
Korczak '90
La Grande Vadrouille '66
La Silence de la Mer '47
The Land Girls '98
Landscape After Battle '70
Lassiter '84
The Last Bastion '84
The Last Bridge '54
The Last Butterfly '92
The Last Chance '45
Last Day of the War '69
The Last Days of Patton '86
The Last Drop '05
The Last Five Days '82
The Last Lieutenant '94
The Last Metro '80
The Last of the Blonde Bombshells '00
The Last Train '74
The Last Warrior '89
Law of the Jungle '42
A League of Their Own '92
Leon Morin, Priest '61
Les Miserables '95
Les Violons du Bal '74
Letters from Iwo Jima '06
Letters to an Unknown Lover '84
The Life and Death of Colonel Blimp '43
Life is Beautiful '98
Lifeboat '44
The Lion Has Wings '40
The Little Thief '89
The Longest Day '62
Lotna '64
A Love in Germany '84
Love Letters '45
Lucie Aubrac '98
MacArthur '77
MacArthur's Children '85
Malaya '49
Malta Story '53
A Man Called Sarge '90
A Man Escaped '57
Manhunt in the African Jungles '43
Manon '50
Map of the Human Heart '93
Maria's Lovers '84
Marine Raiders '43
Massacre in Rome '73
Max and Helen '90
The McConnell Story '55
McHale's Navy '64
McKenzie Break '70
Me and the Colonel '58
Mediterraneo '91
Meet Sexton Blake '44
Memoirs of a Geisha '05
Memories of Hell '87
Memphis Belle '90
The Men '50
Mephisto '81
Merrill's Marauders '62
Merry Christmas, Mr. Lawrence '83
A Midnight Clear '92
Midway '76
Miracle at Midnight '98
Miracle at Moreaux '86
The Miracle of the White Stallions '63
The Mirror '75
The Misfit Brigade '87
Mission Batangas '69
Mission of the Shark '91

Mission to Death '66
Mrs. Henderson Presents '05
Mrs. Miniver '42
Mr. Kingstreet's War '71
Mr. Klein '76
Mister Roberts '55
Mr. Skeffington '44
Mr. Winkle Goes to War '44
The Mortal Storm '40
Moscow Parade '92
Mosley '98
Mother of Kings '82
Mother of Mine '05
The Mountain Road '60
Murderers Among Us: The Simon Wiesenthal Story '89
Murphy's War '71
Music Box '89
Mussolini & I '85
Mutiny '99
My Brother Tom '86
The Naked and the Dead '58
The Nasty Girl '90
The Navy Comes Through '42
Navy Way '44
Never So Few '59
Never Wave at a WAC '52
Night Ambush '57
Night of the Fox '90
The Night of the Shooting Stars '82
The Nightmare Years '89
Nine Men '43
1941 '79
The Ninth Day '04
No Greater Love '43
No Man Is an Island '62
No Regrets for Our Youth '46
None But the Brave '65
The North Star '43
The Notebook '04
Nous N'Irons Plus au Bois '69
November Moon '85
The Nun's Story '59
Objective, Burma! '45
The Odd Squad '86
The Ogre '96
On the Fiddle '61
Once Before I Die '65
One Against the Wind '91
One of Our Aircraft Is Missing '42
One That Got Away '57
The Only Way '70
Open City '45
Operation Bikini '63
The Oppermann Family '82
Overlanders '46
Pacific Inferno '85
Paisan '46
Paradise Road '97
Passage to Marseilles '44
Patton '70
The Pawnbroker '65
Pearl '78
Pearl Harbor '01
The Philadelphia Experiment '84
Piece of Cake '88
Pimpernel Smith '42
Pin-Up Girl '44
Place in Hell '69
Playing for Time '80
Prelude to War '42
Prisoners of the Sun '91
Private Buckaroo '42
Private Contentment '83
Private Navy of Sgt. O'Farrell '68
PT 109 '63
The Purple Heart '44
Pursuit of the Graf Spee '57
Raggedy Man '81
Raid on Rommel '71
Raiders of Leyte Gulf '63
Raiders of Sunset Pass '43
The Ravagers '65
Reach for the Sky '56
Rebel '85
Red Ball Express '52
Red Cherry '95

The Reflecting Skin '91
Rescuers: Stories of Courage "Two Women" '97
Return to Never Land '02
Reunion '88
Reunion in France '42
The Revolt of Job '84
Rodgers & Hammerstein's South Pacific '01
Rosenstrasse '03
Run Silent, Run Deep '58
Running Away '89
Sahara '43
Saint-Ex: The Story of the Storyteller '95
Saints and Soldiers '03
Salo, or the 120 Days of Sodom '75
Salute John Citizen '42
San Demetrio, London '47
Sands of Iwo Jima '49
Saving Private Ryan '98
The Scarlet & the Black '83
Schindler's List '93
Sea Chase '55
Sea of Sand '58
The Sea Shall Not Have Them '55
Sea Wife '57
Sea Wolves '81
The Search '48
The Seventh Cross '44
Second Victory '64
The Secret Invasion '64
The Secret of Santa Vittoria '69
The Secret War of Harry Frigg '68
Seven Beauties '76
Seven Days' Leave '42
Seven Years in Tibet '97
Shadows over Shanghai '38
Shell Shock '63
Sherlock Holmes and the Secret Weapon '42
Sherlock Holmes: The Voice of Terror '42
Ship of Fools '65
The Shop on Main Street '65
Signs of Life '68
The Silent Enemy '58
Silent Raiders '54
Since You Went Away '44
Sink the Bismarck '60
633 Squadron '64
Ski Troop Attack '60
The Sky Is Falling '00
Slaughterhouse Five '72
The Small Back Room '49
Snow Treasure '68
So Proudly We Hail '43
So This Is Washington '43
Soldat Duroc... Ca Va Etre Ta Fete! '75
Soldier of Orange '78
A Soldier's Story '84
A Soldier's Tale '91
Somewhere I'll Find You '42
Son of Lassie '45
Sophie Scholl: The Final Days '05
The Sorrow and the Pity '71
The Sound of Music '65
South Pacific '58
South Sea Woman '53
Special Forces '68
Spitfire '42
SS Girls '77
Stage Door Canteen '43
Stairway to Heaven '46
Stalag Luft '93
Stalingrad '93
Star Spangled Rhythm '42
The Steel Claw '61
Story of a Prostitute '65
The Story of Dr. Wassell '44
The Story of G.I. Joe '45
Straight into Darkness '04
Strayed '03
Strictly G.I. '44
Submarine Attack '54
Submarine Seahawk '59
The Summer of My German Soldier '78

▲ = rated three bones or higher

Sundown '41
Surviving Picasso '96
Sweet Light in a Dark Room '60
Sword of Honour '01
Taking Sides '01►
Tank Commando '59
Task Force '49
A Taste of Hell '73
Tea with Mussolini '99
The Teahouse of the August Moon '56
Tender Comrade '43
The Tenth Man '88
Thank Your Lucky Stars '43
That Long Night in '43 '60
That Summer of White Roses '90
They Were Expendable '45►
The Thin Red Line '64
The Thin Red Line '98►
Thirty Seconds Over Tokyo '44►
36 Hours '64
Thirty-Six Hours of Hell '77
This is the Army '43
This Land is Mine '43
Thousands Cheer '43
Three Came Home '50►
Thunder Birds '42
Tides of War '90
Tiger Fangs '43
A Time of Destiny '88
A Time to Love & a Time to Die '58
The Tin Drum '79►
To Be or Not to Be '42►
To Be or Not to Be '83
To Each His Own '46►
To End All Wars '01
To Have & Have Not '44►
To Hell and Back '55
To the Shores of Tripoli '42
Tobruk '66
Tomorrow Is Forever '46
Tonight and Every Night '45
Too Late the Hero '70►
Tora! Tora! Tora! '70
Torpedo Attack '72
Torpedo Run '58
Tower of Terror '42
A Town Like Alice '85
The Train '65►
Transport from Paradise '65
Treasure Island '99
Triple Echo '77
Triumph of the Spirit '89►
Triumph of the Will '34►
The Truce '96►
True Colors '87
The Tuskegee Airmen '95►
Twelve o'Clock High '49►
25 Fireman's Street '73►
Two Girls and a Sailor '44►
Two Men Went to War '02
The Two of Us '68►
Two Women '61►
U-571 '00
U-Boat Prisoner '44
Uncertain Glory '44
Under the Earth '86►
Under the Flag of the Rising Sun '72►
The Underdog '43
Underground '41
Underground '95►
Until They Sail '57
Up in Arms '44
Uprising '01►
Valiant '05
Varian's War '01
The Victors '63
Victory '81
Von Ryan's Express '65►
Voyage of the Damned '76►
Wackiest Ship in the Army '61
Wake Island '42►
A Walk in the Sun '46►
The Walls of Hell '64
The Wannsee Conference '84►
War & Love '84
War & Remembrance '88
War & Remembrance: The Final Chapter '89
The War Boy '85

War Lover '62
Warkill '65
We Dive at Dawn '43►
We Will Not Enter the Forest '79►
The Weaker Sex '49
Wedding in White '72
Weeping Meadow '04
Well-Digger's Daughter '46►
What Did You Do in the War, Daddy? '66
When Hell Broke Loose '58
When Taekwondo Strikes '83
When Trumpets Fade '98
When Willie Comes Marching Home '50►
The White Cliffs of Dover '44►
The White Rose '83►
The Winds of War '83
Windtalkers '02
A Wing and a Prayer '44►
Wings over the Pacific '43
The Wizard of Loneliness '88
A Woman at War '94
Women of Valor '86
Wooden Horse '50►
World War II: When Lions Roared '94
A Yank in Australia '43
A Yank in the R.A.F. '41
13 Rue Madeleine '46►
The Young Lions '58►
You'll Never Get Rich '41►
Zelary '03►
Zero '84
Zone Troopers '84

World War II Spies
see also Nazis & Other Paramilitary Slugs; Spies & Espionage; World War II
Above Suspicion '43
Action in Arabia '44
Against the Wind '48
Air Raid Wardens '43
All the Queen's Men '02
All Through the Night '42►
Armored Command '61
Background to Danger '43
Bear Island '80
Berlin Express '48►
Betrayed '54►
Black Book '06►
The Black Dragons '42
Bon Voyage '03►
Cairo '42
Call Out the Marines '42
Carve Her Name with Pride '58
Charlotte Gray '01
Clipped Wings '53
Cloak and Dagger '46
Code Name: Emerald '85
Counterblast '48
The Counterfeit Traitor '62►
Cowboy Commandos '43
Dawn Express '42
The Day Will Dawn '42►
Enigma '01
Eye of the Needle '81
A Face in the Rain '63
The Fallen Sparrow '43►
Five Fingers '52►
Five for Hell '67
Five Graves to Cairo '43►
Foreign Correspondent '40►
Head in the Clouds '04
The Heat of the Day '91
Heroes in Hell '73
Hidden Enemy '40
Hotel Reserve '44►
I See a Dark Stranger '46►
International Lady '41
Invisible Agent '42
Journey into Fear '42►
The Lost One '51
Lust, Caution '07

Writers
see also This Is Your Life
Adaptation '02►
The Adventures of Mark Twain '44►
Agatha '79
Agatha Christie: A Life in Pictures '04
Alex & Emma '03
Alias Betty '01
All the Wrong Places '00

The Man Who Never Was '55►
The Mediterranean in Flames '72
Ministry of Fear '44►
Monte Carlo '86
Montuori '65►
Mother Night '96►
My Favorite Blonde '42►
My Name is Ivan '62►
Night Train to Munich '40►
Notorious '46►
Once Upon a Honeymoon '42
Operation Amsterdam '60
Operation Cross Eagles '69
Operation Crossbow '65►
O.S.S. '46►
Panama Hattie '42
Panama Menace '41
Qui Etes Vous, Mr. Sorge? '61
Rio Rita '42
Robot Pilot '41
The Rocketeer '91►
Saboteur '42►
The Second Front '05
Secret Mission '42
Ship Ahoy '42
Spy Smasher '42
Spy Smasher Returns '42
Stalag 17 '53►
The Stranger '46►
36 Hours '64►
13 Rue Madeleine '46►
Triple Cross '67►
Under the Rainbow '81
Underground Agent '42
Up Periscope '59
Watch on the Rhine '43►
Waterfront '44
Where Eagles Dare '68►

Wrestling
...All the Marbles '81
The American Angels: Baptism of Blood '89
Bad Guys '86
Below the Belt '80
Body Slam '87
Chaos Theory '08
Cheaper by the Dozen '03
Chelsea Walls '01
Closer '04►
Closer and Closer '96
Collected Stories '02►
Coming Through '85
Cross Creek '83►
Croupier '97►
Dante's Inferno: Life of Dante Gabriel Rossetti '69
The Dark Half '91►
The Dark Side of the Heart '92
Dash and Lilly '99
Dean Koontz's Mr. Murder '98
Deathtrap '82
Deconstructing Harry '97
Dedication '07
Delirious '91
Dinner and Driving '97
The Disappearance of Garcia Lorca '96
Divine Secrets of the Ya-Ya Sisterhood '02
Doctor Zhivago '65►
Doctor Zhivago '03
The Dog Problem '06
The Door in the Floor '04►
Double Whammy '01
Down With Love '03
Duplex '03
The End of the Affair '99►
Enemies of Laughter '00
Eternity and a Day '97
Eva '62
Evidence of Blood '97
Evil Eyes '04
Evil Lives '92
F. Scott Fitzgerald in Hollywood '76
Factotum '06►
Faithless '00►
Fall '97

Ambition '91
American Dreamer '84
American Splendor '03►
Amuck! '71
Amy's O '02
An Angel at My Table '89►
Anne of Green Gables: The Continuing Story '99
Another Man's Poison '52
Anything Else '03
The Ape '05
As Good As It Gets '97►
Atonement '07►
Author! Author! '82
Batac: A Life of Passion '99►
Bamboozled '00
Barton Fink '91►
Basic Instinct 2 '06
The Basketball Diaries '95
Beau '00
Beautiful Dreamers '92
Becoming Colette '92
Becoming Jane '07
Before Sunset '04►
Before Night Falls '00►
Behind the Lines '97
Beloved Infidel '59
Best Seller '87►
The Best Man '99►
Big Bad Love '02
The Big Slice '90
Bloodhounds '96
Bloodhounds 2 '96
Bone Daddy '97
Boom! '68
Borstal Boy '00
The Brontes of Haworth '73
Breakfast at Tiffany's '61►
Breakfast of Champions '98
Breakin' All The Rules '04
Bright Young Things '03
Burial of the Rats '95
A Business Affair '93
Cabin by the Lake '00
Capote '05►
Casanova '05
Celebrity '98
Celeste '81►
Chapter Two '79

The Man from Elysian Fields '01►
Margot at the Wedding '07
Martian Child '07
The Mask of Dimitrios '44►
Maybe Baby '00
Melissa '97
Men Cry Bullets '00

Father's Day '96
Fear and Loathing in Las Vegas '98
Finding Forrester '00
A Fine Madness '66►
The Flower of My Secret '95►
For Hire '98
Forbidden Passion: The Oscar Wilde Movie '85
Freedom Writers '07
Fresh Cut Grass '04
From Noon Till Three '76
Full Speed '96
The Gambler '97►
Game 6 '05
Ghosts Never Sleep '05
Ghostwriter '84
Glam '97
Goldeneye: The Secret Life of Ian Fleming '89►
Gothic '87►
Hamsun '96
Happy Hour '03
Harriet the Spy '96
Haunted Summer '89
Hav Plenty '97
Heart Beat '80
Heartburn '86►
Heat Wave '54
Henry & June '90►
Her Alibi '88
Hit and Runway '01
The Hoax '07►
The Hours '02►
House of the Long Shadows '82
How to Kill Your Neighbor's Dog '01
How to Lose Your Lover '04
The Human Stain '03
Hustler White '96
I Capture the Castle '02►
Impromptu '90►
In Praise of Love '01
In the Cut '03
In the Deep Woods '91
In the Mouth of Madness '95►
Infamous '06►
Iris '01►
Isn't She Great '00
Jack London '44
James Joyce's Women '35►
James Joyce: A Portrait of the Artist as a Young Man '77►
Jane Doe '96
The Jew '05
Joe Gould's Secret '00
Joshua Then and Now '85►
Just Write '97
Kafka '91►
The Keeper: The Legend of Omar Khayyam '05
Kissing a Fool '98
The Kovak Box '06
Lady in the Water '06
The Life of Emile Zola '37►
Long Day's Journey Into Night '96►
The Lonely Lady '83
Long '04
Love Song for Bobby Long '04
The Lost Boys '78►
Love and Death on Long Island '97
Late August, Early September '98
Letters from a Killer '98
Lies and Whispers '98

A Merry War '97►
Meteor & Shadow '85
Misery '90►
Miss Monday '98
Mission '07
Mr. Jealousy '98
Mr. Woodcock '07
The Moon's Our Home '36
Mother '96
Moulin Rouge '01►
Mrs. Palfrey at the Claremont '05
Mrs. Parker and the Vicious Circle '94►
Murder by the Book '87
A Murder of Crows '99
The Muse '99
The Mystic Masseur '01
Mystery Woman: Mystery Weekend '05
The Mystery of Rampo '94►
My Apprenticeship '39►
My Boy Jack '07
My Brilliant Career '79►
My Childhood '38►
My House in Umbra '03►
My Left Foot '89►
My Universities '40►
Nadja '96
Naked Lunch '91►
Nerolio '96
The Night and the Moment '94
Nim's Island '08
Novel Romance '06
101 Ways (The Things a Girl Will Do to Keep Her Volvo) '00
Our Lady of the Assassins '01
Out of Africa '85►
Out of Order '03
Pandaemonium '00►
Paperback Romance '96
The Passion of Ayn Rand '99
A Perfect Day '06
Personal Velocity: Three Portraits '02►
Personals '00
Petrified Forest '36►
The Pillow Book '95
Pleasure '31
Portraits Chinois '96
Possession '02►
Postmortem '98
The Prize '63►
The Proprietor '96
Pulp '72
Quills '00►
The Real Howard Spitz '98
The Reaper '97
Redeemer '02
Reds '81►
Restaurant '98
Romancing the Stone '84►
Romantic Comedy '83
Rowing with the Wind '88
The Royal Tenenbaums '01►
Russian Dolls '05
Saint-Ex: The Story of the Storyteller '96
Salem's Lot '04
The Savages '07►
The Sculptress '97
Second Best '05
Secret Window '04
Sex and Lucia '01►
Sex and the City: The Movie '08
Shadowlands '85►
Shadowlands '93►
Shakespeare in Love '98►
The Shining '80►
The Singing Detective '03►
Sink or Swim '97
Sitting Pretty '48►
Slam '98
The Sleepy Time Gal '01
Sleuth '07►
Slipstream '07
The Snows of Kilimanjaro '52►
Something's Gotta Give '03►

Writers

Spymaker: The Secret Life of Ian Fleming '90
The Squid and the Whale '05
Stand by Me '86
Starting Out in the Evening '07
The Sticky Fingers of Time '97
Stone Reader '02
Storytelling '01
Stranger Than Fiction '06
Street Smart '87
Swann '96
Sweet and Lowdown '99
Swimming Pool '03
Sylvia '03
Teach Me '97
The Tenants '06
Thanks for the Memory '38
Theodora Goes Wild '36
Things 2 '97
The Third Man '49
301, 302 '94
Time Regained '99
Tom & Viv '94
The Trials of Oscar Wilde '60
The Trip '02
The TV Set '06
2046 '04
Two Ninas '00
Two Shades of Blue '98
Under the Tuscan Sun '03
Undercover Angel '99
United States of Leland '03
Unsane '82
The Weather Man '05
White Badge '97
The Whole Wide World '96
Wilde '97
Winter Passing '05
Wonder Boys '00
The Wonderful World of the Brothers Grimm '62
The World According to Garp '82
A Year Without Love '05
You Stupid Man '02
Your Vice is a Closed Room and Only I Have the Key '72
Zeder '83
Zora Is My Name! '90
Zorba the Greek '64

The Wrong Man
see also Frame-Ups; Mistaken Identity
Absolute Power '97
After Innocence '05
Bad Seed '00
The Bedroom Window '87
The Big Hit '98
Big Steal '49
Black Angel '46
Bloodfist 7: Manhunt '95
Body Heat '81
Catherine Cookson's The Black Candle '92
Chain Reaction '96
Charlie Chan in London '34
Cherish '02
Codename: Jaguar '00
The Confessor '04
Consenting Adults '92
The Contractor '07
Cookie's Fortune '99
Cop-Out '03
The Criminal '00
The Crow: Salvation '00
Dangerous Evidence: The Lori Jackson Story '99
Dead End '98
Deadline '00
Deadlocked '00
Delivered '98
Disorder '06
Double Jeopardy '99
Double Take '01
Extremely Dangerous '99
Fall Guy '47
Fallen '98
Frenzy '72
The Fugitive '93
Girls in Prison '94

High Lonesome '50
The House of the Seven Gables '40
I Confess '53
In Pursuit '00
In the Name of the Father '93
The Jacket '05
Jack's Back '87
Jennifer 8 '92
The Jury's Secret '38
Kansas City Confidential '52
Kept '01
Kick of Death: The Prodigal Boxer '73
Kiss of the Dragon '01
The Last Musketeer '00
Life '99
Life & Times of Grizzly Adams '74
The Lone Rider in Frontier Fury '41
The Long Ride Home '01
The Man Who Knew Too Much '34
The Man Who Knew Too Much '56
Marked Man '96
Melissa '97
Men of America '32
Ministry of Fear '44
Minority Report '02
Mission of Death '97
Most Wanted '97
Murder in Greenwich Village '37
Mystery Street '50
The Negotiator '98
Night of January 16th '41
One Way Out '02
Partners in Crime '99
Perfect Target '98
Phantom Lady '44
Plato's Run '96
Pressure '02
Presumed Innocent '90
Pros & Cons '99
Red Corner '97
Running Woman '98
Saving Shiloh '06
Secret Window '04
The Sentinel '06
Seven Doors to Death '44
Shooter '07
Small Vices: A Spenser Mystery '99
Spoiler '98
Steamboat Round the Bend '35
Storm Catcher '99
A Stranger in the Kingdom '98
Terror Street '54
They Made Me a Criminal '39
The 39 Steps '35
Three Days of the Condor '75
Ticket of Leave Man '37
Time Served '99
Under Suspicion '92
U.S. Marshals '98
We'll Meet Again '02
When Danger Follows You Home '97
Whitewash: The Clarence Brandley Story '02
The Whole Town's Talking '35
The Winslow Boy '98
Winterset '36
The Wrong Guy '96
The Wrong Man '56
The Wrong Man '93
Wrongfully Accused '98

Wrong Side of the Tracks
see also Rags to Riches
Aaron Loves Angela '75
Algiers '38
Alice Adams '35
Amarilly of Clothesline Alley '18
Angel and the Badman '47
Angels with Dirty Faces '38

Anna Christie '30
Bachelor Party '84
Back Door to Heaven '39
Breaking Away '79
The Bride of Frank '96
The Bride Wore Red '37
Camille '36
Cannery Row '82
Captains Courageous '37
Captives '99
Carbon Copy '81
Careful, He Might Hear You '84
Carrie '52
Cat Ballou '65
Chains '89
Cherry Crush '07
China Girl '87
Claudia '85
Cool and the Crazy '94
Cool As Ice '91
The Courtney Affair '47
Courtship '87
crazy/beautiful '01
The Crucified Lovers '54
Cry-Baby '90
The Dark Side of Love '79
Diary of a Chambermaid '46
Dirty Dancing '87
Dragstrip Girl '94
Eegah! '62
Far and Away '92
Federal Hill '94
The Fence '94
Fire with Fire '86
The Flamingo Kid '84
Foxfire Light '82
Fresh Horses '88
Future Kill '85
Grease '78
Great Expectations '97
The Great Gatsby '49
The Great Gatsby '74
The Hairy Ape '44
Hearts of Humanity '32
Here on Earth '00
Hush '98
Iron Maze '91
It '27
It Could Happen to You '37
It Happened One Night '34
Jailbait! '00
Jersey Girl '92
Jungle Fever '91
King Ralph '91
The Lacemaker '77
Last Exit to Brooklyn '90
Liar's Moon '82
Little Minister '34
The Loves of Carmen '48
Luzia '88
Mad About Mambo '00
The Man from Snowy River '82
Manhattan Melodrama '34
Masquerade '88
A Million to One '37
Min & Bill '30
My Forbidden Past '51
My Man Godfrey '36
Naked Youth '59
Night Beat '48
Off Beat '86
Outpost in Morocco '49
Over the Brooklyn Bridge '83
The Phantom in the House '29
The Phantom of the Opera '25
Picnic on the Grass '59
A Place in the Sun '51
The Pope of Greenwich Village '84
Port of New York '49
Pretty in Pink '86
Primrose Path '40
Princess Tam Tam '35
Probation '32
Pygmalion '38
The Rage: Carrie 2 '99
Reckless '84
Reform School Girl '57
Return to Snowy River '88
Rich Girl '91
Riff Raff '92
Rocky '76

Room at the Top '59
Rosewood '96
Ruby Gentry '52
Rumble Fish '83
San Francisco '36
The Second Chance '06
The Servant '63
Set It Off '96
sex, lies and videotape '89
She's All That '99
Show People 28
Small Faces '95
Snow Country '57
Some Kind of Wonderful '87
Somebody Up There Likes Me '56
Starter for Ten '06
Stay Hungry '76
Step Up '06
Stomp the Yard '07
The Story of the Late Chrysanthemum '39
Suburbia '83
The Swan '25
The Swan '56
Sweet Light in a Dark Room '60
The Tamarind Seed '74
Tango '36
That Night '93
This Sporting Life '63
Tortilla Flat '42
A Tree Grows in Brooklyn '45
Under the Boardwalk '89
Uptown Angel '90
Valley Girl '83
The Valley of Decision '45
Virtue's Revolt '24
Vivacious Lady '38
Waterloo Bridge '40
White Palace '90
The White Sin '24
The World of Suzie Wong '60
The Young Philadelphians '59

Yakuza
see also Crime & Criminals; Japan; Organized Crime
Adrenaline Drive '99
American Yakuza '94
Another Lonely Hitman '95
Beautiful Beast '95
Black Rain '89
The Bodyguard '76
Boiling Point '90
Brother '00
Dolls '02
Double Edge '97
Girls of the White Orchid '85
Gozu '03
Graveyard of Honor '02
Hard As Nails '01
Johnny Mnemonic '95
Kill Bill Vol. 1 '03
Minbo—Or the Gentle Art of Japanese Extortion '92
No Way Back '96
Organized Crime & Triad Bureau '93
Overkill '86
Showdown in Little Tokyo '91
Sonatine '96
The Street Fighter's Last Revenge '74
Sympathy for the Underdog '71
Tokyo Drifter '66
War '07
Wasabi '01
Wicked City '92
The Wolves '71
The Yakuza '75
Youth of the Beast '63
Zatoichi: The Life and Opinion of Masseur Ichi '62
Zatoichi: Zatoichi's Flashing Sword '64

Yoga
The Crippled Masters '82
Hollywood Homicide '03

The Next Best Thing '00
What Women Want '00

You are Getting Sleepy!
The Angry Red Planet '59
Blood of Dracula '57
Brainscan '94
Carefree '38
The Curse of the Jade Scorpion '01
Dead Again '91
Devil Doll '36
Devour '05
The Exorcist 2: The Heretic '77
Haunting Fear '91
A Killing in a Small Town '90
The Mask of Dijon '46
The Misadventures of Merlin Jones '63
On a Clear Day You Can See Forever '70
Scared to Death '46
Shallow Hal '01
She Creature '01
Somewhere in Time '80
Stir of Echoes '99
Telefon '77
Threat of Exposure '02
The Three Faces of Eve '57
Thumbsucker '05
A Wind from Wyoming '94

You Big Dummy!
see also Killer Toys
Charlie McCarthy, Detective '39
Dead Silence '07
Devil Doll '64
Dummy '02
The Dummy Talks '43
The Great Gabbo '29
Magic '78
1941 '79
The Ten '07
The Unholy Three 25

You Lose, You Die
see also Post-Apocalypse
Alien vs. Predator '04
Arcade '93
The Arena '73
Arena '89
Blade Boxer '97
Bloodsport 4: The Dark Kumite '98
The Condemned '07
Cruel World '05
Death Race 2000 '75
Deathrow Gameshow '88
DOA: Dead or Alive '06
Dominion '94
Fatal Combat '96
Futuresport '98
Gamebox 1.0 '04
Hostel: Part 2 '07
Mad Max: Beyond Thunderdome '85
Mean Guns '97
Mortal Challenge '97
Nemesis Game '03
Prayer of the Rollerboys '91
Robot Jox '90
Roller Blade '85
Roller Blade Warriors: Taken By Force '90
Rollerball '75
Rollerball '02
The Running Man '87
Sci-Fighter '04
Solarbabies '86
Star Hunter '95
Stay Alive '06
Thr3e '07
Tron '82
Vacancy '07
Webmaster '98
Wrong Turn 2: Dead End '07

Yuppie Nightmares
see also Strained Suburbia
Addams Family Values '93
Alice '90
Almost You '85
Amos and Andrew '93
Baby Boom '87
Bad Influence '90
Barbarians at the Gate '93
Bare Essentials '91
Bedroom Eyes '86
Beetlejuice '88
The Big Chill '83
Blind Date '87
Blind Side '93
Boiler Room '00
The Bonfire of the Vanities '90
The Boost '88
Bright Lights, Big City '88
Cape Fear '91
City of Hope '91
Clara's Heart '88
Clean and Sober '88
Cold Creek Manor '03
Cold Fever '95
Coma '78
Consenting Adults '92
Curly Sue '91
Dead Calm '89
Denise Calls Up '95
Desperately Seeking Susan '85
Diary of a Mad Housewife '70
Down and Out in Beverly Hills '86
Drop Dead Fred '91
Edge of Honor '91
The End of Innocence '90
Eye of the Demon '87
Fatal Attraction '87
The Fisher King '91
Folks! '92
Fun with Dick and Jane '77
The Further Adventures of Tennessee Buck '88
The Game '97
Goodbye, New York '85
The Guardian '90
The Hand that Rocks the Cradle '92
Happiness '98
The Hard Way '91
He Said, She Said '91
Heartbreak '86
Hiding Out '87
In the Company of Men '96
In the Spirit '90
Indian Summer '93
Jungle Fever '91
Key Exchange '85
Kicks '85
L.A. Story '91
Let's Kill All the Lawyers '93
Limit Up '89
Looking for Mr. Goodbar '77
Lost in America '85
Madhouse '90
Maid to Order '87
The Malibu Beach Vampires '91
Maniac '77
Micki & Maude '84
Mifune '99
The Mighty Ducks '92
The Money Pit '86
Mother's Boys '94
Moving '88
My Daughter's Keeper '93
My New Gun '92
Neighbors '81
New Year's Day '89
Next Door '94
Night of the Living Babes '87
Nothing But Trouble '91
Nothing in Common '86
Oasis of the Zombies '82
The Object of Beauty '91
Pacific Heights '90
Perfect Family '92
Permanent Vacation '84
Preppies '82
Private Benjamin '80
Quicksilver '86

★ = rated three bones or higher

The Quiet '05
Reversal of Fortune '90►
Roadhouse 66 '84
Rude Awakening '89
Ruthless People '86►
The Safety of Objects '01
St. Elmo's Fire '85
The Secret of My Success '87
The Secretary '94
September '88
sex, lies and videotape '89►
A Shock to the System '90►
Shattered '91
Six Degrees of Separation '93
A Smile Like Yours '96
Something Wild '86
Stay Tuned '92
Straw Dogs '72►
Summer Rental '85
Taking Care of Business '90
Taking the Heat '93
The Temp '93
Three Men and a Little Lady '90
Through the Eyes of a Killer '92
The Tie That Binds '95
The Toxic Avenger, Part 3: The Last Temptation of Toxie '89
Trading Places '83
Trapped '89
The Trigger Effect '96
Truth or Consequences, N.M. '97
Under Pressure '98
Unlawful Entry '92
The Vagrant '92
Voodoo Dawn '89
Wall Street '87►
The War of the Roses '89►
Westworld '73►
What about Bob? '91►
When a Man Loves a Woman '94
Windy City '84
Wolf '94
Your Friends & Neighbors '98►

Zombie Soldiers
see also Zombies
Akira Kurosawa's Dreams '90
Army of Darkness '92►
The Dark Power '85
Deathdream '72
Hard Rock Zombies '85
House '86►
Oasis of the Zombies '82
Revenge of the Zombies '43
Revolt of the Zombies '36
Scream and Scream Again '70
She Demons '58
Shock Waves '77
The Supernaturals '86
They Saved Hitler's Brain '64
The Zombie Army '93
Zombie Lake '80

Zombies
see also Death & the Afterlife; Ghosts, Ghouls, & Goblins; Zombie Soldiers
The Alchemist '81
Alien Dead '79
Alien Massacre '67
All Souls Day '05
Almost Dead '94
The Astro-Zombies '57
The Beyond '82
Beyond Re-Animator '03
Biozombie '98
Bowery at Midnight '42
Bride of Re-Animator '89
Cabin Fever '03
Carnival of Souls '62►
Cast a Deadly Spell '91►
Cemetery Man '95
Children of the Living Dead '00

Children Shouldn't Play with Dead Things '72
The Chilling '89
Chopper Chicks in Zombietown '91
C.H.U.D. 2: Bud the Chud '89
City of the Walking Dead '80
Creature of the Walking Dead '60
Creatures from the Pink Lagoon '07
The Curse of the Aztec Mummy '59
Dawn of the Dead '78►
Dawn of the Dead '04►
Dawn of the Mummy '82
Day of the Dead '85
Dead Alive '93
Dead Creatures '01
The Dead Don't Die '75
The Dead Hate the Living '99
Dead Heat '88
Dead Heist '07
Dead in the Water '06
Dead Men Don't Die '91
The Dead Next Door '89
The Dead One '07
Dead Pit '89
Death Becomes Her '92►
The Death Curse of Tartu '66
Death Valley: The Revenge of Bloody Bill '04
Deathdream '72
Demon Wind '90
Destroyer '88
Devil's Kiss '75
Diary of the Dead '07
Ed and His Dead Mother '93
Evil Town '87
Fido '06
Flight of the Living Dead: Outbreak on a Plane '07
George A. Romero's Land of the Dead '05►
The Ghost Brigade '93
The Ghoul '75
The Granny '94
The Hanging Woman '72
Haunting Fear '91
Hellgate '89
Horror of the Zombies '74
Horror Rises from the Tomb '72
The House of Seven Corpses '73
House of the Dead '78
House of the Dead '03
House of the Dead 2: Dead Aim '05
I Am Legend '07►
I Eat Your Skin '64
I Walked with a Zombie '43►
I Was a Teenage Zombie '87
Infested: Invasion of the Killer Bugs '02
Invisible Invaders '59
Isle of the Dead '45
The Jitters '88
John Carpenter's Ghosts of Mars '01
King of the Zombies '41
Kiss Daddy Goodbye '81
The Legend of the 7 Golden Vampires '73
Let Sleeping Corpses Lie '74
The Mad Ghoul '43
Messiah of Evil '74
Mortuary '05
The Mummy '32►
The Mummy '59►
The Mummy '99
Mummy & Curse of the Jackal '67
The Mummy's Revenge '73
My Boyfriend's Back '93
Neon Maniacs '86
Night Life '90
Night of Horror '78
Night of the Comet '84
Night of the Creeps '86
Night of the Death Cult '75
Night of the Ghouls '59

Night of the Living Babes '87
Night of the Living Dead '68►
Night of the Living Dead '90
Night of the Living Dead, 25th Anniversary Documentary '93
Nightmare Weekend '86
Oasis of the Zombies '82
Orgy of the Dead '65
The Outing '87
Pet Sematary 2 '92
Phantasm 3: Lord of the Dead '94
Plague of the Zombies '66
Plan 9 from Outer Space '56
Planet Terror '07
Prison '88
Quatermass 2 '57►
Re-Animator '84►
Redneck Zombies '88
Resident Evil '02
Resident Evil: Apocalypse '04
Resident Evil: Extinction '07
Return of the Evil Dead '75
Return of the Living Dead '85
Return of the Living Dead 2 '88
Return of the Living Dead 3 '93
Rave to the Grave '05
Revenge of the Dead '84
Revenge of the Living Zombies '88
Revenge of the Zombies '43
Revolt of the Zombies '36
Ring of Darkness '04
Seedpeople '92
Shaun of the Dead '04►
Shock Waves '77
Slither '06►
Sole Survivor '84
Steps from Hell '92
The Stuff '85
Svengali '31►
Teenage Zombies '58
They Came Back '04
Tomb of the Undead '72
Tomb of the Blind Dead '72
Torture Chamber of Baron Blood '72
28 Days Later '02►
28 Weeks Later '07
Undead '05
Undead or Alive '07
The Vampire's Ghost '45
Vengeance of the Zombies '72
Venom '05
Virgin among the Living Dead '71
Voodoo Dawn '89
Voodoo Woman '57
The White Zombie '32►
Winterbeast '92
Zombie '80
The Zombie Army '93
Zombie High '87
Zombie Honeymoon '04
Zombie Island Massacre '84
Zombie Lake '80
Zombie Nightmare '86
Zombies of Moratau '57
Zombies of the Stratosphere '52
Zombies on Broadway '44

► = rated three bones or higher

Kibbles and Series List

The **Kibbles** and **Series** indexes have been combined into one index. This is where you'll find info on where your favorite movies came from—literary, theatrical, cartoon, and television adaptations to name a few, as well as the behind the scenes talents that make movies possible, such as producers and special effects wizards. Another important feature of this index is the quality check it provides with categories like **Woofs!**, **4 Bones**, and **Top Grossing Films** by year. This index also provides information on recurring characters like James Bond, Jack Ryan, or Mike Hammer, as well as notable screen partnerships. Some examples include Abbott & Costello, Hope & Crosby, and De Niro & Scorsese. **A tipped triangle denotes a three-bone or higher rating** The categories are as follows, with an asterisk (*) denoting a new category:

Adapted from:
a Cartoon
a Fairy Tale
a Game
a Musical
a Play
a Poem
a Song
a Story
an Article
an Opera
*DC/Vertigo Comics
Disney Amusement Park Rides
Comics
*Marvel Comics
Memoirs or Diaries
Saturday Night Live
Television
the Bible
the Radio

Andy Hardy

B/W & Color Combos

***Batman**

Beach Party

Beatlesfilm

Billy the Kid

Blondie

Books to Film:
Richard Adams
Louisa May Alcott
Nelson Algren
Eric Amb·er
Kingsley Amis
Martin Amis
Hans Christian Andersen
Maya Angelou
Isaac Asimov
Eliot Asinof
Jane Austen
Honore de Balzac
Russell Banks
Clive Ba·ker

J.M. Barrie
Peter Benchley
Thomas Berger
Ambrose Bierce
Maeve Binchy
Robert Bloch
Judy Blume
Ray Bradbury
Barbara Taylor Bradford
Max Brand
The Brontes
Pearl S. Buck
Charles Bukowski
Frances Hodgson Burnett
Edgar Rice Burroughs
William Burroughs
James M. Cain
Truman Capote
Forrest Carter
Barbara Cartland
Willa Cather
Raymond Chandler
Paddy Chayefsky
John Cheever
Anton Chechov
Agatha Christie
Tom Clancy
Arthur C. Clarke
Mary Higgins Clark
James Clavell
Jackie Collins
Richard Condon
Joseph Conrad
Pat Conroy
Robin Cook
Catherine Cookson
James Fenimore Cooper
Stephen Crane
Michael Crichton
Michael Cunningham
Clive Cussler
Rcald Dahl
Miguel de Cervantes
Guy de Maupassant
Daniel Defoe
Len Deighton

Phillip K. Dick
Charles Dickens
Willair Diehl
E.L. Doctorow
Sir Arthur Conan Doyle
Daphne Du Maurier
Alexandre Dumas
Lois Duncan
Dominick Dunne
George Eliot
Bret Easton Ellis
James Ellroy
Howard Fast
Edna Ferber
Henry Fielding
F. Scott Fitzgerald
Gustav Flaubert
Ian Fleming
Ken Follett
E.M. Forster
Frederick Forsyth
John ·owles
Nikolai Gogol
William Goldman
David Goodis
Elizabeth Goudge
Kenneth Grahame
Graham Greene
Zane Grey
John Grisham
H. Rider Haggard
Arthur Haley
Alex Haley
Dashiell Hammett
Thomas Hardy
Harlequin Romances
Thomas Harris
Jim Harrison
Nathaniel Hawthorne
Ernest Hemingway
O. Henry
Patricia Highsmith
*Tony Hillerman
James Hilton
S.E. Hinton
Victor Hugo
Joyce Carol Oates
John O'Hara
Marcel Pagnol

Fanny Hurst
John Irving
Washington Irving
Susan Isaacs
Rona Jaffe
John Jakes
Henry James
P.D. James
James Jones
James Joyce
Franz Kafka
Stephen King
W P Kinsella
Rudyard Kipling
Andrew Klavan
Dean R. Koontz
Judith Krantz
Louis L'Amour
Ring Lardner
D.H. Lawrence
John Le Carre
Harper Lee
Elmore Leonard
*C.S. Lewis
Sinclair Lewis
Ira Levin
Astrid Lindgren
Jack London
H.P. Lovecraft
Robert Ludlum
Peter Maas
Alistair MacLean
Norman Mailer
Bernard Malamud
Richard Matheson
W. Somerset Maugham
Colleen McCullough
Ian McEwan
Terry McMillan
Larry McMurtry
Herman Melville
James Michener
Sue Miller
L.M. Montgomery
Vladimir Nabakov
John Nichols

*Robert B. Parker
John Patterson
Nicholas Pileggi
Edgar Allan Poe
Katherine Ann Porter
Richard Price
Mario Puzo
Ruth Rendell
Anne Rice
Mordecai Richler
*Nora Roberts
Harold Robbins
Sax Rohmer
Philip Roth
J.K. Rowling
Damon Runyon
Sir Walter Scott
Erich Segal
Hubert Selby, Jr.
Irwin Shaw
Sidney Sheldon
Mary Shelley
Georges Simenon
Mickey Spillane
Danielle Steel
John Steinbeck
Stendahl
Robert Louis Stevenson
Bram Stoker
Harriet Beecher Stowe
Jacqueline Susann
Jonathan Swift
William Makepeace Thackeray
Paul Theroux
Jim Thompson
Roderick Thorp
James Thurber
J.R.R. Tolkien
Leo Tolstoy
Scott Turow
Mark Twain
John Updike
Jules Verne
Leon Uris
Kurt Vonnegut
Alice Walker

Edgar Wallace
Joseph Wambaugh
Evelyn Waugh
H.G. Wells
Donald Westlake (aka Richard Stark)
Edith Wharton
William Wharton
E.B. White
Oscar Wilde
Thornton Wilder
Ben Ames Williams
Virginia Woolf
Cornell Woolrich
Herman Wouk
Emile Zola

The Bowery Boys

Broken Lizard

Buffalo Bill Cody

Bulldog Drummond

Carry On

Charlie Brown and the Peanuts Gang

Charlie Chan

Cisco Kid

Corman's Mama

Director/Star Teams:
Almodovar & Banderas
*Altman & Gould
*Altman & Murphy
Anderson & Murray
Bergman & Ullmann
Bergman & von Sydow
Boetticher & Scott
Bunuel & F. Rey
Burton & Depp
Capra & Stewart
Carpenter & Russell
*Chabrol & Huppert
Corad & Sandler
Cukor & Hepburn
Donner & Gibson

* = new to this edition

Dugan & Sandler
Ford & Wayne
*Frankenheimer & Lancaster
Hawks & Wayne
Herzog & Kinski
Hill & Newman
Hitchcock & Stewart
Holofcener & Keener
Howard & Hanks
Howard & Keaton
Huston & Bogart
Jordan & Rea
King & Peck
Kurosawa & Mifune
LaBute & Eckart
Lee & Washington
Linklater & Hawke
*Lynch & Nance
Mann & Stewart
Needham & Reynolds
Newman & Woodward
Poitier & Cosby
Pollack & Redford
Rafelson & Nicholson
Raimi & Campbell
Raimi & 1973
Oldsmobile Delta 88
Reiner & Martin
Ritt & Newman
Rodriguez & Banderas
Sayles & Clapp
Sayles & Cooper
Sayles & Strathairn
Scorsese & De Niro
Scorsese & Keitel
Scott (Tony) & Washington
Shadyac & Carrey
Sheridan & Day-Lewis
Siegel & Eastwood
*Sirk & Hudson
Soderburgh & Clooney
Soderburgh & Roberts
Spielberg & Dreyfuss
Spielberg & Hanks
Techine & Deneuve
Truffault & Leaud
*Verhoeven & R. Hauer
von Sternberg & Dietrich
Walsh & Bogart
Woo & Fat
Zemeckis & Hanks

Dirty Harry
Disney Animated Movies
Disney Family Movies
Doc Holliday
Dr. Christian
Dr. Mabuse
Dr. Seuss
Dracula
Dreamworks Animated Movies
Elvisfilm
The Falcon
4 Bones
Francis the Talking Mule
Frankenstein
Fu Manchu
Godzilla and Friends
Hallmark Hall of Fame
Hammer Films: Horror
Hammer Films: Sci Fi & Fantasy
Hercule Poirot
Hercules
Highest Grossing Films of All Time
Hopalong Cassidy
Indiana Jones
Inspector Clouseau
Jack Ryan

Jack the Ripper
James Bond
James Bond Spoofs
Jason Bourne
Jesse James
*John McClane
Lassie
Live Action/Animation Combos
The Lone Rider
Ma & Pa Kettle
The Marx Brothers
MGM Musicals
Mike Hammer
Miss Marple
*Mister Moto
Mr. Wong
Modern Shakespeare
Modern Updates
Monty Python
The Muppets
National Lampoon
Our Gang
*Philip Marlowe
Pixar Animated Movies
The Planet of the Apes
Plays to Film:
Maxwell Anderson
James M. Barrie
Anton Chekov
Noel Coward
Horton Foote
Beth Henley
David Mamet
Arthur Miller
Eugene O'Neill
Rodgers & Hammerstein
Arthur Schnitzler
William Shakespeare
George Bernard Shaw
Sam Shepard
Robert E. Sherwood
Neil Simon
Tom Stoppard
Tennessee Williams

Producers:
Robert Altman
Bruckheimer/Simpson
William Castle
Coppola/American Zoetrope
Roger Corman/New World
Val Lewton
George Lucas
Merchant Ivory
George Pal
Steven Spielberg
Andy Warhol

Rambo
The Rangebusters
Recycled Footage/ Redubbed Dialogue
Renfrew of the Mounties
Restored Footage
The Ritz Brothers
Robin Hood
The Rough Riders
Rusty the Dog
The Saint
Sinbad
Screen Teams:
Abbott & Costello
Allen & Farrow

Allen & Keaton
Astaire & Rogers
Ball & Arnaz
Belushi & Aykroyd
Bogart & Bacall
Bronson & Ireland
Burton & Taylor
Cagney & O'Brien
Cheech & Chong
*Cusack & Piven
Cusack & Robbins
Damon & B. Affleck
De Niro & Keitel
De Niro & Pesci
Depardieu & Deneuve
Douglas & Lancaster
Eastwood & Locke
Eddy & McDonald
Farley & Spade
Favreau & Vaughn
Flynn & de Havilland
Gable & Crawford
Garland & Rooney
Garson & Pidgeon
Gibson & Glover
Hawn & Russell
Hepburn & Grant
Hepburn & Tracy
Hope & Crosby
Ladd & Lake
Laurel & Hardy
Lee & Cushing
Lemmon & Matthau
Loy & Powell
Martin & Lewis
Newman & Woodward
Redford & Newman
Reynolds & DeLuise
Reynolds & Field
Rogers & Evans
Snipes & Harrelson
Stewart & Sullavan
Stiller & O. Wilson
Turner & Douglas
Wayne & O'Hara
Wilder & Pryor

Scrooge
Sexton Blake
Sherlock Holmes
Special FX Extravaganzas
Special FX Extravaganzas: Make-Up
Special FX Wizards:
Rick Baker
Rob Bottin
Anton Furst
Ray Harryhausen
Herschell Gordon Lewis
Tom Savini
Dick Smith
Douglas Trumball

Star Wars
Tarzan
The Texas Rangers
The Thin Man
The Three Mesquiteers
The Three Musketeers
Three Stooges
Tom Ripley
Top Grossing Films: 1939-2007
The Trail Blazers
Trash
Troma Films
Universal Studios' Classic Horror
Wild Bill Hickok
The Wolfman
Wyatt Earp
Zorro
Zucker/Abrahams/Zucker

* = new to this edition

Kibbles and Series Index

Recurrent characters, cinematic collaborations, various adaptations, and important behind-the-scenes personnel information is the focus of the **Kibbles and Series Index**. These categories are listed alphabetically. **A tipped triangle indicates a video rated three bones or higher.**

Adapted from a Cartoon

- The Addams Family '91
- Addams Family Values '93
- The Adventures of Captain Marvel '41
- Adventures of Red Ryder '40
- Adventures of Smilin' Jack '43
- Aeon Flux '05
- Alvin and the Chipmunks '77
- The Amazing Spider-Man '77
- Barbarella '68
- The Belles of St. Trinian's '53 ▶
- Big Zapper '73
- Blondie '38
- Blondie Brings Up Baby '39
- Blondie for Victory '42
- Blondie Goes Latin '42
- Blondie Goes to College '42
- Blondie Has Trouble '40
- Blondie Hits the Jackpot '49
- Blondie in Society '41
- Blondie Knows Best '46
- Blondie Meets the Boss 39
- Blondie On a Budget '40
- Blondie Plays Cupid '40
- Blondie Takes a Vacation '39
- Blondie's Blessed Event '42
- Bratz '07
- Casper '95
- Cool World '92
- Crimewave '85
- Dennis the Menace '93
- Dennis the Menace: Dinosaur Hunter '93
- Dennis the Menace Strikes Again '98
- Dick Tracy '37
- Dick Tracy vs. Cueball '46
- Dick Tracy's Dilemma '47
- Disney's Teacher's Pet '04 ▶
- Dr. Strange 78
- Doogal '05
- Dudley Do-Right '99
- Edward Scissorhands '90 ▶
- Elvira, Mistress of the Dark '88
- Fat Albert '04
- Fatty Finn '84
- The Fighting Redhead '50
- The Flash '90
- Flash Gordon '80
- Flash Gordon 2: Flesh Gordon Meets the Cosmic Cheerleaders '90
- The Flintstones '94
- The Flintstones in Viva Rock Vegas '00
- Footlight Glamour '43
- Friday Foster '75
- Frostbiter: Wrath of the Wendigo '94
- George of the Jungle '97 ▶
- The Great St. Trinian's Train Robbery '66
- The Guyver '91
- Guyver 2: Dark Hero '94
- Heavy Metal '81 ▶
- Hillbilly Blitzkrieg '42
- Inspector Gadget '99
- It's a Great Life '43
- Jene & the Lost City '87
- Josie and the Pussycats '01
- Lil Abner '40
- Little Nemo: Adventures in Slumberland '92
- Little Orphan Annie '32
- The Mask '94 ▶
- Masters of the Universe '87
- Maybe... Maybe Not '94
- Mighty Morphin Power Rangers: The Movie '95
- Mr. Magoo '97
- Office Space '98
- The Perils of Gwendoline '84
- Petit Con '84
- Phantom 2040 Movie: The Ghost Who Walks '95
- Pirates of the Caribbean: Dead Man's Chest '06
- Pirates of the Caribbean: The Curse of the Black Pearl '03 ▶
- Prince Valiant '54
- The Pure Hell of St. Trinian's '61
- Queer Duck: The Movie '06
- Reg'lar Fellers '41
- The Return of Swamp Thing '89
- Richie Rich '94
- The Sad Sack '57
- Scooby-Doo '02
- Scooby-Doo 2: Monsters Unleashed '04
- The SpongeBob SquarePants Movie '04
- Supergirl '84
- Superman 2 '80 ▶
- Tank Girl '94
- Teenage Mutant Ninja Turtles: The Movie '90
- Teenage Mutant Ninja Turtles 2: The Secret of the Ooze '91
- Teenage Mutant Ninja Turtles 3 '93
- Timecop '94
- Tom and Jerry: The Movie '93
- Transformers '07
- Turbo: A Power Rangers Movie '96
- The Villan '79
- Wild Palms '93
- The Wild World of Batwoman '66
- Yu-Gi-Oh! The Movie: Pyramid of Light '04

Adapted from a Disney Amusement Park Ride

- The Country Bears '02
- The Haunted Mansion '03
- Pirates of the Caribbean: Dead Man's Chest '06
- Pirates of the Caribbean: The Curse of the Black Pearl '03 ▶

Adapted from a Fairy Tale

- The Adventures of Pinocchio '96
- Aladdin 86
- Aladdin '92 ▶
- Aladdin and His Wonderful Lamp '84
- Alice in Wonderland '50
- Beanstalk '94
- Beauty and the Beast '46 ▶
- Beauty and the Beast '83 ▶
- Beauty and the Beast '91 ▶
- The Blue Light '32 ▶
- The Boy Who Left Home to Find Out About the Shivers '81
- The Brothers Grimm '05
- Butterfly Ball '76
- Chicken Little '05
- Cinderella '50 ▶
- Cinderella '64
- Cinderella '84 ▶
- Cinderella '97
- A Cinderella Story '04
- Cinderella 2000 '76
- Cinderfella '60
- The Company of Wolves '85 ▶
- The Dancing Princesses '84 ▶
- Deadtime Stories '86
- Donkey Skin '70 ▶
- Ella Enchanted '04 ▶
- The Emperor's New Clothes '84 ▶
- Enchanted '07 ▶
- Ever After: A Cinderella Story '98 ▶
- Fairy Tales '76
- Freeway '95
- Fun & Fancy Free '47 ▶
- George Balanchine's The Nutcracker '93
- The Glass Slipper '55
- Goldilocks & the Three Bears '83
- Green Snake '93
- Hans Christian Andersen '52
- Hansel and Gretel '82
- Happily Ever After '93
- Happily N'Ever After '07
- Hoodwinked '05 ▶
- A Hungarian Fairy Tale '37 ▶
- Irish Cinderella '22
- Jack & the Beanstalk '52
- Jack and the Beanstalk '83 ▶
- Jack and the Beanstalk: The Real Story '01
- La Petite Sirene '80
- Lady in the Water '06 ▶
- Les Visiteurs du Soir '42 ▶
- The Little Match Girl '84
- The Little Match Girl '87
- The Little Mermaid '89 ▶
- The Little Mermaid '75
- The Magic Fountain '61
- The Magic Sword '62
- March of the Wooden Soldiers '34 ▶
- Mother Goose Rock 'n' Rhyme '90
- The Muppets' Wizard of Oz '05
- The NeverEnding Story '84 ▶
- The NeverEnding Story 3: Escape from Fantasia '94
- The Nightingale '83 ▶
- The Nutcracker Prince '91
- The Nutcracker: The Motion Picture '86
- Once Upon a Brothers Grimm '77
- Peau D'Ane '71 ▶
- Peter Pan '53 ▶
- Peter Pan '60 ▶
- The Pied Piper of Hamelin '57
- The Pied Piper of Hamelin '84
- Pin... '88
- Pinocchio '83 ▶
- Pinocchio's Revenge '96
- The Princess and the Pea '33 ▶
- The Princess Bride '87 ▶
- The Princess Who Never Laughed '84 ▶
- Puss 'n Boots '84 ▶
- Rapunzel '82
- Red Riding Hood '88
- Rip van Winkle '85
- Rumpelstiltskin '82 ▶
- Rumpelstiltskin '86
- The Scalawag Bunch '75
- Shrek 2 '04 ▶
- The Singing Princess '49
- Sleeping Beauty '59 ▶
- Sleeping Beauty '83 ▶
- Sleeping Beauty '89
- The Slipper and the Rose '76
- The Snow Queen '83
- The Snow Queen '02
- Snow White '89
- Snow White: A Tale of Terror '97
- Snow White and the Seven Dwarfs '83 ▶
- Snow White and the Three Stooges '61
- Snow White: The Fairest of Them All '02
- The Swan '56 ▶
- The Swan Princess '94 ▶
- Sydney White '07 ▶
- The Tale of the Frog Prince '83 ▶
- The Three Little Pigs '84
- Thumbelina '82 ▶
- Thumbelina '94
- The Tin Soldier '95
- Tom Thumb '58 ▶
- Who Slew Auntie Roo? '71
- The Witches '90 ▶
- The Wonderful World of the Brothers Grimm '62
- The Wonders of Aladdin '61

Adapted from a Game

- Alien vs. Predator '04

▶ = rated three bones or higher

Adapted

Aliens vs. Predator: Requiem '07
Alone in the Dark '05
BloodRayne '06
BloodRayne 2: Deliverance '07
Clue '85
DOA: Dead or Alive '06
Doom '05
Double Dragon '94
Dungeons and Dragons '00
Final Encounter '00
Final Fantasy: The Spirits Within '01
Hitman '07
House of the Dead '03
In the Name of the King: A Dungeon Siege Tale '08
The King of Kong: A Fistful of Quarters '07
Lara Croft: Tomb Raider '01
Lara Croft Tomb Raider: The Cradle of Life '03
Mortal Kombat 1: The Movie '95
Mortal Kombat 2: Annihilation '97
Resident Evil '02
Resident Evil: Apocalypse '04
Resident Evil: Extinction '07
Silent Hill '06
Street Fighter '94
Super Mario Bros. '93
Tag: The Assassination Game '82
Wing Commander '99
Yu-Gi-Oh! The Movie: Pyramid of Light '04

Adapted from a Musical

Annie '82
Annie '99
Babes in Arms '39
Babes in Toyland '61
Beatlemania! The Movie '81
Bells Are Ringing '60
Best Foot Forward '43
The Best Little Whorehouse in Texas '82
Brigadoon '54
Bye, Bye, Birdie '63
Bye Bye Birdie '95
Cabaret '72
Can-Can '60
Charm of La Boheme '36
Chicago '02
A Chorus Line '85
Cool Mikado '63
Damn Yankees '58
The Desert Song '53
Dreamgirls '06
Evita '96
The Fantasticks '95
Fiddler on the Roof '71
Finian's Rainbow '68
Flower Drum Song '61
Follies in Concert '85
Footlight Serenade '42
A Funny Thing Happened on the Way to the Forum '66
The Gay Divorcee '34
Gentlemen Prefer Blondes '53
George White's Scandals '45
Godspell '73
Grease '78
Grease 2 '82
The Guardsman '31
Gypsy '62
Gypsy '93
Hair '79
Hairspray '07
Hello, Dolly! '69
Irma La Douce '63
The King and I '56
Kiss Me Kate '53
Lady Be Good '41
A Little Night Music '77
Mame '74
Mamma Mia! '08
Maytime '37
The Merry Widow '34
The Merry Widow '52
The Music Man '62

My Fair Lady '64
Oh! Calcutta! '72
On a Clear Day You Can See Forever '70
Opera do Malandro '87
Paint Your Wagon '69
The Pajama Game '57
The Phantom of the Opera '04
The Producers '05
1776 '72
Show Boat '36
Show Boat '51
Sweeney Todd: The Demon Barber of Fleet Street '84
Sweeney Todd: The Demon Barber of Fleet Street '07
Sweet Charity '69
The Threepenny Opera '31
West Side Story '61
The Wiz '78

Adapted from a Play

Abe Lincoln in Illinois '40
The Admirable Crichton '57
Aelita: Queen of Mars '24
Age Old Friends '89
Agnes of God '85
Ah, Wilderness! '35
Alfie '66
Alice '86
All My Sons '48
All My Sons '86
All Over the Guy '01
Amadeus '84
Amen '02
American Buffalo '95
Anastasia '56
The Animal Kingdom '32
Anna Christie '23
Anna Christie '30
Annie Get Your Gun '50
The Anniversary '68
Another Country '84
Another Man's Poison '52
Any Wednesday '66
The Architect '06
Arsenic and Old Lace '44
As Is '85
As You Desire Me '32
The Avenger '62
The Awful Truth '37
Babes in Toyland '86
The Baby Dance '98
Baby Doll '56
The Bacchantes '63
Bad Manners '98
The Balcony '63
The Ballad of the Sad Cafe '91
Bar Girls '95
Barefoot in the Park '67
Beau Brummel '24
Beau Brummell '54
Beautiful Thing '95
Becket '64
Becky Sharp '35
Being at Home with Claude '92
The Bells '26
Bent '97
The Best Man '64
Betrayal '83
Beyond Therapy '86
The Big Kahuna '00
The Big Knife '55
Big News '29
Billie '65
Biloxi Blues '88
The Birth of a Nation '15
Bitter Sweet '40
Black Limelight '38
Black Lizard '68
Black Orpheus '58
Blessed Event '32
Blithe Spirit '45
Blood Wedding '81
Bluebeard's Eighth Wife '38
Bodies, Rest & Motion '93
Boesman & Lena '00
Bophal '93
Born Yesterday '50
Born Yesterday '93
Boy Meets Girl '38
The Boys '98

The Boys in the Band '70
The Boys Next Door '96
Breaking the Code '95
Breaking Up '97
Breath of Scandal '60
The Brig '64
Brighton Beach Memoirs '86
Brilliant Lies '96
Broadway Bound '92
Broken Glass '96
A Bronx Tale '93
A Brother's Kiss '97
The Browning Version '51
The Browning Version '94
Bug '06
Bus Stop '56
Butterflies Are Free '72
Cabaret Balkan '98
Cactus Flower '69
Caesar and Cleopatra '46
California Suite '78
Can-Can '60
Caresses '97
Casablanca '42
Casanova Brown '44
Cast a Dark Shadow '55
Casual Sex? '88
The Cat and the Canary '79
The Cat's Meow '01
Cavalcade '33
Cease Fire '85
Ceiling Zero '35
The Chalk Garden '64
Chapter Two '79
Charley's Aunt '41
The Chase '66
The Cheap Detective '78
Chelsea Walls '01
Children of a Lesser God '86
The Children's Hour '61
Chimes at Midnight '67
China '43
A Chorus of Disapproval '89
Clarence, the Cross-eyed Lion '65
Clash by Night '52
The Climax '44
Closer '04
Cock & Bull Story '03
Cold Comfort '90
Collected Stories '02
Columbo: Prescription Murder '67
Come Back, Little Sheba '52
Come Back to the Five & Dime Jimmy Dean, Jimmy Dean '82
Come Blow Your Horn '63
Command Decision '48
Conduct Unbecoming '75
The Connection '61
Coquette '29
The Corn Is Green '45
The Corn Is Green '79
Cosi '95
Counsellor-at-Law '33
The Count of the Old Town '34
Country Girl '54
County Fair '20
Craig's Wife '36
Crimes of the Heart '86
Critic's Choice '63
The Crucible '57
The Crucible '96
Curse of the Golden Flower '06
Curse of the Starving Class '94
Cyrano de Bergerac '85
Cyrano de Bergerac '90
Da '88
Daddy Long Legs '19
Daddy's Dyin'... Who's Got the Will? '90
Dancing at Lughnasa '98
Dangerous Liaisons '88
A Day in the Death of Joe Egg '71
Day of Wrath '43
Daybreak '93
Dead End '37
Dead Heart '96
Death and the Maiden '94
Death of a Salesman '94
Death of a Salesman '51

Death Takes a Holiday '34
Deathtrap '82
The Designated Mourner '97
Desire Under the Elms '58
Desk Set '57
Desperate Hours '55
Detective Story '51
Devil Girl from Mars '54
The Devils '71
The Devil's Brother '33
Dial "M" for Murder '54
Diary of a Hitman '92
Diary of a Mad Black Woman '05
Die Mommie Die! '03
The Dining Room '86
Dinner at Eight '33
Dinner with Friends '01
Disco Pigs '01
Disraeli '30
The Divorce of Lady X '38
The Doctor and the Devils '85
Doctor X '32
Doll Face '46
A Doll's House '59
A Doll's House '73
A Doll's House '73
Don't Drink the Water '69
Double Wedding '37
Dracula '31
The Dresser '83
Driving Miss Daisy '89
Drunks '96
Du Barry Was a Lady '43
Duet for One '86
Dumb Waiter '87
Dutchman '67
The Eagle Has Two Heads '48
Early Days '81
East Is East '99
Easy Virtue '27
Educating Rita '83
Edward II '92
The Effect of Gamma Rays on Man-in-the-Moon Marigolds '73
84 Charing Cross Road '86
Emperor Jones '33
Employees' Entrance '33
The Enchanted Cottage '45
Ensign Pulver '64
The Entertainer '60
Entertaining Mr. Sloane '70
Equus '77
Escanaba in da Moonlight '01
Escapade '55
Escape Me Never '47
Execution of Justice '99
Extremities '86
Eye of the Storm '98
Faithful '95
Far Side of the Moon '03
The Farmer Takes a Wife '53
The Farmer's Wife '28
A Few Good Men '92
The Field '90
Finding Neverland '04
A Fine Romance '92
Five Graves to Cairo '43
Fog Island '45
Fool for Love '86
Footsteps in the Dark '41
Forbidden Planet '56
Forever Female '53
Fortune and Men's Eyes '71
Forty Carats '73
Foxfire '87
Frankenstein Sings... The Movie '95
Frankie and Johnny '91
The Front Page '31
The Fugitive Kind '60
Fun '94
Futz '69
Gangster No. 1 '00
Gaslight '40
Gaslight '44
The Gazebo '59
Generation '69
George Washington Slept Here '42
Get Real '99

Getting Gertie's Garter '45
Getting Out '94
The Ghost Breakers '40
Girl Play '04
Give Me a Sailor '38
The Glass Menagerie '87
Glengarry Glen Ross '92
God Said "Ha!" '99
Golden Boy '39
The Golden Coach '52
Gone Are the Days '63
The Good Fairy '35
Goodbye Charlie '64
The Goodbye Girl '77
The Gorilla '39
Grace & Glorie '98
The Great White Hope '70
Green Pastures '36
The Grey Zone '01
Grown Ups '86
The Guys '02
The Hairy Ape '44
Hamlet '48
Hamlet '69
Hamlet '90
Hamlet '96
The Happiest Days of Your Life '50
Happy Birthday, Gemini '80
Harriet Craig '50
Having Our Say: The Delany Sisters' First 100 Years '99
He Who Gets Slapped '24
Heartbreak House '86
Heaven Can Wait '43
Heaven Can Wait '78
Hedda '75
The Heidi Chronicles '95
Henry IV '85
Henry V '89
Henry V '44
His Double Life '33
His Girl Friday '40
The History Boys '06
Hit the Deck '55
Holiday '38
Holiday Heart '00
Homage '95
Home of the Brave '49
The Honey Pot '67
Hoopla '33
Hotel Paradiso '66
The Hound of London '93
House of the Long Shadows '82
The House of Yes '97
Hurlyburly '98
Hysterical Blindness '02
I Confess '53
I Love You, I Love You Not '97
I Married an Angel '42
I Never Sang for My Father '70
I Ought to Be in Pictures '82
I Remember Mama '48
An Ideal Husband '99
Idiot's Delight '39
I'll Be Yours '47
Illicit '31
Illuminata '98
Illusions '91
I'm Not Rappaport '96
The Importance of Being Earnest '02
The Impossible Years '68
In Celebration '75
In Search of the Castaways '62
In the Good Old Summertime '49
Indiscreet '88
Inherit the Wind '60
Inherit the Wind '99
Intrigue and Love '59
Iphigenia '77
Italian Straw Hat '27
It's the Rage '99
Jacknife '89
Jeffrey '95
Jesus Christ, Superstar '73
Johnny Belinda '82
Jubal '56
Julius Caesar '53
Julius Caesar '70
Key Exchange '85

The Killing of Sister George '69
King and Country '64
The King and I '99
King Lear '71
King Lear '87
King Lear '98
The King on Main Street '25
Kingdom Come '01
Kiss Me, Stupid! '64
The Knack '65
Knocks at My Door '93
K2: The Ultimate High '92
La Cage aux Folles '78
La Cage aux Folles 2 '81
La Cage aux Folles 3: The Wedding '86
Ladies They Talk About '33
The Lady's Not for Burning '87
Lantana '01
The Laramie Project '02
The Last of Mrs. Cheyney '37
Last of the Red Hot Lovers '72
Laughing Sinners '31
Leaving Metropolis '02
Lenny '74
Les Enfants Terrible '50
The Libertine '05
Life '95
A Life in the Theater '93
Life Tastes Good '99
Li'l Abner '59
Lilies '96
Lily Dale '96
The Lion in Winter '68
The Lion in Winter '03
The Little Foxes '41
The Little Murders '71
Little Shop of Horrors '86
Little Voice '98
Long Day's Journey into Night '62
Long Day's Journey into Night '88
Long Day's Journey Into Night '96
The Long Voyage Home '40
Look Back in Anger '58
Look Back in Anger '80
Look Back in Anger '89
Looking for Richard '96
Loot... Give Me Money, Honey! '70
Lost in Yonkers '93
Louisiana Purchase '41
The Lovable Cheat '49
Love and Human Remains '93
Love, Ludlow '05
Love! Valour! Compassion! '96
The Lower Depths '36
The Lower Depths '57
M. Butterfly '93
Macbeth '48
Macbeth '70
Macbeth '71
Madame X '37
Madame X '66
The Madwoman of Chaillot '69
The Magnificent Yankee '50
The Mahabharata '89
Major Barbara '41
A Majority of One '56
Male and Female '19
The Male Animal '42
Mambo Italiano '03
A Man for All Seasons '66
A Man for All Seasons '88
The Man in the Glass Booth '75
Man of La Mancha '72
The Man Who Came to Dinner '41
Marion Bridge '02
Marius '31
Marriage Italian Style '64
Marvin's Room '96
Mass Appeal '84
Master Harold and the Boys '84

♦ = rated three bones or higher

The Matchmaker '58▶
Me and the Colonel '58
Medea '88
Medea '70
The Method '05▶
Merton of the Movies '47
Mexican Hayride '43
Midnight Lace '60
A Midsummer Night's Dream '35▶
A Midsummer Night's Dream '68▶
The Migrants '74▶
The Millionaires '77
Minna von Barnheim or The Soldier's Fortune '77
The Miracle Worker '62▶
The Miracle Worker '79▶
The Miracle Worker '00
Miss Evers' Boys '97
Miss Firecracker '89▶
Miss Julie '50
Miss Julie '99
Miss Rose White '92▶
Mississippi '35
Mister Drake's Duck '50
Mr. Music '50
Mister Roberts '55▶
Mr. Write '92
Mogambo '53▶
Monster in a Box '92▶
Morning Glory '33
Move Over, Darling '63
Much Ado about Nothing '93▶
Murder '30▶
Murder at the Vanities '34
Murder by Death '76
My Big Fat Greek Wedding '02
My Boy Jack '07
My Brother's Wife '89
My Sister Eileen '55▶
Nana and Dani '00
Nell '94
Never Say Die '39
Never Steal Anything Small '59
No '98
Never Too Late to Mend '37
New Faces of 1952 '54
New Moon '40
Nico and Dani '00
Night Must Fall '37▶
Night of January 16th '41
The Night of the Iguana '64▶
No, No, Nanette '40
No Other Woman '33
No Sex Please— We're British '73
No Time for Sergeants '58▶
Noises Off '92
Normal '03
The Norman Conquests, Part 1: Table Manners '78▶
The Norman Conquests, Part 2: Living Together '78▶
The Norman Conquests, Part 3: Round and Round the Garden '78▶
Norman, Is That You? '76
North Shore Fish '97
Nurse Marjorie '20
No. 17 '32▶
The Obsessed '51
The Odd Couple '68▶
Oedipus Rex '67▶
Off the Map '03
Oh Dad, Poor Dad (Momma's Hung You n the Closet & I'm Feeling So Sad) '67
Oh! What a Lovely War '59
Oklahoma! '55▶
The Old Set er '01
Oleanna '94
On Approval '44▶
On Borrowed Time '39▶
On Golden Pond '81▶
On the Town '49▶
Once in the Life '00
Once Upon a Mattress '05
One Night Stand '78
1-900 '94
One of My Wives Is Missing '76
One Touch of Venus '48

One Trick Pony '80
The Only Thrill '97
Only When I Laugh '81▶
Orfeu '99
Ordet '55▶
Orphans '87▶
Orpheus Descending '91
Oscar '91
Othello '22
Othello '52▶
Othello '65▶
Othello '95▶
Other People's Money '91
Our Town '40▶
Our Town '77▶
Our Town '89
Our Town '03
Out of Season '75
The Owl and the Pussycat '70▶
Panama Hattie '42
The Passing of the Third Floor Back '36
Patterns '56▶
Peephole '93
People Will Talk '51▶
A Perfect Murder '98
Period of Adjustment '62▶
Personal Property '37
Petrified Forest '36▶
Phaedra '61
The Phantom of the Opera '90
The Phantom of the Opera '98
The Philadelphia Story '40▶
The Piano Lesson '94▶
Pippin '83
The Pirates of Penzance '83
Play It Again, Sam '72▶
Playboy o' the Western World '62
Plaza Suite '71▶
Plenty '85
The Portrait '93▶
Portrait in Black '60
Prelude to a Kiss '92
The Prime of Miss Jean Brodie '69▶
Prince of Central Park '00
Princess Tam Tam '35▶
Prisoner of Second Avenue '74
Private Fears in Public Places '06
Private Lives '31▶
The Private Secretary '31
Privates on Parade '84
The Producers '05
P.S. Your Cat is Dead! '02
Psycho Beach Party '00
Purlie Victorious '63
Pygmalion '38▶
A Question of Attribution '91
Quiet Day in Belfast '74▶
A Quiet Duel '49
Quills '00

Radiance '98
The Rainmaker '56▶
A Raisin in the Sun '61▶
A Raisin in the Sun '89▶
A Raisin in the Sun '08
Ran '85▶
Real Women Have Curves '02▶
Reckless '95
Red Planet Mars '52
Redwood Curtain '95
Rent '05
The Return of Peter Grimm '35
Rhythm Romance '39
Richard III '55▶
Ride the Wild Fields '00
Riders to the Sea '88
The Right to Remain Silent '95
The Ritz '76▶
The River is Red '48
Rodgers & Hammerstein's South Pacific '01
Roman Spring of Mrs. Stone '61▶
Romance '30
Romantic Comedy '83
Romeo and Juliet '36▶
Romeo and Juliet '54
Romeo and Juliet '68▶
Romy and Michele's High School Reunion '97
The Room '87▶
Roosters '95
Rope '48▶
Rosencrantz & Guildenstern Are Dead '90▶
Roxie Hart '42
Ruby '92
The Runner Stumbles '79
Sabrina '54▶
Sabrina '95
Saint Joan '57
The Saphead '21
Sarafina! '92▶
Scorchers '92
Scum '79▶
The Seagull '71▶
Search and Destroy '94
Secret Honor '85▶
The Secret Rapture '94
Separate Tables '58▶
Separate Tables '83
Seven Chances '25▶
Sex and the Other Man '95
Sextette '78
The Shadow Box '80▶
Shadow of Angels '76
Shadowlands '85
The Shanghai Gesture '42
The Shape of Things '03
Shirley Valentine '89▶
The Shop Around the Corner '40▶
Short Eyes '79▶
The Shot '96
The Show-Off '46
Siberian Lady Macbeth '61▶
The Sicilian '87
The Sign of the Cross '33
Silent Night, Lonely Night '69
Silk Stockings '57▶
A Sinful Life '89
The Singing Blacksmith '38
The Sisters '05
Six Degrees of Separation '93▶

Skin Game '31
Sleuth '72▶
Sleuth '07
A Slight Case of Murder '38
Small Hotel '57
Smart Woman '31
Smoking/No Smoking '94
So Ends Our Night '41▶
A Soldier's Story '84▶
Solid Gold Cadillac '56▶
The Song of Songs '33
Sordid Lives '00
Sorrento Beach '95
South Pacific '58▶
Stage Door '37▶
Stand-Ins '97
Star Spangled Girl '71
Stevie '78
Stolen Hours '63
The Storm Within '48▶
Strange Interlude '32▶
Strange Interlude '90
The Strange Love of Molly Louvain '32
Streamers '83
Street Scene '31
A Streetcar Named Desire '51▶
A Streetcar Named Desire '84▶
A Streetcar Named Desire '95
The Stripper '63
The Student Affair '97
The Subject Was Roses '68▶
The Substance of Fire '96
subUrbia '96
Suddenly, Last Summer '59▶
The Sum of Us '94▶
Summer and Smoke '61▶
Summertime '55▶
Summertree '71
Sunday in New York '63
Sunday in the Park with George '86▶
Sunrise at Campobello '60▶
The Sunshine Boys '75▶
The Sunshine Boys '95
Susan Slept Here '54
Sweet Bird of Youth '62▶
Sweet Bird of Youth '89
Sweet Revenge '98
Sylvia and the Phantom '45▶

Tace '01▶
Taking Slides '01▶
Talk Radio '88▶
Tall Story '60
The Taming of the Shrew '29
The Taming of the Shrew '67▶
Tartuffe '84
Tartuffe '90
A Taste of Honey '61▶
Tea and Sympathy '56▶
Tea for Two '50▶
The Teahouse of the August Moon '56▶
The Tempest '63
The Tempest '82▶
The Terror '38
That Championship Season '82
That Championship Season '99
There's a Girl in My Soup '70
These Girls '05
These Three '36▶
They Knew What They Wanted '40▶
Thin Ice '37▶
This Happy Breed '47▶
This is the Army '43
This Property is Condemned '66▶
Thoroughly Modern Millie '67
Those Endearing Young Charms '45
A Thousand Clowns '65▶
Three Daring Daughters '48
Three for the Show '55
Three Men on a Horse '36▶
Throne of Blood '57▶
Tidy Endings '88
Time Lock '57
The Time of Your Life '48▶
Time Without Pity '57
Tom & Viv '94▶
Tomorrow the World '44
Tonight or Never '31
Too Many Girls '40
Topaze '33▶
Topaze '51▶
Torch Song Trilogy '88▶
Tough Guy '53
Toys in the Attic '63
Trial & Error '62▶
Trial by Media '00
The Trials of Oscar Wilde '60▶
The Trip to Bountiful '85▶
The Triumph of Love '01
Trojan Women '71
Trouble in Paradise '32▶
True West '86▶
The Tunnel of Love '58
The Turning '92
Twelfth Night '96
Twelve Angry Men '57▶
Twelve Angry Men '97
21 Days '37▶
Twin Beds '42
Twisted '86
Two Alone '34
Two for the Seesaw '62▶
Two Small Bodies '93
Tyler Perry's Why Did I Get Married? '07
Un Air de Famille '96
The Unapproachable '82
Under Milk Wood '73
Under the Yum-Yum Tree '63
Up in Central Park '48
Urbania '00
The Visit '64

Volpone '39▶
A Voyage 'Round My Father '89▶
Wait until Dark '67▶
The War at Home '96
The War Lord '65▶
Watch on the Rhine '43▶
Water Drops on Burning Rocks '99
The Water Engine '92
Waterfront '39
Waterloo Bridge '40▶
Weekend at the Waldorf '45▶
We're No Angels '55
We're No Angels '89
We're Not Dressing '34▶
The Whales of August '87▶
What a Girl Wants '03
Where Were You When the Lights Went Out? '68
Who's Afraid of Virginia Woolf? '66▶
Whose Life Is It Anyway? '81▶
Wild Bill '95
The Wild Duck '84
Will Success Spoil Rock Hunter? '57
William Shakespeare's Romeo and Juliet '96▶
Window Shopping '86
The Winner '96
The Winslow Boy '48▶
The Winslow Boy '98▶
The Winter Guest '97▶
Wit '01▶
Without Love '45▶
The Wolves of Kromer '98
The Women '39▶
Woyzeck '78▶
Woyzeck '94
Wozzeck '47
Yellow Dust '36
Yenma '99
You Can't Take It with You '38▶
Young and Willing '42
Zaimen or the Madness of God '75
Zemsta '02
Zooman '95
Zoot Suit '81▶

Adapted from a Poem

The Bells '26▶
Beowulf '98
Beowulf '07▶
Beowulf & Grendel '06▶
Braveheart '95▶
The Castilian '63
The Charge of the Light Brigade '36▶
The Charge of the Light Brigade '68▶
Evangeline '29
Gunga Din '39▶
The Man from Snowy River '82
The Odyssey '97
Old Ironsides '26▶
Perceval '78
The Set-Up '49▶
Troy '04
Ulysses '55
The White Cliffs of Dover '44▶
Wild Party '74

Adapted from a Radio Show

Behind the Mask '46
Big Town '47
Check & Double Check '30
The Devil's Eye '60
Dreaming Out Loud '40
Gang Busters '55
Gang Busters '42
Gildersleeve on Broadway '43
Goin' to Town '44
Goon Movie '52
The Great Gildersleeve '43
Here Come the Nelsons '52
Here We Go Again! '42

Adapted from a Story

A. I.: Artificial Intelligence '01
ABC Stage 67: Truman Capote's A Christmas Memory '66
The Adventures of Ichabod and Mr. Toad '49▶
Alibi Ike '35
Alice in Wonderland '51▶
Alice in Wonderland '99
Amanda and the Alien '95
Ambassador Bill '31
America's Dream '96
Androcles and the Lion '52
The Android Affair '95
The Angel Levine '70
Angels in the Outfield '51▶
Angels with Dirty Faces '38▶
Appointment with Crime '45
Arizona Bushwackers '67
As Young As You Feel '51▶
Ashik Kerib '88▶
The Assassination Bureau '69▶
Ava's Magical Adventure '94
Away From Her '06▶
The Babysitter '95
Babette's Feast '87▶
The Ballad of the Sad Cafe '91
Bartleby '70
The Beast from 20,000 Fathoms '53
Benefit of the Doubt '93
Big Business Girl '31
The Big Stampede '32
Billy the Kid '41
The Birds '63▶

Adapted from a Song

Inner Sanctum '48
International Crime '37
The Invisible Avenger '58▶
Mr. Arkadin '55▶
My Friend Irma '49
Myrt and Marge '33
A Prairie Home Companion '06▶
Queen for a Day '51▶
Renfrew of the Royal Mounted '37
The Shadow '94
The Shadow Strikes '37▶
Sorry, Wrong Number '48▶
Treacherous Crossing '92
The War of the Worlds '53▶

Alice's Restaurant '69▶
The Baron and the Kid '84
Beyond the Wall of Sleep '06
Born in East L.A. '87▶
Convoy '78
Coward of the County '81
Elisa '94
Frankie and Johnny '36▶
Frankie and Johnny '65▶
The Gambler Returns: The Luck of the Draw '93
Girls Just Want to Have Fun '85
The Indian Runner '91▶
Is There Life Out There? '94
Kenny Rogers as the Gambler '80
Kenny Rogers as the Gambler, Part 2: The Adventure Continues '83
Kenny Rogers as the Gambler, Part 3: The Legend Continues '87
Legend of Tom Dooley '59
Love Potion #9 '92
My Boyfriend's Back '93
The Night the Lights Went Out in Georgie '81
Ode to Billy Joe '76
Purple People Eater '88
Single Bars, Single Women '84
Take This Job & Shove It '81▶
Yellow Submarine '68▶
You Light Up My Life '77

▶ = rated three bones or higher

The Black Abbot '63
Blackmail '91
Blood and Roses '61
The Blood Spattered Bride '72
Bloodhounds of Broadway '52
Boots of Destiny '37
Border Caballero '36
Boss of Bullion City '41
A Boy and His Dog '75
Boys '95
Boys' Night Out '62▲
Bram Stoker's Shadowbuilder '98
Breakfast at Tiffany's '61▲
Brief Encounter '46▲
Brigham Young: Frontiersman '40
Bright Angel '91
Bubba Ho-Tep '03▲
Burial of the Rats '95
Burning Daylight '28
Bury Me Not on the Lone Prairie '41
By the Light of the Silvery Moon '53
Call of the Wild '72
Candyman '92
Candyman 2: Farewell to the Flesh '94
The Canterville Ghost '44
The Canterville Ghost '96
Children of the Corn '84
Children On Their Birthdays '02
Cinderella 2000 '78
The Cisco Kid '94
College Swing '38
Comanche Territory '50
Come to the Stable '49▲
Comrade X '40
Cora Unashamed '00
Cosmic Slop '94
Crash Dive '43
Creature from the Black Lagoon '54▲
Creature with the Blue Hand '70
Cricket on the Hearth '23
Cult of the Cobra '55
Curse of the Demon '57▲
Curtis's Charm '96
Dark Eyes '87
Daughter of the Dragon '31
A Day in the Country '46▲
The Day the Earth Stood Still '51▲
The Dead '87▲
The Decameron '70▲
Decameron Nights '53
Department Store '35
Detonator 2: Night Watch '95
The Devil & Daniel Webster '41▲
Diary of a Madman '63
Die, Monster, Die! '65
Dive Bomber '41
Doomed at Sundown '37
Door with the Seven Locks '62
Double Trouble '67
Double Vision '92
D.P. '85
Drift Fence '36
DROP Squad '94
The Dropkick '27▲
Eat a Bowl of Tea '89▲
The Emperor's Club '02▲
Esther Kahn '00
The Eyes of the Amaryllis '82
Eyes of the Panther '90
A Face in the Crowd '57▲
Face to Face '52
Fall Guy '47
Fallen Angels 1 '93▲
Fallen Angels 2 '93▲
Feud Maker '38

The Fig Tree '87
The Fighter '52▲
Fighting Caravans '31
First Love, Last Rites '98
Five Days One Summer '82
The 5000 Fingers of Dr. T '53▲
Flirtation Walk '34
Forger of London '61
Freaks '32▲
From Beyond '86▲
Frontier Uprising '61
Gabrielle '05
Galloping Romeo '33
Gangway '37
A Gentle Woman '69
The Ghost of Frankenstein '42
Ghost Valley '32
The Gift of Love '90
The Girl with the Hungry Eyes '94
The Glass House '72▲
The Go-Between '71▲
Great Adventure '75
The Great Man's Lady '42
Gunfight at the O.K. Corral '57▲
Halfmoon '95
Hands Across the Table '35▲
The Hard Way '91▲
Haunting Fear '91
The Haunting of Hell House '99
The Haunting of Morella '91
Highlander '86▲
Hills of Oklahoma '50
Hole in the Sky '95
Home for the Holidays '95
Homecoming '48
Hondo '53▲
Hostile Guns '67
The House of Usher '88
How to Steal a Million '66▲
H.P. Lovecraft's Necronomicon: Book of the Dead '93
I Don't Want to Talk About It '94
I'm the One You're Looking For '88
The Importance of Being Earnest '52▲
Impostor '02
In Memoriam '76
In Old Chicago '37▲
In the Gloaming '97▲
The Incredible Sarah '76
The Indian Scarf '63
Internes Can't Take Money '37
Into the Badlands '92
Invasion U.S.A. '52
The Invisible Boy '57
The Invisible Woman '40▲
Isaac Asimov's Nightfall '00
Isle of Forgotten Sins '43
It Came from Outer Space 2 '95
It Started with Eve '41▲
It's a Date '40
It's a Dog's Life '55
Jigsaw '49▲
Jindabyne '06
Johnny Eager '42▲
Johnny Mnemonic '95
Johnny Reno '66
Jonathan Livingston Seagull '73
Judgment Night '93
The Jungle Book '42
The Juniper Tree '87
Kaos '85▲
Key to the City '50
The Kill-Off '90
The Killers '46▲
Kim '50▲
Kissed '96
Kull the Conqueror '97
Kurt Vonnegut's Harrison Bergeron '95
Kurt Vonnegut's Monkey House '91
La Chute de la Maison Usher '28▲
La Merveilleuse Visite '74

The Ladies of the Bois de Bologne '44
The Lady Eve '41▲
Lady Killer '33▲
Lady on a Train '45▲
The Land with the Dog '59▲
The Land Unknown '57
Last Mimzy '07
Landscape After Battle '70
Late Chrysanthemums '54
The Lawnmower Man '92
The Lawrenceville Stories '88
Le Plaisir '52▲
The Leech Woman '59
The Legend of Johnny Lingo '03
Legends of the North '95
L'Eleve '95
Life on a String '90
The Little Prince '74
Lone Star '52▲
Lord of Illusions '95
The Lost World '25
The Lost World '92
The Love Letter '98
Love on the Run '36
Love Play '60
Loyalties '86
Lurking Fear '94
Lust, Caution '07▲
Maborosi '95▲
The Magic Fountain '61
The Magnificent Dope '42
Main Street to Broadway '53
The Man Without a Country '73▲
Manfish '56
The Mangler '94
Mapp & Lucia '85
Margaret's Museum '95▲
The Masked Rider '41
Masque of the Red Death '65▲
Masque of the Red Death '89
Masque of the Red Death '90
Maximum Overdrive '86
Menace II Society '93▲
Midnight '39▲
A Million to Juan '94
Miracle in Rome '88
Mr. Deeds Goes to Town '36▲
A Month by the Lake '95
More about the Children of Noisy Village '87
The Most Dangerous Game '32▲
The Mummy's Curse '44
The Mummy's Tomb '42
Murders in the Rue Morgue '71
The Murders in the Rue Morgue '86▲
My Apprenticeship '39▲
My Childhood '38▲
My Favorite Blonde '42
My Foolish Heart '49
My Lucky Star '38
My Mother's Castle '91▲
My Sister Eileen '55▲
My Uncle Silas '01▲
My Universities '40▲
The Mysterious Magician '65
Mystic Circle Murder '39
Naked Jungle '54▲
The Naked Maja '59
Ned Kelly '03
Nevada '44
Never Say Goodbye '46
New Rose Hotel '98
Night Sun '90
Nightfall '88
Nightflyers '87
Noir et Blanc '86
Noon Wine '84▲
Now and Forever '34
Objective, Burma! '45▲
The Oblong Box '69
An Occurrence at Owl Creek Bridge/Coup de Grace '62
Of Human Hearts '38
Old Joy '06▲

On Moonlight Bay '51
One Christmas '95
100 Men and a Girl '37▲
Our Modern Maidens '29
Our Relations '36▲
The Outlaw Deputy '35
The Oval Portrait '88
Peck's Bad Boy '21
Personal Velocity: Three Portraits '02▲
The Pied Piper of Hamelin '84
The Pit and the Pendulum '61▲
Pittsburgh '42
Play Misty for Me '71▲
The Possessed '47▲
Premature Burial '62
The Prince and the Pauper '62
Pudd'nhead Wilson '84
The Purchase Price '32
The Quarrel '93
The Queen of Spades '49▲
Quest for Love '71
Quicksilver Highway '98
Rawhead Rex '87
Re-Animator '84▲
Rear Window '54▲
The Red Shoes '48▲
The Redhead from Wyoming '53
The Report on the Party and the Guests '66▲
Return to Paradise '53
Return to the Lost World '93
Revenge of the Creature '55
Ride Him, Cowboy '32▲
Ridin' Down the Canyon '42
Ridin' the Lone Trail '37
Robbers of the Sacred Mountain '83
Robert Louis Stevenson's The Game of Death '99
Rocket to the Moon '86
The Rocking Horse Winner '49
Roman Holiday '53▲
The Roman Spring of Mrs. Stone '03
Roommate '84
Rough Ridin' Rhythm '37
Ruggles of Red Gap '35▲
Rumpelstiltskin '86
The Safety of Objects '01
St. Michael Had a Rooster '72
Santa Fe '51
Saturday Night Fever '77▲
The Scarlet Tunic '97
Screamers '96
Secret of the Black Trunk '62
Secretary '02▲
Seven Brides for Seven Brothers '54▲
The Seven Hills of Rome '58
Shadow of a Doubt '43▲
Shadrach '98
Shanghai Express '32▲
The Shawshank Redemption '94▲
Shinbone Alley '70
The Shooting Party '77
Shopworn Angel '38▲
Short Cuts '93
The Skull '65
Sleep of Death '79
Sleeping Car to Trieste '45
Smooth Talk '85▲
The Snow Queen '83
The Snow Walker '03▲
Snow White and the Seven Dwarfs '37▲
The Snows of Kilimanjaro '52▲
A Soldier's Sweetheart '98
Sometimes They Come Back... Again '96
Somewhere I'll Find You '42▲
Sorrows of Gin '79
Sorry, Wrong Number '89
The Spectre of Edgar Allen Poe '73
Stagecoach '39▲

Station West '48▲
Stephen King's The Night Flier '96
The Strange Countess '61
The Strange Door '51
Strawberry and Chocolate '93▲
Suicide Kings '97
A Summer Story '88▲
A Summer to Remember '84
Sunset Boulevard '50▲
The Swimmer '68▲
Swept from the Sea '97
Tails You Live, Heads You're Dead '95
Taking Lives '04
Tales from the Darkside: The Movie '90
Tales of Terror '62
Tales of the Klondike: In a Far Country '87
Tales of the Klondike: Race for Number One '87
Tales of the Klondike: The Scorn of Women '87
Tales of the Klondike: The Unexpected '87
The Tell-Tale Heart '60
Tennessee's Partner '55
They Met in Bombay '41
They Watch '93
The Thing '82
This World, Then the Fireworks '97
Three Brothers '80▲
Three Cases of Murder '55▲
Three Days of Rain '03
The Three Little Pigs '84
Three Smart Girls '36▲
3:10 to Yuma '07▲
Through the Eyes of a Killer '92
Thunder Pass '54
The Tin Soldier '95
Today We Live '33
Tomb of Ligeia '64▲
Tomorrow '72▲
Tonto Basin Outlaws '41
Too Far to Go '79▲
The Topeka Terror '45
Torrents of Spring '90
Torture Garden '67
Torture Ship '39
Transmutations '85
Trapped in Space '94
Tribute to a Bad Man '56▲
Trio '50▲
Tropical Heat '93
Trucks '97
Trumps '83
Tully '00▲
The Twelve Chairs '70▲
12:01 '93
Two by Forsyth '86
Two Daughters '61▲
Two Evil Eyes '90
Uncertain Glory '44
Under the Biltmore Clock '85
An Unforgettable Summer '94
The Vampire Lovers '70
Vampyr '31▲
Vanina Vanini '61▲
Ward Six '78
Wee Willie Winkie '37▲
Who Am I This Time? '82▲
Who Slew Auntie Roo? '71
Who's the Man? '93
The Window '49▲
Wintertime '43
A Woman Without Love '51▲
A Woman's World '54▲
Women & Men: In Love There Are No Rules '91
Women & Men: Stories of Seduction '90
The Wonderful Ice Cream Suit '98
Young at Heart '54
The Young Land '59
The Young One '61
Youth Aflame '44

Biker Boyz '03
Blue Crush '02▲
Christiane F. '82▲
City by the Sea '02
Coyote Ugly '00
The Hunting Party '07
The Insider '99▲
Isn't She Great '00
Joe Gould's Secret '00
The Last American Hero '73▲
The Last Shot '04
New Jersey Drive '95
Olivier, Olivier '92▲
Pushing Tin '99▲
Resurrecting the Champ '07
Shattered Glass '03▲
Streetwise '84▲
Trade '07
Two or Three Things I Know about Her '66
Witness Protection '99▲

Adapted from an Opera

Aria '88
Balalaika '39
Baritone '85
Broken Melody '34
Burlesque on Carmen '16
Carmen '83▲
Carmen: A Hip Hopera '01
Carmen, Baby '66
Carmen Jones '54▲
The Chocolate Soldier '41
Farewell My Concubine '93▲
Fitzcarraldo '82▲
For the First Time '59
The Great Caruso '51
The Great Waltz '38▲
Gypsy Blood '18
I Dream Too Much '35
Jesus Christ, Superstar '73▲
La Grande Vadrouille '66▲
Life of Verdi '82
The Magic Flute '73▲
The Marriage of Figaro '49
The Medium '51
Meeting Venus '91
Midnight Girl '25
The Mozart Brothers '86▲
Otello '86▲
The Panther's Claw '42
The Phantom of the Opera '25▲
The Phantom of the Opera '43▲
Rick '03
Rose Marie '36▲
Ruddigore '82
The Tales of Hoffmann '51
The Three Penny Opera '62▲
The Toast of New Orleans '50
The Tsar's Bride '66▲
Verdi '53
Wagner: The Complete Epic '85
Wagner: The Movie '85

Adapted from Comics

American Splendor '03▲
Annie '82
Archie: Return to Riverdale '90
Art School Confidential '06
Barb Wire '96
Batman '66
Batman '89▲
Batman and Robin '97
Batman Begins '05▲
Batman Forever '95▲
Batman Returns '92▲
Black Mask '96
Blade '98
Blade 2 '02
Blade: Trinity '04
Brenda Starr '86
Bulletproof Monk '03
Captain America '44
Captain America '79
Captain America 2: Death Too Soon '79
Casper '95▲

Adapted from an Article

All Mine to Give '56
American Gangster '07▲

Catwoman '04
Constantine '05
Creepshow '82
The Crow '93
The Crow 2: City of Angels '96
The Crow: Salvation '00
The Crow: Wicked Prayer '05
Daredevil '03
The Dead One '07
Dennis the Menace '93
Dennis the Menace Strikes Again '98
Dick Tracy '90▶
Elektra '05
Fantastic Four '05
Fantastic Four: Rise of the Silver Surfer '07
Faust: Love of the Damned '00
"Fist of the North Star '95
Garfield: The Movie '04
Garfield: A Tail of Two Kitties '06
Ghost Rider '07
Ghost World '01▶
Hellboy '04
Hellboy 2: The Golden Army '08
A History of Violence '05▶
Howard the Duck '86
Hulk '03
Immortal '04
The Incredible Hulk '77
The Incredible Hulk Returns '88
Josie and the Pussycats '01
Judge Dredd '95
Killer Condom '95
Kull the Conqueror '97
The League of Extraordinary Gentlemen '03
The Mask '94▶
Men in Black '97▶
Modesty Blaise '66
Monkeybone '0¹
My Name is Modesty: A Modesty Blaise Adventure '03
Mystery Men '99
Over the Hedge '06▶
Persepolis '07▶
The Phantom '96
Prince Valiant '37
The Punisher '90
The Punisher '04
Richie Rich '94
Sabrina the Teenage Witch '96
Sin City '05▶
Spawn '97▶
Spider-Man '02▶
Spider-Man 2 '04▶
Spider-Man 3 '07
Steel '97
Superman: The Movie '78▶
Superman 2 '80▶
Superman 3 '83
Superman 4: The Quest for Peace '87
Superman Returns '06
Swamp Thing '82
Tales from the Crypt '72▶
Tales from the Crypt '89
Tales from the Crypt Presents Bordello of Blood '96
Tales from the Crypt Presents Demon Knight '94
30 Days of Night '07
300 '07
TMNT (Teenage Mutant Ninja Turtles) '07
Todd McFarlane's Spawn '97▶
V for Vendetta '06
Vampirella '96
Vault of Horror '73
Virus '98
Wicked City '92
X-Men '00
X2: X-Men United '03▶
Yu-Gi-Oh! The Movie: Pyramid of Light '04
Zoom '06

Adapted from DC/Vertigo Comics
The Adventures of Captain Marvel '41
Batman '89▶
Batman and Robin '97
Batman Begins '05▶
Batman Forever '95▶
Batman Returns '92
Catwoman '04
The Dark Knight '08
The Flash '90
The League of Extraordinary Gentlemen '03
Superman: The Movie '78▶
Superman 2 '80▶
Superman 3 '83
Superman 4: The Quest for Peace '87
Superman Returns '06
Swamp Thing '82
V for Vendetta '06

Adapted from Marvel Comics
Blade '98
Blade 2 '02
Blade: Trinity '04
Captain America '44
Captain America '79
Captain America '89
Captain America 2: Death Too Soon '79
Daredevil '03
Fantastic Four '05
Fantastic Four: Rise of the Silver Surfer '07
Ghost Rider '07
Hellboy 2: The Golden Army '08
Hulk '03
The Incredible Hulk '08
Iron Man '08▶
Men in Black '97▶
Men in Black 2 '02
The Punisher '04
Spider-Man '02▶
Spider-Man 2 '04▶
Spider-Man 3 '07
X-Men '00
X-Men: The Last Stand '06
X2: X-Men United '03▶

Adapted from Memoirs or Diaries
Angela's Ashes '99
Anna and the King '99
At First Sight '98
Bandit Queen '94
The Basketball Diaries '95
Belles on Their Toes '52
A Business Affair '93
Caro Diario '93
Celeste '81
Churchill and the Generals '81
The Color of Freedom '07
Control '07
The Counterfeiters '07▶
Cowboy '58
Danger UXB '81
The Diary of Anne Frank '59▶
The Diving Bell and the Butterfly '07▶
Downfall '04▶
Edvard Munch '74
The Elegant Criminal '92
The Flame Trees of Thika '81▶
A Free Soul '31
The Gathering Storm '74
Girl, Interrupted '99
God is My Co-Pilot '45
Goodbye, Miss 4th of July '88
Gypsy '62▶
The Happy Hooker '75
The Happy Hooker Goes Hollywood '80
The Happy Hooker Goes to Washington '77
Heart Beat '80
Heartland '81▶
Henry & June '90▶
I Remember Mama '48▶
I Was Nineteen '69
I'll Cry Tomorrow '55▶
I'm Dancing as Fast as I Can '82
In Love and War '96
In Love and War '01
In the Name of the Father '93▶
Inside the Third Reich '82
Iris '01▶
Jacquot '91
Julia '77▶
Just Like a Woman '95
The Kid Stays in the Picture '02▶
Kings in Grass Castles '97
Last Call: The Final Chapter of F. Scott Fitzgerald '02
The Lawless Breed '52▶
Lost for Words '99
Maids of Wilko '79
Meetings with Remarkable Men '79
A Mighty Heart '07▶
Mommie Dearest '81
The Motorcycle Diaries '04▶
My Life and Times with Antonin Artaud '93
My Own Country '98
My Sister's Keeper '02
October Sky '99▶
The Other Side of Heaven '02
Our Lady of the Assassins '01
The Passion of Ayn Rand '99
The Pianist '02▶
The Pillow Book '95
The Road from Coorain '02
Romulus, My Father '07▶
Seven Years in Tibet '97▶
Shot in the Heart '01▶
Sister Kenny '46▶
Stars and Stripes Forever '52▶
The Summer of Aviya '88
Sweet Nothing '96▶
This Boy's Life '93▶
Under the Domim Tree '95
Village of Dreams '97
What's Love Got to Do with It? '93
The Whole Wide World '96▶
Wish You Were Here '87▶

Adapted from Saturday Night Live
Blues Brothers '80▶
Blues Brothers 2000 '98
Coneheads '93
It's Pat: The Movie '94
The Ladies Man '00
A Night at the Roxbury '98
Stuart Saves His Family '94
Superstar '99
Wayne's World '92▶
Wayne's World 2 '93

Adapted from Television
Absolutely Fabulous: The Last Shout '96
The Addams Family '91
Addams Family Values '93
The Adventures of Rocky & Bullwinkle '00
Aeon Flux '05
Alien Nation: Dark Horizon '94
The Avengers '98
Batman '66
Bean '97▶
Beavis and Butt-Head Do America '96
The Beverly Hillbillies '93
Bewitched '05
Big Top Pee-wee '88
Bonanza: The Return '93
Boris and Natasha: The Movie '92
The Brady Bunch Movie '95▶
Car 54, Where Are You? '94
Charlie's Angels '00
Charlie's Angels: Full Throttle '03
Clifford's Really Big Movie '04
Coneheads '93
Corehéads '93
The Crawling Eye '58
Dennis the Menace '93
Dennis the Menace Strikes Again '98
The Defenders: Payback '97
Doctor Who '96
Doctal '05
Dragnet '87
Dudley Do-Right '99
The Dukes of Hazzard '05
The Extreme Adventures of Super Dave '98
Fat Albert '04
The Flintstones '94
The Flintstones in Viva Rock Vegas '00
Flipper '96▶
The Fugitive '93▶
Gargoyles, The Movie: The Heroes Awaken '94
George of the Jungle '97▶
Get Smart '08
Get Smart, Again! '89
Good Burger '97
Here Come the Littles: The Movie '85
The Honeymooners '05
The Invaders '95
I Spy '02
Jackass: The Movie '02
Jetsons: The Movie '90
Jimmy Glick in LaLa Wood '05
Joe's Apartment '96
Kevin & Perry Go Large '00
The Key to Rebecca '85
Kids in the Hall: Brain Candy '96
Lassie '94
Leave It to Beaver '97
The Left-Handed Gun '58▶
The Lizzie McGuire Movie '03
Lost in Space '98
Maverick '94
McHale's Navy '64
McHale's Navy '97
McHale's Navy Joins the Air Force '65
Miami Vice '06
Mission: Impossible '96▶
Mission: Impossible 2 '00▶
The Mod Squad '99
Munster, Go Home! '66
My Favorite Martian '99
Mystery Science Theater 3000: The Movie '96
The Naked Gun: From the Files of Police Squad '88▶
The Naked Gun 2 1/2: The Smell of Fear '91
The Naked Gun 33 1/3: The Final Insult '94
The Nude Bomb '80
Our Miss Brooks '56
Pee-wee's Big Adventure '85▶
Pennies from Heaven '81▶
The People Next Door '70
Phantom 2040 Movie: The Ghost Who Walks '95
Pokemon: The First Movie '99
Pootie Tang '01
Puffnstuf '70
Queen for a Day '51
Reno 911! Miami '07
Requiem for a Heavyweight '62▶
Rescue from Gilligan's Island '78▶
The Return of the Beverly Hillbillies '81
Ringmaster '98
Rugrats Go Wild! '03
Rugrats in Paris: The Movie '00
The Rugrats Movie '98▶
The Saint '68
Salome '53
Sgt. Bilko '95
Sergeant Ryker '68
Serenity '05▶
Sex and the City: The Movie '08
The Simpsons Movie '07▶
The Singing Detective '03▶
South Park: Bigger, Longer and Uncut '99▶
Speed Racer '08
Star Trek: The Motion Picture '79▶
Star Trek 2: The Wrath of Khan '82▶
Star Trek 3: The Search for Spock '84▶
Star Trek 4: The Voyage Home '86▶
Star Trek 5: The Final Frontier '89
Star Trek 6: The Undiscovered Country '91▶
Star Trek: First Contact '96▶
Star Trek: Generations '94▶
Star Trek: Insurrection '98▶
Star Trek: Nemesis '02
Starsky & Hutch '04
Strange Frequency 2 '01
Strangers with Candy '06
S.W.A.T. '03
Tales from the Crypt Presents Bordello of Blood '96
Tales from the Crypt Presents Demon Knight '94
Thomas and the Magic Railroad '00
Thunder in Paradise 2 '94
Thunder in Paradise 3 '94
A Very Brady Sequel '96
Twin Peaks: Fire Walk with Me '92
Underdog '07
The Untouchables '87▶
The Wild Thornberrys Movie '02▶
Wild Wild West '99
The X-Files '98▶
The X-Files: I Want to Believe '08

Adapted from the Bible
Abraham '94
A.D. '85
The Bible '66
David '97
David and Bathsheba '51▶
The Decalogue '88▶
Esther '98
Godspell '73
The Gospel According to St. Matthew '64▶
The Gospel of John '03
Jacob '94
Jeremiah '98
Jesus '00
Jesus Christ, Superstar '73▶
Jesus Christ Superstar '00
Joseph '95
Joseph and the Amazing Technicolor Dreamcoat '00▶
King David '85
King of Kings '27
The King of Kings '61▶
The Last Supper '05
Mary, Mother of Jesus '99
Mary and Joseph: A Story of Faith '79
The Messiah '75▶
The Miracle Maker: The Story of Jesus '00
Moses '76
Moses '96
Noah's Ark '99
The Passion of the Christ '04▶
Peter and Paul '81
Prince of Egypt '98▶
Salome '53
Salome '22
Samson and Delilah '50▶
Samson and Delilah '84
Samson and Delilah '96
Saul and David '64
Sins of Jezebel '54
Solomon '98
The Story of Jacob & Joseph '74▶
The Ten Commandments '23
The Ten Commandments '56▶

Andy Hardy
Andy Hardy Gets Spring Fever '39
Andy Hardy Meets Debutante '40
Andy Hardy's Double Life '42
Andy Hardy's Private Secretary '41▶
Life Begins for Andy Hardy '41▶
Love Finds Andy Hardy '38▶
Love Laughs at Andy Hardy '46

B/W & Color Combos
Amazon Women on the Moon '87
And Now My Love '74
Andrei Rublev '66▶
Awakenings of the Beast '68
The Blue Bird '40▶
Dead Again '91▶
Dixiana '30
D.O.A. '88
Gods and Monsters '98▶
If... '69▶
JFK '91▶
Kafka '91
Made in Heaven '87
A Man and a Woman '66▶
Mishima: A Life in Four Chapters '85▶
The Moon and Sixpence '43▶
Movie, Movie '78
Natural Born Killers '94
A Nightmare on Elm Street 4: Dream Master '88
Nixon '95▶
Portrait of Jennie '48▶
Rumble Fish '83▶
Schindler's List '93▶
She's Gotta Have It '86▶
Stalker '79▶
Transylvania Twist '89
Truth or Dare '91
Unzipped '94▶
Wings of Desire '88▶
The Wizard of Oz '39▶
The Women '39▶
Zelig '83▶

Batman
Batman '66
Batman '89▶
Batman and Robin '97
Batman Begins '05▶
Batman Forever '95▶
Batman Returns '92
Batman: Mask of the Phantasm '93▶
The Dark Knight '08

Beach Party
Back to the Beach '87▶
Beach Blanket Bingo '65▶
Beach Party '63

▶ = rated three bones or higher

Beach

Bikini Beach '64
How to Stuff a Wild Bikini '65
Muscle Beach Party '64
Pajama Party '64

Beatlesfilm

Across the Universe '07
All You Need Is Cash '78
Backbeat '94
A Hard Day's Night '64
Help! '65
The Hours and Times '92
I Wanna Hold Your Hand '78
John & Yoko: A Love Story '85
Let It Be '70
Magical Mystery Tour '67
Yellow Submarine '68

Billy the Kid

Battling Outlaw '40
Billy the Kid '41
Billy the Kid in Texas '40
Billy the Kid Returns '38
Billy the Kid Trapped '42
Billy the Kid Versus Dracula '66
Border Badmen '45
Deadwood '65
Devil Riders '44
Frontier Outlaws '44
Gangster's Den '45
Gore Vidal's Billy the Kid '89
I Shot Billy the Kid '50
Law and Order '42
The Left-Handed Gun '58
The Mysterious Rider '42
Oath of Vengeance '44
The Outlaw '43
Outlaw of the Plains '46
Pat Garrett & Billy the Kid '73
Rustler's Hideout '44
Shadows of Death '45
Texas Trouble '41
Thundering Gunslingers '44
Trigger Men '41
Wild Horse Phantom '44
Young Guns '88
Young Guns 2 '90

Blondie

Blondie '38
Blondie Brings Up Baby '39
Blondie for Victory '42
Blondie Goes Latin '42
Blondie Goes to College '42
Blondie Has Trouble '40
Blondie Hits the Jackpot '49
Blondie in Society '41
Blondie Knows Best '46
Blondie Meets the Boss '39
Blondie On a Budget '40
Blondie Plays Cupid '40
Blondie Takes a Vacation '39
Blondie's Blessed Event '42
Footlight Glamour '43
It's a Great Life '43

Books to Film: Richard Adams
The Girl in a Swing '89
The Plague Dogs '82
Watership Down '78

Books to Film: Louisa May Alcott
Little Men '40
Little Men '33
Little Women '49
Little Women '78
Little Women '94

Books to Film: Nelson Algren
The Man with the Golden Arm '55
Walk on the Wild Side '62

Books to Film: Eric Ambler
Background to Danger '43
Hotel Reserve '44
Journey into Fear '42
The Mask of Dimitrios '44

Books to Film: Kingsley Amis
Lucky Jim '58
That Uncertain Feeling 41

Books to Film: Martin Amis
The Rachel Papers '89

Books to Film: Hans Christian Andersen
The Red Shoes '48
The Snow Queen '02

Books to Film: Maya Angelou
Georgia, Georgia '72
I Know Why the Caged Bird Sings '79

Books to Film: Isaac Asimov
Bicentennial Man '99
I, Robot '04
Isaac Asimov's Nightfall '00
Nightfall '88

Books to Film: Eliot Asinof
Breakout '75
Eight Men Out '88

Books to Film: Jane Austen
Bride & Prejudice '04
Emma '72
Emma '96
Emma '97
Mansfield Park '85
Mansfield Park '99
Mansfield Park '07
Northanger Abbey '87
Northanger Abbey '07
Persuasion '71
Persuasion '95
Persuasion '07
Pride and Prejudice '40
Pride and Prejudice '85
Pride and Prejudice '95
Pride and Prejudice '05
Sense and Sensibility '85
Sense & Sensibility '95
Sense & Sensibility '07

Books to Film: Honore de Balzac
Colonel Chabert '94
Cousin Bette '97
The Duchess of Langeais '07
Passion in the Desert '97
The True and the False '55

Books to Film: Russell Banks
Affliction '97
Sunshine '07
The Sweet Hereafter '96

Books to Film: Clive Barker
Candyman '92
Candyman 2: Farewell to the Flesh '94
Hellbound: Hellraiser 2 '88
Hellraiser '87
Hellraiser 3: Hell on Earth '92
Hellraiser 4: Bloodline '95
Lord of Illusions '95
Nightbreed '90
Rawhead Rex '87
Transmutations '85

Books to Film: Peter Benchley
The Beast '96
The Deep '77
Jaws '75

Books to Film: Thomas Berger
The Feud '90
Little Big Man '70
Neighbors '81

Books to Film: Ambrose Bierce
Eyes of the Panther '90
An Occurrence at Owl Creek Bridge/Coup de Grace '62

Books to Film: Maeve Binchy
Circle of Friends '94
Tara Road '05

Books to Film: Ray Bradbury
The Beast from 20,000 Fathoms '53
Fahrenheit 451 '66
The Illustrated Man '69
It Came from Outer Space '53
The Martian Chronicles: Part 1 '79
The Martian Chronicles: Part 2 '79
The Martian Chronicles: Part 3 '79
Something Wicked This Way Comes '83
A Sound of Thunder '05
Walking on Air '87

Books to Film: Robert Bloch
The Skull '65
Torture Garden '67

Books to Film: Judy Blume
Forever '78

Books to Film: Barbara Taylor Bradford
Hold the Dream '86
A Woman of Substance '84

Books to Film: Max Brand
Branded '50
The Desperadoes '43
Destry Rides Again '39
Justice Rides Again '32
My Outlaw Brother '51
Trailin' '21

Books to Film: The Brontes
Emily Bronte's Wuthering Heights '92
Jane Eyre '34
Jane Eyre '44
Jane Eyre '83
Jane Eyre '96
Jane Eyre '97
Jane Eyre '06
MTV's Wuthering Heights '03
The Tenant of Wildfell Hall '96
Wuthering Heights '39
Wuthering Heights '53
Wuthering Heights '70
Wuthering Heights '98

Books to Film: Pearl S. Buck
China Sky '44
Dragon Seed '44
The Good Earth '37
Pavilion of Women '01

Books to Film: Charles Bukowski
Factotum '06
My Old Man '79

Books to Film: Frances Hodgson Burnett
Little Lord Fauntleroy '36
Little Lord Fauntleroy '80
Little Lord Fauntleroy '95
The Little Princess '39
The Little Princess '87
A Little Princess '95
The Secret Garden '49
The Secret Garden '84
The Secret Garden '87
The Secret Garden '93

Books to Film: Edgar Rice Burroughs
At the Earth's Core '76
Greystoke: The Legend of Tarzan, Lord of the Apes '84
The Land That Time Forgot '75
The People That Time Forgot '77
Tarzan '99
Tarzan and His Mate '34
Tarzan and the Green Goddess '38
Tarzan and the Trappers '58
Tarzan Escapes '36
Tarzan Finds a Son '39
Tarzan, the Ape Man '32
Tarzan, the Ape Man '81
Tarzan the Fearless '33
Tarzan's New York Adventure '42
Tarzan's Revenge '38
Tarzan's Secret Treasure '41

Books to Film: William Burroughs
Naked Lunch '91

Books to Film: James M. Cain
Butterfly '82
Double Indemnity '44
Girl in the Cadillac '94
Mildred Pierce '45
The Postman Always Rings Twice '46
The Postman Always Rings Twice '81
Slightly Scarlet '56

Books to Film: Truman Capote
ABC Stage 67: Truman Capote's A Christmas Memory '66
Breakfast at Tiffany's '61
Children On Their Birthdays '02
The Glass House '72
The Grass Harp '95
In Cold Blood '67
In Cold Blood '96
Other Voices, Other Rooms '95

Books to Film: Forrest Carter
The Education of Little Tree '97
The Outlaw Josey Wales '76

Books to Film: Barbara Cartland
Duel of Hearts '92
The Flame Is Love '79
The Lady and the Highwayman '89

Books to Film: Willa Cather
My Antonia '94
O Pioneers! '91
The Song of the Lark '01

Books to Film: Raymond Chandler
The Big Sleep '46
The Big Sleep '78
The Falcon Takes Over '42
Farewell, My Lovely '75
The Finger Man '55
Lady in the Lake '46
The Long Goodbye '73
Marlowe '69
Murder, My Sweet '44

Books to Film: Paddy Chayefsky
Altered States '80
As Young As You Feel '51
The Catered Affair '56

Books to Film: John Cheever
Sorrows of Gin '79
The Swimmer '68

Books to Film: Agatha Christie
Agatha Christie's A Caribbean Mystery '83
Agatha Christie's Murder is Easy '82
Agatha Christie's Murder with Mirrors '85
Agatha Christie's Sparkling Cyanide '83
Agatha Christie's The Pale Horse '96
Agatha Christie's Thirteen at Dinner '85
The Alphabet Murders '65
And Then There Were None '45
Appointment with Death '88
The Body in the Library '84
Death on the Nile '78
Endless Night '71
Evil under the Sun '82
Love from a Stranger '37
Love from a Stranger '47
The Mirror Crack'd '80
Murder Ahoy '64
Murder at the Gallop '63
A Murder Is Announced '87
Murder Most Foul '65
Murder on the Orient Express '74
Murder She Said '62
Ordeal by Innocence '84
A Pocketful of Rye '87
Ten Little Indians '75
Ten Little Indians '89
Witness for the Prosecution '57

Books to Film: Tom Clancy
Clear and Present Danger '94
The Hunt for Red October '90
Patriot Games '92
The Sum of All Fears '02

Books to Film: Mary Higgins Clark
Before I Say Goodbye '03
A Cry in the Night '93
Double Vision '92
He Sees You When You're Sleeping '02
Terror Stalks the Class Reunion '93
We'll Meet Again '02

Books to Film: Arthur C. Clarke
Trapped in Space '94
2001: A Space Odyssey '68
2010: The Year We Make Contact '84

Books to Film: James Clavell
King Rat '65
Noble House '88
Shogun '80
Tai-Pan '86

Books to Film: Jackie Collins
The Bitch '78
The World Is Full of Married Men '80
Yesterday's Hero '79

Books to Film: Wilkie Collins
Basil '98
The Moonstone '72
The Moonstone '97
The Woman in White '97

Books to Film: Richard Condon
Gun Crazy '69
The Manchurian Candidate '62
The Manchurian Candidate '04
Prizzi's Honor '85
Winter Kills '79

Books to Film: Joseph Conrad
Apocalypse Now '79
The Duellists '77
Face to Face '52
Gabrielle '05
Heart of Darkness '93
Lord Jim '65
Nostromo '96
The Rover '67
Sabotage '36
The Secret Agent '96
Swept from the Sea '97
Victory '95

Books to Film: Pat Conroy
Conrack '74
The Great Santini '80
The Lords of Discipline '83
The Prince of Tides '91

Books to Film: Robin Cook
Coma '78
Robin Cook's Invasion '97
Sphinx '81

Books to Film: Catherine Cookson
Catherine Cookson's Colour Blind '98
Catherine Cookson's The Black Candle '92
Catherine Cookson's The Black Velvet Gown '92
Catherine Cookson's The Cinder Path '94
Catherine Cookson's The Dwelling Place '94
Catherine Cookson's The Fifteen Streets '90
Catherine Cookson's The Gambling Man '98
Catherine Cookson's The Girl '96
Catherine Cookson's The Glass Virgin '95
Catherine Cookson's The Man Who Cried '93
Catherine Cookson's The Moth '96
Catherine Cookson's The Rag Nymph '96
Catherine Cookson's The Round Tower '98

Catherine Cookson's The Secret '00 ▸
Catherine Cookson's The Tide of Life '96
Catherine Cookson's The Wingless Bird '97
Catherine Cookson's Tilly Trotter '99

Books to Film: James Fenimore Cooper
The Deerslayer '78
The Last of the Mohicans '20 ▸
The Last of the Mohicans '32
The Last of the Mohicans '36
The Last of the Mohicans '85
The Last of the Mohicans '92 ▸
The Last of the Mohicans
The Pathfinder '94
The Pioneers '41

Books to Film: Stephen Crane
The Red Badge of Courage '51 ▸
Face to Face '52

Books to Film: Michael Crichton
The Andromeda Strain '71
Congo '95
The Great Train Robbery '79 ▸
Jurassic Park '93 ▸
The Lost World: Jurassic Park 2 '97
Rising Sun '93 ▸
Sphere '97
The Terminal Man '74
The 13th Warrior '99
Timeline '03 ▸
Westworld '73 ▸

Books to Film: Michael Cunningham
The Hours '02 ▸
A Home at the End of the World '04

Books to Film: Clive Cussler
Sahara '05
Raise the Titanic '80

Books to Film: Roald Dahl
Charlie and the Chocolate Factory '05 ▸
James and the Giant Peach '96 ▸
Matilda '96 ▸
Willy Wonka & the Chocolate Factory '71 ▸
The Witches '90 ▸

Books to Film: Miguel de Cervantes
Don Quixote '35 ▸
Man of La Mancha '72

Books to Film: Guy de Maupassant
A Day in the Country '46 ▸
Diary of a Madman '63
The Private Affairs of Bel Ami '47 ▸
Le Plaisir '52
The True and the False '63
A Woman Without Love '51 ▸

Books to Film: Daniel Defoe
The Amorous Adventures of Moll Flanders '65
Crusoe '89
Man Friday '75
Moll Flanders '96
Robinson Crusoe '36
Robinson Crusoe '96
Robinson Crusoe on Mars '64

Books to Film: Len Deighton
Bullet to Beijing '95
Funeral in Berlin '66 ▸
The Ipcress File '65 ▸
Midnight in Saint Petersburg '97

Books to Film: Charles Dickens
An American Christmas Carol '79
Bleak House '85
Bleak House '05 ▸
A Christmas Carol '38 ▸
A Christmas Carol '51 ▸
A Christmas Carol '54
A Christmas Carol '84 ▸
A Christmas Carol '99
Cricket on the Hearth '23
David Copperfield '35 ▸
David Copperfield '70
David Copperfield '99
Great Expectations '34
Great Expectations '46 ▸
Great Expectations '81
Great Expectations '89 ▸
Great Expectations '97
Great Expectations '99
Great Expectations: The Untold Story '87
The Life and Adventures of Nicholas Nickleby '81 ▸
Little Dorrit, Film 1: Nobody's Fault '88 ▸
Little Dorrit, Film 2: Little Dorrit's Story '88 ▸
Martin Chuzzlewit '94
Ms. Scrooge '97
The Muppet Christmas Carol '92 ▸
The Mystery of Edwin Drood '35
The Mystery of Edwin Drood '93
Nicholas Nickleby '46 ▸
Nicholas Nickleby '02 ▸
The Old Curiosity Shop '35
The Old Curiosity Shop '75
The Old Curiosity Shop '94
Oliver & Company '88
Oliver! '68 ▸
Oliver Twist '22 ▸
Oliver Twist '33
Oliver Twist '48 ▸
Oliver Twist '82 ▸
Oliver Twist '85
Oliver Twist '97
Oliver Twist '00
Oliver Twist '05 ▸
Our Mutual Friend '98
The Pickwick Papers '54
Scrooge '35 ▸
Scrooge '70
A Tale of Two Cities '35 ▸
A Tale of Two Cities '58 ▸
A Tale of Two Cities '80
A Tale of Two Cities '89 ▸
A Tale of Two Cities '91
Twist '03 ▸
Twisted '96

Books to Film: Philip K. Dick
Barjo '93
Blade Runner '82 ▸
Impostor '02 ▸
Minority Report '02 ▸
Next '07
Paycheck '03
A Scanner Darkly '06 ▸
Screamers '96
Total Recall '90 ▸
Total Recall 2070: Machine Dreams '99

Books to Film: William Diehl
Primal Fear '96 ▸
Sharky's Machine '81

Books to Film: E.L. Doctorow
Billy Bathgate '91
Ragtime '81 ▸

Books to Film: Fyodor Dostoyevsky
The Brothers Karamazov
Crime and Punishment '35 ▸
Crime and Punishment '70
Crime and Punishment in Suburbia '00
Dostoevsky's Crime and Punishment '99
The Gambler '97
A Gentle Woman '69
La Vengeance d'une Femme '89
L'Idiot '46
Notes from Underground '95
The Possessed '88
White Nights '57 ▸

Books to Film: Sir Arthur Conan Doyle
The Adventures of Sherlock Holmes '39 ▸
The Crucible of Blood '91
Dressed to Kill '46
The Hound of the Baskervilles '39 ▸
The Hound of the Baskervilles '59 ▸
The Hound of the Baskervilles '77
The Hound of the Baskervilles '83
The Hound of the Baskervilles '00
The Hound of the Baskervilles '02
House of Fear '45
The Lost World '25 ▸
The Lost World '92
The Lost World '02
Masks of Death '86
Murder at the Baskervilles '37
The Pearl of Death '44
Return to the Lost World '93
Robbers of the Sacred Mountain '83
Scarlet Claw '44 ▸
Sherlock Holmes and the Deadly Necklace '62
Sherlock Holmes and the Secret Weapon '42 ▸
The Sign of Four '83
The Sign of Four '01
The Silent Mr. Sherlock Holmes '12
Tales from the Darkside: The Movie '90
The Triumph of Sherlock Holmes '35
The Woman in Green '45

Books to Film: Lois Duncan
I Know What You Did Last Summer '97 ▸
I've Been Waiting for You '98
Killing Mr. Griffin '97
Summer of Fear '78

Books to Film: Alexandre Dumas
At Sword's Point '51
Black Magic '49
Camille '21
Camille '36 ▸
Camille 2000 '69
The Corsican Brothers '42
The Count of Monte Cristo '12
The Count of Monte Cristo '34 ▸
The Count of Monte Cristo '75 ▸
The Count of Monte Cristo '02 ▸
The Count of Monte Cristo '98
The Four Musketeers '75 ▸
The Iron Mask '29
The Man in the Iron Mask '77
The Man in the Iron Mask '98
The Man in the Iron Mask '39 ▸
The Prince of Thieves '48
Queen Margot '94 ▸
The Return of the Musketeers '89
Robin Hood '22 ▸
Sword of Monte Cristo '51
The Three Musketeers '16
The Three Musketeers '21 ▸
The Three Musketeers '33
The Three Musketeers '35
The Three Musketeers '39 ▸
The Three Musketeers '48 ▸
The Three Musketeers '74 ▸

Books to Film: Dominick Dunne
An Inconvenient Woman '91

Books to Film: Daphne Du Maurier
The Birds '63 ▸
Don't Look Now '73 ▸
Frenchman's Creek '44
Frenchman's Creek '98
Jamaica Inn '39
Jamaica Inn '82
Rebecca '40 ▸
Rebecca '97

Books to Film: George Eliot
Daniel Deronda '02
Middlemarch '93 ▸
The Mill on the Floss '37
The Mill on the Floss '97
Silas Marner '85 ▸
A Simple Twist of Fate '94

Books to Film: Bret Easton Ellis
American Psycho '99 ▸
Less Than Zero '87
The Rules of Attraction '02

Books to Film: James Ellroy
The Black Dahlia '06
Brown's Requiem '98
Cop '88
Dark Blue '03 ▸
L.A. Confidential '97 ▸
Street Kings '08

Books to Film: William Faulkner
Intruder in the Dust '49 ▸
Land of the Pharaohs '55
The Long, Hot Summer '58 ▸
The Long, Hot Summer '86 ▸
The Reivers '69 ▸
Tarnished Angels '57 ▸
Today We Live '33
Tomorrow '72 ▸
William Faulkner's Old Man '97

Books to Film: Howard Fast
The Crossing '00 ▸
Freedom Road '79

Books to Film: Edna Ferber
Cimarron '31
Cimarron '60
Come and Get It '36 ▸
Dinner at Eight '33 ▸
Giant '56 ▸
Saratoga Trunk '45
Show Boat '36 ▸
Show Boat '51
Stage Door '37 ▸

Books to Film: Henry Fielding
Joseph Andrews '77
Tom Jones '63 ▸
Tom Jones '98 ▸

Books to Film: F. Scott Fitzgerald
The Great Gatsby '49
The Great Gatsby '74
The Great Gatsby '01
The Last Time I Saw Paris '54
The Last Tycoon '76 ▸
Tender Is the Night '55

Books to Film: Ian Fleming
Casino Royale '67
Casino Royale '06 ▸
Chitty Chitty Bang Bang '68 ▸
Diamonds Are Forever '71 ▸
Dr. No '62 ▸
For Your Eyes Only '81 ▸
From Russia with Love '63 ▸
Goldfinger '64 ▸
License to Kill '89 ▸
Live and Let Die '73 ▸
The Living Daylights '87 ▸
The Man with the Golden Gun '74
Moonraker '79
Never Say Never Again '83
Octopussy '83
On Her Majesty's Secret Service '69 ▸
The Poppy Is Also a Flower '66
The Spy Who Loved Me '77
Thunderball '65
A View to a Kill '85
You Only Live Twice '67

Books to Film: Ken Follett
Eye of the Needle '81 ▸
The Key to Rebecca '85
Lie Down with Lions '94

Books to Film: E.M. Forster
Howards End '92 ▸
Maurice '87 ▸
A Passage to India '84 ▸
A Room with a View '86 ▸
Where Angels Fear to Tread '91 ▸

Books to Film: Frederick Forsyth
The Day of the Jackal '73 ▸
The Dogs of War '81
The Fourth Protocol '87 ▸
The Odessa File '74 ▸
Two by Forsyth '86
Wolverine '96

Books to Film: John Fowles
The Collector '65 ▸
Ebony Tower '86
The French Lieutenant's Woman '81 ▸
The Magus '68

Books to Film: Gustav Flaubert
Madame Bovary '34 ▸
Madame Bovary '49 ▸
Madame Bovary '91 ▸
Madame Bovary '00
Salammbo '14

Books to Film: William Goldman
Heat '87
Magic '78
Marathon Man '76 ▸
The Princess Bride '87 ▸

Books to Film: David Goodis
Dark Passage '47 ▸
Moon in the Gutter '83
Nightfall '56 ▸
Shoot the Piano Player '62 ▸

Books to Film: Nikolai Gogol
The Overcoat '59 ▸
Taras Bulba '62

Books to Film: Rumer Godden
Black Narcissus '47 ▸
In This House of Brede '75 ▸
The River '51 ▸

Books to Film: Elizabeth Goudge
Green Dolphin Street '47

Books to Film: Kenneth Grahame
The Adventures of Ichabod and Mr. Toad '49 ▸

Books to Film: Graham Greene
Across the Bridge '57 ▸
Beyond the Limit '83
Brighton Rock '47 ▸
The Comedians '67
The End of the Affair '55 ▸
The End of the Affair '99 ▸
The Fallen Idol '49 ▸
The Fugitive '48 ▸
The Human Factor '79
Ministry of Fear '44 ▸
Monsignor Quixote '91
Our Man in Havana '59 ▸
The Quiet American '02 ▸
Strike It Rich '90
The Tenth Man '88
The Third Man '49 ▸
This Gun for Hire '42 ▸
This Gun for Hire '90
Travels with My Aunt '72

Books to Film: Zane Grey
Arizona Mahoney '36
The Border Legion '40
Desert Gold '36
Drift Fence '36
Dude Ranger '34
Fighting Caravans '31
Forlorn River '37
Helltown '38
The Light of Western Stars '30
Man of the Forest '33
Nevada '27
Nevada '44
Riders of the Purple Sage '25
Riders of the Purple Sage '96 ▸
Roll Along Cowboy '37
Thunder Mountain '35
Thunder Pass '33
To the Last Man '33
The Vanishing American '25 ▸
Wagon Wheels '34
West of the Pecos '45
When the West Was Young '32

▸ = rated three bones or higher

Books to Film: John Grisham
The Chamber '96
Christmas With the Kranks '04
The Client '94
The Firm '93▲
John Grisham's The Rainmaker '97
A Painted House '03
The Pelican Brief '93
Runaway Jury '03▲
A Time to Kill '96▲

Books to Film: H. Rider Haggard
Allan Quatermain and the Lost City of Gold '86
King Solomon's Mines '37▲
King Solomon's Mines '50▲
King Solomon's Mines '85
She '25
She '35

Books to Film: Alex Haley
Malcolm X '92▲
Mama Flora's Family '98
Queen '93▲
Roots '77▲
Roots: The Gift '88
Roots: The Next Generation '79▲

Books to Film: Dashiell Hammett
After the Thin Man '36▲
Another Thin Man '39
The Dain Curse '78
The Glass Key '42▲
Hammett '82
The Maltese Falcon '31▲
The Maltese Falcon '41▲
No Good Deed '02
Satan Met a Lady '36
Shadow of the Thin Man '41▲
Song of the Thin Man '47
The Thin Man '34▲
The Thin Man Goes Home '44
Woman in the Shadows '34

Books to Film: Thomas Hardy
The Claim '00
Far from the Madding Crowd '67▲
Far from the Madding Crowd '97▲
Jude '96▲
Jude the Obscure '71
The Mayor of Casterbridge '03
The Return of the Native '94
The Scarlet Tunic '97
Tess '79▲
Tess of the D'Urbervilles '98
Under the Greenwood Tree '05

Books to Film: Harlequin Romances
Dreams Lost, Dreams Found '87
Love with a Perfect Stranger '86
The Winds of Jarrah '83

Books to Film: Thomas Harris
Black Sunday '77
Hannibal '01
Manhunter '86▲
Red Dragon '02

The Silence of the Lambs '91▲

Books to Film: Jim Harrison
Carried Away '95
Dalva '95
Legends of the Fall '94
Revenge '90
Wolf '94

Books to Film: Nathaniel Hawthorne
The House of the Seven Gables '40
The Scarlet Letter '34
The Scarlet Letter '73▲
The Scarlet Letter '95
Twice-Told Tales '63▲

Books to Film: Ernest Hemingway
After the Storm '01
A Farewell to Arms '32▲
For Whom the Bell Tolls '43▲
Islands in the Stream '77
The Killers '46▲
The Killers '64
My Old Man '79
The Old Man and the Sea '58▲
The Old Man and the Sea '90
The Snows of Kilimanjaro '52▲
To Have & Have Not '44▲
Women & Men: Stories of Seduction '90

Books to Film: O. Henry
The Cisco Kid '94
The Gift of Love '90
Ruthless People '86▲

Books to Film: Patricia Highsmith
The American Friend '77▲
Purple Noon '60▲
Ripley's Game '02▲
Strangers on a Train '51▲
The Talented Mr. Ripley '99

Books to Film: Tony Hillerman
Coyote Waits '03
The Dark Wind '91
Skinwalker '02
A Thief of Time '04

Books to Film: James Hilton
Goodbye, Mr. Chips '02
Lost Horizon '37▲
Random Harvest '42▲
The Story of Dr. Wassell '44

Books to Film: Nick Hornby
About a Boy '02▲
Fever Pitch '96
Fever Pitch '05
High Fidelity '00▲

Books to Film: Victor Hugo
Delusions of Grandeur '76
The Halfback of Notre Dame '96
The Hunchback '97

The Hunchback of Notre Dame '23▲
The Hunchback of Notre Dame '39▲
The Hunchback of Notre Dame '57
The Hunchback of Notre Dame '82▲
The Hunchback of Notre Dame '96▲
Les Miserables '35▲
Les Miserables '52
Les Miserables '57▲
Les Miserables '78▲
Les Miserables '95
Les Miserables '97▲
Ruyblas '48

Books to Film: Evan Hunter (aka Ed McBain)
Blackboard Jungle '55▲
Blood Relatives '77
The Chisholms '79
Fuzz '72
High & Low '62▲
Last Summer '69
Strangers When We Meet '60
Stray Dog '49▲
The Young Savages '61

Books to Film: Fanny Hurst
Back Street '41
Back Street '61
Four Daughters '38▲
Imitation of Life '34▲
Imitation of Life '59▲
Young at Heart '54

Books to Film: John Irving
The Cider House Rules '99▲
The Door in the Floor '04▲
The Hotel New Hampshire '84
The World According to Garp '82▲

Books to Film: Washington Irving
The Adventures of Ichabod and Mr. Toad '49▲
The Legend of Sleepy Hollow '49
The Legend of Sleepy Hollow '79
The Legend of Sleepy Hollow '86▲
Rip van Winkle '85
Sleepy Hollow '99▲

Books to Film: Susan Isaacs
Compromising Positions '85
Shining Through '92

Books to Film: Rona Jaffe
Mazes and Monsters '82

Books to Film: John Jakes
The Bastard '78
Killer Elephants '76
North and South Book 1 '85▲
North and South Book 2 '86▲
The Rebels '79
The Seekers '79

Books to Film: Henry James
The American '01
The Bostonians '84
Celine and Julie Go Boating '74
Daisy Miller '74
The Europeans '79▲
The Golden Bowl '72▲
The Golden Bowl '00

The Green Room '78
The Haunting of Hell House '99
The Heiress '49▲
In the Shadows '98
The Innocents '61▲
L'Eleve '95
Lost Moment '47
The Nightcomers '72
P.D. James: The Murder Room '04
Portrait of a Lady '67
Portrait of a Lady '96▲
The Turn of the Screw '74
The Turn of the Screw '89
The Turn of the Screw '92
The Turn of the Screw '99
Washington Square '97▲
The Wings of the Dove '97▲

Books to Film: P.D. James
A Certain Justice '99
Children of Men '06▲
Devices and Desires '91▲
A Mind to Murder '96
P.D. James: Death in Holy Orders '03
Unsuitable Job for a Woman '82

Books to Film: James Jones
From Here to Eternity '53▲
From Here to Eternity '79
Some Came Running '58▲
The Thin Red Line '64
The Thin Red Line '98▲

Books to Film: James Joyce
Bloom '03
The Dead '87▲
Finnegan's Wake '65
James Joyce: A Portrait of the Artist as a Young Man '77▲
Ulysses '67

Books to Film: Franz Kafka
The Castle '68▲
The Trial '63▲
The Trial '93

Books to Film: Stephen King
Apt Pupil '97
Carrie '76▲
Carrie '02
Cat's Eye '85
Children of the Corn '84
Christine '84
Creepshow '82
Creepshow 2 '87
Cujo '83
The Dark Half '91
Dead Zone '83▲
The Dead Zone '02
Dolores Claiborne '94▲
Dreamcatcher '03
Firestarter '84
1408 '07
Graveyard Shift '90
The Green Mile '99
Hearts in Atlantis '01
The Lawnmower Man '92
The Mangler '94
Maximum Overdrive '86
Misery '90▲
The Mist '07▲
Needful Things '93
Pet Sematary '89
Return to Salem's Lot '87
Riding the Bullet '04
The Running Man '87
Salem's Lot '79
Salem's Lot '04
Secret Window '04
The Shawshank Redemption '94▲
The Shining '80
Silver Bullet '85
Sleepwalkers '92

Sometimes They Come Back '91
Sometimes They Come Back... Again '96
Stand by Me '86▲
Stephen King's Golden Years '91
Stephen King's It '90
Stephen King's Rose Red '02
Stephen King's The Langoliers '95
Stephen King's The Night Flier '96
Stephen King's The Stand '94
Stephen King's The Storm of the Century '99
Stephen King's The Tommyknockers '93
Stephen King's Thinner '96
Tales from the Darkside: The Movie '90
Trucks '97

Books to Film: W.P. Kinsella
Dance Me Outside '95
Field of Dreams '89▲

Books to Film: Rudyard Kipling
Captains Courageous '37▲
Captains Courageous '95
A Fool There Was '14
Gunga Din '39▲
The Jungle Book '42▲
Kim '50▲
Kim '84
The Man Who Would Be King '75▲
Rudyard Kipling's The Jungle Book '94
Rudyard Kipling's the Second Jungle Book: Mowgli and Baloo '97
They Watch '93
Wee Willie Winkie '37▲

Books to Film: Andrew Klavan
Don't Say a Word '01
True Crime '99
White of the Eye '88▲

Books to Film: Dean R. Koontz
Dean Koontz's Black River '01
Dean Koontz's Mr. Murder '98
Demon Seed '77▲
Hideaway '94
Intruder '76
Phantoms '98
Servants of Twilight '91
Watchers '88
Watchers Reborn '98
Whispers '89

Books to Film: Judith Krantz
Mistral's Daughter '84
Princess Daisy '83
Scruples '80

Books to Film: Louis L'Amour
The Burning Hills '56
Cancel My Reservation '72
Conagher '91
Crossfire Trail '01▲
The Diamond of Jeru '01
Heller in Pink Tights '60
Hondo '53▲
The Quick and the Dead '87
The Sacketts '79
The Shadow Riders '82
Shalako '68

Books to Film: Ring Lardner
Alibi Ike '35

Champion '49▲

Books to Film: D.H. Lawrence
Kangaroo '86▲
Lady Chatterley '92
Lady Chatterley '06▲
Lady Chatterley's Lover '55
Lady Chatterley's Lover '81
The Rainbow '89▲
The Rocking Horse Winner '49
Trespasser '81
The Virgin and the Gypsy '70
Women in Love '70▲
Young Lady Chatterly 2 '85

Books to Film: John Le Carre
The Constant Gardener '05▲
The Little Drummer Girl '84▲
The Looking Glass War '69
A Murder of Quality '90
A Perfect Spy '88
The Russia House '90
Smiley's People '82
The Spy Who Came in from the Cold '65▲
The Tailor of Panama '00▲
Tinker, Tailor, Soldier, Spy '80▲

Books to Film: Harper Lee
To Kill a Mockingbird '62▲

Books to Film: Elmore Leonard
The Ambassador '84
Be Cool '05
The Big Bounce '69
The Big Bounce '04
Cat Chaser '90
Elmore Leonard's Gold Coast '97
52 Pick-Up '86
Get Shorty '95▲
Glitz '88
Hombre '67▲
Jackie Brown '97▲
Last Stand at Saber River '96
Mr. Majestyk '74
Out of Sight '98▲
Pronto '97
Stick '85
3:10 to Yuma '57▲
3:10 to Yuma '07▲
Touch '96
Valdez Is Coming '71

Books to Film: Ira Levin
The Boys from Brazil '78
A Kiss Before Dying '91
Rosemary's Baby '68▲
Sliver '93
The Stepford Wives '75▲
The Stepford Wives '04

Books to Film: Sinclair Lewis
Ann Vickers '33
Arrowsmith '32
Dodsworth '36▲
Elmer Gantry '60▲
There Will Be Blood '07▲

Books to Film: C.S. Lewis
The Chronicles of Narnia '89
The Chronicles of Narnia: Prince Caspian '08
The Chronicles of Narnia: The Lion, the Witch and the Wardrobe '05▲

Books to Film: Astrid Lindgren
Brothers Lionheart '77
The Children of Noisy Village '86

- The Land of Faraway '87
- More about the Children of Noisy Village '87
- The New Adventures of Pippi Longstocking '88
- Pippi Goes on Board '69
- Pippi in the South Seas '70
- Pippi Longstocking '69
- Pippi on the Run '70

Books to Film: Jack London
- The Assassination Bureau '69►
- Burning Daylight '29
- Call of the Wild '72
- Call of the Wild '93
- The Fighter '52►
- Great Adventure '75
- Jack London's The Call of the Wild '97
- The Legend of Sea Wolf '75
- The Legend of the Sea Wolf '58
- Legends of the North '95
- The Mutiny of the Elsinore '39
- The Sea Wolf '41►
- The Sea Wolf '93
- Tales of the Klondike: In a Far Country '87
- Tales of the Klondike: Race for Number One '87
- Tales of the Klondike: The Scorn of Women '87
- Tales of the Klondike: The Unexpected '87
- White Fang '91►
- White Fang and the Hunter '85
- Wolf Call '39

Books to Film: H.P. Lovecraft
- Beyond the Wall of Sleep '06
- Blood Island '68
- Bride of Re-Animator '89
- Cthulhu Mansion '91
- The Curse '87
- Die, Monster, Die! '65
- The Dunwich Horror '70
- From Beyond '86►
- H.P. Lovecraft's Necronomicon: Book of the Dead '93
- Lurking Fear '94
- Re-Animator '84►
- The Resurrected '91
- The Sinister Invasion '68
- The Unnamable '88
- The Unnamable 2: The Statement of Randolph Carter '92

Books to Film: Robert Ludlum
- The Apocalypse Watch '97
- The Bourne Identity '88►
- The Bourne Identity '02►
- The Bourne Supremacy '04►
- The Bourne Ultimatum '07►
- The Hades Factor '06
- The Holcroft Covenant '85
- The Osterman Weekend '83►

Books to Film: Peter Maas
- King of the Gypsies '78
- Marie '85►
- Serpico '73►

Books to Film: Alistair MacLean
- Bear Island '80
- Breakheart Pass '76
- Caravan to Vaccares '74
- Detonator '93
- Detonator 2: Night Watch '95
- Force 10 from Navarone '78
- Golden Rendezvous '77
- The Guns of Navarone '61►
- Ice Station Zebra '68
- Puppet on a Chain '72
- River of Death '90
- When Eight Bells Toll '71
- Where Eagles Dare '68►

Books to Film: Bernard Malamud
- The Angel Levine '70
- The Assistant '97
- The Fixer '68►
- The Natural '84►
- The Tenants '06

Books to Film: Norman Mailer
- The Executioner's Song '82
- Marilyn: The Untold Story '80►
- The Naked and the Dead '58
- Tough Guys Don't Dance '87
- Pursuit '72

Books to Film: Richard Matheson
- Cold Sweat '71
- Duel '71►
- I Am Legend '07►
- Icy Breasts '75
- The Incredible Shrinking Man '57►
- The Last Man on Earth '64
- The Legend of Hell House '73►
- Omega Man '71
- Somewhere in Time '80
- Stir of Echoes '99
- What Dreams May Come '98
- Young Warriors '83

Books to Film: W. Somerset Maugham
- Adorable Julia '62
- Beachcomber '38
- Being Julia '04►
- Dirty Gertie from Harlem U.S.A. '46
- Encore '52►
- The Letter '40►
- Miss Sadie Thompson '53►
- The Moon and Sixpence '43►
- Of Human Bondage '34►
- Of Human Bondage '64
- The Painted Veil '34
- The Painted Veil '06
- Rain '32
- The Razor's Edge '46►
- The Razor's Edge '84►
- Sadie Thompson '28►
- Trio '50►
- Up at the Villa '00

Books to Film: Colleen McCullough
- An Indecent Obsession '85
- The Thorn Birds '83►
- Tim '79

Books to Film: Ian McEwan
- The Cement Garden '93
- The Comfort of Strangers '91►
- The Innocent '93

Books to Film: Terry McMillan
- Disappearing Acts '00
- How Stella Got Her Groove Back '98
- Waiting to Exhale '95►

Books to Film: Larry McMurtry
- The Best Little Whorehouse in Texas '82
- Comanche Moon '08
- Hud '63►
- Larry McMurtry's Dead Man's Walk '96
- The Last Picture Show '71►
- Lonesome Dove '89►
- My Father's Glory '91►
- My Mother's Castle '91►
- Terms of Endearment '83►
- Texasville '90

Books to Film: Herman Melville
- Bartleby '70
- Bartleby '01
- Enchanted Island '58
- Moby Dick '56►
- Moby Dick '98
- Pola X '99

Books to Film: James Michener
- The Bridges at Toko-Ri '55►
- Centennial '78►
- Dynasty '76
- Hawaii '66►
- Return to Paradise '53
- Sayonara '57►
- Texas '94
- Until They Sail '57

Books to Film: Sue Miller
- Family Pictures '93
- The Good Mother '88
- Inventing the Abbotts '97

Books to Film: L.M. Montgomery
- Anne of Avonlea '87►
- Anne of Green Gables '34►
- Anne of Green Gables '85►
- Lantern Hill '90

Books to Film: Brian Moore
- Black Robe '91►
- Catholics '73►
- Cold Heaven '92
- The Lonely Passion of Judith Hearne '87►

Books to Film: Vladimir Nabokov
- Despair '78►
- Lolita '62►
- Lolita '97
- The Luzhin Defence '00

Books to Film: John Nichols
- The Milagro Beanfield War '88►
- The Sterile Cuckoo '69►
- The Wizard of Loneliness '88

Books to Film: Joyce Carol Oates
- Blonde '01
- Foxfire '96
- Smooth Talk '85►

Books to Film: John O'Hara
- Butterfield 8 '60►
- From the Terrace '60
- Pal Joey '57►
- Ten North Frederick '58

Books to Film: George Orwell
- Animal Farm '99
- A Merry War '97►
- 1984 '56
- 1984 '84►

Books to Film: Marcel Pagnol
- The Baker's Wife '33
- Fanny '32►
- Jean de Florette '87►
- Marius '31►
- Marion of the Spring '87►
- Topaze '33►

Books to Film: Robert B. Parker
- Jesse Stone: Sea Change '07
- Monte Walsh '03
- Poodle Springs '98
- Small Vices: A Spenser Mystery '99
- Spenser: A Savage Place '94
- Spenser: Ceremony '93
- Spenser: Pale Kings & Princes '94
- Spenser: The Judas Goat '94
- Thin Air '00

Books to Film: James Patterson
- Along Came a Spider '01
- Child of Darkness, Child of Light '91
- Kiss the Girls '97

Books to Film: Nicholas Pileggi
- Casino '95►
- Goodfellas '90►

Books to Film: Edgar Allan Poe
- The Bells '26
- The Black Cat '34►
- The Black Cat '81
- Dr. Tarr's Torture Dungeon '75
- The Fall of the House of Usher '49
- The Fall of the House of Usher '60►
- The Fall of the House of Usher '80
- The Haunted Palace '63
- Haunting Fear '91
- The Haunting of Morella '91
- The House of Usher '88
- The House of Usher '06
- Jaws of Justice '33
- La Chute de la Maison Usher '28►
- The Living Coffin '58
- Manfish '56
- Murders in the Rue Morgue '71
- The Murders in the Rue Morgue '86►
- The Masque of the Red Death '89
- Masque of the Red Death '64►
- Masque of the Red Death '06
- The Oblong Box '69
- The Oval Portrait '88
- The Pit and the Pendulum '61►
- The Pit & the Pendulum '91
- Premature Burial '62
- The Raven '15
- The Raven '35►
- The Raven '63►
- The Spectre of Edgar Allan Poe '73
- Spirits of the Dead '68►
- Tales of Terror '62
- The Tell-Tale Heart '60
- Tomb of Ligeia '64►
- The Torture Chamber of Dr. Sadism '69
- Two Evil Eyes '90
- Web of the Spider '70

Books to Film: Katherine Anne Porter
- Noon Wine '84►
- Ship of Fools '65►

Books to Film: Richard Price
- Bloodbrothers '78
- Clockers '95►
- Freedomland '06
- Wanderers '79►

Books to Film: Mario Puzo
- The Godfather '72►
- The Godfather, Part 2 '74►
- The Godfather, Part 3 '90►
- The Last Don '97
- The Sicilian '87

Books to Film: Ruth Rendell
- Alias Betty '01
- The Bridesmaid '04
- A Dark Adapted Eye '93►
- A Demon in My View '92
- A Fatal Inversion '92
- Gallowglass '95►
- La Ceremonie '95►
- Live Flesh '97►

Books to Film: Anne Rice
- Anne Rice's The Feast of All Saints '01
- Exit to Eden '94
- Interview with the Vampire '94►
- Queen of the Damned '02

Books to Film: Mordecai Richler
- The Apprenticeship of Duddy Kravitz '74►
- Jacob Two Two Meets the Hooded Fang '99
- Joshua Then and Now '55►

Books to Film: Harold Robbins
- The Adventurers '70
- The Betsy '78
- The Carpetbaggers '64
- King Creole '58►
- The Lonely Lady '83
- Nevada Smith '66
- Never Love a Stranger '58
- Stiletto '69
- Where Love Has Gone '64

Books to Film: Nora Roberts
- Angels Fall '07
- Blue Smoke '07
- Carolina Moon '07
- Magic Moments '89
- Montana Sky '07

Books to Film: Sax Rohmer
- The Castle of Fu Manchu '68
- Daughter of the Dragon '31
- The Fiendish Plot of Dr. Fu Manchu '80
- Kiss and Kill '68
- The Mask of Fu Manchu '32►
- The Mysterious Dr. Fu Manchu '29
- The Return of Dr. Fu Manchu '30

Books to Film: Philip Roth
- Goodbye Columbus '69►
- The Human Stain '03
- Portnoy's Complaint '72

Books to Film: J.K. Rowlings
- Harry Potter and the Chamber of Secrets '02►
- Harry Potter and the Goblet of Fire '05►
- Harry Potter and the Prisoner of Azkaban '04►
- Harry Potter and the Sorcerer's Stone '01►
- Untraceable '08

Books to Film: Damon Runyon
- Big Street '42
- Bloodhounds of Broadway '89
- 40 Pounds of Trouble '62
- Guys and Dolls '55►
- It Ain't Hay '43
- Lady for a Day '33►
- The Lemon Drop Kid '51
- Little Miss Marker '34►
- Little Miss Marker '80
- Pocketful of Miracles '61►
- Sorrowful Jones '49

Books to Film: Sir Walter Scott
- Ivanhoe '52►
- Ivanhoe '82
- Ivanhoe '97►
- King Richard and the Crusaders '54
- Oliver's Story '78
- Only Love '98

Books to Film: Erich Segal
- Love Story '70►
- Man, Woman & Child '83
- Oliver's Story '78
- Only Love '98

Books to Film: Hubert Selby, Jr.
- Last Exit to Brooklyn '90►
- Requiem for a Dream '00►

Books to Film: Irwin Shaw
- Easy Living '49
- Two Weeks in Another Town '62
- The Young Lions '58►

Books to Film: Mary Shelley
- The Bride of Frankenstein '35►
- Frankenstein '31►
- Frankenstein '73
- Frankenstein '82
- Frankenstein '93
- Frankenstein Unbound '90►
- Mary Shelley's Frankenstein '94

Books to Film: Jean Shepherd
- A Christmas Story '83►
- My Summer Story '94
- Ollie Hopnoodle's Haven of Bliss '88

Books to Film: Sidney Sheldon
- The Naked Face '84
- The Other Side of Midnight '77
- Rage of Angels '83
- Rage of Angels: The Story Continues '85
- Sidney Sheldon's Bloodline '79
- Windmills of the Gods '88

Books to Film: Georges Simenon
- Betty '92
- Cop-Out '67
- Man on the Eiffel Tower '48►
- Monsieur Hire '89►
- Paris Express '53

► = rated three bones or higher

Books

Red Lights '04▲

Books to Film: Mickey Spillane
Girl Hunters '63
I, the Jury '82
Margin for Murder '81

Books to Film: Danielle Steel
Danielle Steel's Changes '91
Danielle Steel's Daddy '91
Danielle Steel's Fine Things '90
Danielle Steel's Heartbeat '93
Danielle Steel's Kaleidoscope '90
Danielle Steel's Palomino '91
Danielle Steel's Star '93
Now and Forever '82
The Promise '79
Safe Harbour '07

Books to Film: John Steinbeck
Cannery Row '82
East of Eden '54▲
East of Eden '80
The Grapes of Wrath '40▲
Lifeboat '44▲
Of Mice and Men '39▲
Of Mice and Men '81▲
Of Mice and Men '92▲
The Pearl '48▲
The Red Pony '49▲
The Red Pony '76▲
Tortilla Flat '42▲

Books to Film: Robert Louis Stevenson
Abbott and Costello Meet Dr. Jekyll and Mr. Hyde '52
Adventure Island '47
Black Arrow '48▲
The Body Snatcher '45▲
Dr. Jekyll and Mr. Hyde '20▲
Dr. Jekyll and Mr. Hyde '32▲
Dr. Jekyll and Mr. Hyde '41▲
Dr. Jekyll and Mr. Hyde '68
Dr. Jekyll and Mr. Hyde '73
Dr. Jekyll and Sister Hyde '71
The Ebb-Tide '97
I, Monster '71▲
Jekyll '07
Jekyll and Hyde '90
Jekyll & Hyde... Together Again '82
Kidnapped '60
Kidnapped '95
Kidnapped '05▲
Man with Two Heads '72
The Master of Ballantrae '53
Muppet Treasure Island '96
Robert Louis Stevenson's The Game of Death '99
St. Ives '98
Strange Case of Dr. Jekyll & Mr. Hyde '68
Strange Case of Dr. Jekyll & Mr. Hyde '89
The Strange Door '51
Treasure Island '34▲
Treasure Island '50▲
Treasure Island '72
Treasure Island '89
Treasure Island '99
Treasure Planet '02▲
The Wrong Box '66▲

Books to Film: Bram Stoker
Blood from the Mummy's Tomb '71
Bram Stoker's Dracula '92
Bram Stoker's Shadowbuilder '98
Bram Stoker's The Mummy '97
Burial of the Rats '95
Count Dracula '71
Dracula (Spanish Version) '31
Dracula '31▲
Dracula '73
Dracula '79
Dracula '06
The Horror of Dracula '58▲
The Lair of the White Worm '88▲
Nosferatu '22▲
Nosferatu the Vampyre '79
Tomb '86
Van Helsing '04▲

Books to Film: Harriet Beecher Stowe
Uncle Tom's Cabin '14
Uncle Tom's Cabin '27
Uncle Tom's Cabin '69
Uncle Tom's Cabin '87

Books to Film: Jacqueline Susann
The Love Machine '71
Once Is Not Enough '75

Books to Film: Jonathan Swift
Gulliver's Travels '39
Gulliver's Travels '77
Gulliver's Travels '95
The Three Worlds of Gulliver '59

Books to Film: William Makepeace Thackeray
Barry Lyndon '75▲
Becky Sharp '35
Vanity Fair '32
Vanity Fair '67
Vanity Fair '99
Vanity Fair '04▲

Books to Film: Paul Theroux
Half Moon Street '86
The Mosquito Coast '86
Saint Jack '79▲

Books to Film: Jim Thompson
After Dark, My Sweet '90▲
Coup de Torchon '81▲
The Getaway '72
The Getaway '93
The Grifters '90▲
Hit Me '96
The Kill-Off '90
This World, Then the Fireworks '97

Books to Film: Roderick Thorp
The Detective '68▲
Devlin '92
Die Hard '88▲
Rainbow Drive '90

Books to Film: James Thurber
The Battle of the Sexes '60▲
Billy Liar '63▲
The Secret Life of Walter Mitty '47▲

Books to Film: J.R.R. Tolkien
The Hobbit '78▲
The Lord of the Rings '78
Lord of the Rings: The Fellowship of the Rings '01▲
Lord of the Rings: The Two Towers '02▲
Lord of the Rings: The Return of the King '03▲
The Return of the King '80

Books to Film: Leo Tolstoy
Anna Karenina '35▲
Anna Karenina '48
Anna Karenina '85
Anna Karenina '00
Leo Tolstoy's Anna Karenina '96
Night Sun '90
Prisoner of the Mountains '96▲
War and Peace '56
War and Peace '68▲
War and Peace '73

Books to Film: Scott Turow
Presumed Innocent '90▲

Books to Film: Mark Twain
The Adventures of Huck Finn '93▲
The Adventures of Huckleberry Finn '39▲
The Adventures of Huckleberry Finn '60
The Adventures of Huckleberry Finn '78
The Adventures of Huckleberry Finn '85
The Adventures of Tom Sawyer '38▲
The Adventures of Tom Sawyer '73
Ava's Magical Adventure '94
A Connecticut Yankee '31▲
A Connecticut Yankee in King Arthur's Court 49
A Connecticut Yankee in King Arthur's Court '89
Huck and the King of Hearts '93
Huckleberry Finn '74
Huckleberry Finn '75
Huckleberry Finn '81
The Innocents Abroad '84
A Kid in King Arthur's Court '95
A Knight in Camelot '98
A Million to Juan '94
The Modern Adventures of Tom Sawyer '99
The Mysterious Stranger '82
The Prince and the Pauper '37▲
The Prince and the Pauper '62
The Prince and the Pauper '78
The Prince and the Pauper '01
The Prince and the Surfer '99
The Private History of a Campaign That Failed '81
Pudd'nhead Wilson '84
Tom and Huck '95▲
Tom Sawyer '30▲
Tom Sawyer '73
Unidentified Flying Oddball '79
A Young Connecticut Yankee in King Arthur's Court '95

Books to Film: Anne Tyler
The Accidental Tourist '88▲
Breathing Lessons '94▲
Earthly Possessions '99
Saint Maybe '98▲

Books to Film: John Updike
Roommate '84
Too Far to Go '79▲
The Witches of Eastwick '87

Books to Film: Leon Uris
Battle Cry '55▲
Exodus '60▲
QB VII '74▲
Topaz '69▲

Books to Film: Jules Verne
Around the World in 80 Days '56▲
Around the World in 80 Days '89
Around the World in 80 Days '04
Around the World in a Daze '63
800 Leagues Down the Amazon '93
Five Weeks in a Balloon '62
From the Earth to the Moon '58
In Search of the Castaways '62▲
Journey to the Center of the Earth '59▲
Journey to the Center of the Earth '88
Journey to the Center of the Earth '99
Journey to the Center of the Earth 3D '08
Light at the Edge of the World '71
Master of the World '61▲
Mysterious Island '61▲
On the Comet '68▲
Those Fantastic Flying Fools '67
20,000 Leagues under the Sea '16▲
20,000 Leagues under the Sea '54▲
20,000 Leagues Under the Sea 97
Where Time Began '77

Books to Film: Kurt Vonnegut
Breakfast of Champions '98
D.P. '85
Kurt Vonnegut's Harrison Bergeron '95
Mother Night '96▲
Slapstick of Another Kind '84
Slaughterhouse Five '72▲
Who Am I This Time? '82▲

Books to Film: Alice Walker
The Color Purple '85▲

Books to Film: Edgar Wallace
The Black Abbot '63
Chamber of Horrors '40
Creature with the Blue Hand '70
Curse of the Yellow Snake '63
Dead Eyes of London '61
Door with the Seven Locks '62
Forger of London '61
The Human Monster '39
The Indian Scarf '63
Mr. Reeder in Room 13 '38
The Mysterious Magician '65
The Secret Four '40
The Squeaker '37
The Squeaker '65
The Strange Countess '61
The Terror '38

Books to Film: Joseph Wambaugh
The Black Marble '79▲
The Choirboys '77
Echoes in the Darkness '87
The Glitter Dome '84
The New Centurions '72
The Onion Field '79▲

Books to Film: Evelyn Waugh
Brideshead Revisited '81▲
Bright Young Things '03
A Handful of Dust '88
The Loved One '65
Sword of Honour '01

Books to Film: H.G. Wells
Empire of the Ants '77
First Men in the Moon '64
Food of the Gods '76
Food of the Gods: Part 2 '88
Half a Sixpence '67
The History of Mr. Polly '07
The Invisible Man '33▲
The Invisible Man's Revenge '44
The Island of Dr. Moreau '77
The Island of Dr. Moreau '96
Island of Lost Souls '32▲
Kipps '41▲
La Merveilleuse Visite '74
The Man Who Could Work Miracles '37▲
The New Invisible Man '58
Terror Is a Man '59
Things to Come '36▲
The Time Machine '60▲
The Time Machine '02
Village of the Giants '65
The War of the Worlds '53▲
War of the Worlds '05▲

Books to Film: Donald Westlake (aka Richard Stark)
Bank Shot '74▲
Cops and Robbers '73
The Hot Rock '70▲
Made in USA '88
Payback '98▲
Point Blank '67
Slayground '84
A Slight Case of Murder '99
Two Much '96
What's the Worst That Could Happen? '01
Why Me? '90

Books to Film: Edith Wharton
The Age of Innocence '93▲
The Buccaneers '95▲
The Children '90
Ethan Frome '92
House of Mirth '00▲
The Old Maid '39▲

Books to Film: William Wharton
Birdy '84▲
Dad '89

Books to Film: E(lwyn) B(rooks) White
Charlotte's Web '73
Charlotte's Web '06▲
Stuart Little '99
Stuart Little 2 '02▲
The Trumpet of the Swan '01

Books to Film: Oscar Wilde
The Canterville Ghost '44
The Canterville Ghost '96
Dorian Gray '70
A Good Woman '04
An Ideal Husband '99▲
The Importance of Being Earnest '52▲
The Importance of Being Earnest '02
Lady Windermere's Fan '25▲
Picture of Dorian Gray '45▲
Salome '22
Salome '53
Salome '85
The Sins of Dorian Gray '82

Books to Film: Thornton Wilder
The Bridge of San Luis Rey '44▲
The Bridge of San Luis Rey '05
Hello, Dolly! '69
Mr. North '88
The Matchmaker '58▲
Our Town '40▲
Our Town '77▲
Our Town '89

Books to Film: Ben Ames Williams
All the Brothers Were Valiant '53
Leave Her to Heaven '45▲
The Strange Woman '46

Books to Film: Virginia Woolf
Mrs. Dalloway '97▲
To the Lighthouse '83

Books to Film: Cornell Woolrich
Black Angel '46▲
The Bride Wore Black '68▲
The Chase '46
Deadline at Dawn '46
Fall Guy '47
Fear in the Night '47▲
I Married a Dead Man '82
The Leopard Man '43▲
Mississippi Mermaid '69▲
Mrs. Winterbourne '96
Original Sin '01
Phantom Lady '44▲
Rear Window '54▲
Rear Window '98
The Window '49▲

Books to Film: Herman Wouk
The Caine Mutiny '54▲
The Caine Mutiny Court Martial '88▲
Marjorie Morningstar '58
War & Remembrance '88
War & Remembrance: The Final Chapter '89
The Winds of War '83

Books to Film: Emile Zola
The Game Is Over '66
Germinal '93▲
Gervaise '56▲
Human Desire '54▲
La Bete Humaine '38▲
Nana '55▲
Nana '82
Therese Raquin '80

The Bowery Boys
Angels with Dirty Faces '38▲
Blues Busters '50
Bowery Blitzkrieg '41
Bowery Boys Meet the Monsters '54
Bowery Buckaroos '47
Boys of the City '40
Clancy Street Boys '43
Clipped Wings '53
Dead End '37▲
East Side Kids '40
Flying Wild '41
Follow the Leader '44
Ghost Chasers '51
Ghost on the Loose '43
Hard-Boiled Mahoney '47

▲ = rated three bones or higher

Here Come the Marines '52
Kid Dynamite '43
Let's Get Tough '42
Little Tough Guys '38
Master Minds '49
Million Dollar Kid '44
Mr. Muggs Rides Again '45
'Neath Brooklyn Bridge '42
Pride of the Bowery '41
Smart Alecks '42
Smugglers' Cove '48►
Spook Busters '48
Spooks Run Wild '41
That Gang of Mine '40
They Made Me a Criminal '39

Broken Lizard
Beerfest '06
Club Dread '04
The Dukes of Hazzard '05
Super Troopers '01

Buffalo Bill Cody
Annie Oakley '35►
Buffalo Bill '44
Buffalo Bill & the Indians '76►
Buffalo Bill Rides Again '47
The Plainsman '37
Pony Express '53►
Young Buffalo Bill '40

Bulldog Drummond
Arrest Bulldog Drummond '38
Bulldog Drummond '29
Bulldog Drummond at Bay '37
Bulldog Drummond Comes Back '37
Bulldog Drummond Escapes '37
Bulldog Drummond's Bride '39
Bulldog Drummond's Peril '38
Bulldog Drummond's Revenge '37
Bulldog Drummond's Secret Police '39
Bulldog Jack '35►
Deadlier Than the Male '67

Carry On
Carry On at Your Convenience '71
Carry On Behind '75
Carry On Camping '71
Carry On Cleo '65
Carry On Cowboy '66
Carry On Cruising '62
Carry On Dick '75
Carry On Doctor '68►
Carry On Emmanuelle '78
Carry On England '76
Carry On Henry VIII '71
Carry On Nurse '59
Carry On Screaming '66
Follow That Camel '67

Charlie Brown and the Peanuts Gang
Race for Your Life, Charlie Brown '77

Charlie Chan
The Black Camel '31
Castle in the Desert '42
Charlie Chan and the Curse of the Dragon Queen '81
Charlie Chan at Monte Carlo '37
Charlie Chan at the Circus '36
Charlie Chan at the Olympics '37
Charlie Chan at the Opera '36
Charlie Chan at the Race Track '35
Charlie Chan at the Wax Museum '40
Charlie Chan at Treasure Island '39
Charlie Chan in City of Darkness '39
Charlie Chan in Egypt '35
Charlie Chan in Honolulu '38
Charlie Chan in London '34
Charlie Chan in Paris '35
Charlie Chan in Rio '41
Charlie Chan in Shanghai '35
Charlie Chan in the Secret Service '44
Charlie Chan on Broadway '37
Charlie Chan's Secret '35
The Chinese Cat '44
The Jade Mask '45
Meeting at Midnight '44
Murder over New York '40
The Scarlet Clue '45
The Shanghai Cobra '45

Cisco Kid
The Cisco Kid '94
Guns of Fury '49
In Old New Mexico '45
Lucky Cisco Kid '40
Riding the California Trail '47
South of Monterey '47
South of the Rio Grande '45

Corman's Mama
Big Bad Mama '74
Big Bad Mama 2 '87
Bloody Mama '70
Crazy Mama '75

Director/Star Teams: Almodovar & Banderas
Labyrinth of Passion '82
Law of Desire '86►
Matador '86
Tie Me Up! Tie Me Down! '90

Director/Star Teams: Altman & Gould
The Long Goodbye '73►
M*A*S*H '70►
Nashville '75►
The Player '92

Director/Star Teams: Altman & Murphy
Brewster McCloud '70►
The Caine Mutiny Court Martial '88►
Countdown '68
Kansas City '96►
M*A*S*H '70►
McCabe & Mrs. Miller '71►
Nashville '75►
Tanner '88 '88►
Tanner on Tanner '04
That Cold Day in the Park '69

Director/Star Teams: W. Anderson & Murray
The Life Aquatic with Steve Zissou '04
The Royal Tenenbaums '01►
Rushmore '98

Director/Star Teams: Bergman & Ullmann
Cries and Whispers '72►
Face to Face '76►
Hour of the Wolf '68►
The Passion of Anna '70►
Persona '66►
Saraband '03►
Scenes from a Marriage '73►
The Serpent's Egg '78
The Shame '68►

Director/Star Teams: Bergman & von Sydow
Brink of Life '57
Hour of the Wolf '68►
The Magician '58►
The Passion of Anna '70►
The Seventh Seal '56
The Shame '68►
Through a Glass Darkly '61►
The Touch '71
The Virgin Spring '59►
Wild Strawberries '57
The Winter Light '62►

Director/Star Teams: Boetticher & Scott
Comanche Station '60
Ride Lonesome '59
The Tall T '57

Director/Star Teams: Bunuel & F. Rey
The Discreet Charm of the Bourgeoisie '72►
That Obscure Object of Desire '77►
Tristana '70►
Viridiana '61►

Director/Star Teams: Burton & Depp
Ed Wood '94►
Edward Scissorhands '90►
Sleepy Hollow '99►
Sweeney Todd: The Demon Barber of Fleet Street '07
Tim Burton's Corpse Bride '05►

Director/Star Teams: Capra & Stewart
It's a Wonderful Life '46►
Mr. Smith Goes to Washington '39►
You Can't Take It with You '38►

Director/Star Teams: Chabrol & Huppert
Comedy of Power '06
Il Bidone '55
Madame Bovary '91►
Merci pour le Chocolat '00►
The Story of Women '88►

Director/Star Teams: Corací & Sandler
Click '06
The Waterboy '98
The Wedding Singer '97

Director/Star Teams: Cukor & Hepburn
Adam's Rib '50►
A Bill of Divorcement '32
The Corn Is Green '79►
Holiday '38►
Keeper of the Flame '42
Little Women '33►
Love Among the Ruins '75►
Pat and Mike '52►
The Philadelphia Story '40►
Sylvia Scarlett '35

Director/Star Teams: Donner & Gibson
Conspiracy Theory '97►
Lethal Weapon '87►
Lethal Weapon 2 '89►
Lethal Weapon 3 '92
Lethal Weapon 4 '98
Maverick '94

Director/Star Teams: Dugan & Sandler
Big Daddy '99
Happy Gilmore '96

Director/Star Teams: Ford & Wayne
Donovan's Reef '63►
Fort Apache '48►
The Horse Soldiers '59
How the West Was Won '63►
The Long Voyage Home '40►
The Man Who Shot Liberty Valance '62►
The Quiet Man '52►
Rio Grande '50►
The Searchers '56►
She Wore a Yellow Ribbon '49►
Stagecoach '39►
They Were Expendable '45►
Three Godfathers '48►
Wings of Eagles '57

Director/Star Teams: Frankenheimer & Lancaster
Birdman of Alcatraz '62►
The Gypsy Moths '69
The Savage Bees '76
Seven Days in May '64►
The Train '65►
The Young Savages '61

Director/Star Teams: Hawks & Wayne
El Dorado '67►
Hatari! '62►
Red River '48►
Rio Bravo '59►
Rio Lobo '70

Director/Star Teams: Herzog & Kinski
Aguirre, the Wrath of God '72►
Cobra Verde '88
Fitzcarraldo '82►
Nosferatu the Vampyre '79
Woyzeck '78►

Director/Star Teams: Hill & Newman
Butch Cassidy and the Sundance Kid '69►
Slap Shot '77►
The Sting '73►

Director/Star Teams: Hitchcock & Stewart
The Man Who Knew Too Much '56
Rear Window '54►
Rope '48►
Vertigo '58►

Director/Star Teams: Howard & Hanks
Apollo 13 '95►
The Da Vinci Code '06

Director/Star Teams: Howard & Keaton
Gung Ho! '43
Night Shift '82

Director/Star Teams: Holofcener & Keener
Friends with Money '06
Lovely & Amazing '02►
Walking and Talking '96

Director/Star Teams: Huston & Bogart
Across the Pacific '42►
The African Queen '51►
Beat the Devil '53►
Key Largo '48►
The Maltese Falcon '41►
Treasure of the Sierra Madre '48►

Director/Star Teams: Jordan & Rea
The Butcher Boy '97►
The Company of Wolves '85►
The Crying Game '92►
Danny Boy '82►
The End of the Affair '99►
In Dreams '98
Interview with the Vampire '94►
Michael Collins '96►

Director/Star Teams: King & Peck
Beloved Infidel '59
The Bravados '58►
The Gunfighter '50►
The Snows of Kilimanjaro '52►
Twelve o'Clock High '49►

Director/Star Teams: Kurosawa & Mifune
The Bad Sleep Well '60►
Drunken Angel '48►
The Hidden Fortress '58►
High & Low '62►
A Quiet Duel '49
Rashomon '51►
Red Beard '65►
Sanjuro '62►
Scandal '50
Seven Samurai '54►
Stray Dog '49►
Throne of Blood '57►
Yojimbo '61►

Director/Star Teams: LaBute & Eckhart
In the Company of Men '96►
Nurse Betty '00►
Possession '02
Your Friends & Neighbors '98►

Director/Star Teams: Lee & Washington
He Got Game '98
Inside Man '06►
Malcolm X '92►
Mo' Better Blues '90►

Director/Star Teams: Linklater & Hawke
Before Sunrise '94►
Before Sunset '04►
The Newton Boys '97
Tape '01►
Waking Life '01

Director/Star Teams: Lynch & Nance
Blue Velvet '86►
Dune '84
Eraserhead '78►
Lost Highway '96►
Twin Peaks: Fire Walk with Me '92
Wild at Heart '90►

Director/Star Teams: Mann & Stewart
Bend of the River '52►
Far Country '55►
The Man from Laramie '55►
The Naked Spur '53►
Winchester '73 '50►

Director/Star Teams: Needham & Reynolds
Cannonball Run '81
Cannonball Run 2 '84
Hooper '78
Smokey and the Bandit '77
Smokey and the Bandit 2 '80
Stroker Ace '83

Director/Star Teams: Newman & Woodward
The Effect of Gamma Rays on Man-in-the-Moon Marigolds '73►
The Glass Menagerie '87►
Harry & Son '84
Rachel, Rachel '68►
The Shadow Box '80►

Director/Star Teams: Poitier & Cosby
Ghost Dad '90
Let's Do It Again '75
Piece of the Action '77
Uptown Saturday Night '74

Director/Star Teams: Pollack & Redford
The Electric Horseman '79
Havana '90
Jeremiah Johnson '72►
Out of Africa '85►
This Property Is Condemned '66
Three Days of the Condor '75►
The Way We Were '73►

Director/Star Teams: Rafelson & Nicholson
Blood & Wine '96
Five Easy Pieces '70►
Head '68►
The King of Marvin Gardens '72
Man Trouble '92
The Postman Always Rings Twice '81

Director/Star Teams: R. Rodriguez & Banderas
Desperado '95►
Four Rooms '95
Spy Kids '01►
Spy Kids 2: The Island of Lost Dreams '02►

► = rated three bones or higher

Director

Director/Star Teams: Raimi & Campbell
Army of Darkness '92▲
Crimewave '85
Darkman '90▲
Evil Dead '83
Evil Dead 2: Dead by Dawn '87
Spider-Man '02▲
Spider-Man 2 '04▲
Spider-Man 3 '07

Director/Star Teams: Raimi & 1973 Oldsmobile Delta 88
Army of Darkness '92▲
Darkman '90▲
Evil Dead '83
Evil Dead 2: Dead by Dawn '87
For Love of the Game '99
The Gift '00
A Simple Plan '98▲
Spider-Man '02▲
Spider-Man 2 '04▲
Spider-Man 3 '07

Director/Star Teams: Reiner & Martin
All of Me '84
Dead Men Don't Wear Plaid '82
The Jerk '79
The Man with Two Brains '83▲

Director/Star Teams: Ritt & Newman
Hombre '67▲
Hud '63▲
The Long, Hot Summer '58▲
Paris Blues '61

Director/Star Teams: Sayles & Clapp
Eight Men Out '88▲
Matewan '87▲
Return of the Secaucus 7 '80▲
Sunshine State '02▲

Director/Star Teams: Sayles & Cooper
City of Hope '91▲
Lone Star '95▲
Matewan '87▲
Silver City '04

Director/Star Teams: Sayles & Strathairn
The Brother from Another Planet '84▲
City of Hope '91▲
Eight Men Out '88▲
Limbo '99
Matewan '87▲
Passion Fish '92▲
Return of the Secaucus 7 '80▲

Director/Star Teams: Scorsese & De Niro
Cape Fear '91▲
Casino '95▲
Goodfellas '90▲
King of Comedy '82▲
Mean Streets '73▲
New York, New York '77▲
Raging Bull '80▲
Taxi Driver '76▲

Director/Star Teams: Scorsese & DiCaprio
The Aviator '04▲
The Departed '06▲
Gangs of New York '02▲

Director/Star Teams: Scorsese & Keitel
Alice Doesn't Live Here Anymore '74
The Last Temptation of Christ '88▲
Mean Streets '73▲
Taxi Driver '76▲
Who's That Knocking at My Door? '68▲

Director/Star Teams: T. Scott & Washington
Crimson Tide '95▲
Deja Vu '06
Man on Fire '04

Director/Star Teams: Shadyac & Carrey
Ace Ventura: Pet Detective '93
Bruce Almighty '03
Liar Liar '97

Director/Star Teams: Sheridan & Day-Lewis
The Boxer '97
In the Name of the Father '93▲
My Left Foot '89▲

Director/Star Teams: Siegel & Eastwood
The Beguiled '70▲
Coogan's Bluff '68▲
Dirty Harry '71▲
Escape from Alcatraz '79▲
Two Mules for Sister Sara '70▲

Director/Star Teams: Smith & Affleck
Chasing Amy '97
Clerks 2 '06▲
Dogma '99
Jay and Silent Bob Strike Back '01
Jersey Girl '04
Mallrats '95

Director/Star Teams: Soderbergh & Clooney
The Good German '06
The Limey '99▲
Ocean's Eleven '01▲
Ocean's Twelve '04
Solaris '02

Director/Star Teams: Soderbergh & Roberts
Erin Brockovich '00▲
Full Frontal '02
Ocean's Eleven '01▲
Ocean's Twelve '04

Director/Star Teams: Spielberg & Dreyfuss
Always '89
Close Encounters of the Third Kind '77▲
Jaws '75▲

Director/Star Teams: Spielberg & Hanks
Catch Me If You Can '02▲
Saving Private Ryan '98▲
The Terminal '04

Director/Star Teams: Techine & Deneuve
Ma Saison Preferee '93▲

Director/Star Teams: Truffaut & Leaud
Bed and Board '70▲
Day for Night '73▲
The 400 Blows '59▲
Stolen Kisses '68▲
Two English Girls '72▲

Director/Star Teams: Verhoeven & Hauer
Flesh and Blood '85
Katie Tippel '75
Soldier of Orange '78▲
Spetters '80
Turkish Delight '73

Director/Star Teams: von Sternberg & Dietrich
Blonde Venus '32▲
The Blue Angel '30▲
Dishonored '31
Morocco '30▲
Scarlet Empress '34▲
Shanghai Express '32▲

Director/Star Teams: Walsh & Bogart
The Enforcer '51
High Sierra '41▲
The Roaring Twenties '39▲
They Drive by Night '40▲

Director/Star Teams: Woo & Fat
A Better Tomorrow, Part 1 '86▲
A Better Tomorrow, Part 2 '88
A Bullet in the Head '90▲
Hard-Boiled '92▲
The Killer '90▲

Director/Star Teams: Zemeckis & Hanks
Cast Away '00▲
Forrest Gump '94▲
The Polar Express '04

Dirty Harry
The Dead Pool '88
Dirty Harry '71▲
The Enforcer '76
Magnum Force '73
Sudden Impact '83

Disney Animated Movies
Aladdin '92▲
Aladdin and the King of Thieves '96
Alice in Wonderland '51▲
The Aristocats '70▲
Bambi '42▲
Bambi II '06
Beauty and the Beast '91▲
The Black Cauldron '85
Brother Bear '03
Brother Bear 2 '06
Cars '06▲
Chicken Little '05
Cinderella '50▲
Dinosaur '00
Doug's 1st Movie '99▲
DuckTales the Movie: Treasure of the Lost Lamp '90
Dumbo '41▲
The Emperor's New Groove '00▲
Fantasia '40▲
Fantasia/2000 '00
The Fox and the Hound '81▲
The Fox and the Hound 2 '06
A Goofy Movie '94
The Great Mouse Detective '86▲
Hercules '97▲
The Hunchback of Notre Dame '97▲
The Incredibles '04▲
The Jungle Book '67▲
The Jungle Book 2 '03
Lady and the Tramp '55▲
Lilo & Stitch '02▲
The Lion King '94▲
The Lion King 1 1/2 '04▲
The Lion King: Simba's Pride '98
The Little Mermaid '89▲
The Many Adventures of Winnie the Pooh '77
Meet the Robinsons '07
Melody Time '48▲
Mulan '98
The Nightmare before Christmas '93▲
Oliver & Company '88
101 Dalmatians '61▲
Peter Pan '53▲
Piglet's Big Movie '03
Pinocchio '40▲
Pocahontas '95▲
Pooh's Heffalump Movie '05
The Rescuers '77▲
The Rescuers Down Under '90
The Return of Jafar '94
Return to Never Land '02
Robin Hood '73▲
Sleeping Beauty '59▲
Snow White and the Seven Dwarfs '37▲
The Sword in the Stone '63▲
Tarzan '99▲
Tarzan 2 '05
The Three Caballeros '45
Treasure Planet '02
Valiant '05
The Wild '06

Disney Family Movies
The Absent-Minded Professor '61▲
The Adventures of Bullwhip Griffin '66
The Adventures of Huck Finn '93▲
The Adventures of Ichabod and Mr. Toad '49▲
The Air Up There '94
Almost Angels '62
Amy '81
Angels in the Endzone '98
Angels in the Outfield '94
The Apple Dumpling Gang '75
The Apple Dumpling Gang Rides Again '79
Babes in Toyland '61
The Barefoot Executive '71
The Bears & I '74
Bedknobs and Broomsticks '71
Benji the Hunted '87
Big Red '62
Black Arrow '48▲
The Black Arrow '84
The Black Hole '79
Blackbeard's Ghost '67
Blank Check '93
The Blue Yonder '86
Bon Voyage! '62
Breakin' Through '84
Bridge to Terabithia '07
Candleshoe '78
The Castaway Cowboy '74
The Cat from Outer Space '78
Charley and the Angel '73
Charlie, the Lonesome Cougar '67
Cheetah '89
Child of Glass '78
The Chronicles of Narnia: Prince Caspian '08
The Chronicles of Narnia: The Lion, the Witch and the Wardrobe '05
The Computer Wore Tennis Shoes '69
Condorman '81
The Country Bears '02
Darby O'Gill & the Little People '59▲
Davy Crockett and the River Pirates '56
Davy Crockett, King of the Wild Frontier '55▲
The Devil & Max Devlin '81
Dr. Syn, Alias the Scarecrow '64
D3: The Mighty Ducks '96
Emil and the Detectives '64
Enchanted '07
Escapade in Florence '62
Escape to Witch Mountain '75▲
A Far Off Place '93
The Fighting Prince of Donegal '66
Flight of the Grey Wolf '76
Flight of the Navigator '86
Flubber '97
Freaky Friday '76
Freaky Friday '03▲
Fun & Fancy Free '47▲
The Girl Who Spelled Freedom '86▲
The Gnome-Mobile '67
Goal! The Dream Begins '06
Gone Are the Days '84
A Goofy Movie '94
The Great Locomotive Chase '56
Greyfriars Bobby '61
Gus '76
Heavyweights '94
Herbie: Fully Loaded '05
Herbie Goes Bananas '80
Herbie Goes to Monte Carlo '77
Herbie Rides Again '74
High School Musical '06
Homeward Bound: The Incredible Journey '93▲
Honey, I Blew Up the Kid '92
Honey, I Shrunk the Kids '89▲
Honey, We Shrunk Ourselves '97
The Horse in the Gray Flannel Suit '68
The Horse Without a Head '63
Horsemasters '61
Hot Lead & Cold Feet '78
The Hunchback of Notre Dame '96▲
In Search of the Castaways '62▲
The Incredible Journey '63▲
The Incredibles '04▲
Invincible '06▲
Iron Will '93
The Island at the Top of the World '74
Johnny Shiloh '63
Johnny Tremain & the Sons of Liberty '58
The Journey of Natty Gann '85▲
Jump In! '07
Justin Morgan Had a Horse '81
King of the Grizzlies '69
The Last Flight of Noah's Ark '80
Lt. Robinson Crusoe, U.S.N. '66
The Light in the Forest '58
The Littlest Horse Thieves '76
The Littlest Outlaw '54
Lots of Luck '85
The Love Bug '68
Love Leads the Way '84
Mary Poppins '64▲
Menace on the Mountain '70
Million Dollar Duck '71
Miracle Down Under '87
The Miracle of the White Stallions '63
The Misadventures of Merlin Jones '63
Monkeys, Go Home! '66
Monkey's Uncle '65
Moon Pilot '62
The Moon-Spinners '64
Mooncussers '62
Mosby's Marauders '66
My Dog, the Thief '69
My Favorite Martian '98
Napoleon and Samantha '72▲
Never a Dull Moment '68
Newsies '92
Nikki, the Wild Dog of the North '61
The Nine Lives of Elfego Baca '58
No Deposit, No Return '76
The North Avenue Irregulars '79
Now You See Him, Now You Don't '72
Old Yeller '57▲
The One and Only, Genuine, Original Family Band '68▲
101 Dalmatians '96
102 Dalmatians '00
One Little Indian '73
One Magic Christmas '85
One of Our Dinosaurs Is Missing '75
The Parent Trap '61
Pete's Dragon '77
Pocahontas '95▲
Pollyanna '60▲
Return from Witch Mountain '78
Return to Oz '85
Ride a Wild Pony '75▲
Rob Roy—The Highland Rogue '53
The Rocketeer '91▲
Sammy, the Way-Out Seal '62
Savage Sam '63
Scandalous John '71
The Secret of El Zorro '57
The Shaggy D.A. '76
The Shaggy Dog '59
The Shaggy Dog '06
The Sign of Zorro '60
Sky High '05▲
Smith! '69
Smoke '70
Snow Dogs '02
Snowball Express '72
So Dear to My Heart '49▲
Son of Flubber '63
The Story of Robin Hood & His Merrie Men '52▲
The Strongest Man in the World '75
Summer Magic '63
Summer of the Monkeys '98
The Swiss Family Robinson '60▲
The Sword & the Rose '53
Tall Tale: The Unbelievable Adventures of Pecos Bill '95
Ten Who Dared '60
That Darn Cat! '65
That Darn Cat '96
Third Man on the Mountain '59
Those Calloways '65
The Three Lives of Thomasina '63▲
3 Ninjas '92
3 Ninjas Kick Back '94
A Tiger Walks '64
Toby Tyler '59▲

▲ = rated three bones or higher

Tom and Huck '95 ▶
Toothless '97
Toy Story '95 ▶
Treasure Island '50 ▶
The Treasure of Matecumbe '76
20,000 Leagues under the Sea '54 ▶
The Ugly Dachshund '65
Underdog '07
Undergrads '85
Unidentified Flying Oddball '79
Waltz King '63
The Watcher in the Woods '81
The Wild Country '71
The Wild Wolf '34
Westward Ho, the Wagons! '56
White Fang '91 ▶
White Fang 2: The Myth of the White Wolf '94
Wild Hearts Can't Be Broken '91
The World's Greatest Athlete '73

Doc Holliday
Cheyenne Autumn '64
Gunfight at the O.K. Corral '57 ▶
Hour of the Gun '67
My Darling Clementine '46 ▶
Tombstone '93 ▶
Wyatt Earp '94

Dr. Christian
Courageous Dr. Christian '40
Dr. Christian Meets the Women '40
Meet Dr. Christian '39
Remedy for Riches '40
They Meet Again '41

Dr. Mabuse
Dr. Mabuse, The Gambler '22 ▶
Dr. Mabuse vs. Scotland Yard '64
The Invisible Dr. Mabuse '62
The Return of Dr. Mabuse '61
The Thousand Eyes of Dr. Mabuse '60

Dr. Seuss
Dr. Seuss' Horton Hears a Who! '08
Dr. Seuss' How the Grinch Stole Christmas '00
Dr. Seuss' The Cat in the Hat '03
The 5000 Fingers of Dr. T '53 ▶

Dracula
Abbott and Costello Meet Frankenstein '48 ▶
Blood of Dracula '57
Blood of Dracula's Castle '69
Bram Stoker's Dracula '92 ▶
Count Dracula '71
The Brides of Dracula '60
The Creeps '97
Dracula (Spanish Version) '31
Dracula 2: Ascension '03
Dracula 3: Legacy '05
Dracula A.D. 1972 '72
Dracula '31 ▶
Dracula '73
Dracula '79
Dracula 2000 '00
Dracula: Dead and Loving It '95
Dracula Has Risen from the Grave '68 ▶
Dracula and Son '76
Dracula, Prince of Darkness '66 ▶
Dracula: The Dark Prince '07
Dracula Rising '93
Dracula Sucks '79
Dracula vs. Frankenstein '71
Dracula's Daughter '36 ▶
Dracula's Great Love '72
Dracula's Last Rites '79
Dracula's Widow '88
The Horror of Dracula '58 ▶
House of Dracula '45
House of Frankenstein '44
Hysterical '83
Love at First Bite '79
The Legend of the 7 Golden Vampires '73
Lust for Dracula '04
Mad Monster Party '68
The Monster Squad '87
Nocturna '79
Return of Dracula '58
Return of the Vampire '43
The Satanic Rites of Dracula '73
The Scars of Dracula '70
The Screaming Dead '72
Son of Dracula '43
Taste the Blood of Dracula '70
To Die For '89
Transylvania 6-5000 '85
Vampire Circus '71
Van Helsing '04
Waxwork '88
Zoltan... Hound of Dracula '78

Dreamworks Animated Movies
Antz '98
Bee Movie '07
Chicken Run '00 ▶
Kung Fu Panda '08 ▶
Madagascar '05
Over the Hedge '06
Prince of Egypt '98 ▶
The Road to El Dorado '00
Shark Tale '04
Shrek '01 ▶
Shrek 2 '04 ▶
Sinbad: Legend of the Seven Seas '03
Spirit: Stallion of the Cimarron '02
Wallace & Gromit: The Curse of the Were-Rabbit '05 ▶

Elvisfilm
Blue Hawaii '62
Bubba Ho-Tep '03 ▶
Change of Habit '69
Charro! '69
Clambake '67
Double Trouble '67
Easy Come, Easy Go '67
Eddie Presley '92
Elvis and Me '88
Elvis Has Left the Building '04
Elvis in Hollywood '93
Elvis Meets Nixon '98
Elvis: The Movie '79
Finding Graceland '98
Flaming Star '60 ▶
Follow That Dream '61
Frankie and Johnny '65
Fun in Acapulco '63
G.I. Blues '60
Girl Happy '65
Girls! Girls! Girls! '62
Harum Scarum '65
Heartbreak Hotel '88
Honeymoon in Vegas '92
It Happened at the World's Fair '63
Jailhouse Rock '57 ▶
Kid Galahad '62
King Creole '58 ▶
Kissin' Cousins '64
Live a Little, Love a Little '68

Love Me Tender '56
Loving You '57
Paradise, Hawaiian Style '66
Protecting the King '07
Roustabout '64
Six-String Samurai '98
Speedway '68
Spinout '66
Stay Away, Joe '68
This Is Elvis '81 ▶
3000 Miles to Graceland '01
Top Secret! '84 ▶
The Trouble with Girls (and How to Get into It) '69
True Romance '93 ▶
Viva Las Vegas '63
Wild in the Country '61
The Woman Who Loved Elvis '93

The Falcon
The Falcon in Hollywood '44
The Falcon in Mexico '44
The Falcon Takes Over '42
The Falcon's Brother '42

4 Bones
A Nous la Liberté '31 ▶
A Clockwork Orange '71 ▶
Abe Lincoln in Illinois '40 ▶
Adam's Rib '50 ▶
The Adventures of Robin Hood '38 ▶
The African Queen '51 ▶
All About Eve '50 ▶
All Quiet on the Western Front '30 ▶
All the King's Men '49 ▶
An American in Paris '51 ▶
Anatomy of a Murder '59 ▶
Andrei Rublev '66 ▶
An Angel at My Table '89 ▶
Angi Vera '78 ▶
Angels with Dirty Faces '38 ▶
Annie Hall '77 ▶
Apocalypse Now '79 ▶
The Asphalt Jungle '50 ▶
Au Revoir les Enfants '87 ▶
The Awful Truth '37 ▶
The Ballad of Narayama '83 ▶
Bambi '42 ▶
The Bank Dick '40 ▶
The Battleship Potemkin '25 ▶
Beauty and the Beast '46 ▶
Beauty and the Beast '91 ▶
Ben-Hur '26 ▶
Ben-Hur '59 ▶
The Best Years of Our Lives '46 ▶
Best of Youth '03 ▶
The Bicycle Thief '48 ▶
The Big Parade '25 ▶
The Big Sleep '46 ▶
The Birth of a Nation '15 ▶
The Blue Angel '30 ▶
The Boys of St. Vincent '93 ▶
Breathless '59 ▶
Brian's Song '71 ▶
The Bride of Frankenstein '35 ▶
The Bridge on the River Kwai '57 ▶
Brief Encounter '45 ▶
Bringing Up Baby '38 ▶
The Burmese Harp '56 ▶
Butch Cassidy and the Sundance Kid '69 ▶
The Cabinet of Dr. Caligari '19 ▶
The Caine Mutiny '54 ▶
The Cameraman '28 ▶
Casablanca '42 ▶
Cesar '36 ▶
Children of Paradise '44 ▶
Chimes at Midnight '67 ▶
Chinatown '74 ▶
A Christmas Carol '51 ▶
A Christmas Story '83 ▶
Christ Stopped at Eboli '79 ▶
Citizen Kane '41 ▶
City Lights '31 ▶
Close Encounters of the Third Kind '77 ▶
Colonel Redl '84 ▶
Come and See '85 ▶
The Conformist '71 ▶
Crime and Punishment '35 ▶
The Crowd '28 ▶
Cyrano de Bergerac '50 ▶
Cyrano de Bergerac '90 ▶
Danton '82 ▶
Das Boot '81 ▶
David Copperfield '35 ▶
Day for Night '73 ▶
Day of Wrath '43 ▶
The Deer Hunter '78 ▶
Deliverance '72 ▶
Destry Rides Again '39 ▶
Diamonds of the Night '64 ▶
Dinner at Eight '33 ▶
The Discreet Charm of the Bourgeoisie '72 ▶
Dr. Strangelove, or: How I Learned to Stop Worrying and Love the Bomb '64 ▶
Don Quixote '35 ▶
Double Indemnity '44 ▶
Duck Soup '33 ▶
Dumbo '41 ▶
The Earrings of Madame De... '54 ▶
Earth '30 ▶
East of Eden '54 ▶
8 1/2 '63 ▶
El Norte '83 ▶
The Elephant Man '80 ▶
The Empire Strikes Back '80 ▶
The English Patient '96 ▶
E.T.: The Extra-Terrestrial '82 ▶
Every Man for Himself & God Against All '75 ▶
Fanny '32 ▶
Fanny and Alexander '83 ▶
Fantasia '40 ▶
Festival Express '03 ▶
Finding Nemo '03 ▶
Fitzcarraldo '82 ▶
Five Easy Pieces '70 ▶
Forbidden Games '52 ▶
Foreign Correspondent '40 ▶
Forever and a Day '43 ▶
42nd Street '33 ▶
The Four Feathers '39 ▶
The 400 Blows '59 ▶
Frankenstein '31 ▶
The Freshman '25 ▶
From Here to Eternity '53 ▶
The Fugitive '47 ▶
Gallipoli '81 ▶
The Garden of the Finzi-Continis '71 ▶
The General '26 ▶
The General Line '29 ▶
Gigi '58 ▶
The Godfather '72 ▶
The Godfather, Part 2 '74 ▶
The Godfather 1902-1959: The Complete Epic '81 ▶
The Gold Rush '25 ▶
Gone with the Wind '39 ▶
Goodfellas '90 ▶
The Gospel According to St. Matthew '64 ▶
The Graduate '67 ▶
Grand Illusion '37 ▶
The Great Dictator '40 ▶
Great Expectations '46 ▶
Greed '24 ▶
Gunga Din '39 ▶
Hamlet '48 ▶
Harlan County, U.S.A. '76 ▶
Harold and Maude '71 ▶
Harvest '37 ▶
Hearts of Darkness: A Filmmaker's Apocalypse '91 ▶
Henry V '44 ▶
Henry V '89 ▶
Henry: Portrait of a Serial Killer '90 ▶
Here Comes Mr. Jordan '41 ▶
High Noon '52 ▶
Hiroshima, Mon Amour '59 ▶
His Girl Friday '40 ▶
Hollywood Canteen '44 ▶
Hoop Dreams '94 ▶
How Green Was My Valley '41 ▶
Howard's End '92 ▶
Hud '63 ▶
The Hunchback of Notre Dame '39 ▶
I Am a Fugitive from a Chain Gang '32 ▶
The Idiot '51 ▶
If... '69 ▶
Ikiru '52 ▶
The Informer '35 ▶
Intolerance '16 ▶
The Invisible Man '33 ▶
It Happened One Night '34 ▶
It's a Wonderful Life '46 ▶
Ivan the Terrible, Part 1 '44 ▶
James Joyce's A Portrait of the Artist as a Young Man '77 ▶
Jules and Jim '62 ▶
Judgment at Nuremberg '61 ▶
The Killers '46 ▶
King Kong '33 ▶
The King and I '56 ▶
Knife in the Water '62 ▶
Koyaanisqatsi '83 ▶
Kriemhilde's Revenge '24 ▶
Kwaidan '64 ▶
L'Age D'Or '30 ▶
La Chienne '31 ▶
L.A. Confidential '97 ▶
La Dolce Vita '60 ▶
La Strada '54 ▶
The Lady and the Tramp '55 ▶
The Lady Eve '41 ▶
The Lady Vanishes '38 ▶
Last Command '28 ▶
The Last Detail '73 ▶
The Last Emperor '87 ▶
The Last Picture Show '71 ▶
The Last Seduction '94 ▶
Late Spring '49 ▶
Laura '44 ▶
Lawrence of Arabia '62 ▶
Le Trou '59 ▶
Les Misérables '35 ▶
The Letter '40 ▶
A Letter to Three Wives '49 ▶
Letters from Iwo Jima '06 ▶
The Life and Death of Colonel Blimp '43 ▶
The Life and Times of Hank Greenberg '99 ▶
Life Is Beautiful '98 ▶
The Lion in Winter '68 ▶
The Lion King '94 ▶
Little Women '33 ▶
Little Women '94 ▶
The Lives of a Bengal Lancer '35 ▶
Local Hero '83 ▶
Lola Montès '55 ▶
Long Day's Journey into Night '62 ▶
Lord of the Rings: The Two Towers '02 ▶
Lord of the Rings: The Return of the King '03 ▶
Lost Horizon '37 ▶
The Lost Weekend '45 ▶
M '31 ▶
The Magnificent Ambersons '42 ▶
The Magnificent Seven '60 ▶
Male and Female '19 ▶
The Maltese Falcon '41 ▶
A Man for All Seasons '66 ▶
The Man Who Would Be King '75 ▶
The Manchurian Candidate '62 ▶
Manhattan '79 ▶
Marius '31 ▶
The Marriage of Maria Braun '79 ▶
M*A*S*H '70 ▶
Master and Commander: The Far Side of the World '03 ▶
McCabe & Mrs. Miller '71 ▶
Mean Streets '73 ▶
Metropolis '26 ▶
Miracle of Morgan's Creek '44 ▶
Miracle on 34th Street '47 ▶
Mr. & Mrs. Bridge '90 ▶
Mrs. Miniver '42 ▶
Mr. Smith Goes to Washington '39 ▶
Modern Times '36 ▶
Mon Oncle '58 ▶
Monster's Ball '01 ▶
The Mother and the Whore '73 ▶
Murderball '05 ▶
The Music Man '62 ▶
Mutiny on the Bounty '35 ▶
My Left Foot '89 ▶
My Life As a Dog '85 ▶
My Life to Live '62 ▶
My Man Godfrey '36 ▶
Napoleon '27 ▶
Nashville '75 ▶
National Velvet '44 ▶
The New World '05 ▶
The Night of the Hunter '55 ▶
The Night of the Shooting Stars '82 ▶
No Country for Old Men '07 ▶
North by Northwest '59 ▶
Nosferatu '22 ▶
Notorious '46 ▶
O Lucky Man! '73 ▶
Objective, Burma! '45 ▶
Of Mice and Men '39 ▶
Oldboy '03 ▶
Oliver Twist '48 ▶
On the Waterfront '54 ▶
One Flew Over the Cuckoo's Nest '75 ▶
Only Angels Have Wings '39 ▶
Open City '45 ▶
Osama '03 ▶
The Outlaw Josey Wales '76 ▶
The Ox-Bow Incident '43 ▶
Pandora's Box '28 ▶
Pan's Labyrinth '06 ▶
Passion of Joan of Arc '28 ▶
Pather Panchali '54 ▶
Paths of Glory '57 ▶
Pelle the Conqueror '88 ▶
Persona '66 ▶
Petulia '68 ▶
The Philadelphia Story '40 ▶
Pinocchio '40 ▶
Pixote '81 ▶
Poltergeist '82 ▶
Psycho '60 ▶
Pulp Fiction '94 ▶
The Quiet Man '52 ▶
Quiz Show '94 ▶
Raging Bull '80 ▶
Raiders of the Lost Ark '81 ▶
A Raisin in the Sun '61 ▶
Rashomon '51 ▶
Rear Window '54 ▶
Rebecca '40 ▶
Rebel without a Cause '55 ▶
Red River '48 ▶
The Red Shoes '48 ▶
The Reincarnation of Golden Lotus '89 ▶
The Report on the Party and the Guests '66 ▶
Ride the High Country '62 ▶
The River '51 ▶
Road to Perdition '02 ▶
A Room with a View '86 ▶
Roots '77 ▶
Rosemary's Baby '68 ▶
Ruggles of Red Gap '35 ▶
The Rules of the Game '39 ▶
S21: The Khmer Rouge Killing Machine '03 ▶
Sansho the Bailiff '54 ▶
Saving Private Ryan '98 ▶
Scenes from a Marriage '73 ▶
Schindler's List '93 ▶
The Searchers '56 ▶

▶ = rated three bones or higher

Four

Sergeant York '41▸
Seven Beauties '76▸
Seven Samurai '54▸
The Seventh Seal '56▸
Shakespeare in Love '98▸
Shane '53▸
Shin Heike Monogatari '55▸
Shoeshine '47▸
Shoot the Piano Player '62▸
The Shop on Main Street '65▸
Show Boat '36▸
Siegfried '24▸
Singin' in the Rain '52▸
Small Change '76▸
Snow White and the Seven Dwarfs '37▸
Some Like It Hot '59▸
Sounder '72▸
The Southerner '45▸
Spartacus '60▸
Spider '02▸
Stagecoach '39▸
Stalag 17 '53▸
Star Wars '77▸
Storm over Asia '28▸
Strangers on a Train '51▸
A Streetcar Named Desire '51▸
The Stunt Man '80▸
Sullivan's Travels '41▸
Sunrise '27▸
A Tale of Two Cities '36▸
The Third Man '49▸
The 39 Steps '35▸
The Three Burials of Melquiades Estrada '05▸
Throne of Blood '57▸
The Tin Drum '79▸
To Kill a Mockingbird '62▸
To Live '94▸
Tokyo Story '53▸
Tom Jones '63▸
Tootsie '82▸
Top Hat '35▸
Touch of Evil '58▸
Toy Story '95▸
Toy Story 2 '99▸
The Train '65▸
Treasure of the Sierra Madre '48▸
The Triplets of Belleville '02▸
Tristana '70▸
The Truman Show '98▸
Twelve Angry Men '57▸
Twentieth Century '34▸
2001: A Space Odyssey '68▸
Two Women '61▸
Umberto D '55▸
Un Chien Andalou '28▸
Under the Flag of the Rising Sun '72▸
Vampyr '31▸
Variety '25▸
Vertigo '58▸
Viridiana '61▸
Viva Zapata! '52▸
Wages of Fear '55▸
The Wedding March '28▸
Who's Afraid of Virginia Woolf? '66▸
The Wild Bunch '69▸
Wild Strawberries '57▸
The Wind '28▸
The Wizard of Oz '39▸
Woman in the Dunes '64▸
Woman of the Year '42▸
Woodstock '70▸
The World of Apu '59▸
Wuthering Heights '39▸
Yankee Doodle Dandy '42▸
Yojimbo '61▸
Young Frankenstein '74▸
Z '69▸
Zero for Conduct '33▸
Zvenigora '28▸

Francis the Talking Mule

Francis Covers the Big Town '53
Francis Goes to the Races '51
Francis Goes to West Point '52
Francis in the Haunted House '56
Francis in the Navy '55
Francis Joins the WACs '54
Francis the Talking Mule '49▸

Frankenstein

Abbott and Costello Meet Frankenstein '48▸
Andy Warhol's Frankenstein '74
Blackenstein '73
Boltneck '98
The Bride '85
The Bride of Frankenstein '35▸
The Creeps '97
The Curse of Frankenstein '57
Dr. Frankenstein's Castle of Freaks '74
Dracula vs. Frankenstein '69
Dracula vs. Frankenstein '71
The Evil of Frankenstein '64
Frankenstein '73▸
Frankenstein '82
Frankenstein '93
Frankenstein and Me '96
Frankenstein and the Monster from Hell '74
Frankenstein Created Woman '66▸
Frankenstein '80 '79
Frankenstein General Hospital '88
Frankenstein Island '81
Frankenstein Meets the Space Monster '65
Frankenstein Meets the Wolfman '42▸
Frankenstein Must Be Destroyed '69
Frankenstein Reborn '98
Frankenstein Sings... The Movie '95
Frankenstein Unbound '90▸
Frankenstein's Daughter '58
Frankenstein's Great Aunt Tillie '83
Frankenweenie '84
The Ghost of Frankenstein '42
Gothic '87▸
The Horror of Frankenstein '70
House of Dracula '45
House of Frankenstein '44
Jesse James Meets Frankenstein's Daughter '65
Lady Frankenstein '72
Mad Monster Party '68
Mary Shelley's Frankenstein '94
Mr. Stitch '95
The Munsters' Revenge '81
Nosferatu '22▸
Prototype '83▸
The Revenge of Frankenstein '58
Rites of Frankenstein '72
The Screaming Dead '72
Son of Frankenstein '39▸
Subject Two '06
Teenage Frankenstein '58
Van Helsing '04▸
The Vindicator '85
Young Frankenstein '74▸

Fu Manchu

The Castle of Fu Manchu '68
Daughter of the Dragon '31
The Fiendish Plot of Dr. Fu Manchu '80
Kiss and Kill '68
The Mask of Fu Manchu '32
The Mysterious Dr. Fu Manchu '29
The Return of Dr. Fu Manchu '30

Godzilla and Friends

Dagora, the Space Monster '65
Destroy All Monsters '68
Destroy All Planets '68
Gamera vs. Barugon '66
Gamera vs. Gaos '67
Gamera vs. Guiron '69
Gamera vs. Zigra '71
Gappa the Trifibian Monster '67
Ghidrah the Three Headed Monster '65
Godzilla '98
Godzilla, King of the Monsters '56
Godzilla 1985 '85
Godzilla on Monster Island '72
Godzilla Raids Again '55
Godzilla 2000 '99▸
Godzilla vs. Biollante '89
Godzilla vs. King Ghidora '91
Godzilla vs. Mechagodzilla II '93
Godzilla vs. Megalon '76
Godzilla vs. Monster Zero '68
Godzilla vs. Mothra '64
Godzilla vs. the Cosmic Monster '74
Godzilla vs. the Sea Monster '66
Godzilla vs. the Smog Monster '72
Godzilla's Revenge '69
King Kong vs. Godzilla '63
Mothra '62▸
Rebirth of Mothra '96
Rebirth of Mothra 2 '97
Rodan '56
Son of Godzilla '66
Terror of Mechagodzilla '78
Varan the Unbelievable '61
War of the Gargantuas '70
X from Outer Space '67
Yog, Monster from Space '71
Yongkari Monster of the Deep '67

Hallmark Hall of Fame

An American Story '92
Blind Spot '93
The Boys Next Door '96
Breathing Lessons '94▸
Calm at Sunset '96
Caroline? '90▸
Cupid & Cate '00
Decoration Day '90▸
Durango '99
The Echo of Thunder '98
Ellen Foster '97
Fallen Angel '03
The Flamingo Rising '01
Follow the Stars Home '01
Foxfire '87▸
Grace & Glorie '98
Harvest of Fire '95
In Love and War '01
Journey '95
Little John '02
The Locket '02
The Lost Child '00
The Love Letter '98
Miss Rose White '92▸
Missing Pieces '00
My Sister's Keeper '02
Night Ride Home '99
O Pioneers! '91
One Against the Wind '91▸
A Painted House '03
The Piano Lesson '94▸
Pictures of Hollis Woods '07
A Place for Annie '94
Redwood Curtain '95
The Return of the Native '94
Rose Hill '97
The Runaway '00
Saint Maybe '98▸
Sarah, Plain and Tall '91▸
Sarah, Plain and Tall: Skylark '93

Sarah, Plain and Tall: Winter's End '99▸
A Season for Miracles '99
The Secret Garden '87▸
The Seventh Stream '01
The Shell Seekers '89
The Summer of Ben Tyler '96
That Russell Girl '08
To Dance with the White Dog '93▸
20,000 Leagues Under the Sea '97
What the Deaf Man Heard '98▸
William Faulkner's Old Man '97

Hammer Films: Horror

The Abominable Snowman '57
Asylum '72
Blood of the Vampire '58
The Blood on Satan's Claw '71▸
The Brides of Dracula '60
Captain Kronos: Vampire Hunter '74▸
The Creeping Flesh '72
The Curse of Frankenstein '57
The Curse of the Werewolf '61
The Devil Rides Out '68▸
Die Screaming, Marianne '73
Dr. Jekyll and Sister Hyde '71
Dr. Terror's House of Horrors '65
Dracula A.D. 1972 '72
Dracula Has Risen from the Grave '68
Dracula, Prince of Darkness '66
Dynasty of Fear '72
The Evil of Frankenstein '64
Frankenstein and the Monster from Hell '74
Frankenstein Created Woman '66▸
Frankenstein Must Be Destroyed '69
The Ghoul '75
The Gorgon '64
Hands of the Ripper '71
The Horror of Dracula '58▸
The Horror of Frankenstein '70
The Hound of the Baskervilles '59
Hysteria '64
Kiss of the Vampire '62
The Legend of the 7 Golden Vampires '73
Lust for a Vampire '71
Maniac '63
The Mummy '59▸
The Mummy's Shroud '67
The Nanny '65
Nightmare '63
Paranoiac '62
The Phantom of the Opera '62
Plague of the Zombies '66
Rasputin the Mad Monk '66
The Reptile '66
The Revenge of Frankenstein '58
The Satanic Rites of Dracula '73
The Scars of Dracula '70
Tales from the Crypt '72▸
Tales That Witness Madness '73
Taste the Blood of Dracula '70
Theatre of Blood '73▸
To the Devil, a Daughter '76
Twins of Evil '71
The Two Faces of Dr. Jekyll '60
Vampire Circus '71
The Vampire Lovers '70
Vault of Horror '73
The Witches '66

Hammer Films: Sci Fi & Fantasy

Creatures the World Forgot '70
Four Sided Triangle '53
Men of Sherwood Forest '57
One Million Years B.C. '66
Prehistoric Women '67
Quatermass 2 '57▸
Quatermass and the Pit '58
The Quatermass Experiment '56▸
Spaceways '53
Sword of Sherwood Forest '60
The Vengeance of She '68
The Viking Queen '67
When Dinosaurs Ruled the Earth '70
X The Unknown '56

Hercule Poirot

Agatha Christie's Thirteen at Dinner '85
The Alphabet Murders '65
Appointment with Death '88
Death on the Nile '78
Murder on the Orient Express '74▸

Hercules

Conquest of Mycene '63
The Fury of Hercules '61
Hercules '58
Hercules '97▸
Hercules 2 '85
Hercules against the Moon Men '64
Hercules and the Captive Women '63
Hercules in New York '70
Hercules in the Haunted World '64
Hercules, Prisoner of Evil '64
Hercules, the Legendary Journeys, Vol. 1: And the Amazon Women '94
Hercules, the Legendary Journeys, Vol. 2: The Lost Kingdom '94
Hercules, the Legendary Journeys, Vol. 3: The Circle of Fire '94
Hercules, the Legendary Journeys, Vol. 4: In the Underworld '94
Hercules Unchained '59
Hercules vs. the Sons of the Sun '64
Jason and the Argonauts '63▸
The Loves of Hercules '60
Samson and His Mighty Challenge '64
The Three Stooges Meet Hercules '61
The Triumph of Hercules '66
Young Hercules '97

Highest Grossing Films of All Time

Aladdin '92▸
Back to the Future '85▸
Batman '89▸
Beverly Hills Cop '84
The Empire Strikes Back '80▸
E.T.: The Extra-Terrestrial '82▸
Forrest Gump '94▸
Ghost '90▸
Ghostbusters '84▸
Gone with the Wind '39▸
Home Alone '90▸
Indiana Jones and the Last Crusade '89▸
Jaws '75▸
Jurassic Park '93▸
The Lion King '94▸
Mrs. Doubtfire '93
Raiders of the Lost Ark '81▸
Return of the Jedi '83▸
Star Wars '77▸
Terminator 2: Judgment Day '91▸

Titanic '97▸

Hopalong Cassidy

Border Patrol '43
Border Vigilantes '41
Colt Comrades '43
Doomed Caravan '41▸
False Colors '43
The Frontiersmen '38
Hopalong Cassidy '35▸
Hopalong Cassidy: Borrowed Trouble '48
Hopalong Cassidy: Dangerous Venture '48
Hopalong Cassidy: False Paradise '48
Hopalong Cassidy: Hoppy's Holiday '47
Hopalong Cassidy: Renegade Trail '39
Hopalong Cassidy Returns '36
Hopalong Cassidy: Riders of the Deadline '43
Hopalong Cassidy: Silent Conflict '48
Hopalong Cassidy: Sinister Journey '48
Hopalong Cassidy: The Dead Don't Dream '48
Hopalong Cassidy: The Devil's Playground '46
Hopalong Cassidy: The Marauders '47
Hopalong Cassidy: Unexpected Guest '47
Hoppy Serves a Writ '43
In Old Colorado '41
Law of the Pampas '39
Leather Burners '43
Lost Canyon '43
Mystery Man '44
Outlaws of the Desert '41
Renegade Trail '39
Riders of the Timberline '41
Rustler's Valley '37
Santa Fe Marshal '40
Seance '06
The Showdown '40
Texas Masquerade '44
Three on the Trail '36▸
Twilight on the Trail '41
Undercover Man '36

Indiana Jones

Indiana Jones and the Kingdom of the Crystal Skull '08
Indiana Jones and the Last Crusade '89▸
Indiana Jones and the Temple of Doom '84▸
Raiders of the Lost Ark '81▸

Inspector Clouseau

Curse of the Pink Panther '83
Inspector Clouseau '68
The Pink Panther '64▸
The Pink Panther '06
The Pink Panther Strikes Again '76▸
Return of the Pink Panther '74
Revenge of the Pink Panther '78
A Shot in the Dark '64▸
Son of the Pink Panther '93
Trail of the Pink Panther '82

Jack Ryan

Clear and Present Danger '94
The Hunt for Red October '90▸
Patriot Games '92▸
The Sum of All Fears '02

Jack the Ripper

Cosh Boy '61
Deadly Advice '93
Fatal Exposure '90
From Hell '01▸
Hands of the Ripper '71

▸ = rated three bones or higher

He Kills Night After Night
After Night '69
Hall's Gate '01
Jack the Ripper '60
Jack the Ripper '76
Jack the Ripper '88
Jack's Back '87
The Lodger '26
A Man with a Maid '73
The Monster of London City '64
Murder by Decree '79 ►
Night Ripper '86
Phantom Fiend '35
The Ripper '86
The Ripper '97
Ripper: Letter from Hell '01
Room to Let '49
Shanghai Knights '03
A Study in Terror '66 ►
Terror at London Bridge '85
Terror in the Wax Museum '73
Time After Time '79 ►
Waxworks '24 ►

James Bond
Casino Royale '06 ►
Casino Royale '67
Diamonds Are Forever '71 ►
Die Another Day '02
Dr. No '62 ►
For Your Eyes Only '81 ►
From Russia with Love '63 ►
Goldeneye '95 ►
Goldfinger '64 ►
License to Kill '89 ►
Live and Let Die '73 ►
The Living Daylights '87 ►
The Man with the Golden Gun '74
Moonraker '79
Never Say Never Again '83
Octopussy '83
On Her Majesty's Secret Service '69
The Spy Who Loved Me '77
Thunderball '65 ►
Tomorrow Never Dies '97
A View to a Kill '85
The World Is Not Enough '99
You Only Live Twice '67 ►

James Bond Spoofs
The Ambushers '67
Austin Powers: International Man of Mystery '97 ►
Austin Powers 2: The Spy Who Shagged Me '99 ►
Casino Royale '67
Deadlier Than the Male '67
Espionage in Tangiers '65
If Looks Could Kill '91 ►
In Like Flint '67
Murderers' Row '66
Number 1 of the Secret Service '77
Our Man Flint '66
Second Best Secret Agent in the Whole Wide World '65
Where the Bullets Fly '66

Jesse James
American Outlaws '01
The Assassination of Jesse James by the Coward Robert Ford '07 ►
Days of Jesse James '39
Frank and Jesse '94
I Shot Jesse James '49 ►
Jesse James '39 ►
Jesse James at Bay '41 ►
Jesse James Meets Frankenstein's Daughter '65
Jesse James Rides Again '47
Last Days of Frank & Jesse James '86
The Long Riders '80 ►
Return of Jesse James '50

John McClane
Die Hard '88 ►
Die Hard 2: Die Harder '90 ►
Die Hard: With a Vengeance '95
Live Free or Die Hard '07

Lassie
Challenge to Lassie '49
Courage of Lassie '46
The Hills of Home '48 ►
Lassie: Adventures of Neeka '68
Lassie, Come Home '43 ►
Lassie: Well of Love '70
Lassie's Great Adventure '62
Magic of Lassie '78
The Painted Hills '51
The Sun Comes Up '49

Live Action/Animation Combos
The Adventures of Rocky & Bullwinkle '00
Alice '88 ►
Alice in Wonderland '50
Alvin and the Chipmunks '07
Anchors Aweigh '45 ►
Arthur and the Invisibles '06
Bedknobs and Broomsticks '71
Cats & Dogs '01
Cool World '92
Dangerous When Wet '53
Enchanted '07
Fabulous Adventures of Baron Munchausen '61
Fun & Fancy Free '47 ►
Garfield: A Tail of Two Kitties '06
Garfield: The Movie '04
Hollywood Party '34
The Incredible Mr. Limpet '64
James and the Giant Peach '96 ►
Looney Tunes: Back in Action '03
Mary Poppins '64 ►
MirrorMask '05
Monkeybone '01
Osmosis Jones '01
The Pagemaster '94
Pete's Dragon '77
The Polar Express '04
Racing Stripes '05
A Scanner Darkly '06
Scooby-Doo '02
Scooby-Doo 2: Monsters Unleashed '04
Small Soldiers '98
So Dear to My Heart '49
Space Jam '96
The Spiderwick Chronicles '08
The SpongeBob SquarePants Movie '04
Stuart Little '99
Tank Girl '94
Thomas and the Magic Railroad '00
The Three Caballeros '45
Thunderbirds '04
Tron '82
Underdog '07
Volere Volare '92
What the $*! Do We Know? '04
Who Framed Roger Rabbit '88 ►
Xanadu '80

MGM Musicals
An American in Paris '51 ►
Anchors Aweigh '45 ►
Annie Get Your Gun '50 ►
Athena '54
The Band Wagon '53 ►
The Barkleys of Broadway '49 ►
Because You're Mine '52
Bells Are Ringing '60 ►
Big Store '41
Born to Dance '36
Broadway Melody '29
Broadway Melody of 1936 '35 ►
Broadway Melody of 1938 '37
Broadway Melody of 1940 '40
Broadway Rhythm '44
Broadway Serenade '39
The Chocolate Soldier '41
Dancing Lady '33
Deep in My Heart '54
Double Trouble '67
The Duchess of Idaho '50
Easter Parade '48 ►
Easy to Love '53
Everybody Sing '38
The Firefly '37
For Me and My Gal '42
Gigi '58 ►
Girl of the Golden West '38
Give a Girl a Break '53
Going Hollywood '33
Good News '47 ►
Goodbye, Mr. Chips '69 ►
The Great Ziegfeld '36 ►
Harum Scarum '65
Holiday in Mexico '46
Honolulu '39
I Love Melvin '53
I Married an Angel '42
In the Good Old Summertime '49
It Happened at the World's Fair '63
It Happened in Brooklyn '47
The Kissing Bandit '48
Lady Be Good '41
Les Girls '57

The Lone Rider
Border Roundup '41
Death Rides the Plains '44
Law of the Saddle '43
The Lone Rider '42
The Lone Rider in Frontier Fury '41
The Lone Rider in Ghost Town '41
Live a Little, Love a Little '68
Love Me or Leave Me '55
Little Nellie Kelly '40
Lovely to Look At '52
Madam Satan '30
Maytime '37
Meet Me in Las Vegas '56
Meet Me in St. Louis '44 ►
The Merry Widow '34
The Merry Widow '52
Million Dollar Mermaid '52
Mrs. Brown, You've Got a Lovely Daughter '68
On an Island with You '48
On the Town '49 ►
Pagan Love Song '50
Rich, Young and Pretty '51
Rosalie '38
Rose Marie '36
Rose Marie '54
Royal Wedding '51 ►
Seven Brides for Seven Brothers '54 ►
Ship Ahoy '42
Show Boat '51 ►
Singin' in the Rain '52 ►
Skirts Ahoy! '52
Small Town Girl '53
Stay Away, Joe '68
Strike Up the Band '40
The Student Prince '54
Summer Stock '50
Sweethearts '38
Take Me Out to the Ball Game '49
Texas Carnival '51
That Midnight Kiss '49
That's Dancing! '85 ►
That's Entertainment '74 ►
That's Entertainment, Part 2 '76 ►
That's Entertainment, Part 3 '93 ►
Three Little Words '50
Thrill of a Romance '45
Til the Clouds Roll By '46
The Toast of New Orleans '50
The Trouble with Girls (and How to Get into It) '69
The Unsinkable Molly Brown '64 ►
Viva Las Vegas '63 ►
The Wizard of Oz '39 ►
Words and Music '48
Yankee Doodle Dandy '42 ►
Yolanda and the Thief '45
Ziegfeld Follies '46
Ziegfeld Girl '41 ►

Ma and Pa Kettle
Egg and I '47 ►
The Kettles in the Ozarks '56
The Kettles on Old MacDonald's Farm '57
Ma and Pa Kettle '49 ►
Ma and Pa Kettle at Home '54
Ma and Pa Kettle at the Fair '52
Ma and Pa Kettle at Waikiki '55
Ma and Pa Kettle Back On the Farm '51
Ma and Pa Kettle Go to Town '50
Ma and Pa Kettle on Vacation '53

The Marx Brothers
Animal Crackers '30 ►
At the Circus '39 ►
Big Store '41 ►
The Cocoanuts '29
A Day at the Races '37 ►
Duck Soup '33 ►
Go West '40 ►
Horse Feathers '32 ►
Love Happy '50
The Marx Brothers in a Nutshell '90 ►
Monkey Business '31 ►
A Night at the Opera '35 ►
A Night in Casablanca '46 ►
Room Service '38 ►

Mike Hammer
Girl Hunters '63
I, the Jury '82
Kiss Me Deadly '55 ►
Margin for Murder '81

Miss Marple
Agatha Christie's A Caribbean Mystery '83
Agatha Christie's Murder with Mirrors '85
The Body in the Library '84
Murder Ahoy '64
Murder at the Gallop '63 ►
A Murder Is Announced '87
Murder She Said '62 ►

Mr. Moto
Mr. Moto in Danger Island '39
Mr. Moto Takes a Chance '38
Mr. Moto Takes a Vacation '39
Mr. Moto's Gamble '38
Mr. Moto's Last Warning '39
Mysterious Mr. Moto '38
Thank You, Mr. Moto '37
Think Fast, Mr. Moto '37

Mr. Wong
Doomed to Die '40
The Fatal Hour '40
Mr. Wong, Detective '38
Mr. Wong in Chinatown '39
Mysterious Mr. Wong '35
Mystery of Mr. Wong '39
Phantom of Chinatown '40

Modern Shakespeare
Chimes at Midnight '67 ►
A Double Life '47 ►
Forbidden Planet '56 ►
The Godfather '72 ►
The Godfather, Part 2 '74 ►
The Godfather, Part 3 '90 ►
Hamlet '00 ►
Jubal '56
The King Is Alive '00
King Lear '87
King of Texas '02
Kiss Me Kate '53 ►
Let the Devil Wear Black '99
The Lion King 1½ '04
Looking for Richard '96 ►
Love Is All There Is '96
Macbeth '06
Men Are Not Gods '37
Men of Respect '91
A Midsummer Night's Sex Comedy '82 ►
My Own Private Idaho '91 ►
O '01
Othello '86
Othello '01
Prospero's Books '91
Ran '85 ►
Richard III '95 ►
Ring of Fire '91
Ronnie and Julie '97
Rosencrantz & Guildenstern Are Dead '90
Scotland, PA '02
Shakespeare Wallah '65 ►
She's the Man '06
Shiner '00
Siberian Lady Macbeth '61
The Street King '02
The Tempest '82
The Tempest '99
Ten Things I Hate about You '99
Theatre of Blood '73
The Three Weird Sisters '48
Throne of Blood '57 ►
Tromeo & Juliet '95
West Side Story '61 ►
William Shakespeare's Romeo and Juliet '96 ►

Modern Updates
An American Christmas Carol '79
Arthur's Quest '99
Carmen, Baby '66
Clueless '95 ►
Crime and Punishment in Suburbia '00
Cruel Intentions '99
Disturbia '07
Double Play '96
Ebenezer '97
Great Expectations '97
In the Shadows '99
King Lear '87
Les Miserables '95
Loving Annabelle '06
Ms. Scrooge '97
The Modern Adventures of Tom Sawyer '99
The Prince and the Surfer '99
Scrooged '88
Sydney White '07
Ten Things I Hate about You '99
Twisted '96
Whatever It Takes '00
William Shakespeare's Romeo and Juliet '96 ►

Monty Python
The Adventures of Baron Munchausen '89 ►
All You Need Is Cash '78 ►
And Now for Something Completely Different '72 ►
Brazil '85 ►
Clockwise '86
Consuming Passions '68
Down Among the Z Men '52
Erik the Viking '89
A Fish Called Wanda '88 ►
The Fisher King '91 ►
Jabberwocky '77
The Missionary '82
Monty Python and the Holy Grail '75 ►
Monty Python's Life of Brian '79 ►
Monty Python's The Meaning of Life '83 ►
Nuns on the Run '90
The Odd Job '78
Personal Services '87
A Private Function '84
Privates on Parade '84
Rentadick '72
Romance with a Double Bass '74
The Secret Policeman's Other Ball '82
The Secret Policeman's Private Parts '81
Time Bandits '81 ►
Yellowbeard '83

The Muppets
The Adventures of a Gnome Named Gnorm '93
The Great Muppet Caper '81 ►
The Muppet Christmas Carol '92
The Muppet Movie '79 ►
Muppet Treasure Island '96
The Muppets Take Manhattan '84
Muppets from Space '99
Sesame Street Presents: Follow That Bird '85

National Lampoon
National Lampoon's Adam & Eve '05
National Lampoon's Animal House '78 ►
National Lampoon's Attack of the 5 Ft. 2 Women '94
National Lampoon's Christmas Vacation '89 ►
National Lampoon's Christmas Vacation 2: Cousin Eddie's Big Island Adventure '03
National Lampoon's Class Reunion '82
National Lampoon's Class of '86 '86
National Lampoon's European Vacation '85
National Lampoon's Favorite Deadly Sins '95
National Lampoon's Gold Diggers '04
National Lampoon's Golf Punks '99
National Lampoon's Holiday Reunion '03
National Lampoon's Last Resort '94
National Lampoon's Loaded Weapon 1 '93
National Lampoon's Senior Trip '95
National Lampoon's The Don's Analyst '97
National Lampoon's Vacation '83 ►
National Lampoon's Van Wilder '02

Our Gang
General Spanky '36
The Little Rascals '94

Philip Marlowe
The Big Sleep '46 ►
Farewell, My Lovely '75 ►
Lady in the Lake '46
The Long Goodbye '73 ►
Marlowe '69
Murder, My Sweet '44 ►
Poodle Springs '98

★ = rated three bones or higher

Pixar Animated Movies
A Bug's Life '98▲
Cars '06▲
Finding Nemo '03▲
The Incredibles '04▲
Monsters, Inc. '01▲
Ratatouille '07▲
Toy Story '95▲
Toy Story 2 '99▲
WALL-E '08▲

The Planet of the Apes
Battle for the Planet of the Apes '73
Beneath the Planet of the Apes '70
Conquest of the Planet of the Apes '72
Escape from the Planet of the Apes '71▲
Planet of the Apes '68▲

Plays to Film: Maxwell Anderson
Anne of the Thousand Days '69▲
The Bad Seed '56
The Bad Seed '85
The Guardsman '31▲
Joan of Arc '48
Key Largo '48▲
Mary of Scotland '36▲
Meet Joe Black '98
The Private Lives of Elizabeth & Essex '39▲
What Price Glory? '52▲
Winterset '36

Plays to Film: James M. Barrie
The Admirable Crichton '57
Hook '91
Little Minister '34▲
Peter Pan '24
Peter Pan '53▲
Peter Pan '60▲
Peter Pan '03
Quality Street '37
Seven Days' Leave '42

Plays to Film: Anton Chekhov
August '95
Country Life '95
La Petite Lili '03
The Lady with the Dog '59▲
The Seagull '71▲
The Seagull '75
The Shooting Party '77
Three Days of Rain '03
The Three Sisters '65
An Unfinished Piece for a Player Piano '77▲
Vanya on 42nd Street '94▲
Ward Six '78

Plays to Film: Noel Coward
Bitter Sweet '33
Bitter Sweet '40
Blithe Spirit '45▲
Brief Encounter '46▲
Cavalcade '33▲
Private Lives '31▲
Relative Values '99
This Happy Breed '47▲

Plays to Film: Horton Foote
Baby, the Rain Must Fall '64
The Chase '66
Courtship '87▲
Lily Dale '96
1918 '85
The Trip to Bountiful '85▲

Plays to Film: Beth Henley
Crimes of the Heart '86
Miss Firecracker '89▲
Nobody's Fool '86

True Stories '86▲

Plays to Film: David Mamet
About Last Night... '86▲
American Buffalo '95
Glengarry Glen Ross '92▲
Lakeboat '00
Oleanna '94

Plays to Film: Arthur Miller
All My Sons '48▲
All My Sons '86▲
Broken Glass '96
The Crucible '57▲
The Crucible '96▲
Death of a Salesman '86▲
Everybody Wins '90
Focus '01

Plays to Film: Eugene O'Neill
Ah, Wilderness! '35▲
Anna Christie '23▲
Anna Christie '30
Desire Under the Elms '58
Emperor Jones '33
The Hairy Ape '44
The Iceman Cometh '73
Long Day's Journey into Night '62▲
Long Day's Journey into Night '88
Long Day's Journey Into Night '96▲
The Long Voyage Home '40▲
On Borrowed Time '39▲
Strange Interlude '32
Strange Interlude '90
Summer Holiday '48

Plays to Film: Rodgers & Hammerstein
Carousel '56▲
Cinderella '64
Flower Drum Song '61
The King and I '56▲
Oklahoma! '55▲
Rodgers & Hammerstein's South Pacific '01
The Sound of Music '65▲
South Pacific '58▲

Plays to Film: Arthur Schnitzler
Affairs of Anatol '21
Circle of Love '64
Eyes Wide Shut '99
La Ronde '51▲
Liebelei '32

Plays to Film: William Shakespeare
Antony and Cleopatra '73
As You Like It '36
As You Like It '06
Carry On Cleo '65
Hamlet '48▲
Hamlet '69
Hamlet '90▲
Hamlet '96▲
Hamlet '00▲
Henry V '44▲
Henry V '89▲
Julius Caesar '53▲
Julius Caesar '70
King Lear '71▲
King Lear '87
King Lear '98▲
King of Texas '02▲
Looking for Richard '96▲
Love's Labour's Lost '00
Macbeth '48▲
Macbeth '70▲
Macbeth '71▲
Macbeth '06
The Merchant of Venice '73▲

The Merchant of Venice '04▲
The Merry Wives of Windsor '50
A Midsummer Night's Dream '35▲
A Midsummer Night's Dream '68▲
A Midsummer Night's Dream '96
Much Ado about Nothing '93▲
Othello '22
Othello '52▲
Othello '65▲
Othello '95▲
Othello '01▲
Prospero's Books '91▲
Ran '85▲
Richard III '12
Richard III '55▲
Richard III '95▲
Romeo and Juliet '36▲
Romeo and Juliet '54
Romeo and Juliet '68▲
Shakespeare in Love '98▲
The Taming of the Shrew '29
The Taming of the Shrew '67▲
The Tempest '63
The Tempest '82
The Tempest '99
Ten Things I Hate about You '99▲
Titus '99
Tromeo & Juliet '95
Twelfth Night '96▲
William Shakespeare's A Midsummer Night's Dream '99
William Shakespeare's Romeo and Juliet '96▲

Plays to Film: George Bernard Shaw
Androcles and the Lion '52
Caesar and Cleopatra '46
The Devil's Disciple '59▲
Heartbreak House '86
Major Barbara '41▲
The Millionairess '60
Pygmalion '38▲
Saint Joan '57

Plays to Film: Sam Shepard
Curse of the Starving Class '94
Fool for Love '86
Simpatico '99
True West '86▲

Plays to Film: Robert E. Sherwood
Abe Lincoln in Illinois '40▲
Idiot's Delight '39▲
Jupiter's Darling '55
Main Street to Broadway '53
Petrified Forest '36▲
Rebecca '40▲
The Royal Bed '31
Waterloo Bridge '40▲

Plays to Film: Neil Simon
Barefoot in the Park '67▲
Biloxi Blues '88
Brighton Beach Memoirs '86
Broadway Bound '92
California Suite '78▲
Chapter Two '79
The Cheap Detective '78▲
Come Blow Your Horn '63▲
The Goodbye Girl '77▲
The Heartbreak Kid '72▲
I Ought to Be in Pictures '82
Last of the Red Hot Lovers '72
Lost in Yonkers '93
The Marrying Man '91
Max Dugan Returns '83
Murder by Death '76

The Odd Couple '68▲
One Trick Pony '80
Only When I Laugh '81▲
The Out-of-Towners '70▲
Plaza Suite '71▲
Prisoner of Second Avenue '74
Seems Like Old Times '80
The Slugger's Wife '85
Star Spangled Girl '71
The Sunshine Boys '75▲
Sweet Charity '69▲

Plays to Film: Tom Stoppard
Rosencrantz & Guildenstern Are Dead '90▲

Plays to Film: Tennessee Williams
Baby Doll '56▲
Boom! '68
Cat on a Hot Tin Roof '58▲
Cat on a Hot Tin Roof '84
The Fugitive Kind '60
The Glass Menagerie '87▲
The Migrants '74▲
The Night of the Iguana '64▲
Orpheus Descending '91
Period of Adjustment '62▲
Roman Spring of Mrs. Stone '61▲
The Rose Tattoo '55▲
A Streetcar Named Desire '51▲
A Streetcar Named Desire '84▲
A Streetcar Named Desire '95
Suddenly, Last Summer '59▲
Summer and Smoke '61▲
Sweet Bird of Youth '62▲
Sweet Bird of Youth '89
This Property Is Condemned '66

Producers: Robert Altman
Buffalo Bill & the Indians '76▲
Kansas City '95▲
The Late Show '77▲
Nashville '75▲
Quintet '79
Rich Kids '79
A Wedding '78▲
Welcome to L.A. '77▲

Producers: Bruckheimer/Simpson
Bad Boys '95
Beverly Hills Cop '84▲
Beverly Hills Cop 2 '87▲
Crimson Tide '95▲
Dangerous Minds '95
Days of Thunder '90
Flashdance '83
The Ref '93▲
The Rock '96▲
Thief of Hearts '84
Top Gun '86▲

Producers: William Castle
Bug '75
House on Haunted Hill '58▲
Macabre '69
Riot '69
Rosemary's Baby '68▲
Strait-Jacket '64
13 Ghosts '60
Zotz! '62

Producers: Coppola/American Zoetrope
American Graffiti '73▲
The Black Stallion '79▲
The Conversation '74▲
The Escape Artist '82▲
The Godfather, Part 2 '74▲

Hammett '82▲

Producers: Roger Corman/New World
Atlas '60
Attack of the Giant Leeches '59
Avalanche '78
Battle Beyond the Stars '80
Battle Beyond the Sun '63
Beyond the Call of Duty '92
Big Bad Mama '74▲
Big Bad Mama 2 '87
The Big Bird Cage '72
The Big Doll House '71
Bloodfist '89
Bloodfist 2 '90
Bloody Mama '70
Body Waves '92
Boxcar Bertha '72▲
A Bucket of Blood '59▲
Caged Heat '74
Candy Stripe Nurses '74
Carnival Rock '57
Cocaine Wars '86
Cockfighter '74▲
The Corporation '96
Crazy Mama '75
Daddy's Boys '87
Day the World Ended '55
Death Race 2000 '75
Death Sport '78
Dementia 13 '63▲
Dinosaur Island '93
The Dunwich Horror '70
Eat My Dust '76
Eye of the Eagle 3 '91
The Fall of the House of Usher '60▲
Field of Fire '92
Fighting Mad '76
Firehawk '92
Forbidden World '82
Futurekick '91
Galaxy of Terror '81
Gas-s-s-s! '70
Grand Theft Auto '77
The Gunslinger '56
The Haunted Palace '63
Humanoids from the Deep '80
I, Mobster '58▲
I Never Promised You a Rose Garden '77▲
In the Heat of Passion '91
It Conquered the World '56
Jackson County Jail '76▲
Lady in Red '79
The Last Woman on Earth '61
Little Shop of Horrors '60▲
Lords of the Deep '89
Lumiere '76
Machine Gun Kelly '58▲
Masque of the Red Death '65▲
Masque of the Red Death '89
Monster from the Ocean Floor '54
Munchies '87
Nam Angels '88
Night of the Blood Beast '58
Not of This Earth '96
Piranha '78▲
The Pit and the Pendulum '61▲
Premature Burial '62▲
Primary Target '89
Private Duty Nurses '71
Raiders of the Sun '92
The Raven '63▲
Rock 'n' Roll High School '79▲
The St. Valentine's Day Massacre '67▲
Ski Troop Attack '60
Small Change '76▲
Smokey Bites the Dust '81
Stripped to Kill '87
The Student Nurses '70
T-Bird Gang '59
Tales of Terror '62▲
Targets '68▲
Teenage Caveman '58
The Terror '63
Thunder and Lightning '77
Time Trackers '88

Tomb of Ligeia '64▲
Too Hot to Handle '76
The Trip '67
The Undead '57
Unholy Rollers '72
Voyage to the Planet of Prehistoric Women '68
The Wasp Woman '59
The Wasp Woman '96
The Wild Angels '66
The Wild Ride '60
X: The Man with X-Ray Eyes '63▲
The Young Nurses '73

Producers: Val Lewton
Bedlam '45▲
The Body Snatcher '45▲
Cat People '42▲
Isle of the Dead '45
The Leopard Man '43

Producers: George Lucas
The Empire Strikes Back '80▲
The Ewok Adventure '84
More American Graffiti '79
Raiders of the Lost Ark '81▲
Return of the Jedi '83▲

Producers: Merchant Ivory
Autobiography of a Princess '75
The Ballad of the Sad Cafe '91
Bombay Talkie '70
The Courtesans of Bombay '85▲
The Europeans '79▲
Fast Talking '86
Feast of July '95
The Golden Bowl '00
Howard's End '92▲
Hullabaloo over Georgie & Bonnie's Pictures '78
Jane Austen in Manhattan '80
Jefferson in Paris '94
Maurice '87▲
Mr. & Mrs. Bridge '90▲
The Remains of the Day '93▲
A Room with a View '86▲
Roseland '77▲
Shakespeare Wallah '65▲
A Soldier's Daughter Never Cries '98
Surviving Picasso '96
The White Countess '05▲

Producers: George Pal
Atlantis, the Lost Continent '61
Conquest of Space '55
Destination Moon '50
Doc Savage '75
The Great Rupert '50▲
Naked Jungle '54▲
7 Faces of Dr. Lao '63▲
Time Machine '78
The War of the Worlds '53▲
When Worlds Collide '51▲

Producers: Steven Spielberg
Amazing Stories '85
An American Tail '86▲
An American Tail: Fievel Goes West '91
Back to the Future '85▲
The Color Purple '85▲
Empire of the Sun '87▲
The Goonies '85
Gremlins '84▲
Honey, I Shrunk the Kids '89
Innerspace '87▲
Jurassic Park '93▲
Poltergeist '82▲
The Terminal '04
Twilight Zone: The Movie '83

▲ = rated three bones or higher

Who Framed Roger Rabbit '88
Young Sherlock Holmes '85

Producers: Andy Warhol
Andy Warhol's Bad '77
Cocaine Cowboys '79
Flesh '68
Heat '72
Trash '70

Rambo
First Blood '82
Rambo: First Blood, Part 2 '85
Rambo 3 '88

The Rangebusters
Arizona Stagecoach '42
Black Market Rustlers '43
Boot Hill Bandits '42
Cowboy Commandos '43
Fugitive Valley '41
Haunted Ranch '43
Kid's Last Ride '41
Land of Hunted Men '43
Range Busters '40
Rock River Renegades '42
Saddle Mountain Roundup '41
Texas to Bataan '42
Thunder River Feud '42
Tonto Basin Outlaws '41
Trail of the Silver Spurs '41
Trail Riders '42
Trailing Double Trouble '40
Tumbledown Ranch in Arizona '41
Two-Fisted Justice '43
Underground Rustlers '41
West of Pinto Basin '40

Recycled Footage/Redubbed Dialogue
Contact '97
Dead Men Don't Wear Plaid '82
Fast, Cheap & Out of Control '97
Ferocious Female Freedom Fighters '88
Forrest Gump '94
Good Night, and Good Luck '05
J-Men Forever! '79
Last Action Hero '93
The Legend of Drunken Master '94
Mystery Science Theater 3000: The Movie '96
Planet of Blood '66
Twin Dragons '92
Voyage to the Planet of Prehistoric Women '68
Voyage to the Prehistoric Planet '65
What's Up, Tiger Lily? '65
Zelig '83

Renfrew of the Mounties
Danger Ahead '40
Fighting Mad '39
Murder on the Yukon '40
Renfrew of the Royal Mounted '37
Renfrew on the Great White Trail '38
Sky Bandits '40
Yukon Flight '40

Restored Footage
Army of Shadows '69
Beau Revel '21
Crimes of Passion '84
Dr. Jekyll and Mr. Hyde '32
Foolish Wives '22
Frankenstein '31
Isadora '68
Lawrence of Arabia '62
The Leopard '63
Lost Horizon '37
The Lost World '25
New York, New York '77
Othello '52
Que Viva Mexico '32
Red River '48
The Rules of the Game '39
Sadie Thompson '28
Spartacus '60
Spiders '18
A Star Is Born '54
Star Trek: The Motion Picture '79
Sunny Side Up '28
Tarzan and His Mate '34
Twelve O'Clock High '49
Two English Girls '72
Wages of Fear '55
When Time Ran Out '80

The Ritz Brothers
Argentine Nights '40
Blazing Stewardesses '75
The Goldwyn Follies '38
The Gorilla '39

Robin Hood
The Adventures of Robin Hood '38
A Challenge for Robin Hood '68
Men of Sherwood Forest '57
The Prince of Thieves '48
Princess of Thieves '01
Robin and Marian '76
Robin Hood '22
Robin Hood '73
Robin Hood '91
Robin Hood: Men in Tights '93
Robin Hood: Prince of Thieves '91
Robin Hood... The Legend: Herne's Son '85
Robin Hood... The Legend: Robin Hood and the Sorcerer '83
Robin Hood... The Legend: The Swords of Wayland '83
Robin Hood... The Legend: The Time of the Wolf '85
Robin Hood: The Movie '55
Robin of Locksley '95
The Story of Robin Hood & His Merrie Men '52
Sword of Sherwood Forest '60
Tales of Robin Hood '52
Time Bandits '81
Young Ivanhoe '95
The Zany Adventures of Robin Hood '84

The Rough Riders
Arizona Bound '41
Below the Border '42
Dead Man's Gulch (?) '42
Down Texas Way '42
Forbidden Trails '41
Ghost Town Law '42
Gunman from Bodie '41
Riders of the West '42

Rusty the Dog
The Adventures of Rusty '45
Rusty's Birthday '49
Son of Rusty '47

The Saint
Fiction Makers '67
The Saint '68
The Saint '97
The Saint in London '39
The Saint in New York '38
The Saint Strikes Back '39
The Saint Takes Over '40
The Saint's Double Trouble '40
Vendetta for the Saint '68

Screen Teams: Astaire & Rogers
The Barkleys of Broadway '49
Carefree '38
Flying Down to Rio '33
Follow the Fleet '36
The Gay Divorcee '34
Roberta '35
Shall We Dance '37
Swing Time '36
Top Hat '35

Screen Teams: Allen & Keaton
Annie Hall '77
Interiors '78
Love and Death '75
Manhattan '79
Manhattan Murder Mystery '93
Play It Again, Sam '72
Sleeper '73

Screen Teams: Allen & Farrow
Alice '90
Another Woman '88
Broadway Danny Rose '84
Crimes & Misdemeanors '89
Hannah and Her Sisters '86
Husbands and Wives '92
A Midsummer Night's Sex Comedy '82
New York Stories '89
The Purple Rose of Cairo '85
Radio Days '87
September '88
Shadows and Fog '92
Zelig '83

Screen Teams: Abbott & Costello
Abbott and Costello Go to Mars '53
Abbott and Costello in Hollywood '45
Abbott and Costello in the Foreign Legion '50
Abbott and Costello Meet Captain Kidd '52
Abbott and Costello Meet Dr. Jekyll and Mr. Hyde '52
Abbott and Costello Meet Frankenstein '48
Abbott and Costello Meet the Invisible Man '51
Abbott and Costello Meet the Keystone Kops '54
Abbott and Costello Meet the Killer, Boris Karloff '49
Abbott and Costello Meet the Mummy '55
Africa Screams '49
Buck Privates '41
Buck Privates Come Home '47
Comin' Round the Mountain '51
Dance with Me, Henry '56
Here Come the Co-Eds '45
Hit the Ice '43
Hold That Ghost '41
In the Navy '41
It Ain't Hay '43
Jack & the Beanstalk '52
Keep 'Em Flying '41
Little Giant '46
Lost in a Harem '44
Lost in Alaska '52
Mexican Hayride '48
The Naughty Nineties '45
The Noose Hangs High '48
One Night in the Tropics '40
Pardon My Sarong '42
Ride 'Em Cowboy '42
Rio Rita '42
The 30-Foot Bride of Candy Rock '59
The Time of Their Lives '46
Who Done It? '42
The Wistful Widow of Wagon Gap '47

Screen Teams: Ball & Arnaz
The Long, Long Trailer '54

Screen Teams: Belushi & Aykroyd
The Blues Brothers '80
Neighbors '81

Screen Teams: Bogart & Bacall
The Big Sleep '46
Dark Passage '47
To Have & Have Not '44

Screen Teams: Bronson & Ireland
Breakheart Pass '76
Breakout '75
Chino '75
Cold Sweat '71
Death Wish 2 '82
The Family '70
From Noon Till Three '76
Hard Times '75
Love and Bullets '79
The Mechanic '72
Rider on the Rain '70
Someone Behind the Door '71
Villa Rides '68

Screen Teams: Burton & Taylor
Boom! '68
Cleopatra '63
The Comedians '67
Divorce His, Divorce Hers '72
Doctor Faustus '66
Hammersmith Is Out '72
The Sandpiper '65
The Taming of the Shrew '67
Under Milk Wood '73
The V.I.P.s '63
Who's Afraid of Virginia Woolf? '66

Screen Teams: Cagney & O'Brien
Angels with Dirty Faces '38
Boy Meets Girl '38
Ceiling Zero '35
The Fighting 69th '40
Ragtime '81
Torrid Zone '40

Screen Teams: Cheech & Chong
After Hours '85
Cheech and Chong Still Smokin' '83
Cheech and Chong's Next Movie '80
Cheech and Chong's Nice Dreams '81
Cheech and Chong's The Corsican Brothers '84
Cheech and Chong's Up in Smoke '79

Screen Teams: Cusack & Piven
Grosse Pointe Blank '97
One Crazy Summer '86
The Player '92
Runaway Jury '03
Say Anything '89
Serendipity '01

Screen Teams: Cusack & Robbins
Bob Roberts '92
The Cradle Will Rock '99
High Fidelity '00
The Player '92
The Sure Thing '85
Tapeheads '89

Screen Teams: Damon & Affleck
Chasing Amy '97
Dogma '99
Good Will Hunting '97
Jay and Silent Bob Strike Back '01
Jersey Girl '04
School Ties '92

Screen Teams: De Niro & Keitel
A Bronx Tale '93
Falling in Love '84
Mean Streets '73
Taxi Driver '76

Screen Teams: De Niro & Pesci
The Bridge of San Luis Rey '05
Casino '95
Goodfellas '90
Once Upon a Time in America '84
Raging Bull '80

Screen Teams: Depardieu & Deneuve
Changing Times '04
Choice of Arms '83
Fort Saganne '84
The Last Metro '80

Screen Teams: Eastwood & Locke
Any Which Way You Can '80
Bronco Billy '80
Every Which Way But Loose '78
The Gauntlet '77
The Outlaw Josey Wales '76
Sudden Impact '83

Screen Teams: Eddy & McDonald
Bitter Sweet '40
Girl of the Golden West '38
I Married an Angel '42
Maytime '37
New Moon '40
Naughty Marietta '35
Rose Marie '36
Sweethearts '38

Screen Teams: Farley & Spade
Black Sheep '96
Coneheads '93
Tommy Boy '95

Screen Teams: Favreau & Vaughn
The Break Up '06
Made '01
Swingers '96

Screen Teams: Flynn & de Havilland
Captain Blood '35
The Charge of the Light Brigade '36
Dodge City '39
The Private Lives of Elizabeth & Essex '39
Santa Fe Trail '40
They Died with Their Boots On '41

Screen Teams: Gable & Crawford
Chained '34
Dance, Fools, Dance '31
Dancing Lady '33
Forsaking All Others '35
Laughing Sinners '31
Love on the Run '36
Possessed '31
Strange Cargo '40

Screen Teams: Garland & Rooney
Andy Hardy Meets Debutante '40
Babes in Arms '39
Babes on Broadway '41
Girl Crazy '43
Life Begins for Andy Hardy '41
Love Finds Andy Hardy '38
Strike Up the Band '40
Thoroughbreds Don't Cry '37
Words and Music '48

Screen Teams: Garson & Pidgeon
Blossoms in the Dust '41
Julia Misbehaves '48
Madame Curie '43
The Miniver Story '50
Mrs. Miniver '42
Mrs. Parkington '44
That Forsyte Woman '50

Screen Teams: Gibson & Glover
Lethal Weapon '87
Lethal Weapon 2 '89
Lethal Weapon 3 '92
Lethal Weapon 4 '98
Maverick '94

Screen Teams: Hepburn & Grant
Bringing Up Baby '38
Holiday '38
The Philadelphia Story '40

Screen Teams: Hepburn & Tracy
Adam's Rib '50
Desk Set '57
Guess Who's Coming to Dinner '67
Pat and Mike '52
State of the Union '48
Without Love '45
Woman of the Year '42

Screen Teams: Hope & Crosby
Cancel My Reservation '72
My Favorite Blonde '42
My Favorite Brunette '47
The Princess and the Pirate '44
The Road to Bali '53
The Road to Hong Kong '62
The Road to Morocco '42
The Road to Rio '47
The Road to Singapore '40
The Road to Utopia '46
The Road to Zanzibar '41

Screen Teams: Ladd & Lake
The Blue Dahlia '46
The Glass Key '42
This Gun for Hire '42

▸ = rated three bones or higher

Screen Teams: Lancaster & Douglas
The Devil's Disciple '59►
Gunfight at the O.K. Corral '57
The List of Adrian Messenger '63►
Seven Days in May '64►
Tough Guys '86
Victory at Entebbe '76

Screen Teams: Laurel & Hardy
Air Raid Wardens '43
Block-heads '38►
Bohemian Girl '36►
Bonnie Scotland '35
Bullfighters '45
A Chump at Oxford '40
The Devil's Brother '33
The Flying Deuces '39►
Great Guns '41
Hollywood Party '34
Laurel and Hardy and the Family '33
Laurel & Hardy: Another Fine Mess '30
Laurel & Hardy: At Work '32
Laurel & Hardy: Be Big '31
Laurel & Hardy: Below Zero '30
Laurel & Hardy: Berth Marks '29
Laurel & Hardy: Blotto '30
Laurel & Hardy: Brats '30
Laurel & Hardy: Chickens Come Home '31
Laurel & Hardy: Hog Wild '30
Laurel & Hardy: Laughing Gravy '31
Laurel & Hardy: Men O'War '29
Laurel & Hardy: Night Owls '30
Laurel & Hardy On the Lam '30
Laurel & Hardy: Perfect Day '29
Laurel & Hardy Spooktacular '34
Laurel & Hardy: Stan "Helps" Ollie '33
Laurel & Hardy: The Hoose-Gow '29

Screen Teams: Lee & Cushing
The Creeping Flesh '72
The Curse of Frankenstein '57
The Devil's Undead '75
Dr. Terror's House of Horrors '65
Dracula A.D. 1972 '72
The Gorgon '64
Hamlet '48►
Horror Express '72
The Horror of Dracula '58►
The Hound of the Baskervilles '59
The House that Dripped Blood '71
Island of the Burning Doomed '67
Moulin Rouge '52►
The Mummy '59►
Nothing But the Night '72
The Satanic Rites of Dracula '73
Scream and Scream Again '70
The Skull '65

The Golden Stallion '49
Helldorado '46
Home in Oklahoma '47
My Pal Trigger '46
Rainbow over Texas '46
Roll on Texas Moon '46
Song of Arizona '46
Sunset in El Dorado '45
Susanna Pass '49
Trigger, Jr. '50
Twilight in the Sierras '50
Under Nevada Skies '46
Utah '45

Screen Teams: Loy & Powell
After the Thin Man '36►
Another Thin Man '39
Double Wedding '37
Evelyn Prentice '34
The Great Ziegfeld '36►
I Love You Again '40►
Libeled Lady '36►
Love Crazy '41►
Manhattan Melodrama '34►
Shadow of the Thin Man '41►
Song of the Thin Man '47
The Thin Man '34►
The Thin Man Goes Home '44

Screen Teams: Martin & Lewis
Artists and Models '55
At War with the Army '50
The Caddy '53
Hollywood or Bust '56
Jumping Jacks '52
My Friend Irma '49
Pardners '56
The Road to Bali '53►
Sailor Beware '52
Scared Stiff '53►
The Stooge '51

Screen Teams: Newman & Woodward
The Drowning Pool '75
From the Terrace '60
The Long, Hot Summer '58►
Mr. & Mrs. Bridge '90►
A New Kind of Love '63
Paris Blues '61
Rally 'Round the Flag, Boys! '58

Screen Teams: Redford & Newman
Butch Cassidy and the Sundance Kid '69►
The Sting '73►

Screen Teams: Reynolds & DeLuise
The Best Little Whorehouse in Texas '82
Cannonball Run '81
Cannonball Run 2 '84
The End '78►
Smokey and the Bandit '77
Smokey and the Bandit 2 '80

Screen Teams: Reynolds & Field
The End '78►
Hooper '78
Smokey and the Bandit '77
Smokey and the Bandit 2 '80

Screen Teams: Rogers & Evans
Along the Navaho Trail '45
Apache Rose '47
Bells of Coronado '50
Bells of Rosarita '45
Bells of San Angelo '47
Cowboy & the Senorita '44
Don't Fence Me In '45
Down Dakota Way '49

Screen Teams: Lemmon & Matthau
Buddy Buddy '81
The Fortune Cookie '66►
The Front Page '74
The Grass Harp '95
Grumpier Old Men '95
Grumpy Old Men '93►
JFK '91►
Neil Simon's The Odd Couple 2 '98
The Odd Couple '68►
Out to Sea '97

Screen Teams: Snipes & Harrelson
Money Train '95
White Men Can't Jump '92
Wildcats '86

Screen Teams: Stewart & Sullavan
The Mortal Storm '40►
The Shop Around the Corner '40►
Shopworn Angel '38►

Screen Teams: Stiller & O. Wilson
Meet the Fockers '04
Meet the Parents '00►
Permanent Midnight '98
The Royal Tenenbaums '01►
Starsky & Hutch '04
Zoolander '01

Screen Teams: Turner & Douglas
The Jewel of the Nile '85
Romancing the Stone '84►
The War of the Roses '89►

Screen Teams: Wayne & O'Hara
Big Jake '71
McLintock! '63►
The Quiet Man '52►
Rio Grande '50►
Wings of Eagles '57

Screen Teams: Wilder & Pryor
Another You '91
See No Evil, Hear No Evil '89
Silver Streak '76►
Stir Crazy '80

Scrooge
An American Christmas Carol '79
A Christmas Carol '38►
A Christmas Carol '51►
A Christmas Carol '54►
A Christmas Carol '84►
A Christmas Carol '99
Ms. Scrooge '97
Scrooged '88

Sexton Blake
Echo Murders '45
Meet Sexton Blake '44
Sexton Blake and the Hooded Terror '38
Stage Struck '57

Sherlock Holmes
The Adventures of Sherlock Holmes '39
The Adventures of Sherlock Holmes' Smarter Brother '78►
The Crucifer of Blood '91
Dr. Bell and Mr. Doyle: The Dark Beginnings of Sherlock Holmes '00
Dressed to Kill '46
Hands of a Murderer '90
The Hound of London '93
The Hound of the Baskervilles '39►

The Hound of the Baskervilles '59
The Hound of the Baskervilles '77
The Hound of the Baskervilles '83
The Hound of the Baskervilles '00
The Hound of the Baskervilles '02►
House of Fear '45
Masks of Death '86
Murder at the Baskervilles '37
Murder by Decree '79►
The Pearl of Death '44
The Private Life of Sherlock Holmes '70►
Pursuit to Algiers '45
Scarlet Claw '44
The Seven-Per-Cent Solution '76►
Sherlock: Case of Evil '02
Sherlock Holmes and the Deadly Necklace '62►
Sherlock Holmes and the Incident at Victoria Falls '91
Sherlock Holmes and the Secret Weapon '42►
Sherlock Holmes Faces Death '43►
Sherlock Holmes in Washington '43
Sherlock Holmes: The Voice of Terror '42
The Sign of Four '83►
The Sign of Four '01
The Silent Mr. Sherlock Holmes '12
The Speckled Band '31►
Spider Woman '44►
The Strange Case of the End of Civilization As We Know It '93
A Study in Scarlet '33
A Study in Terror '66►
Terror by Night '46
They Might Be Giants '71►
The Triumph of Sherlock Holmes '35
Without a Clue '88
The Woman in Green '45
Young Sherlock Holmes '85

Sinbad
Captain Sinbad '63
Golden Voyage of Sinbad '73
Invitation to the Dance '56
The Magic Voyage of Sinbad '52
The Seventh Voyage of Sinbad '58►
Sinbad and the Eye of the Tiger '77
Sinbad: Legend of the Seven Seas '03
Son of Sinbad '55
What the Moon Saw '90

Special FX Extravaganzas
The Abyss '89►
Alice in Wonderland '85
Alien: Resurrection '97►
Aliens '86►
An American Werewolf in Paris '97
Anaconda '96
The Arrival '96
Baby Geniuses '98
Batman '89►
Batman and Robin '97
Batman Forever '95►
Beetlejuice '88►
Big Trouble in Little China '86
The Black Hole '79
Blithe Spirit '45►
The Borrowers '97
Captain Sinbad '63
The Chronicles of Riddick '04
Crash Dive '43
Dante's Peak '97
Daylight '96

Dragonheart '96
Event Horizon '97
The Ewok Adventure '84
The Exorcist '73►
The Exorcist 2: The Heretic '77
FairyTale: A True Story '97
Fantastic Voyage '66►
The Fifth Element '97
Forbidden Planet '56►
Hideaway '94
Highlander: The Final Dimension '94
Independence Day '96►
Innerspace '87
Judge Dredd '95
Jumanji '95
Jurassic Park '93►
Lifeforce '85
The Lost World: Jurassic Park 2 '97
Mars Attacks! '96
Mary Shelley's Frankenstein '94
The Mask '94►
My Favorite Martian '98
Poltergeist '82►
The Rains Came '39
Return of the Jedi '83►
The Shadow '94
Small Soldiers '98
Solar Crisis '92
Spawn '97►
Species '95
Species 2 '98
Star Trek 2: The Wrath of Khan '82►
Star Trek 4: The Voyage Home '86►
Star Trek: Generations '94►
Superman 2 '80►
The Terminator '84►
Terminator 2: Judgment Day '91►
The Thing '82
Total Recall '90►
Twister '96
2001: A Space Odyssey '68►
2010: The Year We Make Contact '84►
Virtuosity '95
Virus '98
Volcano '97
Who Framed Roger Rabbit '88►
Wolfen '81►

Special FX Extravaganzas: Make-Up
An American Werewolf in London '81►
The Associate '96
Bad Moon '96
Batman and Robin '97
Beetlejuice '88►
Beneath the Planet of the Apes '70
Body Melt '93
Conquest of the Planet of the Apes '72
Darkman 2: The Return of Durant '94
Darkman 3: Die Darkman Die '95
Dawn of the Dead '78►
Day of the Dead '85
Escape from the Planet of the Apes '71►
The Exorcist '73►
The Fly '86►
The Fly 2 '89
Freaked '93
Hocus Pocus '93
The Howling '81►
The Man Without a Face '93
Mary Shelley's Frankenstein '94
The Nutty Professor '96►
The Nutty Professor 2: The Klumps '00
Planet of the Apes '68►
Scanner Cop '94

Scanners '81
Sssssss '73
The Thing '82
Vampire in Brooklyn '95
Warriors of Virtue '97
Wolf '94

Special FX Wizards: Rick Baker
An American Werewolf in London '81►
Food of the Gods '76
The Funhouse '81
The Fury '78
Greystoke: The Legend of Tarzan, Lord of the Apes '84
Harry and the Hendersons '87
Incredible Melting Man '77
The Incredible Shrinking Woman '81
It's Alive '74►
King Kong '76
Men in Black '97►
Mighty Joe Young '98
The Nutty Professor '96►
Octaman '71
Planet of the Apes '01►
Schlock '73
Squirm '76
Star Wars '77►
Tanya's Island '81
Track of the Moonbeast '76
Videodrome '83
Wolf '94

Special FX Wizards: Rob Bottin
Bugsy '91►
Explorers '85
Fear and Loathing in Las Vegas '98
The Fog '78
The Howling '81►
Humanoids from the Deep '80
Innerspace '87
Legend '86
Mission: Impossible '96►
RoboCop '87►
Tanya's Island '81
The Thing '82
Total Recall '90►
Twilight Zone: The Movie '83
The Witches of Eastwick '87

Special FX Wizards: Anton Furst
Alien '79►
Batman '89►
The Company of Wolves '85►
Full Metal Jacket '87►
Moonraker '79
Star Wars '77►

Special FX Wizards: Ray Harryhausen
The Beast from 20,000 Fathoms '53
Clash of the Titans '81
Earth vs. the Flying Saucers '56
First Men in the Moon '64
Golden Voyage of Sinbad '73
It Came from Beneath the Sea '55►
Jason and the Argonauts '63►
Mighty Joe Young '49
Mysterious Island '61►
One Million Years B.C. '66
The Seventh Voyage of Sinbad '58►
Sinbad and the Eye of the Tiger '77
The Three Worlds of Gulliver '59

Tarzan
Greystoke: The Legend of Tarzan, Lord of the Apes '84

Star Wars
The Empire Strikes Back '80►
The Ewok Adventure '84
The Ewoks: Battle for Endor '85
Return of the Jedi '83►
Star Wars '77►
Star Wars: Episode 1—The Phantom Menace '99►
Star Wars: Episode 2—Attack of the Clones '02►
Star Wars: Episode 3—Revenge of the Sith '05►

Special FX Wizards: Douglas Trumbull
The Andromeda Strain '71
Blade Runner '82►
Brainstorm '83
Close Encounters of the Third Kind '77►
Silent Running '71►
Star Trek: The Motion Picture '79
2001: A Space Odyssey '68►

Special FX Wizards: Dick Smith
Altered States '80►
Amadeus '84►
The Exorcist '73►
Ghost Story '81
The Godfather '72►
Deranged '74►
House of Dark Shadows '70►
Little Big Man '70►
Marathon Man '76►
Midnight Cowboy '69►
Scanners '81
The Sentinel '75
Spasms '82
The Stepford Wives '75►
The Sunshine Boys '75►
Taxi Driver '76►
The World of Henry Orient '64►

Special FX Wizards: Tom Savini
Creepshow '82
Dawn of the Dead '78►
Day of the Dead '85
Deathdream '72
Deranged '74►
Friday the 13th '80
Friday the 13th, Part 4: The Final Chapter '84
Knightriders '81
Maniac '80
Martin '77►
Midnight '81
Monkey Shines '88
The Prowler '81
The Ripper '86
The Texas Chainsaw Massacre 2 '86

Special FX Wizards: Herschell Gordon Lewis
Blood Feast '63
Color Me Blood Red '64
Gruesome Twosome '67
Just for the Hell of It '68
Moonshine Mountain '64
The Psychic '68
She-Devils on Wheels '68
Suburban Roulette '67
This Stuff'll Kill Ya! '71
2000 Maniacs '64
The Wizard of Gore '70

20 Million Miles to Earth '57
The Valley of Gwangi '69

Tarzan '35
Tarzan 2 '05
Tarzan and the Green Goddess '38
Tarzan and the Lost City '98
Tarzan and the Trappers '58
Tarzan Escapes '36►
Tarzan Finds a Son '39►
Tarzan of the Apes '17
Tarzan the Ape Man '32►
Tarzan, the Ape Man '81
Tarzan, the Fearless '33
Tarzan the Tiger '29
Tarzan's New York Adventure '42
Tarzan's Revenge '38
Tarzan's Secret Treasure '41
Walk Like a Man '87

The New Adventures of Tarzan '35

The Three Musketeers
The 4 Musketeers '75►
The Four Musketeers '05
The Man in the Iron Mask '98►
The Man in the Iron Mask '16
The Musketeer '01
Ring of the Musketeers '93
The Three Musketeers '16
The Three Musketeers '21
The Three Musketeers '33
The Three Musketeers '35
The Three Musketeers '39
The Three Musketeers '48
The Three Musketeers '74►
The Three Musketeers '93

The Three Mesquiteers
Come on, Cowboys '37
Covered Wagon Days '40
Cowboys from Texas '39
Frontier Horizon '39
Ghost Town Gold '36
Heart of the Rockies '37
Heroes of the Hills '38
Hit the Saddle '37
The Kansas Terrors '39
Outlaws of Sonora '38
Overland Stage Raiders '38
Pals of the Saddle '38
Powdersmoke Range '35
Purple Vigilantes '38
Riders of the Whistling Skull '37
Roarin' Lead '37
Rocky Mountain Rangers '40
Santa Fe Stampede '38
Three Texas Steers '39
The Trigger Trio '37
Wild Horse Rodeo '37
Wyoming Outlaw '39

3.5 Bones
The Leopard '63►
There Will Be Blood '07►

The Thin Man
After the Thin Man '36►
Another Thin Man '39
Shadow of the Thin Man '41►
Song of the Thin Man '47
The Thin Man '34►
The Thin Man Goes Home '44

The Texas Rangers
Boss of Rawhide '44
Comanche Moon '08
Dead or Alive '44
Enemy of the Law '45
Fighting Bullets '43
Flaming Valley '43
Frontier Fugitives '45
Gangsters of the Frontier '44
Guns of the Law '44
Hello Trouble '32
Man of the House '05
Marked for Murder '45
Outlaw Roundup '44
Ranger's Roundup '38
Rangers Take Over '42
Three in the Saddle '45
Trace '07►
Wild West '46

Tom Ripley
The American Friend '77►
Purple Noon '60►
Ripley's Game '02►
The Talented Mr. Ripley '99►

3 Stooges
Around the World in a Daze '63
Dancing Lady '33
Gold Raiders '51
Have Rocket Will Travel '59
Hollywood Party '34
It's a Mad, Mad, Mad, Mad World '63
Johnny Belinda '48
On an Island with You '48
The Outlaws Is Coming! '65
The Paleface '48
Snow White and the Three Stooges '61
Stoogemania '85
Three Stooges in Orbit '62
The Three Stooges Meet Hercules '61

Top Grossing Films of 1939
Gone with the Wind '39►
The Hunchback of Notre Dame '39►
Mr. Smith Goes to Washington '39►
The Wizard of Oz '39►

Top Grossing Films of 1940
Boom Town '40
Fantasia '40►
Pinocchio '40►
Rebecca '40►
Santa Fe Trail '40

Top Grossing Films of 1941
Honky Tonk '41
The Philadelphia Story '40►
Sergeant York '41►
A Yank in the R.A.F. '41

Top Grossing Films of 1942
Bambi '42►
Casablanca '42►
Mrs. Miniver '42►
Random Harvest '42►
Yankee Doodle Dandy '42►

Top Grossing Films of 1943
The Outlaw '43
The Song of Bernadette '43
Stage Door Canteen '43
This Is the Army '43

Top Grossing Films of 1944
Going My Way '44►
Meet Me in St. Louis '44►
Since You Went Away '44►
Thirty Seconds Over Tokyo '44►

Top Grossing Films of 1945
Anchors Aweigh '45►
The Bells of St. Mary's '45►
Spellbound '45►
Weekend at the Waldorf '45►

Top Grossing Films of 1946
The Best Years of Our Lives '46►

Top Grossing Films of 1947
Egg and I '47►
Life with Father '47►

Top Grossing Films of 1948
Johnny Belinda '48
Red River '48►
The Red Shoes '48►
The Three Musketeers '48

Top Grossing Films of 1949
Battleground '49►
Jolson Sings Again '49
Samson and Delilah '50
Sands of Iwo Jima '49►

Top Grossing Films of 1950
Annie Get Your Gun '50►
Cinderella '50►
Father of the Bride '50►
King Solomon's Mines '50►

Top Grossing Films of 1951
Alice in Wonderland '51►
David and Bathsheba '51
The Great Caruso '51►
Quo Vadis '51►
Show Boat '51►

Top Grossing Films of 1952
The Greatest Show on Earth '52►
Hans Christian Andersen '52
Ivanhoe '52►
The Snows of Kilimanjaro '52►

Top Grossing Films of 1953
From Here to Eternity '53►
How to Marry a Millionaire '53►
Peter Pan '53►
The Robe '53►
Shane '53►

Top Grossing Films of 1954
The Caine Mutiny '54►
The Glenn Miller Story '54►
Rear Window '54►
20,000 Leagues under the Sea '54►
White Christmas '54►

Top Grossing Films of 1955
Battle Cry '55►
Lady and the Tramp '55►
Mister Roberts '55►
Oklahoma! '55►

Top Grossing Films of 1956
Around the World in 80 Days '56►
Giant '56►
The King and I '56►
The Ten Commandments '56►

Top Grossing Films of 1957
The Bridge on the River Kwai '57►
Old Yeller '57►
Peyton Place '57
Raintree County '57
Sayonara '57►

Top Grossing Films of 1958
Auntie Mame '58►
Cat on a Hot Tin Roof '58►
Gigi '58►
No Time for Sergeants '58►
South Pacific '58►

Top Grossing Films of 1959
Ben-Hur '59►
Darby O'Gill & the Little People '59►
Operation Petticoat '59►
The Shaggy Dog '59►
Sleeping Beauty '59►

Top Grossing Films of 1960
The Alamo '60►
Exodus '60►
Psycho '60►
Spartacus '60►
The Swiss Family Robinson '60►

Top Grossing Films of 1961
The Absent-Minded Professor '61►
El Cid '61►
The Guns of Navarone '61►
West Side Story '61►

Top Grossing Films of 1962
How the West Was Won '63►
In Search of the Castaways '62►
Lawrence of Arabia '62►
The Longest Day '62►
The Music Man '62►

Top Grossing Films of 1963
Cleopatra '63►
Irma La Douce '63
It's a Mad, Mad, Mad, Mad World '63
The Sword in the Stone '63►
Tom Jones '63►

Top Grossing Films of 1964
The Carpetbaggers '64
From Russia with Love '63►
Goldfinger '64►
Mary Poppins '64►
My Fair Lady '64►

Top Grossing Films of 1965
Doctor Zhivago '65►
The Sound of Music '65►
That Darn Cat '65►
Those Magnificent Men in Their Flying Machines '65►
Thunderball '65►

Top Grossing Films of 1966
Hawaii '66►
Lt. Robin Crusoe, U.S.N. '66
A Man for All Seasons '66►
Who's Afraid of Virginia Woolf? '66►

Top Grossing Films of 1967
Bonnie & Clyde '67►
The Dirty Dozen '67►
The Graduate '67►
Guess Who's Coming to Dinner '67►
The Jungle Book '67►

Top Grossing Films of 1968
Bullitt '68►
Funny Girl '68►
The Odd Couple '68►
Romeo and Juliet '68►
2001: A Space Odyssey '68►

Top Grossing Films of 1969
Butch Cassidy and the Sundance Kid '69►
Easy Rider '69►
Hello, Dolly! '69►
The Love Bug '68►
Midnight Cowboy '69►

Top Grossing Films of 1970
Airport '70►
Love Story '70►
M*A*S*H '70►
Patton '70►

Top Grossing Films of 1971
Billy Jack '71►
Diamonds Are Forever '71►
Fiddler on the Roof '71►
The French Connection '71►
Summer of '42 '71►

Top Grossing Films of 1972
Deliverance '72►
The Godfather '72►
Jeremiah Johnson '72►
The Poseidon Adventure '72►
What's Up, Doc? '72►

Top Grossing Films of 1973
American Graffiti '73►
The Exorcist '73►
Papillon '73►
The Sting '73►
The Way We Were '73►

Top Grossing Films of 1974
Blazing Saddles '74►
Earthquake '74►
The Towering Inferno '74►
The Trial of Billy Jack '74►
Young Frankenstein '74►

Top Grossing Films of 1975
Dog Day Afternoon '75►
Jaws '75►
One Flew Over the Cuckoo's Nest '75►

Top Grossing Films of 1976
All the President's Men '76►
King Kong '76►
Rocky '76►
Silver Streak '76►
A Star Is Born '76►

Top Grossing Films of 1977
Close Encounters of the Third Kind '77►
The Goodbye Girl '77►
Saturday Night Fever '77
Smokey and the Bandit '77
Star Wars '77►

► = rated three bones or higher

Top Grossing Films of 1978
Every Which Way But Loose '78 ►
Grease '78 ►
Jaws 2 '78 ►
National Lampoon's Animal House '78 ►
Superman: The Movie '78 ►

Top Grossing Films of 1979
Alien '79 ►
The Jerk '79 ►
Kramer vs. Kramer '79 ►
Rocky 2 '79 ►
Star Trek: The Motion Picture '79

Top Grossing Films of 1980
Airplane! '80 ►
Any Which Way You Can '80
The Empire Strikes Back '80 ►
9 to 5 '80 ►
Stir Crazy '80

Top Grossing Films of 1981
Arthur '81 ►
Cannonball Run '81
On Golden Pond '81 ►
Raiders of the Lost Ark '81 ►
Stripes '81
Superman 2 '80 ►

Top Grossing Films of 1982
E.T.: The Extra-Terrestrial '82 ►
An Officer and a Gentleman '82 ►
Porky's '82
Rocky 3 '82

Top Grossing Films of 1983
Return of the Jedi '83 ►
Superman 3 '83
Terms of Endearment '83 ►
Trading Places '83 ►
WarGames '83 ►

Top Grossing Films of 1984
Beverly Hills Cop '84 ►
Ghostbusters '84 ►
Gremlins '84 ►
Indiana Jones and the Temple of Doom '84 ►
The Karate Kid '84 ►

Top Grossing Films of 1985
Back to the Future '85 ►
The Color Purple '85 ►
Out of Africa '85 ►
Rambo: First Blood, Part 2 '85
Rocky 4 '85

Top Grossing Films of 1986
Crocodile Dundee '86 ►
The Karate Kid: Part 2 '86
Platoon '86 ►
Star Trek 4: The Voyage Home '86 ►
Top Gun '86 ►

Top Grossing Films of 1987
Beverly Hills Cop 2 '87 ►
Fatal Attraction '87 ►
Good Morning, Vietnam '87 ►
Lethal Weapon '87 ►
Three Men and a Baby '87 ►
The Untouchables '87 ►

Top Grossing Films of 1988
Coming to America '88 ►
Crocodile Dundee 2 '88 ►
Die Hard '88 ►
Rain Man '88 ►
Twins '88
Who Framed Roger Rabbit '88 ►

Top Grossing Films of 1989
Batman '89 ►
Driving Miss Daisy '89 ►
Ghostbusters 2 '89
Honey, I Shrunk the Kids '89 ►
Indiana Jones and the Last Crusade '89 ►
Lethal Weapon 2 '89 ►

Top Grossing Films of 1990
Dances with Wolves '90 ►
Dick Tracy '90 ►
Die Hard 2: Die Harder '90 ►
Ghost '90 ►
Home Alone '90 ►
The Hunt for Red October '90 ►
Pretty Woman '90 ►
Teenage Mutant Ninja Turtles: The Movie '90
Total Recall '90 ►

Top Grossing Films of 1991
The Addams Family '91 ►
Backdraft '91 ►
Boyz N the Hood '91 ►
City Slickers '91 ►
Doc Hollywood '91 ►
Dying Young '91
Hot Shots! '91 ►
Naked Gun 2 1/2: The Smell of Fear '91
New Jack City '91 ►
101 Dalmatians '61 ►
Robin Hood: Prince of Thieves '91 ►
The Rocketeer '91 ►
The Silence of the Lambs '91 ►
Sleeping with the Enemy '91
Teenage Mutant Ninja Turtles 2: The Secret of the Ooze '91
Terminator 2: Judgment Day '91 ►
What about Bob? '91 ►

Top Grossing Films of 1992
Aladdin '92 ►
Alien 3 '92
Basic Instinct '92 ►
Batman Returns '92 ►
The Bodyguard '92
Boomerang '92
Bram Stoker's Dracula '92 ►
Fried Green Tomatoes '91 ►
The Hand that Rocks the Cradle '92
Home Alone 2: Lost in New York '92
The Last of the Mohicans '92 ►
A League of Their Own '92 ►
Lethal Weapon 3 '92 ►
Patriot Games '92 ►
Sister Act '92 ►
Under Siege '92 ►
Unforgiven '92 ►
Wayne's World '92 ►
White Men Can't Jump '92 ►

Top Grossing Films of 1993
Aladdin '92 ►
Cliffhanger '93 ►
A Few Good Men '92 ►
The Firm '93 ►
Free Willy '93 ►
The Fugitive '93 ►
In the Line of Fire '93 ►
Indecent Proposal '93 ►
Jurassic Park '93 ►
Sleepless in Seattle '93 ►

Top Grossing Films of 1994
Ace Ventura: Pet Detective '93 ►
Clear and Present Danger '94 ►
The Client '94 ►
The Flintstones '94 ►
Forrest Gump '94 ►
The Lion King '94 ►
The Mask '94 ►
Maverick '94 ►
Speed '94 ►
True Lies '94 ►

Top Grossing Films of 1995
Ace Ventura: When Nature Calls '95 ►
Apollo 13 '95 ►
Batman Forever '95 ►
Casper '95 ►
Die Hard: With a Vengeance '95 ►
Goldeneye '95 ►
Jumanji '95 ►
Pocahontas '95 ►
Seven '95 ►
Toy Story '95 ►

Top Grossing Films of 1996
The Birdcage '95 ►
Broken Arrow '95 ►
The Cable Guy '96 ►
Courage Under Fire '96 ►
Eraser '96 ►
The First Wives Club '96 ►
The Hunchback of Notre Dame '96 ►
Independence Day '96 ►
Jack '96 ►
Jerry Maguire '96 ►
Mission: Impossible '96 ►
The Nutty Professor '96 ►
101 Dalmatians '96 ►
Phenomenon '96 ►
Ransom '96 ►
The Rock '96 ►
Space Jam '96 ►
Star Trek: First Contact '96 ►
A Time to Kill '96 ►
Twister '96 ►

Top Grossing Films of 1997
Air Force One '97 ►
Batman and Robin '97 ►
Con Air '97 ►
Conspiracy Theory '97 ►
Contact '97 ►
Face/Off '97 ►
Flubber '97 ►
George of the Jungle '97 ►
Hercules '97 ►
I Know What You Did Last Summer '97 ►
Jerry Maguire '96 ►
Liar Liar '97 ►
The Lost World: Jurassic Park 2 '97 ►
Men in Black '97 ►
My Best Friend's Wedding '97 ►
Scream '96 ►
Scream 2 '97 ►
Star Wars '77 ►
Titanic '97 ►
Tomorrow Never Dies '97 ►

Top Grossing Films of 1998
Antz '98 ►
Armageddon '98 ►
As Good As It Gets '97 ►
A Bug's Life '98 ►
Deep Impact '98 ►
Dr. Dolittle '98 ►
Enemy of the State '98 ►
Godzilla '98 ►
Good Will Hunting '97 ►
Lethal Weapon 4 '98 ►
The Mask of Zorro '98 ►
Mulan '98 ►
The Rugrats Movie '98 ►
Saving Private Ryan '98 ►
There's Something about Mary '98 ►
Titanic '97 ►
The Truman Show '98 ►
The Waterboy '98
The X-Files '98 ►

Top Grossing Films of 1999
American Pie '99 ►
Analyze This '99 ►
Austin Powers 2: The Spy Who Shagged Me '99 ►
Big Daddy '99 ►
The Blair Witch Project '99 ►
A Bug's Life '98 ►
Entrapment '99 ►
The Matrix '99 ►
The Mummy '99 ►
Notting Hill '99 ►
Runaway Bride '99 ►
Shakespeare in Love '98 ►
The Sixth Sense '99 ►
Star Wars: Episode 1—The Phantom Menace '99 ►
Tarzan '99 ►
Toy Story 2 '99 ►
Wild Wild West '99
The World Is Not Enough '99 ►
You've Got Mail '98 ►

Top Grossing Films of 2000
Big Momma's House '00 ►
Cast Away '00 ►
Charlie's Angels '00 ►
Chicken Run '00 ►
Dinosaur '00 ►
Dr. Seuss' How the Grinch Stole Christmas '00 ►
Erin Brockovich '00 ►
George Wallace '97 ►
Gladiator '00 ►
Gone in 60 Seconds '00 ►
Me, Myself, and Irene '00 ►
Meet the Parents '00 ►
Mission: Impossible 2 '00 ►
Nutty Professor 2: The Klumps '00 ►
The Patriot '00 ►
The Perfect Storm '00 ►
Remember the Titans '00 ►
Scary Movie '00 ►
What Women Want '00 ►
X-Men '00 ►

Top Grossing Films of 2001
American Pie 2 '01 ►
Cast Away '00 ►
Crouching Tiger, Hidden Dragon '00 ►
Dr. Dolittle 2 '01 ►
The Fast and the Furious '01 ►
Hannibal '01 ►
Harry Potter and the Sorcerer's Stone '01 ►
Jurassic Park 3 '01 ►
Lara Croft: Tomb Raider '01 ►
Lord of the Rings: The Fellowship of the Rings '01 ►
The Matrix Revolutions '03 ►
Monsters, Inc. '01 ►
The Mummy Returns '01 ►
Pearl Harbor '01 ►
Planet of the Apes '01 ►
Rush Hour 2 '01 ►
Shrek '01 ►
Traffic '00 ►

Top Grossing Films of 2002
Austin Powers In Goldmember '02 ►
Die Another Day '02 ►
Harry Potter and the Chamber of Secrets '02 ►
Ice Age '02 ►
Lilo & Stitch '02 ►
Lord of the Rings: The Fellowship of the Rings '01 ►
Lord of the Rings: The Two Towers '02 ►
Men in Black 2 '02 ►
Minority Report '02 ►
Mr. Deeds '02 ►
My Big Fat Greek Wedding '02 ►
The Ring '02 ►
The Santa Clause 2 '02 ►
Scooby-Doo '02 ►
Signs '02 ►
Spider-Man '02 ►
Star Wars: Episode 2—Attack of the Clones '02 ►
Sweet Home Alabama '02 ►

Top Grossing Films of 2003
Anger Management '03 ►
Bad Boys 2 '03 ►
Bringing Down the House '03 ►
Bruce Almighty '03 ►
Chicago '02 ►
Elf '03 ►
Finding Nemo '03 ►
Hulk '03 ►
Lord of the Rings: The Return of the King '03 ►
The Matrix Reloaded '03 ►
Pirates of the Caribbean: The Curse of the Black Pearl '03 ►
Terminator 3: Rise of the Machines '03 ►
2 Fast 2 Furious '03 ►
X2: X-Men United '03 ►

Top Grossing Films of 2004
The Bourne Supremacy '04 ►
The Day After Tomorrow '04 ►
Dodgeball: A True Underdog Story '04 ►
Fahrenheit 9/11 '04 ►
50 First Dates '04 ►
Harry Potter and the Prisoner of Azkaban '04 ►
I, Robot '04 ►
The Incredibles '04 ►
Lord of the Rings: The Return of the King '03 ►
Meet the Fockers '04 ►
National Treasure '04 ►
Ocean's Twelve '04 ►
The Passion of the Christ '04 ►
The Polar Express '04 ►
Shark Tale '04 ►
Shrek 2 '04 ►
Spider-Man 2 '04 ►
Troy '04 ►
Van Helsing '04 ►
The Village '04 ►

Top Grossing Films of 2005
Batman Begins '05 ►
Charlie and the Chocolate Factory '05 ►
Chicken Little '05 ►
The Chronicles of Narnia: The Lion, the Witch and the Wardrobe '05 ►
Fantastic Four '05 ►
The 40 Year Old Virgin '05 ►
Harry Potter and the Goblet of Fire '05 ►
Hitch '05 ►
King Kong '05 ►
The Longest Yard '05 ►
Madagascar '05 ►
Meet the Fockers '04 ►
Million Dollar Baby '04 ►
The Pacifier '05 ►
Robots '05 ►
Star Wars: Episode 3—Revenge of the Sith '05 ►
Walk the Line '05 ►
War of the Worlds '05 ►
Wedding Crashers '05 ►

Top Grossing Films of 2006
Borat: Cultural Learnings of America for Make Benefit Glorious Nation of Kazakhstan '06 ►
The Break-Up '06 ►
Cars '06 ►
Casino Royale '06 ►
Click '06 ►
The Da Vinci Code '06 ►
The Departed '06 ►
The Devil Wears Prada '06 ►
Failure to Launch '06 ►
Happy Feet '06 ►
Ice Age: The Meltdown '06 ►
Mission: Impossible 3 '06 ►
Night at the Museum '06 ►
Over the Hedge '06 ►
Pirates of the Caribbean: Dead Man's Chest '06 ►
The Pursuit of Happyness '06 ►
Scary Movie 4 '06 ►
Superman Returns '06 ►
Talladega Nights: The Ballad of Ricky Bobby '06 ►
X-Men: The Last Stand '06 ►

Top Grossing Films of 2007
Alvin and the Chipmunks '07 ►
American Gangster '07 ►
Bee Movie '07 ►
Blades of Glory '07 ►
Enchanted '07 ►
Fantastic Four: Rise of the Silver Surfer '07 ►
Hairspray '07 ►
Harry Potter and the Order of the Phoenix '07 ►
I Am Legend '07 ►
I Now Pronounce You Chuck and Larry '07 ►
Knocked Up '07 ►
Live Free or Die Hard '07 ►
National Treasure: Book of Secrets '07 ►
Ocean's Thirteen '07 ►
Ratatouille '07 ►
Rush Hour 3 '07 ►
Shrek the Third '07 ►
The Simpsons Movie '07 ►
Spider-Man 3 '07 ►
Superbad '07 ►
300 '07 ►
Transformers '07 ►
Wild Hogs '07 ►

The Trail Blazers
Arizona Whirlwind '44
Death Valley Rangers '44
The Law Rides Again '43
Outlaw Trail '44

Troma Films
Beware! Children at Play '95
Blades '89
Blondes Have More Guns '95
Bloodsucking Freaks '75
Bugged! '96
Cannibal! The Musical '96
Chopper Chicks in Zombietown '91
The Chosen One: Legend of the Raven '98
Christmas Evil '80
Citizen Toxie: The Toxic Avenger 4 '01
Class of Nuke 'Em High '86
Class of Nuke 'Em High 2: Subhumanoid Meltdown '91
Class of Nuke 'Em High 3: The Good, the Bad and the Subhumanoid '94
Combat Shock '84
Cry Uncle! '71
Deadly Daphne's Revenge '93
Escape from Hell '79

Evil Clutch '89
Fat Guy Goes Nutzoid '86
Ferocious Female Freedom Fighters '88
Frostbiter: Wrath of the Wendigo '94
Girls School Screamers '86
I Married a Vampire '87
I Was a Teenage TV Terrorist '87
Invasion of the Space Preachers '90
Maniac Nurses Find Ecstasy '94
A Nymphoid Barbarian in Dinosaur Hell '94
Preacherman '83
Rabid Grannies '89
Redneck Zombies '88
Sgt. Kabukiman N.Y.P.D. '94
Sergio Lapel's Drawing Blood '99
Sizzle Beach U.S.A. '74
Splatter University '84
Squeeze Play '79
Stuck on You '84
Student Confidential '87
Surf Nazis Must Die '87
Teenage Catgirls in Heat '00
The Toxic Avenger '86
The Toxic Avenger, Part 2 '89
The Toxic Avenger, Part 3: The Last Temptation of Toxie '89
Troma's War '88
Tromeo & Juliet '95
Unspeakable '00
Vegas in Space '94
Wizards of the Demon Sword '85
Zombie Island Massacre '84

Universal Studios' Classic Horror

Abbott and Costello Meet Dr. Jekyll and Mr. Hyde '52
Abbott and Costello Meet Frankenstein '48
Abbott and Costello Meet the Killer, Boris Karloff '49
The Black Cat '34
The Bride of Frankenstein '35
Creature from the Black Lagoon '54
The Creature Walks among Us '56
Dracula (Spanish Version) '31
Dracula '31
Dracula's Daughter '36
Frankenstein '31
Frankenstein Meets the Wolfman '42
The Ghost of Frankenstein '42
House of Dracula '45
House of Frankenstein '44
The Hunchback of Notre Dame '23
The Invisible Agent '42
The Invisible Man '33
The Invisible Man Returns '40
The Invisible Woman '40
Island of Lost Souls '32
The Mummy '32
The Mummy's Curse '44
The Mummy's Ghost '44
The Mummy's Hand '40
The Mummy's Tomb '42
Murders in the Rue Morgue '32
The Phantom of the Opera '25
The Phantom of the Opera '43
The Raven '35
Revenge of the Creature '55
Son of Dracula '43
Son of Frankenstein '39
Van Helsing '04
Werewolf of London '35
The Wolf Man '41

The Wolfman

Frankenstein Meets the Wolfman '42
House of Dracula '45
House of Frankenstein '44
The Monster Squad '87
Van Helsing '04
The Wolf Man '41
The Wolfman '82

Wild Bill Hickok

Buffalo Girls '95
Calamity Jane '53
Calamity Jane '82
Dead Man '95
The Plainsman '37
Pony Express '53
The White Buffalo '77
Wild Bill '95
Young Bill Hickok '40

Woofs!

The Adventurers '70
Adventures of a Taxi Driver '76
The Adventures of Ford Fairlane '90
The Adventures of Pluto Nash '02
The Adventurous Knights '35
After the Fall of New York '85
Albino '76
The Alchemist '81
The Alien Agenda: Out of the Darkness '96
Alien Contamination '81
Alien from L.A. '87
Alien Massacre '67
Alien Predators '80
Alien Warrior '85
Almost Human '79
Alone in the Dark '05
The Amazing Transparent Man '60
The Ambushers '67
The Amazing Transplant '70
American Gothic '88
American Ninja 3: Blood Hunt '89
American Ninja 4: The Annihilation '91
American Soldiers '05
Amin: The Rise and Fall '82
Amityville 2: The Possession '82
The Amityville Curse '90
Anatomy of Hell '04
Angel 3: The Final Chapter '88
Angel of Death '86
Angel of H.E.A.T. '82
Angel's Wild Women '72
The Annihilators '85
Another 9 1/2 Weeks '96
A*P*E '76
The Appointment '82
Are You Scared? '06
The Astro-Zombies '67
Atlas in the Land of the Cyclops '61
Atom Age Vampire '61
Attack of the Swamp Creature '75
Auntie '73
Avenging Angel '85
Awakening of Candra '81
Axe '06

Baby Love '69
Baby Love '83
Bachelor Party Vegas '05
Bad Charleston Charlie '73
Bad Girls Do Cry '54
Bad Girls from Mars '90
Bad Girls Go to Hell '65
Bad Medicine '85
Baise Moi '00
Balboa '82
Bananas Boat '78
Bar-B-Q '00
Barn of the Naked Dead '73
Barracuda '78
Basic Training '85
Battlefield Earth '00
Beaks: The Movie '87
Beast of the Yellow Night '70
The Beast of Yucca Flats '61
The Bees '78
Bela Lugosi Meets a Brooklyn Gorilla '52
The Bellboy and the Playgirls '62
Beware! Children at Play '95
Beyond Atlantis '73
Beyond Evil '80
Beyond the Door '75
Beyond the Door 3 '91
Big Foot '72
The Big Bust Out '73
The Bikini Car Wash Company '90
The Birds 2: Land's End '94
The Black Cat '81
The Black Cobra '83
The Black Cobra '87
Black Gestapo '75
Black Magic Woman '91
Black Shampoo '76
Black Venus '83
Blackenstein '73
Blacksnake! '73
Blackwoods '02
Blade of the Ripper '70
Blastfighter '85
Blazing Stewardesses '75
Bleeders '97
Blockhouse '73
Blood Beach '81
Blood Diner '87
Blood Freak '72
Blood Games '90
Blood Orgy of Ghastly Horror '72
Blood Rage '87
Blood Screams '88
Blood Sisters '86
Blood Voyage '77
Bloodmoon '90
Bloodrayne '90
BloodRayne 2: Deliverance '07
Bloodstalkers '76
Bloodstream '00
Bloodsuckers from Outer Space '83
Bloodsucking Freaks '75
Bloodsucking Pharoahs of Pittsburgh '90
The Bloody Brood '59
Bloody Moon '83
Bloody Murder '99
Bloody Murder 2 '03
The Blue Lagoon '80
Blue Movies '88
Boat Trip '03
The Body Beneath '70
Body of Evidence '92
Body Rock '84
The Body Shop '72
Bolero '84
Boogey Man 2 '83
Boom in the Moon '46
Border Radio '88
Bottoms Up '06
Brain of Blood '71
Breeders '97
The Brice & the Beast '58
The Bride & the Monster '55
Brides of the Beast '68
Brotherhood 2: The Young Warlocks '01
The Brotherhood 3: The Young Demons '02
BTK Killer '06
Bug '75
Bullies '86

Bummer '73
Cabin Boy '94
Caged Terror '72
California Casanova '89
Caligula '80
Can I Do It... Till I Need Glasses? '77
Cannibal Apocalypse '80
Can't Stop the Music '80
Carnival of Souls '98
Cartel '90
Castle of Evil '66
Castle of the Creeping Flesh '66
Cave Girl '85
Cave of the Living Dead '65
Cellar Dweller '87
The Centerfold Girls '74
Centipede '05
Chain Gang Women '72
Chain of Souls '00
Chained for Life '51
Challenge of the Board '97
Chaos '05
Charlie McCarthy, Detective '39
Charlie White '04
Creeper to Keep Her '80
Cheech and Chong's The Corsican Brothers '84
Cheering Section '73
Cheerleader Camp '88
The Cheerleaders '72
Cheerleaders' Wild Weekend '85
Cherry Hill High '76
The Children '80
Children of the Living Dead '00
Child's Play 2 '90
The Chilling '89
Chilly Dogs '01
The Chosen '77
Chu Chu & the Philly Flash '81
C.H.U.D. '84
C.H.U.D. 2: Bud the Chud '89
Citizen Toxie: The Toxic Avenger 4 '01
City on Fire '78
Clash of the Titans '81
Class of 1984 '82
Class of Nuke 'Em High 3: The Good, the Bad and the Subhumanoid '94
Class Reunion '72
Class Reunion Massacre '77
Claws '35
Clifford '92
Cop Killers '73
The Corpse Grinders '71
Corruption '70
Cosh Boy '61
Cosmos: War of the Planets '80
Color Me Blood Red '64
Condemned to Hell '84
Confidential '86
The Conqueror '56
The Conqueror & the Empress '64
The Creation of the Humanoids '62
Creatures the World Forgot '70
Creeping Terror '64
The Cremators '72
Crocodile '81
Crocodile 2: Death Swamp '01
The Crater Lake Monster '77
The Cradle Will Fall '83
The Crawling Hand '63
Crazed '82
Crazy Fat Ethel II '85
Cruise into Terror '78
Cruel World '05
Crucible of Terror '72
Crypt of the Living Dead '73
Cthulhu Mansion '91
The Curse of the Aztec Mummy '59
Curse of the Blue Lights '88

Curse of the Stone Hand '64
Curtains '83
Cycle Psycho '72
Cycle Vixens '79
Dagora, the Space Monster '65
Dance of Death '68
Dance Zone '97
Dangerous Love '87
Dark Sanity '82
Dawn of the Mummy '82
The Day It Came to Earth '77
Dead Aim '87
Dead Pit '89
Dead Women in Lingerie '90
Death '94
Deadly Daring '85
Deadly Embrace '88
Deadly Prey '87
Deadly Sanctuary '68
Deadly Twins '85
The Death Curse of Tartu '66
Death Ray '67
Death Spa '87
Death Wish 2 '82
Death Wish 5: The Face of Death '94
Deathstalker '83
Decay '98
Dee Snider's Strangeland '98
Delinquent School Girls '84
Delirium '77
The Demon Lover '77
Demon of Paradise '87
Demonia '90
Demonwarp '87
Deuce Bigalow: European Gigolo '05
The Devil's Rejects '05
Devil's Gift '84
Devil's Son-in-Law '77
Devil's Wedding Night '73
Devil Woman '76
Die Laughing '80
Digging Up Business '91
Dirty Laundry '87
Dirty Love '05
Dirty Mind of Young Sally '72
Doctor Butcher M.D. '80
Doctor of Doom '62
Dr. Orloff's Monster '64
Dr. Tarr's Torture Dungeon '75
The Dolls '83
Don't Go in the Woods '81
Don't Look in the Attic '81
Don't Open the Door '74
Don't Open Till Christmas '84
Doom Asylum '88
Dorm That Dripped Blood '82
Dracula: Dead and Loving It '95
Dracula vs. Frankenstein '72
Dracula's Great Love '72
Dracula's Last Rites '79
Driller Killer '79
Drive-In Massacre '74
Driver's Seat '73
Drop Dead Fred '91
Drum '76
Drums O'Voodoo '34
Dutch Girls '87
Ecstasy '84
Ed '96
Eegah! '62
Emily '77
End of the World '76
Endless Descent '90
Equilibrium '02
Erotic Images '85
Escape from Hell '79
Escape from Safehaven '88
Escape from the KGB '87
Escape 2000 '81
Escapist '83
Eve of Destruction '90
The Evictors '79
Evil Laugh '86
The Evil Within '89
Evilspeak '82

Expose '97
Exterminators in the Year 3000 '83
Eyeball '78
Eyes of a Stranger '81
Fade to Black '80
Fair Game '82
Fair Game '85
Fair Game '89
Fanatic '82
Fanny Hill: Memoirs of a Woman of Pleasure '64
Fantasies '73
Far Out Man '89
Fascination '04
Fat Guy Goes Nutzoid '86
The Fat Spy '66
Fatal Pulse '88
The Fear Chamber '68
Feed '05
Feeders '96
Feelin' Up '76
The Female Bunch '69
Femme Fontaine: Killer Babe for the C.I.A. '95
Fever Pitch '85
Fiend '63
The Fiendish Plot of Dr. Fu Manchu '80
The Fifth Floor '80
Final Exam '81
Final Payback '95
Foolish '99
Fire Serpent '07
The First 9 1/2 Weeks '98
Flesh Feast '69
Flight to Nowhere '46
Food of the Gods '76
Food of the Gods: Part 2 '88
Forbidden World '82
The Forbidden Dance '90
Foreplay '75
Fowl Play '75
Frankenstein '80 '79
Frankenstein General Hospital '88
Frankenstein Island '81
Frankenstein Meets the Space Monster '65
Frankenstein's Great Aunt Tillie '83
Freddy Got Fingered '01
Friday the 13th, Part 2 '81
Friday the 13th, Part 3 '82
Friday the 13th, Part 4: The Final Chapter '84
Friday the 13th, Part 5: A New Beginning '85
Friday the 13th, Part 6: Jason Lives '86
Friday the 13th, Part 7: The New Blood '88
From Justin to Kelly '03
Fun Down There '88
Galactic Gigolo '87
The Gamma People '56
Gangster's Law '86
The Garbage Pail Kids Movie '87
Gas '81
Gates of Hell '80
Getting Away With Murder '95
The Ghastly Ones '68
Ghost Fever '87
Ghost in the Noonday Sun '74
Ghoulies 3: Ghoulies Go to College '91
Giant from the Unknown '58
Giants of Rome '63
Gimme an F '85
The Girl in Room 2A '76
Girl on a Chain Gang '65
Glen or Glenda? '53
Glitter '01
The Glory Stompers '67
Goblin '93
God's Bloody Acre '75
Godzilla vs. the Sea Monster '65
Gone Fishin' '97
Goliath and the Dragon '61
Goof Balls '87
Gore-Met Zombie Chef from Hell '87
Gorp '80
The Green Berets '68

▶ = rated three bones or higher

Woofs

The Green Slime '68
Grotesque '87
Grunt! The Wrestling Movie '85
Guess What We Learned in School Today? '70
Gummo '97
H-Bomb '71
H-Man '59
Hallowed '05
Halloween with the Addams Family '79
Hallucination '67
Hands of Steel '86
Hangmen '87
Hardbodies 2 '86
Hawmps! '76
The Hearse '80
Heart of America '03
Heavenly Bodies '84
Hell Night '81
Hell of the Living Dead '83
Hell Up in Harlem '73
Hellcats '68
Hellgate '89
Hellriders '84
Hell's Belles '95
Hell's Brigade: The Final Assault '80
Helter Skelter Murders '71
High Tension '03
Hillbillies in a Haunted House '67
The Hills Have Eyes '77
His Name Was King '85
Hitchhikers '72
The Hollywood Strangler Meets the Skid Row Slasher '79
Hollywood Zap '86
Hometown U.S.A. '79
Horror House on Highway 5 '86
Horror of Party Beach '64
Horror of the Blood Monsters '70
Hospital Massacre '81
Hot Box '72
Hot T-Shirts '79
Hot Touch '82
The Hound of the Baskervilles '77
House of 1000 Corpses '03
House of Psychotic Women '73
House of the Dead '03
House of Whipcord '75
House on the Edge of the Park '84
How to Seduce a Woman '74
Humanoids from the Deep '80
Humongous '82
Hurricane '79
I Dismember Mama '74
I Eat Your Skin '64
I Spit on Your Corpse '74
I Spit on Your Grave '77
I Was a Teenage TV Terrorist '87
Icebox Murders '82
Idaho Transfer '73
If I Die Before I Wake '98
Ilsa, Harem Keeper of the Oil Sheiks '76
Ilsa, She-Wolf of the SS '74
Ilsa, the Tigress of Siberia '79
Ilsa, the Wicked Warden '78
Impulse '74
In God We Trust '80
In Search of Anna '79
In the Mix '05
In the Shadow of Kilimanjaro '86
In Trouble '67
Incredible Melting Man '77
The Incredible Petrified World '58
The Incredible Two-Headed Transplant '71
Incredibly Strange Creatures Who Stopped Living and Became Mixed-Up Zombies '63
Incubus '82
Infra-Man '76

Inhumanoid '96
Inner Sanctum '91
Inseminoid '80
Invasion of the Animal People '62
Invasion of the Blood Farmers '72
Invasion of the Body Stealers '69
Invasion of the Girl Snatchers '73
Invincible Barbarian '83
Invincible Gladiators '64
The Invisible Maniac '90
Invitation to Hell '82
The Island '80
Island Claw '80
Island of Lost Girls '68
It Waits '05
It's Alive 2: It Lives Again '78
It's All Gone, Pete Tong '04
It's Not the Size That Counts '74
It's Pat: The Movie '94
Jack Frost 2: Revenge of the Mutant Killer Snowman '00
Jason Goes to Hell: The Final Friday '93
Jaws of Satan '81
The Jazz Singer '80
The Jerky Boys '95
Joy Sticks '83
Junior '86
Just for the Hell of It '68
Kidnapped '87
Kill Alex Kill '76
Kill Factor '78
Killer Party '86
Killers from Space '54
Killing Moon '00
Klima, Queen of the Amazons '75
King of Kong Island '78
The King of the Kickboxers '91
King of the Zombies '41
King's Ransom '91
Lake Placid 2 '07
Lap Dancing '95
Larry the Cable Guy: Health Inspector '06
Las Vegas Serial Killer '86
The Las Vegas Story '52
Laserblast '78
Last Days of Planet Earth '74
Last House on Dead End Street '77
Last Mercenary '84
The Last Season '87
The Last Slumber Party '87
The Last Woman on Earth '61
Lauderdale '89
A Legacy for Leonette '85
Legacy of Horror '78
Leprechaun '93
Leprechaun 4: In Space '96
Leprechaun 5: In the Hood '99
Leprechaun 6: Back 2 Tha Hood '03
Lethal '04
The Lifetaker '89
Link '86
Lipstick '76
Lisa and the Devil '75
Lisztomania '75
Little Darlings '80
Loaded Guns '75
The Loch Ness Horror '82
The Lone Runner '88
The Lonely Lady '83
The Long Weekend '05
The Longshot '86
Lords of the Deep '89
Love Thrill Murders '71
The Loves of Hercules '60
Love's Savage Fury '79
Lurkers '88
Lust for Dracula '04
Luther the Geek '90
Machined '06
Mack the Knife '89
Mad About You '90
The Mad Bomber '72

Mad Doctor of Blood Island '68
Mad Dog '84
Mad Youth '40
Madigan's Millions '67
Mama Dracula '80
A Man Called Rage '84
Man from Deep River '77
Maniac '34
Maniac '80
Maniac Nurses Find Ecstasy '94
Mannequin 2: On the Move '91
Manos, the Hands of Fate '66
Mardi Gras Massacre '78
Maslin Beach '97
A Matter of Time '76
Maxim Xul '91
Maximum Thrust '88
Maya '82
Meatballs 3 '87
The Meateater '79
Megaforce '82
Memnon '04
Mesa of Lost Women '52
Meteor '79
Midnight Cabaret '90
The Mighty Peking Man '77
Mindhunters '05
Mirror Wars: Reflection One '05
Mr. Jingles '06
Mistress of the Apes '79
Mom '89
Mondo Trasho '69
Mongrel '83
Monsignor '82
Monster a Go-Go! '65
Monster Dog '82
The Monster of Piedras Blancas '57
Moonshine Mountain '64
Mortuary '05
Moses '76
Motor Psycho '65
Mountain of the Cannibal God '79
Mountaintop Motel Massacre '86
Mummy & Curse of the Jackal '67
Murderer's Keep '88
Murderlust '86
Mutant Hunt '87
Mutants in Paradise '84
The Mutilator '85
My African Adventure '87
My First Wedding '04
My Therapist '84
Myra Breckinridge '70
Nail Gun Massacre '86
Naked Cage '86
The Naked Flame '68
Naked Vengeance '85
Naked Youth '59
The Narcotics Story '58
The New Gladiators '83
New Year's Evil '78
New York Ripper '82
The Night God Screamed '71
A Night in Heaven '83
Night of the Bloody Apes '68
Night of the Bloody Transplant '70
Night of the Demon '80
Night of the Demons 3 '97
Night of the Ghouls '59
Night of the Living Babes '87
Night of the Sharks '87
Night of the Sorcerers '70
Night Patrol '85
Night Train Murders '75
Night Train to Terror '84
Nightmare '82

Nightmare Sisters '87
Nightstalker '81
Nine Deaths of the Ninja '85
1990: The Bronx Warriors '83
Ninja Champion '80
Ninja Fantasy '80s
Ninja Hunt '80s
No One Cries Forever '85
No Way Back '90
Nobody's Perfekt '79
Nocturna '79
Norman's Awesome Experience '88
Nude on the Moon '61
A Nymphoid Barbarian in Dinosaur Hell '94
The Occultist '89
Ocean Drive Weekend '85
Oddballs '84
On Deadly Ground '94
One Brief Summer '70
One Down, Two to Go! '82
One of Them '03
One Russian Summer '73
Orca '77
Orgy of the Dead '65
The Other Side of Midnight '77
Parasite '82
Party Favors '89
People Who Own the Dark '75
Perfect Timing '84
Phobia '80
Pieces '83
Pink Motel '82
Plan 9 from Outer Space '56
Please Don't Eat My Mother '72
Police Academy 5: Assignment Miami Beach '88
Prehistoric Bimbos in Armageddon City '93
Prehistoric Women '50
Pretty Smart '87
Prettykill '87
The Prime Time '60
Private Manoeuvres '83
The Psychic '68
Psychos in Love '87
Puff, Puff, Pass '06
Pulsebeat '85
The Puma Man '80
Python 2 '02
Queen of Outer Space '58
Quick, Let's Get Married '71
Rabid Grannies '89
Raise the Titanic '80
The Rape of the Sabines '61
Rat Pfink a Boo-Boo '66
The Rats Are Coming! The Werewolves Are Here! '72
Razorteeth '05
Rebel Vixens '69
The Red Menace '49
The Return '80
Return to Frogtown '92
Revenge '86
Ridin' the Lone Trail '37
Ring of Darkness '04
Ringmaster '98
The Ripper '85
The Robot vs. the Aztec Mummy '59
Rocket Attack U.S.A. '58
Roller Boogie '79
Rooster: Spurs of Death! '83
Rumpelstiltskin '96
Sabretooth '01
Sahara '83
Sanctimony '01
Santa Claus '59
Sasquatch '76
Satan's Cheerleaders '77
Satan's Touch '84
Satanwar '79
Savage! '73
Savage Is Loose '74
Savage Weekend '80
The Scarlet Letter '95
Scarlet Spear '54
Score '95
Scream Bloody Murder '72
Scream of the Demon Lover '71
Screen Test '85

Screwed '00
Secrets of Sweet Sixteen '74
See Spot Run '01
Senior Week '88
Sensual Partners '87
The Sensuous Teenager '70
Sgt. Kabukiman N.Y.P.D. '94
Sgt. Pepper's Lonely Hearts Club Band '78
The Serpent and the Rainbow '87
The Severed Arm '73
Sex Adventures of the Three Musketeers '71
Sex, Drugs, and Rock-n-Roll '84
The Sex Machine '75
Sex on the Run '78
Sextette '78
She Came on the Bus '69
She Demons '58
She-Devils on Wheels '68
Sheena '84
Showgirls '95
Shriek of the Mutilated '74
Sidney Sheldon's Bloodline '79
Sincerely Yours '56
Single White Female 2: The Psycho '05
The Sinister Urge '60
Skinned Alive '89
Skullduggery '79
Sky Pirates '87
Slashdance '89
The Slasher '72
The Slaughter of the Vampires '62
Slaughterhouse '87
Slaughterhouse Rock '88
The Slayer '82
Sledgehammer '83
Sleepaway Camp 3: Teenage Wasteland '89
The Slime People '63
Slithis '78
Sloane '84
Slugs '87
Slumber Party Massacre 2 '87
Slumber Party Massacre 3 '90
Smashing Time '67
Smooth Talker '90
The Snow Creature '54
Social Intercourse '01
Something Weird '68
Sonny Boy '87
Sorceress '82
Sorority House Massacre '86
Sorority House Massacre 2: Nighty Nightmare '92
Soul Hustler '76
Soul Survivors '01
South Seas Massacre '74
Space Monster '64
Space Riders '83
Spaced Out '80
Spare Parts '79
Spasms '82
Sphinx '81
Splatter University '84
Splitz '84
Spookies '85
The Sporting Club '72
The Squeeze '87
Squeeze Play '79
SS Girls '77
Stalked '99
State Property 2 '05
Stepsisters '74
Stewardess School '86
Stone Cold '91
Stormcatch '87
The Strangeness '85
The Stranger from Venus '54
Street Hero '84
Street Hunter '90
Street People '76
Street Trash '87
Street Warriors '87
Street Warriors, Part 2 '87
Strike Commando '87

Stroker Ace '83
Stryker '83
The Stud '78
Student Affairs '88
Student Bodies '81
Sugar Cookies '77
Summer School Teachers '75
Sunnyside '79
Sunset Strip '91
Superbabies: Baby Geniuses 2 '04
Superchick '71
Superfly T.N.T. '73
Supersonic Man '78
Surf 2 '84
Surfacing '84
Survival Zone '84
Sweater Girls '78
Sweet Insanity '06
Sweet Murder '93
Sweet Spirits '80s
Sweet Trash '70
Switchblade Sisters '75
Tarzan, the Ape Man '81
Teenage Monster '57
Teenage Mother '67
Teenage Strangler '64
Teenage Zombies '58
Teenagers from Outer Space '59
The Telephone '87
The Temp '93
10 Violent Women '79
Tender Flesh '97
Tentacles '77
The Terror '97
Terror House '97
Terror in Beverly Hills '90
Terror in the Wax Museum '73
Terror on Tour '83
The Terronauts '67
Terrovision '86
Test Tube Babies '48
The Texas Chainsaw Massacre 2 '86
The Texas Chainsaw Massacre: The Beginning '06
They Bite '95
They Saved Hitler's Brain '64
They Went That-a-Way & That-a-Way '78
They're Playing with Fire '84
Thieves of Fortune '89
The Thirsty Dead '74
This Stuff'll Kill Ya! '71
Three on a Meathook '72
Three Strikes '00
Threesome '94
The Thrill Killers '65
Throne of Fire '82
Tintorera... Tiger Shark '78
TNT Jackson '75
To All a Goodnight '80
Tomb of Torture '65
Tomboy '85
Tomcats '01
The Tormentors '71
Torso '73
Tower of Evil '72
Treasure of the Moon Goddess '88
The Trial of Billy Jack '74
Trick or Treats '82
Troma's War '88
Turbulence 3: Heavy Metal '00
Twice Dead '88
Twilight People '72
Two Lost Worlds '50
2020 Texas Gladiators '85
The Uncanny '78
Under the Rainbow '81
Underclassman '05
Underground Aces '80
The Uninvited '88
Unknown Powers '80
Vampire Night '00
Vampire Raiders—Ninja Queen '89
Vampire Time Travelers '98
Vasectomy: A Delicate Matter '86
Vegas in Space '94
Vengeance Is Mine '74

▲ = rated three bones or higher

Venom '82
Vice Academy 3 '91
Vice Squad '82
The Video Dead '87
Video Wars '84
Vigilante '83
Viglated '84
Violent Ones '68
The Violent Years '56
Viva Knievel '77
Voyage to the Planet of Prehistoric Women '68
Vulcan God of Fire '62
Wacko '83
Waitress '81
Waiting '05
Wanted: Babysitter '75
Warlords from Hell '87
'Warrior of the Lost World '84
Warriors of the Apocalypse '85
Warriors of the Wasteland '83
Weekend with the Babysitter '70
Werewolves on Wheels '71
Wet and Wild Summer '92
When Lightning Strikes '34
When Nature Calls '85
Where the Boys Are '84, '84
White Pongo '45
Wholly Moses! '80
The Wicker Man '06
The Wild Beasts '85
Wild Guitar '62
Wild Ones on Wheels '62
Wild Orchid 2: Two Shades of Blue '92
Wild Riders '71
Wild Wheels '69
Wing Commander '99
Wired to Kill '86
Witchcraft '88
The Witching '72
Witless Protection '08
Woman Hunt '72
Women in Cell Block 7 '77
Women in Fury '34
Women of the Prehistoric Planet '66
Women Unchained '72
Women's Prison Massacre '85
Woodchipper Massacre '89
The World Is Full of Married Men '80
The Worm Eaters '77
Wrestling Women vs. the Aztec Mummy '59
Xanadu '80
Xtro '83
The Yesterday Machine '63
You Light Up My Life '77
Young Tiger '74
Youth Aflame '44
Zandalee '91
Zero Boys '86
Zombie Nightmare '86
Zombies of Moratau '57

Wyatt Earp
Cheyenne Autumn '64
Four Eyes and Six Guns '93
Gunfight at the O.K. Corral '57 ▲
Hour of the Gun '67
My Darling Clementine '46 ▲
Sunset '88
Tombstone '93 ▲
Wyatt Earp '94
Wyatt Earp: Return to Tombstone '94

Zorro
The Bold Caballero '36
Don Q., Son of Zorro '25
The Legend of Zorro '05
Mark of Zorro '20 ▲
The Mark of Zorro '40 ▲
The Mask of Zorro '98 ▲
The Naked Sword of Zorro '69
The Secret of El Zorro '57
Son of Zorro '47
Zorro '74
Zorro Rides Again '37
Zorro, the Gay Blade '81
Zorro's Black Whip '44
Zorro's Fighting Legion '39

Zucker/Abrahams/Zucker
Airplane! '80 ▲
Kentucky Fried Movie '77 ▲
The Naked Gun: From the Files of Police Squad '88 ▲
Naked Gun 33 1/3: The Final Insult '94
Naked Gun 2 1/2: The Smell of Fear '91
Top Secret! '84 ▲

▲ = rated three bones or higher

The Awards Index lists films honored (or dishonored, in some cases) by nine national and international award bodies, representing over 100 categories of recognition. This information can also be found in the reviews, following the credits. Only features available on video and reviewed in the main section are listed in this index; movies not yet released on video are not covered here. As award-winning and nominated films find their way to video, they will be added to this index. Nominations are once again covered in this index; they are not covered in the individual reviews. The awards covered include:

Academy Awards
British Academy of Film and Television Arts
Directors Guild of America
Golden Globe
Golden Raspberries
Independent Spirit Awards
National Film Registry
Screen Actors Guild Awards
Writers Guild of America

ACADEMY AWARDS

ACTOR

1928
★ Emil Jannings/Last Command
Charlie Chaplin/The Circus

1929
Chester Morris/Alibi

1930
★ George Arliss/Disraeli
Wallace Beery/The Big House
Ronald Colman/Bulldog Drummond
Ronald Colman/Condemned

1931
★ Lionel Barrymore/A Free Soul
Richard Dix/Cimarron
Adolphe Menjou/The Front Page

1932
★ Wallace Beery/The Champ
Fredric March/Dr. Jekyll and Mr. Hyde
Alfred Lunt/The Guardsman

1933
★ Charles Laughton/The Private Life of Henry VIII
Paul Muni/I Am a Fugitive from a Chain Gang

1934
★ Clark Gable/It Happened One Night
William Powell/The Thin Man

1935
★ Victor McLaglen/The Informer
Clark Gable/Mutiny on the Bounty
Charles Laughton/Mutiny on the Bounty
Franchot Tone/Mutiny on the Bounty

1936
★ Paul Muni/The Story of Louis Pasteur
Gary Cooper/Mr. Deeds Goes to Town
Walter Huston/Dodsworth
William Powell/My Man Godfrey
Spencer Tracy/San Francisco

1937
★ Spencer Tracy/Captains Courageous
Charles Boyer/Conquest
Fredric March/A Star is Born
Robert Montgomery/Night Must Fall
Paul Muni/The Life of Emile Zola

1938
★ Spencer Tracy/Boys Town
Charles Boyer/Algiers
James Cagney/Angels with Dirty Faces
Robert Donat/The Citadel
Leslie Howard/Pygmalion

1939
★ Robert Donat/Goodbye, Mr. Chips
Clark Gable/Gone with the Wind
Laurence Olivier/Wuthering Heights
Mickey Rooney/Babes in Arms
James Stewart/Mr. Smith Goes to Washington

1940
★ James Stewart/The Philadelphia Story
Charlie Chaplin/The Great Dictator
Henry Fonda/The Grapes of Wrath
Raymond Massey/Abe Lincoln in Illinois
Laurence Olivier/Rebecca

1941
★ Gary Cooper/Sergeant York
Cary Grant/Penny Serenade
Walter Huston/The Devil & Daniel Webster
Robert Montgomery/Here Comes Mr. Jordan
Orson Welles/Citizen Kane

1942
★ James Cagney/Yankee Doodle Dandy
Ronald Colman/Random Harvest
Gary Cooper/The Pride of the Yankees
Walter Pidgeon/Mrs. Miniver

1943
★ Paul Lukas/Watch on the Rhine
Humphrey Bogart/Casablanca
Gary Cooper/For Whom the Bell Tolls
Walter Pidgeon/Madame Curie
Mickey Rooney/The Human Comedy

1944
★ Bing Crosby/Going My Way
Charles Boyer/Gaslight
Barry Fitzgerald/Going My Way
Cary Grant/None But the Lonely Heart
Alexander Knox/Wilson

1945
★ Ray Milland/The Lost Weekend
Bing Crosby/The Bells of St. Mary's
Gene Kelly/Anchors Aweigh
Gregory Peck/The Keys of the Kingdom
Cornel Wilde/A Song to Remember

1946
★ Fredric March/The Best Years of Our Lives
Laurence Olivier/Henry V
Larry Parks/The Jolson Story
Gregory Peck/The Yearling
James Stewart/It's a Wonderful Life

1947
★ Ronald Colman/A Double Life
John Garfield/Body and Soul
Gregory Peck/Gentleman's Agreement
William Powell/Life with Father

1948
★ Laurence Olivier/Hamlet
Lew Ayres/Johnny Belinda
Montgomery Clift/The Search
Clifton Webb/Sitting Pretty

1949
★ Broderick Crawford/All the King's Men
Kirk Douglas/Champion
Gregory Peck/Twelve o'Clock High
John Wayne/Sands of Iwo Jima

1950
★ Jose Ferrer/Cyrano de Bergerac
Louis Calhern/The Magnificent Yankee
William Holden/Sunset Boulevard
James Stewart/Harvey
Spencer Tracy/Father of the Bride

1951
★ Humphrey Bogart/The African Queen
Marlon Brando/A Streetcar Named Desire
Montgomery Clift/A Place in the Sun

1952
★ Gary Cooper/High Noon
Marlon Brando/Viva Zapata!
Kirk Douglas/The Bad and the Beautiful
Jose Ferrer/Moulin Rouge
Alec Guinness/The Lavender Hill Mob

1953
★ William Holden/Stalag 17
Marlon Brando/Julius Caesar
Richard Burton/The Robe
Montgomery Clift/From Here to Eternity
Burt Lancaster/From Here to Eternity

1954
★ Marlon Brando/On the Waterfront
Humphrey Bogart/The Caine Mutiny
Bing Crosby/Country Girl
James Mason/A Star is Born

1955
★ Ernest Borgnine/Marty
James Cagney/Love Me or Leave Me
James Dean/East of Eden
Frank Sinatra/The Man with the Golden Arm
Spencer Tracy/Bad Day at Black Rock

1956
★ Yul Brynner/The King and I
James Dean/Giant
Kirk Douglas/Lust for Life
Rock Hudson/Giant
Laurence Olivier/Richard III

1957
★ Alec Guinness/The Bridge on the River Kwai
Marlon Brando/Sayonara
Charles Laughton/Witness for the Prosecution

1958
★ David Niven/Separate Tables
Tony Curtis/The Defiant Ones
Paul Newman/Cat on a Hot Tin Roof
Sidney Poitier/The Defiant Ones

1959
★ Charlton Heston/Ben-Hur
Laurence Harvey/Room at the Top
Jack Lemmon/Some Like It Hot
Paul Muni/The Last Angry Man
James Stewart/Anatomy of a Murder

1960
★ Burt Lancaster/Elmer Gantry
Jack Lemmon/The Apartment
Laurence Olivier/The Entertainer
Spencer Tracy/Inherit the Wind

1961
★ Maximilian Schell/Judgment at Nuremberg
Charles Boyer/Fanny
Paul Newman/The Hustler
Spencer Tracy/Judgment at Nuremberg

★ = winner

Academy Awards

Stuart Whitman/The Mark

1962
- ★ Gregory Peck/To Kill a Mockingbird
- Burt Lancaster/Birdman of Alcatraz
- Jack Lemmon/Days of Wine and Roses
- Marcello Mastroianni/Divorce—Italian Style
- Peter O'Toole/Lawrence of Arabia

1963
- ★ Sidney Poitier/Lilies of the Field
- Albert Finney/Tom Jones
- Richard Harris/This Sporting Life
- Rex Harrison/Cleopatra
- Paul Newman/Hud

1964
- ★ Rex Harrison/My Fair Lady
- Richard Burton/Becket
- Peter O'Toole/Becket
- Anthony Quinn/Zorba the Greek
- Peter Sellers/Dr. Strangelove, or: How I Learned to Stop Worrying and Love the Bomb

1965
- ★ Lee Marvin/Cat Ballou
- Richard Burton/The Spy Who Came in from the Cold
- Laurence Olivier/Othello
- Rod Steiger/The Pawnbroker
- Oskar Werner/Ship of Fools

1966
- ★ Paul Scofield/A Man for All Seasons
- Alan Arkin/The Russians Are Coming, the Russians Are Coming
- Richard Burton/Who's Afraid of Virginia Woolf?
- Michael Caine/Alfie
- Steve McQueen/The Sand Pebbles

1967
- ★ Rod Steiger/In the Heat of the Night
- Warren Beatty/Bonnie & Clyde
- Dustin Hoffman/The Graduate
- Paul Newman/Cool Hand Luke
- Spencer Tracy/Guess Who's Coming to Dinner

1968
- ★ Cliff Robertson/Charly
- Alan Arkin/The Heart Is a Lonely Hunter
- Alan Bates/The Fixer
- Ron Moody/Oliver!
- Peter O'Toole/The Lion in Winter

1969
- ★ John Wayne/True Grit
- Richard Burton/Anne of the Thousand Days
- Dustin Hoffman/Midnight Cowboy
- Peter O'Toole/Goodbye, Mr. Chips
- Jon Voight/Midnight Cowboy

1970
- ★ George C. Scott/Patton
- Melvyn Douglas/I Never Sang for My Father
- James Earl Jones/The Great White Hope
- Jack Nicholson/Five Easy Pieces
- Ryan O'Neal/Love Story

1971
- ★ Gene Hackman/The French Connection
- Peter Finch/Sunday, Bloody Sunday
- Walter Matthau/Kotch
- George C. Scott/The Hospital

Chaim Topol/Fiddler on the Roof

1972
- ★ Marlon Brando/The Godfather
- Michael Caine/Sleuth
- Peter O'Toole/The Ruling Class
- Laurence Olivier/Sleuth
- Paul Winfield/Sounder

1973
- ★ Jack Lemmon/Save the Tiger
- Marlon Brando/Last Tango in Paris
- Jack Nicholson/The Last Detail
- Al Pacino/Serpico
- Robert Redford/The Sting

1974
- ★ Art Carney/Harry and Tonto
- Albert Finney/Murder on the Orient Express
- Dustin Hoffman/Lenny
- Jack Nicholson/Chinatown
- Al Pacino/The Godfather, Part 2

1975
- ★ Jack Nicholson/One Flew Over the Cuckoo's Nest
- Walter Matthau/The Sunshine Boys
- Al Pacino/Dog Day Afternoon
- Maximilian Schell/The Man in the Glass Booth
- James Whitmore/Give 'Em Hell, Harry!

1976
- ★ Peter Finch/Network
- Robert De Niro/Taxi Driver
- Giancarlo Giannini/Seven Beauties
- William Holden/Network
- Sylvester Stallone/Rocky

1977
- ★ Richard Dreyfuss/The Goodbye Girl
- Woody Allen/Annie Hall
- Richard Burton/Equus
- Marcello Mastroianni/A Special Day
- John Travolta/Saturday Night Fever

1978
- ★ Jon Voight/Coming Home
- Warren Beatty/Heaven Can Wait
- Gary Busey/The Buddy Holly Story
- Robert De Niro/The Deer Hunter
- Laurence Olivier/The Boys from Brazil

1979
- ★ Dustin Hoffman/Kramer vs. Kramer
- Jack Lemmon/The China Syndrome
- Al Pacino/And Justice for All
- Roy Scheider/All That Jazz
- Peter Sellers/Being There

1980
- ★ Robert De Niro/Raging Bull
- Robert Duvall/The Great Santini
- John Hurt/The Elephant Man
- Jack Lemmon/Tribute
- Peter O'Toole/The Stunt Man

1981
- ★ Henry Fonda/On Golden Pond
- Warren Beatty/Reds
- Burt Lancaster/Atlantic City
- Dudley Moore/Arthur
- Paul Newman/Absence of Malice

1982
- ★ Ben Kingsley/Gandhi
- Dustin Hoffman/Tootsie
- Jack Lemmon/Missing
- Paul Newman/The Verdict
- Peter O'Toole/My Favorite Year

1983
- ★ Robert Duvall/Tender Mercies
- Michael Caine/Educating Rita
- Tom Conti/Reuben, Reuben
- Tom Courtenay/The Dresser
- Albert Finney/The Dresser

1984
- ★ F. Murray Abraham/Amadeus
- Jeff Bridges/Starman
- Albert Finney/Under the Volcano
- Tom Hulce/Amadeus
- Sam Waterston/The Killing Fields

1985
- ★ William Hurt/Kiss of the Spider Woman
- Harrison Ford/Witness
- James Garner/Murphy's Romance
- Jack Nicholson/Prizzi's Honor
- Jon Voight/Runaway Train

1986
- ★ Paul Newman/The Color of Money
- Dexter Gordon/Round Midnight
- Bob Hoskins/Mona Lisa
- William Hurt/Children of a Lesser God
- James Woods/Salvador

1987
- ★ Michael Douglas/Wall Street
- William Hurt/Broadcast News
- Marcello Mastroianni/Dark Eyes
- Jack Nicholson/Ironweed
- Robin Williams/Good Morning, Vietnam

1988
- ★ Dustin Hoffman/Rain Man
- Gene Hackman/Mississippi Burning
- Tom Hanks/Big
- Edward James Olmos/Stand and Deliver
- Max von Sydow/Pelle the Conqueror

1989
- ★ Daniel Day-Lewis/My Left Foot
- Kenneth Branagh/Henry V
- Tom Cruise/Born on the Fourth of July
- Morgan Freeman/Driving Miss Daisy
- Robin Williams/Dead Poets Society

1990
- ★ Jeremy Irons/Reversal of Fortune
- Kevin Costner/Dances with Wolves
- Robert De Niro/Awakenings
- Gerard Depardieu/Cyrano de Bergerac
- Richard Harris/The Field

1991
- ★ Anthony Hopkins/The Silence of the Lambs
- Warren Beatty/Bugsy
- Robert De Niro/Cape Fear
- Nick Nolte/The Prince of Tides
- Robin Williams/The Fisher King

1992
- ★ Al Pacino/Scent of a Woman
- Robert Downey, Jr./Chaplin
- Clint Eastwood/Unforgiven
- Stephen Real/The Crying Game
- Denzel Washington/Malcolm X

1993
- ★ Tom Hanks/Philadelphia
- Daniel Day-Lewis/In the Name of the Father
- Laurence Fishburne/What's Love Got to Do with It?
- Anthony Hopkins/The Remains of the Day
- Liam Neeson/Schindler's List

1994
- ★ Tom Hanks/Forrest Gump
- Morgan Freeman/The Shawshank Redemption
- Nigel Hawthorne/The Madness of King George
- Paul Newman/Nobody's Fool
- John Travolta/Pulp Fiction

1995
- ★ Nicolas Cage/Leaving Las Vegas
- Richard Dreyfuss/Mr. Holland's Opus
- Anthony Hopkins/Nixon
- Sean Penn/Dead Man Walking
- Massimo Troisi/The Postman

1996
- ★ Geoffrey Rush/Shine
- Tom Cruise/Jerry Maguire
- Ralph Fiennes/The English Patient
- Woody Harrelson/The People vs. Larry Flynt
- Billy Bob Thornton/Sling Blade

1997
- ★ Jack Nicholson/As Good As It Gets
- Matt Damon/Good Will Hunting
- Robert Duvall/The Apostle
- Peter Fonda/Ulee's Gold
- Dustin Hoffman/Wag the Dog

1998
- ★ Roberto Benigni/Life Is Beautiful
- Tom Hanks/Saving Private Ryan
- Ian McKellen/Gods and Monsters
- Nick Nolte/Affliction
- Edward Norton/American History X

1999
- ★ Kevin Spacey/American Beauty
- Russell Crowe/The Insider
- Richard Farnsworth/The Straight Story
- Sean Penn/Sweet and Lowdown
- Denzel Washington/The Hurricane

2000
- ★ Russell Crowe/Gladiator
- Javier Bardem/Before Night Falls
- Tom Hanks/Cast Away
- Ed Harris/Pollock
- Geoffrey Rush/Quills

2001
- ★ Denzel Washington/Training Day
- Russell Crowe/A Beautiful Mind
- Sean Penn/I Am Sam
- Will Smith/Ali
- Tom Wilkinson/In the Bedroom

2002
- ★ Adrien Brody/The Pianist
- Nicolas Cage/Adaptation
- Michael Caine/The Quiet American
- Daniel Day-Lewis/Gangs of New York
- Jack Nicholson/About Schmidt

2003
- ★ Sean Penn/Mystic River
- Johnny Depp/Pirates of the Caribbean: The Curse of the Black Pearl
- Ben Kingsley/House of Sand and Fog
- Jude Law/Cold Mountain
- Bill Murray/Lost in Translation

2004
- ★ Jamie Foxx/Ray
- Don Cheadle/Hotel Rwanda
- Johnny Depp/Finding Neverland
- Leonardo DiCaprio/The Aviator
- Clint Eastwood/Million Dollar Baby

2005
- ★ Philip Seymour Hoffman/Capote
- Terrence Howard/Hustle & Flow
- Heath Ledger/Brokeback Mountain
- Joaquin Rafael (Leaf) Phoenix/Walk the Line
- David Strathairn/Good Night, and Good Luck

2006
- ★ Forest Whitaker/The Last King of Scotland
- Leonardo DiCaprio/Blood Diamond
- Ryan Gosling/Half Nelson
- Peter O'Toole/Venus
- Will Smith/The Pursuit of Happyness

2007
- ★ Daniel Day-Lewis/There Will Be Blood
- George Clooney/Michael Clayton
- Johnny Depp/Sweeney Todd: The Demon Barber of Fleet Street
- Tommy Lee Jones/In the Valley of Elah
- Viggo Mortensen/Eastern Promises

ACTOR— SUPPORTING

1936
- ★ Walter Brennan/Come and Get It
- Mischa Auer/My Man Godfrey
- Stuart Erwin/Pigskin Parade
- Basil Rathbone/Romeo and Juliet
- Akim Tamiroff/The General Died at Dawn

1937
- ★ Joseph Schildkraut/The Life of Emile Zola
- Ralph Bellamy/The Awful Truth
- Thomas Mitchell/The Hurricane
- H.B. Warner/Lost Horizon
- Roland Young/Topper

1938
- John Garfield/Four Daughters
- Gene Lockhart/Algiers
- Robert Morley/Marie Antoinette

1939
- ★ Thomas Mitchell/Stagecoach
- Brian Aherne/Juarez
- Harry Carey, Sr./Mr. Smith Goes to Washington
- Brian Donlevy/Beau Geste
- Claude Rains/Mr. Smith Goes to Washington

1940
- ★ Walter Brennan/The Westerner
- Albert Bassermann/Foreign Correspondent
- William Gargan/They Knew What They Wanted
- Jack Oakie/The Great Dictator
- James Stephenson/The Letter

1941
- ★ Donald Crisp/How Green Was My Valley
- Walter Brennan/Sergeant York
- Charles Coburn/The Devil & Miss Jones
- James Gleason/Here Comes Mr. Jordan
- Sydney Greenstreet/The Maltese Falcon

1942
- ★ Van Heflin/Johnny Eager
- William Bendix/Wake Island
- Walter Huston/Yankee Doodle Dandy
- Frank Morgan/Tortilla Flat
- Henry Travers/Mrs. Miniver

1943
- ★ Charles Coburn/The More the Merrier
- Charles Bickford/The Song of Bernadette
- J. Carrol Naish/Sahara
- Claude Rains/Casablanca
- Akim Tamiroff/For Whom the Bell Tolls

1944
- ★ Barry Fitzgerald/Going My Way
- Hume Cronyn/The Seventh Cross
- Claude Rains/Mr. Skeffington
- Clifton Webb/Laura
- Monty Woolley/Since You Went Away

1945
- ★ James Dunn/A Tree Grows in Brooklyn
- Michael Chekhov/Spellbound
- John Dall/The Corn Is Green

1946
- ★ Harold Russell/The Best Years of Our Lives
- William Demarest/The Jolson Story
- Claude Rains/Notorious
- Clifton Webb/The Razor's Edge

1947
- ★ Edmund Gwenn/Miracle on 34th Street
- Charles Bickford/The Farmer's Daughter
- Robert Ryan/Crossfire
- Richard Widmark/Kiss of Death

1948
- ★ Walter Huston/Treasure of the Sierra Madre
- Charles Bickford/Johnny Belinda
- Jose Ferrer/Joan of Arc
- Oscar Homolka/I Remember Mama

1949
- ★ Dean Jagger/Twelve o'Clock High
- John Ireland/All the King's Men
- Arthur Kennedy/Champion
- Ralph Richardson/The Heiress
- James Whitmore/Battleground

1950
- ★ George Sanders/All About Eve
- Jeff Chandler/Broken Arrow
- Sam Jaffe/The Asphalt Jungle
- Erich von Stroheim/Sunset Boulevard

1951
- ★ Karl Malden/A Streetcar Named Desire

★ = winner

1952
Leo Genn/Quo Vadis
Peter Ustinov/Quo Vadis
★ Anthony Quinn/Viva Zapata!
Arthur Hunnicutt/The Big Sky
Victor McLaglen/The Quiet Man
Jack Palance/Sudden Fear

1953
★ Frank Sinatra/From Here to Eternity
Eddie Albert/Roman Holiday
Robert Strauss/Stalag 17
Brandon de Wilde/Shane

1954
★ Edmond O'Brien/The Barefoot Contessa
Lee J. Cobb/On the Waterfront
Karl Malden/On the Waterfront
Rod Steiger/On the Waterfront
Tom Tully/The Caine Mutiny

1955
★ Jack Lemmon/Mister Roberts
Arthur Kennedy/Trial
Joe Mantell/Marty
Sal Mineo/Rebel without a Cause
Arthur O'Connell/Picnic

1956
★ Anthony Quinn/Lust for Life
Don Murray/Bus Stop
Anthony Perkins/Friendly Persuasion
Robert Stack/Written on the Wind

1957
★ Red Buttons/Sayonara
Sessue Hayakawa/The Bridge on the River Kwai
Arthur Kennedy/Peyton Place
Russ Tamblyn/Peyton Place

1958
★ Burl Ives/The Big Country
Theodore Bikel/The Defiant Ones
Lee J. Cobb/The Brothers Karamazov
Arthur Kennedy/Some Came Running
Gig Young/Teacher's Pet

1959
★ Hugh Griffith/Ben-Hur
Arthur O'Connell/Anatomy of a Murder
George C. Scott/Anatomy of a Murder
Robert Vaughn/The Young Philadelphians
Ed Wynn/The Diary of Anne Frank

1960
★ Peter Ustinov/Spartacus
Jack Kruschen/The Apartment
Sal Mineo/Exodus
Chill Wills/The Alamo

1961
★ George Chakiris/West Side Story
Montgomery Clift/Judgment at Nuremberg
Peter Falk/Pocketful of Miracles
Jackie Gleason/The Hustler
George C. Scott/The Hustler

1962
★ Ed Begley, Sr./Sweet Bird of Youth
Victor Buono/What Ever Happened to Baby Jane?
Telly Savalas/Birdman of Alcatraz
Omar Sharif/Lawrence of Arabia
Terence Stamp/Billy Budd

1963
★ Melvyn Douglas/Hud
Bobby Darin/Captain Newman, M.D.
Hugh Griffith/Tom Jones
John Huston/The Cardinal

1964
★ Peter Ustinov/Topkapi
John Gielgud/Becket
Stanley Holloway/My Fair Lady
Edmond O'Brien/Seven Days in May
Lee Tracy/The Best Man

1965
★ Martin Balsam/A Thousand Clowns
Ian Bannen/The Flight of the Phoenix
Tom Courtenay/Doctor Zhivago
Michael Dunn/Ship of Fools
Frank Finlay/Othello

1966
★ Walter Matthau/The Fortune Cookie
Mako/The Sand Pebbles
James Mason/Georgy Girl
George Segal/Who's Afraid of Virginia Woolf?
Robert Shaw/A Man for All Seasons

1967
★ George Kennedy/Cool Hand Luke
John Cassavetes/The Dirty Dozen
Gene Hackman/Bonnie & Clyde
Cecil Kellaway/Guess Who's Coming to Dinner
Michael J. Pollard/Bonnie & Clyde

1968
★ Jack Albertson/The Subject Was Roses
Seymour Cassel/Faces
Daniel Massey/Star!
Jack Wild/Oliver!
Gene Wilder/The Producers

1969
★ Gig Young/They Shoot Horses, Don't They?
Rupert Crosse/The Reivers
Elliott Gould/Bob & Carol & Ted & Alice
Jack Nicholson/Easy Rider
Anthony Quayle/Anne of the Thousand Days

1970
★ John Mills/Ryan's Daughter
Richard S. Castellano/Lovers and Other Strangers
Chief Dan George/Little Big Man
Gene Hackman/I Never Sang for My Father
John Marley/Love Story

1971
★ Ben Johnson/The Last Picture Show
Jeff Bridges/The Last Picture Show
Leonard Frey/Fiddler on the Roof
Richard Jaeckel/Sometimes a Great Notion
Roy Scheider/The French Connection

1972
★ Joel Grey/Cabaret
Eddie Albert/The Heartbreak Kid
James Caan/The Godfather
Robert Duvall/The Godfather
Al Pacino/The Godfather

1973
★ John Houseman/The Paper Chase
Vincent Gardenia/Bang the Drum Slowly
Jack Gilford/Save the Tiger
Jason Miller/The Exorcist
Randy Quaid/The Last Detail

1974
★ Robert De Niro/The Godfather, Part 2
Fred Astaire/The Towering Inferno
Jeff Bridges/Thunderbolt & Lightfoot
Michael V. Gazzo/The Godfather, Part 2
Lee Strasberg/The Godfather, Part 2

1975
★ George Burns/The Sunshine Boys
Brad Dourif/One Flew Over the Cuckoo's Nest
Burgess Meredith/The Day of the Locust
Chris Sarandon/Dog Day Afternoon
Jack Warden/Shampoo

1976
★ Jason Robards, Jr./All the President's Men
Ned Beatty/Network
Burgess Meredith/Rocky
Laurence Olivier/Marathon Man
Burt Young/Rocky

1977
★ Jason Robards, Jr./Julia
Mikhail Baryshnikov/The Turning Point
Peter Firth/Equus
Alec Guinness/Star Wars
Maximilian Schell/Julia

1978
★ Christopher Walken/The Deer Hunter
Bruce Dern/Coming Home
Richard Farnsworth/Comes a Horseman
John Hurt/Midnight Express
Jack Warden/Heaven Can Wait

1979
★ Melvyn Douglas/Being There
Robert Duvall/Apocalypse Now
Frederic Forrest/The Rose
Justin Henry/Kramer vs. Kramer
Mickey Rooney/The Black Stallion

1980
★ Timothy Hutton/Ordinary People
Judd Hirsch/Ordinary People
Michael O'Keefe/The Great Santini
Joe Pesci/Raging Bull
Jason Robards, Jr./Melvin and Howard

1981
★ John Gielgud/Arthur
James Coco/Only When I Laugh
Ian Holm/Chariots of Fire
Jack Nicholson/Reds
Howard E. Rollins, Jr./Ragtime

1982
★ Louis Gossett, Jr./An Officer and a Gentleman
Charles Durning/The Best Little Whorehouse in Texas
John Lithgow/The World According to Garp
James Mason/The Verdict
Robert Preston/Victor/Victoria

1983
★ Jack Nicholson/Terms of Endearment
Charles Durning/To Be or Not to Be
John Lithgow/Terms of Endearment
Sam Shepard/The Right Stuff
Rip Torn/Cross Creek

1984
★ Haing S. Ngor/The Killing Fields
Adolph Caesar/A Soldier's Story
John Malkovich/Places in the Heart
Noriyuki "Pat" Morita/The Karate Kid
Ralph Richardson/Greystoke: The Legend of Tarzan, Lord of the Apes

1985
★ Don Ameche/Cocoon
Klaus Maria Brandauer/Out of Africa
William Hickey/Prizzi's Honor
Robert Loggia/Jagged Edge
Eric Roberts/Runaway Train

1986
★ Michael Caine/Hannah and Her Sisters
Tom Berenger/Platoon
Willem Dafoe/Platoon
Denholm Elliott/A Room with a View
Dennis Hopper/Hoosiers

1987
★ Sean Connery/The Untouchables
Albert Brooks/Broadcast News
Morgan Freeman/Street Smart
Vincent Gardenia/Moonstruck
Denzel Washington/Cry Freedom

1988
★ Kevin Kline/A Fish Called Wanda
Alec Guinness/Little Dorrit, Film 1: Nobody's Fault
Martin Landau/Tucker: The Man and His Dream
River Phoenix/Running on Empty
Dean Stockwell/Married to the Mob

1989
★ Denzel Washington/Glory
Danny Aiello/Do the Right Thing
Dan Aykroyd/Driving Miss Daisy
Marlon Brando/A Dry White Season
Martin Landau/Crimes & Misdemeanors

1990
★ Joe Pesci/Goodfellas
Bruce Davison/Longtime Companion
Andy Garcia/The Godfather, Part 3
Graham Greene/Dances with Wolves
Al Pacino/Dick Tracy

1991
★ Jack Palance/City Slickers
Tommy Lee Jones/JFK
Harvey Keitel/Bugsy
Ben Kingsley/Bugsy
Michael Lerner/Barton Fink

1992
★ Gene Hackman/Unforgiven
Jaye Davidson/The Crying Game
Jack Nicholson/A Few Good Men
Al Pacino/Glengarry Glen Ross
David Paymer/Mr. Saturday Night

1993
★ Tommy Lee Jones/The Fugitive
Leonardo DiCaprio/What's Eating Gilbert Grape
Ralph Fiennes/Schindler's List
John Malkovich/In the Line of Fire
Pete Postlethwaite/In the Name of the Father

1994
★ Martin Landau/Ed Wood
Samuel L. Jackson/Pulp Fiction
Chazz Palminteri/Bullets over Broadway
Paul Scofield/Quiz Show
Gary Sinise/Forrest Gump

1995
★ Kevin Spacey/The Usual Suspects
James Cromwell/Babe
Ed Harris/Apollo 13
Brad Pitt/12 Monkeys
Tim Roth/Rob Roy

1996
★ Cuba Gooding, Jr./Jerry Maguire
William H. Macy/Fargo
Armin Mueller-Stahl/Shine
Edward Norton/Primal Fear
James Woods/Ghosts of Mississippi

1997
★ Robin Williams/Good Will Hunting
Robert Forster/Jackie Brown
Anthony Hopkins/Amistad
Greg Kinnear/As Good As It Gets
Burt Reynolds/Boogie Nights

1998
★ James Coburn/Affliction
Robert Duvall/A Civil Action
Ed Harris/The Truman Show
Geoffrey Rush/Shakespeare in Love
Billy Bob Thornton/A Simple Plan

1999
★ Michael Caine/The Cider House Rules
Tom Cruise/Magnolia
Michael Clarke Duncan/The Green Mile
Jude Law/The Talented Mr. Ripley
Haley Joel Osment/The Sixth Sense

2000
★ Benicio Del Toro/Traffic
Jeff Bridges/The Contender
Willem Dafoe/Shadow of the Vampire
Albert Finney/Erin Brockovich
Joaquin Rafael (Lea) Phoenix/Gladiator

2001
★ Jim Broadbent/Iris
Ethan Hawke/Training Day
Ben Kingsley/Sexy Beast
Ian McKellen/Lord of the Rings: The Fellowship of the Rings
Jon Voight/Ali

2002
★ Chris Cooper/Adaptation
Ed Harris/The Hours
Paul Newman/Road to Perdition
John C. Reilly/Chicago
Christopher Walken/Catch Me If You Can

2003
★ Tim Robbins/Mystic River

2004
★ Morgan Freeman/Million Dollar Baby
Alan Alda/The Aviator
Thomas Haden Church/Sideways
Jamie Foxx/Collateral
Clive Owen/Closer

2005
★ George Clooney/Syriana
Matt Dillon/Crash
Paul Giamatti/Cinderella Man
Jake Gyllenhaal/Brokeback Mountain
William Hurt/A History of Violence

2006
★ Alan Arkin/Little Miss Sunshine
Jackie Earle Haley/Little Children
Djimon Hounsou/Blood Diamond
Eddie Murphy/Dreamgirls
Mark Wahlberg/The Departed

2007
★ Javier Bardem/No Country for Old Men
Casey Affleck/The Assassination of Jesse James by the Coward Robert Ford
Philip Seymour Hoffman/Charlie Wilson's War
Hal Holbrook/Into the Wild
Tom Wilkinson/Michael Clayton

ACTRESS

1928
★ Janet Gaynor/Sunrise
Gloria Swanson/Sadie Thompson

1929
★ Mary Pickford/Coquette
Bessie Love/Broadway Melody

1930
★ Norma Shearer/The Divorcee
Greta Garbo/Anna Christie
Greta Garbo/Romance

1931
★ Marie Dressler/Min & Bill
Marlene Dietrich/Morocco
Irene Dunne/Cimarron
Norma Shearer/A Free Soul

1932
★ Helen Hayes/The Sin of Madelon Claudet
Lynn Fontanne/The Guardsman

1933
★ Katharine Hepburn/Morning Glory
May Robson/Lady for a Day
Diana Wynyard/Cavalcade

1934
★ Claudette Colbert/It Happened One Night
Grace Moore/One Night of Love
Norma Shearer/The Barretts of Wimpole Street

1935
★ Bette Davis/Dangerous
Katharine Hepburn/Alice Adams
Miriam Hopkins/Becky Sharp

1936
★ Luise Rainer/The Great Ziegfeld

Academy Awards

Irene Dunne/Theodora Goes Wild
Carole Lombard/My Man Godfrey
Merle Oberon/The Dark Angel
Norma Shearer/Romeo and Juliet

1937
★ **Luise Rainer**/The Good Earth
Irene Dunne/The Awful Truth
Greta Garbo/Camille
Janet Gaynor/A Star Is Born
Barbara Stanwyck/Stella Dallas

1938
Bette Davis/Jezebel
Wendy Hiller/Pygmalion
Norma Shearer/Marie Antoinette
Margaret Sullavan/Three Comrades

1939
★ **Vivien Leigh**/Gone with the Wind
Bette Davis/Dark Victory
Irene Dunne/Love Affair
Greta Garbo/Ninotchka
Greer Garson/Goodbye, Mr. Chips

1940
★ **Ginger Rogers**/Kitty Foyle
Bette Davis/The Letter
Joan Fontaine/Rebecca
Katharine Hepburn/The Philadelphia Story
Martha Scott/Our Town

1941
★ **Joan Fontaine**/Suspicion
Bette Davis/The Little Foxes
Greer Garson/Blossoms in the Dust
Barbara Stanwyck/Ball of Fire

1942
★ **Greer Garson**/Mrs. Miniver
Bette Davis/Now, Voyager
Katharine Hepburn/Woman of the Year
Teresa Wright/The Pride of the Yankees

1943
★ **Jennifer Jones**/The Song of Bernadette
Jean Arthur/The More the Merrier
Ingrid Bergman/For Whom the Bell Tolls
Greer Garson/Madame Curie

1944
★ **Ingrid Bergman**/Gaslight
Claudette Colbert/Since You Went Away
Bette Davis/Mr. Skeffington
Greer Garson/Mrs. Parkington
Barbara Stanwyck/Double Indemnity

1945
★ **Joan Crawford**/Mildred Pierce
Ingrid Bergman/The Bells of St. Mary's
Greer Garson/The Valley of Decision
Gene Tierney/Leave Her to Heaven

1946
★ **Olivia de Havilland**/To Each His Own
Celia Johnson/Brief Encounter
Jennifer Jones/Duel in the Sun
Rosalind Russell/Sister Kenny
Jane Wyman/The Yearling

1947
★ **Loretta Young**/The Farmer's Daughter

Joan Crawford/Possessed
Susan Hayward/Smash-Up: The Story of a Woman
Dorothy McGuire/Gentleman's Agreement

1948
★ **Jane Wyman**/Johnny Belinda
Ingrid Bergman/Joan of Arc
Irene Dunne/I Remember Mama
Barbara Stanwyck/Sorry, Wrong Number
Olivia de Havilland/The Snake Pit

1949
★ **Olivia de Havilland**/The Heiress
Jeanne Crain/Pinky
Susan Hayward/My Foolish Heart
Loretta Young/Come to the Stable

1950
★ **Judy Holliday**/Born Yesterday
Anne Baxter/All About Eve
Bette Davis/All About Eve
Eleanor Parker/Caged
Gloria Swanson/Sunset Boulevard

1951
★ **Vivien Leigh**/A Streetcar Named Desire
Katharine Hepburn/The African Queen
Eleanor Parker/Detective Story
Shelley Winters/A Place in the Sun

1952
★ **Shirley Booth**/Come Back, Little Sheba
Joan Crawford/Sudden Fear
Julie Harris/The Member of the Wedding
Bette Davis/The Star
Susan Hayward/With a Song in My Heart

1953
★ **Audrey Hepburn**/Roman Holiday
Leslie Caron/Lili
Ava Gardner/Mogambo
Deborah Kerr/From Here to Eternity
Maggie McNamara/The Moon Is Blue

1954
★ **Grace Kelly**/The Country Girl
Dorothy Dandridge/Carmen Jones
Judy Garland/A Star Is Born
Audrey Hepburn/Sabrina
Jane Wyman/Magnificent Obsession

1955
★ **Anna Magnani**/The Rose Tattoo
Susan Hayward/I'll Cry Tomorrow
Katharine Hepburn/Summertime
Jennifer Jones/Love Is a Many-Splendored Thing
Eleanor Parker/Interrupted Melody

1956
★ **Ingrid Bergman**/Anastasia
Carroll Baker/Baby Doll
Katharine Hepburn/The Rainmaker
Nancy Kelly/The Bad Seed
Deborah Kerr/The King and I

1957
★ **Joanne Woodward**/The Three Faces of Eve
Deborah Kerr/Heaven Knows, Mr. Allison
Elizabeth Taylor/Raintree County

Lana Turner/Peyton Place

1958
★ **Susan Hayward**/I Want to Live!
Deborah Kerr/Separate Tables
Shirley MacLaine/Some Came Running
Rosalind Russell/Auntie Mame
Elizabeth Taylor/Cat on a Hot Tin Roof

1959
★ **Simone Signoret**/Room at the Top
Doris Day/Pillow Talk
Audrey Hepburn/The Nun's Story
Katharine Hepburn/Suddenly, Last Summer
Elizabeth Taylor/Suddenly, Last Summer

1960
★ **Elizabeth Taylor**/Butterfield 8
Greer Garson/Sunrise at Campobello
Deborah Kerr/The Sundowners
Shirley MacLaine/The Apartment
Melina Mercouri/Never on Sunday

1961
★ **Sophia Loren**/Two Women
Audrey Hepburn/Breakfast at Tiffany's
Piper Laurie/The Hustler
Geraldine Page/Summer and Smoke
Natalie Wood/Splendor in the Grass

1962
★ **Anne Bancroft**/The Miracle Worker
Bette Davis/What Ever Happened to Baby Jane?
Katharine Hepburn/Long Day's Journey into Night
Geraldine Page/Sweet Bird of Youth
Lee Remick/Days of Wine and Roses

1963
★ **Patricia Neal**/Hud
Shirley MacLaine/Irma La Douce
Rachel Roberts/This Sporting Life
Natalie Wood/Love with the Proper Stranger

1964
★ **Julie Andrews**/Mary Poppins
Anne Bancroft/The Pumpkin Eater
Sophia Loren/Marriage Italian Style
Debbie Reynolds/The Unsinkable Molly Brown
Kim Stanley/Seance on a Wet Afternoon

1965
★ **Julie Christie**/Darling
Julie Andrews/The Sound of Music
Samantha Eggar/The Collector
Elizabeth Hartman/A Patch of Blue
Simone Signoret/Ship of Fools

1966
★ **Elizabeth Taylor**/Who's Afraid of Virginia Woolf?
Anouk Aimée/A Man and a Woman
Ida Kaminska/The Shop on Main Street
Lynn Redgrave/Georgy Girl
Vanessa Redgrave/Morgan: A Suitable Case for Treatment

1967
★ **Katharine Hepburn**/Guess Who's Coming to Dinner
Anne Bancroft/The Graduate
Faye Dunaway/Bonnie & Clyde
Audrey Hepburn/Wait until Dark

1968
★ **Katharine Hepburn**/The Lion in Winter
★ **Barbra Streisand**/Funny Girl
Patricia Neal/The Subject Was Roses
Vanessa Redgrave/Isadora
Joanne Woodward/Rachel, Rachel

1969
★ **Maggie Smith**/The Prime of Miss Jean Brodie
Genevieve Bujold/Anne of the Thousand Days
Jane Fonda/They Shoot Horses, Don't They?
Liza Minnelli/The Sterile Cuckoo
Jean Simmons/The Happy Ending

1970
★ **Glenda Jackson**/Women in Love
Jane Alexander/The Great White Hope
Ali MacGraw/Love Story
Sarah Miles/Ryan's Daughter
Carrie Snodgress/Diary of a Mad Housewife

1971
★ **Jane Fonda**/Klute
Julie Christie/McCabe & Mrs. Miller
Glenda Jackson/Sunday, Bloody Sunday
Vanessa Redgrave/Mary, Queen of Scots
Janet Suzman/Nicholas and Alexandra

1972
★ **Liza Minnelli**/Cabaret
Diana Ross/Lady Sings the Blues
Maggie Smith/Travels with My Aunt
Cicely Tyson/Sounder
Liv Ullmann/The Emigrants

1973
★ **Glenda Jackson**/A Touch of Class
Ellen Burstyn/The Exorcist
Marsha Mason/Cinderella Liberty
Barbra Streisand/The Way We Were
Joanne Woodward/Summer Wishes, Winter Dreams

1974
★ **Ellen Burstyn**/Alice Doesn't Live Here Anymore
Faye Dunaway/Chinatown
Valerie Perrine/Lenny
Gena Rowlands/A Woman under the Influence

1975
★ **Louise Fletcher**/One Flew Over the Cuckoo's Nest
Isabelle Adjani/The Story of Adele H.
Ann-Margret/Tommy
Glenda Jackson/Hedda
Carol Kane/Hester Street

1976
★ **Faye Dunaway**/Network
Marie-Christine Barrault/Cousin, Cousine
Talia Shire/Rocky
Sissy Spacek/Carrie
Liv Ullmann/Face to Face

1977
★ **Diane Keaton**/Annie Hall

Anne Bancroft/The Turning Point
Jane Fonda/Julia
Shirley MacLaine/The Turning Point
Marsha Mason/The Goodbye Girl

1978
★ **Jane Fonda**/Coming Home
Ingrid Bergman/Autumn Sonata
Ellen Burstyn/Same Time, Next Year
Jill Clayburgh/An Unmarried Woman
Geraldine Page/Interiors

1979
★ **Sally Field**/Norma Rae
Jill Clayburgh/Starting Over
Jane Fonda/The China Syndrome
Marsha Mason/Chapter Two
Bette Midler/The Rose

1980
★ **Sissy Spacek**/Coal Miner's Daughter
Ellen Burstyn/Resurrection
Goldie Hawn/Private Benjamin
Mary Tyler Moore/Ordinary People
Gena Rowlands/Gloria

1981
★ **Katharine Hepburn**/On Golden Pond
Diane Keaton/Reds
Marsha Mason/Only When I Laugh
Susan Sarandon/Atlantic City
Meryl Streep/The French Lieutenant's Woman

1982
★ **Meryl Streep**/Sophie's Choice
Julie Andrews/Victor/Victoria
Jessica Lange/Frances
Sissy Spacek/Missing
Debra Winger/An Officer and a Gentleman

1983
★ **Shirley MacLaine**/Terms of Endearment
Jane Alexander/Testament
Meryl Streep/Silkwood
Julie Walters/Educating Rita
Debra Winger/Terms of Endearment

1984
★ **Sally Field**/Places in the Heart
Judy Davis/A Passage to India
Jessica Lange/Country
Vanessa Redgrave/The Bostonians
Sissy Spacek/The River

1985
★ **Geraldine Page**/The Trip to Bountiful
Anne Bancroft/Agnes of God
Whoopi Goldberg/The Color Purple
Jessica Lange/Sweet Dreams
Meryl Streep/Out of Africa

1986
★ **Marlee Matlin**/Children of a Lesser God
Jane Fonda/The Morning After
Sissy Spacek/Crimes of the Heart
Kathleen Turner/Peggy Sue Got Married
Sigourney Weaver/Aliens

1987
★ **Cher**/Moonstruck
Glenn Close/Fatal Attraction

Holly Hunter/Broadcast News
Sally Kirkland/Anna
Meryl Streep/Ironweed

1988
★ **Jodie Foster**/The Accused
Glenn Close/Dangerous Liaisons
Melanie Griffith/Working Girl
Meryl Streep/A Cry in the Dark
Sigourney Weaver/Gorillas in the Mist

1989
★ **Jessica Tandy**/Driving Miss Daisy
Isabelle Adjani/Camille Claudel
Pauline Collins/Shirley Valentine
Jessica Lange/Music Box
Michelle Pfeiffer/The Fabulous Baker Boys

1990
★ **Kathy Bates**/Misery
Anjelica Huston/The Grifters
Julia Roberts/Pretty Woman
Meryl Streep/Postcards from the Edge
Joanne Woodward/Mr. & Mrs. Bridge

1991
★ **Jodie Foster**/The Silence of the Lambs
Geena Davis/Thelma & Louise
Laura Dern/Rambling Rose
Bette Midler/For the Boys
Susan Sarandon/Thelma & Louise

1992
★ **Emma Thompson**/Howard's End
Catherine Deneuve/Indochine
Mary McDonnell/Passion Fish
Michelle Pfeiffer/Love Field
Susan Sarandon/Lorenzo's Oil

1993
★ **Holly Hunter**/The Piano
Angela Bassett/What's Love Got to Do with It?
Stockard Channing/Six Degrees of Separation
Emma Thompson/The Remains of the Day
Debra Winger/Shadowlands

1994
★ **Jessica Lange**/Blue Sky
Jodie Foster/Nell
Miranda Richardson/Tom & Viv
Winona Ryder/Little Women
Susan Sarandon/The Client

1995
★ **Susan Sarandon**/Dead Man Walking
Elisabeth Shue/Leaving Las Vegas
Sharon Stone/Casino
Meryl Streep/The Bridges of Madison County
Emma Thompson/Sense and Sensibility

1996
★ **Frances McDormand**/Fargo
Brenda Blethyn/Secrets and Lies
Diane Keaton/Marvin's Room
Kristin Scott Thomas/The English Patient
Emily Watson/Breaking the Waves

1997
★ **Helen Hunt**/As Good As It Gets

★ = winner

ACTRESS (continued)

1998
★ Gwyneth Paltrow/ Shakespeare in Love
Cate Blanchett/Elizabeth
Fernanda Montenegro/ Central Station
Meryl Streep/One True Thing
Emily Watson/Hilary and Jackie

1999
★ Hilary Swank/Boys Don't Cry
Annette Bening/American Beauty
Janet McTeer/ Tumbleweeds
Julianne Moore/The End of the Affair
Meryl Streep/Music of the Heart

2000
★ Julia Roberts/Erin Brockovich
Joan Allen/The Contender
Juliette Binoche/Chocolat
Ellen Burstyn/Requiem for a Dream
Laura Linney/You Can Count On Me

2001
★ Halle Berry/Monster's Ball
Judi Dench/Iris
Nicole Kidman/Moulin Rouge
Sissy Spacek/In the Bedroom
Renee Zellweger/Bridget Jones's Diary

2002
★ Nicole Kidman/The Hours
Salma Hayek/Frida
Diane Lane/Unfaithful
Julianne Moore/Far from Heaven
Renee Zellweger/Chicago

2003
★ Charlize Theron/Monster
Keisha Castle-Hughes/ Whale Rider
Diane Keaton/Something's Gotta Give
Naomi Watts/21 Grams

2004
★ Hilary Swank/Million Dollar Baby
Annette Bening/Being Julia
Catalina Sandino Moreno/Maria Full of Grace
Imelda Staunton/Vera Drake
Kate Winslet/Eternal Sunshine of the Spotless Mind

2005
★ Reese Witherspoon/Walk the Line
Judi Dench/Mrs. Henderson Presents
Felicity Huffman/ Transamerica
Keira Knightley/Pride and Prejudice
Charlize Theron/North Country

2006
★ Helen Mirren/The Queen
Penelope Cruz/Volver
Judi Dench/Notes on a Scandal
Meryl Streep/The Devil Wears Prada
Kate Winslet/Little Children

2007
★ Marion Cotillard/La Vie en Rose
Cate Blanchett/Elizabeth: The Golden Age
Julie Christie/Away From Her
Helena Bonham-Carter/ The Wings of the Dove
Julie Christie/Afterglow
Judi Dench/Mrs. Brown
Kate Winslet/Titanic
Laura Linney/The Savages
Ellen Page/Juno

ACTRESS—SUPPORTING

1936
★ Gale Sondergaard/ Anthony Adverse
Beulah Bondi/The Gorgeous Hussy
Alice Brady/My Man Godfrey
Bonita Granville/These Three
Maria Ouspenskaya/ Dodsworth

1937
★ Alice Brady/In Old Chicago
Andrea Leeds/Stage Door
Anne Shirley/Stella Dallas
Claire Trevor/Dead End
May Whitty/Night Must Fall

1938
★ Fay Bainter/Jezebel
Beulah Bondi/Of Human Hearts
Spring Byington/You Can't Take It with You
Miliza Korjus/The Great Waltz

1939
★ Hattie McDaniel/Gone with the Wind
Olivia de Havilland/Gone with the Wind
Geraldine Fitzgerald/ Wuthering Heights
Edna May Oliver/Drums Along the Mohawk
Maria Ouspenskaya/Love Affair

1940
★ Jane Darwell/The Grapes of Wrath
Judith Anderson/Rebecca
Ruth Hussey/The Philadelphia Story
Barbara O'Neil/All This and Heaven Too
Marjorie Rambeau/ Primrose Path

1941
★ Mary Astor/The Great Lie
Sara Allgood/How Green Was My Valley
Patricia Collinge/The Little Foxes
Teresa Wright/The Little Foxes
Margaret Wycherly/ Sergeant York

1942
★ Teresa Wright/Mrs. Miniver
Gladys Cooper/Now, Voyager
Agnes Moorehead/The Magnificent Ambersons
Susan Peters/Random Harvest
May Whitty/Mrs. Miniver

1943
★ Katina Paxinou/For Whom the Bell Tolls
Gladys Cooper/The Song of Bernadette
Paulette Goddard/So Proudly We Hail
Anne Revere/The Song of Bernadette
Lucile Watson/Watch on the Rhine

1944
★ Ethel Barrymore/None But the Lonely Heart
Jennifer Jones/Since You Went Away
Angela Lansbury/Gaslight
Aline MacMahon/Dragon Seed
Agnes Moorehead/Mrs. Parkington

1945
★ Anne Revere/National Velvet
Eve Arden/Mildred Pierce
Ann Blyth/Mildred Pierce
Angela Lansbury/Picture of Dorian Gray
Joan Lorring/The Corn Is Green

1946
★ Anne Baxter/The Razor's Edge
Ethel Barrymore/The Spiral Staircase
Lillian Gish/Duel in the Sun
Flora Robson/Saratoga Trunk
Gale Sondergaard/Anna and the King of Siam

1947
★ Celeste Holm/Gentleman's Agreement
Ethel Barrymore/The Paradine Case
Gloria Grahame/Crossfire
Marjorie Main/The Egg and I
Anne Revere/Gentleman's Agreement

1948
★ Claire Trevor/Key Largo
Barbara Bel Geddes/I Remember Mama
Ellen Corby/I Remember Mama
Agnes Moorehead/Johnny Belinda
Jean Simmons/Hamlet

1949
★ Mercedes McCambridge/All the King's Men
Ethel Barrymore/Pinky
Celeste Holm/Come to the Stable
Elsa Lanchester/Come to the Stable
Ethel Waters/Pinky

1950
★ Josephine Hull/Harvey
Hope Emerson/Caged
Celeste Holm/All About Eve
Nancy Olson/Sunset Boulevard
Thelma Ritter/All About Eve

1951
★ Kim Hunter/A Streetcar Named Desire
Lee Grant/Detective Story

1952
★ Gloria Grahame/The Bad and the Beautiful
Jean Hagen/Singin' in the Rain
Colette Marchand/Moulin Rouge
Terry Moore/Come Back, Little Sheba
Thelma Ritter/With a Song in My Heart

1953
★ Donna Reed/From Here to Eternity
Grace Kelly/Mogambo
Marjorie Rambeau/Torch Song
Thelma Ritter/Pickup on South Street

1954
★ Eva Marie Saint/On the Waterfront
Nina Foch/Executive Suite
Katy Jurado/Broken Lance
Jan Sterling/The High and the Mighty
Claire Trevor/The High and the Mighty

1955
★ Jo Van Fleet/East of Eden
Betsy Blair/Marty
Peggy Lee/Pete Kelly's Blues
Marisa Pavan/The Rose Tattoo
Natalie Wood/Rebel without a Cause

1956
★ Dorothy Malone/Written on the Wind
Mildred Dunnock/Baby Doll
Eileen Heckart/The Bad Seed
Mercedes McCambridge/Giant
Patty McCormack/The Bad Seed

1957
★ Miyoshi Umeki/Sayonara
Elsa Lanchester/Witness for the Prosecution
Hope Lange/Peyton Place
Diane Varsi/Peyton Place

1958
★ Wendy Hiller/Separate Tables
Peggy Cass/Auntie Mame
Martha Hyer/Some Came Running
Maureen Stapleton/ Lonelyhearts
Cara Williams/The Defiant Ones

1959
★ Shelley Winters/The Diary of Anne Frank
Hermione Baddeley/Room at the Top
Susan Kohner/Imitation of Life
Juanita Moore/Imitation of Life
Thelma Ritter/Pillow Talk

1960
★ Shirley Jones/Elmer Gantry
Glynis Johns/The Sundowners
Janet Leigh/Psycho

1961
★ Rita Moreno/West Side Story
Fay Bainter/The Children's Hour
Judy Garland/Judgment at Nuremberg
Lotte Lenya/The Roman Spring of Mrs. Stone
Una Merkel/Summer and Smoke

1962
★ Patty Duke/The Miracle Worker
Mary Badham/To Kill a Mockingbird
Shirley Knight/Sweet Bird of Youth
Angela Lansbury/The Manchurian Candidate
Thelma Ritter/Birdman of Alcatraz

1963
★ Margaret Rutherford/The V.I.P.s
Diane Cilento/Tom Jones
Edith Evans/Tom Jones
Joyce Redman/Tom Jones
Lilia Skala/Lilies of the Field

1964
★ Lila Kedrova/Zorba the Greek
Gladys Cooper/My Fair Lady
Edith Evans/The Chalk Garden
Grayson Hall/The Night of the Iguana
Agnes Moorehead/Hush, Hush, Sweet Charlotte

1965
★ Shelley Winters/A Patch of Blue
Ruth Gordon/Inside Daisy Clover
Joyce Redman/Othello
Maggie Smith/Othello
Peggy Wood/The Sound of Music

1966
★ Sandy Dennis/Who's Afraid of Virginia Woolf?
Wendy Hiller/A Man for All Seasons
Jocelyn Lagarde/Hawaii
Vivien Merchant/Alfie
Geraldine Page/You're a Big Boy Now

1967
★ Estelle Parsons/Bonnie & Clyde
Carol Channing/Thoroughly Modern Millie
Mildred Natwick/Barefoot in the Park
Beah Richards/Guess Who's Coming to Dinner
Katharine Ross/The Graduate

1968
★ Ruth Gordon/Rosemary's Baby
Lynn Carlin/Faces
Sondra Locke/The Heart Is a Lonely Hunter
Kay Medford/Funny Girl
Estelle Parsons/Rachel, Rachel

1969
★ Goldie Hawn/Cactus Flower
Catherine Burns/Last Summer
Dyan Cannon/Bob & Carol & Ted & Alice
Sylvia Miles/Midnight Cowboy
Susannah York/They Shoot Horses, Don't They?

1970
★ Helen Hayes/Airport
Karen Black/Five Easy Pieces
Lee Grant/The Landlord
Sally Kellerman/M*A*S*H
Maureen Stapleton/Airport

1971
★ Cloris Leachman/The Last Picture Show
Ann-Margret/Carnal Knowledge
Ellen Burstyn/The Last Picture Show
Margaret Leighton/The Go-Between

1972
★ Eileen Heckart/Butterflies Are Free
Jeannie Berlin/The Heartbreak Kid
Geraldine Page/Pete 'n' Tillie
Susan Tyrrell/Fat City
Shelley Winters/The Poseidon Adventure

1973
★ Tatum O'Neal/Paper Moon
Linda Blair/The Exorcist
Candy Clark/American Graffiti
Madeline Kahn/Paper Moon
Sylvia Sidney/Summer Wishes, Winter Dreams

1974
★ Ingrid Bergman/Murder on the Orient Express
Valentina Cortese/Day for Night
Madeline Kahn/Blazing Saddles
Diane Ladd/Alice Doesn't Live Here Anymore
Talia Shire/The Godfather, Part 2

1975
★ Lee Grant/Shampoo
Ronee Blakley/Nashville
Sylvia Miles/Farewell, My Lovely
Lily Tomlin/Nashville
Brenda Vaccaro/Once Is Not Enough

1976
★ Beatrice Straight/Network
Jane Alexander/All the President's Men
Jodie Foster/Taxi Driver
Lee Grant/Voyage of the Damned
Piper Laurie/Carrie

1977
★ Vanessa Redgrave/Julia
Leslie Browne/The Turning Point
Quinn Cummings/The Goodbye Girl
Melinda Dillon/Close Encounters of the Third Kind
Tuesday Weld/Looking for Mr. Goodbar

1978
★ Maggie Smith/California Suite
Dyan Cannon/Heaven Can Wait
Penelope Milford/Coming Home
Maureen Stapleton/Interiors
Meryl Streep/The Deer Hunter

1979
★ Meryl Streep/Kramer vs. Kramer
Jane Alexander/Kramer vs. Kramer
Barbara Barrie/Breaking Away
Candice Bergen/Starting Over
Mariel Hemingway/Manhattan

1980
★ Mary Steenburgen/Melvin and Howard
Eileen Brennan/Private Benjamin
Eva Le Gallienne/Resurrection
Cathy Moriarty/Raging Bull
Diana Scarwid/Inside Moves

1981
★ Maureen Stapleton/Reds
Melinda Dillon/Absence of Malice
Jane Fonda/On Golden Pond
Joan Hackett/Only When I Laugh
Elizabeth McGovern/Ragtime

1982
★ Jessica Lange/Tootsie
Glenn Close/The World According to Garp
Teri Garr/Tootsie
Kim Stanley/Frances
Lesley Ann Warren/Victor/Victoria

1983
★ Linda Hunt/The Year of Living Dangerously
Cher/Silkwood
Glenn Close/The Big Chill
Amy Irving/Yentl
Alfre Woodard/Cross Creek

1984
★ Peggy Ashcroft/A Passage to India
Glenn Close/The Natural
Lindsay Crouse/Places in the Heart
Christine Lahti/Swing Shift
Geraldine Page/The Pope of Greenwich Village

1985
★ Anjelica Huston/Prizzi's Honor
Margaret Avery/The Color Purple
Amy Madigan/Twice in a Lifetime
Meg Tilly/Agnes of God
Oprah Winfrey/The Color Purple

1986
★ Dianne Wiest/Hannah and Her Sisters
Tess Harper/Crimes of the Heart
Piper Laurie/Children of a Lesser God

★ = winner

Academy Awards

1986
Mary Elizabeth Mastrantonio/The Color of Money
Maggie Smith/A Room with a View

1987
★ Olympia Dukakis/Moonstruck
Norma Aleandro/Gaby: A True Story
Anne Archer/Fatal Attraction
Anne Ramsey/Throw Momma from the Train
Ann Sothern/The Whales of August

1988
★ Geena Davis/The Accidental Tourist
Joan Cusack/Working Girl
Frances McDormand/Mississippi Burning
Michelle Pfeiffer/Dangerous Liaisons
Sigourney Weaver/Working Girl

1989
★ Brenda Fricker/My Left Foot
Anjelica Huston/Enemies, a Love Story
Lena Olin/Enemies, a Love Story
Julia Roberts/Steel Magnolias
Dianne Wiest/Parenthood

1990
★ Whoopi Goldberg/Ghost
Annette Bening/The Grifters
Lorraine Bracco/Goodfellas
Diane Ladd/Wild at Heart
Mary McDonnell/Dances with Wolves

1991
★ Mercedes Ruehl/The Fisher King
Diane Ladd/Rambling Rose
Juliette Lewis/Cape Fear
Kate Nelligan/The Prince of Tides
Jessica Tandy/Fried Green Tomatoes

1992
★ Marisa Tomei/My Cousin Vinny
Judy Davis/Husbands and Wives
Joan Plowright/Enchanted April
Vanessa Redgrave/Howards End
Miranda Richardson/Damage

1993
★ Anna Paquin/The Piano
Holly Hunter/The Firm
Rosie Perez/Fearless
Winona Ryder/The Age of Innocence
Emma Thompson/In the Name of the Father

1994
★ Dianne Wiest/Bullets over Broadway
Rosemary Harris/Tom & Viv
Helen Mirren/The Madness of King George
Uma Thurman/Pulp Fiction
Jennifer Tilly/Bullets over Broadway

1995
★ Mira Sorvino/Mighty Aphrodite
Joan Allen/Nixon
Kathleen Quinlan/Apollo 13
Mare Winningham/Georgia
Kate Winslet/Sense and Sensibility

1996
★ Juliette Binoche/The English Patient
Joan Allen/The Crucible
Lauren Bacall/The Mirror Has Two Faces
Barbara Hershey/Portrait of a Lady
Marianne Jean-Baptiste/Secrets and Lies

1997
★ Kim Basinger/L.A. Confidential
Joan Cusack/In and Out
Minnie Driver/Good Will Hunting
Julianne Moore/Boogie Nights
Gloria Stuart/Titanic

1998
★ Judi Dench/Shakespeare in Love
Kathy Bates/Primary Colors
Brenda Blethyn/Little Voice
Rachel Griffiths/Hilary and Jackie
Lynn Redgrave/Gods and Monsters

1999
★ Angelina Jolie/Girl, Interrupted
Toni Collette/The Sixth Sense
Catherine Keener/Being John Malkovich
Samantha Morton/Sweet and Lowdown
Chloe Sevigny/Boys Don't Cry

2000
★ Marcia Gay Harden/Pollock
Judi Dench/Chocolat
Kate Hudson/Almost Famous
Frances McDormand/Almost Famous
Julie Walters/Billy Elliot

2001
★ Jennifer Connelly/A Beautiful Mind
Helen Mirren/Gosford Park
Maggie Smith/Gosford Park
Marisa Tomei/In the Bedroom
Kate Winslet/Iris

2002
★ Catherine Zeta-Jones/Chicago
Kathy Bates/About Schmidt
Julianne Moore/The Hours
Queen Latifah/Chicago
Meryl Streep/Adaptation

2003
★ Renee Zellweger/Cold Mountain
Shohreh Aghdashloo/House of Sand and Fog
Patricia Clarkson/Pieces of April
Marcia Gay Harden/Mystic River
Holly Hunter/Thirteen
Samantha Morton/In America

2004
★ Cate Blanchett/The Aviator
Laura Linney/Kinsey
Virginia Madsen/Sideways
Sophie Okonedo/Hotel Rwanda
Natalie Portman/Closer

2005
★ Rachel Weisz/The Constant Gardener
Amy Adams/Junebug
Catherine Keener/Capote
Frances McDormand/North Country
Michelle Williams/Brokeback Mountain

2006
★ Jennifer Hudson/Dreamgirls
Adriana Barraza/Babel
Cate Blanchett/Notes on a Scandal
Abigail Breslin/Little Miss Sunshine
Rinko Kikuchi/Babel

2007
★ Tilda Swinton/Michael Clayton
Cate Blanchett/I'm Not There
Ruby Dee/American Gangster
Saoirse Ronan/Atonement
Amy Ryan/Gone Baby Gone

ART DIRECTION

1936
★ The Dark Angel

1957
★ Sayonara
Funny Face
Les Girls
Pal Joey
Raintree County

1958
★ Gigi
Auntie Mame
Bell, Book and Candle
Vertigo

1967
★ Camelot
Doctor Dolittle
Guess Who's Coming to Dinner
The Taming of the Shrew
Thoroughly Modern Millie

1968
★ Oliver!
The Shoes of the Fisherman
Star!
2001: A Space Odyssey
War and Peace

1969
★ Hello, Dolly!
Anne of the Thousand Days
Sweet Charity
They Shoot Horses, Don't They?

1970
★ Patton
Airport
Scrooge
Tora! Tora! Tora!

1971
★ Nicholas and Alexandra
The Andromeda Strain
Bedknobs and Broomsticks
Fiddler on the Roof
Mary, Queen of Scots

1972
★ Cabaret
Lady Sings the Blues
The Poseidon Adventure
Travels with My Aunt
Young Winston

1973
★ The Sting
Brother Sun, Sister Moon
Tom Sawyer
The Way We Were

1974
★ The Godfather, Part 2
Chinatown
Earthquake
The Island at the Top of the World
The Towering Inferno

1975
★ Barry Lyndon
The Hindenburg
The Man Who Would Be King
Shampoo
The Sunshine Boys

1976
★ All the President's Men
The Incredible Sarah
The Last Tycoon
Logan's Run
The Shootist

1977
★ Star Wars
Airport '77
Close Encounters of the Third Kind
The Spy Who Loved Me
The Turning Point

1978
★ Heaven Can Wait
Brink's Job
California Suite
Interiors
The Wiz

1979
★ All That Jazz
Apocalypse Now
The China Syndrome
Star Trek: The Motion Picture

1980
★ Tess
Altered States
Coal Miner's Daughter
The Elephant Man
The Empire Strikes Back
Kagemusha

1981
★ Raiders of the Lost Ark
The French Lieutenant's Woman
Heaven's Gate
Ragtime
Reds

1982
★ Gandhi
Annie
Blade Runner
Victor/Victoria

1983
★ Fanny and Alexander
Return of the Jedi
The Right Stuff
Terms of Endearment
Yentl

1984
★ Amadeus
The Cotton Club
The Natural
A Passage to India
2010: The Year We Make Contact

1985
★ Out of Africa
Brazil
The Color Purple
Ran
Witness

1986
★ A Room with a View
Aliens
The Color of Money
Hannah and Her Sisters
The Mission

1987
★ The Last Emperor
Empire of the Sun
Hope and Glory
Radio Days
The Untouchables

1988
★ Dangerous Liaisons
Beaches
Rain Man
Tucker: The Man and His Dream
Who Framed Roger Rabbit

1989
★ Batman
The Abyss
The Adventures of Baron Munchausen
Driving Miss Daisy
Glory

1990
★ Dick Tracy
Cyrano de Bergerac
Dances with Wolves
The Godfather, Part 3
Hamlet

1991
★ Bugsy
Barton Fink
The Fisher King
Hook
The Prince of Tides

1992
★ Howard's End
Bram Stoker's Dracula
Chaplin
Toys
Unforgiven

1993
★ Schindler's List
Addams Family Values
The Age of Innocence
Orlando
The Remains of the Day

1994
★ The Madness of King George
Bullets over Broadway
Forrest Gump
Interview with the Vampire
Legends of the Fall

1995
★ Restoration
Apollo 13
Babe
A Little Princess
Richard III

1996
★ The English Patient
The Birdcage
Evita
Hamlet
William Shakespeare's Romeo and Juliet

1997
★ Titanic
Gattaca
Kundun
L.A. Confidential
Men in Black

1998
★ Shakespeare in Love
Elizabeth
Pleasantville
Saving Private Ryan
What Dreams May Come

1999
★ Sleepy Hollow
Anna and the King
The Cider House Rules
The Talented Mr. Ripley
Topsy Turvy

2000
★ Crouching Tiger, Hidden Dragon
Dr. Seuss' How the Grinch Stole Christmas
Gladiator
Quills

2001
★ Moulin Rouge
Amelie
Gosford Park
Harry Potter and the Sorcerer's Stone
Lord of the Rings: The Fellowship of the Rings

2002
★ Chicago
Frida
Gangs of New York
Lord of the Rings: The Two Towers
Road to Perdition

2003
★ Lord of the Rings: The Return of the King
Girl with a Pearl Earring
The Last Samurai
Master and Commander: The Far Side of the World
Seabiscuit

2004
★ The Aviator
Finding Neverland
Lemony Snicket's A Series of Unfortunate Events
The Phantom of the Opera
A Very Long Engagement

2005
★ Memoirs of a Geisha
Good Night, and Good Luck
Harry Potter and the Goblet of Fire
King Kong
Pride and Prejudice

2006
★ Pan's Labyrinth
Dreamgirls
The Good Shepherd
Pirates of the Caribbean: Dead Man's Chest
The Prestige

2007
★ Sweeney Todd: The Demon Barber of Fleet Street
American Gangster
Atonement
The Golden Compass
There Will Be Blood

ART DIRECTION (B&W)

1946
★ Anna and the King of Siam

1947
★ Great Expectations

1948
★ Hamlet
Johnny Belinda

1949
★ The Heiress
Come to the Stable
Madame Bovary

1950
★ Sunset Boulevard
All About Eve

1951
★ A Streetcar Named Desire
La Ronde

1952
★ The Bad and the Beautiful
Carrie
Rashomon
Viva Zapata!

1953
★ Julius Caesar
Martin Luther
Roman Holiday
Titanic

1954
★ On the Waterfront
Country Girl
Executive Suite
Le Plaisir
Sabrina

1955
★ The Rose Tattoo
Blackboard Jungle
I'll Cry Tomorrow
The Man with the Golden Arm
Marty

1956
★ Somebody Up There Likes Me
Seven Samurai
Solid Gold Cadillac

1959
★ The Diary of Anne Frank
Career
The Last Angry Man
Some Like It Hot
Suddenly, Last Summer

1960
★ The Apartment
The Facts of Life
Psycho

1961
★ The Hustler
The Absent-Minded Professor
The Children's Hour
Judgment at Nuremberg
La Dolce Vita

1962
★ To Kill a Mockingbird
Days of Wine and Roses
The Longest Day
Period of Adjustment

1963
8 1/2
Hud

★ = winner

(Art Direction — B&W, continued)

Love with the Proper Stranger

1964
★ Zorba the Greek
The Americanization of Emily
Hush, Hush, Sweet Charlotte

1965
Ship of Fools
King Rat
A Patch of Blue
The Slender Thread
The Spy Who Came in from the Cold

1966
Who's Afraid of Virginia Woolf?
The Fortune Cookie
The Gospel According to St. Matthew
Is Paris Burning?

ART DIRECTION (COLOR)

1947
★ Black Narcissus
Life with Father

1948
★ The Red Shoes
Joan of Arc

1949
★ Little Women
Adventures of Don Juan

1950
★ Samson and Delilah
Annie Get Your Gun
Destination Moon

1951
★ An American in Paris
David and Bathsheba
Quo Vadis
The Tales of Hoffmann

1952
★ Moulin Rouge
Hans Christian Andersen
The Merry Widow
The Quiet Man
The Snows of Kilimanjaro

1953
★ The Robe
Knights of the Round Table
Lili
Young Bess

1954
★ 20,000 Leagues under the Sea
Brigadoon
Desiree
Red Garters
A Star is Born

1955
★ Picnic
Daddy Long Legs
Guys and Dolls
Love is a Many-Splendored Thing
To Catch a Thief

1956
★ The King and I
Around the World in 80 Days
Giant
Lust for Life
The Ten Commandments

1957
★ Sayonara
An Affair to Remember
Funny Face
Les Girls
Pal Joey

1959
★ Ben-Hur
Journey to the Center of the Earth
North by Northwest
Pillow Talk
The Big Fisherman

1960
★ Spartacus
Cimarron
It Started in Naples
Pepe
Sunrise at Campobello

1961
★ West Side Story
Breakfast at Tiffany's
El Cid
Flower Drum Song
Summer and Smoke

1962
★ Lawrence of Arabia
The Music Man
Mutiny on the Bounty
That Touch of Mink
The Wonderful World of the Brothers Grimm

1963
★ Cleopatra
The Cardinal
How the West Was Won
Tom Jones

1964
★ My Fair Lady
Becket
Mary Poppins
The Unsinkable Molly Brown

1965
★ Doctor Zhivago
The Agony and the Ecstasy
The Greatest Story Ever Told
Inside Daisy Clover
The Sound of Music

1966
★ Fantastic Voyage
Gambit
Juliet of the Spirits
The Oscar
The Sand Pebbles

CINEMATOGRAPHY

1928
★ Sunrise
My Best Girl
Sadie Thompson
The Tempest

1929
★ White Shadows in the South Seas

1930
★ All Quiet on the Western Front
Anna Christie
Hell's Angels

1931
★ Tabu: A Story of the South Seas
Cimarron
Morocco
Svengali

1932
★ Shanghai Express
Arrowsmith
Dr. Jekyll and Mr. Hyde

1933
★ A Farewell to Arms
The Sign of the Cross

1934
★ Cleopatra

1935
★ A Midsummer Night's Dream
Barbary Coast
The Crusades
Les Miserables

1936
★ Anthony Adverse
The General Died at Dawn
The Gorgeous Hussy

1937
★ The Good Earth
Dead End

1938
★ The Great Waltz
Algiers
Jezebel
Mad About Music
Vivacious Lady
You Can't Take It with You

1959
★ James Wong Howe / The Old Man and the Sea

1960
★ Tess / The Blue Lagoon

1967
★ Bonnie & Clyde
Camelot
Doctor Dolittle
The Graduate
In Cold Blood

1968
★ Romeo and Juliet
Funny Girl
Ice Station Zebra
Oliver!
Star!

1969
★ Butch Cassidy and the Sundance Kid
Anne of the Thousand Days
Bob & Carol & Ted & Alice
Hello, Dolly!
Marooned

1970
★ Ryan's Daughter
Airport
Patton
Tora! Tora! Tora!
Women in Love

1971
★ Fiddler on the Roof
The French Connection
The Last Picture Show
Nicholas and Alexandra
Summer of '42

1972
★ Cabaret
Butterflies Are Free
1776
The Poseidon Adventure
Travels with My Aunt

1973
★ Cries and Whispers
The Exorcist
Jonathan Livingston Seagull
The Sting
The Way We Were

1974
★ The Towering Inferno
Chinatown
Earthquake
Lenny
Murder on the Orient Express

1975
★ Barry Lyndon
The Day of the Locust
Funny Lady
The Hindenburg
One Flew Over the Cuckoo's Nest

1976
★ Bound for Glory
King Kong
Logan's Run
Network
A Star is Born

1977
★ Close Encounters of the Third Kind
Islands in the Stream
Julia
Looking for Mr. Goodbar
The Turning Point

1978
★ Days of Heaven
The Deer Hunter
Heaven Can Wait
Same Time, Next Year
The Wiz

1979
★ Apocalypse Now
All That Jazz
The Black Hole
Kramer vs. Kramer
1941

1980
★ Tess
The Blue Lagoon
Coal Miner's Daughter
The Formula
Raging Bull

1981
★ Reds
Excalibur
On Golden Pond
Ragtime
Raiders of the Lost Ark

1982
★ Gandhi
Das Boot
E.T.: The Extra-Terrestrial
Sophie's Choice
Tootsie

1983
★ Fanny and Alexander
Flashdance
The Right Stuff
WarGames
Zelig

1984
★ The Killing Fields
Amadeus
The Natural
A Passage to India
The River

1985
★ Out of Africa
The Color Purple
Murphy's Romance
Ran
Witness

1986
★ The Mission
Peggy Sue Got Married
Platoon
Star Trek IV: The Voyage Home

1987
★ The Last Emperor
Broadcast News
Empire of the Sun
Hope and Glory
Matewan

1988
★ Mississippi Burning
Rain Man
Tequila Sunrise
The Unbearable Lightness of Being
Who Framed Roger Rabbit

1989
★ Glory
The Abyss
Blaze
Born on the Fourth of July
The Fabulous Baker Boys

1990
★ Dances with Wolves
Avalon
Dick Tracy
Henry & June
The Godfather, Part 3

1991
★ JFK
Bugsy
The Prince of Tides
Terminator 2: Judgment Day
Thelma & Louise

1992
★ A River Runs Through It
Hoffa
Howard's End
The Lover
Unforgiven

1993
★ Schindler's List
Farewell My Concubine
The Fugitive
The Piano
Searching for Bobby Fischer

1994
★ Legends of the Fall
Forrest Gump
The Shawshank Redemption
Trois Couleurs: Rouge
Wyatt Earp

1995
★ Braveheart
Batman Forever
A Little Princess
Sense and Sensibility
Shanghai Triad

1996
★ The English Patient
Evita
Fargo
Fly Away Home
Michael Collins

1997
★ Titanic
Amistad
Kundun
L.A. Confidential
The Wings of the Dove

1998
★ Saving Private Ryan
Elizabeth
A Civil Action
The Thin Red Line

1999
★ American Beauty
The End of the Affair
Sleepy Hollow
Snow Falling on Cedars

2000
★ Crouching Tiger, Hidden Dragon
Gladiator
O Brother, Where Art Thou?
The Patriot

2001
★ Lord of the Rings: The Fellowship of the Ring
Amelie
Black Hawk Down
The Man Who Wasn't There
Moulin Rouge

2002
★ Road to Perdition
Chicago
Far from Heaven
Gangs of New York
The Pianist

2003
★ Master and Commander: The Far Side of the World
City of God
Cold Mountain
Girl with a Pearl Earring
Seabiscuit

2004
★ The Aviator
House of Flying Daggers
The Passion of the Christ
The Phantom of the Opera
A Very Long Engagement

2005
★ Memoirs of a Geisha
Batman Begins
Brokeback Mountain
Good Night, and Good Luck
The New World

2006
★ Pan's Labyrinth
The Black Dahlia
Children of Men
The Illusionist
The Prestige

2007
★ There Will Be Blood
The Assassination of Jesse James by the Coward Robert Ford
Atonement
The Diving Bell and the Butterfly
No Country for Old Men

CINEMATOGRAPHY (B&W)

1939
★ Wuthering Heights
First Love
Gunga Din
Intermezzo
Juarez
Only Angels Have Wings
Stagecoach

1940
★ Rebecca
Abe Lincoln in Illinois
All This and Heaven Too
Boom Town
Foreign Correspondent
The Letter
The Long Voyage Home
Waterloo Bridge

1941
★ How Green Was My Valley
The Chocolate Soldier
Citizen Kane
Dr. Jekyll and Mr. Hyde
Here Comes Mr. Jordan
Sergeant York
Sun Valley Serenade
That Hamilton Woman

1942
★ Mrs. Miniver
Kings Row
The Magnificent Ambersons
The Pride of the Yankees
Ten Gentlemen from West Point

1943
★ The Song of Bernadette
Air Force
Casablanca
Five Graves to Cairo
The Human Comedy
Madame Curie
The North Star
Sahara
So Proudly We Hail

1944
★ Laura
Double Indemnity
Dragon Seed
Gaslight
Going My Way
Lifeboat
Since You Went Away
Thirty Seconds Over Tokyo
The Uninvited
The White Cliffs of Dover

1945
★ The Picture of Dorian Gray
The Keys of the Kingdom
The Lost Weekend
Mildred Pierce
Spellbound

1946
★ Anna and the King of Siam
The Green Years

1947
★ Great Expectations
The Ghost and Mrs. Muir
Green Dolphin Street

1948
★ The Naked City
I Remember Mama
Johnny Belinda
Portrait of Jennie

1949
★ Battleground
Champion
Come to the Stable
The Heiress

1950
★ The Third Man
All About Eve
The Asphalt Jungle
Sunset Boulevard

1951
★ A Place in the Sun
Strangers on a Train
A Streetcar Named Desire

1952
★ The Bad and the Beautiful
The Big Sky
Sudden Fear

1953
★ From Here to Eternity
Julius Caesar
Martin Luther
Roman Holiday

1954
★ On the Waterfront
The Country Girl
Executive Suite
Sabrina

1955
★ The Rose Tattoo
Blackboard Jungle
I'll Cry Tomorrow
Marty
Queen Bee

Foreign Correspondent / The Letter / The Long Voyage Home / Waterloo Bridge

★ = winner

Awards Index | 1299

1956
★ Somebody Up There Likes Me
Baby Doll
The Bad Seed
The Harder They Fall
1958
★ The Defiant Ones
Desire Under the Elms
I Want to Live!
Separate Tables
The Young Lions
1959
★ The Diary of Anne Frank
Anatomy of a Murder
Career
The Gazebo
Some Like It Hot
The Young Philadelphians
1960
The Apartment
The Facts of Life
Inherit the Wind
Psycho
1961
★ The Hustler
The Absent-Minded Professor
The Children's Hour
Judgment at Nuremberg
One, Two, Three
1962
★ The Longest Day
Birdman of Alcatraz
To Kill a Mockingbird
Two for the Seesaw
What Ever Happened to Baby Jane?
1963
★ Hud
The Balcony
Lilies of the Field
Love with the Proper Stranger
1964
★ Zorba the Greek
The Americanization of Emily
Hush, Hush, Sweet Charlotte
The Night of the Iguana
1965
★ Ship of Fools
In Harm's Way
King Rat
Morituri
A Patch of Blue
1966
★ Who's Afraid of Virginia Woolf?
The Fortune Cookie
Georgy Girl
Is Paris Burning?
Seconds

CINEMATOGRAPHY (COLOR)

1939
★ Gone with the Wind
Drums Along the Mohawk
The Four Feathers
The Private Lives of Elizabeth & Essex
The Wizard of Oz
1940
★ The Thief of Bagdad
Bitter Sweet
The Blue Bird
Down Argentine Way
Northwest Passage
1941
★ Blood and Sand
Billy the Kid
Blossoms in the Dust
Dive Bomber
Louisiana Purchase
1942
★ The Black Swan
Arabian Nights
Captains of the Clouds
The Jungle Book
Reap the Wild Wind
To the Shores of Tripoli
1943
★ The Phantom of the Opera

For Whom the Bell Tolls
Heaven Can Wait
Hello, Frisco, Hello
Lassie, Come Home
Thousands Cheer
1944
★ Wilson
Cover Girl
Meet Me in St. Louis
1945
★ Leave Her to Heaven
Anchors Aweigh
National Velvet
A Song to Remember
The Spanish Main
1946
★ The Yearling
The Jolson Story
1947
★ Black Narcissus
Life with Father
Mother Wore Tights
1948
★ Joan of Arc
The Loves of Carmen
The Three Musketeers
1949
★ She Wore a Yellow Ribbon
The Barkleys of Broadway
Jolson Sings Again
Little Women
1950
★ King Solomon's Mines
Annie Get Your Gun
Broken Arrow
The Flame & the Arrow
Samson and Delilah
1951
★ An American in Paris
David and Bathsheba
Quo Vadis
Show Boat
When Worlds Collide
1952
★ The Quiet Man
Hans Christian Andersen
Ivanhoe
Million Dollar Mermaid
The Snows of Kilimanjaro
1953
★ Shane
All the Brothers Were Valiant
Beneath the 12-Mile Reef
Lili
The Robe
1954
★ Three Coins in the Fountain
The Egyptian
Rear Window
Seven Brides for Seven Brothers
The Silver Chalice
1955
★ To Catch a Thief
Guys and Dolls
Love Is a Many-Splendored Thing
A Man Called Peter
Oklahoma!
1956
★ Around the World in 80 Days
The Eddy Duchin Story
The King and I
The Ten Commandments
War and Peace
1958
★ Gigi
Auntie Mame
Cat on a Hot Tin Roof
South Pacific
1959
★ Ben-Hur
The Five Pennies
The Nun's Story
1960
★ Spartacus
The Alamo
Butterfield 8
Exodus
1961
★ West Side Story

Fanny
Flower Drum Song
One-Eyed Jacks
1962
★ Lawrence of Arabia
Gypsy
Hatari!
Mutiny on the Bounty
The Wonderful World of the Brothers Grimm
1963
★ Cleopatra
The Cardinal
How the West Was Won
Irma La Douce
It's a Mad, Mad, Mad, Mad World
1964
★ My Fair Lady
Becket
Cheyenne Autumn
Mary Poppins
The Unsinkable Molly Brown
1965
★ Doctor Zhivago
The Agony and the Ecstasy
The Great Race
The Greatest Story Ever Told
The Sound of Music
1966
★ A Man for All Seasons
Fantastic Voyage
Hawaii
The Professionals
The Sand Pebbles

COSTUME DESIGN

1951
★ The Black Rose
1957
★ Les Girls
An Affair to Remember
Funny Face
Pal Joey
Raintree County
1958
★ Gigi
Bell, Book and Candle
The Buccaneer
Some Came Running
1967
★ Camelot
Bonnie & Clyde
The Happiest Millionaire
The Taming of the Shrew
Thoroughly Modern Millie
1968
★ Romeo and Juliet
The Lion in Winter
Oliver!
Planet of the Apes
Star!
1969
★ Anne of the Thousand Days
Hello, Dolly!
Sweet Charity
They Shoot Horses, Don't They?
1970
★ Cromwell
Airport
Darling Lili
Scrooge
1971
★ Nicholas and Alexandra
Bedknobs and Broomsticks
Death in Venice
Mary, Queen of Scots
What's the Matter with Helen?
1972
★ Travels with My Aunt
The Godfather
Lady Sings the Blues
Young Winston
1973
★ The Sting
Cries and Whispers
Tom Sawyer
The Way We Were

1974
★ The Great Gatsby
Chinatown
Daisy Miller
The Godfather, Part 2
Murder on the Orient Express
1975
★ Barry Lyndon
The Four Musketeers
Funny Lady
The Magic Flute
The Man Who Would Be King
1976
★ Bound for Glory
The Incredible Sarah
The Passover Plot
The Seven-Per-Cent Solution
1977
★ Star Wars
Airport '77
Julia
A Little Night Music
The Other Side of Midnight
1978
★ Death on the Nile
Days of Heaven
The Swarm
The Wiz
1979
★ All That Jazz
Agatha
Butch and Sundance: The Early Days
The Europeans
La Cage aux Folles
1980
★ Tess
The Elephant Man
My Brilliant Career
Somewhere in Time
When Time Ran Out
1981
★ Chariots of Fire
The French Lieutenant's Woman
Pennies from Heaven
Ragtime
Reds
1982
★ Gandhi
Sophie's Choice
Tron
Victor/Victoria
1983
★ Fanny and Alexander
Cross Creek
Heart Like a Wheel
The Return of Martin Guerre
Zelig
1984
★ Amadeus
The Bostonians
A Passage to India
Places in the Heart
2010: The Year We Make Contact
1985
★ Ran
The Color Purple
The Journey of Natty Gann
Out of Africa
Prizzi's Honor
1986
★ A Room with a View
The Mission
Otello
Peggy Sue Got Married
Pirates
1987
★ The Last Emperor
The Dead
Empire of the Sun
Maurice
The Untouchables
1988
★ Dangerous Liaisons
Coming to America
A Handful of Dust
Sunset
Tucker: The Man and His Dream

1989
★ Henry V
The Adventures of Baron Munchausen
Driving Miss Daisy
Harlem Nights
Valmont
1990
★ Cyrano de Bergerac
Avalon
Dances with Wolves
Dick Tracy
Hamlet
1991
★ Bugsy
The Addams Family
Barton Fink
Hook
Madame Bovary
1992
★ Bram Stoker's Dracula
Enchanted April
Howard's End
Malcolm X
Toys
1993
★ The Age of Innocence
Orlando
The Piano
The Remains of the Day
Schindler's List
1994
★ The Adventures of Priscilla, Queen of the Desert
Bullets over Broadway
Little Women
Maverick
Queen Margot
1995
★ Restoration
Braveheart
Richard III
Sense and Sensibility
12 Monkeys
1996
★ The English Patient
Angels and Insects
Emma
Hamlet
Portrait of a Lady
1997
★ Titanic
Amistad
Kundun
Oscar and Lucinda
The Wings of the Dove
1998
★ Shakespeare in Love
Beloved
Elizabeth
Pleasantville
Velvet Goldmine
1999
★ Topsy-Turvy
Anna and the King
The Talented Mr. Ripley
Titus
2000
★ Gladiator
Crouching Tiger, Hidden Dragon
Dr. Seuss' How the Grinch Stole Christmas
102 Dalmatians
Quills
2001
★ Moulin Rouge
The Affair of the Necklace
Gosford Park
Harry Potter and the Sorcerer's Stone
Lord of the Rings: The Fellowship of the Rings
2002
★ Chicago
Frida
Gangs of New York
The Pianist
2003
★ Lord of the Rings: The Return of the King
Girl with a Pearl Earring
The Last Samurai

Master and Commander: The Far Side of the World
Seabiscuit
2004
★ The Aviator
Finding Neverland
Lemony Snicket's A Series of Unfortunate Events
Ray
2005
★ Memoirs of a Geisha
Charlie and the Chocolate Factory
Mrs. Henderson Presents
Pride and Prejudice
Walk the Line
2006
★ Marie Antoinette
Curse of the Golden Flower
The Devil Wears Prada
Dreamgirls
The Queen
2007
★ Elizabeth: The Golden Age
Across the Universe
Atonement
La Vie en Rose
Sweeney Todd: The Demon Barber of Fleet Street

COSTUME DESIGN (B&W)

1948
★ Hamlet
1949
★ The Heiress
1950
★ All About Eve
Born Yesterday
The Magnificent Yankee
Prince of Foxes
1951
★ A Place in the Sun
A Streetcar Named Desire
1952
★ The Bad and the Beautiful
Affair in Trinidad
Carrie
Sudden Fear
1953
★ Roman Holiday
From Here to Eternity
1954
★ Sabrina
The Earrings of Madame De...
Executive Suite
Indiscretion of an American Wife
It Should Happen to You
1955
★ I'll Cry Tomorrow
The Pickwick Papers
Queen Bee
The Rose Tattoo
Ugetsu
1956
★ Solid Gold Cadillac
Seven Samurai
1959
★ Some Like It Hot
Career
The Diary of Anne Frank
The Young Philadelphians
1960
★ The Facts of Life
Never on Sunday
The Rise and Fall of Legs Diamond
Seven Thieves
The Virgin Spring
1961
★ La Dolce Vita
The Children's Hour
Judgment at Nuremberg
Yojimbo
1962
★ Days of Wine and Roses
The Man Who Shot Liberty Valance
The Miracle Worker

★ = winner

COSTUME DESIGN (COLOR)

1963
Phaedra
What Ever Happened to Baby Jane?

1962
★ The Wonderful World of the Brothers Grimm
Pocketful of Miracles
Flower Drum Song
Back Street

1961
★ West Side Story
Babes in Toyland
Sunrise at Campobello

1960
★ Spartacus
Can-Can
Midnight Lace

1959
★ Ben-Hur
The Best of Everything
The Five Pennies

1956
★ The King and I
Around the World in 80 Days
Giant
The Ten Commandments
War and Peace

1955
★ Love Is a Many-Splendored Thing
Guys and Dolls
To Catch a Thief
The Virgin Queen

1954
★ Gate of Hell
Brigadoon
Desiree
A Star Is Born
There's No Business Like Show Business

1953
★ The Robe
The Band Wagon
How to Marry a Millionaire
Young Bess

1952
★ Moulin Rouge
The Greatest Show on Earth
Hans Christian Andersen
The Merry Widow

1951
★ An American in Paris
David and Bathsheba
Quo Vadis
The Tales of Hoffmann

1950
★ Samson and Delilah
That Forsyte Woman

1949
★ Adventures of Don Juan

1948
★ Joan of Arc

1966
★ Who's Afraid of Virginia Woolf?
Morgan: A Suitable Case for Treatment
The Gospel According to St. Matthew

1965
★ Darling
Morituri
Ship of Fools
The Slender Thread

1964
★ The Night of the Iguana
Hush, Hush, Sweet Charlotte
Kisses for My President

Becket
Mary Poppins
Brown
★ My Fair Lady

The Cardinal
How the West Was Won
A New Kind of Love
The Stripper
★ Cleopatra
1963

Bon Voyage!
Gypsy
The Music Man
My Geisha

DIRECTOR

1928
Charlie Chaplin/The Circus
King Vidor/The Crowd
Ted Wilde/Speedy

1929
Harry Beaumont/Broadway Melody

1930
Clarence Brown/Anna Christie
Clarence Brown/Romance
Robert Z. Leonard/The Divorcee
King Vidor/Hallelujah!
★ Lewis Milestone/All Quiet on the Western Front

1931
Clarence Brown/A Free Soul
Lewis Milestone/The Front Page
Wesley Ruggles/Cimarron
Josef von Sternberg/Morocco

1932
King Vidor/The Champ
Josef von Sternberg/Shanghai Express

1933
★ Frank Lloyd/Cavalcade
Frank Capra/Lady for a Day
George Cukor/Little Women

1934
★ Frank Capra/It Happened One Night
Victor Schertzinger/One Night of Love
W.S. Van Dyke/The Thin Man

1935
★ John Ford/The Informer
Henry Hathaway/Lives of a Bengal Lancer
Frank Lloyd/Mutiny on the Bounty

1936
★ Frank Capra/Mr. Deeds Goes to Town
Gregory La Cava/My Man Godfrey
Robert Z. Leonard/The Great Ziegfeld
W.S. Van Dyke/San Francisco
William Wyler/Dodsworth

1937
★ Leo McCarey/The Awful Truth
William Dieterle/The Life of Emile Zola
Sidney Franklin/The Good Earth

1938
★ Frank Capra/You Can't Take It with You
Michael Curtiz/Angels with Dirty Faces
Michael Curtiz/Four Daughters
Norman Taurog/Boys Town
King Vidor/The Citadel

1939
★ Victor Fleming/Gone with the Wind
Frank Capra/Mr. Smith Goes to Washington
John Ford/Stagecoach
Sam Wood/Goodbye, Mr. Chips
William Wyler/Wuthering Heights

1940
★ John Ford/The Grapes of Wrath
George Cukor/The Philadelphia Story
Alfred Hitchcock/Rebecca
Sam Wood/Kitty Foyle
William Wyler/The Letter

1941
★ John Ford/How Green Was My Valley
Alexander Hall/Here Comes Mr. Jordan
Howard Hawks/Sergeant York
Orson Welles/Citizen Kane
William Wyler/The Little Foxes

1942
★ William Wyler/Mrs. Miniver
Michael Curtiz/Yankee Doodle Dandy
John Farrow/Wake Island
Mervyn LeRoy/Random Harvest
Sam Wood/Kings Row

1943
★ Michael Curtiz/Casablanca
Clarence Brown/The Human Comedy
Henry King/The Song of Bernadette
Ernst Lubitsch/Heaven Can Wait
George Stevens/The More the Merrier

1944
★ Leo McCarey/Going My Way
Alfred Hitchcock/Lifeboat
Henry King/Wilson
Otto Preminger/Laura
Billy Wilder/Double Indemnity

1945
★ Billy Wilder/The Lost Weekend
Clarence Brown/National Velvet
Alfred Hitchcock/Spellbound
Leo McCarey/The Bells of St. Mary's
Jean Renoir/The Southerner

1946
★ William Wyler/The Best Years of Our Lives
Clarence Brown/The Yearling
Frank Capra/It's a Wonderful Life
David Lean/Brief Encounter
Robert Siodmak/The Killers

1947
★ Elia Kazan/Gentleman's Agreement
George Cukor/A Double Life
Edward Dmytryk/Crossfire

1948
★ John Huston/Treasure of the Sierra Madre
Anatole Litvak/The Snake Pit
Jean Negulesco/Johnny Belinda
Laurence Olivier/Hamlet
Fred Zinnemann/The Search

1949
★ Joseph L. Mankiewicz/A Letter to Three Wives
Carol Reed/The Fallen Idol
Robert Rossen/All the King's Men
William A. Wellman/Battleground
William Wyler/The Heiress

1950
★ Joseph L. Mankiewicz/All About Eve
George Cukor/Born Yesterday
John Huston/The Asphalt Jungle
Carol Reed/The Third Man
Billy Wilder/Sunset Boulevard

1951
★ George Stevens/A Place in the Sun
John Huston/The African Queen
Elia Kazan/A Streetcar Named Desire
Vincente Minnelli/An American in Paris
William Wyler/Detective Story

1952
★ John Ford/The Quiet Man
Cecil B. DeMille/The Greatest Show on Earth
John Huston/Moulin Rouge
Joseph L. Mankiewicz/Five Fingers
Fred Zinnemann/High Noon

1953
★ Fred Zinnemann/From Here to Eternity
George Stevens/Shane
Charles Walters/Lili
Billy Wilder/Stalag 17
William Wyler/Roman Holiday

1954
★ Elia Kazan/On the Waterfront
Alfred Hitchcock/Rear Window
George Seaton/Country Girl
John Sturges/Bad Day at Black Rock
William A. Wellman/The High and the Mighty

1955
★ Delbert Mann/Marty
Elia Kazan/East of Eden
David Lean/Summertime
Joshua Logan/Picnic
William Wyler/Friendly Persuasion

1956
★ George Stevens/Giant
Michael Anderson, Sr./Around the World in 80 Days
Walter Lang/The King and I
King Vidor/War and Peace
William Wyler/Friendly Persuasion

1957
★ David Lean/The Bridge on the River Kwai
Joshua Logan/Sayonara
Sidney Lumet/Twelve Angry Men
Mark Robson/Peyton Place
Billy Wilder/Witness for the Prosecution

1958
★ Vincente Minnelli/Gigi
Richard Brooks/Cat on a Hot Tin Roof
Stanley Kramer/The Defiant Ones
Mark Robson/The Inn of the Sixth Happiness
Robert Wise/I Want to Live!

1959
★ William Wyler/Ben-Hur
Jack Clayton/Room at the Top
George Stevens/The Diary of Anne Frank
Billy Wilder/Some Like It Hot
Fred Zinnemann/The Nun's Story

1960
★ Billy Wilder/The Apartment
Jules Dassin/Never on Sunday
Alfred Hitchcock/Psycho
Jack Cardiff/Sons and Lovers
Fred Zinnemann/The Sundowners

1961
★ Robert Wise/West Side Story and Jerome Robbins
Federico Fellini/La Dolce Vita
Stanley Kramer/Judgment at Nuremberg
Robert Rossen/The Hustler
J. Lee Thompson/The Guns of Navarone

1962
★ David Lean/Lawrence of Arabia
Pietro Germi/Divorce—Italian Style
Robert Mulligan/To Kill a Mockingbird
Arthur Penn/The Miracle Worker
Frank Perry/David and Lisa

1963
★ Tony Richardson/Tom Jones
Federico Fellini/8 1/2
Otto Preminger/The Cardinal
Martin Ritt/Hud

1964
★ George Cukor/My Fair Lady
Michael Cacoyannis/Zorba the Greek
Peter Glenville/Becket
Stanley Kubrick/Dr. Strangelove, or: How I Learned to Stop Worrying and Love the Bomb
Robert Stevenson/Mary Poppins

1965
★ Robert Wise/The Sound of Music
David Lean/Doctor Zhivago
John Schlesinger/Darling
Hiroshi Teshigahara/Woman in the Dunes
William Wyler/The Collector

1966
★ Fred Zinnemann/A Man for All Seasons
Michelangelo Antonioni/Blow-Up
Richard Brooks/The Professionals
Claude Lelouch/A Man and a Woman
Mike Nichols/Who's Afraid of Virginia Woolf?

1967
★ Mike Nichols/The Graduate
Richard Brooks/In Cold Blood

1968
★ Carol Reed/Oliver!
Anthony Harvey/The Lion in Winter
Stanley Kubrick/2001: A Space Odyssey
Gillo Pontecorvo/The Battle of Algiers
Franco Zeffirelli/Romeo and Juliet

1969
★ John Schlesinger/Midnight Cowboy
Costa-Gavras/Z
George Roy Hill/Butch Cassidy and the Sundance Kid
Arthur Penn/Alice's Restaurant
Sydney Pollack/They Shoot Horses, Don't They?

1970
★ Franklin J. Schaffner/Patton
Robert Altman/M*A*S*H
Federico Fellini/Fellini Satyricon
Arthur Hiller/Love Story
Ken Russell/Women in Love

1971
★ William Friedkin/The French Connection
Peter Bogdanovich/The Last Picture Show
Norman Jewison/Fiddler on the Roof
Stanley Kubrick/A Clockwork Orange
John Schlesinger/Sunday, Bloody Sunday

1972
★ Bob Fosse/Cabaret
John Boorman/Deliverance
Francis Ford Coppola/The Godfather
Joseph L. Mankiewicz/Sleuth
Jan Troell/The Emigrants

1973
★ George Roy Hill/The Sting
Ingmar Bergman/Cries and Whispers
Bernardo Bertolucci/Last Tango in Paris
William Friedkin/The Exorcist
George Lucas/American Graffiti

1974
★ Francis Ford Coppola/The Godfather, Part 2
John Cassavetes/A Woman Under the Influence
Bob Fosse/Lenny
Roman Polanski/Chinatown
Francois Truffaut/Day for Night

1975
★ Milos Forman/One Flew Over the Cuckoo's Nest
Robert Altman/Nashville
Federico Fellini/Amarcord
Stanley Kubrick/Barry Lyndon
Sidney Lumet/Dog Day Afternoon

1976
★ John G. Avildsen/Rocky
Ingmar Bergman/Face to Face
Sidney Lumet/Network
Alan J. Pakula/All the President's Men
Lina Wertmuller/Seven Beauties

★ = winner

1977
★ Woody Allen/Annie Hall
George Lucas/Star Wars
Herbert Ross/The Turning Point
Steven Spielberg/Close Encounters of the Third Kind
Fred Zinnemann/Julia
1978
★ Michael Cimino/The Deer Hunter
Woody Allen/Interiors
Hal Ashby/Coming Home
Warren Beatty/Heaven Can Wait
Alan Parker/Midnight Express
1979
★ Robert Benton/Kramer vs. Kramer
Francis Ford Coppola/Apocalypse Now
Bob Fosse/All That Jazz
Edouard Molinaro/La Cage aux Folles
Peter Yates/Breaking Away
1980
★ Robert Redford/Ordinary People
David Lynch/The Elephant Man
Roman Polanski/Tess
Richard Rush/The Stunt Man
Martin Scorsese/Raging Bull
1981
★ Warren Beatty/Reds
Hugh Hudson/Chariots of Fire
Louis Malle/Atlantic City
Mark Rydell/On Golden Pond
Steven Spielberg/Raiders of the Lost Ark
1982
★ Richard Attenborough/Gandhi
Sidney Lumet/The Verdict
Wolfgang Petersen/Das Boot
Sydney Pollack/Tootsie
Steven Spielberg/E.T.: The Extra-Terrestrial
1983
★ James L. Brooks/Terms of Endearment
Bruce Beresford/Tender Mercies
Ingmar Bergman/Fanny and Alexander
Mike Nichols/Silkwood
Peter Yates/The Dresser
1984
★ Milos Forman/Amadeus
Woody Allen/Broadway Danny Rose
Robert Benton/Places in the Heart
Roland Joffe/The Killing Fields
David Lean/A Passage to India
1985
★ Sydney Pollack/Out of Africa
Hector Babenco/Kiss of the Spider Woman
John Huston/Prizzi's Honor
Akira Kurosawa/Ran
Peter Weir/Witness
1986
★ Oliver Stone/Platoon
Woody Allen/Hannah and Her Sisters
James Ivory/A Room with a View
1987
★ Bernardo Bertolucci/The Last Emperor

John Boorman/Hope and Glory
Lasse Hallstrom/My Life As a Dog
Norman Jewison/Moonstruck
Adrian Lyne/Fatal Attraction
1988
★ Barry Levinson/Rain Man
Charles Crichton/A Fish Called Wanda
Mike Nichols/Working Girl
Alan Parker/Mississippi Burning
Martin Scorsese/The Last Temptation of Christ
1989
★ Oliver Stone/Born on the Fourth of July
Woody Allen/Crimes & Misdemeanors
Kenneth Branagh/Henry V
Jim Sheridan/My Left Foot
Peter Weir/Dead Poets Society
1990
★ Kevin Costner/Dances with Wolves
Francis Ford Coppola/The Godfather, Part 3
Stephen Frears/The Grifters
Barbet Schroeder/Reversal of Fortune
Martin Scorsese/Goodfellas
1991
★ Jonathan Demme/The Silence of the Lambs
Barry Levinson/Bugsy
Ridley Scott/Thelma & Louise
John Singleton/Boyz N the Hood
Oliver Stone/JFK
1992
★ Clint Eastwood/Unforgiven
Robert Altman/The Player
Martin Brest/Scent of a Woman
James Ivory/Howard's End
Neil Jordan/The Crying Game
1993
★ Steven Spielberg/Schindler's List
Robert Altman/Short Cuts
Jane Campion/The Piano
James Ivory/The Remains of the Day
Jim Sheridan/In the Name of the Father
1994
★ Robert Zemeckis/Forrest Gump
Woody Allen/Bullets over Broadway
Krzysztof Kieslowski/Trois Couleurs: Rouge
Robert Redford/Quiz Show
Quentin Tarantino/Pulp Fiction
1995
★ Mel Gibson/Braveheart
Chris Noonan/Babe
Michael Radford/The Postman
Tim Robbins/Dead Man Walking
Mike Leigh/Secrets and Lies
1996
★ Anthony Minghella/The English Patient
Joel Coen/Fargo
Milos Forman/The People vs. Larry Flynt
Scott Hicks/Shine
Mike Leigh/Secrets and Lies
1997
★ James Cameron/Titanic
Peter Cattaneo/The Full Monty

Atom Egoyan/The Sweet Hereafter
Curtis Hanson/L.A. Confidential
Gus Van Sant/Good Will Hunting
1998
★ Steven Spielberg/Saving Private Ryan
Roberto Benigni/Life Is Beautiful
John Madden/Shakespeare in Love
Terrence Malick/The Thin Red Line
Peter Weir/The Truman Show
1999
★ Sam Mendes/American Beauty
Lasse Hallstrom/The Cider House Rules
Spike Jonze/Being John Malkovich
Michael Mann/The Insider
M. Night Shyamalan/The Sixth Sense
2000
★ Steven Soderbergh/Traffic
Stephen Daldry/Billy Elliot
Ang Lee/Crouching Tiger, Hidden Dragon
Ridley Scott/Gladiator
Steven Soderbergh/Erin Brockovich
2001
★ Ron Howard/A Beautiful Mind
Robert Altman/Gosford Park
Peter Jackson/Lord of the Rings: The Fellowship of the Rings
David Lynch/Mulholland Drive
Ridley Scott/Black Hawk Down
2002
★ Roman Polanski/The Pianist
Pedro Almodovar/Talk to Her
Stephen Daldry/The Hours
Rob Marshall/Chicago
Martin Scorsese/Gangs of New York
2003
★ Peter Jackson/Lord of the Rings: The Return of the King
Sofia Coppola/Lost in Translation
Clint Eastwood/Mystic River
Fernando Meirelles/City of God
Peter Weir/Master and Commander: The Far Side of the World
2004
★ Clint Eastwood/Million Dollar Baby
Taylor Hackford/Ray
Mike Leigh/Vera Drake
Alexander Payne/Sideways
Martin Scorsese/The Aviator
2005
★ Ang Lee/Brokeback Mountain
George Clooney/Good Night, and Good Luck
Paul Haggis/Crash
Bennett Miller/Capote
Steven Spielberg/Munich
2006
★ Martin Scorsese/The Departed
Clint Eastwood/Letters from Iwo Jima
Stephen Frears/The Queen
Paul Greengrass/United 93
Alejandro Gonzalez Inarritu/Babel
2007
★ Ethan Coen/No Country for Old Men
★ Joel Coen/No Country for Old Men
Paul Thomas Anderson/There Will Be Blood
Tony Gilroy/Michael Clayton
Jason Reitman/Juno
Julian Schnabel/The Diving Bell and the Butterfly

FILM

1928
★ Wings
Last Command
1929
★ Broadway Melody
Alibi
1930
★ All Quiet on the Western Front
The Big House
Disraeli
The Divorcee
1931
★ Cimarron
The Front Page
Trader Horn
1932
★ Grand Hotel
Arrowsmith
The Champ
Shanghai Express
1933
★ Cavalcade
A Farewell to Arms
42nd Street
I Am a Fugitive from a Chain Gang
Lady for a Day
Little Women
The Private Life of Henry VIII
She Done Him Wrong
Smilin' Through
1934
★ It Happened One Night
The Barretts of Wimpole Street
Cleopatra
Flirtation Walk
The Gay Divorcee
Imitation of Life
One Night of Love
The Thin Man
Viva Villa!
1935
★ Mutiny on the Bounty
Alice Adams
Broadway Melody of 1936
Captain Blood
David Copperfield
The Informer
Les Miserables
The Lives of a Bengal Lancer
A Midsummer Night's Dream
Naughty Marietta
Ruggles of Red Gap
Top Hat
1936
★ The Great Ziegfeld
Anthony Adverse
Dodsworth
Libeled Lady
Mr. Deeds Goes to Town
Romeo and Juliet
San Francisco
A Tale of Two Cities
Three Smart Girls
1937
★ The Life of Emile Zola
The Awful Truth
Captains Courageous
Dead End
The Good Earth
In Old Chicago
Lost Horizon
100 Men and a Girl
Stage Door
A Star Is Born
1938
★ You Can't Take It with You
Alexander's Ragtime Band
Boys Town
The Citadel
Four Daughters
Grand Illusion
Jezebel
Pygmalion
Test Pilot
1939
★ Gone with the Wind
Dark Victory
Goodbye, Mr. Chips
Love Affair
Mr. Smith Goes to Washington
Ninotchka
Of Mice and Men
Stagecoach
The Wizard of Oz
Wuthering Heights
1940
★ Rebecca
All This and Heaven Too
Foreign Correspondent
The Grapes of Wrath
The Great Dictator
Kitty Foyle
The Letter
The Long Voyage Home
Our Town
The Philadelphia Story
1941
★ How Green Was My Valley
Blossoms in the Dust
Citizen Kane
Here Comes Mr. Jordan
The Little Foxes
The Maltese Falcon
Sergeant York
Suspicion
1942
★ Mrs. Miniver
Kings Row
The Magnificent Ambersons
The Pride of the Yankees
Random Harvest
Talk of the Town
Wake Island
Yankee Doodle Dandy
1943
★ Casablanca
For Whom the Bell Tolls
Heaven Can Wait
The Human Comedy
In Which We Serve
Madame Curie
The More the Merrier
The Ox-Bow Incident
The Song of Bernadette
Watch on the Rhine
1944
★ Going My Way
Double Indemnity
Gaslight
Since You Went Away
Wilson
1945
★ The Lost Weekend
Anchors Aweigh
The Bells of St. Mary's
Mildred Pierce
Spellbound
1946
★ The Best Years of Our Lives
Henry V
It's a Wonderful Life
The Razor's Edge
The Yearling
1947
★ Gentleman's Agreement
The Bishop's Wife
Crossfire
Great Expectations
Miracle on 34th Street
1948
★ Hamlet
Johnny Belinda
The Red Shoes
The Snake Pit
Treasure of the Sierra Madre
1949
★ All the King's Men

Battleground
The Heiress
A Letter to Three Wives
Twelve o'Clock High
1950
★ All About Eve
Born Yesterday
Father of the Bride
King Solomon's Mines
Sunset Boulevard
1951
★ An American in Paris
A Place in the Sun
Quo Vadis
A Streetcar Named Desire
1952
★ The Greatest Show on Earth
High Noon
Ivanhoe
Moulin Rouge
The Quiet Man
1953
★ From Here to Eternity
Julius Caesar
The Robe
Roman Holiday
Shane
1954
★ On the Waterfront
The Caine Mutiny
Country Girl
Seven Brides for Seven Brothers
Three Coins in the Fountain
1955
★ Marty
Love Is a Many-Splendored Thing
Mister Roberts
Picnic
The Rose Tattoo
1956
★ Around the World in 80 Days
Friendly Persuasion
Giant
The King and I
The Ten Commandments
1957
★ The Bridge on the River Kwai
Peyton Place
Sayonara
Twelve Angry Men
Witness for the Prosecution
1958
★ Gigi
Auntie Mame
Cat on a Hot Tin Roof
The Defiant Ones
Separate Tables
1959
★ Ben-Hur
Anatomy of a Murder
The Diary of Anne Frank
The Nun's Story
Room at the Top
1960
★ The Apartment
The Alamo
Elmer Gantry
The Sundowners
1961
★ West Side Story
Fanny
The Guns of Navarone
The Hustler
Judgment at Nuremberg
1962
★ Lawrence of Arabia
The Longest Day
The Music Man
Mutiny on the Bounty
To Kill a Mockingbird
1963
★ Tom Jones
Cleopatra
How the West Was Won
Lilies of the Field
1964
★ My Fair Lady
Becket

★ = winner

Best Picture (continued)

1965
★ The Sound of Music
Darling
Doctor Zhivago
Ship of Fools
A Thousand Clowns

Dr. Strangelove, or: How I Learned to Stop Worrying and Love the Bomb
Mary Poppins
Zorba the Greek

1966
★ A Man for All Seasons
Alfie
the Russians Are Coming, the Russians Are Coming
The Sand Pebbles
Who's Afraid of Virginia Woolf?

1967
★ In the Heat of the Night
Bonnie & Clyde
Doctor Dolittle
The Graduate
Guess Who's Coming to Dinner

1968
★ Oliver!
Funny Girl
The Lion in Winter
Rachel, Rachel
Romeo and Juliet

1969
★ Midnight Cowboy
Anne of the Thousand Days
Butch Cassidy and the Sundance Kid
Hello, Dolly!
Z

1970
★ Patton
Airport
Five Easy Pieces
Love Story
M*A*S*H

1971
★ The French Connection
A Clockwork Orange
Fiddler on the Roof
The Last Picture Show
Nicholas and Alexandra

1972
★ The Godfather
Cabaret
Deliverance
The Emigrants
Sounder

1973
★ The Sting
American Graffiti
Cries and Whispers
The Exorcist
A Touch of Class

1974
★ The Godfather, Part 2
Chinatown
The Conversation
Lenny
The Towering Inferno

1975
★ One Flew Over the Cuckoo's Nest
Barry Lyndon
Dog Day Afternoon
Jaws
Nashville

1976
★ Rocky
All the President's Men
Bound for Glory
Network
Taxi Driver

1977
★ Annie Hall
The Goodbye Girl
Julia
Star Wars
The Turning Point

1978
★ The Deer Hunter
Coming Home
Heaven Can Wait

1979
★ Kramer vs. Kramer
All That Jazz
Apocalypse Now
Breaking Away
Norma Rae

Midnight Express
An Unmarried Woman

1980
★ Ordinary People
Coal Miner's Daughter
The Elephant Man
Raging Bull
Tess

1981
★ Chariots of Fire
Atlantic City
On Golden Pond
Raiders of the Lost Ark
Reds

1982
★ Gandhi
E.T.: The Extra-Terrestrial
Missing
Tootsie
The Verdict

1983
★ Terms of Endearment
The Big Chill
The Dresser
The Right Stuff
Tender Mercies

1984
★ Amadeus
The Killing Fields
A Passage to India
Places in the Heart
A Soldier's Story

1985
★ Out of Africa
The Color Purple
Kiss of the Spider Woman
Prizzi's Honor
Witness

1986
★ Platoon
Children of a Lesser God
Hannah and Her Sisters
The Mission
A Room with a View

1987
★ The Last Emperor
Broadcast News
Fatal Attraction
Hope and Glory
Moonstruck

1988
★ Rain Man
The Accidental Tourist
Dangerous Liaisons
Mississippi Burning
Working Girl

1989
★ Driving Miss Daisy
Born on the Fourth of July
Dead Poets Society
Field of Dreams
My Left Foot

1990
★ Dances with Wolves
Awakenings
Ghost
Goodfellas

1991
★ The Silence of the Lambs
Beauty and the Beast
Bugsy
JFK
The Prince of Tides

1992
★ Unforgiven
The Crying Game
A Few Good Men
Howard's End
Scent of a Woman

1993
★ Schindler's List
The Fugitive
In the Name of the Father
The Piano
The Remains of the Day

1994
★ Forrest Gump
Four Weddings and a Funeral
Pulp Fiction
Quiz Show
The Shawshank Redemption

1995
★ Braveheart
Apollo 13
Babe
The Postman
Sense and Sensibility

1996
★ The English Patient
Fargo
Jerry Maguire
Secrets and Lies
Shine

1997
★ Titanic
As Good As It Gets
The Full Monty
Good Will Hunting
L.A. Confidential

1998
★ Shakespeare in Love
Elizabeth
Life is Beautiful
Saving Private Ryan
The Thin Red Line

1999
★ American Beauty
The Cider House Rules
The Green Mile
The Insider
The Sixth Sense

2000
★ Gladiator
Chocolat
Crouching Tiger, Hidden Dragon
Erin Brockovich
Traffic

2001
★ A Beautiful Mind
Gosford Park
In the Bedroom
Lord of the Rings: The Fellowship of the Rings
Moulin Rouge

2002
★ Chicago
Gangs of New York
The Hours
Lord of the Rings: The Two Towers
The Pianist

2003
★ Lord of the Rings: The Return of the King
Lost in Translation
Master and Commander: The Far Side of the World
Mystic River
Seabiscuit

2004
★ Million Dollar Baby
The Aviator
Finding Neverland
Ray
Sideways

2005
★ Crash
Brokeback Mountain
Capote
Good Night, and Good Luck
Munich

2006
★ The Departed
Babel
Letters from Iwo Jima
Little Miss Sunshine
The Queen

2007
★ No Country for Old Men
Atonement
Juno
Michael Clayton
There Will Be Blood

FEATURE DOCUMENTARY

1961 ★ The Sky Above, the Mud Below
1970 ★ Woodstock
1971 ★ The Hellstrom Chronicle
1972 ★ Marjoe
1977 ★ Harlan County, U.S.A.
The Children of Theatre Street
Let's Get Lost
Times of Harvey Milk
When We Were Kings
The War Room
Buena Vista Social Club
Bowling for Columbine
Winged Migration
The Fog of War: Eleven Lessons from the Life of Robert S. McNamara
Capturing the Friedmans
My Architect: A Son's Journey
Born into Brothels: Calcutta's Red Light Kids
The Story of the Weeping Camel
Super Size Me
March of the Penguins
Enron: The Smartest Guys in the Room
An Inconvenient Truth
No End in Sight
Sicko

FILM EDITING

1934
Cleopatra
One Night of Love

1935
★ A Midsummer Night's Dream
David Copperfield
The Informer
Les Miserables
The Lives of a Bengal Lancer
Mutiny on the Bounty

1936
★ Anthony Adverse
Come and Get It
The Great Ziegfeld
Lloyd's of London
A Tale of Two Cities
Theodora Goes Wild

1937
★ Lost Horizon
The Awful Truth
Captains Courageous
The Good Earth
100 Men and a Girl

1938
★ The Adventures of Robin Hood
Alexander's Ragtime Band
The Great Waltz
Test Pilot
You Can't Take It with You

1939
★ Gone with the Wind
Goodbye, Mr. Chips
Mr. Smith Goes to Washington
The Rains Came
Stagecoach

1940
The Grapes of Wrath
The Letter
The Long Voyage Home
Rebecca

1941
★ Sergeant York
Citizen Kane
Dr. Jekyll and Mr. Hyde
How Green Was My Valley
The Little Foxes

1942
★ The Pride of the Yankees
Mrs. Miniver
The Talk of the Town
Yankee Doodle Dandy

1943
★ Air Force
Casablanca
Five Graves to Cairo
For Whom the Bell Tolls
The Song of Bernadette

1944
★ Wilson
Going My Way
None But the Lonely Heart
Since You Went Away

1945
★ National Velvet
The Bells of St. Mary's
The Lost Weekend
A Song to Remember
Objective, Burma!

1946
★ The Best Years of Our Lives
It's a Wonderful Life
The Jolson Story
The Killers
The Yearling

1947
★ Body and Soul
The Bishop's Wife
Gentleman's Agreement
Green Dolphin Street
Odd Man Out

1948
★ The Naked City
Joan of Arc
Johnny Belinda
Red River
The Red Shoes

1949
★ Champion
All the King's Men
Battleground
Sands of Iwo Jima
The Window

1950
★ King Solomon's Mines
Annie Get Your Gun
Sunset Boulevard
The Third Man

1951
★ A Place in the Sun
An American in Paris
Quo Vadis
The Well

1952
★ High Noon
Come Back, Little Sheba
Flat Top
The Greatest Show on Earth
Moulin Rouge

1953
★ From Here to Eternity
The Moon Is Blue
Roman Holiday
The War of the Worlds

1954
★ On the Waterfront
The Caine Mutiny
Seven Brides for Seven Brothers
20,000 Leagues under the Sea

1955
Picnic
Blackboard Jungle
The Bridges at Toko-Ri
Oklahoma!
The Rose Tattoo

1956
★ Around the World in 80 Days
The Brave One
Giant
Somebody Up There Likes Me
The Ten Commandments

1957
★ The Bridge on the River Kwai
Gunfight at the O.K. Corral
Pal Joey
Sayonara
Witness for the Prosecution

1958
★ Gigi
Auntie Mame
Cowboy
The Defiant Ones
I Want to Live!

1959
★ Ben-Hur
Anatomy of a Murder
North by Northwest
The Nun's Story
On the Beach

1960
★ The Apartment
The Alamo
Inherit the Wind
Spartacus

1961
★ West Side Story
Fanny
The Guns of Navarone
Judgment at Nuremberg
The Parent Trap

1962
★ Lawrence of Arabia
The Longest Day
The Manchurian Candidate
The Music Man
Mutiny on the Bounty

1963
★ How the West Was Won
The Cardinal
Cleopatra
The Great Escape
It's a Mad, Mad, Mad, Mad World

1964
★ Mary Poppins
Becket
Father Goose
Hush, Hush, Sweet Charlotte
My Fair Lady

1965
★ The Sound of Music
Doctor Zhivago
The Flight of the Phoenix
The Great Race
The Russians Are Coming, the Russians Are Coming

1966
★ Grand Prix
Fantastic Voyage
The Russians Are Coming, the Russians Are Coming
The Sand Pebbles
Who's Afraid of Virginia Woolf?

1967
★ In the Heat of the Night
The Dirty Dozen
Doctor Dolittle
Guess Who's Coming to Dinner

1968
★ Bullitt
Funny Girl
The Odd Couple
Oliver!
Wild in the Streets

1969
★ Z
Hello, Dolly!
Midnight Cowboy

Academy Awards

1970
- They Shoot Horses, Don't They?
- ★ Patton
- Airport
- M*A*S*H
- Tora! Tora! Tora!
- Woodstock

1971
- ★ The French Connection
- The Andromeda Strain
- A Clockwork Orange
- Kotch
- Summer of '42

1972
- ★ Cabaret
- Deliverance
- The Godfather
- The Hot Rock
- The Poseidon Adventure

1973
- ★ The Sting
- American Graffiti
- The Day of the Jackal
- The Exorcist
- Jonathan Livingston Seagull

1974
- ★ The Towering Inferno
- Blazing Saddles
- Chinatown
- Earthquake
- The Longest Yard

1975
- ★ Jaws
- Dog Day Afternoon
- The Man Who Would Be King
- One Flew Over the Cuckoo's Nest
- Three Days of the Condor

1976
- ★ Rocky
- All the President's Men
- Bound for Glory
- Network
- Two Minute Warning

1977
- ★ Star Wars
- Close Encounters of the Third Kind
- Julia
- Smokey and the Bandit
- The Turning Point

1978
- ★ The Deer Hunter
- The Boys from Brazil
- Coming Home
- Midnight Express
- Superman: The Movie

1979
- ★ All That Jazz
- Apocalypse Now
- The Black Stallion
- Kramer vs. Kramer
- The Rose

1980
- ★ Raging Bull
- Coal Miner's Daughter
- The Competition
- The Elephant Man
- Fame

1981
- ★ Raiders of the Lost Ark
- Chariots of Fire
- The French Lieutenant's Woman
- On Golden Pond
- Reds

1982
- ★ Gandhi
- Das Boot
- E.T.: The Extra-Terrestrial
- An Officer and a Gentleman
- Tootsie

1983
- ★ The Right Stuff
- Blue Thunder
- Flashdance
- Silkwood
- Terms of Endearment

1984
- ★ The Killing Fields
- Amadeus
- The Cotton Club
- A Passage to India
- Romancing the Stone

1985
- ★ Witness
- A Chorus Line
- Out of Africa
- Prizzi's Honor
- Runaway Train

1986
- ★ Platoon
- Aliens
- Hannah and Her Sisters
- The Mission
- Top Gun

1987
- ★ The Last Emperor
- Broadcast News
- Empire of the Sun
- Fatal Attraction
- RoboCop

1988
- ★ Who Framed Roger Rabbit
- Die Hard
- Gorillas in the Mist
- Mississippi Burning
- Rain Man

1989
- ★ Born on the Fourth of July
- The Bear
- Driving Miss Daisy
- The Fabulous Baker Boys
- Glory

1990
- ★ Dances with Wolves
- Ghost
- The Godfather, Part 3
- Goodfellas
- The Hunt for Red October

1991
- ★ JFK
- The Commitments
- The Silence of the Lambs
- Terminator 2: Judgment Day
- Thelma & Louise

1992
- ★ Unforgiven
- Basic Instinct
- The Crying Game
- A Few Good Men
- The Player

1993
- ★ Schindler's List
- The Fugitive
- In the Line of Fire
- In the Name of the Father
- The Piano

1994
- ★ Forrest Gump
- Hoop Dreams
- Pulp Fiction
- The Shawshank Redemption
- Speed

1995
- ★ Apollo 13
- Babe
- Braveheart
- Crimson Tide
- Seven

1996
- ★ The English Patient
- Evita
- Fargo
- Jerry Maguire
- Shine

1997
- ★ Titanic
- Air Force One
- As Good As It Gets
- Good Will Hunting
- L.A. Confidential

1998
- ★ Saving Private Ryan
- Life Is Beautiful
- Out of Sight
- Shakespeare in Love
- The Thin Red Line

1999
- ★ The Matrix
- American Beauty
- The Cider House Rules
- The Insider
- The Sixth Sense

2000
- ★ Traffic
- Almost Famous
- Crouching Tiger, Hidden Dragon
- Gladiator
- Wonder Boys

2001
- ★ Black Hawk Down
- A Beautiful Mind
- Lord of the Rings: The Fellowship of the Rings
- Memento
- Moulin Rouge

2002
- ★ Chicago
- Gangs of New York
- The Hours
- Lord of the Rings: The Two Towers
- The Pianist

2003
- ★ Lord of the Rings: The Return of the King
- City of God
- Cold Mountain
- Master and Commander: The Far Side of the World
- Seabiscuit

2004
- ★ The Aviator
- Collateral
- Finding Neverland
- Million Dollar Baby
- Ray

2005
- ★ Crash
- Cinderella Man
- The Constant Gardener
- Munich
- Walk the Line

2006
- ★ The Departed
- Babel
- Blood Diamond
- Children of Men
- United 93

2007
- ★ The Bourne Ultimatum
- The Diving Bell and the Butterfly
- Into the Wild
- No Country for Old Men
- There Will Be Blood

MAKEUP

1981
- ★ An American Werewolf in London

1982
- ★ Quest for Fire
- Gandhi

1984
- ★ Amadeus
- Greystoke: The Legend of Tarzan, Lord of the Apes
- 2010: The Year We Make Contact

1985
- ★ Mask
- The Color Purple
- Remo Williams: The Adventure Begins

1986
- ★ The Fly
- The Clan of the Cave Bear
- Legend

1987
- ★ Harry and the Hendersons
- Happy New Year

1988
- ★ Beetlejuice

1989
- ★ Driving Miss Daisy
- The Adventures of Baron Munchausen
- Dad

1990
- ★ Dick Tracy
- Cyrano de Bergerac

ORIGINAL DRAMATIC SCORE

1941
- ★ The Devil & Daniel Webster
- Ball of Fire
- Cheers for Miss Bishop
- Citizen Kane
- Dr. Jekyll and Mr. Hyde
- How Green Was My Valley
- King of the Zombies
- The Little Foxes
- Lydia
- Sergeant York
- So Ends Our Night
- Sundown
- Suspicion
- Tanks a Million
- That Uncertain Feeling

1942
- ★ Now, Voyager
- Arabian Nights
- Bambi
- The Black Swan
- The Corsican Brothers
- Flying Tigers
- I Married a Witch
- Joan of Paris
- The Jungle Book
- The Pride of the Yankees
- Random Harvest
- The Shanghai Gesture
- Silver Queen
- Talk of the Town
- To Be or Not to Be

1943
- ★ The Song of Bernadette
- The Amazing Mrs. Holiday
- Casablanca
- Commandos Strike at Dawn
- The Fallen Sparrow
- For Whom the Bell Tolls
- Hangmen Also Die
- Hi Diddle Diddle
- Johnny Come Lately
- The Kansan
- Lady of Burlesque
- Madame Curie
- The Moon and Sixpence
- The North Star
- War of the Wildcats

1944
- ★ Since You Went Away
- The Adventures of Mark Twain
- The Bridge of San Luis Rey
- Casanova Brown
- Double Indemnity
- Fighting Seabees
- The Hairy Ape
- Higher and Higher
- Jack London
- None But the Lonely Heart
- The Princess and the Pirate
- Wilson
- The Woman of the Town

1945
- ★ Spellbound
- The Bells of St. Mary's
- Brewster's Millions
- Captain Kidd
- The Enchanted Cottage
- Flame of the Barbary Coast
- Guest in the House
- Guest Wife
- The Keys of the Kingdom
- The Last Weekend
- Objective, Burma!
- A Song to Remember
- The Southerner
- The Valley of Decision
- Woman in the Window

1946
- ★ The Best Years of Our Lives
- Anna and the King of Siam
- Henry V
- Humoresque
- The Killers

1947
- ★ A Double Life
- The Bishop's Wife
- Captain from Castile
- Forever Amber
- Life with Father
- The Road to Rio

1948
- ★ The Red Shoes
- Hamlet
- Joan of Arc
- Johnny Belinda
- The Snake Pit

1949
- ★ The Heiress
- Beyond the Forest
- Champion

1950
- ★ Sunset Boulevard
- All About Eve
- The Flame & the Arrow
- Samson and Delilah

1951
- ★ A Place in the Sun
- David and Bathsheba
- Quo Vadis
- A Streetcar Named Desire

1952
- ★ High Noon
- Ivanhoe
- Miracle of Our Lady of Fatima
- The Thief
- Viva Zapata!

1953
- ★ Lili
- Above and Beyond
- From Here to Eternity
- Julius Caesar

1954
- ★ The High and the Mighty
- The Caine Mutiny
- Genevieve
- On the Waterfront
- The Silver Chalice

1955
- ★ Love Is a Many-Splendored Thing
- Battle Cry
- The Man with the Golden Arm
- Picnic
- The Rose Tattoo

1956
- ★ Around the World in 80 Days
- Anastasia
- Between Heaven and Hell
- Giant
- The Rainmaker

1958
- ★ The Old Man and the Sea
- The Big Country
- Separate Tables
- The Young Lions

ADAPTED SCORE

1944
- ★ Cover Girl

1962
- ★ The Music Man
- Billy Rose's Jumbo
- Gypsy
- The Wonderful World of the Brothers Grimm

1963
- ★ Irma La Douce
- Bye, Bye, Birdie
- A New Kind of Love
- Sundays & Cybele
- The Sword in the Stone

1964
- ★ My Fair Lady
- A Hard Day's Night
- Robin and the 7 Hoods
- The Unsinkable Molly Brown

1965
- ★ The Sound of Music
- Cat Ballou
- A Thousand Clowns

1966
- ★ A Funny Thing Happened on the Way to the Forum
- The Gospel According to St. Matthew
- Return of the Magnificent Seven
- The Singing Nun

1967
- ★ Camelot
- Guess Who's Coming to Dinner
- Valley of the Dolls

1968
- ★ Oliver!
- Star!

★ = winner

1959
★ Ben-Hur
The Diary of Anne Frank
The Nun's Story
On the Beach
Pillow Talk

1960
★ Exodus
The Alamo
Elmer Gantry
The Magnificent Seven
Spartacus

1961
★ Breakfast at Tiffany's
El Cid
Fanny
The Guns of Navarone
Summer and Smoke

1971
★ Summer of '42
Mary, Queen of Scots
Nicholas and Alexandra
Shaft
Straw Dogs

1972
★ Cabaret
Lady Sings the Blues

1973
★ The Way We Were
Cinderella Liberty
The Day of the Dolphin
Papillon
A Touch of Class

1974
★ The Godfather, Part 2
Chinatown
Murder on the Orient Express
The Towering Inferno

1995
★ The Postman
Apollo 13
Braveheart
Nixon
Sense and Sensibility

1996
★ The English Patient
Hamlet
Michael Collins
Shine
Sleepers

1998
★ Life is Beautiful
Elizabeth
Pleasantville
Saving Private Ryan

ORIGINAL MUSICAL/COMEDY SCORE

1997
★ The Full Monty
Anastasia
As Good As It Gets
Men in Black
My Best Friend's Wedding

1998
★ Shakespeare in Love
A Bug's Life
Mulan
Patch Adams
Prince of Egypt

ORIGINAL SONG SCORE AND/OR ADAPTATION

1957
★ The Bridge on the River Kwai

1970
★ Let It Be
The Baby Maker
Darling Lili
Scrooge

1971
★ Fiddler on the Roof
Bedknobs and Broomsticks
The Boy Friend
Tchaikovsky
Willy Wonka & the Chocolate Factory

1972
★ Cabaret
Lady Sings the Blues

1973
★ The Sting
Jesus Christ, Superstar
Tom Sawyer

1974
★ The Great Gatsby
The Little Prince
Phantom of the Paradise

1975
★ Barry Lyndon
Funny Lady

1976
★ Bound for Glory
A Star is Born

1977
★ A Little Night Music
Pete's Dragon

1978
★ The Buddy Holly Story
Pretty Baby
The Wiz

1979
★ All That Jazz
Breaking Away
The Muppet Movie

1982
★ Victor/Victoria
Annie
One from the Heart

1983
★ Yentl
The Sting 2
Trading Places

1984
★ Purple Rain
The Muppets Take Manhattan
Songwriter

SCORE

1934
★ One Night of Love
The Gay Divorcee
The Lost Patrol

1935
★ The Informer
Mutiny on the Bounty

1936
★ Anthony Adverse
The Charge of the Light Brigade
The Garden of Allah
The General Died at Dawn
Winterset

1937
★ 100 Men and a Girl
The Hurricane
In Old Chicago
The Life of Emile Zola
Lost Horizon
Make a Wish
Maytime
Prisoner of Zenda
Quality Street
Snow White and the Seven Dwarfs
Something to Sing About
Souls at Sea
Way Out West

1938
★ Alexander's Ragtime Band
Carefree
The Goldwyn Follies
Jezebel
Mad About Music
Sweethearts

1939
★ Stagecoach
Babes in Arms
First Love
The Hunchback of Notre Dame
Intermezzo
Mr. Smith Goes to Washington
The Private Lives of Elizabeth & Essex
They Shall Have Music
Way Down South

1940
★ Tin Pan Alley
Our Town

1973
Man of La Mancha

1940
★ Pinocchio
Arizona
Dark Command
The Great Dictator
The Grapes of Wrath
The Howards of Virginia
The Letter
The Long Voyage Home
The Man in the Iron Mask
The Mark of Zorro
My Favorite Wife
One Million B.C.
Rebecca
The Thief of Bagdad
Waterloo Bridge

SCORING OF A MUSICAL

1941
★ Dumbo
Birth of the Blues
Buck Privates
The Chocolate Soldier
Sun Valley Serenade
You'll Never Get Rich

1942
★ Yankee Doodle Dandy
For Me and My Gal
Holiday Inn
It Started with Eve
You Were Never Lovelier

1943
★ This is the Army
The Phantom of the Opera
Stage Door Canteen
Star Spangled Rhythm
Thousands Cheer

1944
★ Hollywood Canteen
Meet Me in St. Louis
Sensations of 1945
Up in Arms

1945
★ Anchors Aweigh
Can't Help Singing
Rhapsody in Blue
State Fair
The Three Caballeros
Tonight and Every Night
Wonder Man

1946
★ The Jolson Story
Blue Skies
Night and Day
The Harvey Girls

1947
★ Mother Wore Tights

1948
★ Easter Parade
Emperor Waltz
The Pirate
Romance on the High Seas

1949
★ On the Town
Jolson Sings Again
Look for the Silver Lining

1950
★ Annie Get Your Gun
Cinderella
Three Little Words
The West Point Story

1951
★ An American in Paris
Alice in Wonderland
The Great Caruso
Show Boat

1952
★ With a Song in My Heart
Hans Christian Andersen
The Medium
The Jolson Story
Singin' in the Rain

1953
★ Call Me Madam
The Band Wagon
Calamity Jane
The 5000 Fingers of Dr. T
Kiss Me Kate

1963
★ Tom Jones
Cleopatra
55 Days at Peking
How the West Was Won

★ = winner

ORIGINAL SCORE

1938
★ The Adventures of Robin Hood

1954
★ Seven Brides for Seven Brothers
Carmen Jones
The Glenn Miller Story
There's No Business Like Show Business
A Star is Born

1955
★ Oklahoma!
Daddy Long Legs
Guys and Dolls
It's Always Fair Weather
Love Me or Leave Me

1956
★ The King and I
The Eddy Duchin Story
High Society
Meet Me in Las Vegas
Umbrellas of Cherbourg

1958
★ Gigi
Damn Yankees
South Pacific

1959
★ The Five Pennies
Li'l Abner
Sleeping Beauty

1960
★ Song Without End
Bells Are Ringing
Can-Can
Let's Make Love

1961
★ West Side Story
Babes in Toyland
Flower Drum Song
Paris Blues

1966
★ A Funny Thing Happened on the Way to the Forum

1967
★ Thoroughly Modern Millie
Doctor Dolittle
Far from the Madding Crowd
In Cold Blood
Thoroughly Modern Millie

1968
★ Oliver!
Finian's Rainbow
Funny Girl
Star!
The Young Girls of Rochefort

1969
★ Hello, Dolly!
Goodbye, Mr. Chips
Paint Your Wagon
Sweet Charity
They Shoot Horses, Don't They?

1968
★ The Lion in Winter
Planet of the Apes
The Shoes of the Fisherman
The Thomas Crown Affair

1969
★ Butch Cassidy and the Sundance Kid
Anne of the Thousand Days
The Reivers
The Wild Bunch

1970
★ Love Story
Airport
Cromwell
Patton

1975
★ Jaws
Bite the Bullet
One Flew Over the Cuckoo's Nest
Birds Do It, Bees Do It
The Wind and the Lion

1976
★ The Omen
Bugsy Malone
Obsession
The Outlaw Josey Wales
Taxi Driver
Voyage of the Damned

1977
★ Star Wars
Close Encounters of the Third Kind
Julia
The Message
The Spy Who Loved Me

1978
★ Midnight Express
The Boys from Brazil
Days of Heaven
Heaven Can Wait
Superman: The Movie

1979
★ A Little Romance
The Amityville Horror
The Champ
Star Trek: The Motion Picture
10

1980
★ Fame
Altered States
The Elephant Man
The Empire Strikes Back
Tess

1981
★ Chariots of Fire
Dragonslayer
On Golden Pond
Ragtime
Raiders of the Lost Ark

1964
★ It's a Mad, Mad, Mad, Mad World

1964
★ Mary Poppins
Becket
The Fall of the Roman Empire
Hush, Hush, Sweet Charlotte
The Pink Panther

1982
★ E.T. The Extra-Terrestrial
Gandhi
An Officer and a Gentleman
Poltergeist
Sophie's Choice

1983
★ The Right Stuff
Cross Creek
Return of the Jedi
Terms of Endearment
Under Fire

1984
★ A Passage to India
Indiana Jones and the Temple of Doom
The Natural
The River
Under the Volcano

1985
★ Out of Africa
Agnes of God
The Color Purple
Silverado
Witness

1986
★ Round Midnight
Aliens
Hoosiers
The Mission
Star Trek 4: The Voyage Home

1987
★ The Last Emperor
Cry Freedom
Empire of the Sun
The Untouchables
The Witches of Eastwick

1988
★ The Milagro Beanfield War
The Accidental Tourist
Dangerous Liaisons
Gorillas in the Mist
Rain Man

1989
★ The Little Mermaid
Born on the Fourth of July
The Fabulous Baker Boys
Field of Dreams
Indiana Jones and the Last Crusade

1990
★ Dances with Wolves
Avalon
Ghost
Havana
Home Alone

1991
★ Beauty and the Beast
Bugsy
The Fisher King
JFK
The Prince of Tides

1992
★ Aladdin
Basic Instinct
Chaplin
Howard's End
A River Runs Through It

1993
★ Schindler's List
The Age of Innocence
The Firm
The Fugitive
The Remains of the Day

1994
★ The Lion King
Forrest Gump
Interview with the Vampire
Little Women
The Shawshank Redemption

1995
★ Pocahontas
The American President
Sabrina
Toy Story
Unstrung Heroes

1996
★ Emma
The First Wives Club

Academy Awards

The Hunchback of Notre Dame
James and the Giant Peach
The Preacher's Wife
1997
★ _Titanic_
Amistad
Good Will Hunting
Kundun
L.A. Confidential
1999
★ _The Red Violin_
American Beauty
Angela's Ashes
The Cider House Rules
The Talented Mr. Ripley
2000
★ _Crouching Tiger, Hidden Dragon_
Chocolat
The Patriot
2003
★ _Lord of the Rings: The Return of the King_
Big Fish
Cold Mountain
Finding Nemo
House of Sand and Fog
The Village
2005
★ _Brokeback Mountain_
The Constant Gardener
Memoirs of a Geisha
Munich
Pride and Prejudice
2006
★ _Babel_
The Good German
Notes on a Scandal
Pan's Labyrinth
The Queen
2007
★ _Atonement_
The Kite Runner
Michael Clayton
Ratatouille
3:10 to Yuma

SONG

1934
★ "The Continental"/_The Gay Divorcee_
"Carioca"/_Flying Down to Rio_
1935
★ "Lullaby of Broadway"/_Gold Diggers of 1935_
"Cheek to Cheek"/_Top Hat_
"Lovely to Look At"/_Roberta_
1936
★ "The Way You Look Tonight"/_Swing Time_
"A Melody from the Sky"/_The Trail of the Lonesome Pine_
"Did I Remember?"/_Suzy_
"I've Got You Under My Skin"/_Born to Dance_
"My Own"/_That Certain Age_
1937
★ "Sweet Leilani"/_Waikiki Wedding_
"That Old Feeling"/_Vogues of 1938_
"They Can't Take That Away From Me"/_Shall We Dance_
1938
★ "Thanks for the Memories"/_The Big Broadcast of 1938_
"Always and Always"/_Mannequin_

"Change Partners and Dance with Me"/_Carefree_
"Now It Can Be Told"/_Alexander's Ragtime Band_
"The Cowboy and the Lady"/_The Cowboy and the Lady_
1939
★ "Over the Rainbow"/_The Wizard of Oz_
"Faithful Forever"/_Gulliver's Travels_
"I Poured My Heart Into Song"/_Second Fiddle_
"Wishing"/_Love Affair_
1940
★ "When You Wish Upon a Star"/_Pinocchio_
"Down Argentine Way"/_Down Argentine Way_
"I'd Know You Anywhere"/_You'll Find Out_
"It's a Blue World"/_Music in My Heart_
"Love of My Life"/_Second Chorus_
"Only Forever"/_Rhythm on the River_
"Our Love Affair"/_Strike Up the Band_
1941
★ "The Last Time I Saw Paris"/_Lady Be Good_
"Baby Mine"/_Dumbo_
"Be Honest With Me"/_Ridin' on a Rainbow_
"Boogie Woogie Bugle Boy of Company B"/_Buck Privates_
"Chattanooga Choo Choo"/_Sun Valley Serenade_
"Since I Kissed My Baby Goodbye"/_You'll Never Get Rich_
1942
★ "White Christmas"/_Holiday Inn_
"Dearly Beloved"/_You Were Never Lovelier_
"How About You?"/_Babes on Broadway_
"I've Got a Gal in Kalamazoo"/_Orchestra Wives_
"Love is a Song"/_Bambi_
1943
★ "You'll Never Know"/_Hello, Frisco, Hello_
"Happiness Is a Thing Called Joe"/_Cabin in the Sky_
"My Shining Hour"/_The Sky's the Limit_
"That Old Black Magic"/_Star Spangled Rhythm_
"They're Either Too Young or Too Old"/_Thank Your Lucky Stars_
"We Mustn't Say Goodbye"/_Stage Door Canteen_
1944
★ "Swinging on a Star"/_Going My Way_
"I Couldn't Sleep A Wink Last Night"/_Higher and Higher_
"I'll Walk Alone"/_Follow the Boys_
"Long Ago and Far Away"/_Cover Girl_
"Now I Know"/_Up in Arms_
"Sweet Dreams Sweetheart"/_Hollywood Canteen_
"The Trolley Song"/_Meet Me in St. Louis_
1945
★ "It Might as Well Be Spring"/_State Fair_
"Accentuate the Positive"/_Here Come the Waves_
"Anywhere"/_Tonight and Every Night_

"Aren't You Glad You're You"/_The Bells of St. Mary's_
"Fall in Love Too Easily"/_Anchors Aweigh_
"More and More"/_Can't Help Singing_
"So in Love"/_Wonder Man_
"Some Sunday Morning"/_San Antonio_
1946
★ "On the Atchison, Topeka and Santa Fe"/_The Harvey Girls_
"I Can't Begin to Tell You"/_The Dolly Sisters_
"You Keep Coming Back Like a Song"/_Blue Skies_
1947
★ "Wish I Didn't Love You So"/_The Perils of Pauline_
"Pass That Peace Pipe"/_Good News_
"You Do"/_Mother Wore Tights_
1948
★ "Buttons and Bows"/_The Paleface_
"For Every Man There's a Woman"/_Casbah_
"It's Magic"/_Romance on the High Seas_
1949
★ "Baby It's Cold Outside"/_Neptune's Daughter_
"It's a Great Feeling"/_It's a Great Feeling_
"Lavender Blue"/_So Dear to My Heart_
"My Foolish Heart"/_My Foolish Heart_
"Through a Long and Sleepless Night"/_Come to the Stable_
1950
★ "Be My Love"/_The Toast of New Orleans_
"Bibbidi-Bobbidi-Boo"/_Cinderella_
1951
★ "In the Cool, Cool, Cool of the Evening"/_Here Comes the Groom_
"Too Late Now"/_Royal Wedding_
"Wonder Why"/_Rich, Young and Pretty_
1952
★ "High Noon (Do Not Forsake Me, Oh My Darlin')"/_High Noon_
"Am I in Love"/_Son of Paleface_
"Because You're Mine"/_Because You're Mine_
"Thumbelina"/_Hans Christian Andersen_
"Zing a Little Zong"/_Just for You_
1953
★ "Secret Love"/_Calamity Jane_
"My Flaming Heart"/_Small Town Girl_
"Sadie Thompson's Song (Blue Pacific Blues)"/_Miss Sadie Thompson_
"That's Amore"/_The Caddy_
"The Moon Is Blue"/_The Moon Is Blue_
1954
★ "Three Coins in the Fountain"/_Three Coins in the Fountain_
"Count Your Blessings Instead of Sheep"/_White Christmas_
"Hold My Hand"/_Susan Slept Here_
"The Man That Got Away"/_A Star Is Born_
1955
★ "Love Is a Many-Splendored Thing"/_Love Is a Many-Splendored Thing_

"(Love Is) The Tender Trap"/_The Tender Trap_
"I'll Never Stop Loving You"/_Love Me or Leave Me_
"Something's Gotta Give"/_Daddy Long Legs_
"The High and the Mighty"/_The High and the Mighty_
1956
★ "Que Sera, Sera"/_The Man Who Knew Too Much_
"Friendly Persuasion (Thee I Love)"/_Friendly Persuasion_
"True Love"/_High Society_
"Written on the Wind"/_Written on the Wind_
1957
★ "An Affair to Remember"/_An Affair to Remember_
"Tammy"/_Tammy and the Bachelor_
1958
★ "Gigi"/_Gigi_
"A Very Precious Love"/_Marjorie Morningstar_
"Almost in Your Arms (Love Song from Houseboat)"/_Houseboat_
"To Love and Be Loved"/_Some Came Running_
1959
★ "High Hopes"/_A Hole in the Head_
"Strange Are the Ways of Love"/_The Young Land_
"The Best of Everything"/_The Best of Everything_
"The Five Pennies"/_The Five Pennies_
"The Hanging Tree"/_The Hanging Tree_
1960
★ "Never on Sunday"/_Never on Sunday_
"The Facts of Life"/_The Facts of Life_
"The Green Leaves of Summer"/_The Alamo_
1961
★ "Moon River"/_Breakfast at Tiffany's_
"Bachelor in Paradise"/_Bachelor in Paradise_
"Love Theme (The Falcon and the Dove)"/_El Cid_
"Pocketful of Miracles"/_Pocketful of Miracles_
"Town without Pity"/_Town without Pity_
1962
★ "Days of Wine and Roses"/_Days of Wine and Roses_
"Love Song (Follow Me)"/_Mutiny on the Bounty_
"Song fromm Two for the Seesaw (Second Chance)"/_Two for the Seesaw_
"Walk on the Wild Side"/_Walk on the Wild Side_
1963
★ "Call Me Irresponsible"/_Papa's Delicate Condition_
"Charade"/_Charade_
"It's a Mad, Mad, Mad, Mad World"/_It's a Mad, Mad, Mad, Mad World_
"More"/_Mondo Cane_
"So Little Time"/_55 Days at Peking_
1964
★ "Chim Chim Cher-ee"/_Mary Poppins_
"Hush, Hush, Sweet Charlotte"/_Hush, Hush, Sweet Charlotte_
"My Kind of Town"/_Robin and the 7 Hoods_

"Where Love Has Gone"/_Where Love Has Gone_
1965
★ "The Shadow of Your Smile"/_The Sandpiper_
"Will Wait for You"/_Umbrellas of Cherbourg_
"The Ballad of Cat Ballou"/_Cat Ballou_
"The Sweetheart Tree"/_The Great Race_
1966
★ "Born Free"/_Born Free_
"Alfie"/_Alfie_
"Georgy Girl"/_Georgy Girl_
"My Wishing Doll"/_Hawaii_
1967
★ "Talk to the Animals"/_Doctor Dolittle_
"The Bare Necessities"/_The Jungle Book_
"The Look of Love"/_Casino Royale_
"Thoroughly Modern Millie"/_Thoroughly Modern Millie_
1968
★ "The Windmills of Your Mind"/_The Thomas Crown Affair_
"Chitty Chitty Bang Bang"/_Chitty Chitty Bang Bang_
"For Love of Ivy"/_For Love of Ivy_
"Funny Girl"/_Funny Girl_
"Star!"/_Star!_
1969
★ "Raindrops Keep Fallin' on My Head"/_Butch Cassidy and the Sundance Kid_
"Come Saturday Morning"/_The Sterile Cuckoo_
"Jean"/_The Prime of Miss Jean Brodie_
"True Grit"/_True Grit_
"What Are You Doing the Rest of Your Life?"/_The Happy Ending_
1970
★ "For All We Know"/_Lovers and Other Strangers_
"Thank You Very Much"/_Scrooge_
"Till Love Touches Your Life"/_Madron_
"Whistling Away the Dark"/_Darling Lili_
1971
★ "Theme from Shaft"/_Shaft_
"All His Children"/_Sometimes a Great Notion_
"Bless the Beasts and the Children"/_Bless the Beasts and Children_
"Life Is What You Make It"/_Kotch_
"The Age of Not Believing"/_Bedknobs and Broomsticks_
1972
★ "The Morning After"/_The Poseidon Adventure_
"Ben"/_Ben_
"Marmalade, Molasses & Honey"/_Life & Times of Judge Roy Bean_
"Strange Are the Ways of Love"/_The Stepmother_
1973
★ "The Way We Were"/_The Way We Were_
"All That Love Went to Waste"/_A Touch of Class_
"Live and Let Die"/_Live and Let Die_
"Love"/_Robin Hood_
"You're So Nice to Be Around"/_Cinderella Liberty_

1974
★ "We May Never Love Like This Again"/_The Towering Inferno_
"Benji's Theme (I Feel Love)"/_Benji_
"Blazing Saddles"/_Blazing Saddles_
"Little Prince"/_The Little Prince_
1975
★ "I'm Easy"/_Nashville_
"How Lucky Can You Get"/_Funny Lady_
"Now That We're in Love"/_Whiffs_
"Richard's Window"/_The Other Side of the Mountain_
"Theme from Mahogany"/_Mahogany_
1976
★ "Evergreen"/_A Star Is Born_
"Ave Satani"/_The Omen_
"Come to Me"/_The Pink Panther Strikes Again_
"Gonna Fly Now"/_Rocky_
1977
★ "You Light Up My Life"/_You Light Up My Life_
"Candle on the Water"/_Pete's Dragon_
"Nobody Does It Better"/_The Spy Who Loved Me_
"Someone's Waiting for You"/_The Rescuers_
1978
★ "Last Dance"/_Thank God It's Friday_
"Hopelessly Devoted to You"/_Grease_
"Ready to Take a Chance Again"/_Foul Play_
"The Last Time I Felt Like This"/_Same Time, Next Year_
"When You're Loved"/_Magic of Lassie_
1979
★ "It Goes Like It Goes"/_Norma Rae_
"Song from 10 (It's Easy to Say)"/_10_
"The Rainbow Connection"/_The Muppet Movie_
"Theme from Ice Castles-Through the Eyes of Love"/_Ice Castles_
"Theme from The Promise: I'll Never Say Goodbye"/_The Promise_
1980
★ "Fame"/_Fame_
"Nine to Five"/_9 to 5_
"On the Road Again"/_Honeysuckle Rose_
"Out Here on My Own"/_Fame_
"People Alone"/_The Competition_
1981
★ "Arthur's Theme"/_Arthur_
"Endless Love"/_Endless Love_
"For Your Eyes Only"/_For Your Eyes Only_
"One More Hour"/_Ragtime_
"The First Time It Happens"/_The Great Muppet Caper_
1982
★ "Up Where We Belong"/_An Officer and a Gentleman_
"Eye of the Tiger"/_Rocky 3_
"How Do You Keep the Music Playing?"/_Best Friends_
"If We Were in Love"/_Yes, Giorgio_
"It Might Be You"/_Tootsie_
1983
★ "Flashdance...What a Feeling"/_Flashdance_
"Maniac"/_Flashdance_

★ = _winner_

Song (continued)

"Over You"/Tender Mercies
"Papa, Can You Hear Me?"/Yentl
"The Way He Makes Me Feel"/Yentl

1984
★ "I Just Called to Say I Love You"/The Woman in Red
"Against All Odds (Take a Look at Me Now)"/Against All Odds
"Footloose"/Footloose
"Ghostbusters"/Ghostbusters
"Let's Hear It for the Boy"/Footloose

1985
★ "Say You, Say Me"/White Nights
"Miss Celie's Blues (Sister)"/The Color Purple
"Surprise, Surprise"/A Chorus Line
"The Power of Love"/Back to the Future

1986
★ "Take My Breath Away"/Top Gun
"Glory of Love"/The Karate Kid: Part 2
"Life in a Looking Glass"/That's Life!
"Mean Green Mother from Outer Space"/Little Shop of Horrors
"Somewhere Out There"/An American Tail

1987
★ "(I've Had) the Time of My Life"/Dirty Dancing
"Cry Freedom"/Cry Freedom
"Nothing's Gonna Stop Us Now"/Mannequin
"Shakedown"/Beverly Hills Cop 2
"Storybook Love"/The Princess Bride

1988
★ "Let the River Run"/Working Girl
"Calling You"/Bagdad Cafe
"Two Hearts"/Buster

1989
★ "Under the Sea"/The Little Mermaid
"After All"/Chances Are
"I Love to See You Smile"/Parenthood
"Kiss the Girl"/The Little Mermaid
"The Girl Who Used to Be Me"/Shirley Valentine

1990
★ "Sooner or Later"/Dick Tracy
"Blaze of Glory"/Young Guns 2
"I'm Checkin' Out"/Postcards from the Edge
"Promise Me You'll Remember"/The Godfather, Part 3
"Somewhere in My Memory"/Home Alone

1991
★ "Beauty and the Beast"/Beauty and the Beast
"Be Our Guest"/Beauty and the Beast
"Belle"/Beauty and the Beast
"When You're Alone"/Hook

1992
★ "A Whole New World"/Aladdin
"Beautiful Maria of My Soul"/The Mambo Kings
"Friend Like Me"/Aladdin
"Have Nothing"/The Bodyguard
"Run to You"/The Bodyguard

1993
★ "Streets of Philadelphia"/Philadelphia
"A Wink and a Smile"/Sleepless in Seattle
"Again"/Poetic Justice
"Philadelphia"/Philadelphia
"The Day I Fall in Love"/Beethoven's 2nd

1994
★ "Can You Feel the Love Tonight"/The Lion King
"Circle of Life"/The Lion King
"Hakuna Matata"/The Lion King
"Look What Love Has Done"/Junior
"Make Up Your Mind"/The Paper

1995
★ "Colors of the Wind"/Pocahontas
"Dead Man Walking"/Dead Man Walking
"Have You Ever Really Loved a Woman?"/Don Juan DeMarco
"Moonlight"/Sabrina
"You've Got a Friend"/Toy Story

1996
★ "You Must Love Me"/Evita
"Because You Loved Me"/Up Close and Personal
"For the First Time"/One Fine Day
"I've Finally Found Someone"/The Mirror Has Two Faces
"That Thing You Do!"/That Thing You Do!

1997
★ "My Heart Will Go On"/Titanic
"Go the Distance"/Hercules
"How Do I Live"/Con Air
"Journey to the Past"/Anastasia
"Miss Misery"/Good Will Hunting

1998
★ "When You Believe"/Prince of Egypt
"A Soft Place to Fall"/The Horse Whisperer
"I Don't Want to Miss a Thing"/Armageddon
"That'll Do"/Babe: Pig in the City
"The Prayer"/Quest for Camelot

1999
★ "You'll Be in My Heart"/Tarzan
"Blame Canada"/South Park: Bigger, Longer and Uncut
"Music of My Heart"/Music of the Heart
"Save Me"/Magnolia
"When She Loved Me"/Toy Story 2

2000
★ "Things Have Changed"/Wonder Boys
"A Fool in Love"/Meet the Parents
"A Love Before Time"/Crouching Tiger, Hidden Dragon
"I've Seen It All"/Dancer in the Dark
"My Funny Friend and Me"/The Emperor's New Groove

2001
★ "If I Didn't Have You"/Monsters, Inc.
"May It Be"/Lord of the Rings: The Fellowship of the Ring
"There You'll Be"/Pearl Harbor
"Until"/Kate & Leopold
"Vanilla Sky"/Vanilla Sky

2002
★ "Lose Yourself"/8 Mile
"Burn It Blue"/Frida
"Father and Daughter"/The Wild Thornberrys Movie
"I Move On"/Chicago
"The Hands That Built America"/Gangs of New York

2003
★ "Into the West"/Lord of the Rings: The Return of the King
"A Kiss at the End of the Rainbow"/A Mighty Wind
"Belleville Rendez-Vous"/The Triplets of Belleville
"Scarlet Tide"/Cold Mountain

2004
★ "Al Otro Lado Del Rio"/The Motorcycle Diaries
"Accidentally in Love"/Shrek 2
"Believe"/The Polar Express
"Learn to be Lonely"/The Phantom of the Opera

2005
★ "It's Hard Out Here for a Pimp"/Hustle & Flow
"In the Deep"/Crash
"Travelin' Thru"/Transamerica

2006
★ "I Need to Wake Up"/An Inconvenient Truth
"Listen"/Dreamgirls
"Love You I Do"/Dreamgirls
"Our Town"/Cars
"Patience"/Dreamgirls

2007
★ "Falling Slowly"/Once
"Happy Working Song"/Enchanted
"Raise It Up"/August Rush
"So Close"/Enchanted
"That's How You Know"/Enchanted

SOUND

1933
★ A Farewell to Arms
42nd Street
Gold Diggers of 1933
I Am a Fugitive from a Chain Gang

1934
★ One Night of Love
Cleopatra
The Gay Divorcee
Imitation of Life
Viva Villa!

1935
★ Naughty Marietta
The Bride of Frankenstein
Captain Blood
I Dream Too Much
The Lives of a Bengal Lancer

1936
★ San Francisco
The Charge of the Light Brigade
The Dark Angel
Dodsworth
General Spanky
Mr. Deeds Goes to Town
The Texas Rangers
That Girl from Paris
Three Smart Girls

1937
★ The Hurricane
The Girl Said No
In Old Chicago
The Life of Emile Zola
Lost Horizon
Maytime
100 Men and a Girl
Topper

1938
★ The Cowboy and the Lady
Four Daughters
Sweethearts
That Certain Age
Vivacious Lady
You Can't Take It with You

1939
★ Balalaika
Gone with the Wind
Goodbye, Mr. Chips
The Hunchback of Notre Dame
Mr. Smith Goes to Washington
Of Mice and Men
The Private Lives of Elizabeth & Essex
The Rains Came

1940
★ Strike Up the Band
Captain Caution
The Grapes of Wrath
The Howards of Virginia
Kitty Foyle
Our Town
The Sea Hawk

1941
★ That Hamilton Woman
Ball of Fire
The Chocolate Soldier
Citizen Kane
The Road to Morocco
Sergeant York
Topper Returns

1942
★ Yankee Doodle Dandy
Arabian Nights
Bambi
Flying Tigers
Mrs. Miniver
Once Upon a Honeymoon
The Pride of the Yankees
You Were Never Lovelier

1943
★ This Land Is Mine
Madame Curie
The North Star
The Phantom of the Opera
Sahara
So This Is Washington
The Song of Bernadette
This Is the Army
War of the Wildcats

1944
★ Wilson
Casanova Brown
Cover Girl
Double Indemnity
His Butler's Sister
Hollywood Canteen

1945
★ The Bells of St. Mary's
Flame of the Barbary Coast
Lady on a Train
Leave Her to Heaven
Rhapsody in Blue
A Song to Remember
The Southerner
They Were Expendable
The Three Caballeros
Wonder Man

1946
★ The Jolson Story
It's a Wonderful Life
The Best Years of Our Lives

1947
★ The Bishop's Wife
Green Dolphin Street
T-Men

1948
★ The Snake Pit
Johnny Belinda
The Smallest Show on Earth

1949
★ Twelve o'Clock High
Sands of Iwo Jima

1950
★ All About Eve

1951
★ The Great Caruso
Two Tickets to Broadway

1952
★ Hans Christian Andersen
The Promoter
The Quiet Man

1953
★ From Here to Eternity
Calamity Jane
Knights of the Round Table
The War of the Worlds
With a Song in My Heart

1954
★ The Glenn Miller Story
Brigadoon
The Caine Mutiny
Rear Window
Susan Slept Here

1955
★ Oklahoma!
Love Is a Many-Splendored Thing
Love Me or Leave Me
Mister Roberts
Not as a Stranger

1956
★ The King and I
The Brave One
The Eddy Duchin Story
Friendly Persuasion
The Ten Commandments

1957
★ Sayonara
Gunfight at the O.K. Corral
Les Girls
Pal Joey
Witness for the Prosecution

1958
★ South Pacific
I Want to Live!
A Time to Love & a Time to Die
Vertigo
The Young Lions

1959
★ Ben-Hur
Journey to the Center of the Earth
The Nun's Story

1960
★ The Alamo
Cimarron
Sunrise at Campobello

1961
★ West Side Story
The Children's Hour
The Guns of Navarone
The Parent Trap

1962
★ Lawrence of Arabia
Bon Voyage!
The Music Man
That Touch of Mink
What Ever Happened to Baby Jane?

1963
★ How the West Was Won
Bye, Bye, Birdie
Captain Newman, M.D.
Cleopatra
It's a Mad, Mad, Mad, Mad World

1964
★ My Fair Lady
Becket
Father Goose
Mary Poppins
The Unsinkable Molly Brown

1965
★ The Sound of Music
The Agony and the Ecstasy
Doctor Zhivago
The Great Race
Shenandoah

1966
★ Grand Prix
Gambit
Hawaii
The Sand Pebbles
Who's Afraid of Virginia Woolf?

1967
★ In the Heat of the Night
Camelot
The Dirty Dozen
Doctor Dolittle
Thoroughly Modern Millie

1968
★ Oliver!
Bullitt
Finian's Rainbow
Funny Girl
Star!

1969
★ Hello, Dolly!
Anne of the Thousand Days
Butch Cassidy and the Sundance Kid
Marooned

1970
★ Patton
Airport
Ryan's Daughter
Tora! Tora! Tora!
Woodstock

1971
★ Fiddler on the Roof
Diamonds Are Forever
The French Connection
Kotch
Mary, Queen of Scots

1972
★ Cabaret
Butterflies Are Free
The Candidate
The Godfather
The Poseidon Adventure

1973
★ The Exorcist
The Day of the Dolphin
The Paper Chase
The Sting

1974
★ Earthquake
Chinatown
The Conversation
The Towering Inferno
Young Frankenstein

1975
★ Jaws
Bite the Bullet
Funny Lady
The Hindenburg
The Wind and the Lion

1976
★ All the President's Men
King Kong
Rocky
Silver Streak
A Star Is Born

1977
★ Star Wars
Close Encounters of the Third Kind
The Deep
Sorcerer
The Turning Point

1978
★ The Deer Hunter
The Buddy Holly Story
Days of Heaven
Hooper
Superman: The Movie

1979
★ Apocalypse Now
The Electric Horseman
Meteor
1941
The Rose

1980
★ The Empire Strikes Back
Coal Miner's Daughter
Fame
Raging Bull

1981
★ Raiders of the Lost Ark
On Golden Pond
Outland
Pennies from Heaven

★ = winner

Academy Awards

Reds

1982
★ Gandhi
Das Boot
E.T.: The Extra-Terrestrial
Tootsie
Tron

1983
★ The Right Stuff
Never Cry Wolf
Return of the Jedi
Terms of Endearment
WarGames

1984
★ Amadeus
Dune
A Passage to India
The River
2010: The Year We Make Contact

1985
★ Out of Africa
Back to the Future
A Chorus Line
Ladyhawke
Silverado

1986
★ Platoon
Aliens
Heartbreak Ridge
Star Trek 4: The Voyage Home
Top Gun

1987
★ The Last Emperor
Empire of the Sun
Lethal Weapon
RoboCop
The Witches of Eastwick

1988
★ Bird
Die Hard
Gorillas in the Mist
Mississippi Burning
Who Framed Roger Rabbit

1989
★ Glory
The Abyss
Black Rain
Born on the Fourth of July
Indiana Jones and the Last Crusade

1990
★ Dances with Wolves
Days of Thunder
Dick Tracy
The Hunt for Red October
Total Recall

1991
★ Terminator 2: Judgment Day
Backdraft
Beauty and the Beast
JFK
The Silence of the Lambs

1992
★ The Last of the Mohicans
Aladdin
A Few Good Men
Under Siege
Unforgiven

1993
★ Jurassic Park
Cliffhanger
The Fugitive
Geronimo: An American Legend
Schindler's List

1994
★ Speed
Clear and Present Danger
Forrest Gump
Legends of the Fall
The Shawshank Redemption

1995
★ Apollo 13
Batman Forever
Braveheart
Crimson Tide
Waterworld

1996
★ The English Patient
Evita
Independence Day
The Rock
Twister

1997
★ Titanic
Air Force One
Con Air
Contact
L.A. Confidential

1998
★ Saving Private Ryan
Armageddon
The Mask of Zorro
Shakespeare in Love
The Thin Red Line

1999
★ The Matrix
The Green Mile
The Insider
The Mummy
Star Wars: Episode 1—The Phantom Menace

2000
★ Gladiator
The Patriot
The Perfect Storm
U-571

2001
★ Black Hawk Down
Amelie
Lord of the Rings: The Fellowship of the Rings
Moulin Rouge
Pearl Harbor

2002
★ Chicago
Gangs of New York
Lord of the Rings: The Two Towers
Road to Perdition
Spider-Man

2003
★ Lord of the Rings: The Return of the King
The Last Samurai
Lord of the Rings: The Return of the King
Master and Commander: The Far Side of the World
Pirates of the Caribbean: The Curse of the Black Pearl
Seabiscuit

2004
★ Ray
The Aviator
The Incredibles
The Polar Express
Spider-Man 2

2005
★ King Kong
The Chronicles of Narnia: The Lion, the Witch and the Wardrobe
Memoirs of a Geisha
Walk the Line
War of the Worlds

2006
★ Dreamgirls
Apocalypto
Blood Diamond
Flags of Our Fathers
Pirates of the Caribbean: Dead Man's Chest

2007
★ The Bourne Ultimatum
No Country for Old Men
Ratatouille
Transformers

SOUND EFFECTS EDITING

1963
★ It's a Mad, Mad, Mad, Mad World

1964
★ Goldfinger

1965
★ The Great Race

1966
★ Grand Prix

1967
★ The Dirty Dozen

1975
★ The Hindenburg

1977
★ Close Encounters of the Third Kind

1979
★ The Black Stallion

1986
★ Aliens

1990
★ The Hunt for Red October

1991
★ Terminator 2: Judgment Day

1992
★ Bram Stoker's Dracula
Aladdin
Under Siege

1993
★ Jurassic Park
Cliffhanger
The Fugitive

1996
★ The Ghost and the Darkness
Daylight
The English Patient

1997
★ Titanic
Face/Off
The Fifth Element

1998
★ Saving Private Ryan
Armageddon
The Mask of Zorro

2000
★ U-571
Space Cowboys

2003
★ Master and Commander: The Far Side of the World
Finding Nemo
Master and Commander: The Far Side of the World

2004
★ The Incredibles
The Polar Express
Spider-Man 2

2006
★ Letters from Iwo Jima
Apocalypto
Blood Diamond
Flags of Our Fathers
Pirates of the Caribbean: Dead Man's Chest

2007
★ The Bourne Ultimatum
No Country for Old Men
Ratatouille
There Will Be Blood
Transformers

ADAPTED SCREENPLAY

1928
★ The Jazz Singer

1931
★ Cimarron
Criminal Code
Little Caesar

1932
★ Arrowsmith
Dr. Jekyll and Mr. Hyde

1933
★ Little Women
Lady for a Day

1934
★ It Happened One Night
The Thin Man
Viva Villa!

1956
★ Around the World in 80 Days
Baby Doll
Friendly Persuasion
Giant
Lust for Life

1957
★ The Bridge on the River Kwai
Heaven Knows, Mr. Allison
Peyton Place
Sayonara
Twelve Angry Men

1958
★ Gigi
Cat on a Hot Tin Roof
The Horse's Mouth
I Want to Live!
Separate Tables

1959
★ Room at the Top
Anatomy of a Murder
Ben-Hur
The Nun's Story
Some Like It Hot

1960
★ Elmer Gantry
Inherit the Wind
The Sundowners
Tunes of Glory

1961
★ Judgment at Nuremberg
Breakfast at Tiffany's
The Guns of Navarone
The Hustler
West Side Story

1962
★ To Kill a Mockingbird
David and Lisa
Lawrence of Arabia
Lolita
The Miracle Worker

1963
★ Tom Jones
Captain Newman, M.D.
Hud
Lilies of the Field
Sundays & Cybele

1964
★ Becket
Dr. Strangelove, or: How I Learned to Stop Worrying and Love the Bomb
Mary Poppins
My Fair Lady
Zorba the Greek

1965
★ Doctor Zhivago
Cat Ballou
The Collector
Ship of Fools
A Thousand Clowns

1966
★ A Man for All Seasons
Alfie
Cool Hand Luke
The Professionals
The Russians Are Coming, the Russians Are Coming

1967
★ In the Heat of the Night
The Graduate
In Cold Blood
Ulysses

1968
★ The Lion in Winter
The Odd Couple
Oliver!
Rachel, Rachel
Rosemary's Baby

1969
★ Midnight Cowboy
Anne of the Thousand Days
Goodbye Columbus
They Shoot Horses, Don't They?
Z

1970
★ M*A*S*H
Airport
I Never Sang for My Father
Lovers and Other Strangers
Women in Love

1971
★ The French Connection
A Clockwork Orange
The Conformist
The Garden of the Finzi-Continis
The Last Picture Show

1972
★ The Godfather
Cabaret
The Emigrants
Pete 'n' Tillie
Sounder

1973
★ The Exorcist
The Last Detail
The Paper Chase
Paper Moon
Serpico

1974
★ The Godfather, Part 2
The Apprenticeship of Duddy Kravitz
Lenny
Murder on the Orient Express
Young Frankenstein

1975
★ One Flew Over the Cuckoo's Nest
Barry Lyndon
The Man Who Would Be King
The Scent of a Woman
The Sunshine Boys

1976
★ All the President's Men
Bound for Glory
The Seven-Per-Cent Solution
Voyage of the Damned

1977
★ Julia
Equus
I Never Promised You a Rose Garden
Oh, God!
That Obscure Object of Desire

1978
★ Midnight Express
Bloodbrothers
California Suite
Heaven Can Wait
Same Time, Next Year

1979
★ Kramer vs. Kramer
Apocalypse Now
La Cage aux Folles
A Little Romance
Norma Rae

1980
★ Ordinary People
Breaker Morant
Coal Miner's Daughter
The Elephant Man
The Stunt Man

1981
★ On Golden Pond
The French Lieutenant's Woman
Pennies from Heaven
Prince of the City
Ragtime

1982
★ Missing
Das Boot
Sophie's Choice
The Verdict
Victor/Victoria

1983
★ Terms of Endearment
Betrayal
The Dresser
Educating Rita
Reuben, Reuben

1984
★ Amadeus
Greystoke: The Legend of Tarzan, Lord of the Apes
The Killing Fields
A Passage to India
A Soldier's Story

1985
★ Out of Africa
The Color Purple
Kiss of the Spider Woman
Prizzi's Honor
The Trip to Bountiful

1986
★ A Room with a View
Children of a Lesser God
The Color of Money
Crimes of the Heart
Stand by Me

1987
★ The Last Emperor
The Dead
Fatal Attraction
Full Metal Jacket
My Life As a Dog

1988
★ Dangerous Liaisons
The Accidental Tourist
Gorillas in the Mist
Little Dorrit, Film 1: Nobody's Fault
The Unbearable Lightness of Being

1989
★ Driving Miss Daisy
Born on the Fourth of July
Enemies, a Love Story
Field of Dreams
My Left Foot

1990
★ Dances with Wolves
Awakenings
Goodfellas
The Grifters
Reversal of Fortune

1991
★ The Silence of the Lambs
Europa, Europa
Fried Green Tomatoes
JFK
The Prince of Tides

1992
★ Howard's End
Enchanted April
The Player
A River Runs Through It
Scent of a Woman

1993
★ Schindler's List
The Age of Innocence
In the Name of the Father
The Remains of the Day
Shadowlands

1994
★ Forrest Gump
The Madness of King George
Nobody's Fool
Quiz Show
The Shawshank Redemption

1995
★ Sense and Sensibility
Apollo 13
Babe
Leaving Las Vegas
The Postman

1996
★ Sling Blade
The Crucible
The English Patient
Hamlet
Trainspotting

1997
★ L.A. Confidential
Donnie Brasco
The Sweet Hereafter
Wag the Dog
The Wings of the Dove

1998
★ Gods and Monsters
Out of Sight
Primary Colors
A Simple Plan
The Thin Red Line

1999
★ The Cider House Rules
Election
The Green Mile
The Insider
The Talented Mr. Ripley

2000
★ Traffic

★ = winner

Chocolat
Crouching Tiger, Hidden Dragon
O Brother Where Art Thou?
Wonder Boys
2001
★ A Beautiful Mind
Ghost World
In the Bedroom
Lord of the Rings: The Fellowship of the Rings
Shrek
2002
★ The Pianist
About a Boy
Adaptation
Chicago
The Hours
2003
★ Lord of the Rings: The Return of the King
American Splendor
City of God
Mystic River
Seabiscuit
2004
★ Sideways
Before Sunset
Finding Neverland
Million Dollar Baby
The Motorcycle Diaries
2005
★ Brokeback Mountain
Capote
The Constant Gardener
A History of Violence
Munich
2006
★ The Departed
Borat Cultural Learnings of America for Make Benefit Glorious Nation of Kazakhstan
Children of Men
Little Children
Notes on a Scandal
2007
★ No Country for Old Men
Atonement
Away From Her
The Diving Bell and the Butterfly
There Will Be Blood

ORIGINAL SCREENPLAY

1940
★ The Great McGinty
Angels Over Broadway
Foreign Correspondent
The Great Dictator
1941
★ Citizen Kane
The Devil & Miss Jones
Sergeant York
1942
★ Woman of the Year
One of Our Aircraft Is Missing
The Road to Morocco
Wake Island
1943
★ Air Force
In Which We Serve
The North Star
So Proudly We Hail
1944
★ Wilson
Hail the Conquering Hero
Miracle of Morgan's Creek
Two Girls and a Sailor
A Wing and a Prayer
1945
★ Dillinger
Marie-Louise
1946
★ The Seventh Veil
The Blue Dahlia
Children of Paradise
Notorious
The Road to Utopia
To Each His Own
1947
★ The Bachelor and the Bobby-Soxer
Body and Soul
1956
★ The Red Balloon
La Strada
The Ladykillers
1974
★ Chinatown
Alice Doesn't Live Here Anymore
Day for Night
Harry and Tonto
The Conversation
1975
★ Dog Day Afternoon
Amarcord
And Now My Love
Lies My Father Told Me
Shampoo
1976
★ Network
Cousin, Cousine
The Front
The Goodbye Girl
The Late Show
1977
★ Annie Hall
The Goodbye Girl
The Late Show
Star Wars
The Turning Point
1978
★ Coming Home
Autumn Sonata
Interiors
1979
★ Breaking Away
All That Jazz
And Justice for All
The China Syndrome
Manhattan
1980
★ Melvin and Howard
Brubaker
Fame
Mon Oncle d'Amerique
Private Benjamin
1981
★ Chariots of Fire
Absence of Malice
Arthur
Atlantic City
Reds
1982
★ Gandhi
Diner
E.T.: The Extra-Terrestrial
An Officer and a Gentleman
Tootsie
1983
★ Tender Mercies
The Big Chill
Fanny and Alexander
Silkwood
WarGames
1984
★ Places in the Heart
Beverly Hills Cop
Broadway Danny Rose
El Norte
Splash
1985
★ Witness
Back to the Future
Brazil
The Official Story
The Purple Rose of Cairo
1986
★ Hannah and Her Sisters
Crocodile Dundee
My Beautiful Laundrette
Platoon
Salvador
1987
★ Moonstruck
Au Revoir les Enfants
Broadcast News
Hope and Glory
Radio Days
1988
★ Rain Man
Big
Bull Durham
A Fish Called Wanda
Running on Empty
1989
★ Dead Poets Society
Crimes & Misdemeanors
Do the Right Thing
sex, lies and videotape
When Harry Met Sally...
1990
★ Ghost
Alice
Avalon
Green Card
Metropolitan
1991
★ Thelma & Louise
Boyz N the Hood
Bugsy
The Fisher King
Grand Canyon
1992
★ The Crying Game
Husbands and Wives
Lorenzo's Oil
Passion Fish
Unforgiven
1993
★ The Piano
Dave
In the Line of Fire
Philadelphia
Sleepless in Seattle
1994
★ Pulp Fiction
Bullets over Broadway
Four Weddings and a Funeral
Heavenly Creatures
Trois Couleurs: Rouge
1995
★ The Usual Suspects
Braveheart
Mighty Aphrodite
Nixon
Toy Story
1996
★ Fargo
Jerry Maguire
Lone Star
Secrets and Lies
Shine
1997
★ Good Will Hunting
As Good As It Gets
Boogie Nights
Deconstructing Harry
The Full Monty
1998
★ Shakespeare in Love
Bulworth
Life Is Beautiful
Saving Private Ryan
The Truman Show
1999
★ American Beauty
Being John Malkovich
Magnolia
The Sixth Sense
Topsy-Turvy
2000
★ Almost Famous
Billy Elliot
Erin Brockovich
Gladiator
You Can Count On Me
2001
★ Gosford Park
Amelie
Memento
Monster's Ball
The Royal Tenenbaums
2002
★ Talk to Her
Far from Heaven
Gangs of New York
My Big Fat Greek Wedding
Y Tu Mama Tambien
2003
★ Lost in Translation
The Barbarian Invasions
2004
★ Eternal Sunshine of the Spotless Mind
Finding Neverland
Hotel Rwanda
The Incredibles
Vera Drake
2005
★ Crash
Good Night, and Good Luck
Match Point
The Squid and the Whale
Syriana
2006
★ Little Miss Sunshine
Babel
Letters from Iwo Jima
Pan's Labyrinth
The Queen
2007
★ Juno
Lars and the Real Girl
Michael Clayton
Ratatouille
The Savages

SCREENPLAY

1935
★ The Informer
The Lives of a Bengal Lancer
Mutiny on the Bounty
1936
★ After the Thin Man
Dodsworth
Mr. Deeds Goes to Town
My Man Godfrey
1937
★ The Life of Emile Zola
The Awful Truth
Captains Courageous
Stage Door
1938
★ Pygmalion
The Citadel
Four Daughters
You Can't Take It with You
1939
★ Gone with the Wind
Goodbye, Mr. Chips
Interrupted Melody
Love Me or Leave Me
1940
★ The Philadelphia Story
The Grapes of Wrath
Kitty Foyle
The Long Voyage Home
Rebecca
1941
★ Here Comes Mr. Jordan
How Green Was My Valley
The Little Foxes
The Maltese Falcon
1942
★ Mrs. Miniver
The Forty-Ninth Parallel
The Pride of the Yankees
Random Harvest
Talk of the Town
1943
★ Casablanca
The Song of Bernadette
Watch on the Rhine
1944
★ Going My Way
Double Indemnity
Gaslight
Laura
Meet Me in St. Louis
1945
★ The Lost Weekend
Mildred Pierce
A Tree Grows in Brooklyn
1946
★ The Best Years of Our Lives
Anna and the King of Siam
Brief Encounter
The Killers
Open City

STORY

1928
★ Underworld
Last Command
1931
★ The Public Enemy
Smart Money
1932
★ The Champ
What Price Hollywood?
1933
★ The Prizefighter and the Lady
Rasputin and the Empress
1934
★ Manhattan Melodrama
Hide-Out
1935
★ Broadway Melody of 1936
1936
★ The Story of Louis Pasteur
Fury
The Great Ziegfeld
San Francisco
Three Smart Girls
1937
★ A Star Is Born
In Old Chicago
100 Men and a Girl
1938
★ Boys Town
Alexander's Ragtime Band
Angels with Dirty Faces
The Black Legion
Mad About Music
Test Pilot
1939
★ Mr. Smith Goes to Washington
Bachelor Mother
Love Affair
Ninotchka
Young Mr. Lincoln
1940
★ Arise, My Love
Comrade X
Edison the Man
My Favorite Wife
The Westerner
1941
★ Here Comes Mr. Jordan
Ball of Fire
The Lady Eve
Meet John Doe
Tom, Dick, and Harry
1942
★ The Forty-Ninth Parallel
Holiday Inn
The Pride of the Yankees
Talk of the Town
Yankee Doodle Candy
1943
★ The Human Comedy
Action in the North Atlantic
Destination Tokyo
Shadow of a Doubt
1944
★ Going My Way
A Guy Named Joe
Lifeboat
1945
★ The House on 92nd Street
Objective, Burma!
A Song to Remember
1946
★ The Dark Mirror
The Strange Love of Martha Ivers
The Stranger
1947
★ Miracle on 34th Street
Kiss of Death
Smash-Up: The Story of a Woman
1948
★ The Search
Louisiana Story
The Naked City
Red River
The Red Shoes
1949
★ The Stratton Story
Come to the Stable
It Happens Every Spring
Sands of Iwo Jima
White Heat
1950
★ Panic in the Streets
Bitter Rice
The Gunfighter
1951
★ Bullfighter & the Lady
Here Comes the Groom
When Willie Comes Marching Home
1952
★ The Greatest Show on Earth
The Narrow Margin
Pride of St. Louis
1953
★ Roman Holiday
Above and Beyond
Captain's Paradise
Hondo
Titanic
1954
★ Broken Lance
Forbidden Games
There's No Business Like Show Business
1955
★ Love Me or Leave Me
The Private War of Major Benson
Rebel without a Cause
The Sheep Has Five Legs
Strategic Air Command

1947
★ Miracle on 34th Street
Boomerang
Crossfire
Gentleman's Agreement
Great Expectations
1948
★ The Treasure of the Sierra Madre
Johnny Belinda
The Search
The Snake Pit
1949
★ A Letter to Three Wives
All the King's Men
The Bicycle Thief
Champion
The Fallen Idol
1950
★ All About Eve
The Asphalt Jungle
Born Yesterday
Broken Arrow
Father of the Bride
1951
★ A Place in the Sun
The African Queen
Detective Story
La Ronde
A Streetcar Named Desire
1952
★ The Bad and the Beautiful
Five Fingers
High Noon
Roman Holiday
Shane
Titanic
1953
★ From Here to Eternity
The Cruel Sea
Lili
Roman Holiday
The Quiet Man
1954
★ Country Girl
The Caine Mutiny
Rear Window
Sabrina
Seven Brides for Seven Brothers
1955
★ Marty
Bad Day at Black Rock
Blackboard Jungle
East of Eden
Interrupted Melody
Love Me or Leave Me

Academy Awards

STORY & SCREENPLAY

1949
- ★ Battleground
- Jolson Sings Again
- Paisan
- Passport to Pimlico

1950
- ★ Sunset Boulevard
- Adam's Rib
- Caged
- The Men
- No Way Out

1951
- ★ An American in Paris
- David and Bathsheba
- Go for Broke!
- The Well

1952
- ★ The Lavender Hill Mob
- The Atomic City
- Pat and Mike
- Viva Zapata!

1953
- ★ Titanic
- The Band Wagon
- The Desert Rats
- The Naked Spur

1954
- ★ On the Waterfront
- The Barefoot Contessa
- Genevieve
- The Glenn Miller Story

1955
- ★ Interrupted Melody
- The Court Martial of Billy Mitchell
- It's Always Fair Weather
- Mr. Hulot's Holiday
- The Seven Little Foys

1956
- ★ The Brave One
- The Eddy Duchin Story
- High Society
- The Proud Ones
- Umberto D

1957
- ★ Designing Woman
- Funny Face
- I Vitelloni
- Man of a Thousand Faces
- The Tin Star

1958
- ★ The Defiant Ones
- The Goddess
- Houseboat
- Teacher's Pet

1959
- ★ Pillow Talk
- The 400 Blows
- North by Northwest
- Operation Petticoat
- Wild Strawberries

1960
- ★ The Apartment
- The Facts of Life
- Hiroshima, Mon Amour
- Never on Sunday

1961
- ★ Splendor in the Grass
- Ballad of a Soldier
- La Dolce Vita
- Lover Come Back

1962
- ★ Divorce—Italian Style
- Last Year at Marienbad
- That Touch of Mink
- Through a Glass Darkly

1963
- ★ How the West Was Won
- 8 1/2
- Love with the Proper Stranger

1964
- ★ Father Goose
- That Man from Rio
- Alun Owen/A Hard Day's Night

1965
- ★ Darling
- Casanova 70
- Those Magnificent Men in Their Flying Machines
- The Train
- Umbrellas of Cherbourg

1966
- ★ A Man and a Woman
- Blow-Up
- The Fortune Cookie
- Khartoum
- The Naked Prey

1967
- ★ Guess Who's Coming to Dinner
- Bonnie & Clyde
- Divorce American Style
- Two for the Road

1968
- ★ The Producers
- The Battle of Algiers
- Faces
- Hot Millions
- 2001: A Space Odyssey

1969
- ★ Butch Cassidy and the Sundance Kid
- Bob & Carol & Ted & Alice
- The Damned
- Easy Rider
- The Wild Bunch

1970
- ★ Patton
- Five Easy Pieces
- Joe
- Love Story
- My Night at Maud's

1971
- ★ The Hospital
- Klute
- Summer of '42
- Sunday, Bloody Sunday

1972
- ★ The Candidate
- The Discreet Charm of the Bourgeoisie
- Lady Sings the Blues
- Murmur of the Heart
- Young Winston

1973
- ★ The Sting
- American Graffiti
- Cries and Whispers
- Save the Tiger
- A Touch of Class

WRITING

1929
- ★ The Leatherneck
- Our Dancing Daughters

1930
- ★ All Quiet on the Western Front
- Disraeli
- The Divorcee

1931
- ★ Smart Money

1938
- ★ The Black Legion

FILM—FOREIGN LANGUAGE

1948
- ★ Monsieur Vincent

1949
- ★ The Bicycle Thief

1950
- ★ The Walls of Malapaga

1951
- ★ Rashomon

1952
- ★ Forbidden Games

1954
- ★ Gate of Hell

1955
- ★ Samurai 1: Musashi Miyamoto

1956
- ★ La Strada
- The Burmese Harp
- Gervaise

1957
- ★ Nights of Cabiria

1958
- ★ Mon Oncle
- Big Deal on Madonna Street

1959
- ★ Black Orpheus
- The Bridge
- The Great War

1960
- ★ The Virgin Spring
- Kapo

1961
- ★ Through a Glass Darkly

1962
- ★ Sundays & Cybele

1963
- ★ 8 1/2
- Knife in the Water

1964
- ★ Yesterday, Today and Tomorrow
- Sallah

1965
- ★ The Shop on Main Street
- Kwaidan
- Umbrellas of Cherbourg
- Woman in the Dunes

1966
- ★ A Man and a Woman
- The Battle of Algiers
- Loves of a Blonde

1967
- ★ Closely Watched Trains

1968
- ★ War and Peace
- The Firemen's Ball
- Stolen Kisses

1969
- ★ Z
- Battle of Neretva
- Tchaikovsky

1970
- ★ First Love
- My Night at Maud's
- Tristana

1971
- ★ The Garden of the Finzi-Continis

1972
- ★ The Discreet Charm of the Bourgeoisie
- I Love You Rosa

1973
- ★ Day for Night
- The Deluge
- The House on Chelouche Street
- The Pedestrian
- Turkish Delight

1974
- ★ Amarcord
- Cat's Play

1975
- ★ Dersu Uzala
- Land of Promise
- Sandakan No. 8
- The Scent of a Woman

1976
- ★ Black and White in Color
- Cousin, Cousine
- Jacob the Liar
- Nights and Days
- Seven Beauties

1977
- ★ Madame Rosa
- Iphigenia
- Operation Thunderbolt
- A Special Day
- That Obscure Object of Desire

1978
- ★ Get Out Your Handkerchiefs

1979
- ★ The Tin Drum
- Maids of Wilko

1980
- Mama Turns a Hundred
- A Simple Story
- To Forget Venice
- ★ Moscow Does Not Believe in Tears
- Kagemusha
- The Last Metro
- The Nest

1981
- ★ Mephisto
- The Boat Is Full
- Man of Iron
- Three Brothers

1982
- ★ Alsino and the Condor
- Coup de Torchon
- Flight of the Eagle
- Private Life

1983
- ★ Fanny and Alexander
- Carmen
- Entre-Nous
- Le Bal

1984
- ★ Dangerous Moves
- Beyond the Walls
- Camila

1985
- ★ The Official Story
- Angry Harvest
- Colonel Redl
- Three Men and a Cradle
- When Father Was Away on Business

1986
- ★ The Assault
- Betty Blue
- The Decline of the American Empire
- My Sweet Little Village

1987
- ★ Babette's Feast
- Au Revoir les Enfants
- The Family
- Pathfinder

1988
- ★ Pelle the Conqueror
- Hanussen
- The Music Teacher
- Salaam Bombay!
- Women on the Verge of a Nervous Breakdown

1989
- ★ Cinema Paradiso
- Camille Claudel
- Jesus of Montreal

1990
- ★ Journey of Hope
- Cyrano de Bergerac
- Ju Dou
- The Nasty Girl
- Open Doors

1991
- ★ Mediterraneo
- The Elementary School
- The Ox
- Raise the Red Lantern

1992
- ★ Indochine
- Children of Nature
- Close to Eden
- Daens
- Schtonk

1993
- ★ Belle Epoque
- Farewell My Concubine
- Hedd Wyn
- The Scent of Green Papaya
- The Wedding Banquet

1994
- ★ Burnt by the Sun
- Before the Rain
- Eat Drink Man Woman
- Farinelli
- Strawberry and Chocolate

1995
- ★ Antonia's Line
- All Things Fair
- Lamerica
- O Quatrilho
- The Star Maker

1996
- ★ Kolya
- A Chef in Love
- The Other Side of Sunday
- Prisoner of the Mountains
- Ridicule

1997
- ★ Character
- Beyond Silence
- Four Days in September
- Secrets of the Heart
- The Thief

1998
- ★ Life Is Beautiful
- Central Station
- The Grandfather
- Tango

1999
- ★ All About My Mother
- East-West
- Himalaya
- Solomon and Gaenor
- Under the Sun

2000
- ★ Crouching Tiger, Hidden Dragon
- Amores Perros
- Divided We Fall
- Everybody's Famous!

2001
- ★ No Man's Land
- Amelie

2002
- ★ Nowhere in Africa
- The Crime of Father Amaro
- Elling
- Lagaan: Once upon a Time in India
- The Man Without a Past
- Mondays in the Sun
- The Son of the Bride
- Zus & Zo

2003
- ★ The Barbarian Invasions

2004
- ★ The Sea Inside

2005
- ★ Tsotsi
- Paradise Now

2006
- ★ The Lives of Others
- Don't Tell
- Pan's Labyrinth

2007
- ★ Beaufort
- The Counterfeiters

VISUAL EFFECTS

1963
- ★ Cleopatra

1964
- ★ Mary Poppins

1965
- ★ Thunderball

1966
- ★ Fantastic Voyage

1967
- ★ Doctor Dolittle

1968
- ★ 2001: A Space Odyssey

1969
- ★ Marooned

1970
- ★ Tora! Tora! Tora!

1971
- ★ Bedknobs and Broomsticks

1972
- ★ The Poseidon Adventure

1974
- ★ Earthquake

1975
- ★ The Hindenburg

1976
- ★ King Kong
- Logan's Run

1977
- ★ Star Wars

1978
- ★ Superman: The Movie

1979
- ★ Alien

1980
- ★ The Empire Strikes Back

1981
- ★ Raiders of the Lost Ark

1982
- ★ E.T.: The Extra-Terrestrial

1983
- ★ Return of the Jedi

1984
- ★ Indiana Jones and the Temple of Doom

1985
- ★ Cocoon

1986
- ★ Aliens

1987
- ★ Innerspace

1988
- ★ Who Framed Roger Rabbit

1989
- ★ The Abyss

1990
- ★ Total Recall

1991
- ★ Terminator 2: Judgment Day
- Backdraft
- Hook

1992
- ★ Death Becomes Her
- Alien 3
- Batman Returns

1993
- ★ Jurassic Park
- Cliffhanger
- The Nightmare before Christmas

1994
- ★ Forrest Gump
- The Mask
- True Lies

1995
- ★ Babe

1996
- ★ Independence Day
- Dragonheart
- Twister

1997
- ★ Titanic
- The Lost World: Jurassic Park 2
- Starship Troopers

1998
- ★ What Dreams May Come
- Armageddon
- Mighty Joe Young

1999
- ★ The Matrix
- Star Wars: Episode 1—The Phantom Menace
- Stuart Little

2000
- ★ Gladiator
- Hollow Man
- The Perfect Storm

2001
- ★ A.I.: Artificial Intelligence
- Lord of the Rings: The Fellowship of the Rings
- Pearl Harbor

2002
- ★ Lord of the Rings: The Two Towers
- Spider-Man
- Star Wars: Episode 2—Attack of the Clones

2003
- ★ Lord of the Rings: The Return of the King

★ = winner

2004
Master and Commander: The Far Side of the World
Pirates of the Caribbean: The Curse of the Black Pearl
2005
King Kong
The Chronicles of Narnia: The Lion, the Witch and the Wardrobe
2006
Pirates of the Caribbean: Dead Man's Chest
Poseidon
Superman Returns
2007
The Golden Compass
Pirates of the Caribbean: At World's End
Transformers

ANIMATED FILM

2001
★ Shrek
Jimmy Neutron: Boy Genius
Monsters, Inc.
2002
★ Spirited Away
Ice Age
Lilo & Stitch
Spirit: Stallion of the Cimarron
Treasure Planet
2003
★ Finding Nemo
Brother Bear
The Triplets of Belleville
2004
★ The Incredibles
Shark Tale
Shrek 2
2005
★ Wallace & Gromit: The Curse of the Were-Rabbit
Howl's Moving Castle
2006
★ Happy Feet
Cars
Monster House
2007
★ Ratatouille
Persepolis
Surf's Up

BRITISH ACADEMY OF FILM AND TELEVISION ARTS

ACTOR

1952 ★ Marlon Brando/Viva Zapata!
1953 ★ Marlon Brando/Julius Caesar
1954 John Gielgud/Julius Caesar
1955 ★ Ernest Borgnine/Marty
Laurence Olivier/Richard III
1956 ★ Francois Perier/Gervaise
1957 Henry Fonda/Twelve Angry Men
1958 ★ Trevor Howard/The Key
Sidney Poitier/The Defiant Ones
1959 ★ Jack Lemmon/Some Like It Hot
Peter Sellers/I'm All Right Jack
1960 ★ Jack Lemmon/The Apartment
1961 ★ Peter Finch/No Love for Johnnie
Paul Newman/The Hustler
1962 ★ Burt Lancaster/Birdman of Alcatraz
Peter O'Toole/Lawrence of Arabia
1963 ★ Dirk Bogarde/The Servant
Marcello Mastroianni/Divorce—Italian Style
1964 ★ Richard Attenborough/Seance on a Wet Afternoon
Marcello Mastroianni/Yesterday, Today and Tomorrow
1965 ★ Dirk Bogarde/Darling
Lee Marvin/Cat Ballou
1966 ★ Richard Burton/Who's Afraid of Virginia Woolf?
1967 ★ Rod Steiger/In the Heat of the Night
Paul Scofield/A Man for All Seasons
1968 ★ Spencer Tracy/Guess Who's Coming to Dinner
1969 ★ Dustin Hoffman/Midnight Cowboy
1970 ★ Robert Redford/Butch Cassidy and the Sundance Kid
1971 ★ Peter Finch/Sunday, Bloody Sunday
1972 ★ Gene Hackman/The French Connection
1973 ★ Walter Matthau/Pete 'n' Tillie
1974 ★ Jack Nicholson/Chinatown
Jack Nicholson/The Last Detail
1975 ★ Al Pacino/Dog Day Afternoon
1976 ★ Jack Nicholson/One Flew Over the Cuckoo's Nest
1977 ★ Peter Finch/Network
1978 ★ Richard Dreyfuss/The Goodbye Girl
1979 ★ Jack Lemmon/The China Syndrome
1980 ★ John Hurt/The Elephant Man
1981 ★ Burt Lancaster/Atlantic City
1982 ★ Ben Kingsley/Gandhi
1983 ★ Michael Caine/Educating Rita
Dustin Hoffman/Tootsie
1984 ★ Haing S. Ngor/The Killing Fields
1985 ★ William Hurt/Kiss of the Spider Woman
1986 ★ Bob Hoskins/Mona Lisa
1987 ★ Sean Connery/The Name of the Rose
1988 ★ John Cleese/A Fish Called Wanda
1989 ★ Daniel Day-Lewis/My Left Foot
1990 ★ Philippe Noiret/Cinema Paradiso
1991 ★ Anthony Hopkins/The Silence of the Lambs
1992 ★ Robert Downey, Jr./Chaplin
1993 ★ Anthony Hopkins/The Remains of the Day
Daniel Day-Lewis/In the Name of the Father
1994 ★ Hugh Grant/Four Weddings and a Funeral
1995 ★ Nigel Hawthorne/The Madness of King George
1996 ★ Geoffrey Rush/Shine
Ralph Fiennes/The English Patient
1997 ★ Robert Carlyle/The Full Monty
Billy Connolly/Mrs. Brown
1998 ★ Roberto Benigni/Life Is Beautiful
Michael Caine/Little Voice
1999 ★ Kevin Spacey/American Beauty
Tom Hanks/Saving Private Ryan
Ralph Fiennes/The End of the Affair
Om Puri/East Is East
2000 ★ Jamie Bell/Billy Elliot
Russell Crowe/Gladiator
2001 ★ Russell Crowe/A Beautiful Mind
Jim Broadbent/Iris
Ian McKellen/Lord of the Rings: The Fellowship of the Ring
Kevin Spacey/The Shipping News
Tom Wilkinson/In the Bedroom
2002 ★ Daniel Day-Lewis/Gangs of New York
Adrien Brody/The Pianist
Nicolas Cage/Adaptation
Michael Caine/The Quiet American
Jack Nicholson/About Schmidt
2003 ★ Johnny Depp/Pirates of the Caribbean: The Curse of the Black Pearl
Bill Murray/Lost in Translation
Benicio Del Toro/21 Grams
Jude Law/Cold Mountain
Sean Penn/Mystic River
Sean Penn/21 Grams
2004 ★ Jamie Foxx/Ray
Gael Garcia Bernal/The Motorcycle Diaries
Jim Carrey/Eternal Sunshine of the Spotless Mind
Johnny Depp/Finding Neverland
Leonardo DiCaprio/The Aviator
2005 ★ Philip Seymour Hoffman/Capote
Ralph Fiennes/The Constant Gardener
Terrence Howard/Hustle & Flow
Heath Ledger/Brokeback Mountain
Joaquin Rafael (Leaf) Phoenix/Walk the Line
David Strathairn/Good Night, and Good Luck
2006 ★ Forest Whitaker/The Last King of Scotland
Daniel Craig/Casino Royale
Leonardo DiCaprio/The Departed
Richard Griffiths/The History Boys
Peter O'Toole/Venus
2007 ★ Daniel Day-Lewis/There Will Be Blood
George Clooney/Michael Clayton
James McAvoy/Atonement
Viggo Mortensen/Eastern Promises
Ulrich Muehe/The Lives of Others

ACTOR—SUPPORTING

1969 ★ Laurence Olivier/Oh! What a Lovely War
1971 ★ Edward Fox/The Go-Between
1972 ★ Ben Johnson/The Last Picture Show
1973 ★ Arthur Lowe/O Lucky Man!
1974 ★ John Gielgud/Murder on the Orient Express
1975 ★ Fred Astaire/The Towering Inferno
1976 ★ Brad Dourif/One Flew Over the Cuckoo's Nest
1977 ★ Edward Fox/A Bridge Too Far
1978 ★ John Hurt/Midnight Express
1979 ★ Robert Duvall/Apocalypse Now
1981 ★ Ian Holm/Chariots of Fire
1982 ★ Jack Nicholson/Reds
1983 ★ Denholm Elliott/Trading Places
1984 ★ Denholm Elliott/A Private Function
1985 ★ Denholm Elliott/Defense of the Realm
1986 ★ Ray McAnally/The Mission
1987 ★ Daniel Auteuil/Jean de Florette
1988 ★ Michael Palin/A Fish Called Wanda
1989 ★ Ray McAnally/My Left Foot
1990 ★ Salvatore Cascio/Cinema Paradiso
1991 ★ Alan Rickman/Robin Hood: Prince of Thieves
1992 ★ Gene Hackman/Unforgiven
1993 ★ Ralph Fiennes/Schindler's List
1994 ★ Samuel L. Jackson/Pulp Fiction
Ben Kingsley/Schindler's List
1995 ★ Tim Roth/Rob Roy
Ian Holm/The Madness of King George
1996 ★ Paul Scofield/The Crucible
John Gielgud/Shine
Alan Rickman/Michael Collins
Edward Norton/Primal Fear
1997 ★ Tom Wilkinson/The Full Monty
Rupert Everett/My Best Friend's Wedding
Burt Reynolds/Boogie Nights
1998 ★ Geoffrey Rush/Shakespeare in Love
Ed Harris/The Truman Show
Geoffrey Rush/Elizabeth
Tom Wilkinson/Shakespeare in Love
2000 ★ Benicio Del Toro/Traffic
Jude Law/The Talented Mr. Ripley
Wes Bentley/American Beauty
Michael Caine/The Cider House Rules
Rhys Ifans/Notting Hill
Timothy Spall/Topsy-Turvy
2001 ★ Jim Broadbent/Moulin Rouge
Hugh Bonneville/Iris
Robbie Coltrane/Harry Potter and the Sorcerer's Stone
Colin Firth/Bridget Jones's Diary
Eddie Murphy/Shrek
2002 ★ Christopher Walken/Catch Me If You Can
Chris Cooper/Adaptation
Ed Harris/The Hours
Alfred Molina/Frida
Paul Newman/Road to Perdition
2003 ★ Bill Nighy/Love Actually
Paul Bettany/Master and Commander: The Far Side of the World
Albert Finney/Big Fish
Ian McKellen/Lord of the Rings: The Return of the King
Tim Robbins/Mystic River
2004 ★ Clive Owen/Closer
Alan Alda/The Aviator
Philip Davis/Vera Drake
Jamie Foxx/Collateral
Rodrigo de la Serna/The Motorcycle Diaries
2005 ★ Jake Gyllenhaal/Brokeback Mountain
Don Cheadle/Crash
George Clooney/Good Night, and Good Luck
George Clooney/Syriana
Matt Dillon/Crash
2006 ★ Alan Arkin/Little Miss Sunshine
James McAvoy/The Last King of Scotland
Jack Nicholson/The Departed
Leslie Phillips/Venus
Michael Sheen/The Queen
2007 ★ Javier Bardem/No Country for Old Men
Paul Franklin Dano/There Will Be Blood
Philip Seymour Hoffman/Charlie Wilson's War
Tommy Lee Jones/No Country for Old Men
Tom Wilkinson/Michael Clayton

ACTRESS

1952 ★ Vivien Leigh/A Streetcar Named Desire
1953 ★ Leslie Caron/Lili
Audrey Hepburn/Roman Holiday
1955 ★ Betsy Blair/Marty
Katie Johnson/The Ladykillers
1956 ★ Anna Magnani/The Rose Tattoo

★ = winner

British Academy Awards

ACTRESS

1958
★ Simone Signoret/Room at the Top

1959
★ Audrey Hepburn/The Nun's Story
★ Shirley MacLaine/Ask Any Girl

1960
★ Shirley MacLaine/The Apartment
★ Rachel Roberts/Saturday Night and Sunday Morning

1961
★ Sophia Loren/Two Women

1962
★ Anne Bancroft/The Miracle Worker

1963
★ Patricia Neal/Hud
★ Rachel Roberts/This Sporting Life

1964
★ Audrey Hepburn/Charade

1965
★ Julie Christie/Darling
★ Patricia Neal/In Harm's Way

1966
★ Elizabeth Taylor/Who's Afraid of Virginia Woolf?

1967
★ Anouk Aimee/A Man and a Woman

1968
★ Katharine Hepburn/Guess Who's Coming to Dinner

1969
★ Maggie Smith/The Prime of Miss Jean Brodie

1970
★ Katharine Ross/Butch Cassidy and the Sundance Kid

1971
★ Glenda Jackson/Sunday, Bloody Sunday

1972
★ Liza Minnelli/Cabaret

1973
★ Delphine Seyrig/The Discreet Charm of the Bourgeoisie

1974
★ Joanne Woodward/Summer Wishes, Winter Dreams

1975
★ Ellen Burstyn/Alice Doesn't Live Here Anymore

1976
★ Louise Fletcher/One Flew Over the Cuckoo's Nest

1977
★ Diane Keaton/Annie Hall

1978
★ Jane Fonda/Julia

1979
★ Jane Fonda/The China Syndrome

1980
★ Judy Davis/My Brilliant Career

1981
★ Meryl Streep/The French Lieutenant's Woman

1982
★ Katharine Hepburn/On Golden Pond

1983
★ Julie Walters/Educating Rita

1984
★ Maggie Smith/A Private Function

1985
★ Peggy Ashcroft/A Passage to India

1986
★ Maggie Smith/A Room with a View

1987
★ Anne Bancroft/84 Charing Cross Road

1988
★ Maggie Smith/The Lonely Passion of Judith Hearne

1989
★ Pauline Collins/Shirley Valentine

1990
★ Jessica Tandy/Driving Miss Daisy

1991
★ Jodie Foster/The Silence of the Lambs

1992
★ Emma Thompson/Howard's End

1993
★ Holly Hunter/The Piano
★ Miranda Richardson/Tom & Viv

1994
★ Susan Sarandon/The Client
★ Emma Thompson/The Remains of the Day
★ Debra Winger/Shadowlands

1995
★ Emma Thompson/Sense and Sensibility
★ Nicole Kidman/To Die For
★ Helen Mirren/The Madness of King George
★ Elisabeth Shue/Leaving Las Vegas

1996
★ Brenda Blethyn/Secrets and Lies
★ Frances McDormand/Fargo
★ Kristin Scott Thomas/The English Patient
★ Emily Watson/Breaking the Waves

1997
★ Judi Dench/Mrs. Brown
★ Kim Basinger/L.A. Confidential
★ Helena Bonham-Carter/The Wings of the Dove
★ Kathy Burke/Nil by Mouth

1998
★ Cate Blanchett/Elizabeth
★ Jane Horrocks/Little Voice
★ Gwyneth Paltrow/Shakespeare in Love
★ Emily Watson/Hilary and Jackie

1999
★ Annette Bening/American Beauty
★ Linda Bassett/East Is East
★ Julianne Moore/The End of the Affair
★ Emily Watson/Angela's Ashes

2000
★ Julia Roberts/Erin Brockovich

2001
★ Judi Dench/Iris
★ Nicole Kidman/The Others
★ Sissy Spacek/In the Bedroom
★ Audrey Tautou/Amelie
★ Renee Zellweger/Bridget Jones's Diary

2002
★ Nicole Kidman/The Hours
★ Halle Berry/Monster's Ball
Salma Hayek/Frida
Meryl Streep/The Hours
Renee Zellweger/Chicago

2003
★ Scarlett Johansson/Lost in Translation
Scarlett Johansson/Girl with a Pearl Earring
Uma Thurman/Kill Bill Vol. 1
Naomi Watts/21 Grams

2004
★ Imelda Staunton/Vera Drake
Charlize Theron/Monster
Kate Winslet/Eternal Sunshine of the Spotless Mind
Kate Winslet/Finding Neverland
Zhang Ziyi/House of Flying Daggers

2005
★ Reese Witherspoon/Walk the Line
Judi Dench/Mrs. Henderson Presents
Keira Knightley/Pride and Prejudice
Charlize Theron/North Country
Zhang Ziyi/Memoirs of a Geisha

2006
★ Helen Mirren/The Queen
Penelope Cruz/Volver
Judi Dench/Notes on a Scandal
Meryl Streep/The Devil Wears Prada
Kate Winslet/Little Children

2007
★ Marion Cotillard/La Vie en Rose
Cate Blanchett/Elizabeth: The Golden Age
Julie Christie/Away From Her
Keira Knightley/Atonement
Ellen Page/Juno

ACTRESS— SUPPORTING

1961
★ Dora Bryan/A Taste of Honey

1969
★ Celia Johnson/The Prime of Miss Jean Brodie
Mary Wimbush/Oh! What a Lovely War

1970
★ Susannah York/They Shoot Horses, Don't They?

1971
★ Margaret Leighton/The Go-Between

1972
★ Cloris Leachman/The Last Picture Show

1973
★ Valentina Cortese/Day for Night

1974
★ Ingrid Bergman/Murder on the Orient Express

1975
★ Diane Ladd/Alice Doesn't Live Here Anymore

1976
★ Jodie Foster/Taxi Driver

1977
★ Jenny Agutter/Equus

1978
★ Geraldine Page/Interiors
Vanessa Redgrave/Julia

1979
★ Rachel Roberts/Yanks

1982
★ Rohini Hattangady/Gandhi
Maureen Stapleton/Reds

1983
★ Jamie Lee Curtis/Trading Places

1984
★ Liz Smith/A Private Function
Tuesday Weld/Once Upon a Time in America

1985
★ Rosanna Arquette/Desperately Seeking Susan

1986
★ Judi Dench/A Room with a View

1987
★ Susan Wooldridge/Hope and Glory

1988
★ Judi Dench/A Handful of Dust

1989
★ Michelle Pfeiffer/Dangerous Liaisons

1990
★ Whoopi Goldberg/Ghost

1991
★ Kate Nelligan/Frankie and Johnny

1992
★ Miranda Richardson/Damage

1993
★ Miriam Margolyes/The Age of Innocence
Holly Hunter/The Firm
Maggie Smith/The Secret Garden

1994
★ Kristin Scott Thomas/Four Weddings and a Funeral
Winona Ryder/The Age of Innocence

1995
★ Kate Winslet/Sense and Sensibility
Joan Allen/Nixon
Mira Sorvino/Mighty Aphrodite
Elizabeth Spriggs/Sense and Sensibility

1996
★ Juliette Binoche/The English Patient
Lauren Bacall/The Mirror Has Two Faces
Marianne Jean-Baptiste/Secrets and Lies
Lynn Redgrave/Shine

1997
★ Sigourney Weaver/The Ice Storm
Jennifer Ehle/Wilde
Lesley Sharp/The Full Monty
Zoe Wanamaker/Wilde

1998
★ Judi Dench/Shakespeare in Love
Kathy Bates/Primary Colors
Brenda Blethyn/Little Voice
Lynn Redgrave/Gods and Monsters

1999
★ Maggie Smith/Tea with Mussolini
Thora Birch/American Beauty
Cate Blanchett/The Talented Mr. Ripley
Cameron Diaz/Being John Malkovich
Mena Suvari/American Beauty

2000
★ Julie Walters/Billy Elliot

2001
★ Jennifer Connelly/A Beautiful Mind
Judi Dench/The Shipping News
Helen Mirren/Gosford Park
Maggie Smith/Gosford Park
Kate Winslet/Iris

2002
★ Catherine Zeta-Jones/Chicago
Toni Collette/About a Boy
Julianne Moore/The Hours
Queen Latifah/Chicago
Meryl Streep/Adaptation

2003
★ Renee Zellweger/Cold Mountain
Holly Hunter/Thirteen
Laura Linney/Mystic River
Judy Parfitt/Girl with a Pearl Earring
Emma Thompson/Love Actually

2004
★ Cate Blanchett/The Aviator
Julie Christie/Finding Neverland
Heather Craney/Vera Drake
Natalie Portman/Closer
Meryl Streep/The Manchurian Candidate

2005
★ Thandie Newton/Crash
Brenda Blethyn/Pride and Prejudice
Catherine Keener/Capote
Frances McDormand/North Country
Michelle Williams/Brokeback Mountain

2006
★ Jennifer Hudson/Dreamgirls
Emily Blunt/The Devil Wears Prada
Abigail Breslin/Little Miss Sunshine
Toni Collette/Little Miss Sunshine
Frances de la Tour/The History Boys

2007
★ Tilda Swinton/Michael Clayton
Cate Blanchett/I'm Not There
Kelly Macdonald/No Country for Old Men
Samantha Morton/Control
Saoirse Ronan/Atonement

ART DIRECTION

1969
★ Oh! What a Lovely War

1997
★ William Shakespeare's Romeo and Juliet

1999
★ Sleepy Hollow
American Beauty
Angela's Ashes
The End of the Affair
The Matrix

CINEMATOGRAPHY

1969
★ Oh! What a Lovely War

1984
Once Upon a Time in America

1995
★ Braveheart
Apollo 13
The Madness of King George
Sense and Sensibility

1996
★ The English Patient

1997
★ The Wings of the Dove
L.A. Confidential
Titanic
William Shakespeare's Romeo and Juliet

1998
★ Elizabeth
Saving Private Ryan
Shakespeare in Love
The Truman Show

1999
★ American Beauty
Angela's Ashes
The End of the Affair
The Matrix
The Talented Mr. Ripley

2000
★ Gladiator

2001
Black Hawk Down
Lord of the Rings: The Fellowship of the Rings
Moulin Rouge

2002
★ Road to Perdition
Chicago
Gangs of New York
Lord of the Rings: The Two Towers
The Pianist

2003
★ Lord of the Rings: The Return of the King
Cold Mountain
Girl with a Pearl Earring
Lost in Translation
Master and Commander: The Far Side of the World

2004
★ Collateral
The Aviator
Finding Neverland
House of Flying Daggers
The Motorcycle Diaries

2005
★ Memoirs of a Geisha
Brokeback Mountain
The Constant Gardener
Crash
March of the Penguins

2006
★ Children of Men
Babel
Casino Royale
Pan's Labyrinth
United 93

2007
★ No Country for Old Men
American Gangster
Atonement
The Bourne Ultimatum
There Will Be Blood

COSTUME DESIGN

1969
★ Oh! What a Lovely War

1984
★ Once Upon a Time in America

1997
★ Mrs. Brown
L.A. Confidential
Titanic
The Wings of the Dove

1998
★ Velvet Goldmine
Elizabeth
The Mask of Zorro
Shakespeare in Love

1999
★ Sleepy Hollow
The End of the Affair
An Ideal Husband
Tea with Mussolini

2001
★ Gosford Park
Harry Potter and the Sorcerer's Stone
Lord of the Rings: The Fellowship of the Rings
Moulin Rouge
Planet of the Apes

★ = winner

2002
- ★ Lord of the Rings: The Two Towers
- ★ Catch Me If You Can
- Chicago
- Gangs of New York

2003
- ★ Master and Commander: The Far Side of the World
- Cold Mountain
- Girl with a Pearl Earring
- Lord of the Rings: The Return of the King
- Pirates of the Caribbean: The Curse of the Black Pearl

2004
- ★ Vera Drake
- The Aviator
- Finding Neverland
- House of Flying Daggers

2005
- ★ Memoirs of a Geisha
- Charlie and the Chocolate Factory
- The Chronicles of Narnia: The Lion, the Witch and the Wardrobe
- Mrs. Henderson Presents
- Pride and Prejudice

2006
- ★ Pan's Labyrinth
- The Devil Wears Prada
- Marie Antoinette
- Pirates of the Caribbean: Dead Man's Chest
- The Queen

2007
- ★ La Vie en Rose
- Elizabeth: The Golden Age
- Lust, Caution
- Sweeney Todd: The Demon Barber of Fleet Street

DIRECTOR

1955
- ★ Laurence Olivier/Richard III

1968
- ★ Mike Nichols/The Graduate

1969
- ★ John Schlesinger/Midnight Cowboy

1970
- ★ George Roy Hill/Butch Cassidy and the Sundance Kid

1971
- ★ John Schlesinger/Sunday, Bloody Sunday

1972
- ★ Bob Fosse/Cabaret

1973
- ★ Francois Truffaut/Day for Night

1974
- ★ Roman Polanski/Chinatown

1975
- ★ Stanley Kubrick/Barry Lyndon

1976
- ★ Milos Forman/One Flew Over the Cuckoo's Nest

1977
- ★ Woody Allen/Annie Hall

1978
- ★ Alan Parker/Midnight Express

1979
- ★ Francis Ford Coppola/Apocalypse Now

1980
- ★ Akira Kurosawa/Kagemusha

1981
- ★ Louis Malle/Atlantic City

1982
- ★ Richard Attenborough/Gandhi

1983
- ★ Bill Forsyth/Local Hero

1984
- ★ Wim Wenders/Paris, Texas

1986
- ★ Woody Allen/Hannah and Her Sisters

1987
- ★ Oliver Stone/Platoon

1988
- ★ Louis Malle/Au Revoir les Enfants

1989
- ★ Kenneth Branagh/Henry V

1990
- ★ Martin Scorsese/Goodfellas

1991
- ★ Alan Parker/The Commitments

1992
- ★ Clint Eastwood/Unforgiven

1993
- ★ Steven Spielberg/Schindler's List

1994
- ★ Mike Newell/Four Weddings and a Funeral

1995
- ★ Michael Radford/The Postman

1996
- ★ Joel Coen/Fargo
- Scott Hicks/Shine
- Mike Leigh/Secrets and Lies
- Anthony Minghella/The English Patient

1997
- ★ Baz Luhrmann/William Shakespeare's Romeo and Juliet
- Nicholas Hytner/The Madness of King George
- Ang Lee/Sense and Sensibility

1998
- ★ Peter Weir/The Truman Show
- Shekhar Kapur/Elizabeth
- John Madden/Shakespeare in Love
- Steven Spielberg/Saving Private Ryan

1999
- ★ Pedro Almodovar/All About My Mother
- Neil Jordan/The End of the Affair
- Sam Mendes/American Beauty
- Anthony Minghella/The Talented Mr. Ripley

2000
- ★ Ang Lee/Crouching Tiger, Hidden Dragon

2001
- ★ Peter Jackson/Lord of the Rings: The Fellowship of the Ring
- Robert Altman/Gosford Park
- Ron Howard/A Beautiful Mind
- Jean-Pierre Jeunet/Amelie
- Baz Luhrmann/Moulin Rouge

2002
- ★ Roman Polanski/The Pianist
- Stephen Daldry/The Hours
- Rob Marshall/Chicago
- Martin Scorsese/Gangs of New York

2003
- ★ Peter Weir/Master and Commander: The Far Side of the World
- Sofia Coppola/Lost in Translation
- Peter Jackson/Lord of the Rings: The Return of the King
- Anthony Minghella/Cold Mountain

2004
- ★ Mike Leigh/Vera Drake
- Marc Forster/Finding Neverland
- Tim Burton/Big Fish
- Michel Gondry/Eternal Sunshine of the Spotless Mind

2005
- ★ George Clooney/Good Night, and Good Luck
- Fernando Meirelles/The Constant Gardener
- Bennett Miller/Capote

2006
- ★ Paul Greengrass/United 93
- Jonathan Dayton/Little Miss Sunshine
- Valerie Faris/Little Miss Sunshine
- Stephen Frears/The Queen
- Alejandro Gonzalez Inarritu/Babel

2007
- ★ Ethan Coen/No Country for Old Men
- Paul Thomas Anderson/There Will Be Blood
- Joel Coen/No Country for Old Men
- Paul Greengrass/The Bourne Ultimatum
- Joe Wright/Atonement
- Florian Henckel von Donnersmarck/The Lives of Others

FILM

1947
- ★ The Best Years of Our Lives

1948
- ★ Odd Man Out

1949
- ★ The Bicycle Thief

1950
- ★ The Third Man

1951
- ★ All About Eve

1953
- ★ The Blue Lamp

1954
- ★ Hobson's Choice

1955
- ★ Richard III

1956
- ★ Gervaise

1957
- ★ Reach for the Sky

1959
- ★ Een-Hur

1960
- ★ Sapphire

1961
- ★ The Apartment

1964
- ★ Tom Jones

1965
- ★ Dr. Strangelove, or: How I Learned to Stop Worrying and Love the Bomb

1966
- ★ King and Country
- The Spy Who Came in from the Cold

1967
- ★ A Man for All Seasons

1968
- ★ The Graduate

1969
- ★ Midnight Cowboy
- Oh! What a Lovely War

1970
- ★ Butch Cassidy and the Sundance Kid

1971
- ★ Sunday, Bloody Sunday

1972
- ★ Cabaret

1973
- ★ Day for Night

1975
- ★ Alice Doesn't Live Here Anymore

1976
- ★ One Flew Over the Cuckoo's Nest

1977
- ★ Annie Hall

1978
- ★ Julia

1979
- ★ Manhattan

1980
- ★ The Elephant Man

1981
- ★ Chariots of Fire

1982
- ★ Gandhi

1983
- ★ Educating Rita

1984
- ★ The Killing Fields

1985
- ★ The Purple Rose of Cairo

1986
- ★ A Room with a View

1987
- ★ Jean de Florette

1988
- ★ The Last Emperor

1989
- ★ Dead Poets Society

1990
- ★ Goodfellas

1991
- ★ The Commitments

1992
- ★ Unforgiven

1993
- ★ Schindler's List
- ★ Shadowlands

1994
- ★ Four Weddings and a Funeral
- The Piano
- The Remains of the Day

1995
- ★ Sense and Sensibility
- Babe
- Carrington
- Land and Freedom
- The Madness of King George

1996
- ★ The English Patient
- Fargo
- Secrets and Lies
- Shine
- The Usual Suspects

1997
- ★ The Full Monty
- L.A. Confidential
- The Borrowers
- Mrs. Brown
- 24-7
- Titanic

1998
- ★ Shakespeare in Love
- Elizabeth
- The Full Monty
- Lock, Stock and 2 Smoking Barrels
- Saving Private Ryan

1999
- ★ American Beauty
- Being John Malkovich
- The Matrix
- The Sixth Sense

2000
- ★ Billy Elliot
- ★ Gladiator

2001
- ★ Gosford Park
- ★ Lord of the Rings: The Fellowship of the Rings
- Amelie
- A Beautiful Mind
- Bridget Jones's Diary
- Harry Potter and the Sorcerer's Stone
- Moulin Rouge
- Shrek

2002
- ★ The Pianist
- Chicago
- Gangs of New York
- The Hours
- Lord of the Rings: The Two Towers

2003
- ★ Lord of the Rings: The Return of the King
- Big Fish
- Cold Mountain
- Lost in Translation
- The Magdalene Sisters
- Master and Commander: The Far Side of the World

2004
- ★ The Aviator
- Eternal Sunshine of the Spotless Mind
- The Motorcycle Diaries
- Vera Drake

2005
- ★ Brokeback Mountain
- Capote
- The Constant Gardener
- Crash
- Good Night, and Good Luck

2006
- ★ The Queen
- Babel
- The Departed
- The Last King of Scotland
- Little Miss Sunshine

2007
- ★ Atonement
- American Gangster
- The Lives of Others
- No Country for Old Men
- There Will Be Blood

FILM EDITING

1969
- ★ Oh! What a Lovely War

1997
- ★ L.A. Confidential
- The Full Monty
- Titanic
- William Shakespeare's Romeo and Juliet

1998
- ★ Shakespeare in Love
- Elizabeth
- Lock, Stock and 2 Smoking Barrels
- Saving Private Ryan

1999
- ★ American Beauty
- Being John Malkovich
- The Matrix
- The Sixth Sense

2001
- ★ Amelie
- Black Hawk Down
- Lord of the Rings: The Fellowship of the Rings
- Moulin Rouge

2002
- ★ Chicago
- Gangs of New York
- The Hours
- Lord of the Rings: The Two Towers

2003
- ★ Lord of the Rings: The Return of the King
- Big Fish
- Cold Mountain
- Lost in Translation
- Master and Commander: The Far Side of the World

2004
- ★ The Aviator
- Collateral
- House of Flying Daggers
- Vera Drake

2005
- ★ The Constant Gardener
- The Aviator
- Brokeback Mountain
- Crash
- Good Night, and Good Luck

2006
- ★ United 93
- Babel
- Casino Royale
- The Departed
- The Queen

★ = winner

British Academy Awards

★ = winner

MAKEUP

1997
- ★ The Wings of the Dove

1999
- ★ Topsy Turvy
- American Beauty
- The End of the Affair
- An Ideal Husband

2002
- ★ Frida
- Chicago
- The Hours
- Lord of the Rings: The Two Towers

2003
- ★ Pirates of the Caribbean: The Curse of the Black Pearl
- Big Fish
- Cold Mountain
- Girl with a Pearl Earring
- Lord of the Rings: The Return of the King

2004
- ★ The Aviator
- Finding Neverland
- Harry Potter and the Prisoner of Azkaban
- House of Flying Daggers
- Vera Drake

2005
- ★ The Chronicles of Narnia: The Lion, the Witch and the Wardrobe
- Charlie and the Chocolate Factory
- Harry Potter and the Goblet of Fire
- Memoirs of a Geisha
- Pride and Prejudice

2006
- ★ Pan's Labyrinth
- The Devil Wears Prada
- Marie Antoinette
- Pirates of the Caribbean: Dead Man's Chest
- The Queen

2007
- ★ La Vie en Rose
- Atonement
- Elizabeth: The Golden Age
- Hairspray
- Sweeney Todd: The Demon Barber of Fleet Street

ORIGINAL SCORE

1984
- ★ Once Upon a Time in America

1999
- ★ Buena Vista Social Club
- The End of the Affair
- The Talented Mr. Ripley

2001
- ★ Moulin Rouge
- Amelie
- Lord of the Rings: The Fellowship of the Rings
- Mulholland Drive
- Shrek

2002
- ★ The Hours
- Catch Me If You Can
- Chicago
- Gangs of New York
- The Pianist

2003
- ★ Cold Mountain
- Girl with a Pearl Earring
- Kill Bill Vol. 1
- Lord of the Rings: The Return of the King
- Lost in Translation

2004
- ★ The Aviator
- Finding Neverland
- Ray

2005
- ★ Memoirs of a Geisha
- The Motorcycle Diaries
- The Constant Gardener
- Mrs. Henderson Presents

2006
- ★ Babel
- Casino Royale
- Dreamgirls
- Happy Feet
- The Queen

2007
- ★ La Vie en Rose
- American Gangster
- Atonement
- The Kite Runner
- There Will Be Blood

SCORE

1993
- Sleepless in Seattle

1994
- The Piano
- Schindler's List

1995
- The Postman
- Braveheart
- The Madness of King George
- Sense and Sensibility

1996
- The English Patient

1997
- William Shakespeare's Romeo and Juliet
- The Full Monty
- L.A. Confidential
- Titanic

1998
- Elizabeth
- Hilary and Jackie
- Saving Private Ryan
- Shakespeare in Love

1999
- ★ American Beauty

2000
- ★ Crouching Tiger, Hidden Dragon

SOUND

1997
- ★ L.A. Confidential
- The Full Monty
- Titanic
- William Shakespeare's Romeo and Juliet

1998
- ★ Saving Private Ryan
- Hilary and Jackie
- Little Voice
- Shakespeare in Love

1999
- ★ The Matrix
- American Beauty
- Buena Vista Social Club

2001
- ★ Moulin Rouge
- Black Hawk Down
- Harry Potter and the Sorcerer's Stone
- Lord of the Rings: The Fellowship of the Rings
- Shrek

2002
- ★ Gangs of New York
- Harry Potter and the Chamber of Secrets
- Lord of the Rings: The Two Towers
- The Pianist

2003
- ★ Chicago
- Master and Commander: The Far Side of the World
- Cold Mountain
- Kill Bill Vol. 1
- Lord of the Rings: The Return of the King
- Pirates of the Caribbean: The Curse of the Black Pearl

2004
- ★ Ray
- The Aviator
- Collateral
- House of Flying Daggers
- Spider-Man 2

2005
- ★ Walk the Line
- Batman Begins
- The Constant Gardener
- Crash
- King Kong

2006
- ★ Casino Royale
- Babel
- Pan's Labyrinth
- Pirates of the Caribbean: Dead Man's Chest
- United 93

2007
- ★ The Bourne Ultimatum
- American Gangster
- Atonement
- Michael Clayton
- No Country for Old Men

ADAPTED SCREENPLAY

1983
- ★ Heat and Dust

1984
- ★ The Killing Fields

1985
- ★ Prizzi's Honor

1986
- ★ Out of Africa

1987
- ★ Jean de Florette

1988
- ★ The Unbearable Lightness of Being

1989
- ★ Dangerous Liaisons

1990
- ★ Goodfellas

1991
- ★ The Commitments

1992
- ★ The Player

1993
- ★ Schindler's List
- In the Name of the Father
- Scent of a Woman

1994
- ★ Quiz Show
- The Remains of the Day
- Schindler's List
- Shadowlands

1995
- ★ Trainspotting
- Babe
- Leaving Las Vegas
- The Madness of King George
- The Postman
- Sense and Sensibility

1996
- ★ The English Patient
- The Crucible
- Evita
- Richard III

1997
- ★ William Shakespeare's Romeo and Juliet
- The Ice Storm
- L.A. Confidential
- The Wings of the Dove

1998
- ★ Primary Colors
- Hilary and Jackie
- Little Voice
- Wag the Dog

1999
- ★ The End of the Affair
- East Is East
- An Ideal Husband
- The Talented Mr. Ripley

2000
- ★ Traffic

2001
- ★ Shrek
- A Beautiful Mind
- Bridget Jones's Diary
- Iris
- Lord of the Rings: The Fellowship of the Rings

2002
- ★ Adaptation
- About a Boy
- Catch Me If You Can
- The Hours
- The Pianist

2003
- ★ Lord of the Rings: The Return of the King
- Big Fish
- Cold Mountain
- Girl with a Pearl Earring
- Mystic River

2004
- ★ Sideways
- Closer
- Finding Neverland
- The Motorcycle Diaries

2005
- ★ Brokeback Mountain
- Capote
- The Constant Gardener
- A History of Violence
- Pride and Prejudice

2006
- ★ The Last King of Scotland
- Casino Royale
- The Departed
- The Devil Wears Prada
- Notes on a Scandal

2007
- ★ The Diving Bell and the Butterfly
- Atonement
- The Kite Runner
- No Country for Old Men
- There Will Be Blood

ORIGINAL SCREENPLAY

1983
- ★ King of Comedy

1984
- ★ Broadway Danny Rose

1985
- ★ The Purple Rose of Cairo

1986
- ★ Hannah and Her Sisters

1987
- ★ Wish You Were Here

1988
- ★ A World Apart

1989
- ★ When Harry Met Sally...

1990
- ★ Cinema Paradiso

1991
- ★ Truly, Madly, Deeply

1992
- ★ Husbands and Wives

1993
- ★ Groundhog Day
- In the Line of Fire
- Sleepless in Seattle

1994
- ★ Pulp Fiction
- The Piano

1995
- ★ The Usual Suspects
- Bullets over Broadway
- Muriel's Wedding
- Seven

1996
- ★ Secrets and Lies
- Brassed Off
- Fargo
- Lone Star
- Shine

1997
- ★ Nil by Mouth
- Boogie Nights
- The Full Monty
- Mrs. Brown

1998
- ★ The Truman Show
- Elizabeth
- Life Is Beautiful
- Shakespeare in Love

1999
- ★ Being John Malkovich
- All About My Mother
- American Beauty
- The Sixth Sense
- Topsy Turvy

2001
- ★ Amelie
- Gosford Park
- Moulin Rouge
- The Others
- The Royal Tenenbaums

2002
- ★ Talk to Her
- Gangs of New York
- Y Tu Mama Tambien

2003
- ★ The Barbarian Invasions
- The Station Agent
- Finding Nemo
- Lost in Translation
- 21 Grams

2004
- ★ Eternal Sunshine of the Spotless Mind
- The Aviator
- Collateral
- Ray
- Vera Drake

2005
- ★ Crash
- Cinderella Man
- Good Night, and Good Luck
- Mrs. Henderson Presents

2006
- ★ Little Miss Sunshine
- Babel
- Pan's Labyrinth
- The Queen
- United 93

2007
- ★ Juno
- American Gangster
- The Lives of Others
- Michael Clayton
- This Is England

SCREENPLAY

1955
- ★ The Ladykillers

1956
- ★ The Man Who Never Was

1957
- ★ The Bridge on the River Kwai

1959
- ★ I'm All Right Jack

1961
- ★ The Day the Earth Caught Fire

1962
- ★ Lawrence of Arabia
- A Taste of Honey

1963
- ★ Tom Jones

1964
- ★ The Pumpkin Eater

1965
- ★ Darling

1966
- ★ Morgan: A Suitable Case for Treatment

1967
- ★ A Man for All Seasons

1968
- ★ The Graduate

1969
- ★ Midnight Cowboy

1970
- ★ Butch Cassidy and the Sundance Kid

1971
- ★ The Go-Between

1972
- ★ The Hospital
- The Last Picture Show

1973
- ★ The Discreet Charm of the Bourgeoisie

1974
- ★ Chinatown
- The Last Detail

1975
- ★ Alice Doesn't Live Here Anymore

1976
- ★ Bugsy Malone

1977
- ★ Annie Hall

1978
- ★ Julia

1979
- ★ Manhattan

1981
- ★ Gregory's Girl

1982
- ★ Missing

2003
- ★ The Magdalene Sisters

FILM—FOREIGN LANGUAGE

1982
- ★ Christ Stopped at Eboli

1983
- ★ Danton

1984
- ★ Carmen

1985
- ★ Colonel Redl

1986
- ★ Ran

1987
- ★ The Sacrifice

1988
- ★ Babette's Feast

1989
- ★ Life and Nothing But

1990
- ★ Cinema Paradiso

1991
- ★ The Nasty Girl

1992
- ★ Raise the Red Lantern

1993
- ★ Farewell My Concubine
- Indochine
- Like Water for Chocolate
- Un Coeur en Hiver

1994
- ★ To Live

1995
- ★ Burnt by the Sun
- The Postman
- Les Miserables
- Queen Margot

1996
- ★ Antonia's Line
- Kolya
- Nelly et Monsieur Arnaud

1997
- ★ Ma Vie en Rose
- The Tango Lesson

1998
- ★ Central Station
- Life Is Beautiful
- Live Flesh

1999
- ★ All About My Mother
- Buena Vista Social Club
- The Celebration
- Run Lola Run

★ = Winner

FOREIGN LANGUAGE FILM

2000
★ Crouching Tiger, Hidden Dragon

2001
★ Amores Perros
★ Behind the Sun
Amelie
Monsoon Wedding

2002
★ Talk to Her
Y Tu Mama Tambien

2003
★ In This World
The Barbarian Invasions
Good Bye, Lenin!
Spirited Away
The Triplets of Belleville

2004
★ The Motorcycle Diaries
Bad Education
House of Flying Daggers
A Very Long Engagement

2005
★ The Beat My Heart Skipped
Tsotsi

2006
★ Pan's Labyrinth
Apocalypto
Volver

2007
★ The Lives of Others
The Diving Bell and the Butterfly
The Kite Runner
Lust, Caution

VISUAL EFFECTS

1997
★ The Fifth Element

1999
★ The Matrix
Sleepy Hollow

2001
★ Lord of the Rings: The Fellowship of the Ring
A.I.: Artificial Intelligence
Harry Potter and the Sorcerer's Stone

2002
★ Lord of the Rings: The Two Towers
Minority Report
Spider-Man

2003
★ Lord of the Rings: The Return of the King
Big Fish
Kill Bill Vol. 1
Master and Commander: The Far Side of the World
Pirates of the Caribbean: The Curse of the Black Pearl

2004
★ The Day After Tomorrow
The Aviator
Harry Potter and the Prisoner of Azkaban
The Chronicles of Narnia: The Lion, the Witch and the Wardrobe
Spider-Man 2

2005
★ King Kong
Batman Begins
Charlie and the Chocolate Factory
Harry Potter and the Goblet of Fire

2006
★ Pirates of the Caribbean: Dead Man's Chest
Casino Royale
Children of Men
Pan's Labyrinth

2007
Superman Returns
★ The Golden Compass
The Bourne Ultimatum
Harry Potter and the Order of the Phoenix
Pirates of the Caribbean: At World's End
Spider-Man 3

ANIMATED FILM

2006
★ Happy Feet
Cars
Flushed Away

2007
★ Ratatouille
Shrek the Third
The Simpsons Movie

DIRECTORS GUILD OF AMERICA

DIRECTOR

1948 ★ Joseph L. Mankiewicz/A Letter to Three Wives
1949 Carol Reed/The Third Man
1950 ★ Joseph L. Mankiewicz/All About Eve
1951 ★ George Stevens/A Place in the Sun
1952 ★ John Ford/The Quiet Man
1953 ★ Fred Zinnemann/From Here to Eternity
1954 ★ Elia Kazan/On the Waterfront
1955 ★ Delbert Mann/Marty
1956 ★ George Stevens/Giant
1957 ★ David Lean/The Bridge on the River Kwai
1958 ★ Vincente Minnelli/Gigi
1959 ★ William Wyler/Ben-Hur
1960 ★ Billy Wilder/The Apartment
1961 ★ Jerome Robbins/West Side Story & Robert Wise/West Side Story
1962 ★ David Lean/Lawrence of Arabia
1963 ★ Tony Richardson/Tom Jones
1964 ★ George Cukor/My Fair Lady
1965 ★ Robert Wise/The Sound of Music
1966 ★ Fred Zinnemann/A Man for All Seasons
1967 ★ Mike Nichols/The Graduate
1968 ★ Anthony Harvey/The Lion in Winter
1969 ★ John Schlesinger/Midnight Cowboy
1970 ★ Franklin J. Schaffner/Patton
1971 ★ William Friedkin/The French Connection
1972 ★ Francis Ford Coppola/The Godfather
1973 ★ George Roy Hill/The Sting
1974 ★ Francis Ford Coppola/The Godfather, Part 2
1975 ★ Milos Forman/One Flew Over the Cuckoo's Nest
1976 ★ John G. Avildsen/Rocky
1977 ★ Woody Allen/Annie Hall
1978 ★ Michael Cimino/The Deer Hunter
1979 ★ Robert Benton/Kramer vs. Kramer
1980 ★ Robert Redford/Ordinary People
1981 ★ Warren Beatty/Reds
1982 ★ Richard Attenborough/Gandhi
1983 ★ James L. Brooks/Terms of Endearment
1984 ★ Milos Forman/Amadeus
1985 ★ Steven Spielberg/The Color Purple
1986 ★ Oliver Stone/Platoon
1987 ★ Bernardo Bertolucci/The Last Emperor
1988 ★ Barry Levinson/Rain Man
1989 ★ Oliver Stone/Born on the Fourth of July
1990 ★ Kevin Costner/Dances with Wolves
1991 ★ Jonathan Demme/The Silence of the Lambs
1992 ★ Clint Eastwood/Unforgiven
1993 ★ Steven Spielberg/Schindler's List
1994 ★ Robert Zemeckis/Forrest Gump

1995 ★ Ron Howard/Apollo 13
Mel Gibson/Braveheart
Ang Lee/Sense and Sensibility
Michael Radford/The Postman
Tim Robbins/Dead Man Walking

1996 ★ Anthony Minghella/The English Patient
Joel Coen/Fargo
Cameron Crowe/Jerry Maguire
Scott Hicks/Shine
Mike Leigh/Secrets and Lies

1997 ★ James Cameron/Titanic
James L. Brooks/As Good As It Gets
Curtis Hanson/L.A. Confidential
Steven Spielberg/Amistad
Gus Van Sant/Good Will Hunting

1998 ★ Steven Spielberg/Saving Private Ryan
Roberto Benigni/Life Is Beautiful
John Madden/Shakespeare in Love
Terrence Malick/The Thin Red Line
Peter Weir/The Truman Show

1999 ★ Sam Mendes/American Beauty
Frank Darabont/The Green Mile
Spike Jonze/Being John Malkovich
Michael Mann/The Insider
M. Night Shyamalan/The Sixth Sense

2000 ★ Ang Lee/Crouching Tiger, Hidden Dragon
Cameron Crowe/Almost Famous
Ridley Scott/Gladiator
Steven Soderbergh/Erin Brockovich
Steven Soderbergh/Traffic

2001 ★ Ron Howard/A Beautiful Mind
Peter Jackson/Lord of the Rings: The Fellowship of the Ring
Christopher Nolan/Memento
Ridley Scott/Black Hawk Down
Steven Soderbergh/Traffic

2002 ★ Rob Marshall/Chicago
Stephen Daldry/The Hours
Peter Jackson/Lord of the Rings: The Two Towers
Baz Luhrmann/Moulin Rouge
Roman Polanski/The Pianist
Martin Scorsese/Gangs of New York

2003 ★ Peter Jackson/Lord of the Rings: The Return of the King
Sofia Coppola/Lost in Translation
Clint Eastwood/Mystic River
Gary Ross/Seabiscuit
Peter Weir/Master and Commander: The Far Side of the World

2004 ★ Clint Eastwood/Million Dollar Baby
Marc Forster/Finding Neverland
Taylor Hackford/Ray
Alexander Payne/Sideways
Martin Scorsese/The Aviator

2005 ★ Ang Lee/Brokeback Mountain
George Clooney/Good Night, and Good Luck
Paul Haggis/Crash
Bennett Miller/Capote
Steven Spielberg/Munich

2006 ★ Martin Scorsese/The Departed
Bill Condon/Dreamgirls
Jonathan Dayton/Little Miss Sunshine
Stephen Frears/The Queen
Alejandro Gonzalez Inarritu/Babel

2007 ★ Ethan Coen/No Country for Old Men, Joel Coen/No Country for Old Men
Paul Thomas Anderson/There Will Be Blood
Tony Gilroy/Michael Clayton
Sean Penn/Into the Wild
Julian Schnabel/The Diving Bell and the Butterfly

FEATURE DOCUMENTARY

1992 ★ Joe Berlinger/Brother's Keeper, Bruce Sinofsky/Brother's Keeper
1995 ★ Steve James/Hoop Dreams
1996 ★ Terry Zwigoff/Crumb
2003 ★ Andrew Jarecki/Capturing the Friedmans
Errol Morris/The Fog of War: Eleven Lessons from the Life of Robert S. McNamara
2004 Born Into Brothels: Calcutta's Red Light Kids
The Story of the Weeping Camel
2005 ★ Werner Herzog/Grizzly Man

GOLDEN GLOBE AWARDS

ACTOR—DRAMA

1944 ★ Alexander Knox/Wilson
1945 ★ Ray Milland/The Lost Weekend
1946 ★ Gregory Peck/The Yearling
1947 ★ Ronald Colman/A Double Life
1948 ★ Laurence Olivier/Hamlet
1949 ★ Broderick Crawford/All the King's Men
1950 ★ Jose Ferrer/Cyrano de Bergerac
1951 ★ Gary Cooper/High Noon
1953 ★ Marlon Brando/On the Waterfront
1955 ★ Ernest Borgnine/Marty
1956 ★ Kirk Douglas/Lust for Life
1957 ★ Alec Guinness/The Bridge on the River Kwai
1958 ★ David Niven/Separate Tables
1959 ★ Anthony (Tony) Franciosa/Career
1960 ★ Burt Lancaster/Elmer Gantry
1961 ★ Maximilian Schell/Judgment at Nuremberg
1962 ★ Gregory Peck/To Kill a Mockingbird
1963 ★ Sidney Poitier/Lilies of the Field
1964 ★ Peter O'Toole/Becket
1965 ★ Omar Sharif/Doctor Zhivago
1966 ★ Paul Scofield/A Man for All Seasons
1967 ★ Rod Steiger/In the Heat of the Night
1968 ★ Peter O'Toole/The Lion in Winter
1970 ★ John Wayne/True Grit
1971 ★ Gene Hackman/The French Connection
1972 ★ Marlon Brando/The Godfather
1973 ★ Al Pacino/Serpico
1974 ★ Jack Nicholson/Chinatown
1975 ★ Jack Nicholson/One Flew Over the Cuckoo's Nest
1976 ★ Peter Finch/Network
1977 ★ Richard Burton/Equus
1978 ★ Jon Voight/Coming Home
1979 ★ Dustin Hoffman/Kramer vs. Kramer
1980 ★ Robert De Niro/Raging Bull
1981 ★ ...

Golden Globe Awards

1982
★ Henry Fonda/On Golden Pond
1983
★ Robert Duvall/Tender Mercies
1984
★ Ben Kingsley/Gandhi
1985
★ Tom Courtenay/The Dresser
1986
★ F. Murray Abraham/Amadeus
1987
★ Jon Voight/Runaway Train
1988
★ Bob Hoskins/Mona Lisa
1989
★ Michael Douglas/Wall Street
1990
★ Dustin Hoffman/Rain Man
1991
★ Tom Cruise/Born on the Fourth of July
1992
★ Jeremy Irons/Reversal of Fortune
1993
★ Nick Nolte/The Prince of Tides
1994
★ Al Pacino/Scent of a Woman
1995
★ Tom Hanks/Philadelphia
1996
★ Tom Hanks/Forrest Gump
1997
★ Nicolas Cage/Leaving Las Vegas
1998
★ Anthony Hopkins/Nixon
Ian McKellen/Richard III
Sean Penn/Dead Man Walking
1997
★ Geoffrey Rush/Shine
Ralph Fiennes/The English Patient
Mel Gibson/Ransom
Woody Harrelson/The People vs. Larry Flynt
Liam Neeson/Michael Collins
1998
★ Peter Fonda/Ulee's Gold
Matt Damon/Good Will Hunting
Daniel Day-Lewis/The Boxer
Leonardo DiCaprio/Titanic
Djimon Hounsou/Amistad
Ian McKellen/Gods and Monsters
1999
★ Jim Carrey/The Truman Show
Stephen Fry/Wilde
Tom Hanks/Saving Private Ryan
Nick Nolte/Affliction
2000
★ Denzel Washington/The Hurricane
Russell Crowe/The Insider

Matt Damon/The Talented Mr. Ripley
Richard Farnsworth/The Straight Story
Kevin Spacey/American Beauty
2002
★ Russell Crowe/A Beautiful Mind
Will Smith/Ali
Kevin Spacey/The Shipping News
Billy Bob Thornton/The Man Who Wasn't There
Denzel Washington/Training Day
2003
★ Jack Nicholson/About Schmidt
Adrien Brody/The Pianist
Michael Caine/The Quiet American
Daniel Day-Lewis/Gangs of New York
Leonardo DiCaprio/Catch Me If You Can
2004
★ Sean Penn/Mystic River
Russell Crowe/Master and Commander: The Far Side of the World
Tom Cruise/The Last Samurai
Ben Kingsley/House of Sand and Fog
Jude Law/Cold Mountain
2005
★ Leonardo DiCaprio/The Aviator
Javier Bardem/The Sea Inside
Don Cheadle/Hotel Rwanda
Liam Neeson/Kinsey
2006
★ Philip Seymour Hoffman/Capote
Russell Crowe/Cinderella Man
Terrence Howard/Hustle & Flow
Heath Ledger/Brokeback Mountain
David Strathairn/Good Night, and Good Luck
2007
★ Forest Whitaker/The Last King of Scotland
Leonardo DiCaprio/Blood Diamond
Leonardo DiCaprio/The Departed
Peter O'Toole/Venus
Will Smith/The Pursuit of Happyness
2008
★ Daniel Day-Lewis/There Will Be Blood
George Clooney/Michael Clayton
James McAvoy/Atonement
Viggo Mortensen/Eastern Promises
Denzel Washington/American Gangster

ACTOR—MUSICAL/COMEDY

1951
★ Fred Astaire/Three Little Words
1953
★ Donald O'Connor/Singin' in the Rain
1954
★ David Niven/The Moon Is Blue
1955
★ James Mason/A Star Is Born
1956
★ Tom Ewell/The Seven Year Itch

1957
★ Cantinflas/Around the World in 80 Days
1958
★ Frank Sinatra/Pal Joey
1960
★ Jack Lemmon/Some Like It Hot
1961
★ Jack Lemmon/The Apartment
1962
★ Glenn Ford/Pocketful of Miracles
1963
★ Marcello Mastroianni/Divorce—Italian Style
1965
★ Rex Harrison/My Fair Lady
1966
★ Lee Marvin/Cat Ballou
1967
★ Alan Arkin/The Russians Are Coming, the Russians Are Coming
1968
★ Richard Harris/Camelot
1969
★ Ron Moody/Oliver!
1970
★ Peter O'Toole/Goodbye, Mr. Chips
1971
★ Albert Finney/Scrooge
1972
★ Chaim Topol/Fiddler on the Roof
1974
★ George Segal/A Touch of Class
1975
★ Art Carney/Harry and Tonto
1976
★ Walter Matthau/The Sunshine Boys
1977
★ Kris Kristofferson/A Star Is Born
1978
★ Richard Dreyfuss/The Goodbye Girl
1979
★ Warren Beatty/Heaven Can Wait
1980
★ Peter Sellers/Being There
1981
★ Ray Sharkey/Idolmaker
1982
★ Dudley Moore/Arthur
1983
★ Dustin Hoffman/Tootsie
1984
★ Michael Caine/Educating Rita
1985
★ Dudley Moore/Micki & Maude
1986
★ Jack Nicholson/Prizzi's Honor
1987
★ Paul Hogan/Crocodile Dundee
1988
★ Robin Williams/Good Morning, Vietnam
1989
★ Tom Hanks/Big

1990
★ Morgan Freeman/Driving Miss Daisy
1991
★ Gerard Depardieu/Green Card
1992
★ Robin Williams/The Fisher King
1993
★ Tim Robbins/The Player
1994
★ Robin Williams/Mrs. Doubtfire
Johnny Depp/Benny & Joon
Tom Hanks/Sleepless in Seattle
Kevin Kline/Dave
Colm Meaney/The Snapper
1995
★ Hugh Grant/Four Weddings and a Funeral
Jim Carrey/The Mask
Johnny Depp/Ed Wood
Arnold Schwarzenegger/Junior
Terence Stamp/The Adventures of Priscilla, Queen of the Desert
1996
★ John Travolta/Get Shorty
Michael Douglas/The American President
Harrison Ford/Sabrina
Steve Martin/Father of the Bride Part 2
Patrick Swayze/To Wong Foo, Thanks for Everything, Julie Newmar
1997
★ Tom Cruise/Jerry Maguire
Antonio Banderas/Evita
Kevin Costner/Tin Cup
Tom Cruise/Jerry Maguire
Nathan Lane/The Birdcage
Eddie Murphy/The Nutty Professor
1998
★ Jack Nicholson/As Good As It Gets
Antonio Banderas/The Mask of Zorro
Jim Carrey/Liar Liar
Dustin Hoffman/Wag the Dog
Samuel L. Jackson/Jackie Brown
Kevin Kline/In and Out
1999
★ Michael Caine/Little Voice
John Travolta/Primary Colors
Robin Williams/Patch Adams
2000
★ Jim Carrey/Man on the Moon
Robert De Niro/Analyze This
Rupert Everett/An Ideal Husband
Hugh Jackman/Kate & Leopold
Ewan McGregor/Moulin Rouge
2001
★ George Clooney/O Brother Where Art Thou?
2002
★ Moulin Rouge
Gene Hackman/The Royal Tenenbaums
Hugh Jackman/Kate & Leopold
John Cameron Mitchell/Hedwig and the Angry Inch
Billy Bob Thornton/Bandits
2003
★ Richard Gere/Chicago

Nicolas Cage/Adaptation
Kieran Culkin/Igby Goes Down
Hugh Grant/About a Boy
Adam Sandler/Punch-Drunk Love
2004
★ Bill Murray/Lost in Translation
Jack Black/School of Rock
Johnny Depp/Pirates of the Caribbean: The Curse of the Black Pearl
Jack Nicholson/Something's Gotta Give
Billy Bob Thornton/Bad Santa
2005
★ Jamie Foxx/Ray
Jim Carrey/Eternal Sunshine of the Spotless Mind
Paul Giamatti/Sideways
Kevin Kline/De-Lovely
Kevin Spacey/Beyond the Sea
2006
★ Joaquin Rafael (Leaf) Phoenix/Walk the Line
Jeff Daniels/The Squid and the Whale
Johnny Depp/Charlie and the Chocolate Factory
Nathan Lane/The Producers
2007
★ Sacha Baron Cohen/Borat: Cultural Learnings of America for Make Benefit Glorious Nation of Kazakhstan
Johnny Depp/Pirates of the Caribbean: Dead Man's Chest
Aaron Eckhart/Thank You for Smoking
Chiwetel Ejiofor/Kinky Boots
Will Ferrell/Stranger Than Fiction
2008
★ Johnny Depp/Sweeney Todd: The Demon Barber of Fleet Street
Ryan Gosling/Lars and the Real Girl
Tom Hanks/Charlie Wilson's War
Philip Seymour Hoffman/The Savages
John C. Reilly/Walk Hard: The Dewey Cox Story

ACTOR—SUPPORTING

1945
★ Barry Fitzgerald/Going My Way
1947
★ Clifton Webb/The Razor's Edge
1948
★ Edmund Gwenn/Miracle on 34th Street
1949
★ Walter Huston/Treasure of the Sierra Madre
1950
★ James Whitmore/Battleground
1952
★ Peter Ustinov/Quo Vadis
1954
★ Frank Sinatra/From Here to Eternity
1955
★ Edmond O'Brien/The Barefoot Contessa
1957
★ Earl Holliman/The Rainmaker
1958
★ Red Buttons/Sayonara

1959
★ Burl Ives/The Big Country
1960
★ Stephen Boyd/Ben-Hur
1961
★ Sal Mineo/Exodus
1962
★ George Chakiris/West Side Story
1963
★ Omar Sharif/Lawrence of Arabia
1964
★ John Huston/The Cardinal
1965
★ Edmond O'Brien/Seven Days in May
1966
★ Oskar Werner/The Spy Who Came in from the Cold
1967
★ Richard Attenborough/The Sand Pebbles
1968
★ David Attenborough/Doctor Dolittle
1970
★ Gig Young/They Shoot Horses, Don't They?
1971
★ John Mills/Ryan's Daughter
1972
★ Ben Johnson/The Last Picture Show
1973
★ Joel Grey/Cabaret
1974
★ John Houseman/The Paper Chase
1975
★ Fred Astaire/The Towering Inferno
1976
★ Richard Benjamin/The Sunshine Boys
1977
★ Laurence Olivier/Marathon Man
1978
★ Peter Firth/Equus
1979
★ John Hurt/Midnight Express
1980
★ Melvyn Douglas/Being There
1981
★ Robert Duvall/Apocalypse Now
1982
★ Timothy Hutton/Ordinary People
1983
★ John Gielgud/Arthur
1984
★ Louis Gossett, Jr./An Officer and a Gentleman
1985
★ Jack Nicholson/Terms of Endearment
1986
★ Haing S. Ngor/The Killing Fields
1987
★ Klaus Maria Brandauer/Out of Africa
1988
★ Sean Connery/The Untouchables

★ = winner

- 1989 ★ Martin Landau/Tucker: The Man and His Dream
- 1990 ★ Denzel Washington/Glory
- Joe Pesci/Goodfellas
- 1991 ★ Bruce Davison/Longtime Companion
- 1992 ★ Jack Palance/City Slickers
- 1993 ★ Gene Hackman/Unforgiven
- 1994 ★ Tommy Lee Jones/The Fugitive
- Leonardo DiCaprio/What's Eating Gilbert Grape
- Ralph Fiennes/Schindler's List
- John Malkovich/In the Line of Fire
- Sean Penn/Carlito's Way
- 1995 ★ Martin Landau/Ed Wood
- Kevin Bacon/The River Wild
- Samuel L. Jackson/Pulp Fiction
- Gary Sinise/Forrest Gump
- John Turturro/Quiz Show
- 1996 ★ Brad Pitt/12 Monkeys
- Ed Harris/Apollo 13
- John Leguizamo/To Wong Foo, Thanks for Everything, Julie Newmar
- 1997 ★ Edward Norton/Primal Fear
- Cuba Gooding, Jr./Jerry Maguire
- 1998 ★ Burt Reynolds/Boogie Nights
- Rupert Everett/My Best Friend's Wedding
- Anthony Hopkins/Amistad
- Burt Reynolds/Boogie Nights
- Jon Voight/John Grisham's The Rainmaker
- Robin Williams/Good Will Hunting
- 1999 ★ Ed Harris/The Truman Show
- Robert Duvall/A Civil Action
- Bill Murray/Rushmore
- Geoffrey Rush/Shakespeare in Love
- Donald Sutherland/Without Limits
- Billy Bob Thornton/A Simple Plan
- 2000 ★ Tom Cruise/Magnolia
- Michael Caine/The Cider House Rules
- Michael Clarke Duncan/The Green Mile
- Jude Law/The Talented Mr. Ripley
- Haley Joel Osment/The Sixth Sense
- 2001 ★ Benicio Del Toro/Traffic
- 2002 ★ Jim Broadbent/Iris
- Steve Buscemi/Ghost World
- Hayden Christensen/Life as a House

- 2003 ★ Chris Cooper/Adaptation
- Ed Harris/The Hours
- Paul Newman/Road to Perdition
- Dennis Quaid/Far from Heaven
- John C. Reilly/Chicago
- 2004 ★ Tim Robbins/Mystic River
- Alec Baldwin/The Cooler
- Albert Finney/Big Fish
- William H. Macy/Seabiscuit
- Peter Sarsgaard/Shattered Glass
- Ken (saku) Watanabe/The Last Samurai
- 2005 ★ Clive Owen/Closer
- David Carradine/Kill Bill Vol. 2
- Thomas Haden Church/Sideways
- Jamie Foxx/Collateral
- Morgan Freeman/Million Dollar Baby
- 2006 ★ George Clooney/Syriana
- Matt Dillon/Crash
- Bob Hoskins/Mrs. Henderson Presents
- 2007 ★ Eddie Murphy/Dreamgirls
- Ben Affleck/Hollywoodland
- Jack Nicholson/The Departed
- Brad Pitt/Babel
- Mark Wahlberg/The Departed
- 2008 ★ Javier Bardem/No Country for Old Men
- Casey Affleck/The Assassination of Jesse James by the Coward Robert Ford
- Philip Seymour Hoffman/Charlie Wilson's War
- John Travolta/Hairspray
- Tom Wilkinson/Michael Clayton

ACTRESS—DRAMA

- 1944 ★ Jennifer Jones/The Song of Bernadette
- 1945 ★ Ingrid Bergman/Gaslight
- 1946 ★ Ingrid Bergman/The Bells of St. Mary's
- 1947 ★ Rosalind Russell/Sister Kenny
- 1949 ★ Jane Wyman/Johnny Belinda
- 1950 ★ Olivia de Havilland/The Heiress
- 1951 ★ Gloria Swanson/Sunset Boulevard
- 1953 ★ Shirley Booth/Come Back, Little Sheba
- 1954 ★ Audrey Hepburn/Roman Holiday
- 1955 ★ Grace Kelly/Country Girl
- 1956 ★ Anna Magnani/The Rose Tattoo
- 1957 ★ Ingrid Bergman/Anastasia

- 1956 ★ Joanne Woodward/The Three Faces of Eve
- 1959 ★ Susan Hayward/I Want to Live!
- 1960 ★ Elizabeth Taylor/Suddenly, Last Summer
- 1961 ★ Greer Garson/Sunrise at Campobello
- 1962 ★ Geraldine Page/Summer and Smoke
- 1963 ★ Geraldine Page/Sweet Bird of Youth
- 1966 ★ Samantha Eggar/The Collector
- 1967 ★ Anouk Aimée/A Man and a Woman
- 1969 ★ Joanne Woodward/Rachel, Rachel
- 1970 ★ Geneviève Bujold/Anne of the Thousand Days
- 1971 ★ Ali MacGraw/Love Story
- 1972 ★ Jane Fonda/Klute
- 1974 ★ Marsha Mason/Cinderella Liberty
- 1975 ★ Gena Rowlands/A Woman under the Influence
- 1976 ★ Louise Fletcher/One Flew Over the Cuckoo's Nest
- 1977 ★ Faye Dunaway/Network
- 1978 ★ Jane Fonda/Julia
- 1979 ★ Jane Fonda/Coming Home
- 1980 ★ Sally Field/Norma Rae
- 1981 ★ Mary Tyler Moore/Ordinary People
- 1982 ★ Meryl Streep/The French Lieutenant's Woman
- 1983 ★ Meryl Streep/Sophie's Choice
- 1984 ★ Shirley MacLaine/Terms of Endearment
- 1985 ★ Sally Field/Places in the Heart
- 1986 ★ Whoopi Goldberg/The Color Purple
- 2000 ★ Hilary Swank/Boys Don't Cry
- 2001 ★ Julia Roberts/Erin Brockovich
- 2002 ★ Sissy Spacek/In the Bedroom
- 2003 ★ Nicole Kidman/The Hours
- Salma Hayek/Frida
- Diane Lane/Unfaithful
- Julianne Moore/Far from Heaven
- Meryl Streep/The Hours

- 1991 ★ Kathy Bates/Misery
- 1992 ★ Jodie Foster/The Silence of the Lambs
- 1993 ★ Emma Thompson/Howard's End
- 1994 ★ Holly Hunter/The Piano
- Juliette Binoche/Trois Couleurs: Bleu
- Michelle Pfeiffer/The Age of Innocence
- Emma Thompson/The Remains of the Day
- Debra Winger/A Dangerous Woman
- 1995 ★ Jessica Lange/Blue Sky
- Jodie Foster/Nell
- Jennifer Jason Leigh/Mrs. Parker and the Vicious Circle
- Miranda Richardson/Tom & Viv
- Meryl Streep/The River Wild
- 1996 ★ Sharon Stone/Casino
- Susan Sarandon/Dead Man Walking
- Elisabeth Shue/Leaving Las Vegas
- Meryl Streep/The Bridges of Madison County
- Emma Thompson/Sense and Sensibility
- 1997 ★ Brenda Blethyn/Secrets and Lies
- Courtney Love/The People vs. Larry Flynt
- Kristin Scott Thomas/The English Patient
- Meryl Streep/Marvin's Room
- Emily Watson/Breaking the Waves
- 1998 ★ Judi Dench/Mrs. Brown
- Helena Bonham-Carter/The Wings of the Dove
- Jodie Foster/Contact
- Jessica Lange/A Thousand Acres
- Emily Watson/Hilary and Jackie
- 1999 ★ Cate Blanchett/Elizabeth
- Fernanda Montenegro/Central Station
- Susan Sarandon/Stepmom
- Meryl Streep/One True Thing

- 2004 ★ Charlize Theron/Monster
- Cate Blanchett/Veronica Guerin
- Scarlett Johansson/Girl with a Pearl Earring
- Nicole Kidman/Cold Mountain
- Uma Thurman/Kill Bill Vol. 1
- 2005 ★ Hilary Swank/Million Dollar Baby
- Imelda Staunton/Vera Drake
- Uma Thurman/Kill Bill Vol. 2
- 2006 ★ Felicity Huffman/Transamerica
- Maria Bello/A History of Violence
- Gwyneth Paltrow/Proof
- Charlize Theron/North Country
- Zhang Ziyi/Memoirs of a Geisha
- 2007 ★ Helen Mirren/The Queen
- Penélope Cruz/Volver
- Judi Dench/Notes on a Scandal
- Maggie Gyllenhaal/Sherrybaby
- Kate Winslet/Little Children
- 2008 ★ Julie Christie/Away From Her
- Cate Blanchett/Elizabeth: The Golden Age
- Jodie Foster/The Brave One
- Angelina Jolie/A Mighty Heart
- Keira Knightley/Atonement

ACTRESS—MUSICAL/COMEDY

- 1951 ★ Judy Holliday/Born Yesterday
- 1955 ★ Judy Garland/A Star Is Born
- 1956 ★ Jean Simmons/Guys and Dolls
- 1957 ★ Deborah Kerr/The King and I
- 1958 ★ Kay Kendall/Les Girls
- 1959 ★ Rosalind Russell/Auntie Mame
- 1960 ★ Marilyn Monroe/Some Like It Hot
- 1961 ★ Shirley MacLaine/The Apartment
- 1963 ★ Shirley MacLaine/Irma La Douce
- 1964 ★ Shirley MacLaine/...
- 1965 ★ Julie Andrews/Mary Poppins
- 1966 ★ Julie Andrews/The Sound of Music
- 1957 ★ Lynn Redgrave/Georgy Girl

- 1968 ★ Anne Bancroft/The Graduate
- 1969 ★ Barbra Streisand/Funny Girl
- 1971 ★ Carrie Snodgress/Diary of a Mad Housewife
- 1972 ★ Twiggy/The Boy Friend
- 1973 ★ Liza Minnelli/Cabaret
- 1974 ★ Glenda Jackson/A Touch of Class
- 1975 ★ Raquel Welch/The Three Musketeers
- 1976 ★ Ann-Margret/Tommy
- 1977 ★ Barbra Streisand/A Star Is Born
- 1978 ★ Diane Keaton/Annie Hall
- 1979 ★ Ellen Burstyn/Same Time, Next Year
- 1980 ★ Bette Midler/The Rose
- 1981 ★ Sissy Spacek/Coal Miner's Daughter
- 1982 ★ Bernadette Peters/Pennies from Heaven
- 1983 ★ Julie Andrews/Victor/Victoria
- 1984 ★ Julie Walters/Educating Rita
- 1985 ★ Kathleen Turner/Romancing the Stone
- 1986 ★ Kathleen Turner/Prizzi's Honor
- 1987 ★ Sissy Spacek/Crimes of the Heart
- 1988 ★ Cher/Moonstruck
- 1989 ★ Melanie Griffith/Working Girl
- 1990 ★ Jessica Tandy/Driving Miss Daisy
- 1991 ★ Julia Roberts/Pretty Woman
- 1992 ★ Bette Midler/For the Boys
- 1993 ★ Miranda Richardson/Enchanted April
- 1994 ★ Angela Bassett/What's Love Got to Do with It?
- Stockard Channing/Six Degrees of Separation
- Anjelica Huston/Addams Family Values
- Diane Keaton/Manhattan Murder Mystery
- Meg Ryan/Sleepless in Seattle

★ = winner

Golden Globe Awards

★ = winner

ACTRESS (continued)

1995
★ Jamie Lee Curtis/True Lies
Geena Davis/Speechless
Andie MacDowell/Four Weddings and a Funeral
Shirley MacLaine/Guarding Tess
Emma Thompson/Junior

1996
★ Nicole Kidman/To Die For
Annette Bening/The American President
Sandra Bullock/While You Were Sleeping
Toni Collette/Muriel's Wedding
Vanessa Redgrave/A Month by the Lake

1997
★ Madonna/Evita
Glenn Close/101 Dalmatians
Frances McDormand/Fargo
Debbie Reynolds/Mother
Barbra Streisand/The Mirror Has Two Faces

1998
★ Helen Hunt/As Good As It Gets
Joey Lauren Adams/Chasing Amy
Pam Grier/Jackie Brown
Jennifer Lopez/Selena
Julia Roberts/My Best Friend's Wedding

1999
★ Gwyneth Paltrow/Shakespeare in Love
Cameron Diaz/There's Something about Mary
Jane Horrocks/Little Voice
Christina Ricci/The Opposite of Sex
Meg Ryan/You've Got Mail

2000
★ Janet McTeer/Tumbleweeds
Julianne Moore/An Ideal Husband
Julia Roberts/Notting Hill
Sharon Stone/The Muse
Reese Witherspoon/Election

2001
★ Renee Zellweger/Nurse Betty

2002
★ Nicole Kidman/Moulin Rouge
Thora Birch/Ghost World
Cate Blanchett/Bandits
Reese Witherspoon/Legally Blonde
Renee Zellweger/Bridget Jones's Diary

2003
★ Renee Zellweger/Chicago
Maggie Gyllenhaal/Secretary
Goldie Hawn/The Banger Sisters
Nia Vardalos/My Big Fat Greek Wedding
Catherine Zeta-Jones/Chicago

2004
★ Diane Keaton/Something's Gotta Give
Jamie Lee Curtis/Freaky Friday
Scarlett Johansson/Lost in Translation
Diane Lane/Under the Tuscan Sun
Helen Mirren/Calendar Girls

2005
★ Annette Bening/Being Julia
Ashley Judd/De-Lovely
Emmy Rossum/The Phantom of the Opera
Kate Winslet/Eternal Sunshine of the Spotless Mind
Renee Zellweger/Bridget Jones: The Edge of Reason

2006
★ Reese Witherspoon/Walk the Line
Judi Dench/Mrs. Henderson Presents
Keira Knightley/Pride and Prejudice
Laura Linney/The Squid and the Whale
Sarah Jessica Parker/The Family Stone

2007
★ Meryl Streep/The Devil Wears Prada
Annette Bening/Running with Scissors
Toni Collette/Little Miss Sunshine
Beyonce Knowles/Dreamgirls
Renee Zellweger/Miss Potter

2008
★ Marion Cotillard/La Vie en Rose
Amy Adams/Enchanted
Nicole Blonsky/Hairspray
Helena Bonham-Carter/Sweeney Todd: The Demon Barber of Fleet Street
Ellen Page/Juno

ACTRESS—SUPPORTING

1945
★ Agnes Moorehead/Mrs. Parkington

1946
★ Angela Lansbury/Picture of Dorian Gray

1947
★ Anne Baxter/The Razor's Edge

1948
★ Celeste Holm/Gentleman's Agreement

1949
★ Ellen Corby/I Remember Mama

1950
★ Mercedes McCambridge/All the King's Men

1951
★ Josephine Hull/Harvey

1952
★ Kim Hunter/A Streetcar Named Desire

1953
★ Katy Jurado/High Noon

1954
★ Grace Kelly/Mogambo

1955
★ Jan Sterling/The High and the Mighty

1956
★ Marisa Pavan/The Rose Tattoo

1957
★ Eileen Heckart/The Bad Seed

1958
★ Elsa Lanchester/Witness for the Prosecution

1959
★ Hermione Gingold/Gigi

1960
★ Susan Kohner/Imitation of Life

1961
★ Janet Leigh/Psycho

1962
★ Rita Moreno/West Side Story

1963
★ Angela Lansbury/The Manchurian Candidate

1964
★ Margaret Rutherford/The V.I.P.'s

1965
★ Agnes Moorehead/Hush, Hush, Sweet Charlotte

1966
★ Ruth Gordon/Inside Daisy Clover

1967
★ Jocelyn Lagarde/Hawaii

1968
★ Carol Channing/Thoroughly Modern Millie

1969
★ Ruth Gordon/Rosemary's Baby

1970
★ Goldie Hawn/Cactus Flower

1971
★ Karen Black/Five Easy Pieces

1972
★ Maureen Stapleton/Airport

1973
★ Shelley Winters/The Poseidon Adventure

1974
★ Linda Blair/The Exorcist

1975
★ Karen Black/The Great Gatsby

1976
★ Brenda Vaccaro/Once Is Not Enough

1977
★ Katharine Ross/Voyage of the Damned

1978
★ Vanessa Redgrave/Julia

1979
★ Dyan Cannon/Heaven Can Wait

1980
★ Meryl Streep/Kramer vs. Kramer

1981
★ Mary Steenburgen/Melvin and Howard

1982
★ Joan Hackett/Only When I Laugh

1983
★ Jessica Lange/Tootsie

1984
★ Cher/Silkwood

1985
★ Peggy Ashcroft/A Passage to India

1986
★ Meg Tilly/Agnes of God

1987
★ Maggie Smith/A Room with a View

1988
★ Olympia Dukakis/Moonstruck

1989
★ Sigourney Weaver/Working Girl

1990
★ Julia Roberts/Steel Magnolias
Lorraine Bracco/Goodfellas

1991
★ Whoopi Goldberg/Ghost
Nicole Kidman/Bathgate

1992
★ Mercedes Ruehl/The Fisher King

1993
★ Joan Plowright/Enchanted April

1994
★ Winona Ryder/The Age of Innocence
Penelope Ann Miller/Carlito's Way
Anna Paquin/The Piano
Rosie Perez/Fearless
Emma Thompson/In the Name of the Father

1995
★ Dianne Wiest/Bullets over Broadway
Kirsten Dunst/Interview with the Vampire
Sophia Loren/Ready to Wear
Uma Thurman/Pulp Fiction
Robin Wright Penn/Forrest Gump

1996
★ Mira Sorvino/Mighty Aphrodite
Anjelica Huston/The Crossing Guard
Kathleen Quinlan/Apollo 13
Kyra Sedgwick/Something to Talk About
Kate Winslet/Sense and Sensibility

1997
★ Lauren Bacall/The Mirror Has Two Faces
Joan Allen/The Crucible
Juliette Binoche/The English Patient
Barbara Hershey/Portrait of a Lady
Marianne Jean-Baptiste/Secrets and Lies
Marion Ross/The Evening Star

1998
★ Kim Basinger/L.A. Confidential
Joan Cusack/In and Out
Julianne Moore/Boogie Nights
Gloria Stuart/Titanic
Sigourney Weaver/The Ice Storm

1999
★ Lynn Redgrave/Gods and Monsters
Kathy Bates/Primary Colors
Brenda Blethyn/Little Voice
Judi Dench/Shakespeare in Love
Sharon Stone/The Mighty

2000
★ Angelina Jolie/Girl, Interrupted
Cameron Diaz/Being John Malkovich
Catherine Keener/Being John Malkovich
Samantha Morton/Sweet and Lowdown
Natalie Portman/Anywhere But Here
Chloe Sevigny/Boys Don't Cry

2001
★ Kate Hudson/Almost Famous

2002
★ Jennifer Connelly/A Beautiful Mind
Cameron Diaz/Vanilla Sky
Helen Mirren/Gosford Park
Maggie Smith/Gosford Park
Marisa Tomei/In the Bedroom
Kate Winslet/Iris

2003
★ Meryl Streep/Adaptation
Kathy Bates/About Schmidt
Cameron Diaz/Gangs of New York
Queen Latifah/Chicago
Susan Sarandon/Igby Goes Down

2004
★ Renee Zellweger/Cold Mountain
Maria Bello/The Cooler
Patricia Clarkson/Pieces of April
Hope Davis/American Splendor
Holly Hunter/Thirteen

2005
★ Natalie Portman/Closer
Cate Blanchett/The Aviator
Laura Linney/Kinsey
Virginia Madsen/Sideways
Meryl Streep/The Manchurian Candidate

2006
★ Rachel Weisz/The Constant Gardener
Scarlett Johansson/Match Point
Will Ferrell/The Producers
Shirley MacLaine/In Her Shoes
Frances McDormand/North Country
Michelle Williams/Brokeback Mountain

2007
★ Jennifer Hudson/Dreamgirls
Adriana Barraza/Babel
Cate Blanchett/Notes on a Scandal
Emily Blunt/The Devil Wears Prada
Rinko Kikuchi/Babel

2008
★ Cate Blanchett/I'm Not There
Julia Roberts/Charlie Wilson's War
Saoirse Ronan/Atonement
Amy Ryan/Gone Baby Gone
Tilda Swinton/Michael Clayton

BEST FILM—DRAMA

1944
★ The Song of Bernadette

1945
★ Going My Way

1946
★ The Lost Weekend

1947
★ The Best Years of Our Lives

1948
★ Gentleman's Agreement

1949
★ Johnny Belinda
Treasure of the Sierra Madre

1950
★ All the King's Men

1951
★ Sunset Boulevard

1952
★ A Place in the Sun

1953
★ The Greatest Show on Earth

1954
★ The Robe

1955
★ On the Waterfront

1956
★ East of Eden

1957
★ Around the World in 80 Days

1958
★ The Bridge on the River Kwai

1959
★ The Defiant Ones

1960
★ Ben-Hur

1961
★ Spartacus

1962
★ The Guns of Navarone

1963
★ Lawrence of Arabia

1964
★ The Cardinal

1965
★ Becket

1966
★ Doctor Zhivago

1967
★ A Man for All Seasons

1968
★ In the Heat of the Night

1969
★ The Lion in Winter

1970
★ Anne of the Thousand Days

1971
★ Love Story

1972
★ The French Connection

1973
★ The Godfather

1974
★ The Exorcist

1975
★ Chinatown

1976
★ One Flew Over the Cuckoo's Nest

1977
★ Rocky

1978
★ The Turning Point

1979
★ Midnight Express

1980
★ Kramer vs. Kramer

1981
★ Ordinary People

1982
★ On Golden Pond

1983
★ E.T.: The Extra-Terrestrial

1984
★ Terms of Endearment

1985
★ Amadeus

1986
★ Out of Africa

1987
★ Platoon

1988
★ The Last Emperor

1989
★ Rain Man

1990
★ Born on the Fourth of July
Goodfellas

1991
★ Dances with Wolves

1992
★ Bugsy

1993
★ Scent of a Woman

1994
★ Schindler's List

Golden Globe Awards

BEST FILM—DRAMA (continued)

1994
- The Age of Innocence
- In the Name of the Father
- The Piano
- The Remains of the Day

1995
- ★ Forrest Gump
- Legends of the Fall
- Nell
- Pulp Fiction
- Quiz Show

1996
- ★ Sense and Sensibility
- Apollo 13
- Braveheart
- The Bridges of Madison County
- Leaving Las Vegas

1997
- ★ The English Patient
- Breaking the Waves
- The People vs. Larry Flynt
- Secrets and Lies
- Shine

1998
- ★ Titanic
- Amistad
- The Boxer
- Good Will Hunting
- L.A. Confidential

1999
- ★ Saving Private Ryan
- Elizabeth
- Gods and Monsters
- The Horse Whisperer
- The Truman Show

2000
- ★ American Beauty
- The End of the Affair
- The Hurricane
- The Insider
- The Talented Mr. Ripley

2001
- ★ Gladiator

2002
- ★ A Beautiful Mind
- In the Bedroom
- Lord of the Rings: The Fellowship of the Ring
- The Man Who Wasn't There
- Mulholland Drive

2003
- ★ The Hours
- About Schmidt
- Gangs of New York
- Lord of the Rings: The Two Towers
- The Pianist

2004
- ★ Lord of the Rings: The Return of the King
- Cold Mountain
- Master and Commander: The Far Side of the World
- Mystic River
- Seabiscuit

2005
- ★ The Aviator
- Closer
- Finding Neverland
- Hotel Rwanda
- Kinsey

2006
- ★ Brokeback Mountain
- The Constant Gardener
- Good Night, and Good Luck
- A History of Violence
- Match Point

2007
- ★ Babel
- Bobby
- The Departed
- Little Children
- The Queen

2008
- ★ Atonement
- American Gangster
- Eastern Promises
- The Great Debaters
- Michael Clayton
- No Country for Old Men
- There Will Be Blood

BEST FILM—MUSICAL/COMEDY

1952 ★ An American in Paris
1955 ★ Carmen Jones
1956 ★ Guys and Dolls
1957 ★ The King and I
1958 ★ Les Girls
1959 ★ Gigi
1960 ★ Some Like It Hot
1961 ★ The Apartment / Song Without End
1962 ★ West Side Story
1963 ★ The Music Man / That Touch of Mink
1964 ★ Tom Jones
1965 ★ My Fair Lady
1966 ★ The Sound of Music
1967 ★ The Russians Are Coming, the Russians Are Coming
1968 ★ The Graduate
1969 ★ Oliver!
1971 ★ M*A*S*H
1972 ★ Fiddler on the Roof
1973 ★ Cabaret
1974 ★ American Graffiti
1975 ★ The Longest Yard
1976 ★ The Sunshine Boys
1977 ★ A Star Is Born
1978 ★ The Goodbye Girl
1979 ★ Heaven Can Wait
1980 ★ Breaking Away
1981 ★ Coal Miner's Daughter
1982 ★ Arthur
1983 ★ Tootsie
1984 ★ Yentl
1985 ★ Romancing the Stone
1988 ★ Hope and Glory
1989 ★ Working Girl
1990 ★ Driving Miss Daisy

1991 ★ Green Card
1992 ★ Beauty and the Beast
1993 ★ The Player
1994
- ★ Mrs. Doubtfire
- Dave
- Much Ado about Nothing
- Sleepless in Seattle
- Strictly Ballroom

1995
- ★ The Lion King
- The Adventures of Priscilla, Queen of the Desert
- Ed Wood
- Four Weddings and a Funeral
- Ready to Wear

1996
- ★ Babe
- The American President
- Get Shorty
- Sabrina
- Toy Story

1997
- ★ Evita
- The Birdcage
- Fargo
- Jerry Maguire

1998
- ★ As Good As It Gets
- The Full Monty
- Men in Black
- My Best Friend's Wedding
- Wag the Dog

1999
- ★ Shakespeare in Love
- Bulworth
- Patch Adams
- Still Crazy
- There's Something about Mary

2000
- ★ Toy Story 2
- Analyze This
- Being John Malkovich
- Man on the Moon
- Notting Hill

2001
- ★ Almost Famous

2002
- ★ Gosford Park
- Bridget Jones's Diary
- Legally Blonde
- Moulin Rouge
- Shrek

2003
- ★ Chicago
- About a Boy
- Adaptation
- My Big Fat Greek Wedding
- Nicholas Nickleby

2004
- ★ Lost in Translation
- Bend It Like Beckham
- Big Fish
- Finding Nemo
- Love Actually

2005
- ★ Sideways
- Eternal Sunshine of the Spotless Mind
- The Incredibles
- The Phantom of the Opera
- Ray

2006
- ★ Walk the Line
- Mrs. Henderson Presents
- Pride and Prejudice
- The Producers
- The Squid and the Whale

2007
- ★ Dreamgirls
- Borat: Cultural Learnings of America for Make Benefit Glorious Nation of Kazakhstan
- The Devil Wears Prada
- Little Miss Sunshine
- Thank You for Smoking

2008
- ★ Sweeney Todd: The Demon Barber of Fleet Street
- Across the Universe
- Charlie Wilson's War
- Hairspray
- Juno

DIRECTOR

1944 ★ Henry King/The Song of Bernadette
1945 ★ Leo McCarey/Going My Way
1946 ★ Billy Wilder/The Lost Weekend
1947 ★ Frank Capra/It's a Wonderful Life
1948 ★ Elia Kazan/Gentleman's Agreement
1949 ★ Robert Rossen/All the King's Men
1950 ★ John Huston/Treasure of the Sierra Madre
1951 ★ Billy Wilder/Sunset Boulevard
1953 ★ Cecil B. DeMille/The Greatest Show on Earth
1954 ★ Fred Zinnemann/From Here to Eternity
1955 ★ Elia Kazan/On the Waterfront
1956 ★ Joshua Logan/Picnic
1957 ★ Elia Kazan/Baby Doll
1958 ★ David Lean/The Bridge on the River Kwai
1959 ★ Vincente Minnelli/Gigi
1960 ★ William Wyler/Ben-Hur
1962 ★ Stanley Kramer/Judgment at Nuremberg
1963 ★ David Lean/Lawrence of Arabia
1965 ★ George Cukor/My Fair Lady
1966 ★ David Lean/Doctor Zhivago
1967 ★ Fred Zinnemann/A Man for All Seasons
1968 ★ Mike Nichols/The Graduate
1969 ★ Paul Newman/Rachel, Rachel
1970 ★ Charles Jarrott/Anne of the Thousand Days
1971 ★ Arthur Hiller/Love Story
1972 ★ William Friedkin/The French Connection
1973 ★ Francis Ford Coppola/The Godfather
1974 ★ William Friedkin/The Exorcist
1975 ★ Roman Polanski/Chinatown
1976 ★ Milos Forman/One Flew Over the Cuckoo's Nest
1977 ★ Sidney Lumet/Network
1978 ★ Herbert Ross/The Turning Point
1979 ★ Michael Cimino/The Deer Hunter
1980 ★ Francis Ford Coppola/Apocalypse Now
1981 ★ Robert Redford/Ordinary People
1982 ★ Warren Beatty/Reds
1983 ★ Richard Attenborough/Gandhi
1984 ★ Barbra Streisand/Yentl
1985 ★ Milos Forman/Amadeus
1986 ★ John Huston/Prizzi's Honor
1987 ★ Oliver Stone/Platoon
1988 ★ Bernardo Bertolucci/The Last Emperor
1989 ★ Clint Eastwood/Bird
1990 ★ Oliver Stone/Born on the Fourth of July
1991 ★ Kevin Costner/Dances with Wolves
1992 ★ Oliver Stone/JFK
1993 ★ Clint Eastwood/Unforgiven
1994 ★ Steven Spielberg/Schindler's List
1995 ★ Robert Zemeckis/Forrest Gump
1996
- ★ Mel Gibson/Braveheart
- Mike Figgis/Leaving Las Vegas
- Ron Howard/Apollo 13
- Ang Lee/Sense and Sensibility
- Rob Reiner/The American President
- Martin Scorsese/Casino

1997
- ★ Milos Forman/The People vs. Larry Flynt
- Joel Coen/Fargo
- Scott Hicks/Shine
- Anthony Minghella/The English Patient
- Alan Parker/Evita

1998
- ★ James Cameron/Titanic
- James L. Brooks/As Good As It Gets
- Curtis Hanson/L.A. Confidential
- Jim Sheridan/The Boxer
- Steven Spielberg/Amistad

1999
- ★ Steven Spielberg/Saving Private Ryan
- Shekhar Kapur/Elizabeth
- John Madden/Shakespeare in Love
- Neil Jordan/The End of the Affair
- Robert Redford/The Horse Whisperer
- Peter Weir/The Truman Show

2000
- ★ Sam Mendes/American Beauty
- Norman Jewison/The Hurricane
- Michael Mann/The Insider
- Anthony Minghella/The Talented Mr. Ripley

2001
- ★ Ang Lee/Crouching Tiger, Hidden Dragon

2002
- ★ Robert Altman/Gosford Park
- Ron Howard/A Beautiful Mind
- Peter Jackson/Lord of the Rings: The Fellowship of the Ring
- Baz Luhrmann/Moulin Rouge
- David Lynch/Mulholland Drive
- David Spielberg/A.I.: Artificial Intelligence

2003
- ★ Martin Scorsese/Gangs of New York
- Stephen Daldry/The Hours
- Peter Jackson/Lord of the Rings: The Two Towers
- Rob Marshall/Chicago
- Alexander Payne/About Schmidt

2004
- ★ Peter Jackson/Lord of the Rings: The Return of the King
- Sofia Coppola/Lost in Translation
- Clint Eastwood/Mystic River
- Peter Weir/Master and Commander: The Far Side of the World
- Anthony Minghella/Cold Mountain

2005
- ★ Clint Eastwood/Million Dollar Baby
- Marc Forster/Finding Neverland
- Mike Nichols/Closer
- Alexander Payne/Sideways
- Martin Scorsese/The Aviator

2006
- ★ Ang Lee/Brokeback Mountain
- Woody Allen/Match Point
- George Clooney/Good Night, and Good Luck
- Peter Jackson/King Kong

★ = winner

Golden Globe Awards

Fernando Meirelles/The Constant Gardener
Steven Spielberg/Munich
2007
★ Martin Scorsese/The Departed
Clint Eastwood/Flags of Our Fathers
Clint Eastwood/Letters from Iwo Jima
Stephen Frears/The Queen
Alejandro Gonzalez Inarritu/Babel
2008
★ Julian Schnabel/The Diving Bell and the Butterfly
Tim Burton/Sweeney Todd: The Demon Barber of Fleet Street
Ethan Coen/No Country for Old Men
Joel Coen/No Country for Old Men
Ridley Scott/American Gangster
Joe Wright/Atonement

SCORE

1948
★ Life with Father
1949
★ The Red Shoes
1950
★ The Inspector General
1951
★ Sunset Boulevard
1952
★ September Affair
1953
★ High Noon
1960
★ On the Beach
1961
★ The Alamo
1962
★ The Guns of Navarone
1963
★ To Kill a Mockingbird
1965
★ The Fall of the Roman Empire
1966
★ Doctor Zhivago
1967
★ Hawaii
1968
★ Camelot
1969
★ The Godfather
1970
★ Butch Cassidy and the Sundance Kid
1971
★ Love Story
1972
★ Shaft
1973
★ The Godfather
1974
★ Jonathan Livingston Seagull
1975
★ The Little Prince
1976
★ Jaws
1977
★ A Star Is Born
1978
★ Star Wars
1979
★ Midnight Express
1980
★ Apocalypse Now
1981
★ The Stunt Man
1983
★ E.T.: The Extra-Terrestrial
1984
★ Flashdance
1985
★ A Passage to India
1986
★ Out of Africa
1987
★ The Mission
1988
★ The Last Emperor
1989
★ Gorillas in the Mist
1990
★ The Little Mermaid
1991
★ The Sheltering Sky
1993
★ Aladdin
1994
★ Heaven and Earth
The Nightmare before Christmas
The Piano
Schindler's List
Trois Couleurs: Bleu
1995
★ The Lion King
Forrest Gump
Interview with the Vampire
Legends of the Fall
Nell
1996
★ A Walk in the Clouds
Braveheart
Don Juan DeMarco
Pocahontas
Sense and Sensibility
1997
★ The English Patient
The Hunchback of Notre Dame
Michael Collins
The Mirror Has Two Faces
Shine
1998
★ Titanic
Gattaca
Kundun
L.A. Confidential
Seven Years in Tibet
1999
★ The Truman Show
A Bug's Life
Mulan
Prince of Egypt
Saving Private Ryan
2000
★ The Legend of 1900
2001
★ Gladiator
2002
★ Moulin Rouge
A.I.: Artificial Intelligence
Ali
A Beautiful Mind
Lord of the Rings: The Fellowship of the Rings
Mulholland Drive
Pearl Harbor
The Shipping News
2003
★ Frida
25th Hour
Far from Heaven
The Hours
Rabbit-Proof Fence

ORIGINAL SCORE

1985
★ Once Upon a Time in America

2000
★ American Beauty
Angela's Ashes
Anna and the King
The End of the Affair
Eyes Wide Shut
The Insider
The Straight Story
The Talented Mr. Ripley
2004
★ Lord of the Rings: The Return of the King
Big Fish
Cold Mountain
Girl with a Pearl Earring
The Last Samurai
2005
★ The Aviator
Finding Neverland
Million Dollar Baby
Sideways
Spanglish
2006
★ Memoirs of a Geisha
Brokeback Mountain
The Chronicles of Narnia: The Lion, the Witch and the Wardrobe
King Kong
Syriana
2007
★ The Painted Veil
Babel
The Da Vinci Code
The Fountain
2008
★ Atonement
Eastern Promises
Grace Is Gone
Into the Wild
The Kite Runner

SONG

1961
★ "Town without Pity"/Town without Pity
1965
★ "Circus World"/Circus World
1968
★ "If Ever I Should Leave You"/Camelot
1969
★ "Life Is What You Make It"/Kotch
1970
★ "Whistling Away the Dark"/Darling Lili
1971
★ "The Windmills of Your Mind"/The Thomas Crown Affair
1972
★ "Ben"/Ben
1973
★ "The Way We Were"/The Way We Were
1974
★ "Jean"/The Prime of Miss Jean Brodie
1975
★ "I Feel Love"/Benji
1976
★ "I'm Easy"/Nashville
1977
★ "Evergreen"/A Star Is Born
1978
★ "You Light Up My Life"/You Light Up My Life
1980
★ "Fame"/Fame
1981
★ "Arthur's Theme"/Arthur
1982
★ "The Rose"/The Rose
1983
★ "Up Where We Belong"/An Officer and a Gentleman
1984
★ "Flashdance...What a Feeling"/Flashdance
1985
★ "I Just Called to Say I Love You"/The Woman in Red
1986
★ "Say You, Say Me"/White Nights
1987
★ "Take My Breath Away"/Top Gun
1988
★ "(I've Had) the Time of My Life"/Dirty Dancing
1989
★ "Let the River Run"/Working Girl
1990
★ "Under the Sea"/The Little Mermaid
1991
★ "Blaze of Glory"/Young Guns 2
1993
★ "A Whole New World"/Aladdin
1994
★ "Streets of Philadelphia"/Philadelphia
"(You Made Me the) Thief of Your Heart"/In the Name of the Father
"Again"/Poetic Justice
"Stay"/Faraway, So Close!
"The Day I Fall in Love"/Beethoven's 2nd
1995
★ "Can You Feel the Love Tonight?"/The Lion King
"Circle of Life"/The Lion King
1996
★ "Colors of the Wind"/Pocahontas
"Have You Ever Really Loved a Woman?"/Don Juan DeMarco
"Hold Me, Thrill Me, Kiss Me, Kill Me"/Batman Forever
"Moonlight"/Sabrina
"You Got a Friend in Me"/Toy Story
1997
★ "You Must Love Me"/Evita
"Because You Loved Me"/Up Close and Personal
"For the First Time"/One Fine Day
"I've Finally Found Someone"/The Mirror Has Two Faces
"That Thing You Do!"/That Thing You Do!
1998
★ "My Heart Will Go On"/Titanic
"Go the Distance"/Hercules
"Journey to the Past"/Anastasia
"Once Upon a December"/Anastasia
"Tomorrow Never Dies"/Tomorrow Never Dies
1999
★ "The Prayer"/Quest for Camelot
"Reflection"/Mulan
"The Flame Still Burns"/Still Crazy
"The Magic Sword"/Quest for Camelot
"The Mighty"/The Mighty
"Uninvited"/City of Angels
"When You Believe"/Prince of Egypt
2000
★ "You'll Be In My Heart"/Tarzan
"Beautiful Stranger"/Austin Powers 2: The Spy Who Shagged Me
"How Can I Not Love You"/Anna and the King
"Save Me"/Magnolia
"When She Loved Me"/Toy Story 2
2001
★ "Things Have Changed"/Wonder Boys
2002
★ "Until"/Kate & Leopold
"Come What May"/Moulin Rouge
"May It Be"/Lord of the Rings: The Fellowship of the Rings
"There You'll Be"/Pearl Harbor
"Vanilla Sky"/Vanilla Sky
2003
★ "The Hands That Built America"/Gangs of New York
"Die Another Day"/Die Another Day
"Father and Daughter"/The Wild Thornberrys Movie
"Here I Am"/Spirit: Stallion of the Cimarron
"Lose Yourself"/8 Mile
2004
★ "Into the West"/Lord of the Rings: The Return of the King
"Man of the Hour"/Big Fish
"The Heart of Every Girl"/Mona Lisa Smile
"Time Enough for Tears"/In America
"You Will Be My Ain True Love"/Cold Mountain
2005
★ "Old Habits Die Hard"/Alfie
"Accidently in Love"/Shrek 2
"Believe"/The Polar Express
"Learn to be Lonely"/The Phantom of the Opera
"Million Voices"/Hotel Rwanda
2006
★ "A Love That Will Never Grow Old"/Brokeback Mountain
"There's Nothing Like a Show on Broadway"/The Producers
"Travelin' Thru"/Transamerica
"Wunderkind"/The Chronicles of Narnia: The Lion, the Witch and the Wardrobe
2007
★ "The Song of the Heart"/Happy Feet
"A Father's Way"/The Pursuit of Happyness
"Listen"/Dreamgirls
"Never Gonna Break My Faith"/Bobby
2008
★ "Guaranteed"/Into the Wild
"Despedida"/Love in the Time of Cholera
"Grace is Gone"/Grace Is Gone
"That's How You Know"/Enchanted
"Walk Hard"/Walk Hard: The Dewey Cox Story

SCREENPLAY

1948
★ Miracle on 34th Street
1949
★ The Search
1950
★ Battleground
1951
★ All About Eve
1953
★ Five Fingers
1954
★ Lili
1955
★ Sabrina
1966
★ Doctor Zhivago
1967
★ A Man for All Seasons
1968
★ In the Heat of the Night
1969
★ Charly
1970
★ Anne of the Thousand Days
1971
★ Love Story
1972
★ The Hospital
1973
★ The Godfather
1974
★ The Exorcist
1975
★ Chinatown
1976
★ One Flew Over the Cuckoo's Nest
1977
★ Network
1978
★ The Goodbye Girl
1979
★ Midnight Express
1980
★ Kramer vs. Kramer
1981
★ The Ninth Configuration
1982
★ On Golden Pond
1983
★ Gandhi
1984
★ Terms of Endearment
1985
★ Amadeus
1986
★ The Purple Rose of Cairo
1987
★ The Mission
1988
★ The Last Emperor
1989
★ Running on Empty
1990
★ Born on the Fourth of July
Goodfellas
1991
★ Dances with Wolves
1993
★ Scent of a Woman
1994
★ Schindler's List

Philadelphia
The Piano
The Remains of the Day
Short Cuts

1995
★ Pulp Fiction
Forrest Gump
Four Weddings and a Funeral
Mr. Holland's Opus
Quiz Show
The Shawshank Redemption

1996
Sense and Sensibility
Braveheart
The American President
Dead Man Walking
Get Shorty

1997
★ The People vs. Larry Flynt
The English Patient
Fargo
Lone Star
Shine

1998
Good Will Hunting
As Good As It Gets
L.A. Confidential
Titanic
Wag the Dog

1999
★ Shakespeare in Love
Bulworth
Happiness
Saving Private Ryan
The Truman Show

2000
★ American Beauty
Being John Malkovich
The Cider House Rules
The Insider
The Sixth Sense

2001
★ Traffic

2002
★ A Beautiful Mind
Gosford Park
The Man Who Wasn't There
Memento
Mulholland Drive

2003
★ About Schmidt
Adaptation
Chicago
Far from Heaven
The Hours

2004
★ Lost in Translation
Cold Mountain
In America
Love Actually
Mystic River

2005
★ Sideways
The Aviator
Closer
Eternal Sunshine of the Spotless Mind
Finding Neverland

2006
★ Brokeback Mountain
Crash
Good Night, and Good Luck
Match Point
Munich

2007
★ The Queen
Babel
The Departed
Little Children
Notes on a Scandal

2008
★ No Country for Old Men
Atonement
Charlie Wilson's War
The Diving Bell and the Butterfly
Juno

FILM—FOREIGN LANGUAGE

1950 ★ The Bicycle Thief
1955 ★ Genevieve
1956 ★ Order
1957 ★ Richard III
★ War and Peace
1959 ★ A Night to Remember
1960 ★ Black Orpheus
Odd Obsession
Wild Strawberries
1961 ★ The Virgin Spring
1962 ★ Two Women
1963 ★ Divorce—Italian Style
1964 ★ Tom Jones
1965 ★ Sallah
1966 ★ Darling
1967 ★ A Man and a Woman
1969 ★ Romeo and Juliet
1970 ★ War and Peace
1971 ★ Z
★ Oh! What a Lovely War
1972 ★ The Sixth Sense
1973 ★ Sunday, Bloody Sunday
1974 ★ Young Winston
1976 ★ Scenes from a Marriage
1977 ★ Lies My Father Told Me
1978 ★ Face to Face
★ The Pedestrian
1984 ★ Fanny and Alexander
1985 ★ A Passage to India
1986 ★ The Official Story
1987 ★ The Assault
1988 ★ My Life As a Dog
1989 ★ Pelle the Conqueror

1990 ★ Cinema Paradiso
1991 ★ Cyrano de Bergerac
1992 ★ Europa, Europa
1993 ★ Indochine
1994 ★ Farewell My Concubine
Eat Drink Man Woman
Queen Margot
To Live
Trois Couleurs: Rouge
1995 ★ The Wedding Banquet
1996 ★ Les Misérables
Brother of Sleep
French Twist
Shanghai Triad
1997 ★ Kolya
The Eighth Day
Artemisia
Lea
The Thief
1998 ★ Ma Vie en Rose
The Best Man
Luna e L'Altra
Prisoner of the Mountains
Ridicule
1999 ★ Central Station
The Celebration
Hombres Armados
2000 ★ All About My Mother
The Red Violin
2001 ★ Crouching Tiger, Hidden Dragon
Amores Perros
The Widow of Saint-Pierre
2002 ★ Amelie
Monsoon Wedding
2003 ★ Talk to Her
City of God
The Crime of Father Amaro
2004 ★ The Barbarian Invasions
2005 ★ The Sea Inside
House of Flying Daggers
The Motorcycle Diaries
A Very Long Engagement
2006 ★ Paradise Now
2007 ★ Tsotsi
2008 ★ The Diving Bell and the Butterfly
The Kite Runner
Lust, Caution

ANIMATED FILM
2000 ★ Chicken Run
2007 ★ Cars
Happy Feet
Monster House
2008 ★ Ratatouille
Bee Movie
The Simpsons Movie

INDEPENDENT SPIRIT AWARDS

ACTOR
1986 ★ M. Emmet Walsh/Blood Simple
1987 ★ James Woods/Salvador
1988 ★ Dennis Quaid/The Big Easy
1989 ★ Edward James Olmos/Stand and Deliver
1990 ★ Matt Dillon/Drugstore Cowboy
1991 ★ Danny Glover/To Sleep with Anger
1992 ★ River Phoenix/My Own Private Idaho
1993 ★ Harvey Keitel/Bad Lieutenant
1994 ★ Jeff Bridges/American Heart
Vincent D'Onofrio/Household Saints
Mitchell Lichtenstein/The Wedding Banquet
Matthew Modine/Equinox
Tyrin Turner/Menace II Society
1995 ★ Samuel L. Jackson/Pulp Fiction
1996 ★ Sean Penn/Dead Man Walking
Nicolas Cage/Leaving Las Vegas
William H. Macy/Oleanna
Campbell Scott/Mrs. Parker and the Vicious Circle
Jon Seda/I Like It Like That
1997 ★ William H. Macy/Fargo
Chris Cooper/Lone Star
Christopher Penn/The Funeral
Tim Roth/Little Odessa
Jimmy Smits/My Family
Kevin Spacey/Swimming with Sharks
1998 ★ Robert Duvall/The Apostle
Peter Fonda/Ulee's Gold
Christopher Guest/Waiting for Guffman
Philip Baker Hall/Hard Eight
John Turturro/Box of Moonlight
1999 ★ Ian McKellen/Gods and Monsters
Dylan Baker/Happiness
Nick Nolte/Affliction
Sean Penn/Hurlyburly
Courtney B. Vance/Blind Faith
2000 ★ Richard Farnsworth/The Straight Story
John Cusack/Being John Malkovich
Terence Stamp/The Limey
David Strathairn/Limbo
Christopher Lloyd/Twenty Bucks
2001 ★ Javier Bardem/Before Night Falls
Adrien Brody/Restaurant
Billy Crudup/Jesus' Son

2002 ★ Tom Wilkinson/In the Bedroom
Brian Cox/L.I.E.
Jake Gyllenhaal/Donnie Darko
John Cameron Mitchell/Hedwig and the Angry Inch
2003 ★ Derek Luke/Antwone Fisher
Graham Greene/Skins
Jeremy Renner/Dahmer
Campbell Scott/Roger Dodger
2004 ★ Bill Murray/Lost in Translation
Peter Dinklage/The Station Agent
Paul Giamatti/American Splendor
Ben Kingsley/House of Sand and Fog
Lee Pace/Soldier's Girl
2005 ★ Paul Giamatti/Sideways
Kevin Bacon/The Woodsman
Jeff Daniels/The Squid and the Whale
Terrence Howard/Hustle & Flow
Liam Neeson/Kinsey
2006 ★ Philip Seymour Hoffman/Capote
Jeff Bridges/The Door in the Floor
Terrence Howard/Hustle & Flow
Heath Ledger/Brokeback Mountain
David Strathairn/Good Night, and Good Luck
2007 ★ Ryan Gosling/Half Nelson
Aaron Eckhart/Thank You for Smoking
Edward Norton/The Painted Veil
Forest Whitaker/American Gun
2008 ★ Philip Seymour Hoffman/The Savages
Don Cheadle/Talk to Me
Tony Leung Chiu-Wai/Lust, Caution

ACTOR—SUPPORTING
1988 ★ Morgan Freeman/Street Smart
1989 ★ Lou Diamond Phillips/Stand and Deliver
1990 ★ Max Perlich/Drugstore Cowboy
1991 ★ Bruce Davison/Longtime Companion
1992 ★ Steve Buscemi/Reservoir Dogs
1993 ★ Christopher Lloyd/Twenty Bucks
1994 ★ Chazz Palminteri/Bullets over Broadway

Independent Spirit Awards

Mark Ruffalo/You Can Count On Me
2002 ★ Tom Wilkinson/In the Bedroom
Giancarlo Esposito/Fresh
Larry Pine/Vanya on 42nd Street
Eric Stoltz/Pulp Fiction
Nicholas Turturro/Federal Hill

1996 ★ Benicio Del Toro/The Usual Suspects
David Morse/The Crossing Guard
James LeGros/Living in Oblivion
Max Perlich/Georgia
Harold Perrineau, Jr./Smoke
1997 ★ Benicio Del Toro/Basquiat
Kevin Corrigan/Walking and Talking
Gary Farmer/Dead Man
Richard Jenkins/Flirting with Disaster
Jason Lee/Chasing Amy
1998 ★ Bill Murray/Rushmore
Gary Farmer/Smoke Signals
Roy Scheider/The Myth of Fingerprints
1999 ★ Steve Zahn/Happy, Texas
Samuel L. Jackson/Hard Eight
2000 ★ Bill Murray/Rushmore
Philip Seymour Hoffman/Happiness
2001 ★ Steve Buscemi/Ghost World
Billy Kay/L.I.E.
Garrett Morris/Jackpot
John C. Reilly/The Anniversary Party
2002 ★ Steve Buscemi/Ghost World
Cole Hauser/Tigerland
Gary Oldman/The Contender
Giovanni Ribisi/The Gift
2003 ★ Dennis Quaid/Far from Heaven
Alan Arkin/Thirteen Conversations About One Thing
Ray Liotta/Narc
John C. Reilly/The Good Girl
2004 ★ Djimon Hounsou/In America
Judah Friedlander/American Splendor
Troy Garity/Soldier's Girl
Alessandro Nivola/Laurel Canyon
Peter Sarsgaard/Shattered Glass
2005 ★ Thomas Haden Church/Sideways
Jonathan Gries/Napoleon Dynamite
Peter Sarsgaard/Kinsey
2006 ★ Matt Dillon/Crash
Jesse Eisenberg/The Squid and the Whale

1991 ★ Bruce Davison/Longtime Companion
Max Perlich/Drugstore Cowboy
1992 ★ David Strathairn/City of Hope
1993 ★ David Chung/Combination Platter
Tate Donovan/Inside Monkey Zetterland
Todd Field/Ruby in Paradise
Edward Furlong/American Heart
1994 ★ Steve Buscemi/Reservoir Dogs
1995 ★ Chazz Palminteri/Bullets over Broadway

★ = winner

2007
★ Alan Arkin/Little Miss Sunshine
Daniel Craig/Infamous
Paul Franklin Dano/Little Miss Sunshine
Channing Tatum/A Guide to Recognizing Your Saints

2008
★ Chiwetel Ejiofor/Talk to Me
Marcus Carl Franklin/I'm Not There
Kene Holliday/Great World of Sound
Irfan Khan/The Namesake
Steve Zahn/Rescue Dawn

ACTRESS

1986
★ Geraldine Page/The Trip to Bountiful

1987
★ Isabella Rossellini/Blue Velvet

1988
★ Sally Kirkland/Anna

1989
★ Jodie Foster/Five Corners

1990
★ Andie MacDowell/sex, lies and videotape

1991
★ Anjelica Huston/The Grifters

1992
★ Judy Davis/Impromptu

1993
★ Fairuza Balk/Gas Food Lodging

1994
★ Ashley Judd/Ruby in Paradise
Suzy Amis/The Ballad of Little Jo
May Chin/The Wedding Banquet
Ariyan Johnson/Just Another Girl on the I.R.T.
Emma Thompson/Much Ado about Nothing

1995
★ Linda Fiorentino/The Last Seduction
Jennifer Jason Leigh/Mrs. Parker and the Vicious Circle
Karen Sillas/What Happened Was...
Lauren Velez/I Like It Like That
Chien-Lien Wu/Eat Drink Man Woman

1996
★ Elisabeth Shue/Leaving Las Vegas
Jennifer Jason Leigh/Georgia
Elina Lowensohn/Nadja
Julianne Moore/Safe
Catherine Keener/Walking and Talking
Renee Zellweger/The Whole Wide World

1997
★ Frances McDormand/Fargo
Maria Conchita Alonso/Caught
Scarlett Johansson/Manny & Lo

1998
★ Julie Christie/Afterglow
Stacy Edwards/In the Company of Men
Alison Folland/All Over Me
Lisa Harrow/Sunday
Robin Wright Penn/Loved

1999
★ Ally Sheedy/High Art

Katrin Cartlidge/Claire Dolan
Christina Ricci/The Opposite of Sex
Robin Tunney/Niagara, Niagara
Alfre Woodard/Down in the Delta

2000
★ Hilary Swank/Boys Don't Cry
Diane Lane/A Walk on the Moon
Janet McTeer/Tumbleweeds
Reese Witherspoon/Election

2001
★ Ellen Burstyn/Requiem for a Dream
Joan Allen/The Contender
Sanaa Lathan/Love and Basketball
Laura Linney/You Can Count On Me
Kelly Macdonald/Two Family House

2002
★ Sissy Spacek/In the Bedroom
Molly Parker/The Center of the World
Tilda Swinton/The Deep End
Kerry Washington/Lift

2003
★ Julianne Moore/Far from Heaven
Jennifer Aniston/The Good Girl
Maggie Gyllenhaal/Secretary
Catherine Keener/Lovely & Amazing
Parker Posey/Personal Velocity: Three Portraits

2004
★ Charlize Theron/Monster
Agnes Bruckner/Blue Car
Zooey Deschanel/All the Real Girls
Laura Linney/The Squid and the Whale
Sienna Miller/Interview

2005
★ Catalina Sandino Moreno/Maria Full of Grace
Kimberly Elise/Woman, Thou Art Loosed

2006
★ Felicity Huffman/Transamerica
Vera Farmiga/Down to the Bone
Angelina Jolie/A Mighty Heart

2007
★ Shareeka Epps/Half Nelson
Catherine O'Hara/For Your Consideration
Michelle Williams/Land of Plenty
Robin Wright Penn/Sorry, Haters

2008
★ Juno
Parker Posey/Broken English
Tang Wei/Lust, Caution

ACTRESS—SUPPORTING

1988
★ Anjelica Huston/The Dead

1989
★ Rosanna Desoto/Stand and Deliver

1990
★ Laura San Giacomo/sex, lies and videotape

1991
★ Sheryl Lee Ralph/To Sleep with Anger

1992
★ Diane Ladd/Rambling Rose

1993
★ Alfre Woodard/Passion Fish

1994
★ Lili Taylor/Household Saints
Lara Flynn Boyle/Equinox
Ah-Leh Gua/The Wedding Banquet
Lucinda Jenney/American Heart
Julianne Moore/Short Cuts

1995
★ Dianne Wiest/Bullets over Broadway
V.S. Brodie/Go Fish
Carla Gallo/Spanking the Monkey
Kelly Lynch/Forbidden Choices
Brooke Smith/Vanya on 42nd Street

1996
★ Mare Winningham/Georgia
Jennifer Lopez/My Family
Vanessa Redgrave/Little Odessa
Chloe Sevigny/Kids
Celia Weston/Dead Man Walking

1997
★ Elizabeth Pena/Lone Star
Mary Kay Place/Manny & Lo
Queen Latifah/Set It Off
Lili Taylor/Girls Town
Lily Tomlin/Flirting with Disaster

1998
★ Debbi (Deborah) Morgan/Eve's Bayou
Farrah Fawcett/The Apostle
Amy Madigan/Loved
Miranda Richardson/The Apostle
Patricia Richardson/Ulee's Gold

1999
★ Lynn Redgrave/Gods and Monsters
Stockard Channing/The Baby Dance
Patricia Clarkson/High Art
Lisa Kudrow/The Opposite of Sex
Joely Richardson/In the Shadows

2000
★ Chloe Sevigny/Boys Don't Cry
Barbara Barrie/Judy Berlin
Vanessa Martinez/Limbo
Julianne Nicholson/Tully
Sarah Polley/Go

2001
★ Zhang Ziyi/Crouching Tiger, Hidden Dragon
Pat Carroll/Songcatcher
Jennifer Connelly/Requiem for a Dream
Marcia Gay Harden/Pollock
Lupe Ontiveros/Chuck & Buck

2002
★ Carrie-Anne Moss/Memento
Uma Thurman/Tape
Tamara Tunie/The Caveman's Valentine

2003
★ Emily Mortimer/Lovely & Amazing
Viola Davis/Antwone Fisher

2004
★ Shohreh Aghdashloo/House of Sand and Fog

2005
★ Hope Davis/The Secret Lives of Dentists
Sarah Bolger/In America
Patricia Clarkson/Pieces of April
Frances McDormand/Laurel Canyon

2006
★ Virginia Madsen/Sideways
Cate Blanchett/Coffee and Cigarettes
Loretta Devine/Woman, Thou Art Loosed
Yenny Paola Vega/Maria Full of Grace

2007
★ Amy Adams/Junebug
Maggie Gyllenhaal/Happy Endings
Michelle Williams/Brokeback Mountain

2008
★ Frances McDormand/Friends with Money
Melonie Diaz/A Guide to Recognizing Your Saints
Marcia Gay Harden/American Gun
★ Cate Blanchett/I'm Not There
Anna Kendrick/Rocket Science
Jennifer Jason Leigh/Margot at the Wedding
Tamara Podemski/Four Sheets to the Wind
Marisa Tomei/Before the Devil Knows You're Dead

CINEMATOGRAPHY

1986
★ Trouble in Mind

1987
★ Platoon

1988
★ Matewan

1989
★ The Unbearable Lightness of Being

1990
★ Drugstore Cowboy

1991
★ Wild at Heart

1992
★ Kafka

1993
★ Night on Earth

1994
★ Menace II Society
American Heart
Chain of Desire
Equinox
Ruby in Paradise

1995
★ Barcelona
Eat Drink Man Woman
Forbidden Choices
I Like It Like That
Suture

1996
★ Leaving Las Vegas
Little Odessa
Nadja
The Underneath
The Usual Suspects

1997
★ Fargo
Bound
Color of a Brisk and Leaping Day
Dead Man
The Funeral

1998
★ Kama Sutra: A Tale of Love
The Bible and Gun Club
Habit
Hard Eight
Sunday

1999
★ Velvet Goldmine
Affliction
Belly
High Art

2000
★ Three Seasons
Judy Berlin
Julien Donkey-boy
Twin Falls Idaho

2001
★ Requiem for a Dream
Before Night Falls
Hamlet
Shadow of the Vampire

2002
★ Mulholland Drive
The Deep End
Hedwig and the Angry Inch
Memento

2003
★ Far from Heaven
Narc
Personal Velocity: Three Portraits

2004
★ In America
Elephant
Northfork
Shattered Glass

2005
★ The Motorcycle Diaries
Saints and Soldiers
We Don't Live Here Anymore

2006
★ Good Night, and Good Luck
Capote
Youth Without Youth

2007
★ Pan's Labyrinth
Brothers of the Head

2008
★ The Diving Bell and the Butterfly
Lust, Caution
The Savages

DIRECTOR

1986
★ Joel Coen/Blood Simple

1987
★ Martin Scorsese/After Hours

1988
★ Oliver Stone/Platoon

1989
★ John Huston/The Dead

1990
★ Ramon Menendez/Stand and Deliver

1991
★ Steven Soderbergh/sex, lies and videotape

1992
★ Charles Burnett/To Sleep with Anger

1993
★ Martha Coolidge/Rambling Rose

1994
★ Carl Franklin/One False Move

1995
★ Robert Altman/Short Cuts
Ang Lee/The Wedding Banquet
Victor Nunez/Ruby in Paradise
Robert Rodriguez/El Mariachi
John Turturro/Mac

1996
★ Quentin Tarantino/Pulp Fiction
John Dahl/Red Rock West
Ang Lee/Eat Drink Man Woman
Roman Polanski/Death and the Maiden
Alan Rudolph/Mrs. Parker and the Vicious Circle
★ Mike Figgis/Leaving Las Vegas
Michael Almereyda/Nadja
Ulu Grosbard/Georgia
Todd Haynes/Safe
John Sayles/The Secret of Roan Inish

1997
★ Joel Coen/Fargo
Abel Ferrara/The Funeral
David O. Russell/Flirting with Disaster
Todd Solondz/Welcome to the Dollhouse
Robert M. Young/Caught

1998
★ Robert Duvall/The Apostle
Larry Fessenden/Habit
Victor Nunez/Ulee's Gold
Paul Schrader/Touch
Wim Wenders/The End of Violence

1999
★ Wes Anderson/Rushmore
Todd Haynes/Velvet Goldmine
Lodge Kerrigan/Claire Dolan
Paul Schrader/Affliction
Todd Solondz/Happiness

2000
★ Alexander Payne/Election
Harmony Korine/Julien Donkey-boy
Doug Liman/Go
David Lynch/The Straight Story
Steven Soderbergh/The Limey

2001
★ Ang Lee/Crouching Tiger, Hidden Dragon
Christopher Nolan/Memento

2002
★ Michael Cuesta/L.I.E.
Richard Linklater/Waking Life
John Cameron Mitchell/Hedwig and the Angry Inch

2003
★ Todd Haynes/Far from Heaven
Joe Carnahan/Narc
Nicole Holofcener/Lovely & Amazing

2004
★ Sofia Coppola/Lost in Translation
Shari Springer Berman/American Splendor
Robert Pulcini/American Splendor
Jim Sheridan/In America
Peter Sollett/Raising Victor Vargas
Gus Van Sant/Elephant

2005
★ Alexander Payne/Sideways
Shane Carruth/Primer
Joshua Marston/Maria Full of Grace
Walter Salles/The Motorcycle Diaries
Mario Van Peebles/Baadasssss!

2006
★ Ang Lee/Brokeback Mountain
Noah Baumbach/The Squid and the Whale
George Clooney/Good Night, and Good Luck

2007
★ Jonathan Dayton/Little Miss Sunshine

[Best Director]

★ Valerie Faris/Little Miss Sunshine
Robert Altman/A Prairie Home Companion
Ryan Fleck/Half Nelson
Steven Soderbergh/Bubble

2008
★ Julian Schnabel/The Diving Bell and the Butterfly
Todd Haynes/I'm Not There
Tamara Jenkins/The Savages
Jason Reitman/Juno

FILM

1986 ★ After Hours
1987 ★ Platoon
1988 ★ River's Edge
1989 ★ Stand and Deliver
1990 ★ sex, lies and videotape
1991 ★ The Grifters
1992 ★ Rambling Rose
1993 ★ The Player
1994 ★ Short Cuts
 Equinox
 Much Ado about Nothing
 Ruby in Paradise
 The Wedding Banquet
1995 ★ Pulp Fiction
 Bullets over Broadway
 Eat Drink Man Woman
 Mrs. Parker and the Vicious Circle
 Wes Craven's New Nightmare
1996 ★ Leaving Las Vegas
 The Addiction
 Living in Oblivion
 Safe
 The Secret of Roan Irish
1997 ★ Fargo
 Dead Man
 The Funeral
 Lone Star
 Welcome to the Dollhouse
1998 ★ The Apostle
 Chasing Amy
 Loved
 Ulee's Gold
 Waiting for Guffman
1999 ★ Gods and Monsters
 Affliction
 Claire Dolan
 A Soldier's Daughter Never Cries
 Velvet Goldmine
2000 ★ Election
 Cookie's Fortune
 The Limey
 The Straight Story
 Sugar Town
2001 ★ Crouching Tiger, Hidden Dragon
 Before Night Falls
 Ghost Dog: The Way of the Samurai
 Requiem for a Dream
2002 ★ Memento
 Hedwig and the Angry Inch
 L.I.E.
 Waking Life
2003 ★ Far from Heaven
 The Good Girl
 Lovely & Amazing
 Secretary
2004 ★ Lost in Translation
 American Splendor
 In America
 Raising Victor Vargas
 Shattered Glass
2005 ★ Sideways
 Baadasssss!
 Kinsey
 Maria Full of Grace
 Primer
2006 ★ Brokeback Mountain
 Capote
 Good Night, and Good Luck
 The Squid and the Whale
2007 ★ Little Miss Sunshine
 American Gun
 Half Nelson
 Pan's Labyrinth
2008 ★ Juno
 The Diving Bell and the Butterfly
 I'm Not There
 A Mighty Heart

FIRST FEATURE

1987 ★ She's Gotta Have It
1988 ★ Dirty Dancing
1989 ★ Mystic Pizza
1990 ★ Heathers
1991 ★ Metropolitan
1992 ★ River's Edge
1993 ★ The Waterdance
1994 ★ Combination Platter
 American Heart
 El Mariachi
 My Own Private Idaho
 To Sleep with Anger
1995 ★ The Brothers McMullen
 Clean, Shaven
 Clerks
 Spanking the Monkey
 Suture
1996 ★ The Waterdance
 Household Saints
 Napoleon Dynamite
 Ruby in Paradise
 The Wedding Banquet
2000 ★ Drugstore Cowboy
2001 ★ Waitress
 Year of the Dog
2003 ★ Straight out of Brooklyn
2004 ★ Garden State
 Brother to Brother
 Napoleon Dynamite
 Saints and Soldiers
 The Woodsman
2005 ★ Transamerica
 Crash
 House of Sand and Fog
 Pieces of April
2006 ★ Monster
2008 ★ The Lookout
 Rocket Science
 2 Days in Paris
 Kinsey
 The Door in the Floor

FEATURE DOCUMENTARY

2003 ★ Bowling for Columbine
2004 ★ The Fog of War: Eleven Lessons from the Life of Robert S. McNamara
 My Architect: A Son's Journey
2005 ★ Metallica: Some Kind of Monster
 Tarnation
2006 ★ Enron: The Smartest Guys in the Room
 Grizzly Man
2007 ★ The Road to Guantanamo
2008 ★ Crazy Love

SCREENPLAY

1986 ★ Platoon
1987 ★ The Trip to Bountiful
1988 ★ Stand and Deliver
1989 ★ sex, lies and videotape
1990 ★ My Own Private Idaho
1991 ★ Rambling Rose
1992 ★ The Player
1993 ★ Short Cuts
1994 ★ Pulp Fiction
1995 ★ Living in Oblivion
1996 ★ Fargo
1997 ★ Chasing Amy
1998 ★ The Opposite of Sex
 Affliction
 Blind Faith
 Gods and Monsters
 The Spanish Prisoner
1999 ★ The Opposite of Sex
 The Apostle
 Touch
 Ulee's Gold
 Waiting for Guffman
2000 ★ Being John Malkovich
 The Blair Witch Project
 Boys Don't Cry
 Twin Falls Idaho
 Xiu Xiu: The Sent Down Girl
2001 ★ You Can Count On Me
 Boiler Room
 Girlfight
 Love and Basketball
2002 ★ Memento
 You Can Count On Me
 Chuck & Buck
 Two Family House
 Waking the Dead
2003 ★ The Good Girl
 Roger Dodger
 Thirteen Conversations About One Thing
2004 ★ Lost in Translation
 American Splendor
 A Mighty Wind
 Pieces of April
 Shattered Glass
2005 ★ Sideways
 Baadasssss!
 Before Sunset
 Kinsey
 Year of the Dog
2006 ★ Capote
 The Squid and the Whale
2007 ★ Thank You for Smoking
 Friends with Money
 The Illusionist
 Sorry, Haters
2008 ★ The Savages
 The Diving Bell and the Butterfly
 Waitress

DEBUT PERFORMANCE

1995 ★ Sean Nelson/Fresh
 Jeff Anderson/Clerks
 Jeremy Davies/Spanking the Monkey
 Renee Zellweger/Love and a .45
 Alicia Witt/Fun
1996 ★ Justin Pierce/Kids
 Jason Andrews/Rhythm Thief
 Lisa Bowman/River of Grass
 Gabriel Casseus/New Jersey Drive

1997 ★ Heather Matarazzo/Welcome to the Dollhouse
 Jena Malone/Bastard out of Carolina
 Brendan Sexton, III/Welcome to the Dollhouse
 Arie Verveen/Caught
 Jeffrey Wright/Basquiat
1998 ★ Aaron Eckhart/In the Company of Men
1999 ★ Evan Adams/Smoke Signals
 Tyrone Burton/Squeeze
 Eddie Cutanda/Squeeze
 Phuong Duong/Squeeze
 Lysa Flores/Star Maps
 Darling Narita/Beng
 Douglas Spain/Star Maps
2000 ★ Kimberly J. Brown/Tumbleweeds
 Rory Culkin/You Can Count On Me
 Emmy Rossum/Songcatcher
 Mike White/Chuck & Buck
2001 ★ Michelle Rodriguez/Girlfight
 Anthony Roth Costanzo/A Soldier's Daughter
 Never Cries
2002 ★ Kimberly J. Brown
 Bob Burrus/Tully
 Jessica Campbell/Election
 Chris Stafford/Edge of Seventeen
2003 ★ Nia Vardalos/My Big Fat Greek Wedding
 America Ferrera/Real Women Have Curves
 Raven Goodwin/Lovely & Amazing
 Artel Kayaru/Dahmer
2004 ★ Nikki Reed/Thirteen
 Anna Kendrick/Camp
 Judy Marte/Raising Victor Vargas
 Victor Rasuk/Raising Victor Vargas
2005 ★ Rodrigo de la Serna/The Motorcycle Diaries
 Anthony Mackie/Brother to Brother
 David Sullivan/Primer

FIRST SCREENPLAY

1995 ★ Spanking the Monkey
 Blessing
 Clerks
 Fun
 What Happened Was...
1996 ★ Big Night
 Girl 6
 Manny & Lo
 Tree's Lounge
 The Whole Wide World
1997 ★ Big Night
 Postcards from America
 River of Grass
 Smoke
1998 ★ The Bible and Gun Club
 Critical Care
 Hard Eight
 Star Maps

FILM—FOREIGN LANGUAGE

1986 ★ Kiss of the Spider Woman
1987 ★ A Room with a View
1988 ★ My Life as a Dog
1989 ★ Wings of Desire
1990 ★ My Left Foot
1992 ★ An Angel at My Table
1993 ★ The Crying Game
1994 ★ The Piano
1995 ★ Like Water for Chocolate
 Naked
 Orlando
 The Story of Qiu Ju
1996 ★ Before the Rain
 The City of Lost Children
 Exotica
 I Am Cuba
 Through the Olive Trees
1997 ★ Breaking the Waves
 Chungking Express
 Lamerica
 Secrets and Lies
 Trainspotting
1998 ★ The Sweet Hereafter
 Happy Together
 Mouth to Mouth
 Nenette and Boni
 Underground
1999 ★ Little Miss Sunshine [In the Company of Men]
 High Art
 Niagara, Niagara
 Sums of Beverly Hills
 Smoke Signals
2000 ★ Being John Malkovich
 The Adventures of Sebastian Cole
 Boys Don't Cry
 Cookie's Fortune
 The Straight Story
2004 ★ Maria Full of Grace
 Blue Car
 Garden State
 Monster
 The Straight Story
2005 ★ Little Miss Sunshine
 Brother to Brother
 Raising Victor Vargas
 Transamerica
2006 ★ Transamerica
 Junebug
2007 ★ Little Miss Sunshine
 Conversations with Other Women
 A Guide to Recognizing Your Saints
 Half Nelson
 Rocket Science
2008 ★ Juno
 Before the Devil Knows You're Dead
 Broken English
 A Mighty Heart
 The Painted Veil

★ = winner

Independent Spirit Awards

1999
- ★ The Celebration
- Central Station
- The Eel
- Fireworks
- The General

2000
- ★ Run Lola Run
- All About My Mother
- My Son the Fanatic
- Rosetta
- Topsy Turvy

2001
- ★ Dancer in the Dark
- In the Mood for Love
- The Terrorist
- The War Zone

2002
- Amelie
- Amores Perros
- Lumumba
- Sexy Beast

2003
- ★ Y Tu Mama Tambien
- Bloody Sunday
- The Fast Runner
- The Piano Teacher
- Time Out

2004
- ★ Whale Rider
- City of God
- The Magdalene Sisters
- The Triplets of Belleville

2005
- ★ The Sea Inside
- Bad Education
- Red Lights

2006
- ★ Paradise Now

2008
- ★ Once
- Persepolis

NATIONAL FILM REGISTRY

1989
- ★ The Best Years of Our Lives
- ★ Casablanca
- ★ Citizen Kane
- ★ Dr. Strangelove, or: How I Learned to Stop Worrying and Love the Bomb
- ★ The General
- ★ Gone with the Wind
- ★ The Grapes of Wrath
- ★ High Noon
- ★ Intolerance
- ★ The Learning Tree
- ★ The Maltese Falcon
- ★ Mr. Smith Goes to Washington
- ★ Modern Times
- ★ On the Waterfront
- ★ The Searchers
- ★ Singin' in the Rain
- ★ Snow White and the Seven Dwarfs
- ★ Some Like It Hot
- ★ Star Wars
- ★ Sunrise
- ★ Sunset Boulevard
- ★ Vertigo
- ★ The Wizard of Oz

1990
- ★ All About Eve
- ★ All Quiet on the Western Front
- ★ Bringing Up Baby
- ★ Dodsworth
- ★ Duck Soup
- ★ Fantasia
- ★ The Freshman
- ★ The Godfather
- ★ Harlan County, U.S.A.
- ★ How Green Was My Valley
- ★ It's a Wonderful Life
- ★ Killer of Sheep
- ★ Ninotchka
- ★ Raging Bull
- ★ Rebel without a Cause
- ★ Red River
- ★ Sullivan's Travels
- ★ Top Hat
- ★ Treasure of the Sierra Madre
- ★ A Woman under the Influence

1991
- ★ Blood of Jesus
- ★ Chinatown
- ★ City Lights
- ★ David Holzman's Diary
- ★ Frankenstein
- ★ Gigi
- ★ Greed
- ★ I Am a Fugitive from a Chain Gang
- ★ The Italian
- ★ King Kong
- ★ Lawrence of Arabia
- ★ The Magnificent Ambersons
- ★ My Darling Clementine
- ★ Out of the Past
- ★ A Place in the Sun
- ★ A Poor Little Rich Girl
- ★ Prisoner of Zenda
- ★ Shadow of a Doubt
- ★ Sherlock, Jr.
- ★ Tevye

1992
- ★ Adam's Rib
- ★ Annie Hall
- ★ The Bank Dick
- ★ The Big Parade
- ★ The Birth of a Nation
- ★ Bonnie & Clyde
- ★ Carmen Jones
- ★ Detour
- ★ Dog Star Man
- ★ Double Indemnity
- ★ Footlight Parade
- ★ The Gold Rush
- ★ Letter from an Unknown Woman
- ★ Morocco
- ★ Nashville
- ★ The Night of the Hunter
- ★ Paths of Glory
- ★ Psycho
- ★ Ride the High Country
- ★ Salt of the Earth

1993
- ★ An American in Paris
- ★ Badlands
- ★ The Black Pirate
- ★ Blade Runner
- ★ Cat People
- ★ The Cheat
- ★ His Girl Friday
- ★ It Happened One Night
- ★ Lassie, Come Home
- ★ A Night at the Opera
- ★ Nothing but a Man
- ★ One Flew Over the Cuckoo's Nest
- ★ Shadows
- ★ Shane
- ★ Sweet Smell of Success
- ★ Touch of Evil
- ★ The Wind
- ★ Yankee Doodle Dandy

1994
- ★ The African Queen
- ★ The Apartment
- ★ The Cool World
- ★ E.T.: The Extra-Terrestrial
- ★ Force of Evil
- ★ Freaks
- ★ Hell's Hinges
- ★ Invasion of the Body Snatchers
- ★ The Lady Eve
- ★ Louisiana Story
- ★ The Manchurian Candidate
- ★ Marty
- ★ Meet Me in St. Louis
- ★ Midnight Cowboy
- ★ Pinocchio
- ★ Safety Last
- ★ Scarface
- ★ Tabu: A Story of the South Seas
- ★ Taxi Driver

1995
- ★ The Adventures of Robin Hood
- ★ All That Heaven Allows
- ★ American Graffiti
- ★ The Band Wagon
- ★ Cabaret
- ★ Chan Is Missing
- ★ The Conversation
- ★ The Day the Earth Stood Still
- ★ El Norte
- ★ The Four Horsemen of the Apocalypse
- ★ Fury
- ★ The Hospital
- ★ The Last of the Mohicans
- ★ North by Northwest
- ★ The Philadelphia Story
- ★ Stagecoach
- ★ To Kill a Mockingbird

1996
- ★ The Awful Truth
- ★ Broken Blossoms
- ★ Destry Rides Again
- ★ The Graduate
- ★ The Heiress
- ★ The Jazz Singer
- ★ M*A*S*H
- ★ Mildred Pierce
- ★ The Outlaw Josey Wales
- ★ The Producers
- ★ The Road to Morocco
- ★ She Done Him Wrong
- ★ Shock Corridor
- ★ Show Boat
- ★ The Thief of Baghdad
- ★ To Be or Not to Be
- ★ Woodstock

1997
- ★ Ben-Hur
- ★ The Big Sleep
- ★ The Bridge on the River Kwai
- ★ The Great Dictator
- ★ Harold and Maude
- ★ How the West Was Won
- ★ The Hustler
- ★ Knute Rockne: All American
- ★ Little Fugitive
- ★ Mean Streets
- ★ The Naked Spur
- ★ Rear Window
- ★ Return of the Secaucus 7
- ★ The Thin Man
- ★ West Side Story
- ★ Wings

1998
- ★ The Bride of Frankenstein
- ★ Easy Rider
- ★ 42nd Street
- ★ From the Manger to the Cross
- ★ Gun Crazy
- ★ The Hitch-Hiker
- ★ The Immigrant
- ★ The Last Picture Show
- ★ Little Miss Marker
- ★ The Lost World
- ★ The Ox-Bow Incident
- ★ The Phantom of the Opera
- ★ Public Enemy
- ★ Sky High
- ★ Tootsie
- ★ Twelve o'Clock High

1999
- ★ Civilization
- ★ Do the Right Thing
- ★ Docks of New York
- ★ Emperor Jones
- ★ Gunga Din
- ★ Kiss Me Deadly
- ★ Laura
- ★ My Man Godfrey
- ★ Night of the Living Dead
- ★ Raiders of the Lost Ark
- ★ Roman Holiday
- ★ The Shop Around the Corner
- ★ A Streetcar Named Desire
- ★ The Ten Commandments
- ★ The Wild Bunch
- ★ Woman of the Year

2000
- ★ Apocalypse Now
- ★ Dracula
- ★ Five Easy Pieces
- ★ Goodfellas
- ★ Koyaanisqatsi
- ★ La Chute de la Maison Usher
- ★ The Life of Emile Zola
- ★ Little Caesar
- ★ Love Finds Andy Hardy
- ★ Network
- ★ Peter Pan
- ★ Regeneration
- ★ Salome
- ★ Shaft
- ★ A Star Is Born
- ★ The Tall T
- ★ Will Success Spoil Rock Hunter?

2001
- ★ Abbott and Costello Meet Frankenstein
- ★ All That Jazz
- ★ All the King's Men
- ★ Hoosiers
- ★ It
- ★ Jaws
- ★ Manhattan
- ★ Miracle of Morgan's Creek
- ★ National Lampoon's Animal House
- ★ Planet of the Apes
- ★ The Sound of Music
- ★ Stormy Weather
- ★ The Thin Blue Line
- ★ The Thing

2002
- ★ Alien
- ★ The Bad and the Beautiful
- ★ Beauty and the Beast
- ★ The Black Stallion
- ★ Boyz N the Hood
- ★ The Endless Summer
- ★ From Here to Eternity
- ★ In the Heat of the Night
- ★ Lady Windermere's Fan
- ★ Melody Ranch
- ★ The Pearl
- ★ Sabrina
- ★ This Is Spinal Tap
- ★ Stranger than Paradise

2003
- ★ Atlantic City
- ★ Butch Cassidy and the Sundance Kid
- ★ Gold Diggers of 1933
- ★ The Hunters
- ★ Medium Cool
- ★ National Velvet
- ★ Naughty Marietta
- ★ Patton
- ★ Show People
- ★ Son of the Sheik
- ★ Tarzan and His Mate
- ★ The Wedding March
- ★ White Heat
- ★ Young Frankenstein
- ★ Young Mr. Lincoln

2004
- ★ Ben-Hur
- ★ Court Jester
- ★ Cool Hand Luke
- ★ D.O.A.
- ★ Enter the Dragon
- ★ Eraserhead
- ★ Fast Times at Ridgemont High
- ★ The French Connection
- ★ Giant
- ★ Hands Up
- ★ Hoop Dreams
- ★ Imitation of Life
- ★ Miracle on 34th Street
- ★ The Music Man
- ★ A Raisin in the Sun
- ★ The Rocky Horror Picture Show
- ★ The Sting
- ★ Toy Story

2005
- ★ Baby Face
- ★ The Cameraman
- ★ Cool Hand Luke
- ★ The Fall of the House of Usher
- ★ Usher

2006
- ★ Applause
- ★ Big Trail
- ★ Blazing Saddles
- ★ Fargo
- ★ The Flesh and the Devil
- ★ Groundhog Day
- ★ Halloween
- ★ Last Command
- ★ Notorious
- ★ Red Dust
- ★ Rocky
- ★ sex, lies and videotape
- ★ Traffic in Souls

SCREEN ACTORS GUILD AWARDS

ACTOR

1994
- ★ Tom Hanks/Forrest Gump
- Morgan Freeman/The Shawshank Redemption
- Paul Newman/Nobody's Fool
- Tim Robbins/The Shawshank Redemption
- John Travolta/Pulp Fiction

1995
- ★ Nicolas Cage/Leaving Las Vegas
- Anthony Hopkins/Nixon
- James Earl Jones/Cry, the Beloved Country
- Sean Penn/Dead Man Walking
- Massimo Troisi/The Postman

1996
- ★ Geoffrey Rush/Shine
- Tom Cruise/Jerry Maguire
- Ralph Fiennes/The English Patient
- Woody Harrelson/The People vs. Larry Flynt
- Billy Bob Thornton/Sling Blade

1997
- ★ Jack Nicholson/As Good As It Gets
- Matt Damon/Good Will Hunting
- Robert Duvall/The Apostle
- Peter Fonda/Ulee's Gold
- Dustin Hoffman/Wag the Dog

1998
- ★ Roberto Benigni/Life Is Beautiful
- Joseph Fiennes/Shakespeare in Love
- Tom Hanks/Saving Private Ryan
- Ian McKellen/Gods and Monsters
- Nick Nolte/Affliction

1999
- ★ Kevin Spacey/American Beauty
- Jim Carrey/Man on the Moon
- Russell Crowe/The Insider
- Philip Seymour Hoffman/Flawless
- Denzel Washington/The Hurricane

2000
- ★ Benicio Del Toro/Traffic
- Jamie Bell/Billy Elliot
- Russell Crowe/Gladiator
- Geoffrey Rush/Quills

2001
- ★ Russell Crowe/A Beautiful Mind
- Kevin Kline/Life as a House
- Sean Penn/I Am Sam
- Denzel Washington/Training Day
- Tom Wilkinson/In the Bedroom

2002
- ★ Daniel Day-Lewis/Gangs of New York
- Adrien Brody/The Pianist
- Nicolas Cage/Adaptation
- Richard Gere/Chicago
- Jack Nicholson/About Schmidt

2003
- ★ Johnny Depp/Pirates of the Caribbean: The Curse of the Black Pearl
- Peter Dinklage/The Station Agent
- Ben Kingsley/House of Sand and Fog
- Bill Murray/Lost in Translation
- Sean Penn/Mystic River

2004
- ★ Jamie Foxx/Ray
- Don Cheadle/Hotel Rwanda
- Johnny Depp/Finding Neverland
- Leonardo DiCaprio/The Aviator
- Paul Giamatti/Sideways

2005
- ★ Philip Seymour Hoffman/Capote
- Russell Crowe/Cinderella Man
- Heath Ledger/Brokeback Mountain
- Joaquin Rafael (Leaf) Phoenix/Walk the Line
- David Strathairn/Good Night, and Good Luck

2006
- ★ Forest Whitaker/The Last King of Scotland
- Leonardo DiCaprio/Blood Diamond
- Ryan Gosling/Half Nelson
- Peter O'Toole/Venus
- Will Smith/The Pursuit of Happyness

2007
- ★ Daniel Day-Lewis/There Will Be Blood
- George Clooney/Michael Clayton
- Ryan Gosling/Lars and the Real Girl
- Emile Hirsch/Into the Wild
- Viggo Mortensen/Eastern Promises

ACTOR—SUPPORTING

1994
- ★ Martin Landau/Ed Wood
- Gary Sinise/Forrest Gump.

1995
- ★ Ed Harris/Apollo 13
- Kevin Bacon/Murder in the First
- Kenneth Branagh/Othello
- Don Cheadle/Devil in a Blue Dress
- Kevin Spacey/The Usual Suspects

1996
- ★ Cuba Gooding, Jr./Jerry Maguire
- Hank Azaria/The Birdcage
- Nathan Lane/The Birdcage
- William H. Macy/Fargo
- Noah Taylor/Shine

1997
- ★ Robin Williams/Good Will Hunting
- Billy Connolly/Mrs. Brown
- Anthony Hopkins/Amistad
- Greg Kinnear/As Good As It Gets
- Burt Reynolds/Boogie Nights

1998
- ★ Robert Duvall/A Civil Action
- James Coburn/Affliction
- David Kelly/Waking Ned Devine
- Geoffrey Rush/Shakespeare in Love

★ = winner

ACTOR — SUPPORTING

Billy Bob Thornton/A Simple Plan

1999
- ★ Michael Caine/The Cider House Rules
- Chris Cooper/American Beauty
- Tom Cruise/Magnolia
- Michael Clarke Duncan/The Green Mile
- Haley Joel Osment/The Sixth Sense

2000
- ★ Albert Finney/Erin Brockovich
- Jeff Bridges/The Contender
- Willem Dafoe/Shadow of the Vampire
- Gary Oldman/The Contender
- Joaquin Rafael (Leaf) Phoenix/Gladiator

2001
- ★ Ian McKellen/Lord of the Rings: The Fellowship of the Rings
- Jim Broadbent/Iris
- Hayden Christensen/Life as a House
- Ethan Hawke/Training Day
- Ben Kingsley/Sexy Beast

2002
- ★ Christopher Walken/Catch Me If You Can
- Chris Cooper/Adaptation
- Ed Harris/The Hours
- Alfred Molina/Frida
- Dennis Quaid/Far from Heaven

2003
- ★ Tim Robbins/Mystic River
- Alec Baldwin/The Cooler
- Chris Cooper/Seabiscuit
- Benicio Del Toro/21 Grams

2004
- ★ Morgan Freeman/Million Dollar Baby
- Thomas Haden Church/Sideways
- Jamie Foxx/Collateral
- James Garner/The Notebook
- Freddie Highmore/Finding Neverland

2005
- ★ Paul Giamatti/Cinderella Man
- Don Cheadle/Crash
- George Clooney/Syria na
- Matt Dillon/Crash
- Jake Gyllenhaal/Brokeback Mountain

2006
- ★ Eddie Murphy/Dreamgirls
- Alan Arkin/Little Miss Sunshine
- Leonardo DiCaprio/The Departed
- Jackie Earle Haley/Little Children
- Djimon Hounsou/Blood Diamond

2007
- ★ Javier Bardem/No Country for Old Men
- Casey Affleck/The Assassination of Jesse James by the Coward Robert Ford
- Hal Holbrook/Into the Wild
- Tommy Lee Jones/No Country for Old Men
- Tom Wilkinson/Michael Clayton

ACTRESS

1994
- ★ Jodie Foster/Nell
- Jessica Lange/Blue Sky
- Meg Ryan/When a Man Loves a Woman
- Susan Sarandon/The Client
- Meryl Streep/The River Wild

1995
- ★ Susan Sarandon/Dead Man Walking
- Joan Allen/Nixon
- Elisabeth Shue/Leaving Las Vegas
- Meryl Streep/The Bridges of Madison County
- Emma Thompson/Sense and Sensibility

1996
- ★ Frances McDormand/Fargo
- Brenda Blethyn/Secrets and Lies
- Diane Keaton/Marvin's Room
- Gena Rowlands/Unhook the Stars
- Kristin Scott Thomas/The English Patient

1997
- ★ Helen Hunt/As Good As It Gets
- Helena Bonham-Carter/The Wings of the Dove
- Judi Dench/Mrs. Brown
- Pam Grier/Jackie Brown
- Robin Wright Penn/She's So Lovely

1998
- ★ Gwyneth Paltrow/Shakespeare in Love
- Cate Blanchett/Elizabeth
- Jane Horrocks/Little Voice
- Meryl Streep/One True Thing
- Emily Watson/Hilary and Jackie

1999
- ★ Annette Bening/American Beauty
- Janet McTeer/Tumbleweeds
- Julianne Moore/The End of the Affair
- Meryl Streep/Music of the Heart
- Hilary Swank/Boys Don't Cry

2000
- ★ Julia Roberts/Erin Brockovich
- Joan Allen/The Contender
- Juliette Binoche/Chocolat
- Ellen Burstyn/Requiem for a Dream
- Laura Linney/You Can Count On Me

2001
- ★ Halle Berry/Monster's Ball
- Jennifer Connelly/A Beautiful Mind
- Judi Dench/Iris
- Sissy Spacek/In the Bedroom
- Renee Zellweger/Bridget Jones's Diary

2002
- ★ Renee Zellweger/Chicago
- Salma Hayek/Frida
- Nicole Kidman/The Hours
- Diane Lane/Unfaithful
- Julianne Moore/Far from Heaven

2003
- ★ Charlize Theron/Monster
- Patricia Clarkson/The Station Agent
- Diane Keaton/Something's Gotta Give
- Naomi Watts/21 Grams
- Evan Rachel Wood/Thirteen

2004
- ★ Hilary Swank/Million Dollar Baby
- Annette Bening/Being Julia
- Catalina Sandino Moreno/Maria Full of Grace
- Imelda Staunton/Vera Drake
- Kate Winslet/Eternal Sunshine of the Spotless Mind

2005
- ★ Reese Witherspoon/Walk the Line
- Judi Dench/Mrs. Henderson Presents
- Felicity Huffman/Transamerica
- Charlize Theron/North Country
- Zhang Ziyi/Memoirs of a Geisha

2006
- ★ Helen Mirren/The Queen
- Penelope Cruz/Volver
- Judi Dench/Notes on a Scandal
- Meryl Streep/The Devil Wears Prada
- Kate Winslet/Little Children

2007
- ★ Julie Christie/Away From Her
- Cate Blanchett/Elizabeth: The Golden Age
- Marion Cotillard/La Vie en Rose
- Angelina Jolie/A Mighty Heart
- Ellen Page/Juno

ACTRESS—SUPPORTING

1994
- ★ Dianne Wiest/Bullets over Broadway
- Sally Field/Forrest Gump
- Robin Wright Penn/Forrest Gump

1995
- ★ Kate Winslet/Sense and Sensibility
- Stockard Channing/Smoke
- Anjelica Huston/The Crossing Guard
- Mira Sorvino/Mighty Aphrodite
- Mare Winningham/Georgia

1996
- ★ Lauren Bacall/The Mirror Has Two Faces
- Juliette Binoche/The English Patient
- Marisa Tomei/Unhook the Stars
- Gwen Verdon/Marvin's Room

1997
- ★ Kim Basinger/L.A. Confidential
- Minnie Driver/Good Will Hunting
- Julianne Moore/Boogie Nights
- Gloria Stuart/Titanic
- Alison Elliott/The Wings of the Dove

1998
- ★ Kathy Bates/Primary Colors
- Brenda Blethyn/Little Voice
- Judi Dench/Shakespeare in Love
- Rachel Griffiths/Hilary and Jackie
- Lynn Redgrave/Gods and Monsters

1999
- ★ Angelina Jolie/Girl, Interrupted
- Cameron Diaz/Being John Malkovich
- Angelina Jolie/Girl, Interrupted
- Catherine Keener/Being John Malkovich
- Chloe Sevigny/Boys Don't Cry

2000
- ★ Judi Dench/Chocolat
- Kate Hudson/Almost Famous
- Julie Walters/Billy Elliot
- Kate Winslet/Quills

2001
- ★ Helen Mirren/Gosford Park
- Cate Blanchett/Bandits
- Judi Dench/The Shipping News
- Cameron Diaz/Vanilla Sky
- Dakota Fanning/I Am Sam

2002
- ★ Catherine Zeta-Jones/Chicago
- Kathy Bates/About Schmidt
- Julianne Moore/The Hours
- Michelle Pfeiffer/White Oleander
- Queen Latifah/Chicago

2003
- ★ Renee Zellweger/Cold Mountain
- Marta Bello/The Cooler
- Keisha Castle-Hughes/Whale Rider
- Patricia Clarkson/Pieces of April
- Holly Hunter/Thirteen

2004
- ★ Cate Blanchett/The Aviator
- Laura Linney/Kinsey
- Virginia Madsen/Sideways
- Sophie Okonedo/Hotel Rwanda

2005
- ★ Rachel Weisz/The Constant Gardener
- Amy Adams/Junebug
- Catherine Keener/Capote
- Frances McDormand/North Country
- Michelle Williams/Brokeback Mountain

2006
- ★ Jennifer Hudson/Dreamgirls
- Adriana Barraza/Babel
- Cate Blanchett/Notes on a Scandal
- Abigail Breslin/Little Miss Sunshine
- Rinko Kikuchi/Babel

2007
- ★ Ruby Dee/American Gangster
- Cate Blanchett/I'm Not There
- Catherine Keener/Into the Wild
- Amy Ryan/Gone Baby Gone
- Tilda Swinton/Michael Clayton

CAST

1995
- ★ Apollo 13
- Get Shorty
- How to Make an American Quilt
- Nixon
- Sense and Sensibility

1996
- ★ The Birdcage
- The English Patient
- Marvin's Room
- Sling Blade

1997
- ★ The Full Monty
- Boogie Nights
- Good Will Hunting
- L.A. Confidential
- Titanic

1998
- ★ Shakespeare in Love
- Life is Beautiful
- Little Voice

WRITERS GUILD OF AMERICA

1999
- ★ American Beauty
- Being John Malkovich
- The Cider House Rules
- The Green Mile
- Magnolia

2000
- ★ Traffic
- Almost Famous
- Billy Elliot
- Chocolat
- Gladiator

2001
- ★ Gosford Park
- A Beautiful Mind
- In the Bedroom
- Lord of the Rings: The Fellowship of the Rings
- Moulin Rouge

2002
- ★ Chicago
- Adaptation
- The Hours
- Lord of the Rings: The Two Towers
- My Big Fat Greek Wedding

2003
- ★ Lord of the Rings: The Return of the King
- Finding Neverland
- Hotel Rwanda
- Million Dollar Baby
- Mystic River

2004
- ★ Sideways
- The Aviator
- Finding Neverland
- Hotel Rwanda
- Million Dollar Baby
- The Station Agent

2005
- ★ Sideways
- Brokeback Mountain
- Capote
- Good Night, and Good Luck
- Hustle & Flow

2006
- ★ Little Miss Sunshine
- Babel
- Bobby
- The Departed
- Dreamgirls

2007
- ★ No Country for Old Men
- American Gangster
- Hairspray
- Into the Wild
- 3:10 to Yuma

Saving Private Ryan
Waking Ned Devine

FEATURE DOCUMENTARY

2005
- ★ Enron: The Smartest Guys in the Room

ADAPTED SCREENPLAY

1995
- ★ Sense and Sensibility
- Apollo 13
- Babe
- Get Shorty
- Leaving Las Vegas

1996
- ★ Sling Blade
- Little Women
- The Madness of King George
- The Joy Luck Club
- The Remains of the Day
- Quiz Show
- The English Patient
- Emma
- The Birdcage
- The Shawshank Redemption
- Trainspotting

1997
- ★ L.A. Confidential
- Donnie Brasco
- The Ice Storm
- Wag the Dog
- The Wings of the Dove

1998
- ★ Out of Sight
- A Civil Action
- Gods and Monsters

1968
1969
- ★ Goodbye Columbus

1970
1971
- ★ M*A*S*H
- ★ I Never Sang for My Father

1972
- ★ The French Connection
- ★ Kotch

1973
- ★ Cabaret
- ★ The Godfather

1974
- ★ The Apprenticeship of Duddy Kravitz
- ★ The Godfather, Part 2

1975
- ★ One Flew Over the Cuckoo's Nest
- ★ The Sunshine Boys

1976
- ★ All the President's Men
- ★ The Pink Panther Strikes Again

1977
- ★ Julia
- ★ Oh, God!

1978
- ★ Heaven Can Wait
- ★ Midnight Express

1979
- ★ Being There
- ★ Kramer vs. Kramer

1980
- ★ Airplane!
- ★ Ordinary People

1981
- ★ On Golden Pond

1982
- ★ Missing
- ★ Victor/Victoria

1983
- ★ Reuben, Reuben
- ★ Terms of Endearment

1984
- ★ The Killing Fields

1985
- ★ Prizzi's Honor

1986
- ★ A Room with a View

1987
- ★ Roxanne

1988
- ★ Dangerous Liaisons

1989
- ★ Driving Miss Daisy

1990
- ★ Dances with Wolves

1991
- ★ The Silence of the Lambs

1992
- ★ The Player

1993
- ★ Schindler's List
- In the Name of the Father
- The Fugitive
- The Joy Luck Club
- The Remains of the Day

1994
- ★ Forrest Gump

★ = winner

Writers Guild of America

Primary Colors
A Simple Plan

1999
★ *Election*
The Cider House Rules
The Insider
October Sky
★ *The Talented Mr. Ripley*

2000
★ *Traffic*
Chocolat
Crouching Tiger, Hidden Dragon
High Fidelity
Wonder Boys

2001
★ *A Beautiful Mind*
Black Hawk Down
Bridget Jones's Diary
Ghost World
Lord of the Rings: The Fellowship of the Rings

2002
★ *The Hours*
About a Boy
About Schmidt
Adaptation
Chicago

2003
★ *American Splendor*
Cold Mountain
Lord of the Rings: The Return of the King
Mystic River
Seabiscuit

2004
★ *Sideways*
Before Sunset
Million Dollar Baby
Mean Girls
The Motorcycle Diaries

2005
★ *Brokeback Mountain*
Capote
The Constant Gardener
A History of Violence
Syriana

2006
★ *The Departed*
The Devil Wears Prada
Little Children
Thank You for Smoking

2007
★ *No Country for Old Men*
The Diving Bell and the Butterfly
Into the Wild
There Will Be Blood
Zodiac

ORIGINAL SCREENPLAY

1967
★ *Bonnie & Clyde*
1968
★ *The Producers*
1969
★ *Bob & Carol & Ted & Alice*
1970
★ *Patton*
1971
★ *The Hospital*
1972
★ *The Candidate*
1973
★ *Save the Tiger*
1974
★ *Chinatown*
1975
★ *Dog Day Afternoon*
1976
★ *Network*
1977
★ *Annie Hall*

2001
★ *Gosford Park*
The Man Who Wasn't There
Monster's Ball
Moulin Rouge
The Royal Tenenbaums

2002
★ *Bowling for Columbine*
Antwone Fisher
Far from Heaven
Gangs of New York
My Big Fat Greek Wedding

2003
★ *Lost in Translation*
Bend It Like Beckham
Dirty Pretty Things
In America
The Station Agent

2004
★ *Eternal Sunshine of the Spotless Mind*
The Aviator
Garden State
Hotel Rwanda
Kinsey

2005
★ *Crash*
Cinderella Man
The 40 Year Old Virgin
Good Night, and Good Luck
The Squid and the Whale

2006
★ *Little Miss Sunshine*
Babel
The Queen
Stranger Than Fiction
United 93

2007
★ *Juno*
Knocked Up
Lars and the Real Girl
Michael Clayton
The Savages

GOLDEN RASPBERRY AWARDS

WORST PICTURE

1980
★ *Can't Stop the Music*
1981
★ *Mommie Dearest*
1983
★ *The Lonely Lady*
1984
★ *Bolero*
1985
★ *Rambo: First Blood, Part 2*
1986
★ *Howard the Duck*
★ *Under the Cherry Moon*
1987
★ *Leonard Part 6*
1988
★ *Cocktail*
1989
★ *Star Trek 5: The Final Frontier*
1990
★ *The Adventures of Ford Fairlane*
Ghosts Can't Do It
1991
★ *Hudson Hawk*
1992
★ *Shining Through*
1993
★ *Indecent Proposal*
1994
★ *Color of Night*
North
On Deadly Ground
The Specialist
Wyatt Earp
1995
★ *Showgirls*

Congo
It's Pat: The Movie
Waterworld
1996
★ *Striptease*
Barb Wire
Ed
The Island of Dr. Moreau
The Stupids
1997
★ *The Postman*
Anaconda
Batman and Robin
Fire Down Below
Speed 2: Cruise Control
1998
★ *An Alan Smithee Film: Burn, Hollywood, Burn*
Armageddon
The Avengers
Godzilla
Spice World: The Movie
1999
★ *Wild Wild West*
Big Daddy
The Blair Witch Project
The Haunting
Star Wars: Episode 1—The Phantom Menace
2000
★ *Battlefield Earth*
Book of Shadows: Blair Witch 2
The Flintstones in Viva Rock Vegas
Little Nicky
The Next Best Thing
2001
★ *Freddy Got Fingered*
2002
★ *Swept Away*
2003
★ *Gigli*
Charlie's Angels: Full Throttle
Dr. Seuss' The Cat in the Hat
From Justin to Kelly
2004
★ *Catwoman*
Alexander
Superbabies: Baby Geniuses 2
Surviving Christmas
White Chicks
2005
★ *Dirty Love*
Deuce Bigalow: European Gigolo
The Dukes of Hazzard
House of Wax
Son of the Mask
2006
★ *Basic Instinct 2*
BloodRayne
Lady in the Water
Little Man
The Wicker Man
2007
★ *I Know Who Killed Me*
Daddy Day Camp
I Now Pronounce You Chuck and Larry
Norbit

WORST REMAKE

2006
★ *Little Man*
The Pink Panther
Poseidon
The Shaggy Dog
The Wicker Man
2007
★ *I Know Who Killed Me*
Are We Done Yet?
Bratz
Epic Movie
Who's Your Caddy?

WORST SEQUEL/PREQUEL

2006
★ *Basic Instinct 2*
Big Momma's House 2

Garfield: A Tail of Two Kitties
The Santa Clause 3: The Escape Clause
The Texas Chainsaw Massacre: The Beginning
2007
★ *Daddy Day Camp*
Aliens vs. Predator: Requiem
Evan Almighty
Hannibal Rising
Hostel: Part 2

WORST REMAKE/SEQUEL

1994
★ *Wyatt Earp*
The Flintstones
1995
★ *The Scarlet Letter*
1997
★ *Speed 2: Cruise Control*
Batman and Robin
Home Alone 3
The Lost World: Jurassic Park 2
McHale's Navy
1998
★ *The Avengers*
Godzilla
Psycho
Lost in Space
Meet Joe Black
Psycho
2000
★ *Book of Shadows: Blair Witch 2*
Dr. Seuss' How the Grinch Stole Christmas
The Flintstones in Viva Rock Vegas
Get Carter
Mission: Impossible 2
2001
★ *Planet of the Apes*
2003
★ *Charlie's Angels: Full Throttle*
Dumb and Dumberer: When Harry Met Lloyd
From Justin to Kelly
The Texas Chainsaw Massacre
2 Fast 2 Furious
2004
★ *Scooby-Doo 2: Monsters Unleashed*
Alien vs. Predator
Anaconda: The Hunt for the Blood Orchid
Around the World in 80 Days
Exorcist: The Beginning
2005
★ *Son of the Mask*
Bewitched
Deuce Bigalow: European Gigolo
The Dukes of Hazzard
House of Wax

WORST ACTOR

1980
★ Neil Diamond/*The Jazz Singer*
1981
★ Klinton Spilsbury/*Legend of the Lone Ranger*
1983
★ Christopher Atkins/*A Night in Heaven*
1984
★ Sylvester Stallone/*Rhinestone*
1985
★ Sylvester Stallone/*Rambo: First Blood, Part 2*
Sylvester Stallone/*Rocky 4*

1986
★ Prince/*Under the Cherry Moon*
1987
★ Bill Cosby/*Leonard Part 6*
1988
★ Sylvester Stallone/*Rambo 3*
1989
★ William Shatner/*Star Trek 5: The Final Frontier*
1990
★ Andrew (Dice Clay) Silverstein/*The Adventures of Ford Fairlane*
1991
★ Kevin Costner/*Robin Hood: Prince of Thieves*
1992
★ Sylvester Stallone/*Stop! or My Mom Will Shoot*
1993
★ Burt Reynolds/*Cop and a Half*
1994
★ Kevin Costner/*Wyatt Earp*
Macaulay Culkin/*Getting Even with Dad*
Macaulay Culkin/*The Pagemaster*
Macaulay Culkin/*Richie Rich*
Bruce Willis/*Color of Night*
Bruce Willis/*North*
1995
★ Pauly Shore/*Jury Duty*
Kevin Costner/*Waterworld*
Kyle MacLachlan/*Showgirls*
Sylvester Stallone/*Assassins*
Sylvester Stallone/*Judge Dredd*
1996
★ Tom Arnold/*Big Bully*
★ Tom Arnold/*Carpool*
★ Tom Arnold/*The Stupids*
Keanu Reeves/*Chain Reaction*
Adam Sandler/*Bulletproof*
Adam Sandler/*Happy Gilmore*
Sylvester Stallone/*Daylight*
1997
★ Kevin Costner/*The Postman*
Val Kilmer/*The Saint*
Shaquille O'Neal/*Steel*
Steven Seagal/*Fire Down Below*
Jon Voight/*Anaconda*
1998
★ Bruce Willis/*Armageddon*
Bruce Willis/*Mercury Rising*
Bruce Willis/*The Siege*
Ralph Fiennes/*The Avengers*
Ryan O'Neal/*An Alan Smithee Film: Burn, Hollywood, Burn*
Ryan Phillippe/*54*
Adam Sandler/*The Waterboy*
1999
★ Adam Sandler/*Big Daddy*
Kevin Costner/*For Love of the Game*
Kevin Costner/*Message in a Bottle*
Kevin Kline/*Wild Wild West*
Arnold Schwarzenegger/*End of Days*
Robin Williams/*Bicentennial Man*
Robin Williams/*Jakob the Liar*
2000
★ John Travolta/*Battlefield Earth*

★ = winner

Leonardo DiCaprio/The Beach
Adam Sandler/Little Nicky
★ Arnold Schwarzenegger/The 6th Day
Sylvester Stallone/Get Carter

2001
★ Tom Green/Freddy Got Fingered

2002
Roberto Benigni'/Pinocchio

2003
★ Ben Affleck/Daredevil
★ Ben Affleck/Gigli
★ Ben Affleck/Paycheck
Cuba Gooding, Jr./Boat Trip
Cuba Gooding, Jr./The Fighting Temptations

2004
Ashton Kutcher/Cheaper by the Dozen
Ashton Kutcher/Just Married
Ashton Kutcher/My Boss's Daughter
Mike Myers/Dr. Seuss' The Cat in the Hat

2005
★ Rob Schneider/Deuce Bigalow: European Gigolo
Tom Cruise/War of the Worlds
Vin Diesel/The Chronicles of Riddick
Colin Farrell/Alexander
Will Ferrell/Bewitched
Dwayne "The Rock" Johnson/Doom

2006
★ M. Night Shyamalan/Lady in the Water
Marlon Wayans/Little Man
Shawn Wayans/Little Man
Tim Allen/The Santa Clause 3: The Escape Clause
Tim Allen/Zoom

2007
★ Eddie Murphy/Norbit
Nicolas Cage/Ghost Rider
Jim Carrey/The Number 23
Cuba Gooding, Jr./Daddy Day Camp
Adam Sandler/I Now Pronounce You Chuck and Larry

WORST ACTRESS

1980
★ Brooke Shields/The Blue Lagoon

1981
★ Bo Derek/Tarzan, the Ape Man
Faye Dunaway/Mommie Dearest

1982
★ Pia Zadora/Butterfly

1983
★ Pia Zadora/The Lonely Lady

1984
★ Bo Derek/Bolero

1985
★ Linda Blair/Night Patrol
Linda Blair/Savage Island
Linda Blair/Savage Streets

1986
★ Madonna/Shanghai Surprise

1987
★ Madonna/Who's That Girl?

1988
★ Liza Minnelli/Rent-A-Cop
Liza Minnelli/Arthur 2: On the Rocks

1990
★ Bo Derek/Ghosts Can't Do It

1991
★ Sean Young/A Kiss Before Dying

1992
★ Melanie Griffith/Shining Through

1993
★ Madonna/Body of Evidence

1994
★ Sharon Stone/Intersection
Sharon Stone/The Specialist

1995
★ Elizabeth Berkley/Showgirls
Uma Thurman/Even Cowgirls Get the Blues

1996
★ Demi Moore/Striptease
Whoopi Goldberg/Bogus
Whoopi Goldberg/Eddie
Whoopi Goldberg/Theodore Rex

1997
★ Demi Moore/The Juror
Melanie Griffith/Two Much
Julia Roberts/Mary Reilly

1998
★ The Spice Girls/Spice World: The Movie
Yasmine Bleeth/BASEketball
Sharon Stone/Gloria
Jessica Lange/Hush
Uma Thurman/The Avengers

1999
★ Heather Donahue/The Blair Witch Project
Melanie Griffith/Crazy in Alabama
Milla Jovovich/The Messenger: The Story of Joan of Arc
Anne Heche/Psycho
Jessica Lange/Hush
Catherine Zeta-Jones/Entrapment
Catherine Zeta-Jones/The Haunting

2000
★ Madonna/The Next Best Thing
Kim Basinger/I Dreamed of Africa
Melanie Griffith/Cecil B. Demented
Bette Midler/Isn't She Great
Demi Moore/Passion of Mind

2001
★ Mariah Carey/Glitter

2002
★ Madonna/Swept Away
Britney Spears/Crossroads

2003
★ Jennifer Lopez/Gigli
Drew Barrymore/Charlie's Angels: Full Throttle
Kelly Clarkson/From Justin to Kelly
Cameron Diaz/Charlie's Angels: Full Throttle
Angelina Jolie/Beyond Borders
Angelina Jolie/Lara Croft Tomb Raider: The Cradle of Life

2004
★ Halle Berry/Catwoman
Hilary Duff/A Cinderella Story
Hilary Duff/Raise Your Voice
Angelina Jolie/Alexander
Angelina Jolie/Taking Lives

2005
★ Jenny McCarthy/Dirty Love
Jessica Alba/Fantastic Four
Jessica Alba/Into the Blue
Hilary Duff/The Perfect Man
Hilary Duff/Cheaper by the Dozen 2
Ashley (Fuller) Olsen/New York Minute
Mary-Kate Olsen/New York Minute

2006
★ Sharon Stone/Basic Instinct 2
Lindsay Lohan/Just My Luck
Kristanna Loken/BloodRayne
Jessica Simpson/Employee of the Month

2007
★ Lindsay Lohan/I Know Who Killed Me
Jessica Alba/Awake
Gabriel Byrne/Bratz
Logan Browning/Bratz
Elisha Cuthbert/Captivity
Diane Keaton/Because I Said So
Janel Parrish/Bratz
Nathalia Ramos/Bratz
Skyler Shaye/Bratz

WORST SUPPORTING ACTOR

1980
★ John Adames/Gloria

1981
★ Laurence Olivier/The Jazz Singer

1982
★ Steve Forrest/Mommie Dearest
Ed McMahon/Butterfly

1983
★ Jim Nabors/Stroker Ace

1985
★ Rob Lowe/St. Elmo's Fire

1986
★ Jerome Benton/Under the Cherry Moon

1987
★ David Mendenhall/Over the Top

1989
★ Christopher Atkins/Listen to Me

1991
★ Dan Aykroyd/Nothing But Trouble

1992
★ Tom Selleck/Christopher Columbus: The Discovery

1993
★ Woody Harrelson'/Indecent Proposal

1994
★ O.J. Simpson/Naked Gun 33 1/3: The Final Insult

1995
★ Dennis Hopper/Waterworld

1996
★ Marlon Brando/The Island of Dr. Moreau
Val Kilmer/The Ghost and the Darkness
Val Kilmer/The Island of Dr. Moreau

1997
★ Dennis Rodman/Double Team
Willem Dafoe/Speed 2: Cruise Control
Chris O'Donnell/Batman and Robin
Arnold Schwarzenegger/Batman and Robin

1998
★ Joe Eszterhas/An Alan Smithee Film: Burn, Hollywood, Burn
Sean Connery/The Avengers
Joe Pesci/Lethal Weapon 4
Sylvester Stallone/An Alan Smithee Film: Burn, Hollywood, Burn

1999
Jake Lloyd/Star Wars: Episode 1 — The Phantom Menace
Rob Schneider/Big Daddy

2000
★ Barry Pepper/Battlefield Earth
Stephen Baldwin/The Flintstones in Viva Rock Vegas
Gabriel Byrne/End of Days
Keanu Reeves/The Watcher
Forest Whitaker/Battlefield Earth

2001
★ Charlton Heston/Planet of the Apes

2002
★ Hayden Christensen/Star Wars: Episode 2 — Attack of the Clones

2003
★ Sylvester Stallone/Spy Kids 3-D: Game Over
Anthony Anderson/Kangaroo Jack
Alec Baldwin/Dr. Seuss' The Cat in the Hat
Al Pacino/Gigli
Christopher Walken/Gigli
Christopher Walken/Kangaroo Jack

2004
★ Donald Rumsfeld/Fahrenheit 9/11
Val Kilmer/Alexander
Elizabeth Taylor/The Flintstones

2005
★ Hayden Christensen/Star Wars: Episode 3 — Revenge of the Sith
Alan Cumming/Son of the Mask
Will Ferrell/Kicking & Screaming
Bob Hoskins/Son of the Mask
Eugene Levy/Cheaper by the Dozen 2
Burt Reynolds/The Dukes of Hazzard
Burt Reynolds/The Longest Yard

2006
★ Danny DeVito/Deck the Halls
Ben Kingsley/BloodRayne
Martin Short/The Santa Clause 3: The Escape Clause

2007
★ Eddie Murphy/Norbit
Orlando Bloom/Pirates of the Caribbean: At World's End
Kevin James/I Now Pronounce You Chuck and Larry
Rob Schneider/I Now Pronounce You Chuck and Larry
Jon Voight/September Dawn

WORST SUPPORTING ACTRESS

1991
★ Sean Young/A Kiss Before Dying

1992
★ Estella Getty/Stop or My Mom Will Shoot

1993
★ Faye Dunaway/The Temp

1994
★ Rosie O'Donnell/Car 54, Where Are You?
Rosie O'Donnell/Exit to Eden

1995
★ Madonna/Four Rooms
Gina Gershon/Showgirls

1996
★ Melanie Griffith/Mulholland Falls
Faye Dunaway/The Chamber

1997
★ Alicia Silverstone/Batman and Robin
Faye Dunaway/Albino Alligator
Milla Jovovich/The Fifth Element

1998
★ Maria Pitillo/Godzilla
Ellen A. Dow/54
Jenny McCarthy/BASEketball
Salma Hayek/54
Salma Hayek/Wild Wild West
Juliette Lewis/The Other Sister

1999
★ Denise Richards/The World Is Not Enough
Sofia Coppola/Star Wars: Episode 1 — The Phantom Menace

2000
★ Kelly Preston/Battlefield Earth
Patricia Arquette/Little Nicky
Joan Collins/The Flintstones in Viva Rock Vegas
Thandie Newton/Mission: Impossible 2
Rene Russo/Adventures of Rocky & Bullwinkle

2001
★ Estella Warren/Planet of the Apes

2002
★ Madonna/Die Another Day

2003
★ Demi Moore/Charlie's Angels: Full Throttle
Lainie Kazan/Gigli
Brittany Murphy/Just Married
Kelly Preston/Dr. Seuss' The Cat in the Hat
Tara Reid/My Boss's Daughter

★ = winner

Golden Raspberry Awards

2004
- ★ Britney Spears/Fahrenheit 9/11
- Carmen Electra/Starsky & Hutch
- Jennifer Lopez/Jersey Girl
- Condoleeza Rice/Fahrenheit 9/11
- Sharon Stone/Catwoman

2005
- ★ Paris Hilton/House of Wax
- Carmen Electra/Dirty Love
- Katie Holmes/Batman Begins
- Jessica Simpson/The Dukes of Hazzard

2006
- ★ Carmen Electra/Date Movie
- Kate (Catherine) Bosworth/Superman Returns
- Kristin Chenoweth/Deck the Halls
- Kristin Chenoweth/The Pink Panther
- Kristin Chenoweth/RV
- Jenny McCarthy/John Tucker Must Die
- Michelle Rodriguez/BloodRayne

2007
- ★ Eddie Murphy/Norbit
- Jessica Biel/I Now Pronounce You Chuck and Larry
- Carmen Electra/Epic Movie
- Julia Ormond/I Know Who Killed Me
- Nicolette Sheridan/Code Name: The Cleaner

WORST DIRECTOR

1980
- ★ Robert Greenwald/Xanadu

1981
- ★ Michael Cimino/Heaven's Gate

1982
- ★ Ken Annakin/Pirate Movie

1983
- ★ Peter Sasdy/The Lonely Lady

1984
- ★ John Derek/Bolero

1985
- ★ Sylvester Stallone/Rocky 4

1986
- ★ Prince/Under the Cherry Moon

1987
- ★ Norman Mailer/Tough Guys Don't Dance
- Elaine May/Ishtar

1988
- ★ Blake Edwards/Sunset
- Stewart Raffill/Mac and Me

1989
- ★ William Shatner/Star Trek 5: The Final Frontier

1990
- ★ John Derek/Ghosts Can't Do It

1991
- ★ Michael Lehmann/Hudson Hawk

1992
- ★ David Seltzer/Shining Through

1993
- ★ Jennifer Lynch/Boxing Helena

1994
- ★ Steven Seagal/On Deadly Ground

1995
- ★ Paul Verhoeven/Showgirls

1996
- ★ Andrew Bergman/Striptease
- John Frankenheimer/The Island of Dr. Moreau
- Stephen Frears/Mary Reilly
- John Landis/The Stupids
- Brian Levant/Jingle All the Way

1997
- ★ Kevin Costner/The Postman
- Jan De Bont/Speed 2: Cruise Control
- Luis Llosa/Anaconda
- Joel Schumacher/Batman and Robin
- Oliver Stone/U-Turn

1998
- ★ Gus Van Sant/Psycho
- Michael Bay/Armageddon
- Jeremiah S. Chechik/The Avengers
- Roland Emmerich/Godzilla
- Arthur Hiller/An Alan Smithee Film: Burn, Hollywood, Burn

1999
- ★ Barry Sonnenfeld/Wild Wild West
- Jan De Bont/The Haunting
- Dennis Dugan/Big Daddy
- Peter Hyams/End of Days
- George Lucas/Star Wars: Episode 1—The Phantom Menace

2000
- ★ Roger Christian/Battlefield Earth
- Brian De Palma/Mission to Mars
- John Schlesinger/The Next Best Thing

2001
- ★ Tom Green/Freddy Got Fingered

2002
- ★ Guy Ritchie/Swept Away

2003
- ★ Martin Brest/Gigli
- Robert Iscove/From Justin to Kelly
- Mort Nathan/Boat Trip
- Andy Wachowski/The Matrix Reloaded
- Andy Wachowski/The Matrix Revolutions
- Larry Wachowski/The Matrix Reloaded
- Larry Wachowski/The Matrix Revolutions
- Bo Welch/Dr. Seuss' The Cat in the Hat

2004
- ★ Pitof/Catwoman
- Bob (Benjamin) Clark/Superbabies: Baby Geniuses 2
- Renny Harlin/Exorcist: The Beginning
- Oliver Stone/Alexander
- Keenen Ivory Wayans/White Chicks

2005
- ★ John Mallory Asher/Dirty Love
- Uwe Boll/Alone in the Dark
- Jay Chandrasekhar/The Dukes of Hazzard
- Nora Ephron/Bewitched
- Lawrence (Larry) Guterman/Son of the Mask

2006
- ★ M. Night Shyamalan/Lady in the Water
- Uwe Boll/BloodRayne
- Michael Caton-Jones/Basic Instinct 2
- Ron Howard/The Da Vinci Code
- Keenen Ivory Wayans/Little Man

2007
- ★ Chris Sivertson/I Know Who Killed Me
- Dennis Dugan/I Now Pronounce You Chuck and Larry
- Roland Joffe/Captivity
- Brian Robbins/Norbit
- Fred Savage/Daddy Day Camp

WORST SCREENPLAY

1980
- ★ Can't Stop the Music

1981
- ★ Mommie Dearest

1983
- ★ The Lonely Lady

1984
- ★ Bolero

1985
- ★ Rambo: First Blood, Part 2
- Rocky 4

1986
- ★ Howard the Duck

1987
- ★ Leonard Part 6

1988
- ★ Cocktail

1989
- ★ Harlem Nights

1990
- ★ The Adventures of Ford Fairlane

1991
- ★ Hudson Hawk

1992
- ★ Stop! Or My Mom Will Shoot

1993
- ★ Indecent Proposal

1994
- ★ The Flintstones

1995
- ★ Showgirls

1996
- ★ Striptease
- Barb Wire
- Ed
- The Island of Dr. Moreau
- The Stupids

1997
- ★ The Postman
- Anaconda
- Batman and Robin
- The Lost World: Jurassic Park 2
- Speed 2: Cruise Control

1998
- ★ An Alan Smithee Film: Burn, Hollywood, Burn
- Armageddon
- The Avengers
- Godzilla
- Spice World: The Movie

1999
- ★ Wild Wild West
- Big Daddy
- The Haunting
- The Mod Squad
- Star Wars: Episode 1—The Phantom Menace

2000
- ★ Battlefield Earth
- Book of Shadows: Blair Witch 2
- Dr. Seuss' How the Grinch Stole Christmas
- Little Nicky
- The Next Best Thing

2001
- ★ Freddy Got Fingered

2003
- ★ Gigli
- Charlie's Angels: Full Throttle
- Dr. Seuss' The Cat in the Hat

2004
- ★ Catwoman
- Alexander
- Superbabies: Baby Geniuses 2
- Surviving Christmas
- White Chicks

2005
- ★ Dirty Love
- Bewitched
- Deuce Bigalow: European Gigolo
- The Dukes of Hazzard
- Son of the Mask

2006
- ★ Basic Instinct 2
- BloodRayne
- Lady in the Water
- Little Man
- The Wicker Man

2007
- ★ I Know Who Killed Me
- Daddy Day Camp
- I Now Pronounce You Chuck and Larry
- Norbit

WORST SONG

1980
- ★ "The Man with Bogart's Face"/The Man with Bogart's Face

1981
- ★ "Baby Talk"/Paternity

1982
- ★ "Drinkenstein"/Rhinestone

1983
- ★ "Pumpin' and Blowin'"/Pirate Movie

1984
- ★ "The Way You Do It"/The Lonely Lady

1985
- ★ "Peace Our Life"/Rambo: First Blood, Part 2

1986
- ★ "Love or Money"/Under the Cherry Moon

1987
- ★ "I Want Your Sex"/Beverly Hills Cop 2

1988
- ★ "Jack Fresh"/Caddyshack 2

1989
- ★ "Bring Your Daughter to the Slaughter"/A Nightmare on Elm Street 5: Dream Child

1990
- ★ "He's Comin' Back (The Devil)"/Repossessed

1991
- ★ "Addams Groove"/The Addams Family

1992
- ★ "High Times, Hard Times"/Newsies

1993
- ★ "WHOOMP! There It Is"/Addams Family Values

1994
- ★ "Marry the Mole"/Thumbelina

1995
- ★ "Walk into the Wind"/Showgirls

1996
- ★ "Pussy, Pussy, Pussy (Whose Kitty Cat Are You?)"/Striptease
- "Welcome to Planet Boom!"/Barb Wire
- "Whenever There is Love"/Daylight

1997
- ★ Entire Song Score/The Postman
- "Fire Down Below"/Fire Down Below
- "How Do I Live"/Con Air
- "My Dream"/Speed 2: Cruise Control
- "The End is The Beginning is The End"/Batman and Robin

1998
- ★ "I Wanna Be Mike Ovitz!"/An Alan Smithee Film: Burn, Hollywood, Burn
- "Barney, The Song"/Barney's Great Adventure
- "I Don't Want to Miss a Thing"/Armageddon
- "Storm"/The Avengers
- "Too Much"/Spice World: The Movie

1999
- ★ "Wild Wild West"/Wild Wild West

2002
- ★ "I'm Not a Girl, Not Yet a Woman"/Crossroads

WORST NEW STAR

1981
- ★ Klinton Spilsbury/Legend of the Lone Ranger

1982
- ★ Pia Zadora/Butterfly

1983
- ★ Lou Ferrigno/Hercules

1984
- ★ Olivia D'Abo/Bolero
- Olivia D'Abo/Conan the Destroyer

1985
- ★ Brigitte Nielsen/Red Sonja
- Brigitte Nielsen/Rocky 4

1987
- ★ David Mendenhall/Over the Top

1990
- ★ Sofia Coppola/The Godfather, Part 3

1991
- ★ Vanilla Ice/Cool As Ice

1992
- ★ Pauly Shore/Encino Man

1993
- ★ Janet Jackson/Poetic Justice

1994
- ★ Anna Nicole Smith/Naked Gun 33 1/3: The Final Insult

1995
- ★ Elizabeth Berkley/Showgirls
- David Caruso/Kiss of Death
- Cindy Crawford/Fair Game
- Julia Sweeney/It's Pat: The Movie

1996
- ★ Pamela Anderson/Barb Wire
- Ellen DeGeneres/Mr. Wrong

1997
- ★ Dennis Rodman/Double Team
- Tori Spelling/The House of Yes
- Howard Stern/Private Parts
- Chris Tucker/The Fifth Element
- Chris Tucker/Money Talks

1998
- ★ Joe Eszterhas/An Alan Smithee Film: Burn, Hollywood, Burn
- ★ Jerry Springer/Ringmaster
- Barney/Barney's Great Adventure
- The Spice Girls/Spice World: The Movie
- Carrot Top/Chairman of the Board

★ = winner

Cast Index

The **Cast Index** provides a complete videography for cast members with more than one appearance on video. The listings for the actor names follow an alphabetical sort by last name (although the names appear in a first name-last name format). The videographies are listed chronologically, from most recent film to earliest appearance, making it easier to trace the development of your favorite actor's career. When a cast member appears in more than one film in the same year, these movies are listed alphabetically within the year. A (V) beside a movie title indicates voice-only work, while an (N) indicates narrator duties.

Beverly Aadland (1943-)
Assault of the Rebel Girls '59

Lee Aaker (1943-)
Courage of Rin Tin Tin, Hero of the West '55
Rin Tin Tin, Hero of the West '55
Hondo '53
Jeopardy '53
The Atomic City '52
Raiders of Sunset Pass '43

Aaliyah (1979-2001)
Queen of the Damned '02
Romeo Must Die '00

Angela Aames (1956-88)
Basic Training '86
Bachelor Party '84
The Lost Empire '83

Willie Aames (1960-)
Cut and Run '85
Paradise '82
Zapped! '82
Scavenger Hunt '79
Frankenstein '73

Caroline Aaron (1952-)
Nancy Drew '07
Grilled '06
Beyond the Sea '04
Cellular '04
A Day Without a Mexican '04
Two Days '03
Amy's O '02
Pumpkin '02
Joe Dirt '01
Never Again '01
Running Mates '00
What Planet Are You From? '00
Anywhere But Here '99
Tuesdays with Morrie '99
Primary Colors '98
Deconstructing Harry '97
Weapons of Mass Distraction '97
House Arrest '96
A Modern Affair '94
Alice '90
Edward Scissorhands '90
Crimes & Misdemeanors '89
Heartburn '86

Judith Abarbanel
The Cantor's Son '37

Silvia Abascal (1979-)
My Mother Likes Women '02

Diego Abatantuono (1955-)
I'm Not Scared '03
Children of Hannibal '98
The Best Man '97
Nirvana '97
Mediterraneo '91

Sean Abbanato
Bikini Med School '98
Bikini House Calls '96

Hiam Abbass (1960-)
The Visitor '07
The Nativity Story '06
Free Zone '05
Munich '05
Paradise Now '05
The Syrian Bride '04
A Loving Father '02

Bruce Abbott (1954-)
Melanie Darrow '97
The Prophecy 2: Ashtown '97
The Demolitionist '95
Dillinger '91
Bride of Re-Animator '89
Bad Dreams '88
Interzone '88
Trapped '89
Re-Animator '84
Summer Heat '87

Bud Abbott (1895-1974)
Dance with Me, Henry '56
Abbott and Costello Meet the Mummy '55
Abbott and Costello Meet the Keystone Kops '55
Abbott and Costello Go to Mars '53
Abbott and Costello Meet Captain Kidd '52
Abbott and Costello Meet Dr. Jekyll and Mr. Hyde '52
Jack & the Beanstalk '52
Lost in Alaska '52
Comin' Round the Mountain '51
Abbott and Costello Meet the Invisible Man '51
Abbott and Costello in the Foreign Legion '50
Africa Screams '49
Mexican Hayride '48
Abbott and Costello Meet Frankenstein '48
The Noose Hangs High '48
Buck Privates Come Home '47
The Wistful Widow of Wagon Gap '47
Little Giant '46
The Time of Their Lives '46
Abbott and Costello in Hollywood '45
Here Come the Co-Eds '45
The Naughty Nineties '45
In Society '44
Lost in a Harem '44
Hit the Ice '43
It Ain't Hay '43
Pardon My Sarong '42
Ride 'Em Cowboy '42
Rio Rita '42
Who Done It? '42
Buck Privates '41
Hold That Ghost '41
In the Navy '41
Keep 'Em Flying '41
One Night in the Tropics '40

Diahnne Abbott (1945-)
Jo Jo Dancer, Your Life is Calling '86
Love Streams '84
King of Comedy '82
New York, New York '77

John Abbott (1905-96)
The Merry Widow '52
Adventure Island '47
Anna and the King of Siam '46
Deception '46
Humoresque '46
Pursuit to Algiers '45
The Vampire's Ghost '45
Cry of the Werewolf '44
The Falcon in Hollywood '44
U-Boat Prisoner '44
Mrs. Miniver '42

Philip Abbott (1923-98)
The Fantastic World of D.C. Collins '84
Hangar 18 '80

Khalid Abdalla (1980-)
The Kite Runner '07
United 93 '06

Nassim Abdi
Secret Ballot '01

Paula Abdul (1962-)
Robots '05 (V)
Mr. Rock 'n' Roll: The Alan Freed Story '99

Kareem Abdul-Jabbar (1947-)
BASEketball '98
Rebound: The Legend of Earl "The Goat" Manigault '96
Slam Dunk Ernest '95
D2: The Mighty Ducks '94
Stephen King's The Stand '94
Purple People Eater '88
Chuck Berry: Hail! Hail! Rock 'n' Roll '87
Fletch '85
Airplane! '80
The Fish that Saved Pittsburgh '79
Game of Death '79

Hiroshi Abe (1964-)
Tokyo Raiders '00
Godzilla 2000 '99
Moon over Tao '97

Alfred Abel (1879-1937)
Metropolis '26
Dr. Mabuse, The Gambler '22
Phantom '22

Walter Abel (1898-1987)
Grace Quigley '84
The Man Without a Country '73
Silent Night, Bloody Night '73
Quick, Let's Get Married '71
Mirage '66
Raintree County '57
The Invisible Boy '57
The Indian Fighter '55
Island in the Sky '53
Curley '47
Fabulous Joe '47
Kid from Brooklyn '46
13 Rue Madeleine '46
Mr. Skeffington '44
So Proudly We Hail '43
Holiday Inn '42
Wake Island '42
Dance, Girl, Dance '40
Michael Shayne: Private Detective '40
Law of the Underworld '38
Fury '36
The Three Musketeers '35

Lionel Abelanski (1964-)
The Grand Role '04
My Wife is an Actress '01
Train of Life '98

Jim Abele (1960-)
Model Behavior '00
Student Affairs '88
Wimps '87

Tim Abell (1968-)
Miracle at Sage Creek '05
Dead Simple '01
Instinct to Kill '01
The Substitute 4: Failure is Not an Option '00
The Base '99
Rapid Assault '99
Death and Desire '97
Hybrid '97
Night Shade '97
Soldier of Fortune Inc. '97
Steel Sharks '97
Sexual Roulette '96
Attack of the 60-Foot Centerfold '95
Masseuse '95
Over the Wire '95

Ian Abercrombie (1933-)
Garfield: A Tail of Two Kitties '06
Inland Empire '06
Marilyn Hotchkiss' Ballroom Dancing & Charm School '06
Scooby-Doo 2: Monsters Unleashed '04 (V)
Rattled '96
Test Tube Teens from the Year 2000 '93
Army of Darkness '92
Zandalee '91

Abercrombie

Curse 4: The Ultimate
Sacrifice '90
Puppet Master 3: Toulon's
Revenge '90
Catacombs '89
Kicks '85
Backstairs at the White
House '79

**Keith Aberdein
(1943-)**
Smash Palace '82
Wild Horses '82

Sivi Aberg (1944-)
Dr. Death, Seeker of Souls
'73
The Killing of Sister George
'69

Abigail (1945-)
Breaking Loose '90
Adventures of Eliza Fraser
'76

**Simon Abkarian
(1962-)**
Persepolis '07 (V)
Casino Royale '06
Yes '04
Almost Peaceful '02
Ararat '02

**F. Murray Abraham
(1939-)**
The Stone Merchant '06
The Bridge of San Luis Rey
'05
Joshua '02
13 Ghosts '01
Finding Forrester '00
Excellent Cadavers '99
Muppets from Space '99
Noah's Ark '99
All New Adventures of
Laurel and Hardy: For
Love or Mummy '98
Esther '98
Star Trek: Insurrection '98
Baby Face Nelson '97
Color of Justice '97
Mimic '97
Larry McMurtry's Dead
Man's Walk '96
Looking for Richard '96
Children of the Revolution
'95
Dillinger and Capone '95
Mighty Aphrodite '95
Surviving the Game '94
By the Sword '93
Last Action Hero '93
National Lampoon's
Loaded Weapon 1 '93
Nostradamus '93
Sweet Killing '93
Mobsters '91
The Bonfire of the Vanities
'90
Beyond the Stars '89
An Innocent Man '89
Intimate Power '89
Slipstream '89
Third Solution '89
The Name of the Rose '86
Amadeus '84
Scarface '83
Madman '79
The Big Fix '78
All the President's Men '76
The Ritz '76
The Sunshine Boys '75
Prisoner of Second Avenue
'74
Serpico '73
They Might Be Giants '71

Ken Abraham
Marked for Murder '89

**Jim Abrahams
(1944-)**
Airplane! '80
Kentucky Fried Movie '77

**Jon Abrahams
(1977-)**
Bottoms Up '06
Deceit '06
House of Wax '05
Prime '05
Standing Still '05

My Boss's Daughter '03
Wes Craven Presents:
They '02
Texas Rangers '01
Boiler Room '00
Meet the Parents '00
Scary Movie '00
Bringing Out the Dead '99
Outside Providence '99
The Faculty '98
Masterminds '96
Dead Man Walking '95
Kids '95

Michele Abrams
Buffy the Vampire Slayer
'92
Cool World '92

**Andrei Abrikosov
(1906-73)**
Sword & the Dragon '56
Alexander Nevsky '38

Victoria Abril (1959-)
Swindled '04
No News from God '01
101 Reykjavik '00
Between Your Legs '99
My Father, My Mother, My
Brothers and My Sisters
'99
French Twist '95
Jimmy Hollywood '94
Kika '94
Intruso '93
High Heels '91
Lovers: A True Story '90
Tie Me Up! Tie Me Down!
'90
If They Tell You I Fell '89
Baton Rouge '88
Max, Mon Amour '86
After Darkness '85
L'Addition '85
Padre Nuestro '85
Moon in the Gutter '83
On the Line '83
I Married a Dead Man '82

Omid Abtahi
Space Chimps '08 (V)
You Don't Mess with the
Zohan '08

Yussef Abu-Warda
Kadosh '99
The Milky Way '97

**Stefano Accorsi
(1971-)**
Blame It on Fidel '06
His Secret Life '01
The Last Kiss '01
The Son's Room '00

Kirk Acevedo (1974-)
Invincible '06
Band of Brothers '01
Bait '00
Boiler Room '00
Dinner Rush '00
The Thin Red Line '98
Witness to the Mob '98
The Sunshine Boys '95

James Acheson
The Garden of Redemption
'97

Sharon Acker (1935-)
Happy Birthday to Me '81
Off Your Rocker '80
The Hanged Man '74
The Stranger '73
Lucky Jim '58

**Forrest J Ackerman
(1916-)**
Attack at the 60-Foot
Centerfold '95
Dead Alive '93
Innocent Blood '92
Hard to Die '90
The Wizard of Speed and
Time '88
Amazon Women on the
Moon '87
Curse of the Queerwolf '87
Evil Spawn '87
Aftermath '85
The Howling '81
Kentucky Fried Movie '77
Schlock '73

Dracula vs. Frankenstein
'71
Planet of Blood '66

**Leslie Ackerman
(1956-)**
Blame It on the Night '84
Shattered Vows '84
Skag '79
Young Love, First Love '79
Joy Ride to Nowhere '78
The First Nudie Musical '75
Law and Disorder '74

Joss Ackland (1928-)
Flawless '07
These Foolish Things '06
Asylum '05
A Different Loyalty '04
I'll Be There '03
K-19: The Widowmaker '02
No Good Deed '02
Passion of Mind '00
Heat of the Sun '99
Firelight '97
Swept from the Sea '97
Deadly Voyage '96
D3: The Mighty Ducks '96
Surviving Picasso '96
Citizen X '95
A Kid in King Arthur's Court
'95
Jacob '94
Miracle on 34th Street '94
Mother's Boys '94
Shameless '94
Nowhere to Run '93
The Strange Case of the
End of Civilization As We
Know It '93
The Mighty Ducks '92
Once Upon a Crime '92
Project: Shadowchaser '92
Bill & Ted's Bogus Journey
'91
Codename Kyril '91
The Object of Beauty '91
The Palermo Connection
'91
A Woman Named Jackie
'91
The Hunt for Red October
'90
Jekyll and Hyde '90
A Murder of Quality '90
Spymaker: The Secret Life
of Ian Fleming '90
Lethal Weapon 2 '89
To Kill a Priest '89
It Couldn't Happen Here '88
White Mischief '88
A Zed & Two Noughts '88
Queenie '87
The Sicilian '87
Lady Jane '85
Shadowlands '85
The Apple '80
Rough Cut '80
Tinker, Tailor, Soldier, Spy
'80
The Big Scam '79
Saint Jack '79
Silver Bears '78
Watership Down '78 (V)
Who Is Killing the Great
Chefs of Europe? '78
Royal Flash '75
The Little Prince '74
S*P*Y*S '74
Mind Snatchers '72
Cry of the Penguins '71
The House that Dripped
Blood '71
Raven '97
Against the Wall '94
Dead On '93
Love, Cheat & Steal '93
The Fear Inside '92
Memories of Me '88

Windmills of the Gods '88
Poor Little Rich Girl: The
Barbara Hutton Story '87
The Children of Times
Square '86
A Smoky Mountain
Christmas '86
Cocaine: One Man's
Seduction '83
When Your Lover Leaves
'83
Sound of Murder '82
A Gun in the House '81
And I Alone Survived '78
The Dark Secret of Harvest
Home '78

**Rodolfo Acosta
(1920-74)**
Savage Run '70
Flaming Star '60
Let No Man Write My
Epitaph '60
Drum Beat '54
Hondo '53
Yankee Buccaneer '52
Pancho Villa Returns '50

Jay Acovone (1955-)
Crash Dive '96
Opposite Corners '96
Showdown '94
Born to Run '93
The Magician '93
Quicksand: No Escape '91
Doctor Mordrid: Master of
the Unknown '90

**Acquanetta (1921-
2004)**
Grizzly Adams: The
Legend Continues '90
The Lost Continent '51
Jungle Woman '44
Captive Wild Woman '43
The Sword '38

Eddie Acuff (1908-56)
G-Men Never Forget '48
It Happened Tomorrow '44
Guadalcanal Diary '43
They Died with Their Boots
On '41
Law of the Underworld '38
The Black Legion '37

**Deborah Adair
(1952-)**
Endless Descent '90
Gore Vidal's Lincoln '88

Dick Adair
Pay or Die '83
Blind Rage '78

Phyllis Adair
Land of Hunted Men '43
Trigger Men '41

**Robert Adair (1900-
54)**
Tomb of Ligeia '64
The Obsessed '51
Seven Days to Noon '50
The Foreman Went to
France '42
Norman Conquest '53
The Face at the Window
'39
Ticket of Leave Man '37

**Ronald Adam (1896-
1979)**
Tomb of Ligeia '64
The Fifth Horseman Is Fear
'64

Amy Adams (1974-)
Miss Pettigrew Lives for a
Day '08
Charlie Wilson's War '07
Enchanted '07
The Ex '07
Underdog '07 (V)
Talladega Nights: The
Ballad of Ricky Bobby '06
Tenacious D in the Pick of
Destiny '06
Junebug '05
Standing Still '05
The Wedding Date '05
Catch Me If You Can '02
Pumpkin '02
Serving Sara '02

The Slaughter Rule '01
Psycho Beach Party '00
Cruel Intentions 2 '99
Drop Dead Gorgeous '99

**Beverly Adams
(1945-)**
The Ambushers '67
Devil's Angels '67
Torture Garden '67
Murderers' Row '66
How to Stuff a Wild Bikini
'65
Roustabout '64

**Brandon Adams
(1979-)**
MacArthur Park '01
Ghost in the Machine '93
The Sandlot '93
The People under the
Stairs '91

**Brooke Adams
(1949-)**
The Legend of Lucy Keyes
'06
The Baby-Sitters' Club '95
The Last Hit '93
The Sandlot '93
Gas Food Lodging '92
Sometimes They Come
Back '91
The Unborn '91
The Lion of Africa '87
Man on Fire '87
Almost You '85
Key Exchange '85
The Stuff '85
The Innocents Abroad '84
Dead Zone '83
Utilities '83
Tell Me a Riddle '80
Cuba '79
A Man, a Woman, and a
Bank '79
Days of Heaven '78
Invasion of the Body
Snatchers '78
Shock Waves '77
James Dean '76

Catlin Adams (1950-)
The Jazz Singer '80
The Jerk '79
Panic in Echo Park '77

**Christine Adams
(1898-)**
Eye of the Dolphin '06
Submerged '05

**Claire Adams (1898-
1978)**
The Big Parade '25
Heart's Haven '22
The Penalty '20

Don Adams (1923-)
Inspector Gadget '99 (V)
Get Smart, Again! '89
Back to the Beach '87
Jimmy the Kid '82
The Nude Bomb '80

**Dorothy Adams
(1899-1988)**
The Prodigal '55
Streets of Sin '49
The Best Years of Our
Lives '46
Laura '44
So Proudly We Hail '43

Edie Adams (1929-)
Armistead Maupin's Tales
of the City '93
Adventures Beyond Belief
'87
Shooting Stars '85
Ernie Kovacs: Between the
Laughter '84
Haunting of Harrington
House '82
Cheech and Chong's Up in
Smoke '79
Racquet '79
The Seekers '79
Evil Roy Slade '71
The Honey Pot '67
The Oscar '66
The Best Man '64
Call Me Bwana '63
It's a Mad, Mad, Mad, Mad
World '63
Love with the Proper
Stranger '63

Under the Yum-Yum Tree
'63
Lover Come Back '61
The Apartment '60

**Ernie Adams (1885-
1946)**
Son of Zorro '47
Sagebrush Law '43
Wings over the Pacific '43
Arizona Gunfighter '37
Gun Lords of Stirrup Basin
'37
Lightning Bill Crandall '37
Ridin' the Lone Trail '37
The Gun Ranger '34
Breed of the Border '33
Galloping Romeo '33
Beyond the Rockies '32
The Tip-Off '31
The Fighting Legion '30
Nevada '27

Evan Adams (1966-)
The Business of
Fancydancing '02
Smoke Signals '98
Lost in the Barrens '91

Jane Adams (1921-)
The Brute Man '46
House of Dracula '45
Lost City of the Jungle '45

Jane Adams (1965-)
Last Holiday '06
Jesse Stone: Stone Cold
'05
Eternal Sunshine of the
Spotless Mind '04
Orange County '02
The Anniversary Party '01
Wonder Boys '00
Mumford '99
Songcatcher '99
A Texas Funeral '99
Day at the Beach '98
Happiness '98
Music from Another Room
'97
Father of the Bride Part 2
'95
Kansas City '95
I Love Trouble '94
Rising Son '90
Vital Signs '90

**Joey Lauren Adams
(1971-)**
The Break-Up '06
Bunny Whipped '06
The Big Empty '04
The Gunman '03
Dr. Dolittle 2 '01 (V)
Harvard Man '01
In the Shadows '01
Jay and Silent Bob Strike
Back '01
Beautiful '00
Big Daddy '99
The Dress Code '99
A Cool, Dry Place '98
Chasing Amy '97
Bio-Dome '96
Mallrats '95
Black Roses '88

The Killer Inside Me '76
The McCullochs '75
Psychic Killer '75
McQ '74
The Last Movie '71
The Trackers '71
Tickle Me '65
The Gunfight at Dodge City
'59
Away All Boats '56
The Private War of Major
Benson '55
Creature from the Black
Lagoon '54
Francis Joins the WACs '54
Man from the Alamo '53
Horizons West '52
The Lawless Breed '52

Blazing Guns '50
Last Bullet '50
Outlaw Fury '50
Sudden Death '50

Ted Adams (1890-1973)
Outlaw Country '49
Billy the Kid '41

Whiskers '96
Steve Adams (1939-)
The Blue Butterfly '04
Strange Fits of Passion '99

Stanley Adams (1915-77)
The Passing of Evil '70
Thunder Alley '67
Lilies of the Field '63
Requiem for a Heavyweight '62

The Juror '96
Celebrity '98
People I Know '02
Uptown Girls '03
United 93 '06

Polly Adams
Mosby's Marauders '66
Mission: Mars '67
'68
Nick Adams (1931-68)
Godzilla vs. Monster Zero '68
Mister Roberts '55
Picnic '55
Our Miss Brooks '56
Teacher's Pet '58
No Time for Sergeants '58
Pillow Talk '59
The FBI Story '59
The Interns '62
Hell Is for Heroes '62
Die, Monster, Die! '65
Killer Force '75
Rollerball '75

Lynne Adams
Dangerous Liaisons '03
Requiem for Murder '99
Time at the Top '99
Psychopath '97
The Ultimate Weapon '97
Silent Hunter '94
The Carpenter '89
Blood Relations '87
Night Zoo '87
Mason Adams (1919-2005)
From the Earth to the Moon '98
Touch '96
Houseguest '94
Son-in-Law '93
F/X '86
Rage of Angels: The Story Continues '86
-alf Slave, Half Free '85
Adam '83
The Kid with the Broken Halo '82
The Final Conflict '81
Revenge of the Stepford Wives '80
Maud Adams (1945-)
Silent Night, Deadly Night 4: Initiation '90
The Kill Reflex '89
Intimate Power '89
Angel 3: The Final Chapter '88
Deadly Intent '88
A Man of Passion '88
Nairobi Affair '88
Hell Hunters '87
Jane & the Lost City '87
Women's Club '87
Target Eagle '84
Octopussy '83
Tattoo '81
The Hostage Tower '80
Playing for Time '80
Rollerball '75
Killer Force '75
The Girl in Blue '74
The Man with the Golden Gun '74

Tracey Adams
See Deborah Blaisdell
Tom Adams (1938-)
License to Kill '89
Fast Kill '73
The House that Dripped Blood '71
Subterfuge '68
Fathom '67
The Fighting Prince of Donegal '66
Where the Bullets Fly '66
Second Best Secret Agent in the Whole Wide World '65
The Great Escape '63
George Adamson (1906-89)
Christian the Lion '76
An Elephant Called Slowly '69
Chris(topher) Adamson
Masters of Horror '06
Masters of Horror: Pelts '06
Tenacious D in the Pick of Destiny '06
Crazy Love '05
Chasing Ghosts '05
Destiny '06
Formula 51 '01
Rustin '01
Crazy in Alabama '99
Fight Club '99
Black Dog '98
Everything That Rises '98
The Mighty '98
Outside Ozona '98
Spice World: The Movie '97
To Catch a Yeti '95
A Hole in One '04
The Salton Sea '02
Focus '01

Meat Loaf Aday (1948-)
BloodRayne '06
Masters of Horror '06
Van Nuys Blvd. '79
Blue Sunshine '78
Pom Pom Girls '76
Roadie '80
Americathon '79
Charles Adler
Switchblade Sisters '75
Tiny Toon Adventures: How I Spent My Vacation '91 (V)

Bill Adler
First Do No Harm '97
Stir '98
Gepetto '00
Resident Evil: Apocalypse '04
Haven '04
Cover '08
Doom '05
Seth Adkins (1989-)
The Story of Adele H. '75
The Slap '75
Barocco '76
The Driver '78
The Tenant '76
Jerry Adler (1929-)
Find Me Guilty '06
In Her Shoes '05
Six Ways to Sunday '99
Manhattan Murder Mystery '93
The Public Eye '92
Jay Adler (1896-1978)
Stage Struck '36
Infamous Crimes '47
The Paleface '48
The Stork Club '45
Carnival Rock '57
The Fast and the Furious '54
G.I. Jane '51
Stop That Cab '51
Hi-Jacked '50
The Lovable Cheat '49
Crime of Passion '57
The Killing '56
Van Gogh? (The Squeeze '87 / Fee the Motion '86 — see above)
Anthony Addabbo (1960-)
A Place Called Truth '98
Red Shoe Diaries 5: Weekend Pass '95
The Gunfighters '87
Dawn Adams (1930-85)
Vault of Horror '73
The Vampire Lovers '70
Zeta One '69
Ballad in Blue '66
Where the Bullets Fly '66
The Liars '64

Isabelle Adjani (1955-)
Bon Voyage '03
Monsieur Ibrahim '03
Diabolique '96
Queen Margot '94
Camille Claudel '89
Ishtar '87
Subway '85
Next Year If All Goes Well '83
One Deadly Summer '83
Possession '81
Quartet '81
Nosferatu the Vampyre '79
Paul Adelstein (1969-)
Be Cool '05
Intolerable Cruelty '03
Mario Adorf (1930-)
The Michigan Kid '29
The Big Parade '25
Renee Adoree (1898-1933)
Smilla's Sense of Snow '96
The Holcroft Covenant '85
Invitation au Voyage '82
Milo Milo '79
The Tin Drum '79
The Lost Honor of Katharina Blum '75
Hired to Kill '73
Hit Men '73
Manhunt '73
Short Night of Glass Dolls '71
The Bird with the Crystal Plumage '70
Brainwashed '60

Raz Adoti
Doom '05
Frank Adonis (1935-)
Suicide Ride '97
True Romance '93
Sarah Adler
Our Music '04
Edvin Adolphson (1893-1979)
Year Zero '04
Boy of Two Worlds '70
Only One Night '42
Dollar '38
The Count of the Old Town '34

Mark Addy (1963-)
Around the World in 80 Days '04
The Order '03
The Time Machine '02
Down to Earth '01
A Knight's Tale '01
The Flintstones in Viva Rock Vegas '00
Jack Frost '98
The Full Monty '97
Nancy Addison (1948-2002)
Somewhere Tomorrow '85
Robert Addie (1960-2003)
Captain Jack '98
A Knight in Camelot '98
Another Country '84
Excalibur '81
Milo Addica
Birth '04
Monster's Ball '01
Luther Adler (1903-84)
Absence of Malice '81
Voyage of the Damned '76
The Man in the Glass Booth '75
Mean Johnny Barrows '75
Murph the Surf '75
The Brotherhood '68
The Three Sisters '66
The Last Angry Man '59
Crashout '55
The Girl in the Red Velvet Swing '55
The Desert Fox '51
Hoodlum Empire '52
Kiss Tomorrow Goodbye '50
D.O.A. '49
House of Strangers '49
Wake of the Red Witch '48
The Loves of Carmen '48
Cornered '45
Wesley Addy (1913-96)
Hiroshima '95
A Modern Affair '94
North Shore '87
White Water Summer '87
Flight of the Navigator '86
The Bostonians '84
The Verdict '82
The Europeans '79
Network '76
The Grissom Gang '71
Tora! Tora! Tora! '70
Seconds '66
The Big Knife '55
Kiss Me Deadly '55
Matt Adler (1966-)
Pearl Harbor '01
Boiler Room '00
Bounce '00
Reindeer Games '00
Glory Daze '96
Mallrats '95
North Shore '87
Doin' Time on Planet Earth '88

Joanna Adler
The Thousand Eyes of Dr. Mabuse '60
The Two Faces of Dr. Jekyll '60
The Event '03
Luther Adler (1903-84) *(see above)*
Patricia Adriani (1958-)
I'm the One You're Looking For '88
The Nest '80
Ljubica Adzovic
Black Cat, White Cat '98
Time of the Gypsies '90
Ben Affleck (1972-)
He's Just Not That into You '08
Smokin' Aces '07
Clerks 2 '06
Hollywoodland '06
Jersey Girl '04
Surviving Christmas '04
Daredevil '03
Gigli '03
Paycheck '03
Changing Lanes '02
The Sum of All Fears '02
The Third Wheel '02
Jay and Silent Bob Strike Back '01
Pearl Harbor '01
Boiler Room '00
Bounce '00
Reindeer Games '00
Daddy & Them '99
Dogma '99
Forces of Nature '99
Armageddon '98
Shakespeare in Love '98
200 Cigarettes '98
Phantoms '97
Good Will Hunting '97
Chasing Amy '97
Going All the Way '97
Glory Daze '96
Mallrats '95
Dazed and Confused '93
Buffy the Vampire Slayer '92
School Ties '92

Casey Affleck (1975-)
The Assassination of Jesse James by the Coward Robert Ford '07
Gone Baby Gone '07
Ocean's Thirteen '07
The Last Kiss '06
Lonesome Jim '06
Ocean's Twelve '04
Gerry '02
American Pie 2 '01
Ocean's Eleven '01
Soul Survivors '01
Drowning Mona '00
Hamlet '00
Attention Shoppers '99
Committed '99
Desert Blue '98
200 Cigarettes '98
Good Will Hunting '97
Race the Sun '96
To Die For '95
John Agar (1921-2002)
Body Bags '93
Invasion of Privacy '92
The Perfect Bride '91
Fear '90
Miracle Mile '89
Perfect Victims '87
King Kong '76
Big Jake '71
Chisum '70
The Undefeated '69
Hell Raiders '68
The St. Valentine's Day Massacre '67
Curse of the Swamp Creature '66
Johnny Reno '66
Women of the Prehistoric Planet '66
Zontar, the Thing from Venus '66
Cavalry Command '63
Invisible Invaders '59
Attack of the Puppet People '58
People '58

Patricia Adriani (1958-) *(see above)*
Ben Affleck (1972-) *(see above)*
Suzanne Ager
Fatal Justice '93
Evil Toons '90
Shohreh Aghdashloo (1952-)
Sisterhood of the Traveling Pants 2 '08
American Dreamz '06
The Lake House '06
The Nativity Story '06
X-Men: The Last Stand '06
The Exorcism of Emily Rose '05
House of Sand and Fog '03
Maryam '00
Teitchie Agbayani
Fort Apache '48
Tarantula '55
Along the Great Divide '51
Sands of Iwo Jima '49
She Wore a Yellow Ribbon '49
Revenge of the Creature '55
Lonesome Trail '55
The Mole People '56
Flesh and the Spur '57
George Aguilar
Lunatics: A Love Story '92
Janet Agren (1949-)
Deathtrap '83
Rikky and Pete '88
Mission Manila '87
Gymkata '85
Night of the Sharks '87
Hands of Steel '86
Aladdin '86
Emerald Jungle '80
Gates of Hell '80
Kris Aguilar
Karate Warrior '88
Magdalene '88
The Nativity Story '06
Jenny Agutter (1952-)
Lunatics: A Love Story '92
The Buccaneers '95
Child's Play 2 '90
Darkman '90
Dark Tower '87
Secret Places '85
Silas Marner '85
An American Werewolf in London '81
Amy '81
Survivor '80
Dominique Is Dead '79
Sweet William '79
Mayflower: The Pilgrims' Adventure '79
The Eagle Has Landed '77
Equus '77
The Man in the Iron Mask '77
Logan's Run '76
The Riddle of the Sands '79
The Railway Children '70
Walkabout '71

Pierre Agostino
Las Vegas Serial Killer '86
The Hollywood Strangler Meets the Skid Row Slasher '79
The Uranium Conspiracy '78
Panic '76
Perfect Crime '79
George Aguilar *(see above)*
Max Adrian (1903-73)
The Boy Friend '71
The Devils '71
The Music Lovers '71
Dr. Terror's House of Horrors '65
Henry V '44
Brian Aherne (1902-86)
Sword of Lancelot '63
Waltz King '63
The Swan '56
A Bullet Is Waiting '54
Prince Valiant '54
I Confess '53
Titanic '53
The Best of Everything '59
Star! '68
The Brain from Planet Arous '57
The Daughter of Dr. Jekyll '57

Forever and a Day '43
A Night to Remember '42
Smilin' Through '41
The Lady in Question '40
My Son, My Son '40
Beloved Enemy '36
I Live My Life '35
Sylvia Scarlett '35
The Song of Songs '33

Borje Ahlstedt (1939-)
Sunday's Children '94
Emma's Shadow '88
I Am Curious (Yellow) '67

Ahmed Ahmed
Iron Man '08

Philip Ahn (1911-78)
Paradise, Hawaiian Style '66
Shock Corridor '63
Battle Hymn '57
Battle Circus '53
His Majesty O'Keefe '53
Impact '49
Back to Bataan '45
They Were Expendable '45
Betrayal from the East '44
China Sky '44
The Story of Dr. Wassell '44
China '43
Across the Pacific '42
Drums of Fu Manchu '40
Hawaii Calls '38
Thank you, Mr. Moto '37
The General Died at Dawn '36

Countdown '68
Hour of the Gun '67
Pork Chop Hill '59

Sung-Ki Ahn (1952-)
White Badge '97

Charles Aidman (1925-93)
Prime Suspect '82
Zoot Suit '81
House of the Dead '78
Zone of the Dead '78
The Barbary Coast '74
The Invasion of Carol Enders '74
Picture of Dorian Gray '74
Adam at 6 a.m. '70
Menace on the Mountain '70

Danny Aiello (1933-)
Lucky Number Slevin '06
Brooklyn Lobster '05
Dinner Rush '00
Mambo Cafe '00
Prince of Central Park '00
Hitman's Journal '99
Dead Silence '98
The Last Don 2 '98
Me and the Kid '93
The Pickle '93
Ruby '92
The Closer '91
Hudson Hawk '91
Mistress '91
Once Around '91
29th Street '91
Jacob's Ladder '90
Do the Right Thing '89
Harlem Nights '89
The January Man '89
The Preppie Murder '89
Third Solution '89
White Hot '88
Alone in the Neon Jungle '87
Man on Fire '87

Moonstruck '87
The Pick-Up Artist '87
Radio Days '87
Key Exchange '85
Protector '85
The Purple Rose of Cairo '85
The Stuff '85
Old Enough '84
Once Upon a Time in America '84
When Angels Fly '84
Chu Chu & the Philly Flash '81
Fort Apache, the Bronx '81
Hide in Plain Sight '80
Question of Honor '80
Defiance '79
Bloodbrothers '78
Fingers '78
The Front '76
Hooch '76
The Godfather, Part 2 '74
Bang the Drum Slowly '73
Deathmask '69

Rick Aiello (1958-)
Brooklyn Lobster '05
Hollywood Confidential '97
Endangered '94
Uncivilized '94
The Closer '91
Jungle Fever '91
29th Street '91

Elaine Aiken (1927-98)
Caddyshack '80
Lonely Man '57

Liam Aiken (1990-)
Fay Grim '06
Lemony Snicket's A Series of Unfortunate Events '04
Good Boy! '03
Road to Perdition '02
Sweet November '01
I Dreamed of Africa '00
Stepmom '98

Anouk Aimee (1932-)
Happily Ever After '04
Napoleon '03
Festival at Cannes '02
Solomon '98
Ready to Wear '94
Dr. Bethune '90
A Man and a Woman: 20 Years Later '86
Success Is the Best Revenge '84
The Tragedy of a Ridiculous Man '81
Justine '69
A Man and a Woman '66
8 1/2 '63
Sodom and Gomorrah '62
Lola '61
La Dolce Vita '60
Modigliani '58
Paris Express '53
The Golden Salamander '51

Anthony Ainley (1932-2004)
The Land That Time Forgot '75

Richard Ainley (1910-67)
Above Suspicion '43
I Dood It '43
White Cargo '42

Holly Aird (1969-)
Scenes of a Sexual Nature '06
Possession '02
The Criminal '00
Dreaming of Joseph Lees '99

Andrew Airlie
Common Ground '00
Hard Evidence '94

Maria Aitken (1945-)
Grave Indiscretions '96

A Fish Called Wanda '88

Spottiswoode Aitken (1868-1933)
The Americano '17
The Birth of a Nation '15

Michael Aitkens (1947-)
Moving Targets '87

Franklin Ajaye (1949-)
The Highest Honor '84
American Yakuza '94
The Wrong Guys '88
Fraternity Vacation '85
Get Crazy '83
The Jazz Singer '80
Convoy '78
Car Wash '76

Denis Akayama
My Baby's Daddy '04
Killing Moon '00
Johnny Mnemonic '95

Chantal Akerman (1950-)
News from Home '76 (N)
Je Tu Il Elle '74

Malin Akerman (1978-)
27 Dresses '08
The Brothers Solomon '07
The Heartbreak Kid '07
The Invasion '07

Andra Akers (1944-2002)
Desert Hearts '86
E. Nick: A Legend in His Own Mind '84

Karen Akers (1945-)
Heartburn '86
The Purple Rose of Cairo '85

Lucy Akhurst (1975-)
Don't Tell '05
The Land Girls '98

Hano Aki
Rebirth of Mothra 2 '97
Rebirth of Mothra '96

Adewale Akinnuoye-Agbaje (1967-)
Get Rich or Die Tryin' '05
The Mistress of Spices '05
Monster in the Closet '86
Pecos Bill '86
The Concrete Cowboys '79
The Bourne Identity '02
The Mummy Returns '01
Lip Service '00
Legionnaire '98

Claude Akins (1918-94)
The Gambler Returns: The Luck of the Draw '93
Falling from Grace '92
The Curse '87
Manhunt for Claude Dallas '86
The Death Squad '73
The Norliss Tapes '73
A Man Called Sledge '71
The Night Stalker '71
The Devil's Brigade '68
Waterhole Number 3 '67
Return of the Magnificent Seven '66
The Killers '64
Merrill's Marauders '62
Comanche Station '60
Inherit the Wind '60
Rio Bravo '59
The Kettles on Old MacDonald's Farm '57
Sea Chase '55
The Caine Mutiny '54
From Here to Eternity '53

Carl Alacchi
Taken '99
The Pianist '91

Marc Alaimo (1942-)
The Fence '94
Quicksand: No Escape '91
Arena '89
Tango and Cash '89
Archer: The Fugitive from the Empire '81

Steve Alaimo (1939-)
Alligator Alley '72
Wild Rebels '71
The Hooked Generation '69

Craig Alan
Endangered '94
Sex Crimes '92

Nelly Alard
Venice, Venice '92
Eating '90

Joe Alaskey (1949-)
Looney Tunes: Back in Action '03 (V)
The Rugrats Movie '98 (V)
Casper '95 (V)
Bank Robber '93
Tiny Toon Adventures: How I Spent My Vacation '91 (V)

Jessica Alba (1981-)
Lucky Stiff '88
The Eye '08
The Love Guru '08
Awake '07
Fantastic Four: Rise of the Silver Surfer '07
Good Luck Chuck '07
The Ten '07
Fantastic Four '05
Into the Blue '05
Sin City '05
Honey '03

Maria Alba (1910-99)
Chandu on the Magic Island '34
Return of Chandu '34
Mr. Robinson Crusoe '32

Javier Albala (1969-)
Between Your Legs '99
Second Skin '99
Zafarinas '94

Carlo Alban (1979-)
Strangers with Candy '06
The Tavern '00

Captain Lou Albano (1933-)
Complex World '92
Body Slam '87
Wise Guys '86

John Albasiny
Have No Fear: The Life of Pope John Paul II '05
Kipperbang '82

Josh Albee
The Runaways '75
The Adventures of Tom Sawyer '73

Kevin Alber (1963-)
Alien Terminator '95
The Showgirl Murders '95

Anna Maria Alberghetti (1936-)
Friends and Family '01
The Whole Shebang '01
Cinderella '60
The Last Command '55
Here Comes the Groom '51
The Medium '51

Luis Alberni (1887-1962)
Harvest Melody '43
The Great Man Votes '38
Hats Off '37
Dancing Pirate '36
Goodbye Love '34
One Night of Love '34
Man from Monterey '33
The Sphinx '33
The Big Stampede '32

Hans Albers (1892-1960)
Die Grosse Freiheit Nr. 7 '45

Baron Munchausen '43
F.P. 1 Doesn't Answer '33
The Blue Angel '30

Eddie Albert (1906-2005)
The Big Picture '89
Out of Sight, Out of Her Mind '89
The Victory '88
Turnaround '87
Brenda Starr '86
Dress Gray '86
Head Office '86
Stitches '85
Burning Rage '84
Dreamscape '84
The Act '82
Yes, Giorgio '82
Goliath Awaits '81
Peter and Paul '81
Take This Job & Shove It '81
Beulah Land '80
Foolin' Around '80
How to Beat the High Cost of Living '80
The Concorde: Airport '79 '79
The Birch Interval '78
The Crash of Flight 401 '78
The Word '78
Moving Violation '76
Devil's Rain '75
Escape to Witch Mountain '75
Whiffs '75
The Longest Yard '74
McQ '74
Fireball Forward '72
The Heartbreak Kid '72
Captain Newman, M.D. '63
The Miracle of the White Stallions '63
Who's Got the Action? '63
The Longest Day '62
Beloved Infidel '59
Attack! '56
The Teahouse of the August Moon '56
I'll Cry Tomorrow '55
Oklahoma! '55
Roman Holiday '53
Actors and Sin '52
Carrie '52
The Fuller Brush Girl '50
You Gotta Stay Happy '48
Smash-Up: The Story of a Woman '47
The Perfect Marriage '46
Bombardier '43
The Wagons Roll at Night '41

Edward Albert (1951-2006)
Extreme Honor '01
Mimic 2 '01
Ablaze '00
The Man in the Iron Mask '97
The Secret Agent Club '96
Space Marines '96
Guarding Tess '94
Hard Drive '94
Red Sun Rising '94
Sorceress '94
Broken Trust '93
The Ice Runner '93
Sexual Malice '93
Shootfighter: Fight to the Death '93
Body Language '92
Exiled in America '90
Accidents '89
Wild Zone '89
Mind Games '89
Fist Fighter '88
The Rescue '88
The Underachievers '88
Distortions '87
Terminal Entry '87
Getting Even '86
Ellie '84
Time to Die '83
Butterfly '82
House Where Evil Dwells '82
Galaxy of Terror '81
The Squeeze '80

When Time Ran Out '80
Silent Victory: The Kitty O'Neil Story '79
The Greek Tycoon '78
The Rip Off '78
The Domino Principle '77
The Purple Taxi '77
Death Cruise '74
Forty Carats '73
Butterflies Are Free '72
The Fool Killer '65

Laura Albert
Blood Games '90

Marv Albert (1941-)
Death by Dialogue '88
The Unnamable '88
The Cookout '04

Shari Albert (1971-)
Remo Williams: The Adventure Begins '85
The Groomsmen '06

Giorgio Albertazzi (1923-)
Eva '62
Last Year at Marienbad '61

Guido Alberti (1909-96)
Ten Days Wonder '72
Casanova '70 '65

Giampiero Albertini (1927-91)
Life of Verdi '82
Zorro '74
Commandos '73
The Case of the Bloody Iris '72
Return of Sabata '71
Burn! '70

Frank Albertson (1909-64)
Psycho '60
Nightfall '56
Killer Dill '47
It's a Wonderful Life '46
Junior G-Men of the Air '42
Underground Agent '42
Wake Island '42
Burma Convoy '41
Louisiana Purchase '41
Man Made Monster '41
Room Service '38
Navy Blue and Gold '37
Fury '36
Ah, Wilderness! '35
Alice Adams '35
Hollywood Mystery '34
Rainbow over Broadway '33
Way Back Home '32
Big Business Girl '31
A Connecticut Yankee '31

Jack Albertson (1907-81)
Charlie and the Great Balloon Chase '82
Dead and Buried '81
The Fox and the Hound '81 (V)
Marriage Is Alive and Well '80
The Poseidon Adventure '72
Where the Eagle Files '72
Willy Wonka & the Chocolate Factory '71
Changes '69
Justine '69
The Subject Was Roses '68
Flim-Flam Man '67
How to Murder Your Wife '64
Kissin' Cousins '64
The Patsy '64
Roustabout '64
Who's Got the Action? '63
Days of Wine and Roses '62
Period of Adjustment '62
Lover Come Back '61
Never Steal Anything Small '59
Teacher's Pet '58
Miracle on 34th Street '47

Mabel Albertson (1901-82)
Barefoot in the Park '67
Ma and Pa Kettle at Waikiki '55

Karl Otto Alberty (1933-)
Battle of the Bulge '65
The Great Escape '63

Jens Albinus
The Boss of It All '06
The Idiots '99

Ariauna Albright (1969-)
Mom's Outta Sight '01
Ancient Evil: Scream of the Mummy '00
Witchouse 2: Blood Coven '00
Witchouse '99

Dan Albright
Bobby Jones: Stroke of Genius '04
I Know What You Did Last Summer '97
To Dance with the White Dog '93

Hardie Albright (1903-75)
Mom & Dad '47
The Jade Mask '45
Sunset in El Dorado '45
Bambi '42 (V)
Champagne for Breakfast '35

Lola Albright (1924-)
Where Were You, When the Lights Went Out? '68
The Way West '67
Lord Love a Duck '66
Joy House '64
Kid Galahad '62
The Monolith Monsters '57
The Tender Trap '55
Champion '49

Wally Albright (1925-99)
Rock All Night '57
Vengeance '37
Law of the Sea '32

Chris Alcaide (1923-2004)
Jupiter's Darling '55

Damian Alcazar (1953-)
Cronicas '04
And Starring Pancho Villa as Himself '03
The Crime of Father Amaro '02

Victor Alcocer (1917-84)
Hombres Armados '97
Pistoleros Asesinos '87
It Happened at Nightmare Inn '70

Alan Alda (1936-)
Resurrecting the Champ '07
The Aviator '04
Club Land '01
The Killing Yard '01
What Women Want '00
The Object of My Affection '98
Mad City '97
Murder at 1600 '97
Everyone Says I Love You '96
Flirting with Disaster '95
Canadian Bacon '94
White Mile '94
And the Band Played On '93
Manhattan Murder Mystery '93
Whispers in the Dark '92
Betsy's Wedding '90
Crimes & Misdemeanors '89
A New Life '88
Sweet Liberty '86
M*A*S*H: Goodbye, Farewell & Amen '83
The Four Seasons '81
The Seduction of Joe Tynan '79
California Suite '78
Same Time, Next Year '78
The Glass House '72
Playmates '72
To Kill a Clown '72
The Mephisto Waltz '71
Jenny '70
Paper Lion '68
Gone Are the Days '63

Antony Alda (1956-)
The Killing Device '92
Homeboy '88

Robert Alda (1914-86)
The Squeeze '80
Express to Terror '79
Every Girl Should Have One '78
The Rip Off '78
Bittersweet Love '76
I Will, I Will for Now '76
Lisa and the Devil '75
Night Flight from Moscow '73
The Devil's Hand '61
Force of Impulse '60
Revenge of the Barbarians '60
Cloak and Dagger '46
The Man I Love '46
Rhapsody in Blue '45

Rutanya Alda (1945-)
Murder Without Conviction '04
The Souler Opposite '97
The Ref '93
Article 99 '92
Prancer '89
Black Widow '87
Girls Night Out '83
Vigilante '83
Amityville 2: The Possession '82
Mommie Dearest '81
Christmas Evil '80
When a Stranger Calls '79
The Deer Hunter '78
The Fury '78
Scarecrow '73

Mary Alden (1883-1946)
Strange Interlude '32
April Fool '26
The Birth of a Nation '15

Norman Alden (1924-)
Ben '72
Total To'al To'al '70
The Devil's Brigade '68
Good Times '67
The Patsy '64
The Nutty Professor '63
The Sword in the Stone '63

Priscilla Alden (1939-2007)
Death Nurse '87
Crazy Fat Ethel II '85
Criminally Insane '75

John Alderman (1933-87)
The Alpha Incident '76
Little Miss Innocence '73

John Alderman
Love Desperados '68
The Quest '96

Erville Alderson (1882-1957)
Objective, Burma! '45
Sergeant York '41
Sally of the Sawdust '25
America '24

John Alderton (1940-)
Calendar Girls '03

Aki Aleong (1934-)
Sci-Fighter '04
Missing Brendan '03
Perfect Assassins '98
Lewis and Clark and George '97
Braddock: Missing in Action 3 '88
On Edge '03 — Hanoi Hilton '87
The Monster Demolisher '60

Julio Aleman (1933-)
The Green Wall '70

Jason Alexander (1959-)
How to Go Out on a Date in Queens '06
Ira & Abby '06
Shallow Hal '01
The Trumpet of the Swan '01 (V)
The Adventures of Rocky & Bullwinkle '00
Love and Action in Chicago '99
Something About Sex '98
Cinderella '97

John Ales (1969-)
Life of the Party '05
Burning Down the House '01
Uprising '01
Nutty Professor 2: The Klumps '00
Ride with the Devil '99

Sarah Alexander (1971-)
Stardust '07
I Could Never Be Your Woman '06

Sasha Alexander (1973-)
Mission: Impossible 3 '06
All Over the Guy '01

Tom Aldredge (1928-)
The Assassination of Jesse James by the Coward Robert Ford '07
Cold Mountain '03
Intolerable Cruelty '03
Message in a Bottle '98
Rounders '98
A Stranger in the Kingdom '98
Commandments '96
Lawn Dogs '96
Andersonville '95
Harvest of Fire '95
The Adventures of Huck Finn '93
O Pioneers! '91
Other People's Money '91
What about Bob? '91
Puddnhead Wilson '84
Gentleman Bandit '81
The Rain People '69

Rhonda Aldrich
Jailbird Rock '88
Saturday the 14th Strikes Back '88

Kay Aldridge (1917-95)
The Phantom of 42nd Street '45
Haunted Harbor '44
Nyoka and the Tigermen '42

Kitty Aldridge (1962-)
Down Argentine Way '40 — no
American Roulette '88
Slipstream '89

Michael Aldridge (1920-94)
Bullshot '83
Tinker, Tailor, Soldier, Spy '80

Norma Aleandro (1936-)
Love for Lydia '79
Live-in Maid '04
The Son of the Bride '01
Autumn Sun '98
One Man's War '90
Vital Signs '90
Cousins '89
Gaby: A True Story '87
The Official Story '85

Mari Aldon (1925-2004)
Race for Life '55
Summertime '55
Distant Drums '51

Ben Alexander (1911-69)
Hired to Kill '91
Dragnet '54
Criminals Within '41
The Western Code '36
Are These Our Parents? '44
All Quiet on the Western Front '30
Hearts of the World '18
Little Orphant Annie '18

Elizabeth (Liz) Alexander (1952-)
The Little American '17

Flex Alexander (1970-)
The Hills Have Eyes 2 '07
Poor Man's Game '06
Snakes on a Plane '06
Arsenic and Old Lace '44

Jane Alexander (1939-)
Feast of Love '07
Fur: An Imaginary Portrait of Diane Arbus '06
The Ring '02
Sunshine State '02
The Cider House Rules '99
A Friendship in Vienna '88
Square Dance '87
Sweet Country '87
City Heat '84
Calamity Jane '82
In the Custody of Strangers '82
Lovey: A Circle of Children '82
Night Crossing '81
Brubaker '80
Playing for Time '80
Kramer vs. Kramer '79
The Betsy '78
A Question of Love '78
Eleanor & Franklin '76
Eleanor & Franklin: The White House Years '76
Death Be Not Proud '75
The New Centurions '72
A Gunfight '71
The Great White Hope '70

Erika Alexander (1969-)
Deja Vu '06
Love Liza '02
30 Years to Life '01
Scalp Merchant '77
Blacksmith '78 — no

Jace Alexander (1964-)
Love and a .45 '94
City of Hope '91
Mistress '91
Matewan '87
Eight Men Out '88
Glory '89
Crocodile Dundee 2 '88

Khandi Alexander (1957-)
Rain '05
Dark Blue '03
Killing Emmett Young '02
The Corner '00
There's Something about Mary '98
Thick as Thieves '99
Greedy '94
Sugar Hill '94
CB4: The Movie '93
What's Love Got to Do with It? '93

Katherine Alexander (1898-1981)
On the Sunny Side '42
Dance, Girl, Dance '40
The Great Man Votes '38
That Certain Woman '37
The Barretts of Wimpole Street '34
Death Takes a Holiday '34

John Alexander (1897-1982)
The Marrying Kind '52
Fancy Pants '50
Where There's Life '47
The Jolson Story '46
The Horn Blows at Midnight '45
A Tree Grows in Brooklyn '45
Mr. Skeffington '44

Jeff Alexander (1910-89)
Twisted Brain '74
Curse of the Swamp Creature '66

Richard Alexander (1902-89)
The Kansas Terrors '39
Renfrew on the Great White Trail '38
S.O.S. Coast Guard '37
Daring Danger '32
Scarlet Dawn '32
Texas Bad Man '32
All Quiet on the Western Front '30

Ross Alexander (1907-37)
Captain Blood '35
A Midsummer Night's Dream '35
Flirtation Walk '34

Peter Alexander
Seamless '00
Color of a Brisk and Leaping Day '95

Muhammad Ali (1942-)
Doin' Time '85
Body & Soul '81
Freedom Road '79
The Greatest '77
Requiem for a Heavyweight '62 — no

Tatyana Ali (1979-)
Nora's Hair Salon 2: A Cut Above '08
Nora's Hair Salon '04
Back in the Day '05
The Brothers '01

Mary Alice (1941-)
The Matrix Revolutions '03
Sunshine State '02
Laurel Avenue '93
Down in the Delta '98
Catfish in Black Bean Sauce '00
He Who Walks Alone '78
The Women of Brewster Place '89

Barbara Lee (Niven) Alexander (1953-)
Psycho Cop 2 '94
Illegal Entry: Formula for Fear '93

Terence Alexander (1923-)
Waterloo '71
What's Good for the Goose '69

Terry Alexander (1947-)
The Runaway Bus 54
Conspiracy Theory '97
Hurricane Streets '96
Amateur '92
Day of the Dead '85

Manuel Alexandre (1917-)
Two Tough Guys '03

Tiana Alexandra
Catch the Heat '87

Charlotta Alexandra
Good-bye, Emmanuelle '77
A Real Young Girl '75

Kristian Alfonso (1964-)
Army of One '94
Blindfold: Acts of Obsession '94

Phillip Alford (1948-)
Shenandoah '65
To Kill a Mockingbird '62

David Alford
The Second Chance '06
A Death in the Family '02

Chuck Alford
The Hollywood Strangler Meets the Skid Row Slasher '79

Lidia Alfonsi (1928-)
Life Is Beautiful '93
Open Doors '89
Black Sabbath '64
The Trojan Horse '62
The Horror Show '89 — no

Hans Alfredson (1931-)
Commando Squad '76
Splendor '35
The Adventures of Picasso '80
The New Land '73
Fippo on the Run '70

Mark Alfred
Rhythm Thief '94
Spare Me '02

Tad Alexander
Rasputin and the Empress '33
Ambassador Bill '31

Sarah Alexander
The Hunchback of Notre Dame '96 (V)
The Last Supper '96
Love! Valour! Compassion! '97

Ana Alicia (1956-)
Romero '89
Coward of the County '81

Lisa Aliff (1960-)
Playroom '90

Damned River '89
Trained to Kill '88

Roger Allam (1953-)
Speed Racer '08
V for Vendetta '06
The Roman Spring of Mrs. Stone '03

Elizabeth Allan (1908-90)
The Haunted Strangler '58
No Highway in the Sky '51
Camille '36
The Shadow '36
A Tale of Two Cities '36
A Woman Rebels '36
Java Head '35
Mark of the Vampire '35
Phantom Fiend '35
Ace of Aces '33
No Marriage Ties '33

Harris Allan
Masters of Horror: Jenifer '05
A Home at the End of the World '04

Jed Allan (1937-)
Suspect Device '95
Lethal Charm '90
Lassie: Adventures of Neeka '68

Louise Allbritton (1920-79)
Sitting Pretty '48
Egg and I '47
Son of Dracula '43
Pittsburgh '42
Who Done It? '42

Michael Alldredge (1938-73)
Robot Jox '90
About Last Night... '86

Catherine Allegret (1946-)
La Vie en Rose '07
Paul and Michelle '74
Last Tango in Paris '73

Aleisha Allen (1991-)
Are We Done Yet? '07
Are We There Yet? '05
School of Rock '03

Bambi Allen (1938-73)
Outlaw Riders '72
Satan's Sadists '69

Barbara Jo Allen (1905-74)
Sleeping Beauty '59 (V)
Girl Rush '44

Bill Allen (1962-)
Sioux City '94
Born on the Fourth of July '89
Rad '86
Streamers '83
Maniac '77

Chad Allen (1974-)
End of the Spear '06
Shock to the System '06
Third Man Out: A Donald Strachey Mystery '05
Murder in New Hampshire: The Pamela Smart Story '91
Camp Cucamonga: How I Spent My Summer Vacation '90
Straight Up '90
The Bad Seed '85

Corey Allen (1934-)
Darby's Rangers '58
Party Girl '58
The Night of the Hunter '55
Rebel without a Cause '55

Debbie Allen (1950-)
All About You '01
The Old Settler '01
Jo Jo Dancer, Your Life Is Calling '86
Ragtime '81
The Fish that Saved Pittsburgh '79
Roots: The Next Generation '79

Elizabeth Allen (1929-2006)
Star Spangled Girl '71
Donovan's Reef '63

Fred Allen (1894-1956)
We're Not Married '52
It's in the Bag '45

Gary Allen
Alice Sweet Alice '76
The Night They Robbed Big Bertha's '75

Ginger Lynn Allen (1962)
The Independent '00
Bound and Gagged: A Love Story '93
Mind, Body & Soul '92
Vice Academy 3 '91
Leather Jackets '90
Vice Academy 2 '90
Young Guns 2 '90
Buried Alive '89
Cleo/Leo '89
Hollywood Boulevard 2 '89
Wild Man '89

Gracie Allen (1902-64)
Two Girls and a Sailor '44
The Gracie Allen Murder Case '39
Honolulu '39
College Swing '38
A Damsel in Distress '37
Here Comes Cookie '35
Love in Bloom '35
Six of a Kind '34
We're Not Dressing '34
International House '33

India Allen (1965-)
Tattoo, a Love Story '02
Seduce Me: Pamela Principle 2 '94
Wild Cactus '92

Jeffrey Allen (1910-79)
This Stuff'll Kill Ya! '71
Something Weird '68
Moonshine Mountain '64

Jo Harvey Allen
The Wendell Baker Story '05
Checking Out '89
Tapeheads '89
True Stories '86

Joan Allen (1956-)
The Bourne Ultimatum '07
Bonneville '06
The Upside of Anger '05
The Bourne Supremacy '04
The Notebook '04
Yes '04
Off the Map '03
Mists of Avalon '01
The Contender '00
It's the Rage '99
When the Sky Falls '99
Pleasantville '98
Face/Off '97
The Ice Storm '97
The Crucible '96
Mad Love '95
Nixon '95
Josh and S.A.M. '93
Searching for Bobby Fischer '93
Ethan Frome '92
In Country '89
Tucker: The Man and His Dream '88
All My Sons '86
Fat Guy Goes Nutzoid! '86
Manhunter '86
Peggy Sue Got Married '86

John Allen (1944-)
The Odd Angry Shot '79
Roses Bloom Twice '77

Jonelle Allen (1944-)
Mr. Barrington '03
Next Time '99
Grave Secrets: The Legacy of Hilltop Drive '92
The Midnight Hour '86
Penalty Phase '86
The River Niger '76

Judith Allen (1911-96)
Train to Tombstone '50
Tough Kid '39
The Port of Missing Girls '38
Boots & Saddles '37
Git Along Little Dogies '37
Healer '36
Bright Eyes '34
Buffalo Stampede '33
Dancing Man '33

Karen Allen (1951-)
Indiana Jones and the Kingdom of the Crystal Skull '08
Plain Dirty '04
Poster Boy '04
When Will I Be Loved '04
In the Bedroom '01
World Traveler '01
The Perfect Storm '00
The Basket '99
Wind River '98
Til There Was You '96
Ghost in the Machine '93
King of the Hill '93
The Sandlot '93
Voyage '93
Malcolm X '92
The Turning '92
Sweet Talker '91
Secret Weapon '90
Animal Behavior '89
Backfire '88
Scrooged '88
The Glass Menagerie '87
Starman '84
Until September '84
Lovey: A Circle of Children 2 '82
Shoot the Moon '82
Split Image '82
Raiders of the Lost Ark '81
Cruising '80
East of Eden '80
A Small Circle of Friends '80
Manhattan '79
Wanderers '79
National Lampoon's Animal House '78

Keith Allen (1953-)
Agent Cody Banks 2: Destination London '04
De-Lovely '04
My Wife is an Actress '01
24 Hour Party People '01
Rancid Aluminium '00
Prince of Poisoners: The Life and Crimes of William Palmer '98
Loch Ness '95
Captives '94
Second Best '94
Shallow Grave '94
Nightscare '93
The Young Americans '93
Kafka '91
Small Time '91
Chicago Joe & the Showgirl '90
A Very British Coup '88

Krista Allen (1972-)
Feast '06
Shut Up and Kiss Me '05
Anger Management '03
Totally Blonde '01
The Haunted Sea '97
Raven '97

Laura Allen
How You Look to Me '05
Sucker Free City '05

Marty Allen (1922-)
Whale of a Tale '76
Harrad Summer '74
Jailbreakin' '72

Mike Allen
Death Driver '78
Hooch '76

Nancy Allen (1950-)
Kiss Toledo Goodbye '00
Children of the Corn 666: Isaac's Return '99
Against the Law '98
Highway Hitcher '98
Out of Sight '98
Secre of the Andes '98
The Last Assassins '96
Acting on Impulse '93
RoboCop 3 '91
Memories of Murder '90
RoboCop 2 '90
Limit Up '89
Poltergeist 3 '88
RoboCop '87
Sweet Revenge '87
The Gladiator '86
Not for Publication '84
The Philadelphia Experiment '84
The Buddy System '83
Strange Invaders '83
Blow Out '81
Dressed to Kill '80
Home Movies '79
1941 '79
I Wanna Hold Your Hand '78
Carrie '76
Forced Entry '75
The Last Detail '73

Parry Allen
See Parry Shen

Patrick Allen (1927-2206)
Bullet to Beijing '95
Body & Soul '93
Full Metal Ninja '89
Thirteenth Day of Christmas '85
Agatha Christie's Murder is Easy '82
Puppet on a Chain '72
When Dinosaurs Ruled the Earth '70
Invasion of the Body Stealers '69
Island of the Burning Doomed '67
Flight from Singapore '62
The Long Haul '57

Penelope Allen (1943-)
The Thin Red Line '98
Looking for Richard '96
Scarecrow '73
Oh! What a Lovely War '69

Penny Allen
Three Days of Rain '03
Three Days of Rain '02

Ray Allen (1975-)
Harvard Man '01
He Got Game '98

Rex Allen (1921-99)
Me, Myself, and Irene '00
The Secret of Navajo Cave '76 (V)
Charlie, the Lonesome Cougar '67 (N)
Legend of Lobo '62 (N)
Phantom Stallion '54
Iron Mountain Trail '53
Shadows of Tombstone '53
Border Saddlemates '52
Colorado Sundown '52
I Dream of Jeannie '52
Rodeo King and the Senorita '51
Silver City Bonanza '51
Thunder in God's Country '51
Hills of Oklahoma '50
Redwood Forest Trail '50
Trail of Robin Hood '50
Arizona Cowboy '49

Robert "Tex" Allen (1906-98)
The Awful Truth '37
The Rangers Step In '37
The Unknown Ranger '36
The Black Room '35
Crime and Punishment '35
Fighting Shadows '35
The Revenge Rider '35
The Perils of Pauline '34

Ronald Allen (1930-91)
Eat the Rich '87
Supergrass '87

Rosalind Allen (1957-)
Pinocchio's Revenge '96
Ticks '93

Children of the Corn 2: The Final Sacrifice '92
To Die For 2: Son of Darkness '91

Sage Allen
Suspended Animation '02
Mr. Saturday Night '92

Sheila Allen (1932-)
Pascall's Island '88
Bouquet of Barbed Wire '76
The Alphabet Murders '65
Children of the Damned '63

Sian Barbara Allen (1946-)
Eric '75
Billy Two Hats '74
You'll Like My Mother '72

Steve Allen (1921-2000)
Casino '95
The St. Tammany Miracle '94
The Player '92
Great Balls of Fire '89
Amazon Women on the Moon '87
Alice in Wonderland '85
Ratings Game '84
Heart Beat '80
Where Were You When the Lights Went Out? '68
The Benny Goodman Story '55

Tanya Allen (1975-)
Silent Hill '06
Lone Hero '02
Tail Lights Fade '99
White Lies '98
Behind the Lines '97
Spenser: Ceremony '93
Redbelt '08
Wild Hogs '07

Tim Allen (1953-)
The Santa Clause 3: The Escape Clause '06
The Shaggy Dog '06
Zoom '06
Big Trouble '02
The Santa Clause 2 '02
Who is Cletis Tout? '02
Joe Somebody '01
Galaxy Quest '99
Toy Story 2 '99 (V)
For Richer or Poorer '97
Toy Story '95 (V)

Todd Allen (1960-)
The Apostle '97
The Postman '97
Pinocchio's Revenge '96
Tall, Dark and Deadly '95
Wyatt Earp '94
Storm and Sorrow '90
Brothers in Arms '88
Witchboard '87

Tom Allen
Clash of the Ninja '86
Shadows '60

Woody Allen (1935-)
Scoop '06
Anything Else '03
Hollywood Ending '02
The Curse of the Jade Scorpion '01
Company Man '00
Small Time Crooks '00
Picking Up the Pieces '99
Sweet and Lowdown '99
Antz '98 (V)
Deconstructing Harry '97
Everyone Says I Love You '96
Mighty Aphrodite '95
The Sunshine Boys '95
Manhattan Murder Mystery '93
Husbands and Wives '92
Shadows and Fog '92
Scenes from a Mall '91
Crimes & Misdemeanors '89
New York Stories '89
King Lear '87
Radio Days '87 (N)
Hannah and Her Sisters '86
Broadway Danny Rose '84
Zelig '83
A Midsummer Night's Sex Comedy '82
Stardust Memories '80
Manhattan '79
Annie Hall '77
The Front '76
Love and Death '75
Sleeper '73
Everything You Always Wanted to Know about Sex (But Were Afraid to Ask) '72
Play It Again, Sam '72
Bananas '71
Take the Money and Run '69
Casino Royale '67
What's Up, Tiger Lily? '66 (N)
What's New Pussycat? '65

Fernando Allende (1954-)
Naked Lies '98
Heartbreaker '83

Kirstie Alley (1951-)
Blonde '01
Drop Dead Gorgeous '99
The Last Don 2 '93
Deconstructing Harry '97
For Richer or Poorer '97
The Last Don '97
Nevada '97
Toothless '97
Sticks and Stones '96
It Takes Two '95
Village of the Damned '95
Look Who's Talking Now '93
Look Who's Talking, Too '90
Madhouse '90
One More Chance '90
Sibling Rivalry '90
Look Who's Talking '89
Loverboy '89
Shoot to Kill '88
Prince of Bel Air '87
Summer School '87
North and South Book 2 '86
A Bunny's Tale '85
North and South Book 1 '85
Blind Date '84
Champions '84
Runaway '84
Star Trek 2: The Wrath of Khan '82

Sara Allgood (1883-1950)
Cheaper by the Dozen '50
Challenge to Lassie '49
The Accused '48
The Fabulous Dorseys '47
Mother Wore Tights '47
The Spiral Staircase '46
The Strange Affair of Uncle Harry '45
Jane Eyre '44
The Keys of the Kingdom '44
City Without Men '43
Roxie Hart '42
Dr. Jekyll and Mr. Hyde '41
How Green Was My Valley '41
That Hamilton Woman '41
Storm in a Teacup '37
Juno and the Paycock '30
Blackmail '29

Jeff Allin
A Matter of Love '78
American Tickler '76

Dorothy Allison (1949-)
Rikky and Pete '88
See No Evil '71
The Third Key '57

Claud Allister (1888-1970)
Lillian Russell '40
Bulldog Drummond at Bay '37
The Dark Angel '35

The Private Life of Henry VIII '33
Monte Carlo '30
Bulldog Drummond '29
Gregg Allman (1947-)
Rush '91
James Allodi (1967-)
Snow Cake '06
Rush Week '88
Christopher Allport
Through None Go With Me '06
Invasion! '99
Jack Frost 2: Revenge of the Mutant Killer Snowman '00
Jack Frost '97
News at Eleven '86
Circle of Power '83
Savage Weekend '80
Corbin Allred (1979-)
Saints and Soldiers '03
Address Unknown '96
Diamonds '99
Josh Kirby...Time Warrior! Chapter 6, Last Battle for the Universe '96
Josh Kirby...Time Warrior! Chapter 5, Journey to the Magic Cavern '96
Josh Kirby...Time Warrior! Chapter 4, Eggs from 70 Million B.C. '95
Josh Kirby...Time Warrior! Chapter 3, Trapped on Toyworld '95
Josh Kirby...Time Warrior! Chapter 2, The Human Pets '95
Josh Kirby...Time Warrior! Chapter 1, Planet of the Dino-Knights '95
Astrid Allwyn (1905-78)
Cracked Nuts '41
Love Affair '39
International Crime '37
It Could Happen to You '37
Stowaway '36
Charlie Chan's Secret '35
Hands Across the Table '35
Beggars in Ermine '34
A Woman's Wo'd '34
Monte Carlo Nights '34
Mystery Liner '34
June Allyson (1917-2006)
The Kid with the Broken Halo '82
Blackout '78
Vegas '78
Curse of the Black Widow '77
They Only Kill Their Masters '72
My Man Godfrey '57
The Opposite Sex '56
The McConnell Story '55
Strategic Air Command '55
Executive Suite '54
The Glenn Miller Story '54
The Stratton Story '49
Little Women '49
The Three Musketeers '48
Words and Music '48
Good News '47
Till the Clouds Roll By '46
Two Girls and a Sailor '44
Best Foot Forward '43
Girl Crazy '43
Thousands Cheer '43
Mario Almada (1922-)
Blood Screams '88
357 Magnum '79
Gila Almagor (1939-)
Munich '05
Under the Domim Tree '95
The Summer of Aviya '88
Every Time We Say Goodbye '86
Hide and Seek '80

The House on Chelouche Street '73
Salah '63
Joaquim Almeida
Deadly Past '07
The Celestine Prophecy '06
Bobby Z '07
Susan Almgren
The Witness '99
Adrian Alonso
Deadly Surveillance '91
Twin Sisters '91
Under the Same Moon '07
The Legend of Zorro '05
The Good, the Bad and the Ugly '67
Son of Samson '62
Ernesto Alonso (1917-2007)
The Criminal Life of Archibaldo de la Cruz '55
Wuthering Heights '53
Jose Alonso
Homework '90
El Diputado '78
Laz Alonso
Captivity '07
This Christmas '07
Stomp the Yard '07
Daniella Alonso (1970-)
The Hills Have Eyes 2 '07
Wrong Turn 2: Dead End '07
Maria Conchita Alonso (1957-)
The Dead One '07
Material Girls '06
Chasing Papi '03
Heart of America '03
High Noon '00
Blind Heat '00
Chain of Command '00
Blackheart '98
Caught '96
Roosters '95
Texas '94
The House of the Spirits '93
Teamster Boss: The Jackie Presser Story '92
Predator 2 '90
McBain '91
Colors '88
Vampire's Kiss '88
Blood Ties '87
Extreme Prejudice '87
The Running Man '87
A Fine Mess '86
Touch and Go '86
Fear City '85
Moscow on the Hudson '84

Body Armor '96
Private Parts '96
Deadly Past '95
Ring of Steel '94
Beyond Justice '92
A Family Matter '91
Millions '90
Bye Bye Baby '88
Portfolio '88
Thunder in Paradise 3 '94
Thunder in Paradise 2 '94
Thunder in Paradise '93
Hector Alterio (1929-)
The Son of the Bride '01
Wild Horses '95
I, the Worst of All '90
The Official Story '85
Camila '84
Basileus Quartet '82
Fridays of Eternity '81
The Nest '80
Cria Cuervos '76
Jeff Altman (1951-)
Russian Roulette '93
Doin' Time '85
In Love with an Older Woman '82
Bruce Altman (1955-)
Running Scared '06
Matchstick Men '03
L.I.E. '01
To Gillian on Her 37th Birthday '96
Vibrations '94
White Mile '94
Mr. Jones '93
Mr. Wonderful '93
The Favor, the Watch, & the Very Big Fish '92
Glengarry Glen Ross '92
My New Gun '92
Walter George Alton (1941-)
Heavenly Bodies '84
The Puma Man '80
Angela Alvarado (1965-)
Boss of Bosses '99
Hollywood Confidential '97
Crox Alvarado (1911-84)
The Curse of the Aztec Mummy '59
The Robot vs. the Aztec Mummy '59
Mummy '59
Dan Alvarado
Shoot to Kill '90
Don Alvarado (1904-67)
Big Steal '49
Demon for Trouble '34
Battle of the Sexes '28
Eisei Amamoto (1926-2003)
Godzilla's Revenge '69
What's Up, Tiger Lily? '65
Attack of the Mushroom People '63
Tom Amandes (1956-)
Bonneville '06
Live from Baghdad '03
When Good Ghouls Go Bad '01
Brokedown Palace '99
Billboard Dad '98
From the Earth to the Moon '98
Second Chances '98
The Long Kiss Goodnight '96
Betty Amann (1906-90)
Nancy Drew, Reporter '39
Rich and Strange '32

Rich Kids '79
Enrique Garcia Alvarez
The Exterminating Angel '62
Invasion of the Vampires '61
Carlos Alvarez-Novoa (1940-)
Lucia, Lucia '03
Solas '99
John Alvin (1917-)
Objective, Burma! '45
Kirk Alyn (1910-99)
Atom Man vs. Superman '50
Radar Patrol vs. Spy King '49
Daughter of Don Q '46
Federal Agents vs. Underworld, Inc. '49
Lyle Alzado (1949-92)
Comrades in Arms '91
Hangfire '91
Neon City '91
Club Fed '90
Tapeheads '89
Who's Harry Crumb? '89
Zapped Again '89
Destroyer '88
Ernest Goes to Camp '87
Oceans of Fire '86
Shigeru Amachi (1931-85)
Zatoichi: The Blind Swordsman's Vengeance '66
Zatoichi: The Life and Opinion of Masseur Ichi '62
The Ghost of Yotsuya '58
Chisco Amado (1962-)
The Situation '06
Said Amadia
A Few Days in September '06
Magali Amadei
Taxi '04
House of D '04
Mathieu Amalric (1965-)
The Diving Bell and the Butterfly '07
La Moustache '05
Munich '05
Kings and Queen '04
Alice et Martin '98
Late August, Early September '98
My Sex Life... Or How I Got into an Argument '96
John Patrick Amedori (1987-)
Stick It '06
Little Athens '05
The Butterfly Effect '04

Audrey Amber
See Andriana Ambesi
Andriana Ambesi (1978-)
Fangs of the Living Dead '68
Stranger in Paso Bravo '68
Secret Agent Super Dragon '66
Lauren Ambrose (1978-)
Starting Out in the Evening '07
Psycho Beach Party '00
Swimming '00
Can't Hardly Wait '98
In and Out '97
Tangie Ambrose
Jackie's Back '99
Don Ameche (1908-93)
Corrina, Corrina '94
Homeward Bound: The Incredible Journey '93
Folks! '92
Sunstroke '92
Oddball Hall '91
Oscar '91
Coming to America '88
Cocoon: The Return '88
Things Change '88
Harry and the Hendersons '87
Cocoon '85
Trading Places '83
The Boatniks '70
Suppose They Gave a War and Nobody Came? '70
Picture Mommy Dead '66
Guest Wife '45
It's in the Bag '45
Greenwich Village '44
A Wing and a Prayer '44
Heaven Can Wait '43
The Magnificent Dope '42
Moon over Miami '41
That Night in Rio '41
Lillian Russell '40
Midnight '39
The Story of Alexander Graham Bell '39
The Three Musketeers '39
Alexander's Ragtime Band '38
Happy Landing '38
In Old Chicago '37
One in a Million '36
Robert Ames (1889-1931)
Behind Office Doors '31
Millie '31
Smart Woman '31
Madchen Amick (1970-)
The Hunted '98
Freed Story '99
The List '00
Hangman '00
The Rats '01
Mr. Rock 'n' Roll: The Alan Freed Story '99
Dream Lover '93
Sleepwalkers '92
Twin Peaks: Fire Walk with Me '92
Don't Tell Her It's Me '90
I'm Dangerous Tonight '90
Trapped in Paradise '94
Love, Cheat & Steal '93
Psychopath '97
Wounded '97
The Courtyard '95
The Great American Sex Scandal '94
Dragon Storm '04
The Mask of Zoro '98
The Dead One '07
Son of the Morning Star '91
Tony Amendola
The Mask of Zorro '98
Three of Hearts '93
Panama Patrol '39
Harmony Lane '35
The Death Kiss '33
Sinners in the Sun '32
Heather Ames
How to Make a Monster '58
Blood of Dracula '57

Leon Ames (1902-93)
Peggy Sue Got Married '86
Testament '83
Claws '77
The Big Push '75
The Meal '75
Tora! Tora! Tora! '70
Monkey's Uncle '65
The Misadventures of Merlin Jones '63
Son of Flubber '63
The Absent-Minded Professor '61
From the Terrace '60
Peyton Place '57
By the Light of the Silvery Moon '53
Angel Face '52
On Moonlight Bay '51
The Big Hangover '50
Watch the Birdie '50
Battleground '49
A Date with Judy '48
On an Island with You '48
Velvet Touch '48
The Postman Always Rings Twice '46
Song of the Thin Man '47
Merton of the Movies '47
Lady in the Lake '45
Son of Lassie '45
Anchors Aweigh '45
They Were Expendable '45
Weekend at the Waldorf '45
Yolanda and the Thief '45
Thirty Seconds Over Tokyo '44
The Iron Major '43
East Side Kids '40
Mr. Moto in Danger Island '39
Mysterious Mr. Moto '38
The Spy Ring '38
Charlie Chan on Broadway '37
Murder in Greenwich Village '37
Murders in the Rue Morgue '32
Uptown New York '32
State's Attorney '31
Ramsay Ames (1919-98)
G-Men Never Forget '48
The Mummy's Ghost '44
Suzy Amis (1962-)
Judgment Day '99
The Usual Suspects '95
Nadja '94
Blown Away '94
The Ballad of Little Jo '93
Two Small Bodies '93
Where the Day Takes You '92
Rocket Gibraltar '88
Fandango '85
Soudad Amidou
Syriana '05
Amidou (1942-)
And Now Ladies and Gentlemen '02
Hot Chocolate '92
Petit Con '84
Sorcerer '77
The Beneficiary '97
Claudio Amendola (1963-)
Caterina in the Big City '03
George American Horse (1944-)
Adrienne Ames (1907-47)
Panama Patrol '39

Firestorm '97
Titanic '97
Cadillac Ranch '96
The Ex '96
Last Stand at Saber River '96
Nadja '95
One Good Turn '95
The Usual Suspects '95
Blown Away '94
The Ballad of Little Jo '93
Rich in Love '93
Two Small Bodies '93
Watch It '93
Where the Heart Is '90
Twister '89
Plain Clothes '88
Rocket Gibraltar '88
Big Town '87
Fandango '85

Christopher Amitrano
Jam '06

Renee Ammann
See Renee Griffin

Luigi Amodeo
Art House '98
B.A.P.'s '97
Red Shoe Diaries 6: How I Met My Husband '95

Christine Amor (1952-)
Bloodmoon '90
Now and Forever '82

David Amos
Flipping '96
The Takeover '94

John Amos (1941-)
Dr. Dolittle 3 '06
Dr. Dolittle 3 '06
Voodoo Moon '05
My Baby's Daddy '04
Disappearing Acts '00
American Flyers '85
Beastmaster '82
Touched by Love '80
Willa '79
Roots '77
Future Cop '76
Let's Do It Again '75
The World's Greatest Athlete '73
Sweet Sweetback's Baadasssss Song '71

John Amplas (1949-)
Midnight '81
Martin '77

Morey Amsterdam (1908-96)
Sooner or Later '78
Muscle Beach Party '64
Beach Party '63
Machine Gun Kelly '58

Eva Amurri (1985-)
Saved! '04
The Banger Sisters '02

Susie Amy (1981-)
House of 9 '05

Kristina Anapau (1979-)
Cruel Intentions 3 '04
Cursed '04
Madison '01

Elena Anaya (1975-)
In the Land of Women '06
Dead Fish '04
Van Helsing '04
Two Tough Guys '03
Sex and Lucia '01

Dominic Anciano (1959-)
Love, Honour & Obey '00
Final Cut '98

Richard Anconina (1953-)
Police '85
Tchao Pantin '84

Avalon Anders
The Portrait '99
Wish Me Luck '95
Great Bikini Off-Road Adventure '94
Bikini Summer 2 '92
Sorority House Party '92

Glenn Anders (1889-1981)
Nancy Goes to Rio '50
The Lady from Shanghai '48

Luana Anders (1938-96)
Limit Up '89
Border Radio '88
Movers and Shakers '85
Irreconcilable Differences '84
Goin' South '78
The Killing Kind '73
Greaser's Palace '72
Manipulator '71
Easy Rider '69
Games '67
The Trip '67
Sex and the College Girl '64
Dementia 13 '63
Night Tide '63
The Pit and the Pendulum '61
Reform School Girl '57

Merry Anders (1932-)
Blood Legacy '73
Women of the Prehistoric Planet '66
The Time Travelers '64
Desk Set '57
Phffft! '54
The Farmer Takes a Wife '53

Rudolph Anders (1895-1987)
36 Hours '64
She Demons '58
Phantom from Space '53
Actors and Sin '52
Under Nevada Skies '46
Junior Army '42
We're in the Legion Now '37

Brigitte Andersen (1975-)
Between Two Women '86
Fever Pitch '85
A Summer to Remember '84
Hansel and Gretel '82
Savannah Smiles '82

Elga Andersen (1939-94)
Night Flight from Moscow '73
Le Mans '71
Your Turn Darling '63
The Twilight Girls '57

Susy Andersen
Gangster's Law '86
Black Sabbath '64

Andy Anderson (1947-)
Salem's Lot '04
Garage Days '03
The Junction Boys '02

Anthony Anderson (1970-)
Transformers '07
Arthur and the Invisibles '06 (V)
The Departed '06
Scary Movie 4 '06
Hoodwinked '05 (V)
Hustle & Flow '05
King's Ransom '05
Agent Cody Banks 2: Destination London '04
Harold and Kumar Go to White Castle '04
My Baby's Daddy '04
Cradle 2 the Grave '03
Malibu's Most Wanted '03
Scary Movie 3 '03
Barbershop '02
Kangaroo Jack '02
Exit Wounds '01
Kingdom Come '01
See Spot Run '01
Two Can Play That Game '01
Big Momma's House '00
Me, Myself, and Irene '00
Romeo Must Die '00
Urban Legends 2: Final Cut '00
Liberty Heights '99
Life '99

Cheryl Anderson
Writer's Block '91
Acorn People '82
Rosie: The Rosemary Clooney Story '82

Donna Anderson (1925-)
Inherit the Wind '60
On the Beach '59

Eddie Anderson (1905-77)
It's a Mad, Mad, Mad, Mad World '63
The Show-Off '46
Brewster's Millions '45
I Love a Bandleader '45
Broadway Rhythm '44
Cabin in the Sky '43
Star Spangled Rhythm '42
Tales of Manhattan '42
Birth of the Blues '41
Topper Returns '41
Gone with the Wind '39
Honolulu '39
You Can't Cheat an Honest Man '39
Jezebel '38
Thanks for the Memory '38
You Can't Take It with You '38
Green Pastures '36
False Faces '32

Erich Anderson
Due East '02
Love Kills '91
Bat 21 '88
Friday the 13th, Part 4: The Final Chapter '84
A Nightmare on Elm Street 5: Dream Child '89

Gillian Anderson (1968-)
The Last King of Scotland '06
Bleak House '05
Tristan Shandy: A Cock and Bull Story '05
House of Mirth '00
Chicago Cab '98
The Mighty '98
Playing by Heart '98
Princess Mononoke '98 (V)
The X-Files '98
The Turning '92

Harry Anderson (1952-)
Spies, Lies and Naked Thighs '91
Mother Goose Rock 'n' Rhyme '90
Stephen King's It '90
I Bury the Living '58
Night Passage '57

Herbert Anderson (1917-94)
Battleground '49
The Male Animal '42
Dive Bomber '41
The Fighting 69th '40

James Anderson (1872-1953)
Sergeant York '41
The Freshman '25

James Anderson (1921-69)
Take the Money and Run '69
The Connection '61

Jean Anderson (1907-2001)
Prince Brat and the Whipping Boy '95
Back Home '90
Death by Prescription '86
Screamtime '83
Lucky Jim '58

Jeff Anderson (1970-)
Clerks 2 '06
Now You Know '02
Dogma '99
Clerks '97

Jo Anderson (1958-)
From the Earth to the Moon '98
Daylight '96
Season of Change '94
Decoration Day '90
Suspicion '87

Joe Anderson
The Ruins '08
Across the Universe '07
Becoming Jane '07
Control '07

John Anderson (1922-92)
Eight Men Out '88
Firehouse '87
Donner Pass: The Road to Survival '84
Ashes and Embers '82
Zoot Suit '81
Smokey and the Bandit 2 '80
Namu, the Killer Whale '66
Geronimo '62
Ride the High Country '62
Psycho '60

Judith Anderson (1898-1992)
Star Trek 3: The Search for Spock '84
Inn of the Damned '74
A Man Called Horse '70
Elizabeth, the Queen '68
Cinderella '60
Cat on a Hot Tin Roof '58
The Ten Commandments '56
Salome '53
Pursued '47
The Red House '47
Tycoon '47
Diary of a Chambermaid '46
Spectre of the Rose '46
The Strange Love of Martha Ivers '46
And Then There Were None '45
Laura '44
Edge of Darkness '43
Stage Door Canteen '43
All Through the Night '42
Kings Row '41
Lady Scarface '41
Rebecca '40

Kevin Anderson (1960-)
Charlotte's Web '06
Carry Me Home '04
Monday Night Mayhem '02
Power and Beauty '02
The Doe Boy '01
Ruby's Bucket of Blood '01
Eye of God '97
Firelight '97
A Thousand Acres '97
The Night We Never Met '93
Rising Sun '93
The Wrong Man '93
Hoffa '92
Liebestraum '91
Orpheus Descending '91
Sleeping with the Enemy '91
In Country '89
Miles from Home '88
Orphans '87
Pink Nights '87
Risky Business '83

Lindsay Anderson (1923-94)
Blame It on the Bellboy '92
Prisoner of Honor '91
Chariots of Fire '81

Lisa Arrindell Anderson (1969-)
Big Momma's House 2 '06
Madea's Family Reunion '06
The Second Chance '06
Disappearing Acts '00
Having Our Say: The Delany Sisters' First 100 Years '99
A Lesson Before Dying '99
Clockers '95
Trial by Jury '94
Livin' Large '91
One Good Cop '91

Loni Anderson (1945-)
A Night at the Roxbury '98
3 Ninjas: High Noon at Mega Mountain '97
Munchie '92
White Hot: The Mysterious Murder of Thelma Todd '91
Blown Away '90
All Dogs Go to Heaven '89 (V)
Sorry, Wrong Number '89
Smile, Jenny, You're Dead '74
The Deerslayer '78
The Specialist '75

Louie Anderson (1953-)
Coming to America '88
The Wrong Guys '88
Ferris Bueller's Day Off '86
Quicksilver '86

Mary Anderson
Dangerous Crossing '53
False Faces '18

Mary Anderson (1921-)
The Underworld Story '50
Whispering City '47
To Each His Own '46
Lifeboat '44
Wilson '44

Melissa Sue Anderson (1962-)
Chattanooga Choo Choo '84
First Affair '83
Happy Birthday to Me '81
On the Edge: The Survival of Dana '79
The Loneliest Runner '76
Little House on the Prairie '74

Melody Anderson (1955-)
Marilyn & Bobby: Her Final Affair '94
Landslide '92
Hitler's Daughter '90
Final Notice '89
Speed Zone '88
Beverly Hills Madam '86
Boy in Blue '86
Firewalker '86
Ernie Kovacs: Between the Laughter '84
Policewoman Centerfold '83
Dead and Buried '81
Flash Gordon '80

Michael Anderson, Jr. (1943-)
Sunset Grill '92
The Great Land of Small '86
A Legacy for Leonette '85
Sons of Katie Elder '65
In Search of the Castaways '62
The Sundowners '60
Tiger Bay '59

Michael J. Anderson (1953-)
Snow White: The Fairest of Them All '02
Mulholland Drive '01
Club Vampire '98

Miles Anderson (1947-)
The King Is Alive '00
A Certain Justice '99
Into the Blue '97
The Rector's Wife '94
A Far Off Place '93
House of Cards '90

Mitchell Anderson (1961-)
If These Walls Could Talk 2 '00
Relax... It's Just Sex! '98
Is There Life Out There? '94
Back to Hannibal: The Return of Tom Sawyer and Huckleberry Finn '90
Deadly Dreams '88
Goodbye, Miss 4th of July '88

Myrtle Anderson
Follow the Sun '51
Green Pastures '36

Nathan Anderson
Alien Siege '05

Pamela Anderson (1967-)
Blonde and Blonder '07
Borat: Cultural Learnings of America for Make Benefit Glorious Nation of Kazakhstan '06
Scary Movie 3 '03
Barb Wire '96
Baywatch the Movie: Forbidden Paradise '95
Naked Souls '95
Raw Justice '93
Snapdragon '93

Pat Anderson
Cover Girl Models '75
Summer School Teachers '75
TNT Jackson '75

Richard Anderson (1926-)
In the Lake of the Woods '96
The Glass Shield '95
Gettysburg '93
The Player '92
Perry Mason Returns '85
Retrievers '82
Murder by Natural Causes '79
Pearl '78
The Bionic Woman '75
The Night Strangler '72
Tora! Tora! Tora! '70
Seconds '66
Kitten with a Whip '64
Seven Days in May '64
Compulsion '59
The Gunfight at Dodge City '59
The Long, Hot Summer '58
Paths of Glory '57
Forbidden Planet '56
The Search for Bridey Murphy '56
Hit the Deck '55
Escape from Fort Bravo '53
Give a Girl a Break '53
I Love Melvin '53

Scaramouche '52
Rich, Young and Pretty '51
The Magnificent Yankee '50
The Vanishing Westerner '50

Richard Dean Anderson (1950-)
Past the Bleachers '95
Through the Eyes of a Killer '92

Shedrack Anderson, III
Ordinary Heroes '05

Stanley Anderson (1945)
Runaway Jury '03
40 Days and 40 Nights '02
Red Dragon '02
Simone '02
Spider-Man '02
Proof of Life '00
Trial by Media '00
Arlington Road '99
Primal Fear '96
The Shadow Conspiracy '96
He Said, She Said '91
Son of the Morning Star '91

Warner Anderson (1911-76)
Armored Command '61
Blackboard Jungle '55
A Lawless Street '55
The Caine Mutiny '54
Drum Beat '54
A Lion is in the Streets '53
The Star '52
Detective Story '51
Go for Broke! '51
Santa Fe '51
Destination Moon '50
Command Decision '48
Song of the Thin Man '47
My Reputation '46
Abbott and Costello in Hollywood '45
Objective, Burma! '45
Weekend at the Waldorf '45
Destination Tokyo '43

Bibi Andersson (1935-)
Babette's Feast '87
I Never Promised You a Rose Garden '77
The Concorde: Airport '79
Quintet '79
Twice a Woman '79
Duel at Diablo '66
Persona '66
The Devil's Eye '60
The Magician '58
Brink of Life '57
Wild Strawberries '57
The Seventh Seal '56

Harriet Andersson (1932-)
Dogville '03
Fanny and Alexander '83
Cries and Whispers '72
Through a Glass Darkly '61
Dreams '55
Smiles of a Summer Night '55
Lesson in Love '54
Sawdust & Tinsel '53
Monika '52

Peter Andersson (1953)
Flickering Lights '01

Anthony Andrews (1948-)
Cambridge Spies '03
Haunted '95

Eiko Ando
III

Noboru Ando
Sympathy for the Underdog '71

Paul Andor (1901-91)
The Wolves '71

Peter Andorai (1948-)
My Twentieth Century '90

Gaby Andre (1920-72)
Goliath and the Dragon '61
The Cosmic Monsters '58

Lona Andre (1915-92)
The Green Glove '52
Verdi '53

Andre 3000
See Andre Benjamin

Andre the Giant (1946-93)
The Princess Bride '87

Marcel Andre (1885-1974)
The Storm Within '48
Beauty and the Beast '46
Maniac '34

Damir Andrei
A Different Loyalty '04

Starr Andreeff (1964-)
Club Vampire '98
Amityville Dollhouse '96
Syngenor '90
Dance of the Damned '88
Out of the Dark '88
The Terror Within '88

Natasha Andreichenko (1956-)
Modern Vampires '98
Operation Intercept '95
Little Odessa '94

Ursula Andress (1936-)
Soft Deceit '04
The Chinatown Murders: Man against the Mob '89
Clash of the Titans '81
Tigers in Lipstick '80
The Fifth Musketeer '79
Loves & Times of Scaramouche '76
The Sensuous Nurse '76
Loaded Guns '75
Stateline Motel '75
Red Sun '71
Casino Royale '67
The Blue Max '66
Once Before I Die '65
10th Victim '65
What's New Pussycat? '65
Four for Texas '63
Fun in Acapulco '63
Dr. No '62

David Andrews (1952-)
Terminator 3: Rise of the Machines '03
Hannibal '01
From the Earth to the Moon '98
Under Pressure '98
Apollo 13 '95
Deconstructing Sarah '94
Wyatt Earp '94
Graveyard Shift '90
Cherry 2000 '88
Wild Horses '84

Dean Andrews
My Summer of Love '05
The Navigators '01

Edward Andrews (1914-85)
Sixteen Candles '84
Avanti! '72
How to Frame a Figg '71
Tora! Tora! Tora! '70
Over the Hill Gang '69
The Trouble with Girls (and How to Get into It) '69
Good Neighbor Sam '64
Kisses for My President '64
The Brass Bottle '63
The Thrill of It All! '63
Hands of a Murderer '90
Strange Case of Dr. Jekyll & Mr. Hyde '89
Hanna's War '88
The Woman He Loved '88
Second Victory '87
A.D. '85
The Holcroft Covenant '84
Under the Volcano '84
Agatha Christie's Sparkling Cyanide '83
Ivanhoe '82
The Scarlet Pimpernel '82
Brideshead Revisited '81
Danger UXB '81

Barry Andrews (1944-)
Dracula Has Risen from the Grave '68
The Blood on Satan's Claw '71

Jewels '92

Dana Andrews (1909-92)
Prince Jack '83
Ike '79
Born Again '78
The Last Tycoon '76
Airport '75 '75
The Cobra '68
The Devil's Brigade '68
Johnny Reno '66
Battle of the Bulge '65
In Harm's Way '65
The Loved One '65
Enchanted Island '58
Curse of the Demon '57
Zero Hour! '57
Beyond a Reasonable Doubt '56
While the City Sleeps '56
Elephant Walk '54
I Want You '51
My Foolish Heart '49
Boomerang '47
Daisy Kenyon '47
The Best Years of Our Lives '46
Canyon Passage '46
A Walk in the Sun '46
State Fair '45
The Purple Heart '44
A Wing and a Prayer '44
Up in Arms '44
Crash Dive '43
The North Star '43
The Ox-Bow Incident '43
Ball of Fire '41
Kit Carson '40
Lucky Cisco Kid '40
The Westerner '40

Jason Andrews
Alexander the Great '55

Advise and Consent '62
40 Pounds of Trouble '62
The Absent-Minded Professor '61
The Young Savages '61
Elmer Gantry '60
Rollercoat '02
Tea and Sympathy '56

Giuseppe Andrews (1979-)
Cabin Fever '03
Detroit Rock City '99
Independence Day '96

Harry Andrews (1911-89)
Cause Celebre '87
Mesmerized '84
Hawk the Slayer '81
Sky Riders '76
The Passover Plot '75
The Story of Jacob & Joseph '74
The Final Programme '73
Internecine Project '73
Mackintosh Man '73
Theatre of Blood '73
I Want What I Want '72
Man of La Mancha '72
The Nightcomers '72
What the Peeper Saw '72
The Ruling Class '72
Nicholas and Alexandra '71
Entertaining Mr. Sloane '70
Too Late the Hero '70
Battle of Britain '69
Nice Girl Like Me '69
The Charge of the Light Brigade '68
Dandy in Aspic '68
The Girl Getters '66
Modesty Blaise '66
The Agony and the Ecstasy '65
The Hill '65
633 Squadron '64
Saint Joan '57
Helen of Troy '56
Moby Dick '56

James Andronica (1945-)
Federal Hill '94
Rhythm Thief '94

Julie Andrews (1935-)
Enchanted '07 (N)
Shrek the Third '07 (V)
The Princess Diaries 2: Royal Engagement '04
Shrek 2 '04 (V)
Eloise at the Plaza '03
The Princess Diaries '01
One Special Night '99
Relative Values '99
A Fine Romance '92
Our Sons '91
Duet for One '86
That's Life! '86
The Man Who Loved Women '83
Victor/Victoria '82
S.O.B. '81
Little Miss Marker '80
10 '79
The Tamarind Seed '74
Darling Lili '70
Star! '68
Thoroughly Modern Millie '67
Torn Curtain '66
Hawaii '66
The Sound of Music '65
The Americanization of Emily '64
Mary Poppins '64
The Singing Princess '49

Naveen Andrews (1963-)
The Brave One '07
Planet Terror '07
Bride & Prejudice '04
The English Patient '96
Kama Sutra: A Tale of Love '96
Wild West '93

Peter Andrews
See Steven Soderbergh

Real Andrews (1963-)
Family of Cops 2: Breach of Faith '97
Soldier of Fortune Inc. '97

Stanley Andrews (1891-1969)
The Adventures of Frank and Jesse James '48
Crash Dive '43
In Old Colorado '41
Brigham Young: Frontiersman '40
Beau Geste '39
Blondie '38
Shine on, Harvest Moon '38

Slim Andrews (1906-)
The Driftin' Kid '41
The Pioneers '41
Riding the Sunset Trail '41

Tod Andrews (1914-72)
In Harm's Way '65
They Died with Their Boots On '41

The Andrews Sisters
Melody Time '48 (V)
The Road to Rio '47
Swingtime Johnny '43
Private Buckaroo '42
Buck Privates '41
Hold That Ghost '41
In the Navy '41
Argentine Nights '40

Russell Andrews
The Punisher '04
The In-Laws '03

Mikel Angel
Evil Spirits '91
Grotesque '87

Vanessa Angel (1963-)
The Perfect Score '04
Superbabes: Baby Geniuses 2 '04
Firetrap '01
Sabretooth '01
Camouflage '00
Enemies of Laughter '00
Made Men '99
Partners '99
Kingpin '96
Kissing a Fool '98
Homicidal Impulse '92
The Cover Girl Murders '93

Chris Angelo
San Franpsycho '06

Pier Angeli (1932-71)
Octaman '71
One Step to Hell '67
Battle of the Bulge '65
Sodom and Gomorrah '62
S.O.S. Pacific '60
Somebody Up There Likes Me '56
The Silver Chalice '54

Maya Angelou (1928-)
Madea's Family Reunion '06
How to Make a American Quilt '95
Roots '77

Muriel Angelus (1909-2004)
The Great McGinty '40
Night Birds '31

Angelyne (1958-)
The Malibu Beach Vampires '91

Michael Angarano (1987-)
Black Irish '07
The Final Season '07
Snow Angels '07
Dear Wendy '05
Lords of Dogtown '05
One Last Thing '05
Sky High '05
Speak '04
Little Secrets '01
The Forbidden Kingdcm '08

Julie Ange (1940-)
Teenage Mother '67
Girl on a Chain Gang '65

Jean-Hugues Anglade (1955-)
Taking Lives '04
Innocents '00
Elective Affinities '96
Maximum Risk '96
Nelly et Monsieur Arnaud '95
Killing Zoe '94
Queen Margot '94
La Femme Nikita '91
Betty Blue '86
Subway '85

Luciana Angiolillo (1925-)
The Easy Life '63
The Trojan Horse '62

Philip Anglim (1953-)
Testament '83
Haunted Summer '88

Heather Angel (1909-86)
Backstairs at the White House '79
Premature Burial '62
Peter Pan '53 (V)
Lifeboat '44
The Undying Monster '42
Shadows on the Stars '41
Suspicion '41
Half a Soldier '40
Bulldog Drummond's Bride '39
Bulldog Drummond's Secret Police '39
Arrest Bulldog Drummond '38
Bulldog Drummond Escapes '37
Western Gold '37
The Bold Caballero '36
The Last of the Mohicans '36
The Informer '35
The Mystery of Edwin Drood '35
The Three Musketeers '35
Daniel Boone '34
Pilgrimage '33

Sally Anglim
Thundering Trail '51
Yes, Sir, Mr. Bones '51

Simon Andreu (1941-)
Beyond Re-Animator '03
At Heist '05
Hidden Assassin '94
Sharpe's Rifles '93
Blood and Sand '89
Fist Fighter '88
The Barcelona Kill '77
Blue Jeans and Dynamite '76
The Blood Spattered Bride '72
Night of the Sorcerers '70
Surprise Attack '70
A Tiger Walks '64
The Glass Bottom Boat '66

Alex Angulo (1953-)
Pan's Labyrinth '06
My Mother Likes Women '02
Live Flesh '97
The Day of the Beast '95

Christien Anholt (1971-)
Dark Corners '06
Flyboys '06
The Waiting Time '99
Appetite '98
Preaching to the Perverted '97
The Blackheath Poisonings '92
Class of '61 '92
One Against the Wind '91
Reunion '88

Jennifer Aniston (1969-)
He's Just Not That Into You '08
The Break-Up '06
Friends with Money '06
Derailed '05
Rumor Has It... '05
Along Came Polly '04
Bruce Almighty '03
The Good Girl '02
Rock Star '01
Iron Giant '99 (V)
The Object of My Affection '98
Office Space '98
Dream for an Insomniac '96
Picture Perfect '96
She's the One '96
Til There Was You '96
Leprechaun '93

Paul Anka (1941-)
Shake, Rattle & Rock! '94
Ordinary Magic '93
The Return of Spinal Tap '92
The Longest Day '62
Girls' Town '59

Evelyn Ankers (1918-85)
Parole, Inc. '49
The Last of the Redmen '47
Black Beauty '46
Flight to Nowhere '46
His Butler's Sister '44
The Invisible Man's Revenge '44
Jungle Woman '44
The Pearl of Death '44
Captive Wild Woman '43
The Mad Ghoul '43
Son of Dracula '43
The Ghost of Frankenstein '42
Sherlock Holmes: The Voice of Terror '42
Burma Convoy '41
Hold That Ghost '41
The Wolf Man '41

Morris Ankrum (1898-1964)
X: The Man with X-Ray Eyes '63
Giant from the Unknown '58
Half Human '58
How to Make a Monster '58
Beginning of the End '57
The Giant Claw '57
Earth vs. the Flying Saucers '56
Crashout '55
Silver Star '55
Invaders from Mars '53
Borderline '50
The Damned Don't Cry '50
Border Vigilantes '41
Doomed Caravan '41
In Old Colorado '41
The Light of Western Stars '40
The Showdown '40
Hopalong Cassidy Returns '36

Ann-Margret (1941-)
The Break-Up '06
Memory '06
Taxi '04
Interstate 60 '02
Blonde '01
A Woman's a Helluva Thing '01
The 10th Kingdom '00
Any Given Sunday '99
The Happy Face Murders '99
Grumpier Old Men '95
Scarlett '94
Grumpy Old Men '93
Queen '93
Newsies '92
Our Sons '91
A New Life '88
A Tiger's Tale '87
52 Pick-Up '86
Twice in a Lifetime '85
A Streetcar Named Desire '84
I Ought to Be in Pictures '82
Lookin' to Get Out '82
Return of the Soldier '82
Middle Age Crazy '80
The Villain '79
The Cheap Detective '78
Magic '78
Joseph Andrews '77
The Last Remake of Beau Geste '77
Twist '76
Tommy '75
The Outside Man '73
Train Robbers '73
Carnal Knowledge '71
C.C. & Company '70
R.P.M.* (*Revolutions Per Minute) '70
Tiger and the Pussycat '67
Murderers' Row '66
The Cincinnati Kid '65
Kitten with a Whip '64
Bye, Bye, Birdie '63
Viva Las Vegas '63
State Fair '62
Pocketful of Miracles '61

Annabella (1909-96)
13 Rue Madeleine '46
Dinner at the Ritz '37
Wings of the Morning '37
Under the Red Robe '36
Le Million '31
Napoleon '27

Amina Annabi (1962-)
The Advocate '93
The Sheltering Sky '90

Frank Annese (1950-)
Another Chance '88
House of the Rising Sun '87

Francesca Annis (1944-)
Jane Eyre '06
The Libertine '05
Revolver '05
Wives and Daughters '01
Onegin '99
Reckless: The Sequel '98
Reckless '97
Doomsday Gun '94
Onassis '88
Under the Cherry Moon '86
The Maze '85
Dune '84
Krull '83
Coming Out of the Ice '82
Lillie '79
Edward the King '75
Macbeth '71
Murder Most Foul '65
Flipper's New Adventure '64
The Guns and the Fury '83
Mission to Glory '80
Centennial '78
The Manitou '78
Day of the Animals '77
The Message '77
The Barbary Coast '74
The Bears & I '74
It's Alive '74
The Doll Squad '73
Dear Dead Delilah '72
Quick, Let's Get Married '71
Powder Keg '70
Guns of the Magnificent Seven '69
Daring Game '68
The Pink Jungle '68
And Now Miguel '66
Texas Across the River '66
Harum Scarum '65
Voyage to the Bottom of the Sea '61
Abbott and Costello Meet the Mummy '55
Diane '55
Jupiter's Darling '55
The Lawless Breed '52
Hill Number One '51
Action in Arabia '44

Zachary Ansley (1972-)
The Spring '00
This Boy's Life '93
Princes in Exile '90
Christmas Comes to Willow Creek '87

Susan Anspach (1939-)
Back to Back '90
The Rutanga Tapes '90
Blood Red '88
Into the Fire '88
Blue Monkey '87
Gone Are the Days '84
Misunderstood '84
The Devil & Max Devlin '81
Gas '81
Montenegro '81
The Big Fix '78
Mad Bull '77
Blume in Love '73
Deadly Encounter '72
Play It Again, Sam '72
Five Easy Pieces '70

Norman Anstey
Queen's Messenger II '01
Scavengers '87
Last Action Hero '93
Sunset Heat '92
Spellcaster '91
Trust Me '89
World Gone Wild '88
Cold Steel '87
Slamdance '87
Nomads '86

Carl Anthony
The Sinister Urge '60
Plan 9 from Outer Space '56

Gerald Anthony (1951-)
To Die Standing '91
Secret of the Ice Cave '89

Lysette Anthony (1963-)
Beneath Loch Ness '01
Russell Mulcahy's Tale of Misbegotten '98
Dead Cold '96
The Fiance '96
Robinson Crusoe '96
Trilogy of Terror 2 '96
Dr. Jekyll and Ms. Hyde '95
Dracula: Dead and Loving It '95
The Hard Truth '94
The Advocate '93
A Brilliant Disguise '93
Look Who's Talking Now '93
Save Me '93
Face the Music '93
Husbands and Wives '92
The Lady and the Highwayman '89
The Bretts '89
Without a Clue '88
Krull '83
Ivanhoe '82
Oliver Twist '82

Marc Anthony (1969-)
El Cantante '06
Man on Fire '04
In the Time of the Butterflies '01
Bringing Out the Dead '99
The Substitute '96
Big Night '95

Paul Anthony (1975-)
Blade: Trinity '04
Eighteen '04
House Party '90

Ray Anthony (1922-)
Girls' Town '59
High School Confidential '58
The Girl Can't Help It '56

Tony Anthony (1937-)
Treasure of the Four Crowns '82
1931: Once Upon a Time in New York '72
Force of Impulse '60

Steve Antin (1956-)
Inside Monkey Zetterland '92
Survival Quest '89
The Accused '88
Penitentiary 3 '87
Last American Virgin '82

Susan Anton (1950-)
Lena's Holiday '90
Options '88
Making Mr. Right '86
The Boy Who Loved Trolls '84
Cannonball Run 2 '84
Spring Fever '81
Goldengirl '79

Laura Antonelli (1941-)
Collector's Item '89
Swashbuckler '84
Passion of Love '82
Tigers in Lipstick '80
Wifemistress '79
How Funny Can Sex Be? '76
The Innocent '76
Malicious '74
High Fashion '72
Divine Nymph '71
A Man Called Sledge '71

Gabriele Antonini
Hero of Rome '63

Jose Antonio
See Anthony (Jose, J. Antonio, J.A.) Mayans

Alexander Antonov
The Battleship Potemkin '25

Omero Antonutti (1935-)
Farinelli '94
The Fencing Master '92
Good Morning, Babylon '87
Kaos '85
Basileus Quartet '82
Life of Verdi '82
The Night of the Shooting Stars '82
Padre Padrone '77

Scott Antony (1950-)
The Freakmaker '73
Savage Messiah '72

Cas Anvar
Shattered Glass '03
Seducing Maarya '99
Psychopath '97

Gabrielle Anwar (1971-)
Crazy Eights '06
Sherlock: Case of Evil '02
If You Only Knew '00
Turbulence 3: Heavy Metal '00
The Guilty '99
My Little Assassin '99
Nevada '97
The Ripper '97
Sub Down '97
The Grave '95
In Pursuit of Honor '95
Innocent Lies '95
Things to Do in Denver When You're Dead '95
Body Snatchers '93
Fallen Angels 2 '93
For Love or Money '93
The Three Musketeers '93
Scent of a Woman '92
If Looks Could Kill '91
Wild Hearts Can't Be Broken '91
A Night of Love '87

Perry Anzilotti
That's Adequate '90
For Us, the Living '88

Rocky Aoki
Air Bud 2: Golden Receiver '98

Devon Aoki (1982-)
DOA: Dead or Alive '06
Sin City '05
D.E.B.S. '04
2 Fast 2 Furious '03

Tsuru Aoki
The Dragon Painter '19

Oscar Apfel (1878-1939)
Shadows of the Orient '37
Bulldog Edition '36
Rainbow's End '35

Apollonia (1961-)
Black Magic Woman '91
Back to Back '90
Ministry of Vengeance '89
Tricks of the Trade '88
Purple Rain '84
Heartbreaker '83

Peter Appel (1959-)
The Navigator '88

Noel Appleby
My Grandpa Is a Vampire '92

Shiri Appleby (1978-)
What Love Is '07
I'm Reed Fish '06
The Killing Floor '06
When Do We Eat? '05
Undertow '04
The Battle of Shaker Heights '03
Swimfan '02

Christina Applegate (1971-)
Anchorman: The Legend of Ron Burgundy '04
Surviving Christmas '04
Grand Theft Parsons '03
Wonderland '03
The Sweetest Thing '02
Just Visiting '01
The Big Hit '98
Out in Fifty '99
Mafia! '98
Nowhere '96
Wild Bill '95
Across the Moon '94
Vibrations '94
Don't Tell Mom the Babysitter's Dead '91
Streets '90
Jaws of Satan '81

Royce D. Applegate (1939-2003)
Gods and Generals '03
Intolerable Cruelty '03
Seabiscuit '03
The Rookie '02
O Brother Where Art Thou? '00
Inherit the Wind '99
Gettysburg '93
Outside Chance '78

John Aprea (1940-)
To the Limit '95
Cyber-Tracker '93
Direct Hit '93
Picasso Trigger '89
Savage Beach '89
Idolmaker '80
Caged Heat '74
The Godfather, Part 2 '74
The Arousers '70

Annabelle Apsion
From Hell '01
My Uncle Silas '01
The War Zone '98
Framed '93

Angelica Aragon (1953-)
La Mujer de Mi Hermano '06
The Crime of Father Amaro '02
Optic Fiber '97
On the Air '95
A Walk in the Clouds '95
Like A Belle '94

Art Aragon (1927-)
To Hell and Back '55
The Ring '52

Julian (Sonny) Arahanga (1972-)
The Matrix '99
Broken English '96
Once Were Warriors '94

Hirofumi Arai (1979-)
The Neighbor No. Thirteen '05

Tomas Arana (1959-)
The Bourne Supremacy '04
Frankenfish '04
Rampage: The Hillside Strangler Murders '04
This Girl's Life '03
Derailed '02
Pearl Harbor '01
Gladiator '00
Wildflowers '99
The Church '98
The Bodyguard '92
The Devil's Daughter '91
Domino '88
The Last Temptation of Christ '88
Captive '87

Angel Aranda (1934-)
Satan's Blood '77
Planet of the Vampires '65

Manuel Aranguiz (1945-)
Levity '03
Eclipse '94
A Paper Wedding '89

Ray Aranha (1939-)
The Kid '97
City of Hope '91

Yoshisaburo Arashi
47 Ronin, Part 1 '42
47 Ronin, Part 2 '42

Julie Araskog
Seven '95

Michiyo Aratama (1930-2001)
The Human Condition: A Soldier's Prayer '61
Kwaidan '64
The Gambling Samurai '60

The Human Condition:
Road to Eternity '59
Saga of the Vagabond '59
The Human Condition: No
Greater Love '58

Alfonso Arau (1932-)
Committed '99
Picking Up the Pieces '99
Dynamite and Gold '88
Three Amigos '86
Romancing the Stone '84
Posse '75
Scandalous John '71

Fatty Arbuckle (1887-1933)
Leap Year '21
Mabel & Fatty '16

Allan Arbus (1918-)
M*A*S*H: Goodbye, Farewell & Amen '83
Americathon '79
Damien: Omen 2 '78
Coffy '73
The Young Nurses '73
Greaser's Palace '72

Gabriel Arcand (1949-)
Post Mortem '99
Blood of the Hunter '94
Suzanne '80

Nathaniel Arcand (1971-)
Montana Sky '07
Clawed: The Legend of Sasquatch '05
Black Cloud '04
Ginger Snaps Back: The Beginning '04
Skins '02
American Outlaws '01
Grey Owl '99

Bernard Archard (1922-)
My Husband's Secret Life '98
The Horror of Frankenstein '70
Village of the Damned '60

Anne Archer (1947-)
End Game '06
Man of the House '05
November '05
The Iris Effect '04
Uncle Nino '03
The Art of War '00
Innocents '00
Rules of Engagement '00
Whispers: An Elephant's Tale '00 (V)
'98
Mojave Moon '96
Clear and Present Danger '94
The Man in the Attic '94
Question of Faith '93
Short Cuts '93
Body of Evidence '92
Nails '92
Patriot Games '92
Eminent Domain '91
Family Prayers '91
Narrow Margin '90
Love at Large '89
Fatal Attraction '87
Check Is in the Mail '85
The Naked Face '84
Waltz across Texas '83
Green Ice '81
Hero at Large '80
Raise the Titanic '80
Good Guys Wear Black '78
Paradise Alley '78
Lifeguard '76
Cancel My Reservation '72

John Archer (1915-99)
Blue Hawaii '62
Santa Fe '51
Best of the Badmen '50
High Lonesome '50
White Heat '49
Crash Dive '43
Guadalcanal Diary '43
Hello, Frisco, Hello '43
Sherlock Holmes in Washington '43
Gangs, Inc. '41
King of the Zombies '41

Leila Arcieri (1973-)
Mammoth '06
King's Ransom '05
Wild Things 2 '04

Fanny Ardant (1949-)
Paris, je t'aime '06
Nathalie '03
Callas Forever '02
8 Women '02
The Family '87
Conseil de Famille '86
Melo '86
Love Unto Death '84
Next Summer '84
Swann in Love '84
Confidentially Yours '83
Life Is a Bed of Roses '83
The Woman Next Door '81

Eve Arden (1907-90)
Cinderella '84
Grease 2 '82
Pandemonium '82
Under the Rainbow '81
Grease '78
A Guide for the Married Woman '78
The Strongest Man in the World '75
Anatomy of a Murder '59
Our Miss Brooks '56
Phone Call from a Stranger '52
We're No; Married '52
Tea for Two '50
Three Husbands '50
My Dream Is Yours '49
One Touch of Venus '48
Song of Scheherazade '47
Kid from Brooklyn '46
My Reputation '46
Night and Day '46
Mildred Pierce '45
Cover Girl '44
That Uncertain Feeling '41
Whistling in the Dark '41
Ziegfeld Girl '41
Comrade X '40
No, No Nanette '40
Slightly Honorable '40
At the Circus '39
Eternally Yours '39
Having Wonderful Time '38
Letter of Introduction '38
Stage Door '37
Dancing Lady '33

Robert Arden (1922-2004)
Mr. Arkadin '55

George Ardisson (1931-)
Hercules in the Haunted World '64
The Invaders '63

Pierre Arditti (1944-)
Private Fears in Public Places '06
Blaise Pascal '71

Rosita (Rosa) Arenas (1933-)
Neutron vs. the Death Robots '62
The Curse of the Crying Woman '61
Neutron and the Black Mask '61
Neutron vs. the Amazing Dr. Caronte '61
The Witch's Mirror '60
The Curse of the Aztec Mummy '59
The Robot vs. the Aztec Mummy '59
El Bruto '52

Lee Arenberg (1962-)
Pirates of the Caribbean: At World's End '07
Pirates of the Caribbean: Dead Man's Chest '06
Pirates of the Caribbean: The Curse of the Black Pearl '03
Dungeons and Dragons '00
The Cradle Will Rock '99
Waterworld '95
Colonel Chabert '94

Geoffrey Arend (1978-)
Loveless in Los Angeles '07

Eddi Arent (1925-)
The Ringer '05
Circus of Fear '67
The Mysterious Magician '65
The Squeaker '65
Door with the Seven Locks '62

Joey Aresco
Circle of Fear '89
Primary Target '89

Niels Arestrup (1949-)
The Diving Bell and the Butterfly '07
The Beat My Heart Skipped '05

Robert Arevalo
The Siege of Firebase Gloria '89

Anna Aries
Invasion of the Bee Girls '73

David Argue (1959-)
Napoleon '96 (V)
Razorback '84
BMX Bandits '83
Gallipoli '81

Yancey Arias (1971-)
Live Free or Die Hard '07
The Time Machine '02

Imanol Arias (1956-)
The Flower of My Secret '95
Camila '84
Demons in the Garden '82
Labyrinth of Passion '82

Ineko Arima (1932-)
Equinox Flower '58
The Human Condition: No Greater Love '58

Ben Aris (1937-2003)
Tommy '75
If... '69
The Charge of the Light Brigade '68

Yareli Arizmendi
A Day Without a Mexican '04

Asia Argento (1975-)
Marie Antoinette '06
George A. Romero's Land of the Dead '05
Last Days '05
The Heart Is Deceitful Above All Things '04
XXX '02
Scarlet Diva '00
The Church '98
New Rose Hotel '98
The Phantom of the Opera '98
B. Monkey '97
Traveling Companion '96
The Stendahl Syndrome '95
Queen Margot '94
Dario Argento's Trauma '93
Palombella Rossa '89
Demons 2 '87

Dario Argento (1940-)
Innocent Blood '92
Demons 2 '87
The Bird with the Crystal Plumage '70

Fiore Argento (1970-)
Demons '86
Creepers '85

Carmen Argenziano (1943-)
Identity '03
Warm Blooded Killers '01
Andersonville '95
Final Combination '93
Unlawful Entry '92
Red Scorpion '89
The Accused '88
Starchaser: The Legend of Orin '85 (V)
When a Stranger Calls '79
Death Force '78

Allison Argo (1953-)
A Cry from the Mountain '80

Victor Argo (1934-2004)
Anything But Love '02
Don't Say a Word '01
Double Whammy '01
Angel Eyes '01
Blue Moon '00
The Yards '00
Ghost Dog: The Way of the Samurai '99
Luu on the Bridge '98
Next Stop, Wonderland '98
Blue in the Face '95
Smoke '95
True Romance '93
Household Saints '93
Bad Lieutenant '92
King of New York '90
Quick Change '90
After Hours '85
Force Five '75
Mean Streets '73
Boxcar Bertha '72

Adam Arkin (1956-)
Marilyn Hotchkiss' Ballroom Dancing & Charm School '06
Hitch '05
Kids in America '05
Stark Raving Mad '02
Off Season '01
Bloody Proof '99
Hanging Up '99
A Slight Case of Murder '99
Halloween: H20 '98
With Friends Like These '98
Not in This Town '97
The Big Green '95
The Doctor '91
Heat Wave '90
Necessary Parties '88
Fourth Wise Man '85
Pearl '78

Alan Arkin (1934-)
Get Smart '08
Rendition '07
Firewall '06
Little Miss Sunshine '06
The Santa Clause 3: The Escape Clause '06
Eros '04
Noel '04
Thirteen Conversations About One Thing '01
Varian's War '01
Blood Money '99
Slums of Beverly Hills '98
Four Days in September '97
Gattaca '97
Grosse Pointe Blank '97
Mother Night '96
Heck's Way Home '95
The Jerky Boys '95
Doomsday Gun '94
North '94
Cooperstown '93
Indian Summer '93
So I Married an Axe Murderer '93
Taking the Heat '93
Glengarry Glen Ross '92
The Rocketeer '91
Edward Scissorhands '90
Havana '90
Coupe de Ville '90
Big Trouble '86
Joshua Then and Now '85
Bad Medicine '85
The Return of Captain Invincible '83
A Matter of Principle '83
Improper Channels '82
Simon '80
Return of Frank Cannon '80
The In-Laws '79
The Magician of Lublin '79
The Seven-Per-Cent Solution '76
Hearts of the West '75
Rafferty & the Gold Dust Twins '75
Freebie & the Bean '74
Last of the Red Hot Lovers '72
Catch-22 '70
Popi '69
The Heart Is a Lonely Hunter '68
Inspector Clouseau '68
Woman Times Seven '67
Wait until Dark '67
The Russians Are Coming, the Russians Are Coming '66

David Arkin (1941-90)
Nashville '75
The Long Goodbye '73
M*A*S*H '70
I Love You, Alice B. Toklas! '68

Matthew Arkin
Raising Flagg '06

Allen Arkus
A Matter of Honor '95

Elizabeth Arlen (1964-)
In the Company of Spies '99
Separate Lives '94
The First Power '89

Richard Arlen (1898-1976)
Hostile Guns '67
Road to Nashville '67
Apache Uprising '66
Johnny Reno '66
To the Shores of Hell '65
The Human Duplicators '64
Don't Be Afraid of the Dark '73
The Crawling Hand '63
Warlock '59
Blonde Blackmailer '58
Hidden Guns '56
The Mountain '56
Return of Wildfire '49
Buffalo Bill Rides Again '47
Accomplice '46
Identity Unknown '45
Timber Queen '44
Wildcat '42
Flying Blind '41
Mutiny on the Blackhawk '39
Village '37
The Light of Western Stars '30
Touchdown '31
Gun Smoke '31
Island of Lost Souls '32
College Humor '33
Let 'Em Have It '35
The Virginian '29
Feel My Pulse '28
Beggars of Life '28
Wings '27
Behind the Front '26

Arletty (1898-1992)
The Longest Day '62
Portrait of an Assassin '49
Children of Paradise '45
Les Visiteurs du Soir '42
Le Jour Se Leve '39
Circonstances Atténuantes '36

Dimitra Arliss (1932-)
Eleni '85
Ski Bum '75
The Sting '73

George Arliss (1868-1946)
Dr. Syn '37
Transatlantic Tunnel '35
The Iron Duke '34
Disraeli '30

Jillian Armenante (1968-)
North Country '05
Delivered '98

Pedro Armendariz, Jr. (1930-)
And Starring Pancho Villa as Himself '03
Once Upon a Time in Mexico '03
The Crime of Father Amaro '02
Original Sin '01
The Mask of Zorro '98
Like A Bride '94
Tombstone '93
Old Gringo '89
La Chevre '81

Pedro Armendariz, Sr. (1912-63)
Captain Sinbad '63
From Russia with Love '63
Flor Silvestre '58
The Conqueror '56
Diane '56
The Littlest Outlaw '54
El Bruto '52
The Torch '50
Tulsa '49
Fort Apache '48
The Fugitive '48
The Pearl '48
Three Godfathers '48
Maria Candelaria '46

Henry Armetta (1888-1945)
Colonel Effingham's Raid '45
Big Store '41
Fisherman's Wharf '39
Let's Sing Again '36
The Black Cat '34
The Cat and the Fiddle '34
The Merry Widow '34

What! No Beer? '33
Speak Easily '32

Armida (1911-89)
Jungle Goddess '49
Bad Men of the Border '45
Border Romance '30

Fred Armisen (1966-)
The Ex '07
Tenacious D in the Pick of Destiny '06
Deuce Bigalow: European Gigolo '05
Anchorman: The Legend of Ron Burgundy '04
Eurotrip '04

Russell Arms (1922-)
By the Light of the Silvery Moon '53
Stage to Mesa City '48

Alun Armstrong (1946-)
Eragon '06
Millions '05
Oliver Twist '05
Carrie's War '04
Van Helsing '04
It's All About Love '03
Harrison's Flowers '02
The Mummy Returns '01
Strictly Sinatra '01
Proof of Life '00
The Aristocrats '99
David Copperfield '99
Onegin '99
Sleepy Hollow '99
The Saint '97
Braveheart '95
An Awfully Big Adventure '94
Black Beauty '94
Split Second '92
White Hunter, Black Heart '90
Get Carter '71

Bess Armstrong (1953-)
Corporate Affairs '07
Diamond Men '01
Forever Love '98
Pecker '98
Big Bully '95
The Perfect Daughter '96
That Darn Cat '96
Dream Lover '93
The Skateboard Kid '93
Second Sight '89
Nothing in Common '86
High Road to China '83
Jaws 3 '83
Jekyll & Hyde... Together Again '82
The Four Seasons '81
Walking Through the Fire '80
How to Pick Up Girls '78

Curtis Armstrong (1953-)
Akeelah and the Bee '06
Southland Tales '06
Man of the House '05
Ray '04
Quigley '03
National Lampoon's Van Wilder '02
Gale Force '01
Elvis Meets Nixon '98
Safety Patrol '98
Big Bully '95
Revenge of the Nerds 4: Nerds in Love '94
The Adventures of Huck Finn '93
Revenge of the Nerds 3: The Next Generation '92
Revenge of the Nerds 2: Nerds in Paradise '87
One Crazy Summer '86
Bad Medicine '85
Better Off Dead '85
Revenge of the Nerds '84
Risky Business '83

Jack Armstrong (1958-)
Eden '93
Eden 2 '93
Eden 3 '93
Eden 4 '93

Katherine Armstrong
Ambition '91
Street Soldiers '91

Kerry Armstrong (1958-)
Lantana '01
Amy '98
The Hunting '92

Lee Armstrong (1970-)
Leprechaun 3 '95
Magic Island '95

Louis Armstrong (1900-71)
Hello, Dolly! '69
A Man Called Adam '66
The Five Pennies '59
High Society '56
The Glenn Miller Story '54
New Orleans '47
Cabin in the Sky '43
Pennies from Heaven '36

Melinda Armstrong
Bikini Summer 2 '92
Bikini Summer '91

R.G. Armstrong (1917-)
Invasion of Privacy '96
Payback '94
Warlock: The Armageddon '93
Dick Tracy '90
Ghetto Blaster '89
Bulletproof '88
Predator '87
Angels Die Hard '84
Children of the Corn '84
The Beast Within '82
Evilspeak '82
The Shadow Riders '82
Steel '80
Where the Buffalo Roam '80
Dear Detective '78
Devil Dog: The Hound of Hell '78
The Car '77
The Pack '77
Texas Detour '77
Dixie Dynamite '76
Race with the Devil '75
Boss '74
My Name Is Nobody '74
Reflections of Murder '74
Final Comedown '72
The Great Northfield Minnesota Raid '72
The Great White Hope '70
El Dorado '67
Ride the High Country '62
The Fugitive Kind '60
No Name on the Bullet '59

R.L. Armstrong (1924-78)
Slumber Party 57 '76
The Hard Ride '71

Robert Armstrong (1890-1973)
Mighty Joe Young '49
The Fugitive '48
The Paleface '48
Fall Guy '47
Criminal Court '46
Decoy '46
G.I. War Brides '46
Blood on the Sun '45
Action in Arabia '44
Mr. Winkle Goes to War '44
Navy Way '44
The Kansan '43
The Mad Ghoul '43
Wings over the Pacific '43
Baby Face Morgan '42
Gang Busters '42
Dive Bomber '41
The Flying Irishman '39
The Girl Said No '37
Three Legionnaires '37
Ex-Mrs. Bradford '36
Without Orders '36
"G" Men '35
The Mystery Man '35
Palooka '34
King Kong '33
Son of Kong '33
Lost Squadron '32
The Most Dangerous Game '32
Panama Flo '32
Suicide Fleet '31
The Tip-Off '31
Be Yourself '30
Danger Lights '30
Big News '29
The Racketeer '29
A Girl in Every Port '28

Samaire Armstrong (1980-)
Just My Luck '06
Stay Alive '06
Darkwolf '03

Todd Armstrong (1939-93)
Dead Heat on a Merry-Go-Round '66
King Rat '65
Jason and the Argonauts '63

John Arnatt (1917-99)
Crucible of Terror '72
A Challenge for Robin Hood '68
Second Best Secret Agent in the Whole Wide World '65

Desi Arnaz, Sr. (1917-86)
The Escape Artist '82
Forever Darling '56
The Long, Long Trailer '54
Holiday in Havana '49
Bataan '43
The Navy Comes Through '42
Four Jacks and a Jill '41
Too Many Girls '40

Desi Arnaz, Jr. (1953-)
The Mambo Kings '92
Fake Out '82
House of the Long Shadows '82
Great American Traffic Jam '80
How to Pick Up Girls '78
A Wedding '78
Joyride '77
Billy Two Hats '74
Marco '73
The Voyage of the Yes '72

Lucie Arnaz (1951-)
Down to You '00
Second Thoughts '83
Mating Season '81
Washington Mistress '81
The Jazz Singer '80
Death Scream '75
Who Is the Black Dahlia? '75

Adelheid Arndt (1952-)
Rosa Luxemburg '86
Chinese Boxes '84

Denis Arndt (1939-)
Anacondas: The Hunt for the Blood Orchid '04
Sniper 3 '04
Undisputed '02
Asteroid '97
The Beast '96
Metro '96
Amelia Earhart: The Final Flight '94
Basic Instinct '92

Peter Arne (1920-83)
Victor/Victoria '82
Straw Dogs '72
The Oblong Box '69
Battle Beneath the Earth '68
The Hellfire Club '61
The Moonraker '58
The Atomic Man '56

James Arness (1923-)
The Alamo: Thirteen Days to Glory '87
Gunsmoke: Return to Dodge '87
Alias Jesse James '59
Flame of the Islands '55
Sea Chase '55
Them! '54
Hondo '53
Island in the Sky '53
Big Jim McLain '52
Horizons West '52
The Thing '51
Stars in My Crown '50
Two Lost Worlds '50
Wagon Master '50
Battleground '49
The Farmer's Daughter '47

Will Arnett (1970-)
Dr. Seuss' Horton Hears a Who! '08 (V)
Semi-Pro '08
Blades of Glory '07
The Brothers Solomon '07
The Comebacks '07
Hot Rod '07
Ratatouille '07 (V)
The Great New Wonderful '06
Ice Age: The Meltdown '06 (V)
Let's Go to Prison '06
RV '06
Wristcutters: A Love Story '06
Monster-in-Law '05
Series 7: The Contenders '01 (N)
The Waiting Game '99

Jeanetta Arnette (1954-)
Snow Angels '07
Sniper 3 '04
The Shipping News '01
The 70s '00
Boys Don't Cry '99
Ladybugs '92
The Shadow Riders '82
Class Reunion Massacre '77

Stefan Arngrim (1955-)
Misbegotten '98
Class of 1984 '82
Fear No Evil '80
Getting Wasted '80

Alice Arno (1946-)
Female Vampire '73

Edward Arnold (1890-1956)
The Ambassador's Daughter '56
City That Never Sleeps '53
Belles on Their Toes '52
Annie Get Your Gun '50
The Yellow Cab Man '50
Dear Wife '49
Take Me Out to the Ball Game '49
Three Daring Daughters '48
The Hucksters '47
Ziegfeld Follies '46
Weekend at the Waldorf '45
Mrs. Parkington '44
Johnny Eager '42
Meet John Doe '41
The Devil & Daniel Webster '41
Johnny Apollo '40
Lillian Russell '40
Slightly Honorable '40
Idiot's Delight '39
Let Freedom Ring '39
Man About Town '39
Mr. Smith Goes to Washington '39
You Can't Take It with You '38
Blossoms on Broadway '37
Easy Living '37
Toast of New York '37
Come and Get It '36
Crime and Punishment '35
Hide-Out '34
Sadie McKee '34
Thirty Day Princess '34
I'm No Angel '33
Roman Scandals '33

Jack Arnold (1916-92)
The Favor, the Watch, & the Very Big Fish '92
Into the Night '85

Mal Arnold
Blood Feast '63
Scum of the Earth '63

Mark Arnold (1957-)
Threesome '94
Trancers 5: Sudden Deth '94
Trancers 4: Jack of Swords '93

Tichina Arnold (1971-)
Wild Hogs '07
Preaching to the Choir '05
Civil Brand '02
Little Shop of Horrors '86

Tom Arnold (1959-)
The Final Season '07
Pride '07
Chasing Christmas '05
Happy Endings '05
Mr. 3000 '04
Soul Plane '04
Cradle 2 the Grave '03
Children On Their Birthdays '02
Exit Wounds '01
Ablaze '00
Animal Factory '00
Bar Hopping '00
Lloyd '00
Shriek If You Know What I Did Last Friday the 13th '00
Blue Ridge Fall '99
Jackie's Back '99
Malicious Intent '99
National Lampoon's Golf Punks '99
Austin Powers: International Man of Mystery '97
McHale's Navy '97
Sink or Swim '97
Carpool '96
Touch '96
Big Bully '95
Nine Months '95
The Stupids '95
True Lies '94
Undercover Blues '93
The Woman Who Loved Elvis '93
Hero '92
Backfield in Motion '91
Freddy's Dead: The Final Nightmare '91

Victor Arnold (1936-)
The Yards '00
The Incident '67
Shaft '71

David Arnott (1976-)
The Last Man '00
Crisscross '92

Mark Arnott (1950-)
Not Quite Human 2 '89
Return of the Secaucus 7 '80

Francoise Arnoul (1931-)
After Sex '97
The Little Theatre of Jean Renoir '71
French Can-Can '55
Forbidden Fruit '52

Charles Arnt (1908-90)
Big Town '47
Big Town After Dark '47
Fall Guy '47
That Brennan Girl '46
Strange Illusion '45
Dangerous Passage '44
Gambler's Choice '44
The Great Gildersleeve '43
Twin Beds '42

Michael J. Aronin (1944-)
Getting Even '92
Miami Cops '89
The Lone Runner '88

Judie Aronson (1964-)
Desert Kickboxer '92
The Sleeping Car '90
After Midnight '89
American Ninja '85
Friday the 13th, Part 4: The Final Chapter '84

Alexis Arquette (1969-)
Spun '02
The Trip '02
Cleopatra's Second Husband '00
Bride of Chucky '98
Children of the Corn 5: Fields of Terror '98
Love Kills '98
I Think I Do '97
The Wedding Singer '97
Never Met Picasso '96
Sometimes They Come Back... Again '96
Things I Never Told You '96
Dead Weekend '95
Frisk '95
Wigstock: The Movie '95
Don't Do It '94
Frank and Jesse '94
Grief '94
Jack Be Nimble '94
Pulp Fiction '94
Threesome '94
The Ghost Brigade '93
Jumpin' at the Boneyard '92
Miracle Beach '92
Terminal Bliss '91
Down and Out in Beverly Hills '86

David Arquette (1971-)
The Darwin Awards '06
The Tripper '06
The Adventures of Sharkboy and Lavagirl in 3-D '05
Never Die Alone '04
Riding the Bullet '04
Stealing Sinatra '04
2 Brothers & a Bride '03
Eight Legged Freaks '02
The Grey Zone '01
See Spot Run '01
3000 Miles to Graceland '01
Ready to Rumble '00
Scream 3 '00
Free Money '99
Muppets from Space '99
Never Been Kissed '99
Ravenous '99
The Alarmist '98
Dream with the Fishes '97
R.P.M. '97
Scream 2 '97
Beautiful Girls '96
johns '96
Larry McMurtry's Dead Man's Walk '96
Scream '96
Wild Bill '95
At Home with the Webbers '94
Fall Time '94
Roadracers '94
The Ghost Brigade '93
Buffy the Vampire Slayer '92
Where the Day Takes You '92

Lewis Arquette (1935-2001)
Little Nicky '00
Ready to Rumble '00
Get a Clue! '98
Kiki's Delivery Service '98 (V)
Almost Heroes '97
A River Made to Drown In '97
Scream 2 '97
Waiting for Guffman '96
Sleep with Me '94
Attack of the 50 Ft. Woman '93

Patricia Arquette (1968)
Fast Food Nation '06
Holes '03
Tiptoes '03
The Badge '02
Human Nature '02
Little Nicky '00
Bringing Out the Dead '99
Goodbye, Lover '99
Stigmata '99
The Hi-Lo Country '98
Infinity '96
Lost Highway '96
Nightwatch '96
The Secret Agent '96
Beyond Rangoon '95
Flirting with Disaster '95
Ed Wood '94
Holy Matrimony '94
Inside Monkey Zetterland '93
True Romance '93
Ethan Frome '92
The Linguini Incident '92
Trouble Bound '92
Book of Love '91
Dillinger '91
The Indian Runner '91
Prayer of the Rollerboys '91
Rock 'n' Roll High School "Forever '91
Wildflower '91
Syngenor '90
Tango and Cash '89
Far North '88
A Nightmare on Elm Street 3: Dream Warriors '87
Pretty Smart '87

Richmond Arquette (1964)
Made of Honor '08
Spent '06
Kids in America '05
Big Bad Love '02
Good Advice '01
Things Behind the Sun '01
The Whole Nine Yards '00
The Treat '98
Search and Destroy '94
Nowhere to Run '93
The Wrong Man '93
Fathers and Sons '92
The Linguini Incident '92
In the Deep Woods '91
Son of the Morning Star '91
...Almost '90
Don't Hang Up '90
Nobody's Fool '86
After Hours '85
The Aviator '85
Desperately Seeking Susan '85
8 Million Ways to Die '85
New York Stories '89
The Big Blue '88
Promised a Miracle '88
Amazon Women on the Moon '87

Rosanna Arquette (1959)
The Tripper '06
Kiss & Tell '99
Sugar Town '99
Hope Floats '98
I'm Losing You '98
Buffalo 66 '97
Gone Fishin' '97
Trading Favors '97
Hell's Kitchen NYC '97
Crash '95
Pulp Fiction '94
Search and Destroy '94
Nowhere to Run '93
The Wrong Man '93
Black Rainbow '91
The Linguini Incident '92

Robert Arthur (1925-)
The Masked Marvel '43
Naked Youth '59
Danger on the Air '38
The Ghost Walks '34
The Monster '25

Maureen Arthur (1934-)
The Love Machine '71
How to Succeed in Business without Really Trying '67

Johnny Arthur (1883-1951)
The Road to Singapore '40
The Plainsman '37
History Is Made at Night '37
Ex-Mrs. Bradford '36
Mr. Deeds Goes to Town '36
The Whole Town's Talking '35
Danger Lights '30
The Return of Dr. Fu Manchu '30
The Silver Horde '30
The Mysterious Dr. Fu Manchu '29

Jean Arthur (1900-91)
A Foreign Affair '48
Shane '53
Lady Takes a Chance '43
The More the Merrier '43
The Devil & Miss Jones '41
Arizona '40
Mr. Smith Goes to Washington '39
Only Angels Have Wings '39
You Can't Take It with You '38
Easy Living '37
History Is Made at Night '37

Indus Arthur (1941-84)
M*A*S*H '70
Alvarez Kelly '66

Jeri Arredondo
Vamping '84
A*P*E* '76

Rod Arrants (1944-)
The Dark Secret of Harvest Home '78

Lisa Arrindell (1954-)
See Lisa Arrindell Anderson

Beatrice Arthur (1923-)
Enemies of Laughter '00
Mame '74
Lovers and Other Strangers '70
How to Commit Marriage '69

Antonin Artaud (1896-1948)
Passion of Joan of Arc '28
Napoleon '27

Carlos Arruza (1920-66)
The Alamo '60
Torero '56

Jayne Ashbourne (1969)
Prince of Poisoners: The Life and Crimes of William Palmer '98
Sharpe's Gold '94

Lorraine Ashbourne (1961-)
Fever Pitch '96
Distant Voices, Still Lives '88

Dana Ashbrook (1967-)
Python 2 '02
Ghost Dad '90
Girlfriend from Hell '89
Return of the Living Dead 2 '88
Waxwork '88
Dragnet '87

Daphne Ashbrook (1966-)
The Love Letter '98
Doctor Who '96
Automatic '94
Intruders '92
Sunset Heat '92

Linden Ashby (1960-)
Resident Evil: Extinction '07
Wild Things 2 '04
A Woman Hunted '03
Sniper 2 '02
Facing the Enemy '00
Tick Tock '00
Where the Truth Lies '99
Murder She Purred: A Mrs. Murphy Mystery '98

Elizabeth Ashley (1939-)
Happiness '98
Just the Ticket '98
The Buccaneers '95
Dangerous Curves '88
A Man of Passion '88
Vampire's Kiss '88
Stagecoach '86
Svengali '83
Paternity '81
Windows '80
Coma '78
Great Scout & Cathouse Thursday '76
One of My Wives Is Missing '76
War Between the Tates '76
Rancho Deluxe '75
Paperback Hero '73
Ship of Fools '65
The Carpetbaggers '64

Jennifer Ashley
Inseminoid '80
Tintorera...Tiger Shark '78
Porn Porn Girls '76

Michael Artura
Apt Pupil '97
Money Train '95
Killer Looks '94
Kiss of Death '94

Douglas Arthurs (1959-)
Wyatt Earp '94
The Perfect Bride '91

William Ash (1977-)
Mad About Mambo '00
All the King's Men '99
Resident Evil: Extinction '07

Ashanti (1980-)
John Tucker Must Die '06
Coach Carter '05
The Muppets' Wizard of Oz '05

Ron Asheton (1948-)
Mosquito '95

Edward Ashley (1904-2000)
Beyond the Next Mountain '87
Dick Tracy Meets Gruesome '47
Nocturne '46
The Black Swan '42
Bitter Sweet '40

Kate Ashfield (1972-)
Fakers '04
Shaun of the Dead '04
Beyond Borders '03
Pure '02
Do or Die '01
The Low Down '00
The Last Minute '01
The War Zone '98

Joseph Ashton (1986-)
Slappy and the Stinkers '97
The Education of Little Tree '97

Roger Ashton-Griffiths (1957-)
Gangs of New York '02
Princess of Thieves '01
Vanity Fair '99
Haunted Honeymoon '86

Desmond Askew (1972-)
The Hills Have Eyes '06
Turistas '06
Fabled '02
Repli-Kate '01
Go '99

Tom Ashworth
Killer Tomatoes Eat France '91
Killer Tomatoes Strike Back '90

Leslie Ash (1960-)
Shadey '87
Murder: Ultimate Grounds for Divorce '84
Curse of the Pink Panther '83
Quadrophenia '79

Neus Asensi (1965-)
Arachnid '01

Oscar Asche (1871-1936)
Don Quixote '35
Scrooge '35

Jane Asher (1946-)
Death at a Funeral '07
The Choir '95
Dreamchild '85
Success Is the Best Revenge '84
Deep End '70
Alfie '66
Masque of the Red Death '65
The Prince and the Pauper '62

Eve Brent Ashe
See Eve Brent

Renee Asherson (1920-)
The Others '01
Grey Owl '99

John Ashton (1948-)
Gone Baby Gone '07
Avalanche '99
Instinct '99
For Which He Stands '98
Meet the Deedles '98
Little Big League '94
Trapped in Paradise '94
Stephen King's The Tommyknockers '93
Dirty Work '92
Love, Lies and Murder '91
L.A. Gangs Rising '89
Midnight Run '88
She's Having a Baby '88
Beverly Hills Cop 2 '87
Some Kind of Wonderful '87
The Deliberate Stranger '86
King Kong Lives '86
The Adventures of Buckaroo Banzai Across the Eighth Dimension '84
Beverly Hills Cop '84

Tadanobu Asano (1973-)
The Doe Boy '01
Color of a Brisk and Leaping Day '95
Tecumseh: The Last Warrior '95
Silent Tongue '92

Ariane Ascaride (1954-)
My Life on Ice '02
The Town Is Quiet '00
The Adventures of Felix '99
Marius and Jeannette '97

Peggy Ashcroft (1907-91)
The Jewel in the Crown '84
A Passage to India '84
Hullabaloo over Georgie & Bonnie's Pictures '78
The Pedestrian '73
The Nun's Story '59
The 39 Steps '35

Shawn Ashmore (1979-)
The Ruins '08
X-Men: The Last Stand '06
Underclassman '05
X2: X-Men United '03
X-Men '00
Melanie Darrow '97
Guitarman '95
Harnessing Peacocks '92

Aaron Ashmore (1979-)
Brave New Girl '04
A Separate Peace '04
The Skulls 2 '02

Ed Asner (1929-)
The Christmas Card '06
Elf '03
Missing Brendan '03
National Lampoon's Christmas Vacation 2: Cousin Eddie's Big Island Adventure '03
The Animal '01
Above Suspicion '00
Common Ground '00
Perfect Game '00
The Bachelor '99
Love and Action in Chicago '99
Hard Rain '97
Gargoyles, The Movie: The Heroes Awaken '94 (V)
Gypsy '93
Happily Ever After '93 (V)
Heads '93
JFK '91
Silent Motive '91
Switched at Birth '91
A Friendship in Vienna '88
Moon over Parador '88
A Case of Libel '83
Daniel '83
O'Hara's Wife '82
Fort Apache, the Bronx '81
A Small Killing '81
The Family Man '79
The Gathering '77
Roots '77
Gus '76

John Ashley (1934-97)
Beyond Atlantis '73
Woman Hunt '72
Brides of the Beast '68
Beach Blanket Bingo '65
How to Stuff a Wild Bikini '65
Bikini Beach '64
Muscle Beach Party '64
Beach Party '63
High School Caesar '60
Dragstrip Girl '57
Motorcycle Gang '57

Leon Askin (1907-2005)
Savage Island '85
Dr. Death, Seeker of Souls '73
Hud '63
Frankenstein's Daughter '58
How to Make a Monster '58

Gregoire Aslan (1908-82)
Golden Voyage of Sinbad '73
Traveller '96
Dune Warriors '91
Kung Fu: The Movie '86
The Warrior & the Sorceress '84
The Red Inn '51

Robin Askwith (1950-)
Flesh and Blood Show '73
Horror Hospital '73
Hans Brinker '69

Luke Askew (1937-)
Just the Ticket '98
Played '05

Fred Asparagus (1947-98)
The Beneficiary '97
Blast '96
Cadillac Ranch '96

Kumiko Aso (1978-)
Shelter '98
Pulse '01
Dr. Akagi '98

Asparagus
Barn of the Naked Dead '73
Hell on Wheels '67
Smoke in the Wind '75
Beyond Atlantis '73
Twilight People '72
Beast of the Yellow Night '70
Mad Doctor of Blood Island '68
Hell on Wheels '67
The Eye Creatures '65
The Devil's Brigade '68
The Green Berets '68
Cool Hand Luke '67
Frailty '02
Minnesota Raid '22
Angel Unchained '70
Easy Rider '69
The Warrior & the Sorceress '84
Sherlock Holmes and the Deadly Necklace '62
Valley of the Kings '54
South Sea Woman '53
Moment to Moment '66
Paris When It Sizzles '64
Our Man in Havana '59
The Red Inn '51
Back to Back '90
The Longest Drive '76
Wanda Nevada '79
Posse '75
Slipstream '73
The Great Northfield Minnesota Raid '72
Nobody's Perfect '90

Armand Assante (1949-)
American Gangster '07
Dead Lenny '06
Soul's Midnight '06
Dot.Kill '05
Mirror Wars: Reflection One '05
Two for the Money '05
Federal Protection '02
After the Storm '01
Last Run '01
On the Beach '00
The Road to El Dorado '00 (V)
The Hunley '99
Looking for an Echo '99
The Odyssey '97
Gotti '96
Striptease '96
Judge Dredd '95
Kidnapped '95
Blind Justice '94
Trial by Jury '94
Fatal Instinct '93
1492: Conquest of Paradise '92
Hoffa '92
The Mambo Kings '92
Fever '91
The Marrying Man '91
Eternity '90
Q & A '90
Animal Behavior '89
Passion in Paradise '89
Jack the Ripper '88
The Penitent '88
Hands of a Stranger '87
Belizaire the Cajun '86
Deadly Business '86
Unfaithfully Yours '84
Rage of Angels '83
I, the Jury '82
Little Darlings '80
Private Benjamin '80
Sophia Loren: Her Own Story '80
Prophecy '79
Lady of the House '78
Paradise Alley '78
The Lords of Flatbush '74

Pat Ast (1942-2001)
Reform School Girls '86
Heat '72

Fred Astaire (1899-1987)
That's Dancing! '85
Ghost Story '81
The Man in the Santa Claus Suit '79
Family Upside Down '78
The Purple Taxi '77
The Amazing Dobermans '76
That's Entertainment, Part 2 '76 (N)
That's Entertainment '74
The Towering Inferno '74
Finian's Rainbow '68
Paris When It Sizzles '64
On the Beach '59
Funny Face '57
Silk Stockings '57
Daddy Long Legs '55
The Band Wagon '53
The Belle of New York '52
Royal Wedding '51
Let's Dance '50
Three Little Words '50
The Barkleys of Broadway '49
Easter Parade '48
Blue Skies '46
Ziegfeld Follies '46
Yolanda and the Thief '45
The Sky's the Limit '43
Holiday Inn '42
You Were Never Lovelier '42
You'll Never Get Rich '41
Broadway Melody of 1940 '40
Second Chorus '40
The Story of Vernon and Irene Castle '39
Carefree '38
A Damsel in Distress '37
Shall We Dance '37
Follow the Fleet '36
Swing Time '36
Roberta '35
Top Hat '35
The Gay Divorcee '34
Dancing Lady '33
Flying Down to Rio '33

Nils Asther (1897-1981)
Son of Lassie '45
Bluebeard '44
Night Monster '42
Flying Blind '41
Make-Up '37
The Bitter Tea of General Yen '33

Adriana Asti (1933-)
Best of Youth '03
Caligula '80
The Sex Machine '75
Phantom of Liberty '74
Zorro '74
Before the Revolution '65

John Astin (1930-)
School of Life '06
The Frighteners '96
Huck and the King of Hearts '93
Silence of the Hams '93
Stepmonster '92
Killer Tomatoes Eat France '91
Gremlins 2: The New Batch '90
Killer Tomatoes Strike Back '90
Night Life '90
Return of the Killer Tomatoes! '88
Adventures Beyond Belief '87
Body Slam '87
Teen Wolf Too '87
National Lampoon's European Vacation '85
Halloween with the New Addams Family '79
The Barcelona Kill '77
Freaky Friday '76
Only with Married Men '74
Brothers O'Toole '73
Pepper and His Wacky Taxi '72

MacKenzie Astin (1973-)
Love's Enduring Promise '04
Off the Lip '04
How to Deal '03
Two Days '03
The Wheeler Dealers '63
The Mating Habits of the Earthbound Human '99
Stranger than Fiction '99
The Last Days of Disco '98
Dream for an Insomniac '96
The Evening Star '96
In Love and War '96
Widow's Kiss '94
Wyatt Earp '94
Iron Will '93
The Garbage Pail Kids Movie '87

Sean Astin (1971-)
The Final Season '07
What Love Is '07
Click '06
Marilyn Hotchkiss' Ballroom Dancing & Charm School '06
Bigger Than the Sky '05
Smile '05
Elvis Has Left the Building '04
50 First Dates '04
Lord of the Rings: The Return of the King '03
The Final Hit '02
Lord of Rings: The Two Towers '02
Lord of the Rings: The Fellowship of the Rings '01
Deterrence '00
Bulworth '98
Dish Dogs '98
Courage Under Fire '96
Kurt Vonnegut's Harrison Bergeron '95
The Low Life '95
Safe Passage '94
Rudy '93
Encino Man '92
Where the Day Takes You '92
Toy Soldiers '91
Memphis Belle '90
The Willies '90
Staying Together '89
The War of the Roses '89
Like Father, Like Son '87
White Water Summer '87
The Goonies '85

John Aston
I Want to Go Home '89
Last Resort '86

Gertrude Astor (1887-1977)
After Midnight '33
Carnival Lady '33
They Never Come Back '32
Be Yourself '30
Dames Ahoy '30
The Cat and the Canary '27
The Cheerful Fraud '27
Strong Man '26
Beyond the Rocks '22

Mary Astor (1906-87)
Hush, Hush, Sweet Charlotte '65
Return to Peyton Place '61
This Happy Feeling '58
Any Number Can Play '49
Little Women '49
Act of Violence '49
Cass Timberlane '47
Meet Me in St. Louis '44
Thousands Cheer '43
Across the Pacific '42
The Palm Beach Story '42
The Great Lie '41
The Maltese Falcon '41
Brigham Young: Frontiersman '40
Midnight '39
Listen, Darling '38
The Hurricane '37
Prisoner of Zenda '37
Dodsworth '36
Lady from Nowhere '36
The Kennel Murder Case '33
Red Dust '32
Behind Office Doors '31
The Royal Bed '31
Smart Woman '31
Don Juan '26
Don Q., Son of Zorro '25
Beau Brummel '24
The Fighting American '24
Mark of Zorro '20

Patti Astor
Assault of the Killer Bimbos '88
Underground U.S.A. '84
The Foreigner '78

Nancy Moore Atchison
The Yearling '94

Hooper Atchley (1887-1943)
Midnight Edition '93
Roarin' Lead '37
Prescott Kid '36
I Can't Escape '34
The Dude Bandit '33
Local Badman '32
Midnight Warning '32
Spirit of the West '32
Arizona Terror '31
Clearing the Range '31

Roscoe Ates (1892-1962)
Hills of Oklahoma '50
Thunder in the Pines '49
Black Hills '48
Check Your Guns '48
The Hawk of Powder River '48
The Tioga Kid '48
West to Glory '47
Wild Country '47
Colorado Serenade '46
Driftin' River '46
Wild West '46
Reg'lar Fellers '41
Robin Hood of the Pecos '41
Three Texas Steers '39
Woman in the Shadows '34
Cheyenne Kid '33
Lucky Devils '33
What! No Beer? '33
Come on Danger! '32
The Champ '32
Freaks '32
Cimarron '31

William Atherton (1947-)
The Last Samurai '03
Headspace '02
Burning Down the House '01
Race to Space '01
The Crow: Salvation '00
Introducing Dorothy Dandridge '99
Executive Power '98
Mad City '97
Bio-Dome '96
Hoodlum '96
Broken Trust '95
Ravenhawk '95
Saints and Sinners '95
Frank and Jesse '94
The Pelican Brief '93
Chrome Soldiers '92
Buried Alive '90
Die Hard 2: Die Harder '90
A Fight for Jenny '90
Intrigue '90
Grim Prairie Tales '89
Die Hard '88
No Mercy '86
Real Genius '85
Ghostbusters '84
Tomorrow's Child '82
Centennial '78
Looking for Mr. Goodbar '77
The Day of the Locust '75
The Hindenburg '75
The Sugarland Express '74
Class of 44 '73

Harvey Atkin (1942-)
Critical Care '97
SnakeEater 2: The Drug Buster '89
Meatballs '79

Feodor Atkine (1948-)
Alexander '04
Angel of Death '02
Carnage '02
Vatel '00
Spy Games '99
Ronin '98
Doctor Chance '97
Sharpe's Revenge '97
Sharpe's Siege '96
Three Lives and Only One Death '96
High Heels '91
Sorceress '88
Pauline at the Beach '83
Le Beau Mariage '82

Christopher Atkins (1961-)
Quigley '03
Malicious Intent '99
Mutual Needs '97
Red Shoe Diaries: Four on the Floor '96
It's My Party '95
Project Shadowchaser 3000 '95
Bullet Down Under '94
Dracula Rising '93
Fatal Charm '92
Shoot '92
Wet and Wild Summer '92
King's Ransom '91
Mortuary Academy '91
Listen to Me '89
Shakma '89
Beaks: The Movie '87
Secret Weapons '85
A Night in Heaven '83
Pirate Movie '82
Child Bride of Short Creek '81
The Blue Lagoon '80

Dave Atkins
The Last Seduction 2 '98
Plunkett & Macleane '98
The Advocate '93
London Kills Me '91
Hellraiser '87
Personal Services '87
Prick Up Your Ears '87
Britannia Hospital '82
Bury Me an Angel '71

Eileen Atkins (1934-)
Evening '07
Ask the Dust '06
Scenes of a Sexual Nature '06
Vanity Fair '04
Cold Mountain '03
What a Girl Wants '03
The Hours '02
Gosford Park '01
Wit '01
The Avengers '98
A Dance to the Music of Time '97
Jack and Sarah '95
Cold Comfort Farm '94
Wolf '94
The Lost Language of Cranes '92
Let Him Have It '91
The Vision '87
The Dresser '83
Oliver Twist '82
Smiley's People '82
I Don't Want to Be Born '75

Essence Atkins (1972-)
Deliver Us from Eva '03
How High '01
Love Song '00

Tom Atkins (1938-)
Out of the Black '01
Bruiser '00
Bob Roberts '92
Two Evil Eyes '90
Dead Man Out '89
The Heist '89
Maniac Cop '88
Lethal Weapon '87
Blind Justice '86
Night of the Creeps '86
Desperate Lives '82
Halloween 3: Season of the Witch '82
Skeezer '82
Escape from New York '81
The Fog '78
Tarantulas: The Deadly Cargo '77
Special Delivery '76
The Detective '68

Beverly Hope Atkinson (1935-2001)
Uforia '81
Heavy Traffic '73

Frank Atkinson (1893-1963)
Pygmalion '38

Jayne Atkinson (1959-)
12 and Holding '05
The Village '04
Our Town '03
Free Willy 2: The Adventure Home '95
Free Willy '93
Capone '89

Rowan Atkinson (1955-)
Mr. Bean's Holiday '07
Keeping Mum '05
Johnny English '03
Love Actually '03
Scooby-Doo '02
Rat Race '01
Maybe Baby '99
Bean '97
Four Weddings and a Funeral '94
The Lion King '94 (V)
Hot Shots! Part Deux '93
Bernard and the Genie '91
The Witches '90
The Tall Guy '89
Never Say Never Again '83

Yvan Attal (1965-)
Rush Hour 3 '07
The Interpreter '05
Munich '05
Happily Ever After '04
Bon Voyage '03
And Now Ladies and Gentlemen '02
My Wife is an Actress '01
The Criminal '00
Love, etc. '96
Portraits Chinois '96

Dave Attell (1965-)
Scary Movie 4 '06
Pootie Tang '01

Richard Attenborough (1923-)
Jack and the Beanstalk: The Real Story '01
Joseph and the Amazing Technicolor Dreamcoat '00
The Railway Children '00
Elizabeth '98
The Lost World: Jurassic Park 2 '97
Hamlet '96
Wavelength '96
Miracle on 34th Street '94
Jurassic Park '93
The Human Factor '79
Brannigan '75
Conduct Unbecoming '75
Rosebud '75
Ten Little Indians '75
10 Rillington Place '71
David Copperfield '70
Loot... Give Me Money, Honey! '70
The Magic Christian '69
The Bliss of Mrs. Blossom '68
Doctor Dolittle '67
The Sand Pebbles '66
The Flight of the Phoenix '65
Guns at Batasi '64
Seance on a Wet Afternoon '64
The Great Escape '63
Only Two Can Play '62
Trial & Error '62
The League of Gentlemen '60
S.O.S. Pacific '60
Sea of Sand '58
Brothers in Law '57
The Baby and the Battleship '56
The Gift Horse '52
Morning Departure '50
The Guinea Pig '48
Brighton Rock '47
Stairway to Heaven '46
In Which We Serve '43

Malcolm Atterbury (1907-92)
Emperor of the North Pole '73
How to Make a Monster '58
Blood of Dracula '57
Crime of Passion '57
I Was a Teenage Werewolf '57

Edward Atterton (1962-)
Children of Dune '03
Mists of Avalon '01
Brittanic '00
Relative Values '99
The Man in the Iron Mask '98
Catherine Cookson's The Wingless Bird '97
The Hunchback '97
Far Harbor '96

The Vacillations of Poppy Carew '94

Michael Attwell (1943-)
Poldark '96
Joseph '95

Barry Atwater (1918-78)
The Night Stalker '71
Night Gallery '69
Pork Chop Hill '59

Edith Atwater (1911-86)
Family Plot '76
Die Sister, Die! '74
Our Time '74
True Grit '69
Strait-Jacket '64
It Happened at the World's Fair '63
The Body Snatcher '45

Hayley Atwell
Cassandra's Dream '07
Mansfield Park '07
The Line of Beauty '06

Lionel Atwill (1885-1946)
Fog Island '45
House of Dracula '45
Lost City of the Jungle '45
Captain America '44
House of Frankenstein '44
Lady in the Death House '44
The Ghost of Frankenstein '42
Junior G-Men of the Air '42
Night Monster '42
Pardon My Sarong '42
Sherlock Holmes and the Secret Weapon '42
To Be or Not to Be '42
Man Made Monster '41
Boom Town '40
Johnny Apollo '40
The Gorilla '39
Balalaika '39
The Hound of the Baskervilles '39
Mr. Moto Takes a Vacation '39
The Secret of Dr. Kildare '39
Son of Frankenstein '39
The Three Musketeers '39
The Great Waltz '38
Three Comrades '38
High Command '37
Captain Blood '35
The Devil is a Woman '35
Mark of the Vampire '35
Murders in the Zoo '33
Mystery of the Wax Museum '33
The Song of Songs '33
The Sphinx '33
Doctor X '32
The Vampire Bat '32
'84

Anat Atzmon (1958-)
From the Life of the Marionettes '80
Double Edge '92
Every Time We Say Goodbye '86
Dead End Street '83
Shell Shock '63

Robert Atzorn (1945-1983)
The Wannsee Conference '84

Brigitte Auber (1928-)
To Catch a Thief '55
Femmes de Paris '53
Rendez-vous de Jui'et '49

Rene Auberjonois (1940-)
Eulogy '04
Burning Down the House '01

Sally Hemings: An American Scandal '00
Inspector Gadget '99
Cats Don't Dance '97 (V)
Los Locos Posse '97
Batman Forever '95
The Player '92
Little Nemo: Adventures in Slumberland '92 (V)
The Feud '90
Wildcard '92
Once Upon a Midnight Scary '90
A Connecticut Yankee in King Arthur's Court '89
Gore Vidal's Billy the Kid '89
The Little Mermaid '89 (V)
My Best Friend Is a Vampire '88
Police Academy 5: Assignment Miami Beach '88
Walker '87
A Smoky Mountain Christmas '86
3:15—The Moment of Truth '86
Where the Buffalo Roam '80
The Dark Secret of Harvest Home '78
Eyes of Laura Mars '78
The Big Bus '76
King Kong '76
Images '72
Pete 'n' Tillie '72
McCabe & Mrs. Miller '71
Brewster McCloud '70
M*A*S*H '70
Petulia '68
Lilith '64

K.D. Aubert (1978-)
In the Mix '05
Frankenfish '04
Soul Plane '04
Friday After Next '02

Lenore Aubert (1913-93)
Abbott and Costello Meet the Killer, Boris Karloff '49
Abbott and Costello Meet Frankenstein '48
Having Wonderful Crime '45
Action in Arabia '44

James Aubrey (1947-)
Buddy's Song '91
Riders of the Storm '88
Forever Young '85
Home Before Midnight '84
The Hunger '83
The Terror '79
Lord of the Flies '63

Jimmy Aubrey (1887-1983)
Bouquet of Barbed Wire '76
The Hound of the Baskervilles '39

Juliet Aubrey (1969-)
The Constant Gardener '05
The Mayor of Casterbridge '03
Iris '01
Still Crazy '98
The Unknown Soldier '98
Welcome to Sarajevo '97
Catherine Cookson's The Moth '96
Go Now '96
Middlemarch '93

Cecile Aubry
The Black Rose '50
Manon '50

Danielle Aubry
Operation C.I.A. '65
Bikini Beach '64

Jacques Aubuchon (1924-91)
Thunder Road '58
Gun Glory '57
Drums of Jeopardy '31

Michel Auclair (1922-88)
Swashbuckler '84
The Story of a Love Story '73
Murder at 45 R.P.M. '65
Head of the Family '71
Manon '50

Maxine Audley (1923-92)
Frankenstein Must Be Destroyed '69
Peeping Tom '60
The Trials of Oscar Wilde '60

Stephane Audran (1932-)
Madeline '98
Maximum Risk '96
Son of Gascogne '95
Betty '92
The Turn of the Screw '92
Sons '89
Faceless '88
Babette's Feast '87
Poor Little Rich Girl: The Barbara Hutton Story '87
La Cage aux Folles 3: The Wedding '86
The Blood of Others '84
Brideshead Revisited '81
Coup de Torchon '81
The Big Red One '80
Eagle's Wing '79
Silver Bears '78
Violette '78
Blood Relatives '77
Twist '76
Vincent, Francois, Paul and the Others '76
The Black Bird '75
Ten Little Indians '75
Wedding in Blood '74
The Discreet Charm of the Bourgeoisie '72
La Rupture '70
La Femme Infidele '69
Le Boucher '69
Les Biches '68
Les Bonnes Femmes '60
Six in Paris '68

Mischa Auer (1905-67)
Arrivederci, Baby! '66
The Christmas That Almost Wasn't '66
Sputnik '61
Mr. Arkadin '55
And Then There Were None '45
Brewster's Millions '45
Around the World '43
Twin Beds '42
Cracked Nuts '41
The Flame of New Orleans '41
Hold That Ghost '41
Seven Sinners '40
Destry Rides Again '39
Vogues of 1938 '37
The Gay Desperado '36
One Woman or Two '85
Grain of Sand '84
A Sunday in the Country '84
The Rage of Paris '38
East Side of Heaven '39
Service De Luxe '38
Sweethearts '38
My Man Godfrey '36
The Princess Comes Across '36

Jean-Pierre Aumont (1913-2001)
The Proprietor '96
Jefferson in Paris '94
Becoming Colette '92
A Tale of Two Cities '80
Catherine & Co. '76
The Happy Hooker '75
Mahogany '75
Day for Night '73
Castle Keep '69
Caudron of Blood '67
The Horse Without a Head '63

Michel Aumont (1936-)
The Closet '00
Alberto Express '92
Napoleon '55
Lili '53
Song of Scheherazade '47
Heartbeat '46
Bizarre Bizarre '39
Maria Chapdelaine '34

Tina Aumont (1946-)
A Matter of Time '76
Lifespan '75
Spoiled Children '77

Daniel Auteuil (1950-)
My Best Friend '06
The Valet '06
Hidden '05
Apres-Vous '03
On Guard! '03
The Closet '00
Sade '00
The Widow of Saint-Pierre '00
The Girl on the Bridge '98
The Lost Son '98
Lucie Aubrac '98
Les Voleurs '96
The Eighth Day '95
Queen Margot '94
The Separation '94
Ma Saison Preferee '93
Un Coeur en Hiver '93
The Elegant Criminal '92

Shaun Austin-Olsen
Suds '20
It '27

Terri Austin (1959-)
False Witness '89
The Vindicator '85

William Austin (1884-1975)
Suckar Money '34
Flaming Signal '33
Woman Condemned '33
Torso '73
Man of Legend '71
Partner '68
The Monster Walks '32

Steve Austin (1964-)
The Condemned '07
The Longest Yard '05

Pam(ela) Austin (1942-)
The Dressmaker '89
Agatha '79
Evil Roy Slade '71
Kissin' Cousins '64
Blue Hawaii '62

Julie Austin
The Flying Scotsman '06
Everyone's Hero '06 (V)
Urban Ghost Story '98
Fatal Exposure '90
Elves '89

Karen Austin (1955-)
When a Stranger Calls Back '93
Far from Home '89
A Girl to Kill For '90
Assassin '86
The Ladies Club '86
Summer Rental '85
The Jagged Edge '85

Jake T. Austin (1994-)
The Ant Bully '06 (V)

Charlotte Austin (1933-)
The Brice & the Beast '58
Daddy Long Legs '55
Desiree '54

Pernilla August (1958-)
Star Wars: Episode 2—Attack of the Clones '02
Mary, Mother of Jesus '99
Star Wars: Episode 1—The Phantom Menace '99
Private Confessions '98
Jerusalem '96
The Best Intentions '92

Lance August (1961-)
Striptease '96

Robert August (1945-)
The Endless Summer 2 '94
The Endless Summer '66

Sherman Augustus (1959-)

Ewa Aulin (1949-)
Start the Revolution without Me '70
Candy '68
Colors '88
ZigZag '02
Virus '99

Karen Austin (1955-) / Monkey Business '52
Les Miserables '52

Jake T. Austin (1994-)

Claudine Auger (1942-)
Secret Places '85
Lobster for Breakfast '82
Rico '74
The Associate '79
Triple Cross '67
Thunderball '65

Marcus Aurelius
Suspect Device '95
A.P.E.X. '94
The Cure '17
One A.M. '16

Albert Austin (1881-1953)
Three Charlies and One Phoney! '18
The Vagabond '16
A Simple Twist of Fate '94

Alana Austin (1982-)
Miracle Dogs Too '06
Miracle Dogs '03

Gene Autry (1907-98)
Alias Jesse James '59
Last of the Pony Riders '53
Winning of the West '53
Blue Canadian Rockies '52
Night Stage to Galveston '52
Hills of Utah '51
Valley of Fire '51
Gene Autry and the Mounties '51
Texans Never Cry '51
Mule Train '50
Ccw Town '50
The Big Sombrero '49
Riders of the Whistling Pines '49
Rim of the Canyon '49
Loaded Pistols '48
The Strawberry Roan '48
Robin Hood of Texas '47
Trail to San Antone '47
Twilight on the Rio Grande '47
Sioux City Sue '46
Bells of Capistrano '42
Call of the Canyon '42
Heart of the Rio Grande '42
Back in the Saddle '41
Down Mexico Way '41
Ridin' on a Rainbow '41
Gaucho Serenade '40
Melody Ranch '40
South of the Border '39
Blue Montana Skies '39
Colorado Sunset '39
In Old Monterey '39
Mexicali Rose '39
Rootin' Tootin' Rhythm '38
Boots & Saddles '37
Git Along Little Dogies '37
Gold Mine in the Sky '38
Melody Trail '35
The Phantom Empire '35
In Old Santa Fe '34
The Big Show '36
Manhattan Merry-Go-Round '37
Public Cowboy No. 1 '37
Round-Up Time in Texas '37
Oh Susannah '36
Prairie Moon '38
Old Barn Dance '38
Old Corral '35
Red River Valley '36
Ride, Ranger, Ride '36
Yodelin' Kid from Pine Ridge '37
Springtime in the Rockies '37
The Man from Music Mountain '38
Mystery Mountain '34

Alan Autry (1952-)
Southern Comfort '81
Proud Men '87
At Close Range '86
Blue De Ville '86
Mama, There's a Man in Your Bed '89
Jean de Florette '87
Manon of the Spring '87

Frankie Avalon (1939-)
Casino '95
I'll Take Sweden '65
Ski Party '65
Bikini Beach '64
Muscle Beach Party '64
Pajama Party '64
Beach Party '63
The Castilan '63
Operation Bikini '63
Panic in the Year Zero! '62
Voyage to the Bottom of the Sea '61
The Alamo '60
Back to the Beach '87
Blood Song '82
Grease '78
Dr. Goldfoot and the Bikini Machine '66
Beach Blanket Bingo '65
Fireball 500 '66
How to Stuff a Wild Bikini '65

Phillip Avalon (1955-)
The Cursed Mountain Mystery '93
Summer City '77

La Grande Bourgeoise '74
Malicious '74

Luis Avalos (1946-)
Noriega: God's Favorite '00
Jungle 2 Jungle '96
Lone Justice 3: Showdown at Plum Creek '96
Lone Justice '93
Lone Justice 2 '93
Ghost Fever '87

Erik Avari (1952-)
Flight of the Living Dead: Outbreak on a Plane '07
Dancing in Twilight '05
Daredevil '03
Three Days of Rain '03
Mr. Deeds '02
Planet of the Apes '01
The Mummy '99
The Undercover Kid '95
Stargate '94
Treacherous Crossing '92
The Beast '88

Loren Avedon (1962-)
Virtual Combat '95
Operation Golden Phoenix '94
The King of the Kickboxers '91
No Retreat, No Surrender 3: Blood Brothers '91
No Retreat, No Surrender 2 '89

Joe Mari Avellana
Deathfight '93
Bloodfist 2 '90
Bloodfist '89

Brian Avenet-Bradley
Jack O'Lantern '04
Ghost of the Needle '03

Brian Avery (1940-)
Forced to Kill '93
The Graduate '67

James Avery (1948-)
Dancing in September '00
The Colony '98
Prince of Egypt '98 (V)
Spirit Lost '96
Home for Christmas '93
Beastmaster 2: Through the Portal of Time '91
Fletch '85
Kicks '85

Linda Avery
Noon Sunday '75
Hitchhikers '72

Margaret Avery
Tyler Perry's Meet the Browns '08
Welcome Home Roscoe Jenkins '08
White Man's Burden '95
Mardi Gras for the Devil '93
The Jacksons: An American Dream '92
Heat Wave '90
Return of Superfly '90
Riverbend '89
Blueberry Hill '88
For Us, the Living '88
The Color Purple '85
The Lathe of Heaven '80
The Amityville Horror '79
Wanderers '79
The Fish that Saved Pittsburgh '79
Which Way Is Up? '77
Hell Up in Harlem '73
Terror at Red Wolf Inn '72
A Dream of Kings '69
Faces '68
Nevada Smith '66

Angel Aviles
Scorpion Spring '96
Mi Vida Loca '94
Somebody to Love '94
Chain of Desire '93

Rick Aviles (1953-95)
Stephen King's The Stand '94
The Saint of Fort Washington '93
Ghost '90
Mystery Train '89
Spike of Bensonhurst '88

Mili Avital (1972-)
When Do We Eat? '05
Colombian Love '04
The Human Stain '03
After the Storm '01
Uprising '01
Arabian Nights '00
Bad Seed '00
Monsoon '99
Kissing a Fool '98
Polish Wedding '97
Invasion of Privacy '96
Dead Man '95
Stargate '94

Natalie Avital
Attack of the Sabretooth '05
Shallow Ground '04

Aviva (1984-)
Superbad '07

Aki Avni (1967-)
Down in the Valley '05
Free Zone '05
Time of Favor '00

Alejandro Awada (1961-)
The Aura '05
The Road '00

Chikage Awashima (1924-)
The Human Condition: No Greater Love '58
Early Summer '51

Eddie Axberg (1947-)
The New Land '73
The Emigrants '72

Nina Axelrod
Cross Country '83
Time Walker '82
Motel Hell '80

Robert Axelrod (1949-)
Repo Jake '90
The Big Turnaround '88
Lensman '84 (V)

Hannelore Axman
Five Fingers '52
The Red Menace '49

Hoyt Axton (1938-99)
King Cobra '98
Kingfish: A Story of Huey P. Long '95
Number One Fan '94
Season of Change '94
Buried Alive '90
The Rousters '90
Disorganized Crime '89
We're No Angels '89
Dixie Lanes '88
Retribution '88
Christmas Comes to Willow Creek '87
Guilty of Innocence '87
Act of Vengeance '86
Gremlins '84
Deadline Auto Theft '83
Goldilocks & the Three Bears '83
Heart Like a Wheel '83
Endangered Species '82
The Junkman '82
The Black Stallion '79

Yano Ayana (1972-)
Better Off Dead '85
A Christmas Story '83

Charlotte Ayanna (1976-)
The Insatiable '06
Push '06
The Thirst '06
Once Upon a Wedding '05
Love the Hard Way '01
Training Day '01

Dancing at the Blue Iguana '00
The Rage: Carrie 2 '99

Nicki Aycox (1975-)
Perfect Stranger '07
Dead Birds '04
Jeepers Creepers 2 '03
Momentum '03

Dan Aykroyd (1952-)
I Now Pronounce You Chuck and Larry '07
Christmas With the Kranks '04
50 First Dates '04
White Coats '04
Bright Young Things '03
Unconditional Love '03
Crossroads '02
The Curse of the Jade Scorpion '01
Earth vs. the Spider '01
Evolution '01
Pearl Harbor '01
House of Mirth '00
Loser '00
Stardom '00
Diamonds '99
Antz '98 (V)
Blues Brothers 2000 '98
Dying to Get Rich '98
Grosse Pointe Blank '97
Celtic Pride '96
Feeling Minnesota '96
Getting Away With Murder '96
My Fellow Americans '96
Casper '95
Sgt. Bilko '95
Tommy Boy '95
Canadian Bacon '94
Exit to Eden '94
My Girl 2 '94
North '94
Coneheads '93
Chaplin '92
Sneakers '92
This Is My Life '92
My Girl '91
Nothing But Trouble '91
Loose Cannons '90
The Masters of Menace '90
Driving Miss Daisy '89
Ghostbusters 2 '89
Caddyshack 2 '88
The Great Outdoors '88
My Stepmother Is an Alien '88
The Couch Trip '87
Dragnet '87
Into the Night '85
Spies Like Us '85
Ghostbusters '84
Doctor Detroit '83
Trading Places '83
Twilight Zone: The Movie '83
Neighbors '81
The Blues Brothers '80
Mr. Mike's Mondo Video '79
1941 '79
All You Need Is Cash '78
Love at First Sight '76

Peter Aykroyd
Kids of the Round Table '96
The Funny Farm '82
Gas '81

Arthur Aylesworth (1883-1946)
Treasure of Fear '45
Beau Geste '39
Sandflow '37

Reiko Aylesworth (1972-)
Aliens vs. Predator: Requiem '07
Mr. Brooks '07
The Killing Floor '06
Magma: Volcanic Disaster '06
Crazylove '05

Felix Aylmer (1889-1979)
The Chalk Garden '64
Victoria Regina '61
Exodus '60
From the Terrace '60
The Hands of Orlac '60
The Mummy '59
Separate Tables '58
Saint Joan '57
Anastasia '56
Knights of the Round Table '53
The Master of Ballantrae '53
Paris Express '53
Ivanhoe '52
Quo Vadis '51
Alice in Wonderland '50
Trio '50
Eye Witness '49
Prince of Foxes '49
Hamlet '48
The October Man '48
Ghosts of Berkeley Square '47
The Magic Bow '47
A Man About the House '47
The Wicked Lady '45
Henry V '44
Mr. Emmanuel '44
The Demi-Paradise '43
Thursday's Child '43
Spellbound '41
Night Train to Munich '40
The Case of the Frightened Lady '39
Action for Slander '38
Dreaming Lips '37
As You Like It '36
Nine Days a Queen '36
The Shadow '36
The Evil Mind '34
The Iron Duke '34

John Aylward (1946-)
Down With Love '03
Path to War '02
Just Visiting '01
Instinct '99
From the Earth to the Moon '98
Three Fugitives '89

Agnes Ayres (1898-1940)
Son of the Sheik '26
Affairs of Anatol '21
The Sheik '21

Leah Ayres (1957-)
Bloodsport '88
Eddie Macon's Run '83
The Burning '82

Lew Ayres (1908-96)
Cast the First Stone '89
Of Mice and Men '81
Salem's Lot '79
Damien: Omen 2 '78
End of the World '76
Francis Gary Powers: The True Story of the U-2 Spy '76
Battle for the Planet of the Apes '73
The Stranger '73
The Carpetbaggers '64
Advise and Consent '62
Donovan's Brain '53
The Capture '50
Johnny Belinda '48
Dark Mirror '46
Dr. Kildare's Strange Case '40
Broadway Serenade '39
The Secret of Dr. Kildare '39
Holiday '38
All Quiet on the Western Front '30
Big News '29
The Kiss '29

Robert Ayres (1914-68)
Battle Beneath the Earth '68
Cat Girl '57
Time Lock '57
River Beat '54

Rosalind Ayres (1946-)
Christmas in the Clouds '01
Beautiful People '99
Gods and Monsters '98
The Slipper and the Rose '76
That'll Be the Day '73

Rochelle Aytes (1976-)
Madea's Family Reunion '06
White Chicks '04

Lubna Azabal
Paradise Now '05
Changing Times '04
Almost Peaceful '02

Hank Azaria (1964-)
Chicago 10 '07 (V)
Run, Fat Boy, Run '07
The Simpsons Movie '07 (V)
Along Came Polly '04
Dodgeball: A True Underdog Story '04
Eulogy '04
Shattered Glass '03
Bark! '02
America's Sweethearts '01
Uprising '01
Fall Safe '00
The Cradle Will Rock '99
Mystery, Alaska '99
Mystery Men '99
Tuesdays with Morrie '99
Celebrity '98
Godzilla '98
Anastasia '97 (V)
Great Expectations '97
Grosse Pointe Blank '97
Homegrown '97
The Birdcage '95
Heat '95
Quiz Show '94
Cool Blue '88

Sabine Azema (1955-)
La Buche '00
Same Old Song '97
Le Bonheur Est Dans le Pre '95
Smoking/No Smoking '94
Life and Nothing But '89
Melo '86
Love Unto Death '84
A Sunday in the Country '84
Life Is a Bed of Roses '83

Ayu Azhari (1970-)
Without Mercy '95
Diamond Run '90

Tony Azito (1949-95)
Bloodhounds of Broadway '89
Chattanooga Choo Choo '84
Private Resort '84
Union City '81

Shabana Azmi (1948-)
Fire '96
In Custody '94
Son of the Pink Panther '93
City of Joy '92
Madame Sousatzka '88

Charles Aznavour (1924-)
Ararat '02
The Truth About Charlie '02
Edith & Marcel '83
The Tin Drum '79
Sky Riders '76
Twist '76
Ten Little Indians '75
Blockhouse '73
The Adventurers '70
Carbon Copy '69
Candy '68
Shoot the Piano Player '62
The Testament of Orpheus '59

Eloy Azorin (1977-)
Warriors '02
Mad Love '01
All About My Mother '99

Candice Azzara (1945-)
In Her Shoes '05
Doin' Time on Planet Earth '88
Easy Money '83
Fatso '80
House Calls '78

Lisa B
See Lisa Barbuscia

B-Real
See Louis Freese

Karin Baal (1940-)
Berlin Alexanderplatz '80
Dead Eyes of London '61
Teenage Wolfpack '57

Obba Babatunde (1951-)
Cover '08
The Eye '08
The Celestine Prophecy '06
Material Girls '06
After the Sunset '04
The Manchurian Candidate '04
John Q '02
Redeemer '02
The Wild Thornberrys Movie '02 (V)
How High '01
The Visit '00
Introducing Dorothy Dandridge '99
Life '99
Apartment Complex '98
The Temptations '98
Miss Evers' Boys '97
Multiplicity '96
Soul of the Game '96
That Thing You Do! '96
A Reason to Believe '95
Philadelphia '93
Undercover Blues '93
The Silence of the Lambs '91
Miami Blues '90
God Bless the Child '88

Barbara Babcock (1937-)
Space Cowboys '00
Far and Away '92
Happy Together '89
The Heart of Dixie '89
News at Eleven '86
Quarterback Princess '85
That Was Then... This Is Now '85
The Lords of Discipline '83
The Black Marble '79
On the Edge: The Survival of Dana '79
The Christmas Coal Mine Miracle '77

Fabienne Babe (1962-)
La Vie Promise '02
Les Voleurs '96
Singing the Blues in Red '87

Lauren Bacall (1924-)
The Walker '07
These Foolish Things '06
Manderlay '05
Birth '04
Howl's Moving Castle '04 (V)
Dogville '03
Gone Dark '03
Diamonds '99
The Mirror Has Two Faces '96
My Fellow Americans '96
From the Mixed-Up Files of Mrs. Basil E. Frankweiler '95
Ready to Wear '94
A Foreign Field '93
The Portrait '93
All I Want for Christmas '91
Innocent Victim '90
Misery '90
Dinner at Eight '89
Appointment with Death '88
Mr. North '88
The Fan '81
The Shootist '76
Murder on the Orient Express '74
Harper '66
Sex and the Single Girl '64
Flame Over India '60
Designing Woman '57
Written on the Wind '56
Blood Alley '55
The Cobweb '55
A Woman's World '54

How to Marry a Millionaire '53
Young Man with a Horn '50
Key Largo '48
Dark Passage '47
The Big Sleep '46
To Have & Have Not '44

Michael Bacall
Death Proof '07
Manic '01
Urban Legends 2: Final Cut '00
Wait until Spring, Bandini '90

Morena Baccarin
Serenity '05
Stargate: The Ark of Truth '08

Salvatore Baccaloni (1900-69)
Full of Life '56
Rock-A-Bye Baby '57

Barbara Bach (1947-)
Give My Regards to Broad Street '84
Caveman '81
The Great Alligator '81
Screamers '80
The Unseen '80
Up the Academy '80
Jaguar Lives '79
Force 10 from Navarone '78
The Spy Who Loved Me '77
The Black Belly of the Tarantula '71
Short Night of Glass Dolls '71

Catherine Bach (1954-)
The Nutt House '95
Rage and Horror '92
The Masters of Menace '90
Street Justice '89
Criminal Act '88
Driving Force '88
Cannonball Run 2 '84
Strange New World '75
Nicole '72

John Bach (1946-)
Chimebroker '93
The Sound and the Silence '93
'04

Dian Bachar (1971-)
The Adventures of Rocky & Bullwinkle '00
BASEketball '98
Orgazmo '98

Burt Bacharach (1928-)
Austin Powers in Goldmember '02
Austin Powers 2: The Spy Who Shagged Me '99

Stephanie Bachelor (1912-96)
Springtime in the Sierras '47
G.I. War Brides '46

Hans Bachman
Invader '97
Star Quest '89

Steve Bacic (1955-)
Afghan Knights '07
The Tooth Fairy '06
Firefight '03
Ballistic: Ecks vs. Sever '02
Bounty Hunters 2: Hardball '97
The 6th Day '00

George Back
The Comebacks '07
Sam & Janet '02

Brian Backer (1956-)
The Money Pit '86
Moving Violations '85
The Burning '82
Fast Times at Ridgemont High '82

Jim Backus (1913-89)
Slapstick of Another Kind '84
Angel's Brigade '79
C.H.O.M.P.S. '79
The Rebels '79
Rescue from Gilligan's Island '78
Pete's Dragon '77
Crazy Mama '75
Now You See Him, Now You Don't '72
Myra Breckinridge '70
Hello Down There '69
Where Were You When the Lights Went Out? '68
Billie '65
Critic's Choice '63
It's a Mad, Mad, Mad, Mad World '63
Operation Bikini '63
Sunday in New York '63
The Wheeler Dealers '63
The Horizontal Lieutenant '62
The Wonderful World of the Brothers Grimm '62
Zotz! '62
Ice Palace '60
Ask Any Girl '59
Man of a Thousand Faces '57
Meet Me in Las Vegas '56
Naked Hills '56
Rebel without a Cause '55
Francis in the Navy '55
Above and Beyond '53
Don't Bother to Knock '52
Here Come the Nelsons '52
Pat and Mike '52
His Kind of Woman '51
I Want You '51
I'll See You in My Dreams '51
Father Was a Fullback '49
The Great Lover '49

Olga Baclanova (1899-1974)
Freaks '32
Docks of New York '28
The Man Who Laughs '27

Irving Bacon (1893-1965)
Ma and Pa Kettle at Home '54

(Kevin Bacon)
Loverboy '05
Where the Truth Lies '05
The Woodsman '04
In the Cut '03
Mystic River '03
Trapped '02
Novocaine '01
Hollow Man '00
My Dog Skip '99
Stir of Echoes '99
Digging to China '99
Wild Things '98
Sleepers '96
Picture Perfect '96
Balto '95 (V)
Murder in the First '95
The Air Up There '94
The River Wild '94
A Few Good Men '92
He Said, She Said '91
JFK '91
Pyrates '91
Queens Logic '91
Flatliners '90
The Big Picture '89
Criminal Law '89
Tremors '89
End of the Line '88
She's Having a Baby '88
Planes, Trains & Automobiles '87
White Water Summer '87
Quicksilver '86
Footloose '84
Enormous Changes '83
Diner '82
Only When I Laugh '81
Friday the 13th '80
Hero at Large '80
National Lampoon's Animal House '78

Lloyd Bacon (1890-1955)
Wagon Tracks '19
Charlie Chaplin .... Our Hero! '15

Jean-Pierre Bacri (1951-)
Look at Me '04
The Housekeeper '02
The Taste of Others '00
Place Vendome '98
Un Air de Famille '96
Entre-Nous '83

Angelo Badalamenti (1937-)
Mulholland Drive '01
Blue Velvet '86

Michael Badalucco (1954-)
Bewitched '05
2B Perfectly Honest '04
13 Moons '02
The Man Who Wasn't There '01
Summer of Sam '99
You've Got Mail '98
Love Walked In '97
The Search for One-Eyed Jimmy '96
Blue in the Face '95
The Sunshine Boys '95
Two If by Sea '95
The Professional '94
Mac '93
Jungle Fever '91

Hermione Baddeley (1906-86)
The Aristocats '70 (V)
Do Not Disturb '65
Marriage on the Rocks '65
Mary Poppins '64
The Unsinkable Molly Brown '64
Brown '64
Cosh Boy '61
Let's Get Married '60
Room at the Top '59
The Pickwick Papers '54
The Belles of St. Trinian's '53
A Christmas Carol '51
The Woman in Question '50
Passport to Pimlico '49
Brighton Rock '47

Alan Badel (1923-82)
Nijinsky '80
The Riddle of the Sands '79
Luther '74
The Day of the Jackal '73
The Adventurers '70
Arabesque '66
Children of the Damned '63
This Sporting Life '63
Three Cases of Murder '55

Sarah Badel (1943-)
Just Visiting '01
Cotton Mary '99
Mrs. Dalloway '97
Not Without My Daughter '90

Diedrich Bader (1966-)
Meet the Spartans '08
Balls of Fury '07
Surf's Up '07 (V)
Miss Congeniality 2: Armed and Fabulous '05
Eurotrip '04
Napoleon Dynamite '04
Ice Age '02 (V)
Jay and Silent Bob Strike Back '01
Office Space '98
The Beverly Hillbillies '93

Rupert Baderman
Shadowlands '85

Russ Badger
1984 '84

Mary Badham (1952-)
This Property Is Condemned '66
To Kill a Mockingbird '62

Mina (Badiyi) Badie
Georgia '95
The Anniversary Party '01

Annette Badland (1950-)
The Kovak Box '06
Secret Society '00
Little Voice '98
Angels and Insects '95

Jane Badler (1953-)
Pictures '80s

Erykah Badu (1971-)
House of D '04
Blues Brothers 2000 '98

Du-na Bae
The Host '06

Buddy Baer (1915-86)
Giant from the Unknown '58
Jack & the Beanstalk '52
Quo Vadis '51

Edouard Baer
Moliere '07
Alias Betty '01

Harry Baer (1947-)
Big Boss '77
Mr. Scarface '77
Fox and His Friends '75
Whity '70

John Baer (1925-)
Night of the Blood Beast '58

Max Baer, Jr. (1937-)
The McCullochs '75
Macon County Line '74

Max Baer, Sr. (1909-59)
The Harder They Fall '56
Riding High '50
Africa Screams '49
The Prizefighter and the Lady '33

Meredith Baer (1945-)
The Chicken Chronicles '77
The Sister-in-Law '74

Parley Baer (1914-2002)
Dave '93
Time Trackers '88
Rodeo Girl '80
The Amazing Dobermans '76
Cash McCall '60
The FBI Story '59
The Young Lions '58

Paloma Baeza (1974-)
The Way We Live Now '02
Anna Karenina '00
A Knight in Camelot '98
Far from the Madding Crowd '97

Rafael Baez
Shanghai Noon '00
Went to Coney Island on a Mission from God... Be Back by Five '98

Regina Baff
Below the Belt '80
Road Movie '72

Larry Bagby (1974-)
Walk the Line '05
Saints and Soldiers '03

William Bagdad (1920-75)
The Doll Squad '73
The Astro-Zombies '67
Blood Orgy of the She-Devils '74

Carol Bagdasarian
The Aurora Encounter '85

Vladas Bagdonas
House of Fools '02
Come and See '85

Lorri Bagley (1973-)
Ice Age '02 (V)
Trick '99

Tim Bagley
Knocked Up '07
Employee of the Month '06
Memnon '04
The Fluffer '01

Vernel Bagneris (1949-)
Down by Law '86
Pennies from Heaven '81

Marcus Bagwell (1970-)
Terror Tract '00
Day of the Warrior '96

Blake Bahner (1959-)
Cyberstalker '96
Wizards of the Demon Sword '94

Maxine Bahns (1971-)
Cutaway '00
Dangerous Curves '99
She's the One '96
The Brothers McMullen '94

Wu Bai (1968-)
Time and Tide '00
The Personals '98

Charles "Chuck" Bail

Bill Bailey (1964-)
Heat and Sunlight '87
On the Edge '86
The Stunt Man '80

Blake Bailey
Head of the Family '96
Lurking Fear '94

Bunty Bailey
Spellcaster '91

Eion Bailey (1976-)
Life of the Party '05
Mindhunters '03
And Starring Pancho Villa as Himself '03
The Home Front '02
Band of Brothers '01
Almost Famous '00
Fight Club '99
Center Stage '00

Fred Bailey
Nam Angels '88

G.W. Bailey (1945-)
Police Academy 6: City under Siege '89
Mannequin '87
A Winner Never Quits '86
Rustler's Rhapsody '85
M*A*S*H: Goodbye, Farewell & Amen '83
The Capture o' Grizzly Adams '82

Jim Bailey (1948-)
Penitentiary 3 '87
Vultures '84

Mark Bailey
Simple Men '92

Pearl Bailey (1918-90)
Peter Gunn '89
The Member of the Wedding '83
The Fox and the Hound '81 (V)
Norman, Is That You? '76
Carmen Jones '54

Raymond Bailey (1904-80)
The Gallant Hours '60
Vertigo '58
The Incredible Shrinking Man '57
Picnic '55

Richard Bailey
Forever Amber '47

Robert Bailey, Jr.
What the #$*! Do We Know? '04
Manhunt of Mystery Island '45
Little John '02

Robin Bailey (1919-99)
Screamtime '83
See No Evil '71

William Bailey (1886-1962)
Thunder Mountain '35
The Lone Avenger '33
Is Money Everything? '23

David Bailie (1937-)
Pirates of the Caribbean: Dead Man's Chest '06
Pirates of the Caribbean: The Curse of the Black Pearl '03

Kirk Baily (1952-)
The Sixth Man '97
3 Ninjas: High Noon at Mega Mountain '97
Voodoo Dawn '89

Barbara Bain (1931-)
American Gun '02
Panic '00
Gideon '99
Spirit of '76 '91
Trust Me '89
Skinheads: The Second Coming of Hate '88
Space: 1999—Alien Attack '79
Destination Moonbase Alpha '75
Murder Once Removed '71

Conrad Bain (1923-)
Postcards from the Edge '90
Child Bride of Short Creek '81
C.H.O.M.P.S. '79
A Pleasure Doing Business '79
The Anderson Tapes '71
Bananas '71
Fury on Wheels '71
Who Killed Mary What's 'Er Name? '71

Jailbreakin' '72

Cynthia Bain (1963-)
Hometown Boy Makes Good '93
The Hard Ride '71
Wild Riders '71

Fay Bainter (1892-1968)
The Children's Hour '61
June Bride '48
The Secret Life of Walter Mitty '47
Kid from Brooklyn '46
The Virginian '46
State Fair '45
Dark Waters '44
The Human Comedy '43
Presenting Lily Mars '43
Journey for Margaret '42
Woman of the Year '42
Babes on Broadway '41
Our Town '40
Young Tom Edison '40
Jezebel '38
The Shining Hour '38
Quality Street '37

Jimmy Baio (1962-)
Kiss and Be Killed '91
Playing for Keeps '86
Brass '85
The Bad News Bears in Breaking Training '77

Scott Baio (1961-)
Cursed '04
Superbabies: Baby Geniuses 2 '04
The Bread, My Sweet '01
Bar Hopping '00
Alice in Wonderland '85
Zapped! '82
Senior Trip '81
Foxes '80

Bugsy Malone '76

Antony Baird (1920-)
The Ghost of Rashmon Hall '47

Diora Baird (1983-)
Dead of Night '45
Hot Tamale '06
The Texas Chainsaw Massacre: The Beginning '06

Harry Baird (1931-2005)
Castle Keep '69
The Oblong Box '69
The Story of a Three Day Pass '68
Tor '64
Thor and the Amazon Women '60

Jimmy Baird (1948-)
Black Orchid '59
Return of Dracula '58

Scott Bairstow (1970-)
New Best Friend '02
Tuck Everlasting '02
Dead in the Water '01
Delivered '98
Black Circle Boys '97
Killing Mr. Griffin '97
The Postman '97
Two for Texas '97
Wild America '97
White Fang 2: The Myth of the White Wolf '94

Mitsuko Baisho (1946-)
The Eel '96
Akira Kurosawa's Dreams '90
Vengeance Is Mine '79

Jon Robin Baitz (1961-)
Last Summer In the Hamptons '96
One Fine Day '96

Sidiki Bakaba (1949-)
Faces of Women '85
Le Professionnel '81

Helmut Bakaitis (1944-)
The Matrix Reloaded '03
The Matrix Revolutions '03

Richard Bakalyan (1931-)
The Fox and the Hound '81
The Strongest Man in the World '75
The Computer Wore Tennis Shoes '69
The St. Valentine's Day Massacre '67
Von Ryan's Express '65
Panic in the Year Zero! '62
Up Periscope '59

Ariyon Bakare (1971-)
After the Rain '99
A Respectable Trade '98

Art Baker (1898-1966)
The Underworld Story '50
Impact '49
Task Force '49
Homecoming '48
A Southern Yankee '48
Shakedown '88
Embassy '85
Cold Feet '84
Sixteen Candles '84
Awakening of Candra '81
French Postcards '79
Mary and Joseph: A Story of Faith '79

Bob Baker (1910-75)
Overland Mail '42
Riders of Pasco Basin '40
Ghost Town Riders '38

Outlaw Express '38
Western Trails '38

Carroll Baker (1931-)
The Game '97
North Shore Fish '97
Just Your Luck '96
Dalva '95
Kindergarten Cop '90
Ironweed '87
Native Son '86
The Secret Diary of Sigmund Freud '84
Star 80 '83
The Watcher in the Woods '81
The World Is Full of Married Men '80
Andy Warhol's Bad '77
You've Got to Have Heart '77
Bloodbath '76
Next Victim '74
Captain Apache '71
Kiss Me, Kill Me '69
Paranoia '69
The Greatest Story Ever Told '65
Harlow '65
The Carpetbaggers '64
Cheyenne Autumn '64
How the West Was Won '63
But Not for Me '59
The Big Country '58
Baby Doll '56
Giant '56
Easy to Love '53

Christopher Baker
The Condemned '07
Ike: Countdown to D-Day '04

Colin Baker (1943-)
The Waiting Time '99
War and Peace '73
The Moonstone '72

David Aaron Baker (1963-)
Kissing Jessica Stein '02
Kate & Leopold '01
The Tao of Steve '00

Diane Baker (1938-)
The Keeper: The Legend of Omar Khayyam '05
Harrison's Flowers '02
Murder at 1600 '97
Baker's Hawk '76
The Horse in the Gray Flannel Suit '68
Mirage '66
Marnie '64
Strait-Jacket '64
The Prize '63
Stolen Hours '63
The 300 Spartans '62
The Best of Everything '59
The Diary of Anne Frank '59
Journey to the Center of the Earth '59

Dylan Baker (1958-)
Chicago 10 '07 (V)
The Hunting Party '07
Spider-Man 3 '07
When a Man Falls in the Forest '07
Fido '06
Let's Go to Prison '06
The Matador '06
Hide and Seek '05
Kinsey '04
Spider-Man 2 '04
Head of State '03
How to Deal '03
Rick '03
Changing Lanes '02
Road to Perdition '02
Along Came a Spider '01

A Gentleman's Game '01
The Cell '00
Thirteen Days '00
Oxygen '99
Random Hearts '99
Simply Irresistible '99
Celebrity '98
From the Earth to the Moon '98
Happiness '98
Disclosure '94
The Last of the Mohicans '92
Love Potion #9 '92
Delirious '91
The Long Walk Home '89
The Wizard of Loneliness '88
Planes, Trains & Automobiles '87

Fay Baker (1917-87)
Sorority Girl '57
The Star '52

Frank Baker (1892-1980)
Run of the Arrow '56
Tarzan and the Green Goddess '38
The New Adventures of Tarzan '35

George Baker (1931-)
Little Lord Fauntleroy '95
The Charmer '87
Robin Hood... The Legend: Herne's Son '85
A Woman of Substance '84
Goodbye, Mr. Chips '69
Sword of Lancelot '63
Dangerous Youth '58
The Moonraker '58

Jay Baker (1961-)
Naked Lies '98
Storm and Sorrow '90
April Fool's Day '86

Jill Baker (1952-)
Catherine Cookson's The Girl '96
Hope and Glory '87

Joby Baker (1934-)
Blackbeard's Ghost '67
Gidget '59

Joe Don Baker (1936-)
Strange Wilderness '08
The Dukes of Hazzard '05
Poodle Springs '98
George Wallace '97
Tomorrow Never Dies '97
Mars Attacks! '96
Congo '95
Felony '95
Goldeneye '95
The Grass Harp '95
The Underneath '95
Reality Bites '94
Ring of Steel '94
Citizen Cohn '92
The Distinguished Gentleman '92
Cape Fear '91
The Children '90
Criminal Law '89
The Living Daylights '87
Edge of Darkness '86
Getting Even '86
Fletch '85
Final Justice '84
The Natural '84
Joy Sticks '83
Wacko '83
Speedtrap '78
The Pack '77
Shadow of Chikara '77
Framed '75
Mitchell '75
Charley Varrick '73
Walking Tall '73
Junior Bonner '72
Wild Rovers '71
Adam at 6 a.m. '70
Guns of the Magnificent Seven '69

Cool Hand Luke '67

Jolyon Baker
Attila '01
Duel of Hearts '92
Final Analysis '92

Jonathan Baker
Great World of Sound '07
Savage Harvest 2: October Blood '06

Josephine Baker (1906-75)
The French Way '40
Princess Tam Tam '35
Zou Zou '34
Siren of the Tropics 27

Kai Baker
American Eagle '90
Stormquest '87

Kathy Baker (1950-)
The Jane Austen Book Club '07
Jesse Stone: Sea Change '07
All the King's Men '06
Nine Lives '05
Sucker Free City '05
13 Going on 30 '04
Assassination Tango '03
Cold Mountain '03
The Glass House '01
A Little Inside '01
Things You Can Tell Just by Looking at Her '00
A Season for Miracles '99
Inventing the Abbotts '97
Not in This Town '97
Weapons of Mass Distraction '97
To Gillian on Her 37th Birthday '96
Lush Life '94
Mad Dog and Glory '93
Article 99 '92
Edward Scissorhands '90
Dad '89
Jacknife '89
Mr. Frost '89
Clean and Sober '88
Permanent Record '88
Street Smart '87
A Killing Affair '85
The Right Stuff '83

Kenny Baker (1934-)
Star Wars: Episode 3—Revenge of the Sith '05
Star Wars: Episode 2—Attack of the Clones '02
Sleeping Beauty '89
Amadeus '84
Return of the Jedi '83
Time Bandits '81
The Elephant Man '80
The Empire Strikes Back '80
Star Wars '77

Kenny L. Baker (1912-85)
The Harvey Girls '46
At the Circus '39

Kirsten Baker (1962-)
Friday the 13th, Part 2 '81
Gas Pump Girls '79
Girls Next Door '79

Max Baker
Constantine '05
The Island '05
Looking for Kitty '04

Phil Baker (1896-1963)
The Gang's All Here '43
The Goldwyn Follies '38

Ray Baker (1948-)
Without a Paddle '04
44 Minutes: The North Hollywood Shootout '03
The Trip '02
Anywhere But Here '99
The Final Cut '96
Camp Nowhere '94
The Hard Truth '94
Speechless '94
Heart Condition '90
Everybody's All American '88

Rockabye '86
Places in the Heart '84

Rick Baker (1950-)
Kentucky Fried Movie '77
King Kong '76
The Thing with Two Heads '72

Robert Baker (1979-)
Seraphim Falls '06
Out of Time '03
Chinese Connection '73

Scott Thompson Baker (1961-)
The Cutting Edge: Going for the Gold '05
Cleo/Leo '89
New York's Finest '87
Rest in Pieces '87

Sharon Baker
Metallica '85
Captive Planet '78

Simon Baker (1969-)
The Devil Wears Prada '06
Something New '06
George A. Romero's Land of the Dead '05
The Ring 2 '05
Book of Love '04
The Missing '03
The Affair of the Necklace '01
Red Planet '00
Ride with the Devil '99
Judas Kiss '98
Restaurant '98
Smoke Signals '98
L.A. Confidential '97
Most Wanted '97

Stanley Baker (1928-76)
Zorro '74
Butterfly Affair '71
A Lizard in a Woman's Skin '71
Queen of Diamonds '70
Accident '67
Robbery '67
Dingaka '65
Zulu '64
Eva '62
Sodom and Gomorrah '62
The Guns of Navarone '61
Helen of Troy '56
Richard III '55
The Cruel Sea '53
Knights of the Round Table '53
The Hidden Room '49

Stephen Baker
Dead Lenny '06
Little Marines '90

Susan Baker
A Wind Named Amnesia '93 (V)
Tommy '75

Timothy Baker
Out for Blood '93
Bloodfist 2 '90

Tom Baker (1934-)
Doogal '05 (V)
Dungeons and Dragons '00
The Chronicles of Narnia '89
Angels Die Hard '84
The Zany Adventures of Robin Hood '84
Fyre '78
Candy Stripe Nurses '74
The Freakmaker '73
Golden Voyage of Sinbad '73
Vault of Horror '73
Nicholas and Alexandra '71

Edward Baker-Duly
Botched '07
De-Lovely '04

Gary Bakewell
Neil Gaiman's NeverWhere '96
Backbeat '94

William "Billy" Bakewell (1908-93)
Davy Crockett, King of the Wild Frontier '55
Lucky Me '54

Radar Men from the Moon
The Capture '50
Romance on the High Seas '48

Bob Balaban (1945-)
Three to Tango '99
Jakob the Liar '99
The Cradle Will Rock '99
Best in Show '00
The Mexican '01
Gosford Park '01
Ghost World '01
A Mighty Wind '03
Capote '05
Lady in the Water '06
For Your Consideration '06
No Reservations '07
Dedication '07

Scott Bakula (1955-)
Sibling Rivalry '90
Necessary Roughness '91
Mercy Mission '93
My Family '94
A Passion to Kill '94
Major League 3: Back to the Minors '98
Mean Streak '99
Luminarias '99
American Beauty '99
The Trial of Old Drum '00
Papa's Angels '00
Above Suspicion '00
Life as a House '01
A Girl Thing '01
Blue Smoke '07

Brigitte Bako (1967-)
Red Shoe Diaries '92
Dark Tide '93
A Man in Uniform '93
Hardbodies 2 '86
Scavengers '87
Death Spa '87
Dangerous Love '87
The Escape '95
Strange Days '95
The Invaders '95
Color of Night '94
Lord of Illusions '95
Beyond the Walls '84
Hanna K. '83

Guilty by Suspicion '91

Muhamad Bakri
Hanna K. '83
Beyond the Walls '84
Cup Final '92
The Milky Way '97

Josiane Balasko (1952-)
French Twist '95
Grosse Fatigue '94
Too Beautiful for You '88
Dinner and Driving '97
Paranoia '98

Nick Baldasare
They Bite '95
Beyond Dream's Door '88

Renato Baldini (1921-)
Four Ways Out '57
Submarine Attack '54
The Wayward Wife '52

Leonor Baldaque
Belle Toujours '06
I'm Going Home '01

A. Michael Baldwin (1965-)
Phantasm 4: Oblivion '98
Vice Girls '96
Phantasm III: Lord of the Dead '94

Adam Baldwin (1962-)
The Thirst '06
Serenity '05
Evil Eyes '04
Lady Jayne Killer '03
Double Bang '01
Jackpot '01
The Patriot '00
The Right Temptation '00
Dr. Jekyll & Mr. Hyde '99
Phoenix '98
On the Border '98
Love Kills '98
Wic Grizzly '99
Silicon Towers '99
Active Stealth '99
Blind Justice '94
Digital Man '94
Wyatt Earp '94
Bitter Harvest '93
Cold Sweat '93
800 Leagues Down the Amazon '93
Deadbolt '92
Radio Flyer '92
Where the Day Takes You '92
Trade Off '95
Sawbones '95
Lover's Knot '96
Independence Day '96
Indiscreet '98
Gargantua '98
From the Earth to the Moon '98

Daniel Baldwin (1960-)
Final Move '06
Anonymous Rex '04
Paparazzi '04
Stealing Candy '04
King of the Ants '03
Water's Edge '03
Homicide: The Movie '00
In Pursuit '00
Killing Moon '00
Desert Thunder '99
Dress Gray '86
Love on the Run '85
Code of Honor '84
Talk Radio '88
Working Girl '88
The Alamo: Thirteen Days to Glory '87
Forever, Lulu '87
New Eden '94
A Simple Twist of Fate '94
Threesome '94
Bitter Harvest '93
Posse '93
Crossing the Bridge '92
Last Exit to Brooklyn '90
Born on the Fourth of July '89
The Beast '88
Mulholland Falls '96
Cat 54, Where Are You? '94
Heaven's Prisoners '96
Vampires '98
Phoenix '98

Brenda Bakke (1963-)
The Quickie '01
Shelter '98
The Fixer '97
Trucks '97
The Iron Mask '97
Lone Justice 3: Showdown at Plum Creek '96
Under Siege 2: Dark Territory '95
Tales from the Crypt Presents Demon Knight '95
Star Quest '94
Lone Justice 2 '93
Hot Shots! Part Deux '93
Fast Getaway '93
Replikator: Cloned to Kill '94

Belinda Balaski (1947-)
Runaway Daughters '94
Gremlins 2: The New Batch '90
Proud Men '87
The Howling '81
Cannonball '76

Liane Balaban (1980-)
Definitely, Maybe '08
Eternal '04
Spliced '03
World Traveler '01
New Waterford Girl '99

Midnight Cowboy '69

Alec Baldwin (1958-)
D.C. Cab '84
Forever, Lulu '87
She's Having a Baby '88
Beetlejuice '88
Married to the Mob '88
Working Girl '88
Talk Radio '88
Great Balls of Fire '89
Miami Blues '90
The Hunt for Red October '90
Alice '90
The Marrying Man '91
Prelude to a Kiss '92
Glengarry Glen Ross '92
Malice '93
The Getaway '94
The Shadow '94
Heaven's Prisoners '95
The Juror '96
Looking for Richard '96
Ghosts of Mississippi '96
The Edge '97
Mercury Rising '98
The Confession '98
Outside Providence '99
Thick as Thieves '99
State and Main '00
Nuremberg '00
Thomas and the Magic Railroad '00
Pearl Harbor '01
Final Fantasy: The Spirits Within '01
The Royal Tenenbaums '01
Cats & Dogs '01
The Cooler '03
Path to War '02
Dr. Seuss' The Cat in the Hat '03
The Aviator '04
The Last Shot '04
Along Came Polly '04
Elizabethtown '05
Running with Scissors '06
The Good Shepherd '06
The Departed '06
Suburban Girl '07
Brooklyn Rules '07

Stephen Baldwin (1966-)
The Beast '88
Last Exit to Brooklyn '90
Born on the Fourth of July '89
Crossing the Bridge '92
Posse '93
8 Seconds '94
Fall Time '94
Threesome '94
New Eden '94
Under the Hula Moon '95
The Usual Suspects '95
Scanda! '94
Dead Weekend '95
Fled '96
Crimetime '96
Bio-Dome '96
Sub Down '97
Half-Baked '97
Scarred City '98
One Tough Cop '98
Table One '00
Xchange '00
Absence of the Good '99
Friends & Lovers '99
The Sex Monster '99
Dean Koontz's Mr. Murder '98
Mercy '00
Rock Vegas '00
The Flintstones in Viva Rock Vegas '00
Cutaway '00
Zebra Lounge '01
Spider's Web '01
Protection '01
Greenmail '01
Shelter Island '03
Firefight '03
Snakeman '05
Bound by Lies '05
Midnight Clear '06
Passage '06
Earthstorm '06
Jesse Stone: Night Passage '06

Janit Baldwin (1955-)
Born on the Fourth of July
The Heroes of Desert Storm '91
Humongous '82
Ruby '77
Gator Bait '73

Peter Baldwin (1929-)
The Ghost '63
Era Notte a Roma '60

Robert Baldwin (1904-96)
Courageous Dr. Christian '40
Meet Dr. Christian '39

Michael Baldwin
see A. Michael Baldwin

William Baldwin (1963-)
Forgetting Sarah Marshall '08
Adrift in Manhattan '07
Yesterday's Target '96
Bodily Harm '95
Family of Cops '95
Fair Game '95
Curdled '96
Virus '98
Relative Values '99
Shattered Image '98
Brotherhood of Murder '99
Double Bang '01
You Stupid Man '02
Say Nothing '01
Art Heist '05
Full Count '06

Walter Baldwin (1889-1977)
Interrupted Melody '55
The Long, Long Trailer '54
I Want You '51
Winter Meeting '48
The Best Years of Our Lives '46
Mr. Winkle Goes to War '44

Michael Balfour (1918-97)
The Canterbury Tales '71
The Private Life of Sherlock Holmes '70
The Flesh and the Fiends '60
Murder on Approval '56
Genevieve '53
Quatermass 2 '57
Murder at the Windmill '49

Eric Balfour (1977-)
Rx '06
The Texas Chainsaw Massacre '03
What Women Want '00

Carla Balenda (1925-)
Outlaw Women '52
Phantom Stallion '54
The Land of Faraway '87
Empire of the Sun '87
Treasure Island '89

Betty Balfour (1903-78)
Evergreen '34
Champagne '28

Jeanne Balibar (1968-)
The Duchess of Langeais '07
Code 46 '03
Va Savoir '01
Clean '04

Jennifer Balgobin
Roadside Prophets '92
Dr. Caligari '89
City Limits '86
Repo Man '83

Frank Ball (1876-1968)
Feud Maker '38
Boothill Brigade '37
Gun Lords of Stirrup Basin '37
Trojan Eddie '96
Brothers in Trouble '95
The Commitments '91

Lucille Ball (1911-89)
Mame '74
Yours, Mine & Ours '68
A Guide for the Married Man '67
The Facts of Life '60
Critic's Choice '63
The Long, Long Trailer '54
Forever Darling '56
The Fuller Brush Girl '50
Fancy Pants '50
Easy Living '49
Miss Grant Takes Richmond '49
Sorrowful Jones '49
Her Husband's Affairs '47
Lured '47
Dark Corner '46
Easy to Wed '46

Angeline Ball (1969-)
Bloom '03
Bait '02
The General '98
The Gambler '97
The Commitments '91

Christian Bale (1974-)
The Dark Knight '08
I'm Not There '07
3:10 to Yuma '07
Rescue Dawn '06
The Prestige '06
The New World '05
Batman Begins '05
Harsh Times '05
Howl's Moving Castle '05
The Machinist '04
Equilibrium '02
Laurel Canyon '02
Reign of Fire '02
Captain Corelli's Mandolin '01
Shaft '00
American Psycho '00
Mary, Mother of Jesus '99
Midsummer Night's Dream '99
All the Little Animals '98
Velvet Goldmine '98
Metroland '97
A Murder of Quality '90
Portrait of a Lady '96
The Secret Agent '96
Pocahontas '95
Little Women '94
Royal Deceit '94
Swing Kids '93
Newsies '92
Henry V '89
Empire of the Sun '87

Peter Baldwin
The Preppie Murder '89
Colonel Redl '84
A Happy New Year! '73
25 Fireman's Street '73
Love Film '70
Father '67

Eszter Balint (1966-)
Tree's Lounge '96
The Linguini Incident '92
Stranger than Paradise '84

Andras Balint (1943-)
Colonel Redl '84
The Comancheros '61
From the Terrace '60
Black Orchid '59

Ina Balin (1937-90)
My Sex Life... Or How I Got into an Argument '96
Vasectomy: A Delicate Matter '86
The Children of An Lac '80
The Projectionist '71
Charro! '69
The Patsy '64
The Comancheros '61
From the Terrace '60
Black Orchid '59

Fairuza Balk (1974-)
Wild Tigers I Have Known '05
Don't Come Knocking '05
Deuces Wild '02
The Waterboy '98
The Maker '98
Almost Famous '00
Life in the Fast Lane '00
American History X '98
The Craft '96
The Island of Dr. Moreau '96
Things to Do in Denver When You're Dead '95
Imaginary Crimes '94
Tollbooth '94
Gas Food Lodging '92
Shame '92
Valmont '89
The Worst Witch '86
Return to Oz '85

Stalin '92
Galyon '77
Citizen X '95
Silver '93

Ball

Ball *(continued)*

Ziegfeld Follies '46
Without Love '45
Best Foot Forward '43
Du Barry Was a Lady '43
Thousands Cheer '43
Big Street '42
Seven Days' Leave '42
Valley of the Sun '42
A Girl, a Guy and a Gob '41
Look Who's Laughing '41
Dance, Girl, Dance '40
Too Many Girls '40
You Can't Fool Your Wife '40
Beauty for the Asking '39
Five Came Back '39
Panama Lady '39
The Affairs of Annabel '38
Having Wonderful Time '38
Joy of Living '38
Next Time I Marry '38
Room Service '38
Stage Door '37
Follow the Fleet '36
That Girl from Paris '36
I Dream Too Much '35
Roberta '35
Top Hat '35
Murder at the Vanities '34
Roman Scandals '33

Nicholas Ball (1946-)
Croupier '97
Claudia '85
Lifeforce '85
The House that Bled to Death '81

Samuel Ball (1973-)
Net Games '03
Pumpkin '02
The Last Castle '01
Urbania '00

Suzan Ball
War Arrow '53
Yankee Buccaneer '52

Vincent Ball (1924-)
Sirens '94
Breaker Morant '80
Demolition '77
Not Tonight Darling '72
Oh! What a Lovely War '69
Where Eagles Dare '68
A Matter of WHO '62
Dead Lucky '60
Blonde Blackmailer '58
Blood of the Vampire '58
Sea of Sand '58
John and Julie '55
Terror Ship '54

Carl Ballantine (1922-)
Dying to Get Rich '98
Mr. Saturday Night '92
Hollywood Chaos '89
World's Greatest Lover '77
Revenge of the Cheerleaders '76
Speedway '68

Jeff(rey) Ballard (1987-)
Dead in a Heartbeat '02
Children of the Corn: Revelation '01

Kaye Ballard (1926-)
Ava's Magical Adventure '94
Eternity '90
Fate '90
Modern Love '90
Tiger Warsaw '87
Freaky Friday '76
The Ritz '76
The Pest '96

Edoardo Ballerini (1970-)
Dinner Rush '00
Romeo Must Die '00
Looking for an Echo '99
I Shot Andy Warhol '96

Smith Ballew (1902-84)
Gun Cargo '49
Hawaiian Buckaroo '38
Panamint's Bad Man '38
Rawhide '38
Roll Along Cowboy '37
Western Gold '37

Timothy Balme
The Vector File '03
Dead Alive '93

Jean-Francois Balmer (1946-)
Comedy of Power '06
Time Regained '99
The Swindle '97
Beaumarchais the Scoundrel '96
Madame Bovary '91
Window Shopping '86

Martin Balsam (1919-96)
Silence of the Hams '93
Cape Fear '91
Two Evil Eyes '90
Innocent Prey '88
P.I. Private Investigations '87
Queenie '87
Delta Force '86
Grown Ups '86
Death Wish 3 '85
Murder in Space '85
St. Elmo's Fire '85
Little Gloria... Happy at Last '84
The Goodbye People '83
The Salamander '82
The People vs. Jean Harris '81
The Warning '80
The House on Garibaldi Street '79
Silver Bears '78
Death Rage '77
Raid on Entebbe '77
All the President's Men '76
The Lindbergh Kidnapping Case '76
Two Minute Warning '76
Mitchell '75
Spaghetti Western '75
Miles to Go Before I Sleep '74
Murder on the Orient Express '74
The Taking of Pelham One Two Three '74
The Stone Killer '73
Summer Wishes, Winter Dreams '73
Brand New Life '72
Confessions of a Police Captain '72
Eyes Behind the Stars '72
The Anderson Tapes '71
Season for Assassins '71
Catch-22 '70
Hard Frame '70
Little Big Man '70
Tora! Tora! Tora! '70
The Good Guys and the Bad Guys '69
Hombre '67
After the Fox '66
Bedford Incident '65
Harlow '65
A Thousand Clowns '65
The Carpetbaggers '64
Seven Days in May '64
Breakfast at Tiffany's '61
Cape Fear '61
Psycho '60
Al Capone '59
Marjorie Morningstar '58
Twelve Angry Men '57

Talia Balsam (1960-)
All the King's Men '06
Into the Fire '05
Coldblooded '94
The Companion '94
Homicidal Impulse '92
Trust Me '89
In the Mood '87
The Kindred '87
P.I. Private Investigations '87
Private Investigations '87
Crawlspace '86
Consenting Adult '85
Mass Appeal '84
Nadia '84
Calamity Jane '82
Kent State '81
On the Edge: The Survival of Dana '79

Sunnyside '79

Humbert Balsan (1954-)
I Married a Dead Man '82
Lancelot of the Lake '74

Kirk Baltz (1959-)
Bloodhounds '96
Natural Born Killers '94
Skin Art '93
Reservoir Dogs '92

Alexander Baluyev (1958-)
Deep Impact '98

David Bamber (1954-)
Miss Potter '06
Daniel Deronda '02
The Railway Children '00
Pride and Prejudice '95
The Buddha of Suburbia '92
High Hopes '88

Jamie Bamber (1973-)
Daniel Deronda '02
Band of Brothers '01
Horatio Hornblower: The Adventure Continues '01
Lady Audley's Secret '00

Judy Bamber (1936-)
The Atomic Brain '64
A Bucket of Blood '59

Firdous Bamji (1966-)
The War Within '05

Gerry Bamman (1941-)
Runaway Jury '03
Home Alone 2: Lost in New York '92
Lorenzo's Oil '92
The Chase '91
The Ten Million Dollar Getaway '91

Janos Ban (1955-)
Fateless '05

Eric Bana (1968-)
The Other Boleyn Girl '08
Lucky You '07
Romulus, My Father '07
Munich '05
Troy '04
Hulk '03
The Nugget '02
Black Hawk Down '01
Chopper '00
The Castle '97

Anne Bancroft (1931-2005)
The Roman Spring of Mrs. Stone '03
Heartbreakers '01
Keeping the Faith '00
Up at the Villa '00
Antz '98 (V)
Critical Care '97
G.I. Jane '97
Great Expectations '97
Homecoming '96
Sunchaser '96
Dracula: Dead and Loving It '95
Home for the Holidays '95
How to Make an American Quilt '95
Malice '93
Mr. Jones '93
Point of No Return '93
Broadway Bound '92
Honeymoon in Vegas '92
Love Potion #9 '92
Bert Rigby, You're a Fool '89
Torch Song Trilogy '88
84 Charing Cross Road '86
'night, Mother '86
Agnes of God '85
Garbo Talks '84
To Be or Not to Be '83
The Elephant Man '80

Fatso '80
The Bell Jar '79
Jesus of Nazareth '77
The Turning Point '77
Silent Movie '76
The Hindenburg '75
Prisoner of Second Avenue '74
Young Winston '72
The Graduate '67
The Slender Thread '65
The Pumpkin Eater '64
The Miracle Worker '62
The Restless Breed '58
Girl in Black Stockings '57
Nightfall '56
Walk the Proud Land '56
Savage Wilderness '55
Demetrius and the Gladiators '54
Treasure of the Golden Condor '53
Don't Bother to Knock '52

Bradford Bancroft
A Time to Die '91
Damned River '89
Bachelor Party '84

Cameron Bancroft (1967-)
Anything But Love '02
He Sees You When You're Sleeping '02
MVP2: Most Vertical Primate '01
Anything for Love '93
Just One of the Girls '93
Love and Human Remains '93

George Bancroft (1882-1956)
Whistling in Dixie '42
Texas '41
Little Men '40
Young Tom Edison '40
Each Dawn I Die '39
Stagecoach '39
Angels with Dirty Faces '38
Hell-Ship Morgan '36
Mr. Deeds Goes to Town '36
Docks of New York '28
White Gold '28
Underworld '27
Old Ironsides '26
The Pony Express '25

Antonio Banderas (1960-)
Shrek the Third '07 (V)
Bordertown '06
Take the Lead '06
The Legend of Zorro '05
Imagining Argentina '04
Shrek 2 '04 (V)
And Starring Pancho Villa as Himself '03
Once Upon a Time in Mexico '03
Spy Kids 3-D: Game Over '03
Ballistic: Ecks vs. Sever '02
Femme Fatale '02
Frida '02
Spy Kids 2: The Island of Lost Dreams '02
The Body '01
Original Sin '01
Spy Kids '01
Play It to the Bone '99
The 13th Warrior '99
White River '99
The Mask of Zorro '98
Evita '96
Never Talk to Strangers '95
Miami Rhapsody '95
Four Rooms '95
Desperado '95
Assassins '95
Two Much '95
Of Love and Shadows '94
Interview with the Vampire '94
The House of the Spirits '93
Outrage '93
Philadelphia '93
The Mambo Kings '92
Terranova '91

Against the Wind '90
Tie Me Up! Tie Me Down! '90
If They Tell You I Fell '89
Baton Rouge '88
Women on the Verge of a Nervous Breakdown '88
Law of Desire '86
Matador '86
Labyrinth of Passion '82

Holly (Mike Ragan) Bane (1918-95)
Ride Clear of Diablo '54
Storm over Wyoming '50
Far Frontier '48
Return of Wildfire '48

Victor Banerjee (1946-)
Bitter Moon '92
Foreign Body '86
The Home and the World '84
A Passage to India '84
Hullabaloo over Georgie & Bonnie's Pictures '78

Lisa Banes (1955-)
Dragonfly '02
Pumpkin '02
Last Exit to Earth '96
Cocktail '88
Marie '85
The Hotel New Hampshire '84
Look Back in Anger '80

Joy Bang (1947-)
Messiah of Evil '74
Night of the Cobra Woman '72
Play It Again, Sam '72

Donatas Banionis
Solaris '72
Adomas Nori Buti Zmogumi '59

Tallulah Bankhead (1902-68)
Die! Die! My Darling! '65
Main Street to Broadway '53
Lifeboat '44
Stage Door Canteen '43

Aaron Banks
Fist of Fear, Touch of Death '80
The Bodyguard '76

Boyd Banks (1964-)
George A. Romero's Land of the Dead '05
Dawn of the Dead '04

Dennis Banks (1937-)
The Last of the Mohicans '92
Thunderheart '92

Elizabeth Banks (1974-)
Comanche Moon '08
Definitely, Maybe '08
Meet Dave '08
Fred Claus '07
Spider-Man 3 '07
Invincible '06
Slither '06
The Baxter '05
Daltry Calhoun '05
The 40 Year Old Virgin '05
The Sisters '05
Heights '04
Spider-Man 2 '04
Seabiscuit '03
Ordinary Sinner '02
Swept Away '02
Wet Hot American Summer '01

Ernie Banks
Finding Buck McHenry '00
Red Shoe Diaries: Luscious Lola '00

Jonathan Banks (1947-)
Reign Over Me '07
R.S.V.P. '02
Crocodile Dundee in Los Angeles '01
Foolish '99

Let the Devil Wear Black '99
Melanie Darrow '97
Dark Breed '96
Flipper '96
Last Man Standing '95
Marilyn & Bobby: Her Final Affair '94
Body Shot '93
Boiling Point '93
Freejack '92
There Goes the Neighborhood '92
Nightmare '91
Honeymoon Academy '90
Cold Steel '87
Armed and Dangerous '86
Assassin '86
The Adventures of Buckaroo Banzai Across the Eighth Dimension '84
Beverly Hills Cop '84
Nadia '84

Leslie Banks (1890-1952)
Madeleine '50
Eye Witness '49
Henry V '44
Cottage to Let '41
Chamber of Horrors '40
The Arsenal Stadium Mystery '39
Jamaica Inn '39
Fire Over England '37
21 Days '37
Wings of the Morning '37
Sanders of the River '35
Transatlantic Tunnel '35
The Man Who Knew Too Much '34
The Most Dangerous Game '32

Tyra Banks (1973-)
Halloween: Resurrection '02
Coyote Ugly '00
Life-Size '00
Love Stinks '99
Higher Learning '94

Vilma Banky (1903-91)
Son of the Sheik '26
The Winning of Barbara Worth '26
The Eagle '25

Ian Bannen (1928-99)
To Walk with Lions '99
Waking Ned Devine '98
Braveheart '95
The Sound and the Silence '93
Blue Ice '92
Damage '92
The Big Man: Crossing the Line '91
George's Island '91
Catherine Cookson's The Fifteen Streets '90
Ghost Dad '90
The Courier '88
Hope and Glory '87
Defense of the Realm '85
Lamb '85
The Prodigal '83
Gandhi '82
Eye of the Needle '81
The Watcher in the Woods '81
The Offence '73
From Beyond the Grave '73
Mackintosh Man '73
Doomwatch '72
Fright '71
Ride to Glory '71
Too Late the Hero '70
The Flight of the Phoenix '65
The Hill '65
Carlton-Browne of the F.O. '59
A Tale of Two Cities '58
The Third Key '57

Jill Banner (1946-82)
Hard Frame '70
The President's Analyst '67
Spider Baby '64

John Banner (1910-73)
Togetherness '70
36 Hours '64
Guilty of Treason '50
The Fallen Sparrow '43
Immortal Sergeant '43
Dead '94

Kanu Bannerjee (1905-85)
Aparajito '58
Pather Panchali '54

Kanu Bannerjee (1956-)
Aparajito '58
Pather Panchali '54

Karuna Bannerjee (1919-2001)
Aparajito '58
Pather Panchali '54

Reggie Bannister (1945-)
The Rage '07
Bubba Ho-Tep '03
Phantasm 4: Oblivion '98
Phantasm 3: Lord of the Dead '94
Phantasm 2 '88
Phantasm '79

Jack Bannon (1940-)
DaVinci's War '92

Jim Bannon (1911-86)
Unknown World '51
The Fighting Redhead '50
Man from Colorado '49

Nina Bara (1920-90)
Missile to the Moon '59
Black Hills '48

Theda Bara (1890-1955)
The Love Goddesses '65
The Unchastened Woman '25

John Baragrey (1918-75)
Gamera, the Invincible '66
Pardners '55

Ari Barak
Waterworld '95
Jericho Fever '93

Christine Baranski (1952-)
Mamma Mia! '08
Bonneville '06
Relative Strangers '06
A Royal Scandal '96
Welcome to Mooseport '04
Eloise at the Plaza '03
Couple 2 '98
The Birdcage '95
Jeffrey '95
New Jersey Drive '95
Addams Family Values '93
The Night We Never Met '93
The Ref '93
To Dance with the White Dog '93
Dr. Seuss' How the Grinch Stole Christmas '00
Bowfinger '99
Bulworth '98
Cruel Intentions '98
Neil Simon's The Odd Couple 2 '98
In Cold Blood '96
Maternal Instincts '96
9 1/2 Weeks '86
Crackers '84
Reversal of Fortune '90
Dog '93

Glynis Barber (1955-)
Deja Vu '98
Edge of Sanity '89
Tangiers '83
The Wicked Lady '83
Yesterday's Hero '79
The Terror '79

Paul Barber (1952-)
The Full Monty '96
The Long Good Friday '80

Katie Barberi (1972-)
Not Quite Human 2 '89
The Garbage Pail Kids Movie '87

Phil Barantini (1980-)
The Boys and Girl From County Clare '03

Ned Kelly '03

Olivia Barash (1965-)
Grave Secrets '89
Dr. Alien '88
Tuff Turf '85
Repo Man '83

Richie Barathy
Body Trouble '92
Caged Fury '89
Child of Glass '78

Luca Barbareschi (1956-)
Private Affairs '89
Bye Bye Baby '88

Adrienne Barbeau (1945-)
Unholy '07
Christmas Do-Over '06
Ring of Darkness '04
Across the Line '00
The Convent '00
Jack Frost 2: Revenge of the Mutant Killer Snowman '00
Silk Degrees '94
Jailbreakers '94
Burial of the Rats '95
Terror at London Bridge '85
Next One '84
Double-Crossed '91
Two Evil Eyes '90
Cannibal Women in the Avocado Jungle of Death '89
Back to School '86
Open House '86
Seduced '85
Creepshow '82
Swamp Thing '82
Cannonball Run '81
Escape from New York '81
The Fog '78
Red Alert '77
Return to Fantasy Island '77
Magic on Love Island '80
The Crash of Flight 401 '78
Charlie and the Great Balloon Chase '82

Urbano Barberini (1962-)
Torrents of Spring '90
Gor '88
Opera '88
Outlaw of Gor '87
Demons '86

Vincent Barbi (1912-98)
The Kettles on Old MacDonald's Farm '57
Runaways '75
Iron Mountain Trail '53
Marshal of Cedar Rock '53
Shadows of Tombstone '53
Border Saddlemates '52
Radar Men from the Moon '52

George Barbier (1864-1945)
Thunder Birds '42
The Man Who Came to Dinner '41
Week-End in Havana '41
The Adventures of Marco Polo '38
Little Miss Broadway '38
My Lucky Star '38
Here Comes Cookie '35
The Crusades '35
The Merry Widow '34
No Man of Her Own '32
On the Avenue '37
Waikiki Wedding '37
Across '36

Christian Barbier (1924-)
Army of Shadows '69

Paula Barbieri (1966-)
The Dangerous '95
Night Eyes 4: Fatal Passion '95
Wife Versus Secretary '36
Eyes of Texas '48
Stagecoach to Denver '46
Alias Billy the Kid '46
Wild Frontier '47
Son of Zorro '47
Lights of Old Santa Fe '47

Richard Barboza
Rites of Frankenstein '72
The Demons '74

Luis Barboo (1927-2001)
The Smiling Lieutenant '31
Strangers in Love '32
One Hour with You '32
No One Man '32
No Man of Her Own '32
Life Begins at Forty '35
Manhunt of Mystery Island '45
The Purple Monster Strikes '45

Lisa Barbuscia (1971-)
Highlander: Endgame '00
Almost Heroes '97
Serpent's Lair '95

Artur Barcis (1956-)
The Decalogue '88
No End '84

Caroline Barclay
Within the Rock '96
American Gothic '88

Don Barclay (1892-1975)
Outlaw Express '38
Thunder in the Desert '38
Border Phantom '37
Sweetheart of the Navy '37
Lion's Den '36

Joan Barclay (1914-2002)
The Shanghai Cobra '45
Sagebrush Law '43
The Black Dragons '42
The Corpse Vanishes '42
Before Night Falls '40
Between Your Legs '99
Second Skin '99
Dance with the Devil '97
Live Flesh '97
Mouth to Mouth '95
Running Out of Time '94
Jamon, Jamon '33

Javier Bardem (1969-)
Love in the Time of Cholera '07
No Country for Old Men '07
Goya's Ghosts '06
Collateral '04
The Sea Inside '04
The Dancer Upstairs '02
Mondays in the Sun '02

Pilar Bardem (1939-)
Alice '86
Holiday Hotel '77
Lost and Found '99
Round Numbers '91

Sophie Barjac (1957-)
Mr. Moto's Gamble '38
Charlie Chan in City of Darkness '39
Kit Carson '40
Lillian Russell '40
Sleepers West '41
Sun Valley Serenade '41
The Magnificent Dope '42
Orchestra Wives '42
The Falcon Takes Over '42
Hello, Frisco, Hello '43

Feud of the West '35
Finishing School '33
God '49

Roy Barcroft (1902-69)
The Secret Code '42
Doomed Caravan '41
Red River Valley '41
Don Daredevil Rides Again '51
Rodeo King and the Senorita '51
Missourians '50
Night Riders of Montana '50
North of the Great Divide '50
The Vanishing Westerner '50
Arizona Cowboy '49
South Dakota Way '49
Federal Agents vs. Underworld, Inc. '49
G-Men Never Forget '48
Jesse James Rides Again '47
Pioneer Marshal '49

Gun Crazy '49
Omoo Omoo, the Shark God '49

Edda Barends (1942-)
Question of Silence '83
Broken Mirrors '85

Sonny Barger (1938-)
Hell's Angels '69
Hell's Angels on Wheels '67

Lynn Bari (1913-89)
Trauma '62
Abbott and Costello Meet the Keystone Kops '54
Francis Joins the WACs '54
I'd Climb the Highest Mountain '51
The Amazing Mr. X '48
Nocturne '46
Shock! '46
The Bridge of San Luis Rey '44

Ashraf Barhoum
Paradise Now '05
The Kingdom '07
The Syrian Bride '04

Brigitte Bardot (1934-)
Don Juan (Or If Don Juan Were a Woman) '73
Legend of Frenchie King '71
Shalako '68
Spirits of the Dead '68
The Women '69
A Coeur Joie '67
Head Over Heels '67
Dear Brigitte '65
Viva Maria! '65
Contempt '64
Ravishing Idiot '64
Le Repos du Guerrier '62
Love on a Pillow '62
A Very Private Affair '62
Please Not Now! '61
The Bride Is Much Too Beautiful '58
Mam'zelle Pigalle '58
That Naughty Girl '58
Une Parisienne '58
And God Created Woman '57
The Night Heaven Fell '57
Doctor at Sea '56
Helen of Troy '56
Plucking the Daisy '56
Les Grandes Manoeuvres '55
Crazy for Love '52

Aleksander Bardini (1913-95)
The Silent Touch '94
Trois Couleurs: Blanc '94
The Double Life of Veronique '91
The Decalogue '88

Yehuda Barkan (1945-)
The Big Gag '87
Eagles Attack at Dawn '70
Lupo '70

Natalie Barish

Clive Barker (1952-)
Quicksilver Highway '98

Sleepwalkers '92

Jess Barker (1912-2000)
Kentucky Rifle '55
Shack Out on 101 '55

Lex Barker (1919-73)
Woman Times Seven '67
A Place Called Glory '66
Apache's Last Battle '64
The Girl in the Black Stockings '57
Away All Boats '56
The Man Outside '68
Mr. Blandings Builds His Dream House '48
Velvet Touch '48
The Farmer's Daughter '47

Ronnie Barker (1929-2005)
My House in Umbria '03
Porridge '79
Robin and Marian '76
The Man Outside '68

Steve Barkett (1950-)
Dark Universe '93
Dinosaur Island '93
The Aftermath '85

Ellen Barkin (1954-)
Ocean's Thirteen '07
Trust the Man '07
Palindromes '04
She Hate Me '04
Someone Like You '01
Crime and Punishment in Suburbia '00
Mercy '00
Drop Dead Gorgeous '99
White River '99
Fear and Loathing in Las Vegas '98
The Fan '96
Trigger Happy '96
Wild Bill '95
This Boy's Life '93
Into the West '92
Man Trouble '92
Switch '91
Johnny Handsome '89
Sea of Love '89
Mac '93
Big Company '94

Marcie Barkin
Fade to Black '80
Kent State '81
Diner '82
Tender Mercies '83
Eddie and the Cruisers '83
Enormous Changes '83
Daniel '83
The Princess Who Never Laughed '84
Harry & Son '84
The Adventures of Buckaroo Banzai Across the Eighth Dimension '84
Terminal Choice '85
Desert Bloom '86
Down by Law '86

Peter Barkworth (1929-2006)
Champions '84
The Littlest Horse Thieves '76
Where Eagles Dare '68

Pat Barlow
Nanny McPhee '06

April Fool's Day '86

Ivor Barnard (1887-1953)
Beat the Devil '53
Madeleine '50

Barry Barnes
Veronica Guerin '03
Bedelia '46

Binnie Barnes (1903-98)
Forty Carats '73
Where Angels Go, Trouble Follows '68
The Trouble with Angels '66
Decameron Nights '53
The Three Musketeers '39
The Time of Their Lives '46
Getting Gertie's Garter '45
It's in the Bag '45
The Spanish Main '45
Call Out the Marines '42
I Married an Angel '42
In Old California '42
Melody Master '41
Man About Town '39
Three Smart Girls '36
Private Life of Don Juan '34
The Private Life of Henry VIII '33
The Divorce of Lady X '38
Holiday '38
Thanks for Everything '38
Broadway Melody of 1938 '37
The Last of the Mohicans '36

Chris Barnes (1965-)
Tut & Tuttle '81
The Bad News Bears in Breaking Training '77
The Bad News Bears '76

Christopher Daniel Barnes (1972-)
Shut Up and Kiss Me '05
A Very Brady Sequel '96
Murder Without Motive '92

Joanna Barnes (1934-)
The Parent Trap '98
I Wonder Who's Killing Her Now? '76
The War Wagon '67
Goodbye Charlie '64
The Parent Trap '61
Spartacus '60

Priscilla Barnes (1955-)
Thr3e '07
The Devil's Rejects '05
Alien 3000 '04
Alone with a Stranger '99
Final Payback '99
Catherine's Grove '98
Implicated '98
The Killing Grounds '97
Mallrats '95
Ava's Magical Adventure '94
Erotique '94
The Crossing Guard '94
National Lampoon's Attack of the 5 Ft. 2 Women '94
Body Trouble '92
Stepfather 3: Father's Day '92
Talons of the Eagle '92
License to Kill '89
Lords of the Deep '89
Traxx '87
The Last Married Couple in America '80
The Seniors '78
Time Machine '78
Beyond Reason '77
Delta Fox '77
Texas Detour '77

Rayford Barnes (1920-2000)
Jesse James Meets Frankenstein's Daughter '65
Sunday in New York '63

Susan Barnes
Nurse Betty '00
Where the Money Is '00
Lover Girl '97
One Night Stand '97
Nothing to Lose '96
Freeway '95
Serving in Silence: The Margarethe Cammermeyer Story '95
The Applegates '89

Charlie Barnett (1954-)
They Bite '95
My Man Adam '86
Nobody's Fool '86
D.C. Cab '83

Chester Barnett (1885-1947)
Trilby '17
The Wishing Ring '14

Griff Barnett (1884-1958)
Holiday Affair '49
Frontier Vengeance '40

Tom Barnett
Niagara Motel '06
The Reagans '04

Vince Barnett (1902-77)
Charade '53
Red Planet Mars '52
Kentucky Jubilee '51
Thunder in the Pines '49
Big Town After Dark '47
Shoot to Kill '47
Captive Wild Woman '43
Baby Face Morgan '42
The Corpse Vanishes '42
I Killed That Man '42
X Marks the Spot '42
Ride 'Em Cowgirl '41
The Singing Cowgirl '39
Boots of Destiny '37
We're in the Legion Now '37
Yellow Cargo '36
I Live My Life '35
Crimson Romance '34
Thirty Day Princess '34
The Death Kiss '33
The Prizefighter and the Lady '33

Jean Marie Barnwell
Blue River '95
Born to Be Wild '95
From the Mixed-Up Files of Mrs. Basil E. Frankweiler '95

Bruce Baron (1949-)
Ninja Hunt '80s
Ninja Champion '80
Fireback '78
Ninja Destroyer '70

Joanne Baron
The Perfect Witness '07
The Prince & Me '04
Burning Down the House '01
Hard Luck '01
Perfume '01
St. Patrick's Day '99
Allie & Me '97
Pet Shop '94
Crazy in Love '92
Leprechaun 2 '94
Motorama '91
Vamp '86
Birdy '84
Broadway Danny Rose '84
The Out-of-Towners '70
If It's Tuesday, This Must Be Belgium '69
Sweet November '68
Targets '68

Sandy Baron (1937-2001)

Elizabeth Barondes
Love to Kill '97
Adrenalin: Fear the Rush '96
Not of This Earth '96
Full Body Massage '95
Night of the Scarecrow '95

Byron Barr (1917-66)
Down Dakota Way '49
Pitfall '48
Big Town '47
Love Letters '45
Double Indemnity '44

Douglas Barr (1949-)
Spaced Invaders '90
Deadly Blessing '81

Jean-Marc Barr (1960-)
Cote d'Azur '05
Manderlay '05
Tara Road '05
Le Divorce '03
Dogville '03
Dancer in the Dark '99
Don't Let Me Die on a Sunday '98
St. Ives '98
The Scarlet Tunic '97
Breaking the Waves '95
The Favorite Son '94
The Plague '92
Zentropa '92
The Big Blue '88
Hope and Glory '87

Patrick Barr (1908-85)
The Godsend '79
House of Whipcord '75
Flesh and Blood Show '73
The Satanic Rites of Dracula '73
The Case of the Frightened Lady '39
Sailing Along '38

Sharon Barr
The Reluctant Agent '95
Spittin' Image '83
Archer: The Fugitive from the Empire '81

Gianfranco Barra (1940-)
Screw Loose '99
Avanti! '72

Maria Barranco (1961-)
Gaudi Afternoon '01
The Girl of Your Dreams '99
Mouth to Mouth '95
Zafarinas '94
The Red Squirrel '93
Don Juan, My Love '90
Tie Me Up! Tie Me Down! '90
Women on the Verge of a Nervous Breakdown '88

Robert Barrat (1889-1970)
Distant Drums '51
Riders of the Range '50
Magnificent Doll '46
The Road to Utopia '46
Strangler of the Swamp '46
They Were Expendable '45
The Adventures of Mark Twain '44
Captain Caution '40
Go West '40
Northwest Passage '40
Bad Lands '39
Union Pacific '39
Charlie Chan in Honolulu '38
Shadows over Shanghai '38
The Texans '38
The Black Legion '37
The Charge of the Light Brigade '36
Mary of Scotland '36
The Trail of the Lonesome Pine '36
Devil Dogs of the Air '35
Village Tale '35
Massacre '34
Heroes for Sale '33
King of the Jungle '33

Beethoven '36

Marie-Christine Barrault (1944-)
Obsession '97
Jesus of Montreal '89
Le Jupon Rouge '87
Swann in Love '84
Table for Five '83
Stardust Memories '80
L'Etat Sauvage '78
The Medusa Touch '78
Perceval '78
Cousin, Cousine '76
The Daydreamer '75
Chloe in the Afternoon '72
My Night at Maud's '69

Adriana Barraza (1956-)
Babel '06
Amores Perros '00

Amy Barrett
House Where Evil Dwells '82

Claudia Barrett
Robot Monster '53
Night Riders of Montana '50

Edith Barrett (1907-77)
Jane Eyre '44
The Ghost Ship '43
I Walked with a Zombie '43
Lady for a Night '42

Jacinda Barrett (1972-)
The Last Kiss '06
The Namesake '06
Poseidon '06
School for Scoundrels '06
Bridget Jones: The Edge of Reason '04
Ladder 49 '04

Jane Barrett (1923-69)
The Human Stain '03
Yellowstone '36

John Barrett (1952-)
To the Death '93
American Kickboxer 1 '91
Lights! Camera! Murder! '89

Judith Barrett (1914-2000)
The Road to Singapore '40

Tony Barrett (1916-74)
Impact '49
Dick Tracy Meets Gruesome '47

Barbara Barrie (1931-)
Second Best '05
Spent '00
Judy Berlin '99
Hercules '97 (V)
Scarlett '94
End of the Line '88
Real Men '87
The Execution '85
Two of a Kind '82
Private Benjamin '80
To Race the Wind '80
Backstairs at the White House '79
The Bell Jar '79
Breaking Away '79
Child of Glass '78

Chris (Christopher) Barrie (1960-)
When Evil Calls '06
Lara Croft Tomb Raider: The Cradle of Life '03
Lara Croft: Tomb Raider '01

Judith Barrie
Hidden Gold '33
Party Girls '29

Mona Barrie (1909-64)
Cass Timberlane '47
Dawn on the Great Divide '42
Today I Hang '42
Charlie Chan in London '34
One Night of Love '34

Wendy Barrie (1912-78)
The Saint Strikes Back: Criminal Court '46
Follies Girl '43
The Saint Takes Over '40
Five Came Back '39
The Hound of the Baskervilles '39
The Saint Strikes Back '39
I Am the Law '38
Dead End '37
Vengeance '37
If I Were Rich '33
The Private Life of Henry VIII '33
Wedding Rehearsal '32

Edgar Barrier (1907-64)
The Giant Claw '57
Cobra Woman '44
The Phantom of the Opera '43
Arabian Nights '42

Pat (Barringer) Barrington (1941-)
Mantis in Lace '67
The Acid Eaters '67
Agony of Love '66
Orgy of the Dead '65

Phyllis Barrington
Sucker Money '34
The Drifter '32

Chuck Barris (1929-)
Confessions of a Dangerous Mind '02
Hugo Pool '97

Desmond Barrit (1944-)
Northanger Abbey '07
A Christmas Carol '99
A Midsummer Night's Dream '96

Bob (Robert) Barron (1922-2002)
Ballad of a Gunfighter '64
Tank Commando '59
Sea Hound '47
The Caravan Trail '46
Song of Old Wyoming '45
Guns of the Law '44

Dana Barron (1968-)
National Lampoon's Christmas Vacation 2: Cousin Eddie's Big Island Adventure '03
The Perfect Nanny '00
The Man in the Iron Mask '97
City of Industry '96
National Lampoon's Vacation '83

John Barron (1920-2004)
Agatha Christie's Thirteen at Dinner '85
Whoops Apocalypse '83

Keith Barron (1936-)
Take Me '01
Madame Bovary '00
Catherine Cookson's The Round Tower '98
At the Earth's Core '76
Nothing But the Night '72
Freelance '71
Baby Love '69

Robert V. Barron (1932-2000)
Bill & Ted's Excellent Adventure '89

Barta Barry (1911-)
Dr. Jekyll and the Wolfman '71
Gladiators 7 '62

Bruce Barry (1934-)
The Good Wife '86
Plunge Into Darkness '77

Donald (Don "Red") Barry (1912-80)
Blazing Stewardesses '75
Johnny Got His Gun '71
Hard Frame '70
The Shakiest Gun in the West '68
Hostile Guns '67
Iron Angel '64
Born Reckless '59
Square Dance Jubilee '51
Border Rangers '50
Gunfire '50
I Shot Billy the Kid '50
Red Desert '50
Train to Tombstone '50
Outlaw Gang '49
Ringside '49
Tough Assignment '49
The Purple Heart '44
California Joe '43
Sundown Kid '43
The Sombrero Kid '42
Sundown Fury '42
Adventures of Red Ryder '40
Frontier Vengeance '40
Days of Jesse James '39
Panama Patrol '39
Saga of Death Valley '39
Wyoming Outlaw '39
The Duke of West Point '38
Sinners in Paradise '38

Gene Barry (1921-)
War of the Worlds '05
These Old Broads '01
The Gambler Returns: The Luck of the Draw '93
Perry Mason: The Case of the Lost Love '87
The Adventures of Nellie Bly '81
A Cry for Love '80
Second Coming of Suzanne '80
Subterfuge '68
Columbo: Prescription Murder '67
Maroc 7 '67
Thunder Road '58
China Gate '57
Forty Guns '57
The 27th Day '57
Back from Eternity '56
Soldier of Fortune '55
Red Garters '54
The War of the Worlds '53
The Atomic City '52

Jason Barry (1975-)
The Still Life '07
Honor '06
MirrorMask '05
Beyond Re-Animator '03
Conspiracy of Silence '03
When the Sky Falls '99
Monument Ave. '98
Joey '85
Old Enough '84

Neill Barry (1965-)
The Last of the High Kings '96
Friends & Lovers '99
O.C. and Stiggs '87
Bogie: The Last Hero '80
Kitten with a Whip '64
Sammy, the Way-Out Seal '62

Patricia Barry (1930-)
Twilight Zone: The Movie '83

Phyllis Barry (1908-54)
Cry Wolf '47
Goodbye Love '34
What No Beer? '33

Raymond J. Barry (1939-)
Flight of the Living Dead:
Outbreak on a Plane '07
Walk Hard: The Jewey Cow...
Steel City '06
Just Married '03
Interview with the Assassin '02
The Deep End '01
Training Day '01
Year of the Dragon '85
Dead Man Walking '95
Sudden Death '95
Cool Runnings '93
Flubber '97
The Chamber '96
Scream '96
Headless Body in Topless Bar '96
Wishful Thinking '96
The Ref '93
K2: The Ultimate High '92
Rapid Fire '92
The Turning '92
Drug Wars: The Camarena Story '90
Cop '88
Daddy's Boys '87
Born on the Fourth of July '89

Roukietou Barry
Tilai '90

Thom Barry
Yaaba '89

Toni Barry

Tony Barry (1941-)
Paperback Hero '99
Doing Time for Patsy Cline '97
Road to Nhill '97
Shame '87
The Quest '86
We of the Never Never '82
Goodbye Pork Pie '81
Hard Knocks '80
The Odd Angry Shot '79
Little Boy Lost '78

Wendy Barry
Evil Lives '92
Knights of the City '85

Wesley Barry (1907-94)
Blind Fools '40
Sunny Skies '30
Battling Bunyon '24
The Country Kid '23

Deborah Barrymore
See Deborah Maria Moore

Drew Barrymore (1975-)
He's Just Not That Into You '08
Lucky You '07
Music & Lyrics '07
Curious George '06 (V)
Fever Pitch '05
Charlie's Angels: Full Throttle '03
Duplex '03
Confessions of a Dangerous Mind '02
Donnie Darko '01
Riding in Cars with Boys '01
Charlie's Angels '00
Skipped Parts '00
Titan A.E. '00 (V)
Never Been Kissed '99
Best Men '98
Ever After: A Cinderella Story '98
Home Fries '98
The Wedding Singer '97
Everyone Says I Love You '96
Scream '96
Wishful Thinking '96
Batman Forever '95
Mad Love '95
Bad Girls '94
Boys on the Side '94
The Amy Fisher Story '93
No Place to Hide '93
Wayne's World 2 '93
Guncrazy '92
Poison Ivy '92
Sketch Artist '92
Motorama '91
Waxwork 2: Lost in Time '91
Doppelganger: The Evil Within '90
Far from Home '89
See You in the Morning '89
A Conspiracy of Love '87
Babes in Toyland '86
Cat's Eye '85
Firestarter '84
Irreconcilable Differences '84
E.T.: The Extra-Terrestrial '82
Altered States '80

Ethel Barrymore (1879-1959)
Young at Heart '54
Main Street to Broadway '53
Just for You '52
That Midnight Kiss '49
Pinky '49
Portrait of Jennie '48
The Smallest Show on Earth '48
Moss Rose '47
The Farmer's Daughter '47
The Paradine Case '47
The Spiral Staircase '46
None But the Lonely Heart '44
Rasputin and the Empress '33

John Barrymore (1882-1942)
Playmates '41
The Invisible Woman '40
Midnight '39
The Great Man Votes '38
Marie Antoinette '38
Spawn of the North '38
Bulldog Drummond Comes Back '37
Bulldog Drummond's Revenge '37
Maytime '37
Romeo and Juliet '36
Twentieth Century '34
Counsellor-at-Law '33
Dinner at Eight '33
Topaze '33
A Bill of Divorcement '32
Grand Hotel '32
State's Attorney '31
Svengali '31
The Beloved Rogue '27
Don Juan '26
Beau Brummel '24
Dr. Jekyll and Mr. Hyde '20

John Drew Barrymore, Jr. (1932-2004)
Americana '81
Smokey Bites the Dust '81
The Trojan Horse '62
High School Confidential '58
Never Love a Stranger '58
High Lonesome '50

Lionel Barrymore (1878-1954)
Main Street to Broadway '53
Lone Star '52
Malaya '49
Key Largo '48
Duel in the Sun '46
It's a Wonderful Life '46
The Valley of Decision '45
A Guy Named Joe '44
Since You Went Away '44
Thousands Cheer '43
Dr. Kildare's Strange Case '40
Let Freedom Ring '39
On Borrowed Time '39
The Secret of Dr. Kildare '39
Test Pilot '38
You Can't Take It with You '38
Captains Courageous '37
Navy Blue and Gold '37
Camille '36
Devil Doll '36
The Gorgeous Hussy '36
Ah, Wilderness! '35
David Copperfield '35
The Little Colonel '35
Mark of the Vampire '35
The Return of Peter Grimm '35
The Girl from Missouri '34
Treasure Island '34
Night Flight '33
Rasputin and the Empress '33
Grand Hotel '32
Mata Hari '32
A Free Soul '31
Free and Easy '30
West of Zanzibar '28
The Bells '26
America '24

Judith Barsi (1977-88)
All Dogs Go to Heaven '89
The Land Before Time '88
Jaws: The Revenge '87

Roger Bart (1962-)
The Producers '05
The Stepford Wives '04

Paul Bartel (1938-2000)
Hamlet '00
Billy's Hollywood Screen Kiss '98
American Gangster '07
Hostel: Part 2 '07
Harold & Kumar Escape from Guantanamo Bay '08
The Usual Suspects '95

Freddie Bartholomew (1924-92)
St. Benny the Dip '51
Sepia Cinderella '47
Junior Army '42
Tom Brown's School Days '40
Listen, Darling '38
Captains Courageous '37
Lord Fauntleroy '36
Lloyds of London '36
Anna Karenina '35
David Copperfield '35

Logan Bartholomew (1984-)
Love's Long Journey '05
Love's Enduring Promise '04

J Barton
Beau Geste '39
The Fighting Westerner '35
Feud of the West '35
Powdersmoke Range '35
The Tonto Kid '35
The Lone Defender '32
Mystery Trooper '32
Apache Kid's Escape '30

Richard Barthelmess (1895-1963)
The Spoilers '42
Only Angels Have Wings '39
Massacre '34
Heroes for Sale '33
The Cabin in the Cotton '32
The Dropkick '27
Just Suppose '26
Ranson's Folly '26
Shore Leave '25
Soul-Fire '25
Tol'able David '21
The Idol Dancer '20
The Love Flower '20
Way Down East '20

Eddie Barth (1931-)
Mr. White '92
Twenty Dollar Star '91
Thunder and Lightning '77
Hollywood Boulevard '76

Isolde Barth
Rosenstrasse '03
Club Extinction '89

Justin Bartha (1978-)
National Treasure: Book of Secrets '07
Failure to Launch '06
National Treasure '04
Gigli '03

Jayce Bartok (1974-)
Spy of Napoleon '36
The Gamma People '56
Norman Conquest '53
S.O.S. Pacific '50
Naked in the Night '56
The Gamma People '56
Crimson Pirate '52
Speedways '53

Eva Bartok (1926-98)
Blood and Black Lace '64
Operation Amsterdam '60
S.O.S. Pacific '50
A Midsummer Night's Dream '35
The Undead '57
Mickey the Great '39
The Bride of Frankenstein '35

Siri Baruc (1978-)
Megasnake '07

Jay Baruchel (1982-)
Tropic Thunder '08
Knocked Up '07
I'm Reed Fish '06
The Foursome '06
Unholy '07
Million Dollar Baby '04
Nemesis Game '03

Gary Basaraba (1959-)
Charlotte's Web '06
Jesse Stone: Death in Paradise '06
K-9: P.I. '01
Untalent '02
Dead Silence '96
The Turning Point '77
The War '94

Lynsey Bartilson (1983-)
A Rat's Tale '98 (V)
Mrs. Santa Claus '96

Bennie Bartlett (1924-99)
Bowery Boys Meet the Monsters '54
Clipped Wings '53
Master Minds '49

Bonnie Bartlett (1929-)
Shiloh 2: Shiloh Season '99
Tuesdays with Morrie '99
Primary Colors '98
Shiloh '97
Ghosts of Mississippi '96
Dave '93

Jamie Bartlett
Beyond Borders '03
Ernest Goes to Africa '97

Martine Bartlett (1925-2006)
Sybil '76

Richard Bartlett (1922-94)
Lord Love a Duck '66
Silent Raiders '54
Silver Star '55
Lonesome Trail '55

Robin Bartlett (1951-)
City of Angels '98
Honey, We Shrunk Ourselves '97
Dangerous Minds '95
Fallen Angels 1 '93
If Looks Could Kill '91
Regarding Henry '91
Alice '90
Postcards from the Edge '90
Lean on Me '89
Baby Boom '87

Diana Barton (1966-)
Body of Influence '93
Sexual Malice '93

Charles T. Barton (1902-81)

Buzz Barton (1913-90)
The Riding Avenger '36

Luciano Bartoli
Henry IV '85

James Barton (1890-1962)
The Death Artist '95
The Jerky Boys '95
The Usual Suspects '95
Grief '94
Number One Fan '94
The Tempest '28
Armistead Maupin's Tales of the City '93
Acting on Impulse '93
Posse '93
Desire and Hell at Sunset Motel '92
Evil Lives '92
Liquid Dreams '92
The Pope Must Diet '91
Gremlins 2: The New Batch '90
Far Out Man '89
Mortuary Academy '91
Pucker Up and Bark Like a Dog '89
Scenes from the Class Struggle in Beverly Hills '89
Out of the Dark '88
Amazon Women on the Moon '87
Chopping Mall '86
Munchies '87
Killer Party '86
Into the Night '85
Eating Raoul '82
Get Crazy '83
Heartbeeps '81
Trick or Treats '82
Rock 'n' Roll High School '79
Piranha '78
Grand Theft Auto '77
Cannonball '76
Eat My Dust '76
Hollywood Boulevard '76

Lynsey Bartilson

Billy Barty (1924-2000)
The Rescuers Down Under '90 (V)
Digging Up Business '90
Life Stinks '91
Lobster Man from Mars '89
Snow White '89
UHF '89
Willow '88
Body Slam '87
Masters of the Universe '87
Legend '86
Tough Guys '86
Night Patrol '85
Rumpelstiltskin '86
Under the Rainbow '81
Foul Play '78
The Amazing Dobermans '76
The Day of the Locust '75
Harum Scarum '65
Roustabout '64
Pufnstuf '70

Peter Barton (1956-)
The Patriot '00
Friday the 13th, Part 4: The Final Chapter '84
Hell Night '81

Skye McCole Bartusiak (1992-)
Kill Your Darlings '06
Boogeyman '05
Love Comes Softly '03
Firestarter 2: Rekindled '02
Don't Say a Word '01
The Sixth Sense '99
The Patriot '00
Riding in Cars with Boys '01

Mischa Barton (1986-)
Pulse '06
Decameron '07
The Misfits '61
Naked Hills '56
Here Comes the Groom '51
The Time of Your Life '48
Lost and Delirious '01
Notting Hill '99
Skipped Parts '00
Pups '99
Lawn Dogs '96
The Sixth Sense '99
The Shepherd of the Hills '41

Gregg Barton (1912-2000)
Apache Kid's Escape '30

Mikhail Baryshnikov (1948-)
Company Business '91
Dancers '87
White Nights '85
The Turning Point '77
That's Dancing! '85
Company Business '91

Gary Basaraba

David Alan Basche (1968-)
United 93 '06
Crazylove '05
War of the Worlds '05
Carry Me Home '04

Dante Basco (1975-)
Take the Lead '06
Extremedays '01
Riot in the Streets '96
Hook '91

Richard Basehart (1914-84)
Marilyn: The Untold Story '80
Being There '79
The Rebels '79
Great Bank Hoax '78
The Island of Dr. Moreau '77
Flood! '76
The Bounty Man '72
Rage '72
Chato's Land '71
The Andersonville Trial '70
Hans Brinker '69
Kings of the Sun '63
Hitler '62
Portrait in Black '60
The Brothers Karamazov '58
Moby Dick '56
Il Bidone '55
La Strada '54
Titanic '53
Fixed Bayonets! '51
Tension '50
Reign of Terror '49
He Walked by Night '48
Cry Wolf '47

Alain Bashung (1947-)
Confusion of Genders '00
My Father, My Mother, My Brothers and My Sisters '99

Kim Basinger (1953-)
Even Money '06
The Sentinel '06
Cellular '04
The Door in the Floor '04
Elvis Has Left the Building '04
8 Mile '02
People I Know '02
Bless the Child '00
I Dreamed of Africa '00
L.A. Confidential '97
The Getaway '93
The Real McCoy '93
Wayne's World 2 '93
Cool World '92
Final Analysis '92
The Marrying Man '91
Batman '89
My Stepmother Is an Alien '88
Blind Date '87
Nadine '87
Fool for Love '86
9 1/2 Weeks '86
No Mercy '86
The Natural '84
The Man Who Loved Women '83
Never Say Never Again '83
Mother Lode '82
Hard Country '81
Killjoy '81
From Here to Eternity '79

Elya Baskin (1951-)
Thirteen Days '00
Running Mad '99
Air Force One '97
Spy Trap '92
Deepstar Six '89
Enemies, a Love Story '89
The Name of the Rose '86
Moscow on the Hudson '84

Antoine Basler
Irma Vep '96

Marianne Basler (1964-)
Rendezvous in Paris '95
Va Savoir '01
A Soldier's Tale '91
Overseas: Three Women with Man Trouble '90

Lena Basquette (1907-94)
Heroes of the Heart '94
A Night for Crime '42
Rose of Rio Grande '38
Hello Trouble '32
Arizona Terror '31
Hard Hombre '31
Pleasure '31

Alfie Bass (1921-87)
The Fearless Vampire Killers '67
Alfie '66
Help! '65
Blackout '54
Made in Heaven '52
The Lavender Hill Mob '51
Man on the Run '49

Bobby Bass (1936-2001)
The Squeeze '87
Blood Beach '81

Tamara La Seon Bass (1978-)
Baby Boy '01
Bellyfruit '99

Albert Bassermann (1862-1952)
The Red Shoes '48
The Private Affairs of Bel Ami '47
Rhapsody in Blue '45
Since You Went Away '44
Madame Curie '43
The Moon and Sixpence '43
Invisible Agent '42
Reunion in France '42
Melody Master '41
A Woman's Face '41
Foreign Correspondent '40

Angela Bassett (1958-)
Tyler Perry's Meet the Browns '08
Meet the Robinsons '07 (V)
Akeelah and the Bee '06
Mr. 3000 '04
Masked and Anonymous '03
The Rosa Parks Story '02
Sunshine State '02
Ruby's Bucket of Blood '01
The Score '01
Boesman & Lena '00
Whispers: An Elephant's Tale '00 (V)
Music of the Heart '99
Supernova '99
How Stella Got Her Groove Back '98
Contact '97
Strange Days '95
Vampire in Brooklyn '95
Waiting to Exhale '95
What's Love Got to Do with It? '93
Innocent Blood '92
The Jacksons: An American Dream '92
Malcolm X '92
Passion Fish '92
Boyz N the Hood '91
City of Hope '91
Critters 4 '91
The Heroes of Desert Storm '91
F/X 86

Linda Bassett (1950-)
Kinky Boots '06
Calendar Girls '03
The Hours '02
Beautiful People '99
East Is East '99
Oscar and Lucinda '97
Mary Reilly '95
Waiting for the Moon '87

Steve Bassett (1955-)
The Jackal '97
Spring Break '83

Alexandra Bastedo (1946-)
Draw! '81
Find the Lady '76
The Ghoul '75
The Blood Spattered Bride '72
Kashmiri Run '69

Billy Bastiani
Blood & Concrete: A Love Story '90
Salvation! '87

Steve Bastoni (1966-)
Macbeth '06
The Crocodile Hunter: Collision Course '02
Rodgers & Hammerstein's South Pacific '01
Dr. Jekyll & Mr. Hyde '99
15 Amore '98

Othon Bastos (1933-)
Behind the Sun '01
Central Station '98
Antonio Das Mortes '68
Black God, White Devil '64

Michal Bat-Adam
The Impossible Spy '87
Atalia '85
Madame Rosa '77
Rachel's Man '75
The House on Chelouche Street '73
I Love You Rosa '72

Sylvia Bataille (1908-93)
A Day in the Country '46
The Crime of Monsieur Lange '36

Alexei Batalov (1928-)
Moscow Does Not Believe in Tears '80
The Lady with the Dog '59
The Cranes Are Flying '57

Nikolai Batalov (1899-1937)
The Road to Life '31
Bed and Sofa '27
Mother '26

Pierre Batcheff (1901-32)
Un Chien Andalou '28
The Chess Player '27
Napoleon '27
Siren of the Tropics '27

Anthony Bate (1929-)
Philby, Burgess and MacLean: Spy Scandal of the Century '84
Smiley's People '82
Tinker, Tailor, Soldier, Spy '80
Madhouse Mansion '74

Geoffrey Bateman
Manderlay '05
Another Country '84

Jason Bateman (1969-)
Forgetting Sarah Marshall '08
Hancock '08
Juno '07
The Ex '07
The Kingdom '07
Mr. Magorium's Wonder Emporium '07
Smokin' Aces '07
Arthur and the Invisibles '06 (V)
The Break-Up '06
Dodgeball: A True Underdog Story '04
Starsky & Hutch '04
One Way Out '02
The Sweetest Thing '02
Sol Goode '01
Love Stinks '99
Breaking the Rules '92
A Taste for Killing '92
Necessary Roughness '91
Teen Wolf Too '87
Can You Feel Me Dancing? '85

Justine Bateman (1966-)
The TV Set '06
Out of Order '03
Kiss & Tell '99
Highball '97
God's Lonely Man '96
The Night We Never Met '93
Deadbolt '92
Primary Motive '92
The Closer '91
The Fatal Image '90
Satisfaction '88
Can You Feel Me Dancing? '85

Alan Bates (1934-2003)
Hollywood North '03
The Statement '03
Evelyn '02
The Mothman Prophecies '02
The Sum of All Fears '02
Gosford Park '01
The Prince and the Pauper '01
Arabian Nights '00
St. Patrick: The Irish Legend '00
Grave Indiscretions '96
Silent Tongue '92
Unnatural Pursuits '91
Hamlet '90
Club Extinction '89
Mr. Frost '89
A Voyage 'Round My Father '89
We Think the World of You '88
Pack of Lies '87
Prayer for the Dying '87
Duet for One '86
An Englishman Abroad '83
Separate Tables '83
The Wicked Lady '83
Britannia Hospital '82
Return of the Soldier '82
Hands Up '81
Trespasser '81
Nijinsky '80
The Shout '78
An Unmarried Woman '78
In Celebration '75
Royal Flash '75
The Story of Jacob & Joseph '74 (N)
The Story of a Love Story '73
A Day in the Death of Joe Egg '71
The Go-Between '71
Women in Love '70
The Fixer '68
Far from the Madding Crowd '67
Georgy Girl '66
The King of Hearts '66
Zorba the Greek '64
A Kind of Loving '62
Whistle down the Wind '61
The Entertainer '60

Barbara Bates (1925-69)
Rhapsody '54
The Caddy '53
Belles on Their Toes '52
I'd Climb the Highest Mountain '51
Let's Make It Legal '51
Cheaper by the Dozen '50
The Inspector General '49
June Bride '48

Florence Bates (1888-1954)
Lullaby of Broadway '51
The Judge Steps Out '49
A Letter to Three Wives '49
My Dear Secretary '49
I Remember Mama '48
Portrait of Jennie '48
Winter Meeting '48
The Secret Life of Walter Mitty '47
Diary of a Chambermaid '46
San Antonio '45
Saratoga Trunk '45
His Butler's Sister '44
The Mask of Dimitrios '44
Since You Went Away '44
Heaven Can Wait '43
Mr. Lucky '43
The Moon and Sixpence '43
Mexican Spitfire at Sea '42
The Tuttles of Tahiti '42
The Chocolate Soldier '41
Love Crazy '41
Road Show '41
Rebecca '40

Granville Bates (1882-1940)
My Favorite Wife '40
The Great Man Votes '38
The Jury's Secret '38
Next Time I Marry '38
Larceny On the Air '37
Waikiki Wedding '37

Jeanne Bates (1918-2007)
Mom '89
Eraserhead '78
The Strangler '64
Sabaka '55

Kathy Bates (1948-)
Bee Movie '07 (V)
Fred Claus '07
The Golden Compass '07
P.S. I Love You '07
Bonneville '06
Charlotte's Web '06 (V)
Failure to Launch '06
Relative Strangers '06
The Bridge of San Luis Rey '05
Around the World in 80 Days '04
Little Black Book '04
Popeye's Voyage: The Quest for Pappy '04
Unconditional Love '03
About Schmidt '02
Dragonfly '02
Love Liza '02
My Sister's Keeper '02
American Outlaws '01
Annie '99
The Dress Code '99
Primary Colors '98
The Waterboy '98
Swept from the Sea '97
Titanic '97
Diabolique '96
The Late Shift '96
The War at Home '96
Angus '95
Curse of the Starving Class '94
Dolores Claiborne '94
North '94
Stephen King's The Stand '94
A Home of Our Own '93
Hostages '93
Prelude to a Kiss '92
Shadows and Fog '92
Used People '92
At Play in the Fields of the Lord '91
Fried Green Tomatoes '91
Dick Tracy '90
Misery '90
White Palace '90
High Stakes '89
Men Don't Leave '89
Roe vs. Wade '89
Signs of Life '89
My Best Friend Is a Vampire '88
Murder Ordained '87
Summer Heat '87
The Morning After '86
Come Back to the Five & Dime, Jimmy Dean, Jimmy Dean '82
Straight Time '78

Michael Bates (1920-78)
No Sex Please—We're British '73
Frenzy '72
A Clockwork Orange '71
Patton '70
Oh! What a Lovely War '69
Bedazzled '68

Paul Bates
8 Mile '02
Instinct '99
The Preacher's Wife '96
Mr. Wonderful '93
True Romance '93
Crazy People '90
Coming to America '88

Ralph Bates (1940-91)
Letters to an Unknown Lover '84
Second Chance '80
I Don't Want to Be Born '75
Poldark '75
Poldark 2 '75
The Graveyard '74
Murder Motel '74
Dynasty of Fear '72
Dr. Jekyll and Sister Hyde '71
Lust for a Vampire '71
The Horror of Frankenstein '70
Taste the Blood of Dracula '70

R(ichard) C(arlos) Bates (1946-)
Werewolf '95
...And God Spoke '94

Timothy Bateson (1926-)
The 10th Kingdom '00
Joseph '95
Heart of Darkness '93
The Mouse That Roared '59

Randall Batinkoff (1968-)
Touched '05
April's Shower '03
As Good As It Gets '97
The Curve '97
The Peacemaker '97
Walking and Talking '96
Christy '94
Buffy the Vampire Slayer '92
The Player '92
School Ties '92
For Keeps '88
Streetwalkin' '85

Stiv Bators (1949-90)
Tapeheads '89
Polyester '81

Susan Batson (1944-)
Bamboozled '00
Girl 6 '96

Matt Battaglia (1965-)
Half Past Dead '02
Universal Soldier 2: Brothers in Arms '98
Universal Soldier 3: Unfinished Business '98
Raven '97

Rick (Rik) Battaglia (1930-)
'Tis a Pity She's a Whore '73
Cold Steel for Tortuga '65
Apache's Last Battle '64
Roland the Mighty '56

Cyia Batten (1975-)
At Any Cost '00
Red Shoe Diaries: Swimming Naked '00

Sins of the Mind '97

Guiseppe Battiston (1968-)
Don't Tell '05
Bread and Tulips '01

Hinton Battle (1956-)
Child Star: The Shirley Temple Story '01
Foreign Student '94

Texas Battle (1976-)
Coach Carter '05
Wrong Turn 2: Dead End '07

Patrick Bauchau (1938-)
Boy Culture '06
Karla '06
Ray '04
Shade '03
Panic Room '02
Secretary '02
The Cell '00
Jackpot '01 (V)
King of Texas '02
Double Identity '09
The Music Teacher '88
Creepers '85
Choose Me '84
Emmanuelle 4 '84
Entre-Nous '83
State of Things '82
La Collectionneuse '67

Vanessa Bauche (1973-)
The Three Burials of Melquiades Estrada '05
Amores Perros '00
A Lost Year '92
Highway Patrolman '91

Belinda Bauer (1951-)
Poison Ivy 2: Lily '95
A Case for Murder '93
H.P. Lovecraft's Necronomicon: Book of the Dead '93
Servants of Twilight '91
RoboCop 2 '90
Act of Piracy '89
The Rosary Murders '87
Samson and Delilah '84
Flashdance '83
Timerider '83
The Sins of Dorian Gray '82
Archer: The Fugitive from the Empire '81
Winter Kills '79

Chris Bauer (1966-)
Flags of Our Fathers '06
Masters of Horror: Sounds Like '06
The Notorious Bettie Page '06
Broken Flowers '05
61* '01
Flawless '99
The Hunley '99
8mm '99
The Devil's Advocate '97

David Bauer (1917-73)
Tropic of Cancer '70
Inspector Clouseau '68

Michelle (McClellan) Bauer (1958-)
Assault of the Party Nerds 2: Heavy Petting Detective '95
Attack of the 60-Foot Centerfold '95
Vampire Vixens from Venus '94
Dinosaur Island '93
Evil Toons '90
Assault of the Party Nerds '89
Lady Avenger '89
Wild Man '89
Beverly Hills Vamp '88
Deadly Embrace '88
Death Row Diner '88
Hollywood Chainsaw Hookers '88
Night of the Living Babes '87
Tomb '86
Roller Blade '85
Screen Test '85

Steven Bauer (1956-)
Dead Lenny '06
The Lost City '05
Pit Fighter '05
The Learning Curve '01
Along for the Ride '00
For Love or Country: The Arturo Sandoval Story '00
Hooded Angels '00
Traffic '00
Bloody Proof '99
Boss of Bosses '99
Naked Lies '98
Navajo Blues '97
Star Portal '97
Plato's Run '96
Primal Fear '96
Body Count '95
Wild Side '95
Improper Conduct '94
Star Quest '94
Stranger by Night '94
Woman of Desire '93
Snapdragon '93
False Arrest '92
Raising Cain '92
Double Dare '92
A Climate for Killing '91
Sweet Poison '91
Drug Wars: The Camarena Story '90
Gleaming the Cube '89
The Beast '88
Wildfire '88
Running Scared '86
Sword of Gideon '86
Thief of Hearts '84
Scarface '83

Ricardo Bauleo
Lost Diamond '67
The Curious Dr. Humpp '70

Katharine Baumann (1948-)

Marie Baumer
Beethoven '36
Crime and Punishment '35

Harry Baur (1880-1943)
Volpone '39
Beethoven '36

Frances Bavier (1902-89)
It Started with a Kiss '59
Man in the Attic '53
Horizons West '52
The Day the Earth Stood Still '51
The Lady Says No '51
The Stooge '51

Barbara Baxley (1923-90)
A Shock to the System '90
Come Along with Me '84
Nashville '75
Countdown '68
All Fall Down '62

David Baxt
Cloud Waltzing '87
The Shining '80

George L. Baxt (1923-2003)
Which Way to the Front? '70

Warner Baxter (1889-1951)
Adam Had Four Sons '41
Vogues of 1938 '37
The Prisoner of Shark Island '36
Under the Pampas Moon '35
Broadway Bill '34
42nd Street '33
Penthouse '33
West of Zanzibar '28
Linda '29

Alan Baxter (1908-76)
Inside Monkey Zetterland '93
The Set-Up '49
She Shoulda Said No '49
Behind Prison Walls '43
Saboteur '42
Shadow of the Thin Man '41
Abe Lincoln in Illinois '40
Each Dawn I Die '39
Wide Open Faces '38
It Could Happen to You '37
Big Brown Eyes '36

Anne Baxter (1923-85)
Masks of Death '86
East of Eden '80
Jane Austen in Manhattan '80
The Return of Martin Guerre '83
Walk on the Wild Side '62
Cimarron '60
Three Violent People '57
The Ten Commandments '56
The Come On '56
Carnival Story '54
The Blue Gardenia '53
I Confess '53
Follow the Sun '51
All About Eve '50
Ticket to Tomahawk '50
Homecoming '48
Angel on My Shoulder '46
The Razor's Edge '46
Guest in the House '44
The North Star '43
Crash Dive '43
Five Graves to Cairo '43
The Magnificent Ambersons '42
The Fighting Sullivans '42
Charley's Aunt '41

Amy Lynn Baxter (1967-)
Broadcast Bombshells '95
Bikini Bistro '94

Nathalie Baye (1948-)
Le Petit Lieutenant '05
Catch Me If You Can '02
An Affair of Love '99
Venus Beauty Institute '98
The Return of Martin Guerre '83
I Married a Dead Man '82
A Balance '82
Beau Pere '81
The Green Room '78
The Man Who Loved Women '77
Day for Night '73

Sara Bay
See Rosalba Neri

Gary Bayer
Promised a Miracle '88
Will: G. Gordon Liddy '82
Not My Kid '85

Nathalie Baye (1948-)
Le Petit Lieutenant '05
Catch Me If You Can '02
An Affair of Love '99
Venus Beauty Institute '98
The Return of Martin Guerre '83
I Married a Dead Man '82
A Balance '82
Beau Pere '81
The Green Room '78
The Man Who Loved Women '77
Day for Night '73

Geoffrey Bayldon (1924-)
Porridge '79
Madame Sousatzka '88
Cause Célèbre '87
After the Deluge '03
The Crocodile Hunter: Collision Course '02
Chopper '00
Casino Royale '67
The Bushbaby '70
Asylum '72
King Rat '65
Emperor of the North Pole '73
To the Lighthouse '83
The Girl in a Swing '89
Island in the Sky '58
Sands of Iwo Jima '49

Lynsey Baxter (1965-)
The Gospel of John '03
Clarissa '91
The French Lieutenant's Woman '81

Keith Baxter (1933-)
Berlin Blues '89
Ash Wednesday '73
George A. Romero's Land of the Dead '05
Chimes at Midnight '67

Jennifer Baxter
Dark Water '05

Meredith Baxter (1947-)
The Counterfeiters '07
Dresden, Texas '05
Devil's Pond '03
Crash Course '00
Till Murder Do Us Part '92
Jezebel's Kiss '90
Broken Badge '85
Take Your Best Shot '82
Beulah Land '80
The Family Man '79
Little Women '78
All the President's Men '76
Bittersweet Love '76
Ben '72

Jordan Bayne
Under Hellgate Bridge '99
A Stranger in the Kingdom '98

Lawrence Bayne
Getting Gotti '94
Lakota Woman: Siege at Wounded Knee '94
Black Robe '91

Adam Beach (1972-)
Flags of Our Fathers '06
The Big Empty '04
A Thief of Time '04
Windtalkers '02
Posers '02
Now & Forever '02
Coyote Waits '03
Skinwalkers '02
Joe Dirt '01
Comanche Moon '08
Bury My Heart at Wounded Knee '07
Luna: Spirit of the Whale '07
Smoke Signals '98
Coyote Summer '96
Dance Me Outside '95
Squanto: A Warrior's Tale '94

Stephanie Beacham (1947-)
Unconditional Love '03
Sketch Artist 2: Hands That See '95
Bad Company '94
Wedding Bell Blues '96
Foreign Affairs '93
The Dying Truth '91
Troop Beverly Hills '89
Riders '88
Schizo '77
Inseminoid '80
The Confessional '75
And Now the Screaming Starts '73
Super Bitch '73
Dracula A.D. 1972 '72
The Nightcomers '72

Frances Bay (1918-)
The Operator '01
Finder's Fee '01
Goodbye, Lover '99
Inspector Gadget '99
Charging Habits '96
Happy Gilmore '96
In the Mouth of Madness '95
The Neighbor '93
The Set-Up '49
Inside Monkey Zetterland '93
Single White Female '92
The Karate Kid: Part 3 '89
The Attic '80
Foul Play '78

John Beal (1909-97)
The Firm '93
The North Star '43
Amityville 3: The Demon '83
Ten Who Dared '60
Edge of Darkness '43
The Great Commandment '41
I Am the Law '38
Double Wedding '37
Madame X '37
Break of Hearts '35
Les Misérables '35
The Little Minister '34

Simon Russell Beale (1961-)
The Gathering '02
Persuasion '95
Hamlet '96
A Dance to the Music of Time '97

Kate Beahan (1969-)
The Return '06
Flightplan '05
The Wicker Man '06

Jennifer Beals (1963-)
The Grudge 2 '06
Catch That Kid '04
Runaway Jury '03
Roger Dodger '02
13 Moons '02
The Anniversary Party '01
Anne Rice's The Feast of All Saints '01
A House Divided '00
Militia '99
The Last Stop '99
Something More '99
Turbulence 2: Fear of Flying '99
Body and Soul '98
The Last Days of Disco '98
The Prophecy 2: Ashtown '98
The Twilight of the Golds '97
The Spree '96
The Wishful Thinking '96 (V)
Devil in a Blue Dress '95
Four Rooms '95
Dead on Sight '94
Mrs. Parker and the Vicious Circle '94
Terror Stalks the Class Reunion '93
Day of Atonement '93
Blood & Concrete: A Love Story '90
Club Extinction '89
Sons '89
Vampire's Kiss '88
Split Decisions '88
The Gamble '88
The Bride '85
That's Dancing! '85
Cinderella '84
Flashdance '83

Lee Ann Beaman
Improper Conduct '94
Bad Company '94
Sketch Artist 2: Hands That See '95
Final Appeal '93
True Romance '93
The Dying Truth '91
One False Move '91
Internal Affairs '90

Michael Beach (1963-)
First Sunday '08
Stargate: The Ark of Truth '08
Full Count '06
Crazy as Hell '02
Asunder '99
Made Men '99
Ruby Bridges '98
Casualties '97
Ms. Scrooge '97
Soul Food '97
A Family Thing '96
Rebound: The Legend of Earl "The Goat" Manigault '96
Indecency '92
In the Soup '92
Cadence '89
Lean on Me '89
In a Shallow Grave '88
Weekend War '88
Waiting to Exhale '95

Orson Bean (1928-)
Being John Malkovich '99
Final Judgment '92
Instant Karma '90
Innerspace '87
My Bodyguard '80
Anatomy of a Murder '59

Robert Bean
Creature from the Haunted Sea '60
The Wild Ride '60

Sean Bean (1959-)
The Hitcher '07
Silent Hill '06
The Return '06
Outlaw '07
North Country '05
The Island '05
Flightplan '05
The Big Empty '04
National Treasure '04
Troy '04
The Lord of the Rings: The Return of the King '03
Equilibrium '02
Don't Say a Word '01
The Lord of the Rings: The Fellowship of the Rings '01
Essex Boys '99
Airborne '98
Ronin '98
When Saturday Comes '95
Black Beauty '94
Scarlet '94
Jacob '94
Leo Tolstoy's Anna Karenina '96
Sharpe's Justice '97
Sharpe's Waterloo '97
Sharpe's Revenge '97
Sharpe's Mission '96
Sharpe's Siege '96
Sharpe's Regiment '96
Sharpe's Gold '95
Sharpe's Honour '94
Sharpe's Sword '94
Sharpe's Company '94
Sharpe's Enemy '94
Sharpe's Battle '94
Sharpe's Eagle '93

Sharpe's Rifles '93
Shopping '93
A Woman's Guide to Adultery '93
Fool's Gold: The Story of the Brink's-Mat Robbery '92
Lady Chatterley '92
Patriot Games '92
Clarissa '91
Catherine Cookson's The Fifteen Streets '90
The Field '90
Lorna Doone '90
Stormy Monday '88
Troubles '88
Caravaggio '86

Matthew "Stymie" Beard (1925-81)
Sophisticated Gents '81
East of Eden '80
Backstairs at the White House '79
Dead Reckoning '47
Broken Strings '40
Way Down South '39
Two-Gun Man from Harlem '38

Amanda Bearse (1958-)
Fraternity Vacation '85
Fright Night '85
Protocol '84

Emmanuelle Beart (1965-)
The 4 Musketeers '05
Nathalie '03
Strayed '03
8 Women '02
La Buche '00
Les Destinees '00
Time Regained '99
Mission: Impossible '96
Nelly et Monsieur Arnaud '95
L'Enfer '93
Un Coeur en Hiver '93
La Belle Noiseuse '90
Date with an Angel '87
Manon of the Spring '87

Allyce Beasley (1954-)
2 Brothers & a Bride '03
Dream with the Fishes '97
Entertaining Angels: The Dorothy Day Story '96
Rumpelstiltskin '96
National Lampoon's Loaded Weapon 1 '93
Stephen King's The Tommyknockers '93
Motorama '91
Silent Night, Deadly Night 4: Initiation '90
Moonlighting '85
Ratings Game '84

John Beasley (1943-)
Walking Tall '04
The Sum of All Fears '02
Freedom Song '00
The Gift '00
Lost Souls '00
Crazy in Alabama '99
The General's Daughter '99
The Apostle '97

Norman Beaton (1934-94)
The Mighty Quinn '89
Playing Away '87

Stephanie Beaton (1972-)
Blood Gnome '02
Witchcraft 11: Sisters in Blood '00
Witchcraft 10: Mistress of the Craft '98

Ian Beattie
Alexander '04
Stray Bullet '98

Clyde Beatty (1903-65)
Africa Screams '49
Darkest Africa '36
The Lost Jungle '34

Debra Beatty
Caged Heat 3000 '95
Hollywood Dreams '94

May (Mae) Beatty (1880-1945)
I Wake Up Screaming '41
Mad Love '35

Nancy Beatty
Lars and the Real Girl '07
The Confessor '04
Eye '96

Ned Beatty (1937-)
Charlie Wilson's War '07
Shooter '07
The Walker '07
Sweet Land '05
Homicide: The Movie '00
Cookie's Fortune '99
Life '99
Spring Forward '99
He Got Game '98
Crazy Horse '96
The Curse of Inferno '96
The Affair '95
Gulliver's Travels '95
Larry McMurtry's Streets of Laredo '95
Black Water '94
Just Cause '94
Radioland Murders '94
Replikator: Cloned to Kill '94
Ed and His Dead Mother '93
Rudy '93
Angel Square '92
Prelude to a Kiss '92
T Bone N Weasel '92
Blind Vision '91
Going Under '91
Hear My Song '91
Illusions '91
Tragedy of Flight 103: The Inside Story '91
Back to Hannibal: The Return of Tom Sawyer and Huckleberry Finn '90
Big Bad John '90
A Cry in the Wild '90
Repossessed '90
Robert Kennedy and His Times '90
Captain America '89
Chattahoochee '89
Ministry of Vengeance '89
Physical Evidence '89
Spy '89
Purple People Eater '88
Shadows in the Storm '88
Switching Channels '88
Time Trackers '88
The Unholy '88
The Big Easy '87
The Fourth Protocol '87
Midnight Crossing '87
Rolling Vengeance '87
The Trouble with Spies '87
Back to School '86
Charlotte Forten's Mission: Experiment in Freedom '85
Konrad '85
Stroker Ace '83
Pray TV '82
Rumpelstiltskin '82
Touched '82
The Toy '82
A Woman Called Golda '82
The Incredible Shrinking Woman '81
All God's Children '80
The Guyana Tragedy: The Story of Jim Jones '80
Hopscotch '80
Superman 2 '80
Friendly Fire '79
1941 '79
Promises in the Dark '79
Wise Blood '79
Great Bank Hoax '78
A Question of Love '78
Superman: The Movie '78
The Exorcist 2: The Heretic '77
Gray Lady Down '77
Our Town '77
All the President's Men '76
The Big Bus '76
Hunter '76
Mikey & Nicky '76
Network '76
Silver Streak '76
Nashville '75
Sniper '75
The Execution of Private Slovik '74
Dying Room Only '73
The Last American Hero '73
The Thief Who Came to Dinner '73
White Lightning '73
Deliverance '72

Robert Beatty (1909-92)
2001: A Space Odyssey '68
Where Eagles Dare '68
Time Lock '57
Postmark for Danger '56
The Love of Three Queens '54
Wings of Danger '52
Captain Horatio Hornblower '51
Against the Wind '48
Counterblast '48
San Demetrio, London '47
Appointment with Crime '45

Warren Beatty (1937-)
Town and Country '01
Bulworth '98
Love Affair '94
Bugsy '91
Dick Tracy '90
Ishtar '87
Reds '81
Heaven Can Wait '78
Shampoo '75
The Parallax View '74
Dollars '71
McCabe & Mrs. Miller '71
Bonnie & Clyde '67
Promise Her Anything '66
Mickey One '65
Lilith '64
All Fall Down '62
Roman Spring of Mrs. Stone '61
Splendor in the Grass '61

Michelle Beaudoin (1975-)
Escape Velocity '99
Sabrina the Teenage Witch '96
Live Bait '95

Hugh Beaumont (1909-82)
The Human Duplicators '64
Night Passage '57
The Mole People '56
Bugles in the Afternoon '52
Phone Call from a Stranger '52
Cavalry Scout '51
Danger Zone '51
The Lost Continent '51
Pier 23 '51
Roaring City '51
Savage Drums '51
Money Madness '47
Railroaded '47
The Blue Dahlia '46
The Lady Confesses '45
Objective, Burma! '45
Mr. Winkle Goes to War '44
The Fallen Sparrow '43
The Seventh Victim '43
To the Shores of Tripoli '42
Wake Island '42
Panama Menace '41

Kathryn Beaumont (1937-)
Peter Pan '53 (V)
Alice in Wonderland '51 (V)

Lucy Beaumont (1873-1937)
Condemned to Live '35
A Free Soul '31
The Crowd '28

Garcelle Beauvais (1966-)
I Know Who Killed Me '07
American Gun '05
Barbershop 2: Back in Business '04
Bad Company '02
Double Take '01
Wild Wild West '99
Manhunter '86

Nicolas Beauvy (1958-)
Take Down '79
The Toolbox Murders '78
The Cowboys '72
Rage '72
Shoot Out '71

Jim Beaver (1950-)
Next '07
Bad Girls '94
Twogether '94
In Country '89

Terry Beaver (1948-)
To Dance with the White Dog '93
Impure Thoughts '86

Louise Beavers (1902-62)
Tammy and the Bachelor '57
Goodbye, My Lady '56
The Jackie Robinson Story '50
My Blue Heaven '50
Tell It to the Judge '49
Mr. Blandings Builds His Dream House '48
Delightfully Dangerous '45
Dixie Jamboree '44
Du Barry Was a Lady '43
Big Street '42
Reap the Wild Wind '42
General Spanky '36
It Happened in New Orleans '36
Imitation of Life '34
In the Money '34
She Done Him Wrong '33
Woman Condemned '33
Too Busy to Work '32
Coquette '29

Davide Bechini (1962-)
Days '02

Damian Bechir (1963-)
No News from God '01
Solo '96

Jennifer Beck (1974-)
Gypsy '93
Troll '86
Tightrope '84

John Beck (1943-)
Timecop 2: The Berlin Decision '03
Extreme Limits '01
Agent of Death '99
Militia '99
Black Day Black Night '95
Suspect Device '95
Honor Thy Father and Mother: The True Story of the Menendez Brothers '94
Last Time Out '94
A Climate for Killing '91
Fire and Rain '89
In the Cold of the Night '89
Deadly Illusion '87
Great American Traffic Jam '80
Time Machine '78
Audrey Rose '77
The Other Side of Midnight '77
The Big Bus '76
Sky Riders '76
Rollerball '75
Paperback Hero '73
Sleeper '73
Lawman '71
Three in the Attic '68

John (Jack) Beck
Everyman's Law '36
King of the Pecos '36

Julian Beck (1925-85)
Poltergeist 2: The Other Side '86
Oedipus Rex '67

Kimberly Beck (1956-)
In the Deep Woods '91
Private War '90
Nightmare at Noon '87
Friday the 13th, Part 4: The Final Chapter '84
Roller Boogie '79
Massacre at Central High '76

Michael Beck (1949-)
Fade to Black '93
Deadly Game '91
Blackout '85
Celebrity '85
The Golden Seal '83
Megaforce '82
Warlords of the 21st Century '82
Xanadu '80
Madman '79
Mayflower: The Pilgrims' Adventure '79
The Warriors '79
Holocaust '78

Thomas Beck (1909-95)
Thank you, Mr. Moto '37
Think Fast, Mr. Moto '37
Charlie Chan at the Opera '36
Charlie Chan at the Race Track '36
Charlie Chan in Egypt '35
Charlie Chan in Paris '35
Life Begins at Forty '35

Graham Beckel (1955-)
Brokeback Mountain '05
Northfork '03
Two Days '03
Hardball '01
Pearl Harbor '01
The '70s '00
Blue Streak '99
No Vacancy '99
True Crime '99
Black Dog '98
Bulworth '98
Lost in the Bermuda Triangle '98
L.A. Confidential '97
Jennifer 8 '92
O Pioneers! '91
Separate but Equal '91
Rising Son '90
Lost Angels '89
The Money '75

Ben Becker (1964-)
Gloomy Sunday '02
The Harmonists '99
Samson and Delilah '96
Brother of Sleep '95

Gerry Becker (1950-)
Blood Work '02
Spider-Man '02
Mickey Blue Eyes '99
Donnie Brasco '96
Eraser '96
Legacy of Lies '92
The Public Eye '92

Gretchen Becker
Huck and the King of Hearts '93

Hartmut Becker (1948-)
The Waiting Time '99
Escape from Sobibor '87
Jenny's War '85

Jacques Becker (1906-60)
Grand Illusion '37
Boudu Saved from Drowning '32

Josh Becker (1958-)
Army of Darkness '92
Evil Dead 2: Dead by Dawn '87

Kuno Becker (1978-)
Sex and Breakfast '07
Goal! The Dream Begins '06
Once Upon a Wedding '05
Lucia, Lucia '03

Meret Becker (1969-)
Munich '05
The Harmonists '99
The Wicked, Wicked West '97
The Promise '94

Randy Becker (1970-)
American Adobo '02
Love! Valour! Compassion! '96

Tony Becker (1963-)
Lie Down with Dogs '95
Agent Red '00
Cody '77

Scotty Beckett (1929-68)
The Oklahoman '56
Nancy Goes to Rio '50
Battleground '49
The Jolson Story '46
The Climax '44
Ali Baba and the Forty Thieves '43
Heaven Can Wait '43
Kings Row '41
My Favorite Wife '40
My Son, My Son '40
Love Affair '39
Devil's Party '38
Listen, Darling '38
Marie Antoinette '38
Conquest '37
The Charge of the Light Brigade '36
I Dream Too Much '35
Stand Up and Cheer '34

Tyson Beckford (1970-)
Into the Blue '05
Searching for Bobby D '05
Biker Boyz '03

Kate Beckinsale (1974-)
Snow Angels '07
Vacancy '07
Click '06
Underworld: Evolution '05
The Aviator '04
Van Helsing '04
Tiptoes '03
Underworld '03
Laurel Canyon '02
Pearl Harbor '01
Serendipity '01
The Golden Bowl '00
Brokedown Palace '99
The Last Days of Disco '98
Shooting Fish '98
Emma '97
Haunted '95
Cold Comfort Farm '94
Royal Deceit '94
Uncovered '94
Much Ado about Nothing '93
One Against the Wind '91

Tony Beckley (1927-80)
When a Stranger Calls '79
The Fiend '71
Get Carter '71
Assault '70
The Italian Job '69

William Beckley (1930-)
Too Late the Hero '70
The Killing of Sister George '69

Claire Beckman (1961-)
The Thing About My Folks '05
Fallout '01

Henry Beckman (1925-)
The Man Upstairs '93
Family Reunion '88
Marnie '64

Reginald Beckwith (1908-65)
Burn Witch, Burn! '62
Genevieve '53
Lucky Jim '58
Curse of the Demon '57
Men of Sherwood Forest '57
The Runaway Bus '54

William Beckwith
Escape from Safehaven '88
Prime Evil '88

Irene Bedard (1967-)
Love's Long Journey '05
Miracle at Sage Creek '05
The New World '05
The Lost Child '00
Wildflowers '99
Smoke Signals '98
Navajo Blues '97
True Women '97
Two for Texas '97
Crazy Horse '96
Grand Avenue '96
Pocahontas '95 (V)
Lakota Woman: Siege at Wounded Knee '94
Squanto: A Warrior's Tale '94

Don Beddoe (1891-1991)
Nickel Mountain '85
Jack the Giant Killer '62
The Night of the Hunter '55
The Enforcer '51
The Narrow Margin '52
Caged '50
Gun Crazy '49
Buck Privates Come Home '47
Welcome Stranger '47
The Best Years of Our Lives '46
O.S.S. '46
Junior Army '42
Before I Hang '40
Golden Boy '39

Bonnie Bedelia (1950-)
Sordid Lives '00
Anywhere But Here '99
Locked in Silence '99
Bad Manners '98
Gloria '98
Homecoming '96
Judicial Consent '94
Speechless '94
Fallen Angels 2 '93
The Fire Next Time '93
Needful Things '93
Switched at Birth '91
When the Time Comes '91
Die Hard 2: Die Harder '90
Presumed Innocent '90
Somebody Has to Shoot the Picture '90
Fat Man and Little Boy '89
Die Hard '88
Prince of Pennsylvania '88
The Boy Who Could Fly '86
The Stranger '87
Death of an Angel '86
Violets Are Blue '86
Heart Like a Wheel '83
Memorial Day '83
Lady from Yesterday '85
Walking Through the Fire '80
Salem's Lot '79
The Big Fix '78
A Question of Love '78
Lovers and Other Strangers '70
The Gypsy Moths '69
They Shoot Horses, Don't They? '69

Brian Bedford (1935-)
Mr. St. Nick '02
Cavalry Charge '51
War Arrow '53
Jubal '56
Terminal Entry '87
Nixon '95
The Beast '88
Beyond Justice '92
Grand Prix '66
The Last Best Year '90
Robin Hood '73 (V)

Kabir Bedi (1945-)
Gung Ho! '43
The Lost Empire '01
Lie Down with Lions '94
Forty Days of Musa Dagh '85
Octopussy '83
Demon Rage '82
Archer: The Fugitive from the Empire '81

Guy Bedos (1934-)
Pardon Mon Affaire '76
Pardon Mon Affaire, Too! '77

Alfonso Bedoya (1904-57)
The Stranger Wore a Gun '53
Border Incident '49
Treasure of the Sierra Madre '48

Janet Beecher (1884-1955)
I'd Give My Life '36
The Dark Angel '35
Village Tale '35

David Beecroft (1956-)
Octopus '00
Kidnapped in Paradise '98
The Rain Killer '90
Shadowzone '89

Daniel Beer
The Last Best Sunday '98
Talking about Sex '94
Point Break '91
Creepshow 2 '87

Noah Beery, Sr. (1884-1945)
Overland Mail '42
The Last of the Mohicans '20

Noah Beery, Jr. (1913-94)
Savages '75
Walking Tall: Part 2 '75
Walking Tall '73
Richard Petty Story '72
7 Faces of Dr. Lao '63
Inherit the Wind '60
Fastest Gun Alive '56
Red River '48
Million Dollar Kid '44
'Neath Brooklyn Bridge '42
Overland Mail '42
Sergeant York '41
Tanks a Million '41
Carson City Kid '40
Bad Lands '39
Of Mice and Men '39
Only Angels Have Wings '39
Ace Drummond '36
The Avenging Hand '36
Tailspin Tommy '34
Trail Beyond '34
Fighting with Kit Carson '33
Rustler's Roundup '33
The Three Musketeers '33
Mark of Zoro '20

Wallace Beery (1885-1949)
A Date with Judy '48
Ah, Wilderness! '35
China Seas '35
Viva Villa! '34
Dinner at Eight '33
The Bowery '33
The Champ '32
Grand Hotel '32
The Big House '30
Min & Bill '30
Beggars of Life '28
We're in the Navy Now '27
Behind the Front '26
Old Ironsides '26
The Lost World '25
The Night Club '25
The Pony Express '25
Three Ages '23
White Tiger '23
Robin Hood '22
The Four Horsemen of the Apocalypse '21
The Last of the Mohicans '20
The Mollycoddle '20
Teddy at the Throttle '16

Max Beesley (1971-)
Bloodlines '05
Glitter '01
Hotel '01
Kill Me Later '01
The Last Minute '01
The Match '99
Tom Jones '98

Chris Beetem (1969-)
Black Hawk Down '01
Grace & Glorie '98

Jason Beghe (1960-)
One Missed Call '08
Baby Monitor: Sound of Fear '97
G.I. Jane '97
The Chinatown Murders: Man against the Mob '89
Monkey Shines '88

Bibiana Beglau (1971-)
The Ninth Day '04
The Legend of Rita '99

Ed Begley, Sr. (1901-70)
The Dunwich Horror '70
Firecreek '68
Road to Salina '68
Wild in the Streets '68
Hang 'Em High '67
The Oscar '66
The Unsinkable Molly Brown '64

Ed Begley, Jr. (1949-)
Boomerang '47
For Your Consideration '06
Pittsburgh '06
Relative Strangers '06
Sixteside '04
A Mighty Wind '03
Net Games '03
Auto Focus '02
Get Over It! '01
Best in Show '00
I'm Losing You '98
Joey '98
Murder She Purred: A Mrs. Murphy Mystery '98
Ms. Bear '97
Horton Foote's Alone '97
Not in This Town '97
The Student Affair '97
The Late Shift '96
Santa with Muscles '96
Batman Forever '95
Hourglass '95
Rave Review '95
Children of Fury '94
The Crazysitter '94
Even Cowgirls Get the Blues '94
Greedy '94
Incident at Deception Ridge '94
The Pagemaster '94
Renaissance Man '94
Sensation '94
World War II: When Lions Roared '94
Cooperstown '93
The Story Lady '93
Dark Horse '92
Mastergate '92
Running Mates '92
The Great Los Angeles Earthquake '91
Opportunity Knocks '90
Spies, Lies and Naked Thighs '91
The Applegates '89
Scenes from the Class Struggle in Beverly Hills '89
She-Devil '89
The Accidental Tourist '88
Amazon Women on the Moon '87
The Legend of Sleepy Hollow '86
Elvis: The Movie '79
The In-Laws '79
A Shining Season '79
Blue Collar '78
Goin' South '78
Citizens Band '77
Private Lessons '75
Cockfighter '74

Dani Behr (1970-)
Alvin Rides Again '74
Infamous Crimes '47
It's a Date '40
Rancid Aluminium '00
Like It Is '98

Jason Behr (1973-)
Skinwalkers '07
Shooting Livien '05
Dead of Night '77
The Midnight Hour '86
If You Could See What I Hear '82

Briony Behets (1951-)
Cassandra '87

Leon Belasco (1902-88)
Can-Can '60
Abbott and Costello in the Foreign Legion '50
Fisherman's Wharf '39

Shari Belafonte (1954-)
Mars '95
The Heidi Chronicles '95
French Silk '92
The Player '92
Fire, Ice and Dynamite '91
Murder by Numbers '89
Speed Zone '88
The Midnight Hour '86
If You Could See What I Hear '82

Harry Belafonte (1927-)
Bobby '06
Kansas City '95
White Man's Burden '95
Ready to Wear '94
The Player '92
Grambling's White Tiger '81
Uptown Saturday Night '74
Buck and the Preacher '72
The Angel Levine '70
Odds Against Tomorrow '59
Island in the Sun '57
Carmen Jones '54

Charles Belcher (1872-1943)
King of Kings '27

Sweet Bird of Youth '62
Odds Against Tomorrow '59

Melissa Behr
Twelve Angry Men '57
Patterns '56
Me & Will '99

Doris Belack
Doug's 1st Movie '99 (V)
Krippendorf's Tribe '98
Neil Simon's The Odd Couple 2 '98
What about Bob? '91

Bernard Behrens
Invasion! '99
Mother Night '96
The Man with Two Brains '83

Sam Behrens (1950-)
Galaxy of Terror '81

Richard Bekins (1954-)
United '33 '06
George Washington: The Forging of a Nation '86
Model Behavior '82

Barbara Bel Geddes (1922-)
Summertree '71
The Todd Killings '71
The Five Pennies '59
Vertigo '58
Panic in the Streets '50
Caught '49
Blood on the Moon '48
I Remember Mama '48
The Long Night '47

Leila Bekhti
Paris, je t'aime '06
Sheitan '06

Ana Belen (1951-)
Love Can Seriously Damage Your Health '96
The Perfect Husband '92
Demons in the Garden '82

Christine Belford (1949-)
Christine '84
Agatha Christie's Sparkling Cyanide '83
Kenny Rogers as the Gambler '80
The Groundstar Conspiracy '72

Ann Bell (1940-)
When Saturday Comes '95
Christabel '89
Champions '84
The Lost Boys '78
Fahrenheit 451 '66
The Witches '66
Dr. Terror's House of Horrors '65

Yerye Beirut
The Fear Chamber '68
The Sinister Invasion '68
Battle Shock '56

Brendan Beiser (1970-)
The Fear: Halloween Night '99
Savage Island '03

Catherine Bell (1968-)
Bruce Almighty '03
Thrill Seekers '99
Men with Two Brains

Christopher Bell
Pocket Money '72

Cassandra Bell
Goal! The Dream Begins '06

Dan Bell
The Shot '96
Terror Eyes '87

Darryl M. Bell (1963-)
Mr. White '92
School Daze '88

Drake Bell (1986-)
Superhero Movie '08
Yours, Mine & Ours '05
The Jack Bull '99

Edward Bell
Image of Passion '86
The Premonition '75

E.E. Bell (1955-)
The Neon Bible '95
Sarah, Plain and Tall: Winter's End '99
Sarah, Plain and Tall: Skylark '93
James Brady Story '91
Without Warning: The James Brady Story '91

Geoff Bell (1963-)
Green Street Hooligans '05
Image of Passion '86

Hank Bell (1892-1950)
Valley of the Sun '42
Border Vengeance '35
The Fiddlin' Buckaroo '33
Beyond the Rockies '32
The Big Stampede '32
South of Santa Fe '32
Whistlin' Dan '32

James Bell (1891-1973)
Tribute to a Bad Man '56
A Lawless Street '55
Teenage Crime Wave '55
Flying Leathernecks '51
My Friend Flicka '43
The Leopard Man '43

Jamie Bell (1986-)
Jumper '08
Flags of Our Fathers '06
The Chumscrubber '05
Dear Wendy '05
King Kong '05
Undertow '04
Deathwatch '02
Nicholas Nickleby '02
Billy Elliot '00

Jeannie Bell (1944-)
Fass Black '77
The Muthers '76
TNT Jackson '75

The Thief of Baghdad '24
Shooting Livien '05

The Grudge '04
The Shipping News '01
Rites of Passage '99

Cold and Dark '05
'06

AKA '02
'03

Sarah, Plain and Tall: '93
'94

Galaxy of Terror '81
'83

Dollman vs Demonic Toys '93

Policewomen '73

Kristen Bell (1980-)
Forgetting Sarah Marshall '08
Pulse '06
Roman '06
Deepwater '05
Gracie's Choice '04
Spartan '04
Pootie Tang '01
Polish Wedding '97

Lake Bell
Over Her Dead Body '08
What Happens in Vegas '08
Rampage: The Hillside Strangler Murders '04

Marie Bell (1900-85)
Phedre 68
Hotel Paradiso 66
Sandra of a Thousand Delights '65

Marshall Bell (1944-)
The Final Season '07
Nancy Drew '07
Rescue Dawn '06
Identity '03
Northfork '03
Mercy '00
Sand '00
Black & White '99
A Slipping Down Life '99
Virus '98
The End of Violence '97
Starship Troopers '97
Too Fast, Too Young '96
When You're Dead '95
Payback '88
Twins '88
Wildfire '88
No Way Out '87
A Nightmare on Elm Street 2: Freddy's Revenge '85

Michael Bell (1938-)
Rugrats Go Wild! '03 (V)
Rugrats in Paris: The Movie '00 (V)
The Rugrats Movie '98 (V)

Nicholas Bell
Attack of the Sabretooth '05
Dead Letter Office '98
Sorrento Beach '95

Rex Bell (1905-62)
Stormy '36
West of Nevada '36
The Tonto Kid 35
Diamond Trail '33
Fighting Texans '33
Rainbow Ranch '33
Broadway to Cheyenne '32
Law of the Sea '32
Battling with Buffalo Bill '31

Rini Bell (1981-)
The Terminal '04
Bring It On '00

Tobin Bell (1942-)
Boogeyman 2 '07
Saw 4 '07
Saw III '06
Saw II '05
Saw '04
Power Play '02
The 4th Floor '99
Best of the Best: Without Warning '98
Brown's Requiem '98
Overnight Delivery '96
Serial Killer '95
New Eden '94
The Firm '93
Sex, Love and Cold Hard Cash '93
Ruby '92
False Identity '90

Tom Bell (1932-)
The Last Minute '01

Dive Bomber '41
Footsteps in the Dark '41
The Wolf Man '41
Brother Orchid '40
Dance, Girl, Dance '40
His Girl Friday '40
Boy Meets Girl '38
Carefree '38
The Awful Truth '37
Healer '36
Hands Across the Table '35
Spitfire '34
Woman in the Shadows '34
Ace of Aces '33
Picture Snatcher '33

Clara Bellar
Kill the Poor '06
Dominion: Prequel to the Exorcist '05
A.I.: Artificial Intelligence '01
The First 9 1/2 Weeks '98
David '97
Romance and Rejection '96
Rendezvous in Paris '95

Harry Bellaver (1905-93)
The Old Man and the Sea 58
From Here to Eternity '53
The Lemon Drop Kid '51
No Way Out '50
House on 92nd Street '45

Annie Belle (1956-)
House on the Edge of the Park '84
Naked Paradise '78
Forever Emmanuelle 75
Lips of Blood 75

Camilla Belle (1986-)
10,000 B.C. '08
When a Stranger Calls '06
The Ballad of Jack and Rose '05
The Chumscrubber '05
The Quiet '05
Back to the Secret Garden '01
Secre of the Andes '98
Annie: A Royal Adventure '95

Kathleen Beller (1955-)
Time Trackers '88
Cloud Waltzing '87
Surfacing '84
Sword & the Sorcerer '82
Touched '82
The Betsy '78
Mary White '77

Agostina Belli (1949-)
The Chosen '77
The Scent of a Woman '75
The Sex Machine '75
Seduction of Mimi '72

Melvin Belli (1907-96)
Ground Zero 88
Gimme Shelter 70

Cynthia Belliveau
The Dark '94
The Spider and the Fly 94
The Dream Team '88

Gina Gellman (1966-)
Jekyll '07
Seven Days to Live '01
David '97
Silent Trigger '97
Leon the Pig Farmer '93

Maria Bello (1967-)
The Mummy: Tomb of the Dragon Emperor 08
The Jane Austen Book Club '07
Shattered '07
Flicka '06
Thank You for Smoking '06

World Trade Center '06
Assault on Precinct 13 '05
A History of Violence '05
The Sisters '05
Secret Window '04
Silver City '04
The Cooler '03
Auto Focus '02
100 Mile Rule '02
Coyote Ugly '00
Duets '00
Payback '98
Permanent Midnight '98

Sara Bellomo (1974-)
Beach Babes 2: Cave Girl Island '95
Bikini Drive-In '94
Beach Babes from Beyond '93

Gil Bellows (1967-)
The Weather Man '05
Blind Horizon '04
Whitewash: The Clarence Brandley Story '02
She Creature '01
Beautiful Joe '00
Chasing Sleep '00
The Courage to Love '00
Judas Kiss '98
The Assistant '97
Snow White: A Tale of Terror 97
The Substance of Fire '96
Black Day Blue Night '95
Miami Rhapsody '95
Silver Strand '95
Love and a .45 '94
The Shawshank Redemption '94

Monica Bellucci (1968-)
Shoot 'Em Up '07
Irreversible '02
The Matrix Reloaded '03
The Matrix Revolutions '03
Tears of the Sun '03
Brotherhood of the Wolf '01
Malena '00
Under Suspicion '00
How Much Do You Love Me? '05
Like a Fish Out of Water '99
Bram Stoker's Dracula '92

Pamela Bellwood (1951-)
Going Shopping '05
Double Standard '88
Cellar Dweller '87
Agatha Christie's Sparkling Cyanide '83
Cocaine: One Man's Seduction 83
Hangar 18 '80
Deadman's Curve '78

Jean-Paul Belmondo (1933-)
Les Miserables '95
Swashbuckler '84
Le Professional '81
Stuntwoman '81
Le Magnifique 76
Stavisky 74
High Heels 72
La Scoumoune 72
Borsalino 70
The Brain '69
Mississippi Mermaid 69
Casino Royale '67
Is Paris Burning? '66
Pierrot le Fou '65
That Man from Rio 64
Cartouche '62
Un Singe en Hiver 62
Le Doulos '61
Leon Morin, Priest '61
Two Women 61
Love and the Frenchwoman 60
A Woman Is a Woman 60
Breathless 59
Sois Belle et Tais-Toi '58

Lionel Belmore (1867-1953)
My Son, My Son '40
Son of Frankenstein '39
Police Court '32
Frankenstein '31
Monte Carlo '30
The Love Parade '29
Oliver Twist 22

Robert Beltran (1953-)
Fire Serpent '07
Manticore '05
Luminarias '99
Managua '97
Bugsy '91
The Chase '91
Kiss Me a Killer '91
To Die Standing '91
El Diablo '90
Scenes from the Class Struggle in Beverly Hills '89
Gaby: A True Story '87
Latino '85
Night of the Comet '84
Eating Raoul '82

Mark Beltzman (1960-)
Billy Madison '94
Mo' Money '92

James Belushi (1954-)
Snow Buddies '08 (V)
Underdog '07
The Wild '06 (V)
Hoodwinked '05 (V)
One Way Out '02
Joe Somebody '01
K-9: P.I. '01
Return to Me '00
Angel's Dance '99
Backlash 99
K-911 99
Made Men '99
The Florentine '98
Living in Peril '97
Retroactive '97
Gang Related '96
Jingle All the Way '96
Race the Sun 96
Destiny Turns on the Radio '95
Canadian Bacon '94
Parallel Lives '94
The Pebble and the Penguin '94 (V)
Separate Lives '94
Last Action Hero '93
Royce '93
Wild Palms 93
Once Upon a Crime '92
Traces of Red '92
Curly Sue '91
Diary of a Hitman '91
Only the Lonely '91
The Palermo Connection '91
Abraxas: Guardian of the Universe '90
The Masters of Menace '90
Mr. Destiny '90
Taking Care of Business '90
Homer and Eddie '89
K-9 '89
Wedding Band '89
Who's Harry Crumb? '89
Red Heat '88
The Principal '87
Real Men '87
Jumpin' Jack Flash '86
Little Shop of Horrors '86
Salvador '86
Birthday Boy '85
The Man with One Red Shoe 85
Pinocchio '83
Trading Places '83
Thief '81
The Fury '78

John Belushi (1949-82)
Continental Divide '81
Neighbors '81
The Blues Brothers '80
1941 '79
Old Boyfriends '79
All You Need Is Cash '78
Goin' South '78
National Lampoon's Animal House '78
Shame of the Jungle '75

Richard Belzer (1944-)
Homicide: The Movie '00
Get On the Bus '96
Girl 6 '96
Not of This Earth '96
A Very Brady Sequel '96
The Invaders '95
The Puppet Masters '94
Mad Dog and Glory '93
Off and Running '90
The Big Picture 89
Fletch Lives '89
Freeway '88
The Wrong Guys 88
America '86
Flicks '85
Scarface 83
Night Shift '82
Fame 80

Paul Ben-Victor (1965-)
Daredevil '03
Drowning Mona '00
Gun Shy '00
Kiss Toledo Goodbye '00
The Corruptor '99
Crazy in Alabama '99
I Come in Peace '90
Maximum Risk 96
Mortal Sins '90
Metro '96
Houseguest '94
True Romance 93
Body Parts '91

Brian Benben (1956-)
Surf's Up '07 (V)
It's in the Bag '45
Weekend at the Waldorf '45
The Sky's the Limit 43
I Married a Witch '42
The Major and the Minor '42
Young and Willing '42
Nice Girl? '41
You'll Never Get Rich '41
Foreign Correspondent '40
China Seas '35
Dancing Lady '33
Radioland Murders '94

Russ Bender (1910-69)
Navy vs. the Night Monsters '66
Space Monster 64
Anatomy of a Psycho '61
I Bury the Living '58
The War of the Colossal Beast '58
The Amazing Colossal Man '57
Invasion of the Saucer Men '57
It Conquered the World '56
The Stork Club '45

Michael C. Bendetti (1967-)
Red Shoe Diaries:
Luscious Lola '00
Amanda and the Alien '95
Netherworld '90

William Bendix (1906-64)
For Love or Money 63
Johnny Nobody '61
Deep Six 58
Crashout 55
Dangerous Mission '54
Blackbeard the Pirate '52
A Girl in Every Port '52
Macao 52

Detective Story '51
Kill the Umpire '50
Big Steal '49
A Connecticut Yankee in King Arthur's Court '49
Johnny Holiday '49
Babe Ruth Story '48
The Time of Your Life '48
I'll Be Yours '47
Where There's Life '47
The Blue Dahlia '46
Dark Corner '46
Two Years before the Mast '46
It's in the Bag '45
Abroad with Two Yanks '44
Greenwich Village '44
The Hairy Ape '44
China '43
Guadalcanal Diary '43
The Glass Key '42
Star Spangled Rhythm '42
Wake Island '42
Who Done It? '42
Woman of the Year '42
A Place in the World '92
Condemned to Hell '84

Leonor Benedetto (1941-)

Brooks Benedict (1896-1968)
Gun Smoke '31
The Dropkick '27
Ranson's Folly '26
The Freshman '25

Dirk Benedict (1945-)
Earthstorm '06
Alaska '96
November Conspiracy '96
Official Denial '93
Shadow Force '92
Blue Tornado '90
Body Slam '87
Ruckus '81
Follow That Car! '80
Underground Aces '80
Scavenger Hunt '79
Battlestar Galactica '78
Cruise into Terror '78
Mission Galactica: The Cylon Attack '78
W '74
Sssssss '73
Georgia, Georgia '72

Jay Benedict (1951-)
Mosquitoman '05
Double Team '97
'93

Paul Benedict (1938-)
Waiting for Guffman '96
The Freshman '90
Babycakes '89
Cocktail '88
The Chair '87
Desperate Moves '86
This Is Spinal Tap '84
The Man with Two Brains '83
Mandingo '75
Jeremiah Johnson '72

Richard Benedict (1916-84)
Beginning of the End '57
Breakdown '53
Ghost Chasers '55
Master Minds '49
Spook Busters '48
Bowery Buckaroos '47
Hard-Boiled Mahoney '47
O.S.S. '46
A Walk in the Sun '46
Mr. Muggs Rides Again '45
The Story of G.I. Joe '45
Follow the Leader '44
On the Sunny Side '42
Wildcat '42
Legion of the Lawless '40

Yves Beneyton (1946-)
Rogue Trader '98
Letters to an Unknown Lover '84

John Benfield (1938-)
Cassandra's Dream '07
Endgame '01
In the Name of the Father '93

Maurice Benichou (1943-)
Hidden '05
Amelie '01

Jean Benguigui (1944-)
Control '87
Buffet Froid '79

Norma Bengell (1935-)
Hellbenders '67
Planet of the Vampires '65

Leonor Benedetto

Murilo Benicio (1972-)
The Adventures of Felix '99

Roberto Benigni (1952-)
Coffee and Cigarettes '03
Fellini: I'm a Born Liar '03
Pinocchio '02
Life is Beautiful '98
The Monster '96
Son of the Pink Panther '93
Johnny Stecchino '92
Night on Earth '91
Down by Law '86

Benigno
'95

Wilson Benge (1875-1955)
Hidden Agenda '90
By the Blood of Others '73
The Lacemaker '77
Weekend '67
'06

Richard Benjamin (1938-)
The Deadly Trackers '73
Across 110th Street '72
The Anderson Tapes '71
Diary of a Mad Housewife '70
Catch-22 '70
Goodbye Columbus '69

Benji
Benji the Hunted '87
For the Love of Benji '77
Benji '74

Heinz Bennent (1921-)
Possession '81
From the Life of the Marionettes '80
The Last Metro '80
The Tin Drum '79

David Bennent (1966-)
Legend '86
The Tin Drum '79
Nea '78

John Bennes
Stephen King's The Night Flier '96
Black Rainbow '91

Alan Bennett (1934-)
A Dance to the Music of Time '97

Bruce Bennett (1906-2007)
Fortunes of War '87
The Cosmic Man '59
Three Violent People '57
Daniel Boone: Trail Blazer '56
Hidden Guns '56
Dragonfly Squadron '54
Sudden Fear '52
Angels in the Outfield '51
Cavalry Charge '51
Mystery Street '50
Task Force '49
Silver River '48
Treasure of the Sierra Madre '48
Dark Passage '47
The Man I Love '46
A Stolen Life '46
Mildred Pierce '45
I'm from Arkansas '44
U-Boat Prisoner '44
Fighting Devil Dogs '43
The More the Merrier '43
Sahara '43
Underground Agent '42
Before I Hang '40
Daredevils of the Red Circle '38
Hawk of the Wilderness '38
Tarzan and the Green Goddess '38
A Million to One '37
Shadow of Chinatown '36
The New Adventures of Tarzan '35

Jill Bennett (1931-90)
The Sheltering Sky '90
Hawks '89
Murders at Lynch Cross '85
For Your Eyes Only '81
The Old Curiosity Shop '75
I Want What I Want '72
The Charge of the Light Brigade '68
The Nanny '65
The Skull '65
Lust for Life '56

Jimmy Bennett (1996-)
Snow Buddies '08 (V)
Evan Almighty '07
Firewall '06
Poseidon '06
The Amityville Horror '05
Hostage '05
The Heart is Deceitful Above All Things '04

Joan Bennett (1910-90)
Suspiria '77
House of Dark Shadows '70
We're No Angels '55

David Bennent
Looney Tunes: Back in Action '03 (V)
Return to Never Land '02 (V)

Jeff Glenn Bennett (1962-)
The Land Before Time 7: The Stone of Cold Fire '00 (V)
Kiki's Delivery Service '98
The Land Before Time 6: The Secret of Saurus Rock '98 (V)
The Land Before Time 5: The Mysterious Island '97 (V)
The Land Before Time 4: Journey Through the Mists '96 (V)
The Land Before Time 3: The Time of the Great Giving '95 (V)
Gargoyles, The Movie: The Heroes Awaken '94 (V)
The Land Before Time 2: The Great Valley Adventure '94 (V)

Nigel Bennett (1949-)
Jesse Stone: Sea Change '07
The State Within '06
Cypher '02
Widows '02
The Pilot's Wife '01
Anne of Green Gables: The Continuing Story '99
Naked City: A Killer Christmas '98
Rescuers: Stories of Courage—Two Couples '98
Gotti '96
Darkman 3: Die Darkman Die '95
Degree of Guilt '95
Kurt Vonnegut's Harrison Bergeron '95
Macroni: Innocence Lost '95
Where's the Money, Noreen? '95
Back in Action '94
Soft Deceit '94

Ray Bennett (1895-1957)
Thundering Trail '51
Border Badmen '45
Death Rides the Plains '44
'06

Sonja Bennett
Fido '06

Tony Bennett (1926-)
Where the Truth Lies '05
The Scout '94
The Oscar '66

Zachary Bennett (1980-)
Stir of Echoes 2: The Homecoming '07

Hywel Bennett (1944-)
Vatel '00
Mary, Mother of Jesus '99
A Mind to Kill '95
Deadline '87
Murder Elite '86
Tinker, Tailor, Soldier, Spy '80
Endless Night '71
Loot... Give Me Money, Honey! '70

Elizabeth Bennett
Scout's Midnight '06

Darlene Bennett
Bad Girls Go to Hell '65

Eliza Bennett (1992-)
The Contractor '07
Nanny McPhee '06
The Prince & Me '04

Constance Bennett (1904-65)
Madame X '66
As Young As You Feel '51
Two-Faced Woman '41
Topper Takes a Trip '39
Service De Luxe '38
Topper '37
What Price Hollywood? '32
Sin Takes a Holiday '30
Married? '26

Lela Bennett (1890-1965)
No Other Woman '33
Doctor X '32

Marjorie Bennett (1896-1982)
Stacey '73
The Love God? '70
Games '67
36 Hours '64
Promises! Promises! '63
Kiss Me Deadly '55
Abbott and Costello Meet Dr. Jekyll and Mr. Hyde '52

Jonathan Bennett (1981-)
Bachelor Party Vegas '05
Cheaper by the Dozen 2 '05
Mean Girls '04

John Bennett (1928-2005)
Chaos & Cadavers '03
Priest '94
Antonia and Jane '91
Eye of the Needle '81
The House that Dripped Blood '71
Victim '61
It Takes a Thief '59

Amber Bennett
The White Rose '83
From the Life of the Marionettes '80
'06

Deborah Benson
Danger of Love '95
Mutant on the Bounty '89
Just Before Dawn '80

George Benson (1911-83)
The Creeping Flesh '72
Convoy '40

Jodi Benson (1961-)
Toy Story 2 '99 (V)
Thumbelina '94 (V)
The Little Mermaid '89 (V)

Robby Benson (1956-)
MXP: Most Xtreme Primate '03
Dragonheart: A New Beginning '00 (V)
At Home with the Webbers '94

Martin Benson (1918-)
The Omen '76
Tiffany Jones '75
A Matter of WHO '62
Exodus '60
The Cosmic Monsters '58
Istanbul '57
The King and I '56

Lucille Benson (1914-84)
Huckleberry Finn '74
Reflections of Murder '74
Nashville '74
Cactus in the Snow '72
Private Parts '72
Duel '71

Lucille Benson

Abraham Benrubi (1969-)
Charlotte's Web '06 (V)
Wristcutters: A Love Story '06

Martin Benrath (1926-2000)
Twister '96
Wagic Island '95
The Shadow '94
The Program '93
U-Turn '97
George of the Jungle '97
Under Oath '97
Miss Congeniality 2: Armed and Fabulous '05
Without a Paddle '04
Open Range '03
Medicine Man '92
Transatlantic Merry-Go-Round '35

Jack Benny (1894-1974)
A Guide for the Married Man '67
It's a Mad, Mad, Mad, Mad World '63
The Great Lover '49
George Washington Slept Here '42
Charley's Aunt '41
Man About Town '39
Broadway Melody of 1936 '35

Amy Benson
Father's Little Dividend '51
Father of the Bride '50
Reckless Moment '49
The Scar '48
Secret Beyond the Door '48
Colonel Effingham's Raid '45
The Texans '38
Vogues of 1938 '37
Big Brown Eyes '36
Wedding Present '36
Mississippi '35
Little Women '33
Disraeli '30
Bulldog Drummond '29
Power '28

John Benson (1928-2005)

Cube: Zero '04
Verdict in Blood '02
Bonanno: A Godfather's Story '99
By Way of the Stars '92
Looking for Miracles '90
The Great Lover '49
'45
Scarlet Street '45
Woman in the Window '44
Twin Beds '42
House Across the Bay '40
The Son of Monte Cristo '40
The Man in the Iron Mask '39
'45
It's in the Bag '45
Hollywood Canteen '44
George Washington Slept Here '42

Deadly Exposure '93

Homewrecker '92
Invasion of Privacy '92
Beauty and the Beast '91 (V)
Modern Love '90
Rent-A-Cop '88
White Hot '85
City Limits '85
Harry & Son '84
Running Brave '83
Two of a Kind '82
The Chosen '81
Tribute '80
Ice Castles '79
The End '78
One on One '77
Our Town '77
The Death of Richie '76
The Last of Mrs. Lincoln '76
Ode to Billy Joe '76
The Virginia Hill Story '76
Death Be Not Proud '75
All the Kind Strangers '74
Jory '72

Wendy Benson (1971-)
Luck of the Draw '00
Wishmaster '97

Lyriq Bent
Saw 4 '07
Saw III '06

Timothy Bentinck (1953-)
Sharpe's Rifles '93
Year of the Comet '92

Michael Bentine (1922-96)
Rentadick '72
Down Among the Z Men '52

Fabrizio Bentivoglio (1957-)
Eternity and a Day '97
The Real Thing '97
Elective Affinities '96
Apartment Zero '88
Vatican Conspiracy '81

Dana Bentley
Sorority House Massacre 2: Nighty Nightmare '92
Karate Cop '91
Bad Girls from Mars '90

John Bentley (1916-)
Submarine Seahawk '59
Istanbul '57
White Huntress '57
Flight from Vienna '56
The Way Out '56
Profile '54
River Beat '54
Scarlet Spear '54
The Happiest Days of Your Life '50
Calling Paul Temple '48

Lamont Bentley (1973-)
The Wash '01
Tales from the Hood '95

Wes Bentley (1978-)
Ghost Rider '07
P2 '07
The Perfect Witness '07
Weirdsville '07
The Game of Their Lives '05
The Four Feathers '02
Soul Survivors '01
The Claim '00
American Beauty '99
White River '99

Barbi Benton (1950-)
Deathstalker '83
Hospital Massacre '81

Dean Benton
Cocaine Fiends '36
Thunder Mountain '35

Eddie Benton
Prom Night '80
Dr. Strange '78

Jerome Benton
Graffiti Bridge '90
Under the Cherry Moon '86

Mark Benton (1965-)
Topsy Turvy '99
Career Girls '97

Susanne Benton (1948-)
A Boy and His Dog '75
Catch-22 '70
That Cold Day in the Park '69

Michael Bentt (1965-)
State Property 2 '05
Ali '01

Femi Benussi (1948-)
Hit Men '73
M'Lady's Court '73
The Slasher '72
Hatchet for the Honeymoon '70
Rattler Kid '68

Luke Benward (1995-)
How to Eat Fried Worms '06
Because of Winn-Dixie '05

Julie Benz (1972-)
Rambo '08
Kill Your Darlings '06
Taken '02
The Brothers '01
Shriek If You Know What I Did Last Friday the 13th '00
Darkdrive '98
Jawbreaker '98

A.J. Benza (1962-)
Rocky Balboa '06
P.S. Your Cat is Dead! '02

Daniel Benzali (1950-)
Believers '07
Dead Heat '01
The Grey Zone '01
Screwed '00
Boss of Bosses '99
All the Little Animals '98
The End of Violence '97
Murder at 1600 '97
A Day in October '92

George Beranger (1893-1973)
Flirting with Fate '16
The Birth of a Nation '15

Iris Berben (1950-)
Killer Condom '95

Ady Berber (1913-66)
Door with the Seven Locks '62
Dead Eyes of London '61

Marcel Berbert
The Green Room '78
Mississippi Mermaid '69

Luca Bercovici (1957-)
Burning Down the House '01
Dirt Boy '01
Hard Luck '01
The Big Squeeze '96
Drop Zone '94
Scanner Cop '94
Inside Monkey Zetterland '93
Mirror Images 2 '93
K2: The Ultimate High '92
Mission of Justice '92
Mortal Passions '90
Pacific Heights '90
Clean and Sober '88
American Flyers '85
Parasite '82
Frightmare '81

Blaze Berdahl (1980-)
We're Back! A Dinosaur's Story '93 (V)
Pet Sematary '89

Tom Berenger (1950-)
The Christmas Miracle of Jonathan Toomey '07
Sniper 3 '04
Johnson County War '02
The Junction Boys '02
Sniper 2 '02
Cruel and Unusual '01
Eye See You '01
The Hollywood Sign '01
Training Day '01
True Blue '01
Cutaway '00
Diplomatic Siege '99
In the Company of Spies '99
A Murder of Crows '99
Turbulence 2: Fear of Flying '99
One Man's Hero '99
Shadow of Doubt '98
The Gingerbread Man '97
Rough Riders '97
An Occasional Hell '96
The Substitute '96
The Avenging Angel '95
Body Language '95
The Last of the Dogmen '95
Chasers '94
Major League 2 '94
Gettysburg '93
Silver '93
Sniper '92
At Play in the Fields of the Lord '91
Shattered '91
The Field '90
Born on the Fourth of July '89
Love at Large '89
Major League '89
Betrayed '88
Last Rites '88
Shoot to Kill '88
Someone to Watch Over Me '87
Platoon '86
Fear City '85
Rustler's Rhapsody '85
The Big Chill '83
Eddie and the Cruisers '83
Beyond Obsession '82
The Dogs of War '81
Butch and Sundance: The Early Days '79
In Praise of Older Women '78
Johnny We Hardly Knew Ye '77
Looking for Mr. Goodbar '77
Rush It '77
The Sentinel '76

Marisa Berenson (1948-)
Women '97
Night of the Cyclone '90
White Hunter, Black Heart '90
Trade Secrets '86
The Secret Diary of Sigmund Freud '84
S.O.B. '81
Killer Fish '79
Sex on the Run '78
Barry Lyndon '75
Cabaret '72
Death in Venice '71

Harry Beresford (1864-1944)
Klondike Annie '36
Murders in the Zoo '33
The Sign of the Cross '33

Justin Berfield (1986-)
Max Keeble's Big Move '01
The Kid with the X-Ray Eyes '99
Mom, Can I Keep Her? '98
Invisible Mom '96

Peter Berg (1964-)
Lions for Lambs '07
Smokin' Aces '07
Collateral '04
Corky Romano '01
Cop Land '97
Sisters '97
Girl 6 '96
The Great White Hype '96
Across the Moon '94
The Last Ride '94
The Last Seduction '94
Aspen Extreme '93
A Case for Murder '93
Fire in the Sky '93
A Midnight Clear '92
Crooked Hearts '91
Late for Dinner '91
Genuine Risk '89
Going Overboard '89
Race for Glory '89
Shocker '89
Tale of Two Sisters '89
Never on Tuesday '88

Judith-Marie Bergan
Never Pick Up a Stranger '79
Abduction '75

Francine Berge (1940-)
The Nun '66
Circle of Love '64
Judex '64

Candice Bergen (1946-)
The In-Laws '03
View from the Top '03
Sweet Home Alabama '02
Miss Congeniality '00
Mayflower Madam '87
Merlin and the Sword '85
My Sweet Victim '85
Stick '85
2010: The Year We Make Contact '84 (V)
Gandhi '82
Rich and Famous '81
Starting Over '79
A Night Full of Rain '78
Oliver's Story '78
The Domino Principle '77
Bite the Bullet '75
The Wind and the Lion '75
11 Harrowhouse '74
Carnal Knowledge '71
The Adventurers '70
Getting Straight '70
Soldier Blue '70
The Group '66
The Sand Pebbles '66

Edgar Bergen (1903-78)
The Muppet Movie '79
Homecoming: A Christmas Story '71
I Remember Mama '48
Fun & Fancy Free '47 (N)
Stage Door Canteen '43
Here We Go Again! '42
Look Who's Laughing '41
Charlie McCarthy, Detective '39
You Can't Cheat an Honest Man '39
The Goldwyn Follies '38
Letter of Introduction '38

Frances Bergen (1922-2006)
Eating '90
The Morning After '86

Polly Bergen (1930-)
A Very Serious Person '06
Paradise, Texas '05
Dr. Jekyll and Ms. Hyde '95
Once Upon a Time... When We Were Colored '95
The Lightning Incident '91
Cry-Baby '90
Haunting of Sarah Hardy '89
My Brother's Wife '89
War & Remembrance: The Final Chapter '89
War & Remembrance '88
Making Mr. Right '86
The Winds of War '83
Born Beautiful '82
How to Pick Up Girls '78
Murder on Flight 502 '75
Anatomy of Terror '74
Death Cruise '74
A Guide for the Married Man '67
Kisses for My President '64
Move Over, Darling '63
Cape Fear '61
Escape from Fort Bravo '53
The Stooge '51
At War with the Army '50

Tushka Bergen (1969-)
Invisible Child '99
Journey to the Center of the Earth '99
Lovelife '97
Voices from a Locked Room '95
Barcelona '94
Swing Kids '93
Wrangler '88

Deborah Berger
Rosebud '75
La Merveilleuse Visite '74

Harris Berger (1921-83)
East Side Kids '40
Junior G-Men '40

Helmut Berger (1944-)
The Godfather, Part 3 '90
Faceless '88
Code Name: Emerald '85
Mad Dog '84
Deadly Game '83
Fatal Fix '80
Battleforce '78
Victory at Entebbe '76
Conversation Piece '75
Romantic Englishwoman '75
Ash Wednesday '73
Order to Kill '73
Ludwig '72
The Garden of the Finzi-Continis '71
Dorian Gray '70
The Damned '69

Katya Berger (1964-)
Tales of Ordinary Madness '83
Nana '82

Michael Berger (1935-)
Sarah's Child '96
Allonsanfan '73

Nicole Berger (1935-67)
The Story of a Three Day Pass '68
Shoot the Piano Player '62

Sarah Berger (1960-)
Element of Doubt '96
The Green Man '91

Senta Berger (1947-)
Blitz '85
Swiss Conspiracy '77
The Boss is Served '76
Cross of Iron '76
Smugglers '75
When Women Lost Their Tails '75
The Scarlet Letter '73
Cobra '71
When Women Had Tails '70
The Ambushers '67
Diabolically Yours '67
Cast a Giant Shadow '66
The Quiller Memorandum '66
Full Hearts & Empty Pockets '63
The Victors '63
Waltz King '63
Secret of the Black Trunk '62
Sherlock Holmes and the Deadly Necklace '62
Testament of Dr. Mabuse '62

Sidney Berger (1936-)
Carnival of Souls '98
Carnival of Souls '62

William Berger (1928-93)
I'm Dangerous Tonight '90
Dial Help '88
Django Strikes Again '87
Hell Hunters '87
Hercules 2 '85
Day of the Cobra '84
Devilfish '84
Hercules '83
Oil '78
Slaughterday '77
Superfly T.N.T. '73
Today We Kill, Tomorrow We Die '71
Five Dolls for an August Moon '70
What a Way to Die '70
Sabata '69

Thommy Berggren (1937-)
Sunday's Children '94
The Adventurers '70
Elvira Madigan '67

Herbert Berghof (1909-90)
Harry and Tonto '74
Master Mind '73
Five Fingers '52
Red Planet Mars '52

Patrick Bergin (1954-)
False Prophets '06
The Far Side of Jericho '06
Played '06
Secret of the Cave '06
Frederick Forsyth's Icon '05
Johnny Was '05
Ella Enchanted '04
The Boys and Girl From County Clare '03
Brush with Fate '03
King of Texas '02
Amazons and Gladiators '01
Beneath Loch Ness '01
The Devil's Prey '01
Cause of Death '00
Deadline '00
Invisible Circus '00
St. Patrick: The Irish Legend '00
Durango '99
Escape Velocity '99
Eye of the Beholder '99
Treasure Island '99
When the Sky Falls '99
One Man's Hero '99
Sir Arthur Conan Doyle's The Lost World '98
The Apocalypse Watch '97
The Island on Bird Street '97
The Ripper '97
The Proposition '96
Suspicious Minds '96
Lawnmower Man 2: Beyond Cyberspace '95
Triplecross '95
Double Cross '94
Soft Deceit '94
Frankenstein '93
Map of the Human Heart '93
They Watch '93
Highway to Hell '92
Love Crimes '92
Patriot Games '92
The Real Charlotte '91
Robin Hood '91
Sleeping with the Enemy '91
Mountains of the Moon '90
The Courier '88
Taffin '88

Emily Bergl (1975-)
Taken '02
Happy Campers '01
Chasing Sleep '00
The Rage: Carrie 2 '99

Erik "Bullen" Berglund (1887-1946)
Only One Night '42
Walpurgis Night '41
Intermezzo '36

Henry Bergman (1868-1946)
Modern Times '36
City Lights '31
Pawnshop '16

Ingrid Bergman (1915-82)
A Woman Called Golda '82
Autumn Sonata '78
A Matter of Time '76
Murder on the Orient Express '74
The Hideaways '73
Walk in the Spring Rain '70
Cactus Flower '69
Goodbye Again '61
24 Hours in a Woman's Life '61
Indiscreet '58
The Inn of the Sixth Happiness '58
Anastasia '56
Elena and Her Men '56
Voyage in Italy '53
Europa 51 '52
Stromboli '50
Under Capricorn '49
Arch of Triumph '48
Joan of Arc '48
Notorious '46
The Bells of St. Mary's '45
Saratoga Trunk '45
Spellbound '45
Gaslight '44
For Whom the Bell Tolls '43
Casablanca '42
Adam Had Four Sons '41
Dr. Jekyll and Mr. Hyde '41
Walpurgis Night '41
June Night '40
Intermezzo '39
Dollar '38
A Woman's Face '38
Intermezzo '36
Swedenhielms '35
The Count of the Old Town '34

Jaime Bergman (1975-)
Darkwolf '03
Daybreak '01

Peter Bergman (1953-)
Phantom of the Ritz '88
J-Men Forever '79

Sandahl Bergman (1951-)
The P.A.C.K. '96
Ice Cream Man '95
Inner Sanctum 2 '94
Possessed by the Night '93
Raw Nerve '91
Hell Comes to Frogtown '88
Programmed to Kill '86
Stewardess School '86
Red Sonja '85
Getting Physical '84
She '83
Airplane 2: The Sequel '82
Conan the Barbarian '82
Xanadu '80

Elisabeth Bergner (1900-86)
The Pedestrian '73
Cry of the Banshee '70
As You Like It '36
Catherine the Great '34

Helena Bergstrom (1964-)
Under the Sun '98
Still Crazy '98
The Last Dance '93
House of Angels '92
The Women on the Roof '89
Noisy Village '87
The Children of Noisy Village '86

Linda Bergstrom
More about the Children of Noisy Village '87

Luis Beristain (1918-62)
The Exterminating Angel '62
El '52

Christian Berkel (1957-)
Black Book '06
Downfall '04
Guys and Balls '04
The Experiment '01

Xander Berkeley (1958-)
Fracture '07
Magna: Volcanic Disaster '06
Deepwater '05
Standing Still '05
In Enemy Hands '04
Quicksand '03
Shanghai Noon '00
Universal Soldier: The Return '99
Phoenix '98
Air Force One '97
One Night Stand '97
Barb Wire '96
Bulletproof '96
If These Walls Could Talk '96
The Killing Jar '96
Persons Unknown '96
The Rock '96
Within the Rock '96
Apollo 13 '95
Heat '95
Safe '95
Roswell: The U.F.O. Cover-Up '94
Attack of the 50 Ft. Woman '93
Dead to Rights '93
Candyman '92
A Few Good Men '92
The Gun in Betty Lou's Handbag '92
Internal Affairs '90
Short Time '90
Assassin '89
Tapeheads '89
Deadly Dreams '88
The Lawless Land '88
Sid & Nancy '86

Elizabeth Berkley (1972-)
Roger Dodger '02
The Curse of the Jade Scorpion '01
Any Given Sunday '99
Tail Lights Fade '99
Random Encounter '98
The Taxman '98
The First Wives Club '96
Showgirls '95
White Wolves 2: Legend of the Wild '94

Steven Berkoff (1937-)
Charlie '04
Head in the Clouds '04
Children of Dune '03
Attila '01
Rancid Aluminium '00
Legionnaire '98
Another 9 1/2 Weeks '96
Flynn '96
The Krays '90
Prisoner of Rio '89
Intruders '92
The Flying Scotsman '06
Fair Game '95

Busby Berkeley (1895-1976)
Million Dollar Mermaid '52
Babes on Broadway '41
Dames '34
Fashions of 1934 '34
42nd Street '33
Roman Scandals '33

Terri Berland
The Strangeness '85

Milton Berle (1908-2002)
Storybook '95
Driving Me Crazy '91
Side by Side '88
Broadway Danny Rose '84
Cracking Up '83
Off Your Rocker '80
The Muppet Movie '79
Legend of Valentino '75
Lepke '75
Evil Roy Slade '71 (V)
Where Angels Go, Trouble Follows '68
Who's Minding the Mint? '67
The Oscar '66
The Loved One '65
It's a Mad, Mad, Mad, Mad World '63
The Bellboy '60
Let's Make Love '60
Sun Valley Serenade '41
Mark of Zorro '20

Francois Berleand (1952-)
Comedy of Power '06
Transporter 2 '05
The Chorus '04
The Grand Role '04
The Transporter '02
Romance '99
Place Vendome '98
Seventh Heaven '98
Capitaine Conan '96
May Fools '90
Au Revoir les Enfants '87

Jeannie Berlin (1932-)
In the Spirit '90
The Heartbreak Kid '72
Housewife '72
Portnoy's Complaint '72
The Baby Maker '70
Getting Straight '70
The Strawberry Statement '70

Charles Berling (1958-)
The Man of My Life '06
How I Killed My Father '03
Demonlover '02
The Bridge '00
Comedy of Innocence '00
Les Destinees '00
Stardom '00
L'Ennui '98
Those Who Love Me Can Take the Train '98
Dry Cleaning '97
Obsession '97
Love, etc. '96
Ridicule '96
Nelly et Monsieur Arnaud '95

Peter Berling (1934-)
Francesco '93
Cobra Verde '88
Hit Men '73
Aguirre, the Wrath of God '72

Warren Berlinger (1937-)
Backlash '99
The Feminine Touch '95
Hero '92
Take Two '87
Sex and the Single Parent '82
The World According to Garp '82
Four Deuces '75
The Long Goodbye '73
Thunder Alley '67
Spinout '66
Billie '65
Platinum High School '60

Shelley Berman (1926-)
Noir et Blanc '86
Outland '81
The Passenger '01
A Clockwork Orange '75
You Don't Mess with the Zohan '08
The Holiday '06
Meet the Fockers '04
Motorama '91
Beware! The Blob '72
Think Dirty '70
Divorce American Style '67
The Best Man '64

Susan Berman
Smithereens '82

Gael Garcia Bernal (1978-)
Babel '06
The Science of Sleep '06
Bad Education '04
The Motorcycle Diaries '04
Dot the I '03
Cuban Blood '03
The Crime of Father Amaro '02
I'm with Lucy '02
No News from God '01
Y Tu Mama Tambien '01
Amores Perros '00

Ed Bernard (1939-)
Welcome to Paradise '07
Jackpot '01
A Face to Kill For '99
Gideon '99
As Good as Dead '95
Siringo '94
Slumber Party Massacre 2 '87

Jason Bernard (1938-96)
Liar Liar '97
Down, Out and Dangerous '95
While You Were Sleeping '95
Cosmic Slop '94
Paint It Black '89
No Way Out '87
All of Me '84
Square '86
Wilma '77

Paul Bernard (1898-1958)
Pattes Blanches '49
The Ladies of the Bois de Boulogne '44

Susan Bernard (1948-)
Teenager '74
Faster, Pussycat! Kill! Kill! '65

Herschel Bernardi (1923-86)
Actor: The Paul Muni Story '78
The Front '76
The Story of Jacob & Joseph '74
No Place to Run '72
Irma La Douce '63
Love with the Proper Stranger '63
Stranger '63
1001 Arabian Nights '59 (V)
Green Fields '37

Michael Bernardo (1964-)
Shootfighter 2: Kill or Be Killed '96
Virtual Combat '95
Shootfighter: Fight to the Death '93

Lynn Bernay (1931-)
The Pit and the Pendulum '61
I Bury the Living '58

Marc Berman
The Girl from Paris '02

Sandra Bernhard (1955-)
Dinner Rush '00
Playing Mona Lisa '00
Footsteps '98
Wrongfully Accused '98
An Alan Smithee Film: Burn, Hollywood, Burn '97
Somewhere in the City '97
Plump Fiction '97
Lover Girl '97
Marry Me, Marry Me '69
Please Not Now! '61
The Apocalypse '96
The Late Shift '96
Inside Monkey Zetterland '93
Hudson Hawk '91
Heavy Petting '89
Track 29 '88
Le Sex Shop '73
La Savoir '21
Five Corners '86
Amadeus '84
Go, Johnny Go! '59
Rock, Rock, Rock '56

Daniel Bernhardt (1965-)
The Matrix Reloaded '03
G2: Mortal Conquest '99
True Vengeance '97
Bloodsport 3 '97
Perfect Target '98
Bloodsport 4: The Dark Kumite '98
Bloodsport 2: The Next Kumite '95

Mara Berni (1934-)
The Fury of Hercules '61
Samson '61

Kevin Bernhardt (1961-)
The Immortals '95
Beauty School '93
Hellraiser 3: Hell on Earth '92
Midnight Warrior '89
Counterforce '87

Collin Bernsen
Hangfire '91
Puppet Master 2 '90

Corbin Bernsen (1954-)
Masters of Horror: Right to Die '07
Kiss Kiss Bang Bang '05
Call Me: The Rise and Fall of Heidi Fleiss '04
Love Comes Softly '03
The Tomorrow Man '01
The Santa Trap '02
Rangers '00
An American Affair '99
Final Payback '99
The Dentist 2: Brace Yourself '98
Major League 3: Back to the Minors '98
Spacejacked '98
Bloodhounds '96
Bloodhounds 2 '96
The Dentist '96
The Great White Hype '96
Inhumanoid '96
Kounterfeit '96
Menno's Mind '96
Baja '95
Cover Me '95
Operation Intercept '95
Someone to Die For '95
Tails You Live, Heads You're Dead '95
Tales from the Hood '95
Temptress '95
The New Age '94
Major League 2 '94
True Lies '94
Radioland Murders '94
Savage Land '94
The Soft Kill '94
A Brilliant Disguise '93
Final Mission '93
The Ghost Brigade '93
Frozen Assets '92
Dead on the Money '91
Shattered '91
Bert Rigby, You're a Fool '89

David Beron
East Side Story '07
Honor Thy Father and Mother: The True Story of the Menendez Brothers '94

Olinka (Schoberova) Berova (1943-)
Togetherness '70
The Vengeance of She '68

Claude Berri (1934-)
Happily Ever After '04

Elizabeth Berridge (1962-)
Hidalgo '04
When the Party's Over '91
Five Corners '86
Amadeus '84
The Funhouse '81

Elizabeth Berrington (1970-)
Tristram Shandy: A Cock and Bull Story '05
Urban Ghost Story '98

Chuck Berry (1926-)
Chuck Berry: Hail! Hail! Rock 'n' Roll! '87

Halle Berry (1968-)
Perfect Stranger '07
Things We Lost in the Fire '07
X-Men: The Last Stand '06
Robots '05 (V)
Catwoman '04
Gothika '03
X2: X-Men United '03
Die Another Day '02
Monster's Ball '01
Swordfish '01
X-Men '00
Introducing Dorothy Dandridge '99
Bulworth '98
Why Do Fools Fall in Love? '98
B.A.P.'s '97
Executive Decision '96
Girl 6 '96
Race the Sun '96
The Rich Man's Wife '96
Losing Isaiah '94
The Flintstones '94
The Program '93
Father Hood '93
Queen '93
Boomerang '92
Jungle Fever '91
Strictly Business '91

Ken Berry (1930-)
The Cat from Outer Space '78
Mountain Man '77
Herbie Rides Again '74
Hello Down There '69

Mark Berry
Blade: Trinity '04
Delivered '98

Michael Berry
Beyond the Law '92

Richard Berry (1950-)
The Valet '06
Pedale Douce '96
L'Appat '94

Jules Berry (1883-1951)
Les Visiteurs du Soir '42
Le Jour Se Leve '39
The Crime of Monsieur Lange '36

Day of Atonement '93
Honeymoon '87
A Man and a Woman: 20 Years Later '86
L'Addition '85
Special Police '85

Vincent Berry
Baby '00
Sugar Town '99
The Fury Within '98
Free Willy 3: The Rescue '97
Amnesia '96

Dorothee Berryman (1948-)
The Barbarian Invasions '03
Taken '99
Winter Lily '98
The Pianist '91
Scanners 2: The New Order '91
A Paper Wedding '89
The Decline of the American Empire '86

Michael Berryman (1948-)
The Devil's Rejects '05
Wizards of the Demon Sword '94
Teenage Exorcist '93
Auntie Lee's Meat Pies '92
Beastmaster 2: Through the Portal of Time '91
Evil Spirits '91
The Guyver '91
Haunting Fear '91
Cut and Run '85
The Hills Have Eyes, Part 2 '84
Deadly Blessing '81
Aftershock '88
Saturday the 14th Strikes Back '88
The Barbarians '87
Voyage of the Rock Aliens '87
Star Trek 4: The Voyage Home '86
Wolfen '81
Sweet Hostage '75
The Hills Have Eyes '77
One Flew Over the Cuckoo's Nest '75
Gator King '70

Julien Bertheau (1910-95)
That Obscure Object of Desire '77
Phantom of Liberty '74

Anders W. Berthelsen (1969-)
Italian for Beginners '01
The Weight of Water '00
Mifune '99

Dehl Berti (1921-91)
Bullies '86
Don't Drink the Water '69
Billie '65
McHale's Navy Joins the Air Force '65

Marina Berti (1925-2002)
Night Train Murders '75
Torture Train '75
A Face in the Rain '63
Quo Vadis '51
Prince of Foxes '49

Francoise Bertin
Dad On the Run '00
Happenstance '00

Roland Bertin (1930-)
Pas Tres Catholique '93
The Hairdresser's Husband '92
Cyrano de Bergerac '90
L'Homme Blesse '83
Diva '82

Valerie Bertinelli (1960-)
Saved! '04
Taken Away '89
Pancho Barnes '88
Number One with a Bullet '87
Rockabye '86
Ordinary Heroes '85
Silent Witness '85
Aladdin and His Wonderful Lamp '84
Shattered Vows '84
C.H.O.M.P.S. '79
Young Love, First Love '79

Jane Bertish
The Roman Spring of Mrs. Stone '03
Dance with a Stranger '85

Suzanne Bertish (1953-)
The Roman Spring of Mrs. Stone '03
The Scarlet Pimpernel 3: The Kidnapped King '99
Venice, Venice '92
The Hunger '83
To the Lighthouse '83

Juliet Berto (1947-90)
Mr. Klein '76
Celine and Julie Go Boating '74
Le Sex Shop '73
The Joy of Knowledge '65

Paul Bertoya
Angels from Hell '68
Cop-Out '67

Gene Bervoets (1956-)
The Vanishing '88

Bibi Besch (1940-96)
Rattled '96
Doing Time on Maple Drive '92
Crazy from the Heart '91
Betsy's Wedding '90
Kill Me Again '89
Date with an Angel '87
The Lonely Lady '83
The Beast Within '82
Star Trek 2: The Wrath of Khan '82
Death of a Centerfold '81
Sophisticated Gents '81
Backstairs at the White House '79
Peter Lundy and the Medicine Hat Stallion '77

Melchior Beslon
Paris, je t'aime '06

Dominique Besnehard (1954-)
Beaumarchais the Scoundrel '96
A Nos Amours '84

Ardon Bess
Moving Target '96
Spenser: The Judas Goat '94

Ted Bessell (1935-96)
Acorn People '82
Breaking Up Is Hard to Do '79

Eugenie Besserer (1868-1934)
The Flesh and the Devil '27
The Jazz Singer '27
Anna Christie '23

Joe Besser (1907-88)
Savage Intruder '68
Sins of Jezebel '54
Africa Screams '49

Matt Besser
Undead or Alive '07
Walk Hard: The Dewey Cox Story '07

Ahmed Best (1973-)
The Greatest Question '19
Little Orphan Annie '18
Star Wars: Episode 3—Revenge of the Sith '05
Star Wars: Episode 2—Attack of the Clones '02 (V)
Star Wars: Episode 1—The Phantom Menace '99 (V)

Edna Best (1900-74)
The Ghost and Mrs. Muir '47
Intermezzo '39
South Riding '37
The Man Who Knew Too Much '34

James Best (1926-)
Moondance Alexander '07
Death Mask '98
Ode to Billy Joe '76
The Savage Bees '76
The Runaway Barge '75
Mind Warp '72
Sounder '72
Savage Run '70
Shenandoah '65
Shock Corridor '63
The Killer Shrews '59
Ride Lonesome '59
Verboten! '59
The Naked and the Dead '58
Ma and Pa Kettle at the Fair '52

Wayne Best
Mean Streak '99
Summer's Children '79

Willie Best (1913-62)
The Kansan '43
The Ghost Breakers '40
The Bride Walks Out '36
The Littlest Rebel '35
Kentucky Kernels '34
The Monster Walks '32

Martine Beswick (1941-)
Night of the Scarecrow '95
Wide Sargasso Sea '92
Evil Spirits '91
Miami Blues '90
Trancers 2: The Return of Jack Deth '90
Cyclone '87
The Offspring '87
Balboa '82
The Happy Hooker Goes Hollywood '80
Devil Dog: The Hound of Hell '78
Strange New World '75
Seizure '74
Dr. Jekyll and Sister Hyde '71
A Bullet for the General '68
Prehistoric Women '67
One Million Years B.C. '66
Thunderball '65
From Russia with Love '63

Anne Betancourt
Bless the Child '00
Fools Rush In '97

Sabine Bethmann (1931-)
Dr. Mabuse vs. Scotland Yard '64
The Indian Tomb '59
Journey to the Lost City '58

Zena Bethune (1945-)
Who's That Knocking at My Door? '68

Paul Bettany (1971-)
The Da Vinci Code '06
Firewall '06
Wimbledon '04
Dogville '03
Master and Commander: The Far Side of the World '03
The Reckoning '03
The Heart of Me '02
A Beautiful Mind '01
A Knight's Tale '01
Gangster No. 1 '00
After the Rain '99
Every Woman Knows a Secret '99
Robert Louis Stevenson's The Game of Death '99
Coming Home '98
The Land Girls '98
Bent '97
Sharpe's Waterloo '97

Lyle Bettger (1915-2003)
Johnny Reno '66
Nevada Smith '66
Lone Ranger '56
Sea Chase '55
Carnival Story '54
All I Desire '53
Union Station '50

Laura Betti (1934-)
Courage Mountain '89
Lovers and Liars '81
1900 '76
Allonsanfan '73
Sonny and Jed '73
The Canterbury Tales '71
Twitch of the Death Nerve '71
Teorema '68

Val Bettin (1916-)
The Return of Jafar '94 (V)
The Great Mouse Detective '86 (V)

Angela Bettis (1975-)
Masters of Horror: Sick Girl '06
Carrie '02
Coastlines '02
May '02
The Flamingo Rising '01
Perfume '01
The Ponder Heart '01
Bless the Child '00
The Last Best Sunday '98

Robert Bettles (1962-)
Fourth Wish '75
Ride a Wild Pony '75

Franca Bettoya (1936-)
Marauder '65
The Last Man on Earth '64

Daniel Betts (1970-)
Heat of the Sun '99
The Magical Legend of the Leprechauns '99
The Canterville Ghost '96

Jack Betts
Spider-Man '02
Southern Man '99
Gods and Monsters '98
Dead Men Don't Die '91
Fistful of Death '71
The Bloody Brood '59

Carl Betz (1921-78)
The Meal '75
Spinout '66
Dangerous Crossing '53

Matthew Betz (1881-1938)
Little Red Schoolhouse '36
The Fighting Rookie '34
Tarzan the Fearless '33
Broadway to Cheyenne '32
The Fighting Marshal '32
The Wrong Road '34
The Lost Patrol '34
Cavalcade '33
Vanity Fair '32
High Voltage '29
The White Sin '24
The Wedding March '28
The Unholy Three '25

Billy Bevan (1887-1957)
The Woman in Green '45
The Man Who Wouldn't Die '42
Mrs. Miniver '42
Dr. Jekyll and Mr. Hyde '41
Girl of the Golden West '38
The Wrong Road '37

Clem Bevans (1879-1963)
Gold Raiders '51
Silver City Bonanza '51
Rim of the Canyon '49
Highway 13 '48
The Kansan '43
Sergeant York '41
Abe Lincoln in Illinois '40

Helen Beverly
Meeting at Midnight '44
Overture to Glory '40
The Light Ahead '39
Green Fields '37

Leslie Bevis (1957-)
The November Men '93
Alien Nation '88

Nathan Bexton (1977-)
The In Crowd '00
Psycho Beach Party '00
Go '99
Nowhere '96

Turhan Bey (1920-)
Virtual Combat '95
Parole, Inc. '49
The Amazing Mr. X '48
Out of the Blue '47
The Climax '44
Dragon Seed '44
Ali Baba and the Forty Thieves '43
Background to Danger '43
The Mad Ghoul '43
Arabian Nights '42
Junior G-Men of the Air '42
The Mummy's Tomb '42
Footsteps in the Dark '41
Shadows on the Stairs '41

Alexander Beyer (1973-)
Good Bye, Lenin! '03
The Legend of Rita '99

Brad Beyer (1973-)
Monday Night Mayhem '02
Sorority Boys '02
Crazy in Alabama '99
The General's Daughter '99
Trick '99

Troy Beyer (1965-)
John Q '02
A Light in the Darkness '02
Let's Talk About Sex '98
B.A.P.'s '97
The Little Death '95
Weekend at Bernie's 2 '93
Rooftops '89

Richard Beymer (1939-)
Elvis Meets Nixon '98
Foxfire '96
The Disappearance of Kevin Johnson '95
The Little Death '95
Under Investigation '93
Black Belt '92
Silent Night, Deadly Night 3: Better Watch Out! '89
Cross Country '83
Free Grass '69
The Stripper '63
The Longest Day '62
West Side Story '61
The Diary of Anne Frank '59

Didier Bezace (1946-)
The Chambermaid on the Titanic '97
Les Voleurs '96
Between Heaven and Earth '93
L.627 '92

Dante Beze
See Mos Def

Raoul Bhaneja
Weirdsville '07
Touch of Pink '04

Bhasker (1930-2003)
Wild West '93
Drachenfutter '87
I Drink Your Blood '71

Daniela Bianchi (1942-)
Dirty Heroes '71
Secret Agent 00 '67
From Russia with Love '63
The Sword of El Cid '62

Yuen Biao (1957-)
Robin-B-Hood '06
Once Upon a Time in China '91
Miracles '89
Dragons Forever '88
Eastern Condors '87
The Millionaire's Express '86
Project A '83
Zu: Warriors from the Magic Mountain '83
The Prodigal Son '82

Leslie Bibb (1974-)
Iron Man '08
Talladega Nights: The Ballad of Ricky Bobby '06
Wristcutters: A Love Story '06
See Spot Run '01
The Skulls '00

Charles K. Bibby
Order of the Black Eagle '87
Unmasking the Idol '86

Abner Biberman (1909-77)
Elephant Walk '54
Roaring City '51
Betrayal from the East '44
The Keys of the Kingdom '44
The Leopard Man '43
His Girl Friday '40
Gunga Din '39
Panama Patrol '39
The Rains Came '39

Robert Bice (1914-68)
Invasion U.S.A. '52
Loan Shark '52
Tales of Robin Hood '52
Gunplay '51
Bandit King of Texas '49
The Ghost and the Guest '43

Bruno Bichir (1967-)
La Mujer de Mi Hermano '06
No News from God '01
Midaq Alley '95
A Lost Year '93
Highway Patrolman '91

Stewart Bick
The Reagans '04
Danger Beneath the Sea '02
Life with Judy Garland—Me and My Shadows '01
Lip Service '00
Mercy '00
Sex & Mrs. X '00
One Special Night '99
Captive '97

Charles Bickford (1889-1967)
A Big Hand for the Little Lady '66
Fatal Confinement '64
Days of Wine and Roses '62
The Unforgiven '60
The Big Country '58
The Court Martial of Billy Mitchell '55
Not as a Stranger '55
A Star Is Born '54
Jim Thorpe: All American '51
Branded '50
Guilty of Treason '50
Riding High '50
Babe Ruth Story '48
Command Decision '48
Four Faces West '48
Johnny Belinda '48
Brute Force '47
The Farmer's Daughter '47
Duel in the Sun '46
A Wing and a Prayer '44
Mr. Lucky '43
The Song of Bernadette '43
Reap the Wild Wind '42
Tarzan's New York Adventure '42
Burma Convoy '41
Mutiny in the Big House '39
Of Mice and Men '39
The Plainsman '37
Thunder Pass '37
Thunder Trail '37
The Farmer Takes a Wife '35
Little Miss Marker '34
No Other Woman '33

Panama Flo '32
East of Borneo '31
Anna Christie '30

Andrew Bicknell
Attack Force '06

Jean-Luc Bideau (1940-)
The Red Violin '98
Revenge of the Musketeers '94
Jonah Who Will Be 25 in the Year 2000 '76
La Salamandre '71

Michael Biehn (1956-)
Planet Terror '07
The Insatiable '06
Sundance '04
Borderline '02
Clockstoppers '02
The Art of War '00
Chain of Command '00
Cherry Falls '00
Dying to Get Rich '98
The Magnificent Seven '98
Silver Wolf '98
Asteroid '97
Dead Men Can't Dance '97
Double Edge '97
Mojave Moon '96
The Rock '96
Breach of Trust '95
Jade '95
Blood of the Hunter '94
Deep Red '94
In the Kingdom of the Blind the Man with One Eye Is King '94
Deadfall '93
Strapped '93
Tombstone '93
K2: The Ultimate High '92
A Taste for Killing '92
Timebomb '91
Navy SEALS '90
The Abyss '89
In a Shallow Grave '88
The Seventh Sign '88
Rampage '87
Aliens '86
The Terminator '84
The Lords of Discipline '83
The Fan '81
Hog Wild '80
Coach '78
Grease '78

Dick Biel
Slime City '89

Jessica Biel (1982-)
I Now Pronounce You Chuck and Larry '07
Next '07
Home of the Brave '06
The Illusionist '06
Elizabethtown '05
London '05
Stealth '05
Blade: Trinity '04
Cellular '04
The Texas Chainsaw Massacre '03
The Rules of Attraction '02
Summer Catch '01
I'll Be Home for Christmas '98
Ulee's Gold '97

Josef Bierbichler (1948-)
Winter Sleepers '97
Woyzeck '78
Heart of Glass '74

Ramon Bieri (1929-2001)
Love, Lies and Murder '91
Grandview U.S.A. '84
A Matter of Life and Death '80
A Christmas Without Snow '80

Craig Bierko (1965-)
Scary Movie 4 '06
Cinderella Man '05
Dickie Roberts: Former Child Star '03
The Suburbans '99
The Thirteenth Floor '99
Fear and Loathing in Las Vegas '98
Sour Grapes '98
The Long Kiss Goodnight '96

Adam Biesk
The Applegates '91

Big Boi
See Antwan Andre Patton

Big Pun (1971-2000)
Urban Menace '99

Claudio Bigagli (1955-)
Fiorile '93
Mediterraneo '91
Kaos '85
The Night of the Shooting Stars '82

Scott "Bam Bam" Bigelow (1961-)
Major Payne '95

Dan Biggers
SnakeEater 3: His Law '92

Sean Biggerstaff (1983-)
Cashback '06
Harry Potter and the Sorcerer's Stone '01
The Winter Guest '97

Jason Biggs (1978-)
Over Her Dead Body '08
Eight Below '06
Wedding Daze '06
Jersey Girl '04
American Wedding '03
Anything Else '03
American Pie 2 '01
Saving Silverman '01
Prozac Nation '01
Boys and Girls '00
Loser '00
Jay and Silent Bob Strike Back '01

Richard Biggs (1960-2004)
Forever Love '98
Ablaze '00

Roxann Biggs-Dawson (1964-)
Darkman 3: Die Darkman Die '95

Theodore Bikel (1924-)
Shattered '91
The Final Days '89
See You in the Morning '89
Dark Tower '87
Very Close Quarters '84
The Return of the King '80
Victory at Entebbe '76
200 Motels '71
Darker than Amber '70
My Side of the Mountain '69
Sweet November '68
The Russians Are Coming, the Russians Are Coming '66
My Fair Lady '64
A Dog of Flanders '59
The Defiant Ones '58
I Bury the Living '58
I Want to Live! '58
Enemy Below '57
The Pride and the Passion '57
The African Queen '51

Vincent Bilancio
Blood Gnome '02

Fernando Bilbao
The Screaming Dead '72
Fangs of the Living Dead '68

Nicole Bilderback (1975-)
Bring It On '00
Paper Bullets '99

Leo Bill
Becoming Jane '07
Lethal Dose '03

Tony Bill (1940-)
Two Men Went to War '02
Naked City: Justice with a Bullet '98
Barb Wire '96
The Killing Mind '90
Pee-wee's Big Adventure '85
Washington Mistress '81
Heart Beat '80
Little Dragons '80
Are You in the House Alone? '78
Initiation of Sarah '78
Shampoo '75
Haunts of the Very Rich '72
Castle Keep '69
Ice Station Zebra '68
Never a Dull Moment '68
You're a Big Boy Now '66
Marriage on the Rocks '65
None But the Brave '65
Come Blow Your Horn '63
Soldier in the Rain '63

Raoul Billerey (1920-)
Revenge of the Musketeers '94

Don Billett
Gloria '98
Prince of the City '81

Roy Billing
Aquamarine '06
Strange Bedfellows '04
Siam Sunset '99

Dawn Ann Billings
Stakeout '87

Earl Billings (1945-)
Something New '06
Christmas at Water's Edge '04
Mr. 3000 '04
American Splendor '03
Antwone Fisher '02
One False Move '91

Beau Billingslea (1953-)
Silent Predators '99
Indecent Behavior 3 '95

Barbara Billingsley (1922-)
Back to the Beach '87
Airplane! '80

Jennifer Billingsley (1942-)
Hollywood Man '76
The Thirsty Dead '74
White Lightning '73
C.C. & Company '70
Lady in a Cage '64

John Billingsley (1960-)
The Man from Earth '07
The Twelve Dogs of Christmas '05
Out of Time '03

Peter Billingsley (1971-)
Iron Man '08
The Break-Up '06
Arcade '93
Beverly Hills Brats '89
Russkies '87
Dirt Bike Kid '86
A Christmas Story '83
Death Valley '81

Stephen Billington (1969-)
Dracula 2: Ascension '03
The Black Cobra '87

Bruno Bilotta
Excellent Cadavers '99

Rachel Bilson
The Last Kiss '05
Jumper '08

Mike Binder (1958-)
Reign Over Me '07
The Upside of Anger '05
Minority Report '02
The Sex Monster '99
Indian Summer '93
Crossing the Bridge '92

Sybilla Binder (1898-1962)
The Golden Salamander '51
Counterblast '48
Blanche Fury '49

John Bindon (1943-93)
Performance '70

Herman Bing (1889-1947)
Dumbo '41 (V)
Bitter Sweet '40
Bluebeard's Eighth Wife '38
Every Day's a Holiday '38
The Great Waltz '38
Maytime '37
Tango '36
That Girl from Paris '36
Crimson Romance '34
The Merry Widow '34
The Guardsman '31

Barbara Bingham
Beyond Darkness '92
Soldier's Fortune '91
Friday the 13th, Part 8: Jason Takes Manhattan '89

S.J. Bingham
Wolfheart's Revenge '25
Three Word Brand '21
Home Alone '90

Geoffrey Binney
Raw Force '81
Hot Potato '76

Edward Binns (1916-90)
Return to Eden '89
The Verdict '82
Oliver's Story '78
Night Moves '75
Hunter '73
Patton '70
The Americanization of Emily '64
A Public Affair '62
Judgment at Nuremberg '61
Compulsion '59
Curse of the Undead '59
Twelve Angry Men '57
Beyond a Reasonable Doubt '56
Without Warning '52

Juliette Binoche (1964-)
Dan in Real Life '07
Breaking and Entering '06
A Few Days in September '06
Code Unknown '00
Chocolat '00
The Widow of Saint-Pierre '00
Children of the Century '99
Alice et Martin '98
The English Patient '96
A Couch in New York '96
The Horseman on the Roof '95
Trois Couleurs: Rouge '94
Trois Couleurs: Blanc '94
Trois Couleurs: Bleu '93
Damage '92
Emily Brontë's Wuthering Heights '92
Women & Men: In Love '91
The Lovers on the Bridge '91
The Unbearable Lightness of Being '88
Mauvais Sang '86
Rendez-vous '85
Hail Mary '85

Thora Birch (1982-)
Silver City '04
Ghost World '01
The Hole '01
Dungeons and Dragons '00
The Smokers '00
American Beauty '99
Night Ride Home '99
Alaska '96
Now and Then '95
Clear and Present Danger '94
Monkey Trouble '94
Hocus Pocus '93
Patriot Games '92
All I Want for Christmas '91
Paradise '91
The End of Innocence '90
Home Alone '90

Billie Bird (1908-2002)
Dennis the Menace '93
Ernest Saves Christmas '88
Sixteen Candles '84

Brad Bird (1957-)
Ratatouille '07 (V)
The Incredibles '04 (V)

Larry Bird (1956-)
Blue Chips '94
Celtic Pride '96

Norman Bird (1924-2005)
The Slipper and the Rose '76
Hands of the Ripper '71
The Hill '65
Burn, Witch, Burn! '62
Victim '61
Whistle Down the Wind '61

Paul Birch (1913-69)
The Man Who Shot Liberty Valance '62
Queen of Outer Space '58
Apache Woman '55
Day the World Ended '55
Ride Clear of Diablo '54

Maurice Biraud (1922-82)
A Slightly Pregnant Man '79
The Last Train '74
Any Number Can Win '63

Thelma Biral (1941-)
Rendez-vous '85

Len Birman (1932-)
Web of Deceit '90
Undergrads '85
Captain America 2: Death Too Soon '79
Captain America '79
Lies My Father Told Me '75
Back in Action '94

Matt Birman
Family of Cops 2: Breach of Faith '97

Serafina Birman (1890-1976)
Ivan the Terrible, Part 2 '46
Ivan the Terrible, Part 1 '44
The Girl with the Hat Box '27

David Birney (1939-)
Nightfall '88
Prettykill '87
The Five of Me '81
Mom, the Wolfman and Me '80
Oh, God! Book 2 '80
Choice of Weapons '76
Caravan to Vaccares '74
Murder or Mercy '74

Reed Birney (1954-)
Crimewave '85
Four Friends '81

Jane Birkin (1946-)
Merci Docteur Rey '04
The Last September '99
A Soldier's Daughter Never Cries '98
Jet Lag '02
Dust '85
Evil under the Sun '82
Make Room for Tomorrow '81
Death on the Nile '78
Catherine & Co. '75
Don Juan (Or If Don Juan Were a Woman) '73
Seven Deaths in the Cat's Eye '72
Too Pretty to Be Honest '72
Romance of a Horsethief '71
French Intrigue '77
Swimming Pool '70
La Piscine '69
Wonderwall: The Movie '69
Blow-Up '66

David Birkin
Sylvia '03
All the Queen's Men '01
Charlotte Gray '01

Tala Birell (1907-58)
Song of Love '47
The Purple Heart '44
Crime and Punishment '35
The White Legion '36

Mary Birdsong
Reno 911!: Miami '07
Pizza '05

Jesse Birdsall (1963-)
Getting It Right '89
Wish You Were Here '87

Christopher Birt
A Soldier's Sweetheart '98

Eva Birthistle
Imagine Me & You '06
The State Within '06
A Fond Kiss '04
The American '01

Borstal Boy '00

Olga Bisera
Women in Cell Block 7 '77
Castle Keep '69

Debbie Bishop
Sid & Nancy '86
Scrubbers '82

Ed Bishop (1932-)
Saturn 3 '80
S.O.S. Titanic '79
Brass Target '78
The Devil's Web '74
Journey to the Far Side of the Sun '69

Jennifer Bishop (1942-)
We Don't Live Here Anymore '04
Jaws of Death '76
Jessi's Girls '75
Impulse '74
House of Terror '72
Horror of the Blood Monsters '70
The Female Bunch '69

Joey Bishop (1918-2007)
Trigger Happy '96
Betsy's Wedding '90
Delta Force '86
Valley of the Dolls '67
Who's Minding the Mint? '67
Texas Across the River '66
Ocean's 11 '60
Deep Six '58
The Naked and the Dead '58

Julie Bishop (1914-2001)
The High and the Mighty '54
Westward the Women '51
Sands of Iwo Jima '49
The Last of the Redmen '47
Rhapsody in Blue '45
Action in the North Atlantic '43
Northern Pursuit '43
Her First Romance '40
Young Bill Hickok '40
The Kansas Terrors '39
Torture Ship '39
Bohemian Girl '36
The Black Cat '34
Tarzan the Fearless '33

Kelly Bishop (1944-)
Private Parts '96
Miami Rhapsody '95
Queens Logic '91
Dirty Dancing '87

Kevin Bishop (1980-)
Russian Dolls '05
Food of Love '02
L'Auberge Espagnole '02
Muppet Treasure Island '96

Pat Bishop
Women of Valor '86
Don's Party '76

Stephen Bishop (1951-)
Someone to Love '87
Twilight Zone: The Movie '83
The Blues Brothers '80
National Lampoon's Animal House '78

Wes Bishop (1933-93)
Dixie Dynamite '76
Black Gestapo '75
Chain Gang Women '72
The Thing with Two Heads '72
Chrome and Hot Leather '71
Rebel Vixens '69
Love Desperados '68

William Bishop (1918-59)
Breakdown '53
The Redhead from Wyoming '53
Harriet Craig '50
Coroner Creek '48

Thor Bishopric
Breaking All the Rules '85
The Little Mermaid '75 (V)

Claudio Bisio

Steve Bisley
Fast Talking '86
The Highest Honor '84
Chain Reaction '80
Mad Max '80

Whit Bissell (1909-96)
Soylent Green '73
Seven Days in May '64
Spencer's Mountain '63
The Manchurian Candidate '62
The Time Machine '60
No Name on the Bullet '59
Teenage Frankenstein '58
I Was a Teenage Werewolf '57
Invasion of the Body Snatchers '56
Shack Out on 101 '55
The Atomic Kid '54
The Caine Mutiny '54
Creature from the Black Lagoon '54
Devil's Canyon '53
Boots Malone '52
Tales of Robin Hood '52
The Lost Continent '51
He Walked by Night '48
Raw Deal '48
Brute Force '47

Jacqueline Bisset (1944-)
Carolina Moon '07
Domino '05
Fascination '04
Latter Days '04
Britannic '00
Jesus '00
Sex & Mrs. X '00
Britannic '99
Joan of Arc '99
Let the Devil Wear Black '99
Dangerous Beauty '98
End of Summer '97
La Ceremonie '95
Crime Broker '94
Crimebroker '93
The Maid '90
Wild Orchid '90
Scenes from the Class Struggle in Beverly Hills '89
High Season '88
Choices '86
Anna Karenina '85
Forbidden '85
Under the Volcano '84
Class '83
Rich and Famous '81
When Time Ran Out '80
Together? '79
The Greek Tycoon '78
Who Is Killing the Great Chefs of Europe? '78
The Deep '77
Le Magnifique '76
St. Ives '76
Spiral Staircase '75
Murder on the Orient Express '74
Day for Night '73
The Thief Who Came to Dinner '73
Life & Times of Judge Roy Bean '72
The Mephisto Waltz '71
Secrets '71
Airport '70
The Passing of Evil '70
The First Time '69
Bullitt '68
The Detective '68
Casino Royale '67
Two for the Road '67
Cul de Sac '66

Josie Bissett (1970-)
Baby Monitor: Sound of Fear '97
Mikey '92
All-American Murder '91
Book of Love '91

Joel Bissonnette
Suspicious River '00
Boulevard '94

Chhabi Biswas (1900-62)
Devi '60
Jalsaghar '58

Seema Biswas
Water '05
Bandit Queen '94

Bill Bixby (1934-93)
Death of the Incredible Hulk '90
The Trial of the Incredible Hulk '89
The Incredible Hulk Returns '88
Agatha Christie's Murder is Easy '82
The Incredible Hulk '77
Kentucky Fried Movie '77
Fantasy Island '76
Rich Man, Poor Man '76
The Apple Dumpling Gang '75
The Barbary Coast '74
Speedway '68
Clambake '67
Under the Yum-Yum Tree '63
Lonely Are the Brave '62

Denise Bixler
The Assassination Game '92
Evil Dead 2: Dead by Dawn '87

Dragan Bjelogric (1963-)
The Wounds '98
Pretty Village, Pretty Flame '96

Halvar Bjork (1928-)
Autumn Sonata '78
The New Land '73

Irina Bjorklund
Lost '05
Ambush '99

Anna Bjorn
Sword & the Sorcerer '82
More American Graffiti '79

Gunnar Bjornstrand (1909-86)
Autumn Sonata '78
Face to Face '76
The Rite '69
The Shame '68
Persona '66
The Winter Light '62
Through a Glass Darkly '61
The Magician '58
Wild Strawberries '57
The Seventh Seal '56
Dreams '55
Smiles of a Summer Night '55
Lesson in Love '54
Torment '44

Backstairs at the White House '79

Isobel Black (1943-)
10 Rillington Place '71
Kiss of the Vampire '62

Jack Black (1969-)
Be Kind Rewind '08
Kung Fu Panda '08 (V)
Tropic Thunder '08
Margot at the Wedding '07
Danny Roane: First Time Director '06
The Holiday '06
Nacho Libre '06
Tenacious D in the Pick of Destiny '06
King Kong '05
Envy '04
Shark Tale '04 (V)
School of Rock '03
Ice Age '02 (V)
Orange County '02
Saving Silverman '01
Shallow Hal '01
High Fidelity '00
The Cradle Will Rock '99
Jesus' Son '99
The Love Letter '99
Bongwater '98
Enemy of the State '98
I Still Know What You Did Last Summer '98
The Jackal '97
Johnny Skidmarks '97
Bio-Dome '96
The Cable Guy '96
Crossworlds '96
The Fan '96
Mars Attacks! '96
Dead Man Walking '95
Waterworld '95
Blind Justice '94
Bye Bye, Love '94
The NeverEnding Story 3: Escape from Fantasia '94
Airborne '93
Demolition Man '93
Bob Roberts '92

James Black
Unshackled '00
Standing on Fishes '99
The Substitute 3: Winner Takes All '99
Men '97
Children of the Corn 4: The Gathering '96
Crimetime '96
Dinosaur Valley Girls '96
Movies Money Murder '96
Plan 10 from Outer Space '95
Armistead Maupin's Tales of the City '93
Bound and Gagged: A Love Story '93
Auntie Lee's Meat Pies '92
Caged Fear '92
Children of the Night '91
Final Judgment '92
The Player '92
Rubin & Ed '92
Evil Spirits '91
Haunting Fear '91
Quiet Fire '91

The Children '90
Club Fed '90
The Killer's Edge '90
Mirror, Mirror '90
Night Angel '90
Overexposed '90
Hitz '89
Homer and Eddie '89
Twisted Justice '89
Zapped Again '89
Dixie Lanes '88
The Invisible Kid '88
Out of the Dark '88
Eternal Evil '87
Hostage '87
It's Alive 3: Island of the Alive '87
Invaders from Mars '86
Cut and Run '85
Martin's Day '85
Bad Manners '84
Killing Heat '84
Savage Dawn '84
Can She Bake a Cherry Pie? '83
Come Back to the Five & Dime Jimmy Dean, Jimmy Dean '82
Separate Ways '82
Chanel Solitaire '81
Miss Right '81
The Last Word '80
The Squeeze '80
Killer Fish '79
Mr. Horn '79
Capricorn One '78
In Praise of Older Women '78
Love Under Pressure '78
The Rip Off '78
Burnt Offerings '76
Family Plot '76
Airport '75 '75
Crime & Passion '75
The Day of the Locust '75
Nashville '75
Trilogy of Terror '75
The Great Gatsby '74
Law and Disorder '74
Little Laura & Big John '73
The Pyx '73
A Gunfight '71
Five Easy Pieces '70
Easy Rider '69
You're a Big Boy Now '66
The Prime Time '60

Lewis Black (1948-)
Accepted '06
Man of the Year '06
Unaccompanied Minors '06

Lucas Black (1982-)
The Fast and the Furious: Tokyo Drift '06
Deepwater '05
Jarhead '05
Friday Night Lights '04
Killer Diller '04
Cold Mountain '03
All the Pretty Horses '00
The Miracle Worker '00
Crazy in Alabama '99
Flash '98
The X-Files '98
Ghosts of Mississippi '96
Sling Blade '96
The War '94

Maurice Black (1891-1938)
Three Legionnaires '37
Sixteen Fathoms Deep '34
Marked Money '28

Michael Ian Black (1971-)
The Baxter '05
Wet Hot American Summer '01
The Bogus Witch Project '00

Ryan Black (1973-)
Stryker '04
Dance Me Outside '95
Geronimo '93

Shane Black (1961-)
An Alan Smithee Film: Burn, Hollywood, Burn '97
As Good As It Gets '97
Predator '87

Richard Blackburn
Eating Raoul '82
Lemora, Lady Dracula '73

Richard Blackburn
Blue State '07
Stephen King's The Storm of the Century '99
Down in the Delta '98
Murder at 1600 '97
In Love and War '96
Sugartime '95
A Man in Uniform '93

Don Blackman
The Old Man and the Sea '58
Serpent Island '54

Honor Blackman (1926-)
Russell Mulcahy's Tale of the Mummy '99
To Walk with Lions '99
The First Olympics: Athens 1896 '84
The Cat and the Canary '79
To the Devil, a Daughter '76
Fright '71
The Virgin and the Gypsy '70
Lola '69
Shalako '68
Moment to Moment '66
Goldfinger '64
Jason and the Argonauts '63
A Matter of WHO '62
A Night to Remember '58
Suspended Alibi '56
Glass Tomb '55
Green Grow the Rushes '51
Conspirator '49

Jeremy Blackman
Crown Heights '02
Magnolia '99

Joan Blackman (1938-)
Macon County Line '74
Daring Game '68
Blue Hawaii '62
Kid Galahad '62
Career '59
Good Day for a Hanging '58

Sidney Blackmer (1895-1973)
Rosemary's Baby '68
How to Murder Your Wife '64
Tammy and the Bachelor '57
Beyond a Reasonable Doubt '56
High Society '56
The High and the Mighty '54
People Will Talk '51
Buffalo Bill '44
Wilson '44
War of the Wildcats '43
The Panther's Claw '42
Love Crazy '41
Law of the Pampas '39
Charlie Chan at Monte Carlo '37
Heidi '37
The House of Secrets '37
In Old Chicago '37
Shadows of the Orient '37
Thank you, Mr. Moto '37
The President's Mystery '36
The Little Colonel '35
The Count of Monte Cristo '34
Goodbye Love '34
Transatlantic Merry-Go-Round '34
Deluge '33
Little Caesar '30

David Blackwell
The Rookie '02
China O'Brien '88

Taurean Blacque (1941-)
Deepstar Six '89
Oliver & Company '88 (V)
The $5.20 an Hour Dream '80

Ruben Blades (1948-)
Imagining Argentina '04
Spin '04
Assassination Tango '03
The Maldonado Miracle '03
Once Upon a Time in Mexico '03
All the Pretty Horses '00
The Cradle Will Rock '99
Chinese Box '97
The Devil's Own '96
The Two Jakes '90
Predator 2 '90
Scorpion Spring '96
Color of Night '94
A Million to Juan '94
Life with Mikey '93
Crazy from the Heart '91
The Super '91
The Josephine Baker Story '90
Fatal Beauty '87
Critical Condition '86
Crossover Dreams '85
The Last Fight '82

Estella Blain (1936-81)
The Diabolical Dr. Z '65
Pirates of the Coast '61
The Twilight Girls '57

Gerard Blain (1930-2000)
Hatari! '62
The American Friend '77
The Cousins '59
Le Beau Serge '58
Les Mistons '57

Vivian Blaine (1921-95)
Parasite '82
The Cracker Factory '79
The Dark '79
Guys and Dolls '55
Doll Face '46
Skirts Ahoy! '52
State Fair '45
Greenwich Village '44
Something for the Boys '44

Betsy Blair (1923-)
Scarlet '94
Suspicion '87
Il Grido '57
Marty '55
The Match '99
The Final Cut '95
Betrayal '74
The Glass Slipper '55
Sabre Jet '53

Isla Blair (1944-)
Taste the Blood of Dracula '70

Linda Blair (1959-)
Gang Boys '97
Prey of the Jaguar '96
Scream '96
Sorceress '94
Dead Sleep '91
Fatal Bond '91
Ball Out '90

Janet Blair (1921-2007)
The One and Only, Genuine, Original Family Band '68
Boys' Night Out '62
Burn Witch, Burn! '62
Black Arrow '48
The Fuller Brush Man '48
The Fabulous Dorseys '47
Tonight and Every Night '45
Blondie Goes to College '42

Repossessed '90
Bedroom Eyes 2 '89
Moving Target '89
The Chilling '89
Up Your Alley '89
Hair Show '89
Zapped Again! '89
Silent Assassins '88
Witchery '88
Grotesque '87
Nightforce '86
Night Patrol '85
Red Heat '85
Savage Island '85
Chained Heat '83
Savage Streets '83
Hell Night '81
Ruckus '81
Roller Boogie '79
Wild Horse Hank '79
Summer of Fear '78
The Exorcist 2: The Heretic '77
Victory at Entebbe '76
Airport '75 '75
Sweet Hostage '75
Born Innocent '74
The Exorcist '73
The Sporting Club '72

Nicky Blair (1926-98)
The Crossing Guard '94
Viva Las Vegas '63

Pamela Blair (1949-)
Beavis and Butt-Head Do America '96 (V)

Selma Blair (1972-)
Hellboy 2: The Golden Army '08
Feast of Love '07
Kill Me Later '01
Legally Blonde '01
Lies & Alibis '06
Storytelling '01
Down to You '00
Brown's Requiem '98
Cruel Intentions '98
Girl '98
No Laughing Matter '97
A Guy Thing '03
The Sweetest Thing '02
Highway '01
The Bed You Sleep In '93

Tom Blair
Sure Fire '90
Singin' in the Rain '52
The Game '89

Isabelle Blais
Human Trafficking '05

Nesbitt Blaisdell (1928-)
The Mothman Prophecies '02

Deborah Blaisdell (1959-)
Wildest Dreams '90
Student Affairs '88
Wimps '87
Screen Test '85

Amanda Blake (1929-89)
The Boost '88
B.O.R.N. '88
Gunsmoke: Return to Dodge '87

Robert (Bobby) Blake (1933-)
Lost Highway '96
Money Train '95
The Heart of a Champion: The Ray Mancini Story '85
Coast to Coast '80

The Duchess of Idaho '50
Stars in My Crown '50

Andre B. Blake
Hair Show '04
The Other Brother '02
Just the Ticket '98
Philadelphia '93
Who's the Man? '93

Ellen Blake
Suspect Zero '04
Last Resort '86

Geoffrey Blake (1962-)
Life Without Dick '01
Cast Away '00
Contact '97
Entertaining Angels: The Dorothy Day Story '96
The War at Home '96
Dominion '94
Forrest Gump '94
Marilyn & Bobby: Her Final Affair '94
Philadelphia Experiment 2 '93
Fatal Exposure '91
The Abduction of Kari Swanson '87

Jon Blake (1958-)
The Lighthorsemen '87
Anzacs: The War Down Under '85

Madge Blake (1899-1969)
Batman '66

Larry J. Blake (1914-82)
Demon Seed '77
Beginning of the End '57
Holiday Affair '49
The Jury's Secret '38

Marie Blake (1896-1978)
Sensations of 1945 '44
Prowler '51

Noah Blake (1964-)
The Base '99
Class of Fear '91
Trapper County War '89
My Brilliant Career '79
The Long, Long Trailer '54

Oliver Blake (1905-92)
Ma and Pa Kettle at Waikiki '55

Pamela Blake (1918-)
Casablanca '42
Gunfire '50
Border Rangers '50
Sky Liner '49
Highway 13 '48
Rolling Home '48
Son of God's Country '48
Hat Box Mystery '47
Sea Hound '47
Kid Dynamite '43
Pop Always Pays '40
Wyoming Outlaw '39

Rachael Blake
Perfect Strangers '03
Lantana '01

Busting '74
Electra Glide in Blue '73
Counter Punch '71
Tell Them Willie Boy Is Here '69
In Cold Blood '67
This Property Is Condemned '66
PT 109 '63
Town without Pity '61
Pork Chop Hill '59
Treasure of the Sierra Madre '48
Humoresque '46
Homesteaders of Paradise Valley '47

Ronee Blakley (1946-)
Murder by Numbers '89
Return to Salem's Lot '87
Someone to Love '87
Student Confidential '87
A Nightmare on Elm Street '84
The Baltimore Bullet '80
Desperate Women '78
The Driver '78
The Private Files of J. Edgar Hoover '77
She Came to the Valley '77
Nashville '75

Colin Blakely (1930-87)
Operation Julie '85
Loophole '83
Evil under the Sun '82
The Dogs of War '81
Nijinsky '80
The Big Sleep '78
Equus '77
Love Among the Ruins '75
Murder on the Orient Express '74
Galileo '74
The Private Life of Sherlock Holmes '70
The Vengeance of She '68
This Sporting Life '63

Donald Blakely
In the Shadow of Kilimanjaro '86
Vigilante '83

Susan Blakely (1950-)
Hate Crime '05
Extreme Limits '01
The Perfect Nanny '00
Honor Thy Father and Mother: The True Story of the Menendez Brothers '94
Russian Roulette '93
Intruders '92
Blackmail '91
Wildflower '91
Dead Reckoning '89
The Incident '89
My Mom's a Werewolf '89
Out of Sight, Out of Her Mind '89
Broken Angel '88
Hiroshima Maiden '88
Ladykillers '88
The Survivalist '87
Over the Top '86
A Cry for Love '80
Make Me an Offer '80
The Concorde: Airport '79 '79
Dreamer '79
Secrets '77
Rich Man, Poor Man '76
The Lords of Flatbush '74
Report to the Commissioner '74
The Towering Inferno '74
The Way We Were '73
Savages '72

James Blakely (1910-)
The Shadow Strikes '37
Small Town Boy '37
Fans in a Spring '35

Susan Blakely (1950-)

Jennifer Blanc
Fish Without a Bicycle '03
Kiss Tomorrow Goodbye '00

Mel Blanc (1908-89)
Cool and the Crazy '94
Strange Brew '83 (V)
Looney Looney Looney Bugs Bunny Movie '81
Jetsons: The Movie '90 (V)
Who Framed Roger Rabbit '88 (V)
Buck Rogers in the 25th Century '79 (V)
Phantom Tollbooth '69 (V)
Hey There, It's Yogi Bear '64 (V)
Kiss Me, Stupid! '64
Gay Pur-ee '62 (V)
Neptune's Daughter '49

Michel Blanc (1952-)
The Monster '96
Grosse Fatigue '94
Ready to Wear '94
The Favor, the Watch, & the Very Big Fish '92
Prospero's Books '91
Uranus '91
Monsieur Hire '89
Menage '86
French Fried Vacation '79
The Tenant '76

Sean Blakemore
Woman, Thou Art Loosed '04
Motives '03

Michael Blakemore (1928-)
Country Life '95
The Last Bastion '84

Olive Blakeney (1903-59)
Billy the Kid '41
Gangway '37

Claudie Blakley
Severance '06
Pride and Prejudice '05
Gosford Park '01

Erika Blanc (1942-)
His Secret Life '01
Sweet Spirits '96
The Boss Is Served '76
Mark of the Devil 2 '72
The Night Evelyn Came Out of the Grave '71
Kill, Baby, Kill '66
Special... Forces '68
Your Pistol for a Coffin '68
Santana's Here... Trade Your Pistol for a Coffin '67
Indochine '92
May Fools '90

Dominique Blanc (1962-)
A Soldier's Daughter Never Cries '98
Those Who Love Me Can Take the Train '58
Total Eclipse '95
Queen Margot '94

Jolene Blalock (1969-)
Shadow Puppets '07
Slow Burn '05
Jason and the Argonauts '00

Cate Blanchett (1969-)
Elizabeth: The Golden Age '07
Hot Fuzz '07
I'm Not There '07
Babel '06
The Good German '06
Notes on a Scandal '06
Little Fish '05
The Life Aquatic with Steve Zissou '04
The Aviator '04
Coffee and Cigarettes '03
Lord of the Rings: The Return of the King '03
The Missing '03
Veronica Guerin '03
Charlotte Gray '01
The Shipping News '01
Lord of the Rings: The Two Towers '02
Bandits '01
Heaven '01
The Man Who Cried '00
An Ideal Husband '99
Pushing Tin '99
The Talented Mr. Ripley '99
Elizabeth '98
Oscar and Lucinda '97
Paradise Road '97
The Wedding Party '97

Mari Blanchard (1927-70)
Son of Sinbad '55
Abbott and Costello Go to Mars '53

Jarred Blanchard
The Boys Club '96

Pierre Blanchar (1892-1963)
La Symphonie Pastorale '46
Man from Nowhere '37

Rachel Blanchard (1976-)
Snakes on a Plane '06
Where the Truth Lies '05
Without a Paddle '04
Chasing Holden '01
Sugar & Spice '01
Road Trip '00
The Rage: Carrie 2 '99
Iron Eagle 4 '95
Young Ivanhoe '95

Francis Blanche
The Good Shepherd '06
Stealing Harvard '02
Life with Judy Garland—Me and My Shadows '01

Bruno Blanchet
Scandal Man '67

Susan Blanchard
Prince of Darkness '87
She's in the Army Now '81
President's Mistress '78

Tammy Blanchard
Seducing Doctor Lewis '03

Sandrine Blancke
The Son of the Shark '93

Dorothee Blanck

Jewel Blanch
Against a Crooked Sky '75
Baffled! '72

Joyce Bland (1906-63)
Dreaming Lips '37
Spy of Napoleon '36

Peter Bland (1983-)
Tearaway '87
Dangerous Orphans '86
Came a Hot Friday '85

Clara Blandick (1880-1962)
Umbrellas of Cherbourg '64
Cleo from 5 to 7 '61

Michael Blakemore (1928-)

Crime and Punishment '35
The Chess Player '27

Toto le Héros '91

Blandick (cont.)
Tomboy '40
The Wizard of Oz '39
Small Town Boy '37
The Girl from Missouri '34
The Bitter Tea of General Yen '33
Murder at Midnight '31
Romance '30

Sally Blane (1910-97)
Charlie Chan at Treasure Island '39
Fighting Mad '39
The Story of Alexander Graham Bell '39
Way Down South '39
No More Women '34
The Silver Streak '34
Heritage of the Desert '33
Night of Terror '33
Cross Examination '32
Law of the Sea '32
Local Badman '32
Phantom Express '32
Probation '32
When the West Was Young '32
Vagabond Lover '29

Mark Blankfield (1950-)
Dracula: Dead and Loving It '95
The Great American Sex Scandal '94
Robin Hood: Men in Tights '93
Angel 3: The Final Chapter '88
Frankenstein General Hospital '88
The Midnight Hour '86
Jack & the Beanstalk '83
Jekyll & Hyde... Together Again '82

Billy Blanks (1956-)
Shadow Warriors '97
Balance of Power '96
Expect No Mercy '95
Back in Action '94
Tough and Deadly '94
Showdown '93
TC 2000 '93
Talons of the Eagle '92
The King of the Kickboxers '91
The Last Boy Scout '91
Timebomb '91
Bloodfist '89

Arell Blanton
Assault of the Killer Bimbos '88
House of Terror '72
Wild Riders '71

Rosa Blasi (1972-)
The Grudge '04
Noriega: God's Favorite '00

Maddie (Madeleine) Blaustein (1960-)
Yu-Gi-Oh! The Movie: Pyramid of Light '04 (V)
Pokemon 3: The Movie '01 (V)

Charles Blavette (1902-67)
The Horror Chamber of Dr. Faustus '59
Toni '34

Hans-Christian Blech (1915-93)
Colonel Redl '84
The Wrong Move '78
Innocents with Dirty Hands '76

Jonah Blechman (1975-)
Luster '02
Treasure Island '99
Fall Time '94
This Boy's Life '93

Alexis Bledel (1981-)
Sisterhood of the Traveling Pants 2 '08
I'm Reed Fish '06
Sin City '05
Sisterhood of the Traveling Pants '05
Tuck Everlasting '02

Tempestt Bledsoe (1973-)
Johnny B. '00
Dream Date '93

Debra Blee (1961-)
Malibu Bikini Shop '86
Sloane '84
Savage Streets '83
Beach Girls '82

Yasmine Bleeth (1968-)
Coming Soon '99
Undercover Angel '99
BASEketball '98
Heaven or Vegas '98
It Came from the Sky '98
Baywatch the Movie: Forbidden Paradise '95

Moritz Bleibtreu (1971-)
The Walker '07
The Keeper: The Legend of Omar Khayyam '05
Munich '05
Agnes and His Brothers '04
The Experiment '01
Taking Sides '01
Invisible Circus '00
Run Lola Run '98

Claudiu Bleont (1959-)
Vlad '03
An Unforgettable Summer '94

Brian Blessed (1937-)
As You Like It '06
Day of Wrath '06
Alexander '04
Star Wars: Episode 1—The Phantom Menace '99
Tarzan '99 (V)
Tom Jones '98
The Bruce '96
Hamlet '96
Catherine the Great '95
Kidnapped '95
Chasing the Deer '94
Much Ado about Nothing '93
Back in the USSR '92
Freddie the Frog '92 (V)
Prisoner of Honor '91
Robin Hood: Prince of Thieves '91
Henry V '89
The Hound of the Baskervilles '83
Flash Gordon '80
King Arthur, the Young Warlord '75
Young Warlord '75
Man of La Mancha '72
Trojan Women '71

Jack Blessing (1951-)
Above Suspicion '00
The Last of His Tribe '92
Galaxy of Terror '81

Billy Bletcher (1894-1979)
Boss of Rawhide '44
God's Country and the Man '37

Brenda Blethyn (1946-)
Atonement '07
Introducing the Dwights '07
On a Clear Day '05
Pooh's Heffalump Movie '05 (V)
Pride and Prejudice '05
Beyond the Sea '04
A Way of Life '04
Lovely & Amazing '02
Pumpkin '02
The Sleeping Dictionary '02
Sonny '02
The Wild Thornberrys Movie '02 (V)
Saving Grace '00
Daddy & Them '99
RKO 281 '99
In the Winter Dark '98
Little Voice '98
Girls' Night '97
Music from Another Room '97
Secrets and Lies '95
The Buddha of Suburbia '92
A River Runs Through It '92
The Witches '90
Grown Ups '80

Corbin Bleu (1989-)
High School Musical 2 '07
Jump In! '07
High School Musical '06
Catch That Kid '04

Bill Blewitt
Johnny Frenchman '46
Nine Men '43
The Foreman Went to France '42

Jason Blicker
Earthstorm '06
Owning Mahowny '03
Crown Heights '02
Naked City: A Killer Christmas '98
African Journey '89
American Boyfriends '89

Bernard Blier (1916-89)
The Possessed '88
Buffet Froid '79
The Daydreamer '75
By the Blood of Others '73
The Tall Blond Man with One Black Shoe '72
Catch Me a Spy '71
Casanova '70 '65
The Organizer '64
Les Miserables '57
The Man in the Raincoat '57
Dedee d'Anvers '49
Passion for Life '48
Jenny Lamour '47

Ian Bliss
Stealth '05
The Matrix Reloaded '03
The Matrix Revolutions '03
Siam Sunset '99

Hunt Block (1955-)
The Dirty Dozen: The Fatal Mission '88
Secret Weapons '85

Larry Block (1943-)
Dead Man Out '89
High Stakes '89
After Hours '85

Dan Blocker (1928-72)
Lady in Cement '68
The Errand Boy '61

Dirk Blocker (1957-)
Inherit the Wind '99
Night of the Scarecrow '95
Bonanza: The Return '93
Prince of Darkness '87
Trouble in Mind '86

Michael Blodgett (1940-2007)
The Ultimate Thrill '74
The Velvet Vampire '71
Beyond the Valley of the Dolls '70
The Trip '67

Sebastian Blomberg (1972-)
Go for Zucker '05
What to Do in Case of Fire '02
Anatomy '00

Susan Blommaert (1947-)
United 93 '06
Henry Hill '00

Joan Blondell (1909-79)
The Baron '88
The Woman Inside '83
The Champ '79
The Rebels '79
The Glove '79
Grease '78
Opening Night '77
The Dead Don't Die '75
Death at Love House '75
Support Your Local Gunfighter '71
Stay Away, Joe '68
Waterhole Number 3 '67
The Cincinnati Kid '65
Angel Baby '61
Desk Set '57
This Could Be the Night '57
Will Success Spoil Rock Hunter? '57
The Opposite Sex '56
Christmas Eve '47
Nightmare Alley '47
Adventure '45
A Tree Grows in Brooklyn '45
Lady for a Night '42
Topper Returns '41
East Side of Heaven '39
Bullets or Ballots '38
Stand-in '37
Stage Struck '36
Three Men on a Horse '36
Dames '34
Footlight Parade '33
Gold Diggers of 1933 '33
Havana Widows '33
Three Broadway Girls '32
Three on a Match '32
Big Business Girl '31
Blonde Crazy '31
Illicit '31
Millie '31
Night Nurse '31
Public Enemy '31

Simone Blondell
Dr. Frankenstein's Castle of Freaks '74
Jungle Master '56

Moon Bloodgood (1975-)
Pathfinder '07
Eight Below '06

Anne Bloom
That's Adequate '90

Brian Bloom (1970-)
Across the Line '00
Blood Money '99
Knocking on Death's Door '99
Extramarital '98
The Sender '98
Escape from Atlantis '97
Melanie Darrow '97
Vampirella '96
At Home with the Webbers '94

Claire Bloom (1931-)
The Chatterley Affair '06
Imagining Argentina '04
The Lady in Question '99
What the Deaf Man Heard '98
Daylight '96
Mighty Aphrodite '95
A Village Affair '95
The Princess and the Goblin '94 (V)
Shadowlands '93
Brideshead Revisited '81
Clash of the Titans '81
Backstairs at the White House '79
Islands in the Stream '77
A Doll's House '73
The Illustrated Man '69
Charly '68
Soldier in Love '67
The Spy Who Came in from the Cold '65
The Haunting '63
The Wonderful World of the Brothers Grimm '62
Brainwashed '60
The Brothers Karamazov '58
The Buccaneer '58
Look Back in Anger '58
Alexander the Great '55
Richard III '55
Innocents in Paris '53
Limelight '52

John Bloom (1945-99)
Frozen Assets '92
The Great Outdoors '88
Harry and the Hendersons '87
Runaway Train '85
Bachelor Party '84
The Hills Have Eyes, Part 2 '84
The Dark '79
Brain of Blood '71
Dracula vs. Frankenstein '71
The Incredible Two-Headed Transplant '71

John (Joe Bob Briggs) Bloom (1953-)
Casino '95
Stephen King's The Stand '94
The Texas Chainsaw Massacre 2 '86

Lindsay Bloom (1952-)
French Quarter '78
Hughes & Harlow: Angels in Hell '77
Cover Girl Models '75

Orlando Bloom (1977-)
Pirates of the Caribbean: At World's End '07
Pirates of the Caribbean: Dead Man's Chest '06
Elizabethtown '05
Kingdom of Heaven '05
Haven '04
Troy '04
Lord of the Rings: The Return of the King '03
Ned Kelly '03
Pirates of the Caribbean: The Curse of the Black Pearl '03
Lord of the Rings: The Two Towers '02
Black Hawk Down '01
Lord of the Rings: The Fellowship of the Rings '01

Verna Bloom (1939-)
The Last Temptation of Christ '88
The Journey of Natty Gann '85
Honkytonk Man '82
Playing for Time '80
National Lampoon's Animal House '78
The Blue Knight '75
Where Have All the People Gone? '74
Badge 373 '73
High Plains Drifter '73
Hired Hand '71
Medium Cool '69

Eric Blore (1887-1959)
Fancy Pants '50
Love Happy '50
The Adventures of Ichabod and Mr. Toad '49 (V)
Romance on the High Seas '48
The Moon and Sixpence '43
The Shanghai Gesture '42
The Lady Eve '41
Lady Scarface '41
The Road to Zanzibar '41
Sullivan's Travels '41
Music in My Heart '40
Joy of Living '38
Swiss Miss '38
Quality Street '37
Shall We Dance '37
Ex-Mrs. Bradford '36
Swing Time '36
I Dream Too Much '35
I Live My Life '35
Top Hat '35
The Gay Divorcee '34
Flying Down to Rio '33

Roberts Blossom (1924-)
Balloon Farm '97
The Quick and the Dead '95
Doc Hollywood '91
Home Alone '90
Always '89
The Last Temptation of Christ '88
Candy Mountain '87
Vision Quest '85
Christine '84
Flashpoint '84
Reuben, Reuben '83
Johnny Belinda '82
Resurrection '80
Escape from Alcatraz '79
Citizens Band '77
Deranged '74
Slaughterhouse Five '72
The Hospital '71

Lisa Blount (1957-)
Box of Moonlight '96
Judicial Consent '94
Stalked '94
An American Story '92
Blind Fury '90
Femme Fatale '90
Great Balls of Fire '89
Nightflyers '87
Prince of Darkness '87
South of Reno '87
Radioactive Dreams '86
Cease Fire '85
Cut and Run '85
An Officer and a Gentleman '82
Dead and Buried '81
September 30, 1955 '77

Kurtis Blow (1959-)
The Show '95
Krush Groove '85

Marc Blucas (1972-)
Meet Dave '08
The Jane Austen Book Club '07
Thr3e '07
The Alamo '04
First Daughter '04
Prey for Rock and Roll '03
I Capture the Castle '03
Sunshine State '02
We Were Soldiers '02
Wes Craven Presents: They '02
Jay and Silent Bob Strike Back '01
Summer Catch '01

Ben Blue (1901-75)
Where Were You When the Lights Went Out? '68
The Russians Are Coming, the Russians Are Coming '66
Easy to Wed '46
Broadway Rhythm '44
Two Girls and a Sailor '44
For Me and My Gal '42
Panama Hattie '42
The Big Broadcast of 1938 '38
College Swing '38

Erin Blunt (1963-)
The Bad News Bears Go to Japan '78
The Bad News Bears in Breaking Training '77
The Bad News Bears '76

Emily Blunt (1983-)
Charlie Wilson's War '07
Dan in Real Life '07
The Jane Austen Book Club '07
Wind Chill '07
The Devil Wears Prada '06
Irresistible '06
Gideon's Daughter '06
My Summer of Love '05
Warrior Queen '03

Callum Blue (1977-)
The Princess Diaries 2: Royal Engagement '04
In Love and War '01

Monte Blue (1890-1963)
Silver River '48
Across the Pacific '42
Casablanca '42
Bad Man of Deadwood '41
Young Bill Hickok '40
Helltown '38
Prison Shadows '36
Desert Gold '36
Thunder Pass '37
Thunder Trail '37
A Million to One '37
Rootin' Tootin' Rhythm '38
Ride, Ranger, Ride '36
Song of the Gringo '36
Orphans of the Storm '21
Undersea Kingdom '36
The Man from Painted Post '17
The Lives of a Bengal Lancer '35
Social Error '35
Wagon Wheels '34
White Shadows in the South Seas '29
So This Is Paris '26
The Marriage Circle '24
Affairs of Anatol '21

Trevor Blumas (1984-)
Ice Princess '05
The Unsaid '01
The Year My Voice Broke '87

Alan Blumenfeld
The Wall '99

Ina Blum
The Crazysitter '94

Brady Bluhm (1983-)
Alone in the Woods '95

Ralph Bluemke
Invader '91
Kid and the Killers '74
Waterhole Number 3 '67

Mark Blum (1950-)
Worth Winning '89
Blind Date '87
The Presidio '88
Crocodile Dundee '86
Desperately Seeking Susan '85

Jack Blum
SnakeEater 2: The Drug Buster '89
Happy Birthday to Me '81

Ann Blyth (1928-)
The King's Thief '55
Kismet '55
Rose Marie '54
The Student Prince '54
All the Brothers Were Valiant '53
One Minute to Zero '52
The World in His Arms '52
The Great Caruso '51
Our Very Own '50
Mr. Peabody & the Mermaid '48
Brute Force '47
Mildred Pierce '45

Margaret Blye (1939-)
Silhouette '91
Little Darlings '80
Mischief '85

John Bluthal (1929-)
Dark City '97
The Fifth Element '97
Leapin' Leprechauns '95
Help! '65

Stanley Blystone (1894-1956)
Fighting Parson '35
Man of Action '33
The Fighting Legion '30

Betty Blythe (1893-1972)
They Were Expendable '45
Girls in Chains '43
Dawn on the Great Divide '42
The Wild Life '84
Having It All '82
Rich and Famous '81
East of Eden '80
Mr. Destiny '90
Fellow Traveler '89
War & Remembrance: The Final Chapter '89
Apartment Zero '88
Die Hard '88
Making Mr. Right '86
Supergirl '84

Graeme Blundell (1945-)
Idiot Box '97
Alvin Purple '73
Alvin Rides Again '74
Don's Party '76
Weekend of Shadows '77
The Odd Angry Shot '79
Doctors and Nurses '82

Benedick Blythe
The Apocalypse Watch '97
One Against the Wind '91

Domini Blythe (1947-2004)
Savage Messiah '02
Afterglow '97
Vampire Circus '71

Janus Blythe
Soldier's Fortune '91
The Hills Have Eyes, Part 2 '84
The Hills Have Eyes '77
Eaten Alive '76

Peter Blythe (1934-2004)
Carrington '95
A Challenge for Robin Hood '68
Frankenstein Created Woman '66

Bruce Boa (1930-2004)
The Neighbor '93
White Light '90

Lothaire Bluteau (1957-)
Disappearances '06
Snow Buddies '08 (V)
The Crowd '28
Dead Heat '02
The Healer '02
Urbania '00
Restless Spirits '99
Conquest '98
Bent '97
I Shot Andy Warhol '96
Nostromo '96
The Confessional '95
Other Voices, Other Rooms '95
The Silent Touch '94
Urban Crossfire '94
China Beach '88
Hamburger Hill '87
Black Robe '91
Jesus of Montreal '89
Orlando '92

Eleanor Boardman (1898-1991)
She Goes to War '29
The Crowd '28

Virginia True Boardman (1889-1971)
Brand of the Outlaws '36
Test of Donald Norton '26

Michael Boatman (1964-)
And Then Came Love '07
Woman, Thou Art Loosed '04
The Peacemaker '97
The Glass Shield '95
Urban Crossfire '94
China Beach '88
Hamburger Hill '87

Anne Bobby (1967-)
The Spectator '04
In Love and War '01
Beautiful Girls '96
Scott Turow's The Burden of Proof '92
Nightbreed '90
Baby of the Bend '04
Around the Bend '04

Jonah Bobo (1997-)
Zathura '05

Barbara Bobulova (1974-)
A Happy New Year '79

Hart Bochner (1956-)
Ring of Death '09
Inspector Clouseau '68
The Break Up '98
A Good Day to Die '95
Batman: Mask of the Phantasm '93 (V)
The Innocent '93
Mad at the Moon '92
Anywhere But Here '99
Urban Legends 2: Final Cut '00
Terminator 2: Judgment Day '91

Delia Boccardo (1948-)
A Woman at Her Window '77
Tentacles '83

Lloyd Bochner (1924-2005)
Morning Glory '93
Landslide '92
Naked Gun 2 1/2: The Smell of Fear '91
Millennium '89
Fine Gold '88
Crystal Heart '87
Mazes and Monsters '82
Louisiana '87
Terraces '77
It Seemed Like a Good Idea at the Time '75
Satan's School for Girls '73
Ulzana's Raid '72
They Call It Murder '71
The Dunwich Horror '68
The Detective '68
The Night Walker '64
Point Blank '67
Tony Rome '67
The Horse in the Gray Flannel Suit '68

Beatrice Boepple (1962-)
A Nightmare on Elm Street 5: Dream Child '89
Quarantine '89

Dirk Bogarde (1920-)
Daddy Nostalgia '90
The Vision '87
A Bridge Too Far '77
Providence '77
Permission To Kill '75
Night Flight from Moscow '73
Death in Venice '71
The Damned '69
Justine '69
Oh! What a Lovely War '69
The Fixer '68
Sebastian '68
Accident '67
Modesty Blaise '66
Darling '65
King and Country '64
Doctor in Distress '63
I Could Go on Singing '63
The Servant '63
Damn the Defiant! '62
Victim '61
A Tale of Two Cities '58
Doctor at Large '57
The Spanish Gardener '57
Doctor at Sea '55

Earl Boen (1945-)
Friend of the Family 2 '96
The Portrait '99
The Quickie '01
East-West '99
Brother '97
Prisoner of the Mountains '96
Nutty Professor 2: The Klumps '00
Within the Rock '96
Norma Jean and Marilyn '95
Peeping Tom '60
Unnatural '52
Clifford's Really Big Movie '04 (V)
Fox and His Friends '75
Brothers Grimm '62
The Wonderful World of the Brothers Grimm '62
Mother Kusters Goes to Heaven '76

Karl-Heinz Boehm (1928-)
Conflict '45
The Big Sleep '46
The Two Mrs. Carrolls '47
Passage to Marseilles '44
To Have & Have Not '44
Action in the North Atlantic '43
All Through the Night '42
Casablanca '42
The Maltese Falcon '41
High Sierra '41
They Drive by Night '40
Virginia City '40
Dark Victory '39
Oklahoma Kid '39
The Roaring Twenties '39
Amazing Dr. Clitterhouse '38
Angels with Dirty Faces '38
Bullets or Ballots '36
The Black Legion '37
Dead End '37
Kid Galahad '37
Marked Woman '37
San Quentin '37
Stand-In '37
Petrified Forest '36
Midnight '34
Three on a Match '32
Up the River '30

Sergei Bodrov, Jr. (1971-2002)
Sisters '01
Brother 2 '00
Brother '97
Prisoner of the Mountains '96

Jenna Bodnar
Amanac of Fall '85

Erika Bodnar (1948-)
Amanac of Fall '85

Wolfgang Bodison (1966-)
Freeway '95
A Few Good Men '92

Jose Bodalo (1916-85)
Garringo '69
Django '68

Martin Boddey (1908-75)
Black Glove '54
Valley of the Eagles '51

Robert Bockstael
Snap Decision '01
Nero Wolfe Mystery: A Woman in Question '99
Invasion! '99
All I Wanna Do '98

Humphrey Bogart (1899-1957)
The Harder They Fall '56
The Desperate Hours '55
The Left Hand of God '55
We're No Angels '55
The Caine Mutiny '54
The Barefoot Contessa '54
Sabrina '54
Battle Circus '53
Beat the Devil '53
The African Queen '51
The Enforcer '51
Sirocco '51
Chain Lightning '50
In a Lonely Place '50
Knock on Any Door '49
Tokyo Joe '49
Key Largo '48
Treasure of the Sierra Madre '48
Dead Reckoning '47
Dark Passage '47
Conflict '45
The Big Sleep '46
The Two Mrs. Carrolls '47
Passage to Marseilles '44
To Have & Have Not '44
Action in the North Atlantic '43
All Through the Night '42
Casablanca '42
The Maltese Falcon '41
High Sierra '41
They Drive by Night '40
Virginia City '40
Dark Victory '39
Oklahoma Kid '39
The Roaring Twenties '39
Amazing Dr. Clitterhouse '38
Angels with Dirty Faces '38
Bullets or Ballots '36
The Black Legion '37
Dead End '37
Kid Galahad '37
Marked Woman '37
San Quentin '37
Stand-In '37
Petrified Forest '36
Midnight '34
Three on a Match '32
Up the River '30

Stephen Bogardus (1954-)
States of Control '98
Love! Valour! Compassion! '96

Elizabeth Bogush
Believers '07
Jam '06

Hark Bohm (1939-)
Underground '95
The Promise '94
Wyatt Earp '94
Movie '95

Karlheinz Bohm
See Karl-Heinz Boehm
Carbide and Screel '63
Minna von Barnhelm or The Soldier's Fortune '62
On the Sunny Side '62
The Hairy Ape '44

Ian Bohen (1976-)
Eric Bogosian '91
Young Hercules '97
Frankenstein Sings... The Movie '95

Roman Bohnen (1894-1949)
Open Secret '48
Song of Love '47
The Best Years of Our Lives '46

Marita Bonne (1939-)

Corinne Bohrer (1959-)
Big Eden '00
Kisses in the Dark '97
Star Kid '97
Revenge of the Nerds 4: Nerds in Love '94
Dead Solid Perfect '88
Vice Versa '88
Stewardess School '86

Richard Bohringer (1942-)
Crime Spree '03
Transfixed '01
The Accompanist '93
Baijo '93
The Cook, the Thief, His Wife & Her Lover '90
Le Grand Chemin '87
L'Addition '85
Peril '85
Subway '85
Diva '82
I Married a Dead Man '82

Romane Bohringer (1974-)
He Died With a Felafel in His Hand '01
The Life Is Alive '01
The Chambermaid on the Titanic '97
Portraits Chinois '96
Total Eclipse '95
Mina Tannenbaum '93
Les Nuits Fauves '92

Jean Boht (1936-)
Heaven's a Drag '94

Peter Bogdanovich (1939-)
Dedication '07
Infamous '06
Out of Order '03
Festival at Cannes '02
The Independent '00
Rated X '00
Coming Soon '99
Mr. Jealousy '98
Bella Mafia '97
Highball '97
Sant Jack '79
Targets '68

Eric Bogosian (1953-)
Blade: Trinity '04
Heights '04
King of the Corner '04
Wonderland '03
Ararat '02
Igby Goes Down '02
Blonde '01
Gossip '99
A Bright Shining Le '98
Deconstructing Harry '97
Office Killer '97
Beavis and Butt-Head Do America '96 (V)
Under Siege 2: Dark Territory '95
Witch Hunt '94
Naked in New York '93
Sex, Drugs, Rock & Roll: Eric Bogosian '91
Last Flight Out: A True Story '90
Suffering Bastards '90
Special Effects '85
Talk Radio '88
Eastside '99
Tweek City '05
Under Siege 2: Dark

Karlheinz Bohm
Cast a Dark Shadow '55
The Sea Shall Not Have Them '55
Simba '55
The Sleeping Tiger '54
Doctor in the House '53
The Blue Lamp '49
The Woman in Question '49

Roman Bohnen
Charlie's Angels: Full Throttle '03

Arthur's Hallowed Ground '84

Samuel Boidin
Flanders '06

Curt Bois (1901-91)
The Life of Jesus '96
Wings of Desire '88
The Boat Is Full '81
Caught '49
Blue, White and Perfect '42
Casablanca '42
The Tuttles of Tahiti '42
That Night in Rio '41
Bitter Sweet '40
Boom Town '40
The Lady in Question '40
The Hunchback of Notre Dame '39
Amazing Dr. Clitterhouse '38
The Great Waltz '38

Christine Boisson (1957-)
The Truth About Charlie '02
Pas Tres Catholique '93
Sorceress '88
Unsettled Land '88
Identification of a Woman '82

James Bolam (1938-)
Stella Does Tricks '96
The Maze '85
In Celebration '75
Dressed for Death '74
Crucible of Terror '72
A Kind of Loving '62
The Loneliness of the Long Distance Runner '62

Eamon Boland (1947-)
All the King's Men '99
Business As Usual '88

Joanne Boland (1975-)
George A. Romero's Land of the Dead '05
Brave New Girl '04

Mary Boland (1880-1965)
Julia Misbehaves '48
Nothing But Trouble '44
New Moon '40
One Night in the Tropics '40
Pride and Prejudice '40
The Women '39
Ruggles of Red Gap '35
Six of a Kind '34
Personal Maid '31

Philip Daniel Bolden (1995-)
Are We Done Yet? '07
Are We There Yet? '05
Johnson Family Vacation '04

John Boles (1895-1969)
Thousands Cheer '43
Sinners in Paradise '38
Stella Dallas '37
Craig's Wife '36
Curly Top '35
The Littlest Rebel '35
Stand Up and Cheer '34
Frankenstein '31
King of Jazz '30

Ray Bolger (1904-87)
That's Dancing! '85
For Heaven's Sake '79
The Runner Stumbles '79
Babes in Toyland '61
April in Paris '52
Look for the Silver Lining '49
Sunny '41
The Harvey Girls '46
Stage Door Canteen '43
Four Jacks and a Jill '41
The Wizard of Oz '39
Rosalie '38
Sweethearts '38
The Great Ziegfeld '36

Sarah Bolger (1991-)
The Spiderwick Chronicles '08
Alex Rider: Operation Stormbreaker '06
In America '02
A Love Divided '01

Florinda Bolkan (1941-)
Collector's Item '89
Some Girls '88
Acqua e Sapone '83
The Day That Shook the World '78
The Word '78
Royal Flash '75
Master Touch '74
Primal Impulse '74
Don't Torture a Duckling '72
The Last Valley '71
A Lizard in a Woman's Skin '71
Black Lemons '70
Ring of Death '69

Tiffany Bolling (1947-)
Ecstasy '84
Kingdom of the Spiders '77
The Centerfold Girls '74
Wild Party '74
Bonnie's Kids '73

Ryan Bollman (1972-)
No Vacancy '99
The NeverEnding Story 3: Escape from Fantasia '94
Children of the Corn 2: The Final Sacrifice '92

Joseph Bologna (1938-)
Ice Age: The Meltdown '06 (V)
The Boynton Beach Club '05
Players '03
Big Daddy '99
National Lampoon's The Don's Analyst '97
Heaven Before I Die '96
Love Is All There Is '96
Danger of Love '95
Revenge of the Nerds 4: Nerds in Love '94
Citizen Cohn '92
Deadly Rivals '92
Jersey Girl '92
My Favorite Year '82
Chapter Two '79
Tom Between Two Lovers '79
The Big Bus '76
Cops and Robbers '73
Honor Thy Father '73

Christopher Bolton
Killing Moon '00
City Boy '93
Ordeal in the Arctic '93

Jon Bon Jovi (1962-)
CryWolf '05
John Carpenter Presents Vampires: Los Muertos '02
Pay It Forward '00
U-571 '00
No Looking Back '98
Row Your Boat '98
Homegrown '97
Little City '97
The Leading Man '96
Moonlight and Valentino '95
Young Guns 2 '90

Ronaldo Bonacchi (1950-)
Orchestra Rehearsal '78
The Wide Blue Road '57

Paolo Bonacelli (1939-)
The Stendahl Syndrome '95
Francesco '93
Mille Bolle Blu '93
Johnny Stecchino '92
Night on Earth '91
Henry IV '85
Caligula '80
Christ Stopped at Eboli '79
Salo, or the 120 Days of Sodom '75
Baker's Hawk '76
Charlotte's Web '73 (V)

Danny Bonaduce (1959-)
America's Deadliest Home Video '91
H.O.T.S. '79

Louie Bonanno (1961-)
Student Affairs '88
Night of the Living Babes '87
Wimps '87

Fortunio Bonanova (1895-1969)
An Affair to Remember '57
Double Indemnity '44
Ali Baba and the Forty Thieves '43
Five Graves to Cairo '43
For Whom the Bell Tolls '43
The Black Swan '42

Ivan Bonar (1924-88)
The Haunting Passion '83
MacArthur '77

Derek Bond (1920-2006)
When Eight Bells Toll '71
The Hand '60
Black Tide '58
Rogue's Yarn '56
Svengali '55
The Stranger from Venus '54
Tony Draws a Horse '51
The Weaker Sex '49
Scott of the Antarctic '48
Inheritance '47
Nicholas Nickleby '46

James Bond, III
Def by Temptation '90
School Daze '88
Go Tell It on the Mountain '84
The Fish that Saved Pittsburgh '79

Lillian Bond (1908-91)
Man in the Attic '53
The Westerner '40
China Seas '35
The Old Dark House '32

Renee Bond (1950-96)
Class Reunion '72
Please Don't Eat My Mother '72

Samantha Bond (1962-)
P.D. James: The Murder Room '04
Yes '04
Die Another Day '02
The World Is Not Enough '99
Emma '97
Tomorrow Never Dies '97
Goldeneye '95
Catherine Cookson's The Black Candle '92
Tryst '94
To Die For 2: Son of Darkness '91
L.A. Gangs Rising '89
Picasso Trigger '89
To Die For '89
Magdalene '88
The Prey '80
Gas Pump Girls '79
H.O.T.S. '79
Massacre at Central High '76

Sudie Bond (1928-84)
I Am the Cheese '83
Trumps '83
Come Back to the Five & Dime Jimmy Dean, Jimmy Dean '82
Where the Lilies Bloom '74
Tomorrow '72
Fury on Wheels '71

Ward Bond (1903-60)
Alias Jesse James '59
Rio Bravo '59
Wings of Eagles '57
Dakota Incident '56
The Searchers '56
The Long Gray Line '55
A Man Alone '55
Mister Roberts '55
Blowing Wild '54
Gypsy Colt '54
Hondo '53
Johnny Guitar '53
The Quiet Man '52
Great Missouri Raid '51
On Dangerous Ground '51
Kiss Tomorrow Goodbye '50
Only the Valiant '50
Riding High '50
Wagon Master '50
Fort Apache '48
The Fugitive '48
Three Godfathers '48
The Time of Your Life '48
Unconquered '47
Canyon Passage '46
It's a Wonderful Life '46
My Darling Clementine '46
Dakota '45
They Were Expendable '45
A Guy Named Joe '44
Tall in the Saddle '44
Hello, Frisco, Hello '43
Hitler: Dead or Alive '42
The Falcon Takes Over '42
The Fighting Sullivans '42
Gentleman Jim '42
The Maltese Falcon '41
Sergeant York '41
The Shepherd of the Hills '41
Wheel of Fortune '41
Kit Carson '40
Drums Along the Mohawk '39
Gone with the Wind '39
Oklahoma Kid '39
Young Mr. Lincoln '39
Waterfront '39
Amazing Dr. Clitterhouse '38
Born to Be Wild '38
Bringing Up Baby '38
Hawaii Calls '38
Mr. Moto's Gamble '38
Prison Break '38
Park Avenue Logger '37
You Only Live Once '37
Without Orders '36
The Crimson Trail '35
Devil Dogs of the Air '35
Fighting Shadows '35
It Happened One Night '34
Heroes for Sale '33
Hello Trouble '32
White Eagle '32
Big Trail '30
Sister Kenny '46
Back to Bataan '45
The Southerner '45
Watch on the Rhine '43
Penny Serenade '41
The Shepherd of the Hills '41
Our Town '40
Remember the Night '40
Mr. Smith Goes to Washington '39
On Borrowed Time '39
Of Human Hearts '38
The Sisters '38
Vivacious Lady '38
The Invisible Ray '36
The Moon's Our Home '36
The Trail of the Lonesome Pine '36
The Good Fairy '35
Two Alone '34
Finishing School '33
Rain '32
Street Scene '31

De'Aundre Bonds (1976-)
Lockdown '00
Three Strikes '00
The Wood '99
Get On the Bus '96
Sunset Park '96
Tales from the Hood '95

Christopher Bondy
The Jesse Ventura Story '99
The Dark '94
Deadly Surveillance '91

Peter Bonerz (1938-)
Man on the Moon '99
Your Place or Mine '83
Serial '80
The Bastard '78
How to Break Up a Happy Divorce '76
Catch-22 '70
Medium Cool '69
A Session with The Committee '68

Ken Bones
Bellman and True '88
Jack the Ripper '88

Charles Bonet
Way of the Black Dragon '81
Death Promise '78

Lisa Bonet (1967-)
Biker Boyz '03
The Lathe of Heaven '02
High Fidelity '00
Enemy of the State '98
Dead Connection '94
New Eden '94
Bank Robber '93
Final Combination '93
Angel Heart '87

Nai Bonet (1940-)
Gangsters '79
Nocturna '79
Fairy Tales '76
Soul Hustler '76
Devil's Angels '67

Sergei Bondarchuk (1920-94)
Battle of Neretva '69
War and Peace '68
A Summer to Remember '61
Era Notte a Roma '60

Beulah Bondi (1892-1981)
The Wonderful World of the Brothers Grimm '62
A Summer Place '59
Unholy Wife '57
Back from Eternity '56
Latin Lovers '53
Lone Star '52
Baron of Arizona '51
So Dear to My Heart '49
The Snake Pit '48
Breakfast in Hollywood '46
It's a Wonderful Life '46

Massimo Bonetti (1954-)
The Story of Boys & Girls '91
Terranova '91
Night Sun '90
Kaos '85
The Night of the Shooting Stars '82

Crispin Bonham Carter (1969-)
Wuthering Heights '98
Catherine Cookson's The Rag Nymph '96
Pride and Prejudice '95

Helena Bonham-Carter (1966-)
Harry Potter and the Order of the Phoenix '07
Sweeney Todd: The Demon Barber of Fleet Street '07
Charlie and the Chocolate Factory '05
Conversations with Other Women '05
Tim Burton's Corpse Bride '05 (V)
Wallace & Gromit: The Curse of the Were-Rabbit '05 (V)
Big Fish '03
Live from Baghdad '03
The Heart of Me '02
Till Human Voices Wake Us '02
Novocaine '01
Planet of the Apes '01
Fight Club '99
Merlin '98
Sweet Revenge '98
The Theory of Flight '98
A Merry War '97
The Wings of the Dove '97
Portraits Chinois '96
Twelfth Night '96
Margaret's Museum '95
Mighty Aphrodite '95
Mary Shelley's Frankenstein '94
A Dark Adapted Eye '93
Francesco '93
Howard's End '92
Where Angels Fear to Tread '91
Hamlet '90
Getting It Right '89
Maurice '87
The Vision '87
A Room with a View '86
Lady Jane '85

Alessio Boni (1966-)
Don't Tell '05
Best of Youth '03

Gabrielle Boni (1985-)
Time at the Top '99
Little Men '98
Daddy's Girl '96

Luisella Boni (1935-)
The Fury of Hercules '61
Samson '61

Evan Bonifant (1985-)
Blues Brothers 2000 '98
Breakout '98
3 Ninjas Kick Back '94

Paul Bonifas (1902-75)
The Train '65
The Foreman Went to France '42

Jacques Bonnaffe (1958-)
Cote d'Azur '05
Lemming '05
Va Savoir '01
Jeanne and the Perfect Guy '98
Venus Beauty Institute '98
First Name: Carmen '83

Sandrine Bonnaire (1967-)
Intimate Strangers '04
East-West '99
Circle of Passion '97
La Ceremonie '95
Jeanne la Pucelle '94
The Plague '92
Monsieur Hire '89
Under Satan's Sun '87
La Puritaine '86
Police '85
Vagabond '85
A Nos Amours '84

Lee Bonnell (1918-86)
The Navy Comes Through '42
Look Who's Laughing '41

Vivian Bonnell (1924-2003)
Christmas in Connecticut '92
The Josephine Baker Story '90

Beverly Bonner
Basket Case 2 '90
Frankenhooker '90
Brain Damage '88
Basket Case '82

Bill Bonner
Outlaw Riders '72
Satan's Sadists '69

Frank Bonner (1942-)
Shut Up and Kiss Me '05
You Can't Hurry Love '88
The Colony '95
Equinox '71

Priscilla Bonner (1898-1996)
Long Pants '27
Charley's Aunt '25

Tony Bonner (1943-)
Joyeux Noel '05
Dead Sleep '91
Quigley Down Under '90
The Lighthorsemen '87
Money Movers '78
Alternative '76
Inn of the Damned '74

Dina Bonnevie (1961-)
American Adobo '02
Fight for Us '89

Maria Bonnevie (1973-)
I Am David '04
Insomnia '97
Reconstruction '03

Hugh Bonneville (1963-)
Asylum '05
Underclassman '05
Conspiracy of Silence '03
Daniel Deronda '02
The Gathering Storm '02
Iris '01
Notting Hill '99
Mansfield Park '99
The Emperor's New Clothes '01
Tipping the Velvet '02
The Man Who Made Husbands Jealous '98
Mosley '98
Stalag Luft '93
The Vals '85
Dirty Laundry '87
Hairspray '88
Troll '86

Celine Bonnier (1965-)
Human Trafficking '05
Far Side of the Moon '03
The Assignment '97
A Wind from Wyoming '94

Sonny Bono (1935-98)
Under the Boardwalk '89
Airplane 2: The Sequel '82
Balboa '82
Escape to Athena '79
Good Times '67
Murder on Flight 502 '75

Deanna (Dee) Booher (1951-)
Brain Smasher... A Love Story '93

Brian Bonsall (1981-)
Father and Scout '94
Lily in Winter '94
Blank Check '93
Father Hood '93
Desperate McLives '92
Mikey '92

Charley Boorman (1966-)
The Patriot '00
Smile '05
Dirty Dancing: Havana Nights '04
Sleepover '04
Blue Crush '02
Along Came a Spider '01
Hope and Glory '87
The Serpent's Kiss '97
Picture Windows '95
The Emerald Forest '85
Excalibur '81
Deliverance '72
Hearts in Atlantis '01
Riding in Cars with Boys '01

Katrine Boorman (1958-)
Camille Claudel '89

The Iceman Cometh '73
Up the Down Staircase '67
A Fine Madness '66
Joy House '64

Elayne Boosler (1952-)
Mother Goose Rock 'n' Rhyme '90

Dany Boon (1966-)
Meatballs 2 '84
Son of God's Country '48

Adrian Booth (1918-)
Under Colorado Skies '47
Daughter of Don Q '46
The Valet '06
My Best Friend '06

Debbie Boone (1956-)
Treehouse Hostage '99
Hollywood Safari '96

Mark Boone, Jr. (1955-)
30 Days of Night '07
The Legend of Lucy Keyes '06
Lonesome Jim '06
Wristcutters: A Love Story '06
Batman Begins '05
Dead Birds '04
Frankenfish '04
2 Fast 2 Furious '03
Animal Factory '00
Memento '00
Buddy Boy '99
The Treat '98
The General's Daughter '99
John Carpenter's Vampires '97
Rosewood '96
Tree's Lounge '96
Fever '91

Pat Boone (1934-)
Roger & Me '89
The Cross & the Switchblade '72
The Greatest Story Ever Told '65
Goodbye Charlie '64
State Fair '62
Journey to the Center of the Earth '59

Richard Boone (1916-81)
The Bushido Blade '80
Winter Kills '79
The Big Sleep '78
The Hobbit '78 (V)
The Shootist '76
Against a Crooked Sky '75
God's Gun '75
Big Jake '71
Madron '70
The Arrangement '69
The Night of the Following Day '69
Hombre '67
The War Lord '65
Rio Conchos '64
The Alamo '60
The Tall T '57
I Bury the Living '58
Away All Boats '56
Dragnet '54
Ten Wanted Men '54
Beneath the 12-Mile Reef '53
The Robe '53
The Halls of Montezuma '50

Connie Booth (1941-)
The Buccaneers '95
Leon the Pig Farmer '93
The Strange Case of the End of Civilization As We Know It '93
American Friends '91
Hawks '89
Monty Python and the Holy Grail '75
Romance with a Double Bass '74
And Now for Something Completely Different '72
John Cleese on How to Irritate People '68

Connie Booth (1941-)

James Booth (1927-2005)
Trader Horn '31
Keeping Mum '05
American Ninja 4: The Annihilation '91
Bad Guys '86
Programmed to Kill '86
Pray for Death '85
Zorro, the Gay Blade '81
That'll Be the Day '73
Rentadick '72
Revenge '71
Darker than Amber '70
Man Who Had Power Over Women '70
Robbery '67
Zulu '64
90°in the Shade '65

Edwina Booth (1909-91)
The Last of the Mohicans '32

Mika Boorem (1987-)
Winter Kills '79
Zorro, the Gay Blade '81
Hotline '82
I'm with Lucy '02
Valentine '01
These Girls '05
The Bliss of Mrs. Blossom '68
Day '69
The Trials of Oscar Wilde '60

Karin (Karen, Katharine) Booth (1919-92)
Beloved Infidel '59
Tobor the Great '54
My Foolish Heart '49

Lindy Booth (1979-)
CryWolf '05
Dawn of the Dead '04
Hollywood North '03
Wrong Turn '03
American Psycho 2: All American Girl '02
The Skulls 2 '02

Shirley Booth (1907-92)
Hot Spell '58
The Matchmaker '58
Main Street to Broadway '53
Come Back, Little Sheba '52

Powers Boothe (1949-)
The Final Season '07
Sin City '05
Frailty '02
Attila '01
Men of Honor '00
Joan of Arc '99
True Women '97
U-Turn '97
The Spree '96

Nelly Borgeaud (1931-2004)
Tattoo '81
I Take This Oath '40
Melody Ranch '40
Kid Galahad '37
San Quentin '37
The Corsican Brothers '42
I Married an Angel '42
Honky Tonk '41
Dr. Christian Meets the Women '40

Rikke Borge
Amityville 3: The Demon '83

Nick Boraine
Cape of Good Hope '04
Queen's Messenger II '01
A Cry for Love '80
The Guyana Tragedy: The Story of Jim Jones '80
Skag '80

Caterina Boratto (1916-)
Salo, or the 120 Days of Sodom '75
8 1/2 '63

Cornell Borchers (1925-)
Istanbul '57
The Big Lift '50

David Boreanaz (1971-)
Mr. Fix It '06
'05
These Girls '05

Lynn Borden (1939-)
Hellhole '85
This Is a Hijack '73
Frogs '72

Rene Borden
Kid Courageous '35
Western Justice '35

Carla Borelli (1942-)
Charlotte Forten's Mission: Experiment in Freedom '85

Veda Ann Borg (1915-73)
The Alamo '60
Wings of Eagles '57
Guys and Dolls '55
I'll Cry Tomorrow '55
Love Me or Leave Me '55
Big Jim McLain '52
Rider from Tucson '50
The Bachelor and the Bobby-Soxer '47
Big Town '47
Blonde Savage '47
Accomplice '46
Fog Island '45
Treasure of Fear '45
The Falcon in Hollywood '44
Marked Trails '44
Isle of Forgotten Sins '43
Revenge of the Zombies '43

Nixon '95
Sudden Death '95
Tombstone '93
Rapid Fire '92
Wildcard '92
Blue Sky '91
By Dawn's Early Light '89
Extreme Prejudice '87
Into the Homeland '87
A Breed Apart '84
Red Dawn '84
Southern Comfort '81
Plutonium Incident '82
Cruising '80
'95 (V)
Mistress '91
Laser Mission '90
Moving Target '89
The Opponent '89
Adios, Sabata '71
Find Me Guilty '06

Ernest Borgnine (1917-)
Strange Wilderness '08
The Long Ride Home '01
BASEketball '98
Small Soldiers '98 (V)
Gattaca '97
McHale's Navy '97
All Dogs Go to Heaven 2 '96
Codename: Wildgeese '84
Love Leads the Way '84
Young Warriors '83
Deadly Blessing '81
Escape from New York '81
High Risk '81
Super Fuzz '81
When Time Ran Out '80
All Quiet on the Western Front '79
Fire '77
The Greatest '77
Jesus of Nazareth '77
Future Cop '76
Love by Appointment '76
Devil's Rain '75
Law and Disorder '74
Vengeance Is Mine '74
Emperor of the North Pole '73
The Poseidon Adventure '72
Hannie Caulder '72
Willard '71
The Adventurers '70
The Wild Bunch '69
Suppose They Gave a War and Nobody Came? '70
Ice Station Zebra '68
Chuka '67
The Dirty Dozen '67
The Oscar '66
The Flight of the Phoenix '65

Paul Borghese
Flight of the Innocent '93
Thundersquad '85
Private Parts '96

Sal Borgese (1937-)
Dragon Storm '04
Epoch: Evolution '03
Interceptor Force '99
Warlock 3: The End of Innocence '99

Angel Boris (1974-)
Bio Hazard '85

Carroll Borland (1914-94)
Desperate Crimes '93
Mille Bolle Blu '93

Nicoletta Boris
Mark of the Vampire '35

Matt Borlenghi
Strange Wilderness '08
Laser Mission '90

Katherine Borowitz
The Man Who Wasn't There '01
Illuminata '98
Mac '93

Roscoe Born (1950-)
The American Scream '80s
Haunting of Sarah Hardy '89

Jesse Borrego (1962-)
The Maldonado Miracle '03
The Crew '00
Con Air '97
Retroactive '97
Fellow Traveler '89

Dieter Borsche (1909-82)
The Mad Executioners '65
The Phantom of Soho '64
The Black Abbot '63
Dead Eyes of London '61

Alex Borstein (1972-)
Catwoman '04
Good Night, and Good Luck '05
Seeing Other People '04
The Lizzie McGuire Movie '03
Dawg '02

Rangers: The Movie '95

Bobby Borriello
Night Is My Future '47
The Phantom Chariot '20

Bobby Boriello
A Walk on the Moon '99
Enemy of the State '98

Angel Boris (1974-)
Kare's Addiction '99

Alexandre Borges (1966-)
Bossa Nova '99
Foreign Land '95

Hilda Borgstrom
There '01
Mi Vida Loca '94
Blood in ... Blood Out: Bound by Honor '93

Jason Bortz (1970-)
The Lookout '07
Little Man '06

Jean-Mark Bory (1934-2001)
Le Repos du Guerrier '62
Love on a Pillow '62

Frank Borzage (1893-1962)
A Mormon Maid '17
The Wrath of the Gods '14

John Yong Bosch (1976-)
Devon's Ghost: Legend of the Bloody Boy '05
Turbo: A Power Rangers Movie '96
Mighty Morphin Power Rangers: The Movie '95

Philip Bosco (1930-)
The Savages '07
Abandon '02
Cupid & Cate '00
Kate & Leopold '01

Roscoe Born (1950-)
Tecumseh: The Last Warrior '95
I Like It Like That '94
The Lovers '59
RoGoPaG '62
Movie '96

Matt Borlenghi
Bio Hazard '85

Katherine Borowitz
Bank Shot '74
Special Delivery '76
Devil Times Five '74
Rock-a-Doodle '92 (V)
The Other Side of Midnight '77

Sorrell Booke (1930-94)

Shaft '00
Wonder Boys '00
Bonanno: A Godfather's Story '99
Borough of Kings '98
Moon over Broadway '98
Critical Care '97
Deconstructing Harry '97
My Best Friend's Wedding '97
The First Wives Club '96
It Takes Two '95
Against the Wall '94
Angie '94
Milk Money '94
Nobody's Fool '94
Safe Passage '94
Shadows and Fog '92
Straight Talk '92
F/X 2: The Deadly Art of Illusion '91
The Return of Eliot Ness '91
True Colors '91
Blue Steel '90
Quick Change '90
The Dream Team '89
Another Woman '88
Working Girl '88
Suspect '87
Three Men and a Baby '87
Children of a Lesser God '86
The Money Pit '86
Heaven Help Us '85
Walls of Glass '85
The Pope of Greenwich Village '84

Lucia Bose (1931-)
Harem '99
Lumiere '76
The Legend of Blood Castle '72
The Lady Without Camellias '53
Story of a Love Affair '50

Miguel Bose (1956-)
Queen Margot '94
High Heels '91

Andrea Bosic (1919-)
Hornet's Nest '70
Pirates of the Seven Seas '62
Maciste in Hell '60

Todd Bosley (1984-)
Lloyd '00
Treehouse Hostage '99
Jack '96

Tom Bosley (1927-)
Hidden Places '06
Christmas at Water's Edge '04
Fire and Rain '89
Wicked Stepmother '89
Million Dollar Mystery '87
The Jesse Owens Story '84
O'Hara's Wife '82
For the Love of It '80
The Rebels '79
The Triangle Factory Fire Scandal '79
The Bastard '78
Gus '76
Death Cruise '74
The Streets of San Francisco '72
Night Gallery '69
The Secret War of Harry Frigg '68
Yours, Mine & Ours '68
Bang Bang Kid '67
Divorce American Style '67
The World of Henry Orient '64
Love with the Proper Stranger '63

Simon Bossell
Better Than Sex '00
Cut '00
Aberration '97
Hotel de Love '96

Barbara Bosson (1939-)
The Great American Sex Scandal '94
Little Sweetheart '90

The Last Starfighter '84
Mame '74
A Session with The Committee '68

Barry Bostwick (1945-)
Evening '07
Nancy Drew '07
Tales from a Parallel Universe: I Worship His Shadow '97
The Secret Agent Club '96
Spy Hard '96
In the Heat of Passion 2: Unfaithful '94
Project Metalbeast: DNA Overload '94
The Secretary '94
800 Leagues Down the Amazon '93
Praying Mantis '93
Russian Roulette '93
Weekend at Bernie's 2 '93
War & Remembrance '88
George Washington: The Forging of a Nation '86
Jailbait: Betrayed By Innocence '86
George Washington '84
A Woman of Substance '84
Megaforce '82
Red Flag: The Ultimate Game '81
Scruples '80
Murder by Natural Causes '79
Movie Movie '78
The Rocky Horror Picture Show '75
Fantastic Planet '73 (V)
Road Movie '72

Jackson Bostwick
A Matter of Honor '95
Escape from DS-3 '81

Charles Boswell
Dangerous Passion '95
Kiss Me a Killer '91

Brian Bosworth (1965-)
The Longest Yard '05
Mach 2 '00
Back in Business '96
Black Out '96
Virus '96
One Man's Justice '95
Stone Cold '91

Hobart Bosworth (1867-1943)
King of the Sierras '38
Rollin' Plains '38
The Dark Hour '36
The Crusades '35
Steamboat Round the Bend '35
The Last of the Mohicans '32
Phantom Express '32
Abraham Lincoln '30
Dubarry '30
Annapolis '28
Hangman's House '28
A Woman of Affairs '28
My Best Girl '27
The Nervous Wreck '26
Spangles '26

Kate (Catherine) Bosworth (1983-)
Superman Returns '06
Bee Season '05
Beyond the Sea '04
Win a Date with Tad Hamilton! '04
Wonderland '03
Blue Crush '02
The Rules of Attraction '02
Remember the Titans '00
The Horse Whisperer '97

Wade Boteler (1888-1943)
The Green Hornet '39
Southward Ho! '39
The Mandarin Mystery '37
You Only Live Once '37
Come on Danger! '32
Big News '29
Let 'er Go Gallegher '28

Niki Botelho
No Turning Back '01
Nancy Drew '07
Tales from a Parallel Universe: I Worship His Shadow '97

Rodrigo Botero
True Friends '98

Sara Botsford (1951-)
The Fog '05
Jumpin' Jack Flash '86
The Gunrunner '84
By Design '82
Deadly Eyes '82
Murder by Phone '82
Still of the Night '82

Juan Diego Botto (1975-)
The Dancer Upstairs '02
Broken Silence '01
Martin (Hache) '97
If They Tell You I Fell '89

Maria Botto (1974-)
Broken Silence '01
Jealousy '99

Benjamin Bottoms (1960-)
A Shining Season '79
Stalk the Wild Child '76

Joseph Bottoms (1954-)
Liar's Edge '92
Treacherous Crossing '92
Inner Sanctum '91
Born to Race '88
Open House '86
Celebrity '85
Blind Date '84
Surfacing '84
The Sins of Dorian Gray '82
Intruder Within '81
King of the Mountain '81
Cloud Dancer '80
The Black Hole '79
Holocaust '78
Return Engagement '78
High Rolling in a Hot Corvette '77
Stalk the Wild Child '76
Crime & Passion '75
The Dove '74

Sam Bottoms (1955-)
Sherrybaby '06
Shopgirl '05
The Unsaid '01
Angel Blue '97
Mercenary 2: Thick and Thin '97
Project Shadowchaser 3000 '95
The Witching of Ben Wagner '95
Dolly Dearest '92
Desperate Lives '82
Bronco Billy '80
East of Eden '80
Apocalypse Now '79
The Outlaw Josey Wales '76
Savages '75
Zandy's Bride '74
Class of 44 '73
The Last Picture Show '71

Timothy Bottoms (1950-)
Shanghai Kiss '07
Paradise, Texas '05
DC 9/11: Time of Crisis '04
The Girl Next Door '04
Ike: Countdown to D-Day '04
Elephant '03
Diamondbacks '99
The Prince and the Surfer '99
Total Force '98
The Man in the Iron Mask '97
Mortal Challenge '97
Ripper Man '96
Uncle Sam '96
Hourglass '95
The Prince '95
Top Dog '95
Ava's Magical Adventure '94
Digger '94
The Gift of Love '90
Istanbul '90
Texasville '90
The Fantasist '89
The Drifter '88
The Land of Faraway '87
Husbands, Wives, Money, and Murder '86
In the Shadow of Kilimanjaro '86
Invaders from Mars '86
The Sea Serpent '85
Hambone & Hillie '84
Love Leads the Way '84
Tin Man '83
What Waits Below '83
High Country '81
East of Eden '80
Hurricane '79
A Shining Season '79
The Other Side of the Mountain, Part 2 '78
Rollercoaster '77
A Small Town in Texas '76
The Story of David '76
The White Dawn '75
The Paper Chase '73
Johnny Got His Gun '71
The Last Picture Show '71

Sami Bouajila (1966-)
Days of Glory '06
The Adventures of Felix '99
The Siege '98
Bye-Bye '96

Savannah Smith Boucher
Last Summer in the Hamptons '96
The Applegates '89

Barbara Bouchet (1943-)
Rogue '76
Surabaya Conspiracy '75
Mean Machine '73
Cry of a Prostitute: Love Kills '72
Don't Torture a Duckling '72
Amuck! '71
The Black Belly of the Tarantula '71
Casino Royale '67
In Harm's Way '65

Willis Bouchey (1907-77)
The Man Who Shot Liberty Valance '62
Panic in the Year Zero! '62
The Horse Soldiers '59
Zero Hour! '57
Battle Cry '55
The Bridges at Toko-Ri '55
Suddenly '54
Dangerous Crossing '53

Elodie Bouchez (1973-)
Sorry, Haters '05
CQ '01
Don't Let Me Die on a Sunday '98
The Dreamlife of Angels '98
Full Speed '96
Wild Reeds '94

Chill Bouchier (1909-99)
Old Mother Riley's New Venture '49
The Ghost Goes West '36

Patrick Bouchitey (1946-)
Life Is a Long Quiet River '88
The Best Way '76

Jacques Boudet
The Town Is Quiet '00
Marius and Jeannette '97
Farinelli '94
Waiting for the Moon '87

Jean Bouise (1929-89)
La Femme Nikita '91
Le Dernier Combat '84
Hothead '78
Old Gun '76
I Am Cuba '64

Michel Boujenah (1952-)
Les Miserables '95
Three Men and a Cradle '85

Daniel Boulanger (1922-)
Bed and Board '70
The Bride Wore Black '68
The King of Hearts '66
Breathless '59

Sam Bould (1985-)
The End of the Affair '99
Hollow Reed '95

Ingrid Boulting (1947-)
Deadly Passion '85
The Last Tycoon '76

Matthew Boulton (1883-1962)
Night Must Fall '37
Sabotage '36

Carole Bouquet (1957-)
Red Lights '04
Wasabi '01
Lucie Aubrac '98
Grosse Fatigue '94
A Business Affair '93
New York Stories '89
Too Beautiful for You '88
Special Police '85
Dagger Eyes '83
For Your Eyes Only '81
Buffet Froid '79
That Obscure Object of Desire '77

Michel Bouquet (1926-)
How I Killed My Father '03
Tous les Matins du Monde '92
Toto le Heros '91
Le Complot '73
Borsalino '70
La Rupture '70
La Femme Infidele '69
Mississippi Mermaid '69
The Bride Wore Black '68
This Special Friendship '67
Pattes Blanches '49
Monsieur Vincent '47

Sacha Bourdo (1962-)
The Science of Sleep '06
Western '96

John Bourgeois
A Different Loyalty '04
The Prince & Me '04
Rudy: The Rudy Giuliani Story '03
Ginger Snaps '01
Ms. Scrooge '97
Dead Silence '96

Stacie Bourgeois
See Stacie Randall

J.R. Bourne (1970-)
The Butterfly Effect 2 '06
Everything's Gone Green '06
The Exorcism of Emily Rose '05
The Ginger Snaps Back: The Beginning '04
13 Ghosts '01

Andre Bourvil (1917-70)
Le Cercle Rouge '70
The Brain '69
When Wolves Cry '69
La Grande Vadrouille '66
Jailbird's Vacation '65
The Sucker '65
Les Miserables '57
Four Bags Full '56
Crazy for Love '52
Mr. Peek-A-Boo '50

Joy Boushel (1959-)
The Fly '86
Humongous '82

Nathalie Boutefeu (1968-)
Kings and Queen '04
Irma Vep '96
Barjo '93

Dennis Boutsikaris (1952-)
Cherry Crush '07
They Crawl '01
Perfect Murder, Perfect Town '00
Taken '99
In Dreams '98
The Three Lives of Karen '97
The Yarn Princess '94
The Dream Team '89
*batteries not included '87

Denise Boutte (1982-)
Tyler Perry's Why Did I Get Married? '07
Bram Stoker's Way of the Vampire '05
Death Valley; The Revenge of Bloody Bill '04

Duane Boutte
Brother to Brother '04
Stonewall '95

Jean-Pierre Bouvier (1948-)
Ma Saison Preferee '93
Good-bye, Emmanuelle '77

Joe (Joseph) Bova (1924-2006)
Roboman '75
Pretty Poison '68

Raoul Bova (1971-)
The Company '07
Alien vs. Predator '04
Facing Windows '03
Under the Tuscan Sun '03
Avenging Angelo '02

Julie Bovasso (1930-91)
Article 99 '92
Betsy's Wedding '90
Moonstruck '87
Wise Guys '86
The Verdict '82
Gentleman Bandit '81
Willie & Phil '80

Brunella Bovo (1932-)
The White Sheik '52
Miracle in Milan '51

Clara Bow (1905-65)
Hoopla '33
Hula '28
It '27
Dancing Mothers '26
Mantrap '26
Free to Love '25
My Lady of Whims '25
Parisian Love '25
The Plastic Age '25
Down to the Sea in Ships '22

Simmy Bow (1922-88)
Zoltan... Hound of Dracula '78
The Doberman Gang '72

Bow Wow (1987-)
The Fast and the Furious: Tokyo Drift '06
Roll Bounce '05
Johnson Family Vacation '04
All About the Benjamins '02
Like Mike '02
Carmen: A Hip Hopera '01

Dorris Bowdon (1914-2005)
The Grapes of Wrath '40
Drums Along the Mohawk '39

David Bowe
Dark Justice '00

John Bowe (1950-)
Tipping the Velvet '02
UHF '89
Back to the Beach '87
Wildrose '85

Christopher Bowen
Prime Suspect '92

Dennis Bowen
The Shell Seekers '89
Gas Pump Girls '79
Van Nuys Blvd. '79

Julie Bowen (1970-)
Kids in America '05
Joe Somebody '01
The Killing Club '01
An American Werewolf in Paris '97
Happy Gilmore '96
Multiplicity '96
Runaway Daughters '94

Michael Bowen (1953-)
Walking Tall '04
Kill Bill Vol. 1 '03
Magnolia '99
Jackie Brown '97
Cupid '96
Excess Baggage '96
True Crime '95
New Eden '94
Casualties of Love: The "Long Island Lolita" Story '93
The Player '92
The Taking of Beverly Hills '91
Mortal Passions '90
Season of Fear '89
The Abduction of Kari Swenson '87
Echo Park '86
Iron Eagle '86
Night of the Comet '84
Valley Girl '83
Forbidden World '82

Roger Bowen (1932-96)
What about Bob? '91
Zapped! '82
Prom Night '80
Die Sister, Die! '74
M*A*S*H '70
Petulia '68

Malick Bowens
Tears of the Sun '03
Ali '01
Bopha! '93
The Believers '87
Out of Africa '85

Antoinette Bower (1932-)
The Evil That Men Do '84
Blood Song '82
Prom Night '80

Tom Bower
Thr3e '07
Flannel Pajamas '06
The Hills Have Eyes '06
The Badge '02
High Crimes '02
Hearts in Atlantis '01
The Million Dollar Hotel '99
A Slipping Down Life '96
The Killing Jar '96
The Last Time I Committed Suicide '96
Buffalo Soldiers '97
White Man's Burden '95
Against the Wall '94
Far from Home: The Adventures of Yellow Dog '94
Relentless 3 '93
Teenage Bonnie & Klep'o Clyde '93
Raising Cain '92
Love, Lies and Murder '91
True Believer '89
Promised a Miracle '88

John Bowers (1899-1936)
The White Sin '24
Lorna Doone '22
The Sky Pilot '21

David Bowie (1947-)
Arthur and the Invisibles '06 (V)
The Prestige '06
Mr. R.ce's Secret '00
B.U.S.T.E.D. '99
Gunsinger's Revenge '98
Basquiat '96
The Linguini Incident '92
Twin Peaks: Fire Walk with Me '92
The Last Temptation of Christ '88
Absolute Beginners '86
Labyrinth '86
Into the Night '85
Merry Christmas, Mr. Lawrence '83
Yellowbeard '83
Christiane F. '82
Just a Gigolo '79
The Man Who Fell to Earth '75

Aldrich Bowker (1875-1947)
I Married a Witch '42
Nancy Drew—Trouble Shooter '39

Judi Bowker (1954-)
Anna Karenina '85
The Shooting Party '85
Clash of the Titans '81
East of Elephant Rock '76
Brother Sun, Sister Moon '73

Paul Bowles (1910-99)
Halfmoon '95 (N)
The Sheltering Sky '90

Peter Bowles (1936-)
Co.or Me Kubrick '05
In Love and War '01
The Offence '73
A Day in the Death of Joe Egg '71
Endless Night '71
The Charge of the Light Brigade '68
Blow-Up '66

Sully Boyar (1923-2001)
In the Soup '92
The Manhattan Project '86
Car Wash '76

Alan Boyce (1961-)
Nowhere '96
Where the Day Takes You '92
Permanent Record '88

Todd Boyce
Spy Game '01
Jefferson in Paris '94
Great Expectations: The Untold Story '87

Beverly Boyd
Dog Gone Love '03
Ghost Rider '43
Jive Junction '43

Boy George (1961-)
I Love You Baby '01

Alexandra Boyd
Karla '06
In Love and War '01

William Boyd (1898-1972)
Borrowed Trouble '48
Dangerous Venture '48
Hopalong Cassidy: The Dead Don't Dream '48
Hopalong Cassidy: Silent Conflict '48
Hopalong Cassidy: Sinister Journey '48
Hoppy's Holiday '47
Unexpected Guest '47
Hopalong Cassidy: The Marauders '47
Hopalong Cassidy: The Devil's Playground '46
Mystery Man '44
Texas Masquerade '44
Border Patrol '43
Colt Comrades '43
False Colors '43
Hopalong Cassidy: Riders of the Deadline '43
Leather Burners '43
Lost Canyon '43
Bar 20 '43
Hoppy Serves a Writ '43
Prairie Pals '42
Tumbleweed Trail '42
Border Vigilantes '41
Doomed Caravan '41
In Old Colorado '41
Outlaws of the Desert '41
Riders of the Timberline '41
Twilight on the Trail '41
Santa Fe Marshal '40
The Showdown '40
Hopalong Cassidy: Renegade Trail '39
Law of the Pampas '39

Tanya Boyd (1951-)
Roots '77
Black Shampoo '76
Ilsa, Harem Keeper of the Oil Sheiks '76
The Man Who Never Was '55

John Boxer (1909-82)
The Bridge on the River Kwai '57

Bruce Boxleitner (1950-)
Pandemic '07
Gods and Generals '03
Dickie Roberts: Former Child Star '03
The Secret '93
The Babe '92
Double Jeopardy '92
Kuffs '92
Perfect Family '92
Murderous Vision '91
Diplomatic Immunity '91
From the Dead of Night '89
Kenny Rogers as the Gambler, Part 3: The Legend Continues '87
Passion Flower '86
Kenny Rogers as the Gambler, Part 2: The Adventure Continues '83
Tron '82
The Baltimore Bullet '80
East of Eden '80
Kenny Rogers as the Gambler '80

Jenna Boyd (1993-)
Sisterhood of the Traveling Pants '05
The Missing '03

Lynda Boyd (1965-)
The Fast and the Furious: Tokyo Drift '06
Final Destination 2 '03
Leaving Metropolis '02

Stephen Boyd (1928-77)
The Squeeze '77
Imperial Venus '72
Hannie Caulder '72
Black Brigade '69
Shalako '68
The Oscar '66
Fantastic Voyage '66
The Bible '66
The Fall of the Roman Empire '64
Billy Rose's Jumbo '62
Lisa '62
Ben-Hur '59
The Best of Everything '59
The Bravados '58
Abandon Ship '57
The Night Heaven Fell '57
The Man Who Never Was '57

Charles Boyer (1897-1978)
A Matter of Time '76
Stavisky '74
Barnaby and Me '77
The Madwoman of Chaillot '69
The Hot Line '69
How to Steal a Million '66
Is Paris Burning? '66
Casino Royale '67
Barefoot in the Park '67
Adorable Julia '62
The Four Horsemen of the Apocalypse '62
Fanny '61
The Buccaneer '58
Une Parisienne '58
Around the World in 80 Days '56
What a Woman! '56
The Cobweb '55
Nana '55
The Earrings of Madame de... '54
First Legion '51
Arch of Triumph '48
Gaslight '44
Heart of a Nation '43 (N)
Tales of Manhattan '42
Back Street '41
Hold Back the Dawn '41
All This and Heaven Too '40
Love Affair '39
Algiers '38
Conquest '37
History Is Made at Night '37
The Garden of Allah '36
Mayerling '36
Break of Hearts '35
Private Worlds '35
Liliom '34
Red Headed Woman '32

William "Stage" Boyd (1889-1935)
The Lost City '34

Sally Boyden (1965-)
Barnaby and Me '77
Little Dragons '80

Christopher Boyer
Conspiracy: The Trial of the Chicago Eight '87
Echoes in the Darkness '87

Katy Boyer
White Dwarf '95
Tapeheads '89
Trapped '89
Long Gone '87

Miriam Boyer (1948-)
Un Coeur en Hiver '93
Tous les Matins du Monde '92
Window Shopping '86
Jonah Who Will Be 25 in the Year 2000 '76

William Boyett (1927-2004)
Levitation '97
Uninvited '93

Jessica Bowman (1980-)
Derailed '02

Laura Bowman (1881-1957)
Drums O'Voodoo '34

Lee Bowman (1914-79)
My Dream Is Yours '49
Smash-Up: The Story of a Woman '47
Tonight and Every Night '45
Cover Girl '44
Bataan '43
Buck Privates '41
Love Affair '39
Next Time I Marry '38
Internes Can't Take Money '37

Lisa Bowman
River of Grass '94

Paul Bown (1957-)
Butterfly Kiss '94
Anne of Green Gables '85

Guy Boyd (1943-)
Cries of Silence '97
Retroactive '97
Past Midnight '92
Kiss Me a Killer '91
Drug Wars: The Camarena Story '90

Blake Boyd
First Kid '96
Raiders of the Sun '92
Dune Warriors '91
Joy Ride '01

Billy Boyd (1968-)
Seed of Chucky '04 (V)
On a Clear Day '05
Lord of the Rings: Return of the King '03 (V)
The Lord of the Rings: The Two Towers '02
The Lord of the Rings: The Fellowship of the Rings '01

Cameron Boyd (1984-)
Manny & Lo '96

Darren Boyd (1971-)
Imagine Me & You '06
High Heels and Low Lifes '01

Lara Flynn Boyle (1971-)
Land of the Blind '06
Men in Black 2 '02
Chain of Fools '00
Dying to Get Rich '98
Happiness '98
The Big Squeeze '95
Farmer & Chase '96
Baby's Day Out '94
Jacob '94
Past Tense '94
The Road to Wellvile '94
Threesome '94
Equinox '93
Red Rock West '93
The Temp '93
Wayne's World '92
Where the Day Takes You '92

Lisa Boyle (1968-)
The Last Marshal '99
Friend of the Family '95
I Like to Play Games '95
Poltergeist 3 '88

Peter Boyle (1933-2006)
The Santa Clause 3: The Escape Clause '06
Scooby-Doo 2: Monsters Unleashed '04
The Adventures of Pluto Nash '02
Monster's Ball '01
Dr. Dolittle '98
In the Lake of the Woods '96
That Darn Cat '96
While You Were Sleeping '95
Born to Be Wild '95
Bulletproof Heart '95
The Shadow '94
The Surgeon '94
Urban Crossfire '94
Nervous Ticks '93
Royce '93
Taking the Heat '93
Malcolm X '92
Honeymoon in Vegas '92
Solar Crisis '92
Men of Respect '91
Kickboxer 2: The Road Back '90
The Dream Team '89
Disaster at Silo 7 '88
Red Heat '88
Speed Zone '88
Walker '87
Surrender '87
Turk 182! '85
Johnny Dangerously '84
Yellowbeard '83
Hammett '82
Outland '81
In God We Trust '80
Where the Buffalo Roam '80
Beyond the Poseidon Adventure '79
From Here to Eternity '79
Hardcore '79
Brink's Job '78
F.I.S.T. '78
Swashbuckler '76

Taxi Driver '76
Ghost in the Noonday Sun '74
Young Frankenstein '74
Slither '73
Steelyard Blues '73
The Candidate '72
Joe '70
Medium Cool '69

Max Bozyk (1899-1970)
The Jolly Paupers '38
Mamele '38
Yidl Mitn Fidl '36

Marcel Bozzuffi (1929-88)
La Cage aux Folles 2 '81
Le Gitan '75
Images '72
The French Connection '71
Carbon Copy '69
Z '69

Teda Bracci
The Big Bird Cage '72
C.C. & Company '70

Elizabeth Bracco (1959)
13 Moons '02
Analyze This '98
The Imposters '98
Tree's Lounge '96
Money for Nothing '93
In the Soup '92
Mystery Train '89
Sons '89

Lorraine Bracco (1954-)
Riding in Cars with Boys '01
Tangled '01
The Basketball Diaries '95
Hackers '95
Being Human '94
Even Cowgirls Get the Blues '94
Getting Gotti '94
Scam '93
Medicine Man '92
Radio Flyer '92
Traces of Red '92
Switch '91
Talent for the Game '91
Goodfellas '90
The Dream Team '89
Sing '89
The Pick-Up Artist '87
Someone to Watch Over Me '87
Camorra: The Naples Connection '85

Eddie Bracken (1920-2002)
Home Alone 2: Lost in New York '92
National Lampoon's Vacation '83
Shinbone Alley '70 (V)
We're Not Married '52
Summer Stock '50
Too Many Girls '40
Hail the Conquering Hero '44
Miracle of Morgan's Creek '44
Star Spangled Rhythm '42
Young and Willing '42
Caught in the Draft '41

Sidney Bracy (1877-1942)
Tangled Destinies '32
The Cameraman '28

Kitty Bradbury (1875-1945)
Our Hospitality '23
The Immigrant '17

Lane Bradbury
The Ultimate Warrior '75
Maybe I'll Be Home in the Spring '70

Kim Braden (1949-)
Bloodsuckers from Outer Space '83
That'll Be the Day '73

Greg Bradford (1955-)
Lovelines '84
Zapped! '82

Jesse Bradford (1979-)
Flags of Our Fathers '06
Happy Endings '05
Eulogy '04
Heights '04
Clockstoppers '02
Swimfan '02
Bring It On '00
Cherry Falls '00
Speedway Junky '99
A Soldier's Daughter Never Cries '98
William Shakespeare's Romeo and Juliet '96
Hackers '95
Far from Home: The Adventures of Yellow Dog '94
King of the Hill '93

Lane Bradford (1922-73)
Gun Glory '57
Ride Clear of Diablo '54
The Fighting Redhead '50
The Invisible Monster '50
Missourians '50
Bandit King of Texas '49
Far Frontier '48
The Hawk of Powder River '48

Richard Bradford (1937-)
The Lost City '05
The Man from Elysian Fields '01
Just the Ticket '98
Elmore Leonard's Gold Coast '97
Hoodlum '96
Indictment: The McMartin Trial '95
The Crossing Guard '94
Arctic Blue '93
Cold Heaven '92
Ambition '91
Servants of Twilight '91
Internal Affairs '90
The Chinatown Murders: Man against the Mob '89
The Heart of Dixie '89
Little Nikita '88
A Rumor of War '80
More American Graffiti '79
Goin' South '78

Cathleen Bradley
About Adam '00
American Women '00

Charlotte Bradley
The Boys and Girl From County Clare '03
About Adam '00

Christopher Bradley (1961-)
Leather Jacket Love Story '98
Killer Instinct '92

David Bradley
Total Reality '97
White Cargo '96
Exit '95
Hard Justice '95
Outside the Law '95
Cyborg Soldier '94
Blood Warriors '93
Cyborg Cop '93
American Samurai '92
American Ninja 4: The Annihilation '91
Lower Level '91
American Ninja 3: Blood Hunt '89

David Bradley (1942-)
Harry Potter and the Order of the Phoenix '07
Harry Potter and the Goblet of Fire '05

Red Mercury '05
Exorcist: The Beginning '04
Harry Potter and the Chamber of Secrets '02
The Intended '02
This Is Not a Love Song '02
The Way We Live Now '02
Harry Potter and the Sorcerer's Stone '01
The King Is Alive '00
Vanity Fair '99
Our Mutual Friend '98
Reckless: The Sequel '98
Reckless '97
Catherine Cookson's The Moth '96
Kiss and Tell '96
Martin Chuzzlewit '94
The Buddha of Suburbia '92

Doug Bradley (1954-)
Pumpkinhead 3: Ashes to Ashes '06
Hellraiser: Deader '05
Hellraiser: Hellworld '05
Hellraiser: Hellseeker '02
Hellraiser 5: Inferno '00
Killer Tongue '96
Hellraiser 4: Bloodline '95
Proteus '95
Hellraiser 3: Hell on Earth '92
Hellbound: Hellraiser 2 '88
Hellraiser '87

Grace Bradley (1913-)
The Invisible Killer '40
Larceny On the Air '37

Leslie Bradley (1907-74)
Teenage Caveman '58
The Conqueror '56
Lady Godiva '55
Man in the Attic '53

Olympe Bradna (1920-)
The Night of Nights '39
Souls at Sea '37

Carl Bradshaw
Third World Cop '99
The Lunatic '92
The Harder They Come '72

Cathryn Bradshaw
The Mother '03
Bert Rigby, You're a Fool '89
Oranges Are Not the Only Fruit '89

Terry Bradshaw (1948-)
Failure to Launch '06
Robots '05 (V)
Smokey and the Bandit 2 '80

Alice Brady (1892-1939)
Young Mr. Lincoln '39
Joy of Living '38
In Old Chicago '37
100 Men and a Girl '37
Go West, Young Man '36
My Man Godfrey '36
Three Smart Girls '36
Gold Diggers of 1935 '35
The Gay Divorcee '34
Her Silent Sacrifice '18

Orla Brady (1961-)
Jesse Stone: Death in Paradise '06
The Debt '03
A Love Divided '01
The Luzhin Defence '00
The Magical Legend of the Leprechauns '99
Wuthering Heights '98

Pat Brady (1914-72)
Bells of Coronado '50
Trigger, Jr. '50
Twilight in the Sierras '50
Down Dakota Way '49
The Golden Stallion '49
Song of Texas '43
Texas Legionnaires '43
Call of the Canyon '42
Sunset on the Desert '42

Scott Brady (1924-85)
Gremlins '84

Strange Behavior '81
The China Syndrome '79
When Every Day Was the Fourth of July '78
Bonnie's Kids '73
Loners '72
Cain's Cutthroats '71
Dollars '71
Gun Riders '69
Satan's Sadists '69
Arizona Bushwackers '67
Journey to the Center of Time '67
Castle of Evil '66
Operation Bikini '63
The Restless Breed '58
Storm Rider '57
Mohawk '56
The Maverick Queen '55
They Were So Young '55
Party Girls for Sale '54
Johnny Guitar '53
White Fire '53
Bloodhounds of Broadway '52
Montana Belle '52
Yankee Buccaneer '52
Port of New York '49
He Walked by Night '48

Wayne Brady (1972-)
Crossover '06
Roll Bounce '05
Clifford's Really Big Movie '04 (V)
Gepetto '00

Eric (Hans Gudegast) Braeden (1943-)
Meet the Deedles '98
The Ambulance '90
Happily Ever After '82
Aliens Are Coming '80
The Power Within '79
The Adultress '77
Death Scream '75
The Ultimate Thrill '74
Lady Ice '73
Escape from the Planet of the Apes '71
Colossus: The Forbin Project '70
Dayton's Devils '68

Zach Braff (1975-)
The Last Kiss '06
Chicken Little '05 (V)
Garden State '04
The Broken Hearts Club '00
Manhattan Murder Mystery '93

Alice Braga (1983-)
Crossing Over '08
I Am Legend '07
Redbelt '08

Sonia Braga (1951-)
Bordertown '06
The Hottest State '06
Marilyn Hotchkiss' Ballroom Dancing & Charm School '06
Testosterone '03
Empire '02
Angel Eyes '01
Perfume '01
From Dusk Till Dawn 3: The Hangman's Daughter '99
Tieta of Agreste '96
Larry McMurtry's Streets of Laredo '95
Roosters '95
The Burning Season '94
Two Deaths '94
The Last Prostitute '91
The Rookie '90
The Milagro Beanfield War '88
Moon over Parador '88
The Man Who Broke 1,000 Chains '87
Kiss of the Spider Woman '85
Gabriela '84
I Love You '81
Dona Flor and Her Two Husbands '78
Lady on the Bus '78

Richard Brake
Doom '05
Subterfuge '98

Wilfrid Brambell (1912-85)
Sword of the Valiant '83
The Adventures of Picasso '80
The Conqueror Worm '68
A Hard Day's Night '64
The 39 Steps '35

Virgile Bramly
Four Last Songs '06
Manderlay '05

Francisco (Frank) Brana (1934-)
Cthulhu Mansion '91
Street Warriors '87
Kilma, Queen of the Amazons '75
Crypt of the Living Dead '73
Graveyard of Horror '71
Emerald of Artama '67

Kenneth Branagh (1960-)
Harry Potter and the Chamber of Secrets '02
Rabbit-Proof Fence '02
Shackleton '02
Conspiracy '01
How to Kill Your Neighbor's Dog '01
Love's Labour's Lost '00
The Road to El Dorado '00 (V)
Wild Wild West '99
Celebrity '98
The Theory of Flight '98
The Gingerbread Man '97
The Proposition '97
Hamlet '96
Looking for Richard '96
Othello '95
Mary Shelley's Frankenstein '94
Much Ado about Nothing '93
Swing Kids '93
Peter's Friends '92
Dead Again '91
Henry V '89
Look Back in Anger '89
High Season '88
Fortunes of War '87
The Lady's Not for Burning '87
A Month in the Country '87
Coming Through '85
To the Lighthouse '83

Rustam Branaman
Love to Kill '97

Lillo Brancato (1976-)
In the Shadows '01
'R Xmas '01
Blue Moon '00
Enemy of the State '98
Sticks '98
Provocateur '96
Crimson Tide '95
Renaissance Man '94
A Bronx Tale '93

Christopher Brand
Dracula: The Dark Prince '01
Voyage to the Prehistoric Planet '65

Neville Brand (1921-92)
Evils of the Night '85
The Return '80
The Ninth Configuration '79
The Seekers '79
Hi-Riders '77
Eaten Alive '76
The Longest Drive '76
Psychic Killer '75
The Barbary Coast '74
Death Stalk '74
Cahill: United States Marshal '73
The Deadly Trackers '73
This Is a Hijack '73
The Mad Bomber '72

No Place to Run '72
Tora! Tora! Tora! '70
Desperados '69
That Dam Cat '65
Birdman of Alcatraz '62
Scarface Mob '62
The Adventures of Huckleberry Finn '60
Lonely Man '57
The Tin Star '57
Love Me Tender '56
Mohawk '56
The Prodigal '55
Riot in Cell Block 11 '54
Stalag 17 '53
Kansas City Confidential '52
The Halls of Montezuma '50
Only the Valiant '50
D.O.A. '49

Steven Brand (1969-)
The Diary of Ellen Rimbauer '03
The Scorpion King '02

Klaus Maria Brandauer (1944-)
The Crown Prince '06
Between Strangers '02
Druids '01
Introducing Dorothy Dandridge '99
Jeremiah '98
Becoming Colette '92
White Fang '91
The Russia House '90
Burning Secret '89
Hanussen '88
The Lightship '86
Streets of Gold '86
Out of Africa '85
Quo Vadis '85
Colonel Redl '84
Kindergarten '84
Never Say Never Again '83
Mephisto '81
The Salzburg Connection '72

Larry Brandenburg (1948-)
What the #$*! Do We Know? '04
The Mod Squad '99
Major League 3: Back to the Minors '98
Mo' Money '92
Victimless Crimes '90

Walter Brandi (-1996)
Terror Creatures from the Grave '66
The Bloody Pit of Horror '65
The Slaughter of the Vampires '62

Jonathan Brandis (1976-2003)
Puerto Vallarta Squeeze '04
Hart's War '02
Outside Providence '99
Ride with the Devil '99
Sidekicks '93
Ladybugs '92
NeverEnding Story 2: The Next Chapter '91
Stephen King's It '90
Stepfather 2: Make Room for Daddy '89

Thomas Brandise (1976)
The Jesse Ventura Story '99
Gravesend '97

Jocelyn Brando (1919-2005)
A Question of Love '78
Nightfall '56
Ten Wanted Men '54
The Big Heat '53

Luisina Brando
The Longest Drive '76

Marlon Brando (1924-2004)
Superman Returns '06
The Score '01

Free Money '99
The Island of Dr. Moreau '96
Don Juan DeMarco '94
Christopher Columbus: The Discovery '92
The Freshman '90
A Dry White Season '89
The Godfather 1902-1959: The Complete Epic '81
The Formula '80
The Nightcomers '72
Burn! '70
The Night of the Following Day '69
Superman: The Movie '78
Apocalypse Now '79
Roots: The Next Generation '79
The Appaloosa '66
The Chase '66
Missouri Breaks '76
Last Tango in Paris '73
The Godfather '72
Mutiny on the Bounty '62
One-Eyed Jacks '61
The Fugitive Kind '60
The Young Lions '58
Sayonara '57
Julius Caesar '53
Viva Zapata! '52
A Streetcar Named Desire '51
The Men '50
The Teahouse of the August Moon '56
Guys and Dolls '55
Desiree '54
On the Waterfront '54
The Wild One '54
Julius Caesar '53

Rikki Brando
Reflections in a Golden Eye '67

David Brandon
Beyond Darkness '92
Good Morning, Babylon '87
Stagefright '87

Henry (Kleinbach) Brandon (1912-90)
Assault on Precinct 13 '75
When the North Wind Blows '74
He Lives: The Search for the Evil One '67
The Searchers '56
War Arrow '53
The Land Unknown '57
Buford's Beach Bunnies '92
Zipperface '92
Bad Man of Deadwood '41
Drums of Fu Manchu '40
The Black Legion '37
Big Brown Eyes '36
The Garden of Allah '36
March of the Wooden Soldiers '34

Michael Brandon (1945-)
The Detonator '06
The Contaminated Man '01
Deja Vu '98
The Disappearance of Kevin Johnson '95
Rich and Famous '81
A Change of Seasons '80
Promises in the Dark '79
Red Alert '77
James Dean '76
Heavy Traffic '73
Lovers and Other Strangers '70

Luis Brandoni (1940-)
A Shadow You Soon Will Be '94
Made in Argentina '86

Carlo Brandt
Ridicule '96
Indochine '92

Carolyn Brandt
The Hollywood Strangler Meets the Skid Row Slasher '79
Rat Pfink a Boo-Boo '66
The Thrill Killers '65
Incredibly Strange Creatures Who Stopped Living and Became Mixed-Up Zombies '63
Eegah! '62
Wild Guitar '62

Brandy
See Brandy Norwood

Brigid Brannah (1972-)
Candy '68

Jennifer Bransford (1968-)
Amy's O '02
Rift '96

Betsy Brantley (1955-)
Deep Impact '98
From the Earth to the Moon '93
Havana '90
I Come in Peace '90
Dreams Lost, Dreams Found '87
Another Country '84
Five Days One Summer '82

Albert Bras (1865-1942)
Vampyr '31
Napoleon '27

Nicoletta Braschi (1960-)
Pinocchio '02
Life Is Beautiful '98
The Monster '96
Mystery Train '89
Johnny Stecchino '92
Down by Law '86
No '98
Le Polygraphe '96

Steve Braun
Wrong Turn 2: Dead End '07

Bart Braverman (1946-)
Running Red '99
From the Earth to the Moon '98

How the West Was Won '63
Rio Bravo '59
Tammy and the Bachelor '57
Glory '56
Goodbye, My Lady '56
At Gunpoint '55
Far Country '55
Bad Day at Black Rock '54
Along the Great Divide '51
Best of the Badmen '50
The Showdown '50
Ticket to Tomahawk '50
The Green Promise '49
Task Force '49
Blood on the Moon '48
Red River '48
My Darling Clementine '46
A Stolen Life '46
Dakota '45
The Princess and the Pirate '44
To Have & Have Not '44
The North Star '43
Hangmen Also Die '42
The Pride of the Yankees '42
Meet John Doe '41
Nice Girl? '41
Sergeant York '41
Northwest Passage '40
The Westerner '40
Stanley and Livingstone '39
The Story of Vernon and Irene Castle '39
They Shall Have Music '39
The Adventures of Tom Sawyer '38
The Cowboy and the Lady '38
The Texans '38
Come and Get It '36
Fury '36
The Moon's Our Home '36
Prescott Kid '36
These Three '36
Barbary Coast '35
The Bride of Frankenstein '35
The Invisible Man '33
Man of Action '33
Phantom of the Air '33
Texas Cyclone '32
Two-Fisted Law '32

Amy Brenneman (1964-)
88 Minutes '08
Nine Lives '05
Off the Map '03
Things You Can Tell Just by Looking at Her '00
The Suburbans '99
Your Friends & Neighbors '98
Nevada '97
Daylight '96
Fear '96
Casper '95
Heat '95
Bye Bye, Love '94

Dori Brenner (1946-2000)
Infinity '96
Silent Victim '92
For the Boys '91
Baby Boom '87
Sex and the Single Parent '82
Altered States '80
Summer Wishes, Winter Dreams '73

Eve Brenner
The Great Mouse Detective '86 (V)
Torment '85

Lisa Brenner (1974-)
The Diary of Ellen Rimbauer '03
Finding Home '03
Brainwash '08
Fade to Black '80
Stakeout '62

Eve Brent (1930-)
The Green Mile '99
Tarzan and the Trappers '58
Forty Guns '57
Gun Girls '56

Evelyn Brent (1899-1975)
The Payoff '43
The Seventh Victim '43
Holt of the Secret Service '42
Robot Pilot '41
Daughter of the Tong '39
Panama Lady '39
Law West of Tombstone '38
Hopalong Cassidy Returns '36
The President's Mystery '36
Song of the Trail '36
The Silver Horde '30
Last Command '28
Underworld '27
Love 'Em and Leave 'Em '26
Trapped by the Mormons '22

George Brent (1904-79)
Born Again '78
FBI Girl '52
Montana Belle '52
Christmas Eve '47
Out of the Blue '47
My Reputation '46
The Spiral Staircase '46
Tomorrow Is Forever '46
Experiment Perilous '45
In This Our Life '42
Silver Queen '42
Twin Beds '42
The Great Lie '41
International Lady '41
The Fighting 69th '40
Dark Victory '39
The Old Maid '39
The Rains Came '39
Jezebel '38
In Person '35
The Painted Veil '34
Baby Face '33
Female '33
42nd Street '33
The Purchase Price '32
They Call It Sin '32
Lightning Warrior '31

Linda Brent
Death Valley Rangers '44
Below the Border '42

Romney Brent (1902-76)
The Sign of Zorro '60
The Virgin Queen '55
Adventures of Don Juan '49
Dreaming Lips '37
Under the Red Robe '36

Timothy Brent
See Giancarlo Prete

Amy Brentano
Blood Sisters '86

Edmund Breon (1882-1951)
Forever Amber '47
Dressed to Kill '46
Casanova Brown '44
Gaslight '44
The White Cliffs of Dover '44
Woman in the Window '44
The Scarlet Pimpernel '34

Bobbie Bresee (1950-)
Pre-Madonnas: Rebels Without a Clue '95
Evil Spawn '87
Surf Nazis Must Die '87
Ghoulies '84
Mausoleum '83

Abigail Breslin (1996-)
Definitely, Maybe '08
Nim's Island '08
No Reservations '07
The Ultimate Gift '07
Air Bud 6: Air Buddies '06 (V)
Little Miss Sunshine '06
The Family Plan '05
Keane '04
Raising Helen '04
Signs '02

Spencer Breslin (1992-)
Sublime '07
The Big Bad Swim '06
A Perfect Day '06
Unaccompanied Minors '06
Man of the House '05
The Santa Clause 3: The Escape Clause '06
The Shaggy Dog '06
Zoom '06
Raising Helen '04
Dr. Seuss' The Cat in the Hat '03
Return to Never Land '02 (V)
The Santa Clause 2 '02
Disney's The Kid '00

Felix Bressart (1895-1949)
Portrait of Jennie '48
A Song Is Born '48
Without Love '45
Greenwich Village '44
The Seventh Cross '44
Iceland '42
To Be or Not to Be '42
Blossoms in the Dust '41
Ziegfeld Girl '41
Bitter Sweet '40
Comrade X '40
Edison the Man '40
The Shop Around the Corner '40
Ninotchka '39

Bernard Bresslaw (1934-93)
Carry On Camping '71
Carry On Cowboy '66
Morgan: A Suitable Case for Treatment '66

Martin Brest (1951-)
Spies Like Us '85
Fast Times at Ridgemont High '82

Jean Bretonniere (1924-2001)
Mam'zelle Pigalle '58
That Naughty Girl '58
The Green Glove '52

Danielle Brett
Road Rage '01
Jill the Ripper '00
Rated X '00

Jeremy Brett (1935-95)
Moll Flanders '96
Shameless '94
The Medusa Touch '78
Haunted: The Ferryman '74
One Deadly Owner '74
The Merchant of Venice '73
My Fair Lady '64
The Very Edge '63
War and Peace '56

Jim Breuer (1967-)
Once in the Life '00
Titan A.E. '00 (V)
Dick '99
Half-Baked '97

Marita Breuer (1953-)
The Princess and the Warrior '00
Heimat 1 '84

Juliette Brewer
Balto '95 (V)
The Little Rascals '94

Diane Brewster (1931-91)
Torpedo Run '58
Courage of Black Beauty '57
The Invisible Boy '57

Jordana Brewster (1980-)
Annapolis '06
The Texas Chainsaw Massacre: The Beginning '06
Nearing Grace '05
D.E.B.S. '04
The Fast and the Furious '01
Invisible Circus '00
The 60s '99
The Faculty '98

Paget Brewster (1969-)
Now You Know '02
The Adventures of Rocky & Bullwinkle '00
The Specials '00
Let's Talk About Sex '98

Maia Brewton (1977-)
Adventures in Babysitting '87
Back to the Future '85

Kevin Breznahan (1968-)
SLC Punk! '99
I Love Trouble '94
Alive '93

Tom Breznahan (1965-)
Terrified '94
Ski School '91
The Brain '88
Twice Dead '88

Jean-Claude Brialy (1933-2007)
The Count of Monte Cristo '99
Beaumarchais the Scoundrel '96
The Monster '96
Portraits Chinois '96
Queen Margot '94
Son of Gascogne '95
No Fear, No Die '90
La Nuit de Varennes '82
Robert et Robert '78
Barocco '76
Catherine & Co. '76
L'Annee Sainte '76
The Judge and the Assassin '75
Phantom of Liberty '74
Claire's Knee '71
The Bride Wore Black '68
The King of Hearts '66
Tonio Kroger '65
Circle of Love '64
The Burning Court '62
Cleo from 5 to 7 '61
Paris Belongs to Us '60
A Woman Is a Woman '60
The Cousins '59
The 400 Blows '59
Le Beau Serge '58

David Brian (1914-93)
Confessions of Tom Harris '72
Castle of Evil '66
Pocketful of Miracles '61
The High and the Mighty '54
Ambush at Tomahawk Gap '53
Million Dollar Mermaid '52
Springfield Rifle '52
The Damned Don't Cry '50
Beyond the Forest '49
Flamingo Road '49
Intruder in the Dust '49

Mary Brian (1908-2002)
Amazing Adventure '37
Charlie Chan in Paris '35
Monte Carlo Nights '34
Blessed Event '32
Gun Smoke '31
The Light of Western Stars '30
Running Wild '27
Behind the Front '26
Peter Pan '24

Shane Briant (1946-)
Twisted '96
Tunnel Vision '95
Till There Was You '91
Darlings of the Gods '90
Wrangler '88
Cassandra '87
The Lighthorsemen '87
Moving Targets '87
True Colors '87
Agatha Christie's Murder is Easy '82
Lady Chatterley's Lover '81
The Flame Is Love '79
Captain Kronos: Vampire Hunter '74
Dressed for Death '74
Frankenstein and the Monster from Hell '74
Picture of Dorian Gray '74
Demons of the Mind '72

Fanny Brice (1891-1951)
Ziegfeld Follies '46
Everybody Sing '38
The Great Ziegfeld '36
Be Yourself '30

Pierre Brice (1929-)
Lady of the Evening '75
A Place Called Glory '66
Apache's Last Battle '64
The Bacchantes '63
Sweet Ecstasy '62
Mill of the Stone Women '60

Ron Brice
Ripe '97
Tar '97
A Horse for Danny '95
Fresh '94
Little Odessa '94
Fly by Night '93

Alexander Brickel
Palindromes '04

Beth Brickell (1941-)
Satan's Little Helper '04
Seducers '77

Alan Bridge (1891-1957)
Miracle of Morgan's Creek '44
Sullivan's Travels '41
Fast Bullets '36
Outlaw Rule '36
Silent Valley '35
Sucker Money '34
Cheyenne Kid '33
Cowboy Counselor '33
The Lone Avenger '33
When a Man Rides Alone '33
Broadway to Cheyenne '32
The Forty-Niners '32
Man's Land '32

Beau Bridges (1941-)
Stargate: The Ark of Truth '08
Charlotte's Web '06
The Good German '06
The Ballad of Jack and Rose '05
Smile '05
Common Ground '00
Sordid Lives '00
Inherit the Wind '99
P.T. Barnum '99
White River '99
The Defenders: Taking the First '98
Meeting Daddy '98
The Defenders: Payback '97
The Second Civil War '97
RocketMan '97
Hidden in America '96
Kissinger and Nixon '96
Losing Chase '96
Nightjohn '96
The Outer Limits: Sandkings '95
Married to It '93
The Positively True Adventures of the Alleged Texas Cheerleader-Murdering Mom '93
Sidekicks '93
Wildflower '91
Without Warning: The James Brady Story '91
Daddy's Dyin'... Who's Got the Will? '90
Women & Men: Stories of Seduction '90
The Fabulous Baker Boys '89
The Iron Triangle '89
Signs of Life '89
The Wizard '89
Seven Hours to Judgment '88
The Killing Time '87
The Wild Pair '87
Outrage! '86
Alice in Wonderland '85
The Hotel New Hampshire '84
The Red Light Sting '84
Heart Like a Wheel '83
Silver Dream Racer '83
Love Child '82
Honky Tonk Freeway '81
Night Crossing '81
The Fifth Musketeer '79
The Runner Stumbles '79
The Four Feathers '78
President's Mistress '78
Greased Lightning '77
Mutual Respect '77
One Summer Love '76
Swashbuckler '76
Two Minute Warning '76
The Other Side of the Mountain '75
The Stranger Who Looks Like Me '74
The Man Without a Country '73
Hammersmith Is Out '72
For Love of Ivy '68
The Incident '67
Village of the Giants '65
The Red Pony '49

Chris Bridges
See Ludacris
Fred Claus '07

Jeff Bridges (1949-)
Iron Man '08
Surf's Up '07 (V)
Stick It '06
Tideland '05
The Door in the Floor '04
Lost in La Mancha '03 (N)
Masked and Anonymous '03
Seabiscuit '03
K-PAX '01
The Contender '00
Arlington Road '99
The Muse '99
Simpatico '99
Hidden in America '96
The Mirror Has Two Faces '96
White Squall '96
Wild Bill '95
Blown Away '94
Fearless '93
The Vanishing '93
American Heart '92
The Fisher King '91
Texasville '90
Cold Feet '89
The Fabulous Baker Boys '89
See You in the Morning '89
Tucker: The Man and His Dream '88
Nadine '87
The Morning After '86
8 Million Ways to Die '85
The Jagged Edge '85
Against All Odds '84
Starman '84
Kiss Me Goodbye '82
The Last Unicorn '82 (V)
Rapunzel '82
Tron '82
Cutter's Way '81
Heaven's Gate '81
Winter Kills '79
King Kong '76
Stay Hungry '76
Hearts of the West '75
Rancho Deluxe '75
Thunderbolt & Lightfoot '74
The Iceman Cometh '73

The Last American Hero '73
Bad Company '72
Fat City '72
The Last Picture Show '71
Yin & Yang of Mr. Go '71
Silent Night, Lonely Night '69

Jordan Bridges (1973-)
The Family Plan '05
Mcna Lisa Smile '03
Frequency '00
Inhumanity '00

Krista Bridges
George A. Romero's Land of the Dead '05
Nerc '02
Twice Dead '88

Lloyd Bridges (1913-98)
Mafia! '98
Meeting Daddy '98
The Outer Limits: Sandkings '95
Blown Away '94
Hot Shots! Part Deux '93
Devlin '92
Honey, I Blew Up the Kid '92
Hot Shots! '91
Joe Versus the Volcano '90
Cousins '89
Winter People '89
Tucker: The Man and His Dream '88
The Wild Pair '87
The Grace Kelly Story '83
Dress Gray '86
North and South Book 2 '86
Weekend Warriors '86
Alice in Wonderland '85
George Washington '84
Loving '84
The Goddess '58
The Rainmaker '56
Wetbacks '56
Apache Woman '55
Big Deadly Game '54
The Limping Man '53
Tall Texan '53
High Noon '52
Last of the Comanches '52
Little Big Horn '51
Rocketship X-M '50
Try and Get Me '50
Home of the Brave '49
Trapped '49
The Smallest Show on Earth '48
Ramrod '47
Abilene Town '46
Canyon Passage '46
A Walk in the Sun '46
Strange Confession '45
Louisiana Hayride '44
Master Race '44
The Heat's On '43
Sahara '43
Blondie Goes to College '42
Harmon of Michigan '41

Spencir Bridges (1998)
Daddy Day Camp '07

Todd Bridges (1965-)
The Reading Room '05
San Franpsycho '06
I Got Five on It '05
Inhumanity '00
Homebodys '01
P.T. Barnum '99
Silent Night, Lonely Night '59
Nerc '02
Roots '77

Richard Briers (1934-2006)
Peter Pan '03
Unconditional Love '03
Love's Labour's Lost '00
Spice World: The Movie '97
Hamlet '96
A Midwinter's Tale '95
Frankenstein (Mary Shelley's Frankenstein) '94
Much Ado about Nothing '93
Henry V '89
The Norman Conquests, Part 1: Table Manners '78
The Norman Conquests, Part 2: Living Together '78
The Norman Conquests, Part 3: Round and Round the Garden '78
Watership Down '78 (V)
Rentadick '72
Fathom '67

Johnny Briggs (1935-)
Au Pair Girls '72
The Leather Boys '63

Julie Briggs
Brotherhood 2: The Young Warlocks '01

Bernard Brieux
A Matter of WHO '62
Petit Con '84

Cameron Bright (1993-)
Witness to the Mob '98
Beautiful Girls '96
The Ref '93
Running Scared '06
Thank You for Smoking '06
Ultraviolet '06
X-Men: The Last Stand '06
Birth '04
Godsend '04

Richard Bright (1937-2006)
Bowery Buckaroos '47
Petit Con '84
The Leather Boys '63
The Rascals '81
The Great Waliendas '78
Cylon Attack '78
The Godfather, Part 3 '90
Red Heat '88
Once Upon a Time in America '84
Vigilante '83
Idolmaker '80
Marathon Man '76
Rancho Deluxe '75
Panic in Needle Park '71
Odds Against Tomorrow '59

Nancy Brinckman
Detour to Danger '45

Michele Brin
Sexual Intent '94

Paul Brinegar (1918-95)
Wyatt Earp: Return to Tombstone '94
Lily Was Here '89
Waterloo '77

Adrian Brine (1936-)
Mr. Muggs Rides Again '45
War and Peace '56
There Goes Barder '54

Charlotte Brittain
Secret Society '00

Morgan Brittany (1951-)
Get Real '99
How to Make a Monster '58
The Young Lions '58
The Hunters '58
The Untalthus '60
Haunts '77
Bound '96
Virgin Machine '88

Susie Bright (1958-)
Vegas Vacation '96
National Lampoon's Vacation '83
Charol '69

Fran Brill (1946-)
What about Bob? '91
Old Enough '84

Charlie Brill (1938-)
Bail Out '90

Steven Brill (1962-)
Bloodstone '88

Nick Brimble
Submerged '05
Seven Days to Live '01
Fortress 2: Re-Entry '99
Gone Fishin' '97

Patti Brill (1923-63)
Girl Rush '44
Hard-Boiled Mahoney '47
The Lawnmower Man '92
Dead Man '95
Soldier '98

Mark Bringleson (1957-)
The Creature Wasn't Nice '81

John Brinkley (1954-)
A Bucket of Blood '59
T-Bird Gang '59
Teenage Doll '57

Christie Brinkley (1954-)
Now and Forever '82
My Brilliant Career '79

Barbara Britton (1919-30)
Dragonfly Squadron '54
Ride the Man Down '53
Bandit Queen '51
Champagne for Caesar '50

Cynthia Brimhall (1964-)
Fit to Kill '93
Hard Ticket to Hawaii '87

Wilford Brimley (1934-)
Brigham City '01
Crossfire Trail '01
Progeny '98
In and Out '97
My Fellow Americans '96
The Good Old Boys '95
The Last of the Dogmen '95
Mutant Species '95
Hard Target '93
The Firm '93
Cocoon: The Return '88
End of the Line '88
American Justice '86
Cocoon '85
Remo Williams: The Adventure Begins '85
Country '84
Harry & Son '84
The Thing '32
Absence of Malice '81
Borderline '80
Death Valley '81
Rodeo Girl '80
Roughnecks '80
The China Syndrome '79
The Electric Horseman '79
True Grit '69

Charles Brinley (1880-1946)
The Crimson Trail '35
Moran of the Lady Letty '22

Bo Brinkman (1956-)
Gods and Generals '03
Gettysburg '93
Ice House '89

Virginia Brissac (1894-1979)
Phantom Lady '44
Black Friday '40

Danielle Brisebois (1969-)
As Good As It Gets '97
Killcrazy '89
Big Bad Mama 2 '87
Mom, the Wolfman and Me '80

Carl Brisson (1893-1958)
Murder at the Vanities '34
The Ring '27

May Britt (1936-)
The Blue Angel '59
The Hunters '58
The Young Lions '58
War and Peace '56

Aileen Britton (1916-86)
Yours, Mine & Ours '68
Life Is Sweet '90
The Birds '63

Kent Broadhurst (1940-)
A Couch in New York '95
The Dark Half '91
Silver Bullet '85

Peter Brocco (1903-92)
One Flew Over the Cuckoo's Nest '75
Homebodies '74

David Brisbin
Goodbye, Lover '99

Brent Briscoe (1951-)
The Big Empty '04
Double Take '01
Waking Up in Reno '02
Beautiful '00
A Simple Plan '98
Sling Blade '96

Syd Brisbane
Dead Letter Office '98
Alien Visitor '95

Vera Briole
A Single Girl '96
Pigalle '95

Françoise Brion (1938-)
Dangerous Liaisons '03
Neily et Monsieur Arnaud '95

Bill Brinsfield
Warbirds '88
Slaughterhouse '87

Brent Briscoe (listings above)

Herman Brix
See Bruce Bennett

Nicolas Bro
Adam's Apples '05
The Green Butchers '03

Jim Broadbent (1949-)
Indiana Jones and the Kingdom of the Crystal Skull '08
Hot Fuzz '07
Art School Confidential '05
Longford '06
The Chronicles of Narnia: The Lion, the Witch and the Wardrobe '05
Robots '05 (V)
Valiant '05 (V)
Around the World in 80 Days '04
Bridget Jones: The Edge of Reason '04
Vanity Fair '04
And Starring Pancho Villa as Himself '03
Bright Young Things '03
Gangs of New York '02
The Gathering Storm '02
Nicholas Nickleby '02
Bridget Jones's Diary '01
Iris '01
Moulin Rouge '01
Topsy Turvy '99
Little Voice '98
The Avengers '98
Widow's Peak '94
The Wedding Gift '93
The Crying Game '92
Enchanted April '92
The Borrowers '97
The Secret Agent '96
Smilla's Sense of Snow '96
Richard III '95
Rough Magic '95
Bullets over Broadway '94
Princess Caraboo '94

Syd Brisbane (above)

Charles Brinley (1880-1946)
(above)

Ritch Brinkley (1944-)
Breakdown '96
Cabin Boy '94
Silhouette '91

Connie Britton (1968-)
The Lather Effect '06
Friday Night Lights '04
Looking for Kitty '04
The Next Big Thing '02
Child Star: The Shirley Temple Story '01
No Looking Back '98
Escape Clause '96
The Brothers McMullen '95

Tony Britton (1924-)
Agatha '79
The Day of the Jackal '73
Cry of the Penguins '71
Sunday, Bloody Sunday '71
Dr. Syn, Alias the Scarecrow '64
Operation Amsterdam '60

Stan Brock (1931-91)
Return to Africa '89

Roy Brocksmith (1945-2001)
Mercy '96
Gayon '77
Arachnophobia '90
Total Recall '90
Big Business '88
Tales of Ordinary Madness '83

Phil Brock (1953-)
Cyrano de Bergerac '90
The Balcony '63
Ma and Pa Kettle on Vacation '53

Anne Brochet (1966-)
Intimate Strangers '04
Dust '01
Barjo '93

Pamela Britton (1923-74)
If It's Tuesday, This Must Be Belgium '69
D.O.A. '49
Anchors Aweigh '45

Erin Broderick (1985-)
Weekend '02

Beth Broderick (1959-)
Mystery Woman: Mystery Weekend '05
Psycho Beach Party '00
French Exit '97
Maternal Instincts '96
Are You Lonesome Tonight '92
Thousand Pieces of Gold '91

Gladys Brockwell (1894-1929)
The Drake Case '29
Spangles '26
Oliver Twist '22

James Broderick (1927-82)
The Group '66
Alice's Restaurant '69
Two Three '74

Matthew Broderick (1962-)
Bee Movie '07 (V)
Deck the Halls '06
Strangers with Candy '05
The Producers '05
The Last Shot '04
The Lion King 1 1/2 '04 (V)
The Stepford Wives '04
Election '99
Inspector Gadget '99
You Can Count On Me '99
Godzilla '98
The Lion King: Simba's Pride '98 (V)
Addicted to Love '96
The Cable Guy '96

Helen Broderick (1891-1959)
Nice Girl? '41
The Rage of Paris '38
Service De Luxe '38
The Bride Walks Out '36
Swing Time '36
Top Hat '35

Johnny Got His Gun '71
The Virginian '46
Captain Kidd '45
The Story of Dr. Wassell '44
So Proudly We Hail '43
Reap the Wild Wind '42
Wake Island '42
Young and Willing '42
The Brothers McMullen '95

Killer Fish '79
King of the Gypsies '78
Thunder Alley '85
A Climate for Killing '91

Tin Men '87
UHF '89

Nickel & Dime '92
Bill & Ted's Bogus Journey '91
Dolman vs Demonic Toys '93

Kull the Conqueror '97
Cons of Breathing '04
The Road to Weilville '94
The Road to Wellville '94

Tous les Matins du Monde

Infinity '96
The Lion King '94 (V)

The Thief and the Cobbler '96 (V)
The Lion King '94 (V)
Mrs. Parker and the Vicious Circle '94
A Life in the Theater '93
The Night We Never Met '93
Out on a Limb '92
The Freshman '90
Family Business '89
Glory '89
Biloxi Blues '88
Torch Song Trilogy '88
Project X '87
Ferris Bueller's Day Off '86
On Valentine's Day '86
Ladyhawke '85
1918 '85
Cinderella '84
Master Harold and the Boys '84
Max Dugan Returns '83
WarGames '83

Don Brodie (1899-2001)
Eat My Dust '76
Detour '46
Pinocchio '40 (V)

Helen Brodie
Tales of the Kama Sutra 2: Monsoon '98
Monsoon '97

Steve Brodie (1919-92)
The Wizard of Speed and Time '88
The Giant Spider Invasion '75
The Wild World of Batwoman '66
Roustabout '64
Blue Hawaii '62
The Caine Mutiny '54
The Beast from 20,000 Fathoms '53
Donovan's Brain '53
Three for Bedroom C '52
The Steel Helmet '51
The Saint Strikes Back: Criminal Court '46
A Walk in the Sun '46
The Admiral Was a Lady '50
Armored Car Robbery '50
Kiss Tomorrow Goodbye '50
Treasure of Monte Cristo '50
Home of the Brave '49
Tough Assignment '49
Desperate '47
Out of the Past '47
Badman's Territory '46
Criminal Court '46

Adam Brody (1980-)
Smiley Face '07
The Ten '07
In the Land of Women '06
Thank You for Smoking '06
Mr. & Mrs. Smith '05
Grind '03

Adrien Brody (1973-)
Missing Brendan '03
The Darjeeling Limited '07
Hollywoodland '06
The Jacket '05
King Kong '05
The Village '04
The Singing Detective '03
Dummy '02
Harrison's Flowers '02
The Pianist '02
The Affair of the Necklace '01
Love the Hard Way '01
Bread and Roses '00
Liberty Heights '99
Oxygen '99
Six Ways to Sunday '99
Summer of Sam '99
Restaurant '98
Ten Benny '98
The Thin Red Line '98

The Undertaker's Wedding '97
The Last Time I Committed Suicide '96
Solo '96
Bullet '94
Jailbreakers '94
King of the Hill '93
Home at Last '88

Harry Brogan (1905-77)
Broth of a Boy '59
Shake Hands with the Devil '59

Giulio Brogi (1935-)
St. Michael Had a Rooster '72
The Spider's Stratagem '70

Tom Brokaw (1940-)
Tanner on Tanner '04
Journeys with George '02

James Brolin (1940-)
The Hunting Party '07
Lies & Alibis '06
Wedding Wars '06
Category 7: The End of the World '05
The Reagans '04
A Guy Thing '03
Catch Me If You Can '02
Master of Disguise '02
Traffic '00
The Haunted Sea '97
Lewis and Clark and George '97
My Brother's War '97
Terminal Virus '96
The Expert '95
The Fighter '95
Relative Fear '95
Tracks of a Killer '95
Final Justice '94
Indecent Behavior 2 '94
Parallel Lives '94
Cheatin' Hearts '93
City Boy '93
Ted & Venus '93
Gas Food Lodging '92
Twin Sisters '92
Backstab '90
Nightmare on the 13th Floor '90
Bad Jim '89
Finish Line '89
Hold the Dream '86
Pee-wee's Big Adventure '85
Mae West '84
The Ambush Murders '82
High Risk '81
Night of the Juggler '80
The Amityville Horror '79
Capricorn One '78
Steel Cowboy '78
The Car '77
Class of '63 '73
Westworld '73
The Boston Strangler '68
Fantastic Voyage '66
Our Man Flint '66
Von Ryan's Express '65

Josh Brolin (1968-)
American Gangster '07
In the Valley of Elah '07
No Country for Old Men '07
Planet Terror '07
The Dead Girl '06
Into the Blue '05
Milwaukee, Minnesota '03
Coastlines '02
Hollow Man '00
Slow Burn '00
Best Laid Plans '99
It's the Rage '99
The Mod Squad '99
Mimic '97
My Brother's War '97
Nightwatch '96
Bed of Roses '95
Flirting with Disaster '95
Prison for Children '93
Finish Line '89
Thrashin' '86
The Goonies '85

Shane Brolly (1970-)
48 Angels '06

Underworld: Evolution '05
Underworld '03
Flypaper '97

J. Edward Bromberg (1903-51)
A Song Is Born '48
Queen of the Amazons '47
Cloak and Dagger '46
The Missing Corpse '45
The Phantom of the Opera '43
Son of Dracula '43
Invisible Agent '42
Reunion in France '42
The Mark of Zorro '40
Return of Frank James '40
Strange Cargo '40
Four Men and a Prayer '38
Mr. Moto Takes a Chance '38
Charlie Chan on Broadway '37

John Bromfield (1922-)
Manfish '56
Big Bluff '55
Revenge of the Creature '55
Easy to Love '53
Flat Top '52

Valri Bromfield (1949-)
Nothing But Trouble '91
Who's Harry Crumb? '89
Home Is Where the Hart Is '88
Mr. Mom '83

Sheila Bromley
See Sheila (Manors)
Mannors

Sydney Bromley (1909-87)
Crystalstone '88
The NeverEnding Story '84
Frankenstein and the Monster from Hell '74

Eleanor Bron (1934-)
Wimbledon '04
The Heart of Me '02
Iris '01
House of Mirth '00
Vanity Fair '99
A Little Princess '95
Saint-Ex: The Story of the Storyteller '95
Black Beauty '94
Intrigue '90
The Attic: The Hiding of Anne Frank '80
Little Dorrit, Film 1: Nobody's Fault '88
Little Dorrit, Film 2: Little Dorrit's Story '88
Turtle Diary '86
Women in Love '70
Bedazzled '68
Two for the Road '67
Alfie '66
Help! '65

William Bronder (1928-)
Return to Me '00
Flush '81

Brick Bronsky
Class of Nuke 'Em High 3: The Good, the Bad and the Subhumanoid '94
Sgt. Kabukiman N.Y.P.D. '94
Class of Nuke 'Em High 2: Subhumanoid Meltdown '91

Betty Bronson (1906-71)
Naked Kiss '64
Yodelin' Kid from Pine Ridge '37
Medicine Man '30
Ben-Hur '26
Are Parents People? '25
Peter Pan '24

Charles Bronson (1921-2003)
Family of Cops 3 '98

Family of Cops 2: Breach of Faith '97
Family of Cops '95
Death Wish 5: The Face of Death '94
Dead to Rights '93
The Sea Wolf '93
The Indian Runner '91
Kinjite: Forbidden Subjects '89
Messenger of Death '88
Assassination '87
Death Wish 4: The Crackdown '87
Act of Vengeance '86
Murphy's Law '86
Death Wish 3 '85
The Evil That Men Do '84
Ten to Midnight '83
Death Wish 2 '82
Cabo Blanco '81
Death Hunt '81
Borderline '80
Love and Bullets '79
Raid on Entebbe '77
Telefon '77
The White Buffalo '77
Breakheart Pass '76
From Noon Till Three '76
St. Ives '76
Chino '75
Hard Times '75
Death Wish '74
Mr. Majestyk '74
The Stone Killer '73
The Mechanic '72
Bull of the West '71
Chato's Land '71
Cold Sweat '71
Red Sun '71
Someone Behind the Door '71
The Family '70
Rider on the Rain '70
Lola '69
Honor Among Thieves '68
Once Upon a Time in the West '68
Villa Rides '68
The Dirty Dozen '67
The Meanest Men in the West '67
This Property Is Condemned '66
Battle of the Bulge '65
The Sandpiper '65
Guns of Diablo '65
Four for Texas '63
The Great Escape '63
Kid Galahad '62
Master of the World '61
The Magnificent Seven '60
Never So Few '59
Machine Gun Kelly '58
Showdown at Boot Hill '58
When Hell Broke Loose '58
Jubal '56
Run of the Arrow '56
Apache '54
Crime Wave '54
Drum Beat '54
House of Wax '53
Miss Sadie Thompson '53
Vera Cruz '53
Pat and Mike '52

Lillian Bronson (1903-95)
Spencer's Mountain '63
The Next Voice You Hear '50

Claudio Brook (1929-95)
Cronos '94
The Bees '78
Devil's Rain '75
Dr. Tarr's Torture Dungeon '75
Sisters of Satan '75
The Peking Blond '68
Simon of the Desert '66
Viva Maria! '65
Samson in the Wax Museum '63
The Exterminating Angel '62
Neutron and the Black Mask '61

The Young One '61
Daniel Boone: Trail Blazer '56

Clive Brook (1887-1974)
On Approval '44
Convoy '40
Action for Slander '38
Cavalcade '33
Shanghai Express '32
Hula 28
Underworld '27

Faith Brook (1922-)
Eye of the Needle '81
After Julius '78
Bloodbath '76
War and Peace '73
To Sir, with Love '67
Uneasy Terms '48

Irina Brook (1962-)
Captive '87
The Girl in the Picture '86
Transmutations '85

Isabel Brook
About a Boy '02
Faust: Love of the Damned '00

Jayne Brook (1962-)
Gattaca '97
Ed '96
Last Dance '96
Bye Bye, Love '94
Clean Slate '94
Doing Time on Maple Drive '92

Lyndon Brook (1926-2004)
Invasion '65
The Spanish Gardener '57
Above Us the Waves '56

Elwyn Brook-Jones (1911-62)
Rogue's Yarn '56
The Gilded Cage '54
Bonnie Prince Charlie '48

Bunny Brooke (1920-2000)
Dawn! '83
Alison's Birthday '79

Hillary Brooke (1914-99)
The Man Who Knew Too Much '56
Heat Wave '54
Invaders from Mars '53
Abbott and Costello Meet Captain Kidd '52
Never Wave at a WAC '52
The Lost Continent '51
Africa Screams '49
Big Town '47
Big Town After Dark '47
Underworld Scandal '48
The Road to Utopia '46
Strange Impersonation '46
The Strange Woman '46
The Enchanted Cottage '45
The Woman in Green '45
Jane Eyre '44
Ministry of Fear '44
Sherlock Holmes Faces Death '43
Sherlock Holmes: The Voice of Terror '42
Wake Island '42
The Lone Rider in Frontier Fury '41
The Philadelphia Story '40

Paul Brooke (1944-)
The Affair of the Necklace '01
Dead of Night '99
The Lair of the White Worm '88

Sandy Brooke
Crazed Cop '88
Miami Vendetta '87
Star Slammer '87
Terror on Alcatraz '86

Tyler Brooke
The Divorcee '30
Monte Carlo '30

Walter Brooke (1914-86)
The Return of Count Yorga '71
Tora! Tora! Tora! '70
Conquest of Space '55

Richard Brooker (1955-)
Friday the 13th, Part 4: The Final Chapter '84
Deathstalker '83
Friday the 13th, Part 3 '82

Jacqueline Brookes (1930-)
Naked Gun 2 1/2: The Smell of Fear '91
Silent Witness '85
Hardhat & Legs '80
Rodeo Girl '80
The Gambler '74

Michelle Brookhurst
Recipe for Disaster '03
Can't Hardly Wait '98

Aimee Brooks (1974-)
The Hillside Strangler '04
Monster Man '03
Critters 3 '91
Say Anything '89

Albert Brooks (1947-)
The Simpsons Movie '07 (V)
Looking for Comedy in the Muslim World '06
Finding Nemo '03 (V)
The In-Laws '03
My First Mister '01
The Muse '99
Dr. Dolittle '98 (V)
Out of Sight '98
Critical Care '97
Mother '96
I'll Do Anything '93
Defending Your Life '91
Broadcast News '87
Lost in America '85
Unfaithfully Yours '84
Twilight Zone: The Movie '83
Modern Romance '81
Private Benjamin '80
Real Life '79
Taxi Driver '76

Avery Brooks (1948-)
15 Minutes '01
American History X '98
The Big Hit '98
Spenser: A Savage Place '94
Spenser: Pale Kings & Princes '94
Spenser: The Judas Goat '94
The Ernest Green Story '93
Spenser: Ceremony '93
Roots: The Gift '88
Uncle Tom's Cabin '87
Half Slave, Half Free '85

Carroll Brooks
Mauvais Sang '86
Boy Meets Girl '84

Clarence Brooks (1896-1969)
Bronze Buckaroo '39
Harlem Rides the Range '39

Conrad Brooks (1931-)
The Alien Agenda: Under the Skin '97
Bikini Drive-In '94
Ed Wood '94
Test Tube Teens from the Year 2000 '93
Curse of the Queerwolf '87
The Beast of Yucca Flats '61
The Sinister Urge '60
Plan 9 from Outer Space '56
Bride of the Monster '55
Jail Bait '54
Glen or Glenda? '53

David Allan Brooks (1947-)
Cast Away '00

Jack Frost 2: Revenge of
the Mutant Killer
Snowman '00
The Kindred '87
Manhunter '86

**Elisabeth Brooks
(1951-97)**
The Forgotten One '89
The Howling '81

**Foster Brooks (1912-
2001)**
Oddballs '84
Cracking Up '83
The Villain '79
Super Seal '77

**Geraldine Brooks
(1925-77)**
Johnny Tiger '66
Challenge to Lassie '49
Reckless Moment '49
Cry Wolf '47
The Possessed '47

**Golden Brooks
(1970-)**
Something New '06
Beauty Shop '05
Motives '03

Hildy Brooks
Forbidden Love '82
The Chosen '81

**Jean Brooks (1916-
63)**
The Iceman Cometh 73
Boss of Big Town '43
The Leopard Man '43
The Seventh Victim '43
Boot Hill Bandits '42

Jennifer Brooks
The Man with Two Brains
'83

Joel Brooks (1949-)
Bound by Lies '05
The Man Who Captured
Eichmann '95
Indecent Proposal '93
Are You Lonesome Tonight
'92

Leslie Brooks (1922-)
The Cobra Strikes '48
Romance on the High Seas
'48

**Louise Brooks (1906-
85)**
Overland Stage Raiders 38
Prix de Beaute '30
Diary of a Lost Girl 29
Beggars of Life 28
A Girl in Every Port 28
Pandora's Box 28
It's the Old Army Game 26
Love 'Em and Leave 'Em
'26
The Show Off '26

Mel Brooks (1926-)
The Producers '05
Robots '05 (V)
Screw Loose '99
Robin Hood: Men in Tights
'93
Life Stinks '91
Look Who's Talking, Too
'90 (V)
Spaceballs '87
To Be or Not to Be '83
History of the World: Part 1
'81
The Muppet Movie 79
High Anxiety 77
Silent Movie '76
Blazing Saddles '74
The Twelve Chairs '70
Putney Swope '69
The Producers '68

**Phyllis Brooks (1915-
95)**
Dangerous Passage '44
The Shanghai Gesture '42
Slightly Honorable '40
Charlie Chan in Honolulu
'38
Little Miss Broadway '38
Rebecca of Sunnybrook
Farm '38
In Old Chicago '37

**Rand Brooks (1918-
2003)**
Comanche Station '60
To Hell and Back '55
The Vanishing Westerner
'50
Ladies of the Chorus '49
Hopalong Cassidy:
Borrowed Trouble '48
Hopalong Cassidy:
Dangerous Venture '48
Hopalong Cassidy: False
Paradise '48
Hopalong Cassidy: Silent
Conflict '48
Hopalong Cassidy: Sinister
Journey '48
Hopalong Cassidy: The
Dead Don't Dream '48
Hopalong Cassidy: The
Marauders '47
Hopalong Cassidy:
Unexpected Guest '47
Hopalong Cassidy: The
Devil's Playground '46
The Sombrero Kid '42
Gone with the Wind '39

Randi Brooks (1956-)
Colors '88
Cop '88
Hamburger... The Motion
Picture '86
Tightrope '84

Ray Brooks (1939-)
Office Romances '86
House of Whipcord '75
Daleks—Invasion Earth
2150 A.D. '66
The Knack '65

Randy Brooks
Reservoir Dogs '92
Black Snow '89

Richard Brooks (1962-)
Johnny B. '00
The Crow 2: City of Angels
'96
The Substitute '96
Wolverine '96
Chameleon '96
Machine Gun Blues '95
Memphis '91
To Sleep with Anger '90
84 Charlie MoPic '89
Shocker '89
Shakedown '88
Short Fuse '88
The Hidden '87

Terron Brooks
The Temptations '98

Van Brooks
The Substitute '96
Blood Simple '85

Anthony Brophy
The Informant '97
The Run of the Country '95

Brian Brophy
Brain Dead '89
Skinheads: The Second
Coming of Hate '88

**Edward Brophy
(1895-1960)**
Last Hurrah '58
Pier 23 '51

**Dr. Joyce Brothers
(1928-)**
When Evil Calls '07
Surveillance 24/7 '07
The Naked Gun: From the
Files of Police Squad! '88
Love at Stake '87
The Lonely Guy '84

Sean Brosnan
Surveillance 24/7 '07

Kevin Brophy (1953-)
Delos Adventure '86
The Seduction '82
Time Walker '82
Hell Night '81

**Pierce Brosnan
(1953-)**
Mamma Mia! '08
Married Life '07
Seraphim Falls '06
The Matador '06
After the Sunset '04
Laws of Attraction '04
Die Another Day '02
Evelyn '02
The Tailor of Panama '00
The Thomas Crown Affair
'99
The World Is Not Enough
'99
Grey Owl '99
The Nephew '97
Dante's Peak '97
Tomorrow Never Dies '97
Mars Attacks! '96
The Mirror Has Two Faces
'96
Robinson Crusoe '96
Goldeneye '95
Detonator 2: Night Watch
'95
The Disappearance of
Kevin Johnson '95
Love Affair '94
Don't Talk to Strangers '94
Victim of Love '91
Mister Johnson '91
Murder 101 '91
Around the World in 80
Days '89
The Heist '89
The Deceivers '88
Noble House '88
Taffin '88
The Fourth Protocol '87
Nomads '86
The Carpathian Eagle '81
The Manions of America
'81

Bobby Brown (1969-)
Nora's Hair Salon 2: A Cut
Above '08
Nora's Hair Salon '04
Gang of Roses '03
Two Can Play That Game
'01
A Thin Line Between Love
and Hate '96
Mother Goose Rock 'n'
Rhyme '90
The Choirboys '77

Bruce Brown (1938-)
The Endless Summer 2 '94
Zipperface '92
The Endless Summer '66

Desperate Lives '82
Embryo '76

Amelda Brown
Little Dorrit, Film 1:
Nobody's Fault '88
Little Dorrit, Film 2: Little
Dorrit's Story '88

Barbara Brown (1902-
My Sister Eileen '55
Ma and Pa Kettle on
Vacation '53
Jack & the Beanstalk '52
Home Town Story '51
Ma and Pa Kettle Back On
the Farm '51
Born Yesterday '50
Hollywood Canteen '44

**Barry Brown (1951-
78)**
He Who Walks Alone '78
The Disappearance of
Aimee '76
The Ultimate Thrill '74
Bad Company '72

Billie Brown (1952-)
The Dish '01
Oscar and Lucinda '97
Fierce Creatures '96
Flesh '68

Billy Aaron Brown
Jeepers Creepers 2 '03
Attack of the Sabretooth
'05

Blair Brown (1948-)
The Sentinel '06
The Treatment '06
Loverboy '05
Dogville '03
Follow the Stars Home '01
Hamlet '01
In His Life: The John
Lennon Story '00
Space Cowboys '00
The Astronaut's Wife '99
The Day My Parents Ran
Away '93
Passed Away '92
Strapless '90
Stealing Home '88
Hands of a Stranger '87
The Bad Seed '85
A Flash of Green '85
Kennedy '83
Continental Divide '81
Altered States '80
One Trick Pony '80
And I Alone Survived '78

Ben Browder (1962-)
Stargate: The Ark of Truth
'08
Boogie Boy '98
A Kiss Before Dying '91

Jordan Brower (1981-)
Night Ride Home '99
Speedway Junky '99

Alan Brough
The Nugget '02

Liliane Brousse
Paranoiac '63
Maniac '63

Bryan Brown (1947-)
The Adventures of
Buckaroo Banzai Across
the Eighth Dimension '84
Along Came Polly '04
Dirty Deeds '02
On the Beach '00
Risk '00
Two Hands '98
Dead Heart '96
Grizzly Falls '99
Journey to the Center of
the Earth '99
Styx '00
Full Body Massage '95
Blame It on the Bellboy '92
Devlin '92
Twisted '96 (V)
Tracked '98
F/X 2: The Deadly Art of
Illusion '91
Prisoners of the Sun '91
Sweet Talker '91
Gorillas in the Mist '88
Cocktail '88
F/X '86
The Good Wife '86
Tai-Pan '86
The Empty Beach '85
Rebel '85
Far East '85
Give My Regards to Broad
Street '84
Kim '84
Parker '84
The Thorn Birds '83
A Town Like Alice '85
The Winter of Our Dreams
'82
The Odd Angry Shot '79
Palm Beach '79
The Chant of Jimmie
Blacksmith '78
The Irishman '78
Newsfront '78
Money Movers '79
Blood Money '80
Breaker Morant '80

**Charles D. Brown
(1887-1949)**
Follow Me Quietly '49
Merton of the Movies '47
Having Wonderful Crime
'45
International Lady '41
Brother Orchid '40
Old Swimmin' Hole '40
Mr. Moto in Danger Island
'39

Christopher Brown
This Christmas '07
Alien Avengers '96

Clancy Brown (1959-)
The Reading Room '05
The Guardian '06
The SpongeBob
SquarePants Movie '04
(V)
Normal '03
Snow White: The Fairest of
Them All '02
The Hurricane '99
In the Company of Spies
'99
Starship Troopers '97
Female Perversions '96
Flubber '97
Cabin Boy '94
The Shawshank
Redemption '94
Last Light '93
Past Midnight '92
Waiting for the Light '90
Season of Fear '89
Shoot to Kill '88
Extreme Prejudice '87
Highlander '86
The Bride '85
Thunder Alley '85

**Drew "Bundini"
Brown (1928-87)**
Shaft's Big Score '72
Shaft '71

David G. Brown
Chasing Dreams '81
Deadly Harvest '72
Bad Boys '83

D.W. Brown
Mischief '85
Weekend Pass '84

Dwier Brown (1959-)
Deconstructing Sarah '94
The Cutting Edge '92
Galaxies Are Colliding '92
Gettysburg '93
Lily in Winter '94
Same River Twice '96
Intimate Betrayal '96
Mom and Dad Save the
World '92
Field of Dreams '89
The Guardian '90

Eric Brown (1964-)
Video Murders '87
They're Playing with Fire
'84
Private Lessons '75

Erin Brown
See Misty Mundae

Gary Brown
Invasion of the Space
Preachers '90

Gaye Brown (1941-)
An American Haunting '05
The Glory Boys '84
Space Monster '64
Masque of the Red Death
'65

**Georg Stanford
Brown (1943-)**
Roots: The Next
Generation '79
Roots '77
Colossus: The Forbin
Project '70
Dayton's Devils '68
The Man in the Glass
Booth '75
Bullitt '68

**Georgia Brown (1933-
92)**
Victim of Love '91
Love at Stake '87
The Fixer '68
Nothing But the Night '72
Long Ago Tomorrow '71
Tales That Witness
Madness '73

Henry Brown
Cash '93

**James Brown (1920-
93)**
Adios Amigo '75
Targets '68
Rin Tin Tin, Hero of the
West '55
Courage of Rin Tin Tin '57
Objective, Burma! '45
Sands of Iwo Jima '49

Air Force '43
Wake Island '42

James Brown (1933-2006)
Undercover Brother '02
Blues Brothers 2000 '98
Doctor Detroit '83
The Blues Brothers '80

Jim Brown (1935-)
Animal '05
She Hate Me '04
Any Given Sunday '99
He Got Game '98
Small Soldiers '98 (V)
Mars Attacks! '96
Original Gangstas '96
The Divine Enforcer '91
Crack House '89
L.A. Vice '89
Twisted Justice '89
I'm Gonna Git You Sucka '88
L.A. Heat '88
The Running Man '87
Pacific Inferno '85
One Down, Two to Go! '82
Fingers '78
Kid Vengeance '75
Take a Hard Ride '75
Three the Hard Way '74
Slaughter's Big Ripoff '73
Slaughter '72
El Condor '70
The Passing of Evil '70
100 Rifles '69
Riot '69
Dark of the Sun '68
Ice Station Zebra '68
The Dirty Dozen '67
Rio Conchos '64

Joe E. Brown (1892-1973)
The Comedy of Terrors '64
It's a Mad, Mad, Mad, Mad World '63
Some Like It Hot '59
Around the World in 80 Days '56
Show Boat '51
The Tender Years '47
Pin-Up Girl '44
The Gladiator '38
Wide Open Faces '38
Fit for a King '37
Riding on Air '37
When's Your Birthday? '37
Earthworm Tractors '36
Alibi Ike '35
A Midsummer Night's Dream '35
Lottery Bride '30

Johnny Mack Brown (1904-74)
Apache Uprising '66
Border Bandits '46
Gentleman from Texas '46
The Stranger from Pecos '45
Lawmen '44
Partners of the Trail '44
Raiders of the Border '44
Range Law '44
Ghost Rider '43
Six Gun Gospel '43
Texas Kid '43
Ride 'Em Cowboy '42
The Masked Rider '41
Boss of Bullion City '41
Pony Post '40
Riders of Pasco Basin '40
Flaming Frontiers '38
Man from Montana '41
Boothill Brigade '37
The Gambling Terror '37
Guns in the Dark '37
A Lawman Is Born '37
Crooked Trail '36
Desert Phantom '36
Everyman's Law '36
Rogue of the Range '36
Undercover Man '36
Valley of the Lawless '36
Between Men '35
Branded a Coward '35
Courageous Avenger '35
Rustlers of Red Dog '35
Belle of the Nineties '34
Female '33
Fighting with Kit Carson '33
Fire Alarm '32
Undertow '30
Coquette '29
The Single Standard '29
Annapolis '28
Our Dancing Daughters '28
A Woman of Affairs '28

Juanita Brown
Black Starlet '74
Caged Heat '74
Foxy Brown '74

Judy (Judith) Brown (1944)
The Manhandlers '73
The Big Doll House '71

Julie Brown (1958-)
Plump Fiction '97
Clueless '95
Fist of the North Star '95
Out There '95
National Lampoon's Attack of the 5 Ft. 2 Women '94
Nervous Ticks '93
The Opposite Sex and How to Live With Them '93
Raining Stones '93
Shakes the Clown '92
Spirit of '76 '91
Earth Girls Are Easy '89
Bloody Birthday '80

Downtown Julie Brown (1963-)
Bug Buster '99
Ride '98

Kimberly J. Brown (1984-)
Bringing Down the House '03
My Sister's Keeper '02
Stephen King's Rose Red '02
Tumbleweeds '98

Lou Brown (1952-)
Death Games '80
Alison's Birthday '79
The Irishman '78

Lowell Brown
Wuthering Heights '70
Secret Ceremony '69

Marcus Lyle Brown
Mammoth '06
Venom '05

Melanie (Scary Spice) Brown (1975-)
Lethal Dose '03
Spice World: The Movie '97
Max Keeble's Big Move '01 (V)

Murray Brown (1937-)
Vampyres '74
Dracula '73

Olivia Brown
Memories of Murder '90
Streets of Fire '84

Orlando Brown
The Proud Family Movie '05 (V)

Pamela Brown (1917-75)
In This House of Brede '75
Dracula '73
Wuthering Heights '70
Secret Ceremony '69
Cleopatra '63
Victoria Regina '61
Lust for Life '56
Alice in Wonderland '50
I Know Where I'm Going '45
One of Our Aircraft Is Missing '41

Pat Crawford Brown (1929-)
Stuck On You '03
Elvira, Mistress of the Dark '88

Peter Brown (1935-)
Three Bad Men '05
Asylum '97
The Aurora Encounter '85
The Concrete Jungle '82
Act of Vengeance '74
Foxy Brown '74
Memory of Us '74
Slashed Dreams '74
Chrome and Hot Leather '71
Eagles Attack at Dawn '70
Hard Frame '70
Kitten with a Whip '64
Ride the Wild Surf '64
A Tiger Walks '64
Merrill's Marauders '62
Darby's Rangers '58
The Commies Are Coming, the Commies Are Coming '57

Phil Brown (1916-2006)
Tropic of Cancer '70
Operation Cross Eagles '69
The Hidden Room '49
Without Reservations '46
Jungle Captive '45

Philip Brown (1958-)
Wild Zone '89
Eye of the Needle '81
Special Olympics '78

P.J. Brown (1956-)
Double Parked '00
Rick '03

Ralph Brown (1913-90)
Star Wars: Episode 1—The Phantom Menace '99
Ivanhoe '97
Wayne's World 2 '93
Alien 3 '92
The Crying Game '92
Impromptu '90
Christabel '89
Buster '88
Withnail and I '87

Ralph Brown (1960-)
Closure '07
The Contractor '07
I'll Be There '03
Mean Machine '01
Extremely Dangerous '99

Reb Brown (1948-)
Cage 2: The Arena of Death '94
The Firing Line '91
Last Flight to Hell '91
Street Hunter '90
The Cage '89
Mercenary Fighters '88
Space Mutiny '88
White Ghost '88
Strike Commando '87
Death of a Soldier '85
Howling 2: Your Sister Is a Werewolf '85
Uncommon Valor '83
Yor, the Hunter from the Future '83
Captain America '79
Captain America 2: Death Too Soon '79

Ritza Brown
The McGuffin '85
Ator the Fighting Eagle '83

Rob Brown (1984-)
Stop-Loss '08
Take the Lead '06
Coach Carter '05
Finding Forrester '00

Robert Brown (1918-2003)
License to Kill '89
The Living Daylights '87
A View to a Kill '85
Octopussy '83
Pilgrim, Farewell '82
One Million Years B.C. '66
Tower of London '62
It Takes a Thief '59
Shake Hands with the Devil '59
The Abominable Snowman '57

Roger Aaron Brown (1949-)
Miracle in Lane Two '00
Tall Tale: The Unbelievable Adventures of Pecos Bill '95
Undesirable '92
Don't Cry, It's Only Thunder '82

Ron Brown
The Legend of Black Thunder Mountain '79
Charlie, the Lonesome Cougar '67

Samantha Brown (1976-)
Lift '01
New Jersey Drive '95

Sara Suzanne Brown
Killer Looks '94
Secret Games 2: The Escort '93
Test Tube Teens from the Year 2000 '93
The Bikini Car Wash Company 2 '92
The Bikini Car Wash Company '90

Stanley Brown (1914-2001)
Blondie's Blessed Event '42
Blondie Meets the Boss '39

Stephen Brown (1917-98)
Beyond Darkness '92
Metamorphosis '90

Thomas Wilson Brown (1972-)
Skeletons '96
Diggstown '92
Honey, I Shrunk the Kids '89
Welcome Home '89

Timothy Brown (1937-)
Pacific Inferno '85
Code Name: Zebra '84
Losin' It '82
The Dynamite Brothers '74
Girls Are for Loving '73
A Place Called Today '72
Sweet Sugar '72
M*A*S*H '70

Tom Brown (1913-90)
The Choppers '61
Operation Haylift '50
Ringside '49
Buck Privates Come Home '47
Adventures of Smilin' Jack '43
The Payoff '43
The Duke of West Point '38
In Old Chicago '37
Maytime '37
Navy Blue and Gold '37
I'd Give My Life '36
Anne of Green Gables '34
Two Alone '34

Vanessa Brown (1928-99)
Witch Who Came from the Sea '76
The Fighter '52
Three Husbands '50
The Heiress '49
The Ghost and Mrs. Muir '47
Mother Wore Tights '47

W. Earl Brown (1963-)
The Big White '05
Killer Diller '04
Dancing at the Blue Iguana '00
Lost Souls '00
Meat Loaf: To Hell and Back '00
There's Something about Mary '98
Scream '96
Excessive Force '93
Dead Air '94

Wally Brown (1904-61)
The Absent-Minded Professor '61
The High and the Mighty '54
Girl Rush '44
Seven Days Ashore '44
Zombies on Broadway '44

Woody Brown (1956-)
Animal Instincts 2 '94
Dominion '94
Secret Games 3 '94
Alligator 2: The Mutation '90
The Rain Killer '90
The Accused '88
Killer Party '86

Charles A. Browne
Federal Agent '36
Tailspin Tommy '34

Coral Browne (1913-91)
Dreamchild '85
American Dreamer '84
An Englishman Abroad '83
Eleanor: First Lady of the World '82
Theatre of Blood '73
The Ruling Class '72
The Killing of Sister George '69
Auntie Mame '58
The Courtney Affair '47

Leslie Browne (1958-)
Dancers '87
Nijinsky '80
The Turning Point '77

Lucille Browne (1907-76)
Cheyenne Rides Again '38
Crooked Trail '36
Texas Terror '35
Western Frontier '35
Brand of Hate '34
Law of the Wild '34
The Devil's Brother '33
Mystery Squadron '33
Battling with Buffalo Bill '31

Roscoe Lee Browne (1925-2007)
Garfield: A Tail of Two Kitties '06 (V)
Treasure Planet '02 (V)
Hamlet '01
Morgan's Ferry '99
Babe: Pig in the City '98 (N)
Dear God '96
Last Summer In the Hamptons '96
Babe '95 (N)
Forest Warrior '95
The Pompatus of Love '95
Naked in New York '93
Eddie Presley '92
The Mambo Kings '92
Moon 44 '90
For Us, the Living '88
Oliver & Company '88 (V)
Jumpin' Jack Flash '86
Legal Eagles '86
Haunting of Harrington House '82
Nothing Personal '80
Unknown Powers '80
King '78
Twilight's Last Gleaming '77
Logan's Run '76
Superfly T.N.T. '73
The World's Greatest Athlete '73
The Cowboys '72
The Liberation of L.B. Jones '70
Black Like Me '64
The Connection '61

Suzanne Browne
See Sara Suzanne Brown

Zachary Browne (1985-)
Shiloh 2: Shiloh Season '99
Shiloh '97
Man of the House '95

Alistair Browning
Rain '01

Emily Browning (1988-)
Lemony Snicket's A Series of Unfortunate Events '04
Ned Kelly '03
Ghost Ship '02

Ricou Browning (1930-)
Flipper's New Adventure '64
The Creature Walks among Us '56
Creature from the Black Lagoon '54

Rod Browning (1942-)
The Life & Times of the Chocolate Killer '88
When Hell Was in Session '82

Ryan Browning (1974-)
The Legend of Butch & Sundance '04
Stealing Sinatra '04
Extremedays '01
The Smokers '00

Frank Brownlee (1874-1948)
Sundown Fury '42
Tombstone Canyon '32

Brenda Bruce (1919-96)
Splitting Heirs '93
Antonia and Jane '91
December Bride '91
Back Home '90
The Tenth Man '88
Mad Death '83
That'll Be the Day '73
Nightmare '63
Peeping Tom '60

Cheryl Lynn Bruce
Daughters of the Dust '91
Victimless Crimes '90
Music Box '89

Colin Bruce
Chicago Joe & the Showgirl '90
Crusoe '89
Gotham '88

David Bruce (1916-76)
Jungle Hell '55
Pier 23 '51
Hi-Jacked '50
Can't Help Singing '45
Lady on a Train '45
Salome, Where She Danced '45
Son of Lassie '45
The Woman in Green '45
Frenchman's Creek '44
The Pearl of Death '44
Scarlet Claw '44

Nigel Bruce (1895-1953)
Limelight '52
Julia Misbehaves '48
The Two Mrs. Carrolls '47
Dressed to Kill '46
Terror by Night '46
The Corn Is Green '45
House of Fear '45
Pursuit to Algiers '45
The Woman in Green '45
Frenchman's Creek '44
The Pearl of Death '44
Scarlet Claw '44
Spider Woman '44
Lassie, Come Home '43
Sherlock Holmes Faces Death '43
Sherlock Holmes in Washington '43
Journey for Margaret '42
Roxie Hart '42
Sherlock Holmes and the Secret Weapon '42
Sherlock Holmes: The Voice of Terror '42
The Chocolate Soldier '41
Suspicion '41
The Blue Bird '40
Lillian Russell '40
Rebecca '40
Susan and God '40

Kate Bruce (1858-1946)
Struggle '31
The Idol Dancer '20
Way Down East '20
Judith of Bethulia '14

The Adventures of Sherlock Holmes '39
The Hound of the Baskervilles '39
The Rains Came '39
The Last of Mrs. Cheyney '37
Thunder in the City '37
The Charge of the Light Brigade '36
The Trail of the Lonesome Pine '36
Becky Sharp '35
She '35
The Scarlet Pimpernel '34
Treasure Island '34

Virginia Bruce (1910-82)
Strangers When We Meet '60
State Department File 649 '49
Action in Arabia '44
Pardon My Sarong '42
The Invisible Woman '40
Let Freedom Ring '39
Born to Dance '36
The Great Ziegfeld '36
Let 'Em Have It '35
Dangerous Corner '34
Jane Eyre '34

Agnes Bruckner (1985-)
Blood & Chocolate '07
Dreamland '06
Peaceful Warrior '06
Venom '05
Haven '04
The Iris Effect '04
Stateside '04
Blue Car '03
Rick '03
The Woods '03
Home Room '02
Murder by Numbers '02

Amy Bruckner (1991-)
Nancy Drew '07
Rebound '05

Patrick Bruel (1959-)
Comedy of Power '06
Lost and Found '99
Sabrina '95
Secret Obsession '88
Bandits '86
Magic Island '95

Eddie Brugman (1943-)
Broken Mirrors '85
Katie Tippel '75

Alex Bruhanski
Black Point '01
Showdown at Williams Creek '91

Daniel Bruhl (1978-)
The Bourne Ultimatum '07
Joyeux Noel '05
The Educators '04
Good Bye, Lenin! '03

John Brumpton
Dance Me to My Song '98
Life '95

Bo Brundin (1937-)
Headless Eyes '83
Shoot the Sun Down '81
Russian Roulette '75

Robert Bruning
The Night After Halloween '79

Dylan Bruno (1972-)
Fresh Cut Grass '04
Going Greek '01
The One '01
Where the Heart Is '00
The Rage: Carrie 2 '99

Nando (Fernando) Bruno (1895-1963)
Time Out for Love '61
Two Nights with Cleopatra '54

Philip Bruns (1931-)
The Opposite Sex and How to Live with Them '93
Dead Men Don't Die '91
Return of the Living Dead 2 '88
The Stunt Man '80
Harry and Tonto '74

Keith Brunsmann
Tweek City '05
Tropix '02
Sticks '98

Eric Bruskotter (1966-)
Major League 3: Back to the Minors '98
Starship Troopers '97
The Fan '96
Major League 2 '94
Can't Buy Me Love '87

Dora Bryan (1924-)
Apartment Zero '88
Screamtime '83
Hands of the Ripper '71
The Great St. Trinian's Train Robbery '66
A Taste of Honey '61
Small Hotel '57
Made in Heaven '52
My Son, the Vampire '52
No Trace '50
The Fallen Idol '49

Jane Bryan (1918-)
Each Dawn I Die '39
The Old Maid '39
The Sisters '38
A Slight Case of Murder '38
Kid Galahad '37
Marked Woman '37

Zachery Ty Bryan (1981-)
Annapolis '06
The Fast and the Furious: Tokyo Drift '06
The Game of Their Lives '05
A Killing Spring '02
Rustin '01
The Rage: Carrie 2 '99
The Principal Takes a Holiday '98
True Heart '97
First Kid '96
Bigfoot: The Unforgettable Encounter '94

Bill Bryant
A Bullet for Joey '55

John Bryant (1916-89)
Run Silent, Run Deep '58
Courage of Black Beauty '57

Pamela Bryant (1959-)
Tigershark '87
Lunch Wagon '81

Virginia Bryant
The Barbarians '87
Demons 2 '87

William (Bill) Bryant (1924-2001)
Mountain Family Robinson '79
Corvette Summer '78
Green Eyes '76

Paul Bryar (1910-85)
Sky High '51
The Night of the Hunter '55
McLintock! '63
Move Over, Darling '63
Ride the High Country '62
It Started with a Kiss '59
The Devil's Partner '58
Lonesome Trail '55
Rage at Dawn '55
Silver Star '55
Human Desire '54
Make Haste to Live '54
Shane '53
Big Trees '52
She Couldn't Say No '52
The Big Hangover '50
Cheaper by the Dozen '50
Rawhide '50
Lust for Gold '49
Man from Colorado '49
Black Arrow '48
Coroner Creek '48
Abilene Town '46
If I'm Lucky '46
Talk of the Town '42
Penny Serenade '41
Texas '41
Arizona '40

Claudia Bryar (1918-)
Psycho 2 '83
Yuma '70

Rob Brydon (1965-)
Tristram Shandy: A Cock and Bull Story '05

Scott Bryce (1958-)
Up Close and Personal '96
Stalking Laura '93

Larry Bryggman (1938-)
Spy Game '01
Die Hard: With a Vengeance '95
Hollywood Shootout '03
44 Minutes: The North Hollywood Shootout '03

Andrew Bryniarski (1969-)
The Texas Chainsaw Massacre: The Beginning '06
The Program '93
The Texas Chainsaw Massacre '03
Cyborg 3: The Recycler '95
Batman Returns '92

Greg Bryk
Weirdsville '07
Poor Man's Game '06

Yul Brynner (1915-85)
Death Rage '77
Futureworld '76
The Ultimate Warrior '75
Night Flight from Moscow '73
Westworld '73
Fuzz '72
Adios, Sabata '71
Catlow '71
Light at the Edge of the World '71
The Poppy Is Also a Flower '66
Return of the Magnificent Seven '66
Kings of the Sun '63
Taras Bulba '62

Michael Bryant (1928-2002)
The Miracle Maker: The Story of Jesus '00 (V)
Half Slave, Half Free '94

Lee Bryant (1945-)
Alien Nation: Dark Horizon '94
The Skeleton Key '05
Get Rich or Die Tryin' '05
London '05
Bobby '06
3-Way '04
Baadasssss! '03
Antwone Fisher '02
Honey '03

Joyce Bryant
East Side Kids '40
Across the Plains '39
Fighting Renegade '39

Robert Buchanan
Monte Carlo '30

Jack Buchanan (1891-1957)
The Band Wagon '53
When Knights Were Bold '36

Sherry Buchanan
Doctor Butcher M.D. '80
Emmanuelle & Joanna '78
Eyes Behind the Stars '72

Simone Buchanan (1968-)
Shame '87
Run, Rebecca, Run '81

Ian Buchanan (1957-)
Panic Room '02
Ivory Tower '97
Marilyn & Bobby: Her Final Affair '94
Blue Flame '93
Double Exposure '93
The Cool Surface '92

King Lear '98
Hamlet '96
Sakharov '84
The Ruling Class '72
Girly '70

Nana Bryant (1888-1955)
The Private War of Major Benson '55
Harvey '50
Inner Sanctum '48
Big Town '47
The Possessed '47
If I Had My Way '40
Give Me a Sailor '38

Scott Bryce
Sinners in Paradise '38
Pennies from Heaven '36

Claudia Bryar
Convette Summer '78
Moll Flanders '96

Edgar Buchanan (1903-79)
Over the Hill Gang '69
Man from Button Willow '65
The Rounders '65
McLintock! '63
Cimarron '60
Shane '53

Colin Buchanan (1967-)
Catherine Cookson's The Secret '00
Robinson Crusoe of Clipper Island '36

Buck
Robinson Crusoe of Clipper Island '36
Teenage Wolfpack '57

Michael Buble (1975-)
The Snow Walker '03
Totally Blonde '01

Flavio Bucci (1947-)
Suspiria '77
Night Train Murders '75
Torture Train '75

Samantha Buck (1974-)
Wirey Spindell '99
The Sticky Fingers of Time '97

John Buckler (1906-36)
Tarzan Escapes '36
The Black Room '35

A.J. Buckley (1978-)
The Box '07
Eye '06
Mon Amie Max '94
Oh, What a Night '92
A Paper Wedding '90
Dead Ringers '88

Betty Buckley (1947-)
The Happening '08
Simply Irresistible '99
Critical Choices '97
Last Time Out '94
Wyatt Earp '94
Rain Without Thunder '93
Another Woman '88
Frantic '88
Babycakes '89
Tender Mercies '83
Carrie '76

Keith Buckley (1941-)
Deadly Blessing '81
Grease '78
Excalibur '81

Robert Budaska
Grizzly Mountain '97
Ice Pawn '92

Susan Buckner (1951-)
Deadly Blessing '81
Grease '78

Donald Buka (1921-)
The King of Hearts '66
The Street with No Name '48
Watch on the Rhine '43

Helen Buday (1963-)
Dingo '90
For Love Alone '86

Gustavo Bueno
The Motorcycle Diaries '04
La Boca del Lobo '89
Thunderdome '85

Jack Buetel (1915-89)
The Half-Breed '51
Best of the Badmen '50
The Outlaw '43

Marilyn Buferd (1925-90)
Queen of Outer Space '58
Machine to Kill Bad People '48

Christopher Buchholz
Eros '04

Horst Buchholz (1932-2003)
The Enemy '01
Life Is Beautiful '98
Faraway, So Close! '93
Aces: Iron Eagle 3 '92
Code Name: Emerald '85
Sahara '83
Berlin Tunnel 21 '81
From Hell to Victory '79
Avalanche Express '79
Raid on Entebbe '77
Return to Fantasy Island '77
The Savage Bees '76
The Catamount Killing '74
Empty Canvas '64
Fanny '61
One, Two, Three '61
The Magnificent Seven '60
Tiger Bay '59

Jimmy Buffett (1946-)
Hoot '06
FM '78
From the Earth to the Moon '98

Celso Bugallo (1947-)
The Sea Inside '04
Mondays in the Sun '02

Monica Bugajski
Rancho Deluxe '75
The Three Lives of Karen '97

Niall Buggy (1948-)
The Playboys '92
Zardoz '73

Joe Bugner (1950-)
The Cursed Mountain '97

Genevieve Bujold (1942-)
Finding Home '03
Jericho Mansions '03
Disappearances '06
Trouble in Mind '86
Choose Me '84
Tightrope '84
Monsignor '82
The House of Yes '97
Earthquake '74
Swashbuckler '76
Obsession '76
Journey '77
Another Man, Another Chance '77
Coma '78
Murder by Decree '79
Anne of the Thousand Days '69

Gerard Buhr (1928-88)
The Night of the Following Day '69
Boo le Flambeur '55

Valerie Buhagiar (1963-)
Highway 61 '91
Roadkill '89

Peter Bull (1912-84)
Doctor Dolittle '67
The Adventures of Nellie Bly '81
The Jayne Mansfield Story '80
Dr. Strangelove, or: How I Learned to Stop Worrying and Love the Bomb '64
Tom Jones '63
The African Queen '51
A Christmas Carol '51
Marie Antoinette '38

Raymond Buktenica (1943-)
My Girl '91
Wait Till Your Mother Gets Home '83
Second Best Secret Agent in the Whole Wide World '65

Buffalo Bill, Jr. (1896-1961)
Lightning Bill '35
Powdersmoke Range '35

Sabotage '36

Richard Bull (1924-)
Normal '03
Different Story '78
Lawman '71

Amelia Bullmore (1964-)
State of Play '03
Catherine Cookson's Tilly Trotter '99
Mrs. Dalloway '97

Jeremy Bulloch (1945-)
Return of the Jedi '83
The Empire Strikes Back '80
Hoffman '70

Donna Bullock (1955-)
The Girl Next Door '04
Air Force One '97

Sandra Bullock (1964)
Premonition '07
Infamous '06
The Lake House '06
Crash '05
Loverboy '05
Miss Congeniality 2: Armed and Fabulous '05
Divine Secrets of the Ya-Ya Sisterhood '02
Murder by Numbers '02
Two Weeks Notice '02
Lisa Picard Is Famous '01
Gun Shy '00
Miss Congeniality '00
28 Days '00
Forces of Nature '99
Hope Floats '98
Practical Magic '98
Prince of Egypt '98 (V)
Speed 2: Cruise Control '97
In Love and War '96
A Time to Kill '96
The Net '95
Two If by Sea '95
While You Were Sleeping '95
Me and the Mob '94
Speed '94
Demolition Man '93
Fire on the Amazon '93
The Thing Called Love '93
The Vanishing '93
Wrestling Ernest Hemingway '93
Love Potion #9 '92
Who Shot Pat? '92
When the Party's Over '91
A Fool and His Money '88
Hangmen '87

William Bumiller (1956)
Dark Justice '00
The Heroes of Desert Storm '91
Death Spa '87

Rodger Bumpass (1951-)
The SpongeBob SquarePants Movie '04 (V)
National Lampoon's Class of '86 '86
Heavy Metal '81 (V)

Stuart Bunce (1971-)
The Gospel of John '03
All the King's Men '99
Behind the Lines '97

Brooke Bundy (1944-)
Beverly Hills Bodysnatchers '89
A Nightmare on Elm Street 4: Dream Master '88
Twice Dead '88
A Nightmare on Elm Street 3: Dream Warriors '87
Explorers '85
Two Fathers' Justice '85
The Crash of Flight 401 '78
Francis Gary Powers: The True Story of the U-2 Spy '76
The Gay Deceivers '69

Marie Bunel (1964-)
The Chorus '04
Close to Leo '02
Ma Vie en Rose '97
La Discrete '90

Edward (Eddie) Bunker (1933-2005)
The Longest Yard '05
Animal Factory '00
Final Cut '98
Shadrach '98
Somebody to Love '94
Best of the Best 2 '93
Desperate Motives '92
Reservoir Dogs '92
Best of the Best '89
Miracle Mile '89
Relentless '89
Fear '89
The Running Man '87
Shy People '87
Runaway Train '85
Straight Time '78

Avis Bunnage (1923-90)
The Krays '90
No Surrender '86
Forbidden '85
The L-Shaped Room '62
The Loneliness of the Long Distance Runner '62

Luis Buñuel (1900-83)
The Discreet Charm of the Bourgeoisie '72
Un Chien Andalou '28

Cara Buono (1974-)
From Other Worlds '04
Hulk '03
Happy Accidents '00
Two Ninas '00
Attention Shoppers '99
Chutney Popcorn '99
In a Class of His Own '99
Man of the Century '99
Next Stop, Wonderland '98
Kicking and Screaming '95
Killer: A Journal of Murder '95
The Cowboy Way '94
Gladiator '92
Waterland '92

Victor Buono (1938-82)
The River Is Red '48
Arnold '73
The Mad Butcher '72
Northeast of Seoul '72
Beneath the Planet of the Apes '70
Boot Hill '69
The Silencers '66
Hush, Hush, Sweet Charlotte '65
Robin and the 7 Hoods '64
The Strangler '64
Four for Texas '63
What Ever Happened to Baby Jane? '62

Sonny Bupp (1928-2007)
Citizen Kane '41
Three Faces West '40
Hopalong Cassidy '39
Renegade Trail '39

Tommy Bupp (1924-83)
Roarin' Lead '37
Tex Rides with the Boy Scouts '37
It's a Gift '34

Hugh Burden (1913-85)
Blood from the Mummy's Tomb '71
Funeral in Berlin '66
Ghost Ship '53
Fame Is the Spur '47

Immortal Battalion '44

Suzanne Burden (1958-)
A Mind to Murder '96
Strapless '90

Ray Burdis (1958-)
Love, Honour & Obey '00
Final Cut '98

Alexander Burejev
Prisoner of the Mountains '96

Kim Burfield
Freedom Is Paradise '89
Treasure Island '72
The Hero '71

Michael J. Burg (1968-)
The Audrey Hepburn Story '00
Impostors '80

Christopher Burgard
Full Body Massage '95
84 Charlie MoPic '89
Twice Dead '88

Gregg Burge (1957-98)
School Daze '88
A Chorus Line '85

Dorothy Burgess (1907-61)
Girls in Chains '43
Village Tale '35
Hold Your Man '33
Ladies They Talk About '33

John Burgess
Rosencrantz & Guildenstern Are Dead '90
Christabel '89

Scott Burgess
Dead Easy '82
1915 '82

Gary Burghoff (1943-)
Small Kill '80
Casino '80
M*A*S*H '70

Richard Burgi (1958-)
Hostel: Part 2 '07
Fun With Dick and Jane '05
In Her Shoes '05
Cellular '04
I Married a Monster '98

Zlatko Buric (1953-)
Dirty Pretty Things '03
Pusher '96

MyAnna Buring
Doomsday '08
The Descent '05

Alfred Burke (1918-)
The House on Garibaldi Street '79
The Brontes of Haworth '73
One Day in the Life of Ivan Denisovich '71
Night Caller from Outer Space '66
The Nanny '65
Children of the Damned '63
Dead Lucky '60
Sergeant Rutledge '60
The Young Philadelphians '59
Small Town Girl '53
Father's Little Dividend '51
Father of the Bride '50
The Barkleys of Broadway '49

Everybody Sing '38
The Young in Heart '38
The Bride Wore Red '37
Navy Blue and Gold '37
Topper '37
Craig's Wife '36
Becky Sharp '35
Doubting Thomas '35
Forsaking All Others '35
Splendor '35
Christopher Strong '33
Dinner at Eight '33
Finishing School '33
A Bill of Divorcement '32

Billy Burke (1966-)
Untraceable '08
Feast of Love '07
Fracture '07
Ladder 49 '04
Lost Junction '03
Along Came a Spider '01
The Independent '00
Komodo '99
Don't Look Down '98
Mafia! '98
Without Limits '97
To Cross the Rubicon '91

Brandon Burke
Best Enemies '86
The Odd Angry Shot '79

David Burke
King Lear '94
Vibrations '94

Delta Burke (1956-)
Good Boy! '03 (V)
Dangerous Child '01
Sordid Lives '00
What Women Want '00
Melanie Darrow '97
Maternal Instincts '96
Dynamite and Gold '88
A Bunny's Tale '85
First & Ten: The Team Scores Again '85
The Seekers '79

J. Frank Burke (1867-1918)
The Bargain '15
The Italian '15

James Burke (1886-1968)
In Enemy Hands '04
Lucky Me '54
Cavalry Charge '51
Down to Earth '47
At the Circus '39
Beau Geste '39
Dawn Patrol '38
Dead End '37
Make a Million '35
The Mystery Man '35
Ruggles of Red Gap '35
Lady by Choice '34

Michelle Burke
See Michelle Rene Thomas

Patricia Burke (1917-2003)
While I Live '47
Murder in the Footlights '46

Paul Burke (1926-)
The Red Light Sting '84
Wild & Wooly '78
Psychic Killer '75
Anatomy of Terror '74
Daddy's Gone A-Hunting '69
Valley of the Dolls '67
Fatal Confinement '64
Francis in the Navy '55
Francis Goes to West Point '52

Robert John Burke (1961-)
Good Night, and Good Luck '05
Hide and Seek '05
Connie and Carla '04
Speak '04
No Such Thing '01
A Bright Shining Lie '98
First Love, Last Rites '98
Somewhere in the City '97
Fled '96
Stephen King's Thinner '96
Killer: A Journal of Murder '95
Dust Devil '93
Tombstone '93
Simple Men '92
Rambling Rose '91
RoboCop 3 '91
The Unbelievable Truth '90

Robert Karl Burke
The Basket '99
Big and Hairy '98

Simon Burke (1961-)
The Alice '04
After the Deluge '03
Rodgers & Hammerstein's South Pacific '01
Pitch Black '00
Passion '99
The One That Got Away '96
Class of '61 '92
House 4: Home Deadly Home '91
The Inshman '78
The Devil's Playground '76

Tom Burke (1981-)
Dracula '06
All the King's Men '99

Laura Burkett
Daddy's Boys '87
Overkill '86

Scott Burkholder
Sketch Artist 2: Hands That See '94

Dennis Burkley (1945-)
Possums '99
The First 9 1/2 Weeks '98
Father's Day '96
Tin Cup '96
Son-in-Law '93
Stop! or My Mom Will Shoot '92
The Doors '91
Lambada '90
Pass the Ammo '88
Murphy's Romance '85
Bummer '73

Tom Burlinson (1957-)
Landslide '92
Showdown at Williams Creek '91
Piece of Cake '88
Return to Snowy River '88
The Time Guardian '87
Windrider '86
Flesh and Blood '85
Phar Lap '84
The Man from Snowy River '82

Leo Burmester (1944-)
Carry Me Home '04
City by the Sea '02
Limbo '99
Speed of Life '99
Eye of the Storm '98
Switchback '97
William Faulkner's Old Man '97
Mistral '96
The Great Elephant Escape '95
The Neon Bible '95
Truman '95
Fly by Night '93
A Perfect World '93
Passion Fish '92
The Abyss '89 *
The River Is Red '48

Tam Dean Burn
Longford '06
The Acid House '98

Caesar Burner
Green Inferno '72

Carol Burnett (1933-)
Dr. Seuss' Horton Hears a Who! '08 (V)
The Trumpet of the Swan '01 (V)
Moon over Broadway '98
Noises Off '92
Follies in Concert '85
Between Friends '83
Annie '82
Chu Chu & the Philly Flash '81
The Four Seasons '81
Friendly Fire '79
Tenth Month '79
The Grass Is Always Greener Over the Septic Tank '78
A Wedding '78
Pete 'n' Tillie '72

Olivia Burnette (1977-)
Flourish '06
The Thorn Birds: The Missing Years '96
Final Verdict '91

Smiley Burnette (1911-67)
Last of the Pony Riders '53
On Top of Old Smoky '53
Winning of the West '53
Bonanza Town '51
Blazing Across the Pecos '48
Call of the Rockies '44
Idaho '43
King of the Cowboys '43
Raiders of Sunset Pass '43
Silver Spurs '43
Bells of Capistrano '42
Call of the Canyon '42
Heart of the Golden West '42
Heart of the Rio Grande '42
Back in the Saddle '41
Down Mexico Way '41
Ridin' on a Rainbow '41
Gaucho Serenade '40
South of the Border '39
Billy the Kid Returns '38
Hollywood Stadium Mystery '38
The Man from Music Mountain '38
Old Barn Dance '38
Prairie Moon '38
Rootin' Tootin' Rhythm '38
Under Western Stars '38
Big Show '37
Boots & Saddles '37
Dick Tracy '37
Dick Tracy: The Spider Strikes '37
Git Along Little Dogies '37
Larceny On the Air '37
Public Cowboy No. 1 '37
Round-Up Time in Texas '37

(continued from previous page)
Springtime in the Rockies '37
Yodelin' Kid from Pine Ridge '37
Old Corral '36
Red River Valley '36
Ride, Ranger, Ride '36
Undersea Kingdom '36
Harmony Lane '35
Melody Trail '35
The Phantom Empire '35
In Old Santa Fe '34
Mystery Mountain '34

Alex Burns (1977-)
National Lampoon's Van Wilder '02
Thirteen Conversations About One Thing '01

Bob Burns (1890-1956)
Waikiki Wedding '37
Rhythm on the Range '36

Brooke Burns (1978-)
The Salon '05
Bad Blood '07
Single White Female 2: The Psycho '05
Shallow Hal '01

Carol Burns (1947-)
Dusty '85

Catherine Lloyd Burns (1961-)
Everything Put Together '00

Edmund Burns (1892-1989)
Reform School Girl '57
Sea Devils '31
Sunny Side Up '28
Made for Love '26

Edward Burns (1968-)
One Missed Call '08
27 Dresses '08
The Groomsmen '06
The Holiday '06
The River King '05
She's the One '96
The Brothers McMullen '94
Confidence '03
Ash Wednesday '02
Life or Something Like It '02
15 Minutes '01
Sidewalks of New York '01
No Looking Back '98
Saving Private Ryan '98

George Burns (1896-1996)
Radioland Murders '94
18 Again! '88
Oh, God! You Devil '84
Two of a Kind '82
Oh, God! Book 2 '80
Going in Style '79
Sgt. Pepper's Lonely Hearts Club Band '78
Oh, God! '77
The Sunshine Boys '75
Solid Gold Cadillac '56 (N)
Honolulu '39
College Swing '38
A Damsel in Distress '37
Here Comes Cookie '35
Love in Bloom '34
Six of a Kind '34
We're Not Dressing '34
College Humor '33
International House '33

Heather Burns (1974-)
The Groomsmen '06
Kill the Poor '06
Bewitched '05
Brooklyn Lobster '05
Miss Congeniality 2: Armed and Fabulous '05
Miss Congeniality '00
Two Weeks Notice '02
You've Got Mail '98

Helen Burns
Utilities '83

Jennifer Burns
Isaac Asimov's Nightfall '00
Zorro, the Gay Blade '81

Jere Burns (1954-)
Crocodile Dundee in Los Angeles '01
Life-Size '00
Santa Fe '97
Greedy '94
The Gambler Returns: The Luck of the Draw '91

Marilyn Burns (1956-)
The Texas Chainsaw Massacre 4: The Next Generation '95
Future Kill '85
Kiss Daddy Goodbye '81
Eaten Alive '76
Helter-Skelter '76
The Texas Chainsaw Massacre '74

Marion Burns (1907-93)
Dawn Rider '35
Paradise Canyon '35

Mark Burns (1936-)
Bullseye! '90
House of the Living Dead '73
Death in Venice '71
The Virgin and the Gypsy '70
The Charge of the Light Brigade '68

Martha Burns
Slings & Arrows: Season 2 '05
Slings & Arrows '05

Megan Burns (1986-)
28 Days Later '02
Liam '00

Michael Burns (1947-)
The Life Before This '99
Santee '73
That Cold Day in the Park '69

Robert Burns (1884-1957)
Western Trails '38
Gun Law '33
When a Man Rides Alone '33

Tim Burns (1953-)
Freaked '93
Mad Max '80

Raymond Burr (1917-93)
Delirious '91
Showdown at Williams Creek '91
Perry Mason: The Case of the Lost Love '87
Godzilla 1985 '85
Perry Mason Returns '85
Airplane 2: The Sequel '82
Peter and Paul '81
The Curse of King Tut's Tomb '80
Crime of Passion '57
Godzilla, King of the Monsters '56
A Man Alone '55
Great Day in the Morning '56
They Were So Young '55
Casanova's Big Night '54
Party Girls for Sale '54
Passion '54
Thunder Pass '54
Rear Window '54
Gorilla at Large '54
The Blue Gardenia '53
FBI Girl '52
Horizons West '52
Meet Danny Wilson '52
Bride of the Gorilla '51
His Kind of Woman '51
A Place in the Sun '51
Borderline '50
Key to the City '50
Love Happy '50
Adventures of Don Juan '49
Black Magic '49
Pitfall '48
Raw Deal '48
Station West '48
Desperate '47

Robert Burr (1926-2000)
Netherworld '90
Look Back in Anger '80
The Possession of Joel Delaney '72

Ty Burrell (1967-)
The Incredible Hulk '08
The Darwin Awards '06
Friends with Money '06
Fur: An Imaginary Portrait of Diane Arbus '06
Dawn of the Dead '04
In Good Company '04
Black Hawk Down '01
Evolution '01

Sheila Burrell (1922-)
Paranoiac '62
Cold Comfort Farm '94

Maryedith Burrell (1952-)
Camp Nowhere '94

Bonnie Burroughs
One Small Hero '99
Hard to Kill '89

Jackie Burroughs (1938-)
Siblings '04
King's Ransom '05
A Guy Thing '03
Willard '03
Elvis Meets Nixon '98
Last Night '98
Lost and Delirious '01
Overdrawn at the Memory Bank '83
125 Rooms of Comfort '83
The Grey Fox '83
Undergrads '85
Anne of Green Gables '85
The Housekeeper '86
John and the Missus '87
A Winter Tan '88

Hedy Burress (1973-)
Valentine '01
Foxfire '96

Ellen Burstyn (1932-)
The Wicker Man '06
Mrs. Harris '05
The Fountain '06
Requiem for a Dream '00
The Yards '00
Night Ride Home '99
Playing by Heart '98
Flash '98
Deceiver '97
The Baby-Sitters' Club '95
Roommates '95
The Color of Evening '95
How to Make an American Quilt '95
My Brother's Keeper '95
Getting Gotti '94
Getting Out '94
Grand Isle '92
Dying Young '91
Hanna's War '88
Something in Common '86
Act of Vengeance '86
Twice in a Lifetime '85
Into Thin Air '85
The People vs. Jean Harris '81
Silence of the North '81
Resurrection '80
A Dream of Passion '78
Same Time, Next Year '78
Providence '77
Alice Doesn't Live Here Anymore '74
Harry and Tonto '74
Thursday's Game '74
The Exorcist '73
The King of Marvin Gardens '72
The Last Picture Show '71
Tropic of Cancer '70
Alex in Wonderland '70
Pit Stop '67

Luigi Burruano
Luna e L'Altra '96
The Sicilian Connection '85

William S. Burroughs (1914-97)
Wax, or the Discovery of Television among the Bees '93
Bloodhounds of Broadway '89
Drugstore Cowboy '89
Twister '89

Saffron Burrows (1973-)
The Bank Job '08
Reign Over Me '07
Klimt '06
Fay Grim '06
Troy '04
Peter Pan '03 (N)
Frida '02
Enigma '01
Hotel '01
The Seventh Stream '01
Gangster No. 1 '00
Time Code '00
Deep Blue Sea '99
Miss Julie '99
Wing Commander '99
The Loss of Sexual Innocence '95
Circle of Friends '94

Darren E. Burrows (1966-)
Class of 1999 '90
Cry-Baby '90
The Hi-Lo Country '98
Casualties of War '89
Forty Shades of Blue '05

Corey Burton (1955-)
Return to Never Land '02 (V)
Treasure Planet '02 (V)
Atlantis: The Lost Empire '01 (V)

Benny Burt (1900-80)
Goodbye Charlie '64
Hawaiian Buckaroo '38
Sea Racketeers '37

John Burton (1904-)
Mrs. Miniver '42

Harry Burton (1961-)
Devices and Desires '91

Frederick Burton
Dudley Do-Right '99 (N)
Too Busy to Work '32

Jennifer Burton
Death and Desire '97
Watch Me '96
Play Time '94

Julian Burton (1932-2006)
Masque of the Red Death '65
A Bucket of Blood '59

Kate Burton (1957-)
Empire Falls '05
The Diary of Ellen Rimbauer '03
Stay '05
Celebrity '98
Unfaithful '02
Swimfan '02
Ellen Foster '97
The Ice Storm '97
August '95
Love Matters '93
Big Trouble in Little China '87
Uncle Tom's Cabin '87

LeVar Burton (1957-)
Ali '01
Star Trek: Nemesis '02
Star Trek: Insurrection '98
Yesterday's Target '96
Star Trek: First Contact '96
Parallel Lives '94
Star Trek Generations '94
Firestorm: 72 Hours in Oakland '93
Roots: The Gift '88
The Midnight Hour '86
The Supernaturals '86
The Jesse Owens Story '84
Acorn People '82
Grambling's White Tiger '81
The Hunter '80
The Guyana Tragedy: The Story of Jim Jones '80
One in a Million: The Ron LeFlore Story '78
Billy: Portrait of a Street Kid '77
Roots '77

Marie Burton
Outlaws of the Range '36
Pinto Rustlers '36

Norman Burton (1935-)
Bloodsport '88
Bad Guys '86
Crimes of Passion '84
Mausoleum '83
Fade to Black '80
The Terminal Man '74
Save the Tiger '73
Diamonds Are Forever '71
Jud '71

Richard Burton (1925-84)
Wagner: The Movie '85
Wagner: The Complete Epic '85
1984 '84
Absolution '81
Circle of Two '80
Lovespell '79
Breakthrough '78
The Medusa Touch '78
Wild Geese '78
Equus '77
The Exorcist 2: The Heretic '77
The Gathering Storm '74
The Klansman '74
Massacre in Rome '73
Under Milk Wood '73
Assassination of Trotsky '72
Hammersmith Is Out '72
Divorce His, Divorce Hers '72
Bluebeard '72
Raid on Rommel '71
Villain '71
Anne of the Thousand Days '69
Staircase '69
Where Eagles Dare '68
Doctor Faustus '68
The Comedians '67
The Taming of the Shrew '67
Who's Afraid of Virginia Woolf? '66
The Spy Who Came in from the Cold '65
The Sandpiper '65
Becket '64
The Night of the Iguana '64
Zulu '64 (N)
Cleopatra '63
The V.I.P.'s '63
The Longest Day '62
The Bramble Bush '60
Ice Palace '60
Look Back in Anger '58
Sea Wife '57
Alexander the Great '55
A Man Called Peter '55
Above and Beyond '53
The Desert Rats '53
The Robe '53
Green Grow the Rushes '51
The Last Days of Dolwyn '49

Robert Burton (1895-1962)
The Slime People '63
Invasion of the Animal People '62
The Gallant Hours '60
Compulsion '59
Teenage Frankenstein '58
The Tall T '57
All the Brothers Were Valiant '53

Robert (Skip) Burton
Bucktown '75

Steve (Stephen) Burton (1970-)
Taken '02

Tony Burton (1937-)
Hack! '07
The Last Castle '01
Cyber-Tracker 2 '95
Rocky Balboa '06
The Magnificent Seven '98
Rocky 5 '90
Flipping '96
Mission of Justice '92
House Party 2: The Pajama Jam! '91
Armed and Dangerous '86
Oceans of Fire '86
The Shining '80
Blackjack '78
Rocky '76
Assault on Precinct 13 '76

Warren Burton (1944-)
Bloodfist 8: Hard Way Out '96
Humanoids from the Deep '96

Gettysburg '93

Wendell Burton (1947-)
East of Eden '80
Fortune and Men's Eyes '71
The Sterile Cuckoo '69

Sean Bury (1954-)
Paul and Michelle '74
Friends '71
I... '69

Steve Buscemi (1957-)
I Now Pronounce You Chuck and Larry '07
I Think I Love My Wife '07
Interview '07
Art School Confidential '06
Charlotte's Web '06 (V)
Monster House '06 (V)
Paris, je t'aime '06
The Island '05
Romance & Cigarettes '05
Home on the Range '04 (V)
Tanner on Tanner '04
Big Fish '03
Coffee and Cigarettes '03
Spy Kids 3-D: Game Over '03
The Laramie Project '02
Love in the Time of Money '02
Mr. Deeds '02
Spy Kids 2: The Island of Lost Dreams '02
13 Moons '02
Domestic Disturbance '01
Double Whammy '01
Final Fantasy: The Spirits Within '01 (V)
Ghost World '01
The Grey Zone '01
Monsters, Inc. '01 (V)
Animal Factory '00
28 Days '00
Big Daddy '99
Armageddon '98
The Imposters '98
The Big Lebowski '97
Con Air '97
The Real Blonde '97
The Wedding Singer '97
Escape from L.A. '96
Fargo '96
Jimmy '96
Tree's Lounge '96
Desperado '95
Kansas City '95
Things to Do in Denver When You're Dead '95
Airheads '94
Billy Madison '94
Floundering '94
In the Soup '92
Reservoir Dogs '92
Trusting Beatrice '92
Barton Fink '91
Billy Bathgate '91
King of New York '90
Tales from the Darkside: The Movie '90
Mystery Train '89
New York Stories '89
Slaves of New York '89
Heart '87
Parting Glances '86

Charles Busch (1954-)
A Very Serious Person '06
Die Mommie Die! '03
Psycho Beach Party '00

Ernst Busch (1900-80)
Kameradschaft '31

Mae Busch (1897-1946)
The Threepenny Opera '31
The Mad Monster '42
Ziegfeld Girl '41
Marie Antoinette '38
Bohemian Girl '36
The Clutching Hand '36
Sucker Money '34
Sons of the Desert '33
Doctor X '32
Without Honors '32
Defenders of the Law '31
Alibi '29
The Unholy Three '25
Foolish Wives '22

Gary Busey (1944-)
Chasing Ghosts '05
Border Blues '03
Latin Dragon '03
Quigley '03
Sam & Janet '02
Slap Shot 2: Breaking the Ice '02
A Crack in the Floor '00
Hooded Angels '00
Tribulation '00
Detour '99
Jacob Two Two Meets the Hooded Fang '99
No Tomorrow '99
Fear and Loathing in Las Vegas '98
The Girl Next Door '98
Soldier '98
Two Shades of Blue '98
Universal Soldier 2: Brothers in Arms '98
Diary of a Serial Killer '97
The Real Thing '97
Rough Riders '97
Steel Sharks '97
Black Sheep '96
Lethal Tender '96
Lost Highway '96
Plato's Run '96
The Rage '96
Strays '91
Field of Dreams '89
Revenge of the Nerds II: Nerds in Paradise '87
Revenge of the Nerds '84

Billy Green Bush (1935-)
Jason Goes to Hell: The Final Friday '93
Conagher '91
Elvis and Me '88
Critters '86
The Deliberate Stranger '86
The Hitcher '86
The River '84
Tom Horn '80
Alice Doesn't Live Here Anymore '74
Electra Glide in Blue '73
Culpepper Cattle Co. '72
Five Easy Pieces '70

James Bush (1907-87)
King of the Cowboys '43
Children of the Wild '37
The Glory Trail '36
The Return of Peter Grimm '35
A Shot in the Dark '35
Beggars in Ermine '34
Crimson Romance '34

Jovita Bush
Foxstyle '73
The Cheerleaders '72

Sophia Bush (1982-)
The Hitcher '07
John Tucker Must Die '06
Stay Alive '06

Anthony Bushell (1904-97)
A Night to Remember '58
Angel with the Trumpet '50

Jake Busey (1972-)
Comanche Moon '08
Road House 2: Last Call '06
Wristcutters: A Love Story '06
Christmas With the Kranks '04
The Hitcher II: I've Been Waiting '03
Identity '03
Lost Junction '03
The First $20 Million is Always the Hardest '02
Fast Sofa '01
Tomcats '01
Held Up '00
Tail Lights Fade '99
Black Cat Run '98
Enemy of the State '98
Home Fries '98
Contact '97
Starship Troopers '97
The Frighteners '96
Twister '96
P.C.U. '94
S.F.W. '94
Windrunner '94

Timothy Busfield (1957-)
National Security '03
Dead in a Heartbeat '02
Terminal Error '02
Time at the Top '99
Dream House '98
Wanted '98
Buffalo Soldiers '97
Shadow of a Scream '97
The Souler Opposite '97
Trucks '97
First Kid '96
Little Big League '94
Fade to Black '93
The Skateboard Kid '93
Striking Distance '93
Sneakers '92
Point Break '91
Hider in the House '90
Predator 2 '90
Act of Piracy '89
Dangerous Life '89
The Neon Empire '89
Bulletproof '88
Lethal Weapon '87
Let's Get Harry '87
Eye of the Tiger '86
Half a Lifetime '86
Insignificance '85
Silver Bullet '85
D.C. Cab '84
Didn't You Hear? '83
Barbarosa '82
Carny '80
Foolin' Around '80
Big Wednesday '78
The Buddy Holly Story '78
Straight Time '78
Gumball Rally '76
A Star Is Born '76
The Execution of Private Slovik '74
Thunderbolt & Lightfoot '74
The Shrieking '73
Angels Hard As They Come '71

The Miniver Story '50
The Small Back Room '49
The Arsenal Stadium Mystery '39
Dark Journey '37
The Ghoul '34
The Scarlet Pimpernel '34
Vanity Fair '32
The Royal Bed '31
Disraeli '30

Francis X. Bushman (1883-1966)
The Phantom Planet '61
Sabrina '54
David and Bathsheba '51
Honky Tonk '41
Dick Tracy: The Spider Strikes '37
When Lightning Strikes '34
The Three Musketeers '33
Last Frontier '32
Ben-Hur '26
Eyes Right! '26
Midnight Faces '26

Akosua Busia (1968-)
Tears of the Sun '03
Larry McMurtry's Dead Man's Walk '96
Rosewood '96
The Seventh Sign '88
Hard Lessons '86
Native Son '86
The Color Purple '85
The Final Terror '83

Marion Busia
Deadline Auto Theft '83
Gone in 60 Seconds '74

Pascale Bussieres (1968-)
The Blue Butterfly '04
Xchange '00
The Five Senses '99
Girls Can't Swim '99
Set Me Free '99
Jack Higgins' Thunder Point '97
The Twilight of the Ice Nymphs '97
When Night Is Falling '95

Raymond Bussieres (1907-82)
Jonah Who Will Be 25 in the Year 2000 '76
Paris When It Sizzles '64
Beauties of the Night '52
Casque d'Or '52

Budd Buster (1891-1965)
Outlaw of the Plains '46
Border Badmen '45
Frontier Outlaws '44
Cowboy Commandos '43
Raiders of Sunset Pass '43
Thunder River Feud '42
The Lone Rider in Frontier Fury '41
The Lone Rider in Ghost Town '41
Trigger Men '41
Covered Wagon Trails '40
Pinto Canyon '40
Zorro's Fighting Legion '39
Feud Maker '38
Songs and Bullets '38
Thunder in the Desert '38
Roaring Six Guns '37
Gun Girl '36
Texas Jack '35
The Gun Ranger '34

Mitchell Butel
The Bank '01
Strange Fits of Passion '99
Dark City '97

Dick Butkus (1942-)
Spontaneous Combustion '89
Hamburger... The Motion Picture '86
Cracking Up '83
Deadly Games '80
Mother, Jugs and Speed '76
Spaghetti Western '75

Brett Butler (1958-)
The Dress Code '99
Militia '99

Cindy Butler
Boggy Creek II '83
Grayeagle '77

Dan E. Butler (1954-)
The First $20 Million is Always the Hardest '02
Sniper 2 '02
Enemy of the State '98
From the Earth to the Moon '98
Armistead Maupin's More Tales of the City '97
The Assassination File '96
The Fan '96
I Love Trouble '94
Dave '93
Rising Sun '93
Captain Ron '92
The Silence of the Lambs '91
Longtime Companion '90
The Long Walk Home '89
The Manhattan Project '86
Manhunter '86

David Butler
Rhodes '97
Prey for the Hunter '92
Crucible of Horror '69

David Butler (1927-2006)
The Man on the Box '25
The Sky Pilot '21
County Fair '20

Daws Butler (1916-88)
The Good, the Bad, and Huckleberry Hound '88 (V)
Hey There, It's Yogi Bear '64 (V)

Dean Butler (1956-)
The Final Goal '94
Desert Hearts '86
The Kid with the 200 I.Q. '83
Forever '78

Frank Butler (1890-1967)
Made for Love '26

Gerard Butler (1969-)
Nim's Island '08
P.S. I Love You '07
Shattered '07
300 '07
Beowulf & Grendel '06
The Game of Their Lives '05
Dear Frankie '04
The Phantom of the Opera '04
Lara Croft Tomb Raider: The Cradle of Life '03
Timeline '03
Harrison's Flowers '02
Reign of Fire '02
Attila '01
Dracula 2000 '00
Shooters '00
One More Kiss '99
Mrs. Brown '97

Lois Butler (1931-89)
High Lonesome '50
Mickey '48

Patrick Butler
Frostbiter: Wrath of the Wendigo '94

Paul Butler
Romeo is Bleeding '93
Zebrahead '92
To Sleep with Anger '90

Roy Butler (1893-1973)
My Dinner with Andre '81
House of Errors '42

Tom Butler (1951-)
Everything's Gone Green '06
Every Mother's Worst Fear '98
Ronnie and Julie '97
Dead Ahead '96
Maternal Instincts '96
Ernest Rides Again '93
Scanners 2: The New Order '91
Tales of the Klondike: The Scorn of Women '87
Confidential '86
July Group '81

William Butler
Inner Sanctum '91

Yancy Butler (1970-)
The Last Letter '04
Thin Air '00
The Witness Files '00
The Treat '98
Ravager '97
The Ex '96
Fast Money '96
Drop Zone '94
Hard Target '93
The Hit List '93

Merritt Butrick (1959-89)
From the Dead of Night '89
Death Spa '87
Shy People '87
When the Bough Breaks '86
Wired to Kill '86
Code of Honor '84
Star Trek 3: The Search for Spock '84
Star Trek 2: The Wrath of Khan '82
Zapped! '82

Johnny Butt (-1930)
Blackmail '29
Q Ships '28

Lawson Butt (1883-1956)
Lady of the Lake '28
Dante's Inferno '24

Charles Butterworth (1896-1946)
Dixie Jamboree '44
Follow the Boys '44
Road Show '41
Second Chorus '40
Let Freedom Ring '39
Every Day's a Holiday '38
Thanks for the Memory '38
Swing High, Swing Low '37
It Happened in New Orleans '36
The Moon's Our Home '36
Forsaking All Others '35
The Cat and the Fiddle '34
Hollywood Party '34
Penthouse '33
Illicit '31

Donna Butterworth (1956-)
Paradise, Hawaiian Style '66
Family Jewels '65

Jorg Butgereit (1963-)
Der Todesking '89
Nekromantik '87

Stephanie Buttle
Urban Ghost Story '98
A Couch in New York '95

Red Buttons (1919-2006)
The Story of Us '99
It Could Happen to You '94
The Ambulance '90
18 Again! '88
Alice in Wonderland '85
Side Show '84
Leave 'Em Laughing '81
Off Your Rocker '80
When Time Ran Out '80
C.H.O.M.P.S. '79
Movie, Movie '78
Users '78
Pete's Dragon '77
Viva Knievel '77

The Poseidon Adventure '72
Who Killed Mary What's 'Er Name? '71
They Shoot Horses, Don't They? '69
Harlow '65
Five Weeks in a Balloon '62
Gay Purr-ee '62 (V)
Hatari! '62
The Longest Day '62
Sayonara '57
13 Rue Madeleine '46

Pat Buttram (1917-94)
Back to the Future, Part 3 '90
The Fox and the Hound '81 (V)
Robin Hood '73 (V)
The Gatling Gun '72
Evil Roy Slade '71 (N)
The Aristocats '70 (V)
Roustabout '64
Blue Canadian Rockies '52
Night Stage to Galveston '52
Hills of Utah '51
Valley of Fire '51

Margherita Buy (1962-)
Caterina in the Big City '03
His Secret Life '01
Not of This World '99
The Favorite Son '94
The Station '92

Sarah Buxton (1972-)
The Climb '97
Listen '96
Fast Getaway 2 '94
Rock 'n' Roll High School Forever '91
Primal Rage '90
Welcome to Spring Break '89

Ruth Buzzi (1939-)
Boys Will Be Boys '97
Troublemakers '94
Wishful Thinking '92
Digging Up Business '92
My Mom's a Werewolf '89
Up Your Alley '89
Dixie Lanes '88
Pound Puppies and the Legend of Big Paw '88 (V)
Bad Guys '86
Surf 2 '84
The Being '83
Chu Chu & the Philly Flash '81
The North Avenue Irregulars '79
Scavenger Hunt '79
The Villain '79
Once Upon a Brothers Grimm '77
Freaky Friday '76

Dave Buzzotta
The Prophecy 3: The Ascent '99
Children of the Corn 5: Fields of Terror '98
Gang Boys '97
The Real Thing '97

Bobbie Byers
Wild Rebels '71

Kate Byers
The Man Who Made Husbands Jealous '93
Career Girls '97

Spring Byington (1893-1971)
Please Don't Eat the Daisies '60
Because You're Mine '52
Angels in the Outfield '51
Walk Softly, Stranger '50
The Big Wheel '49
In the Good Old Summertime '49
Singapore '47
Thrill of a Romance '45
Heaven Can Wait '42
Roxie Hart '42

Amanda Bynes (1986-)
Hairspray '07
Sydney White '07
She's the Man '06
Robots '05 (V)
What a Girl Wants '03
Big Fat Liar '02

John Byner (1938-)
My 5 Wives '00
Transylvania 6-5000 '85 (V)
The Man in the Santa Claus Suit '79
A Pleasure Doing Business '79
Great Smokey Roadblock '76

Dan Byrd (1985-)
The Hills Have Eyes '06
Jam '06
Outlaw Trail '06
Salem's Lot '04
A Cinderella Story '04

David Byrd (1933-2001)
Thick as Thieves '99

Eugene Byrd (1975-)
Rails & Ties '07
Confess '05
Anacondas: The Hunt for the Blood Orchid '04
Paranoia 1.0 '04
8 Mile '02
Survival Island '02
Lift '01
Color of Justice '97
Sleepers '98

Ralph Byrd (1909-52)
Dick Tracy Meets Gruesome '47
Dick Tracy's Dilemma '47
Guadalcanal Diary '43
The Jungle Book '42
Dick Tracy vs. Crime Inc. '41
Dick Tracy's G-Men '39
Born to Be Wild '38
Dick Tracy Returns '38
Dick Tracy '37
S.O.S. Coast Guard '37
Blake of Scotland Yard '37
Border Caballero '36
Hell-Ship Morgan '36

Thomas Jefferson Byrd (1960-)
Ray '04
MacArthur Park '01
Bamboozled '00
He Got Game '98
Get On the Bus '96
Set It Off '96

Jenna Byrne (1970-)
Club Land '01
Lip Service '00

The Devil & Miss Jones '41
When Ladies Meet '41
The Blue Bird '40
Lucky Partners '40
The Story of Alexander Graham Bell '39
Jezebel '38
You Can't Take It with You '38
The Charge of the Light Brigade '36
Theodora Goes Wild '36
Ah, Wilderness! '35
Mutiny on the Bounty '35
Little Women '33

Rolan Bykov (1929-98)
Ivan and Abraham '94
Commissar '68
The Overcoat '59

Antony Byrne
Svengali '83

Catherine Byrne (1954-)
Eat the Peach '86
S.O.S. Titanic '79

Gabriel Byrne (1950-)
Jindabyne '06
Played '06
Assault on Precinct 13 '05
The Bridge of San Luis Rey '05
Wah-Wah '05
Vanity Fair '04
Shade '03
Ghost Ship '02
Spider '02
End of Days '99
Stigmata '99
Enemy of the State '98
The Man in the Iron Mask '98
Quest for Camelot '98 (V)
The End of Violence '97
Polish Wedding '97
Weapons of Mass Distraction '97
The Brylcreem Boys '96
The Last of the High Kings '96
Smilla's Sense of Snow '96
Somebody Is Waiting '96
Trigger Happy '96
Dead Man '95
Frankie Starlight '95
The Usual Suspects '95
Little Women '94
Royal Deceit '94
A Simple Twist of Fate '94
Trial by Jury '94
A Dangerous Woman '93
Point of No Return '93
Into the West '92
Cool World '92
A Soldier's Tale '91
Dark Obsession '90
Miller's Crossing '90
Siesta '87
Gothic '87
Hello Again '87
Julia and Julia '87
Lionheart '87
The Courier '88
Shipwrecked '90
Christopher Columbus '85
Hanna K. '83
The Keep '83
Excalibur '81
Defense of the Realm '85

David Byron
My Brother's Wife '89
Fade to Black '93

David Byron
The Mummy '32

Jeffrey Byron (1955-)
Dungeonmaster '83
Metalstorm: The Destruction of Jared-Syn '83

Kathleen Byron (1922-)
From a Far Country: Pope John Paul II '81
The Golden Bowl '72
The Moonstone '72
Twins of Evil '71
Burn Witch, Burn! '62
Young Bess '53

Girls of the White Orchid '84

Miriam Byrd-Nethery (1929-2003)
Civil War Diary '90
Leatherface: The Texas Chainsaw Massacre 3 '89

Bill Byrge
Ernest Goes to School '94
Ernest Goes to Jail '90

Anne Byrne (1943-)
Manhattan '79

Antoine Byrne
I Went Down '97
Oliver Twist '97

Barbara Byrne
Sunday in the Park with George '86

David Byrne (1952-)
Heavy Petting '89
True Stories '86

Eddie Byrne (1911-81)
The Mummy '59
Dangerous Youth '58
Abandon Ship! '57

David Byrnes (1952-)
Witchcraft 7: Judgement Hour '95
Witchcraft 9: Bitter Flesh '96

Edd Byrnes (1933-)
Troop Beverly Hills '89
Back to the Beach '87
Mankillers '87
Grease '78
Go Kill and Come Back '68
Any Gun Can Play '67
Darby's Rangers '58
The Secret Invasion '64
Stardust '74

Jim Byrnes (1948-)
Highlander: Endgame '00
Bloodhounds 2 '96
Starlight '97
Suspicious Agenda '94
Dirty Work '92

Arthur Byron (1872-1943)
The Whole Town's Talking '35
Two Alone '34
Gabriel Over the White House '33
The Mummy '32

Josephine Byrnes (1966-)
Oscar and Lucinda '97
Frauds '93
Brides of Christ '91

Martha Byrne (1969-)
Anna to the Infinite Power '84
The Eyes of the Amaryllis '82

Michael Byrne (1943-)
Mists of Avalon '01
The Sum of All Fears '02
Battlefield Earth '00
Gunshy '98
Apt Pupil '98
The Musketeer '01
Heat of the Sun '99
Saint-Ex '97
The Saint '97
Agatha Christie's The Pale Horse '96
The Infiltrator '95
Sharpe's Enemy '94
Sharpe's Honour '94
Indiana Jones and the Last Crusade '89

Susan Byun
Deadly Target '94
Sgt. Kabukiman N.Y.P.D. '94

Rose Byrne (1979-)
Sunshine '07
28 Weeks Later '07
The Dead Girl '06
Marie Antoinette '06
The Tenants '05
Troy '04
Wicker Park '04
City of Ghosts '03
The Night We Called It a Day '03
I Capture the Castle '02
Star Wars: Episode 2— Attack of the Clones '02
Two Hands '98

David Byrnes (1952-)
Dead Simple '01
A Glimpse of Hell '01
In the Shadows '01
Warden of Red Rock '01
The Lathe of Heaven '02
Night at the Golden Eagle '02
Dogville '03
Elf '03
Dallas 362 '03

James Caan (1939-)
Crime Lords '91
The Incredible Mrs. Ritchie '03
Jericho Mansions '03
This Thing of Ours '03
Blood Crime '02
The Yards '00
Way of the Gun '00
Luckytown '00
Mickey Blue Eyes '99
This Is My Father '99
Poodle Springs '98
Bulletproof '96
Eraser '96
Bottle Rocket '96
North Star '96
A Boy Called Hate '95
Flesh and Bone '93
The Program '93
Honeymoon in Vegas '92
For the Boys '91
Dick Tracy '90
Misery '90
Alien Nation '88
Gardens of Stone '87
Kiss Me Goodbye '82
Bolero '82
Thief '81
Hide in Plain Sight '80
Chapter Two '79
Comes a Horseman '78
Little Moon & Jud McGraw '78
Another Man, Another Chance '77
A Bridge Too Far '77
Harry & Walter Go to New York '76
Silent Movie '76
The Killer Elite '75
Rollerball '75
Funny Lady '75
Freebie & the Bean '74
The Gambler '74
The Godfather, Part 2 '74
Cinderella Liberty '73
Slither '73
The Godfather '72
Brian's Song '71
The Rain People '69
Countdown '68
El Dorado '67
Games '67
Red Line 7000 '65
Lady in a Cage '64
The Godfather Epic 1902-1959: The Complete Epic '81

Scott Caan (1976-)
Meet Dave '08
The Incredible Hulk '08
Ocean's Thirteen '07
Brooklyn Rules '07
Friends with Money '06
The Dog Problem '06
Lonely Hearts '06
Into the Blue '05
In Enemy Hands '04
Ocean's Twelve '04
Dallas 362 '03
Sonny '02
Novocaine '01
American Outlaws '01
Ocean's Eleven '01
Gone in 60 Seconds '00
Boiler Room '00
Ready to Rumble '00
Black and White '99
Varsity Blues '98
Enemy of the State '98
Nowhere '96

Christina Cabot (1969-)
The Incredible Hulk '08
The Italian Job '03

Sebastian Cabot (1918-77)
The Many Adventures of Winnie the Pooh '77 (V)
The Jungle Book '67 (V)
Family Jewels '65
The Sword in the Stone '63
Twice-Told Tales '63
Seven Thieves '60
The Time Machine '60
Johnny Tremain & the Sons of Liberty '58
Terror in a Texas Town '58
Omar Khayyam '57
Westward Ho, the Wagons! '56
Romeo and Juliet '54
Captain's Paradise '53
Old Mother Riley's Jungle Treasure '51
Dick Barton Strikes Back '48
Dual Alibi '47
Old Mother Riley's New Venture '49

Susan Cabot (1927-86)
The Wasp Woman '59

Marion Byron (1911-85)
Steamboat Bill, Jr. '28
The Savage Girl '32

Walter Byron (1899-1972)
Breed of the Border '33
Blood Crime '02

Katia Caballero
Madeline '98
Sharpe's Eagle '93
Beyond Innocence '87

Bruce Cabot (1904-72)
Diamonds Are Forever '71
Chisum '70
The Undefeated '69
The Green Berets '68
Hellfighters '68
The War Wagon '67
In Harm's Way '65
McLintock! '63
Hatari! '62
The Comancheros '61
Goliath and the Cregon '61
Goliath and the Barbarians '60
John Paul Jones '59
Kid Monk Baroni '52
Lost in Alaska '52
Best of the Badmen '50
Fancy Pants '50
Sorrowful Jones '49
Angel and the Badman '47
Silver Queen '42
The Flame of New Orleans '41
Sundown '41
Captain Caution '40
Susan and God '40
Dodge City '39
Sinners in Paradise '38
Smashing the Rackets '38
Ann Vickers '33
King Kong '33
Fury '36
The Last of the Mohicans '36

The Gambler & the Lady '52
The Small Back Room '49
Black Narcissus '47
Stairway to Heaven '46

Cabot
Machine Gun Kelly '58
Carnival Rock '57
Sorority Girl '57
Ride Clear of Diablo '54
Gunsmoke '53
Duel at Silver Creek '52
Son of Ali Baba '52
Flame of Araby '51

Manuel Cabral
Apartment 12 '06
Manito '03

Jesus Cabrero (1965-)
Km. 0 '00
Yerma '99

Jean Cadell (1884-1967)
The Obsessed '51
Madeleine '50
Pygmalion '38
Love from a Stranger '37

Anne-Marie Cadieux
Far Side of the Moon '03
Four Days '99
No '98
Street Heart '98
The Confessional '95

Jason Cadieux
Lilies '96
Iron Eagle 4 '95

Rita Cadillac (1936-95)
Das Boot '81
It Means That to Me '60

Michael Cadman (1942-)
Poldark 2 '75
If... '69

Frank Cady (1915-)
Zandy's Bride '74
The Bad Seed '56
Ace in the Hole '51
Let's Make It Legal '51

Adolph Caesar (1933-86)
Club Paradise '86
Fortune Dane '86
The Color Purple '85
A Soldier's Story '84
Fist of Fear, Touch of Death '80
The Hitter '79

Harry Caesar (1928-94)
Bird on a Wire '90
Ghetto Blaster '89
The Offspring '87
The Longest Yard '74
Emperor of the North Pole '73

Sid Caesar (1922-)
Comic Book: The Movie '04
The Wonderful Ice Cream Suit '98
Vegas Vacation '96
Side by Side '88
Stoogemania '85
Cannonball Run 2 '84
Over the Brooklyn Bridge '83
Grease 2 '82
History of the World: Part 1 '81
The Munsters' Revenge '81
The Fiendish Plot of Dr. Fu Manchu '80
The Cheap Detective '78
Grease '78
Barnaby and Me '77
Curse of the Black Widow '77
Silent Movie '76
Airport '75 '75
A Guide for the Married Man '67
It's a Mad, Mad, Mad, Mad World '63

Cheri Caffaro (1945-)
Too Hot to Handle '76
Girls Are for Loving '73
The Abductors '72
Ginger '72
A Place Called Today '72

Peter Caffrey (1949-2008)
A Love Divided '01
I Went Down '97

Stephen Caffrey (1961-)
Danny Boy '82
Blowback '99
Buried Alive 2 '97
The Babe '92
Longtime Companion '90
Tour of Duty '87

Andrea Cagan
Teenager '74
Hot Box '72

Nicolas Cage (1964-)
Bangkok Dangerous '08
Ghost Rider '07
National Treasure: Book of Secrets '07
Next '07
The Ant Bully '06 (V)
The Wicker Man '06
World Trade Center '06
Lord of War '05
The Weather Man '05
National Treasure '04
Matchstick Men '03
Adaptation '02
Sonny '02
Windtalkers '02
Captain Corelli's Mandolin '01
Family Man '00
Gone in 60 Seconds '00
Bringing Out the Dead '99
City of Angels '98
8mm '98
Snake Eyes '98
Con Air '97
Face/Off '97
The Rock '96
Leaving Las Vegas '95
Guarding Tess '94
It Could Happen to You '94
Kiss of Death '94
Trapped in Paradise '94
Amos and Andrew '93
Deadfall '93
Red Rock West '93
Honeymoon in Vegas '92
Zandalee '91
Fire Birds '90
Wild at Heart '90
Time to Kill '89
Vampire's Kiss '88
Moonstruck '87
Raising Arizona '87
Boy in Blue '86
Peggy Sue Got Married '86
Birdy '84
The Cotton Club '84
Racing with the Moon '84
Rumble Fish '83
Valley Girl '83
Fast Times at Ridgemont High '82

James Cagney (1899-1986)
Ragtime '81
One, Two, Three '61
The Gallant Hours '60
Never Steal Anything Small '59
Shake Hands with the Devil '59
Man of a Thousand Faces '57
Tribute to a Bad Man '56
Love Me or Leave Me '55
Mister Roberts '55
The Seven Little Foys '55
A Lion Is in the Streets '53
What Price Glory? '52
Kiss Tomorrow Goodbye '50
The West Point Story '50
White Heat '49
The Time of Your Life '48
13 Rue Madeleine '46
Blood on the Sun '45
Johnny Come Lately '43
Captains of the Clouds '42
Yankee Doodle Dandy '42
The Bride Came C.O.D. '41
Strawberry Blonde '41
City for Conquest '40
The Fighting 69th '40
Torrid Zone '40
Each Dawn I Die '39
Oklahoma Kid '39
The Roaring Twenties '39
Angels with Dirty Faces '38
Boy Meets Girl '38
Great Guy '36
Something to Sing About '36
Ceiling Zero '35
Devil Dogs of the Air '35
"G" Men '35
A Midsummer Night's Dream '35
Footlight Parade '33
Lady Killer '33
The Mayor of Hell '33
Picture Snatcher '33
Blonde Crazy '31
Public Enemy '31
Smart Money '31

Jeanne Cagney (1908-84)
Kentucky Rifle '55
A Lion Is in the Streets '53
Don't Bother to Knock '52
Quicksand '50
The Time of Your Life '48
Yankee Doodle Dandy '42

William Cagney (1902-88)
Palooka '34
Ace of Aces '33

Stan Cahill (1964-)
Goldrush: A Real Life Alaskan Adventure '98
JFK: Reckless Youth '93

Dean Cain (1966-)
September Dawn '07
Bailey's Billion$ '05
Lost '05
Out of Time '03
Boa '02
Firetrap '01
Rat Race '01
The Broken Hearts Club '00
Final Encounter '00
No Alibi '00
The Runaway '00
Militia '99
Best Men '98
Futuresport '98
Tracked '98

Howard Caine (1926-93)
Watermelon Man '70
Pressure Point '62

Michael Caine (1933-)
The Dark Knight '08
Flawless '07
Sleuth '07
Children of Men '06
The Prestige '06
Batman Begins '05
Bewitched '05
The Weather Man '05
Around the Bend '04
Secondhand Lions '03
The Statement '03
Austin Powers In Goldmember '02
The Quiet American '02
Last Orders '01
Quicksand '01
Get Carter '00
Miss Congeniality '00
Quills '00
Shiner '00
The Cider House Rules '99
Little Voice '98
Curtain Call '98
Mandela and de Klerk '97
Midnight in Saint Petersburg '97
Blood & Wine '96
Bullet to Beijing '95
On Deadly Ground '94
World War II: When Lions Roared '94
Blue Ice '92
Death Becomes Her '92
The Muppet Christmas Carol '92
Noises Off '92
Bullseye! '90
Jekyll and Hyde '90
Mr. Destiny '90
A Shock to the System '90
Dirty Rotten Scoundrels '88
Jack the Ripper '88
Without a Clue '88
The Fourth Protocol '87
Jaws: The Revenge '87
Surrender '87
The Whistle Blower '87
Half Moon Street '86
Hannah and Her Sisters '86
Mona Lisa '86
Sweet Liberty '86
The Holcroft Covenant '85
Water '85
Blame It on Rio '84
The Jigsaw Man '84
Beyond the Limit '83
Educating Rita '83
Deathtrap '82
The Hand '81
Victory '81
Dressed to Kill '80
The Island '80
Ashanti, Land of No Mercy '79
Beyond the Poseidon Adventure '79
California Suite '78
Silver Bears '78
The Swarm '78
A Bridge Too Far '77
The Eagle Has Landed '77
Harry & Walter Go to New York '76
The Man Who Would Be King '75
Romantic Englishwoman '75
The Wilby Conspiracy '75
The Black Windmill '74
The Destructors '74
Pulp '72
Sleuth '72
X, Y & Zee '72
Get Carter '71
The Last Valley '71
Too Late the Hero '70
Battle of Britain '69
The Italian Job '69
Woman Times Seven '67
Alfie '66
Funeral in Berlin '66
Gambit '66
The Wrong Box '66
The Ipcress File '65
Zulu '64
Room 43 '58

John Cairney (1930-)
The Flesh and the Fiends '60
A Night to Remember '58

Jonathan Cake (1968-)
Noah's Ark '99
Mosley '98
A Dance to the Music of Time '97
Rebecca '97
Catherine Cookson's The Girl '96
The Tenant of Wildfell Hall '96

Thomas Calabro
Ice Spiders '07
Ladykillers '88

Clara Calamai (1915-98)
Deep Red: Hatchet Murders '75
White Nights '57
Ossessione '42

David Calder (1946-)
Love or Money '01
The King Is Alive '00
The Murder of Stephen Lawrence '99
The World Is Not Enough '99
Cracker: Brotherly Love '95
A Question of Attribution '91

Anna Calder-Marshall (1947-)
The Two Faces of Evil '82
Wuthering Heights '70

Paul Calderon
Pistol Whipped '08
Kill the Poor '06
The Sentinel '06
21 Grams '03
The Last Castle '01
3 A.M. '01
Once in the Life '00
Girlfight '99
Sweet Nothing '96
The Addiction '95
Condition Red '95
Four Rooms '95
Lotto Land '95
Pulp Fiction '94
Bad Lieutenant '92
Crisscross '92
Q & A '90
The Chair '87

Sergio Calderon (1945-)
The Missing '03
Men in Black '97
Border Shootout '90
Old Gringo '89
Erendira '83

L. Scott Caldwell (1944-)
Twilight Man '96
Down Came a Blackbird '94
God Bless the Child '88

Zoe Caldwell (1933-)
Birth '04
Just a Kiss '02
Lilo & Stitch '02 (V)
Lantern Hill '90
The Purple Rose of Cairo '85

Paula Cale (1970-)
Brian's Song '01
Milo '98

Anthony Calf (1959-)
Sirens '02
Inspector Lynley Mysteries: A Great Deliverance '01

Don Calfa (1940-)
Terrified '94
H.P. Lovecraft's Necronomicon: Book of the Dead '93
Foul Play '78

Louis Calhern (1895-1956)
Forever Darling '56
High Society '56
Blackboard Jungle '55
The Prodigal '55
Athena '54
Betrayed '54
Executive Suite '54
Men of the Fighting Lady '54
Rhapsody '54
The Student Prince '54
Julius Caesar '53
Latin Lovers '53
Prisoner of Zenda '52
We're Not Married '52
Annie Get Your Gun '50
The Asphalt Jungle '50
A Life of Her Own '50
The Magnificent Yankee '50
Nancy Goes to Rio '50
Two Weeks with Love '50
The Red Pony '49
Arch of Triumph '48
Notorious '46
The Bridge of San Luis Rey '44
Up in Arms '44
Heaven Can Wait '43
Charlie McCarthy, Detective '39
The Gorgeous Hussy '36
Last Days of Pompeii '35
Sweet Adeline '35
The Count of Monte Cristo '34
Duck Soup '33
The World Gone Mad '33
Night After Night '32
They Call It Sin '32
Blonde Crazy '31
The Blot '21
Too Wise Wives '21

Alice Calhoun (1904-66)
Tentacles of the North '26
The Man on the Box '25

Monica Calhoun (1971-)
The Salon '05
Gang of Roses '03
Civil Brand '02
The Best Man '99
The Players Club '98
Rebound: The Legend of Earl "The Goat" Manigault '96
Bagdad Cafe '88

Rory Calhoun (1922-99)
Pure Country '92
Roller Blade Warriors: Taken By Force '90
Night of the Lepus '72
Operation Cross Eagles '69
Dayton's Devils '68
Apache Uprising '66
Finger on the Trigger '65
A Face in the Rain '63
Hard Drivin' '60
Treasure of Pancho Villa '55
A Bullet Is Waiting '54
River of No Return '54
With a Song in My Heart '52
I'd Climb the Highest Mountain '51
Ticket to Tomahawk '50
Adventure Island '47
The Red House '47

Joseph Cali (1950-)
The Lonely Lady '83
The Competition '80
Saturday Night Fever '77

Brandon Call (1976-)
For the Boys '91
The Adventures of Ford Fairlane '90
Blind Fury '90

R.D. Call
Murder by Numbers '02
Last Man Standing '96
Waterworld '95
Other People's Money '91
Stephen King's Golden Years '91
Young Guns 2 '90
Colors '88
The Children of Times Square '86

James Callahan (1930-2007)
Freddy vs. Jason '03
Blood for Blood '95
Prison for Children '93
Outlaw Blues '77
Missiles of October '74
Lady Sings the Blues '72
Tropic of Cancer '70

Margaret Callahan (1910-81)
Special Investigator '36
Hot Tip '35

Mars Callahan (1972-)
What Love Is '07

Poolhall Junkies '02

K. Callan (1942-)
Crazylove '05
Midnight Clear '06
Saved by the Light '95
Donner Pass: The Road to Survival '84
Double Exposure '82
Blind Ambition '79
The Cat and the Canary '79
Lepke '75
Photographer '75
Frasier the Sensuous Lion '73

Michael Callan (1938-)
Leprechaun 3 '95
Freeway '88
Cat Ballou '65
The Victors '63
Bon Voyage! '62
The Interns '62
Gidget Goes Hawaiian '61
Mysterious Island '61

Charlie Callas (1924-)
Vampire Vixens from Venus '94
Amazon Women on the Moon '87
History of the World: Part 1 '81
Pete's Dragon '77 (V)
Big Mouth '67

Rebecca Callard (1976-)
The Miracle Maker: The Story of Jesus '00 (V)
The Return of the Borrowers '96
The Borrowers '93

Joseph Calleia (1897-1975)
The Alamo '60
The Light in the Forest '58
Touch of Evil '58
The Littlest Outlaw '54
The Caddy '53
Yankee Buccaneer '52
Branded '50
The Noose Hangs High '48
Gilda '46
For Whom the Bell Tolls '43
The Glass Key '42
The Jungle Book '42
The Monster and the Girl '41
Sundown '41
My Little Chickadee '40
Five Came Back '39
Golden Boy '39
Algiers '38
Marie Antoinette '38
After the Thin Man '36
Riff Raff '35

Bryan Callen (1967-)
Scary Movie 4 '06
Fish Without a Bicycle '03
Terror Squad '87

Dayton Callie
When Willie Comes Marching Home '50

Sarah Wayne Callies
Whisper '07
The Celestine Prophecy '06

James Callis (1971-)
Bridget Jones: The Edge of Reason '04
Helen of Troy '03
Bridget Jones's Diary '01

Simon Callow (1949-)
Surveillance 24/7 '07
Bob the Butler '05
Merci Docteur Rey '04
The Phantom of the Opera '04
Angels in America '03

Cab Calloway (1907-94)
The Blues Brothers '80
The Littlest Angel '69
The Cincinnati Kid '65
Sensations of 1945 '44
Stormy Weather '43
Manhattan Merry-Go-Round '37
Hi-De-Ho '35
International House '33

Kirk Calloway (1960-)
Cinderella Liberty '73
Summertree '71

Vanessa Bell Calloway (1957-)
Love Don't Cost a Thing '03
Cheaper by the Dozen '03
Biker Boyz '03
Dawg '02
All About You '01
The Red Sneakers '01
Love Song '00
The Temptations '98
Daylight '96
Crimson Tide '95
America's Dream '95
What's Love Got to Do with It '93
Bebe's Kids '92 (V)
Memphis '91
Coming to America '88
Number One with a Bullet '87

Michael Caloz (1985-)
Escape from Wildcat Canyon '99
Little Men '98
Screamers '96
Whiskers '97

Donald Calthrop (1888-1940)
The Phantom Light '35
Scrooge '35
No. 17 '32
Blackmail '29

Bill Calvert (1966-)
Body Waves '92
C.H.U.D. 2: Bud the Chud '89

Corinne Calvet (1925-2001)
Dr. Heckyl and Mr. Hype '80
Too Hot to Handle '76
Apache Uprising '66
Indiscreet '58
The Man in Grey '45
Kipps '41

Phyllis Calvert (1915-2002)
Mandy '53
Man of Evil '48
The Magic Bow '47
Men of Two Worlds '46
The Man in Grey '45
The Young and the Guilty '58

Dean Cameron (1962-)
Highball '97
Ski School 2 '94
Sleep with Me '94
The Ghost Brigade '93
Miracle Beach '92
Ski School '91
Bad Dreams '88
Summer School '87

Candace Cameron (1976-)
Last Action Hero '93
Some Girl '94

James Cameron (1954-)
Submarine Attack '54

Earl Cameron (1917-)
The Interpreter '05
Revolver '05
The Queen '06

Kirk Cameron (1970-)
The Unborn '91
Listen to Me '89
Like Father, Like Son '87

Henry Calvin (1918-75)
The Sign of Zorro '60
Toby Tyler '59

John Calvin
Dragonworld '94
The Magic Bubble '93
Primary Target '89

Armando Calvo (1919-96)
Satanik '69
The Witch's Mirror '62

Pablito Calvo (1949-)
The Man Who Wagged His Tail '57
The Miracle of Marcelino '55

Mark Camacho (1965-)
Bad Education '04
Nowhere in Sight '01
Jericho Mansions '03

Javier Cámara (1967-)
Torremolinos 73 '03
Talk to Her '02
Sex and Lucía '01

Roberto Camardiel (1933-76)
Guns for San Sebastian '68
Challenge of McKenna '70
Whiffs '75
Beware! The Blob '72
Cotton Comes to Harlem '70

Christian Camargo (1971-)
K-19: The Widowmaker '02

Godfrey Cambridge (1933-76)
Friday Foster '75
Watermelon Man '70
The President's Analyst '67
Gone Are the Days '63
Purlie Victorious '63

Juan José Camero (1947-)
Veronico Cruz '87
Far Away and Long Ago '74

Joan Camden (1929-2000)
Gunfight at the O.K. Corral '57
Stolen Identity '53

Candice Cameron
Tales of the City '93

Colleen Camp (1953-)
Die, Mommie, Die! '03
Last Holiday '50 ... (various)
Apocalypse Now '79
Smile '75

Jesse Cameron-Glickenhaus
Timemaster '95
Slaughter of the Innocents '93

Trent Cameron
Shot '01
The Wood '99

Rod Cameron (1910-83)
The Best of Times '86
Psychic Killer '75
Evel Knievel '72
The Electronic Monster '57

Terry Camilleri (1949-)
Siblings '04
The Truman Show '98
Bill & Ted's Excellent Adventure '89

Adam Campbell (1984-)
Epic Movie '07
Date Movie '06

Alex Campbell
Killer Workout '86

Beatrice Campbell (1922-79)
Last Holiday '50
The Master of Ballantrae '53

Billy Campbell (1959-)
The Rising Place '02
Armistead Maupin's More Tales of the City '97
Armistead Maupin's Tales of the City '93
The Night We Never Met '93

Bruce Campbell (1958-)
Aqua Teen Hunger Force Colon Movie Film for Theaters '07 (V)
Spider-Man 3 '07 (V)
The Ant Bully '06 (V)
Sky High '05
Spider-Man 2 '04
Comic Book: The Movie '04
Bubba Ho-Tep '03
The Woods '03
Serving Sara '02
Spider-Man '02
The Majestic '01

Eric Campbell (1879-1917)
The Cure '17
The Immigrant '17
Easy Street '17

J. Kenneth Campbell
U.S. Seals '98
Operation Delta Force 2: Mayday '97

Jessica Campbell (1982-)
The Safety of Objects '01
Election '99

Judy Campbell (1916-2004)
Cry of the Penguins '71
Bonnie Prince Charlie '48
The World Owes Me a Living '47

Julia Campbell (1963-)
Stephen King's Rose Red '02

Frank Campanella (1919-2006)
Blood Red '88
Chesty Anderson USN '76
The Producers '68

Bernard Campan
Eating Raoul '82

Joseph Campanella (1927-)
James Dean: Live Fast, Die Young '97
The Glass Cage '96

Christian Campbell (1972-)
Trick '99

Cheryl Campbell (1949-)
Chariots of Fire '81
McVicar '80
Testament of Youth '79

David James Campbell
KillZone '85

Emma Campbell (1971-)
Nightwaves '03

Elizabeth Campbell (1942-)
Doctor of Doom '62
Wrestling Women vs. the Aztec Mummy '59

Glen Campbell (1936-)
Rock-a-Doodle '92 (V)
Uphill All the Way '85
True Grit '69

Kate Campbell
Monte Carlo Nights '34
Come on Tarzan '32
Ghost Valley '32

Ken Campbell (1941-)
Smart Money '88
Letter to Brezhnev '86
Joshua Then and Now '85
The Big Red One '80

Ken H. Campbell (1963-)
Breakfast of Champions '98
Down Periscope '96

Larry Joe Campbell (1970-)
Jiminy Glick in LaLa Wood '05
Wedding Crashers '05

Louise Campbell (1911-97)
Bulldog Drummond's Peril '38
Bulldog Drummond Comes Back '37
Bulldog Drummond's Revenge '37

Maia Campbell (1976-)
Trippin' '99
Parental Guidance '98

Michael Leydon Campbell
Knots '05

Naomi Campbell (1970-)
Prisoner of Love '99
Girl 6 '96
Invasion of Privacy '96
Miami Rhapsody '95
Cool As Ice '91

Nell Campbell (1953-)
Great Expectations '97
I Wanna Be a Beauty Queen '85
Pink Floyd: The Wall '82
Shock Treatment '81
Lisztomania '75
The Rocky Horror Picture Show '75

Neve Campbell (1973-)
I Really Hate My Job '07
Partition '07
Relative Strangers '06
When Will I Be Loved '04
The Company '03
Lost Junction '03
Three to Tango '99
54 '98
The Lion King; Simba's Pride '98 (V)
Too Smooth '98
Wild Things '98
Scream 2 '97
The Canterville Ghost '96
The Craft '96
Scream '96
Northern Passage '95
The Dark '94

Nicholas (Nick) Campbell (1952-)
Cinderella Man '05
Siblings '04
Prozac Nation '01
Full Disclosure '00
The Happy Face Murders '99
New Waterford Girl '99
The Boys Club '96
Gutterman '95
No Contest '94
Naked Lunch '91
The Big Slice '90
The Victory '88
Rampage '87
Going Home '86
Certain Fury '85
Knights of the City '85

Peggy Campbell (1912-85)
Big Calibre '35
Stone of Silver Creek '35
When a Man Sees Red '34

Rob Campbell
Hedwig and the Angry Inch '00
Boys Don't Cry '99
Hostile Waters '97
The Crucible '96
Lone Justice 2 '93
Unforgiven '92

Scott Michael Campbell (1971-)
Brothers Three '07
Brokeback Mountain '05
Just like Heaven '05
Wedding Crashers '05
Flight of the Phoenix '04
The Maldonado Miracle '03
The Hunted '03
United States of Leland '03
Dean Koontz's Black River '01
Hart's War '02
Radioland Murders '94

Sean Campbell
Blackwoods '02
He Sees You When You're Sleeping '02

Tisha Campbell (1968-)
The Sweetest Gift '98
Sprung '96
House Party 3 '94
Boomerang '92
House Party 2: The Pajama Jam '91
House Party '90
Rooftops '89
School Daze '88
Rags to Riches '87
Little Shop of Horrors '86

Torquil Campbell
Heaven on Earth '89
The Golden Seal '83

William Campbell (1926-)
Portrait in Terror '66
Track of the Vampire '66
The Secret Invasion '64
Dementia 13 '63
Night of Evil '62
The Sheriff of Fractured Jaw '59
Love Me Tender '56
Battle Cry '55
Man Without a Star '55
The High and the Mighty '54
Battle Circus '53
Escape from Fort Bravo '53

Frank Campeau (1864-1943)
Everyman's Law '36
Abraham Lincoln '30
Battling Bunyon '24
His Majesty, the American '19
When the Clouds Roll By '19
Heart of Texas Ryan '17
The Man from Painted Post '17

Cris Campion (1966-)
Field of Honor '87
Pirates '86

Tom Campitelli
Gates of Hell 2: Dead Awakening '96

Wally Campo (1923-)
The Beast from Haunted Cave '60
Ski Troop Attack '60
Tank Commando '59
Hell Squad '58
Machine Gun Kelly '58

Bruno Campos (1974-)
Crazylove '05
Dopamine '03
Mimic 2 '01

O Quatrilho '95

Rafael Campos (1936-85)
The Return of Josey Wales '86
A Streetcar Named Desire '84
V '83
Where the Buffalo Roam '80
Centennial '78
Slumber Party '57 '76
The Hanged Man '74
The Doll Squad '73
The Astro-Zombies '67
Lady in a Cage '64
This Could Be the Night '57

Victor Campos
Scarface '83
Archer: The Fugitive from the Empire '81

Ron Canada
Cinderella Man '05
Just like Heaven '05
Wedding Crashers '05
The Human Stain '03
The Hunted '03
United States of Leland '03
Dean Koontz's Black River '01
Lost in the Bermuda Triangle '98
Pinocchio's Revenge '96
The American President '95
Lone Star '95
Man of the House '95
Play Nice '92

Gianna Maria Canale (1927-)
Marauder '65
Colossus and the Amazon Queen '64
Tiger of the Seven Seas '62
Hercules '58
I, Vampiri '56
Man from Cairo '54
Sins of Rome '54
Go for Broke! '51

Lee Canalito
The Glass Jungle '88
Paradise Alley '78

Maria Canals (1966-)
Imagining Argentina '04
Master of Disguise '02
My Family '94

David Canary (1938-)
King of America '80
Johnny Firecloud '75
Posse '75
Sharks' Treasure '75
Melvin Purvis: G-Man '74

John Henry Canavan (1969-)
Torso '01
The Crossing '00

Urbain Cancellier
Intimate Strangers '04
Amelie '01

Stelio Candelli
A Man Called Rage '84
Planet of the Vampires '65

Candy Candido (1913-99)
The Great Mouse Detective '86 (V)
Peter Pan '53 (V)
Rhythm Parade '43

John Candy (1950-94)
Canadian Bacon '94
Hostage for a Day '94
Wagons East '94
Cool Runnings '93
Boris and Natasha: The Movie '92
Once Upon a Crime '92
Career Opportunities '91
Delirious '91
JFK '91
Nothing But Trouble '91
Only the Lonely '91
Home Alone '90
The Masters of Menace '90
The Rescuers Down Under '90 (V)
Uncle Buck '89
Who's Harry Crumb? '89
The Great Outdoors '88
Hot to Trot! '88 (V)
Speed Zone '88
Planes, Trains & Automobiles '87
Spaceballs '87
Tales of the Klondike: The Unexpected '87
Armed and Dangerous '86
Little Shop of Horrors '86
Really Weird Tales '86
Brewster's Millions '85
Sesame Street Presents: Follow That Bird '85
Summer Rental '85
Volunteers '85
The Last Polka '84
Splash '84
Going Berserk '83
National Lampoon's Vacation '83
Heavy Metal '81 (V)
Stripes '81
The Blues Brothers '80
The Double Negative '80
Lost and Found '79
1941 '79
The Silent Partner '78
Find the Lady '76
Tunnelvision '76
It Seemed Like a Good Idea at the Time '75
Class of 44 '73

Charles Cane (1899-1973)
Revenge of the Creature '55
Lucky Me '54
Native Son '51
Dead Reckoning '47

Natalie Canerday (1962-)
Tully '00
October Sky '99
Gunshy '98
Sling Blade '96
One False Move '91

Guillaume Canet (1973-)
Joyeux Noel '05
Love Me if You Dare '03
The Beach '00

Ridge Canipe
Pictures of Hollis Woods '07
The Bad News Bears '05

Bobby Cannavale (1971-)
Dedication '07
The Take '07
The Ten '07
The Night Listener '06
Snakes on a Plane '06
10 Items or Less '06
Happy Endings '05
Romance & Cigarettes '05
The Breakup Artist '04
Fresh Cut Grass '04
Haven '04
Shall We Dance? '04
The Station Agent '03
Washington Heights '02
3 A.M. '01
The Bone Collector '99

Stephen J. Cannell (1942-)
Ice Spiders '07
Half Past Dead '02
Posse '93

Dyan Cannon (1937-)
The Boynton Beach Club '05
The Sender '98
Allie & Me '97
Beverly Hills Family Robinson '97
Out to Sea '97
8 Heads in a Duffel Bag '96
That Darn Cat '96
Based on an Untrue Story '93
The Pickle '93
Christmas in Connecticut '92
The End of Innocence '90
Caddyshack '88
Jenny's War '85
Merlin and the Sword '85
Author! Author! '82
Deathtrap '82
Having It All '82
Coast to Coast '80
Honeysuckle Rose '80
Heaven Can Wait '78
Lady of the House '78
Revenge of the Pink Panther '78
The Virginia Hill Story '76
The Last of Sheila '73
Shamus '73
The Anderson Tapes '71
The Love Machine '71
Doctors' Wives '70
Bob & Carol & Ted & Alice '69

Esma Cannon (1896-1972)
Crow Hollow '52
I Met a Murderer '39

J.D. Cannon (1922-)
Street Justice '89
Death Wish 2 '82
The Adventures of Nellie Bly '81
Pleasure Palace '80
Raise the Titanic '80
Walking Through the Fire '80
Scorpio '73
Lawman '71
Cotton Comes to Harlem '70
Cool Hand Luke '67

Katherine (Kathy) Cannon (1953-)
Matters of the Heart '90
The Red Fury '84
Will: G. Gordon Liddy '82
High Noon: Part 2 '80
Private Duty Nurses '71

Nick Cannon (1980-)
Bobby '06
Even Money '06
Monster House '06 (V)
Roll Bounce '05
Underclassman '05
Garfield: The Movie '04 (V)
Shall We Dance? '04
Love Don't Cost a Thing '03
Drumline '02

Wanda Cannon (1960-)
The Christmas Blessing '05
Masters of Horror: Homecoming '05
The 6th Day '00
For the Moment '94
The Last Winter '89
Overdrawn at the Memory Bank '83

Sibylle Canonica (1957-)
Mostly Martha '01
Beyond Silence '96

Diana Canova (1953-)
Night Partners '83

Judy Canova (1913-83)
Cannonball '76
The Adventures of Huckleberry Finn '60
Carolina Cannonball '55
Oklahoma Annie '51
Louisiana Hayride '44

Anne Canovos
Ready to Wear '94
High Frequency '88
Zeder '83

Antonio Cantafora (1943-)
Intervista '87
Gabriela '84
Torture Chamber of Baron Blood '72
And God Said to Cain '69

Aldo Canti
Reactor '85
Five for Hell '67

Jose Pablo Cantillo (1979-)
Cleaner '07
Disturbia '07
Crank '06

Marilyne Canto (1963-)
Comedy of Power '06
Apres-Vous '03

Toni Canto (1965-)
All About My Mother '99
I'm the One You're Looking For '88

Mario Cantone (1959-)
Sex and the City: The Movie '08
Surf's Up '07 (V)

Eddie Cantor (1892-1964)
If You Knew Susie '48
Hollywood Canteen '44
Show Business '44
Thank Your Lucky Stars '43
Strike Me Pink '36
Kid Millions '34
Roman Scandals '33
Kid from Spain '32
Palmy Days '31
Glorifying the American Girl '30
Whoopee! '30

Yakima Canutt (1895-1986)
The Showdown '50
Calling Wild Bill Elliott '43
For Whom the Bell Tolls '43
Frontier Vengeance '40
Gone with the Wind '39
The Kansas Terrors '39
Wyoming Outlaw '39
Overland Stage Raiders '38
Santa Fe Stampede '38
Heart of the Rockies '37
Hit the Saddle '37
The Painted Stallion '37
Riders of the Rockies '37
Riders of the Whistling Skull '37
Roarin' Lead '37
Trouble in Texas '37
Circle of Death '36
King of the Pecos '36
Outlaw Rule '36
Winds of the Wasteland '36
Branded a Coward '35
Cyclone of the Saddle '35
Dawn Rider '35
Pals of the Range '35
Paradise Canyon '35
Rough Riding Ranger '35
Lucky Texan '34
The Man from Hell '34
Man from Utah '34
The Star Packer '34
Law and Lawless '33
Sagebrush Trail '33
Telegraph Trail '33
West of the Divide '33
Last Frontier '32
Battling with Buffalo Bill '31
The Fighting Stallion '26
Wild Horse Canyon '25
Branded a Bandit '24

Peter Capaldi (1958-)
Pinochet's Last Stand '06
House of 9 '05
Modigliani '04
Max '02
Shooting Fish '98
Bean '97
The Crow Road '96
Neil Gaiman's NeverWhere '96
Smilla's Sense of Snow '96
Captives '96
Dangerous Liaisons '88
The Lair of the White Worm '88
John & Yoko: A Love Story '85
Local Hero '83

Jad Capelja (1964-)
Freedom '82
Puberty Blues '81

Peter Capell (1912-86)
For the First Time '59
Paths of Glory '57

Virginia Capers (1925-2004)
The Feminine Touch '95
Ferris Bueller's Day Off '86
Jo Jo Dancer, Your Life Is Calling '86
White Mama '80
The North Avenue Irregulars '79

Lizzy Caplan (1982-)
Cloverfield '08
Mean Girls '04

Carmine Capobianco (1958-)
Galactic Gigolo '87
Psychos in Love '87

John Capodice (1938-)
Shut Up and Kiss Me '05
Double Bang '01
Out of the Black '01
Enemy of the State '98
Executive Power '98
Ringmaster '98
True Friends '98
Independence Day '96
Wedding Bell Blues '96
Honeymoon in Vegas '92
Fever '91
The Hard Way '91
Internal Affairs '90
Family Business '89
Square '86

Nadia Capone (1943-)
Traveling Companion '96
Flottie '93

Lino Capolicchio (1943-)
The Garden of the Finzi-Continis '71
The Bloodstained Shadow '78

Truman Capote (1924-84)
Murder by Death '76
ABC Stage 67: Truman Capote's A Christmas Memory '66 (N)

Carl Capotorto
Mac '93

Joolia Cappleman
American Blue Note '89
Who's Who '73

Pier Paolo Capponi (1938-)
Man of Legend '71
Super Brother '68

Francis Capra (1983-)
The King of Hearts '66
A Bronx Tale '93
Kazaam '96
A Simple Wish '97
Black Irish '07

Jordanna Capra
Watch It '93

Tony Caprari
Hired to Kill '91

Vittorio Caprioli (1921-89)
Le Magnifique '76

Jessica Capshaw (1976-)
The Groomsmen '06
Minority Report '02

Valentine '01
Something About Sex '98

Kate Capshaw (1953-)
Due East '02
A Girl Thing '01
The Love Letter '99
The Alarmist '98
The Locusts '97
How to Make an American Quilt '95
Just Cause '94
Love Affair '94
Next Door '94
My Heroes Have Always Been Cowboys '91
Black Rain '89
Love at Large '89
Private Affairs '89
Code Name: Dancer '87
The Quick and the Dead '87
Power '86
SpaceCamp '86
Best Defense '84
Dreamscape '84
Indiana Jones and the Temple of Doom '84
Windy City '84
A Little Sex '82

Capucine (1933-90)
Scandalous '88
Curse of the Pink Panther '83
Trail of the Pink Panther '82
The Con Artists '80
From Hell to Victory '79
Jaguar Lives '79
The Switch '76
Fellini Satyricon '69
The Honey Pot '67
What's New Pussycat? '65
The Pink Panther '64
The Seventh Dawn '64
Walk on the Wild Side '62
North to Alaska '60
Song Without End '60

Irène Cara (1959-)
Happily Ever After '93 (V)
The Magic Voyage '93 (V)
Caged in Paradiso '89
For Us, the Living '88
Busted Up '86
Certain Fury '85
Killing 'Em Softly '85
City Heat '84
D.C. Cab '84
Fame '80

Nestor Carbonell (1967-)
The Dark Knight '08
Smokin' Aces '07

The Lost Command '66

Flora Carabella (1926-99)
A Night Full of Rain '78
The Messiah '75

Paul Carafotes (1963-)
Journey to the Center of the Earth '88
All the Right Moves '83
Choices '81

Ion Caramitru (1942-)
Amen '02
Citizen X '95
Two Deaths '94

Joseph Carberry (1948-)
The Ten Million Dollar Getaway '91
Vigilante '83

Antony Carbone (1927-)
Skateboard '77
The Last Porno Flick '74
Sex Through a Window '72
The Last Woman on Earth '61
The Pit and the Pendulum '61
Creature from the Haunted Sea '60
A Bucket of Blood '59

Claudia Cardinale (1939-)
And Now Ladies and Gentlemen '02
Nostromo '96
Son of the Pink Panther '93
A Man in Love '87
Henry IV '85
Next Summer '84
Princess Daisy '83
Fitzcarraldo '82
The Gift '82
The Salamander '82
Midnight at the Wax Museum '36
Corleone '79
Escape to Athena '79
The Snicer '78
Blonde in Black Leather '77
Jesus of Nazareth '77
Blood Brothers '74
Conversation Piece '75
One Russian Summer '73
La Scoumoune '72
Legend of Frenchie King '71
L'Udienza '71
Queen of Diamonds '70
Red Tent '69
Once Upon a Time in the West '68

Linda Cardellini (1975-)
The Lost City '05
The Laramie Project '02
Noriega: God's Favorite '00
Attention Shoppers '99
Circus World '64
The Pink Panther '64
8 1/2 '63
The Leopard '63
Cartouche '62
Rocco and His Brothers '60
The Girl with a Suitcase '60
Il Bell'Antonio '60
Big Deal on Madonna Street '58
Blood of a Thousand '59

Stephen Antonio Cardenas (1974-)
Turbo: A Power Rangers Movie '96
Mighty Morphin Power Rangers: The Movie '95
Dee Snider's Strangeland '98

Linda Cardellini
Comanche Moon '08
Grandma's Boy '06
American Gun '05
Brokeback Mountain '05
Jiminy Glick in LaLa Wood '05
Scooby-Doo 2: Monsters Unleashed '04
Scooby-Doo '02
Legally Blonde '01
The Prince and the Surfer '99

Tantoo Cardinal (1951-)
Luna: Spirit of the Whale '07
Edge of Madness '02
Dodson's Journey '01
The Lost Child '00
Big Bear '98
Smoke Signals '98
Dances with Wolves '90
Loyalties '86
Lakota Woman: Siege at Wounded Knee '94
Legends of the Fall '94
Where the Rivers Flow North '94
Spirit Rider '93
By Way of the Stars '92
Silent Tongue '92
Black Robe '91
The Lightning Incident '91
Grand Avenue '96
Tecumseh: The Last Warrior '95

Ben Cardinal
Night of the Living Dead '90
Saan's Sadists '59
Down Dakota Way '49
Fear '46
A Walk in the Sun '46
The Devil on Wheels '47

Bill "Chilly Billy" Cardille (1928-)
Night of the Living Dead '68

Pat Cardi (1952-)
Twisted Brain '74

Stephen Antonio Cardenas
Blood of Dracula's Castle '69

Nathalie Cardone (1967-)
L'Enfer '93

John Cardos (1928-)
The Little Thief '89
Kid Galahad '37
Souls at Sea '37
Last Outlaw '36

Anthony Cardoza (1930-)
The Beast of Yucca Flats '61
Night of the Ghouls '59

Pedro Cardoso (1962-)
Bossa Nova '99
Four Days in September '97

David Cardy
Fool's Gold: The Story of the Brink's-Mat Robbery '92

James B. Cardwell (1920-54)
The Devil's Brigade '68
The 40 Year Old Virgin '05
Bewitched '06 (V)
Over the Hedge '06 (V)
Little Miss Sunshine '06
Evan Almighty '07
Dan in Real Life '07
Get Smart '08
Vulture '67
The Tell-Tale Heart '60

Steven Carell (1963-)
Dr. Seuss' Horton Hears a Who! '08 (V)

Annette Carell (1929-67)
The Two of Us '68
Xtro '83

Roger Carel (1927-)
Soldat Duroc... Ca Va Etre Ta Fete! '75

Harry Carey, Jr. (1921-)
Last Stand at Saber River '96
Sunchaser '96
Wyatt Earp: Return to Tombstone '94
Tombstone '93
Back to the Future, Part 3 '90
Bad Jim '89
Breaking In '89
The Whales of August '87
Challenge to White Fang '86
Crossroads '86
Mask '85
Endangered Species '82
Uforia '81
The Long Riders '80
Trinity Is Still My Name '75
Cahill: United States Marshal '73
Death of a Gunfighter '69
The Undefeated '69
Bandolero! '68
Alvarez Kelly '66
Billy the Kid Versus Dracula '66
Shenandoah '65
A Public Affair '52
Rio Bravo '59
The Searchers '56
Seventh Cavalry '56
House of Bamboo '55
Mister Roberts '55
Island in the Sky '53
Niagara '52
Copper Canyon '50
Rio Grande '50
Wagon Master '50
She Wore a Yellow Ribbon '49
Red River '48
The Smallest Show on Earth '48
Three Godfathers '48
Pursued '47
King of Alcatraz '38

Harry Carey, Sr. (1878-1947)
Robots '05 (V)
Gepetto '00
So Dear to My Heart '49
Angel and the Badman '47
Red River '48
Duel in the Sun '46

Drew Carey (1958-)
Geppetto '00

Amie Carey
Dog Park '98
suburbia '96

Julien Carette (1897-1966)
The Red Inn '51
The Rules of the Game '39
La Bete Humaine '38
Grand Illusion '37

James Carew (1876-1938)
Non-Stop New York '37

Arthur Edmund Carewe (1884-1937)
Doctor X '32
The Cat and the Canary '27
The Phantom of the Opera '25

Joyce Carey (1898-1993)
Cry, the Beloved Country '51
The October Man '48

Timothy Carey (1925-94)
Echo Park '86
Fast Walking '82
Speedtrap '78
The Killing of a Chinese Bookie '76
Fatso '80
High Anxiety '77
Who Killed Mary What's 'Er Name? '71
Minnie and Moskowitz '71
The World's Greatest Sinner '62
One-Eyed Jacks '61
The Killing '56
East of Eden '55

Sandy Carey
Mysterious Jane '81
Wham-Bam, Thank You Spaceman '7

Roland Carey (1933-)
Revolt of the Barbarians '64
The Sword of El Cid '62
The Giants of Thessaly '60

Ron Carey (1935-2007)
Fatso '80
History of the World: Part 1 '81
High Anxiety '77
Silent Movie '76

Phil Carey (1925-)
Monster '78
Fighting Mad '76
Scream of the Wolf '74
Dead Ringer '64
The Time Travelers '64
Tonka '58
The Long Gray Line '55
Mister Roberts '55
Gun Fury '53
Springfield Rifle '52

Michele Carey (1943-)
In the Shadow of Kilimanjaro '86
The Banger Sisters '02
Scandalous John '71
The Desperados '70
Changes '69
El Dorado '67
Live a Little, Love a Little '68

Olive Carey (1896-1988)
Billy the Kid Versus Dracula '66
The Alamo '60
The Searchers '56
Run of the Arrow '56
Night Passage '57
Gunfight at the O.K. Corral '57

Matthew Carey (1980-)
November '05
Old School '03

Mariah Carey (1970-)
Glitter '01
Wisegirls '02
You Don't Mess with the Zohan '08

MacDonald Carey (1913-94)
It's Alive 3: Island of the Alive '87
Access Code '84
The Rebels '79
Summer of Fear '78
Roots '77
Enc of the World '76
Who Is the Black Dahlia? '75
Tammy and the Doctor '63
John Paul Jones '59
Man or Gun '58
The Great Gatsby '49
Shadow of a Doubt '43
Wake Island '42
Let's Make It Legal '51
Comanche Territory '50
Copper Canyon '50
South Sea Sinner '50
Streets of Laredo '49
Great Missouri Rad '51

Leonard Carey (1887-1977)
The Greatest Gamble '34
His Greatest Gamble '34
The Snows of Kilimanjaro '52
Sundown '41
Beyond Tomorrow '40
They Knew What They Wanted '40
Mr. Smith Goes to Washington '39
Law West of Tombstone '38
The Port of Missing Girls '38
The Prisoner of Shark Island '36
You and Me '38
Aces Wild '37
Ghost Town '37
The Spoilers '42
The Shepherd of the Hills '41
Air Force '43
The Great Moment '44
Blithe Spirit '45
Brief Encounter '46

Night Rider '32
Without Honors '32
Cavalier of the West '31
Last of the Clintons '35
Powdersmoke Range '35
Rustler's Paradise '35
Wagon Trail '35
Wild Mustang '35
Buffalo Stampede '33
Man of the Forest '33
Border Devils '32
Devil Horse '32
The Last of the Mohicans '32
The Last of the Living Dead '68
W:segilts '02

The Profess onals '66
Sandra of a Thousand Delights '65

Minnie and Moskowitz 71
Head 68
Beach Blanket Bingo 65
Bikini Beach 64
The Mermaids of Tiburon 62
One-Eyed Jacks 61
Paths of Glory 57
Poor White Trash 57
The Killing 56
The Finger Man 55
Crime Wave 54

Patrick Cargill (1918-96)
Inspector Clouseau 68
A Countess from Hong Kong 67
Help! 65

Timothy Carhart (1953-)
Black Sheep 96
America's Dream 95
Beverly Hills Cop 3 94
Candyman 2: Farewell to the Flesh 94
Red Rock West 93
Quicksand: No Escape 91
Thelma & Louise 91
Pink Cadillac 89
The Manhattan Project 86
Ghostbusters 84
Party Animal 83

Gia Carides (1964-)
Backlash 86
Midnite Spares 85

Zoe Carides (1962-)
Brilliant Lies 96
Death in Brunswick 90
Stones of Death 88

Carmine Caridi (1933-)
Stick It 06
Exposed 03
My Big Fat Greek Wedding 02
Maze 01
Austin Powers 2: The Spy Who Shagged Me 99
The Extreme Adventures of Super Dave 98
Letters from a Killer 98
Primary Colors 98
Brilliant Lies 96
Last Breath 96
Paperback Romance 96
Bad Company 94
Strictly Ballroom 92

Len Cariou (1939-)
Flags of Our Fathers 06
The Boynton Beach Club 05
The Greatest Game Ever Played 05
Secret Window 04
About Schmidt 02
Nuremberg 00
Thirteen Days 00
In the Company of Spies 99
Executive Decision 96
The Summer of Ben Tyler 96
Never Talk to Strangers 95
The Man in the Attic 94
Witness to the Execution 94
Class of '61 92
Kurt Vonnegut's Monkey House 91
The Lady in White 88
Louisiana 87
Who'll Save Our Children? 82
The Four Seasons 81
A Little Night Music 77
Drying Up the Streets 76

Richard Carle (1871-1941)
Little Red Schoolhouse 36
Mistaken Identity 36
Love in Bloom 35
The Ghost Walks 34
One Hour with You 32
Sin Takes a Holiday 30

Claire Carleton (1913-79)
The Devil's Partner 58
The Fighter 52
Gildersleeve on Broadway 43

George Carlin (1937-)
Happily N'Ever After '07 (V)
Cars '06 (V)
Tarzan 2 '05 (V)
Jersey Girl '04
Scary Movie 3 '03
Jay and Silent Bob Strike Back '01
Dogma '99
Larry McMurtry's Streets of Laredo '95
Bill & Ted's Bogus Journey '91
The Prince of Tides '91
Bill & Ted's Excellent Adventure '89
Outrageous Fortune '87
Americathon '79 (N)
Car Wash '76
Goldenrod '77

Gloria Carlin
Varian's War '01
Color of Justice '97
Hanoi Hilton '87

Lynn Carlin (1930-)
Forbidden Love '82
Superstition '82
Deathdream '72
Wild Rovers '71
Silent Night, Lonely Night '69
Faces '68

Anne Carlisle (1956-)
Perfect Strangers '84
Liquid Sky '83

Jodi Carlisle (1960-)
Rugrats Go Wild! '03 (V)
The Wild Thornberrys Movie '02 (V)

Mary Carlisle (1912-)
Dead Men Walk 43
Baby Face Morgan '42
Dance, Girl, Dance '40
Double or Nothing '37
Champagne for Breakfast '35
One Frightened Night '35
Kentucky Kernels '34
College Humor '33
Held for Murder '32

Kitty Carlisle Hart (1910-2007)
Six Degrees of Separation '93
Radio Days '87
A Night at the Opera '35
Here is My Heart '34
Murder at the Vanities '34

Christine Carlo
Nora's Hair Salon 2: A Cut Above '08
Nora's Hair Salon '04

Ismael Carlo (1942-)
Y2K '99
One Man Out '89

Johann Carlo (1942-)
Fair Game '95
Quiz Show '94
Nadia '84

Margit Carlquist (1932-)
Smiles of a Summer Night '55
To Joy '50

Amy Carlson (1968-)
Winning Girls Through Psychic Mind Control '02
If These Walls Could Talk 2 '00

Jeff Carlson (1953-)
The Killing Floor '06
Slap Shot 2: Breaking the Ice '02
Slap Shot '77

June Carlson (1924-96)
The Hawk of Powder River '48
Mom & Dad '47
Delinquent Daughters '44

Karen Carlson (1945-)
A Horse for Danny '95
Teen Vamp '88
On Wings of Eagles '86
Brotherly Love '85
Fleshburn '84
Wild Horses '84
In Love with an Older Woman '82
American Dream '81
Octagon '80
Black Oak Conspiracy '77
The Candidate '72
The Student Nurses '70

Kelly Carlson (1976-)
Made of Honor '08
The Marine '06

Leslie (Les) Carlson (1933-)
A Christmas Story '83
Deranged '74

Richard Carlson (1912-77)
Change of Habit '69
The Valley of Gwangi '69
The Doomsday Flight '66
Tormented '60
The Last Command '55
Creature from the Black Lagoon '54
All I Desire '53
It Came from Outer Space '53
Flat Top '52
Retreat, Hell! '52
King Solomon's Mines '50
Try and Get Me '50
The Amazing Mr. X '48
Behind Locked Doors '48
Human Gorilla '48
White Cargo '42
Presenting Lily Mars '43
Back Street '41
Hold That Ghost '41
The Little Foxes '41
Beyond Tomorrow '40
The Ghost Breakers '40
The Howards of Virginia '40
No, No Nanette '40
Too Many Girls '40
The Duke of West Point '38
The Young in Heart '38

Steve Carlson (1943-)
Brothers O'Toole '73
The Horror of Frankenstein '70
Deadlier Than the Male '67

Steve Carlson (1955-)
Slap Shot 2: Breaking the Ice '02
Slap Shot '77

Veronica Carlson (1945-)
Freakshow '95
The Horror of Frankenstein '70
Frankenstein Must Be Destroyed '69
Dracula Has Risen from the Grave '68

Karin Carlsson (1906-90)
Walpurgis Night '41
A Woman's Face '38

Hope Marie Carlton (1966-)
Bloodmatch '91
Round Numbers '91
Slumber Party Massacre 3 '90
Picasso Trigger '89
Savage Beach '89
Terminal Exposure '89
Slaughterhouse Rock '88
Hard Ticket to Hawaii '87

Richard Carlyle (1879-1942)
The Lion Man '36
Sons of Steel '35
Playing Around '30

Robert Carlyle (1961-)
28 Weeks Later '07
Eragon '06
Marilyn Hotchkiss' Ballroom Dancing & Charm School '06
Human Trafficking '05
Dead Fish '04
Hitler: The Rise of Evil '03
Once Upon a Time in the Midlands '02
Formula 51 '01
To End All Wars '01
The Beach '00
Angela's Ashes '99
Ravenous '99
The World Is Not Enough '99
Plunkett & Macleane '98
Carla's Song '97
Face '97
The Full Monty '96
Go Now '96
Trainspotting '95
Being Human '94
Cracker: To Be a Somebody '94
Priest '94
Riff Raff '92

Roger C. Carmel (1932-86)
Hardly Working '81
Thunder and Lightning '77
Skullduggery '70
My Dog, the Thief '69
Alvarez Kelly '66
Gambit '66
The Silencers '66
Goodbye Charlie '64

Jeanne Carmen (1930-2007)
The Monster of Piedras Blancas '57
In Old Montana '39

Jewel Carmen (1897-1984)
The Bat '26
American Aristocracy '17
Flirting with Fate '16

Julie Carmen (1960-)
King of the Jungle '01
Gargantua '98
True Women '97
In the Mouth of Madness '95
Seduced by Evil '94
Deadly Currents '93
Drug Wars 2: The Cocaine Cartel '92
The Hunt for the Night Stalker '91
Kiss Me a Killer '91
Gore Vidal's Billy the Kid '89
The Neon Empire '89
Paint It Black '89
Fright Night 2 '88
The Milagro Beanfield War '88
The Penitent '88
Blue City '86
Last Plane Out '83
She's in the Army Now '81
Gloria '80
Night of the Juggler '80
Can You Hear the Laughter? The Story of Freddie Prinze '79

Jean Carmet (1920-94)
Germinal '93
Secret Obsession '88
Sorceress '88
Buffet Froid '79
Violette '78
Black and White in Color '76
Dupont Lajoie '74
Return of the Tall Blond Man with One Black Shoe '74
The Tall Blond Man with One Black Shoe '72
The Little Theatre of Jean Renoir '71
La Rupture '70
Any Number Can Win '63
There Goes Barder '54
Monsieur Vincent '47

Hoagy Carmichael (1899-1981)
Belles on Their Toes '52
The Las Vegas Story '52
Young Man with a Horn '50
The Best Years of Our Lives '46
Johnny Angel '45
Canyon Passage '46
To Have & Have Not '44
Topper '37

Ian Carmichael (1920-)
Wives and Daughters '01
Dark Obsession '90
Smashing Time '67
Heavens Above '63
I'm All Right Jack '59
Lucky Jim '58
Brothers in Law '57
The Colditz Story '55
Betrayed '54

Tullio Carminati (1894-1971)
War and Peace '56
Roman Holiday '53
London Melody '37
Paris in Spring '35
One Night of Love '34

Michael Carmine (1959-89)
Leviathan '89
*batteries not included '87
Band of the Hand '86

Primo Carnera (1906-67)
Hercules Unchained '59
A Kid for Two Farthings '55
The Iron Crown '41
The Prizefighter and the Lady '33

Alan Carney (1911-73)
Girl Rush '44
Seven Days Ashore '44
Zombies on Broadway '44

Art Carney (1918-2003)
Last Action Hero '93
Night Friend '87
The Night They Saved Christmas '87
The Blue Yonder '86
Miracle of the Heart: A Boys Town Story '86
The Naked Face '84
Better Late Than Never '83
St. Helen's, Killer Volcano '82
Izzy & Moe '85
Undergrads '85
The Emperor's New Clothes '84
Firestarter '84
The Muppets Take Manhattan '84
Defiance '79
Going in Style '79
Sunburn '79
House Calls '78
Movie, Movie '78
The Late Show '77
Death Scream '75
Katherine '75
Harry and Tonto '74
Pot o' Gold 41

George Carney (1887-1942)
Brighton Rock '47
I Know Where I'm Going '45
In Which We Serve '43
Love on the Dole '41

Morris Carnovsky (1897-1992)
Joe's Bed-Stuy Barbershop: We Cut Heads '83
Cyrano de Bergerac '50
Gun Crazy '49
Dead Reckoning '47
Our Vines Have Tender Grapes '45
Rhapsody in Blue '45

Cindy Carol (1944-)
Dear Brigitte '65
Gidget Goes to Rome '63

Linda Carol (1970-)
Carnal Crimes '91
Future Hunters '88
Reform School Girls '86

Martine Carol (1920-67)
The Battle of Austerlitz '60
Around the World in 80 Days '56
Lola Montes '55
Nana '55
Beauties of the Night '52
Voyage Suprise '46

Sheila Carol
The Beast from Haunted Cave '60
Ski Troop Attack '60

Sue Carol (1907-82)
The Lone Star Ranger '30
Walking Back '26
Captain Swagger '25

Adam Carolla (1964-)
The Hammer '07
Art House '98
Too Smooth '98

Leslie Caron (1931-)
Le Divorce '03
Chocolat '00
The Last of the Blonde Bombshells '00
Funny Bones '94
Damage '92
Courage Mountain '89
Dangerous Moves '84
The Unapproachable '82
Contract '80
Goldengirl '79
The Man Who Loved Women '77
Valentino '77
Fanny '61
Gigi '58
Daddy Long Legs '55
The Glass Slipper '55
Lili '53
An American in Paris '51

Memmo Carotenuto (1908-80)
Big Deal on Madonna Street '58
Too Bad She's Bad '54

Todd Carpent
Razorteeth '05
Feeders '96

Carleton Carpenter (1926-)
Up Periscope '59
Summer Stock '50
Two Weeks with Love '50
Lost Boundaries 49

David Carpenter
Spiders '00
Amelia Earhart: The Final Flight '94
Gettysburg '93
Warlock '91

Fred Carpenter (1954-)
Murdered Innocence '94
Small Kill '93

Horace Carpenter (1875-1945)
Range Riders '35
Maniac '34
The Dude Bandit '33

Jennifer Carpenter (1979-)
The Exorcism of Emily Rose '05
White Chicks '04

John Carpenter (1914-2003)
Night of the Ghouls '45
Song of Old Wyoming '45
Waxwork 2: Lost in Time '91

John Carpenter (1948-)
Masters of Horror: Pro-Life '05
The Cradle Will Rock '99
Body Bags '93
Silence of the Hams '93

Paul Carpenter (1921-64)
Call Me Bwana '63
Fire Maidens from Outer Space '56
Black Glove '54
Heat Wave '54
Paid to Kill '54
Unholy Four '54
Uneasy Terms '48

Peter Carpenter
Point of Terror '71*
Blood Mania '70

Camilla Carr
Making Love '82
Keep My Grave Open '80
Logan's Run '76
Poor White Trash 2 '75
Don't Look in the Basement '73

Carole Carr (1928-97)
Scream Dream '89
Down Among the Z Men '52
Goon Movie '52

Darlene Carr (1950-)
Piranha '95
Death of a Gunfighter '69
The Jungle Book '67 (V)

Mary Carr (1874-1973)
The World Accuses '35
Gun Law '33
Kept Husbands '31
The Fighting Marshal '32
Red Kimono '25

Paul Carr (1934-)
Sisters of Death '76
Sniper '75
The Bat People '74
Truck Stop Women '74
The Severed Arm '73
Ben '72
Dirt Gang '71

Thomas Carr (1907-97)
S.O.S. Coast Guard '37
The Idol Dancer '20

Raffaella Carra
Von Ryan's Express '65
Mole Men Against the Son of Hercules '61

David Carradine (1936-)
Epic Movie '07
Final Move '06
Miracle at Sage Creek '05
Kill Bill Vol. 2 '04
Kill Bill Vol. 1 '03 (V)
The Outsider '02
Warden of Red Rock '01*
By Dawn's Early Light '00
Codename: Jaguar '00
Isaac Asimov's Nightfall '00
Cybercity '99
Dangerous Curves '99
Knocking on Death's Door '99
Children of the Corn 5: Fields of Terror '98
Capital Punishment '96
Last Stand at Saber River '96
The Rage '96
The Gambler Returns: The Luck of the Draw '91
Animal Instincts '92
Distant Justice '92
Field of Fire '91
Night Rhythms '92
Roadside Prophets '92
Deadly Surveillance '91
Double Trouble '91
Dune Warriors '91
The Dying Truth '91
Karate Cop '91
Project: Eliminator '91
Sundown '91
Waxwork 2: Lost in Time '91

John Carradine (1906-88)
Jack-O '95
Buried Alive '89
Evil Spawn '87
Star Slammer '87
Monster in the Closet '86
Peggy Sue Got Married '86
Revenge '86
Tomb '86
Evils o' the Night '85
The Vals '85
Ice Pirates '84
Boogey Man 2 '83
Demon Rage '82
House of the Long Shadows '82
The Secret of NIMH '82 (V)
Frankenstein Island '81
Goliath Awaits '81
The Howling '81
The Boogey Man '80
The Nesting '80
Nocturna '79
The Seekers '79
The Bees '78
Monster '78
The Vampire Hookers '78
The Christmas Coal Mine Miracle '77
Golden Rendezvous '77
Satan's Cheerleaders '77
Shock Waves '77
The White Buffalo '77
The Killer Inside Me '76
The Last Tycoon '76
Mary, Mary, Bloody Mary '76
The Sentinel '76
The Shootist '76
Death at Love House '75
Blood Legacy '73
The House of Seven Corpses '73
The Shrieking '73
Silent Night, Bloody Night '73
Terror in the Wax Museum '73
Big Foot '72
Blood of Ghastly Horror '72
Boxcar Bertha '72
Everything You Always Wanted to Know about Sex (But Were Afraid to Ask) '72
The Night Strangler '72
Cain's Cutthroats '71
Horror of the Blood Monsters '70
The McMasters '70
Myra Breckinridge '70
Shinbone Alley '70 (V)
Blood of Dracula's Castle '69
The Good Guys and the Bad Guys '69
Gun Riders '69
The Trouble with Girls (and How to Get into It) '69
The Astro-Zombies '67
Autopsy of a Ghost '67
Hillbillies in a Haunted House '67
The Hostage '67
Mummy & Curse of the Jackal '67
Billy the Kid Versus Dracula '66
Munster, Go Home! '66
The Cosmic Man '59
Invisible Invaders '59
Half Human '58
The Incredible Petrified World '58
Last Hurrah '58
Showdown at Boot Hill '58
Hell Ship Mutiny '57
The Unearthly '57
Around the World in 80 Days '56
The Black Sleep '56
Court Jester '56
The Female Jungle '56
Hidden Guns '56
The Ten Commandments '56
The Kentuckian '55
Casanova's Big Night '54
The Egyptian '54
Thunder Pass '54
Johnny Guitar '53
The C-Man '49
The Private Affairs of Bel Ami '47
Captain Kidd '45
House of Dracula '45
The Adventures of Mark Twain '44
Bluebeard '44
House of Frankenstein '44
The Invisible Man's Revenge '44
The Mummy's Ghost '44
Return of the Ape Man '44
Waterfront '44
Captive Wild Woman '43
Isle of Forgotten Sins '43
Revenge of the Zombies '43
Silver Spurs '43
Reunion in France '42
Son of Fury '42
Blood and Sand '41
Western Union '41
Brigham Young '40
The Grapes of Wrath '40
Return of Frank James '40
Drums Along the Mohawk '39
Five Came Back '39
The Hound of the Baskervilles '39
Jesse James '39
Mr. Moto's Last Warning '39
Stagecoach '39
The Three Musketeers '39
Alexander's Ragtime Band '38
Four Men and a Prayer '38
Of Human Hearts '38
Captains Courageous '37
The Hurricane '37
Thank you, Mr. Moto '37
Dimples '36
The Garden of Allah '36
Mary of Scotland '36
The Prisoner of Shark Island '36
Winterset '36
Les Miserables '35
The Black Cat '34
Daniel Boone '34
The Invisible Man '33
To the Last Man '33
The Bride of Frankenstein '35

Keith Carradine (1951-)
All Hat '07
Bobby Z '07
Coyote Waits '03
Monte Walsh '03
The Outsider '02
The Diamond of Jeru '01
Baby '00
Hostage Hotel '00
Night Ride Home '99
Out of the Cold '99
Sirens '99
Hunter's Moon '97
Standoff '97
A Thousand Acres '97
Larry McMurtry's Dead Man's Walk '96
Last Stand at Saber River '96
Two Days in the Valley '96
The Tie That Binds '95
Wild Bill '95
Andre '94
Is There Life Out There? '94
The Bachelor '93
Crisscross '92
The Ballad of the Sad Cafe '91
Eye on the Sparrow '91
Daddy's Dyin'... Who's Got the Will? '90
Cold Feet '89
Capone '89
The Forgotten '89
Backfire '88
The Moderns '88
The Inquiry '87
Murder Ordained '87
Half a Lifetime '86
Trouble in Mind '86
A Winner Never Quits '86
Blackout '85
Choose Me '84
Maria's Lovers '84
Chiefs '83
Southern Comfort '81
The Long Riders '80
An Almost Perfect Affair '79
Old Boyfriends '79
Pretty Baby '78
The Duellists '77
Welcome to L.A. '77
Lumiere '76
Nashville '75
Thieves Like Us '74
Emperor of the North Pole '73
Idaho Transfer '73
Kung Fu '72
A Gunfight '71
McCabe & Mrs. Miller '71
Man on a String '71

Robert Carradine (1954-)
Tooth and Nail '07
Attack of the Sabretooth '05
Supercross: The Movie '05
The Lizzie McGuire Movie '03
Max Keeble's Big Move '01
Dangerous Curves '99
Shepherd '99
Breakout '98
Gunfighter '98
Stray Bullet '98
Scorpio One '97
Humanoids from the Deep '96
Bird of Prey '95
Body Bags '93
The Kid with the X-Ray Eyes '99
Revenge of the Nerds 2: Nerds in Paradise '87
Tales of the Klondike: In a Far Country '87
Number One with a Bullet '87
Conspiracy: The Trial of the Chicago Eight '87
Rude Awakening '89
The Incident '89
Buy & Cell '89
Ali's Fair '89
As Is '85
Aladdin and His Wonderful Lamp '84
Monte Carlo '86
Just the Way You Are '84
Revenge of the Nerds '84
Wavelength '83
Heartaches '82
Tag: The Assassination Game '82
The Big Red One '80
The Long Riders '80
Coming Home '78
Joyride '77
Orca '77
Cannonball '76
Jackson County Jail '76
Massacre at Central High '76
Pom Pom Girls '76
Aloha, Bobby and Rose '74
Mean Streets '73
The Cowboys '72

Jim Carrey (1962-)
Dr. Seuss' Horton Hears a Who! '08 (V)
The Number 23 '07
Fun With Dick and Jane '05
Eternal Sunshine of the Spotless Mind '04
Lemony Snicket's A Series of Unfortunate Events '04
Bruce Almighty '03
The Majestic '01
Dr. Seuss' How the Grinch Stole Christmas '00
Me, Myself, and Irene '00
Man on the Moon '99
Simon Birch '98 (V)
The Truman Show '98
The Cable Guy '96
Liar Liar '97
Ace Ventura: When Nature Calls '95
Batman Forever '95
Dumb & Dumber '94
The Mask '94
Ace Ventura: Pet Detective '94
Doing Time on Maple Drive '92
High Strung '91
Earth Girls Are Easy '89
Pink Cadillac '89
The Dead Pool '88
Peggy Sue Got Married '86
Once Bitten '85
Finders Keepers '84
Club Med '83
Rubberface '81

Tia Carrere (1967-)
Back in the Day '05
Lilo & Stitch 2: Stitch Has a Glitch '05 (V)
Lilo & Stitch '02 (V)
Scared City '98
Top of the World '97
Kull the Conqueror '97
High School High '96
Natural Enemy '96
The Immortals '95
Jury Duty '95
My Teacher's Wife '95
Hostile Intentions '94
True Lies '94
Quick '93
Rising Sun '93
Wayne's World 2 '93
Wayne's World '92
Showdown in Little Tokyo '91
Fatal Mission '89
Aloha Summer '88
Noble House '88
Zombie Nightmare '86

Barbara Carrera (1945-)
Love Is All There Is '96
Sawbones '95
Tryst '94
Point of Impact '93
Loverboy '89
Wicked Stepmother '89
The Underachievers '88
Love at Stake '87
Wild Geese 2 '85
Lone Wolf McQuade '83
Never Say Never Again '83
Condorman '81
Masada '81
When Time Ran Out '80
Centennial '78
The Island of Dr. Moreau '77
Embryo '76
The Master Gunfighter '75

Carlos Carrasco
Double Take '01
Speed '94
Bone Man's Hero '98
The Cowboys '72

Dany Carrel (1935-)
The Hands of Orlac '60
Mill of the Stone Women '60
The Bay Boy '85

Isabelle Carre (1971-)
Private Fears in Public Places '06
He Loves Me... He Loves Me Not '02
Children of the Century '99

Corey Carrier (1980-)
Savage Land '94
After Dark, My Sweet '90
Men Don't Leave '90

Matthieu Carriere (1950-)
Luther '03
Christopher Columbus: The Discovery '92
The Bay Boy '85

Carriere
A Woman in Flames '84
La Passante '83
The Aviator's Wife '80
Coup de Grace '78
Born for Hell '76
Germicide '74
Don Juan (Or if Don Juan Were a Woman) '73
An Occurrence at Owl Creek Bridge/Coup de Grace '62

Elpidia Carrillo (1963-)
Nine Lives '05
Forces of Nature '99
The Omega Code '99
Bread and Roses '00
Dangerous Passion '95
Family Business '89
My Family '94
The Lightning Incident '91
Memories of Me '88
Assassin '89
Bluffing It '87
Let's Get Harry '87
Risky Business '83
Predator '87
Salvador '86
Beyond the Limit '83
The Border '82

Leo Carrillo (1880-1961)
Pancho Villa Returns '50
Guns of Fury '48
The Fugitive '48
The Phantom of the Opera '43
American Empire '42
Riders of Death Valley '41
Lillian Russell '40
One Night in the Tropics '40
Wolf Call '39
Rose of Rio Grande '38
Zorro Rides Again '37
Fisherman's Wharf '39
Girl of the Golden West '38
Too Hot to Handle '38
Fit for a King '37
History Is Made at Night '37
I Promise to Pay '37
The Gay Desperado '36
Manhattan Melodrama '34
Viva Villa! '34
Before Morning '33

Debbie Lee Carrington (1959-)
Tiptoes '03
Club Fed '90
Spaced Invaders '90

Regina Carrol (1943-92)
Blazing Stewardesses '75
Jessi's Girls '75
Angels' Wild Women '72
Blood of Ghastly Horror '72
Brain of Blood '71
Dracula vs. Frankenstein '71
The Female Bunch '69
Satan's Sadists '69

Barbara Carroll
Goliath Against the Giants '63

Beeson Carroll
Coming Home '78
Werewolf of Washington '73

Diahann Carroll (1935-)
The Courage to Love '00
Livin' for Love: The Natalie Cole Story '00
Sally Hemings: An American Scandal '00
The Private Lives of Elizabeth & Essex '39
The Tower of London '39
Wuthering Heights '39
A Christmas Carol '38

Madeleine Carroll (1906-87)
When a Stranger Calls '06
Bahama Passage '42
My Favorite Blonde '42
My Son, My Son '40
My Love For Yours '39
On the Avenue '37
Prisoner of Zenda '37
The General Died at Dawn '36
Lloyds of London '36
The Secret Agent '36
The 39 Steps '35

Helen Carroll
The Man Upstairs '93
The Dead '87
Backstairs at the White House '79

James Carroll
DC 9/11: Time of Crisis '04
Police Academy 4: Citizens on Patrol '87
Girls Night Out '83
Senior Trip '81
He Knows You're Alone '80

James Dennis (Jim) Carroll (1950-)
The Basketball Diaries '95
The Unholy '88

Janet Carroll (1940-)
Enough '02

Joan Carroll (1932-)
Tomorrow the World '44
Primrose Path '40

John Carroll (1905-79)
Rock, Baby, Rock It '57
The Farmer Takes a Wife '53
Susan and God '40
Go West '40
Only Angels Have Wings '39

Justin Carroll
Dark Secrets '95
Stormswept '95

Kevin Carroll
The Notorious Bettie Page '06
Paid in Full '02
Pipe Dream '02
The Secret Lives of Dentists '02
Ed's Next Move '96

Leo G. Carroll (1892-1972)
That Funny Feeling '65
The Prize '63
One Plus One '61
The Parent Trap '61
North by Northwest '59
Tarantula '55
We're No Angels '55
The Paradine Case '47
Forever Amber '47
Song of Love '47
House on 92nd Street '45
Spellbound '45
Suspicion '41
Rebecca '40
Bulldog Drummond's Secret Police '39
Charlie Chan in City of Darkness '39
The World Moves On '34

Nancy Carroll (1904-65)
That Certain Age '38
Transatlantic Merry-Go-Round '34
Scarlet Dawn '32
Personal Maid '31
Dance of Life '29

Pat Carroll (1927-)
Freedom Writers '07
Redacted '07
Songcatcher '99
The Little Mermaid '89 (V)
My Neighbor Totoro '88 (V)
Brothers O'Toole '73
With Six You Get Eggroll '68

Peter Carroll (1943-)
Who Killed Baby Azaria? '83
Cass '78
The Chant of Jimmie Blacksmith '78
The Last Wave '77

Rocky Carroll (1963-)
Best Laid Plans '99
The Great White Hype '96
Crimson Tide '95

Carrot Top (1967-)
Dennis the Menace Strikes Again '98
Chairman of the Board '97

Ben Carruthers (1936-83)
Riot '69
Shadows '60

Julius J. Carry, III (1952-)
The New Guy '02
The Last Dragon '85
Avenging Disco Godfather '76

Charles Carson (1886-1977)
Beau Brummel '54
Cry, the Beloved Country '51
The Courageous Mr. Penn '41
Dreaming Lips '37
The Secret Agent '36
Broken Melody '34

Crystal Carson (1967-)
Killer Tomatoes Strike Back '90

Glen Carson
Ninja Death Squad '87
Ninja Phantom Heroes '87

Hunter Carson (1975-)
Mr. North '88
Invaders from Mars '86
Paris, Texas '83

Jack Carson (1910-63)
The King of the Roaring 20s: The Story of Arnold Rothstein '61
The Bramble Bush '60
Cat on a Hot Tin Roof '58
Rally 'Round the Flag, Boys! '58
Tarnished Angels '57
Phffft! '54
Red Garters '54
A Star Is Born '54
Dangerous When Wet '53
It's a Great Feeling '49
My Dream Is Yours '49
Romance on the High Seas '48
Mildred Pierce '45
Arsenic and Old Lace '44
Hollywood Canteen '44
Thank Your Lucky Stars '43
Gentleman Jim '42
The Male Animal '42
The Bride Came C.O.D. '41
Love Crazy '41
Mr. & Mrs. Smith '41
Strawberry Blonde '41
Lucky Partners '40
Destry Rides Again '39
Mr. Smith Goes to Washington '39
Carefree '38
The Saint in New York '38
Vivacious Lady '38
Stage Door '37
Stand-In '37

John Carson (1927-)
An African Dream '90
After Julius '78
Captain Kronos: Vampire Hunter '74
Emma '72
Taste the Blood of Dracula '70
Plague of the Zombies '66
Night of the Blood Beast '58

John David Carson (1952-)
Empire of the Ants '77
Charge of the Model T's '76
Creature from Black Lake '76
Savage Is Loose '74

Lisa Nicole Carson (1969-)
Life '99
Eve's Bayou '97
Love Jones '96
Devil in a Blue Dress '95

L.M. Kit Carson (1947-)
Hurricane Streets '96
Running on Empty '88
David Holzman's Diary '67

Shawn Carson
Something Wicked This Way Comes '83
The Funhouse '81

Silas Carson (1965-)
Star Wars: Episode 3—Revenge of the Sith '05
Hidalgo '04

Sunset Carson (1922-90)
Battling Marshal '48
Alias Billy the Kid '46
Rio Grande Raiders '45
Bells of Rosarita '45
Rough Riders of Cheyenne '45
Call of the Rockies '44
Stage Door Canteen '43

Terrence "T.C." Carson
Final Destination 2 '03
U-571 '00
Relax... It's Just Sex! '98
Gang Related '96
Livin' Large '91

Peter Carsten (1929-)
Zeppelin '71
Black Lemons '70
Web of the Spider '70
And God Said to Cain '69
Dark of the Sun '68
Secret of the Black Trunk '62

Margit Carstensen (1940-)
Terror 2000 '92
Chinese Roulette '86
Angry Harvest '85
Possession '81
Berlin Alexanderplatz '80
Mother Kusters Goes to Heaven '76
Satan's Brew '76
Fear of Fear '75
Tenderness of the Wolves '73
The Bitter Tears of Petra von Kant '72

Alex Carter (1964-)
Out of Time '03
Hitched '01

Alice Carter
The Man in the Attic '94
Dangerous Heart '93
Gross Anatomy '89

Ann Carter (1936-)
Song of Love '47
The Two Mrs. Carrolls '47
Curse of the Cat People '44
I Married a Witch '42

Ben Carter (1907-46)
Crash Dive '43
Sleepers West '41

Dixie Carter (1939-)
The Big Day '99
Going Berserk '83
Killing of Randy Webster '81

Finn Carter (1960-)
Missing Pieces '00
Sweet Justice '92
How I Got into College '89
Tremors '89

Gary Carter
Late Bloomers '95
Ninja Strike Force '88

Georgianna Carter
The Wild Ride '60

Helena Carter (1923-2000)
Invaders from Mars '53
Bugles in the Afternoon '52
Double Crossbones '51
Kiss Tomorrow Goodbye '50
Something in the Wind '47

Jack Carter (1923-)
One Last Ride '03
Play It to the Bone '99
In the Heat of Passion '91
Satan's Princess '90
Arena '89
Robo-Chic '89
Deadly Embrace '88
Sexpot '88
Death Blow '87
Red Nights '87
Ecstasy '84
Hambone & Hillie '84
History of the World: Part 1 '81
Alligator '80
Octagon '80
The Glove '80
Rainbow '78
The Happy Hooker Goes to Washington '77
The Amazing Dobermans '76
Resurrection of Zachary Wheeler '71
Viva Las Vegas '63
The Horizontal Lieutenant '62

Janis Carter (1913-94)
Flying Leathernecks '51
The Half-Breed '51
Santa Fe '51
Miss Grant Takes Richmond '49
Lady of Burlesque '43
I Married an Angel '42

Jason Carter (1960-)
Behind the Red Door '02
The Dark Dancer '95
A Merry War '97
Brassed Off '96
Grave Indiscretions '96
Black Beauty '94
Cracker: The Big Crunch '94

Jim Carter (1948-)
The Secret Life of Mrs. Beeton '06
The Thief Lord '06
Bright Young Things '03
Dinotopia '02
The Way We Live Now '02
The Little Vampire '00
102 Dalmatians '00
Legionnaire '98
Shakespeare in Love '98

Joelle Carter (1972-)
When Will I Be Loved '04
High Fidelity '00
It Had to Be You '00
Just One Time '00
Swimming '00

Karen Carter
The Legend of the Wolf Woman '77

Lynda Carter (1951-)
Slayer '06
The Dukes of Hazzard '05
Sky High '05
Super Troopers '01
A Prayer in the Dark '97
Danielle Steel's Daddy '91
I Posed for Playboy '91
Rita Hayworth: The Love Goddess '83
Hotline '82
Last Song '80
Bobbie Jo and the Outlaw '76

Neil Carter (1948-2003)
The Proprietor '96
The Grass Harp '95
The Crazysitter '94
Bebe's Kids '92 (V)
Final Shot: The Hank Gathers Story '92
Modern Problems '81
Hair '79

Nick Carter
The Hollow '04
Class Reunion Massacre '77

Sarah Carter (1980-)
DOA: Dead or Alive '06
Final Destination 2 '03

Terry Carter (1929-)
Battlestar Galactica '78
Black Force 2 '78
Mission Galactica: The Cylon Attack '78
Foxy Brown '74
Man on the Run '74

Thomas Carter (1953-)
Whose Life Is It Anyway? '81
Monkey Hustle '77

T.K. Carter (1956-)
Domino '05
Baadasssss! '03
The Corner '00
Yesterday's Target '96
A Rage in Harlem '91
Ski Patrol '89
Amazon Women on the Moon '87
He's My Girl '87
Runaway Train '85
Doctor Detroit '83
The Thing '82
The Hollywood Knights '80
Seems Like Old Times '80

Anna Carteret (1942-)
Mrs. Palfrey at the Claremont '05

Katrin Cartlidge (1961-2002)
From Hell '01
No Man's Land '01
Sword of Honour '01
The Weight of Water '00
Hi-Life '98
The Lost Son '98
Career Girls '97
Claire Dolan '97
The Heat of the Day '91
The Shell Seekers '89
Before the Rain '94
Naked '93

Angela Cartwright (1952-)
Lost in Space '98
High School USA '84
Scout's Honor '80
The Sound of Music '65

Lynn Cartwright (1928-2004)
The Wasp Woman '59
Queen of Outer Space '58

Nancy Cartwright (1959-)
The Simpsons Movie '07
Rugrats Go Wild! '03 (V)
The Land Before Time 6: The Secret of Saurus Rock '98 (V)
The Little Mermaid '89 (V)
Pound Puppies and the Legend of Big Paw '88 (V)
Twilight Zone: The Movie '83

Veronica Cartwright (1950-)
Kinsey '04
Just Married '03
The Invasion '07
Scary Movie 2 '01
A Slipping Down Life '99
Sparkler '99
Quicksilver Highway '98
Money Talks '97
My Brother's Keeper '95
Candyman 2: Farewell to the Flesh '94
Dead Air '94
Man Trouble '92
Dead Again '91
False Identity '90
Hitler's Daughter '90
Robert Kennedy and His Times '90
Valentino Returns '88
Wisdom '87
The Witches of Eastwick '87
Flight of the Navigator '86
My Man Adam '85
Nightmares '83
The Right Stuff '83
Prime Suspect '82
Alien '79
Goin' South '78
Invasion of the Body Snatchers '78
Inserts '76
One Man's Way '63
The Birds '63
Spencer's Mountain '63
The Children's Hour '61

David Caruso (1956-)
Black Point '01
Session 9 '01
Deadlocked '00
Proof of Life '00
Body Count '97
Cold Around the Heart '97
Kiss of Death '95
Jade '95
Mad Dog and Glory '93
King of New York '90
Rainbow Drive '90
China Girl '87
Blue City '86
First Blood '82
An Officer and a Gentleman '82
Getting Wasted '80

Max Casella (1967-)
Analyze This '98
Trial and Error '96
Ed Wood '95
Newsies '92

Kathleen Case (1933-79)
Human Desire '54

Betty Carvalho
Man '72
Orloff and the Invisible Man '70

Brent Carver (1952-)
The Event '03
Ararat '02
Deeply '99
Lilies '96
Whiskers '96
Millennium '89
Crossbar '79
One Night Stand '78

Lynne Carver (1909-55)
Bataan '43
Man from Cheyenne '42
Sunset on the Desert '42
Huckleberry Finn '39
A Christmas Carol '38
Everybody Sing '38
The Bride Wore Red '37
Maytime '37

Dana Carvey (1955-)
Master of Disguise '02
Little Nicky '00
The Shot '96
Clean Slate '94
The Road to Wellville '94
Trapped in Paradise '94
Wayne's World 2 '93
Wayne's World '92
Opportunity Knocks '90
Moving '88
Tough Guys '86
Racing with the Moon '84
This Is Spinal Tap '84

James Carville
The Assassination of Jesse James by the Coward Robert Ford '07
The People vs. Larry Flynt '96

Johnny Cash (1932-2003)
Last Days of Frank & Jesse James '86
Stagecoach '86
The Baron and the Kid '84
Murder in Coweta County '83
The Pride of Jesse Hallam '81
A Gunfight '71
Road to Nashville '67
Door to Door Maniac '61

Anthony Caruso (1913-2003)
Claws '77
Zebra Force '76
Legend of Earl Durand '74
Never Steal Anything Small '59
When Gangland Strikes '56
Cattle Queen of Montana '54
Drum Beat '54
The Asphalt Jungle '50
Objective, Burma! '45
The Ghost and the Guest '43

Lisa Marie Caruk
Blood Angels '05
Call Me: The Rise and Fall of Heidi Fleiss '04

Maria Casares (1922-96)
Someone Else's America '96
La Lectrice '88
Sand and Blood '87
The Testament of Orpheus '59
Orpheus '49
La Chartreuse de Parme '48
Children of Paradise '44
The Ladies of the Bois de Bologne '44

Amira Casar (1971-)
Piano Tuner of Earthquakes '05
Anatomy of Hell '04
Sylvia '03
How I Killed My Father '03

Eloy Casados (1949-)
Grand Avenue '96
A Climate for Killing '91

Salvatore Cascio (1979-)
The Pope Must Diet '91
Everybody's Fine '90
Cinema Paradiso '88

Antonio Casas (1911-82)
Blood at Sundown '88
Tristana '70
The Texican '66

Rosalind Cash (1938-95)
Tales from the Hood '95
The Mighty Pawns '87
The Offspring '87
The Adventures of Buckaroo Banzai Across the Eighth Dimension '84
Go Tell It on the Mountain '84
Wrong Is Right '82
Keeping On '81
Sophisticated Gents '81
The Class of Miss MacMichael '78
Monkey Hustle '77
Dr. Black, Mr. Hyde '76
Cornbread, Earl & Me '75
Amazing Grace '74
Omega Man '71

June Carter Cash (1929-2003)
The Apostle '97
Last Days of Frank & Jesse James '86
The Baron and the Kid '84
Murder in Coweta County '83

Nick Cassavetes (1959-)
The Astronaut's Wife '99
Life '99
Face/Off '97
Twogether '94
Body of Influence '93
Broken Trust '93
Class of 1999 2: The Substitute '93

Chiara Caselli (1967-)
Ripley's Game '02
Sleepless '01
Forgotten City '98
Beyond the Clouds '95
Fiorile '93
My Own Private Idaho '91

Lawrence Casey (1941-)
The Hunted Lady '77
The Student Nurses '70
The Gay Deceivers '69

Maurice Cass (1884-1954)
Rocky Jones, Space Ranger: Renegade Satellite '54
Spook Busters '48
Thin Ice '37

Katrina Caspary
My Mom's a Werewolf '89
Mac and Me '88

Peggy Cass (1924-99)
Cheaters '84
Paddy '70
If It's Tuesday, This Must Be Belgium '69
Gidget Goes Hawaiian '61
Auntie Mame '58
The Marrying Kind '52

John Cassavetes (1929-89)
Love Streams '84
Marvin & Tige '84
The Tempest '82
Incubus '82
Whose Life Is It Anyway? '81
Brass Target '78
The Fury '78
Opening Night '77
Mikey & Nicky '76
Two Minute Warning '76
Minnie and Moskowitz '71
Husbands '70
Rosemary's Baby '68
Devil's Angels '67
The Dirty Dozen '67
The Killers '64

Seymour Cassel (1935-)
The Life Aquatic with Steve Zissou '04
Stealing Harvard '02
Sonny '02
The Royal Tenenbaums '01
Animal Factory '00
The Crew '00
Just One Night '00
Me & Will '99
Rushmore '98
The Treat '98
Relax... It's Just Sex! '98
This World, Then the Fireworks '97
Obsession '97
Trees Lounge '96
Dream for an Insomniac '96
Things I Never Told You '96
Indecent Proposal '93
When Pigs Fly '93
Adventures in Spying '92
Honeymoon in Vegas '92
In the Soup '92
There Goes My Baby '92
Trouble Bound '92
Diary of a Hitman '91
White Fang '91
Dick Tracy '90
Sweet Bird of Youth '89
Wicked Stepmother '89
Colors '88
Johnny Be Good '88
Plain Clothes '88
Track 29 '88
Best Seller '87
Survival Game '87
Tin Men '87
Eye of the Tiger '86
Love Streams '84
Double Exposure '82
The Mountain Men '80
California Dreaming '79
Valentino '77
Black Oak Conspiracy '77
The Killing of a Chinese Bookie '76
Minnie and Moskowitz '71
Faces '68
The Killers '64

Isadore Cashier (1887-1948)
The Light Ahead '39
The Cantor's Son '37
His Wife's Lover '31

Graciela Casillas
American Streetfighter '92

Philip Casnoff (1955-)
Chameleon '98
The Defenders: Taking the First '98
Sinatra '92
Ironclads '90
Hands of a Stranger '87
North and South Book 2 '86

John Cason (1918-61)
Last Bullet '50
Outlaw of the Plains '46

Stefania Casini (1948-)
The Bloodstained Shadow '73
Andy Warhol's Bad '77
Suspiria '77
Blood for Dracula '74

Jean-Pierre Cassel (1932-2007)
The Crimson Rivers '01
La Ceremonie '95
L'Elève '95
Cafe au Lait '94
Ready to Wear '94
Between Heaven and Earth '93
The Favor, the Watch, & the Very Big Fish '92
The Maid '90
The Phantom of the Opera '90
Mr. Frost '89
The Return of the Musketeers '89
Alice '86
La Truite '83
Nudo di Donna '83
La Vie Continue '82
From Hell to Victory '79
Les Rendez-vous D'Anna '78
Murder on the Orient Express '74
The Three Musketeers '74
The Discreet Charm of the Bourgeoisie '72
La Rupture '70
Army of Shadows '69
Oh! What a Lovely War '69
Is Paris Burning? '66
Those Magnificent Men in Their Flying Machines '65

Vincent Cassel (1967-)
Eastern Promises '07
Ocean's Thirteen '07
Sheitan '06
Derailed '05
Ocean's Twelve '04
The Reckoning '03
Birthday Girl '02
Irreversible '02
Brotherhood of the Wolf '01
The Crimson Rivers '01
Read My Lips '01
Shrek '01 (V)
The Messenger: The Story of Joan of Arc '99
Elizabeth '98
Hate '95

Andrew Cassese
Revenge of the Nerds II: Nerds in Paradise '87
Revenge of the Nerds '84

Gabriel Casseus (1962-)
Black Hawk Down '01
Bedazzled '00
Lockdown '00
Black Dog '98
Don King: Only in America '97
New Jersey Drive '95

Alan Cassell (1932-)
Strange Bedfellows '04
Breakdown '97
Squizzy Taylor '84
The Club '81
Breaker Morant '80
Money Movers '78

Wally Cassell (1915-92)
Sands of Iwo Jima '49
White Heat '49
The Story of G.I. Joe '45

David Cassidy (1950-)
Instant Karma '90
The Night the City Screamed '80
Spirit of '76 '90

Edward Cassidy (1893-1968)
Buffalo Bill Rides Again '47
Son of Zorro '47
Boss of Rawhide '44
Devil Riders '44
Frontier Outlaws '44

Rustler's Hideout '44
Wild Horse Phantom '44
Raiders of Red Gap '43
Sagebrush Law '43
Aces Wild '37
Boothill Brigade '37
Boots of Destiny '37
Roaring Six Guns '37
Santa Fe Bound '37
A Face in the Fog '36
Feud of the West '35
Pecos Kid '35
Toll of the Desert '35

Elaine Cassidy (1979-)
The Lost World '02
Disco Pigs '01
The Others '01
Felicia's Journey '99

Jack Cassidy (1927-76)
The Eiger Sanction '75
Columbo: Murder by the Book '71
The Andersonville Trial '70

Joanna Cassidy (1944-)
Larry the Cable Guy: Health Inspector '06
The Reading Room '05
Witches of the Caribbean '05
John Carpenter's Ghosts of Mars '01
Dangerous Beauty '98
Executive Power '98
Loved '97
The Second Civil War '97
Chain Reaction '96
Barbarians at the Gate '93
Stephen King's The Tommyknockers '93
Landslide '92
Livel From Death Row '92
Perfect Family '92
All-American Murder '91
Don't Tell Mom the Babysitter's Dead '91
Lonely Hearts '91
Nightmare at Bittercreek '91
A Girl of the Limberlost '90
May Wine '90
Wheels of Terror '90
Where the Heart Is '90
1969 '89
The Package '89
A Father's Revenge '88
Who Framed Roger Rabbit '88
The Fourth Protocol '87
The Children of Times Square '86
Club Paradise '86
Codename: Foxfire '85
Invitation to Hell '84
Under Fire '83
Blade Runner '82
Night Games '80
The Glove '78
The Late Show '77
Prime Time '77
Stunts '77
Bank Shot '74

Katie Cassidy (1986-)
Black Christmas '06

Patrick Cassidy (1961-)
The Fiance '96
How the West Was Fun '95
Hitler's Daughter '90
Longtime Companion '90
Love at Stake '87
Dress Gray '86
Something in Common '86
Fever Pitch '85
Nickel Mountain '85
Just the Way You Are '84
Off the Wall '82

Shaun Cassidy (1958-)
Texas Guns '90
Roots: The Gift '88

Ted Cassidy (1932-79)
Halloween with the Addams Family '77

Sunshine Run '79
Goin' Coconuts '78
Planet Earth '74
Thunder County '74
Women's Prison Escape '74
Poor Pretty Eddie '73
Butch Cassidy and the Sundance Kid '69
MacKenna's Gold '69

Claudio Cassinelli (1938-85)
Hands of Steel '86
Hercules 2 '85
The New Gladiators '83
Scorpion with Two Tails '82
The Great Alligator '81
Mountain of the Cannibal God '79
Allonsanfan '73

John Cassini
Catwoman '04
Window Theory '04
Break a Leg '03
Chain of Fools '00
Get Carter '00
The Spree '96

Nadia Cassini (1949-)
Star Crash '78
Pulp '72

Carla Cassola (1947-)
The Devil's Daughter '91
Demonia '90

Jean-Pierre Castaldi (1944-)
Extreme Ops '02
The Musketeer '01
A Fine Romance '92
La Merveilleuse Visite '74

France Castel (1943-)
Karmina '96
A Wind from Wyoming '94

Lou Castel (1943-)
Irma Vep '96
Three Lives and Only One Death '96
Rorret '87
The Eyes, the Mouth '83
The American Friend '77
The Scarlet Letter '73
Beware of a Holy Whore '70
Paranoia '69
A Bullet for the General '68

Dan Castellaneta (1958-)
The Simpsons Movie '07 (V)
The Pursuit of Happyness '06
The Settlement '99
Plump Fiction '97
Hey Arnold! The Movie '02 (V)
The Return of Jafar '94 (V)
The War of the Roses '89
Nothing in Common '86

Richard S. Castellano (1933-88)
The Godfather 1902-1959: The Complete Epic '81
Night of the Juggler '80
Honor Thy Father '73
The Godfather '72
Lovers and Other Strangers '70
A Fine Madness '66

Vincent Castellanos (1962-)
Mulholland Drive '01
K-911 '99
The Last Marshal '99
Anaconda '96
The Crow 2: City of Angels '96

Sergio Castellitto (1953-)
The Chronicles of Narnia: Prince Caspian '08
Paris, je t'aime '06
Caterina in the Big City '03
My Mother's Smile '02
Va Savoir '01
For Sale '98

Pronto '97
Portraits Chinois '96
The Star Maker '95
Alberto Express '92
The Big Blue '88

Willy Castello (1910-53)
Confessions of a Vice Baron '42
Mad Youth '40
Cocaine Fiends '36

Nino Castelnuovo (1936-)
The English Patient '96
Camille 2000 '69
Umbrellas of Cherbourg '64
Dishonorable Discharge '57
Nana '55
Forbidden Fruit '52

Movita Castenada
See Movita

Movita Castendada
See Movita

Movita Casteneda
See Movita

Christopher Castile (1980-)
Beethoven's 2nd '93
Beethoven '92

Enrique Castillo (1949-)
The Hi-Lo Country '98
The End of Violence '97
My Family '94
Blood In … Blood Out: Bound by Honor '93

Gloria Castillo (1933-)
Invasion of the Saucer Men '57
Reform School Girl '57
Teenage Monster '57
The Night of the Hunter '55

Don Castle (1917-66)
Motor Patrol '50
Who Killed Doc Robbin? '48
Wake Island '42

John Castle (1940-)
The Crucifer of Blood '91
RoboCop 3 '91
The Bretts '88
Lillie '78
Antony and Cleopatra '73
Man of La Mancha '72
The Lion in Winter '68
Blow-Up '66

Maggie Castle
Weirdsville '07

Mary Castle (1931-98)
Gunsmoke '53
White Fire '53

Nick Castle (1947-)
Halloween '78

Robert Castle
The Manchurian Candidate '04

Peggy Castle (1927-73)
The Seven Hills of Rome '58
Beginning of the End '57
The Finger Man '55
The White Orchid '54
Invasion U.S.A. '52
Dr. Terror's House of Horrors '65

William Castle (1914-77)
Bug '75
Shampoo '75
Rosemary's Baby '68

Keisha Castle-Hughes (1990-)
The Nativity Story '06

Star Wars: Episode 3— Revenge of the Sith '05
Whale Rider '02

Coralina Cataldi-Tassoni (1971-)
Ghost Son '06
The Phantom of the Opera '98
Evil Clutch '89
Opera '88
Demons 2 '87

Patrick Catalifo
Don't Let Me Die on a Sunday '98
Sand and Blood '87

Antonio Catania (1952-)
Bread and Tulips '01
Mediterraneo '91

Luciano Catenacci (1933-90)
Crime Busters '78
La Scoumoune '72

John Cater (1932-)
The Duchess of Duke Street '78
Captain Kronos: Vampire Hunter '74

Georgina Cates (1975-)
Big City Blues '99
Clay Pigeons '98
Illuminata '98
A Soldier's Sweetheart '98
The Treat '98
Stiff Upper Lips '96
Frankie Starlight '95
An Awfully Big Adventure '94

Helen Cates
The Whole Wide World '96
The Underneath '95
A Taste for Killing '92

Phoebe Cates (1963-)
The Anniversary Party '01
My Life's in Turnaround '94
Princess Caraboo '94
Bodies, Rest & Motion '93
Drop Dead Fred '91
Gremlins 2: The New Batch '90
I Love You to Death '90
The Heart of Dixie '89
Shag: The Movie '89
Bright Lights, Big City '88
Date with an Angel '87
Gremlins '84
Private School '83
Fast Times at Ridgemont High '82
Paradise '82

Reg E. Cathey (1958-)
The Machinist '04
S.W.A.T. '03
Boycott '02
Pootie Tang '01
Seven '95

Mary Jo Catlett (1938-)
The SpongeBob SquarePants Movie '04 (V)
Ablaze '00
Bram Stoker's The Mummy '97

Walter Catlett (1889-1960)
The Inspector General '49
I'll Be Yours '47
I Love a Bandleader '45
His Butler's Sister '44

They Got Me Covered '43
Yankee Doodle Dandy '42
It Started with Eve '41
Pinocchio '40 (V)
Pop Always Pays '40
Remedy for Riches '40
Bringing Up Baby '38
Every Day's a Holiday '38
On the Avenue '37
Sing Me a Love Song '37
Mr. Deeds Goes to Town '36
A Tale of Two Cities '36
Rain '32
The Front Page '31
Maker of Men '31

Victoria Catlin
Howling 5: The Rebirth '89
Mutant on the Bounty '89

Juliette Caton (1975-)
Lady Audley's Secret '00
Courage Mountain '89
The Last Temptation of Christ '88

Michael Caton (1943-)
Strange Bedfellows '04
The Animal '01
The Echo of Thunder '98
The Interview '98
The Castle '97
The Thorn Birds: The Missing Years '96

Christine Cattall
Bedroom Eyes '86
Screwball Academy '86

Kim Cattrall (1956-)
Sex and the City: The Movie '08
My Boy Jack '07
Ice Princess '05
Crossroads '02
15 Minutes '01
36 Hours to Die '99
Baby Geniuses '98
Modern Vampires '98
Robin Cook's Invasion '97
Unforgettable '96
Where Truth Lies '96
Above Suspicion '95
The Heidi Chronicles '95
Live Nude Girls '95
Breaking Point '94
Running Delilah '93
Wild Palms '93
Double Vision '92
Split Second '92
Miracle in the Wilderness '91
Star Trek 6: The Undiscovered Country '91
The Bonfire of the Vanities '90
Honeymoon Academy '90
Smokescreen '90
Goodnight, Michelangelo '89
The Return of the Musketeers '89
Masquerade '88
Palais Royale '88
Mannequin '87
Midnight Crossing '87
Big Trouble in Little China '86
City Limits '85
Turk 182! '85
Police Academy '84
Porky's '82
Ticket to Heaven '81
Scruples '80
Tribute '80
The Rebels '79
The Bastard '78
Rosebud '75

Philippe Caubere (1950-)
My Father's Glory '91
My Mother's Castle '91

Daniel Cauchy (1930-)
Bob le Flambeur '55
Grisbi '53

Lane Caudell (1952-)
Archer: The Fugitive from the Empire '81

Hanging on a Star '78

Jessica Cauffiel (1976-)
Hoot '06
Guess Who '05
D.E.B.S. '04
White Chicks '04
Legally Blonde 2: Red White & Blonde '03
You Stupid Man '02
Legally Blonde '01
Valentine '01
Urban Legends 2: Final Cut '00

Joan Caulfield (1922-91)
Pony Express Rider '76
Daring Dobermans '73
Buckskin '68
The Lady Says No '51
Dear Wife '49
Welcome Stranger '47
Blue Skies '46
Monsieur Beaucaire '46

Maxwell Caulfield (1959-)
Dragon Storm '04
The Hit '01
Facing the Enemy '00
Missing Pieces '00
Submerged '00
Perfect Tenant '99
The Real Blonde '97
Prey of the Jaguar '96
Backlash: Oblivion 2 '95
Empire Records '95
Inevitable Grace '94
Alien Intruder '93
Gettysburg '93
In a Moment of Passion '93
Midnight Witness '93
No Escape, No Return '93
Animal Instincts '92
Dance with Death '91
Sundown '91
Exiled in America '90
Mind Games '89
Project: Alien '89
The Supernaturals '86
The Boys Next Door '85
Electric Dreams '84
Grease 2 '82

Tony Caunter (1937-)
S.O.S. Titanic '79
The Hill '65

Catherine Cavadini (1967-)
The Powerpuff Girls Movie '02 (V)
An American Tail: Fievel Goes West '91 (V)

Gary Cavagnaro (1963-)
The Bad News Bears '76
Drive-In '76

Michael Cavalieri
Seduced: Pretty When You Cry '01

Megan Cavanagh (1960-)
Jimmy Neutron: Boy Genius '01 (V)
Meet the Deedles '98
For Richer or Poorer '97
Dracula: Dead and Loving It '95
I Love Trouble '94
Robin Hood: Men in Tights '93
A League of Their Own '92

Paul Cavanagh (1895-1959)
Francis in the Haunted House '56
The Prodigal '55
Charade '53

House of Wax '53
Tales of Robin Hood '52
Bride of the Gorilla '51
The Strange Door '51
Hi-Jacked '50
Black Arrow '48
Humoresque '46
House of Fear '45
The Woman in Green '45

Tom Cavanagh (1963-)
Sublime '07
Gray Matters '06
How to Eat Fried Worms '06
Something More '99
Bloodhounds 2 '96
A Vow to Kill '94

Robert Cavanah (1964-)
Wuthering Heights '98
Cracker: True Romance '95

Christine Cavanaugh (1963-)
Rugrats in Paris: The Movie '00 (V)
The Rugrats Movie '98 (V)
Babe '95 (V)

Hobart Cavanaugh (1886-1950)
Up in Central Park '48
Black Angel '46
Gildersleeve on Broadway '43
The Kansan '43
The Magnificent Dope '42
Rose of Washington Square '39
Wife Versus Secretary '36
Wings in the Dark '35
I Cover the Waterfront '33

Michael Cavanaugh (1942-)
Poison '01
Dancing in September '00
Black Thunder '98
Full Fathom Five '90

Patrick Cavanaugh
Gamebox 1.0 '04
Bloody Murder '99

Elise Cavanna (1902-63)
The Barber Shop '33
The Dentist '32
Pharmacist '32

Lumi Cavazos (1969-)
Exposed '03
In the Time of the Butterflies '01
Bless the Child '00
Sugar Town '99
Bottle Rocket '95
Manhattan Merengue! '95
Like Water for Chocolate '93

Ingrid Caven (1943-)
Malou '83
In a Year of 13 Moons '78
Mother Küsters Goes to Heaven '76
Satan's Brew '76
Shadow of Angels '76
Tenderness of the Wolves '73
The American Soldier '70
Beware of a Holy Whore '70

Dick Cavett (1936-)
Duane Hopwood '05
The Marx Brothers in a Nutshell '90
Beetlejuice '88
Moon over Parador '88
A Nightmare on Elm Street 3: Dream Warriors '87
Annie Hall '77

James (Jim) Caviezel (1968-)
Deja Vu '06
Bobby Jones: Stroke of Genius '04
The Final Cut '04
I Am David '04
The Passion of the Christ '04
Highwaymen '03
The Count of Monte Cristo '02
High Crimes '02
Angel Eyes '01
Madison '01
Frequency '00
Pay It Forward '00
Ride with the Devil '99
The Thin Red Line '98
G.I. Jane '97
Ed '96
The Rock '96
Wyatt Earp '94

Henry Cavill (1983-)
Stardust '07
Tristan & Isolde '06
Hellraiser: Hellworld '05
I Capture the Castle '02
The Count of Monte Cristo '02

Joseph Cawthorn (1869-1949)
Harmony Lane '35
Sweet Adeline '35
The Cat and the Fiddle '34
The White Zombie '32
The Taming of the Shrew '29

Elizabeth Cayton
See Elizabeth Kaitan

John Cazale (1936-78)
The Godfather 1902-1959: The Complete Epic '81
The Deer Hunter '78
Dog Day Afternoon '75
The Conversation '74
The Godfather, Part 2 '74
The Godfather '72

Christopher Cazenove (1945-)
Johnson County War '02
A Knight's Tale '01
The Proprietor '96
Aces: Iron Eagle 3 '92
Lady '90
Three Men and a Little Lady '90
The Fantasist '89
The Man Who Guards the Greenhouse '88
Windmills of the Gods '88
Tears in the Rain '88
Souvenir '88
Jenny's War '85
Mata Hari '85
Children of the Full Moon '84
Until September '84
Heat and Dust '82
Eye of the Needle '81
From a Far Country: Pope John Paul II '81
The Duchess of Duke Street '78
East of Elephant Rock '76
Royal Flash '75

Carlo Cecchi (1939-)
The Red Violin '98
Stealing Beauty '96
Steam: The Turkish Bath '96
La Scorta '94

Fulvio Cecere (1960-)
John Tucker Must Die '06
Assault on Precinct 13 '05
The Perfect Score '04

Sandra Ceccarelli
The Crown Prince '06
Light of My Eyes '01

Daniel Ceccaldi (1927-2003)
Twisted Obsession '90
Charles et Lucie '79
Holiday Hotel '77
Chloe in the Afternoon '72
Bed and Board '70
The Soft Skin '64

Adolfo Celi (1922-86)
Cafe Express '83
The Con Artists '80
Perfect Crime '79
The Switch '76
The Arab Conspiracy '76
Intruder '76
Phantom of Liberty '74
Ten Little Indians '75
Hit Men '73
Hired to Kill '73

Edward Cecil (1888-1940)
Desert of the Lost '27
Wild Horse Canyon '25

Jonathan Cecil (1939-)
The Rector's Wife '94
Agatha Christie's Thirteen at Dinner '85

Jon Cedar (1931-)
Kiss Daddy Goodbye '81
The Manitou '78
Day of the Animals '77
The King of Hearts '66
Target for Killing '66
The Agony and the Ecstasy '65

Larry Cedar (1955-)
Constantine '05
Boris and Natasha: The Movie '92
C.H.U.D. 2: Bud the Chud '89
Feds '88

Giuseppe Cederna (1957-)
For Roseanna '97
Mediterraneo '91

Cedric the Entertainer (1964-)
Street Kings '08
Welcome Home Roscoe Jenkins '08
Code Name: The Cleaner '07
Talk to Me '07
Charlotte's Web '06 (V)
Be Cool '05
Madagascar '05 (V)
Man of the House '05
The Honeymooners '05
Johnson Family Vacation '04
Barbershop 2: Back in Business '04
Intolerable Cruelty '03
Barbershop '02
Ice Age '02 (V)
Serving Sara '02
Kingdom Come '01

Pablo Cedron (1958-)
The Aura '05

Elisa Cegani (1911-96)
Medusa Against the Son of Hercules '62
Saul and David '64
What a Woman! '56
Nana '55
The Iron Crown '41

Violeta Cela (1959-)
Conquest '83

Clementine Celarie (1957-)
Lawless Heart '01
Les Miserables '95
Sand and Blood '87
Betty Blue '86

Henry Cele (1949-)
The Ghost and the Darkness '96
Curse 3: Blood Sacrifice '90
The Last Samurai '90
The Rutanga Tapes '90
Rage to Kill '88
Shaka Zulu '83

Nicholas Celozzi
Hidden Obsession '92
Slaughterhouse Rock '88

Angie Cepeda (1974-)
The Dead One '07
Love for Rent '05

Petr Cepek (1940-94)
The Elementary School '91
My Sweet Little Village '86
Adelheid '69

Maria Celedonio
Freeway 2: Confessions of a Trickbaby '99
How to Make an American Quilt '95

Michael Cera (1988-)
Juno '07
Superbad '07
My Louisiana Sky '01

Daniel Cerny (1981-)
Children of the Corn 3: Urban Harvest '95
Demonic Toys '92

Mike Cerrone
Me, Myself, and Irene '00
Outside Providence '99
Kingpin '96

Claude Cerval (1921-72)
Any Number Can Win '63
The Cousins '59

Carlos Cervantes
Fugitive Champion '99
Wheels of Terror '90
Full Hearts & Empty Pockets '63
Return to Fantasy Island '77

Teco Celio
The Truce '96

Teresa Celli (1924-)
Tre Colori: Rouge '94
The Black Hand '50
The Asphalt Jungle '50
Border Incident '49

Stanislawa Celinska (1947-)
Maids of Wilko '79
Landscape After Battle '70

Richard Cetrone
Underworld: Evolution '05
John Carpenter's Ghosts of Mars '01

Renzo Cesana (1907-70)
For the First Time '59
The Naked Maja '59
Stromboli '50

Antoinette Cellier (1913-81)
River of Unrest '36
Late Extra '35

Caroline Cellier (1945-)
L'Eleve '95
Farinelli '94
Petit Con '84
Pain in the A— '77
This Man Must Die '70

Frank Cellier (1884-1948)
The Magic Bow '47
Cottage to Let '41
Non-Stop New York '37
O.H.M.S. '37
Rhodes '36
The 39 Steps '35
The Man Who Lived Again '36

Peter Cellier (1928-)
Fergie & Andrew: Behind the Palace Doors '92

Michael Ceveris
A New Wave '07
The Mexican '01
A Woman, Her Men and Her Futon '92
Rock 'n' Roll High School Forever '91

Valentina Cervi
James Dean '01
Children of Hannibal '98
Artemisia '98

Alain Chabat (1958-)
The Science of Sleep '06
Happily Ever After '04
The Taste of Others '00
French Twist '95

Lacey Chabert (1982-)
Black Christmas '06
Mean Girls '04
Daddy Day Care '03
Rugrats Go Wild! '03 (V)
The Wild Thornberrys Movie '02 (V)
Not Another Teen Movie '01
Lost in Space '98

Tom Chabon (1946-)
The Rascals '81

Amadee Chabot (1945-)
Autopsy of a Ghost '67
Muscle Beach Party '64

Thomas Chabrol (1963-)
Comedy of Power '06

Dead in a Heartbeat '02
Valentine '01

Alexsei Chadov
Day Watch '06
Night Watch '04
War '02

Cyril Chadwick
Peter Pan '24
The Iron Horse '24

June Chadwick (1950-)
This Is Spinal Tap '84
Forbidden World '82
Golden Lady '79

Sarah Chadwick (1960-)
The Adventures of Priscilla, Queen of the Desert '94
Gross Misconduct '93

Suzy Chaffee (1946-)
Fire and Ice '87
Snowball '78

George Chakiris (1933-)
Pale Blood '91
Return to Fantasy Island '77
Why Not Stay for Breakfast? '79
Is Paris Burning? '66
633 Squadron '64
Kings of the Sun '63
Diamond Head '62
West Side Story '61

Kathleen Chalfant (1945-)
Perfect Stranger '07
Kinsey '04
A Death in the Family '02
David Searching '97

Feodor Chaliapin, Jr. (1907-92)
The Church '91
The Inner Circle '91
Stanley and Iris '90
Moonstruck '87
The Name of the Rose '86
A Price above Rubies '97
Bob Roberts '92
Jumpin' at the Boneyard '92

Sarah Chalke (1977-)
Chaos Theory '08
Alchemy '05
Cake '05
Y2K '99
I've Been Waiting for You '98
My Mother's Murder '97
The Spree '98

Garry Chalk (1953-)
Popeye's Voyage: The Quest for Pappy '04 (V)
Video Voyeur: The Susan Wilson Story '02
Take Me Home: The John Denver Story '00
Dead Ahead '96
Robin of Locksley '96
City Boy '93

Andrew Chalmers
A Home at the End of the World '04
Siblings '04

Georges Chamarat (1901-82)
Diabolique '55
The French Touch '54

William Challee (1904-89)
Billy the Kid Versus Dracula '66
Zachariah '70

Thomas Chabrol
Fernandel the Dressmaker '57

Howland Chamberlain (1911-84)
Francis the Talking Mule '49
The Best Years of Our Lives '46

Richard Chamberlain (1935-)
I Now Pronounce You Chuck and Larry '07
A River Made to Drown In '97
The Thorn Birds: The Missing Years '96
Bird of Prey '95
Ordeal in the Arctic '93
The Return of the Musketeers '89
Casanova '87
Allan Quatermain and the Lost City of Gold '86
King Solomon's Mines '85
The Thorn Birds '83
Murder by Phone '82
Shogun '80
Centennial '78
The Swarm '78
The Last Wave '77

Hitler: The Last Ten Days '73
1931: Once Upon a Time in New York '72
Who Saw Her Die? '72
Dirty Heroes '71
Murders in the Rue Morgue '71
'65

The Naked Maja '59
The Lady Without Camelias '53
The Young Girls of Rochefort '67
The Hot Line '69
Les Miserables '52
Little World of Don Camillo '51
The Forbidden Christ '50
The Iron Crown '41
Fabiola '48
West Side Story '61
Diamond Head '62

The Man in the Iron Mask '77
The Slipper and the Rose '76
The Four Musketeers '75
The Count of Monte Cristo '74
The Three Musketeers '74
The Towering Inferno '74
Lady Caroline Lamb '73
The Music Lovers '71
Julius Caesar '70
The Madwoman of Chaillot '69
Petulia '68
Portrait of a Lady '67

Kevin Chamberlin (1963-)
Lucky Number Slevin '06
Bound by Lies '05
Suspect Zero '04

Carrie Chambers
The Divine Enforcer '91
Karate Cop '91

Faune A. Chambers (1976)
Epic Movie '07
White Chicks '04
Bring It On Again '03

Justin Chambers (1970)
Southern Belles '05
The Zodiac '05
Hysterical Blindness '02
Leo '02
The Musketeer '01
The Wedding Planner '01
Liberty Heights '99
Rose Hill '97

Marilyn Chambers (1952-)
Bikini Bistro '94
Party Incorporated '89
My Therapist '84
Cassie '83
Angel of H.E.A.T. '82
Rabid '77

Michael "Boogaloo Shrimp" Chambers (1967-)
Breakin' '84
Breakin' 2: Electric Boogaloo '84

Wheaton Chambers (1888-1958)
Big Chase '54
Prowler '51

Jo Champa (1969-)
The Whole Shebang '01
Direct Hit '93
Beretta's Island '92
The Family '87
Salome '85

Gower Champion (1921-80)
Jupiter's Darling '55
Three for the Show '55
Give a Girl a Break '53
Lovely to Look At '52
Show Boat '51
Mr. Music '50

Marge Champion (1921-)
The Party '68
The Swimmer '68
Jupiter's Darling '55
Three for the Show '55
Give a Girl a Break '53
Lovely to Look At '52

Michael Champion
Dead Cold '96
Operation Intercept '95
Private Wars '93
The Swordsman '92
The Heroes of Desert Storm '91
One Man Out '89

Dennis Chan
Kickboxer 3: The Art of War '92
Kickboxer

Jackie Chan (1954-)
The Forbidden Kingdom '08
Kung Fu Panda '08 (V)
Rush Hour 3 '07
Robin-B-Hood '06
Around the World in 80 Days '04
New Police Story '04
The Medallion '03
Shanghai Knights '03
Vampire Effect '03
The Tuxedo '02
The Accidental Spy '01
Rush Hour 2 '01
Shanghai Noon '00
Gen-X Cops '99
Gorgeous '99
Jackie Chan's Who Am I '98
Mr. Nice Guy '98
Rush Hour '98
An Alan Smithee Film: Burn, Hollywood, Burn '97
Downdraft '96
Jackie Chan's First Strike '96
Rumble in the Bronx '96
The Legend of Drunken Master '94
Crime Story '93
Supercop 2 '93
Supercop '92
Twin Dragons '92
Operation Condor '91
The Prisoner '90
Miracles '89
Dragons Forever '88
Project A: Part 2 '87
Operation Condor 2: The Armour of the Gods '86
Heart of Dragon '85
Police Story '85
Protector '85
Cannonball Run 2 '84
Eagle's Shadow '84
Fantasy Mission Force '84
Project A '83
Dragon Lord '82
The Big Brawl '80
Young Master '80
Half a Loaf of Kung Fu '78
New Fist of Fury '76
Young Tiger '74
Enter the Dragon '73
Master with Cracked Fingers '71

Kim Chan (1917-)
The Honeymooners '05
Shanghai Knights '03
The Corruptor '99
The Insider '99
Molly '99
U.S. Marshals '98
Falling Down '93
The Joy Luck Club '93
Rapid Fire '92
Thousand Pieces of Gold '91

Philip Chan (1945-)
Hard-Boiled '92
Twin Dragons '92

Naomi Chance (1930-2003)
Terror Ship '54
Three Stops to Murder '53
The Gambler & the Lady '52
Wings of Danger '52

Anna Chancellor (1965)
The Secret Life of Mrs. Beeton '06
Agent Cody Banks 2: Destination London '04
The Dreamers '03
What a Girl Wants '03
Crush '02
Tipping the Velvet '02
Longitude '00
Heart '99
The Man Who Knew Too Little '97
Pride and Prejudice '95

Norman Chancer
Local Hero '83
Victor/Victoria '82

Chick Chandler (1905-88)
The Lost Continent '51
Seven Doors to Death '44
Action in the North Atlantic '43
Rhythm Parade '43
Baby Face Morgan '42
Blondie in Society '41
I Wake Up Screaming '41
Mr. Moto Takes a Chance '38
Mistaken Identity '36
Tango '36
Circumstantial Evidence '35
Melody Cruise '32

David Chandler (1950-)
Hide and Seek '05
The Grey Zone '01

George Chandler (1898-1985)
Dead Ringer '64
The High and the Mighty '54
Island in the Sky '53
Westward the Women '51
The Next Voice You Hear '50
Behind the Mask '46
Strange Impersonation '46
Roxie Hart '42
Arizona '40
Beau Geste '39
Lady Killer '33

Helen Chandler (1906-65)
Mr. Boggs Steps Out '38
Christopher Strong '33
Dracula '31

Jeff Chandler (1918-61)
Merrill's Marauders '62
Return to Peyton Place '61
The Jayhawkers '59
Man in the Shadow '57
Away All Boats '56
War Arrow '53
Because of You '52
Red Ball Express '52
Yankee Buccaneer '52
Flame of Araby '51
Broken Arrow '50

John Davis Chandler (1937-)
The Color of Evening '95
Convict Cowboy '95
Pure Country '92
The Ultimate Thrill '74
Alligator Alley '72
Shoot Out '71
Ride the High Country '62
The Young Savages '61

Kyle Chandler (1965-)
King Kong '05
And Starring Pancho Villa as Himself '03
Angel's Dance '99

Lane Chandler (1899-1972)
Money Madness '47
Wild Horse Phantom '44
Law of the Saddle '43
Sergeant York '41
Pony Post '40
Southward Ho! '39
Heroes of the Alamo '37
Sea Racketeers '37
The Lawless Nineties '36
Stormy Trails '36
Winds of the Wasteland '36
Deluge '33
Lone Bandit '33
The Outlaw Tamer '33
Trouble Busters '33
The Single Standard '29

Simon Chandler
Incognito '97
The Man Who Knew Too Little '97
Middlemarch '93
Who's Who '78

Tanis Chandler (1924-)
Spook Busters '48
Lured '47

Jay Chandrasekhar (1968-)
Beerfest '06
Club Dread '04
Super Troopers '01

Helene Chanel (1941-)
Place in Hell '69
Samson and the 7 Miracles of the World '62
Maciste in Hell '60

Lon Chaney, Sr. (1883-1930)
The Unholy Three '30
Where East Is East '29
West of Zanzibar '28
The Unknown '27
The Monster '25
The Phantom of the Opera '25
The Unholy Three '25
He Who Gets Slapped '24
The Hunchback of Notre Dame '23
The Shock '23
Flesh and Blood '22
The Light of Faith '22
Oliver Twist '22
Shadows '22
The Trap '22
Outside the Law '21
Nomads of the North '20
The Penalty '20
False Faces '18
The Scarlet Car '17
Oubliette '14

Lon Chaney, Jr. (1906-73)
Dracula vs. Frankenstein '71
The Female Bunch '69
Buckskin '68
Alien Massacre '67
Hillbillies in a Haunted House '67
Apache Uprising '66
Johnny Reno '66
House of the Black Death '65
Spider Baby '64
The Haunted Palace '63
Face of the Screaming Werewolf '59
The Defiant Ones '58
The Black Sleep '56
Cyclops '56
Daniel Boone: Trail Blazer '56
The Indestructible Man '56
Manfish '56
Pardners '56
I Died a Thousand Times '55
The Indian Fighter '55
Not as a Stranger '55
Silver Star '55
Big Chase '54
Passion '54
A Lion Is in the Streets '53
Behave Yourself! '52
The Black Castle '52
The Bushwackers '52
High Noon '52
Springfield Rifle '52
Bride of the Gorilla '51
Flame of Araby '51
Only the Valiant '51
Abbott and Costello Meet Frankenstein '48
My Favorite Brunette '47
Here Come the Co-Eds '45
House of Dracula '45
Strange Confession '45
Cobra Woman '44
House of Frankenstein '44
The Mummy's Curse '44
The Mummy's Ghost '44
Son of Dracula '43
Frankenstein Meets the Wolfman '42
The Ghost of Frankenstein '42
The Mummy's Tomb '42
Overland Mail '42
Billy the Kid '41
Man Made Monster '41
Riders of Death Valley '41
The Wolf Man '41
One Million B.C. '40
Charlie Chan in City of Darkness '39
Of Mice and Men '39
Cheyenne Rides Again '38
Mr. Moto's Gamble '38
Undersea Kingdom '36
Sixteen Fathoms Deep '34
The Three Musketeers '33
Bird of Paradise '32
Last Frontier '32

Jason Chang
The Heirloom '05
Formula 17 '04

Sylvia Chang (1953-)
The Red Violin '98
Eat Drink Man Woman '94
Twin Dragons '92
Mad Mission 3 '84

Carol Channing (1921-)
Thumbelina '94 (V)
Happily Ever After '93 (V)
Alice in Wonderland '85
Shinbone Alley '70 (V)
Thoroughly Modern Millie '67

Stockard Channing (1944-)
Must Love Dogs '05
Red Mercury '05
Anything Else '03
Bright Young Things '03
Hitler: The Rise of Evil '03
Le Divorce '03
Behind the Red Door '02
Life or Something Like It '02
The Business of Strangers '01
A Girl Thing '01
Isn't She Great '00
The Truth About Jane '00
Where the Heart Is '00
Edie & Pen '95
Smoke '95
To Wong Foo, Thanks for Everything, Julie Newmar '95
Married to It '93
Six Degrees of Separation '93
Bitter Moon '92
The Applegates '89
Perfect Witness '89
Staying Together '89
Tidy Endings '88
A Time of Destiny '88
Echoes in the Darkness '87
Heartburn '86
The Men's Club '86
Not My Kid '85
Table Settings '84
Without a Trace '83
The Fish that Saved Pittsburgh '79
Silent Victory: The Kitty O'Neil Story '79
Grease '78
The Big Bus '76
The Hospital '71

Rosalind Chao (1949-)
Just like Heaven '05
Life of the Party '05
Freaky Friday '03
Enemies of Laughter '00
What Dreams May Come '98
The End of Violence '97
The Joy Luck Club '93
Memoirs of an Invisible Man '92
Thousand Pieces of Gold '91
Drug Wars: The Camarena Story '90
White Ghost '88
M*A*S*H: Goodbye, Farewell & Amen '83
The Terry Fox Story '83
Twirl '81
The Big Brawl '80
Chinese Web '78

Winston Chao (1960-)
Eat Drink Man Woman '94
The Wedding Banquet '93

Damian Chapa (1963)
Lady Jayne Killer '03
Hell's Gate '01
U.S. Seals 2 '01
Cypress Edge '99
Hitman's Run '99
Sometimes They Come Back... For More '99
Footsteps '98
Midnight Blue '96
Saints and Sinners '95
Street Fighter '94
Blood In ... Blood Out: Bound by Honor '93
Final Combination '93

Billy Chapin (1943-)
The Night of the Hunter '55
Tobor the Great '54

Jonathan Chapin
Prison for Children '93
Twice Dead '88

Miles Chapin (1954-)
The People vs. Larry Flynt '96
Get Crazy '83
Pandemonium '82
The Funhouse '81
French Postcards '79
Bless the Beasts and Children '71

Robert Chapin (1964-)
Dragon Fury 2 '96
Dragon Fury '95
Ring of Steel '94

Ben Chaplin (1970-)
The Water Horse: Legend of the Deep '07
Two Weeks '06
Stage Beauty '04
Birthday Girl '02
Murder by Numbers '02
Lost Souls '00
The Thin Red Line '98
Washington Square '97
The Return of the Borrowers '96
The Truth about Cats and Dogs '96
Feast of July '95
A Fatal Inversion '92

Carmen Chaplin
All About the Benjamins '02
Snapshots '02
The Serpent's Kiss '97
Ma Saison Preferee '93

Charles Chaplin, Jr. (1925-68)
Girls' Town '59
High School Confidential '58
Fangs of the Wild '54

Charlie Chaplin (1889-1977)
Man in the Silk Hat '83

Days of Thrills and Laughter '61
The Chaplin Revue '58
A King in New York '57
Limelight '52
Monsieur Verdoux '47
The Great Dictator '40
Modern Times '36
City Lights '31
The Gold Rush '25
The Kid '21
The Circus '19
Three Charlies and One Phoney! '18
The Adventurer '17
The Cure '17
The Floorwalker '17
The Immigrant '17
The Rink '16
Pawnshop '16
One A.M. '16
Easy Street '16
The Count '16
The Fireman '16
Burlesque on Carmen '16
the Show '15
Charlie Chaplin: Night at the Show '15
Charlie Chaplin ... Our Hero! '15
Tillie's Punctured Romance '14

Sydney Chaplin (1885-1965)
Cria Cuervos '76
The Chaplin Revue '58
Charley's Aunt '25
The Man on the Box '25

Josephine Chaplin (1949-)
Jack the Ripper '76
Shadow Man '75
Escape to the Sun '72
Nashville '75
The Canterbury Tales '71
Scandal Man '67
L'Odeur des Fauves '66
I Killed Rasputin '67
Doctor Zhivago '65

Lonny (Lonnie) Chapman (1920-2007)
Scorpio One '97
Fire on the Amazon '93
Dead Space '90
And God Created Woman '88
Moving Violation '76
Witch Who Came from the Sea '76

Three Charlies and One Phoney! '18
I Walk the Line '70
Take the Money and Run '69
The Birds '63

Marguerite Chapman (1918-99)
The Amazing Transparent Man '60
Kong '67
Destroyer '43
Double Face '70
The Woman Hunter '72
The Sibling '72

Sydney Chaplin (1926-)
Satan's Cheerleaders '77
The Sibling '72

Alexander Chapman (1976-)
Exquisite Corpses '88
Lilies '96
Princes in Exile '90

Constance Chapman (1912-2003)
My Friend Walter '93
Charlie Chan at the Wax Museum '40

Daniel Chapman
Philadelphia '93
Death Collector '89

Geraldine Chaplin (1944-)
The Orphanage '07
BloodRayne '05
The Bridge of San Luis Rey '05

Dolores Chaplin
The Counterfeiters '07

Edward Chapman (1901-77)
The Young and the Guilty '58

Sean Chapman
Hellraiser '87
Hellraiser: Hellraiser 2 '88

Georgina Chapman
Derailed '05
Awake '07

Graham Chapman (1941-89)
Yellowbeard '83
The Secret Policeman's Other Ball '82
The Secret Policeman's Private Parts '81
Chaplin '92
A Foreign Field '93
Monty Python's Life of Brian '79
The Odd Job '78
And Now for Something Completely Different '72
Monty Python and the Holy Grail '75

Edythe Chapman (1863-1948)
The Ten Commandments '23

Patricia Charbonneau (1559-)
Dark Corners '06
One Special Night '99
Kiss the Sky '98
Portraits of a Killer '95
K2: The Ultimate High '92
RoboCop 2 '90
Brain Dead '89
Call Me '88
Shakedown '88
Disaster at Silo 7 '88
Desert Hearts '86

Ray Charleson
Chariots of Fire '81

Antoine Chappey (1960-)
Le Petit Lieutenant '05
5x2 '04
I'm Going Home '00

Charo (1942-)
Moon over Parador '88
The Concorde: Airport '79

Dave Chappelle (1973-)
Dave Chappelle's Block Party '05
Undercover Brother '02
Screwed '00
Blue Streak '99
200 Cigarettes '98
You've Got Mail '98
Con Air '97
Half-Baked '97
Woo '97
The Nutty Professor '96
Getting In '94
Robin Hood: Men in Tights '93

Mark Lindsay Chapman (1954-2004)
Beethoven's 4th '01
Ballad in Blue '66
Bram Stoker's The Mummy '97
Stephen King's The Langoliers '95
Separate Lives '95
American Gothic '88

Ian Charleson (1949-90)
Codename Kyril '91
Opera '88
Troubles '88
Louisiana '87
Car Trouble '86
United 93 '06
Greystoke: The Legend of Tarzan, Lord of the Apes '84
Gandhi '82
Chariots of Fire '81

Henri Charriere (1906-73)
Butterfly Affair '71
Queen of Diamonds '70

Where the Red Fern Grows '74

Josh Charles (1971-)
The Ex '07
Four Brothers '05
Seeing Other People '04
S.W.A.T. '03
Muppets from Space '99
Meeting Daddy '98
Little City '97
Crossworlds '96
The Grave '95
Don't Tell Mom the Babysitter's Dead '91
Dead Poets Society '89
Crossing the Bridge '92

Ray Charles (1930-)
Blue in the Face '95
The Blues Brothers '80
Limit Up '89
The Brady Bunch Movie '95
A Mother's Prayer '95
Smoke '95
To Wong Foo, Thanks for Everything, Julie Newmar '95
Who Is Cletis Tout? '02
The Truth About Jane '00
EDtv '99
An Unexpected Life '97
A Very Brady Sequel '96
Blue in the Face '95

RuPaul Charles (1960-)
Starstruck '98
Skinwalker '02

Cheryl Chase
Rugrats Go Wild! '03 (V)
Rugrats in Paris: The Movie '00 (V)
Phoney! '18

Chevy Chase (1943-)
Zoom '06
Kelly the Second '36
When You're Dead '95
Three Charlies and One '05
Karate Dog '04 (V)
Our Italian Husband '04
Orange County '02
Snow Day '00
Dirty Work '97
Vegas Vacation '6
Man of the House '95
Cops and Robbersons '94
Last Action Hero '93
Memoirs of an Invisible Man '92
Nothing But Trouble '91
Fletcher Lives '89
National Lampoon's Christmas Vacation '89
Caddyshack 2 '68
Funny Farm '88
Three Amigos '86
Fletch '85
National Lampoon's European Vacation '85
Sesame Street Presents: Follow That Bird '85
Spies Like Us '85
Deal of the Century '83
National Lampoon's Vacation '83
Modern Problems '81
Under the Rainbow '81
Caddyshack '80
Oh, Heavenly Dog! '80
Seems Like Old Times '80
Foul Play '78
Tunnelvision '76
The Groove Tube '72

Charley Chase (1893-1940)
Block-heads '38
Sons of the Desert '33
King of the Wild Horses '24
Three Charlies and One Phoney! '18

Annazette Chase
Truck Turner '74
Fist '76

Steve Chase
Eden '93
Eden 2 '93
Eden 3 '93
Eden 4 '93

Soumitra Chatterjee (1934-)
Distant Thunder '73
Days and Nights in the Forest '70
The Home and the World '84

Anil Chatterjee (1928-66)
The Big City '63

Alden Chase (1902-82)
Having It All '82
Buried Alive '39
Prescott Kid '36
Rogue of the Range '36

Courtney Chase
Queen of Diamonds '70

Davleigh Chase (1990-)
Mean Girls '04
13 Going on 30 '04
Nick of Time '95
The Ring 2 '05
Beethoven's 5th '03
Lilo & Stitch '02 (V)
The Ring '02

James Chase (1940-)
The Big Knife '55
Now, Voyager '42
The Animal Kingdom '32

Spencer Charters (1875-1943)
Mr. Boggs Steps Out '38
Lady from Nowhere '36
The Moon's Our Home '36
The Ghost Walks '34
Palmy Days '31

Frank Chase (1923-2004)
Attack of the 50 Foot Woman '58
The Creature Walks among Us '56

Ilka Chase (1905-78)
The Big Knife '55
The Victors '63

Jeffrey Chase (1968-)
Transporter 2 '05
Kids in America '05

Melanie Chartoff (1955-)
The Rugrats Movie '98 (V)
Rugrats Go Wild! '03 (V)
The Bat Whispers '30
Doin' Time '85
Stoogemania '85

Cyd Charisse (1921-)
Swimsuit '89
That's Dancing! '85
Maroc 7 '67
The Silencers '66
Two Weeks in Another Town '62
Black Tights '60
Party Girl '58
Silk Stockings '57
Meet Me in Las Vegas '56
It's Always Fair Weather '55
Brigadoon '54
Deep in My Heart '54
The Band Wagon '53
Singin' in the Rain '52
Tension '50
On an Island with You '48
Words and Music '48
The Harvey Girls '46

Andre Charles
See RuPaul Charles

House of Death '82

Stephan Chase (1900-78)
The Dying Truth '91
The Black Arrow '84
Macbeth '71
Guns of Fury '49

Peter Chatel (1943-86)
Fox and His Friends '75
Who Saw Her Die? '72

Tom Chatterton (1881-1952)
Overland Mail '42
Drums of Fu Manchu '40
Flash Gordon Conquers the Universe '40
The Chumscrubber '05
War of the Worlds '05
Nobody's Fault '88
Little Dorrit, Film 1: Nobody's Fault '88
Little Dorrit, Film 2: Little Dorrit's Story '88

Ruth Chatterton (1893-1961)
Female '33
Dodsworth '36

Charlotte Chatton
Stand-Ins '97
Hellraiser 4: Bloodline '96

Daniel Chatto (1957-)
The Incredible Mrs. Ritchie '03

Justin Chatwin (1982-)
The Invisible '07
Taking Lives '04
Superbabies: Baby Geniuses 2 '04

Francois Chau (1959-)
Beverly Hills Ninja '96
Teenage Mutant Ninja Turtles 2: The Secret of the Ooze '91

Emmanuelle Chaulet
Boyfriends & Girlfriends '88

Lilyan Chauvin (1931-)
Silent Night, Deadly Night '84

Maury Chaykin (1949-)
Heavens Fall '06
Where the Truth Lies '05
Being Julia '04
White Coats '04
Owning Mahowny '03
Bartleby '01
The Docktell Rang: A Nero Wolfe Mystery '01
Varian's War '01
The Art of War '00
The Golden Spiders: A Nero Wolfe Mystery '00
What's Cooking? '00

Richard Chaves (1951-)
Night Eyes 2 '91
Predator '87

Jennifer Chase
Death Screams '83

Entrapment '99
Jacob Two Two Meets the Hooded Fang '99
Joan of Arc '99
Let the Devil Wear Black '99
Mystery, Alaska '99
Jerry and Tom '98
The Mask of Zorro '98
A Life Less Ordinary '97
Love and Death on Long Island '97
Mouse Hunt '97
Pale Saints '97
Strip Search '97
The Sweet Hereafter '96
Cutthroat Island '95
Devil in a Blue Dress '95
Sugartime '95
Unstrung Heroes '95
Camilla '94
Whale Music '94
Money for Nothing '93
Northern Extremes '93
Sommersby '93
Hero '92
Leaving Normal '92
The Adjuster '91
The Pianist '91
George's Island '91
Cold Comfort '90
Dances with Wolves '90
Mr. Destiny '90
Where the Heart Is '90
Breaking In '89
Millennium '89
Higher Education '88
Iron Eagle 2 '88
Stars and Bars '88
Wild Thing '87
Canada's Sweetheart: The Saga of Hal C. Banks '85
Def-Con 4 '85
Mrs. Soffel '84
Overdrawn at the Memory Bank '83
July Group '81

Suzanne Chazelle
See Dany Carrel

Don Cheadle (1964-)
Ocean's Thirteen '07
Reign Over Me '07
Talk to Me '07
The Dog Problem '06
Rebound: The Legend of Earl "The Goat" Manigault '96
Rosewood '96
Devil in a Blue Dress '95
Things to Do in Denver When You're Dead '95
Lush Life '94
Colors '88
Hamburger Hill '87

Andrea Checchi (1916-74)
Waterloo '71
Diary of a Rebel '68
The Invaders '63
Black Sunday '60

The Hit Man '60
The Lady Without Camelias '53
The Walls of Malapaga '49

Chubby Checker (1941-)
Calendar Girl '93
Purple People Eater '88

Molly Cheek (1950-)
A Lot Like Love '05
American Wedding '03
April's Shower '03
American Pie 2 '01
Smoke Signals '98

Derk Cheetwood (1973-)
Frailty '02
U-571 '00

Micheline Cheirel (1917-2002)
Cornered '45
Carnival in Flanders '35

Michael Chekhov (1891-1955)
Rhapsody '54
Spectre of the Rose '46
Spellbound '45

Tsilla Chelton (1918-)
Tatie Danielle '91
Peppermint Soda '77

Chang Chen (1976-)
Three Times '05
Eros '04
2046 '04
Crouching Tiger, Hidden Dragon '00
Happy Together '96

Daoming Chen (1955-)
Silver Hawk '04
Hero '03

Edison Chen (1980-)
Dog Bite Dog '06
The Grudge 2 '06
Vampire Effect '03

Joan Chen (1961-)
Lust, Caution '07
Saving Face '04
What's Cooking! '00
In a Class of His Own '99
Precious Find '96
Judge Dredd '95
Wild Side '95
The Hunted '94
On Deadly Ground '94
Temptation of a Monk '94
Golden Gate '93
Heaven and Earth '93
The Killing Beach '92
Deadlock '91
Strangers '91
The Blood of Heroes '89
The Last Emperor '87
Night Stalker '87
Tai-Pan '86
Dim Sum: A Little Bit of Heart '85

Terry Chen
Memory '06
Snakes on a Plane '06
Ballistic: Ecks vs. Sever '02
Stark Raving Mad '02
Almost Famous '00
Crash & Byrnes '99

Tina Chen (1945-)
Lady from Yesterday '85
Paper Man '71
Alice's Restaurant '69

Adam Cheng (1947-)
Painted Skin '93
Fantasy Mission Force '84
Zu: Warriors from the Magic Mountain '83

Ekin Cheng (1967-)
Vampire Effect '03
Tokyo Raiders '00

Kent Cheng (1951-)
The Bodyguard from Beijing '94
Crime Story '93
Sex and Zen '93
Once Upon a Time in China '91

Kristin Chenoweth (1968-)
Space Chimps '08 (V)

Deck the Halls '06
The Pink Panther '06
Running with Scissors '06
RV '06
Bewitched '05
Annie '99

Cher (1946-)
Stuck On You '03
Tea with Mussolini '99
If These Walls Could Talk '96
Faithful '95
Ready to Wear '94
The Player '92
Mermaids '90
Moonstruck '87
Suspect '87
The Witches of Eastwick '87
Mask '85
Silkwood '83
Come Back to the Five & Dime Jimmy Dean, Jimmy Dean '82
Good Times '67

Patrice Chereau (1944-)
Time of the Wolf '03
Time Regained '99 (V)
Lucie Aubrac '98
The Last of the Mohicans '92
Danton '82

Nikolai Cherkassov (1903-66)
Don Quixote '57
Ivan the Terrible, Part 2 '46
Ivan the Terrible, Part 1 '44
Alexander Nevsky '38
Peter the First: Part 2 '38
Baltic Deputy '37
Peter the First: Part 1 '37
Happiness '32

Jonas Chernick (1973-)
Eloise at the Plaza '03
Edge of Madness '02
A Woman's a Helluva Thing '01

Virginia Cherrill (1908-96)
Late Extra '35
City Lights '31

Jonathan Cherry
Final Destination 2 '03
House of the Dead '03

George Chesebro (1888-1959)
Check Your Guns '48
Stage to Mesa City '48
Cheyenne Takes Over '47
Fighting Vigilantes '47
Homesteaders of Paradise Valley '47
Return of the Lash '47
Boss of Rawhide '44
Devil Riders '44
Raiders of Red Gap '43
Two-Fisted Justice '43
Holt of the Secret Service '42
Sundown Fury '42
Thunder River Feud '42
The Pioneers '41
Saddle Mountain Roundup '41
Trigger Men '41
Lightning Strikes West '40
West of Pinto Basin '40
Purple Vigilantes '38
Roarin' Lead '37
S.O.S. Coast Guard '37
Fast Bullets '36
Pinto Rustlers '36
Red River Valley '36
Roamin' Wild '36
Fighting Caballero '35
Laramie Kid '35
The Miracle Rider '35
Pals of the Range '35
Rough Riding Ranger '35
Wild Mustang '35
In Old Santa Fe '34
The Silver Bullet '34
Fighting Champ '33
Wolf Blood '25

Elizabeth Cheshire (1967-)
Awakening of Candra '81
Melvin and Howard '80

Harry Cheshire (1891-1968)
Impact '49
Shoot to Kill '47

Patrick Chesnais (1947-)
The Diving Bell and the Butterfly '07
After Sex '00
La Lectrice '88

Craig Chester (1965-)
Adam & Steve '05
Kiss Me, Guido '97
I Shot Andy Warhol '96
Frisk '95
Grief '94
Swoon '91

Vanessa Lee Chester (1984-)
The Lost World: Jurassic Park 2 '97
Harriet the Spy '96
A Little Princess '95

Morris Chestnut (1969-)
The Game Plan '07
The Perfect Holiday '07
The Cave '05
Anacondas: The Hunt for the Blood Orchid '04
Breakin' All The Rules '04
Ladder 49 '04
Confidence '03
Half Past Dead '02
Like Mike '02
The Brothers '01
The Killing Yard '01
Two Can Play That Game '01
The Best Man '99
G.I. Jane '97
Under Siege 2: Dark Territory '95
The Ernest Green Story '93
Boyz N the Hood '91
The Last Boy Scout '91

Cecilia Cheung (1980-)
The Promise '05
Shaolin Soccer '01
Tokyo Raiders '00

Cindy Cheung
Lady in the Water '06
Robot Stories '03

Daphne Cheung
Jack Higgins' Midnight Man '96
Jack Higgins' On Dangerous Ground '95

George Kee Cheung
Starsky & Hutch '04
High Voltage '98
Opposing Force '87

Jacky Cheung (1961-)
Meltdown '95
Wicked City '92

Leslie Cheung (1956-2003)
Happy Together '96
Temptress Moon '96
The Phantom Lover '95
The Bride with White Hair '93
The Bride with White Hair 2 '93
Farewell My Concubine '93
Once a Thief '90
A Better Tomorrow, Part 2 '88
A Better Tomorrow, Part 1 '86

Maggie Cheung (1964-)
Clean '04
Hero '03
In the Mood for Love '00
Irma Vep '96

The Executioners '93
Green Snake '93
The Heroic Trio '93
Supercop '92
Twin Dragons '92
Song of the Exile '90
Paper Marriage '88
Project A: Part 2 '87
Police Story '85

Roy Cheung (1964-)
Exiled '06
The Mission '99
Organized Crime & Triad Bureau '93
Wicked City '92
City on Fire '87

Kevin Timothy Chevalia (1986-)
Homeward Bound 2: Lost in San Francisco '96
Homeward Bound: The Incredible Journey '93
Folks! '92

Maurice Chevalier (1888-1972)
The Sorrow and the Pity '71
Monkeys, Go Home! '66
A New Kind of Love '63
In Search of the Castaways '62
Panic Button '62
Fanny '61
Black Tights '60 (N)
Breath of Scandal '60
Can-Can '60
Gigi '58
Love in the Afternoon '57
The Merry Widow '34
One Hour with You '32
The Smiling Lieutenant '31
The Love Parade '29

Richard Chevolleau (1966-)
Narc '02
Who is Cletis Tout? '02
True Blue '01
No Alibi '00
The Wall '99
Tracked '98
Blood Brothers '97
Rude '96

Arno Chevrier
Agnes Browne '99
The Red Dwarf '99

Laureen Chew
Dim Sum: A Little Bit of Heart '85

Minoru Chiaki (1917-99)
Face of Another '66
The Human Condition: Road to Eternity '59
The Hidden Fortress '58
Throne of Blood '57
Godzilla Raids Again '55
Seven Samurai '54
Rashomon '51

Dominic Chianese (1931-)
Adrift in Manhattan '07
King of the Corner '04
When Will I Be Loved '04
Unfaithful '02
Once in the Life '00
Under Hellgate Bridge '99
Went to Coney Island on a Mission from God... Be Back by Five '98
Gotti '96
Looking for Richard '96
Love Is All There Is '96
Night Falls on Manhattan '96
The Public Eye '92
Out for Justice '91
Q & A '90
Second Sight '89
And Justice for All '79
Firepower '79
On the Yard '79

All the President's Men '76
Dog Day Afternoon '75
The Godfather, Part 2 '74

David Chiang (1947-)
The Kumite '03
Duel of Fists '71

Roy Chiao (1927-99)
Summer Snow '94
Bloodsport '88

Walter Chiari (1924-91)
Girl Under the Sheet '61
Bonjour Tristesse '57
Nana '55
Bellissima '51

Stephen Chiau
See Stephen (Chiau) Chow

Sofiko Chiaureli (1937-)
Ashik Kerib '88
The Color of Pomegranates '69

Sonny Chiba (1939-)
The Fast and the Furious: Tokyo Drift '06
Kill Bill Vol. 2 '04
Kill Bill Vol. 1 '03
Body Count '95
Immortal Combat '94
Aces: Iron Eagle 3 '92
Shogun's Ninja '83
Fall Guy '82
Virus '82
Samurai Reincarnation '81
Hunter in the Dark '80
The Bodyguard '76
Sister Street Fighter '76
Return of the Street Fighter '74
The Street Fighter '74
The Street Fighter's Last Revenge '74
Terror Beneath the Sea '66

Etienne Chicot (1949-)
The Da Vinci Code '06
36 Fillete '88
Osa '85

Caroline Chikezie (1979-)
Eragon '06
Aeon Flux '05

Michael Chiklis (1963-)
Fantastic Four: Rise of the Silver Surfer '07
Rise: Blood Hunter '07
Fantastic Four '05
Spirited Away '01 (V)
Silent Witness '99
Body and Soul '98
Soldier '98
The Taxman '98
Wired '89

Jeremy Child (1944-)
Frenchman's Creek '98
Mosley '98
Behind the Lines '97
Sharpe's Enemy '94
Fool's Gold: The Story of the Brink's-Mat Robbery '92

Patricia Childress (1971-)
Larry McMurtry's Dead Man's Walk '96
Shake, Rattle & Rock! '94

Linden Chiles (1933-)
Deadline Assault '90
To Heal a Nation '88
Forbidden World '82
Red Flag: The Ultimate Game '81
Death Be Not Proud '75
Who Is the Black Dahlia? '75
Texas Across the River '66

Lois Chiles (1947-)
Speed 2: Cruise Control '97
Bliss '96
Wish upon a Star '96
The Babysitter '95
Curdled '95
Diary of a Hitman '91
Twister '89

Broadcast News '87
Creepshow 2 '87
Raw Courage '84
Moonraker '79
Coma '78
Death on the Nile '73
The Way We Were '73

Simon Chilvers (1939-)
Ground Zero '88
The Big Hurt '87
Windrider '86
The Dunera Boys '85

Andre Chimene
Computer Beach Party '88

Joey Chin
The Outing '87
King of New York '90
China Girl '87

Tsai Chin (1938-)
The Joy Luck Club '93
Red Corner '97
Rentadick '72
The Virgin Soldiers '69
The Castle of Fu Manchu '68
Kiss and Kill '68
You Only Live Twice '67
The Diary of Ellen Rimbauer '03
Memoirs of a Geisha '05

William Ching (1913-39)
Terror in the Haunted House '58
Give a Girl a Break '53
Never Wave at a WAC '52
Pat and Mike '52
D.O.A. '49
The Wistful Widow of Wagon Gap '47

Kieu Chinh (1939-)
Green Dragon '01
Catfish in Black Bean Sauce '00
Riot in the Streets '96
The Joy Luck Club '93
Hamburger Hill '87
The Girl Who Spelled Freedom '86
Operation C.I.A. '65

Nicholas Chinlund (1961-)
Ultraviolet '06
The Legend of Zorro '05
The Chronicles of Riddick '04
Tears of the Sun '03
Below '02
Amy's O '02
100 Mile Rule '02
Training Day '01
Beyond Suspicion '00
Disney's The Kid '00
Once in the Life '00
Chutney Popcorn '99
Frogs for Snakes '98
A Brother's Kiss '97
Con Air '97
Mr. Magoo '97
Rough Riders '97
Eraser '96
Letter to My Killer '95
Bad Girls '94
Unveiled '94
Red Shoe Diaries 4: Auto Erotica '93

Jimmy Chisholm (1956-)
Strictly Sinatra '01
Ivanhoe '97
Lethal Weapon 3 '92
The Ambulance '90

Erik Chitty (1907-77)
Doctor Zhivago '65
First Men in the Moon '64

Anna Chlumsky (1980-)
Gold Diggers: The Secret of Bear Mountain '95
My Girl 2 '94
Trading Mom '94
My Girl '91

Thomas Chong (1938-)
The Wash '01
Half-Baked '97
McHale's Navy '97

John Cho (1972-)
Harold & Kumar Escape from Guantanamo Bay '08
American Dreamz '06
Bickford Shmeckler's Cool Ideas '06
Bam Bam & Celeste '05
Harold and Kumar Go to White Castle '04
Better Luck Tomorrow '02
Earth vs. the Spider '01
Pavilion of Women '01
The Doom Generation '95

Margaret Cho (1969-)
Yellow '98
One Missed Call '08
Bam Bam & Celeste '05
Spent '00
The Tavern '00
Ground Control '98
Face/Off '97
Sweethearts '97
It's My Party '95

Tim Choate (1954-2004)
Pearl Harbor '01
Live Nude Girls '95
Blind Witness '89
The Discovery Program '89
Spy '89
Def-Con 4 '85
First Time '82

Charlene (Cheuk-Yin) Choi (1982-)
New Police Story '04

Min-Sik Choi (1962-)
Lady Vengeance '05
Oldboy '03

Jun Chong
Street Soldiers '91
Silent Assassins '88

Marcus Chong (1967-)
The Matrix '99
Panther '95

Rae Dawn Chong (1962-)
The Visit '00
Highball '97
Mask of Death '97
Protector '97
Starlight '97
Smalltime '96
The Break '95
Boca '94
Boulevard '94
Hideaway '94
Power of Attorney '94
Dangerous Relations '93
Time Runner '92
Common Bonds '91
Denial: The Dark Side of Passion '91
Prison Stories: Women on the Inside '91
When the Party's Over '91
Amazon '90
Curiosity Kills '90
Tales from the Darkside: The Movie '90
The Borrower '89
Far Out Man '89
The Principal '87
The Squeeze '87
Soul Man '86
Running out of Luck '86
American Flyers '85
Badge of the Assassin '85
City Limits '85
The Color Purple '85
Fear City '85
Beat Street '84
Cheech and Chong's The Corsican Brothers '84
Choose Me '84

Sarita Choudhury (1966-)
Lady in the Water '06
The War Within '05
The Breakup Artist '04
It Runs in the Family '03
Just a Kiss '02
A Perfect Murder '98
Subway Stories '97
Kama Sutra: A Tale of Love '96
Down Came a Blackbird '94
The House of the Spirits '93
Wild West '93
Mississippi Masala '92

China Chow (1974-)
Frankenfish '04
Head Over Heels '01
The Big Hit '98

Stephen (Chiau) Chow (1962-)
Kung Fu Hustle '04
Shaolin Soccer '01

Valerie Chow (1970-)
Chungking Express '95

Collin Chou (1967-)
The Forbidden Kingdom '08
DOA: Dead or Alive '06
Jet Li's Fearless '06
The Matrix Revolutions '03
The Matrix Reloaded '03
Jet Li's The Enforcer '95
The Bodyguard from Beijing '94

Etchika Choureau (1923-)
Darby's Rangers '58
Lafayette Escadrille '58

Claudia Christian (1965-)
Half Past Dead '02
Atlantis: The Lost Empire '01 (V)
Final Voyage '99
The Substitute 3: Winner Takes All '99
The Haunting of Hell House '99
Mercenary 2: Thick and Thin '97
Sisters '97
The Adventures of a Gnome Named Gnorm '93
Hexed '93
The Dark Backward '91
Strays '91
Mad About You '90
Maniac Cop 2 '90
Arena '89
Clean and Sober '88
Never on Tuesday '88
The Hidden '87

Hayden Christensen (1981-)
Jumper '08
Awake '07
Factory Girl '06
The Interpreter '05
Star Wars: Episode 3—Revenge of the Sith '05
Shattered Glass '03
Star Wars: Episode 2—Attack of the Clones '02
Life as a House '01

Jesper Christensen (1948-)
Casino Royale '06
The Interpreter '05
Uprising '01
The White Lioness '96

Morven Christie
The Flying Scotsman '06

Katia Christine (1946-)
Cosmos: War of the Planets '80
Spirits of the Dead '68
Doctor Zhivago '65

Marilyn Chris (1938-)
Joe Torre: Curveballs Along the Way '97
Backstairs at the White House '79
Honeymoon Killers '70

Erika Christensen (1982-)
Flightplan '05
The Upside of Anger '05
The Perfect Score '04
Swimfan '02
Traffic '00

David Christensen
Turn of the Blade '97
Over the Wire '95

Chad Christ (1976-)
Jawbreaker '97
No Laughing Matter '98
MTV's Wuthering Heights '03

Mady Christians (1900-51)
All My Sons '48
Letter from an Unknown Woman '48
Tender Comrade '43

Benjamin Christensen (1879-1959)
The Only Way '70
Haxan: Witchcraft through the Ages '22

Francoise Christophe (1925-)
Borsalino '70
The King of Hearts '66
The Invaders '63

Bojesse Christopher
Point Break '91

Dennis Christopher (1955-)
Circuitry Man 2 '94
It's My Party '95
Meatballs 4 '92
Mind Lies '00
Out in Fifty '99
Circuitry Man '90
Doppelganger: The Evil Within '92
Boys Life '90
Breaking Away '79
Didn't You Hear? '83
Jack & the Beanstalk '83
Don't Cry, It's Only Thunder '82

Audrey Christie (1912-89)
Harper Valley P.T.A. '78
Mame '74
Frankie and Johnny '85
Splendor in the Grass '61
Keeper of the Flame '42

Julie Christie (1941-)
Away From Her '06
Finding Neverland '04
Harry Potter and the Prisoner of Azkaban '04
Troy '04
I'm with Lucy '02
Snapshots '02
No Such Thing '01
Secret Obsession '68
Miss Mary '86
Power '86
Separate Tables '83
Heat and Dust '82
Return of the Soldier '82
Heaven Can Wait '78
Demon Seed '77
Nashville '75
Shampoo '75
Don't Look Now '73
McCabe & Mrs. Miller '71
The Go-Between '71
Petulia '68
Far from the Madding Crowd '67
Fahrenheit 451 '66
Darling '65
Doctor Zhivago '65
Billy Liar '63

Virginia Christine (1920-96)
Billy the Kid Versus Dracula '66
One Man's Way '63
The Cobweb '55
The Inner Circle '46
The Killers '46
The Mummy's Curse '44

Eric Christmas (1916-2000)
Air Bud '97
Mouse Hunt '97
Home Is Where the Hart Is '88
The Challengers '89
Child of Darkness, Child of Light '91
Porky's Revenge '85
All of Me '84
The Philadelphia Experiment '84
Porky's II: The Next Day '83
Porky's '82
Middle Age Crazy '80
Attack of the Killer Tomatoes '77

Linda Christian (1924-)
Athena '54
The V.I.P.'s '63
The Devil's Hand '61

Michael Christian (1947-)
Private Obsession '94
Hard Knocks '79
Mid Knight Rider '79
The Legend of Frank Woods '77
Poor Pretty Eddie '73

John Christian (1957-)
Full Hearts & Empty Pockets '63
Blood Relic '05
Covert Action '88
Comrades in Arms '91
The Outfit '93
Mob War '88
The Hidden '87
The Night We Never Met '93
Bleeding Hearts '94
Fire '96
Last Holiday '06

Joseph Chrest
You Don't Mess with the Zohan '08
Deceit '06
The Crow: Wicked Prayer '05
In the Mix '05

Emmanuelle Chriqui (1977-)
Waiting '05
Rick '03
Wrong Turn '03
A.I.: Artificial Intelligence '01
On the Line '01

Navin Chowdhry (1971-)
Red Mercury '05
The Seventh Coin '92
Madame Sousatzka '88

Ranjit (Chaudry) Chowdhry
The Night We Never Met '93
Mississippi Masala '92
Lonely in America '90

Shawn Christian
Meet Dave '08
Snow Day '00
100 Girls '00

Debra Christofferson
Jesse Stone: Death n Paradise '06
Harold and Maude '71
Johnny Got His Gun '71

Kathy Christopherson
Executive Target '97
Guyver 2: Dark Hero '94

Tyler Christopher (1972-)
Out of the Black '01
Alive '02
U.S. Navy SEALs: Dead or Alive '02

Thom Christopher
Chariots of Fire '81
Alien Predators '87
Fade to Black '80
The Last Word '80
Breaking Away '79
California Dreaming '79
Elvis: The Movie '79
A Wedding '78
A Sinful Life '89
Jake Speed '86
September 30, 1955 '77
3 Women '77
The Young Graduates '71
Deathstalker 3 '89
Wizards of the Lost Kingdom '85

William (Bill) Christopher (1932-)
M*A*S*H: Goodbye, Farewell & Amen '83
For the Love of It '80
With Six You Get Eggroll '68

Dorothy Christy (1906-77)
Sons of the Desert '33
Convicted '32
Big Business Girl '31
Night Life in Reno '31

Emily Chu (1960-)
A Better Tomorrow '86
A Better Tomorrow, Part 1 '86

Paul Chubb (1949-2002)
Road to Nhill '97
The Well '97
Cosi '95
Heart of Dragon '85

Sweet Talker '91

Babz Chula (1946-)
Connie and Carla '04
Live Bait '95

Christy Chung (1970-)
The Medallion '03
The Bodyguard from Beijing '94
The Bride with White Hair 2 '93

David Chung (1946-2006)
Color of a Brisk and Leaping Day '95
The Ballad of Little Jo '93
Combination Platter '93

Mok Siu Chung (1960-)
Once Upon a Time in China III '93
Once Upon a Time in China II '92

Fred Church (1888-1983)
Apache Kid's Escape '30
Son of a Gun '19

Thomas Haden Church (1960-)
Smart People '08
Spider-Man 3 '07
Broken Trail '06
Charlotte's Web '06 (V)
Idiocracy '06
Over the Hedge '06 (V)
Serial Killing 101 '04
Sideways '04
Spanglish '04
Lone Star State of Mind '02
3000 Miles to Graceland '01
The Specials '00
Free Money '99
Dean Koontz's Mr. Murder '98
Dying to Get Rich '98
George of the Jungle '97
One Night Stand '97
Tales from the Crypt Presents Demon Knight '94
Tombstone '93

Berton Churchill (1876-1940)
Stagecoach '39
Danger on the Air '38
Four Men and a Prayer '38
Wide Open Faces '38
In Old Chicago '37
The Dark Hour '36
Dimples '36
Mistaken Identity '36
Sing Sing Nights '35
Steamboat Round the Bend '35
Bachelor Bait '34
Badmen of Nevada '33
Doctor Bull '33
The Mysterious Rider '33
So This Is Africa '33
The Big Stampede '32
False Faces '32

Donald Churchill (1930-91)
The Hound of the Baskervilles '83
Charlie Muffin '79
Victim '61

Marguerite Churchill (1909-2000)
Dracula's Daughter '36
Ambassador Bill '31
Big Trail '30

Chyna
See Joanie Laurer

Julien Ciamaca (1978-)
My Father's Glory '91

Eduardo Ciannelli (1889-1969)
MacKenna's Gold '69
Houseboat '58
Monster from Green Hell '58
Mambo '55
The Creeper '48
Heartbeat '46
The Mask of Dimitrios '44
Passage to Marseilles '44
They Got Me Covered '43
Cairo '42
They Met in Bombay '41
Doctor Satan's Robot '40
Foreign Correspondent '40
Kitty Foyle '40
The Mummy's Hand '40
Mysterious Doctor Satan '40
Strange Cargo '40
Bulldog Drummond's Bride '39
Gunga Din '39
Law of the Underworld '38
Marked Woman '37

Eddie Cibrian (1973-)
The Cave '05
Say It Isn't So '01
But I'm a Cheerleader '99

Robert Cicchini (1966-)
The Watcher '00
Devlin '92

Jude Ciccolella (1947-)
A Perfect Day '06
Sin City '05
The Manchurian Candidate '04
The Terminal '04
Head of State '03
High Crimes '02
Star Trek: Nemesis '02
Washington Heights '02
Beloved '98
Mad Love '95
Glengarry Glen Ross '92
Shakedown '88

Phyllis Cicero
America's Dream '95
Steele's Law '91

Anna Ciepielewska (1936-2006)
Passenger '61
Mother Joan of the Angels '60

Jennifer Clesar (1968-)
Red Shoe Diaries 7: Burning Up '96
Red Shoe Diaries: Strip Poker '96
Inner Sanctum 2 '94
Lovers' Lovers '94
True Love '89

Maria Cina
April's Shower '03
Suspended Animation '02

Kelly Cinnante
Christmas in Connecticut '92

Luis Miguel Cintra (1949-)
The Dancer Upstairs '02
The Convent '95
Abraham's Valley '93

Diane Cilento (1933-)
Winner Takes All '84
The Wicker Man '73
Zero Population Growth '72
Negatives '68
Hombre '67
The Agony and the Ecstasy '65
Rattle of a Simple Man '64
Tom Jones '63
The Naked Edge '61
The Admirable Crichton '57

Leonardo Cimino (1917-)
Trusting Beatrice '92
Penn and Teller Get Killed '90

Charles Cioffi (1935-)
Amy's O '02
The Shadow Conspiracy '96
Newsies '92
Used People '92
Peter Gunn '89
Remo Williams: The Adventure Begins '85
All the Right Moves '83
Missing '82
Time After Time '79
The Arab Conspiracy '76
Return to Earth '76
The Don Is Dead '73
The Thief Who Came to Dinner '73
Klute '71
Shaft '71

Augusta Ciolli (1901-67)
Love with the Proper Stranger '63
Marty '55

Greg Cipes (1980-)
The Wild '06 (V)
Ring of Darkness '04

Roberto Citran (1955-)
Nora '00
The Truce '96

Franco Citti (1935-)
Watch Me When I Kill '77
Arabian Nights '74
The Decameron '70
Porcile '69
Super Brother '68
Oedipus Rex '67
Accatone! '61

Jany Clair (1938-)
Hercules against the Moon Men '64
Conquest of Mycene '63
Planets Against Us '61

Cyrielle Claire (1955-)
The Worker and the Hairdresser '96
Control '87
Code Name: Emerald '85
Sword of the Valiant '83
Le Professionnel '81

Ina Claire (1892-1985)
Ninotchka '39
Three Broadway Girls '32

Tom Clancy (1924-90)
Backstairs at the White House '79
Eric '75

Rony Clanton
Def by Temptation '90
The Education of Sonny Carson '74

Gordon Clapp (1948-)
The Game Plan '07
Sunshine State '02
Skeletons in the Closet '00
The Rage: Carrie 2 '99
Stand Off '93
Fever '91
Kurt Vonnegut's Monkey House '91
Small Sacrifices '89
Termini Station '89
Eight Men Out '88
Matewan '87
Return of the Secaucus 7 '80

Eric Clapton (1945-)
Chuck Berry: Hail! Hail! Rock 'n' Roll '87
Water '85
Tommy '75

Diane Clare (1938-)
Vulture '67
Beast of Morocco '66
Plague of the Zombies '66
The Haunting '63
Whistle down the Wind '61
The Reluctant Debutante '58
Murder on the Campus '52

Mary Clare (1894-1970)
Moulin Rouge '52
The Night Has Eyes '42
The Mill on the Floss '37
Young and Innocent '37
Lorna Doone '34
Power '34

O.B. Clarence (1870-1955)
Great Expectations '46
On Approval '44
The Courageous Mr. Penn '41
Pygmalion '38
The Scarlet Pimpernel '34
A Shot in the Dark '33

Hans Clarin
Pippi Goes on Board '69
Pippi Longstocking '69

Aime Clariond (1894-1960)
Monsieur Vincent '47
De Mayerling a Sarajevo '40
La Marseillaise '37

Anthony Clark (1964-)
Say Uncle '05
Paid in Full '02
The Rock '96
Hourglass '95
Teresa's Tattoo '94
The Thing Called Love '93
Dogfight '91

Blake Clark (1946-)
I Now Pronounce You Chuck and Larry '07
The Benchwarmers '06
50 First Dates '04
The Ladykillers '04
Mr. Deeds '02
Critical Mass '00
Little Nicky '00
The Waterboy '98
Grave Secrets: The Legacy of Hilltop Drive '92
Ladybugs '92
Shakes the Clown '92
Johnny Handsome '89

Bob (Benjamin) Clark (1941-2007)
A Christmas Story '83
Porky's '82

Brett (Baxter) Clark
Stormy Nights '97
Deathstalker 4: Match of Titans '92
Inner Sanctum '91
Eye of the Eagle '87
Alien Warrior '85

Buddy Clark (1912-49)
Melody Time '48 (V)
Seven Days' Leave '42

Candy Clark (1947-)
Zodiac '07
Cherry Falls '00
Buffy the Vampire Slayer '92
Cool As Ice '91
Original Intent '91
The Blob '88
At Close Range '86
Cat's Eye '85
Amityville 3: The Demon '83
Blue Thunder '83
Johnny Belinda '82
Q (The Winged Serpent) '82
National Lampoon Goes to the Movies '81
Rodeo Girl '80
More American Graffiti '79
The Big Sleep '78
Citizens Band '77
James Dean '76
The Man Who Fell to Earth '76
American Graffiti '73
Fat City '72

Cliff Clark (1889-1953)
Home of the Brave '49
The Wagons Roll at Night '41

Dane Clark (1913-98)
Last Rites '88
Blood Song '82
James Dean '76
Say Goodbye, Maggie Cole '72
The McMasters '70
Blackout '54
Paid to Kill '54
Thunder Pass '54
The Gambler & the Lady '52
The Smallest Show on Earth '48
A Stolen Life '46
God Is My Co-Pilot '45
Hollywood Canteen '44
Action in the North Atlantic '43
Destination Tokyo '43
The Glass Key '42

Daniel Clark (1985-)
That Russell Girl '08
Model Behavior '00
Grizzly Falls '99

Davison Clark (1881-1972)
Rogue's Gallery '44
Dishonored '31

Dick Clark (1929-)
Deadman's Curve '78
Wild in the Streets '68

Ernest Clark (1912-94)
Castle Keep '69
Sink the Bismarck '60
1984 '56

Eugene Clark (1955-)
George A. Romero's Land of the Dead '05
Man in the Mirror: The Michael Jackson Story '04
Jasper, Texas '03
Turn It Up '00
Wilder '00
TekWar '94
Trial and Error '92

Frank Clark (1857-1945)
Roaring Ranch '30
The Spoilers '14

Fred Clark (1914-68)
The Horse in the Gray Flannel Suit '68
Dr. Goldfoot and the Bikini Machine '66
Move Over, Darling '63
Zotz! '62
Bells Are Ringing '60
Joyful Laughter '60
Passionate Thief '60
It Started with a Kiss '59
The Mating Game '59
Don't Go Near the Water '57
Solid Gold Cadillac '56
The Court Martial of Billy Mitchell '55
Daddy Long Legs '55
Abbott and Costello Meet the Keystone Kops '54
The Caddy '53
Here Come the Girls '53
Three for Bedroom C '52
The Lemon Drop Kid '51
The Jackpot '50
Sunset Boulevard '50
Flamingo Road '49

Greydon Clark (1943-)
Bad Bunch '76
Satan's Sadists '69

Harvey Clark (1885-1938)
Law for Tombstone '35
Peck's Bad Boy '34
Shriek in the Night '33
Red Headed Woman '32

Judy Clark
Kid Sister '45
South of Santa Fe '42

Ken Clark (1927-)
Tarzana, the Wild Girl '69
Desert Commandos '67
Attack of the Giant Leeches '59
Between Heaven and Hell '56

Liddy Clark (1953-)
Deadly Possession '88
Kitty and the Bagman '82
The Chant of Jimmie Blacksmith '78

Marlene Clark
The Baron '88
The Beast Must Die '75
Switchblade Sisters '75
Ganja and Hess '73
Night of the Cobra Woman '72
Slaughter '72

Matt Clark (1936-)
Kiss of Fire '98
Homegrown '97
Trilogy of Terror 2 '96
Barbarians at the Gate '93
Frozen Assets '92
The Harvest '92
Class Action '91
Back to the Future, Part 3 '90
Blind Witness '89
The Horror Show '89
Kenny Rogers as The Gambler, Part 3: The Legend Continues '87
Let's Get Harry '87
The Quick and the Dead '87
Out of the Darkness '85
Return to Oz '85
Tuff Turf '85
The Adventures of Buckaroo Banzai Across the Eighth Dimension '84
Country '84
Love Letters '83
In the Custody of Strangers '82
Chasing Dreams '81
An Eye for an Eye '81
Legend of the Lone Ranger '81
Ruckus '81
The Driver '78
The Outlaw Josey Wales '76
The Execution of Private Slovik '74
Melvin Purvis: G-Man '74
Emperor of the North Pole '73
The Great Northfield Minnesota Raid '72

Mystro Clark (1966-)
Storm Catcher '99
Chairman of the Board '97

Oliver Clark (1939-)
Nightlife '90
Ernest Saves Christmas '88
One Cooks, the Other Doesn't '83
Mikey & Nicky '76
A Star Is Born '76

Petula Clark (1932-)
Goodbye, Mr. Chips '69
Finian's Rainbow '68
The Runaway Bus '54
Made in Heaven '52
The Promoter '52

Roger Clark (1909-78)
Monster '78
Girls in Chains '43
The Lady Is Willing '42

Spencer (Treat) Clark (1987-)
Mystic River '03
Minority Report '02
Gladiator '00
Unbreakable '00
Arlington Road '99
Double Jeopardy '99

Steve Clark (1891-1954)
Range Renegades '48
Fighting Vigilantes '47
Border Bandits '46
The Stranger from Pecos '45
Range Law '44
Land of Hunted Men '43
Pinto Canyon '40
Boothill Brigade '37
Gun Lords of Stirrup Basin '37
Paroled to Die '37
West of Nevada '36
No Man's Range '35

Susan Clark (1940-)
Snowbound: The Jim and Jennifer Stolpa Story '94
The Choice '81
Porky's '82
The Double Negative '80
Murder by Decree '79
Nobody's Perfekt '80
The North Avenue Irregulars '79
Promises in the Dark '79
City on Fire '78
Airport '75 '75
The Apple Dumpling Gang '75
Babel '75
Night Moves '75
Showdown '73
Skin Game '71
Valdez Is Coming '71
Colossus: The Forbin Project '70
Skullduggery '70
Coogan's Bluff '68
Madigan '68

Ted Clark
Here '69
"Tell Them Willie Boy Is Here '69

Wallis (Clarke) Clark (1886-1961)
Star Reporter '39
Postal Inspector '36

Andrew Clarke (1954-)
Les Patterson Saves the World '90
Anzacs: The War Down Under '85

Angela (Clark) Clarke (1912-)
Letter to Brezhnev '86
Harrad Summer '74
The Interns '62
The Seven Little Foys '55
The Egyptian '54
Beneath the 12-Mile Reef '53
Houdini '53
House of Wax '53
Miracle of Our Lady of Fatima '52
The Great Caruso '51
The Gunfighter '50
Mrs. Mike '49
Bedlam '45

Brian Patrick Clarke (1952-)
Sleepaway Camp 2: Unhappy Campers '88

Caitlin Clarke (1952-2004)
Penn and Teller Get Killed '90
Dragonslayer '81

Cameron Clarke (1957-)
The Pirates Who Don't Do Anything: A Veggie Tales Movie '08 (V)
Clifford's Really Big Movie '04 (V)

Gary Clarke (1936-)
Confessions of Tom Harris '72
Bull of the West '71
Date Bait '60
Missile to the Moon '59
How to Make a Monster '58

Graham Clarke
Armageddon: The Final Challenge '94
Laser Mission '90
Lights! Camera! Murder! '89

Hope Clarke (1943-)
Seventeen Again '00
Piece of the Action '77

Jason Clarke
The Outsider '02
Rabbit-Proof Fence '02

Justine Clarke (1971-)
Look Both Ways '05
Danny Deckchair '03
Japanese Story '03
Risk '00

Lenny Clarke (1953-)
Fever Pitch '05
What's the Worst That Could Happen? '01
Me, Myself, and Irene '00
There's Something about Mary '98

Mae Clarke (1907-92)
Because of You '52
Pat and Mike '52
King of the Rocketmen '49
Lost Planet Airmen '49
Here Come the Waves '45
Flying Tigers '42
Hats Off '37
Great Guy '36
Lady Killer '33
Penthouse '33
Frankenstein '31
The Front Page '31
Public Enemy '31

Melinda (Mindy) Clarke (1969-)
Spawn '97
Killer Tongue '96
Return of the Living Dead 3 '93

Richard Clarke (1930-2005)
Return to Two Moon Junction '93
Hot Under the Collar '91

Robert Clarke (1920-2005)
Identity Crisis '90
Alienator '89
Secret File of Hollywood '62
Terror of the Bloodhunters '62
Beyond the Time Barrier '60
Hideous Sun Demon '59
The Astounding She-Monster '58
A Night to Remember '58
Sword of Venus '53
Tales of Robin Hood '52
The Man from Planet X '51
Riders in the Range '50
Bedlam '45

Sarah Clarke (1972-)
The Lather Effect '06
Happy Endings '05
Thirteen '03

Warren Clarke (1947-)
The Debt '03
Blow Dry '00
Greenfingers '00
A Respectable Trade '98
Enigma '82
Firefox '82
From a Far Country: Pope John Paul II '81
Tinker, Tailor, Soldier, Spy '80
Mandela '87
Joseph '95
Hands of a Murderer '90
The Enchanted Cottage '45
Cyberzone '95
White Wolves 3: Cry of the White Wolf '98
Inseminoid '80

D.A. Clarke-Smith (1888-1959)
The Ghoul '34
The Man Who Knew Too Much '34

Lana Clarkson (1962-2003)
Vice Girls '96
The Haunting of Morella '91
Barbarian Queen 2: The Empress Strikes Back '89
Wizards of the Lost Kingdom 2 '89
Barbarian Queen '85
Deathstalker '84
Blind Date '84

Patricia Clarkson (1960-)
Lars and the Real Girl '07
Married Life '07
No Reservations '07
All the King's Men '06
Good Night, and Good Luck '05
The Dying Gaul '05
Miracle '04
All the Real Girls '03
Dogville '03
Pieces of April '03
The Station Agent '03
The Woods '03
Carrie '02
Welcome to Collinwood '02
Far from Heaven '02
The Safety of Objects '01
Joe Gould's Secret '00
The Pledge '00
Wendigo '01
The Green Mile '99
Simply Irresistible '99
High Art '98
Playing by Heart '98
Four Eyes and Six Guns '93
Caught in the Act '93
An American Story '92
Legacy of Lies '92
Blind Man's Bluff '91
The Old Man and the Sea '90
Tune in Tomorrow '90
The Dead Pool '88
Rocket Gibraltar '88

John Clayton (1940-)

June Clayworth (1912-93)
At Sword's Point '51
Dick Tracy Meets Gruesome '47

Charles Clary (1873-1931)
The Sea Lion '21
The Penalty '20

Robert Clary (1926-)
Remembrance of Love '82
New Faces of 1952 '54

Garance Clavel (1973-)
When the Cat's Away '96

Kira Clavell
Apres-Vous '03

Christian Clavier (1952-)
The Crown Prince '06
Napoleon '03
Just Visiting '01
The Visitors '01

Jill Clayburgh (1944-)
Running with Scissors '06
Never Again '01
My Little Assassin '99
Fools Rush In '97
Whispers in the Dark '92
Rich in Love '93
Naked in New York '93
Day of Atonement '93
Shy People '87
Where Are the Children? '85
Hanna K. '83
I'm Dancing as Fast as I Can '82
First Monday in October '81
Starting Over '79
An Unmarried Woman '78
Semi-Tough '77
It's My Turn '80
Silver Streak '76
The Art of Crime '75
Hustling '75
The Terminal Man '74
The Thief Who Came to Dinner '73
Portnoy's Complaint '72
The Wedding Party '69

Nicholas Clay (1946-2000)
Merlin '98
The Odyssey '97
Sleeping Beauty '89
Lionheart '87
The Hound of the Baskervilles '83
Evil under the Sun '82
Excalibur '81
Lady Chatterley's Lover '81
Lovespell '79

John Cleese (1939-)
Shrek the Third '07 (V)
Charlotte's Web '06 (V)
Valiant '05 (V)
Around the World in 80 Days '04
Shrek 2 '04 (V)
Charlie's Angels: Full Throttle '03
The Adventures of Pluto Nash '02
Die Another Day '02
Harry Potter and the Chamber of Secrets '02
Pinocchio '02 (V)
Scorched '02
Rat Race '01
Isn't She Great '00
The Out-of-Towners '99
The World Is Not Enough '99
George of the Jungle '97
Fierce Creatures '96
Mr. Toad's Wild Ride '96
Frankenstein '94
Rudyard Kipling's The Jungle Book '94
The Swan Princess '94 (V)
Splitting Heirs '93
The Strange Case of the End of Civilization As We Know It '77
An American Tail: Fievel Goes West '91 (V)
Bullseye! '90
The Big Picture '89
Erik the Viking '89
A Fish Called Wanda '88
Clockwise '86
Silverado '85
Privates on Parade '84
Yellowbeard '83
Monty Python's The Meaning of Life '83
Whoops Apocalypse '83
The Secret Policeman's Other Ball '82
The Great Muppet Caper '81
Time Bandits '81
The Secret Policeman's Private Parts '81
Monty Python's Life of Brian '79
Romance with a Double Bass '74
And Now for Something Completely Different '72
Monty Python and the Holy Grail '75
The Statue '71
The Magic Christian '69
The Bliss of Mrs. Blossom '68
Interlude '68

Ellen Cleghorne (1965-)
MacArthur Park '01
Coyote Ugly '00
Little Nicky '00
Mr. Wrong '96

Jimmy Clem
The Town That Dreaded Sundown '76
Winterhawk '76

Paul Clemens (1958-)
The Beast Within '82
Promises in the Dark '79

Christian Clemenson (1959-)
United 93 '06
Hero '92
Bad Influence '90

Aurore Clement (1945-)
The Bridesmaid '04
Bon Voyage '03
For Sale '98
The Eighties '83
Paris, Texas '83
Invitation au Voyage '82
Toute Une Nuit '82
Les Rendez-vous D'Anne '78
Le Crabe Tambour '77

Suzanne Clement
2 Seconds '98
The Confessional '95

Pierre Clementi (1942-99)
Hideous Kinky '99
Sweet Movie '75
Steppenwolf '74
The Conformist '71
Partner '68
Belle de Jour '67
The Leopard '63

Corinne Clery (1950-)
Dangerous Obsession '88
Yor, the Hunter from the Future '83
Love by Appointment '76
The Story of O '75
Moonraker '79

Carol Cleveland (1943-)
Monty Python's The Meaning of Life '83
Monty Python's The Life of Brian '79
Monty Python and the Holy Grail '75
And Now for Something Completely Different '72

George Cleveland (1886-1957)
Miss Grant Takes Richmond '49
Trigger, Jr. '50
Rimfire '49
The Wistful Widow of Wagon Gap '47
Little Giant '46
The Show-Off '46
Abroad with Two Yanks '44
It Happened Tomorrow '44
Texas Legionnaires '43
Valley of the Sun '42
Nevada City '41
Two-Faced Woman '41
Playmates '41
Drums of Fu Manchu '40
Hidden Enemy '40
Midnight Limited '40
The Abe Lincoln of Ninth Avenue '40
Tomboy '40
Mutiny in the Big House '39
Ghost Town Riders '38
I Conquer the Sea '36
Revolt of the Zombies '36
Monte Carlo Nights '34

Clarence Clemons (1941-)
Swing '98
Fatal Instinct '93

John Clements (1910-88)
Oh! What a Lovely War '69
The Silent Enemy '58
Train of Events '49
This England '42
Convoy '40
The Four Feathers '39
South Riding '37

Stanley Clements (1926-81)
Timber Tramp?
The Harder They Come '72
A Bullet for Joey '55
The Finger Man '55
Hercules '61
Teenage Frankenstein '58
The Three Stooges Meet Hercules '62
Boating '74

David Clennon (1943-)
Saving Sarah Cain '07
Life of the Party '05
Syriana '05
Silver City '04
The Visit '00
From the Earth to the Moon '98
Tecumseh: The Last Warrior '95
And the Band Played On '93
Matinee '93
Light Sleeper '92
Man Trouble '92
The Trouble with Dick '88
Conspiracy: The Trial of the Chicago Eight '87
The Couch Trip '87
Legal Eagles '86
Sweet Dreams '85
Falling in Love '84
Hanna K. '83
The Right Stuff '83
Star 80 '83
The Thing '82
Missing '82
The Con Artists '80
Fatal Fix '80
Moonraker '79
Insanity '76
Going All the Way '97
Sins of the Mind '97
Honor Thy Father and Mother: The True Story of the Menendez Brothers '94

Philippe Clevenot (1942-2001)
Place Vendome '98
The Hairdresser's Husband '92
Celine and Julie Go Boating '74

Jimmy Cliff (1948-)
Club Paradise '86
The Harder They Come '72
Rude Boy: The Jamaican Don '03

John Cliff (1918-2001)
Johnny Holiday '49
Underworld Scandal '47
On the Sunny Side '42

David Clennon (1943-)
The Four Feathers '39
Convoy '40
This England '42

Jack Clifford (1880-1956)
King of the Pecos '36
The Revenge Rider '35
The Man from Gun Town '36
Law of the Sea '32
South of Santa Fe '32

Sunrise Trail '31
Sweet Adeline '26

Richard Clifford
Carrington '95
Much Ado about Nothing '93
Henry V '89

Faith Clift
Savage Journey '83
Cataclysm '81

Montgomery Clift (1920-66)
Judgment at Nuremberg '61
The Misfits '61
Suddenly, Last Summer '59
Lonelyhearts '58
The Young Lions '58
Raintree County '57
Indiscretion of an American Wife '54
From Here to Eternity '53
I Confess '53
A Place in the Sun '51
The Big Lift '50
The Heiress '49
Red River '48
The Search '48

Elmer Clifton (1892-1949)
Intolerance '16
The Birth of a Nation '15

Brett Climo (1964-)
Double Vision '02

Emily Cline (1969-)
Dead Dog '00
In the Company of Men '96

Renee Cline
Fatal Exposure '90
Invasion Force '90
Lock 'n' Load '90

George Clinton (1941-)
Good Burger '97
P.C.U. '94
Graffiti Bridge '90

Colin Clive (1898-1937)
History Is Made at Night '37
The Bride of Frankenstein '35
Mad Love '35
Jane Eyre '34
Christopher Strong '33
Frankenstein '31

E.E. Clive (1879-1940)
The Adventures of Sherlock Holmes '39
Bulldog Drummond's Bride '39
Bulldog Drummond's Secret Police '39
The Hound of the Baskervilles '39
The Little Princess '39
The Bride of Frankenstein '35
The Mystery of Edwin Drood '35
The Invisible Man '33

John Clive (1938-)
A Clockwork Orange '71
Yellow Submarine '68 (V)

Teagan Clive
Vice Academy 2 '90
Alienator '89
Sinbad of the Seven Seas '89
Interzone '88

Al Cliver (1951-)
Demonia '90
2020 Texas Gladiators '85
The Beyond '81
Alien Contamination '81
The Black Cat '81
Zombie '80
Naked Paradise '78
Big Boss '77
Mr. Scarface '77
Rulers of the City '76
Forever Emmanuelle '75

Kristen Cloke (1970-)
Black Christmas '06
Final Destination '00

George Clooney (1961-)
Leatherheads '08
Michael Clayton '07
Ocean's Thirteen '07
The Good German '06
Good Night, and Good Luck '05
Syriana '05
Ocean's Twelve '04
Intolerable Cruelty '03
Spy Kids 3-D: Game Over '03
Confessions of a Dangerous Mind '02
Solaris '02
Welcome to Collinwood '02
Ocean's Eleven '01
Spy Kids '01
Fail Safe '00
O Brother Where Art Thou? '00
The Perfect Storm '00
South Park: Bigger, Longer and Uncut '99 (V)
Three Kings '99
Out of Sight '98
The Thin Red Line '98
Batman and Robin '97
The Peacemaker '97
One Fine Day '96
From Dusk Till Dawn '95
The Magic Bubble '93
Red Surf '90
Return of the Killer Tomatoes! '88
Return to Horror High '87
Combat Academy '86

Rosemary Clooney (1928-2002)
Deep in My Heart '54
Red Garters '54
White Christmas '54
Here Come the Girls '53

Del Close (1935-99)
Mommy 2: Mommy's Day '96
Opportunity Knocks '90
The Blob '88
Big Town '87
Ferris Bueller's Day Off '86

Eric Close (1967-)
Taken '02
Follow the Stars Home '01
The Magnificent Seven '98

Glenn Close (1947-)
Evening '07
The Chumscrubber '05
Hoodwinked '05 (V)
Nine Lives '05
Tarzan 2 '05 (V)
Heights '04
The Stepford Wives '04
Brush with Fate '03
Le Divorce '03
The Lion in Winter '03
Pinocchio '02 (V)
The Safety of Objects '01
102 Dalmatians '00
Baby '00 (N)
Things You Can Tell Just by Looking at Her '00
Cookie's Fortune '99
Sarah, Plain and Tall: Winter's End '99
Tarzan '99 (V)
Air Force One '97
In the Gloaming '97
Paradise Road '97
Mars Attacks! '96
101 Dalmatians '96
Mary Reilly '95
Serving in Silence: The Margarethe Cammermeyer Story '95
The Paper '94
The House of the Spirits '93
Sarah, Plain and Tall '91
Hook '91
Meeting Venus '91
Hamlet '90
Reversal of Fortune '90
Immediate Family '89
Dangerous Liaisons '88
Light Years '88 (V)
Fatal Attraction '87
The Jagged Edge '85
Maxie '85
The Natural '84
The Stone Boy '84
The Big Chill '83
The World According to Garp '82
Orphan Train '79
Too Far to Go '79

John Close (1921-63)
The Slime People '63
Beginning of the End '57
The Finger Man '55
Above and Beyond '53

Joshua Close (1981-)
Diary of the Dead '07
Full of It '07
The Exorcism of Emily Rose '05
Twist '05

John Scott Clough (1960-)
Phantoms '97
What Ever Happened To... '93
Gross Anatomy '89
Fast Forward '84

Raymond Cloutier (1945-)
Karmina '96
Riel '79

Vera Clouzot (1921-60)
Diabolique '55
Wages of Fear '55

David Clover
Zipperface '92
Ten Speed '76

Jennifer Cluff (1956-)
Death Games '80

Martin Clunes (1963-)
Goodbye, Mr. Chips '02
Rock My World '02
Lorna Doone '01
Saving Grace '00
The Acid House '98
Shakespeare in Love '98
Sweet Revenge '98

George Clutesi (1905-88)
Nightwing '79
Prophecy '79

Francois Cluzet (1955-)
Late August, Early September '98
The Swindle '97
French Kiss '95
The Horseman on the Roof '95
Les Apprentis '95
Ready to Wear '94
A Wind from Wyoming '94
L'Enfer '93
Olivier, Olivier '92
Chocolat '88
The Story of Women '88
Too Beautiful for You '88
Round Midnight '86
Elsa, Elsa '85
The Horse of Pride '80

Andy Clyde (1892-1967)
Carolina Cannonball '55
Hopalong Cassidy: Borrowed Trouble '48
Hopalong Cassidy: Dangerous Venture '48
Hopalong Cassidy: False Paradise '48
Hopalong Cassidy: Silent Conflict '48
Hopalong Cassidy: Sinister Journey '48
Hopalong Cassidy: The Dead Don't Dream '48
Sundown Riders '48
Hopalong Cassidy: Hoppy's Holiday '47
Hopalong Cassidy: The Marauders '47
Hopalong Cassidy: Unexpected Guest '47
Hopalong Cassidy: The Devil's Playground '46
Mystery Man '44
Texas Masquerade '44
Border Patrol '43
Colt Comrades '43
False Colors '43
Hopalong Cassidy: Riders of the Deadline '43
Hoppy Serves a Writ '43
Leather Burners '43
Lost Canyon '43
Border Vigilantes '41
Doomed Caravan '41
In Old Colorado '41
Outlaws of the Desert '41
Riders of the Timberline '41
Twilight on the Trail '41
Bad Lands '39
Red Lights Ahead '36
Yellow Dust '36
Annie Oakley '35
Village Tale '35
Ships in the Night '28

Jeremy Clyde (1944-)
The Musketeer '01
Kaspar Hauser '93
Splitting Heirs '93

June Clyde (1909-87)
Behind the Mask '46
Seven Doors to Death '44
Make-Up '37
She Shall Have Music '36
Hollywood Mystery '34
A Study in Scarlet '33
Wayne Murder Case '32
Branded Men '31
Morals for Women '31

Kim Coates (1959-)
Hero Wanted '08
Alien Agent '07
Grilled '06
Silent Hill '06
Assault on Precinct 13 '05
Hostage '05
The Island '05
Hollywood North '03
Open Range '03
Black Hawk Down '01
Pearl Harbor '01
Battlefield Earth '00
Beyond Suspicion '00
Full Disclosure '00
Killing Moon '00
Xchange '00
Carpool '96
Dead Silence '96
Lethal Tender '96
Unforgettable '96
Breach of Trust '95
Waterworld '95
Black Fox: Good Men and Bad '94
The Club '94
The Spider and the Fly '94
Innocent Blood '92
The Last Boy Scout '91
The Amityville Curse '90
Red Blooded American Girl '90
Smokescreen '90
Blind Fear '89
Cold Front '89

Phyllis Coates (1927-)
The Incredible Petrified World '58
Teenage Frankenstein '58
El Paso Stampede '53
Jungle Drums of Africa '53
Marshal of Cedar Rock '53
Invasion U.S.A. '52
Superman & the Mole Men '51
Blues Busters '50

Edmund Cobb (1892-1974)
Tales of Terror '62
Guns of Fury '49
Far Frontier '48
Buffalo Bill Rides Again '47
Son of Zorro '47
Renegade Girl '46
Santa Fe Uprising '46
Sunset in El Dorado '45
Lawmen '44
Texas Kid '43
Tonto Basin Outlaws '41
Wild Horse Rodeo '37
Darkest Africa '36
Danger Trails '35
Rustler's Paradise '35
Gunners & Guns '34
Gun Law '33
Wild Horse '31
Riders of the Range '24

Irvin S. Cobb
Hawaii Calls '38
Steamboat Round the Bend '35

Lee J. Cobb (1911-76)
That Lucky Touch '75
The Exorcist '73
Macho Callahan '70
The Liberation of L.B. Jones '70
Lawman '71
Bull of the West '71
Coogan's Bluff '68
MacKenna's Gold '69
In Like Flint '67
The Meanest Men in the West '67
Our Man Flint '66
Come Blow Your Horn '63
How the West Was Won '63
The Four Horsemen of the Apocalypse '62
Exodus '60
But Not for Me '59
Green Mansions '59
The Trap '59
The Brothers Karamazov '58
Man of the West '58
Party Girl '58
The Three Faces of Eve '57
Twelve Angry Men '57
The Man in the Gray Flannel Suit '56
The Left Hand of God '55
The Racers '55
Day of Triumph '54
On the Waterfront '54
Tall Texan '53
The Fighter '52
Sirocco '51
The Dark Past '49
Call Northside 777 '48
The Miracle of the Bells '48
Boomerang! '47
Captain from Castile '47
Anna and the King of Siam '46
Buckskin Frontier '43
The Song of Bernadette '43
Men of Boys Town '41
Golden Boy '39
Danger on the Air '38
Rustler's Valley '37

Randall "Tex" Cobb (1950-)
Liar Liar '97
Diggstown '92
Raw Nerve '91
Blind Fury '90
Ernest Goes to Jail '90
Buy & Cell '89
Fletch Lives '89
Raising Arizona '87
The Golden Child '86
Uncommon Valor '83

Bill Cobbs (1935-)
The Ultimate Gift '07
Night at the Museum '06
Enough '02
Sunshine State '02
Random Hearts '99
Always Outnumbered Always Outgunned '98
Hope Floats '98
I Still Know What You Did Last Summer '98
Paulie '98
Air Bud '97
Ed '96
First Kid '96
Ghosts of Mississippi '96
Nightjohn '96
That Thing You Do! '96
Fluke '95
Kingfish: A Story of Huey P. Long '95
Man with a Gun '95
Out There '95
Pocahontas '95 (V)
Things to Do in Denver When You're Dead '95
Demolition Man '93
The Hudsucker Proxy '93
The Bodyguard '92
Carolina Skeletons '92
Decoration Day '90
Dominick & Eugene '88
Trading Places '83

Roberto Cobo (1930-2002)
Santitos '99
Esmeralda Comes by Night '98
Cabeza de Vaca '90
Los Olvidados '50

German Cobos
Cria Cuervos '76
Hawk and Castile '67

Charles Coburn (1877-1961)
John Paul Jones '59
Around the World in 80 Days '56
Gentlemen Prefer Blondes '53
Trouble along the Way '53
Monkey Business '52
Mr. Music '50
Impact '49
Lured '47
The Paradine Case '47
Colonel Effingham's Raid '45
Rhapsody in Blue '45
Wilson '44
Heaven Can Wait '43
The More the Merrier '43
George Washington Slept Here '42
In This Our Life '42
The Devil & Miss Jones '41
Kings Row '41
The Lady Eve '41
Edison the Man '40
The Road to Singapore '40
Three Faces West '40
Bachelor Mother '39
Idiot's Delight '39
In Name Only '39
Made for Each Other '39
Stanley and Livingstone '39
The Story of Alexander Graham Bell '39
Of Human Hearts '38
Vivacious Lady '38

James Coburn (1928-2002)
American Gun '02
Snow Dogs '02
The Man from Elysian Fields '01
Monsters, Inc. '01 (V)
Walter and Henry '01
Missing Pieces '00
Proximity '00
Noah's Ark '99
Dean Koontz's Mr. Murder '98
Payback '99
Affliction '97
The Second Civil War '97
The Cherokee Kid '96
Eraser '96

[James Coburn, continued]
Keys to Tulsa '96 · The Nutty Professor '96 · Skeletons '96 · A Christmas Reunion '93 · The Avenging Angel '95 · The Disappearance of Kevin Johnson '95 · The Set Up '95 · Maverick '94 · Deadfall '93 · The Hit List '93 · Hudson Hawk '91 · Sister Act 2: Back in the Habit '93 · Hugh Hefner: Once Upon a Time '92 (N) · Masterpiece '92 · The Player '92 · A Thousand Heroes '92 · Young Guns 2 '90 · Death of a Soldier '85 · Martin's Day '85 · Pinocchio '83 · Crossover '82 · Drawl '81 · High Risk '81 · Looker '81 · Loving Couples '80 · Firepower '79 · Goldengirl '79 · The Muppet Movie '79 · The Dain Curse '78 · Cross of Iron '76 · The Last Hard Men '76 · Midway '76 · Sky Riders '76 · Bite the Bullet '75 · Hard Times '75 · Internecine Project '73 · Pat Garrett & Billy the Kid '73 · A Reason to Live, a Reason to Die '73 · A Fistful of Dynamite '72 · Candy '68 · In Like Flint '67 · The President's Analyst '67 · Waterhole Number 3 '67 · Dead Heat on a Merry-Go-Round '66 · Our Man Flint '66 · What Did You Do in the War, Daddy? '66 · The Loved One '65 · Major Dundee '65 · The Americanization of Emily '64 · Charade '63 · The Great Escape '63 · Hell Is for Heroes '62 · The Magnificent Seven '60 · Ride Lonesome '59

Michael Coby (1943-)
The Bitch '79 · Supersonic Man '78

Imogene Coca (1908-2001)
Alice in Wonderland '85 · National Lampoon's Vacation '83 · The Return of the Beverly Hillbillies '81 · Rabbit Test '78 · Under the Yum-Yum Tree '63

Richard Coca
The Truth about Cats and Dogs '96 · Street Knight '93 · Dogs '96

Eddie Cochran (1938-60)
Go, Johnny Go! '59 · The Girl Can't Help It '56

Robert Cochran (1904-99)
I Stand Condemned in Room 13 '38 · Sanders of the River '35

Shannon Cochran (1958-)
The Ring '02 · Star Trek: Nemesis '02

Steve Cochran (1917-65)
Deadly Companions '61

Michael Cochrane
Sharpe's Challenge '06 · A Different Loyalty '04 · Incognito '97 · Sharpe's Regiment '96 · Sharpe's Eagle '93

Rory Cochrane (1972-)
The Company '07 · Right at Your Door '06 · A Scanner Darkly '06 · Hart's War '02 · The Prime Gig '00 · Black & White '99 · Flawless '99 · Dogtown '97 · The Last Don '97 · Empire Records '95 · The Low Life '95 · Love and a .45 '94 · Dazed and Confused '93 · Fathers and Sons '92

Arlene Cockburn
The Acid House '98 · The Governess '98 · The Winter Guest '97

Gary Cockrell
Lolita '62 · War Lover '62

James Coco (1929-87)
That's Adequate '90 · The Chair '87 · Hunk '87 · You Can't Take It with You '84 · Only When I Laugh '81 · Wholly Moses! '80 · Scavenger Hunt '79 · The Cheap Detective '78 · Murder by Death '76 · Man of La Mancha '72 · A New Leaf '71 · End of the Road '70 · The Strawberry Statement '70 · Generation '69 · Ensign Pulver '64

Jean Cocteau (1889-1963)
The Testament of Orpheus '59

Camille Coduri (1966-)
King Ralph '91 · Nuns on the Run '90 · Strapless '89 · Hawks '89

Bill Cody (1891-1948)
Outlaws of the Range '36 · Frontier Days '34 · Ghost City '32 · Texas Pioneers '32 · Mason of the Mounted '32

Iron Eyes Cody (1904-99)
Spirit of '76 '91 · Ernest Goes to Camp '87 · Grayeagle '77 · The Longest Drive '76 · El Condor '70 · Sitting Bull '54 · Son of Paleface '52 · Bowery Buckaroos '47 · Under Nevada Skies '46 · King of the Stallions '42 · Texas Pioneers '32

Kathleen (Kathy) Cody (1953-)
Charley and the Angel '73 · Girls on the Road '73 · Superdad '73 · Dr. Death, Seeker of Souls '73

Lew Cody (1884-1934)
Dishonored '31

Frederick Coffin (1943-2003)
Identity '03 · The Base '99 · Andersonville '95

Tristram Coffin (1909-90)
Good Neighbor Sam '64 · Ma Barker's Killer Brood '60 · Queen for a Day '51 · Rodeo King and the Senorita '51 · King of the Rocketmen '49 · Lost Planet Airmen '49 · Tonto Basin Outlaws '41 · Us in the Air '40 · West of Pinto Basin '40 · Under Nevada Skies '46 · The Corpse Vanishes '42 · Holt of the Secret Service '42 · Whistlin' Dan '32 · The Road to Yesterday '25 · There Goes My Baby '92 · Hard to Kill '89 · Shoot to Kill '88 · The Bedroom Window '87 · One Summer Love '76

Barry Coe (1934-)
The 300 Spartans '62 · But Not for Me '59 · The Bravados '58 · Peyton Place '57 · Love Me Tender '56 · House of Bamboo '55 · Lady Grey '82

David Allan Coe (1939-)
Take This Job & Shove It '81

George Coe
Corporate Affairs '07 · Diamond Men '01 · Big Eden '00 · The Omega Code '99 · Nick and Jane '96 · The End of Innocence '90 · The Hollywood Detective '89 · Best Seller '87 · Blind Date '87 · Uncle Tom's Cabin '87 · A Flash of Green '85 · Remo Williams: The Adventure Begins '85 · Rage of Angels '83 · Sessions '83 · Bustin' Loose '81 · Red Flag: The Ultimate Game '81

Peter Coe (1918-93)
Sands of Iwo Jima '49 · House of Frankenstein '44 · The Mummy's Curse '44

Paul Coeur
White Fang 2: The Myth of the White Wolf '94

Colleen T. Coffey
Indecent Behavior 3 '95 · Relentless 4 '94

David Coffey
Lawless Heart '01

Denise Coffey (1936-)
Boyfriends '96 · Start the Revolution without Me '70 · Georgy Girl '66

Elizabeth Coffey
Female Trouble '74 · Pink Flamingos '72

Scott Coffey (1967-)
Inland Empire '06 (V) · Ellie Parker '05 · Mulholland Drive '01 · Route 9 '98 · Lost Highway '96 · Breaking Free '95 · Tank Girl '94 · Dream Lover '93 · The Temp '93 · Shag: The Movie '89 · Satisfaction '88 · Zombie High '87

Peter Coffield (1945-83)
Times Square '80 · The Man Without a Country '73

Frank "Junior" Coghlan (1917-)
The Adventures of Captain Marvel '41

Nikki Coghill (1964-)
Dark Age '88

Henri Cogan (1914-2003)
As If It Were Raining '63 · It Means That to Me '60

Helen Coker
Vera Drake '04 · All or Nothing '02

Catero Colbert
Up Against the Wall '91

Claudette Colbert (1903-96)
The Love Goddesses '65 · Parrish '61 · Texas Lady '56 · Let's Make It Legal '51 · Three Came Home '50 · The Egg and I '47 · Tomorrow Is Forever '46 · Without Reservations '46 · Guest Wife '45 · Since You Went Away '44 · So Proudly We Hail '43 · The Palm Beach Story '42 · Boom Town '40 · Drums Along the Mohawk '39 · Midnight '39 · Bluebeard's Eighth Wife '38 · Cleopatra '34 · Imitation of Life '34 · It Happened One Night '34 · I Cover the Waterfront '33 · The Sign of the Cross '33 · Misleading Lady '32 · The Smiling Lieutenant '31

Stephen Colbert (1964-)
Strangers with Candy '06 · Bewitched '05

Nicholas Colasanto (1924-85)
Raging Bull '80 · Mad Bull '77 · Family Plot '76 · Fat City '72

Enrico Colantoni (1963-)
The First $20 Million Is Always the Hardest '02 · Full Frontal '02 · A.I.: Artificial Intelligence '01 · Galaxy Quest '99 · Stigmata '99 · James Dean '01

Sammy Cohen (1902-81)
The Fighting 69th '40

Scott Cohen (1964-)
For One More Day '07 · Fatal Contact: Bird Flu in America '06 · Kissing Jessica Stein '02 · Vibrations '94 · The Wrong Guy '95 · Money Train '95 · The Wharf Rat '95 · Sweet Evil '95 · Gia '98 · Gotti '96 · The 10th Kingdom '00

Sacha Baron Cohen (1971-)
Sweeney Todd: The Demon Barber of Fleet Street '07 · Borat: Cultural Learnings of America for Make Benefit Glorious Nation of Kazakhstan '06 · Talladega Nights: The Ballad of Ricky Bobby '06 · Madagascar '05 (V) · The Jolly Boys' Last Stand '00

J.J. (Jeffrey Jay) Cohen (1965-)
The Principal '87 · Back to the Future, Part 3 '90 · Back to the Future, Part 2 '89 · Back to the Future '85

Emma Cohen (1946-)
Spaghetti Western '75 · Bronson's Revenge '72 · Horror Rises from the Tomb '72 · Cannibal Man '71

Alain Cohen (1958-)
Happily Ever After '04 · The Two of Us '68

Assi Cohen (1974-)
Yossi & Jagger '02

Kaipo Cohen (1978-)
Under the Domim Tree '95 · The Summer of Aviya '88

Lynn Cohen
Sex and the City: The Movie '08 · Munich '05 · The Jimmy Show '01 · Hurricane Streets '96 · I Shot Andy Warhol '96 · Walking and Talking '96 · Vanya on 42nd Street '94 · Manhattan Murder Mystery '93

Ben Cole
Edge of Sanity '89

Christina Cole (1982-)
Miss Pettigrew Lives for a Day '08 · Jane Eyre '06

Dennis Cole (1940-)
Dead End City '88 · Death House '88 · Pretty Smart '87 · Amateur Night '85 · The Barbary Coast '74 · The Connection '73 · Powder Keg '70

Eric Michael Cole (1976-)
Snapshots '02 · Outrage '98 · White Squall '96

Gary Cole (1957-)
Conspiracy '08 · Pineapple Express '08 · Breach '07 · One Hour Photo '02 · The Rising Place '02 · The Gift '00 · Office Space '99 · From the Earth to the Moon '98 · A Simple Plan '98 · Santa Fe '97 · Gang Related '96 · A Very Brady Sequel '96 · The Brady Bunch Movie '95 · Fall from Grace '94 · In the Line of Fire '93 · Son of the Morning Star '91 · The Old Man and the Sea '90 · Echoes in the Darkness '87 · Fatal Vision '84

George Cole (1925-)
Station Jim '01 · Mary Reilly '95 · Deadline Auto Theft '83 · Gone in 60 Seconds '74 · Fright '71 · The Vampire Lovers '70 · Dr. Syn, Alias the Scarecrow '64 · The Pure Hell of St. Trinian's '61 · Too Many Crooks '59 · Blue Murder at St. Trinian's '56 · The Adventures of Sadie '55 · The Belles of St. Trinian's '54 · A Christmas Carol '51 · The Spider and the Fly '49 · Cottage to Let '41

Jacqulin Cole
Satan's Cheerleaders '77

Kevin Anthony Cole (1945-)
Asylum '97 · Bad Bunch '76 · Undercover Cop '94

Michael Cole (1945-)
Mr. Brooks '07 · The Apostate '98 · Nickel Mountain '85 · Chuka '67

Nat King Cole (1919-65)
Cat Ballou '65 · China Gate '57 · Istanbul '57 · The Blue Gardenia '53 · Small Town Girl '53 · Killer Diller '48

Tim Colceri (1951-)
Leprechaun 4: In Space '96 · Full Metal Jacket '87

Helen Coker
Vera Drake '04 · All or Nothing '02

Natalie Cole (1950-)
De-Lovely '04
Livin' for Love: The Natalie Cole Story '00
Always Outnumbered Always Outgunned '98
Cats Don't Dance '97 (V)
Lily in Winter '94

Olivia Cole (1942-)
The Women of Brewster Place '89
The Fig Tree '87
North and South Book 1 '85
Go Tell It on the Mountain '84
Some Kind of Hero '82
Backstairs at the White House '79
Coming Home '78
Roots '77

Robert Coleby (1947-)
The Phantom '96
In Pursuit of Honor '95
Great Expectations: The Untold Story '87
The Blue Lightning '86
Now and Forever '82
Plumber '79

Bobby Coleman (1997-)
Martian Child '07
Glass House: The Good Mother '06

Charles Coleman (1885-1951)
Grand Canyon Trail '48
Twin Beds '42
It Started with Eve '41
Michael Shayne: Private Detective '40
First Love '39
That Certain Age '38
Bachelor Apartment '31

Charlotte Coleman (1968-2001)
Beautiful People '99
Bodywork '99
Sweet Revenge '98
Twice upon a Yesterday '98
Different for Girls '96
Four Weddings and a Funeral '94

Dabney Coleman (1932-)
Domino '05
Moonlight Mile '02
Giving It Up '99
Inspector Gadget '99
Must Be Santa '99
Stuart Little '99
Taken '99
My Date with the President's Daughter '98
You've Got Mail '98
Judicial Consent '94
Amos and Andrew '93
The Beverly Hillbillies '93
Clifford '92
Guilty of Innocence '87
Murrow '86
The Man with One Red Shoe '85
Cloak & Dagger '84
The Muppets Take Manhattan '84
WarGames '83
Tootsie '82
Young Doctors in Love '82
Callie and Son '81
Modern Problems '81
On Golden Pond '81
How to Beat the High Cost of Living '80
Melvin and Howard '80
9 to 5 '80
Nothing Personal '80
Pray TV '80
North Dallas Forty '79
Viva Knievel '77
Fist '76
Midway '76
Bite the Bullet '75
Homeboy '75
The Other Side of the Mountain '75
The Dove '74
Bad Ronald '74
Cinderella Liberty '73
Dying Room Only '73
The President's Plane Is Missing '71
Downhill Racer '69
The Trouble with Girls (and How to Get into It) '69
The Scalphunters '68

Gary Coleman (1968-)
Dirty Work '97
The Fantastic World of D.C. Collins '84
The Kid with the 200 I.Q. '83
Jimmy the Kid '82
The Kid with the Broken Halo '82
On the Right Track '81
Scout's Honor '80
The Kid from Left Field '79

Holliston Coleman (1992-)
Love's Unending Legacy '07
Lilo & Stitch 2: Stitch Has a Glitch '05 (V)
Bless the Child '00

Jack Coleman (1958-)
Beneath the Bermuda Triangle '98
The Landlady '98
Foreign Student '94
Trapped in Space '94
Rubdown '93
The Return of Eliot Ness '91
Daughter of Darkness '89
Return to Eden '89
Who's Harry Crumb? '89

Jimmy Coleman
Priest '94
Riff Raff '92

Monique Coleman
High School Musical 2 '07
High School Musical '06

Nancy Coleman (1912-2000)
Edge of Darkness '43
Desperate Journey '42
Kings Row '41

Oliver Coleman
The Other Boleyn Girl '08

Renee Coleman
The Line of Beauty '06
Pentathlon '94

Rosalyn Coleman (1965-)
Our Song '01
Mixing Nia '98
The Piano Lesson '94

Signy Coleman (1960-)
Miss Monday '98

Michael Coles (1936-)
The Satanic Rites of Dracula '73
Dracula A.D. 1972 '72

Mildred Coles (1920-95)
Oklahoma Badlands '48
So This Is Washington '43
Hurry, Charlie, Hurry '41
Lady Scarface '41

Caia Coley (1968-)
Are You Scared? '06
A Dead Calling '06

Eileen Colgan
The Secret of Roan Inish '94
Quackser Fortune Has a Cousin in the Bronx '70

John Colicos (1928-2000)
Jack Higgins' The Windsor Protocol '97
Jack Higgins' Thunder Point '97
The Last Don '97
Love and Hate: A Marriage Made in Hell '90
Shadow Dancing '88
The Changeling '80
Battlestar Galactica '78
Mission Galactica: The Cylon Attack '78
Scorpio '73
Raid on Rommel '71
Doctors' Wives '70
Anne of the Thousand Days '69
Murder on Approval '56

David Colin, Jr. (1968-)
Shock '79
Beyond the Door '75

Gregoire Colin (1975-)
The Intruder '04
Sade '00
Beau Travail '98
The Dreamlife of Angels '98
Nenette and Boni '96
Fiesta '95
Son of Gascogne '95
Before the Rain '94
Pas Tres Catholique '93
Olivier, Olivier '92

Ian Colin (1910-)
Never Too Late to Mend '37
Late Extra '35

Margaret Colin (1957-)
Deception '08
First Daughter '04
Blue Car '03
Unfaithful '02
My Husband's Double Life '01
The Adventures of Sebastian Cole '99
The Devil's Own '96
Independence Day '96
The Butcher's Wife '91
Martians Go Home! '90
Traveling Man '89
True Believer '89
Like Father, Like Son '87
Three Men and a Baby '87
Pretty in Pink '86
Something Wild '86

Christopher Collet (1968-)
Stephen King's The Langoliers '95
Prayer of the Rollerboys '91
The Manhattan Project '86
First Born '84
Sleepaway Camp '83

Toni Collette (1972-)
Evening '07
The Dead Girl '06
Little Miss Sunshine '06
Murderous Intent '06
The Night Listener '06
In Her Shoes '05
Connie and Carla '04
The Last Shot '04
Japanese Story '03
About a Boy '02
Changing Lanes '02
Dirty Deeds '02
The Hours '02
Dinner with Friends '01
Shaft '00
8 1/2 Women '99
The Sixth Sense '99
The Boys '98
Velvet Goldmine '98
Clockwatchers '97
Emma '96
The Thief and the Cobbler '96 (V)
Cosi '95
Lilian's Story '95
The Pallbearer '96
Muriel's Wedding '94
The Efficiency Expert '92

Kenneth Colley (1937-)
Prisoner of Honor '91
The Rainbow '89
A Summer Story '88
Casanova '87
And Nothing But the Truth '82
Firefox '82
Lisztomania '75
The Music Lovers '71

Ombretta Colli
Terror of the Steppes '64
Gladiator of Rome '63

Mark Collie (1956-)
The Punisher '04
Jericho '01
The Kid with the X-Ray Eyes '99
Fire Down Below '97

Constance Collier (1878-1955)
Rope '48
The Perils of Pauline '47
Dark Corner '46
Monsieur Beaucaire '46
Half a Soldier '40
Thunder in the City '37
Wee Willie Winkie '37

Lois Collier (1919-99)
A Night in Casablanca '46
The Naughty Nineties '45
Cobra Woman '44
Jungle Woman '44

William "Buster" Collier, Jr. (1902-87)
Phantom Express '32
Cimarron '31
Street Scene '31

John Collin (1901-80)
Tess '79
The Witches '66
Start '68

Patricia Collinge (1892-1974)
Casanova Brown '44
Tender Comrade '43

Anne Collings
Return to Africa '89
The Mask '61

Peter Collingwood
The Wacky World of Wills & Burke '85
Morgan: A Suitable Case for Treatment '66

Alan Collins (1927-)
Exterminators in the Year 3000 '83
Tornado '83
Ark of the Sun God '82
Hunters of the Golden Cobra '82
The Last Hunter '80
Hatchet for the Honeymoon '70
And God Said to Cain '69
Hyena of London '62

Chris Collins
Detention '03
Owning Mahowny '03

Clifton (Gonzalez) Collins, Jr. (1970-)
Capote '05
Dirty '05
Life of the Party '05
Mindhunters '05
Rampage: The Hillside Strangler Murders '04
Undefeated '03
I Witness '03
The Rules of Attraction '02
The Last Castle '01
Price of Glory '00
Tigerland '00
Traffic '00
Light It Up '99
The Replacement Killers '98
The Wonderful Ice Cream Suit '98

Cora Sue Collins (1927-)
The World Accuses '35
Evelyn Prentice '34
The Scarlet Letter '34

Dean Collins (1990-)
Hoot '06
Yours, Mine & Ours '05

Eddie Collins (1884-1940)
The Blue Bird '40
Drums Along the Mohawk '39
Young Mr. Lincoln '39
Charlie Chan in Honolulu '38

G. Pat Collins (1895-1959)
Above and Beyond '53
All Quiet on the Western Front '30
Be Yourself '30

Gary Collins (1938-)
Beautiful '00
Watchers Reborn '98
Hangar 18 '80
Airport '70

Greg Collins
Operation Delta Force 3: Clear Target '98
U.S. Seals '98

Jessica Collins (1971-)
Dirty Love '05
Best of the Best: Without Warning '98

Joan Collins (1933-)
These Old Broads '01
The Flintstones in Viva Rock Vegas '00
Joseph and the Amazing Technicolor Dreamcoat '00
Annie: A Royal Adventure '95
A Midwinter's Tale '95
Game for Vultures '86
Monte Carlo '86
Sins '85
Cartier Affair '84
Nutcracker Sweet '84
Her Life as a Man '83
Hansel and Gretel '82
Homework '82
Sunburn '79
The Big Sleep '78
The Bitch '78
The Stud '78
Zero to Sixty '78
Empire of the Ants '77
Fearless '77
The Bawdy Adventures of Tom Jones '76
Great Adventure '75
I Don't Want to Be Born '75
Oh, Alfie '75
Dark Places '73
Tales That Witness Madness '73
Dynasty of Fear '72
Tales from the Crypt '72
Quest for Love '71
Revenge '71
The Executioner '70
Three in the Cellar '70
Subterfuge '68
The Road to Hong Kong '62
Esther and the King '60
Seven Thieves '60
The Bravados '58
Rally 'Round the Flag, Boys! '58
Sea Wife '57
Stopover Tokyo '57
The Opposite Sex '56
The Adventures of Sadie '55
The Girl in the Red Velvet Swing '55
Land of the Pharaohs '55
The Virgin Queen '55
Decameron Nights '53
Tough Guy '53

Judy Collins (1939-)
A Town Has Turned to Dust '98
Junior '94

K.C. Collins
Animal 2 '07
Poor Man's Game '06

Kevin Collins
Edward II '92
The Garden '90

Lewis Collins (1946-)
Jack the Ripper '88
Codename: Wildgeese '84
The Final Option '82

Lynn Collins (1979-)
Numb '07
The Number 23 '07
Bug '06
The Dog Problem '06
The Lake House '06
The Merchant of Venice '04

Misha Collins
Karla '06
Finding Home '03

Mo Collins
Danny Roane: First Time Director '06
Jiminy Glick in LaLa Wood '05

Monte (Monty) Collins (1856-1929)
King of Kings '27
Our Hospitality '23

Monte (Monty) Collins, Jr. (1898-1951)
House of Errors '42
Midnight Limited '40

Patricia Collins
Speaking Parts '89
Pin... '88
When Angels Fly '82
Summer's Children '79

Patrick Collins
Friends and Family '01
Dirt Bike Kid '86

Pauline Collins (1940-)
My Mother's Courage '95
Paradise Road '97
City of Joy '92
Shirley Valentine '89

Phil Collins (1951-)
The Jungle Book 2 '03 (V)
Balto '95 (V)
And the Band Played On '93
Frauds '93
Hook '91
Buster '88
Secret Policeman's Private Parts '81

Ray Collins (1889-1965)
Touch of Evil '58
Solid Gold Cadillac '56
Desperate Hours '55
The Go-Getter '54
The Desert Song '53
Ma and Pa Kettle on Vacation '53
I Want You '51
Ma and Pa Kettle Back On the Farm '51
The Racket '51
Kill the Umpire '50
Ma and Pa Kettle Go to Town '50
Summer Stock '50
The Fountainhead '49
Francis the Talking Mule '49
The Heiress '49
It Happens Every Spring '49
Man from Colorado '49
Command Decision '48
For the Love of Mary '48
Good Sam '48
Homecoming '48
The Bachelor and the Bobby-Soxer '47

A Double Life '47
The Best Years of Our Lives '46
Crack-Up '46
Can't Help Singing '45
Leave Her to Heaven '45
The Seventh Cross '44
Commandos Strike at Dawn '43
The Human Comedy '43
Whistling in Brooklyn '43
The Magnificent Ambersons '42
The Navy Comes Through '42
Citizen Kane '41

Rick Collins
The Toxic Avenger, Part 3: The Last Temptation of Toxie '89
The Toxic Avenger, Part 2 '89

Roberta Collins (1946-)
Hardbodies '84
Whiskey Mountain '77
Eaten Alive '76
Death Race 2000 '75
Caged Heat '74
The Deadly and the Beautiful '73
Unholy Rollers '72
The Big Doll House '71
The Arousers '70

Russell Collins (1897-1965)
The Matchmaker '58
Enemy Below '57
Savage Wilderness '55
Soldier of Fortune '55
Niagara '52

Ruth (Coreen) Collins (1947-)
Because I Said So '07
Blood Diamond '06
Wildest Dreams '90
Cemetery High '89
Death Collector '89
Doom Asylum '86
Exquisite Corpses '88
Scarlet '94
Sexpot '88
High Stakes '89
Galactic Gigolo '87
New York's Finest '87

Stephen Collins (1947-)
The Big Picture '89
Stella '89
Weekend War '88
Choke Canyon '86
Hold the Dream '86
Jumpin' Jack Flash '86
Brewster's Millions '85
Chiefs '83
Inside the Third Reich '82
Summer Solstice '81
The Henderson Monster '80
Loving Couples '80
The Promise '79
Star Trek: The Motion Picture '79
Between the Lines '77
All the President's Men '76

Wayne Collins
Way Past Cool '00
Bebe's Kids '92 (V)

Madeleine Collinson (1952-)
Twins of Evil '71

Mary Collinson (1952-)
The Love Machine '71
Twins of Evil '71

Frank Collison (1950-)
The Happening '08
Hidalgo '04
The Village '04
The Whole Ten Yards '04
O Brother Where Art Thou? '00
Dollman '90

Silvia Colloca (1977-)
The Detonator '06
Van Helsing '04

Mark Collver
Bix '90

Roy Collodi
The Girl, the Body and the Pill '67

June Collyer (1907-68)
A Face in the Fog '36
The Ghost Walks '34
Drums of Jeopardy '31
Four Sons '28
Hangman's House '28

Ronald Colman (1891-1958)
Around the World in 80 Days '56
Champagne for Caesar '50
A Double Life '47
Random Harvest '42
Talk of the Town '42
Lucky Partners '40
If I Were King '38
Lost Horizon '37
Prisoner of Zenda '37
A Tale of Two Cities '36
Arrowsmith '32
Raffles '30
Bulldog Drummond '29
Condemned '29
The Winning of Barbara Worth '26
Romola '25
The White Sister '23

Olivia Colman (1974-)
Hot Fuzz '07
Confetti '06

Pamela Collyer
The Kiss '88
Evil Judgment '85

Scott Colomby (1952-)
Caddyshack '80
Porky's '82
Porky's Revenge '85
Porky's 2: The Next Day '83

Alex Colon (1941-95)
Death of an Angel '86
Invasion U.S.A. '85

Miriam Colon (1945-)
Goal! The Dream Begins '05
All the Pretty Horses '00
Lone Star '95
Sabrina '95
The House of the Spirits '93
A Life of Sin '92

Jerry Colonna (1904-86)
Meet Me in Las Vegas '56
Alice in Wonderland '51 (V)
Kentucky Jubilee '51
Strictly G.I. '44
The Road to Singapore '40
Rosalie '38

Franco (Columbo) Columbu (1941-)
Pretty Persuasion '05
Desperate Crimes '93
Beretta's Island '92
Circle Man '87
Last Man Standing '87

Anjanette Comer (1942-)
Larry McMurtry's Streets of Laredo '95
The Underneath '95
Netherworld '90
Dead of Night '77
Death Stalk '74
Terror on the 40th Floor '74
The Baby '72
Night of a Thousand Cats '72
The Appaloosa '66

Robbie Coltrane (1950-)
Harry Potter and the Order of the Phoenix '07
Alex Rider: Operation Stormbreaker '06
Harry Potter and the Goblet of Fire '05
Harry Potter and the Prisoner of Azkaban '04
Ocean's Twelve '04
Van Helsing '04
Harry Potter and the Chamber of Secrets '02
From Hell '01
Harry Potter and the Sorcerer's Stone '01
The World Is Not Enough '99
Frogs for Snakes '98
Message in a Bottle '98
Buddy '97
The Ebb-Tide '97
Montana '97
Cracker: Best Boys '95
Cracker: Brotherly Love '95
Cracker: True Romance '95
Goldeneye '95
Cracker: Men Should Weep '94
Cracker: The Big Crunch '94
Cracker: To Be a Somebody '94
The Adventures of Huck Finn '93
Oh, What a Night '92
Perfectly Normal '91
The Pope Must Die '91
Nuns on the Run '90
Where the Heart Is '90
Bert Rigby, You're a Fool '89
Henry V '89
Let It Ride '89
Slipstream '89
Wonderland '88
Loose Connections '87
Caravaggio '86
Mona Lisa '86
Defense of the Realm '85
National Lampoon's European Vacation '85
Chinese Boxes '84

Jacque Lynn Colton (1939-)
Heartbreak Hotel '88

Mike Colter (1976-)
Million Dollar Baby '04
The Dreamers '03

Jeffrey Combs (1954-)
Sweet Hearts Dance '88
Born on the Fourth of July '89
House on Haunted Hill '99
I Still Know What You Did Last Summer '98
Spoiler '98
Time Tracers '97
Cyberstalker '96
The Frighteners '96
Castle Freak '95
Love and a .45 '94
Lurking Fear '94
H.P. Lovecraft's Necronomicon: Book of the Dead '93
The Guyver '91
The Pit & the Pendulum '91
Doctor Mordrid: Master of the Unknown '90
Trancers 2: The Return of Jack Deth '90
Bride of Re-Animator '89
Cellar Dweller '87
Cyclone '87
Phantom Empire '87
From Beyond '86
Re-Animator '84

Ryan Combs (1974-)
Straight out of Compton '99
I Accidentally Domed Your Son '04

Muriel Combeau
Near Misses '91
Marra, There's a Man in Your Bed '94

Holly Marie Combs (1973-)
Ocean's Eleven '01
Our Mother's Murder '97
Chain of Desire '93
Dr. Giggles '92
Simple Men '92
Born on the Fourth of July '89

Sean (Puffy, Puff Daddy, P. Diddy) Combs (1969-)
A Raisin in the Sun '08
Carlito's Way: Rise to Power '05
Made '01
Monster's Ball '01

Andy Comeau
One Hour Photo '02
8 Heads in a Duffel Bag '96

Maurice Compte
All the Real Girls '03

Joyce Compton (1907-97)
A Southern Yankee '48
Scared to Death '46
Christmas in Connecticut '45
Silver Spurs '43
I Take This Oath '40
Balalaika '39
Escape to Paradise '39
Rose of Washington Square '39
The Awful Truth '37
Sea Racketeers '37
Small Town Boy '37
County Gentlemen '36
Let 'Em Have It '35
Rustlers of Red Dog '35
King Kelly of the U.S.A. '34

Fay Compton (1894-1978)
Cold Comfort Farm '71
The Haunting '63
The Story of Esther Costello '57
Othello '52
The Mill on the Floss '37
Robinson Crusoe '36
Fidel '02

Joyce Compton (1907-97)
The Dream Catcher '99

Martin Compston (1984-)
A Guide to Recognizing Your Saints '06
Red Road '06
Sweet Sixteen '02
The Great Gabbo '29
The Port of Missing Girls '28

Betty Compson (1897-1974)
Hard-Boiled Mahoney '47
The Invisible Ghost '41
Mad Youth '40
Mystic Circle Murder '39
God's Country and the Man '37
A Slight Case of Murder '38
Bulldog Edition '36
The Lady Refuses '31
Inside the Lines '30
The Great Gabbo '29
The Docks of New York '28
The Barker '28
Paths to Paradise '25
The Pony Express '25

Jack Colvin (1934-2005)
Child's Play '88
The Incredible Hulk Returns '88
The Incredible Hulk '77

Michael Colyar
House Party 3 '94
Hot Shots! Part Deux '93

Richard Comar
Eberezer '97

Perry Como (1912-2001)
Words and Music '48
Doll Face '46
If I'm Lucky '46
Something for the Boys '44

Rosella Como (1939-86)
How to Kill 400 Duponts '68
The Seven Hills of Rome '58

Oliver Conant (1955-)
Class of '44 '73
Summer of '42 '71

Juliette Compton (1899-1989)
No One Man '32
Strangers in Love '32
Square '39
The Awful Truth '37
False Faces '32

O'Neal Compton (1951-)
Kill Me... Later '01
Big Eden '00
Life '99
Deep Impact '98
Roadracers '94
Attack of the 50 Ft. Woman '93

Danny Comden
Pretty Persuasion '05
Sol Goode '01

Franco (Columbo) Columbu (1941-)
Taken Alive '95

Coluche (1944-86)
My Best Friend's Girl '84
Tchao Pantin '84

Catherine Colvey
Captive '03
Levity '03

Peter Colvey
Dead Silent '99
Silent Hunter '94

Pinto Colvig (1892-1967)
Sleeping Beauty '59 (V)
Snow White and the Seven Dwarfs '37 (V)

Clara Colosimo (1922-94)
Orchestra Rehearsal '78
Alfredo, Alfredo '72

Vince Colosimo (1966-)
After the Deluge '03
The Hard Word '02
Walking on Water '02
Lantana '01
Chopper '00

Dorothy Comingore (1913-71)
The Big Night '51
The Hairy Ape '44
Citizen Kane '41

Common
Street Kings '08
Wanted '08
American Gangster '07
Smokin' Aces '06

Cristi Conaway (1965-)
The Colony '98
Batman Returns '92

Jeff Conaway (1950-)
My Brother's War '97
Intimate Betrayal '96
Nina Takes a Lover '94
Almost Pregnant '92
Bikini Summer 2 '92
Mirror Images '91
Sunset Strip '91
A Time to Die '91
Total Exposure '91
The Sleeping Car '90
The Banker '89
Ghost Writer '89
The Patriot '86
Covergirl '83
For the Love of It '80
Grease '78
Breaking Up Is Hard to Do '79

James Congdon (1929-)
Summerdog '78
The 4D Man '59

Kerry Condon (1983-)
Ned Kelly '03
How Harry Became a Tree '01

Chester Conklin (1888-1971)
The Great Dictator '40
Modern Times '36
Hallelujah, I'm a Bum '33
The Virginian '29
We're in the Navy Now '27
Behind the Front '26
The Nervous Wreck '26
Battling Bunyon '24
Greed '24
Anna Christie '23
Charlie Chaplin... Our Hero! '15
Tillie's Punctured Romance '14

Brigid Conley Walsh
See Brigid Brannagh

Jimmy Conlin (1884-1962)
Operation Haylift '50
Dick Tracy's Dilemma '47
Miracle of Morgan's Creek '44
Sullivan's Travels '41

Joe Conley (1928-)
A Day for Thanks on Walton's Mountain '82
The Waltons '72

Jack Conley
Collateral '04
Payback '98

Didi Conn (1951-)
Thomas and the Magic Railroad '00
Grease '78
You Light Up My Life '77

Grease 2 '82
Grease '78
You Light Up My Life '77

Maureen Connell (1931-)
Black Tide '58
Lucky Jim '58
The Abominable Snowman '57

Christopher Connelly (1941-88)
Django Strikes Again '87
The Messenger '87
Mines of Kilimanjaro '87
Night of the Sharks '87
Strike Commando '87
Foxtrap '85
Jungle Raiders '85
Operation 'Nam '85
1990: The Bronx Warriors '83
Raiders of Atlantis '83
Liar's Moon '82
Manhattan Baby '82
Return of the Rebels '81
Fantastic Seven '79
The Martian Chronicles: Part 3 '79
The Crash of Flight 401 '78
Norseman '78
The Incredible Rocky Mountain Race '77
Hawmps! '76
Benji '74
The Invasion of Carol Enders '73
They Only Kill Their Masters '72

Edward Connelly (1855-1928)
The Mysterious Lady '28
The Saphead '21

Jennifer Connelly (1970-)
He's Just Not That Into You '08
Reservation Road '07
Blood Diamond '06
Little Children '06
Dark Water '05
House of Sand and Fog '03
Hulk '03
A Beautiful Mind '01
Pollock '00
Requiem for a Dream '00
Waking the Dead '00
Dark City '97
Inventing the Abbotts '97
Far Harbor '96
Mulholland Falls '95
Higher Learning '94
Of Love and Shadows '94
Career Opportunities '91
The Rocketeer '91
The Hot Spot '90
Some Girls '88
Labyrinth '86
Seven Minutes in Heaven '86
Creepers '85
Once Upon a Time in America '84
When Angels Fly '84

Marc Connelly (1890-1980)
Tall Story '60
Spirit of St. Louis '57

Bart Conner (1958-)
Stick It '06
Rad '86

Jason Connery (1962-)
The Far Side of Jericho '06
Wishmaster 3: Beyond the Gates of Hell '01
Shanghai Noon '00
Urban Ghost Story '98
Midnight in Saint Petersburg '97
Bullet to Beijing '95
Double Cross '92
Spymaker: The Secret Life of Ian Fleming '90
Casablanca Express '89
Bye Bye Baby '88
Robin Hood... The Legend: Herne's Son '85

Robin Hood... The Legend: The Time of the Wolf '85
The First Olympics: Athens 1896 '84
Winner Takes All '84

Sean Connery (1930-)
The League of Extraordinary Gentlemen '03
Finding Forrester '00
Entrapment '99
The Avengers '98
Playing by Heart '98
Dragonheart '96 (V)
The Rock '96
First Knight '95
A Good Man in Africa '94
Just Cause '94
Rising Sun '93
Medicine Man '92
Highlander 2: The Quickening '91
Robin Hood: Prince of Thieves '91
The Hunt for Red October '90
The Russia House '90
Family Business '89
Indiana Jones and the Last Crusade '89
Memories of Me '88
The Presidio '88
Highlander '86
The Name of the Rose '86
Never Say Never Again '83
Sword of the Valiant '83
Five Days One Summer '82
Wrong Is Right '82
Outland '81
Time Bandits '81
Cuba '79
The Great Train Robbery '79
Meteor '79
A Bridge Too Far '77
The Arab Conspiracy '76
Robin and Marian '76
The Man Who Would Be King '75
The Wind and the Lion '75
Murder on the Orient Express '74
The Terrorists '74
The Offence '73
Zardoz '73
The Anderson Tapes '71
Diamonds Are Forever '71
Molly Maguires '70
Red Tent '69
Shalako '68
You Only Live Twice '67
A Fine Madness '66
The Hill '65
Thunderball '65
Marnie '64
Woman of Straw '64
From Russia with Love '63
Dr. No '62
The Longest Day '62
The Frightened City '61
On the Fiddle '61
Darby O'Gill & the Little People '59
Another Time, Another Place '58
Time Lock '57

Harry Connick, Jr. (1967-)
P.S. I Love You '07
Bug '06
Basic '03
Life Without Dick '01
Rodgers & Hammerstein's South Pacific '01
Iron Giant '99 (V)
My Dog Skip '99 (N)
The Simian Line '99
Hope Floats '98
Excess Baggage '96
Independence Day '96
Copycat '95
Little Man Tate '91
Memphis Belle '90

Billy Connolly (1942-)
The X-Files: I Want to Believe '08

Fido '06
Garfield: A Tail of Two Kitties '06
Open Season '06 (V)
Lemony Snicket's A Series of Unfortunate Events '04
The Last Samurai '03
Timeline '03
White Oleander '02
Who is Cletis Tout? '02
Gentlemen's Relish '01
Beautiful Joe '00
An Everlasting Piece '00
Boondock Saints '99
Deacon Brodie '98
The Imposters '98
Still Crazy '98
Mrs. Brown '97
Muppet Treasure Island '96
Pocahontas '95 (V)
Indecent Proposal '93
The Big Man: Crossing the Line '91
The Return of the Musketeers '89
Blue Money '84
The Secret Policeman's Other Ball '82
Absolution '81

Kevin Connolly (1974-)
The Notebook '04
Antwone Fisher '02
John Q '02
The Beverly Hillbillies '93
Alan & Naomi '92

Walter Connolly (1887-1940)
The Adventures of Huckleberry Finn '39
Fifth Avenue Girl '39
Too Hot to Handle '38
The Good Earth '37
Nothing Sacred '37
Libeled Lady '36
Broadway Bill '34
It Happened One Night '34
Lady by Choice '34
Twentieth Century '34
The Bitter Tea of General Yen '33
Lady for a Day '33

Kenneth Connor (1915-92)
Carry On England '76
Carry On Henry VIII '71
Carry On Cleo '65
What a Carve-Up! '62
Dentist In the Chair '60
Carry On Nurse '59
The Ladykillers '55

Buck Connors (1880-1947)
The Law Rides '36
No Man's Range '35
The Phantom Flyer '28

Chuck Connors (1921-92)
The Gambler Returns: The Luck of the Draw '93
Last Flight to Hell '91
Salmonberries '91
Three Days to a Kill '91
High Desert Kill '90
Texas Guns '90
One Last Run '89
Skinheads: The Second Coming of Hate '88
Trained to Kill '88
Terror Squad '87
Summer Camp Nightmare '86
The Vals '85
Target Eagle '84
Airplane 2: The Sequel '82
Balboa '82
The Capture of Grizzly Adams '82
Virus '82
Day of the Assassin '81
Tourist Trap '79
Roots '77
Nightmare in Badham County '76

The Legend of Sea Wolf '75
99 & 44/100 Dead '74
Soylent Green '73
Embassy '72
The Mad Bomber '72
Pancho Villa '72
The Proud and the Damned '72
Ride to Glory '71
Flipper '63
Move Over, Darling '63
Geronimo '62
The Big Country '58
Designing Woman '57
Old Yeller '57
Hot Rod Girl '56
South Sea Woman '53
Pat and Mike '52

Mike Connors (1925-)
Gideon '99
James Dean: Live Fast, Die Young '97
Fist Fighter '88
Too Scared to Scream '85
Casino '80
Nightkill '80
Avalanche Express '79
Long Journey Back '78
Harlow '65
Good Neighbor Sam '64
Panic Button '62
Flesh and the Spur '57
Shake, Rattle and Rock '57
Voodoo Woman '57
Jaguar '56
Day the World Ended '55
Swamp Women '55
Island in the Sky '53
Sudden Fear '52

Chris Conrad (1971-)
Young Hercules '98
Airborne '93

David Conrad (1967-)
Wedding Crashers '05
Anything Else '03
Men of Honor '00
The Weekend '00
A Season for Miracles '99
Return to Paradise '98
The Wizard of Speed and Time '88

Michael Conrad (1925-83)
Bordello '79
The Longest Yard '74
Scream Blacula Scream '73
Gone with the West '72
Thumb Tripping '72
Castle Keep '69
They Shoot Horses, Don't They? '69
Blackbeard's Ghost '67
The War Lord '65

Mikel Conrad (1919-82)
The Flying Saucer '50
Abbott and Costello Meet the Killer, Boris Karloff '49

Robert Conrad (1935-)
Jingle All the Way '96
Samurai Cowboy '93
Assassin '86
Two Fathers' Justice '85
Hard Knox '83
Will: G. Gordon Liddy '82
Wrong Is Right '82
More Wild, Wild West '80
Breaking Up Is Hard to Do '79
Lady in Red '79
Wild, Wild West Revisited '79
Centennial '78
Sudden Death '77
Murph the Surf '75
The Bandits '67
Palm Springs Weekend '63
The Commies Are Coming, the Commies Are Coming '57

William Conrad (1920-94)
Vengeance '89
Blitz '85
Return of Frank Cannon '80
The Return of the King '80 (V)
The Rebels '79 (N)
Night Cries '78
Moonshine County Express '77
The Ride Back '57
Zero Hour! '57 (N)
The Conqueror '56
Naked Jungle '54
The Desert Song '53
Cry Danger '51
The Racket '51
Tension '50
Body and Soul '47
The Killers '46

Hans Conried (1917-82)
Tut & Tuttle '81
Oh, God! Book 2 '80
The Hobbit '78 (V)
Brothers O'Toole '73
Phantom Tollbooth '69 (V)
The Patsy '64
Robin and the 7 Hoods '64
1001 Arabian Nights '59 (V)
Jet Pilot '57
The Monster That Challenged the World '57
Rock-A-Bye Baby '57
Birds & the Bees '56
Bus Stop '56
Davy Crockett, King of the Wild Frontier '55
The Affairs of Dobie Gillis '53
The 5000 Fingers of Dr. T '53
Peter Pan '53 (V)
Behave Yourself! '52
Three for Bedroom C '52
The World in His Arms '52
Rich, Young and Pretty '51
Nancy Goes to Rio '50
Summer Stock '50
My Friend Irma '49
The Senator Was Indiscreet '47
His Butler's Sister '44
Hitler's Children '43
Blondie's Blessed Event '42
Underground Agent '42

Frances Conroy (1953-)
The Seeker: The Dark Is Rising '07
Ira & Abby '06
A Perfect Day '06
The Wicker Man '06
Broken Flowers '05
Shopgirl '05
The Aviator '04
Catwoman '04
Die Mommie Die! '03
Maid in Manhattan '02
Murder in a Small Town '99
The Crucible '96
The Neon Bible '95
The Adventures of Huck Finn '93
Scent of a Woman '92
Another Woman '88
Rocket Gibraltar '88

Frank Conroy (1890-1964)
The Bramble Bush '60
The Day the Earth Stood Still '51
All My Sons '48
Crash Dive '43
The Ox-Bow Incident '43
I Live My Life '35
The Cat and the Fiddle '34
Manhattan Melodrama '34
Ace of Aces '33

Kevin Conroy (1955-)
Batman: Mask of the Phantasm '93 (V)
Chain of Desire '93
The Secret Passion of Robert Clayton '92

Neili Conroy
Bloom '03
The Van '95
Family '94

Ruaidhri Conroy (1979-)
Deathwatch '02
When the Sky Falls '99
Moondance '95
Nothing Personal '95
The Van '95
Into the West '92

Charlotte Considine
See Charlotte Stewart

John Considine (1938-)
Gia '98
Tinseltown '97
Breathing Lessons '94
Opposing Force '87
Trouble in Mind '86
Dixie: Changing Habits '85
Choose Me '84
Circle of Power '83
Rita Hayworth: The Love Goddess '83
Endangered Species '82
Forbidden Love '82
The Shadow Box '80
See How She Runs '78
A Wedding '78
The Late Show '77
Welcome to L.A. '77
The Thirsty Dead '74
Dr. Death, Seeker of Souls '73
Reunion in France '42

Paddy Considine (1974-)
Hot Fuzz '07
PU-239 '06
Cinderella Man '05
My Summer of Love '05
Stoned '05
Dead Man's Shoes '04
Close Your Eyes '02
In America '02
24 Hour Party People '01
Born Romantic '00

Tim Considine (1940-)
Patton '70
Daring Dobermans '73
Sunrise at Campobello '60
The Shaggy Dog '59
The Private War of Major Benson '55
Clown '53

Michel Constantin (1924-2003)
Beyond Fear '75
La Scoumoune '72
The Family '70
A Very Curious Girl '69
Le Trou '59

Eddie Constantine (1917-93)
Zentropa '92
The Long Good Friday '80
It's Alive 2: It Lives Again '78
Beware of a Holy Whore '70
Attack of the Robots '66
Alphaville '65
License to Kill '64
As If It Were Raining '63
Your Turn Darling '63
Cleo from 5 to 7 '61
Keep Talking Baby '61
It Means That to Me '60
S.O.S. Pacific '60
Room 43 '58
Dishonorable Discharge '57
There Goes Barder '54

Michael Constantine (1927-)
My Big Fat Greek Wedding '02
Winds of Terror '01
The Juror '96
Stephen King's Thinner '96
My Life '93
Question of Faith '93
Prancer '89
In the Mood '87

Forty Days of Musa Dagh '85
Silent Rebellion '82
Fear in the Night '81
The North Avenue Irregulars '79
Billy: Portrait of a Street Kid '77
Voyage of the Damned '76
Conspiracy of Terror '75
Death Cruise '74
Killing in the Sun '73
Say Goodbye, Maggie Cole '72
The Reivers '69
The Hustler '61

Mark Consuelos (1971-)
My Super Ex-Girlfriend '06
Wedding Daze '06

John Conte (1915-2006)
Trauma '62
The Man with the Golden Arm '55
Lost in a Harem '44

Richard Conte (1914-75)
The Godfather 1902-1959: The Complete Epic '81
Violent Professionals '73
The Godfather '72
1931: Once Upon a Time in New York '72
Explosion '69
Operation Cross Eagles '69
Lady in Cement '68
The Fighter '52
House of Strangers '49
Hotel '67
Tony Rome '67
Assault on a Queen '66
13 Rue Madeleine '46
Call Northside 777 '48
A Walk in the Sun '46
The Purple Heart '44
Ocean's 11 '60
They Came to Cordura '59
Circus World '64
Full of Life '56
Big Combo '55
I'll Cry Tomorrow '55
Race for Life '55
Guadalcanal Diary '43

Steve Conte (1920-97)
The Wild World of Batwoman '67
Attack of the Mayan Mummy '63
Terror of the Bloodhunters '62

Albert Conti (1887-1967)
The Black Cat '34
State's Attorney '31

Tom Conti (1941-)
Derailed '05
The Enemy '01
Sub Down '97
Someone Else's America '96
That Summer of White Roses '90
Shirley Valentine '89
Deep Cover '88
Dumb Waiter '87
The Quick and the Dead '87
Beyond Therapy '86
Miracles '86
Saving Grace '86
American Dreamer '84
Merry Christmas, Mr. Lawrence '83
Reuben, Reuben '83
The Princess and the Pea '83

The Norman Conquests, Part 1: Table Manners '78
The Norman Conquests, Part 2: Living Together '78
The Norman Conquests, Part 3: Round and Round the Garden '78

Patricio Contreras (1947-)
Of Love and Shadows '94
Old Gringo '89
The Official Story '85

Ugo Conti (1955-)
Goodbye, Miss 4th of July '88

Chantal Contouri (1949-)
Thirst '87
The Night After Halloween '79

Frank Converse (1938-)
Our Town '03
Brother Future '91
Everybody Wins '90
Home at Last '88
Alone in the Neon Jungle '87
Anne of Avonlea '87
Spring Fever '81
The Bushido Blade '80
Marilyn: The Untold Story '80
Danger in the Skies '79
Cruise into Terror '78
Sergeant Matlovich vs. the U.S. Air Force '78
Killer on Board '77
The Tattered Web '71

William Converse-Roberts
The Margarethe Cammermeyer Story '95
Courtship '87

Bert Convy (1933-91)
Help Wanted: Male '82
Cannonball Run '81
Hero at Large '80
The Man in the Santa Claus Suit '79
Racquet '79
Jennifer '78
Semi-Tough '77
The Love Bug '68
A Bucket of Blood '59
Gunman's Walk '58

Gary Conway (1936-)
Blast-Off Girls '67
The Falcon's Brother '42

Dan Conway
Things Change '88

Angell Conwell (1982-)
What About Your Friends: Weekend Getaway '02
Baby Boy '01
The Wash '01

Jackie Coogan (1914-84)
The Escape Artist '82
Dr. Heckyl and Mr. Hype '80
The Prey '80
Halloween with the Addams Family '79

Kevin Conway (1942-)
Invincible '06
Gods and Generals '03
Black Knight '01
Thirteen Days '00
Two Family House '99
The Confession '98
Mercury Rising '98
Looking for Richard '96
How to Make a Monster '58
Teenage Frankenstein '58
The Bronx Is Burning '07

Lawnmower Man 2: Beyond Cyberspace '95
Prince Brat and the Whipping Boy '95
The Quick and the Dead '95
Gettysburg '93
Jennifer 8 '92
One Good Cop '91
Rambling Rose '91
Homeboy '88
Rage of Angels '83
The Funhouse '81
F.I.S.T. '78
The Scarlet Letter '79
The Lathe of Heaven '80
Paradise Alley '78
Johnny We Hardly Knew Ye '77

Tim Conway (1933-)
Air Bud 2: Golden Receiver '98
Speed 2: Cruise Control '97
Dear God '96
The Longshot '86
Cannonball Run 2 '84
The Private Eyes '80
The Apple Dumpling Gang Rides Again '79
The Billion Dollar Hobo '78
They Went That-a-Way & That-a-Way '78
Gus '76
The Shaggy D.A. '76
The Apple Dumpling Gang '75
The World's Greatest Athlete '73
McHale's Navy Joins the Air Force '65
McHale's Navy '64

Tom Conway (1904-67)
Atomic Submarine '59
Voodoo Woman '57
Murder on Approval '56
Norman Conquest '53
Peter Pan '53 (V)
Three Steps to Murder '53
Bride of the Gorilla '51
One Touch of Venus '48
Criminal Court '46
The Saint Strikes Back: Criminal Court '46
Sixteen Candles '84
The Incredible Mr. Limpet '64

Pat Conway (1931-81)
Brightly of the Grand Canyon '67
Geronimo '62
An Annapolis Story '55

Russ Conway (1913-)
The Deadly Mantis '57
The Private Eyes '80
Tristan Shandy: A Cock and Bull Story '05
Around the World in 80 Days '04
Ella Enchanted '04 (V)
Coffee and Cigarettes '03
24 Hour Party People '01
Mr. Toad's Wild Ride '96

A.J. Cook (1978-)
Final Destination 2 '03
I'm Reed Fish '06
The House Next Door '01
Out Cold '01
Ripper: Letter from Hell '01
Wishmaster 3: Beyond the Gates of Hell '01

Carole Cook (1928-)
Home on the Range '04 (V)
Lost and Found '99
Fast Money '96
Sixteen Candles '84

Clyde Cook (1891-1984)
The White Cliffs of Dover '44
White Cargo '42
Through the Breakers '28
White Gold '28

Dale "Apollo" Cook (1958-)
Dan in Real Life '07
Good Luck Chuck '07
Mr. Brooks '07
Employee of the Month '06
London '05
Waiting '05
Mystery Men '99
Simon Sez '99

Ben Cook
Restless Spirits '99

Marianne Cook
See Marianne Koch

Dane Cook (1972-)
Dan in Real Life '07
Good Luck Chuck '07
Mr. Brooks '07
Employee of the Month '06
London '05
Waiting '05
Mystery Men '99
Simon Sez '99

Rachael Leigh Cook (1979-)
All Hat '07
Blonde Ambition '07
The Final Season '07
Nancy Drew '07
The Big Empty '04
My First Wedding '04
Stateside '04
Bookies '03
11:14 '03
Scorched '02

Morgan Conway (1903-81)
Dick Tracy vs. Cueball '46
Dick Tracy, Detective '45

Pat Conway
The Saint Takes Over '40
Sinners in Paradise '38

Russ Conway (1913-)
The Screaming Skull '58
Love Me Tender '56
Twelve o'Clock High '49

Keith Coogan (1970-)
Ivory Tower '97
Downhill Willie '96

Doria Cook
Public Enemy '31

Elisha Cook, Jr. (1906-95)
Hammett '82
Carny '80
1941 '79
Salem's Lot '79
St. Ives '76
The Champ '79
The Kid '21
The Power Within '95
Forever, A Ghost of a Love Story '92
Book of Love '91
Life 101 '95
My Boy '21
Peck's Bad Boy '21
Mesa of Lost Women '52
Outlaw Women '52
College Swing '38
Free and Easy '30
Oliver Twist '22
Baby Face '33
Viva Villa! '34
Confidential '35
Show Boat '36
High School Confidential '58
Girl Happy '65
A Fire Madness '66

Roderick Cook (1932-)
The Champ '79
Tom and Huck '95
The Naked Man '96
The Defenders: Payback '97

Steve Coogan (1965-)
Tropic Thunder '08
Hot Fuzz '07
Lies & Alibis '06
Night at the Museum '06
Happy Endings '05

Ron Cook (1948-)
On a Clear Day '05
The Merchant of Venice '04
Thunderbirds '04
The Other Boleyn Girl '03
Dead Gorgeous '02
The Hound of the Baskervilles '02
Charlotte Gray '01
102 Dalmatians '00
Secrets and Lies '95
Sharpe's Honour '94

Tommy Cook (1930-)
Missile to the Moon '59
Night Passage '57
Battle Cry '55
Teenage Crime Wave '55
Adventures of Red Ryder '40

Donald Cook (1901-61)
Our Very Own '50
Here Come the Co-Eds '45
Show Boat '36
Blow Dry '00
Get Carter '00
She's All That '99
All I Wanna Do '98
Anyway '98
Evil Town '87
Mame '74

Keith Cooke (1959-)
Heatseeker '95
The King of the Kickboxers '91
China, O'Brien 2 '89
China O'Brien '88

Christopher Cooke
Rhythm Thief '94

Alan Cooke
Young Adam '03
Defenders of the Law '31

Tracy Cook
Killing Moon '00
Gimme an F '85

Jennifer Cooke (1964-)
Friday the 13th, Part 6: Jason Lives '86

Peter Cook (1938-95)
Black Beauty '94
Getting It Right '89
Great Balls of Fire '89
Without a Clue '88
The Princess Bride '87
Yellowbeard '83
Secret Policeman's Private Parts '81
The Hound of the Baskervilles '77
Find the Lady '76
Those Daring Young Men in Their Jaunty Jalopies '69
Bedazzled '68
Dandy in Aspic '68
The Wrong Box '66

Peter Cookson (1913-90)
Black Tower '50
Fear '46

Jennifer Coolidge (1963-)
Epic Movie '07
American Dreamz '06
Click '06
Date Movie '06
For Your Consideration '06
Robots '05 (V)
American Wedding '03
Legally Blonde 2: Red, White & Blonde '03
A Mighty Wind '03
Testosterone '03
A Cinderella Story '04
American Pie 2 '01
Down to Earth '01
Legally Blonde '01

Spade Cooley (1910-69)
Everybody's Dancin' '50
Swingtime Johnny '43
Kid from Gower Gulch '50
Silver Bandit '50

Josie and the Pussycats '01
Tangled '01
Texas Rangers '01
Antitrust '00

Best in Show '00
American Pie '99
Slappy and the Stinkers '97
Trial and Error '96
Philip Coolidge (1908-67)
Inherit the Wind '60
The Tingler '59
Coolio (1963-)
Stealing Candy '04
Exposed '03
Get Over It! '01
Perfume '01
Red Water '01
The Convent '00
Dope Case Pending '00
In Pursuit '00
Shriek If You Know What I Did Last Friday the 13th '00
Submerged '00
Judgment Day '99
Leprechaun 5: In the Hood '99
An Alan Smithee Film: Burn, Hollywood, Burn '97
Phat Beach '96
James Coombes
A Knight in Camelot '98
Norman Coombes
The House of Usher '88
Kill or Be Killed '80
Kevin Cooney (1945-)
Bring It On Again '03
Clockwatchers '97
If These Walls Could Talk '96
Full Moon in Blue Water '88
Alice Cooper (1948-)
Wayne's World '92
Roadie '80
Sextette '78
Ben Cooper (1930-)
The Rose Tattoo '55
Johnny Guitar '53
Bradley Cooper (1975-)
He's Just Not That Into You '08
The Comebacks '07
Failure to Launch '06
Wedding Crashers '05
Wet Hot American Summer '01
Camille (Cami) Cooper
Lawnmower Man 2: Beyond Cyberspace '95
The Applegates '89
Shocker '89
Chris Cooper (1951-)
Breach '07
The Kingdom '07
Married Life '07
Capote '05
Jarhead '05
Silver City '04
Syriana '05
My House in Umbria '03
Adaptation '02
Seabiscuit '03
Interstate 60 '02
The Bourne Identity '02
Me, Myself, and Irene '00
The Patriot '00
American Beauty '99
October Sky '99
Breast Men '97
Great Expectations '97
The Horse Whisperer '97
Horton Foote's Alone '97
A Time to Kill '96
Lone Star '96
Money Train '95
Pharoah's Army '95
Lone Justice '93

Return to Lonesome Dove '93
This Boy's Life '93
City of Hope '91
Guilty by Suspicion '91
Thousand Pieces of Gold '91
Matewan '87
Clancy Cooper (1906-75)
Naked Youth '59
A Time to Love & a Time to Die '58
Girls in Chains '43
The Secret Code '42
Dominic Cooper (1978-)
Mamma Mia! '08
Sense & Sensibility '07
The History Boys '06
Starter for Ten '06
Garry Cooper (1955-)
My Beautiful Laundrette '85
Quadrophenia '79
Gary Cooper
Naked Gun 33 1/3: The Final Insult '94
Dark Before Dawn '89
Garden of Evil '54
Gary Cooper (1901-61)
The Naked Edge '61
Alias Jesse James '59
The Hanging Tree '59
They Came to Cordura '59
The Wreck of the Mary Deare '59
Man of the West '58
Ten North Frederick '58
Love in the Afternoon '57
Friendly Persuasion '56
The Court Martial of Billy Mitchell '55
Blowing Wild '54
Return to Paradise '53
Vera Cruz '53
High Noon '52
Springfield Rifle '52
Distant Drums '51
The Fountainhead '49
It's a Great Feeling '49
Task Force '49
Good Sam '48
Unconquered '47
Cloak and Dagger '46
Along Came Jones '45
Saratoga Trunk '45
Casanova Brown '44
The Story of Dr. Wassell '44
For Whom the Bell Tolls '43
The Pride of the Yankees '42
Ball of Fire '41
Meet John Doe '41
Sergeant York '41
The Westerner '40
Beau Geste '39
The Real Glory '39
The Adventures of Marco Polo '38
Bluebeard's Eighth Wife '38
The Cowboy and the Lady '38
The Plainsman '37
Souls at Sea '37
Desire '36
The General Died at Dawn '36
Mr. Deeds Goes to Town '36
The Lives of a Bengal Lancer '35
Now and Forever '34
Today We Live '33
A Farewell to Arms '32
Fighting Caravans '31
Morocco '30
Doomsday '28
It '27
The Last Outlaw '27
Nevada '27
Wings '27
The Winning of Barbara Worth '26

George Cooper (1892-1943)
Federal Agent '36
The Phantom Rider '36
Uptown New York '32
Smouldering Fires '25
Little Church Around the Corner '23
Gladys Cooper (1888-1971)
Nice Girl Like Me '69
My Fair Lady '64
Separate Tables '58
At Sword's Point '51
Madame Bovary '49
The Secret Garden '49
Homecoming '48
The Pirate '48
The Bishop's Wife '47
Beware of Pity '46
Love Letters '45
The Valley of Decision '45
Mrs. Parkington '44
The White Cliffs of Dover '44
Mr. Lucky '43
The Song of Bernadette '43
Now, Voyager '42
The Black Cat '41
That Hamilton Woman '41
Kitty Foyle '40
Rebecca '40
The Iron Duke '34
Inez Cooper (1922-)
'Neath Canadian Skies '46
Wings over the Pacific '43
I Married an Angel '42
Jackie Cooper (1921-)
Surrender '87
Superman 3 '83
Superman 2 '80
Superman: The Movie '78
The Love Machine '71
The Navy Comes Through '42
Ziegfeld Girl '41
Return of Frank James '40
The Abe Lincoln of Ninth Avenue '39
That Certain Age '38
Peck's Bad Boy '34
Treasure Island '34
The Bowery '33
The Champ '32
Jeanne Cooper (1928-)
Sweet Hostage '75
Shame '61
Let No Man Write My Epitaph '60
The Commies Are Coming, the Commies Are Coming '57
Plunder Road '57
The Redhead from Wyoming '53
Shadows of Tombstone '53
Jeff Cooper
Circle of Iron '78
Fantastic Balloon Voyage '76
The Impossible Years '68
Born Losers '67
Justin Cooper (1988-)
Dennis the Menace Strikes Again '98
Liar Liar '97
Maggie Cooper
Death Ray 2000 '81
An Eye for an Eye '81
And Baby Makes Six '79
Melville Cooper (1896-1973)
Around the World in 80 Days '56
The King's Thief '55
Let's Dance '50
The Underworld Story '50
Heartbeat '46
13 Rue Madeleine '46
Immortal Sergeant '43
The Lady Eve '41
Murder over New York '40
Rebecca '40

The Adventures of Robin Hood '38
Dawn Patrol '38
Thin Ice '37
Private Life of Don Juan '34
The Scarlet Pimpernel '34
Miriam Cooper (1894-1976)
Is Money Everything? '23
The Birth of a Nation '15
Pat Cooper (1929-)
Analyze That '02
Analyze This '98
Ralph Cooper (1908-92)
Gang War '40
The Duke Is Tops '38
Stan Cooper
See Stelvio Rosi
Ted Cooper
The Caine Mutiny '54
Phantom from Space '53
Terence Cooper (1928-97)
Hell's Belles '95
Heart of the Stag '84
Casino Royale '67
Trevor Cooper (1953-)
The History of Mr. Polly '07
Ivanhoe '97
Framed '93
Wendy Cooper
24 Hours in London '00
Witchcraft 10: Mistress of the Craft '98
Robert Coote (1909-82)
Theatre of Blood '73
Alice Through the Looking Glass '66
My Fair Lady '64
The Horse's Mouth '58
The Merry Widow '52
Othello '52
Scaramouche '52
The Elusive Pimpernel '50
Macbeth '48
The Three Musketeers '48
Forever Amber '47
The Ghost and Mrs. Muir '47
Lured '47
Stairway to Heaven '46
Commandos Strike at Dawn '43
You Can't Fool Your Wife '40
Bad Lands '39
Gunga Din '39
Mr. Moto's Last Warning '39
Nurse Edith Cavell '39
Kenneth Cope (1931-)
Rentadick '72
Carry On at Your Convenience '71
Joan Copeland (1922-)
Brother Bear '03 (V)
The Adventures of Sebastian Cole '99
The Peacemaker '97
The Laserman '90
Her Alibi '88
Happy New Year '87
Roseland '77
Zane R. (Lil' Zane) Copeland, Jr. (1982-)
Dr. Dolittle 2 '01
Finding Forrester '00
Focus '01
Michael Copeman
His Bodyguard '98
Circle Man '87
Geoffrey Copleston
The Belly of an Architect '91
The Black Cat '81
Peter Copley (1915-)
Oliver Twist '05
A Dangerous Man: Lawrence after Arabia '91
Help! '65
King and Country '64

The Golden Salamander '51
Teri Copley (1961-)
Brain Donors '92
Frozen Assets '92
Down the Drain '89
Transylvania Twist '89
In the Line of Duty: The FBI Murders '88
I Married a Centerfold '84
Alicia Coppola (1968-)
National Treasure: Book of Secrets '07
Fresh Cut Grass '04
Sin '02
Double Down '01
Blood Money '99
Velocity Trap '99
Christopher Coppola (1962-)
BloodRayne 2: Deliverance '07
Loveless in Los Angeles '07
Undead or Alive '07
Dog Gone Love '03
Francis Ford Coppola (1939-)
Hearts of Darkness: A Filmmaker's Apocalypse '91
Apocalypse Now '79
Sofia Coppola (1971-)
Star Wars: Episode 1—The Phantom Menace '99
Inside Monkey Zetterland '93
The Godfather, Part 3 '90
Peggy Sue Got Married '86
Vincent Corazza (1972-)
Leaving Metropolis '02
Hangman '00
Brady Corbett (1988-)
Funny Games '07
Mysterious Skin '04
Thunderbirds '04
Thirteen '03
Ben (Benny) Corbett (1892-1961)
Fighting Renegade '39
Outlaw's Paradise '39
Texas Wildcats '39
Circle of Death '36
Coyote Trails '35
Glenn Corbett (1934-93)
Shadow Force '92
Midway '76
Ride in a Pink Car '74
The Stranger '73
Dead Pigeon on Beethoven Street '72
Chisum '70
Shenandoah '65
Homicidal '61
All the Young Men '60
The Mountain Road '60
The Violent Years '56
Gretchen Corbett (1947-)
Change of Heart '98
Jaws of Satan '81
PSI Factor '80
Secrets of Three Hungry Wives '78
The Savage Bees '76
Let's Scare Jessica to Death '71
Harry H. Corbett (1925-82)
Silver Dream Racer '83
Jabberwocky '77
Carry On Screaming '66
Rattle of a Simple Man '64
Ladies Who Do '63
The Unstoppable Man '59
John Corbett (1962-)
Street Kings '08
The Messengers '07
Montana Sky '07
Dreamland '06
Bigger Than the Sky '05

Elvis Has Left the Building '04
Raise Your Voice '04
Raising Helen '04
My Big Fat Greek Wedding '02
Prancer Returns '01
Serendipity '01
Dinner Rush '00
Volcano '97
Don't Look Back '96
Wedding Bell Blues '96
Tombstone '93
Ronnie Corbett (1930-)
British '73
Barry Corbin (1940-)
In the Valley of Elah '07
No Country for Old Men '07
Hidden Places '06
Monte Walsh '03
Hope Ranch '02
Crossfire Trail '01
Race to Space '01
Held Up '00
A Face to Kill For '99
Solo '96
Curdled '95
Career Opportunities '91
The Chase '91
Conagher '91
The Hot Spot '90
Short Time '90
Who's Harry Crumb? '89
Critters 2: The Main Course '88
It Takes Two '88
LBJ: The Early Years '88
Permanent Record '88
Undercover '87
Nothing in Common '86
Hard Traveling '85
My Science Project '85
What Comes Around '85
Fatal Vision '84
Ellen Corby (1913-99)
A Day for Thanks on Walton's Mountain '82
Homecoming: A Christmas Story '71
Support Your Local Gunfighter '71
The Glass Bottom Boat '66
The Strangler '64
Vertigo '58
Night Passage '57
All Mine to Give '56
Illegal '55
Angels in the Outfield '51
On Moonlight Bay '51
Caged '50
Harriet Craig '50
Ma and Pa Kettle Go to Town '50
I Remember Mama '48
Forever Amber '47
It's a Wonderful Life '46
Bedlam '45
Urban Cowboy '80
Donna Corcoran (1942-)
Gypsy Colt '54
Don't Bother to Knock '52
Angels in the Outfield '51
Kevin Corcoran (1949-)
A Tiger Walks '64
Johnny Shiloh '63
Savage Sam '63
Mooncussers '62
Pollyanna '60
The Swiss Family Robinson '60
The Shaggy Dog '59
Toby Tyler '59
Old Yeller '57

Alex Cord (1931-)
Air Rage '01
To Be the Best '93
C.I.A.: Code Name Alexa '92
Grayeagle '77
Inn of the Damned '74
Jungle Warriors '84
Sidewinder One '77
Stiletto '69
The Brotherhood '68
The Dead Are Alive '72
The Dirty Dozen: The Fatal Mission '88
The Last Don '97
The Uninvited '88

Nick(y) Corello
Lansky '99
The Last Don '97

Raymond Cordy (1898-1956)
Beauties of the Night '52
Beauty and the Devil '50
A Nous la Liberte '31
Le Chat '75
La Rupture '70

Annie Cordy (1928-)

Allan Corduner (1951-)
Bigger Than the Sky '05
De-Lovely '04
Food of Love '02
Friends & Crocodiles '05
Heart of Darkness '93
Mandela '87
Room '05
The Grey Zone '01
The History Boys '06
The Impostors '98
The Merchant of Venice '04
The Way We Live Now '02
Topsy-Turvy '99
Voices from a Locked Room '95
Yentl '83

James Corden (1980-)
All or Nothing '02
The History Boys '06

Harry Cording (1891-1954)

Pancho Cordova

Mara Corday (1932-)
The Black Scorpion '57
The Giant Claw '57
Tarantula '55
Francis Joins the WACs '54

Rita (Paula) Corday (1920-92)
Because You're Mine '52
The Black Castle '52
Sword of Monte Cristo '51
The Body Snatcher '45
West of the Pecos '45
The Falcon in Hollywood '44
The Leopard Man '43

Rob Corddry (1971-)
Harold & Kumar Escape from Guantanamo Bay '08
Semi-Pro '08
What Happens in Vegas '08
The Heartbreak Kid '07
I Now Pronounce You Chuck and Larry '07
The Ten '07
Unaccompanied Minors '06
Wedding Daze '06

Devil in a Blue Dress '95
Blankman '94
Sugar Hill '94
Casualties of Love: The "Long Island Lolita" Story '93
Colors '88

Prof. Irwin Corey (1912-)
The Curse of the Jade Scorpion '01
Stuck on You! '84
Fairy Tales '76
How to Commit Marriage '69

Brigitte Corey
See Luisella Boni

Isabel Corey (1939-)
Bob le Flambeur '55

Jeff Corey (1914-2002)
The Invincible Gladiator '63
Color of Night '94
Surviving the Game '94
Deception '92
Secret Ingredient '92
Sinatra '92
Payoff '91
Bird on a Wire '90
Messenger of Death '88
Creator '85
Conan the Destroyer '84
Sword & the Sorcerer '82
Battle Beyond the Stars '80
Butch and Sundance: The Early Days '79
The Two Worlds of Jenny Logan '79
Coming Home '79
Early Days '79
Up River '79
Jennifer '78
Wild Geese '78
Curse of the Black Widow '77
Moonshine County Express '77
Oh, God! '77
Banjo Hackett '76
The Premonition '75
Catlow '71
Shoot Out '71
Beneath the Planet of the Apes '70
Getting Straight '70
Little Big Man '70
They Call Me Mr. Tibbs! '70
Butch Cassidy and the Sundance Kid '69
True Grit '69
The Boston Strangler '68
In Cold Blood '67
Seconds '66
Mickey One '65
Lady in a Cage '64
The Balcony '63
Superman & the Mole Men '51
The Nevadan '50
The Next Voice You Hear '50
Rawhide '50
Bagdad '49
Follow Me Quietly '49
Home of the Brave '49
A Southern Yankee '48
Brute Force '47
Hopalong Cassidy: Hoppy's Holiday '47
My Friend Flicka '43
The Man Who Wouldn't Die '42
Superman & the Mole Men '51

Wendell Corey (1914-68)
Buckskin '68
The Astro-Zombies '67
Women of the Prehistoric Planet '66
Agent for H.A.R.M. '66
Alias Jesse James '59
The Light in the Forest '58
Loving You '57
The Rainmaker '56
The Big Knife '55
Rear Window '54
Great Missouri Raid '51
Harriet Craig '50
Rich, Young and Pretty '51
Any Number Can Play '49
Holiday Affair '49
The Accused '48
The Search '48

Lee Cormie

December Boys '07
Darkness Falls '03

Michael Cornelison (1952-)
Real Time: Siege at Lucas Street Market '00
No Way Back '74

Ellie Cornell (1963-)
All Souls Day '05
House of the Dead '03
Chips, the War Dog '90
The Departed '06
Anchorman: The Legend of Ron Burgundy '04

Don Cornelius (1936-)
Tapeheads '89

Danielle Cormack
The Price of Milk '00

Maddie Corman (1969-)
Seven Minutes in Heaven '86
Some Girls '88

Roger Corman (1926-)
Apollo 13 '95
The Manchurian Candidate '04
The Godfather, Part 2 '74
The Silence of the Lambs '91

Lords of the Deep '89
Swing Shift '84
State of Things '82
The Complete Epic 1902-1959: The Godfather '81
Rawhide '50

Sorry, Wrong Number '48

Danny Corkill (1974-)
Between Two Women '86
Desperate Lives '82

Al Corley (1956-)
Cowboy Up '00
A Kiss Goodnight '94
Incident at Channel Q '86
Torchlight '85
Squeeze Play '79

Annie Corley
Monster '03
Sealsuit '03
Juwanna Mann '02
Along for the Ride '00
Here on Earth '00
If You Only Knew '00
The '60s '99
Free Willy 3: The Rescue '97
Box of Moonlight '96
The Bridges of Madison County '95

Pat Corley (1930-2006)
Come Early Morning '06
Mr. Destiny '90
Poker Alice '87
Silent Witness '85
Night Shift '82

Sharron Corley (1971-)
The Substitute '96
New Jersey Drive '95

Jose Coronado (1957-)
Goya in Bordeaux '99
The Disappearance of Garcia Lorca '96

Antoni Corone
Reservation Road '07
We Own the Night '07

Georges Corraface (1953-)
Escape from L.A. '96
Impromptu '90
Not Without My Daughter '90
Christopher Columbus: The Discovery '92

Mady Correll (1907-81)
Monsieur Verdoux '47
Texas Masquerade '44

Ray Corrigan (1907-76)
It! The Terror from Beyond Space '58
Renegade Girl '46
The Painted Stallion '37
The Thin Man Goes Home '44

Lloyd Corrigan (1900-69)
The Manchurian Candidate '62
Bowery Boys Meet the Monsters '54
Cavalry Charge '51
Ghost Chasers '51
When Willie Comes Marching Home '50
Blondie Hits the Jackpot '49
The Chase '46
She Wolf of London '46
Gambler's Choice '44
Since You Went Away '44
The Thin Man Goes Home '44
Captive Wild Woman '43
Hitler's Children '43
A Girl, a Guy and a Gob '41
King of the Cowboys '43
The Lady in Question '40
Young Tom Edison '40

Abbie Cornish (1982-)
Stop-Loss '08
Elizabeth: The Golden Age '07
A Good Year '06
Candy '06
Somersault '04

Robert Cornthwaite (1917-2006)
Matinee '92
The Thing '51
The War of the Worlds '53

Charlotte Cornwell
The Saint '97
White Hunter, Black Heart '90

Judy Cornwell (1942-)
Prince of Poisoners: The Life and Crimes of William Palmer '93
Santa Claus: The Movie '85
Persuasion '95
Wuthering Heights '70
Two for the Road '67

Anne Cornwall (1897-1980)
Laurel & Hardy: Men O'War '29

Clovis Cornillac (1967-)
A Very Long Engagement '04
The Unbearable Lightness of Being '88

Carnage '02

Antoni Corone — (see above)

Kevin Corrigan (1969-)
Definitely, Maybe '08
American Gangster '07
Superbad '07
The Departed '06
The Dog Problem '06
Lonesome Jim '06

Sergio Corrieri (1939-)

Nick Corri
See Jsu Garcia

Adrienne Corri (1930-)
Rosebud '75
Madhouse '74
A Clockwork Orange '71
Vampire Circus '71
Africa Texas Style '67
The Viking Queen '67
Doctor Zhivago '65
The Hellfire Club '60
The Tell-Tale Heart '60
Corridors of Blood '58
Make Me an Offer '55
Devil Girl from Mars '54
The River '51

William Cort (1936-93)
Elvira, Mistress of the Dark '88

Bill Cort (1950-)

Bud Cort (1950-)
The Big Empty '04
The Life Aquatic with Steve Zissou '04
Coyote Ugly '00
Pollock '00
South of Heaven, West of Hell '00
But I'm a Cheerleader '99
Dogma '99
The Million Dollar Hotel '99
Sweet Jane '98
Heat '95
Girl in the Cadillac '94
Ted & Venus '91
Going Under '91
Brain Dead '89
Out of the Dark '88
The Chocolate War '88
Love at Stake '87
Invaders from Mars '86
Electric Dreams '84
Maria's Lovers '84
The Secret Diary of Sigmund Freud '84
Hysterical '83
Love Letters '83
The Nightingale '83
Why Shoot the Teacher '79
Brewster McCloud '71
Harold and Maude '71
Gas-s-s-s! '70
M*A*S*H '70
The Strawberry Statement '70
Sweet Charity '69
Die Laughing '80
Rumpelstiltskin '22

Silvana Corsini (1962-)
Mamma Roma '62

Aneta Corsaut (1933-95)
Return to Mayberry '85
The Toolbox Murders '78
The Blob '58

Rowena Cortes
To Live and Die in Hong Kong '89

Joe Cortese (1949-)
At First Sight '95
Demolition Man '93
Against the Ropes '04
American History X '98
Malevolence '95
Born to Run '93
Ruby '92
The Closer '91
To Protect and Serve '92
Python Wolf '88
Deadly Illusion '87
Assault and Matrimony '87
Stalking Danger '86
Windows '80
Evilspeak '82
Heroes Three '84
Kong '92
Heroes Three '84

Dan Cortese (1967-)
Volcano: Fire on the Mountain '97
Public Enemies '96
A Weekend in the Country '96

Valentina Cortese (1924-)
The Adventures of Baron Munchausen '89
When Time Ran Out '80
Widow's Nest '77
Brother Sun, Sister Moon '73
Day for Night '73
Assassination of Trotsky '72
First Love '70
The Secret of Santa Vittoria '69

Shirley Corrigan
The Devil's Nightmare '71
Dr. Jekyll and the Wolfman '71

Cortese (continued)
Juliet of the Spirits '65
The Girl Who Knew Too Much '63
The Barefoot Contessa '54
Les Miserables '52
Malaya '49

Bella Cortez (1944-)
Tor '64
Vulcan God of Fire '62
The Giant of Metropolis '61

Ricardo Cortez (1899-1977)
Last Hurrah '58
The Inner Circle '46
I Killed That Man '42
Murder over New York '40
Mr. Moto's Last Warning '39
The Gentleman from California '37
No One Man '32
Behind Office Doors '31
Big Business Girl '31
Illicit '31
The Maltese Falcon '31
Lost Zeppelin '29
The Phantom in the House '29
Mockery '27
The Sorrows of Satan '26
The Pony Express '25
The Swan '25

Jesse Corti
Beauty and the Beast '91 (V)
Nightlife '90
High Stakes '89

Bill Cosby (1937-)
Fat Albert '04
Jack '96
The Meteor Man '93
Ghost Dad '90
Leonard Part 6 '87
The Devil & Max Devlin '81
California Suite '78
Piece of the Action '77
Mother, Jugs and Speed '76
Let's Do It Again '75
Uptown Saturday Night '74
Man & Boy '71
To All My Friends on Shore '71

Howard Cosell (1920-95)
Broadway Danny Rose '84
The World's Greatest Athlete '73
Bananas '71

Daniel Cosgrove (1970-)
National Lampoon's Van Wilder '02
They Crawl '01
Valentine '01

Miranda Cosgrove (1993-)
Keeping Up with the Steins '06
Yours, Mine & Ours '05
School of Rock '03

James Cosmo (1948-)
The Last Legion '07
The Seeker: The Dark Is Rising '07
The Chronicles of Narnia: The Lion, the Witch and the Wardrobe '05
Troy '04
All the Queen's Men '02
To End All Wars '01
The Match '99
One More Kiss '99
Split Second '99
Babe: Pig in the City '98 (V)
Urban Ghost Story '98
Ivanhoe '97
Emma '96
Braveheart '95
Stormy Monday '88
Orde Wingate '76

Ernest Cossart (1876-1951)
Love from a Stranger '47
Kings Row '41
Kitty Foyle '40
Three Smart Girls Grow Up '39
Desire '36

James Cossins (1933-97)
Dynasty of Fear '72
Wuthering Heights '70
The Anniversary '68

Pierre Cosso (1961-)
An American Werewolf in Paris '97
My Wonderful Life '90

James Costa
L.I.E. '01
Joe the King '99

Marina Costa
Jungle Raiders '85

Constantin Costa-Gavras (1933-)
The Stupids '95
Spies Like Us '85

Suzanne Costallos
Lotto Land '95
True Love '89

Paulo Costanzo (1978-)
Everything's Gone Green '06
40 Days and 40 Nights '02
Scorched '02
Gypsy 83 '01
Josie and the Pussycats '01
Road Trip '00

Robert Costanzo
In the Mix '05
61* '01
Air Bud 2: Golden Receiver '98
For Which He Stands '98
With Friends Like These '98
Plump Fiction '97
Underworld '96
For Better or Worse '95
Storybook '95
Lady in Waiting '94
Ring of Fire 3: Lion Strike '94

Bob Costas (1951-)
Pootie Tang '01
BASEketball '98
The Scout '94

Dolores Costello (1905-79)
The Magnificent Ambersons '42
Breaking the Ice '38
Little Lord Fauntleroy '36

Don Costello (1901-45)
The Blue Dahlia '46
Mystery Man '44
Texas Masquerade '44
Sleepers West '41
Whistling in the Dark '41

Elvis Costello (1954-)
De-Lovely '04
I Love Your Work '03
Austin Powers 2: The Spy Who Shagged Me '99
200 Cigarettes '98
Spice World: The Movie '97
Straight to Hell '87
No Surrender '86
Americathon '79

Helene Costello (1903-57)
Don Juan '26
The Man on the Box '25

Lou Costello (1906-59)
The 30-Foot Bride of Candy Rock '59
Dance with Me, Henry '56
Abbott and Costello Meet the Mummy '55
Abbott and Costello Meet the Keystone Kops '54
Abbott and Costello Go to Mars '53
Abbott and Costello Meet Captain Kidd '52
Abbott and Costello Meet Dr. Jekyll and Mr. Hyde '52
Jack & the Beanstalk '52
Lost in Alaska '52
Abbott and Costello Meet the Invisible Man '51
Comin' 'Round the Mountain '51
Abbott and Costello in the Foreign Legion '50
Abbott and Costello Meet the Killer, Boris Karloff '49
Africa Screams '49
Abbott and Costello Meet Frankenstein '48
Mexican Hayride '48
The Noose Hangs High '48
Buck Privates Come Home '47
The Wistful Widow of Wagon Gap '47
Little Giant '46
The Time of Their Lives '46
Abbott and Costello in Hollywood '45
Here Come the Co-Eds '45
The Naughty Nineties '45
In Society '44
Lost in a Harem '44
Hit the Ice '43
It Ain't Hay '43
Pardon My Sarong '42
Ride 'Em Cowboy '42
Rio Rita '42
Who Done It? '42
Buck Privates '41
Hold That Ghost '41
In the Navy '41
Keep 'Em Flying '41
One Night in the Tropics '40

Mariclare Costello
Heart of a Champion: The Ray Mancini Story '85
Skeezer '82
Coward of the County '81
All God's Children '80
Conspiracy of Terror '75
The Execution of Private Slovik '74

Ward (Edward) Costello (1919-)
MacArthur '77
The City '76
The Gallant Hours '60

John A. Costelloe
Kazaam '96
Me and the Mob '94
Billy Bathgate '91

Nicolas Coster (1934-)
Betsy's Wedding '90
The Solitary Man '82
Stir Crazy '80
The Electric Horseman '79
MacArthur '77
The Sporting Club '72

Ritchie Coster
The Sentinel '06
The Tuxedo '02
Rear Window '98

Nikolaj Coster-Waldau (1970-)
Firewall '06
Kingdom of Heaven '05
Wimbledon '04
Black Hawk Down '01
Bent '97

George Costigan (1947-)
Calendar Girls '03
Love or Money '01
Girls' Night '97
The Hawk '93
Rita, Sue & Bob Too '87

Kevin Costner (1955-)
Swing Vote '08
Mr. Brooks '07
The Guardian '06
Rumor Has It... '05
The Upside of Anger '05
Open Range '03
Dragonfly '02
3000 Miles to Graceland '01
Thirteen Days '00
For Love of the Game '99
Message in a Bottle '98
The Postman '97
Tin Cup '96
Waterworld '95
The War '94
Wyatt Earp '94
A Perfect World '93
The Bodyguard '92
JFK '91
Robin Hood: Prince of Thieves '91
Dances with Wolves '90
Revenge '90
Field of Dreams '89
Bull Durham '88
No Way Out '87
The Untouchables '87
Amazing Stories '85
American Flyers '85
Fandango '85
Silverado '85
The Gunrunner '84
Shadows Run Black '84
Stacy's Knights '83
Table for Five '83
Testament '83
Night Shift '82
Chasing Dreams '81
Sizzle Beach U.S.A. '74

Laurence Cote (1966-)
Les Voleurs '96
Up/Down/Fragile '95
Nouvelle Vague '90

Tina Cote
Mean Guns '97
Omega Doom '96
Nemesis 2: Nebula '94

John Cothran, Jr. (1947-)
Black Snake Moan '07
Ricochet '91

Marion Cotillard (1975-)
La Vie en Rose '07
A Good Year '06
A Very Long Engagement '04
Big Fish '03
Love Me if You Dare '03

Kami Cotler (1965-)
A Day for Thanks on Walton's Mountain '82
The Waltons '72

Jonathon Cott
Above and Beyond '53
Battle Circus '53

Joseph Cotten (1905-94)
Delusion '84
Churchill and the Generals '81
Heaven's Gate '81
Casino '80
The Hearse '80
Screamers '80
Survivor '80
Perfect Crime '79
Airport '77 '77
Return to Fantasy Island '77
Twilight's Last Gleaming '77
The Lindbergh Kidnapping Case '76
The Big Push '75
Soylent Green '73
Lady Frankenstein '72
Torture Chamber of Baron Blood '72
The Abominable Dr. Phibes '71
The Passing of Evil '70
Toral Toral Toral '70
Petulia '68
Brighty of the Grand Canyon '67
Hellbenders '67
White Comanche '67
The Oscar '66
Tramplers '66
Hush, Hush, Sweet Charlotte '65
From the Earth to the Moon '58
Touch of Evil '58
Niagara '52
Othello '52
September Affair '50
Walk Softly, Stranger '50
Beyond the Forest '49
The Third Man '49
Under Capricorn '48
Portrait of Jennie '48
The Farmer's Daughter '47
Duel in the Sun '46
Love Letters '45
Gaslight '44
Since You Went Away '44
Shadow of a Doubt '43
Journey into Fear '42
The Magnificent Ambersons '42
Citizen Kane '41
Lydia '41

Fanny Cottencon (1957-)
Window Shopping '86
Special Police '85

Catherine Cotter
See Marie Burton

Chrissie Cotterill (1955-)
Nil by Mouth '96
Scrubbers '82

Ralph Cotterill (1932-)
Bad Boy Bubby '93
Crimebroker '93
Howling 3: The Marsupials '87
Starship '87
Burke & Wills '85

Mia Cottet (1968-)
Dawg '02

Oliver Cotton (1944-)
Shanghai Knights '03
The Dancer Upstairs '02
Beowulf '98
Christopher Columbus: The Discovery '92
Eleni '85
Robin Hood... The Legend: Herne's Son '85

Erin Cottrell
Love's Unending Legacy '07
Love's Long Journey '05

Paul Coufos
Mortal Danger '94
Boxcar Blues '90
Dragonfly '90
Thunderground '89
Food of the Gods: Part 2 '88
Busted Up '86
City of Shadows '86

Marisa Coughlan (1973-)
Already Dead '07
I Love Your Work '03
Pumpkin '02
Freddy Got Fingered '01
Super Troopers '01
Gossip '99
Teaching Mrs. Tingle '99

George Coulouris (1903-89)
The Long Good Friday '80
It's Not the Size That Counts '74
Murder on the Orient Express '74
The Tempter '74
Papillon '73
The Stranger '73
Tower of Evil '72
Blood from the Mummy's Tomb '71
Arabesque '66
The Skull '65
The Womaneater '59
Race for Life '55
The Runaway Bus '54
Doctor in the House '53
A Southern Yankee '48
Where There's Life '47
Lady on a Train '45
A Song to Remember '45
Master Race '44
Mr. Skeffington '44
None But the Lonely Heart '44
For Whom the Bell Tolls '43
This Land Is Mine '43
Watch on the Rhine '43
Citizen Kane '41
The Lady in Question '40

Keith Coulouris (1967-)
Beastmaster 3: The Eye of Braxus '95
Dead Man's Revenge '93
Take Down '92

Bernie Coulson (1965-)
Cabin by the Lake '00
The Highway Man '99
Hard Core Logo '96
Adventures in Spying '92
Eddie and the Cruisers 2: Eddie Lives! '89
The Accused '88

Clare Coulter (1942-)
Coast to Coast '04
Hollywood North '03

Raymond Coulthard (1968-)
Agatha Christie: A Life in Pictures '04
Emma '97
Rhodes '97

Barbara Couper (1903-92)
Vanity Fair '67
The Last Days of Dolwyn '49

Clotilde Courau (1969-)
La Vie en Rose '07
Almost Peaceful '02
Deep in the Woods '00
Deterrence '00
Elisa '94
The Pickle '93

Nicole Courcel (1930-)
Sundays & Cybele '62
Le Cas du Dr. Laurent '57
Rendez-vous de Juillet '49

Hazel Court (1926-2008)
Masque of the Red Death '65
The Raven '63
Doctor Blood's Coffin '62
Premature Burial '62
The Curse of Frankenstein '57
Hour of Decision '57
Devil Girl from Mars '54
Ghost Ship '53
Dear Murderer '47

Jason Court
A Night in the Life of Jimmy Reardon '88
Grandview U.S.A. '84

Margaret Courtenay (1923-96)
The Mirror Crack'd '80
Hot Millions '68

Tom Courtenay (1937-)
The Golden Compass '07
Nicholas Nickleby '02
Last Orders '01
A Rather English Marriage '98
The Old Curiosity Shop '94
The Last Butterfly '92

Let Him Have It '91
Happy New Year '87
Leonard Part 6 '87
The Dresser '83
I Heard the Owl Call My Name '73
Catch Me a Spy '71
One Day in the Life of Ivan Denisovich '71
Dandy in Aspic '66
Night of the Generals '66
Doctor Zhivago '65
Operation Crossbow '65
King and Country '64
Billy Liar '63
The Loneliness of the Long Distance Runner '62

Jerome Courtland (1926-)
Tharus Son of Attila '62
Tonka '58
Santa Fe '51
The Texas Rangers '51
Battleground '49
Man from Colorado '49
Tokyo Joe '49

Alex Courtney (1940-)
And the Band Played On '93
Fatal Pulse '88
Enter the Ninja '81

Chuck Courtney (1931-2000)
Billy the Kid Versus Dracula '66
Teenage Monster '57

Inez Courtney (1908-75)
The Thirteenth Man '37
Let's Sing Again '36
The Reckless Way '36
Suzy '36
Wedding Present '36

Jeni Courtney
Nothing Personal '95
The Secret of Roan Inish '94

Brian Cousins (1959-)
Soldier of Fortune Inc. '97
Invisible: The Chronicles of Benjamin Knight '93

Christopher Cousins (1960-)
Twinsitters '95

Christian Cousins (1983-)
Danielle Steel's Heartbeat '93

Allen Covert (1964-)
Strange Wilderness '08
I Now Pronounce You Chuck and Larry '07
Grandma's Boy '05
50 First Dates '04
Anger Management '03
Mr. Deeds '02
Little Nicky '00
The Wedding Singer '97
Longtime Companion '90

Jerome Cowan (1897-1972)
Critic's Choice '63
Have Rocket Will Travel '59
The West Point Story '50
Blondie Hits the Jackpot '49
June Bride '48
Cry Wolf '47
Riff-Raff '47
Blondie Knows Best '46
My Reputation '46
The Perfect Marriage '46
Fog Island '45
Getting Gertie's Garter '45
Jungle Captive '45
Guest in the House '44
Silver Spurs '43
Who Done It? '42
The Great Lie '41
The Maltese Falcon '41
Torrid Zone '40
East Side of Heaven '39
The Gracie Allen Murder Case '39
The Saint Strikes Back '39

Noel Coward (1899-1973)
The Italian Job '69
Boom! '68
Paris When It Sizzles '64
Our Man in Havana '59
Around the World in 80 Days '56
In Which We Serve '43
Hearts of the World '18

Jack Cowell
A Face in the Fog '36

Bruce Cowling (1919-86)
To Hell and Back '55
Cause for Alarm '51
The Painted Hills '51
Battleground '49

Nicola Cowper (1967-)
Devices and Desires '91
Journey to the Center of the Earth '88
Lionheart '87
Dreamchild '85
Transmutations '85
Winter Flight '84

Alan Cox (1970-)
Mrs. Dalloway '97
The Odyssey '97
An Awfully Big Adventure '94
Young Sherlock Holmes '85

Alex Cox (1954-)
Dance with the Devil '97
Dead Beat '94

Beau Cox (1971-)
Nowhere to Hide '83
On the Run '83

Brian Cox (1946-)
The Water Horse: Legend of the Deep '07
Zodiac '07
Running with Scissors '06
The Flying Scotsman '06
Match Point '05
Red Eye '05
The Ringer '05
The Bourne Supremacy '04
Troy '04
X2: X-Men United '03
Adaptation '02
The Ring '02
The Rookie '02
The Affair of the Necklace '01
L.I.E. '01
Strictly Sinatra '01
Super Troopers '01
Longitude '00
Mad About Mambo '00
Nuremberg '00
Sin '02
25th Hour '02
The Corruptor '99
For Love of the Game '99
The Minus Man '99
Desperate Measures '98
Poodle Springs '98
Rushmore '98
The Boxer '97
Kiss the Girls '97
Chain Reaction '96
The Glimmer Man '96
The Long Kiss Goodnight '96
Braveheart '95
Rob Roy '95
Royal Deceit '94
Sharpe's Eagle '93
Sharpe's Rifles '93
The Lost Language of Cranes '92
Murder by Moonlight '91
Hidden Agenda '90
Secret Weapon '90
Manhunter '86
Pope John Paul II '84
Silent Scream '84
Therese Raquin '80
In Celebration '75

Charlie Cox (1982-)
Stardust '07
Casanova '05
The Merchant of Venice '04
Dot the I '03

Christina Cox (1971-)
Better Than Chocolate '99

Claire Cox (1975-)
Street Law '95
Luther '03

Courteney Cox (1964-)
Zoom '06
Barnyard '06 (V)
The Longest Yard '05
November '05
Get Well Soon '01
3000 Miles to Graceland '01
Scream 3 '00
The Runner '99
Scream 2 '97
Commandments '96
Scream '96
The Opposite Sex and How to Live With Them '93
Ace Ventura: Pet Detective '93
Shaking the Tree '92
Mr. Destiny '90
Curiosity Kills '90
Down Twisted '87
Cocoon: The Return '88
Masters of the Universe '87
Misfits of Science '85

David Cox
Extreme Vengeance '90

Jennifer Elise Cox (1973-)
The Last Season '87

Julie Cox (1973-)
The Brady Bunch Movie '95
Second in Command '05
Byron '03
Children of Dune '03
King of Texas '02
Dune '00
The Scarlet Pimpernel 2: Mademoiselle Guillotine '99
20,000 Leagues Under the Sea '97

Mitchell Cox
Crossfire '98
A.P.E.X. '94
Red Snow '91
Rule #3 '93

Nikki Cox (1978-)
Nutty Professor 2: The Klumps '00
The Glimmer Man '96

Richard Cox (1948-)
Missing Brendan '03
American Tragedy '00
Street Justice '89
Zombie High '87
The Vindicator '85
King of the Mountain '81
Cruising '80

Jonathan Coy (1953-)
Conspiracy '01
The Scarlet Pimpernel '99
The Scarlet Pimpernel 2: Mademoiselle Guillotine '99

Ruth Cox
The Attic '80
Swap Meet '79

Tony Cox (1958-)
Date Movie '06
I Accidentally Domed Your Son '04
Bad Santa '03
Me, Myself, and Irene '00
Spaced Invaders '90

Veanne Cox (1963-)
Marci X '03
Beethoven's 4th '01
Big Eden '00

Wally Cox (1924-73)
The Night Strangler '72
The Barefoot Executive '71
The Boatniks '70
Bard '68
A Guide for the Married Man '67
Bedford Incident '65
Spencer's Mountain '63
State Fair '62

Ronny Cox (1938-)
Crazy as Hell '02
Point of Origin '02
American Outlaws '01
Perfect Murder, Perfect Town '00
Forces of Nature '99
Frog and Wombat '98
From the Earth to the Moon '98
Murder at 1600 '97
Todd McFarlane's Spawn '97 (V)
Rebound: The Legend of Earl "The Goat" Manigault '96
Scissors '91
Loose Cannons '90
Martians Go Home! '90
Total Recall '90
Captain America '89
One Man Force '89
Scandal in a Small Town '88
In the Line of Duty: The FBI Murders '88
The Abduction of Kari Swenson '87
Beverly Hills Cop 2 '87
RoboCop '87
Steele Justice '87
Vision Quest '85
Beverly Hills Cop '84
Raw Courage '84
Reckless Disregard '84
Tangiers '83
The Beast Within '82
Some Kind of Hero '82
Two of a Kind '82
When Hell Was in Session '82
Taps '81
Fallen Angel '81
The Onion Field '79
Harper Valley P.T.A. '78
Gray Lady Down '77
The Car '77
Last Song '80
Kavik the Wolf Dog '80
Bound for Glory '76
Our Town '77
Who Is the Black Dahlia? '75
The Connection '73
Deliverance '72

Peter Coyote (1942-)
Resurrecting the Champ '07
Deepwater '05
Bon Voyage '03
Northfork '03
Femme Fatale '02
Purpose '02
A Walk to Remember '02
A Time for Dancing '00
More Dogs Than Bones '00
Erin Brockovich '00
Red Letters '00
Execution of Justice '99
Random Hearts '99
Indiscreet '98
Patch Adams '98
Seeds of Doubt '96
Buffalo Girls '95
Moonlight and Valentino '95
Terminal Justice: Cybertech P.D. '95
Breach of Conduct '94
Kika '94
Bitter Moon '92
Keeper of the City '92
Crooked Hearts '91
Exposure '91
The Man Inside '90
Heart of Midnight '89
Echoes in the Darkness '87
A Man in Love '87
Outrageous Fortune '87
Stacking '87
Slayground '84
Cross Creek '83
Strangers Kiss '83
Timerider '83
Endangered Species '82
E.T.: The Extra-Terrestrial '82
The People vs. Jean Harris '81
Southern Comfort '81
Die Laughing '80
Tell Me a Riddle '80

Cylk Cozart (1957-)
16 Blocks '06
Play It to the Bone '99
Three to Tango '99
White Men Can't Jump '92

Richard Coyle (1972-)
The History of Mr. Polly '07
The Libertine '05
Othello '01

Brendan Coyle (1963-)
Conspiracy '01
The Mapmaker '01
Catherine Cookson's The Glass Virgin '95
Prince of Foisoners: The Life and Crimes of William Palmer '98

Susan Coyne
Slings & Arrows: Season 2 '05

Carolyn Craig (1934-70)
Studs Lonigan '60
House on Haunted Hill '58

Daniel Craig (1968-)
The Golden Compass '07
The Invasion '07
Casino Royale '06
Infamous '06
Renaissance '06 (V)
Archangel '05
Fateless '05
The Jacket '05
Layer Cake '05
Munich '05
Enduring Love '04
The Mother '03
Sylvia '03
Road to Perdition '02
Lara Croft: Tomb Raider '01
Sword of Honour '01
I Dreamed of Africa '00
Love and Rage '99
The Trench '99
Elizabeth '98
Love Is the Devil '98
The Ice House '97
Obsession '97
Kiss and Tell '96
Moll Flanders '96
The Power of One '92

Buster Crabbe (1907-83)
The Scarlet Pimpernel 3: The Kidnapped King '99
The Rector's Wife '94
Alien Dead '79
Swim Team '79
Arizona Raiders '65
King of the Congo '52
Pirates of the High Seas '50
The Last of the Redmen '47
Sea Hound '47
Outlaw of the Plains '46
Swamp Fire '46
Border Badmen '45
Gangster's Den '45
His Brother's Ghost '45
Lightning Raiders '45
Shadows of Death '45
Devil Riders '44
Frontier Outlaws '44
Nabonga '44
Oath of Vengeance '44
Rustler's Hideout '44
Thundering Gunslingers '44
Wild Horse Phantom '44
Billy the Kid Trapped '42
Jungle Siren '42
Law and Order '42
The Mysterious Rider '42
Wildcat '42
Flash Gordon Conquers the Universe '40
Red Barry '38
Forlorn River '37
Desert Gold '36
Drift Fence '36
Flash Gordon '36
Buffalo Stampede '33
King of the Jungle '33
Tarzan the Fearless '33
Island of Lost Souls '32
To the Last Man '33

Ruth Cracknell (1925-2002)
Joey '98
Lilian's Story '95
Alice to Nowhere '86
The Chant of Jimmie Blacksmith '78
Island Trader '71

Diane Craig (1949-)
All the Rivers Run '84
The Mango Tree '77
Ned Kelly '70
Roses Bloom Twice '77

Helen Craig (1912-86)
They Live by Night '49
The Snake Pit '48
James Craig (1912-85)
The Tormentors '71
The Devil's Brigade '68
Man or Gun '58
Naked in the Sun '57
Cyclops '56
Drums in the Deep South '51
Side Street '50
Our Vines Have Tender Grapes '45
The Human Comedy '43
Valley of the Sun '42
The Devil & Daniel Webster '41
Black Friday '40
Kitty Foyle '40
Winners of the West '40
Thunder Trail '37
Michael Craig (1928-)
Robin Hood... The Legend: Herne's Son '85
Escape 2000 '81
The Irishman '78
Night of the Assassin '77
Roses Bloom Twice '77
Ride a Wild Pony '75
Inn of the Damned '74
Vault of Horror '73
Lola '69
Star! '68
Modesty Blaise '66
Sandra of a Thousand Delights '65
Stolen Hours '63
Mysterious Island '61
Sapphire '59
Sea of Sand '58
The Silent Enemy '58
Philip Craig
Behind the Red Door '02
Spider '02
Wendy Craig (1934-)
The Nanny '65
The Servant '63
The Young Land '59
Jeanne Crain (1925-2003)
The Night God Screamed '71
Nefertiti; Queen of the Nile '64
Fastest Gun Alive '56
Man Without a Star '55
Dangerous Crossing '53
Belles on Their Toes '52
People Will Talk '51
Cheaper by the Dozen '50
A Letter to Three Wives '49
Pinky '49
Leave Her to Heaven '45
State Fair '45
Grant Cramer (1961-)
Addicted to Murder 3: Bloodlust '99
Leapin' Leprechauns '95
Killer Klowns from Outer Space '88
Hardbodies '84
New Year's Evil '78
Joey Cramer (1974-)
Stone Fox '87
Flight of the Navigator '86
Marc Cramer (1910-88)
First Yank into Tokyo '45
Isle of the Dead '45
Richard Cramer (1889-1960)
Saps at Sea '40
Santa Fe Bound '37
Slaves in Bondage '37
Speed Reporter '36
Frontier Justice '35
Barbara Crampton (1962-)
Poison '01
Cold Harvest '98
The Godson '98
Space Truckers '97
Castle Freak '95
Robot Wars '93
Trancers 2: The Return of Jack Deth '90
Puppet Master '89
Kidnapped '87
Chopping Mall '86
Fraternity Vacation '85
Body Double '84
Re-Animator '84
Bob Crane (1928-78)
Gus '76
Superdad '73
Return to Peyton Place '61
Norma Crane (1928-73)
Fiddler on the Roof '71
They Call Me Mr. Tibbs! '70
Night Gallery '69
Tea and Sympathy '56
Richard Crane (1918-69)
The Devil's Partner '58
Guns Don't Argue '57
Rocky Jones, Space Ranger: Renegade Satellite '54
Winning of the West '53
Cavalry Charge '51
Dynamite '49
Tony Crane (1972-)
Wishmaster '97
An American Summer '90
In the Line of Duty: A Cop for the Killing '90
Kenneth Cranham (1944-)
A Good Year '06
Layer Cake '05
Two Men Went to War '02
Born Romantic '00
Gangster No. 1 '00
Lady Audley's Secret '00
Shiner '00
The Murder of Stephen Lawrence '99
Deep in the Heart (of Texas) '98
Our Mutual Friend '98
The Boxer '97
Jack Higgins' Midnight Man '96
The Tenant of Wildfell Hall '96
Jack Higgins' On Dangerous Ground '95
Tale of a Vampire '92
Under Suspicion '92
Prospero's Books '91
Monkey Boy '90
Oranges Are Not the Only Fruit '89
Chocolat '88
Hellbound: Hellraiser 2 '88
Stealing Heaven '88
Danger UXB '81
Therese Raquin '80
Brother Sun, Sister Moon '73
Lorcan Cranitch (1959-)
Shackleton '02
Dancing at Lughnasa '98
Deacon Brodie '98
Cracker: Brotherly Love '95
Cracker: Men Should Weep '94
Cracker: To Be a Somebody '94
Patrick Cranshaw (1919-2005)
Air Bud 5: Buddy Spikes '03
Bubble Boy '01
Best in Show '00
Broken Vessels '98
Nothing to Lose '96
The Amazing Transparent Man '60
Bryan Cranston (1956-)
Little Miss Sunshine '06
Seeing Other People '04
National Lampoon's Holiday Reunion '03
Terror Tract '00
From the Earth to the Moon '98
Saving Private Ryan '98
That Thing You Do! '96
The Companion '94
Erotique '94
High Stakes '93
Dead Space '90
The Big Turnaround '88
Paul Crauchet (1920-)
Beyond Fear '75
Army of Shadows '69
Nick Cravat (1911-94)
The Island of Dr. Moreau '77
The Scalphunters '68
Run Silent, Run Deep '58
Crimson Pirate '52
The Flame & the Arrow '50
Noel Cravat (1910-60)
The 5000 Fingers of Dr. T '53
Pirate Ship '49
The Razor's Edge '46
G-Men vs. the Black Dragon '43
Frank Craven (1875-1945)
Colonel Effingham's Raid '45
Jack London '44
Son of Dracula '43
In This Our Life '42
Keeper of the Flame '42
Pittsburgh '42
City for Conquest '40
Dreaming Out Loud '40
Our Town '40
James Craven (1892-1955)
D-Day on Mars '45
Immortal Sergeant '43
Sherlock Holmes and the Secret Weapon '42
Today I Hang '42
Green Archer '40
Matt Craven (1956-)
The Longshots '08
Assault on Precinct 13 '05
The Life of David Gale '03
The Statement '03
Timeline '03
Dragonfly '02
Varian's War '01
Nuremberg '00
Things You Can Tell Just by Looking at Her '00
From the Earth to the Moon '98
Paulie '98
The Final Cut '96
The Juror '96
Masterminds '96
Breach of Trust '95
Bulletproof Heart '95
Crimson Tide '95
K2: The Ultimate High '92
Jacob's Ladder '90
Smokescreen '90
Chattahoochee '89
Palais Royale '88
Agent on Ice '86
Happy Birthday to Me '81
'Till Death Do Us Part '72
Mimi (Meyer) Craven
Dogwatch '97
Daddy's Girl '96
Midnight Heat '95
The Last Gasp '94
Open Fire '94
Mikey '92
Wes Craven (1939-)
Red Eye '05
Jay and Silent Bob Strike Back '01
Scream '96
ShadowZone: The Undead Express '96
The Fear '94
Wes Craven's New Nightmare '94
Body Bags '93
Andrew Crawford (1917-94)
The Gay Lady '49
Dear Murderer '47
Anne Crawford (1920-56)
Knights of the Round Table '53
Tony Draws a Horse '51
Night Beat '48
Bedelia '46
Broderick Crawford (1911-86)
Ransom Money '88
Dark Forces '83
The Uppercrust '81
Express to Terror '79
A Little Romance '79
The Private Files of J. Edgar Hoover '77
Hunter '76
Proof of the Man '77
Terror in the Wax Museum '73
Embassy '72
The Tattered Web '71
Yin & Yang of Mr. Go '71
Vulture '67
The Oscar '66
The Texican '66
The Castilian '63
Goliath and the Dragon '61
Between Heaven and Hell '56
Fastest Gun Alive '56
Il Bidone '55
Not as a Stranger '55
Human Desire '54
Last of the Comanches '52
Lone Star '52
Born Yesterday '50
All the King's Men '49
The Time of Your Life '48
Black Angel '46
The Black Cat '41
Seven Sinners '40
Slightly Honorable '40
The Texas Rangers Ride Again '40
Beau Geste '39
Eternally Yours '39
The Real Glory '39
Chace Crawford
Loaded '08
Cindy Crawford (1966-)
The Simian Line '99
Fair Game '95
Clayne Crawford (1978-)
Swimfan '02
A Walk to Remember '02
Ellen Crawford
The Man from Earth '07
Cries of Silence '97
Ulterior Motives '92
H. Marion Crawford
See Howard Marion-Crawford
Howard Crawford
See Howard Marion-Crawford
Joan Crawford (1904-77)
Night Gallery '69
Berserk! '67
Fatal Confinement '64
Strait-Jacket '64
What Ever Happened to Baby Jane? '62
The Best of Everything '59
The Story of Esther Costello '57
Autumn Leaves '56
Queen Bee '55
Johnny Guitar '53
Torch Song '53
Sudden Fear '52
The Damned Don't Cry '50
Harriet Craig '50
Flamingo Road '49
It's a Great Feeling '49
Daisy Kenyon '47
The Possessed '47
Humoresque '46
Mildred Pierce '45
Hollywood Canteen '44
Above Suspicion '43
Reunion in France '42
They All Kissed the Bride '42
When Ladies Meet '41
A Woman's Face '41
Strange Cargo '40
Susan and God '40
The Women '39
The Shining Hour '38
The Bride Wore Red '37
The Last of Mrs. Cheyney '37
Mannequin '37
The Gorgeous Hussy '36
Love on the Run '36
Forsaking All Others '35
I Live My Life '35
Chained '34
Sadie McKee '34
Dancing Lady '33
Today We Live '33
Grand Hotel '32
Rain '32
Dance Fools Dance '31
Laughing Sinners '31
Possessed '31
Our Modern Maidens '29
Our Dancing Daughters '28
The Unknown '27
Tramp, Tramp, Tramp '26
John Crawford (1926-)
Hard Knocks '79
The Enforcer '76
The Severed Arm '73
John Paul Jones '59
Actors and Sin '52
Zombies of the Stratosphere '52
Ringside '49
Night Time in Nevada '48
O.S.S. '46
Meeting at Midnight '44
Phantom Lady '44
Hands Across the Border '43
Johnny Crawford (1946-)
The Gambler Returns: The Luck of the Draw '93
Kenny Rogers as the Gambler, Part 2: The Adventure Continues '83
Outlaw Blues '77
The Great Texas Dynamite Chase '76
El Dorado '67
Village of the Giants '65
Indian Paint '64
Courage of Black Beauty '57
Katherine Crawford (1944-)
Riding with Death '76
Walk in the Spring Rain '70
The Doomsday Flight '66
Kathryn Crawford (1908-80)
The Concentratin' Kid '30
Mountain Justice '30
King of the Rodeo '30
Michael Crawford (1942-)
Once Upon a Forest '93 (V)
Condorman '81
Hello, Dolly! '69
How I Won the War '67
A Funny Thing Happened on the Way to the Forum '66
The Knack '65
Rachael Crawford (1969-)
The Man '05
Love Songs '99
In His Father's Shoes '97
Pale Saints '97
Curtis's Charm '96
Rude '96
When Night Is Falling '95
Sophia Crawford (1966-)
U.S. Seals 2 '01
Sword of Honor '94
Wayne Crawford
American Cop '94
Crime Lords '91
Rebel Storm '90
Headhunter '89
White Ghost '88
The Evil Below '87
Quiet Thunder '87
Jake Speed '86
Barracuda '78
Charlie Creed-Miles (1972-)
King Arthur '04
Station Jim '01
Essex Boys '99
Nil by Mouth '96
The Young Poisoner's Handbook '94
Monica Creel (1970-)
Possums '99
Rattled '96
Laird Cregar (1916-44)
Hangover Square '45
Heaven Can Wait '43
Hello, Frisco, Hello '43
The Black Swan '42
Joan of Paris '42
This Gun for Hire '42
Charley's Aunt '41
I Wake Up Screaming '41
Joseph Crehan (1886-1966)
Red Desert '50
The Invisible Monster '50
The Fighting 69th '40
Music in My Heart '40
Stanley and Livingstone '39
Star Reporter '39
Francis Creighton (1955-2003)
Barcelona '94
The Malibu Beach Vampires '91
Jack Creley (1926-2004)
Dr. Strangelove, or: How I Learned to Stop Worrying and Love the Bomb '64
Bruno Cremer (1929-)
Under the Sand '00
Menage '86
Josepha '82
A Simple Story '79
Sorcerer '77
Is Paris Burning? '66
Richard Crenna (1926-2003)
The Day Reagan Was Shot '01
By Dawn's Early Light '00
Wrongfully Accused '98
20,000 Leagues Under the Sea '97
Jade '95
A Pyromaniac's Love Story '95
Sabrina '95
Hot Shots! Part Deux '93
Intruders '92

Last Flight Out: A True Story '90
Montana '90
The Hillside Strangler '89
Leviathan '89
Rambo 3 '88
A Case of Deadly Force '86
On Wings of Eagles '86
Rambo: First Blood, Part 2 '85
Summer Rental '85
The Flamingo Kid '84
Table for Five '83
First Blood '82
Body Heat '81
Death Ship '80
Stone Cold Dead '80
Mayflower: The Pilgrims' Adventure '79
Wild Horse Hank '79
Centennial '78
Devil Dog: The Hound of Hell '78
The Evil '78
Breakthrough Pass '76
War Between the Tates '76
Catlow '71
Ride to Glory '71
Thief '71
Doctors' Wives '70
Marooned '69
Star! '68
Wait until Dark '67
The Sand Pebbles '66
Our Miss Brooks '56
Pride of St. Louis '52

Pierre Cressoy (1924-80)
Blood for a Silver Dollar '66
The Triumph of Hercules '66

Laura Hope Crews (1879-1942)
The Lion of Thebes '64
The Flame of New Orleans '41
Gone with the Wind '39
The Rains Came '39
Thanks for the Memory '39
Angel '37
Camille '36

Terry Crews (1968-)
Get Smart '08
Street Kings '08
Balls of Fury '07
Norbit '07
The Benchwarmers '06
Idiocracy '06
Harsh Times '05
The Longest Yard '05
White Chicks '04
Baadasssss! '03
Friday After Next '02
Serving Sara '02

Wendy Crewson (1956-)
The Seeker: The Dark Is Rising '07
Away From Her '06
The Covenant '06
Eight Below '06
Niagara Motel '06
The Clearing '04
Between Strangers '02
A Killing Spring '02
The Santa Clause 2 '02
Verdict in Blood '02
Mercy '00
The 6th Day '00
Better Than Chocolate '99
Bicentennial Man '99
Escape Velocity '99
Summer's End '99
From the Earth to the Moon '98
Air Force One '97
The Eighteenth Angel '97

Amanda Crew
Final Destination 3 '06
Meltdown '06

Verdi '53

Ed Crick
Future Hunters '88
Eye of the Eagle '87

Missy (Melissa) Crider (1974-)
Gigli '03
Frailty '02
Instinct to Kill '01
Mulholland Drive '01
Alien Cargo '99
Quicksilver Highway '98
The Sex Monster '99
Sins of the Mind '97
Powder '95
Girls in Prison '94

Erno Crisa (1924-68)
The Duke Is Tops '38
Miracle in Harlem '48
Gang War '40

Donald Crisp (1880-1974)
Spencer's Mountain '63
Greyfriars Bobby '61
Pollyanna '60
A Dog of Flanders '59
Last Hurrah '58
The Long Gray Line '55
The Man from Laramie '55
Prince Valiant '54
Home Town Story '51
Challenge to Lassie '49
The Hills of Home '48
Ramrod '47
Son of Lassie '45
The Valley of Decision '45
The Adventures of Mark Twain '44
National Velvet '44
Lassie, Come Home '43
How Green Was My Valley '41
Brother Orchid '40
City for Conquest '40
Knute Rockne: All American '40
The Sea Hawk '40
Oklahoma Kid '39
The Old Maid '39
The Private Lives of Elizabeth & Essex '39
Wuthering Heights '38
Amazing Dr. Clitterhouse '38

Bernard Cribbins (1928-)
The Adventures of Picasso '80
Frenzy '72
The Railway Children '70
The Wrong Arm of the Law '63
The Mouse on the Moon '62

Mik Cribben
Beware! Children at Play '95

Nightmare '82

Peter Criss (1947-)
Detroit Rock City '99
KISS Meets the Phantom of the Park '78

Anthony Criss
See Treach

Quentin Crisp (1908-99)
Naked in New York '93
Philadelphia '93
Orlando '92
The Bride '85

Criswell (1907-82)
White Comanche '67
Orgy of the Dead '65
Night of the Ghouls '59
Plan 9 from Outer Space '56

Anthony Crivello (1955-)
Running Woman '98
Star Portal '97
Twisted '96
Frankenstein Sings... The Movie '95
The Lost Capone '90

Karlene Crockett
Massive Retaliation '85
Eyes of Fire '84
Diary of a Teenage Hitchhiker '82

Jamie Croft (1981-)
Joey '98
The Real Macaw '98
Napoleon '96 (V)
That Eye, the Sky '94

Peter Croft (1917-)
O.H.M.S. '37

Jeanette Cronin
Danny Deckchair '03
Mr. Accident '00
The Boys '98

Laurel Cronin (1939-92)
Beethoven '92
Housesitter '92

Hume Cronyn (1911-2003)
Marvin's Room '96
Camilla '94
The Pelican Brief '93
Broadway Bound '92
To Dance with the White Dog '93
Age Old Friends '89

Perla Cristal (1937-)
The Fury of the Wolfman '70
The Christmas Kid '68
A Witch Without a Broom '68

Linda Cristal (1934-)
Mr. Majestyk '74
Two Rode Together '61
The Alamo '60
The Perfect Furlough '59
The Fiend Who Walked the West '58

Richard Cromwell (1910-60)
Baby Face Morgan '42
Riot Squad '41
Young Mr. Lincoln '39
The Wrong Road '37
Life Begins at Forty '35
The Lives of a Bengal Lancer '35
Hoopla '33
The Strange Love of Molly Louvain '32
Maker of Men '31

James Cromwell (1940-)
Becoming Jane '07
Spider-Man 3 '07
The Queen '06
The Longest Yard '05
I, Robot '04
Salem's Lot '04
Angels in America '03
A Death in the Family '02
The Magnificent Ambersons '02
RFK '02
Spirit: Stallion of the Cimarron '02 (V)
Space Cowboys '00
The Bachelor '99
The General's Daughter '99
The Green Mile '99
Snow Falling on Cedars '99
A Slight Case of Murder '99
Babe: Pig in the City '98
Deep Impact '98
Species 2 '98
The Education of Little Tree '97
L.A. Confidential '97
Eraser '96
Star Trek: First Contact '96
The People vs. Larry Flynt '96
The Babe '92
A Christmas Without Snow '80

David Cronenberg (1943-)
Jason X '01
Resurrection '99
Last Night '98
Blood & Donuts '95
Extreme Measures '96
The Stupids '95
Henry & Verin '94
Nightbreed '90
Into the Night '85

Neil Crone
Carried Away '95
Hit & Run '82

Gail Cronauer
The Newton Boys '97

Claudia Cron
Running Brave '83

Leland Crooke
Scorchers '92
Dead Man Walking '88

Anna Cropper (1938-2007)
Praying Mantis '83
The Lost Boys '78

Linda Cropper
Blackrock '97
The Seventh Floor '93
Passion '99

Annette Crosbie (1934-)
Calendar Girls '03
Oliver Twist '00
Shooting Fish '98
Hawks '89
Miracle Mile '89
Double Dare '92
Desperate Crimes '93
Black Water '94
Relative Fear '95
Mutant Species '95
Red Shoe Diaries 2: Double Dare '92
Arizona Heat '87
Skin Deep '89
Pet Sematary '89

Tandy Cronyn (1945-)
Getting Out '94
Age Old Friends '89
Twisted '86

Mackenzie Crook (1971-)
Pirates of the Caribbean: At World's End '07
Land of the Blind '06
Pirates of the Caribbean: Dead Man's Chest '06
The Merchant of Venice '04
Pirates of the Caribbean: The Curse of the Black Pearl '03
Once Upon a Time in America '84

Peter Crook (1958-)
Clean Slate '94
The Yarn Princess '94
Peephole '93
Chaplin '92
Bird '88
Coach '78
The Dark '79

David Crosby (1941-)
Thunderheart '92
Backdraft '91
Hook '91
Gimme Shelter '70

Cathy Lee Crosby (1944-)
Ablaze '00
The Big Tease '99
The Real Howard Spitz '98
The Player '92
World War III '86
Roughnecks '80

Denise Crosby (1957-)
Mortuary '05
Deep Impact '98
Executive Power '98
Red Shoe Diaries: Four on the Floor '96
Mutant Species '95
Relative Fear '95
Black Water '94
Desperate Crimes '93
Double Dare '92
Miracle Mile '89
Pet Sematary '89
Skin Deep '89
Arizona Heat '87
Desert Hearts '86
The Eliminators '86
Curse of the Pink Panther '83
48 Hrs. '82

Gary Crosby (1933-95)
That's Entertainment '74
Cancel My Reservation '72
Robin and the 7 Hoods '64
Girl Happy '65
Operation Bikini '63
The Night Stalker '87
Justin Morgan Had a Horse '81
Chill Factor '90

Lindsay Crosby (1938-89)
The Glory Stompers '67
Free Grass '69

Lucinda Crosby (1952-)
Blue Movies '88
Naked Cage '86

Mary Crosby (1959-)
The Night Caller '97
Cupid '96
Desperate Motives '92

Bing Crosby (1904-77)
That's Entertainment '74
Cancel My Reservation '72
Stagecoach '66
Robin and the 7 Hoods '64
High Society '56
Anything Goes '56
White Christmas '54
The Country Girl '54
Little Boy Lost '53
Scared Stiff '53
Just for You '52
Here Comes the Groom '51
Mr. Music '50
Riding High '50
The Adventures of Ichabod and Mr. Toad '49 (V)
A Connecticut Yankee in King Arthur's Court '49
The Bells of St. Mary's '46
Blue Skies '46
The Road to Utopia '46
Welcome Stranger '47
My Favorite Brunette '47
Emperor Waltz '48
Holiday Inn '42
Road to Morocco '42
Here Is My Heart '34

Cleopatra '63
The Arrangement '69
The Parallax View '74
There Was a Crooked Man '70
Strictly G.I. '44
They Got Me Covered '43
The Phantom of the Opera '43
Shadow of a Doubt '43
Lifeboat '44
The Seventh Cross '44
Ziegfeld Follies '46
Twice '46
The Postman Always Rings Twice '46
Brute Force '47
People Will Talk '51
Conrack '74
The World According to Garp '82
Honky Tonk Freeway '81
Rollover '81
The Road to Zanzibar '41
Road to Rio '47
Blue Skies '46
Birth of the Blues '41
Star Spangled Rhythm '42
Rhythm on the River '40
Rhythm on the Range '36
Pennies from Heaven '36
Waikiki Wedding '37
If I Had My Way '40
Going Hollywood '33
College Humor '33
Reaching for the Moon '31
King of Jazz '30
Double or Nothing '37
Mississippi '35
East Side of Heaven '39
The Road to Singapore '40
Going My Way '44
The Princess and the Pirate '44
A Connecticut Yankee in King Arthur's Court '49
The Legend of Sleepy Hollow '49 (N)
Brewster's Millions '85
Cocoon '85
Gin Game '84
Impulse '84
The World According to Garp '82
Blue Skies '46
Welcome Stranger '47

Day One '89
Cocoon: The Return '88
"batteries not included" '87
Foxfire '87

Gary Crosby (1933-95)

Bing Crosby (1904-77)

The Berlin Conspiracy '91
Body Chemistry '90
Corporate Affairs '90
Eating '90
Tapeheads '89
Deadly Innocence '88
Quicker Than the Eye '88
Stagecoach '86
Ice Pirates '84
Last Plane Out '83
Pearl '78

Norm Crosby (1927-)
Adam Sandler's 8 Crazy Nights '02 (V)
Amore! '93

Wade Crosby (1905-75)
Invasion U.S.A. '52
Tales of Robin Hood '52
Rough Riders of Cheyenne '45

Henrietta Crosman (1861-1944)
Personal Property '37
The Moon's Our Home '36
Charlie Chan's Secret '35
The Dark Angel '35
Pilgrimage '33

Ben Cross (1947-)
Hero Wanted '08
Species 4: The Awakening '07
Undisputed II: Last Man Standing '06
Frederick Forsyth's Icon '05
Exorcist: The Beginning '04
Solomon '98
The Corporate Ladder '97
20,000 Leagues Under the Sea '97
The Invader '96
Turbulence '96
First Knight '95
Temptress '95
The Ascent '94
Haunted Symphony '94
Cold Sweat '93
The Criminal Mind '93
Diamond Fleece '92
Live Wire '92
The Jeweller's Shop '90
Nightlife '90
Paperhouse '89
Steal the Sky '88
The Unholy '88
The Assisi Underground '84
The Far Pavilions '84
Coming Out of the Ice '82
Chariots of Fire '81
The Flame Trees of Thika '81

David Cross (1964-)
Kung Fu Panda '08 (V)
Alvin and the Chipmunks '07
I'm Not There '07
Curious George '06 (V)
School for Scoundrels '06
She's the Man '06
Eternal Sunshine of the Spotless Mind '04
Men in Black 2 '02
Scary Movie 2 '01
Chain of Fools '00
Small Soldiers '98
The Cable Guy '96

Dennis Cross (1924-)
How to Make a Monster '58
Crime of Passion '57

Flora Cross
Margot at the Wedding '07
Bee Season '05

Harley Cross (1978-)
Shriek If You Know What I Did Last Friday the 13th '00
Dance with the Devil '97
To Dance with the White Dog '93
Stanley and Iris '90
The Fly 2 '89
Cohen and Tate '88
The Believers '87
Where Are the Children? '85

Joseph Cross (1986-)
Untraceable '08
Flags of Our Fathers '06
Running with Scissors '06
Strangers with Candy '06
The Spring '00
Desperate Measures '98
Jack Frost '98
Wide Awake '97

Larry Cross (1913-76)
The Wind and the Lion '75

Paul Cross
The Return of the Borrowers '96
The Borrowers '93
Ice Pawn '92

Peter Cross
See Pierre Cressoy

Rebecca Cross
The Bachelor '99

TJ Cross
The Last Warrior '99
Leprechaun 4: In Space '96
Wet and Wild Summer '92

Rupert Crosse (1927-73)
The Reivers '69
Ride in the Whirlwind '66
Shadows '60

Syd Crossley (1885-1960)
Young and Innocent '37
The Deputy Drummer '35
That Certain Thing '28

Scatman Crothers (1910-86)
The Journey of Natty Gann '85
Twilight Zone: The Movie '83
Two of a Kind '83
Deadly Eyes '82
Zapped! '82
Bronco Billy '80
The Shining '80
Scavenger Hunt '79
Mean Dog Blues '78
Chesty Anderson USN '76
The Shootist '76
Silver Streak '76
Stay Hungry '76
One Flew Over the Cuckoo's Nest '75
Streetfight '75
Black Belt Jones '74
Truck Turner '74
Detroit 9000 '73
The King of Marvin Gardens '72
Bloody Mama '70
The Great White Hope '70
Lady in a Cage '64
The Patsy '64
Between Heaven and Hell '56
Yes, Sir, Mr. Bones '51

Brian Croucher
I'll Sleep When I'm Dead '03
Fool's Gold: The Story of the Brink's-Mat Robbery '92
The House that Bled to Death '81

Lindsay Crouse (1948-)
Mr. Brooks '07
Cherish '02
Impostor '02
The Insider '99
Progeny '98
The Arrival '96
If These Walls Could Talk '96
The Juror '96
Prefontaine '96
The Indian in the Cupboard '95
Norma Jean and Marilyn '96
Being Human '94
Bye Bye, Love '94
Parallel Lives '94

Chantilly Lace '93
Final Appeal '93
Desperate Hours '90
Communion '89
House of Games '87
Iceman '84
Places in the Heart '84
Daniel '83
The Verdict '82
Prince of the City '81
Summer Solstice '81
Between the Lines '77
Slap Shot '77
All the President's Men '76
Eleanor & Franklin '76

Roger Crouzet (1927-2000)
Blue Country '77
Double Agents '59
Letters from My Windmill '54

Ashley Crow (1960-)
Minority Report '02
Little Big League '94
Final Appeal '93

Emilia Crow
Grand Tour: Disaster in Time '92
Hitz '89

Graham Crowden (1922-)
Calendar Girls '03
Possession '02
I Want You '98
The Innocent Sleep '95
Monsignor Quixote '91
Code Name: Emerald '85
The Company of Wolves '85
Out of Africa '85
Britannia Hospital '82
The Little Prince '74
Romance with a Double Bass '74
Naughty Knights '71
If.... '69
Morgan: A Suitable Case for Treatment '66

Russell Crowe (1964-)
American Gangster '07
3:10 to Yuma '07
A Good Year '06
Cinderella Man '05
Master and Commander: The Far Side of the World '03
A Beautiful Mind '01
Gladiator '00
Proof of Life '00
The Insider '99
Mystery, Alaska '99
Breaking Up '97
Heaven's Burning '97
L.A. Confidential '97
No Way Back '96
The Quick and the Dead '95
Rough Magic '95
Virtuosity '95
The Sum of Us '94
For the Moment '94
The Silver Stallion: King of the Wild Brumbies '93
The Crossing '92
The Efficiency Expert '92
Romper Stomper '92
Hammers over the Anvil '91
Proof '91

Josephine Crowell (1849-1932)
The Man Who Laughs '27
The Greatest Question '19
Hearts of the World '18
The Birth of a Nation '15

Dermot Crowley (1947-)
Dead Gorgeous '02
Falling for a Dancer '98
The Sculptress '97
Echoes '88

Jeananne Crowley (1946-)
The Real Charlotte '91
Reilly: Ace of Spies '87

Kathleen Crowley (1931-)
Curse of the Undead '59
The Rebel Set '59
The Female Jungle '56
Westward Ho, the Wagons! '56
The Farmer Takes a Wife '53

Pat(ricia) Crowley (1929-)
61* '01
Force of Evil '77
Return to Fantasy Island '77
Menace on the Mountain '70
Hollywood or Bust '56
Walk the Proud Land '56
Red Garters '54
Forever Female '53

Suzan Crowley
Devices and Desires '91
Christabel '89

Marie Josee Croze (1970-)
The Diving Bell and the Butterfly '07
Munich '05
The Barbarian Invasions '03
Ararat '02
Battlefield Earth '00
Maelstrom '00

Billy Crudup (1968-)
Dedication '07
The Good Shepherd '06
Mission: Impossible 3 '06
Trust the Man '06
Stage Beauty '04
Big Fish '03
Charlotte Gray '01
World Traveler '01
Almost Famous '00
Waking the Dead '00
Jesus' Son '99
The Hi-Lo Country '98
Monument Ave. '98
Princess Mononoke '98 (V)
Inventing the Abbotts '97
Without Limits '97
Grind '96
Sleepers '96

Tom Cruise (1962-)
Tropic Thunder '08
Lions for Lambs '07
Mission: Impossible 3 '06
War of the Worlds '05
Collateral '04
The Last Samurai '03
Austin Powers in Goldmember '02
Minority Report '02
Vanilla Sky '01
Mission: Impossible 2 '00
Eyes Wide Shut '99
Magnolia '99
Jerry Maguire '96
Mission: Impossible '96
Interview with the Vampire '94
The Firm '93
Far and Away '92
A Few Good Men '92
Days of Thunder '90
Born on the Fourth of July '89
Cocktail '88
Rain Man '88
The Color of Money '86
Legend '86
Top Gun '86
All the Right Moves '83
The Outsiders '83
Risky Business '83
Losin' It '82
Endless Love '81
Taps '81

Rosalie Crutchley (1920-97)
A Village Affair '95
Four Weddings and a Funeral '94
The Franchise Affair '88
Eleni '85
The Hunchback of Notre Dame '82
Smiley's People '82
Testament of Youth '79
Night of the Laughing Dead '75
And Now the Screaming Starts '73
Elizabeth R '72
Cold Comfort Farm '71
Six Wives of Henry VIII '71
Creatures the World Forgot '70
Wuthering Heights '70
The Haunting '63
Make Me an Offer '55

Abigail Cruttenden (1969-)
Charlotte Gray '01
Hideous Kinky '99
Into the Blue '97
Jane Eyre '97
Sharpe's Justice '97
Sharpe's Revenge '97
Sharpe's Mission '96
Sharpe's Regiment '96
Sharpe's Siege '96
Intimate Contact '87
Kipperbang '82

Greg Cruttwell (1962-)
George of the Jungle '97
Two Days in the Valley '96
Naked '93

Alexis Cruz (1974-)
Slayer '06
Darkwolf '03
Why Do Fools Fall in Love? '98
Hostage High '97
Grand Avenue '96
Riot in the Streets '96
Larry McMurtry's Streets of Laredo '95
Stargate '94
The Old Man and the Sea '90
Gryphon '88

Brandon Cruz (1962-)
Safe '95
The Bad News Bears '76

Celia Cruz (1924-2003)
The Perez Family '94
The Mambo Kings '92

Ernesto Cruz
Midaq Alley '95
El Norte '83
Erendira '83

Penelope Cruz (1974-)
The Good Night '07
Volver '06
Sahara '05
Head in the Clouds '04
Noel '04
Gothika '03
Masked and Anonymous '03
Waking Up in Reno '02
Blow '01
Captain Corelli's Mandolin '01
No News from God '01
All the Pretty Horses '00
Woman on Top '00
All About My Mother '99
The Girl of Your Dreams '99
The Hi-Lo Country '98
Twice upon a Yesterday '98
Live Flesh '97
Open Your Eyes '97
Love Can Seriously Damage Your Health '96
Talk of Angels '96
Framed '93
Jamon, Jamon '93
Belle Epoque '92

Raymond Cruz
Training Day '01
The Last Marshal '99
From Dusk Till Dawn 2: Texas Blood Money '99
Alien: Resurrection '97
The Rock '96
The Substitute '96
Up Close and Personal '96
Clear and Present Danger '94
Dragstrip Girl '94

Vladimir Cruz (1965-)
A Paradise Under the Stars '99
Strawberry and Chocolate '93

Wilson Cruz (1973-)
He's Just Not That Into You '08
Coffee Date '06
Bam Bam & Celeste '05
Party Monster '03
Supernova '99
Joyride '97
All Over Me '96

Jon Cryer (1965-)
johns '96
Holy Man '98
Went to Coney Island on a Mission from God... Be Back by Five '98
Glam '97
Plan B '97
The Pompatus of Love '95
Heads '93
Hot Shots! '91
Dudes '87
Hiding Out '87
Morgan Stewart's Coming Home '87
O.C. and Stiggs '87
Superman 4: The Quest for Peace '87
Pretty in Pink '86
No Small Affair '84
Noon Wine '84

Suzanne Cryer (1967-)
Friends & Lovers '99
Dead Silence '98
Wag the Dog '97
Some Folks Call It a Sling Blade '94

Billy Crystal (1947-)
Howl's Moving Castle '04 (V)
Analyze That '02
America's Sweethearts '01
Monsters, Inc. '01 (V)
The Adventures of Rocky & Bullwinkle '00
Analyze This '99
My Giant '98
Deconstructing Harry '97
Father's Day '96
Hamlet '96
Forget Paris '95
City Slickers 2: The Legend of Curly's Gold '94
Mr. Saturday Night '92
City Slickers '91
When Harry Met Sally... '89
Memories of Me '88
The Princess Bride '87
Throw Momma from the Train '87
Running Scared '86
This Is Spinal Tap '84
The Three Little Pigs '84
Enola Gay: The Men, the Mission, the Atomic Bomb '80
Breaking Up Is Hard to Do '79
Rabbit Test '78

Jennifer Crystal Foley (1973-)
61* '01

Sandor Csanyi (1975-)
Kontroll '03
I Love Budapest '01

Gyorgy Cserhalmi (1948-)
Flowers of Reverie '84
Mephisto '81
Hungarian Rhapsody '78

Marton Csokas (1966-)
Romulus, My Father '07
Aeon Flux '05
Asylum '05

The Great Raid '05
Kingdom of Heaven '05
The Bourne Supremacy '04
Garage Days '03
Broken English '96

David Cubitt (1965-)
Ali '01
The Perfect Son '00
I Shot a Man in Vegas '96
Swann '96

Michael Cudlitz (1964-)
Running Scared '06
Live from Baghdad '03
Band of Brothers '01
Grosse Pointe Blank '97

Daniel Cudmore (1981-)
X-Men: The Last Stand '06
X2: X-Men United '03

Xavier Cugat (1900-90)
Neptune's Daughter '49
A Date with Judy '48
Holiday in Mexico '45
Two Girls and a Sailor '44
Stage Door Canteen '43
You Were Never Lovelier '42

Maria Grazia Cucinotta (1969-)
Our Italian Husband '04
Just One Night '00
Picking Up the Pieces '99
The World Is Not Enough '99
Solomon '98
A Brooklyn State of Mind '97
The Postman '94

Michael Culkin
Cold and Dark '05
Dangerous Beauty '98
Into the Blue '97
Candyman '92

Rory Culkin (1989-)
Signs '02
Off Season '01
Down in the Valley '05
The Chumscrubber '05
You Can Count On Me '99

Kieran Culkin (1982-)
The Dangerous Lives of Altar Boys '02
Igby Goes Down '02
The Cider House Rules '99
The Mighty '98
She's All That '99
Father of the Bride Part 2 '95
My Summer Story '94
Home Alone 2: Lost in New York '92
Father of the Bride '91
Home Alone '90

Macaulay Culkin (1980-)
Sex and Breakfast '07
Saved! '04
Party Monster '03
Getting Even with Dad '94
Richie Rich '94
The Pagemaster '94
George Balanchine's The Nutcracker '93
The Good Son '93
The Great Raid '05

Home Alone 2: Lost in New York '92
My Girl '91
Only the Lonely '91
Home Alone '90
Jacob's Ladder '90
See You in the Morning '89
Uncle Buck '89
Rocket Gibraltar '88

Rory Culkin
The Liar's Club '93

Vladimir Cuk (1975-)
Celtic Pride '96
The Sixth Man '97

Frances Cuka (1936-)
Oliver Twist '05
The Watcher in the Woods '81

John Cullum (1930-)
The Night Listener '06
The Notorious Bettie Page '06
Held Up '99
Inherit the Wind '99
Undesirable '92
Ricochet River '98
Marie '85
The Day After '83
The Prodigal '83
The Man Without a Country '73

Frederick Culley (1879-1942)
The Four Feathers '39
The Private Life of Henry VIII '33

Peter Cullen (1944-)
Transformers '07 (V)
Pooh's Heffalump Movie '05 (V)

Max Cullen (1940-)
The Nugget '02
Kings in Grass Castles '97
Lightning Jack '94
Hard Knocks '80
The Odd Angry Shot '79

Daniel Cudmore
A Kiss Goodnight '94
Prehysteria '93
In a Stranger's Hand '92
Leaving Normal '92
The Last Exit to Earth '96

Running Mates '00
Running Mates '92

Robert Culp (1930-)
Newsbreak '00
Innocents '00

Joseph Culp (1963-)
Baadasssss! '03
Innocents '00
The Arrival '90
Iguana '89
Dream Lover '85
Home '87
Morgan Stewart's Coming Home '87
Glory '89
Reversal of Fortune '90
Ambition '91
Fever '91
Sweet Country '87
The Day After '83
To Each His Own '46
Dead of Night '45
On Approval '44
The Day Will Dawn '42
Secret Mission '42
Spitfire '42
Night Train to Munich '40

John David (J.D.) Cullum (1966-)
Good Night, and Good Luck '05
Forever Young '92
Roadside Prophets '92
Down to Earth '47
Emperor Waltz '48
The Great Lover '49
The Lion King '94 (V)
A Goofy Movie '94 (V)
Balto '95 (V)

Ji-Tu Cumbuka (1942-)
Midnight Edition '93

Benedict Cumberbatch (1977-)
Atonement '07
Amazing Grace '06
Starter for Ten '06
The Other Boleyn Girl '08

Roland Culver (1900-84)
The Legend of Hell House '73
Fast Kill '73
The Devil's Web '74
Conduct Unbecoming '75
Philby, Burgess and Maclean: Spy Scandal of the Century '84
Singapore '47
The Goodbye Girl '77
The Babysitter '80
(1967-)
The Obsessed '51
Encore '52
Betrayed '54

Michael Culver (1938-)
The Green Man '91
Alamut Ambush '86
Deadly Recruits '86
Hidgoblins '87
VIII '33
The Emperor's Club '02
How to Make a Monster '01
Thirteen Days '00
Norma Jean and Marilyn '95
Jason Goes to Hell: The Final Friday '93
Demon with a Glass Hand '64

Jeffrey Culver
Bad Girls from Mars '90

Calvin Culver (1943-87)
Ginger '72
Score '72

Steven Culp (1955-)
Firehouse Dog '07
The Sisters '05
Spartan '04
Thursday '98
Sky Riders '76
Inside Out '75
Hannie Caulder '72
A Name for Evil '70
Bob & Carol & Ted & Alice '69

PT 109 '63
Sunday in New York '63
The Castaway Cowboy '74
Goldengirl '79
Hot Rod '79
Flood! '76
Great Scout & Cathouse Thursday '76
Her Life as a Man '83
Killjoy '81
The Night the City Screamed '80
Calendar Girl Murders '84
The Zodiac '05

Dorothy (Dorothy G.) Cumming
The Wind '28
King of Kings '27

Constance Cummings (1910-2005)
Applause '29
The Battle of the Sexes '60
John and Julie '55
Blithe Spirit '45
The Foreman Went to France '42
This England '42
American Madness '32
Night After Night '32
Criminal Code '31
The Saphead '21
Sex '20
Uncle Tom's Cabin '14

Alan Cumming (1965-)
Mandingo '75

Glitch! '88
Mercenary '96
Xtro 3: Watch the Skies '95
The Pelican Brief '93
Murderous Vision '91
Timebomb '91
Voyage of Terror: The Achille Lauro Affair '90
Sweet Land '05
Son of the Mask '05
Bam Bam & Celeste '05
Spy Kids 3-D: Game Over '03
Spy Kids 2: The Island of Lost Dreams '02
Spy Kids '01
Company Man '00
The Flintstones in Viva Rock Vegas '00
Get Carter '00
Urbania '00
Annie '99
Eyes Wide Shut '99
Titus '99
Plunkett & Macleane '98
Buddy '97
Romy and Michele's High School Reunion '97
Spice World: The Movie '97
Emma '96
Goldeneye '95
Circle of Friends '95
Second Best '94
Bernard and the Genie '91

Gregory Scott Cummins (1956-)
Harley '90
Dakota '88

Eli Cummins
Swamp Women '55
Verboten! '59

Susan Cummings (1930-)
The Naked Gun: The Movie '04 (V)
Pooh's Heffalump Movie
The Return of the Borrowers '96
24-7 '97
Intimate Strangers '77
Night Terror '76
The Carpetbaggers '64
Beach Party '63
My Geisha '62
Lucky Me '54
Dial "M" for Murder '54
Reign of Terror '49
Tell It to the Judge '49
Lost Moment '47
The Accused '48
The Chase '46
Forever and a Day '43
Saboteur '42

James (Jimmy) Cummings (1968-)
Southie '98
Ed's Next Move '96

Jim (Jonah) Cummings (1953-)
Ground Zero '88
Blue Fire Lady '73
Salute John Citizen '42

Irving Cummings (1888-1959)
The Saphead '21

Peter Cummings
The Dark Knight '08
Half Nelson '06
Three Seasons '98

Pamela Cundell

Rusty Cundieff (1965-)
Sprung '96
Tales from the Hood '95
Fear of a Black Hat '94

Peggy Cummins (1925-)
Devour '05
Ice Men '04
Liberty Stands Still '02
Love Come Down '00
Poltergeist: The Legacy '96
Born to Run '93
Friday the 13th, Part 8: Jason Takes Manhattan '89

Martin Cummins (1969-)
Running Hot '83
New Beginning '85

Juliette Cummins (1964-)
Deadly Dreams '86
Slumber Party Massacre 2 '87
Friday the 13th, Part 5: A New Beginning '85
Watchers II '90
The Last of the Dogmen '95

Kaley Cuoco (1985-)
Cougar Club '07
The Hollow '04
Alley Cats Strike '00

Emma Cunniffe (1973-)
Love or Money '01
Plain Jane '01
All the King's Men '99
Great Expectations '99

Cecil Cunningham (1888-1959)
Above Suspicion '43
Twin Beds '42
Hurry, Charlie, Hurry '41
The Awful Truth '37

Colin Cunningham (1967-)
The League of Extraordinary Gentlemen '03
The 13th Warrior '99
Blade 2 '02
Pearl Harbor '01
Split Second '99

Monique Gabriela Curnen
The Dark Knight '08
Half Nelson '06
Three Seasons '98

Barbara Cupisti
The Church '98
Opera '88
Stagefright '87

Tran Manh Cuong
The Vertical Ray of the Sun '00

Alain Cuny (1908-94)
Bloodmatch '91
Camille Claudel '89
Detective '85
Basileus Quartet '82
Christ Stopped at Eboli '79
Emmanuelle '74
Fellini Satyricon '69
The Milky Way '68
La Dolce Vita '60
The Lovers '59
The Hunchback of Notre Dame '57
The Lady Without Camellias '53
Les Visiteurs du Soir '42

The Devil & Miss Jones '41
It Started with Eve '41
Kings Row '41
Moon over Miami '41
One Night in the Tropics '40
Charlie McCarthy, Detective '39
Everything Happens at Night '39
Three Smart Girls Grow Up '39

Danny Cunningham
The 6th Day '00

John Cunningham (1932-)
24 Hour Party People '01
Loaded '94

Liam Cunningham (1961-)
Northanger Abbey '07
The Wind That Shakes the Barley '06
Attila '01
Dog Soldiers '01
A Love Divided '01
RKO 281 '99
First Knight '95
Jude '96
Cracker: Best Boys '95
A Little Princess '95
War of the Buttons '95

Peter "Sugarfoot" Cunningham
Bloodfist 3: Forced to Fight '92

Paul Curran (1913-86)
Merlin '98
Poldark '75

Tony Curran (1969-)
Beowulf & Grendel '06
The Good German '06
Red Road '06
The Boys '98
Road to Nhill '97
The Year My Voice Broke '87
Bliss '85

Lynette Curran (1945-)
Somersault '04
Japanese Story '03
The Boys '98
Return of the Family Man '89
Reason to Die '90

Robert Cumming

Roland Curram (1932-)
Parting Shots '98
Darling '65

Masters of Horror: We All Scream for Ice Cream '07
Stealing Sinatra '04
Being Human '94

Cherie Currie (1959-)
- Rosebud Beach Hotel '85
- Twilight Zone: The Movie '83
- Wavelength '83
- Parasite '82
- Foxes '80

Finlay Currie (1878-1968)
- Billy Liar '63
- The Adventures of Huckleberry Finn '60
- Ben-Hur '59
- Corridors of Blood '58
- Abandon Ship '57
- Make Me an Offer '55
- Big Deadly Game '54
- Ivanhoe '52
- Stars and Stripes Forever '52
- People Will Talk '51
- Quo Vadis '51
- The Black Rose '50
- Treasure Island '50
- Trio '50
- Bonnie Prince Charlie '48
- Great Expectations '46
- Murder in the Footlights '46
- I Know Where I'm Going '45

Gordon Currie (1965-)
- Possessed '05
- Highwaymen '03
- The Fraternity '01
- Left Behind: The Movie '00
- The Fear: Halloween Night '99
- Laserhawk '99
- Dog Park '98
- Ripe '97
- Listen '96
- Blood & Donuts '95
- Puppet Master 5: The Final Chapter '94
- Puppet Master 4 '93

Michael Currie
- The Dead Pool '88
- Halloween 3: Season of the Witch '82

Bernard Curry
- The Junction Boys '02

Christopher Curry (1948-)
- City of Ghosts '03
- Home Alone 3 '97
- C.H.U.D. '84

Don "DC" Curry
- Friday After Next '02
- Next Friday '00

Julian Curry (1937-)
- Sky Captain and the World of Tomorrow '04
- Rasputin: Dark Servant of Destiny '96

Stephen Curry
- Cut '00

Tim Curry (1946-)
- Garfield: A Tail of Two Kitties '06 (V)
- Queer Duck: The Movie '06 (V)
- Bailey's Billion$ '05 (V)
- Valiant '05 (V)
- Kinsey '04
- Sorted '04
- Rugrats Go Wild! '03 (V)
- The Home Front '02
- The Wild Thornberrys Movie '02 (V)
- Attila '01
- Scary Movie 2 '01
- Charlie's Angels '00
- Four Dogs Playing Poker '00
- Jackie's Back '97
- Doom Runners '97
- McHale's Navy '97
- The Shadow '94
- National Lampoon's Loaded Weapon 1 '93
- The Three Musketeers '93
- Ferngully: The Last Rain Forest '92 (V)
- Home Alone 2: Lost in New York '92
- Passed Away '92
- Oscar '91
- The Hunt for Red October '90
- Stephen King's It '90
- Pass the Ammo '88
- Legend '86
- The Worst Witch '86
- Clue '85
- Blue Money '84
- The Ploughman's Lunch '83
- Annie '82
- Oliver Twist '82
- Times Square '80
- The Shout '78
- The Rocky Horror Picture Show '75
- Mr. Mike's Mondo Video '79

Louise Currie (1921-)
- Wild West '46
- Million Dollar Kid '44
- Pray TV '82

Sondra Currie (1952-)
- The Concrete Jungle '82
- Jessi's Girls '75
- Runaways '75
- Mama's Dirty Girls '74
- Policewomen '73

Mary Currier (1904-57)
- Return of the Ape Man '44
- Frolics on Ice '39

Billy Curtis (1909-88)
- Eating Raoul '82
- The Incredible Shrinking Man '57
- Terror of Tiny Town '38

Clifford Curtis (1968-)
- Crossing Over '08
- 10,000 B.C. '08
- Fracture '07
- Live Free or Die Hard '07
- Sunshine '07
- The Fountain '06
- Runaway Jury '03
- Collateral Damage '02
- Point of Origin '02
- Whale Rider '02
- Blow '01
- The Majestic '01
- Training Day '01
- Bringing Out the Dead '99
- Three Kings '99
- Virus '98
- Desperate Remedies '93

Dick Curtis
- What Waits Below '83
- Motel Hell '80

Dick Curtis (1902-52)
- Government Agents vs. Phantom Legion '51
- Santa Fe Uprising '46
- Billy the Kid '41
- Valley of Terror '38
- Boothill Brigade '37
- A Lawman Is Born '37
- Racing Luck '35

Donald Curtis (1915-97)
- Night Passage '57
- Earth vs. the Flying Saucers '56
- Seventh Cavalry '56
- It Came from Beneath the Sea '55
- The Amazing Mr. X '48
- Son of Lassie '45
- They Were Expendable '45
- Thirty Seconds Over Tokyo '44
- Bataan '43
- Criminals Within '41

Jack Curtis (1880-1956)
- Lawless Range '35
- The Sea Lion '21

Jackie Curtis (1947-85)
- WR: Mysteries of the Organism '71
- Flesh '68

Jamie Lee Curtis (1958-)
- Christmas With the Kranks '04
- Freaky Friday '03
- Halloween: Resurrection '02
- Drowning Mona '00
- The Tailor of Panama '00
- Daddy & Them '99
- Halloween: H20 '98
- Virus '98
- Homegrown '97
- Fierce Creatures '96
- House Arrest '96
- The Heidi Chronicles '95
- Mother's Boys '94
- My Girl 2 '94
- True Lies '94
- Forever Young '92
- The Return of Spinal Tap '92
- My Girl '91
- Queens Logic '91
- Blue Steel '90
- Dominick & Eugene '88
- A Fish Called Wanda '88
- Amazing Grace & Chuck '87
- A Man in Love '87
- As Summers Die '86
- Perfect '85
- The Adventures of Buckaroo Banzai Across the Eighth Dimension '84
- Grandview U.S.A. '84
- Love Letters '83
- Trading Places '83
- Death of a Centerfold '81
- Escape from New York '81 (V)
- Halloween 2: The Nightmare Isn't Over! '81
- Road Games '81
- She's in the Army Now '81
- Prom Night '80
- Terror Train '80
- The Fog '78
- Halloween '78

Alan Curtis (1909-53)
- Apache Chief '50
- Flight to Nowhere '46
- Renegade Girl '46
- The Naughty Nineties '45
- The Invisible Man's Revenge '44
- Phantom Lady '44
- Gung Ho! '43
- Buck Privates '41
- Melody Master '41
- The Duke of West Point '38
- Shopworn Angel '38
- Mannequin '37
- Last Outlaw '36

Peter Curtin
- Darkness Falls '03

Jane Curtin (1947-)
- The Shaggy Dog '06
- Brooklyn Lobster '05
- Our Town '03
- Antz '98 (V)
- Coneheads '93
- O.C. and Stiggs '87
- Suspicion '87
- Maxie '85
- How to Beat the High Cost of Living '80
- A Christmas Without Snow '80
- Different Story '78

Valerie Curtin (1945-)
- Big Trouble '86
- Down and Out in Beverly Hills '86

Keene Curtis (1925-2002)
- Mother Teresa: In the Name of God's Poor '97
- Silver '93
- The Buddy System '83
- Strange New World '75
- Missiles of October '74

Ken Curtis (1916-91)
- Conagher '91
- Texas Guns '90
- Lost '83
- California Gold Rush '81
- Pony Express Rider '76
- Robin Hood '73 (V)
- The Alamo '60
- The Killer Shrews '59
- The Young Land '59
- Wings of Eagles '57
- Mister Roberts '55
- The Quiet Man '52
- Don Daredevil Rides Again '51
- Call of the Forest '49

Liane (Alexandra) Curtis (1965-)
- Wild Orchid 2: Two Shades of Blue '92
- Rock 'n' Roll High School Forever '91
- Girlfriend from Hell '89
- Critters 2: The Main Course '88
- Sixteen Candles '84

Robin Curtis (1956-)
- Scorpio One '97
- Dark Breed '96
- Santa with Muscles '96
- Star Trek 3: The Search for Spock '84

Sonia Curtis
- Evil Lives '92

Thomas Curtis (1991-)
- The Chumscrubber '05
- North Country '05

Todd Curtis
- Chain of Command '95
- Out for Blood '93

Tony Curtis (1925-)
- Bounty Hunters 2: Hardball '97
- The Immortals '95
- Last Action Hero '93
- The Mummy Lives '93
- Naked in New York '93
- Center of the Web '92
- Christmas in Connecticut '92
- Prime Target '91
- Lobster Man from Mars '89
- Midnight '89
- The Last of Philip Banter '87
- Club Life '86
- Mafia Princess '86
- Insignificance '85
- Balboa '82
- Brainwaves '82
- Portrait of a Showgirl '82
- Title Shot '81
- Little Miss Marker '80
- The Mirror Crack'd '80
- The Bad News Bears Go to Japan '78
- It Rained All Night the Day I Left '78
- The Manitou '78
- Sex on the Run '78
- Sextette '78
- Users '78
- Vegas '78
- The Last Tycoon '76
- Lepke '75

Vondie Curtis-Hall (1956-)
- Honeydripper '07
- Talk to Me '07
- Freedom Song '00
- Turn It Up '00
- Sirens '99
- Don King: Only in America '97
- Eve's Bayou '97
- Gridlock'd '96
- William Shakespeare's Romeo and Juliet '96
- Heaven's Prisoners '95
- Zooman '95
- Crooklyn '94
- DROP Squad '94
- Sugar Hill '94
- Fallen Angels 2 '93
- Falling Down '93
- In a Stranger's Hand '92
- Passion Fish '92
- Die Hard 2: Die Harder '90
- Mystery Train '89
- Coming to America '88

Pierre Curzi (1946-)
- The Barbarian Invasions '03
- Stand Off '93
- Pouvoir intime '87
- Maria Chapdelaine '84

George Curzon (1898-1976)
- Woman of Straw '64
- Clouds over Europe '39
- The Hooded Terror '38
- Sexton Blake and the Hooded Terror '38
- Young and Innocent '37
- Java Head '35
- The Man Who Knew Too Much '34

Aria Noelle Curzon (1987-)
- The Land Before Time 7: The Stone of Cold Fire '00 (V)
- Treehouse Hostage '99
- The Land Before Time 6: The Secret of Saurus Rock '98 (V)
- The Land Before Time 5: The Mysterious Island '97 (V)

Joan Cusack (1962-)
- Martian Child '07
- Friends with Money '06
- Chicken Little '05 (V)
- Ice Princess '05
- The Last Shot '04
- Raising Helen '04
- A Smile Like Yours '96
- Two Much '96
- Mr. Wrong '95
- Nine Months '95
- Addams Family Values '93
- Hero '92
- Toys '92
- My Blue Heaven '90
- Men Don't Leave '89
- Say Anything '89
- Married to the Mob '88
- Stars and Bars '88
- Working Girl '88
- The Allnighter '87
- Broadcast News '87
- Grandview U.S.A. '84
- Sixteen Candles '84
- My Bodyguard '80

Ann Cusack (1961-)
- Accepted '06
- Fatal Contact: Bird Flu in America '06
- Dean Koontz's Black River '01
- What Planet Are You From? '00
- Stigmata '99
- From the Earth to the Moon '98
- Grosse Pointe Blank '97
- Multiplicity '96
- Tank Girl '94
- A League of Their Own '92

Cyril Cusack (1910-93)
- Far and Away '92
- My Left Foot '89
- Little Dorrit, Film 1: Nobody's Fault '88
- Little Dorrit, Film 2: Little Dorrit's Story '88
- The Tenth Man '88
- Two by Forsyth '86
- 1984 '84
- The Golden Bowl '72
- Harold and Maude '71
- King Lear '71
- Sacco & Vanzetti '71
- David Copperfield '70
- The Taming of the Shrew '67
- Fahrenheit 451 '66
- The Spy Who Came in from the Cold '65
- Waltz of the Toreadors '62
- Johnny Nobody '61
- Night Ambush '57
- The Spanish Gardener '57
- The Elusive Pimpernel '50
- The Small Back Room '49
- Odd Man Out '47
- Late Extra '35

John Cusack (1966-)
- The Contract '07
- 1408 '07
- Grace Is Gone '07
- Martian Child '07
- The Ice Harvest '05
- Must Love Dogs '05
- Identity '03
- Runaway Jury '03
- Max '02
- America's Sweethearts '01
- Serendipity '01
- High Fidelity '00

[John Cusack, cont.]
Being John Malkovich '99
The Cradle Will Rock '99
The Jack Bull '99
Pushing Tin '99
This is My Father '99
Chicago Cab '98
The Thin Red Line '98
Anastasia '97 (V)
Con Air '97
Grosse Pointe Blank '97
Midnight in the Garden of Good and Evil '97
Floundering '94
Bullets over Broadway '94
City Hall '95
Money for Nothing '93
Bob Roberts '92
The Player '92
Roadside Prophets '92
Shadows and Fog '92
True Colors '91
The Grifters '90
Say Anything '89
Tapeheads '89
Fat Man and Little Boy '89
Eight Men Out '88
Stars and Bars '88
Broadcast News '87
Hot Pursuit '87
One Crazy Summer '86
Stand by Me '86
Better Off Dead '85
The Journey of Natty Gann '85

Richard (Dick) Cusack (1925-2003)
The Playboys '92

Niamh Cusack (1959-)
Catherine Cookson's American Women '00
Colour Blind '98

Sinead Cusack (1948-)
Eastern Promises '07
V for Vendetta '06
I Capture the Castle '02
Passion of Mind '00
The Nephew '97
Stealing Beauty '96
Uncovered '94
Crazy People '90

Susie Cusack (1971-)
The Company '03
Hero '92

Peter Cushing (1913-94)
Masks of Death '86
Biggles '85
Silent Scream '84
Top Secret! '84
Sword of the Valiant '83
House of the Long Shadows '83
A Tale of Two Cities '80
The Uncanny '77
Land of the Minotaur '77
Shock Waves '77
Star Wars '77
At the Earth's Core '76
Choice of Weapons '76
The Beast Must Die '76
The Ghoul '75
The Devil's Undead '75
Legend of the Werewolf '75
Call Him Mr. Shatter '74
Frankenstein and the Monster from Hell '74
Madhouse '74
And Now the Screaming Starts '73
From Beyond the Grave '73
The Legend of the 7 Golden Vampires '73
The Satanic Rites of Dracula '73
The Creeping Flesh '72
Doctor Phibes Rises Again '72
Asylum '72
Dracula A.D. 1972 '72
Horror Express '72
Dynasty of Fear '72
Nothing But the Night '72
Tales from the Crypt '72
The House that Dripped Blood '71
I, Monster '71
Blood '71
Twins of Evil '71
The Vampire Lovers '70
Scream and Scream Again '70
The Bloodsuckers '70
Frankenstein Must Be Destroyed '69
Blood Beast Terror '67
Island of the Burning Doomed '67
Torture Garden '67
2150 A.D. '66
Daleks—Invasion Earth 2150 A.D. '66
Frankenstein Created Woman '66
Island of Terror '66
Dr. Terror's House of Horrors '65
The Skull '65
The Evil of Frankenstein '64
The Gorgon '64
The Hellfire Club '61
The Naked Edge '61
The Brides of Dracula '60
The Flesh and the Fiends '60
Sword of Sherwood Forest '60
The Mummy '59
John Paul Jones '59
The Hound of the Baskervilles '59
The Revenge of Frankenstein '58
The Abominable Snowman '57
The Curse of Frankenstein '57
Alexander the Great '55
End of the Affair '55
Moulin Rouge '52
Hamlet '48

Henry Ian Cusick (1969-)
Half Light '05
The Gospel of John '03

Bob Custer (1898-1974)
Law of the Wild '34
Mark of the Spur '32

Lou (Cutel) Cutell (1930-)
The Odd Couple 2 '98
Glam '97
Frankenstein General Hospital '88

Charles Cyphers (1939-)
Major League '89
Big Bad Mama 2 '87
Escape from New York '81
Halloween 2: The Nightmare Isn't Over! '81
Coming Home '78
Halloween '78
Assault on Precinct 13 '76
Missiles of October '74

Isabelle Cyr
Savage Messiah '02
Karmina '96

Billy Ray Cyrus (1961-)
Mulholland Drive '01
Wish You Were Dead '00

Myriam Cyr (1960-)
Species 2 '98
Frankenstein and Me '96
I Shot Andy Warhol '96
Savage Hearts '95
Gothic '87

Henry Czerny (1959-)
The Exorcism of Emily Rose '05
The Pink Panther '06
Fido '06
Gone Dark '03
Klepto '03
The Girl Next Door '04
The Quiet '05
Rose '05
Double Obsession '93
Helen of Troy '03
An American Affair '99
Timelock '99
Romance and Rejection '96
The Browning Version '94
Notes from Underground '95
A Texas Funeral '99
Soccer Dog: The Movie '98
The Velocity of Gary '98

Jon Cypher (1932-)
The Invaders '95
Memory of Us '74
Valdez Is Coming '71

Augusta Dabney (1918-)
The Portrait '93
Running on Empty '88
Violets Are Blue '86
Cold River '81

Maryam D'Abo (1960-)
The Browning Version '94
Solitaire for 2 '94
Double Obsession '93
Leon the Pig Farmer '93
An American Affair '99
Timelock '99
Immortal Sins '91
Nightlife '90
The Living Daylights '87
Xtro '83

Olivia D'Abo (1967-)
The Triangle '01
The Enemy '01
It Had to Be You '00
Seven Girlfriends '00
Tropical Heat '93
Lipstick '93
Immortal Sins '91
Nightlife '90
Point of No Return '93
Really Weird Tales '86
Conan the Destroyer '84
Bolero '84

Zbigniew Cybulski (1927-67)
The Saragossa Manuscript '65
Innocent Sorcerers '60
Ashes and Diamonds '58
A Generation '54

Iain Cuthbertson (1930-)
Strictly Sinatra '01
Nobody's Daughter '04
Gorillas in the Mist '88
The Railway Children '70

Allan Cuthbertson (1920-88)
Performance '70
Agatha Christie's Thirteen at Dinner '85

Jon Cuthbert

Elisha Cuthbert (1982-)
Captivity '07
He Was a Quiet Man '07
House of Wax '05
The Quiet '05
The Girl Next Door '04
Old School '03
Believe '99
Time at the Top '99

Victor Cutler (1913-79)
The Best Years of Our Lives '46

Ryan Cutrona
A Walk in the Sun '46
Number One Fan '94

Lise Cutter
The Glimmer Man '96
Fleshtone '94
Nickel & Dime '92
Shadow Force '92
Havana '90
Buy & Cell '89

Zsuzsi Czinkoczi
An American Rhapsody '01

Chris D (1950-)
Border Radio '88
No Way Out '87

Victor Cypher (1913-79)
The Best Years of Our Lives '46

Da Brat (1974-)
Civil Brand '02
Carmen: A Hip Hopera '01
Glitter '01 (V)

Deezer D
Fear of a Black Hat '94
CB4: The Movie '93

Eric (DaRe) Da Re (1965-)
Twin Peaks: Fire Walk with Me '92

Erick Da Silva
Delta of Venus '95
It's Son of the Shark '93

Howard da Silva (1909-86)
Garbo Talks '84
Mommie Dearest '81
The Great Gatsby '74
1776 '72
Nevada Smith '66
David and Lisa '62
The Blue Dahlia '46
Two Years before the Mast '46
The Lost Weekend '45
Keeper of the Flame '42
Reunion in France '42
The Sea Wolf '41
Sergeant York '41
Abe Lincoln in Illinois '40

Yaya DaCosta
Honeydripper '07
Take the Lead '06

Jacques Dacqmine
Germinal '93
Melo '86
Piedre '68

Cameron Daddo (1965-)
Category 7: The End of the World '05
Zebra Lounge '01
Anne of Green Gables: The Continuing Story '99

Andrew Daddo (1967-)
Body Melt '93
A Kink in the Picasso '90

Mark Dacascos (1964-)
The Hunt for Eagle One: Crash Point '06
Final Approach '04
Cradle 2 the Grave '03
Scorcher '02
Brotherhood of the Wolf '01
Instinct to Kill '01
The Base '99
Boogie Boy '98
No Code of Conduct '98
Sanctuary '98
DNA '97
Redline '97
Drive '96
Sabotage '96
Crying Freeman '95
Only the Strong '93
Double Dragon '94
American Samurai '92

Willem Dafoe (1955-)
Mr. Bean's Holiday '07
The Walker '07
American Dreamz '06
Inside Man '06
Paris, je t'aime '06
The Black Widow '05
XXX: State of the Union '05
Manderlay '05
The Life Aquatic with Steve Zissou '04
The Aviator '04
The Clearing '04
Once Upon a Time in Mexico '03
Finding Nemo '03 (V)
Spider-Man 2 '04
Auto Focus '02
Spider-Man '02
The Reckoning '03
Pavilion of Women '02
The Animal Factory '00
Shadow of the Vampire '00
American Psycho '00
Boondock Saints '99
eXistenZ '99
New Rose Hotel '98
Lulu on the Bridge '98
Affliction '97
Speed 2: Cruise Control '97
Basquiat '96
The English Patient '96
Victory '95
Clear and Present Danger '94
Body of Evidence '92
Light Sleeper '92
White Sands '92
Cry-Baby '90
Flight of the Intruder '90
Wild at Heart '90
Born on the Fourth of July '89
Triumph of the Spirit '89
The Last Temptation of Christ '88
Off Limits '87
Mississippi Burning '88
Platoon '86
To Live & Die in L.A. '85
Roadhouse 66 '84
Streets of Fire '84
The Hunger '83
The Loveless '83

Werner Daehn (1965-)
Shadow Man '06
Stalked '06

Frances Dade (1910-68)
Dracula '31
Raffles '30

Lil Dagover (1897-1980)
Destiny '21
The Cabinet of Dr. Caligari '19
Spiders '18

Nicholas D'Agosto
Rocket Science '07

Jean-Michel Dagory
Clowning Around 2 '93
Clowning Around '92

Alice Dahl
When Lightning Strikes '34

Arlene Dahl (1924-)
Night of the Warrior '91
Land Raiders '69
Journey to the Center of the Earth '59
Slightly Scarlet '56
A Woman's World '54
Here Come the Girls '53
Three Little Words '50
Watch the Birdie '50
Reign of Terror '49
A Southern Yankee '48

Eva Dahlbeck (1920-)
Brink of Life '57
Dreams '55
Secrets of Women '52
Smiles of a Summer Night '55
Lesson in Love '54

Jensen (Jennifer) Daggett
Friday the 13th, Part 8: Jason Takes Manhattan '89

Paul Dahlke (1904-84)
The Head '59
The Third Sex '57
The Private Files of J. Edgar Hoover '77

Dan Dailey (1914-78)
Meet Me in Las Vegas '56
It's Always Fair Weather '55

There's No Business Like Show Business '54
The Girl Next Door '53
Pride of St. Louis '52
What Price Glory? '52
My Blue Heaven '50
Ticket to Tomahawk '50
When Willie Comes Marching Home '50
Mother Wore Tights '47
Panama Hattie '42
Lady Be Good '41
Ziegfeld Girl '41

Bill Daily (1928-)
Alligator 2: The Mutation '90
Magic on Love Island '80

Elizabeth (E.G. Dailey) Daily (1961-)
Happy Feet '06 (V)
The Devil's Rejects '05
Rugrats Go Wild! '03 (V)
The Powerpuff Girls Movie '02 (V)
Rugrats in Paris: The Movie '00 (V)
Babe: Pig in the City '98 (V)
The Rugrats Movie '98 (V)
Lorenzo's Oil '92
Dogfight '91
Dutch '91
Loverboy '89
Bad Dreams '88
Better Off Dead '85
Fandango '85
Pee-wee's Big Adventure '85
No Small Affair '84
Streets of Fire '84
Valley Girl '83
Diabolique '55

Alberto Dalbes (1922-83)
Bronson's Revenge '72
Rites of Frankenstein '72
The Screaming Dead '72

Cynthia Dale (1961-)
P.T. Barnum '99
Spenser: A Savage Place '94
Boy in Blue '86
Heavenly Bodies '84
My Bloody Valentine '81

Dick Dale (1937-)
Back to the Beach '87
Muscle Beach Party '64
Beach Party '63

Esther Dale (1885-1961)
Ma and Pa Kettle at the Fair '52
On Moonlight Bay '51
Ma and Pa Kettle Go to Town '50
Holiday Affair '49
Ma and Pa Kettle '49
A Stolen Life '46
Back Street '41
Blondie Has Trouble '40
The Awful Truth '37
Curly Top '35
In Old Kentucky '35

James Dale
The Departed '06
Federal Agents vs. Underworld, Inc. '49

Janet Dale
The Tenant of Wildfell Hall '96

The Buddha of Suburbia '92
Prick Up Your Ears '87

Jennifer Dale (1955-)
Love Come Down '00
The Life Before This '99
Dream House '98
Trail of a Serial Killer '98
Once a Thief '96
Whale Music '94
Cadillac Girls '93
The Adjuster '91
Separate Vacations '86
Of Unknown Origin '83
When Angels Fly '82
Ticket to Heaven '81
Suzanne '80

Jim Dale (1935-)
The Hunchback '97
The Adventures of Huckleberry Finn '85
Scandalous '84
Unidentified Flying Oddball '79
Hot Lead & Cold Feet '78
Joseph Andrews '77
Pete's Dragon '77
Digby, the Biggest Dog in the World '73
Carry On Doctor '68
Follow That Camel '67
Carry On Cowboy '66
Carry On Screaming '66
Carry On Cleo '65

Virginia Dale (1917-94)
Danger Zone '51
Fall Guy '47
Holiday Inn '42

Fabienne Dali (1941-)
Mayerling '68
Kill, Baby, Kill '66
Erotic Touch of Hot Skin '65

Tracy Dali (1966-)
American Streetfighter '96
Virgin High '90

David DaLie
Mighty Jungle '64

Marcel Dalio (1900-83)
The Mad Adventures of Rabbi Jacob '73
How Sweet It Is! '68
How to Steal a Million '66
Lady L '65
The Monocle '64
Can-Can '60
The Perfect Furlough '59
Lafayette Escadrille '58
China Gate '57
Lucky Me '54
Sabrina '54
Lovely to Look At '52
The Merry Widow '52
The Snows of Kilimanjaro '52
Captain Blackjack '51
Rich, Young and Pretty '51
Dedee d'Anvers '49
To Have & Have Not '44
Casablanca '42
The Rules of the Game '39
Grand Illusion '37
Beethoven '36

Ewa Dalkowska (1947-)
Korczak '90
Provincial Actors '79
Without Anesthesia '78

John Dall (1918-71)
Atlantis, the Lost Continent '61
Gun Crazy '49
Rope '48
Something in the Wind '47
The Corn Is Green '45

Night on Earth '91
La Vengeance d'une Femme '89
Betty Blue '86

Joe Dallesandro (1948-)
The Limey '99
Bad Love '95
Sugar Hill '94
Guncrazy '92
Wild Orchid 2: Two Shades of Blue '92
Cry-Baby '90
Private War '90
Double Revenge '89
The Hollywood Detective '89
Sunset '88
The Cotton Club '84
Seeds of Evil '76
Andy Warhol's Dracula '74
Andy Warhol's Frankenstein '74
Heat '72
Trash '70
Flesh '68

Maurice Dallimore (1912-73)
Johnny Got His Gun '71
The Collector '65

Francesca D'Aloja (1963-)
Scarlet Diva '00
Steam: A Turkish Bath '96
Apartment Zero '88

Abby Dalton (1935-)
Buck and the Magic Bracelet '97
Cyber-Tracker '93
Roller Blade Warriors: Taken By Force '90
Whale of a Tale '76
Rock All Night '57

Audrey Dalton (1934-)
Kitten with a Whip '64
Mr. Sardonicus '61
Separate Tables '58
The Monster That Challenged the World '57
The Prodigal '55
Casanova's Big Night '54
Titanic '53

Darren Dalton (1965-)
The Wolves '95
Montana '90
Brotherhood of Justice '86

Dorothy Dalton (1894-1972)
Moran of the Lady Letty '22
The Three Musketeers '16

Kristen Dalton (1966-)
The Disciple '15
The Departed '06
The Wolves '95
Bitter Vengeance '94
Digital Man '94

Timothy Dalton (1944-)
Hot Fuzz '07
Looney Tunes: Back in Action '03
American Outlaws '01
Possessed '00
Cleopatra '99
Made Men '99
The Beautician and the Beast '97
The Informant '97
Lie Down with Lions '94
Scarlett '94
Framed '93
Last Action Hero '93
Naked in New York '93
The Rocketeer '91
The King's Whore '90
Hawks '89
License to Kill '89
The Living Daylights '87
Brenda Starr '86
The Doctor and the Devils '85
Sins '85
The Emperor's New Clothes '84 (N)
Mistral's Daughter '84
Jane Eyre '83

Chanel Solitaire '81
Flash Gordon '80
Agatha '79
The Flame Is Love '79
Centennial '78
Sextette '78
Permission To Kill '75
Mary, Queen of Scots '71
Cromwell '70
Wuthering Heights '70
The Lion in Winter '68

Roger Daltrey (1945-)
Johnny Was '05
Dracula: The Dark Prince '01
Strange Frequency 2 '01
Chasing Destiny '00
The Magical Legend of the Leprechauns '99
Like It Is '98
Vampirella '96
Lightning Jack '94
Buddy's Song '91
If Looks Could Kill '91
Forgotten Prisoners '90
Cold Justice '89
Mack the Knife '89
Murder: Ultimate Grounds for Divorce '80
McVicar '80
The Kids Are Alright '79
The Legacy '79
Lisztomania '75
Tommy '75

Candice Daly (1963-2004)
Where Truth Lies '96
Liquid Dreams '92
Hell Hunters '87

Eileen Daly (1963-)
Razor Blade Smile '98
Witchcraft 10: Mistress of the Craft '98

James Daly (1918-78)
Resurrection of Zachary Wheeler '71
The Big Bounce '69
Planet of the Apes '68
The Court Martial of Billy Mitchell '55
Tender Is the Night '55

Mark Daly (1887-1957)
Lassie from Lancashire '38
The Ghost Goes West '36

Timothy Daly (1956-)
Against the Ropes '04
Convicted '04
Basic '03
The Outsider '02
A House Divided '00
Seven Girlfriends '00
Execution of Justice '99
Stephen King's The Storm of the Century '99
From the Earth to the Moon '98
The Object of My Affection '98
The Associate '96
Caroline at Midnight '93
Dangerous Heart '93
In the Line of Duty: Ambush in Waco '93
Queen '93
Year of the Comet '92
For Love or Money '88
My Neighbor Totoro '88 (V)
The Spellbinder '88
Made in Heaven '87
The Rise & Rise of Daniel Rocket '86
Mirrors '85
I Married a Centerfold '84
Just the Way You Are '84
Diner '82

Tyne Daly (1947-)
Absence of the Good '99
Execution of Justice '99
The Simian Line '99
Money Plays '98
The Student Affair '97
Tricks '97
Bye Bye Birdie '95

Christy '94
On the Town '91
The Aviator '85
Movers and Shakers '85
Your Place or Mine '83
A Matter of Life and Death '81
Zoot Suit '81
Better Late Than Never '79
Speedtrap '78
The Adultress '77
Intimate Strangers '77
Telefon '77
The Enforcer '76
Larry '74
Angel Unchained '70

Jacqueline Dalya (1918-80)
Miss Melody Jones '73
Behind Prison Walls '43

Susan Damante-Shaw (1950-)
Image of Passion '86
Mountain Family Robinson '79
Further Adventures of the Wilderness Family, Part 2 '77
The Adventures of the Wilderness Family '76
The Student Teachers '73

Bertila Damas
True Friends '98
Mi Vida Loca '94
Nothing But Trouble '91

Paul D'Amato
The Deer Hunter '78
Slap Shot '77

Charlotte d'Amboise (1964-)
Lost in the Bermuda Triangle '98
American Blue Note '89

Leo Damian
Hard Drive '94
Ghosts Can't Do It '90

Marcus D'Amico (1965-)
Armistead Maupin's Tales of the City '93
Full Metal Jacket '87

Blackie Dammett
The American Scream '80s
Nine Deaths of the Ninja '85

Cathryn Damon (1933-87)
She's Having a Baby '88
First Time '82
How to Beat the High Cost of Living '80

Gabriel Damon (1976-)
Social Misfits '00
Journey to Spirit Island '92
Little Nemo: Adventures in Slumberland '92 (V)
Iron Maze '91
RoboCop 2 '90
The Land Before Time '88 (V)
Call to Glory '84

Mark Damon (1933-)
Ocean's Thirteen '07
The Departed '06
The Good Shepherd '06
The Brothers Grimm '05
Syriana '05
Black Sabbath '64
Anzio '68

Matt Damon (1970-)
The Bourne Ultimatum '07
Ocean's Thirteen '07
The Departed '06
The Good Shepherd '06
The Brothers Grimm '05
Syriana '05
Eurotrip '04
Jersey Girl '04
Ocean's Twelve '04
Stuck On You '03
The Bourne Supremacy '04
The Bourne Identity '02
Confessions of a Dangerous Mind '02
Gerry '02
Spirit: Stallion of the Cimarron '02 (V)
The Third Wheel '02
Jay and Silent Bob Strike Back '01
Ocean's Eleven '01
All the Pretty Horses '00
The Legend of Bagger Vance '00
Titan A.E. '00 (V)
Dogma '99
Rounders '98
Saving Private Ryan '98
Chasing Amy '97
Good Will Hunting '97
John Grisham's The Rainmaker '97
Courage Under Fire '96
Glory Daze '96
The Good Old Boys '95
Geronimo: An American Legend '93
School Ties '92
Rising Son '90
The Good Mother '88
Mystic Pizza '88

Vic Damone (1928-)
Hell to Eternity '60
Meet Me in Las Vegas '56
Hit the Deck '55
Kismet '55
Athena '54
Rich, Young and Pretty '51

JoJo D'Amore (1931-2005)
Zoltan... Hound of Dracula '78

Barbara Dana (1940-)
Raising Flagg '06
Necessary Parties '88
A Matter of Principle '83
Inspector Clouseau '68

Bill Dana (1924-)
Lena's Holiday '90
I Wonder Who's Killing Her Now? '76
Harrad Summer '74

Leora Dana (1923-83)
Amityville 3: The Demon '83
Baby It's You '82
Tora! Tora! Tora! '70
Change of Habit '69
Kings Go Forth '58
3:10 to Yuma '57

Viola Dana (1897-1987)
That Certain Thing '28
The Ice Flood '26

Malcolm Danare (1962-)
Godzilla '98
Popcorn '89
Heaven Help Us '85

Charles Dance (1946-)
The Contractor '07
Scoop '06
Starter for Ten '06
Bleak House '05
Swimming Pool '03
Dark Blue World '01
Gosford Park '01
Dr. Bell and Mr. Doyle: The Dark Beginnings of Sherlock Holmes '00
Hilary and Jackie '98
The Blood Oranges '97
In the Presence of Mine Enemies '97
Rebecca '97
Space Truckers '97
Michael Collins '96
The Stranger: Kabloonak '95
Undertow '95
Century '94
The Surgeon '94
Last Action Hero '93
Alien 3 '92
China Moon '91

[Charles Dance — continued]
Tales of the Unexpected '91
The Phantom of the Opera '90
Goldeneye: The Secret Life of Ian Fleming '90
Out of the Shadows '88
Pascali's Island '88
White Mischief '88
Good Morning, Babylon '87
Hidden City '87
Out on a Limb '87
The Golden Child '86
The McGuffin '85
Plenty '85

Hugh Dancy (1975-)
Blood & Chocolate '07
Evening '07
The Jane Austen Book Club '07
Basic Instinct 2 '06
Elizabeth I '05
Shooting Dogs '05
Ella Enchanted '04
King Arthur '04
Daniel Deronda '02
The Sleeping Dictionary '02
Black Hawk Down '01
Madame Bovary '00

Evan Dando (1967-)
Heavy '94
Reality Bites '94

Tom D'Andrea (1909-98)
Kill the Umpire '50
The Next Voice You Hear '50
Silver River '48
Dark Passage '47
Humoresque '45
Never Say Goodbye '46

Dorothy Dandridge (1922-65)
Tamango '59
Island in the Sun '57
Carmen Jones '54
Since You Went Away '44
Bahama Passage '42
Lady from Louisiana '42
Sun Valley Serenade '41
Sundown '41

Eric Dane (1972-)
Feast '06
Wedding Wars '06
X-Men: The Last Stand '05
The Basket '99

Karl (Daen) Dane (1886-1934)
The Big House '30
Son of the Sheik '26
The Big Parade '25

Lawrence Dane (1937-)
Waking the Dead '00
Thrill Seekers '99
Bride of Chucky '98
It Takes Two '95
National Lampoon's Senior Trip '95
Devlin '92
The Good Fight '92
Lethal Lolita—Amy Fisher: My Story '92
Rolling Vengeance '87
Clown Murders '83
Of Unknown Origin '83
Happy Birthday to Me '81
Scanners '81
Fatal Attraction '80
Rituals '79
Find the Lady '76
It Seemed Like a Good Idea at the Time '75

Patricia Dane (1918-95)
I Dood It '43
Johnny Eager '42
Rio Rita '42
Somewhere I'll Find You '42

Paul Daneman (1925-2001)
Tears in the Rain '88

Claire Danes (1979-)
Evening '07
The Flock '07
Stardust '07
Shopgirl '05
The Family Stone '05
Stage Beauty '04
It's All About Love '03
Terminator 3: Rise of the Machines '03
The Hours '02
Igby Goes Down '02
Brokedown Palace '99
The Mod Squad '99
Princess Mononoke '98 (V)
I Love You, I Love You Not '97
John Grisham's The Rainmaker '97
Les Miserables '97
Polish Wedding '97
U-Turn '97
To Gillian on Her 37th Birthday '96
William Shakespeare's Romeo and Juliet '96
Home for the Holidays '95
How to Make an American Quilt '95
Little Women '94

Shera Danese (1950-)
Enemies of Laughter '00

Jean Danet (1924-2001)
The Hunchback of Notre Dame '57
There Goes Barder '54

Beverly D'Angelo (1953-)
Harold & Kumar Escape from Guantanamo Bay '08
Relative Strangers '06
King of the Corner '04
Lansky '99
Sugar Town '99
American History X '98
Illuminata '98
A Rat's Tale '98
With Friends Like These '98
Pterodactyl Woman from Beverly Hills '97
Vegas Vacation '96
Nowhere '96
An Eye for an Eye '95
The Crazysitter '94
Lightning Jack '94
Widow's Kiss '94
Man Trouble '92
Lonely Hearts '91
The Pope Must Diet '91
The Miracle '91
Daddy's Dyin'... Who's Got the Will? '90
Pacific Heights '90
Cold Front '89
Christmas Vacation '89
Aria '88
High Spirits '88
Hands of a Stranger '87
In the Mood '87
Maid to Order '87
Trading Hearts '87
Big Trouble '86
Slow Burn '86
National Lampoon's European Vacation '85
Finders Keepers '84
National Lampoon's Vacation '83
A Streetcar Named Desire '84
Sleeping Beauty '83
Honky Tonk Freeway '81
Paternity '81
Coal Miner's Daughter '80
Highpoint '80
Hair '79

Carlo D'Angelo (1919-73)
Secret Agent Super Dragon '66

Laura D'Angelo (1956-)
Night Train Murders '75
Torture Train '75

Mirella D'Angelo (1956-)
Apartment Zero '88
Unsane '82

Rodney Dangerfield (1921-2004)
The 4th Tenor '02
Little Nicky '00
My 5 Wives '00
The Godson '98
Meet Wally Sparks '97
Casper '95
Natural Born Killers '94
Ladybugs '92
Rover Dangerfield '91 (V)
Moving '88
Back to School '86
Easy Money '83
Caddyshack '80
The Projectionist '71

Dani (1944-)
Day for Night '73

Brittany Daniel (1976-)
Loveless in Los Angeles '07
Little Man '06
Club Dread '04
Rampage: The Hillside Strangler Murders '04
White Chicks '04
Joe Dirt '01

Jennifer Daniel (1939-)
The Reptile '66
Kiss of the Vampire '62

Isa Danieli (1937-)
Ciao, Professore! '94
Macaroni '85

Henry Daniell (1894-1963)
Les Girls '57
Witness for the Prosecution '57
Lust for Life '56
The Man in the Gray Flannel Suit '56
Diane '55
The Prodigal '55
The Egyptian '54
Wake of the Red Witch '49
Song of Love '47
The Body Snatcher '45
The Woman in Green '45
Jane Eyre '44
Sherlock Holmes in Washington '43
Watch on the Rhine '43
Castle in the Desert '42
Reunion in France '42
A Woman's Face '41
All This and Heaven Too '40
The Great Dictator '40
The Philadelphia Story '40
The Sea Hawk '40
The Firefly '37
Madame X '37
Camille '36

Gary Daniels (1963-)
Queen's Messenger II '01
No Tomorrow '99
Cold Harvest '98
Spoiler '98
Recoil '97
Bloodmoon '97
American Streetfighter 2
Capital Punishment '96
Hawk's Vengeance '96
Riot '96
Fist of the North Star '95
Heatseeker '95
Rage '95
White Tiger '95
Deadly Target '94
Firepower '93
Knights '93
Reds '81

Erin Daniels (1973-)
House of 1000 Corpses '03
One Hour Photo '02

Ben Daniels (1964-)
The State Within '06
Doom '05
Conspiracy '01
The Aristocrats '99
Britannic '99
I Want You '98
Madeline '98
Passion in the Desert '97
Beautiful Thing '95

Bebe Daniels (1901-71)
Counsellor-at-Law '33
42nd Street '33
The Maltese Falcon '31
Reaching for the Moon '31
Dixiana '30
Feel My Pulse '28
Monsieur Beaucaire '24
Affairs of Anatol '21
Why Change Your Wife? '20
Male and Female '19

Jeff Daniels (1955-)
RV '06
Infamous '06
Because of Winn-Dixie '05
Good Night, and Good Luck '05
Imaginary Heroes '05
The Squid and the Whale '05
Gods and Generals '03
I Witness '03
The Hours '02
Blood Work '02
Cheaters '00
Chasing Sleep '00
It's the Rage '99
My Favorite Martian '99
Pleasantville '98
Trial and Error '96
101 Dalmatians '96
Fly Away Home '96
Two Days in the Valley '96
Redwood Curtain '95
Dumb & Dumber '94
Speed '94
Gettysburg '93
Rain Without Thunder '93
Grand Tour: Disaster in Time '92

J.D. Daniels (1980-)
Beanstalk '94
Roswell: The U.F.O. Cover-Up '94

Anthony Daniels (1946-)
Star Wars: Episode 3—Revenge of the Sith '05
Star Wars: Episode 2—Attack of the Clones '02
Return of the Jedi '83
The Empire Strikes Back '80
Star Wars '77

John Daniels
Getting Over '81
Bare Knuckles '77
Black Shampoo '76
Candy Tangerine Man '75

Phil Daniels (1958-)
Chicken Run '00 (V)
Still Crazy '98
Bad Behavior '92
The Bride '85
Meantime '81
Breaking Glass '80
Quadrophenia '79
Scum '79

William Daniels (1927-)
Her Alibi '88
Blind Date '87
The Blue Lagoon '80
City in Fear '80
Sunburn '79
The One and Only '78
Sergeant Matlovich vs. the U.S. Air Force '78
Black Sunday '77
Oh, God! '77
The Parallax View '74
1776 '72
Marlowe '69
The Graduate '67
Two for the Road '67
A Thousand Clowns '65

Mark Daniels
Candyman '92
Mr. Holland's Opus '95

Mickey Daniels (1914-70)
The Great Ziegfeld '36
The Adventurous Knights '35
Roaring Roads '35
Social Error '35

[Blythe Danner entries]
Terms of Endearment '83
Ragtime '81
A Rumor of War '80
The Purple Rose of Cairo '85
Marie '85
Something Wild '86
Heartburn '86
Radio Days '87
Sweet Hearts Dance '88
Love Notes '88
Checking Out '89
Arachnophobia '90
Welcome Home, Roxy Carmichael '90
The Butcher's Wife '91
Love Hurts '91
The Neighborhood '92
There Goes the Neighborhood '92
Teamster Boss: The Jackie Presser Story '92

Blythe Danner (1944-)
Sisterhood of the Traveling Pants 2 '08
The Last Kiss '06
Howl's Moving Castle '04
Meet the Fockers '04
Sylvia '03
Three Days of Rain '03
Invisible Circus '01
Meet the Parents '00
Forces of Nature '99
The Love Letter '99
The X-Files '98
No Looking Back '98
Saint Maybe '98
Eye of the Storm '98
From the Earth to the Moon '98
Murder She Purred: A Mrs. Murphy Mystery '98 (V)
The Myth of Fingerprints '97
Mad City '97
A Call to Remember '97
Getting Up and Going Home '96
Homage '95
To Wong Foo, Thanks for Everything, Julie Newmar '95
Husbands and Wives '92
Never Forget '91
The Prince of Tides '91
Alice '90
Mr. & Mrs. Bridge '90
Judgment '90
Another Woman '88
Brighton Beach Memoirs '86
Guilty Conscience '85
Man, Woman & Child '83
Inside the Third Reich '82
The Great Santini '80
Too Far to Go '79
Love Affair: The Eleanor & Lou Gehrig Story '77
Futureworld '76
Hearts of the West '75
The Seagull '75
1776 '72
To Kill a Clown '72

Sybil Danning (1952-)
L.A. Bounty '89
Amazon Women on the Moon '87
Phantom Empire '87
Warrior Queen '87
Reform School Girls '86
Young Lady Chatterly 2 '85
Malibu Express '85
Private Passions '85
Howling II: Your Sister Is a Werewolf '85
Jungle Warriors '84
Day of the Cobra '84
Panther Squad '84
S.A.S. San Salvador '84
Seven Magnificent Gladiators '84
They're Playing with Fire '84
Chained Heat '83
Hercules '83
Daughter of Death '82
The Salamander '82
Separate Ways '82
Battle Beyond the Stars '80
Kill Castro '80
The Man with Bogart's Face '80
The Mercenaries '80
Nightkill '80
The Concorde: Airport '79
Meteor '79
The Prince and the Pauper '78
Albino '76
God's Gun '75
Bluebeard '72
Cat in the Cage '68

Lynn Danielson-Rosenthal
Nickel & Dime '92
Mortuary Academy '91

Eli Danker
Undisputed II: Last Man Standing '06
Impulse '90
The Flight '89
The Taking of Flight 847: The Uli Derickson Story '88

Rick Danko (1943-99)
Man Outside '88
The Kids Are Alright '79
The Last Waltz '78

Roger Dann (1910-67)
Two for the Road '67

I Confess '53

Paul Franklin Dano (1984-)
There Will Be Blood '07
Fast Food Nation '06
Little Miss Sunshine '06
The Ballad of Jack and Rose '05
The Girl Next Door '04
Taking Lives '04
The Emperor's Club '02
L.I.E. '01

Royal Dano (1922-94)
The Dark Half '91
Big Score '83
Spaced Invaders '90
Texas Guns '90
Killer Klowns from Outer Space '88
Ghoulies 2 '87
Cocaine Wars '86
Teachers '84
The Right Stuff '83
Something Wicked This Way Comes '83
Bad Georgia Road '77
Hughes & Harlow: Angels in Hell '77
The Killer Inside Me '76
The Outlaw Josey Wales '76
Huckleberry Finn '75
Big Bad Mama '74
Messiah of Evil '74
Wild Party '74
Electra Glide in Blue '73
Moon of the Wolf '72
Death of a Gunfighter '69
7 Faces of Dr. Lao '63
The Adventures of Huckleberry Finn '60
Never Steal Anything Small '59
Man of the West '58
Crime of Passion '57
Man in the Shadow '57
All Mine to Give '56
Tribute to a Bad Man '56
The Trouble with Harry '55
Johnny Guitar '53
Bend of the River '52
Flame of Araby '51
The Red Badge of Courage '51

Leslie Danon
Hail Caesar '94
The Whispering '94

Cesare Danova (1926-92)
St. Helen's, Killer Volcano '82
National Lampoon's Animal House '78
Tentacles '78
Scorchy '76
Mean Streets '73
Boy, Did I Get a Wrong Number! '66
Gidget Goes to Rome '63
Viva Las Vegas '63

Ted Danson (1947-)
Mad Money '08
Knights of the South Bronx '05
The Moguls '05
Mumford '99
Jerry and Tom '98
Saving Private Ryan '98
Homegrown '97
Gulliver's Travels '95
Loch Ness '95
Getting Even with Dad '94
Pontiac Moon '94
Made in America '93
Three Men and a Little Lady '90
Cousins '89
Dad '89
Three Men and a Baby '87
We Are the Children '87
A Fine Mess '86
Just Between Friends '86
When the Bough Breaks '86
Little Treasure '85
Creepshow '82
Body Heat '81
Our Family Business '81
The Onion Field '79
Chinese Web '78

Joe Dante (1946-)
Silence of the Hams '93
Sleepwalkers '92
Code Name: Zebra '84
Cannonball '76

Michael Dante (1931-)
Crazy Horse and Custer: "The Untold Story" '90
The Cage '89
Beyond Evil '80
Cruise Missile '78
Winterhawk '76
Willard '71
Naked Kiss '64
Operation Bikini '63
Seven Thieves '60

Peter Dante (1968-)
Strange Wilderness '08
Grandma's Boy '06
Mr. Deeds '02

Helmut Dantine (1917-82)
The Fifth Musketeer '79
The Killer Elite '75
The Wilby Conspiracy '75
Bring Me the Head of Alfredo Garcia '74
Operation Crossbow '65
War and Peace '56
Alexander the Great '55
The Stranger from Venus '54
Whispering City '47
Hollywood Canteen '44
Passage to Marseilles '44
Edge of Darkness '43
Northern Pursuit '43
Watch on the Rhine '43
Casablanca '42
Desperate Journey '42
Mrs. Miniver '42
The Navy Comes Through '42
To Be or Not to Be '42

Ray Danton (1931-92)
Apache Blood '75
The Centerfold Girls '74
Jailbreakin' '72
Secret Agent Super Dragon '66
The Conqueror & the Empress '64
The Longest Day '62
The Rise and Fall of Legs Diamond '60
A Majority of One '56
I'll Cry Tomorrow '55

Mark Danvers
Rude Boy: The Jamaican Don '03
Third World Cop '99

Tony Danza (1951-)
The Garbage-Picking, Field Goal-Kicking Philadelphia Phenomenon '98
Noah '98
A Brooklyn State of Mind '97
Glam '97
Love to Kill '97
North Shore Fish '97
Twelve Angry Men '97
Illtown '96
Angels in the Outfield '94
Last Action Hero '93
She's Out of Control '89
Truth or Die '86
Going Apel '81
The Hollywood Knights '80

Maia Danziger (1950-)
The Ice Storm '97
Last Exit to Brooklyn '90
High Stakes '89
Dr. Heckyl and Mr. Hype '80

Ho Chung Dao
See Bruce Li

Ingeborga Dapkounaite (1963-)
Seven Years in Tibet '97
Jack Higgins' On Dangerous Ground '95
Burnt by the Sun '94

Patti D'Arbanville (1951-)
A Tale of Two Pizzas '03
Personal Velocity: Three Portraits '02
Celebrity '98
The Fan '96
Father's Day '96
Blind Spot '93
Deadly Conspiracy '91
Snow Kill '90
Wired '89
Call Me '88
Fresh Horses '88
The Boys Next Door '85
Real Genius '85
Modern Problems '81
The Fifth Floor '80
Hog Wild '80
Time After Time '79
Big Wednesday '78
Bilitis '77
Flesh '68

Patrika Darbo (1948-)
Madhouse '04
Speed 2: Cruise Control '97
Fast Money '96
Leaving Normal '92
Daddy's Dyin'... Who's Got the Will? '90

Kim Darby (1947-)
Newsbreak '00
The Last Best Sunday '98
Halloween 6: The Curse of Michael Myers '95
Teen Wolf Too '87
Better Off Dead '85
The Capture of Grizzly Adams '82
Enola Gay: The Men, the Mission, the Atomic Bomb '80
Flatbed Annie and Sweetiepie: Lady Truckers '79
The One and Only '78
Rich Man, Poor Man '76
Don't Be Afraid of the Dark '73
The Streets of San Francisco '72
The Grissom Gang '71
The People '71
The Strawberry Statement '70
Generation '69
True Grit '69

Mireille Darc (1938-)
Intruder '76
Icy Breasts '75
Return of the Tall Blond Man with One Black Shoe '74
The Tall Blond Man with One Black Shoe '72
The Peking Blond '68
Weekend '67

Denise Darcel (1925-)
Vera Cruz '53
Westward the Women '51
Battleground '49
Thunder in the Pines '49

Alexander D'Arcy (1908-96)
Dead Pigeon on Beethoven Street '72
Blood of Dracula's Castle '69
Fanny Hill: Memoirs of a Woman of Pleasure '64
Horrors of Spider Island '59
Abdulla the Great '56
Soldier of Fortune '55
The Awful Truth '37
Prisoner of Zenda '37

Jake D'Arcy
Gregory's Girl '80

James D'Arcy (1975-)
A Sense of Freedom '78
Mansfield Park '07
Rise: Blood Hunter '07
An American Haunting '05
Exorcist: The Beginning '04
Dot the I '03
Master and Commander: The Far Side of the World '03
Sherlock: Case of Evil '02
The Trench '99
A Dance to the Music of Time '97

Roy D'Arcy (1894-1969)
Legion of Missing Men '37
Revolt of the Zombies '36
Kentucky Blue Streak '35
Murder on the High Seas '32

Sheila Darcy (1914-2004)
Tumbleweed Ranch in Arizona '41
Irish Luck '39
Zorro's Fighting Legion '39

Severn Darden (1929-95)
Once Upon a Midnight Scary '90
Back to School '86
Real Genius '85
Saturday the 14th '81
In God We Trust '80
Wanda Nevada '79
The Disappearance of Aimee '76
I Wonder Who's Killing Her Now? '76
Jackson County Jail '76
Battle for the Planet of the Apes '73
The Day of the Dolphin '73
The Legend of Hillbilly John '73
Conquest of the Planet of the Apes '72
Playmates '72
Hired Hand '71
Vanishing Point '71
Werewolves on Wheels '71
They Shoot Horses, Don't They? '69
The President's Analyst '67
Dead Heat on a Merry-Go-Round '66
Goldstein '64

Debra (Deborah Dutch) Dare (1951-)
Hard to Die '90

Florence Darel (1968-)
The Count of Monte Cristo '99
Don't Let Me Die on a Sunday '98
A la Mode '94
The Stolen Children '92
A Tale of Springtime '89

Ricardo Darin (1957-)
The Aura '05
The Son of the Bride '01
Nine Queens '00

Johnny Dark
Wishful Thinking '92
Up Your Alley '89
Rip-Off '77

Samantha Dark
Malevolence '04

Gigi Darlene
Bad Girls Go to Hell '65
The Beast That Killed Women '65

Candy Darling (1947-74)
Silent Night, Bloody Night '73
Flesh '68

Joan Darling (1935-)
Sunnyside '79
The Two Worlds of Jenny Logan '79

Linda Darlow
Angels Fall '07
Masters of Horror: The Screwfly Solution '06
Connie and Carla '04
The Amy Fisher Story '93
Immediate Family '89

Gerard Darmon (1948-)
The Good Thief '03
Obsession: A Taste for Fear '89
Betty Blue '86
Diva '82

Linda Darnell (1921-65)
Zero Hour! '57
Dakota Incident '56
Second Chance '53
Blackbeard the Pirate '52
Island of Desire '52
No Way Out '50
A Letter to Three Wives '49
Unfaithfully Yours '48
Forever Amber '47
Anna and the King of Siam '46
My Darling Clementine '46
Hangover Square '45
Buffalo Bill '44
It Happened Tomorrow '44
City Without Men '43
Blood and Sand '41
Brigham Young: Frontiersman '40
The Mark of Zorro '40

Steve Darrell (1904-70)
The Adventures of Frank and Jesse James '48
Lightning Raiders '45

James Darren (1936-)
Boss' Son '78
Venus in Furs '70
Hey There, It's Yogi Bear '64 (V)
Gidget Goes to Rome '63
Diamond Head '62
Gidget Goes Hawaiian '61
The Guns of Navarone '61
All the Young Men '60
Let No Man Write My Epitaph '60
The Gene Krupa Story '59
Gidget '59
Gunman's Walk '58

Danielle Darrieux (1917-)
Persepolis '07 (V)
Dangerous Liaisons '03
8 Women '02
Scene of the Crime '87
Le Cavaleur '78
L'Annee Sainte '76
The Young Girls of Rochefort '68
Murder at 45 R.P.M. '65
Bluebeard '63
The Red and the Black '57
Alexander the Great '55
Lady Chatterley's Lover '55
The Earrings of Madame De... '54
Five Fingers '52
Le Plaisir '52
La Ronde '51
Rich Young and Pretty '51
Ruy Blas '48
The Rage of Paris '38
Mayerling '36
Mauvaise Graine '33

Frankie Darro (1917-76)
Runaways '75
Forbidden Planet '56
Westward the Women '51
Riding High '50
Junior G-Men of the Air '42
Let's Go Collegiate '41
The Gang's All Here '40
Pinocchio '40 (V)
Up in the Air '40
Boy's Reformatory '39
Irish Luck '39
Tough Kid '39
Anything for a Thrill '37
Devil Diamond '37
Tough to Handle '37
Black Gold '36
The Phantom Empire '35
Valley of Wanted Men '35
Broadway Bill '34
The Mayor of Hell '33
Wolf Dog '33
Devil Horse '32
Lightning Warrior '31
Vanishing Legion '31

Jean-Pierre Darroussin (1953-)
How Much Do You Love Me? '05
Red Lights '04
La Buche '00

Barbara Darrow (1931-)
Tall Story '60
Queen of Outer Space '58

Henry Darrow (1933-)
Tequila Body Shots '99
Mom, Can I Keep Her? '98
The Last of the Finest '90
L.A. Bounty '89
In Dangerous Company '88
Death Blow '87
Computer Wizard '77
Where's Willie? '77

John Darrow (1907-80)
Monte Carlo Nights '34
The Lady Refuses '31
Ten Nights in a Bar-Room '31

Oliver Darrow
Hell's Angels '30

Tony Darrow (1946-)
Bad Girls from Mars '90
Spirits '90
The Channeler '89

Ivan Darvas
Love '71

Lili Darvas (1906-74)
Love '71
Cold Days '66
24 Hours in a Woman's Life '61
Meet Me in Las Vegas '56

Bella Darvi (1927-71)
The Racers '55
The Egyptian '54

Jane Darwell (1879-1967)
Last Hurrah '58
Girls in Prison '56
The Bigamist '53
We're Not Married '52
The Lemon Drop Kid '51
Caged '50
Redwood Forest Trail '50
Wagon Master '50
Three Husbands '50
Three Godfathers '48
The Red Stallion '47
I Live in Grosvenor Square '46
My Darling Clementine '46
The Great Gildersleeve '43
The Ox-Bow Incident '43
Tender Comrade '43
All Through the Night '42
The Loves of Edgar Allen Poe '42
On the Sunny Side '42
The Devil & Daniel Webster '41
Brigham Young: Frontiersman '40
The Grapes of Wrath '40
Gone with the Wind '39

Jesse James '39
The Rains Came '39
The Jury's Secret '38
Little Miss Broadway '38
Captain January '36
Craig's Wife '36
Curly Top '35
Life Begins at Forty '35
Bright Eyes '34
One Night of Love '34
Finishing School '33

Stacey Dash (1966-)
Above '08
I Could Never Be Your Woman '06
Soldiers of Change '06
Getting Played '06
Gang of Roses '03
Personals '05
Cold Around the Heart '97
Clueless '95
Illegal in Blue '95
Black Water '94
Renaissance Man '94
Mo' Money '92
Moving '88

Nandita Das (1969-)
Earth '98
Fire '96

Jules Dassin (1911-2008)
Phaedra '61
Never on Sunday '60
Rififi '54

Alex Datcher (1962-)
The Expert '95
Body Bags '93
Passenger 57 '92
Rage and Honor '92

Kristin Dattilo-Hayward (1970-)
Child of Darkness, Child of Light '91
Pyrates '91
Mirror, Mirror '90

James Daughton (1950-)
Girlfriend from Hell '89
Blind Date '84
Swim Team '79
Malibu Beach '78

Claude Dauphin (1903-78)
Les Miserables '78
Madame Rosa '77
The Tenant '76
Rosebud '75
The Madwoman of Chaillot '69
Two for the Road '67
Is Paris Burning? '66
Lady L '65
Tiara Tahiti '62
April in Paris '52
Casque d'Or '52
Le Plaisir '52

Jean Daste (1904-94)
Love Unto Death '84
The Green Room '78
The Wild Child '70
La Guerre Est Finie '66
Grand Illusion '37
The Crime of Monsieur Lange '36
L'Atalante '34
Zero for Conduct '33
Boudu Saved from Drowning '32

Alexa Davalos (1982-)
Feast of Love '07
The Mist '07
The Chronicles of Riddick '04
And Starring Pancho Villa as Himself '03

Dominique Davalos (1965-)
Salvation '87
A House in the Hills '93

Elyssa Davalos (1959-)
Howard the Duck '86
Jericho Fever '93
Wild & Wooly '78

Richard (Dick) Davalos (1935-)
Something Wicked This Way Comes '83
Soul Patrol '80
Zulu Dawn '79
The Island of Dr. Moreau '77
Blood Legacy '73
Kelly's Heroes '70
Cool Hand Luke '67
Pit Stop '67
All the Young Men '60
Sea Chase '55
East of Eden '54

Harry Davenport (1866-1949)
December 7th: The Movie '91
Riding High '50
That Forsyte Woman '50
Tell It to the Judge '49
For the Love of Mary '48
Three Daring Daughters '48
The Bachelor and the Bobby-Soxer '47
The Farmer's Daughter '47
Courage of Lassie '46
G.I. War Brides '46
The Enchanted Forest '45
Jack London '44
Meet Me in St. Louis '44
The Thin Man Goes Home '44
The Amazing Mrs. Holiday '43
The Ox-Bow Incident '43
Son of Fury '42
Kings Row '41
That Uncertain Feeling '41
All This and Heaven Too '40
Foreign Correspondent '40
Lucky Partners '40
Gone with the Wind '39
The Hunchback of Notre Dame '39
The Story of Alexander Graham Bell '39
The Cowboy and the Lady '38
Marie Antoinette '38
You Can't Take It with You '38
Fit for a King '37

Jack Davenport (1973-)
Pirates of the Caribbean: At World's End '07
Pirates of the Caribbean: Dead Man's Chest '06
The Incredible Journey of Mary Bryant '05
The Libertine '05
The Wedding Date '05
Pirates of the Caribbean: The Curse of the Black Pearl '03
The Wyvern Mystery '00
The Talented Mr. Ripley '99
Ultraviolet '98
Catherine Cookson's The Moth '96

Lucy Davenport
Sylvia '03
Soho Square '00

Mary Davenport
Home Movies '79
Sisters '73

Nigel Davenport (1928-)
Without a Clue '88
Caravaggio '86
Mountbatten: The Last Viceroy '86
Greystoke: The Legend of Tarzan, Lord of the Apes '84
A Christmas Carol '84
Chariots of Fire '81
Nighthawks '81

Joanna David (1947-)
The Way We Live Now '02
Cotton Mary '99
Murder at Lynch Cross '85

Eleanor David (1956-)
Topsy Turvy '99
Slipstream '89
84 Charing Cross Road '86
Sylvia '86
Comfort and Joy '84
Pink Floyd: The Wall '82
The Scarlet Pimpernel '82

Keith David (1954-)
First Sunday '08
The Last Sentinel '07
Delta Farce '07
Transformers '07 (V)
ATL '06
Crash '05

Angel David
Two Girls and a Guy '98
The Substitute 2: School's Out '98
The Crow '93
Mixed Blood '84

Thayer David (1927-78)
The Duchess and the Dirtwater Fox '76
Rocky '76
The Eiger Sanction '75
Save the Tiger '73
Savages '72
Night of Dark Shadows '71
House of Dark Shadows '70
The Story of Ruth '60
Journey to the Center of the Earth '59
A Time to Love & a Time to Die '58

Robert Davi (1953-)
Transporter 2 '05
Mr. & Mrs. Smith '05
In the Mix '05
Agent Cody Banks 2: Destination London '04
The Chronicles of Riddick '04
Agent Cody Banks '03
Head of State '03
Hollywood Homicide '03
Kaena: The Prophecy '03
Call Me: The Rise and Fall of Heidi Fleiss '04
One Last Ride '03
The 4th Tenor '02
The Hot Chick '02
Verdict in Blood '02
My Little Assassin '99
The Bad Pack '98
For Which He Stands '97
The Beneficiary '97
Mutual Needs '97
An Occasional Hell '96
Body Count '95
The Dangerous '95
The Dogfighters '95
Showgirls '95
Blind Justice '94
Cops and Robbersons '94
No Contest '94
Maniac Cop 3: Badge of Silence '93
Mardi Gras for the Devil '93
The November Men '93
Quick '93
Center of the Web '92
Christopher Columbus: The Discovery '92
Wild Orchid 2: Two Shades of Blue '92
Illicit Behavior '91
The Taking of Beverly Hills '91
White Hot: The Mysterious Murder of Thelma Todd '91
Amazon '90
Legal Tender '90
Maniac Cop 2 '90
Peacemaker '90
Predator 2 '90
License to Kill '89
Die Hard '88
Traxx '87
Wild Thing '87
The Goonies '85
Gangster Wars '81
The $5.20 an Hour Dream '80
Cry of the Innocent '80
The Ordeal of Dr. Mudd '80

Lolita (David) Davidovich (1961-)
September Dawn '07
Hollywood Homicide '03
Dark Blue '03
Snow in August '01
Mystery, Alaska '99
No Vacancy '99
Play It to the Bone '99
Four Days '99
Gods and Monsters '98
Santa Fe '97
The Garden of Redemption '97
Jungle 2 Jungle '96
Dead Silence '96
Touch '96
For Better or Worse '95
Harvest of Fire '95
Indictment: The McMartin Trial '95
Now and Then '95
Cobb '94
Keep the Change '92
Leap of Faith '92
Raising Cain '92
The Inner Circle '91
JFK '91
The Object of Beauty '91
Prison Stories: Women on the Inside '91
Blaze '89
Blindside '88
Adventures in Babysitting '87
Big Town '87
Recruits '86

Alan Davidson
Frailty '02
Rift '96

Ben Davidson (1940-)
Conan the Barbarian '82

Diana Davidson
Around the World in 80 Ways '86
Scared to Death '80

Eileen Davidson (1959-)
Eternity '90
Easy Wheels '89
The House on Sorority Row '83

Jack Davidson (1936-)
You Tell Me '06
Baby It's You '82
Shock Waves '77

Jaye Davidson (1968-)
Stargate '94
The Crying Game '92

John Davidson (1886-1969)
Tailspin Tommy '34
Monsieur Beaucaire '24

John Davidson (1941-)
Edward Scissorhands '90
The Squeeze '87
The Concorde: Airport '79 '79
The Happiest Millionaire '67

John Davidson (1953-)
Positive I.D. '87
Interface '84

Max Davidson (1875-1950)
Roamin' Wild '36
Daring Danger '32
Hotel Imperial '27

Tommy Davidson (1965-)
The Proud Family Movie '05 (V)
Juwanna Mann '02
Bamboozled '00
Pros & Cons '99
Plump Fiction '97
Booty Call '96
Ace Ventura: When Nature Calls '95
Strictly Business '91

William B. Davidson (1888-1947)
They Were Expendable '45
I'm No Angel '33
Held for Murder '32
Vice Squad '31
The Silver Horde '30

Embeth Davidtz (1966-)
Fracture '07
Junebug '05
The Emperor's Club '02
Bridget Jones's Diary '01
13 Ghosts '01
The Hole '01
Bicentennial Man '99
Mansfield Park '99
Last Rites '98
Fallen '98
The Gingerbread Man '97
Matilda '96
Feast of July '95
Murder in the First '95
Schindler's List '93
Army of Darkness '92

Betty Ann Davies (1910-55)
The Belles of St. Trinian's '53
The Blue Lamp '49

Geraint Wyn Davies (1957-)
Conspiracy of Fear '96
Slings & Arrows: Season 2 '05

Gwen Ffrangcon Davies (1891-)
The Witches '66
The Devil Rides Out '68

Jackson Davies
Dead Ahead: The Exxon Valdez Disaster '92

James Davies
The Rocking Horse Winner '49

Jeremy Davies (1969-)
Rescue Dawn '06
Mandalay '05
Dogville '03
The Laramie Project '02
Secretary '02
Solaris '02
CQ '01
Intimate Affairs '01
Up at the Villa '00
The Million Dollar Hotel '00
Ravenous '99
Saving Private Ryan '98
Going All the Way '97
The Locusts '97
Twister '96
Spanking the Monkey '94

John (Howard) Davies (1939-)
Tom Brown's School Days '51
Oliver Twist '48

Kimberly Davies (1973-)
Psycho Beach Party '00

Lindy Davies (1946-)
Malcolm '86

Marion Davies (1897-1961)
Going Hollywood '33
Show People '28

Oliver Ford Davies (1939-)
Star Wars: Episode 3 — Revenge of the Sith '05
Johnny English '03
Star Wars: Episode 2 — Attack of the Clones '02
The Way We Live Now '02
Star Wars: Episode 1 — The Phantom Menace '99
A Royal Scandal '96

Rachel Davies
Band of Gold '95
Cause Celebre '87

Ray Davies (1944-)
Absolute Beginners '86
Return to Waterloo '85

Rudi Davies (1967-)
The Object of Beauty '91
Maria's Child '93
The Lonely Passion of Judith Hearne '87

Rupert Davies (1916-76)
Frightmare '74
Waterloo '71
Zeppelin '71

The Conqueror Worm '68
The Crimson Cult '68
Dracula Has Risen from the Grave '68
Target for Killing '66
The Spy Who Came in from the Cold '65

Stephen Davies
Tattoo, a Love Story '02
Star Portal '97
Bloodfist 7: Manhunt '95
Dillinger and Capone '95
The Berlin Conspiracy '91
The Nest '88
Hanoi Hilton '87

Tamara Davies
Scorcher '02
Decay '98

Luis Davila (1927-98)
The Scalawag Bunch '75
The Mummy's Revenge '73
Pancho Villa '72
Espionage in Tangiers '65

Alex Davion (1929-)
The Bloodsuckers '70
Valley of the Dolls '67
Plague of the Zombies '66
Paranoiac '62

Ann B. Davis (1926-)
The Brady Bunch Movie '95
Naked Gun 33 1/3: The Final Insult '94
A Very Brady Christmas '88

Art Davis (1987-)
Along the Sundown Trail '42
Prairie Pals '42
Tumbleweed Trail '42
Phantom Gold '38

Bette Davis (1908-89)
Wicked Stepmother '89
The Whales of August '87
As Summers Die '86
Agatha Christie's Murder with Mirrors '85
Little Gloria... Happy at Last '84
Right of Way '84
A Piano for Mrs. Cimino '82
The Watcher in the Woods '81
White Mama '80
Strangers: The Story of a Mother and Daughter '79
The Dark Secret of Harvest Home '78
Death on the Nile '78
Return from Witch Mountain '78
Burnt Offerings '76
The Disappearance of Aimee '76
Madame Sin '71
The Anniversary '68
Hush, Hush, Sweet Charlotte '65
The Nanny '65
Dead Ringer '64
Empty Canvas '64
Where Love Has Gone '64
What Ever Happened to Baby Jane? '62
Pocketful of Miracles '61
John Paul Jones '59
The Catered Affair '56
The Virgin Queen '55
Another Man's Poison '52
Phone Call from a Stranger '52
The Star '52
All About Eve '50
Beyond the Forest '49
June Bride '48
Winter Meeting '48
Deception '46
A Stolen Life '46
The Corn Is Green '45
Hollywood Canteen '44
Mr. Skeffington '44
Thank Your Lucky Stars '43
Watch on the Rhine '43
In This Our Life '42
Now, Voyager '42
The Bride Came C.O.D. '41
The Great Lie '41

The Little Foxes '41
The Man Who Came to Dinner '41
All This and Heaven Too '40
The Letter '40
Dark Victory '39
Juarez '39
The Old Maid '39
The Private Lives of Elizabeth & Essex '39
Jezebel '38
The Sisters '38
Kid Galahad '37
Marked Woman '37
That Certain Woman '37
Petrified Forest '36
Satan Met a Lady '36
Dangerous '35
Fashions of 1934 '34
Bureau of Missing Persons '33
Ex-Lady '33
The Cabin in the Cotton '32
Hell's House '32
Three on a Match '32
Way Back Home '32

Brad Davis (1949-91)
Child of Darkness, Child of Light '91
The Habitation of Dragons '91
Hangfire '91
When the Time Comes '91
Robert Kennedy and His Times '90
Rosalie Goes Shopping '89
Vengeance '89
The Caine Mutiny Court Martial '88
Blood Ties '87
Cold Steel '87
Heart '87
Chiefs '83
Querelle '83
Chariots of Fire '81
A Rumor of War '80
A Small Circle of Friends '80
Midnight Express '78
The Campus Corpse '77
Sybil '76

Bud Davis
Andersonville '95
House of the Rising Sun '87

Carole (Raphaelle) Davis (1958-)
If Looks Could Kill '91
The Shrimp on the Barbie '90
Mannequin '87
Princess Academy '87

Chet Davis
The Eye Creatures '65
Yes, Sir, Mr. Bones '51

Clifton Davis (1945-)
Cover '08
Soldiers of Change '06
Kingdom Come '01
Max Keeble's Big Move '01
Dream Date '93
Don't Look Back: The Story of Leroy "Satchel" Paige '81
The Night the City Screamed '80
Little Ladies of the Night '77

Dana Davis
Prom Night '08
Raise Your Voice '04

DeRay Davis
License to Wed '07
The Hit '06
The Fog '05
Jiminy Glick in LaLa Wood '05
Who Made the Potatoe Salad? '05
Beneath '07
The Still Life '07
Savage Island '03

Suspicious River '00

Duane Davis
Paparazzi '04
Angels in the Infield '00
Rocky Marciano '99
The Program '93
Diggstown '92
Final Shot: The Hank Gathers Story '92

Eddie Davis (1895-1987)
Fighting Pilot '35
Gunners & Guns '34

Essie Davis
Charlotte's Web '06
After the Deluge '03
Code 46 '03
Girl with a Pearl Earring '03
The Matrix Reloaded '03
The Matrix Revolutions '03
Kings in Grass Castles '97
The Ripper '97
Lilian's Story '95
River Street '95

Frank Davis
Killer Tomatoes Strike Back '90
Return of the Killer Tomatoes! '88

G. Paul Davis
See Litefoot

Gail Davis (1925-97)
Race for Your Life, Charlie Brown '77 (V)
Alias Jesse James '59
On Top of Old Smoky '53
Winning of the West '53
Blue Canadian Rockies '52
Flying Leathernecks '51
Valley of Fire '51
Cow Town '50
Brand of Fear '49
Far Frontier '48

Geena Davis (1957-)
Stuart Little 2 '02
Stuart Little '99
The Long Kiss Goodnight '96
Cutthroat Island '95
Angie '94
Speechless '94
Hero '92
A League of Their Own '92
Thelma & Louise '91
Quick Change '90
Earth Girls Are Easy '89
The Accidental Tourist '88
Beetlejuice '88
The Fly '86
Fletch '85
Secret Weapons '85
Transylvania 6-5000 '85
Tootsie '82

Gene Davis
Messenger of Death '88
Night Games '80

Hope Davis (1964-)
Charlie Bartlett '07
The Nines '07
The Hoax '06
Infamous '06
The Matador '06
Duma '05
Proof '05
The Weather Man '05
American Splendor '03
About Schmidt '02
The Secret Lives of Dentists '02
Final '01
Hearts in Atlantis '01
Joe Gould's Secret '00
Arlington Road '99
Mumford '99
The Imposters '98
Next Stop, Wonderland '98
The Myth of Fingerprints '97

Jim Davis (1915-81)
Inferno in Paradise '88
Don't Look Back: The Story of Leroy "Satchel" Paige '81
Day Time Ended '80
Comes a Horseman '78

Killing Stone '78
The Choirboys '77
Law of the Land '76
The Runaway Barge '75
Bad Company '72
Dracula vs. Frankenstein '71
The Trackers '71
Monte Walsh '70
Gun Riders '69
El Dorado '67
Jesse James Meets Frankenstein's Daughter '65
Zebra in the Kitchen '65
Iron Angel '64
Frontier Uprising '61
Alias Jesse James '59
Monster from Green Hell '58
The Restless Breed '58
Guns Don't Argue '57
The Maverick Queen '55
Big Chase '54
The Outcast '54
The Big Sky '52
Little Big Horn '51
Hi-Jacked '50
The Showdown '50
Three Desperate Men '50
Hellfire '48

Joan Davis (1907-61)
The Outcast '54
The Traveling Saleswoman '50
If You Knew Susie '48
George White's Scandals '45
Show Business '44
Around the World '43
Hold That Ghost '41
Sun Valley Serenade '41
Just Around the Corner '38
My Lucky Star '38
The Holy Terror '37
On the Avenue '37
Thin Ice '37

Judy Davis (1956-)
The Starter Wife '07
The Break-Up '06
Marie Antoinette '06
Seeing Other People '04
Swimming Upstream '03
Coast to Coast '04
Gaudi Afternoon '01
Life with Judy Garland—Me and My Shadows '01
A Cooler Climate '99
Dash and Lily '99
Celebrity '98
The Echo of Thunder '98
Absolute Power '97
Deconstructing Harry '97
Blood & Wine '96
Children of the Revolution '95
Serving in Silence: The Margarethe Cammermeyer Story '95
The New Age '94
The Ref '93
Husbands and Wives '92
On My Own '92
Barton Fink '91
Naked Lunch '91
One Against the Wind '91
Where Angels Fear to Tread '91
Alice '90
Impromptu '90
Georgia '87
High Tide '87
Kangaroo '86
Rocket to the Moon '86
A Passage to India '84
Heatwave '83
The Final Option '82
The Winter of Our Dreams '82
A Woman Called Golda '82
My Brilliant Career '79
High Rolling in a Hot Corvette '77

Julia Davis (1966-)
Persuasion '07
Power Play '02
Wilbur Wants to Kill Himself '02

Kristen Davis (1965-)
Sex and the City: The Movie '08
Deck the Halls '06
The Shaggy Dog '06
The Adventures of Sharkboy and Lavagirl in 3-D '05
Take Me Home: The John Denver Story '00
Atomic Train '99
Alien Nation: Body and Soul '95
Nine Months '95
Doom Asylum '88

Lisa Davis
Edge of Sanity '89
101 Dalmatians '61 (V)
Queen of Outer Space '58

Lucy Davis (1973-)
Garfield: A Tail of Two Kitties '06
The TV Set '06
Shaun of the Dead '04
Angel's Dance '99
Possums '99
Blackmail '91

Mac Davis (1942-)
Jackpot '01
The Sting 2 '83
Cheaper to Keep Her '80
North Dallas Forty '79

Marvin Davis (1931-2005)
Tomorrow the World '44
The Fighting Sullivans '42

Matthew Davis (1978-)
BloodRayne '06
Heights '04
Blue Crush '02
Below '02
Lone Star State of Mind '02
Legally Blonde '01
Tigerland '00
Urban Legends 2: Final Cut '00

Michael Davis
Ballad of a Gunfighter '64
All the Young Men '60
Let No Man Write My Epitaph '60

Nancy Davis (1921-)
Hellcats of the Navy '57
Donovan's Brain '53
The Next Voice You Hear '50
East Side, West Side '49

Nathan Davis (1917-)
Holes '03
Dunston Checks in '95
Shaking the Tree '92
Code of Silence '85

Ossie Davis (1917-2005)
She Hate Me '04
Baadasssss! '03
Bubba Ho-Tep '03
Anne Rice's The Feast of All Saints '01
Dinosaur '00 (V)
Finding Buck McHenry '00
Dr. Dolittle '98
Miss Evers' Boys '97
Twelve Angry Men '97
Get On the Bus '96
I'm Not Rappaport '96
The Android Affair '95
The Client '94
Stephen King's The Stand '94
The Ernest Green Story '93
Grumpy Old Men '93
Queen '93
Gladiator '92
Jungle Fever '91
Joe Versus the Volcano '90
Do the Right Thing '89
School Daze '88
Avenging Angel '85
Harry & Son '84
Don't Look Back: The Story of Leroy "Satchel" Paige '81
All God's Children '80
Hot Stuff '80

King '78
Billy: Portrait of a Street Kid '77
Roots '77
Let's Do It Again '75
Night Gallery '69
Sam Whiskey '69
The Scalphunters '68
A Man Called Adam '66
The Hill '65
Gone Are the Days '63
Purlie Victorious '63
No Way Out '50

Owen Davis, Jr. (1907-49)
It Could Happen to You '37
Special Investigator '36
All Quiet on the Western Front '30

Patricia (Patti) Davis (1952-)
Night Partners '83
For Ladies Only '81

Philip Davis (1953-)
Five Days '07
Like Father Like Son '05
Vera Drake '04
Still Crazy '98
Face '97
Photographing Fairies '97
Howling 5: The Rebirth '89
High Hopes '88
The Bounty '84
Grown Ups '80
Quadrophenia '79
Who's Who '78

Phyllis E. Davis (1947-)
Terminal Island '73
Sweet Sugar '72
Beyond the Valley of the Dolls '70

Roger Davis (1939-)
Ruby '77
Flash & Firecat '75
House of Dark Shadows '70

Sammi Davis (1964-)
Stand-Ins '97
Four Rooms '95
Indecency '92
The Horseplayer '91
The Perfect Bride '91
Shadow of China '91
Final Warning '90
The Rainbow '89
Consuming Passions '88
The Lair of the White Worm '88
Hope and Glory '87
Pack of Lies '87
Prayer for the Dying '87
Mona Lisa '86

Sammy Davis, Jr. (1925-90)
Ocean's 11 '60
Moon over Parador '88
Alice in Wonderland '85
That's Dancing! '85
Cannonball Run 2 '84
Cracking Up '83
Cannonball Run '81
Little Moon & Jud McGraw '78
Gone with the West '72
Sweet Charity '69
A Man Called Adam '66
Robin and the 7 Hoods '64
The Trackers '71
The Three Penny Opera '62

Scott Davis
The Abomination '88
Tabloid! '88

Sonny Carl Davis
Bad Channels '92
Seedpeople '92
Pair of Aces '90
Verne Miller '88
Fast Money '83
Last Night at the Alamo '83
The Whole Shootin' Match '79

Stringer Davis (1896-1973)
Murder at the Gallop '63
The Smallest Show on Earth '57

Tom Davis (1952-)
The Runaway Bus '54
'86
One More Saturday Night

Tracy Davis
Tumelvision '76
All You Need Is Cash 78

Ursula Davis
Nemesis 2: Nebula '94
Star Quest '89

Viola Davis (1952-)
An Angel for Satan '66
Battle of Valiant '63
'05
Jesse Stone: Sea Change
Jesse Stone: Stone Cold '05
Jesse Stone: Night Passage '06
Get Rich or Die Tryin' '05
Antwone Fisher '02
Far from Heaven '02
Solaris '02
'07
The Architect '06

Viveka Davis
Cast Away '00
Time Code '00
EDtv '99
Message in a Bottle '99
Home '97
Morgan Stewart's Coming Hood '85
Not My Kid '85

Warwick Davis (1970-)
Shoot the Moon '82
Ray '04
Prince Valiant '97
Harry Potter and the Chamber of Secrets '02
Snow White: The Fairest of Them All '02
The 10th Kingdom '00
Harry Potter and the Phoenix '07
Harry Potter and the Sorcerer's Stone '01
The Hitchhiker's Guide to the Galaxy '05
Leprechaun 3: In the Hood '99
Leprechaun 6: Back 2 Tha Hood '03
Harry Potter and the Goblet of Fire '05
Leprechaun 4: In Space '96
Gulliver's Travels '95
Leprechaun 2 '94
Leprechaun '93
Willow '88
The Ewoks: Battle for Endor '85
The Ewok Adventure '24

William B. Davis (1938-)
Numb '07
Mindstorm '01
The Proposal '00
Perpetrator's of the Crime '98
The X-Files '98

Bruce Davison (1946-)
Breach '07
The Dead Girl '06
Going Shopping '05
Hate Crime '05
Evergreen '04
Runaway Jury '03
X2: X-Men United '03
Dahmer '02
High Crimes '02
crazy/beautiful '01

His Majesty, the American '19

Marjorie Daw (1902-79)
Something to Sing About '36

Andrew Davoli (1973-)
Spartan '04
Welcome to Collinwood '02
Knockaround Guys '01
The Yards '00

Ninetto Davoli (1948-)
Arabian Nights '74
The Canterbury Tales '71
The Decameron '70
The Hawks & the Sparrows '67

Evelyn Daw (1912-70)
Paramount's Bad Man '38

Ken Davitian
Get Smart '08
Meet the Spartans '08
Borat: Cultural Learnings of America for Make Benefit Glorious Nation of Kazakhstan '06

Davey Davison (1942-)
When the Line Goes Through '73
No Drums, No Bugles '71

Peter Davison (1951-)
Parting Shots '98
Wuthering Heights '98
Black Beauty '94
Harnessing Peacocks '92
Love for Lydia '79

The Ewok Adventure '24

The Strawberry Statement '70
Last Summer '69
The Affair '73
Ulzana's Raid '72
Willard '71
Mame '74

Warwick Davis (1970-)
The Chronicles of Narnia: Prince Caspian '08

Jesse Stone: Death in Paradise '06
The Crucible '96
Lovelife '97
Color of Justice '97
Apt Pupl '97
Paulie '98
At First Sight '98
Vendetta '99
Locked in Silence '99
X-Men '00
The King Is Alive '00
Off Season '01
Summer Catch '01

Dog '94
The Skateboard Kid 2 '94
Widow's K.ss '94
Short Cuts '93
Six Degrees of Separation '93

The Ladies Club '86
Spies Like Us '85
Crimes of Passion '84
Lies '83
Kiss My Grits '82
Tomorrow's Child '82
High Risk '81
The Lathe of Heaven '80
The Gathering: Part 2 '79
Short Eyes '78
Brass Target '78
Deadman's Curve '78
French Quarter '78
The Summer of My German Soldier '78
The Gathering '77
Mother, Jugs and Speed '76

Live! From Death Row '92
Longtime Companion '90
Steel and Lace '90
The Misfit Brigade '87
Poor Little Rich Girl: The Barbara Hutton Story '87

Richard Dawson (1932-)
Death Proof '07
Descent '07
Clerks 2 '06
A Guide to Recognizing Your Saints '06
Rent '05
Sin City '05
This Revolution '05
Alexander '04
The Rundown '03
Shattered Glass '03

Rosario Dawson (1979-)
The Running Man '87
How to Pick Up Girls '78
The Devil's Brigade '68
Munster, Go Home! '66
King Rat '65
War and Peace '56
The Voyeur '94

The Adventures of Yellow Homage '95
It's My Party '95
Far from Home: The Adventures of Yellow

Marpessa Dawn (1934-)
The Womaneater '59
Black Orpheus '58

Sugar Dawn (1931-)
Arizona Roundup '42
Lone Star Law Men '42
Dynamite Canyon '41

Kamala Dawson
The Queen of Spades '49

Kim (Kimberly Dawn) Dawson (1963-)
Jimmy Zip '99
Bikini House School '98
Bikini House Calls '96
The Perfect Gift '95

Anthony Dawson (1916-92)
Dr. No '62
The Curse of the Werewolf '61
Tiger Bay '59
Hour of Decision '57
Dial "M" for Murder '54
The Woman in Question '50

Josette Day (1914-78)
The Storm Within '48
Beauty and the Beast '46
Well-Digger's Daughter '46

Gary Day (1941-)
They Got Me Covered '43

Laraine Day (1920-2007)
Murder on Flight 502 '75
Return to Fantasy Island '77
The High and the Mighty '54
My Dear Secretary '49
Tycoon '47
Those Endearing Young Charms '45
Nash '24
Mr. Lucky '43
Journey for Margaret '42
Foreign Correspondent '40
My Son, My Son '40
The Secret of Dr. Kildare '39
Calamity Jane '53
April in Paris '52
By the Light of the Silvery Moon '53
Young at Heart '54
Lucky Me '54
Love Me or Leave Me '55
Young Man with a Horn '50
The West Point Story '50
Tea for Two '50
On Moonlight Bay '51
Lullaby of Broadway '51
My Dream Is Yours '49
It's a Great Feeling '49
Romance on the High Seas '48
I'll See You in My Dreams '51
The Winning Team '52

Pam Dawber (1951-)
Rebecca of Sunnybrook Farm '17
Through Naked Eyes '87
Stay Tuned '92
Storm Warning '51
Turf Boy '42

Doris Day (1924-98)
Where Were You When the Lights Went Out? '68
With Six You Get Eggroll '68
Caprice '67
The Glass Bottom Boat '66
Do Not Disturb '65
Send Me No Flowers '64
Move Over, Darling '63
The Thrill of It All! '63
Billy Rose's Jumbo '62
That Touch of Mink '62
Lover Come Back '61
Midnight Lace '60
Please Don't Eat the Daisies '60
Pillow Talk '59
Teacher's Pet '58
The Tunnel of Love '58
The Pajama Game '57
The Man Who Knew Too Much '56

Dennis Day (1916-88)
Melody Time 48 (V)
I'll Remember April '99
The Baskervilles '02
Lady Be Good '41
Doing Time for Patsy Cline '97

Patrick Day (1968-)
Hollywood Hot Tubs 2: Educating Crystal '89

Stuart Garrison Day
The Adventures of Huckleberry Finn '85
Covert Action '88
Search and Destroy '88

Vera Day (1939-)
The Womaneater '59
The Haunted Strangler '58
Up the Creek '58
Quatermass 2 '57

Daniel Day-Lewis (1957-)
There Will Be Blood '07
The Ballad of Jack and Rose '05
Gangs of New York '02
The Boxer '97
The Crucible '96
The Age of Innocence '93
In the Name of the Father '93
A Room with a View '86
My Beautiful Laundrette '85
The Bounty '84
Gandhi '82
Sunday, Bloody, Sunday '71

Morris Day (1957-2000)
Muriel's Wedding '94
Graffiti Bridge '90
Purple Rain '84

Brenda de Banzie (1915-81)
The Entertainer '60
The Pink Panther '64
Come September '61
The Mark '61

Antje de Boeck (1964-)
Daens '92

Nikki de Boer (1970-)
The Dead Zone '02
Cube '98
Rated X '00
Family of Cops 3 '98
JFK: Reckless Youth '93
Prom Night 4: Deliver Us from Evil '91

Koen de Bouw (1964-)
So This Is Paris '26
The Bat '26

Andre de Beranger (1895-1973)

James De Bello
See James De Bello

Burr de Benning (1936-2003)
Incredible Melting Man '77
Iron Horsemen '68
Sweet November '71

Isaach de Bankole (1957-)
The Diving Bell and the Butterfly '07
Casino Royale '06
Manderlay '05
Coffee and Cigarettes '03
Ghost Dog: The Way of the Samurai '99
Chocolat '88

Jean De Baer
The Cremators '72
Blood Mania '70
Broken Vows '87

Matt(hew) Day (1971-)
The Beloved Rogue '27
And Starring Pancho Villa as Himself '03

Yvonne de Bray (1889-1954)
The Storm Within '48
Eternal Return '43

Nigel de Bruller (1877-1948)
In Celebration '75
10 Rillington P'ace '71
Ben-Hur '26
The Iron Mask '29
The Four Ho'semen o' the Apocalypse '21
The Three Musketeers '21

Margit Dayka (1907-86)
Nice Neighbor '97
Cat's Play '74
The Story of Dr. Wassell '44

Gabrielle Daye (1911-2005)
Operation Thunderbolt '77
The Uranium Conspiracy '78

Assaf Dayan (1945-)
Babylon? '82
How Many Miles to Babylon? '82

William De Acutis (1957-91)
Chattahoochee '89
Trust Me '89

Joaquim de Almeida (1957-)
Behind Enemy Lines '01
La Cucaracha '99
No Vacancy '99
Vendetta '99
One Man's Hero '99
Women '97
Nostromo '96
Man's Walk '96
Desperado '95
Clear and Present Danger '94
Only You '94

Yvonne De Carlo (1922-2007)
American Gothic '88
Cellar Dweller '87
Vultures '84
House of Shadows '83
The Munsters' Revenge '81
The Munster's Revenge '81
Play Dead '81
Silent Scream '80
Nocturna '79
Satan's Cheerleaders '77
Blazing Stewardesses '75
It Seemed Like a Good Idea at the Time '75
Arizona Bushwackers '67
Hostile Guns '67
Munster, Go Home! '66
A Global Affair '63
McLintock! '63
The Sword and the Cross '58

Celia de Burgh (1958-)
Phar Lap '84
Sound of Love '78

Maria de Aragon (1942-)
The Deadly and the Beautiful '73

Band of Angels '57
Death of a Scoundrel '56
The Ten Commandments '56
Flame of the Islands '55
Shotgun '55
Passion '54
Captain's Paradise '53
Sea Devils '53
Tomahawk '51
Buccaneer's Girl '50
Casbah '48
Criss Cross '48
Brute Force '47
Song of Scheherazade '47
Salome, Where She Danced '45
For Whom the Bell Tolls '43
Rhythm Parade '43
The Road to Morocco '42
This Gun for Hire '42

Emma de Caunes (1976-)
Mr. Bean's Holiday '07
The Science of Sleep '06

Pedro de Cordoba (1881-1950)
Guns of Fury '49
Omoo Omoo, the Shark God '49
Mexican Hayride '48
Swamp Fire '46
They Were Expendable '45
For Whom the Bell Tolls '43
Son of Fury '42
Before I Hang '40
The Ghost Breakers '40
Law of the Pampas '39
Condemned to Live '35
The Crusades '35

Arturo de Cordova (1908-73)
The New Invisible Man '58
El '52
New Orleans '47
Frenchman's Creek '44
For Whom the Bell Tolls '43

Ted de Corsia (1903-73)
The Outside Man '73
The Conqueror '56
Dance with Me, Henry '56
The Kettles in the Ozarks '56
The Killing '56
Slightly Scarlet '56
Crime Wave '54
The Enforcer '51
It Happens Every Spring '49
Neptune's Daughter '49
Variety Lights '51

Calvert De Forest
See Calvert Deforest

Helene de Fougerolles (1973-)
Va Savoir '01
The Fall '98

Cecile de France (1975-)
Avenue Montaigne '06
Russian Dolls '05
Around the World in 80 Days '04
High Tension '03
L'Auberge Espagnole '02

Louis de Funes (1914-83)
Delusions of Grandeur '76
The Mad Adventures of Rabbi Jacob '73
La Grande Vadrouille '66
The Sucker '65
The Gendarme of Saint-Tropez '64
Belle Americaine '61

Four Bags Full '56
The Sheep Has Five Legs '54
Seven Deadly Sins '53

Sam De Grasse (1875-1953)
Robin Hood '22
The Scarlet Car '17
The Birth of a Nation '15

Gianfranco de Grassi
Night Train Murders '75
Torture Train '75

Julio de Grazia (1920-89)
The Stranger '87
Deadly Revenge '83
Funny, Dirty Little War '83
Time for Revenge '82
The Lion's Share '79

Xavier De Guillebon
Bon Voyage '03
L'Auberge Espagnole '02
The Taste of Others '00

Gloria De Haven (1924)
Out to Sea '97
Bog '84
Banjo Hackett '76
Two Tickets to Broadway '51
Summer Stock '50
Three Little Words '50
The Yellow Cab Man '50
Summer Holiday '48
Broadway Rhythm '44
The Thin Man Goes Home '44
Two Girls and a Sailor '44
Best Foot Forward '43
Susan and God '40
Modern Times '36

Consuelo de Haviland
Barjo '93
The Unbearable Lightness of Being '88
Betty Blue '86

Olivia de Havilland (1916)
The Woman He Loved '88
Anastasia: The Mystery of Anna '86
Agatha Christie's Murder is Easy '82
The Fifth Musketeer '79
Roots: The Next Generation '79
The Swarm '78
Airport '77 '77
The Adventurers '70
Hush, Hush, Sweet Charlotte '65
Lady in a Cage '64
Proud Rebel '58
The Ambassador's Daughter '56
Not as a Stranger '55
The Heiress '49
The Snake Pit '48
Dark Mirror '46
To Each His Own '46
Thank Your Lucky Stars '43
In This Our Life '42
The Male Animal '42
Strawberry Blonde '41
They Died with Their Boots On '41
Santa Fe Trail '40
Dodge City '39
Gone with the Wind '39
The Private Lives of Elizabeth & Essex '39
The Adventures of Robin Hood '38
Anthony Adverse '36
The Charge of the Light Brigade '36
Alibi Ike '35
Captain Blood '35
A Midsummer Night's Dream '35

Wanda De Jesus (1960-)
Illegal Tender '07
Blood Work '02
Flawless '99

Elmore Leonard's Gold Coast '97

David de Keyser (1927-)
The Statement '03
The Designated Mourner '97

Frank De Kova (1910-81)
Johnny Firecloud '75
Frasier the Sensuous Lion '73
Heavy Traffic '73
Cat in the Cage '68
Atlantis, the Lost Continent '61
The Jayhawkers '59
Machine Gun Kelly '58
Teenage Caveman '58
Run of the Arrow '56
Shack Out on 101 '55

Viktor de Kowa (1904-73)
Forger of London '61
The Embezzled Heaven '58

Agathe de la Boulaye
Alien vs. Predator '04
The Girl '01

Simon de la Brosse (1965-98)
Strike It Rich '90
The Little Thief '89
Pauline at the Beach '83

Agathe de la Fontaine (1972-)
Train of Life '98
Another 9 1/2 Weeks '96
King of the Airwaves '94

Christian de la Fuente (1974-)
Once Upon a Wedding '05
Basic '03
John Carpenter Presents Vampires: Los Muertos '02
Driven '01

Joel de la Fuente
The Happening '08
From Other Worlds '04
Personal Velocity: Three Portraits '02

Danny De La Paz (1957-)
Picking Up the Pieces '99
American Me '92
Miracle Mile '89
3:15—The Moment of Truth '86
Boulevard Nights '79

George de la Pena (1955-)
Brain Donors '92
Kuffs '92
The Cowboy & the Ballerina '84
Nijinsky '80

Antonio de la Torre
Dark Blue Almost Black '06
Volver '06

Frances de la Tour (1944-)
The History Boys '06
Harry Potter and the Goblet of Fire '05
Tom Jones '98
Flickers '80

John de Lancie (1948-)
Pathology '08
Woman on Top '00

Schemes '95
Deep Red '94
Evolver '94
Arcade '93
Fearless '93
The Hand that Rocks the Cradle '92
The Fisher King '91

Derek de Lint (1950-)
Black Book '06
When a Stranger Calls '06
Soul Assassin '01
The Man Who Made Husbands Jealous '98
Poltergeist: The Legacy '96
The Endless Game '89
Diary of a Mad Old Man '88
Stealing Heaven '88
The Unbearable Lightness of Being '88
Mascara '87
Three Men and a Baby '87
The Assault '86
Soldier of Orange '78

Michael De Lorenzo
See Michael Delorenzo

Kamar De Los Reyes (1967-)
Undefeated '03
Mambo Cafe '00
Nixon '95
DaVinci's War '92
Coldfire '90
East L.A. Warriors '89
Ghetto Blaster '89
Salsa '88

Alvaro de Luna (1935-)
Broken Silence '01
Hawk and Castile '67

Donna De Mario
See Donna (Dona Martel) Martel

Terence de Marney (1909-71)
Beast of Morocco '66
Die, Monster, Die! '65
Dual Alibi '47

Drea De Matteo (1973-)
Broken English '07
Assault on Precinct 13 '05
Prey for Rock and Roll '03
Crazy Little Thing '02
Deuces Wild '02
Made '01
'R Xmas '01
Swordfish '01

Maria De Medeiros (1965-)
My Life Without Me '03
The Saddest Music in the World '03
Le Polygraphe '96
Pulp Fiction '94
Meeting Venus '91
Henry & June '90

Nieve De Medina (1962-)
Mondays in the Sun '02
El Bola '00

Carlo De Mejo (1945-)
Other Hell '85
Alien Contamination '81
Gates of Hell '80
The Outside Man '73

Alberto De Mendoza (1923-)
Bossa Nova '99
Horror Express '72
The Case of the Scorpion's Tail '71
A Lizard in a Woman's Skin '71
Blade of the Ripper '70

Jo de Meyere (1939-)
The Memory of a Killer '03

Laurence De Monaghan
The Story of Love Story '73
Claire's Knee '71

Rebecca De Mornay (1962-)
Music Within '07
Lords of Dogtown '05

Wedding Crashers '05
Raise Your Voice '04
Identity '03
A Girl Thing '01
Range of Motion '00
The Right Temptation '00
Night Ride Home '99
Thick as Thieves '99
Wicked Ways '99
The Con '98
The Winner '96
Never Talk to Strangers '95
Getting Out '94
Blind Side '93
Guilty as Sin '93
The Three Musketeers '93
The Hand that Rocks the Cradle '92
Backdraft '91
An Inconvenient Woman '91
By Dawn's Early Light '89
Dealers '89
And God Created Woman '88
Feds '88
Morgue '86
Pecos Bill '86
Runaway Train '85
The Slugger's Wife '85
The Trip to Bountiful '85
Risky Business '83
Testament '83
One from the Heart '82

Drena De Niro
Ghetto Dawg '02
Showtime '02

Robert De Niro (1943-)
Stardust '07
Arthur and the Invisibles '06 (V)
The Good Shepherd '06
The Bridge of San Luis Rey '05
Hide and Seek '05
Godsend '04
Meet the Fockers '04
Shark Tale '04 (V)
Analyze That '02
City by the Sea '02
Showtime '02
15 Minutes '01
The Score '01
The Adventures of Rocky & Bullwinkle '00
Meet the Parents '00
Men of Honor '00
Flawless '99
Analyze This '98
Ronin '98
Cop Land '97
Great Expectations '97
Jackie Brown '97
Wag the Dog '97
The Fan '96
Marvin's Room '96
Sleepers '96
Casino '95
Heat '95
Mary Shelley's Frankenstein '94
A Bronx Tale '93
Mad Dog and Glory '93
This Boy's Life '93
Night and the City '92
Backdraft '91
Cape Fear '91
Guilty by Suspicion '91
Mistress '91
Awakenings '90
Goodfellas '90
Stanley and Iris '90
Jacknife '89
We're No Angels '89
Midnight Run '88
Angel Heart '87
The Untouchables '87
The Mission '86
Brazil '85
Falling in Love '84
Once Upon a Time in America '84
When Angels Fly '84
King of Comedy '82
The Godfather 1902-1959: The Complete Epic '81

True Confessions '81
Raging Bull '80
The Deer Hunter '78
New York, New York '77
America at the Movies '76
The Last Tycoon '76
1900 '76
Taxi Driver '76
The Godfather, Part 2 '74
Bang the Drum Slowly '73
Mean Streets '73
Born to Win '71
The Swap '71
Bloody Mama '70
Hi, Mom! '70
Greetings '68

Ana Christine de Oliveira (1973-)
Two Drifters '05
Taxi '04

Rossy de Palma (1965-)
Talk of Angels '96
The Flower of My Secret '95
Kika '94
Ready to Wear '94
Don Juan, My Love '90
Tie Me Up! Tie Me Down! '90
Women on the Verge of a Nervous Breakdown '88

Josse De Pauw (1952-)
Everybody's Famous! '00
Hombres Complicados '97

Miranda de Pencier (1968-)
Anne of Green Gables: The Continuing Story '99
Kurt Vonnegut's Harrison Bergeron '95
Anne of Green Gables '85

Teresa De Priest (1970-)
Hit and Runway '01
The Doorway '00

Lya de Putti (1897-1931)
The Informer '29
The Sorrows of Satan '26
Variety '25
Othello '22
Phantom '22
The Indian Tomb '21

Emilie de Ravin (1981-)
Brick '06
The Hills Have Eyes '06
Carrie '02

Chris De Rose (1948-)
Breakaway '95
Aftershock '88

Portia de Rossi (1973-)
Cursed '04
I Witness '03
The Night We Called It a Day '03
Who is Cletis Tout? '02
The Invisibles '99
Stigmata '99
Girl '98
Scream 2 '97
Sirens '94

Anna De Sade
Arizona '86
Sorceress '82

Anthony De Sando (1965-)
Beer League '06
Hysterical Blindness '02
Double Parked '00
Cement '99
Kiss Me, Guido '97
Federal Hill '94
Party Girl '94
Whispers of White '93
Grand Isle '92
The Return of Eliot Ness '91

Joe De Santis (1909-89)
- Blue '68
- And Now Miguel '66
- Al Capone '59

Lorraine (De Sette) De Selle (1951-)
- The Wild Beasts '85
- Women's Prison Massacre '85

Christian de Sica (1951)
- Men Men Men '95
- Detective School Dropouts '85

Vittorio De Sica (1902-74)
- The Sex Machine '75
- Andy Warhol's Dracula '74
- 12 Plus 1 '70
- The Shoes of the Fisherman '68
- Scandal Man '67
- L'Odeur des Fauves '66
- An Almost Perfect Affair '79
- The Amorous Adventures of Moll Flanders '65
- The Wonders of Aladdin '61
- The Battle of Austerlitz '60
- Generale Della Rovere '60
- It Started in Naples '60
- Pardon My Trunk '52
- Peddlin' in Society '47
- Teresa Venerdi '41
- The Gold of Naples '54
- Too Bad She's Bad '54
- The Earrings of Madame De... '54
- The Millionairess '60
- Angel in a Taxi '59

Brandon de Wilde (1942-72)
- The Member of the Wedding '52
- Shane '53
- Goodbye My Lady '56
- Night Passage '57
- Missouri Traveler '58
- All Fall Down '62
- Hud '63
- Those Calloways '65
- In Harm's Way '65

Jose-Luis De Villalonga (1920-2007)
- Blood and Sand '89
- Darling '65

Werner De Smedt
- The Memory of a Killer '03

Melissa De Sousa (1967-)
- 30 Years to Life '01
- Lockdown '00
- Miss Congeniality '00
- The Best Man '99
- Ride '98

Edward De Souza (1933-)
- A Question of Attribution '91
- Kiss of the Vampire '62
- The Phantom of the Opera '62

Guiliana de Sio (1957-)
- Private Affairs '89
- Pool Hustlers '83

Jacqueline De Witt
See Jacqueline DeWitt

Francis De Wolff (1913-84)
- Devil Doll '64
- The Two Faces of Dr. Jekyll '60
- The Smallest Show on Earth '57

Marie Dea (1912-92)
- Orpheus '49
- Les Visiteurs du Soir '42

Brian Deacon (1949-)
- A Zed & Two Noughts '88
- Jesus '79

Richard Deacon (1921-84)
- Bad Manners '84
- Piranha '78
- The One and Only, Genuine, Original, Family Band '68
- Billie '65
- The Patsy '64
- Blackbeard's Ghost '67
- The Gnome-Mobile '67
- Carousel '56
- Critic's Choice '63
- Invasion of the Body Snatchers '56
- The Kettles in the Ozarks '56
- Francis in the Haunted House '56
- Abbott and Costello Meet the Mummy '55

Lucy Deakins (1971-)
- The Boy Who Could Fly '86
- Cheetah '89
- There Goes My Baby '92
- Little Nikita '88

Sarah Deakins
- Possessed '05

Allison Dean
- Where's Marlowe? '98
- Ruby in Paradise '93
- Coming to America '88

Eddie Dean (1907-99)
- Check Your Guns '48
- Black Hills '48
- Renegade Trail '39
- Law of the Pampas '40
- Santa Fe Marshal '40
- Knights of the Range '40
- Wildfire '45
- Song of Old Wyoming '45
- Driftin' River '46
- Colorado Serenade '46
- The Caravan Trail '46
- Wild Country '47
- West to Glory '47
- The Tioga Kid '48
- The Hawk of Powder River '48

Felicity Dean (1959-)
- The Last of the Blonde Bombshells '00
- Persuasion '95

Howard Dean (1948-)
- Tanner on Tanner '04

Ron Dean
- Wild Things 2 '04
- The Wild Card '03
- Rudy '93
- The Client '94
- Legacy of Lies '92
- Above the Law '88
- Cocktail '88
- Big Score '83

Isabel Dean (1918-97)
- Journeys with George '02
- Weather in the Streets '84

James Dean (1931-55)
- Oh! What a Lovely War '69
- America at the Movies '76
- Giant '56
- Rebel without a Cause '55
- East of Eden '54

Jeanne Dean (1925-93)
- Fixed Bayonets! '51
- Hill Number One '51

Jimmy Dean (1928-)
- Big Bad John '90
- Diamonds Are Forever '71
- The Ballad of Andy Crocker '69

Loren Dean (1969-)
- Space Cowboys '00
- Mumford '99
- The War Bride '01

Justin Deas (1948-)
- Prairie Moon '03
- Charlie Chan at the Circus '36

Jamel Debbouze
- Days of Glory '06
- Angel-A '05
- She Hate Me '04
- Amelie '01

Shirley Deane (1913-)
- Girlfriend from Hell '89
- 976-EVIL '88

Lezlie (Dean) Deane (1964-)
- Freddy's Dead: The Final Nightmare '91
- To Protect and Serve '92

Kristine DeBell (1954-)
- Cheerleaders' Wild Weekend '85

Rick Dean (1953-2006)
- Carnosaur 3: Primal Species '96
- Max Is Missing '95
- Striptease '95
- Cheyenne Warrior '94
- Peephole '93
- Bloodfist 3: Forced to Fight '92
- Saturday Night Special '92
- Naked Obsession '91
- Raiders of the Sun '92
- Heroes Stand Alone '89
- Nam Angels '88
- Island of Blood '82

Priscilla Dean (1896-1987)
- Law of the Sea '32
- White Tiger '23
- Outside the Law '21

Nathaniel Dean
- Somersault '04

Man Mountain Dean (1891-1953)
- The Gladiator '38
- Three Legionnaires '37

Margia Dean (1921-)
- The Quatermass Experiment '56
- Lonesome Trail '55
- Fangs of the Wild '54
- Kentucky Jubilee '51
- Leave It to the Marines '51
- Sins of Jezebel '54
- Loan Shark '52
- Mr. Walkie Talkie '52
- Savage Drums '51
- Sky High '51
- Red Desert '50
- Rimfire '49
- Pier 23 '51
- Ringside '49
- Shep Comes Home '49

Lee DeBroux (1941-)
- L.I.E. '01
- 12 and Holding '05
- Death Benefit '96
- Out of the Dark '88
- Attack of the Killer Tomatoes '78

James DeBello (1980-)
- Cabin Fever '03
- Players '03
- Swimfan '02
- Detroit Rock City '99
- 100 Girls '00

John DeBello (1952-)
- Killer Tomatoes Eat France '90
- Killer Tomatoes Strike Back '91

David Deblinger
- Club Land '01
- Intern '00

Marcia DeBonis (1960-)
- Frogs for Snakes '98
- Intern '00
- 12 and Holding '05

Rosemary DeCamp (1910-2001)
- Saturday the 14th '81
- 13 Ghosts '60
- By the Light of the Silvery Moon '53
- On Moonlight Bay '51
- Look for the Silver Lining '49
- The Story of Seabiscuit '49
- Rhapsody in Blue '45
- Commandos Strike at Dawn '43
- The Jungle Book '42
- Yankee Doodle Dandy '42
- Cheers for Miss Bishop '41

Amanda DeCadenet (1972-)
- Fall '97
- Four Rooms '95

Jean Debucourt (1894-1958)
- Nana '55
- Monsieur Vincent '47
- La Chute de la Maison Usher '28

Joe Decker
- Bloodstream '01

Mark DeCarlo (1962-)
- The Ant Bully '06 (V)
- Jimmy Neutron: Boy Genius '01 (V)
- Buffy the Vampire Slayer '92

Eugene Deckers
- Chain of Souls '00
- Madeleine '50
- The Golden Salamander '51
- The Alamo '60
- Lady L '65
- Flame Over India '60

Edward "Blue" Deckert
- Home Fries '98
- The Rookie '02
- Envy '04

Janie Dee (1966-)
- P.D. James: The Murder Room '04
- P.D. James: Death in Holy Orders '03

Ruby Dee (1924-)
- American Gangster '07
- Anne Rice's The Feast of All Saints '01
- Finding Buck McHenry '00
- Delany Sisters' First 100 Years '99
- Passing Glory '99
- The Wall '99
- Baby Geniuses '98
- A Simple Wish '97
- Mr. & Mrs. Loving '96
- Just Cause '94
- Stephen King's The Stand '94
- Cop and a Half '93
- The Ernest Green Story '93
- Jungle Fever '91
- The Court Martial of Jackie Robinson '90
- Decoration Day '90
- Do the Right Thing '89
- Zora Is My Name! '90
- Love at Large '89
- Gore Vidal's Lincoln '88
- Windmills of the Gods '88
- Go Tell It on the Mountain '84
- Cat People '82
- All God's Children '80
- I Know Why the Caged Bird Sings '79
- Roots: The Next Generation '79
- It's Good to Be Alive '74
- Buck and the Preacher '72
- A Raisin in the Sun '61
- The Incident '67
- Gone Are the Days '63
- The Balcony '63
- Purlie Victorious '63
- A Raisin in the Sun '61
- The Jackie Robinson Story '50
- No Way Out '50

Guy Decomble (1910-64)
- Gypsy Colt '54
- Because of You '52
- Four Faces West '48
- Bob le Flambeur '55

Frances Dee (1907-2004)
- I Walked with a Zombie '43
- So Ends Our Night '41
- If I Were King '38
- The Private Affairs of Bel Ami '47
- Finishing School '33
- Becky Sharp '35
- Of Human Bondage '34
- King of the Jungle '33
- Little Women '33

Xavier DeClie
- Gangster World '98
- The Survivor '98

Rick Dees (1950-)
- Jetsons: The Movie '90 (V)
- La Bamba '87

Olive Deering (1918-86)
- Caged '50
- Samson and Delilah '50

Eddie Deezen (1958-)
- The Polar Express '04
- Teenage Exorcist '93
- Rock-a-Doodle '92 (V)
- Mob Boss '90
- Hollywood Boulevard 2 '89
- Assault of the Killer Bimbos '88
- Beverly Hills Vamp '88
- Million Dollar Mystery '87
- Desperate Moves '86
- Mugsy's Girls '85
- Surf 2 '84
- Grease '78
- 1941 '79

Felix Defauce
- Hawk and Castle '67
- Magnificent Adventurer '63

Don DeFore (1917-93)
- Battle Hymn '57
- A Girl in Every Port '52
- Too Late for Tears '49
- A Time to Love & a Time to Die '58
- Romance on the High Seas '48
- Ramrod '47
- Without Reservations '46
- The Stork Club '45
- Thirty Seconds Over Tokyo '44
- The Male Animal '42

Ellen DeGeneres (1958-)
- EDtv '99
- Goodbye, Lover '99
- The Love Letter '99
- Mr. Wrong '95
- If These Walls Could Talk 2 '00

Pia Degermark (1949-)
- The Looking Glass War '69
- Elvira Madigan '67

Calvert DeForest (1921-2007)
- Mr. Write '92
- Leader of the Band '87
- Heaven Help Us '85

Sam DeGrasse
See Sam De Grasse

Raffaello Degruttola
- Dot.Kill '05
- House of 9 '05
- Pulse '03

John Dehner (1915-92)
- Creator '85
- The Jagged Edge '85
- Airplane 2: The Sequel '82
- California Gold Rush '81
- Nothing Personal '80
- Mountain Man '77
- The Killer Inside Me '76
- Missiles of October '74
- The Day of the Dolphin '73
- Support Your Local Gunfighter '71
- The Cheyenne Social Club '70
- That Funny Feeling '65
- The Hallelujah Trail '65 (N)
- Critic's Choice '63
- Tammy and the Doctor '63
- Come September '61
- The Left-Handed Gun '58
- The Halliday Brand '57

Jan Decleir (1946-)
- The Memory of a Killer '03
- Rosenstrasse '03
- Running Free '00
- Molokai: The Story of Father Damien '99
- Character '97
- Antonia's Line '95
- Daens '92

Sandra Dee (1942-)
See also Sandra Dee

A Summer Place '59
- The Reluctant Debutante '58
- Until They Sail '57

Dehner
Man of the West '58
Girl in Black Stockings '57
Fastest Gun Alive '56
The King's Thief '55
The Prodigal '55
Apache '54
Hot Lead '51
Big Town '47
Vigilantes of Boom Town '46

Khigh (Kaie Deei) Deigh (1910-91)
Noble House '88
Seconds '66
The Manchurian Candidate '62

Tim DeKay (1963-)
That Russell Girl '08
Peaceful Warrior '06
The Chumscrubber '05
Big Eden '00

David DeKeyser
See David de Keyser

Albert Dekker (1904-68)
Gamera, the Invincible '66
Suddenly, Last Summer '59
Illegal '55
Kiss Me Deadly '55
East of Eden '54
As Young As You Feel '51
Cass Timberlane '47
Gentleman's Agreement '47
The Killers '46
Two Years before the Mast '46
Experiment Perilous '45
The Woman of the Town '44
Buckskin Frontier '43
The Kansan '43
War of the Wildcats '43
In Old California '42
Once Upon a Honeymoon '42
Wake Island '42
The Great Commandment '41
Honky Tonk '41
Dr. Cyclops '40
Seven Sinners '40
Strange Cargo '40
Beau Geste '39
Marie Antoinette '38

Thomas Dekker (1987-)
Land Before Time 7: The Stone of Cold Fire '00 (V)
The Land Before Time 6: The Secret of Saurus Rock '98 (V)
The Land Before Time 5: The Mysterious Island '97 (V)

Frank DeKova
See Frank De Kova

Louis Del Grande
Sugartime '95
Northern Extremes '93
Of Unknown Origin '83
Eclipse '94

Angel Del Pozo (1934-)
Horror Express '72
Pancho Villa '72

Duilio Del Prete (1938-98)
Voices from Beyond '90
How Funny Can Sex Be? '76
Redneck '73
The Sensuous Nurse '76
Alfredo, Alfredo '72

Armando Del Rio (1970-)
Km. 0 '00
Amor de Hombre '97

Dolores Del Rio (1905-83)
Children of Sanchez '79
Cheyenne Autumn '64
Flaming Star '60
Flor Silvestre '58
Torero '56
The Fugitive '48
Maria Candelaria '46
Journey into Fear '42
Accused '36
Flying Down to Rio '33
Bird of Paradise '32
Evangeline '29

Laura Del Sol (1961-)
El Amor Brujo '86
The Hit '85
The Stilts '84
Carmen '83

Benicio Del Toro (1967-)
Things We Lost in the Fire '07
Sin City '05
The Hunted '03
21 Grams '03
The Pledge '00
Snatch '00
Traffic '00
Way of the Gun '00
Fear and Loathing in Las Vegas '98
Joyride '97
Basquiat '96
Excess Baggage '96
The Fan '96
The Funeral '96
The Usual Suspects '95
Swimming with Sharks '94
Fearless '93
Money for Nothing '93
Christopher Columbus: The Discovery '92
China Moon '91
The Indian Runner '91
Drug Wars: The Camarena Story '90
License to Kill '89

Michel Delahaye (1929-)
Simone Barbes '80
Alphaville '65

Suzy Delair (1916-)
The Mad Adventures of Rabbi Jacob '73
Is Paris Burning? '66
Fernandel the Dressmaker '57
Gervaise '56
Utopia '51
Pattes Blanches '49
Jenny Lamour '47

Lisa (Lise) Delamare (1913-2006)
Monsieur Vincent '47
La Marseillaise '37

Louise Delamere (1969-)
The Chatterley Affair '06
Shameless '94

Cassandra Delaney (1961-)
Hurricane Smith '92
Fair Game '85
One Night Stand '84

Charles Delaney (1892-1959)
Captured in Chinatown '35
The Fighting Trooper '34
Hearts of Humanity '32

Joan Delaney
Don't Drink the Water '69
The President's Analyst '67

Kim Delaney (1961-)
Mission to Mars '00
Closer and Closer '96
Serial Killer '95
Tail, Dark and Deadly '95
Temptress '95
Darkman 2: The Return of Durant '94
The Force '94
Project Metalbeast: DNA Overload '94
The Disappearance of Christina '93
Body Parts '91
Hangfire '91
The Drifter '88
Campus Man '87
Christmas Comes to Willow Creek '87
Hunter's Blood '87
Delta Force '86
That Was Then... This Is Now '85

Pat Delaney
Iron Horsemen '71

Diane Delano (1957-)
The Wicker Man '06
The Ladykillers '04
A Painted House '03

Michael Delano (1940-)
Out for Blood '93
Private Wars '93
Ring of Fire 2: Blood and Steel '92
Ring of Fire '91
Not of This Earth '88
Catlow '71

Dana Delany (1956-)
Spin '04
Conviction '02
The Right Temptation '00
Sirens '99
Rescuers: Stories of Courage—Two Couples '98
The Curve '96
True Women '97
Wide Awake '97
Fly Away Home '96
Live Nude Girls '95
The Enemy Within '94
Exit to Eden '94
Batman: Mask of the Phantasm '93 (V)
Dead to Rights '93
Tombstone '93
Wild Palms '93
Housesitter '92
Light Sleeper '92
China Beach '88
Masquerade '88
Moon over Parador '88
Patty Hearst '88
A Winner Never Quits '86
Almost You '85

Brian Delate (1949-)
Buffalo Soldiers '01
The Truman Show '98

Cyril Delevanti (1889-1975)
The Killing of Sister George '69
Oh Dad, Poor Dad (Momma's Hung You in the Closet & I'm Feeling So Sad) '67
Dead Ringer '64
The Night of the Iguana '64
I Bury the Living '58
Red Barry '38

Majandra Delfino (1981-)
R.S.V.P. '02
The Learning Curve '01
Shriek If You Know What I Did Last Friday the 13th '00
The Secret Life of Girls '99
Zeus and Roxanne '96

George DelHoyo (1953-)
Dead Letter Office '98
The Crying Child '96

Jorge d'Elia (1938-)
The Aura '05
Lost Embrace '04

Debra Deliso
Iced '88
Slumber Party Massacre '82

Claudia Dell (1910-77)
Boots of Destiny '37
We're in the Legion Now '37
Yellow Cargo '36
The Midnight Phantom '35
The Lost City '34
Woman Condemned '33
Hearts of Humanity '32
Justice Rides Again '32
Midnight Warning '32
Bachelor Apartment '31

Gabriel Dell (1919-88)
Mars '96
The Escape Artist '82
Framed '75
The 300 Year Weekend '71
Blues Busters '50
Master Minds '49
Smugglers' Cove '48
Spook Busters '48
Bowery Buckaroos '47
Hard-Boiled Mahoney '47
Follow the Leader '44
Million Dollar Kid '44
Kid Dynamite '43
Junior G-Men of the Air '42
Let's Get Tough '42
'Neath Brooklyn Bridge '42
Smart Alecks '42
Pride of the Bowery '41
Junior G-Men '40
They Made Me a Criminal '39
Angels with Dirty Faces '38
Little Tough Guys '38
Dead End '37

Myrna Dell (1924-)
Ma Barker's Killer Brood '60
Naked Hills '56
The Bushwackers '52
The Judge Steps Out '49
Fighting Father Dunne '48
Nocturne '46
Raiders of Red Gap '43

Ottaviano Dell'Acqua
Days of Hell '84
Rats '83

Michael DellaFemina
Bloodlust: Subspecies 3 '93
Invisible: The Chronicles of Benjamin Knight '93
Italian Movie '93
Mandroid '93

Erik Todd Dellums (1964-)
Boycott '02
Blackmale '99
She's Gotta Have It '86

Edouard Delmont (1893-1955)
The Sheep Has Five Legs '54
Passion for Life '48
Harvest '37
Angele '34
Toni '34

Nikki Deloach (1979-)
The Net 2.0 '06
Gunfighters' Moon '96
Traveller '96

Genevieve Deloir
The Screaming Dead '72
The Red Half-Breed '70

Alain Delon (1935-)
Nouvelle Vague '90
Notre Histoire '84
Swann in Love '84
The Concorde: Airport '79 '79
Boomerang '76
Mr. Klein '76
Gypsy '75
Icy Breasts '75
Le Gitan '75
Widow Couderc '74
Zorro '74
Scorpio '73
Assassination of Trotsky '72
Red Sun '71
Borsalino '70
Le Cercle Rouge '70
Swimming Pool '70
La Piscine '69
The Girl on a Motorcycle '68
Honor Among Thieves '68
Spirits of the Dead '68
Diabolically Yours '67
The Last Adventure '67
Le Samourai '67
The Eclipse '66
Is Paris Burning? '66
The Lost Command '66
Texas Across the River '66
Joy House '64
Any Number Can Win '63
The Leopard '63
Purple Noon '60
Rocco and His Brothers '60
Sois Belle et Tais-Toi '58

Nathalie Delon (1941-)
Game of Seduction '86
Le Sex Shop '73
Bluebeard '72
Eyes Behind the Stars '72
When Eight Bells Toll '71
Le Samourai '67

Jennifer Delora (1962-)
Bedroom Eyes 2 '89
Deranged '87
New York's Finest '87
Robot Holocaust '87
Sensations '87

Michael Delorenzo (1959-)
Border Patrol '01
Gun Shy '00
The Wall '99
My Family '94
Somebody to Love '94
Platoon Leader '87

Daniele Delorme (1926-)
November Moon '85
Pardon Mon Affaire '76
Les Miserables '57

Julie Delpy (1969-)
The Air I Breathe '07
2 Days in Paris '07
The Hoax '06
The Legend of Lucy Keyes '06
Broken Flowers '05
Before Sunset '04
Intimate Affairs '01
MacArthur Park '01
Waking Life '01
Sand '00
Before Sunrise '94
Killing Zoe '94
Trois Couleurs: Blanc '94
Trois Couleurs: Rouge '94
Younger & Younger '94
The Three Musketeers '93
Europa, Europa '91
Voyager '91
Beatrice '88
Mauvais Sang '86

Rene Deltgen (1909-79)
Black and White as Day and Night '78

Xavier DeLuc
The Other Side of the Law '95

Rudy DeLuca
Life Stinks '91
The Return of Count Yorga '71

David DeLuise (1971-)
Jam '06
Terror Tract '00
Too Smooth '98

Dom DeLuise (1933-)
Girl Play '04
Baby Geniuses '98
The Godson '98
Boys Will Be Boys '97
Red Line '96
All Dogs Go to Heaven 2 '95 (V)
The Tin Soldier '95
A Troll in Central Park '94 (V)
Happily Ever After '93 (V)
The Magic Voyage '93 (V)
Silence of the Hams '93
The Skateboard Kid '93 (V)
Munchie '92 (V)
Almost Pregnant '91
An American Tail: Fievel Goes West '91 (V)
Driving Me Crazy '91
Loose Cannons '90
All Dogs Go to Heaven '89 (V)
Going Bananas '88
Oliver & Company '88 (V)
My African Adventure '87
Spaceballs '87
An American Tail '86 (V)
Haunted Honeymoon '86
Cannonball Run 2 '84
Johnny Dangerously '84
The Best Little Whorehouse in Texas '82
The Secret of NIMH '82 (V)
Cannonball Run '81
History of the World: Part 1 '81
Fatso '80
Hot Stuff '80
The Last Married Couple in America '80
Smokey and the Bandit 2 '80
Wholly Moses! '80
Diary of a Young Comic '79
The Muppet Movie '79
The Adventures of Sherlock Holmes' Smarter Brother '78
The Cheap Detective '78
The End '78
Sextette '78
World's Greatest Lover '77
Silent Movie '76
Blazing Saddles '74
Evil Roy Slade '71
Who Is Harry Kellerman and Why Is He Saying Those Terrible Things About Me? '71
The Twelve Chairs '70
The Glass Bottom Boat '66
Fail-Safe '64

Michael DeLuise (1970-)
Boys Will Be Boys '97
Midnight Edition '93
The Shot '96
Children of the Night '92
Encino Man '92

Peter DeLuise (1966-)
Before I Say Goodbye '03
National Lampoon's Attack of the 5 Ft. 2 Women '94
Rescue Me '93
Free Ride '86
The Midnight Hour '86

Gordon DeMain (1886-1954)
The Mad Monster '42
International Lady '41
Lucky Texan '34
The Dude Bandit '33
Fighting Texans '33
High Gear '33
Rainbow Ranch '33

William Demarest (1892-1983)
The McCullochs '75
Don't Be Afraid of the Dark '73
It's a Mad, Mad, Mad, Mad World '63
Viva Las Vegas '63
The Mountain '56
Sincerely Yours '56
The Far Horizons '55
Hell on Frisco Bay '55
Jupiter's Darling '55

The Private War of Major Benson '55
Dangerous When Wet '53
Escape from Fort Bravo '53
Here Come the Girls '53
Behave Yourself! '52
What Price Glory? '52
First Legion '51
Never a Dull Moment '50
Riding High '50
Jolson Sings Again '49
Sorrowful Jones '49
On Our Merry Way '48
The Perils of Pauline '47
Along Came Jones '45
The Jolson Story '46
Christmas in July '40
Sullivan's Travels '41
The Lady Eve '41
The Devil & Miss Jones '41
Pardon My Sarong '42
The Palm Beach Story '42
All Through the Night '42
Miracle of Morgan's Creek '44
Hail the Conquering Hero '44
Rebecca of Sunnybrook Farm '38
The Great Man Votes '38
The Great McGinty '40
Charlie Chan at the Opera '36
The Great Ziegfeld '36
Love on the Run '36
Wedding Present '36
Hands Across the Table '35
The Jazz Singer '27

Donna DeMario
See Donna (Dona Martell) Martell

Derrick DeMarney (1906-78)
Inheritance '47
Frenzy '46
Dangerous Moonlight '41
Young and Innocent '37
Things to Come '36

Orane Demazis (1904-91)
Le Schpountz '38
Harvest '37
Cesar '36
Angele '34
Fanny '32
Marius '31

Alla Demidova (1936-)
The Seagull '71
Tchaikovsky '71

Katherine DeMille (1911-95)
The Judge '49
Unconquered '47
In Old Caliente '39
Charlie Chan at the Olympics '37
The Gentleman from California '37
Drift Fence '36
Sky Parade '36
The Black Room '35
The Crusades '35
Belle of the Nineties '34
Viva Villa! '34

Jonathan Demme (1944-)
That Thing You Do! '96
Married to the Mob '88
Into the Night '85
Incredible Melting Man '77

William DeMeo
Searching for Bobby D '05
Wannabes '01

William Demerest
When Willie Comes Marching Home '50
Easy Living '37

Ellen Dennerus
More about the Children of Noisy Village '87
The Children of Noisy Village '86

Mylene Demongeot (1936-)
12 Plus 1 '70
Uncle Tom's Cabin '69
The Rape of the Sabines '61
Sois Belle et Tais-Toi '58
Bonjour Tristesse '57
The Crucible '57

Darcy Demoss (1964-)
Forbidden Zone: Alien Abduction '96
The Death Artist '95

Brendan F. Dempsey
About Adam '00
Waking Ned Devine '98

Patrick Dempsey (1966-)
Made of Honor '08
Enchanted '07
Freedom Writers '07
Brother Bear 2 '06 (V)
Lucky Seven '03
The Emperor's Club '02
Sweet Home Alabama '02
The Treat '98
Something About Sex '98
Jeremiah '98
Me & Will '99
Hugo Pool '97
Bloodknot '95
The Escape '95
The Right to Remain Silent '95
With Honors '94
Bank Robber '93
JFK: Reckless Youth '93
Face the Music '92
For Better and for Worse '92
Mobsters '91
Run '91
Coupe de Ville '90
Happy Together '89
Loverboy '89
Some Girls '88
Can't Buy Me Love '87
In the Mood '87
Meatballs 3 '87
Heaven Help Us '85

Richard Dempsey
Catherine Cookson's Tilly Trotter '99
The Chronicles of Narnia '89

Tanya Dempsey
Witchouse 3: Demon Fire '01
Witchouse '97
Shrieker '97

Carol Dempster (1901-91)
The Sorrows of Satan '26
Sally of the Sawdust '25
America '24
Isn't Life Wonderful '24
Dream Street '23
The White Rose '23
Dancer in the Dark '21
The Love Flower '20

Catherine Deneuve (1943-)
Changing Times '04
Kings and Queen '04
Dangerous Liaisons '03
8 Women '02
I'm Going Home '00
The Musketeer '01
East-West '99
Pola X '99
Place Vendome '98
Time Regained '99
Genealogies of a Crime '97
Les Voleurs '96
The Convent '95
Ma Saison Preferee '93
Indochine '92
Scene of the Crime '87
Fort Saganne '84
Le Choc '83
The Hunger '83
I Love All of You '83
The Last Metro '80
A Slightly Pregnant Man '79
March or Die '77
The Hustle '75
Lovers Like Us '75
La Grande Bourgeoise '74
Act of Aggression '73
Peau d'Ane '71
Donkey Skin '70
Tristana '70
April Fools '69
Mayerling '69
The Young Girls of Rochefort '68
Belle de Jour '67
Repulsion '65
Umbrellas of Cherbourg '64
The Twilight Girls '57

Jake Dengel (1933-94)
Prayer of the Rollerboys '91
Bloodsucking Pharaohs of Pittsburgh '90
Ironweed '87

Jacques Denis (1943-)
This Sweet Sickness '77
Jonah Who Will Be 25 in the Year 2000 '76
The Clockmaker '73
La Salamandre '71

Alexis Denisof (1966-)
Rip It Off '02
Noah's Ark '99
Sharpe's Justice '97
Sharpe's Revenge '97

Jeffrey DeMunn (1947-)
The Mist '07
The Hades Factor '06
Hollywoodland '06
Indochine '92
Empire Falls '05
Our Town '03
Cash Crop '01
The Majestic '01
Noriega: God's Favorite '00
The Green Mile '99
Stephen King's The Storm of the Century '99
Harvest '98
The X-Files '98
RocketMan '97
Turbulence '96
Citizen X '95
Hiroshima '95
Down Came a Blackbird '94
Barbarians at the Gate '93
Treacherous Crossing '92
The Hitcher '86
Windy City '84
A Time to Live '85
Eyes of an Angel '91
Blaze '89
Betrayed '88
The Blob '88
Gore Vidal's Lincoln '88
Windmills of the Gods '88
Trumps '83
Frances '82
Ragtime '81
Christmas '81
Sessions '83

Mathieu Demy (1972-)
A Few Days in September '06
Jeanne and the Perfect Guy '98
One Hundred and One Nights '95
Le Petit Amour '87

Maggie Dence
Look Both Ways '05
Danny Deckchair '03

Judi Dench (1934-)
Casino Royale '06
Notes on a Scandal '06
Mrs. Henderson Presents '05
Pride and Prejudice '05
The Chronicles of Riddick '04
Home on the Range '04 (V)
Ladies in Lavender '04
Die Another Day '02
The Importance of Being Earnest '02
The Shipping News '01
Iris '01
Chocolat '00
The Last of the Blonde Bombshells '00
Tea with Mussolini '99
The World Is Not Enough '99
Shakespeare in Love '98
Mrs. Brown '97
Tomorrow Never Dies '97
Hamlet '96
Goldeneye '95
Jack and Sarah '95
Henry V '89
A Handful of Dust '88
Saigon: Year of the Cat '87
84 Charing Cross Road '86
A Room with a View '86
Wetherby '85
Luther '74
A Midsummer Night's Dream '68
A Study in Terror '66

Mathieu Demy (1972-)
Ironweed '87

Maurice Denham (1909-2002)
Monsignor Quixote '91
84 Charing Cross Road '86
Mr. Love '86
From a Far Country: Pope John Paul II '81
Luther '74
Sunday, Bloody Sunday '71
Negatives '68
Night Caller from Outer Space '66
The Alphabet Murders '65
The Nanny '65
The Seventh Dawn '64
Hysteria '64
The Very Edge '63
Damn the Defiant! '62
Paranoiac '62
The Mark '61
Sink the Bismarck '60
Our Man in Havana '59
Curse of the Demon '57
Animal Farm '55 (V)
Captain Boycott '47
Blanche Fury '48

Marianne (Cuau) Denicourt (1966-)
Me Without You '01
Sade '00
The Lost Son '98
She Hate Me '04
My Sex Life... Or How I Got into an Argument '96
Up/Down/Fragile '95
Doomsday Gun '94
Guardian Angel '94
La Sentinelle '92
La Belle Noiseuse '90

Lydie Denier (1964-)
White Cargo '96
Guardian Angel '94
Mardi Gras for the Devil '93
Red Shoe Diaries 3: Another Woman's Lipstick '93
Uncut Investigation '93
Invasion of Privacy '92
Satan's Princess '90
Midnight Cabaret '90
Blood Relations '87

Leslie Denison (1905-92)
The Snow Creature '54
O.S.S. '46
Five Graves to Cairo '43
The Franchise Affair '52
Sherlock Holmes and the Secret Weapon '42
To Be or Not to Be '42
The Great Escape 2: The Untold Story '88

Michael Denison (1915-98)
Shadowlands '93
Angels One Five '54
The Importance of Being Earnest '52
The Franchise Affair '51

Marie Denn
Bury Me an Angel '71
Wild Guitar '62

Brian Dennehy (1939-)
Marco Polo '07
Ratatouille '07 (V)
The Ultimate Gift '07
Welcome to Paradise '07
Everyone's Hero '06 (V)
10th & Wolf '06
Assault on Precinct 13 '05
Category 6: Day of Destruction '04
She Hate Me '04
The Roman Spring of Mrs. Stone '03
A Season on the Brink '02
Stolen Summer '02
Summer Catch '01
Warden of Red Rock '01
Fail Safe '00
Out of the Cold '99
Silicon Towers '99
Sirens '99
Dish Dogs '98
Tom Clancy's Netforce '98
Larry McMurtry's Dead Man's Walk '96
Nostromo '96
William Shakespeare's Romeo and Juliet '96
Tommy Boy '95
The Stars Fell on Henrietta '94
Final Appeal '93
Foreign Affairs '93
Diamond Fleece '92
Gladiator '92
Scott Turow's The Burden of Proof '92
Teamster Boss: The Jackie Presser Story '92
To Catch a Killer '92
The Belly of an Architect '91

Anthony John (Tony) Denison (1950-)
Wild Things 2 '04
Now You Know '02
Looking for an Echo '99
For Which He Stands '98
The Corporate Ladder '97
Opposite Corners '96
Getting Gotti '94
The Amy Fisher Story '93
Men of War '94
A Brilliant Disguise '93
Full Eclipse '93
Sex, Love and Cold Hard Cash '93
Child of Darkness, Child of Light '91
City of Hope '91
Light '91
Little Vegas '90
Full Exposure: The Sex Tape Scandals '89

David Denman (1973-)
Shutter '08
When a Stranger Calls '06
Big Fish '03
The Replacements '00

Tony Denman (1979-)
Sorority Boys '02
Poor White Trash '00

Barry Dennen (1938-)
Liquid Dreams '92
The Shining '80
Jesus Christ, Superstar '73
Paul Bartel's The Secret Cinema '69

Charles Denner (1926-95)
Window Shopping '86
Robert et Robert '78
The Man Who Loved Women '77
Mado '76
The Holes '72
Les Assassins de L'Ordre '71
Z '69
The Bride Wore Black '68
The Two of Us '68
Life Upside Down '64
Landru '63

Richard Denning (1914-98)
Alice Through the Looking Glass '66
Twice-Told Tales '63
An Affair to Remember '57
The Black Scorpion '57
Girls in Prison '56
Creature from the Black Lagoon '54
Hangman's Knot '52
Double Deal '50
Unknown Island '48
Black Beauty '46
The Glass Key '42
Adam Had Four Sons '41

Kat Dennings (1986-)
Charlie Bartlett '07
Big Momma's House 2 '06
Down in the Valley '05
The 40 Year Old Virgin '05
Raise Your Voice '04

John Dennis (1919-2004)
Tomb of the Undead '72
From Here to Eternity '53

F/X 2: The Deadly Art of Illusion '91
A Killing in a Small Town '90
The Last of the Finest '90
Presumed Innocent '90
Rising Son '90
Day One '89
Perfect Witness '89
A Father's Revenge '88
Cocoon: The Return '88
Return to Snowy River '88
Miles from Home '88
The Lion of Africa '87
Best Seller '87
Acceptable Risks '86
F/X '86
Legal Eagles '86
Check Is in the Mail '86
Cocoon '85
Twice in a Lifetime '85
Silverado '85
Finders Keepers '84
The River Rat '84
Gorky Park '83
Never Cry Wolf '83
First Blood '82
Split Image '82
Foul Play '78
F.I.S.T. '78
Pearl '78
A Real American Hero '79
Johnny We Hardly Knew Ye '77
Semi-Tough '77
Ants '77
Women '77
10 '79
O'Neil Story '79
Silent Victory: The Kitty O'Neil Story '79
The Jericho Mile '79
Butch and Sundance: The Early Days '79
To Love Again '80
A Rumor of War '80

Sandy Dennis (1937-92)
The Indian Runner '91
Parents '89
Another Woman '88
976-EVIL '88
The Execution '85
Come Back to the Five & Dime Jimmy Dean, Jimmy Dean '82
The Four Seasons '81
Nasty Habits '77
God Told Me To '76
Mr. Sycamore '74
The Out-of-Towners '70
That Cold Day in the Park '69
Sweet November '68
Up the Down Staircase '67
Who's Afraid of Virginia Woolf? '66
The Three Sisters '65
Splendor in the Grass '61

Leslie Denniston (1950-)
Blue Heaven '84
Pippin '81

Reginald Denny (1891-1967)
Assault on a Queen '66
Batman '66
Cat Ballou '65
Around the World in 80 Days '56
Escape to Burma '55
Sabaka '55
Abbott and Costello Meet Dr. Jekyll and Mr. Hyde '52
Mr. Blandings Builds His Dream House '48
Escape Me Never '47
My Favorite Brunette '47
Love Letters '45
Captains of the Clouds '42
Sherlock Holmes: The Voice of Terror '42
Thunder Birds '42
Rebecca '40
Bulldog Drummond Escapes '37
Bulldog Drummond's Revenge '37
Bulldog Drummond's Bride '39
Bulldog Drummond's Secret Police '39
Arrest Bulldog Drummond '38
Bulldog Drummond's Peril '38
Four Men and a Prayer '38
Bulldog Drummond Comes Back '37
The World Moves On '34
Dancing Man '33
Parlor, Bedroom and Bath '31
Private Lives '31
Madam Satan '30
The Cheerful Fraud '27
Skinner's Dress Suit '26
California Straight Ahead '25

Catherine Dent (1965-)
Taken '02
The Majestic '01
Replicant '01
Someone Like You '01
Venomous '01

Vernon Dent (1895-1963)
House of Errors '42
Texas Cyclone '32
The Cameraman '28
His First Flame '26
Extra Girl '23

Christa Denton (1972-)
Scandal in a Small Town '88
Convicted: A Mother's Story '87
The Gate '87
The Bad Seed '85

Donna Denton
Slaughterhouse Rock '88
Death Blow '87
Glory Years '87
Outlaw of Gor '87

Graham Denton (1914-66)
The Young One '61
The Great St. Louis Bank Robbery '59

Bob Denver (1935-)
Back to the Beach '87
High School USA '84
Rescue from Gilligan's Island '78

John Denver (1943-97)
Walking Thunder '94
Fire and Ice '87 (N)
Foxfire '87
Oh, God! '77

Elisabeth Depardieu (1941-)
Jean de Florette '87
Manon of the Spring '87
Tartuffe '84

Gerard Depardieu (1948-)
Babylon AD '08
La Vie en Rose '07
Last Holiday '06
Paris, je t'aime '06
How Much Do You Love Me? '05
Changing Times '04
Bon Voyage '03
City of Ghosts '03
Crime Spree '03
Napoleon '03
Nathalie '03
Between Strangers '02
A Loving Father '02
CQ '01
The Bridge '00
The Closet '00
102 Dalmatians '00
Vatel '00
Balzac: A Life of Passion '99
The Count of Monte Cristo '99
The Man in the Iron Mask '98
Bogus '96
Hamlet '96
The Machine '96
The Secret Agent '96
Unhook the Stars '96
The Horseman on the Roof '95
Colonel Chabert '94
Elisa '94
Helas pour Moi '94
A Pure Formality '94
Germinal '93
My Father the Hero '93
1492: Conquest of Paradise '92
Tous les Matins du Monde '92
Uranus '91
Cyrano de Bergerac '90
Green Card '90
Camille Claudel '89
I Want to Go Home '89
Too Beautiful for You '88
Jean de Florette '87
Under Satan's Sun '87
Menage '86
One Woman or Two '85
Police '85
Fort Saganne '84
Tartuffe '84
Choice of Arms '83
I Love All of You '83

Les Comperes '83
Moon in the Gutter '83
The Return of Martin Guerre '83
Danton '82
La Chevre '81
The Woman Next Door '81
The Last Metro '80
Loulou '80
Mon Oncle d'Amerique '80
Buffet Froid '79
Get Out Your Handkerchiefs '78
This Sweet Sickness '77
Barocco '76
Maitresse '76
1900 '76
Vincent, Francois, Paul and the Others '76
Going Places '74
Stavisky '74
The Holes '72

Guillaume Depardieu (1971-)
The Duchess of Langeais '07
Napoleon '03
A Loving Father '02
The Count of Monte Cristo '99
Pola X '99
Les Apprentis '95
Tous les Matins du Monde '92

Julie Depardieu (1973-)
Rush Hour 3 '07
Blame It on Fidel '06
La Petite Lili '03
Les Destinees '00
The Count of Monte Cristo '99

Johnny Depp (1963-)
Pirates of the Caribbean: At World's End '07
Sweeney Todd: The Demon Barber of Fleet Street '07
Pirates of the Caribbean: Dead Man's Chest '06
Charlie and the Chocolate Factory '05
The Libertine '05
Tim Burton's Corpse Bride '05 (V)
Finding Neverland '04
Happily Ever After '04
Secret Window '04
Once Upon a Time in Mexico '03
Pirates of the Caribbean: The Curse of the Black Pearl '03
Blow '01
From Hell '01
Before Night Falls '00
The Man Who Cried '00
The Astronaut's Wife '99
The Ninth Gate '99
Sleepy Hollow '99
Fear and Loathing in Las Vegas '98
Donnie Brasco '96
Dead Man '95
Nick of Time '95
Arizona Dream '94
Don Juan DeMarco '94
Ed Wood '94
Benny & Joon '93
What's Eating Gilbert Grape '93
Freddy's Dead: The Final Nightmare '91
Cry-Baby '90
Edward Scissorhands '90
Platoon '86
A Nightmare on Elm Street '84
Private Resort '84

Emilie Dequenne (1981-)
The Bridge of San Luis Rey '05
The Housekeeper '02
Brotherhood of the Wolf '01
Rosetta '99

Gregori Derangere
The 4 Musketeers '05
Bon Voyage '03

Bo Derek (1956-)
Malibu's Most Wanted '03
Sunstorm '01
Tommy Boy '95
Shattered Image '93
Woman of Desire '93
Hot Chocolate '92
Ghosts Can't Do It '90
Bolero '84
Tarzan, the Ape Man '81
A Change of Seasons '80
10 '79

John Derek (1926-98)
Once Before I Die '65
Exodus '60
Omar Khayyam '57
The Ten Commandments '56
An Annapolis Story '55
The Outcast '54
Ambush at Tomahawk Gap '53
All the King's Men '49
Knock on Any Door '49

Joe DeRita (1909-93)
The Outlaws Is Coming! '65
Around the World in a Daze '63
Four for Texas '63
It's a Mad, Mad, Mad, Mad World '63
Three Stooges in Orbit '62
Snow White and the Three Stooges '61
The Three Stooges Meet Hercules '61
Have Rocket Will Travel '59

Edouard Dermithe (1915-95)
The Testament of Orpheus '59
Les Enfants Terrible '50
Orpheus '49

Bruce Dern (1936-)
The Astronaut Farmer '07
Believe in Me '06
Down in the Valley '05
Masked and Anonymous '03
Milwaukee, Minnesota '03
Monster '03
Madison '01
All the Pretty Horses '00
The Haunting '99
Small Soldiers '98 (V)
Down Periscope '96
Last Man Standing '96
Mrs. Munck '95
A Mother's Prayer '95
Mulholland Falls '95
Wild Bill '95
Amelia Earhart: The Final Flight '94
Dead Man's Revenge '93
Carolina Skeletons '92
Diggstown '92
Into the Badlands '92
After Dark, My Sweet '90
The Court Martial of Jackie Robinson '90
1969 '89
World Gone Wild '88
Big Town '87
On the Edge '86
Toughlove '85
Harry Tracy '83
That Championship Season '82
Tattoo '81
Middle Age Crazy '80
Coming Home '78
The Driver '78
Black Sunday '77
Family Plot '76
Twist '76
Posse '75
Smile '75
The Great Gatsby '74

The Laughing Policeman '74
The Cowboys '72
The King of Marvin Gardens '72
Thumb Tripping '72
The Incredible Two-Headed Transplant '71
Silent Running '71
Bloody Mama '70
Castle Keep '69
Rebel Rousers '69
Support Your Local Sheriff '69
They Shoot Horses, Don't They? '69
Psych-Out '68
The St. Valentine's Day Massacre '67
The Trip '67
The War Wagon '67
Waterhole Number 3 '67
Will Penny '67
The Wild Angels '66
Hush, Hush, Sweet Charlotte '65
Marnie '64

Laura Dern (1966-)
Year of the Dog '07
Inland Empire '06
Lonely Hearts '06
Happy Endings '05
The Prize Winner of Defiance, Ohio '05
We Don't Live Here Anymore '04
Focus '01
I Am Sam '01
Jurassic Park 3 '01
Novocaine '01
Dr. T & the Women '00
Daddy & Them '99
A Season for Miracles '99
The Baby Dance '98
October Sky '99
Citizen Ruth '96
Down Came a Blackbird '94
Fallen Angels 1 '93
Jurassic Park '93
A Perfect World '93
Afterburn '92
Rambling Rose '91
Wild at Heart '90
Fat Man and Little Boy '89
Strange Case of Dr. Jekyll & Mr. Hyde '89
Haunted Summer '88
Blue Velvet '86
Mask '85
Smooth Talk '85
Teachers '84
Foxes '80
Alice Doesn't Live Here Anymore '74

Barbara DeRossi (1960-)
Blood Ties '87
Mussolini & I '85
Quo Vadis '85

Richard Derr (1918-92)
Adam at 6 a.m. '70
Terror Is a Man '59
The Invisible Avenger '58
When Worlds Collide '51
Guilty of Treason '50
Castle in the Desert '42
The Man Who Wouldn't Die '42

Cleavant Derricks (1953-)
World Traveler '01
Carnival of Souls '98
Bluffing It '87
Off Beat '86
The Slugger's Wife '85
Moscow on the Hudson '84

Donna D'Errico (1968-)
Comic Book: The Movie '04
Austin Powers In Goldmember '02
Candyman 3: Day of the Dead '98

Debi Derryberry
Comic Book: The Movie '04

Jimmy Neutron: Boy Genius '01 (V)
Whispers: An Elephant's Tale '00 (V)
Kiki's Delivery Service '98 (V)

Mark Derwin (1960-)
Accepted '06
Evil Obsession '96

Janos Derzsi (1954-)
Almanac of Fall '85
Bad Guys '79

Michael Des Barres (1948-)
Catch That Kid '04
The Man from Elysian Fields '01
Mulholland Drive '01
Sugar Town '99
Poison Ivy 3: The New Seduction '97
Silk Degrees '94
A Simple Twist of Fate '94
Widow's Kiss '94
The High Crusade '92
Waxwork 2: Lost in Time '91
Midnight Cabaret '90
Pink Cadillac '89
Nightflyers '87
I, Monster '71

Jean Desailly (1920-)
Le Professionnel '81
Assassination of Trotsky '72
The Soft Skin '64
Les Grandes Manoeuvres '55
La Symphonie Pastorale '46

Anne DeSalvo (1949-)
Hi-Life '98
National Lampoon's Attack of the 5 Ft. 2 Women '94
Casualties of Love: The "Long Island Lolita" Story '93
Dead in the Water '91
Taking Care of Business '90
Spike of Bensonhurst '88
Burglar '87
Compromising Positions '85
Perfect '85
Bad Manners '84
D.C. Cab '84
My Favorite Year '82

Jaclyn DeSantis
Bomb the System '05
Carlito's Way: Rise to Power '05

Stanley DeSantis (1954-)
The Aviator '04
Head Over Heels '01
I Am Sam '01
Lansky '99
Uranus '91

Alex Descas (1958-)
Coffee and Cigarettes '03
Lumumba '01
Harem '99
Late August, Early September '98
Irma Vep '96
Nenette and Boni '96
I Can't Sleep '93
No Fear, No Die '90

Gerard Desarthe (1945-)
Daens '92
Uranus '91

Jerome Deschamps (1945-)
La Separation '98
The Separation '94

Emily Deschanel (1978)
Glory Road '06
Boogeyman '05
The Alamo '04

Mary Jo Deschanel (1945-)
Bark! '02
The Patriot '00
2010: The Year We Make Contact '84
The Right Stuff '83

Zooey Deschanel (1980-)
The Happening '09
The Assassination of Jesse James by the Coward Robert Ford '07
Bridge to Terabithia '07
Surf's Up '07 (V)
Tin Man '07
The Good Girl '02
The New Guy '02
Manic '01
Almost Famous '00
Mumford '99
Failure to Launch '06
The Hitchhiker's Guide to the Galaxy '05
Winter Passing '05
Eulogy '04
All the Real Girls '03
Elf '03
Abandon '02
Big Trouble '02

Alex Desert (1968-)
Pretty Persuasion '05
Swingers '96
P.C.U. '94
Oh, God! You Devil '84

Robert Desiderio (1951-)
No Laughing Matter '97
Gross Anatomy '89
Maximum Security '87

Florence Desmond (1905-93)
Accused '36
Three Came Home '50

William Desmond (1878-1949)
The Cobweb '55
The Prodigal '55
Them! '54
Hidden Assassin '94
Hanna's War '88
Devil in the Flesh '87
A Little Inside '01
Saving Silverman '01
Boys and Girls '00
Final Destination '00
Drop Dead Gorgeous '99
The Galaxy '05

Ivan Desny (1928-2002)
Les Voleurs '96
The Disenchanted '90
Quicker Than the Eye '88
Escape from the KGB '87
Song Without End '61
Daniella by Night '61
Deadly Necklace '62
Escaped in Florence '62
End of Desire '62
Sherlock Holmes and the Deadly Necklace '62
Anastasia '56
Lola Montès '55
The Lady Without Camelias '53
'53
The Respectful Prostitute '50
Madeleine '52

Sandy Descher (1948-)
The Prodigal '55
Them! '54

Maruschka Detmers (1962-)
Hidden Assassin '94
The Mambo Kings '92
Hanna's War '88
Devil in the Flesh '87
First Name: Carmen '83

Tamara DeTreaux (1959-90)
Ghoulies '84
Don't Be Afraid of the Dark '73

Ernst Deutsch (1891-1969)
The Third Man '49
The Golem '20

Geoffrey Deuel (1943-)
Chisum '70

William Devane (1939-)
Jesse Stone: Sea Change '07
Jesse Stone: Death in Paradise '06
The Badge '02
Threat of Exposure '02
Race to Space '01
Hollow Man '00
Poor White Trash '00
Payback '98
Detonator 2: Night Watch '95

Patti Deutsch (1945-)
Groove '00 (V)
Jetsons: The Movie '90 (V)

Amanda Detmer (1971-)
Final Move '06
Jam '06
You, Me and Dupree '06
Extreme Dating '04
Big Fat Liar '02
The Majestic '01

Natalie Desselle
B.A.P.'S '97
Def Jam's How to Be a Player '97

Nathaniel DeVeaux
In a Class of His Own '99

Alan Deveau
Recruits '86
Loose Screws '85

Natalie Desselle
Babycakes '89
Taken Away '89

Nada Despotovich (1967-)
Series 7: The Contenders '01
The In-Laws '79

Devin Devasquez (1963-)
Society '92
Can't Buy Me Love '87
House 2: The Second Story '87

Joanna DeVarona
See Joanna Kerns

George Devine (1910-66)
Tom Jones '63
Lock Back in Anger '58
Time Without Pity '57

Loretta Devine (1949-)
First Sunday '08
Cougar Club '07
Dirty Laundry '07
This Christmas '07
Dreamgirls '06
Crash '05
King's Ransom '05
Woman, Thou Art Loosed '04

Marie Devereux (1941-)
In a Class of His Own '99
The Escape '95
The Spree '96
Outrage '98

Renee Devillers (1902-2000)
What Women Want '00
The Breaks '99
Freedom Song '00
Urban Legends 2: Final Cut '00

Ed Devereaux (1925-)
Goldeneye: The Secret Life of Ian Fleming '89
The Breakup Artist '04
Dinner and Driving '97

Paula DeVicq (1965-)
Lover Girl '97
Hoodlum '96
The Preacher's Wife '96
Rebound: The Legend of Earl 'The Goat' Manigault '96
Waiting to Exhale '95
Caged Fear '92

Kamala Devi
The Brass Bottle '63
Geronimo '62

Aidan Devine
Everything's Gone Green '06

Andy Devine (1905-77)
Mouse and His Child '77 (V)
Whale of a Tale '76
Robin Hood '73 (V)
Myra Breckinridge '70
Smoke '70
Over the Hill Gang '69
Zebra in the Kitchen '65
How the West Was Won '63
The Man Who Shot Liberty Valance '62
Two Rode Together '61
The Adventures of Huckleberry Finn '60
Around the World in 80 Days '56
Thunder Pass '54
Island in the Sky '53
Montana Belle '52
The Red Badge of Courage '51
Slaughter Trail '51
Never a Dull Moment '50
The Traveling Saleswoman '50
Eyes of Texas '48
Far Frontier '48
Grand Canyon Trail '48
Night Time in Nevada '48
Under California Stars '48
On the Old Spanish Trail '47
Springtime in the Sierras '47
Canyon Passage '46
Ali Baba and the Forty Thieves '43
The Gay Ranchero '43
Torrid Zone '40

Danny DeVito (1944-)
The Good Night '07
Reno 911!: Miami '07
Deck the Halls '06
Even Money '06
Relative Strangers '06
10 Items or Less '06
Be Cool '05
Anything Else '03
Big Fish '03
My Sex Life... Or How I Got into an Argument '96
Goldmember '02
Death to Smoochy '02
Heist '01
What's the Worst That Could Happen? '01
The Big Kahuna '00
Drowning Mona '00
Screwed '00
Man on the Moon '99
The Virgin Suicides '99
Living Out Loud '98
Look Who's Talking Now '93 (V)
Batman Returns '92
Hoffa '92
Other People's Money '91
Twins '88
L.A. Confidential '97
Mars Attacks! '96
Matilda '96
Space Jam '96 (V)
Get Shorty '95
Junior '94
Renaissance Man '94
Jack the Bear '93
Hercules '97 (V)
John Grisham's The Rainmaker '97

Sean Devine (1970-)
The Rendering '02
Dead Silent '99
Perpetrators of the Crime '98

Richard Devon (1931-)
The Battle of Blood Island '60
Machine Gun Kelly '58
Blood of Dracula '57
Teenage Doll '57
The Undead '57
The Prodigal '55

Laura Devon (1940-)
Red Line 7000 '65
Goodbye Charlie '64

Dean Devlin (1962-)
Moon 44 '90
Real Genius '85

Gordon Devol (1946-)
Killings at Outpost Zeta '80

J.G. Devlin (1909-91)
The Miracle '91
The Raggedy Rawney '90

Don Devlin (1930-2000)
Operation Dames '59
Blood of Dracula '57

Alan Devlin
Bloom '03
Danny Boy '82

Matthew Devitt
Waking Ned Devine '98
Funnyman '94

Felicity Devonshire
Lisztomania '75
Whose Child Am I? '75

Emmanuelle Devos (1964-)
The Beat My Heart Skipped '05
La Moustache '05
Kings and Queen '04
Read My Lips '01
Dac On the Run '00
Esther Kahn '00
Sarah, Plain and Tall: Skylark '93
Grand Isle '92
Sarah, Plain and Tall '91
Rachel River '87
Truth or Die '86
Act of Passion: The Lost Honor of Kathryn Beck '83

Jon (John) DeVries (1947-)

Jacqueline DeWit (1912-98)
The Story of Jacob & Joseph '74
A Fine Madness '66
The Nun's Story '59
Little Giant '46
Lady on a Train '45

Rosemarie DeWitt
The Great New Wonderful '06

Billy DeWolfe (1907-74)
Billie '65
Lullaby of Broadway '51
Tea for Two '50
Dear Wife '49
The Perils of Pauline '47
Blue Skies '46

Richard Devon / **Patrick Dewaere** (1947-82)
Heat of Desire '84
Beau Pere '81
Get Out Your Handkerchiefs '78
Hothead '78

Eddie Dew (1909-72)
Raiders of Sunset Pass '43
Pagan Island '60
Six Gun Gospel '43
The Fighting 69th '40

Elaine Devry (1935-)
The Cheyenne Social Club '70
A Guide for the Married Man '67
Diary of a Madman '63

Noureen DeWulf (1984-)
The Comebacks '07
Ocean's Thirteen '07
American Dreamz '06

Anthony Dexter (1913-2001)
Married Too Young '62
Fire Maidens from Outer Space '56

Brad Dexter (1917-2002)
Secret Ingredient '92
Winter Kills '79
None But the Brave '65
Von Ryan's Express '65
Kings of the Sun '63
The Magnificent Seven '60
Last Train from Gun Hill '59
Run Silent, Run Deep '58
Between Heaven and Hell '56
The Oklahoman '56
House of Bamboo '55
The Las Vegas Story '52
Blue River '95
That's Adequate '90

Susan Dey (1952-)
Disappearance '02

William Dewhurst (1888-1937)
Non-Stop New York '37
Sabotage '36

Jenna Dewan (1980-)
Take the Lead '06
Step Up '06
Love Lies Bleeding '07
The Best Way '76

Colleen Dewhurst (1924-93)
Bed & Breakfast '92
Dying Young '91
Going Places '74
The French Detective '75
The Boy Who Could Fly '86
Between Two Women '86
Obsessed '88
Termini Station '89
Kaleidoscope '90
Lantern Hill '90
A.D. '85
Anne of Green Gables '85
Anne of Avonlea '87
And Baby Makes Six '79
Ice Castles '79
Silent Victory: The Kitty O'Neil Story '79
Third Walker '79
When a Stranger Calls '79
You Can't Take It with You '84
The Guyana Tragedy: The Story of Jim Jones '80
The Blue and the Gray '82
Final Assignment '80
Mary and Joseph: A Story of Faith '79
The Cowboys '72
The Nun's Story '59
Annie Hall '77
McQ '74
The Glitter Dome '24
The Story of Jacob & Joseph '74
A Fine Madness '66
Sword of Gideon '86

George Devine (1910-66)
Doctor Bull '33
Yellowstone '36
Johnny Dangerously '84
The Jewel of the Nile '85
Terms of Endearment '83
Romancing the Stone '84
Ratings Game '84
Amazing Stories '85
Wise Guys '86
Ruthless People '86
Head Office '86
Tin Men '87
The Playboys '92
The Lonely Passion of Judith Hearne '87
Hurry Up or I'll Be Thirty '73
One Flew Over the Cuckoo's Nest '75
Going Ape! '81
Goin' South '78
The Van '77
The Money '75

Rosanna Desoto (1950-)
Mambo Cafe '00
Family Business '89
Stand and Deliver '88
La Bamba '87
Ballad of Gregorio Cortez '83
The In-Laws '79
Red Alert '77
Rolling Thunder '77
Never Say Die '39
Stagecoach '39
Double or Nothing '37
In Old Chicago '37
A Star is Born '37
The Undiscovered Country '91
My Old Man's Place '71
McCabe & Mrs. Miller '71
The 300 Year Weekend '71
Mutiny on the Blackhawk '39

The Trouble with Dick '88
Echo Park '86
L.A. Law '86
Love Leads the Way '84
Sunset Limousine '83
Looker '81
Comeback Kid '80
Little Women '78
First Love '77

Cliff DeYoung (1945-)
Path to War '02
Deliberate Intent '01
Gale Force '01
The Runaway '00
Get a Clue! '98
George Wallace '97
The Last Don '97
Suicide Kings '97
The Substitute '96
Andersonville '95
JAG '95
Carnosaur 2 '94
Star Quest '94
Revenge of the Red Baron '93
Stephen King's The Tommyknockers '93
Dr. Giggles '92
Nails '92
Immortal Sins '91
To Die Standing '91
Fourth Story '90
Robert Kennedy and His Times '90
Flashback '89
Forbidden Sun '89
Glory '89
Rude Awakening '89
Bulldance '88
Fear '88
In Dangerous Company '88
Pulse '88
Code Name: Dancer '87
The Survivalist '87
F/X '86
Flight of the Navigator '86
Secret Admirer '85
Protocol '84
Reckless '84
The Hunger '83
Independence Day '83
Awakening of Candra '81
Shock Treatment '81
Blue Collar '78
Centennial '78
King '78
The Lindbergh Kidnapping Case '76
Harry and Tonto '74

Ayesha Dharker (1977-)
The Mistress of Spices '05
The Mystic Masseur '01
The Terrorist '98
City of Joy '92

Caroline Dhavernas (1978-)
Breach '07
Niagara Motel '06
These Girls '05
Edge of Madness '02
Out Cold '01

Bernard Dheran (1926-)
Ridicule '96
Bernadette '90

Dalia di Lazzaro (1953-)
Creepers '85
Lady of the Evening '75
Andy Warhol's Frankenstein '74

Melissa Di Marco (1969-)
Hustle '04
No Alibi '00

Andrea Di Stefano (1972-)
Angela '02
Before Night Falls '00

Rick Dial (1955-)
Beyond the Wall of Sleep '06
The General's Daughter '99
The Apostle '97
Sling Blade '96

Chris Diamantopoulos
The Starter Wife '07
Wedding Daze '06

Don Diamond (1921-)
The Old Man and the Sea '58
Borderline '50

Harold Diamond
Picasso Trigger '89
Trained to Kill '88
Hard Ticket to Hawaii '87

Marcia Diamond (1942-)
Love Letters '99
Deranged '74

Neil Diamond (1941-)
Keeping Up with the Steins '06
Saving Silverman '01
The Jazz Singer '80

Reed Edward Diamond (1964-)
Good Night, and Good Luck '05
S.W.A.T. '03
Madison '01
High Noon '00
Homicide: The Movie '00
Secrets '94
Blind Spot '93
O Pioneers! '91
Ironclads '90
Memphis Belle '90

Selma Diamond (1920-85)
All of Me '84
Ratings Game '84
Twilight Zone: The Movie '83
Bang the Drum Slowly '73

Sheryl Lee Diamond
See Sheryl Lee

John DiAquino (1958-)
Pumpkinhead '88
Slipping into Darkness '88

Cameron Diaz (1972-)
What Happens in Vegas '08
Shrek the Third '07 (V)
The Holiday '06
In Her Shoes '05
Shrek 2 '04 (V)
Charlie's Angels: Full Throttle '03
Gangs of New York '02
Slackers '02
The Sweetest Thing '02
Shrek '01 (V)
Vanilla Sky '01
Charlie's Angels '00
Invisible Circus '00
Things You Can Tell Just by Looking at Her '00
Any Given Sunday '99
Being John Malkovich '99
Fear and Loathing in Las Vegas '98
There's Something about Mary '98
Very Bad Things '98
A Life Less Ordinary '97
My Best Friend's Wedding '97
Feeling Minnesota '96
Head Above Water '96
Keys to Tulsa '96
The Last Supper '96
She's the One '96
The Mask '94

Chico Diaz (1959-)
Mango Yellow '02

Guillermo Diaz (1975-)
The Terminal '04
Undefeated '03
Fidel '02
Just One Time '00
200 Cigarettes '98
Half-Baked '97
I Think I Do '97
I'm Not Rappaport '96
Nowhere '96
Freeway '95
Girls Town '95
Stonewall '95
Party Girl '94

Maria Isabel Diaz
Volver '06
Extramarital '98

Melonie Diaz (1984-)
Be Kind Rewind '08
Feel the Noise '07
A Guide to Recognizing Your Saints '06
Raising Victor Vargas '03

Vic Diaz (1932-)
Caged Heat 2: Stripped of Freedom '94
The Children of An Lac '80
Project: Kill! '77
Too Hot to Handle '76
Deathhead Virgin '74
The Deadly and the Beautiful '73
Savage! '73
The Big Bird Cage '72
Night of the Cobra Woman '72
Beast of the Yellow Night '70
Flight to Fury '66
Blood Thirst '65

Tony DiBenedetto (1944-)
Gloria '98
Dangerous Passion '95
Family Business '89
Someone to Watch Over Me '87

George DiCenzo (1940-)
Hustle '04
Tempted '01
Down, Out and Dangerous '95
Exorcist 3: Legion '90
Sing '89
18 Again! '88
The New Adventures of Pippi Longstocking '88
Omega Syndrome '87
Walk Like a Man '87
About Last Night... '86
Back to the Future '85
The Night the City Screamed '80
The Frisco Kid '79
The Ninth Configuration '79
Helter Skelter '76
Las Vegas Lady '76

Bobby DiCicco (1955-)
All Dogs Go to Heaven 2 '95 (V)
Killing Obsession '94
Ghoulies 4 '93
Maniac Cop 3: Badge of Silence '93
The Baby Doll Murders '92
Frame Up '91
The Last Hour '91
A Man Called Sarge '90
Double Revenge '89
She's Back '88
Number One with a Bullet '87
Tiger Warsaw '87
The Supernaturals '86
The Philadelphia Experiment '84
Splash '84
Wavelength '83
Night Shift '82
National Lampoon Goes to the Movies '81
The Big Red One '80
1941 '79
I Wanna Hold Your Hand '78

Andy Dick (1965-)
Blonde Ambition '07
The Comebacks '07
Happily N'Ever After '07 (V)
Danny Roane: First Time Director '06
Employee of the Month '06
Hoodwinked '05 (V)
Old School '03
Scotland, PA '01
Dr. Dolittle 2 '01 (V)
The Independent '00
Loser '00
Road Trip '00
Inspector Gadget '99
Picking Up the Pieces '99
Best Men '98
Bongwater '98

Bryan Dick (1978-)
Blood & Chocolate '07
Brothers of the Head '06

Douglas Dick (1920-)
Flaming Star '60
The Oklahoman '56
The Red Badge of Courage '51
Home of the Brave '49
The Accused '48
Casbah '48

Kim Dickens (1965-)
Thank You for Smoking '06
Wild Tigers I Have Known '06
House of Sand and Fog '03
Out of Order '03
Things Behind the Sun '01
The Gift '00
Hollow Man '00
Committed '99
White River '99
Mercury Rising '98
Great Expectations '97
Truth or Consequences, N.M. '97
Zero Effect '97
Palookaville '95

Bonnie Dickenson
Bellyfruit '99
Little Shots of Happiness '97

Beach Dickerson (1924-2005)
The Dunwich Horror '70
The Trip '67
Creature from the Haunted Sea '60
T-Bird Gang '59
Rock All Night '57

George Dickerson (1933-)
After Dark, My Sweet '90
Death Warrant '90
Blue Velvet '86
Cutter's Way '81

Lucinda Dickey
Cheerleader Camp '88
Breakin' '84
Breakin' 2: Electric Boogaloo '84
Ninja 3: The Domination '84

Angie Dickinson (1931-)
Elvis Has Left the Building '04
Big Bad Love '02
Ocean's Eleven '01
Duets '00
Pay It Forward '00
National Lampoon's The Don's Analyst '97
The Maddening '95
Sabrina '95
Even Cowgirls Get the Blues '94
Wild Palms '93
Treacherous Crossing '92
Texas Guns '90
Fire and Rain '89
Big Bad Mama 2 '87
Jealousy '84
One Shoe Makes It Murder '82
Charlie Chan and the Curse of the Dragon Queen '81
Death Hunt '81
Dressed to Kill '80
Klondike Fever '79
Pearl '78
Big Bad Mama '74
Pray for the Wildcats '74
The Norliss Tapes '73
The Outside Man '73
Resurrection of Zachary Wheeler '71
Thief '71
Sam Whiskey '69
Point Blank '67
Cast a Giant Shadow '66
The Chase '66
The Poppy Is Also a Flower '66
The Killers '64
Captain Newman, M.D. '63
Rome Adventure '62
The Bramble Bush '60
Ocean's 11 '60
Rio Bravo '59
China Gate '57
Hidden Guns '56
I Married a Woman '56
Run of the Arrow '56 (V)
Lucky Me '54

Neil Dickson
It Couldn't Happen Here '88
The Murders in the Rue Morgue '86
Biggles '85

Bo Diddley (1928-)
Rockula '90
Eddie and the Cruisers 2: Eddie Lives! '89
Chuck Berry: Hail! Hail! Rock 'n' Roll '87

Evelyne Didi
Hell's Angels Forever '83
Celestial Clockwork '94
La Vie de Boheme '93

Gabino Diego (1966-)
Love Can Seriously Damage Your Health '96
Belle Epoque '92
Ay, Carmela! '90

Juan Diego (1942-)
Torremolinos 73 '03
Between Your Legs '99
Yerma '99
Jamon, Jamon '93
Cabeza de Vaca '90

August Diehl (1976-)
The Counterfeiters '07
The Ninth Day '04
Love the Hard Way '01

Hans Diehl
Ancient Relic '92
The Boat Is Full '81

John Diehl (1958-)
The Far Side of Jericho '06
Hidden Places '06
Jesse Stone: Death in Paradise '06
Down in the Valley '05
Land of Plenty '04
Bookies '03
Jurassic Park 3 '01
Pearl Harbor '01
Fail Safe '00
Lost Souls '00
Tully '00
Anywhere But Here '99
The Hi-Lo Country '98
Monument Ave. '98
Casualties '97
The End of Violence '97
Managua '97
The Destiny of Marty Fine '96
Foxfire '96
The Lazarus Man '96
A Time to Kill '96
Buffalo Bills '95
Color of a Brisk and Leaping Day '95
The Grave '95
Three Wishes '95
Wes Craven Presents Mind Ripper '95
Almost Dead '94
Stargate '94
Falling Down '93
Gettysburg '93
Remote '93
Mikey '92
Mo' Money '92
A Climate for Killing '91
Motorama '91
Dark Side of the Moon '90
Kickboxer 2: The Road Back '90
Madhouse '90
Cool Blue '88
Glitz '88
Angel '84
Miami Vice '84
National Lampoon's Vacation '83

John Dierkes (1905-75)
Omega Man '71
The Haunted Palace '63
Premature Burial '62
The Alamo '60
The Daughter of Dr. Jekyll '57
Abbott and Costello Meet Dr. Jekyll and Mr. Hyde '52
The Red Badge of Courage '51
The Thing '51

Charles Dierkop (1936-)
SuperGuy: Behind the Cape '02
Invisible Dad '97
Roots of Evil '91
Banzai Runner '86
The Fix '84
Angels Hard As They Come '07

Vin Diesel (1967-)
Babylon AD '08
The Fast and the Furious: Tokyo Drift '06
Find Me Guilty '06
The Pacifier '05
The Chronicles of Riddick '04
A Man Apart '03
XXX '02
The Fast and the Furious '01
Knockaround Guys '01
Boiler Room '00
Pitch Black '00
Iron Giant '99 (V)
Saving Private Ryan '98
Awakenings '90

Gustav Diesl (1899-1948)
Crimes of Dr. Mabuse '32
Westfront 1918 '30
Pandora's Box '28

William Dieterle (1893-1972)
Waxworks '24

Backstairs '21

Daniel Dietrich
Crossfire '89

Marlene Dietrich (1901-92)
Dawn of the Dead '78
Just a Gigolo '79
The Love Goddesses '65
Paris When It Sizzles '64
Judgment at Nuremberg '61
Touch of Evil '58
Witness for the Prosecution '57
Around the World in 80 Days '56
Rancho Notorious '52
No Highway in the Sky '51
Stage Fright '50
Jigsaw '49
A Foreign Affair '48
Golden Earrings '47
Pittsburgh '42
The Spoilers '42
The Lady Is Willing '42
The Flame of New Orleans '41
Seven Sinners '40
Destry Rides Again '39
Angel '37
Knight Without Armour '37
Desire '36
The Garden of Allah '36
The Devil Is a Woman '35
Scarlet Empress '34
The Song of Songs '33
Blonde Venus '32
Shanghai Express '32
Dishonored '31
The Blue Angel '30
Morocco '30

Nade Dieu
Our Music '04
The Butterfly '02

Anton Diffring (1918-89)
Faceless '88
S.A.S. San Salvador '84
The Winds of War '83
Zeppelin '71
Little Mother '71
Eye '72
Where Eagles Dare '68
The Blue Max '66
Fahrenheit 451 '66
The Heroes of Telemark '65
Circus of Horrors '60
The Colditz Story '55

Frank Dietz
The Jitters '88
Zombie Nightmare '86
Rock 'n' Roll Nightmare '85

Uschi Digart (1948-)
Kentucky Fried Movie '77
Black Gestapo '75
Supervixens '75
Ilsa, She-Wolf of the SS '74
Superchick '71

Dudley Digges (1879-1947)
Son of Fury '42
The General Died at Dawn '36
China Seas '35
Mutiny on the Bounty '35
Massacre '34
The World Moves On '34
The Invisible Man '33
Emperor Jones '33
The Mayor of Hell '33
Devotion '31
The Maltese Falcon '31
Condemned '29

Robert Diggs
See The RZA

Taye Diggs (1972-)
Cake '05
Rent '05
Slow Burn '05
Basic '03
Malibu's Most Wanted '03
Brown Sugar '02
Chicago '02
Equilibrium '02
Just a Kiss '02
New Best Friend '02
Way of the Gun '00
The Best Man '99
Go '99
House on Haunted Hill '99
The Wood '99
How Stella Got Her Groove Back '98

Arthur Dignam (1939-)
Gods and Monsters '98
The Nostradamus Kid '92
The Everlasting Secret Family '88
We of the Never Never '82
Grendel, Grendel, Grendel '82 (V)
The Devil's Playground '76

Basil Dignam (1905-79)
The Moonstone '72
Persuasion '71

Mark Dignam (1909-89)
Disraeli '79
The Charge of the Light Brigade '68
Sink the Bismarck '60

Bogdan Diklic (1953-)
Grbavica: The Land of My Dreams '06
Fuse '03
Cabaret Balkan '96

Irasema Dilian (1925-96)
Wuthering Heights '53

Stephen (Dillon) Dillane (1956-)
John Adams '08
Goal! The Dream Begins '06
Klimt '06
Nine Lives '05
Haven '04
King Arthur '04
The Gathering '02
The Hours '02
The Rector's Wife '94
An Affair in Mind '89

Richard Dillane (1964-)
De-Lovely '04
Solomon '98

Garret Dillahunt
The Assassination of Jesse James by the Coward Robert Ford '07
No Country for Old Men '07

Denny Dillon (1951-)
United 93 '06
Roseanne: An Unauthorized Biography '94

Hugh Dillon (1963-)
Assault on Precinct 13 '05
Down to the Bone '04
Ginger Snaps Back: The Beginning '04
Hard Core Logo '96

Kevin Dillon (1965-)
The Foursome '06
Poseidon '06
Hidden Agenda '99
Misbegotten '98
Stag '97
Criminal Hearts '95
True Crime '95
No Escape '94
The Pathfinder '94
A Midnight Clear '92
The Doors '91
Immediate Family '89
War Party '89
When He's Not a Stranger '89
The Blob '88
Remote Control '88
The Rescue '88
Platoon '86
Heaven Help Us '85
No Big Deal '83

Matt Dillon (1964-)
You, Me and Dupree '06
Crash '05
Happily Ever After '05 (V)
Herbie: Fully Loaded '05
Heartstrings '03
City of Ghosts '03
Deuces Wild '02
One Night at McCool's '01
There's Something about Mary '98
In and Out '97
Albino Alligator '96
Beautiful Girls '96
Grace of My Heart '96
Frankie Starlight '95
To Die For '95
Golden Gate '93
Mr. Wonderful '93
The Saint of Fort Washington '93
Singles '92
A Kiss Before Dying '91
Women & Men: In Love There Are No Rules '91
Drugstore Cowboy '89
Kansas '88
Big Town '87
Native Son '86
Rebel '85
The Flamingo Kid '84
Target '85
The Outsiders '83
Rumble Fish '83
Liar's Moon '82
Tex '82
Little Darlings '80
My Bodyguard '80
Over the Edge '79

Melinda Dillon (1939-)
Reign Over Me '07
A Painted House '03
Cowboy Up '00
Magnolia '99
How to Make an American Quilt '95
Sioux City '94
Staying Together '89
Spontaneous Combustion '89
Harry and the Hendersons '87
Shattered Spirits '86
Songwriter '84
A Christmas Story '83
Absence of Malice '81
Fallen Angel '81
Marriage Is Alive and Well '80
The Shadow Box '80
F.I.S.T. '78
Close Encounters of the Third Kind '77
Slap Shot '77
Bound for Glory '76
April Fools '69

Mia Dillon (1955-)
Gods and Generals '03
Our Town '03

Paul Dillon
Chicago Cab '98
Austin Powers: International Man of Mystery '97
Blink '93
The Beat '88
Kiss Daddy Goodnight '87

Tom Dillon (1896-1962)

John DiMaggio (1968-)
Extreme Dating '04
The Pirates of Silicon Valley '99

Bradford Dillman (1930-)
The Bone Yard '90
Mad Monster Party '68 (V)
Private Navy of Sgt. O'Farrell '68
Eight on the Lam '67
Sudden Impact '83
Running Scared '79
Love and Bullets '79
The Amsterdam Kill '78
Piranha '78
The Swarm '78
The Enforcer '76
The Iceman Cometh '73
The Way We Were '73
Escape from the Planet of the Apes '71
The Mephisto Waltz '71
The Resurrection of Zachary Wheeler '71
Brother John '70
Suppose They Gave a War and Nobody Came? '70
Black Water Gold '69
The Bridge at Remagen '69
Sergeant Ryker '68
Compulsion '59

Peter Dinklage (1969-)
The Chronicles of Narnia: Prince Caspian '08
Death at a Funeral '07
Underdog '07
Find Me Guilty '06
Penelope '06
The Baxter '05
Lassie '05
Elf '03
The Station Agent '03
Tiptoes '03
Human Nature '02
13 Moons '02
Living in Oblivion '94

Joe DiNicol
Diary of the Dead '07
Weirdsville '07

Shaun Dingwall (1972-)
On a Clear Day '05
Touching Evil '97
Around the World in 80 Ways '86

Kelly Dingwall
The Fringe Dwellers '86
The Custodian '94

Ernie Dingo (1956-)
The Echo of Thunder '98
Kings in Grass Castles '97
Crocodile Dundee 2 '88
A Waltz Through the Hills '88

Charles Dingle (1887-1956)
The Court-Martial of Billy Mitchell '55
If You Knew Susie '48
A Southern Yankee '48
The Beast with Five Fingers '46
Guest Wife '45
Here Come the Co-Eds '45
Johnny Eager '42
The Little Foxes '41

Yi Ding
Pavilion of Women '01
The Amazing Panda Adventure '95

Paul Dinello (1962-)
Strangers with Candy '06

Alan Dinehart (1889-1944)
The Heat's On '43
It's a Great Life '43
Sweet Rosie O'Grady '43
Everything Happens at Night '39
Second Fiddle '39
Charlie Chan at the Race Track '36
In Old Kentucky '35
Baby, Take a Bow '34
After Midnight '33
Supernatural '33
A Study in Scarlet '33

Victor Dimattia (1979-)
Nightwaves '03
Deadline '00
Psychopath '97
Stranger in the House '97
Dennis the Menace: Dinosaur Hunter '93
Ghost Ship '92

Alex Dimitriades (1973-)
Ghost Ship '02
Subterano '01
Head On '98
The Heartbreak Kid '93

Stefano Dionisi (1966-)
Gloomy Sunday '02
Sleepless '01
Children of the Century '99
Kiss of Fire '98
The Loss of Sexual Innocence '98
The Truce '96
Joseph '95
Farinelli '94
Hercules '62

Silvia Dionisio (1951-)
Street War '76
The Scalawag Bunch '75
Mille Bolle Blu '93

Dante DiPaolo (1926-)
Blood and Black Lace '64
Venus Against the Son of Hercules '62

Kim Director (1977-)
Inside Man '06
Book of Shadows: Blair Witch 2 '01

John DiResta (1951-)
15 Minutes '01

Bob (Robert) Dishy (1943-)
Along Came Polly '04
Judy Berlin '99
Don Juan DeMarco '94
My Boyfriend's Back '93
Used People '92
Brighton Beach Memoirs '86
Lovers and Other Strangers '70

John Disanti (1938-)
Miss Congeniality '00
Eyes of a Stranger '81

Walt Disney (1901-66)
Fantasia '40 (V)
Fun & Fancy Free '47 (V)

Harry Ditson
The Big Bus '76
Tragedy of Flight 103: The Inside Story '91

Barbara Dittus (1939-2001)
Anton, the Magician '78

Madame Rose (Dion) Dione (1875-1936)
Freaks '32
Salome '22

Divine (1945-88)
Divine '90
Hairspray '88
Out of the Dark '88
Trouble in Mind '86
Lust in the Dust '85
Polyester '81
Female Trouble '74
Pink Flamingos '72
Multiple Maniacs '70
Mondo Trasho '69

Reece Dinsdale (1959-)
Hamlet '96
Romance and Rejection '94
Threads '84

Bruce Dinsmore
Danielle Steel's Heartbeat '93

Andrew Divoff (1955-)
Indiana Jones and the Kingdom of the Crystal Skull '08
The Rage '07
Faust: Love of the Damned '00
Captured '99
Stealth Fighter '99
Crossfire '98
Wishmaster 2: Evil Never Dies '98
Nemesis 4: Cry of Angels '97
Wishmaster '97
Blast '96

[continued]

Deadly Voyage '96
Backlash: Oblivion 2 '95
Magic Island '95
The Stranger '95
Xtro 3: Watch the Skies '95
A Low Down Dirty Shame '94
Oblivion '94
Running Cool '93
Back in the USSR '92
Interceptor '92
Toy Soldiers '91
Graveyard Shift '90

Billy Dix
She Demons '58
Red Rock Outlaw '47

Richard Dix (1894-1949)
Buckskin Frontier '43
The Ghost Ship '43
The Kansan '43
American Empire '42
Special Investigator '36
Yellow Dust '36
Transatlantic Tunnel '35
His Greatest Gamble '34
Ace of Aces '33
No Marriage Ties '33
Lost Squadron '32
Cimarron '31
Seven Keys to Baldpate '29
Lucky Devil '25
The Vanishing American '25
The Ten Commandments '23

Robert Dix (1934-)
Killers '88
Cain's Cutthroats '71
Horror of the Blood Monsters '70
Blood of Dracula's Castle '69
Satan's Sadists '69
Wild Wheels '69
Deadwood '65
Forty Guns '57
Forbidden Planet '56

Donna Dixon (1957-)
Wayne's World '92
Lucky Stiff '88
Speed Zone '88
The Couch Trip '87
Beverly Hills Madam '86
Spies Like Us '85
Doctor Detroit '83

James Dixon
The Ambulance '90
Maniac Cop 2 '90
Wicked Stepmother '89
It's Alive 3: Island of the Alive '87
Return to Salem's Lot '87
The Stuff '85
Q (The Winged Serpent) '82
It's Alive 2: It Lives Again '78
It's Alive '74
Black Caesar '73
Hell Up in Harlem '73

Jean Dixon (1896-1981)
Joy of Living '38
You Only Live Once '37

Joan Dixon (1930-92)
Gunplay '51
Hot Lead '51

MacIntyre Dixon (1931-)
Gettysburg '93
Funny Farm '88
Ghostwriter '84

Michael Dixon
Cashback '06
Chains '89

Pamela Dixon
C.I.A. 2: Target Alexa '94
C.I.A.: Code Name Alexa '92
Magic Kid '92
Chance '89

Steve Dixon
L.A. Crackdown 2 '88
Hollywood in Trouble '87
L.A. Crackdown '87
Mayhem '87
The Carrier '87

Omid Djalili (1965-)
The Love Guru '08
Over the Hedge '06 (V)
Casanova '05
Modigliani '04
The Mummy '99

Badja (Medu) Djola (1948-2005)
Deterrence '00
Gunshy '98
Rosewood '96
Heaven's Prisoners '95
Who's the Man? '93
A Rage in Harlem '91
An Innocent Man '89
Mississippi Burning '88
The Serpent and the Rainbow '87
Penitentiary '79

Shae D'Lyn (1963-)
Vegas Vacation '96
Secrets '94

DMX (1970-)
Father of Lies '07
Never Die Alone '04
Cradle 2 the Grave '03
Exit Wounds '01
Romeo Must Die '00
Belly '98

Peter J. D'Noto (1947-)
The Best Man '97
Escape from the Bronx '85
Passion of Love '82

Alan Dobie (1932-)
White Mischief '88
War and Peace '72
Brigade 68

Lawrence (Larry) Dobkin (1919-2002)
Hotwire '80
Patton '70
Geronimo 62
Above and Beyond '53
Loan Shark '52
Twelve o'Clock High 49

Karel Dobry (1969-)
The Ninth Day '04

Gosia Dobrowolska (1958-)
Lust and Revenge '95
The Custodian '94
Careful '92
A Woman's Tale '92
Around the World in 80 Ways 86
Silver City 84
The Girl of Your Dreams '99

James Dobson (1920-87)
Impulse 74
Flying Leathernecks '51

Kevin Dobson (1943-)
Mom, Can I Keep Her? '98
Dirty Work '92
Code of Honor '84
All Night Long 81
Margin for Murder '81
Hardhat & Legs '80
Orphan Train 79
Midway '76

Peter Dobson (1964-)
Protecting the King '07
Lady Jayne Killer '03
Players '03
Double Down '01
Drowning Mona '00
Wicked Ways '99
Nowhere Land '98
Quiet Days in Hollywood '97
The Big Squeeze '96
Dead Cold '96
The Frighteners '96
Riot in the Streets '96
Norma Jean and Marilyn '95
Forrest Gump '94
Where the Day Takes You '92
The Marrying Man '91
Sing '89
Plain Clothes '88

Tamara Dobson (1947-2006)
The Amazons '84
Chained Heat 83
Norman, Is That You? '76
Cleopatra Jones & the Casino of Gold '75
Cleopatra Jones '73

Vernon Dobtcheff (1934-)
Priceless '06
The Body '01
Deja Vu 98
Hilary and Jackie '98
M. Butterfly '93
Pascall's Island '88
Nijinsky '80
The Messiah '75
Murder on the Orient Express '74
Darling Lili '70
The Assassination Bureau 69

Gina Doctor
Shopgirl '05
Dead Pet '01

Claire Dodd (1908-64)
The Black Cat '41
If I Had My Way 40
Charlie Chan in Honolulu 38
Massacre '34
Ex-Lady '33

Jimmie Dodd (1910-64)
Too Late for Tears 49
Snuffy Smith, Yard Bird '42

K.K. Dodds
Soldier '98

Anna Dodge (1867-1945)
A Life Less Ordinary '97

Megan Dodds (1971-)
The Contract '07
Purpose '02
Sword of Honour '01
Bait '00
Urbania '00
Ever After: A Cinderella Story '98
The Rat Pack '98

Jack Dodson (1931-94)
A Climate for Killing '91
Return to Mayberry 85
The Getaway 72

John Doe (1954-)
Torque '04
Players '03
The Good Girl '02
Gypsy 83 '01
Drowning on Dry Land '00
Brokedown Palace '99
Forces of Nature '99
Knocking on Death's Door '99
The Rage: Carrie 2 '99
Sugar Town '99
Wildflowers '99
Highway Hitcher '98
Black Circle Boys '97
Boogie Nights '97
Scorpion Spring '96
Touch '96
Georgia '95
Shake, Rattle & Rock! '94
Wyatt Earp '94
Liquid Dreams '91
Pure Country '92
Roadside Prophets '92
A Matter of Degrees '90
Great Balls of Fire '89
Slamdance 87

Christian Doermer
Oh! What a Lovely War 69
Teenage Wolfpack '57

Darrick Doerner
Riding Giants '04
In God's Hands '98

Tatiana Dogileva (1957-)
East-West '99
A Forgotten Tune for the Flute 88

Matt Doherty (1977-)
D3: The Mighty Ducks '96
So I Married an Axe Murderer '93
The Mighty Ducks '92

Shannen Doherty (1971-)
Category 7: The End of the World '05
The Rendering '02
Jay and Silent Bob Strike Back '01
The Ticket '97
Nowhere '96
Mallrats '95
Almost Dead '94
Blindfold: Acts of Obsession '94
Jailbreakers '94
Freeze Frame '92
Heathers '89
Girls Just Want to Have Fun '85
Night Shift '82

Lexa Doig (1973-)
Jason X '01
No Alibi '00

Lou Doillon (1982-)
Le Petit Amour 87

Michael Dolan (1965-)
The Hunley '99
The Turning '92
Biloxi Blues '88
Hamburger Hill '87
Light of Day '87

Thomas Dolby (1958-)
Rockula '90

Guy Doleman (1924-96)
Funeral in Berlin 66
The Ipcress File '65
Thunderball '65

Ami Dolenz (1969-)
Witchboard 2: The Devil's Doorway '93
Children of the Night '92
Miracle Beach '92
Stepmonster 92
Faith '90
She's Out of Control 89
Can't Buy Me Love '87
The Children of Times Square '86

Mickey Dolenz (1945-)
The Love Bug '97
Invisible Mom '96
The Brady Bunch Movie '95
Night of the Strangler 73
Head '68

Damon D'Oliveira
My Teacher Ate My Homework '98
Back in Action '94

Dora Doll (1922-)
Black and White in Color 76
Boomerang '76
The Young Lions '58

Patrick Dollaghan
The Bad Pack '98
Circle of Fear '89
Kill Slade '89
Murphy's Fault '88

John Doman (1945-)
Gracie '07
Fatwa '06
Sniper 3 '04
City by the Sea '02
Killing Emmett Young '02
The Opponent '01

Larry Domasin (1955-)
Island of the Blue Dolphins '64
Fun in Acapulco 63

Arielle Dombasle (1955-)
Vatel '00
Time Regained '99
L'Ennui 98
Three Lives and Only One Death '96
Little Indian, Big City '95
Raging Angels 95
Celestial Clockwork '94
Twisted Obsession '90
Around the World in 80 Days '89
The Boss' Wife '86
Trade Secrets '86
Pauline at the Beach '83
Le Beau Mariage '82
Perceval 78

Faith Domergue (1925-99)
Blood Legacy 73
The House of Seven Corpses '73
The Sibling '72
Voyage to the Prehistoric Planet 65
The Atomic Man '56
Cult of the Cobra '55
It Came from Beneath the Sea 55
This Island Earth '55
Duel at Silver Creek 52
Where Danger Lives '50

Dagmara Dominczyk (1976-)
Trust the Man '06
Kinsey '04
The Count of Monte Cristo '02

Adriana Dominguez (1976-)
The Bridge of San Luis Rey '05

Wade Dominguez (1966-98)
Virtual Seduction '96
Life 101 '95
Mortal Danger '94
Pumpkinhead 2: Blood Wings 94
Rescue Me '93
Ticks '93

Arturo Dominici (1918-92)
The Trojan Horse '62
Black Sunday '60
Hercules '58

Fats Domino (1928-)
The Girl Can't Help It '56
Rock, Rock, Rock 56

Solveig Dommartin (1961-2007)
Faraway, So Close! '93
Until the End of the World '91
No Fear, No Die '90
Wings of Desire 88

Angelica Domrose (1941-)
The Scorpion Woman '89
Girls Riot '88
The Legend of Paul and Paula 73
Under the Pear Tree '73

Linda Dona
Delta Heat '92
Final Embrace '92
Futurekick '91

Ron Donachie
The Flying Scotsman '06
Extremely Dangerous 99

Elinor Donahue (1937-)
The Princess Diaries 2: Royal Engagement '04
The Invaders '95
Freddy's Dead: The Final Nightmare '91
Pretty Woman '90
High School USA '84
Going Berserk '83
Girls' Town '59
Love Is Better Than Ever '52
My Blue Heaven '50
Three Daring Daughters '48

Heather Donahue (1974-)
Manticore '05
Boys and Girls '00
The Blair Witch Project '99

Troy Donahue (1936-2001)
Showdown '93
Deadly Diamonds '91
The Pamela Principle '91
Sounds of Silence '91
Cry-Baby 90
Nudity Required! '90
Omega Cop '90
Shock 'Em Dead '90
Assault of the Party Nerds '89
The Chilling '89
Deadly Spygames '89
Dr. Allen '89
Hawkeye '88
Sexpot '88
Terminal Force 88
A Woman Obsessed '88
Cyclone '87
Deadly Prey '87
Hollywood Cop 87
Grandview U.S.A. '84
Tin Man 83
The Godfather 1902-1959: The Complete Epic '81
The Legend of Frank Woods 77
Cockfighter 74
The Godfather, Part 2 '74
Seizure 74
South Seas Massacre 74
Love Thrill Murders 71
Those Fantastic Flying Fools '67
Palm Springs Weekend '63
Rome Adventure '62
Parrish 61
Imitation of Life 59
Monster on the Campus '59
A Summer Place '59
Tarnished Angels '57

James Donald (1917-93)
The Big Sleep 78
Cast a Giant Shadow 66
King Rat '65
The Great Escape 63
Victoria Regina 61
The Vikings '58
The Bridge on the River Kwai 57
Lust for Life '56
Beau Brummel 54
The Pickwick Papers 54
The Gay Lady 49
Immortal Battalion '44
In Which We Serve 43

Arthur Donaldson (1869-1955)
- The Broadway Drifter '27
- America '24

Lesleh Donaldson (1964-)
- Funeral Home '82
- Happy Birthday to Me '81
- Staying Alive '83

Norma Donaldson (1928-94)
- Poetic Justice '93
- The Five Heartbeats '91
- 9 to 5 '80

Peter Donaldson
- Invasion! '99
- Escape Clause '96
- Long Day's Journey Into Night '96
- The Sweet Hereafter '96

Ted Donaldson (1933-)
- The Green Promise '49
- Rusty's Birthday '49
- The Red Stallion '47
- Son of Rusty '47
- The Adventures of Rusty '45
- A Tree Grows in Brooklyn '45
- Mr. Winkle Goes to War '44

Peter Donat (1928-)
- The Deep End '01
- The Game '97
- Red Corner '97
- The Babe '92
- School Ties '92
- Tucker: The Man and His Dream '88
- Honeymoon '87
- The Bay Boy '85
- Massive Retaliation '85
- The China Syndrome '79
- Different Story '78
- F.I.S.T. '78
- Mirrors '78
- Return Engagement '78
- The Godfather, Part 2 '74
- Missiles of October '74

Robert Donat (1905-58)
- Happiness '58
- The Inn of the Sixth Happiness '58
- The Winslow Boy '48
- Captain Boycott '47
- The Adventures of Tartu '43
- Goodbye, Mr. Chips '39
- The Citadel '38
- Knight Without Armour '37
- The Ghost Goes West '36
- The 39 Steps '35
- The Count of Monte Cristo '34
- If I Were Rich '33
- The Private Life of Henry VIII '33

Ludwig Donath (1900-67)
- Sins of Jezebel '54
- The Great Caruso '51
- The Lovable Cheat '49
- The Jolson Story '46
- The Secret Code '42

Marc Donato (1989-)
- The Blue Butterfly '04
- Dangerous Child '01
- Locked in Silence '99

Len Doncheff
- Nuremberg '00
- Moving Target '96
- One Night Stand '78

Manuel Dondé
- Swamp of the Lost Monster '65
- Savage Wilderness '55

Chad E. Donella (1978-)
- Hate Crime '05
- Shattered Glass '03
- SuperFire '02
- Final Destination '00
- Disturbing Behavior '98

Yolande Donlan (1920-)
- The Adventurers '70
- Expresso Bongo '59
- Mister Drake's Duck '50
- The Devil Bat '41

Brian Donlevy (1899-1972)
- Arizona Bushwackers '67
- Five Golden Dragons '67
- Hostile Guns '67
- The Fat Spy '66
- Gamera, the Invincible '66
- How to Stuff a Wild Bikini '65
- The Errand Boy '61
- Cowboy '58
- Quatermass 2 '57
- The Quatermass Experiment '56
- Big Combo '55
- Ride the Man Down '53
- Hoodlum Empire '52
- Slaughter Trail '51
- Impact '49
- Command Decision '48
- A Southern Yankee '48
- Kiss of Death '47
- Canyon Passage '47
- Two Years before the Mast '46
- The Virginian '46
- Miracle of Morgan's Creek '44
- A Gentleman After Dark '42
- The Glass Key '42
- The Great Man's Lady '42
- Hangmen Also Die '42
- Wake Island '42
- Billy the Kid '41
- Birth of the Blues '41
- Brigham Young: Frontiersman '40
- The Great McGinty '40
- Allegheny Uprising '39
- Beau Geste '39
- Destry Rides Again '39
- Jesse James '39
- In Old Chicago '37
- Strike Me Pink '36
- Barbary Coast '35
- The Affairs of Annabel '38
- Holiday '38
- A Slight Case of Murder '38
- Mr. Deeds Goes to Town '36
- George '34

Steve Donmyer
- Glitch! '88

Barnard Pierre Donnadieu (1949-)
- Beatrice '88
- The Vanishing '88
- The Return of Martin Guerre '83

Connor Donne
- In Enemy Hands '04

Jeff Donnell (1921-88)
- Gidget Goes to Rome '63
- My Man Godfrey '57
- The Blue Gardenia '53
- Because You're Mine '52
- Three Guys Named Mike '51
- The Fuller Brush Girl '50
- In a Lonely Place '50
- Redwood Forest Trail '50
- Walk Softly, Stranger '50
- Outcasts of the Trail '49
- The Boogie Man Will Get You '42

Donal Donnelly (1931-)
- The Dead '87
- Waterloo '71
- The Knack '65

Ruth Donnelly (1896-1982)
- A Lawless Street '55
- I'd Climb the Highest Mountain '51
- My Little Chickadee '40

Amanda Donohoe (1962-)
- Circus '00
- Hooded Angels '00
- I'm Losing You '98
- A Knight in Camelot '98
- The Real Howard Spitz '98
- Liar Liar '97
- Mad Dog Time '96?
- The Blood of Heroes '89
- Signs of Life '89
- Mystic Pizza '88

Tim Donnelly (1944-)
- The Toolbox Murders '79
- The Clonus Horror '79

Robert Donner (1931-2006)
- The Toolbox Murders '78
- Secret Policeman's Private Parts '81
- Under the Rainbow '81
- The Last Hard Men '76
- The Young Pioneers '76
- Dancing '73
- Vanishing Point '71
- Lassie: Well of Love '70
- Cool Hand Luke '67

Joseph (Joe) D'Onofrio
- Goodfellas '90
- Jungle Fever '91
- A Bronx Tale '93
- I Love Trouble '94
- The Pallbearer '95
- Caught '96
- The Deli '97

Vincent D'Onofrio (1959-)
- The Break-Up '06
- Thumbsucker '05
- Bark! '02
- The Dangerous Lives of Altar Boys '02
- Impostor '02
- The Salton Sea '02
- Sherlock: Case of Evil '02
- Chelsea Walls '01
- The Cell '00
- Steal This Movie! '00
- Happy Accidents '00
- That Championship Season '99
- Spanish Judges '99
- The Thirteenth Floor '99
- The Velocity of Gary '98
- Claire Dolan '97
- Men in Black '97
- The Newton Boys '97
- Feeling Minnesota '96
- Good Luck '96
- The Whole Wide World '96
- The Winner '96
- Strange Days '95
- Being Human '94
- Ed Wood '94
- Imaginary Crimes '94
- Stuart Saves His Family '94
- Mr. Wonderful '93
- The Player '92
- Crooked Hearts '91
- Dying Young '91
- Fires Within '91
- JFK '91
- Naked Tango '91
- Adventures in Babysitting '87
- Full Metal Jacket '87
- First Turn On '83

King Donovan (1918-87)
- The Hanging Tree '59
- The Perfect Furlough '59
- Cowboy '58
- Private Hell 36 '54
- Easy to Love '53
- Forever Female '53
- The Merry Widow '52
- Singin' in the Rain '52
- The Enforcer '51

Martin Donovan (1957-)
- Masters of Horror: Right to Die '07
- Wind Chill '07
- The Sentinel '06
- The Quiet '05
- Saved! '04
- Agent Cody Banks '03
- United States of Leland '03
- Insomnia '02
- RFK '02
- Heaven '99
- In a Savage Land '99
- Onegin '99
- Living Out Loud '98
- The Opposite of Sex '98
- Rescuers: Stories of Courage—Two Couples '98
- When Trumpets Fade '98
- Portrait of a Lady '96
- Flirt '95
- Hollow Reed '95
- Nadja '95
- Amateur '94
- Quick '93
- Simple Men '92
- Surviving Desire '91
- Trust '91

Daisy Donovan (1975-)
- Death at a Funeral '07
- Millions '05

Elisa Donovan (1971-)
- Loving Jezebel '99
- A Night at the Roxbury '98
- Clueless '95

Jeffrey Donovan (1968-)
- Believe in Me '06
- Come Early Morning '06
- Purpose '02
- Bait '00
- Book of Shadows: Blair Witch 2 '00
- Catherine's Grove '98

Ryan Donowho (1980-)
- Strangers with Candy '06
- Imaginary Heroes '05
- A Home at the End of the World '04

Robert Donovan
- The Affairs of Annabel '38

Tate Donovan (1963-)
- Shooter '07
- Nancy Drew '07
- One Night Stand '97
- The Thorn Birds: The Missing Years '96
- The Madness of King George '94
- George '94
- The Substitute '93
- A Woman's Guide to Adultery '93
- Murder at 1600 '97
- Hercules '97 (V)
- Get Well Soon '01
- Exposed '03
- The Pacifier '05
- Good Night, and Good Luck '05
- The Lather Effect '06
- My Boyfriend's Back '93
- Shakes the Clown '92
- White Hot: The Mysterious Murder of Thelma Todd '91
- The Court Martial of Jackie Robinson '90
- Flashback '90
- When He's Not a Stranger '89
- Dark Obsession '90
- Shame '92
- Double Cross '92
- Paper Mask '91
- A Woman's Guide to Adultery '93
- The Substitute '93
- Castaway '87
- Foreign Body '86
- Dead at a Funeral '07
- Clean and Sober '88
- Dangerous Curves '88
- SpaceCamp '86
- Into Thin Air '85
- Not My Kid '85

Terence Donovan (1942-)
- The Winds of Jarrah '83
- The Man from Snowy River '82

James Doohan (1920-2005)
- Bug Buster '99
- The Duke '99
- Storybook '95
- National Lampoon's Loaded Weapon 1 '93
- Double Trouble '91
- Star Trek 6: The Undiscovered Country '91
- Star Trek 5: The Final Frontier '89
- Star Trek 4: The Voyage Home '86
- Star Trek 3: The Search for Spock '84
- Star Trek 2: The Wrath of Khan '82
- Star Trek: The Motion Picture '79
- Man in the Wilderness '71
- 36 Hours '64

Alison Doody (1966-)
- Major League 2 '94
- Temptation '94
- Indiana Jones and the Last Crusade '89
- A View to a Kill '85
- Duel of Hearts '92

Paul Dooley (1928-)
- Hairspray '07
- Cars '06 (V)
- Crazy Little Thing '02
- Insomnia '02
- Madison '01
- A Woman's a Helluva Thing '01
- Guinevere '99
- Happy, Texas '99
- I'll Remember April '99
- Runaway Bride '99
- Angels in the Endzone '98
- Clockwatchers '97
- God's Lonely Man '96
- Telling Lies in America '96
- Waiting for Guffman '96
- Out There '95
- The Underneath '95
- Evolver '94
- State of Emergency '94
- Cooperstown '93
- A Dangerous Woman '93

Patric Doonan (1927-58)
- John and Julie '55
- The Blue Lamp '49
- Blackout '50
- The Blue Lamp '49

Lucinda Dooling
- Lovely... But Deadly '82
- The Alchemist '81

Mike Dopud
- In the Name of the King: A Dungeon Siege Tale '08
- White Noise 2: The Light '07

Karin Dor (1936-)
- A Dream for Christmas '73
- Prisoner in the Middle '74
- The Screaming, Marianne '73
- Dracula vs. Frankenstein '69
- Topaz '69
- You Only Live Twice '67
- The Torture Chamber of Dr. Sadism '69
- The Last Tomahawk '65
- Carpet of Horror '62
- Strangler of Blackmoor Castle '63
- The FBI Story '59
- The Brass Bottle '63
- The Painted Hills '51
- Tomahawk '51
- Never a Dull Moment '50
- The Clay Pigeon '49
- The Fountainhead '49
- Rusty's Birthday '49
- Holiday in Havana '49
- Love Is Better Than Ever '52
- Island in the Sky '53
- Kitten with a Whip '64
- The Accused '48
- Pitfall '48
- Fear in the Night '47

Robert DoQui (1934-)
- Glam '97
- Original Intent '91
- Miracle Mile '89
- Short Fuse '88
- RoboCop 2 '90
- RoboCop '87
- Nashville '75
- Coffy '73

Ann Doran (1911-2000)
- Backstairs at the White House '79
- The Brass Bottle '63
- Kitten with a Whip '64
- The Last Tomahawk '65
- Carpet of Horror '62
- The Painted Hills '51
- Tomahawk '51
- Never a Dull Moment '50
- The Clay Pigeon '49
- The Fountainhead '49
- Holiday in Havana '49
- The Accused '48
- Pitfall '48
- Fear in the Night '47
- The High and the Mighty '54
- Rebel without a Cause '55
- Island in the Sky '53
- Love Is Better Than Ever '52
- Space '58
- Forger of London '61
- The Invisible Dr. Mabuse '62

Son of Rusty '47
Here Come the Waves '45
Air Force '43
Gildersleeve on Broadway '43
The More the Merrier '43
So Proudly We Hail '43
Mr. Wise Guy '42
Criminals Within '41
Dive Bomber '41
Meet John Doe '41
Penny Serenade '41
Blondie '38
Little Red Schoolhouse '36

Jesse Doran
Street Asylum '90
Heart '87

Mary Doran (1907-95)
Sing Sing Nights '35
Sunset Range '35
The Strange Love of Molly Louvain '32
Criminal Code '31
The Divorcee '30
Broadway Melody '29

Richard Doran
Hollywood Boulevard '76
Harrad Summer '74

Edna Dore (1922-)
Nil by Mouth '96
High Hopes '88

Johnny Dorelli (1937-)
The Odd Squad '86
Bread and Chocolate '73

Stephen Dorff (1973-)
Botched '07
.45 '06
The Hades Factor '06
Shadowboxer '06
World Trade Center '06
Alone in the Dark '05
Cold Creek Manor '03
Deuces Wild '02
Feardotcom '02
The Last Minute '01
Rescue Me '93
The Power of One '92
The Gate '87

David Dorfman (1993-)
Drillbit Taylor '08
The Ring 2 '05
Blood & Wine '96
City of Industry '96
I Shot Andy Warhol '96
Innocent Lies '95
Reckless '95
Backbeat '94
S.F.W. '94
Judgment Night '93
Invisible Child '99
The Ring '02
Bounce '00
Panic '00

Diogo Doria (1953-)
Voyage to the Beginning of the World '96
Abraham's Valley '93

Pierre Doris (1919-)
Overseas: Three Women with Man Trouble '90
The Story of a Three Day Pass '68

Françoise Dorléac (1942-67)
The Young Girls of Rochefort '68
Cul de Sac '66
The Soft Skin '64
That Man from Rio '64

Dolores Dorn (1935-)
Truck Stop Women '74
Underworld, U.S.A. '60
Lucky Me '54

Michael Dorn (1952-)
Shade '03
The Santa Clause 2 '02
Star Trek: Nemesis '02
Ali '01
Mach 2 '00
The Prophet's Game '99
Star Trek: Insurrection '98
Menno's Mind '96
Star Trek: First Contact '96
Amanda and the Alien '95
Timemaster '95
Star Trek: Generations '94
Star Trek 6: The Undiscovered Country '91
The Jagged Edge '85
Rocky '76

Philip Dorn (1901-75)
The Fighting Kentuckian '49
I've Always Loved You '46
Random Harvest '42
Reunion in France '42
Tarzan's Secret Treasure '41
Underground '41
Ziegfeld Girl '41

Robert Dornan (1933-)
Hell on Wheels '67
The Starfighters '63

Sandra Dorne (1925-92)
Eat the Rich '87
Devil Doll '64
The House in Marsh Road '60
Alias John Preston '56
Roadhouse Girl '53
Happy Go Lovely '51

Lester Dorr (1893-1980)
Meet the Mob '42
Panama Menace '41
Red Salute '35

Diana Dors (1931-84)
Steaming '86
Children of the Full Moon '84
Adventures of a Taxi Driver '76
Craze '74
The Devil's Web '74
From Beyond the Grave '73
A Man with a Maid '73
Theatre of Blood '73
Amazing Mr. Blunden '72
Hannie Caulder '72
Nothing But the Night '72
Deep End '70
There's a Girl in My Soup '70
Baby Love '69
Berserk! '67
The King of the Roaring '20s: The Story of Arnold Rothstein '61
Room 43 '58
The Long Haul '57
Unholy Wife '57
I Married a Woman '56
A Kid for Two Farthings '55
Man Bait '52
Oliver Twist '48

Brooke D'Orsay (1982-)
King's Ransom '05
Harold and Kumar Go to White Castle '04

Fifi d'Orsay (1904-83)
The Gangster '47
Delinquent Daughters '44
Nabonga '44
Three Legionnaires '37
Going Hollywood '33
Girl from Calgary '32

Jimmy Dorsey (1904-57)
The Fabulous Dorseys '47
Hollywood Canteen '44

Tommy Dorsey (1905-56)
The Fabulous Dorseys '47
Presenting Lily Mars '43

Adrien Dorval
Ginger Snaps Back: The Beginning '04
Pressure '02

Gabrielle Dorziat (1880-1979)
The Storm Within '48
Monsieur Vincent '47
De Mayerling a Sarajevo '40

Susana Dosamantes (1948-)
Counterforce '87
Target Eagle '84
Remolino de Pasiones '68

John Dossett
Nick and Jane '96
That Night '93

Angela Dotchin (1974-)
Beyond Justice '01
Dead Evidence '00

Karen Dotrice (1955-)
The Thirty-Nine Steps '79
The Gnome-Mobile '67
Mary Poppins '64
The Three Lives of Thomasina '63

Michele Dotrice (1947-)
Vanity Fair '99
And Soon the Darkness '70
The Witches '66

Roy Dotrice (1925-)
Hellboy 2: The Golden Army '08
Played '06
The Scarlet Letter '95
The Cutting Edge '92
Suburban Commando '91
The Eliminators '86
Amadeus '84
Cheech and Chong's The Corsican Brothers '84
The Dancing Princesses '84
Space: 1999—Alien Attack '79
The Heroes of Telemark '65

Attilio Dottesio
Jungle Inferno '72
Man with a Cross '43

David Doty
Nancy Drew '07
Full Moon in Blue Water '88

Catherine Doucet (1875-1958)
It Started with Eve '41
These Three '36

John Doucette (1921-94)
Fighting Mad '76
Patton '70
True Grit '69
Nevada Smith '66
Paradise, Hawaiian Style '66
The Hunters '58
House of Bamboo '55
Seven Cities of Gold '55
Fixed Bayonets! '51

Doug E. Doug (1970-)
Shark Tale '04
Eight Legged Freaks '02
That Darn Cat '96
Operation Dumbo Drop '95
Cool Runnings '93
Class Act '91
Jungle Fever '91

Suzi Dougherty
Chameleon 3: Dark Angel '00
Love and Other Catastrophes '95

Kenny Doughty (1975-)
My First Wedding '04
Crush '02

Angela Douglas (1940-)
Digby, the Biggest Dog in the World '73
Carry On Cowboy '66
Carry On Screaming '66

Brandon Douglas (1968-)
Journey to Spirit Island '92
Chips, the War Dog '90
The Children of Times Square '86

Burt Douglas (1930-2000)
High School Confidential '58
The Law and Jake Wade '58

Cameron Douglas (1978-)
National Lampoon's Adam & Eve '05
It Runs in the Family '03

Damon Douglas (1954-)
From Noon Till Three '76
Massacre at Central High '76

Diana Douglas (1923-)
It Runs in the Family '03
Loving '70
The Indian Fighter '55

Don Douglas (1905-45)
Club Havana '46
Behind the Rising Sun '43
Whistling in the Dark '41
Law of the Texan '38
Tomorrow's Children '34
The Great Gabbo '29

Donald Douglas (1905-45)
A Mind to Murder '96
Diana: Her True Story '93
Murder, My Sweet '44
Action in the North Atlantic '43
On the Sunny Side '42
Sergeant York '41
Sleepers West '41

Donna Douglas (1939-)
The Return of the Beverly Hillbillies '81
Frankie and Johnny '65
Career '59

Earl Douglas
Tim Tyler's Luck '37
Fighting Caballero '35

Eric Douglas (1958-2004)
Delta Force 3: The Killing Game '91
Student Confidential '87
Tomboy '85

Illeana Douglas (1965-)
Factory Girl '06
Pittsburgh '06
Alchemy '05
Missing Brendan '03
The Adventures of Pluto Nash '02
Dummy '02
The New Guy '02
Point of Origin '02
Ghost World '01
The Next Best Thing '00
Happy, Texas '99
Lansky '99
Stir of Echoes '99
Message in a Bottle '98
Bella Mafia '97
Flypaper '97
Rough Riders '97
Sink or Swim '97
Weapons of Mass Distraction '97
Grace of My Heart '96
Picture Perfect '96
Wedding Bell Blues '96
To Die For '95
Grief '95
Search and Destroy '94
Alive '93
Household Saints '93
Cape Fear '91
Guilty by Suspicion '91
Goodfellas '90
The Last Temptation of Christ '88

James B. Douglas (1933-)
Men with Brooms '02
Boy in Blue '86
The Changeling '80

John Douglas
Violent Zone '89
Hell's Brigade: The Final Assault '80

Kirk Douglas (1916-)
It Runs in the Family '03
Diamonds '99
Greedy '94
The Secret '93
Oscar '91
Queenie '87
Tough Guys '86
Amos '85
Eddie Macon's Run '83
Remembrance of Love '83
The Man from Snowy River '82
Draw! '81
The Final Countdown '80
Saturn 3 '80
Home Movies '79
The Villain '79
The Fury '78
The Chosen '77
Victory at Entebbe '76
Once Is Not Enough '75
Posse '75
Master Touch '74
Dr. Jekyll and Mr. Hyde '73
Catch Me a Spy '71
A Gunfight '71
Light at the Edge of the World '71
There Was a Crooked Man '70
The Arrangement '69
The Brotherhood '68
The War Wagon '67
The Way West '67
Cast a Giant Shadow '66
Is Paris Burning? '66
The Heroes of Telemark '65
In Harm's Way '65
Seven Days in May '64
For Love or Money '63
The List of Adrian Messenger '63
Lonely Are the Brave '62
Two Weeks in Another Town '62
Town without Pity '61
Spartacus '60
Strangers When We Meet '60
The Devil's Disciple '59
Last Train from Gun Hill '59
The Vikings '58
Gunfight at the O.K. Corral '57
Paths of Glory '57
Lust for Life '56
The Indian Fighter '55
Man Without a Star '55
The Racers '55
Ulysses '55
20,000 Leagues under the Sea '54
The Bad and the Beautiful '52
The Big Sky '52
Big Trees '52
Ace in the Hole '51
Along the Great Divide '51
Detective Story '51
Young Man with a Horn '50
Champion '49
A Letter to Three Wives '49
My Dear Secretary '49
Out of the Past '47
The Strange Love of Martha Ivers '46

Mark Douglas
Moonshine Mountain '64
2000 Maniacs '64

Melvyn Douglas (1901-81)
Hot Touch '82
Ghost Story '81
The Changeling '80
Tell Me a Riddle '80
Being There '79
The Seduction of Joe Tynan '79
Intimate Strangers '77
Twilight's Last Gleaming '77
The Tenant '76
Murder or Mercy '74
The Death Squad '73
The Candidate '72
Hard Frame '70
I Never Sang for My Father '70
Hotel '67
Lamp at Midnight '66
The Americanization of Emily '64
Hud '63
Billy Budd '62
My Forbidden Past '51
A Woman's Secret '49
Mr. Blandings Builds His Dream House '48
They All Kissed the Bride '42
That Uncertain Feeling '41
Two-Faced Woman '41
A Woman's Face '41
Ninotchka '39
The Shining Hour '38
That Certain Age '38
Angel '37
Captains Courageous '37
The Gorgeous Hussy '36
Theodora Goes Wild '36
Annie Oakley '35
Dangerous Corner '34
Woman in the Shadows '34
Counsellor-at-Law '33
As You Desire Me '32
The Old Dark House '32
The Vampire Bat '32
Tonight or Never '31

Michael Douglas (1944-)
King of California '07
The Sentinel '06
You, Me and Dupree '06
The In-Laws '03
It Runs in the Family '03
Don't Say a Word '01
One Night at McCool's '01
Traffic '00
Wonder Boys '00
A Perfect Murder '98
The Game '97
The Ghost and the Darkness '96
The American President '95
Disclosure '94
Falling Down '93
Basic Instinct '92
Shining Through '92
Black Rain '89
The War of the Roses '89
Fatal Attraction '87
Wall Street '87
A Chorus Line '85
The Jewel of the Nile '85
Romancing the Stone '84
The Star Chamber '83
It's My Turn '80
The China Syndrome '79
Coma '78
Napoleon and Samantha '72

Mike Douglas (1925-2006)
Nasty Habits '77
Gator '76

Paul Douglas (1907-59)
The Mating Game '59
This Could Be the Night '57

The Gamma People '56
Solid Gold Cadillac '56
Green Fire '55
Executive Suite '54
Forever Female '53
Clash by Night '52
Never Wave at a WAC '52
We're Not Married '52
Angels in the Outfield '51
The Big Lift '50
Panic in the Streets '50
It Happens Every Spring '49
A Letter to Three Wives '49

Robert Douglas (1909-99)
Helen of Troy '56
King Richard and the Crusaders '54
The Desert Rats '53
At Sword's Point '51
Buccaneer's Girl '50
The Flame & the Arrow '50
Adventures of Don Juan '49
The Fountainhead '49
The Challenge '38
London Melody '37

Sarah Douglas (1952-)
Chained Heat 3: Hell Mountain '98
Asylum '97
The Demolitionist '95
Voodoo '95
Spitfire '94
Meatballs 4 '92
Beastmaster 2: Through the Portal of Time '91
Puppet Master 3: Toulon's Revenge '90
Superman: The Movie '78
Tagget '90
The Return of Swamp Thing '89
Nightfall '88
Steele Justice '87
Solarbabies '86
Conan the Destroyer '84
'98

Susan Douglas (1926-)
Johnny's Girl '95
Dead Ringers '88
Shadow Dancing '88
Lolita '62

Shirley Douglas (1934-)
The Christmas Shoes '02
A House Divided '00
Barney's Great Adventure '98

Warren Douglas (1911-97)
The Inner Circle '46
The Man I Love '46
God Is My Co-Pilot '45

Kent Douglass
See Douglass Montgomery

Robyn Douglass (1953-)
Her Life as a Man '83
Partners '82

Suzanne Douglass (1957-)
How Stella Got Her Groove Back '98
Jason's Lyric '94
Chain of Desire '93
Tap '89

Gary Dourdan (1966-)
Perfect Stranger '07
Impostor '02

Brad Dourif (1950-)
Halloween '07
Pulse '06
Drop Dead Sexy '05
Philadelphia '93
Towers '02
Cypress Edge '99
Interceptor Force '99
The Prophecy 3: The Ascent '99
Silicon Towers '99
Best Men '98
Bride of Chucky '98 (V)
Brown's Requiem '98
Progeny '98
Senseless '98
Urban Legend '98
Alien: Resurrection '97
Sworn to Justice '97
Black Out '96
Nightwatch '96
Death Machine '95
Murder in the First '95
Phoenix '95
Color of Night '94
Amos and Andrew '93
Dario Argento's Trauma '93
Body Parts '91
Child's Play 3 '91 (V)
Common Bonds '91
Critters 4 '91
The Horseplayer '91
Jungle Fever '91
London Kills Me '91
Child's Play 2 '90 (V)
Exorcist 3: Legion '90
Graveyard Shift '90
Sonny Boy '87
Blue Velvet '86
Impure Thoughts '86
Mardi Gras for the Devil '93
Rage of Angels: The Story Continues '86
Grim Prairie Tales '89
Spontaneous Combustion '89
Dune '84
Ragtime '81
Heaven's Gate '81
The Guyana Tragedy: The Story of Jim Jones '80
Wise Blood '79
Eyes of Laura Mars '78
Sergeant Matlovich vs. the U.S. Air Force '78
One Flew Over the Cuckoo's Nest '75

Billie Dove (1900-97)
All the Brothers Were Valiant '53
The Black Pirate '26

Ann Dowd
Garden State '04
Baby '00
Shiloh 2: Shiloh Season '99
Shiloh '97
The Thing About My Folks '05
All Over Me '96
Bushwhacked '95
The Notorious Bettie Page '06

Peggy Dow (1928-)
I Want You '51
Harvey '50

Tony Dow (1945-)
Back to the Beach '87
High School USA '84
Kentucky Fried Movie '77
Death Scream '75

Ellen A. Dow (1918-)
Wedding Crashers '05
The Wedding Singer '97

Ned Dowd (1950-)
Test Tube Teens from the Year 2000 '93
Slap Shot '77

Don Dowe (1961-)
Southern Comfort '81
Popeye '80

Raye Dowell (1961-)
She's Gotta Have It '86

Garrick Dowhen
Land of Doom '84

Freda Dowie (1928-)
Distant Voices, Still Lives '88

Constance Dowling (1923-69)
Black Angel '46
Up in Arms '44

Doris Dowling (1923-2004)
Othello '52
Bitter Rice '49
The Blue Dahlia '46
The Lost Weekend '45

Joan Dowling (1928-54)
Train of Events '49
Hue and Cry '47

Lesley-Anne Down (1954-)
The King's Guard '01
The Perfect Wife '00
The Secret Agent Club '96
Beastmaster 3: The Eye of Braxus '95
Death Wish 5: The Face of Death '94
In the Heat of Passion 2: Unfaithful '94
Indiscreet '88
Ladykillers '88
Scenes from the Goldmine '87
Nomads '86
North and South Book 2 '86
Arch of Triumph '85
North and South Book 1 '85
Agatha Christie's Murder is Easy '82
The Hunchback of Notre Dame '82
Sphinx '81
Rough Cut '80
Hanover Street '79
The Great Train Robbery '79
The Betsy '78
A Little Night Music '77
The Pink Panther Strikes Again '76
Brannigan '75
From Beyond the Grave '73
Assault '70

Brian Downey (1044-)
Hercules the Legendary Journeys, Vol. 1: And the Amazon Women '94
Getting Up and Going Home '92
A Woman Named Jackie '91

Penny Downie (1954-)
The Girl in the Cafe '05
A Certain Justice '99
Dostoevsky's Crime and Punishment '99
Lost for Words '99
Home '92

J. Downing
Robot Wars '93
Ghoulies 2 '87

David Dowling (1943-)
Backstairs at the White House '79
Universe: I Worship His Shadow '97
Tales from a Parallel Universe '97
Gordon's War '73

Morton Downey, Jr. (1933-2001)
Revenge of the Nerds 3: The Next Generation '92
The Silencer '92
Universe: Super Nova '97
George's Island '91

Cathy Downs (1924-76)
Missile to the Moon '59
The Amazing Colossal Man '57
The Curfew Breakers '57

Robert Downey (1936-)
It Could Happen to You '94
Driving Me Crazy '91
Legal Tender '90
Predator 2 '90
Too Much Sun '90

Robert Downey, Jr. (1965-)
Iron Man '08
The Incredible Hulk '08
Charlie Bartlett '07
Zodiac '07
Lucky You '07
Fur: An Imaginary Portrait of Diane Arbus '06
A Guide to Recognizing Your Saints '06
A Scanner Darkly '06
The Shaggy Dog '06
Good Night, and Good Luck '05
Kiss Kiss Bang Bang '05
Game 6 '05
Gothika '03
The Singing Detective '03
Wonder Boys '00
Black and White '99
Bowfinger '99
Friends & Lovers '99
In Dreams '99
Two Girls and a Guy '98
U.S. Marshals '98
Hugo Pool '97
One Night Stand '97
Richard III '95
Home for the Holidays '95
Danger Zone '95
Natural Born Killers '94
Only You '94
Restoration '94
Short Cuts '93
Heart and Souls '93
Chaplin '92
Soapdish '91
Air America '90
Chances Are '89
True Believer '89
1969 '88
Johnny Be Good '88
Less Than Zero '87
The Pick-Up Artist '87
America '86
Back to School '86
Tuff Turf '85
Weird Science '85
First Born '84
Baby It's You '82
To Live & Die in L.A. '85
A Love Divided '01
I Went Down '97

Roma Downey (1960-)
A Love Divided '01
I Went Down '97
Hercules the Legendary Journeys, Vol. 1: And the Amazon Women '94
Devlin '92
Getting Up and Going Home '92
A Woman Named Jackie '91

Maria Doyle Kennedy (1964-)
Miss Julie '99
The General '98
The Break '97
The Matchmaker '97
Nothing Personal '95
The Commitments '91

Maxine Doyle (1915-73)
Come on, Cowboys '37
S.O.S. Coast Guard '37
Condemned to Live '35
The Mystery Man '35

Shawn Doyle (1968-)
A Killing Spring '02
Verdict in Blood '02
Don't Say a Word '01
The Majestic '01
Stiletto Dance '01
Frequency '00

Tony Doyle (1941-2000)
Eat the Peach '86
The Final Option '82

John (Roy Slaven) Doyle (1953-)
Rock & Roll Cowboys '92
The Wicked '89

Denise Dowse (1958-)
Coach Carter '05
Guess Who '05
Ray '04
What About Your Friends: Weekend Getaway '02
Killing Mr. Griffin '97
Bio-Dome '96

David Doyle (1925-97)
Wild & Wooly '78
The Comeback '78
My Boys Are Good Boys '78
Who Killed Mary What's 'Er Name? '71
Loving '70
Paper Lion '68

Brian Doyle-Murray (1945-)
Daddy Day Camp '07
Snow Dogs '02
A Gentleman's Game '01
Bedazzled '00
Stuart Little '99
Dennis the Menace Strikes Again '98
As Good As It Gets '97
Multiplicity '96
Waiting for Guffman '96
Cabin Boy '94
Groundhog Day '93
Wayne's World '92
JFK '91
The Phantom from 10,000 Leagues '56
Ghostbusters 2 '89
How I Got Into College '89
National Lampoon's Christmas Vacation '89
The Experts '89
Scrooged '88
Club Paradise '86
The Razor's Edge '84
Sixteen Candles '84
National Lampoon's Vacation '83
Modern Problems '81
Caddyshack '80

Pamela D'Pella (1967-)
Circus of Fear '67
The Mysterious Magician '64
Shame of the Jungle '75 (V)
Caged Heat 2: Stripped of Freedom '94
Uncaged '91

Heinz Drache (1923-2002)
The Squeaker '65
The Indian Scarf '63
Door with the Seven Locks '62
The Avenger '60

Billy Drago (1949-)
Masters of Horror: Imprint '05
Mysterious Skin '04
Convict 762 '98
Shadow Warriors '97
Deadly Heroes '96
Naked in the Night '58
Phoenix '95
Never Say Die '94
Solar Force '94
The Takeover '94
The Hills Have Eyes '06
Blood Relic '05
Sci-Fighters '96
Lady Dragon 2 '93
In Self Defense '93
Death Ring '93
Guncrazy '92
Secret Games '92
China White '91
Martial Law 2: Undercover '91
Diplomatic Immunity '91
Cyborg 2 '93
Delta Force 2: Operation Stranglehold '90
Dark Before Dawn '89
Freeway '88
Hero and the Terror '88
Prime Suspect '88
The Untouchables '87
Vamp '86
Invasion U.S.A. '85

Charles Drake (1914-94)
Hail, Hero! '69
Valley of the Dolls '67
No Name on the Bullet '59
Until They Sail '57
Walk the Proud Land '56
To Hell and Back '55
Tobor the Great '54
Gunsmoke '53
Comanche Territory '50
Harvey '50
Winchester '73 '50
Air Force '43

Betsy Drake (1923-94)
Will Success Spoil Rock Hunter? '57
Clarence, the Cross-eyed Lion '65
Every Girl Should Be Married '48

BeBe Drake
Friday After Next '02
Backstairs at the White House '79

A Night in Casablanca '46
Conflict '45
Air Force '43
Dive Bomber '41

Claudia Drake (1918-97)
Detour '46
Gentleman from Texas '46
Renegade Girl '46
The Lady Confesses '45
Enemy of Women '44
Border Patrol '43

David Drake (1963-)
David Searching '97
Philadelphia '93

Dona Drake (1914-89)
The Road to Morocco '42
Louisiana Purchase '41

Frances Drake (1908-2000)
I'd Give My Life '36
The Invisible Ray '36
Forsaking All Others '35
Les Miserables '35
Mad Love '35

Gabrielle Drake (1944-)
Au Pair Girls '72
Cry Terror '76

Larry Drake (1950-)
Dark Asylum '01
Desert Heat '99
Paranoia '98
The Treat '98
Bean '97
The Beast '96
Overnight Delivery '96
Power 98 '96
The Journey of August King '95
Darkman 2: The Return of Durant '94
Dr. Giggles '92
Murder in New Hampshire: The Pamela Smart Story '91
Darkman '90
Tales from the Crypt '89
Dark Night of the Scarecrow '81
This Stuff'll Kill Ya! '71

Tom Drake (1918-82)
Savage Abduction '73
The Spectre of Edgar Allen Poe '73
Cycle Psycho '72
Johnny Reno '66
The Singing Nun '66
Warkill '65
The Bramble Bush '60
Cyclops '56
FBI Girl '52
The Great Rupert '50
The Hills of Home '48
Words and Music '48
Cass Timberlane '47
I'll Be Yours '47
Courage of Lassie '46
Meet Me in St. Louis '44
Two Girls and a Sailor '44
The White Cliffs of Dover '44
The Howards of Virginia '40

Polly Draper (1957-)
Second Best '05
Shooting Livien '05
Dinner Rush '00
Hitman's Journal '99
The Tic Code '99
Gold Diggers: The Secret of Bear Mountain '95
Schemes '95
A Million to Juan '94
Danielle Steel's Heartbeat '93
The Pick-Up Artist '87
Making Mr. Right '86

Thomas Draper
Bikini Med School '98
Bikini House Calls '96

Rachel Dratch
I Now Pronounce You Chuck and Larry '07
The Pleasure Drivers '05
Down With Love '03

Milena Dravic (1940-)
WR: Mysteries of the Organism '71
Steel Arena '72
Man Is Not a Bird '65

Alfred Drayton (1881-1949)
Things Happen at Night '48
Nicholas Nickleby '46
First a Girl '35
Jack Ahoy '34

Dr. Dre (1965-)
Training Day '01
The Wash '01
The Show '95
Gunmen '93

Alex Dreier (1916-2000)
Lady Cocoa '75
Loners '72

Fran Drescher (1957-)
Picking Up the Pieces '99
The Beautician and the Beast '97
Jack '96
Car 54, Where Are You? '94
We're Talkin' Serious Money '92
Cadillac Man '90
UHF '89
Wedding Band '89
Rosebud Beach Hotel '85
This Is Spinal Tap '84
Doctor Detroit '83
Ragtime '81
The Hollywood Knights '80
Summer of Fear '78
Saturday Night Fever '77

Sonia Dresdel (1909-76)
The Clouded Yellow '51
The Fallen Idol '49
While I Live '47

Curley Dresden (1900-53)
Fighting Valley '43
Law of the Saddle '43
Trigger Men '41
Wyoming Outlaw '39
Pals of the Saddle '38
Santa Fe Stampede '38
Rough Ridin' Rhythm '37

John Dresden
No Dead Heroes '87
Final Mission '84
Raw Force '81

Louise Dresser (1878-1965)
David Harum '34
Scarlet Empress '34
The World Moves On '34
Doctor Bull '33
The Garden of Eden '28
The Eagle '25

Lieux Dressler (1930)
Truck Stop Women '74
Grave of the Vampire '72

Marie Dressler (1869-1934)
Dinner at Eight '33
Anna Christie '30
Min & Bill '30
Vagabond Lover '29
Tillie Wakes Up '17
Tillie's Punctured Romance '14

Gene Drew (1926-90)
Truck Stop Women '74
Steel Arena '72
Sweet Georgia '72

Griffin (Griffen) Drew (1968-)
The Kid with the X-Ray Eyes '99
Dinosaur Valley Girls '96
Friend of the Family '95
Masseuse '95
Sinful Intrigue '95
Dinosaur Island '93

Roland (Walter Goss) Drew (1900-88)
Across the Pacific '42
The Invisible Killer '40
Evangeline '29

Nancy Drexel (1910-89)
Man from Hell's Edges '32
Mason of the Mounted '32
Texas Buddies '32

James Dreyfus (1968-)
Color Me Kubrick '05
Notting Hill '99
Boyfriends '96

Jean-Claude Dreyfus (1946-)
Two Brothers '04
A Very Long Engagement '04
The Lady and the Duke '01
The City of Lost Children '95
Son of Gascogne '95
Delicatessen '92

Julie Dreyfus (1972-)
Kill Bill Vol. 2 '04
Kill Bill Vol. 1 '03

Lorin Dreyfuss (1944-)
Dutch Treat '86
Detective School Dropouts '85

Richard Dreyfuss (1947-)
Tin Man '07
Poseidon '06
Coast to Coast '04
Silver City '04
Who is Cletis Tout? '02
The Day Reagan Was Shot '01
The Crew '00
Fail Safe '00
Lansky '99
Krippendorf's Tribe '98
Jack London's The Call of the Wild '97 (N)
Oliver Twist '97
James and the Giant Peach '96 (V)
Night Falls on Manhattan '96
Trigger Happy '96
The American President '95
The Last Word '95
Mr. Holland's Opus '95
Another Stakeout '93
Silent Fall '94
Lost in Yonkers '93
Once Around '91
Prisoner of Honor '91
What about Bob? '91
Postcards from the Edge '90
Rosencrantz & Guildenstern Are Dead '90
Always '89
Let It Ride '89
Moon over Parador '88
Nuts '87
Stakeout '87
Tin Men '87
Down and Out in Beverly Hills '86
Stand by Me '86
The Buddy System '83
Whose Life Is It Anyway? '81
The Competition '80
Second Coming of Suzanne '80
The Big Fix '78
Close Encounters of the Third Kind '77
The Goodbye Girl '77
Inserts '76
Victory at Entebbe '76
Jaws '75
The Apprenticeship of Duddy Kravitz '74
American Graffiti '73
Dillinger '73
Hello Down There '69
The Graduate '67
Valley of the Dolls '67

Moosie Drier (1964-)
Charlie and the Great Balloon Chase '82
The Hollywood Knights '80
Homeward Bound '80
Ants '77

Deborah Driggs (1963-)
Night Rhythms '92
Total Exposure '91

Brian Drillinger (1960-)
How to Go Out on a Date in Queens '06
I Shot a Man in Vegas '96
Brighton Beach Memoirs '86

Carol Drinkwater (1948-)
An Awfully Big Adventure '94
Father '53 (V)
Peter Pan '53 (V)
Treasure Island '50
So Dear to My Heart '49
The Window '49
O.S.S. '46
Identity Unknown '45

Bobby Driscoll (1937-68)
The Fighting Sullivans '42

Robert Drivas (1938-86)
God Told Me To '76
Road Movie '72
The Illustrated Man '69
Cool Hand Luke '67

Minnie Driver (1971-)
Ella Enchanted '04
The Phantom of the Opera '04
Owning Mahowny '03
High Heels and Low Lifes '01
Beautiful '00
Return to Me '00
Slow Burn '00
An Ideal Husband '99
South Park: Bigger, Longer and Uncut '99 (V)
Tarzan '99 (V)
The Governess '98
Princess Mononoke '98 (V)
Uncorked '98
Good Will Hunting '97
Grosse Pointe Blank '97
Hard Rain '97
Sleepers '96
Big Night '95
Goldeneye '95
Circle of Friends '94

Jean-Claude Drouot (1938-)
La Rupture '70
Le Bonheur '65

Joanne Dru (1923-96)
Super Fuzz '81
The Light in the Forest '58
Sincerely Yours '56
Hell on Frisco Bay '55
The Warriors '55
Thunder Bay '53
Pride of St. Louis '52
Vengeance Valley '51
Wagon Master '50
All the King's Men '49
She Wore a Yellow Ribbon '49
Red River '48

Dinara Drukarova (1976-)
Of Freaks and Men '98
Son of Gascogne '95
Freeze-Die-Come to Life '90

Alice Drummond (1929-)
For One More Day '07
House of D '04
Pieces of April '03
The Rising Place '02
Joe Gould's Secret '00
I'll Take You There '99
The Love Letter '99
Office Killer '97
Commandments '96
Til There Was You '96
Daybreak '93
Awakenings '90

James Drury (1934-)
The Gambler Returns: The Luck of the Draw '93
Walker: Texas Ranger: One Riot, One Ranger '93
Bull of the West '71
The Meanest Men in the West '67
Ride the High Country '62
Ten Who Dared '60
Good Day for a Hanging '58
Love Me Tender '56
The Tender Trap '55

Fred (John F.) Dryer (1946-)
Shakedown '02
The Independent '00
Wild Grizzly '99
Stray Bullet '98
Death Before Dishonor '87
The Fantastic World of D.C. Collins '84
Fantasy Man '84
Prime Time '77

Robert Dryer
Fast Gun '93
Heartbreaker '83
Savage Streets '83

Jeanie Drynan
Paperback Hero '99
Soft Fruit '99
Muriel's Wedding '94

Gerald du Maurier (1873-1934)
Power '34

Carmen (De Sautoy) Du Sautoy (1952-)
It Couldn't Happen Here '88
Deadly Recruits '86
Praying Mantis '83

Michael Duane (1914-)
The Prince of Thieves '48
City Without Men '43

Don Dubbins (1928-91)
The Illustrated Man '69
From the Earth to the Moon '58
D.I. '57
Tribute to a Bad Man '56

Conor Dubin
A Tale of Two Pizzas '03
Wannabes '01

Ellen Dubin
Tales from a Parallel Universe: I Worship His Shadow '97
Tales from a Parallel Universe: Super Nova '97

Jessica Dublin
The Toxic Avenger, Part 3: The Last Temptation of Toxie '89
The Rejuvenator '88
Troma's War '88
The Slasher '72

Danielle Dublino
Emmanuelle & Joanna '78
St. Michael Had a Rooster '72

Ja'net DuBois (1945-)
Charlie's Angels: Full Throttle '03
Waterproof '99
Magic Island '95
Heart Condition '90
I'm Gonna Git You Sucka '88
Sophisticated Gents '81
Piece of the Action '77

Marie DuBois (1937-)
La Petite Sirene '80
Mon Oncle d'Amerique '80
Vincent, Francois, Paul and the Others '76
Night Flight from Moscow '73
Jailbird's Vacation '65
Circle of Love '64
Jules and Jim '62
Shoot the Piano Player '62
A Woman Is a Woman '60

Marta DuBois
Luminarias '99
Black Out '96
Dead Badge '94
Fear '90
The Trial of the Incredible Hulk '89
The Grace Kelly Story '83
Boulevard Nights '79

Paulette Dubost (1911-)
May Fools '90
Jupiter's Thigh '81
The Last Metro '80
Viva Maria! '65
The Sheep Has Five Legs '54
The Rules of the Game '39

Paul Dubov (1918-79)
Shock Corridor '63
Ma Barker's Killer Brood '60
Underworld, U.S.A. '60
Atomic Submarine '59
Verboten! '59
China Gate '57
Guns Don't Argue '57
Apache Woman '55
Day the World Ended '55

Kristie Ducati
The Bikini Car Wash Company 2 '92
The Bikini Car Wash Company '90

Michel Duchaussoy (1938-)
The Bridesmaid '04
Intimate Strangers '04
Amen '02
The Widow of Saint-Pierre '00
Road to Ruin '91
May Fools '90
Fort Saganne '84
Return of the Tall Blond Man with One Black Shoe '74
This Man Must Die '70
La Femme Infidele '69
The Killing Game '67

David Duchovny (1960-)
The X-Files: I Want to Believe '08
Things We Lost in the Fire '07
Queer Duck: The Movie '06 (V)
Trust the Man '06
The TV Set '06
Connie and Carla '04
House of D '04
Full Frontal '02
Evolution '01
Zoolander '01
Red Shoe Diaries: Luscious Lola '00
Red Shoe Diaries: Swimming Naked '00
Return to Me '00
The X-Files '98
Red Shoe Diaries 8: Night of Abandon '97
Playing God '96

Red Shoe Diaries 7: Burning Up '96
Red Shoe Diaries: Four on the Floor '96
Red Shoe Diaries: Strip Poker '96
Red Shoe Diaries 6: How I Met My Husband '95
Red Shoe Diaries 3: Another Woman's Lipstick '93
Red Shoe Diaries 4: Auto Erotica '93
Red Shoe Diaries '92
Red Shoe Diaries 2: Double Dare '92
Ruby '92
Venice, Venice '92
Julia Has Two Lovers '91
The Rapture '91
New Year's Day '89

Ric(k) Ducommun (1949)
MVP (Most Valuable Primate) '00
Final Voyage '99
Blank Check '93
Ghost in the Machine '93
Encino Man '92
Class Act '91
The 'Burbs '89
Little Monsters '89
Die Hard '88
No Small Affair '84

Louis Ducreux (1901-92)
The Double Life of Veronique '91
The Story of Women '88
A Sunday in the Country '84

Anne Dudek (1975-)
10 Items or Less '06
White Chicks '04
Quicksand '01

Neil Dudgeon
Breathtaking '00
Speedy Death '99
Different for Girls '96
Piece of Cake '88

Marc Dudicourt
Jupiter's Thigh '81
The King of Hearts '66

Michael Dudikoff (1954-)
Black Horizon '01
Gale Force '01
Quicksand '01
Ablaze '00
Counter Measures '99
Fugitive Mind '99
The Silencer '99
Black Thunder '98
Freedom Strike '98
Ringmaster '98
Bounty Hunters 2: Hardball '97
The Shooter '97
Bounty Hunters '96
Crash Dive '96
Moving Target '96
Chain of Command '95
Soldier Boyz '95
The Human Shield '92
Midnight Ride '92
The American Ninja 4: The Annihilation '91
River of Death '90
American Ninja 2: The Confrontation '87
Platoon Leader '87
Avenging Force '86
Radioactive Dreams '86
American Ninja '85
Bachelor Party '84
I Ought to Be in Pictures '82
Making Love '82
Bloody Birthday '80
The Black Marble '79

Florence Dudley (1902-53)
Teenage '44

Jacques Dufilho (1914-2005)
The Horse of Pride '80
Le Crabe Tambour '77

William Duell (1923-)
Rogue of the Rio Grande '30

Lola Duenas (1971-)
Volver '06
The Sea Inside '04

Anne-Marie Duff (1970-)
The History of Mr. Polly '07
The Magdalene Sisters '02

Denice Duff (1965-)
The Aristocrats '99
Bloodstorm: Subspecies 4 '98
Bloodlust 5: Human Target '93
Bloodlust: Subspecies 3 '93
Bloodstone: Subspecies 2 '92

Hilary Duff (1987-)
Material Girls '06
Cheaper by the Dozen 2 '05
The Perfect Man '05
A Cinderella Story '04
Raise Your Voice '04
Agent Cody Banks '03
Cheaper by the Dozen '03
The Lizzie McGuire Movie '03

Haylie Duff (1985-)
Material Girls '06
Napoleon Dynamite '04

Thomas F. Duffy
Varsity Blues '98
The Lost World: Jurassic Park 2 '97
Wagons East '94
Eye of the Stranger '93

Patrick Duffy (1949-)
Perfect Game '00
The Man from Atlantis '77

Karen Duffy (1962-)
The 24 Hour Woman '99
Dumb & Dumber '94

Kevin Duffis
The Expendables '89

Julia Duffy (1951-)
Dumb and Dumberer: When Harry Met Lloyd '03
Intolerable Cruelty '03
Children in the Crossfire '84
Night Warning '82

Dennis Dugan (1946-)
I Now Pronounce You Chuck and Larry '07
The Benchwarmers '06
Strange Relations '02
The Last of the Blonde Bombshells '00
Club Paradise '86
Norman, Is That You? '76
The New Adventures of Pippi Longstocking '88
She's Having a Baby '88
Can't Buy Me Love '87
The Howling '81
Unidentified Flying Oddball '79
Night Call Nurses '72
Mighty Aphrodite '95
Digger '94
Moonstruck '87
Picture Perfect '96
Happy Gilmore '96
Parenthood '89

John Dugan (1940-)
The Texas Chainsaw Massacre 4: The Next Generation '95
The Texas Chainsaw Massacre '74

Michael Dugan
Armistead Maupin's Tales of the City '93

Tom Dugan (1889-1955)
Gun Glory '57
I've Been Waiting for You '49

Andrew Duggan (1923-88)
J. Edgar Hoover '87
Return to Salem's Lot '87
Doctor Detroit '83
The Winds of War '83
Frankenstein Island '81
The Long Days of Summer '80
Backstairs at the White House '79
It's Alive 2: It Lives Again '78
Time Machine '78
The Hunted Lady '77
The Bears & I '74
It's Alive '74
Missiles of October '74
Pueblo Affair '73
Firehouse '72
Housewife '72
The Streets of San Francisco '72
Jigsaw '71
Skin Game '71
The Secret War of Harry Frigg '68
In Like Flint '67
The Incredible Mr. Limpet '64
Seven Days in May '64
Palm Springs Weekend '63
Merrill's Marauders '62
The Commies Are Coming, the Commies Are Coming '57

Patty Duke (1946-)
Little John '02
A Season for Miracles '99
Harvest of Fire '95
Grave Secrets: The Legacy of Hilltop Drive '92
Prelude to a Kiss '92
Amityville 4: The Evil Escapes '89
Best Kept Secrets '88
George Washington '84
September Gun '83
By Design '82
The Babysitter '80
Mom, the Wolfman and Me '80
The Miracle Worker '79
Family Upside Down '78
The Swarm '78
Curse of the Black Widow '77
Fire '77
Killer on Board '77
You'll Like My Mother '72
She Waits '71
My Sweet Charlie '70
Valley of the Dolls '67
Billie '65
The Daydreamer '66
The Miracle Worker '62
4D Man '59
Happy Anniversary '59
The Goddess '58

Bill Duke (1943-)
X-Men: The Last Stand '06
Get Rich or Die Tryin' '05
National Security '03
Red Dragon '02
Exit Wounds '01
Never Again '01
Payback '99
Foolish '99
The Limey '99
Menace II Society '93
Bird on a Wire '90
Predator '87
Commando '85
American Gigolo '79
Car Wash '76

Caitlin Dulany
Class of 1999 II: The Substitute '93
Maniac Cop 3: Badge of Silence '93

Keir Dullea (1936-)
The Good Shepherd '06
The Audrey Hepburn Story '00
Oh, What a Night '92
Blind Date '84
Next One '84
2010: The Year We Make Contact '84
Brainwaves '82
No Place to Hide '81
The Hostage Tower '80
Leopard in the Snow '78
Love Under Pressure '73
Full Circle '77
Welcome to Blood City '77
Black Christmas '75
Paul and Michelle '74
Paperback Hero '73
Black Water Gold '69
2001: A Space Odyssey '68
Madame X '66
The Thin Red Line '64
David and Lisa '62
The Hoodlum Priest '61

Josh Duhamel (1972-)
Transformers '07
Turistas '06
Win a Date with Tad Hamilton! '04

Olympia Dukakis (1931-)
Away From Her '06
The Great New Wonderful '06
In the Land of Women '05
The Thing About My Folks '05
Time of the Gypsies '95

Davor Dujmovic (1969-99)
Underground '95
Time of the Gypsies '88

Douglass Dumbrille (1890-1974)
Shake, Rattle and Rock! '57
Son of Paleface '52
Abbott and Costello in the Foreign Legion '50
Riding High '50
Last of the Wild Horses '49
Spook Busters '48
Blondie Savage '47
The Road to Utopia '46
Under Nevada Skies '46
Jungle Woman '44
Lost in a Harem '44
Uncertain Glory '44
Castle in the Desert '42
A Gentleman After Dark '42
I Married an Angel '42
Ride 'Em Cowboy '42
Big Store '41
Michael Shayne: Private Detective '40
Virginia City '40
Charlie Chan in City of Darkness '39
Charlie Chan at Treasure Island '39
The Three Musketeers '39
The Mysterious Rider '38
The Firefly '37
A Day at the Races '37
Mr. Deeds Goes to Town '36
The Princess Comes Across '36
Crime and Punishment '35
The Lives of a Bengal Lancer '35
Naughty Marietta '35
Treasure Island '34
Baby Face '33
Heroes for Sale '33
King of the Jungle '33
Rustler's Roundup '33

David Dukes (1945-2000)
Tick Tock '00
Supreme Sanction '99
Gods and Monsters '98
The Love Letter '98
Tinseltown '97
Last Stand at Saber River '97
Norma Jean and Marilyn '96
And the Band Played On '93
Me and the Kid '93
Held Hostage '91
War and Remembrance '88
Date with an Angel '87
Rawhead Rex '86
The Men's Club '86
George Washington '84
The Winds of War '83
Without a Trace '83
Miss All-American Beauty '82
Only When I Laugh '81
The First Deadly Sin '80
The Strawberry Statement '70

Robin Duke (1954-)
Hostage for a Day '94
I Love Trouble '94
Motorama '91
Club Paradise '86
The Last Polka '84

Margaret Dumont (1889-1965)
Zotz! '62
Shake, Rattle and Rock! '57
Three for Bedroom C '52
The Horn Blows at Midnight '45
Up in Arms '44
Rhythm Parade '43
Sing Your Worries Away '42
The Big Store '41
A Day at the Races '37
A Night at the Opera '35
Duck Soup '33
Animal Crackers '30
The Cocoanuts '29

Jose Dumont (1950-)
Behind the Sun '01
At Play in the Fields of the Lord '91

James DuMont (1955-)
Fast Girl '07
Combination Platter '93

Denise Dumont
Heart of Midnight '89
Kiss of the Spider Woman '85

Ulises Dumont (1937-)
Time for Revenge '82
The Lion's Share '79

Steffi Duna (1910-92)
Law of the Pampas '39
Panama Lady '39
Way Down South '39
Dancing Pirate '36
I Conquer the Sea '36

Dennis Dun (1954-)
The Last Emperor '87
Prince of Darkness '87
Big Trouble in Little China '86

Donnie Dunagan (1934-)
Bambi '42 (V)
Son of Frankenstein '39

Faye Dunaway (1941-)
Cougar Club '07

Cast Index 1433

Dunaway (continued)
Pandemic '07
Rain '06
Ghosts Never Sleep '05
Anonymous Rex '04
Blind Horizon '04
Chronicle of the Raven '04
The Rules of Attraction '02
Running Mates '00
The Yards '00
The Messenger: The Story of Joan of Arc '99
The Thomas Crown Affair '99
Gia '98
Rebecca '97
The Twilight of the Golds '97
Albino Alligator '96
The Chamber '96
Drunks '96
Dunston Checks In '95
Arizona Dream '94
Don Juan DeMarco '94
The Temp '93
Double Edge '92
Scorchers '92
Silhouette '91
The Handmaid's Tale '90
Wait until Spring, Bandini '90
Burning Secret '89
Cold Sassy Tree '89
The Gamble '88
Barfly '87
Casanova '87
Midnight Crossing '87
Beverly Hills Madam '86
Agatha Christie's Thirteen at Dinner '85
Christopher Columbus '85
Ordeal by Innocence '84
Supergirl '84
The Wicked Lady '83
Country Girl '82
Mommie Dearest '81
The First Deadly Sin '80
The Champ '79
Eyes of Laura Mars '78
The Disappearance of Aimee '76
Network '76
Voyage of the Damned '76
The Four Musketeers '75
Three Days of the Condor '75
Chinatown '74
The Three Musketeers '74
The Towering Inferno '74
Oklahoma Crude '73
The Deadly Trap '71
Little Big Man '70
The Arrangement '69
The Thomas Crown Affair '68
Bonnie & Clyde '67

Adrian Dunbar (1958-)
Eye of the Dolphin '06
Kidnapped '05
Suspicion '03
Triggermen '02
How Harry Became a Tree '01
Shooters '00
The General '98
Melissa '97
Innocent Lies '95
Widow's Peak '94
A Woman's Guide to Adultery '93
The Crying Game '92
The Playboys '92
Hear My Song '91
My Left Foot '89
The Gig '85

Rockmond Dunbar
Dirty Laundry '07
Kiss Kiss Bang Bang '05

Andrew Duncan
Morgan Stewart's Coming Home '87
Slap Shot '77
Shame of the Jungle '75 (V)
Loving '70
The Rain People '69

Angus Duncan (1936-)
How to Seduce a Woman '74
Hard Frame '70

Arletta Duncan (1914-95)
Roaring Speedboats '37
Fighting Champ '33
The Gallant Fool '33
Frankenstein '31

Bob Duncan (1904-67)
Border Feud '47

Bud Duncan (1883-1960)
Hillbilly Blitzkrieg '42
Snuffy Smith, Yard Bird '42

Carmen Duncan (1942-)
Counterstrike '03
Moving Targets '87
Bootleg '85
Dark Forces '83
Now and Forever '82

Julie Duncan
Haunted Ranch '43
Along the Sundown Trail '42
Fugitive Valley '41

Kenne Duncan (1903-72)
Revenge of the Virgins '62 (N)
The Sinister Urge '60
Night of the Ghouls '59
The Astounding She-Monster '58
Flesh and the Spur '57
Cyclotrode "X" '46
Manhunt of Mystery Island '45
Rough Riders of Cheyenne '45
Raiders of Sunset Pass '43
Dynamite Canyon '41
Riding the Sunset Trail '41
Pinto Canyon '40
Make-Up '37

Lindsay Duncan (1950-)
Longford '06
Starter for Ten '06
Under the Tuscan Sun '03
Almost Strangers '01
Oliver Twist '99
An Ideal Husband '99
Mansfield Park '99
Shooting the Past '99
A Midsummer Night's Dream '99
City Hall '96
The Rector's Wife '94
Body Parts '91
Traffik '90
A Year in Provence '89
Loose Connections '87
Prick Up Your Ears '87
Grown Ups '80

Mary Duncan (1895-1993)
Morning Glory '33
State's Attorney '31
City Girl '30

Michael Clarke Duncan (1957-)
Kung Fu Panda '08 (V)
Welcome Home Roscoe Jenkins '08
The Last Mimzy '07
Slipstream '07
Air Bud 6: Air Buddies '06
School for Scoundrels '06
Talladega Nights: The Ballad of Ricky Bobby '06
The Island '05
Racing Stripes '05 (V)
Sin City '05
D.E.B.S. '04
Brother Bear '03 (V)
Daredevil '03
The Scorpion King '02
Cats & Dogs '01 (V)
Planet of the Apes '01
See Spot Run '01
They Call Me Sirr '00
The Whole Nine Yards '00
The Green Mile '99
Armageddon '98

Neil Duncan (1958-)
Sleeping with Strangers '94
Split Second '92
Murder on Line One '90

Peter Duncan (1954-)
The Lifetaker '89
The Old Curiosity Shop '75

Rachel Duncan (1985-)
Amityville Dollhouse '96
Last Stand at Saber River '96

Sandy Duncan (1946-)
The Crazysitter '94
Never Again '01
The Swan Princess '94 (V)
Rock-a-Doodle '92 (V)
The Fox and the Hound '81 (V)
The Cat from Outer Space '78
Roots '77
Million Dollar Duck '71
Star Spangled Girl '71
Mrs. Soffel '84
The Beniker Gang '83

Claude Duneton
Trois Couleurs: Bleu '93
The Double Life of Veronique '91

Christine Dunford
How to Go Out on a Date in Queens '06
Ulee's Gold '97

Katherine Dunham (1909-2006)
Mambo '55
Casbah '48

Robert Dunham (1931-2001)
Godzilla vs. Megalon '76
The Green Slime '68
Face of Another '66

Rosemary Dunham
The Wolves of Kromer '98
Mistress Pamela '74

Stephen Dunham (1964-)
Monster-in-Law '05
The Mummy '99

Dawn Dunlap (1962-)
Barbarian Queen '85
Heartbreaker '83
Forbidden World '82

Lesley Dunlop (1956-)
Tess of the D'Urbervilles '98
The Dying Truth '91
Agatha Christie's Thirteen '85

Vic Dunlop
Wishful Thinking '92
Martians Go Home! '90
Jud '71

Carolyn Dunn
Hitler's Daughter '90
Breaking All the Rules '85

Conrad Dunn
Animal 2 '07
The Last Don 2 '98
Mask of Death '97
Silent Trigger '92
Inside Edge '92

Eddie Dunn (1896-1951)
Call Northside 777 '48
Mexican Spitfire at Sea '42
Billy the Kid '41
South of Santa Fe '32
Sunrise Trail '31

Emma Dunn (1875-1966)
I Married a Witch '42
Talk of the Town '42
The Great Dictator '40
You Can't Fool Your Wife '40
The Secret of Dr. Kildare '39
Son of Frankenstein '39
The Duke of West Point '38
Madame X '37
Hell's House '32
Blessed Event '32
Morals for Women '31

Geoffrey Dunn
Voyage of the Heart '90
The Leather Boys '63

Harvey B. Dunn (1894-1968)
The Sinister Urge '60
Teenagers from Outer Space '59
Bride of the Monster '55

James Dunn (1905-67)
The Oscar '66
The Bramble Bush '60
That Brennan Girl '46
A Tree Grows in Brooklyn '45
The Ghost and the Guest '43
Shadows over Shanghai '38
Baby, Take a Bow '34
Bright Eyes '34
Stand Up and Cheer '34
365 Nights in Hollywood '34

Josephine Dunn (1906-83)
Between Fighting Men '32
Our Modern Maidens '29

Kevin Dunn (1956-)
Lions for Lambs '07
Transformers '07
All the King's Men '06
The Black Dahlia '06
Gridiron Gang '06
A Perfect Day '06
Stir of Echoes '99
Godzilla '98
Small Soldiers '98
Snake Eyes '98
Almost Heroes '97
The Second Civil War '97
The Sixth Man '97
Chain Reaction '96
Picture Perfect '96
JAG '95
Mad Love '95
Nixon '95
Little Big League '94
Dave '93
Hot Shots! '91
Only the Lonely '91
Taken Away '89
Mississippi Burning '88

Liam Dunn (1917-76)
Blazing Saddles '74
Young Frankenstein '74
Catch-22 '70

Michael Dunn (1934-73)
Dr. Frankenstein's Castle of Freaks '74
Werewolf of Washington '73
House of the Damned '71
Murders in the Rue Morgue '71
Boom! '68
Madigan '68
You're a Big Boy Now '66
Ship of Fools '65

Nora Dunn (1952-)
Pineapple Express '08
Southland Tales '06
Love for Rent '05
November '05
Laws of Attraction '04
Bruce Almighty '03
Die Mommie Die! '03
Runaway Jury '03
Cherish '02
Heartbreakers '01
Max Keeble's Big Move '01
What's the Worst That Could Happen? '01
What Planet Are You From? '00
Drop Dead Gorgeous '99
Three Kings '99
Air Bud 2: Golden Receiver '98
Bulworth '98
The Last Supper '96
I Love Trouble '94

Roger Dunn
Owning Mahowny '03
Ignition '01

Ryan Dunn (1977-)
Jackass Number Two '06
Jackass: The Movie '02

John Dunn-Hill
Secret Window '04
Varian's War '01
Wilder '00
La Deroute '98
Bleeders '97

Dominick Dunne (1925-)
An Alan Smithee Film: Burn, Hollywood, Burn '97
Addicted to Love '96

Dominique Dunne (1959-82)
Diary of a Teenage Hitchhiker '82
Haunting of Harrington House '82
Poltergeist '82

Griffin Dunne (1955-)
Snow Angels '07
Game 6 '05
40 Days and 40 Nights '02
Blonde '01
Lisa Picard Is Famous '01
The Android Affair '95
I Like It Like That '94
Quiz Show '94
Search and Destroy '94
Hotel Room '93
Love Matters '93
The Pickle '93
Big Girls Don't Cry... They Get Even '92
Straight Talk '92
My Girl '91
Once Around '91
Secret Weapon '90
White Palace '90
Me and Him '89
The Big Blue '88
Lip Service '88
Amazon Women on the Moon '87
Who's That Girl? '87
After Hours '85
Almost You '85
From Here to Maternity '85
Cold Feet '84
An American Werewolf in London '81
The Fan '81
Chilly Scenes of Winter '79
The Other Side of the Mountain '75

Irene Dunne (1898-1990)
Never a Dull Moment '50
I Remember Mama '48
Life with Father '47
Anna and the King of Siam '46
A Guy Named Joe '44
The White Cliffs of Dover '44
Penny Serenade '41
My Favorite Wife '40
Love Affair '39
Joy of Living '38
The Awful Truth '37
Show Boat '36
Theodora Goes Wild '36
Roberta '35
Sweet Adeline '35
Ann Vickers '33
No Other Woman '33
Bachelor Apartment '31
Consolation Marriage '31

Murphy Dunne (1942-)
Live from Baghdad '03
Blues Brothers 2000 '98
Bad Manners '84
Going Berserk '83
The Blues Brothers '80
The Big Bus '76

Robin Dunne (1976-)
The Snow Walker '03
American Psycho 2: All American Girl '02
The Skulls 2 '02
The Fraternity '01
Cruel Intentions 2 '99

Steve (Stephen) Dunne (1918-77)
I Married a Woman '56
Above and Beyond '53
The Underworld Story '50
The Big Sombrero '49
Son of Rusty '47
Colonel Effingham's Raid '45

Mildred Dunnock (1901-91)
The Pick-Up Artist '87
And Baby Makes Six '79
One Summer Love '76
Spiral Staircase '75
Murder or Mercy '74
Brand New Life '72
Whatever Happened to Aunt Alice? '69
Behold a Pale Horse '64
Sweet Bird of Youth '62
Butterfield 8 '60
The Nun's Story '59
Peyton Place '57
Baby Doll '56
Love Me Tender '56
The Trouble with Harry '55
Viva Zapata! '52
Death of a Salesman '51
I Want You '51
The Corn Is Green '45

Rosemary Dunsmore (1953-)
Wedding Wars '06
Dreamcatcher '03
Breaking the Surface: The Greg Louganis Story '96
Personals '90
Blades of Courage '88
After the Promise '87
Anne of Avonlea '87
Dancing in the Dark '86

Kirsten Dunst (1982-)
Spider-Man 3 '07
Marie Antoinette '06
Elizabethtown '05
Eternal Sunshine of the Spotless Mind '04
Spider-Man 2 '04
Wimbledon '04
Kaena: The Prophecy '03 (V)
Levity '03
Mona Lisa Smile '03
Spider-Man '02
The Cat's Meow '01
crazy/beautiful '01
Get Over It! '01
Bring It On '00
The Crow: Salvation '00
Luckytown '00
Deeply '99
The Devil's Arithmetic '99
Dick '99
Drop Dead Gorgeous '99

(continued)
Lover's Prayer '99
The Virgin Suicides '99
Anastasia '97 (V)
All I Wanna Do '98
Kiki's Delivery Service '98 (V)
Small Soldiers '98
Tower of Terror '97 (V)
True Heart '97
Wag the Dog '97
Mother Night '96
Jumanji '95
Interview with the Vampire '94

Wilson Dunster
Yankee Zulu '95
The Rutanga Tapes '90
Swift Justice '88

Don Duong (1957-)
We Were Soldiers '02
Green Dragon '01
Three Seasons '98

Anny (Annie Legras) Duperey (1947-)
Charlemagne '95
Germinal '93
Les Comperes '83
From Hell to Victory '79
Bobby Deerfield '77
Pardon Mon Affaire '76
No Problem '75
Stavisky '74
The Women '68
Two or Three Things I Know about Her '66

Daphne Lynn Duplaix (1976-)
Foolish '99
Lost and Found '99

Starletta DuPois
Friday After Next '02
Big Momma's House '00
Three Strikes '00
The Road to Galveston '96
A Raisin in the Sun '89
Hollywood Shuffle '87

Albert Dupontel (1964-)
Irreversible '02
Avenue Montaigne '06
A Very Long Engagement '04
A Self-Made Hero '95

June Duprez (1918-84)
And Then There Were None '45
Brighton Strangler '45
None But the Lonely Heart '44
Tiger Fangs '43
The Lion Has Wings '40
The Thief of Bagdad '40
The Four Feathers '39
The Spy in Black '35

Paul Dupuis (1913-76)
Against the Wind '48
Johnny Frenchman '46
None But the Lonely Heart '44

Roy Dupuis (1963-)
That Beautiful Somewhere '06
The Rocket '05
Bleeders '97
Entangled '93
Being at Home with Claude '92

Jack Durant
Four Jacks and a Jill '41

Jimmy Durante (1893-1980)
Alice Through the Looking Glass '66
It's a Mad, Mad, Mad, Mad World '63
Billy Rose's Jumbo '62
The Great Rupert '50
On an Island with You '48
It Happened in Brooklyn '47
Ziegfeld Follies '46
Two Girls and a Sailor '44
The Man Who Came to Dinner '41
Melody Ranch '40
Little Miss Broadway '38
Hollywood Party '34
Palooka '34
The Lost Stooges '33
What! No Beer? '33
Speak Easily '32
365 Nights in Hollywood '34

Deanna Durbin (1921-)
For the Love of Mary '48
Up in Central Park '48
I'll Be Yours '47
Something in the Wind '47
Because of Him '46
Can't Help Singing '45
Lady on a Train '45
His Butler's Sister '44
The Amazing Mrs. Holliday '43
It Started with Eve '41
Nice Girl? '41
It's a Date '40
First Love '39
Three Smart Girls Grow Up '39
Mad About Music '38
That Certain Age '38
100 Men and a Girl '37
Three Smart Girls '36

Richard Durden
The First 9 1/2 Weeks '98

Minta Durfee (1889-1975)
Pumpkinhead 4: Blood Feud '07
Tapeheads '89
Dr. Caligari '89
Savage Intruder '68
Miracle Kid '42
Mickey '17

Romain Duris (1974-)
Moliere '07
Inside Paris '06
The Beat My Heart Skipped '05
Russian Dolls '05
Le Divorce '03
L'Auberge Espagnole '02
The Crazy Stranger '98
When the Cat's Away '96

Anna Marie Duringer (1925-)
Veronika Voss '82
The Lacemaker '77

Charles Durning (1933-)
Forget About It '06
Miracle Dogs Too '06
One Last Ride '03
Mr. St. Nick '02
L.A.P.D.: To Protect and Serve '01
Hostage Hotel '00
Lakeboat '00
O Brother, Where Art Thou? '00
State and Main '00
One Fine Day '96
Spy Hard '96
The Grass Harp '95
Home for the Holidays '95
The Kennedys of Massachusetts '95
A Woman of Independent Means '94
The Hudsucker Proxy '93
The Music of Chance '93
The Story Lady '93
When a Stranger Calls Back '93
V.I. Warshawski '91
Cat Chaser '90
Dick Tracy '90
Project: Alien '89
Cop '88
Far North '88
Happy New Year '87
The Man Who Broke 1,000 Chains '87
A Tiger's Tale '87
Big Trouble '86
Brenda Starr '86
Death of a Salesman '86
Stick '85
Stand Alone '85
The Man with One Red Shoe '85
Hadley's Rebellion '84
Mass Appeal '84
Two of a Kind '83
To Be or Not to Be '83
The Best Little Whorehouse in Texas '82
Tootsie '82
The Best Little Girl in the World '81
Killjoy '81
Crisis at Central High '80
Die Laughing '80
Attica '80
True Confessions '81
Sharky's Machine '81
The Final Countdown '80
The Muppet Movie '79
North Dallas Forty '79
When a Stranger Calls '79
The Fury '78
Special Olympics '78
Tilt '78
The Choirboys '77
Twilight's Last Gleaming '77
Breakheart Pass '76
Harry & Walter Go to New York '76
Dog Day Afternoon '75
The Hindenburg '75
The Front Page '74
The Sting '73
The Connection '73
Sisters '73

Dick Durock (1938-)
The Return of Swamp Thing '89
Swamp Thing '82
I Walk the Line '70

Jason Durr (1968-)
Killer Tongue '96
Sharpe's Battle '94
A Dark Adapted Eye '93

Michael Durrell (1943-)
Magma: Volcanic Disaster '06
Illegal in Blue '95
Family Sins '87

Nancy Dussault (1936-)
The In-Laws '79

Marta Dusseldorp
After the Deluge '03
Innocence '00

Andre Dussollier (1946-)
Private Fears in Public Places '06
Lemming '05
A Very Long Engagement '04
Amelie '01 (N)
Same Old Song '97
Colonel Chabert '94
Love Unto Death '84
Life Is a Bed of Roses '83
Le Beau Mariage '82
Perceval '78
And Now My Love '74

Fred Durst (1970-)
Population 436 '06
Sorry, Haters '05

Ian Dury (1942-2000)
The Crow 2: City of Angels '95
Split Second '92
The Raggedy Rawney '90
Number One '84
Roll '84

Dan Duryea (1907-68)
Five Golden Dragons '67
The Bamboo Saucer '68
The Flight of the Phoenix '65
Platinum High School '60
Battle Hymn '57
Silver Lode '54
Ride Clear of Diablo '54
Thunder Bay '53
Terror Street '53
Winchester '73 '50
The Underworld Story '50
Too Late for Tears '49
Criss Cross '48
Black Angel '46
Scarlet Street '45
The Valley of Decision '45
Lady on a Train '45
Along Came Jones '45
Ministry of Fear '44
None But the Lonely Heart '44
Woman in the Window '44
Great Flamarion '45
Sahara '43
Ball of Fire '41
The Little Foxes '41
The Pride of the Yankees '42

George Duryea
See Tom Keene

Mari Dusay (1936-)
Love Walked In '97
Pendulum '69
Sweet November '68

Jaroslav Dusek (1961-)
Up and Down '04
Divided We Fall '00

Ann Dusenberry (1953-)
Basic Training '86
Long Time Gone '86
The Men's Club '86
Lies '83
Cutter's Way '81
Heart Beat '80
Desperate Women '78
The Possessed '77

Eliza Dushku (1980-)
Sex and Breakfast '07
Wrong Turn '03
City by the Sea '02
The New Guy '02
Soul Survivors '01
Bring It On '00
Race the Sun '96
Journey '95
True Lies '94
That Night '93
This Boy's Life '93
Bye Bye, Love '94
Jay and Silent Bob Strike Back '01

Charles S. Dutton (1951-)
The Bronx Is Burning '07
Honeydripper '07
Against the Ropes '04
Secret Window '04
Gothika '03
Conviction '02
Eye See You '01
Deadlocked '00
For Love or Country: The Arturo Sandoval Story '00
Aftershock: Earthquake in New York '99
Cookie's Fortune '99
Random Hearts '99
The '30s '99
Black Dog '98
Blind Faith '98
Mimic '97
True Women '97
Get on the Bus '96
A Time to Kill '96
Nick of Time '95
Zooman '95
Foreign Student '94
A Low Down Dirty Shame '94
The Piano Lesson '94
Surviving the Game '94
Menace II Society '93
Rudy '93
Alien 3 '92
The Distinguished Gentleman '92
Mississippi Masala '92
Q & A '90
Jacknife '89
An Unremarkable Life '89
Crocodile Dundee 2 '88
The Murder of Mary Phagan '87
Cat's Eye '85

Tim Dutton (1964-)
The Bourne Identity '02
Oliver Twist '99
Darkness Falls '98
Frenchman's Creek '98
St. Ives '98
Melissa '97
Rhodes '96
Tom & Viv '94

Jacques Dutronc (1943-)
Merci pour le Chocolat '00
Place Vendome '98
Van Gogh '92
L'Etat Sauvage '78

Clea DuVall (1977-)
Two Weeks '06
The Grudge '04
Identity '03
21 Grams '03
The Slaughter Rule '01
How to Make a Monster '01
John Carpenter's Ghosts of Mars '01
Thirteen Conversations About One Thing '01
The Astronaut's Wife '99
Girl, Interrupted '99
Committed '99
But I'm a Cheerleader '99
The Faculty '98
Wildflowers '99

Daniel Duval (1944-)
Time to Leave '05
Time of the Wolf '03
Will It Snow for Christmas? '96

Diane Duval
See Julie Bishop

James Duval (1973-)
Mad Cowgirl '06
Roman '06
Chasing Ghosts '05
Window Theory '04
Comic Book Villains '02
May '02
The Doe Boy '01
Donnie Darko '01
Gone in 60 Seconds '00
The Weekend '99
Go '99
SLC Punk! '99
Nowhere '97
Independence Day '96
The Doom Generation '95
Totally F***ed Up '94
Sex, Drugs, and Rock-n-Roll '84

Josey Duval
New York's Finest '87

Maria Duval (1939-)
Samson vs. the Vampire Women '61

Robert Duvall (1931-)
We Own the Night '07
Lucky You '07
Broken Trail '06
Thank You for Smoking '06
Kicking & Screaming '05
Assassination Tango '03
Secondhand Lions '03
Open Range '03
Gods and Generals '03
John Q '02
21 Grams '03
Gone in 60 Seconds '00
A Shot at Glory '00
The 6th Day '00
A Civil Action '98
Deep Impact '98
The Apostle '97
The Gingerbread Man '97
A Family Thing '96
The Man Who Captured Eichmann '96
Phenomenon '96
Sling Blade '96
The Scarlet Letter '95
Something to Talk About '95
The Paper '94
The Stars Fell on Henrietta '94
Falling Down '93
Geronimo: An American Legend '93
Wrestling Ernest Hemingway '93
Newsies '92
Rambling Rose '91
Days of Thunder '90
The Handmaid's Tale '90
Lonesome Dove '89
Colors '88
Hotel Colonial '88
Let's Get Harry '87
Belizaire the Cajun '86
The Lightship '86
The Natural '84
The Stone Boy '84
The Terry Fox Story '83
Tender Mercies '83
True Confessions '81
The Great Santini '80
The Pursuit of D.B. Cooper '81
Apocalypse Now '79
The Betsy '78
Ike '78
Invasion of the Body Snatchers '78
The Eagle Has Landed '77
The Greatest '77
Network '76

The Seven-Per-Cent Solution '76
Breakout '75
The Killer Elite '75
The Conversation '74
The Godfather, Part 2 '74
Badge 373 '73
Lady Ice '73
The Godfather '72
The Great Northfield Minnesota Raid '72
Joe Kidd '72
Tomorrow '72
Lawman '71
THX 1138 '71
M*A*S*H '70
The Rain People '69
True Grit '69
Bullitt '68
Countdown '68
The Detective '68
The Chase '66
Captain Newman, M.D. '63
To Kill a Mockingbird '62

Shelley Duvall (1949-)
The 4th Floor '99
Russell Mulcahy's Tale of the Mummy '99
Boltneck '98
Home Fries '98
My Teacher Ate My Homework '98
Horton Foote's Alone '97
The Twilight of the Ice Nymphs '97
Changing Habits '96
Portrait of a Lady '96
The Underneath '95
Suburban Commando '91
Mother Goose Rock 'n' Rhyme '90
Roxanne '87
Frankenweenie '84
Rapunzel '82
Rumpelstiltskin '82
Time Bandits '81
Popeye '80
The Shining '80
Annie Hall '77
3 Women '77
Nashville '75
Thieves Like Us '74
McCabe & Mrs. Miller '71
Brewster McCloud '70

Wayne Duvall (1958-)
Leatherheads '08
Killing Emmett Young '02
A Better Way to Die '00
O Brother Where Art Thou? '00

Janine Duvitsky (1952-)
Grown Ups '80
Dracula '79

Pierre Dux (1908-90)
La Lectrice '88
La Vie Continue '82
The Day and the Hour '63
Les Grandes Manoeuvres '55
Monsieur Vincent '47

Ann Dvorak (1912-79)
A Life of Her Own '50
Our Very Own '50
Return of Jesse James '50
The Long Night '47
Out of the Blue '47
The Private Affairs of Bel Ami '47
Abilene Town '46
Flame of the Barbary Coast '45
Manhattan Merry-Go-Round '37
"G" Men '35
Massacre '34
The Strange Love of Molly Louvain '32
Three on a Match '32
Scarface '31
The Guardsman '31

Peter Dvorsky
Mesmer '94
The Kiss '88

Videodrome '83

Dorothy Dwan (1906-81)
The Fighting Legion '30
The Peacock Fan '29
Great K & A Train Robbery '26
The Wizard of Oz '25

Earl Dwire (1883-1940)
Purple Vigilantes '38
Lightning Bill Crandall '37
Riding On '37
Trouble in Texas '37
Cavalcade of the West '36
Pinto Rustlers '36
Stormy Trails '36
Assassin of Youth '35
Between Men '35
Big Calibre '35
Lawless Frontier '35
Lawless Range '35
Pecos Kid '35
Rider of the Law '35
Toll of the Desert '35
Wagon Trail '35
The Star Packer '34
Tombstone Terror '34

Bill Dwyer
Little Shots of Happiness '97

Hilary Dwyer (1935-)
Cry of the Banshee '70
Wuthering Heights '70
The Oblong Box '69
The Conqueror Worm '68

Leslie Dwyer (1906-86)
Die, Monster, Die! '65
Black Tide '58
Roadhouse Girl '53
Immortal Battalion '44

Franklin Dyall (1874-1950)
The Private Life of Henry VIII '33
Easy Virtue '27

Valentine Dyall (1908-85)
The Body in the Library '84
The Haunting '63
Horror Hotel '60
Suspended Alibi '56
The Golden Salamander '51
Room to Let '49
The Ghost of Rashmon Hall '47
Brief Encounter '46
Frenzy '46
Pink String and Sealing Wax '45
Henry V '44
Hotel Reserve '44

Cameron Dye (1967-)
The Tavern '00
The Apocalypse '96
Out of the Dark '88
Heated Vengeance '87
Scenes from the Goldmine '87
Stranded '87
Body Rock '84
Joy of Sex '84
The Last Starfighter '84
Valley Girl '83

Dale Dye (1944-)
The Great Raid '05
44 Minutes: The North Hollywood Shootout '03
Missing Brendan '03
Band of Brothers '01
Rules of Engagement '00
Saving Private Ryan '98
Operation Delta Force 2: Mayday '97
Rough Riders '97
Starship Troopers '97
Mission: Impossible '96
Within the Rock '96
Sgt. Bilko '95
Trial and Error '96

Natural Born Killers '94
Outbreak '94
Uncivilized '94
Heaven and Earth '93
Sniper '92
Under Siege '92
Blue Sky '91
JFK '91
Relentless 2: Dead On '91
Servants of Twilight '91
The Court Martial of Jackie Robinson '90
Fire Birds '90
The Fourth War '90
Kid '90
Always '89
Born on the Fourth of July '89
Casualties of War '89
Spontaneous Combustion '89
Billionaire Boys Club '87
Invaders from Mars '86
Platoon '86

John Dye (1963-)
Best of the Best '89
Campus Man '87

Danny Dyer (1977-)
Closure '07
Outlaw '07
Severance '06
High Heels and Low Lifes '01
Mean Machine '01
Borstal Boy '00
Greenfingers '00
Human Traffic '99
The Trench '99

Karen Dyer
Corrupt '99
Urban Menace '99

Russell Dykstra
Introducing the Dwights '07
Romulus, My Father '07
Garage Days '03
Ned Kelly '03
Soft Fruit '99

Matthew Dyktynski
Japanese Story '03
Heaven's Burning '97
Road to Nhill '97
Love and Other Catastrophes '95

Bob Dylan (1941-)
Masked and Anonymous '03
Backtrack '89
Hearts of Fire '87
Pat Garrett & Billy the Kid '73

Peter Dyneley (1921-77)
Soul Patrol '80
The Manster '59
Strange Awakening '58
Beau Brummel '54

Richard Dysart (1929-)
Panther '95
Truman '95
Marilyn & Bobby: Her Final Affair '94
Back to the Future, Part 3 '90
Day One '89
Wall Street '87
L.A. Law '86
The Last Days of Patton '86
The Falcon and the Snowman '85
Mask '85
Pale Rider '85
The Thing '82
Warning Sign '85
Bitter Harvest '81
The People vs. Jean Harris '81
Bogie: The Last Hero '80
Being There '79

Meteor '79
Prophecy '79
Riding with Death '76
The Day of the Locust '75
The Hindenburg '75
The Autobiography of Miss Jane Pittman '74
The Terminal Man '74
The Hospital '71
The Lost Man '69
Petulia '68

Richard Dyszel (1947-)
Night Beast '83
The Alien Factor '78

Alexis Dziena (1984-)
Fool's Gold '08
Sex and Breakfast '07
Broken Flowers '05
Pizza '05
Mimic 3: Sentinel '03

George Dzundza (1945-)
National Lampoon's Adam & Eve '05
City by the Sea '02
Above Suspicion '00
Instinct '99
Species 2 '98
Trading Favors '97
The Limbic Region '96
That Darn Cat '96
Crimson Tide '95
Dangerous Minds '95
The Enemy Within '94
Basic Instinct '92
The Butcher's Wife '91
Impulse '90
White Hunter, Black Heart '90
The Beast '88
Glory Years '87
No Way Out '87
Broken Badge '85
Brotherly Love '85
Best Defense '84
Act of Passion: The Lost Honor of Kathryn Beck '83
Streamers '83
A Long Way Home '81
The Deer Hunter '78
Loose in New York '74

Sheila E (1957-)
The Adventures of Ford Fairlane '90
Krush Groove '85

Nicholas Eadie (1958-)
Celia: Child of Terror '89
Return to Snowy River '88

Angela Eads
Things 2 '97

George Eads (1967-)
Dead Girls '90
Monte Walsh '03
The Spring '00

James Eagles (1907-59)
Heroes of the Hills '38
Sunset Range '35

Michael Ealy (1973-)
November '05
Sleeper Cell '05
Barbershop 2: Back in Business '04
Never Die Alone '04
2 Fast 2 Furious '03
Barbershop '02

Edward Earle (1882-1972)
Command Decision '48
I Accuse My Parents '45
Bordertown Gunfighters '43
California Joe '43
The Duke of West Point '38
The Revenge Rider '35
Spite Marriage '29
The Wind '28

Harry Earles (1902-85)
Freaks '32
The Unholy Three '30
The Unholy Three '25

Bo Eason
Tornado! '96

Miami Rhapsody '95

Carlos East (1942-94)
Fearmaker '89
Fantastic Balloon Voyage '76
The Fear Chamber '68
The Snake People '68

Jeff East (1957-)
Another Chance '88
Pumpkinhead '88
Deadly Blessing '81
Mary and Joseph: A Story of Faith '79
Summer of Fear '78
The Campus Corpse '77
Flight of the Grey Wolf '76
Huckleberry Finn '74
Tom Sawyer '73

Leslie Easterbrook (1951-)
A Dead Calling '06
The Devil's Rejects '05
The Biggest Fan '02
Police Academy 7: Mission to Moscow '94
Police Academy 6: City under Siege '89
Police Academy 5: Assignment Miami Beach '88
Police Academy 3: Back in Training '86
Police Academy '84
Private Resort '84

Steve Eastin
When a Stranger Calls '06
A Man Apart '03
Matchstick Men '03
Catch Me If You Can '02
Agent Red '00
Peril '00
Stealth Fighter '99
Last Man Standing '95

Todd Eastland
Mommy 2: Mommy's Day '96
Pledge Night '90

George Eastman (1854-1932)
Hands of Steel '86
After the Fall of New York '85
Blastfighter '85
Detective School Dropouts '85
Ironmaster '82
Grim Reaper '81
Bloody Avenger '80
Belle Starr '79
Call of the Wild '72
Kiss Me, Kill Me '69

Rodney Eastman (1967-)
The Caveman's Valentine '01
Sand '00
Blue Ridge Fall '99
Beverly Hills Bodysnatchers '89
Deadly Weapon '88
A Nightmare on Elm Street 4: Dream Master '88
A Nightmare on Elm Street 3: Dream Warriors '87

Michael Easton (1967-)
The '70s '00

Richard Easton (1933-)
Pizza '05
Dead Again '91
Henry V '89

Robert Easton (1930-)
Just One Night '00
Working Girl '88
The Giant Spider Invasion '75
Heavy Traffic '73

Johnny Got His Gun '71
When Hell Broke Loose '58
Belles on Their Toes '52

Sheena Easton (1959-)
All Dogs Go to Heaven 2 '95 (V)
Body Bags '93
Indecent Proposal '93

Alison Eastwood (1972-)
How to Go Out on a Date in Queens '06
Don't Tell '05
The Lost Angel '04
Poolhall Junkies '02
Power Play '02
If You Only Knew '00
The Spring '00
Black & White '99
Friends & Lovers '99
Just a Little Harmless Sex '99
Breakfast of Champions '98
Midnight in the Garden of Good and Evil '97
Tightrope '84

Clint Eastwood (1930-)
Million Dollar Baby '04
Blood Work '02
Space Cowboys '00
True Crime '99
Absolute Power '97
The Bridges of Madison County '95
Casper '95
In the Line of Fire '93
A Perfect World '93
Unforgiven '92
The Rookie '90
White Hunter, Black Heart '90
Pink Cadillac '89
The Dead Pool '88
Heartbreak Ridge '86
Pale Rider '85
City Heat '84
Tightrope '84
Sudden Impact '83
Firefox '82
Honkytonk Man '82
Any Which Way You Can '80
Bronco Billy '80
Escape from Alcatraz '79
Every Which Way But Loose '78
Dirty Harry '71
Play Misty for Me '71
The Beguiled '70
Kelly's Heroes '70
Two Mules for Sister Sara '70
The Gauntlet '77
The Enforcer '76
The Outlaw Josey Wales '76
The Eiger Sanction '75
Thunderbolt & Lightfoot '74
High Plains Drifter '73
Magnum Force '73
Joe Kidd '72
Hang 'Em High '67
For a Few Dollars More '65
A Fistful of Dollars '64
Lafayette Escadrille '58
Escapade in Japan '57
Away All Boats '56
Francis in the Navy '55
Revenge of the Creature '55
Tarantula '55

Jayne (Jane) Eastwood (1946-)
You Kill Me '07
Wedding Wars '06
Dawn of the Dead '04
Life with Judy Garland—Me and My Shadows '01
That Old Feeling '96
Hostile Takeover '88

Kidnapping of Baby John Doe '88
Night Friend '87
My Pleasure Is My Business '74

Kyle Eastwood (1968-)
Honkytonk Man '82
The Outlaw Josey Wales '76

Marjorie Eaton (1901-86)
Street Music '81
The Attic '80
The Atomic Brain '64
Night Tide '63

Mary Eaton (1901-48)
Glorifying the American Girl '30

Roberta Eaton
The Cocoanuts '29

Shirley Eaton (1936-)
Around the World Under the Sea '65
Eight on the Lam '67
Kiss and Kill '68
The Naked Truth '58
Girl Hunters '63
Goldfinger '64
What a Carve-Up! '62
Carry On Nurse '59
Doctor at Large '57
Doctor in the House '53

Wallace (Wallas) Eaton (1917-95)
Isadora '68
Plunge Into Darkness '77

Christine Ebersole (1953-)
Double Platinum '99
True Crime '99
My Favorite Martian '98
An Unexpected Life '97
Black Sheep '96
My Girl 2 '94
Richie Rich '94
Gypsy '93
Folks! '92
Dead Again '91
Ghost Dad '90
Mac and Me '88
Acceptable Risks '86
Amadeus '84
Tootsie '82

Buddy Ebsen (1908-2003)
The Beverly Hillbillies '93
Stone Fox '87
The Return of the Beverly Hillbillies '81
The Bastard '78
The Adventures of Tom Sawyer '73
The President's Plane Is Missing '71
The Andersonville Trial '70
The One and Only, Genuine, Original Family Band '68
The Interns '62
Breakfast at Tiffany's '61
Attack! '56
Between Heaven and Hell '56
Davy Crockett and the River Pirates '56
Davy Crockett, King of the Wild Frontier '55
Red Garters '54
Rodeo King and the Senorita '51
Silver City Bonanza '51
Thunder in God's Country '51
Sing Your Worries Away '42

Eriq Ebouaney
Femme Fatale '02
Lumumba '00

Maude Eburne (1875-1960)
The Boogie Man Will Get You '42
The Border Legion '40
Courageous Dr. Christian '40
Doughnuts & Society '36
Ruggles of Red Gap '35
Ladies They Talk About '33
Panama Flo '32
The Vampire Bat '32
The Guardsman '31

Aimee (Amy) Eccles (1949-)
Humanoid Defender '85
Lovelines '84
The Concrete Jungle '82
Group Marriage '72
Little Big Man '70

Christopher Eccleston (1964-)
The Seeker: The Dark Is Rising '07
28 Days Later '02
Othello '01
The Others '01
Gone in 60 Seconds '00
eXistenZ '99
Heart '99
Elizabeth '98
A Price above Rubies '97
Jude '96
'95
Shallow Grave '94
Cracker: To Be a Somebody '94
Let Him Have It '91

Alonso Echanove (1954-)
'93

Juan Echanove (1961-)
No News from God '01
The Flower of My Secret '95
In the Middle of Nowhere '93

Emilio Echeverria
The Alamo '04
Die Another Day '02
Amores Perros '00

Jean-Philippe Ecoffey (1959-)
Cold Showers '05
From the Terrace '60
Ma Vie en Rose '97

Billy Eckstine (1914-93)
Jo Jo Dancer, Your Life Is Calling '86
Skirts Ahoy! '52

Aaron Eckhart (1968-)
In the Company of Men '96
Your Friends & Neighbors '98
Thursday '98
Molly '99
Any Given Sunday '99
Nurse Betty '00
Erin Brockovich '00
The Pledge '01
Possession '02
Paycheck '03
The Missing '03
The Core '03
Suspect Zero '04
Women '05
Conversations with Other Women '05
Thank You for Smoking '06
The Black Dahlia '06
No Reservations '07
The Dark Knight '08

James Eckhouse (1955-)
Jimmy & Judy '06
One True Thing '98
Robin Cook's Terminal '96

Guy Ecker (1959-)
Night Terror '06
Devil Wears White '86

Gregg Edelman (1958-)
Green Card '90
Little Children '06

Herb Edelman (1930-)
Cracking Up '83
On the Right Track '81
Strike Force '81
A Cry for Love '80
Marathon '80
Goin' Coconuts '78
Special Olympics '78
Charge of the Model T's '76
The Yakuza '75
The Way We Were '73
I Love You, Alice B. Toklas! '68
The Odd Couple '68
Barefoot in the Park '67

Alfred Edel (1932-93)
Terror 2000 '92
My Father Is Coming '91

Barbara Eden (1934-)
Loco Love '03
A Very Brady Sequel '96
Lethal Charm '90
Chattanooga Choo Choo '84
Return of the Rebels '81
Harper Valley P.T.A. '78
How to Break Up a Happy Divorce '76
The Amazing Dobermans '76
The Stranger Within '74
The Woman Hunter '72
7 Faces of Dr. Lao '64
The Brass Bottle '63
Ride the Wild Surf '64
Flaming Star '60
From the Terrace '60
Voyage to the Bottom of the Sea '61
The Wonderful World of the Brothers Grimm '62
Five Weeks in a Balloon '62

Lisa Edelstein (1966-)
Grilled '06
Say Uncle '05
Dean Koontz's Black River '01
Keeping the Faith '00
What Women Want '00

Bobby Edner (1988-)
Welcome to Paradise '07
Spy Kids 3-D: Game Over '03

Adrian Edmondson
Miss Austen Regrets '07
Supergrass '87

Elizabeth Edmonds
Experience Preferred... But Not Essential '83

Dartanyan Edmonds (1972-)
Deliver Us from Eva '03
Rangers '00
Ride '98

Louis Edmonds (1923-2001)
Next Year in Jerusalem '98
House of Dark Shadows '70

Beatie Edney (1962-)
Highlander: Endgame '00
The Affair '95
'93
In the Name of the Father '93
Mister Johnson '91
Diary of a Mad Old Man '88
Highlander '86

Valerie Edmond (1969-)
Saving Grace '00
Love and Rage '99
One More Kiss '99

Jerome (Jerry Stallion) Eden
The Defilers '65
2000 Maniacs '64
Color Me Blood Red '64
Blood Feast '63

Paul Eddington (1927-95)
The Camomile Lawn '92
The Devil Rides Out '68

Helen Jerome Eddy (1897-1990)
Klondike Annie '36
A Shot in the Dark '35
The Country Kid '23
The County Fair '20
Pollyanna '20
The Tong Man '19
Rebecca of Sunnybrook Farm '17

Mark Eden (1928-)
The Crimson Cult '68
Doctor Zhivago '65
Seance on a Wet Afternoon '64

Harry Eden (1990-)
Oliver Twist '05
Pure '02

Nelson Eddy (1901-67)
Northwest Outpost '47
The Phantom of the Opera '43
I Married an Angel '42
Bitter Sweet '40
New Moon '40
Balalaika '39
Let Freedom Ring '39
Girl of the Golden West '38
Sweethearts '38
Rosalie '38
Maytime '37
Rose Marie '36
Naughty Marietta '35
Dancing Lady '33

Richard Eden (1956-)
Whitewash: The Clarence Brandley Story '02
Undercover Angel '99
Public Enemies '96
Liberty & Bash '90
Let It Ride '89

Robert Edeson (1868-1931)
King of Kings '27
Walking Back '28
Braveheart '25
On the Night Stage '15
Kinky Boots '06
King Arthur '04
Ned Kelly '03

George Edgely
Common Law Wife '63

Joel Edgerton (1974-)
Smokin' Aces '07
King Arthur '04
The Hard Word '02
Erskineville Kings '99

Allan Edwall (1924-97)
The Sacrifice '86
Fanny and Alexander '83
Brothers Lionheart '77
The New Land '73
The Emigrants '72

Anthony Edwards (1962-)
The Forgotten '04
Thunderbirds '04
Northfork '03
Jackpot '01
Playing by Heart '98
In Cold Blood '96
Charlie's Ghost: The Secret of Coronado '94
The Client '94
Hometown Boy Makes Good '90
Downtown '90
El Diablo '90
Delta Heat '92
Landslide '92
Pet Sematary 2 '92
Miracle Mile '89
Hawks '89
How I Got into College '89
Mr. North '88
Summer Heat '87
Revenge of the Nerds 2: Nerds in Paradise '87
Gotcha! '85
The Sure Thing '85
Revenge of the Nerds '84
Heart Like a Wheel '83
Fast Times at Ridgemont High '82

Richard Edson (1954-)
The Kid and I '05
Frankenfish '04
Land of Plenty '04
Starsky & Hutch '04
Destiny Turns on the Radio '95
Jury Duty '95
Strange Days '95
Super Mario Bros. '93
Posse '93
Joey Breaker '93
Eight Men Out '88
Tougher Than Leather '88
Good Morning, Vietnam '87
Ferris Bueller's Day Off '86
Howard the Duck '86
Platoon '86
Do the Right Thing '89
Desperately Seeking Susan '85
Stranger Than Paradise '84

Bruce Edwards (1914-2002)
Federal Agents vs. Underworld, Inc. '49
The Black Widow '47
Queen of the Amazons '47
The Fallen Sparrow '43
Hitler: Dead or Alive '43
The Iron Major '43

Cliff Edwards (1895-1971)
Fun & Fancy Free '47
Sagebrush Law '43
Dumbo '41 (V)
His Girl Friday '40 (V)
Pinocchio '40 (V)
Gone with the Wind '39 (V)
Girl of the Golden West '38
Saratoga '37
Rec Salute '35
Dance Fools Dance '31
Laughing Sinners '31
Parlor, Bedroom and Bath '31
Doughboys '30

Edward Edwards
A Perfect Little Murder '90
Jesse Stone: Death in Paradise '06
Noriega: God's Favorite '00
The Sin of Madelon Claudet '31

Gail Edwards
A Perfect Little Murder '90

Glynn Edwards (1931-)
Get Carter '71
Zulu '64
'62

Henry Edwards (1882-1952)
The Golden Salamander '50
Madeleine '50
'51

Hilton Edwards (1903-82)
Victim '61
Othello '52

James Edwards (1918-70)
Patton '70
The Manchurian Candidate '62
Pork Chop Hill '59
Men in War '57
The Killing '56
The Member of the Wedding '52
The Steel Helmet '51
Home of the Brave '49
The Set-Up '49

Jennifer Edwards (1959-)
Overexposed '90
All's Fair '89
Peter Gunn '89
Perfect Match '88
Sunset '88
That's Life! '86
The Man Who Loved Women '83
S.O.B. '81
Heidi '67

Lance Edwards
A Woman, Her Men and Her Futon '92
Peacemaker '90

Luke Edwards (1980-)
Cheaters '00
Little Big League '94
Mother's Boys '94
Newsies '92
Guilty by Suspicion '91
The Wizard '89

Mark Edwards (1942-)
Tower of Evil '72
Blood from the Mummy's Tomb '71
The Bloodiest Job in the West '71

Megan Edwards
Tattoo, a Love Story '02
Poison Ivy 3: The New Seduction '97

Richard Edson (1954-)

Barbara (Lee) Edwards (1960-)
House Party 3 '94
Another Chance '88
Malibu Express '85

Bill Edwards (1918-99)
War Lover '62
First Man into Space '59
Ladies of the Chorus '49

Meredith Edwards (1917-99)
A Christmas Reunion '93
The Electronic Monster '57
Race for Life '55
The Gambler & the Lady '52

Penny Edwards (1928-98)
Heart of the Rockies '51
North of the Great Divide '50
Sunset in the West '50
Trail of Robin Hood '50

Ronnie Clair Edwards (1933-)
8 Seconds '94
A Day for Thanks on Walton's Mountain '82
Future Cop '76

Sam Edwards (1915-2004)

Snitz Edwards (1862-1937)
April Fool 26
Battling Butler 26
The Phantom of the Opera 25
Seven Chances 25
The Thief of Baghdad '24

Stacy Edwards (1965-)
Superbad '07
Joshua '02
Local Boys '02
Driven '01
The Gumshoe Kid '89
Cellar Dweller '87
The Dirty Dozen: The Deadly Mission '87
Return to Horror High '87

Vince Edwards (1926-96)
The Fear '94
Jailbreakers '94
Dillinger '91
Motorama '91
Original Intent '91
To Die For 2: Son of Darkness '91
Andy and the Airwave Rangers '89 *
Desperados '69
The Mad Bomber '72
The Devil's Brigade '68
The Victors '63
The Three Faces of Eve '57
The Killing '56
Sailor Beware '52

Zac Efron (1987-)
Hairspray '07
High School Musical 2 '07
High School Musical '06
The Derby Stallion '05

Marshall Efron (1938-)
Home on the Range '04 (V)
First Time '82
Is There Sex After Death? '71

Aeryk Egan
The Secret Life of Girls '99

Christopher Egan (1984-)
Resident Evil: Extinction '07
Alpha Male '06
Eragon '06

Eddie Egan (1930-95)
Out of the Darkness '85
Badge 373 '73
The French Connection '71

Peter Egan (1946-)
Death at a Funeral '07
The Wedding Date '05
A Perfect Spy '88
A Woman of Substance '84
Lillie '79
Hennessy '75
Cold Comfort Farm '71
One Brief Summer '70

Richard Egan (1921-87)
Mission to Glory '80
Sweet Creek County War '79
The Amsterdam Kill '78
The 300 Spartans '62
Esther and the King '60
Pollyanna '60
A Summer Place '59
The Hunters '58
Love Me Tender '56
Tension at Table Rock '56
Seven Cities of Gold '55
Underwater! '55
Demetrius and the Gladiators '54
Split Second '53
Blackbeard the Pirate '52
One Minute to Zero '52
Flame of Araby '51
The Damned Don't Cry '50

Susan Egan (1970-)
Spirited Away '01 (V)
Man of the Century '99
Hercules '97 (V)

Will Egan
Ninja Academy '90
Glitch! 88

Julie Ege (1943-)
Craze '74
It's Not the Size That Counts '74
The Freakmaker '73
The Legend of the 7 Golden Vampires '73
Rentadick '72
Creatures the World Forgot '70
On Her Majesty's Secret Service '69

Tamsin Egerton (1988-)
The Marine '06
Driving Lessons '06
Keeping Mum '05

Samantha Eggar (1939-)
The Astronaut's Wife '99
Hercules '97 (V)
The Phantom '96
Inevitable Grace '94
The Magic Voyage '93 (V)
Dark Horse '92
Round Numbers '91
Tales of the Unexpected '91
Ragin' Cajun '90
Curtains '83
Hot Touch '82
Demonoid, Messenger of Death 81
Exterminator '80
Unknown Powers '80
The Brood '79
Why Shoot the Teacher 79
Battleforce '78
The Uncanny '78
Welcome to Blood City '77
The Seven-Per-Cent Solution '76
All the Kind Strangers '74
Man of Destiny '73
Dead Are Alive '72
Light at the Edge of the World 71
Molly Maguires '70
A Name for Evil '70
Doctor Dolittle '67
Walk, Don't Run '66
The Collector '65
Doctor in Distress '63

Nicole Eggert (1972-)
Dead Lenny '06
Submerged '00
The Demolitionist '95
Amanda and the Alien '95
Anything for Love '93
Blown Away '93
Just One of the Girls '93
The Double O Kid '92
The Haunting of Morella '91
When Hell Was in Session '82

Martha Eggerth (1912-)
For Me and My Gal '42
Charm of La Boheme '36

Stan(ford) Egi
Paradise Road '97
Escape Clause '96
Golden Gate '93
Rising Sun '93
Come See the Paradise '90
Hiroshima: Out of the Ashes '90

Atom Egoyan (1960-)
The Stupids '95
Calendar '93

Jennifer Ehle (1969-)
That Russell Girl '08
Alpha Male '06
The River King '05
Possession '02
Sunshine '99
Melissa '97
Paradise Road '97
Wilde '97
Pride and Prejudice '95
Backbeat '94
The Camomile Lawn '92

Jerome Ehlers (1958-)
The Marine '06
Fatal Bond '91
Darlings of the Gods '90
Quigley Down Under '90
Grim Prairie Tales '89
Opposing Force '87
Blind Justice '86
Wildrose '85
Weather in the Streets '84
Cutter's Way '81
The Europeans '79
Yanks '79

Gard B. Eidsvold (1966-)
Zero Degrees Kelvin '95
The Last Lieutenant '94

Christopher Eigeman (1965-)
The Treatment '06
Crazy Little Thing '02
Maid in Manhattan '02
The Next Big Thing '02
Path to War '02
The Last Days of Disco '98
Mr. Jealousy '98
Highball '97
Kicking and Screaming '95
Barcelona '94
Metropolitan '90

David Eigenberg (1964-)
Sex and the City: The Movie '08
Love, Ludlow '05
Garfield: The Movie '04 (V)
The Mothman Prophecies '02
Daybreak '93

Jill Eikenberry (1946-)
Manna from Heaven '02
My Very Best Friend '96
Parallel Lives '94
Chantilly Lace '93
An Inconvenient Woman '91
Cast the First Stone '89
Assault and Matrimony '87
Family Sins '87
L.A. Law '86
The Manhattan Project '86
Grace Quigley '84
Sessions '83
Arthur '81
Hide in Plain Sight '80
Butch and Sundance: The Early Days '79
Orphan Train '79
Rich Kids '79
Between the Lines '77
Rush It '77

Cynthia Eilbacher (1958-)
Thunder Alley '85
The Big Bounce '69

Lisa Eilbacher (1957-)
Live Wire '92
Blind Man's Bluff '91
The Hunt for the Night Stalker '91
The Last Samurai '90
Never Say Die '90
Leviathan '89
Deadly Intent '88
Monte Carlo '86
Beverly Hills Cop '84
Ten to Midnight '83
An Officer and a Gentleman '82
On the Right Track '81
To Race the Wind '80
Run for the Roses '78
The Amazing Spider-Man '77

Sally Eilers (1908-78)
Coroner Creek '48
Strange Illusion '45
Strike Me Pink '36
Without Orders '36
The Black Camel '31
Clearing the Range '31
Doughboys '30
Roaring Ranch '30
Trigger Tricks '30

Bob Einstein (1940-)
Ocean's Thirteen '07
The Extreme Adventures of Super Dave '98
Modern Romance '81

Aron Eisenberg (1969-)
Pterodactyl Woman from Beverly Hills '97
Playroom '90
The Horror Show '89

Hallie Kate Eisenberg (1992-)
Wild Child '08
How to Eat Fried Worms '06
A Little Inside '01
Beautiful '00
The Miracle Worker '00
Bicentennial Man '99
The Insider '99
Paulie '98

Jesse Eisenberg (1983-)
The Hunting Party '07
The Squid and the Whale '05
Cursed '04
The Emperor's Club '02
Roger Dodger '02

Ned Eisenberg (1957-)
Dash and Lilly '99
Path to Paradise '97
Last Man Standing '96
The Burning '82

Ike Eisenmann (1962-)
The Bastard '78
Devil Dog: The Hound of Hell '78
Return from Witch Mountain '78
Terror Out of the Sky '78
Banjo Hackett '76
Escape to Witch Mountain '75

Debra Eisenstadt
The Heidi Chronicles '95
Oleanna '94

Andre Eisermann (1967-)
Brother of Sleep '95
Kaspar Hauser '93

Anthony Eisley (1925-2003)
Monster '78
Secrets '77
Dracula vs. Frankenstein '71
The Tormentors '71
The Witchmaker '69
Star! '68
Journey to the Center of Time '67
Lightning Bolt '67
Mummy & Curse of the Jackal '67
Navy vs. the Night Monsters '66
Frankie and Johnny '65
Naked Kiss '64
The Wasp Woman '59

David Eisner
Family Reunion '88
Happy Birthday to Me '81

Felix Eittner (1967-)
The Tunnel '01
The Trio '97

Chiwetel Ejiofor (1976-)
Redbelt '08
American Gangster '07
Talk to Me '07
Children of Men '06
Inside Man '06
Kinky Boots '06
Four Brothers '05
Serenity '05
Slow Burn '05
She Hate Me '04
Dirty Pretty Things '03
Love Actually '03
I Want You '98
Metro '96

Carmen Ejogo (1975-)
The Brave One '07
Boycott '02
What's the Worst That Could Happen? '01
Love's Labour's Lost '00
Sally Hemings: An American Scandal '00
The Avengers '98
Catherine Cookson's Colour Blind '98
Three Blind Mice '02

Anita Ekberg (1931-)
The Red Dwarf '99
Intervista '92
Gold of the Amazon Women '79
S*H*E '79
We All Loved Each Other So Much '77
Northeast of Seoul '72
The Cobra '68
Fangs of the Living Dead '68
Woman Times Seven '67
How I Learned to Love Women '66
The Alphabet Murders '65
Call Me Bwana '63
Four for Texas '63
Bocaccio '70 '62
La Dolce Vita '60
The Mongols '60
Paris Holiday '57
Back from Eternity '56
Hollywood or Bust '56
War and Peace '56
Artists and Models '55
Blood Alley '55
Abbott and Costello Go to Mars '53

Britt Ekland (1942-)
The Children '90
Cold Heat '90
Scandal '89
Beverly Hills Vamp '88
Moon in Scorpio '86
Erotic Images 85
Fraternity Vacation '85
Marbella '85
The Monster Club '85
Ecstasy 84
Dead Wrong '83
Demon Rage '82
The Hostage Tower '80
The Great Wallendas '78
Sex on the Run '78
Slayers '77
High Velocity '76
King Solomon's Treasure '76
Royal Flash 75
The Wicker Man '75
The Man with the Golden Gun '74
The Ultimate Thrill '74
Asylum '72
What the Peeper Saw '72
Endless Night '71
Get Carter '71
The Night They Raided Minsky's '69
Stiletto '69
The Bobo 67
After the Fox '66

Michael Eklund
BloodRayne 2: Deliverance '07
House of the Dead '03
We'll Meet Again '02

Gosta Ekman (1890-1938)
Intermezzo '36
Swedenhielms '35
Faust 26

Gosta Ekman, Jr. (1939-)
The Inside Man 84
The Adventures of Picasso '80

Hasse (Hans) Ekman (1915-2004)
Devil's Wanton '49
Intermezzo '36

Nour (el-Sherif) el-Cherif (1946-)
Destiny '97

Jack Elam (1916-2003)
An Egyptian Story '82
Bonanza: The Return '93
Uninvited '93
Shadow Force '92
Suburban Commando '91
Big Bad John '90
Dynamite and Gold 88
Hawken's Breed '87
The Aurora Encounter '85
Cannonball Run 2 '84
Lost '83
Sacred Ground '83
Cannonball Run '81
The Apple Dumpling Gang Rides Again '79
The Sacketts '79
The Villain '79
Norseman '78
Grayeagle '77
Creature from Black Lake '76
Pony Express Rider '76
The Red Pony '76
Huckleberry Finn '75
Hannie Caulder '72
Support Your Local Gunfighter '71
Rio Lobo '70
Over the Hill Gang '69

Support Your Local Sheriff '69
Firecreek '68
Never a Dull Moment '68
Once Upon a Time in the West '68
The Way West '67
The Rare Breed '66
Kiss Me Deadly '55
The Man from Laramie '55
Cattle Queen of Montana '54
Ride Clear of Diablo '54
'Vera Cruz '53
The Bushwackers '52
Kansas City Confidential '52
Rancho Notorious '52
The Ring '52
High Lonesome '50
Rawhide '50
Ticket to Tomahawk '50
She Shoulda Said No '49

Idris Elba (1972-)
American Gangster '07
Daddy's Little Girls '07
The Reaping '07
This Christmas '07
28 Weeks Later '07
The Gospel '05
Sometimes in April '05
Ultraviolet '98

Vincent Elbaz
The 4 Musketeers '05
Almost Peaceful '02

Dana Elcar (1927-2005)
Inside Out '91
Toughlove '85
All of Me '84
Code of Honor '84
Blue Skies Again '83
Forbidden Love '82
Help Wanted: Male '82
Condorman '81
The Nude Bomb '80
Missiles of October '74
Dying Room Only '73
The Fool Killer '65
The Learning Tree '69
Fireball Forward '72
A Gunfight '71
Adam at 6 a.m. '70
Soldier Blue '70

Ron Eldard (1965-)
Diggers '06
Already Dead '07
Freedomland '05
Ghost Ship '02
House of Sand and Fog '03
Just a Kiss '02
Black Hawk Down '01
Mystery, Alaska '99
The Runner '99
Deep Impact '98
When Trumpets Fade '98
Delivered '98
Bastard out of Carolina '96
The Last Supper '96
Sleepers '96
Sex and the Other Man '95
Scent of a Woman '92
Drop Dead Fred '91
True Love '89

Take Me Back to Oklahoma '40

George Eldredge (1914-92)
An Annapolis Story '55
Hi-Jacked '50
Sonora Stagecoach '44
Sherlock Holmes and the Secret Weapon '42
Buzzy Rides the Range '40
Mom & Dad '47

Kevin Eldon (1960-)
Hot Fuzz '07
High Heels and Low Lifes '01

Florence Eldridge (1901-88)
Inherit the Wind '60
Christopher Columbus '49
Mary of Scotland '36
Les Misérables '35

John Eldridge (1917-60)
I Married a Monster from Outer Space '58
Square Dance Jubilee '51
Bad Men of the Border '45

Jenna Elfman (1971-)
Touched '05
Clifford's Really Big Movie '04 (V)
Looney Tunes: Back in Action '03
Keeping the Faith '00
EDtv '99
Can't Hardly Wait '98
Krippendorf's Tribe '98

Danny Elfman (1953-)
Tim Burton's Corpse Bride '05 (V)
Forbidden Zone '80
The Nightmare before Christmas '93 (V)

Bodhi (Pine) Elfman (1969-)
Collateral '04
The Celestine Prophecy '06
Coyote Waits '03
The Princess Diaries 2: Royal Engagement '04
Keeping the Faith '00
Gone in 60 Seconds '00
Sand '00
The Mod Squad '99
The Princess Diaries '01
The Pirates of Silicon Valley '99
Enemy of the State '98

Sandor Eles (1936-2002)
And Soon the Darkness '70
The Evil of Frankenstein '64

Erika Eleniak (1969-)
Chasers '94
Girl in the Cadillac '94
The Beverly Hillbillies '93
Under Siege '92
Broken Angel '88

Karra Elejalde (1960-)
Tierra '95
Running Out of Time '94
Lady Jayne Killer '03
He Sees You When You're Sleeping '02
Shakedown '02
Love Actually '03
American Pie 2 '01
Jay and Silent Bob Strike Back '01
13 Ghosts '01
Tomcats '01
Scary Movie '00
Seamless '00
American Pie '99
Dish Dogs '98

Carmen Electra (1972-)
Meet the Spartans '08
Epic Movie '07
Full of It '07
Date Movie '06
Hot Tamale '06
Scary Movie 4 '06
Cheaper by the Dozen 2 '05
Dirty Love '05
Getting Played '05
Searching for Bobby D '05
Starsky & Hutch '04
My Boss's Daughter '03
Get Over It! '01
Perfume '01
Sol Goode '01
Scary Movie '00

Nicholas Elia
When a Man Falls in the Forest '07
White Noise '05

Alix Elias
Munchies '87
True Stories '86
Citizens Band '77

Hector Elias
Envy '04
Buddy Boy '99

Christine Elise (1965-)
The Hit '01
Nowhere to Land '00
Escape from Mars '99
Boiling Point '93
Child's Play 2 '90

Kimberly Elise (1971-)
Pride '07
Diary of a Mad Black Woman '05
The Manchurian Candidate '04
Woman, Thou Art Loosed '04
John Q '02
Bojangles '01
Bait '00
The Loretta Claiborne Story '00
Beloved '98
Set It Off '96

Arie Elias (1921-)
Bonjour Monsieur Shlomi '03
James' Journey to Jerusalem '03

Jeremie Elkaim
Come Undone '00

Ronit Elkabetz (1966-)
The Band's Visit '07
Or (My Treasure) '04
Late Marriage '01

Harry Ellerbe (1901-92)
The Fall of the House of Usher '60
Desk Set '57

Taina Elg (1930-)
Hercules in New York '70
The Bacchantes '63
Les Girls '57
Diane '55
The Prodigal '55

Nicholas Elia
When a Man Falls in the Forest '07

Duke Ellington (1899-1974)
Anatomy of a Murder '59
Cabin in the Sky '43
Check & Double Check '30

Shannon Elizabeth (1973-)
The Kid and I '05
Cursed '04
Johnson Family Vacation '04
Love Actually '03
American Pie 2 '01
Jay and Silent Bob Strike Back '01
13 Ghosts '01
Tomcats '01
Scary Movie '00
Seamless '00
American Pie '99
Dish Dogs '98

Hector Elizondo (1936-)
Georgia Rule '07
Love in the Time of Cholera '07
Music Within '07
Raising Helen '04
The Princess Diaries 2: Royal Engagement '04
How High '01
The Princess Diaries '01
Tortilla Soup '01
Entropy '99
Runaway Bride '99
Safe House '98
The Other Sister '98
Dear God '96
Being Human '94
Beverly Hills Cop 3 '94
The Flamingo Kid '84
Exit to Eden '94
Backstreet Justice '94
Chains of Gold '92
Samantha '92

Jane Elliot (1947-)
The Dark '79
The Hard Ride '71
Pork Chop Hill '59
House of Bamboo '55
Change of Habit '69

Biff (Elliott) Elliot (1923-)
I, the Hard Case '...
The Dark '79

Shawn Elliot
Honkytonk Nights '78
Roadie '80

Ramblin' Jack Elliot (1931-)
The Assassination of Jesse James by the Coward Robert Ford '07

Alison Elliott (1970-)
Hurricane Streets '96
Indictment: The McMartin Trial '95
The Spitfire Grill '95
The Buccaneers '95
The Underneath '95
The Wings of the Dove '97
The Eternal '99
Wyatt Earp '94
Home Before Midnight '84

Beverley Elliott
Voyage of the Damned '76
We'll Meet Again '02
My Very Best Friend '96

Chris Elliott (1960-)
Scary Movie 4 '06
Osmosis Jones '01
Scary Movie 2 '01
The Nutty Professor 2: The Klumps '00
Snow Day '00
There's Something about Mary '98
Kingpin '96
Cabin Boy '94
CB4: The Movie '93
Groundhog Day '93
The Abyss '89
New York Stories '89
Manhunter '86

Bob Elliott (1923-)
Cabin Boy '94
Quick Change '90

David Elliott
Ali '01
Pearl '78

David James Elliott (1960-)
Delaney '72
The Possession of Joel Delaney '72
Dodson's Journey '01
Clockwatchers '97
Holiday Affair '96
Degree of Guilt '95
JAG '95
Lethal Charm '90

Denholm Elliott (1922-92)
Catherine Cookson's The Black Candle '92
Noises Off '92
Scorchers '92
One Against the Wind '91
Toy Soldiers '91
A Murder of Quality '90
Indiana Jones and the Last Crusade '89
Deep Cover '88
Hanna's War '88
September '88
Stealing Heaven '88
Maurice '87
Over Indulgence '87
Hotel du Lac '86
A Room with a View '86
Bleak House '85
Defense of the Realm '85
Transmutations '85
A Private Function '84
The Razor's Edge '84
The Hound of the Baskervilles '83
Trading Places '83
The Wicked Lady '83
Brimstone & Treacle '82
The Missionary '82
The Two Faces of Evil '82
Raiders of the Lost Ark '81
Rude Awakening '81
Cuba '79
Saint Jack '79
Zulu Dawn '79
The Boys from Brazil '78
Watership Down '78 (V)
A Bridge Too Far '77
The Hound of the Baskervilles '77
Robin and Marian '76
To the Devil, a Daughter '76
Voyage of the Damned '76
Russian Roulette '75
The Apprenticeship of Duddy Kravitz '74
It's Not the Size That Counts '74
A Doll's House '73
Vault of Horror '73
The House that Dripped Blood '71
Too Late the Hero '70
The Night They Raided Minsky's '69
Dr. Jekyll and Mr. Hyde '68
Strange Case of Dr. Jekyll & Mr. Hyde '68
Alfie '66
King Rat '65
Holy Terror '65
The Leather Boys '63
The Cruel Sea '53
The Night They Raided Minsky's '69

Sam Elliott (1944-)
Ghost Rider '07
The Golden Compass '07
Barnyard '06 (V)
Thank You for Smoking '06
Off the Map '03
Hulk '03
We Were Soldiers '02
The Contender '00
You Know My Name '99
The Big Lebowski '98
The Hi-Lo Country '98
Dogwatch '97
Rough Riders '97
The Final Cut '96
Buffalo Girls '95
Blue River '95
Hole in the Sky '95
Woman Undone '95
The Desperate Trail '94
Gettysburg '93
Tombstone '93
Conagher '91
Rush '91
Sibling Rivalry '90
Prancer '89
Road House '89
Shakedown '88
Fatal Beauty '87
The Quick and the Dead '87
The Blue Lightning '86
Mask '85
The Legacy '79
The Sacketts '79
The Shadow Riders '82
Murder in Texas '81
Frogs '72
Molly & Lawless John '72
Butch Cassidy and the Sundance Kid '69
Lifeguard '76
I Will Fight No More Forever '75

Scott Elliott
The French Line '54
Homesteaders of Paradise Valley '47
Santa Fe Uprising '46

Peter Elliott (1913-75)
Missing Link '88
Curse of the Demon '57

Robert Elliott (1879-1951)
The Great Mike '44

Ross Elliott (1917-99)
The Indestructible Man '56
Carolina Cannonball '55
Tarantula '55
Paper Man '71

Edythe Elliott (1888-1978)
Ma and Pa Kettle at Home '54
Hot Lead '51
Ghost Rider '07

John Elliott (1876-1956)
The Great Mike '44
Riding On '37
A Face in the Fog '36
Rogue's Tavern '36
Big Calibre '35
Bulldog Courage '35
Danger Trails '35
The Midnight Phantom '35
Rider of the Law '35
Sunset Range '35
Toll of the Desert '35
The Gallant Fool '33
Riders of the Desert '32
Mother and Son '31
Two Fisted Justice '31
The Return of Casey Jones '34
White Eagle '32
The Maltese Falcon '31
Murder at Midnight '31
Lies & Alibis '06 (V)
Codename Kyril '91
One Against the Wind '91
Death Rides the Range '40
Phantom Rancher '39
The Phantom of the Range '38
'39
Law of Gore '70
Two-Fisted Justice '43
Two-Fisted Justice '43
Saddle Mountain Roundup '41
Two-Gun Man '31

King of the Forest Rangers '46

Shawn Elliott
Double Take '01
Thirteen Conversations About One Thing '01
Bloodsucking Pharaohs of Pittsburgh '90
Impulse '90
Crossover Dreams '85
Short Eyes '79

Stephen Elliott (1945-)
Taking Care of Business '90
Arthur 2: On the Rocks '88
Assassination '87
Perry Mason: The Case of the Lost Love '87
Beverly Hills Cop '84
Days of Hell '84
Roadhouse 66 '84
Beauty and the Beast '83
Arthur '81
Cutter's Way '81
Jacqueline Bouvier Kennedy '81
Can You Hear the Laughter? The Story of Freddie Prinze '79
Mrs. R's Daughter '79
Betrayal '78
Sergeant Matlovich vs. the U.S. Air Force '78
Report to the Commissioner '74
The Hospital '71

William (Bill) Elliott (1934-83)
Coffy '73
Night of the Lepus '72
They Call It Murder '71
Change of Habit '69

William (Wild Bill) Elliott (1903-65)
Hellfire '48
Bordertown Gunfighters '43
Calling Wild Bill Elliott '43
Death Valley Manhunt '43
Man from Thunder River '43

Aunjanue Ellis (1969-)
Cover '08
Freedomland '06
Brother to Brother '04
Ray '04
Lovely & Amazing '02
Undercover Brother '02
The Caveman's Valentine '01
The Opponent '01
Disappearing Acts '00
Men of Honor '00
Girls Town '96

Chris Ellis (1956-)
The Devil's Rejects '05
In Enemy Hands '04
Catch Me If You Can '02
The Watcher '00
October Sky '99
Home Fries '98
Apollo 13 '95

Edward Ellis (1870-1952)
Wheel of Fortune '41
Fury '36
The Texas Rangers '36
The Return of Peter Grimm '35
Village Tale '35
The Thin Man '34
I Am a Fugitive from a Chain Gang '32

Frank Ellis (1897-1969)
Wildfire '45
Two-Fisted Justice '43
Rock River Renegades '42
The Big Stampede '32
Whistlin' Dan '32

Greg Ellis (1968-)
To End All Wars '01
Crash & Byrnes '99

James Ellis (1931-)
Conspiracy of Silence '03
Resurrection Man '97
Spellbreaker: Secret of the Leprechauns '96
Leapin' Leprechauns '95
Priest '94
No Surrender '86

Mary Ellis (1897-2003)
The Three Worlds of Gulliver '59
Paris in Spring '35

Patricia Ellis (1916-70)
Back Door to Heaven '39
Block-heads '38
Sing Me a Love Song '37
Postal Inspector '36
The Case of the Lucky Legs '35
Picture Snatcher '33
Three on a Match '32

Paul Ellis (1896-1974)
Marihuana '36
Woman Condemned '33
No Man of Her Own '32

Robert Ellis (1892-1974)
The Green Promise '49
Captured in Chinatown '35
American Madness '32
Broadway vs Cheyenne '32
Come on Danger! '32
Daring Danger '32
Fighting Fool '32
White Eagle '32
The Fighting Sheriff '31
Undertow '30
The Love Trap '29

Robin Ellis (1943-)
A Dark Adapted Eye '93
The Curse of King Tut's Tomb '80
The Europeans '79
Poldark '75
Poldark 2 '75
Elizabeth R '72
The Moonstone '72

Tracey Ellis
The Crow: City of Angels '96
The NeverEnding Story 3: Escape from Fantasia '94
This Boy's Life '93
The Last of the Mohicans '92

Chase Ellison (1993-)
End of the Spear '06
Mysterious Skin '04

James Ellison (1910-93)
Kentucky Jubilee '51
Blazing Guns '50
Guns of Justice '50
Last Bullet '50
Marshal of Heldorado '50
Outlaw Fury '50
Rangeland Empire '50
Sudden Death '50
Last of the Wild Horses '49
G.I. War Brides '46
The Gang's All Here '43
I Walked with a Zombie '43
Charley's Aunt '41
You Can't Fool Your Wife '40
Fifth Avenue Girl '39
Next Time I Marry '38
Vivacious Lady '38
23 1/2 Hours Leave '37
Three on the Trail '36
Hopalong Cassidy '35

Greg Ellwand
DC 9/11: Time of Crisis '04
Eclipse '94

Gad Elmaleh (1971-)
Priceless '06
The Valet '06

Rebekah Elmaloglou (1974-)
Back of Beyond '95
The Sum of Us '94
In Too Deep '90

Nicoletta Elmi (1964-)
Demons '86
Deep Red: Hatchet Murders '75
Andy Warhol's Frankenstein '74
Primal Impulse '74
Who Saw Her Die? '72

Michael Elphick (1946-2002)
Buddy's Song '91
Let Him Have It '91
Little Dorrit, Film 1: Nobody's Fault '88
Little Dorrit, Film 2: Little Dorrit's Story '88
Withnail and I '87
Arthur's Hallowed Ground '84
The Element of Crime '84
Ordeal by Innocence '84
The Elephant Man '80
Cry of the Banshee '70

Hannelore Elsner (1942-)
Go for Zucker '05
Time Troopers '89

Isobel Elsom (1893-1981)
Love is a Many-Splendored Thing '55
Escape Me Never '47
The Ghost and Mrs. Muir '47
Love from a Stranger '47
Monsieur Verdoux '47
Casanova Brown '44
The White Cliffs of Dover '44

June Elvidge (1893-1965)
Beyond the Rocks '22
A Girl's Folly '17

Cary Elwes (1962-)
Georgia Rule '07
Edison Force '05
Ella Enchanted '04
Saw '04
Comic Book Villains '02
The Cat's Meow '01
Uprising '01
Race Against Time '00
Shadow of the Vampire '00
Wish You Were Dead '00
The Cradle Will Rock '99
From the Earth to the Moon '98
The Pentagon Wars '98
Quest for Camelot '98 (V)
The Informant '97
Kiss the Girls '97
Liar Liar '97
Twister '96
Rudyard Kipling's The Jungle Book '94
The Crush '93
Robin Hood: Men in Tights '93
Bram Stoker's Dracula '92
Hot Shots! '91
Days of Thunder '90
Leather Jackets '90
Glory '89
The Princess Bride '87
The Bride '85
Lady Jane '85
Another Country '84
Oxford Blues '84

Chris Elwood
Dog Gone Love '03
How High '01

Ron Ely (1938-)
Slavers '77
Doc Savage '75
Once Before I Die '65
The Fiend Who Walked the West '58

Sallee Elyse
Demented '80
Home Sweet Home '80

Ouassini Embarek
The Good Thief '03
Bye-Bye '96

Ethan (Randall) Embry (1978-)
Vacancy '07
Pizza '05
Standing Still '05
Harold and Kumar Go to White Castle '04
Timeline '03
Sweet Home Alabama '02
Wes Craven Presents: They '02
The Independent '00
Can't Hardly Wait '98
Dancer, Texas—Pop. 81 '98
Disturbing Behavior '98
Montana '97
That Thing You Do! '96
Vegas Vacation '96
White Squall '96
Empire Records '95
Evolver '94
Season of Change '94
A Far Off Place '93
All I Want for Christmas '91
Dutch '91

Faye Emerson (1917-83)
The Mask of Dimitrios '44
Uncertain Glory '44
Air Force '43
Destination Tokyo '43

Hope Emerson (1891-1960)
All Mine to Give '56
Westward the Women '51
Adam's Rib '50
Caged '50

Karrie Emerson (1960-)
Chopping Mall '86
Evils of the Night '85

Michael Emerson
The Legend of Zorro '05
29th & Gay '05

Roy Emerton (1892-1944)
Henry V '44
Nine Days a Queen '36
Lorna Doone '34

Dick Emery (1915-83)
Find the Lady '76
Yellow Submarine '68 (V)

Gideon Emery (1972-)
Primeval '07

Gilbert Emery (1875-1945)
Queen's Messenger II '01
The Spanish Main '45
Mademoiselle Fifi '44
Ship Ahoy '42
Here Comes Mr. Jordan '41
Return of the Vampire '43
Wife Versus Secretary '36
Goin' to Town '35
Now and Forever '34
The Lady Refuses '31
The Royal Bed '31

John Emery (1905-64)
Kronos '57
Forever Darling '56
The Girl Can't Help It '56
A Lawless Street '55
Double Crossbones '51
Rocketship X-M '50
Mademoiselle Fifi '44

Julie Ann Emery
Pictures of Hollis Woods '07
Hitch '05

Katherine Emery (1907-80)
The Private Affairs of Bel Ami '47
Isle of the Dead '45

Lisa Emery
Cash Crop '01
Harvest '98

David Emge (1946-)
Hellmaster '92
Dawn of the Dead '78

Robert Emhardt (1914-94)
Die Sister, Die! '74
Change of Habit '69
Shame '61
Underwood, U.S.A. '60
3:10 to Yuma '57

Michael Emil
Adventures in Spying '92
In the Spirit '90
New Year's Day '89
Someone to Love '87
Always '85
Insignificance '85
Can She Bake a Cherry Pie? '83
Sitting Ducks '80
Tracks '76

Daniel Emilfork (1924-)
The City of Lost Children '95
The Devil's Nightmare '71
Lady L '65

Eminem (1972-)
8 Mile '02
Da Hip Hop Witch '00

Alphonsia Emmanuel
Peter's Friends '92
Under Suspicion '92

Takis Emmanuel (1933-)
Kostas '79
Caddie '76
Young Aphrodites '63

Noah Emmerich (1965-)
Little Children '06
Sometimes in April '05
Cellular '04
Miracle '04
Beyond Borders '03
Windtalkers '02
Frequency '00
Love & Sex '00
Crazy in Alabama '99
Life '99
Monument Ave. '98
The Truman Show '98
Tumbleweeds '98
Cop Land '97
Beautiful Girls '96

Michael Emmet
Attack of the Giant Leeches '59
Night of the Blood Beast '58

Fern Emmett (1896-1946)
Dead Men Walk '43
Assassin of Youth '35
Texas Terror '35
Trail Drive '33
The Forty-Niners '32

Cliff Emmich (1936-)
Jackson County Jail '76
Invasion of the Bee Girls '73

Akira (Tsukamoto) Emoto (1948-)
Dr. Akagi '98
The Eel '96
Shall We Dance? '96

Kyoko Enami
The Wolves '71
Gamera vs. Barugon '66

Lena Endre (1955-)
Faithless '00
Jerusalem '96
Sunday's Children '94
The Best Intentions '92
The Visitors '89

Georgia Engel (1948-)
Open Season '06 (V)
Signs of Life '89
The Day the Women Got Even '80

Tina Engel (1950-)
The Promise '94
The Boat Is Full '81
The Second Awakening of Christa Klages '78

Constanze Engelbrecht (1955-2000)
The Count of Monte Cristo '99

Wera Engels (1909-88)
Hong Kong Nights '35
Fugitive Road '34

Audie England (1971-)
Free Enterprise '98
Legion '98
A Place Called Truth '98
Shame, Shame, Shame '98
Red Shoe Diaries 8: Night of Abandon '97
Delta of Venus '95
Miami Hustle '95
Venus Rising '95

Randall England
Asylum of the Damned '03
Dream Machine '91

Bradford English
Halloween 6: The Curse of Michael Myers '95
Sex, Love and Cold Hard Cash '93
Capone '89

Marla English (1935-)
Flesh and the Spur '57
Voodoo Woman '57

Zach English (1983-)
The Missing Years '96
The Real McCoy '93

Robert Englund (1947-)
Freddy vs. Jason '03
Python '00
Wish You Were Dead '00
The Prince and the Surfer '99
Dee Snider's Strangeland '98
Meet the Deedles '98
Perfect Target '98
Urban Legend '98
Wishmaster '97
Killer Tongue '96
The Paper Brigade '96
The Mangler '94
Wes Craven's New Nightmare '94
Dance Macabre '91
Freddy's Dead: The Final Nightmare '91
The Adventures of Ford Fairlane '90
A Nightmare on Elm Street 5: Dream Child '89
A Nightmare on Elm Street 4: Dream Master '88
A Nightmare on Elm Street 3: Dream Warriors '87
A Nightmare on Elm Street 2: Freddy's Revenge '85
A Nightmare on Elm Street '84
V: The Final Battle '84
V '83
Mysterious Two '82
Dead and Buried '81
Galaxy of Terror '81
Eaten Alive '76
A Star Is Born '76
Stay Hungry '76
Buster and Billie '74
Slashed Dreams '74

Takaaki Enoki (1956-)
Moon over Tao '97
Heaven & Earth '90

John Enos (1962-)
Missionary Man '07
Love Thy Neighbor '02
Phone Booth '02
Brigham City '01
Dead Sexy '01
Red Shoe Diaries: Luscious Lola '00
Stealth Fighter '99
Miami Hustle '95
Ravenhawk '95
Red Shoe Diaries 6: How I Met My Husband '95
Bullet '94
Till the End of the Night '94

Rene Enriquez (1933-90)
Bulletproof '88
The Evil That Men Do '84
Ants '77
Harry and Tonto '74

Michael Ensign (1944)
Born Yesterday '93
Life Stinks '91
House '86

John Entwhistle (1944-2002)
Tommy '75

Brenda Epperson (1965)
Storybook '95
Amore! '93

Dieter Eppler (1927-)
The Sprinter '84
The Torture Chamber of Dr. Sadism '69
Strangler of Blackmoor Castle '63
The Slaughter of the Vampires '62

Mike Epps (1970-)
Welcome Home Roscoe Jenkins '08
Resident Evil: Extinction '07
Talk to Me '07
Something New '06
Guess Who '05
Roll Bounce '05
Resident Evil: Apocalypse '04
The Fighting Temptations '03
All About the Benjamins '02
Friday After Next '02
Dr. Dolittle 2 '01 (V)
How High '01
Bait '00
Next Friday '00

Omar Epps (1973-)
Against the Ropes '04
Alfie '04
Big Trouble '02
Conviction '02
Perfume '01
Brother '00
Dracula 2000 '00
Love and Basketball '00
In Too Deep '99
The Mod Squad '99
The Wood '99
Breakfast of Champions '99
First Time Felon '97
Scream 2 '97
Deadly Voyage '96
Higher Learning '94
Major League 2 '94
Daybreak '93
The Program '93
Juice '92

Kathryn Erbe (1966-)
The Runaway '00
Stir of Echoes '99
Naked City: Justice with a Bullet '98
Dream with the Fishes '97
The Addiction '95
Breathing Lessons '94
D2: The Mighty Ducks '94
Kiss of Death '94
Rich in Love '93
What about Bob? '91

Andoni Erburu (1988-)
Secrets of the Heart '97

Richard Erdman (1925-)
Stalag 17 '53
Cry Danger '51
The Stooge '51
Objective, Burma! '45

Ethan Erickson (1973-)
Fear Runs Silent '99
Jawbreaker '99

Kandis Erickson
Seance '06
Death Valley: The Revenge of Bloody Bill '04

Leif Erickson (1911-86)
D.C. Cab '84
Penitentiary 2 '82
Rocky 3 '82
Winterhawk '76
Abduction '75
Force Five '75
The Carpetbaggers '64
Roustabout '64
Strait-Jacket '64
A Gathering of Eagles '63
Istanbul '57
Tea and Sympathy '56
Fastest Gun Alive '56
On the Waterfront '54
Trouble along the Way '53
Abbott and Costello Meet Captain Kidd '52
Never Wave at a WAC '52
Sailor Beware '52
With a Song n My Heart '52
Hill Number One '51
The Showdown '50
Three Secrets '50
Joan of Arc '48
The Snake Pit '48
Blonde Savage '47
Arabian Nights '42
Night Monster '42
Pardon My Sarong '42
One Third of a Nation '39
The Big Broadcast of 1938 '38

John Ericson (1927-)
Primary Target '89
House of the Dead '78
Hustler Squad '76
The Bounty Man '72
The Bamboo Saucer '68
7 Faces of Dr. Lao '63
Forty Guns '57
Green Fire '55
Bad Day at Black Rock '54
Rhapsody '54
The Student Prince '54

Devon Ericson (1952-)
Can You Hear the Laughter? The Story of Freddie Prinze '79
The Runaway Barge '75

Kaj-Erik Eriksen (1979-)
Captains Courageous '95
Kurt Vonnegut's Monkey House '91
Short Time '90

R. Lee Ermey (1944-)
The Texas Chainsaw Massacre: The Beginning '06
Man of the House '05
Willard '03
Massacre '03
The Texas Chainsaw Massacre '03
Dreaming of Julia '03
The Salton Sea '02
The Visitors '89
Saving Silverman '01
Taking Sides '01
On the Borderline '01
Chaos Factor '00
Skipped Parts '00
Avalanche '99
Life '99
Toy Story 2 '99 (V)
You Know My Name '99
Switchback '97
Prefontaine '97
The Frighteners '96
Distraction '97
Weapons of Mass Distraction '97
Dead Man Walking '95
Leaving Las Vegas '95
Murder in the First '95
Seven '95
Killer Dill '47

George Ernest (1921-86)
Conquest '37
Waikiki Wedding '37
Desert Gold '36

Leon Errol (1881-1951)
The Noose Hangs High '48
Higher and Higher '44
The Invisible Man's Revenge '44
Slightly Terrific '44
Mexican Spitfire at Sea '42
Hurry, Charlie, Hurry '41
Never Give a Sucker an Even Break '41
Mexican Spitfire '40
Pop Always Pays '40
Make a Wish '37
The Great Ziegfeld '36
We're Not Dressing '34

Melissa Errico (1970-)
Loverboy '05
Life or Something Like It '02
Frequency '00

Krista Erickson (1964-)
Mockingbird Don't Sing '01

Patrick Ersgard
Backlash '99
Living in Peril '97

Homayon Ershadi
The Kite Runner '07
The Taste of Cherry '96

Victor Ertmanis
Holiday Affair '96
Brainscan '94
Paris, France '94

Marilyn Erskine (1924-)
Above and Beyond '53
Westward the Women '51

Eileen Erskine (1914-95)
This Happy Breed '47
Great Expectations '46

Bill Erwin (1914-)
Chairman of the Board '97
Dead Men Can't Dance '97
Rough Riders '97
The Color of Evening '95
Fallen Angels 1 '93

Mike Erwin (1978-)
Chaos Theory '08
Huckleberry Finn '75
Hard Knox '83
Hulk '03

Gianni Esposito (1930-74)
Paris Belongs to Us '60
Les Miserables '57

Dead Man Walking '95 — *(see listings above)*

The Fighter '95
Leaving Las Vegas '95
Murder in the First '95
Seven '95
Killer Dill '47
Winterhawk '76
French Silk '94
Under the Hula Moon '95
Love Is a Gun '94
On Deadly Ground '94
Body Snatchers '93
Hexed '93
Sommersby '93
The Terror Within 2 '91
Endless Descent '90
I'm Dangerous Tonight '90
Kid '90
The Take '90
Demonstone '89
Fletch Lives '89
The Siege of Firebase Gloria '89
Going Hollywood '33
Hold Your Man '33
Misleading Lady '32
Strangers in Love '32
Apocalypse Now '79
The Boys in Company C '77

George Ernest (1921-86)
The Showdown '50
Three Secrets '50
Joan of Arc '48
The Snake Pit '48
Blonde Savage '47
Arabian Nights '42
Night Monster '42

Mario Erpichini
The Best Man '97
Escape from Death Row '73

Krista Erickson (1964-)
The Navy Comes Through '42
Panama Hattie '42
Dawn Patrol '38

Jill Esmond (1908-90)
The World in His Arms '52
Without Love '45
Ministry of Fear '44
The Story of Dr. Wassell '44
The White Cliffs of Dover '44
Casanova Brown '44
Bedelia '46
A Man Called Peter '55
Journey for Margaret '42
On the Sunny Side '42
F.P. 1 '33
Skin Game '31
State's Attorney '31

Bella Esperance
Lady Dragon 2 '93
Lady Dragon '92

Giancario Esposito (1958-)
Queens '06
For Love or Country: The Arturo Sandoval Story '00
Music of the Heart '99
Trapper County War '89
Phantom of the Mall: Eric's Revenge '89
Aces: Iron Eagle 3 '92
Countersink '03
Sleepaway Camp 2: Unhappy Campers '88
Maximum Overdrive '86

Carl Esmond (1908-2004)
The Bad News Bears in Breaking Training '77

Jaime Escobedo
The Bad News Bears '76

Stuart Erwin (1902-67)
The Misadventures of Merlin Jones '63
Heading for Heaven '47

Robert Estes (1963-)
Suspended Animation '02
Awakenings '90

Laura Esterman
Music of the Heart '99

Gloria Estefan (1957-)
For Love or Country: The Arturo Sandoval Story '00
Almost You '85

David Essex (1947-)
Journey of Honor '91
Silver Dream Racer '83
That'll Be the Day '73
Octaman '71

Eileen Essell (1922-)
Charlie and the Chocolate Factory '05
Finding Neverland '04
Duplex '03

Paul Esser (1913-88)
Daughters of Darkness '71
The Kaiser's Lackey '51
The Merry Wives of Windsor '50

Christine Estabrook (1952-)
Presumed Innocent '90
Second Sight '89

Ato Essandoh (1972-)
Garden State '04
Saving Face '04

Eileen Essell — *(see above)*

Emilio Estevez (1962-)
Arthur and the Invisibles '06
Bobby '06
Rated X '00 (V)
U-571 '00
Terror Tract '00
The Road Home '95
Mission: Impossible '96
D3: The Mighty Ducks '96
The War at Home '96
Another Stakeout '93
Judgment Night '93
National Lampoon's Loaded Weapon 1 '93
Freejack '92
The Mighty Ducks '92
Men at Work '90
Young Guns 2 '90
Young Guns '88
Never on Tuesday '88
Stakeout '87
Wisdom '87
Maximum Overdrive '86
That Was Then... This Is Now '85
St. Elmo's Fire '85
The Breakfast Club '85
Repo Man '83
Nightmares '83
The Outsiders '83
In the Custody of Strangers '82
Tex '82

Will Estes (1978-)
Blue Ridge Fall '95
Terror Tract '00
Mimic 2 '01
My Husband's Double Life '01

Jennifer Esposito (1973-)
Conspiracy '08
Crash '05
Breakin' All The Rules '04
Taxi '04
Master of Disguise '02
Welcome to Collinwood '02
Don't Say a Word '01
Dracula 2000 '00
Just One Time '00
The Proposal '00
The Bachelor '99
Summer of Sam '99
I Still Know What You Did Last Summer '98
No Looking Back '98

Ines Estevez (1964-)

Joe Estevez (1950-)
San Franpsycho '06
Autopsy: A Love Story '02
Killing Grandpa '91

Erik Estrada (1949-)
Kickin' It Old Skool '07
Border Blues '03
Gang Justice '94
The Final Goal '94
Panic in the Skies '96
The Modern Adventures of Tom Sawyer '99
The Divine Enforcer '91
The Last Riders '90
Night of the Wilding '90
A Show of Force '90
Spirits '90
Allen Seed '89
Andy and the Airwave Rangers '89
Twisted Justice '89
Caged Fury '90
Guns '90
Do or Die '91
The Repo Man '83

Renee Estevez (1967-)
Storm Tracker '99
Good Girls Don't '95
Endangered '94
Uncivilized '94
Eddie Presley '92
Forbidden Sun '89
Heathers '89
Marked for Murder '89
Bulldance '88
Intruder '88

Ramon Estevez (1963-)
Cadence '89

Jennifer Esposito (1973-) — *(see above)*

Ato Essandoh (1972-)
Garden State '04
The Sunshine Boys '55
Last Summer '98

Ines Estevez (1964-)
Killing Grandpa '91
Autopsy: A Love Story '02
San Franpsycho '06

Joe Estevez (1950-)
Tex '82
The Outsiders '83
Repo Man '83
In the Custody of Strangers '82
Nightmares '83

St. Elmo's Fire '85
Maximum Overdrive '86
The Line '80
Midway '76
The Cross & the Switchblade '72
Honeyboy '82
Lightblast '85
Hour of the Assassin '86
Mission '88
Night of the Wilding '90
Never on Tuesday '88
Young Guns '88
Judgment Night '93
Loaded Weapon 1 '93
The Breakfast Club '85
That Was Then... This Is
Now '85
Jailbreakin' '72
The New Centurions '72

Alberto Estrella (1962-)
Esmeralda Comes by Night '98
Optic Fiber '97
On the Air '95

Pat Estrin
Dennis the Menace: Dinosaur Hunter '93
Act of Vengeance '74
America First '70

Pierre Etaix (1928-)
Max, Mon Amour '86
Pickpocket '59

Alex(ander Nathan) Etel
The Water Horse: Legend of the Deep '07
Millions '05

Treva Etienne
Pirates of the Caribbean: The Curse of the Black Pearl '03
Black Hawk Down '01
Eyes Wide Shut '99

Ruth Etting (1896-1978)
Hips, Hips, Hooray '34
Roman Scandals '33

Cynthia Ettinger
Frailty '02
Down, Out and Dangerous '95

Shari Eubank (1947-)
Chesty Anderson USN '76
Supervixens '75

Bob Eubanks (1938-)
Roger & Me '89

Corey Michael Eubanks
School Daze '88
White of the Eye '88
Mom '89
Jo Jo Dancer, Your Life Is Calling '86
Native Son '86
Fright Night '85
A Soldier's Story '84
The In-Laws '79
King '78

Chris Evans (1981-)
Street Kings '08
Fantastic Four: Rise of the Silver Surfer '07
The Nanny Diaries '07
Sunshine '07
TMNT (Teenage Mutant Ninja Turtles) '07 (V)
Fantastic Four '05
Fierce People '05
London '05
Cellular '04
The Perfect Score '04
Not Another Teen Movie '01

Clifford Evans (1912-85)
One Brief Summer '70
Kiss of the Vampire '62
The Curse of the Werewolf '61
The Gilded Cage '54
I'll Get You '53
While I Live '47
The Foreman Went to France '42
The Courageous Mr. Penn '41
Love on the Dole '41
The Mutiny of the Elsinore '39
River of Unrest '36

Dale Evans (1912-2001)
Bells of Coronado '50
Trigger, Jr. '50
Twilight in the Sierras '50
Down Dakota Way '49
The Golden Stallion '49
Susanna Pass '49
Apache Pass '47
Bells of San Angelo '47
Home in Oklahoma '47
Lights of Old Santa Fe '47
Helldorado '46
My Pal Trigger '46
Rainbow over Texas '46
Roll on Texas Moon '46
Song of Arizona '46
Under Nevada Skies '46
Along the Navaho Trail '45
Bells of Rosarita '45
Don't Fence Me In '45
Sunset in El Dorado '45
Utah '45
Cowboy & the Senorita '44
San Fernando Valley '44
Song of Nevada '44
The Yellow Rose of Texas '44

Daniel Evans (1973-)
Daniel Deronda '02
Great Expectations '99

Douglas Evans (1904-68)
Actors and Sin '52
Leave It to the Marines '51
Sky High '51
North of the Great Divide '50
The Golden Stallion '49
My Dog Shep '46
The Green Hornet '39

Edith Evans (1888-1976)
Nasty Habits '77
The Slipper and the Rose '76
Craze '74
A Doll's House '73
David Copperfield '70
Scrooge '70
Crooks & Coronets '69
The Madwoman of Chaillot '69
The Chalk Garden '64
Tom Jones '63
The Nun's Story '59
Look Back in Anger '58
The Importance of Being Earnest '52
The Last Days of Dolwyn '49

Joan Evans (1934-)
No Name on the Bullet '59
Skirts Ahoy! '52
Our Very Own '50

John Evans (1934-)
UKM: The Ultimate Killing Machine '06
Escape Clause '96
Long Road Home '91
I've Heard the Mermaids Singing '87

Josh Evans (1971-)
The Doors '91
Ricochet '91
Born on the Fourth of July '89

Josh Ryan Evans (1982-2002)
Dr. Seuss' How the Grinch Stole Christmas '00
P.T. Barnum '99

Lee Evans (1965-)
The History of Mr. Polly '07
Doogal '05 (V)
Freeze Frame '04
The Medallion '03
Dinotopia '02 (V)
The Ladies Man '00
There's Something about Mary '98
The Fifth Element '97
Mouse Hunt '97
Funny Bones '94

Linda Evans (1942-)
The Stepsister '97
The Gambler Returns: The Luck of the Draw '93
Kenny Rogers as the Gambler, Part 2: The Adventure Continues '83
Tom Horn '80
Avalanche Express '79
Standing Tall '78
Hunter '76
Mitchell '75
The Klansman '74
Confessions of Tom Harris '72
Beach Blanket Bingo '65
Those Calloways '65

Madge Evans (1909-81)
Sinners in Paradise '38
Pennies from Heaven '36
David Copperfield '35
Transatlantic Tunnel '35
Stand Up and Cheer '34
Dinner at Eight '33
Hallelujah, I'm a Bum '33
The Mayor of Hell '33
Three Broadway Girls '32

Maurice Evans (1901-89)
Terror in the Wax Museum '73
Beneath the Planet of the Apes '70
Planet of the Apes '68
Rosemary's Baby '68
The War Lord '65
The Tempest '63
Androcles and the Lion '52
Scrooge '35
Wedding Rehearsal '32

Mike Evans (1949-2006)
The House on Skull Mountain '74

Monica Evans (1940-)
Robin Hood '73 (V)
The Odd Couple '68

Muriel Evans (1910-2000)
Roll, Wagons, Roll '39
The House of Secrets '37
King of the Pecos '36
Law for Tombstone '35
The New Frontier '35
The Throwback '35
Manhattan Melodrama '34
The Prizefighter and the Lady '33

Rex Evans (1903-69)
The Matchmaker '58
The Wrong Road '37

Robert Evans (1930-)
The Kid Stays in the Picture '02 (N)
An Alan Smithee Film: Burn, Hollywood, Burn '97
The Best of Everything '59
The Fiend Who Walked the West '58
Man of a Thousand Faces '57

Robin Evans
Rage of Honor '87
One Dark Night '82

Shaun Evans (1980-)
Cashback '06
Being Julia '04
The Boys and Girl From County Clare '03

Terrence Evans
Mr. Fix It '06
The Texas Chainsaw Massacre '03
Curse 2: The Bite '88

Terry Evans
Mongrel '83
Cody '77

Troy Evans (1948-)
The Black Dahlia '06
Alien Fury: Countdown to Invasion '00
I'll Remember April '99
The Frighteners '96
Bodily Harm '95
Father and Scout '94
My Summer Story '94
Ace Ventura: Pet Detective '94
Article 99 '92
Kuffs '92
The Lawnmower Man '92

Edith Evanson (1900-80)
The Girl in the Red Velvet Swing '55
Silver Star '55
The Day the Earth Stood Still '51
Caged '50
The Damned Don't Cry '50
The Magnificent Yankee '50

Eve (1979-)
Barbershop 2: Back in Business '04
The Cookout '04
The Woodsman '04
Barbershop '02

Alice Eve
Crossing Over '08
Big Nothing '06
Starter for Ten '06

Trevor Eve (1951-)
Troy '04
Possession '02
David Copperfield '99
Heat of the Sun '99
Appetite '98
Dracula '79

Judith Evelyn (1913-67)
The Tingler '59
The Egyptian '54
Rear Window '54

Kimberly Evenson (1932-)
Kandyland '87
The Big Bet '85
Porky's Revenge '85

Barbara Everest (1890-1968)
Madeleine '50
The Valley of Decision '45
Gaslight '44
Jane Eyre '44
Phantom Fiend '35

Chad Everett (1936-)
Anchorman: The Legend of Ron Burgundy '04
Mulholland Drive '01
Psycho '98
When Time Expires '97
Official Denial '93
The Rousters '90
Heroes Stand Alone '89
Jigsaw Murders '89
Fever Pitch '85
Airplane 2: The Sequel '82
Intruder Within '81
Centennial '78
The Impossible Years '68
Johnny Tiger '66
The Singing Nun '66
Rome Adventure '62

Francine Everett (1920-99)
Dirty Gertie from Harlem U.S.A. '46
Tall, Tan and Terrific '46

Rupert Everett (1959-)
Shrek the Third '07 (V)
Stardust '07
The Chronicles of Narnia: The Lion, the Witch and the Wardrobe '05 (V)
A Different Loyalty '04
Shrek 2 '04 (V)
Stage Beauty '04
Dangerous Liaisons '03
Unconditional Love '03
The Importance of Being Earnest '02
The Wild Thornberrys Movie '02 (V)
The Next Best Thing '00
An Ideal Husband '99
Inspector Gadget '99
William Shakespeare's A Midsummer Night's Dream '99
Shakespeare in Love '98
B. Monkey '97
My Best Friend's Wedding '97
Cemetery Man '95
Dunston Checks In '95
The Madness of King George '94
Ready to Wear '94
Inside Monkey Zetterland '93
The Comfort of Strangers '91
Hearts of Fire '87
The Right Hand Man '87
Dance with a Stranger '85
Another Country '84

Todd Everett
Blood on the Badge '92
The Capture of Grizzly Adams '82

Tom Everett (1948-)
The Alamo '04
XXX '02
Air Force One '97
My Fellow Americans '96
Best of the Best '89
Leatherface: The Texas Chainsaw Massacre 3 '89
Prison '88
Friday the 13th, Part 4: The Final Chapter '84

Nancy Everhard (1959-)
The China Lake Murders '90
This Gun for Hire '90
Deepstar Six '89
Demonstone '89
Double Revenge '89
The Trial of the Incredible Hulk '89

Angie Everhart (1969-)
Heart of Stone '00
The Stray '00
The Substitute 4: Failure is Not an Option '00
Welcome to Hollywood '00
D.R.E.A.M. Team '99
Running Red '99
Bitter Sweet '98
Something About Sex '98
Executive Target '97
Another 9 1/2 Weeks '96
Tales from the Crypt Presents Bordello of Blood '96
Trigger Happy '96
Jade '95

Rex Everhart (1920-2000)
Beauty and the Beast '91 (V)
Family Business '89

Jason Evers (1922-2005)
Basket Case 2 '90
Barracuda '78
Claws '77
Fer-De-Lance '74
Escape from the Planet of the Apes '71
The Green Berets '68

Cory (Corinna) Everson (1959-)
Felony '95
Double Impact '91

Greg Evigan (1953-)
Arizona Summer '03
He Sees You When You're Sleeping '02
One of Her Own '97
Spectre '96
TekWar '94
Lies Before Kisses '92
Deepstar Six '89
Private Road: No Trespassing '87
Stripped to Kill '87

Pat Evison (1924-)
What the Moon Saw '90
Starstruck '82
Tim '79

John Ewart (1928-94)
Which Way Home '90
The Quest '86
Prince and the Great Race '83
Blue Fire Lady '78
Newsfront '78
Island Trader '71

Dwight Ewell
Jay and Silent Bob Strike Back '01
Intern '00
Man of the Century '99
Chasing Amy '97
Flirt '95

Tom Ewell (1909-94)
Easy Money '83
They Only Kill Their Masters '72
State Fair '62
The Girl Can't Help It '56
The Seven Year Itch '55
Lost in Alaska '52
Adam's Rib '50
A Life of Her Own '50
Mr. Music '50

Barbara Ewing (1944-)
Brothers of the Head '06
Guardian of the Abyss '82
Dracula Has Risen from the Grave '68

Peter Eyre (1942-)
The Affair of the Necklace '01
Don Quixote '00
The Golden Bowl '00
Dangerous Beauty '98
The Tango Lesson '97
Surviving Picasso '96
Joseph '95
Princess Caraboo '94
Scarlett '94
Sharpe's Gold '94

Orlando '92
Diamond's Edge '83
Hedda '75

William Eythe (1918-57)
Colonel Effingham's Raid '45
House on 92nd Street '45
Wilson '44
A Wing and a Prayer '44
The Ox-Bow Incident '43

Bessie Eyton (1890-1965)
Heart of Texas Ryan '17
The Spoilers '14

Maynard Eziashi (1965-)
Ace Ventura: When Nature Calls '95
Bophal '93
Mister Johnson '91
Twenty-One '91

Shelley Fabares (1944-)
The Canterville Ghost '91
For Love or Money '88
Hot Pursuit '87
Memorial Day '83
Great American Traffic Jam '80
Sky Feist '75
Brian's Song '71
Clambake '67
Spinout '66
Girl Happy '65
Ride the Wild Surf '64

Matthew Faber
Palindromes '04
Hard Luck '01
Welcome to the Dollhouse '95

Fabian (1942-)
Mr. Rock 'n' Roll: The Alan Freed Story '99
Runaway Daughters '94
Get Crazy '83
Kiss Daddy Goodbye '81
Soul Hustler '76
Little Laura & Big John '73
Thunder Alley '67
Fireball 500 '66
Dear Brigitte '65
Ride the Wild Surf '64
Five Weeks in a Balloon '62
The Longest Day '62
Mr. Hobbs Takes a Vacation '62
North to Alaska '60

Ava Fabian (1962-)
Quigley '03
The Reluctant Agent '95
Gargoyles: The Movie: The Heroes Awaken '94 (V)
Stephen King's The Stand '94
Welcome Home, Roxy Carmichael '90
To Die For '89

Francoise Fabian (1935-)
5x2 '04
La Euche '00
Reunion '88
The French Woman '79
Love by Appointment '76
Salut l'Artiste '74
Happy New Year '73
My Night at Mauri's '69
Belle de Jour '67
Mam'zelle Pigalle '58
That Naughty Girl '58
Fernandel the D'essmaker '57
Dressmaker '56

Patrick Fabian
Twitches Too '07
Twitches '05

Joel Fabiani (1936-)
Snake Eyes '98
Reuben, Reuben '83
President's Mistress '78

Fabio (1961-)
Bubble Boy '01
Death Becomes Her '92
Scenes from a Mall '91
Exorcist 3: Legion '90

Nanette Fabray (1920-)
Teresa's Tattoo '94
Personal Exemptions '88
Amy '81
The Man in the Santa Claus Suit '79
Harper Valley P.T.A. '78
The Happy Ending '69
Alice Through the Looking Glass '66
The Band Wagon '53

Pierre Fabre (1933-2006)
The 317th Platoon '65

Aldo Fabrizi (1905-90)
The Flowers of St. Francis '50
Open City '45

Franco Fabrizi (1916-95)
Ginger & Fred '86
Aurora '84
Act of Aggression '73
A Woman of Rome '56
Il Bidone '55
I Vitelloni '53

Valeria Fabrizi (1938-)
Women in Cell Block 7 '77
Beauty on the Beach '61

Peter Facinelli (1973-)
Hollow Man 2 '06
The Lather Effect '06
The Scorpion King '02
Riding in Cars with Boys '01
Tempted '01
The Big Kahuna '00
Blue Ridge Fall '99
Supernova '99
Can't Hardly Wait '98
Dancer, Texas—Pop. 81 '98
Telling You '98
Calm at Sunset '96
Foxfire '96

Robert Factor
Below '02
Bad Channels '92
Ninja Academy '90
Fear '88

Bill Fagerbakke (1957-)
The Scarlet Pimpernel '99
The Kidnapped King '99
The SpongeBob SquarePants Movie '04
How Many Miles to Babylon? '82

Jeff Fahey (1954-)
Planet Terror '07
The Hunt for Eagle One: Crash Point '06
Frederick Forsyth's Icon '05
No Witness '04
Inferno '01
Blind Heat '00
Revelation '00
Detour '99
Johnny 2.0 '99
No Tomorrow '99
Time Served '99
Beneath the Bermuda Triangle '99
Catherine's Grove '98
When Justice Falls '98
Operation Delta Force '97
The Underground '97
Lethal Tender '96
Smalltime '96
Virtual Seduction '96
Die '95
Eye of the Wolf '95
Darkman 3: Die Darkman '96
Northern Passage '95
Serpent's Lair '95
The Sweeper '95
Firetail '94
Sketch Artist 2: Hands That See '94
Temptation '94
Wyatt Earp '94
Blindsided '93
The Hit List '93
Quick '93
Woman of Desire '93
Sketch Artist '92
Body Parts '91
Iron Maze '91
Curiosity Kills '90
Impulse '90
The Last of the Finest '90
White Hunter, Black Heart '90
True Blood '89
Backfire '88
Split Decisions '88
Psycho 3 '86
Silverado '85
Execution of Raymond Graham '85

Mary-Anne Fahey (1956-)
Celia: Child of Terror '89
Mutant Hunt '87
The Dunera Boys '85

Matty Fain (1905-71)
Social Error '35
The Thirteenth Man '37

Elinor Fair (1903-57)
Yankee Clipper '27
Kismet '20

Jody Fair
The Brain Eaters '58
High School Confidential '58

Bruce Fairbairn (1947-99)
Cyclone '87
Nightstick '87
The Vampire Hookers '78

Christopher Fairbank

Douglas Fairbanks, Sr. (1883-1939)
Private Life of Don Juan '34
Mr. Robinson Crusoe '32
Reaching for the Moon '31
The Iron Mask '29
The Taming of the Shrew '29
The Gaucho '27
A Kiss for Mary Pickford '27
The Black Pirate '26
Don Q, Son of Zorro '25
The Thief of Baghdad '24
Robin Hood '22
The Nut '21
The Three Musketeers '21
The Mark of Zorro '20
The Mollycoddle '20
His Majesty, the American '19
When the Clouds Roll By '19
American Aristocracy '17
The Americano '17
Down to Earth '17
The Man from Painted Post '17
A Girl of the Limberlost '90
Reaching for the Moon '17
His Picture in the Papers '16
Flirting with Fate '16
The Matrimaniac '16
Reggie Mixes In '16
The Lamb '15

Douglas Fairbanks, Jr. (1909-2000)
Ghost Story '81
The Hostage Tower '80
Mister Drake's Duck '50
Sinbad the Sailor '47
The Corsican Brothers '42
Angels Over Broadway '40
Having Wonderful Time '38
Joy of Living '38
The Rage of Paris '38
The Young in Heart '38
When Thief Meets Thief '37
Accused '36
Mimi '35
Catherine the Great '34
Morning Glory '33
Scarlet Dawn '32
Our Modern Maidens '29
Party Girls '29
A Woman of Affairs '28
Little Caesar '30

Virginia Brown Faire (1904-80)
Peter Pan '24
Cricket on the Hearth '23

Heather Fairfield (1934-)
No Secrets '91
I'll Never Forget What's 'Isname '67

Michael Fairman (1934-)
Dead Silence '07
Thirteen Days '00
Forces of Nature '99
The Nurse '97
The Banker '89
Double Whammy '01

Craig Fairbrass (1954-)
White Noise 2: The Light '07

Mary-Anne Fahey ...

Morgan Fairchild (1950-)
Shock to the System '06
Arizona Summer '03
Peril '00
Unshackled '00
Nice Guys Sleep Alone '99
Criminal Hearts '95
Venus Rising '95
Gospa '94
Based on an Untrue Story '93
Body Chemistry 3: Point of Seduction '93
Freaked '93
Test Tube Teens from the Year 2000 '93
Writer's Block '91
Even Angels Fall '90
Mob Boss '90
Haunting of Sarah Hardy '89
Phantom of the Mall: Eric's Revenge '89
Sleeping Beauty '89
Midnight Cop '88
Campus Man '87
Deadly Illusion '87
Red Headed Stranger '87
North and South Book 2 '86
Pee-wee's Big Adventure '85
The Zany Adventures of Robin Hood '84
Honeyboy '82
The Seduction '82
The Concrete Cowboys '79
Initiation of Sarah '78

Matthew Faison
The Long Weekend '05
Killing Time '97
Galaxis '95
Proteus '95
Cliffhanger '93
Nightscare '93

Donald Adeosun Faison (1974-)
Something New '06
Bachelor Party Vegas '05
King's Ransom '05
Good Boy! '03 (V)
Uptown Girls '03
Big Fat Liar '02

Dolores Faith (1942-)
The Phantom Planet '61
The Human Duplicators '64

Adam Faith (1940-2003)
McVicar '80
Yesterday's Hero '79
Beat Girl '60

Marianne Faithfull (1946-)
Marie Antoinette '05
Paris, je t'aime '06
Intimacy '00
Absolutely Fabulous: The Last Shout '96
Crimetime '96
Moondance '95
Shopping '93
When Pigs Fly '93
Assault on Agathon '75
Madhouse Mansion '74
Hamlet '69
The Girl on a Motorcycle '68
I'll Never Forget What's 'Isname '67

Eduardo Fajardo (1918-)
The Killer Must Kill Again '75
Lisa and the Devil '75
Mean Machine '73
Sting of the West '72
Django '68
Stranger in Paso Bravo '68
The Klansman '74
Lady Cocoa '75
The Liberation of L.B. Jones '70
A Man Called Adam '66

Lola Falana (1942-)

Edie Falco (1954-)
Freedomland '06

The Hostage Tower '80
Supreme Sanction '99
Trippin' '99
Never 2 Big '98
Clueless '95
New Jersey Drive '95
Waiting to Exhale '95
Sugar Hill '93

Frankie Faison (1949-)
Tyler Perry's Meet the Browns '08
The Cookout '04
In Good Company '04
White Chicks '04
Gods and Generals '03
Highwaymen '03
Red Dragon '02
Showtime '02
Night on Earth '91
Hannibal '01
A Little Inside '01
The Sleepy Time Gal '01
Thirteen Conversations About One Thing '01
The Thomas Crown Affair '99
Julian Po '97
Mother Night '96
The Rich Man's Wife '96
Stephen King's The Langoliers '95
The Stupids '95
I Love Trouble '94
The Silence of the Lambs '91
Betsy's Wedding '90
Do the Right Thing '89
Coming to America '88
Mississippi Burning '88
Manhunter '86
The Money Pit '86
Ragtime '81

Adam Faith (1940-2003)

Lisanne Falk
Shark Tale '04 (V)
Three Days of Rain '03
A Price above Rubies '98
The Lost World '02
Three Days of Rain '02
Undisputed '02
Corky Romano '01
Night on Earth '91
Heathers '89

Andre Falcon (1924-)
A Slightly Pregnant Man '79
Happy New Year '73
The Mad Adventures of Rabbi Jacob '73

Peter Falk (1927-)
Next '07
The Thing About My Folks '05
Shark Tale '04 (V)
Three Days of Rain '03
The Lost World '02
Undisputed '02
Corky Romano '01
Made '01
Enemies of Laughter '00
Lakeboat '00
Money Kings '98
Pronto '97
The Sunshine Boys '95
Roommates '95
Faraway, So Close! '93
The Player '92
In the Spirit '90
Tune in Tomorrow '90
Cookie '89
Vibes '88
Wings of Desire '88
Happy New Year '87
The Princess Bride '87
Big Trouble '86
...All the Marbles '81
The Great Muppet Caper '81
The In-Laws '79
Brink's Job '78
The Cheap Detective '78
Murder by Death '76
Mikey & Nicky '76
A Woman under the Influence '74
Columbo: Murder by the Book '71
Husbands '70
Castle Keep '69
Anzio '68
Luv '67
Murder '67
The Great Race '65
Robin and the 7 Hoods '64
The Balcony '63
It's a Mad, Mad, Mad, Mad World '63
Pressure Point '62
Pocketful of Miracles '61
The Bloody Brood '59
Wind Across the Everglades '58

Rossella Falk (1926-)
The Black Belly of the Tarantula '71
Modesty Blaise '66
8 1/2 '63

Deborah Fallender
Jabberwocky '77

Jimmy Fallon (1974-)
Factory Girl '06 (V)
Fever Pitch '05
Taxi '04
Anything Else '03
Band of Brothers '01
Almost Famous '00

Siobhan Fallon (1972-)
Charlotte's Web '06

Fallon

Fever Pitch '05
Dogville '03
Holes '03
What's the Worst That Could Happen? '01
Krippendorf's Tribe '98
The Negotiator '98
Men in Black '97
Forrest Gump '94

Roger Fan
Annapolis '06
Better Luck Tomorrow '02
Corky Romano '01
Demon Queen '80

Al Fann (1925-)
Frankie and Johnny '91
Parasite '82
Sophisticated Gents '81

Dakota Fanning (1994-)
Charlotte's Web '06
Dreamer: Inspired by a True Story '05
Hide and Seek '05
Lilo & Stitch 2: Stitch Has a Glitch '05 (V)
Nine Lives '05
War of the Worlds '05
Man on Fire '04
Dr. Seuss' The Cat in the Hat '03
Uptown Girls '03
Sweet Home Alabama '02
Taken '02 (N)
Trapped '02
I Am Sam '01

Elle Fanning (1998-)
Reservation Road '07
Babel '06
Because of Winn-Dixie '05
The Door in the Floor '04

Franco Fantasia (1928-)
Emerald Jungle '80
Mountain of the Cannibal God '79
Adios, Sabata '71

Ennio Fantastichini (1955-)
Napoleon '03
The Blonde '92
The Station '92
Open Doors '89

Sergio Fantoni (1930-)
The Belly of an Architect '91
Hornet's Nest '70
What Did You Do in the War, Daddy? '66
Do Not Disturb '65
Von Ryan's Express '65
The Prize '63
Atom Age Vampire '61
Esther and the King '60
The Giant of Marathon '60
The Hit Man '60

Stephanie Faracy (1952-)
Flightplan '05
Safety Patrol '98
Hocus Pocus '93
Blind Date '87

Daniel Faraldo
Full Fathom Five '90
Above the Law '88

Debrah Farentino (1961-)
Stephen King's The Storm of the Century '99
Dead Air '94
Son of the Pink Panther '93
Bugsy '91
Mortal Sins '90
Capone '89

James Farentino (1938-)
Termination Man '97
Bulletproof '96
Honor Thy Father and Mother: The True Story of the Menendez Brothers '94

In the Line of Duty: A Cop for the Killing '90
Naked Lie '89
Her Alibi '88
Family Sins '87
Sins '85
License to Kill '84
A Summer to Remember '84
The Cradle Will Fall '83
Dead and Buried '81
The Final Countdown '80
Silent Victory: The Kitty O'Neil Story '79
The Possessed '77
The War Lord '65
Ensign Pulver '64
Psychomania '63

Debra Fares
Killer Tomatoes Eat France '91
Killer Tomatoes Strike Back '90

Antonio Fargas (1946-)
Extreme Honor '01
Three Strikes '00
The Suburbans '99
Milo '98
Howling 6: The Freaks '90
The Borrower '89
I'm Gonna Git You Sucka '88
Shakedown '88
Florida Straits '87
Night of the Sharks '87
Crimewave '85
Streetwalkin' '85
Firestarter '84
The Ambush Murders '82
Nurse '80
Pretty Baby '78
Car Wash '76
Cornbread, Earl & Me '75
Huckleberry Finn '75
Busting '74
Foxy Brown '74
Across 110th Street '72
Shaft '71

Betty Faria (1941-)
The Story of Fausta '88
Bye Bye Brazil '79

Carolyn Farina
Metropolitan '90

Dennis Farina (1944-)
What Happens in Vegas '08
You Kill Me '07
Empire Falls '04
Paparazzi '04
Big Trouble '02
Stealing Harvard '02
Sidewalks of New York '01
Bad Seed '00
Reindeer Games '00
Snatch '00
The Mod Squad '99
Out of Sight '98
Saving Private Ryan '98
Bella Mafia '97
Eddie '96
That Old Feeling '96
Get Shorty '95
Little Big League '94
Out of Annie's Past '94
Another Stakeout '93
High Stakes '93
Mac '93
Striking Distance '93
Drug Wars 2: The Cocaine Cartel '92
Street Crimes '92
We're Talkin' Serious Money '92
Men of Respect '91
The Hillside Strangler '89
Midnight Run '88
Jo Jo Dancer, Your Life Is Calling '86
Manhunter '86
Code of Silence '85
Thief '81

Daniela Farinacci
Look Both Ways '05

Lantana '01

Pierfrancesco Farino
The Chronicles of Narnia: Prince Caspian '08
Our Italian Husband '04

Gabriella Farinon (1941-)
Assignment Outer Space '61
Blood and Roses '61

Anna Faris (1976-)
Smiley Face '07
My Super Ex-Girlfriend '06
Scary Movie 4 '06
Brokeback Mountain '05
Just Friends '05
Southern Belles '05
Waiting '05
Lost in Translation '03
Scary Movie 3 '03
The Hot Chick '02
May '02
Scary Movie 2 '01
Scary Movie '00

Sean Faris (1982-)
Never Back Down '08
Yours, Mine & Ours '05
Sleepover '04
Brotherhood 2: The Young Warlocks '01

Albert Farley
See Alberto (Albert Farley) Farnese

Chris Farley (1964-97)
Almost Heroes '97
Dirty Work '97
Beverly Hills Ninja '96
Black Sheep '96
Tommy Boy '95
Airheads '94
Billy Madison '94
Coneheads '93
Wayne's World 2 '93
The Midnight Phantom '35

John Farley
The General '26
Believers '07
Blonde and Blonder '07

Kevin Farley
Blonde and Blonder '07
Danny Roane: First Time Director '06

Morgan Farley (1898-1988)
Abbott and Costello Meet the Killer, Boris Karloff '49
Open Secret '48

Sean Farley (1976-)
Tainted '98

Teresa Farley
Crimewave '85

Frances Farmer (1913-70)
Son of Fury '42
South of Pago Pago '40
Toast of New York '37
Come and Get It '36
Rhythm on the Range '36

Gary Farmer (1953-)
All Hat '07
Disappearances '06
The Big Empty '04
Evergreen '04
A Thief of Time '04
Twist '03
Adaptation '02
Skins '02
The Score '01
Angels Don't Sleep Here '00
Heater '99
Smoke Signals '98
Moonshine Highway '96
Dead Man '95
Henry & Verlin '94
Sioux City '94

Powwow Highway '89
Big Town '87

Mimsy Farmer (1945-)
Codename: Wildgeese '84
The Black Cat '81
Autopsy '74
Allonsanfan '73
More '69
Road to Salina '68
Devil's Angels '67
Spencer's Mountain '63

Suzan Farmer (1943-)
Death in Deep Water '74
The Graveyard '74
Dracula, Prince of Darkness '66
Rasputin the Mad Monk '66
Die, Monster, Die! '65

Vera Farmiga (1973-)
Joshua '07
Breaking and Entering '06
The Departed '06
Running Scared '06
Down to the Bone '04
The Manchurian Candidate '04
Dummy '02
Love in the Time of Money '02
15 Minutes '01
Autumn in New York '00
Return to Paradise '98

Alberto (Albert Farley) Farnese (1926-96)
The Conqueror & the Empress '64
Gladiator of Rome '63
The Giants of Thessaly '60

Richard Farnsworth (1920-2000)
The Straight Story '99
Lassie '94
The Natural '84
Rhinestone '84
The Grey Fox '83
Independence Day '83
Waltz across Texas '83
Legend of the Lone Ranger '81
Ruckus '81
Resurrection '80
Tom Horn '80
Comes a Horseman '78
Strange New World '75
Texas Across the River '66

Franklyn Farnum (1878-1961)
Prison Train '38
Ghost Rider '35
Hopalong Cassidy '35
Powdersmoke Range '35
The Silver Bullet '34
Mark of the Spur '32
Battling with Buffalo Bill '31
The Scarlet Car '17

William Farnum (1876-1953)
Jack & the Beanstalk '52
Lone Star '52
Trail of Robin Hood '50
Gun Cargo '49
God's Country '46
My Dog Shep '46
Wildfire '45
Today I Hang '42
Adventures of Red Ryder '40
South of the Border '39
Santa Fe Stampede '38
Git Along Little Dogies '37
Public Cowboy No. 1 '37

The Clutching Hand '36
Custer's Last Stand '36
Kid Ranger '36
Undersea Kingdom '36
Between Men '35
The Crusades '35
Powdersmoke Range '35
The Silver Streak '34
Supernatural '33
The Drifter '32
Law of the Sea '32
Mr. Robinson Crusoe '32
A Connecticut Yankee '31
Painted Desert '31
Ten Nights in a Bar-Room '31
Dubarry '30
The Spoilers '14

Derek Farr (1912-86)
Truth about Women '58
Man on the Run '49
Spellbound '41

Felicia Farr (1932-)
Charley Varrick '73
Kotch '71
Kiss Me, Stupid! '64
3:10 to Yuma '57
Jubal '56

Jamie Farr (1936-)
Fearless Tiger '94
Curse 2: The Bite '88
Scrooged '88
Speed Zone '88
Happy Hour '87
Combat Academy '86
Cannonball Run 2 '84
For Love or Money '84
M*A*S*H: Goodbye, Farewell & Amen '83
Cannonball Run '81
Return of the Rebels '81
Arnold '73
Heavy Traffic '73
With Six You Get Eggroll '68
Who's Minding the Mint? '67
The Loved One '65
No Time for Sergeants '58
Blackboard Jungle '55

Judi Farr
Walking on Water '02
The Year My Voice Broke '87

Patricia Farr (1915-48)
Mistaken Identity '36
Tailspin Tommy '34

David Farrar (1908-95)
The 300 Spartans '62
Beat Girl '60
John Paul Jones '59
Let's Make Up '55
Pearl of the South Pacific '55
Sea Chase '55
The Black Shield of Falworth '54
The Obsessed '51
The Small Back Room '49
Black Narcissus '47
Frieda '47
The World Owes Me a Living '47
Murder in the Footlights '46
Echo Murders '45
Meet Sexton Blake '44
The Hooded Terror '38

Charles Farrell (1901-88)
The Abominable Dr. Phibes '71
The Vampire Lovers '70
Girl Hunters '63
The Sheriff of Fractured Jaw '59
Crimson Pirate '52
Night and the City '50
They Made Me a Fugitive '47
Meet Sexton Blake '44

Charles Farrell (1901-90)
Just Around the Corner '38
Moonlight Sonata '38

Aggie Appleby, Maker of Men '33
City Girl '30
Old Ironsides '26

Colin Farrell (1938-)
A Bridge Too Far '77
The Land That Time Forgot '75

Colin Farrell (1976-)
Oh! What a Lovely War '69
In Bruges '08
Cassandra's Dream '07
Ask the Dust '06
Miami Vice '06
The New World '05
Alexander '04
A Home at the End of the World '04
Daredevil '03
The Recruit '03
S.W.A.T. '03
Veronica Guerin '03
Hart's War '02
Minority Report '02
Phone Booth '02
American Outlaws '01
Tigerland '00
Ordinary Decent Criminal '99
Falling for a Dancer '98
The War Zone '98

Glenda Farrell (1904-71)
Disorderly Orderly '64
Kissin' Cousins '64
The Girl in the Red Velvet Swing '55
Heading for Heaven '47
City Without Men '43
Johnny Eager '42
A Night for Crime '42
Talk of the Town '42
Twin Beds '42
Prison Break '38
Gold Diggers of 1935 '35
Bureau of Missing Persons '33
Gambling Ship '33
Havana Widows '33
Lady for a Day '33
Mystery of the Wax Museum '33
I Am a Fugitive from a Chain Gang '32
Little Caesar '30

Mike Farrell (1939-)
Sins of the Mind '97
Silent Motive '91
Dark River: A Father's Revenge '90
Lockdown '90
Vanishing Act '88
M*A*S*H: Goodbye, Farewell & Amen '83
Memorial Day '83
Prime Suspect '82
Sex and the Single Parent '82
Damien: The Leper Priest '80
Targets '68
Escape from Planet Earth '67
The Graduate '67

Nicholas Farrell (1955-)
Amazing Grace '06
Driving Lessons '06
Bait '02
Bloody Sunday '01
Charlotte Gray '01
Beautiful People '99
Legionnaire '98
Hamlet '96
Sharpe's Regiment '96
Twelfth Night '96
The Choir '95
A Midwinter's Tale '95
Othello '95
To Play the King '93
Hold the Dream '86

Sharon Farrell (1946-)
Beyond '93
Arcade '93
One Man Force '89
Can't Buy Me Love '87
Night of the Comet '84

Flage '80
The Stunt Man '80
The Premonition '75
It's Alive '74
The Love Machine '71
Marlowe '69
The Reivers '69
40 Pounds of Trouble '62

Terry Farrell (1963-)
Legion '98
Red Sun Rising '94
Danielle Steel's Star '93
Hellraiser 3: Hell on Earth '92
Off the Mark '87
Back to School '86
Beverly Hills Madam '86

Timothy Farrell (1923-89)
Gun Girls '56
Jail Bait '54
The Devil's Sleep '51
Pin Down Girls '51
Test Tube Babies '48
Pirates of the High Seas '50

Tommy Farrell (1921-2004)
Kissin' Cousins '64
Meet Danny Wilson '52

Mia Farrow (1945-)
Be Kind Rewind '08
The Ex '07
Arthur and the Invisibles '06
The Omen '06
Purpose '02
A Girl Thing '01
Coming Soon '99
Miracle at Midnight '98
Miami Rhapsody '95
Reckless '95
Widow's Peak '94
Husbands and Wives '92
Shadows and Fog '92
Alice '90
Crimes & Misdemeanors '89
New York Stories '89
Another Woman '88
September '88
Radio Days '87
Hannah and Her Sisters '86
The Purple Rose of Cairo '85
Broadway Danny Rose '84
Supergirl '84
Zelig '83
A Midsummer Night's Sex Comedy '82
Hurricane '79
Avalanche '78
Death on the Nile '78
A Wedding '78
The Great Gatsby '74
High Heels '72
See No Evil '71
Secret Ceremony '69
Dandy in Aspic '68
Rosemary's Baby '68
Guns at Batasi '64

Tisa Farrow (1951-)
Grim Reaper '81
Search and Destroy '81
The Last Hunter '80
Zombie '80
Manhattan '79
Winter Kills '79
Fingers '78
Initiation of Sarah '78
Strange Shadows in an Empty Room '76
Some Call It Loving '73
And Hope to Die '72
The American Soldier '70
Beware of a Holy Whore '70
Whity '70

Rainer Werner Fassbinder (1946-82)
Kamikaze '89 '83
Shadow of Angels '76
Fox and His Friends '75
Tenderness of the Wolves '73

Ron Fassler (1957-)
Alien Nation: The Enemy Within '96
Alien Nation: Dark Horizon '94

Fat Joe (1970-)
Empire '02
Thicker than Water '99
The Cooler '03

Joey Fatone (1977-)
My Big Fat Greek Wedding '02
On the Line '01

Andrew Faulds (1922-2000)
Lisztomania '75
The Devils '71

James Faulkner (1948-)
The Bank Job '08
Agent Cody Banks 2: Destination London '04
I Capture the Castle '02
The Target '02
Conduct Unbecoming '75
Flashpoint Africa '84
Albino '76
A Kid in Aladdin's Palace '97
All the Little Animals '98

Sally Faulkner (1944-)
Alien Prey '83
Vampyres '74

Stephanie Faulkner
Virus '82

Renee Faure (1918-2005)
The Judge and the Assassin '75
La Chartreuse de Parme '48

Chad Faust (1974-)
Saved! '04

David Faustino (1974-)
Descent '07
Nearing Grace '05
MacArthur Park '01
Killer Bud '00
Alien Nation: Millennium '96
Perfect Harmony '91

Jon Favreau (1966-)
Iron Man '08
The Break-Up '06
Open Season '06 (V)
The Big Empty '04
Wimbledon '04
Daredevil '03
Elf '03
Something's Gotta Give '03
Made '01
Love & Sex '00
The Replacements '00
Rocky Marciano '99
Deep Impact '98
Very Bad Things '98
Dogtown '97
Just Your Luck '96
Persons Unknown '96
Swingers '96
Batman Forever '95
Notes from Underground '95
P.C.U. '94
Rudy '93

Farrah Fawcett (1946-)
The Cookout '04
Baby '00
Dr. T & the Women '00
The Apostle '97
Dalva '95
A Good Day to Die '95
Man of the House '95
The Substitute Wife '94
Double Exposure: The Story of Margaret Bourke-White '89
See You in the Morning '89
Small Sacrifices '89
Poor Little Rich Girl: The Barbara Hutton Story '87
Between Two Women '86
Extremities '86
The Burning Bed '85
The Red Light Sting '84
Murder in Texas '81
Cannonball Run '81
Saturn 3 '80
Logan's Run '76
Murder on Flight 502 '75
Myra Breckinridge '70

Alan Fawcett
Blindside '88
A Conspiracy of Love '87

George Fawcett (1860-1939)
Personal Maid '31
Drums of Jeopardy '31
The Wedding March '28
The Flesh and the Devil '27
Son of the Sheik '26
The Mad Whirl '25
Heart of Texas Ryan '17

William "Bill" Fawcett (1894-1974)
Jesse James Meets Frankenstein's Daughter '65
Gun Glory '57
Storm Rider '57
Black Hills '48
Check Your Guns '48
The Tioga Kid '48
Driftin' River '46
Death Journey '76
King Rat '65

Dorothy Fay (1915-2003)
Trigger Pals '38
Law of the Texan '38

Frank Fay (1897-1961)
Love Nest '51
Spotlight Scandals '43

Meagen Fay
The County Bears '02

Alice Faye (1915-98)
Every Girl Should Have One '78
State Fair '62
The Gang's All Here '43
Hello, Frisco, Hello '43
That Night in Rio '41
Week-End in Havana '41
Tin Pan Alley '40
Lillian Russell '40
Rose of Washington Square '39
Alexander's Ragtime Band '38
In Old Chicago '37
On the Avenue '37
The Poor Little Rich Girl '36
Stowaway '36
365 Nights in Hollywood '34

Denise Faye
American Pie 2 '01
Square '39

Frank Faylen (1905-85)
Gunfight at the O.K. Corral '57
Seventh Cavalry '56
The McConnell Story '55
Red Garters '54
Riot in Cell Block 11 '54
Hangman's Knot '52
Detective Story '51
Copper Canyon '50
The Nevadan '50
Francis the Talking Mule '49
The Road to Rio '47
Welcome Stranger '47
Blue Skies '46
It's a Wonderful Life '46
The Lost Weekend '45
Across the Pacific '42
Wake Island '42
Sergeant York '41
Tanks a Million '41
Gone with the Wind '39
Waterfront '39

Louise Fazenda (1895-1962)
The Old Maid '39
Doughnuts & Society '36
Gun Smoke '31
The Bat '26
The Night Club '25

Ron Fazio
Basket Case 2 '90
The Toxic Avenger, Part 2 '89
The Toxic Avenger, Part 3: The Last Temptation of Toxie '89

Michael Feast (1946-)
Penelope '06
Velvet Goldmine '98
Touching Evil '97

Angela Featherstone (1965-)
Family of Cops 2: Breach of Faith '97
Con Air '97
200 Cigarettes '98
Zero Effect '97
The Wedding Singer '97
Dark Angel: The Ascent '94
The Guilty '00
One Way Out '02
Skipped Parts '00
Pressure '02
Palmetto '98

Birgitte Federspiel (1925-2005)
Babette's Feast '87
Ordet '55

Andrea Feldman (1948-72)
Heat '72
Trash '70

Clarence Felder (1938-)
The Hidden '87
Killing Floor '85

Corey Feldman (1971-)
The Million Dollar Kid '99
Legion '98
Storm Trooper '98
Born Bad '97
Evil Obsession '96
Red Line '96
No Witness '04
Tales from the Crypt Presents Bordello of Blood '96
South Beach Academy '96
A Dangerous Place '94
Dream a Little Dream 2 '94
National Lampoon's Last Resort '94
Blown Away '93
Lipstick Camera '93
The Magic Voyage '93 (V)
National Lampoon's Loaded Weapon 1 '93
Meatballs 4 '92
Round Trip to Heaven '92
Edge of Honor '91
Rock 'n' Roll High School Forever '91
Teenage Mutant Ninja Turtles: The Movie '90
The 'Burbs '89
Dream a Little Dream '89
License to Drive '88
The Lost Boys '87
Stand by Me '86
Friday the 13th, Part 5: A New Beginning '85
The Goonies '85
Friday the 13th, Part 4: The Final Chapter '84
Gremlins '84

Brendan Fehr (1977-)
The Long Weekend '05
Biker Boyz '03
Nemesis Game '03
Edge of Madness '02
The Forsaken '01
Kill Me Later '01
Christina's House '01
The Mummy Returns '01
Texas Rangers '01

Oded Fehr (1970-)
Resident Evil: Extinction '07
Deuce Bigalow: European Gigolo '05
Dreamer: Inspired by a True Story '05
Sleeper Cell '05
Resident Evil: Apocalypse '04
The Mummy Returns '01
Deuce Bigalow: Male Gigolo '99
The Mummy '99

Bekim Fehmiu (1936-)
Battle of the Eagles '79
Ride to Glory '71
The Adventurers '70

Caroleen Feeney
Happy Hour '03
Avalanche '99
Bad Manners '98
Cadillac Ranch '96
Denise Calls Up '95

Ben Feldman (1980-)
The Perfect Man '05
When Do We Eat? '05

Trevor Fehrman
Clerks 2 '06
Now You Know '02
The Mummy '99

Martin Feifel (1964-)
Rosenstrasse '03
What to Do in Case of Fire '02

Halley Feiffer
Margot at the Wedding '07
Stephanie Daley '06

Michael Feast [see above]

The Squid and the Whale '05
J.J. Feild (1978-)
Northanger Abbey '07
Ruby in the Smoke '06
The Secret Life of Mrs. Beeton '06
The Intended '02
Last Orders '01

Alan Feinstein (1941-)
Get Smart, Again! '89
The Hunt for the Night Stalker '91
Stalker '91

Fritz Feld (1900-93)
Get Smart, Again! '89
Barfly '87
Herbie Goes Bananas '80
World's Greatest Lover '77
The Strongest Man in the World '75
Promises! Promises! '63
The Errand Boy '61
Kentucky Jubilee '51
Sky High '51
The Lovable Cheat '49
The Noose Hangs High '48
Mexican Hayride '48
Iceland '42
Four Jacks and a Jill '41
At the Circus '39
Everything Happens at Night '39
Bringing Up Baby '38
The Affairs of Annabel '38

History of the World: Part 1 '81

Tibor Feldman (1947-)
Fat Guy Goes Nutzoid '86
The River Is Red '48

Barbara Feldon (1941-)
Get Smart, Again! '89
The Two Worlds of Jenny Logan '79
No Deposit, No Return '76
Smile '75
Playmates '72

Tovah Feldshuh (1952-)
Just My Luck '06
Lady in the Water '06
The Tollbooth '04
Kissing Jessica Stein '02
Happy Accidents '01
Friends and Family '01
A Walk on the Moon '99
The Corruptor '99
A Day in October '92
Brewster's Millions '85
Blue Iguana '88
Cheaper to Keep -ier '80
Idolmaker '80
Holocaust '78
Terror Out of the Sky '78
The Amazing Howard Hughes '77

Jose Feliciano (1945-)
Aaron Loves Angela '75

Mario Feliciani (1918-)
Assassination in Rome '65
Revolt of the Barbarians '64

Norman Fell (1924-98)
The Destiny of Marty Fine '96
Hexed '93
For the Boys '91
The Bone Yard '90
Stripped to Kill '87
Transylvania 6-5000 '85
On the Right Track '81
Paternity '81
For the Love of It '80
The End '78
Cleopatra Jones & the Casino of Gold '75
Death Stalk '74
Charley Varrick '73
The Stone Killer '73
The Boatniks '70
Catch-22 '70
If It's Tuesday, This Must Be Belgium '69
Bullitt '68
The Graduate '67
The Killers '64
It's a Mad, Mad, Mad, Mad World '63
Inherit the Wind '60
Ocean's 11 '60
Pork Chop Hill '59

Barbara Feldon [see above]

The Fox and the Hound '81
Marty Feldman (1933-82)
(V),
Slapstick of Another Kind '84
Yellowbeard '83
In God We Trust '80
The Adventures of Sherlock Holmes' Smarter Brother '78
The Last Remake of Beau Geste '77
Sex with a Smile '76
Silent Movie '76
Young Frankenstein '74
Think Dirty '70

Tom Fellegi
Hornet's Nest '70
Revenge of the Barbarians '60

Federico Fellini (1920-93)
Fellini: I'm a Born Liar '03
Intervista '87

We All Loved Each Other So Much '77
Fellini's Roma '72 (V)
Alex in Wonderland '70
Ciao Federico! Fellini Directs Satyricon '69
The Miracle '48

Julian Fellowes (1950-)
The Aristocrats '99
Behind the Lines '97
The Final Cut '95
Sharpe's Rifles '93
Damage '92
Goldeneye: The Secret Life of Ian Fleming '89
Baby... Secret of the Lost Legend '85

Rockliffe Fellowes (1885-1950)
Monkey Business '31

Edith Fellows (1923-)
Regeneration '15
In the Mood '87
The Grace Kelly Story '83
Heart of the Rio Grande '42
Her First Romance '40
Music in My Heart '40
Pennies from Heaven '36

Hansjorg Felmy (1931-2007)
The Mad Executioners '65
The Monster of London City '64
Brainwashed '60

Tom Felton (1987-)
Harry Potter and the Order of the Phoenix '07
Harry Potter and the Goblet of Fire '05
Harry Potter and the Prisoner of Azkaban '04
Harry Potter and the Chamber of Secrets '02
Harry Potter and the Sorcerer's Stone '01
Anna and the King '99
The Borrowers '97

Verna Felton (1890-1966)
The Jungle Book '67 (V)
Sleeping Beauty '59 (V)
The Oklahoman '56
Lady and the Tramp '55 (V)
Picnic '55
Belles on Their Toes '52
Cinderella '50 (V)
Dumbo '41 (V)

Freddy Fender (1937-2006)
The Milagro Beanfield War '88

Edwige Fenech (1948-)
Hostel: Part 2 '07
Phantom of Death '87
You've Got to Have Heart '77

Tanya Fenmore
Lisa '90
My Stepmother Is an Alien '88

Sherilyn Fenn (1965-)
Novel Romance '06
Nightwaves '03
United States of Leland '03
Swindle '02
Off Season '01
Cement '99
Darkness Falls '98
Just Write '97

Lovelife '97
National Lampoon's The Don's Analyst '97
The Assassination File '96
Boxing Helena '93
Fatal Instinct '93
Three of Hearts '93
Desire and Hell at Sunset Motel '92
Of Mice and Men '92
Ruby '92
Diary of a Hitman '91
Dillinger '91
Backstreet Dreams '90
Meridian: Kiss of the Beast '90
Wild at Heart '90
True Blood '89
Crime Zone '88
Two Moon Junction '88
The Wraith '87
Zombie High '87
Just One of the Guys '85
The Wild Life '84

Tod Fennell (1984-)
The Kid '97
Stalked '94

Parker Fennelly (1891-1988)
How to Frame a Figg '71
The Kettles on Old MacDonald's Farm '57

George Fenneman (1919-97)
The Marx Brothers in a Nutshell '90
How to Succeed in Business without Really Trying '67
The Thing '51

Shelby Fenner (1978-)
The Guardian '06
Local Boys '02

Frank Fenton (1906-57)
Naked Hills '56
Island in the Sky '53
The Glass Pigeon '49
The Golden Stallion '49
Mexican Hayride '48
Isle of Forgotten Sins '43

Lance Fenton (1966-)
Heathers '89
Night of the Demons '88

Leslie Fenton (1902-78)
The House of Secrets '37
Fugitive Road '34
Marie Galante '34
F.P. 1 '33
Lady Killer '33
The Strange Love of Molly Louvain '32
Murder at Midnight '31
Public Enemy '31

Simon Fenton (1976-)
A Knight in Camelot '98
The Rector's Wife '94
Matinee '92

Perry Fenwick (1962-)
The Winslow Boy '98
The Raggedy Rawney '90
Party! Party! '83

Colm Feore (1958-)
Bury My Heart at Wounded Knee '07
The Exorcism of Emily Rose '05
Slings & Arrows: Season 2 '05
The Chronicles of Riddick '04
And Starring Pancho Villa as Himself '03
Highwaymen '03
National Security '03
Paycheck '03
Chicago '02
Point of Origin '02
The Sum of All Fears '02
Widows '02
The Caveman's Valentine '01

The Day Reagan Was Shot '01
Ignition '01
Pearl Harbor '01
Sins of the Father '01
The Perfect Son '00
The Insider '99
Stephen King's The Storm of the Century '99
Titus '99
Airborne '98
City of Angels '98
The Red Violin '98
Critical Care '97
Face/Off '97
The Lesser Evil '97
Night Falls on Manhattan '96
The Wrong Guy '96
The Escape '95
Truman '95
Where's the Money, Noreen? '95
The Spider and the Fly '94
32 Short Films about Glenn Gould '93
Beautiful Dreamers '90
Dr. Bethune '90
Personals '90
Blades of Courage '88

Heino Ferch (1963-)
The 4 Musketeers '05
Downfall '04
Napoleon '03
Extreme Ops '02
The Tunnel '01
The Harmonists '99
Straight Shooter '99
Lucie Aubrac '98
Winter Sleepers '97

Pamelyn Ferdin (1959-)
Rockula '90
Night Children '89
Angel 3: The Final Chapter '88

Adam Ferency (1951-)
The Interrogation '82
Mother of Kings '82
Fever '81

Al Ferguson (1888-1971)
Rose Marie '54
Lightning Raiders '45
Law of the Saddle '43
Roamin' Wild '36
Laramie Kid '35
The Three Musketeers '33
Mystery Trooper '32
Near the Rainbow's End '30
Tarzan the Tiger '29
Tentacles of the North '26

Chloe Ferguson (1989-)
The Quiet Room '96
Alien Visitor '95

Craig Ferguson (1962-)
Niagara Motel '06
I'll Be There '03
Life Without Dick '02
Born Romantic '00
Chain of Fools '00
Saving Grace '00
The Big Tease '99

Frank Ferguson (1899-1978)
Battle Cry '55

Johnny Guitar '53
Abbott and Costello Meet Frankenstein '48

J. Don Ferguson
The Second Chance '06
Running Mates '86
Loveless '83

Jay R. Ferguson (1989-)
Blue Ridge Fall '99
Campfire Tales '98

Mark Ferguson (1961-)
Hercules the Legendary Journeys, Vol. 3: The Circle of Fire '94
Hercules the Legendary Journeys, Vol. 4: In the Underworld '94

Matthew Ferguson (1973-)
Cube 2: Hypercube '02
The Wall '99
Lilies '96
The Club '94
Eclipse '94
Love and Human Remains '93
On My Own '92

Phoebe Ferguson (1993-)
The Lost City '05
The Quiet Room '96

Stacy "Fergie" Ferguson (1975-)
Planet Terror '07
Poseidon '06

Tom Ferguson (1946-)
Biohazard: The Alien Force '95

Anouk Ferjac (1932-)
Dark Universe '93
Peppermint Soda '77
This Man Must Die '70

Jodelle Ferland (1994-)
Pictures of Hollis Woods '07
Silent Hill '06

Vanessa Ferlito (1970-)
Death Proof '07
Shadowboxer '06
Man of the House '05
Spider-Man 2 '04
Undefeated '03
OnLine '01

Fernando Fernan-Gomez (1921-2007)
Butterfly '98
The Grandfather '98
Belle Epoque '92
The Stilts '84
Mama Turns a Hundred '79
Spirit of the Beehive '73

Fernandel (1903-71)
Fernandel the Dressmaker '57
The Man in the Raincoat '57
Pantaloons '57
Paris Holiday '57
Around the World in 80 Days '56
The French Touch '54
The Sheep Has Five Legs '54
Forbidden Fruit '52
Little World of Don Camillo '51
The Red Inn '51
Topaze '51
Well-Digger's Daughter '46
Nais '45
Le Schpountz '38
Harvest '37
Angele '34

Miguel Fernandes
Sorry, Wrong Number '89
True Believer '89

Spasms '82
The Kidnapping of the President '80

Abel Fernandez (1930-)
Pork Chop Hill '59
Rose Marie '54

Emilio Fernandez (1904-86)
Bring Me the Head of Alfredo Garcia '74
The Wild Bunch '69
Return of the Magnificent Seven '66
The Night of the Iguana '64

Esther Fernandez (1917-99)
Pancho Villa Returns '50
Two Years before the Mast '46

Evelina Fernandez (1973-)
Gabriela '01
Luminarias '99
American Me '92

Jesus Fernandez
Tristana '70
Nazarin '58

Juan Fernandez (1973-)
Bad Education '04
A Man Apart '03
Dead Tides '97
Fire on the Amazon '93
Liquid Dreams '92
Cat Chaser '90
Kinjite: Forbidden Subjects '89
Crocodile Dundee 2 '88
Salvador '86

Rudolf Fernau (1898-1985)
Strangler of Blackmoor Castle '63
The Invisible Dr. Mabuse '62

Abel Ferrara (1952-)
Ms. 45 '81
Driller Killer '79

Ashley Ferrare
Cyclone '87
Revenge of the Ninja '83

Christina Ferrare (1950-)
Mary, Mary, Bloody Mary '76

Conchata Ferrell (1943-)
Mr. Deeds '02
Crime and Punishment in Suburbia '00
Erin Brockovich '00
My Fellow Americans '96
The Buccaneers '95
Heaven and Earth '93
Samurai Cowboy '93
True Romance '93
Backfield in Motion '91
Eye on the Sparrow '91
Family Prayers '91
Edward Scissorhands '90
Goodbye, Miss 4th of July '88
Mystic Pizza '88
Where the River Runs Black '86

Who'll Save Our Children? '82
Heartland '81
Rape and Marriage: The Rideout Case '80
To Love Again '80
Lost Legacy: A Girl Called Hatter Fox '77
Network '76
Deadly Hero '75

Tyra Ferrell (1962-)
The Perfect Score '04
The Corner '00
Equinox '93
Poetic Justice '93
White Men Can't Jump '92
Boyz N the Hood '91
Jungle Fever '91
School Daze '88
Lady Beware '87

Will Ferrell (1968-)
Semi-Pro '08
Step Brothers '08
Blades of Glory '07
Curious George '06 (V)
Stranger Than Fiction '06
Talladega Nights: The Ballad of Ricky Bobby '06
Bewitched '05
Kicking & Screaming '05
Melinda and Melinda '05
The Producers '05
Wedding Crashers '05
The Wendell Baker Story '05
Winter Passing '05
Anchorman: The Legend of Ron Burgundy '04
Starsky & Hutch '04
Boat Trip '03
Elf '03
Old School '03
Jay and Silent Bob Strike Back '01
Zoolander '01
Austin Powers 2: The Spy Who Shagged Me '99
Dick '99
The Suburbans '99
Superstar '99
A Night at the Roxbury '98
Austin Powers: International Man of Mystery '97

Andrea Ferreol (1947-)
Iris Blond '98
Francesco '93
Sweet Killing '93
The Phantom of the Opera '90
Stroke of Midnight '90
The Sleazy Uncle '89
A Zed & Two Noughts '88
Control '87
The Last Metro '80
Three Brothers '80
Milo Milo '79
The Tin Drum '79
Despair '78
La Grande Bouffe '73

Jose Ferrer (1909-92)
A Life of Sin '92
Hired to Kill '91
Old Explorers '90
Strange Interlude '90
Christopher Columbus '85
Seduced '85
Dune '84
The Evil That Men Do '84
George Washington '84
Samson and Delilah '84
The Being '83
Bloody Birthday '80
Blood Tide '82
A Midsummer Night's Sex Comedy '82
Berlin Tunnel 21 '81
Peter and Paul '81
The Big Brawl '80
Gideon's Trumpet '80
Pleasure Palace '80
The Fifth Musketeer '79
Natural Enemies '79

The Swarm '78
Zoltan... Hound of Dracula '78
The Private Files of J. Edgar Hoover '77
Who Has Seen the Wind? '77
The Big Bus '76
The Sentinel '76
Voyage of the Damned '76
The Art of Crime '75
Paco '75
Order to Kill '73
Enter Laughing '67
The Greatest Story Ever Told '65
Ship of Fools '65
Lawrence of Arabia '62
The Caine Mutiny '54
Deep in My Heart '54
Moulin Rouge '53
Miss Sadie Thompson '53
Cyrano de Bergerac '50
Joan of Arc '48

Leilani Sarelle Ferrer (1966-)
Breach of Trust '95
Sketch Artist 2: Hands That See '94
Barbarians at the Gate '93
Basic Instinct '92
Shag: The Movie '69

Mel Ferrer (1917-)
Catherine the Great '95
Outrage! '86
Deadly Game '83
One Shoe Makes It Murder '82
The Great Alligator '81
City of the Walking Dead '80
The Fifth Floor '80
The Visitor '80
Norseman '78
Hi-Riders '77
Eaten Alive '76
The Tempter '74
The Fall of the Roman Empire '64
Paris When It Sizzles '64
Sex and the Single Girl '64
The Longest Day '62
Return to Peyton Place '61
Blood and Roses '61
The Hands of Orlac '60
Elena and Her Men '56
War and Peace '56
Knights of the Round Table '53
Lili '53
Rancho Notorious '52
Scaramouche '52
Born to Be Bad '50
Lost Boundaries '49

Miguel Ferrer (1954-)
The Man '05
The Manchurian Candidate '04
Silver City '04
Sunshine State '02
Traffic '00
Mulan '98 (V)
Where's Marlowe? '98
Mr. Magoo '97
The Disappearance of Garcia Lorca '96
Point of No Return '93
It's All True '93 (V)
Royce '93
Scam '93
The Harvest '92
Twin Peaks: Fire Walk with Me '92
Drug Wars: The Camarena Story '90
Revenge '90
The Guardian '90
Deepstar Six '89
Python Wolf '88
RoboCop '87
Flashpoint '84
Lovelines '84
Star Trek 3: The Search for Spock '84

Dan Ferro (1960-)
Blow '01
Sgt. Bilko '95

America Ferrera (1984-)
Sisterhood of the Traveling Pants 2 '08
Steel City '06
Sisterhood of the Traveling Pants '05
Real Women Have Curves '02

Martin Ferrero (1947-)
Air Bud 3: World Pup '00
The Tailor of Panama '00
Gods and Monsters '98
Stop! or My Mom Will Shoot '92
Jurassic Park '93
High Spirits '88
Planes, Trains & Automobiles '87

Eve Ferret
Foreign Body '86
Haunted Honeymoon '86

Claudia Ferri
Mambo Italiano '03

Lupita Ferrer (1947-)
Balboa '82
Children of Sanchez '79

Noel Ferrier (1930-97)
Great Expectations: The Untold Story '87
Return of Captain Invincible '83
The Year of Living Dangerously '82
Adventures of Eliza Fraser '76

Carla Ferrigno
Black Roses '88
Seven Magnificent Gladiators '84

Lou Ferrigno (1952-)
Hulk '03
The Godson '98
...And God Spoke '94
Cage 2: The Arena of Death '94
Return to Frogtown '92
Hangfire '91
Death of the Incredible Hulk '90
Liberty & Bash '90
All's Fair '89
The Cage '89
Sinbad of the Seven Seas '89
The Trial of the Incredible Hulk '89
The Incredible Hulk Returns '88
Desert Warrior '88
Hercules 2 '85
Hercules '83
The Incredible Hulk '77

Turi Ferro (1921-2001)
Malicious '74
Seduction of Mimi '72

Gabriele Ferzetti (1925-)
Othello '95
Julia and Julia '87
Basileus Quartet '82
Vatican Conspiracy '81
The Psychic '78
The Night Porter '74
Counter Punch '71
French Intrigue '70
On Her Majesty's Secret Service '69
L'Avventura '60

David Ferry (1951-)
Thin Air '00
Boondock Saints '99
The Passion of Ayn Rand '99

Mark Feuerstein (1971-)
In Her Shoes '05
Rules of Engagement '00
What Women Want '00
Woman on Top '00
Giving It Up '99
The Muse '99

Debra Feuer
Night Angel '90
Homeboy '88

Darrell Fetty
Blood Beach '81
Stunts '77

Stepin Fetchit (1902-85)
Amazing Grace '74
The Sun Shines Bright '53
Miracle in Harlem '48
Charlie Chan in Egypt '35
Steamboat Round the Bend '35
Bend '35
David Harum '34
Judge Priest '34
Stand Up and Cheer '34
The World Moves On '34
Wild Horse '31

Larry Fessenden (1963-)
Broken Flowers '05
Headspace '05
Margarita Happy Hour '01
You Are Here '00
Habit '95
River of Grass '94

Adam Fiduslewicz (1985-)
In Desert and Wilderness '01

John Fiedler (1925-2005)
Pooh's Heffalump Movie '05 (V)
Piglet's Big Movie '03 (V)
The Emperor's New Groove '00 (V)
I Am the Cheese '83
The Fox and the Hound '81 (V)
Sharky's Machine '81
Harper Valley P.T.A. '78
The Many Adventures of Winnie the Pooh '77 (V)
Bad Ronald '74
True Grit '69
The Odd Couple '68
A Fine Madness '66
Kiss Me, Stupid! '64
A Raisin in the Sun '61
Twelve Angry Men '57

Shelby Fiddis
Cheech and Chong's The Corsican Brothers '84
Cheech and Chong: Things Are Tough All Over '82

William Fichtner (1956-)
The Dark Knight '08
Blades of Glory '07
First Snow '07
Ultraviolet '05
The Chumscrubber '05
Crash '05
Empire Falls '05
The Longest Yard '05
The Moguls '05
Nine Lives '05
Equilibrium '02
The Settlement '99
Armageddon '98
Contact '97
Switchback '97
Albino Alligator '96
Heat '95
Strange Days '95
The Underneath '95
Virtuosity '95

Kveta Fialova (1929-)
Murder Czech Style '66
Lemonade Joe '64

William Fichtner (1956-)
Project: Genesis '93
The Last Winter '89
Men of Steel '88

Laurence Fevrier
Time Regained '99
Tatie Danielle '91

Tina Fey (1970-)
Baby Mama '08
Mean Girls '04

Edwige Feuillere (1907-98)
Woman Hater '49
The Eagle Has Two Heads '48
L'Idiot '46
De Mayerling a Sarajevo '40
Topaze '33

Peggy (Margaret) Feury (1924-85)
All of Me '84
The Orphan '79
Kings Row '41

Norman Feusier (1886-1945)
Border Vengeance '35
Diamond Trail '33

Chelsea Field (1957-)
The Unsaid '01
Tom Clancy's Netforce '98
Wicked '98
Flipper '96

David Field
Command '85
The Night We Called It a Day '03
Blood Crime '02
Chopper '00
Mr. Accident '99
Two Hands '98
Blackrock '97

Karin (Karen) Field
The Demons '74
The Mad Butcher '72
Web of the Spider '70
The Alley Cats '65
Cave of the Living Dead '65

Mary Field (1896-1968)
To Hell and Back '55
I Married a Witch '42

Sally Field (1946-)
Two Weeks '06
Legally Blonde 2: Red, White & Blonde '03
Say It Isn't So '01
Where the Heart Is '00
A Cooler Climate '99
Forrest Gump '94
A Woman of Independent Means '94
Mrs. Doubtfire '93
Homeward Bound: The Incredible Journey '93
Soapdish '91
Not Without My Daughter '91 (V)
Steel Magnolias '89
Punchline '88
Surrender '87
Murphy's Romance '85
Places in the Heart '84
Kiss Me Goodbye '82
Absence of Malice '81
Back Roads '81
Beyond the Poseidon Adventure '79
Norma Rae '79
The End '78
Hooper '78
Heroes '77
Smokey and the Bandit '77
Smokey and the Bandit 2 '80
Stay Hungry '76
Sybil '76
Home for the Holidays '72
Maybe I'll Be Home in the Spring '70
The Way West '67

Todd Field (1964-)
Saturday Night and Sunday Morning '60
Rip It Off '02
Eyes Wide Shut '99
The Haunting '99
Broken Vessels '98
Farmer & Chase '96
Walking and Talking '96
Sleep with Me '94
Ruby in Paradise '93
Back to Back '90
Full Fathom Five '90
Gross Anatomy '89
Eye of the Eagle 2 '89

Virginia Field (1917-92)
A Connecticut Yankee in King Arthur's Court '49
Christmas Eve '47
Dance, Girl, Dance '40
Waterloo Bridge '40
Mr. Moto's Last Warning '39
Mr. Takes a Vacation '39

Dorothy Fielding
Inspector Lynley Mysteries: A Great Deliverance '01

Fenella Fielding (1930-)
Pandaemonium '00
Arrivederci, Baby! '66
Carry On Screaming '66
Doctor in Clover '66

Emma Fielding (1966-)
Pandaemonium '00

Margaret Fleicing (1895-1974)
Swenson '87
Fright Night '85

Marjorie Fielding (1892-1956)
A Respectable Trade '98
The Scarlet Tunic '97
The Demi-Paradise '43
The Franchise Affair '52
The Lavender Hill Mob '51
Conspirator '49
The Moon's Our Home '36
A Woman in Grey '20

Betty Field (1918-73)
Coogan's Bluff '68
Birdman of Alcatraz '62
Butterfield 8 '60
Peyton Place '57
Picnic '55
Bus Stop '56
The Great Gatsby '49
The Southerner '45
The Great Moment '44
Tomorrow the World '44
Kings Row '41
The Shepherd of the Hills '41
Of Mice and Men '39

Arabella Field (1970-)
Blowin' Smoke '99
Godzilla '98
Dante's Peak '97
The Pompatus of Love '95
Laws of Gravity '92

Shirley Anne Field (1936-)
Lady Chatterley '92
Hear My Song '91
Getting It Right '89
Shag: The Movie '89
Two by Forsyth '86
My Beautiful Laundrette '85
House of the Living Dead '73
Alfie '66
Kings of the Sun '63
War Lover '62
Beat Girl '60
The Entertainer '60
Peeping Tom '60

Holly Fields
Runaway Daughters '94
Seedpeople '92

Christopher John Fields
Alien 3 '92
The Gun in Betty Lou's Handbag '92

Charlie (Charles) Fields (1971-)
The Beniker Gang '83
Fish Hawk '79

Kim Fields (1969-)
The Kid with the Broken Halo '82

Norman Fields
Dirty Mind of Young Sally '73

Robert Fields (1938-)
Anna '87

Stanley Fields (1884-1941)
Wide Open Faces '38
Three Legionnaires '37
The Gay Desperado '36
Island of Lost Souls '32
Justice Rides Again '32
Cimarron '31

Indictment: The McMartin Trial '95
The Wrong Woman '95
Andre '94
A Passion to Kill '94
The Birds 2: Land's End '94
Texas '94
Dust Devil '93
Extreme Justice '93
Hotel Room '93
Royce '93
Snapdragon '93
The Dark Half '91
Harley Davidson and the Marlboro Man '91
Skin Deep '89
Prison '88
Walking and Talking '96
Sleep with Me '94

The Night We Called It a Day '03

Octavia '72

Fields

Tony Fields (1958-95)
Across the Moon '94
Backstreet Dreams '90
Body Beat '88
Trick or Treat '86

W.C. Fields (1879-1946)
Sensations of 1945 '44
Tales of Manhattan '42
Never Give a Sucker an Even Break '41
The Bank Dick '40
My Little Chickadee '40
You Can't Cheat an Honest Man '39
The Big Broadcast of 1938 '38
David Copperfield '35
Mississippi '35
It's a Gift '34
Six of a Kind '34
The Barber Shop '33
International House '33
The Dentist '32
Pharmacist '32
Running Wild '27
It's the Old Army Game '26
Sally of the Sawdust '25
Pool Sharks '15

Joseph Fiennes (1970-)
The Color of Freedom '07
The Darwin Awards '06
Running with Scissors '06
The Great Raid '05
Luther '03
Sinbad: Legend of the Seven Seas '03 (V)
Leo '02
Dust '01
Killing Me Softly '00
Enemy at the Gates '00
Rancid Aluminium '00
Forever Mine '99
Elizabeth '98
Shakespeare in Love '98
The Very Thought of You '98
Stealing Beauty '96
The Vacillations of Poppy Carew '94

Ralph Fiennes (1962-)
Bernard and Doris '08
In Bruges '08
Harry Potter and the Order of the Phoenix '07
Land of the Blind '06
The Chumscrubber '05
The Constant Gardener '05
Harry Potter and the Goblet of Fire '05
Wallace & Gromit: The Curse of the Were-Rabbit '05 (V)
The White Countess '05
The Good Thief '03
Maid in Manhattan '02
Red Dragon '02
Spider '02
The Miracle Maker: The Story of Jesus '00 (V)
The End of the Affair '99
Onegin '99
Sunshine '99
The Avengers '98
Prince of Egypt '98 (V)
Oscar and Lucinda '97
The English Patient '96
Strange Days '95
Quiz Show '94
Schindler's List '93
Emily Bronte's Wuthering Heights '92
Prime Suspect '92
A Dangerous Man: Lawrence after Arabia '91

Harvey Fierstein (1954-)
Duplex '03
Death to Smoochy '02
Common Ground '00
Playing Mona Lisa '00
Double Platinum '99
Mulan '98 (V)
Safe Men '98
Kull the Conqueror '97
Independence Day '96
Bullets over Broadway '94
Mrs. Doubtfire '93
The Harvest '92
Tidy Endings '88
Torch Song Trilogy '88
Apology '86
Garbo Talks '84

Mike Figgis (1948-)
Me Without You '01
Wives and Daughters '01
Internal Affairs '90

George Figgs (1947-)
Polyester '81

Efrain Figueroa
The Visit '00
Eastside '98
The Apostate '98
Desperate Measures '98
Star Maps '97

Kasia (Katarzyna) Figura (1962-)
Zemsta '02

Nathan Fillion (1971-)
Waitress '07
White Noise 2: The Light '07
Slither '06
Serenity '05
Outing Riley '04
Water's Edge '03

Clyde Fillmore (1875-1946)
Laura '44
Watch on the Rhine '43
Nurse Marjorie '20

Dennis Fimple (1940-2002)
House of 1000 Corpses '03
My Heroes Have Always Been Cowboys '91
Of Mice and Men '81
The $5.20 an Hour Dream '80
The Evictors '79
Creature from Black Lake '76
King Kong '76
Winterhawk '76
Truck Stop Women '74

Jon Finch (1941-)
Kingdom of Heaven '05
Lurking Fear '94
Unexplained Laughter '89
Game of Seduction '86
Witching Time '84
And Nothing But the Truth '82
Peter and Paul '81
Breaking Glass '80
Death on the Nile '78
The Final Programme '73
Lady Caroline Lamb '73
Frenzy '72
Macbeth '71
First Men in the Moon '64
Girl with Green Eyes '64
The Pumpkin Eater '64
Kidnapped '60

Peter Finch (1916-77)
Raid on Entebbe '77
Network '76
Shattered '72
Sunday, Bloody Sunday '71
Red Tent '69
Far from the Madding Crowd '67
The Flight of the Phoenix '65
First Men in the Moon '64
The Nun's Story '59
Pursuit of the Graf Spee '57
Robbery under Arms '57
Windom's Way '57
Make Me an Offer '55
The Detective '54
Elephant Walk '54
The Story of Robin Hood & His Merrie Men '52
Wooden Horse '50
Eureka Stockade '49
Train of Events '49
The Fighting Rats of Tobruk '44

Deborah Findlay
Me Without You '01

Larry Fine (1902-75)
The Outlaws Is Coming! '65
Around the World in a Daze '63
Four for Texas '63
It's a Mad, Mad, Mad, Mad World '63
Three Stooges in Orbit '62
Snow White and the Three Stooges '61
The Three Stooges Meet Hercules '61
Have Rocket Will Travel '59
Gold Raiders '51
Hollywood Party '34
Dancing Lady '33
The Lost Stooges '33
Myrt and Marge '33

Travis Fine (1968-)
Tomcats '01
My Antonia '94
Child's Play 3 '91

Anthony Finetti
Prime Time Murder '92
The Expendables '89

Sticky Fingaz
See Kirk "Sticky Fingaz" Jones

Fyvush Finkel (1923-)
The Crew '00
Q & A '90

Frank Finlay (1926-)
The Statement '03
The Pianist '02
Station Jim '01
Longitude '00
Dreaming of Joseph Lees '99
The Magical Legend of the Leprechauns '99
A Mind to Murder '96
Romance and Rejection '96
Stiff Upper Lips '96
Gospa '92
Stalin '92
Cthulhu Mansion '91
The Return of the Musketeers '89
Casanova '87
Arch of Triumph '85
In the Secret State '85
Lifeforce '85
A Christmas Carol '84
The Death of Adolf Hitler '84
The Ploughman's Lunch '83
Enigma '82
Return of the Soldier '82
Murder by Decree '79
The Thief of Baghdad '78
Wild Geese '78
Bouquet of Barbed Wire '76
The Four Musketeers '75
The Three Musketeers '74
Shaft in Africa '73
Gumshoe '72
Assault '72
Cromwell '70
Molly Maguires '70
Inspector Clouseau '68
I'll Never Forget What's 'Isname '67
Robbery '67
A Study in Terror '66
Othello '65

James Finlayson (1887-1953)
To Be or Not to Be '42
A Chump at Oxford '40
Saps at Sea '40
The Flying Deuces '39
Block-heads '38
All Over Town '37
Pick a Star '37
Way Out West '37
Bohemian Girl '36
Our Relations '36
Bonnie Scotland '35
The Devil's Brother '33
Pack Up Your Troubles '32
Laurel & Hardy: Chickens Come Home '31
Pardon Us '31
No Man's Law '27

Jon Finlayson
Lonely Hearts '82

Cameron Finley (1987-)
Perfect Game '00
Hope Floats '98
Leave It to Beaver '97

Evelyn Finley (1916-89)
Trail Riders '42
Dynamite Canyon '41

Margot Finley (1980-)
Tourist Trap '98
Ronnie and Julie '97
In Cold Blood '96

William Finley (1944-)
The Black Dahlia '06
The Funhouse '81
The Fury '78
Eaten Alive '76
Phantom of the Paradise '74
Sisters '73

John Finn (1952-)
The Hunted '03
Analyze That '02
Catch Me If You Can '02
Deadlocked '00
Atomic Train '99
True Crime '99
Crazy Horse '96
Turbulence '96
Cover-Up '91
Glory '89

John Finnegan
Finish Line '89

Warren Finnerty (1925-74)
Cockfighter '74
Panic in Needle Park '71
Easy Rider '69
Free Grass '69
Cool Hand Luke '67
The Brig '64
The Connection '61

Albert Finney (1936-)
Before the Devil Knows You're Dead '07
The Bourne Ultimatum '07
Amazing Grace '06
A Good Year '06
Tim Burton's Corpse Bride '05 (V)
Big Fish '03
The Gathering Storm '02
My Uncle Silas '01
Erin Brockovich '00
Traffic '00
Simpatico '99
Breakfast of Champions '98
A Rather English Marriage '98
Washington Square '97
Nostromo '96
The Run of the Country '95
The Browning Version '94
A Man of No Importance '94
Rich in Love '93
The Playboys '92
The Green Man '91
Miller's Crossing '90
The Endless Game '89
The Image '89
Orphans '87
Pope John Paul II '84
Under the Volcano '84
The Dresser '83
Loophole '83
Annie '82
Shoot the Moon '82
Looker '81
Wolfen '81
The Duellists '77
Murder on the Orient Express '74
Alpha Beta '73
Gumshoe '72
Scrooge '70
Two for the Road '67
Tom Jones '63
The Victors '63
The Entertainer '60
Saturday Night and Sunday Morning '60

Shirley Jo Finney
Echo Park '86
Wilma '77

Angela Finocchiaro (1955-)
Don't Tell '05
Volere Volare '92

Elena Fiore
Seven Beauties '76
Seduction of Mimi '72

Linda Fiorentino (1960-)
Liberty Stands Still '02
What Planet Are You From? '00
Where the Money Is '00
Dogma '99
Ordinary Decent Criminal '99
Body Count '97
Kicked in the Head '97
Men in Black '97
Larger Than Life '96
Unforgettable '96
Bodily Harm '95
Jade '95
Charlie's Ghost: The Secret of Coronado '94
The Desperate Trail '94
The Last Seduction '94
Acting on Impulse '93
Chain of Desire '93
Beyond the Law '92
Queens Logic '91
Shout '91
Strangers '91
The Neon Empire '89
The Moderns '88
Wildfire '88
After Hours '85
Gotcha! '85
Vision Quest '85

Ann(e) Firbank (1933-)
Flame to the Phoenix '85
Lillie '79
Asylum '72
Persuasion '71

Eddie Firestone (1920-2007)
Duel '71
Two for the Seesaw '62
The Law and Jake Wade '58

MacKenzie Firgens (1975-)
Sweet Insanity '06
Against the Wall '04
Groove '00

Colin Firth (1961-)
The Accidental Husband '08
Mamma Mia! '08
The Last Legion '07
Nanny McPhee '06
Where the Truth Lies '05
Bridget Jones: The Edge of Reason '04
Girl with a Pearl Earring '03
Love Actually '03
What a Girl Wants '03
The Importance of Being Earnest '02
Bridget Jones's Diary '01
Conspiracy '01
Relative Values '99
The Turn of the Screw '99
My Life So Far '98
Shakespeare in Love '98
A Thousand Acres '97
The English Patient '96
Fever Pitch '96
Nostromo '96
Pride and Prejudice '95
Circle of Friends '94
Playmaker '94
The Advocate '93
Hostages '93
Wings of Fame '93
Femme Fatale '90
Valmont '89
Apartment Zero '88
Dutch Girls '87
A Month in the Country '87
The Secret Garden '87
Another Country '84

Jonathan Firth (1967-)
The Prince & Me 2: Royal Wedding '06
Luther '03
Bait '02
Victoria & Albert '01
Far from the Madding Crowd '97
Middlemarch '93
Emily Bronte's Wuthering Heights '92

Peter Firth (1953-)
The Greatest Game Ever Played '05
Me & Mrs. Jones '02
Pearl Harbor '01
Chill Factor '99
The Garden of Redemption '97
An Awfully Big Adventure '94
Shadowlands '93
The Perfect Husband '92
Prisoner of Honor '91
The Hunt for Red October '90
Innocent Victim '90
Burndown '89
The Incident '89
Born of Fire '87
Northanger Abbey '87
Letter to Brezhnev '86
Lifeforce '85
Fire and Sword '82
Tess '79
Equus '77
Joseph Andrews '77
King Arthur, the Young Warlord '75

Jenna Fischer (1974-)
Blades of Glory '07
The Brothers Solomon '07
Walk Hard: The Dewey Cox Story '07
Slither '06

Kai (Kay) Fischer (1934)
The Goalie's Anxiety at the Penalty Kick '71
The Hellfire Club '61
Uncle Was a Vampire '59

Kate Fischer (1973-)
Blood Surf '00
Sirens '94

Vera Fischer (1950-)
Quilombo '84
Love Strange Love '82
I Love You '81

Nancy Fish (1938-)
Reflections in the Dark '94
Ghost in the Machine '93
Death Becomes Her '92
Exorcist 3: Legion '90

Laurence Fishburne (1963-)
21 '08
Bobby Z '07
Fantastic Four: Rise of the Silver Surfer '07 (V)
Akeelah and the Bee '06
Bobby '06
Mission: Impossible 3 '06
Assault on Precinct 13 '05
Biker Boyz '03
The Matrix Reloaded '03
The Matrix Revolutions '03
Mystic River '03
Osmosis Jones '01 (V)

Once in the Life '00
The Matrix '99
Always Outnumbered
Always Outgunned '98
Event Horizon '97
Fled '96
Hoodlum '96
Othello '95
The Tuskegee Airmen '95
Bad Company '94
Higher Learning '94
Just Cause '94
Searching for Bobby
Fischer '93
What's Love Got to Do with
It? '93
Deep Cover '92
Boyz N the Hood '91
Class Action '91
Hearts of Darkness: A
Filmmaker's Apocalypse
'91
Decoration Day '90
King of New York '90
Cadence '89
For Us, the Living '88
Red Heat '88
School Daze '88
Gardens of Stone '87
A Nightmare on Elm Street
3: Dream Warriors '87
Quicksilver '86
A Rumor of War '82
Death Wish 2 '82
Willie & Phil '80
Apocalypse Now '79
Cornbread, Earl & Me '75

Carrie Fisher (1956-)
Wonderland '03
Jay and Silent Bob Strike
Back '01
Scream 3 '00
Austin Powers:
International Man of
Mystery '97
This is My Life '92
Drop Dead Fred '91
Soapdish '91
Sibling Rivalry '90
Sweet Revenge '90
Loverboy '89
When Harry Met Sally...
'89
Appointment with Death '88
She's Back '88
Amazon Women on the
Moon '87
The Time Guardian '87
Hannah and Her Sisters '86
Hollywood Vice Squad '86
From Here to Maternity '85
The Man with One Red
Shoe '85
Garbo Talks '84
Return of the Jedi '83
Under the Rainbow '81
The Blues Brothers '80
The Empire Strikes Back
'80
Hollywood Chaos '89
Star Wars '77
Shampoo '75
Mr. Mike's Mondo Video '79

Frances Fisher (1952-)
In the Valley of Elah '07
Mrs. Harris '05
Laws of Attraction '04
Blue Car '03
House of Sand and Fog '03
The Rising Place '02
The Audrey Hepburn Story
'00
Gone in 60 Seconds '00
The Big Tease '99
True Crime '99
Titanic '97
Trading Favors '97
Wild America '97
Female Perversions '96
Babyfever '94
Molly and Gina '94
The Stars Fell on Henrietta
'94
Praying Mantis '93
Devlin '92
Unforgiven '92
Deadly Conspiracy '91
Frame Up '91
Lucy and Desi: Before the
Laughter '91
Sudie & Simpson '90
Cold Sassy Tree '89
Patty Hearst '88
Heart '87

Eddie Fisher (1928-)
Butterfield 8 '60
Bundle of Joy '56

Cindy Fisher
Liar's Moon '82
Hometown U.S.A. '79

Schuyler Fisk (1982-)
I'm Reed Fish '06
Orange County '02
Snow Day '00
The Baby-Sitters Club '95

Robert (Fisk) Fiske
(1899-1944)
Before I Hang '40
Green Archer '40
Mystic Circle Murder '39
Purple Vigilantes '38
Devil Diamond '37
Roaring Six Guns '37
Sky Parade '36

Alan Fisler
Student Affairs '88
New York's Finest '87
If Looks Could Kill '86

Gregor Fisher (1953-)
Love Actually '03
The Merchant of Venice '04
The Railway Children '00
The Girl in the Picture '86

Isla Fisher (1976-)
Definitely, Maybe '08
Dr. Seuss' Horton Hears a
Who! '08 (V)
Hot Rod '07
The Lookout '07
Wedding Daze '06
London '05
Wedding Crashers '05
Scooby-Doo 2 '03
Scooby-Doo '02

Joely Fisher (1967-)
Inspector Gadget '99
Kidnapped in Paradise '98
The Companion '94

Kay Fisher
See Kai (Kay) Fischer

Noel Fisher (1984-)
Holiday Reunion '03
Max Keeble's Big Move '01

Rashiya Fisher
See Rah Digga

Shug Fisher (1907-84)
Huckleberry Finn '75
The Giant Gila Monster '59

Stephen H. Fisher
Smoke '07

Thomas (Tom)
Fisher (1968-)
Van Helsing '04

Tricia Leigh Fisher
(1969-)
Arizona Dream '94
Hostile Intentions '94
Book of Love '91
C.H.U.D. 2: Bud the Chud
'89

Ella Fitzgerald (1917-
96)
Let No Man Write My
Epitaph '60
Pete Kelly's Blues '55
Ride 'Em Cowboy '42

Ciaran Fitzgerald
(1983-)
Into the West '92

Ella Fitzgerald (1917-
96)

Mark Fite
Off the Lip '04
Stuart Bliss '98
Department Store '35

Rick Fitts
Hanoi Hilton '87
Border Patrol '01
Pitch Black '00
Dead Heat '95
A Cry in the Dark '88
The Four Minute Mile '88

Peter Fitz (1931-)
Club Extinction '89
Au Revoir les Enfants '87
The Wannsee Conference
'84

Lewis Fitz-Gerald
(1958-)
The Oppenheim Family '82
Attack of the 50 Ft. Woman
'93

Barry Fitzgerald
(1888-1961)
Broth of a Boy '59
The Catered Affair '56
The Quiet Man '52
Union Station '50
The Story of Seabiscuit '49
The Naked City '48
Welcome Stranger '47
The Saint Strikes Back:
Criminal Court '46
Two Years before the Mast
'46
And Then There Were
None '45
The Stork Club '45
Going My Way '44
None But the Lonely Heart
'44
The Long Voyage Home
'40
The Saint Strikes Back '39
Bringing Up Baby '38
Dawn Patrol '38
Four Men and a Prayer '38
Marie Antoinette '38
Juno and the Paycock '30

Geraldine Fitzgerald
(1913-2005)
Arthur 2: On the Rocks '88
Poltergeist 2: The Other
Side '86
Easy Money '83
Arthur '81
The Mango Tree '77
Harry and Tonto '74
Rachel, Rachel '68
The Pawnbroker '65
Ten North Frederick '58
The Obsessed '51
O.S.S. '46
The Strange Affair of Uncle
Harry '45
Watch on the Rhine '43
Wilson '44
Wuthering Heights '39
Dark Victory '39

Walter Fitzgerald
(1896-1976)
The Camomile Lawn '92
The Adventures of Sadie
'55
Treasure Island '50
The Fallen Idol '49
Blanche Fury '48
San Demetrio, London '47
Great Day '46
Mutiny on the Blackhawk
'39

Colleen (Ann)
Fitzpatrick (1972-)
Get Over It! '01
Rock Star '01
Scary Movie 2 '01 (V)
Da Hip Hop Witch '00
Dracula 2000 '00
St. Patrick's Day '99
Higher Learning '94
Hairspray '88

Gabrielle Fitzpatrick
(1967-)
Desert Heat '99
Mr. Nice Guy '98

Jim (James)
Fitzpatrick (1959-)
Operation Delta Force 3:
Clear Target '98
U.S. Seals '98

Tara Fitzgerald (1968-)
Jane Eyre '06
Like Father Like Son '05
I Capture the Castle '03
Dark Blue World '01
Rancid Aluminium '00
New World Disorder '99
Conquest '98
Frenchman's Creek '98
The Woman in White '97
Brassed Off '96
The Englishman Who Went
up a Hill But Came down
a Mountain '95
A Man of No Importance
'94
Sirens '94
The Camomile Lawn '92
Catherine Cookson's The
Black Candle '92
Hear My Song '91

Sean Fitzgerald
Poltergeist: The Legacy '96

Patrick Fitzgerald
(1962-)
Day at the Beach '98
A Price above Rubies '98
Baby Geniuses '98

Myles Fitzgerald
Superbabies: Baby
Geniuses 2 '04
Baby Geniuses '98

Leo Fitzgerald
Superbabies: Baby
Geniuses 2 '04
Baby Geniuses '98

Tac Fitzgerald (1981-)
Black Hawk Down '01
Here on Earth '00

Gerry Fitzgerald
Superbabies: Baby
Geniuses 2 '04
Baby Geniuses '98

Glenn Fitzgerald
(1971-)
Confess '05
40 Days and 40 Nights '02
The Believer '01
Series 7: The Contenders
'01
101 Ways (The Things a
Girl Will Do to Keep Her
Volvo) '00
Tully '00
The Sixth Sense '99
A Price above Rubies '97

Leo Fitzpatrick (1978-)
Personal Velocity: Three
Portraits '02
Bully '01
Storytelling '01
Kids '95

Michael Fitzpatrick
Fay Grim '06
Pay Off '89
Take It to the Limit '00

Neil Fitzpatrick (1934-
2005)
Wedding Band '89
Who's Harry Crumb? '89
Blue Monkey '87

Richard Fitzpatrick
A Cry in the Dark '88
Ground Zero '88

Emily Fitzroy (1860-
1954)
The Frontiersmen '38
Don Quixote '35
The Bat '26

Paul Fix (1901-83)
Grayeagle '77
Night of the Lepus '72
Zabriskie Point '70
El Dorado '67
Nevada Smith '66
Shenandoah '65
Sons of Katie Elder '65
To Kill a Mockingbird '62
Lafayette Escadrille '58
Jet Pilot '57
Man in the Shadow '57
Night Passage '57
The Bad Seed '56
Blood Alley '55
The High and the Mighty
'54
Hondo '53
Island in the Sky '53
Johnny Guitar '53
She Wore a Yellow Ribbon
'49
Red River '48
Tycoon '47
Fighting Seabees '44
Captive Wild Woman '43
Hitler: Dead or Alive '43
Sherlock Holmes and the
Secret Weapon '42
South of Santa Fe '42
Black Friday '40
Dr. Cyclops '40
The Great Plane Robbery
'40
Mutiny on the Blackhawk
'39
Star Reporter '39
Mannequin '37
Phantom Patrol '36
The Prisoner of Shark
Island '36
Desert Trail '35
His Fighting Blood '35
The Throwback '35
Gun Law '33
Valley of Wanted Men '35
Somewhere in Sonora '33
Fargo Express '32
The Fighting Sheriff '31

Georges Flament
(1903-90)
The 400 Blows '59
La Chienne '31

Cash Flagg
See Ray Dennis Steckler

Fannie Flagg (1944-)
Crazy in Alabama '99

Kate Fitzpatrick (1948-)
Fantasy Man '84
Return of Captain Invincible
'83
Night Nurse '77

Leo Fitzpatrick (1978-)
Blood Tracks '86

Joe Flaherty (1941-)
National Security '03
Home on the Range '04 (V)
Slackers '02
Happy Gilmore '96
Snowboard Academy '96
Stuart Saves His Family '94
Looking for Miracles '90
Back to the Future, Part 2
'89
Speed Zone '89
One Crazy Summer '86
Really Weird Tales '86
Sesame Street Presents:
Follow That Bird '85
Going Berserk '83
Heavy Metal '81 (V)
Used Cars '80
1941 '79
Stripes '81
Tunnelvision '76

Lanny Flaherty (1935-)
Home Fries '98
Tom and Huck '95
Sommersby '93
The Ballad of the Sad Cafe
'91

Pat Flaherty (1903-70)
The Red House '47
Sergeant York '41
Midnight Limited '40
My Son, My Son '40
The Crimson Rivers '01
Women '97

Didier Flamand
(1947-)
Factotum '06
Love '05
The Chorus '04
The Chateau '01

Fionnula Flanagan
(1941-)
Transamerica '05
Four Brothers '05
Shinstream '07
The Others '01
Divine Secrets of the Ya-Ya
Sisterhood '02
Tears of the Sun '03
For Love or Country: The
Arturo Sandoval Story
'00
Waking Ned Devine '98
Kings in Grass Castles '97
Some Mother's Son '96
White Mile '94
Money for Nothing '93
Mad at the Moon '92
A Winner Never Quits '86
Youngblood '86
James Joyce's Women '85
The Ewok Adventure '84
Young Love, First Love '79
Mary White '77

Tommy Flanagan
(1965-)
Hero Wanted '08
Smokin' Aces '07
When a Stranger Calls '06
The Last Drop '05
Picture of Dorian Gray '04
Cold Comfort Farm '71
All About the Benjamins '02
Attila '01
Strictly Sinatra '01
Gladiator '00
Ratcatcher '99
Braveheart '95

Ed Flanders (1934-95)
Bye Bye, Love '94
Citizen Cohn '92
Exorcist 3: Legion '90
The Final Days '89
Special Bulletin '83
Tomorrow's Child '82
The Pursuit of D.B. Cooper '81
True Confessions '81
Sophia Loren: Her Own Story '80
Backstairs at the White House '79
Blind Ambition '79
The Ninth Configuration '79
Salem's Lot '79
The Amazing Howard Hughes '77
Mary White '77
Eleanor & Franklin '76
Things in Their Season '74
Trial of the Catonsville Nine '72
The Passing of Evil '70

Sean Patrick Flanery (1965-)
The Insatiable '06
Into the Fire '05
The Gunman '03
Borderline '02
Lone Hero '02
Acceptable Risk '01
Eye See You '01
Ride the Wild Fields '00
Body Shots '99
Boondock Saints '99
Simply Irresistible '99
Best Men '98
Eden '98
Girl '98
Zack & Reba '98
Pale Saints '97
Suicide Kings '97
Just Your Luck '96
The Grass Harp '95
Powder '95
Raging Angels '95

Susan Flannery (1943-)
Anatomy of a Seduction '79
Gumball Rally '76

Maureen Flannigan (1973-)
A Day Without a Mexican '04
At Any Cost '00
Teenage Bonnie & Klepto Clyde '93

Barry Flatman
Saw III '06
The Witness Files '00
Random Encounter '98
Open Season '95

John Flaus (1934-)
Lilian's Story '95
In Too Deep '90
Bootleg '85
Blood Money '80

James Flavin (1906-76)
In Cold Blood '67
Night Passage '57
Francis in the Haunted House '56
Abbott and Costello Go to Mars '53
Armored Car Robbery '50
Abbott and Costello Meet the Killer, Boris Karloff '49
Blondie Hits the Jackpot '49
Cloak and Dagger '46
Easy to Wed '46
The Shanghai Cobra '45
Abroad with Two Yanks '44
Hollywood Canteen '44
Laura '44
Uncertain Glory '44
Air Force '43
So Proudly We Hail '43
Brand of Hate '34
King Kong 33

Flea (1962-)
Rugrats Go Wild! '03 (V)
The Wild Thornberrys Movie '02 (V)

Ian Fleming (1888-1969)
The Trials of Oscar Wilde '60
Land of Fury '55
Norman Conquest '53
Butler's Dilemma '43
Murder at the Baskervilles '37
When Thief Meets Thief '37
The Triumph of Sherlock Holmes '35

Lone Fleming (1949-)
Return of the Evil Dead '75
Tombs of the Blind Dead '72
It Happened at Nightmare Inn '70

Rhonda Fleming (1923-)
The Nude Bomb '80
Alias Jesse James '59
Bullwhip '59
Gun Glory '57
Gunfight at the O.K. Corral '57
Slightly Scarlet '56
While the City Sleeps '56
Tennessee's Partner '55
Pony Express '53
Cavalry Charge '51
Cry Danger '51
A Connecticut Yankee in King Arthur's Court '49
The Great Lover '49
Adventure Island '47
Out of the Past '47
Abilene Town '46
The Spiral Staircase '46
Spellbound '45
Since You Went Away '44

Jason Flemyng (1966-)
Bobby Z '07
Stardust '07
PU-239 '06
Layer Cake '05
Transporter 2 '05
Seed of Chucky '04
The League of Extraordinary Gentlemen '03
Below '02
The Body '01
From Hell '01
Mean Machine '01
Rock Star '01
Bruiser '00
Snatch '00
Deep Rising '98
Lock, Stock and 2 Smoking Barrels '98
The Red Violin '98
Tess of the D'Urbervilles '98
Spice World: The Movie '97
Alive and Kicking '96
Stealing Beauty '96
Hollow Reed '95
Rob Roy '95
A Question of Attribution '91

Robert Flemyng (1912-95)
The Choir '95
Kafka '91
Oh! What a Lovely War '69
Blood Beast Terror '67
Vanity Fair '67
The Horrible Dr. Hichcock '62
Cast a Dark Shadow '55
The Man Who Never Was '55
The Blue Lamp '49
The Guinea Pig '48

Flesh N Bone
Thicker than Water '99
Winner Takes All '98

Alan Fletcher (1957-)
Gross Misconduct '93
Fran '85

Bramwell Fletcher (1904-88)
Random Harvest '42
The Undying Monster '42
White Cargo '42
The Scarlet Pimpernel '34
The Mummy '32
Daughter of the Dragon '31
Raffles '30

Brendan Fletcher (1981-)
BloodRayne 2: Deliverance '07
RV '06
Tideland '05
Eighteen '04
The Final Cut '04
Ginger Snaps Back: The Beginning '04
Freddy vs. Jason '03
Heart of America '03
The Unsaid '01
Jimmy Zip '00
The Five Senses '99
Summer's End '99
Air Bud '97
Trucks '97

Dexter Fletcher (1966-)
Doom '05
Layer Cake '05
Stander '03
Below '02
Lock, Stock and 2 Smoking Barrels '98
The Raggedy Rawney '90
Twisted Obsession '90
The Rachel Papers '89
Lionheart '87
The Long Good Friday '80

Diane Fletcher (1944-)
The Aristocrats '99
The Final Cut '95
To Play the King '93
House of Cards '90

Dusty Fletcher (1897-1954)
Boardinghouse Blues '48
Killer Diller '48

Louise Fletcher (1934-)
A Dennis the Menace Christmas '07
Aurora Borealis '06
Dancing in Twilight '05
Finding Home '03
A Time to Remember '03
Big Eden '00
More Dogs Than Bones '00
The Devil's Arithmetic '99
A Map of the World '99
Time Served '99
Cruel Intentions '98
Love Kills '98
Breast Men '97
Love to Kill '97
Sins of the Mind '97
Frankenstein and Me '96
High School High '96
Two Days in the Valley '96
Edie & Pen '95
Virtuosity '95
Strange Invaders '83
Strange Behavior '81
Mama Dracula '80
Lady in Red '79
The Magician of Lublin '79
Natural Enemies '79
The Cheap Detective '78
The Exorcist 2: The Heretic '77
One Flew Over the Cuckoo's Nest '75
Russian Roulette '75
Thieves Like Us '74

Neil Fletcher
Creature of Destruction '67
Zontar, the Thing from Venus '66

Page Fletcher
Ordeal in the Arctic '93
Friends, Lovers & Lunatics '89
Humongous '82

Suzanne Fletcher
Bloodsucking Pharoahs of Pittsburgh '90
Sleepwalk '88

Sam Flint (1882-1980)
Leave It to the Marines '51
Sky High '51
Command Decision '48
Lights of Old Santa Fe '47
The Chinese Cat '44
Spy Smasher '42
Spy Smasher Returns '42
Roaring Six Guns '37
A Face in the Fog '36
The Lawless Nineties '36
Red Lights Ahead '36
Red River Valley '36
Evelyn Prentice '34

Jay C. Flippen (1900-71)
Firecreek '68
Hellfighters '68
Studs Lonigan '60
The Restless Breed '58
Jet Pilot '57
Night Passage '57
The Killing '56
The King and Four Queens '56
Run of the Arrow '56
Seventh Cavalry '56
Far Country '55
Oklahoma! '55
The Wild One '54
Devil's Canyon '53
Flying Leathernecks '51
The Lemon Drop Kid '51
Buccaneer's Girl '50
Winchester '73 '50
They Live by Night '49
A Woman's Secret '49
Marie Galante '34

Josh Flitter (1994-)
The Last Shot '04
Snow Buddies '08 (V)
License to Wed '07
Nancy Drew '07
Air Bud 6: Air Buddies '06
Big Momma's House 2 '06
The Greatest Game Ever Played '05

Bjorn Floberg (1947-)
Uno '04
Kitchen Stories '03
Insomnia '97

Calista Flockhart (1964-)
Things You Can Tell Just by Looking at Her '00
William Shakespeare's A Midsummer Night's Dream '99
Drunks '96
Jane Doe '96
Telling Lies in America '96
The Birdcage '96

Suzanne Flon (1918-2005)
Avenue Montaigne '06
Joyeux Noel '05
One Deadly Summer '83
Mr. Klein '76
The Train '65
Un Singe en Hiver '62
Moulin Rouge '52

Michael Flood
Death Nurse '87

Sheila Florance (1916-91)
A Woman's Tale '92
Cactus '86

Dann Florek (1950-)
Beautiful Joe '00
From the Earth to the Moon '98
Hard Rain '97
The Flintstones '94
Getting Even with Dad '94
Angel Heart '87

Fiorelle (1901-74)
The Crime of Monsieur Lange '36
Liliom '35

Stefano Satta Flores
The Sniper '78
We All Loved Each Other So Much '77

Von Flores (1960-)
The Confessor '04
Tracked '98
The Assignment '97
Frame by Frame '95
Eclipse '94

Holly Floria (1966-)
Private Wars '93
Bikini Island '91
Presumed Guilty '91
Netherworld '90

George "Buck" Flower (1936-)
Relentless '89
Cheerleader Camp '88
Pumpkinhead '88
They Live '88
Sorority Babes in the Slimeball Bowl-A-Rama '87
In Search of a Golden Sky '84
Escape from New York '81
The Capture of Bigfoot '79
Mountain Family Robinson '79
Further Adventures of the Wilderness Family, Part 2 '77
Across the Great Divide '76
Candy Tangerine Man '75
Devil & Leroy Basset '73
Dirty Mind of Young Sally '72

Kim Flowers
Alien: Resurrection '97
Nobody's Perfect '90

Robert Floyd
Soul's Midnight '06
The Song of the Lark '01
Cold Hearts '99
The Darwin Conspiracy '99

Roger Floyd
Big City Blues '99
The Walking Dead '94

Susan Floyd (1968-)
Domestic Disturbance '01
Random Hearts '99
Breathing Room '96

Darlanne Fluegel (1956-)
Darkman 3: Die Darkman Die '95
Relative Fear '95
Breaking Point '94
Scanner Cop '94
Slaughter of the Innocents '93
Pet Sematary 2 '92
Lock Up '89
Project: Alien '89
Bulletproof '88
Deadly Stranger '88
Freeway '88
Running Scared '86
Tough Guys '86
To Live & Die in L.A. '85
Concrete Beat '84
Once Upon a Time in America '84

When Angels Fly '84
The Last Fight '82
Battle Beyond the Stars '80
Eyes of Laura Mars '78

Joel Fluellen (1907-90)
Man Friday '75
A Dream for Christmas '73
The Great White Hope '70
Fun in Silent, Run Deep '58
Sitting Bull '54
The Jackie Robinson Story '50
No Time for Romance '48

Barbara Flynn (1948-)
Miss Potter '06
Elizabeth I '05
Lorna Doone '01
Wives and Daughters '01
King Lear '98
Cracker: Best Boys '95
Cracker: Brotherly Love '95
Cracker: True Romance '95
Cracker: To Be a Somebody '94
The Temp '93

Errol Flynn (1909-59)
Assault of the Rebel Girls '59
Istanbul '57
The King's Rhapsody '55
Let's Make Up '55
The Warriors '48
The Master of Ballantrae '53
Against All Flags '52
Adventures of Captain Fabian '51
Kim '50
That Forsyte Woman '50
Adventures of Don Juan '49
It's a Great Feeling '49
Silver River '48
Cry Wolf '47
Escape Me Never '47
Never Say Goodbye '46
Objective, Burma! '45
San Antonio '45
Uncertain Glory '44
Edge of Darkness '43
Northern Pursuit '43
Thank Your Lucky Stars '43
Desperate Journey '42
Gentleman Jim '42
Dive Bomber '41
Footsteps in the Dark '41
They Died with Their Boots On '41
The Adventures of Robin Hood '38
Dawn Patrol '38
The Sisters '38
The Prince and the Pauper '37
The Charge of the Light Brigade '36
Captain Blood '35

Jerome Flynn (1963-)
A Mind to Murder '96
Edward II '92
A Summer Story '88

Joe Flynn (1924-74)
The Rescuers '77 (V)
The Strongest Man in the World '75
Superdad '73
Gentle Savage '73
Now You See Him, Now You Don't '72
Million Dollar Duck '71
How to Frame a Figg '71
The Barefoot Executive '71
The Computer Wore Tennis Shoes '69
My Dog, the Thief '69

Kimberly Flynn
Boys Life '94
Rhythm Thief '94
Revolution! A Red Comedy '91

Michael Flynn (1944-)
Partners in Crime '99
Address Unknown '96

Miriam Flynn (1952-)
National Lampoon's Christmas Vacation 2: Cousin Eddie's Big Island Adventure '03
National Lampoon's Vacation '83

Neil Flynn (1960-)
Hoot '06
Mean Girls '04

Sean Flynn (1943-70)
Mission to Venice '63
Son of Captain Blood '62
The Jewel of the Nile '85
Rocco and His Brothers '60

Nina Foch (1924-)
How to Deal '03
Hush '98
Pumpkin '02
Til There Was You '96
Armistead Maupin's Tales of the City '93
Morning Glory '93
Silver '93
Dixie Lanes '88
Skin Deep '89
Child of Glass '78
Jennifer '78
Mahogany '75
Salty '73
Columbo: Prescription Murder '67
Cash McCall '60
Spartacus '60
The Ten Commandments '56
Illegal '55
Executive Suite '54
Scaramouche '52
An American in Paris '51
St. Benny the Dip '51
The Dark Past '49
A Song to Remember '45
Return of the Vampire '44

Megan Follows (1968-)
2 Brothers & a Bride '03
Anne of Green Gables: The Continuing Story '99
The Chase '91
The Nutcracker Prince '91 (V)
Back to Hannibal: The Return of Tom Sawyer and Huckleberry Finn '90
Termini Station '89
Anne of Avonlea '87
A Time of Destiny '88
Anne of Green Gables '85
Silver Bullet '85
Hockey Night '84

Joe Folau
The Legend of Johnny Lingo '03

Dennis Folbigge
Howling 4: The Original Nightmare '88
Zulu '64

Dave Foley (1963-)
California Dreaming '07
Sky High '05
White Coats '04
Stark Raving Mad '02
Swindle '02
Monkeybone '01
On the Line '01
Dick '99
Blast from the Past '98
The Wrong Guy '96
It's Pat: The Movie '94

Ellen Foley (1951-)
Married to the Mob '88
Fatal Attraction '87

Jeremy Foley (1983-)
Soccer Dog: The Movie '98

Scott Foley (1973-)
Below '02
Scream 3 '00
Forever Love '98

Abel Folk (1959-)
Art Heist '05
Sharpe's Gold '94

Michael Foley (1954-)
Prison Planet '92
The Divine Enforcer '91
Karate Cop '91

Macka Foley
WarCat '88

Sink or Swim '97
Kids in the Hell: Brain Candy '96
The Wrong Guy '96

Ellen Foley
Sometimes a Great Notion '71
There Was a Crooked Man '70
The Cheyenne Social Club '70

Henry Fonda (1905-82)
On Golden Pond '81
Summer Solstice '81
Gideon's Trumpet '80
Oldest Living Graduate '80
Home to Stay '79
Meteor '79
Roots: The Next Generation '79
Wanda Nevada '79
Battleforce '78
City on Fire '78
The Swarm '78
Tentacles '77
Rollercoaster '77
Great Smokey Roadblock '76
Midway '76
The Red Pony '76
My Name Is Nobody '74
Ash Wednesday '73
Night Flight from Moscow '73
The Serpent '73
Too Late the Hero '70
The Boston Strangler '68
Firecreek '68
Madigan '68
Once Upon a Time in the West '68
Yours, Mine & Ours '68
A Big Hand for the Little Lady '66
Battle of the Bulge '65
In Harm's Way '65
The Rounders '65
The Best Man '64
The Longest Day '62
Advise and Consent '62
Spencer's Mountain '63
Warlock '59
Stage Struck '57
The Tin Star '57
The Wrong Man '56
Twelve Angry Men '57
War and Peace '56
Mister Roberts '55
The Magnificent Dope '42
Tales of Manhattan '42
The Male Animal '42
The Ox-Bow Incident '43
Immortal Sergeant '43
My Darling Clementine '46
The Big Street '42
The Grapes of Wrath '40
Return of Frank James '40
Lillian Russell '40
Drums Along the Mohawk '39
Jesse James '39

Jane Fonda (1937-)
Georgia Rule '07
Monster-in-Law '05
Stanley and Iris '90
Old Gringo '89
The Morning After '86
Agnes of God '85
On Golden Pond '81
Rollover '81
The Dollmaker '84
Nine to Five '80
The China Syndrome '79
The Electric Horseman '79
California Suite '78
Comes a Horseman '78
Coming Home '78
Fun with Dick and Jane '77
Julia '77
A Doll's House '73
Steelyard Blues '73
Klute '71
They Shoot Horses, Don't They? '69
Barbarella '68
Spirits of the Dead '68
Barefoot in the Park '67
Any Wednesday '66
The Chase '66
The Game Is Over '66
Cat Ballou '65
Circle of Love '64
Joy House '64
Sunday in New York '63
Period of Adjustment '62
Walk on the Wild Side '62
Tall Story '60

Peter Fonda (1939-)
Ghost Rider '07
3:10 to Yuma '07
The Heart Is Deceitful Above All Things '04
A Thief of Time '04
The Maldonado Miracle '03
The Laramie Project '02
Second Skin '00
South of Heaven, West of Hell '00
Thomas and the Magic Railroad '00
The Limey '99
The Passion of Ayn Rand '99
The Tempest '99
Ulee's Gold '97
Escape from L.A. '96
Grace of My Heart '96 (V)
Nadja '95
Love and a .45 '94
Molly and Gina '94
Deadfall '93
South Beach '93
Bodies, Rest & Motion '93
Fatal Mission '89
The Rose Garden '89
Mercenary Fighters '88
Hawken's Breed '87
Certain Fury '85
Jungle Heat '84
Spasms '82
Split Image '82
Cannonball Run '81
The Hostage Tower '80
Wanda Nevada '79
High Ballin' '78
Outlaw Blues '77
Fighting Mad '76
Futureworld '76
92 in the Shade '76
Race with the Devil '75
Dirty Mary Crazy Larry '74
Killer Force '75
The Last Movie '71
Hired Hand '71

Spiros Focas (1937-)
White Palace '90
Rambo 3 '88
The Jewel of the Nile '85

Alison Folland (1978-)
Milwaukee, Minnesota '03
Things Behind the Sun '01
Boys Don't Cry '99
All Over Me '96
Before and After '95
To Die For '95

Steve Flynn
Jesse Stone: Death in Paradise '06
Scarred City '98
Ulee's Gold '97

Colleen Flynn (1962-)
Serving in Silence: The Margarethe Cammermeyer Story '95
Incident at Deception Ridge '94

Vegas Vacation '96
18 Again! '88

Dan Fogler
Dr. Seuss' Horton Hears a Who! '08 (V)
Balls of Fury '07
Good Luck Chuck '07
Kung Fu Panda '08 (V)

Vladimir Fogel (1902-29)
Bed and Sofa '27
The Girl with the Hat Box '27

Brenda Fogarty
Fairy Tales '76
Deadly Fieldtrip '74

Freda Foh Shen
Red Doors '05
Mulan '98 (V)

Bridget Fonda (1964-)
The Snow Queen '02
Kiss of the Dragon '01
Monkeybone '01
The Whole Shebang '01
South of Heaven, West of Hell '00
Lake Placid '99
The Break Up '98
Finding Graceland '98
Mr. Jealousy '98
A Simple Plan '98
In the Gloaming '97
Jackie Brown '97
Grace of My Heart '96
Touch '96
Balto '95 (V)
City Hall '95
Rough Magic '95
Camilla '94
It Could Happen to You '94

The Road to Wellville '94
Bodies, Rest & Motion '93
Little Buddha '93
Army of Darkness '92
Single White Female '92
Singles '92
Doc Hollywood '91
Iron Maze '91
Frankenstein Unbound '90
The Godfather, Part 3 '90
Leather Jackets '90
Scandal '89
Shag: The Movie '89
Strapless '90
Aria '88
Jacob Have I Loved '88
Light Years '88 (V)
You Can't Hurry Love '88

The Story of Alexander Graham Bell '39
Young Mr. Lincoln '39
Jezebel '38
Blockade '38
I Dream Too Much '35
Spawn of the North '38
Mad Miss Manton '38
Lilith '64
Tammy and the Doctor '63
The Victors '63
Wings of the Morning '37
You Only Live Once '37
The Moon's Our Home '36
The Trail of the Lonesome Pine '36
The Farmer Takes a Wife '35

Phil Fondacaro (1958-)
George A. Romero's Land of the Dead '05
The Creeps '97
Meridian: Kiss of the Beast '90
Troll '86
Ghoulies 2 '87

Benson Fong (1916-87)
Kung Fu: The Movie '86
The Strongest Man in the World '75
Our Man Flint '66
Girls! Girls! Girls! '62
His Majesty O'Keefe '53
Conquest of Space '55
The Scarlet Clue '45
Charlie Chan in the Secret Service '44
The Chinese Cat '44
The Purple Heart '44

Leo Fong (1928-)
Showdown '93
Killpoint '84
The Last Reunion '80
Blind Rage '78
Enforcer from Death Row '78

Joan Fontaine (1917-)
The Witches '66
Voyage to the Bottom of the Sea '61
Until They Sail '57
Island in the Sun '57
Beyond a Reasonable Doubt '56
Casanova's Big Night '54
The Bigamist '53
Decameron Nights '53
Ivanhoe '52
Othello '52
Born to Be Bad '50
September Affair '50
Letter from an Unknown Woman '48
You Gotta Stay Happy '48
Frenchman's Creek '44
Jane Eyre '44
Suspicion '41
Rebecca '40
Gunga Din '39
The Women '39
A Damsel in Distress '37
A Million to One '37

Frank Fontaine (1920-)
Nightwaves '03
Random Encounter '98

Joan Fontaine (1917-)

Genevieve Fontanel (1936-)
The Man Who Loved Women '77

Shawn Fonteno
The Wash '01
Grain of Sand '84

Dolores Fonzi (1978-)
The Aura '05
Burnt Money '00
The Bottom of the Sea '03

Hallie Foote (1953-)
Horton Foote's Alone '97
Courtship '87
The Little Match Girl '87
On Valentine's Day '86
1918 '85
The Habitation of Dragons '91

Easy Rider '69
Spirits of the Dead '68
The Trip '67
The Wild Angels '66
Lilith '64
Tammy and the Doctor '63
The Victors '63

Horton Foote, Jr. (1954-)
Blood Red '88
On Valentine's Day '86
1918 '85

Dick Foran (1910-79)
Brighty of the Grand Canyon '67
Studs Lonigan '60
Atomic Submarine '59
Deputy Marshal '50
Guest Wife '45
The Mummy's Tomb '42
Private Buckaroo '42
Ride 'Em Cowboy '42
Riders of Death Valley '41
The Fighting 69th '40
The House of the Seven Gables '40
The Mummy's Hand '40
My Little Chickadee '40
Winners of the West '40
Boy Meets Girl '38
Four Daughters '38
The Sisters '38
The Black Legion '37
Earthworm Tractors '36
Petrified Forest '36
Dangerous '35

June Foray (1919-)
The Adventures of Rocky & Bullwinkle '00 (V)
Mulan '98 (V)
Thumbelina '94 (V)
DuckTales the Movie: Treasure of the Lost Lamp '90 (V)
Who Framed Roger Rabbit '88 (V)
Looney Looney Looney Bugs Bunny Movie '81 (V)
Sabaka '55

Brenda Forbes (1909-96)
The Man Upstairs '93
The White Cliffs of Dover '44
Mrs. Miniver '42

Bryan Forbes (1926-)
December Flower '84

Mary Forbes (1883-1974)
You Gotta Stay Happy '48
Tender Comrade '43
You Can't Cheat an Honest Man '39
You Can't Take It with You '38
The Awful Truth '37
Vanity Fair '32

Michelle Forbes (1967-)
Johnson County War '02
Perfume '01
Homicide: The Movie '00
Escape from L.A. '96
Black Day Blue Night '95
Swimming with Sharks '94
Kalifornia '93

Ralph Forbes (1902-51)
Frenchman's Creek '44
Convicts at Large '38
Legion of Missing Men '37
Make a Wish '37
I'll Name the Murderer '36
Riptide '34
Twentieth Century '34
The Phantom Broadcast '33
Smilin' Through '33
Inside the Lines '30

Anitra Ford (1942-)
The Longest Yard '74
Invasion of the Bee Girls '73
Stacey '73
The Big Bird Cage '72

Ann Ford
Logan's Run '76
The Love Machine '71

Constance Ford (1923-93)
All Fall Down '62
Rome Adventure '62
Home from the Hill '60
A Summer Place '59
The Last Hunt '56

Dorothy Ford (1923-)
Jack & the Beanstalk '52
On Our Merry Way '48

Faith Ford (1960-)
The Pacifier '05
Beethoven's 5th '03
Sometimes They Come Back... For More '99
A Weekend in the Country '96
North '94
Murder So Sweet '93
You Talkin' to Me? '87

Francis Ford (1881-1953)
The Quiet Man '52
She Wore a Yellow Ribbon '49
Far Frontier '48
Accomplice '46
Girls in Chains '43
Lucky Cisco Kid '40
Stagecoach '39
The Texans '38
Charlie Chan at the Circus '36
Steamboat Round the Bend '35
Man from Monterey '33
Justice Rides Again '32
Battling with Buffalo Bill '31

Glenn Ford (1916-2006)
Final Verdict '91
Raw Nerve '91
Border Shootout '90
Casablanca Express '89
Virus '82
Day of the Assassin '81
Happy Birthday to Me '81
The Visitor '80
The Sacketts '79
Superman: The Movie '78
Midway '76
Santee '73
Smith! '69
Is Paris Burning? '66
The Rounders '65
The Courtship of Eddie's Father '62
Experiment in Terror '62
The Four Horsemen of the Apocalypse '62
Pocketful of Miracles '61
Cimarron '60
The Gazebo '59
It Started with a Kiss '59
Cowboy '58
Torpedo Run '58
Don't Go Near the Water '57
3:10 to Yuma '57
Fastest Gun Alive '56
Jubal '56
The Teahouse of the August Moon '56
Americano '55
Blackboard Jungle '55
Interrupted Melody '55
The Violent Men '55
Human Desire '54
Appointment in Honduras '53
The Big Heat '53
Man from the Alamo '53
Affair in Trinidad '52
The Green Glove '52
Follow the Sun '51
The White Tower '50
Lust for Gold '49
Man from Colorado '49
The Loves of Carmen '48
Gilda '46
A Stolen Life '46
The Desperadoes '43
Destroyer '43
So Ends Our Night '41
Texas '41
Blondie Plays Cupid '40
The Lady in Question '40

Harrison Ford (1884-1957)
The Nervous Wreck '26
The Average Woman '24
Foolish Wives '22
Shadows '22
Hawthorne of the USA '19
The Primitive Lover '16

Harrison Ford (1942-)
Crossing Over '08
Indiana Jones and the Kingdom of the Crystal Skull '08
Firewall '06
Hollywood Homicide '03
K-19: The Widowmaker '02
What Lies Beneath '00
Random Hearts '99
Six Days, Seven Nights '98
Air Force One '97
The Devil's Own '96
Sabrina '95
Clear and Present Danger '94
The Fugitive '93
Patriot Games '92
Regarding Henry '91
Presumed Innocent '90
Indiana Jones and the Last Crusade '89
Frantic '88
Working Girl '88
The Mosquito Coast '86
Witness '85
Indiana Jones and the Temple of Doom '84
Return of the Jedi '83
Blade Runner '82
Raiders of the Lost Ark '81
The Empire Strikes Back '80
Apocalypse Now '79
The Frisco Kid '79
Hanover Street '79
More American Graffiti '79
Force 10 from Navarone '78
Heroes '77
Star Wars '77
Dynasty '76
The Conversation '74
American Graffiti '73
Getting Straight '70
Zabriskie Point '70
Dead Heat on a Merry-Go-Round '66

Maria Ford (1966-)
Dark Planet '97
Future Fear '97
The Glass Cage '96
The Wasp Woman '96
Alien Terminator '95
Burial of the Rats '95
Machine Gun Blues '95
Night Fever '95
The Showgirl Murders '95
The Unnamable 2: The Statement of Randolph Carter '92
Futurekick '91
The Haunting of Morella '91
Naked Obsession '91
The Rain Killer '90
Slumber Party Massacre 3 '90
Masque of the Red Death '89
Stripped to Kill II: Live Girls '89
Dance of the Damned '88

Mick Ford (1957-)
How to Get Ahead in Advertising '89
Scum '79

Paul Ford (1901-76)
Lola '69
The Comedians '67
The Russians Are Coming, the Russians Are Coming '66
Who's Got the Action? '63
Advise and Consent '62
The Music Man '62
The Matchmaker '58
Missouri Traveler '58
The Teahouse of the August Moon '56
Lust for Gold '49

Peter Ford
The Thorn Birds: The Missing Years '96
Fair Game '85

Ross Ford (1923-88)
Reform School Girl '57
Project Moon Base '53
Blue Canadian Rockies '52
Jungle Patrol '48

Ruth Ford (1915-)
The Eyes of the Amaryllis '82
Strange Impersonation '46
The Woman Who Came Back '45
The Lady Is Willing '42

Steven Ford (1956-)
Black Hawk Down '01
Against the Law '98
When Harry Met Sally... '89
Body Count '87

Trent Ford
September Dawn '07
How to Deal '03

Wallace Ford (1898-1966)
A Patch of Blue '65
Warlock '59
Last Hurrah '58
The Matchmaker '58
The Rainmaker '56
A Lawless Street '55
The Man from Laramie '55
The Maverick Queen '55
She Couldn't Say No '52
Harvey '50
Great Jesse James Raid '49
The Set-Up '49
Coroner Creek '48
Dead Reckoning '47
T-Men '47
Black Angel '46
Crack-Up '46
Blood on the Sun '45
Spellbound '45
The Ape Man '43
Shadow of a Doubt '43
All Through the Night '42
Inside the Law '42
The Mummy's Tomb '42
Seven Days' Leave '42
Wheel of Fortune '41
The Mummy's Hand '40
Back Door to Heaven '39
Jericho '38
Exiled to Shanghai '37
Mad About Money '37
O.H.M.S. '37
Swing It, Sailor! '37
Rogue's Tavern '36
Get That Man '35
The Informer '35
Mysterious Mr. Wong '35
One Frightened Night '35
The Whole Town's Talking '35
The Lost Patrol '34
Employees' Entrance '33
Night of Terror '33
Freaks '32
Skyscraper Souls '32
Possessed '31

Ken Foree (1948-)
The Devil's Rejects '05
The Dentist '96
Leatherface: The Texas Chainsaw Massacre 3 '89
Glitz '88
From Beyond '86
Dawn of the Dead '78

Deborah Foreman (1962-)
Lunatics: A Love Story '92
Sundown '91
The Experts '89
Friends, Lovers & Lunatics '89
Lobster Man from Mars '89
Destroyer '88
Waxwork '88
April Fool's Day '86
My Chauffeur '86
3:15—The Moment of Truth '86
Real Genius '85
Valley Girl '83

Jamie Foreman (1958-)
Botched '07
Layer Cake '05
Oliver Twist '05
I'll Sleep When I'm Dead '03

Michelle Foreman
Sunset Strip '91
Stripped to Kill '87

Mark Forest (1933-)
Goliath and the Sins of Babylon '64
Hercules vs. the Sons of the Sun '64
The Lion of Thebes '64
Terror of Rome Against the Son of Hercules '64
Colossus of the Arena '62
Son of Samson '62
Goliath and the Dragon '61
Mole Men Against the Son of Hercules '61

Michael Forest (1929-)
Cast Away '00
Body of Evidence '92
Lensman '84 (V)
The Message '77
Dirt Gang '71
Atlas '60
The Beast from Haunted Cave '60
Ski Troop Attack '60

Sara Forestier
A Few Days in September '06
Games of Love and Chance '03

Maud Forget (1982-)
La Vie Promise '02
Bad Company '99

Farrah Forke (1967-)
Kate's Addiction '99
Ground Control '98
National Lampoon's Favorite Deadly Sins '95

Claire Forlani (1972-)
In the Name of the King: A Dungeon Siege Tale '08
Carolina Moon '07
Green Street Hooligans '05
Bobby Jones: Stroke of Genius '04
Memron '04
Gone '03
The Medallion '03
Northfork '03
Triggermen '02
Antitrust '00
Boys and Girls '00
Mystery Men '99
Basil '98
Meet Joe Black '98
Basquiat '96
The Last Time I Committed Suicide '96
The Rock '96
Mallrats '95
JFK: Reckless Youth '93

Carol Forman (1919-97)
Federal Agents vs. Underworld, Inc. '49
The Black Widow '47

Milos Forman (1932-)
Keeping the Faith '00
New Year's Day '89
Heartburn '86

Richard Foronjy (1937-)
Man of the House '95
DaVinci's War '92
The Public Eye '92
Midnight Run '88
The Morning After '86
Prince of the City '81

Veronica Forque (1955-)
I Love You Baby '01
Kika '94
Why Do They Call It Love When They Mean Sex? '92

Alan Forrest
The Phantom Bullet '26
Eyes of Julia Deep '18

Christine Forrest
Monkey Shines '88
Martin '77

Frederic Forrest (1936-)
All the King's Men '06
Path to War '02
The House Next Door '01
Militia '00
Sweetwater: A True Rock Story '99
Black Thunder '98
Boogie Boy '98
The First 9 1/2 Weeks '98
Implicated '98
Point Blank '98
Whatever '98
The End of Violence '97
Horton Foote's Alone '97
Crash Dive '96
Andersonville '95
One Night Stand '95
Against the Wall '94
Chasers '94
Lassie '94
Dario Argento's Trauma '93
Double Obsession '93
Falling Down '93
Hidden Fears '93
Rain Without Thunder '93
Citizen Cohn '92
Music Box '89
Best Kept Secrets '88
Gotham '88
Return '88
Shadow on the Sun '88
Tucker: The Man and His Dream '88
Valentino Returns '88
Saigon: Year of the Cat '87
Stacking '87
The Deliberate Stranger '86
The Adventures of Huckleberry Finn '85
Quo Vadis '85
Where Are the Children? '85
The Stone Boy '84
Valley Girl '83
Calamity Jane '82
Hammett '82
One from the Heart '82
Apocalypse Now '79
The Rose '79
It's Alive 2: It Lives Again '78
Missouri Breaks '76
Permission To Kill '75

The Conversation '74
Larry '74
The Don Is Dead '73
When the Legends Die '72

Irene Forrest
Jackie Brown '97
Hindsight '97
Night Vision '97
Amazon Women on the Moon '87

Sally Forrest (1928-)
Sitting Ducks '80
Son of Sinbad '55
Vengeance Valley '51
Mystery Street '50

Steve Forrest (1924-)
S.W.A.T. '03
Killer: A Journal of Murder '95
The Last of the Mohicans '85
Spies Like Us '85
Sahara '83
Hotline '82
Mommie Dearest '81
Roughnecks '80
A Rumor of War '80
North Dallas Forty '79
Captain America '79
The Deerslayer '78
The Hatfields & the McCoys '75
The Hanged Man '74
The Wild Country '71
Flaming Star '60
Heller in Pink Tights '60
Battle Circus '53
Clown '53
The Ghost Ship '43

William Forrest (1902-89)
Billy the Kid Versus Dracula '66
Good Neighbor Sam '64
Fighting Seabees '44
Air Force '43
The Masked Marvel '43
Wake Island '42
Dive Bomber '41
International Lady '41
I'll See You in My Dreams '51

Kathrine (Kate) Forster (1969)

Cay Forrester (1921-2005)
Dead Reckoning '47
D.O.A. '49
Door to Door Maniac '61

Constance Forslund
A Shining Season '79

Robert Forster (1950-)
Cleaner '07
Rise: Blood Hunter '07
Firewall '06
Confidence '03
Grand Theft Parsons '03
Undefeated '03
Due East '02
Human Nature '02
Like Mike '02
Lone Hero '02
Murder in Greenwich '02
Diamond Men '01
Finder's Fee '01
Road to Riches '01
Mulholland Drive '01
Family Tree '00
Lakeboat '00
Me, Myself, and Irene '00
Kiss Toledo Goodbye '00
It's the Rage '99
Supernova '99
Outside Ozona '98
Psycho '98
Rear Window '98
Hindsight '97
Jackie Brown '97
Night Vision '97
Amazon Women on the Moon '87
Hollywood Harry '86
Goliath Awaits '81
Alligator '80
The Black Hole '79
Avalanche '78
Stunts '77
Vigilante '83
Walking the Edge '83
In Between '92
Committed '91
Diplomatic Immunity '91
29th Street '91
Peacemaker '90
Satan's Princess '90
The Banker '89
Once a Hero '88
Delta Force '86
The City '76
The Death Squad '73
The Don Is Dead '73
Journey Through Rosebud '72
The Stalking Moon '69
Medium Cool '69

Rosemary Forsyth (1945-)
A Time to Remember '03
Columbo: Murder by the Book '71
Whatever Happened to Aunt Alice? '69
Texas Across the River '66
Shenandoah '65
The War Lord '65
Disclosure '94
Daylight '96
Girl '98
Mars '91
Star! '68
A Friendship in Vienna '88
The Gladiator '86
Gray Lady Down '77

Drew Forsythe

John Forsythe (1918-)
Charlie's Angels: Full Throttle '03
Charlie's Angels '00
Sessions '83
Scrooged '88
Midnight Murders '91
Crisis at Central High '80
A Time for Miracles '80
And Justice for All '79
Cruise into Terror '78
Users '78

Henderson Forsythe (1917-2006)
Carolina Skeletons '92
Teamster Boss: The Jackie Presser Story '92
Dead Bang '89
Raising Arizona '87
Silkwood
Weeds '87
The Lightship '86
The Long, Hot Summer '86
Once Upon a Time in America '84
The Gun in Betty Lou's Handbag '92
The Namesake '06

Bruce Forsyth (1928-)
Bedknobs and Broomsticks '71

Rudolph Forster (1884-1968)
The Mad Executioners '65
The Return of Dr. Mabuse '61
The Threepenny Opera '31

Josef Forte (1896-1967)
Reefer Madness '38

Marlene Forte
Our Song '01
Mob Queen '98
The Bronx War '90

Will Forte (1970-)
Beerfest '06
The Brothers Solomon '07
Around the World in 80 Days '04

Albert Fortell (1952-)
Time Troopers '85
Scandalous '88

Robert Fortier (1926-2005)
3 Women '77
Incubus '65

William Forsythe (1955-)
Sniper '75
Cry Panic '74
Terror on the 40th Floor '74
Murder Once Removed '71
The Happy Ending '69
88 Minutes '08
Hack! '07
Halloween '07
Masters of Horror: We All Scream for Ice Cream '07
Freedomland '06
Jam '06
The Devil's Rejects '05
The Last Letter '04
City by the Sea '02
Hard Cash '01
Camouflage '00
Luck of the Draw '00
Big City Blues '99
Blue Streak '99
Deuce Bigalow: Male Gigolo '99
Four Days '99
Hitman's Journal '99
The Last Marshal '99
Malicious Intent '99
Soundman '99
Virtuosity '95
For Which He Stands '96
Beyond Desire '94
Direct Hit '93
Relentless 3 '93
American Me '92
Stone Cold '91
The Waterdance '91
Dick Tracy '90
Torrents of Spring '90
Dead Bang '89
Sons '89
Patty Hearst '88
Extreme Prejudice '87
Raising Arizona '87
Weeds '87
The Lightship '86
The Long, Hot Summer '86
Once Upon a Time in America '84
The Gun in Betty Lou's Handbag '92

Frances Foster (1924-97)
Crooklyn '94
Enemy Territory '87
Savage Dawn '84

Dianne Foster (1928-)
The King of the Roaring '20s: The Story of Arnold Rothstein '61
The Kentuckian '55
The Violent Men '55
Night Passage '57
Last Hurrah '58

Ben Foster (1980-)
30 Days of Night '07
3:10 to Yuma '07
Alpha Dog '06
X-Men: The Last Stand '06
Hostage '05
The Heart Is Deceitful Above All Things '04
The Punisher '04
11:14 '03
Northfork '03
Big Trouble '02
Get Over It! '01
Liberty Heights '99

Gloria Foster (1936-2001)
The Matrix Reloaded '03
The Matrix '99
Percy & Thunder '53
City of Hope '91
The House of Dies Drear '84
Leonard Part 6 '87
Man & Boy '71
To All My Friends on Shore '71
The Angel Levine '70
Nothing but a Man '64
The Cool World '63

George Foster
Centipede '05
Killer Me '01

Helen Foster (1906-82)
Young Blood '32
Boiling Point '32
Ghost City '32

John Fortune (1939-)
Calendar Girls '03
The Tailor of Panama '00

Bob Fosse (1927-87)
Bloodbath at the House of Death '85
The Little Prince '74
My Sister Eileen '55
The Affairs of Dobie Gillis '53
Give a Girl a Break '53
Kiss Me Kate '53

Brigitte Fossey (1946-)
The Last Butterfly '92
Enigma '82
Chanel Solitaire '81
La Boum '81
Quintet '79
Blue Country '77
The Man Who Loved Women '77
Going Places '74
Honor Among Thieves '68
The Wanderer '67
Forbidden Games '52

Nicole Fosse (1963-)
All That Jazz '79
A Chorus Line '85

Anthony Foster
See Anthony (Jose, J. Antonio, J.A.) Mayans

Barry Foster (1931-2002)
After Pilkington '88
Beyond the Next Mountain '87
Maurice '87
The Whistle Blower '87
Heat and Dust '82
Smiley's People '82
Orde Wingate '76
Quiet Day in Belfast '74
Frenzy '72
Inspector Clouseau '68
Robbery '67
King and Country '64
The Family Way '66

Jon Foster (1984-)
Stay Alive '06
The Door in the Floor '04
Murder in Greenwich '02

Julia Foster (1942-)
Half a Sixpence '67
Alfie '66
Thirteenth Reunion '81
F. Scott Fitzgerald in Hollywood '76
Great McGonagall '75

Meg Foster (1948-)
Alfie '66
Space Marines '96
Backlash: Oblivion 2 '95
Immortal Combat '94
Lady in Waiting '94
Oblivion '94
Shrunken Heads '94
Undercover '94
Best of the Best 2 '93
Hidden Fears '93
Project: Shadowchaser '92
To Catch a Killer '92
Diplomatic Immunity '91
Blind Fury '90
Futurekick '91
Backstab '90
Jezebel's Kiss '90
Stepfather 2: Make Room for Daddy '89
Leviathan '89
Relentless '89
They Live '88
Tripwire '89

Kimberly Foster (1961-)
Broken Trust '93
It Takes Two '88
Spoiler '98
The Man in the Iron Mask '97

Robert Fotre
See Anthony (Jose, J. Antonio, J.A.) Mayans

Stacie Foster
Cyber-Tracker 2 '95
Steel Frontier '94
D.E.B.S. '04

Susanna Foster (1924-)
The Climax '44
The Phantom of the Opera '43

Sara Foster (1981-)
Bachelor Party 2: The Last Temptation '08
The Big Bounce '04
D.E.B.S. '04

Jodie Foster (1963-)
The Brave One '07
Inside Man '06
Flightplan '05
A Very Long Engagement '04
The Dangerous Lives of Altar Boys '02
Panic Room '02
Anna and the King '99
Contact '97
Maverick '94
Nell '94
Sommersby '93
Shadows and Fog '92
Little Man Tate '91
The Silence of the Lambs '91
Backtrack '89
The Accused '88
Five Corners '88
Stealing Home '88
Siesta '87
The Blood of Others '84
The Hotel New Hampshire '84
Svengali '83
O'Hara's Wife '82
Carny '80
Foxes '80
Candleshoe '78
Bugsy Malone '76
The Little Girl Who Lives down the Lane '76
Taxi Driver '76
Alice Doesn't Live Here Anymore '74
Smile, Jenny, You're Dead '74
One Little Indian '73
Tom Sawyer '73
Napoleon and Samantha '72

Norman Foster (1900-76)
Journey into Fear '42
Pilgrimage '33
Skyscraper Souls '32

Phil Foster (1914-85)
Bang the Drum Slowly '73

Preston Foster (1902-70)
The Time Travelers '64
The Marshal's Daughter '53
Kansas City Confidential '52
Tomahawk '51
Three Desperate Men '50
The Big Cat '49
I Shot Jesse James '49
Ramrod '47
The Harvey Girls '46
The Valley of Decision '45
Guadalcanal Diary '43
My Friend Flicka '43
American Empire '42
A Gentleman After Dark '42
Thunder Birds '42
The Roundup '41
Annie Oakley '35
Sea Devils '37
The Informer '35
The Last Days of Pompeii '35
Hoopla '33
Ladies They Talk About '33
Doctor X '32
I Am a Fugitive from a Chain Gang '32
The Last Mile '32

Robert Foulk (1908-89)
Saddle Buster '32

Byron Foulger (1899-1968)
The Devil's Partner '58
Red Desert '50
Outlaw Gang '49
Bells of San Fernando '47
The Panther's Claw '42
Sullivan's Travels '41
Prisoner of Zenda '37
Frankenstein Created Woman '66
Hotel Paradiso '66
Flight from Singapore '62
Over the Hill '31

Robert Foulk (1908-89)
Emperor of the North Pole '73
Robin and the 7 Hoods '64

Derek Fowlds (1937-)
Frankenstein Created Woman '66
Hotel Paradiso '66

Harry Fowler (1926-)
Flight from Singapore '62
Over the Hill '31

Douglas Fowley (1911-98)
The Emerald Forest '85
From Noon Till Three '76
The White Buffalo '77
Masters of the Universe '87
The Wind '87

The Osterman Weekend '83
Ticket to Heaven '81
Carny '80
The Legend of Sleepy Hollow '79
The Scarlet Letter '79
Different Story '78
James Dean '76
Things in Their Season '74
Thumb Tripping '72
Adam at 6 a.m. '70
Conquest of Space '55

The Good Guys and the Bad Guys '69
Poor White Trash '57
Lonesome Trail '55
The High and the Mighty '54
Cat Women of the Moon '53
Singin' in the Rain '52
Armored Car Robbery '50
Rider from Tucson '50
Battleground '49
Susanna Pass '49
Behind Locked Doors '48
Desperate '47
Fall Guy '47
Wild Country '47
Scared to Death '46
Along the Navaho Trail '45
One Body Too Many '44
Shake Hands with Murder '44

Bernard Fox (1927-)
The Mummy '99
Titanic '97
The Private Eyes '80
House of the Dead '78
Zone of the Dead '78
Arnold '73
Munster, Go Home! '66
Strange Bedfellows '65

Colin Fox (1938-)
The Doorbell Rang: A Nero Wolfe Mystery '01
Angels in the Infield '00
A House Divided '00
Left Behind: The Movie '00
Daylight '96
Beautiful Dreamers '92
Canada's Sweetheart: The Saga of Hal C. Banks '85
War Between the Tates '76
My Pleasure Is My Business '74

David Fox (1941-)
Population 436 '06
That Beautiful Somewhere '06
The Saddest Music in the World '03
Grey Owl '99
Conquest '98
When Night Is Falling '95
Black Fox: Good Men and Bad '94
Ordinary Magic '93

Edward Fox (1937-)
Lassie '05
Stage Beauty '04
All the Queen's Men '02
Daniel Deronda '02
The Importance of Being Earnest '02
Nicholas Nickleby '02
Lost in Space '98
A Dance to the Music of Time '97
Prince Valiant '97
Gulliver's Travels '95
A Month by the Lake '95
The Crucifer of Blood '91
Robin Hood '91
Anastasia: The Mystery of Anna '86
The Shooting Party '85
Wild Geese 2 '85
The Bounty '84
The Dresser '83
Never Say Never Again '83
Shaka Zulu '83
Gandhi '82
Edward and Mrs. Simpson '80
The Mirror Crack'd '80
The Cat and the Canary '79
The Big Sleep '78
Force 10 from Navarone '78
Soldier of Orange '78
A Bridge Too Far '77
The Duellists '77
The Day of the Jackal '73
A Doll's House '73
The Go-Between '71
Skullduggery '70
Battle of Britain '69
Oh! What a Lovely War '69
Portrait of a Lady '67
Morgan: A Suitable Case for Treatment '66

Emilia Fox (1974-)
Cashback '06
Keeping Mum '05
Helen of Troy '03
The Pianist '02
Three Blind Mice '02
David Copperfield '99
The Scarlet Pimpernel '99
Shooting the Past '99
Catherine Cookson's The Round Tower '98
Rebecca '97

Huckleberry Fox (1975-)
Pharoah's Army '95
The Blue Yonder '86
A Winner Never Quits '86
Konrad '85
Misunderstood '84

James Fox (1939-)
Charlie and the Chocolate Factory '05
The Prince & Me '04
Cambridge Spies '03
The Lost World '02
The Mystic Masseur '01
The Golden Bowl '00
Sexy Beast '00
Up at the Villa '00
Lover's Prayer '99
Mickey Blue Eyes '99
Circle of Passion '97
Kings in Grass Castles '97
Leo Tolstoy's Anna Karenina '96
The Choir '95
Catherine Cookson's The Dwelling Place '94
Doomsday Gun '94
Fall from Grace '94
Hostage '92
Patriot Games '92
A Question of Attribution '91
Afraid of the Dark '92
The Russia House '90
Farewell to the King '89
The Mighty Quinn '89
High Season '88
Shadow on the Sun '88
The Whistle Blower '87
Absolute Beginners '86
Greystoke: The Legend of Tarzan, Lord of the Apes '84
A Passage to India '84
Performance '70
Isadora '68
Thoroughly Modern Millie '67
The Chase '66
King Rat '65
Those Magnificent Men in Their Flying Machines '65
The Servant '63

Jerry Fox
Hollywood Chainsaw Hookers '88
Evil Spawn '87

Jorja Fox (1968-)
Memento '00
Happy Hell Night '92

Kerry Fox (1966-)
P.D. James: The Murder Room '04
The Gathering '02
Intimacy '00
To Walk with Lions '99
Immortality '98
The Hanging Garden '97
Welcome to Sarajevo '97
The Affair '95
Country Life '95
Friends '95
A Village Affair '95
Rainbow Warrior '94
Shallow Grave '94
The Last Days of Chez Nous '92
An Angel at My Table '89

Lauren Fox (1977-)
Standing on Fishes '99
I Love You, I Love You Not '97

Laurence Fox (1978-)
Becoming Jane '07
The Last Drop '05
Deathwatch '02
The Hole '01

Matthew Fox (1966-)
Speed Racer '08
Vantage Point '08
Smokin' Aces '07
We Are Marshall '06
Behind the Mask '99
My Boyfriend's Back '93

Megan Fox (1986-)
Transformers '07
Confessions of a Teenage Drama Queen '04

Michael Fox (1921-96)
The Longest Yard '74
Bloody Mama '70
The Dunwich Horror '70

Michael J. Fox (1961-)
Interstate 60 '02
Stuart Little 2 '02 (V)
Atlantis: The Lost Empire '01 (V)
Stuart Little '99 (V)
The Frighteners '96
Homeward Bound 2: Lost in San Francisco '96 (V)
Mars Attacks! '96
The American President '95
Blue in the Face '95
Coldblooded '94
Greedy '94
Where the Rivers Flow North '94
For Love or Money '93
Homeward Bound: The Incredible Journey '93 (V)
Life with Mikey '93
Doc Hollywood '91
The Hard Way '91
Back to the Future, Part 3 '90
Back to the Future, Part 2 '89
The Secret of My Success '87
Back to the Future '85
Poison Ivy '85
Teen Wolf '85
High School USA '84
Class of 1984 '82
Midnight Madness '80

Peter Fox
Diamond Run '90
A Minor Miracle '83

Rick Fox (1969-)
Tyler Perry's Meet the Browns '08
Holes '03
Resurrection '99
The Collectors '99

Samantha Fox (1951-)
Warrior Queen '87
Delivery Boys '84
Violated '84

Sidney (Sydney) Fox (1910-42)
Don Quixote '35
Midnight '34
Murders in the Rue Morgue '32

Spencer Fox (1993-)
Air Bud 6: Air Buddies '06 (V)
The Groomsmen '06
The Incredibles '04 (V)

Vivica A. Fox (1964-)
Cover '08
Father of Lies '07
Kickin' It Old Skool '07
Getting Played '05
The Salon '05
Blast '04
Ella Enchanted '04
Kill Bill Vol. 2 '04
Boat Trip '03
Kill Bill Vol. 1 '03
Motives '03
Juwanna Mann '02
Little Secrets '02
Kingdom Come '01
Two Can Play That Game '01
Hendrix '00
Idle Hands '99
A Saintly Switch '99
Teaching Mrs. Tingle '99
Solomon '98
Why Do Fools Fall in Love? '98
Batman and Robin '97
Soul Food '97
Booty Call '96
Independence Day '96
Set It Off '96
The Tuskegee Airmen '95
Born on the Fourth of July '89

Earle Foxe (1891-1973)
Justice Rides Again '32
They Never Come Back '32
Four Sons '28
Hangman's House '28

Robert Foxworth (1941-)
Transformers '07 (V)
Syriana '05
Beyond the Stars '88
Double Standard '88
Peter and Paul '81
The Black Marble '79
Prophecy '79
Damien: Omen 2 '78
Deathmoon '78
Ants '77
The Invisible Strangler '76
The Treasure of Matecumbe '76
Frankenstein '73

Jeff Foxworthy (1958-)
The Fox and the Hound 2 '06 (V)
Racing Stripes '05 (V)

Jamie Foxx (1967-)
The Kingdom '07
Dreamgirls '06
Miami Vice '06
Jarhead '05
Stealth '05
Breakin' All The Rules '04
Collateral '04
Ray '04
Shade '03
Ali '01
Bait '00
Held Up '00
Any Given Sunday '99
The Players Club '98
Booty Call '96
The Great White Hype '96
The Truth about Cats and Dogs '96

Redd Foxx (1922-91)
Harlem Nights '89
Norman, Is That You? '76
Cotton Comes to Harlem '70

Charles Foy (1898-1984)
The Wagons Roll at Night '41

Eddie Foy, Jr. (1905-83)
30 Is a Dangerous Age, Cynthia '68
Gidget Goes Hawaiian '61
Bells Are Ringing '60
The Pajama Game '57
Lucky Me '54
The Farmer Takes a Wife '53
Wilson '44
Yankee Doodle Dandy '42
Four Jacks and a Jill '41
Myrt and Marge '33

Victoria Foyt
Going Shopping '05
Deja Vu '98
Last Summer In the Hamptons '96
Babyfever '94

Carla Fracci (1936-)
Life of Verdi '82
Nijinsky '80

Tracy Fraim
Best Men '98
Fear '96

James Frain (1969-)
The Front Line '06
Into the Blue '05
The Count of Monte Cristo '02
Path to War '02
Arabian Nights '00
The Miracle Maker: The Story of Jesus '00 (V)
Reindeer Games '00
Where the Heart Is '00
Sunshine '99
Titus '99
Elizabeth '98
Hilary and Jackie '98
Red Meat '98
The Mill on the Floss '97
Rasputin: Dark Servant of Destiny '96
The Buccaneers '95
Loch Ness '95
Nothing Personal '95

Jonathan Frakes (1952-)
Star Trek: Nemesis '02
Star Trek: Insurrection '98
Star Trek: First Contact '96
Gargoyles, The Movie: The Heroes Awaken '94 (V)
Star Trek: Generations '94
North and South Book 1 '85

David "Shark" Fralick (1962-)
Clawed: The Legend of Sasquatch '05
Uncle Sam '96
Femme Fontaine: Killer Babe for the C.I.A. '95
The Legend of Wolf Mountain '92
Dark Rider '91
Invasion Force '90
Soultaker '90

Peter Frampton (1950-)
Almost Famous '00
Sgt. Pepper's Lonely Hearts Club Band '78

C.V. France (1868-1949)
Night Train to Munich '40
If I Were King '38
Skin Game '31

Richard France (1930-)
Vortex '81
Dawn of the Dead '78
The Crazies '73

Victor Francen (1888-1977)
The Beast with Five Fingers '46
San Antonio '45
The Mask of Dimitrios '44
Madame Curie '43
The Tuttles of Tahiti '42
J'Accuse '37

Anthony (Tony) Franciosa (1928-2006)
City Hall '95
Double Threat '92
Backstreet Dreams '90
Ghost Writer '89
Death House '88
Blood Vows: The Story of a Mafia Wife '87
Stagecoach '86
Side Show '84
La Cicada '83
Daughter of Death '82
Death Wish 2 '82
Kiss My Grits '82
Unsane '82
The World Is Full of Married Men '80
Curse of the Black Widow '77
The Drowning Pool '75
Ghost in the Noonday Sun '74
Across 110th Street '72
Web of the Spider '70
Fathom '67
Assault on a Queen '66
Rio Conchos '64
Period of Adjustment '62
Career '59
The Naked Maja '59
The Long, Hot Summer '58
A Face in the Crowd '57
This Could Be the Night '57

Alec B. Francis (1867-1934)
His Private Secretary '33
Mata Hari '32
Evangeline '29
Tramp, Tramp, Tramp '26
Charley's Aunt '25
The Mad Whirl '25
Beau Brummel '24
Little Church Around the Corner '23
Beyond the Rocks '22
The Wishing Ring '14

Anne Francis (1930-)
Lover's Knot '96
The Double O Kid '92
Little Vegas '90
Return '88
Laguna Heat '87
Poor Little Rich Girl: The Barbara Hutton Story '87
Mazes and Monsters '82
The Rebels '79
Born Again '78
Banjo Hackett '76
Cry Panic '74
Fireball Forward '72
Haunts of the Very Rich '72
Pancho Villa '72
The Love God? '70
Wild Women '70
Funny Girl '68
More Dead Than Alive '68
Don't Go Near the Water '57
Forbidden Planet '56
Battle Cry '55
Blackboard Jungle '55
Bad Day at Black Rock '54
Susan Slept Here '54
A Lion Is in the Streets '53
Portrait of Jennie '48
Summer Holiday '48

Arlene Francis (1908-2001)
The Thrill of It All! '63
One, Two, Three '61
All My Sons '48
Murders in the Rue Morgue '32

Clive Francis (1946-)
Longitude '00
Sharpe's Company '94
The Bretts '88
Poldark '75
Man Who Had Power Over Women '70

Derek Francis (1923-84)
Murder Motel '74
What's Good for the Goose '69
Rasputin the Mad Monk '66

Tomb of Ligeia '64

Genie Francis (1960-)
Disney's Teacher's Pet '04 (V)
Thunderbirds '04

Ivor Francis (1918-86)
House of the Dead '78
Zone of the Dead '78
Wackiest Wagon Train in the West '77
Hard Frame '70

Jan Francis (1951-)
Champions '84

Jon Francis
See Jon(athan) Gries

Kay Francis ('899-1968)
Charley's Aunt '41
It's a Date '40
Little Men '40
In Name Only '39
One Way Passage '32
Strangers in Love '32
Trouble in Paradise '32
Vice Squad '31
Raffles '30
The Cocoanuts '29

Paul Francis
Smart Woman '31
The River Pirates '0C
Social Misfits '0C
Straight into Darkness '04

Ryan Francis (1977-)
The Caine Mutiny '54
The Long Gray Line '55

Robert Francis (1930-55)
Warlock 3: The End of Innocence '98

Noel Francis (1906-59)
Stone of Silver Creek '35
Fire Alarm '32
My Pal, the King '32
Bachelor Apartment '31

James Franciscus (1934-91)
The Amazing Dobermans '76
Butterfly '82
Jacqueline Bouvier Kennedy '81
Nightkill '80
Killer Fish '79
Good Guys Wear Black '78
The Greek Tycoon '78
Puzzle '78
Secrets of Three Hungry Wives '78
Hunter '76
The Man Inside '76
One of My Wives Is Missing '76

Don Francks (1932-)
Summer of the Monkeys '98
Bogus '96
Conspiracy of Fear '96
Degree of Guilt '95
Madonna: Innocence Lost '95
The Christmas Wife '88
Big Town '87
Rock & Rule '83 (V)
Heavy Metal '81 (V)
My Bloody Valentine '81
Summer's Children '81
Fast Company '78
Drying Up the Streets '78
Finian's Rainbow '68

Rainbow Sun Francks (1979-)
Love Come Down '00
Love Song '00

James Franco (1978-)
Pineapple Express '08
In the Valley of Elah '07
Spider-Man 3 '07
Annapolis '06
Flyboys '06
The Dead Girl '06
The Great Raid '05
The Company '03
City by the Sea '03
Deuces Wild '02
Sonny '02
Spider-Man '02
James Dean '01
Whatever It Takes '00

Margarita Franco
Venus in Furs '70
The Diabolical Dr. Z '65

Ramon Franco (1963-)
Shattered Image '93

Deborah Francois
The Page Turner '06
The Child '05

Jacques Francois (1920-2003)
The Gift '82
The Barkleys of Broadway '49

Billy Franey (1885-1940)
Somewhere in Sonora '33
Ghost Valley '32

Astrid Frank (1945-)
Au Pair Girls '72

Ben Frank (1934-90)
Her and S.te and Him '69
Hollywood Vice Squad '86
Hollywood Zap '86
Don't Answer the Phone '80

Billy Frank
Track 16 '02

Charles Frank (1947-)
Nudity Required '90
Grotesque '87
LBJ: The Early Years '88
CSA: The Confederate States of America '04
Danielle Steel's Changes '91

Dan Frank (1959-)
Tarantulas: The Deadly Cargo '77

Diana Frank (1965-)
Snowblind '78
Adventure '94

Jess (Jesus) Franco (1930-)
Ilsa, the Wicked Warden '78

Joanna Frank (1941-)
The Savage Seven '68
Always '85

Tony Frank (1943-2000)
Rush '91
Riverbend '89

Mark Frankel (1962-96)
For Roseanna '96
Solitaire for 2 '94
Young Catherine '91
Leon the Pig Farmer '93

Al Franken (1951-)
When Stuart Saves His Family '94
Harvard Man '01
From the Earth to the Moon '98
One More Saturday Night '86
Trading Places '83
All You Need Is Cash '78

Steve Franken (1932-)
Freeway '88
The Fiendish Plot of Dr. Fu Manchu '80
Terror Out of the Sky '78
Which Way to the Front? '70

William Frankfather (1944-98)
Born Yesterday '93
Cool World '92
Defense Play '88
Un Singe en Hiver '62
Nana '55

Paul Frankeur (1905-75)
Bogie: The Last Hero '80
The Caine Mutiny '54
Le Gentleman D'Epsom '62

Aretha Franklin (1942-)
Blues Brothers 2000 '98
The Blues Brothers '80

Bonnie Franklin (1944-)
Your Place or Mine '83
Portrait of a Rebel: Margaret Sanger '80
Breaking Up Is Hard to Do '79

David Franklin (1962-)
Rock & Roll Cowboys '92
Early Frost '84

Diane Franklin (1963-)
Terrorvision '86
Better Off Dead '85
Second Time Lucky '84
Amityville 2: The Possession '82

Eduard Franz (1902-83)
Johnny Got His Gun '71

Enola Gay: The Men, the Mission, the Atomic Bomb '80
The Night the City Screamed '80

Horst Frank (1929-99)
Albino '76
Cold Blood '75
The Grand Duel '73
Dead Are Alive '72
Code Name Alpha '67
Desert Commandos '67
The Head '59

Joe Franklin (1926-)
29th Street '91
Ghoul School '90
Broadway Danny Rose '84

Jason David Frank (1973-)
Turbo: A Power Rangers Movie '96
Mighty Morphin Power Rangers: The Movie '95

Jerry Frank
The Company '03
Sweet Lies '88

Marilyn Dodds Frank
The Game of Their Lives '05

Gloria Franklin (1923-84)
Without Warning '52
Drums of Fu Manchu '40

John Franklin (1967-)
Children of the Corn 666: Isaac's Return '99
The Addams Family '91
Children of the Corn '84

Pamela Franklin (1950-)
Satan's School for Girls '73
The Witching '72
And Soon the Darkness '70
David Copperfield '70
The Night of the Following Day '69
The Prime of Miss Jean Brodie '69
The Nanny '65
Flipper's New Adventure '64
A Tiger Walks '64
The Horse Without a Head '63
The Innocents '61

William Franklyn (1925-2006)
Splitting Heirs '93
The Satanic Rites of Dracula '73
Quatermass 2 '57

Chloe Franks (1963-)
Ivanhoe '82

Mary Frann (1943-98)
Fatal Charm '92
I'm Dangerous Tonight '90

Adrienne Frantz
Hack! '07
Jimmy Zip '00

Arthur Franz (1920-2006)
Sisters of Death '76
Dream No Evil '75
The Human Factor '75
Missiles of October '74
Atomic Submarine '59
Monster on the Campus '59
The Young Lions '58
-relicats of the Navy '57
Beyond a Reasonable Doubt '56
The Caine Mutiny '54
Invaders from Mars '53
Flight to Mars '52
The Member of the Wedding '52
Abbott and Costello Meet the Invisible Man '51
Sands of Iwo Jima '49
Jungle Patrol '48

Dennis Franz (1944-)
City of Angels '98
American Buffalo '95
The Player '92
Die Hard 2: Die Harder '90
Kiss Shot '89
The Package '89
Body Double '84
Psycho 2 '83
Blow Out '81
Dressed to Kill '80
The Fury '78
A Wedding '78

Last American Virgin '82

Don Franklin (1960-)
Asteroid '97
Fast Forward '84

Daniel Franzese
Mean Girls '04
Bully '01

Francis Frappat
The Butterfly '02

Bill Fraser (1908-87)
Little Dorrit, Film 1: Nobody's Fault '88
Little Dorrit, Film 2: Little Dorrit's Story '88

Brendan Fraser (1968-)
Journey to the Center of the Earth 3D '08
The Mummy: Tomb of the Dragon Emperor '08
The Air I Breathe '07
The Last Time '06
Crash '05
Looney Tunes: Back in Action '03
The Quiet American '02
Monkeybone '01
The Mummy Returns '01
Bedazzled '00
Dudley Do-Right '99
The Mummy '99
Blast from the Past '98
Gods and Monsters '98
George of the Jungle '97
Still Breathing '97
The Twilight of the Golds '97
Glory Daze '96
Mrs. Winterbourne '96
Now and Then '95
The Passion of Darkly Noon '95
Airheads '94
Dark Side of Genius '94
The Scout '94
With Honors '94
Younger & Younger '94
Twenty Bucks '93
Encino Man '92
School Ties '92
Dogfight '91

Brent Fraser (1967-)
The Little Death '95
Wild Orchid 2: Two Shades of Blue '92

Duncan Fraser
Masters of Horror: The Washingtonians '07
Merlin's Apprentice '06
The Exorcism of Emily Rose '05
Octopus 2: River of Fear '02

The Story of Ruth '60
The Burning Hills '56
The Indian Fighter '55

Elizabeth Franz (1941-)
Christmas With the Kranks '04

Stephen King's Thinner '96
The Substance of Fire '96
Sabrina '95

Outpost in Morocco '49

Francis the Talking Mule '50
The Magnificent Yankee '50

Noir et Blanc '86
The Breits '88

Leo Fraser (1533-)
Chicago Joe & the Showgirl '90
Adventures of a Taxi Driver '76
The Americanization of Emily '64
A Christmas Carol '99
Kevin & Perry Go Large '00
Carry On Cruising '62
Two-Way Stretch '60
The Match '99
Titus '99
Virtual Sexuality '99
Left Luggage '98
Neil Gaiman's NeverWhere '96
Small Faces '95

Laura Fraser (1976-)
The Flying Scotsman '06
Casanova '05
16 Years of Alcohol '03
A Knight's Tale '01
A Station '01

John Fraser (1931-)
Isadora '68
Repulsion '65
Horsemasters '61

Hugh Fraser
Sharpe's Challenge '06
Chaos & Cadavers '03
P.D. James: Death in Holy Orders '03
Sharpe's Waterloc '97
Sharpe's Mission '96
Sharpe's Siege '96
Sharpe's Battle '94
Sharpe's Company '94
Sharpe's Enemy '94
Sharpe's Gold '94
Sharpe's Honour '94

Liz Fraser (1933-)

Phyllis Fraser (1911-2006)
The Little Valentino '79
Tough to Handle '37

Richard Fraser (1913-71)
The Cobra Strikes '48
The Private Affairs of Bel Ami '47
Bedlam '45
White Pongo '45

Sally Fraser
Dangerous Charter '62
Giant from the Unknown '58
The War of the Colossal Beast '58
It Conquered the World '56

Timescop '94
Call of the Wild '93
The Reflecting Skin '91
Watchers '88

Elisabeth Fraser (1920-2005)
Latin Lovers '54
One Minute to Zero '52
The Thing '51
The Great Caruso '51
Ask Any Girl '59
The Tunnel of Love '58
Young at Heart '54
Hills of Oklahoma '50
The Man Who Came to Dinner '41

Helen Fraser (1942-)
Start the Revolution without Me '70
Repulsion '65

Ronald Fraser (1930-97)
The Blackheath Poisonings '92
Let Him Have It '91
Rentadick '72
Too Late the Hero '70
The Killing of Sister George '69

Eduard Franz (1902-83)
When Danger Follows You Home '97
Unforgettable '96
Captains Courageous '95

Stuart Fratkin (1963-)
Prehysteria '93
Remote '93
Ski School '91
Dr. Alien '88

William Frawley (1887-1966)
Rancho Notorious '52
Abbott and Costello Meet the Invisible Man '51
The Lemon Drop Kid '51
Kill the Umpire '50
East Side, West Side '49
Babe Ruth Story '48
Down to Earth '47
Miracle on 34th Street '47
Monsieur Verdoux '47
Mother Wore Tights '47
The Inner Circle '46
The Virginian '46
Flame of the Barbary Coast '45
Lady on a Train '45
Fighting Seabees '44
Whistling in Brooklyn '43
Gentleman Jim '42
Roxie Hart '42
Wildcat '42
Blondie in Society '41
The Bride Came C.O.D. '41
Cracked Nuts '41
Footsteps in the Dark '41
One Night in the Tropics '40
Rhythm on the River '40
The Adventures of Huckleberry Finn '39
Rose of Washington Square '39
Strike Me Pink '36
Alibi Ike '35
Harmony Lane '35
Here is My Heart '34
Mad About Music '38
Blossoms on Broadway '37
Double or Nothing '37
Desire '36
The General Died at Dawn '36
The Princess Comes Across '36
Something to Sing About '36
The Gay Ranchero '42

Dan Frazer (1921-)
Lord Love a Duck '66
Lilies of the Field '63

Liz Frazer
See Liz Fraser

Robert Frazer (1891-1944)
Lawmen '44
Partners of the Trail '44
Dawn Express '42
Renfrew on the Great White Trail '38
We're in the Legion Now '37
The Clutching Hand '36
Death from a Distance '36
Fighting Parson '35
Fighting Pilot '35
The Miracle Rider '35
The Fighting Trooper '34
Found Alive '34
Monte Carlo Nights '34
Mystery Trooper '32
Saddle Buster '32
The White Zombie '32
Ten Nights in a Bar-Room '31
The Drake Case '29

Rupert Frazer (1947-)
Back Home '90
The Girl in a Swing '89
Empire of the Sun '87
Testament of Youth '79

Joe Frazier (1944-)
Just the Ticket '98
Home of Angels '94

Sheila Frazier (1948-)
The Hitter '79
The Lazarus Syndrome '79
Three the Hard Way '74
Superfly T.N.T. '73
Firehouse '72
Superfly '72

Stan Freberg (1926-)
It's a Mad, Mad, Mad, Mad World '63
Lady and the Tramp '55 (V)

Peter Frechette (1956-)
Paint It Black '89
The Kindred '87
The Hills Have Eyes, Part 2 '84
No Small Affair '84

Richard Frechette
No '98
The Confessional '95

Blanche Frederici (1878-1933)
Buffalo Stampede '33
A Farewell to Arms '32
Night Nurse '31
Sadie Thompson '28

Lynne Frederick (1955-94)
Prisoner of Zenda '79
Schizo '77
Voyage of the Damned '76
Phase 4 '74
Amazing Mr. Blunden '72
Vampire Circus '71

Pauline Frederick (1881-1938)
Thank you, Mr. Moto '37
Smouldering Fires '25

Vicki Frederick (1954-)
Chopper Chicks in Zombietown '91
A Chorus Line '85
Body Rock '84
...All the Marbles '81

Alan Freed (1922-65)
Go, Johnny Go! '59
Rock, Rock, Rock '56

Sam Freed (1948-)
Brooklyn Lobster '05
Stephen King's Thinner '96
Call Me '88

Al Freeman, Jr. (1934-)
Down in the Delta '98
Once Upon a Time .... When We Were Colored '95
Assault at West Point: The Court-Martial of Johnson Whittaker '94
Malcolm X '92
Seven Hours to Judgment '88
Roots: The Next Generation '79
My Sweet Charlie '70
Castle Keep '69
The Lost Man '69
The Detective '68
Finian's Rainbow '68
Dutchman '67
Ensign Pulver '64

Alfonso Freeman
The Bucket List '07
Ten 'Til Noon '06

Howard Freeman (1899-1967)
Million Dollar Mermaid '52
Scaramouche '52
Double Dynamite '51
The Long Night '47
The Blue Dahlia '46
House of Horrors '46
Mr. Winkle Goes to War '44
Air Raid Wardens '43

J.E. Freeman (1946-)
44 Minutes: The North Hollywood Shootout '03
Go '99
Alien: Resurrection '97
Dream with the Fishes '97
It Could Happen to You '94
Mother's Boys '94
Casualties of Love: The "Long Island Lolita" Story '93
Fallen Angels 2 '93
Aces: Iron Eagle 3 '92
There Goes My Baby '92
Memphis '91
Miller's Crossing '90
Wild at Heart '90
Hard Traveling '85

Jennifer Freeman (1985-)
Johnson Family Vacation '04
You Got Served '04

Joan Freeman (1941-)
Fastest Guitar Alive '68
The Reluctant Astronaut '67
The Rounders '65
Roustabout '64
Panic in the Year Zero! '62
Tower of London '62

K. Todd Freeman
The Cider House Rules '99
The End of Violence '97
Grosse Pointe Blank '97
Grand Canyon '91

Kathleen Freeman (1919-2001)
Shrek '01 (V)
Nutty Professor 2: The Klumps '00
Ready to Rumble '00
Blues Brothers 2000 '98
At First Sight '95
Naked Gun 33 1/3: The Final Insult '94
Reckless Kelly '93
The Willies '90
Hollywood Chaos '89
Dragnet '87
In the Mood '87
Innerspace '87
Malibu Bikini Shop '86
Heartbeeps '81
The Blues Brothers '80
The Strongest Man in the World '75
Death of a Gunfighter '69
The Rounders '65
That Funny Feeling '65
Disorderly Orderly '64
The Nutty Professor '63
The Errand Boy '61
The Fly '58
Kid Monk Baroni '52
Love Is Better Than Ever '52
Let's Make It Legal '51

Martin Freeman (1971-)
Dedication '07
The Good Night '07
Hot Fuzz '07
Breaking and Entering '06
Confetti '06
The Hitchhiker's Guide to the Galaxy '05
The Debt '03
Love Actually '03

Mona Freeman (1926-)
The Way Out '56
Battle Cry '55
Angel Face '52
Jumping Jacks '52
Branded '50
Copper Canyon '50
Dear Wife '49
The Heiress '49
Mother Wore Tights '47
Black Beauty '46
That Brennan Girl '46

Morgan Freeman (1937-)
The Dark Knight '08
A Raisin in the Sun '08 (N)
Wanted '08
The Bucket List '07
The Contract '07
Evan Almighty '07
Feast of Love '07
Gone Baby Gone '07
Lucky Number Slevin '06
10 Items or Less '06
Batman Begins '05
Edison Force '05
March of the Penguins '05 (N)
An Unfinished Life '05
Unleashed '05
War of the Worlds '05 (N)
The Big Bounce '04
Bruce Almighty '03
Dreamcatcher '03
Guilty by Association '03
Levity '03
High Crimes '02
The Sum of All Fears '02
Along Came a Spider '01
Nurse Betty '00
Under Suspicion '00
Deep Impact '98
Amistad '97
Hard Rain '97
Kiss the Girls '97
Chain Reaction '96
Moll Flanders '96
Seven '95
Outbreak '94
The Shawshank Redemption '94
The Power of One '92
Unforgiven '92
Robin Hood: Prince of Thieves '91
The Bonfire of the Vanities '90
Driving Miss Daisy '89
Glory '89
Johnny Handsome '89
Lean on Me '89
Blood Money; The Story of Clinton and Nadine '88
Clean and Sober '88
Street Smart '87
Execution of Raymond Graham '85
Marie '85
Teachers '84
Harry & Son '84
Eyewitness '81
Brubaker '80
Death of a Gunfighter '69

Paul Freeman (1943-)
Hot Fuzz '07
Bobby Jones: Stroke of Genius '04
The Devil's Arithmetic '99
Only Love '98
Double Team '97
Samson and Delilah '96
The Final Cut '95
Just Like a Woman '95
Mighty Morphin Power Rangers: The Movie '95
Aces: Iron Eagle 3 '92
A Dangerous Man: Lawrence after Arabia '91
Eminent Domain '91
May Wine '90
Murderers Among Us: The Simon Wiesenthal Story '89
Prisoner of Rio '89
Without a Clue '88
A World Apart '88
Shanghai Surprise '86
The Sender '82
Unsuitable Job for a Woman '82
The Dogs of War '81
Raiders of the Lost Ark '81
The Long Good Friday '80
Whose Child Am I? '75

Rob Freeman (1931-)
Pumpkinhead 4: Blood Feud '07
New Blood '99

Paul Frees (1920-86)
The Return of the King '80 (V)
The Hobbit '78 (V)
The Milpitas Monster '75 (N)
The Point '71 (V)
The Time Machine '60
Atlantis, the Lost Continent '61 (N)
Francis in the Haunted House '56 (V)
Suddenly '54
The War of the Worlds '53
The Star '52

Louis Freese (1970-)
Shade '03
How High '01
MacArthur Park '01
Thicker than Water '99
Winner Takes All '98
The Meteor Man '93
Who's the Man? '93

Ace Frehley (1951-)
Detroit Rock City '99
KISS Meets the Phantom of the Park '78

Alice Freindlikh (1934-)
Rasputin '85
Stalker '79

Stephane Freiss (1960-)
5x2 '04
The Grand Role '04
Crime Spree '03
Monsieur N. '03
Alias Betty '01
Does This Mean We're Married? '90
Vagabond '85

Phyllis Frelich (1944-)
Children On Their Birthdays '02
Santa Fe '97

Andrew French
Dominion: Prequel to the Exorcist '05

Bruce French (1945-)
Coming Home '78
Terror Out of the Sky '78
Ants '77
Pipe Dreams '76
The Savage Bees '76

Charles French (1860-1952)
Where Trails Divide '37
Gun Play '36
The Crimson Trail '35
No Man's Range '35
Trail of Terror '35
The Live Wire '34
The Man from Hell '34
When a Man Sees Red '34
Man of Action '33
King of the Rodeo '28
The Bargain '15

Dawn French (1957-)
The Chronicles of Narnia: The Lion, the Witch and the Wardrobe '05 (V)
Maybe Baby '99
Supergrass '87

Leigh French
The Hollywood Knights '80
Aloha, Bobby and Rose '74

Valerie French (1931-90)
The 27th Day '57
Jubal '56

Victor French (1934-89)
Choices '81
Spencer's Mountain '63

Pierre Fresnay (1897-1975)
Monsieur Vincent '47
Le Corbeau '43
Grand Illusion '37
Cesar '36
The Man Who Knew Too Much '34
Fanny '32
Marius '31

Bernard Fresson (1931-2002)
Brotherhood of the Wolf '01
Place Vendome '98
Germinal '93
Sons '89
Intruder '76
The Tenant '76
French Connection 2 '75
Honor Among Thieves '68
Please Not Now! '61
Hiroshima, Mon Amour '59

Matt Frewer (1958-)
Weirdsville '07
Dawn of the Dead '04
A Home at the End of the World '04
White Coats '04
Taken '02
The Sign of Four '01
The Hound of the Baskervilles '00
Jailbait! '00
Dead Fire '98
In the Doghouse '98
Quicksilver Highway '98
Breast Men '97
Hercules '97 (V)
Kissinger and Nixon '96
Lawnmower Man 2: Beyond Cyberspace '95
National Lampoon's Senior Trip '95
Stephen King's The Stand '94
The Day My Parents Ran Away '93
The Positively True Adventures of the Alleged Texas Cheerleader-Murdering Mom '93
Twenty Bucks '93
The Taking of Beverly Hills '91
Short Time '90
Far from Home '89
Honey, I Shrunk the Kids '89
Speed Zone '88
The Fourth Protocol '87
Ishtar '87
Supergirl '84
The Lords of Discipline '83
Monty Python's The Meaning of Life '83

Glenn Frey (1948-)
Jerry Maguire '96
Let's Get Harry '87

Leonard Frey (1938-88)
Sound of Murder '82
Tattoo '81
Where the Buffalo Roam '80
Fiddler on the Roof '71
The Boys in the Band '70
The Magic Christian '69

Sami Frey (1937-)
Revenge of the Musketeers '94
My Life and Times with Antonin Artaud '93
Traps '93
War & Remembrance: The Final Chapter '89
War & Remembrance '88
Black Widow '87
Sand and Blood '87
The Little Drummer Girl '84
Nea '78
Sweet Movie '75
Cesar & Rosalie '72
Chato's Land '71
Charrol '69
Cleo from 5 to 7 '61
Death of a Gunfighter '69

Giovanni Frezza (1972)
The House by the Cemetery '83

Grayson Fricke '82
Manhattan Baby '82

Brenda Fricker (1944-)
Tara Road '05
Call Me: The Rise and Fall of Heidi Fleiss '04
Rory O'Shea Was Here '04
Conspiracy of Silence '03
Veronica Guerin '03
The Intended '02
The American '01
Torso '01
The War Bride '01
Cupid & Cate '00
Durango '99
Pete's Meteor '98
Resurrection Man '97
The Wicked, Wicked West '97
Masterminds '96
Moll Flanders '96
Swann '96
A Time to Kill '96
Journey '95
Angels in the Outfield '94
A Man of No Importance '94
A Woman of Independent Means '94
Deadly Advice '93
So I Married an Axe Murderer '93
The Sound and the Silence '93
Utz '93
Home Alone 2: Lost in New York '92
Brides of Christ '91
The Field '90
My Left Foot '89
Seizure '74

John Friedrich
The Final Terror '83
A Rumor of War '80
Wanderers '79
Forever '78
The Boy in the Plastic Bubble '76

Anna Friel (1976-)
Goal! The Dream Begins '06
Niagara Motel '06
Irish Jam '05
Timeline '03
The War Bride '01
Me Without You '01
An Everlasting Piece '00
Our Mutual Friend '98
The Land Girls '98
A Midsummer Night's Dream '99
William Shakespeare's A Midsummer Night's Dream '99

Colin Friels (1952-)
Child Star: The Shirley Temple Story '01
Dark City '97
Angel Baby '95
Back of Beyond '95
Cosi '95
Mr. Reliable: A True Story '95
A Good Man in Africa '94
Class Action '91
Dingo '90
Grievous Bodily Harm '89
Ground Zero '88
High Tide '87
Kangaroo '86
Warm Nights on a Slow-Moving Train '87
Malcolm '86
Monkey Grip '82

Alex Frost
Drillbit Taylor '08
Elephant '03

Lindsay Frost (1962-)
The Ring '02
Collateral Damage '02
Monolith '93
Danielle Steel's Palomino '91

Lee Frost (1935-2007)
The St. Valentine's Day Massacre '67
Batman '66

Ewa Froling (1952-)
The Last Dance '93
The Ox '91
Fanny and Alexander '83

Samuel Froler (1957-)
Pulse '03
Private Confessions '98
The Best Intentions '92

Gustav Froehlich (1902-87)
Homecoming '28
Metropolis '26

John Fujioka (1925-)
Pearl Harbor '01
American Samurai '92
The Last Samurai '90
The Maltese Falcon '31
Frankenstein '31
Dracula '31

Milton Frome (1908-89)
The Nutty Professor '63

Dwight Frye (1899-1943)
Dead Men Walk '43
Frankenstein Meets the Wolfman '42
The Ghost of Frankenstein '42
The Crime of Dr. Crespi '35
The Invisible Man '33
The Vampire Bat '32
Tha Black Camel '31
The Bride of Frankenstein '35

Brittain Frye
Slumber Party Massacre 3 '88

Hiroshi Fujioka (1931-2005)
Godzilla vs. Mothra '64
King Kong vs. Godzilla '63
Gappa the Trifibian Monster '67

Yu Fujiki
Yog, Monster from Space '71

Susumu Fujita (1912-91)
The Battle of the Japan Sea '70
Yojimbo '61
The Human Condition: Road to Eternity '59
The Hidden Fortress '58
No Regrets for Our Youth '46

Toyo Fujita
The Dragon Painter '19
The Tong Man '19

Virgil Frye
Born in America '90
Revenge of the Ninja '83
Running Hot '83
Dr. Heckyl and Mr. Hype '80
Hot Moves '84

Gaby Fuchs
Up from the Depths '79
The Werewolf vs. the Vampire Woman '70
Mark of the Devil '69

Christopher Fulford
Millions '05
Goodbye, Mr. Chips '02
Eye See You '01
Bedrooms and Hallways '98
The Sculptress '97
Moll Flanders '96
Immortal Beloved '94
Prayer for the Dying '87
Zombie '80
Gates of Hell '80

Robert Fuller (1934-)
Donner Pass: The Road to Survival '84
Seven Samurai '54

Lucio Fulci (1927-96)
Demonia '90
Manhattan Baby '82
The Black Cat '81

Kamatari Fujiwara (1905-85)
Yojimbo '61
The Hidden Fortress '58
Seven Samurai '54

Alan Fudge (1944-)
Nightmare on the 13th Floor '90
Too Young to Die? '90
The Children of An Lac '80
Bug '75

Patrick Fugit (1982-)
Bickford Shmeckler's Cool Ideas '06
Saved! '04
White Oleander '02
Spun '02
Almost Famous '00

Athol Fugard (1932-)
Gandhi '82
The Killing Fields '84

Miguel Angel Fuentes
Fitzcarraldo '82

Frances Fuller (1907-80)
Homebodies '74
The Puma Man '80

Penny Fuller (1940-)
The Beverly Hillbillies '93
Danielle Steel's Star '93
Lies Before Kisses '92
Miss Rose White '92
Fire and Rain '89
As Summers Die '86
George Washington: The Forging of a Nation '86
Cat on a Hot Tin Roof '84
License to Kill '84
Your Place or Mine '83
Lois Gibbs and the Love Canal '82
A Piano for Mrs. Cimino '82
All the President's Men '76

Nancy Belle Fuller
Sky Heist '75
Hard Part Begins '73

Olive Fuller
See Olive Carey

Lance Fuller (1928-2001)
The Bride & the Beast '58
Voodoo Woman '57
Girls in Prison '56
Apache Woman '55
Kentucky Rifle '55
Cattle Queen of Montana '54

Kurt Fuller (1952-)
The Pursuit of Happyness '06
Don't Come Knocking '05
Ray '04
Anger Management '03
Auto Focus '02
Bingo '91
Wayne's World '92
Eye of Destruction '90
Miracle Mile '89
No Holds Barred '89
Elvira, Mistress of the Dark '88

Drew Fuller
Blonde Ambition '07
The Ultimate Gift '07

Frances Fuller (1907-80)
(see above)

Dolores Fuller (1923-)
Bride of the Monster '55
The Girl in the Red Velvet Swing '55
Glen or Glenda? '53
Mesa of Lost Women '52

Jonathan Fuller
Castle Freak '95
Last Man Standing '95
Suspect Device '95
Arcade '93
The Pit & the Pendulum '91

Samuel Fuller (1911-97)
The End of Violence '97
La Vie de Boheme '93
Sons '89
Return to Salem's Lot '87
Slapstick of Another Kind '84
State of Things '82
1941 '79
The American Friend '77

Alex Frost
(see above)

Samuel Fuller (1911-97)
(see above)

Peter Friedman (1949-)
The Savages '07
Power and Beauty '02
Blood Feast '63
'91

David Friedman (1923-)
Sex and Buttered Popcorn '91

Will Friedle (1976-)
National Lampoon's Gold Diggers '04
Trojan War '97
My Date with the President's Daughter '96

Judah Friedlander (1969-)
(see left)
Meet Dave '08
Date Movie '06
Feast '06
Duane Hopwood '05
Pizza '05
Along Came Polly '04
American Splendor '03
Showtime '02
My Date with the President's Daughter '96

Joel Friedkin (1885-1954)
Impact '49
Money Madness '47

Anthony Fridjhon
Kill Slade '89

Tom Fridley
Navajo Blues '97
Vegas Vice '94
Friday the 13th, Part 5: A New Beginning '85
Jason Lives '86
Summer Camp Nightmare '86

Jonathan Frid (1924-)
Seizure '74
House of Dark Shadows '70

Bonita Friedericy
Sleeping Dogs Lie '05
The Twelve Dogs of Christmas '05

Rupert Friend (1981-)
The Last Legion '07
Outlaw '07
The Libertine '05
Mrs. Palfrey at the Claremont '05
Pride and Prejudice '05

Philip Friend (1915-87)
Vulture '67
Buccaneer's Girl '50
Great Day '46

Trixie Friganza (1870-1955)
Myrt and Marge '33
Free and Easy '30

Arno Frisch (1975-)
Funny Games '07
Benny's Video '92

Willy Fritsch (1901-73)
The Bellboy and the Playgirls '62
Congress Dances '31
Woman in the Moon '29
Spies '28

Lou Frizzell (1920-79)
Devil Dog: The Hound of Hell '78
Steel Cowboy '78
The Other '72
Duel '71

Gert Frobe (1912-88)
Sidney Sheldon's Bloodline '79
Shadow Man '75
The Serpent's Egg '78
Ten Little Indians '75
Ludwig '72
Dollars '71
Those Daring Young Men in Their Jaunty Jalopies '69
Chitty Chitty Bang Bang '68

Sadie Frost (1967-)
Shaun of the Dead '04
The Ring '02
Final Cut '98
Captain Jack '98
Crimetime '96
Magic Hunter '96
A Pyromaniac's Love Story '95
Uprising '01
Love, Honour & Obey '00
Rancid Aluminium '00
Flypaper '97
Shopping '93
Splitting Heirs '93
Bram Stoker's Dracula '92
Dark Obsession '90

Nick Frost (1972-)
Hot Fuzz '07
Wild Child '08
Dead Heat '88
Piranha '95
Pumpkinhead 2: Blood Wings '94
Kinky Boots '06

Terry Frost (1906-93)
The Dinner Game '98
The Page Turner '06
Chaos '01
The Krays '90
The Cisco Kid '94
Paper Marriage '93

Catherine Frot (1956-)
The Monster Maker '44
Waterfront '44
California Joe '43
The Last Tomahawk '65
The Mysterious Magician '65

Leo Fuchs (1910-94)
Trail of the Mounties '47
The New Eve '98
Un Air de Famille '96
American Matchmaker '40
Avalon '90

Joachim Fuchsberger (1927-)
The Black Abbot '63
Curse of the Yellow Snake '63
Inn on the River '62

Taylor Fry (1981-)
Lone Justice '93
A Little Princess '95

Stephen Fry (1957-)
V for Vendetta '06
The Hitchhiker's Guide to the Galaxy '05 (V)
Cold Comfort Farm '94
Tristram Shandy: A Cock and Bull Story '05
Le Divorce '03
Gosford Park '01
Relative Values '99
Spice World: The Movie '97
Wilde '97

Jordan Fry (1993-)
Meet the Robinsons '07 (V)
Charlie and the Chocolate Factory '05

Soleil Moon Frye (1976-)
The Proud Family Movie '05 (V)
I've Been Waiting for You '98
Motel Blue '98
The St. Tammany Miracle '94
The Liar's Club '93
Invitation to Hell '84
Secret of the Ice Cave '89
Body Beat '88

Sean Frye (1966-)
Deadline Assault '90
E.T.: The Extra-Terrestrial '82

Tatsuya Fuji (1941-)
Bright Future '03
The Empire of Passion '76
In the Realm of the Senses '76

Takako Fujii (1972-)
The Grudge '04
The Grudge 2 '06
Ju-On: The Grudge '03

Dale Fuller (1885-1948)
Greed '25
The Unchastened Woman '25
The Marriage Circle '24

The Young Nurses '73
Pierrot le Fou '65

Fiona Fullerton (1956-)
Spymaker: The Secret Life of Ian Fleming '90
The Charmer '87
Shaka Zulu '83

Christina (Kristina) Fulton (1967-)
Red Shoe Diaries: Luscious Lola '00
The Girl with the Hungry Eyes '94
Hard Drive '94
Red Shoe Diaries 3: Another Woman's Lipstick '93

Julie Fulton
My Brother's Keeper '95
Lethal Charm '90

Rad Fulton
See James Westmoreland

Soren Fulton
Saving Sarah Cain '07
Thunderbirds '04

Eiji Funakoshi (1933-2007)
Gamera vs. Guiron '69
Gamera, the Invincible '66
Being Two Isn't Easy '62
Fires on the Plain '59

Willie Fung (1896-1945)
Burma Convoy '41
Saddle Mountain Roundup '41
Come on, Cowboys '37

Annette Funicello (1942-)
Back to the Beach '87
Lots of Luck '85
Head '68
Thunder Alley '67
Dr. Goldfoot and the Bikini Machine '66
Fireball 500 '66
Beach Blanket Bingo '65
How to Stuff a Wild Bikini '65
Monkey's Uncle '65
Bikini Beach '64
Muscle Beach Party '64
Pajama Party '64
Beach Party '63
The Misadventures of Merlin Jones '63
Babes in Toyland '61
Horsemasters '61
The Shaggy Dog '59

Joseph Fuqua (1963-)
David Searching '97
Gettysburg '93

John Furey
A Killing Spring '02
The Wolves '95
Mutant on the Bounty '89
Friday the 13th, Part 2 '81

Edward Furlong (1977-)
Living & Dying '07
Jimmy & Judy '06
The Crow: Wicked Prayer '05
Cruel World '05
Three Blind Mice '02
Animal Factory '00
Detroit Rock City '99
American History X '98
Pecker '98
Before and After '95
The Grass Harp '95
Brainscan '94
Little Odessa '94
A Home of Our Own '93
Last Action Hero '93
American Heart '92
Pet Sematary 2 '92
Terminator 2: Judgment Day '91

Benno Furmann (1972-)
Speed Racer '08
Joyeux Noel '05
My House in Umbria '03
The Order '03
Anatomy '00
The Princess and the Warrior '00

Yvonne Furneaux (1928-)
Frankenstein's Great Aunt Tillie '83
Repulsion '65
The Lion of Thebes '64
La Dolce Vita '60
The Mummy '59
The Warriors '55
The House of the Arrow '53
The Master of Ballantrae '53

Betty Furness (1916-94)
The President's Mystery '36
Swing Time '36
Here Comes Cookie '35
Beggars in Ermine '34
Aggie Appleby, Maker of Men '33

Deborra-Lee Furness (1960-)
Sleepwalking '08
Jindabyne '06
The Real Macaw '98
Angel Baby '95
Voyager '91
The Last of the Finest '90
Shame '87

Joseph Furst (1916-2005)
The Dunera Boys '85
Diamonds Are Forever '71

Stephen Furst (1955-)
National Lampoon's Christmas Vacation 2: Cousin Eddie's Big Island Adventure '03
Magic Kid 2 '94
Magic Kid '92
The Dream Team '89
Up the Creek '84
Silent Rage '82
Getting Wasted '80
Midnight Madness '80
The Unseen '80
Swim Team '79
Take Down '79
The Bastard '78
National Lampoon's Animal House '78
Prime Time '77

Toru Furuya
Paprika '06 (V)
Toward the Terra '80 (V)

Ed Fury (1934-)
Dinosaur Valley Girls '96
Colossus and the Amazon Queen '64
Samson Against the Sheik '62
Ursus in the Valley of the Lions '62
Wild Women of Wongo '59

Dan Futterman (1967-)
A Mighty Heart '07
Enough '02
Urbania '00
1999 '98
Shooting Fish '98
When Trumpets Fade '98
Breathing Room '96
Far Harbor '96
The Birdcage '95
Class of '61 '92

Herbert (Fuchs) Fux (1927-2007)
The Uranium Conspiracy '78
Jack the Ripper '76
Lady Frankenstein '72
Mark of the Devil '69
Island of Lost Girls '68

Jim Fyfe
Tanner on Tanner '04
The Frighteners '96

Robert Fyfe
Around the World in 80 Days '04
Xtro '83

Franky G. (1965-)
Saw II '05
Confidence '03
The Italian Job '03
Manito '03
Wonderland '03

Marianne Gaba (1939-)
How to Stuff a Wild Bikini '65
The Choppers '61

Richard Gabai (1964-)
Black Horizon '01
Virtual Girl '00
Sexual Roulette '96
Vice Girls '96
Assault of the Party Nerds 2: Heavy Petting Detective '95
Bikini Drive-In '94
Dinosaur Island '93
Hot Under the Collar '91
Virgin High '90
Assault of the Party Nerds '89

Sasson Gabai
The Band's Visit '07
Escape: Human Cargo '98
Blink of an Eye '92

Martin Gabel (1912-86)
Smile, Jenny, You're Dead '74
Lady in Cement '68
Divorce American Style '67
Goodbye Charlie '64
Marnie '64
The Thief '52

Scilla Gabel (1937-)
Colossus of the Arena '62
Mill of the Stone Women '60

Jean Gabin (1904-76)
L'Annee Sainte '76
Le Chat '75
Any Number Can Win '63
Duke of the Derby '62
Le Gentleman D'Epsom '62
Un Singe en Hiver '62
Le Cas du Dr. Laurent '57
Les Miserables '57
Four Bags Full '56
French Can-Can '55
Napoleon '55
Grisbi '53
Le Plaisir '52
The Walls of Malapaga '49
Stormy Waters '41
Le Jour Se Leve '39
La Bete Humaine '38
Grand Illusion '37
Pepe Le Moko '37
The Lower Depths '36
Maria Chapdelaine '34
Zou Zou '34

Christopher Gable (1940-98)
The Rainbow '89
The Lair of the White Worm '88
A Woman of Substance '84
The Slipper and the Rose '76
The Boy Friend '71
The Music Lovers '71

Clark Gable (1901-60)
The Misfits '61
It Started in Naples '60
Run Silent, Run Deep '58
But Not for Me '59
Teacher's Pet '58
Band of Angels '57
The King and Four Queens '56
Soldier of Fortune '55
The Tall Men '55
Betrayed '54
Mogambo '53
Never Let Me Go '53
Lone Star '52
Across the Wide Missouri '51
Key to the City '50
To Please a Lady '50
Any Number Can Play '49
Command Decision '48
Homecoming '48
The Hucksters '47
Adventure '45
Somewhere I'll Find You '42
Honky Tonk '41
They Met in Bombay '41
Boom Town '40
Comrade X '40
Strange Cargo '40
Gone with the Wind '39
Idiot's Delight '39
Test Pilot '38
Too Hot to Handle '38
Saratoga '37
Love on the Run '36
San Francisco '36
Wife Versus Secretary '36
China Seas '35
Forsaking All Others '35
Mutiny on the Bounty '35
Chained '34
It Happened One Night '34
Manhattan Melodrama '34
Dancing Lady '33
Hold Your Man '33
The Lost Stooges '33
Night Flight '33
No Man of Her Own '32
Red Dust '32
Strange Interlude '32
Dance Fools Dance '31
A Free Soul '31
Laughing Sinners '31
Night Nurse '31
Painted Desert '31
Possessed '31
Susan Lenox: Her Fall and Rise '31

Eva Gabor (1924-95)
Naked Gun 2 1/2: The Smell of Fear '91
The Rescuers Down Under '90 (V)
Princess Academy '87
Tales of the Klondike: The Scorn of Women '87
The Rescuers '77
The Aristocats '70 (V)
A New Kind of Love '63
It Started with a Kiss '59
Gigi '58
Truth about Women '58
Don't Go Near the Water '57
My Man Godfrey '57
Artists and Models '55
The Last Time I Saw Paris '54

Zsa Zsa Gabor (1919-)
A Very Brady Sequel '96
The Beverly Hillbillies '93
Happily Ever After '93 (V)
A Nightmare on Elm Street 3: Dream Warriors '87
Movie Maker '86
Frankenstein's Great Aunt Tillie '83
Every Girl Should Have One '78
Arrivederci, Baby! '66
Picture Mommy Dead '66
Boys' Night Out '62
For the First Time '59
Queen of Outer Space '58
Touch of Evil '58
Death of a Scoundrel '56
Lili '53
Lovely to Look At '52
Moulin Rouge '52
We're Not Married '52

Ruth Gabriel (1975-)
Nostromo '96
Running Out of Time '94

Monique Gabrielle (1963-)
Evil Toons '90
Silk 2 '89
Not of This Earth '88
Amazon Women on the Moon '87
Deathstalker 2: Duel of the Titans '87
Emmanuelle 5 '87
Screen Test '85
Bachelor Party '84
Hard to Hold '84
Hot Moves '83
Black Venus '83

Gabriel Gabrio (1887-1946)
Harvest '37
Pepe Le Moko '37

James Gaddas (1960-)
Girls' Night '97
Catherine Cookson's The Black Candle '91

Ariel Gade (1997-)
Aliens vs. Predator: Requiem '07
Dark Water '05
Envy '04

John Gaden (1941-)
A Little Bit of Soul '97
The Wedding Party '97

Antonio Gades (1936-2004)
El Amor Brujo '86
Carmen '83
Blood Wedding '81

Anna Gael (1943-)
Zeta One '69
Therese & Isabelle '67

Jim Gaffigan (1966-)
The Great New Wonderful '06
Stephanie Daley '06
13 Going on 30 '04
No Sleep 'Til Madison '02
Final '01
Super Troopers '01
30 Years to Life '01
Jailbait! '00

Mo Gaffney (1958-)
Drop Dead Gorgeous '99
The Shot '96

Kevin Gage (1959-)
Chaos '05
Paparazzi '04
May '02
Blow '01
Dee Snider's Strangeland '98
Double Tap '98
Gunshy '98
Point Blank '98
Heat '95

Patricia Gage
The Little Kidnappers '90
Rabid '77

Holly Gagnier (1962-)
The Undertaker's Wedding '97
Alligator 2: The Mutation '90
Girls Just Want to Have Fun '85

Jenny Gago (1953-)
Alien Nation: Millennium '96
Grand Avenue '96
My Family '94
Sweet 15 '90
Old Gringo '89

Max Gail (1943-)
Facing the Enemy '00
Mind Lies '00
Not in This Town '97
Good Luck '96
Forest Warrior '95
Deadly Target '94
Pontiac Moon '94
Street Crimes '92
Sodbusters '94
The Game of Love '90
Judgment in Berlin '88
Where Are the Children? '85
D.C. Cab '84
Heartbreakers '84
Aliens Are Coming '80
Pearl '78
Night Moves '75
Cardiac Arrest '74

Boyd Gaines (1953-)
Second Best '05
The Confession '98
I'm Not Rappaport '96
The Discovery Program '89
Call Me '88
Piece of Cake '88
Heartbreak Ridge '86
The Sure Thing '85
Porky's '82

Jim Gaines (1955-)
Fist of Steel '93
Codename: Terminate '90
Commando Invasion '87
Blood Debts '83

Richard Gaines (1904-75)
Ace in the Hole '51
Humoresque '46
The Enchanted Cottage '45
Mr. Winkle Goes to War '44
The More the Merrier '43

M.C. Gainey (1948-)
Unearthed '07
Wild Hogs '07
Beerfest '06
Are We There Yet? '05
The Dukes of Hazzard '05
Club Dread '04
Sideways '04
The Cooler '03
Wonderland '03
The New Guy '02
Happy, Texas '99
Con Air '97
Breakdown '96
Citizen Ruth '96
The Fan '96
Leap of Faith '92
El Diablo '90

Courtney Gains (1965-)
Sweet Home Alabama '02
King Cobra '98
No Code of Conduct '98
The Killing Grounds '97
Behind Enemy Lines '96
Memphis Belle '90
The 'Burbs '89
Colors '88
Can't Buy Me Love '87
The Children of Times Square '86
Back to the Future '85
Lust in the Dust '85
Children of the Corn '84
Hardbodies '84

Charlotte Gainsbourg (1972-)
I'm Not There '07
The Science of Sleep '06
Lemming '05
Happily Ever After '04
21 Grams '03
My Wife is an Actress '01
La Buche '00
Jane Eyre '96
Love, etc. '96
Grosse Fatigue '94
The Cement Garden '93
Night Sun '90
The Little Thief '89
Le Petit Amour '87

Serge Gainsbourg (1928-91)
I Love All of You '83
Too Pretty to Be Honest '72
French Intrigue '70
The Fury of Hercules '61
Samson '61
Voulez-Vous Danser avec Moi? '59

Cristina Gajoni
Andy Warhol's Frankenstein '74
Ursus in the Valley of the Lions '62

Janusz Gajos (1939-)
Zemsta '02
Trois Couleurs: Blanc '94
The Decalogue '88
The Interrogation '82

Michel Galabru (1924-)
Belle Epoque '92
Uranus '91

(La Cage aux Folles 3: The Wedding '86 ...)
La Cage aux Folles 3: The Wedding '86
Subway '85
La Cage aux Folles 2 '81
La Cage aux Folles '78
L'Amour en Herbe '77
Assassin '75
Soldat Duroc... Ca Va Etre Ta Fete! '75
The Gendarme of Saint-Tropez '64

David Gale (1936-91)
The Guyver '91
Syngenor '90
Bride of Re-Animator '89
The Brain '88
Re-Animator '84
Savage Weekend '80
The Judge and the Assassin '75

Ed Gale (1963-)
O Brother Where Art Thou? '00
Chopper Chicks in Zombietown '91

Eddra Gale (1921-2001)
Revenge of the Cheerleaders '76
8 1/2 '63

Joan Gale (1915-82)
Devil Diamond '37
The Miracle Rider '35

June Gale (1918-96)
Charlie Chan at Treasure Island '39
It Could Happen to You '39
Rainbow's End '35
Swifty '35

Vincent Gale
Firewall '06
Meltdown '06
The Final Cut '04
The Twelve Days of Christmas Eve '04
Brotherhood of Murder '99
Every Mother's Worst Fear '98
Baby Monitor: Sound of Fear '97

Johnny Galecki (1975-)
Happy Endings '05
Bookies '03
Vanilla Sky '01
Bounce '00
Playing Mona Lisa '00
Morgan's Ferry '99
The Opposite of Sex '98
Bean '97
I Know What You Did Last Summer '97
Suicide Kings '97
Backfield in Motion '91
National Lampoon's Christmas Vacation '89

Michael Galeota (1984-)
Clubhouse Detectives '96
Rattled '96

Juan Luis Gallardo (1940-)
The Girl of Your Dreams '99
Tango '98
Don Juan, My Love '90

Anna Galiena (1954-)
Excellent Cadavers '99
The Leading Man '96
Moses '96
Three Lives and Only One Death '96
Being Human '94
Jamon, Jamon '93
The Hairdresser's Husband '92

Rorret '87

Zach Galifianakis (1969-)
Below '08
Out Cold '01

Kelly Galindo
The Malibu Beach Vampires '07
High Spirits '88

Nacho Galindo (1908-73)
Angels of the City '89
Born Reck ess '59
Wetbacks '56
Green Fire '55
Borderline '50

Annie Galipeau (1979-)
Grey Owl '99
Map of the Human Heart '93

Frank Gallacher (1948-)
December Boys '07
My Little Girl '87
Dreamchild '85
Private Contentment '83
Summer Lovers '82
Idolmaker '80
Skag '79

Richard "Skeets" Gallagher (1891-1955)
Zis Boom Bah '41
Danger on the Air '38
Hats Off '37
Bachelor Bait '34
Riptide '34
Possessed '31

Bronagh Gallagher (1972-)
Botched '07
Tristan & Isolde '06
The Wicked, Wicked West '98
Mary Reilly '95
Pulp Fiction '94
The Commitments '91

David Gallagher (1985-)
Us '02
Mr. Reliable: A True Story

Megan Gallagher (1960-)
Waterfront '83

Peter Gallagher (1955-)
How to Deal '03
Mr. Deeds '02
Anne Rice's The Feast of All Saints '01
Perfume '01
Protection '01
Center Stage '00
Cupid & Cate '00
The Last Debate '00
American Beauty '99
Brotherhood of Murder '99
House on Haunted Hill '99
Cafe Society '97
Johnny Skidmarks '97
The Man Who Knew Too Little '97
Path to Paradise '97
Last Dance '96
Titanic '96
To Gillian on Her 37th Birthday '96
The Underneath '95
While You Were Sleeping '95
Mrs. Parker and the Vicious Circle '94
Mother's Boys '94
White Mile '94
Fallen Angels 1 '93
Fallen Angels 2 '93
The Hudsucker Proxy '93
Malice '93
Short Cuts '93
Watch It '93
Bob Roberts '92
The Player '92
An Inconvenient Woman '91
Late for Dinner '91
Tune in Tomorrow '91
sex, lies and videotape '89

The Caine Mutiny Court Martial '88
High Spirits '88
Long Day's Journey into Night '88
The Murder of Mary Phagan '87

Patrick Gallagher (1968-)
Night at the Museum '06
Silent Partner '05
In Enemy Hands '04
The Ambulance '90

Georges Galley (1926-)
Gorilla '56
Femmes de Paris '53
A Gentleman's Game '61
Arlington Road '99
Rushmore '98
Bad Moon '96
Dennis the Menace '93
Babel '07

Gina Gallego (1959-)
Personals '90
My Demon Lover '87
Lust in the Dust '85

Ely Galleani
Redneck '73
Five Dolls for an August Moon '70

Ketti Gallian (1912-72)
Under the Pampas Moon '35
Marie Galante '34

Zach Galligan (1963-)
Infested: Invasion of the Killer Bugs '02
Gabriela '01
Carnage '02
Dr. Akagi '98
Pedale Douce '96
Zandalee '91
Gremlins 2: The New Batch '90
Mortal Passions '90
Rebel Storm '90
The Lawrenceville Stories '88
Waxwork '88
Waxwork 2: Lost in Time '91
Psychic '91
Round Trip to Heaven '92
All Tied Up '92
Gremlins '84

Carlos Gallardo
Planet Terror '07
Eastside '99
Desperado '95
El Mariachi '93

Rosa Maria Gallardo
Creature of the Walking Dead '60

Silvania Gallardo (1953-)
Prison Stories: Women on the Inside '91
Out of the Dark '88

John Gallaudet (1903-83)
In Cold Blood '67
Outcasts of the Trail '49

Jack Galloway
A Different Loyalty '04

Anna Galvin
Codename: Icarus '85

Don Galloway (1937-)
Two Moon Junction '88
Snowbird '78

Tom Gallop
The Bourne Ultimatum '07
The Bourne Supremacy '04

Camillo Gallardo
The House of the Spirits '94
Arizona Dream '94
Angela '94

Rita Gam (1928-)
Inhumanoid '96
Sinatra '92
Guilty by Suspicion '91
Gore Vidal's Lincoln '88
Project X '87
Klute '71
Shoot Out '71
The King of Kings '61
Mohawk '56
The Thief '52

Robert Gallo (1945-)
Sinners '89

Michaela Gallo (1990-)
Beethoven's 4th '01
Beethoven's 3rd '00

Vincent Gallo (1961-)
Mayhem '89
The Brown Bunny '03
Get Well Soon '01
H de and Seek '00
Freeway 2: Confessions of a Trickbaby '99
Buffalo 66 '97
Truth or Consequences, N.M. '97

Carla Gallo (1975-)
Mission: Impossible 3 '06
Spanking the Monkey '94

Kyle Gallner
The Last September '99

Mason Gamble (1986-)
Arthur's Quest '99
Raw Nerve '99
Storm Trooper '98
Prince Valiant '97
Cyborg 3: The Recycler '95
Caroline at Midnight '93
Ice '93
Warlock: The Armageddon '93

Nathan Gamble
Babel '07

Michael Gambon (1940-)
Harry Potter and the Order of the Phoenix '07
Amazing Grace '06
The Good Shepherd '06
The Omen '06
Harry Potter and the Goblet of Fire '05
Being Julia '04
Harry Potter and the Prisoner of Azkaban '04
The Life Aquatic with Steve Zissou '04
Sky Captain and the World of Tomorrow '04
Angels in America '03
Deep Blue '03 (N)
Open Range '03
Sylvia '03
Path to War '02
Charlotte Gray '01
Gosford Park '01
High Heels and Low Lifes '01

Jacques Gamblin (1957-)

James Gammon (1940-)
The Cell '00
Iron Giant '99 (V)
You Know My Name '99
The Hi-Lo Country '98
One Man's Hero '98
The Man in the Iron Mask '97
Traveller '96
Wild Bill '95
Cabin Boy '94
Hard Vice '94
Major League 2 '94
Natural Born Killers '94
Wyatt Earp '94
Leaving Normal '92
Coupe de Ville '90
I Love You to Death '90
Revenge '90
Major League '89
Roe vs. Wade '89
Milagro Beanfield War '88
Ironweed '87

James Gandolfini (1961-)
See also Jean-Pierre Eouvier
All the King's Men '06
Lonely Hearts '06
Romance & Cigarettes '05
Surviving Christmas '04
The Last Castle '01
The Man Who Wasn't There '01
The Mexican '01
Wildflowers '99
A Civil Action '98
8mm '98
The Mighty '98
Fallen '97
She's So Lovely '97
Twelve Angry Men '97
The Juror '96
Night Falls on Manhattan '96
Crimson Tide '95
Get Shorty '95
New World '95
Angie '94
Terminal Velocity '94
Italian Movie '93
Mr. Wonderful '93
Money for Nothing '93
True Romance '93
A Stranger Among Us '92

Robin Gammell
Waist Deep '06
Street Kings '08

The Game (1979-)
Waist Deep '06

Marguerite Gance
La Chute de la Maison Usher '28
Napoleon '27

Michel Ganci
See also Jean-Pierre Eouvier

Nitin Ganatra (1967-)
The Mistress of Spices '05
Pure '02

Tony Ganios (1959-)
Die Hard 2: Die Harder '90
Porky's Revenge '85
Porky's 2: The Next Day '83
Porky's '82
Continental Divide '81
Wanderers '79

Richard Ganoung
Billy's Hollywood Screen Kiss '98
Parting Glances '86

Richard Gant (1940-)
Daddy Day Camp '07
Kingdom Come '01
Johnny B. '00
Nutty Professor 2: The Klumps '00
Leaving Las Vegas '95
Sour Grapes '98
Blade '98
Raven '97
The Glimmer Man '96
Jason Goes to Hell: The Final Friday '93
The Freshman '90
Krush Groove '85

Ken Gampu (1929-2003)
American Ninja 4: The Annihilation '91
Enemy Unseen '91
Act of Piracy '89
Scavengers '87
Flashpoint Africa '84
Kill and Kill Again '81
Chain Gang Killings '80
Soul Patrol '80
African Rage '78
The Naked Prey '66
Dingaka '65

Chester Gan (1908-59)
Across the Pacific '43
Crash Dive '43
Carson City Kid '40
The McCullochs '75
Deadly Encounter '72
Cool Hand Luke '57

Longitude '00
The Insider '99

Yvonne Garny
Manon of the Spring '87
Jean de Florette '86

Joseph (Joe) Gallison
Critic's Choice '63

The Girl Next Door '98
His Bodyguard '98
Last Night '98
Bone Daddy '97
If These Walls Could Talk '96

The House of Mary Phagan '87

Hard Traveling '85
Vision Quest '85
Ballad of Gregorio Cortez '83

Wives and Daughters '01

Peter Gantzler
The Boss of It All '06
Italian for Beginners '01
Paul Ganus (1961-)
The Silencer '92
Crash and Burn '90
Bruno Ganz (1941-)
Youth Without Youth '07
Have No Fear: The Life of Pope John Paul II '05
Downfall '04
The Manchurian Candidate '04
Luther '03
Bread and Tulips '01
Eternity and a Day '97
Saint-Ex: The Story of the Storyteller '95
Faraway, So Close! '93
The Last Days of Chez Nous '92
Children of Nature '91
Strapless '90
Wings of Desire '88
In the White City '83
Nosferatu the Vampyre '79
Black and White As Day and Night '78
Knife in the Head '78
The American Friend '77
Lumiere '76
The Marquise of O '76
Teresa Ganzel (1957-)
Clifford's Really Big Movie '04 (V)
C.O.D. '83
Yehoram Gaon (1939-)
Dead End Street '83
Operation Thunderbolt '77
Eagles Attack at Dawn '70
Siqin Gaowa (1949-)
The Day the Sun Turned Cold '94
Women from the Lake of Scented Souls '94
Romola Garai (1982-)
Atonement '07
Amazing Grace '06
Renaissance '06
Scoop '06
The Incredible Journey of Mary Bryant '05
Dirty Dancing: Havana Nights '04
Rory O'Shea Was Here '04
Vanity Fair '04
Daniel Deronda '02
I Capture the Castle '02
Nicholas Nickleby '02
Kaz Garas (1940-)
Humanoids from the Deep '96
Puppet Master 5: The Final Chapter '94
Fast Gun '93
Naked Vengeance '85
Final Mission '84
Ben '72
The Last Safari '67
Matthew Garber (1956-77)
The Gnome-Mobile '67
Mary Poppins '64
The Three Lives of Thomasina '63
Terri Garber (1960-)
North and South Book 2 '86
North and South Book 1 '85
Victor Garber (1949-)
Home Room '02
Tuck Everlasting '02
Call Me Claus '01
Legally Blonde '01
Life with Judy Garland—Me and My Shadows '01
Torso '01
Annie '99
Invisible Child '99
Cinderella '97
Titanic '97
The First Wives Club '96
Jeffrey '95
Exotica '94
Kleptomania '94
Life with Mikey '93
Queen '93

Sleepless in Seattle '93
Godspell '73
Greta Garbo (1905-90)
The Love Goddesses '65
Two-Faced Woman '41
Ninotchka '39
Conquest '37
Camille '36
Anna Karenina '35
The Painted Veil '34
Queen Christina '33
Grand Hotel '32
Mata Hari '32
Susan Lenox: Her Fall and Rise '31
Anna Christie '30
Romance '30
The Kiss '29
The Single Standard '29
The Mysterious Lady '28
Wild Orchids '28
A Woman of Affairs '28
Joyless Street '25
Ingrid Garbo
Touch Me Not '74
Dracula's Great Love '72
John Garces
Kid and the Killers '74
Robby '68
Mauricio Garces (1926-89)
The Brainiac '61
The Living Head '59
Paula Garces (1974-)
Harold & Kumar Escape from Guantanamo Bay '08
Man of the House '05
Harold and Kumar Go to White Castle '04
Spin '04
Marci X '03
Clockstoppers '02
Cash Crop '01
Adam Garcia (1973-)
Standing Still '05
Confessions of a Teenage Drama Queen '04
Fascination '04
The First $20 Million is Always the Hardest '02
Riding in Cars with Boys '01
Bootmen '00
Coyote Ugly '00
Aimee Garcia (1978-)
A Lot Like Love '05
Dirty '05
Allan Garcia (1887-1938)
South of Santa Fe '32
The Circus '19

Dead Again '91
The Godfather, Part 3 '90
Internal Affairs '90
A Show of Force '90
Black Rain '89
American Roulette '88
Blood Money: The Story of Clinton and Nadine '88
Stand and Deliver '88
The Untouchables '87
8 Million Ways to Die '85
Mean Season '85
Blue Skies Again '83
A Night in Heaven '83
Darnell Garcia
Blind Rage '78
Enforcer from Death Row '78
Eddie Garcia (1921-)
Relax... It's Just Sex! '98
Twilight People '72
Woman Hunt '72
Beast of the Yellow Night '70
Jeff Garcia
Barnyard '06 (V)
Jimmy Neutron: Boy Genius '01 (V)
Jerry Garcia (1942-95)
Hell's Angels Forever '83
Gimme Shelter '70
Jesse Garcia
The Comebacks '07
Quinceanera '06
Jorge Garcia (1973-)
Deck the Halls '06
The Good Humor Man '05
Little Athens '05
Jsu Garcia (1963-)
The Lost City '05
Sueno '05
Along Came Polly '04
Klepto '03
Collateral Damage '02
We Were Soldiers '02
The Quickie '01
Devil in the Flesh 2 '00
Traffic '00
Candyman 3: Day of the Dead '98
Woo '97
Red Shoe Diaries: Four on the Floor '96
Vampire in Brooklyn '95
In the Heat of Passion '91
Predator 2 '90
Slaves of New York '89
The Lawless Land '88
Tropical Snow '88
Wildcats '86
Gotcha! '85
A Nightmare on Elm Street '84
Juan Garcia
Bounce '00
The Banker '89
Nicole Garcia (1946-)
La Petite Lili '03
Alias Betty '01
Overseas: Three Women with Man Trouble '90
Peril '85
Corrupt '84
Bolero '82
Mon Oncle d'Amerique '80
Le Cavaleur '78
Stenio Garcia (1933-)
Me You Them '00
At Play in the Fields of the Lord '91
Ginette Garcin (1928-)
Charles et Lucie '79
Blue Country '77
Cousin, Cousine '76
Henri Garcin (1929-)
The Dress '96
The Eighth Day '95
One Hundred and One Nights '95
Someone Behind the Door '71
Betty Garde
Caged '50
Call Northside 777 '48

Micah Gardener
Atomic Dog '98
Carpool '96
Vincent Gardenia (1922-92)
The Super '91
Tragedy of Flight 103: The Inside Story '91
Age Old Friends '89
Skin Deep '89
Moonstruck '87
Little Shop of Horrors '86
The Odd Squad '86
Brass '85
Movers and Shakers '85
Kennedy '83
Death Wish 2 '82
The Last Flight of Noah's Ark '80
Home Movies '79
Marciano '79
Greased Lightning '77
Death Wish '74
The Front Page '74
Lucky Luciano '74
Bang the Drum Slowly '73
Cold Turkey '71
Little Murders '71
Jenny '70
Where's Poppa? '70
The Hustler '61
Parrish '61
Reginald Gardiner (1903-80)
Do Not Disturb '65
Mr. Hobbs Takes a Vacation '62
Rock-A-Bye Baby '57
Birds & the Bees '56
Black Widow '54
The Halls of Montezuma '50
The Dolly Sisters '46
Christmas in Connecticut '45
The Horn Blows at Midnight '45
Immortal Sergeant '43
Sweet Rosie O'Grady '43
Captains of the Clouds '42
The Man Who Came to Dinner '41
Sundown '41
A Yank in the R.A.F. '41
Doctor Takes a Wife '40
The Great Dictator '40
The Flying Deuces '39
Everybody Sing '38
Marie Antoinette '38
A Damsel in Distress '37
Born to Dance '36
Arthur Gardner (1910-)
Mystic Circle Murder '39
Assassin of Youth '35
Ava Gardner (1922-90)
Harem '86
The Long, Hot Summer '86
A.D. '85
Regina '83
The Kidnapping of the President '80
City on Fire '79
The Cassandra Crossing '76
The Sentinel '76
Permission To Kill '75
Earthquake '74
Life & Times of Judge Roy Bean '72
Mayerling '68
The Bible '66
The Night of the Iguana '64
Seven Days in May '64
55 Days at Peking '63
The Naked Maja '59
On the Beach '59
Around the World in 80 Days '56
Bhowani Junction '56
The Barefoot Contessa '54
Knights of the Round Table '53
Mogambo '53
Lone Star '52

The Snows of Kilimanjaro '52
My Forbidden Past '51
Pandora and the Flying Dutchman '51
Show Boat '51
East Side, West Side '49
One Touch of Venus '48
The Hucksters '47
Singapore '47
The Killers '46
Whistle Stop '46
Reunion in France '42
David Gardner
When Angels Fly '82
Bethune '77
Joan Gardner (1915-99)
The Challenge '38
Dark Journey '37
The Man Who Could Work Miracles '37
Private Life of Don Juan '34
The Scarlet Pimpernel '34
Wedding Rehearsal '32
Katya Gardner
Stir of Echoes 2: The Homecoming '07
Careful '92
Jennifer Gareis (1970-)
Boat Trip '03
Luckytown '00
Miss Congeniality '00
The 6th Day '00
Night Visitor '89
Allen (Goorwitz) Garfield (1939-)
The Majestic '01
Absence of the Good '99
Obsession '97
Crime of the Century '96
Diabolique '96
Destiny Turns on the Radio '95
Jack and His Friends '92
Family Prayers '91
Club Fed '90
Let It Ride '89
Beverly Hills Cop 2 '87
Desert Bloom '86
The Cotton Club '84
Irreconcilable Differences '84
Get Crazy '83
State of Things '82
Continental Divide '81
Leave 'Em Laughing '81
One Trick Pony '80
The Stunt Man '80
Brink's Job '78
Fyre '78
Sketches of a Strangler '78
Skateboard '77
Mother, Jugs and Speed '76
The Virginia Hill Story '76
Nashville '75
Paco '75
Busting '74
The Conversation '74
Slither '73
The Candidate '72
Bananas '71
Cry Uncle '71
Hi, Mom! '70
The Owl and the Pussycat '70
Greetings '68
John Garfield (1913-52)
Force of Evil '49
Jigsaw '49
Body and Soul '47
Gentleman's Agreement '47
Humoresque '46
The Postman Always Rings Twice '46
Hollywood Canteen '44
Air Force '43
Destination Tokyo '43
The Fallen Sparrow '43
Thank Your Lucky Stars '43
Tortilla Flat '42
The Sea Wolf '41
Juarez '39

They Made Me a Criminal '39
Four Daughters '38
John David Garfield (1943-94)
The Other Side of the Mountain '75
White Line Fever '75
Golden Voyage of Sinbad '73
The Stepmother '71
MacKenna's Gold '69
That Cold Day in the Park '69
Savage Intruder '68
The Swimmer '68
Art Garfunkel (1941-)
Boxing Helena '93
Mother Goose Rock 'n' Rhyme '90
Short Fuse '88
Carnal Knowledge '71
Catch-22 '70
Edward (Ed) Gargan (1902-64)
San Fernando Valley '44
The Falcon Takes Over '42
The Saint Strikes Back '39
Hands Across the Table '35
Belle of the Nineties '34
William Gargan (1905-79)
Dynamite '49
Strange Impersonation '46
Till the End of Time '46
The Canterville Ghost '44
Miss Annie Rooney '42
Who Done It? '42
Cheers for Miss Bishop '41
I Wake Up Screaming '41
They Knew What They Wanted '40
Broadway Serenade '39
Devil's Party '38
You Only Live Once '37
Milky Way '36
Sky Parade '36
Aggie Appleby, Maker of Men '33
Lucky Devils '33
Night Flight '33
The Animal Kingdom '32
Rain '32
Troy Garity (1973-)
Sunshine '07
After the Sunset '04
Barbershop 2: Back in Business '04
Milwaukee, Minnesota '03
Soldier's Girl '03
Barbershop '02
Bandits '01
Steal This Movie! '00
Gabriel Garko (1974-)
Callas Forever '02
His Secret Life '01
Gianni "John" Garko (1935-)
Devilfish '84
The Psychic '78
Waterloo '71
Gunslinger '70
Five for Hell '67
Saul and David '64
The Avenger '62
The Mongols '60
Kapo '59
Beverly Garland (1926-)
National Lampoon's Christmas Vacation 2: Cousin Eddie's Big Island Adventure '03
Haunted Symphony '94
The World's Oldest Living Bridesmaid '92
Gamble on Love '86
It's My Turn '80
Roller Boogie '79
Where the Red Fern Grows '74
The Voyage of the Yes '72
Pretty Poison '68
Twice-Told Tales '63
The Gunslinger '56
It Conquered the World '56
Desperate Hours '55

Swamp Women '55
The Go-Getter '54

Judy Garland (1922-69)
That's Entertainment '74
A Child Is Waiting '63
Gay Purr-ee '62 (V)
Judgment at Nuremberg '61
A Star Is Born '54
Summer Stock '50
In the Good Old Summertime '49
The Pirate '48
Easter Parade '48
The Harvey Girls '46
Till the Clouds Roll By '46
Ziegfeld Follies '46
The Clock '45
Meet Me in St. Louis '44
Girl Crazy '43
Presenting Lily Mars '43
Thousands Cheer '43
For Me and My Gal '42
Babes on Broadway '41
Life Begins for Andy Hardy '41
Ziegfeld Girl '41
Andy Hardy Meets Debutante '40
Little Nellie Kelly '40
Strike Up the Band '40
Babes in Arms '39
The Wizard of Oz '39
Everybody Sing '38
Listen, Darling '38
Love Finds Andy Hardy '38
Broadway Melody of 1938 '37
Thoroughbreds Don't Cry '37
Pigskin Parade 36

Richard Garland (1927-69)
Panic in the Year Zero! '62
The Undead '57

Jeff Garlin (1962-)
WALL-E '08 (V)
I Want Someone to Eat Cheese With '06
Sleepover '04
Daddy Day Care '03
The Hot Chick '02
The Sum of All Fears '02
Along for the Ride '00
Can of Worms '00
The Babysitter '95

Lee Garlington (1953-)
A Lot Like Love '05
Guarding Eddy '04
Johnson Family Vacation '04

Monkey Grip '82

James Garner (1928-)
The Ultimate Gift '07
The Notebook '04
Divine Secrets of the Ya-Ya Sisterhood '02
Atlantis: The Lost Empire '01 (V)
The Last Debate '00
Space Cowboys '00
One Special Night '99
Legalese '98
Twilight '98
Dead Silence '96
My Fellow Americans '96

Alice Garr (1969-)
Jindabyne '06
Strange Planet '99
Love and Other Catastrophes '95

Larry McMurtry's Streets of Laredo '95
Breathing Lessons '94
Maverick '94
Barbarians at the Gate '93
Fire in the Sky '93
The Distinguished Gentleman '92
Decoration Day '90
My Name Is Bill W. '89
Sunset '88
Murphy's Romance '85
The Glitter Dome '84
Tank '83
The Fan '81
The Castaway Cowboy '74
One Little Indian '73
They Only Kill Their Masters '72
A Man Called Sledge '71
Skin Game '71
Support Your Local Gunfighter '71
Marlowe '69
Support Your Local Sheriff '69
How Sweet It Is! '68
The Pink Jungle '68
The Great Escape '63
Move Over, Darling '63
The Thrill of It All! '63
The Wheeler Dealers '63
Boys' Night Out '62
The Children's Hour '61
Cash McCall '60
Alias Jesse James '59
Up Periscope '59
Darby's Rangers '58
Sayonara '57

Jennifer Garner (1972-)
Catch and Release '07
Juno '07
The Kingdom '07
Elektra '05
13 Going on 30 '04
Daredevil '03
Catch Me If You Can '02
Pearl Harbor '01
Dude, Where's My Car? '00
Aftershock: Earthquake in New York '99
1999 '98
Mr. Magoo '97
Rose Hill '97
Washington Square '97
Larry McMurtry's Dead Man's Walk '96

Katrina Garner
Halloween Night '90
Hack O'Lantern '87

Kelli Garner (1984-)
Man's Walk '96
Havoc 2: Normal Adolescent Behavior '07
Lars and the Real Girl '07
Dreamland '06
London '05
Man of the House '05
Thumbsucker '05
The Aviator '04
Bully '01

Teri Garr (1949-)
Unaccompanied Minors '06
Ghost World '01
Life Without Dick '01
Dick '99
NightScreams '97
Ronnie and Julie '97
The Pacifier '05
Underdog '07 (V)
Dumb & Dumber '94
Michael '96
Perfect Alibi '94
Ready to Wear '94
Mom and Dad Save the World '92
The Player '92
Take Down '92
A Bug's Life '98 (V)
Going Postal '98
Casper '95 (V)
Club Land '01
Stuart Little 2 '02
The Country Bears '02 (V)
Finding Nemo '03 (V)
Tarzan 2 '05 (V)
Garfield: The Movie '04 (V)
A Simple Wish '97
Changing Habits '96
Waiting for the Light '90
Short Time '90
A Perfect Little Murder '90
Mother Goose Rock 'n' Rhyme '90
The Black Stallion Returns '83
Mr. Mom '83
The Sting 2 '83
To Catch a King '84
First Born '84
Tootsie '82
Honky Tonk Freeway '81
One from the Heart '82
The Escape Artist '82
The Black Stallion '79

Peggy Ann Garner (1931-84)
Betrayal '78
A Wedding '78
The Cat '66
Black Widow '54
Eight Witnesses '54
The Big Cat '49
The Lovable Cheat '49
Daisy Kenyon '47
A Tree Grows in Brooklyn '45
Jane Eyre '44
The Keys of the Kingdom '44
Blondie Brings Up Baby '39

Gale Garnett (1942-)
32 Short Films about Glenn Gould '93

Janeane Garofalo (1964-)
Ratatouille '07 (V)
The Wild '06 (V)
Duane Hopwood '05
Jimmy Glick in Lala Wood '05
Stay '05
Wonderland '03
Big Trouble '02
The Independent '00
Steal This Movie! '00
Titan A.E. '00 (V)
What Planet Are You From? '00
Dogma '99
The Minus Man '99
Mystery Men '99
Thick as Thieves '99
The Bumblebee Flies Anyway '98
Clay Pigeons '98
Dog Park '98
Permanent Midnight '98
200 Cigarettes '98
Cop Land '97
Half-Baked '98
The Matchmaker '97
Romy and Michele's High School Reunion '97
Sweethearts '97
The Cable Guy '96
I Shot a Man in Vegas '96
Kids in the Hall: Brain Candy '96
Larger Than Life '96
Touch '96
The Truth about Cats and Dogs '96
Bye Bye, Love '94
Coldblooded '94
Reality Bites '94

Tay Garnett (1898-1977)
The Children '80
Witches' Brew '79
Challenge To Be Free '76
Strong Man '26

Mr. & Mrs. Bridge '90

Mr. Mike's Mondo Video '79
The Outsiders '83

Teri Garr (1949-)
Unaccompanied Minors '06
Ghost World '01
Take Me Out to the Ball Game '49
On the Town '49
Neptune's Daughter '49
My Sister Eileen '55

Betty Garrett (1919-)
Words and Music '48

Beau Garrett
Made of Honor '08
Unearthed '07
Turistas '06

Brad Garrett (1960-)
Music & Lyrics '07
Ratatouille '07 (V)

Eliza (Simons) Garrett
Love Is a Gun '94
Terraces '77
Schlock '73
Child Star '03

Leif Garrett (1961-)
Dickie Roberts: Former Child Star '03
The Whispering '94
Spirit of '76 '91
The Banker '89
Cheerleader Camp '88
Party Line '88

Jordan Garrett (1992-)
Death Sentence '07
Saving Shiloh '06
Final Approach '04

Hank Garrett (1931-)
Blood Frenzy '87
The Boys Next Door '85
Roseboad Beach Hotel '85

Willie Garson (1964-)
Sex and the City: The Movie '08
Zoom '06
Fever Pitch '05
Little Manhattan '05
Freaky Friday '03
Taken '02
Luster '02
Out Cold '01
What Planet Are You From? '00
Play It to the Bone '99
The Rock '96
Untamed Heart '93

Jennie Garth (1972-)
Telling You '98

Louis Garrel (1983-)
Love Songs '07
Inside Paris '06
The Dreamers '03

Maurice Garrel (1923-)
Kings and Queen '04
Artemisia '97
Un Coeur en Hiver '93
La Discrète '90

Jean-Françoise Garreaud (1947-)
Betty '92
Violette '78

Ivo Garrani (1924-)
Waterloo '71
Atom Age Vampire '61
Black Sunday '60
The Giant of Marathon '60
The Day the Sky Exploded '57

Martin Garralaga (1894-1981)
I Know Who Killed Me '07
Night of the Cobra Woman '72
The Firm '93

Patsy Garrett (1921-)
Dennis the Menace: Dinosaur Hunter '93
For the Love of Benji '77
Benji '74

Roger Garrett (1921-)
The Passing of Evil '70

Spencer Garrett (1963-)
Brooklyn Lobster '05
Armistead Maupin's More Tales of the City '97

Martin Garralaga
Bela Lugosi Meets a Brooklyn Gorilla '52
For Whom the Bell Tolls '43
Casablanca '42
Boots of Destiny '37

Greer Garson (1906-96)
The Happiest Millionaire '67
The Singing Nun '66
Sunrise at Campobello '60
Pepe '60
Julius Caesar '53
Scandal at Scourie '53
The Miniver Story '50
That Forsyte Woman '49
Julia Misbehaves '48
Desire Me '47
Adventure '45
The Valley of Decision '45
Mrs. Parkington '44
Madame Curie '43
Random Harvest '42
Mrs. Miniver '42
When Ladies Meet '41
Blossoms in the Dust '41
Pride and Prejudice '40
Goodbye, Mr. Chips '39

How to Kill 400 Duponts '68
Terror Creatures from the Grave '66
Eva '62
Two Nights with Cleopatra '54

Riccardo Garrone (1926-)
Havoc 2: Normal Adolescent Behavior '07

Barbara Garrick (1965-)
Sleepless in Seattle '93
The Firm '93
Armistead Maupin's More Tales of the City '95

John Garrick (1902-66)
Lily of Killarney '34
Lottery Bride '30
Song of My Heart '29

David Garrison
Homeboys '92

Julia Garro
On the Town '91
Gracie '07

Greer Garson (1906-96)
Little Women '78

Alessandro Gassman (1965-)
Transporter 2 '05
Steam: A Turkish Bath '96
A Month by the Lake '95
Sacrilege '86

Vittorio Gassman (1922-2000)
Sleepers '96
Abraham '94
The Sleazy Uncle '89
The Family '87
Life Is a Bed of Roses '83
The Tempest '82
Sharky's Machine '81
Immortal Bachelor '80
Quintet '79
A Wedding '78
We All Loved Each Other So Much '77
The Scent of a Woman '75
12 Plus 1 '70
Catch as Catch Can '68
Tiger and the Pussycat '67
Woman Times Seven '67
The Easy Life '63
Il Sorpasso '63
Barabbas '62
The Great War '59
Big Deal on Madonna Street '56
War and Peace '56
Rhapsody '54
Anna '51
Bitter Rice '49
Lure of the Sila '49

Kyle Gass (1960-)
Tenacious D in The Pick of Destiny '06
The Cable Will Rock '99
Bio-Dome '96

Vincent Gaskins
The Dark Dealer '95
The Underneath '95

Christopher Gartin (1968-)
Friends and Family '01
Tremors 3: Back to Perfection '01
Tremors 2: Aftershocks '96

Steve Garvey (1948-)
BASEketball '95

Elizabeth Garvie
Diana: Her True Story '93
Pride and Prejudice '85

John Garwood
A Taste of Hell '73
The Losers '70
Hell's Angels on Wheels '67

Linda Gary
The Land Before Time 4: Journey Through the Mists '96 (V)
The Land Before Time 3: The Time of the Great Giving '95 (V)
The Land Before Time 2: The Great Valley Adventure '94 (V)

Lorraine Gary (1937-)
Jaws: The Revenge '87
1941 '79
Jaws 2 '78
Car Wash '76
Jaws '75

The Black Stallion '79
Shaker Run '85
Thunder Alley '85

My Brother's War '97
Power '98 '96
Danielle Steel's Star '93
The Outsiders '83
Long Shot Kids '81
Peter Lundy and the Medicine Hat Stampede '77
Skateboard '77
Walking Tall: The Final Chapter '77
Kid Vengeance '77
Matters of Evil '70

Pajama Party '64
Speedway '68
Shep Comes Home '49
Susanna Pass '49
Riding the California Trail '47
In Old New Mexico '45
South of Monterey '47
The Fighter '52
Young Frankenstein '74
The Conversation '74
Grimm '77
Oh, God! '77
Once Upon a Brothers Grimm '77
Third Kind '77
Close Encounters of the Third Kind '77
The Children '80

Ana Gasteyer (1967-)
Mean Girls '04
What's the Worst That Could Happen? '01
Gepetto '00
What Women Want '00
Dick '99
Meet the Deedles '98
Michael Gaston
The Notorious Bettie Page '06
Stay '05
High Crimes '02
Bless the Child '00
Cora Unashamed '00
Ransom '96
Lisa Gastoni (1935-)
Tharus Son of Attila '87
Submission '77
Wild, Wild Planet '65
The Great Armored Car Swindle '64
Messalina vs. the Son of Hercules '64
RoGoPaG '62
The Baby and the Battleship '56
The Runaway Bus '54
Larry Gates (1915-96)
The Henderson Monster '80
Backstairs at the White House '79
Funny Lady '75
Missiles of October '74
Death of a Gunfighter '69
The Sand Pebbles '66
Toys in the Attic '63
The Hoodlum Priest '61
The Young Savages '61
Underworld, U.S.A. '60
The Strange One '57
Invasion of the Body Snatchers '56
Above and Beyond '53
Francis Covers the Big Town '53
Nancy Gates (1926-)
Comanche Station '60
The Gunfight at Dodge City '59
Some Came Running '58
The Search for Bridey Murphy '56
Wetbacks '56
Suddenly '53
Torch Song '53
The Atomic City '52
The Member of the Wedding '52
At Sword's Point '51
Check Your Guns '48
Master Race '44
Nevada '44
The Great Gildersleeve '43
Marjorie Gateson (1891-1977)
International Lady '41
The Duke of West Point '38
Arizona Mahoney '36
Big Brown Eyes '36
Goin' to Town '35
John Gatins
The Ambulance '90
Return to Salem's Lot '87
Jennifer Gatti (1968-)
Blood Money '99
Double Exposure '93
Street Knight '93
Valerie Gaunt (1933-)
The Horror of Dracula '58
The Curse of Frankenstein '57
Mikkel Gaup (1968-)
Breaking the Waves '95
Pathfinder '87

Chris Gauthier
The Foursome '06
40 Days and 40 Nights '02
Dan Gauthier (1963-)
Excessive Force 2: Force on Force '95
Illegal in Blue '95
Son-in-Law '93
Shame '92
Teen Witch '89
Dick Gautier (1937-)
Get Smart, Again! '89
Glitch! '88
Marathon '80
Divorce American Style '67
Jean-Yves Gautier
A Chef in Love '96
Three Lives and Only One Death '96
Voyage to the Beginning of the World '96
The Promise '94
Jean Gaven (1922-)
The Story of O '75
The Crucible '57
Erica Gavin (1947-)
Caged Heat '74
Beyond the Valley of the Dolls '70
John Gavin (1928-)
House of Shadows '83
History of the World: Part 1 '81
Sophia Loren: Her Own Story '80
Jennifer '78
The Madwoman of Chaillot '69
Murder for Sale '68
Thoroughly Modern Millie '67
Back Street '61
Breath of Scandal '60
Midnight Lace '60
Psycho '60
Spartacus '60
Imitation of Life '59
A Time to Love & a Time to Die '58
Cassandra Gaviola (1959-)
The Black Room '82
Conan the Barbarian '82
Peter Gawthorne (1884-1962)
Seven Doors to Death '44
The Secret Code '42
Phantom Fiend '35
William Gaxton (1890-1963)
Best Foot Forward '43
The Heat's On '43
It's the Old Army Game '26
Gregory Gay (1900-93)
Ticket of Leave Man '37
Ramon Gay (1917-60)
The Curse of the Aztec Mummy '59
The Robot vs. the Aztec Mummy '59
Howard Gaye (1878-1955)
Dante's Inferno '24
Flirting with Fate '16
The Birth of a Nation '15
Lisa Gaye
Class of Nuke 'Em High 3: The Good, the Bad and the Subhumanoid '94
Class of Nuke 'Em High 2: Subhumanoid Meltdown '91
The Toxic Avenger, Part 2 '89
The Toxic Avenger, Part 3: The Last Temptation of Toxie '89
Lisa Gaye (1935-)
Castle of Evil '66
Night of Evil '62
The Sign of Zorro '60
Shake, Rattle and Rock '57

Marvin Gaye (1939-84)
Chrome and Hot Leather '71
The Ballad of Andy Crocker '69
Nona Gaye (1974-)
Crash '05
The Gospel '05
XXX: State of the Union '05
The Polar Express '04
The Matrix Reloaded '03
The Matrix Revolutions '03
Ali '01
Julie Gayet (1972-)
My Best Friend '06
Confusion of Genders '00
One Hundred and One Nights '95
Rebecca Gayheart (1972-)
Bunny Whipped '06
The Christmas Blessing '05
Pipe Dream '02
Harvard Man '01
From Dusk Till Dawn 3: The Hangman's Daughter '99
Jawbreaker '98
Too Smooth '98
Urban Legend '98
Robin Cook's Invasion '97
Scream 2 '97
Nothing to Lose '96
Somebody Is Waiting '96
Jackie Gayle (1926-2002)
Bulworth '98
Mr. Saturday Night '92
Bert Rigby, You're a Fool '89
Plain Clothes '88
Tin Men '87
Pepper and His Wacky Taxi '72
Monica Gayle
Nashville Girl '76
Switchblade Sisters '75
Anna Gaylor (1932-)
The Killing Game '67
Life Upside Down '64
Mitch Gaylord (1961-)
Animal Instincts '92
American Tiger '89
George Gaynes (1917-)
The Crucible '96
Police Academy 7: Mission to Moscow '94
Vanya on 42nd Street '94
Stepmonster '93
Police Academy 6: City under Siege '89
Police Academy 5: Assignment Miami Beach '88
Police Academy 4: Citizens on Patrol '87
Police Academy 3: Back in Training '86
Police Academy 2: Their First Assignment '85
It Came Upon a Midnight Clear '84
Micki & Maude '84
Police Academy '84
Dead Men Don't Wear Plaid '82
Tootsie '82
Breaking Up Is Hard to Do '79
Trilogy of Terror '75
The Way We Were '73
Janet Gaynor (1906-84)
The Young in Heart '38
A Star Is Born '37
The Farmer Takes a Wife '35
Sunrise '27
Mitzi Gaynor (1930-)
For Love or Money '63
South Pacific '58
Les Girls '57
Birds & the Bees '56

There's No Business Like Show Business '54
Bloodhounds of Broadway '52
We're Not Married '52
My Blue Heaven '50
Eunice Gayson (1931-)
From Russia with Love '63
Dr. No '62
The Revenge of Frankenstein '58
Carry On Admiral '57
Gwen Gaze (1909-)
Two-Fisted Justice '43
West of Pinto Basin '40
Wendy Gazelle
The Net '95
Crooked Hearts '91
Triumph of the Spirit '89
Understudy: The Graveyard Shift 2 '88
Hot Pursuit '87
Sammy & Rosie Get Laid '87
Ben Gazzara (1930-)
Paris, je t'aime '06
Dogville '03
Hysterical Blindness '02
Brian's Song '01
Blue Moon '00
Believe '99
The List '99
Summer of Sam '99
The Thomas Crown Affair '99
Happiness '98
Illuminata '98
The Big Lebowski '97
Buffalo 66 '97
Lady Killer '97
Protector '97
The Spanish Prisoner '97
Quicker Than the Eye '88
Secret Obsession '88
Control '87
An Early Frost '85
Tales of Ordinary Madness '83
They All Laughed '81
Question of Honor '80
Saint Jack '79
Sidney Sheldon's Bloodline '79
Opening Night '77
The Trial of Lee Harvey Oswald '77
The Death of Richie '76
High Velocity '76
The Killing of a Chinese Bookie '76
Voyage of the Damned '76
QB VII '74
Neptune Factor '73
Fireball Forward '72
Pursuit '72
Sicilian Connection '72
Shattered Silence '71
Husbands '70
The Bridge at Remagen '69
Joyful Laughter '60
Anatomy of a Murder '59
The Strange One '57
Michael V. Gazzo (1923-95)
Cookie '89
The Godfather 1902-1959: The Complete Epic '81
Alligator '80
Kill Castro '80
The Mercenaries '80
Gangsters '79
Love and Bullets '79
Fingers '78
King of the Gypsies '78

Black Sunday '77
The Godfather, Part 2 '74
Devon Gearhart (1995-)
Funny Games '07
Canvas '06
Bobby Jones: Stroke of Genius '04
Valerie Gearon (1937-2003)
Persuasion '71
Invasion '65
Anthony Geary (1947-)
Disney's Teacher's Pet '04 (V)
Scorchers '92
Night of the Warrior '91
High Desert Kill '90
Crack House '89
UHF '89
It Takes Two '88
Pass the Ammo '88
You Can't Hurry Love '88
Dangerous Love '87
Penitentiary 3 '87
Kicks '85
The Impostor '84
Johnny Got His Gun '71
Bud Geary (1898-1946)
D-Day on Mars '45
The Topeka Terror '45
Bataan '43
Bordertown Gunfighters '43
Immortal Sergeant '43
Cynthia Geary (1965-)
The Business of Fancydancing '02
Smoke Signals '98
The Killing Grounds '97
When Time Expires '97
The Heist '96
8 Seconds '94
To Grandmother's House We Go '94
Karl Geary (1972-)
Mimic 3: Sentinel '03
Hamlet '00
Gordon Gebert (1941-)
To Hell and Back '55
The Narrow Margin '52
Flying Leathernecks '51
Martina Gedeck (1961-)
The Good Shepherd '06
The Lives of Others '06
Mostly Martha '01
Jew-Boy Levi '99
Jason Gedrick (1965-)
Hidden Places '06
Strange Frequency 2 '01
Summer Catch '01
The Last Don 2 '98
The Last Don '97
Power '98
The Force '94
Crossing the Bridge '92
Still Life '92
Backdraft '91
Rooftops '89
Promised Land '88
Stacking '87
Iron Eagle '86
Prunella Gee (1950-)
Witching Time '84
Never Say Never Again '83
The Wilby Conspiracy '75
Robbie Gee (1970-)
Underworld '03

Mean Machine '01
Snatch '00
Ellen Geer (1941-)
Neil Simon's The Odd Couple 2 '98
Satan's Princess '90
Hard Traveling '85
Bloody Birthday '80
Over the Edge '79
A Shining Season '79
Babel '75
Memory of Us '74
Silence '73
Harold and Maude '71
Petulia '68
Kevin Geer
The Tavern '00
Sweet Bird of Youth '89
Will Geer (1902-78)
Unknown Powers '80
The Billion Dollar Hobo '78
My Sister, My Love '78
A Woman Called Moses '78
Bunco '77
Moving Violation '76
The Hanged Man '74
Hurricane '74
Memory of Us '74
Executive Action '73
Silence '73
Dear Dead Delilah '72
Jeremiah Johnson '72
Napoleon and Samantha '72
Brother John '70
The Reivers '69
Bandolero! '68
In Cold Blood '67
The President's Analyst '67
Seconds '66
Black Like Me '64
Salt of the Earth '54
Double Crossbones '51
Broken Arrow '50
Comanche Territory '50
To Please a Lady '50
Winchester '73 '50
Lust for Gold '49
Spitfire '34
Judy Geeson (1948-)
The Duke '99
Houdini '99
The Plague Dogs '82 (V)
Danger UXB '81
Inseminoid '80
Adventures of a Taxi Driver '76
Carry On England '76
Poldark 2 '75
Poldark '75
It's Not the Size That Counts '74
Murder on the Midnight Express '74
Doomwatch '72
Dynasty of Fear '72
10 Rillington Place '71
It Happened at Nightmare Inn '70
Twinsanity '70
Berserk! '67
To Sir, with Love '67
Sally Geeson (1950-)
Cry of the Banshee '70
The Oblong Box '69
What's Good for the Goose '69
Deborah Geffner (1952-)
Exterminator 2 '84
All That Jazz '79
Martha Gehman
Going Shopping '05
Threesome '94
Unveiled '94
Father of the Bride '91
A Kiss Before Dying '91
F/X '86
The Flamingo Kid '84
Leap Year '21
Clarence Geldart (1867-1935)
Go-Get-'Em-Haines '35
Jungle Bride '33
Bob Geldof (1954-)
Spice World: The Movie '97

The Return of Spinal Tap '92
Pink Floyd: The Wall '82
The Secret Policeman's Other Ball '82
Secret Policeman's Private Parts '81

Alan Gelfant (1956-)
Apartment 12 '06
The Destiny of Marty Fine '96
Next Stop, Wonderland '98

Daniel Gélin (1921-2002)
Forced to Kill '33
Is Paris Burning? '66
Life is a Long Quiet River '88
La Ronde '51
The Man Who Knew Too Much '56
Murmur of the Heart '71
Rendez-vous de Juillet '49
The Testament of Orpheus '59

Sarah Michelle Gellar (1977-)
The Air I Breathe '07
Happily N'Ever After '07 (V)
Suburban Girl '07
TMNT (Teenage Mutant Ninja Turtles) '07 (V)
The Grudge 2 '06
The Return '06
The Grudge '04
Scooby-Doo 2: Monsters Unleashed '04
Scooby-Doo '02
Harvard Man '01
Simply Irresistible '99
Small Soldiers '98 (V)
Cruel Intentions '98
Beverly Hills Family Robinson '97
I Know What You Did Last Summer '97
Scream 2 '97
Summer '97
High Stakes '89

Larry Gelman (1930-)
Prime Time '77
Chatterbox '76
Slumber Party '57 '76

Grant Gelt (1980-)
Mutant Species '95
Avalon '90

Rhoda Gemignani (1940-)
Rocky Marciano '99
Concrete Beat '84

Giuliano Gemma (1938-)
Mad Love '01
Blood at Sundown '68
Unsane '82
The Warning '80
Corleone '79
Battleforce '78
The Desert of the Tartars '76
Smugglers '75
Master Touch '74
Erik, the Viking '65
Goliath and the Sins of Babylon '64
Hercules vs. the Sons of the Sun '64

Ruth Gemmell (1967-)
The Alchemists '99
Fever Pitch '96
Band of Gold '95

Laura Gemser (1950-)
Women's Prison Massacre '85
Caged Women '84
Ator the Fighting Eagle '83
Black Cobra '83
Love Camp '81
Emmanuelle, the Queen '79
Emmanuelle's Daughter '79
Crime Busters '78
Emmanuelle in the Country '78
'78
Fury '78
Naked Paradise '78
Trap Them & Kill Them '77
Emmanuelle on Taboo Island '76
Emmanuelle, the Joys of a Woman '76

Bryan Genesse (1967-)
Cloud Waltzing '87
Live Wire: Human Timebomb '95
Terminal Impact '95
Night Siege Project: Shadowchaser 2 '94
California Casanova '89
Loose Screws '85
Clear Target '98
Spoiler '98
Terminal Virus '96

François-Eric Gendron (1954-)
Boyfriends & Girlfriends '88
Americathon '79
A Woman of Rome '56
Plucking the Daisy '56

Bill George
Excalibur '81

Brian George (1952-)
Employee of the Month '06
Touch of Pink '04
On the Run '73

Christopher George (1929-83)
Pieces '83
AngKor: Cambodia Express '83
Enter the Ninja '81
Graduation Day '81
Mortuary '81
Exterminator '80
Gates of Hell '80
Grizzly '76
Midway '76
Train Robbers '73
Man on a String '71
Chisum '70
El Dorado '67

Stephen Geoffreys (1964-)
Moon 44 '90
976-EVIL '88
The Chair '87
Fraternity Vacation '85
Fright Night '85

Paul Geoffrey
Emily Brontë's Wuthering Heights '92
Excalibur '81

Carrie Genzel (1971-)
Virtual Seduction '96
Caged Hearts '95

Maud(e) George (Ford) (1888-1963)
The Wedding March '28
Foolish Wives '22
Blind Husbands '19

Roger Gentry
Georgia, Georgia '72

Troy Gentile
Drillbit Taylor '08
Destiny '06
Tenacious D in the Pick of Destiny '06

Minnie Gentry (1916-93)
The Bad News Bears '05
When Thief Meets Thief '37

Melissa George (1976-)
Music Within '07
30 Days of Night '07
Turistas '06
Derailed '05
Down With Love '03
Mulholland Drive '01
Sugar & Spice '01
The Limey '99
Dark City '97

Rita George
Hollywood Boulevard '76

Susan George (1950-)
That Summer of White Roses '90
Jack the Ripper '88
Lightning: The White Stallion '86
The Jigsaw Man '84
Pajama Tops '83
House Where Evil Dwells '82
Kiss My Grits '82
Venom '82
Enter the Ninja '81
Tintorera... Tiger Shark '78
Tomorrow Never Comes '77
A Small Town in Texas '76
Mandingo '75
Out of Season '75
Dirty Mary Crazy Larry '74
Die Screaming, Marianne '73
Sonny and Jed '73
Straw Dogs '71
Eye Witness '70
Lola '69
The Looking Glass War '69
Fright '71

Steven Geray (1904-73)
Verboten! '58
Affair in Trinidad '52
Tobor the Great '54
The Big Sky '52
Frankenstein's Daughter '58
Gilda '46
Blondie Knows Best '46
Ladies of the Chorus '48
Savage Drums '51
Sky Liner '49
In Society '44

Chief Dan George (1899-1981)
The Outlaw Josey Wales '76
The Bears & I '74
Harry and Tonto '74
Dan Candy's Law '73
Cancel My Reservation '72
Little Big Man '70

Gladys George (1900-54)
Detective Story '51
Lullaby of Broadway '51
Flamingo Road '49
The Best Years of Our Lives '46
The Maltese Falcon '41
The Roaring Twenties '39
Marie Antoinette '38
Madame X '37

Goetz George (1938-)
Schtonk! '92
Out of Order '84

Heinrich George (1893-1946)
Kolberg '45
Metropolis '25

Chief Leonard George
Smoke Signals '98

Lynda Day George (1946-)
Pieces '83
Young Warriors '83
The Junkman '82
Mortuary '81
Beyond Evil '80
Casino '80
Racquet '79
Cruise into Terror '78
Aliens from Spaceship Earth '77
Ants '77
Day of the Animals '77
Roots '77

Carmelita Geraghty (1901-66)
Flaming Signal '33
Night Life in Reno '31
Fightin' Ranch '30
Rogue of the Rio Grande '30
My Best Girl '27
Cyclone Cavalier '25
My Lady of Whims '25

Marita Geraghty
Groundhog Day '93
Past Tense '94

Brian Geraghty (1974-)
We Are Marshall '06
Bobby '06
The Guardian '06
Conversations with Other Women '05
Jarhead '05
Cruel World '05

Aliki Georgouli (1933-95)
Landscape in the Mist '88
The Traveling Players '75

Charles Gerard
Bandits '86
Happy New Year '73
Robot in the Family '94

Danny Gerard (1977-)
Leatherheads '08
Charlie Wilson's War '07
Inside Man '06
Second Best '05
Virgin '03
Hollywood Ending '02
The Curse of the Jade Scorpion '01
K-PAX '01
Homicide: The Movie '00
The Legend of Bagger Vance '00
Went to Coney Island on a Mission from God... Be Back by Five '99
Killing Zone '79

Gil Gerard (1943-)
Air Rage '01
The Stepdaughter '00
Mom, Can I Keep Her? '98
Soldier's Fortune '91
Final Notice '89
Fury to Freedom: The Life Story of Raul Ries '85
For Love or Money '84
Help Wanted: Male '82
Buck Rogers in the 25th Century '79

Georges Geret (1924-96)
Killer '73
A Very Curious Girl '69
Z '69
Diary of a Chambermaid '64

Peter Gerety (1940-)
The Mask of Dimitrios '44
The Seventh Cross '44
The Moon and Sixpence '43
Blue, White and Perfect '42

Claudia Gerini (1971-)
The Passion of the Christ '04
Iris Blond '98

Louise Germaine (1971-)
Lipstick on Your Collar '94

Lauren German (1978-)
Hostel: Part 2 '07
Rx '06
Standing Still '05
A Walk to Remember '02

Jeanne Gerson (1905-92)
Sharp's Company '94
Voodoo Dawn '89

Betty Lou Gerson (1914-99)
101 Dalmatians '61 (V)
The Fly '58
An Annapolis Story '55
The Red Menace '49

Tom Georgeson (1941-)
Bleak House '05
The Land Girls '98
Swing '98
Devices and Desires '91
A Fish Called Wanda '88
No Surrender '86

Olga Georges-Picot (1944-97)
Children of Rage '75
The Graveyard '74
The Day of the Jackal '73

Richard Gere (1949-)
The Flock '07
The Hunting Party '07
I'm Not There '07
The Hoax '06
Bee Season '05
Shall We Dance? '04
Chicago '02
The Mothman Prophecies '02
Unfaithful '02
Autumn in New York '00
Dr. T & the Women '00
Runaway Bride '99
Red Corner '97
The Jackal '97
Primal Fear '96
First Knight '95
And the Band Played On '93
Intersection '93
Mr. Jones '93
Sommersby '93
Final Analysis '92
Rhapsody in August '91
Internal Affairs '90
Pretty Woman '90
Miles from Home '88
No Mercy '86
Power '86
King David '85
The Cotton Club '84
Beyond the Limit '83
Breathless '83
An Officer and a Gentleman '82
American Gigolo '79
Yanks '79
Bloodbrothers '78
Days of Heaven '78
Looking for Mr. Goodbar '77
Strike Force '75
Report to the Commissioner '74

George Gerdes
Jailbreakers '94
Iron Will '93

Joan Gerber (1935-)
DuckTales the Movie: Treasure of the Lost Lamp '90 (V)

Greg Germann (1962-)
Friends with Money '06
Kill Your Darlings '06
Bigger Than the Sky '05
Down to Earth '01
Sweet November '01
Jesus' Son '99
Once Around '91

Richard Gere — (continued entries)

Daniel Gerroll (1951-)
Far from Heaven '02
Heart of Texas Ryan '17
The Nervous Wreck '26
Down to Earth '17
Big Business '88
Drop Dead Fred '91
84 Charing Cross Road '86

Charles Gerrard (1883-1969)
War Bus Commando '89
Beyond the Door 3 '51
Curse 2: The Bite '92
She Gods of Shark Reef '56

Savina Gersak
Midnight Ride '92
War Bus Commando '89
Iron Warrior '87
Sonny Boy '87

Gina Gershon (1962-)
P.S. I Love You '07
What Love Is '07
Dreamland '06
One Last Thing '05
Category 7: The End of the World '05
3-Way '04
Prey for Rock and Roll '03
Demonlover '02
Borderline '02
Driven '01
Picture Claire '01
Black & White '99
Guinevere '99
The Insider '99
I'm Losing You '99
Lulu on the Bridge '98
Legalese '98
Palmetto '98
Face/Off '97
This World, Then the Fireworks '97
Bound '96
Touch '96
City of Hope '91
Cocktail '88
Red Heat '88
Pretty in Pink '86
Sinatra '92
The Player '92
Joey Breaker '93
Love Matters '93
Snowgirls '95
Flinch '94
Cut for Justice '91
Turning Back '95

Gaia Germani (1942-)
Castle of the Living Dead '64
Your Turn Darling '63

Lisa Gerstein
Border Blues '03
My Life's in Turnaround '94

Berta Gersten (1894-1972)
A Brivele der Mamen '38
Mirele Efros '38

Frank Gerstle (1915-70)
Hell on Wheels '67
The Atomic Brain '64
Submarine Seahawk '59
The Wasp Woman '59
Gang Busters '55
Above and Beyond '53

Valeska Gert (1892-1978)
Juliet of the Spirits '65
An Occurrence at Owl Creek Bridge/Coup de Grace '62
The Threepenny Opera '31
Joyless Street '25

Jami Gertz (1965-)
Keeping Up with the Steins '06
Lip Service '00
Seven Girlfriends '00
Twister '96
Jersey Girl '92
Don't Tell Her It's Me '90
Sibling Rivalry '90
Silence Like Glass '90
Listen to Me '89
Renegades '89
Less Than Zero '87
The Lost Boys '87
Crossroads '86
Quicksilver '86
Solarbabies '86
Mischief '85
Alphabet City '84
Sixteen Candles '84
Endless Love '81

Ricky Gervais (1961-)
Stardust '07
For Your Consideration '06
Night at the Museum '06
Valiant '05 (V)

Erwin Geschonneck (1906-)
Jacob the Liar '74
Carbide and Sorrel '63
Five Cartridges '60

Zen Gesner (1970-)
Fever Pitch '05
The Breed '01
Shallow Hal '01
Me, Myself, and Irene '00
There's Something about Mary '98
Kingpin '96
Wish Me Luck '95

Malcolm Gets (1964-)
Adam & Steve '05
Love in the Time of Money '02

Balthazar Getty (1975-)
Feast '06
The Tripper '06
Ladder 49 '04
Deuces Wild '02
The Center of the World '01
Hard Cash '01
MacArthur Park '01
Sol Goode '01
Four Dogs Playing Poker '00
Big City Blues '99
Out in Fifty '99
Voodoo Dawn '99
Habitat '02
Lost Highway '96
White Squall '96
Red Hot '95
Dead Beat '94
Don't Do It '94
Natural Born Killers '94
Terrified '94
Where the Day Takes You '92
December '91
My Heroes Have Always Been Cowboys '91
The Pope Must Diet '91
Young Guns 2 '90
Lord of the Flies '90

Estelle Getty (1923-)
Stuart Little '99
Stop! or My Mom Will Shoot '92
Mannequin '87
Mask '85
Tootsie '82

John Getz (1947-)
Zodiac '07
A Day Without a Mexican '04
The Late Shift '96
A Passion to Kill '94
Playmaker '94
Curly Sue '91
Don't Tell Mom the Babysitter's Dead '91
Born on the Fourth of July '89
The Fly 2 '89
The Fly '86
Blood Simple '85
Concrete Beat '84
Thief of Hearts '84
Kent State '81
Tattoo '81

Stan Getz (1927-91)
Exterminator '80
The Benny Goodman Story '55

Stephen Gevedon (1966-)
Session 9 '01
Blue in the Face '95
Smoke '95

Luminita Gheorghiu (1949-)
The Death of Mr. Lazarescu '05
Code Unknown '00

Massimo Ghini (1954-)
CQ '01
Up at the Villa '00
Tea with Mussolini '99
The Truce '96
Men Men Men '95

Alice Ghostley (1926-2007)
Whispers: An Elephant's Tale '00 (V)
Neil Simon's The Odd Couple 2 '98
Not for Publication '84
Blue Sunshine '78
Grease '78
Gator '76
With Six You Get Eggroll '68
The Graduate '67
To Kill a Mockingbird '62
New Faces of 1952 '54

Paul Giamatti (1967-)
John Adams '08
Fred Claus '07
The Nanny Diaries '07
Shoot 'Em Up '07
The Ant Bully '06 (V)
The Hawk Is Dying '06
The Illusionist '06
Lady in the Water '06
Cinderella Man '05
Robots '05 (V)
Sideways '04
American Splendor '03
Confidence '03
Paycheck '03
Big Fat Liar '02
Planet of the Apes '01
Storytelling '01
Big Momma's House '00
Duets '00
If These Walls Could Talk 2 '00
The Cradle Will Rock '99
Man on the Moon '99
The Negotiator '98
Safe Men '98
Saving Private Ryan '98
The Truman Show '98
Winchell '98
The Break '97
My Best Friend's Wedding '97
Private Parts '96

Louis Giambalvo (1945-)
Gun Shy '00
Gia '98
Illegal in Blue '95
Dead to Rights '93
Fade to Black '93
Question of Faith '93
Mastergate '92
Weekend at Bernie's '89
The Jagged Edge '85
Ratings Game '84
The Ambush Murders '82
Blackout '89
Night Stalker '87

Rick Gianasi
Sgt. Kabukiman N.Y.P.D. '94
The Occultist '89
Posed for Murder '89
Escape from Safehaven '88
Maximum Thrust '88
Mutant Hunt '87
Robot Holocaust '87

Adriano Giannini (1971-)
Sinbad: Legend of the Seven Seas '03 (V)
Swept Away '02

Giancarlo Giannini (1942-)
Casino Royale '06
Man on Fire '04
Incantato '03
My House in Umbria '03
Darkness '02
Joshua '02
Hannibal '01
The Whole Shebang '01
CQ '01
Dune '00
Mimic '97
The Disappearance of Garcia Lorca '96
Heaven Before I Die '96
A Walk in the Clouds '95
Jacob '94
Once Upon a Crime '92
Goodnight, Michelangelo '89
New York Stories '89
The Sleazy Uncle '89
Time to Kill '89
Blood Red '88
Saving Grace '86
Fever Pitch '85
American Dreamer '84
Where's Piccone '84
Lovers and Liars '81
Immortal Bachelor '80
Blood Feud '79
Life Is Beautiful '79
A Night Full of Rain '78
How Funny Can Sex Be? '76
The Innocent '76
Seven Beauties '76
Swept Away... '75
La Grande Bourgeoise '74
The Sensual Man '74
Love and Anarchy '73
Seduction of Mimi '72
The Black Belly of the Tarantula '71
The Secret of Santa Vittoria '69
Anzio '68

Cynthia Gibb (1963-)
Life with Judy Garland—Me and My Shadows '01 (N)
Volcano: Fire on the Mountain '97
Holiday Affair '96
Sin and Redemption '94
Gypsy '93
The Woman Who Loved Elvis '93
Death Warrant '90
Short Circuit 2 '88
Jack's Back '87
Malone '87
Modern Girls '86
Salvador '86
Youngblood '86
Stardust Memories '80

Donald Gibb
Magic Kid 2 '94
Revenge of the Nerds 4: Nerds in Love '94
Bloodsport '88

Robyn Gibbes (1957-)
What the Moon Saw '90
Wild Horses '82
Gone to Ground '76

Leeza Gibbons (1957-)
The Player '92
Soapdish '91

Marla Gibbs (1946-)
The Brothers '01
The Visit '00
Foolish '99
Lost and Found '99
Lily in Winter '94
The Meteor Man '93
Up Against the Wall '91

Timothy Gibbs (1967-)
Witchboard 2: The Devil's Doorway '93
The Kindred '87
Huckleberry Finn '81 (V)

Josianne Gibert
Sensual Partners '87

Rebecca Gibney (1965-)
Introducing the Dwights '07
Joey '98
Paperback Romance '96
Jigsaw '90
Among the Cinders '83

Susan Gibney
Cabin by the Lake '00
And You Thought Your Parents Were Weird! '91

Deborah Gibson (1970-)
Coffee Date '06
Heat Street '87

Henry Gibson (1935-)
Wedding Crashers '05
A Stranger in the Kingdom '98
Asylum '97
Bio-Dome '96
Mother Night '96
Color of a Brisk and Leaping Day '95
Tom and Jerry: The Movie '93 (V)
Gremlins 2: The New Batch '90
Tune in Tomorrow '90
Around the World in 80 Days '89
Night Visitor '89
Switching Channels '88
Innerspace '87
Long Gone '87
Brenda Starr '86
Monster in the Closet '86
The Incredible Shrinking Woman '81
Tulips '81
The Blues Brothers '80
For the Love of It '80
Kentucky Fried Movie '77
Nashville '75
Charlotte's Web '73 (V)
The Long Goodbye '73
Evil Roy Slade '71
The Outlaws Is Coming! '65
Kiss Me, Stupid! '64
The Nutty Professor '63

Hoot Gibson (1892-1962)
The Horse Soldiers '59
The Marshal's Daughter '53
Arizona Whirlwind '44
Death Valley Rangers '44
Marked Trails '44
Outlaw Trail '44
Sonora Stagecoach '44
The Law Rides Again '43
The Painted Stallion '37
Cavalcade of the West '36
Last Outlaw '36
Lucky Terror '36
The Riding Avenger '36
Feud of the West '35
Fighting Parson '35
Frontier Justice '35
Powdersmoke Range '35
Rainbow's End '35
Sunset Range '35
Swifty '35
Cowboy Counselor '33
The Dude Bandit '33
Boiling Point '32
Local Badman '32
Man's Land '32
Spirit of the West '32
Clearing the Range '31
Hard Hombre '31
Wild Horse '31
The Concentratin' Kid '30
Roaring Ranch '30
Spurs '30
Trailing Trouble '30
Trigger Tricks '30
Courtin' Wildcats '29
King of the Rodeo '28
The Prairie King '27
The Phantom Bullet '26
Straight Shootin' '17

Mel Gibson (1956-)
Paparazzi '04
The Singing Detective '03
Signs '02
We Were Soldiers '02
Chicken Run '00 (V)
The Patriot '00
What Women Want '00
The Million Dollar Hotel '99
Lethal Weapon 4 '98
Payback '98
Conspiracy Theory '97
FairyTale: A True Story '97
Ransom '96
Braveheart '95
Casper '95
Pocahontas '95 (V)
Maverick '94
The Man Without a Face '93
Forever Young '92
Lethal Weapon 3 '92
Air America '90
Bird on a Wire '90
Hamlet '90
Lethal Weapon 2 '89
Tequila Sunrise '88
Lethal Weapon '87
Mad Max: Beyond Thunderdome '85
Attack Force Z '84
The River '84
Mrs. Soffel '84
The Road Warrior '82
The Year of Living Dangerously '82
Gallipoli '81
Mad Max '80
Tim '79
Summer City '77

Mimi Gibson (1948-)
Courage of Black Beauty '57
The Monster That Challenged the World '57

Thomas Gibson (1962-)
Category 6: Day of Destruction '04
Brush with Fate '03
The Lost Empire '01
The Flintstones in Viva Rock Vegas '00
Psycho Beach Party '00
Stardom '00
Eyes Wide Shut '99
Armistead Maupin's More Tales of the City '97
Barcelona '94
Secrets '94
Sleep with Me '94
Armistead Maupin's Tales of the City '93
Love and Human Remains '93
Far and Away '92

Tyrese Gibson (1978-)
The Take '07
Transformers '07
Annapolis '06
Waist Deep '06
Four Brothers '05
Flight of the Phoenix '04
2 Fast 2 Furious '03
Baby Boy '01
Love Song '00

Virginia Gibson (1928-)
Athena '54
Seven Brides for Seven Brothers '54
Tea for Two '50

Wynne Gibson (1899-1987)
Motorcycle Squad '41
Aggie Appleby, Maker of Men '33
Night After Night '32
Man of the World '31

Bond Gideon
Gold of the Amazon Women '79
Stepsisters '74
Storyville '74

Pamela Gidley (1966-)
Luster '02
The Little Vampire '00
Kiss & Tell '99
Liar's Poker '99
Mafia! '98
The Treat '98
Aberration '97
Bombshell '97
Bad Love '95
The Crew '95
The Little Death '95
Firefall '94
S.F.W. '94
Cheatin' Hearts '93
Highway to Hell '92
Liebestraum '91
Disturbed '90
Blue Iguana '88
Cherry 2000 '88
Permanent Record '88
Thrashin' '86

John Gielgud (1904-2000)
Elizabeth '98
Merlin '98
Quest for Camelot '98 (V)
A Dance to the Music of Time '97
Dragonheart '96 (V)
Hamlet '96
The Leopard Son '96 (N)
Looking for Richard '96
Portrait of a Lady '96
First Knight '95
Gulliver's Travels '95
Haunted '95
Shine '95
Scarlett '94
The Power of One '92
Shining Through '92
Prospero's Books '91
Strike It Rich '90
Getting It Right '89
Romance on the Orient Express '89
War & Remembrance: The Final Chapter '89
Appointment with Death '88
Arthur 2: On the Rocks '88
A Man for All Seasons '88
War & Remembrance '88
The Whistle Blower '87
Plenty '85
The Shooting Party '85
Wagner: The Complete Epic '85
Wagner: The Movie '85
The Far Pavilions '84
Scandalous '84
The Scarlet & the Black '83
The Wicked Lady '83
Frankenstein '82
Gandhi '82
The Hunchback of Notre Dame '82
Inside the Third Reich '82
Arthur '81
Brideshead Revisited '81
Chariots of Fire '81
Lion of the Desert '81
Priest of Love '81
Sphinx '81

Caligula '80
The Conductor '80
The Elephant Man '80
The Formula '80
The Human Factor '79
Murder by Decree '79
Les Misérables '78
James Joyce: A Portrait of the Artist as a Young Man '77
Providence '77
Edward the King '75
11 Harrowhouse '74
Murder on the Orient Express '74
QB VII '74
Invitation to the Wedding '73
Probe '72
Julius Caesar '70
Oh! What a Lovely War '69
The Charge of the Light Brigade '68
Sebastian '68
The Shoes of the Fisherman '68
Chimes at Midnight '67
The Loved One '65
Becket '64
Saint Joan '57
Around the World in 80 Days '56
Richard III '55
Romeo and Juliet '54
Julius Caesar '53
Hamlet '48 (V)
The Secret Agent '36

Stefan Gierasch (1926-)
Murder in the First '95
Brainwashed '60
Time Lock '57

Frances Gifford (1919-94)
Riding High '50
Our Vines Have Tender Grapes '45
Thrill of a Romance '45
American Empire '42
Border Vigilantes '41

Frank Gifford (1930-)
Viva Knievel '77

Gloria Gifford
Vice Versa '88
D.C. Cab '84

Alan Gifford (1905-89)
Isadora '68
Town without Pity '61
36 Hours '64

Belle Epoque '92
Celestial Clockwork '94
Talk of Angels '96
Second Skin '99
Pan's Labyrinth '06

Ariadna Gil (1969-)
No '98

Marie Gignac
The Confessional '95

Sandro Giglio (1900-79)
The Student Nurses '70
Gas-s-s-s! '70
The Wrestler '73
Tut & Tuttle '81
Angel '84

Elaine Gittos (1945-)
Sammy & Rosie Get Laid '87

Kathie Lee Gifford (1953-)
Model Behavior '00
Dudley Do-Right '99

Roland Gift (1963-)
Scandal '89
The Painted Lady '97

Marcus Gilbert (1958-)
Army of Darkness '92
Riders '88

Melissa Gilbert (1964-)
Sylvester '85
Penalty Phase '86
Choices '86
Blood Vows: The Story of a Mafia Wife '87
Ice House '89
The Lookalike '90
Undesirable '92
Dying to Remember '93
Safe Harbour '07

Lou Gilbert
The Great White Hope '70
Goldstein '64

John Gilbert (1895-1936)
Queen Christina '33
A Woman of Affairs '28
The Flesh and the Devil '27
The Big Parade '25
He Who Gets Slapped '24
The Busher '19

Jody Gilbert (1916-79)
Willard '71
Actors and Sin '52
The Secret of Dr. Kildare '39

Helen Gilbert (1915-95)
Girls in Prison '56
Death Valley '46
God's Country '46
The Falcon Takes Over '42
Andy Hardy Gets Spring Fever '39

Eugenia Gilbert (1902-78)

Edmund Gilbert (1932-99)
Tom and Jerry: The Movie '93 (V)

Bob Gilbert
Silver Bandit '50
Red Rock Outlaw '47

Billy Gilbert (1894-1971)
The Kissing Bandit '48
Fun & Fancy Free '47 (V)
Trouble Chasers '45
Cooking Up Trouble '44
Ghost Crazy '44
Spotlight Scandals '43
Mr. Wise Guy '42
The Great Dictator '40
Destry Rides Again '39
Block-heads '38
Breaking the Ice '38
Happy Landing '38
Joy of Living '38
Maid's Night Out '38
Circus '38
The Firefly '37
100 Men and a Girl '37
Snow White and the Seven Dwarfs '37 (V)
Toast of New York '37
Kelly the Second '36
Seven Sinners '40
No, No Nanette '40
His Girl Friday '40
Week-End in Havana '41
Melody Master '41
The Great Dictator '40
Valley of the Sun '42
Song of the Islands '42

Andrew S. Gilbert
Look Both Ways '05
Dirty Deeds '02
Paperback Hero '99
Idiot Box '97
Kiss or Kill '97

Vincent (Vince) Gill (1939-)
Body Melt '93
Mad Max '80
Solo '77

Aidan Gillen (1968-)
Shanghai Knights '03
Buddy Boy '99
Some Mother's Son '96
Circle of Friends '94
L'Appat '94
Elective Affinities '96

Marie Gillain (1975-)
On Guard! '03
Harem '99
Last Breath '96
Barcelona '94

Dana Gillespie (1949-)
Scrubbers '82
The People That Time Forgot '77

Thea Gill
Masters of Horror: Homecoming '05

Dana Gilhooley
Grace is Gone '07
Outing Riley '04

Jack Gilford (1907-90)
Cocoon: The Return '88
Cocoon '85
Caveman '81
Wholly Moses! '80
Max '79
Harry & Walter Go to New York '76
Save the Tiger '73
They Might Be Giants '71
Catch-22 '70
Enter Laughing '67
The Incident '67
A Funny Thing Happened on the Way to the Forum '66

Sara Gilbert (1975-)
Riding in Cars with Boys '01

Taylor Gilbert
Alone in the T-Shirt Zone '86

Pamela Gilbert
Demonwarp '87
Evil Spawn '87

Connie Gilchrist (1901-85)
The Misadventures of Merlin Jones '63
Long John Silver '54
Houdini '53
The Half-Breed '51
Here Comes the Groom '51
Stars in My Crown '50
A Ticket to Tomahawk '50
A Letter to Three Wives '49
Nothing But Trouble '44
Tortilla Flat '42

Richard Gilden
The Black Klansman '66

Sandra Giles (1932-)
Daddy-O '59
Lost, Lonely, and Vicious '59

Nancy Giles (1960-)
Loverboy '05
States of Control '98

Gwynne Gifford (1946-)
Fade to Black '80
Satan's School for Girls '73
Beware! The Blob '72

Seth Gilliam
The Great New Wonderful '06
Personal Velocity: Three Portraits '02
Starship Troopers '97
Tar '97
Courage Under Fire '96
Assault at West Point: The Court-Martial of Johnson Whittaker '94
Jefferson in Paris '94

David Gilliam (1948-)
Gunpowder '87

Terry Gilliam (1940-)
Spies Like Us '85
Monty Python's The Meaning of Life '83
Monty Python's Life of Brian '79
Monty Python and the Holy Grail '75

Larry (Lawrence) Gilliard, Jr.
The Machinist '04
Gangs of New York '02
Cecil B. Demented '00
Simply Irresistible '99
Next Stop, Wonderland '98
The Waterboy '98
The Substitute 2: School's Out '97
Straight out of Brooklyn '91

Aden (John) Gillett (1958-)
Shadow of the Vampire '00
The 10th Kingdom '00
The Winslow Boy '98
The Borrowers '97
Ivanhoe '97
Under the Lighthouse Dancing '97

Rebecca Gilling (1953-)
Heaven Tonight '93
The Blue Lightning '86
The Naked Country '85

James Gillis (1943-)
Alien Space Avenger '91
Deranged '87
Night of the Zombies '81

Denis Gilmore (1949-)
Winter Lily '98
Lilies '96

Danny Gilmore (1973-)

Kenneth Gilman
A Woman's World '54
Cause for Alarm! '51

Hermione Gingold (1897-1987)
Garbo Talks '84
A Little Night Music '77
Gigi '58
Bell, Book and Candle '58
The Music Man '62
The Naked Edge '61
Around the World in 80 Days '56

Lowell Gilmore (1906-60)
Ma and Pa Kettle at Waikiki '55
Lone Star '52
King Solomon's Mines '50
Johnny Angel '45
Picture of Dorian Gray '45
Days of Glory '43

Art Gilmore (1912-)
The Narcotics Story '58 (N)
The Gallant Hours '60

Danny Gilmore (1973-)

Margalo Gillmore (1897-1986)
Sayonara '57
High Society '56
Gaby '56
Woman's World '54

Caroline Gillmer
The Monkey's Mask '00
Sorrento Beach '95

Ann Gillis (1927-)
Big Town After Dark '47
In Society '44
Nice Girl? '41
Bambi '42 (V)
The Adventures of Tom Sawyer '38
Peck's Bad Boy with the Circus '38

Anita Gillette (1936-)
Shall We Dance? '04
Larger Than Life '96
She's the One '96
Boys on the Side '95
Bob Roberts '92
Moonstruck '87
Brass '85
Marathon '80
Ants! '77

Claude Gillingwater (1870-1939)
The Prisoner of Shark Island '36
Mississippi '35
Illicit '31
My Boy '21

Linda Gillin (1948-)
Terror at Red Wolf Inn '72

Tom Gilroy
Spring Forward '99

Virginia Gilmore (1919-86)
The Loves of Edgar Allen Poe '42
Orchestra Wives '42
Western Union '41

Peter Gilmore
The Abominable Dr. Phibes '71

Fiona Gillies
Frankenstein '93

Andrew Gillies
DC 9/11: Time of Crisis '04

Daniel Gillies (1976-)
Captivity '07
Spider-Man 2 '04
Bride & Prejudice '04

Isabel Gillies (1970-)
Metropolitan '90

Ian Gilmour

Jack Gilpin (1951-)
101 Ways (The Things a Girl Will Do to Keep Her Volvo) '00
From the Earth to the Moon '98
Commandments '96
Last Breath '96
Barcelona '94
White Mile '94
Unnatural Pursuits '91
A Killing in a Small Town '90
Quick Change '90
Reversal of Fortune '90
Funny Farm '88
Something Wild '86

Richard Gilliland (1950-)
Audrey's Rain '03
Home Room '02
Online '01
I Shot Andy Warhol '96
One Way Out '95

Marc Gilpin (1966-)
Computer Wizard '77
Where's Willie? '77

Peri Gilpin (1961-)
Final Fantasy: The Spirits Within '01 (V)

Jessalyn Gilsig

Clarence Gilyard, Jr. (1955-)
Left Behind: The Movie '00
Walker: Texas Ranger: One Riot, One Ranger '93
Die Hard '88
Off the Mark '87
Top Gun '86

Daniel Gimenez Cacho (1961-)
Bad Education '04
Jealousy '99
Deep Crimson '96
Midaq Alley '95
Cabeza de Vaca '90

Teresa Gimpera (1936-)
The Fence '94
Smoke '95

Erica Gimpel (1964-)
Impostor '02

Jack Ging (1931-)
Where the Red Fern Grows '74
High Plains Drifter '73
Play Misty for Me '71
Macabre '69

Allen Ginsberg (1926-97)
Superstar: The Life and Times of Andy Warhol '90
Heavy Petting '89

Robert Ginty (1948-)
The Prophet's Game '99
Vietnam, Texas '90
Madhouse '90
Marlboro Man '91
Harley Davidson and the Marlboro Man '91

Robert Ginnaven
One False Move '91

Bob Ginnaven
The Day It Came to Earth '77
Visions of Evil '75

Loverboy '89
Out on Bail '89
Codename: Vengeance '87
Three Kinds of Heat '87
Programmed to Kill '86
Mission... Kill '85
Exterminator 2 '84
Warrior of the Lost World '84
White Fire '84
Gold Raiders '83
The Act '82
The Alchemist '81
Exterminator '80
Coming Home '78

Frank Gio
La Vie Continue '82
Jupiter's Thigh '81
Le Cavaleur '78
Dear Detective '77
Gypsy '75
Le Gitan '75

Vahina Giocante (1981-)
Lila Says '04
Marie Baie des Anges '97

Rocky Giordani
Cop and a Half '93
After Dark, My Sweet '90
Tapeheads '89

Daniela Giordano (1948-)
Assassination Tango '03
Analyze That '02
Backtrack '89
Once Upon a Time in America '84

Domiziana Giordano (1960-)
Interview with the Vampire '94
Nouvelle Vague '90
Nostalghia '83
Inquisition '76
Gunslinger '70
Four Times That Night '69

Florence Giorgetti (1944-)
The Lacemaker '77
Monique '76

Elenora Giorgi (1953-)
Creepers '85
Nudo di Donna '83
Beyond Obsession '82
Inferno '80
To Forget Venice '79
The Sex Machine '75

Ty(rone) Giordano (1976-)
Untraceable '08
A Lot Like Love '05
The Family Stone '05
For Love of the Game '99
Terror Tract '00

Chaim Girafi
The Monster '96

Carmine D. Giovinazzo (1973-)
More Dogs Than Bones '00
The Impossible Spy '87
In Enemy Hands '04
Players '03

Joseph Girard (1871-1949)
Sergeant York '41
Mystery of the Hooded Horseman '37
Aces and Eights '36
His Fighting Blood '35
The Ivory Handled Gun '35
Kentucky Blue Streak '35
Social Error '35
The Tonto Kid '35
The Fighting Trooper '34
Hurricane Express '32
Defenders of the Law '31
King of the Rodeo '28
Tentacles of the North '26
Laughing at Danger '24

Remy Girard (1950-)
Human Trafficking '05
The Barbarian Invasions '03
Varian's War '01
The Boys '97
Jesus of Montreal '89

Simone-Elise Girard
Shattered Glass '03
After the Storm '01

Michele Girardon (1938-75)
Devil of the Desert Against the Son of Hercules '62
Death in the Garden '56

Annie Girardot (1931-)
Hidden '05
The Piano Teacher '01
Les Miserables '95
Mussolini & I '85
Jacko & Lise '82
La Vie Continue '82
Jupiter's Thigh '81
Le Cavaleur '78
Dear Detective '77
Gypsy '75
Le Gitan '75
Love and the Frenchwoman '60

Hippolyte Girardot (1955-)
Flight of the Red Balloon '08
Lady Chatterley '06
Paris, je t'aime '06
House of 9 '05
La Moustache '05
Kings and Queen '04
Modigliani '04
Love After Love '94
Barjo '93
Love Without Pity '91
Manon of the Spring '87

Claude Giraud (1936-)
The Mad Adventures of Rabbi Jacob '73
Phedre '68
Circle of Love '64

Joyce Giraud (1975-)
Miss Cast Away '04
Latin Dragon '03

Roland Giraud (1942-)
Mr. Frost '89
La Boum '81
Bilitis '77

Bernard Giraudeau (1947-)
La Petite Lili '03
Water Drops on Burning Rocks '99
Ridicule '96
The Favorite Son '94
Passion of Love '82

Cindy Girling
Devotion '95

Ennio Girolami (1934-)
Beauty on the Beach '61

Massimo Girotti (1918-2003)
Facing Windows '03
The Monster '96
Quo Vadis '85
Mr. Klein '76
Last Tango in Paris '73
Torture Chamber of Baron Blood '72
Red Tent '69
Teorema '68
The Giants of Thessaly '60
Senso '54
Sins of Rome '54
Story of a Love Affair '50
Ossessione '42
The Iron Crown '41

Jackie Giroux
Trick or Treats '82
The Cross & the Switchblade '72

Annabeth Gish (1972-)
The Celestine Prophecy '06
Knots '05
Buying the Cow '02
A Death in the Family '02
Pursuit of Happiness '01
Race to Space '01
Double Jeopardy '99
SLC Punk! '99
Steel '97
True Women '97
Beautiful Girls '96
Don't Look Back '96
The Last Supper '96
Nixon '95
Scarlett '94
Wyatt Earp '94
Coupe de Ville '90
Shag: The Movie '89
When He's Not a Stranger '89
Mystic Pizza '88
Hiding Out '87
Desert Bloom '86

Dorothy Gish (1898-1968)
The Cardinal '63
Romola '25
Orphans of the Storm '21
Hearts of the World '18
Home Sweet Home '14
Judith of Bethulia '14

Lillian Gish (1896-1993)
The Whales of August '87
Sweet Liberty '86
The Adventures of Huckleberry Finn '85
Hambone & Hillie '84
Hobson's Choice '83
A Wedding '78
The Comedians '67
Follow Me, Boys! '66
The Love Goddesses '65
The Unforgiven '60
The Cobweb '55
The Night of the Hunter '55
Portrait of Jennie '48
Duel in the Sun '46
Commandos Strike at Dawn '43
His Double Life '33
The Wind '28
Romola '25
The White Sister '23
Orphans of the Storm '21
Way Down East '20
Broken Blossoms '19
The Greatest Question '19
True Heart Susie '19
Hearts of the World '18
The Birth of a Nation '15
Home Sweet Home '14
Judith of Bethulia '14

Sheila Gish (1942-2005)
Highlander: Endgame '00
Mansfield Park '99
Jewels '92
Highlander '86

Neil Giuntoli
Henry: Portrait of a Serial Killer 2: Mask of Sanity '96
Memphis Belle '90
Capone '89

Paul(o) Giusti
Emmanuelle on Taboo Island '76
L'Annee Sainte '76

Adele Givens
Beauty Shop '05
Queens of Comedy '01
The Players Club '98

Robin Givens (1964-)
Head of State '03
Antibody '02
Blankman '94
Foreign Student '94
Boomerang '92
The Penthouse '92
A Rage in Harlem '91
The Women of Brewster Place '89

George Givot (1903-84)
China Gate '57
Lady and the Tramp '55 (V)
April in Paris '52
Du Barry Was a Lady '43
Leather Burners '43
Thin Ice '37
Hollywood Party '34

Liliana Glabczynska
See Liliana Komorowska

Frances Gladwin
Frontier Outlaws '44
Thundering Gunslingers '44

Etienne Glaser (1937-)
Speak Up! It's So Dark '93
The Mozart Brothers '86

Paul Michael Glaser (1943-)
Starsky & Hutch '04
Something's Gotta Give '03
Jealousy '84
Single Bars, Single Women '84
Wait Till Your Mother Gets Home '83
Phobia '80
Fiddler on the Roof '71

Ned Glass (1906-84)
Street Music '81
Kid Galahad '62
West Side Story '61
The Rebel Set '59
Fright '56
Requiem for a Heavyweight '56

Ron Glass (1945-)
Serenity '05
Back in Business '96
It's My Party '95
Houseguest '94
Deep Space '94

Seamon Glass (1925-)
The Surgeon '94
Death Ring '93
Forever Young '92
Pure Country '92
Winterhawk '76
This Is Not a Test '62

Isabel Glasser (1958-)
Tactical Assault '99
Second Chances '98
Mother '96
Circumstances Unknown '95

Phillip Glasser (1978-)
Voodoo Dawn '99
A Troll in Central Park '94 (V)
An American Tail: Fievel Goes West '91 (V)
Satan's Princess '90
An American Tail '86 (V)

Summer Glau (1982-)
Mammoth '06
Serenity '05

Bob Giaudini
Coastlines '02
Parasite '82
The Alchemist '81

Lola Giaudini (1971-)
Invincible '06
Groove '00

Louise Glaum (1900-70)
The Leopard Woman '20
Sex '20
Return of Draw Egan '16
The Three Musketeers '16

Karen Glave
Blind Faith '98
Last Night '98

Matthew Glave
Corky Romano '01
Rock Star '01
Mutiny '99
Ricochet River '98
Plump Fiction '97
True Women '97
The Wedding Singer '97
Baby's Day Out '94

Eugene Robert Glazer (1942-)
New Blood '99
It's My Party '95
Bounty Tracker '93
The Substitute '93
The Five Heartbeats '91
Stepping Out '91
Dollman '90
Eve of Destruction '90
Harlem Nights '89
I'm Gonna Git You Sucka '88
Stand and Deliver '88
Hollywood Shuffle '87
Hunter's Blood '87
No Way Out '87
Vendetta '85

Jackie Gleason (1916-87)
Nothing in Common '86
Izzy & Moe '85
Smokey and the Bandit, Part 3 '83
The Sting 2 '83
The Toy '82
Smokey and the Bandit 2 '80
Mr. Billion '77
Smokey and the Water '69
Don't Drink the Water '69
How to Commit Marriage '69
Papa's Delicate Condition '63
Soldier in the Rain '63
Requiem for a Heavyweight '62
The Hustler '61
All Through the Night '42
Orchestra Wives '42
Springtime in the Rockies '42

James Gleason (1886-1959)
Last Hurrah '58
Man or Gun '58
Loving You '57
Man in the Shadow '57
Rock-A-Bye Baby '57
The Night of the Hunter '55
Suddenly '54
Forever Female '53
Movie Stuntmen '53
We're Not Married '52
Down to Earth '47
The Bishop's Wife '47
Tycoon '47
The Clock '45
A Tree Grows in Brooklyn '45
Arsenic and Old Lace '44
A Guy Named Joe '44
The Keys of the Kingdom '44
Crash Dive '43
The Falcon Takes Over '42
Footlight Serenade '42
Tales of Manhattan '42
Here Comes Mr. Jordan '41
Meet John Doe '41
Tanks a Million '41
Ex-Mrs. Bradford '36
Hot Tip '35
Hoopla '33
The Crooked Circle '32
A Free Soul '31
Suicide Fleet '31

Joanna Gleason (1950-)
Wedding Daze '06
The Wedding Planner '01
Road Ends '98
Boogie Nights '97
If These Walls Could Talk '96
Edie & Pen '95
For Richer, for Poorer '92
F/X 2: The Deadly Art of Illusion '91
Crimes & Misdemeanors '89
Heartbeat '86

Mary Pat Gleason
I Now Pronounce You Chuck and Larry '07
Marilyn Hotchkiss' Ballroom Dancing & Charm School '06
Wristcutters: A Love Story '06
Underclassman '05
A Cinderella Story '04
Memron '04

Pat Gleason
Battling Marshal '48
Criminal Court '46
Detour '46
Rogue's Gallery '44
I Killed That Man '42
Swing It, Professor '37

Paul Gleason (1939-2006)
National Lampoon's Van Wilder '02
Not Another Teen Movie '01
Social Misfits '00
The Brutal Truth '99
No Code of Conduct '98
The Thin Red Line '98
Money Talks '97
The Shadow Conspiracy '96
Digital Man '94
I Love Trouble '94
Boiling Point '93
Maniac Cop 3: Badge of Silence '93
Running Cool '93
Wishman '93
There Goes My Baby '92
Wild Cactus '92
Rich Girl '91
Fourth Story '90
Miami Blues '90
Night Game '89
Die Hard '88
Ghost Chase '88
Johnny Be Good '88
She's Having a Baby '88
Forever, Lulu '87
Morgan Stewart's Coming Home '87
The Breakfast Club '85
Challenge of a Lifetime '85
The Ewoks: Battle for Endor '85
Trading Places '83
He Knows You're Alone '80
Doc Savage '75
Private Duty Nurses '71

Russell Gleason (1908-45)
Condemned to Live '35
Hot Tip '35
I Can't Escape '34
All Quiet on the Western Front '30
The Flying Fool '29

Nicholas Gleaves
Half Light '05
Poldark '96

Robert Gleckler (1887-1939)
Defenders of the Law '31
The Sea God '30

Brendan Gleeson (1954-)
In Bruges '08
Black Irish '07
Harry Potter and the Order of the Phoenix '07
Harry Potter and the Goblet of Fire '05
Kingdom of Heaven '05
In My Country '04
Troy '04
The Village '04
Cold Mountain '03
Dark Blue '03

Gangs of New York '02
Harrison's Flowers '02
28 Days Later '02
A. I.: Artificial Intelligence '01
Mission: Impossible 2 '00
The Tailor of Panama '01
Lake Placid '99
This Is My Father '98
The General '98
The Break '97
The Butcher Boy '97
Michael Collins '96
Trojan Eddie '96
Turbulence '96
Braveheart '95

Paul Gleeson
Komodo '99
Idiot Box '97

Redmond M. Gleeson
St. Patrick's Day '03
2 Brothers & a Bride '03

Iain Glen (1961-)
The Last Legion '07
Resident Evil: Extinction '07
Kingdom of Heaven '05
Tara Road '05
Resident Evil: Apocalypse '04
Darkness '02
Lara Croft: Tomb Raider '01
Beautiful Creatures '00
The Wyvern Mystery '00
Mararia '98
The Painted Lacy '97
The Young Americans '93
Fools of Fortune '90
Mountains of the Moon '90
Rosencrantz & Guildenstern Are Dead '90

J. Frank Glendon (1886-1937)
Lion's Den '36
Sucker Money '34
Border Romance '30
Horatio Hornblower: The Adventure Continues '01

Philip Glenister (1963)
Byron '03
Calendar Girls '03
The Other Boleyn Girl '03
State of Play '03
Vanity Fair '99

Robert Glenister (1960)
Sirens '02
Just Visiting '01

Montgomery Glenn
See Silvano Tranquilli

Roy Glenn (1905-71)
Guess Who's Coming to Dinner '67
Carmen Jones '54

Scott Glenn (1942-)
Jungle Drums of Africa '53
The Bourne Ultimatum '07
Freedom Writers '07
Puerto Vallarta Squeeze '04
A Painted House '03
Buffalo Soldiers '01
The Seventh Stream '01
The Shipping News '01
Training Day '01
Vertical Limit '00
The Virgin Suicides '99
The Last Marshal '99
Naked City: A Killer Christmas '98
Naked City: Justice with a Bullet '98
Absolute Power '97
Carla's Song '97
Firestorm '97
Courage Under Fire '96
Edie & Pen '95
Reckless '95

Tall Tale: The Unbelievable Adventures of Pecos Bill '95
Night of the Running Man '94
Past Tense '94
The Spy Within '94
Extreme Justice '93
Shadowhunter '93
Slaughter of the Innocents '93
The Player '92
Backdraft '91
My Heroes Have Always Been Cowboys '91
The Silence of the Lambs '91
Women & Men: In Love There Are No Rules '91
The Hunt for Red October '90
Intrigue '90
Miss Firecracker '89
Verne Miller '88
Man on Fire '87
Off Limits '87
As Summers Die '86
Silverado '85
Wild Geese 2 '85
The River '84
The Keep '83
The Right Stuff '83
The Challenge '82
Personal Best '82
Urban Cowboy '80
Apocalypse Now '79
More American Graffiti '79
She Came to the Valley '77
Fighting Mad '76
Nashville '75
The Shrieking '73
Angels Hard As They Come '71
The Baby Maker '70

Sharon Gless (1943-)
The State Within '06
Tales of the Unexpected '91

Stacey Glick (1971-)
The Crash of Flight 401 '78
Centennial '78

Brian Glover (1934-97)
Stiff Upper Lips '96
Royal Deceit '94
Leon the Pig Farmer '93
Alien 3 '92
Kafka '91
The Company of Wolves '85
The McGuffin '85
An American Werewolf in London '81
Brighton Beach Memoirs '86
Letting Go '85
Hobson's Choice '83
The Star Chamber '83
Hardhat & Legs '80
Revenge of the Stepford Wives '80
Come '71

Bruce Glover (1932-)
Night of the Scarecrow '95
Warlock: The Armageddon '93
Hider in the House '90
Killcrazy '89
Ghost Town '88
Big Bad Mama 2 '87
Stunts '77
Diamonds Are Forever '71
C.C. & Company '70
Chisum '70

Crispin Glover (1964-)
Beowulf '07 (V)
Epic Movie '07
Drop Dead Sexy '05
Charlie's Angels: Full Throttle '03
Willard '03
Like Mike '02
Bartleby '01
Charlie's Angels '01
Nurse Betty '00

The People vs. Larry Flynt '96
Dead Man '95
Chasers '94
Even Cowgirls Get the Blues '94
Hotel Room '93
What's Eating Gilbert Grape '93
Rubin & Ed '92
The Doors '91
Little Noises '91
Where the Heart Is '90
Back to the Future, Part 2 '89
Twister '89
River's Edge '87
At Close Range '86
Friday the 13th, Part 4: The Final Chapter '84
Racing with the Moon '84
Teachers '84
My Tutor '83

Danny Glover (1947-)
Be Kind Rewind '08
Honeydripper '07
Shooter '07
Barnyard '06 (V)
Dreamgirls '06
Poor Man's Game '06
The Shaggy Dog '06
Manderlay '05
The Cookout '04
Saw '04
Good Fences '03
The Royal Tenenbaums '01
3 A.M. '01
Boesman & Lena '00
Freedom Song '00
Antz '98 (V)
Beloved '98
Prince of Egypt '98 (V)
Buffalo Soldiers '97
Gone Fishin' '97
Switchback '97
America's Dream '95
Operation Dumbo Drop '95
Angels in the Outfield '94
Maverick '94
Bophal '93
Queen '93
The Saint of Fort Washington '93
Lethal Weapon 3 '92
Grand Canyon '91
Pure Luck '91
A Rage in Harlem '91
Predator 2 '90
To Sleep with Anger '90
Dead Man Out '89
Lethal Weapon 2 '89
Lonesome Dove '89
A Raisin in the Sun '89
Bat 21 '88
Out '88
Lethal Weapon '87
Mandela '87
The Color Purple '85
Silverado '85
Stand-In '85
Witness '85
Iceman '84
Places in the Heart '84
Memorial Day '83
Chu Chu & the Philly Flash '81
Keeping On '81
Escape from Alcatraz '79

Jamie Glover (1969-)
In His Life: The John Lennon Story '00

John Glover (1944-)
Joseph '95
On Edge '03
Dead Broke '99
Payback '99
Batman and Robin '97
Love! Valour! Compassion! '96
In the Mouth of Madness '95

Schemes '95
Assault at West Point: The Court-Martial of Johnson Whittaker '94
Night of the Running Man '94
Automatic '94
Ed and His Dead Mother '93
What Ever Happened To... '93
Drug Wars 2: The Cocaine Cartel '92
Dead on the Money '91
El Diablo '90
Gremlins 2: The New Batch '90
Meet the Hollowheads '89
Traveling Man '89
The Chocolate War '88
Masquerade '88
Rocket Gibraltar '88
Scrooged '88
Apology '86
52 Pick-Up '86
Something Special '86
An Early Frost '85
A Killing Affair '85
Ernie Kovacs: Between the Laughter '84
The Evil That Men Do '84
A Little Sex '82
The Mountain Men '80
Last Embrace '79
Annie Hall '77
Julia '77

Julian Glover (1935-)
Troy '04
Harry Potter and the Chamber of Secrets '02
Vatel '00
The Infiltrator '95
Indiana Jones and the Last Crusade '89
Treasure Island '89
Tusks '89
The Fourth Protocol '87
Hearts of Fire '87
Mandela '87
The Secret Garden '87
Kim '84
Heat and Dust '82
Ivanhoe '82
For Your Eyes Only '81
The Empire Strikes Back '80
Luther '74
The Story of Jacob & Joseph '74
Antony and Cleopatra '73
Theatre of Death '67
The Alphabet Murders '65
Girl with Green Eyes '64
Tom Jones '63

Kara Glover
The Beat '88
Caribe '87

Savion Glover (1973-)
Bojangles '01
Bamboozled '00
The Wall '99
Tap '89

Susan Glover
Jericho Mansions '03
Random Encounter '98
Eye '96

Vadim Glowna (1941-)
Agnes and His Brothers '04
Advertising Rules! '01
Cross of Iron '76

Carlin Glynn (1940-)
Judy Berlin '99
Blessing '94
Night Game '89
Blood Red '88
Gardens of Stone '87
The Trip to Bountiful '85
Sixteen Candles '83
Continental Divide '81

Mathias Gnaedinger (1941-)
Journey of Hope '90
The Boat Is Full '81

Hiromi Go (1955-)
Samurai Cowboy '93

George Gobel (1919-91)
MacArthur's Children '85
Ellie '84
Better Late Than Never '79
Rabbit Test '78
The Fantastic World of D.C. Collins '84

Justin Gocke (1978-)
Birds & the Bees '56
I Married a Woman '56

Jean-Luc Godard (1930-)
King Lear '87
First Name: Carmen '83
Contempt '64
Cleo from 5 to 7 '61
Le Petit Soldat '60

Alf Goddard (1897-1981)
Butler's Dilemma '43
Non-Stop New York '37

Mark Goddard (1936-)
Lost in Space '98
Strange Invaders '83
Roller Boogie '79
Blue Sunshine '78
The Death Squad '73

John Goddard
The Last Seduction 2 '98

Paul Goddard
Holy Smoke '99
The Matrix '99

Beth Goddard (1969-)
Take Me '01

Vanda Godsell (1919-90)
This Sporting Life '63
The Victors '63
Naked Youth '59
Storm Rider '57

Adam Godley
The X-Files: I Want to Believe '08

Alexander Godunov (1949-95)
The Runestone '91
North '94
Waxwork 2: Lost in Time '91
Die Hard '88
The Money Pit '86
Witness '85

Maurice Godin
Boat Trip '03
Double Take '97

Jacques Godin (1930-)
Being at Home with Claude '92

Judith Godreche (1972-)
L'Auberge Espagnole '02
Entropy '99
Quicksand '01
The Man in the Iron Mask '98

Ridicule '96
The Disenchanted '90
Sons '89

Patrick Godfrey (1933-)
The Importance of Being Earnest '02
Ever After: A Cinderella Story '98

Dave Goetz
Muppets from Space '99

Angela Goethals (1977-)
V.I. Warshawski '91
Home Alone '90
Heartbreak Hotel '88

Peter Michael Goetz (1941-)
The Empty Mirror '99
Infinity '96
The Buccaneers '95
Father of the Bride Part 2 '95
Father of the Bride '91
The Water Engine '92
Father of the Bride '91
My Girl '91
Tagget '90
Glory '89
Jumpin' Jack Flash '86
King Kong Lives '86
Beer '85
Wolfen '81

Trevor Goddard (1965-2003)
Pirates of the Caribbean: The Curse of the Black Pearl '03
Deac Tides '97
First Encounter '97
Shadow Warriors '97
Fast Money '96
Prey of the Jaguar '96
Yesterday's Target '96
Men of War '94

Arthur Godfrey (1903-83)
Angel's Brigade '79
Flatbed Annie and Sweetiepie: Lady Truckers '79
Great Bank Hoax '78
Where Angels Go, Trouble Follows '68
The Glass Bottom Boat '66
Four for Texas '63

Godfrey (1969-)
Soul Plane '06
Phat Girlz '06

Derek Godfrey (1924-83)
The Tempest '80
The Vengeance of She '68
A Midsummer Night's Dream '68
Hands of the Ripper '71

Bernhard Goetzke (1884-1964)
Dr. Mabuse, The Gambler '22
The Indian Tomb '21
Destiny '21

John Goff
Party Plane '90
Night Stalker '87
Getting Over '81

Norris Goff (1906-78)
Goin' to Town '44
Two Weeks to Live '43
So This Is Washington '43
The Bashful Bachelor '42

Dreaming Out Loud '40

Walton Goggins (1971-)
The Architect '06
House of 1000 Corpses '03
The Bourne Identity '02
Shanghai Noon '00
Daddy & Them '99
Red Dirt '99
Major League 3: Back to the Minors '98
The Apostle '97

Joanna Going (1963-)
Runaway Jury '03
Cupid & Cate '00
Heaven '99
Eden '98
Tom Clancy's Netforce '98
Inventing the Abbotts '97
Little City '97
Phantoms '97
Still Breathing '97
Commandments '96
Keys to Tulsa '96
A Good Day to Die '95
How to Make an American Quilt '95
Wyatt Earp '94

Gila Golan (1940-)
The Valley of Gwangi '69
Catch as Catch Can '68
Our Man Flint '66

Tracey Gold (1969-)
Dirty Little Secret '98
Wanted '98
The Perfect Daughter '96
Shoot the Moon '82

Adam Goldberg (1970-)
2 Days in Paris '07
Zodiac '07
Deja Vu '06
Keeping Up with the Steins '06
Stay Alive '06
How to Lose a Guy in 10 Days '03
The Salton Sea '02
All Over the Guy '01
A Beautiful Mind '01
Fast Sofa '01
Waking Life '01
EDtv '99
Babe: Pig in the City '98 (V)
Saving Private Ryan '98
Homeward Bound 2: Lost in San Francisco '96 (V)
Dazed and Confused '93

Whoopi Goldberg (1949-)
Everyone's Hero '06 (V)
Jiminy Glick in LaLa Wood '05
Racing Stripes '05 (V)
The Lion King 1 1/2 '04 (V)
Good Fences '03
Call Me Claus '01
Kingdom Come '01
Monkeybone '01
Rat Race '01
The Adventures of Rocky & Bullwinkle '00
More Dogs Than Bones '00
Alice in Wonderland '99
Girl, Interrupted '99
Jackie's Back '99
The Magical Legend of the Leprechauns '99
The Deep End of the Ocean '98
How Stella Got Her Groove Back '98
A Knight in Camelot '98
An Alan Smithee Film: Burn, Hollywood, Burn '97
Cinderella '97
In the Gloaming '97
The Associate '96
Bogus '96
Eddie '96
Ghosts of Mississippi '96
Moonlight and Valentino '95
The Sunshine Boys '95
Theodore Rex '95
Boys on the Side '94
Corrina, Corrina '94
The Lion King '94 (V)
The Little Rascals '94
The Pagemaster '94 (V)
Star Trek: Generations '94
Made in America '93
Naked in New York '93
Sister Act 2: Back in the Habit '93
The Player '92
Sarafina! '92
Sister Act '92
Soapdish '91
Ghost '90
Homer and Eddie '89
Kiss Shot '89
The Long Walk Home '89
Clara's Heart '88
Burglar '87
Fatal Beauty '87
The Telephone '87
Jumpin' Jack Flash '86
The Color Purple '85

Jeff Goldblum (1952-)
Fay Grim '06
Man of the Year '06
Pittsburgh '06
The Life Aquatic with Steve Zissou '04
Dallas 362 '03
Igby Goes Down '02
Cats & Dogs '01
Perfume '01
Beyond Suspicion '00
Chain of Fools '00
Holy Man '98
Prince of Egypt '98 (V)
The Lost World: Jurassic Park 2 '97
The Great White Hype '96
Independence Day '96
Trigger Happy '96
Nine Months '95
Powder '95
Hideaway '94
Lush Life '94
Jurassic Park '93
Deep Cover '92
Fathers and Sons '92
The Favor, the Watch, & the Very Big Fish '92
The Player '92
Shooting Elizabeth '92
Framed '90
Twisted Obsession '90
Earth Girls Are Easy '89
Mr. Frost '89
The Tall Guy '89
Vibes '88
Beyond Therapy '86
The Fly '86
Into the Night '85
Silverado '85
Transylvania 6-5000 '85
The Adventures of Buckaroo Banzai Across the 8th Dimension '84
Ernie Kovacs: Between the Laughter '84
The Sentinel '76
Special Delivery '76
Nashville '75
Death Wish '74

Annie Golden (1951-)
Tom and Francie '05
It Runs in the Family '03
One Way Out '95
The Pebble and the Penguin '94 (V)
Baby Boom '87
Forever, Lulu '87
Love at Stake '87
National Lampoon's Class of '86 '86
Desperately Seeking Susan '85
Key Exchange '85
Streetwalkin' '85
Hair '79

Norman D. Golden, II (1984-)
Moby Dick '98
America's Dream '95
Cop and a Half '93

Olive Golden
See Olive Carey

Devin Goldenberg
Fanatic '82
Cry Uncle '71
Guess What We Learned in School Today? '70

Heather Goldenhersch (1973-)
Wedding Daze '06
Southern Belles '05
Kinsey '04
The Merchant of Venice '04
Spin the Bottle '97

Goldie (1965-)
B.U.S.T.E.D. '99
The World Is Not Enough '99

Ricky Paull Goldin (1968-)
Pastime '91
Mirror, Mirror '90
Lambada '89
The Blob '88

Danny Goldman
Where the Buffalo Roam '80
Swap Meet '79

Lelia Goldoni (1937-)
Choices '81
Bloodbrothers '78
Fatal Chase '77
The Spell '77
The Disappearance of Aimee '76
Theatre of Death '67
Shadows '60

Renee Goldsberry
Pistol Whipped '08
All About You '01

Clio Goldsmith (1957-)
Heat of Desire '84
La Cicada '83
Honey '81

Jonathan Goldsmith
Phantom of the Mall: Eric's Revenge '89
Go Tell the Spartans '78

Jenette Goldstein (1960-)
Home Room '02
Fair Game '95
Dead to Rights '93
Lethal Weapon 2 '89
The Presidio '88
Near Dark '87
Aliens '86

Bob(cat) Goldthwait (1962-)
Blow '01
Hercules '97 (V)
Sweethearts '97
Back to Back '96
Destiny Turns on the Radio '95
Out There '95
Radioland Murders '94
Freaked '93 (V)
Shakes the Clown '92
Little Vegas '90
Tapeheads '89
Hot to Trot! '88
Scrooged '88
Burglar '87
Police Academy 4: Citizens on Patrol '87
One Crazy Summer '86
Police Academy 3: Back in Training '86

Tony Goldwyn (1960-)
American Gun '05
Ghosts Never Sleep '05
The Sisters '05
The Last Samurai '03
Abandon '02
Joshua '02
An American Rhapsody '01
The Song of the Lark '01
Bounce '00
The 6th Day '00
Tarzan '99 (V)
From the Earth to the Moon '98
Kiss the Girls '97
The Lesser Evil '97
The Boys Next Door '96
The Substance of Fire '96
The Last Word '95
Nixon '95
Pocahontas: The Legend '95
Reckless '95
Truman '95
Doomsday Gun '94
A Woman of Independent Means '94
Love Matters '93
The Pelican Brief '93
Taking the Heat '93
Kuffs '92
Traces of Red '92
Iran: Days of Crisis '91
Ghost '90
Gaby: A True Story '87

Valeria Golino (1966-)
Frida '02
Respiro '02
Things You Can Tell Just by Looking at Her '00
Harem '99
Spanish Judges '99
Escape from L.A. '96
An Occasional Hell '96
Four Rooms '95
Leaving Las Vegas '95
Clean Slate '94
Immortal Beloved '94
Hot Shots! Part Deux '93
Year of the Gun '91
The Indian Runner '91
The King's Whore '90
Torrents of Spring '90
Rain Man '88
A Joke of Destiny, Lying in Wait Around the Corner Like a Bandit '84

Lisa Golm (1891-1964)
Come Back, Little Sheba '52
The Hoodlum '51

Arlene Golonka (1939-)
A Family Affair '01
The Gumshoe Kid '89
Dr. Alien '88
Trained to Kill '88
Foxtrap '85
My Tutor '82
Long Shot Kids '81
The In-Laws '79

Marina Golovine
Olivier, Olivier '92
The Stolen Children '92

Yekaterina (Katia) Golubeva
The Intruder '04
Twentynine Palms '03
Pola X '99
I Can't Sleep '93

Minna Gombell (1892-1973)
I'll See You in My Dreams '51
Pagan Love Song '50
The Best Years of Our Lives '46
Doomed Caravan '41
Second Fiddle '39
The Great Waltz '38
The Merry Widow '34
No More Women '34
The Thin Man '34
Hoopla '33

Carlos Gomez (1962-)
House of Sand and Fog '03
The Negotiator '98
The Replacement Killers '98
Asteroid '97
Fools Rush In '97
The Peacemaker '97
Desperado '95
Bitter Vengeance '94
Hostile Intentions '94
Silhouette '91

Carmelo Gomez
The Method '05
Between Your Legs '99
Maraia '98
Secrets of the Heart '97
Tierra '95
Running Out of Time '94
The Red Squirrel '93
Vacas '91

Ian Gomez (1964-)
Underclassman '05
Connie and Carla '04
The Last Shot '04
Chasing Papi '03
Get a Clue '02
My Big Fat Greek Wedding '02

Jaime Gomez (1965-)
Devil's Knight '03
Gabriela '01
Training Day '01
Solo '96

Jose Luis Gomez (1940-)
Goya's Ghosts '06
Rowing with the Wind '88
Roads to the South '78
In Memoriam '76

Panchito Gomez (1963-)
Saints and Sinners '95
Mi Vida Loca '94
Sweet 15 '90
Paco '75

Rick Gomez (1972-)
Sin City '05
Ray '04
11:14 '03
Band of Brothers '01

Thomas Gomez (1905-71)
Beneath the Planet of the Apes '70
Stay Away, Joe '68
Summer and Smoke '61
But Not for Me '59
The Conqueror '56
Trapeze '56
The Magnificent Matador '55
The Merry Widow '52
Force of Evil '49
Sorrowful Jones '49
Casbah '48
Key Largo '48
Captain from Castile '47
Singapore '47
Can't Help Singing '45
The Climax '44
In Society '44
Phantom Lady '44
Pittsburgh '42

Marina Goncalves (1933-)
Carandiru '03
Orfeu '99
Subway to the Stars '87
Kiss of the Spider Woman '85

Stella Gonet (1963-)
Nicholas Nickleby '02
The Crow Road '96
The House of Eliott '92

Mascha Gonska
Tea for Three '84
The Infernal Trio '74

George Gonzales (1967-)
The Bad News Bears Go to Japan '78
The Bad News Bears in Breaking Training '77
The Bad News Bears '76

Augustin Gonzalez (1930-2005)
Caresses '97
The Nest '80

Rick Gonzalez (1979-)
Illegal Tender '07
Pulse '06
Coach Carter '05
Roll Bounce '05
War of the Worlds '05
Biker Boyz '03
Old School '03
The Rookie '02

Pedro Gonzalez-Gonzalez (1925-2006)
Lust in the Dust '85
Rio Bravo '59
The Young Land '59

Julie Gonzalo (1981-)
Cherry Crush '07
Must Love Dogs '05
Christmas With the Kranks '04
A Cinderella Story '04

Christopher Good
Bullshot '83
A Bridge Too Far '77

Meagan Good (1981-)
The Love Guru '08
One Missed Call '08
Stomp the Yard '07
Brick '06
Waist Deep '06
Roll Bounce '05
Venom '05
The Cookout '04
D.E.B.S. '04
You Got Served '04
Biker Boyz '03
Deliver Us from Eva '03
Three Strikes '00
The Secret Life of Girls '99
Eve's Bayou '97

Caroline Goodall (1959-)
The Thief Lord '06
The Chumscrubber '05
Chasing Liberty '04
The Princess Diaries 2: Royal Engagement '04
Harrison's Flowers '02
Me & Mrs. Jones '02
Mists of Avalon '01
The Princess Diaries '01
Casualties '97
The Sculptress '97
White Squall '96
Sorrento Beach '95
At Home with the Webbers '94
Disclosure '94
Cliffhanger '93
Schindler's List '93
The Silver Stallion: King of the Wild Brumbies '93
Hook '91
The Moon Stallion '85

Matthew Goode (1978-)
The Lookout '07
Imagine Me & You '06
Match Point '05

Grant Goodeve (1952-)
Take Two '87
Hot Rod '79
Last Cry for Help '79

Cuba Gooding, Jr. (1968-)
Hero Wanted '08
American Gangster '07
Daddy Day Camp '07
Norbit '07
What Love Is '07
End Game '06
Shadowboxer '06
Dirty '05
Home on the Range '04 (V)
Boat Trip '03
The Fighting Temptations '03
Radio '03
Snow Dogs '02
In the Shadows '01
Pearl Harbor '01
Rat Race '01
Men of Honor '00
Chill Factor '99
Instinct '99

A Murder of Crows '99
What Dreams May Come '98
Jerry Maguire '96
As Good As It Gets '97
The Tuskegee Airman '95
Lightning Jack '94
Losing Isaiah '94
Outbreak '95
Daybreak '93
Judgment Night '93
A Few Good Men '92
Gladiator '92
Murder Without Motive '92
Boyz N the Hood '91
Hitz '89
Coming to America '88

Omar Gooding (1976-)
The Gospel '05
Baby Boy '01

Michael Goodliffe (1914-76)
To the Devil, a Daughter '76
Macbeth '70
Von Ryan's Express '65
The Gorgon '64
The Seventh Dawn '64
The Battle of the Sexes '60
Sink the Bismarck '60
A Night to Remember '58
Up the Creek '58
The Way Out '56

Benny Goodman (1909-86)
A Song is Born '48
The Gang's All Here '43
Stage Door Canteen '43

Brian Goodman
Annapolis '06

Dody Goodman (1929-)
Frozen Assets '92
Cool As Ice '91
Private Resort '84
Splash '84
Grease '78
Bedtime Story '63

Henry Goodman
Hannibal '01
Deconstructing Harry '97

Hazelle Goodman (1959-)

John Goodman (1952-)
Beyond the Sea '04
Green Street Hooligans '05
Clifford's Really Big Movie '04 (V)
Masked and Anonymous '03
Dirty Deeds '02
Monsters, Inc. '01 (V)
My First Mister '01
One Night at McCool's '01
Storytelling '01
The Adventures of Rocky & Bullwinkle '00
Coyote Ugly '00
O Brother Where Art Thou? '00
What Planet Are You From? '00
Bringing Out the Dead '99
The Jack Bull '99
The Runner '99
Blues Brothers 2000 '98
The Borrowers '97
The Big Lebowski '98 (V)
The Real Macaw '98 (V)
Dirty Work '97
Fallen '97
Mother Night '96
Kingfish: A Story of Huey P. Long '95
Pie in the Sky '95
A Streetcar Named Desire '95
The Flintstones '94
Born Yesterday '93
We're Back! A Dinosaur's Story '93 (V)
The Babe '92
Matinee '92
Barton Fink '91
King Ralph '91
Arachnophobia '90
Always '89
Sea of Love '89
Stella '89
Everybody's All American '88
Punchline '88
The Wrong Guys '88
The Big Easy '87
Burglar '87
Raising Arizona '87
True Stories '86
Sweet Dreams '85
C.H.U.D. '84
Maria's Lovers '84
Revenge of the Nerds '84
Survivors '83

Julia Goodman
Twenty-One '91
This Lightning Always Strikes Twice '85

Deborah Goodrich
Remote Control '88
Survival Game '87
April Fool's Day '86

Joe Goodrich
Axe '06
Monster Man '03

Garry Goodrow (1938-)
The Hollywood Knights '80
Cardiac Arrest '74
Steelyard Blues '73
A Session with The Committee '68
The Connection '61

Bernard Gorcey (1886-1955)
Bowery Boys Meet the Monsters '54
Clipped Wings '53
Ghost Chasers '51
Blues Busters '50
Spook Busters '48
Bowery Buckaroos '47
Hard-Boiled Mahoney '47

Leo Gorcey (1915-69)
It's a Mad, Mad, Mad, Mad World '63
Bowery Boys Meet the Monsters '54
Clipped Wings '53
Here Come the Marines '52
Ghost Chasers '51
Blues Busters '50
Master Minds '49
She Shoulda Said No '49
Spook Busters '48
Bowery Buckaroos '47
Hard-Boiled Mahoney '47
Junior G-Men of the Air '42
Mr. Wise Guy '42
Flying Wild '41
Pride of the Bowery '41
Prairie Moon '38

Bill Goodwin (1910-58)
The Atomic Kid '54
Lucky Me '54
It's a Great Feeling '49
Jolson Sings Again '49
Mickey '48
House of Horrors '46
The Jolson Story '46
To Each His Own '46
The Stork Club '45
Bathing Beauty '44
So Proudly We Hail '43
Wake Island '42

Angela Goodwin (1925-)
Julia and Julia '87
Autopsy '74

Alexander Goodwin
The Prince '95
Mimic '97
Box of Moonlight '96

David Gorcey (1921-84)
Bowery Boys Meet the Monsters '54
Clipped Wings '53
Ghost Chasers '51
Blues Busters '50
Master Minds '49
Spook Busters '48
Bowery Buckaroos '47
Hard-Boiled Mahoney '47
Junior G-Men of the Air '42
Mr. Wise Guy '42
Flying Wild '41
Pride of the Bowery '41
Prairie Moon '38

Harold Goodwin (1902-87)
The Bridge on the River Kwai '57
Abbott and Costello Meet the Keystone Kops '54
Million Dollar Kid '44
Clancy Street Boys '43
Destroyer '43
Ghost on the Loose '43
Kid Dynamite '43
Let's Get Tough '42
Mr. Wise Guy '42
'Neath Brooklyn Bridge '42
Smart Alecks '42
Bowery Blitzkrieg '41
Flying Wild '41
Spooks Run Wild '41
Boys of the City '40
That Gang of Mine '40
Pleasure '31
All Quiet on the Western Front '30
College '27
Front '30

Kia Joy Goodwin

Laurel Goodwin (1942-)
Swinian '02
Strapped '93
Sizzle '81

Raven Goodwin (1992-)
The Station Agent '03
Lovely & Amazing '02

Malcolm Goodwin
The Longshots '08

Michael Goodwin
Color of Justice '97
The Dead Pool '88
Date with an Angel '87

Michael Goorjian (1971-)
Deal of a Lifetime '99
The Invisibles '99
Silent Witness '99
Hard Rain '97
Something More '99
SLC Punk! '99

Barbara Gordon
Skinwalkers '07
Cube 2: Hypercube '02
Men with Brooms '02
Deadline Assault '90
Mannequin '87

Howard Goorney (1921-2007)
The Hill '65
Bedazzled '68

Allen Goorwitz
See Allen (Goorwitz) Garfield

Alicia (Lecy) Goranson (1974-)
Love, Ludlow '05
Boys Don't Cry '99
How to Make an American Quilt '95

C. Henry Gordon (1883-1940)
Charlie Chan at the Wax Museum '40
Charlie Chan in City of Darkness '39
Charlie Chan at the Olympics '37
The Charge of the Light Brigade '36
The Crusades '35
Gabriel Over the White House '33
Penthouse '33
Rasputin and the Empress '33
The Crooked Circle '32
Mata Hari '32
Th'e Strange Love o' Nolly Louvain '32
State's Attorney '31

Ben Gordon
Goof Balls '87
Utilities '83

Barry J. Gordon (1948-)
Body Slam '87
A Thousand Clowns '65

Del Gordon

Dexter Gordon (1923-90)
Awakenings '90
Round Midnight '86

Colin Gordon (1911-72)
The Body Beneath '70
Burn Witch, Burn! '62
The Key Man '57
One That Got Away '57
John and Julie '55

Carl Gordon (1932-)
Love Songs '99
The Piano Lesson '94

Don Gordon (1926-)
The Borrower '89
The Beast Within '82
The Final Conflict '81
The Education of Sonny Carson '74
The Mack '73
Slaughter '72
Zero Population Growth '72
Bullitt '68

Dorothy Gordon (1924-)
Where the Money Is '00

Eve Gordon
I'll Be Home for Christmas '98

Elizabeth Gorcey (1962-)
Iced '88
The Trouble with Dick '88

Gavin Gordon (1901-83)
Angels with Dirty Faces '38
Little Tough Guys '38
Dead End '37
Love at First Bite '79
A Thousand Clowns '65
The Girl Can't Help It '56
Pressure Point '62
The Bat '59
Speedway '68
The Matchmaker '58
I Killed That Man '42
Turf Boy '42
Gangs, Inc. '41
The Bride of Frankenstein '35
The Bitter Tea of General Yen '33
Female '33
American Madness '32
Romance '30
The Silver Horde '30
His First Command '29

Gerald Gordon (1934-2001)
Ants '77
Force Five '75
Hell Up in Harlem '73

James Gordon (1881-1941)
Trailin' '21
The Last of the Mohicans '20

Keith Gordon (1961-)
I Love Trouble '94
Wings '27
Static '87
Back to School '86
Combat Academy '86
Legend of Billie Jean '85
Christine '84
Single Bars, Single Women '84
Dressed to Kill '80
Home Movies '79
Jaws 2 '78

Julia Swayne Gordon (1879-1933)
It '27
Wings '27

Susan Gordon (1949-)
Picture Mommy Dead '66
Tormented '60
Attack of the Puppet People '58
People '58
Stop-Loss '08

Serena Gordon (1963-)
The Aristocrats '93
GoldenEye '95
A Tale of Two Cities '89

Gale Gordon (1906-95)
The 'Burbs '89
Speedway '68
The 30-Foot Bride of Candy Rock '59
Rock '59
Rally 'Round the Flag, Boys! '58
Our Miss Brooks '56
Francis Covers the Big Town '53
Here We Go Again! '42
They Made Me a Criminal '39

Roy Gordon (1896-1978)
The Wasp Woman '59
Attack of the 50 Foot Woman '58
The Real Glory '39

Ruth Gordon (1896-1985)
The Big Bus '76
Harold and Maude '71
Where's Poppa? '70
Whatever Happened to Aunt Alice? '69
Rosemary's Baby '68
Lord Love a Duck '66
Inside Daisy Clover '65
Action in the North Atlantic '43
Edge of Darkness '43
Two-Faced Women '41
Abe Lincoln in Illinois '40

Philip Gordon
Boogeyman '05
The Bridge to Nowhere '86
Came a Hot Friday '85

Pamela Gordon (1937-2003)
Baadasssss! '03
Bloodtight: Subspecies 3 '93
Bloodstone: Subspecies 2 '92

Leo Gordon (1922-2000)
Alienator '89
Bog '84
Devil's Angels '67
Kitten with a Whip '64
The Haunted Palace '63
Kings of the Sun '63
Shane '67
The Jayhawkers '59
Seventh Cavalry '56
Soldier of Fortune '55
Riot in Cell Block 11 '54
Ten Wanted Men '54
Hondo '53

Lucy Gordon (1980-)
Russian Dolls '05
Spider-Man 3 '07

Mary Gordon (1882-1963)
Little Giant '46
The Woman in Green '45
Follow the Leader '44
Million Dollar Kid '44
Boss of Big Town '43
Sherlock Holmes and the Secret Weapon '43
Sherlock Holmes and the Voice of Terror '42
The Adventures of Sherlock Holmes '39
Double Wedding '37
Texas Cyclone '32

Charles Gordone (1925-95)
Angel Heart '87
Streetfight '75

Joseph Gordon-Levitt (1981-)
The Lookout '07
Brick '06
Shadowboxer '06
Latter Days '04
Mysterious Skin '04
Treasure Planet '02 (V)
Manic '01
Along for the Ride '00
Picking Up the Pieces '99
Ten Things I Hate about You '99
Halloween: H20 '98
Sweet Jane '98
The Juror '96
The Great Elephant '95
Escape '95
Angels in the Outfield '94
Holy Matrimony '94

Honey, We Shrunk Ourselves '97
The Heidi Chronicles '95
Leaving Normal '92
The Secret Passion of Robert Clayton '92
Paradise '91
Switched at Birth '91
Avalon '90

Sandy Gore (1950-)
Wrangler '88
Street Hero '84

Galyn Gorg (1964-)
Angel Heart '87
Streetfight '75
RoboCop 2 '90
Body Beat '88
Malibu Bikini Shop '86

Mel Gorham (1959-)
The Center of the World '01
Wishful Thinking '96
Blue in the Face '95
Curdled '95
Smoke '95

Marius Goring (1012-1998)
Charlie Boy '81
Holocaust '78
Zeppelin '71
Exodus '60
The Unstoppable Man '59
The Moonraker '58
Night Ambush '57
The Barefoot Contessa '54
Paris Express '53
The Red Shoes '48
Stairway to Heaven '46
The Case of the Frightened Lady '39
Spy in Black '39

Esther Gorintin (1913-)
Since Otar Left...' '03
Carnage '02

Buddy Gorman (1921-)
Ghost Chasers '51
Mr. Muggs Rides Again '45

Cliff Gorman (1936-2002)
King of the Jungle '01
Ghost Dog: The Way of the Samurai '99
The '60s '99
Down Came a Blackbird '94
Hoffa '92
Night and the City '92
Angel '84
Night of the Juggler '80
All That Jazz '79
An Unmarried Woman '78
Rosebud '75
Strike Force '75
Class of 63 '73
Cops and Robbers '73
The Boys in the Band '70

Jonathan Gorman
Gang Justice '94
Street Soldiers '91

Patrick Gorman
Gods and Generals '03
Gettysburg '93

Robert Gorman (1980-)
Leprechaun '93
Mr. Nanny '93

Eydie Gorme (1931-)
Ocean's Eleven '01

Peggy Gormley
The Sleepy Time Gal '01
Bad Lieutenant '92

Karen (Lynn) Gorney (1945-)
Ripe '97
The Hard Way '91
Saturday Night Fever '77

Walt Gorney (1912-2004)
Friday the 13th, Part 2 '81
Friday the 13th '80

Frederic Gorny (1973-)
Jeanne and the Perfect Guy '98
Wild Reeds '94

Irene Gorovaia (1989-)
The Butterfly Effect '04
It Runs in the Family '03

Ashley Gorrell
Mail to the Chief '00

Frank Gorshin (1934-2005)
Beethoven's 3rd '00
Luck of the Draw '00
Man of the Century '99
Bloodmoon '97
The Twilight of the Ice Nymphs '97
12 Monkeys '95
Hail Caesar '94
Amorel '93
The Meteor Man '93
Body Trouble '92
Sweet Justice '92
Beverly Hills Bodysnatchers '89
Midnight '89
Hollywood Vice Sqaud '86
Hot Resort '85
The Uppercrust '81
Underground Aces '80
Sky Heist '75
Batman '66
That Darn Cat '65
The Great Impostor '61
Studs Lonigan '60
Where the Boys Are '60
Dragstrip Girl '57
Invasion of the Saucer Men '57
Between Heaven and Hell '56

Marjoe Gortner (1944-)
Wild Bill '95
Fire, Ice and Dynamite '91
American Ninja 3: Blood Hunt '89
The Survivalist '87
Hellhole '85
Jungle Warriors '84
Mausoleum '83
Acapulco Gold '78
Star Crash '78
Sidewinder One '77
Viva Knievel '77
Bobbie Jo and the Outlaw '76
Food of the Gods '76
Earthquake '74
Pray for the Wildcats '74
Marjoe '72

Ryan Gosling (1980-)
Fracture '07
Lars and the Real Girl '07
Half Nelson '06
Stay '05
The Notebook '04
United States of Leland '03
Murder by Numbers '02
The Believer '01
The Slaughter Rule '01
Remember the Titans '00

David Goss
Hollywood Cop '87
She '83

Luke Goss (1968-)
Hellboy 2: The Golden Army '08
Unearthed '07
Cold and Dark '05
The Man '05
Charlie '04
Silver Hawk '04
Blade 2 '02
ZigZag '02

Jean-Rene Gossart
Emmanuelle 6 '88
Panther Squad '84

Mark Paul Gosselaar (1974-)
Dead Man on Campus '97
Specimen '97
Kounterfeit '96
Twisted Love '95
The St. Tammany Miracle '94

Louis Gossett, Jr. (1936-)
Cover '08
Daddy's Little Girls '07
All In '06
Jasper, Texas '03
Momentum '03
What About Your Friends: Weekend Getaway '02
The Inspectors 2: A Shred of Evidence '00
The Highway Man '99
Love Songs '99
Strange Justice: The Clarence Thomas and Anita Hill Story '99
Y2K '99
The Inspectors '98
Bram Stoker's The Mummy '97
In His Father's Shoes '97
Inside '96
Run for the Dream: The Gail Devers Story '96
Iron Eagle 4 '95
Zooman '95
Curse of the Starving Class '94
Flashfire '94
A Good Man in Africa '94
Dangerous Relations '93
Return to Lonesome Dove '93
Diggstown '92
Keeper of the City '92
Cover-Up '91
Murder on the Bayou '91
Toy Soldiers '91
El Diablo '90
The Josephine Baker Story '90
The Punisher '90
Straight Up '90
Sudie & Simpson '90
Zora Is My Name! '90
Goodbye, Miss 4th of July '88
Iron Eagle 2 '88
Roots: The Gift '88
The Father Clements Story '87
The Principal '87
Firewalker '86
Iron Eagle '86
Enemy Mine '85
Finders Keepers '84
The Guardian '84
Jaws 3 '83
Sadat '83
Don't Look Back: The Story of Leroy "Satchel" Paige '81
Backstairs at the White House '79
The Lazarus Syndrome '79
He Who Walks Alone '78
It Rained All Night the Day I Left '78
The Choirboys '77
The Deep '77
Little Ladies of the Night '77
J.D.'s Revenge '76
The River Niger '76
The White Dawn '75
It's Good to Be Alive '74
The Laughing Policeman '74
Travels with My Aunt '72
Skin Game '71
The Bushbaby '70
A Raisin in the Sun '61

Robert Gossett (1954-)
Jimmy Zip '00
Arlington Road '99

Roland Got (1916-48)
G-Men vs. the Black Dragon '43
Across the Pacific '42

Walter Gotell (1925-97)
Prince Valiant '97
Puppet Master 3: Toulon's Revenge '90
Sleepaway Camp 2: Unhappy Campers '88
The Living Daylights '87
Basic Training '86
For Your Eyes Only '81
Moonraker '79
The Spy Who Loved Me '77
Lord Jim '65
From Russia with Love '63
The Guns of Navarone '61

Michael Gothard (1939-93)
Lifeforce '85
For Your Eyes Only '81
King Arthur, the Young Warlord '75
Young Warlord '75
The Devils '71
The Valley Obscured by the Clouds '70

Gilbert Gottfried (1955-)
Dr. Dolittle '98 (V)
Def Jam's How to Be a Player '97
Aladdin and the King of Thieves '96 (V)
The Return of Jafar '94 (V)
Silk Degrees '94
Thumbelina '94 (V)
Aladdin '92 (V)
Highway to Hell '92
Problem Child 2 '91
Problem Child '90
Beverly Hills Cop 2 '87
Bad Medicine '85

Carl Gottlieb (1938-)
The Jerk '79
Cannonball '76
Jaws '75
M*A*S*H '70
A Session with The Committee '68

Theodore Gottlieb
See Brother Theodore

John Gottowt (1881-1942)
Waxworks '24
Nosferatu '22

Ferdinand Gottschalk (1869-1944)
Sing Sing Nights '35
King Kelly of the U.S.A. '34
Ex-Lady '33
Female '33
Tonight or Never '31

Thomas Gottschalk (1950-)
Ring of the Musketeers '93
Sister Act 2: Back in the Habit '93
Driving Me Crazy '91

Jetta Goudal (1891-1985)
White Gold '28
The Coming of Amos '25
The Road to Yesterday '25

Lloyd Gough
Storm Warning '51
Tension '50

Michael Gough (1917-)
A Southern Yankee '48
Uncovered '94
The Advocate '93
The Age of Innocence '93
Nostradamus '93
Wittgenstein '93
Batman Returns '92
Let Him Have It '91
Strapless '90
Batman '89
The Shell Seekers '89
Batman and Robin '97
Batman Forever '95
A Village Affair '95
The Fourth Protocol '87
The Serpent and the Rainbow '87
Caravaggio '86
Out of Africa '85
Oxford Blues '84
Top Secret! '84
To the Lighthouse '83
Venom '82
Smiley's People '82
Horror Hospital '73
The Legend of Hell House '73
Savage Messiah '72
The Go-Between '71
Women in Love '70
Crucible of Horror '69
The Crimson Cult '68
They Came from Beyond Space '67
Dr. Terror's House of Horrors '65
The Skull '65
The Phantom of the Opera '62
What a Carve-Up! '62
The Horror of Dracula '58
The Horse's Mouth '58
Richard III '55
Rob Roy—The Highland Rogue '53
The Sword & the Rose '53
The Small Back Room '49
Anna Karenina '48
Blanche Fury '48

Alexander Gould (1994-)
Bambi II '06 (V)
How to Eat Fried Worms '06
Finding Nemo '03 (V)
Wes Craven Presents: They '02

Ben Gould (1980-)
Mexico City '00
Home Room '02
Frankenstein Reborn '98

Dominic Gould (1964-)
The Butterfly '02
Close to Leo '02

Elliott Gould (1938-)
Ocean's Thirteen '07
Saving Sarah Cain '07
Masters of Horror: The Screwfly Solution '06
Ocean's Twelve '04
Ocean's Eleven '01
Playing Mona Lisa '00
Picking Up the Pieces '99
American History X '98
The Big Hit '98
City of Industry '96
November Conspiracy '96
A Boy Called Hate '95
Cover Me '95
The Dangerous '95
The Feminine Touch '95
The Glass Shield '95
Kicking and Screaming '95
Bleeding Hearts '94
Amore! '93
Beyond Justice '92
The Player '92
Wet and Wild Summer '92
Bugsy '91
Dead Men Don't Die '91
Inside Out '91
The Lemon Sisters '90
My Wonderful Life '90
Hitz '89
Night Visitor '89
Vanishing Act '88
Conspiracy: The Trial of the Chicago Eight '87
Dangerous Love '87
Lethal Obsession '87
The Telephone '87
The Naked Face '84
Jack & the Beanstalk '83
Over the Brooklyn Bridge '83
The Devil & Max Devlin '81
Dirty Tricks '81
Falling in Love Again '80
The Last Flight of Noah's Ark '80
Escape to Athena '79
The Lady Vanishes '79
The Muppet Movie '79
Capricorn One '78
Matilda '78
The Silent Partner '78
A Bridge Too Far '77
Harry & Walter Go to New York '76
I Will, I Will for Now '76
Mean Johnny Barrows '75
Nashville '75
Roboman '75
Whiffs '75
Busting '74
S*P*Y*S '74
The Long Goodbye '73
Little Murders '71
Quick, Let's Get Married '71
The Touch '71
Getting Straight '70
I Love My... Wife '70
M*A*S*H '70
Bob & Carol & Ted & Alice '69
The Night They Raided Minsky's '69

Harold Gould (1923-)
Brother Bear '03 (V)
Freaky Friday '03
Master of Disguise '02
Brown's Requiem '98
My Giant '98
Patch Adams '98
The Love Bug '97
Killer: A Journal of Murder '95
Get Smart, Again! '89
Romero '89
Playing for Keeps '86
Fourth Wise Man '85
The Red Light Sting '84
Kenny Rogers as the Gambler, Part 2: The Adventure Continues '83
Dream Chasers '82
Help Wanted: Male '82
Kenny Rogers as the Gambler '80
Seems Like Old Times '80
Better Late Than Never '79
Actor: The Paul Muni Story '78
The One and Only '78
How to Break Up a Happy Divorce '76
Love and Death '75
The Strongest Man in the World '75
The Sting '73

Jason Gould (1966-)
Subterfuge '98
The Prince of Tides '91
The Big Picture '89
Say Anything '89

William (Bill) Gould (1915-60)
Man from Montana '41
Tanks a Million '41
Lightning Strikes West '40
Wild Horse Rodeo '37
Fast Bullets '36
Pinto Rustlers '36
Rio Rattler '35
Swifty '35
Phantom Thunderbolt '33
The Phantom '31

Robert Goulet (1933-2007)
Toy Story 2 '99 (V)
Mr. Wrong '95
Based on an Untrue Story '93
Naked Gun 2 1/2: The Smell of Fear '91
Beetlejuice '88
Scrooged '88
Gay Purr-ee '62 (V)

Olivier Gourmet (1963-)
The Child '05
Time of the Wolf '03
Read My Lips '01
Rosetta '99
La Promesse '96
The Confessional '95

Gibson Gowland (1877-1951)
Gun Cargo '49
The Secret of the Loch '34
Without Honors '32
Hell Harbor '30
The Phantom of the Opera '25
Greed '24

Patrick Goyette
Four Days '99
Le Polygraphe '96

Harry Goz (1932-2003)
The Underneath '95

Rappin' '85
Bill: On His Own '83
Bill '81
Mommie Dearest '81

GQ (1976-)
Drumline '02
On the Line '01
What's the Worst That Could Happen? '01
Traffic '00

Jody Graber
Edward II '92

Betty Grable (1916-73)
How to Marry a Millionaire '53
Three for the Show '55
The Farmer Takes a Wife '53
My Blue Heaven '50
The Beautiful Blonde from Bashful Bend '49
Mother Wore Tights '47
The Dolly Sisters '46
Pin-Up Girl '44
Sweet Rosie O'Grady '43
Footlight Serenade '42
Song of the Islands '42
Springtime in the Rockies '42
I Wake Up Screaming '41
Moon over Miami '41
A Yank in the R.A.F. '41
Tin Pan Alley '40
Down Argentine Way '40
Day the Bookies Wept '39
Man About Town '39
College Swing '38
Give Me a Sailor '38
Campus Confessions '38
Follow the Fleet '36
Pigskin Parade '36
The Gay Divorcee '34
Hold 'Em Jail '32
Probation '32
Whoopee! '30

Maggie Grace (1983-)
The Jane Austen Book Club '07
Suburban Girl '07
The Fog '05
Murder in Greenwich '02

Sofie Grabol (1968-)
The Boss of It All '06
Flickering Lights '01
Mifune '99
The Silent Touch '94

April Grace (1962-)
Girls Town '95

Anna Grace
Fiona '98

Nickolas Grace (1949-)
Casanova '05
Shooting Fish '98
The Final Cut '95
Tom & Viv '94
The Green Man '91
Two Deaths '94
Diamond's Edge '86
Salome's Last Dance '88
Robin Hood... The Legend: The Time of the Wolf '85
Robin Hood... The Legend: Herne's Son '85
Robin Hood... The Legend: The Legend: Sorcerer '83
Robin Hood... The Legend: The Swords of Wayland '83

Topher Grace (1978-)
Spider-Man 3 '07
In Good Company '04
P.S. '04
Win a Date with Tad Hamilton! '04

Heat and Dust '82

Wayne Grace
The Lazarus Man '96
My Summer Story '94
Fallen Angels 2 '93
Heroes Stand Alone '89

Elizabeth (Ward) Gracen (1960-)
The Expert '95
Discretion Assured '93
Final Mission '93
Lower Level '91
Death of the Incredible Hulk '90

Sancho Gracia (1936-)
The Crime of Father Amaro '02

Sally Gracie (1920-2001)
Opportunity Knocks '90
The Rain People '69

Paulo Gracindo
Amor Bandido '79

Paul Graetz (1887-1937)
Heart's Desire '37
Bulldog Jack '35
Power '34

Gary (Rand) Graham (1950-)
Running Woman '98
Alien Nation: The Enemy Within '96
Alien Nation: Body and Soul '95
Alien Nation: Dark Horizon '94
Alien Nation: Millennium '96

David Graf (1950-2001)
The Trial of Old Drum '00
Citizen Ruth '96
The Brady Bunch Movie '95
Father and Scout '94
Police Academy 7: Mission to Moscow '94
Police Academy 6: City under Siege '89
Police Academy 5: Assignment Miami Beach '88
Police Academy 4: Citizens on Patrol '87
Police Academy 3: Back in Training '86
Police Academy 2: Their First Assignment '85

Robert Graf (1923-66)
The Great Escape '63
Forger of London '61

Ilene Graf (1949-)
Rodgers & Hammerstein's South Pacific '01
Loving Annabelle '06

Todd Graff (1959-)
Fly by Night '93
City of Hope '91
Opportunity Knocks '90
The Abyss '89
Dominick & Eugene '88
Five Corners '88
Sweet Lorraine '87

Wilton Graff (1903-69)
Bloodlust '59
Compulsion '59
The Mozart Story '48
The West Point Story '50

Aimee Graham
Bark! '02
Shriek If You Know What I Did Last Friday the 13th '00
Time Code '00
Brokedown Palace '99
Dance with the Devil '97
Jackie Brown '97
Fallen Angels 1 '93
Amos and Andrew '93

Heather Graham (1970-)
Adrift in Manhattan '07
Bobby '06
Gray Matters '06
Cake '05
Anger Management '03
The Guru '02
From Hell '01
Killing Me Softly '01
Say It Isn't So '01
Committed '00
Bowfinger '99
Kiss & Tell '98
Lost in Space '98
Two Girls and a Guy '98
Boogie Nights '97
The Doors '91
Gardens of Stone '87
Gimme Shelter '07 (V)

Bill Graham (1931-91)
Bugsy '91

C.J. Graham
Jason Lives: Friday the 13th, Part 6 '86

Billy Graham (1918-)
The Prodigal '83

Currie Graham (1967-)
Stargate: The Ark of Truth '08

Fred Graham (1918-79)
The Last Hunt '56
Trader Tom of the China Seas '54
Escape from Fort Bravo '53
Heart of the Rockies '51
The Fuller Brush Girl '50

Gerrit Graham (1948-)
One True Thing '98
The Love Letter '98
Stuart Saves His Family '94
Philadelphia Experiment 2 '93
This Boy's Life '93
Frozen Assets '92
Child's Play 2 '90
Martians Go Home! '90
Night of the Cyclone '90
Big Man on Campus '89
C.H.U.D. 2: Bud the Chud '89
It's Alive 3: Island of the Alive '87
Chopping Mall '86
Last Resort '86
Terrorvision '86
The Annihilators '85
The Man with One Red Shoe '85
Ratings Game '84
National Lampoon's Class Reunion '82
Home Movies '79
Pretty Baby '78
Demon Seed '77
Cannonball '76
Special Delivery '76
Phantom of the Paradise '74
Beware! The Blob '72
Hi, Mom! '70

Julie Graham (1965-)
The History of Mr. Polly '07
Bedrooms and Hallways '98
Preaching to the Perverted '97

Lauren Graham (1967-)
Evan Almighty '07
The Moguls '05
The Pacifier '05
Seeing Other People '04
Bad Santa '03
Sweet November '01
Chasing Destiny '00
One True Thing '98
Nightwatch '96

Marcus Graham (1963-)
Mulholland Drive '01
Animal Instincts 3: The Seductress '96

Morland Graham (1891-1949)
Bonnie Prince Charlie '48
The Ghost Train '41
Night Train to Munich '40
The Scarlet Pimpernel '34

Ronny Graham (1919-99)
The Substance of Fire '96
World's Greatest Lover '77
New Faces of 1952 '54

Sasha Graham
Addicted to Murder 3: Blood Lust '00
Addicted to Murder 2: Tainted Blood '97
Addicted to Murder '96

Stephen Graham (1973-)
This Is England '06
Pit Fighter '05
Snatch '00
Gangs of New York '02

Stuart Graham (1967-)
The Ox '91

Gloria Grahame (1925-81)
The Nesting '80
The Big Scam '79
Chilly Scenes of Winter '79
Mama's Dirty Girls '74
Loners '72
The Todd Killings '71
Odds Against Tomorrow '59

Daisy Granados (1942-)
A Paradise Under the Stars '99
Portrait of Teresa '79

Rosario Granados
Pelle the Conqueror '88
A Woman Without Love '51
The Great Madcap '49

Bjorn Granath (1946-)
Gun Glory '57

Omari (Omarion) Grandberry (1984-)
Feel the Noise '07

Stuart Grandberry
You Got Served '04

Dario Grandinetti (1959-)
Talk to Her '02
The Day Silence Died '98
The Dark Side of the Heart '92

Pippa Grandison (1970-)
Hotel de Love '96

The Doors '91
Gardens of Stone '87
Gimme Shelter '07

S. Sidewalks of New York '01
Austin Powers 2: The Spy Who Shagged Me '99

Nowhere '96
Swingers '96
Desert Winds '95
Don't Do It '94
Terrified '94
The Ballad of Little Jo '93
Six Degrees of Separation '93
Diggstown '92
Guilty as Charged '92
Twin Peaks: Fire Walk with Me '92
O Pioneers! '91
Shout '91
I Love You to Death '90
Drugstore Cowboy '89

Entertaining Angels: The Dorothy Day Story '96

Margot Grahame (1911-82)
Broken Melody '34
The Informer '35
The Three Musketeers '35
Fabulous Joe '47
Sudden Fear '52
Macao '52
Crossfire '47
A Woman's Secret '49
In a Lonely Place '50

Gawn Grainger (1940-)
Love and Death on Long Island '97
August '95

Kelsey Grammer (1954-)
Swing Vote '08
Ever Money '06
X-Men: The Last Stand '06
The Good Humor Man '05
Disney's Teacher's Pet '04 (V)
Benedict Arnold: A Question of Honor '03
Mr. St. Nick '02
15 Minutes '01
Animal Farm '99 (V)
Standing on Fishes '99
Toy Story 2 '99 (V)
The Pentagon Wars '98
The Real Howard Spitz '98
Anastasia '97 (V)
Down Periscope '96
Galaxies Are Colliding '92

Sam Grana
The Boys of St. Vincent '93
90 Days '86

Alexander Granach (1893-1945)
The Seventh Cross '44
For Whom the Bell Tolls '43
Hangmen Also Die '43
Joan of Paris '42
Kameradschaft '31
Warning Shadows '23
Nosferatu '22

Philip Granger
Possessed '05
Sasquatch '02

Stewart Granger (1913-93)
The Army Fisher Story '93
Young Bess '53
Salome '53
King Solomon's Mines '50
Scaramouche '52
Prisoner of Zenda '52
The Magic Bow '47
Caesar and Cleopatra '46
The Man in Grey '45
Thursday's Child '43
Waterloo Road '45
Captain Boycott '47
Moonfleet '55
Man of Evil '48
Beau Brummel '54
Blanche Fury '48
Woman Hater '49
Green Fire '55
The Last Hunt '56
Gun Glory '57
The Secret Invasion '64
North to Alaska '60
Sodom and Gomorrah '62
Bhowani Junction '56
Code Name Alpha '67
Hell Hunters '87
Wild Geese '78
Target for Killing '66
The Last Safari '67
The Wild Geese '78
All the Brothers Were Valiant '53
Harry Black and the Tiger '58

Farley Granger (1925-)
The Prowler '81
Arnold '73
Night Flight from Moscow '73
The Slasher '72
They Call Me Trinity '72
Amuck! '71
Deathmask '69
The Girl in the Red Velvet Swing '55
Senso '54
Small Town Girl '53
Behave Yourself! '52
Hans Christian Andersen '52
I Want You '51
Strangers on a Train '51
Our Very Own '50
Side Street '50
They Live by Night '49
Rope '48
The Purple Heart '44
The North Star '43
The Next Big Thing '02
Sweet Spirits '80s
Imagemaker '86
Very Close Quarters '84
The Widow '76

Philip Granger
The Deal '05

Nils T. Granlund (1882-1957)
Take It Big '44
Rhythm Parade '43

William Grannel
The Perfect Witness '07

Greta Granstedt (1907-87)
Return of Dracula '53
Girls Are for Loving '73
Welcome to Paradise '07
Factory Girl '06

Beth Grant (1949-)
The Abductors '72

Dorothy Granger (1912-95)
Killer Dill '47
One Body Too Many '44
The Dentist '32
Fighting Fool '32

Dating the Enemy '95
Over the Hill '93
The Man Who Never Was '55
The Cobweb '55
Oklahoma! '55
Human Desire '54
Not as a Stranger '55
The Big Heat '53
The Bad and the Beautiful '52
The Greatest Show on Earth '52
It's a Wonderful Life '46
It Happened in Brooklyn '47
Mentor of the Movies '47
Song of the Thin Man '47

The House of Usher '06
Little Miss Sunshine '06
Matchstick Men '03
The Rookie '02
Rock Star '01
Sordid Lives '00
Dance with Me '98
Under Oath '97
Lawn Dogs '96
Speed '94
White Sands '92
The Dark Half '91
Love Field '91
Rain Man '88

Cary Grant (1904-86)
Walk, Don't Run '66
Father Goose '64
Charade '63
That Touch of Mink '62
The Grass Is Greener '61
North by Northwest '59
Operation Petticoat '59
Houseboat '58
Indiscreet '58
An Affair to Remember '57
The Pride and the Passion '57
To Catch a Thief '55
Monkey Business '52
People Will Talk '51
I Was a Male War Bride '49
Every Girl Should Be Married '48
Mr. Blandings Builds His Dream House '48
The Bachelor and the Bobby-Soxer '47
The Bishop's Wife '47
Night and Day '46
Notorious '46
Without Reservations '46
Arsenic and Old Lace '44
My Favorite Wife '40
The Howards of Virginia '40
The Philadelphia Story '40
Gunga Din '39
In Name Only '39
Only Angels Have Wings '39
Bringing Up Baby '38
Holiday '38
Amazing Adventure '37
The Awful Truth '37
Toast of New York '37
Topper '37
Big Brown Eyes '36
Suzy '36
Wedding Present '36
Sylvia Scarlett '35
Wings in the Dark '35
Kiss and Make Up '34
Thirty Day Princess '34
The Eagle and the Hawk '33
Gambling Ship '33
I'm No Angel '33
She Done Him Wrong '33
Blonde Venus '32
Sinners in the Sun '32

Cy Grant
At the Earth's Core '76
Sea Wife '57

David Marshall Grant (1955-)
The Devil Wears Prada '06
The Stepford Wives '04
Kids in America '05
Noriega: God's Favorite '00
Teenage Caveman '01
The Chamber '96
The Lazarus Man '96
The Rock '96
Three Wishes '95

And the Band Played On '93
Forever Young '92
Through the Eyes of a Killer '92
Air America '90
Bat 21 '88
Big Town '87
American Flyers '85
Sessions '83
End of August '82
Happy Birthday, Gemini '80

Faye Grant (1957-)
Manna from Heaven '02
Drive Me Crazy '99
Omen 4: The Awakening '91
Internal Affairs '90
V '83

Frances Grant (1909-82)
Oh Susannah '38
Cavalry '36
Red River Valley '36
The Traitor '36
Thunder Mountain '35

Hugh Grant (1960-)
Music & Lyrics '07
American Dreamz '06
Bridget Jones: The Edge of Reason '04
Love Actually '03
About a Boy '02
Two Weeks Notice '02
Bridget Jones's Diary '01
Small Time Crooks '00
Mickey Blue Eyes '99
Notting Hill '99
Extreme Measures '96
The Englishman Who Went up a Hill But Came down a Mountain '95
Nine Months '95
Sense and Sensibility '95
An Awfully Big Adventure '94
Four Weddings and a Funeral '94
Restoration '94
Sirens '94
Night Train to Venice '93
The Remains of the Day '93
Bitter Moon '92
The Big Man: Crossing the Line '91
Our Sons '91
Impromptu '90
The Lady and the Highwayman '89
The Dawning '88
The Lair of the White Worm '88
Rowing with the Wind '88
White Mischief '88
Maurice '87

James Grant (1936-)
The Innocent '93
Prick Up Your Ears '87

Jennifer Grant (1966-)
Blood Relic '05
Savage '96

Kathryn Grant (1933-)
Anatomy of a Murder '59
1001 Arabian Nights '59 (V)
Gunman's Walk '58
The Seventh Voyage of Sinbad '58

Kirby Grant (1914-85)
Comin' Round the Mountain '51
Bad Men of the Border '45
The Stranger from Pecos '45
Hi, Good Lookin'! '44
In Society '44
Lawmen '44

Lawrence Grant (1870-1952)
Son of Frankenstein '39
S.O.S. Coast Guard '37
Werewolf of London '35
The Mask of Fu Manchu '32
Shanghai Express '32

Speak Easily '32
Bulldog Drummond '29
Doomsday '28
The Grand Duchess and the Waiter '26

Lee Grant (1927-)
Going Shopping '05
Mulholland Drive '01
Dr. T & the Women '00
It's My Party '96
Citizen Cohn '92
Defending Your Life '91
A Billion for Boris '90
Big Town '87
Teachers '84
Visiting Hours '82
Charlie Chan and the Curse of the Dragon Queen '81
For Ladies Only '81
Little Miss Marker '80
Backstairs at the White House '79
Damien: Omen 2 '78
My Sister, My Love '78
The Swarm '78
Airport '77
The Spell '77
Voyage of the Damned '76
The Seagull '75
Shampoo '75
Internecine Project '73
Portnoy's Complaint '72
Plaza Suite '71
There Was a Crooked Man '70
The Big Bounce '69
Marooned '69
Buona Sera, Mrs. Campbell '68
Divorce American Style '67
In the Heat of the Night '67
Valley of the Dolls '67
The Balcony '63
Detective Story '51

Leon Grant
Playing for Keeps '86
Beat Street '84

Micah Grant
Terminal Bliss '91
High Desert Kill '90

Richard E. Grant (1957-)
Garfield: A Tail of Two Kitties '06 (V)
Penelope '06
Color Me Kubrick '05
Tim Burton's Corpse Bride '05 (V)
The Story of an African Farm '04
Bright Young Things '03
Monsieur N. '03
The Hound of the Baskervilles '02
Sherlock: Case of Evil '02
Gosford Park '01
Strictly Sinatra '01
The Little Vampire '00
The Miracle Maker: The Story of Jesus '00 (V)
A Christmas Carol '99
The Match '99
The Scarlet Pimpernel '99
The Scarlet Pimpernel 2: Mademoiselle Guillotine '99
The Scarlet Pimpernel 3: The Kidnapped King '99
St. Ives '98
A Merry War '97
The Serpent's Kiss '97
Spice World: The Movie '97
Portrait of a Lady '96
A Royal Scandal '96
Twelfth Night '96
Cold Light of Day '95
Jack and Sarah '95
Ready to Wear '94
The Age of Innocence '93
Bram Stoker's Dracula '92
The Player '92
Codename Kyril '91
Hudson Hawk '91
L.A. Story '91
Warlock '91
Henry & June '90
Mountains of the Moon '90

How to Get Ahead in Advertising '89
Withnail and I '87

Rodney A. Grant (1959-)
Don't Come Knocking '05
The Jack Bull '99
Wild Wild West '99
White Wolves 3: Cry of the White Wolf '98
The Killing Grounds '97
Two for Texas '98
The Substitute '96
The Last Ride '94
Wagons East '94
Geronimo: An American Legend '93
Son of the Morning Star '91
Dances with Wolves '90

Salim Grant (1977-)
What About Your Friends: Weekend Getaway '02
The Hitman '91

Schuyler Grant (1971-)
Anne of Green Gables: The Continuing Story '99
Wrestling with Alligators '98
Anne of Avonlea '87
Anne of Green Gables '85

Shelby Grant (1940-)
The Witchmaker '69
Fantastic Voyage '66
Our Man Flint '66

Stacy Grant
The Fear: Halloween Night '99
One Special Night '99

Allan Granville
Prey for the Hunter '92
Black Terrorist '85

Bonita Granville (1923-88)
Lone Ranger '56
Guilty of Treason '50
Breakfast in Hollywood '46
Love Laughs at Andy Hardy '46
Hitler's Children '43
The Glass Key '42
Now, Voyager '42
The Mortal Storm '40
Nancy Drew, Reporter '39
Nancy Drew—Trouble Shooter '39
Nancy Drew—Detective '38
Quality Street '37
These Three '36

Charley Grapewin (1869-1956)
Follow the Boys '44
They Died with Their Boots On '41
The Grapes of Wrath '40
Johnny Apollo '40
Rhythm on the River '40
The Texas Rangers Ride Again '40
The Wizard of Oz '39
Of Human Hearts '38
Shopworn Angel '38
Three Comrades '38
Captains Courageous '37
The Good Earth '37
Libeled Lady '36
Petrified Forest '36
Without Orders '36
Ah, Wilderness! '35
Alice Adams '35
One Frightened Night '35
Anne of Green Gables '34
Two Alone '34
Heroes for Sale '33
Pilgrimage '33
Hell's House '32

Karen Grassle (1944-)
Wyatt Earp '94
Harry's War '84
Cocaine: One Man's Seduction '83
President's Mistress '78
Little House on the Prairie '74

Bill Gratton
Devil in the Flesh 2 '00

Syngenor '90

Ernest Graves (1919-83)
Hercules in New York '70
One Plus One '61

Karron Graves
The Crucible '96
The Fig Tree '87

Peter Graves (1911-94)
The Adventurers '70
The Magic Christian '69
The Admirable Crichton '57
Encore '52
Maytime in Mayfair '49

Peter Graves (1925-)
Men in Black 2 '02
These Old Broads '01
Number One with a Bullet '87
Mad Mission 3 '84
The Guns and the Fury '83
The Winds of War '83
Airplane 2: The Sequel '82
Savannah Smiles '82
Airplane! '80
Survival Run '80
The Clonus Horror '79
The Rebels '79
Cruise Missile '78
The Slipper and the Rose '76
Scream of the Wolf '74
Where Have All the People Gone? '74
The President's Plane Is Missing '71
Sergeant Ryker '68
Texas Across the River '66
The Legend of the Sea Wolf '58
Beginning of the End '57
Poor White Trash '57
It Conquered the World '56
The Court Martial of Billy Mitchell '55
Let's Make Up '55
The Night of the Hunter '55
Beneath the 12-Mile Reef '53
Stalag 17 '53
Red Planet Mars '52

Ralph Graves (1900-77)
Three Texas Steers '39
That Certain Thing '28
Extra Girl '23
Dream Street '21
The Greatest Question '19

Rupert Graves (1963-)
Death at a Funeral '07
V for Vendetta '06
Extreme Ops '02
All My Loved Ones '00
Cleopatra '99
Dreaming of Joseph Lees '99
Sweet Revenge '98
Bent '97
Mrs. Dalloway '97
Different for Girls '96
The Tenant of Wildfell Hall '96
The Innocent Sleep '95
Intimate Relations '95
The Madness of King George '94
Damage '92
Where Angels Fear to Tread '91
The Children '90
A Handful of Dust '88
Fortunes of War '87
Maurice '87
A Room with a View '86

Teresa Graves (1949-2002)
Get Christie Love! '74
That Man Bolt '73

Fernand Gravey (1905-70)
The Madwoman of Chaillot '69
La Ronde '51

The Fantastic Night '42
The Great Waltz '38
Bitter Sweet '33

Carla Gravina (1941-)
Boomerang '76
And Now My Love '74
Salut l'Artiste '74
The Tempter '74
Alfredo, Alfredo '72

Cesare Gravina (1858-1954)
The Wedding March '28
Merry-Go-Round '23
Foolish Wives '22

Billy Gray (1938-)
Werewolves on Wheels '71
Two for the Seesaw '62
By the Light of the Silvery Moon '53
The Girl Next Door '53
The Day the Earth Stood Still '51
On Moonlight Bay '51

Bruce Gray (1939-)
Chasing Freedom '04
A Killing Spring '02
My Big Fat Greek Wedding '02
The Last Debate '00
Dangerous Evidence: The Lori Jackson Story '99
The Happy Face Murders '99
Odd Birds '85

Charles Gray (1928-2000)
Mr. & Mrs. Loving '96
Dreams Lost, Dreams Found '87
The Jigsaw Man '84
An Englishman Abroad '83
Shock Treatment '81
The Mirror Crack'd '80
The House on Garibaldi Street '79
Silver Bears '78
The Devil Rides Out '68
The Man Outside '68
Night of the Generals '67
You Only Live Twice '67
The Rocky Horror Picture Show '75
Murder on the Midnight Express '74
Diamonds Are Forever '71
Nine Ages of Nakedness '69 (N)
The Executioner '70
The Phantom Planet '61
The Leech Woman '59
The Killing '56
Kansas City Confidential '52
The Seven-Per-Cent Solution '76
The Beast Must Die '75

Coleen Gray (1922-)
A Cry from the Mountain '85

David Barry Gray
Lawn Dogs '96
Soldier Boyz '95
Cops and Robbersons '94
S.F.W. '94

Dolores Gray (1924-2002)
Designing Woman '57
The Opposite Sex '56
Kismet '55

Donald Gray (1914-78)
Flight from Vienna '56
Island of Desire '52
Murder on the Campus '52
The Four Feathers '39

Dorian Gray (1934-)
Colossus and the Amazon Queen '64
Il Grido '57
Nights of Cabiria '57

Dulcie Gray (1919-)
Angels One Five '54

The Franchise Affair '52
À Man About the House '52
Mine Own Executioner '47
Mother: The True Story of the Menendez Brothers '94
T-Force '94
Jason Goes to Hell: The Final Friday '93
Official Denial '93
Breaking Home Ties '87
Born Beautiful '82
Six Pack '82
Buck Rogers in the 25th Century '79
The Ultimate Imposter '79

Eve Gray (1900-83)
Department Store '35
Night Birds '31

Gary Gray (1936-2006)
The Painted Hills '51
The Next Voice You Hear '50
Two Weeks with Love '50
Rachel and the Stranger '48

Lawrence Gray (1898-1970)
A Face in the Fog '36
Man of the World '31
Love 'Em and Leave 'Em '26

Linda Gray (1940-)
Are Parents People? '25
Accidental Meeting '93
Bonanza: The Return '93
Kenny Rogers as the Gambler, Part 3: The Legend Continues '87
The Wild and the Free '80
The Two Worlds of Jenny Logan '79
The Grass Is Always Greener Over the Septic Tank '78

MacKenzie Gray (1957-)
My Teacher Ate My Homework '98
Strip Search '97

Macy Gray (1967-)
Idlewild '06
Shadowboxer '06
The Crow: Wicked Prayer '05
Domino '05
Around the World in 80 Days '04
Scary Movie 3 '03
Training Day '01

Marc Gray
Which Way Home '90
Flirting '89

Nadia Gray (1923-94)
Two for the Road '67
Maniac '63
The Captain's Table '60
La Dolce Vita '60
Une Parisienne '58
Valley of the Eagles '51

Pamela Gray
Corn '02
The Devil's Advocate '97
Commandments '96

Rebecca Gray
The Coroner '98
Tinseltown '97
A Matter of Honor '95

Sally Gray (1916-2006)
Keeper '84
I'll Get You '53
The Hidden Room '49
They Made Me a Fugitive '47
Dangerous Moonlight '41

Elspet Gray (1929-)
Lady in Distress '39
The Saint in London '39
Mr. Reeder in Room 13 '38

Sam Gray (1923-)
Burnzy's Last Call '95
Heart '87
Wolfen '81
Christmas Evil '80

Spalding Gray (1941-2004)
How High '01
Kate & Leopold '01
Revolution #9 '01
Coming Soon '99
Bliss '96
Diabolique '96
Drunks '96
Glory Daze '96
Gray's Anatomy '96
Beyond Rangoon '95
Bad Company '94
The Paper '94
King of the Hill '93
The Pickle '93
Twenty Bucks '93
Monster in a Box '92
Straight Talk '92
Heavy Petting '89
The Image '89
Our Town '89
Beaches '88
Clara's Heart '88
Spalding Gray: Terrors of Pleasure '88
Stars and Bars '88
Swimming to Cambodia '87
True Stories '86
Almost You '85
Hard Choices '84
The Killing Fields '84

Vivean Gray (1924-)
The Last Wave '77
Picnic at Hanging Rock '75

Willoughby Gray (1916-93)
Absolution '81
Waterloo '71

Ari Graynor (1983-)
The Great New Wonderful '06
Game 6 '05
Book of Love '04

Denise Grayson
Though None Go With Me '06

Kathryn Grayson (1922-)
The Desert Song '53
Kiss Me Kate '53
Lovely to Look At '52
Show Boat '51
The Toast of New Orleans '50
That Midnight Kiss '49
The Kissing Bandit '48
It Happened in Brooklyn '47
Till the Clouds Roll By '46
Anchors Aweigh '45
Thousands Cheer '43
Rio Rita '42
Andy Hardy's Private Secretary '41

Jerry Grayson
Corn '02
Pushing Tin '99
Mob Queen '98

Irene Grazioli
The Red Violin '98
Mediterraneo '91

Jose Greco (1918-2000)
Ship of Fools '65
Goliath and the Sins of Babylon '64

Juliette Greco (1927-)
Uncle Tom's Cabin '69
Elena and Her Men '56
The Green Glove '52
Orpheus '49

Adolph Green (1915-2002)
I Want to Go Home '89
Follies in Concert '85
Lily in Love '85
My Favorite Year '82
Simon '80

Kerri Green (1967-)
School of Rock '03
Blue Flame '93
Tainted Blood '93
Three for the Road '87
Lucas '86
The Goonies '85
Summer Rental '85

Marika Green (1922-)
Emmanuelle '74
Pickpocket '59

Mitzie Green (1920-69)
Lost in Alaska '52
Little Orphan Annie '32
Tom Sawyer '30

Nigel Green (1924-72)
The Ruling Class '72
The Pink Jungle '68
The Wrecking Crew '68
Africa - Texas Style '67
Deadlier Than the Male '67
Khartoum '66
Tobruk '66
The Ipcress File '65
Masque of the Red Death '65
The Skull '65
Zulu '64
Jason and the Argonauts '63
Mysterious Island '61
Beat Girl '60
Sword of Sherwood Forest '60
Corridors of Blood '58
Reach for the Sky '56

Robson Green (1964-)
Like Father Like Son '05
Me & Mrs. Jones '02

Janet-Laine Green
Anne of Green Gables: The Continuing Story '00
When the Dark Man Calls '95

Shon Greenblatt
Freddy's Dead: The Final Nightmare '91

William Greenblatt (1987-)
Ms. Scrooge '97
The Abduction '96
Homecoming '96

Angela Greene (1923-78)
The Cosmic Man '59
Night of the Blood Beast '58

Billoah Greene
Preaching to the Choir '05
Levity '03

Daniel Greene
American Tiger '89
Me, Myself, and Irene '00
The Opponent '96
Skeleton Coast '89
Elvira, Mistress of the Dark '88
Hands of Steel '86
Weekend Warriors '86
Pulsebeat '85

Ellen Greene (1952-)
The Cooler '03
States of Control '98
One Fine Day '96
Killer: A Journal of Murder '95
Murdered Innocence '94
The Professional '94
Wagons East '94
Fathers and Sons '92
Rock-a-Doodle '92 (V)
Stepping Out '91
Glory! Glory! '90
Pump Up the Volume '90
Dinner at Eight '89
Me and Him '89
Talk Radio '88
Little Shop of Horrors '86

Harry Green (1892-1958)
A King in New York '57
Be Yourself '30

Eva Green (1980-)
The Golden Compass '07
Casino Royale '06
Kingdom of Heaven '05
The Dreamers '03

Danny Green (1903-73)
The Seventh Voyage of Sinbad '58
The Ladykillers '55
Non-Stop New York '37

Brian A(ustin) Green (1973-)
Domino '05
Cook & Bull Story '03
Fish Without a Bicycle '03
Laws of Deception '97
An American Summer '90
Kid '90

Seth Green (1974-)
Scooby-Doo 2: Monsters Unleashed '04
Without a Paddle '04
The Italian Job '03
Party Monster '03
Austin Powers in Goldmember '02
America's Sweethearts '01
Knockaround Guys '01
Rat Race '01
Josie and the Pussycats '01
The Trumpet of the Swan '01 (V)
Austin Powers: International Man of Mystery '97
Can't Buy Me Love '87
My Stepmother Is an Alien '88
Arcade '93
Airborne '93
Radio Days '87
Something Special '86
The Hotel New Hampshire '84

Tom Green (1971-)
Bob the Butler '05
Stealing Harvard '02
Freddy Got Fingered '01
Charlie's Angels '00
Road Trip '00

Brian Lane Green (1962-)
Friends and Family '01
Circuit '02

Al Green (1946-)
On the Line '01

Anthony Green (1970-)
The Scarlet Pimpernel '99
The Scarlet Pimpernel 2: Mademoiselle Guillotine '99

Scott Green
Paranoid Park '07

Esther Greenberg
Lupo '70
Sallah '63

James Greene (1926-)
The Moon Stallion '85
Pals '87
Powwow Highway '89
Philadelphia Experiment 2 '93

Joe "Mean Joe" Greene (1946-)
Smokey and the Bandit 2 '80

Kim Morgan Greene (1960-)
Grizzly Mountain '97
The Corporation '96
The Soft Kill '94
Scorned '93

Jon Greene
Swift Justice '88
Alley Cat '84

Leon Greene (1933-)
The Devil Rides Out '68
A Challenge for Robin Hood '68

Lorne Greene (1915-87)
The Alamo: Thirteen Days to Glory '87
Earthquake '74
Tidal Wave '75
The Errand Boy '61
The Trap '55
The Buccaneer '58
Peyton Place '57
Autumn Leaves '56
Tight Spot '55
The Silver Chalice '54

Richard Greene (1918-85)
Special Effects '85
Tales from the Crypt '72
The Castle of Fu Manchu '69
Island of the Lost '68
Kiss and Kill '68
Sword of Sherwood Forest '60
Robin Hood: The Movie '55
Captain Scarlett '53
The Black Castle '52
Forever Amber '47
The Hound of the Baskervilles '39
The Little Princess '39
Stanley and Livingstone '39
Four Men and a Prayer '38
My Lucky Star '38

Shecky Greene (1926-)
Splash '84
Lovelines '84

Graham Greene (1952-)
Next Stop, Greenwich Village '76
Johnny Bee Good '88
Gambling Man '98
All Hat '07
Reckless: The Sequel '98
Luna: Spirit of the Whale '07
Transamerica '05
A Thief of Time '04
Coyote Waits '03
Skins '02
Snow Dogs '02
Christmas in the Clouds '01
Lost and Delirious '01
The Green Mile '99
Grey Owl '99
Shattered Image '98
The Education of Little Tree '97
Wounded '97
Die Hard: With a Vengeance '95
Camilla '94
Maverick '94
Medicine River '94
North '94
The Pathfinder '94
Savage Land '94
Benefit of the Doubt '93
Cooperstown '93
The Broken Chain '93
Rain Without Thunder '93
Clearcut '92
The Last of His Tribe '92
Thunderheart '92
Dances with Wolves '90
Lost in the Barrens '91
Powwow Highway '89

Michele Greene (1962-)
Nightmare on the 13th Floor '90
Moon over Parador '88
A Woman Hunted '03
Redeemer '02
A Family Affair '01
Fugitive Mind '99
Wild Grizzly '99
Stranger in the House '97
Daddy's Girl '96
How the West Was Fun '95
Stranger by Night '94
The Unborn 2 '94
The Naked Angels '69

Peter Greene (1965-)
I Posed for Playboy '91
Double Standard '88
End Game '06
Black Cloud '04
The Mask '94
The Usual Suspects '95
Nobody's Baby '01
Pulp Fiction '94
Clean, Shaven '93
Judgment Night '93
Laws of Gravity '92
Bang '95
Blue Streak '99
Out in Fifty '99
Black Cat Run '98
Double Tap '98
Permanent Midnight '98
Trading Favors '97
The Rich Man's Wife '96
Sworn Enemies '96

Kate Greenhouse
Crime and Punishment in Suburbia '00

Raymond Greenleaf (1892-1963)
When Gangland Strikes '56
Storm Warning '51
Harriet Craig '50

Kate Greenfield (1987-)
The Love Machine '71

Brad Greenquist (1959-)
The Diary of Ellen Rimbauer '03
Pet Sematary '89

Michael Greene (1934-)
Last Man Standing '95
The Trial of Lee Harvey Oswald '77
The Khartoum Worker '00
Roots '77
The Assistant '97
Cylon Attack '78
Battlestar Galactica: The Mission Galactica: The Cylon Attack '78
A Time for Miracles '80
Klondike Fever '79
The Bastard '78
Battlestar Galactica '78
Lost Souls '00
Inherit the Wind '99
The Yearling '94
Gang Related '96
In the Heat of Passion '91

The Bedroom Window '87
Mutants In Paradise '84

Sydney Greenstreet (1879-1954)
Flamingo Road '49
It's a Great Feeling '49
Malaya '49
Velvet Touch '48
The Hucksters '47
Christmas in Connecticut '45
Conflict '45
Hollywood Canteen '44
The Mask of Dimitrios '44
Passage to Marseilles '44
Background to Danger '43
Across the Pacific '42
Casablanca '42
The Maltese Falcon '41
They Died with Their Boots On '41

Bruce Greenwood (1956-)
Firehouse Dog '07
I'm Not There '07
National Treasure: Book of Secrets '07
Deja Vu '06
Eight Below '06
Capote '05
Racing Stripes '05
Being Julia '04
I, Robot '04
The Core '03
Hollywood Homicide '03
Ararat '02
Below '02
The Magnificent Ambersons '02
Swept Away '02
A Girl Thing '01
Here on Earth '00
Hide and Seek '00
Rules of Engagement '00
Thirteen Days '00
Double Jeopardy '99
Thick as Thieves '99
The Color of Courage '98
Disturbing Behavior '98
The Lost Son '98
Father's Day '96
The Climb '87
Striker's Mountain '87
Malibu Bikini Shop '86

Charlotte Greenwood (1890-1978)
Glory '56
Oklahoma! '55
Dangerous When Wet '53
Great Dan Patch '49
The Gang's All Here '43
Springtime in the Rockies '42
Moon over Miami '41
Down Argentine Way '40
Young People '40
Palmy Days '31
Parlor, Bedroom and Bath '31

Joan Greenwood (1921-87)
Little Dorrit, Film 1: Nobody's Fault '88
Little Dorrit, Film 2: Little Dorrit's Story '88
The Hound of the Baskervilles '77
The Moon-Spinners '64
Tom Jones '63
Mysterious Island '61
Stage Struck '57

Moonfleet '55
The Detective '54
The Importance of Being Earnest '52
The Man in the White Suit '51
A Stolen Face '52
The Woman in Question '50
Mr. Peek-A-Boo '49
Kind Hearts and Coronets '49
The October Man '48
Whiskey Galore '48
Frenzy '46
A Girl in a Million '46

Dabbs Greer (1917-2007)
The Green Mile '99
Little Giants '94
Pacific Heights '90
Two Moon Junction '88
Rage '72
The Cheyenne Social Club '70
Shenandoah '65
Roustabout '64
Cash McCall '60
The Day of the Outlaw '59
It! The Terror from Beyond Space '58
Invasion of the Body Snatchers '56
An Annapolis Story '55
Private Hell 36 '54
Rose Marie '54
Above and Beyond '53
Trouble along the Way '53

Jane Greer (1924-2001)
Immediate Family '89
Just Between Friends '86
Against All Odds '84
Billie '65
Where Love Has Gone '64
Man of a Thousand Faces '57
Clown '53
Prisoner of Zenda '52
Big Steal '49
Station West '48
Out of the Past '47
Sinbad, the Sailor '47
They Won't Believe Me '47
Dick Tracy, Detective '45
George White's Scandals '45

Judy Greer (1971-)
27 Dresses '08
American Dreamz '06
The Great New Wonderful '06
The TV Set '06
Elizabethtown '05
Cursed '04
13 Going on 30 '04
The Village '04
I Love Your Work '03
The Wedding Planner '01
The Specials '00
What Planet Are You From? '00
What Women Want '00
Three Kings '99
Jawbreaker '98
Kissing a Fool '98

Michael Greer (1943-2002)
Messiah of Evil '74
Fortune and Men's Eyes '71

Bradley Gregg (1966-)
Eye of the Storm '91
Class of 1999 '90
Madhouse '90

Clark Gregg (1964-)
Iron Man '08
Hoot '06
In the Land of Women '06
When a Stranger Calls '06
In Enemy Hands '04
In Good Company '04
Spartan '04
11:14 '03

Tyson '95
I Love Trouble '94
Lana in Love '92

Everley Gregg (1903-59)
A Stolen Face '52
The Woman in Question '50
Brief Encounter '46
Great Expectations '46
Pygmalion '38
The Ghost Goes West '36
The Private Life of Henry VIII '33

John Gregg (1940-)
To End All Wars '01
Ebbtide '94
Trouble in Paradise '88
Heatwave '83

Julie Gregg (1944-)
The Seekers '79
From Hell to Borneo '64

Virginia Gregg (1916-86)
No Way Back '74
Walk in the Spring Rain '70
Columbo: Prescription Murder '67
Spencer's Mountain '63
Psycho '60 (V)
The Hanging Tree '59
Operation Petticoat '59
D.I. '57
Love Is a Many-Splendored Thing '55
The Amazing Mr. X '48

Ezio Greggio (1954-)
2001: A Space Travesty '00
Screw Loose '99
Silence of the Hams '93

Pascal Greggory (1954-)
La Vie en Rose '07
The Page Turner '06
Gabrielle '05
La Vie Promise '02
Confusion of Genders '00
The Messenger: The Story of Joan of Arc '99
Time Regained '99
Those Who Love Me Can Take the Train '98
Queen Margot '94
Pauline at the Beach '83
Le Beau Mariage '82

Rose Gregorio (1932-)
Maze '01
Tarantella '95
City of Hope '91
Five Corners '88
The Last Innocent Man '87
Desperate Characters '71
The Swimmer '68

Andre Gregory (1934-)
Goodbye, Lover '99
Celebrity '98
Last Summer in the Hamptons '96
The Shadow '94
Vanya on 42nd Street '94
The Linguini Incident '92
The Bonfire of the Vanities '90
The Last Temptation of Christ '88
Some Girls '88
Street Smart '87
The Mosquito Coast '86
Always '85
Follies in Concert '85
Protocol '84
Author! Author! '82
My Dinner with Andre '81

Celia Gregory (1952-)
Children of the Full Moon '84
Agatha '79

Dorian Gregory (1971-)
Getting Played '05
Deliver Us from Eva '03

James Gregory (1911-2002)
Wait Till Your Mother Gets Home '83
Great American Traffic Jam '80
The Bastard '78
The Strongest Man in the World '75
Shoot Out '71
Beneath the Planet of the Apes '70
The Love God? '70
The Ambushers '67
Clambake '67
Murderers' Row '66
The Silencers '66
Sons of Katie Elder '65
Captain Newman, M.D. '63
PT 109 '63
The Manchurian Candidate '62
Two Weeks in Another Town '62
Gun Glory '57
Nightfall '56

Leo Gregory (1978-)
Green Street Hooligans '05
Stoned '05
Pulse '03

Mark Gregory (1965-)
War Bus Commando '89
Thunder Warrior 3 '88
Escape from the Bronx '85
Thunder Warrior '85
Thunder Warrior 2 '85

Mary Gregory
Coming Home '78
Sleeper '73
Lassie: Well of Love '70

Michael Gregory (1944-)
Spider's Web '01
Zero Tolerance '93

Natalie Gregory (1975-)
Oliver & Company '88 (V)
Alice in Wonderland '85

Nick Gregory
Last Summer in the Hamptons '96
Happy Hell Night '92

Sebastian Gregory
See Anthony (Tony) Vorno

Thea Gregory (1929-)
Paid to Kill '54
Profile '54

John Gregson (1919-75)
Fright '71
Hans Brinker '69
Night of the Generals '67
The Frightened City '61
The Captain's Table '60
S.O.S. Pacific '60
Sea of Sand '58
Above Us the Waves '56
Three Cases of Murder '55
Angels One Five '54
Genevieve '53
The Lavender Hill Mob '51

Stephen Greif (1944-)
Casanova '05
The Dying Truth '91
The Great Riviera Bank Robbery '79

Robert Greig (1880-1958)
Sullivan's Travels '41
The Great Ziegfeld '36
Trouble in Paradise '32
Tonight or Never '31
Animal Crackers '30

Kim Greist (1958-)
Zoe '01
Homeward Bound 2: Lost in San Francisco '96
Last Exit to Earth '96
Houseguest '94
Roswell: The U.F.O. Cover-Up '94
Homeward Bound: The Incredible Journey '93
Duplicates '92
Payoff '91
Why Me? '90

Punchline '88
Throw Momma from the Train '87
Manhunter '86
Brazil '85
C.H.U.D. '84

Joyce Grenfell (1910-79)
The Americanization of Emily '64
The Pure Hell of St. Trinian's '61
Blue Murder at St. Trinian's '56
Genevieve '53
The Happiest Days of Your Life '50

Adrian Grenier (1976-)
The Devil Wears Prada '06
Anything Else '03
Hart's War '02
Love in the Time of Money '02
A.I.: Artificial Intelligence '01
Harvard Man '01
Cecil B. Demented '00
The Adventures of Sebastian Cole '99
Drive Me Crazy '99

Zach Grenier (1954-)
Zodiac '07
Pulse '06
Rescue Dawn '06
Swordfish '01
Chasing Sleep '00
Shaft '00
Ride with the Devil '99
Donnie Brasco '96
Maximum Risk '96
Twister '96

Macha Grenon (1968-)
Cafe Ole '00
Jack Higgins' The Windsor Protocol '97
Sworn Enemies '96
Legends of the North '95
The Pianist '91

Googy Gress
Bloodhounds of Broadway '89
Promised Land '88
Vibes '88
Babes in Toyland '86
First Turn On '83

Joel Gretsch (1963-)
National Treasure: Book of Secrets '07
Glass House: The Good Mother '06
The Emperor's Club '02
Taken '02
The Legend of Bagger Vance '00

Laurent Grevill (1961-)
Look at Me '04
I Can't Sleep '93
Camille Claudel '89

Denise Grey (1896-1996)
La Boum '81
Sputnik '61

Jennifer Grey (1960-)
Bounce '00
Outrage '98
Red Meat '98
Since You've Been Gone '97
Lover's Knot '96
Portraits of a Killer '95
Eyes of a Witness '94
A Case for Murder '93
Wind '92
Criminal Justice '90
Stroke of Midnight '90

Ferris Bueller's Day Off '86
American Flyers '85
The Cotton Club '84
Reckless '84
Red Dawn '84

Joel Grey (1932-)
A Christmas Carol '99
Dancer in the Dark '99
The Empty Mirror '99
The Dangerous '95
The Fantasticks '95
The Music of Chance '93
The Player '92
Kafka '91
Queenie '87
Remo Williams: The Adventure Begins '85
Buffalo Bill & the Indians '76
The Seven-Per-Cent Solution '76
Cabaret '72
Man on a String '71
Come September '61

Nan Grey (1918-93)
The House of the Seven Gables '40
The Invisible Man Returns '40
Three Smart Girls Grow Up '39
The Tower of London '39
The Black Doll '38
Danger on the Air '38
Dracula's Daughter '36
Three Smart Girls '36

Shirley Grey (1910-81)
Circumstantial Evidence '35
The Mystery of the Mary Celeste '35
Green Eyes '34
His Greatest Gamble '34
Cornered '32
Drifting Souls '32
Get That Girl '32
Hurricane Express '32
The Riding Tornado '32
Texas Cyclone '32
Uptown New York '32

Virginia Grey (1917-2004)
Bachelor in Paradise '69
Madame X '66
Love Has Many Faces '65
Naked Kiss '64
Portrait in Black '60
Crime of Passion '57
All That Heaven Allows '55
The Last Command '55
The Rose Tattoo '55
Slaughter Trail '51
Bullfighter & the Lady '50
Three Desperate Men '50
Threat '49
Mexican Hayride '48
Unknown Island '48
Who Killed Doc Robbin? '48
Unconquered '47
House of Horrors '46
Swamp Fire '46
Idaho '43
Sweet Rosie O'Grady '43
Bells of Capistrano '42
Tarzan's New York Adventure '42
Big Store '41
Whistling in the Dark '41
Another Thin Man '39
Broadway Serenade '39
The Michigan Kid '28
Uncle Tom's Cabin '27

Zena Grey (1988-)
The Shaggy Dog '06
In Good Company '04
Max Keeble's Big Move '01
Summer Catch '01

Michael Greyeyes (1967-)
The New World '05
Sunshine State '02
ZigZag '02
The Lost Child '00
Skipped Parts '00
The Magnificent Seven '98

Light Years '88 (V)
Dirty Dancing '87

The Minion '98
Smoke Signals '98
Firestorm '97
True Women '97
Crazy Horse '96
Dance Me Outside '95
Geronimo '93

Clinton Greyn (1936-)
The Love Machine '71
Raid on Rommel '71

Bill Gribble
Dogs of Hell '83

Eddie Gribbon (1890-1965)
The Phantom Rider '36
Flo Rattler '35
Dames Ahoy '30

Harry Gribbon (1885-1961)
Ride Him, Cowboy '32
The Cameraman '28
The Tomboy '24

Richard Grieco (1965-)
Forget About It '06
Final Payback '99
Harold Robbins' Body Parts '99
Against the Law '98
The Apostate '98
Blackheart '98
Heaven or Vegas '98
A Night at the Foxbury '98
Mutual Needs '97
When Time Expires '97
Inhumanoid '96
The Demolitionist '95
Rebel Run '94
Sin and Redemption '94
Suspicious Agenda '94
A Vow to Kill '94
Born to Run '93
Tomcat: Dangerous Desires '93
If Looks Could Kill '91
Mobsters '91

Helmut Griem (1932-2004)
Escape '90
La Passante '83
Les Rendez-vous D'Anna '78
The Desert of the Tartars '76
Voyage of the Damned '76
Children of Rage '75
Cabaret '72
Ludwig '72
McKenzie Break '70
The Damned '69
The Thing with Two Heads '72

David Alan Grier (1955-)
Bewitched '05
The Muppets' Wizard of Oz '05
The Woodsman '04
Baadasssss! '03
King of Texas '02
15 Minutes '01
The Adventures of Rocky & Bullwinkle '00
Angels in the Infield '00
Return to Me '00
The Rundown '03
The Snow Walker '03
Three Strikes '00
A Saintly Switch '99
The '60s '99
Stuart Little '99 (V)
McHale's Navy '97
Top of the World '97
Blankman '94
In the Army Now '94
Jumanji '95
Tales from the Hood '95
The Player '92
Boomerang '92
Loose Cannons '90
I'm Gonna Git You Sucka '88

Pam Grier (1949-)
Back in the Day '05
The Adventures of Pluto Nash '02
Anne Rice's The Feast of All Saints '01
Bones '01
John Carpenter's Ghosts of Mars '01
Love the Hard Way '01
3 A.M. '01
Snow Day '00
Wilder '00
Fortress 2: Re-Entry '99
In Too Deep '99
No Tomorrow '99
Holy Smoke '99
Jackie Brown '97
Strip Search '97
Woo '97
Escape from L.A. '96
Mars Attacks! '96
Original Gangstas '96
Serial Killer '95
Posse '93
Bill & Ted's Bogus Journey '91
Class of 1999 '90
The Package '89
Above the Law '88
On the Edge '86
Badge of the Assassin '85
Stand Alone '85
The Vindicator '85
Something Wicked This Way Comes '83
Tough Enough '83
Fort Apache, the Bronx '81
Greased Lightning '77
Drum '76
Bucktown '75
Friday Foster '75
Sheba, Baby '75
Foxy Brown '74
The Arena '73
Coffy '73
Scream Blacula Scream '73
The Big Bird Cage '72
Twilight People '72
The Big Doll House '71
Beyond the Valley of the Dolls '70

Roosevelt "Rosie" Grier (1932-)
Sophisticated Gents '81
The Seekers '79
The Glove '78
The Big Push '75
The Treasure of Jamaica Reef '74

Jon(athan) Gries (1957-)
The Astronaut Farmer '07
The Comebacks '07
September Dawn '07
Stick It '06
The Big Empty '04
Napoleon Dynamite '04
Northfork '03
The Runaway '03
Angels in the Infield '00
Freeway 2: Confessions of a Trickbaby '99
Twin Falls Idaho '99
Casualties '97
Fever '91
Rainbow Drive '90
Kill Me Again '89
Pucker Up and Bark Like a Dog '89
Fright Night 2 '88
Number One with a Bullet '87
Real Genius '85
Joy Sticks '83
Swap Meet '79

Kathy Griffin (1960-)
Dirty Love '05
Beethoven's 5th '03
On Edge '03
Enemies of Laughter '00
Intern '00
Muppets from Space '99
The Cable Guy '96
It's Pat: The Movie '94
Pulp Fiction '94

Josephine Griffin (1928-)
The Spanish Gardener '57
Postmark for Danger '56
The Man Who Never Was '55

Lorie Griffin
Aloha Summer '88
Cheerleader Camp '88

Lynne Griffin (1952-)
Santa Baby '06
Obsessed '88
Strange Brew '83
Curtains '83

Merv Griffin (1925-2007)
Alice in Wonderland '85
The Lonely Guy '84

John Griesemer (1947-)
Henry Hill '00
Where the Rivers Flow North '94

Joe Grifasi (1944-)
13 Going on 30 '04
Bought and Sold '03
61* '01
Looking for an Echo '99
The Naked Man '98
One Fine Day '96
Sunday '96
Batman Forever '95
Money Train '95
Heavy '94
Natural Born Killers '94
Benny & Joon '93
Household Saints '93
City of Hope '91
The Feud '90
Presumed Innocent '90
Chances Are '89
Perfect Witness '89
Ironweed '87
Matewan '87
F/X '86
Bad Medicine '85
The Pope of Greenwich Village '84
Still of the Night '82
Gentleman Bandit '81
On the Yard '79
The Deer Hunter '78

Simone Griffeth (1955-)
Hot Target '85
Delusion '84
Death Race 2000 '75
Sixteen '72

Ethel Griffies (1878-1975)
The Birds '63
The Mystery of Edwin Drood '35

Eddie Griffin (1968-)
Norbit '07
Redline '07
Urban Justice '07
Date Movie '06
Deuce Bigalow: European Gigolo '05
Irish Jam '05
The Wendell Baker Story '05
Who Made the Potatoe Salad? '05
Blast '04
My Baby's Daddy '04
Scary Movie 3 '03
John Q '02
The New Guy '02
Pinocchio '02 (V)
Undercover Brother '02
Double Take '01

Anthony Griffith
Masters of Horror: Deer Woman '05
Panther '95
Tales from the Hood '95

Charles B. Griffith (1930-2007)
Hollywood Boulevard '76
At as '60
It Conquered the World '56

Eva Griffith (1962-)
Ride a Wild Pony '75

Gordon Griffith (1907-58)
Outlaws of the Range '36
Little Annie Rooney '25

Hugh Griffith (1912-80)
The Abominable Dr. Phibes '71
The Canterbury Tales '71
Who Slew Auntie Roo? '71
Cry of the Banshee '70
The Passover Plot '75
Craze '74
Luther '74
Diary of Forbidden Dreams '73
The Final Programme '73
Doctor Phibes Rises Again '72
Start the Revolution without Me '70
The Abominable Dr. Phibes '71
Oliver! '68
Oh Dad, Poor Dad (Momma's Hung You in the Closet & I'm Feeling So Sad) '67
The Counterfeit Traitor '62
Tom Jones '63
Mutiny on the Bounty '62
Exodus '60
Ben-Hur '59
Lucky Jim '58
The Sleeping Tiger '54
Kind Hearts and Coronets '49

The Big Scam '79
Legend of the Werewolf '75

Nikki Griffin (1978-)
The Fast and the Furious: Tokyo Drift '06
The Dukes of Hazzard '05
Death Match '94
Number One Fan '94

Renee Griffin (1968-)
Monster from Green Hell '58
Crime of Passion '57
I Was a Teenage Werewolf '57

Robert E. (Bob) Griffin (1902-60)
Hideous '97
The Creeps '97

Rhonda Griffin

Tim Griffin (1969-)
The Bourne Supremacy '04
Lover Girl '97

Andy Griffith (1926-)
Waitress '07
Daddy & Them '01
Spy Hard '96
Return to Mayberry '86
Rustler's Rhapsody '85
Fatal Vision '84
Murder in Coweta County '83
Murder in Texas '81
From Here to Eternity '79
Centennial '78
Hearts of the West '75
Savages '75
Pray for the Wildcats '74
No Time for Sergeants '58
A Face in the Crowd '57

Tony Griffin (1959-)
Rodin Hooc: Men in Tights '93

Evil Laugh '86
The Englishman Who Went up a Hill But Came down a Mountain '95
Four Weddings and a Funeral '94
The Final Option '82
Night of the Laughing Dead '75

Melanie Griffith (1957-)
The Night We Called It a Day '03
Shade '03
Stuart Little 2 '02 (V)
Tart '01
Along for the Ride '00
Cecil B. Demented '00
Crazy in Alabama '99
RKO 281 '99
Another Day in Paradise '98
Celebrity '98
Shadow of Doubt '98
Lolita '97
Two Much '96
Buffalo Girls '95
Mulholland Falls '95
Now and Then '95
Milk Money '94
Nobody's Fool '94
Born Yesterday '93
Shining Through '92
A Stranger Among Us '92
Paradise '91
The Bonfire of the Vanities '90
In the Spirit '90
Pacific Heights '90
Women & Men: Stories of Seduction '90
Stormy Monday '88
Working Girl '88
Something Wild '86
Fear City '85
Body Double '84
She's in the Army Now '81
Underground Aces '80
Joyride '77
One on One '77
The Drowning Pool '75
Night Moves '75
Smile '75
Harrad Experiment '73

Rachel Griffiths (1968-)
Step Up '06
All Tied Up '93
Comanche Moon '08
Skeeter '93
Blow Dry '01
Very Annie Mary '00
Me Myself I '99
Among Giants '98
Amy '98
Hilary and Jackie '98
My Best Friend's Wedding '97
Welcome to Woo:) Woop Woop '97
Children of the Revolution '96
Cosi '95
Muriel's Wedding '94

Katherine Griffith (1921-2006)
Discontent '16
Pollyanna '20
Mid-Channel '20

Kenneth Griffith
Night Beast '83

Nam Angels '88

Jeff Griffith
The 13th Mission '91

Tom Griffith (1945-)
The Alien Factor '78

Tracy Griffith (1965-)
The Good Mother '86
Excessive Force '93
Crackerjack '94
Beyond Forgiveness '94
Hollow Point '95
Behind Enemy Lines '96
Kill the Conqueror '97
Sleepaway Camp 5: Teenage Wasteland '89
The Karate Kid: Part 3 '89
The First Power '89
The Finest Hour '91
Fast Food '89

Linda Griffiths (1956-)
Lianna '83
Reno and the Doc '84

Michael Griffiths
Timeless '96

James J. Griffith (1916-93)
The Last Days of Dolwyn '49

Richard Griffiths (1947-)
Harry Potter and the Order of the Phoenix '07
The History Boys '06
Venus '06
The Hitchhiker's Guide to the Galaxy '05 (V)
Harry Potter and the Chamber of Secrets '02
Harry Potter and the Sorcerer's Stone '01
Vatel '00
Sleepy Hollow '99
Guarding Tess '94
Blame It on the Bellboy '92
The Naked Gun 2 1/2: The Smell of Fear '91
Withnail and I '87
Shanghai Surprise '86
A Private Function '84
Whoops Apocalypse '83
Breaking Point '94

Johanna Grika
Vice Academy 3 '91
Visitants '87

Jeff Griggs (1963-)
Forbidden Games '95

Dan Grimaldi
Joey '86

Thomas Ian Griffith (1962-)
Timecop 2: The Berlin Decision '03
Black Point '01
Final Encounter '00
Avalanche '99
John Carpenter's Vampires '97
The Karate Kid: Part 3 '89
Excessive Force '93
Hollow Point '95
Night Beast '83
Ulterior Motives '92
The Man with Two Brains '83
The Legend of Sleepy Hollow '79
The Amazing Transparent Man '58
Tribute to a Bad Man '56
Bullwhip '58

Don't Go in the House '80

Frank Grimes (1947-)
Catherine Cookson's The Wingless Bird '97
The Dive '89
Crystalstone '88

Gary Grimes (1955-)
Cahill: United States Marshal '73
Class of '44 '73
Culpepper Cattle Co. '72
Summer of '42 '71

Scott Grimes (1971-)
Band of Brothers '01
Mystery, Alaska '99
Night Life '90
Critters 2: The Main Course '88
Critters '86
It Came Upon a Midnight Clear '84

Tammy Grimes (1934-)
High Art '98
A Modern Affair '94
Backstreet Justice '93
Mr. North '88
America '86
The Stuff '85
No Big Deal '83
The Last Unicorn '82 (V)
The Runner Stumbles '79

Jim Grimshaw
Chill Factor '99
Basket Case 3: The Progeny '92

Herbert Grimwood (1875-1929)
Romola '25
When the Clouds Roll By '19

Anouk Grinberg (1963-)
Mon Homme '96
A Self-Made Hero '95

Nikolai Grinko (1920-89)
Stalker '79
Solaris '72
Andrei Rublev '66

Rupert Grint (1988-)
Harry Potter and the Order of the Phoenix '07
Driving Lessons '06
Harry Potter and the Goblet of Fire '05
Harry Potter and the Prisoner of Azkaban '04
Harry Potter and the Chamber of Secrets '02
Harry Potter and the Sorcerer's Stone '01

Stephen Grives (1951-)
Scooby-Doo '02
Inseminoid '80
Flambards '78

George Grizzard (1928-2007)
Flags of Our Fathers '06
Small Time Crooks '00
Scarlett '94
Iran: Days of Crisis '91
Caroline? '90
False Witness '89
The Deliberate Stranger '86
Embassy '85
Bachelor Party '84
Wrong Is Right '82
Attica '80
Oldest Living Graduate '80
Seems Like Old Times '80
Comes a Horseman '78
The Stranger Within '74
Pueblo Affair '73
Advise and Consent '62
From the Terrace '60
So I Married an Axe Murderer '93
Beethoven '92
Clifford '92
Taking Care of Business '90
Midnight Run '88
You Can't Hurry Love '88
The Couch Trip '87
Ishtar '87
Grown Ups '86
Last Resort '86
Movers and Shakers '85
The Lonely Guy '84
The Woman in Red '84
The Great Muppet Caper '81
The Incredible Shrinking Woman '81
It's My Turn '80
Seems Like Old Times '80
Real Life '79
Sunburn '79
The Grass Is Always Greener Over the Septic Tank '78
Heaven Can Wait '78
Just Me & You '78
King Kong '76
11 Harrowhouse '74
The Heartbreak Kid '72
Catch-22 '70
Rosemary's Baby '68
The Meanest Men in the West '67
Sex and the College Girl '64

Kathryn Grody (1946-)
Limbo '99
Hombres Armados '97
The Lemon Sisters '90
Quick Change '90
Parents '89

Harry Groener (1951-)
Manna from Heaven '02
Buddy Boy '99

Clare Grogan (1962-)
Comfort and Joy '84
Gregory's Girl '80

David Groh (1941-)
Blowback '99
Acts of Betrayal '98
Spoiler '98
Last Exit to Earth '96
White Cargo '96
Illegal in Blue '95
Broken Vows '87
Hot Shot '86
Zertigo Diamond Caper '82
A Hero Ain't Nothin' but a Sandwich '78
Victory at Entebbe '76

Ake Gronberg (1914-69)
Sawdust & Tinsel '53
Monika '52
Boris and Natasha: The Movie '92
A Midnight Clear '92
Shaking the Tree '92
For the Boys '91
A Matter of Degrees '90
The Experts '89
Tequila Sunrise '88
The Couch Trip '87
House 2: The Second Story '87
Soul Man '86

Edan Gross (1978-)
Best of the Best 2 '93
And You Thought Your Parents Were Weird! '91

Mary Gross (1953-)
40 Days and 40 Nights '02
The Santa Clause '94
There Goes the Neighborhood '92
Troop Beverly Hills '89
Big Business '88
Casual Sex? '88
Feds '88
Baby Boom '87
The Couch Trip '87
Club Paradise '86

Michael Gross (1947-)
Mrs. Harris '05
Tremors 3: Back to Perfection '01
Ground Control '98
True Heart '97
Kounterfeit '96
Tremors 2: Aftershocks '96
Sometimes They Come Back... Again '96
In the Heat of Passion 2: Unfaithful '94
Snowbound: The Jim and Jennifer Stolpa Story '94
Firestorm: 72 Hours in Oakland '93
Alan & Naomi '92
Undesirable '92
Cool As Ice '91
Midnight Murders '91
A Connecticut Yankee in King Arthur's Court '89
Tremors '89
Big Business '88
In the Line of Duty: The FBI Murders '88
Summer Fantasy '84

Paul Gross (1959-)
Slings & Arrows: Season 2 '05
Men with Brooms '02
20,000 Leagues Under the Sea '97
Whale Music '94
Armistead Maupin's Tales of the City '93
Aspen Extreme '93
Northern Extremes '93
Buffalo Jump '90
Cold Comfort '90

Brigitte Grothum (1933-)
Inn on the River '62
The Strange Countess '61

Deborah Grover
Where the Truth Lies '05
The Christmas Wife '88

Gulshan Grover (1955-)
Eastside '99
Tales of the Kama Sutra 2: Monsoon '98
Monsoon '97
Rudyard Kipling's the Second Jungle Book: Mowgli and Baloo '97

Robin Groves
Silver Bullet '85
The Nesting '80

Robert Grubb (1950-)
Salem's Lot '04
Mad Max: Beyond Thunderdome '85
Remember Me '85
Gallipoli '81
My Brilliant Career '79

Gary Grubbs
Double Take '01
Gone Fishin' '97
The Ernest Green Story '93
Without Warning: The James Brady Story '91
Foxfire '87
Fatal Vision '84

Franz Gruber
X from Outer Space '67
Terror Beneath the Sea '66
Deutschland im Jahre Null '47

Ioan Gruffudd (1974-)
Fantastic Four: Rise of the Silver Surfer '07
Amazing Grace '06
The TV Set '06
Fantastic Four '05
King Arthur '04
This Girl's Life '03
The Gathering '02
Black Hawk Down '01
Horatio Hornblower: The Adventure Continues '01
102 Dalmatians '00
Shooters '00
Very Annie Mary '00
Great Expectations '99
Horatio Hornblower '99
Solomon and Gaenor '98
Poldark '96

Greg Grunberg (1966-)
Mission: Impossible 3 '06
The Ladykillers '04
The Medicine Show '01
Hollow Man '00
Dinner and Driving '97

Gustav Grundgens (1899-1963)
Liebelei '32
M '31

Olivier Gruner (1960-)
Extreme Honor '01
Crackerjack 3 '00
Interceptor Force '99
Velocity Trap '99
T.N.T. '98
Mercenary 2: Thick and Thin '97
Mercenary '96
Savage '96
The Fighter '95
Automatic '94
Nemesis '93
Angel Town '89

Ilka Gruning (1876-1964)
Desperate '47
Casablanca '42
Underground '41
Joyless Street '25

Stefan Gryff (1939-)
One Against the Wind '91
Legend of the Werewolf '75

Ah-Leh Gua (1944-)
Fleeing by Night '00
Eat Drink Man Woman '94
The Wedding Banquet '93

Nicky Guadagni
The Golden Spiders: A Nero Wolfe Mystery '00
Cube '98

Christopher Guard (1953-)
A Woman of Substance '84
The Lord of the Rings '78

Dominic Guard (1956-)
Absolution '81
Picnic at Hanging Rock '75
The Go-Between '71

Kit Guard (1894-1961)
El Diablo Rides '39
Six Gun Rhythm '39
Carnival Lady '33
Fighting Champ '33

Pippa Guard (1952-)
Scarlett '94
All or Nothing at All '93
Unsuitable Job for a Woman '82

Harry Guardino (1925-95)
Fist of Honor '92
The Neon Empire '89
Sophisticated Gents '81
Any Which Way You Can '80
Goldengirl '79
Matilda '78
Rollercoaster '77
The Enforcer '76
St. Ives '76
Whiffs '75
Get Christie Love! '74
They Only Kill Their Masters '72
Dirty Harry '71
Octaman '71
Lovers and Other Strangers '70
Madigan '68
The Adventures of Bullwhip Griffin '66
Hell Is for Heroes '62
The Five Pennies '59
Pork Chop Hill '59
Houseboat '58

Justin Guarini (1978-)
Fast Girl '07
From Justin to Kelly '03

Vincent Guastaferro
Liberty Heights '99
Sweet and Lowdown '99
Nitti: The Enforcer '88

Irina Gubanova (1940-)
War and Peace '68

Florence Guerin (1965-)
Bizarre '87
Black Venus '83

Blanca Guerra (1953-)
In the Middle of Nowhere '93
Danzon '91
Santa Sangre '90
Erendira '83

Alvaro Guerrero
Amores Perros '00
In the Country Where Nothing Happens '99

Evelyn Guerrero (1949-)
Cheech and Chong: Things Are Tough All Over '82
Cheech and Chong's Nice Dreams '81
Cheech and Chong's Next Movie '80

Franco Guerrero
Deathfight '93
The Kick Fighter '91
Warriors of the Apocalypse '85
American Commandos '84
One Armed Executioner '80

Monica Guerritore (1958-)
The Endless Game '89
Together? '79

Fausto Guerzoni (1904-)
Black Orpheus '58
The Bicycle Thief '48

Christopher Guest (1948-)
For Your Consideration '06
Mrs. Henderson Presents '05
A Mighty Wind '03
Best in Show '00
Small Soldiers '98 (V)
Waiting for Guffman '96
A Few Good Men '92
The Return of Spinal Tap '92
Sticky Fingers '88
The Princess Bride '87
Beyond Therapy '86
Little Shop of Horrors '86
This Is Spinal Tap '84
A Piano for Mrs. Cimino '82
Heartbeeps '81
The Last Word '80
The Long Riders '80
Blind Ambition '79
Girlfriends '78
Shame of the Jungle '75 (V)

Lance Guest (1960-)
Mach 2 '00
Plan B '97
The Wizard of Loneliness '88
Jaws: The Revenge '87
My Father, My Rival '85
Just the Way You Are '84
The Last Starfighter '84
Roommate '84
I Ought to Be in Pictures '82
Halloween 2: The Nightmare Isn't Over! '81

Nicholas Guest (1955-)
Nemesis 4: Cry of Angels '97
Night Hunter '95
Kickboxer 4: The Aggressor '94
Puppet Master 5: The Final Chapter '94
Brain Smasher... A Love Story '93
My Daughter's Keeper '93
Nemesis '93
Chrome Soldiers '92
Forever: A Ghost of a Love Story '92
Grand Tour: Disaster in Time '92
Dollman '90
Assassin '89
National Lampoon's Christmas Vacation '89
Strange Case of Dr. Jekyll & Mr. Hyde '89
Criminal Act '88
Trading Places '83
The Long Riders '80

Carla Gugino (1971-)
American Gangster '07
The Lookout '07
Rise: Blood Hunter '07
Even Money '06
Night at the Museum '06
Sin City '05
The Singing Detective '03
Spy Kids 3-D: Game Over '03
Spy Kids 2: The Island of Lost Dreams '02
The Center of the World '01
The Jimmy Show '01
The One '01
She Creature '01
Spy Kids '01
A Season for Miracles '99
Judas Kiss '98
Snake Eyes '98
Lovelife '97
Homeward Bound 2: Lost in San Francisco '96 (V)
Jaded '96
The War at Home '96
Wedding Bell Blues '96
The Buccaneers '95
Miami Rhapsody '95
Red Hot '95
Son-in-Law '93
This Boy's Life '93
Murder Without Motive '92

Noel Guglielmi
Splinter '06
Harsh Times '05

Wandisa Guida (1937-)
Gladiator of Rome '63
I, Vampiri '56

Giovanni Guidelli (1966-)
Fiorile '93
Where Angels Fear to Tread '91

Anthony Guidera
L.A. Dicks '05
Red Shoe Diaries 7: Burning Up '96
Undercover '94

Darrel Guilbeau (1962-)
Murder-in-Law '92
Lauderdale '89

Ann Guilbert (1928-)
Sour Grapes '98
Grumpier Old Men '95

Nancy Guild (1925-99)
Francis Covers the Big Town '53
Abbott and Costello Meet the Invisible Man '51
Black Magic '49

Paul Guilfoyle (1902-61)
Apache '54
Actors and Sin '52
Follow Me Quietly '49
The Judge '49
The Missing Corpse '45
It Happened Tomorrow '44
The Seventh Cross '44
The Saint Takes Over '40
The Crime of Dr. Crespi '35

Paul Guilfoyle (1955-)
Live from Baghdad '03
Session 9 '01
Anywhere But Here '99
In Dreams '99
The Negotiator '98
One Tough Cop '98
Primary Colors '98
Air Force One '97
Amistad '97
Cafe Society '97
L.A. Confidential '97
Path to Paradise '97
Celtic Pride '96
Extreme Measures '96
Looking for Richard '96
Curiosity Kills '90
Dealers '89
Beverly Hills Cop 2 '87
The Serpent and the Rainbow '88
Three Men and a Baby '87
Wall Street '87
Howard the Duck '86

Robert Guillaume (1937-)
The Lion King 1 1/2 '04 (V)
Big Fish '03
Silicon Towers '99
His Bodyguard '98
A Good Day to Die '95
Cosmic Slop '94
The Lion King '94 (V)
The Meteor Man '93
The Penthouse '92
First Kid '96
Panic in the Skies! '96
Run for the Dream: The Gail Devers Story '95
Death Warrant '90
Fire and Rain '89
You Must Remember This '92

Paul Guilfoyle / Sophie Guillemin (1977-)
He Loves Me ... He Loves Me Not '02
With a Friend Like Harry '00
L'Ennui '98

Paul Guilleaumin (1955-)
Women on the Verge of a Nervous Breakdown '88

Sienna Guillory (1975-)
Eragon '05
Sorted '04
Helen of Troy '03
Love Actually '03
Resident Evil: Apocalypse '04
The Time Machine '02
Stargate: The Ark of Truth '08

Francis Guinan
Hannibal '01
Guinevere '99
Lansky '99
Shining Through '92

Tim Guinee (1962-)
Iron Man '08
Oliver Twist '48
Great Expectations '46
The Lavender Hill Mob '51
The Man in the White Suit '51
Last Holiday '50
Kind Hearts and Coronets '49

Alec Guinness (1914-2000)
Mute Witness '95
A Foreign Field '93
Kafka '91
Monsignor Quixote '91
A Handful of Dust '88
Little Dorrit, Film 1: Nobody's Fault '88
Little Dorrit, Film 2: Little Dorrit's Story '88
Edwin '84
A Passage to India '84
Lovesick '83
Return of the Jedi '83 (V)
Smiley's People '82
Lean on Me '89
They Still Call Me Bruce '86
Wanted Dead or Alive '86
North and South Book 1 '85
The Kid with the 200 I.Q. '83
Prince Jack '83
The Kid with the Broken Halo '82
Star Wars '77
Murder by Death '76
Brother Sun, Sister Moon '73
Hitler: The Last Ten Days '73
Cromwell '70
Scrooge '70
The Comedians '67
Hotel Paradiso '66
The Quiller Memorandum '66
Doctor Zhivago '65
The Fall of the Roman Empire '64
Damn the Defiant '62
Lawrence of Arabia '62
Tunes of Glory '60
Our Man in Havana '59
The Horse's Mouth '58
The Bridge on the River Kwai '57
The Swan '56
The Ladykillers '55
The Prisoner '55
The Detective '54
To Paris with Love '55
Father Brown '54
Captain's Paradise '53
Malta Story '53
The Promoter '52

Tito Guizar (1908-99)
On the Old Spanish Trail '47
Blondie Goes Latin '42
The Gay Ranchero '42

Clu Gulager (1928-)
Feast '06
Gunfighter '98
Eddie Presley '92
The Killing Device '92
My Heroes Have Always Been Cowboys '91
Tapeheads '89
I'm Gonna Git You Sucka '88
Teen Vamp '88
The Uninvited '88
The Hidden '87
Hunter's Blood '87
The Offspring '87
The Sandlot '93
Lange '36

Henri Guisol (1904-94)
Murder at 45 R.P.M. '65
Murder at the Twilight Girls '57
Bizarre Bizarre '39
The Crime of Monsieur Lange '36

Tom Guiry (1981-)
Black Irish '07
Steel City '06
The Mudge Boy '03
Mystic River '03
Scotland, PA '02
Black Hawk Down '01
Tigerland '00
U-571 '00
Ride with the Devil '99
All I Wanna Do '98
Wrestling with Alligators '98
The Sandlot '93

Julien Guiomar (1928-)
Leolo '92
My New Partner '84
Swashbuckler '84
A Very Curious Girl '69
The King of Hearts '66

David Gulpilil (1954-)
The Proposition '05
Rabbit-Proof Fence '02
Until the End of the World '91
Dark Age '88
Crocodile Dundee '86
The Last Wave '77
Mad Dog Morgan '76
Walkabout '71

Mamie Gummer
Stop-Loss '08
Evening '07

Devon Gummersall (1978-)
Earth vs. the Spider '01
Dick '99
When Trumpets Fade '98
Lured Innocence '97
Trading Favors '97
Independence Day '96
It's My Party '95
Nobody's Baby '01
Enemy of the State '98
Without Evidence '96

Anna Gunn (1968-)
Enemy of the State '98
Without Evidence '96

David Gunn (1972-)
The Convent '00
Vampire Journals '96

Janet Gunn (1961-)
Inferno '01
Lost Voyage '01
The Nurse '97

Moses Gunn (1929-93)
Memphis '91
Perfect Harmony '91
The Women of Brewster Place '89
The House of Dies Drear '88
The Quest '96
Marquis de Sade '96
Carnosaur 3: Primal Species '96
The Adventures of Marco Polo '38
Aigiers '38

Neena Gupta
Cotton Mary '99
In Custody '94

Sean Gullette (1968-)
Happy Accidents '00
Requiem for a Dream '00
Pi '98

Leo Gullotta (1946-)
Men Men Men '95
La Scorta '94
Sinbad of the Seven Seas '89

Dorothy Gulliver (1908-97)
Faces '68
Fighting Caballero '35
The Fighting Marshal '32
Outlaw Justice '32
Shadow of the Eagle '32
The Galloping Ghost '31
Under Montana Skies '30

Sean Gunn (1974-)
The Specials '00
Stricken '07

Dan Gunther (1945-)
Dead Silence '07

Bob Gunton (1945-)
Fracture '07
Numb '07
Pandemic '07
Believe in Me '06
Boat Trip '03
Dallas 362 '03
61* '01
The Perfect Storm '00
Running Mates '00
Bats '99
Calls '95
Broken Arrow '95
In Pursuit of Honor '95
Kingfish: A Story of Huey P. Long '95
Roswell: The U.F.O. Cover-Up '94
The Shawshank Redemption '94
Demolition Man '93
Patch Adams '98
Buffalo Soldiers '97
Changing Habits '96
The Glimmer Man '96
Ace Ventura: When Nature Calls '95
Father Hood '93
Lone Justice '93
Wild Palms '93
Don't Tell Her It's Me '90
Three Men and a Little Lady '90
Cocoon: The Return '88
High Spirits '88
Pecos Bill '86

Sean Guist (?) / Ray Guth
Wonderland Cove '75
Hit Lady '74
McQ '74
Smile, Jenny, You're Dead '74
Snowblind '78
The Other Side of Midnight '77
Touched by Love '80
Force of One '79
Willa '79
He Who Walks Alone '78
A Question of Love '78
Amazing Grace '74
Rollerball '75
Rollerball '75
Black Brigade '69
Wild Rovers '71
The Iceman Cometh '73
Haunts of the Very Rich '72
Shaft's Big Score '72
The Great White Hope '70
The Hot Rock '70
Willie & Phil '80
Moonstruck '87
Pizza Man '91
Bright Lights, Big City '88
Masterminds '96
The Cable Guy '96
One Night Stand '97
Not Like Us '96

Steve Guttenberg (1958-)
P.S. Your Cat Is Dead! '02
Airborne '98
Home Team '99
Tower of Terror '97
Zeus and Roxanne '96
The Big Green '95
It Takes Two '95
Home for the Holidays '95
The Bedroom Window '87
Police Academy 4: Citizens on Patrol '87
Police Academy 3: Back in Training '86
Short Circuit '86
Bad Medicine '85
Cocoon '85
Police Academy 2: Their First Assignment '85
Police Academy '84
Amazon Women on the Moon '87
The Day After '83
The Man Who Wasn't There '83
Diner '82
Miracle on Ice '81
Can't Stop the Music '80
To Race the Wind '80
The Boys from Brazil '78
The Chicken Chronicles '77
Rollercoaster '77

Tani Phelps Guthrie (1928-)
Beachcomber '38

Arlo Guthrie (1947-)
Roadside Prophets '92
Alice's Restaurant '69

Tyrone Guthrie (1900-71)
In the Country Where Nothing Happens '39

Antonio Gutierrez
Sidewalks of London '38
El Norte '83

Emilio Gutierrez-Caba (1942-)
No News from God '01

Zaide Silvia Gutierrez
Highway Patrolman '91

Annabelle Gurwitch (1961-)
The Shaggy Dog '06
Melvin Goes to Dinner '03
The 4th Tenor '02
The Medicine Show '01

Louis Guss (1918-)
A Tale of Two Pizzas '03
American Blue Note '89
The Cemetery Club '93
Nitti: The Enforcer '88

Sigrid Gurie (1911-69)
Enemy of Women '44
Three Faces West '40
The Adventures of Marco Polo '38

Alizia Gur (1942-)
Beast of Morocco '66
From Russia with Love '63

Eric Gurry (1966-)
Cold Comfort Farm '71
Crucible of Horror '69

Sharon Gurney
Something Special '66
The Zoo Gang '85
Bad Boys '83

Lucy Gutteridge (1956-)
Tusks '89
Grief '94
The Woman He Loved '86
The Secret Garden '87

Kick (Christopher) Gurry
Daltry Calhoun '05
Spartan '04

Gutteridge

The Trouble with Spies '87
A Christmas Carol '84
Top Secret! '84

Ronald Guttman
The Tollbooth '04
Just the Ticket '98
Kisses in the Dark '97
The Beast '96
The Pillow Book '95
And the Band Played On '93
Josh and S.A.M. '93
Iran: Days of Crisis '91

DeJuan Guy (1981-)
One Man's Justice '95
Candyman '92

Jasmine Guy (1964-)
Carrie '02
Anne Rice's The Feast of All Saints '01
Diamond Men '01
Guinevere '99
Cats Don't Dance '97 (V)
Perfect Crime '97
America's Dream '95
Queen '93
Harlem Nights '89
School Daze '88

Henri Guybet (1936-)
No Problem '75
The Mad Adventures of Rabbi Jacob '73

Sheila Guyse (1925-)
Miracle in Harlem '48
Sepia Cinderella '47
Boy! What a Girl '45

Joe Guzaldo (1960-)
Evil Has a Face '96
Hoodlum '96
The Woman Who Loved Elvis '93
Bingo '91
Smooth Talker '90

Luis Guzman (1956-)
Cleaner '07
War '07
The Adventures of Pluto Nash '02
Disappearances '06
Fast Food Nation '06
School for Scoundrels '06
Carlito's Way: Rise to Power '05
Dreamer: Inspired by a True Story '05
Waiting '05
Anger Management '03
Confidence '03
Dumb and Dumberer: When Harry Met Lloyd '03
Punch-Drunk Love '02
The Salton Sea '02
Welcome to Collinwood '02
Double Whammy '01
Luckytown '00
Table One '00
Thin Air '00
Traffic '00
The Bone Collector '99
The Limey '99
One Tough Cop '98
Out of Sight '98
Snake Eyes '98
Boogie Nights '97
Pronto '97
The Substitute '96
Lotto Land '95
Stonewall '95
The Burning Season '94
Carlito's Way '93
Guilty as Sin '93
Mr. Wonderful '93
Jumpin' at the Boneyard '92
The Hard Way '91
Q & A '90
Family Business '89
Crocodile Dundee 2 '88

Teri Guzman
Escape from Cell Block 3 '74
Women Unchained '72

Jack Gwaltney (1960-)
Love Thy Neighbor '02
The Siege '98
One Way Out '95
Risk '94
Vital Signs '90

Edmund Gwenn (1875-1959)
It's a Dog's Life '55
The Trouble with Harry '55
The Student Prince '54
Them! '54
The Bigamist '53
A Woman of Distinction '50
Challenge to Lassie '49
The Hills of Home '48
Green Dolphin Street '47
Life with Father '47
Miracle on 34th Street '47
Undercurrent '46
Charley's Aunt '41
Forever and a Day '43
Lassie, Come Home '43
Cheers for Miss Bishop '41
The Devil & Miss Jones '41
Doctor Takes a Wife '40
Foreign Correspondent '40
Pride and Prejudice '40
South Riding '37
Anthony Adverse '36
Java Head '35
Sylvia Scarlett '35
If I Were Rich '33
Skin Game '31

David Gwillim (1948-)
Peter and Paul '81
If It's a Man, Hang Up '75
The Island at the Top of the World '74

Jack (Gwyllam) Gwillim (1912-2001)
The Bushbaby '70
Jason and the Argonauts '63

Anne Gwynne (1918-2003)
Adam at 6 a.m. '70
Teenage Monster '57
Breakdown '53
King of the Bullwhip '51
Black Tower '50
Dick Tracy Meets Gruesome '47
Killer Dill '47
Fear '46
House of Frankenstein '44
Ride 'Em Cowboy '42
The Black Cat '41
Nice Girl? '41
Black Friday '40
Flash Gordon Conquers the Universe '40

Michael Gwynn (1916-76)
The Scars of Dracula '70
Jason and the Argonauts '63
Village of the Damned '60
The Revenge of Frankenstein '58

Fred Gwynne (1926-93)
My Cousin Vinny '92
Shadows and Fog '92
Disorganized Crime '89
Pet Sematary '89
Vanishing Act '88
Fatal Attraction '87
Ironweed '87
Murder by the Book '87
The Secret of My Success '87
The Boy Who Could Fly '86
Off Beat '86
Water '85
The Cotton Club '84
The Mysterious Stranger '82
The Munsters' Revenge '81
Simon '80
Sanctuary of Fear '79
The Littlest Angel '69
Munster, Go Home! '66

Michael C. Gwynne (1942-)
The Last of the Finest '90
Cherry 2000 '88
Seduced '85
Harry Tracy '83
The Streets of L.A. '79
Special Delivery '76
Payday '73

Peter Gwynne
Tim '79
Puzzle '78
The Dove '74

Jake Gyllenhaal (1980-)
Rendition '07
Zodiac '07
Brokeback Mountain '05
Jarhead '05
Proof '05
The Day After Tomorrow '04
The Good Girl '02
Lovely & Amazing '02
Moonlight Mile '02
Bubble Boy '01
Donnie Darko '01
Highway '01
October Sky '99

Maggie Gyllenhaal (1977-)
The Dark Knight '08
The Great New Wonderful '06
Monster House '06 (V)
Paris, je t'aime '06
Sherrybaby '06
Stranger Than Fiction '06
Trust the Man '06
World Trade Center '06
Happy Endings '05
Criminal '04
Casa de los Babys '03
Mona Lisa Smile '03
Adaptation '02
Confessions of a Dangerous Mind '02
40 Days and 40 Nights '02
Secretary '02
Donnie Darko '01
Riding in Cars with Boys '01
Cecil B. Demented '00

Kim Gyngell (1952-)
The Hard Word '02
Love and Other Catastrophes '95
Heaven Tonight '93
The Wacky World of Wills & Burke '85

Greta Gynt (1916-2000)
Dear Murderer '47
Mr. Emmanuel '44
The Arsenal Stadium Mystery '39
Mystery '39
The Human Monster '39
The Hooded Terror '38
Sexton Blake and the Hooded Terror '38

Johnathan Haagensen
City of Men '07
City of God '02

Christina Haag
Lost in the Bermuda Triangle '98
Shaking the Tree '92

Charles S. Haas (1952-)
Matinee '92
Gremlins 2: The New Batch '90
Tex '82

Dolly Haas (1910-94)
I Confess '53
Spy of Napoleon '36

Hugo Haas (1902-68)
King Solomon's Mines '50
The Fighting Kentuckian '49
Casbah '48
For the Love of Mary '48
My Girl Tisa '48
Merton of the Movies '47
Northwest Outpost '47
The Private Affairs of Bel Ami '47
Holiday in Mexico '46
Days of Glory '43

Lukas Haas (1976-)
Alpha Dog '06
Brick '06
Material Girls '06
The Tripper '06
Last Days '05
Bookies '03
The Lathe of Heaven '02
Running Free '00
Breakfast of Champions '99
Everyone Says I Love You '96
johns '96
Mars Attacks! '96
Boys '95
Warrior Spirit '94
Alan & Naomi '92
Leap of Faith '92
Rambling Rose '91
Music Box '89
See You in the Morning '89
The Lady in White '88
The Wizard of Loneliness '88
Shattered Spirits '86
Solarbabies '86
Witness '85

Alessandro Haber (1947-)
Men Men Men '95
The Story of Boys & Girls '91

Eva Habermann (1976-)
Tales from a Parallel Universe: Eating Pattern '97
Tales from a Parallel Universe: Giga Shadow '97
Tales from a Parallel Universe: I Worship His Shadow '97
Tales from a Parallel Universe: Super Nova '97

Matthias Habich (1940-)
Downfall '04
Nowhere in Africa '02
Enemy at the Gates '00
The Savage Woman '91
Straight for the Heart '88
Coup de Grace '78
An Occurrence at Owl Creek Bridge/Coup de Grace '62

Olivia Hack (1983-)
A Very Brady Sequel '96
The Brady Bunch Movie '95

Shelley Hack (1952-)
The Finishing Touch '92
Me, Myself & I '92
A Casualty of War '89
Blind Fear '89
The Stepfather '87
Troll '86
Kicks '85
Single Bars, Single Women '84

George Hackathorne (1895-1940)
Merry-Go-Round '23
The Worldly Madonna '22
The Last of the Mohicans '20

Joseph Hacker
Little Treasure '85
The Ultimate Imposter '79

Buddy Hackett (1924-2003)
Paulie '98
The Little Mermaid '89 (V)
Scrooged '88
Bud and Lou '78
Muscle Beach Party '64
It's a Mad, Mad, Mad, Mad World '63
The Music Man '62
The Wonderful World of the Brothers Grimm '62
God's Little Acre '58

Claire Hackett
Liam '00
Gallowglass '95

Joan Hackett (1942-83)
Flicks '85
The Escape Artist '82
Only When I Laugh '81
The Long Days of Summer '80
One Trick Pony '80
Dead of Night '77
The Possessed '77
The Treasure of Matecumbe '76
Reflections of Murder '74
The Terminal Man '74
Class of '63 '73
The Last of Sheila '73
Rivals '72
Support Your Local Sheriff '69
Will Penny '67
The Group '66

Karl Hackett (1893-1948)
Outlaw of the Plains '46
His Brother's Ghost '45
Lightning Raiders '45
Shadows of Death '45
Sonora Stagecoach '44
Bordertown Gunfighters '43
Sagebrush Law '43
Sundown Fury '42
The Lone Rider in Frontier Fury '41
Texas Trouble '41
Take Me Back to Oklahoma '40
Yukon Flight '40
Feud Maker '38
Phantom Ranger '38
Rollin' Plains '38
Songs and Bullets '38
Border Phantom '37
Gun Lords of Stirrup Basin '37
Paroled to Die '37
The Red Rope '37
Sing, Cowboy, Sing '37
Tex Rides with the Boy Scouts '37
Cavalry '36
Stormy Trails '36
The Traitor '36

Sandy Hackett
Ex-Cop '93

Penne Hackforth-Jones (1943-)
Paradise Road '97
Image of Death '77
Alvin Purple '73

Gene Hackman (1930-)
Welcome to Mooseport '04
Runaway Jury '03
Behind Enemy Lines '01
Heartbreakers '01
Heist '01
The Mexican '01
The Royal Tenenbaums '01
The Replacements '00
Under Suspicion '00
Antz '98
Enemy of the State '98
Twilight '98
Absolute Power '97
The Chamber '96
Extreme Measures '96
The Birdcage '96
Crimson Tide '95
Get Shorty '95
The Quick and the Dead '95
Wyatt Earp '94
The Firm '93
Geronimo: An American Legend '93
Unforgiven '92
Class Action '91
Company Business '91
Loose Cannons '90
Narrow Margin '90
Postcards from the Edge '90
The Package '89
Another Woman '88
Bat 21 '88
Full Moon in Blue Water '88
Mississippi Burning '88
Split Decisions '88
No Way Out '87
Superman 4: The Quest for Peace '87
Hoosiers '86
Power '86
Target '85
Twice in a Lifetime '85
Misunderstood '84
Uncommon Valor '83
Under Fire '83
All Night Long '81
Eureka! '81
Reds '81
Superman 2 '80
Superman: The Movie '78
A Bridge Too Far '77
The Domino Principle '77
March or Die '77
America at the Movies '76
Bite the Bullet '75
French Connection 2 '75
Night Moves '75
The Conversation '74
Young Frankenstein '74
Zandy's Bride '74
Scarecrow '73
The Poseidon Adventure '72
Prime Cut '72
The French Connection '71
Doctors' Wives '70
I Never Sang for My Father '70
Downhill Racer '69
The Gypsy Moths '69
Marooned '69
Riot '69
Bonnie & Clyde '67
Hawaii '66
Lilith '64

Michiko Hada (1968-)
Flowers of Shanghai '98
Rowing Through '96
The Mystery of Rampo '94

Jonathan Hadary (1948-)
Intolerable Cruelty '03
A Simple Wish '97
Private Parts '96
The New Age '94
As Is '85

Suheil Haddad
The Milky Way '97

Ellie Haddington
Lawless Heart '01
The Wyvern Mystery '00

Dayle Haddon (1949-)
Fiesta '95
Cyborg '89
Bedroom Eyes '86
North Dallas Forty '79
The Cheaters '76
Paperback Hero '73
The World's Greatest Athlete '73

Peter Haddon (1898-1962)
Secret of Stamboul '36
The Silent Passenger '35

Ron Haddrick (1929-)
Quigley Down Under '90
The Great Expectations: The Untold Story '87
Camel Boy '84 (V)
Dawn! '83

Sara Haden (1897-1981)
The Great Rupert '50
A Life of Her Own '50
Love Laughs at Andy Hardy '46

Mr. Ace '46
She Wolf of London '46
Our Vines Have Tender Grapes '45
Andy Hardy's Double Life '42
Somewhere I'll Find You '42
Andy Hardy Meets Debutante '40
The Shop Around the Corner '40
Andy Hardy Gets Spring Fever '39
The Poor Little Rich Girl '36
Spitfire '34
Finishing School '33

Bill Hader (1978-)
Forgetting Sarah Marshall '08
Pineapple Express '08
Tropic Thunder '08
Hot Rod '07
Supe bad '07

Reed Hadley (1911-74)
Brain of Blood '71
Kansas Pacific '53
Baron of Arizona '51
The Half-Breed '51
Little Big Horn '51
Motor Patrol '50
Return of Jesse James '50
Ziegfeld Girl '41
Whistling in the Dark '41
Guadalcanal Diary '43
Dark Corner '46
I'll Ir. Lucky '46
Doll Face '46
A Southern Yankee '48
Return of Wildfire '48
Last of the Wild Horses '49
I Shot Jesse James '49
Zorro's Fighting Legion '39
Hollywood Stadium Mystery '38

Angel '84
Night Creature '79
Fowl Play '75
Bad Charleston Charlie '73
The Deadly and the Beautiful '73
Hell is for Heroes '62
The Gunfight at Dodge City '59

Uta Hagen (1919-2004)
Reversal of Fortune '90
The Boys from Brazil '78
The Other '72

Kristi Hager
Wanted '08
Sure Fire '90
Spare Me '92

Julie Hagerty (1955-)
She's the Man '06
Storytelling '01
Freddy Got Fingered '01
The Badge '02
A Guy Thing '03
Pizza '05
Just Friends '05
U-Turn '97
The Wife '95
Noises Off '92
What about Bob? '91
Reversal of Fortune '90
Bloodhounds of Broadway '89
Rude Awakening '89
Necessary Parties '88
Beyond Therapy '86
Bad Medicine '85
Goodbye, New York '85
Lost in America '85
Airplane 2: The Sequel '82
A Midsummer Night's Sex Comedy '82
Airplane! '80
The Day the Women Got Even '80

Michael Hagiwara
Indio '90
Indio 2: The Revolt '92

Sean Haggerty
Rhythm Thief '94

Dylan Haggerty (1984-)
The Boys from Brazil '78

Grizzly Mountain '97
Spare Me '92
Hell is for Heroes '62
The Gunfight at Dodge City '59
Command Decision '48

Larry Hagman (1939-)
Primary Colors '98
Nixon '95
S.O.B. '81
President's Mistress '78
The Eagle Has Landed '77
Mother, Jugs and Speed '76
The Big Bus '76
Harry and Tonto '74
Hurricane '74
Antonio '73
Beware! The Blob '72
No Place to Run '72
Hired Hand '71
Three in the Cellar '70
The Group '66
In Harm's Way '65
Ensign Pulver '64
Fail-Safe '64

Marvin Hagler (1954-)
Indio '90
Indio 2: The Revolt '92

Kenichi Hagiwara (1950-)
Kagemusha '80

Michael Hagiwara
Traffic Jam '91

Sid Haig (1939-)
The Devil's Rejects '05
A Dead Calling '06
House of the Dead 2: Dead Aim '05
The House of 1000 Corpses '03
Jackie Brown '97
The Forbidden Dance '90
Wizards of the Lost Kingdom 2 '89
Warlords '88
Commando Squad '87
Galaxy of Terror '81
Aftermath '85
Busting '74
Foxy Brown '74
Coffy '73
The Big Bird Cage '72
The Big Doll House '71
Pit Stop '67
C.C. & Company '70
Emperor of the North Pole

Don Haggerty (1914-88)
The Killers '64
Horre on the Range '04 (V)
The Third Miracle '99
Broken Trust '95
Cooperstown '93
The Fire Next Time '93
Freeze Frame '92
Storyville '92
Fire and Rain '89
Ccp '88
The Great Escape 2: The Untold Story '88
The Rescue '88
Weekend War '88
The Beneficiary '97
Desert Thunder '99
The Darwin Conspiracy '99
The Moon Stallion '85
Station Jim '01
Two Weeks Notice '02

Charles Haid (1943-)
How to Lose a Guy in 10 Days '03
Blown Away '93
Just One of the Girls '93
Thin Ice '37
Oh, What a Night '92
Dream Machine '91
Fast Getaway '91
Prayer of the Rollerboys '91
Dream a Little Dream '89
Watchers '88
License to Drive '88
The Lost Boys '87

Stacy Haiduk (1968-)
The Girl Said No '37
Way Out West '37
Free and Easy '30
Show People '28
Little Annie Rooney '25

David Haig (1955-)
Two Weeks Notice '02

Ion Haiduc
Cyborg 3: The Recycler '95
Scanner Cop 2: Volkin's Revenge '94
Scanners: The Showdown '94

Khrystyne Haje (1968-)

Jester Hairston (1901-2000)
I'm Gonna Git You Sucka '88

Jeanette Hain (1969-)
The Rescue '88
The Journey to Kafiristan '01

William Haines (1900-73)
The Girl Said No '37
Way Out West '37
Free and Easy '30
Show People '28
Little Annie Rooney '25

Richard Haines (1990-)
An African Dream '90
Alien from L.A. '87
Space '66

Patricia Haines (1936-)
The Virgin Witch '72
Night Caller from Outer Space '66

Alan Hale (1892-1950)
The Prince and the Pauper '37
Stella Dallas '37
When Thief Meets Thief '37
Our Relations '36
The Crusades '35
The Good Fairy '35
Great Expectations '34
It Happened One Night '34
Little Minister '34
The Lost Patrol '34
The Scarlet Letter '34
The Sin of Madelon Claudet '31
Susan Lenox: Her Fall and Rise '31

Barbara Hale (1921-)
Perry Mason: The Case of...
Airport '70
Buckskin '68
The Oklahoman '56
Seventh Cavalry '56
The Far Horizons '55
A Lion is in the Streets '53
Last of the Comanches '52
The Jackpot '50
The Clay Pigeon '49
Jolson Sings Again '49
The Window '49
The Boy with the Green Hair '48
First Yank into Tokyo '45
West of the Pecos '45
The Falcon in Hollywood '44
Goin' to Town '44

Alan Hale, Jr. (1918-90)
Back to the Beach '87
Hambone & Hillie '84
Johnny Dangerously '84
The Fifth Musketeer '79
The North Avenue Irregulars '79
Rescue from Gilligan's Island '78
The Giant Spider Invasion '75

Binnie Hale (1899-1984)
Love from a Stranger '37

Creighton Hale (1882-1965)
Action in the North Atlantic '43
The Adventures of Robin Hood '38
Algiers '38
Listen, Darling '38

The Shrieking '73
Starbirc and Sweet William '73
The Adventures of Frontier Fremont '75
Terror Out of the Sky '78
Desperate Women '78
King of the Mountain '81
California Gold Rush '81
The Capture of Grizzly Adams '82
Angels Die Hard '84
Abducted '86
The Grand Duel '73
Sicilian Connection '72
The Night of the Following Day '69
Topkapi '64
Triple Cross '67
Secret Agent Super Dragon '66

Jessica Hahn (1959-)
Bikini Summer 2 '92
Thunder & Mud '89

Kathryn Hahn (1974-)
The Holiday '06
Step Brothers '08
A Lot Like Love '05
Win a Date with Tad Hamilton! '04

Corey Haim (1972-)
Snowboard Academy '96
Demolition High '95
Life 101 '95
Dream a Little Dream 2 '94
National Lampoon's Last Resort '94

Marian Hailey (1941-)
Lovers and Other Strangers '70
Jenny '70

Louisa Haigh
Shipwrecked '90

Kenneth Haigh [1929-]
Cleopatra '63
The Bitch '78

Jean Hagen (1923-77)
Dead Ringer '64
Panic in the Year Zero! '62
Sunrise at Campobello '60
The Shaggy Dog '59
The Big Knife '55
Latin Lovers '53
Singin' in the Rain '52
Adam's Rib '50
The Asphalt Jungle '50
A Life of Her Own '50
Side Street '50

Ross Hagen (1938-)
Midnight Tease 2 '95
Bikini Drive-In '94
Dinosaur Island '93
B-ood Games '90
Alienator '89
Marked for Mu.der '89
B.O.R.N. '88
Commando Squad '87
Phantom Empire '87
Star Slammer '87
Avenging Angel '85

Richard Hageman (1882-1966)
The Great Caruso '51
New Orleans '47

Marianne Hagan
Rick '03
I Think I Do '97
Halloween 6: The Curse of Michael Myers '95

Molly Hagan (1962-)
Playing Mona Lisa '00
Election '99
Ringmaster '98
French Exit '97
Some Kind of Wonderful '87

Merle Haggard (1937-)
Huckleberry Finn '75
Hillbillies in a Haunted House '67

Michael G. (Mike) Hagerty (1953-)
Rampage: The Hillside Strangler Murders '04
Best Laid Plans '99
Inspector Gadget '99
Speed 2: Cruise Control '97
This is Spinal Tap '84
Cannonball '76
Phantom of the Paradise '74

Dan Haggerty (1941-)
Cheyenne Warrior '94
The Magic Voyage '93 (V)
Ice Pawn '92
Deadly Diamonds '91
Mind Trap '91
Soldier's Fortune '91
The Inheritor '90
Repo Jake '90
Spirit of the Eagle '90
Chance '89
The Channeler '89
The Chilling '89
Elves '88
Night Wars '88
Escape from Death Row '73
Jungle Inferno '72
Mr. Scarface '77
Rulers of the City '76
Pray TV '80

Jess Hahn (1922-98)
Cannonball '76
Warlords '88
The Devil's Rejects '05

Eric Hahn
Fist of Glory '95
Crossfire '89

Gisela Hahn (1943-)
Nam Angels '88
Alien Contamination '81
Big Boss '77

Archie Hahn
Amazon Women on the Moon '87
Glory Years '87
Meatballs 2 '84
Protocol '84
This is Spinal Tap '84

Kenneth Haigh [1929-]
Teenage Bad Girl '59
Spider Baby '64
Murders Among Us: The Simon Wiesenthal Story '89

Louisa Haigh
The Private Lives of Elizabeth & Essex '39
The Adventures of Marco Polo '38
The Man in the Iron Mask '39
Dodge City '39
Virginia City '40
The Sea Hawk '40
They Drive by Night '40
The Fighting 69th '40
Santa Fe Trail '41
Strawberry Blonde '41
Gentleman Jim '42
Desperate Journey '42
Captains of the Clouds '42
This is the Army '43
Thank Your Lucky Stars '43
Adventures of Don Juan '49
The Inspector General '49
My Girl Tisa '48
South of St. Louis '48
Pursued '47
The Man I Love '46
Night and Day '45
God is My Co-Pilot '45
The Adventures of Mark Twain '44
Action in the North Atlantic '43
Destination Tokyo '43

Hai'j (1946-)
Ilsa, Harem Keeper of the Oil Sheiks '76
Supervixens '75
Beyond the Valley of the Dolls '70
Faster, Pussycat! Kill! Kill! '65
Motor Psycho '65

Khrystyne Haje (1968-)
Cyborg 3: The Recycler '95
Up Periscope '59
Battle Hymn '57
Al Mine to Give '56
The Indian Fighter '55
Young at Heart '54
Big Trees '52
Mr. Walkie Talkie '52
At Sword's Point '51
To the Shores of Tripoli '42
Watch on the Rhine '43
The Spirit of West Point '47
Rim of the Canyon '49
Wake Island '42
Dive Bomber '41
Four Men and a Prayer '38

Jeanette Hain (1969-)
The Alamo '60
Hard Drivin' '60
The Crawling Hand '63
Robin Hood '22
The Covered Wagon '23
Dick Turpin '25
Power '28
The Giant Spider Invasion '75
Island '78
The Leatherneck '28
Rise '31
Claudet '31

Patricia Haines (1936-)
Apocalypse 21
The Four Horsemen of the...
The Trap '22
The Phantom _ight '35
The Falcon in Hollywood
West of the Pecos '45
First Yank into Tokyo '45
The Boy with the Green Hair '48

The Tender Warrior '71
Bury Me an Angel '71
Win a Date with Tad Hamilton! '04
A Lot Like Love '05

Watch on the Rhine '43
Dive Bomber '41
Sergeant York '41
Shop Angel '32
The Cat and the Canary '27
The Marriage Circle '24
Broken Hearts of Broadway '23

Doug Hale
The Idol Dancer '20
Way Down East '20

Georgina Hale (1943-)
Preaching to the Perverted '97
Castaway '87
Mahler '74
The Boy Friend '71
The Devils '71

Jean Hale (1938-)
In Like Flint '67
The St. Valentine's Day Massacre '67
Psychomania '63

Jonathan Hale (1891-1966)
The Judge '49
Call Northside 777 '48
Silver River '48
Blondie Knows Best '46
Easy to Wed '46
Hollywood Canteen '44
It's a Great Life '43
Blondie for Victory '42
Blondie Goes Latin '42
Blondie Goes to College '42
Hangmen Also Die '42
Blondie in Society '41
Blondie Has Trouble '40
Blondie Plays Cupid '40
Johnny Apollo '40
The Saint Takes Over '40
The Saint's Double Trouble '40
Blondie Brings Up Baby '39
Blondie Meets the Boss '39
Blondie Strikes Back '39
The Story of Alexander Graham Bell '39
Blondie '38
Breaking the Ice '38
Bringing Up Baby '38
The Duke of West Point '38
Exiled to Shanghai '37
Saratoga '37
You Only Live Once '37

Louise Closser Hale (1872-1933)
Today We Live '33
Shanghai Express '32
Devotion '31
Platinum Blonde '31

Monte Hale (1921-)
Missourians '50
Trail of Robin Hood '50
The Vanishing Westerner '50
Outcasts of the Trail '49
Pioneer Marshal '49
Son of God's Country '48
Under Colorado Skies '47
Rough Riders of Cheyenne '45

Sonnie Hale (1902-59)
It's Love Again '36
First a Girl '35
Evergreen '34

Tony Hale (1970-)
Because I Said So '07
Larry the Cable Guy: Health Inspector '06
RV '06
Stranger Than Fiction '06
Fortunes '05

Brian Haley (1963-)
Pearl Harbor '01
McHale's Navy '97
That Darn Cat '96

Baby's Day Out '94
Little Giants '94

Jack Haley (1899-1979)
People Are Funny '46
George White's Scandals '45
Treasure of Fear '45
Higher and Higher '44
One Body Too Many '44
Take It Big '44
Moon over Miami '41
The Wizard of Oz '39
Alexander's Ragtime Band '38
Pick a Star '37
Pigskin Parade '36
The Poor Little Rich Girl '36

Jackie Earle Haley (1961-)
Semi-Pro '08
All the King's Men '06
Little Children '06
Maniac Cop 3: Badge of Silence '93
Dollman '90
The Zoo Gang '85
Losin' It '82
Breaking Away '79
The Bad News Bears Go to Japan '78
The Bad News Bears in Breaking Training '77
Damnation Alley '77
The Bad News Bears '76

H.B. Halicki (1941-89)
Deadline Auto Theft '83
The Junkman '82
Gone in 60 Seconds '74

Albert Hall (1937-)
Ali '01
Beloved '98
Get On the Bus '96
Devil in a Blue Dress '95
Major Payne '95
Malcolm X '92
Hearts of Darkness: A Filmmaker's Apocalypse '91
Separate but Equal '91
Betrayed '88
Uncle Tom's Cabin '87
The Long, Hot Summer '86
Sophisticated Gents '81
Apocalypse Now '79

Anthony Michael Hall (1968-)
The Dark Knight '08
Funny Valentine '05
All About the Benjamins '02
The Dead Zone '02
The Caveman's Valentine '01
Freddy Got Fingered '01
Hitched '01
61* '01
Happy Accidents '00
Fallen Angel '99
The Pirates of Silicon Valley '99
Bomb Squad '97
Exit in Red '97
The Killing Grounds '97
Trojan War '97
The Death Artist '95
The Grave '95
Hail Caesar '94
Me and the Mob '94
Texas '94
The Adventures of a Gnome Named Gnorm '93
Six Degrees of Separation '93
Into the Sun '92
Edward Scissorhands '90
Johnny Be Good '88
Out of Bounds '86
The Breakfast Club '85
Weird Science '85
Sixteen Candles '84
National Lampoon's Vacation '83
Six Pack '82

Arch Hall, Jr. (1945-)
Deadwood '65
Nasty Rabbit '64
The Sadist '63
Eegah! '62
Wild Guitar '62
The Choppers '61

Arch (Archie) Hall, Sr. (1908-78)
The Thrill Killers '65
Wild Guitar '62
Border Badmen '45
His Brother's Ghost '45
The Lone Rider in Frontier Fury '41

Arsenio Hall (1956-)
The Proud Family Movie '05 (V)
Harlem Nights '89
Coming to America '88
Amazon Women on the Moon '87

Brad Hall (1958-)
Must Love Dogs '05
Bye Bye, Love '94
The Guardian '90
Limit Up '89
Worth Winning '89
Troll '86

Bug Hall (1985-)
Mortuary '05
Arizona Summer '03
Get a Clue '02
Skipped Parts '00
Safety Patrol '98
Honey, We Shrunk Ourselves '97
The Big Green '95
The Stupids '95
The Little Rascals '94

Craig Hall
Eagle vs. Shark '07
Ike: Countdown to D-Day '04
The Vector File '03

Delores Hall
Leap of Faith '92
Lethal Weapon 3 '92

Ellen Hall (1922-99)
Raiders of the Border '44
Range Law '44

Evelyn Hall
Hell's Angels '30
The Return of Dr. Fu Manchu '30

Gabriella Hall (1966-)
The Seductress '00
The Portrait '99
Lolida 2000 '97
Sexual Roulette '96
Shadow Dancer '96

Grayson Hall (1927-85)
Night of Dark Shadows '71
Adam at 6 a.m. '70
House of Dark Shadows '70
The Night of the Iguana '64
Satan in High Heels '61

Hanna Hall (1987-)
The Virgin Suicides '99
Homecoming '96
Forrest Gump '94

Harriet Hall (1948-2007)
The Witching of Ben Wagner '95
Foxfire '87

Henry Hall (1898-1989)
Command Decision '48
Lightning Raiders '45
The Ape Man '43
The Ape '40
Circle of Death '36
Inside Information '34
Rainbow Ranch '33
Midnight Warning '32

Huntz Hall (1920-99)
Auntie Lee's Meat Pies '92
Cyclone '87
Ratings Game '84
The Escape Artist '82
Gas Pump Girls '79
Valentino '77
Gentle Giant '67
Bowery Boys Meet the Monsters '54
Clipped Wings '53
Here Come the Marines '52
Ghost Chasers '51
Blues Busters '50
Master Minds '49
Smugglers' Cove '48
Spook Busters '48
Bowery Buckaroos '47
Hard-Boiled Mahoney '47
A Walk in the Sun '46
Mr. Muggs Rides Again '45
Follow the Leader '44
Million Dollar Kid '44
Clancy Street Boys '43
Ghost on the Loose '43
Kid Dynamite '43
Junior Army '42
Junior G-Men of the Air '42
Let's Get Tough '42
Mr. Wise Guy '42
'Neath Brooklyn Bridge '42
Smart Alecks '42
Bowery Blitzkrieg '41
Pride of the Bowery '41
Spooks Run Wild '41
Zis Boom Bah '41
Junior G-Men '40
They Made Me a Criminal '39
Angels with Dirty Faces '38
Little Tough Guys '38
Dead End '37

Irma P. Hall (1937-)
Tyler Perry's Meet the Browns '08
Collateral '04
The Ladykillers '04
A Lesson Before Dying '99
A Slipping Down Life '99
Beloved '98
The Love Letter '98
Patch Adams '98
Buddy '97
Midnight in the Garden of Good and Evil '97
Soul Food '97
Steel '97
A Family Thing '96
Nothing to Lose '96

James Hall (1900-40)
Millie '31
Hell's Angels '30
Four Sons '28
Hotel Imperial '27

Jerry Hall (1956-)
Merci Docteur Rey '04
R.P.M. '97
Savage Hearts '95
Batman '89
Running out of Luck '86

Jon Hall (1913-79)
The Beach Girls and the Monster '65
Hell Ship Mutiny '57
Deputy Marshal '50
Pirate Ship '49
The Prince of Thieves '48
The Last of the Redmen '47
Cobra Woman '44
The Invisible Man's Revenge '44
Ali Baba and the Forty Thieves '43
Arabian Nights '42
Invisible Agent '42
The Tuttles of Tahiti '42
Kit Carson '40
South of Pago Pago '40
The Hurricane '37

Juanita Hall (1901-68)
Flower Drum Song '61
South Pacific '58
Paradise in Harlem '40

Kevin Peter Hall (1955-91)
Highway to Hell '92
Predator 2 '90
Harry and the Hendersons '87
Predator '87
Misfits of Science '85

Landon Hall
The Escort '97
Witchcraft 9: Bitter Flesh '96
Over the Wire '95
Stolen Hearts '95

Lois Hall (1926-2006)
Kalifornia '93
Dead Again '91
Pirates of the High Seas '50

Michael Keys Hall
Flight of Black Angel '91
Blackout '88

Philip Baker Hall (1931-)
You Kill Me '07
Zodiac '07
The Matador '06
The Shaggy Dog '06
The Amityville Horror '05
The Zodiac '05
In Good Company '04
Bruce Almighty '03
Die Mommie Die! '03
Dogville '03
Path to War '02
The Sum of All Fears '02
A Gentleman's Game '01
The Contender '00
Lost Souls '00
Rules of Engagement '00
The Cradle Will Rock '99
The Insider '99
Let the Devil Wear Black '99
Magnolia '99
The Talented Mr. Ripley '99
Enemy of the State '98
Psycho '98
Rush Hour '98
Sour Grapes '98
The Truman Show '98
Witness to the Mob '98
Boogie Nights '97
Hard Eight '96
Hit Me '96
The Rock '96
Kiss of Death '94
A Thousand Heroes '92
Blue Desert '91
Dark River: A Father's Revenge '90
Three o'Clock High '87
Secret Honor '85
The Last Reunion '80
The Bastard '78
Terror Out of the Sky '78

Porter Hall (1888-1953)
Ace in the Hole '51
The Half-Breed '51
The Beautiful Blonde from Bashful Bend '49
Intruder in the Dust '49
Miracle on 34th Street '47
Singapore '47
Unconquered '47
Murder, He Says '45
Weekend at the Waldorf '45
Double Indemnity '44
Going My Way '44
The Great Moment '44
Miracle of Morgan's Creek '44
The Woman of the Town '44
The Desperadoes '43
Sullivan's Travels '41
Arizona '40
His Girl Friday '40
Mr. Smith Goes to Washington '39
They Shall Have Music '39
Bulldog Drummond's Peril '38
Bulldog Drummond Escapes '37
The Plainsman '37
Souls at Sea '37
The General Died at Dawn '36
Petrified Forest '36
The Princess Comes Across '36
Satan Met a Lady '36
The Story of Louis Pasteur '36
The Case of the Lucky Legs '35
The Thin Man '34

Rebecca Hall (1982-)
The Prestige '06
Starter for Ten '06
Like a Brother '05
The Camomile Lawn '92

Regina Hall (1971-)
First Sunday '08
Scary Movie 4 '06
The Honeymooners '05
King's Ransom '05
Malibu's Most Wanted '03
Scary Movie 3 '03
The Other Brother '02
Paid in Full '02
Scary Movie 2 '01
Disappearing Acts '00
Scary Movie '00

Ron Hall
Vampire Assassin '05
Raw Target '95
Triple Impact '92

Ruth Hall (1910-2003)
The Return of Casey Jones '34
Man from Monterey '33
Strawberry Roan '33
The Three Musketeers '33
Between Fighting Men '32
Dynamite Ranch '32
Kid from Spain '32
Ride Him, Cowboy '32
Monkey Business '31

Scott H. Hall
Color Me Blood Red '64
Blood Feast '63

Shannah Hall
The Princess & the Call Girl '84
Boogey Man 2 '83

Thurston Hall (1883-1958)
The Go-Getter '54
Night Stage to Galveston '52
Rim of the Canyon '49
Up in Central Park '48
Colonel Effingham's Raid '45
West of the Pecos '45
In Society '44
Something for the Boys '44
Song of Nevada '44
Crash Dive '43
Footlight Glamour '43
The Great Gildersleeve '43
I Dood It '43
Call of the Canyon '42
Twin Beds '42
The Invisible Woman '40
Each Dawn I Die '39
Jeepers Creepers '39
Mutiny on the Blackhawk '39
You Can't Cheat an Honest Man '39
Amazing Dr. Clitterhouse '38
Campus Confessions '38
I Promise to Pay '37
Murder in Greenwich Village '37
Lady from Nowhere '36
Theodora Goes Wild '36
The Black Room '35

William Hall (1903-86)
Harmon of Michigan '41
The Spy Ring '38

Zooey Hall (1947-)
I Dismember Mama '74
Fortune and Men's Eyes '71

Lillian Hall-Davis (1896-1933)
The Farmer's Wife '28
The Ring '27
The Last of the Mohicans '20

Charles Hallahan (1943-97)
Mind Lies '00
Dante's Peak '97
The Fan '96
The Pest '96
The Rich Man's Wife '96
Warlock: The Armageddon '93
Wild Palms '93
Body of Evidence '92
True Believer '89
Dangerous Obsession '88
A Winner Never Quits '86
Pale Rider '85
Vision Quest '85
The Thing '82
Margin for Murder '81
Nightwing '79

John Hallam (1941-)
Lifeforce '85
Under Capricorn '82
Dragonslayer '81
The Offence '73

Jane Hallaren
A Night in the Life of Jimmy Reardon '88
Lianna '83
Body Heat '81

May Hallatt (1876-1969)
Separate Tables '59
Black Narcissus '47

Gisli Halldorsson (1927-98)
Devil's Island '96
Cod Fever '95
Children of Nature '91

Tom Hallick (1941-)
A Rare Breed '81

John Halliday (1880-1947)
The Philadelphia Story '40
That Certain Age '38
Desire '36
The Dark Angel '35
Finishing School '33
Consolation Marriage '31
Millie '31
Smart Woman '31

Lori Hallier (1959-)
Running Wild '99
Blacklight '98
Night of the Twisters '95
Blindside '88

Johnny Hallyday (1943-)
Crimson Rivers 2: Angels of the Apocalypse '05
Crime Spree '03
The Man on the Train '02
Conseil de Famille '86
Detective '85

Billy Halop (1920-76)
Too Late for Tears '49
Junior Army '42
Junior G-Men of the Air '42
Pride of the Bowery '41
Junior G-Men '40
They Made Me a Criminal '39
Angels with Dirty Faces '38
Little Tough Guys '38
Dead End '37

Luke Halpin (1948-)
Flipper '96
Matinee '92
Shock Waves '77
If It's Tuesday, This Must Be Belgium '69
Island of the Lost '68
Flipper's Odyssey '66
Flipper's New Adventure '64
Flipper '63
Peter Pan '60

Brett Halsey (1933-)
First Degree '95
Taking Care of Business '90
The Crash of Flight 401 '78
Four Times That Night '69
Magnificent Adventurer '63
Twice-Told Tales '63
The Girl in Lover's Lane '60
Atomic Submarine '59
Jet Over the Atlantic '59
Return of the Fly '59
Submarine Seahawk '59
To Hell and Back '55
Ma and Pa Kettle at Home '54

Michael Halsey
Postmortem '98
Mean Guns '97
Dollman '90
Treasure Island '89
Under the Gun '88

Rodger Halston
Carnosaur 3: Primal Species '95
Alien Terminator '95

Julie Halston (1954-)
A Very Serious Person '06
Joe Gould's Secret '00
David Searching '97

Charles Halton (1876-1959)
Here Comes the Groom '51
My Dear Secretary '49
A Star is Born '54
Carrie '52
If You Knew Susie '48
The Best Years of Our Lives '46
It's a Wonderful Life '46
Sister Kenny '46
Rhapsody in Blue '45
A Tree Grows in Brooklyn '45
Enemy of Women '44
The Thin Man Goes Home '44
Up in Arms '44
Wilson '44
Heaven Can Wait '43
Across the Pacific '42
Captains of the Clouds '42
In Old California '42
The Lady is Willing '42
Saboteur '42
The Spoilers '42
To Be or Not to Be '42
Dance Hall '41
Mr. & Mrs. Smith '41
Look Who's Laughing '41
Dr. Cyclops '40
Doctor Takes a Wife '40
Foreign Correspondent '40
The Shop Around the Corner '40
Stranger on the Third Floor '40
They Drive by Night '40
Virginia City '40
Young Mr. Lincoln '39
The Westerner '40
I Am the Law '38
Mad Miss Manton '38
Room Service '38
Dodge City '39
Golden Boy '39
Jesse James '39
Juarez '39
Nancy Drew, Reporter '39
Dead End '37
The Young in Heart '38
The Saint in New York '38
Prisoner of Zenda '37
Pick a Star '37
Come and Get It '36
Dodsworth '36
The Adventurer '17

Mie Hama (1943-)
You Only Live Twice '67
What's Up, Tiger Lily? '67
King Kong vs. Godzilla '63

Mark Hamill (1952-)
Comic Book: The Movie '04
Jay and Silent Bob Strike Back '01
Laserhawk '99
Watchers Reborn '98
When Time Expires '97
Ghost Who Walks '95 (V)
Village of the Damned '95
The Raffle '94
Silk Degrees '94
Batman: Mask of the Phantasm '93 (V)
Black Magic Woman '91
The Guyver '91
Slipstream '89
The Night the Lights Went Out in Georgia '81
Britannia Hospital '82
Return of the Jedi '83
The Big Red One '80
The Empire Strikes Back '80
Corvette Summer '78
Star Wars '77
The City '76
Eric '75

Pete Hamill (1935-)
The Insider '99
One Fine Day '96

Antony (Tony) Hamilton (1953-95)
Fatal Instinct '92
Howling 4: The Original Nightmare '88
Mirrors '85
Samson and Delilah '84
Nocturna '79

Bernie Hamilton (1929-)
Bucktown '75
Scream Blacula Scream '73
The Losers '70
The Lost Man '69
Captain Sinbad '63
The Young One '61

Derek Hamilton
Hollywood Ending '02
Angels Fall '07
Nightstalker '02
Taboo '02

Carrie Hamilton (1963-2002)
Cool World '92
Shag: The Movie '89
Tokyo Pop '88
Fanatic '82
Star Crash '78
Gun Crazy '69

Linda Hamilton (1956-)
The Kid and I '05
Smile '05
A Girl Thing '01
Sex & Mrs. X '00
Skeletons in the Closet '00
The Secret Life of Girls '99
The Color of Courage '98
Rescuers: Stories of Courage—Two Couples '98
Shadow Conspiracy '97
Dante's Peak '97
A Mother's Prayer '95
Separate Lives '94
Silent Fall '94
Terminator 2: Judgment Day '91
Mr. Destiny '90
Black Moon Rising '86
King Kong Lives '86
Secret Weapons '85
Children of the Corn '84
The Terminator '84
The Stone Boy '84
Tag: The Assassination Game '82
Rape and Marriage: The Rideout Case '80

Judd Hamilton
Hollywood Ending '02
P.T. Barnum '99
Rough Riders '97
8 Heads in a Duffel Bag '96
Vanished '95
Amore! '93
Once Upon a Crime '92
The Godfather, Part 3 '90
Doc Hollywood '91
Poker Alice '87
Monte Carlo '86
Two Fathers' Justice '85
Zorro, the Gay Blade '81

Josh Hamilton (1968-)
Broken English '07
Diggers '06
Four and a Half Women '05
The Bourne Identity '02
Urbania '00
OnLine '02
The '60s '99
Don't Look Back '96
The Proprietor '96
The House of Yes '97
Kicking and Screaming '95
With Honors '94
Alive '93

John Hamilton (1886-1958)
The Wizard of Oz '39
The Adventures of Tom Sawyer '38
Nothing Sacred '37
You Only Live Once '37
The Moon's Our Home '36

Jane (Veronica Hart) Hamilton (1962-)
Bloodsucking Pharaohs of Pittsburgh '90
Wildest Dreams '90
Bedroom Eyes 2 '89
Cleo/Leo '89
Deranged '87
New York's Finest '87
Slammer Girls '87
Beauty School '93

Murray Hamilton (1923-86)
The Last Days of Patton '86
Too Scared to Scream '85
Mazes and Monsters '82
Brubaker '80
The Amityville Horror '79
Last Cry for Help '79
Casey's Shadow '78
Jaws 2 '78
The Drowning Pool '75
Jaws '75
The Way We Were '73
1941 '79
Seconds '66
The Graduate '67
The Hustler '61
Anatomy of a Murder '59
The FBI Story '59
The Spirit of St. Louis '57
No Time for Sergeants '58
The Brotherhood '68
The Boston Strangler '68
No Way to Treat a Lady '68
Sergeant Ryker '68

Neil Hamilton (1899-1984)
Batman '66
Good Neighbor Sam '64
The Patsy '64
The Devil's Hand '61
The Saint Strikes Back '39
Hollywood Stadium Mystery '38
King of the Texas Rangers '41
X Marks the Spot '42

Veronica Hamel (1945-)
Secrets '95
High Stakes '93
Users '78
The Happy Hooker Goes to Washington '77
A New Life '88
Sessions '83
The Gathering: Part 2 '79
Killer on Board '77
The Dead Don't Die '75
Once is Not Enough '75

George Hamilton (1939-)
Love at First Bite '79
The Seekers '79
Sextette '78
Nine Lives '77
The Terminator '84
The Stone Boy '84
Evel Knievel '72
Medusa '74
Togetherness '70
Viva Maria! '65
The Victors '63
Two Weeks in Another Town '62
Angel Baby '61
By Love Possessed '61
Home from the Hill '60
Where the Boys Are '60
Town '62
True Crime '99

Hale Hamilton (1883-1942)
The Champ '32
Murder at Midnight '31
Susan Lenox: Her Fall and Rise '31

Mahlon Hamilton (1880-1960)
Peg o' My Heart '22
Daddy Long Legs '19

Margaret Hamilton (1902-85)
The Anderson Tapes '71
Brewster McCloud '70
13 Ghosts '60
Comin' Round the Mountain '51
People Will Talk '51
Riding High '50
The Red Pony '49
The Sin of Harold Diddlebock '47
George White's Scandals '45
Guest in the House '44
City Without Men '43
Twin Beds '42
The Invisible Woman '40
My Little Chickadee '40
The Wizard of Oz '39
The Adventures of Tom Sawyer '38
Nothing Sacred '37
Way Back Home '31

Harry Hamlin (1951-)
The Hunted '98
Allie & Me '97
Ebbtide '94
Save Me '93
Take Down '90
Deceptions '90
Dinner at Eight '89
Laguna Heat '87
Blue Skies Again '83
Making Love '82
Clash of the Titans '81
King of the Mountain '81
Movie, Movie '78

Wendy Hamilton
The Dallas Connection '94
Ski School 2 '94

Lisa Gay Hamilton (1964-)
Honeydripper '07
Nine Lives '05
The Sum of All Fears '02
The Truth About Charlie '02
A House Divided '00
Hamlet '01
Beloved '98
Jackie Brown '97
True Crime '99
Drunks '96
Palookaville '95
Krush Groove '85

Richard Hamilton (1920-2004)
Duel of Hearts '92
Tale of a Vampire '92
Out of Africa '85
Sommersby '93
In Country '89
Greetings '68

Patricia Hamilton
Anne of Green Gables: The Continuing Story '99
Holiday Affair '96
The Christmas Wife '88
Anne of Avonlea '87
Anne of Green Gables '85
Who Has Seen the Wind? '77

Suzanna Hamilton (1960-)
Brimstone & Treacle '82
1984 '84
Wetherby '85
Out of Africa '85

Victoria Hamilton (1971-)
Scoop '06
Goodbye, Mr. Chips '02
Victoria & Albert '01
Mansfield Park '99
Persuasion '95
King Lear '98

Warren Hammack
Zontar, the Thing from Venus '66
Mars Needs Women '66

Ben Hammer (1925-)
Subterfuge '98
Crazy People '90
Survival Quest '89

Alvin Hammer (1915-93)
Command Decision '48
A Walk in the Sun '46

Hammer (1962-)
The Eye Creatures '65
One Man's Justice '95
Last Action Hero '93

Beastmaster '82
The Execution of Private Slovik '74
Invasion of the Bee Girls '73
Johnny Got His Gun '71
John Hammil (1948-)
Phantoms '97
Brandon Hammond (1984-)
Soul Food '97
The Fan '96
Tales from the Hood '95
Darrell Hammond (1955-)
Epic Movie '07
Ira & Abby '06
New York Minute '04
Agent Cody Banks '03
The King and I '99 (V)
Blues Brothers 2000 '98
John Hammond
The Prodigal '83
The Blue and the Gray '82
Enforcer from Death Row '78
Kay Hammond (1909-80)
The Girl in the Red Velvet Swing '55
Blithe Spirit '45
Nicholas Hammond (1950-)
Stealth '05
Salem's Lot '04
Black Cobra 2 '89
Trouble in Paradise '88
The Martian Chronicles: Part 1 '79
The Martian Chronicles: Part 3 '79
Chinese Web '78
Spiderman: The Deadly Dust '78
The Amazing Spider-Man '77
The Sound of Music '65
Roger Hammond (1936-)
Around the World in 80 Days '04
A Good Woman '04
Lady Chatterley '92
A Dangerous Man: Lawrence after Arabia '91
Olivia Hamnett
The Ripper '97
Deadly Possession '88
Earthling '80
The Last Wave '77
Plunge Into Darkness '77
Emily Hampshire (1981-)
Snow Cake '06
Posers '02
The Happy Face Murders '99
Love Letters '99
Eye '96
Susan Hampshire (1938-)
Coming Home '98
Cry Terror '76
The Story of David '76
Baffled '72
Living Free '72
David Copperfield '70
Those Daring Young Men in Their Jaunty Jalopies '69

Vanity Fair '67
The Fighting Prince of Donegal '66
The Three Lives of Thomasina '63
Danielle Hampton (1978-)
Detention '03
Ginger Snaps '01
James Hampton (1936-)
Sling Blade '96
World War III '86
Teen Wolf '85
Condorman '81
Tut & Tuttle '81
Hangar 18 '80
The China Syndrome '79
The Amazing Howard Hughes '77
Bunco '77
Hawmps! '76
Force Five '75
The Longest Yard '74
Lionel Hampton (1908-2002)
Force of Impulse '60
The Benny Goodman Story '55
Paul Hampton (1945-)
Deadly Exposure '93
They Came from Within '75
Hitl '73
Lady Sings the Blues '72
Private Duty Nurses '71
Maggie Han (1959-)
Open Season '95
The Last Emperor '87
Master Bong Soo Han (1933-2007)
Force: Five '81
Kill the Golden Goose '79
Herbie Hancock (1940-)
Indecent Proposal '93
Round Midnight '86
John Hancock (1939-)
Why Me? '90
Traxx '87
In the Custody of Strangers '82
Archer: The Fugitive from the Empire '81
Lou Hancock
Miracle Mile '89
Evil Dead 2: Dead by Dawn '87
Sheila Hancock (1933-)
Yes '04
Bait '02
Love or Money '01
Love and Death on Long Island '97
The Buccaneers '95
A Business Affair '93
Three Men and a Little Lady '90
Hawks '89
Buster '88
The Anniversary '68
The Moon-Spinners '64
Irene Handl (1901-87)
Adventures of a Private Eye '87
Riding High '78
The Private Life of Sherlock Holmes '70
Wonderwall: The Movie '69
Smashing Time '67
Morgan: A Suitable Case for Treatment '66
Small Hotel '57
A Kid for Two Farthings '55
The Belles of St. Trinian's '53
Brief Encounter '46
Mr. Emmanuel '44
Night Train to Munich '40
Evan Handler (1961-)
Sex and the City: The Movie '08
Cash Crop '01
Harvest '98

Ransom '96
Natural Born Killers '94
Sweet Lorraine '87
Ruby's Dream '82
Taps '81
Taylor Handley
September Dawn '07
The Texas Chainsaw Massacre: The Beginning '06
Marina Hands
Lady Chatterley '06
The Barbarian Invasions '03
James Handy
Ash Wednesday '02
15 Minutes '01
Unbreakable '00
K-911 '99
Time Served '99
Gang Related '96
Rave Review '95
The O.J. Simpson Story '94
False Arrest '92
The Rocketeer '91
Arachnophobia '90
K-9 '89
The Preppie Murder '89
Bird '88
Burglar '87
The Verdict '82
Anne Haney (1934-2001)
Psycho '98
The Lesser Evil '97
Liar Liar '97
Midnight in the Garden of Good and Evil '97
Changing Habits '96
The American President '95
The Bad Seed '85
Daryl Haney (1963-)
Concealed Weapon '94
Lords of the Deep '89
Daddy's Boys '87
Perla Haney-Jardine
Untraceable '08
Spider-Man 3 '07
Dark Water '05
Kill Bill Vol. 2 '04
Helen Hanft (1934-)
Used People '92
Stardust Memories '80
Roger Hanin (1925-)
Day of Atonement '93
My Other Husband '85
Rocco and His Brothers '60
Sois Belle et Tais-Toi '58
Larry Hankin (1945-)
The Independent '00
Money Talks '97
Billy Madison '94
Prehysteria 2 '94
Out on a Limb '92
T Bone N Weasel '92
Black Magic Woman '91
Armed and Dangerous '86
Escape from Alcatraz '79
Colin Hanks (1977-)
Untraceable '08
Alone With Her '07
Rx '06
Tenacious D in the Pick of Destiny '06
King Kong '05
Standing Still '05
11:14 '03
Orange County '02
Band of Brothers '01
Get Over It! '01
Whatever It Takes '00
That Thing You Do! '96
Jim Hanks (1961-)
Purgatory House '04
Xtro 3: Watch the Skies '95
Buford's Beach Bunnies '92
Tom Hanks (1956-)
Charlie Wilson's War '07
The Simpsons Movie '07 (V)
The Da Vinci Code '06
Elvis Has Left the Building '04
The Ladykillers '04
The Polar Express '04

The Terminal '04
Catch Me If You Can '02
Road to Perdition '02
Cast Away '00
The Green Mile '99
Toy Story 2 '99 (V)
Saving Private Ryan '98
You've Got Mail '98
That Thing You Do! '96
Apollo 13 '95
Toy Story '95 (V)
Forrest Gump '94
Philadelphia '93
Sleepless in Seattle '93
A League of Their Own '92
Radio Flyer '92 (N)
The Bonfire of the Vanities '90
Joe Versus the Volcano '90
The 'Burbs '89
Turner and Hooch '89
Big '88
Punchline '88
Dragnet '87
Every Time We Say Goodbye '86
The Money Pit '86
Nothing in Common '86
The Man with One Red Shoe '85
Volunteers '85
Bachelor Party '84
Splash '84
Mazes and Monsters '82
He Knows You're Alone '80
Jenny Hanley (1947-)
Flesh and Blood Show '73
The Scars of Dracula '70
On Her Majesty's Secret Service '69
Jimmy Hanley (1918-70)
The Blue Lamp '49
Room to Let '49
Captive Heart '47
Immortal Battalion '44
Salute John Citizen '42
Gaslight '40
Housemaster '38
Bert Hanlon (1890-1972)
A Slight Case of Murder '38
Park Avenue Logger '37
Wings in the Dark '35
Too Busy to Work '32
Adam Hann-Byrd (1982)
Halloween: H20 '98
The Ice Storm '97
Diabolique '96
Jumanji '95
Digger '94
Little Man Tate '91
Daryl Hannah (1960-)
Keeping Up with the Steins '06
The Big Empty '04
Kill Bill Vol. 2 '04
Silver City '04
Casa de los Babys '03
The Job '03
Kill Bill Vol. 1 '03
Northfork '03
A Walk to Remember '02
Hard Cash '01
Jack and the Beanstalk: The Real Story '01
Jackpot '01
Cowboy '00
Dancing at the Blue Iguana '00
Hide and Seek '00
Diplomatic Siege '99
Speedway Junky '99
Wildflowers '99
Hi-Life '98
My Favorite Martian '98
Rear Window '98
The Gingerbread Man '97
The Last Don '97
The Last Days of Frankie the Fly '96
Grumpier Old Men '95
Two Much '96
The Tie That Binds '95

The Little Rascals '94
Attack of the 50 Ft. Woman '93
Grumpy Old Men '93
Memoirs of an Invisible Man '92
At Play in the Fields of the Lord '91
Crazy People '90
Crimes & Misdemeanors '89
Steel Magnolias '89
High Spirits '88
Roxanne '87
Wall Street '87
The Clan of the Cave Bear '86
Legal Eagles '86
The Pope of Greenwich Village '84
Reckless '84
Splash '84
The Final Terror '83
Blade Runner '82
Summer Lovers '82
Hard Country '81
The Fury '78
John Hannah (1962-)
The Mummy: Tomb of the Dragon Emperor '08
The Last Legion '07
Ghost Son '06
I'm with Lucy '02
Circus '00
The Mummy Returns '01
Pandaemonium '00
The Mummy '99
The Love Bug '97
Resurrection Man '97
Sliding Doors '97
The Final Cut '96
Romance and Rejection '96
The Innocent Sleep '95
Madagascar Skin '95
Faith '94
Four Weddings and a Funeral '94
Page Hannah (1964-)
Shag: The Movie '89
Creepshow 2 '87
My Man Adam '86
Racing with the Moon '84
Alyson Hannigan (1974-)
Date Movie '06
American Wedding '03
Rip It Off '02
American Pie 2 '01
Boys and Girls '00
American Pie '99
Dead Man on Campus '97
My Stepmother Is an Alien '88
Donna Hanover (1950-)
Series 7: The Contenders '01
Just the Ticket '98
The People vs. Larry Flynt '96
Lawrence Hanray (1874-1947)
On Approval '44
Mimi '35
The Private Life of Henry VIII '33
Glen Hansard
Once '06
The Commitments '91
Gale Hansen (1969-)
Double Vision '92
Shaking the Tree '92
The Finest Hour '91
Dead Poets Society '89
The Deadly and the Beautiful '73
Gunnar Hansen (1947-)
Hellblock 13 '97
Freakshow '95
Mosquito '95
Hollywood Chainsaw Hookers '88
The Demon Lover '77
The Texas Chainsaw Massacre '74

Heidi Hansen
Superbug Super Agent '76
Fanny Hill: Memoirs of a Woman of Pleasure '64
Holger Juul Hansen (1924-)
The Kingdom 2 '97
The Kingdom '95
Joachim Hansen (1930-2007)
Anne of Green Gables '85
Frozen Alive '64
Secret of the Black Trunk '62
Patti Hansen (1956-)
Hard to Hold '84
They All Laughed '81
Paul Hansen
The Return of Count Yorga '71
Count Yorga, Vampire '70
Peter Hansen (1921-)
Cavalry Charge '51
When Worlds Collide '51
Valda Hansen (1932-93)
Wham-Bam, Thank You Spaceman '75
Cain's Cutthroats '71
Night of the Ghouls '59
William Hansen (1911-75)
Homebodies '74
Willard '71
The Member of the Wedding '52
Dave Hanson
Slap Shot 2: Breaking the Ice '02
Slap Shot '77
Lars Hanson (1886-1965)
Walpurgis Night '41
The Informer '29
Homecoming '28
The Wind '28
The Flesh and the Devil '27
The Atonement of Gosta Berling '24
Katy Hansz
Fresh Cut Grass '04
Coffee and Cigarettes '03
Thomas Hanzon (1962-)
Faithless '00
Private Confessions '98
Setsuko Hara (1920-)
Tokyo Story '53
Early Summer '51
The Idiot '51
Late Spring '49
No Regrets for Our Youth '46
Kiwako Harada (1965-)
Godzilla vs. King Ghidora
Days of Hell '84
Meiko Harada (1958-)
Akira Kurosawa's Dreams '90
Ran '85
Nomugi Pass '79
Haya Harareet (1931-)
The Interns '62
Journey Beneath the Desert '61
Ben-Hur '59
Hill 24 Doesn't Answer '55
Clement Harari (1919-)
Train of Life '98
Flight of the Eagle '82
The Fiendish Plot of Dr. Fu Manchu '80
Monkeys, Go Home! '66
Double Agents '59
Matthew Harbour (1990-)
Equilibrium '02
The Witness Files '00
Time at the Top '99
James Harcourt (1873-1951)
The Hidden Room '49

Johnny Frenchman '46
Night Train to Munich '40
I Met a Murderer '39
The Avenging Hand '36

Ty Hardin (1930-)
Bad Jim '89
Rooster: Spurs of Death '83

Diana Hardcastle
A Good Woman '04
If Only '04
Catherine Cookson's The Tide of Life '96
Fortunes of War '87

Ernest Harden, Jr. (1952-)
The Hit '06
Gang Boys '97
White Men Can't Jump '92
The Final Terror '83
White Mama '80

Marcia Gay Harden (1959)
Into the Wild '07
The Invisible '07
The Mist '07
Rails & Ties '07
Canvas '06
American Dreamz '06
The Dead Girl '06
The Hoax '06
American Gun '05
The Bad News Bears '05
Welcome to Mooseport '04
P.S. '04
Mona Lisa Smile '03
Casa de los Babys '03
Mystic River '03
Pollock '00
Space Cowboys '00
Thin Air '00
Desperate Measures '98
Meet Joe Black '98
Curtain Call '97
Flubber '97
Path to Paradise '97
The Daytrippers '96
Far Harbor '96
The First Wives Club '96
Spy Hard '96
Convict Cowboy '95
The Spitfire Grill '95
Safe Passage '94
Crush '93
Sinatra '92
Used People '92
Fever '91
Late for Dinner '91
Miller's Crossing '90

Crofton Hardester
Devastator '85
Android '82

Kate Hardie (1969-)
Heart '99
Croupier '97
The Krays '90
Conspiracy '89
Mona Lisa '86

Jerry Hardin (1929-)
Hidalgo '04
The Firm '93
The Hot Spot '90
Blaze '89
Wanted Dead or Alive '86
Cujo '83
Wolf Lake '79

Melora Hardin (1967-)
27 Dresses '08
The Comebacks '07
The Hot Chick '02
Seven Girlfriends '00
Absolute Power '97
Chameleon '95
The Undercover Kid '95
Reckless Kelly '93
The Rocketeer '91
Big Man on Campus '89
Dead Poets Society '89
Lambada '89
Iron Eagle '86
The North Avenue Irregulars '79

Ann Harding (1901-81)
The Man in the Gray Flannel Suit '56
Two Weeks with Love '50
The Magnificent Yankee '50
Christmas Eve
Mission to Moscow '43
The North Star '43
Love from a Stranger '37
The Animal Kingdom '32
Devotion '31
Condemned '29

John Harding
The Impossible Years '68
This Property Is Condemned '66

Kay Harding (1924-84)
The Mummy's Curse '44
Scarlet Claw '44

Lyn Harding (1876-1952)
The Man Who Lived Again '37
Spy of Napoleon '36
Old Spanish Custom '36
The Speckled Band '31

Kadeem Hardison (1965-)
Made of Honor '08
Biker Boyz '03
Showtime '02
Instinct to Kill '01
30 Years to Life '01
Dancing in September '00
Blind Faith '98
The Sixth Man '97
Drive '96
Panther '95
Vampire in Brooklyn '95
Renaissance Man '94
Dream Date '93
Gunmen '93
White Men Can't Jump '92
Def by Temptation '90
I'm Gonna Git You Sucka '88
School Daze '88
Beat Street '84

Chris Hardwick (1971-)
House o' 1000 Corpses '03
Art House '98

Derek Hardwick
Among the Cinders '83

Cedric Hardwicke (1883-1964)
Five Weeks in a Balloon '62
The Magic Fountain '61
Around the World in 80 Days '56
Helen of Troy '56
The Ten Commandments '56
Richard III '55
Salome '53
Botany Bay '53
Diane '55
The War of the Worlds '53
The Green Glove '52
The Desert Fox '51
The White Tower '50
A Connecticut Yankee in King Arthur's Court '49
I Remember Mama '48
The Winslow Boy '48
Rope '48
Tycoon '47
Nicholas Nickleby '47
Beware of Pity '46
You're Jinxed, Friend, You've Met Sacramento '70
The Keys of the Kingdom '44
Wilson '44
A Wing and a Prayer '44
The Moon Is Down '43
The Ghost of Frankenstein '42
Invisible Agent '42
Valley of the Sun '42
Suspicion '41
Sundown '41
The Howards of Virginia '40
The Invisible Man Returns '40
Tom Brown's School Days '40
The Hunchback of Notre Dame '39
On Borrowed Time '39
Stanley and Livingstone '39
King Solomon's Mines '37
Nine Days a Queen '36
Things to Come '36
Becky Sharp '35
Les Miserables '35
Power '34

Edward Hardwicke (1932-)
Oliver Twist '05
The Alchemists '99
Appetite '98
Elizabeth '98
Parting Shots '98
Photographing Fairies '97
Hollow Reed '95
The Scarlet Letter '95
Shadowlands '93

Jonathan Hardy (1940-)
The Thorn Birds: The Missing Years '96
The Wacky World of Wills & Burke '85
Lonely Hearts '82

Oliver Hardy (1892-1957)
The Devil's Playground '76
Utopia '51
Riding High '50
The Fighting Kentuckian '49
The Flying Deuces '39
Swiss Miss '38
Block-heads '38
Way Out West '37
Pick a Star '37
Saps at Sea '40
A Chump at Oxford '40
Great Guns '41
Air Raid Wardens '43
Nothing But Trouble '44
Bullfighters '45
Our Relations '36
The Bohemian Girl '36
Bonnie Scotland '35
Hollywood Party '34
March of the Wooden Soldiers '34
The Devil's Brother '33
Sons of the Desert '33
Laurel & Hardy: Stan "Helps" Ollie '33
Laurel & Hardy and the Family '33
Laurel & Hardy: At Work '32
Pack Up Your Troubles '32
Laurel & Hardy: Be Big '31
Laurel & Hardy: Chickens Come Home '31
Laurel & Hardy: Laughing Gravy '31
Pardon Us '31
Laurel & Hardy: Another Fine Mess '30
Laurel & Hardy: Below Zero '30
Laurel & Hardy: Blotto '30
Laurel & Hardy: Brats '30
Laurel & Hardy: Hog Wild '30
Laurel & Hardy: Night Owls '30
Laurel & Hardy On the Lam '30
Laurel & Hardy: Berth Marks '29
Laurel & Hardy: Men O'War '29
Laurel & Hardy: Perfect Day '29

Sam Hardy (1883-1935)
Break of Hearts '35
Powdersmoke Range '35
King Kong '33
Big News '29

Thomas (Tom) Hardy (1977-)
Scenes of a Sexual Nature '06
The Mysterious Magician '65
Star Trek: Nemesis '02
Band of Brothers '01
Black Hawk Down '01

Sophie Hardy (1940-)
Erotic Touch of Hot Skin '65

Robert Hardy (1925-)
Harry Potter and the Order of the Phoenix '07
Harry Potter and the Goblet of Fire '05
Lassie '05
P.D. James: Death in Holy Orders '03
The Gathering '02
Mrs. Dalloway '97
Gulliver's Travels '95
Mary Shelley's Frankenstein '94
Middlemarch '93
The Woman He Loved '88
War & Remembrance '88
War & Remembrance: The Final Chapter '89
The Shooting Party '85
Jenny's War '85
Edward the King '75
Dark Places '73
Demons of the Mind '72

Mariska Hargitay (1964-)
Perfume '01
Lake Placid '99
Leaving Las Vegas '95
Hotel R.com '93
Finish Line '89
Welcome to 18 '87
Ghoulies '84

Mickey Hargitay (1927-2006)
Lady Frankenstein '72
The Bloody Pit of Horror '65
Promised! Promised! '63
The Loves of Hercules '60
Will Success Spoil Rock Hunter? '57

Corinna Harfouch (1954-)
Downfall '04
Murder '06
An American Christmas Carol '79
Roots: The Next Generation '79

Doris Hardgrave
The Reckoning '03
Dot the I '03
Lethal Dose '03

Dorian Harewood (1950-)
Assault on Precinct 13 '05
Gothika '03
Full Metal Jacket '87
God Bless the Child '88
Strike Force '81
Beulah Land '80
Against All Odds '84
The Jesse Owens Story '84
Sudden Death '85
Pacific Heights '90
Kiss Shot '89

David Harewood
Blood Diamond '06
Ruby in the Smoke '06

Mark Harelik (1951-)
Election '99
Jurassic Park 3 '01
My Brother's Keeper '95
The Swan Princess '94 (V)

Robertson Hare (1891-1979)
The World Moves On '34
The Lives of a Bengal Lancer '35

Lumsden Hare (1875-1964)
Rose Marie '54
That Forsyte Woman '50
The White Cliffs of Dover '44
Shadows on the Stairs '41
Northwest Passage '40
Gunga Din '39
The Princess Comes Across '36
The Crusades '35
The Lives of a Bengal Lancer '35

Amy Hargreaves (1970-)
Saint Maybe '98
Brainscan '94

John Hargreaves (1945-96)
Country Life '95
Lust and Revenge '95
Sorrento Beach '95
Cry Freedom '87
Sky Pirates '87
Malcolm '86
Careful, He Might Hear You '84
My First Wife '84
Beyond Reasonable Doubt '81
Killing of Angel Street '81
The Odd Angry Shot '79
Little Boy Lost '78
Deathcheaters '76
Don's Party '76

Tsui Hark (1951-)
Twin Dragons '92
Mad Mission 3 '84

Gordon Harker (1885-1967)
Small Hotel '57
Things Happen at Night '48
Inspector Hornleigh '39
The Phantom Light '35
Champagne '28
The Ring '27
The Farmer's Wife '28

Susannah Harker
Intimacy '00
Heat of the Sun '99
Ultraviolet '98
Faith '94
Pride and Prejudice '95

John Harkins (1932-99)
Crime of the Century '96
This Gun for Hire '90
Slaves of New York '89
City Killer '87
Rampage '87
Birdy '84
Amityville 3: The Demon '83
The Lady's Not for Burning '87

Kenneth Harlan (1895-1967)
Paradise Island '30
San Francisco '36
The Shadow Strikes '37
Dawn Express '42
Phantom Killer '42

Otis Harlan (1865-1940)
Mr. Boggs Steps Out '38
Outlaws of Sonora '38
Snow White and the Seven Dwarfs '37
Western Gold '37
The Virginian '23

Jean Harlow (1911-37)
Saratoga '37
Personal Property '37
Libeled Lady '36
Suzy '36
Wife Versus Secretary '36
China Seas '35
Reckless '35
Riff Raff '35
The Girl from Missouri '34
Bombshell '33
Dinner at Eight '33
Hold Your Man '33
Red Dust '32
Red Headed Woman '32
The Public Enemy '31
Platinum Blonde '31
City Lights '31
Hell's Angels '30

Shalom Harlow (1973-)
Game 6 '05
How to Lose a Guy in 10 Days '03
I Love Your Work '03
The Salton Sea '02
Head Over Heels '01

Angie Harmon (1971-)
End Game '06
Glass House: The Good Mother '06
Agent Cody Banks '03
Video Voyeur: The Susan Wilson Story '02

Good Advice '01

Deborah Harmon (1951-)
Prince of Bel Air '87
Bachelor Party '84
Used Cars '80

John Harmon (1905-85)
The Monster of Piedras Blancas '57
A Slight Case of Murder '38

Mark Harmon (1951-)
Chasing Liberty '04
Freaky Friday '03
Local Boys '02
Crossfire Trail '01
I'll Remember April '99
Fear and Loathing in Las Vegas '98
From the Earth to the Moon '98
Casualties '97
The First to Go '97
The Last Supper '96
Magic in the Water '95
Natural Born Killers '94
Wyatt Earp '94
Cold Heaven '92
Dillinger '91
Long Road Home '91
Till There Was You '91
Fourth Story '90
Sweet Bird of Youth '89
Worth Winning '89
The Presidio '88
Stealing Home '88
After the Promise '87
Let's Get Harry '87
Prince of Bel Air '87
Summer School '87
The Deliberate Stranger '86
Goliath Awaits '81
Beyond the Poseidon Adventure '79
Centennial '78
Comes a Horseman '78

Renee Harmon (1922-2006)
Night of Terror '87
Lady Street Fighter '86
The Executioner, Part 2: Frozen Scream '84
Hellriders '84

Ricci Harnett
A Certain Justice '99
The Object of Beauty '91

Elisabeth Harnois (1979-)
Chaos Theory '08
Strangers with Candy '06
Pretty Persuasion '05
My Date with the President's Daughter '98
One Magic Christmas '85
Where Are the Children? '85

Christina Harnos
Hollywood Confidential '97
Bloodhounds '96
Hellraiser 4: Bloodline '95
Cool and the Crazy '94
Denial: The Dark Side of Passion '91
The Rescue '88

Ralf Harolde (1899-1974)
Behind Locked Doors '48
Manhunt in the African Jungles '43
Baby Face Morgan '42
Gang Busters '42
I Killed That Man '42
The Sea Wolf '41
Little Red Schoolhouse '36
I'm No Angel '33
Picture Snatcher '33
Night Nurse '31
Smart Money '31
Hook, Line and Sinker '30

Frank Harper (1962-)
Bend It Like Beckham '02
Lucky Break '01
Shiner '00
Lock, Stock and 2 Smoking Barrels '98
24-7 '97
In the Name of the Father '93

Gerald Harper (1929-)
If It's a Man, Hang Up '75
The Admirable Crichton '57

Hill Harper (1973-)
The Breed '06
The Badge '02
The Skulls '00
The Visit '00
In Too Deep '99
Loving Jezebel '99
Slaves of Hollywood '99
He Got Game '98
Mama Flora's Family '98
Hav Plenty '97
The Nephew '97
Steel '97
Get On the Bus '96
Zooman '95

Jessica Harper (1954)
Minority Report '02
Safe '95
Mr. Wonderful '93
Big Man on Campus '89
Eat a Bowl of Tea '89
Blue Iguana '88
Imagemaker '88
My Favorite Year '82
Pennies from Heaven '81
Shock Treatment '81
Stardust Memories '80
The Evictors '79
Suspiria '77
Inserts '75
Phantom of the Paradise '74

Kyra Harper
Swann '96
Buffalo Jump '90

Robert Harper (1951-)
Molly '99
The Wrong Man '93
Final Analysis '92
Running Mates '92
Held Hostage '91
Not Quite Human '87
Once Upon a Time in America '84

Tess Harper (1950-)
No Country for Old Men '07
Saving Sarah Cain '07
Jam '06
Karla '06
Loggerheads '05
The Rising Place '02
The In Crowd '00
The Jackal '97
The Road to Galveston '96
Children of Fury '94
Christy '94
My New Gun '92
The Turning '92
The Man in the Moon '91
My Heroes Have Always Been Cowboys '91
Daddy's Dyin'... Who's Got the Will? '90
Dark River: A Father's Revenge '90
Criminal Law '89
Far North '88
Her Alibi '88
Ishtar '87
Crimes of the Heart '86
Flashpoint '84
Reckless Disregard '84
A Summer to Remember '84
Amityville 3: The Demon '83
Chiefs '83
Tender Mercies '83

Valerie Harper (1940-)
Drop-Out Mother '88
The Execution '85
Blame It on Rio '84
Don't Go to Sleep '82
The Last Married Couple in America '80
The Shadow Box '80
Chapter Two '79
Night Terror '76
Freebie & the Bean '74
Thursday's Game '74

Cindy Harrel
The Final Terror '83
Model Behavior '82

Jim Harrell (1918-2000)
A Family Thing '96
Don't Open the Door! '74

Rebecca Harrell (1980-)
Suspended Animation '02
Prancer '89

Brett Harrelson
Dee Snider's Strangeland '98
From Dusk Till Dawn 2: Texas Blood Money '98
The People vs. Larry Flynt '96

Woody Harrelson (1962-)
Semi-Pro '08
Sleepwalking '08
No Country for Old Men '07
The Walker '07
A Prairie Home Companion '06
A Scanner Darkly '06
The Big White '05
North Country '05
The Prize Winner of Defiance, Ohio '05
After the Sunset '04
She Hate Me '04
Anger Management '03
Go Further '03
Scorched '02
Austin Powers 2: The Spy Who Shagged Me '99
EDtv '99
Play It to the Bone '99
The Hi-Lo Country '98
Palmetto '98
The Thin Red Line '98
Wag the Dog '97
Welcome to Sarajevo '97
Kingpin '96
The People vs. Larry Flynt '96
Sunchaser '96
Money Train '95
The Cowboy Way '94
Natural Born Killers '94
Indecent Proposal '93
Ted & Venus '93
White Men Can't Jump '92
Doc Hollywood '91
Mother Goose Rock 'n' Rhyme '90
Cool Blue '88
Eye of the Demon '87
Wildcats '86

William Harrigan (1894-1966)
Flying Leathernecks '51
Exiled to Shanghai '37
"G" Men '35
The Invisible Man '33

Laura Elena Harring (1964-)
Love in the Time of Cholera '07
Nancy Drew '07
Ghost Son '06
Inland Empire '06
All Souls Day '05
The Punisher '04
Loco Love '03
Willard '03
Derailed '02
John Q '02
Mulholland Drive '01
Black Scorpion 2: Ground Zero '96
Exit to Eden '94
Rio Diablo '93
Dead Women in Lingerie '90
The Forbidden Dance '90
Silent Night, Deadly Night 3: Better Watch Out! '89
The Alamo: Thirteen Days to Glory '87

Cheryl Francis Harrington
Legal Deceit '95
Perfume '91

Desmond Harrington (1976-)
3-Way '04
Wrong Turn '03
Ghost Ship '02
We Were Soldiers '02
The Hole '01
My First Mister '01
Riding in Cars with Boys '01
The Messenger: The Story of Joan of Arc '99

Jay Harrington (1971-)
A Little Inside '01
Octopus '00

Laura Harrington (1958-)
Paulie '98
The Devil's Advocate '97
Dead Air '94
Linda '93
The Secret '93
What's Eating Gilbert Grape '93
Perfect Witness '89
Maximum Overdrive '86

Pat Harrington (1929-)
These Old Broads '01
Ablaze '00
The Affair '73
Easy Come, Easy Go '67
The President's Analyst '67

Peter Harrington
Diamond Run '00
Time Chasers '95

Barbara Harris (1937-)
Grosse Pointe Blank '97
Dirty Rotten Scoundrels '88
Nice Girls Don't Explode '87
Peggy Sue Got Married '86
The North Avenue Irregulars '79
Nashville '75
Plaza Suite '71
Who Is Harry Kellerman and Why Is He Saying Those Terrible Things About Me? '71
Oh Dad, Poor Dad (Momma's Hung You in the Closet & I'm Feeling So Sad) '67
A Thousand Clowns '65

Baxter Harris (1940-)
Species 2 '98
Home Alone 3 '97

Brad Harris (1933-)
Seven Magnificent Gladiators '84
Hercules '83
King of Kong Island '78
Jungle Inferno '72
Island of Lost Girls '68
Rattler Kid '68
Goliath Against the Giants '63
Samson '61

Cynthia Harris (1934-)
Pancho Barnes '88
Three Men and a Baby '87
Izzy & Moe '85
Reuben, Reuben '83
Edward and Mrs. Simpson '80
Isadora '68

Danielle Harris (1977-)
Halloween '07
Rugrats Go Wild! '03 (V)
The Wild Thornberrys Movie '02 (V)
Killer Bud '00
Urban Legend '98
Back to Back '96
Daylight '96
Wish upon a Star '96
Roseanne: An Unauthorized Biography '94
The Woman Who Loved Elvis '93
The Last Boy Scout '91
Nightmare '91
Marked for Death '90
Halloween 5: The Revenge of Michael Myers '89
Halloween 4: The Return of Michael Myers '88

David Harris (1959-)
Undercover '87
Badge of the Assassin '85
The Warriors '79
She-Devils on Wheels '68

Ed Harris (1949-)
Cleaner '07
Gone Baby Gone '07
National Treasure: Book of Secrets '07
Empire Falls '05
A History of Violence '05
Winter Passing '05
The Human Stain '03
Masked and Anonymous '03
Radio '03
The Hours '02
A Beautiful Mind '01
Buffalo Soldiers '01
Enemy at the Gates '00
Pollock '00
The Prime Gig '00
The Third Miracle '99
Stepmom '98
The Truman Show '98
Absolute Power '97
Riders of the Purple Sage '96
The Rock '96
Apollo 13 '95
An Eye for an Eye '95
Nixon '95
Just Cause '94
Milk Money '94
Stephen King's The Stand '94
The Firm '93
Needful Things '93
Glengarry Glen Ross '92
Running Mates '92
China Moon '91
Paris Trout '91
State of Grace '90
The Abyss '89
Jacknife '89
To Kill a Priest '89
The Last Innocent Man '87
Walker '87
Alamo Bay '85
Code Name: Emerald '85
Sweet Dreams '85
Places in the Heart '84
Swing Shift '84
The Right Stuff '83
Under Fire '83
Creepshow '82
Knightriders '81
Borderline '80
Coma '78

Edna Mae Harris (1910-97)
Paradise in Harlem '40
Lying Lips '39
The Spirit of Youth '37

Estelle Harris (1926-)
Tarzan 2 '05 (V)
Disney's Teacher's Pet '04 (V)
Home on the Range '04 (V)
Brother Bear '03 (V)
Good Advice '01
Playing Mona Lisa '00
What's Cooking? '00
Lost and Found '99
Toy Story 2 '99 (V)
Chairman of the Board '97
Downhill Willie '96
Once Upon a Time in America '84

Fox Harris (1936-88)
Alienator '89
Dr. Caligari '89
Warlords '89
Repo Man '83

Gail Harris (1964-)
Cellblock Sisters: Banished Behind Bars '95
Forbidden Games '95
Virtual Desire '95

George Harris (1949-)
Eye of the Dolphin '06
The Interpreter '05
Layer Cake '05
Black Hawk Down '01
Soul Survivor '95

Hank Harris
Milwaukee, Minnesota '03
Pumpkin '02

Harriet Sansom Harris (1955-)
Memento '00
Nurse Betty '00

Jamie Harris (1963-)
The New World '05
Rick '03
The Next Big Thing '02
Lost Battalion '01

Jared Harris (1961-)
Lady in the Water '06
The Notorious Bettie Page '06
Ocean's Twelve '04
Resident Evil: Apocalypse '04
I Love Your Work '03
The Other Boleyn Girl '03
Sylvia '03
Igby Goes Down '02
Mr. Deeds '02
How to Kill Your Neighbor's Dog '01
Lush '01
Perfume '01
Shadow Magic '00
Two of Us '00
The Weekend '00
The Eternal '99
The External '99
Happiness '98
Lost in Space '98
B. Monkey '97
Father's Day '96
I Shot Andy Warhol '96
Sunday '96
Blue in the Face '95
Dead Man '95
Nadja '95
Smoke '95
Tall Tale: The Unbelievable Adventures of Pecos Bill '95
Natural Born Killers '94
The Public Eye '92

Jim Harris
Waitress '81
Squeeze Play '79

Jo Ann Harris (1949-)
Deadly Games '80
Act of Vengeance '74
The Beguiled '70

Jonathan Harris (1914-2002)
Toy Story 2 '99 (V)
A Bug's Life '98 (V)

Julie Harris (1925-)
Bad Manners '98
Ellen Foster '97
Carried Away '95
One Christmas '95
Scarlett '94
Secrets '94
Housesitter '92
The Dark Half '91
The Christmas Wife '88

Gorillas in the Mist '88
The Woman He Loved '88
Backstairs at the White House '79
The Bell Jar '79
America at the Movies '76
Voyage of the Damned '76
The Hiting Place '75
Home for the Holidays '72
The People Next Door '70
Reflections in a Golden Eye '67
Harper '66
You're a Big Boy Now '66
Holy Terror '65
The Haunting '63
Requiem for a Heavyweight '62

Julius W. Harris (1923-2004)
Shrunken Heads '94
Murder on the Bayou '91
Prayer of the Rollerboys '91
Crimewave '85
Missing Pieces '83
Victory at Entebbe '76
Two Three '74
Black Caesar '73
Hell Up in Harlem '73
Live and Let Die '73
Shaft's Big Score '72
Superfly '72
Nothing but a Man '64

Kirk Harris
Harc Luck '01
Loser '97

Laura Harris (1976-)
April's Shower '03
I'll Take You There '99
Habitat '97
Inhumanoid '96
All Tied Up '92
The Fourth War '90
Blood Red '88
No Man's Land '87

Leigh Anne Harris (1954-)
I, the Jury '82
Sorceress '82

Lynette Harris (1954-)
I, the Jury '82
Sorceress '82

Mel Harris (1957-)
Hangman's Curse '03
Firetrap '01
Out of Time '00
Sonic Impact '99
Suicide Kings '97
The Pagemaster '94
The Spider and the Fly '94
Suture '93
Desperate Motives '92
Raising Cain '92
Scott Turow's The Burden of Proof '92
Cameron's Closet '89
K-9 '89
My Brother's Wife '89
Wanted Dead or Alive '86

Michael (M.K.) Harris
I Love You, Don't Touch Me! '97
Mel '97
Mr. Stitch '95
Dead Air '94
Sleepstalker: The Sandman's Last Rites '94
The Soft Kill '94

Shattered Image '93
Suture '93
The Horseplayer '91
Satan's Princess '90
Slumber Party Massacre 3

Naomie Harris (1976-)
Street Kings '08
Pirates of the Caribbean: At World's End '07
Miami Vice '06
Shriek of the Mutilated '74

Neil Patrick Harris (1973-)
Harold & Kumar Escape from Guantanamo Bay '08
The Christmas Blessing '05
Harold and Kumar Go to White Castle '04
Undercover Brother '02
The Next Best Thing '00
The Proposition '97
Starship Troopers '97
Animal Rocm '95
The Man in the Attic '94
My Antonia '94
Snowbound: The Jim and Jennifer Stolpa Story '94
Cold Sassy Tree '89
Clara's Heart '88
Purple People Eater '88

Phil Harris (1906-95)
Rock-a-Doodle '92 (V)
Robin Hood '73 (V)
The Gatling Gun '72
The Aristocats '70 (V)
The Jungle Book '67 (V)
The Patsy '64
The Wheeler Dealers '63
Goodbye, My Lady '56
The High and the Mighty '54

Richard Harris (1932-2002)
Kaena: The Prophecy '03
The Count of Monte Cristo '02
Harry Potter and the Chamber of Secrets '02
Harry Potter and the Sorcerer's Stone '01
Gladiator '00
Grizzly Falls '99
To Walk with Lions '99
The Hunchback '97
Smilla's Sense of Snow '96
This Is the Sea '96
Trojan Eddie '96
Cry, the Beloved Country '95
Savage Hearts '95
Abraham '94
King of the Wind '93
Wrestling Ernest Hemingway '93
Patriot Games '92
Silent Tongue '92
Unforgiven '92
The Field '90
Mack the Knife '89
Game for Vultures '86
Your Ticket Is No Longer Valid '84
Triumphs of a Man Called Horse '83

The Christmas Blessing '05

Rossie (Ross) Harris (1969-)
Zapped Again! '89
Two Kinds of Love '85
Testament '83
Amber Waves '82
Airplane! '80
The Plougman's Lunch '83
To the Lighthouse '83
The Chisholms '79
Beau Brummel '54

Sean Harris
Outlaw '07
Brothers of the Head '06
Asylum '05
24 Hour Party People '01

Shawntae Harris
See Da Brat

Stacy Harris (1918-73)
Bloody Mama '70
The Hunters '58
New Orleans After Dark '58

Rosalind Harris
Mrs. Santa Claus '96
Fiddler on the Roof '71

Rosemary Harris (1930-)
Before the Devil Knows You're Dead '07
Spider-Man 3 '07
Being Julia '04
Spider-Man 2 '04
Spider-Man '02
The Gift '00
Sunshine '99
My Life So Far '98
Hamlet '96
Tom & Viv '94
The Camomile Lawn '92
Crossing Delancey '88
Heartbreak House '86
The Ploughman's Lunch '83

Robin Harris (1953-90)
Sorority House Massacre 2: Nighty Nightmare '92
Hard to Die '90
House Party '90
Mo' Better Blues '90
I'm Gonna Git You Sucka '88

Robert H. Harris (1909-81)
Valley of the Dolls '67
Apache Uprising '66
Rock-a-Doodle '92 (V)

Ricky Harris (1962-)
How to Make a Monster '58
The Invisible Boy '57
Woman, Thou Art Loosed '04
Bones '01
Simon Sez '99
Trick as Thieves '99
Heat of the Sun '99

A Christmas Carol '51
Trio '50
The Pickwick Papers '54
Let's Make Up '55
A Cry from the Streets '57
Cast a Dark Shadow '55

Kathleen Harrison (1892-1995)
Curse 3: Blood Sacrifice '90
Tank '83
Razorback '84
Seduced '85
Oceans of Fire '86
The Hasty Heart '86
North Shore '87
Dangerous Pursuit '89
Body Chemistry 2: Voice of a Stranger '91
Duplicates '92
Caught in the Act '93

Jenilee Harrison (1959-)
Fists of Iron '94
Prime Target '91
Gunfight at the O.K. Corral
Bomb '80
Centennial '78
Trilogy of Terror '75

Gregory Harrison (1952-)
First Daughter '99
Running Wild '99
Air Bud 2: Golden Receiver '98
It's My Party '95
Hard Evidence '94
Cadillac Girls '93
Bare Essentials '91
For Ladies Only '81
Enola Gay: The Mer, the Mission, the Atomic Bomb '80
Centennial '78

George Harrison (1943-2001)
Shanghai Surprise '86
Water '85
Monty Python's Life of Brian '79
All You Need Is Cash '78
Let It Be '70
Yellow Submarine '68 (V)
Magical Mystery Tour '67
Help! '65
A Hard Day's Night '64

Cathryn Harrison (1960-)
Images '72
House of the Dead '03
Blackwoods '02
Paid in Full '02
Remember the Titans '00
Small Vices: A Spenser Mystery '99
The Choir '95
Clarissa '91
A Handful of Dust '89
The Dresser '83
Blue Fire Lady '78

Anthony Harrison (1961-)
My Fair Lady '64
Cleopatra '63
Midnight Lace '60
The Reluctant Debutante '58

Zelda Harris (1985-)
He Got Game '98
The Baby-Sitters Club '95
Crooklyn '94
The Piano Lesson '94

Ted Harris (1938-91)
Ufoira '81
Blacula '72
Southland Tales '06
A Man Called Horse '70
Molly Maguires '70
Camelot '67
Caprice '67
The Bible '66
Hawaii '66
The Heroes of Telemark '65
Major Dundee '65
The Red Desert '64
This Sporting Life '63
Mutiny on the Bounty '62
The Guns of Navarone '61
The Wreck of the Mary Deare '59
Dirty '05
Come as You Are '05
Pressure '02

Wood Harris (1969-)
Sugar Hill '94

Steve Harris (1965-)
Bringing Down the House '03
Minority Report '02
Rip It Off '02
The Skulls '00
The Mod Squad '99
The Rock '96

The House on Todville Road '95
Magic Island '95
Interlocked '98
The Thin Red Line '98

David Harrod
Union City '81
Videodrome '83
Forever, Lulu '97
Satisfaction '88
New York Stories '89
Tales from the Darkside: The Movie '90
Hairspray '88
Heavy '94
Body Bags '93
Dead Beat '94
Cop Land '97
Six Ways to Sunday '99
Shaker Run '85
Under Capricorn '82
The Final Conflict '81
From a Far Country: Pope John Paul II '81
All Creatures Great and Small '74

Lisa Harrow (1943-)
Sunday '96
That Eye, the Sky '94
The Last Days of Chez Nous '92
The Citadel '38
Sidewalks of London '38
Men Are Not Gods '37
Storm in a Teacup '37

Richard Harrison (1935-)
Ninja Powerforce '90
Ninja Showdown '90
The Channeler '89
Ninja Strike Force '88
Terminal Force '88
Ninja Commandments '87
Ninja Operation: Licensed to Terminate '87
His Name Was King '85
Blood Debts '83
Fireback '78
Thirty-Six Hours of Hell '77
Between God, the Devil & a Winchester '72
Messalina vs. the Son of Hercules '64
Giants of Rome '63
Gunfight at Red Sands '63
The Invincible Gladiator '63
Gladiators 7 '62
Medusa Against the Son of Hercules '62

The Tuskegee Airmen '95
Armed for Action '92
Blood on the Badge '92

Jamie Harrold
Flannel Pajamas '06
Corn '02
Cocoon '85
Beneath the Planet of the Apes '70
Planet of the Apes '68
Henry Hill '00
101 Ways (The Things a Girl Will Do to Keep Her Volvo) '00
Swimming '00
I Think I Do '97
I Shot Andy Warhol '96
Chain of Desire '93
Family Pictures '93

Kathryn Harrold (1950-)
A Woman's a Helluva Thing '01
The '70s '00
Outrage '98
Tagget '90
Deja Vu '98
The Companion '94
Deadly Desire '91
Rainbow Drive '90
Dead Solid Perfect '88
Raw Deal '86
Into the Night '85
Heartbreakers '84
The Sender '82
Yes, Giorgio '82
Modern Romance '81
The Pursuit of D.E. Cooper '81
Bogie: The Last Hero '80
The Hunter '80
Nightwing '79

Noel Harrison (1936-)
See Mya
Take It Off '07
The Fifth Musketeer '79
Deadly Thief '79
The Prince and the Pauper '78

Michelle Harrison
Luna: Spirit of the Whale '07
Diffin' River '46
Lost in a Harem '44

Lottie Harrison
Lost in a Harem '44

Linda Harrison (1945-)
Cocoon '85
Beneath the Planet of the Apes '70
Planet of the Apes '68

The Foreigner '78
Mr. Mike's Mondo Video '79
The Winslow Boy '48
The Ghost Train '41
Night Must Fall '37
The Ghoul '34

Jackee Harry
See Jackee

John Harron (1903-39)
Midnight Warning '32
The White Zombie '32
The Night Cry '26
West-Bound Limited 23

Rex Harrison (1908-90)
Anastasia: The Mystery of Anna '86
Heartbreak House '86
Time to Die '83
Ashanti, Land of No Mercy '79
The Prince and the Pauper '78
Behind the Iron Mask '77
The Flight of the Doves '71
Doctor Dolittle '67
The Honey Pot '67
The Agony and the Ecstasy '65
My Fair Lady '64
Cleopatra '63
Midnight Lace '60
The Reluctant Debutante '58

Robert "Bobbie" Harron (1893-1920)
The Greatest Question '19
True Heart Susie '19
Hearts of the World '18
Hoodoo Ann '16
The Birth of a Nation '15
Home Sweet Home '14
Judith of Bethulia '14
Battle of Elderbush Gulch '13

Deborah Harry (1945-)
My Life Without Me '03
All I Want '02
Deuces Wild '02
The Fluffer '01
Six Ways to Sunday '99
Cop Land '97
Heavy '94
Body Bags '93
Dead Beat '94
Intimate Stranger '91
Mother Goose Rock 'n' Rhyme '90
Tales from the Darkside: The Movie '90
New York Stories '89
Satisfaction '88
Hairspray '88
Forever, Lulu '97
Union City '81
Videodrome '83

Ray Harryhausen (1920-)
Comic Book: The Movie '04
Mighty Joe Young '98
Spies Like Us '85

Christina Hart
Helter Skelter '76
Games Girls Play '75
Johnny Firecloud '75
The Runaway Barge '75

Christopher Hart
Idle Hands '99
Addams Family Values '93
The Addams Family '91

Dianne Lee Hart
Pom Pom Girls '76

Dolores Hart (1938-)
Where the Boys Are '60
King Creole '58
Lonelyhearts '58
Loving You '57

Dorothy Hart (1923-2004)
Loan Shark '52
The Naked City '48

Ian Hart (1964-)
Tristram Shandy: A Cook and Bull Story '05
Finding Neverland '04
The Hound of the Baskervilles '02
Harry Potter and the Sorcerer's Stone '01
Killing Me Softly '01
Strictly Sinatra '01
Aberdeen '00
American Women '00
Born Romantic '00
Liam '00
Longitude '00
The End of the Affair '99
Spring Forward '99
Wonderland '99
Frogs for Snakes '98
Monument Ave. '98
B. Monkey '97
The Butcher Boy '97
Michael Collins '96
Robinson Crusoe '96
The Englishman Who Went up a Hill But Came down a Mountain '95
Hollow Reed '95
Land and Freedom '95
Nothing Personal '95
Backbeat '94
The Hours and Times '92

John Hart (1917-)
Blackenstein '73
The Fighting Redhead '50

Kevin Hart
Lone Wolf '88
Mindkiller '87

Kevin Hart (1980-)
Fool's Gold '08
Scary Movie 4 '06
In the Mix '05
Along Came Polly '04
Soul Plane '04
Scary Movie 3 '03

Linda Hart
The First $20 Million is Always the Hardest '02
Crazy in Alabama '99
Tin Cup '96
Gypsy '93
A Perfect World '93

Melissa Joan Hart (1976-)
Backflash '01
Drive Me Crazy '99
Sabrina the Teenage Witch '96

Neal Hart (1870-1949)
The Dude Bandit '33
Trigger Tricks '30
Sands of Sacrifice '21

Pamela Hart
Changing Lanes '02
Next Stop, Wonderland '98
Pi '98

Roxanne Hart (1952-)
The Good Girl '02
Home Room '02
Moonlight Mile '02
Follow the Stars Home '01
The Runaway '00
Horton Foote's Alone '97
Our Mother's Murder '97
Once Around '91
Tagget '90
Vengeance '89
Pulse '88
The Last Innocent Man '87
Highlander '86
Samaritan: The Mitch Snyder Story '86
Oh, God! You Devil '84
Old Enough '84
The Tender Age '84
Special Bulletin '83
The Verdict '82

Shad Hart
The Reagans '04
Big Brother Trouble '00

Susan Hart (1941-)
Dr. Goldfoot and the Bikini Machine '66
Pajama Party '64
Ride the Wild Surf '64
The Slime People '63

Teddy Hart (1897-1971)
Mickey One '65
Ma and Pa Kettle at Waikiki '55

William S. Hart (1864-1946)
Show People '28
Tumbleweeds '25
Three Word Brand '21
The Toll Gate '20
Wagon Tracks '19
Blue Blazes Rawden '18
Narrow Trail '17
Hell's Hinges '16
Return of Draw Egan '16
The Bargain '15
The Disciple '15
The Fugitive: Taking of Luke McVane '15
On the Night Stage '15

Douglas Harter
Invasion Force '90
White Fury '90

Pat Hartigan (1881-1951)
Ranson's Folly '26
King of the Wild Horses '24

Clabe Hartley
Trancers 5: Sudden Deth '94
Trancers 4: Jack of Swords '93

Mariette Hartley (1940-)
Novel Romance '06
Encino Man '92
1969 '89
Passion in Paradise '89
Silence of the Heart '84
M.A.D.D.: Mothers Against Drunk Driving '83
Improper Channels '82
O'Hara's Wife '82
No Place to Hide '81
Nightmare at 43 Hillcrest '74
The Return of Count Yorga '71
Marnie '64
Ride the High Country '62

Pat Hartley
Edie in Ciao! Manhattan '72
Rainbow Bridge '71

Steven Hartley
The Walker '07

Elizabeth Hartman (1941-87)
The Secret of NIMH '82 (V)
Walking Tall '73
The Beguiled '70
The Fixer '68
The Group '66
You're a Big Boy Now '66
A Patch of Blue '65

Margot Hartman
Voyage to the Planet of Prehistoric Women '68
Curse of the Living Corpse '64

Phil Hartman (1948-98)
Kiki's Delivery Service '98 (V)
Small Soldiers '98
The Second Civil War '97
Jingle All the Way '96
Sgt. Bilko '95
The Crazysitter '94
Greedy '94
Houseguest '94
CB4: The Movie '93
Coneheads '93
Daybreak '93
National Lampoon's Loaded Weapon 1 '93
So I Married an Axe Murderer '93
Quick Change '90
Fletch Lives '89
How I Got into College '89
Amazon Women on the Moon '87
Blind Date '87
Jumpin' Jack Flash '86
Last Resort '86
Three Amigos '86
Pee-wee's Big Adventure '85
Weekend Pass '84
The Pee-wee Herman Show '82
Cheech and Chong's Next Movie '80

Lisa Hartman Black (1956-)
Bare Essentials '91
Red Wind '91
The Return of Eliot Ness '91
The Take '90
Full Exposure: The Sex Tape Scandals '89
The Seventeenth Bride '84
Where the Boys Are '84 '84
Deadly Blessing '81
Just Tell Me You Love Me '80
Magic on Love Island '80

William Hartnell (1908-75)
This Sporting Life '63
The Mouse That Roared '59
Brighton Rock '47
Appointment with Crime '45
Immortal Battalion '44

Rona Hartner (1973-)
Le Divorce '03
Time of the Wolf '03
Dad On the Run '00
The Crazy Stranger '98

Josh Hartnett (1978-)
Resurrecting the Champ '07
30 Days of Night '07
The Black Dahlia '06
Lucky Number Slevin '06
Mozart and the Whale '05
Sin City '05
Wicker Park '04
Hollywood Homicide '03
40 Days and 40 Nights '02
Black Hawk Down '01
O '01
Pearl Harbor '01
Town and Country '01
Blow Dry '00
Here on Earth '00
The Virgin Suicides '99
The Faculty '98
Halloween: H20 '98

Joshua Harto (1979-)
The Dark Knight '08
Iron Man '08

Rainbow Harvest
Fever '91
Mirror, Mirror '90
Old Enough '84

Alex Harvey
Fire Down Below '97
Gettysburg '93

Don Harvey
Corn '02
Sparkler '99
The Con '98
The Thin Red Line '98
Crime of the Century '96
Last Dance '96
Sawbones '95
Better Off Dead '94
Men of War '94
Tank Girl '94
American Heart '92
Mission of the Shark '91
Prey of the Chameleon '91
Die Hard 2: Die Harder '90
Casualties of War '89
The Beast '88
Eight Men Out '88

Forrester Harvey (1890-1945)
Mrs. Miniver '42
The Wolf Man '41
Thoroughbreds Don't Cry '37
The Eagle and the Hawk '33

Harry Harvey (1901-85)
The Narrow Margin '52
Ace in the Hole '51
Tea for Two '50
I'm from Arkansas '44
Ridin' the Trail '40
Code of the Fearless '39
In Old Montana '39
Phantom Rancher '39
King of the Sierras '38
The Reckless Way '36

Harry Harvey, Jr. (1929-78)
King of the Sierras '38
Reefer Madness '38

Laurence Harvey (1928-73)
Escape to the Sun '72
Night Watch '72
The Magic Christian '69
Dandy in Aspic '68
Spy with a Cold Nose '66
Darling '65
Of Human Bondage '64
The Manchurian Candidate '62
Walk on the Wild Side '62
The Wonderful World of the Brothers Grimm '62
Summer and Smoke '61
The Alamo '60
Butterfield 8 '60
Expresso Bongo '59
Room at the Top '59
The Silent Enemy '58
Truth about Women '58
I Am a Camera '55
Romeo and Juliet '54
Innocents in Paris '53

Paul Harvey (1882-1955)
Three for the Show '55
April in Paris '52
Thunder in God's Country '51
Riding High '50
Side Street '50
The Yellow Cab Man '50
Call Northside 777 '48
A Southern Yankee '48
Easy to Wed '46
Helldorado '46
A Blondie in Casablanca '46
Blondie's Blessed Event '42
The Man Who Wouldn't Die '42
Arizona '40
Meet Dr. Christian '39
A Slight Case of Murder '38
23 1/2 Hours Leave '37
Alibi Ike '35
The Whole Town's Talking '35

Rodney Harvey (1967-98)
Guncrazy '92
My Own Private Idaho '91
Five Corners '88
Salsa '88

Steve Harvey (1956-)
Racing Stripes '05 (V)
Johnson Family Vacation '04
You Got Served '04
The Fighting Temptations '03
Love Don't Cost a Thing '03

Terence Harvey
From Hell '01
The Phantom of the Opera '89

Tom Harvey
Moving Target '96
And Then You Die '88
Second Wind '76

Verna Harvey (1952-)
That'll Be the Day '73
The Nightcomers '72

Kazuo Hasegawa (1908-84)
An Actor's Revenge '63
Gate of Hell '54

David Haskell (1948-2000)
Body Double '84
Godspell '73

Peter Haskell (1934-)
Robot Wars '93
Child's Play 3 '91
In Old Montana '39
Phantom Rancher '39
Fantastic Seven '79
Christina '74
Legend of Earl Durand '74
The Ballad of Andy Crocker '69

Susan Haskell (1968-)
Black Point '01
No Turning Back '01
Smart House '00
Mrs. Winterbourne '96

Imogen Hassall (1942-80)
The Bloodsuckers '70
When Dinosaurs Ruled the Earth '70

O.E. Hasse (1903-78)
State of Siege '73
The Elusive Corporal '62
Above Us the Waves '56
Betrayed '54
I Confess '53
The Big Lift '50

Danny Hassel (1967-)
A Nightmare on Elm Street 5: Dream Child '89
A Nightmare on Elm Street 4: Dream Master '88

David Hasselhoff (1952-)
Kickin' It Old Skool '07
Click '06
A Dirty Shame '04
Dodgeball: A True Underdog Story '04
The SpongeBob SquarePants Movie '04
Baywatch the Movie: Forbidden Paradise '95
Ring of the Musketeers '93
Bail Out '90
The Final Alliance '89
Fire and Rain '89
Witchery '88
Terror at London Bridge '85
Cartier Affair '84
Star Crash '78
Revenge of the Cheerleaders '76

Marilyn Hassett (1947-)
Twenty Dollar Star '91
Messenger of Death '88
Body Count '87
The Bell Jar '79
The Other Side of the Mountain, Part 2 '78
The Other Side of the Mountain '75

Signe Hasso (1910-2002)
The True and the False '55
A Double Life '47
Where There's Life '47
A Scandal in Paris '46
House on 92nd Street '45
Johnny Angel '45
The Seventh Cross '44
The Story of Dr. Wassell '44
Heaven Can Wait '43
Journey for Margaret '42

Bob Hastings (1925-)
Shadow Force '92
Snowballing '85
The Munsters' Revenge '81
Harper Valley P.T.A. '78
McHale's Navy Joins the Air Force '65
McHale's Navy '64

Richard Hatch (1945-)
Unseen Evil '99
Delta Force Commando 2 '90
Ghetto Blaster '89
Party Line '88
Heated Vengeance '87
Prisoners of the Lost Universe '84
Charlie Chan and the Curse of the Dragon Queen '81
Battlestar Galactica '78
Deadman's Curve '78
Mission Galactica: The Cylon Attack '78
The Hatfields & the McCoys '75

Mary Hatcher (1929-)
Tales of Robin Hood '52
The Big Wheel '49
Holiday in Havana '49
Variety Girl '47

Teri Hatcher (1964-)
Resurrecting the Champ '07
Momentum '03
Spy Kids '01
Running Mates '00
Fever '99
Since You've Been Gone '97
Tomorrow Never Dies '97
Two Days in the Valley '96
Heaven's Prisoners '95
Brain Smasher... A Love Story '93
All Tied Up '92
The Cool Surface '92
Straight Talk '92
Dead in the Water '91
Soapdish '91
The Big Picture '89
Tango and Cash '89

Hurd Hatfield (1918-98)
Her Alibi '88
Crimes of the Heart '86
King David '85
The Word '78
Thief '71
The Boston Strangler '68
Lamp at Midnight '66
Mickey One '65
Invincible Mr. Disraeli '63
El Cid '61
The King of Kings '61
Diary of a Chambermaid '46
Picture of Dorian Gray '45
Dragon Seed '44

Amy Hathaway
Smiling Fish & Goat on Fire '99
Joyride '97

Anne Hathaway (1982-)
Get Smart '08
Becoming Jane '07
The Devil Wears Prada '06
Brokeback Mountain '05
Hoodwinked '05 (V)
Ella Enchanted '04
The Princess Diaries 2: Royal Engagement '04
Nicholas Nickleby '02

Noah Hathaway (1971-)
The NeverEnding Story '84
Troll '86
Mortal Danger '94

Shawn Hatosy (1975-)
The Other Side of Heaven '02
The Princess Diaries '01
Alpha Dog '06
Factory Girl '06
The Cooler '03
Dallas 362 '03
11:14 '03
A Guy Thing '03
Soldier's Girl '03
John Q '02
Tangled '01
Borstal Boy '00
Down to You '00
Anywhere But Here '99
Outside Providence '99
Simpatico '99
Witness Protection '99
The Thin Red Line '98
In and Out '97
The Postman '97

Raymond Hatton (1887-1971)
Peg o' My Heart '22
Invasion of the Saucer Men '57
Flesh and the Spur '57
Motorcycle Gang '57
Shake, Rattle and Rock '57
Girls in Prison '56
Day the World Ended '55
Kentucky Jubilee '51
Rolling Home '48
Land of the Lawless '47
Border Bandits '46
Blazing Guns '50
Gentleman from Texas '46
Northwest Trail '46
The Stranger from Pecos '45
Lawmen '44
Partners of the Trail '44
Raiders of the Border '44
Range Law '44
Ghost Rider '43
Six Gun Gospel '43
Texas Kid '43
Arizona Bound '41
Forbidden Trails '41
Gunman from Bodie '41
Covered Wagon Days '40
Rocky Mountain Rangers '40
Cowboys from Texas '39
Frontier Horizon '39
The Kansas Terrors '39
Rough Riders' Roundup '39
Wyoming Outlaw '39
Come on Rangers '38
West of the Law '42
Riders of the West '42
Reap the Wild Wind '42
Down Texas Way '42
Below the Border '42
Dawn on the Great Divide '42
The Texans '38
Desert Gold '36
The Vigilantes Are Coming '36
Rustlers of Red Dog '35
Buffalo Stampede '33
Hidden Gold '33
Terror Trail '33
Lady Killer '33
The Three Musketeers '33
Cornered '32
The Crooked Circle '32
Drifting Souls '32

D.R.O. Hatswell (1898-1976)

Rondo Hatton (1894-1946)
The Brute Man '46
House of Horrors '46
Jungle Captive '45
The Pearl of Death '44
The Little American '17
Male and Female '19
The Virginian '23
The Fighting American '24
Behind the Front '26

Rutger Hauer (1944-)
Moving McAllister '07
Batman Begins '05
Crash Point '06
Dracula 3: Legacy '05
Dangerous Mind '02
Scorcher '02
The 10th Kingdom '00
Turbulence 3: Heavy Metal '00
New World Disorder '99
Partners in Crime '99
Tactical Assault '99
Merlin '98
Bleeders '97
Bone Daddy '97
Hostile Waters '97
Jack London's The Call of the Wild '97
Redline '97
Mr. Stitch '95
Nostradamus '93
Beyond Justice '92
Voyage '93
Beyond Forgiveness '94
Fatherland '94
Forbidden Choices '94
Surviving the Game '94
Arctic Blue '93
Blind Side '93
Past Midnight '92
Split Second '92
Blind Fury '90
Deadlock '92
The Blood of Heroes '90
Bloodhounds of Broadway '89
Wanted Dead or Alive '86
The Hitcher '86
Escape from Sobibor '87
Flesh and Blood '85
Ladyhawke '85
A Breed Apart '84
Nighthawks '81
Eureka! '81
Chanel Solitaire '81
Blade Runner '82
The Osterman Weekend '83
Inside the Third Reich '82
Spetters '80
Soldier of Orange '78

Didier Haudepin (1951-)
This Special Friendship '67
The Devil '92

Aysha Hauer (1966-)
Married People, Single Sex '93
Welcome Says the Angel '01

Rutger Hauer / **Fay Hauser**
Witchcraft 5: Dance with the Devil '92
One '05
Dracula 2: Ascension '03
Confessions of a Scorcher '02

Cole Hauser (1975-)
Tears of the Sun '03
2 Fast 2 Furious '03
White Oleander '02
Hart's War '02
Pitch Black '00
A Shot at Glory '00
The Hi-Lo Country '98
Good Will Hunting '97
Higher Learning '94
Dazed and Confused '93
School Ties '92

Fay Hauser
The Hot Chick '02
Candyman 2: Farewell to the Flesh '94
Jo Jo Dancer, Your Life Is Calling '86

Wings Hauser (1948-)
Marvin & Tige '84
Jimmy the Kid '82
The Insider '99
Gang Boys '97
Tales from the Hood '95
Victim of Desire '94
Watchers 3 '94
In Between '92
Mind, Body & Soul '92
Beastmaster 2: Through the Portal of Time '91
Deadly Conspiracy '91
Frame Up '91
Living to Die '91
Pale Blood '91
Coldfire '90
Exiled in America '90
The Killer's Edge '90
Reason to Die '90
Street Asylum '90
Wilding '90
Bedroom Eyes 2 '89
The Carpenter '89
L.A. Bounty '89
Marked for Murder '89
Out of Sight, Out of Her Mind '89
The Siege of Firebase Gloria '89
Dead Man Walking '88
Hostage '87
Nightmare at Noon '87
No Safe Haven '87
Tough Guys Don't Dance '87
The Wind '87

Robin Hawdon (1939-)
When Dinosaurs Ruled the Earth '70
Zeta One '69
Bedazzled '68

Jeremy Hawk (1918-2002)

Ethan Hawke (1971-)
Lucky Jim '58
Who to Done It? '56
Race for Life '55
A Shot in the Dark '33

Keeley Hawes (1977-)
Death at a Funeral '07
Tristram Shandy: A Cock and Bull Story '05
The Last September '99
The Avengers '98
The Moonstone '97
Retribution '98
Chaos & Cadavers '03
Me & Mrs. Jones '02
Tipping the Velvet '02
Othello '01
Wives and Daughters '01

Ullrich Haupt (1887-1931)
Morocco '30
The Iron Mask '29
Captain Swagger '25

Angelika Hauff (1923-83)
The Life and Loves of Mozart '59
The Marriage of Figaro '49

Thomas Hauff
DC 9/11: Time of Crisis '04
My Father, My Rival '85
Look for the Silver Lining '49

Vicky Haughton
Whale Rider '02
Her Majesty '01

Darla Haun (1964-)
Dracula: Dead and Loving It '95

June Havoc (1916-)
Brewster's Millions '45
Timser Queen '44
Hello, Frisco, Hello '43
Gentleman's Agreement '47
Four Jacks and a Jill '41
Sing Your Worries Away '42

Alex Hayler (1911-45)
They Were Expendable '45
Bataan '43

Thom Haverstock
Watch It '93

Nigel Havers (1949-)
Penelope '06
Element of Doubt '96
Empire of the Sun '87
The Charmer '87
The Little Princess '87
The Whistle Blower '87
The Burning Season '94
Lie Down with Lions '94
Farewell to the King '89
A Passage to India '84
Chariots of Fire '81

Phyllis Haver (1899-1960)
Battle of the Sexes '28
The Nervous Wreck '26

June Haver (1926-2005)
The Girl Next Door '53
Love Nest '51

Richie Havens (1941-)
Street Hunter '90
Boss' Son '78
Vice Squad '82

Thom Haverstock (cont.)
Tales That Witness Madness '73
Theatre of Blood '73
Escape to the Sun '72

Jack Hawkins (1910-73)
The Killing Man '94
Waterloo '71
When Eight Bells Toll '71
Lola '69
Oh! What a Lovely War '69
Those Daring Young Men in Their Jaunty Jalopies '69
Guns at Batasi '64
Lord Jim '65
Zulu '64
Lawrence of Arabia '62
The League of Gentlemen '60
Ben-Hur '59
The Bridge on the River Kwai '57
The Third Key '57
Land of Fury '55
The Prisoner '55
Angels One Five '54
The Cruel Sea '53
Mandy '53
The Adventurers '51
No Highway in the Sky '51
The Elusive Pimpernel '50
The Black Rose '50
The Fallen Idol '49
The Small Back Room '49
Bonnie Prince Charlie '48
Phantom Fiend '35

Screamin' Jay Hawkins (1929-2000)
A Rage in Harlem '91
Two Moon Junction '88
Mystery Train '89

Jimmy Hawkins (1941-)
Zotz! '62
Cell Me Claus '01
Spartacus '60
Junior G-Men of the Air '42

Sally Hawkins (1976-)
Cassandra's Dream '07
Persuasion '07
Layer Cake '05
Vera Drake '04
All or Nothing '02
Tipping the Velvet '02

Terri Hawkes
The Perfect Storm '00
We Know '05

John Hawkes (1959-)
Miami Vice '06
Wristcutters: A Love Story '06
Me and You and Everyone We Know '05
Identity '03
Hardball '01
The Perfect Storm '00
Sand '00
A Slipping Down Life '99
I Still Know What You Did Last Summer '98
Playing God '96
Night of the Scarecrow '95
Roadracers '94
Murder Rap '87

Jill Haworth (1945-)
The Freakmaker '73
Tower of Evil '72
The Ballad of Andy Crocker '69
In Harm's Way '65
Exodus '60

Nigel Hawthorne (1929-2001)
Tarzan '99 (V)
The Big Brass Ring '99
The Madness of King George '94
Twelfth Night '96
Richard III '95
Inside '96
Madeline '98
The Object of My Affection '98
Amistad '97
Murder in Mind '97
The Winslow Boy '98
Victoria & Albert '01
Demolition Man '93

Elizabeth Hawthorne
The Chronicles of Narnia: The Lion, the Witch and the Wardrobe '05
Without Orders '36

Goldie Hawn (1945-)
The Banger Sisters '02
Town and Country '01
The Out-of-Towners '99
Everyone Says I Love You '96
The First Wives Club '96
Crisscross '92
The Girl from Petrovka '74
Housesitter '92
Deceived '91
Bird on a Wire '90
Overboard '87
Wildcats '86
Protocol '84
Swing Shift '84
Best Friends '82
Lovers and Liars '81
Private Benjamin '80
Seems Like Old Times '80
Foul Play '78
The Duchess and the Dirtwater Fox '76
Shampoo '75
The Sugarland Express '74
Butterflies Are Free '72
Dollars '71
There's a Girl in My Soup '70
Cactus Flower '69

Wanda (Petit) Hawley (1895-1963)
The Smoldering Fires '25
American Pluck '25
Affairs of Anatol '21

Richard Hawley
The Duke is Tops '38

Monte Hawley (1901-50)
Look Out Sister '48
Miracle in Harlem '48
Tall, Tan and Terrific '48
Gang War '40
Mystery in Swing '40
Double Deal '39

Demolition Man '93
Freddie the Frog '92 (V)
Tartuffe '90
The Black Cauldron '85 (V)
Jenny's War '85
Mapp & Lucia '85
Pope John Paul II '84
Firefox '82
Gandhi '82
S*P*Y*S '74

Charles Hawtrey (1914-88)
Carry On at Your Convenience '71
Carry On Camping '71
Carry On Henry VIII '71
Zeta One '69
The Terronauts '67
Carry On Cowboy '66
Carry On Screaming '66
Carry On Cleo '65
Room to Let '49
A Canterbury Tale '44
Sabotage '36

Kay Hawtrey (1926-)
Focus '01
Funeral Home '82

Alexandra Hay (1944-93)
How Come Nobody's On Our Side? '73
The Love Machine '71

Christian Hay (1944-)
Autopsy '74
You're Jinxed, Friend, You've Met Sacramento '70

Colin Hay (1953-)
The Wild '06 (V)
Heaven's Burning '97
Cosi '95

Sessue Hayakawa (1889-1973)
Hell to Eternity '60
The Swiss Family Robinson '60
Green Mansions '59
The Geisha Boy '58
The Bridge on the River Kwai '57
House of Bamboo '55
Three Came Home '50
Tokyo Joe '49
Daughter of the Dragon '31
The Dragon Painter '19
The Tong Man '19
The Cheat '15
The Wrath of the Gods '14

Marc Hayashi
The Laserman '90
White of the Eye '88
Chan Is Missing '82

Harry Hayden (1884-1955)
Double Dynamite '51
Pier 23 '51
Gun Crazy '49
Merton of the Movies '47
The Rains Came '39
Baby Love '69

Russell Hayden (1912-81)
Apache Chief '50
Blazing Guns '50
Guns of Justice '50
Last Bullet '50
Marshal of Heldorado '50
Outlaw Fury '50
Rangeland Empire '50
Sudden Death '50

James Hayden (1954-83)
Once Upon a Time in America '84
Don't Go in the Woods '81

Linda Hayden (1953-)
Therese: The Story of Saint Therese of Lisieux '04
The Barcelona Kill '77
The House on Straw Hill '76
Madhouse '74
The Blood on Satan's Claw '71
Taste the Blood of Dracula '70

Rolling Home '48
Trail of the Mounties '47
Where the North Begins '47
'Neath Canadian Skies '46
Lost City of the Jungle '45
Gambler's Choice '44
Frontier Law '43
Border Vigilantes '41
Doomed Caravan '41
In Old Colorado '41
Knights of the Range '40
The Light of Western Stars '40
Santa Fe Marshal '40
The Showdown '40
Hopalong Cassidy: Renegade Trail '39
Law of the Pampas '39
Renegade Trail '39
The Frontiersmen '38
The Mysterious Rider '38

Sterling Hayden (1916-86)
The Blue and the Gray '82
Deadly Strangers '82
Venom '82
Gas '81
The Godfather 1902-1959: The Complete Epic '81
9 to 5 '80
Winter Kills '79
King of the Gypsies '78
1900 '76
Spaghetti Western '75
The Long Goodbye '73
The Final Programme '73
The Godfather '72
Cobra '71
Loving '70
Dr. Strangelove, or: How I Learned to Stop Worrying and Love the Bomb '64
Terror in a Texas Town '58
Crime of Passion '57
Zero Hour! '57
The Killing '56
The Last Command '55
Shotgun '55
Crime Wave '54
Prince Valiant '54
Suddenly '54
Fighter Attack '53
Johnny Guitar '53
Kansas Pacific '53
Flat Top '52
The Star '52
The Denver & Rio Grande '51
The Asphalt Jungle '50
Bahama Passage '42

Richard Haydn (1905-85)
Young Frankenstein '74
Clarence, the Cross-eyed Lion '65
The Sound of Music '65
Mutiny on the Bounty '62
Please Don't Eat the Daisies '60
Jupiter's Darling '55
Never Let Me Go '53
The Merry Widow '52
Emperor Waltz '48
Sitting Pretty '48
Forever Amber '47
Singapore '47
Adventure '45
Thunder Birds '42
Charley's Aunt '41

Julie Haydon (1910-94)
It's Pat: The Movie '94
Come on Danger! '32

Helen Haye (1874-1957)
Man of Evil '48
The Case of the Frightened Lady '39
Spy in Black '39
Sidewalks of London '38
The 39 Steps '35
Skin Game '31

Salma Hayek (1966-)
Ask the Dust '06
Lonely Hearts '06
After the Sunset '04
Once Upon a Time in Mexico '03
Spy Kids 3-D: Game Over '03
Frida '02
Hotel '01
In the Time of the Butterflies '01
Chain of Fools '00
Time Code '00
Traffic '00
Dogma '99
Wild Wild West '99
The Faculty '98
54 '98
The Velocity of Gary '98
Breaking Up '97
Fools Rush In '97
The Hunchback '97
Fled '96
Desperado '95
Fair Game '95
Four Rooms '95
From Dusk Till Dawn '95
Midaq Alley '95
Mi Vida Loca '94
Roadracers '94

Jeff Hayenga
The Unborn '91
Prince of Pennsylvania '88

Allan Hayes
Neon Maniacs '86
Sam's Son '84

Allison Hayes (1930-77)
The Crawling Hand '63
Attack of the 50 Foot Woman '58
The Undead '57
The Unearthly '57
Zombies of Moratau '57
The Gunslinger '56
Francis Joins the WACs '54

Anthony Hayes (1977-)
Look Both Ways '05
The Boys '98

Bernadene Hayes (1903-87)
Santa Fe Marshal '40
Heroes in Blue '39
Panama Lady '39
Sweetheart of the Navy '37

Billie Hayes (1924-)
Pufnstuf '70
Li'l Abner '59

George "Gabby" Hayes (1885-1969)
The Cariboo Trail '50
Return of the Bad Men '48
Home in Oklahoma '47
Lights of Old Santa Fe '47
Trail Street '47
Badman's Territory '46
Great Expectations '46
Helldorado '46
My Pal Trigger '46
Rainbow over Texas '46
Roll on Texas Moon '46
Song of Arizona '46
Under Nevada Skies '45
Along the Navajo Trail '45
Bells of Rosarita '45
Don't Fence Me In '45
Sunset in El Dorado '45
Utah '45
Tall in the Saddle '44
Bordertown Gunfighters '43
Calling Wild Bill Elliott '43
Death Valley Manhunt '43
Man from Thunder River '43
Red River Valley '41
Robin Hood of the Pecos '41
Sheriff of Tombstone '41
The Border Legion '40
Carson City Kid '40
Colorado '40
Dark Command '40
Melody Ranch '40
Ranger and the Lady '40
Wagon's Westward '40
Young Buffalo Bill '40
Arizona Kid '39
Days of Jesse James '39
Hopalong Cassidy: Renegade Trail '39
In Old Caliente '39
Renegade Trail '39
Saga of Death Valley '39
Southward Ho! '39
Wall Street Cowboy '39
Billy the Kid Returns '38
Come on Rangers '38
The Frontiersmen '38
The Plainsman '37
Rustler's Valley '37
Hopalong Cassidy Returns '36
The Lawless Nineties '36
Smokey Smith '36
Song of the Trail '36
The Texas Rangers '36
Three on the Trail '36
Hopalong Cassidy '35
Lawless Frontier '35
Swifty '35
Texas Terror '35
The Throwback '35
Thunder Mountain '35
Beggars in Ermine '34
Blue Steel '34
Brand of Hate '34
House of Mystery '34
In Old Santa Fe '34
The Lost City '34
Lucky Texan '34
The Man from Hell '34
Man from Utah '34
Monte Carlo Nights '34
Mystery Liner '34
'Neath the Arizona Skies '34
Randy Rides Alone '34
The Return of Casey Jones '34
The Star Packer '34
Tombstone Terror '34
Breed of the Border '33
Fighting Champ '33
The Gallant Fool '33
Galloping Romeo '33
The Outlaw Tamer '33
The Phantom Broadcast '33
Riders of Destiny '33
The Sphinx '33
West of the Divide '33
Boiling Point '32
Border Devils '32
Broadway to Cheyenne '32
Man from Hell's Edges '32
Night Rider '32
Riders of the Desert '32
Texas Buddies '32
Without Honors '32
Cavalier of the West '31
Pleasure '31

Gloria Hayes
Judgment Day '88
Witchboard '87

Grace Hayes (1895-1989)
Zis Boom Bah '41
Rainbow over Broadway '33

Helen Hayes (1900-93)
Agatha Christie's Murder with Mirrors '85
Agatha Christie's A Caribbean Mystery '83
Agatha Christie's Murder is Easy '82
Candleshoe '78
Family Upside Down '78
Victory at Entebbe '76
One of Our Dinosaurs Is Missing '75
Herbie Rides Again '74
Airport '70
Third Man on the Mountain '59
Anastasia '56
Main Street to Broadway '53
Stage Door Canteen '43
Night Flight '33
Arrowsmith '32
A Farewell to Arms '32
The Sin of Madelon Claudet '31

Isaac Hayes (1942-)
Hustle & Flow '05
Anonymous Rex '04
Dr. Dolittle 2 '01 (V)
Reindeer Games '00
Shaft '00
Six Ways to Sunday '99
South Park: Bigger, Longer and Uncut '99 (V)
Woo '97
Flipper '96
Illtown '96
Uncle Sam '96
Backlash: Oblivion 2 '95
It Could Happen to You '94
Oblivion '94
Acting on Impulse '93
Deadly Exposure '93
Posse '93
Robin Hood: Men in Tights '93
Final Judgment '92
Guilty as Charged '92
Prime Target '91
I'm Gonna Git You Sucka '88
Counterforce '87
Dead Aim '87
Nightstick '87
Jailbait: Betrayed By Innocence '86
Escape from New York '81
It Seemed Like a Good Idea at the Time '75
Truck Turner '74

Linda Hayes (1922-95)
Ridin' Down the Canyon '42
Romance on the Range '42
South of Santa Fe '42
Mexican Spitfire '42
Danger on the Air '38

Margaret (Maggie) Hayes (1916-77)
Girls' Town '59
Good Day for a Hanging '58
Omar Khayyam '57
Blackboard Jungle '55
Sullivan's Travels '41

Patricia Hayes (1909-98)
A Fish Called Wanda '88
Little Dorrit, Film 1: Nobody's Fault '88
Little Dorrit, Film 2: Little Dorrit's Story '88
Willow '88
The NeverEnding Story '84
The Corn Is Green '79
Super Bitch '73

Peter Lind Hayes (1915-98)
The 5000 Fingers of Dr. T '53
Seven Days' Leave '42
Playmates '41
Zis Boom Bah '41

Sean P. Hayes (1970-)
The Bucket List '07
Win a Date with Tad Hamilton! '04
Pieces of April '03
Cats & Dogs '01 (V)
Billy's Hollywood Screen Kiss '98

Tony Haygarth (1945-)
Under the Greenwood Tree '05
Fakers '04
Chicken Run '00 (V)
Don Quixote '00
Swept from the Sea '97
The Return of the Borrowers '96
The Infiltrator '95
Royal Deceit '94
The Borrowers '93
Devices and Desires '91
A Month in the Country '87
A Private Function '84
Dracula '79

Lisa Hayland
Fatal Passion '94
Novel Desires '92

Grace Hayle (1888-1963)
Loving You '57
The Great Dictator '40
The Moon's Our Home '36

Cyd Hayman (1944-)
The Godsend '79
After Julius '78
Rogue Male '76

David Hayman (1950-)
Where the Truth Lies '05
The Tailor of Panama '00
Vertical Limit '00
The Match '99
My Name Is Joe '98
Behind the Lines '97
The Jackal '97
Rob Roy '95
Hope and Glory '87
Sid & Nancy '86
A Sense of Freedom '78

Dick Haymes (1916-80)
Betrayal '74
St. Benny the Dip '51
One Touch of Venus '48
Up in Central Park '48
State Fair '45
Du Barry Was a Lady '43

Cal Haynes
Fyre '78
Kemek '70

Linda Haynes (1947-)
Human Experiments '79
Rolling Thunder '77
The Fighter '52

Loren Haynes
Eve of Destruction '90
The Expendables '89

Roberta Haynes (1929-)
The Adventurers '70
Hell Ship Mutiny '57
Return to Paradise '53

Jim Haynie (1940-)
The Peacemaker '97
The Bridges of Madison County '95
Danielle Steel's Star '93
Grand Tour: Disaster in Time '92
Sleepwalkers '92
Too Much Sun '90
From Hollywood to Deadwood '89
Men Don't Leave '89
Out '88
Jack's Back '87
On the Edge '86
Hard Traveling '85
Bitter Harvest '81

Robert Hays (1947-)
The Santa Trap '02
Dr. T & the Women '00
The Abduction '96
Homeward Bound 2: Lost in San Francisco '96
Vanished '95
Cyber Bandits '94
No Dessert Dad, 'Til You Mow the Lawn '94
Homeward Bound: The Incredible Journey '93
Honeymoon Academy '90
Running Against Time '90
Murder by the Book '87
Cat's Eye '85

Scandalous '84
Trenchcoat '83
Utilities '83
Airplane 2: The Sequel '82
Touched '83
Airplane! '80
California Gold Rush '81
Take This Job & Shove It '81
The Fall of the House of Usher '80
Initiation of Sarah '78
The Young Pioneers '76

Dennis Haysbert (1955-)
Breach '07
The Color of Freedom '07
Jarhead '05
Sinbad: Legend of the Seven Seas '03 (V)
Far from Heaven '02
Love and Basketball '00
What's Cooking? '00
The Minus Man '99
Random Hearts '99
The Thirteenth Floor '99
Major League 3: Back to the Minors '98
Absolute Power '97
Standoff '97
Heat '95
Waiting to Exhale '95
Major League 2 '94
Widow's Kiss '94
Return to Lonesome Dove '93 (V)
Suture '93
Mr. Baseball '92
Love Field '91
Navy SEALS '90
Major League '89

David Hayter (1969-)
Guyver 2: Dark Hero '94
The Castle of Cagliostro '80 (V)

James Hayter (1907-83)
Not Tonight Darling '72
The Blood on Satan's Claw '71
A Challenge for Robin Hood '68
Cop-Out '67
Abandon Ship! '57
Beau Brummel '54
The Pickwick Papers '54
Four Sided Triangle '53
Tom Brown's School Days '51
Morning Departure '50
Trio '50
The Fallen Idol '49

Chard Hayward (1949-)
Violent Zone '89

David Hayward
Accidental Meeting '93
Thousand Pieces of Gold '91
Delusion '84
Who'll Save Our Children? '82

Louis Hayward (1909-85)
Terror in the Wax Museum '73
Chuka '67
Promise to Murder '56
The Search for Bridey Murphy '56
Black Arrow '48
The Strange Woman '46
And Then There Were None '45
Dance, Girl, Dance '40
My Son, My Son '40
The Son of Monte Cristo '40
The Man in the Iron Mask '39
The Duke of West Point '38
The Saint in New York '38
Anthony Adverse '36

Rachel Hayward
Cruel and Unusual '01
The Fear: Halloween Night '99
Anything for Love '93
Breaking All the Rules '85

Susan Hayward (1918-75)
Say Goodbye, Maggie Cole '72
The Honey Pot '67
Valley of the Dolls '67
Where Love Has Gone '64
Stolen Hours '63
Back Street '61
I Want to Live! '58
The Conqueror '56
I'll Cry Tomorrow '55
Soldier of Fortune '55
Demetrius and the Gladiators '54
Garden of Evil '54
The Lusty Men '52
The Snows of Kilimanjaro '52
With a Song in My Heart '52
David and Bathsheba '51
I'd Climb the Highest Mountain '51
Rawhide '50
House of Strangers '49
My Foolish Heart '49
Tulsa '49
Smash-Up: The Story of a Woman '47
Lost Moment '47
They Won't Believe Me '47
Deadline at Dawn '46
Canyon Passage '46
Fighting Seabees '44
The Hairy Ape '44
Jack London '44
I Married a Witch '42
Reap the Wild Wind '42
Star Spangled Rhythm '42
Young and Willing '42
Adam Had Four Sons '41
Beau Geste '39

Chris Haywood (1949-)
Jindabyne '06
Innocence '00
Blackrock '97
Kiss or Kill '97
Lust and Revenge '95
Shine '95
Alex '92
A Woman's Tale '92
The Navigator '88
The Tale of Ruby Rose '87
Malcolm '86
Burke & Wills '85
Attack Force Z '84
Man of Flowers '84
The Coca-Cola Kid '84
Razorback '84
Heatwave '83
Waterfront '83
Breaker Morant '80
Newsfront '78

Rita Hayworth (1918-87)
Road to Salina '68
The Rover '67
The Poppy Is Also a Flower '66
The Love Goddesses '65
Circus World '64
They Came to Cordura '59
Separate Tables '58
Pal Joey '57
Fire Down Below '57
Miss Sadie Thompson '53
Salome '53
Affair in Trinidad '52
The Lady from Shanghai '48
The Loves of Carmen '48
Down to Earth '47
Gilda '46
Tonight and Every Night '45
Cover Girl '44
Tales of Manhattan '42
You Were Never Lovelier '42
Blood and Sand '41
Strawberry Blonde '41
You'll Never Get Rich '41
Angels Over Broadway '40
Blondie On a Budget '40
The Lady in Question '40
Music in My Heart '40
Only Angels Have Wings '39
Hit the Saddle '37
Trouble in Texas '37
Charlie Chan in Egypt '35

Lena Headey (1976-)
300 '07
The Contractor '07
Imagine Me & You '06
The Brothers Grimm '05
The Cave '05
The Gathering Storm '02
Possession '02
Ripley's Game '02
Aberdeen '00
Gossip '00
Onegin '99
Merlin '98
Twice upon a Yesterday '98
Face '97
Mrs. Dalloway '97
Grave Indiscretions '96
Century '94
Rudyard Kipling's The Jungle Book '94
The Summer House '94
Waterland '92

Murray Head (1946-)
Beaumarchais the Scoundrel '96
White Mischief '88
Freedom '82
Sunday, Bloody Sunday '71

Anthony Head (1954-)
Persuasion '07
Imagine Me & You '06
Scoop '06
And Starring Pancho Villa as Himself '03
I'll Be There '03

Saifei He (1953-)
Temptress Moon '96
Blush '95

James Hazeldine (1948-2002)

Noni Hazlehurst (1954-)
Candy '06
Little Fish '05
True Colors '87
Fran '85
Waterfront '83
Monkey Grip '82

Jonathan Haze (1929-)
The St. Valentine's Day Massacre '67
The Terror '63
X: The Man with X-Ray Eyes '63
Little Shop of Horrors '60
The Gunslinger '56
It Conquered the World '56
Apache Woman '55
Day the World Ended '55
Swamp Women '55
Monster from the Ocean Floor '54

Shari Headley (1964-)
Johnson Family Vacation '04
The Preacher's Wife '96
Coming to America '88

Glenne Headly (1955-)
Raising Flagg '06
The Moguls '05
Around the Bend '04
Confessions of a Teenage Drama Queen '04
Eulogy '04
Women vs. Men '02
Bartleby '01
2 Days in the Valley '96
Bastard out of Carolina '96
Ordinary Magic '93
Hotel Room '93
Grand Isle '92
Mortal Thoughts '91
Dick Tracy '90
Paperhouse '89
Stars and Bars '88
Nadine '87
Making Mr. Right '86
Seize the Day '86
Fandango '85
The Purple Rose of Cairo '85

Darin Heames
Cock & Bull Story '03
The Fear '94
Night of the Demons 2 '94

Amber Heard
Never Back Down '08
Pineapple Express '08
North Country '05

Ted Healy (1896-1937)
San Francisco '36
Mad Love '35
Reckless '35
Hollywood Party '34
Dancing Lady '33
Myrt and Marge '33

Patricia Healy
Mr. Fix It '06
Undertow '04
Sweet Poison '91
Ultraviolet '91

Pat Healy (1971-)
Great World of Sound '07
Rescue Dawn '06

Mary Healy (1918-)
The 5000 Fingers of Dr. T '53
Zis Boom Bah '41
Second Fiddle '39

David Healy (1932-95)
Unnatural Pursuits '91
Supergirl '84
Lust for a Vampire '71

Myron Healey (1922-2005)
Pulse '88
Claws '77
Smoke in the Wind '75
Cavalry Command '63
Varan the Unbelievable '61
Guns Don't Argue '57
The Unearthly '57
Gang Busters '55
Bonanza Town '51
Down to Earth '47

Anthony Heald (1944-)
Accepted '06
X-Men: The Last Stand '06
Red Dragon '02
Proof of Life '00
Deep Rising '98
8mm '98
A Time to Kill '96
Bushwhacked '95
The Client '94
Kiss of Death '94
The Ballad of Little Jo '93
Whispers in the Dark '92
The Silence of the Lambs '91
Postcards from the Edge '90

John Heard (1946-)
The Guardian '06
Dead Lenny '06
Steel City '06
The Chumscrubber '05
The Deal '05
Sweet Land '05
Tracks '05
White Chicks '04
Mind the Gap '04
A Girl Thing '01
O '01
The Pilot's Wife '01
What's the Worst That Could Happen? '01
The Sandy Bottom Orchestra '00
Time Code '00
Animal Factory '00
Perfect Murder, Perfect Town '00
Pollock '00
The Pact '99
The Witness '99
Babe: Pig in the City '98 (V)
Breakfast of Champions '98
My Own Country '98
The X-Files '98
Winchell '98
Men '97
187 '97
My Fellow Americans '96
Two Days in the Valley '96
Before and After '95
Mr. Holland's Opus '95
Sgt. Bilko '95
Pie in the Sky '95
Me & Veronica '93
The Pelican Brief '93
Gladiator '92
Home Alone 2: Lost in New York '92
Radio Flyer '92
Waterland '92
Deceived '91
Rambling Rose '91
Awakenings '90
Home Alone '90
The End of Innocence '90
The Package '89
Beaches '88
Big '88
Betrayed '88
The Milagro Beanfield War '88
The Seventh Sign '88
Out on a Limb '87
The Telephone '87
After Hours '85
Heaven Help Us '85
Too Scared to Scream '85
The Trip to Bountiful '85
C.H.U.D. '84
Violated '84
Best Revenge '83
Cutter's Way '81
Heart Beat '80
Chilly Scenes of Winter '79
On the Yard '79
The Scarlet Letter '79
Between the Lines '77
First Love '77
Rush It '77

Daphne Heard (1904-83)
Jude the Obscure '71
Macbeth '70

Ann Heard (1953-)
The War at Home '96
A Woman of Independent Means '95

George Hearn (1934-)
Barney's Great Adventure '98
The Devil's Own '96
The Vanishing '93
Sneakers '92
See You in the Morning '89

Anne Heche (1969-)
What Love Is '07
Birth '04
Gracie's Choice '04
John Q '02
Prozac Nation '01
Beyond Suspicion '00
One Kill '00
The Third Miracle '99
Psycho '98
Return to Paradise '98
Six Days, Seven Nights '98
I Know What You Did Last Summer '97
Volcano '97
Subway Stories '97
Wag the Dog '97
Donnie Brasco '96
If These Walls Could Talk '96
The Juror '96
Walking and Talking '96
Kingfish: A Story of Huey P. Long '95
Wild Side '95
Against the Wall '94

Patty (Patricia Campbell) Hearst (1954-)
A Dirty Shame '04
Cecil B. Demented '00
Pecker '98
Serial Mom '94
Cry-Baby '90

Rick Hearst (1965-)
Warlock 3: The End of Innocence '98
Crossing the Line '90

Jean Heather (1921-95)
Murder, He Says '45
Double Indemnity '44

Clifford Heatherley (1888-1937)
Bitter Sweet '33
If I Were Rich '33

Darrell Heath
Woo '97
Don't Be a Menace to South Central While Drinking Your Juice in the Hood '96

Thomas Heathcote (1917-86)
Luther '74
Demons of the Mind '72
Village of the Damned '60

Joey Heatherton (1944-)
The Happy Hooker Goes to Washington '77
Bluebeard '72
The Ballad of Andy Crocker '69

Patricia Heaton (1959-)
The New Age '94
Beethoven '92
Memoirs of an Invisible Man '92

Tom Heaton
Mermaid '00
Call of the Wild '93
April Fool's Day '86

David Heavener
The Catcher '98
Fugitive X '96
Eye of the Stranger '93
Kill or Be Killed '93
L.A. Goddess '92
Prime Target '91
Ragin' Cajun '90
Deadly Reactor '89
Killcrazy '89
Twisted Justice '89
Outlaw Force '87

Heavy D See Dwight "Heavy D" Myers

Girls in Prison '94
Milk Money '94
A Simple Twist of Fate '94
The Adventures of Huck Finn '93
O Pioneers! '91

Jessica Hecht (1965-)
Starting Out in the Evening '07
The Forgotten '04
Saving Face '04
Sideways '04
Intimate Betrayal '96

Paul Hecht (1941-)
Last Call: The Final Chapter of F. Scott Fitzgerald '02
Private Parts '96
Mary and Joseph: A Story of Faith '79
The Savage Bees '76
The Reincarnation of Peter Proud '75
Riding the California Trail '47
So Proudly We Hail '43

Ted Hecht (1908-69)

Eileen Heckart (1919-2001)
The First Wives Club '96
Breathing Lessons '94
Heartbreak Ridge '86
Table Settings '84
White Mama '80
Backstairs at the White House '79
Sorrows of Gin '79
The Hiding Place '75
Zandy's Bride '74
Butterflies Are Free '72
No Way to Treat a Lady '68
Up the Down Staircase '67
Heller in Pink Tights '60
A Doll's House '59
Hot Spell '58
The Bad Seed '56
Bus Stop '56
Somebody Up There Likes Me '56

Andrew Heckler
Time Code '00
Stir '98

Dan Hedaya (1940-)
Strangers with Candy '06
Robots '05 (V)
American Cousins '02
Swimfan '02
Mulholland Drive '01
Quicksand '01
The Crew '00
Shaft '00
Dick '99
The Hurricane '99
Locked in Silence '99
The Extreme Adventures of Super Dave '00
A Night at the Roxbury '98
Alien: Resurrection '97
The Garden of Redemption '97
A Life Less Ordinary '97
The Second Civil War '97
Daylight '96
The First Wives Club '96
Marvin's Room '96
Ransom '96
Clueless '95
Freeway '95
The Reluctant Agent '95
To Die For '95
Maverick '94
Based on an Untrue Story '93
Benny & Joon '93
Boiling Point '93
Fallen Angels 2 '93
For Love or Money '93
Four Eyes and Six Guns '93
Tune in Tomorrow '90
Mr. Wonderful '93
Rookie of the Year '93
The Addams Family '91
Joe Versus the Volcano '90
Pacific Heights '90
Courage '86
Running Scared '86
Slow Burn '86
A Smoky Mountain Christmas '86
Wise Guys '86
Blood Simple '85
Commando '85
The Adventures of Buckaroo Banzai Across the Eighth Dimension '84
Reckless '84
Tightrope '84
The Hunger '83
Endangered Species '82
The Prince of Central Park '77

Jon Heder (1977-)
Blades of Glory '07
Moving McAllister '07
The Benchwarmers '06
Monster House '06 (V)
School for Scoundrels '06
Just like Heaven '05
Napoleon Dynamite '04

Amel Hedhili
Honey & Ashes '96
The Silences of the Palace '94

Serene Hedin
Hawken's Breed '87
Boggy Creek II '83

David Hedison (1928-)
Fugitive Mind '99
Undeclared War '91
License to Kill '89
A.D. '85
The Naked Face '84
Kenny Rogers as the Gambler, Part 2: The Adventure Continues '83
ffolkes '80
The Power Within '79
The Art of Crime '75
Live and Let Die '73
Kemek '70
The Fly '58
Enemy Below '57

Jack Hedley (1930-)
New York Ripper '82
For Your Eyes Only '81
Goodbye, Mr. Chips '69
The Anniversary '68
The Very Edge '63

Garrett Hedlund (1984-)
Death Sentence '07
Georgia Rule '07
Eragon '06
Four Brothers '05
Friday Night Lights '04
Troy '04

Tippi Hedren (1935-)
The Last Confederate: The Story of Robert Adams '05
Raising Genius '04
Darkwolf '03
Mind Lies '00
The Break Up '98
Footsteps '98
Citizen Ruth '96
The Birds 2: Land's End '94
Inevitable Grace '94
Teresa's Tattoo '94
Through the Eyes of a Killer '92
Pacific Heights '90
Deadly Spygames '89
In the Cold of the Night '89
Foxfire Light '82
Harrad Experiment '73
Mr. Kingstreet's War '71
A Countess from Hong Kong '67
Satan's Harvest '65
Marnie '64
The Birds '63

Deborah Hedwall
Shadrach '98
Sessions '83

Astrid Heeren
Silent Night, Bloody Night '73
Castle Keep '69

Richard Heffer
Mad Death '83
Waterloo '71

Meghan Heffern
American Pie Presents: Beta House '07
Insecticidal '05

Kevin Heffernan (1968-)
Strange Wilderness '08
Beerfest '06
The Lather Effect '06
The Dukes of Hazzard '05
Sky High '05
Club Dread '04
Super Troopers '01

Wayne Heffley (1927-)
Johnny Got His Gun '71
Submarine Seahawk '59

Kyle T. Heffner
Asylum of the Damned '03
Mutant on the Bounty '89
Flashdance '83

Marta Heflin (1945-)
Come Back to the Five & Dime Jimmy Dean, Jimmy Dean '82
A Star Is Born '76

Nora Heflin (1950-)
Chilly Scenes of Winter '79
Our Time '74

Van Heflin (1910-71)
Airport '70
The Ruthless Four '70
The Big Bounce '69
The Man Outside '68
The Greatest Story Ever Told '65
Cry of Battle '63
They Came to Cordura '59
Gunman's Walk '58
3:10 to Yuma '57
Patterns '56
Battle Cry '55
Black Widow '54
A Woman's World '54
Shane '53
Prowler '51
Tomahawk '51
East Side, West Side '49
Madame Bovary '49
Act of Violence '48
The Three Musketeers '48
Green Dolphin Street '47
The Possessed '47
The Strange Love of Martha Ivers '46
Till the Clouds Roll By '46
Presenting Lily Mars '43
Johnny Eager '42
Santa Fe Trail '40
Back Door to Heaven '39
Flight from Glory '37
A Woman Rebels '36

Hugh Hefner (1926-)
Comic Book: The Movie '04
Hugh Hefner: Once Upon a Time '92
Beverly Hills Cop 2 '87
History of the World: Part 1 '81

Rene Heger (1978-)
In Enemy Hands '04

O.P. Heggie (1879-1936)
The Bride of Frankenstein '35
Anne of Green Gables '34
The Count of Monte Cristo '34
Midnight '34
Peck's Bad Boy '34
Smilin' Through '33
Devotion '31
The Return of Dr. Fu Manchu '30
The Mysterious Dr. Fu Manchu '29

Robert Hegyes (1951-)
Bob Roberts '92
Just Tell Me You Love Me '80
Underground Aces '80

Peter Hehir (1949-)
Sweet Talker '91
Fast Talking '86
I Live with Me Dad '86
Two Friends '86

Sasha Hehn
Melody in Love '78
Secrets of Sweet Sixteen '74

Katherine Heigl (1978-)
27 Dresses '08
Knocked Up '07
The Ringer '05
Side Effects '05
Love's Enduring Promise '04
Love Comes Softly '03
MTV's Wuthering Heights '03
Valentine '01
100 Girls '00
Bug Buster '99
The Tempest '99
Bride of Chucky '98
Prince Valiant '97
Stand-Ins '97
Wish upon a Star '96
Under Siege 2: Dark Territory '95
King of the Hill '93
My Father the Hero '93

Elayne Heilveil
The Adventures of Nellie Bly '81
Birds of Prey '72

Laurie Heineman
Lady in Red '79
Save the Tiger '73

Amelia Heinle (1973-)
Earth vs. the Spider '01
Liar's Poker '99
The Limey '99
Black Cat Run '98
Quicksilver Highway '98
Uncorked '98

Jayne Heitmeyer (1960-)
Snakeman '05
Voodoo Moon '05
An American Affair '99
Believe '99
Beyond Redemption '99
Requiem for Murder '99
Dead End '98
Sir Arthur Conan Doyle's The Lost World '98
Face the Evil '97
Hawk's Vengeance '96
Sci-Fighters '96
Suspicious Minds '96

Brit Helfer (1959-)
Body Trouble '91
Alley Cat '84

Tricia Helfer
Spiral '07
Memory '06

Marg Helgenberger (1958-)
Mr. Brooks '07
In Good Company '04
Erin Brockovich '00
Perfect Murder, Perfect Town '00
The Happy Face Murders '99
Species 2 '98
Elmore Leonard's Gold Coast '97
Fire Down Below '97
The Last Time I Committed Suicide '96
Bad Boys '95
Frame by Frame '95
Species '95
The Cowboy Way '94
Lie Down with Lions '94
Fallen Angels 2 '93
Stephen King's The Tommyknockers '93
Death Dreams '92
Desperate Motives '92
Through the Eyes of a Killer '92
Crooked Hearts '91
Blind Vengeance '90
After Midnight '89
Always '89
China Beach '88

Erik Hell (1911-73)
The Passion of Anna '70
The Rite '69
Port of Call '48

Richard Hell (1949-)
Desperately Seeking Susan '85
Geek Maggot Bingo '83
Smithereens '82

Thomas Hellberg
Man from Mallorca '84
The Assignment '78

Randee Heller
Matter of Trust '98
Danielle Steel's Changes '91
The Karate Kid '84
Can You Hear the Laughter? The Story of Freddie Prinze '79
Fast Break '79

Anne Helm (1938-)
Nightmare in Wax '69
The Unkissed Bride '66
Follow That Dream '61

Brigitte Helm (1906-96)
The Love of Jeanne Ney '27
Metropolis '26

Fay Helm (1913-2003)
One Body Too Many '44
Phantom Lady '44
The Wolf Man '41
Blondie On a Budget '40
Blondie Brings Up Baby '39

Levon Helm (1943-)
Shooter '07
The Three Burials of Melquiades Estrada '05
Fire Down Below '97
Feeling Minnesota '96
End of the Line '88
Man Outside '88
Smooth Talk '85
The Dollmaker '84
Best Revenge '83
The Right Stuff '83
Coal Miner's Daughter '80

Charlotte J. Helmkamp (1961-)
Frankenhooker '90
Posed for Murder '89

Katherine Helmond (1934-)
Cars '06 (V)
Beethoven's 5th '03
Mr. St. Nick '02
The Perfect Nanny '00
Fear and Loathing in Las Vegas '98
The Spy Within '94
Amore! '93
Inside Monkey Zetterland '93
The Lady in White '89
Overboard '87
Shadey '87
World War III '86
Brazil '85
Time Bandits '81
Scout's Honor '80
Pearl '78
Family Plot '76
Rosie: The Rosemary Clooney Story '82
The Autobiography of Miss Jane Pittman '74
Larry '71
The Hospital '71

Tom Helmore (1904-95)
Flipper's New Adventure '64
Vertigo '58
Designing Woman '57
This Could Be the Night '57
The Tender Trap '55
Trouble along the Way '53

Ed Helms
Harold & Kumar Escape from Guantanamo Bay '08
Meet Dave '08
Evan Almighty '07

Frits Helmuth (1931-2004)
Flickering Lights '01
Memories of a Marriage '90

Robert Helpmann (1909-86)
Patrick '78
Puzzle '78
The Mango Tree '77
The Tales of Hoffmann '51
The Red Shoes '48
Henry V '44

Sheila Helpmann (1916-94)
The Getting of Wisdom '77
Image of Death '77

Percy Helton (1894-1971)
Crashout '55
Kiss Me Deadly '55

David Hemblen
Rollerball '02

Mark Hembrow (1955-)
Swimming Upstream '03
Desperate Prey '94
Out of the Body '88
Return to Snowy River '88
High Tide '87

Margaux Hemingway (1955-96)
Bad Love '95
Inner Sanctum 2 '94
Double Obsession '93
Deadly Rivals '92
Deadly Conspiracy '91
Inner Sanctum '91
The Adjuster '91
Speaking Parts '89
Short Circuit 2 '88
Family Viewing '87
The Room '87

Mariel Hemingway (1961-)
Perfume '01
First Daughter '99
The Sex Monster '99
Little Men '98
Road Ends '98
Deconstructing Harry '97
Bad Moon '96
The Crying Child '96
Deceptions 2: Edge of Deception '94
Falling from Grace '92
Into the Badlands '92
Delirious '91
Steal the Sky '88
Sunset '88
Creator '85
Mean Season '85
Star 80 '83
Personal Best '82
Manhattan '79
Lipstick '76

Toby Hemingway (1983-)
Feast of Love '07
The Covenant '06

David Hemmings (1941-2003)
The League of Extraordinary Gentlemen '03

Don Henderson (1931-97)
The Adventures of Baron Munchausen '89
The Ghoul '75

Dell Henderson (1883-1956)
Love Affair '39
Rainbow over Broadway '33
The Crowd '28
Show People '28

Doug(las) Henderson (1918-78)
The Manchurian Candidate '62

Florence Henderson (1934-)
The Brady Bunch Movie '95
Shakes the Clown '92
A Very Brady Christmas '88
Song of Norway '70

Jo Henderson (1934-88)
Matewan '87
Rachel River '87
Lianna '83

Marcia Henderson (1930-87)
Naked Hills '56
Thunder Bay '53

Martin Henderson (1974-)
Smokin' Aces '07
Flyboys '06
Little Fish '05
Bride & Prejudice '04
Torque '04
The Ring '02
Windtalkers '02

Sarah Henderson
Kids '95

Shirley Henderson (1966-)
Miss Pettigrew Lives for a Day '08
Wild Child '08
I Really Hate My Job '07
Marie Antoinette '06
Harry Potter and the Goblet of Fire '05
Tristram Shandy: A Cock and Bull Story '05
Bridget Jones: The Edge of Reason '04
Yes '04
American Cousins '02
Close Your Eyes '02
Harry Potter and the Chamber of Secrets '02
Once Upon a Time in the Midlands '02
24 Hour Party People '01
Topsy Turvy '99
Wonderland '99
Rob Roy '95
Clarissa '91

Ty Henderson
Happy Hour '87

Daniel Hendler (1976-)
Lost Embrace '04
The Bottom of the Sea '03

Tony Hendra (1941-)
Life with Mikey '93
This is Spinal Tap '84

Benjamin Hendrickson (1950-2006)
Spanking the Monkey '94
Manhunter '86

Elaine Hendrix (1971-)
Coffee Date '06
Bam Bam & Celeste '05
What the #$*! Do We (K)now!? '04
Inspector Gadget 2 '02
Mr. St. Nick '02
Wish You Were Dead '00
Molly '99

Anouska (Anoushka) Hempel (1941-)
Tiffany Jones '75
Blacksnake '73
The Scars of Dracula '70
On Her Majesty's Secret Service '69

John Hemphill (1955-)
Screwed '00
Home of Angels '94
Mr. Nanny '93
Camp Cucamonga: How I Spent My Summer Vacation '90

Sherman Hemsley (1938-)
Screwed '00
Sodbusters '94
Club Fed '90
Ghost Fever '87
Combat Academy '86
Alice in Wonderland '85
Ghost Dance '83
Love at First Bite '79

George Henare (1945-)
The Legend of Johnny Lingo '03
The Vector File '03
The Silent One '86

Richard Hench (1955-)
Endangered '94
Uncivilized '94
Tomb '86
Bio Hazard '85

Bill Henderson (1925-)
Trippin' '99
City Slickers '91
Movie Maker '86
Murphy's Law '86
Clue '85
The Adventures of Buckaroo Banzai Across the Eighth Dimension '84
Get Crazy '83

Gloria Hendry (1949-)
Pumpkinhead 2: Blood Wings '94
Black Belt Jones '74
Black Caesar '73
Hell Up in Harlem '73
Live and Let Die '73
Slaughter's Big Ripoff '73

Ian Hendry (1931-84)
The Bitch '78
The Passenger '75
Captain Kronos: Vampire Hunter '74
Theatre of Blood '73
Get Carter '71
McKenzie Break '70
Journey to the Far Side of the Sun '69
The Saint '68
Vendetta for the Saint '68
The Hill '65
Repulsion '65

Wanda Hendrix (1928-81)
My Outlaw Brother '51
The Admiral Was a Lady '50
Prince of Foxes '49
Welcome Stranger '47

Sonja Henie (1912-69)
Wintertime '43
Iceland '42
Sun Valley Serenade '41
Everything Happens at Night '39
Second Fiddle '39
Happy Landing '38
My Lucky Star '38
Thin Ice '37
One in a Million '36

Eva Henning (1920-)
Devil's Wanton '49
Three Strange Loves '49

Andre Hennicke
Youth Without Youth '07
Antibodies '05
Days '05

Sam Hennings
Indecent Behavior 3 '95
Seedpeople '92
Night Angel '90
Mission Manila '87

Monika Henreid
Omega Man '71

Paul Henreid (1908-92)
Dead Ringer '64
Network '76

Jill(ian) Hennessey (1969-)
Wild Hogs '07
Exit Wounds '01
Jackie, Ethel, Joan: The Kennedy Women '01
Autumn in New York '00
Nuremberg '00
A Smile Like Yours '96

Lance Henriksen (1940-)
Pistol Whipped '08
Pumpkinhead 4: Blood Feud '07
Pumpkinhead 3: Ashes to Ashes '06
When a Stranger Calls '06
Hellraiser: Hellworld '05
Tarzan 2 '05 (V)
Alien vs. Predator '04
Modigliani '04
Paranoia 1.0 '04
Starkweather '04
The Invitation '03
Mimic 3: Sentinel '03
Nature of the Beast '94
No Escape '94
Boulevard '94
Color of Night '94
The Criminal Mind '93
Excessive Force '93
Knights '93
Man's Best Friend '93
Super Mario Bros. '93
Alien 3 '92
Delta Heat '92
Jennifer 8 '92
The Linguini Incident '92
Mastergate '92
Comrades in Arms '91
Stone Cold '91
The Pit & the Pendulum '91
The Horror Show '89
Johnny Handsome '89
Survival Quest '89
The Jagged Edge '85
Savage Dawn '84
The Terminator '84
Nightmares '83
The Right Stuff '83
The Hit List '88
Pumpkinhead '88
Near Dark '87
Aliens '86
Choke Canyon '86
Prince of the City '81
The Visitor '80
Damien: Omen 2 '78
Dog Day Afternoon '75

Buck Henry (1930-)
The Last Shot '04
Town and Country '01
Breakfast of Champions '98
I'm Losing You '98
1999 '98
Curtain Call '97
The Real Blonde '97
Kurt Vonnegut's Harrison Bergeron '95
To Die For '95
Short Cuts '93
Keep the Change '92
Grumpy Old Men '93
Defending Your Life '91
The Player '92
Tune in Tomorrow '90
Dark Before Dawn '89
Rude Awakening '89
Aria '88
Eating Raoul '82
Gloria '80
Old Boyfriends '79
Heaven Can Wait '78
The Man Who Fell to Earth '76

Anders Henrikson (1896-1965)
Miss Julie '51
Intermezzo '36
A Woman's Face '38

Krister Henriksson (1946-)
Reconstruction '03
Faithless '00

Brad William Henke (1971-)
Hollywoodland '06
Sherrybaby '06
Must Love Dogs '05
The Zodiac '05
Mr. Wrong '95

Barry (Shabaka) Henley (1954-)
Miami Vice '06
Collateral '04
The Terminal '04
Ali '01
Life '99
How Stella Got Her Groove Back '98
Patch Adams '98
Fear of a Black Hat '94

Georgie Henley
The Chronicles of Narnia: Prince Caspian '08
The Chronicles of Narnia: The Lion, the Witch and the Wardrobe '05

Marilu Henner (1952-)
Enemies of Laughter '00
Man on the Moon '99
Titanic '96
Chasers '94
Chains of Gold '92
Grand Larceny '92
Noises Off '92
L.A. Story '91
Ladykillers '88
Grown Ups '86
Stranger '86
Perfect '85
Stark '85
Rustler's Rhapsody '85
Cannonball Run 2 '84
Johnny Dangerously '84
The Man Who Loved Women '83
Hammett '82
Bloodbrothers '78
Between the Lines '77

Charlotte Henry (1913-80)
Bowery Blitzkrieg '41
God's Country and the Man '37
The Mandarin Mystery '37
Charlie Chan at the Opera '36
March of the Wooden Soldiers '34

Pat Henry (1924-82)
The Detective '68
Lady in Cement '68

Mike Henry (1939-)
Smokey and the Bandit 3 '83
Smokey and the Bandit 2 '80
Smokey and the Bandit '77
Adios Amigo '75
The Longest Yard '74
The Green Berets '68
More Dead Than Alive '68

Martha Henry (1938-)
Clean '04
Anne of Green Gables: The Continuing Story '99
Long Day's Journey Into Night '96
Dancing in the Dark '86
White Light '90

Louise Henry
Charlie Chan on Broadway '37

Hank Henry (1906-81)
Robin and the 7 Hoods '64
Pal Joey '57

Judith Henry
Germinal '93
La Discrete '90

Justin Henry (1971-)
Lost '05
Finding Home '03
Chasing Destiny '00
Andersonville '95
Sweet Hearts Dance '88
Martin's Day '85
Sixteen Candles '84
Tiger Town '83
Kramer vs. Kramer '79

Lenny Henry (1958-)
Penelope '06
Bernard and the Genie '91
True Identity '91

Gregg Henry (1952-)
The Black Dahlia '05
In the Land of Women '06
Slither '06
United '06
Silent Partner '05
Ballistic: Ecks vs. Sever '02
Femme Fatale '02
Sin '02
Sleep Easy, Hutch Rimes '00
The Big Brass Ring '99
Payback '98
Star Trek: Insurrection '98
Robin Cook's Terminal '96
Sharon's Secret '95
Kiss of a Killer '93
The Positively True Adventures of the Alleged Texas Cheerleader-Murdering Mom '93
Fever '91
Fair Game '89
Mean Dog Blues '78
Pearl '78

Gloria Lynne Henry (1952-)
The Devil's Advocate '97
Phantasm 3: Lord of the Dead '94

Gloria Henry (1923-)
Kill the Umpire '50

Robert "Buzzy" Henry (1931-71)
Buzzy Rides the Range '40
The Unknown Ranger '36
Western Frontier '35

Thomas B(rowne). Henry (1907-80)
Showdown at Boot Hill '58
Beginning of the End '57
Blood of Dracula '57
The Brain from Planet Arous '57
20 Million Miles to Earth '57

Tim Henry
Masters of Horror: We All Scream for Ice Cream '07

William Henry (1918-82)
The Alamo '60
Mister Roberts '55
Marshal of Cedar Rock '53
Movie Stuntmen '53
Motor Patrol '50
Trail to San Antone '47
G.I. War Brides '46
The Adventures of Mark Twain '44
Navy Way '44
Dance Hall '41
Campus Confessions '38
Four Men and a Prayer '38
Double or Nothing '37
Madame X '37
Tarzan Escapes '36
China Seas '35

Douglas Henshall (1965-)
It's All About Love '03
Gentlemen's Relish '01
Lawless Heart '01
Anna Karenina '00
Twice upon a Yesterday '98
Kull the Conqueror '97
Orphans '97
Sharpe's Justice '97
Angels and Insects '95

John Hensley
Shutter '08
Teeth '07

Lisa Hensley
15 Amore '98
Paradise Road '97
Dating the Enemy '95
Mr. Reliable: A True Story '95

Pamela Hensley (1950-)
Double Exposure '82
The Nude Bomb '80
Buck Rogers in the 25th Century '79
The Rebels '79
Doc Savage '75

Shuler Hensley (1967-)
The Legend of Zorro '05
Van Helsing '04

Darrin Dewitt Henson (1972-)
Life Support '07
The Salon '05

Elden (Ratliff) Henson (1977-)
Deja Vu '06
Marilyn Hotchkiss' Ballroom Dancing & Charm School '06
The Butterfly Effect '04
The Battle of Shaker Heights '03
Dumb and Dumberer: When Harry Met Lloyd '03
Manic '01
O '01
She's All That '99
The Mighty '98
D3: The Mighty Ducks '96

Gladys Henson (1897-1983)
The Leather Boys '63
Train of Events '49

Jim Henson (1936-90)
Into the Night '85
Sesame Street Presents: Follow That Bird '85 (V)
The Muppets Take Manhattan '84 (V)
The Dark Crystal '82 (V)
The Muppet Movie '79 (V)

John Henson (1967-)
Bar Hopping '00
Stag '97

Nicky Henson (1945-)
Love or Money '01
Me Without You '01
Parting Shots '98
Number 1 of the Secret Service '77
Psychomania '73
The Conqueror Worm '68

Taraji P. Henson (1970-)
Smokin' Aces '07
Talk to Me '07
Something New '06
Four Brothers '05
Hustle & Flow '05
Hair Show '04
Baby Boy '01

Natasha Henstridge (1974-)
Deception '08
The Whole Ten Yards '04
Power and Beauty '02
Chilly Dogs '01
John Carpenter's Ghosts of Mars '01
A Better Way to Die '00
Bounce '00
Caracara '00
It Had to Be You '00
Second Skin '00
Dog Park '98
Species 2 '98
Standoff '97
Adrenalin: Fear the Rush '96
Maximum Risk '96
Species '95

Audrey Hepburn (1929-93)
Always '89
They All Laughed '81
Sidney Sheldon's Bloodline '79
Robin and Marian '76
Two for the Road '67
Wait until Dark '67
How to Steal a Million '66
My Fair Lady '64
Paris When It Sizzles '64
Charade '63
Breakfast at Tiffany's '61
The Children's Hour '61
The Unforgiven '60
Green Mansions '59
The Nun's Story '59
Funny Face '57
Love in the Afternoon '57
War and Peace '56
Sabrina '54
Roman Holiday '53

Katharine Hepburn (1907-2003)
One Christmas '95
Love Affair '94
The Man Upstairs '93
Grace Quigley '84
On Golden Pond '81
The Corn Is Green '79
Olly Olly Oxen Free '79
Love Among the Ruins '75
Rooster Cogburn '75
Trojan Women '71
The Madwoman of Chaillot '69
The Lion in Winter '68
Guess Who's Coming to Dinner '67
Long Day's Journey into Night '62
Suddenly, Last Summer '59
Desk Set '57
The Rainmaker '56

Summertime '55
Pat and Mike '52
The African Queen '51
Adam's Rib '50
State of the Union '48
Song of Love '47
Undercurrent '46
Without Love '45
Dragon Seed '44
Stage Door Canteen '43
Keeper of the Flame '42
Woman of the Year '42
The Philadelphia Story '40
Bringing Up Baby '38
Holiday '38
Quality Street '37
Stage Door '37
Mary of Scotland '36
A Woman Rebels '36
Alice Adams '35
Break of Hearts '35
Sylvia Scarlett '35
Little Minister '34
Spitfire '34
Christopher Strong '33
Little Women '33
Morning Glory '33
A Bill of Divorcement '32

Bernard Hepton (1925-)
Emma '97
Eminent Domain '91
Woman in Black '89
Stealing Heaven '88
The Charmer '87
The Lady's Not for Burning '87
Shadey '87
Mansfield Park '85
Smiley's People '82
Tinker, Tailor, Soldier, Spy '80
Orde Wingate '76
Get Carter '71

Charles Herbert (1948-)
13 Ghosts '60
The Fly '58
Gun Glory '57

Holmes Herbert (1883-1956)
Command Decision '48
Invisible Agent '42
Sherlock Holmes and the Secret Weapon '42
British Intelligence '40
Bad Boy '39
Stanley and Livingstone '39
The House of Secrets '37
Sons of Steel '35
Dangerous Appointment '34
The Invisible Man '33
Mystery of the Wax Museum '33
Dr. Jekyll and Mr. Hyde '32
Shop Angel '32
Daughter of the Dragon '31
The Kiss '29
Through the Breakers '28

Hugh Herbert (1887-1952)
The Beautiful Blonde from Bashful Bend '49
On Our Merry Way '48
It's a Great Life '43
Sherlock Holmes and the Secret Weapon '42
The Black Cat '41
The Villain Still Pursued Her '41
Eternally Yours '39
The Great Waltz '38
Sing Me a Love Song '37
One Rainy Afternoon '36
Gold Diggers of 1935 '35
A Midsummer Night's Dream '35
Sweet Adeline '35
Fashions of 1934 '34
Bureau of Missing Persons '33
Diplomaniacs '33
Lost Squadron '32
Hook, Line and Sinker '30

Percy Herbert (1920-92)
Blacksnake! '73
The Fiend '71
Man in the Wilderness '71
Too Late the Hero '70
Carry On Cowboy '66
One Million Years B.C. '66
Call Me Bwana '63
Mutiny on the Bounty '62
The Guns of Navarone '61
Mysterious Island '61
The Bridge on the River Kwai '57

Becky Herbst (1977-)
Donor Unknown '95
Shrunken Heads '94

Carla Herd
Deathstalker 3 '89
Wild Zone '89

Richard Herd (1932-)
I Married a Monster '98
The Survivor '98
Cosmic Slop '94
The Judas Project: The Ultimate Encounter '94
V '83

Dolores Heredia (1966-)
Santitos '99
On the Air '95

Eileen Herlie (1920-)
Angel with the Trumpet '50
Hamlet '48

Jacques Herlin (1932-)
Torrents of Spring '90
Ironmaster '82

Roberto Herlitzka (1937-)
The Favorite Son '94

David Herman (1967-)
Idiocracy '06
Dude, Where's My Car? '00
Table One '00
Office Space '98

Jack Herman
The Naked Witch '64
The Yesterday Machine '63

Jimmy Herman
Coyote Waits '03
Crazy Horse '96
Medicine River '94
Warrior Spirit '94
Geronimo '93
Dances with Wolves '90

Paul Herman (1946-)
Somebody to Love '94
New York Stories '89
The Last Temptation of Christ '88
The Squeeze '87

Pee-wee Herman
See Paul (Pee-wee Herman) Reubens

Woody Herman (1913-87)
New Orleans '47
Sensations of 1945 '44
Wintertime '43

Irm Hermann (1942-)
The Last Five Days '82
Mother Kusters Goes to Heaven '76
Fear of Fear '75
Ali: Fear Eats the Soul '74
The Bitter Tears of Petra von Kant '72
The Merchant of Four Seasons '71

Jay Hernandez (1978-)
Hostel: Part 2 '07
Hostel '06
World Trade Center '06
Carlito's Way: Rise to Power '05
Friday Night Lights '04
Torque '04

The Rookie '02
crazy/beautiful '01

Jonathan Hernandez (1983-)
The Hammer '07
A Million to Juan '94
My Family '94

Juan Carlos Hernandez
Carlito's Way: Rise to Power '05
High Crimes '02

Juano Hernandez (1901-70)
They Call Me Mr. Tibbs! '70
Sergeant Rutledge '60
The Mark of the Hawk '57
Something of Value '57
Stars in My Crown '50
Intruder in the Dust '49

Vicky Hernandez
Proof of Life '00

Blake Heron (1982-)
11:14 '03
We Were Soldiers '02
Cheaters '00
Wind River '98
Shiloh '97

Marcel Herrand (1897-1953)
Fanfan la Tulipe '51
Children of Paradise '44
Les Visiteurs du Soir '42

Mark Herrier (1954-)
Porky's Revenge '85
Sprague '84
Porky's 2: The Next Day '83
Tank '83
Porky's '82

Aggie Herring (1876-1939)
That Certain Thing '28
Oliver Twist '22

Laura (Martinez) Herring
See Laura Elena Haring

Edward Herrmann (1943-)
I Think I Love My Wife '07
Relative Strangers '06
Wedding Daze '06
The Aviator '04
Intolerable Cruelty '03
The Emperor's Club '02
The Cat's Meow '01
Double Take '01
James Dean '01
The Shaft '01
Atomic Train '99
Vendetta '99
Saint Maybe '98
Big Business '91
Sweet Poison '91
My Boyfriend's Back '93
A Foreign Field '93
Born Yesterday '93
Richie Rich '94
Foreign Student '94
Nixon '95
Soul of the Game '96
Critical Care '97
The Lost Boys '87
Overboard '87
Murrow '86
Compromising Positions '85
The Man with One Red Shoe '85
The Purple Rose of Cairo '85

The North Avenue Irregulars '79
Portrait of a Stripper '79
Sorrows of Gin '79
Take Down '79
The Betsy '78
Brass Target '78
Love Affair: The Eleanor & Lou Gehrig Story '77
Eleanor & Franklin '76
The Great Waldo Pepper '75
The Great Gatsby '74
The Day of the Dolphin '73
The Paper Chase '73

Mark Herron
Girl in Gold Boots '69
8 1/2 '63

Gary Hershberger (1964-)
The Siege of Firebase Gloria '89
Free Ride '86
Paradise Motel '84

Barbara Hershey (1948-)
Riding the Bullet '04
11:14 '03
Daniel Deronda '02
Lantana '01
Drowning on Dry Land '00
Passion '99
Breakfast of Champions '98
Frogs for Snakes '98
A Soldier's Daughter Never Cries '98
Portrait of a Lady '96
The Last of the Dogmen '95
The Pallbearer '95
Abraham '94
A Dangerous Woman '93
Falling Down '93
Return to Lonesome Dove '93
Splitting Heirs '93
Swing Kids '93
The Public Eye '92
Defenseless '91
Paris Trout '91
A Killing in a Small Town '90
Tune in Tomorrow '90
Beaches '88
The Last Temptation of Christ '88
A World Apart '88
Shy People '87
Tin Men '87
Hannah and Her Sisters '86
Hoosiers '86
Passion Flower '86
My Wicked, Wicked Ways '84
The Natural '84
The Entity '83
The Nightingale '83
The Right Stuff '83
Americana '81
The Last Hard Men '76
Boxcar Bertha '72
Diamonds '72
The Baby Maker '70
The Liberation of L.B. Jones '70
The Pursuit of Happiness '70
Last Summer '69
With Six You Get Eggroll '68

Jean Hersholt (1886-1956)
Melody for Three '41
They Meet Again '41
Courageous Dr. Christian '40
The Private History of a Campaign That Failed '81
Reds '81
Freedom Road '79
Dr. Christian Meets the Women '40
Remedy for Riches '40
Meet Dr. Christian '39

Mr. Moto in Danger Island '39
Alexander's Ragtime Band '38
Happy Landing '38
Heidi '37
One in a Million '36
Reunion '36
Break of Hearts '35
Mark of the Vampire '35
The Cat and the Fiddle '34
The Painted Veil '34
Dinner at Eight '33
Grand Hotel '32
The Sin of Madelon Claudet '31
Susan Lenox: Her Fall and Rise '31
Hell Harbor '30
Battle of the Sexes '28
Greed '24
Heart's Haven '22
Tess of the Storm Country '22
The Disciple '15

Gerard Herter
Adios, Sabata '71
Hornet's Nest '70
Last Day of the War '69
Any Gun Can Play '67

Brighton Hertford (1986-)
Mystery Kids '99

Irene Hervey (1910-98)
Play Misty for Me '71
Mickey '48
Mr. Peabody & the Mermaid '48
Gang Busters '42
Night Monster '42
Destry Rides Again '39
East Side of Heaven '39
The Girl Said No. '37
Charlie Chan in Shanghai '35
The Count of Monte Cristo '34

Dude Ranger '34

Jason Hervey (1972-)
Back to School '86
Back to the Future '85
Pee-wee's Big Adventure '85
Frankenweenie '84

Werner Herzog (1942-)
Julian Donkey-boy '99
Man of Flowers '84
Burden of Dreams '82

Kam Heskin (1973-)
The Prince & Me 2: Royal Wedding '06
Dirty Love '05
This Girl's Life '03
Vlad '03

Grant Heslov (1963-)
Good Night, and Good Luck '05
Sleeper Cell '05
The Scorpion King '02
Dante's Peak '97
Black Sheep '96
Congo '95
True Lies '94

Annelise Hesme (1976-)
Avenue Montaigne '06
Priceless '06
Alexander '04

David A(lexander) Hess (1942-)
Alexander '04
Avalanche Express '79
House on the Edge of the Park '84
Left It Rock '86
Park '84
Last House on the Left '72

Joe Hess
Bloodmoon '97
Master Blaster '85

Sandra Hess (1968-)
Annihilation '97
Mortal Kombat 2: Annihilation '97
Beastmaster 3: The Eye of Braxus '95
Endangered '94
Uncivilized '94

Howard Hesseman (1940-)
About Schmidt '02
Gridlock'd '96
Out of Sync '95
Home for Christmas '93
Hot Chocolate '92
The Diamond Trap '92
Rubin & Ed '92
Murder in New Hampshire: The Pamela Smart Story '91
Amazon Women on the Moon '87
Heat '87
Flight of the Navigator '86
My Chauffeur '86
Clue '85
Police Academy 2: Their First Assignment '85
This Is Spinal Tap '84
Doctor Detroit '83
One Shoe Makes It Murder '82
Honky Tonk Freeway '81
Americathon '79
Tarantulas: The Deadly Cargo '77
The Big Bus '76
Jackson County Jail '76
Tunnelvision '76
Shampoo '75
The Sunshine Boys '75
Steelyard Blues '73
Billy Jack '71
A Session with The Committee '68

Catherine Hessling (1900-79)
Renoir Shorts '27
Charleston '26

Charlton Heston (1924-2008)
Planet of the Apes '01 (V)
Cats & Dogs '01 (V)
Town and Country '01
Any Given Sunday '99
Gideon '99
Hercules '97 (V)
Alaska '96
Hamlet '96
The Avenging Angel '95
In the Mouth of Madness '95
True Lies '94
Tombstone '93
Wayne's World 2 '93
Solar Crisis '92
A Thousand Heroes '92
Almost an Angel '90
A Man for All Seasons '88
Treasure Island '89
The Little Kidnappers '90
Nairobi Affair '88
Proud Men '87
Chiefs '83
Mother Lode '82
The Awakening '80
The Mountain Men '80
The Prince and the Pauper '78
Gray Lady Down '77
America at the Movies '76
The Last Hard Men '76
Midway '75
Two Minute Warning '76
Airport '75 '75
The Four Musketeers '75

Sean Hewitt
Battlefield Earth '00
My Own Country '98

Earthquake '74
The Three Musketeers '74
Antony and Cleopatra '73
Soylent Green '73
Call of the Wild '72
Omega Man '71
Beneath the Planet of the Apes '70
Julius Caesar '70
The War Lord '65
Major Dundee '65
The Greatest Story Ever Told '65
The Agony and the Ecstasy '65
Khartoum '66
Will Penny '67
Planet of the Apes '68
Diamond Head '62
55 Days at Peking '63
El Cid '61
Ben-Hur '59
The Wreck of the Mary Deare '59
The Big Country '58
The Buccaneer '58
Touch of Evil '58
Three Violent People '57
The Ten Commandments '56
The Private War of Major Benson '55
The Far Horizons '55
Naked Jungle '54
Arrowhead '53
Pony Express '53
The Greatest Show on Earth '52
Ruby Gentry '52

Lori Heuring (1973-)
False Prophets '06
The Locket '02
Taboo '02
Seduced: Pretty When You Cry '01
True Blue '01
The In Crowd '00
Kitties '06

Jennifer Love Hewitt (1979-)
Garfield: A Tail of Two Kitties '06
Confessions of a Sociopathic Social Climber '05
Garfield: The Movie '04
If Only '04
The Tuxedo '02
Heartbreakers '01
The Audrey Hepburn Story '00
The Suburbans '99
Can't Hardly Wait '98
I Still Know What You Did Last Summer '98
I Know What You Did Last Summer '97
Trojan War '97
House Arrest '96
Sister Act 2: Back in the Habit '93
Let's Scare Jessica to Death '71

Swann '96
The Sender '82
Big Zapper '73

David Hewlett (1968-)
A Dog's Breakfast '07
Ice Men '04
Cypher '02
The Triangle '01
The Life Before This '99
Cube '98
Scanners 2: The New Order '91
Where's the Heart Is '90
Pin... '88

Virginia Hey (1952-)
Bullet Down Under '94
Obsession: A Taste for Fear '89
The Road Warrior '82

Weldon Heyburn (1904-51)
The Chinese Cat '44
Rock River Renegades '42
Criminals Within '41
Panama Patrol '39
Sea Racketeers '37

Louis Jean Heydt (1905-60)
Island in the Sky '53
The Big Sleep '46
Our Vines Have Tender Grapes '45
They Were Expendable '45
Thirty Seconds Over Tokyo '44

Chris Heyerdahl
Blade: Trinity '04
Calvonman '04
Varian's War '01
Requiem for Murder '99
The Witness '99

Barton Heyman (1937-96)
Dead Man Walking '95
Raising Cain '92
Roadside Prophets '92
Awakenings '90
Teenage '44
The Cobra Strikes '48
Calling Wild Bill Elliott '43

Herbert (Hayes) Heyes (1889-1958)
The Far Horizons '55
Bedtime for Bonzo '51
A Place in the Sun '51
Behind Locked Doors '48

Pat Heywood (1927-)
Wish You Were Here '87

Herbert Heywood (1881-1964)
Swingtime Johnny '43
Legion of the Lawless '40

Anne Heywood (1932-)
Sedat '83
I Want What I Want '72
Scenes from a Murder '72
The Shaming '71
The Very Edge '63
The Brain '62
Carthage in Flames '60
Doctor at Large '85
Valdez Is Coming '71
The Naked Flame '68

Zombies on Broadway '44
Sleepers West '41
The Great McGinty '40
Charlie Chan at Treasure Island '39

William Hickey (1928-)
Mouse Hunt '97
Love Is All There Is '96
Twisted '96
Forget Paris '95
The Jerky Boys '95
The Maddening '95
Major Payne '95
The Runestone '91
Christmas '93 (V)
Any Man's Death '90
Mob Boss '90
My Blue Heaven '90
Tales from the Darkside: The Movie '90
National Lampoon's Christmas Vacation '89
Pink Cadillac '89
Puppet Master '89
Sea of Love '89
Sons '89
Bright Lights, Big City '88
Da '88
Hobo's Christmas '87
The Name of the Rose '86
One Crazy Summer '86
Prizzi's Honor '85
Remo Williams: The Adventure Begins '85
Walls of Glass '85
Mikey & Nicky '76
The Boston Strangler '68
Invitation to a Gunfighter '64

Tom Hickey (1944-)
Rory O'Shea Was Here '04
Possession '02
Raining Stones '93
Unnatural Pursuits '91
Nuns on the Run '90

Marguerite Hickey (1963-)
Grizzly Mountain '97
Mirrors '85

Catherine Hickland (1956-)
Millions '90
Ghost Town '88
Witchery '88

Darryl Hickman (1931-)
Johnny Shiloh '63
Geronimo's Revenge '60
Texas John Slaughter: Geronimo's Revenge '60
The Tingler '59
Tea and Sympathy '56
Island in the Sky '53
Fighting Father Dunne '48
The Devil on Wheels '47
Underwood Scandal '47
Two Years before the Mast '46
Leave Her to Heaven '45
Keeper of the Flame '42
Men of Boys Town '41

Ruth Hiatt
Ridin' Thru '35
Sunset Trail '32

Edward Hibbert (1955-)
A Different Loyalty '04
The Lion King 1 1/2 '04 (V)
Friends and Family '01
Hamlet '01
The Anniversary Party '01

John Benjamin Hickey (1963-)
Flags of Our Fathers '06
Infamous '06
Changing Lanes '02
Rising '07
The Seeker: The Dark Is Rising '07
The Lady in Question '99
The General's Daughter '99
The Bone Collector '99
She's Out of Control '89
Spy '89
Child's Play '88
Souvenir '88
Laguna Heat '87
Animal Room '95
Dillinger and Capone '95
Redwood Curtain '95
Secret Ingredient '92
Running Against Time '90
The Razor's Edge '84
Death Valley '81
The Ice Storm '97

Dan Hicks
Class Action '91
Evil Dead 2: Dead by Dawn '87

James Hicks
Miss Monday '98
Swing '98

Kevin Hicks
Final Notice '89

Michele Hicks (1973-)
Northfork '03

Russell Hicks (1895-1957)
Seventh Cavalry '56
Mr. Walkie Talkie '52
As You Were '51
Kentucky Jubilee '51
Air Raid Wardens '43
Hitler: Dead or Alive '43
Tarzan's New York Adventure '42
Dive Bomber '41
Sergeant York '41*
The Bank Dick '40
Blind Fools '40
Johnny Apollo '40
The Real Glory '39
Stanley and Livingstone '39
The Big Broadcast of 1938 '38
Pick a Star '37
Charlie Chan in Shanghai '35
Devil Dogs of the Air '35
Before Morning '33

Dwayne Hickman (1934-)
A Night at the Roxbury '98
High School USA '84

Howard Hickman (1880-1949)
My Dog, the Thief '69
Dr. Goldfoot and the Bikini Machine '66
Cat Ballou '65
Gone with the Wind '39
Western Gold '37
Hell-Ship Morgan '36
Civilization '16

Anthony Hickox (1959-)
Blast '04
Prince Valiant '97
Lobster Man from Mars '89

Catherine Hicks (1951-)
Eight Days a Week '97
Turbulence '96
Like Father, Like Son '87
Peggy Sue Got Married '86
Star Trek 4: The Voyage Home '86
Fever Pitch '85
Garbo Talks '84
The Razor's Edge '84
Better Late Than Never '83
Death Valley '81

Sir Seymour Hicks (1891-1949)
Fame Is the Spur '47
Scrooge '35
The Secret of the Loch '34
Taral Hicks (1975-)
The Salon '05
Belly '98
Subway Stories '97
A Bronx Tale '93
Tommy Redmond Hicks (1962-)
Daughters of the Dust '91
She's Gotta Have It '86
Joe's Bed-Stuy Barbershop: We Cut Heads '83
William T. Hicks
Order of the Black Eagle '87
Unmasking the Idol '86
Death Screams '83
House of Death '82
Day of Judgment '81
Challenge '74
Joan Hickson (1906-98)
Century '94
A Murder Is Announced '87
A Pocketful of Rye '87
The Body in the Library '84
Great Expectations '81
A Day in the Death of Joe Egg '71
Sea Wife '57
Doctor in the House '53
Seven Days to Noon '50
She and He '63
The Guinea Pig '48
Bokuzen Hidari (1894-1971)
The Lower Depths '57
Seven Samurai '54
Sachiko Hidari (1930-2001)
Under the Flag of the Rising Sun '72
The Insect Woman '63
She and He '63
Chieko Higashiyama (1890-1980)
Tokyo Story '53
Early Summer '51
Wilbur Higby (1867-1934)
David Anthony Higgens (1961-)
The Wrong Guy '96
Coldblooded '94
Anthony (Corlan) Higgins (1947-)
The Last Minute '01
Alive and Kicking '96
Moses '96
For Love or Money '93
Nostradamus '93
Sweet Killing '93
One Against the Wind '91
Darlings of the Gods '90
Max, Mon Amour '86
The Bride '85
Cold Room '84
Raiders of the Lost Ark '81
Vampire Circus '71
Something for Everyone '70
Clare Higgins (1955-)
Cassandra's Dream '07
Bigger Than the Sky '05
The Libertine '05
Catherine Cookson's The Secret '00
Small Faces '95
Circle of Deceit '94
Fatherland '94
Bad Behavior '92

Hellbound: Hellraiser 2 '88
Wonderland '88
Hellraiser '87
Colin Higgins (1941-88)
Hope and Glory '87
Into the Night '85
Joe Higgins (1925-98)
Milo Milo '79
Namu, the Killer Whale '66
Flipper's New Adventure '64
John Michael Higgins (1962-)
Evan Almighty '07
Fred Claus '07
The Break-Up '06
For Your Consideration '06
Fun With Dick and Jane '05
Jiminy Glick in LaLa Wood '05
Blade: Trinity '04
A Mighty Wind '03
Best in Show '00
Bicentennial Man '99
From the Earth to the Moon '98
Wag the Dog '97
The Late Shift '96
Vampire's Kiss '88
National Lampoon's Class of '86 '86
Jonathan Higgins
A Woman Hunted '03
No Good Deed '02
Michael Higgins (1925-)
Swimfan '02
School Ties '92
Crusoe '89
Dead Bang '89
Angel Heart '87
Courtship '87
On Valentine's Day '86
1918 '85
Born Beautiful '82
The Conversation '74
Desperate Characters '71
Jane Higginson
Silent Night, Deadly Night 5: The Toymaker '91
Devil Wears White '86
Torri Higginson (1969-)
Family of Cops 3 '98
Double Take '97
Jungleground '95
TekWar '94
Family Pictures '93
Freddie Highmore (1992-)
The Spiderwick Chronicles '08
August Rush '07
The Golden Compass '07 (V)
Arthur and the Invisibles '06
A Good Year '06
Charlie and the Chocolate Factory '05
Finding Neverland '04
Two Brothers '04
Gerald Hiken (1927-)
The Three Sisters '65
Jennifer Hilary (1942-)
Miss A & Miss M '86
One Brief Summer '70
Lise Hilboldt (1954-)
A Married Man '84
Noon Wine '84
Amy Hill (1953-)
Kids in America '05
50 First Dates '04
Cheaper by the Dozen '03
Dr. Seuss' The Cat in the Hat '03
Big Fat Liar '02
Lilo & Stitch '02 (V)
Max Keeble's Big Move '01
Next Friday '00
Yellow '98
Rising Sun '93

Arthur Hill (1922-2006)
Tales of the Unexpected '91
One Magic Christmas '85
The Guardian '84
Love Leads the Way '84
The Amateur '82
Making Love '82
Tomorrow's Child '82
Churchill and the Generals '81
Dirty Tricks '81
The Ordeal of Dr. Mudd '80
Return of Frank Cannon '80
Revenge of the Stepford Wives '80
The Champ '79
Riel '79
A Bridge Too Far '77
Futureworld '76
Judge Horton and the Scottsboro Boys '76
Death Be Not Proud '75
The Killer Elite '75
The Andromeda Strain '71
The Pursuit of Happiness '70
Petulia '68
Harper '66
Moment to Moment '66
The Ugly American '63
Benny Hill (1925-92)
The Italian Job '69
Chitty Chitty Bang Bang '68
Those Magnificent Men in Their Flying Machines '65
Who Done It? '56
Bernard Hill (1944-)
Wimbledon '04
The Boys and Girl From County Clare '03
Gothika '03
Lord of the Rings: The Return of the King '03
Lord of the Rings: The Two Towers '02
The Scorpion King '02
The Criminal '00
Great Expectations '99
True Crime '99
William Shakespeare's A Midsummer Night's Dream '99
Catherine Cookson's The Gambling Man '98
The Mill on the Floss '97
Titanic '97
The Ghost and the Darkness '96
Mr. Toad's Wild Ride '96
Madagascar Skin '95
Lipstick on Your Collar '94
Mountains of the Moon '90
Shirley Valentine '89
Bellman and True '88
Drowning by Numbers '87
No Surrender '86
The Bounty '84
Dana Hill (1964-96)
Tom and Jerry: The Movie '93 (V)
Jetsons: The Movie '90 (V)
National Lampoon's European Vacation '85
Silence of the Heart '84
Cross Creek '83
The Member of the Wedding '83
Shoot the Moon '82
The Boy Who Left Home to Find Out About the Shivers '81
Fallen Angel '81

The $5.20 an Hour Dream '80
Dennis Hill (1949-)
The Underneath '95
Confessions of a Serial Killer '87
Doris Hill (1905-76)
Galloping Romeo '33
Tangled Destinies '32
Dule Hill (1974-)
Whisper '07
The Guardian '06
Holes '03
Love Songs '99
She's All That '99
Color of Justice '97
Sugar Hill '94
Gil Hill (1931-)
Beverly Hills Cop 3 '94
Beverly Hills Cop 2 '87
Jack Hill (1933-)
Dance of Death '68
The Sinister Invasion '68
The Brain Eaters '58
The Female Jungle '56
Jean Hill
Polyester '81
Desperate Living '77
Jonah Hill (1983-)
Dr. Seuss' Horton Hears a Who! '08 (V)
Forgetting Sarah Marshall '08
Strange Wilderness '08
Evan Almighty '07
Knocked Up '07
Superbad '07
Accepted '06
Grandma's Boy '06
10 Items or Less '06
Lauryn Hill (1975-)
Restaurant '98
King of the Hill '93
Sister Act 2: Back in the Habit '93
Marianna Hill (1941-)
Blood Beach '81
Schizoid '80
The Invisible Strangler '76
The Godfather, Part 2 '74
The Last Porno Flick '74
Messiah of Evil '74
High Plains Drifter '73
The Baby '72
Thumb Tripping '72
El Condor '70
Medium Cool '69
Paradise, Hawaiian Style '66
Red Line 7000 '65
Roustabout '64
Married Too Young '62
Mary Hill
The Beast from 20,000 Fathoms '53
Mesa of Lost Women '52
Matt Hill (1968-)
Contagious '96
Teenage Mutant Ninja Turtles 3 '93 (V)
Nick (Nicholas, Niko) Hill
Mistaken Identity '41
Pygmalion '38
Nellie Hill (1922-)
Murder with Music '45
Richard (Rick) Hill
Storm Trooper '98
Class of 1999 2: The Substitute '93
Fast Gun '93
Deathstalker 4: Match of Titans '92
Dune Warriors '91
Bloodfist 2 '90
Warrior Queen '87
Devastator '85
Deathstalker '83
Steven Hill (1922-)
The Firm '93
Billy Bathgate '91
White Palace '90
The Boost '88

Running on Empty '88
Between Two Women '86
Heartburn '86
Legal Eagles '86
On Valentine's Day '86
Raw Deal '86
Garbo Talks '84
Yentl '83
Go for It '83
Super Fuzz '81
Crime Busters '78
Odds and Evens '78
March or Die '77
Mr. Billion '77
Eyewitness '81
Rich and Famous '81
It's My Turn '80
The Slender Thread '65
A Child Is Waiting '63
Terence Hill (1941-)
Lucky Luke '94
Troublemakers '94
Miami Supercops '85
Trinity Is Still My Name '75
My Name Is Nobody '74
All the Way, Boys '73
They Call Me Trinity '72
Boot Hill '69
Ace High '68
The Leopard '63
Teresa Hill (1969-)
Twin Falls Idaho '99
Bio-Dome '96
Nowhere '96
In the Heat of Passion 2: Unfaithful '94
Puppet Master 5: The Final Chapter '94
Puppet Master 4 '93
Thomas Hill (1927-)
An Empty Bed '90
The NeverEnding Story '84
Victoria Hill
December Boys '07
Macbeth '06
Marcel Hillaire
Siam Sunset '99
Take the Money and Run '69
Seven Thieves '60
Wendy Hiller (1912-2003)
Anne of Avonlea '87
The Lonely Passion of Judith Hearne '87
Mountbatten: The Last Viceroy '86
A Man for All Seasons '66
Toys in the Attic '63
Separate Tables '58
Something of Value '57
I Know Where I'm Going '45
Major Barbara '41
Pygmalion '38
John Hillerman (1932-)
A Very Brady Sequel '96
Hands of a Murderer '90
Around the World in 80 Days '89
Assault and Matrimony '87
Little Gloria... Happy at Last '84
Up the Creek '84
History of the World: Part 1 '81
Magnum P.I.: Don't Eat the Snow in Hawaii '80
Marathon '80
Betrayal '78
Audrey Rose '77
Blazing Saddles '74
Chinatown '74
The Outside Man '73
Paper Moon '73
The Thief Who Came to Dinner '73

The Last Picture Show '71
Lawman '71
Harriet Hilliard
See Harriet Hilliard Nelson
Verna Hillie (1914-97)
House of Mystery '34
Trail Beyond '34
Man of the Forest '33
Candace Hilligoss (1935-)
Curse of the Living Corpse '64
Carnival of Souls '62
Ali Hillis (1978-)
The Ultimate Gift '07
Must Love Dogs '05
All the Wrong Places '00
Richard Hillman (1974-)
Teenage Caveman '01
Bring It On '00
Men '97
Beverly Hills
See Beverly (Hills) Powers
Gillian Hills (1946-)
Demons of the Mind '72
Blow-Up '66
Beat Girl '60
Daisy Hilton (1908-69)
Chained for Life '51
Freaks '32
George Hilton (1934-)
Day of the Maniac '77
Guns for Dollars '73
The Case of the Bloody Iris '72
The Ruthless Four '70
Sartana's Here... Trade Your Pistol for a Coffin '70
The Next Victim? '71
The Scorpion's Tail '71
Blade of the Ripper '70
Bullet for Sandoval '70
Dead for a Dollar '70
Fistful of Lead '70
Violet Hilton (1908-69)
Chained for Life '51
Freaks '32
Liberators '69
The Battle of El Alamein '68
Any Gun Can Play '67
Paris Hilton (1981-)
Bottoms Up '06
House of Wax '05
May '02
Amazons and Gladiators '01
Pippa Hinchley (1966-)
Fergie & Andrew: Behind Palace Doors '93
Tyler Hilton (1983-)
Charlie Bartlett '07
Walk the Line '05
Violet Hilton (1908-69)
Chained for Life '51
Freaks '32
Nichole Hiltz (1978-)
All Souls Day '05
May '02
Madeline Hinde (1949-)
The Fiend '71
The Bloodsuckers '70
And a Nightingale Sang '91
Art Hindle (1948-)
The Trip '02
Black Horizon '01
The World's Oldest Living Bridesmaid '92
Dixie Lanes '88
Into the Fire '88
Surrogate '88
The Gunfighters '87
J. Edgar Hoover '87
Say Yes! '86
Raw Courage '84
The Man Who Wasn't There '83
Porky's 2: The Next Day '83
Wild Pony '83
Desperate Lives '82
Porky's '82
Octagon '80
The Brood '79
The Power Within '79

Invasion of the Body
Snatchers '78
Black Christmas '75

**Earl Hindman (1942-
2003)**
The Ballad of the Sad Cafe '91
Murder in Coweta County '83
Taps '81
Shoot It Black, Shoot It Blue '74
The Taking of Pelham One Two Three '74

Aisha Hinds (1975-)
Mr. Brooks '07

Ciaran Hinds (1953-)
Miss Pettigrew Lives for a Day '08
Stop-Loss '08
Margot at the Wedding '07
There Will Be Blood '07
Amazing Grace '06
Miami Vice '06
The Nativity Story '06
Munich '05
The Phantom of the Opera '04
Calendar Girls '03
Lara Croft Tomb Raider: The Cradle of Life '03
The Mayor of Casterbridge '03
Veronica Guerin '03
Road to Perdition '02
The Sum of All Fears '02
Jason and the Argonauts '00
The Weight of Water '00
The Lost Son '99
Ivanhoe '97
Jane Eyre '97
Oscar and Lucinda '97
Some Mother's Son '96
The Affair '95
Mary Reilly '95
Persuasion '95
Catherine Cookson's The Man Who Cried '93
A Dark Adapted Eye '93
Hostages '93
December Bride '91

Cindy Hines
The Brood '79

**Samuel S. Hinds
(1875-1948)**
It's a Wonderful Life '46
Scarlet Street '45
The Strange Affair of Unce Harry '45
Weekend at the Waldorf '45
Cobra Woman '44
Jungle Woman '44
Son of Dracula '43
Pardon My Sarong '42
Ride 'Em Cowboy '42
Back Street '41
Man Made Monster '41
Blossoms in the Dust '41
It's a Date '40
Charlie McCarthy, Detective '39
Destry Rides Again '39
The Secret of Dr. Kildare '39
Devil's Party '38
The Jury's Secret '38
Test Pilot '38
You Can't Take It with You '38

Cheryl Hines (1965-)
Waitress '07
Space Chimps '08 (V)
Bickford Shmeckler's Cool Ideas '06
Keeping Up with the Steins '06
RV '06
Cake '05
Herbie: Fully Loaded '05

Damon Hines
Once Upon a Time ... When We Were Colored '95
What's Love Got to Do with It? '93
Lethal Weapon 4 '98
Lethal Weapon 3 '92
Lethal Weapon 2 '89
Scrooged '88
Bartly '87
Lethal Weapon '87
The Adventures of Buckaroo Banzai Across the Eighth Dimension '84

Gregory Hines (1946-2003)
Bojangles '01
The Red Sneakers '01
Running Scared '86
White Nights '85
The Cotton Club '84
The Muppets Take Manhattan '84
Deal of the Century '83
Eubie! '82
History of the World: Part 1 '81
Wolfen '81

Johnny Hines (1895-1970)
The Speed Spook '24
A Girl's Folly '17
Tillie Wakes Up '17

Pat Hingle (1923-)
The Runaway '00
Shaft '00
Muppets from Space '99
Batman and Robin '97
Hunter's Moon '97
A Thousand Acres '97
Larger Than Life '96
Batman Forever '95
One Christmas '95
The Quick and the Dead '95
Truman '95
Lightning Jack '94
Batman Returns '92
Citizen Cohn '92
The Habitation of Dragons '91
The Grifters '90
Batman '89
The Land Before Time '88
Baby Boom '87
LBJ: The Early Years '88 (V)
In 'n Out '86
'06

Michael Hinz (1939-)
Firecracker '71
The Bridge '59

Bill (William) Heinzman Hinzman (1936-)
Night of the Living Dead '68
The Majorettes '87
The Treasure of Jamaica Reef '74
Revenge of the Living Zombies '88
Echoes '88
Devices and Desires '91
Puss 'n Boots '84

Darby Hinton (1957-)
Malibu Express '85
Firecracker '71

Tommy Hinkle
The Little Vampire '00
The Human Shield '92

Skip Hinnant (1940-)
Nine Lives of Fritz the Cat '74 (V)
Fritz the Cat '72 (V)

Brent Hinkley (1962-)
Say It Isn't So '01
The Silence of the Lambs '91

Martin Hinkle (1966-)
Rails & Ties '07
Four and a Half Women '05
The Next B g Thing '02
Winds of Terror '01

Ronald Hines (1929-)
Pack of Lies '87
We'll Meet Again '82
Elizabeth R '72

Paul Hipp (1963-)
Firestorm '97
For the Moment '94
Teenage Caveman '01
Cleopatra's Second Husband '00
More Dogs Than Bones '00
Waking the Dead '00
Another Day in Paradise '98
Midnight in the Garden of Good and Evil '97
Vicious Circles '97
The Funeral '96
Bad Channels '92

Akihiko Hirata (1927-84)
Godzilla vs. the Cosmic Monster '74
Son of Godzilla '66
King Kong vs. Godzilla '63
Mothra '62
The Secret of the Telegian '61
H-Man '59
Godzilla, King of the Monsters '56
Samurai 2: Duel at Ichijoji Temple '55

Michael Hinz
Manhunt for Claude Dallas '86
Maximum Overdrive '86
Brewster's Millions '85
Broken Badge '85
The Falcon and the Snowman '85
Lady from Yesterday '85
Going Berserk '83
Running Brave '83
Sudden Impact '83
The Act '82
When Hell Was in Session '82
Of Mice and Men '81
The Ugly American '63
The Strange One '57

Tommy Hinkle
Norma Rae '79
Running Scared '79
Wild Times '79
The Gauntlet '77
Tarantulas: The Deadly Cargo '77
Hazel's People '73
Running Wild '73
Bloody Mama '70
The Ballad of Andy Crocker '69

Brent Hinkley (1962-)
Elvis: The Movie '79
Hang 'Em High '67
Nevada Smith '66
Invitation to a Gunfighter '64

Darby Hinton (1957-)
Untold Story '88
Color of Justice '97
Independence Day '96
The Great Escape 2: The Untold Story '88
Brotherly Love '85
The Goodbye People '83
Without a Trace '83

Robert Hirsch (1929-)
The Hunchback of Notre Dame '57
Plucking the Daisy '56

Lou Hirsch
Who Framed Roger Rabbit '88

Daniel Hirsch
Conspirator '49
Dangerous Youth '58
The Entertainer '60
A Kind of Loving '62
Rattle of a Simple Man '64
The Nightcomers '72
Sky High '84
Zero Boys '86
Lady Avenger '89

Emile Hirsch (1985-)
Speed Racer '08
Into the Wild '07
Alpha Dog '06
Imaginary Heroes '05
The Girl Next Door '04
Lords of Dogtown '05
The Mudge Boy '03
The Emperor's Club '02
The Dangerous Lives of Altar Boys '02
Gargantua '98

Judd Hirsch (1935-)
A Beautiful Mind '01
Man on the Moon '99
Out of the Cold '99
Running on Empty '88
Teachers '84
Ordinary People '80
King of the Gypsies '78
Sooner or Later '78
Legend of Valentino '75
Fury on Wheels '71

Hallee Hirsh (1987-)
Happy Endings '05
Speak '04
My Sister's Keeper '02
Joe Gould's Secret '00
Spring Forward '99
You've Got Mail '98

Alice Hirson (1929-)
Blind Date '87
The Majorettes '87

Alfred Hitchcock (1899-1980)
Family Plot '76
Frenzy '72
Psycho '60
The Birds '63
The Lady Vanishes '38
Blackmail '29
The Lodger '26

Christianne Hirt
Next One '84
Gooc Neighbor Sam '64

Paul Hirt
In the Mood '87

Patricia Hitchcock (1928-)
Strangers on a Train '51
Psycho '60
Stage Fright '50

William Hobbs (1939-)
The Three Musketeers '74

Rebecca Hobbs
Siam Sunset '99

Katrina Hobbs (1971-)
The Ugly '98

Peter Hobbs (1918-)
Absent Without Leave '95
Super-Fire '97
Blades of Courage '88

Michael Hitchcock (1958-)
Danny Roane: First Time Director '06
Pretty Persuasion '05
A Mighty Wind '03
Best in Show '00

Valerie Hobson (1917-98)
The Promoter '52
The Interrupted Journey '49
Kind Hearts and Coronets '49
The Rocking Horse Winner '49
Train of Events '49
Blanche Fury '48
Great Expectations '46
The Adventures of Tartu '43

Mara Hobel (1971-)
Personal Velocity: Three Portraits '02
Broadway Damage '98
Mommie Dearest '81
Sorrows of Gin '79

Rebecca Hobbs
Clawed: The Legend of Sasquatch '05

Chelsea Hobbs (1984-)
Clawed: The Legend of Sasquatch '05

Alice Hirson (1929-)
Casanova Brown '44
Gaslight '44
Sherlock Holmes Faces Death '43
Dr. Jekyll and Mr. Hyde '32
Charlie Chan in Shanghai '38
You Can't Take It with You '38

Thora Hird (1911-2003)
Lost for Words '99
The Wedding Gift '93
Consuming Passions '88

Josie Ho
Roman '06

Jesse Hlubik
Masters of Horror: Sick Girl '06

Iben Hjejle (1971-)
The Boss of It All '06

Patricia Hodge
The Leading Man '96
The Heat of the Day '91
The Shell Seekers '90
Diamond's Edge '88
Sunset '88
Betrayal '83

William Hobbs (1939-)
The Three Musketeers '74

Hallwell Hobbes (1877-1962)
You Gotta Stay Happy '48
Casanova Brown '44
Gaslight '44
Sherlock Holmes Faces Death '43
Dr. Jekyll and Mr. Hyde '32

Cuban Blood '03

Judith Hoag (1968-)
Acting on Impulse '93
Switched at Birth '91
White Boyz '99
Subway Stories '97
Teenage Mutant Ninja Turtles: The Movie '90

Josie Ho
Exiled '06
Vampire Effect '03

Jesse Hlubik
The Emperor's New Clothes '01
Flickering Lights '01
High Fidelity '00

Daniel Hirsch
Things '90
A Matter of Degrees '90
Danielle Steel's Fine Things '90

Kristen Hocking
See Kristen Dalton

Kane Hodder (1951-)
Hatchet '07
Jason X '01
Watchers Reborn '98
Wishmaster '97
Pumpkinhead 2: Blood Wings '94
Jason Goes to Hell: The Final Friday '93
Friday the 13th, Part 8: Jason Takes Manhattan '89
Friday the 13th, Part 7: The New Blood '88

Florence Hoath (1984-)
Back to the Secret Garden '01
The Governess '96
FairyTale: A True Story '97
The Death Curse of Tartu '66

Rose Hobart (1906-2000)
The Professor '58
Cass Timberlane '47
Conflict '45
The Farmer's Daughter '47
The Mad Ghoul '43
Susan and God '40
East of Borneo '31
Dr. Jekyll and Mr. Hyde '32

Doug Hobart
Death '43
Journey for Margaret '42
Son of Fury '42
To Be or Not to Be '42
The Undying Monster '42
My Teacher Ate My Homework '93

Douglas Hodge
Mansfield Park '07
Scenes of a Sexual Nature '06
Office Killer '97
Coastlines '02
Salome's Last Dance '88

Mike Hodge (1947-)
Boycott '02
Fiona '98

Kate Hodge (1966-)
Desire '95
The Hidden 2 '94
Rapid Fire '92
Love Kills '91
Leatherface: The Texas Chainsaw Massacre 3 '89

Edwin Hodge (1985-)
Hangman's Curse '03
Buddy's Song '91
Middlemen '93
A Fatal Inversion '92
Dark Obsession '90

Danny Hoch (1970-)
We Own the Night '07
Washington Heights '02
Black Hawk Down '01

Kane Hodder (1951-)
The Mystery of Edwin Drood '35
Werewolf of London '35
Contraband '40
Clouds over Europe '39
Spy in Black '39
Drums '38
When Thief Meets Thief '37
Secret of Stamboul '36
The Bride of Frankenstein '35

Eddie Hodges (1947-)
Live a Little, Love a Little '68
Summer Magic '63
The Adventures of Huckleberry Finn '60
A Hole in the Head '59

Earle Hodgins (1893-)
The Baby Doll Murders '92
Vanity Fair '04
The Way We Live Now '02
Hollow Reed '95
The Man Who Shot Liberty Valance '62
The Topeka Terror '45
Colt Comrades '43
Hoppy Serves a Writ '43

Tom (Thomas E.) Hodges (1965-)
Since You've Been Gone '97

The Bashful Bachelor '42
Inside the Law '42
Boss of Bullion City '41
Range Busters '40
Santa Fe Marshal '40
Purple Vigilantes '38
Heroes of the Alamo '37
A Lawman Is Born '37
Aces and Eights '36
Law for Tombstone '35

Leyland Hodgson (1894-1949)
Bedlam '45
International Lady '41
My Son, My Son '40
The Eagle and the Hawk '33

John Hodiak (1914-55)
Dragonfly Squadron '54
Ambush at Tomahawk Gap '53
Conquest of Cochise '53
Across the Wide Missouri '51
The Miniver Story '50
Battleground '49
Malaya '49
Command Decision '48
Homecoming '48
Love from a Stranger '47
The Harvey Girls '46
Lifeboat '44

Biddy Hodson
Hellboy '04
Loaded '94

Heinz Hoenig
Antibodies '05
Judgment in Berlin '88

Paul Hoerbiger (1894-1981)
The Third Man '49
The Mozart Story '48

Dennis Hoey (1893-1960)
David and Bathsheba '51
Golden Earrings '47
Where There's Life '47
Anna and the King of Siam '46
Roll on Texas Moon '46
She Wolf of London '46
Terror by Night '46
House of Fear '45
A Thousand and One Nights '45
Son of Fury '42
The Mystery of the Mary Celeste '35
Power '34

Abbie Hoffman (1936-89)
Born on the Fourth of July '89
Heavy Petting '89

Basil Hoffman (1941-)
The Ice Runner '93
The Double O Kid '92
Communion '89
Lambada '89
Ratings Game '84
Love at First Bite '79

Bridget Hoffman
Time Trackers '88
The Castle of Cagliostro '80 (V)

David Hoffman (1904-61)
Children in the Crossfire '84
Wolf Lake '79
A Woman's World '54

Dustin Hoffman (1937-)
Kung Fu Panda '08 (V)
Mr. Magorium's Wonder Emporium '07
Perfume: The Story of a Murderer '07
Stranger Than Fiction '06
The Lost City '05
Racing Stripes '05 (V)
Finding Neverland '04
I Heart Huckabees '04
Meet the Fockers '04
Confidence '03
Runaway Jury '03
Moonlight Mile '02
The Messenger: The Story of Joan of Arc '99
Mad City '97
Sphere '97
Wag the Dog '97
Sleepers '96
American Buffalo '95
Outbreak '94
Hero '92
Billy Bathgate '91
Hook '91
Dick Tracy '90
Family Business '89
Rain Man '88
Ishtar '87
Death of a Salesman '86
Tootsie '82
Agatha '79
Kramer vs. Kramer '79
Straight Time '78
All the President's Men '76
Marathon Man '76
Lenny '74
Papillon '73
Alfredo, Alfredo '72
Straw Dogs '72
Who Is Harry Kellerman and Why Is He Saying Those Terrible Things About Me? '71
Little Big Man '70
Midnight Cowboy '69
The Graduate '67
Madigan's Millions '67

Elizabeth Hoffman (1927-)
Dante's Peak '97
Fear No Evil '80

Erika Hoffman
The Final Cut '95
To Play the King '93

Gaby Hoffman (1982-)
Perfume '01
Black and White '99
Coming Soon '99
All I Wanna Do '00
200 Cigarettes '98
Volcano '97
Everyone Says I Love You '96
Now and Then '95
The Man Without a Face '93
Sleepless in Seattle '93
This Is My Life '92
Field of Dreams '89
Uncle Buck '89

Gertrude Hoffman
The Ape '40
Caged '50

Jackie Hoffman (1960-)
Queer Duck: The Movie '06 (V)
Robots '05 (V)
A Dirty Shame '04
Garden State '04
Kissing Jessica Stein '02

Jake Hoffman (1981-)
Jiminy Glick in LaLa Wood '05
National Lampoon's Adam & Eve '05
Static '87

Jane Hoffman (1911-2004)
Sybil '76
Senior Trip '81

Jenna Hoffman
See Jenna Byrne

Linda Hoffman
Captured '99
Beneath the Bermuda Triangle '98
The Dentist 2: Brace Yourself '98
Mission of Death '97
The Dentist '96

Philip Seymour Hoffman (1967-)
Before the Devil Knows You're Dead '07
Charlie Wilson's War '07
The Savages '07
Mission: Impossible 3 '06
Strangers with Candy '06
Capote '05
Empire Falls '05
Along Came Polly '04
Cold Mountain '03
Owning Mahowny '03
Love Liza '02
Punch-Drunk Love '02
Red Dragon '02
25th Hour '02
Almost Famous '00
State and Main '00
Flawless '99
Magnolia '99
The Talented Mr. Ripley '99
Happiness '98
Patch Adams '98
The Big Lebowski '97
Boogie Nights '97
Montana '97
Hard Eight '96
Twister '96
Nobody's Fool '94
When a Man Loves a Woman '94
The Yearling '94
Joey Breaker '93
Leap of Faith '92
Scent of a Woman '92

Rick Hoffman (1970-)
The Condemned '07
Hostel '06
Cellular '04
Blood Work '02

Robert Hoffman
Joe Panther '76
Eyes Behind the Stars '72
A Black Veil for Lisa '68
How I Learned to Love Women '66

Shawn Hoffman
Karla '06
Adventures in Dinosaur City '92

Susan Lee Hoffman
Acts of Betrayal '98
Wizards of the Lost Kingdom 2 '89

Thom Hoffman (1957-)
Black Book '06
Dogville '03
Soul Assassin '01
Orlando '92
Lily Was Here '89
The 4th Man '79

Jutta Hoffmann (1941-)
Bandits '99

Susanna Hoffs (1959-)
Austin Powers In Goldmember '02
The Allnighter '87

Charlie Hofheimer (1981-)
Black Hawk Down '01
Music of the Heart '99
Father's Day '96

Isabella Hofmann (1958-)
Homicide: The Movie '00
Atomic Dog '98
The Colony '96
Tripwire '89

Marco Hofschneider (1969-)
Urban Legends 2: Final Cut '00
The Island of Dr. Moreau '96
Europa, Europa '91
Foreign Student '94
Immortal Beloved '94

Bosco Hogan (1949-)
In the Name of the Father '93
James Joyce: A Portrait of the Artist as a Young Man '77
Zardoz '73

Chris Hogan
On Edge '03
Dancing at the Blue Iguana '00

Dick Hogan (1917-95)
Action in the North Atlantic '43
So Proudly We Hail '43

Gabriel Hogan (1973-)
Head in the Clouds '04
Show Me '04
The Halfback of Notre Dame '96

Heather Hogan
The Land Before Time 4: Journey Through the Mists '96 (V)
The Land Before Time 3: The Time of the Great Giving '95 (V)
The Land Before Time 2: The Great Valley Adventure '94 (V)

Hulk Hogan (1953-)
Shadow Warriors '97
Shadow Warriors 2: Hunt for the Death Merchant '97
3 Ninjas: High Noon at Mega Mountain '97
The Ultimate Weapon '97
Santa with Muscles '96
The Secret Agent Club '96
Thunder in Paradise 2 '94
Thunder in Paradise 3 '94
Mr. Nanny '93
Thunder in Paradise '93
Suburban Commando '91
Gremlins 2: The New Batch '90
No Holds Barred '89

Michael Hogan
Coffee and Cigarettes '03
End of Summer '97
Clearcut '92
Smokescreen '90
Lost '86
The Peanut Butter Solution '85

Pat Hogan (1920-66)
Indian Paint '64
Seventh Cavalry '56
Davy Crockett, King of the Wild Frontier '55
Savage Wilderness '55

Paul Hogan (1939-)
Strange Bedfellows '04
Crocodile Dundee in Los Angeles '01
Flipper '96
Lightning Jack '94
Almost an Angel '90
Crocodile Dundee 2 '88
Crocodile Dundee '86
Anzacs: The War Down Under '85

Robert Hogan (1936-)
Maze '01
Gone Are the Days '84
Lady in Red '79
Memory of Us '74

Susan Hogan
Everything's Gone Green '06
Take Me Home: The John Denver Story '00
Rupert's Land '98
When Danger Follows You Home '97
Impolite '92
White Fang '91
Title Shot '81
Phobia '80
One Night Stand '78

B.J. Hogg (1955-)
Resurrection Man '97

Brian Hogg
Eden Valley '94
Catherine Cookson's The Black Candle '91

Ian Hogg (1937-)
Rasputin: Dark Servant of Destiny '96
The Legacy '79

Arthur Hohl (1889-1964)
Mystery of the Riverboat '44
Son of Fury '42
Blondie Has Trouble '40
Devil Doll '36
Village Tale '35
The Whole Town's Talking '35
Massacre '34
The Sign of the Cross '33
Island of Lost Souls '32

Solbjorg Hojfeldt (1947-)
The Kingdom 2 '97
The Kingdom '95

Allen Holbrook
Lightning Bill '35
Circle Canyon '33
Fighting Cowboy '33

David Holbrook
Creepshow 2 '87
Return to Salem's Lot '87

Hal Holbrook (1925-)
Into the Wild '07
Shade '03
Purpose '02
The Majestic '01
Men of Honor '00
Waking the Dead '00
The Bachelor '99
Hush '98
Judas Kiss '98
My Own Country '98
Cats Don't Dance '97 (V)
Eye of God '97
Hercules '97 (V)
Operation: Delta Force '97
Carried Away '95
The Firm '93
A Killing in a Small Town '90
Day One '89
Fletch Lives '89
Sorry, Wrong Number '89
The Unholy '88
Wall Street '87
Dress Gray '86
North and South Book 2 '86
Behind Enemy Lines '85
North and South Book 1 '85
George Washington '84
Girls Night Out '83
The Star Chamber '83
Creepshow '82
When Hell Was in Session '82
Killing of Randy Webster '81
The Kidnapping of the President '80
Murder by Natural Causes '79
Natural Enemies '79
Rituals '79
Capricorn One '78
The Fog '78
Julia '77
Our Town '77
All the President's Men '76
Midway '76
The Girl from Petrovka '74
Magnum Force '73
Pueblo Affair '73
They Only Kill Their Masters '72
The Great White Hope '70
The People Next Door '70
Wild in the Streets '68
The Group '66

Kristin Holby
Manhunter '86
Trading Places '83

Kathryn Holcomb
Skag '79

Sarah Holcomb (1960-)
Caddyshack '80
Happy Birthday, Gemini '80

National Lampoon's Animal House '78

Alexandra Holden (1977-)
A Dead Calling '06
Window Theory '04
How to Deal '03
American Gun '02
The Hot Chick '02
Sugar & Spice '01
Uprising '01
Dancer, Texas—Pop. 81 '98
In and Out '97

Diane Holden
Black Starlet '74

Fay Holden (1895-1973)
The Big Hangover '50
Samson and Delilah '50
Love Laughs at Andy Hardy '46
Andy Hardy's Double Life '42
Andy Hardy's Private Secretary '41
Blossoms in the Dust '41
Life Begins for Andy Hardy '41
Ziegfeld Girl '41
Andy Hardy Meets Debutante '40
Bitter Sweet '40
Andy Hardy Gets Spring Fever '39
Love Finds Andy Hardy '38
Double or Nothing '37

Frankie J. Holden (1952-)
Introducing the Dwights '07
Ebbtide '94

Gina Holden (1975-)
The Butterfly Effect 2 '06
Final Destination 3 '06

Gloria Holden (1908-91)
The Adventures of Rusty '45
Having Wonderful Crime '45
Behind the Rising Sun '43
A Gentleman After Dark '42
Hawaii Calls '38
The Life of Emile Zola '37
Dracula's Daughter '36
Wife Versus Secretary '36

Jan Holden (1931-2005)
One Brief Summer '70
Fire Maidens from Outer Space '56

Laurie Holden (1972-)
The Mist '07
Silent Hill '06
Bailey's Billion$ '05
Fantastic Four '05
The Magnificent Seven '98
Past Perfect '98
The Pathfinder '94

Marjean Holden
Hostage '05
Mortal Kombat 2: Annihilation '97
Ballistic '94
Philadelphia Experiment 2 '93
Secret Agent 00-Soul '89
Stripped to Kill II: Live Girls '89

Rebecca Holden (1953-)
Twenty Dollar Star '91
The Sisterhood '88

William Holden (1918-81)
S.O.B. '81
Earthling '80
When Time Ran Out '80
Ashanti, Land of No Mercy '79
Escape to Athena '79
Damien: Omen 2 '78

Network '76
21 Hours at Munich '76
Wild Rovers '71
When Wolves Cry '69
The Towering Inferno '74
The Wild Bunch '69
The Devil's Brigade '68
Casino Royale '67
Alvarez Kelly '64
Paris When It Sizzles '64
The Seventh Dawn '64
The Counterfeit Traitor '62
The World of Suzie Wong '60
The Horse Soldiers '59
The Key '58
The Bridge on the River Kwai '57
The Moon Is Blue '53
Stalag 17 '53
Boots Malone '52
Born Yesterday '50
Sunset Boulevard '50
Union Station '50
The Dark Past '49
Dear Wife '49
Man from Colorado '49
Rachel and the Stranger '48
Arizona '40
Our Town '40
Golden Boy '39

Roy Holder (1946-)
Swashbuckler '76
The Man Without a Country '73
Live and Let Die '73

Kris Holden-Ried
Niagara Motel '06
Waking Up Wally '05
Touch of Pink '02
Hendrix '00
Night of the Demons 3 '97

Philip Holder
Doctor Dolittle '67
Gremlins '84
Lots of Luck '85

Geoffrey Holder (1930-)
Charlie and the Chocolate Factory '05 (N)
Boomerang '92
Swashbuckler '76
Live and Let Die '73

Kene Holliday
Great World of Sound '07

Edna Holland (1895-1982)
Blood of Dracula '57
Shep Comes Home '49

Eric Holland (1933-)
Masquerade '88
Gardens of Stone '87

John Holland (1908-93)
They Saved Hitler's Brain '64
Girl in Black Stockings '57
House of Errors '42
Gentleman from Dixie '41
Up in the Air '40
Defenders of the Law '31
Morals for Women '31
Hell Harbor '30

Tom Hollander (1969-)
Elizabeth: The Golden Age '07
The Company '07
Pirates of the Caribbean: At World's End '07
The Darwin Awards '06
A Good Year '06
Land of the Blind '06
Pirates of the Caribbean: Dead Man's Chest '06
The Libertine '05
Pride and Prejudice '05
Paparazzi '04
Cambridge Spies '03
Possession '02
Enigma '01
Gosford Park '01
Lawless Heart '01
Wives and Daughters '01
Maybe Baby '99
Bedrooms and Hallways '98

Kris Holden-Ried (cont.)
The Very Thought of You '98

Judy Holliday (1922-65)
Bells Are Ringing '60
Full of Life '56
Solid Gold Cadillac '56
It Should Happen to You '54
Phffft! '54
The Marrying Kind '52
Adam's Rib '50
Born Yesterday '50

Kene Holliday
All the President's Men '76

Polly Holliday (1937-)
Stick It '06
The Parent Trap '98
Mr. Wrong '95
Mrs. Doubtfire '93
Moon over Parador '88
Konrad '85
Gremlins '84

Earl Holliman (1928-)
Perfect Tenant '99
Gunsmoke: Return to Dodge '87
The Solitary Man '82
Sharky's Machine '81
Alexander: The Other Side of Dawn '77
Cry Panic '74
The Desperate Mission '69
Last Train from Gun Hill '59
The Trap '59
Hot Spell '58
Don't Go Near the Water '57
Gunfight at the O.K. Corral '57
Forbidden Planet '56
Giant '56
The Rainmaker '56
Big Combo '55

Sterling Holloway (1905-92)
The Many Adventures of Winnie the Pooh '77 (V)
Super Seal '77
Thunder and Lightning '77
The Aristocats '70 (V)
Live a Little, Love a Little '68
The Jungle Book '67 (V)
The Adventures of Huckleberry Finn '60
Shake, Rattle and Rock '57
Kentucky Rifle '55
Alice in Wonderland '51 (V)
The Beautiful Blonde from Bashful Bend '49
Robin Hood of Texas '47
Trail to San Antone '47
Death Valley '46
Sioux City Sue '46
A Walk in the Sun '46
The Three Caballeros '45
Wildfire '45
Bambi '42 (V)
The Lady Is Willing '42
Cheers for Miss Bishop '41
Dumbo '41 (V)
Melody Master '41
Twilight on the Rio Grande '41
Remember the Night '40
Doubting Thomas '35
I Live My Life '35
Life Begins at Forty '35
The Merry Widow '34
Tomorrow's Children '34

Ellen Holly (1931-)
School Daze '88
Cops and Robbers '73

Carol Holloway (1892-1979)
The Rising Place '02
Lush '01
Loving Jezebel '99
Tumbleweeds '98
Boogie Nights '97
The First to Go '97
Sabrina '95
Turbulence '96
A Smile Like Yours '96
Down Periscope '96

Julian Holloway (1944-)
Porridge '91
Carry On Henry VIII '71

Stanley Holloway (1890-1982)
The Private Life of Sherlock Holmes '70
Mrs. Brown, You've Got a Lovely Daughter '68
In Harm's Way '65
My Fair Lady '64
On the Fiddle '61
No Love for Johnnie '60
The Lavender Hill Mob '51
Passport to Pimlico '49
This Happy Breed '47
Brief Encounter '46
Nicholas Nickleby '46
Immortal Battalion '44
Salute John Citizen '42
Cotton Queen '37

Astrid Holm
Seducing Maarya '99
Master of the House '25
Häxan: Witchcraft through the Ages '22

Celeste Holm (1919-)
Alchemy '05
Still Breathing '97
Murder by the Book '87
Three Men and a Baby '87
Backstairs at the White House '79
Bittersweet Love '76
Death Cruise '74
Tom Sawyer '73
Cinderella '64
High Society '56
The Tender Trap '55
All About Eve '50
Champagne for Caesar '50
Come to the Stable '49
A Letter to Three Wives '49
Road House '48
The Snake Pit '48
Gentleman's Agreement '47

Ryan Hollyman
The Audrey Hepburn Story '00

Lauren Holly (1963-)
Fatwa '06
Raising Flagg '06
The Chumscrubber '05
The Pleasure Drivers '05
In Enemy Hands '04
The Final Hit '02
King of Texas '02
Jackie, Ethel, Joan: The Women of Camelot '01 (V)
Spirited Away '01 (V)
What Women Want '00
Any Given Sunday '99
Money Kings '98
No Looking Back '98
Beautiful Girls '96
Down Periscope '96
A Smile Like Yours '96
Sabrina '95
Dumb & Dumber '94
Dragon: The Bruce Lee Story '93

Ian Holm (1931-)
Ratatouille '07 (V)
Renaissance '06
Strangers with Candy '06
The Aviator '04
Lord of War '05
The Day After Tomorrow '04
Garden State '04
Lord of the Rings: The Return of the King '03
The Emperor's New Clothes '01
From Hell '01
Lord of the Rings: The Fellowship of the Rings '01
Beautiful Joe '00
Bless the Child '00
Esther Kahn '00
Joe Gould's Secret '00
The Last of the Blonde Bombshells '00
The Miracle Maker: The Story of Jesus '00 (V)
Animal Farm '99 (V)
eXistenZ '99
The Match '99
King Lear '98
The Fifth Element '97
A Life Less Ordinary '97
Night Falls on Manhattan '96

Clare Holman (1964-)
Dot Kill '05
Tom & Viv '94
Afraid of the Dark '92

Harry Holman (1874-1947)
Inside the Law '42
Mexican Spitfire at Sea '42
Fugitive Road '34

Rex Holman (1928-)
Panic in the Year Zero! '62
The Choppers '61

Ashton Holmes (1978-)
Smart People '08
Havoc 2: Normal Adolescent Behavior '07
Wind Chill '07
Peaceful Warrior '06
A History of Violence '05

Katie Holmes (1978-)
Mad Money '08
Thank You for Smoking '06
Batman Begins '05
First Daughter '04
Pieces of April '03
The Singing Detective '03
Abandon '02
Phone Booth '02
The Gift '00
Wonder Boys '00
Go '99
Teaching Mrs. Tingle '99
Disturbing Behavior '98
The Ice Storm '97

Luree Holmes (1942-)
How to Stuff a Wild Bikini '65
Pajama Party '64
Beach Party '63

Phillips Holmes (1909-42)
Housemaster '38
General Spanky '36
Great Expectations '34
Dinner at Eight '33
Penthouse '33
Criminal Code '31

Taylor Holmes (1872-1959)
Sleeping Beauty '59 (V)
Tobor the Great '54
Beware, My Lovely '52
Hoodlum Empire '52
Copper Canyon '50
Double Deal '50
Act of Violence '48
Boomerang '47
Nightmare Alley '47
Before Morning '33

Teck Holmes (1976-)
National Lampoon's Van Wilder '02
Love Song '00

Tina Holmes (1973-)
Taken '02
Half Nelson '06

Stuart Holmes (1887-1971)
People Will Talk '51
My Pal, the King '32
Beyond the Trail '26
The Four Horsemen of the Apocalypse '21

Karen Holmes
Lost Boundaries '49

Rosie Holotik
Encounter with the Unknown '75
Twisted Brain '74
Don't Look in the Basement '73

Wendell Holmes (1915-62)
Edge of Seventeen '99
Good Day for a Hanging '58
Professor '61
Elmer Gantry '60
Compulsion '59
Never Steal Anything Small '59

Rex Holman ...
Mary, Queen of Scots '71
Oh! What a Lovely War '69
The Fixer '68
A Midsummer Night's Dream '68
Alien '79
S.O.S. Titanic '79
Holocaust '78
The Lost Boys '78
The Thief of Baghdad '78
The Man in the Iron Mask '77
March or Die '77
Robin and Marian '76
Shout at the Devil '76
Return of the Soldier '82
Chariots of Fire '81
Time Bandits '81
Brazil '85
Another Woman '88
Henry V '89
Hamlet '90
The Advocate '93
The Borrowers '93
Dance with a Stranger '85
Dreamchild '85
Wetherby '85
Greystoke: The Legend of Tarzan, Lord of the Apes '84
Singleton's Pluck '84
Inside the Third Reich '82

Hans Holt (1909-2002)
Almost Angels '62
The Embezzled Heaven '58
The Mozart Story '48

Jack Holt (1888-1951)
Across the Wide Missouri '51
King of the Bullwhip '51
Red Desert '50
Trail of Robin Hood '50
Task Force '49
Loaded Pistols '48
Wild Frontier '47
The Chase '46
Flight to Nowhere '46
My Pal Trigger '46
Renegade Girl '46
They Were Expendable '45
Cat People '42
San Francisco '36
The Littlest Rebel '35
Maker of Men '31
Thunder Birds '42
The Great Plains Robbery '40

David Holt (1927-2003)
El Dorado '67
Red Line 7000 '65
Man's Favorite Sport? '63
Last Days of Pompeii '35
The Adventures of Tom Sawyer '38

Charlene Holt (1939-96)
The Return of the Borrowers '96
In Dreams '98
Big Night '95
Loch Ness '95
The Madness of King George '94
Mary Shelley's Frankenstein '94
The Borrowers '93
Kafka '91
Naked Lunch '91
Hamlet '90
The Endless Game '89
The Advocate '93

Wendell Holmes ...
King of the Gypsies '78
The Man Who Fell to Earth
The Rainmaker '56
The Lonely Lady '83
Oh, God! Book 2 '80
All That Jazz '79

Prudence Wright Holmes
The Sweet Hereafter '96
Kingpin '96

Jennifer Holt (1920-97)
The Hawk of Powder River '48
Range Renegades '48
Stage to Mesa City '48
The Tioga Kid '48

Bridget Holloman (1958-2006)
Evils of the Night '85
Slumber Party '57 '76
Love '95

Tommy Hollis (1954-2001)
Primary Colors '98
The Piano Lesson '94
Malcolm X '92

Laurel Holloman (1971-)
Pretoriane '96
The Incredibly True Adventure of Two Girls in Love '95

Anthony Holland (1928-88)
The Rounders '65
The Apartment '60

Hope Holiday (1938-)
Delicatessen '92

Ticky Holgado (1944-2004)
A Very Long Engagement '04
And Now Ladies and Gentlemen '02
French Twist '95

Harry Holman ...
Champagne for Caesar '50

Lauren Holly ...
The Bridges at Toko-Ri '55
I Died a Thousand Times '55
Broken Lance '54
George '94

Buffalo Bill Rides Again '47
Fighting Vigilantes '47
Ghost Town Renegades '47
Trail of the Mounties '47
Where the North Begins '47
Song of Old Wyoming '45
Outlaw Trail '44
Frontier Law '43
Raiders of Sunset Pass '43

Jim Holt (1956-)
The Prince & Me 2: Royal Wedding '06
The Monkey's Mask '00
Fever '88

Patrick Holt (1912-93)
Psychomania '73
When Dinosaurs Ruled the Earth '70
Vulture '67
Flight from Singapore '62
It Takes a Thief '59
Men of Sherwood Forest '57
Alias John Preston '56
Suspended Alibi '56
Unholy Four '54

Sandrine Holt (1971-)
Fire Serpent '07
Resident Evil: Apocalypse '04
Happy Hour '03
Ballistic: Ecks vs. Sever '02
Loving Jezebel '99
Gunslinger's Revenge '98
1999 '98
Once a Thief '96
Legends of the North '95
Pocahontas: The Legend '95

Tim Holt (1918-73)
This Stuff'll Kill Ya! '71
The Yesterday Machine '63
The Monster That Challenged the World '57
Gunplay '51
His Kind of Woman '51
Hot Lead '51
Dynamite Pass '50
Rider from Tucson '50
Riders of the Range '50
Storm over Wyoming '50
Mysterious Desperado '49
Treasure of the Sierra Madre '48
My Darling Clementine '46
Hitler's Children '43
Sagebrush Law '43
The Magnificent Ambersons '42
Back Street '41
Fifth Avenue Girl '39
Stagecoach '39
Law West of Tombstone '38
Stella Dallas '37

Sean Holton
Presumed Guilty '91
White Fury '90
Operation Warzone '89

Maria Holvoe
The Last Warrior '89
Worth Winning '89

Arabella Holzbog (1966-)
Red Shoe Diaries: Swimming Naked '00
Carnosaur 2 '94
Evil Lives '92
Stone Cold '91
The Last Samurai '90

Robert E. Homans (1874-1947)
The Scarlet Clue '45
Rogue's Gallery '44
X Marks the Spot '42
I Take This Oath '40
Man from Hell's Edges '32
The Concentratin' Kid '30
Spurs '30
Trigger Tricks '30

Liuis Homar (1957-)
Bad Education '04
Celestial Clockwork '94
If They Tell You I Fell '89

David Homb
Street Soldiers '91
The Channeler '89

Skip Homeier (1930-)
Starbird and Sweet William '73
Bethune '77
The Voyage of the Yes '72
The Ghost and Mr. Chicken '66
Johnny Shiloh '63
Comanche Station '60
The Tall T '57
The Burning Hills '56
Black Widow '54
Cry Vengeance '54
Ten Wanted Men '54
Fixed Bayonets! '51
The Gunfighter '50
The Halls of Montezuma '50
Tomorrow the World '44

Oscar Homolka (1898-1978)
The Executioner '70
Song of Norway '70
The Madwoman of Chaillot '69
Dr. Jekyll and Mr. Hyde '68
Strange Case of Dr. Jekyll & Mr. Hyde '68
Funeral in Berlin '66
The Long Ships '64
Boys' Night Out '62
I Remember Mama '48
Ball of Fire '41
Comrade X '40
The Invisible Woman '40
Seven Sinners '40
Rhodes '36
Sabotage '36

James Hong (1929-)
Kung Fu Panda '08 (V)
Balls of Fury '07
Shanghai Kiss '07
Latin Dragon '03
The Art of War '00
Epoch '00
G2: Mortal Conquest '99
Breakout '98
Broken Vessels '98
Mulan '98 (V)
Bloodsport 3 '97
Red Corner '97
The Secret Agent Club '96
South Beach Academy '96
Bloodsport 2: The Next Kumite '95
Femme Fontaine: Killer Babe for the C.I.A. '95
Gladiator Cop: The Swordsman 2 '95
Bad Company '94
Operation Golden Phoenix '94
The Shadow '94
Wayne's World 2 '93
Body Trouble '92
L.A. Goddess '92
Merlin '92
Talons of the Eagle '92
Crime Lords '91
Caged Fury '90
Dragonfight '90

Tax Season '90
The Brotherhood of the Rose '89
Shadowzone '89
Tango and Cash '89
The Vineyard '89
The Jitters '88
Black Widow '87
Revenge of the Nerds 2: Nerds in Paradise '87
Big Trouble in Little China '86
The Golden Child '86
When Hell Was in Session '82
Yes, Giorgio '82
Airplane! '80
Go Tell the Spartans '78
The Dynamite Brothers '74
Missiles of October '74
The Sand Pebbles '66
China Gate '57

Kojiro Hongo (1938-)
Destroy All Planets '68
Gamera vs. Gaos '67
Gamera vs. Barugon '66

Darla Hood (1931-79)
The Bat '59
Bohemian Girl '36

Don Hood (1940-2003)
Dean Koontz's Mr. Murder '98
Blind Vengeance '90
Marie '85
Absence of Malice '81

Morag Hood (1942-2002)
A Shot at Glory '00
War and Peace '73

Brian Hooks (1973-)
Fool's Gold '08
Soul Plane '04
Nothin' 2 Lose '00
Three Strikes '00
Phat Beach '96

Jan Hooks (1957-)
Jiminy Glick in LaLa Wood '05
Simon Birch '98
Coneheads '93
A Dangerous Woman '93
Batman Returns '92
Pee-wee's Big Adventure '85

Kevin Hooks (1958-)
Backstairs at the White House '79
Can You Hear the Laughter? The Story of Freddie Prinze '79
Take Down '79
Aaron Loves Angela '75
Sounder '72

Robert Hooks (1937-)
Seventeen Again '00
Free of Eden '98
Posse '93
Passenger 57 '92
Heat Wave '90
The Execution '85
Words by Heart '84
Fast Walking '82
Sophisticated Gents '81
Backstairs at the White House '79
A Woman Called Moses '78
Aaron Loves Angela '75
Black Brigade '69
Sweet Love, Bitter '67

Ewan Hooper (1935-)
Kinky Boots '06
Dracula Has Risen from the Grave '68

Tobe Hooper (1946-)
Body Bags '93
Sleepwalkers '92

Peter Hooten (1950-)
2020 Texas Gladiators '85
Deadly Mission '78
Dr. Strange '78
Slashed Dreams '74
Fantasiers '73

Sweet Killing '93
The Abduction of Allison Tate '92
The Big Slice '90

William Hootkins (1948-2005)
Color Me Kubrick '05
The Magnificent Ambersons '02
The Omega Code '99
This World, Then the Fireworks '97
Death Machine '95
Dust Devil '93
Hear My Song '91
American Gothic '88
Valentino '77

Joseph Hoover
The Astro-Zombies '67
Hell Is for Heroes '62
The Man Who Shot Liberty Valance '62

Phil Hoover
Acapulco Gold '78
Black Gestapo '75
Policewomen '73
Chain Gang Women '72

Bob Hope (1903-2003)
The Muppet Movie '79
Cancel My Reservation '72
Bachelor in Paradise '69
How to Commit Marriage '69
Private Navy of Sgt. O'Farrell '68
Eight on the Lam '67
Boy, Did I Get a Wrong Number! '66
The Oscar '66
I'll Take Sweden '65
Critic's Choice '63
A Global Affair '63
The Road to Hong Kong '62
The Facts of Life '60
Alias Jesse James '59
Paris Holiday '57
The Seven Little Foys '55
Casanova's Big Night '54
Here Come the Girls '53
Off Limits '53
Scared Stiff '53
Son of Paleface '52
The Lemon Drop Kid '51
Fancy Pants '50
The Great Lover '49
Sorrowful Jones '49
The Paleface '48
My Favorite Brunette '47
Where There's Life '47
Monsieur Beaucaire '46
The Road to Utopia '46
The Road to Zanzibar '41
The Ghost Breakers '40
The Road to Singapore '40
Never Say Die '39
The Big Broadcast of 1938 '38
College Swing '38
Give Me a Sailor '38
Thanks for the Memory '38

Leslie Hope (1965-)
Never Back Down '08
The Incredible Mrs. Ritchie '03
Bruiser '00
The Life Before This '99
Restless Spirits '99
Bram Stoker's Shadowbuilder '98
Summer of the Monkeys '98
Conspiracy of Fear '96
Rowing Through '96
First Degree '95
Schemes '95
Fun '94
Paris, France '94
Caught in the Act '93

The Night We Called It a Day '03
Lust and Revenge '95
Bad Boy Bubby '93

Richard Hope
Antonia and Jane '91
A Casualty of War '90
Bellman and True '88
Piece of Cake '88
Singleton's Pluck '84

Tamara Hope (1984-)
September Dawn '07
A Different Loyalty '04
Saint Ralph '04
Shall We Dance? '04
The Deep End '01
The Sandy Bottom Orchestra '00

Vida Hope (1918-63)
Angels One Five '54
Roadhouse Girl '54
The Woman in Question '50
They Made Me a Fugitive '47

William Hope (1955-)
The Detonator '06
Submerged '05
Hellbound: Hellraiser 2 '88
Aliens '86

Alan Hopgood (1934-)
Hotel de Love '96
Road Games '81
My Brilliant Career '79

Anthony Hopkins (1937-)
Beowulf '07 (V)
Fracture '07
Slipstream '07
All the King's Men '06
Bobby '06
Proof '05
The World's Fastest Indian '05
Alexander '04
The Human Stain '03
Bad Company '02
Red Dragon '02
Hannibal '01
Hearts in Atlantis '01
Mission: Impossible 2 '00
Instinct '99
Titus '99
The Mask of Zorro '98
Meet Joe Black '98
Amistad '97
The Edge '97
Surviving Picasso '96
August '95
Nixon '95
Legends of the Fall '94
The Road to Wellville '94
The Innocent '93
The Remains of the Day '93
Shadowlands '93
Bram Stoker's Dracula '92
Chaplin '92
The Efficiency Expert '92
Freejack '92
Howard's End '92
The Silence of the Lambs '91
Desperate Hours '90
One Man's War '90
A Chorus of Disapproval '89
Great Expectations '89
The Dawning '88
The Tenth Man '88

The Good Father '87
84 Charing Cross Road '86
Arch of Triumph '85
Guilty Conscience '85
Mussolini & I '85
The Bounty '84
A Married Man '84
The Hunchback of Notre Dame '82
Peter and Paul '81
A Change of Seasons '80
The Elephant Man '80
Mayflower: The Pilgrims' Adventure '79
International Velvet '78
Magic '78
Audrey Rose '77
A Bridge Too Far '77
The Lindbergh Kidnapping Case '76
Victory at Entebbe '76
All Creatures Great and Small '74
The Girl from Petrovka '74
Juggernaut '74
QB VII '74
A Doll's House '73
War and Peace '73
Young Winston '72
When Eight Bells Toll '71
Hamlet '69
The Looking Glass War '69
The Lion in Winter '68

Bo Hopkins (1942-)
Shade '03
Big Brother Trouble '00
Cowboy Up '00
A Crack in the Floor '00
Time Served '99
From Dusk Till Dawn 2: Texas Blood Money '98
U-Turn '97
November Conspiracy '96
Uncle Sam '96
The Feminine Touch '95
Painted Hero '95
Texas Payback '95
Cheyenne Warrior '94
Wyatt Earp: Return to Tombstone '94
The Ballad of Little Jo '93
Inside Monkey Zetterland '93
President's Target '93
Blood Ties '92
Center of the Web '92
The Legend of Wolf Mountain '92
Big Bad John '90
Bounty Hunters '89
The Final Alliance '89
Trapper County War '89
Nightmare at Noon '87
A Smoky Mountain Christmas '86
What Comes Around '85
Mutant '83
The Day of the Locust '75
The Killer Elite '75
Posse '75
The Runaway Barge '75
American Graffiti '73
Man Who Loved Cat Dancing '73
White Lightning '73
Culpepper Cattle Co. '72
The Getaway '72
The Only Way Home '72
The Wild Bunch '69

Bruce Hopkins (1955-)
You Move You Die '07
Beyond Justice '01
Dead Evidence '00

Harold Hopkins (1944-)
Joey '98
Resistance '92
Fantasy Man '84

McKey Grip '82
Gallipoli '81
Saara Dane '81
Demonstrator '71

Jermaine "Huggy" Hopkins (1973-)
Def Jam's How to Be a Player '97
Phat Beach '96
Juice '92

Joan Hopkins (1915-2002)
Man on the Run '49
The Weaker Sex '49

Josh Hopkins (1970-)
The Hades Factor '06
Love & Sex '00
The Perfect Storm '00
The Pirates of Silicon Valley '99

Miriam Hopkins (1902-72)
The Chase '66
Fanny Hill: Memoirs of a Woman of Pleasure '64
The Children's Hour '61
Carrie '52
The Heiress '49
A Gentleman After Dark '42
Virginia City '40
Men Are Not Gods '37
These Three '36
Becky Sharp '35
Splendor '35
Dr. Jekyll and Mr. Hyde '32
The Smiling Lieutenant '31
Trouble in Paradise '32

Nikita Hopkins
Piglet's Big Movie '03 (V)
Poon's Heffalump Movie '05 (V)

Paul Hopkins (1968-)
My First Wedding '04
Armistead Maupin's More Tales of the City '97
A Young Connecticut Yankee in King Arthur's Court '95
Halo '82
The Kid with the Broken Halo '82

Rolf Hoppe (1930-)
Go for Zucker '05
Palmetto '98
Schtonk '92
Mephisto '81

Dennis Hopper (1936-)
Sleepwalking '08
Swing Vote '08
Spring Symphony '86
Memory '06
10th & Wolf '06
Americano '05
The Crow: Wicked Prayer '05
George A. Romero's Land of the Dead '05
House of 9 '05
The Night We Called It a Day '03
Firestarter 2: Rekindled '02
Leo '02
The Target '02
Unspeakable '02
Knockaround Guys '01
L.A.P.D.: To Protect and Serve '01
Ticker '01
Choke '00

Jeson and the Argonauts '00
Luck of the Draw '00
EDtv '99
Jesus' Son '99
The Prophet's Game '99
Straight Shooter '99
The Apostate '98
Meet the Deedles '98
Road Ends '98
Tycus '98
The Blackout '97
Lured Innocence '97
Space Truckers '97
Top of the World '97
Basquiat '96
Carried Away '95
Samson and Delilah '96
Waterworld '95
Chasers '94
Search and Destroy '94
Speed '94
Witch Hunt '94
Boiling Point '93
Red Rock West '93
Super Mario Bros. '93
True Romance '93
Nails '92
Sunset Heat '92
Double-Crossed '91
Eye of the Storm '91
Hearts of Darkness: A Filmmaker's Apocalypse '91
The Indian Runner '91
Paris Trout '91
Superstar: The Life and Times of Andy Warhol '90
Backtrack '89
Chattahoochee '89
Flashback '89
Blood Red '88
Black Widow '88
Riders of the Storm '88
The Pick-Up Artist '87
O.C. and Stiggs '87
River's Edge '87
Straight to Hell '87
Blue Velvet '86
Hoosiers '86
Let It Rock '86
Running out of Luck '86
The Texas Chainsaw Massacre 2 '86
My Science Project '85
Stark '85
The Inside Man '84
The Osterman Weekend '83
Rumble Fish '83
King of the Mountain '81
Reborn '81
Out of the Blue '80
Apocalypse Now '79
Wild Times '79
The American Friend '77
Bloodbath '76
Mad Dog Morgan '76
Tracks '76
The Last Movie '71
Easy Rider '69
Head '68
True Grit '69
Cool Hand Luke '67
The Trip '67
The Glory Stompers '67
Planet of Blood '66
Sons of Katie Elder '65
Night Tide '63
The Young Land '59
Gunfight at the O.K. Corral '57
Giant '56
Rebel without a Cause '55

Hedda Hopper (1890-1966)
Breakfast in Hollywood '46
Reap the Wild Wind '42
Midnight '39
Maid's Night Out '38
Tarzan's Revenge '38
Thanks for the Memory '38
Dangerous Holiday '37
Vogues of 1938 '37
The Dark Hour '36
Doughnuts & Society '36
Dracula's Daughter '36
Alice Adams '35
I Live My Life '35
One Frightened Night '35
Pilgrimage '33
As You Desire Me '32
Speak Easily '32
The Racketeer '29
Don Juan '26
Skinner's Dress Suit '26
Seven Keys to Baldpate '17

Tim Hopper
School of Rock '03
Pipe Dream '02

Victoria Hopper (1909-2007)
The Mill on the Floss '37
Lorna Doone '34

William Hopper (1915-70)
The Deadly Mantis '57
20 Million Miles to Earth '57
The Bad Seed '56
Conquest of Space '55
Rebel without a Cause '55
The High and the Mighty '54
Sitting Bull '54

Russell Hopton (1900-45)
The Fighting 69th '40
The Girl from Missouri '34
The World Accuses '35
Last Outlaw '36
Death from a Distance '36
Renegade Trail '39
Hopalong Cassidy: Renegade Trail '39
Zombies on Broadway '45
West of the Pecos '45

Gerard Horan
Bayou Romance '86
Malibu Bikini Shop '86

Barbara Horan
Nicholas Nickleby '02
A Midwinter's Tale '95
Much Ado about Nothing '93
I'm No Angel '33

James Horan (1954-)
Look Back in Anger '89
Counter Measures '99
The Haunting of Seacliff Inn '94
Image of Passion '86

Michael Hordern (1911-95)
Middlemarch '93
Freddie the Frog '92 (V)
The Green Man '91
Dark Obsession '90
The Secret Garden '87
Suspicion '87
The Trouble with Spies '87
Lady Jane '85
Young Sherlock Holmes '85
Yellowbeard '83
Ivanhoe '82
The Missionary '82
Oliver Twist '82
The Medusa Touch '78
Watership Down '78 (V)
Joseph Andrews '77
The Slipper and the Rose '76
The Taming of the Shrew '67
'67

Harvey '50
Abbot and Costello Meet the Killer, Boris Karloff '49

Wil Horneff (1979-)
Cash Crop '01
Harvest '98
Born to Be Wild '95
Ghost in the Machine '93
The Yearling '94

Victoria Horne (1911-2003)
Oldest Confederate Widow Tells All '95
St. Elmo's Fire '85
Times Square '80
Harvey '50

Craig Horner
See No Evil '06
Swimming Upstream '03

Penelope Horner
Dracula '73
Man Who Had Power Over Women '70
Half a Sixpence '67

Russell Hornsby
Get Rich or Die Tryin' '05
After the Sunset '04

Lena Horne (1917-)
The Wiz '78
Death of a Gunfighter '69
The Duchess of Idaho '50
Till the Clouds Roll By '46
Words and Music '48
Ziegfeld Follies '46
Broadway Rhythm '44
Two Girls and a Sailor '44
Cabin in the Sky '43
I Dood It '43
Stormy Weather '43
Thousands Cheer '43
Panama Hattie '42
The Duke Is Tops '38

Geoffrey Horne (1933-)
Bonjour Tristesse '57
The Bridge on the River Kwai '57

A Funny Thing Happened on the Way to the Forum '66

David Horne (1898-1970)
Kung Pow! Enter the Fist '02
Men of Two Worlds '46
Spitfire '42
Night Train to Munich '40
Late Extra '35

Michelle Horn (1987-)
Hostage '05
Little Athens '05

Sacha Horler
Look Both Ways '05
Soft '99
Praise '98

Sharon Horgan (1970-)
Imagine Me & You '06
Valiant '05 (V)

Tad Horino (1921-2002)
Life Is Sweet '90

David Horne (1898-1970)
Galaxina '80

Tim Horton
The Promoter '52
A Christmas Carol '51
Train of Events '49

The Warriors '55
The Man Who Never Was '55
Battleship '56
The Baby and the Battleship '56
The Spaniard's Curse '58
The Spanish Gardener '57
Sink the Bismarck '60

The Avenging '82
The Witches '90
Memphis Belle '90
The Dressmaker '89
Getting It Right '89

Michael Horse (1951-)
Navajo Blues '97
Lakota Woman: Siege at Wounded Knee '94
Wagons East '94
Border Shootout '90
Deadly Weapon '88
Buckeye and Blue '87
Legend of the Lone Ranger '81

Ivanhoe '97
The Sculptress '97
Paper Marriage '93
Piece of Cake '88

Adam Horovitz (1966-)
Roadside Prophets '92
A Kiss Before Dying '91
Long Road Home '91

Sam Horrigan (1981-)
Brink '98
Little Giants '94

Jane Horrocks (1964-)
Brothers of the Head '06
Garfield: A Tail of Two Kitties '06 (V)
Tim Burton's Corpse Bride '05 (V)
Lost Horizon '37
Angel '37
Lost Angels '89

Born Romantic '00
Chicken Run '00 (V)
Little Voice '98
Second Best '94
Deadly Advice '93
Catherine Cookson's The House of Cards '92
Passenger 57 '92
The Witches '90
Life Is Sweet '90
Memphis Belle '90
The Dressmaker '89
Getting It Right '89

Sharon Horgan
Here Comes Mr. Jordan '41
Ziegfeld Girl '41
College Swing '38
Holiday '38

The Gay Divorcee '34
The Merry Widow '34
Sing and Like It '34
Trouble in Paradise '32
The Front Page '31
Lonely Wives '31
Reaching for the Moon '31
Smart Woman '31
Amazon Women or the Moon '87

Peter Horton (1953-)
The End of Violence '97
Into Thin Air: Death on Everest '97
Where the River Runs Black '86
61* '01

Bobby Hosea
Shooting Dogs '05
Stalingrad '94
Come See the Paradise '90

Dominique Horwitz
Shooting Dogs '05
Stalingrad '94

Anna Maria Horsford (1948-)
Friday After Next '02
How High '01
Dancing in September '00
Lockdown '00
Nutty Professor 2: The Klumps '00
Dear God '96
One Fine Day '96
Set It Off '96
Friday '95
Widow's Kiss '94
Murder Without Motive '92
Presumed Innocent '90
Taken Away '89
Street Smart '87
Heartburn '86
The O.J. Simpson Story '94
The Green Slime '68
Men of the Fighting Lady '54

Michael Horse (1951-)
Children of the Corn '84
Black '86
The Veteran '06
All About You '01
Gargantua '98
Independence Day '96
French Silk '94
Times Square '80

Robert Horton (1924-)
The Green Slime '68
Men of the Fighting Lady '54

Bob Hoskins (1942-)
Last War '68
Last Orders '01
Godzilla vs. Mothra '64
Don Quixote '00
Enemy at the Gates '00
Noriega: God's Favorite '00

Yuriko Hoshi (1943-)
Godzilla vs. Mothra '64
Monster '65

Shizuko Hoshi
Memoirs of a Geisha '05
Charlotte Sometimes '02
M. Butterfly '93
Come See the Paradise '90

John David Horsley
The Girl from Missouri '34
Finishing School '33
Outlaw '07
Garfield: A Tail of Two Kitties '06 (V)
Hollywoodland '06
Paris, je t'aime '06
Mrs. Henderson Presents '05
Son of the Mask '05
Stay '05
Unleashed '05
Beyond the Sea '04
Vanity Fair '04
The Lost World '04
Maid in Manhattan '02
The Sleeping Dictionary '02
Last Orders '01
Enemy at the Gates '00
Don Quixote '00
Noriega: God's Favorite '00
Felicia's Journey '99
White River '99
American Virgin '98

Arsenic and Old Lace '44
Forever and a Day '43
The Gang's All Here '43
Thank Your Lucky Stars '43
I Married an Angel '42
The Magnificent Dope '42
Springtime in the Rockies '42

Penelope Horner
Agatha Christie's Thirteen at Dinner '85
Sword & the Sorcerer '82
Pocketful of Miracles '61
Down to Earth '47
Her Husband's Affairs '47
Lady on a Train '45

Edward Everett Horton (1886-1970)
Cold Turkey '71
Sex and the Single Girl '64
It's a Mad, Mad, Mad, Mad World '63

Jochen Horst (1961-)
Luther '03
The Cement Garden '93

Lee Horsley (1955-)
French Silk '94
Danielle Steel's Palomino '91

Hoskins

Captain Jack '98
Parting Shots '98
Cousin Bette '97
Spice World: The Movie '97
24-7 '97
Michael '96
The Secret Agent '96
Balto '95 (V)
Nixon '95
World War II: When Lions Roared '94
Super Mario Bros. '93
Blue Ice '92
The Favor, the Watch, & the Very Big Fish '92
Passed Away '92
Hook '91
The Inner Circle '91
Shattered '91
Heart Condition '90
Mermaids '90
The Raggedy Rawney '90
Who Framed Roger Rabbit '88
The Lonely Passion of Judith Hearne '87
Prayer for the Dying '87
Mona Lisa '86
Sweet Liberty '86
Brazil '85
The Dunera Boys '85
Mussolini & I '85
The Cotton Club '84
Lassiter '84
Beyond the Limit '83
Pink Floyd: The Wall '82
Flickers '80
The Long Good Friday '80
Zulu Dawn '79
Cry Terror '76
Inserts '76
Royal Flash '75

Allison Hossack (1965-)
Escape from Mars '99
White Light '90

Robert Hossein (1927-)
Venus Beauty Institute '98
Wax Mask '97
Bolero '82
Le Professionnel '81
Don Juan (Or If Don Juan Were a Woman) '73
Carbon Copy '69
The Battle of El Alamein '68
Murder for Sale '68
Le Repos du Guerrier '62
Love on a Pillow '62
Double Agents '59

Barry Hostetler
Mystery Mansion '83
The Worm Eaters '77

Emil Hostina
Catacombs '07
Vlad '03

Yukihiro Hotaru
Zeram 2 '94
Zeram '91

Donald Hotton
The Freeway Maniac '88
The Hearse '80

Germain Houde (1952-)
Night Zoo '87
Les Bons Debarras '81

Serge Houde (1953-)
The Invisible '07
Eighteen '04
The Lathe of Heaven '02
Hidden Agenda '01
Wilder '00
Legends of the North '95

James Houghton (1948-)
Superstition '82
More American Graffiti '79

Katharine Houghton (1945-)
The Night We Never Met '93
Ethan Frome '92
Billy Bathgate '91
Mr. North '88
The Eyes of the Amaryllis '82
Seeds of Evil '76
Guess Who's Coming to Dinner '67

Nicholas Hoult (1989-)
Wah-Wah '05
The Weather Man '05
About a Boy '02

Djimon Hounsou (1964-)
Never Back Down '08
Blood Diamond '06
Eragon '06
Beauty Shop '05
Constantine '05
The Island '05
Biker Boyz '03
Lara Croft Tomb Raider: The Cradle of Life '03
The Four Feathers '02
In America '02
Gladiator '00
Deep Rising '98
Amistad '97

Ned Hourani
Fist of Steel '92
Raiders of the Sun '92
Triple Impact '92

Billy House (1890-1961)
People Will Talk '51
Santa Fe '51
Where Danger Lives '50
Egg and I '47
Bedlam '45

Ron House
Stoogemania '85
Bullshot '83

Arthur Houseman (1889-1942)
The Bat '26
Manhandled '24

John Houseman (1902-88)
Another Woman '88
Bright Lights, Big City '88
Gore Vidal's Lincoln '88
The Naked Gun: From the Files of Police Squad '88
Scrooged '88
A.D. '85
The Winds of War '83
Murder by Phone '82
Ghost Story '81
The Babysitter '80
A Christmas Without Snow '80
Gideon's Trumpet '80
My Bodyguard '80
Wholly Moses! '80
Old Boyfriends '79
The Cheap Detective '78
The Fog '78
Our Town '77
St. Ives '76
Rollerball '75
Three Days of the Condor '75
The Paper Chase '73
Seven Days in May '64

Jerry Houser (1952-)
A Very Brady Christmas '88
Forbidden Love '82
Magic '78
Slap Shot '77
Class of 44 '73
Summer of '42 '71

Allan Houston (1971-)
Laws of Attraction '04
Black and White '99

Donald Houston (1923-91)
Tales That Witness Madness '73
The Bushbaby '70
Where Eagles Dare '68
The Viking Queen '67
A Study in Terror '66
Maniac '63
The 300 Spartans '62
The Mark '61
Room at the Top '59
Doctor in the House '53
Crow Hollow '52

George Houston (1898-1944)
The Lone Rider in Cheyenne '42
Texas Justice '42
Border Roundup '41
The Lone Rider in Frontier Fury '41
The Lone Rider in Ghost Town '41
Frontier Scout '38
The Great Waltz '38
Wallaby Jim of the Islands '37
Let's Sing Again '36
Conspiracy '89
River Beat '54

Joff Houston
Ninja: American Warrior '90
Ninja Death Squad '87

Marques Houston (1981-)
Fat Albert '04
You Got Served '04
Bebe's Kids '92 (V)

Renee Houston (1902-)
Legend of the Werewolf '75
Repulsion '65
The Flesh and the Fiends '60
The Horse's Mouth '58
Time Without Pity '57
The Belles of St. Trinian's '53

Whitney Houston (1963-)
Cinderella '97
The Preacher's Wife '96
Waiting to Exhale '95
The Bodyguard '92

Anders (Tofting) Hove (1956-)
Mifune '99
Bloodstorm: Subspecies 4 '98
Bloodlust: Subspecies 3 '93
Bloodstone: Subspecies 2 '92
Subspecies '91

Adrian Hoven (1922-81)
Fear of Fear '75
Fox and His Friends '75
Mark of the Devil '69
Castle of the Creeping Flesh '68
Cave of the Living Dead '65
Tromba, the Tiger Man '52

Natasha Hovey (1967-)
Demons '86
Acqua e Sapone '83

Adam Coleman Howard
No Secrets '91
Slaves of New York '89
Quiet Cool '86

Alan Howard (1937-)
P.D. James: Death in Holy Orders '03
The Secret Rapture '94
A Casualty of War '90
The Cook, the Thief, His Wife & Her Lover '90
Strapless '90

Andrew Howard
Revolver '05
The Lion in Winter '03
Below '02
Shooters '00

Anne Howard (1925-91)
The Ghost of Rashmon Hall '47
All This and Heaven Too '40
Little Men '40
The Prince and the Pauper '37
Anthony Adverse '36
Lloyds of London '36
Great Expectations '34
Jane Eyre '34

Anne Marie Howard (1960-)
Shopgirl '05
The Weather Man '05
Blue Streak '99
Prince of Darkness '87
Model Behavior '82

Arliss Howard (1955-)
Awake '07
Birth '04
Big Bad Love '02
The Song of the Lark '01
A Map of the World '99
You Know My Name '99
The Lesser Evil '99
The Lost World: Jurassic Park 2 '97
William Faulkner's Old Man '97
Beyond the Call '96
johns '96
The Man Who Captured Eichmann '96
The Infiltrator '95
To Wong Foo, Thanks for Everything, Julie Newmar '95
Natural Born Killers '94
The Sandlot '93 (V)
Tales of Erotica '93
Wilder Napalm '93
Crisscross '92
Ruby '92
Till Death Do Us Part '92
For the Boys '91
Iran: Days of Crisis '91
Somebody Has to Shoot the Picture '90
Men Don't Leave '89
Plain Clothes '88
Tequila Sunrise '88
Full Metal Jacket '87
Hands of a Stranger '87
The Lightship '86
Door to Door '84
The Prodigal '83

Arthur Howard (1910-95)
Another Country '84
Paradisio '61

Bob Howard (1906-86)
Junction 88 '47
Murder with Music '45

Boothe Howard (1887-1936)
Oh Susannah '38
Red River Valley '36
Mystery Liner '34

Brie Howard
The Runnin' Kind '89
Android '82

Bryce Dallas Howard (1981-)
Spider-Man 3 '07
As You Like It '06
Lady in the Water '06
Manderlay '05
Book of Love '04
The Village '04

Clint Howard (1959-)
Curious George '06 (V)
Beethoven's 5th '03
Heart of America '03
House of the Dead '03
The Missing '03
Austin Powers in Goldmember '02
Blackwoods '02
Dr. Seuss' How the Grinch Stole Christmas '00
Little Nicky '00
Arthur's Quest '99
Austin Powers 2: The Spy Who Shagged Me '99
EDtv '99
The Million Dollar Kid '99
Ping! '99
From the Earth to the Moon '98
The Waterboy '98
Under Oath '97
Barb Wire '96
Body Armor '96
Humanoids from the Deep '96
Rattled '96
Santa with Muscles '96
That Thing You Do! '96
Apollo 13 '95
Dillinger and Capone '95
Ice Cream Man '95
Bigfoot: The Unforgettable Encounter '94
Cheyenne Warrior '94
Leprechaun 2 '94
Carnosaur '93
Forced to Kill '93
Far and Away '92
Backdraft '91
Disturbed '90
Silent Night, Deadly Night 4: Initiation '90
Tango and Cash '89
B.O.R.N. '88
End of the Line '88
Freeway '88
The Wraith '87
Cocoon '85
Get Crazy '83
Cotton Candy '82
Evilspeak '82
Night Shift '82
Rock n' Roll High School '79
Grand Theft Auto '77
The Death of Richie '76
Eat My Dust '76
The Red Pony '76
Huckleberry Finn '75
Salty '73
The Wild Country '71
Gentle Giant '67

Curly Howard (1903-52)
Hollywood Party '34
Dancing Lady '33
The Lost Stooges '33
Myrt and Marge '33

Esther Howard (1892-1965)
Detour '46
Murder, My Sweet '44
Klondike Annie '36
Vice Squad '31

Frank Howard (1970-)
That Was Then... This Is Now '85
Hard Knox '83

Jeffrey Howard
The Wedding Banquet '93
Simple Men '92

John Howard (1913-95)
The High and the Mighty '54
Make Haste to Live '54
Radar Secret Service '50
The Fighting Kentuckian '49
Love from a Stranger '47
The Undying Monster '42
The Invisible Woman '40
The Philadelphia Story '40
The Texas Rangers Ride Again '40
Bulldog Drummond's Bride '39
Bulldog Drummond's Secret Police '39
Arrest Bulldog Drummond '38
Bulldog Drummond's Peril '38
Bulldog Drummond Comes Back '37
Bulldog Drummond's Revenge '37
Lost Horizon '37

John Howard (1952-)
Jindabyne '06
Japanese Story '03
The Road from Coorain '02
Dating the Enemy '95
Young Einstein '89
The Highest Honor '84
Prince and the Great Race '83
The Club '81

Joyce Howard (1922-)
Appointment with Crime '45
The Night Has Eyes '42

Kathleen Howard (1879-1956)
Crash Dive '43
Blossoms in the Dust '41
Young People '40
First Love '39
It's a Gift '34

Ken Howard (1944-)
Rambo '08
Michael Clayton '07
Dreamer: Inspired by a True Story '05
In Her Shoes '05
Perfect Murder, Perfect Town '00
Tactical Assault '99
At First Sight '98
The Net '95
Mastergate '92
Ulterior Motives '92
Murder in New Hampshire: The Pamela Smart Story '91
Oscar '91
Strange Interlude '90
Rage of Angels: The Story Continues '86
Pudd'nhead Wilson '84
Rage of Angels '83
Second Thoughts '83
The Thorn Birds '83
Country Girl '82
Damien: The Leper Priest '80
Manhunter '74
1776 '72

Kevyn Major Howard
Alien Nation '88
Full Metal Jacket '87

Kyle Howard (1978-)
Orange County '02
Baby Geniuses '98
Address Unknown '96
House Arrest '96
The Paper Brigade '96
Robo Warriors '96
Skeletons '96

Leslie Howard (1893-1943)
Pimpernel Smith '42
Spitfire '42
The Forty-Ninth Parallel '41
Gone with the Wind '39
Intermezzo '39
Pygmalion '38
Stand-In '37
Petrified Forest '36
Romeo and Juliet '34
Of Human Bondage '34
The Scarlet Pimpernel '34
Smilin' Through '33
The Animal Kingdom '32
Devotion '31
A Free Soul '31

Lisa Howard (1963-)
Bounty Hunters 2: Hardball '97
Bounty Hunters '96
Rolling Vengeance '87
Sabaka '55

Mary Howard (1912-89)
The Loves of Edgar Allen Poe '42
Billy the Kid '41
Abe Lincoln in Illinois '40
All Over Town '37

Moe Howard (1897-1975)
Dr. Death, Seeker of Souls '73
The Outlaws Is Coming! '65
Around the World in a Daze '63

Four for Texas '63
It's a Mad, Mad, Mad, Mad World '63
Three Stooges in Orbit '62
Snow White and the Three Stooges '61
The Three Stooges Meet Hercules '61
Have Rocket Will Travel '59
Gold Raiders '51
Swing Parade of 1946 '46
Hollywood Party '34
Dancing Lady '33
The Lost Stooges '33

Rance Howard (1929-)
The Alamo '04
Eye See You '01
A Crack in the Floor '00
Me '00
The Best Man '99
Psycho '98
The Student Affair '97
Dark Before Dawn '89
B.O.R.N. '88
Grand Theft Auto '77
Eat My Dust '76
Cool Hand Luke '67

Ron Howard (1954-)
Osmosis Jones '01 (V)
Return to Mayberry '86
Bitter Harvest '81
More American Graffiti '79
Grand Theft Auto '77
The Shootist '76
The First Nudie Musical '76
Huckleberry Finn '75
The Migrants '74
American Graffiti '73
Run, Stranger, Run '73
The Wild Country '71
Smoke '70
Village of the Giants '65
The Courtship of Eddie's Father '62
The Music Man '62
Door to Door Maniac '61

Ronald Howard (1918-96)
Pattern for Plunder '62
The Naked Edge '61
The Queen of Spades '49
Night Beat '48

Shawn Michael Howard (1969-)
Boycott '02

Susan Howard (1944-)
The Power Within '79
Moonshine County Express '77
Sidewinder One '77

Terrence Howard (1969-)
Iron Man '08
August Rush '07
Awake '07
The Brave One '07
The Hunting Party '07
The Perfect Holiday '07
Pride '07
Idlewild '06
Animal '05
Crash '05
Four Brothers '05
Get Rich or Die Tryin' '05
Hustle & Flow '05
The Salon '05
Ray '04
Biker Boyz '03
Boycott '02
Hart's War '02
Angel Eyes '01
Glitter '01
Intimate Affairs '01
Big Momma's House '00
Love Beat the Hell Outta Me '00
Spark '98
johns '96
Sunset Park '96
The Jacksons: An American Dream '92

Traylor Howard (1966-)
Me, Myself, and Irene '00
Dirty Work '97

Trevor Howard (1916-88)
The Dawning '88
The Unholy '88
White Mischief '88
Foreign Body '86
Dust '85
Gandhi '82
Inside the Third Reich '82
Sea Wolves '81
Windwalker '81
Staying On '80
Hurricane '79
Meteor '79
Stevie '78
Superman: The Movie '78
Slavers '77
Adventures of Eliza Fraser '76
Albino '76
The Bawdy Adventures of Tom Jones '76
Conduct Unbecoming '75
Hennessy '75
Roboman '75
The Count of Monte Cristo '74
Craze '74
11 Harrowhouse '74
Catholics '73
A Doll's House '73
The Offence '73
Ludwig '72
Catch Me a Spy '71
Mary, Queen of Scots '71
The Night Visitor '70
Ryan's Daughter '70
Battle of Britain '69
Lola '69
The Charge of the Light Brigade '68
Triple Cross '67
The Poppy Is Also a Flower '66
Morituri '65
Operation Crossbow '65
Von Ryan's Express '65
Father Goose '64
The Golden Salamander '51
The Third Man '49

Shemp Howard (1895-1955)
Gold Raiders '51
Africa Screams '49
Blondie Knows Best '46
Trouble Chasers '45
Cooking Up Trouble '44
Ghost Crazy '44
It Ain't Hay '43
Pittsburgh '42
Private Buckaroo '42
Buck Privates '41
Cracked Nuts '41
The Bank Dick '40
Hold That Ghost '41
The Invisible Woman '40

Hoke Howell (1930-97)
Vice Girls '96
Alienator '89

Green for Danger '47
They Made Me a Fugitive '47

Vanessa Howard (1948-)
Picture of Dorian Gray '74
Girly '70

Walker Howard
Blood Beast Terror '67

Brian Howe
The Pursuit of Happyness '06

Kevin Howarth
Cold and Dark '05
Razor Blade Smile '98

Clark Howat (1917-)
Billy Jack '71
The Giant Claw '57

Anthony Howell
The Other Boleyn Girl '03
Wives and Daughters '01

C. Thomas Howell (1966-)
The Far Side of Jericho '06
The Keeper: The Legend of Omar Khayyam '05
The Glass Trap '04
Hidalgo '04
The Hillside Strangler '04
The Lost Angel '04
Gods and Generals '03
The Hitcher 2: I've Been Waiting '03
Net Games '03
Catch Me If You Can '02
Burning Down the House '01
Dead Evidence '00
Avalanche '99
The Crimson Code '99
Cybercity '99
The Million Dollar Kid '99
The Prince and the Surfer '99
Shepherd '99
Dead Fire '98
First Degree '98
Last Lives '98
Matter of Trust '98
Stalker '97
Baby Face Nelson '97
Dilemma '97
Laws of Deception '97
The Big Fall '96
Pure Danger '96
Hourglass '95
Suspect Device '95
The Sweeper '95
Dangerous Indiscretion '94
Payback '94
Shameless '94
Teresa's Tattoo '94
Acting on Impulse '93
Gettysburg '93
Jailbait '93
That Night '93
Breaking the Rules '92
Nickel & Dime '92
Tattle Tale '92
To Protect and Serve '92
Curiosity Kills '90
Eyes of the Panther '90
Kid '90
Side Out '90
Far Out Man '89
The Return of the Musketeers '89
Into the Homeland '87
A Tiger's Tale '87
The Hitcher '86
Soul Man '86
Secret Admirer '85
Grandview U.S.A. '84
Red Dawn '84
The Outsiders '83
Tank '83
E.T.: The Extra-Terrestrial '82

B.O.R.N. '88
Humanoids from the Deep '80

Jean Howell (1927-96)
Crime of Passion '57
The Fast and the Furious '54

Kenneth Howell (1913-66)
Hurry, Charlie, Hurry '41
Junior G-Men '40
Little Red Schoolhouse '36
The Eagle and the Hawk '33

Ursula Howells (1922-2005)
Jewels '92
Girly '70
The Gilded Cage '54

Peter Howell
Almost Strangers '01
Shadowlands '93

Virginia Howell
Star Reporter '39
Spitfire '34

Frankie Howerd (1922-92)
Night of the Laughing Dead '75
Naughty Knights '71
Carry On Doctor '68
The Great St. Trinian's Train Robbery '66
Cool Mikado '63
The Runaway Bus '54

Bobby Howes (1895-1972)
Happy Go Lovely '51
Murder in the Footlights '46

Reed Howes (1900-64)
The Sinister Urge '60
My Dog Shep '46
Dead or Alive '44
Law of the Saddle '43
Fugitive Valley '41
Covered Wagon Days '40
Lightning Strikes West '40
Phantom Rancher '39
Roll, Wagons, Roll '39
Six Gun Rhythm '39
A Million to One '37
The Clutching Hand '36
Custer's Last Stand '36
Confidential '35
Feud of the West '35
Queen of the Jungle '35

Sally Ann Howes (1930-)
Death Ship '80
Chitty Chitty Bang Bang '68
The Admirable Crichton '57
Anna Karenina '48
Nicholas Nickleby '46
Dead of Night '45
Pink String and Sealing Wax '45
Thursday's Child '43
Wax '45

Steve Howey (1977-)
DOA: Dead or Alive '06
Supercross: The Movie '05

Peter Howitt (1957-)
Kiss and Tell '96
The Magician '93

Chris Howland
The Mad Executioners '65
Fanny Hill: Memoirs of a Woman of Pleasure '64

Jobyna Howland (1880-1936)
Topaze '33

Noel Howlett (1901-84)
Hook, Line and Sinker '30

Woman of Straw '64
Victim '61
The Doors '91

Olin Howlin (1886-1959)
The Blob '58
Storm Rider '57
Last of the Wild Horses '49
Apache Rose '47

David Huband (1958-)
Cinderella Man '05
Cube: Zero '04
Wrong Turn '03
Dirty Pictures '00

Kelly Hu (1967-)
Shanghai Kiss '07
Underclassman '05
X2: X-Men United '03
Cradle 2 the Grave '03
The Scorpion King '02
No Way Back '96
Strange Days '95
Surf Ninjas '93
The Doors '91

Hsia
See Brigitte Lin

Vera Hruba Ralston
See Vera Hruba Ralston

Rudolf Hrusinsky (1921-94)
The Elementary School '91
My Sweet Little Village '86
Larks on a String '68
Murder Czech Style '66

Brigitte Lin Ching Hsia
See Brigitte Lin

The Wistful Widow of Wagon Gap '47
Nancy Drew, Reporter '39
Girl of the Golden West '38
Earthworm Tractors '36
Satan Met a Lady '36
Road Show '41

Karl Howman
Party! Party! '83
The House on Straw Hill '76

Leonard Earl Howze
Barbershop 2: Back in Business '04
Barbershop '02
The Ringer '05

Cork Hubbert (1952-2003)
The Ballad of the Sad Cafe '91
Caveman '81

Cristina Hoyos (1946-)
El Amor Brujo '86
Carmen '83
Blood Wedding '81

Carol Hoyt
Midnight Confessions '95
Illegal Entry: Formula for Fear '93

Arthur Hoyt (1874-1953)
The Great McGinty '40
In the Money '34
His Private Secretary '33
American Madness '32
Dynamite Ranch '32
Backfire '22
Blue Blazes Rawden '18

Jack Hoxie (1885-1965)
Gun Law '33
Law and Lawless '33
Trouble Busters '33
Outlaw Justice '32
Men of Daring '35

John Hoyt (1905-91)
Flesh Gordon '72
The Time Travelers '64
X: The Man with X-Ray Eyes '63
Merrill's Marauders '62
Curse of the Undead '59
Attack of the Puppet People '58
The Conqueror '56
Forever Darling '56
Wetbacks '56
Blackboard Jungle '55
The Girl in the Red Velvet Swing '55
Sins of Jezebel '53
Julius Caesar '53
The Black Castle '52
Loan Shark '52
The Lost Continent '51
Great Dan Patch '49
Trapped '49
Winter Meeting '48
O.S.S. '46

Whip Hubley (1957-)
Kiss the Sky '98
Stepfather 3: Father's Day '92
Total Exposure '91
Child in the Night '90
Prettykill '87
Russkies '87
Top Gun '86

Season Hubley (1951-)
A Cinderella Story '04
Armistead Maupin's More Tales of the City '97
Black Scorpion 2: Ground Zero '96
Vice Squad '82
Escape from New York '81
Mrs. R's Daughter '79
Hardcore '79
Elvis: The Movie '79
The Key to Rebecca '85
Agatha Christie's A Caribbean Mystery '83

Elizabeth Hubbard (1933-)
Center Stage '00
Cold River '81

John Hubbard (1914-88)
Mexican Hayride '48
Cowboy & the Senorita '44
The Mummy's Tomb '42
Road Show '41

Harold Huber (1904-59)
A Gentleman After Dark '42
Charlie Chan in Rio '41
Charlie Chan in City of Darkness '39
Mysterious Mr. Moto '38
Mr. Moto's Gamble '38
A Slight Case of Murder '38
Charlie Chan at Monte Carlo '37
Charlie Chan on Broadway '37

Janet Hubert-Whitten (1956-)
30 Years to Life '01
New Eden '94

Henry Hubchen (1947-)
Go for Zucker '05
Jacob the Liar '74

Paul (Christian) Hubschmid (1917-2001)
Funeral in Berlin '66
The Indian Tomb '59
Journey to the Lost City '58

Cooper Huckabee (1951-)
Gettysburg '93
Love Field '91
Night Eyes '90
Cohen and Tate '88
The Curse '87
The Funhouse '81
Getting Wasted '80
Fathoms '53
The Beast from 20,000 Fathoms '53
Bagdad '49
Top Gun '86

Joni '79

Steffany Huckaby
Death Tunnel '05
The Pleasure Drivers '05

Walter Hudd (1897-1963)
Sink the Bismarck '60
Cast a Dark Shadow '55
I Know Where I'm Going '45
Black Limelight '38
Housemaster '38
Elephant Boy '37
Rembrandt '36

David Huddleston (1930-)
The Producers '05
The Big Lebowski '97
Life with Mikey '93
Double Exposure: The Story of Margaret Bourke-White '89
Frantic '88
The Tracker '88
When the Bough Breaks '86
Santa Claus: The Movie '85
Finnegan Begin Again '84
Go for It '83
Smokey and the Bandit 2 '80
Crime Busters '78
Billy Two Hats '74
Blazing Saddles '74
McQ '74
On the Run '73
Rio Lobo '70

Michael Huddleston
Wyatt Earp '94
Bad Channels '92
Bombs Away! '86
Four Friends '81
World's Greatest Lover '77

Vanessa Anne Hudgens (1988-)
High School Musical 2 '07
High School Musical '06
Thunderbirds '04

Reginald (Reggie) Hudlin (1961-)
Joe's Apartment '96 (V)
Posse '93
She's Gotta Have It '86

Bill Hudson (1949-)
Hysterical '83
KISS Meets the Phantom of the Park '78

Ernie Hudson (1945-)
All Hat '07
Marilyn Hotchkiss' Ballroom Dancing & Charm School '06
Miss Congeniality 2: Armed and Fabulous '05
Clifford's Really Big Movie '04 (V)
Miss Congeniality '00
Nowhere to Land '00
Red Letters '00
The Watcher '00
Corrupt '99
Interceptor Force '99
Paper Bullets '99
Shark Attack '99
Stealth Fighter '99
Urban Menace '99
Best of the Best: Without Warning '98
For Which He Stands '98
Never 2 Big '98
A Stranger in the Kingdom '98
Congo '95
Airheads '94
The Cowboy Way '94
In the Army Now '94
No Escape '94
Speechless '94
Sugar Hill '94
Levitation '97
Mr. Magoo '97
Operation: Delta Force '97
The Cherokee Kid '96
Just Your Luck '96
The Substitute '96
Tornado! '96
The Basketball Diaries '95
Leviathan '89
Trapper County War '89
The Wrong Guys '88
Ghostbusters 2 '89
Ghostbusters '84
Joy of Sex '84
Going Berserk '83
Spacehunter: Adventures in the Forbidden Zone '83
Penitentiary 2 '82
The $5.20 an Hour Dream '80
The Jazz Singer '80
Dolemite 2: Human Tornado '76

Gary Hudson (1956-)
Angels Fall '07
Snakeman '05
Extreme Limits '01
My Husband's Double Life '01
The Stepdaughter '00
Bridge of Dragons '99
Eye of the Killer '99
Black Thunder '98
Serial Killer '95
Texas Payback '95
The Wrong Woman '95
The Force '94
Scanner Cop '94
Sexual Intent '94
Indecent Behavior '93
Martial Outlaw '93
Mind Twister '93
Wild Cactus '92
Night Angel '90

Jennifer Hudson
Sex and the City: The Movie '08
Dreamgirls '06

John Hudson (1922-96)
When Gangland Strikes '56
Return to Paradise '53

Kate Hudson (1979-)
Fool's Gold '08
You, Me and Dupree '06
The Skeleton Key '05
Raising Helen '04
Alex & Emma '03
How to Lose a Guy in 10 Days '03
Le Divorce '03
The Four Feathers '02
About Adam '00
Almost Famous '00
Dr. T & the Women '00
Gossip '99
Desert Blue '98
Ricochet River '98
200 Cigarettes '98

Larry Hudson (1921-61)
Tank Commando '59
The Creature Walks among Us '56

Rochelle Hudson (1914-72)
Alien Massacre '67
The Night Walker '64
Strait-Jacket '64
Rebel without a Cause '55
Sky Liner '49
The Devil's Cargo '48
Bush Pilot '47
Mr. Moto Takes a Chance '38
Reunion '36
Curly Top '35
Les Miserables '35
Life Begins at Forty '35
Show Them No Mercy '35
Bachelor Bait '34
Imitation of Life '34
Mr. Skitch '33
Beyond the Rockies '32
The Savage Girl '32

Rock Hudson (1925-85)
World War III '86
The Ambassador '84
The Vegas Strip Wars '84
The Mirror Crack'd '80
The Martian Chronicles: Part 1 '79
The Martian Chronicles: Part 2 '79
The Martian Chronicles: Part 3 '79
Avalanche '78
Embryo '76
Showdown '73
Darling Lili '70
Hornet's Nest '70
The Undefeated '69
Ice Station Zebra '68
Seconds '66
Tobruk '66
Strange Bedfellows '65
Send Me No Flowers '64
A Gathering of Eagles '63
Man's Favorite Sport? '63
Come September '61
Lover Come Back '61
Pillow Talk '59
Battle Hymn '57
Something of Value '57
Tarnished Angels '57
Giant '56
Written on the Wind '56
All That Heaven Allows '55
Magnificent Obsession '54
Gun Fury '53
Sea Devils '53
Bend of the River '52
Here Come the Nelsons '52
Horizons West '52
The Lawless Breed '52
Tomahawk '51
Winchester '73 '50

Toni Hudson
The Uninvited '88
Just One of the Guys '85
Prime Risk '84

William (Bill) Hudson (1925-74)
Attack of the 50 Foot Woman '58
The Screaming Skull '58
The Amazing Colossal Man '57

Jon Huertas
Believers '07
The Insatiable '06

Matthias Hues (1959-)
Suicide Ride '07
Alone in the Woods '95
Cyberzone '95
Death Match '94
Digital Man '94
Final Justice '94
Fists of Iron '94
Bounty Tracker '93
TC 2000 '93
Black Belt '92
Falling from Grace '92
Mission of Justice '92
Talons of the Eagle '92
Fist Fighter '88
Stormquest '87
Armed Response '86
Deadly Passion '85
Nine Deaths of the Ninja '85

Brent Huff (1961-)
The Glass Trap '04
New Best Friend '02
Going Greek '01
Submerged '00
The Bad Pack '98
The Perils of Gwendoline '84

David Huffman (1945-85)
Agatha Christie's Sparkling Cyanide '83
Last Plane Out '83
Firefox '82
St. Helen's, Killer Volcano '82
Blood Beach '81
Ice Castles '79
The Onion Field '79
F.I.S.T. '78
The Winds of Kitty Hawk '78

Felicity Huffman (1962-)
Georgia Rule '07
Transamerica '05
Christmas With the Kranks '04
Raising Helen '04
Out of Order '03
Path to War '02
Snap Decision '01
A Slight Case of Murder '97
The Spanish Prisoner '97
Hackers '95
Quicksand: No Escape '91
Stephen King's Golden Years '91

Kymberley Huffman
K-9:3: P.I. '01
Sleeping with Strangers '94

Billy Hufsey (1958-)
Magic Kid '92
Off the Wall '82

Daniel Hugh-Kelly (1954-)
Jackie, Ethel, Joan: The Kennedy Women '01
Chill Factor '99
Passing Glory '99
Atomic Dog '98
From the Earth to the Moon '98
Star Trek: Insurrection '98
The Tuskegee Airmen '95
Bad Company '94
The Good Son '93
Cujo '83
Nowhere to Hide '83

Andrew Hughes (1908-85)
Destroy All Monsters '68
Terror Beneath the Sea '66

Barnard Hughes (1915-2006)
The Cradle Will Rock '99
Neil Simon's The Odd Couple 2 '98
The Fantasticks '95
Past the Bleachers '95
Primal Secrets '94
Sister Act 2: Back in the Habit '93
Doc Hollywood '91
Day One '89
The Incident '89
Da '88
Hobo's Christmas '87
The Lost Boys '87
The Adventures of Huckleberry Finn '85
Maxie '85
Under the Biltmore Clock '85
Where Are the Children? '85
Oh, God! '77
Sisters '73
Rage '72
Cold Turkey '71
The Hospital '71
Where's Poppa? '70
Midnight Cowboy '69

Brendan Hughes
Howling 6: The Freaks '90
To Die For '89
Return to Horror High '87

Carol Hughes (1915-85)
Home in Oklahoma '47
Miracle Kid '42
Desperate Cargo '41
Robot Pilot '41
Silver Stallion '41
The Border Legion '40
Flash Gordon Conquers the Universe '40
Space Soldiers Conquer the Universe '40
Love Affair '39
The Man from Music Mountain '38
Renfrew of the Royal Mounted '37
Earthworm Tractors '36
Three Men on a Horse '36

Charles Hughes
Call of the Forest '49
The Frontiersmen '38

Finola Hughes (1960-)
Tycus '98
Prison of Secrets '97
The Crying Child '96
Dark Side of Genius '94
Aspen Extreme '93
Soapdish '91
Nutcracker Sweet '84
Staying Alive '83

Frank John Hughes (1967-)
Catch Me If You Can '02
Band of Brothers '01
Deranged '01
Angel's Dance '99
Happy Hell Night '92

Heather Hughes
Blood Freak '72
Flesh Feast '69

Helen Hughes (1929-)
Night of the Twisters '95
The Amityville Curse '90
Kidnapping of Baby John Doe '88
My Father, My Rival '85
The Peanut Butter Solution '85
Incubus '82
Off Your Rocker '80
Outrageous! '77

Jason Hughes (1971-)
Killing Me Softly '01
Plain Jane '01
Shooters '00

Kathleen Hughes (1928-)
Cult of the Cobra '55
It Came from Outer Space '53

Kay Hughes (1914-98)
Dick Tracy: The Spider Strikes '37
The Mandarin Mystery '37
Ride, Ranger, Ride '36
The Vigilantes Are Coming '36

Lloyd Hughes (1897-1958)
Blake of Scotland Yard '36
A Face in the Fog '36
Kelly of the Secret Service '36
Little Red Schoolhouse '36
The Midnight Phantom '35
Social Error '35
Drums of Jeopardy '31
Where East is East '29
Ella Cinders '26
The Lost World '25
Tess of the Storm Country '22
Beau Revel '21
Dangerous Hours '19

Mary Beth Hughes (1919-95)
Square Dance Jubilee '51
Holiday Rhythm '50
Last of the Wild Horses '49
Rimfire '49
Return of Wildfire '48
Inner Sanctum '48
Great Flamarion '45
I Accuse My Parents '45
The Lady Confesses '45
Take It Big '44
Timber Queen '44
The Ox-Bow Incident '43
Blue, White and Perfect '42
Orchestra Wives '42
Charlie Chan in Rio '41

Miko Hughes (1986-)
Fly Boy '99
Mercury Rising '98
Spawn '97
Zeus and Roxanne '96
Apollo 13 '95
Cops and Robbersons '94
Wes Craven's New Nightmare '94
Jack the Bear '93
Pet Sematary '89

Roddy Hughes (1891-1970)
Old Mother Riley's Jungle Treasure '51
The Last Days of Dolwyn '49

Sharon Hughes
Grotesque '87
Chained Heat '83

Tresa Hughes
Sarah, Plain and Tall: Skylark '93
Coming Home '78

Wendy Hughes (1952-)
Paradise Road '97
Lust and Revenge '95
Princess Caraboo '94
Wild Orchid 2: Two Shades of Blue '92
A Woman Named Jackie '91
The Heist '89
Happy New Year '87
Warm Nights on a Slow-Moving Train '87
Echoes of Paradise '86
An Indecent Obsession '85
Remember Me '85
Careful, He Might Hear You '84
My First Wife '84
Dangerous Summer '82
Lonely Hearts '82
Touch & Go '80
Kostas '79
My Brilliant Career '79
Newsfront '78
Puzzle '78
High Rolling in a Hot Corvette '77
Alternative '76
Jock Petersen '74

D.L. Hughley (1964-)
Soul Plane '04
Chasing Papi '03
Scary Movie 3 '03
The Brothers '01
Inspector Gadget '99 (V)

Michael Hui
Robin-B-Hood '06
Chinese Box '97

Steve Huison (1963-)
Chaos & Cadavers '03
The Navigators '01
The Full Monty '96

Claude Hulbert (1900-64)
The Dummy Talks '43
Bulldog Jack '35

Jack Hulbert (1892-1978)
Bulldog Jack '35
Jack Ahoy '34

Tom Hulce (1953-)
Stranger Than Fiction '06
The Hunchback of Notre Dame '96 (V)
The Heidi Chronicles '95
Mary Shelley's Frankenstein '94
Fearless '93
Black Rainbow '91
The Inner Circle '91
Parenthood '89
Dominick & Eugene '88
Slamdance '87
Echo Park '86
The Rise & Rise of Daniel Rocket '86
Amadeus '84

Those Lips, Those Eyes '80
National Lampoon's Animal House '78

Dianne Hull (1948-)
The New Adventures of Pippi Longstocking '88
Christmas Evil '80
The Fifth Floor '80
The Onion Field '79
Aloha, Bobby and Rose '74
Girls on the Road '73

Henry Hull (1890-1977)
The Fool Killer '65
Master of the World '61
The Sheriff of Fractured Jaw '59
The Buccaneer '58
Return of Jesse James '50
The Fountainhead '49
Great Dan Patch '49
The Great Gatsby '49
Rimfire '49
Portrait of Jennie '48
Objective, Burma! '45
Lifeboat '44
The Woman of the Town '44
High Sierra '41
My Son, My Son '40
Return of Frank James '40
Jesse James '39
Stanley and Livingstone '39
Boys Town '38
Three Comrades '38
Werewolf of London '35
Great Expectations '34
Midnight '34

Josephine Hull (1884-1957)
Harvey '50
Arsenic and Old Lace '44

Lachy Hulme (1971-)
Macbeth '06
The Matrix Revolutions '03
The Crocodile Hunter: Collision Course '02

Warren Hull (1903-74)
Bowery Blitzkrieg '41
Hidden Enemy '40
Yukon Flight '40
Star Reporter '39

George Humbert (1880-1963)
Music in My Heart '40
Hearts of Humanity '32

Benita Hume (1906-67)
It Happened in New Orleans '36
Suzy '36
Tarzan Escapes '36
Power '34
Private Life of Don Juan '34
Gambling Ship '33
Lady of the Lake '28

Renee Humphrey (1975-)
Hard Luck '01
Jay and Silent Bob Strike Back '01
Chicks, Man '99
The Sex Monster '99
Lover Girl '97
Cadillac Ranch '96
The Cure '95
Devil in a Blue Dress '95
French Kiss '95
Mallrats '95
Fun '94
Jailbait '93

Alf Humphreys
X2: X-Men United '03
The Stickup '01
My Bloody Valentine '81

Cecil Humphreys (1883-1947)
The Razor's Edge '46
Accused '36

William Humphreys (1874-1942)
The Unholy Three '25
Beau Brummel '24

Barry Humphries (1934-)
Finding Nemo '03 (V)
Spice World: The Movie '97
Welcome to Woop Woop '97
The Leading Man '96
Immortal Beloved '94
Les Patterson Saves the World '90
Shock Treatment '81
The Getting of Wisdom '77
Barry McKenzie Holds His Own '74
Bedazzled '68

Tessa Humphries
Paradise Road '97
Cassandra '87

Robert Hundar
See Claudio Undari

Sammo Hung (1952-)
Around the World in 80 Days '04
Mr. Nice Guy '98
Painted Skin '93
Dragons Forever '90
Paper Marriage '88
Eastern Condors '87
The Millionaire's Express '86
Heart of Dragon '85
Project A '83
Zu: Warriors from the Magic Mountain '83
The Prodigal Son '82
Spooky Encounters '80

Charlie Hunnam (1980-)
Children of Men '06
Green Street Hooligans '05
Cold Mountain '03
Abandon '02
Nicholas Nickleby '02

Arthur Hunnicutt (1911-79)
Winterhawk '76
Harry and Tonto '74
The Bounty Man '72
Shoot Out '71
El Dorado '67
Apache Uprising '66
Born Reckless '59
The Tall T '57
The Kettles in the Ozarks '56
The French Line '54
Devil's Canyon '53
The Big Sky '52
The Lusty Men '52
She Couldn't Say No '52
Distant Drums '51
The Red Badge of Courage '51
Broken Arrow '50
Stars in My Crown '50
Ticket to Tomahawk '50
Border Incident '49
Great Dan Patch '49
Abroad with Two Yanks '44
Wildcat '42

Gayle Hunnicutt (1943-)
Turnaround '87
Dream Lover '85
Target '85
Flashpoint Africa '84
A Woman of Substance '84
Return of the Man from U.N.C.L.E. '83
The Martian Chronicles: Part 2 '79
The Martian Chronicles: Part 3 '79
Once in Paris... '79
Sell Out '77
Strange Shadows in an Empty Room '76
Shadow Man '75
Spiral Staircase '75
The Legend of Hell House '73
Scorpio '73
The Golden Bowl '72
Freelance '71

The Love Machine '71
Marlowe '69
The Wild Angels '66

Bonnie Hunt (1964-)
Cars '06 (V)
I Want Someone to Eat Cheese With '06
Cheaper by the Dozen 2 '05
Loggerheads '05
Cheaper by the Dozen '03
Stolen Summer '02
Monsters, Inc. '01 (V)
Return to Me '00
The Green Mile '99
Random Hearts '99
A Bug's Life '98 (V)
Kissing a Fool '98
Getting Away With Murder '96
Jerry Maguire '96
Jumanji '95
Now and Then '95
Only You '94
Beethoven's 2nd '93
Dave '93
Rain Man '88
Beethoven '92

Brad Hunt
Cherish '02
Dream with the Fishes '97
Fire Down Below '97

Crystal Hunt
Sydney White '07
The Derby Stallion '05

David Hunt
The Dead Pool '88
Date with an Angel '87

Eleanor Hunt (-1981)
We're in the Legion Now '37

Helen Hunt (1963-)
Bobby '06
Empire Falls '05
A Good Woman '04
The Curse of the Jade Scorpion '01
Cast Away '00
Dr. T & the Women '00
Pay It Forward '00
What Women Want '00
As Good As It Gets '97
Twister '96
Kiss of Death '94
Bob Roberts '92
Into the Badlands '92
Mr. Saturday Night '92
Only You '92
Trancers 2: The Return of Jack Deth '90
Next of Kin '89
Bill: On His Own '83
Desperate Lives '82
The Best Little Girl in the World '81

Gareth Hunt (1943-)
Parting Shots '98
A Chorus of Disapproval '89
It Couldn't Happen Here '88
Bloodbath at the House of Death '85
Funny Money '82
The World Is Full of Married Men '80

Jimmy Hunt (1939-)
Pioneer Woman '73
Invaders from Mars '53
Belles on Their Toes '52
The Capture '50
Pitfall '48

Linda Hunt (1945-)
Stranger Than Fiction '06
Yours, Mine & Ours '05
Dragonfly '02
Pocahontas '95 (V)
Ready to Wear '94
Twenty Bucks '93
If Looks Could Kill '91
Kindergarten Cop '90
The Room '87
Waiting for the Moon '87
Eleni '85
Silverado '85
The Bostonians '84
Dune '84
The Year of Living Dangerously '82
Popeye '80

Marsha Hunt (1917-)
Johnny Got His Gun '71
The Valley of Decision '45
Blossoms in the Dust '41
Actors and Sin '52
Star Reporter '39
Smash-Up: The Story of a Woman '47
Carnegie Hall '47
Raw Deal '48
Thunder Trail '37
Desert Gold '36

Marsha A. Hunt (1947-)
Howling 2: Your Sister Is a Werewolf '85
Britannia Hospital '82
The Sender '82
Dracula A.D. 1972 '72

Martita Hunt (1900-69)
Brown '64
The Unsinkable Molly Brown '64
The Wonderful World of the Brothers Grimm '62
The Brides of Dracula '60
Song Without End '60
Me and the Colonel '58
The Admirable Crichton '57
Anastasia '56
The King's Rhapsody '55
The Story of Robin Hood & His Merrie Men '52
Little Ballerina '47
Anna Karenina '47
Great Expectations '46
Nine Days a Queen '36
Sabotage '36
When Knights Were Bold '36
First a Girl '35

Bill Hunter (1940-)
Finding Nemo '03 (V)
Kangaroo Jack '02
The Echo of Thunder '98
Road to Nhill '97
Race the Sun '96
River Street '95
The Adventures of Priscilla, Queen of the Desert '94
Muriel's Wedding '94
The Last Days of Chez Nous '92
Strictly Ballroom '92

William Dennis Hunt
Flesh Gordon 2: Flesh Gordon Meets the Cosmic Cheerleaders '90

Holly Hunter (1958-)
The Big White '05
Nine Lives '05
The Incredibles '04 (V)
Little Black Book '04
Levity '03
Thirteen '03
Moonlight Mile '02
Harlan County War '00
O Brother, Where Art Thou? '00
Things You Can Tell Just by Looking at Her '00
Time Code '00
Jesus '99
Woman Wanted '98
A Life Less Ordinary '97
Crash '95
Copycat '95
Home for the Holidays '95
Crazy in Love '92
Once Around '91
The Firm '93
The Positively True Adventures of the Alleged Texas Cheerleader-Murdering Mom '93
Raising Arizona '87
Broadcast News '87
Always '89
Animal Behavior '89
Miss Firecracker '89
Roe vs. Wade '89
End of the Line '88
Swing Shift '84
Urge to Kill '84
Svengali '83
The Burning '82

Dirk Hunter
Undead '05

Ian Hunter (1900-75)
Unmasking the Idol '86
Doctor Blood's Coffin '62
Pursuit of the Graf Spee '57
Bedelia '46
Andy Hardy's Private Secretary '41
Billy the Kid '41
Dr. Jekyll and Mr. Hyde '41
Smilin' Through '41
Ziegfeld Girl '41
Bitter Sweet '40
Broadway Melody of 1940 '40
The Long Voyage Home '40
Strange Cargo '40
Broadway Serenade '39
The Little Princess '39
Tarzan Finds a Son '39
The Tower of London '39
The Adventures of Robin Hood '38
The Sisters '38
That Certain Woman '37
A Midsummer Night's Dream '35

Ian Hunter
Order of the Black Eagle '87
Two Shades of Blue '98
Just a Little Harmless Sex '98

Rachel Hunter (1969-)
MacArthur Park '01

Ronald Hunter
Jakarta '88
Adventure of the Action Hunters '87
Rage of Angels '83
The Lazarus Syndrome '79

Ross Hunter (1916-96)
Louisiana Hayride '44
Reform School Girl '57

Kaki Hunter (1955-)
Porky's Revenge '85
Just the Way You Are '84
Porky's 2: The Next Day '83
Porky's '82
Whose Life Is It Anyway? '81

Kim Hunter (1922-2002)
Out of the Cold '99
Midnight in the Garden of Good and Evil '97
A Price above Rubies '98
Two Evil Eyes '90
The Kindred '87
Backstairs at the White House '79
Dark August '76
Bad Ronald '74
Born Innocent '74
Escape from the Planet of the Apes '71
Beneath the Planet of the Apes '70
Planet of the Apes '68
The Swimmer '68
Lilith '64
Requiem for a Heavyweight '56
A Streetcar Named Desire '51
Stairway to Heaven '46
The Seventh Victim '43
Tender Comrade '43

Tab Hunter (1931-)
Out of the Dark '88
Cameron's Closet '89
Grotesque '87
Lust in the Dust '85
Pandemonium '82
Grease 2 '82
Polyester '81
The Arousers '70
The Loved One '65
Ride the Wild Surf '64
Operation Bikini '63
They Came to Cordura '59
The Big Push '75
Gunman's Walk '58
Damn Yankees '58
Lafayette Escadrille '58
The Burning Hills '56
Battle Cry '55
The Sea Chase '55
Island of Desire '52

Thomas Hunter (1932-)
Escape from the KGB '87

Jeffrey Hunter (1925-69)
Private Navy of Sgt. O'Farrell '68
The Christmas Kid '68
A Witch Without a Broom '68
A Guide for the Married Man '67
The Longest Day '62
No Man Is an Island '62
The King of Kings '61
Hell to Eternity '60
Sergeant Rutledge '60
Last Hurrah '58
The Great Locomotive Chase '56
The Searchers '56
Seven Cities of Gold '55
Belles on Their Toes '52

Fever '88
Rikky and Pete '88
The Hit '85
An Indecent Obsession '85
Rebel '85
Heatwave '83
Return of Captain Invincible '83
1915 '82
Hard Knocks '80
In Search of Anna '79
Newsfront '78

The Searchers '56
Seven Cities of Gold '55
Belles on Their Toes '52
The Great Locomotive Chase '56
Last Hurrah '58
Sergeant Rutledge '60
Hell to Eternity '60
The King of Kings '61
No Man Is an Island '62
The Longest Day '62

Battle of the Commandos '71
The Vampire Happening '71
Web of Deception '71

Sam Huntington (1982-)
Superman Returns '06
In Enemy Hands '04
Sleepover '04
Not Another Teen Movie '01
Detroit Rock City '99
Jungle 2 Jungle '96

G.P. (Tim) Huntley, Jr. (1904-71)
Journey for Margaret '42
They Died with Their Boots On '41
Beau Geste '39
Mr. Takes a Vacation '39
The Charge of the Light Brigade '36

Raymond Huntley (1904-90)
Hot Millions '68
The Mummy '59
Our Man in Havana '59
Room at the Top '59
The Prisoner '55
The Long Dark Hall '51
I See a Dark Stranger '46
Immortal Battalion '44
Night Train to Munich '40

Isabelle Huppert (1955-)
Comedy of Power '06
Private Property '06
Gabrielle '05
I Heart Huckabees '04
Time of the Wolf '03
8 Women '02
La Vie Promise '02
The Piano Teacher '01
Comedy of Innocence '00
Les Destinees '00
Merci pour le Chocolat '00
La Separation '98
The Swindle '97
Elective Affinities '96
La Ceremonie '95
Amateur '94
Love After Love '94
The Separation '94
Madame Bovary '91
La Vengeance d'une Femme '89
The Possessed '88
The Story of Women '88
The Bedroom Window '87
Cactus '86
Sincerely Charlotte '86
My Best Friend's Girl '84
Entre-Nous '83
La Truite '83
Passion '82
Coup de Torchon '81
Heaven's Gate '81
Loulou '80
Violette '78
The Lacemaker '77
The Judge and the Assassin '75
Rosebud '75
Going Places '74

Paige Hurd (1992-)
Beauty Shop '05
Cradle 2 the Grave '03

Rachel Hurd-Wood (1990-)
Perfume: The Story of a Murderer '06
An American Haunting '05
Peter Pan '03

Elizabeth Hurley (1965-)
Dawg '02
Serving Sara '02
Double Whammy '01
Bedazzled '00
The Weight of Water '00
Austin Powers 2: The Spy Who Shagged Me '99
EDtv '99
My Favorite Martian '98
Permanent Midnight '98
Austin Powers: International Man of Mystery '97
Dangerous Ground '96
Samson and Delilah '96
Shameless '94
Sharpe's Enemy '94
Nightscare '93
Passenger 57 '92
Kill Cruise '90
Christabel '89
Rowing with the Wind '88

Richard Hurndall
Running Blind '78

Brandon Hurst (1866-1947)
Stanley and Livingstone '39
House of Mystery '34
The Lost Patrol '34
Murders in the Rue Morgue '32
The White Zombie '32
Murder at Midnight '31
The Man Who Laughs '27
Made for Love '26
The Thief of Baghdad '24
The Hunchback of Notre Dame '23
Dr. Jekyll and Mr. Hyde '20

David Hurst (1926-)
Kelly's Heroes '70
Tony Draws a Horse '51

Michael Hurst (1957-)
Hercules the Legendary Journeys, Vol. 1: And the Amazon Women '94
Hercules the Legendary Journeys, Vol. 2: The Lost Kingdom '94
Hercules the Legendary Journeys, Vol. 3: The Circle of Fire '94
Hercules the Legendary Journeys, Vol. 4: In the Underworld '94
Desperate Remedies '93
Death Warmed Up '85

Paul Hurst (1888-1953)
Missourians '50
The Vanishing Westerner '50
Outcasts of the Trail '49
Pioneer Marshal '49
Who Killed Doc Robbin? '48
Under Colorado Skies '47
Treasure of Fear '45
Girl Rush '44
Caught in the Draft '41
Bad Lands '39
Gone with the Wind '39
It Could Happen to You '39
Alexander's Ragtime Band '38
Prison Break '38
Legion of Missing Men '37
Hold Your Man '33
The Sphinx '33
The Big Stampede '32
My Pal, the King '32
Panama Flo '32
13th Guest '32
Mountain Justice '30
Paradise Island '30
Battling Bunyon '24

Ryan Hurst (1976-)
The Ladykillers '04
Lone Star State of Mind '02
Taken '02
We Were Soldiers '02

Veronica Hurst (1931-)
Second Best Secret Agent in the Whole Wide World '65
Peeping Tom '60
Angels One Five '54
The Gilded Cage '54

John Hurt (1940-)
Hellboy 2: The Golden Army '08
Indiana Jones and the Kingdom of the Crystal Skull '08
Perfume: The Story of a Murderer '06 (N)
V for Vendetta '06
Manderlay '05
The Proposition '05
Shooting Dogs '05
The Skeleton Key '05
Valiant '05 (V)
Hellboy '04
Dogville '03 (N)
Owning Mahowny '03
Bait '02
Captain Corelli's Mandolin '01
Harry Potter and the Sorcerer's Stone '01
Miranda '01
Lost Souls '00
New Blood '99
All the Little Animals '98
Brute '97
The Climb '97
Contact '97
Love and Death on Long Island '97
Dead Man '95
Rob Roy '95
Wild Bill '95
Even Cowgirls Get the Blues '94
Second Best '94
Thumbelina '94 (V)
Monolith '93
Shades of Fear '93
King Ralph '91
The Field '90
Frankenstein Unbound '90
Little Sweetheart '90
Scandal '89
Aria '88
White Mischief '88
Spaceballs '87
Vincent: The Life and Death of Vincent van Gogh '87 (V)
From the Hip '86
Jake Speed '86
After Darkness '85
The Black Cauldron '85 (V)
The Hit '85
Champions '84
1984 '84
Success Is the Best Revenge '84
The Osterman Weekend '83
Partners '82
The Plague Dogs '82 (V)
Disappearance '81
Heaven's Gate '81
History of the World: Part 1 '81
Night Crossing '81
The Elephant Man '80
Alien '79
The Lord of the Rings '78 (V)
Midnight Express '78
The Shout '78
Watership Down '78 (V)
East of Elephant Rock '76
The Ghoul '75
The Naked Civil Servant '75
Cry of the Penguins '71
10 Rillington Place '71

Mary Beth Hurt (1948-)
Untraceable '08
The Walker '07
The Dead Girl '06
Lady in the Water '06
The Exorcism of Emily Rose '05
Red Dragon '02
Family Man '00
Bringing Out the Dead '99
Affliction '97
From the Journals of Jean Seberg '95
The Age of Innocence '93
My Boyfriend's Back '93
Six Degrees of Separation '93
Light Sleeper '92
Defenseless '91
Parents '89
Slaves of New York '89
Baby Girl Scott '87
Compromising Positions '85
D.A.R.Y.L. '85
The World According to Garp '82
A Change of Seasons '80
Chilly Scenes of Winter '79
Interiors '78

William Hurt (1950-)
The Incredible Hulk '08
Vantage Point '08
Into the Wild '07
Mr. Brooks '07
The Good Shepherd '06
A History of Violence '05
Syriana '05
The Blue Butterfly '04
The Village '04
Changing Lanes '02
Master Spy: The Robert Hanssen Story '02
Tuck Everlasting '02
A.I.: Artificial Intelligence '01
The Contaminated Man '01
The Flamingo Rising '01
Rare Birds '01
Varian's War '01
Dune '00
The Miracle Maker: The Story of Jesus '00 (V)
The Big Brass Ring '99
The 4th Floor '99
Silent Witness '99
The Simian Line '99
Sunshine '99
Lost in Space '98
One True Thing '98
Dark City '97
Loved '97
The Proposition '97
Jane Eyre '96
Michael '96
A Couch in New York '95
Smoke '95
Second Best '94
Trial by Jury '94
Mr. Wonderful '93
The Plague '92
The Doctor '91
Until the End of the World '91
Alice '90
I Love You to Death '90
The Accidental Tourist '88
A Time of Destiny '88
Broadcast News '87
Children of a Lesser God '86
Kiss of the Spider Woman '85
The Big Chill '83
Gorky Park '83
Body Heat '81
Eyewitness '81
Altered States '80

Ferlin Husky (1927-)
Hillbillies in a Haunted House '67
Las Vegas Hillbillys '66

Toby Huss (1966-)
Rescue Dawn '06
Dogs: The Rise and Fall of an All-Girl Bookie Joint '96
Down Periscope '96

Olivia Hussey (1951-)
Headspace '02
Bloody Proof '99
Shame, Shame, Shame '98
Ice Cream Man '95
Quest of the Delta Knights '93
Save Me '93
Undeclared War '91
The Jeweller's Shop '90
Psycho 4: The Beginning '90
Stephen King's It '90
Distortions '87
Ivanhoe '82
Virus '82
Escape 2000 '81
The Man with Bogart's Face '80
The Cat and the Canary '79
The Bastard '78
Death on the Nile '78
Black Christmas '75
Rico '74
H-Bomb '71
Romeo and Juliet '68

Ruth Hussey (1911-2005)
The Facts of Life '60
Stars and Stripes Forever '52
Hill Number One '51
Mr. Music '50
The Great Gatsby '49
The Uninvited '44
Marine Raiders '43
Tender Comrade '43
Northwest Passage '40
The Philadelphia Story '40
Susan and God '40
Another Thin Man '39
The Women '39
Madame X '37

Francis Huster (1947-)
The Dinner Game '98
I Married a Dead Man '82
Another Man, Another Chance '77
Lumiere '76

Anjelica Huston (1951-)
The Darjeeling Limited '07
Martian Child '07
Art School Confidential '06
The Hades Factor '06
Material Girls '06
Seraphim Falls '06
These Foolish Things '06
The Life Aquatic with Steve Zissou '04
Daddy Day Care '03
Kaena: The Prophecy '03 (V)
Blood Work '02
The Man from Elysian Fields '01
Mists of Avalon '01
The Royal Tenenbaums '01
The Golden Bowl '00
Agnes Browne '99
Ever After: A Cinderella Story '98
Phoenix '98
Buffalo 66 '97
Buffalo Girls '95
The Crossing Guard '94
The Perez Family '94
Addams Family Values '93
And the Band Played On '93
Family Pictures '93
Manhattan Murder Mystery '93
The Player '92
The Addams Family '91
The Grifters '90
The Witches '90
Crimes & Misdemeanors '89
Enemies, a Love Story '89
Lonesome Dove '89
A Handful of Dust '88
Mr. North '88
The Dead '87
Gardens of Stone '87
Prizzi's Honor '85
The Cowboy & the Ballerina '84
Ice Pirates '84
This Is Spinal Tap '84
Beauty and the Beast '83
Comic Book Kids '82
The Postman Always Rings Twice '81
The Last Tycoon '76
Hamlet '69

Danny Huston (1962-)
John Adams '08
I Really Hate My Job '07
The Number 23 '07
30 Days of Night '07
Alpha Male '06
Children of Men '06
The Hades Factor '06
Marie Antoinette '06
The Constant Gardener '05
The Proposition '05
The Aviator '04
Birth '04
Silver City '04
21 Grams '03
Time Code '00
Leo Tolstoy's Anna Karenina '96

John Huston (1906-87)
Mr. Corbett's Ghost '90
The Black Cauldron '85 (N)
Lovesick '83
A Minor Miracle '83
Cannery Row '82 (N)
Fatal Attraction '80
The Return of the King '80 (V)
The Visitor '80
Jaguar Lives '79
Winter Kills '79
Wise Blood '79
Battleforce '78
The Hobbit '78 (V)
The Word '78
Angela '77
Tentacles '77
Breakout '75
The Wind and the Lion '75
Chinatown '74
Battle for the Planet of the Apes '73
Man in the Wilderness '71
Ride to Glory '71
Myra Breckinridge '70
Candy '68
Casino Royale '67
The Bible '66 (N)
The Cardinal '63

Virginia Huston (1925-81)
Flight to Mars '52
Night Stage to Galveston '52
Sudden Fear '52
The Doolins of Oklahoma '49
Flamingo Road '49
Out of the Past '47
Nocturne '46

Walter Huston (1884-1950)
December 7th: The Movie '91
Summer Holiday '48
Treasure of the Sierra Madre '48
Duel in the Sun '46
And Then There Were None '45
Dragon Seed '44
Edge of Darkness '43
The North Star '43
The Outlaw '43
In This Our Life '42
The Shanghai Gesture '42
Yankee Doodle Dandy '42
The Devil & Daniel Webster '41
The Maltese Falcon '41
Of Human Hearts '38
Dodsworth '36
Rhodes '36
Transatlantic Tunnel '35
Ann Vickers '33
Gabriel Over the White House '33
The Prizefighter and the Lady '33
American Madness '32
Rain '32
Criminal Code '31
Abraham Lincoln '30
The Virginian '29

Michael Hutchence (1960-97)
Frankenstein Unbound '90
Dogs in Space '87

Josh Hutcherson (1992-)
Journey to the Center of the Earth 3D '08

Bridge to Terabithia '07
Firehouse Dog '07
RV '06
Kicking & Screaming '05
Little Manhattan '05
Zathura '05
Howl's Moving Castle '04 (V)
Miracle Dogs '03

David Hutcheson (1905-76)
The Abominable Dr. Phibes '71
No Highway in the Sky '51
Murder in the Footlights '46

Geoffrey Hutchings (1939-)
It's All About Love '03
Heart of Darkness '93

Will Hutchins (1932-)
Maverick '94
Slumber Party '57 '76
Clambake '67
The Shooting '66
Spinout '66
Merrill's Marauders '62

Eleanor Hutchins
Wish You Were Here '87

Fiona Hutchinson
Rage '95

Josephine Hutchinson (1904-98)
The Adventures of Huckleberry Finn '60
North by Northwest '59
Love Is Better Than Ever '52
Cass Timberlane '47
The Tender Years '47
My Son, My Son! '40
Son of Frankenstein '39
The Story of Louis Pasteur '36

Ken Hutchison (1948-)
Ladyhawke '85
Deadly Strangers '82

Candy Hutson
The Land Before Time 3: The Time of the Great Giving '95 (V)
The Land Before Time 2: The Great Valley Adventure '94 (V)

Doug Hutchison (1960-)
No Good Deed '02
The Salton Sea '02
I Am Sam '01
Bait '00
The Green Mile '99

Marion Hutton (1919-87)
Love Happy '50
In Society '44

Robert Hutton (1920-94)
Cry of the Banshee '70
They Came from Beyond Space '67
Vulture '67
The Slime People '63
Cinderfella '60
Invisible Invaders '59
Naked Youth '59
Showdown at Boot Hill '58
Outcasts of the City '58
Big Bluff '55
The Steel Helmet '51
Slaughter Trail '51
Hollywood Canteen '44
Destination Tokyo '43

Timothy Hutton (1960-)
The Last Mimzy '07
When a Man Falls in the Forest '07
The Good Shepherd '06
Heavens Fall '06
The Kovak Box '06
Last Holiday '06
Stephanie Daley '06
Kinsey '04
Secret Window '04
Sunshine State '02
Deliberate Intent '01
The Doorbell Rang: A Nero Wolfe Mystery '01
Wints of Terror '01
Deterrence '00
The Golden Spiders: A Nero Wolfe Mystery '00
Just One Night '00
The General's Daughter '99
Aldrich Ames: Traitor Within '98
Money Kings '98
Beautiful Girls '96
City of Industry '96
Mr. & Mrs. Loving '96
Playing God '96
The Substance of Fire '96
French Kiss '95
The Last Word '95
The Temp '93
The Dark Half '91
Strangers '91
Q & A '90
Everybody's All American '88
Made in Heaven '87
The Falcon and the Snowman '85
Turk 182! '85
Iceman '84
Daniel '83
A Long Way Home '81
Taps '81
Father Figure '80
Ordinary People '80
And Baby Makes Six '79
Friendly Fire '79
Young Love, First Love '79

William Hutt (1920-2007)

Betty Hutton (1921-2007)
The Greatest Show on Earth '52
Annie Get Your Gun '50
Let's Dance '50
The Perils of Pauline '47
Here Come the Waves '45
The Stork Club '45
Miracle of Morgan's Creek '44
Star Spangled Rhythm '42

Brian Hutton
Last Train from Gun Hill '59
Carnival Rock '57

Jim Hutton (1933-79)
Psychic Killer '75
Nightmare at 43 Hillcrest '74
Don't Be Afraid of the Dark '73
They Call It Murder '71
Bachelor in Paradise '61
The Green Berets '68
Hellfighters '68
Walk, Don't Run '66
The Hallelujah Trail '65
Major Dundee '65
The Honeymoon Machine '61
Sunday in New York '63
The Horizontal Lieutenant '62
Period of Adjustment '62
Where the Boys Are '60

Lauren Hutton (1943-)
Caracara '00
Just a Little Harmless Sex '99
54 '98
A Rat's Tale '98
My Father the Hero '93
Guilty as Charged '92
Missing Pieces '91
Fear '90
Millions '90
Forbidden Sun '89
Scandalous '88
Malone '87
Timestalkers '87
Monte Carlo '86
Trade Secrets '86
From Here to Maternity '85
Once Bitten '85
Scandal Sheet '85
Lassiter '84
The Cradle Will Fall '83
The Snow Queen '83
Starflight One '83
Paternity '81
Zorro, the Gay Blade '81
American Gigolo '79
A Wedding '78
Viva Knievel! '77
Welcome to L.A. '77
Gator '76
Nashville '75
The Gambler '74
Paper Lion '68

Richard Huw
A Certain Justice '99

Jonathan Hyde (1947-)
The Contract '07
Attila '01
The Prince and the Pauper '01
Princess of Thieves '01
Joan of Arc '99
The Mummy '99
Titanic '97
Anaconda '96
Jumanji '95
Richie Rich '94
Fellow Traveler '89
An Indecent Obsession '85

Alex Hyde-White (1958-)
Pursuit of Happiness '01
Silent Victim '92
Unknown Origin '95
Mars '96
Wyatt Earp: Return to Tombstone '94
Pretty Woman '90
Indiana Jones and the Last Crusade '89
The Phantom of the Opera '89
Time Trackers '88
Echoes in the Darkness '87
Biggles '85
The First Olympics: Athens 1896 '84
The Seekers '79

Jacquelyn Hyde (1930-92)
House of Terror '72
Take the Money and Run '69

Pam Hyatt
He Sees You When You're Sleeping '02
Holiday Affair '96

Leila Hyams (1905-77)
Yellow Dust '36
Ruggles of Red Gap '35
Freaks '32
Island of Lost Souls '32
Red Headed Woman '32
The Big House '30
Spite Marriage '29

Martha Hyer (1924-)
The Chase '66
Night of the Grizzly '66
Picture Mommy Dead '66
Sons of Katie Elder '65
The Carpetbaggers '64
First Men in the Moon '64
Bikini Beach '64
Ice Palace '60
The Best of Everything '59
Some Came Running '58
Houseboat '58
Mister Cory '57
Battle Hymn '57
My Man Godfrey '57
Paris Holiday '58
The Delicate Delinquent '56
Francis in the Navy '55
Cry Vengeance '54
Lucky Me '54
Sabrina '54
Scarlet Spear '54
Abbott and Costello Go to Mars '53
Geisha Girl '52

Diana Hyland (1936-77)
The Boy in the Plastic Bubble '76
Hercules and the Princess of Troy '65
One Man's Way '63

Frances Hyland (1927-2004)
When the Dark Man Calls '95
The Lotus Eaters '93
Happy Birthday to Me '81
Home to Stay '79

Scott Hylands (1943-)
Decoy '95
Ordeal in the Arctic '93
Coming Out Alive '84
Savage Hunger '84
The Winds of Kitty Hawk '78
The Boys in Company C '78
Earthquake '74
Slipstream '73
Fools '70
Daddy's Gone A-Hunting '69

Mirta Ibarra
Maria '98
Guantanamera '95
Strawberry and Chocolate '93
Up to a Certain Point '83

Stanislav Ianevski (1985-)
Hostel: Part 2 '07
Harry Potter and the Goblet of Fire '05

Ice Cube (1969-)
First Sunday '08
The Longshots '08
Are We Done Yet? '07
Are We There Yet? '05
XXX: State of the Union '05
Torque '04
Barbershop 2: Back in Business '04
Friday After Next '02
All About the Benjamins '02
Ghosts of Mars '01
Next Friday '00
Thicker than Water '99
Three Kings '99
I Got the Hook-Up '98
The Players Club '98
Dangerous Ground '96
Anaconda '96
The Glass Shield '95
Friday '95
Higher Learning '95
Trespass '92
Boyz N the Hood '91

Ice-T (1958-)
Tracks '05
Air Rage '01
Black Horizon '01
Guardian '01
Kept '01 (V)
'R Xmas '01
Rhapsody '01
3000 Miles to Graceland '01
Ticker '01
Ablaze '00
Luck of the Draw '00
The Guardian '00
Agent of Death '99
Final Voyage '99
Corrupt '99
Judgment Day '99
Leprechaun 5: In the Hood '99
Sonic Impact '99
Stealth Fighter '99
Urban Menace '99
Jacob Two Two Meets the Hooded Fang '99
The Deli '97
Mean Guns '97
Johnny Mnemonic '95
Surviving the Game '94
Tank Girl '94
Who's the Man? '93
Trespass '92
New Jack City '91
Ricochet '91
The Wrecking Crew '99
Crazy Six '98
Body Count '97

Jane Hylton (1925-79)
Circus of Horrors '60
The Manster '59
Dear Murderer '47

Richard Hylton (1920-62)
Fixed Bayonets! '51
The Halls of Montezuma '50

Phyllis Hyman (1949-95)
School Daze '88

Warren Hymer (1906-48)
Hitler: Dead or Alive '43
Baby Face Morgan '42
Lure of the Islands '42
Meet the Mob '42
Mr. Wise Guy '42
Phantom Killer '42
Birth of the Blues '41
Mr. Moto in Danger Island '39
Joy of Living '38
You and Me '38
Sea Racketeers '37
You Only Live Once '37
Rhythm on the Range '36
San Francisco '36
Confidential '35
Hong Kong Nights '35
Show Them No Mercy '35
In the Money '34
Badmen of Nevada '33
The Mysterious Rider '33
One Way Passage '32
The Lone Star Ranger '30
Up the River '30

Joyce Hyser (1956-)
Wedding Band '89
Just One of the Guys '85
The Hollywood Knights '80

Steve Hytner
Eurotrip '04
Forces of Nature '99
Love Stinks '99
The Prophecy 3: The Ascent '99
The Prophecy 2: Ashtown '97

Etsuko Ichihara (1936-)
The Eel '96
Black Rain '88
Snow Country '57

Raizo Ichikawa (1931-69)
Sleepy Eyes of Death: The Chinese Jade '63
Enjo '58
Shin Heike Monogatari '55

Utaemon Ichikawa (1904-99)
47 Ronin, Part 1 '42
47 Ronin, Part 2 '42

Eric Idle (1943-)
Shrek the Third '07 (V)
Ella Enchanted '04 (V)
Hollywood Homicide '03
National Lampoon's Christmas Vacation 2: Cousin Eddie's Big Island Adventure '03
Pinocchio '02 (V)
102 Dalmatians '00
South Park: Bigger, Longer and Uncut '99 (V)
Dudley Do-Right '99
An Alan Smithee Film: Burn, Hollywood, Burn '97
Quest for Camelot '98 (V)
Mr. Toad's Wild Ride '96
Casper '95
Splitting Heirs '93
The Adventures of Baron Munchausen '89
Around the World in 80 Days '89
Transformers: The Movie '86 (V)
National Lampoon's European Vacation '85
The Pied Piper of Hamelin '84
Monty Python's The Meaning of Life '83
Yellowbeard '83
Secret Policeman's Private Parts '81
Monty Python's Life of Brian '79
All You Need Is Cash '78
Jabberwocky '77
Monty Python and the Holy Grail '75
And Now for Something Completely Different '72

Cinnamon Idles (1975-)
Sixteen Candles '84
Kidco '83

Billy Idol (1955-)
Heavy Metal 2000 '00 (V)
The Wedding Singer '97
Trigger Happy '96

Rhys Ifans (1968-)
Elizabeth: The Golden Age '07
Hannibal Rising '07
Four Last Songs '06
Garfield: A Tail of Two Kitties '06 (V)
Enduring Love '04
Vanity Fair '04
Danny Deckchair '03
Human Nature '02
Once Upon a Time in the Midlands '02
Formula 51 '01
Hotel '01
Girl 6 '96
Kevin & Perry Go Large '00
Little Nicky '00
Love, Honour & Obey '00
Rancid Aluminium '00
The Replacements '00
Heart '99
Janice Beard '99
Notting Hill '99
Dancing at Lughnasa '98
Twin Town '97

Hisashi Igawa (1936-)
Hiroshima '95
Rhapsody in August '91
Akira Kurosawa's Dreams '90
Boiling Point '90
Ran '85
Harakiri '62

Togo Igawa (1946-)
The Last Samurai '03
Incognito '97

James Iglehart
Death Force '78
Fighting Mad '77
Savage! '73
Angels Hard As They Come '71

Igor Ilyinsky (1904-87)
A Kiss for Mary Pickford '27
The Cigarette Girl of Mosselprom '24

Iman (1955-)
The Deli '97
Exit to Eden '94
Heart of Darkness '93
The Linguini Incident '92
House Party 2: The Pajama Jam '91
L.A. Story '91
Lies of the Twins '91
Star Trek 6: The Undiscovered Country '91
No Way Out '87
Surrender '87
Out of Africa '85
The Human Factor '79

Roger Imhof (1875-1958)
Sweetheart of the Navy '37
Red Lights Ahead '36

San Francisco '36
Life Begins at Forty '35
Riff Raff '35
Steamboat Round the Bend '35
David Harum '34
Hoopla '33

Gary Imhoff (1952-)
Thumbelina '94 (V)
The Seniors '78

Michael Imperioli (1966-)
For One More Day '07
My Baby's Daddy '04
Shark Tale '04 (V)
Love in the Time of Money '02
Hamlet '01
Disappearing Acts '00
Witness to the Mob '98
Office Killer '97
A River Made to Drown In '97
I Shot Andy Warhol '96
Last Man Standing '96
Sweet Nothing '96
The Addiction '95
Bad Boys '95
The Basketball Diaries '95
Postcards from America '95
Household Saints '93
Jungle Fever '91
Goodfellas '90

Celia Imrie (1952-)
Imagine Me & You '06
Nanny McPhee '06
Wah-Wah '05
Calendar Girls '03
Doctor Zhivago '03
Daniel Deronda '02
Lucky Break '01
Station Jim '01
A Christmas Carol '99
Hilary and Jackie '98
The Borrowers '97
Into the Blue '97
A Midwinter's Tale '95
Mary Shelley's Frankenstein '94
The Return of the Native '94
A Dark Adapted Eye '93

Yoshio Inaba (1921-98)
Harakiri '62
Seven Samurai '54

Francesca Inaudi (1977-)
Don't Tell '05
After Midnight '04

Ada Ince (1913-)
Rainbow's End '35
The Fighting Rookie '34
Frontier Days '34

Ralph Ince (1887-1937)
Law of the Sea '32
Lost Squadron '32
Men of America '32
State's Attorney '31

Frieda Inescort (1901-76)
A Place in the Sun '51
The Underworld Story '50
The Judge Steps Out '49
The Amazing Mrs. Holiday '43

Pride and Prejudice '40
Beauty for the Asking '39
Tarzan Finds a Son '39
The Dark Angel '35

Eddie Infante
Ethan '71
Warkill '65

Marty Ingels (1936-)
Cavalry Command '63
Round Numbers '91
Instant Karma '90
How to Seduce a Woman '74
If It's Tuesday, This Must Be Belgium '69

Mariah Inger
Lost Junction '03

Randi Ingerman (1967-)
Screw Loose '99
Let's Talk About Sex '98
Desperate Crimes '93
Deadly Rivals '92

Barrie Ingham (1934-)
Josh Kirby... Time Warrior: Chapter 5, Journey to the Magic Cavern '96
Josh Kirby... Time Warrior: Chapter 6, Last Battle for the Universe '96
Josh Kirby... Time Warrior: Chapter 3, Trapped on Toyworld '95
Josh Kirby... Time Warrior: Chapter 4, Eggs from 70 Million B.C. '95
The Great Mouse Detective '86 (V)
A Challenge for Robin Hood '68
Invasion 65

John Ingle
The Land Before Time 5: The Mysterious Island '97 (V)
The Land Before Time 4: Journey Through the Mists '96 (V)
The Land Before Time 3: The Time of the Great Giving '95 (V)
The Land Before Time 2: The Great Valley Adventure '94 (V)

Lee Ingleby (1976-)
Master and Commander: The Far Side of the World '03
Borstal Boy '00

Lloyd Ingraham (1885-1956)
The Caravan Trail '46
Partners of the Trail '44
Range Law '44
Park Avenue Logger '37
Everyman's Law '36
Red River Valley '36
Stormy Trails '36
Undercover Man '36
Between Men '35
Ghost Rider '35
Go-Get-'Em-Haines '35
Rider of the Law '35
Sons of Steel '35
Trail of Terror '35
Peck's Bad Boy '34

Jack Ingram (1902-69)
Texas Gunfighter '32
Lost in Alaska '52
Frontier Fugitives '45
Boss of Rawhide '44
Devil Riders '44
Frontier Outlaws '44
Guns of the Law '44
Oath of Vengeance '44
Outlaw Roundup '44
Range Law '44
Thundering Gunslingers '44
Frontier Law '43
Raiders of Sunset Pass '43
Arizona Roundup '42
The Mysterious Rider '42
Sheriff of Tombstone '41
Ridin' the Trail '40
Wyoming Outlaw '39
Valley of Terror '38

The Rangers Step In '37
Wild Horse Rodeo '37
Whistling Bullets '36

Rex Ingram (1892-1950)
Elmer Gantry '60
The Smallest Show on Earth '48
A Thousand and One Nights '45
Dark Waters '44
Cabin in the Sky '43
Sahara '43
Talk of the Town '42
The Thief of Bagdad '40
The Adventures of Huckleberry Finn '39
Green Pastures '36

Frankie Ingrassia
Election '99
The Positively True Adventures of the Alleged Texas Cheerleader-Murdering Mom '93

Valeri Inkizhinov (1895-1973)
Samson and the 7 Miracles of the World '62
Journey to the Lost City '58
Storm over Asia '28

George Innes (1938-)
Master and Commander: The Far Side of the World '03
Agatha Christie's A Caribbean Mystery '83
Ivanhoe '82
Archer: The Fugitive from the Empire '81
Danger UXB '81

Laura Innes
Deep Impact '98
Just Like Dad '96

Neil Innes (1944-)
Erik the Viking '89
Monty Python's Life of Brian '79
All You Need Is Cash '78
Jabberwocky '77
Monty Python and the Holy Grail '75
Magical Mystery Tour '67

Harold Innocent (1933-93)
Fergie & Andrew: Behind Palace Doors '93
Robin Hood: Prince of Thieves '91
Henry V '89

Annie Shizuka Inoh (1969-)
8 1/2 Women '99
Flowers of Shanghai '98
Goodbye South, Goodbye '96

Tino Insana (1948-)
The Masters of Menace '90
Wedding Band '89

Antonella Interlenghi (1960-)
New York Ripper '82
Gates of Hell '80

Franco Interlenghi (1931-)
I Vitelloni '53
The Wayward Wife '52
Shoeshine '47

Steve Inwood (1947-)
The Human Shield '92
Hurry Up or I'll Be Thirty '73

Aharon Ipale (1941-)
The Mummy '99
A Kid in Aladdin's Palace '97
Invisible: The Chronicles of Benjamin Knight '93
Tragedy of Flight 103: The Inside Story '91
One Man Out '89
Too Hot to Handle '76

Michael Irby
Flightplan '05
Pinero '01

Jill Ireland (1936-90)
Assassination '87
Death Wish 2 '82
Love and Bullets '79
Breakheart Pass '76
From Noon Till Three '76
Breakout '75
Chino '75
Hard Times '75
The Mechanic '72
Cold Sweat '71
Someone Behind the Door '71
The Family '70
Rider on the Rain '70
Villa Rides '68

John Ireland (1914-92)
Waxwork 2: Lost in Time '91
Messenger of Death '88
Miami Horror '87
Tales of the Klondike: Race for Number One '87
Flying from the Hawk '86
Thunder Run '86
Martin's Day '85
The Treasure of the Amazon '84
Incubus '82
Kavik the Wolf Dog '80
Marilyn: The Untold Story '80
Mission to Glory '80
Bordello '79
Crossbar '79
Midnight Auto Supply '78
Delta Fox '77
Maniac '77
Perfect Killer '77
Satan's Cheerleaders '77
Tomorrow Never Comes '77
Farewell, My Lovely '75
The House of Seven Corpses '73
Escape to the Sun '72
Northeast of Seoul '72
Dirty Heroes '71
The Adventurers '70
Challenge of McKenna '70
Dead for a Dollar '70
Diary of a Rebel '68
Taste of Death '68
Arizona Bushwackers '67
The Fall of the Roman Empire '64
55 Days at Peking '63
Wild in the Country '61
Spartacus '60
Black Tide '58
Party Girl '58
Gunfight at the O.K. Corral '57
The Gunslinger '56
Glass Tomb '55
Queen Bee '55
The Fast and the Furious '54
The Bushwackers '52
Little Big Horn '51
Vengeance Valley '51
Return of Jesse James '50
The Doolins of Oklahoma '49
All the King's Men '49
I Shot Jesse James '49
Joan of Arc '48
Open Secret '48
Raw Deal '48
Red River '48
A Southern Yankee '48
The Gangster '47
Railroaded '47
My Darling Clementine '46
A Walk in the Sun '46

Kathy Ireland (1963-)
Miami Hustle '95
Backfire! '94
Amore! '93
National Lampoon's Loaded Weapon 1 '93
Mom and Dad Save the World '92
The Player '92
Necessary Roughness '91
Mr. Destiny '90
Side Out '90
Alien from L.A. '87

Vincent Irizarry (1959-)
Heartbreak Ridge '86
Marie '85

Jeremy Irons (1948-)
Eragon '06
Inland Empire '06
Casanova '05
Elizabeth I '05
Kingdom of Heaven '05
Being Julia '04
The Merchant of Venice '04
And Now Ladies and Gentlemen '02
Callas Forever '02
Last Call: The Final Chapter of F. Scott Fitzgerald '02
The Time Machine '02
The Fourth Angel '01
Dungeons and Dragons '00
Longitude '00
The Man in the Iron Mask '98
Chinese Box '97
Lolita '97
Stealing Beauty '96
Die Hard: With a Vengeance '95
The Lion King '94 (V)
The House of the Spirits '93
M. Butterfly '93
Damage '92
Waterland '92
Kafka '91
Reversal of Fortune '90
A Chorus of Disapproval '89
Dead Ringers '88
The Mission '86
Swann in Love '84
The Wild Duck '84
Betrayal '83
Moonlighting '82
Brideshead Revisited '81
The French Lieutenant's Woman '81
Nijinsky '80
Love for Lydia '79

Michael Ironside (1950-)
The Veteran '05
Deepwater '05
Masters of Horror: The V Word '05
The Machinist '04
Children of the Corn: Revelation '01
Extreme Honor '01
Ignition '01
Mindstorm '01
The Shaft '01
Cause of Death '00
Crime and Punishment in Suburbia '00
Heavy Metal 2000 '00 (V)
Nuremberg '00
The Perfect Storm '00
Beyond Redemption '99
Johnny 2.0 '99
The Omega Code '99
Blacklight '98
Blood Money '98
Chicago Cab '98
Bomb Squad '97
Captive '97
Ivory Tower '97
Starship Troopers '97
The Destiny of Marty Fine '96
Kids of the Round Table '96
Robin Cook's Terminal '96
Too Fast, Too Young '96
The Glass Shield '95
One Way Out '95
Portraits of a Killer '95
Probable Cause '95
Fortunes of War '94
The Killing Man '94
Rebel Run '94
Red Scorpion 2 '94
Red Sun Rising '94
Tokyo Cowboy '94
Dead Man's Revenge '93
Father Hood '93
Forced to Kill '93

Mardi Gras for the Devil '93
Point of Impact '93
Save Me '93
Sweet Killing '93
Black Ice '92
Guncrazy '92
Killer Image '92
The Vagrant '92
Common Bonds '91
Highlander 2: The Quickening '91
Deadly Surveillance '91
Murder by Night '89
Mindfield '89
Hostile Takeover '88
Surrogate '88
Watchers '88
Extreme Prejudice '87
Ford: The Man & the Machine '87
Hello Mary Lou: Prom Night 2 '87
Top Gun '86
The Falcon and the Snowman '85
Murder in Space '85
Coming Out Alive '84
V: The Final Battle '84
Cross Country '83
Nowhere to Hide '83
Spacehunter: Adventures in the Forbidden Zone '83
Visiting Hours '82
American Nightmare '81
Scanners '81
The Family Man '79
Hot Rod '07

Brittney Irvin (1984-)
National Lampoon's Snow White: The Fairest of Them All '02
Exposed '03

Amy Irving (1953-)
Hide and Seek '05
Tuck Everlasting '02
Thirteen Conversations About One Thing '01
Traffic '00
Blue Ridge Fall '99
Bossa Nova '99
The Rage: Carrie 2 '99
One Tough Cop '98
The Confession '98
Deconstructing Harry '97
I'm Not Rappaport '96
Carried Away '95
Kleptomania '94
Benefit of the Doubt '93
An American Tail: Fievel Goes West '91 (V)
A Show of Force '90
The Turn of the Screw '89
Crossing Delancey '88
Who Framed Roger Rabbit '88 (V)
Anastasia: The Mystery of Anna '86
Rumpelstiltskin '86
Heartbreak House '86
The Far Pavilions '84
Micki & Maude '84
Yentl '83
The Competition '80
Honeysuckle Rose '80
The Fury '78
Carrie '76
James Dean '76
Dynasty '76

George Irving (1874-1961)
Sergeant York '41
The Abe Lincoln of Ninth Avenue '39
Maid's Night Out '38
The Mandarin Mystery '37
Captain January '36
Touchdown '31
The Divorcee '30
Coquette '29

Margaret Irving (1898-1988)
In Society '44
San Francisco '36

Animal Crackers '30

Penny Irving (1950-)
House of Whipcord '75
Big Zapper '73

Bill Irwin (1950-)
Lady in the Water '06
Dr. Seuss' How the Grinch Stole Christmas '00
William Shakespeare's A Midsummer Night's Dream '99
Illuminata '98
Just the Ticket '98
Subway Stories '97
Silent Tongue '92
Hot Shots '91
Scenes from a Mall '91
Stepping Out '91

Tom Irwin (1956-)
Exposed '03
Snow White: The Fairest of Them All '02
The Sandy Bottom Orchestra '00
Holiday Affair '96
My Very Best Friend '96
Mr. Jones '93
Deceived '91
Ladykiller '92

Steve Irwin (1962-2006)
The Crocodile Hunter: Collision Course '02
Happy Feet '06 (V)

Boyd Irwin (1880-1957)
Madam Satan '30
The Three Musketeers '21

January Isaac
Doomsdayer '01

Oscar Isaac
The Nativity Story '06

Jason Isaacs (1963-)
Harry Potter and the Order of the Phoenix '07
Friends with Money '06
The State Within '06
The Chumscrubber '05
Harry Potter and the Goblet of Fire '05
Nine Lives '05
Peter Pan '03
Harry Potter and the Chamber of Secrets '02
The Tuxedo '02
Windtalkers '02
Black Hawk Down '01
Hotel '01
The Last Minute '01
Sweet November '01
The Patriot '00
The End of the Affair '99
Armageddon '98
The Last Don 2 '98
St. Ives '98
Soldier '98
Event Horizon '97
Dragonheart '96
Solitaire for 2 '94

Chris Isaak (1956-)
A Dirty Shame '04
Blue Ridge Fall '99
From the Earth to the Moon '98
Grace of My Heart '96
That Thing You Do! '96
Little Buddha '93
Twin Peaks: Fire Walk with Me '92
Married to the Mob '88

Margarita Isabel
Lucia, Lucia '03
Cronos '94

Katharine Isabelle (1982-)
Everything's Gone Green '06
Ginger Snaps Back: The Beginning '04
Ginger Snaps: Unleashed '04
Show Me '04
Freddy vs. Jason '03
Carrie '02
Due East '02
Insomnia '02
Bones '01
Ginger Snaps '01

Tom Isbell (1957-)
Behind Enemy Lines '86
A Case of Deadly Force '86

Ryo Ishibashi (1956-)
War '07
The Grudge '04
Gozu '03
Suicide Club '02
Audition '99

Takaaki Ishibashi (1961-)
Major League 3: Back to the Minors '98
Major League 2 '94

Akira Ishihama (1935-)
The Summer of Ben Tyler '98
Harakiri '62

Dale Ishimoto (1923-2004)
The Human Condition: No Greater Love '58

Hisaya Ito (1938-)
Godzilla vs. Mothra '64
Monster '65
Mothra '62

Robert Ito (1931-)
Destroy All Monsters '68
Ghidrah the Three Headed Monster '65

Emilo Ito (1946-)
Ghidrah the Three Headed Monster '65
Mothra '62

Juzo Itami (1933-97)
MacArthur's Children '85
The Family Game '83

Ravil Isyanov
The Good German '06
K-19: The Widowmaker '02
Octopus '00
Doomsday Man '99

Gregory Itzin (1948-)
I Know Who Killed Me '07
DC 9/11: Time of Crisis '04
Life or Something Like It '02

Jose Iturbi (1895-1980)
That Midnight Kiss '49
Three Daring Daughters '48
Holiday in Mexico '46
Anchors Aweigh '45
Two Girls and a Sailor '44

Yumi Ito (1946-)
Godzilla vs. Mothra '64
Monster '65
Mothra '62

Yunosuke Ito (1919-80)
The Burmese Harp '56
Ikiru '52

Toshiya Ito (1947-)
Ran '85
The Omega Code '99
The Adventures of Buckaroo Banzai Across the Eighth Dimension '84
Midway '76
Women of the Prehistoric Planet '66

Burt Ives (1909-95)
Two Moon Junction '88
Poor Little Rich Girl: The Barbara Hutton Story '87
Uphill All the Way '85
The Ewok Adventure '84 (V)
Roots '77
Baker's Hawk '76
Hugo the Hippo '76 (V)
The McMasters '70
Those Fantastic Flying Fools '67
Ensign Pulver '64
The Brass Bottle '63
Summer Magic '63
The Day of the Outlaw '59
Our Man in Havana '59
The Big Country '58
Cat on a Hot Tin Roof '58
Desire Under the Elms '58
East of Eden '54
So Dear to My Heart '49
Station West '48

Victor Izay (1923-2003)
The Delicate Delinquent '56

Robert Ivers (1934-2003)
G.I. Blues '60

Evolution '01
Original Sin '01
Fly Boy '99
Goal! The Dream Begins '06

Marcel Iures (1951-)
The Cave '05
Layer Cake '05
Amen '02
Hart's War '02
The Peacemaker '97

Rosalind Ivan (1880-1959)
The Corn Is Green '45

Zeljko Ivanek (1957-)
John Adams '08
The Manchurian Candidate '04
The Reagans '04
Dogville '03
Unfaithful '02
Black Hawk Down '01
Hannibal '01
Homicide: The Movie '00
Dancer in the Dark '00
A Civil Action '98
From the Earth to the Moon '98
The Rat Pack '98
Donnie Brasco '96
Courage Under Fire '96
White Squall '96
Infinity '96
My Brother's Keeper '95
School Ties '92
Echoes in the Darkness '87
Rachel River '87
Mass Appeal '84
The Sender '82

Mark Ivanir (1968-)
The Good Shepherd '06
Schindler's List '93

Stan Ivar
High Stakes '89
Creature '85

Terri Ivens (1967-)
Trancers 5: Sudden Death '94
Trancers 4: Jack of Swords '93

Daniel Ivernel (1920-99)
High Heels '72
Diary of a Chambermaid '64

Dana Ivey (1942-)
Rush Hour 3 '07
A Very Serious Person '06

Legally Blonde 2: Red, White & Blonde '03
Orange County '02
Two Weeks Notice '02
Mumford '99
Simon Birch '98
The Impostors '98
Sabrina '95
Addams Family Values '93
The Adventures of Huck Finn '93
The Scarlet Letter '95
Home Alone 2: Lost in New York '92
The Addams Family '91
Dirty Rotten Scoundrels '88
Explorers '85

Judith Ivey (1951-)
Pictures of Hollis Woods '07
Flags of Our Fathers '06
Washington Square '97
Without Limits '97
In Country '89
Everybody Wins '90
Miles from Home '88
Hello Again '87
Sister, Sister '87
Brighton Beach Memoirs '86
The Long, Hot Summer '86
Compromising Positions '85
Harry & Son '84
The Woman in Red '84
Piaf '81
There Goes the Neighborhood '92
Love Hurts '91
We Are the Children '87

Bob Ivy
Bubba Ho-Tep '03
Phantasm 4: Oblivion '98

Moshe Ivgi (1953-)
Munich '05
Cup Final '92

Tommy "T.V." Ivo (1936-)
Belles on Their Toes '52

Victor Izay (1923-2003)
The Trial of Billy Jack '74
Billy Jack '71

Eddie Izzard (1962-)
The Chronicles of Narnia: Prince Caspian '08
Ocean's Thirteen '07
My Super Ex-Girlfriend '06
The Wild '06 (V)
Romance & Cigarettes '05
Ocean's Twelve '04
All the Queen's Men '02
The Cat's Meow '01
Circus '00
The Criminal '00
Shadow of the Vampire '00
Mystery Men '99

Shima Iwashita (1941-)
Gonza the Spearman '86
MacArthur's Children '85
Double Suicide '69
Red Lion '69
An Autumn Afternoon '62
Harakiri '62

The Avengers '98
Velvet Goldmine '98

Ja Rule (1976-)
Assault on Precinct 13 '05
Back in the Day '05
The Cookout '04
Scary Movie 3 '03
Half Past Dead '02
The Fast and the Furious '01
Turn It Up '00

Michael Jace (1965-)
Cradle 2 the Grave '03
Planet of the Apes '01
The Replacements '00
Thick as Thieves '99
Boogie Nights '97
Bombshell '97
The Fan '96
The Great White Hype '96
Strange Days '95
Forrest Gump '94

Jackee (1956-)
You Got Served '04
Ladybugs '92
The Women of Brewster Place '89

Ian Jacklin
American Streetfighter '96
Capital Punishment '96
Warrior of Justice '96
Death Match '94
Expert Weapon '93
Kickboxer 3: The Art of War '92

Hugh Jackman (1968-)
Deception '08
Scoop '06
X-Men: The Last Stand '06
The Prestige '06
The Fountain '06
Flushed Away '06 (V)
Happy Feet '06 (V)
Van Helsing '04
X2: X-Men United '03
Kate & Leopold '01
Someone Like You '01
Swordfish '01
X-Men '00
Erskinville Kings '99
Paperback Hero '99

Bo Jackson (1962-)
The Chamber '96

Brandon T. Jackson (1975-)
Tropic Thunder '08
Roll Bounce '05

Curtis "50 Cent" Jackson (1975-)
Home of the Brave '06
Get Rich or Die Tryin' '05

Anne Jackson (1926-)
Rescuers: Stories of Courage "Two Women" '97
Folks! '92
Funny About Love '90
Out on a Limb '87
Sam's Son '84
Blood Debts '83
Blinded by the Light '82
A Woman Called Golda '82
Leave 'Em Laughing '81
The Shining '80
The Bell Jar '79
The Family Man '79
Nasty Habits '77
The Angel Levine '70
Lovers and Other Strangers '70
Tall Story '60

Andrew Jackson (1962-)
Merlin's Apprentice '06
Category 6: Day of Destruction '04
We'll Meet Again '02
Bram Stoker's Shadowbuilder '98
The Last Don 2 '98
Family of Cops 2: Breach of Faith '97
Twists of Terror '96
Specimen '97

Get Rich or Die Tryin' '05

Eugene Jackson (1916-2001)
Shenandoah '65
Red River Valley '36

Freda Jackson (1909-90)
The Valley of Gwangi '69
Die, Monster, Die! '65
The Brides of Dracula '60
Bhowani Junction '56
Beware of Pity '46
Great Expectations '46
Henry V '44

Glenda Jackson (1936-)
King of the Wind '93
A Murder of Quality '90
Strange Interlude '90
The Rainbow '89
Business As Usual '88
Salome's Last Dance '88
Beyond Therapy '86
Turtle Diary '86
Sakharov '84
And Nothing But the Truth '82
Return of the Soldier '82
Hopscotch '80
Lost and Found '79
The Class of Miss MacMichael '78
House Calls '78
Stevie '78
Nasty Habits '77
Triple Echo '77
The Incredible Sarah '76
Hedda '75
Romantic Englishwoman '75

Gordon Jackson (1923-90)
Noble House '88
Gunpowder '87
The Whistle Blower '87
My Brother Tom '86
A Town Like Alice '85
Hamlet '69
The Fighting Prince of Donegal '66
The Ipcress File '65
Those Magnificent Men in Their Flying Machines '65
The Great Escape '63
Abandon Ship '57
The Baby and the Battleship '56
Death Goes to School '53
Against the Wind '48
Whiskey Galore '48
Pink String and Sealing Wax '45
Nine Men '43

Howard Jackson (1900-66)
The Foreman Went to France '42

Janet Jackson (1966-)
Tyler Perry's Why Did I Get Married? '07
Nutty Professor 2: The Klumps '00
Poetic Justice '93

Jenie Jackson (1921-76)
How Sweet It Is! '68
Ride the High Country '62

Jeremy Jackson (1980-)
Ring of Darkness '04
Baywatch the Movie: Forbidden Paradise '95

John M. Jackson (1950-)
The Invasion '07
The Spitfire Grill '95
Roswell: The U.F.O. Cover-Up '94
An American Story '92
A Thousand Heroes '92
Career Opportunities '91
Love, Lies and Murder '91
Switched at Birth '91
Eve of Destruction '90
Sudie & Simpson '90
Cold Sassy Tree '89
Ginger Ale Afternoon '89
The Hitcher '86

Jonathan Jackson (1982-)
Dirty Dancing: Havana Nights '04
Riding the Bullet '04
Insomnia '02
Tuck Everlasting '02
On the Edge '00
Skeletons in the Closet '00
The Deep End of the Ocean '98
Double Play '96
Camp Nowhere '94

Joshua Jackson (1978-)
Shutter '08
Aurora Borealis '06
Bobby '06
Americano '05
Racing Stripes '05 (V)
Venom '05
Cursed '04
I Love Your Work '03
Lone Star State of Mind '02
Ocean's Eleven '01
The Safety of Objects '01
The Skulls '00
Gossip '99
Cruel Intentions '98
Urban Legend '98
Apt Pupil '97
Ronnie and Julie '97
D3: The Mighty Ducks '96
Magic in the Water '95
Robin of Locksley '95
Andre '94
Digger '94
The Mighty Ducks '92

Kate Jackson (1949-)
Miracle Dogs '03
Panic in the Skies '96
Adrift '93
Homewrecker '92 (V)
Loverboy '89
Listen to Your Heart '83
Making Love '82
Dirty Tricks '81
Thunder and Lightning '77
Death at Love House '75
Death Scream '75
Death Cruise '74
Satan's School for Girls '73
Night of Dark Shadows '71

Leonard Jackson (1928-)
Basket Case 2 '90
Ganja and Hess '73

Linda Jackson
Black Bikers from Hell '70
The Outlaw Bikers—Gang Wars '70

Mary Jackson (1910-2005)
A Family Thing '96
Skinned Alive '89
Terror at Red Wolf Inn '72
Targets '68

Mel Jackson (1970-)
Deliver Us from Eva '03
Motives '03
Little Richard '00
Uninvited Guest '99
Soul Food '97

Michael Jackson (1958-)
The Wiz '78

Neil Jackson
The Thirst '06
Alexander '04

Peter Jackson (1961-)
Hot Fuzz '07
Dead Alive '93
Bad Taste '88

Philip Jackson (1948-)
The Intended '02
Little Voice '98
Girls' Night '97
Brassed Off '96
Bad Behavior '92
High Hopes '88

Reggie Jackson (1946-)
The Benchwarmers '06
BASEketball '98
Richie Rich '94
The Naked Gun: From the Files of Police Squad '88

Richard Lee Jackson (1979-)
Love's Long Journey '05
Bring It On Again '03
Hope Ranch '02
Madison '01

Sammy Jackson (1937-95)
Shame, Shame on the Bixby Boys '82
Fastest Guitar Alive '68
None But the Brave '65

Samuel L. Jackson (1948-)
Iron Man '08
Jumper '08
Black Snake Moan '07
Cleaner '07
1408 '07
Resurrecting the Champ '07
Freedomland '06
Home of the Brave '06
Snakes on a Plane '06
Coach Carter '05
The Man '05
Star Wars: Episode 3—Revenge of the Sith '05
XXX: State of the Union '05
In My Country '04
The Incredibles '04 (V)
Kill Bill Vol. 2 '04
Twisted '04
Basic '03
S.W.A.T. '03
Changing Lanes '02
No Good Deed '02
Star Wars: Episode 2—Attack of the Clones '02
XXX '02
The Caveman's Valentine '01
Formula 51 '01
Rules of Engagement '00
Shaft '00
Unbreakable '00
Deep Blue Sea '99
Star Wars: Episode 1—The Phantom Menace '99
The Negotiator '98
Out of Sight '98
The Red Violin '98
Eve's Bayou '97
Jackie Brown '97
187 '97
Sphere '97
The Great White Hype '96
Hard Eight '96
The Long Kiss Goodnight '96
The Search for One-Eyed Jimmy '96
A Time to Kill '96
Tree's Lounge '96
Die Hard: With a Vengeance '95
Fluke '95 (V)
Against the Wall '94
Assault at West Point: The Court-Martial of Johnson Whittaker '94
Fresh '94
Hail Caesar '94
Kiss of Death '94
Losing Isaiah '94
The New Age '94
Pulp Fiction '94
Amos and Andrew '93
Jurassic Park '93
Menace II Society '93
National Lampoon's Loaded Weapon 1 '93
True Romance '93
Fathers and Sons '92
Johnny Suede '92
Juice '92
Jumpin' at the Boneyard '92
Patriot Games '92
White Sands '92
Jungle Fever '91
Betsy's Wedding '90
Def by Temptation '90
Goodfellas '90
Mo' Better Blues '90
Return of Superfly '90
Dead Man Out '89
Coming to America '88
School Daze '88
Ragtime '81

Selmer Jackson (1888-1971)
The Gallant Hours '60
We're Not Married '52
Pitfall '48
Guadalcanal Diary '43
The Fighting Sullivans '42
Gangs, Inc. '41
International Lady '41
Sergeant York '41
They Died with Their Boots On '41
Brigham Young: Frontiersman '40
Johnny Apollo '40
The Thirteenth Man '37
Alibi Ike '35

Sherry Jackson (1942-)
Daughters of the Dust '91
Stingray '78
Bare Knuckles '77
Cotter '72
The Adventures of Huckleberry Finn '60
Trouble along the Way '53
Miracle of Our Lady of Fatima '52

Stoney Jackson (1960-)
Trippin' '99
Black Scorpion 2: Ground Zero '96
The Disappearance of Kevin Johnson '95
Up Against the Wall '91
Sweet Perfection '90
Knights of the City '85
Streets of Fire '84
Roller Boogie '79

Tom Jackson (1948-)
Skinwalkers '07
Grizzly Falls '99
Medicine River '94
Spirit Rider '93

Victoria Jackson (1959-)
Midnight Clear '06
Shut Up and Kiss Me '05
Wedding Bell Blues '96
The Undercover Kid '95 (V)
Based on an Untrue Story '93
I Love You to Death '90
Dream a Little Dream '89
Family Business '89
UHF '89
Casual Sex? '88
Baby Boom '87
The Pick-Up Artist '87
Stoogemania '85

Catherine Jacob (1956-)
Who Killed Bambi? '03
The Green House '96
Tatie Danielle '91

Irene Jacob (1966-)
The Big Brass Ring '99
Spy Games '99
My Life So Far '98
U.S. Marshals '98
Incognito '97
Beyond the Clouds '95
Othello '95
Victory '95
Trois Couleurs: Rouge '94
Trusting Beatrice '92
The Double Life of Veronique '91
Au Revoir les Enfants '87

Derek Jacobi (1938-)
The Golden Compass '07
Nanny McPhee '06
Pinochet's Last Stand '06
Underworld: Evolution '05
The Gathering Storm '02
Two Men Went to War '02
The Body '01
Gladiator '00
Up at the Villa '00
The Wyvern Mystery '00
Molokai: The Story of Father Damien '99
Basil '98
Love is the Devil '98
Hamlet '96
Breaking the Code '95
Circle of Deceit '94
Dead Again '91
Henry V '89
Little Dorrit, Film 1: Nobody's Fault '88
Little Dorrit, Film 2: Little Dorrit's Story '88
The Tenth Man '88
The Secret Garden '87
Cyrano de Bergerac '85
Philby, Burgess and MacLean: Spy Scandal of the Century '84
Enigma '82
Inside the Third Reich '82 (V)
The Secret of NIMH '82 (V)
The Human Factor '79
The Medusa Touch '78
The Odessa File '74
Blue Blood '73
The Day of the Jackal '73
The Strauss Family '73
Othello '65

Ernst Jacobi (1933-)
Hamsun '96
Germany, Pale Mother '80

Lou Jacobi (1913-)
I.Q. '94
I Don't Buy Kisses Anymore '92
Avalon '90
Amazon Women on the Moon '87
The Boss' Wife '86
My Favorite Year '82
Arthur '81
Chu Chu & the Philly Flash '81
Off Your Rocker '80
Better Late Than Never '79
The Magician of Lublin '79
Roseland '77
Next Stop, Greenwich Village '76
Everything You Always Wanted to Know about Sex (But Were Afraid to Ask) '72
Little Murders '71
Cotton Comes to Harlem '70
Song Without End '60
The Diary of Anne Frank '59
A Kid for Two Farthings '55

Andre Jacobs
Curse of the Crystal Eye '93
Prey for the Hunter '92
Pursuit '90
Emissary '89

Danny A. Jacobs (1979-)
Bachelor Party 2: The Last Temptation '08
The Cavern '05

Jon Jacobs (1966-)
Hard Luck '01
Welcome Says the Angel '01

Lawrence-Hilton Jacobs (1953-)
Sublime '07
Indecent Behavior '93
The Jacksons: An American Dream '92
Quiet Fire '91
Angels of the City '89
Chance '89
East L.A. Warriors '89
Killcrazy '89
L.A. Vice '89
L.A. Heat '88
Paramedics '88
The Annihilators '85
For the Love of It '80
Cooley High '75

Mark Evan Jacobs
Bleeding Hearts '92
Trusting Beatrice '92

Steve Jacobs (1967-)
Father '90
Alice to Nowhere '86
Echoes of Paradise '86

Colombe Jacobsen (1979-)
Men in Black 2 '02
D3: The Mighty Ducks '96

Peter Jacobson (1965-)
The Starter Wife '07
Transformers '07
Failure to Launch '06
Domino '05
Good Night, and Good Luck '05
Pipe Dream '02
Hit and Runway '01
61* '01
The Cradle Will Rock '99
A Civil Action '98
It Could Happen to You '94

Ulla Jacobsson (1929-82)
Fox and His Friends '75
The Heroes of Telemark '65
Zulu '64
Smiles of a Summer Night '55

Billy Jacoby (1969-)
Dr. Alien '88
Party Camp '87
Just One of the Guys '85
Cujo '83
Beastmaster '82
Bloody Birthday '80

Bobby Jacoby (1973-)
Fear Runs Silent '99
Night of the Demons 2 '94
The Day My Parents Ran Away '93
The Applegates '89
Tremors '89
Wizards of the Lost Kingdom 2 '89
Iron Eagle '86

Dale Jacoby
Guardian Angel '94
Ring of Fire 2: Blood and Steel '92
Bloodmatch '91
Ring of Fire '91

Scott Jacoby (1956-)
To Die For 2: Son of Darkness '91
To Die For '89
Return to Horror High '87
Midnight Auto Supply '78
The Little Girl Who Lives down the Lane '76
Bad Ronald '74
Rivals '72

Carlos Jacott
Fun With Dick and Jane '05
Jiminy Glick in LaLa Wood '05
Bats '99
Mr. Jealousy '98
Kicking and Screaming '95

Hattie Jacques (1924-80)
Carry On at Your Convenience '71
Make Mine Mink '60
Carry On Nurse '59

A Christmas Carol '51

Yves Jacques (1956-)
The Barbarian Invasions '03
La Petite Lili '03
Napoleon '03

Claude Jade (1948-2006)
Love on the Run '78
Bed and Board '70
Stolen Kisses '68

Richard Jaeckel (1926-97)
Martial Outlaw '93
The King of the Kickboxers '91
Delta Force 2: Operation Stranglehold '90
Ghetto Blaster '89
Black Moon Rising '86
The Dirty Dozen: The Next Mission '85
Pacific Inferno '85
The Fix '84
Starman '84
Airplane 2: The Sequel '82
Blood Song '82
Grizzly '76
Jaws of Death '76
The Drowning Pool '75
Surabaya Conspiracy '75
The Dirty Dozen '67
Born Innocent '74
The $5.20 an Hour Dream '80
Herbie Goes Bananas '80
The Dark '79
Speedtrap '78
Day of the Animals '77
Twilight's Last Gleaming '77
Firehouse '72
Ulzana's Raid '72
Sometimes a Great Notion '71
Chisum '70
The Devil's Brigade '68
The Green Slime '68
Once Before I Die '65
The Gallant Hours '60
Cowboy '58
When Hell Broke Loose '58
3:10 to Yuma '57
Attack! '56
Come Back, Little Sheba '52
Hoodlum Empire '52
Battleground '49
Sands of Iwo Jima '49
Jungle Patrol '48
Town without Pity '61
Flaming Star '60
Platinum High School '60
Guadalcanal Diary '43
A Wing and a Prayer '44

Scott Jaeck (1954-)
Killing Mr. Griffin '97
Washington Square '97
JAG '95

Chapelle Jaffe
Sin and Redemption '94
Confidential '86
Overdrawn at the Memory Bank '83
One Night Stand '78
Who Has Seen the Wind? '77

Sam Jaffe (1891-1984)
On the Line '83
Battle Beyond the Stars '80
Gideon's Trumpet '80
Bedknobs and Broomsticks '71
The Dunwich Horror '70
Night Gallery '69
A Guide for the Married Man '67
Ben-Hur '59
Barbarian and the Geisha '58
The Day the Earth Stood Still '51
The Asphalt Jungle '50
13 Rue Madeleine '46
Gunga Din '39
Lost Horizon '37
Scarlet Empress '34

Melissa Jaffer (1936-)
Weekend of Shadows '77
The Cars That Ate Paris '74

Seth Jaffe
Scorned 2 '96
Beverly Hills Bodysnatchers '89

Madhur Jaffrey (1933-)
Partition '07
Chutney Popcorn '99
Cotton Mary '99
Vanya on 42nd Street '94
Heat and Dust '82
Autobiography of a Princess '75
Shakespeare Wallah '65

Saeed Jaffrey (1929-)
Masala '91
The Deceivers '88
The Courtesans of Bombay '85
My Beautiful Laundrette '85
The Razor's Edge '84
Gandhi '82
Hullabaloo over Georgie & Bonnie's Pictures '78
The Man Who Would Be King '75
The Wilby Conspiracy '75

Sakina Jaffrey (1962-)
The Manchurian Candidate '04
Raising Helen '04
Revolution #9 '01
Chutney Popcorn '99
Cotton Mary '99
Masala '91

Anthony James (1942-)
Unforgiven '92
Slow Burn '90
The Teacher '74
Sam Whiskey '69
Rambling Rose '91
The Phone Call '89
Murder '67
The Last Days of Dolwyn '49

Brenda James
Slither '06
Masters of Horror: Jenifer '05

Bianca Jagger (1945-)
C.H.U.D. 2: Bud the Chud '89
All You Need Is Cash '78

Dean Jagger (1903-91)
Evil Town '87
Gideon's Trumpet '80
Game of Death '79
End of the World '76
The Lindbergh Kidnapping Case '76
Visions of Evil '75
The Hanged Man '74
I Heard the Owl Call My Name '73
The Stranger '73
The Glass House '72
Vanishing Point '71
Firecreek '68
Alligator '80
King Creole '58
Proud Rebel '58
Forty Guns '57
X The Unknown '56
It's a Dog's Life '55
White Christmas '54
Executive Suite '54
Private Hell 36 '54
The Robe '53
The Denver & Rio Grande '51
Rawhide '50
The C-Man '49
Twelve o'Clock High '49
Pursued '47
I Live in Grosvenor Square '46
Sister Kenny '46
Brigham Young: Frontiersman '40
Western Union '41
Valley of the Sun '42
The North Star '43

Brion James (1945-99)
The Operator '01
The King Is Alive '00
Arthur's Quest '99
Brown's Requiem '98
In God's Hands '98
A Place Called Truth '98
Bombshell '97
The Fifth Element '97
Hunter's Moon '97
Precocity Woman from Beverly Hills '97
The Killing Jar '96
Nemesis '93
Cabin Boy '94
The Companion '94
The Dark '94
Dominion '94
Hong Kong '97 '94
The Last Ride '94
Nature of the Beast '94
Radioland Murders '94
Savage Land '94
Scanner Cop '94
Sketch Artist 2: Hands That See '94
The Soft Kill '94
Steel Frontier '94
Brain Smasher... A Love Story '93
Rio Diablo '93
Striking Distance '93
Wishman '93
Black Magic '92
The Player '92
The Runner '92
Future Shock '93
Ultimate Desires '91
Another 48 Hrs. '90
Beyond the Silhouette '90
The Horror Show '89
Mom '89
Red Scorpion '89
Tango and Cash '89
48 Hrs. '82
Southern Comfort '81
Blade Runner '82
Dead Man Walking '88
Nightmare at Noon '87
Steel Dawn '87
Armed and Dangerous '86
Crimewave '86
Enemy Mine '85
Flesh and Blood '85
A Breed Apart '84
Ballad of Gregorio Cortez '83

Mick Jagger (1943-)
The Man from Elysian Fields '01
Running out of Luck '86
The Nightingale '83
Burden of Dreams '82
All You Need Is Cash '78
Gimme Shelter '70
Ned Kelly '70
Performance '70

Henry Jaglom (1943-)
Sympathy for the Devil '70
Last Summer in the Hamptons '96
Venice, Venice '92
New Year's Day '89
Someone to Love '87
Always '85
Sitting Ducks '80
Psych-Out '68

Lisa Jakub (1978-)
Dream House '98
The Beautician and the Beast '97
The Wicked, Wicked West '96
Mrs. Doubtfire '93
The Story Lady '93
Matinee '92

Clifton James (1921-)
Raising Flagg '06
The Summer of Ben Tyler '96
Lone Star '95
Carolina Skeletons '92
Eight Men Out '88
Where Are the Children? '85
Talk to Me '84
The Bad News Bears in Breaking Training '77
Rancho Deluxe '75
Sniper '75
Bank Shot '74
Buster and Billie '74
The Man with the Golden Gun '74
The Iceman Cometh '73
The Last Detail '73
Live and Let Die '73
Werewolf of Washington '73
Cool Hand Luke '67
Will Penny '67
David and Lisa '62
The Strange One '57

Colton James
The Cell '00
The Derby Stallion '05

Dalton James (1971-)
My Father the Hero '93
The Substitute '93

Etta James (1938-)
Tao '89
Chuck Berry: Hail! Hail! Rock 'n' Roll '87

Gennie James (1977-)
The River Pirates '88
Broadcast News '87
The Secret Garden '87
A Smoky Mountain Christmas '86

Hawthorne James
Campfire Tales '98
Heaven's Prisoners '95
Speed '94

Ida James
The Devil's Daughter '39
Hi-De-Ho '35

Jesse James (1989-)
The Amityville Horror '05
The Butterfly Effect '04
Fear of the Dark '02
Blow '01
A Dog of Flanders '99
Hanging Up '99
Message in a Bottle '98
The Gingerbread Man '97

Jessica James (1929-90)
Immediate Family '89
Diner '82
I, the Jury '82

John James (1956-)
Peril '00
Secret Passions '78
Night of the Death Cult '75

Julie James
Terror Beach '75

John James (1914-60)
Range Renegades '48
Homesteaders of Paradise Valley '47
The Devil Bat's Daughter '46
Man from Thunder River '43

Ken James (1948-)
Verdict in Blood '02
The Third Miracle '99
Tracked '98
Landslide '92
Switching Channels '88
Summer's Children '79
I Now Pronounce You Chuck and Larry '07

Gerald James (1917-2006)
Tess of the D'Urbervilles '98

Geraldine James (1950-)
Hope and Glory '87
Northanger Abbey '07 (N)
The Fever '04
Calendar Girls '03
Lucky Break '01
24 Hour Party People '01
Snatch '00
Among Giants '98
Lost in Space '98
The Tall Guy '89
If Looks Could Kill '91
Gandhi '82

Harry James (1916-83)
The Benny Goodman Story '55
If I'm Lucky '46
Strictly G.I. '44
Two Girls and a Sailor '44
Best Foot Forward '43
Private Buckaroo '42

Jesse James (1989-) — see above

Gladden James (1892-1948)
Paradise Island '30
The Social Secretary '16
The Peacock Fan '29

Godfrey James (1931-)
Spellbreaker: Secret of the Leprechauns '96
Leapin' Leprechauns '95
At the Earth's Core '76
The Land That Time Forgot '75

Pell James
Broken Flowers '05
Undertow '04

Paul James
The Architect '06

Oliver James (1980-)
Raise Your Voice '04
What a Girl Wants '03

Michael James (1959-)
Command Invasion '87
Warriors of the Apocalypse

Lennie James (1965-)
Outlaw '07
The State Within '06
Sahara '05
The Rosa Parks Story '02
Snatch '00

Lee James
The Taking of Beverly Hills '91

Peter Francis James (1956-)
CryWolf '05
The St. Francisville Experiment '00

Ron James
Love Song '00

Sidney James (1913-76)
Carry On Behind '75
Carry On Dick '75
Carry On at Your Convenience '71
Carry On Camping '71
Carry On Henry VIII '71
Carry On Cowboy '66
Carry On Cleo '65
Carry On Cruising '62
Carry On Constable... '62
The Silent Enemy '58
Quatermass 2 '57
The Smallest Show on Earth '57
Glass Tomb '55
John and Julie '55
Heat Wave '54
The Belles of St. Trinian's '53
Norman Conquest '53
The Lavender Hill Mob '51

Sonny James (1929-)
Las Vegas Hillbillys '66
Hillbillys in a Haunted House '67

Steve James (1955-93)
Bloodfist 5: Human Target '93
Weekend at Bernie's 2 '93
The Player '92
McBain '91
Street Hunter '90
Avenging Force '86
The P.O.W. Escape '86
American Ninja 3: Blood Hunt '89
Stalking Danger '86
Hunter '84
Riverbend '89
Hero and the Terror '88
I'm Gonna Git You Sucka '88
Johnny Be Good '88
Python Wolf '88
American Ninja 2: The Confrontation '87
American Ninja '85
The Brother from Another Planet '84
The Exterminator '80

Walter James (1882-1946)
Police Court '32
The Kid Brother '27

Kevin James (1965-)
Monster House '06 (V)
Hitch '05
Barnyard '06 (V)
Grilled '06

Battling Butler '26
Little Annie Rooney '25
The Monster '25
The Idol Dancer '20

Joyce Jameson (1932-87)
Hardbodies '84
Pray TV '80
Savage Run '70
The Comedy of Terrors '64
Good Neighbor Sam '64
The Balcony '63
Tales of Terror '62

Malcom Jamieson
Meridian: Kiss of the Beast '90
Pictures '80s

Tadeusz Janczar (1926-97)
Landscape After Battle '70
Kanal '56

Krystyna Janda (1955-)
The Decalogue '88
The Interrogation '82
Man of Iron '81
Mephisto '81
The Conductor '80
Without Anesthesia '78
Man of Marble '76

Thomas Jane (1969-)
The Mist '07
The Tripper '06
The Punisher '04
Dreamcatcher '03
Stander '03
The Sweetest Thing '02
Original Sin '01
61* '01
Under Suspicion '00
Deep Blue Sea '99
Molly '99
Boogie Nights '97
Hollywood Confidential '97
The Crow 2: City of Angels '96
The Last Time I Committed Suicide '96
Buffy the Vampire Slayer '92

Dong-Kun Jang (1972-)
Typhoon '06
The Promise '05
Tae Guk Gi: The Brotherhood of War '04

Conrad Janis (1928-)
The Cable Guy '96
November Conspiracy '96
The Feminine Touch '95
Mr. Saturday Night '92
My Twentieth Century '90
Nostalghia '83
Sonny Boy '87
Oh, God! Book 2 '80

Petr Janis
Hostel '06
The Ninth Day '04

Oleg (Yankovsky) Jankowsky (1944-)
Mute Witness '95

Allison Janney (1960-)
Hairspray '07
Juno '07
Over the Hedge '06 (V)
Strangers with Candy '06
The Chumscrubber '05
Winter Solstice '04
Finding Nemo '03 (V)
How to Deal '03
The Hours '02
A Girl Thing '01
Nurse Betty '00
American Beauty '99
Drop Dead Gorgeous '99
Ten Things I Hate about You '99

Celebrity '98
The Imposters '98
The Object of My Affection '98
Primary Colors '98
Six Days, Seven Nights '98
First Do No Harm '97
The Ice Storm '97
Julian Po '97
Private Parts '96
Big Night '95

Leon Janney (1917-80)
Charly '68
Police Court '32

William Janney (1908-92)
Hopalong Cassidy Returns '36
Coquette '29

Emil Jannings (1884-1950)
The Blue Angel '30
Last Command '28
Faust '26
Variety '25
The Last Laugh '24
Waxworks '24
Othello '22
Fortune's Fool '21
Passion '19

Walter Janovitz (1913-97)
The Hollywood Knights '80
Billy the Kid Versus Dracula '66

Thom Jansen (1945-)
The Gambler '97
Suite 16 '94

Horst Janson (1935-)
To Catch a King '84
Captain Kronos: Vampire Hunter '74
McKenzie Break '70

David Janssen (1930-80)
City in Fear '80
High Ice '80
S.O.S. Titanic '79
Centennial '78
The Word '78
Golden Rendezvous '77
Swiss Conspiracy '77
Stalk the Wild Child '76
Two Minute Warning '76
Once Is Not Enough '75
Fer-De-Lance '74
Prisoner in the Middle '74
Smile, Jenny, You're Dead '74
Pioneer Woman '73
Birds of Prey '72
Moon of the Wolf '72
Macho Callahan '70
Generation '69
Marooned '69
The Green Berets '68
The Shoes of the Fisherman '68
The King of the Roaring '20s: The Story of Arnold Rothstein '61
Hell to Eternity '60
Darby's Rangers '58
Lafayette Escadrille '58
Francis in the Haunted House '56
Francis in the Navy '55
To Hell and Back '55
Francis Goes to West Point '52
Yankee Buccaneer '52
Swamp Fire '46

Eilene Janssen (1937-)
On Our Merry Way '48
Who Killed Doc Robbin? '48
Curley '47
Song of Love '47

Famke Janssen (1964-)
The Ten '07
The Treatment '06
X-Men: The Last Stand '06
Hide and Seek '05

Eulogy '04
X2: X-Men United '03
I Spy '02
Don't Say a Word '01
Made '01
Circus '00
Love & Sex '00
X-Men '00
House on Haunted Hill '99
Celebrity '98
Deep Rising '98
The Faculty '98
Monument Ave. '98
Rounders '98
The Gingerbread Man '97
R.P.M. '97
City of Industry '96
Goldeneye '95
Lord of Illusions '95
Model by Day '94
Relentless 4 '94
Fathers and Sons '92

Walther Jansson (1887-1976)
The Mozart Story '48
Destiny '21

Lois January (1912-2006)
Lightning Bill Crandall '37
The Red Rope '37
The Roamin' Cowboy '37
Border Caballero '36
Cocaine Fiends '36
Rogue of the Range '36
Bulldog Courage '35
Skull & Crown '35

Agnes Jaoui (1964-)
Look at Me '04
The Taste of Others '00
Same Old Song '97
Un Air de Famille '96

Ernst-Hugo Jaregard (1928-98)
The Kingdom 2 '97
The Kingdom '95
The Slingshot '93

Claude Jarman, Jr. (1934-)
Hangman's Knot '52
Rio Grande '50
Intruder in the Dust '49
The Sun Comes Up '49
The Yearling '46

Jim Jarmusch (1953-)
Sling Blade '96
Blue in the Face '95
In the Soup '92
Leningrad Cowboys Go America '89
Straight to Hell '87
American Autobahn '84

John Jarratt (1952-)
Wolf Creek '05
Dead Heart '96
Talk '94
Dark Age '88
Next of Kin '82
The Odd Angry Shot '79
The Karate Kid: Part 3 '89

Catherine Jarrett
A Fine Romance '92
Quicker Than the Eye '88
S.A.S. San Salvador '84

Paul Jarrett
The Foursome '06
Suspicious River '00
Apollo 13 '95
Real Genius '85
The Chant of Jimmie Blacksmith '78
Sound of Love '78
Summer City '77

Stig Jarrel (1910-98)
The Devil's Eye '60
Torment '44

Gabe Jarret (1970-)
Poseidon '06
The American President '95

Graham Jarvis (1930-2003)
Misery '90
Parents '89
Vanishing Act '88
Doin' Time '85

Mischief '85
Drawl '81
Middle Age Crazy '80
Cold Turkey '71
Alice's Restaurant '69

Martin Jarvis (1941-)
Ruby in the Smoke '06 (V)
Lorna Doone '01
Buster '88
The Moonstone '72
Taste the Blood of Dracula '70

Chona Jason (1963-)
Dragon Fury '95
Knock Outs '92

Donna Jason
Abducted 2: The Reunion '94
Undefeatable '94
Honor and Glory '92

Harvey Jason (1940-)
The Lost World: Jurassic Park 2 '97
I Wonder Who's Killing Her Now? '76
Oklahoma Crude '73
The Witching '72
Too Late the Hero '70
Star! '68

Peter Jason (1944-)
The Christmas Card '06
Adaptation '02
The Demolitionist '95
In the Mouth of Madness '95
Rage '95
Village of the Damned '95
Deconstructing Sarah '94
Arachnophobia '90
Alien Nation '88
They Live '88
Heartbreak Ridge '86
Hyper-Sapien: People from Another Star '86
Trick or Treats '82
Texas Lightning '81

Rick Jason (1926-2000)
Partners '82
Witch Who Came from the Sea '76
Eagles Attack at Dawn '70
Color Me Dead '69

Sybil Jason (1929-)
The Blue Bird '40
The Little Princess '39

Star Jasper (1966-)
Jersey Girl '92
True Love '89

Mark Jax
Mystery Men '99
Boogie Nights '97
Sink or Swim '97
The Spanish Prisoner '97
Tomorrow Never Dies '97
Hole in the Sky '95
Things Change '88
House of Games '87

Tony Jay (1933-2006)
The Jungle Book 2 '03 (V)
Treasure Planet '02 (V)
The Hunchback of Notre Dame '96 (V)
Rainbow Drive '90

Michael Jayston (1936-)
20,000 Leagues Under the Sea '97
Element of Doubt '96
Macbeth '88
From a Far Country: Pope John Paul II '81 (N)
Tinker, Tailor, Soldier, Spy '80
Craze '74
The Merchant of Venice '73

Nicholas and Alexandra '71
A Midsummer Night's Dream '94

Gregory Jbara (1961-)
The First $20 Million Is Always the Hardest '02
William Shakespeare's A Midsummer Night's Dream '99
In and Out '97

Gloria Jean (1927-)
The Ladies' Man '61
Copacabana '47
Never Give a Sucker an Even Break '41
If I Had My Way '40

Nelust Wyclef Jean (1972-)
Dirty '05
One Last Thing '05
Carmen: A Hip Hopera '01

Marianne Jean-Baptiste (1967-)
Jam '06
Spy Game '01
The Cell '00
28 Days '00
A Murder of Crows '99
The 24 Hour Woman '99
The Murder of Stephen Lawrence '99
Mr. Jealousy '98
Secrets and Lies '95

Jimmy Jean-Louis
Phat Girlz '06
The Game of Their Lives '05

Zizi Jeanmaire (1924-)
Black Tights '60
Hans Christian Andersen '52

Marcel Jeannin
The Sign of Four '01
The Audrey Hepburn Story '00

Isabel Jeans (1891-1985)
The Magic Christian '69
Heavens Above '63
Gigi '58
Elizabeth of Ladymead '48
Great Day '46
Easy Virtue '27

Ursula Jeans (1906-73)
Flame Over India '60
Dam Busters '55
The Weaker Sex '49
Mr. Emmanuel '44
The Life and Death of Colonel Blimp '43
Dark Journey '37
Cavalcade '33

Colin Jeavons (1929-)
World War III '86
Mission Galactica: The Cylon Attack '78
Detroit 9000 '73
Private Duty Nurses '71

Allan Jeayes (1885-1963)
The Hidden Room '49
The Four Feathers '39
The Scarlet Pimpernel '34

Eve Jihan Jeffers
See Eve

Herbert Jefferson, Jr. (1946-)

Barbara Jefford (1930-)
The Ninth Gate '99
A Village Affair '95

Where Angels Fear to Tread '91
When the Whales Came '89
Reunion '88
Murders at Lynch Cross '85
And the Ship Sails On '83
Lust for a Vampire '71
A Midsummer Night's Dream '68
Ulysses '67

Myles Jeffrey (1990-)
The Ant Bully '06 (V)
Hoodlum & Son '03
Tart '01
Babe: Pig in the City '98 (V)

Peter Jeffrey (1929-99)
The Scarlet Pimpernel 2: Mademoiselle Guillotine '99
Rasputin: Dark Servant of Destiny '96
Middlemarch '93
Hands of a Murderer '90
The Adventures of Baron Munchausen '89
The Odessa File '74
Doctor Phibes Rises Again '72
Elizabeth R '72
The Abominable Dr. Phibes '71
The Horsemen '70
Twinsanity '70
If... '69
The Fixer '68

Anne Jeffreys (1923-)
Return of the Bad Men '48
Riff-Raff '47
Trail Street '47
Dick Tracy vs. Cueball '46
Dick Tracy, Detective '45
Dillinger '45
Those Endearing Young Charms '45
Nevada '44
Step Lively '44
Zombies on Broadway '44
Bordertown Gunfighters '43
Calling Wild Bill Elliott '43
Death Valley Manhunt '43
Man from Thunder River '43
Billy the Kid Trapped '42
I Married an Angel '42
X Marks the Spot '42

Chuck Jeffreys (1958-)
Bloodmoon '97
Deathfight '93
Honor and Glory '92
Aftershock '88
Hawkeye '88

Fran Jeffries (1939-)
Harum Scarum '65
Sex and the Single Girl '64

Herbert Jeffries (1911-)
Chrome and Hot Leather '71
Bronze Buckaroo '39
Harlem Rides the Range '39
Harlem on the Prairie '38
Two-Gun Man from Harlem '38

Lang Jeffries (1930-87)
Deadline Auto Theft '83
Mission Stardust '68
Alone Against Rome '62

Lionel Jeffries (1926-)
Jekyll and Hyde '90
A Chorus of Disapproval '89
Letting the Birds Go Free '86
Prisoner of Zenda '79
Bananas Boat '78
Royal Flash '75
Who Slew Auntie Roo? '71
Eye Witness '70
Lola '69
Chitty Chitty Bang Bang '68
Camelot '67

Oh, Dad, Poor Dad
(Momma's Hung You in
the Closet & I'm Feeling
So Sad) '67
Those Fantastic Flying
Fools '67
Arrivederci, Baby! '66
Spy with a Cold Nose '66
First Men in the Moon '64
Murder Ahoy '64
Call Me Bwana '63
The Wrong Arm of the Law
'63
Fanny '61
The Trials of Oscar Wilde
'60
The Revenge of
Frankenstein '58
Up the Creek '58
Hour of Decision '57
The Vicious Circle '57
The Baby and the
Battleship '56
Bhowani Junction '56
Blue Murder at St. Trinian's
'56
Lust for Life '56

Edith Jehanne
The Chess Player '27
The Love of Jeanne Ney
'27

Rudolf Jelinek (1935-)
Fabulous Adventures of
Baron Munchausen '61
The Original Fabulous
Adventures of Baron
Munchausen '61

Anna Jemison
See Anna Maria Monticelli

Edward Jemison
Ocean's Thirteen '07
Ocean's Twelve '04
Ocean's Eleven '01

George Jenesky
See Conrad Dunn

Richard Jeni (1957-2007)
An Alan Smithee Film:
Burn, Hollywood, Burn
'97
National Lampoon's Dad's
Week Off '97

Alien Jenkins (1900-74)
Robin and the 7 Hoods '64
Chained for Life '51
Oklahoma Annie '51
The Big Wheel '49
Hat Box Mystery '47
Lady on a Train '45
The Falcon Takes Over '42
They All Kissed the Bride
'42
Dive Bomber '41
Brother Orchid '40
Tin Pan Alley '40
Destry Rides Again '39
Amazing Dr. Clitterhouse
'38
A Slight Case of Murder '38
Dead End '37
Marked Woman '37
Sing Me a Love Song '37
The Mayor of Hell '33
Havana Widows '33
Three Men on a Horse '36
Tomorrow at Seven '33
Blessed Event '32
I Am a Fugitive from a
Chain Gang '32

**Burgess Jenkins
(1973-)**
Remember the Titans '00
Unshackled '00

**Carter Jenkins
(1991-)**
Keeping Up with the Steins
'06
The Bad News Bears '05

Daniel H. Jenkins
Infested: Invasion of the
Killer Bugs '02
The Cradle Will Rock '99
The Caine Mutiny Court
Martial '88
Florida Straits '87

**Larry "Flash"
Jenkins**
EDtv '99
Ferris Bueller's Day Off '86
Fletch '85

**Megs Jenkins (1917-
98)**
Asylum '72
Murder Most Foul '65
The Innocents '61
Tiger Bay '59
John and Julie '55
Trouble in Store '53

Noam Jenkins
All Hat '07
The State Within '06
First Love '39
That Girl from Paris '36

**Jackie "Butch"
Jenkins (1937-2001)**
Summer Holiday '48
Our Vines Have Tender
Grapes '45
National Velvet '44
The Human Comedy '43

Ken Jenkins (1940-)
Welcome to Paradise '07
The Sum of All Fears '02
Home Room '02
Courage Under Fire '96
Last Man Standing '96
Hiroshima '95
Past the Beachers '95
White Mile '94
And the Band Played On
'93
Edge of Honor '91
Matewan '87

Sam Jenkins (1966-)
Fortunes of War '94
That Brennan Girl '46
Kid Sister '45
The Missing Corpse '45
His Butler's Sister '44
The Navy Comes Through
'42
Zombies on Broadway '44
Corregidor '43
Back Street '41
The Flame of New Orleans
'41
His Girl Friday '40

Frank Jenks (1902-62)
The Amazing Colossal Man
'57
Motor Patrol '50
Shep Comes Home '49
Blonde Savage '47
Gator Bait '73
Group Marriage '72
Unholy Rollers '72

**DeWitt Jennings
(1879-1937)**
Kelly the Second '36
The Fighting Rookie '34
Criminal Code '31
The Bat Whispers '30
The Big House '30
The Little American '17

Byron Jennings
Hamlet '07
The Ice Storm '97
A Simple Twist of Fate '94

**Claudia Jennings
(1949-79)**
Death Sport '78
Fast Company '78
Moonshine County Express
'77
The Great Texas Dynamite
Chase '76
Sisters of Death '76
Truck Stop Women '74

Rita Jenrette (1949-)
End of the Line '88
Malibu Bikini Shop '86
Zombie Island Massacre
'84

Salome Jens (1935-)
Cats & Dogs '01 (V)
I'm Losing You '98
The Grace Kelly Story '83
Tomorrow's Child '82
A Matter of Life and Death
'81
Diary of the Dead '80
Savages '72
Seconds '66
The Fool Killer '65
Angel Baby '61

**Waylon Jennings
(1937-2002)**
The Dukes '83
Nashville Rebel '66

Juanita Jennings
Runaway Jury '03
Spirit Lost '96
Laurel Avenue '93

Tom Jennings
Stones of Death '88
Night Master '87
My Brother Tom '86

Byron Jennings
The Manhattan Project '86
On Valentine's Day '86

**Adele Jergens (1917-
2002)**
Girls in Prison '56
The Cobweb '55
Day the World Ended '55
Lonesome Trail '55
Pirate Ship '49
Ladies of the Chorus '49
The Fuller Brush Man '48
The Dark Past '49

Diane Jergens (1937-)
The FBI Story '59
High School Confidential
'58
Desk Set '57

Jimmy Jerman
Vampire Night '00

**Mary Jerrold (1877-
1955)**
Woman Hater '49

**George Jessel (1898-
1981)**
Diary of a Young Comic '79
Valley of the Dolls '67

Tim Jerome (1943-)
Thirteen Days '00

**Hector Jimenez
(1973-)**
Epic Movie '07
Nacho Libre '06

Yolanda Jilot
Diving In '90

Joyce Jillson (1938-)
Slumber Party '57 '76
Superchick '71

**Jose Luis Jimenez
(1900-78)**
The Vampire '57

Lucia Jimenez (1978-)
The Kovak Box '06
Broken Silence '01

**Soledad Jimenez
(1874-1966)**
For Whom the Bell Tolls '43
The Real Glory '39
The Phantom of the Range
'38

Ann Jillian (1950-)
Little White Lies '89
Convicted: A Mother's
Story '87
Alice in Wonderland '85
Mr. Mom '83
Gypsy '62

Penn Jillette (1955-)
Fear and Loathing in Las
Vegas '98
Hackers '95
Penn and Teller Get Killed
'90

**Isabel Jewell (1909-
72)**
Eddie in Clao! Manhattan '72
The Arousers '70
Man in the Attic '53
The Leopard Man '43
Gone with the Wind '39
Lost Horizon '37
Marked Woman '37
Big Brown Eyes '36
Ceiling Zero '35
A Tale of Two Cities '36

**Jimmy Jewel (1913-
95)**
The Krays '90
Arthur's Hallowed Ground
'84

Joan Jett (1958-)
Boogie Boy '98
Light of Day '87
Dubeat-E-O '84

Ma Jingwu
Cold '94
The Day the Sun Turned
Cold '94
Raise the Red Lantern '91

Kenzaburo Jo
See Tomisaburo Wakayama

Ebony Jo-Ann
The Other Brother '02
Fly by Night '93

Suzy Joachim
White Chicks '04

Marlene Jobert (1943-)
Ten Days Wonder '72
Catch Me a Spy '71
Rider on the Rain '70
Masculine Feminine '66

Maz Jobrani (1972-)
The Interpreter '05
13 Going on 30 '04
The Medicine Show '01

Adan Jodorowsky
2 Days in Paris '07
Santa Sangre '90

Zita Johann (1904-93)
The Mummy '32
Struggle '31

David Johansen (1950-)
The Tic Code '99
Cats Don't Dance '97 (V)
Nick and Jane '96
Burnzy's Last Call '95
Car 54, Where Are You? '94
Mr. Nanny '93
Naked in New York '93 (V)
Desire and Hell at Sunset Motel '92
Freejack '92
Tales from the Darkside: The Movie '90
Let It Ride '89
Light Years '88 (V)
Married to the Mob '88
Scrooged '88
Candy Mountain '87

Paul Johansson (1964-)
Novel Romance '06
Dark Side '02
Edge of Madness '02
John Q '02
Hooded Angels '00
Carnival of Souls '98
Wishmaster 2: Evil Never Dies '98
Midnight Witness '93
Martial Law 2: Undercover '91
Soapdish '91

Scarlett Johansson (1984-)
He's Just Not That Into You '08
The Other Boleyn Girl '07
The Nanny Diaries '07
The Black Dahlia '06
The Prestige '06
Scoop '06
The Island '05
Match Point '05
A Good Woman '04
In Good Company '04
A Love Song for Bobby Long '04
The Perfect Score '04
Girl with a Pearl Earring '03
Lost in Translation '03
Eight Legged Freaks '02
An American Rhapsody '01
Ghost World '01
The Man Who Wasn't There '01
Home Alone 3 '97
The Horse Whisperer '97
Manny & Lo '96

I.S. Johar (1920-)
Maya 66
Flame Over India '60

Elton John (1947-)
The Road to El Dorado '00 (N)

Spice World: The Movie '97
Tommy '75
Born to Boogie '72

Gottfried John (1942-)
Plano Tuner of Earthquakes '05
Proof of Life '00
The Ogre '96
Goldeneye '95
Institue Benjamenta or This Dream People Call Human Life '95
Abraham '94
Mata Hari '85
Berlin Alexanderplatz '80
The Marriage of Maria Braun '79
In a Year of 13 Moons 78
Mother Kusters Goes to Heaven '76

Karl John (1905-77)
The Mysterious Magician '65

The Lost One '51

Rosamund John (1913-98)
Fame Is the Spur 47
Spitfire '42

Glynis Johns (1923-)
Superstar '99
While You Were Sleeping '95
Nukie '93
The Ref '93
Zelly & Me '88
Sprague '84
Under Milk Wood '73
Vault of Horror '73
Dear Brigitte '65
Mary Poppins '64
The Sundowners '60
All Mine to Give '56
Around the World in 80 Days, '56
Court Jester '56
Land of Fury '55
Rob Roy—The Highland Rogue 53
The Sword & the Rose 53
Encore '52
The Promoter '52
No Highway in the Sky 51
Frieda '47

Marcus Johns (1993-)
Canvas '06

Mervyn Johns (1899-1992)
Day of the Triffids '63
The Victors '63
No Love for Johnnie '60
1984 56
Romeo and Juliet '54
The Master of Ballantrae '53
A Christmas Carol '51
Tony Draws a Horse 51
Counterblast '48
Captain Boycott '47
Captive Heart '47
San Demetrio, London '47
Dead of Night '45
Pink String and Sealing Wax 45
The Foreman Went to France '42

Stratford Johns (1925-2002)
Neil Gaiman's NeverWhere '96
Splitting Heirs '93
The Strange Case of the End of Civilization As We Know It '93
A Demon in My View '92

The Lair of the White Worm '88
Salome's Last Dance '88
Dance with a Stranger '85
Great Expectations '05
The Fiendish Plot of Dr. Fu Manchu '80
Who Done It? '56

Tracy C. Johns (1963-)
New Jack City '91
Mo' Better Blues '90
She's Gotta Have It '86

Aaron Johnson (1990-)
The Illusionist '06
The Thief Lord '06
Shanghai Knights '03

A.J. (Anthony) Johnson (1967-)
O '01
I Got the Hook-Up '98
Cold Hearts '99
The Players Club '98
B.A.P.'s '97
Def Jam's How to Be a Player '97

Amy Jo Johnson (1970-)
Magma: Volcanic Disaster '06
Infested: Invasion of the Killer Bugs '02
Pursuit of Happiness '01
Down in the Delta '98
Asteroid '97
Dream Date 93
True Identity '91
Robot Jox 90
Mighty Morphin Power Rangers: The Movie '95

Anne-Marie Johnson (1960-)
Pursuit of Happiness '01
I'm Gonna Git You Sucka '88
Hollywood Shuffle 87

Arch Johnson (1922-97)
The Cheyenne Social Club '70
Gun Glory 57

Ariyan Johnson
Bulworth '98
Just Another Girl on the I.R.T. '93

Arnold Johnson (1922-2000)
My Demon Lover '87
Putney Swope '69

Arte Johnson (1934-)
Assault of the Party Nerds 2: Heavy Petting Detective '95
Munchie '92
Evil Spirits '91
Evil Toons '90
The Red Raven Kiss-Off '90
Tax Season '90
Alice in Wonderland '85
What Comes Around '85
If Things Were Different 79
Bud and Lou 78
Bunco 77
Charge of the Model T's 76
The President's Analyst '67
That Funny Feeling '65

Ashley Johnson (1983-)
Fast Food Nation '06
Nearing Grace '05
Killer Diller '04
King of the Corner '04
Rustin '01
What Women Want '00
Anywhere But Here '99

Dancer, Texas—Pop. 81 '98
Annie: A Royal Adventure '95
Nine Months '95
Lionheart '90

Ben Johnson (1920-96)
The Evening Star '96
Ruby Jean and Joe '96
Angels in the Outfield '94
Bonanza: The Return '93
Radio Flyer '92
The Chase '91
My Heroes Have Always Been Cowboys '91
Back to Back '90
Dark Before Dawn '89
Cherry 2000 '88
Let's Get Harry '87
Trespasses 86
Champions 84
Red Dawn '84
Soggy Bottom U.S.A. '84
Wild Horses '84
The Shadow Riders '82
Tex 82
Ruckus 81
Terror Train 80
The Sacketts '79
Wild Times 79
The Swarm 78
Grayeagle 77
Breakheart Pass '76
The Red Pony 76
The Savage Bees 76
Town That Dreaded Sundown 76
Bite the Bullet 75
The Sugarland Express 74
Dillinger 73
Train Robbers '73
The Getaway 72
Junior Bonner 72
Bull of the West 71
The Last Picture Show '71
Chisum 70
The Undefeated '69
The Wild Bunch 69
Will Penny '67
The Rare Breed 66
Major Dundee '65
One-Eyed Jacks '61
Tomboy & the Champ '58
Shane '53
Rio Grande '50
Wagon Master '50
Mighty Joe Young 49
She Wore a Yellow Ribbon 49
Three Godfathers 48

Beverly Johnson (1952-)
Crossroads '02
Def Jam's How to Be a Player '97
True Vengeance '97
The Cover Girl Murders '93
Ashanti, Land of No Mercy '79

Brad Johnson (1959-)
Safe Harbour '07
Alien Siege '05
Crossfire Trail '01
Left Behind: The Movie '00
Across the Line '00
Soldier of Fortune Inc, '97
Lone Justice 3: Showdown at Plum Creek '96
The Birds 2: Land's End '94
Dominion '94
Siringo '94
Lone Justice 2 '93
Philadelphia Experiment 2 '93
An American Story '92
Flight of the Intruder '90
Always 89
Nam Angels 88

Bryce Johnson
Sleeping Dogs Lie '06
Harry and Max '04
Bring It On Again 03

C. David Johnson (1955-)
Aldrich Ames: Traitor Within '98
The Legend of Gator Face '96

Candy Johnson (1944-)
Bikini Beach '64
Muscle Beach Party '64
Pajama Party '64
Beach Party 63

Celia Johnson (1908-82)
The Hostage Tower '80
Staying On '80
Les Miserables 78
The Prime of Miss Jean Brodie 69
A Kid for Two Farthings '55
Captain's Paradise '53
This Happy Breed '47
Brief Encounter '46
In Which We Serve 43

Chic Johnson (1891-1962)
Crazy House '43
All Over Town '37
Country Gentlemen '36

Clark Johnson (1954-)
The Sentinel '06
S.W.A.T. '03
Boycott '02
Deliberate Intent '01
Disappearing Acts '00
Homicide: The Movie '00
Love Come Down '00
Blood Brothers '00
Junior's Groove '97
Rude '96
Soul Survivor '95
Final Round '93
The Finishing Touch 92
Personals '90
Colors '88

Corey Johnson (1961-)
The Bourne Ultimatum '07
The Contract '07
A Sound of Thunder '05
Hellboy '04
Endgame '01
Last Run '01
The Mummy '99

Don Johnson (1950-)
Moondance Alexander '07
Goodbye, Lover '99
Tin Cup '96
In Pursuit of Honor '95
Born Yesterday '93
Guilty as Sin 93
Harley Davidson and the Marlboro Man '91
Paradise '91
Tales of the Unexpected '91
The Hot Spot '90
Dead Bang 89
Sweet Hearts Dance '88
The Long, Hot Summer '86
Cease Fire '85
Miami Vice '84
Soggy Bottom U.S.A. '84
Melanie '82
Beulah Land 80
Revenge of the Stepford Wives 80
The Rebels '79
Snowblind 78
The City 76
Law of the Land 76
A Boy and His Dog 75
Return to Macon County '75
Harrad Experiment 73
Zachariah '70

Dots Johnson (1913-86)
Paisan '46

Dwayne "The Rock" Johnson (1972-)
Get Smart '08
The Game Plan '07
Reno 911!: Miami '07

Gridiron Gang '06
Southland Tales '06
Be Cool '05
Doom '05
Walking Tall '04
The Rundown '03
The Scorpion King '02
The Mummy Returns '01

Geordie Johnson (1953-)
Charms for the Easy Life '02
Dangerous Evidence: The Lori Jackson Story '99
Spenser: The Judas Goat '94

Georgann Johnson (1926-)
Twilight Man '96
Shattered Dreams '90
Murphy's Romance '85

Helen Johnson (1954-)
Vice Squad '31
The Divorcee '30
Sin Takes a Holiday '30

Jack Johnson (1987-)
Sleep Easy, Hutch Rimes '00
Lost in Space '98

Jerry Johnson
Code of Honor '82
Kill Squad '81

Joey Johnson
Courier of Death '84
Grad Night '81

Julie Johnson
Barney's Great Adventure '98 (V)

Karl Johnson (1924-93)
The Islander '88
Night of the Ghouls '59
The Unearthly '57
Plan 9 from Outer Space '56

Karl Johnson (1948-)
The Chatterley Affair '06
Four Last Songs '06
Pure '02
Love Is the Devil '98
Saint-Ex: The Story of the Storyteller '95
Wittgenstein '93
Close My Eyes '91

Katie Johnson (1878-1957)
John and Julie '55
The Ladykillers '55

Kay Johnson (1904-75)
Son of Fury '42
The Real Glory '39
Village Tale '35
American Madness '32
Madam Satan 30

Kelly Johnson
Utu '83
Carry Me Back '82
Goodbye Pork Pie '81

Kenneth Johnson (1942-)
The Veteran '06

Kurt Johnson (1952-86)
Sole Survivor '84
Jane Austen in Manhattan '80

Kyle Johnson (1951-)
Man on the Run 74
The Learning Tree 69

Lamont Johnson (1955-)
Waiting to Exhale '95
Fear of a Black Hat '94
The Five Heartbeats '91

Laura Johnson (1957-)
Hope Ranch '02
Judge & Jury '96
Cheatin' Hearts '93
Dario Argento's Trauma '93
Deadly Exposure '93

Fatal Instinct '92
Red Shoe Diaries 2: Double Dare '92
Murderous Vision '91
Nick Knight '89
Beyond Reason '77
Opening Night '77

Lynn-Holly Johnson (1958-)
Fugitive X '96
The Criminal Mind '93
Digging Up Business '91
Hyper Space '89
The Sisterhood '88
Where the Boys Are '84, '84
For Your Eyes Only '81
The Watcher in the Woods '81
Alien Predators '80
Ice Castles '79

Mel Johnson, Jr.
Total Recall '90

Melody Johnson (1982-)
Eubie! '82
Jason X '01
Jailbait '00

Michael Johnson (1939-2001)
Lust for a Vampire '71
Anne of the Thousand Days '69

Michelle Johnson (1965-)
Fallen Angel '99
Specimen '97
The Glimmer Man '96
Moving Target '96
When the Bullet Hits the Bone '96
Body Shot '93
Blood Ties '92
Death Becomes Her '92
Till Murder Do Us Part '92
Wishful Thinking '92
Driving Me Crazy '91
Genuine Risk '89
Slipping into Darkness '88
Jigsaw Murders '89
Waxwork '88
Beaks: The Movie '87
A Chorus Line '85
Gung Ho '85
Blame It on Rio '84

Noble Johnson (1881-1973)
The Most Dangerous Game '32
King Kong '33
Lancer '35
The Lives of a Bengal Lancer '35
Murders in the Rue Morgue '32
The Mummy '32
The Navigator '24
The Leopard Woman '20

Penny Johnson (1961-)
DC 9/11: Time of Crisis '04
Deliberate Intent '01
The Road to Galveston '96
Fear of a Black Hat '94
What's Love Got to Do with It? '93

Rebekah Johnson (1976-)
Liberty Heights '99
Ruby Jean and Joe '96

Reggie Johnson
Platoon '86
Seven Hours to Judgment '88

Richard Johnson (1927-)
Lara Croft, Tomb Raider '01
Breaking the Code '95
The Camomile Lawn '92
Duel of Hearts '92
The Crucifer of Blood '91
Diving In '90
Spymaker: The Secret Life of Ian Fleming '90
Treasure Island '89
A Man for All Seasons '88
Turtle Diary '86
Lady Jane '86
The Great Alligator '81
Screamers '80
Zombie '80
The Big Scam '79
The Four Feathers '78
The Comeback '77
Beyond the Door '75
Hennessy '75
Fifth Day of Peace '72
Restless '72
Deadlier Than the Male '67
The Rover '67
Khartoum '66
The Witch '66
The Amorous Adventures of Moll Flanders '65
Operation Crossbow '65
The Pumpkin Eater '64
The Haunting '63
Never So Few '59
Men of the Fighting Lady '54

Rita Johnson (1913-65)
All Mine to Give '56
The Big Clock '48
They Won't Believe Me '47
The Perfect Marriage '46
The Naughty Nineties '45
My Friend Flicka '43
Here Comes Mr. Jordan '41
Edison the Man '40
Broadway Serenade '39
Honolulu '39

Robin Johnson (1964-)
Splitz '84
Times Square '80

Ron Johnson (1973-)
Shadow Dancer '96
Zebrahead '92

Russell Johnson (1924-)
Starship Invasions '77
Grizzly '76
The Human Comedy '43

Victoria (Vicki) Johnson

Bobby Johnston
DC 9/11: Time of Crisis '04
Sandy Strokes '95
Sinful Intrigue '95
Hollywood's New Blood '88

Grace Johnston
One Good Cop '91
God Bless the Child '88

James Johnston
Clean '04
Never Pick Up a Stranger '79

J.J. Johnston (1933-)
Lakeboat '00
K-911 '99
The Fixer '97
Stranger by Night '94
Mad Dog and Glory '93
Things Change '88
Fatal Attraction '87

John Dennis Johnston
Firestarter 2: Rekindled '02
Mercenary 2: Thick and Thin '97
In Pursuit of Honor '95
Wyatt Earp '94
Fever '91
Miracle in the Wilderness '91
Big Bad John '90

Tor Johnson (1903-71)
The Beast of Yucca Flats '61
Night of the Ghouls '59
The Unearthly '57
The Black Sleep '56
Carousel '56
Plan 9 from Outer Space '56
Bride of the Monster '55
Houdini '53
Abbott and Costello in the Foreign Legion '50
Behind Locked Doors '48
Human Gorilla '48

Van Johnson (1916-)
Three Days to a Kill '91
Delta Force Commando 2 '90
The Purple Rose of Cairo '85
Scorpion with Two Tails '82
The Kidnapping of the President '80
Where Angels Go, Trouble Follows '68
Yours, Mine & Ours '68
Divorce American Style '67
The Doomsday Flight '66
The Pied Piper of Hamelin '57
End of the Affair '55
Brigadoon '54
The Caine Mutiny '54
The Last Time I Saw Paris '54
Easy to Love '53
Go for Broke! '51
Three Guys Named Mike '51
The Big Hangover '50
The Duchess of Idaho '50
Battleground '49
In the Good Old Summertime '49
Command Decision '48
State of the Union '48
Easy to Wed '46
Thrill of a Romance '45
Weekend at the Waldorf '45
A Guy Named Joe '44
Thirty Seconds Over Tokyo '44
Two Girls and a Sailor '44
The White Cliffs of Dover '44
The Human Comedy '43
Madame Curie '43
Too Many Girls '40

Angelina Jolie (1975-)
Beowulf '08 (V)
Wanted '08
A Mighty Heart '07
The Good Shepherd '06
Mr. & Mrs. Smith '05
Alexander '04
The Fever '04
Sky Captain and the World of Tomorrow '04
Taking Lives '04
Beyond Borders '03
Lara Croft Tomb Raider: The Cradle of Life '03
Life or Something Like It '02
Original Sin '01
Gone in 60 Seconds '00
Girl, Interrupted '99
The Bone Collector '99
Pushing Tin '99
Gia '98
Playing by Heart '98
Hell's Kitchen NYC '98
George Wallace '97
True Women '97
Foxfire '96
Love Is All There Is '96
Mojave Moon '96
Playing God '95
Without Evidence '96
Hackers '95
Cyborg 2 '93

I. Stanford Jolley (1900-78)
The Rebel Set '59
The Violent Years '56
Ghost Town Law '42
Outlaw Fury '50
King of the Rocketmen '49
Rimfire '49
Sands of Iwo Jima '49
Check Your Guns '48
Wild Country '47
Ambush Trail '46
Cyclotrode "X" '46

Kristen Johnston (1967-)
Music & Lyrics '07
Strangers with Candy '06
The Flintstones in Viva Rock Vegas '00
Austin Powers 2: The Spy Who Shagged Me '99
KISS Meets the Phantom of the Park '78

Margaret Johnston (1918-2002)
Sebastian '68
Burn Witch, Burn! '52
A Man About the House '47

Shawn Johnston
September Dawn '07
The Christmas Blessing '05

Oliver Johnston (1888-1966)
Tomb of Ligeia '64
A King in New York '57

Kim Johnston-Ulrich (1955-)
Rumpelstiltskin '96
Blood Ties '92

Marilyn Joi
Hospital of Terror '78
Kentucky Fried Movie '77
Black Samurai '77

Mirjana Jokovic (1967-)
Vukovar '94
Underground '95

Al Jolson (1886-1950)
Rhapsody in Blue '45
The Jazz Singer '27
Hallelujah, I'm a Bum '33
Midnight Limited '40

Wesley Jonathan (1978-)
Crossover '06
Roll Bounce '05
Baadasssss! '03

Carolyn Jones (1929-83)
Halloween with the Addams Family '79
Little Ladies of the Night '77
Eaten Alive '76
The Shaming '71
Color Me Dead '69
How the West Was Won '63
Ice Palace '60
Career '59
A Hole in the Head '59
Last Train from Gun Hill '59
King Creole '58
The Man Who Knew Too Much '56
The Seven Year Itch '55
The Tender Trap '55
The Big Heat '53
House of Wax '53
The War of the Worlds '53
The Road to Bali '53

Angela Jones
The Debt '98
Curdled '96
Pulp Fiction '94

Angus T. Jones (1993-)
The Christmas Blessing '05
Audrey's Rain '03
Bringing Down the House '03
See Spot Run '01
The Rookie '02

Andras Jones (1968-)
The Demolitionist '95
Far from Home '89
A Nightmare on Elm Street 4: Dream Master '88
Sorority Babes in the Slimeball Bowl-A-Rama '87

Allison Jones
Ellen Foster '97

Allan Jones (1908-92)
A Swingin' Summer '65
One Night in the Tropics '40
Everybody Sing '38
A Day at the Races '37
The Firefly '37
Rose Marie '36
Show Boat '36
A Night at the Opera '35

Ashley Jones (1976-)
The Devil's Prey '01
The King's Guard '01
The Fire Next Time '93

Barry Jones (1893-1981)
War and Peace '56
The Glass Slipper '55
Brigadoon '54
Demetrius and the Gladiators '54
Prince Valiant '54
Return to Paradise '53
The Clouded Yellow '51
Madeleine '50
Seven Days to Noon '50
Uneasy Terms '48

Ben Jones (1941-)
Joe Gould's Secret '00
Primary Colors '98
Deep in the Heart '83
Don't Change My World '83

Billy "Red" Jones (1913-2000)
Ninja Death Squad '87
The Phantom Flyer '28

Bruce Jones (1953-)
24-7 '97
Raining Stones '93

Buck Jones (1889-1942)
Below the Border '42
Dawn on the Great Divide '42
Down Texas Way '42
Arizona Bound '41
Forbidden Trails '41
Gunman from Bodie '41
Riders of Death Valley '41
Riders of the West '42
West of the Law '42
The Phantom Rider '36
Sandflow '37
The Crimson Trail '35
The Ivory Handled Gun '35
Stone o' Silver Creek '35
Law for Tombstone '35
When a Man Sees Red '34
The Throwback '35
The Fighting Sheriff '31
The Big Hop '31
Range Feud '31
Border Law '31
Hello Trouble '32
White Eagle '32
Trail of the Silver Spurs '41
Rangers Take Over '42
The Black Raven '43
Outlaw Roundup '44
Flaming Bullets '45
Frontier Fugitives '45
Lightning Raiders '45

Cherry Jones (1956-)
Ocean's Twelve '04
Signs '02
Erin Brockovich '00
The Perfect Storm '00
Cradle Will Rock '99
The Horse Whisperer '97
Julian Po '97
Big Town '87

Christopher Jones (1941-)
Ryan's Daughter '70
The Looking Glass War '69
Three in the Attic '68
Wild in the Streets '68

Claude Earl Jones
Bride of Re-Animator '89
Miracle Mile '89
Impulse '84
Evilspeak '62

Clyde Jones
Father of Lies '07
Love Beat the Hell Outta Me '00

Cody Jones (1985-)
Running Wild '99
Rent-A-Kid '95

Darby Jones (1910-86)
Zombies on Broadway '44
I Walked with a Zombie '43

Davy Jones (1946-)
The Brady Bunch Movie '95
Head '68

Dean Jones (1935-)
The Love Bug '97
That Darn Cat '96
Clear and Present Danger '94
Beethoven '92
Other People's Money '91
Fire and Rain '89
The Long Days of Summer '80
Born Again '78
When Every Day Was the Fourth of July '78

[continued]
Herbie Goes to Monte Carlo '77
Once Upon a Brothers Grimm '77
The Shaggy D.A. '76
Mr. Superinvisible '73
Snowball Express '72
Million Dollar Duck '71
The Horse in the Gray Flannel Suit '68
The Love Bug '68
Blackbeard's Ghost '67
Any Wednesday '66
Monkeys, Go Home! '66
That Darn Cat '65
The Ugly Dachshund '65
Under the Yum-Yum Tree '63
Torpedo Run '58
Jailhouse Rock '57
Tea and Sympathy '56

Dick(ie) Jones (1927-)
Pinocchio '40 (V)
Nancy Drew, Reporter '39
The Frontiersmen '38
Trail of the Hawk '37

Doug Jones (1960-)
Hellboy 2: The Golden Army '08
Fantastic Four: Rise of the Silver Surfer '07
Pan's Labyrinth '06
Hellboy '04
Hocus Pocus '93
Night Angel '90

Duane Jones (1937-88)
Fright House '89
To Die For '89
Beat Street '84
Ganja and Hess '73
Night of the Living Dead '68

Eddie Jones
The Terminal '04
Seabiscuit '03
Return to Me '00

Evan Jones (1927-)
Lucky You '07
Glory Road '06
Rescue Dawn '06
Jarhead '05
The Last Shot '04
Mr. 3000 '04
8 Mile '02

Freddie Jones (1927-)
Ladies in Lavender '04
The Count of Monte Cristo '02
Prince of Poisoners: The Life and Crimes of William Palmer '98
Neil Gaiman's Neverwhere '96
Cold Comfort Farm '94
The NeverEnding Story 3: Escape from Fantasia '94
Hotel Room '93
The Mystery of Edwin Drood '93
The Last Butterfly '92
Wild at Heart '90
Consuming Passions '88
The Black Cauldron '85 (V)
Young Sherlock Holmes '85
Dune '84
Firestarter '84
And the Ship Sails On '83
Krull '83
Agatha Christie's Murder is Easy '82
Firefox '82
The Elephant Man '80
Zulu Dawn '79
All Creatures Great and Small '74

Napoleon and Samantha '72
Pete n' Tillie '72
Support Your Local Gunfighter '71
Butch Cassidy and the Sundance Kid '69
Stay Away, Joe '68
Angel Baby '61
The Bramble Bush '60
Cash McCall '60
Vertigo '58
3:10 to Yuma '57
Will Success Spoil Rock Hunter? '57
The Bad Seed '56
The Girl Can't Help It '56
The Lady Says No '51

Jack Jones (1938-)
Airplane 2: The Sequel '82

James Earl Jones (1931-)
Welcome Home Roscoe Jenkins '08
The Benchwarmers '06 (V)
Scary Movie 4 '06 (N)
The Reading Room '05
Star Wars: Episode 3—Revenge of the Sith '05 (V)
Anne Rice's The Feast of All Saints '01
Finder's Fee '01
Summer's End '99
Undercover Angel '99
The Lion King: Simba's Pride '98 (V)
Merlin '98 (V)
What the Deaf Man Heard '98
Horton Foote's Alone '97
The Second Civil War '97
A Family Thing '96
Gang Related '96
Good Luck '96
Looking for Richard '96
Rebound: The Legend of Earl "The Goat" Manigault '96
Cry, the Beloved Country '95
Clean Slate '94
Clear and Present Danger '94
Jefferson in Paris '94
The Lion King '94 (V)
Naked Gun 33 1/3: The Final Insult '94
Excessive Force '93
The Meteor Man '93
Percy & Thunder '93
The Sandlot '93
Sommersby '93
Freddie the Frog '92 (N)
Patriot Games '92
Scorchers '92
Sneakers '92
The Ambulance '90
Heat Wave '90
The Hunt for Red October '90
Ivory Hunters '90
Last Flight Out: A True Story '90
Terrorgram '90 (N)
Best of the Best '89
By Dawn's Early Light '89
Field of Dreams '89
Grim Prairie Tales '89
Three Fugitives '89
Coming to America '88
Lone Star Kid '88
Gardens of Stone '87
Matewan '87
My Little Girl '87
Allan Quatermain and the Lost City of Gold '86
Soul Man '86
City Limits '85
Aladdin and His Wonderful Lamp '84
The Vegas Strip Wars '84
Return of the Jedi '83
Blood Tide '82
Conan the Barbarian '82
Flight of Dragons '82 (V)

The Bushido Blade '80
The Empire Strikes Back '80 (V)
The Guyana Tragedy: The Story of Jim Jones '80
Roots: The Next Generation '79
The Exorcist 2: The Heretic '77
The Greatest '77
The Last Remake of Beau Geste '77
Paul Robeson '77
Piece of the Action '77
Star Wars '77
Bingo Long Traveling All-Stars & Motor Kings '76
The River Niger '76
Swashbuckler '76
Deadly Hero '75
End of the Road '70
The Great White Hope '70
Dr. Strangelove, or: How I Learned to Stop Worrying and Love the Bomb '64

Janet Jones (1961-)
Police Academy 5: Assignment Miami Beach '88
American Anthem '86
A Chorus Line '85
The Flamingo Kid '84

January Jones (1978-)
We Are Marshall '06
The Three Burials of Melquiades Estrada '05
Dirty Dancing: Havana Nights '04
Love's Enduring Promise '04
American Wedding '03
Anger Management '03
Taboo '02
Bandits '01

Jedda Jones
Jeremy's Family Reunion '04
Talkin' Dirty after Dark '91

Jeffrey Jones (1947-)
Who's Your Caddy? '07
Dr. Dolittle 2 '01
Heartbreakers '01
Hanoi Hilton '87
Kenny Rogers as the Gambler, Part 3: The Legend Continues '87
Ferris Bueller's Day Off '86
George Washington: The Forging of a Nation '86
Howard the Duck '86
Transylvania 6-5000 '85
Amadeus '84
Valmont '89
Houseguest '94
Mom and Dad Save the World '92
Out on a Limb '92
Stay Tuned '92
The Hunt for Red October '90

Madame Bovary '49
Portrait of Jennie '48
Duel in the Sun '46
Love Letters '45
Since You Went Away '44
The Song of Bernadette '43
Frontier Horizon '39
Dick Tracy '37

Jerry Jones
Dolemite 2: Human Tornado '76
Dolemite '75

Jill Jones
The Perfect Holiday '07
Graffiti Bridge '90

Jocelyn Jones
Tourist Trap '79
The Enforcer '76
The Great Texas Dynamite Chase '76

John Marshall Jones (1962-)
Sgt. Bilko '95
Tapeheads '89

John Simon Jones
U.S. Navy SEALS: Dead or Alive '02
Mission of Death '97

Josephine Jacqueline Jones (1960-)
Warrior Queen '87
Black Venus '83

Kidada Jones
Black and White '99
Thicker than Water '99

Kimberly (Lil' Kim) Jones (1974-)
Nora's Hair Salon '04
You Got Served '04
Gang of Roses '03
Juwanna Mann '02
She's All That '99

Kirk "Sticky Fingaz" Jones (1973-)
House of the Dead 2: Dead Aim '05
Flight of the Phoenix '04
Leprechaun 6: Back 2 Tha Hood '03

L.Q. Jones (1927-)
A Prairie Home Companion '06
Route 666 '01
The Patriot '99
The Mask of Zorro '98
In Cold Blood '96
Tornado! '96
Casino '95
Lightning Jack '94
Grizzly Adams: The Legend Continues '90
River of Death '90
Bulletproof '88
Lone Wolf McQuade '83
Sacred Ground '83
Timerider '83
The Beast Within '82
Standing Tall '78
Banjo Hackett '76
Mother, Jugs and Speed '76
Winterhawk '76
A Boy and His Dog '75
White Line Fever '75
Manhunter '74
A Strange and Deadly Occurrence '74
Fireball Forward '72
Richard Petty Story '72
The Brotherhood of Satan '71
Ballad of Cable Hogue '70
The McMasters '70

The Wild Bunch '69
Stay Away, Joe '68
Iron Angel '64
Hell Is for Heroes '62
Ride the High Country '62
Flaming Star '60
Torpedo Run '58
The Young Lions '58
Men in War '57
Between Heaven and Hell '56
Love Me Tender '56
An Annapolis Story '55
Battle Cry '55

Marcia Mae Jones (1924-2007)
The Way We Were '73
Lady in the Death House '44
Let's Go Collegiate '41
The Gang's All Here '40
Old Swimmin' Hole '40
Tomboy '40
The Little Princess '39
The Adventures of Tom Sawyer '38
Mad About Music '38
Heidi '37
These Three '36
The Champ '32

Mark Jones (1953-)
Don't Open Till Christmas '84

Mark Lewis Jones (1964-)
Master and Commander: The Far Side of the World '03
Mists of Avalon '01
Solomon and Gaenor '98

Mickey Jones (1941-)
Sling Blade '96
Tin Cup '96
It Came from Outer Space 2 '95
Drop Zone '94
Forced to Kill '93
National Lampoon's Vacation '83

Morgan Jones
The Giant Claw '57
Apache Woman '55

Nathan Jones (1969-)
The Condemned '07

Orlando Jones (1968-)
Primeval '07
House of D '04
Biker Boyz '03
Drumline '02
The Time Machine '02
Double Take '01
Evolution '01
Say It Isn't So '01
Bedazzled '00
Chain of Fools '00
The Replacements '00
Liberty Heights '99
Waterproof '99
Miracle Mile '89
Office Space '98

Neal Jones (1960-)
Zombie Honeymoon '04
Day at the Beach '98

Nicholas Jones (1946-)
Horatio Hornblower: The Adventure Continues '01
Black Beauty '94
A Dangerous Man: Lawrence after Arabia '91

O-lan Jones (1950-)
American Virgin '98
Natural Born Killers '94
Pacific Heights '90

Peter Jones (1920-2000)
Whoops Apocalypse '83
Hot Millions '68

Gemma Jones (1942-)
The Contractor '07
Bridget Jones: The Edge of Reason '04
Shanghai Knights '03
Harry Potter and the Chamber of Secrets '02
Bridget Jones's Diary '01
Longitude '00
Cotton Mary '99
Captain Jack '98
The Theory of Flight '98
The Winslow Boy '98
Jane Eyre '97
Wilde '97
Wilderness '96
Feast of July '95
Sense and Sensibility '95
Devices and Desires '91
Paperhouse '89
The Duchess of Duke Street '78
The Devils '71

Gillian Jones (1947-)
Shame '87
Echoes of Paradise '86

Gordon Jones (1911-63)
McLintock! '63
The Monster That Challenged the World '57
Island in the Sky '53
Heart of the Rockies '51
North of the Great Divide '50
Sunset in the West '50
Trail of Robin Hood '50
Trigger, Jr. '50
Arizona Cowboy '49

Grace Jones (1948-)
Cyber Bandits '94
Boomerang '92
Siesta '87
Straight to Hell '87
Vamp '86
A View to a Kill '85
Conan the Destroyer '84
Deadly Vengeance '81
Gordon's War '73

Griffith Jones (1909-2007)
They Made Me a Fugitive '47
The Wicked Lady '45
Henry V '44
The Secret Four '40
The Mill on the Floss '37
First a Girl '35

Harold W. Jones
Provoked '89
The Crazies '73

Helen Jones
Resistance '92
Bliss '85

Henry Jones (1912-99)
Breathing Lessons '94
Arachnophobia '90
The Grifters '90
Nowhere to Run '88
Codename: Foxfire '85 (V)
Balboa '82
Deathtrap '82

Jennifer Jones (1919-)
The Towering Inferno '74
The Man in the Gray Flannel Suit '56
Love Is a Many-Splendored Thing '55
Indiscretion of an American Wife '54
Beat the Devil '53
Carrie '52
Ruby Gentry '52

,John and Julie '55
Man of Evil '48
Gideon '00
Ping! '96

Rashida Jones (1976-)
Little Black Book '04
Now You Know '02

Richard Jones (1946-)
Where the Heart Is '00
The Newton Boys '97
Two for Texas '97
The Good Old Boys '95
Lone Star '95
Under Siege '92
Another Pair o' Aces: Three of a Kind '91
Blue Sky '91

Richard T. Jones (1972-)
Vantage Point '09
Tyler Perry's Why Did I Get Married? '07
Twisted '04
G '02
Moonlight Mile '02
Phone Booth '02
Beyond Suspicion '00
Lockdown '00
The Wood '99
Event Horizon '97
Hollywood Confidential '97
Kiss the Girls '97
The Trigger Effect '96
Renaissance Man '94

Robert Earl Jones (1911-2006)
Rein Without Thunder '93
Maniac Cop 2 '90
Sleepaway Camp '83
Trading Places '83
C.old River '81
Sophisticated Gents '81
The Sting '73
Cockfighter '74

Rosie Jones
Ganjasaurus Rex '87
Alice to Nowhere '86

Sam Jones (1954-)
Strange Fruit '04
Dead Sexy '01
T.N.T. '98
American Strays '96
Where Truth Lies '96
Texas Payback '95
Ballistic '94
Fists of Iron '94
-tard Vice '94
Vegas Vice '94
Expert Weapon '93
Lady Dragon 2 '93
Thunder in Paradise '93
DaVinci's War '92
Maximum Force '92
Night Rhythms '92
The Other Woman '92
In Gold We Trust '91
One Man Force '88
Driving Force '88
Silent Assassins '88
Under the Gun '88
WhiteForce '88
Jane & the Lost City '87
My Chauffeur '86
Flash Gordon '80

Sam Jones, III (1983-)
Glory Road '06
Home of the Brave '05
ZigZag '02
Snipes '01

Sharon Lee Jones
Josh Kirby... Time Warrior: Chapter 3, Trapped on Toyworld '95

Shirley Jones (1934-)
Grandma's Boy '06
Hidden Places '06
Raising Genius '04
Manna from Heaven '02
Shriek If You Know What I Did Last Friday the 13th '00

Simon Jones (1950-)
The Hitchhiker's Guide to the Galaxy '05
Operation Delta Force 2: Mayday '97
The Devil's Own '96
Miracle on 34th Street '94
Green Card '90
Club Paradise '86
Privates on Parade '84
Monty Python's The Meaning of Life '83
The Hitchhiker's Guide to the Galaxy '81

Steve Jones (1955-)
The Big Bounce '04
The Filth and the Fury '99

Tamala Jones (1974-)
Daddy Day Camp '07
What Love Is '07
Who's Your Caddy? '07
Nora's Hair Salon '04
Head of State '03
The Brothers '01
On the Line '01
Two Can Play That Game '01
The Ladies Man '00
Little Richard '00
Next Friday '00
Turn It Up '00
Blue Streak '99
The Wood '99
Booty Call '96

Terry Jones (1942-)
Mr. Toad's Wild Ride '96
Erik the Viking '89
Monty Python's The Meaning of Life '83
The Secret Policeman's Other Ball '82
Secret Policeman's Private Parts '81
Monty Python's Life of Brian '79
Jabberwocky '77
Monty Python and the Holy Grail '75
And Now for Something Completely Different '72

Toby Jones (1967-)
The Mist '07
Amazing Grace '06
Infamous '06
The Painted Veil '06
Elizabeth I '05
Harry Potter and the Chamber of Secrets '02

Tom Jones (1940-)
Agnes Browne '99
Mars Attacks! '96
The Jerky Boys '95
The Last Days of Dolwyn '49

Tommy Lee Jones (1946-)
In the Valley of Elah '07
No Country for Old Men '07

Black Devil Doll from Hell '84
Tank '83
Who'll Save Our Children? '82

Samson Jorah
The Snow Walker '03

Richard Jordahl
To the Shores of Hel! '65
The Starfighters '63

Bobby Jordan (1923-65)
Spook Busters '48
Bowery Buckaroos '47
Hard-Boiled Mahoney '47
Clancy Street Boys '43

Betsy Jones-Moreland (1930-2006)
The Last Woman on Earth '61
Creature from the Haunted Sea '60

Patrick Jordan (1923-)
See Aldo Canti

Nick Jordan
Lady Godiva Rides '68
Count Yorga, Vampire '70
Sweet Georgia '72
Class Reunion '72

Marsha Jordan (1939-)
Dodge City '39
Each Dawn I Die '39
Gone with the Wind '39
Susannah of the Mounties '39
The Adventures of Tom Sawyer '38

Marian Jordan (1897-1961)
Here We Go Again! '42
Look Who's Laughing '41

Louis Jordan (1908-75)
Look Out Sister '48
Reet, Petite and Gone '47
Beware '46

Lydia Grace Jordan
Pistol Whipped '08
Into the Fire '05
The Thing About My Folks '05

Tyler Patrick Jones (1994-)
Ski Patrol '89
Frankenstein General Hospital '88

Jason Goes to Hell: The Final Friday '93
Madhouse '04
Eliza's Horoscope '70
Love Story '70

Leslie Jordan (1955-)
I Dismember Mama '74
Faces '68

Joanne Jordan / Joanne Moore
(various)

A Prairie Home Companion '06
Man of the House '05
'Neath Brooklyn Bridge '42
Bowery Blitzkrieg '41
Flying Wild '41
Pride of the Bowery '41
Spooks Run Wild '41
Boys of the City '40
That Gang of Mine '40
Young Tom Edison '40
They Made Me a Criminal '39
Angels with Dirty Faces '38
A Slight Case of Murder '38

Men in Black '97
U.S. Marshals '98 (V)
Small Soldiers '98 (V)
Double Jeopardy '99
Space Cowboys '00
Rules of Engagement '00
Men in Black 2 '02
The Missing '03
The Hunted '03
The Three Burials of Melquiades Estrada '05

Clint Jordan (1906-88)
Down to the Bone '04

Dorothy Jordan (1906-88)
The Searchers '56
The Cabin in the Cotton '32
Min & Bill '30

James Carroll Jordan (1950-)
Tales of the Unexpected '91

Jeremy Jordan (1973-)
Never Been Kissed '99
Nowhere '96

Jim Jordan (1896-1988)
Here We Go Again! '42
Look Who's Laughing '41

The Rescuers '77 (V)
Diary of a Teenage Hitchhiker '82

Kid Dynamite '43
Junior Army '42
Let's Get Tough! '42

Slashdance '89
Gotham '88
Big Town '87
Stormy Monday '88
Broken Vows '87
Yuri Nosenko, KGB '86
Moon Rising '86
The Park Is Mine '85
The River Rat '84
Cat on a Hot Tin Roof '84
Nate and Hayes '83
The Executioner's Song '82
Coal Miner's Daughter '80
The Betsy '78
Fire Birds '90
Blue Sky '91
JFK '91
Natural Born Killers '94
House of Cards '93
Heaven and Earth '93
Under Siege '92
The Good Old Boys '95

Blown Away '94
The Client '94
Cobb '94
The Fugitive '93
The Client '94
Batman Forever '95
Volcano '97

James Carroll Jordan

Victor Jory (1902-82)
Papillon '73
Cheyenne Autumn '64
The Miracle Worker '62
The Fugitive Kind '60
Death of a Scoundrel '56
Manfish '56
Sabaka '55
Valley of the Kings '54
Cat Women of the Moon '53
Man from the Alamo '53
Son of Ali Baba '52
The Capture '50
The Cariboo Trail '50
A Woman's Secret '49
The Loves of Carmen '48
South of St. Louis '48
Buckskin Frontier '43
Colt Comrades '43
Hoppy Serves a Writ '43
The Kansan '43
Leather Burners '43
Border Vigilantes '41
Charlie Chan in Rio '41
Riders of the Timberline '41
Green Archer '40
Knights of the Range '40
The Light of Western Stars '40

Daniel Jordano
Playing for Keeps '86
Alphabet City '84

William Jordan
Kingpin '96
The Men's Club '86
Solarbabies '86
A Flash of Green '85
Mean Season '85
Dune '84

The Murder of Mary Phagan '87
The Secret of My Success '87

Chato's Land '71
Lawman '71
Valdez Is Coming '71
Les Misérables '78
Logan's Run '76
Rooster Cogburn '75
The Yakuza '75
Trial of the Catonsville Nine '72
Interiors '78
Old Boyfriends '79
The Big Scam '79
Raise the Titanic '80
Washington Mistress '81

William Jordan
Kingpin '96

Larry Joshua
Spider-Man '02
The Shadow '94
Sugar Hill '94
Romeo is Bleeding '93
A Midnight Clear '92
Svengali '83
The Burning '81

Allyn Joslyn (1901-81)
Heaven Can Wait '43
Immortal Sergeant '43
I Wake Up Screaming '41
Fastest Gun Alive '56
I Love Melvin '53
Island in the Sky '53
As Young As You Feel '51
Harriet Craig '50
If I Had My Way '40
Only Angels Have Wings '39
The Shining Hour '38
They Won't Forget '37

Darwin Joston (1937-98)
Eraserhead '76
Assault on Precinct 13 '76
Cain's Cutthroats '71

Jennifer Jostyn
House of 1000 Corpses '03
Shot '01
Murder at Devil's Glen '99
Milo '98
Telling You '98
The First to Go '97
Midnight Blue '96
The Brother's McMullen '94
Omega Cop '90

Jacques Jouanneau (1926-)
Judex '64

Louis Jourdan (1919-)
Grand Larceny '92
Year of the Comet '92
The Return of Swamp Thing '89
Counterforce '87
Beverly Hills Madam '86
Double Deal '84
The First Olympics: Athens 1896 '84
Octopussy '83
Escape to Love '82
For the Love of Angela '82
Swamp Thing '82
Silver Bears '78

Ron Joseph
Mexican Blow '02
Navy SEALS '90

Erland Josephson (1923-)
Saraband '03
Faithless '00
Ulysses' Gaze '95
Good Evening, Mr. Wallenberg '93
Sofie '92
Meeting Venus '91
The Ox '91
Prospero's Books '91
Hanussen '88
The Unbearable Lightness of Being '88
Control '87
The Sacrifice '86
Saving Grace '86
After the Rehearsal '84
Fanny and Alexander '83
Nostalghia '83
Montenegro '81
To Forget Venice '79
Autumn Sonata '78
Face to Face '76
Scenes from a Marriage '73
Cries and Whispers '72
The Passion of Anna '70
Hour of the Wolf '68
The Smallest Show on Earth '48
Colonel Effingham's Raid '45
The Horn Blows at Midnight '45

Jackie Joseph (1934-)
Gremlins 2: The New Batch '90
Gremlins '84
Get Crazy '83
The Cheyenne Social Club '70
Little Shop of Horrors '60

Paterson Joseph (1964-)
Greenfingers '00
Neil Gaiman's NeverWhere

Hell-Ship Morgan '26
A Midsummer Night's Dream '35
Bulldog Drummond at Bay
The Beach '00
Bed and Board '70

Jourdan

The Man in the Iron Mask '77
The Count of Monte Cristo '74
The V.I.P.'s '63
Can-Can '60
The Best of Everything '59
The Bride Is Much Too Beautiful '58
Gigi '58
The Swan '56
Three Coins in the Fountain '54
Decameron Nights '53
Madame Bovary '49
Letter from an Unknown Woman '48
The Paradine Case '47

Louis Jouvet (1887-1951)
Jenny Lamour '47
Heart of a Nation '43
Bizarre Bizarre '39
Volpone '39
La Marseillaise '37
Carnival in Flanders '35
Topaze '33

Meto Jovanovski (1946-)
The Great Water '04
Stalked '99

Arly Jover
April's Shower '03
John Carpenter Presents Vampires: Los Muertos '02
Fish in a Barrel '01
Blade '98

Milla Jovovich (1975-)
Resident Evil: Extinction '07
.45 '06
Ultraviolet '06
Resident Evil: Apocalypse '04
Dummy '02
No Good Deed '02
Resident Evil '02
You Stupid Man '02
Zoolander '01
The Claim '00
The Messenger: The Story of Joan of Arc '99
The Million Dollar Hotel '99
He Got Game '98
The Fifth Element '97
Dazed and Confused '93
Chaplin '92
Kuffs '92
Return to the Blue Lagoon '91
The Night Train to Kathmandu '88
Two Moon Junction '88

Leatrice Joy (1893-1985)
Old Swimmin' Hole '40
First Love '39
Made for Love '26

Mark Joy
Crazy Like a Fox '04
Pecker '98
The Perfect Daughter '96
Black Rainbow '91

Nicholas Joy (1894-1964)
Desk Set '57
Native Son '51
Abbott and Costello Meet the Killer, Boris Karloff '49
Daisy Kenyon '47
Gentleman's Agreement '47

Robert Joy (1951-)
Aliens vs. Predator: Requiem '07
The Hills Have Eyes '06
George A. Romero's Land of the Dead '05
Pretty Persuasion '05
Whole New Thing '05
Joe Somebody '01
Perfume '01
The Shipping News '01
61* '01
Sweet November '01
The '70s '00
Resurrection '99
Fallen '97
Harriet the Spy '96
Waterworld '95
Henry & Verlin '94
A Modern Affair '94
The Dark Half '92
Longtime Companion '90
Millennium '89
The Lawrenceville Stories '88
She's Back '88
Big Shots '87
Miracle at Moreaux '86
Sword of Gideon '86
Desperately Seeking Susan '85
Joshua Then and Now '85
Amityville 3: The Demon '83
Atlantic City '81
Ragtime '81

Alice Joyce (1890-1955)
Song of My Heart '29
Dancing Mothers '26

Brenda Joyce (1917-)
Little Giant '46
The Enchanted Forest '45
Strange Confession '45
The Rains Came '39

Elaine Joyce (1945-)
Honor Thy Father and Mother: The True Story of the Menendez Brothers '94

Ella Joyce (1954-)
How to Frame a Figg '71
Motel Hell '80
Trick or Treat '86

Odette Joyeux (1917-2000)
La Ronde '51
Sylvia and the Phantom '45

Mario Joyner (1961-)
Pootie Tang '01
Bubba Ho-Tep '03
What About Your Friends: Weekend Getaway '02
Set It Off '96

Natalie Joyce (1902-92)
A Girl in Every Port '28
Through the Breakers '28

William Joyce (1930-)
The Young Nurses '73
I Eat Your Skin '64

Yootha Joyce (1927-80)
Horrors of Burke & Hare '71
Diel Diel My Darling! '65

Michelle Joyner
Painted Hero '95
Cliffhanger '93
Traces of Red '92

Kevin Jubinville (1967-)
Twitches Too '07
Nightwaves '03
The Courage to Love '00

Ashley Judd (1968-)
Crossing Over '08
Bug '06
Come Early Morning '06
De-Lovely '04
Twisted '04
Divine Secrets of the Ya-Ya Sisterhood '02
Frida '02
High Crimes '02
Someone Like You '01
Where the Heart Is '00
Double Jeopardy '99
Eye of the Beholder '99
Simon Birch '98
Kiss the Girls '97
The Locusts '97
Normal Life '96
A Time to Kill '96
Heat '95
Norma Jean and Marilyn '95
The Passion of Darkly Noon '95
Smoke '95
Ruby in Paradise '93

Carolyn Judd
Escape from Cell Block 3 '74
Women Unchained '72

Edward Judd (1932-)
The Kitchen Toto '87
Early Days '81
Flambards '78
Whose Child Am I? '75
Murder Motel '74
The Vengeance of She '68
Island of Terror '66
Invasion '65
Strange Bedfellows '65
First Men in the Moon '64
The Long Ships '64
Stolen Hours '63
The Day the Earth Caught Fire '61

Naomi Judd (1946-)
Family Tree '00
Rio Diablo '93
Living Proof: The Hank Williams Jr. Story '83
More American Graffiti '79

Robert Judd (1986-)
Crossroads '86
Fight for Your Life '77

Charles (Judel, Judells) Judels (1882-1969)
Baby Face Morgan '42
Down Argentine Way '40
Pinocchio '40 (V)
Love on the Run '36

Arline Judge (1912-74)
The Crawling Hand '63
Take It Big '44
Girls in Chains '43
Song of Texas '43
The Lady Is Willing '42
Law of the Jungle '42
Wildcat '42
One in a Million '36
Pigskin Parade '36
Mysterious Mr. Wong '35

Christopher Judge
Stargate: The Ark of Truth '08
A Dog's Breakfast '07

Mike Judge (1962-)
Spy Kids 3-D: Game Over '03
Spy Kids 2: The Island of Lost Dreams '02
South Park: Bigger, Longer and Uncut '99 (V)
Office Space '98
Beavis and Butt-Head Do America '96 (V)

Heather Juergensen
The Hammer '07
Kissing Jessica Stein '02

Arno Juerging (1947-83)
Andy Warhol's Dracula '74
Andy Warhol's Frankenstein '74

Gerard Jugnot (1951-)
The Chorus '04
French Fried Vacation '79
Spoiled Children '77

Aurora Julia
See Monica Randall

Raul Julia (1940-94)
The Burning Season '94
Down Came a Blackbird '94
Street Fighter '94
Addams Family Values '93
A Life of Sin '92
The Plague '92
The Addams Family '91
Frankenstein Unbound '90
Havana '90
Presumed Innocent '90
The Rookie '90
Mack the Knife '89
Romero '89
Moon over Parador '88
Onassis '88
The Penitent '88
Tango Bar '88
Tequila Sunrise '88
The Alamo: Thirteen Days to Glory '87
Florida Straits '87
Trading Hearts '87
The Morning After '86
Kiss of the Spider Woman '85
Strong Medicine '84
Overdrawn at the Memory Bank '83
The Escape Artist '82
One from the Heart '82
The Tempest '82
Eyes of Laura Mars '78
Gumball Rally '76
Death Scream '75
The Organization '71
Panic in Needle Park '71
Stiletto '69

Janet (Johnson) Julian (1959-)
King of New York '90
Ghostwarrior '86
Humongous '82
Smokey Bites the Dust '81
Def Jam's How to Be a Player '97
The Mack '73
Getting Straight '70

Sandra Julien (1950-)
I Am Frigid... Why? '72
The Sensuous Teenager '70

Julissa (1945-)
Dance of Death '68
The Fear Chamber '68
The Snake People '68

Gordon Jump (1932-2003)
Bitter Vengeance '94
Honeymoon Academy '90
Ransom Money '88
Dirkham Detective Agency '83
Conquest of the Planet of the Apes '72

Hu Jun (1968-)
Lan Yu '01
East Palace, West Palace '97

Tito Junco (1915-83)
The Exterminating Angel '62
Invasion of the Vampires '61
Death in the Garden '56
A Woman Without Love '51

Calvin Jung (1945-)
American Ninja 3: Blood Hunt '89
In the Shadow of Kilimanjaro '86

Eric Jungmann (1981-)
Killer Pad '06
Happy Endings '05
Monster Man '03
Not Another Teen Movie '01

John Junkin (1930-2006)
A Handful of Dust '88
A Hard Day's Night '64

Katy Jurado (1924-2002)
The Hi-Lo Country '98
Under the Volcano '84
Children of Sanchez '79
Once Upon a Scoundrel '73
Pat Garrett & Billy the Kid '73
Stay Away, Joe '68
Barabbas '62
One-Eyed Jacks '61
The Badlanders '58
Trapeze '56
Broken Lance '54
Arrowhead '53
El Bruto '52
High Noon '52
Bullfighter & the Lady '50

Peter Jurasik (1950-)
The Late Shift '96
Problem Child '90
Full Exposure: The Sex Tape Scandals '89
Peter Gunn '89
Scandal Sheet '85
Tron '82

Curt Jurgens (1912-82)
Smiley's People '82
Goldengirl '79
Just a Gigolo '79
Sleep of Death '79
Breakthrough '78
Cruise Missile '78
The Spy Who Loved Me '77
Twist '76
Vault of Horror '73
Battle of the Commandos '71
Dirty Heroes '71
The Mephisto Waltz '71
Nicholas and Alexandra '71
French Intrigue '70
The Assassination Bureau '69
Battle of Britain '69
Battle of Neretva '69
The Invincible Six '68
Murder for Sale '68
Target for Killing '66
Lord Jim '65
The Miracle of the White Stallions '63
The Longest Day '62
The Three Penny Opera '62
Brainwashed '60
Ferry to Hong Kong '59
Tamango '59
The Inn of the Sixth Happiness '58
Me and the Colonel '58
This Happy Feeling '58
And God Created Woman '57
Enemy Below '57
The Devil in Silk '56
The Mozart Story '48

Deana Jurgens (1957-)
Code Name: Zebra '84
Tin Man '83

James Robertson Justice (1905-75)
Zeta One '69
Mayerling '68
A Coeur Joie '67
Doctor in Distress '63
Le Repos du Guerrier '62
Murder She Said '62
The Guns of Navarone '61
Doctor at Large '57
Above Us the Waves '56
Doctor at Sea '55
Land of the Pharaohs '55
Doctor in the House '53
Rob Roy—The Highland Rogue '53
The Sword & the Rose '53
David and Bathsheba '51
The Lady Says No '51
Whiskey Galore '48

Katherine Justice (1942-)
Captain America 2: Death Too Soon '79
Frasier the Sensuous Lion '73
The Stepmother '71
Five Card Stud '68
Columbo: Prescription Murder '67

John Justin (1917-2002)
Lisztomania '75
The Thief of Bagdad '40

William Justine
Trauma '62

Jeff Kaake (1959-)
D.R.E.A.M. Team '99
Border Shootout '90

Suzanne Kaaren (1912-2004)
The Devil Bat '41
Phantom Ranger '38
Undercover Man '36

Nikolaj Lie Kaas (1973-)
PU-239 '06
Adam's Apples '05
Brothers '05
Reconstruction '03
Flickering Lights '01
The Idiots '99

Jane Kaczmarek (1955-)
Pleasantville '98
All's Fair '89
D.O.A. '88
Vice Versa '88
The Heavenly Kid '85
Door to Door '84
Falling in Love '84

Karen Kadler (1934-84)
The Beatniks '60
It Conquered the World '56

Piotr Kadochnikev
Ivan the Terrible, Part 2 '46
Ivan the Terrible, Part 1 '44

Charlotte Kady
Revenge of the Musketeers '94
L.627 '92

Heather Kafka
Three Days of Rain '03
Three Days of Rain '02

Diane Kagan
Mr. & Mrs. Bridge '90

Elaine Kagan
Sharon's Secret '95
Babyfever '94

Kyoko Kagawa (1931-)
Mothra '62
The Lower Depths '57
The Crucified Lovers '54
Sansho the Bailiff '54
Mother '52

David Kagen (1948-)
Body Chemistry '90
Conspiracy: The Trial of the Chicago Eight '87
Friday the 13th, Part 6: Jason Lives '86

Steve Kahan (1930-)
Lethal Weapon 4 '98
Demolition Man '93
Warlock: The Armageddon '93
Lethal Weapon 3 '92
Predator 2 '90
Lethal Weapon 2 '89
Scrooged '88
Lethal Weapon '87

Wolf Kahler (1946-)
One Against the Wind '91
Raiders of the Lost Ark '81

Madeline Kahn (1942-99)
Judy Berlin '99
A Bug's Life '98 (V)
Nixon '95
Mixed Nuts '94
For Richer, for Poorer '92
Kurt Vonnegut's Monkey House '91
Betsy's Wedding '90
An American Tail '86 (V)
Wanted: The Perfect Guy '86
Clue '85
City Heat '84
Slapstick of Another Kind '84
Yellowbeard '83
History of the World: Part 1 '81
First Family '80

Happy Birthday, Gemini '80
Simon '80
Wholly Moses! '80
The Muppet Movie '79
The Adventures of Sherlock Holmes' Smarter Brother '78
The Cheap Detective '78
High Anxiety '77
Blazing Saddles '74
Young Frankenstein '74
The Hideaways '73
Paper Moon '73
What's Up, Doc? '72

Alexander Kaidanovsky (1946-95)
Magic Hunter '96
Stalker '79

Chen Kaige (1952-)
Together '02
The Emperor and the Assassin '99

Khalil Kain (1965-)
Baadasssss! '03
Bones '01
Execution of Justice '99
Passing Glory '99
The Tiger Woods Story '98
Love Jones '96
Zooman '94
Renaissance Man '94
Juice '92

Joel Kaiser (1956-)
Dead Certain '92
Home for Christmas '92

Suki Kaiser (1967-)
Bloodhounds 2 '96
Virtual Assassin '95

Elizabeth Kaitan (1960-)
South Beach Academy '95
Virtual Encounters '96
Desperate Crimes '93
Beretta's Island '92
Vice Academy 3 '91
Roller Blade Warriors: Taken By Force '90
Nightwish '89
Aftershock '88
Assault of the Killer Bimbos '88
Friday the 13th, Part 7: The New Blood '88
Necromancer: Satan's Servant '79
Silent Night, Deadly Night 2 '87
Slave Girls from Beyond Infinity '87

Bonita Kalem
Escape from Cell Block 3 '74

Toni Kalem (1956-)
Women Unchained '72
American Strays '96
Billy Galvin '86
Silent Rage '82
Wanderers '79

Patricia Kalember (1957-)
Path to War '02
Signs '02
A Time for Dancing '00
Degree of Guilt '95
A Far Off Place '93
Big Girls Don't Cry... They Get Even '92
Jacob's Ladder '90
Fletch Lives '89

Helena Kallianiotes
Backtrack '89
Five Easy Pieces '70

Alexander Kalyagin (1942-)
A Slave of Love '78
An Unfinished Piece for a Player Piano '77

Jean-Pierre Kalfon (1938-)
The Cry of the Owl '87
Condorman '81
The Valley Obscured by the Clouds '70
Weekend '67

Danny Kamekona (1926-96)
Tree's Lounge '96
Big Bully '95
Robot Jox '90
The Karate Kid: Part 2 '86

Stanley Kamel (1943-2008)
Domino '05
Escape under Pressure '00
Running Red '99
Stonebrook '98
Honor Thy Father and Mother: The True Story of the Menendez Brothers '94
Murder by Numbers '89

Antoine Kamerling (1966-)
Dominion: Prequel to the Exorcist '05
Soul Assassin '01
Suite 16 '94

Dan Kamin (1947-)
The Rookie '02
America's Dream '95
Another Pair of Aces: Three of a Kind '91

Ida Kaminska (1899-1980)
The Angel Levine '70
The Shop on Main Street '65

Kris Kamm (1964-)
Andersonville '95
Wyatt Earp '94
Born to Ride '91
When the Party's Over '91

Fritz Kampers (1891-1950)
Kameradschaft '31
Westfront 1918 '30

Akiko Kana
The Imperial Japanese Empire '85
Samurai Reincarnation '81

Melina Kanakaredes (1967-)
Into the Fire '05
15 Minutes '01
Rounders '98
Saint Maybe '98
The Long Kiss Goodnight '96

Anna Kanakis (1962-)
After the Fall of New York '85
Warriors of the Wasteland '83

Ivan Kane
Bound '96
Gettysburg '93
Platoon '86

Steve Kanaly (1946-)
Scorpio One '97
Midnight Blue '96
Pumpkinhead 2: Blood Wings '94
Double Trouble '91
Driving Me Crazy '91
Eye of the Eagle 3 '91
Headhunter '89
Fleshburn '84
Balboa '82
Midway '76

Michael Kane
The Gunfighters '87
Lonely Are the Brave '62

Sandra Kane
Hack! '07
Chasing Holden '01
Chaos Factor '00
Rich Girl '91

Nobuo Kaneko (1923-)
The Human Condition: A Soldier's Prayer '61
Ikiru '52

Takeshi Kaneshiro (1911-)
House of Flying Daggers '04
Chungking Express '95
Fallen Angels '95

Hye-Jeong Kang (1982-)
Three ... Extremes '04
Oldboy '03

Sean Kanan (1966-)
Dead Heist '07
Gunmen '93
Posse '93

Carol Kane (1952-)
The Pacifier '05
Confessions of a Teenage Drama Queen '04
Audrey's Rain '03
Love in the Time of Money '02
My First Mister '01
Noah's Ark '99
The Tic Code '99
Jawbreaker '98
Gone Fishin' '97
Office Killer '97
American Strays '96
Trees Lounge '96
Big Bully '95
The Pallbearer '95
The Crazysitter '94
Addams Family Values '93
Ted & Venus '93
When a Stranger Calls Back '93
Baby on Board '92
In the Soup '92
The Lemon Sisters '90
My Blue Heaven '90
Flashback '90
Scrooged '88
License to Drive '88
Sticky Fingers '88
Ishtar '87
The Princess Bride '87
Jumpin' Jack Flash '86
Transylvania 6-5000 '85
Racing with the Moon '84
The Secret Diary of Sigmund Freud '84
Over the Brooklyn Bridge '83
Norman Loves Rose '82
Pandemonium '82
Keeping On '81
The Muppet Movie '79
When a Stranger Calls '79
My Sister, My Love '78
Annie Hall '77
Valentino '77
Harry & Walter Go to New York '76
Dog Day Afternoon '75
Hester Street '75
The Last Detail '73
Wedding in White '72
Carnal Knowledge '71
Desperate Characters '71

Christian Kane (1974-)
Four Sheets to the Wind '07
Just Married '03
Life or Something Like It '02
Summer Catch '01
Crossfire Trail '01
Love Song '00

Marjorie "Babe" Kane (1909-92)
Hollywood Boulevard '76
Teenage Gang Debs '66
Mutiny on the Blackhawk '39

Tom Kane (1962-)
Rugrats Go Wild! '03 (V)
The Powerpuff Girls Movie '02 (V)
The Wild Thornberrys Movie '02 (V)

Marvin Kaplan (1924-)
The Severed Arm '73
Angels in the Outfield '51
Adam's Rib '50

Mady Kaplan (1956-)
The Falcon and the Snowman '85
The Deer Hunter '78

Jonathan Kaplan (1947-)
Heat and Dust '82
Cannonball '76

Gabe Kaplan (1945-)
Tulips '81
Fast Break '79
Nobody's Perfekt '79

John Kapelos (1956-)
Shallow Ground '04
Mimic 3: Sentinel '03
Cold Blooded '00
The Deep End of the Ocean '98
The Late Shift '96
The Shadow '94
Man Trouble '92
Internal Affairs '90
All's Fair '89
Nick Knight '89
The Boost '88
Roxanne '87
Nothing in Common '86
The Breakfast Club '85

Ivar Kants (1949-)
A River Made to Drown In '97
Silver City '84

Jack Kao (1958-)
Flowers of Shanghai '98
Goodbye South, Goodbye '96

China Kantner (1971-)
The Evening Star '96
The Stoned Age '94

Alexis Kanner (1942-)
Nightfall '88
Kings and Desperate Men '83

James Karen (1923-)
The Pursuit of Happyness '06
Mulholland Drive '01
Thirteen Days '00
Fly Boy '59
Joyride '97
Up Close and Personal '96
Piranha '95
A Kiss Goodnight '94
Tough and Deadly '94
The Closer '91
The Unborn '91
Shattered Dreams '90
Vital Signs '90
The Willies '90
Wall Street '87
Billionaire Boys Club '87
Hardbodies 2 '86
The Jagged Edge '85
Latino '85
Return of the Living Dead '85
Sam's Son '84
Poltergeist '82
Time Walker '82
All the President's Men '76
Hercules in New York '70
Return of the Living Dead 2 '88
Frankenstein Meets the Space Monster '65

Sung Kang (1972-)
War '07
Tokyo Drift '06
Better Luck Tomorrow '02

Tim Kang
Rambo '08

John Kani
Robot Stories '03
The Ghost and the Darkness '96
An African Dream '90
Sarafina! '92
Options '88
Killing Heat '84
Master Harold and the Boys '85

Mirjana Karanovic (1957-)
Grbavica: The Land of My Dreams '06
Go West '05
Underground '95
When Father Was Away on Business '85

Manfred Karge (1938-)
Under the Pear Tree '73
The Adventures of Werner Holt '65

Anna Karin
The Fear '94
Body of Influence '93
Wild Cactus '92

Rita Karin (1919-93)
Enemies, a Love Story '89
Sophie's Choice '82

Anna Karina (1940-)
The Truth About Charlie '02
Chinese Roulette '76
Bread and Chocolate '73
The Salzburg Connection '72
The Nun '66
Alphaville '65
Pierrot le Fou '65
Band of Outsiders '64
Les Carabiniers '63
My Life to Live '62
Cleo from 5 to 7 '61
Le Petit Soldat '60
A Woman Is a Woman '60

Valerie Kaprisky
The Deceivers '88
L'Année des Méduses '86
Breathless '83

Shashi Kapoor (1938-)
Gulliver's Travels '95
In Custody '94
Siddhartha '72
Bombay Talkie '70
Shakespeare Wallah '65
The Householder '63

Mitzi Kapture (1964-)
His Bodyguard '98
Perfect Crime '97
Liberty & Bash '90

Richard Karlan (1919-)
Missiles of October '74

Vassilli Karis
Animal Called Man '87

Ron Karabatsos
The Crew '00
Rich Girl '91
29th Street '91
Hollywood Heartbreak '89
Missing Pieces '83

John Karlen (1933-)
Roseanne: An Unauthorized Biography '94
Racing with the Moon '84
Impulse '84
Surf Ninjas '93
Native Son '86
Gimme an F '85
Daughters of Darkness '71
Trilogy of Terror '75
House of Dark Shadows '70

Olga Karlatos (1947-)
Purple Rain '84
Zombie '80

Miriam Karlin (1925-)
The Attic: The Hiding of Anne Frank '86
A Clockwork Orange '71
Ladies Who Do '63
Room at the Top '59

Boris Karloff (1887-1969)
Targets '68
The Sorcerers '67
Mad Monster Party '68 (V)
The Snake People '68
The Sinister Invasion '68
The Fear Chamber '68
The Crimson Cult '68
Die, Monster, Die! '65
Black Sabbath '64
Bikini Beach '64
The Comedy of Terrors '64
Monco Bajordo '64 (N)
The Raven '63
The Terror '63
Corridors of Blood '58
The Haunted Strangler '58
Island Monster '53
Sabaka '55
Abbott and Costello Meet Dr. Jekyll and Mr. Hyde '53
The Strange Door '51
The Black Castle '52
The Boogie Man Will Get You '42
The Man They Could Not Hang '39
Mr. Wong in Chinatown '39
Mystery of Mr. Wong '39
Son of Frankenstein '39
Bedlam '45
Unconquered '47
The Secret Life of Walter Mitty '47
Lured '47
Dick Tracy Meets Gruesome '47
Isle of the Dead '45
The Body Snatcher '45
The Climax '44
House of Frankenstein '44
The Fatal Hour '40
Doomed to Die '40
British Intelligence '40
Black Friday '40
Before I Hang '40
The Ape '40
You'll Find Out '40
Devil's Island '40
Mr. Wong, Detective '38
Juggernaut '37
Charlie Chan at the Opera '36
The Invisible Ray '36
The Man Who Lived Again '36
The Black Room '35
The Bride of Frankenstein '35
Angel 3: The Final Chapter '88
Private Road: No Trespassing '87
Abbott and Costello Meet the Mummy '55
Start! '68

Karloff
The Raven '35
The Black Cat '34
The Ghoul '34
The Lost Patrol '34
The Mask of Fu Manchu '32
The Mummy '32
The Old Dark House '32
Criminal Code '31
Frankenstein '31
Scarface '31
Smart Money '31
Tonight or Never '31
King of the Kongo '29
The Bells '26
Old Ironsides '26
Dynamite Dan '24
The Last of the Mohicans '20

John Karlsen
Waterfront '83
Maciste in Hell '60

Oscar Karlweis (1895-1956)
Meet Me in Las Vegas '56
Five Fingers '52

Richard Karn (1956-)
Snow Buddies '08
Air Bud 4: Seventh Inning Fetch '02
MVP2: Most Vertical Primate '01

Roscoe Karns (1893-1970)
The Devil's Cargo '48
Vigilantes of Boom Town '46
Hi, Good Lookin'! '44
His Butler's Sister '44
Navy Way '44
Woman of the Year '42
Footsteps in the Dark '41
His Girl Friday '40
They Drive by Night '40
Frolics on Ice '39
You and Me '38
Alibi Ike '35
Wings in the Dark '35
It Happened One Night '34
Twentieth Century '34
Gambling Ship '33
Today We Live '33
The Crooked Circle '32
Night After Night '32
Laughing Sinners '31
Pleasure '31
Beggars of Life '28
Wings '27

Sarah Rose Karr (1984-)
Beethoven's 2nd '93
Beethoven '92
Homewrecker '92

Alex Karras (1935-)
Against All Odds '84
Goldilocks & the Three Bears '83
Porky's '82
Victor/Victoria '82
Nobody's Perfekt '79
Centennial '78
FM '78
Mad Bull '77
Babel '77
Hooch Country Boys '75
Blazing Saddles '74
Win, Place, or Show '72
Paper Lion '68

Sabine Karsenti
Battlefield Earth '00
Silent Hunter '94

Buck Kartalian (1922-)
Josh Kirby... Time Warrior: Chapter 3, Trapped on Toywrold '95
Please Don't Eat My Mother '72
The Acid Eaters '67
Cool Hand Luke '67

Vincent Kartheiser (1979-)
Alpha Dog '06

Linda Kash
The Unsaid '01
Bad Seed '00
Crime and Punishment in Suburbia '00
Luckytown '00
All I Wanna Do '98
Another Day in Paradise '98
Alaska '96
Masterminds '96

Claudia Karvan (1973-)
Aquamarine '06
Risk '00
Paperback Hero '99
Passion '99
Strange Planet '99
Flynn '96
Dating the Enemy '95
Lust and Revenge '95
Desperate Prey '94
High Tide '87

Tcheky Karyo (1953-)
The 4 Musketeers '05
Taking Lives '04
A Very Long Engagement '04
The Core '03
The Good Thief '03
Kiss of the Dragon '01
Arabian Nights '00
The Patriot '00
Saving Grace '00
Like a Fish Out of Water '99
The Messenger: The Story of Joan of Arc '99
Wing Commander '99
From the Earth to the Moon '98
My Life So Far '98
Habitat '97
Addicted to Love '96
Bad Boys '95
Foreign Land '95
Goldeneye '95
And the Band Played On '93

Alex Karzis
Detention '03
Stalked '94

Max Kasch (1985-)
A Man in Uniform '93
Waiting '05
Holes '03

Lawrence Kasdan (1949-)
As Good As It Gets '97
Into the Night '85

Casey Kasem (1933-)
Wedding Wars '06
Cinderella Man '05
Ernest Goes to Africa '97
Ernest Goes to School '94
Ernest Rides Again '93

Anna Kashfi (1934-)
Cowboy '58
Battle Hymn '57

Harold Kasket (1916-2002)
The Seventh Voyage of Sinbad '58
Moulin Rouge '52

Gary Kasper (1958-)
The Hunt for Eagle One: Crash Point '06

John Kassir (1957-)
Pocahontas '95 (V)
Final Equinox '95
Josh Kirby... Time Warrior: Chapter 4, Eggs from 70 Million B.C. '95
Ring of Steel '94

Mathieu Kassovitz (1967-)
Munich '05
Amen '02
Birthday Girl '02
Amelie '01
Jakob the Liar '99
The Fifth Element '97
Mon Homme '96
A Self-Made Hero '95
Cafe au Lait '94

Daphna Kastner (1961-)
Time Code '00
Lana '92
Venice, Venice '92
Julia Has Two Lovers '91
Eating '90

Peter Kastner (1944-)
Unfinished Business '89
Frightmare '81
You're a Big Boy Now '66

Kurt Kasznar (1913-79)
The Ambushers '67
Casino Royale '67
For the First Time '59
Legend of the Lost '57
Flame of the Islands '55
My Sister Eileen '55
Valley of the Kings '54
All the Brothers Were Valiant '53
Lili '53
Lovely to Look At '52

Anna (Katerina) Katarina
The Game '97
Omega Doom '96
The Blood of Heroes '89
Slaves of New York '89

Kurt Katch (1896-1958)
Abbott and Costello Meet the Mummy '55
The Mask of Dimitrios '44
The Mummy's Curse '44
The Seventh Cross '44
Ali Baba and the Forty Thieves '43
Background to Danger '43
Watch on the Rhine '43

Bernard Kates (1922-)
Robo Warriors '96
The Babe '92
Seedpeople '92

Kimberley Kates (1971-)
Highway '01
First Degree '98
Bad Blood '94

Branka Katic (1970-)
Chained Heat 2 '92
The Truth About Love '04
Black Cat, White Cat '98
The Wounds '98

Stana Katic
Feast of Love '07
Pit Fighter '05

Daisuke Kato (1910-75)
Yojimbo '61
Snow Country '57
Samurai 2: Duel at Ichijoji Temple '55
Seven Samurai '54
Rashomon '51

Haruhiko Kato
Carved '07
Pulse '01

Kazuo Kato (1928-)
Hiroshima '95
Ran '85

Masaya Kato (1963-)
Brother '00
Nobody '99
Drive '96
Crime Broker '94
Crimebroker '93
The Seventh Floor '93

Takeshi Kato (1929-)
Ran '85
None But the Brave '65

Rosanne Katon (1954-)
Bachelor Party '84
Zapped! '82
Lunch Wagon '81
Motel Hell '80
Chesty Anderson USN '76
The Muthers '76
She Devils in Chains '76
The Swinging Cheerleaders '74

Shintaro Katsu (1932-97)
The Razor: Sword of Justice '72
Zatoichi vs. Yojimbo '70
Zatoichi: The Blind Swordsman and the Fugitives '68
Zatoichi: The Blind Swordsman's Vengeance '66
Zatoichi: The Blind Swordsman and the Chess Expert '65
Zatoichi: Master Ichi and a Chest of Gold '64
Zatoichi: Zatoichi's Flashing Sword '64
Zatoichi: The Life and Opinion of Masseur Ichi '62

Andreas Katsulas (1947-2006)
Path to Paradise '97
The Fugitive '93
Blame It on the Bellboy '92
Communion '89
Next of Kin '89
Someone to Watch Over Me '87
Milo Milo '79

Nicky Katt (1970-)
The Brave One '07
Death Proof '07
Planet Terror '07
Snow Angels '07
Sin City '05
I Love Your Work '03
School of Rock '03
Secondhand Lions '03
Full Frontal '02
Insomnia '02
Waking Life '01
Boiler Room '00
Way of the Gun '00
The Limey '99
Delivered '98
One True Thing '98
Phantoms '97
johns '96
suBUrbia '96

William Katt (1950-)
The Man from Earth '07
Circuit '02
Twin Falls Idaho '99
Deadly Game '98
Jawbreaker '98
Mother Teresa: In the Name of God's Poor '97
Rough Riders '97
Daddy's Girl '96
Rattled '96
Piranha '95
American Cop '94
The Paperboy '94
Stranger by Night '94
Tollbooth '94
Desperate Motives '92
House 4: Home Deadly Home '91
Naked Obsession '91
Last Call '90
Swimsuit '89
Wedding Band '89
White Ghost '88
Perry Mason: The Case of the Lost Love '87
House '86
Baby... Secret of the Lost Legend '85
Perry Mason Returns '85
Thumbelina '82
Pippin '81
Butch and Sundance: The Early Days '79
Big Wednesday '78
First Love '77
Carrie '76

Chris Kattan (1970-)
Undead or Alive '07
Adam & Steve '05
Undercover Brother '02
Corky Romano '01
Monkeybone '01
House on Haunted Hill '99
A Night at the Roxbury '98

Jonathan Katz (1946-)
Daddy Day Care '03
The Independent '00

Judah Katz (1960-)
Crown Heights '02
Dirty Pictures '00

Omri Katz (1976-)
Adventures in Dinosaur City '92
Hocus Pocus '93
Matinee '92

Yftach Katzur (1958-)
Young Love—Lemon Popsicle 7 '87
Atalia '85
Baby Love '83
Hot Bubblegum '81

Andy Kaufman (1949-84)
Heartbeeps '81
In God We Trust '80
God Told Me To '76

David Kaufman (1969-)
Invisible: The Chronicles of Benjamin Knight '93
The Last Prostitute '91

Gunther Kaufman (1947-)
Kamikaze '89 '83
In a Year of 13 Moons '78
Whity '70

Christine Kaufmann (1944-)
Bagdad Cafe '88
Welcome to 18 '87
Murders in the Rue Morgue '71

Joseph Kaufman
Heavy Traffic '73
Johnny Got His Gun '71
Jud '71
Private Duty Nurses '71

Maurice Kaufman (1928-97)
Next Victim '74
The Abominable Dr. Phibes '71
Fright '71
The Hero '71
Die! Die! My Darling! '65

Caroline Kava
Born on the Fourth of July '89
Little Nikita '88

Christine Kavanagh
In His Life: The John Lennon Story '00
Catherine Cookson's The Glass Virgin '95
The Blackheath Poisonings '92

John Kavanagh
The Black Dahlia '06
Alexander '04
Benedict Arnold: A Question of Honor '03
The Informant '97
Sharpe's Sword '94
Widow's Peak '94
Bellman and True '88
Cal '84

Julie Kavner (1951-)
The Simpsons Movie '07 (V)
Click '06
The Lion King 1 1/2 '04 (V)
Judy Berlin '99
Dr. Dolittle '98 (V)
Deconstructing Harry '97
Forget Paris '95
I'll Do Anything '93
Shadows and Fog '92
This Is My Life '92
Alice '90
Awakenings '90
New York Stories '89
Radio Days '87
Surrender '87
Hannah and Her Sisters '86
Bad Medicine '85
Revenge of the Stepford Wives '80
Katherine '75

Tamio Kawaji (1938-)
Gappa the Triffian Monster '67
Tokyo Drifter '66
Story of a Prostitute '65

Chojuro Kawarazaki (1903-81)
47 Ronin, Part 1 '42
47 Ronin, Part 2 '42

Kunitaro Kawarazaki
47 Ronin, Part 1 '42
47 Ronin, Part 2 '42

Hiroyuki Kawase (1964-)
Godzilla vs. Megalon '76
Godzilla vs. the Smog Monster '72

Seizaburo Kawazu (1908-83)
Yojimbo '61

Yusuke Kawazu (1935-)
A Geisha '53
Fighting Elegy '66
The Human Condition: A Soldier's Prayer '61
The Cruel Story of Youth '60
The Human Condition: Road to Eternity '59

Barnaby Kay
Conspiracy '01

Bernard Kay (1928-)
Oscar and Lucinda '97
The Conqueror Worm '68
Doctor Zhivago '65

Billy Kay (1984-)
The Battle of Shaker Heights '03
L.I.E. '01

Dianne Kay (1955-)
Andy and the Airwave Rangers '89
Portrait of a Showgirl '82

Charles Kay (1930-)
Have No Fear: The Life of Pope John Paul II '05
The Importance of Being Earnest '02
Beautiful People '99
Henry V '89
Fortunes of War '87

1941 '79

Jody Kay
Death Screams '63
House of Death '82
One Armed Executioner '80

Mary Ellen Kay (1929-)
Thunder Pass '54
Border Saddlemates '52
Colorado Sundown '52
Government Agents vs. Phantom Legion '51
Rodeo King and the Senorita '51
Silver City Bonanza '51
Thunder in God's Country '51

Melody Kay
Camp Nowhere '94
The NeverEnding Story 3: Escape from Fantasia '94

Yuzo Kayama (1937-)
Zero '84
The Battle of the Japan Sea '70
Red Beard '65
Attack Squadron '63
Sanjuro '62

Danny Kaye (1913-87)
The Madwoman of Chaillot '69
The Five Pennies '59
Me and the Colonel '58
Court Jester '56
White Christmas '54
Help Wanted: Male '82
Hans Christian Andersen '52
The Inspector General '49
It's a Great Feeling '49
A Song Is Born '48
The Secret Life of Walter Mitty '47
Kid from Brooklyn '46
Wonder Man '45
Up in Arms '44

Caren Kaye (1951-)
Satan's Princess '90
My Tutor '82
Kill Castro '80
The Mercenaries '80

Celia Kaye (1941-)
Island of the Blue Dolphins '64

David Kaye (1964-)
3000 Miles to Graceland '01
Mermaid '00

Lila Kaye (1929)
Dragonworld '94
Mrs. 'Arris Goes to Paris '92
Antonia and Jane '91
Nuns on the Run '90
An American Werewolf in London '81

Norman Kaye (1927-2007)
Innocence '00
Heaven's Burning '97
Lust and Revenge '95
Bad Boy Bubby '93
A Woman's Tale '92
Frenchman's Farm '87
Warm Nights on a Slow Moving Train '87
Cactus '86
Man of Flowers '84
Where the Green Ants Dream '84
Lonely Hearts '82

Stubby Kaye (1918-97)
Who Framed Roger Rabbit '88
The Way West '67
Cat Ballou '65
Cool Mikado '63
40 Pounds of Trouble '62
Li'l Abner '59
Guys and Dolls '55

Lainie Kazan (1942-)
My Big Fat Greek Wedding '02
Gigli '03
Bratz '07
The Crew '00
If You Only Knew '00
What's Cooking? '00
The Big Hit '98
Safety Patrol '98
Allie & Me '97
Love Is All There Is '96
Movies Money Murder '96
The Cemetery Club '93
I Don't Buy Kisses Anymore '92
29th Street '91
Beaches '88
Out of the Dark '88
Harry and the Hendersons '87
Sunset Limousine '83
My Favorite Year '82
One from the Heart '82
Obsessive Love '84
Lust in the Dust '85
Delta Force '86
The Journey of Natty Gann '85

Tim Kazurinsky (1950-)
Poor White Trash '00
Shakes the Clown '92
A Billion for Boris '90
Wedding Band '89
Dinner at Eight '89
Hot to Trot '88
Police Academy 4: Citizens on Patrol '87
Police Academy 3: Back in Training '86
The Princess and the Pea '83
Continental Divide '81
My Bodyguard '80

James Keach (1948-)
The Experts '89
Options '88
The Dance Goes On '92
Wildcats '86
Moving Violations '85
Stand Alone '85
The Razor's Edge '84
Love Letters '83
National Lampoon's Vacation '83
The Long Riders '80
Hurricane '79
Smokey & the Hotwire Gang '79
Slashed Dreams '74
Till Death Do Us Part '72

Stacy Keach (1941-)
Honeydripper '07
Come Early Morning '06
Fatal Contact: Bird Flu in America '06
The Hollow '04
Miracle Dogs '03
The Santa Trap '02
Sunstorm '01
The Courage to Love '00
Children of the Corn 666: Isaac's Return '99
Fear Runs Silent '99
Militia '99
American History X '98
Prey of the Jaguar '96
Legend of the Lost Tomb '97
Escape from L.A. '96
Amanda and the Alien '95
Future Fear '97
Young Ivanhoe '95
Alien Nation: The Enemy Within '96
Alien Nation: Millennium '96

Staci Keanan (1975-)
Lisa '90

Kerrie Keane
Nowhere '96
Downhill Willie '96
Steel '97
Spasms '82
Incubus '82
Hot Pursuit '84
Kung Fu: The Movie '86
Nightstick '87
Obsessed '88
Distant Thunder '88
Malarek '89

Edward (Ed Kean, Keene) Keane (1884-1959)
Rogue's Gallery '44
Midnight Limited '40
Forever and a Day '43
Two Girls and a Sailor '44

James Keane (1952-)
Assassination Tango '03
Cannery Row '82
Apocalypse Now '79

Robert Emmett Keane (1883-1981)
Spasms '82
Incubus '82
Hills of Oklahoma '50
Susanna Pass '49

Marie Kean (1922-94)
The Lonely Passion of Judith Hearne '87
The Dead '87
Girl with Green Eyes '64

Betty Kean (1915-86)
Hi, Good Lookin'! '44
Slightly Terrific '44

Stacy Keach, Sr. (1914-2003)
Mission of the Shark '91
Ants '77
Watched '73
Fat City '72
Life & Times of Judge Roy Bean '72
The New Centurions '72
Brewster McCloud '70
End of the Road '70
The Heart Is a Lonely Hunter '68

Buster Keaton (1895-1966)
Man in the Silk Hat '83
A Funny Thing Happened on the Way to the Forum '66
Beach Blanket Bingo '65
How to Stuff a Wild Bikini '65
Pajama Party '64
Railrodder '65
It's a Mad, Mad, Mad, Mad World '63
Days of Thrills and Laughter '61
The Adventures of Huckleberry Finn '60
Around the World in 80 Days '56
Limelight '52
Sunset Boulevard '50
In the Good Old Summertime '49
Boom in the Moon '46
God's Country '46
Summertime '49
Two Girls and a Sailor '44
Li'l Abner '40
New Moon '40
Old Spanish Custom '36
What No Beer? '33
Speak Easily '32
Night Shift '32
Steamboat Bill, Jr. '28
The Cameraman '28
College '27
Battling Butler '26
The General '26
Sherlock, Jr. '24
The Navigator '24
Seven Chances '25
Our Hospitality '23
Three Ages '23
Sidewalks of New York '31
Doughboys '30
Free and Easy '30
Spite Marriage '29
The Villain Still Pursued Her '41
Her '41

Joe Keaton (1867-1946)
The General '26
The Last Time '06
Our Hospitality '23
Sherlock, Jr. '24

Michael Keaton (1951-)
Cars '06 (V)
The Company '07
Herbie: Fully Loaded '05
White Noise '05
First Daughter '04
Live from Baghdad '03
Quicksand '01
A Shot at Glory '00
Desperate Measures '98
Jack Frost '98
Out of Sight '98
Jackie Brown '97
Multiplicity '96
The Paper '94
Speechless '94
Much Ado about Nothing '93
My Life '93
Batman Returns '92
One Good Cop '91
Pacific Heights '90
Batman '89
The Dream Team '89
Beetlejuice '88
Clean and Sober '88
The Squeeze '87
Touch and Go '86
Gung Ho '85
Johnny Dangerously '84
Mr. Mom '83
Night Shift '82

James Kee
Coast to Coast '04
Double Standard '88
Shadow Dancing '88

Don Keefer (1916-)
Candy Stripe Nurses '74
The Young Nurses '73
Sleeper '73
The Adorable Cheat '28
Man from Headquarters '28

Cornelius Keefe (1900-72)
The Trigger Trio '37
Death from a Distance '36
Hong Kong Nights '35
Kentucky Blue Streak '35
Mystery Liner '34
The War Wagon '67
Man for Button Willow '65 (V)

Andrew Keegan (1979-)
A New Wave '07
Cruel World '05
Extreme Dating '04
O '01
Teenage Caveman '01
The Broken Hearts Club '00
10 Things I Hate About You '99
You '95

Howard Keel (1917-2004)
Day of the Triffids '63
Armored Command '61
Kismet '55
Jupiter's Darling '55
Deep in My Heart '54
Rose Marie '54
Seven Brides for Seven Brothers '54

Caitlin Keats (1972-)
The Lather Effect '06
Kill Bill Vol. 2 '04

Ele Keats (1973-)
Eros '04
White Dwarf '95
Mother '94

Charles Keating (1941-)
Deuce Bigalow: European Gigolo '05
The Thomas Crown Affair '99
The Bodyguard '92
Brideshead Revisited '81
God '79

Fred Keating (1897-1961)
The Ninth Configuration '79
Battleforce '78
Diary of a Young Comic '79
Mountain of the Cannibal God '79

Larry Keating (1896-1963)
The Incredible Mr. Limpet '64
The New Interns '64
Stopover Tokyo '57
Daddy Long Legs '55
Gypsy Colt '54
Above and Beyond '53
Give a Girl a Break '53
A Lion Is in the Streets '53
Monkey Business '52
Francis Goes to the Races '51
When Worlds Collide '51

Billy Kearns (1923-92)
The Nutt House '95
Ricky and Pete '88
Princess Daisy '83
Mistral's Daughter '84
The Blue and the Gray '82
Butterfly '82
That Championship Season '82
Road Games '81
Saturday the 14th '81
The Long Riders '80
A Rumor of War '80

Stephen Kearney
In His Life: The John Lennon Story '00

Gillian Kearney (1972-)
Catherine Cookson's The Tide of Life '96

Diane Keaton (1946-)
Mad Money '08
Because I Said So '07
The Family Stone '05
Something's Gotta Give '03
Town and Country '01
Hanging Up '99
The Other Sister '99
The Only Thrill '97
The First Wives Club '96
Marvin's Room '96
Father of the Bride Part 2 '95
Running Mates '92
Father of the Bride '91
The Godfather, Part 3 '90
The Lemon Sisters '90
The Good Mother '88
Baby Boom '87
Radio Days '87
The Little Drummer Girl '84
Mrs. Soffel '84
Crimes of the Heart '86
Shoot the Moon '82
Reds '81
The Godfather 1902-1959: The Complete Epic '81
Manhattan '79
Interiors '78
Annie Hall '77
Looking for Mr. Goodbar '77
Harry & Walter Go to New York '76
I Will, I Will...for Now '76
Love and Death '75
The Godfather, Part 2 '74
Sleeper '73
Play It Again, Sam '72
Lovers and Other Strangers '70
The Godfather '72

Hugh Keays-Byrne (1947-)
Journey to the Center of the Earth '99
Moby Dick '98
Resistance '92
Kangaroo '86
Mad Max '80
Death Train '79

Lila Kedrova (1918-2000)
Some Girls '88
Sword of the Valiant '83
Tell Me a Riddle '80
Le Cavaleur '78
Widow's Nest '77
The Tenant '76
Torn Curtain '66
Zorba the Greek '64
Modigliani '58

Arielle Kebbel (1985-)
Aquamarine '06
The Grudge 2 '06
John Tucker Must Die '06
Outlaw Trail '06
American Pie Presents Band Camp '05
The Kid and I '05
Soul Plane '04

Toby Kebbell
Control '07
Dead Man's Shoes '04

White Wolves 2: Legend of the Wild '94
Lipstick Camera '93

Steven Keats (1946-94)
Lipstick '76

Brian L. Keaulana (1961-)
Black Sunday '77
Hester Street '75
For Ladies Only '81
Mysterious Island of Beautiful Women '79
Silent Rage '82
The Executioner's Song '82
Badge of the Assassin '85
In Dangerous Company '88
The Spring '89
Eternity '90

Andrew Keegan (1979-)

Howard Keel (1917-2004)

Calamity Jane '53
I Love Melvin '53
Kiss Me Kate '53
Lovely to Look At '52
Across the Wide Missouri '51 (N)
Show Boat '51
Texas Carnival '51
Three Guys Named Mike '51
Annie Get Your Gun '50
Pagan Love Song '50

Ruby Keeler (1909-93)
That's Dancing! '85
Dames '34
Flirtation Walk '34
Footlight Parade '33
42nd Street '33
Gold Diggers of 1933 '33

Diane Keen (1946-)
Jekyll and Hyde '90

Geoffrey Keen (1916-2005)
The Living Daylights '87
Amin: The Rise and Fall '82
For Your Eyes Only '81
Moonraker '79
Number 1 of the Secret Service '77
The Spy Who Loved Me '77
Sacco & Vanzetti '71
Taste the Blood of Dracula '70
Doctor Zhivago '65
Dr. Syn, Alias the Scarecrow '64
A Matter of WHO '62
Sink the Bismarck '60
The Third Key '57
Postmark for Danger '56
The Man Who Never Was '55
Angels One Five '54
Black Glove '54
Doctor in the House '53
Genevieve '53
Scotland Yard Inspector '52
The Clouded Yellow '51
Cry, the Beloved Country '51
The Fallen Idol '49
The Third Man '49

Malcolm Keen (1888-1970)
Mr. Reeder in Room 13 '38
The Manxman '29
The Lodger '26

Pat Keen
Without a Clue '88
A Kind of Loving '81

Monica Keena (1979-)
Loaded '08
Brooklyn Rules '07
Corporate Affairs '07
Left in Darkness '06
Man of the House '05
Freddy vs. Jason '03
Crime and punishment in Suburbia '00
First Daughter '99
The Simian Line '99
All I Wanna Do '98
Ripe '97
Snow White: A Tale of Terror '97
While You Were Sleeping '95

Caroline Keenan (1970-)
Killer Bud '00
Vice Girls '96

Will Keenan
Margarita Happy Hour '01
Waiting '00

Tom Keene (1898-1963)
Plan 9 from Outer Space '56
Storm over Wyoming '50
Trail of Robin Hood '50
Lights of Old Santa Fe '47
Navy Way '44

Arizona Roundup '42
Lone Star Law Men '42
Western Mail '42
The Driftin' Kid '41
Dynamite Canyon '41
Riding the Sunset Trail '41
God's Country and the Man '37
Where Trails Divide '37
Desert Gold '36
Drift Fence '36
The Glory Trail '36
Hong Kong Nights '35
Beyond the Rockies '32
Our Daily Bread '34
Come on Danger! '32
Ghost Valley '32
Saddle Buster '32
Pardon My Gun '30
Marked Money '28

Catherine Keener (1961-)
Into the Wild '07
Friends with Money '06
The Ballad of Jack and Rose '05
Capote '05
The 40 Year Old Virgin '05
The Interpreter '05
Death to Smoochy '02
Full Frontal '02
Lovely & Amazing '02
Simone '02
Being John Malkovich '99
Simpatico '99
8mm '98
Out of Sight '98
Your Friends & Neighbors '98
The Real Blonde '97
Box of Moonlight '96
The Destiny of Marty Fine '96
If These Walls Could Talk '96
Walking and Talking '96
Living in Oblivion '94
Johnny Suede '92
Survival Quest '89

Eliott Keener (1949-99)
Running Wild '94
Hard Target '93
Angel Heart '87

Eric Keenleyside
Blue Smoke '07
The Interpreter '05

Matt Keeslar (1972-)
Art School Confidential '06
The Thirst '06
Masters of Horror: Family '05
Live from Baghdad '03
Stephen King's Rose Red '02
Texas Rangers '01
Dune '00
Psycho Beach Party '00
Scream 3 '00
Urbania '00
Durango '99
Splendor '99
The Last Days of Disco '98
Sour Grapes '98
The Deli '97
Mr. Magoo '97
Waiting for Guffman '96
The Run of the Country '95
The Stupids '95
Safe Passage '94

Jack Kehler
Grilled '06
Invincible '06
Fever Pitch '05
Big Trouble '02
Love Liza '02
Men in Black 2 '02
Beyond Suspicion '00
Austin Powers 2: The Spy Who Shagged Me '99
Dudley Do-Right '99
Forces of Nature '99
The Mating Habits of the Earthbound Human '99
True Crime '99

Lethal Weapon 4 '98
Sour Grapes '98
The Big Lebowski '97
The Lesser Evil '97
187 '97
American Strays '96
Death Benefit '96
Lost Highway '96
My Fellow Americans '96
The Shot '96
Desert Winds '95
The Invaders '95
Serpent's Lair '95
Waterworld '95
Across the Moon '94
Cops and Robbersons '94
Love Is a Gun '94
Wyatt Earp '94
Blindsided '93
Casualties of Love: The "Long Island Lolita" Story '93
The Positively True Adventures of the Alleged Texas Cheerleader-Murdering Mom '93
White Sands '92
Grand Canyon '91
The Last Boy Scout '91
Point Break '91
I Love You to Death '90
Bloodstone '88
Year of the Dragon '85
Strange Invaders '83

Jack Kehoe (1938-)
Falling Down '93
Servants of Twilight '91
Young Guns 2 '90
The Untouchables '87
A Winner Never Quits '86
The Pope of Greenwich Village '84
On the Nickel '80
The Fish that Saved Pittsburgh '79
Law and Disorder '74
Serpico '73
The Sting '73

Claire Keim (1975-)
The Girl '01

Andrew Keir (1926-97)
Ripper: Letter from Hell '01
Rob Roy '95
Dragonworld '94
Absolution '81
The Thirty-Nine Steps '79
Blood from the Mummy's Tomb '71
Zeppelin '71
The Night Visitor '70
The Viking Queen '67
Daleks—Invasion Earth 2150 A.D. '66
Dracula, Prince of Darkness '66
The Fighting Prince of Donegal '66
Lord Jim '65
Cleopatra '63
Suspended Alibi '56

Harvey Keitel (1947-)
National Treasure: Book of Secrets '07
Arthur and the Invisibles '06 (V)
The Stone Merchant '06
Be Cool '05
The Bridge of San Luis Rey '05
National Treasure '04
Puerto Vallarta Squeeze '04
Crime Spree '03
Cuban Blood '03
Red Dragon '02
The Grey Zone '01
Taking Sides '01
Fail Safe '00
Little Nicky '00
U-571 '00
Holy Smoke '99
Finding Graceland '98
Gunslinger's Revenge '98
Lulu on the Bridge '98
Shadrach '98
Three Seasons '98

Cop Land '97
FairyTale: A True Story '97
City of Industry '96
Head Above Water '96
Blue in the Face '95
Clockers '95
From Dusk Till Dawn '95
Get Shorty '95
Smoke '95
Ulysses' Gaze '95
Imaginary Crimes '94
Monkey Trouble '94
Pulp Fiction '94
Somebody to Love '94
Dangerous Game '93
The Piano '93
Point of No Return '93
Rising Sun '93
The Young Americans '93
Bad Lieutenant '92
Reservoir Dogs '92
Sister Act '92
Bugsy '91
Mortal Thoughts '91
Thelma & Louise '91
Two Evil Eyes '90
The Two Jakes '90
The January Man '89
Blindside '88
The Last Temptation of Christ '88
The Inquiry '87
The Pick-Up Artist '87
The Men's Club '86
Off Beat '86
Camorra: The Naples Connection '85
Star Knight '85
Corrupt '84
Falling in Love '84
Exposed '83
The Border '82
La Nuit de Varennes '82
Death Watch '80
Saturn 3 '80
Eagle's Wing '79
Blue Collar '78
Fingers '78
The Duellists '77
Welcome to L.A. '77
Buffalo Bill & the Indians '76
Mother, Jugs and Speed '76
Taxi Driver '76
The Virginia Hill Story '76
Shining Star '75
Alice Doesn't Live Here Anymore '73
Mean Streets '73
Who's That Knocking at My Door? '68

Alexander Keith
The Capitol Conspiracy '99
Counter Measures '98

Brian Keith (1921-97)
Rough Riders '97
Entertaining Angels: The Dorothy Day Story '96
National Lampoon's Favorite Deadly Sins '95
Picture Windows '95
Walking Thunder '94 (N)
The Gambler Returns: The Luck of the Draw '93
Escape '90
Welcome Home '89
Young Guns '88
The Alamo: Thirteen Days to Glory '87
Death Before Dishonor '87
World War III '86
Charlie Chan and the Curse of the Dragon Queen '81
Sharky's Machine '81
The Mountain Men '80
The Chisholms '79
Meteor '79
The Seekers '79
Centennial '78
Hooper '78
Joe Panther '76
The Loneliest Runner '76
The Longest Drive '76
The Wind and the Lion '75
The Yakuza '75
Bull of the West '71

Scandalous John '71
McKenzie Break '70
Suppose They Gave a War and Nobody Came? '70
With Six You Get Eggroll '68
Reflections in a Golden Eye '67
Nevada Smith '66
The Rare Breed '66
The Russians Are Coming, the Russians Are Coming '66
The Hallelujah Trail '65
Those Calloways '65
A Tiger Walks '64
Johnny Shiloh '63
Savage Sam '63
Moon Pilot '62
Deadly Companions '61
The Parent Trap '61
Ten Who Dared '60
The Young Philadelphians '59
Dino '57
Nightfall '56
Run of the Arrow '56
Tight Spot '55
The Violent Men '55
Arrowhead '53

David Keith (1954-)
Bottoms Up '06
Miracle Dogs Too '06
All Souls Day '05
Raise Your Voice '04
Daredevil '03
Epoch: Evolution '03
Hangman's Curse '03
Carrie '02
Behind Enemy Lines '01
Burning Down the House '01
Sabretooth '01
The Stickup '01
World Traveler '01
Epoch '00
Men of Honor '00
U-571 '00
Hot Blooded '98
Poodle Springs '98
Secre of the Andes '98
Invasion of Privacy '96
Judge & Jury '96
Red Blooded 2 '96
Born Wild '95
Deadly Sins '95
Gold Diggers: The Secret of Bear Mountain '95
The Indian in the Cupboard '95
Major League 2 '94
Temptation '94
Texas '94
Raw Justice '93
Caged Fear '92
Desperate Motives '92
Liar's Edge '92
Off and Running '90
The Further Adventures of Tennessee Buck '88
Heartbreak Hotel '88
White of the Eye '88
The Curse '87
Gulag '85
Firestarter '84
Independence Day '83
The Lords of Discipline '83
An Officer and a Gentleman '82
Back Roads '81
Take This Job & Shove It '81
Brubaker '80
The Great Santini '80
The Rose '79

Donald Keith (1903-69)
Outlaw Justice '32
Branded Men '31
Bare Knees '28
We're in the Navy Now '27
Dancing Mothers '26
Free to Love '25
My Lady of Whims '25
Parisian Love '25
The Plastic Age '25

Ian Keith (1899-1960)
It Came from Beneath the Sea '55
The Black Shield of Falworth '54
Dick Tracy's Dilemma '47
Nightmare Alley '47
Dick Tracy vs. Cueball '46
Song of Old Wyoming '45
The Chinese Cat '44
Bordertown Gunfighters '43
Corregidor '43
Five Graves to Cairo '43
Man from Thunder River '43
The Payoff '43
Sundown Kid '43
Mary of Scotland '36
The White Legion '36
The Crusades '35
The Three Musketeers '35
Queen Christina '33
The Sign of the Cross '33
Abraham Lincoln '30
Manhandled '24

Penelope Keith (1940-)
Coming Home '98
The Norman Conquests, Part 1: Table Manners '78
The Norman Conquests, Part 2: Living Together '78
The Norman Conquests, Part 3: Round and Round the Garden '78
Madhouse Mansion '74

Robert Keith (1898-1966)
Cimarron '60
Men in War '57
My Man Godfrey '57
Between Heaven and Hell '56
Written on the Wind '56
Love Me or Leave Me '55
Drum Beat '54
The Wild One '54
Young at Heart '54
Battle Circus '53
Devil's Canyon '53
Small Town Girl '53
Here Comes the Groom '51
I Want You '51
My Foolish Heart '49
Boomerang '47

Rosalind Keith (1916-2000)
Bad Boy '39
Theodora Goes Wild '36

Sheila Keith (1920-2004)
House of the Long Shadows '82
The Comeback '77
The Confessional '75
Frightmare '74

Peter Keleghan (1959-)
Niagara Motel '06
Jericho Mansions '03
Ginger Snaps '01
Angels in the Infield '00
Escape from Wildcat Canyon '99
Screwballs '83

Joseph Kell (1960-)
White Lies '98
Bone Daddy '97
Cupid '96

Robert Kellard (1915-81)
Gentleman from Dixie '41
Drums of Fu Manchu '40

Cecil Kellaway (1893-1973)
Quick, Let's Get Married '71
Getting Straight '70
Guess Who's Coming to Dinner '67
Spinout '66
Hush, Hush, Sweet Charlotte '65
The Cardinal '63
Zotz! '62

Interrupted Melody '55
The Prodigal '55
The Beast from 20,000 Fathoms '53
Young Bess '53
Francis Goes to the Races '51
Harvey '50
Kim '50
Portrait of Jennie '48
Unconquered '47
Easy to Wed '46
Monsieur Beaucaire '46
The Postman Always Rings Twice '46
Love Letters '45
Frenchman's Creek '44
It Ain't Hay '43
Bahama Passage '42
I Married a Witch '42
Birth of the Blues '41
Burma Convoy '41
Night of January 16th '41
Brother Orchid '40
The House of the Seven Gables '40
The Letter '40
Mexican Spitfire '40
Gunga Din '39
Wuthering Heights '39
Maid's Night Out '38

Tina Kellegher (1967-)
The Snapper '93
Scarlet '94

Tim Kelleher
Thirteen Days '00
Understudy: The Graveyard Shift 2 '88

Hiram Keller (1944-97)
Countryman '83
Lifespan '75
A Real Young Girl '75
Ciao Federico Fellini
Directs Satyricon '69
Fellini Satyricon '69

Joel S. Keller
Brotherhood of Murder '99
The Life Before This '99
The Hanging Garden '97

Marthe Keller (1945-)
Women '97
Mon Amie Max '94
Young Catherine '91
The Nightmare Years '89
Dark Eyes '87
Red Kiss '85
The Amateur '82
The Formula '80
Bobby Deerfield '77
Black Sunday '77
Marathon Man '76
And Now My Love '74

Mary Page Keller (1961-)
Timecop 2: The Berlin Decision '03
Venomous '01

DeForest Kelley (1920-99)
Star Trek V: The Final Frontier '89
Star Trek 4: The Voyage Home '86
Star Trek 3: The Search for Spock '84
Star Trek: The Motion Picture '79
Night of the Lepus '72
Apache Uprising '66
Warlock '59
The Law and Jake Wade '58
Gunfight at the O.K. Corral '57
The Man in the Gray Flannel Suit '56
House of Bamboo '55
Illegal '55
Fear in the Night '47
Variety Girl '47

Kimberly Kelley
Midnight Tease 2 '95
Hard Bounty '94

Boris and Natasha: The Movie '92
The Player '92
Doppelganger: The Evil Within '90

Ryan Kelley
Outlaw Trail '06
Mean Creek '04

Sheila Kelley (1961-)
Mozart and the Whale '05
Matchstick Men '03
Secret Weapons '85
Passion Fish '92
Dancing at the Blue Iguana '00
Nurse Betty '00
One Fine Day '96
Deconstructing Sarah '94
A Passion to Kill '94
The Secretary '94
Singles '92
The Chase '91
Pure Luck '91
Soapdish '91
Mortal Passions '90
Where the Heart Is '90
Breaking In '89
Some Girls '88
A Little Romance '79

Walter Kelley
Men in War '57
Marty '55

Mike Keilin (1922-83)
Sleepaway Camp '83
On the Yard '79
Girlfriends '78
God Told Me To '76
Next Stop Greenwich Village '76
Freebie and the Bean '74
The Last Porno Flick '74
Riot '69
The Boston Strangler '68
The Incident '67
Hell Is for Heroes '62
The Great Impostor '61
Crooklyn '94
Café Society '97
Songcatcher '99
In Too Deep '99
Agent Cody Banks 2: Destination London '04
Greenfingers '00
Waking Ned Devine '98
The Run of the Country '95
A Man of No Importance '94

David Patrick Kelly (1952-)
Stardust '07
Charlie and the Chocolate Factory '05
The Longest Yard '05
Personal Velocity: Three Portraits '02
K-PAX '01
Mean Machine '01
The Crow '94
Malcolm X '92
Cheap Shots '91
The Adventures of Ford Fairlane '90
The Misfit Brigade '87
Commando '85
Dreamscape '84
The Warriors '79

Nathalie Kelley
Loaded '08
The Fast and the Furious: Tokyo Drift '06

Claire Kelly (1934-)
Dressed for Death '74
And Soon the Darkness '70
A Guide for the Married Man '67
Georgy Girl '66
Ask Any Girl '59
The Badlanders '58
Party Girl '58

Craig Kelly (1970-)
When Saturday Comes '95
Nightscare '93
The Young Americans '93

Darragh Kelly
48 Angels '06

David Kelly (1929-)
Stardust '07
Charlie and the Chocolate Factory '05
Agent Cody Banks 2: Destination London '04
Greenfingers '00
Waking Ned Devine '98
The Run of the Country '95
A Man of No Importance '94
Into the West '92
The Kovak Box '06

Jim Kelly (1946-)
One Down, Two to Go! '82
Black Eliminator '78
Kill Factor '78
Hot Potato '76
Take a Hard Ride '75
Black Belt Jones '74
Three the Hard Way '74
Enter the Dragon '73

Judy Kelly (1913-91)
Dead of Night '45
Butler's Dilemma '43
House of Mystery '41
Make-Up '37
The Private Life of Henry VIII '33

Kathleen Kelly (1912-)
The Mutiny of the Elsinore '39
Heart's Desire '37
The Avenging Hand '36
The Deputy Drummer '35
An Empty Bed '90
The Amazing Transparent Man '60

Bruce Kellogg (1918-66)
Unknown World '51
They Were Expendable '45

John Kellogg (1916-2000)
Jacob Have I Loved '88
Violets Are Blue '86
The Enforcer '51
Twelve O'Clock High '49
Hopalong Cassidy: Borrowed Trouble '48
To Be or Not to Be '42

Gene Kelly (1912-96)
The Low Down '00
The Marx Brothers in a Nutshell '90 (N)
North and South Book 1 '85
Sins '85
That's Dancing! '85
Xanadu '80
Viva Knievel! '77
That's Entertainment, Part 2 '76 (N)
That's Entertainment '74
Forty Carats '73
The Young Girls of Rochefort '68
Inherit the Wind '60
Let's Make Love '60
Marjorie Morningstar '58
Les Girls '57
Invitation to the Dance '56
It's Always Fair Weather '55
Brigadoon '54
Deep in My Heart '54
Singin' in the Rain '52
An American in Paris '52
The Black Hand '50
Summer Stock '50
On the Town '49
Take Me Out to the Ball Game '49
The Pirate '48
The Three Musketeers '48
Words and Music '48
Anchors Aweigh '45
Ziegfeld Follies '46
Cover Girl '44
Du Barry Was a Lady '43
Thousands Cheer '43
For Me and My Gal '42

Grace Kelly (1928-82)
The Children of Theatre Street '77 (N)
High Society '56
The Swan '56
The Bridges at Toko-Ri '55
Green Fire '55
To Catch a Thief '55
Country Girl '54
Dial "M" for Murder '54
Rear Window '54
Mogambo '53
High Noon '52

Jack Kelly (1927-92)
The Gambler Returns: The Luck of the Draw '91
Commandos '73
Forbidden Planet '56
Cult of the Cobra '55
To Hell and Back '55
Gunsmoke '53
The Redhead from Wyoming '53
Red Ball Express '52

Jean (Louisa) Kelly (1972-)
A Stranger in the Kingdom '98
The Fantasticks '95
Harvest of Fire '95
Mr. Holland's Opus '95
Breathing Lessons '94
Uncle Buck '89

James F. Kelly
Marilyn & Bobby: Her Final Affair '94

Sinatra '92

Patsy Kelly (1910-81)
The North Avenue Irregulars '79
Freaky Friday '75
Rosemary's Baby '68
Naked Kiss '64
Please Don't Eat the Daisies '60
Broadway Limited '41
Playmates '41
Road Show '41
The Gorilla '39
In Old California '42
Sing Your Worries Away '42
Swiss Miss '38
Pick a Star '37
Pigskin Parade '36
Going Hollywood '33
Gunsmoke '53
Split Second '53
Springfield Rifle '52
The Curfew Breakers '57
The High and the Mighty '54

Paul Kelly (1899-1956)
Bail Out at 43,000 '57
Tarzan's New York Adventure '42
Ziegfeld Girl '41
The Roaring Twenties '39
Fit for a King '37

Patrick Kelly
Twitches Too '07
Twitches '05
White Coats '04

Nancy Kelly (1921-95)
The Woman Who Came Back '45
Betrayal from the East '44
Gambler's Choice '44
To the Shores of Tripoli '42
One Night in the Tropics '40
Stanley and Livingstone '39
Tarzan's New York Adventure '42
Submarine Patrol '38

Lew Kelly (1879-1944)
Death from a Distance '36
Mistaken Identity '36

Kevin Kelly

Kitty Kelly (1902-68)
So Proudly We Hail '43
Bachelor Apartment '31

Lisa Robin Kelly (1970-)
Late Last Night '99
Amityville Dollhouse '96

Michael Kelly (1969-)
Tooth and Nail '07
Invincible '06

Barbara Kellerman (1949-)
The Chronicles of Narnia '89
Mad Death '83
Quatermass Conclusion '79

Sally Kellerman (1936-)
The Prince and the Pauper '07
I Could Never Be Your Woman '06
The Boynton Beach Club '05
Back by Midnight '02
Ready to Wear '94
Dance '94
Mirror, Mirror 2: Raven Dance '94
American Virgin '98
Bar Hopping '00
Verdict in Blood '02
Boris and Natasha: The Movie '92

Barry Kelley (1908-91)
Jack the Giant Killer '62
The Manchurian Candidate '62
South Sea Woman '53
Carrie '52
Francis Goes to the Races '51
The Well '51
The Asphalt Jungle '50
Ma and Pa Kettle '49
Too Late for Tears '49

Susan Kellerman
Last Holiday '06
Elvira, Mistress of the Dark '88
Oh, Heavenly Dog! '80
Where the Buffalo Roam '80

Catherine Kellner (1970-)
Pearl Harbor '01
Shaft '00
Tully '00
Spring Forward '99
Day at the Beach '98
Restaurant '98
200 Cigarettes '98
Highball '97
No Way Home '96
Rosewood '96
Six Degrees of Separation '93

Brett Kelly (1993-)
Bad Santa '03

Brian Kelly (1932-)
Flipper's Odyssey '66
Around the World Under the Sea '65
Flipper's New Adventure '64

Brendan Kelly (1964-)
Cellular '04
The Lizzie McGuire Movie '03
The Rock '96
Angels Hard As They Come '71

Dean Lennox Kelly (1975-)
Deathwatch '02

Jim Kelly
Carlito's Way: Rise to Power '05
Loggerheads '05
Dawn of the Dead '04
The River Is Red '84

Moira Kelly (1968-)
To Live and Die in Hong Kong '89
Heroes Three '84

Mike Kelly
The Lion King 1 1/2 '04 (V)
The Safety of Objects '01
Henry Hill '00
Dangerous Beauty '98
Hi-Life '98
Love Walked In '97
Changing Habits '96
Entertaining Angels: The Dorothy Day Story '96
Unhook the Stars '96
The Tie That Binds '95
The Lion King '94 (V)
Little Odessa '94
With Honors '94
Daybreak '93
Chaplin '92
The Cutting Edge '92
Twin Peaks: Fire Walk with Me '92
Love, Lies and Murder '91
Billy Bathgate '91

Navy Blue and Gold '37
Star of Midnight '35
Girl from Calgary '32

Paula Kelly (1943-)
Once Upon a Time...
When We Were Colored '95

Rae'ven (Alyia Larrymore) Kelly (1985-)
Freedom Song '00
Milo '98
Ms. Scrooge '97
A Time to Kill '96
America's Dream '95
Lily in Winter '94
What's Love Got to Do with It? '93

Roz Kelly (1943-)
American Pop '81 (V)
New Year's Evil '78
Curse of the Black Widow '77

Sharon Kelly
Ilsa, Harem Keeper of the Oil Sheiks '76
Supervixens '75
Ilsa, She-Wolf of the SS '74
Dirty Mind of Young Sally '72

Terence Kelly
The Silencer '99
Accident '83

Tommy Kelly (1928-)
People's Choice '46
Paths to Paradise '25

Linda Kelsey (1946-)
Baby Girl Scott '87
Eleanor & Franklin '76
Picture of Dorian Gray '74

Kate Kelton (1978-)
Cake '05
Harold and Kumar Go to White Castle '04

Pert Kelton (1907-68)
The Comic '69
The Music Man '62
Kelly the Second '36
Annie Oakley '35
Bachelor Bait '34
Sing and Like It '34
The Bowery '33

Richard Kelton (1943-78)
The Ultimate Warrior '75
Silence '73

Edward Kemmer (1921-2004)
Earth vs. the Spider '58
Giant from the Unknown '58
Trauma '62

Warren Kemmerling (1924-2005)
The Dark '79
Eat My Dust '76
Family Plot '76
The Execution of Private Slovik '74
Hit! '73
The Cheyenne Social Club '70

Brandis Kemp (1951-)
South of Reno '87
Surf 2 '84
Goldilocks & the Three Bears '83

Elizabeth Kemp (1951-)
Eating '90
Killing Hour '84
He Knows You're Alone '80

Gary Kemp (1960-)
Magic Hunter '96
Killing Zoe '94
Paper Marriage '93
The Bodyguard '92
The Krays '90

Jeremy Kemp (1935-)
Angels and Insects '95
Four Weddings and a Funeral '94
The Magician '93
Duel of Hearts '92
Prisoner of Honor '91
War & Remembrance: The Final Chapter '89
When the Whales Came '89
War & Remembrance '88
Top Secret! '84
Sadat '83
The Winds of War '83
Prisoner of Zenda '79
The Treasure Seekers '79
East of Elephant Rock '76
The Seven-Per-Cent Solution '76
The Belstone Fox '73
Blockhouse '73
Darling Lili '70
The Blue Max '66
Operation Crossbow '65

Lindsay Kemp (1940-)
Sebastiane '79
The Wicker Man '75
Savage Messiah '72

Will(iam) Kemp (1977-)
Mindhunters '05
Van Helsing '04

Will Kempe (1963-)
Hit the Dutchman '92
Metropolitan '90
Pledge Night '90

Charles Kemper (1900-50)
On Dangerous Ground '51
Mr. Music '50
The Nevadan '50
Stars in My Crown '50
Ticket to Tomahawk '50
Where Danger Lives '50
The Doolins of Oklahoma '49
Fighting Father Dunne '48

Gerhard Kempinski (1947-)
Beware of Pity '46
Thursday's Child '43

Rachel Kempson (1910-2003)
Deja Vu '98
Stealing Heaven '88
Out of Africa '85
Little Lord Fauntleroy '80
Love for Lydia '79
The Virgin Soldiers '69
The Charge of the Light Brigade '68
Georgy Girl '66
Captive Heart '47

Felicity Kendal (1946-)
Parting Shots '98
We're Back! A Dinosaur's Story '93 (V)
The Camomile Lawn '92
Valentino '77
Shakespeare Wallah '65

Jennifer Kendal (1934-84)
Heat and Dust '82
Bombay Talkie '70

Cy Kendall (1898-1953)
Girl Rush '44
Outlaw Trail '44
Johnny Eager '42
Tarzan's New York Adventure '42
Billy the Kid '41
The Saint Takes Over '40
The Green Hornet '39
The Shadow Strikes '37
Bulldog Edition '36
King of the Pecos '36

Henry Kendall (1897-1962)
Butler's Dilemma '43
Amazing Adventure '37
The Shadow '36
The Ghost Camera '33
Rich and Strange '32

Katherine Kendall (1969-)
Devil in the Flesh 2 '00
Eye of the Storm '98
Swingers '96

Kay Kendall (1926-59)
The Reluctant Debutante '58
Les Girls '57
Abdulla the Great '56
Doctor in the House '53
Genevieve '53
The Shadow Man '53
Wings of Danger '52

Suzy Kendall (1944-)
Adventures of a Private Eye '87
Craze '74
Tales That Witness Madness '73
Torso '73
Assault '70
The Bird with the Crystal Plumage '70
Darker than Amber '70
30 Is a Dangerous Age, Cynthia '68
Circus of Fear '67
To Sir, with Love '67

Tony Kendall (1936-)
Oll '78
People Who Own the Dark '75
Return of the Evil Dead '75
When the Screaming Stops '73
Island of Lost Girls '68
Hyena of London '62

Anna Kendrick
Rocket Science '07
Camp '03

Alexa Kenin (1962-85)
Pretty in Pink '86
Honkytonk Man '82
A Piano for Mrs. Cimino '82
My Old Man's Place '71
The President's Plane Is Missing '71
Hail, Hero! '69
Anzio '68
Shark! '68

Arthur Kennedy (1914-90)
A Minute to Pray, a Second to Die '67
Fantastic Voyage '66
Nevada Smith '66
Cheyenne Autumn '64
Barabbas '62
Lawrence of Arabia '62
Murder She Said '62
A Summer Place '59
Some Came Running '58
Peyton Place '57
Crashout '55
Desperate Hours '55
Impulse '55
The Man from Laramie '55
Bend of the River '52
The Lusty Men '52
Rancho Notorious '52
Champion '49
Too Late for Tears '49
The Window '49
Boomerang '47
Air Force '43
Desperate Journey '42
High Sierra '41
They Died with Their Boots On '41
City for Conquest '40

Beth Kennedy
The Tomorrow Man '01
Jerome '98

Bill Kennedy (1909-97)
Silver City Bonanza '51
Storm over Wyoming '50
Two Lost Worlds '50
People's Choice '46

David Kennedy
Attack Force '06
Reign of Fire '02
Shiner '00

Deborah Kennedy
Swimming Upstream '03
Idiot Box '97
The Wedding Party '97
The Sum of Us '94

Douglas Kennedy (1915-73)
The Amazing Transparent Man '60
The Land Unknown '57
Big Chase '54
Sitting Bull '54
South of St. Louis '48

Edgar Kennedy (1890-1948)
My Dream Is Yours '49
Unfaithfully Yours '48
The Sin of Harold Diddlebock '47
It Happened Tomorrow '44
Air Raid Wardens '43
Hillbilly Blitzkrieg '42
Snuffy Smith, Yard Bird '42
Blondie in Society '41
Dr. Christian Meets the Women '40
Remedy for Riches '40
Charlie McCarthy, Detective '39
Frolics on Ice '39
The Black Doll '38
Peck's Bad Boy with the Circus '38
Double Wedding '37
When's Your Birthday? '37
San Francisco '36
Cowboy Millionaire '35
King Kelly of the U.S.A. '34
The Silver Streak '34
Twentieth Century '34
Duck Soup '33
Hold 'Em Jail '32
Little Orphan Annie '32
Laurel & Hardy: Night Owls '30
Laurel & Hardy: Perfect Day '29

George Kennedy (1925-)
Don't Come Knocking '05
Three Bad Men '05
Dennis the Menace Strikes Again '98
Small Soldiers '98 (V)
Cats Don't Dance '97 (V)
Naked Gun 33 1/3: The Final Insult '94
Distant Justice '92
Final Shot: The Hank Gathers Story '92
Driving Me Crazy '91
Hangfire '91
Hired to Kill '91
Naked Gun 2 1/2: The Smell of Fear '91
Brain Dead '89
Ministry of Vengeance '89
Born to Race '88
The Naked Gun: From the Files of Police Squad '88
The Terror Within '88
The Uninvited '88
Counterforce '87
Creepshow 2 '87
Demonwarp '87
The Gunfighters '87
Kenny Rogers as the Gambler, Part 3: The Legend Continues '87
Nightmare at Noon '87
Private Road: No Trespassing '87
Delta Force '86
Radioactive Dreams '86
Bolero '84
Chattanooga Choo Choo '84
The Jesse Owens Story '84
Savage Dawn '84
Wacko '83
Virus '82
Archer: The Fugitive from the Empire '81
Modern Romance '81
A Rare Breed '81
Search and Destroy '81
Death Ship '80
Hotwire '80
Just Before Dawn '80
Steel '80
Backstairs at the White House '79
The Concorde: Airport '79 '79
The Double McGuffin '79
Brass Target '78
Death on the Nile '78
Mean Dog Blues '78
Airport '77 '77
Proof of the Man '77
Airport '75 '75
The Blue Knight '75
The Eiger Sanction '75
The Human Factor '75
Earthquake '74
Thunderbolt & Lightfoot '74
Cahill: United States Marshal '73
Bull of the West '71
Airport '70
The Good Guys and the Bad Guys '69
Guns of the Magnificent Seven '69
Bandolero! '68
The Boston Strangler '68
The Pink Jungle '68
Cool Hand Luke '67
The Dirty Dozen '67
Mirage '66
The Flight of the Phoenix '65
In Harm's Way '65
Shenandoah '65
Sons of Katie Elder '65
Island of the Blue Dolphins '64
McHale's Navy '64
Strait-Jacket '64
Charade '63
Lonely Are the Brave '62

Gerald Kennedy
Puzzle '78
The Mango Tree '77

Gerard Kennedy (1932-)
Body Melt '93
The Lighthorsemen '87
Panic Station '82
Newsfront '78

Graham Kennedy (1934-)
Return of Captain Invincible '83
The Club '81
The Odd Angry Shot '79
Don's Party '76

Jamie Kennedy (1970-)
Kickin' It Old Skool '07
Son of the Mask '05
Malibu's Most Wanted '03
Max Keeble's Big Move '01
Seduced: Pretty When You Cry '01
Sol Goode '01
Bait '00
Boiler Room '00
Scream 3 '00
The Specials '00
Bowfinger '99
Sparkler '99
Three Kings '99
Bongwater '98
Enemy of the State '98
Highway Hitcher '98
Stricken '98
Clockwatchers '97
Scream 2 '97
Scream '95

Jayne Kennedy (1951-)
Body & Soul '81
Mysterious Island of Beautiful Women '79
Death Force '78
Fighting Mad '77
The Muthers '76
Group Marriage '72

Joey Kennedy
Innocence '00
Dance Me to My Song '98

Leon Isaac Kennedy (1949-)
Skeleton Coast '89
Penitentiary 3 '87
Hollywood Vice Squad '86
Too Scared to Scream '85
Lone Wolf McQuade '83
Penitentiary 2 '82
Body & Soul '81
Penitentiary '79
Death Force '78
Fighting Mad '77

Marklen Kennedy (1967-)
Magenta '96
Witchcraft 5: Dance with the Devil '92

Merle Kennedy (1967-)
Three Days of Rain '03
Three Days of Rain '02
Switchback '97
Night of the Demons 2 '94
Nemesis '93

Merna Kennedy (1908-44)
Come on Tarzan '32
Ghost Valley '32
The Circus '19

Mimi Kennedy (1949-)
Death Becomes Her '92
Pump Up the Volume '90
Immediate Family '89

Patricia Kennedy (1917-)
Road to Nhill '97
Country Life '95
My Brilliant Career '79
The Getting of Wisdom '77

Patrick Kennedy (1977-)
Atonement '07
Bleak House '05
Cambridge Spies '03

Rigg Kennedy
Hostile Intentions '94
Perfect Alibi '94
Dangerous Relations '93
Maid to Order '87
Slumber Party Massacre '82
Jessi's Girls '75
Girls on the Road '73

R.P.M.* (*"Revolutions Per Minute') '70
Daytor's Devils '68
Pirate Ship '49
The Devil's Cargo '48

Sheila Kennedy
Dead Boyz Can't Fly '93
Hollywood Party '34
Indiscreet '31
Ellie '84
First Turn On '83

Tom Kennedy (1885-1965)
Invasion U.S.A. '52
The Flesh and the Devil '27
The Dropkick '27
Feel First '30
The Matchmaker '27
We're in the Navy Now '27
Marked Money '28
Big News '29
Monkey Business '31
Behind the Mask '46
Mantrap '26

Kari Kennell
See Kari Whitman

Donald Kenney

James Kenney (1930-82)
Above Us the Waves '56
Tough Guy '53

June Kenney
Bloodlust '59
Attack of the Puppet People '58
Earth vs. the Spider '58
Sorority Girl '57
Teenage Doll '57

Kerri Kenney
The Comebacks '07

Patsy Kensit (1968-)
Shelter Island '03
Playd '06
Hell's Gate '01
Strange Frequency 2 '01
Things Behind the Sun '01
Janice Beard '99
Speedway Junky '99
Human Bomb '97
The Last Don 2 '98
Grace of My Heart '96
Angels and Insects '95
Tunnel Vision '95
Dream Man '94
Fall from Grace '94
Kleptomania '94
Bitter Harvest '93
Full Eclipse '93
Blame It on the Bellboy '92
The Turn of the Screw '92
Timebomb '91
Twenty-One '91
Blue Tornado '90
Bullseye! '90
Chicago Joe & the Showgirl '90
Does This Mean We're Married? '90
Kill Cruise '90
A Chorus of Disapproval '89
Lethal Weapon 2 '89
Absolute Beginners '86
Silas Marner '85
Monty Python and the Holy Grail '75
The Great Gatsby '74

Anne Kent
Catherine Cookson's The Gambling Man '93
Widow's Peak '94

Barbara Kent (1906-)
Oliver Twist '33
Vanity Fair '32
Chinatown After Dark '31
Feel First '30
The Dropkick '27
No Man's Law '27

Crauford Kent (1881-1953)
Tea for Two '50
Seven Keys to Baldpate '29
Virtue's Revolt '24

Dorothea Kent (1916-90)
Behind the Mask '46

Jean Kent (1921-)
The Magic Bow '47
Sleeping Car to Trieste '45
The Haunted Stranger '58
The Browning Version '51
Bonjour Tristesse '57
The Woman in Question '50
The Gay Lady '49
Man of Evil '48

Julie Kent
Center Stage '00
Dancers '87

Kenneth Kent (1892-1963)
Dangerous Moonlight '41
House of Mystery '41
Night Train to Munich '40
Hangman's House '28
Eyes Right! '26

Marjorie Kent
See Marjorie Ann Mutchie

Robert Kent (1908-55)
Big Town After Dark '47
Shoot to Kill '47
The Phantom Rider '46
East Side of Heaven '39
Gang Bullets '38
The Gladiator '38
Mr. Moto Takes a Chance '38
Charlie Chan at Monte Carlo '37
Dimples '36

Doug Kenney
Heavy Metal '81 (V)
National Lampoon's Animal House '78

Tom Kenny (1962-)
Comic Book: The Movie '04
The SpongeBob SquarePants Movie '04 (V)
The Powerpuff Girls Movie '02 (V)

Sean Kenney (1942-)
Savage Abduction '73
The Corpse Grinders '71

Larry Kent (1900-67)
Viva Las Vegas '63

Gary Kent (1933-)
Satan's Sadists '69

Kerri Kenney '77

Kenneth Kent (1892-1963)

Elizabeth Kent
Trapped Alive '93

Joey Kern (1976-)
The Sasquatch Gang '06
Pizza '05
Cabin Fever '03
Grind '03

Roger Kern (1948-)
The Preppie Murder '89
Street Justice '89
An American Summer '90
Earthquake '91
Cross My Heart '88
Broken Badge '85
A Bunny's Tale '85
A*P*E '76

Jean Kent (1921-)

Joanna Kerns (1954-)
Memorial Valley Massacre '88
Bad Georgia Road '77
Mrs. Mike '49
Fighting Seabees '44
Action in the North Atlantic '43
The Flying Irishman '39
The Great Man Votes '38
Hot Tip '35
The Informer '35
Lost Patrol '34
The Black Camel '31
Song of My Heart '29

Delos Kent (1976-)
Delos Adventure '86

Evelyne Ker (1935-2005)
A Nos Amours '84
Power '86

Ken Kercheval (1935-)
Beretta's Island '92
California Casanova '89
Calamity Jane '82
Corporate Affairs '90
Magic Island '95
Above Suspicion '95
Legalese '98

Edward Kerr (1966-)
Reunion '88
The Destructors '74

Maureen Kerr

John Kerr (1931-)
The Pit and the Pendulum '61
South Pacific '58
Tea and Sympathy '56
The Cobweb '55

Linda Kerridge (1959-)
Down Twisted '89
Alien from L.A. '87
Mixed Blood '84
Surf 2 '84
Strangers Kiss '83
Fade to Black '80

J.M. Kerrigan (1884-1964)
Fastest Gun Alive '56
Beverly Hills Vamp '88
Trick or Treats '82
Zardoz '73

Danny Keogh (1948-)
Operation Delta Force 3: Clear Target '98
Kill Slade '89

Jimmy Keogh
Bloom '03

E. Katherine Kerr (1937-)
Songcatcher '99
The Siege '98
The Buccaneers '95

Deborah Kerr (1921-2007)
Hold the Dream '86
A Woman of Substance '84
America at the Movies '76
The Arrangement '69
The Gypsy Moths '69
Casino Royale '67
Marriage on the Rocks '65
The Chalk Garden '64
The Night of the Iguana '64
The Grass Is Greener '61
The Innocents '61
The Sundowners '60
Beloved Infidel '59
Separate Tables '58
An Affair to Remember '57
Bonjour Tristesse '57
Heaven Knows, Mr. Allison '57
The King and I '56
Tea and Sympathy '56
From Here to Eternity '53
Julius Caesar '53
Young Bess '53
Prisoner of Zenda '52
Quo Vadis '51
King Solomon's Mines '50
Edward, My Son '49
The Hucksters '47
Black Narcissus '47
I See a Dark Stranger '46
The Life and Death of Colonel Blimp '43
The Day Will Dawn '42
The Courageous Mr. Penn '41

Bill Kerr (1924-)
Sweet Talker '91
The Lighthorsemen '87
Miracle Down Under '87
Dusty '85
The Coca-Cola Kid '84
Razorback '84
Vigil '84
Pirate Movie '82
The Year of Living Dangerously '82
Gallipoli '81
The Night of the Following Day '69
Appointment in London '53

Paul Kersey (1970-)
Hulk '03
Missing Pieces '00

Brian Kerwin (1949-)
27 Dresses '08
Flash '98
Common Ground '00
The Desperados '43
Here Comes Mr. Jordan '41
Before I Hang '40
The Lady in Question '40
Slightly Honorable '40
Gone with the Wind '39
Union Pacific '39
The Seven Year Itch '55
Prowler '51
The Jolson Story '46
A Thousand and One Nights '45

Norman Kerry (1889-1956)
Tanks a Million '41
Bachelor Apartment '31
The Claw '27
The Unknown '27
The Phantom of the Opera '25
The Hunchback of Notre Dame '23
Merry-Go-Round '23

John Kerry

Janet Key (1945-92)
Fire Birds '90
Dracula A.D. 1972 '72

Evelyn Keyes (1919-)
Wicked Stepmother '89
Return to Salem's Lot '87
Around the World in 80 Days '56

Bryan Kestner (1964-)
In Dark Places '97

Irwin Keyes (1952-)
Intolerable Cruelty '03
Backlash: Oblivion 2 '95
The Flintstones '94
Frankenstein General Hospital '88
Gimme an F '85
Mike's Murder '84

Mark Keyloun (1960-)
Separate Vacations '86
Hard Promises '92
Love Field '91
Switched at Birth '91
Code Name: Chaos '90
Torch Song Trilogy '88
King Kong Lives '86
Murphy's Romance '85
Nickel Mountain '85
Wet Gold '84
Jack '96
Gold Diggers: The Secret of Bear Mountain '95
It Came from Outer Space 2 '95

Skander Keynes
The Chronicles of Narnia: Prince Caspian '08
The Chronicles of Narnia: The Lion, the Witch and the Wardrobe '05

Alicia Keys
The Nanny Diaries '07
Smokin' Aces '07

Lance Kerwin (1960-)
Enemy Mine '85
Fourth Wise Man '85
Side Show '84

William Kerwin (1927-89)
A Taste of Blood '67
Playgirl Killer '66
2000 Maniacs '64
Blood Feast '63

Boyd Kestner (1964-)
The Insatiable '06
Black Hawk Down '01
The General's Daughter '99
The Art of Murder '99

Sara Kestelman (1944-)
Lady Jane '85
Lisztomania '75
Zardoz '73

Quin Kessler
Firecracker '71

Jillian Kesner (1950-2007)
Roots of Evil '91
The Warrior '01
The Namesake '06

Chulpan Khamatova (1975-)
Good Bye, Lenin! '03
A Thin Line Between Love and Hate '96

Maureen Kerwin (1949-)
Reunion '88

Persis Khambatta (1950-98)
Deadly Intent '88
Phoenix the Warrior '88
First Strike '85
Warrior of the Lost World '84
Megaforce '82
Nighthawks '81
Star Trek: The Motion Picture '79

Irfan Khan
A Mighty Heart '07
Partition '07
The Namesake '06
The Warrior '01

Aamir Khan (1965-)
The Rising: Ballad of Mangal Pandey '05
Lagaan: Once upon a Time in India '01

Shaheen Khan
Bend It Like Beckham '02
Bhaji on the Beach '94

Sajid Khan (1952-)
Heat and Dust '82
Maya '66

Arsinee Khanjian (1958-)
Ararat '02
Felicia's Journey '99
Late August, Early September '98
Exotica '94
Calendar '93
The Adjuster '91
Speaking Parts '89
Family Viewing '87

Rahul Khanna (1972-)
Bollywood Hollywood '02
The Emperor's Club '02
Earth '98

Kulbhushan Kharbanda
Lagaan: Once upon a Time in India '01

Makram Khoury (1945-)
Free Zone '05
Munich '05
The Body '01
The Milky Way '97
Double Edge '92
Cup Final '92

Nozha Khouadra
The New Eve '98
Bye-Bye '96
Honey & Ashes '96

Anupam Kher (1955-)
Bride & Prejudice '04
Bend It Like Beckham '02

Leleti Khumalo
Sarafina! '92

Malika Khadijah
ATL '06

Simbi Khali (1971-)
We Were Soldiers '02

Konstantin Khabensky
Day Watch '06
Night Watch '04

Doris Kenyon (1897-1979)
Counsellor-at-Law '33
No Marriage Ties '33
Burning Daylight '28
Monsieur Beaucaire '24
A Girl's Folly '17

Gwen Kenyon (1916-99)
In Old New Mexico '45
Charlie Chan in the Secret Service '44
The Great Mike '44
Meet the Mob '42

Sandy Kenyon (1924-)
The Arousers '70
The Loch Ness Horror '82

Leila Kenzle (1960-)
Identity '03
Enemies of Laughter '00

Michael Kenworthy
Dead Weekend '95
Shakes the Clown '92
Friends '95

Dambisa Kente (1950-2002)
Cry, the Beloved Country '95

Lance Kerwin (1960-)
Love on the Dole '41
Major Barbara '41

Evelyn Keyes (1919-)
The Seven Year Itch '55

Guy Kibbee (1882-1956)
Fort Apache '48
Three Godfathers '48
The Horn Blows at Midnight '45
It's a Wonderful Life '46
Dixie Jamboree '44
Miss Annie Rooney '42
Whistling in Dixie '42
It Started with Eve '41
Our Town '40
Babes in Arms '39
Let Freedom Ring '39

Mr. Smith Goes to Washington '39
Joy of Living '38
Of Human Hearts '38
Three Comrades '38
Captain January '36
Earthworm Tractors '36
Little Lord Fauntleroy '36
Three Men on a Horse '36
Captain Blood '35
Dames '34
Footlight Parade '33
42nd Street '33
Gold Diggers of 1933 '33
Havana Widows '33
Lady for a Day '33
Rain '32
Scarlet Dawn '32
The Strange Love of Molly Louvain '32
Laughing Sinners '31
Man of the World '31

Milton Kibbee (1896-1970)
Homesteaders of Paradise Valley '47
Jungle Siren '42

Sandrine Kiberlain (1968-)
Apres-Vous '03
Alias Betty '01
For Sale '98
Seventh Heaven '98
Beaumarchais the Scoundrel '96
A Self-Made Hero '95

Kid Rock (1971-)
Larry the Cable Guy: Health Inspector '06
Biker Boyz '03
Joe Dirt '01

Jonathan Kidd
The 7th Commandment '61
Seven Thieves '60

Janet Kidder
Ginger Snaps: Unleashed '04
Dark Side '02

Margot Kidder (1948-)
Common Ground '00
Tribulation '00
My Teacher Ate My Homework '98
Junior's Groove '97
Never Met Picasso '96
Bloodknot '95
Phantom 2040 Movie: The Ghost Who Walks '95 (V)
Young Ivanhoe '95
Beanstalk '94
Henry & Verlin '94
Windrunner '94
To Catch a Killer '92
Mob Story '90
Vanishing Act '88
Louisiana '87
Superman 4: The Quest for Peace '87
Keeping Track '86
Little Treasure '85
The Glitter Dome '84
Superman 3 '83
Trenchcoat '83
Heartaches '82
Some Kind of Hero '82
Miss Right '81
Shoot the Sun Down '81
Superman 2 '80
Willie & Phil '80
The Amityville Horror '79
Mr. Mike's Mondo Video '79
Superman: The Movie '78
92 in the Shade '76
Black Christmas '75
The Great Waldo Pepper '75
The Reincarnation of Peter Proud '75
Quiet Day in Belfast '74
Sisters '73
The Bounty Man '72

Quackser Fortune Has a Cousin in the Bronx '70

Nicole Kidman (1966-)
The Golden Compass '07
The Invasion '07
Margot at the Wedding '07
Fur: An Imaginary Portrait of Diane Arbus '06
Happy Feet '06 (V)
Bewitched '05
The Interpreter '05
Birth '04
The Stepford Wives '04
Cold Mountain '03
Dogville '03
The Human Stain '03
Birthday Girl '02
The Hours '02
Moulin Rouge '01
The Others '01
Eyes Wide Shut '99
Practical Magic '98
The Peacemaker '97
The Leading Man '96
Portrait of a Lady '96
Batman Forever '95
To Die For '95
Malice '93
My Life '93
Far and Away '92
Billy Bathgate '91
Days of Thunder '90
Dead Calm '89
Flirting '89
Night Master '87
Windrider '86
Archer's Adventure '85
BMX Bandits '83
Prince and the Great Race '83

James Kidnie
Resurrection '99
Rescuers: Stories of Courage—Two Couples '98
Hostile Intent '97
Gate 2 '92
Body Parts '91

Richard Kiel (1939-)
Happy Gilmore '96
Think Big '90
Pale Rider '85
Mad Mission 3 '84
Hysterical '83
War of the Wizards '83
So Fine '81
Moonraker '79
Force 10 from Navarone '78
They Went That-a-Way & That-a-Way '78
The Spy Who Loved Me '77
Silver Streak '76
Flash & Firecat '75
The Longest Yard '74
The Human Duplicators '64
Roustabout '64
Eegah! '62
The Phantom Planet '61

Sue Kiel
Survivor '87
Red Heat '85

Wolfgang Kieling (1924-85)
Out of Order '84
The Oppermann Family '82

Udo Kier (1944-)
BloodRayne '06
Manderlay '05
Masters of Horror: Cigarette Burns '05
Evil Eyes '04
Modigliani '04
Paranoia 1.0 '04
Dogville '03
All the Queen's Men '02
Feardotcom '02
He Sees You When You're Sleeping '02
Headspace '02
Doomsdayer '01
Invincible '01
The Last Minute '01
Critical Mass '00
Just One Night '00
Life in the Fast Lane '00

Red Letters '00
Shadow of the Vampire '00
Dancer in the Dark '99
Doomsdayer '99
End of Days '99
Spy Games '99
Blade '98
Modern Vampires '98
Betty '97
The End of Violence '97
The Kingdom 2 '97
Prince Valiant '97
The Adventures of Pinocchio '96
Barb Wire '96
Red Shoe Diaries 7: Burning Up '96
Breaking the Waves '95
Johnny Mnemonic '95
The Kingdom '95
Ace Ventura: Pet Detective '93
For Love or Money '93
Terror 2000 '92
Zentropa '92
My Own Private Idaho '91
Seduction: The Cruel Woman '89
Medea '88
The Stationmaster's Wife '77
Suspiria '77
The House on Straw Hill '76
The Story of O '75
Andy Warhol's Dracula '74
Andy Warhol's Frankenstein '74
Mark of the Devil '69

Robbie Kiger (1973-)
Welcome Home, Roxy Carmichael '90
Children of the Corn '84
Table for Five '83

Susan Kiger (1953-)
Death Screams '83
House of Death '82
The Return '80
H.O.T.S. '79
Seven '79

Laura Kightlinger (1969)
The Shaggy Dog '06
Kicking & Screaming '05
Must Love Dogs '05
Anchorman: The Legend of Ron Burgundy '04
Down With Love '03
Old School '03

Rya Kihlstedt (1970-)
She Creature '01
Deep Impact '98
Home Alone 3 '97
Jaded '96

Jorgen Kiil (1931-2003)
Webmaster '98
Parallel Corpse '83

Nicholas Kilbertus
Rescuers: Stories of Courage—Two Couples '98
The Defenders: Payback '97

Craig Kilborn (1962-)
Full of It '07
The Benchwarmers '06
The Shaggy Dog '06
Old School '03

Percy Kilbride (1888-1964)
Ma and Pa Kettle at Waikiki '55
Ma and Pa Kettle at Home '54
Ma and Pa Kettle on Vacation '53
Ma and Pa Kettle at the Fair '52
Ma and Pa Kettle Back On the Farm '51
Ma and Pa Kettle Go to Town '50
Riding High '50
Ma and Pa Kettle '49
You Gotta Stay Happy '48

The Kiss '88

Egg and I '47
Riff-Raff '47
Welcome Stranger '47
The Southerner '45
State Fair '45
The Adventures of Mark Twain '44
Guest in the House '44
The Woman of the Town '44
George Washington Slept Here '42
Keeper of the Flame '42

Terence (Terry) Kilburn (1926-)
Lolita '62
Fiend without a Face '58
National Velvet '44
Goodbye, Mr. Chips '39
They Shall Have Music '39
A Christmas Carol '38

Richard Kiley (1922-99)
Patch Adams '98
Phenomenon '96
Secrets '94
Jurassic Park '93 (V)
Mastergate '92
The Canterville Ghost '91
Separate but Equal '91
The Final Days '89
Howard the Duck '86 (V)
A.D. '85
The Adventures of Huckleberry Finn '85
The Bad Seed '85
George Washington '84
The Thorn Birds '83
Pray TV '82
Endless Love '81
Angel on My Shoulder '80
Looking for Mr. Goodbar '77
The Little Prince '74
Jigsaw '71
Murder Once Removed '71
Night Gallery '69
Pendulum '69
Blackboard Jungle '55
Pickup on South Street '53

Victor Kilian (1891-1979)
One Too Many '51
Unknown World '51
Rimfire '49
Dangerous Passage '44
Dr. Cyclops '40
Young Tom Edison '40
The Adventures of Tom Sawyer '38
Prison Break '38
Lady from Nowhere '36
Riff Raff '35

Val Kilmer (1959-)
Comanche Moon '08
Conspiracy '08
Deja Vu '06
Played '06
10th & Wolf '06
Kiss Kiss Bang Bang '05
Mindhunters '05
Alexander '04
Spartan '04
Stateside '04
The Missing '03
Wonderland '03
The Salton Sea '02
Hard Cash '01
Pollock '00
Joe the King '99
At First Sight '98
Prince of Egypt '98 (V)
The Saint '97
The Ghost and the Darkness '96
The Island of Dr. Moreau '96
Batman Forever '95
Heat '95
The Real McCoy '93
Tombstone '93
True Romance '93
Thunderheart '92
The Doors '91
Gore Vidal's Billy the Kid '89

Kill Me Again '89
Willow '88
The Man Who Broke 1,000 Chains '87
The Murders in the Rue Morgue '86
Top Gun '86
Real Genius '85
Top Secret! '84

Kevin Kilner (1958-)
Inside '06
A Cinderella Story '04
Raising Helen '04
Smart House '00
Home Alone 3 '97
Music from Another Room '97
Danielle Steel's Heartbeat '93

Lincoln Kilpatrick (1932-2004)
Piranha '96
Fortress '93
Prison '88
Deadly Force '83
Omega Man '71

Patrick Kilpatrick (1949-)
Already Dead '07
Gamebox 1.0 '04
Minority Report '02
The Substitute 4: Failure is Not an Option '00
Free Willy 3: The Rescue '97
Last Stand at Saber River '96
Riot '96
Beastmaster 3: The Eye of Braxus '95
3 Ninjas Knuckle Up '95
Open Fire '94
Scanner Cop 2: Volkin's Revenge '94
Scanners: The Showdown '94
Showdown '93
The Cellar '90
Class of 1999 '90
Death Warrant '90
Roanoak '86
Remo Williams: The Adventure Begins '85

Bobby Kim
Kill Line '91

Daniel Dae Kim (1968-)
The Cave '05
Momentum '03
Charlotte Sometimes '02
American Shaolin: King of the Kickboxers 2 '92
The Hollywood Sign '01
The Operator '01
Brokedown Palace '99
Volcano '97

Evan C. Kim
The Dead Pool '88
Go Tell the Spartans '78

Jacqueline Kim (1965-)
Red Doors '05
Charlotte Sometimes '02

Joon Kim
Gang Justice '94
Street Soldiers '91

Joy Kim
Blood Alley '55

Randall Duk Kim (1943-)
Kung Fu Panda '08 (V)
Memoirs of a Geisha '05
The Matrix Reloaded '03

Bruce (Kemp) Kimball
Cain's Cutthroats '71
Rebel Vixens '69

Billy Kimbley
Silver City Bonanza '51
Shep Comes Home '49

Charles Kimbrough (1936-)
The Wedding Planner '01

The Hunchback of Notre Dame '96 (V)
The Good Mother '88
Switching Channels '88
Sunday in the Park with George '86

Clinton Kimbrough (1933-96)
Night Call Nurses '72
Bloody Mama '70

Bruce Kimmel (1947-)
The Creature Wasn't Nice '81
Spaceship '81
The First Nudie Musical '75

Dana Kimmell (1959-)
Friday the 13th, Part 3 '82
Sweet 16 '81

Kenneth Kimmins (1941-)
My Best Friend Is a Vampire '88
Eleanor: First Lady of the World '82

Isao Kimura (1923-81)
Black Lizard '68
Stray Dog '49

Aron Kincaid (1943-)
The Proud and the Damned '72
Creature of Destruction '67
Ski Party '65

Richard Kind (1956-)
Raising Flag '06
The Wild '06 (V)
Bewitched '05
Elvis Has Left the Building '04
Dog Gone Love '03
Quicksand '01
A Bug's Life '98 (V)
Sink or Swim '97
Tom and Jerry: The Movie '93 (V)
All-American Murder '91

Helmo Kinderman
The Secret Invasion '64
The Magic Fountain '61

Kevin Kindlin
Heartstopper '92
Revenge of the Living Zombies '88
The Majorettes '87

Adrienne King (1960-)
Friday the 13th, Part 2 '81
Friday the 13th '80

Alan King (1927-2004)
Mind the Gap '04
Sunshine State '02
Rush Hour 2 '01
Casino '95
The Infiltrator '95
Night and the City '92
The Bonfire of the Vanities '90
Enemies, a Love Story '89
Memories of Me '88
Cat's Eye '85
Author! Author! '82
I, the Jury '82
Just Tell Me What You Want '80
Pleasure Palace '80
How to Pick Up Girls '78
The Anderson Tapes '71

Andrea King (1919-2003)
Inevitable Grace '94
The Linguini Incident '92
Blackenstein '73
House of the Black Death '65
Band of A'ngels '57
Red Planet Mars '52
The World in His Arms '52
The Lemon Drop Kid '51
Buccaneer's Girl '50
Mr. Peabody & the Mermaid '48
The Beast with Five Fingers '46
The Man I Love '46
God Is My Co-Pilot '45

Atlas King
The Thrill Killers '65

Incredibly Strange Creatures Who Stopped Living and Became Mixed-Up Zombies '63

B.B. King (1925-)
Blues Brothers 2000 '98
Amazon Women on the Moon '87

Benjamin King
A Little Inside '01
Spider's Web '01

Brad King (1917-91)

Brett King (1920-99)
Flying Leathernecks '51
Battleground '49

Cammie King (1934-)
Bambi '42 (V)
Gone with the Wind '39

Charles King (1889-1944)
The Silver Bullet '34
Broadway Melody '29

Charles "Blackie" King (1895-1957)
Law of the Lash '47

Charles King
The Unnamable '88

Chris Thomas King (1962-)
Ray '04
O Brother Where Art Thou? '00

Riders of the Desert '41
Twilight on the Timberline '41
Range Law '31
Two Gun Man '31
Oklahoma Cyclone '30
Outlaw of the Plains '46
Border Badmen '45
Flaming Bullets '45
Gangster's Den '45
His Brother's Ghost '45
Shadows of Death '45
Three in the Saddle '45
Boss of Rawhide '44
Dead or Alive '44
Devil Riders '44
Frontier Outlaws '44
Oath of Vengeance '44
Rustler's Hideout '44
Thundering Gunslingers '44
Wild Horse Phantom '44
California Joe '43
Raiders of Red Gap '43
...and of Hunted Men '43
Trigger Men '41
Where Trails End '42
Texas Kid '43
Two-Fisted Justice '43
Death Rides the Range '40
Lightning Strikes West '40
Along the Sundown Trail '42
Arizona Stagecoach '42
Below the Border '42
Prairie Pals '42
Rangers Take Over '42
Down the Wyoming Trail '39
Mesquite Buckaroo '39
Wild Horse Canyon '39
Gun Packer '38
The Phantom of the Range '38
Songs and Bullets '38
Thunder in the Desert '38
The Gambling Terror '37
God's Country and the Man '37
Hittin' the Trail '37
A Lawman Is Born '37
Lightning Bill Crandall '37
Mystery of the Hooded Horseman '37
The Red Rope '37
Riders of the Rockies '37
Ridin' the Lone Trail '37
Santa Fe Bound '37
Sing, Cowboy, Sing '37
Tex Rides with the Boy Scouts '37
Desert Phantom '36
Headin' for the Rio Grande '36
Last of the Warrens '36
The Law Rides '36

The Lawless Nineties '36
Lucky Terror '36
Red River Valley '36
Rip Roarin' Buckaroo '36
Fighting Parson '35
His Fighting Blood '35
Silent Valley '35
Trail of Terror '35
Fighting Champ '33
The Lone Avenger '33
Young Blood '33
Outlaw Justice '32
Branded Men '31
The Pocatello Kid '31

Trail Riders '42
Texas to Bataan '42
Thunder River Feud '42
Fugitive Valley '41
Kid's Last Ride '41
Tonto Basin Outlaws '41
Trail of the Silver Spurs '41
Tumbledown Ranch in Arizona '41
Saddle Mountain Roundup '41

Claude King (1875-1941)
Three on the Trail '36
The Mysterious Dr. Fu Manchu '29

Damu King (1917-91)
Blackjack '78
Black Godfather '74

Dave King (1929-2002)
Revolution '85
The Long Good Friday '80

Erik King
Casualties of War '89
Joey Breaker '93
True Crime '99
Atomic Train '99

Jaime (James) King (1979-)
Pretty Persuasion '05
The River King '05
Sin City '05
Two for the Money '05
White Chicks '04
Bulletproof Monk '03
Slackers '02
Blow '01
Happy Campers '01
Pearl Harbor '01
Danielle Steel's Kaleidoscope '90

Joe King (1883-1951)
Alexander's Ragtime Band '38

John "Dusty" King (1909-87)
The Outlaw Bikers—Gang Wars '70
Black Bikers from Hell '70
Psycho from Texas '81
San Quentin '37
Woman in the Shadows '34
Shifting Sands '18
Until They Get Me '18

John King, III (1909-87)

A Time to Remember '87
The Godfather, Part 2 '74
The Godfather '72
Cheaper by the Dozen 2 '05
The Day After Tomorrow '04
The Perfect Wife '00
A Cry in the Night '93
Jericho Fever '93
The Hasty Heart '86
Killing Hour '84
Class of 1984 '82
Search and Destroy '81
City in Fear '80
The Prize Pulitzer '89
Disaster at Silo 7 '88
The Cracker Factory '79
Love's Savage Fury '79
Different Story '78
Andy Warhol's Bad '77
The Choirboys '77
Lipstick '76
Mandingo '75
The Lords of Flatbush '74
Wild Party '74
The Possession of Joel Delaney '72
Slaughterhouse Five '72

Kent Masters King (1974-)

Kenneth King
Ace Drummond '36

Larry King (1933-)
Shrek the Third '07 (V)
Bee Movie '07 (V)
Shrek 2 '04 (V)
America's Sweethearts '01
An Alan Smithee Film: Burn, Hollywood, Burn '97

Leslie King
Pink Nights '85
Eddie and the Cruisers 2: Eddie Lives! '89

Mabel King (1932-99)
Cotton Candy '82
Gas Pump Girls '79
Dead Men Don't Die '91
Scrooged '88
The Jerk '79
The Wiz '78

Meegan King
Ganja and Hess '73

Morgana King (1930-)
Sweater Girls '78
A Brooklyn State of Mind '97

Perry King (1948-)
The Day After Tomorrow '04

Regina King (1971-)
Year of the Dog '07
The Ant Bully '06 (V)
Miss Congeniality 2: Armed and Fabulous '05
A Cinderella Story '04
Ray '04
Daddy Day Care '03
Legally Blonde 2: Red White & Blonde '03
Down to Earth '01
If These Walls Could Talk 2 '00
A.I.: Artificial Intelligence '01 (V)

Rowena King
The Bucket List '07
A Perfect Day '06
Romance and Rejection '95

Stephen King (1947-)
To Play the King '93
Wide Sargasso Sea '93
Framed '93
Creepshow 2 '87
Maximum Overdrive '86
Creepshow '82

Tony King
Cannibal Apocalypse '80
Sparkle '76
Report to the Commissioner '74
Gordon's War '73
Hell Up in Harlem '73

Walter Woolf King (1899-1984)
Today I Hang '42
Yank in Libya '42
Go West '40
Swiss Miss '38
A Night at the Opera '35

Wright King (1923-)
Humanoids from the Deep '80
King Rat '65
Dangerous Charter '62
Invasion of the Bee Girls '73

Yolanda King (1955-)
Selma, Lord, Selma '99
Ghosts of Mississippi '96
America's Dream '96

Zalman King (1941-)
Galaxy of Terror '81
Blue Sunshine '78
The Passover Plot '75
Ski Bum '75
Deadly Fieldtrip '74
Smile, Jenny, You're Dead '74
Some Call It Loving '73

Jerry Maguire '96
Half a Soldier '40
Midnight Limited '40
Range Busters '40
Trailing Double Trouble '40
West of Pinto Basin '40
Poetic Justice '93
Mr. Takes a Vacation '39
Charlie Chan in Honolulu '38

Kenneth King

Rowena King

Kathleen Kinmont (1965-)
Sweet Justice '92
Final Impact '91
Night of the Warrior '91
The Art of Dying '90
Texas Payback '95
C.I.A. 2: Target Alexa '94
Final Round '93
C.I.A.: Code Name Alexa '92
The Corporate Ladder '97
That Thing You Do! '96
Stormswept '95
C.I.A.: Code Name Alexa '92

Laurence Kinlan (1983-)
An Everlasting Piece '00
Ned Kelly '03

Guy Kingsford (1911-86)
House of Errors '42
The Invisible Ray '36
The Story of Louis Pasteur '36

Walter Kingsford (1881-1958)
The Love Guru '08
The Last Legion '07
You Kill Me '07
BloodRayne '06
Lucky Number Slevin '06
Mrs. Harris '05
Oliver Twist '05
A Sound of Thunder '05
Suspect Zero '04
Thunderbirds '04
House of Sand and Fog '03

Ben Kingsley (1943-)
Sexy Beast '00
What Planet Are You From? '00
Alice in Wonderland '99

Regina King (1971-)

Danitza Kingsley
Jack's Back '87
Amazons '86

Alex Kingston (1963-)
Alpha Dog '06
Warrior Queen '03
Essex Boys '99
Croupier '97
Moll Flanders '96
Carrington '95
The Infiltrator '95

Susan Kingsley
The Dollmaker '84
Old Enough '84

Natalie Kingston (1905-91)
His Private Secretary '33
Tarzan the Tiger '29
His First Flame '26

Amelia Kinkade
Night of the Demons 3 '97
Night of the Demons 2 '94
Night of the Demons '86

Greg Kinnear (1963-)
Baby Mama '08
Feast of Love '07
Fast Food Nation '06
Invincible '06
Little Miss Sunshine '06
The Matador '05
The Bad News Bears '05
Robots '05 (V)
Godsend '04
Stuck On You '03
Auto Focus '02
We Were Soldiers '02
Dinner with Friends '01
Someone Like You '01
The Gift '00
Loser '00
Nurse Betty '00
What Planet Are You From? '00
Mystery Men '99
You've Got Mail '98
As Good As It Gets '97
Dear God '96
A Smile Like Yours '96
Sabrina '95

Roy Kinnear (1934-88)
The Return of the Musketeers '89
Pirates '86
The Zany Adventures of Robin Hood '84
Hawk the Slayer '81
The Hound of Dracula '77
Herbie Goes to Monte Carlo '77
The Four Musketeers '75
Juggernaut '74
Melody '71
Willy Wonka & the Chocolate Factory '71
Help! '65
How I Won the War '67
The Hill '65

Leonid Kinskey (1903-98)
Can't Help Singing '45
Fighting Seabees '44
Casablanca '42
Broadway Limited '41
That Night in Rio '41
Down Argentine Way '40
Everything Happens at Night '39
The Great Waltz '38
Les Miserables '35
The Lives of a Bengal Lancer '35
Duck Soup '33

Klaus Kinski (1926-91)
Cobra Verde '88
Rough Justice '87

Kathy Kinney (1954-)
This Boy's Life '93
Three Fugitives '89
Parting Glances '86

Terry Kinney (1954-)
Parting Shots '98
The Assignment '97
The Laramie Project '02
Save the Last Dance '01
House of Mirth '00
Luminous Motion '00
Oxygen '99
That Championship Season '99
Sleepers '96
Devil in a Blue Dress '95
The Firm '93
Body Snatchers '93
Critical Choices '97
The Good Old Boys '95
Talent for the Game '91
Murder Ordained '87
Sleepers '96

Dostoevsky's Crime and Punishment '99
The Confession '98
The Contessa '98
A Thin Line Between Love and Hate '96
Higher Learning '94
Photographing Fairies '97
Weapons of Mass Distraction '97
Species '95
Schindler's List '93
Dave '93
Death and the Maiden '94
Searching for Bobby Fischer '93
Bugsy '91
Sneakers '92
Freddie the Frog '92 (V)
Stephen King's The Langoliers '95
Stephen King's The Stand '94
Stephen King's Golden Years '91
Pet Sematary '89
Sleepwalkers '92
Stephen King's Thinner '96
The Last Hunter '80
The Children '90
The Fifth Monkey '90
Murderers Among Us: The Simon Wiesenthal Story '89
Slipstream '89
Pascali's Island '88
Without a Clue '88
Maurice '86
Turtle Diary '86
Harem '85
Silas Marner '85
Betrayal '83
Gandhi '82
Hard Labour '73
The Bucket List '07
Moses '96
Joseph '95
Twelfth Night '96
Dead God '96
Carlo '77
The Adventures of Sherlock Holmes' Smarter Brother '78
Taste the Blood of Dracula '71
George Wallace '97
Fly Away Home '96
The Young Girl and the Monsoon '99
Don't Look Down '98
JFK: Reckless Youth '93
The Last of the Mohicans '92
A Man for All Seasons '88
Lady for a Night '42
Married an Angel '42
Somewhere I'll Find You '42

Kinski

Timestalkers '87
Crawlspace '86
Gangster's Law '86
Creature '85
His Name Was King '85
Star Knight '85
Codename: Wildgeese '84
The Little Drummer Girl '84
The Secret Diary of Sigmund Freud '84
Beauty and the Beast '83
Android '82
Burden of Dreams '82
Fitzcarraldo '82
The Soldier '82
Venom '82
Schizoid '80
Buddy Buddy '81
The French Woman '79
Nosferatu the Vampyre '79
Woyzeck '78
Night of the Assassin '77
Operation Thunderbolt '77
Jack the Ripper '76
Lifespan '75
Primal Impulse '74
Heroes in Hell '73
Aguirre, the Wrath of God '72
Count Dracula '71
Fistful of Death '71
Slaughter Hotel '71
Creature with the Blue Hand '71
Double Face '70
The Ruthless Four '70
Shoot the Living, Pray for the Dead '70
Venus in Furs '70
Web of the Spider '70
And God Said to Cain '69
Liberators '69
Twice a Judas '69
A Bullet for the General '68
Deadly Sanctuary '68
Psychopath '68
Circus of Fear '67
Five for Hell '67
Five Golden Dragons '67
Target for Killing '66
Doctor Zhivago '65
Fighting Fists of Shanghai Joe '65
For a Few Dollars More '65
The Squeaker '65
The Indian Scarf '63
Door with the Seven Locks '62
Inn on the River '62
Dead Eyes of London '61
The Avenger '60
A Time to Love & a Time to Die '58

Nastassja Kinski (1959-)
Dangerous Liaisons '03
Rip It Off '02
An American Rhapsody '01
The Day the World Ended '01
Say Nothing '01
Town and Country '01
The Claim '00
Red Letters '00
Dying to Get Rich '98
The Lost Son '98
Playing by Heart '98
Savior '98
Your Friends & Neighbors '98
Bella Mafia '97
Little Boy Blue '97
One Night Stand '97
Father's Day '96
Somebody is Waiting '96
Crackerjack '94
Terminal Velocity '94
Faraway, So Close! '93
The Blonde '92
Torrents of Spring '90
Magdalene '88
Spring Symphony '86
Harem '85
Revolution '85
The Hotel New Hampshire '84
Maria's Lovers '84
Unfaithfully Yours '84
Boarding School '83
Exposed '83
Moon in the Gutter '83
Paris, Texas '82
Cat People '82
One from the Heart '82
For Your Love Only '79
Tess '79
Stay As You Are '78
The Wrong Move '78
To the Devil, a Daughter '76

Nikolai Kinski (1976-)
Klimt '06
Aeon Flux '05
Tortilla Soup '01

Bruce Kirby (1928-)
Blood Money '99
Interlocked '98
Rave Review '95
Mr. Wonderful '93
Getting Up and Going Home '92
Throw Momma from the Train '87
Armed and Dangerous '86
Fyre '78
Cinderella Liberty '73
The Young Graduates '71
Catch-22 '70

Bruno Kirby (1949-2006)
Played '06
American Tragedy '00
A Slipping Down Life '99
Spy Games '99
Stuart Little '99 (V)
Donnie Brasco '96
Sleepers '96
The Basketball Diaries '95
Fallen Angels 2 '93
Golden Gate '93
Mastergate '92
City Slickers '91
The Freshman '90
Bert Rigby, You're a Fool '89
We're No Angels '89
When Harry Met Sally... '89
Nitti: The Enforcer '88
Good Morning, Vietnam '87
Tin Men '87
Flesh and Blood '85
Birdy '84
This Is Spinal Tap '84
Kiss My Grits '82
The Godfather 1902-1959: The Complete Epic '81
Modern Romance '81
Borderline '80
Where the Buffalo Roam '80
Between the Lines '77
The Godfather, Part 2 '74
Harrad Experiment '73

George Kirby (1924-95)
Trouble in Mind '86
Oh Dad, Poor Dad (Momma's Hung You in the Closet & I'm Feeling So Sad) '67

Jay Kirby (1920-64)
Sundown Riders '48
Border Patrol '43
Colt Comrades '43
Hoppy Serves a Writ '43
Leather Burners '43
Lost Canyon '43

Luke Kirby (1978-)
All Hat '07
Window Theory '04
Mambo Italiano '03
Shattered Glass '03
Halloween: Resurrection '02
Lost and Delirious '01

Michael Kirby (1925-97)
Shadows and Fog '92
Swoon '91
Another Woman '88
Find the Lady '76
The Girl in Blue '74

James Kirk (1986-)
She's the Man '06
X2: X-Men United '03
National Lampoon's Golf Punks '99

Joe (Joseph) Kirk (1903-75)
Abbott and Costello Go to Mars '53
Impact '49
The Noose Hangs High '48
The Naughty Nineties '45
Smart Alecks '42

Justin Kirk (1969-)
Ask the Dust '06
Flannel Pajamas '06
Puccini for Beginners '06
Angels in America '03
Love! Valour! Compassion! '96

Pamela Kirk
See Pam(ela) Austin

Phyllis Kirk (1926-2006)
The Sad Sack '57
Back from Eternity '56
Crime Wave '54
River Beat '54
House of Wax '53
Three Guys Named Mike '51
A Life of Her Own '50
Our Very Own '50
Two Weeks with Love '50

Tommy Kirk (1941-)
Attack of the 60-Foot Centerfold '95
Blood of Ghastly Horror '72
It's Alive! '68
Mars Needs Women '66
The Unkissed Bride '66
Monkey's Uncle '65
Village of the Giants '65
Pajama Party '64
The Misadventures of Merlin Jones '63
Savage Sam '63
Son of Flubber '63
Bon Voyage! '62
Escapade in Florence '62
Moon Pilot '62
The Absent-Minded Professor '61
Babes in Toyland '61
Horsemasters '61
The Swiss Family Robinson '60
The Shaggy Dog '59
Old Yeller '57

Donald Kirke (1901-71)
A Night for Crime '42
Oh Susannah! '38
Country Gentlemen '36

Sally Kirkland (1944-)
Coffee Date '06
Adam & Steve '05
Out of the Black '01
Another Woman's Husband '00
Wish You Were Dead '00
EDtv '99
Starry Night '99
Dead Silence '98
Get a Clue! '98
Paranoia '96
Amnesia '96
Excess Baggage '96
Cheatin' Hearts '93
Eye of the Stranger '93
Gunmen '93
The Woman Who Loved Elvis '93
Double Jeopardy '92
Double Threat '92
Forever: A Ghost of a Love Story '92
Hit the Dutchman '92
The Player '92
Primary Motive '92
Prime Time Murder '92
In the Heat of Passion '91
JFK '91
Bullseye! '90
Heat Wave '90
Revenge '90
Superstar: The Life and Times of Andy Warhol '90
Two Evil Eyes '90
Best of the Best '89
Cold Feet '89
High Stakes '89
Paint It Black '89
White Hot '88
Anna '87
Talking Walls '85
Fatal Games '84
Love Letters '83
Private Benjamin '80
Hometown U.S.A. '79
Breakheart Pass '76
Pipe Dreams '76
A Star Is Born '76
Bite the Bullet '75
Crazy Mama '75
Death Scream '75
The Noah '75 (V)
Big Bad Mama '74
Candy Stripe Nurses '74
Cinderella Liberty '73
The Sting '73
The Way We Were '73
The Young Nurses '73
Fury on Wheels '71
Coming Apart '69
Futz '69
Blue '68

Gene Kirkwood (1945-)
The Crossing Guard '94
Night and the City '92

Jack Kirkwood (1895-1964)
Fancy Pants '50
Never a Dull Moment '50

Stan Kirsch (1968-)
Shallow Ground '04
Highlander: The Gathering '92

Rudiger Kirschstein (1941-)
Coup de Grace '78
An Occurrence at Owl Creek Bridge/Coup de Grace '62

Mia Kirshner (1976-)
The Black Dahlia '06
The Iris Effect '04
New Best Friend '02
Now & Forever '02
Not Another Teen Movie '01
Cowboys and Angels '00
Innocents '00
Out of the Cold '99
Speed of Life '99
Mad City '97
Pet Shop '94
Tammy and the T-Rex '93
Weekend at Bernie's 2 '93
Into the Sun '92
Mannequin 2: On the Move '91
Weekend at Bernie's '89
Friday the 13th, Part 7: The New Blood '88
The Offspring '87
Surf 2 '84
Starflight One '83
Making Love '82
Steel '80
Snow Country '57

Kyoko Kishida (1930-2006)
Face of Another '66
Woman in the Dunes '64
The Human Condition: A Soldier's Prayer '61

Shin Kishida (1939-82)
Shogun Assassin '80
Murders in the Doll House '79

Charles Kissinger (1925-91)
Grizzly '76
Sheba, Baby '75
Asylum of Satan '72
Three on a Meathook '72

Tawny Kitaen (1961-)
Dead Tides '97
Playback '95
Hercules the Legendary Journeys, Vol. 3: The Circle of Fire '94
Hercules the Legendary Journeys, Vol. 4: In the Underworld '94
White Hot '88
Crystal Heart '87
Glory Years '87
Happy Hour '87
Witchboard '87
Instant Justice '86
Bachelor Party '84
The Perils of Gwendoline '84

Kazuo Kitamura (1927-2007)
Black Rain '88
Toral Toral Toral '70

Takeshi "Beat" Kitano (1948-)
Zatoichi '03
Brother '00
Kikujiro '99
Taboo '99
Fireworks '97
Johnny Mnemonic '95
Boiling Point '90
Violent Cop '89
Merry Christmas, Mr. Lawrence '83

Michael Kitchen (1948-)
Loma Doone '01
Oliver Twist '00
Proof of Life '00
The Railway Children '00
The World Is Not Enough '99
Reckless: The Sequel '98
Mrs. Dalloway '97
Reckless '97
A Royal Scandal '96
Wilderness '96
The Buccaneers '95
Goldeneye '95
Kidnapped '95
Doomsday Gun '94
Fatherland '94
To Play the King '93
Enchanted April '92
Fools of Fortune '90
The Russia House '90
The Dive '89
Out of Africa '85

Taylor Kitsch (1981-)
The Covenant '06
Snakes on a Plane '06

Eartha Kitt (1928-)
And Then Came Love '07
Preaching to the Choir '05
Holes '03
Anything But Love '02
Two Weeks Notice '02
The Safety of Objects '01
Labor Pains '99
Next Stop, Wonderland '98
Primary Colors '98
One Fine Day '96
Mixed Nuts '94
Radioland Murders '94
The Marx Brothers in a Nutshell '90
Tales from the Darkside: The Movie '90
Dangerous Curves '88
A Secret Space '88
Poison Ivy '85
Table Settings '84
Pajama Tops '83
Your Place or Mine '83
The Last Unicorn '82 (V)
The Bell Jar '79
Nobody's Perfekt '79
Hooper '78
Rivals '72
The Owl and the Pussycat '70
The Pursuit of Happiness '70

Tory Kittles
Next '07
Get Rich or Die Tryin' '05
Frankenfish '04
Big Shot: Confessions of a Campus Bookie '02

John Kitzmiller (1913-65)
Uncle Tom's Cabin '69
Cave of the Living Dead '65
Dr. No '62
Jungle Master '56
The Victors '63

Barry Kivel
Bound '96
One Fine Day '96

Alf Kjellin (1920-88)
The Victors '63
Summer Interlude '50
Torment '44

Bjorn Kjellman (1963-)
All Things Fair '95
The Best Intentions '92

Gary Klar (1947-)
Devlin '92
Chattahoochee '89

Uri Klauzner
Free Zone '05
Year Zero '04
Kippur '00
Kadosh '99

Martin Klebba (1969-)
Pirates of the Caribbean: At World's End '07
Pirates of the Caribbean: Dead Man's Chest '06
El Matador '03

Chris Klein (1979-)
Day Zero '07
American Dreamz '06
Full Count: '06
Just Friends '05
The Long Weekend '05
United States of Leland '03
We Were Soldiers '02 -
American Pie 2 '01
Say It Isn't So '01
Here on Earth '00
American Pie '99
Election '99

Erik S. Klein (1926-2002)
Anton, the Magician '78
Under the Pear Tree '73
The Second Track '62

Gerard Klein
Frantic '88
La Passante '83

Nita Klein
Dr. Petiot '90
Muriel '63

Robert Klein (1942-)
Reign Over Me '07
Ira & Abby '06
How to Lose a Guy in 10 Days '03
People I Know '02

Silke Klein (1974-)
Felicidades '00
Tierra '95

Rudolf Klein-Rogge (1888-1955)
Crimes of Dr. Mabuse '32
Spies '28
Metropolis '26
Kriemhilde's Revenge '24
Warning Shadows '23
Dr. Mabuse, The Gambler '22
Destiny '21
The Cabinet of Dr. Caligari '19

Werner Klemperer (1920-2000)
Judgment at Nuremberg '61
Istanbul '57

Kevin Kline (1947-)
Definitely, Maybe '08
Trade '07
As You Like It '06
The Pink Panther '06
A Prairie Home Companion '06
Jimmy Glick in LaLa Wood '05 (V)
De-Lovely '04
The Emperor's Club '02
Orange County '02
The Anniversary Party '01
Life as a House '01
The Road to El Dorado '00 (V)
Wild Wild West '99
William Shakespeare's A Midsummer Night's Dream '99
The Ice Storm '97
In and Out '97
Fierce Creatures '96
The Hunchback of Notre Dame '96 (V)
Looking for Richard '96
I Love You to Death '90
French Kiss '95
A Fish Called Wanda '88
Cry Freedom '87
Princess Caraboo '94
Dave '93
George Balanchine's The Nutcracker '93 (N)
Chaplin '92
Consenting Adults '92
Grand Canyon '91
Soapdish '91
Silverado '85
Violets Are Blue '86
The Big Chill '83
The Pirates of Penzance '83
Sophie's Choice '82

Richard Kline (1944-)
I Now Pronounce You Chuck and Larry '07
Liberty Heights '99
The Feminine Touch '95
Treehouse Hostage '99

Heidi Kling (1962-)
D3: The Mighty Ducks '96
The Mighty Ducks '92
Out on a Limb '92

Evan J. Klisser
Prey for the Hunter '92
Hellgate '89

Jack Klugman (1922-)
When Do We Eat? '05
The Twilight of the Golds '97
Dear God '96
Parallel Lives '94
Around the World in 80 Days '89
Two Minute Warning '76
One of My Wives Is Missing '76
Goodbye Columbus '69
The Detective '68
I Could Go on Singing '63
Days of Wine and Roses '62
Twelve Angry Men '57

Heidi Klum (1973-)
Ella Enchanted '04

Vincent Klyn
Blow Dry '00
Mexican Blow '02
Urban Menace '99
Nemesis '93
Bloodmatch '91
Point Break '91
Dollman '90
Cyborg '89

Skelton Knaggs (1911-55)
Dick Tracy Meets Gruesome '47
Forever Amber '47
Dick Tracy vs. Cueball '46
Bedlam '45
Isle of the Dead '45
The Strange Love of Molly Louvain '32

Evalyn Knapp (1908-81)
Hawaiian Buckaroo '38
Rawhide '38
Bulldog Edition '36
Mistaken Identity '36
Confidential '35
In Old Santa Fe '34
The Perils of Pauline '34
His Private Secretary '33
Smart Money '31

Herbert Knaup (1956-)
The Three Penny Opera '62
Bluebeard '63

Robert Knepper (1959-)
Hitman '07
Good Night, and Good Luck '05
Jackie, Ethel, Joan: The Kennedy Women '01
Hostage '05
Gas Food Lodging '92
Where the Day Takes You '92
Young Guns 2 '90
Renegades '89
Wild Thing '87
That's Life! '86

Bobby Knight (1940-)
Anger Management '03
Blue Chips '94

Christopher Knight (1957-)
Nowhere '96
The Brady Bunch Movie '95
The Doom Generation '95
Good Girls Don't '95
A Very Brady Christmas '88
Diary of a Teenage Hitchhiker '82
Cotter '72

David Knight (1927-)
Nightmare '63
Across the Bridge '57

David Edwin Knight (1972-)
Who Shot Pat? '92
Demons 2 '87

Esmond Knight (1906-87)
The Element of Crime '84
Peeping Tom '60
Sink the Bismarck '60
Hamlet '48
The River '51
The Red Shoes '48
Black Narcissus '47
A Canterbury Tale '44
Henry V '44
Contraband '40
The Rain People '69
Petulia '68
Duchman '67

Fuzzy Knight (1901-76)
Hostile Guns '67
Naked Hills '56
Oklahoma Annie '51
Apache Chief '50
Blazing Guns '50
Hills of Oklahoma '50
Last Bullet '50
Marshal of Heldorado '50
Rangeland Empire '50
Sudden Death '50
Rimfire '49
The Adventures of Gallant Bess '48
Bad Men on the Border '45
Hi, Good Lookin'! '44
Take It Big '44
Frontier Law '43
Boss of Bullion City '41
Man from Montana '41
Prairie '41
The Masked Rider '41
The Shepherd of the Hills '41
Song of the Gringo '36
Song of the Trail '36
The Trail of the Lonesome Pine '36
Kelly of the Secret Service '36
Spawn of the North '38
The Cowboy and the Lady '38
To the Last Man '33
My Little Chickadee '40
Pony Post '40
Riders of Pasco Basin '40

Gladys Knight (1944-)
Hollywood Homicide '03
Twenty Bucks '93
Spring Break '83
Pipe Dreams '76

Harlan E. Knight
Whistlin' Dan '32
The Fighting Sheriff '31

Lily Knight (1956-)
The Assassination of Richard Nixon '05
An Unremarkable Life '89
Static '87

Keira Knightley (1985-)
Atonement '07
Pirates of the Caribbean: At World's End '07
Silk '07
Pirates of the Caribbean: Dead Man's Chest '06
Domino '05
The Jacket '05
Pride and Prejudice '05
King Arthur '04
Doctor Zhivago '03
Love Actually '03
Pirates of the Caribbean: The Curse of the Black Pearl '03
Bend It Like Beckham '02
Pure '02
The Hole '01
Princess of Thieves '01
Oliver Twist '00
The Bubble '06

Michael E. Knight (1959-)
Hexed '93

Matthew Knight
Skinwalkers '07
The Greatest Game Ever Played '05

Sandra Knight (1940-)
Track of the Vampire '66
The Terror '63
Tower of London '62
Frankenstein's Daughter '58
Date with an Angel '87

Shirley Knight (1937-)
Grandma's Boy '06
Divine Secrets of the Ya-Ya Sisterhood '02
My Louisiana Sky '02
P.S. Your Cat is Dead! '02
The Salton Sea '02
Thunder Road '58

Wyatt Knight (1955-)
Porky's Revenge '85
Porky's 2: The Next Day '83
Porky's '82

William Knight (1934-)
Action U.S.A. '89

Zachery Knighton (1978-)
The Hitcher '07
The Mudge Boy '03
Angel Eyes '01
75 Degrees '00
As Good As It Gets '97
Little Boy Blue '97
Diabolique '96
If These Walls Could Talk '96

Ohad Knoller (1976-)
The Bubble '06
Yossi & Jagger '02
Under the Domim Tree '95

Sascha Knopf (1971-)
He Was a Quiet Man '07
What's the Worst That Could Happen? '01
Blackmale '99

Andrew Knott (1979-)
The History Boys '06

The Sender '82
Endless Love '81
Beyond the Poseidon Adventure '79

Don Knotts (1924-2006)
Air Bud 6: Air Buddies '06 (V)
Chicken Little '05 (V)
Pleasantville '98
Cats Don't Dance '97 (V)
Big Bully '95
Return to Mayberry '86 (V)
Cannonball Run 2 '84
The Private Eyes '80
The Apple Dumpling Gang Rides Again '79
Hot Lead & Cold Feet '78
Herbie Goes to Monte Carlo '77
No Deposit, No Return '76
The Apple Dumpling Gang '75
How to Frame a Figg '71
The Love God? '70
The Shakiest Gun in the West '58
The Reluctant Astronaut '67
The Ghost and Mr. Chicken '66
The Incredible Mr. Limpet '64
Move Over, Darling '63
It's a Mad, Mad, Mad, Mad World '63
No Time for Sergeants '58

Beyonce Knowles (1981-)
Dreamgirls '06
The Pink Panther '06
The Fighting Temptations '03
Austin Powers in Goldmember '02
Carmen: A Hip Hopera '01
The Theory of the Leisure Class '01

Trenton Knight (1982-)
Invisible Mom '96
The Tin Soldier '95

Ted (Edward) Knight (1923-86)
Caddyshack '80
Countdown '68
Psycho '60

Tuesday Knight (1969-)

Wayne Knight (1955-)
Master Spy: The Robert Hanssen Story '02
Rat Race '01
Tarzan '99 (V)
Toy Story 2 '99 (V)
For Richer or Poorer '97
Space Jam '96
Chameleon '95
To Die For '95
Fallen Angels 2 '93
Jurassic Park '93
Basic Instinct '92
Dead Again '91
JFK '91

Patric Knowles (1911-95)
Arnold '73
Chisum '70
The Devil's Brigade '68
Auntie Mame '58
Band of Angels '57
Mutiny '52
Three Came Home '50
Monsieur Beaucaire '46
O.S.S. '46
Hit the Ice '43
Frankenstein Meets the Wolfman '42
Who Done It? '42
How Green Was My Valley '41
The Wolf Man '41
Beauty for the Asking '39
Five Came Back '39
The Adventures of Robin Hood '38
The Sisters '38
The Charge of the Light Brigade '36

Black Beauty '94
The Secret Garden '93

Gustav Knuth (1901-87)
Heidi '65
Tromba, the Tiger Man '52

Johnny Knoxville (1971-)
Jackass Number Two '06
Daltry Calhoun '05
The Dukes of Hazzard '05
Lords of Dogtown '05
The Ringer '05
A Dirty Shame '04
Walking Tall '04
Grand Theft Parsons '03
The Big Empty '03
Big Trouble '02
Deuces Wild '02
Jackass: The Movie '02
Men in Black 2 '02
Life Without Dick '01

Terence Knox (1946-)
The Invaders '95
The Spy Within '95
Murder So Sweet '93
Children of the Corn 2: The Final Sacrifice '92
Forever: A Ghost of a Love Story '92
Tour of Duty '87
Humanoid Defender '85

Patricia Knox
Flaming Bullets '45
I Accuse My Parents '45

Mickey Knox (1922-)
Frankenstein Unbound '90
Western Pacific Agent '51

Elyse Knox (1917-)
Hit the Ice '43
Guard '43
Man in the Saddle '51
The Judge Steps Out '49
Tokyo Joe '49
Sister Kenny '46
Wilson '44
Commandos Strike at Dawn '43
The Sea Wolf '41
The Four Feathers '39
Don Winslow of the Coast '43

Peggy Knudsen (1923-80)
Istanbul '57
Copper Canyon '50
The Big Sleep '46
Humoresque '46
Never Say Goodbye '46
A Stolen Life '46

Mpho Koaho
Saw III '06
Get Rich or Die Tryin' '05
Detention '03
Crown Heights '02
Snipes '01
Down in the Delta '98

Keiju Kobayashi (1923-)
Rebirth of Mothra 2 '97
Godzilla 1985 '85
Tidal Wave '75
Sanjuro '62

Nenji Kobayashi (1943-)
The Hidden Blade '04

Megumi Kobayashi (1977-)
Rebirth of Mothra 3 '97
Rebirth of Mothra 2 '97
Rebirth of Mothra '96

Shoji Kobayashi (-1996)
The Twilight Samurai '02
Godzilla vs. King Ghidora '91
Youth of the Beast '63

Yukiko Kobayashi (1946-)
Yog, Monster from Space '71
Destroy All Monsters '68
Jeff Kober (1953-)
A Man Apart '03
Lost Voyage '01
American Tragedy '00
Militia '99
The Colony '98
The Maker '98
Elmore Leonard's Gold Coast '97
The Big Fall '96
Demolition High '95
One Man's Justice '95
Automatic '94
Tank Girl '94
Lone Justice '93
The Baby Doll Murders '92
Keep the Change '92
The First Power '89
Alien Nation '88
China Beach '88
Lucky Stiff '88
Out of Bounds '86
Bogumil Kobiela
Hands Up '81
Ashes and Diamonds '58
Edward I. Koch (1924-)
Somewhere in the City '97
New York Stories '89
Marianne Koch (1931-)
A Place Called Glory '66
A Fistful of Dollars '64
Frozen Alive '64
The Monster of London City '64
Pete Koch
Adventures in Dinosaur City '92
Heartbreak Ridge '86
Sebastian Koch (1962-)
Black Book '06
Napoleon '03
Gloomy Sunday '02
The Tunnel '01
Barbara Kodetova (1970-)
Children of Dune '03
Dune '00
Boris Kodjoe (1973-)
Madea's Family Reunion '06
The Gospel '05
Brown Sugar '02
David Koechner (1962-)
Get Smart '08
Semi-Pro '08
The Brothers Solomon '07
The Comebacks '07
Larry the Cable Guy: Health Inspector '06
Let's Go to Prison '06
Snakes on a Plane '06
Thank You for Smoking '06
Unaccompanied Minors '06
Daltry Calhoun '05
The Dukes of Hazzard '05
The 40 Year Old Virgin '05
Waiting... '05
Yours, Mine & Ours '05
Anchorman: The Legend of Ron Burgundy '04
A Guy Thing '03
My Boss's Daughter '03
Frederick Koehler (1975-)
Touched '05
Divine Secrets of the Ya-Ya Sisterhood '02
Walter Koenig (1936-)
Mad Cowgirl '06
Star Trek: Generations '94
Star Trek 6: The Undiscovered Country '91
Moontrap '89
Star Trek 5: The Final Frontier '89

Star Trek 4: The Voyage Home '86
Star Trek 3: The Search for Spock '84
Star Trek 2: The Wrath of Khan '82
Star Trek: The Motion Picture '79
Michiyo Kogure (1918-90)
Street of Shame '56
Shin Heike Monogatari '55
A Geisha '53
Fred Kohler, Sr. (1889-1938)
The Texas Rangers '36
Mississippi '35
Honor of the Range '34
Deluge '33
The Fiddlin' Buckaroo '33
Texas Bad Man '32
Fighting Caravans '31
Underworld '27
Riders of the Purple Sage '25
Fred Kohler, Jr. (1912-93)
Daniel Boone: Trail Blazer '56
Tough Assignment '49
Calling Wild Bill Elliott '43
Bahama Passage '42
Western Mail '42
Nevada City '41
Pigskin Parade '36
The Prisoner of Shark Island '36
Pecos Kid '35
Toll of the Desert '35
The Man from Hell '34
The Iron Horse '24
Juliane Kohler (1965-)
Nowhere in Africa '02
Aimee & Jaguar '98
Lee Kohlmar (1873-1946)
Death from a Distance '36
Love in Bloom '35
Night of January 16th '41
His Girl Friday '40
Michael Shayne: Private Detective '40
Honolulu '39
Give Me a Sailor '38
Susan Kohner (1936-)
The Gene Krupa Story '59
Imitation of Life '59
Dino '57
To Hell and Back '55
Scott Kolk (1905-93)
Murder in Greenwich Village '37
All Quiet on the Western Front '30
Henry Kolker (1870-1947)
The Real Glory '39
Union Pacific '39
The Cowboy and the Lady '38
Charlie Chan in Paris '35
Mad Love '35
The Mystery Man '35
The Ghost Walks '34
Baby Face '33
Rasputin and the Empress '33
Coquette '29

Amos Kollek (1947-)
Whore 2 '94
Double Edge '92
Goodbye, New York '85
Tetsu Komai (1893-1970)
The Real Glory '39
The Princess Comes Across '36
Hong Kong Nights '35
Bulldog Drummond '29
Hosei Komatsu (1924-2003)
A Taxing Woman's Return '88
Double Suicide '69
Rich Komenich
The Amityville Horror '05
Henry: Portrait of a Serial Killer 2: Mask of Sanity '96
Two Wrongs Make a Right '89
Liliana Komorowska (1956-)
Extreme Ops '02
The Art of War '00
The Assignment '97
Martial Outlaw '93
Scanners 3: The Takeover '92
Maja Komorowska (1937-)
The Decalogue '88
Year of the Quiet Sun '84
Contract '80
Maids of Wilko '79
Family Life '71
Magda Konopka (1943-)
When Dinosaurs Ruled the Earth '70
Satanik '69
Karin Konoval
The Tooth Fairy '06
Alone in the Dark '05
We'll Meet Again '02
Phyllis Konstam (1907-76)
Skin Game '31
Murder '30
Guich Koock (1944-)
Picasso Trigger '89
Square Dance '87
American Ninja '85
Seven '79
Kool Moe Dee (1962-)
Crossroads '02
Storm Trooper '98
Thomas Kopache
Ten Til Noon '06
Stigmata '99
Milos Kopecky (1922-96)
Lemonade Joe '64
Fabulous Adventures of Baron Munchausen '61
The Original Fabulous Adventures of Baron Munchausen '61
Bernie Kopell (1933-)
Get Smart '08
Bug Buster '99
Get Smart, Again! '89
Combat Academy '86
The Loved One '65
Good Neighbor Sam '64
Kim Kopf
Stormswept '95
Witchcraft 8: Salem's Ghost '95
Karen Kopins
Lady in Waiting '94
Archie: Return to Riverdale '90
Jake Speed '86
Creator '85
Once Bitten '85
Aya Koren (1979-)
Bonjour Monsieur Shlomi '03
Yossi & Jagger '02
Mia Korf
Blood Brothers '97
Color of Justice '97

Arnold Korff (1870-1944)
Doughboys '30
The Haunted Castle '21
Jon Korkes
Syngenor '90
Jaws of Satan '81
The Day of the Dolphin '73
Little Murders '71
Catch-22 '70
Baltasar Kormakur (1966-)
No Such Thing '01
101 Reykjavik '00
Devil's Island '96
Harvey Korman (1927-)
The Flintstones in Viva Rock Vegas '00
Gideon '99
Jingle All the Way '96
Dracula: Dead and Loving It '95
The Flintstones '94 (V)
Radioland Murders '94
Based on an Untrue Story '93
Betrayal of the Dove '92
Munchies '87
The Longshot '86
Alice in Wonderland '85
Gone Are the Days '84
Curse of the Pink Panther '83
History of the World: Part 1 '81
Herbie Goes Bananas '80
Americathon '79
Bud and Lou '78
High Anxiety '77
Blazing Saddles '74
Huckleberry Finn '74
April Fools '69
Lord Love a Duck '66
Mary Korman (1915-73)
Swing It, Professor '37
The Adventurous Knights '35
Desert Trail '35
Roaring Roads '35
Alix Koromzay (1971-)
Blood Work '02
Mimic 2 '01
Children of the Corn 666: Isaac's Return '99
The Haunting '99
Nightwatch '96
Charlie Korsmo (1978-)
Can't Hardly Wait '98
The Doctor '91
Hook '91
What about Bob? '91
Dick Tracy '90
Heat Wave '90
Men Don't Leave '89
Robert F. (Bob) Kortman (1887-1967)
Guns of the Law '44
Fugitive Valley '41
Hopalong Cassidy: Renegade Trail '39
Law of the Texan '38
The Rangers Step In '37
Sandflow '37
Robinson Crusoe of Clipper Island '36
The Crimson Trail '35
Feud of the West '35
Swifty '35
Wild Mustang '35
When a Man Sees Red '34
The Fiddlin' Buckaroo '33
Phantom Thunderbolt '33
Rainbow Ranch '33
Terror Trail '33
Trail Drive '33
Come on Tarzan '32
Island of Lost Souls '32
The Lone Defender '32

Fritz Kortner (1892-1970)
Woman in Brown '48
Pandora's Box '28
Warning Shadows '23
Backstairs '23
Charles Korvin (1907-98)
Ship of Fools '65
Berlin Express '48
Sylva Koscina (1933-94)
Lisa and the Devil '75
Hit Men '73
The Slasher '72
Hornet's Nest '70
Deadly Sanctuary '68
The Secret War of Harry Frigg '68
Deadlier Than the Male '67
Juliet of the Spirits '65
The Hit Man '60
Hercules Unchained '59
Uncle Was a Vampire '59
Hercules '58
Martin Kosleck (1907-94)
The Flesh Eaters '64
36 Hours '64
House of Horrors '46
The Wolf of London '46
Pursuit to Algiers '45
The Mummy's Curse '44
All Through the Night '42
International Lady '41
Underground '41
Foreign Correspondent '40
Paul Koslo (1944-)
Downdraft '96
Judge & Jury '96
Chained Heat 2 '92
Project: Shadowchaser '92
Xtro 2: The Second Encounter '91
Robot Jox '90
A Night in the Life of Jimmy Reardon '88
The Annihilators '85
Roots: The Next Generation '79
Maniac '77
Rooster Cogburn '75
Joe Kidd '72
Omega Man '71
Vanishing Point '71
The Losers '70
David Kossoff (1919-2005)
The Mouse on the Moon '62
The Two Faces of Dr. Jekyll '60
1984 '56
Who Done It? '56
A Kid for Two Farthings '55
Svengali '55
Maria Kosti (1951-)
Night of the Death Cult '75
Exorcism '74
Nick Kostopoulos
Addicted to Murder 3: Bloodlust '99
The Alien Agenda: Under the Skin '97
Kane (Takeshi) Kosugi (1973-)
DOA: Dead or Alive '06
Journey of Honor '91
Nine Deaths of the Ninja '85
Sho Kosugi (1948-)
Journey of Honor '91
Blind Fury '90
Aloha Summer '88
Black Eagle '88
Rage of Honor '87
Nine Deaths of the Ninja '85
Pray for Death '85
Ninja 3: The Domination '84
Revenge of the Ninja '83

Enter the Ninja '81
Kingfisher the Killer '81
Yoshio Kosugi (1903-68)
The Human Condition: No Greater Love '58
Seven Samurai '54
The Men Who Tread on the Tiger's Tail '45
Eva Kotamanidou (1936-)
Weeping Meadow '04
Landscape in the Mist '88
The Travelling Players '75
Elias Koteas (1961-)
Shooter '07
Skinwalkers '07
Zodiac '07
The Greatest Game Ever Played '05
Ararat '02
Collateral Damage '02
Harrison's Flowers '02
Simone '02
Novocaine '01
Shot in the Heart '01
Dancing at the Blue Iguana '00
Lost Souls '00
Living Out Loud '98
The Thin Red Line '98
Apt Pupil '97
Fallen '97
Gattaca '97
Hit Me '96
Crash '95
The Prophecy '95
Sugartime '95
Camilla '94
Exotica '94
Power of Attorney '94
Chain of Desire '93
Cyborg 2 '93
Teenage Mutant Ninja Turtles 3 '93
The Adjuster '91
Almost an Angel '90
Desperate Hours '90
Look Who's Talking, Too '90
Teenage Mutant Ninja Turtles: The Movie '90
Friends, Lovers & Lunatics '89
Malarek '89
Blood Red '88
Full Moon in Blue Water '88
Tucker: The Man and His Dream '88
Gardens of Stone '87
Some Kind of Wonderful '87
Oded Kotler (1937-)
Hanna K. '83
My Michael '75
Yaphet Kotto (1937-)
Witless Protection '08
Stiletto Dance '01
Homicide: The Movie '00
The Defenders: Payback '97
Out of Sync '95
Two If by Sea '96
Dead Badge '94
Almost Blue '93
Extreme Justice '93
In Self Defense '93
Chrome Soldiers '92
Freddy's Dead: The Final Nightmare '91
Hangfire '91
After the Shock '90
Jigsaw Murders '89
Ministry of Vengeance '89
Tripwire '89
Midnight Run '88
A Whisper to a Scream '88
Prettykill '87
The Running Man '87
Terminal Entry '87
Eye of the Tiger '86
Harem '86
Badge of the Assassin '85
The Park Is Mine '85
Warning Sign '85
The Star Chamber '83

Fighting Back '82
Brubaker '80
Rage '80
Alien '79
Blue Collar '78
Monkey Hustle '77
Raid on Entebbe '77
Report to the Commissioner '74
Truck Turner '74
Friday Foster '75
Sharks' Treasure '75
Drum '76
Across 110th Street '72
Live and Let Die '73
Man & Boy '71
Five Card Stud '68
The Thomas Crown Affair '68
Nothing but a Man '64

Adam Kotz (1962-)
Suspicion '03
All the King's Men '99
Shot Through the Heart '98
Touching Evil '97
Max and Helen '90

Hubert Kounde (1970-)
The Constant Gardener '05
How I Killed My Father '03
Simon the Magician '99
Hate '95
Cafe au Lait '94

The Karate Kid '84
Laboratory '80
Seven '79
Death Face 2000 '75
Last House on the Left '72

Jeff Kovski
Life '95
Zone 39 '96

Koyuki (1976-)
The Last Samurai '03
Pulse '01

Andras Kozak (1943-2005)
The Red and the White '68
The Round Up '66

Harley Jane Kozak (1957-)
Titanic '96
The Android Affair '95
Magic in the Water '95
The Amy Fisher Story '93
The Favor '92
All I Want for Christmas '91
Necessary Roughness '91
The Taking of Beverly Hills '91
Arachnophobia '90
Side Out '90
Parenthood '89
When Harry Met Sally... '89

Ernie Kovacs (1919-62)
North to Alaska '60
Strangers When We Meet '60
Our Man in Havana '59
Bell, Book and Candle '58

Geza Kovacs
Return to the Lost World '93
Con Games '02
Crocodile 2: Death Swamp '01
Baby on Board '92

Lajos Kovacs (1944-)
Kontroll '03
Woyzeck '94

Martin Kove (1946-)
Devil's Knight '03
Extreme Honor '01
Under Heavy Fire '01
Final Payback '99
Timelock '99
Nowhere Land '98
Baby Face Nelson '97
Grizzly Mountain '97
Shadow Warriors '97
Shadow Warriors 2: Hunt for the Death Merchant '97
Top of the World '97
Judge & Jury '96
Mercenary '96
Final Equinox '96
Without Mercy '95
Death Match '94
Endangered '94
Uncivilized '94
Wyatt Earp '94
Wyatt Earp: Return to Tombstone '94
Tombstone '94
Future Shock '93
The Outfit '93
President's Target '93
Shootfighter: Fight to the Death '93
To Be the Best '93
Death '93
Firehawk '93
Project Shadowchaser '92
White Light '90
Steele Justice '87
The Karate Kid: Part 3 '89
The Karate Kid: Part 2 '86
Rambo: First Blood, Part 2 '85

Nancy Kovack (1935-)
The Silencers '66
Frankie and Johnny '65
The Outlaws Is Coming! '65
Diary of a Madman '63
Jason and the Argonauts '63

Linda Kozlowski (1958-)
Crocodile Dundee in Los Angeles '01
Village of the Damned '95
Backstreet Justice '93
The Neighbor '93
Almost an Angel '90
Pass the Ammo '88
Crocodile Dundee 2 '88
Target: Favorite Son '87
Crocodile Dundee '86

Jeroen Krabbe (1944-)
Ocean's Twelve '04
Jesus '00
The Sky Is Falling '00
An Ideal Husband '99
Dangerous Beauty '98
Ever After: A Cinderella Story '98
Left Luggage '98
Only Love '98
The Odyssey '97
The Fugitive '93
For a Lost Soldier '93
King of the Hill '93
Stalin '92
Kafka '91
The Prince of Tides '91
Robin Hood '91
Till There Was You '91
The Punisher '90
Secret Weapon '90
Scandal '90
Crossing Delancey '88
A World Apart '88
Code Name: Dancer '87
The Living Daylights '87
Jumpin' Jack Flash '86
No Mercy '86
Turtle Diary '86
A Flight of Rainbirds '81
The 4th Man '79
Soldier of Orange '78

Jane Krakowski (1966-)
Surf's Up '07 (V)
Open Season '06 (V)
Pretty Persuasion '05
Alfie '04
Marci X '03
Ice Age '02 (V)
Go '99
Dance with Me '98
Stepping Out '91

Deuce Bigalow: European Gigolo '05

John Krasinski (1979-)
Leatherheads '08
License to Wed '07
A New Wave '07
Shrek the Third '07 (V)
Smiley Face '07
The Holiday '06
Duane Hopwood '05
Jarhead '05
Kinsey '04

Brian Krause (1972-)
Protecting the King '07
Return to Cabin by the Lake '01
Within the Rock '96
Breaking Free '95
Naked Souls '95
The Liar's Club '93
Sleepwalkers '92
December '91
Return to the Blue Lagoon '91
An American Summer '90

Fran Kranz
The TV Set '06
The Village '04
Whirlygirl '04

Robert Krantz
A Man Like Eva '83
Basileus Quartet '82
The American Friend '77
Kings of the Road—In the Course of Time '76
Alice in the Cities '74
The Man with Two Brains '83
Terror at London Bridge '85
The Cutting Edge: Going for the Gold '05
Leatherheads '08
License to Wed '07

Werner Krauss (1884-1959)
Jud Süss '40
Joyless Street '25
Secrets of a Soul '25
Variety '25
Waxworks '24
Othello '22
The Cabinet of Dr. Caligari '19

Peter Krause (1965-)
Civic Duty '06
We Don't Live Here Anymore '04
Lovelife '97

Nicolette Krebitz (1971-)
All the Queen's Men '02
The Tunnel '01
Bandits '99

Hans Kremer (1954-)
Mendel '98
The Promise '94

Connie Kreski (1946-95)
Black Bird '73
The Trackers '71

Harry Krimer (1896-)
Heart of a Nation '43
Napoleon '27

Thomas Kretschmann (1962-)
Hellboy 2: The Golden Army '08 (V)
Dracula's Widow '88

Sylvia Kristel (1952-)
Beauty School '93
Hot Blood '89
Dracula's Widow '88
Emmanuelle 4 '84
Mata Hari '85
Red Heat '85
Private School '83
The Nude Bomb '80
The Concorde: Airport '79
Emmanuelle, the Joys of a Woman '77
Emmanuelle '74

Grant Kramer See Grant Cramer

Jeffrey Kramer (1952-)
Halloween 2: The Nightmare Isn't Over! '81
Jaws 2 '78
Hollywood Boulevard '76
Jaws '75

Clare Kramer
The Thirst '06
Bring It On '00

Eric Allen Kramer (1962-)
Grilled '06
American Wedding '03
The Colony '98
Robin Hood: Men in Tights '93
The Comedians of Summer '92
Quest for the Mighty Sword '90

Stephanie Kramer (1956-)
The Cutting Edge: Going for the Gold '05
Twin Sisters '91

Anneline Kriel
Reason to Die '90
Kill and Kill Again '81

Alice Krige (1955-)
Silent Hill '06
Lonely Hearts '06
The Contract '07
The Line of Beauty '06
Lake '01
Molokai: The Story of Father Damien '99
Donor Unknown '95
Institute Benjamenta, or This Dream People Call Human Life '95
Joseph '95
Sleepwalkers '92
-ladykiller '92
Iran: Days of Crisis '91
Code Name: Chaos '90
See You in the Morning '89
Haunted Summer '88
Barfly '87
King David '85
Chariots of Fire '81
Ghost Story '81
A Tale of Two Cities '80

Kristen Kreuk (1982-)
Partition '07
Eurotrip '04
Snow White: The Fairest of Them All '02

Jason Kristofer
Speed '94
Alive '93
Quest of the Delta Knights '93

David Kriegel
Speed '94
The Jacket '05
The Wendell Baker Story '05

Marta Kristen (1945-)
Lost in Space '98
Body Count '97
Battle Beyond the Stars '80
Gemini Affair '74
Terminal Island '73
Beach Blanket Bingo '65
Savage Sam '63

Kurt Kreuger (1916-2006)
Unfaithfully Yours '48
Dark Corner '46
Mademoiselle Fifi '44
Manhunt in the African Jungles '43
Sahara '43

Elisabeth (Lisa) Kreuzer (1945-)
Brigitte Haas Must Be Killed '83
A Man Like Eva '83
Basileus Quartet '82
The American Friend '77
Kings of the Road—In the Course of Time '76
Alice in the Cities '74

Romano Kristoff
Slash '87
Warbus '85

Kris Kristofferson (1936-)
He's Just Not That Into You '08
Disappearances '06
Fast Food Nation '06
Dreamer: Inspired by a True Story '05
The Jacket '05
The Wendell Baker Story '05
Blade: Trinity '04
Silver City '04
Blade 2 '02
Chelsea Walls '01
Planet of the Apes '01
Perfect Murder, Perfect Town '00
Payback '98
Outlaw Justice '98
Rock '98 (V)
The Land Before Time 6: The Secret of Saurus Rock '98 (V)
Dance with Me '98
Blade '98
Molokai: The Story of Father Damien '99
Limbo '99
Tom Clancy's Netforce '98
Fire Down Below '97
Girls' Night '97
Two for Texas '97
Lone Star '95
Pharaoh's Army '95
The Road Home '95
Sodbusters '94
Cheatin' Hearts '93
Knights '93
No Place to Hice '93
Christmas in Connecticut '92
Another Pair of Aces: Three of a Kind '91
Pair of Aces '90
Night of the Cyclone '90
Original Intent '91
Welcome Home '89
Millennium '89
Big Top Pee-wee '88
Amerika '87
Trouble in Mind '86
Stagecoach '86
James '86
Songwriter '84
Flashpoint '84
Heaven's Gate '81
Rollover '81
Freedom Road '79
Convoy '78
Semi-Tough '77
A Star Is Born '76
The Sailor Who Fell from Grace with the Sea '76
Alice Doesn't Live Here Anymore '74
Bring Me the Head of Alfredo Garcia '74
Blume in Love '73
Pat Garrett & Billy the Kid '73
The Last Movie '71

Joachim Krol (1957-)
Gloomy Sunday '02
The Princess and the Warrior '00
Run Lola Run '98
Maybe... Maybe Not '94

Josef Kroner (1924-98)
Another Way '82
The Shop on Main Street '65

Gary Kroeger (1957-)
Secret Ingredient '92
Archie: Return to Riverdale '90

Berry Kroeger (1912-91)
Demon Seed '77
The Incredible Two-Headed Transplant '71
Seven Thieves '60
Blood Alley '55
Yellowneck '55
Guilty of Treason '49
Gun Crazy '49
Act of Violence '48
The Dark Corner '46

National Lampoon's Vacation '83
Next '07
Wanted '08
The Celestine Prophecy '06
Have No Fear: The Life of Pope John Paul II '05
King Kong '05
Downfall '04
Head in the Clouds '04
In Enemy Hands '04
Resident Evil: Apocalypse '04
Blade 2 '02
The Pianist '02
U-571 '00
Esther '98
Prince Valiant '97
Total Reality '97
The Stendahl Syndrome '96
Stalingrad '94

Margareta Krook (1925-2001)
Pay Off '89

Chad Krowchuk
Persona '66
Warbus '85
Another Way '82
The Shop on Main Street '65

Christiane Kruger (1945-)
Forever Amber 47
A Scandal in Paris '46
The Great Waltz '38
100 Men and a Girl '37
These Three '36
Craig's Wife '36
On the Sunny Side '62
Five Cartridges '60
National Treasure: Book of Secrets '07
National Treasure '04
Joyeux Noel '05

Hardy Kruger (1928-)
The Inside Man '84
Wrong Is Right '82
Blue Fin '78
Wild Geese '78
A Bridge Too Far '77
Barry Lyndon '75
Paper Tiger '76
What the Peeper Saw '72
Battle of Neretva '69

Diane Kruger (1976-)
The Hunting Party '07
National Treasure: Book of Secrets '07
The Color of Freedom '07
Joyeux Noel '05
Troy '04
Wicker Park '04
The Target '02

Alma Kruger (1868-1960)
Forever Amber 47
A Scandal in Paris '46
Anne of Green Gables '85
Le Dernier Combat '84
Little Mother '7'
Double Face '77

Manfred Krug (1937-)
Trace of Stones '66
The Boxer and Death '63
Minna von Barnhelm or The Soldier's Fortune '62

Kruger
Act of Passion: The Lost Honor of Kathryn Beck '83
Casanova '87
Game of Seduction '83
The Big Bet '85

Kruger _(continued)_
Red Tent 69
The Secret of Santa Vittoria 69
The Flight of the Phoenix 65
Hatari! 62
Sundays & Cybele '62
Bachelor of Hearts '58
One That Got Away '57
Liane, Jungle Goddess '56

Otto Kruger (1885-1974)
The Wonderful World of the Brothers Grimm '62
Meet Danny Wilson '52
Cash McCall '60
The Young Philadelphians '59
Black Widow '54
High Noon '52
Jungle Captive '45
Wonder Man '45
Cover Girl '44
Murder, My Sweet '44
Corregidor '43
Hitler's Children '43
Saboteur '42
Another Thin Man '39
Black Eyes '39
Housemaster '38
I Am the Law '38
Thanks for the Memory '37
They Won't Forget '37
Dracula's Daughter '36
Chained '34
Treasure Island '34
The Prizefighter and the Lady '33

David Krumholtz (1978-)
Harold & Kumar Escape from Guantanamo Bay '08
Walk Hard: The Dewey Cox Story '07
Bobby '06
Kill the Poor '06
Tenacious D in the Pick of Destiny '06
Guess Who '05
Harold and Kumar Go to White Castle '04
Looking for Kitty '04
Ray '04
Big Shot: Confessions of a Campus Bookie '02
Scorched '02
You Stupid Man '02
The Mexican '01
Sidewalks of New York '01
Liberty Heights '99
Ten Things I Hate about You '99
Slums of Beverly Hills '98
The Ice Storm '97
The Santa Clause '94
Addams Family Values '93
Life with Mikey '93
Mac '93
Home Alone 3 '97
Kicked in the Head '97
Ivory Hunters '90

Gene Krupa (1909-73)
The Benny Goodman Story '55
The Glenn Miller Story '54
Ball of Fire '41
Rhythm Romance '39

Jack Kruschen (1922-2002)
Cheaters '84
Money to Burn '83
Mountain Man '77
Satan's Cheerleaders '77
Freebie & the Bean '74
Caprice '67
Dear Brigitte '65
McLintock! '63
Cape Fear '61
Follow That Dream '61
The Ladies' Man '61
Lover Come Back '61
The Apartment '60
The Last Voyage '60
Where the Boys Are '60
The Angry Red Planet '59
Reform School Girl '57
Carolina Cannonball '55
Soldier of Fortune '55
Abbott and Costello Go to Mars '53
The War of the Worlds '53

Line Kruse
The Green Butchers '03
Emma's Shadow '88

Michelle Krusiec (1974-)
What Happens in Vegas '08
Saving Face '04
Dumb and Dumberer: When Harry Met Lloyd '03

Boris Krutonog
Thirteen Days '00
My Antonia '94

Nikolai Kryuchkov
Ballad of a Soldier '60
The Patriots '33

Khalid Ksouri
Halfmoon '95
Man of Ashes '86

Alex Kubik
Trapped Alive '93
Carnal Crimes '91

Akira Kubo (1926-)
Yog, Monster from Space '71
Destroy All Monsters '68
Godzilla vs. Monster Zero '68
Son of Godzilla '66
Attack of the Mushroom People '63
Gorath '62
Snow Country '57
Throne of Blood '57

Youki Kudoh (1971-)
Rush Hour 3 '07
Masters of Horror: Imprint '05
Bark! '02
All Over the Guy '01
Dr. Dolittle 2 '01 (V)
Lucky Numbers '00
Hanging Up '99
Analyze This '98
The Opposite of Sex '98
Clockwatchers '97
Romy and Michele's High School Reunion '97
Mother '96

Yoshiko Kuga (1931-)
The Cruel Story of Youth '60
Shin Heike Monogatari '55
The Idiot '51

Nikolina Kujaca
The Great Water '04
Dust '01

Nutsa Kukhianidze (1983-)
Bad City '06
The Good Thief '03

Vladimir Kulich (1956-)
Smokin' Aces '07
The 13th Warrior '99
Firestorm '97

Jarl Kulle (1927-97)
Babette's Feast '87
Fanny and Alexander '83
The Devil's Eye '60
Smiles of a Summer Night '55
Secrets of Women '52

Nancy Kulp (1921-91)
The Return of the Beverly Hillbillies '81
The Aristocats '70 (V)
Strange Bedfellows '65
The Patsy '64
Who's Minding the Store? '63
The Three Faces of Eve '57
Forever Darling '56

Will Kuluva (1917-90)
Missiles of October '74
Odds Against Tomorrow '59

William J. Kulzer
Lust for Freedom '87
Shadows Run Black '84

Pravesh Kumar
Tales of the Kama Sutra: The Perfumed Garden '98
Brothers in Trouble '95

Magda Kun (1912-45)
Dead of Night '45
Meet Sexton Blake '44

Vusi Kunene
Queen's Messenger II '01
The King Is Alive '00
Cry, the Beloved Country '95

Jun Kunimura (1955-)
Kill Bill Vol. 1 '03

Mila Kunis (1983-)
Audition '99
Forgetting Sarah Marshall '08

William Kunstler (1919-95)
Malcolm X '92
The Doors '91

Simon Kunz
The Affair of the Necklace '01
The Parent Trap '98

Sakari Kuosmanen (1956-)
The Man Without a Past '02
Night on Earth '91

Komake Kurihara
Sandakan No. 8 '74
The Wolves '71

Chiaki Kuriyama (1984-)
Kill Bill Vol. 2 '04
Kill Bill Vol. 1 '03

Ron Kurowski (1953-)
The Creature Wasn't Nice '81
Spaceship '81

Akbar Kurtha
Syriana '05
My Son the Fanatic '97

Alwyn Kurts (1915-2000)
Road to Nhill '97
The Efficiency Expert '92
Earthling '80
Tim '79

Mehmet Kurtulus (1972-)
Head On '04
The Tunnel '01

Marcia Jean Kurtz
Find Me Guilty '06
Inside Man '06
Once Upon a Time in America '84

Swoosie Kurtz (1944-)
Category 7: The End of the World '05
Duplex '03
The Rules of Attraction '02
Bubble Boy '01
Get Over It! '01
Sleep Easy, Hutch Rimes '00
White River '99
Cruel Intentions '98
My Own Country '98
Outside Ozona '98
Armistead Maupin's More Tales of the City '97
Liar Liar '97
Citizen Ruth '96
One Christmas '95
Storybook '95
Reality Bites '94
And the Band Played On '93
The Positively True Adventures of the Alleged Texas Cheerleader-Murdering Mom '93
A Shock to the System '90
Stanley and Iris '90
The Image '89
Bright Lights, Big City '88
Dangerous Liaisons '88
Vice Versa '88
Baja Oklahoma '87
True Stories '86
Wildcats '86
Guilty Conscience '85
A Time to Live '85
Against All Odds '84
Agatha Christie's A Caribbean Mystery '83
The World According to Garp '82
Marriage Is Alive and Well '80
Walking Through the Fire '80
Slap Shot '77

Katy Kurtzman (1965-)
Diary of a Teenage Hitchhiker '82
Child of Glass '78
Long Journey Back '78
When Every Day Was the Fourth of July '78

Kurupt (1972-)
I Accidentally Domed Your Son '04
Johnson Family Vacation '04
Dark Blue '03
Hollywood Homicide '03
Half Past Dead '02

Olga Kurylenko (1979-)
Hitman '07
Paris, je t'aime '06

Clyde Kusatsu (1948-)
Pandemic '07
The Interpreter '05
Shopgirl '05
Hollywood Homicide '03
United States of Leland '03
American Tragedy '00
Paradise Road '97
Top Dog '95
Dream Lover '93
Made in America '93
Rising Sun '93
Bird on a Wire '90
Dr. Strange '78
Go Tell the Spartans '78
Black Sunday '77
The Choirboys '77
Midway '76

Richard Kuss
Warlock '91
The Deer Hunter '78

Dylan Kussman
Ten 'Til Noon '06
Wild Things 2 '04
Wild Things '98
Way of the Gun '00
Journey of Honor '91
Wild Hearts Can't Be Broken '91
Dead Poets Society '89

Emir Kusturica (1954-)
The Good Thief '03
The Widow of Saint-Pierre '00
Underground '95

Ashton Kutcher (1978-)
What Happens in Vegas '08
Bobby '06
The Guardian '06
Open Season '06 (V)
A Lot Like Love '05
Guess Who '05
The Butterfly Effect '04
Cheaper by the Dozen '03
Just Married '03
My Boss's Daughter '03
Texas Rangers '01
Down to You '00
Dude, Where's My Car? '00

Miyuki Kuwano (1942-)
The Cruel Story of Youth '60
Equinox Flower '58

Alexander Kuznitsov (1959-)
Agent Red '00
The Ice Runner '93

Mimi Kuzyk (1952-)
A Different Loyalty '04
The Final Cut '04
The Human Stain '03
Lost and Delirious '01
The Golden Spiders: A Nero Wolfe Mystery '00
Thrill Seekers '99
The Defenders: Payback '97
Family of Cops 2: Breach of Faith '97
Dead Silence '96
Malicious '95
The Kiss '88
Family Sins '87
Striker's Mountain '87
Blind Justice '86
Miles to Go '86

Nancy Kwan (1939-)
Dragon: The Bruce Lee Story '93
Night Children '89
Stickfighter '89
Blade in Hong Kong '85
Walking the Edge '83
Night Creature '79
The Deadly and the Beautiful '73
The McMasters '70
The Wrecking Crew '68
The Corrupt Ones '67
Arrivederci, Baby! '66
Lt. Robin Crusoe, U.S.N. '66
Flower Drum Song '61
The World of Suzie Wong '60

Rosamund Kwan (1962-)
Big Shot's Funeral '01
Once Upon a Time in China III '93
Once Upon a Time in China II '92
Once Upon a Time in China '91
Operation Condor 2: The Armour of the Gods '86

Ryan Kwanten (1976-)
Dead Silence '07
Flicka '06

Philip Kwok (1951-)
The Phantom Lover '95
Hard-Boiled '92

Burt Kwouk (1930-)
Beyond Borders '03
Kiss of the Dragon '01
Bullet to Beijing '95
Son of the Pink Panther '93
Empire of the Sun '87
Plenty '85
Trail of the Pink Panther '82
Revenge of the Pink Panther '78
The Pink Panther Strikes Again '76
Casino Royale '67

Sam Kydd (1917-82)
Eye of the Needle '81
Too Late the Hero '70
Island of Terror '66
The House in Marsh Road '60

David Kyle (1951-)
L.A. Gangs Rising '89
Halloween '78
Cruisin' High '75

Machiko Kyo (1924-)
Face of Another '66
Odd Obsession '60
Drifting Weeds '59
Street of Shame '56
The Teahouse of the August Moon '56
Princess Yang Kwei Fei '55
Gate of Hell '54
Ugetsu '53
Rashomon '51

Kay Kyser (1897-1995)
Around the World '43
Stage Door Canteen '43
Thousands Cheer '43
Playmates '41
You'll Find Out '40

David La Haye (1966-)
Ginger Snaps Back: The Beginning '04
The Courage to Love '00
L'Enfant d'Eau '95

Jake La Motta
See Jake LaMotta

Alison La Placa (1959-)
Madhouse '90
Voyage of the Rock Aliens '87
Fletch '85

Rosemary La Planche (1923-79)
Federal Agents vs. Underworld, Inc. '49
The Devil Bat's Daughter '46
Strangler of the Swamp '46

Laura La Plante (1904-96)
Hold Your Man '33
Lonely Wives '31
The Love Trap '29
The Cat and the Canary '27
Skinner's Dress Suit '26
Show People '28
Stand and Deliver '28
Bravehear '25
Captain Swagger '25

Rod La Rocque (1898-1969)
Meet John Doe '41
Beyond Tomorrow '40
Dr. Christian Meets the Women '40
The Hunchback of Notre Dame '39
International Crime '37
The Shadow Strikes '37
Our Modern Maidens '29
The Coming of Amos '25
The Ten Commandments '23

Rita La Roy (1907-93)
The Mandarin Mystery '37
Sin Takes a Holiday '30

Jack La Rue (1902-84)
The Young Nurses '73
Robin and the 7 Hoods '64
Ride the Man Down '53
The Road to Utopia '46
Santa Fe Uprising '46
Dangerous Passage '44
Follow the Leader '44
The Law Rides Again '43
The Payoff '43
X Marks the Spot '42
Footsteps in the Dark '41
Gentleman from Dixie '41
In Old Caliente '39
Captains Courageous '37
Dangerous Holiday '37
Dancing Pirate '36
Strike Me Pink '36
Yellow Cargo '36

Headline Woman, 35
The Fighting Rookie '34
The Kennel Murder Case '33
To the Last Man '33
A Farewell to Arms '32

Eriq La Salle (1962-)
Inside Out '05
Johnny Was '05
Biker Boyz '03
Crazy as Hell '02
One Hour Photo '02
Rebound: The Legend of Earl "The Goat" Manigault '96
Color of Night '94
DROP Squad '94
Jacob's Ladder '90
Coming to America '88
Cut and Run '85

Lucille La Verne
See Lucille LaVerne
Pilgrimage '33

John La Zar
See John Lazar

Barbara Laage (1920-88)

Samuel Labarthe
Strayed '03
The Green House '96
The Accompanist '93

Patti LaBelle (1944-)
Cover '08
Preaching to the Choir '05
Fire and Rain '89
Sing '89
Unnatural Causes '86
A Soldier's Story '84

Shia LaBeouf (1986-)
Indiana Jones and the Kingdom of the Crystal Skull '08
Disturbia '07
Surf's Up '07 (V)
Transformers '07
A Guide to Recognizing Your Saints '06
Bobby '06
Constantine '05
The Greatest Game Ever Played '05
I, Robot '04
The Battle of Shaker Heights '03
Charlie's Angels: Full Throttle '03
Holes '03

Halina Labonarska (1947-)
A Woman and a Woman '80

Matthew Laborteaux (1966-)
Deadly Friend '86
Shattered Spirits '86
Aliens Are Coming '80
Tarantulas: The Deadly Cargo '77
A Woman under the Influence '74

Patrick Laborteaux (1965-)
JAG '95
3 Ninjas '92
Heathers '89
Prince of Bel Air '87

Elina Labourdette (1919-)
The Ladies of the Bois de Bologne '44
Lola '61

Dominique Labourier (1943-)
Jonah Who Will Be 25 in the Year 2000 '76
Celine and Julie Go Boating '74

Catherine Lacey (1904-79)
The Private Life of Sherlock Holmes '70
The Servant '63
Pink String and Sealing Wax '45
Cottage to Let '41
The Lady Vanishes '38

Ingrid Lacey
In Love and War '96
Funnyman '94
A Woman's Guide to Adultery '93

Margaret Lacey (1910-88)
Our Town '03
Diamonds Are Forever '71
Seance on a Wet Afternoon '64

Ronald Lacey (1935-91)
Landslide '92
The Lone Runner '88
Into the Darkness '86
Sahara '83
Firefox '82
Raiders of the Lost Ark '81
Nijinsky '80
Next Victim '74
Crucible of Terror '72
Disciple of Death '72
The Fearless Vampire Killers '67

Stephen Lack (1946-)
All the Vermeers in New York '91
Dead Ringers '88
Perfect Strangers '84
Scanners '81
Fatal Attraction '80

Elizabeth Lackey (1971-)
Blood Crime '02

Frank Lackteen (1894-1968)
Red Barry '38
Rustler's Roundup '33
Texas Pioneers '32
The Pony Express '25

Andre Lacombe
Dr. Petiot '90
The Bear '89

Ghalia Lacroix
For Ever Mozart '96

John Lacy (1965-)
The Silences of the Palace '94

Alan Ladd (1913-64)
Duel of Champions '64
The Carpetbaggers '64
All the Young Men '60
The Badlanders '58
The Deep Six '58
The Proud Rebel '58
Hell on Frisco Bay '55
The McConnell Story '55
Drum Beat '54
Botany Bay '53
Shane '53
Branded '50
The Great Gatsby '49
My Favorite Brunette '47
The Blue Dahlia '46
O.S.S. '46
Two Years before the Mast '46
China '43
The Glass Key '42
Joan of Paris '42
Star Spangled Rhythm '42
This Gun for Hire '42
The Black Cat '41
Citizen Kane '41
Gangs, Inc. '41
They Met in Bombay '41
Captain Caution '40
Her First Romance '40
The Howards of Virginia '40
Island of Lost Souls '32

Cheryl Ladd (1951-)
A Dog of Flanders '99
Every Mother's Worst Fear '98
Permanent Midnight '98
Dancing with Danger '93
Poison Ivy '92
Danielle Steel's Changes '91
Jekyll and Hyde '90
Lisa '90
Millennium '89
Fulfillment '89
Romance on the Orient Express '85
The Hasty Heart '86
Purple Hearts '84
The Grace Kelly Story '83
Now and Forever '82
Satan's School for Girls '73

David Ladd (1947-)
Inland Empire '06
The World's Fastest Indian '05
The Treasure of Jamaica Reef '74
The Adventures of Buckaroo Banzai Across the Eighth Dimension '84
Making the Grade '84
The Hound of the Baskervilles '83
Catlow '71
Misty '61
A Dog of Flanders '59

Diane Ladd (1939-)
Montana Sky '07
Come Early Morning '06
Inland Empire '06
Forever Young '03
Gracie's Choice '04
Forever Together '00
28 Days '00
Daddy & Them '99
Get a Clue! '98
Primary Colors '98
The Cemetery Club '93
Citizen Ruth '96
Ghosts of Mississippi '96
Mrs. Munck '95
Raging Angels '95
Mother '94
Carnosaur '93
James Dean: Live Fast, Die Young '97
Father Hood '93
Hold Me, Thrill Me, Kiss Me '93
Hush Little Baby '93
A Kiss Before Dying '91
Rambling Rose '91
Wild at Heart '90
The Lookalike '90
National Lampoon's Christmas Vacation '89
Plain Clothes '88
Black Widow '87
I Married a Centerfold '84
The Grace Kelly Story '83
Something Wicked This Way Comes '83
Desperate Lives '82
All Night Long '81
Willa '79
Embryo '76
Alice Doesn't Live Here Anymore '74
Chinatown '74
Rebel Rousers '69
The Wild Angels '66
Morgan the Pirate '60

Jordan Ladd (1975-)
Hostel: Part 2 '07
Death Proof '07
Waiting '05
Madhouse '04
Club Dread '04
Cabin Fever '03
Dog Gone Love '03
The Specials '00
Never Been Kissed '99

Walter Ladengast (1899-1980)
Nosferatu the Vampyre '79
Every Man for Himself & God Against All '75

Art LaFleur (1944-)
The Santa Clause 2 '02
The Replacements '00
The Garbage-Picking, Field Goal-Kicking Philadelphia Phenomenon '98
Jack the Bear '93
The Sandlot '93
Man of the House '95
Live! From Death Row '92
Oscar '91
Rampage '87
Trancers '84
Zone Troopers '84

Pat Laffan
How Harry Became a Tree '01
American Women '00
The Snapper '93

Patricia Laffan (1919-)
Devil Girl from Mars '54
Quo Vadis '51

Bernadette LaFont (1938-)
Genealogies of a Crime '97
Son of Gascogne '95
Dingo '92
Waiting for the Moon '87
Violette '78
The Mother and the Whore '73
Too Pretty to Be Honest '72
Catch Me a Spy '71
A Very Curious Girl '69
Les Bonnes Femmes '60
Le Beau Serge '58
Les Mistons '57

Roc Lafortune (1956-)
The List '99
The Minion '98
The Boys '97

John Lafayette (1950-)
Loverboy '05
White Sands '92
Full Fathom Five '90

Alicia Lagano
Believe in Me '06
All Things Fair '95
The Truth About Jane '00

Marika Lagercrantz (1954-)

Valerie Lagrange (1942-)
Cat and Mouse '78
Weekend '67
A Man and a Woman '66

Caroline Lagerfelt (1947-)
Glam '97
Home at Last '88
Iron Eagle '86

Ernesto Laguardia
Esmeralda Comes by Night '98

Bert Lahr (1895-1967)
Like A Bride '94
The Night They Raided Minsky's '69
Rose Marie '54
Ship Ahoy '42

Christine Lahti (1950-)
Women vs. Men '02
The Pilot's Wife '01
Hope '97
Subway Stories '97
A Weekend in the Country '96
Pie in the Sky '95
Hideaway '94
Leaving Normal '92
The Good Fight '92
The Fear Inside '92
The Doctor '91
Crazy from the Heart '91
Funny About Love '90
Gross Anatomy '89
Miss Firecracker '89
Running on Empty '88
Housekeeping '87
Stacking '87
Just Between Friends '86
Single Bars, Single Women '84
Swing Shift '84
Whose Life Is It Anyway? '81
The Executioner's Song '82
The Henderson Monster '80
And Justice for All '79

Me Me Lai (1952-)
The Element of Crime '84
Emerald Jungle '80
Au Pair Girls '72

Leon Lai (1966-)
Fallen Angels '95

Leah Lai (1966-)
Late Last Night '99
Body Waves '93

Cleo Laine (1927-)
The Last of the Blonde Bombshells '00

Robin Laing
On the Town '91
Borstal Boy '00
Dr. Bell and Mr. Doyle: The Dark Beginnings of Sherlock Holmes '00

Stuart Laing (1969-)
Cambridge Spies '03
Sharpe's Challenge '06

Jenny Laird (1917-2001)
Village of the Damned '60
Beware of Pity '46
Black Narcissus '47

Alan Lake (1941-84)
Don't Open Till Christmas '84

Arthur Lake (1905-87)
Blondie's Blessed Event '42
Broken Hearts of Broadway '23
Playing Dead '15
Blondie in Society '41
Blondie Hits the Jackpot '49
Blondie Knows Best '45
It's a Great Life '43
Footlight Glamour '43
Blondie for Victory '42
Blondie Goes Latin '42
Blondie Goes to College '42
Blondie Plays Cupid '40
Blondie Has Trouble '40
Blondie on a Budget '40
Blondie Brings Up Baby '39
Blondie Meets the Boss '39
Blondie Takes a Vacation '39
Blondie '38

Alice Lake (1889-1967)

Lorena Lalazquez (1937-)
Doctor of Doom '62
Samson vs. the Vampire Women '61
Wrestling Women vs. the Aztec Mummy '59

Padma Lakshmi
Glitter '01
The Mistress of Spices '05

Christine Lakin (1979-)
Mystery Kids '99
Boltneck '98

Veronica Lake (1919-73)
Flesh Feast '69
Ramrod '47
The Blue Dahlia '46
So Proudly We Hail '43
I Married a Witch '42
The Glass Key '42
Star Spangled Rhythm '42
This Gun for Hire '42
Sullivan's Travels '41
Hold That Blonde '45

Sanoe Lake
Cruel World '05
Blue Crush '02

Don Lake (1956-)
Skinner's Dress Suit '26
Best in Show '00
Hostage for a Day '94
Sodbusters '94
Crash Dive '43
Big Town '47
Next Time I Marry '38
Quality Street '37
Romance '30

Florence Lake (1904-80)
Savage Intruder '68
Goin' to Town '44

Ricki Lake (1968-)
A Dirty Shame '04
Cecil B. Demented '00
Murder She Purred: A Mrs. Murphy Mystery '98
Mrs. Winterbourne '96
Serial Mom '94
Cabin Boy '94
Based on an Untrue Story '93
Inside Monkey Zetterland '92
Last Exit to Brooklyn '90
Cry-Baby '90
Where the Day Takes You '92
Buffy the Vampire Slayer '92
Hairspray '88
Working Girl '88
Babycakes '89
Cookie '89

James Lally (1956-)
Working Girl '88
Critical Care '97
Focus of Fortune '90

Michael David Lally (1942-)
Cool World '92
The Nesting '80

Nick (Michael) Lally (1945-)
Circle of Friends '94
The Prodigal Son '82
A Man of No Importance '94

Ching-Ying Lam (1952-97)
Mr. Vampire '96

Suet Lam
Big Bite Dog '06

Maurice LaMarche (1958-)
Barnyard '06 (V)
Queer Duck: The Movie '06 (V)
The Silver Streak '34

Sing Your Worries Away '42
Every Mott's Worst Fear '98
Stand-Ins '97
Nowhere '96
Embrace of the Vampire '95
Just Around the Corner '38
The Wizard of Oz '39
Exiled to Shanghai '37
23 1/2 Hours Leave '37
Blondie Goes Latin '42
The Secret of Roan Inish '94
'39

Inspector Gadget's Biggest Caper Ever '05 (V)
Team America: World Police '04 (V)
Hey Arnold! The Movie '02

Hedy Lamarr (1913-2000)
The Love of Three Queens '54
Copper Canyon '50
Samson and Delilah '50
Dishonored Lady '47
The Strange Woman '46
Experiment Perilous '45
Tortilla Flat '42
White Cargo '42
Ziegfeld Girl '41
Boom Town '40
Comrade X '40
Algiers '38
Ecstasy '33

Phil LaMarr (1967-)
Shark Tale '04 (V)
Free Enterprise '98
Pulp Fiction '94

Jean LaMarre
Deadly Voyage '96
Fresh '94
Malcolm X '92

Fernando Lamas (1915-82)
The Cheap Detective '78
Murder on Flight 502 '75
Powder Keg '70
100 Rifles '69
Violent Ones '68
Rose Marie '54
Dangerous When Wet '53
The Girl Who Had Everything '53
The Merry Widow '52
Rich, Young and Pretty '51

Lorenzo Lamas (1958-)
Blood Angels '05
18 Fingers of Death '05
Alien 3000 '04
Lethal '04
Sci-Fighter '04
Latin Dragon '03
Hope Ranch '02
The Immortal '01
The Muse '99
Undercurrent '99
Final Impact '91
Killing Streets '91
Night of the Warrior '91
The Debt '98
Mask of Death '97
The Rage '96
Blood for Blood '95
Gladiator Cop: The Swordsman 2 '95
Terminal Justice: Cybertech P.D. '95
Bad Blood '94
C.I.A. 2: Target Alexa '94
Bounty Tracker '93
Final Round '93
C.I.A.: Code Name Alexa '92
SnakeEater 3: His Law '92
The Swordsman '92
SnakeEater 2: The Drug Buster '89
SnakeEater '89
Beverly Hills Vamp '88
B.O.R.N. '88
Body Rock '84
Take Down '79
Grease '78

Larry Lamb
Essex Boys '99
Fool's Gold: The Story of the Brink's-Mat Robbery '92
Buster '88
Shadey '87
Transmutations '85

Debra Lamb (1963-)
Evil Spirits '91
The Invisible Maniac '90
Rock & the Money-Hungry Party Girls '89
Stripped to Kill II: Live Girls '89

Adam Lamberg (1984-)
When Do We Eat? '05
The Lizzie McGuire Movie '03

Anne Louise Lambert (1956-)
Napoleon '96 (V)
Lilian's Story '95
Great Expectations: The Untold Story '87
The Draughtsman's Contract '82
Picnic at Hanging Rock '75

Christopher Lambert (1959-)
Day of Wrath '06
The Target '02
Druids '01
Highlander: Endgame '00
Fortress 2: Re-Entry '99
Gideon '99
Resurrection '99
Beowulf '98
Mean Guns '97
Nirvana '97
Adrenalin: Fear the Rush '96
North Star '96
Mortal Kombat 1: The Movie '95
The Road Killers '95
Highlander: The Final Dimension '94
The Hunted '94
Fortress '93
Gunmen '93
Knight Moves '93
Highlander: The Gathering '92
Highlander 2: The Quickening '91
Priceless Beauty '90
Why Me? '90
To Kill a Priest '89
The Sicilian '87
Highlander '86
Love Songs '85
Subway '85
Greystoke: The Legend of Tarzan, Lord of the Apes '84

Jack Lambert (1899-1976)
Three Cases of Murder '55
Hue and Cry '47
Nine Men '43

Jack Lambert (1920-2002)
The Day of the Outlaw '59
Machine Gun Kelly '58
Kiss Me Deadly '55
Montana Belle '52
North of the Great Divide '50
Stars in My Crown '50
Dick Tracy's Dilemma '47

Mark Lambert
Durango '99

Paul Lambert (1922-97)
Soldier's Revenge '84
Mama's Dirty Girls '74
Missiles of October '74

Heath Lamberts (1941-2005)
Tom and Huck '95
Ordinary Magic '93
To Kill a Clown '72

Ellie Lambetti (1926-83)
A Matter of Dignity '57
Girl in Black '56

Lloyd Lamble
Sea Wife '57
The Belles of St. Trinian's '53

Vassili Lambrinos
Last Rites '88
That Man Bolt '73

Anne Lambton (1954-)
A Different Loyalty '04
American History X '98
Love Is the Devil '98

Karen Lamm (1952-2001)
Ants '77
The Hatfields & the McCoys '75

Duncan Lamont (1918-78)
The Creeping Flesh '72
Frankenstein Created Woman '66
The Evil of Frankenstein '64
Murder at the Gallop '63
The Golden Coach '52
The Woman in Question '50

Marten Lamont (1911-)
Redwood Forest Trail '50
Federal Operator 99 '45
Son of Fury '42
International Lady '41

Molly Lamont (1910-2001)
The Devil Bat's Daughter '46
Somewhere I'll Find You '42
The Awful Truth '37

Pascal Lamorisse (1950-)
Voyage en Ballon '59
The Red Balloon '56

Jake LaMotta (1921-)
Mob War '88
Hangmen '87
The Hustler '61

John Lamotta
Showdown '94
We're Talkin' Serious Money '92
One More Chance '90
Revenge of the Ninja '83

Dorothy Lamour (1914-96)
Creepshow 2 '87
The Love Goddesses '65
Pajama Party '64
Donovan's Reef '63
The Road to Hong Kong '62
The Road to Bali '53
The Greatest Show on Earth '52
Here Comes the Groom '51
On Our Merry Way '48
My Favorite Brunette '47
The Road to Rio '47
The Road to Utopia '46
They Got Me Covered '43
The Road to Morocco '42
Star Spangled Rhythm '42
Caught in the Draft '41
The Road to Zanzibar '41
Johnny Apollo '40
The Road to Singapore '40
Man About Town '39
The Big Broadcast of 1938 '38
Spawn of the North '38
The Hurricane '37
Swing High, Swing Low '37
Dixiana '30

Lisa Lampanelli
Delta Farce '07

Jutta Lampe (1937-)
Rosenstrasse '03
The Possessed '88
Marianne and Juliane '82
Sisters, Or the Balance of Happiness '79

Zohra Lampert (1937-)
Alan & Naomi '92
Stanley and Iris '90
American Blue Note '89
Izzy & Moe '85
Alphabet City '84
Teachers '84
Isle of Secret Passion '82
Opening Night '77
The Connection '73
Let's Scare Jessica to Death '71
A Fine Madness '66
Splendor in the Grass '61

Chus (Maria Jesus) Lampreave (1930-)
Volver '06
The Flower of My Secret '95
I'm the One You're Looking For '88
Matador '86
What Have I Done to Deserve This? '85

Gunter Lamprecht (1930-)
Red Kiss '85
Berlin Alexanderplatz '80

Sarah Lancashire (1964-)
Gentlemen's Relish '01
Seeing Red '99

Ann Lancaster (1920-70)
The Railway Children '70
Hot Millions '68

Burt Lancaster (1913-94)
Separate but Equal '91
The Jeweller's Shop '90
The Phantom of the Opera '90
Voyage of Terror: The Achille Lauro Affair '90
Field of Dreams '89
Rocket Gibraltar '88
Control '87
Barnum '86
On Wings of Eagles '86
Tough Guys '86
Little Treasure '85
Scandal Sheet '85
Local Hero '83
The Osterman Weekend '83
Atlantic City '81
Zulu Dawn '79
Go Tell the Spartans '78
The Island of Dr. Moreau '77
Twilight's Last Gleaming '77
1900 '76
America at the Movies '76
Buffalo Bill & the Indians '76
The Cassandra Crossing '76
Moses '76
Victory at Entebbe '76
Conversation Piece '75
Executive Action '73
Scorpio '73
Ulzana's Raid '72
Lawman '71
Valdez Is Coming '71
Airport '70
Castle Keep '69
The Gypsy Moths '69
The Scalphunters '68
The Swimmer '68
The Professionals '66
The Hallelujah Trail '65
The Train '65
Seven Days in May '64
The Leopard '63
The List of Adrian Messenger '63
Birdman of Alcatraz '62
Judgment at Nuremberg '61
The Young Savages '61
Elmer Gantry '60
The Unforgiven '60
The Devil's Disciple '59
Run Silent, Run Deep '58
Separate Tables '58
Gunfight at the O.K. Corral '57
Sweet Smell of Success '57
The Rainmaker '56
Trapeze '56
The Kentuckian '55
The Rose Tattoo '55
Apache '54
From Here to Eternity '53
His Majesty O'Keefe '53
South Sea Woman '53
Vera Cruz '53
Come Back, Little Sheba '52
Crimson Pirate '52
Jim Thorpe: All American '51
Vengeance Valley '51
The Flame & the Arrow '50
All My Sons '48
Criss Cross '48
Sorry, Wrong Number '48
Brute Force '47
The Killers '46

James Lancaster
Leprechaun 2 '94
Gettysburg '93

Stuart Lancaster (1920-2000)
Beneath the Valley of the Ultra-Vixens '79
Mistress in Lace '79
Mantis in Lace '68
Born Losers '67
Faster, Pussycat! Kill! Kill! '65

Karl Lanchbury (1944-)
Vampyres '74
The House that Vanished '73

Elsa Lanchester (1902-86)
Die Laughing '80
Murder by Death '76
Arnold '73
Terror in the Wax Museum '73
Willard '71
My Dog, the Thief '69
Blackbeard's Ghost '67
Easy Come, Easy Go '67
That Darn Cat '65
Pajama Party '64
Bell, Book and Candle '58
Witness for the Prosecution '57
The Glass Slipper '55
Androcles and the Lion '52
Buccaneer's Girl '50
Mystery Street '50
Come to the Stable '49
The Inspector General '49
The Secret Garden '49
The Big Clock '48
The Bishop's Wife '47
Northwest Outpost '47
The Razor's Edge '46
The Spiral Staircase '46
Forever and a Day '43
Lassie, Come Home '43
Son of Fury '42
Tales of Manhattan '42
Beachcomber '38
The Ghost Goes West '36
Rembrandt '36
The Bride of Frankenstein '35
David Copperfield '35
Naughty Marietta '35
The Private Life of Henry VIII '33

Micheline Lanctot (1947-)
Blood Relatives '77
The Apprenticeship of Duddy Kravitz '74

Addie Land
The Sasquatch Gang '06
Evergreen '04

Geoffrey Land
Hospital of Terror '78
Against a Crooked Sky '75
The Female Bunch '69

Paul Land (1956-)
Spring Break '83
Idolmaker '80

Rodolfo Landa
Neutron vs. the Maniac '62
Neutron vs. the Amazing Dr. Caronte '61
The Criminal Life of Archibaldo de la Cruz '55

David Landau (1878-1935)
Gabriel Over the White House '33
No Marriage Ties '33
False Faces '32
Horse Feathers '32
The Purchase Price '32
Street Scene '31

Juliet Landau (1965-)
Hack! '07
Going Shopping '05
Ravager '97
Theodore Rex '95
Ed Wood '94
Direct Hit '93
Neon City '91

Martin Landau (1931-)
Hollywood Homicide '03
The Majestic '01
Ready to Rumble '00
Shiner '00
Bonanno: A Godfather's Story '99
EDtv '99
Sleepy Hollow '99
Rounders '98
The X-Files '98
B.A.P.'s '97
The Adventures of Pinocchio '96
City Hall '95
The Color of Evening '95
Joseph '95
Ed Wood '94
Eye of the Stranger '93
Intersection '93
No Place to Hide '93
Sliver '93
12:01 '93
Legacy of Lies '92
Mistress '91
Firehead '90
Max and Helen '90
Real Bullets '90
By Dawn's Early Light '89
Crimes & Misdemeanors '89
The Neon Empire '89
Paint It Black '89
Tucker: The Man and His Dream '88
Cyclone '87
Death Blow '87
Empire State '87
Run If You Can '87
Sweet Revenge '86
Kung Fu: The Movie '86
Access Code '84
The Being '83
Alone in the Dark '82
The Fall of the House of Usher '80
The Last Word '80
The Return '80
Meteor '79
Space: 1999—Alien Attack '79
Strange Shadows in an Empty Room '76
Destination Moonbase Alpha '75
A Town Called Hell '72
They Call Me Mr. Tibbs! '70
The Hallelujah Trail '65
Cleopatra '63
The Gazebo '59
North by Northwest '59
Pork Chop Hill '59

Dinsdale Landen (1931-2003)
Catherine Cookson's The Wingless Bird '97
Morons from Outer Space '85
Anatomy of Terror '74
Digby, the Biggest Dog in the World '73

David Lander (1947-)
Scary Movie '00
Ava's Magical Adventure '94
Tom and Jerry: The Movie '93 (V)
Betrayal of the Dove '92

A League of Their Own '92
Steel and Lace '90
Funland '89
The Man with One Red Shoe '85
1941 '79
The Tell-Tale Heart '60
Used Cars '80

Audrey Landers (1959-)
Bachelor Party 2: The Last Temptation '08
California Casanova '89
Getting Even '86
A Chorus Line '85
Deadly Twins '85
Underground Aces '80
1941 '79
Dr. Alien '88
Ghost Writer '89
The Black Marble '79
Hellhole '85
Doin' Time '85
Deadly Twins '85
Stewardess School '86
Armed and Dangerous '86
Tennessee Stallion '78
The Yum-Yum Girls '78

Harry Landers (1921-)
The Gallant Hours '60
The Indian Fighter '55
Phantom from Space '53
The C-Man '49

Judy Landers (1961-)
Expert Weapon '93
The Divine Enforcer '91
Club Fed '90
Ghost Writer '89

Michael Landes (1972-)
Final Destination 2 '03
Rescuers: Stories of Courage: "Two Women" '97
Dream for an Insomniac '96
An American Summer '90

Steve Landesberg (1945-)
Forgetting Sarah Marshall '08
The Souler Opposite '97
The Crazysitter '94
Sodbusters '94
Home for Christmas '93
Final Notice '89
Leader of the Band '87
Blade '72

Clayton Landey
Assault of the Killer Bimbos '88
First & Ten: The Team Scores Again '85

Gudrun Landgrebe (1950-)
Advertising Rules! '01
The Berlin Affair '85
Colonel Redl '84
A Woman in Flames '84

Janet Landgard
Land Raiders '69
The Swimmer '68

Sonny Landham (1941-)
Best of the Best 2 '93
Taxi Dancers '93
Three Days to a Kill '91
Lock Up '89
Predator '87
The Dirty Dozen: The Next Mission '87
Fleshburn '84
48 Hrs. '82
Southern Comfort '81

Nina Landi
Kcmodo '99

Elissa Landi (1904-48)
Corregidor '43
After the Thin Man '36
The Count of Monte Cristo '34
The Sign of the Cross '33

Maria Landi (1937-)
First Man into Space '59
Across the Bridge '57

Sal Landi
Xtro 3: Watch the Skies '95

Back to Back '90
Savage Streets '83

D.W. Landingham
Karate Cop '91
Omega Cop '90

Carole Landis (1919-48)
Out of the Blue '47
A Scandal in Paris '46
Having Wonderful Crime '45
Wintertime '43
Orchestra Wives '42
Dance Hall '41
I Wake Up Screaming '41
Moon over Miami '41
Road Show '41
Topper Returns '41
One Million B.C. '40
Cowboys from Texas '39
Three Texas Steers '39
Daredevils of the Red Circle '38

Cullen Landis (1895-1975)
The Broken Mask '28

Forrest Landis (1994-)
Cheaper by the Dozen 2 '05
Cheaper by the Dozen '03

Jessie Royce Landis (1904-72)
Airport '70
Critic's Choice '63
Gidget Goes to Rome '63
Bon Voyage! '62
Goodbye Again '61
North by Northwest '59
My Man Godfrey '57
The Swan '56
To Catch a Thief '55
I Married a Woman '56
It Happens Every Spring '49
My Foolish Heart '49

John Landis (1950-)
Diamonds '99
Freeway 2: Confessions of a Trickbaby '99
Laws of Deception '97
Silence of the Hams '93
Sleepwalkers '92
Venice, Venice '92
Body Chemistry 2: Voice of a Stranger '91
Darkman '90
Spontaneous Combustion '89
The Muppets Take Manhattan '84
The Blues Brothers '80
1941 '79
Death Race 2000 '75
Battle for the Planet of the Apes '73
Schlock '73

Margaret Landis (1890-1981)
The Confession '20

Monte Landis (1936-)
Yellowbeard '83

Abbe Lane (1932-)
Americano '55

David Landsberg
Dutch Treat '86
Detective School Dropouts '85

Valerie Landsburg (1958-)
The Triangle Factory Fire Scandal '79
Thank God It's Friday '78

Allan "Rocky" Lane (1904-73)
Trail of Robin Hood '50
Bandit King of Texas '49
Oklahoma Badlands '48
Homesteaders of Paradise Valley '47
Wild Frontier '47
Santa Fe Uprising '46
Stagecoach to Denver '46
Vigilantes of Boom Town '47
Silver City Kid '45
The Topeka Terror '45
Perils of the Darkest Jungle '44
Night Riders of Montana '50

Rosalyn Landor (1958-)
Disney's Teacher's Pet '04
The Unbearable Lightness of Being '88
The Uppercrust '81

Ali Landry (1973-)
Outta Time '01
Repli-Kate '01

Tamara Landry (1962-)
Bikini Med School '98
Bikini House Calls '96
Beach Babes from Beyond '93

Karen Landry
Roadracers '94
Patti Rocks '88
Heartbreak Hotel '88

The Personals '83

Michael Landon (1936-91)
Sam's Son '84
I, the Jury '82
It's Alive 3: Island of the Alive '87
America 3000 '86
Hundra '85
The Legend of Tom Dooley '59
God's Little Acre '58
High School Confidential '58
Legend of the Lone Ranger '81 [?]

The Leather Boys '63
Maid's Night Out '38
Charlie Chan at the Olympics '37
Night Nurse '31

Hal Landon, Jr. (1941-)
Bill & Ted's Bogus Journey '91
Eraserhead '78

Laurene Landon (1958-)
The Ambulance '90
Maniac Cop 2 '90
Wicked Stepmother '89
Maniac Cop '88
America 3000 '86
It's Alive 3: Island of the Alive '87
Hundra '85
Yellow Hair & the Fortress of Gold '84

Charles Lane (1905-2007)
Acting on Impulse '93
War & Remembrance '88
Date with an Angel '87
Murphy's Romance '85
Strange Invaders '83
Sunset Limousine '83
The Winds of War '83
Strange Behavior '81
Little Dragons '80
Billie '65
Good Neighbor Sam '64
But Not for Me '59
The Mating Game '59
Teacher's Pet '58
The Affairs of Dobie Gillis '53
Borderline '50
Riding High '50
Call Northside 777 '48
I Wake Up Screaming '41
The Invisible Woman '40
It's a Date '40
Rhythm on the River '40
Mr. Smith Goes to Washington '39
Twentieth Century '34

Charles Lane (1953-)
Posse '93
True Identity '91

Pavel Landovsky (1936-)
The Unbearable Lightness of Being '88

Colin Lane
The Blood Oranges '97
Broken Harvest '94

Diane Lane (1965-)
Untraceable '08
Hollywoodland '06
Fierce People '05
Must Love Dogs '05
Under the Tuscan Sun '03
Unfaithful '02
Hardball '01
The Perfect Storm '00
My Dog Skip '00
The Virginian '99
A Walk on the Moon '99
Gunshy '98
Grace & Glory '98
Murder at 1600 '97
The Only Thrill '97
Jack '96
Judge Dredd '95
Wild Bill '95
Indian Summer '93
Knight Moves '93
Chaplin '92
My New Gun '92
Descending Angel '90
Priceless Beauty '90
Vital Signs '90
Lonesome Dove '89
Big Town '87
The Cotton Club '84
Streets of Fire '84
The Outsiders '83
Rumble Fish '83
Miss All-American Beauty '82
Six Pack '82
Child Bride of Short Creek '81
National Lampoon Goes to the Movies '81
Touched by Love '80
A Little Romance '79

Hercules Against the Son of Hercules '62

Kent Lane
Changes '69
Defiant '70

Krista Lane (1959-)
Thrilled to Death '88
Sensations '87

Lola Lane (1909-81)
Deadline at Dawn '45
Buckskin Frontier '43
Lost Canyon '43
Four Daughters '38
Marked Woman '37
Woman Condemned '33
Death from a Distance '36

Lupino Lane (1892-1959)
The Deputy Drummer '35
The Love Parade '29
Isn't Life Wonderful '24

Mike Lane (1931-)
Curse of the Crystal Eye '93
Cold War Killers '86
Zebra Force '76
A Name for Evil '70

Nathan Lane (1956-)
Swing Vote '08
The Producers '05
Disney's Teacher's Pet '04
The Lion King 1 1/2 '04 (V)
Win a Date with Tad Hamilton! '04
Austin Powers in Goldmember '02
Nicholas Nickleby '02
Stuart Little 2 '02 (V)
Isn't She Great '00
Love's Labour's Lost '00
Titan A.E. '00 (V)
Trixie '00
Stuart Little '99 (V)
At First Sight '98
The Lion King: Simba's Pride '98 (V)
The Boys Next Door '96
The Birdcage '95
Jeffrey '95
The Lion King '94 (V)
Life with Mikey '93
Frankie and Johnny '91
He Said, She Said '91
Ironweed '87

Nora Lane (1905-48)
The Outlaw Deputy '35
Western Frontier '35

Priscilla Lane (1917-95)
Arsenic and Old Lace '44
Saboteur '42
Silver Queen '42
The Roaring Twenties '39
Four Daughters '38

Richard Lane (1900-82)
Take Me Out to the Ball Game '49
Sioux City Sue '46
Bullfighters '45
Louisiana Hayride '44
Slightly Terrific '44
Air Force '43
Arabian Nights '42
Mr. Winkle Goes to War '44
Junior G-Men of the Air '42
Ride 'Em Cowboy '42
Sunny '41
The Jackie Robinson Story '50

Panama Lady '39

Rosemary Lane (1914-74)
Harvest Melody '43
Oklahoma Kid '39
Four Daughters '38

Jackie Lane (1947-)
See Frederic Lehne

Frederic Lane
See Frederic Lehne

Venus Against the Son of Hercules '62

Stephen Lang (1952-)
The Treatment '06
Gods and Generals '03
After the Storm '01
Eye See You '01
The Proposal '00
Fire Down Below '97
Niagara, Niagara '97
Gang in Blue '96
An Occasional Hell '96
The Shadow Conspiracy '96
Tall Tale: The Unbelievable Adventures of Pecos Bill '95
The Amazing Panda Adventure '95
Gettysburg '93
Guilty as Sin '93
Tombstone '93
Another Woman '91 [?]
The Hard Way '91
Last Exit to Brooklyn '90
Project X '87
Band of the Hand '86
Death of a Salesman '86
Manhunter '86
King of America '80

k.d. lang (1961-)
Eye of the Beholder '99
The Last Don '97
Teresa's Tattoo '94
Salmonberries '91

June Lang (1915-)
Wee Willie Winkie '37
Captain January '36
Bonnie Scotland '35

Katherine Kelly Lang (1961-)
The Corporation '96
Subliminal Seduction '96
Mortuary Academy '91
Little Vegas '90
Eight Men Out '88
Jailbird Rock '88

Doreen Lang (1918-99)
Almost an Angel '90
Missiles of October '74
Omega Man '71

Judith Lang
Count Yorga, Vampire '70

Eric Laneuville (1952-)
Fear of a Black Hat '94
Love at First Bite '79
Shoot It Black, Shoot It Blue '74

Matthew Lang
The Rules of Attraction '02

Robert Lang (1934-2004)
Mrs. Palfrey at the Claremont '05
Cider with Rosie '99
I'm the Girl He Wants to Kill '74

Perry Lang (1959-)
We Were Soldiers '02
Jocks '87
Sahara '83
Spring Break '83
O'Hara's Wife '82
Game '82
Body & Soul '81
Alligator '80
The Big Red One '80
A Rumor of War '80
Girls Next Door '79
1941 '79

Glenn Langan (1917-91)
The Amazing Colossal Man '57
Big Chase '54
Hangman's Knot '52
Treasure of Monte Cristo '50
The Snake Pit '48
Hangover Square '45
Something for the Boys '44

Harry Langdon (1884-1944)
House of Errors '42
Double Trouble '41
Misbehaving Husbands '41
Mad About Money '37
Long Pants '27
Ella Cinders '26
His First Flame '26
Strong Man '26
Tramp, Tramp, Tramp '26

Libby Langdon
Corn '02
A Shot at Glory '00
Federal Hill '94

Lillian Langdon (1884-1944)
Daddy Long Legs '19
His Majesty, the American '19
Shifting Sands '18
The Americano '17
Flirting with Fate '16
The Lamb '15

Sue Ane Langdon (1936-)
Zapped! '82
The Evictors '79
The Cheyenne Social Club '70
A Guide for the Married Man '67
A Fine Madness '66
Frankie and Johnny '65
The Rounders '65
Roustabout '64

Carl Lange (1909-99)
Creature with the Blue Hand '70
The Torture Chamber of Dr. Sadism '69
Carpet of Horror '64

Hope Lange (1931-2003)
Cooperstown '93
Tune in Tomorrow '90
Ford: The Man & the Machine '87
Blue Velvet '86
A Nightmare on Elm Street 2: Freddy's Revenge '85
I Am the Cheese '83
The Prodigal '83
Beulah Land '80
Pleasure Palace '80
Death Wish '74
Fer-De-Lance '74
I Love You, Goodbye '74
The Love Bug '68
Pocketful of Miracles '61
Wild in the Country '61
The Best of Everything '59
The Young Lions '58
Peyton Place '57
Bus Stop '56

Jessica Lange (1949-)
Bonneville '06
Broken Flowers '05
Don't Come Knocking '05
Big Fish '03
Masked and Anonymous '03
Normal '03
Prozac Nation '01
Titus '99
Hush '98
Cousin Bette '97
A Thousand Acres '97
Rob Roy '95
A Streetcar Named Desire '95
Losing Isaiah '94
Night and the City '92
Blue Sky '91
Cape Fear '91
O Pioneers! '91
Men Don't Leave '89
Music Box '89
Everybody's All American '88
Far North '88
Crimes of the Heart '86
Sweet Dreams '85
Cat on a Hot Tin Roof '84
Country '84
Frances '82
Tootsie '82
The Postman Always Rings Twice '81
How to Beat the High Cost of Living '80
All That Jazz '79
King Kong '76

Ted Lange (1947-)
Perfume '91
Terminal Exposure '89
Glitch! '88

Jack Langedijk
One Way Out '02
Codename: Jaguar '00
Left Behind: The Movie '00
The Pact '99
Dead End '98
A Young Connecticut Yankee in King Arthur's Court '95
Blind Fear '89
Evil Judgment '85

Frank Langella (1940-)
Starting Out in the Evening '07
The Hillside Strangler '04
Out of the Black '01
Christina's House '99
Cutthroat Island '95
Bad Company '94
Brainscan '94
Doomsday Gun '94
Junior '94
Dave '93
Body of Evidence '92
1492: Conquest of Paradise '92
Kurt Vonnegut's Monkey House '91
True Identity '91
And God Created Woman '88
Masters of the Universe '87
The Men's Club '86
Sphinx '81
Dracula '79
The Seagull '75
The Deadly Trap '71
Diary of a Mad Housewife '70
The Twelve Chairs '70

Sarah Langenfeld
Bloodlink '86
Gold Raiders '83
The Act '82

Heather Langenkamp (1964-)
Fugitive Mind '99
The Demolitionist '95
Wes Craven's New Nightmare '94
Shocker '89
A Nightmare on Elm Street 3: Dream Warriors '87
Nickel Mountain '85
A Nightmare on Elm Street '84

A.J. (Allison Joy) Langer (1974-)
On Edge '03
Meet the Deedles '98
Escape from L.A. '96
The Ghost Brigade '93
The People under the Stairs '91

Frances Langford (1913-2005)
Deputy Marshal '50
Melody Time '48 (V)
Dixie Jamboree '44
Girl Rush '44
Yankee Doodle Dandy '42
Dreaming Out Loud '40
Too Many Girls '40
Born to Dance '36

Wallace (Wally) Langham (1965-)
I Want Someone to Eat Cheese With '06
Little Miss Sunshine '06
On Edge '03
God's Lonely Man '96
The Chocolate War '88
The Invisible Kid '88
Thunder Run '86

Amanda Langlet
Triple Agent '04
A Summer's Tale '96
Pauline at the Beach '83

Lisa Langlois (1959-)
Boxcar Blues '90
Cold Comfort '90
American Boyfriends '89
Thunderground '89
The Nest '88
Transformations '88
Truth or Die '86
Joy of Sex '84
The Man Who Wasn't There '83
Class of 1984 '82
Deadly Eyes '82
Blood Relatives '77

Margaret Langrick (1971-)
Wishful Thinking '92
Digging Up Business '91
Up Your Alley '89
Night Patrol '85

Brooke Langton (1970-)
Primeval '07
The Benchwarmers '06
Playing Mona Lisa '00
The Replacements '00
Reach the Rock '98
Listen '96
Swingers '96

David Langton (1912-94)
The Whistle Blower '87
Quintet '79
Abandon Ship '57

Jeff Langton
Maximum Force '92
Final Impact '91

Paul Langton (1913-80)
The Cosmic Man '59
It! The Terror from Beyond Space '58
The Incredible Shrinking Man '57
The Big Knife '55
To Hell and Back '55
The Snow Creature '54
They Were Expendable '45
Thirty Seconds Over Tokyo '44

Kim Lankford (1962-)
Street Corner Justice '96
Cameron's Closet '89
Octagon '80
Malibu Beach '78

Frank Lanning (1872-1945)
The Lone Defender '32
Stand and Deliver '28
The Unknown '27

Les Lannom
Southern Comfort '81
Centennial '78
Stingray '78

Jenya Lano
Ten 'Til Noon '06
Stealing Candy '04

Victor Lanoux (1936-)
Louisiana '87
Scene of the Crime '87
National Lampoon's European Vacation '85
Dog Day '83
Make Room for Tomorrow '81
Investigation '79
One Wild Moment '78
A Woman at Her Window '77
Cousin, Cousine '76
Pardon Mon Affaire '76
The French Detective '75

Angela Lansbury (1925-)
The Nest '88
The Company of Wolves '85
The First Olympics: Athens 1896 '84
Little Gloria... Happy at Last '84
Sweeney Todd: The Demon Barber of Fleet Street '84
The Pirates of Penzance '83
The Last Unicorn '82 (V)
The Mirror Crack'd '80
The Lady Vanishes '79
Death on the Nile '78
Bedknobs and Broomsticks '71
Something for Everyone '70
The Amorous Adventures of Moll Flanders '65
The Greatest Story Ever Told '65
Harlow '65
The World of Henry Orient '64
All Fall Down '62
Blue Hawaii '62
The Manchurian Candidate '62
Breath of Scandal '60
The Long, Hot Summer '58
The Reluctant Debutante '58
Court Jester '56
A Lawless Street '55
Mutiny '52
Samson and Delilah '50
State of the Union '48
The Three Musketeers '48
The Private Affairs of Bel Ami '47
The Harvey Girls '46
Picture of Dorian Gray '45
Gaslight '44
National Velvet '44

David Lansbury (1961-)
From Other Worlds '04
Cupid & Cate '00
A Stranger in the Kingdom '98
Truman '95
Parallel Lives '94
Gas Food Lodging '92

John Lansing
More American Graffiti '79
Sunnyside '79

Joi Lansing (1928-72)
Big Foot '72
Hillbillies in a Haunted House '67
Atomic Submarine '59
A Hole in the Head '59
Touch of Evil '58
The Brave One '56
The Finger Man '55
Son of Sinbad '55
The French Line '54
The Merry Widow '52
Singin' in the Rain '52
Pier 23 '51
Two Tickets to Broadway '51
Neptune's Daughter '49
Easter Parade '48
Julia Misbehaves '48

Robert Lansing (1929-94)
The Nest '88
Island Claw '80
S*H*E '79
Acapulco Gold '78
Empire of the Ants '77
Bittersweet Love '76
Scalpel '76
The Widow '76
The Grissom Gang '71
Namu, the Killer Whale '66
Talion '66
Under the Yum-Yum Tree '63
The 4D Man '59

Virginia Lantry
No Way Back '90
Ain't No Way Back '89

Gerard Lanvin (1950-)
The Taste of Others '00
Mon Homme '96
The Favorite Son '94

Mario Lanza (1921-59)
For the First Time '59
The Seven Hills of Rome '58
Because You're Mine '52
The Great Caruso '51
The Toast of New Orleans '50
That Midnight Kiss '49

Fabio Lanzoni
See Fabio

Anthony LaPaglia (1959-)
The Architect '06
Happy Feet '06 (V)
Played '06
Winter Solstice '04
Happy Hour '03
The Guys '02
I'm with Lucy '02
The Salton Sea '02
The Bank '01
Dead Heat '01
Lantana '01
Autumn in New York '00
Company Man '00
House of Mirth '00
Lansky '99
Summer of Sam '99
Sweet and Lowdown '99
Phoenix '98
The Garden of Redemption '97
Brilliant Lies '96
Commandments '96
Paperback Romance '96
Tree's Lounge '96
Bulletproof Heart '95
Chameleon '95
Empire Records '95
The Client '94
The Custodian '94
Mixed Nuts '94
Past Tense '94
So I Married an Axe Murderer '93
Black Magic '92
Innocent Blood '92
Keeper of the City '92
Whispers in the Dark '92
He Said, She Said '91
One Good Cop '91
29th Street '91
Betsy's Wedding '90
Criminal Justice '90
Mortal Sins '90
Slaves of New York '89
Nitti: The Enforcer '88

Jonathan LaPaglia (1967-)
Under Hellgate Bridge '99
Inferno '98

Daniel Lapaine (1971-)
The 10th Kingdom '00
Brokedown Palace '99
Dangerous Beauty '98
1999 '98
Polish Wedding '97
Muriel's Wedding '94

Francine Lapensee
Bounty Hunter 2002 '94
Demon Wind '90
Born Killer '89
Hollywood's New Blood '88

Andrzej Lapicki (1924-)
The Deluge '73
Everything for Sale '68

Peter Lapis
Undeclared War '91
Death Blow '87

Victor Laplace (1943-)
Letters from the Park '88
Under the Earth '86

Jane Lapotaire (1944-)
Shooting Fish '98
Surviving Picasso '96
The Dark Angel '91
Murder by Moonlight '91
Eureka! '81
Piaf '81
The Asphyx '72

Joe Lara (1962-)
Doomsdayer '01
Operation: Delta Force '97
Warhead '96
Final Equinox '95
Hologram Man '95
Live Wire: Human Timebomb '95
American Cyborg: Steel Warrior '94
Steel Frontier '94

John Larch (1922-94)
The Amityville Horror '79
Future Cop '76
Bad Ronald '74
Santee '73
Dirty Harry '71
Play Misty for Me '71
Hail, Hero! '69
The Wrecking Crew '68
Man in the Shadow '57

Vincent Laresca (1974-)
El Cantante '06
The Fast and the Furious: Tokyo Drift '06
.45 '06
The Aviator '04
Empire '02
Hard Cash '01

Just One Time '00
Forever Mine '99
Music from Another Room '97
Ripe '97
Money Train '95
Juice '92

Corey Large (1975-)
Loaded '08
Chasing Ghosts '05
Window Theory '04

Bryan Larkin
Born on the Fourth of July '89

Veronica Lario (1956-)
Sotto, Sotto '85
Unsane '82

Chris Larkin (1967-)
Friends & Crocodiles '05
Hitler: The Rise of Evil '03
Master and Commander: The Far Side of the World '03
Shackleton '02

Linda Larkin (1970-)
The Flamingo Rising '01
Angels and Insects '95
Aladdin and the King of Thieves '96 (V)
The Return of Jafar '94 (V)
Aladdin '92 (V)

Mary Laroche (1920-99)
Psychomania '73
Gidget '59

Michele Laroque (1960-)
Ma Vie en Rose '97
Pedale Douce '96
Nelly et Monsieur Arnaud '95

Scott LaRose
Booty Call '96

Pierre Larquey (1884-1962)
Topaze '51
Le Corbeau '43

Tito Larriva
Just a Little Harmless Sex '99
True Stories '86
Show '82

John Larroquette (1947-)
Kill Your Darlings '06
Southland Tales '06
Beethoven's 5th '03
Recipe for Disaster '03
The Texas Chainsaw Massacre '03 (N)
Walter and Henry '01
Isn't She Great '00
The 10th Kingdom '00
The Defenders: Payback '97
Richie Rich '94
Madhouse '90
Tune in Tomorrow '90
Second Sight '89
Blind Date '87
Convicted '86
Summer Rental '85
Choose Me '84
Meatballs 2 '84
Star Trek 3: The Search for Spock '84
Twilight Zone: The Movie '83
Cat People '82
Green Ice '81
Stripes '81
Altered States '80
Heart Beat '80
The Texas Chainsaw Massacre '74 (N)

Larry the Cable Guy (1963-)
Witless Protection '08
Delta Farce '07
Cars '06

She-Devil '89

Keith Larsen (1924-)
Mission Batangas '69

Ham Larsen
Mountain Family Robinson '79
Further Adventures of the Wilderness Family, Part 2 '77

Eric Larsen (1961-)
Young & Free '78

.arry the Cable Guy: Health Inspector '06

Wolf Larson (1959-)
The Closet '00
Shakedown '02
Crash & Byrnes '99
Storm Chasers: Revenge of the Twister '98
The Heist '96
Expect No Mercy '95
Tracks of a Killer '95
Back '01

Eric Larson (1905-88)
Demon Wind '90
The Uninvited '88

Darrell Larson (1951-)
Dirty '05
Latin Dragon '03
Double Tap '98
The Real Thing '96
Under Oath '97
City Limits '85
Mike's Murder '84
Red, White & Busted '75

Bobby Larson (1930-2002)
Leather Burners '43
The Underdog '43

David Lascher (1972-)
A Call to Remember '97
White Squall '96

Dieter Laser (1942-)
The Man Inside '90
The Lost Honor of Katharina Blum '75

Eva LaRue (1966-)
Crash and Burn '90
The Barbarians '87

Frank LaRue (1878-1960)
Range Renegades '48
Border Bandits '45
Devil Riders '44
Battling Outlaw '40
Range Busters '40
Riders of Pasco Basin '40
Mesquite Buckaroo '39
Overland Stage Raiders '38
Songs and Bullets '38
Boothill Brigade '37
Gun Lords of Stirrup Basin '37
A Lawman Is Born '37
Lightning Bill Crandall '37
The Phantom Rider '36
Red River Valley '36
His Fighting Blood '35
The Throwback '35
Law of the Sea '32

Jack LaRue (1902-84)
Gangs, Inc. '41
Under the Pampas Moon '35
Gambling Ship 33

Louise Lasser (1939-)
National Lampoon's Gold Diggers '04
Club Land '01
Requiem for a Dream '00
Mystery Men '99
Happiness '98
Sudden Manhattan '96
The Night We Never Met '93
Frankenhooker '90
Modern Love '90
Rude Awakening '89
Sing '89
Blood Rage '87
Surrender '87
Crimewave '85
For Ladies Only '81
In God We Trust '80
Just Me & You '78
Slither '73
Everything You Always Wanted to Know about Sex (But Were Afraid to Ask) '72
Bananas '71
Take the Money and Run '69

Dagmar Lassander (1943-)
S.A.S. San Salvador '84
Flattout '78
The Frightened Woman '71
Hatchet for the Honeymoon '70

Tommy Lasorda (1927-)
Homeward Bound 2: Lost in San Francisco '96 (V)
Ladybugs '92

Louise Latham (1922-)
Love & Murder '91
My Story '92
Toughlove '85
Mass Appeal '84
Love Field '91
Paradise '91
Crazy from the Heart '91
In Cold Blood '96
Lois Gibbs and the Love Canal '82
Pray TV '82
Dying Room Only '73
White Lightning '73
Adam at 6 a.m. '70
Marnie '64

Anne Latham
Thieves Like Us '74
Mind Warp '72

Michael Laskin (1951-)
Bounce '00
Limbo '99

Kathleen Lasky
Getting Gotti '94

Dick Latessa (1930-)
Arlie '04
The Event '03
Stigmata '99
Rockabye '86
Izzy & Moe '85
Puddn'head Wilson '84

Lyle Latell (1904-67)
Dick Tracy Meets Gruesome '47
Dick Tracy vs. Cueball '46
Dick Tracy's Dilemma '47
Dick Tracy, Detective '45

Lash LaRue (1917-96)
Pair of Aces '90
The Dark Power '85
King of the Bullwhip '51
Thundering Trail '51
Nowhere '96
Outlaw Country '49
Stage to Mesa City '48
Border Feud '47
Cheyenne Takes Over '47
Fighting Vigilantes '47
Ghost Town Renegades '47
Heartaches '47
Law of the Lash '47
Return of the Lash '47
The Caravan Trail '46
Wild West '46
Song of Old Wyoming '45
Master Key '44

Robert LaSardo (1963-)
Never Down '06
Dirty '05
Committed '91
Shakes the Clown '92
Monaco Forever '83
Roxanne '87
My Tutor '82
Rich and Famous '81
Out on Bail '89
Smooth Talker '90
The Art of Dying '90
Cool as Ice '91

Sarah Lassez
Mac 'Cowgirl '06
In Pursuit '00
The Blackout '97
Malicious '95
Nowhere '96
Diving In '90
Catch Me... If You Can '89

Sydney Lassick (1922-2003)
American Vampire '97
Sisters '97
Freeway '95
Money to Burn '94
Sonny Boy '87
Night Patrol '85
Silent Madness '84
Alligator '80
The Unseen '80
The Billion Dollar Hobo '78
Carrie '76

Rolf Lassgard (1955-)
After the Wedding '06
Under the Sun '98
The White Lioness '96

Zoltan Latanovits

Ney Latorraca (1944-)
Pigeon Fancier '88
Opera do Malandro '87

Andy Lau (1961-)
House of Flying Daggers '04
Infernal Affairs '02
Running out of Time '99
The Legend of Drunken Master '94

Matt Lattanzi (1959-)
Diving In '90
Catch Me... If You Can '89
13 Rue Madeleine '46

Carina Lau (1964-)
2046 '04
Project A: Part 2 '87

Damian Lau (1949-)
Jet Li's The Enforcer '95
The Heroic Trio '93

Tak-Wah Lau
See Andy Lau

Philippe Laudenbach (1936-)
Four Adventures of Reinette and Mirabelle '89

Andrew Lauer (1965-)
Confidentially Yours '83
Gun Shy '00
I'll Be Home for Christmas '98

Jack Laufer
Screamers '96
The Learning Curve '01
The Man Who Captured Eichmann '96
And the Band Played On '93

John Laughlin
Lost in Yonkers '93
Storm Trooper '98
Back to Back '96
Improper Conduct '94
Night Fire '94
Sexual Malice '93
The Lawnmower Man '92
Memphis '91
Motorama '91
Midnight Crossing '87
Space Rage '86
Crimes of Passion '84
Footloose '84
The Hills Have Eyes, Part 2 '84

Hugh Latimer (1913-2006)
The Cosmic Monsters '58
Rogue's Yarn '56

Michael Latimer (1941-)
Prehistoric Women '67
Man of Violence '71
Someone at the Door '50

Philip Latham (1927-)
The Two Faces of Evil '82
Dracula, Prince of Darkness '66

Sanaa Lathan (1971-)
A Raisin in the Sun '08
Something New '06
Alien vs. Predator '04
Out of Time '03
Brown Sugar '02
Catfish in Black Bean Sauce '00
Disappearing Acts '00
Love and Basketball '00
The Best Man '99
The Wood '99
Blade '98

Tom Laughlin (1939-)
The Trial of Billy Jack '74
Billy Jack '71
The Born Losers '67
South Pacific '58
Tall Story '60

Chester Lauck (1901-80)
Goin' to Town '44
So This Is Washington '43
Two Weeks to Live '43
Dreaming Out Loud '40

Carole Laure (1951-)
Surrogate '88
Sweet Country '87
Heartbreakers '84
Victory '81
Get Out Your Handkerchiefs '78

Frank Latimore (1925-98)
Patton '70
The Dolly Sisters '46
The Razor's Edge '46
The Big Clock '48
Man on the Eiffel Tower '48
The Paradine Case '47
13 Rue Madeleine '46
Shock! '46

Charles Laughton (1899-1962)
Advise and Consent '62
Spartacus '60
Witness for the Prosecution '57
Hobson's Choice '53
Salome '53
Young Bess '53
The Canterville Ghost '44
The Hunchback of Notre Dame '39
Jamaica Inn '39
Beachcomber '38
Sidewalks of London '38
Rembrandt '36
Les Miserables '35
Mutiny on the Bounty '35
Ruggles of Red Gap '35
The Barretts of Wimpole Street '34
The Private Life of Henry VIII '33
The Sign of the Cross '33
Island of Lost Souls '32
The Old Dark House '32
Because of Him '45
Captain Kidd '45
This Land Is Mine '43
The Tuttles of Tahiti '42
It Started with Eve '41
They Knew What They Wanted '40

Rik Launspach (1958-)
Mandolay '05
The Delivery '99

Cyndi Lauper (1953-)
Life with Mikey '93
Vibes '88
Off and Running '90

S. John Launer (1919-2006)
Crime of Passion '57
I Was a Teenage Werewolf '57

Matthew Laurance (1950-)
Perfect Assassins '98
Eddie and the Cruisers 2: Eddie Lives! '89
Eddie and the Cruisers '83

Mitchell Laurance (1950-)
Vibes '88

Stan Laurel (1890-1965)
Days of Thrills and Laughter '61
Utopia '51
Bullfighters '45
Nothing But Trouble '44
Air Raid Wardens '43
Great Guns '41
A Chump at Oxford '40
Saps at Sea '40
The Flying Deuces '39
Block-heads '38
Swiss Miss '38
Pick a Star '37
Way Out West '37
Bohemian Girl '36
Our Relations '36
Bonnie Scotland '35
Hollywood Party '34
Abbott and Costello Meet Captain Kidd '52
The Strange Door '51
Arch of Triumph '48

Laurel & Hardy
Laurel & Hardy Spooktacular '34
March of the Wooden Soldiers '34
The Devil's Brother '33
Laurel & Hardy and the Family '33
Laurel & Hardy: Stan "Helps" Ollie '33
Sons of the Desert '33
Laurel & Hardy: At Work '32
Pack Up Your Troubles '32
Laurel & Hardy: Be Big '31
Laurel & Hardy: Chickens Come Home '31
Laurel & Hardy: Laughing Gravy '31
Pardon Us '31
Laurel & Hardy: Another Fine Mess '30
Laurel & Hardy: Below Zero '30
Laurel & Hardy: Blotto '30
Laurel & Hardy: Brats '30
Laurel & Hardy: Hog Wild '30
Laurel & Hardy: Night Owls '30
Laurel & Hardy On the Lam '30
Laurel & Hardy: Berth Marks '29
Laurel & Hardy: Men O'War '29
Laurel & Hardy: Perfect Day '29
Laurel & Hardy: The Hoose-Gow '29

Andrew Lauren (1969-)
G '02
Far Harbor '96

Ashley Lauren
See Ashley Laurence

Greg Lauren (1970-)
Friends and Family '01
The Prophet's Game '99
Boys Life '94

Rod Lauren (1940-)
Once Before I Die '65
The Crawling Hand '63

Tammy Lauren (1969-)
Wishmaster '97
The Real Thing '97
Cupid '96
Felony '95
The Fighter '95
Outside the Law '95
Triplecross '95
American Cop '94
Lurking Fear '94
Mikey '92
One Last Run '89

Veronica Lauren (1980-)
Homeward Bound 2: Lost in San Francisco '96
Homeward Bound: The Incredible Journey '93

Ashley Laurence (1971-)
Hellraiser: Hellseeker '02
Cypress Edge '99
Warlock 3: The End of Innocence '98
Hellraiser 3: Hell on Earth '92
Hellbound: Hellraiser 2 '88
Hellraiser '87

Phil Laurenson
The Gore-Gore Girls '72
The Wizard of Gore '70

James Laurenson (1935)
Three Blind Mice '02
The Cat's Meow '01
Sharpe's Mission '96
Sharpe's Regiment '96
Sharpe's Siege '96
Cold Light of Day '95
A House in the Hills '93
Codename Kyril '91
Rainbow Drive '90

Heartbreakers '84
Pink Floyd: The Wall '82
Rude Awakening '81
Assault '70

Agnes Laurent
Girl in His Pocket '57
The Twilight Girls '57

Remy Laurent (1957-89)
The Gift '82
La Cage aux Folles '78

Joanie Laurer (1970-)
Cougar Club '07
Frank McKlusky, C.I. '02
Alien Fury: Countdown to Invasion '00

Dan Lauria (1947-)
The Bronx Is Burning '07
Big Momma's House 2 '06
Common Ground '00
Full Disclosure '00
Hangman '00
Fear Runs Silent '99
Dean Koontz's Mr. Murder '98
From the Earth to the Moon '98
Ricochet River '98
True Friends '98
Dogwatch '97
Prison of Secrets '97
Wide Awake '97
Independence Day '96
In the Line of Duty: Ambush in Waco '93
In the Line of Duty: A Cop for the Killing '90
Skin '90
Stakeout '87

Hugh Laurie (1959-)
Street Kings '08
Valiant '05 (V)
Flight of the Phoenix '04
Stuart Little 2 '02
Life with Judy Garland—Me and My Shadows '01
Maybe Baby '99
Stuart Little '99
The Man in the Iron Mask '98
The Borrowers '97
Cousin Bette '97
Spice World: The Movie '97
101 Dalmatians '96
Sense and Sensibility '95
All or Nothing at All '93
Peter's Friends '92
Strapless '90

John Laurie (1897-1980)
The Reptile '66
Devil Girl from Mars '54
Encore '52
Madeleine '50
No Trace '50
Trio '50
Bonnie Prince Charlie '48
Hamlet '48
Man of Evil '48
Mine Own Executioner '47
The World Owes Me a Living '47
Henry V '44
Immortal Battalion '44
Dangerous Moonlight '41
Clouds over Europe '39
The Four Feathers '39
Edge of the World '37
Nine Days a Queen '36
The 39 Steps '35
Juno and the Paycock '30

Piper Laurie (1932-)
The Dead Girl '06
Eulogy '04
Possessed '00
Inherit the Wind '99
St. Patrick's Day '99
The Faculty '98
Horton Foote's Alone '97
The Road to Galveston '96
The Grass Harp '95
The Crossing Guard '94
Dario Argento's Trauma '93
Rich in Love '93
Wrestling Ernest Hemingway '93
Storyville '92
Other People's Money '91
Rising Son '90
Dream a Little Dream '89
Appointment with Death '88
Distortions '87
Tiger Warsaw '87
Children of a Lesser God '86
Return to Oz '85
Toughlove '85
Mae West '84
The Thorn Birds '83
Skag '79
Tim '79
Boss' Son '78
Ruby '77
Carrie '76
Days of Wine and Roses '58
Until They Sail '57
Dangerous Mission '54
Son of Ali Baba '52
Francis Goes to the Races '51

Charlotte Laurier (1966-)
2 Seconds '98
Les Bons Debarras '81

Lucie Laurier (1975-)
Seducing Doctor Lewis '03
Stiletto Dance '01
Strip Search '97

Ed Lauter (1940-)
The Number 23 '07
The Prince and the Pauper '07
Seraphim Falls '06
Art Heist '05
Into the Fire '05
The Longest Yard '05
Seabiscuit '03
Not Another Teen Movie '01
Thirteen Days '00
Malicious Intent '99
A Bright Shining Lie '98
For Which He Stands '98
Allie & Me '97
Coyote Summer '96
Mercenary '96
Rattled '96
Breach of Trust '95
Leaving Las Vegas '95
Mulholland Falls '95
Ravenhawk '95
The Sweeper '95
Black Water '94
Digital Man '94
Girl in the Cadillac '94
Trial by Jury '94
Extreme Justice '93
Murder So Sweet '93
True Romance '93
Under Investigation '93
School Ties '92
The Rocketeer '91
Stephen King's Golden Years '91
Goodbye, Miss 4th of July '88
Revenge of the Nerds 2: Nerds in Paradise '87
The Last Days of Patton '86
Youngblood '86
Yuri Nosenko, KGB '86
Death Wish 3 '85
Girls Just Want to Have Fun '85
Nickel Mountain '85
Real Genius '85
Cartier Affair '84
Finders Keepers '84
Lassiter '84
Big Score '83
Cujo '83
Timerider '83
The Amateur '82
In the Custody of Strangers '82
Death Hunt '81
Eureka! '81
Love's Savage Fury '79
Magic '78
The Chicken Chronicles '77
Breakheart Pass '76
Family Plot '76
King Kong '76
The Longest Yard '74
The Migrants '74
Class of '63 '73
Rage '72

Harry Lauter (1914-90)
Escape from the Planet of the Apes '71
Trader Tom of the China Seas '54
Thunder in God's Country '51
Bandit King of Texas '49

Heiner Lauterbach
Dresden '06
Men... '85

Kathrin Lautner
Two Bits & Pepper '95
The Last Riders '90
Night of the Wilding '90
Spirits '90

Taylor Lautner (1992-)
The Adventures of Sharkboy and Lavagirl in 3-D '05
Cheaper by the Dozen 2 '05

Rene Lavan (1968-)
Christmas With the Kranks '04
Dirty Dancing: Havana Nights '04
Bitter Sugar '96

Dominique Lavanant (1944-)
The Monster '96
Three Men and a Cradle '85
French Fried Vacation '79

Denis Lavant (1961-)
A Very Long Engagement '04
Beau Travail '98
The Lovers on the Bridge '91
Mauvais Sang '86
Boy Meets Girl '84

Lucille LaVerne (1872-1945)
Snow White and the Seven Dwarfs '37 (V)
Kentucky Kernels '34
Hearts of Humanity '32
Wayne Murder Case '32
The White Rose '23

Daliah Lavi (1942-)
Those Fantastic Flying Fools '67
The Silencers '66
Spy with a Cold Nose '66
Lord Jim '65
Apache's Last Battle '64
The Whip and the Body '63
Two Weeks in Another Town '62
The Return of Dr. Mabuse '61

Gabriele Lavia (1942-)
Revenge of the Dead '84
Zeder '83
Deep Red: Hatchet Murders '75

Avril Lavigne (1984-)
The Flock '07
Fast Food Nation '06
Over the Hedge '06 (V)

Linda Lavin (1937-)
Collected Stories '02
I Want to Go Home '89
See You in the Morning '89
Maricela '88
The Muppets Take Manhattan '84
A Matter of Life and Death '81
The $5.20 an Hour Dream '80

Marc Lavoine (1962-)
The Good Thief '03
Fiesta '95
L'Enfer '93

Adam LaVorgna (1981-)
Outside Providence '99
I'll Be Home for Christmas '98

John Phillip Law (1937-)
CQ '01
Hindsight '97
My Magic Dog '97
Cold Heat '90
Alienator '89
Space Mutiny '88
Thunder Warrior 3 '88
Moon in Scorpio '86
L.A. Bad '85
American Commandos '84
Attack Force Z '84
Night Train to Terror '84
No Time to Die '84
Overthrow '82
Tarzan, the Ape Man '81
African Rage '78
The Cassandra Crossing '76
Spiral Staircase '75
Golden Voyage of Sinbad '73
The Last Movie '71
The Love Machine '71
Barbarella '68
Danger: Diabolik '68
The Russians Are Coming, the Russians Are Coming '66

Jude Law (1972-)
My Blueberry Nights '07
Sleuth '07
All the King's Men '06
Breaking and Entering '06
The Holiday '06
Alfie '04
The Aviator '04
Closer '04
I Heart Huckabees '04
Lemony Snicket's A Series of Unfortunate Events '04
Sky Captain and the World of Tomorrow '04
Cold Mountain '03
Road to Perdition '02
A. I.: Artificial Intelligence '01
Enemy at the Gates '00
Love, Honour & Obey '00
eXistenZ '99
Final Cut '98
Immortality '98
Bent '97
Gattaca '97
I Love You, I Love You Not '97
Midnight in the Garden of Good and Evil '97
Music from Another Room '97
Wilde '97
Shopping '93

Phyllida Law (1932-)
Miss Austen Regrets '07
Day of Wrath '06
Miss Potter '06
Pinochet's Last Stand '06
Brush with Fate '03
The Time Machine '02
Two Men Went to War '02
The Magical Legend of the Leprechauns '99
I Want You '98
The Winter Guest '97
Emma '96
Leo Tolstoy's Anna Karenina '96
Before the Rain '94
All or Nothing at All '93
Much Ado about Nothing '93
Peter's Friends '92
Hitler: The Last Ten Days '73

Christopher Lawford (1955-)
The World's Fastest Indian '05
Counterstrike '03
The 6th Day '00
Thirteen Days '00
Mary, Mother of Jesus '99
The Confession '98
Kiss Me, Guido '97
The Abduction '96
The Russia House '90
Mr. North '88

Peter Lawford (1923-84)
Body & Soul '81
Angel's Brigade '79
Mysterious Island of Beautiful Women '79
Fantasy Island '76
Rosebud '75
They Only Kill Their Masters '72
Togetherness '70
April Fools '69
Buona Sera, Mrs. Campbell '68
A Man Called Adam '66
The Oscar '66
Harlow '65
Dead Ringer '64
Advise and Consent '62
The Longest Day '62
Exodus '60
Ocean's 11 '60
Never So Few '59
It Should Happen to You '54
Royal Wedding '51
Little Women '49
Easter Parade '48
Julia Misbehaves '48
On an Island with You '48
Good News '47
It Happened in Brooklyn '47
Picture of Dorian Gray '45
Son of Lassie '45
The Canterville Ghost '44
The White Cliffs of Dover '44
Immortal Sergeant '43
Sahara '43
Junior Army '42
Mrs. Miniver '42
Thunder Birds '42

Lucy Lawless (1968-)
Boogeyman '05
Eurotrip '04
Spider-Man '02
Hercules, Vol. 1: And the Legendary Journeys... '94
Hercules and the Amazon Women '94

Yvonne Lawley (1914-99)
Death in Brunswick '90
Among the Cinders '83

Stephanie Lawlor
Hot T-Shirts '79
Cherry Hill High '76

Barbara Lawrence (1928-)
Kronos '57
Man in the Shadow '57
Oklahoma! '55
Here Come the Nelsons '52
The Star '52
A Letter to Three Wives '49
The Street with No Name '48

Bruno Lawrence (1941-95)
Jack Be Nimble '94
Rainbow Warrior '94
The Efficiency Expert '92
Grievous Bodily Harm '89
Rikky and Pete '88
The Bridge to Nowhere '86
An Indecent Obsession '85
The Quiet Earth '85
Heart of the Stag '84
Treasure of the Yankee Zephyr '83
Utu '83
Smash Palace '82

Carol Lawrence (1934-)
Shattered Image '93
Summer of Fear '78
New Faces of 1952 '54

Carolyn Lawrence (1964-)
The SpongeBob SquarePants Movie '04 (V)
Jimmy Neutron: Boy Genius '01 (V)

Cary Lawrence
Canvas: The Fine Art of Crime '92
The Dance Goes On '92

Delphi Lawrence (1926-2002)
Frozen Alive '64
Murder on Approval '56
Three Stops to Murder '53

Elizabeth Lawrence (1922-2000)
Unbreakable '00
The Crucible '96
Sleeping with the Enemy '91

Gertrude Lawrence (1898-1952)
Stage Door Canteen '43
Men Are Not Gods '37
Rembrandt '36

Joey Lawrence (1976-)
Killer Pad '06
Tequila Body Shots '99
Radioland Murders '94
Mrs. Doubtfire '93
Chains of Gold '92
Oliver & Company '88 (V)
Pulse '88
Wait Till Your Mother Gets Home '83

John Lawrence (1931-92)
They Live '88
The Asphyx '72
The Manchurian Candidate '62

Joseph Lawrence
Confessions of a Sociopathic Social Climber '05
Urban Legends 2: Final Cut '00

Marc Lawrence (1910-2005)
Gotti '96
Ruby '92
The Big Easy '87
Night Train to Terror '84
Cataclysm '81
Foul Play '78
Goin' Coconuts '78
King of Kong Island '78
Marathon Man '76
Dream No Evil '75
The Man with the Golden Gun '74
Frasier the Sensuous Lion '73
Pigs '73
Abbott and Costello in the Foreign Legion '50
The Asphalt Jungle '50
The Black Hand '50
Jigsaw '49
Tough Assignment '49
Cloak and Dagger '46
'Neath Brooklyn Bridge '42
This Gun for Hire '42
The Monster and the Girl '41
Brigham Young: Frontiersman '40
Charlie Chan at the Wax Museum '40
Johnny Apollo '40
I Am the Law '38
Murder in Greenwich Village '37
San Quentin '37
Vengeance '37

Mark Christopher Lawrence (1964-)
That Darn Cat '96
Fear of a Black Hat '94

Martin Lawrence (1965-)
Welcome Home Roscoe Jenkins '08
Wild Hogs '07
Open Season '06 (V)
Big Momma's House 2 '06
Rebound '05
Bad Boys 2 '03
National Security '03
Black Knight '01
What's the Worst That Could Happen? '01
Big Momma's House '00
Blue Streak '99
Life '99
Nothing to Lose '96
A Thin Line Between Love and Hate '96
Bad Boys '95
You So Crazy '94
House Party 2: The Pajama Jam '91
House Party '90
The Movie '90

Matthew Lawrence (1980-)
The Hot Chick '02
Family Tree '00
All I Wanna Do '98
Angels in the Endzone '98
Boltneck '98
Kiki's Delivery Service '98 (V)
Undesirable '92
Tales from the Darkside: The Movie '90

Michael Lawrence (1980-)
The Price of Milk '00
Othello '52

Peter Lee Lawrence (1943-73)
Garringo '69
They Paid with Bullets: Chicago 1929 '69
Special Forces '68

Rosina Lawrence (1913-97)
Pick a Star '37
Way Out West '37
General Spanky '36
Charlie Chan's Secret '35

Scott Lawrence
Laurel Avenue '93
God's Bloody Acre '75

Sharon Lawrence (1963-)
Lies & Alibis '06
Aftershock: Earthquake in New York '99
Gossip '99
The Only Thrill '97
Degree of Guilt '95
The Heidi Chronicles '95

Sheldon Lawrence
Sweet Beat '59
Black Tide '58

Stephanie Lawrence (1949-2000)
The Phantom of the Opera '89

Steve Lawrence (1935-)
Ocean's Eleven '01
Blues Brothers 2000 '98
Alice in Wonderland '85
The Lonely Guy '84
The Blues Brothers '80

Steven Anthony Lawrence (1995-)
Kicking & Screaming '05
Rebound '05
Cheaper by the Dozen '03

Marlene Lawston
Flightplan '05
Dan in Real Life '07

Bianca Lawson (1979-)
Breakin' All The Rules '04
Anne Rice's The Feast of All Saints '01
Bones '01

Chas Lawther
Urban Legends 2: Final Cut '00
Love Letters '99

Save the Last Dance '01
Boltneck '98

Denis Lawson (1947-)
Jekyll '07
Bleak House '05
The Winslow Boy '99
Horatio Hornblower '98
The Mill on the Floss '97
Local Hero '83
Return of the Jedi '83

Leigh Lawson (1945-)
Casanova '05
Being Julia '04
Back to the Secret Garden '01
Charlie Boy '81
Disraeli '79
Tess '79
Love Among the Ruins '75
It's Not the Size That Counts '74
Madhouse Mansion '74
Brother Sun, Sister Moon '73

Louise Lawson
Creeping Terror '64

Maggie Lawson (1980-)
Cleaner '07
Winter Break '02
Model Behavior '00

Priscilla Lawson (1914-58)
Flash Gordon: Rocketship '40

Sarah Lawson (1928-)
The Devil Rides Out '68
Island of the Burning Doomed '67

Shannon Lawson
Last Call: The Final Chapter of F. Scott Fitzgerald '02
Possessed '00
Anne of Green Gables: The Continuing Story '99
Heck's Way Home '95

Wilfred Lawson (1900-66)
Room at the Top '59
War and Peace '56
The Prisoner '55
Man of Evil '48
Thursday's Child '43
The Night Has Eyes '42
Tower of Terror '42
Pygmalion '38
The Terror '38

Frank Lawton (1904-69)
Wrongfully Accused '98
Tracks of a Killer '95
Hard Bounty '94
Betrayal of the Dove '92

John Lazar (1934-)
Attack of the 60-Foot Centerfold '95
Night of the Scarecrow '95
Over the Wire '95
Devil Doll '36

Justin Lazard (1967-)
The Brutal Truth '99
Species 2 '98
The Big Fall '96
Deathstalker 2: Duel of the Titans '87

Eugene (Yevgeny) Lazarev
Lord of War '05
The Sum of All Fears '02
The Saint '97
The Ice Runner '93

Eusebio Lazaro (1942-)
Twice upon a Yesterday '98
Soldier's Web '01
Four Dogs Playing Poker '00

Evelyn Laye (1900-96)
Say Hello to Yesterday '71
Theatre of Death '67

John Le Mesurier (1912-83)
A Married Man '84
Brideshead Revisited '81
The Fiendish Plot of Dr. Fu Manchu '80
Jabberwocky '77
Brothers in Law '57
The Baby and the Battleship '56

Steve Le Marquand
The Brush-Off '04
Risk '00

Jake Le Doux
See Jake LeDoux

Bernard Le Coq (1950-)
Hidden '05
Joyeux Noel '05
The Bridesmaid '04
Capitaine Conan '96
Van Gogh '92

Nicholas Le Prevost (1947-)
P.D. James: The Murder Room '04
Amazing Grace '06
Catherine Cookson's The Gambling Man '98

Sylvestria Le Touzel
Northanger Abbey '07
The Girl in a Swing '89
A Fatal Inversion '92
Mansfield Park '85

George Lazenby (1939-)
Fatally Yours '95
Twinsitters '95
Gettysburg '93
Eyes of the Beholder '92
Hell Hunters '87
Never Too Young to Die '86
Saint Jack '79
Kill Factor '78
Kentucky Fried Movie '77
Who Saw Her Die? '72
On Her Majesty's Secret Service '69

Samuel Le Bihan (1965-)
Vertical Limit '00
Once a Thief '96
The Raffle '94
Xtro 2: The Second Encounter '91

Becky Le Beau
See Becky LeBeau

Isild Le Besco (1982-)
Sade '00
Girls Can't Swim '99

Malwenn Le Besco (1976-)
High Tension '03
The Fifth Element '97
The Elegant Criminal '92

Bruce Le
Clones of Bruce Lee '80
The Young Bruce Lee '80
Bruce Lee Fights Back from the Grave '76

Hiep Thi Le (1970-)
Green Dragon '01

Ron Lea
A Different Loyalty '04
Sea People '00
A Map of the World '99
The Neighbor '93
Clearcut '92
The Phone Call '89

Rosemary Leach (1925-)
Catherine Cookson's Tilly Trotter '99
Berkeley Square '98
The Buccaneers '95
The Hawk '93
The Mystery of Edwin Drood '93
The Children '90
The Charmer '87
A Room with a View '86
That'll Be the Day '73

Cloris Leachman (1930-)
Lake Placid 2 '07
Beerfest '06
Scary Movie 4 '06
The Longest Yard '05
Mrs. Harris '05
Sky High '05
Spanglish '04
Alex & Emma '03
Bad Santa '03
Manna from Heaven '02
Hanging Up '99
Iron Giant '99 (V)
Music of the Heart '99
Beavis and Butt-Head Do America '96 (V)
Now and Then '95
A Troll in Central Park '94 (V)
The Beverly Hillbillies '93
Fade to Black '93
My Boyfriend's Back '93
Double Double Toil and Trouble '93
Danielle Steel's Fine Things '90
Texasville '90
Prancer '89
The Victory '88
Walk Like a Man '87
Shadow Play '86
Dixie: Changing Habits '85
Ernie Kovacs: Between the Laughter '84
The Woman Who Willed a Miracle '83
Acorn People '82
Miss All-American Beauty '82
History of the World: Part 1 '81
Foolin' Around '80
Herbie Goes Bananas '80
Oldest Living Graduate '80
Backstairs at the White House '79
The North Avenue Irregulars '79
The Muppet Movie '79
Mrs. R's Daughter '79
Willa '79
Long Journey Back '78
High Anxiety '77
Mouse and His Child '77 (V)
Crazy Mama '75
Death Scream '75
Someone I Touched '75
Daisy Miller '74
The Migrants '74
Death Sentence '74
Thursday's Game '74
Young Frankenstein '74
Dillinger '73
Dying Room Only '73
Charley and the Angel '73
Run, Stranger, Run '73
Brand New Life '72
Haunts of the Very Rich '72
The People Next Door '70
The Last Picture Show '71
The Steagle '71
Lovers and Other Strangers '70
Butch Cassidy and the Sundance Kid '69
Silent Night, Lonely Night '69
Kiss Me Deadly '55

Kelly Le Brock (1960-)
Hard to Kill '89
Weird Science '85
The Woman in Red '84

Gene Le Brock (1961-)
Beyond Darkness '92
Metamorphosis '90
Fortress of Amerikkka '89

Viv Leacock (1974-)
White Coats '04
I Spy '02

Damien Leake
Killing Floor '85
Apocalypse Now '79

Sharon Leal (1972-)
This Christmas '07
Tyler Perry's Why Did I Get Married? '07
Dreamgirls '06
Face the Music '00

Michael Learned (1939-)
Loggerheads '05
Dragon: The Bruce Lee Story '93
Murder in New Hampshire: The Pamela Smart Story '91

Deadly Business '86
Power '86
A Christmas Without Snow '80
Nurse '80
The Widow '76

Denis Leary (1957-)
Ice Age: The Meltdown '06
Dawg '02
Ice Age '02 (V)
The Secret Lives of Dentists '02
Double Whammy '01
Final '01
Company Man '00
Lakeboat '00
Sand '00
Jesus' Son '99
Silent Witness '99
The Thomas Crown Affair '99
True Crime '99
A Bug's Life '98 (V)
Monument Ave. '98
Small Soldiers '98
Love Walked In '97
The Matchmaker '97
The Real Blonde '97
The Second Civil War '97
Subway Stories '97
Suicide Kings '97
Wag the Dog '97
Wide Awake '97
Underworld '96
National Lampoon's Favorite Deadly Sins '95
The Neon Bible '95
Operation Dumbo Drop '95
Two If by Sea '95
Natural Born Killers '94
Demolition Man '93
Gunmen '93
Judgment Night '93
National Lampoon's Loaded Weapon 1 '93
The Ref '93
The Sandlot '93
Who's the Man? '93

Timothy Leary (1920-96)
Conceiving Ada '97
Hold Me, Thrill Me, Kiss Me '93
Ted & Venus '93
Roadside Prophets '92
Fatal Skies '90
Shocker '89
Cheech and Chong's Nice Dreams '81

The Mother and the Whore '73
Two English Girls '72
Bed and Board '70
Porcile '69
Stolen Kisses '68
Weekend '67
Masculine Feminine '66
Alphaville '65
The Joy of Knowledge '65
Pierrot le Fou '65
The 400 Blows '59
The Testament of Orpheus '59

Becky LeBeau (1962-)
The Malibu Beach Vampires '91

Madeleine LeBeau (1921-)
8 1/2 '63
Une Parisienne '58
Casablanca '42

Ivan Lebedeff (1894-1953)
Love on the Run '36
Goin' to Town '35
Bachelor Apartment '31
The Lady Refuses '31
Walking Back '26

Matt LeBlanc (1967-)
Charlie's Angels: Full Throttle '03
All the Queen's Men '02
Charlie's Angels '00
Lost in Space '98
Ed '96
Showdown '94
The Ghost Brigade '93
Red Shoe Diaries 3: Another Woman's Story '93

Geno Lechner (1965-)
Love '05
8 Women '02
Flirt '95

Brian Leckner (1967-)
Joy Ride '01
Sgt. Bilko '96
Bonanza: The Return '93

Michael LeClair
Leave 'Em Laughing '81
Anatomy of a Seduction '79

Ginette LeClerc (1912-92)
Le Corbeau '43
Man from Nowhere '37
The Baker's Wife '33

Jean LeClerc (1948-)
Blown Away '93
Whispers '89

Friedrich Ledebur (1900-86)
The 27th Day '57
Moby Dick '56

Erwin Leder (1951-)
Underworld '03
Das Boot '81

Paul Leder (1926-96)
How to Succeed with Girls '64

Francis Lederer (1899-2000)
Terror Is a Man '59
Return of Dracula '58
The Ambassador's Daughter '56
Lisbon '56
Stolen Identity '53
A Woman of Distinction '50
Diary of a Chambermaid '46
The Bridge of San Luis Rey '44
Midnight '39
One Rainy Afternoon '36
Romance in Manhattan '34
Pandora's Box '28

Suzanne Lederer (1948-)
Women of Valor '86
Judge Horton and the Scottsboro Boys '76

Brandy Ledford (1969-)
Ice Men '04

We'll Meet Again '02
Zebra Lounge '01

Heath Ledger (1979-2008)
The Dark Knight '08
I'm Not There '07
Candy '06
Brokeback Mountain '05
The Brothers Grimm '05
Casanova '05
Lords of Dogtown '05
Ned Kelly '03
The Order '03
The Four Feathers '02
A Knight's Tale '01
Monster's Ball '01
The Patriot '00
Ten Things I Hate about You '99
Two Hands '98

Fernand Ledoux (1897-1993)
Pattes Blanches '49
Les Visiteurs du Soir '42
Volpone '39
La Bete Humaine '38

Jake LeDoux (1985-)
Love Come Down '00
Summer's End '99

Virginie Ledoyen (1976-)
The Valet '06
Bon Voyage '03
8 Women '02
The Beach '00
Jeanne and the Perfect Guy '98
Late August, Early September '98
A Soldier's Daughter Never Cries '98
A Single Girl '96
La Ceremonie '95

Richard Leduc
We Will Not Enter the Forest '79
Nous N'Irons Plus au Bois '69

Anna Lee (1913-2004)
Eleanor & Franklin '76
In Like Flint '67
The Sound of Music '65
Jack the Giant Killer '62
What Ever Happened to Baby Jane? '62
The Horse Soldiers '59
Fort Apache '48
The Ghost and Mrs. Muir '47
G.I. War Brides '46
Bedlam '45
Commandos Strike at Dawn '43
Flying Tigers '42
Hangmen Also Die '42
How Green Was My Valley '41
The Secret Four '40
King Solomon's Mines '37
Non-Stop New York '37
O.H.M.S. '37
The Man Who Lived Again '36
The Passing of the Third Floor Back '36
First a Girl '35

Belinda Lee (1935-61)
The Hit Man '60
That Long Night in '43 '60
Who Done It? '56
Blackout '54
The Runaway Bus '54
The Belles of St. Trinian's '53

Bernard Lee (1908-81)
Moonraker '79
The Spy Who Loved Me '77
Frankenstein and the Monster from Hell '74
It's Not the Size That Counts '74
The Man with the Golden Gun '74
Live and Let Die '73
Diamonds Are Forever '71
Long Ago Tomorrow '71
10 Rillington Place '71

On Her Majesty's Secret Service '69
You Only Live Twice '67
Thunderball '65
Goldfinger '64
From Russia with Love '63
The Brain '62
Dr. No '62
The L-Shaped Room '62
Whistle down the Wind '61
Across the Bridge '57
The Spanish Gardener '57
The Detective '54
Beat the Devil '53
The Gift Horse '52
The Adventurers '51
Last Holiday '50
Morning Departure '50
The Blue Lamp '49
The Fallen Idol '49
The Third Man '49
Elizabeth of Ladymead '48
The Courtney Affair '47
The Terror '38
Rhodes '36

Billy Lee (1929-89)
Nevada City '41
Reg'lar Fellers '41
Wagon Wheels '34

Brandon Lee (1965-93)
The Crow '93
Rapid Fire '92
Showdown in Little Tokyo '91
Laser Mission '90
Kung Fu: The Movie '86
Legacy of Rage '86

Britton Lee
Ironheart '92
The Power of the Ninjitsu '88

Bruce Lee (1940-73)
The Three Avengers '80
Game of Death '79
Chinese Connection 2 '77
Chinese Connection '73
Enter the Dragon '73
Fists of Fury '73
Return of the Dragon '73
Marlowe '69

Canada Lee (1907-52)
Cry, the Beloved Country '51
Lost Boundaries '49
Body and Soul '47
Lifeboat '44
Keep Punching '39

Carl Lee (1926-86)
Keeping On '87
Gordon's War '73
Superfly '72
The Cool World '63
The Connection '61

Casey Lee
White Chicks '04

China Lee (1942-)
Good Times '67
What's Up, Tiger Lily? '66

Christopher Lee (1922-)
The Golden Compass '07
Charlie and the Chocolate Factory '05
Crimson Rivers 2: Angels of the Apocalypse '05
Star Wars: Episode 3—Revenge of the Sith '05 (V)
Lord of the Rings: The Two Towers '02
Star Wars: Episode 2—Attack of the Clones '02
Lord of the Rings: The Fellowship of the Rings '01
Russell Mulcahy's Tale of the Mummy '99
Sleepy Hollow '99
Ivanhoe '97
The Odyssey '97
Moses '96
The Stupids '95
Funnyman '94

Police Academy 7: Mission to Moscow '94
Detonator '93
Double Vision '92
Journey of Honor '91
Sherlock Holmes and the Incident at Victoria Falls '91
Curse 3: Blood Sacrifice '90
Gremlins 2: The New Batch '90
Around the World in 80 Days '89
Murder Story '89
The Return of the Musketeers '89
Treasure Island '89
Jocks '87
The Land of Faraway '87
Desperate Moves '86
The Girl '86
Many Faces of Sherlock Holmes '86
Howling 2: Your Sister Is a Werewolf '85
Rosebud Beach Hotel '85
The Far Pavilions '84
Keeper '84
Return of Captain Invincible '83
Shaka Zulu '83
House of the Long Shadows '82
The Last Unicorn '82 (V)
Safari 3000 '82
The Salamander '82
The Boy Who Left Home to Find Out About the Shivers '81
An Eye for an Eye '81
Goliath Awaits '81
Bear Island '80
Serial '80
Captain America 2: Death Too Soon '79
Jaguar Lives '79
1941 '79
Circle of Iron '78
Return from Witch Mountain '78
Airport '77 '77
Starship Invasions '77
Albino '76
Dracula and Son '76
End of the World '76
To the Devil, a Daughter '76
The Devil's Undead '75
The Four Musketeers '75
The Man with the Golden Gun '74
The Three Musketeers '74
Dark Places '73
The Satanic Rites of Dracula '73
The Creeping Flesh '72
Dracula A.D. 1972 '72
Hannie Caulder '72
Horror Express '72
Nothing But the Night '72
Count Dracula '71
The House that Dripped Blood '71
I, Monster '71
The Private Life of Sherlock Holmes '70
The Scars of Dracula '70
Scream and Scream Again '70
Taste the Blood of Dracula '70
The Magic Christian '69
The Oblong Box '69
Five Golden Dragons '67
The Torture Chamber of Dr. Sadism '69
The Crimson Cult '68
The Devil Rides Out '68
Dracula Has Risen from the Grave '68
Kiss and Kill '68
Circus of Fear '67
Island of the Burning Doomed '67
Theatre of Death '67

Dracula, Prince of Darkness '66
Rasputin the Mad Monk '66
Dr. Terror's House of Horrors '65
The Skull '65
The Virgin of Nuremberg '65
Castle of the Living Dead '64
The Gorgon '64
Hercules in the Haunted World '64
The Whip and the Body '63
The Longest Day '62
Sherlock Holmes and the Deadly Necklace '62
Scream of Fear '61
Beat Girl '60
The Hands of Orlac '60
Horror Hotel '60
The Two Faces of Dr. Jekyll '60
The Hound of the Baskervilles '59
The Mummy '59
Uncle Was a Vampire '59
Corridors of Blood '58
The Horror of Dracula '58
A Tale of Two Cities '58
The Curse of Frankenstein '57
Night Ambush '57
Alias John Preston '56
Crimson Pirate '52
Moulin Rouge '52
Captain Horatio Hornblower '51
Valley of the Eagles '51
Hamlet '48
Scott of the Antarctic '48

Cinque Lee (1966-)
Rapturious '07
Coffee and Cigarettes '03
Mystery Train '89

Conan Lee
The Eliminators '86
Gymkata '85

Cosette Lee (1910-76)
The Fly '86
Deranged '74

Danny Lee (1952-)
Organized Crime & Triad Bureau '93
The Untold Story '93
The Killer '90
City on Fire '87
The Mighty Peking Man '77

DeWitt Lee
The Legend of Jedediah Carver '76
Apache Blood '75

Dixie Lee (1911-52)
Love in Bloom '35
Night Life in Reno '31

Dorothy Lee (1911-99)
Cockeyed Cavaliers '34
Hips, Hips, Hooray '34
Half-Shot at Sunrise '30
Hook, Line and Sinker '30

Dragon Lee
Clones of Bruce Lee '80
The Three Avengers '80

Elizabeth Lee
Organized Crime & Triad Bureau '93

Eric Lee (1948-)
Something Weird '68
Out for Blood '93
Ring of Fire '91

Etta Lee (1906-56)
The Thief of Baghdad '24
The Untamable '23

Florence Lee
City Lights '31
Road Agent '25
Virtue's Revolt '24

Gypsy Rose Lee (1914-70)
Over the Hill Gang '69
The Trouble with Angels '66
The Stripper '63
My Lucky Star '38

Jason Lee (1971-)
Alvin and the Chipmunks '07
Underdog '07 (V)
Clerks 2 '06
Monster House '06 (V)
The Ballad of Jack and Rose '05
Drop Dead Sexy '05
Jersey Girl '04
Dreamcatcher '03
A Guy Thing '03
I Love Your Work '03
Big Trouble '02
Stealing Harvard '02
Heartbreakers '01
Jay and Silent Bob Strike Back '01
Vanilla Sky '01
Almost Famous '00
Dogma '99
Mumford '99
Enemy of the State '98
Kissing a Fool '98
Chasing Amy '97
Weapons of Mass Distraction '97
Mallrats '95

Jesse Lee (1984-)
Dracula 3: Legacy '05
Lilo & Stitch 2: Stitch Has a Glitch '05 (V)
Dracula 2: Ascension '03
Timecop 2: The Berlin Decision '03
Lilo & Stitch '02 (V)
Arabian Nights '00
Russell Mulcahy's Tale of the Mummy '99
Soldier '98
Murder in Mind '97
Rudyard Kipling's The Jungle Book '94
Dragon: The Bruce Lee Story '93
Map of the Human Heart '93
Rapa Nui '93
The Lookalike '90
Back to the Future, Part 2 '89

Joanna Lee (1931-2003)
Making the Grade '84
Sem's Son '84
The Brain Eaters '58
Plan 9 from Outer Space '56

Joie Lee (1962-)
Coffee and Cigarettes '03
Crooklyn '94
Fathers and Sons '92
Mo' Better Blues '90
School Daze '88
She's Gotta Have It '86

Jon Kit Lee (1967-)
Guess Who '05
Killer Diller '04
The Corruptor '99
Vacation '97

Ruta Lee (1936-)
Christmas Do-Over '06
Funny Bones '94
Sweet Bird of Youth '89
First & Ten: The Team Scores Again '85
Rooster: Spurs of Death! '83

Sam Lee (1975-)
Dog Bite Dog '06
Gen-X Cops '99
Biozombie '98

Shannon Lee (1969-)
Epoch '00

Lila Lee (1901-73)
A Nation Aflame '37
Country Gentlemen '36
Champagne for Breakfast '35

Jason Scott Lee (1966-)
Dracula 3: Legacy '05
Lilo & Stitch 2: Stitch Has a Glitch '05 (V)

Margaret Lee (1943-)
Rogue '76
Slaughter Hotel '71
Dorian Gray '70
Circus of Fear '67
Five for Hell '67
Five Golden Dragons '67
Secret Agent Super Dragon '66
Casanova 70 '65
Venus in Furs '70
Murder for Sale '68
How to Kill 400 Duponts '68
Fire Monsters Against the Son of Hercules '62
Love, Lies and Murder '91

Mark Lee (1958-)
The Everlasting Secret Family '88
The City's Edge '83
Gallipoli '81

Mary Lee (1925-96)
Blackwater Trail '95
The Junction Boys '02
Nowhere to Land '00
Chameleon 2: Death Match '99
Bootmen '00
Holy Smoke '99
The Castle '97
Muriel's Wedding '94

Michele Lee (1942-)
Back in the Saddle '41
Ridin' on a Rainbow '41
Gaucho Serenade '40
Nancy Drew, Reporter '39
South of the Border '39
Murder in Mind '97
DROP Squad '94
Crooklyn '94
Malcolm X '92
Jungle Fever '91
Do the Right Thing '89
School Daze '88
Mo' Better Blues '90
She's Gotta Have It '86

Moon Lee (1965-)
Mr. Vampire '86
Zu: Warriors from the Magic Mountain '83

Peggy Lee (1920-2002)
Lady and the Tramp '55 (V)
Pete Kelly's Blues '55
Mr. Music '50
Stage Door Canteen '43
Switchblade Sisters '75

Robbie Lee (1955-)
Switchblade Sisters '75
Big Bad Mama '74

Robine Lee (1974-)
13 Going on 30 '04
Deliver Us from Eva '03
National Security '03
Hav Plenty '97

RonReaco Lee (1977-)

Waise Lee (1959-)
The New Guy '02
10th & Wolf '06

Tommy Lee (1962-)
A Better Tomorrow, Part 1 '86

Tommy Lee (1901-76)
The Sand Pebbles '66

Will Yun Lee (1971-)
Elektra '05
Torque '04
Die Another Day '02
Running out of Time '99
Wing Chun '94
Fatal Chase '92
A Bullet in the Head '90
A Better Tomorrow, Part 1 '86

Andrea Leeds (1914-74)
The Real Glory '39
They Shall Have Music '39
The Goldwyn Follies '38
Letter of Introduction '38

Stephen Leeder
Resistance '92
Fatal Bond '91

Alison Leggatt (1904-90)
Day of the Triffids '63
This Happy Breed '47

Michael Legge (1978-)
Cowboys & Angels '04
Angela's Ashes '99

Sheryl Lee (1967-)
Paradise, Texas '05
Children On Their Birthdays '02
Hitched '01
Angel's Sky '93
Kiss the Sky '98
The Blood Oranges '97
David '97
John Carpenter's Vampires '97
This World, Then the Fireworks '97
Bliss '96
Mother Night '96
Follow the River '95
Homage '95
Notes from Underground '95
Backbeat '94
Don't Do It '94
Fall Time '94
Red Shoe Diaries 4: Auto Erotica '93
Jersey Girl '92
Twin Peaks: Fire Walk with Me '92

Sophie Lee (1968-)
Wild at Heart '90
He Died With a Felafel in His Hand '01
Muriel's Wedding '94
Holy Smoke '99

Spike Lee (1957-)
Lisa Picard is Famous '01
Summer of Sam '99
Girl 6 '96
Crooklyn '94
DROP Squad '94
Malcolm X '92
Jungle Fever '91
Mo' Better Blues '90
Do the Right Thing '89
School Daze '88
She's Gotta Have It '86

Stan Lee (1922-)
Fantastic Four '05
Comic Book: The Movie '04
Daredevil '03
Hulk '03
Mallrats '95

Stephen Lee (1951-)
The Ambulence '90
Me and the Mob '94
Prehysteria '93
The Pit & the Pendulum '91
Dolls '87
Purple Hearts '84

Richard Leech (1922-2004)
The Garden '90
The Moonraker '58
The Third Key '57

Phoebe Legere
The Toxic Avenger, Part 2 '89
The Toxic Avenger, Part 3: The Last Temptation of Toxie '89

Sheila LeGay
See Sheila (Manors)

Erica Leerhsen (1976-)
The Texas Chainsaw Massacre '03
Book of Shadows: Blair Witch 2 '00

Jane Leeves (1962-)
Miracle on 34th Street '94
James and the Giant Peach '96 (V)
Mr. Write '92
L.I.E. '01

Adam LeFevre (1950-)
Duke of the Derby '02
Tadpole '02
Hearts in Atlantis '01
Arthur and the Invisibles '06
Return of the Secaucus 7 '80

Rachel Lefevre
The River King '05
The Legend of Butch & Sundance '04

Rene Lefevre (1898-1991)
The Crime of Monsieur Lange '36
Le Million '31

Christian Leffler
Madhouse '04
A Girl, 3 Guys and a Gun '01

Eva LeGallienne (1899-1991)
Resurrection '80
The Devil's Disciple '59

Lance LeGault (1935-)
Home on the Range '04 (V)
Roadracers '94
Shadow Force '92
Welcome to Spring Break '88
Stripes '81

Lila Leeds (1928-99)
She Shoulda Said No '49
The Show-Off '46

Phil Leeds (1916-98)
Vantage Point '08
Trust the Man '06
November '05
Sleeper Cell '05
Catch That Kid '04
Straight into Darkness '04
Big Shot: Confessions of a Campus Bookie '02
Lovely & Amazing '02
Scotland, PA '02
Enemies, a Love Story '89
Ghost '90
He Said, She Said '91
Frankie and Johnny '91
Lost and Found '99

Jean (Lefevre) Lefebvre (1919-2004)
The Gendarme of Saint-Tropez '64
No Problem '75

John Leguizamo (1964-)
The Take '07
The Groomsmen '06
Ice Age: The Meltdown '06
Lies & Alibis '06
Assault on Precinct 13 '05
George A. Romero's Land of the Dead '05
The Honeymooners '05
Sueno '05
Cronicas '04
Undefeated '03
Collateral Damage '02
Empire '02
Ice Age '02 (V)
Point of Origin '02
Spun '02
ZigZag '02
King of the Jungle '01
Moulin Rouge '01
What's the Worst That Could Happen? '01
Titan A.E. '00 (V)
Summer of Sam '99
Joe the King '99
Dr. Dolittle '98 (V)
Frogs for Snakes '98
Body Count '97
A Brother's Kiss '97
Spawn '97
Executive Decision '96
The Fan '96
The Pest '96

Meme Lei
See Me Me Lai

Fritz Leiber (1882-1949)
Bagdad '49

Ron Leibman (1937-)
Garden State '04
Auto Focus '02
Dummy '02
Personal Velocity: Three Portraits '02
Just the Ticket '98
Don King: Only in America '97
Night Falls on Manhattan '97
Seven Hours to Judgment '88
Door to Door '84
Phar Lap '84
Rhinestone '84
Romantic Comedy '83
Zorro, the Gay Blade '81
Up the Academy '80
Norma Rae '79
A Question of Guilt '78
Slaughterhouse Five '72
The Hot Rock '70
Where's Poppa? '70

Don Leifert
Deadly Neighbor '91
Galaxy Invader '85
Fiend '83

Barbara Leigh (1946-)
The Alien Factor '78
Mistress of the Apes '79
Boss '74

James LeGros (1962-)
See Amy (Annie Legras)
Duperey

Kristen Lehman (1970-)
Out for Justice '91
Regarding Henry '91
Die Hard 2: Die Harder '90
Street Hunter '90
Casualties of War '89

Beatrix Lehmann (1903-79)
The Cat and the Canary '79
Love for Lydia '79
The Myth of Fingerprints '97

Frederic Lehne
Octopus 2: River of Fear '02

John Lehne
A Long Way Home '81
The Disappearance of Aimee '76
Griffin and Phoenix: A Love Story '76
Roboman '75

Carla Lehmann (1917-90)
Fame is the Spur '47
Secret Mission '42
Cottage to Let '41

Hudson (Heidi) Leick (1969-)
Chill Factor '99
Something About Sex '98

Annie Legras
To Wong Foo, Thanks for Everything, Julie Newmar '95
Carlito's Way '93
Super Mario Bros. '93
Whispers in the Dark '92
Hangin' with the Homeboys '91

Phil Leeds (continued)
Sleeper Cell '05

Kang-sheng Lee
Goodbye, Dragon Inn '03
What Time Is It There? '01
Cujo '83

Karen Lee
Eye on the Sparrow '91
Roadhouse 66 '84
Zelly & Me '88

Kaiulani Lee
Hush '98
Before and After '95

Julia Lee
The Hillside Strangler '04
Asylum of the Damned '03
Romeo Must Die '00
G ory '89

Kyung-Young Lee
White Badge '97
White Badge '92

Cassandra Leigh (1968-) *(continued)*
- Smile, Jenny, You're Dead '74
- Junior Bonner '72
- The Student Nurses '70

Cassandra Leigh (1968-)
- Alien Terminator '95
- Caged Heat 3000 '95
- Midnight Tease '94

Frank Leigh (1876-1948)
- Below the Deadline '29
- American Pluck '25
- Nurse Marjorie '20

Janet Leigh (1926-2004)
- Halloween: H20 '98
- The Fog '78
- Night of the Lepus '72
- Hello Down There '69
- Harper '66
- Bye, Bye, Birdie '63
- Psycho '60
- The Perfect Furlough '59
- Touch of Evil '58
- The Vikings '58
- Jet Pilot '57
- My Sister Eileen '55
- Pete Kelly's Blues '55
- The Black Shield of Falworth '54
- Prince Valiant '54
- Houdini '53
- The Naked Spur '53
- Scaramouche '52
- Angels in the Outfield '51
- Two Tickets to Broadway '51
- That Forsyte Woman '50
- Holiday Affair '49
- Little Women '49
- Act of Violence '48
- The Hills of Home '48
- Words and Music '48

Jennifer Jason Leigh (1963-)
- Margot at the Wedding '07
- The Jacket '05
- The Quickie '01
- The King Is Alive '00
- The Machinist '04
- Palindromes '04
- Skipped Parts '00
- In the Cut '03
- Hey Arnold! The Movie '02 (V)
- Road to Perdition '02
- The Anniversary Party '01
- eXistenZ '99
- The Love Letter '98
- A Thousand Acres '97
- Washington Square '97
- Bastard out of Carolina '96
- Georgia '95
- Kansas City '95
- Dolores Claiborne '94
- Mrs. Parker and the Vicious Circle '94
- The Hudsucker Proxy '93
- Short Cuts '93
- Single White Female '92
- Backdraft '91
- Crooked Hearts '91
- Rush '91
- Buried Alive '90
- Last Exit to Brooklyn '90
- Miami Blues '90
- The Big Picture '89
- Heart of Midnight '89
- Sister, Sister '87
- Undercover '87
- The Hitcher '86
- The Men's Club '86
- Flesh and Blood '85
- Girls of the White Orchid '85
- Grandview U.S.A. '84
- Easy Money '83
- Fast Times at Ridgemont High '82
- Wrong Is Right '82
- The Best Little Girl in the World '81
- Eyes of a Stranger '81
- Killing of Randy Webster '81
- Angel City '80

John Leigh (1965-)
- Kidnapped '05
- Stickmen '01

Nelson Leigh (1905-85)
- The Gallant Hours '60
- Ma Barker's Killer Brood '60
- Texas Masquerade '44

Spencer Leigh
- Smart Money '88
- The Last of England '87
- Caravaggio '86

Steven Leigh
- Sword of Honor '94
- To Be the Best '93
- China White '91
- Deadly Bet '91

Suzanna Leigh (1945-)
- The Fiend '71
- Lust for a Vampire '71
- Deadlier Than the Male '67
- Paradise, Hawaiian Style '66
- Boeing Boeing '65

Vivien Leigh (1913-67)
- Ship of Fools '65
- Roman Spring of Mrs. Stone '61
- A Streetcar Named Desire '51
- Anna Karenina '48
- Caesar and Cleopatra '46
- That Hamilton Woman '41
- Waterloo Bridge '40
- Gone with the Wind '39
- Sidewalks of London '38
- Dark Journey '37
- Fire Over England '37
- Storm in a Teacup '37
- 21 Days '37

Barbara Leigh-Hunt (1935-)
- Wives and Daughters '07
- Longitude '00
- A Merry War '97
- Pride and Prejudice '95
- Paper Mask '90
- The Plague Dogs '82 (V)
- Frenzy '72

Laura Leighton (1968-)
- We'll Meet Again '02
- Seven Girlfriends '00
- Naked City: A Killer Christmas '98

Lillian (Lillianne, Lyllian) Leighton (1874-1956)
- Man from Monterey '33
- $50,000 Reward '25
- Parisian Love '25
- Peck's Bad Boy '21
- The Jack Knife Man '20

Margaret Leighton (1922-76)
- Choice of Weapons '76
- From Beyond the Grave '73
- The Go-Between '71
- The Madwoman of Chaillot '69
- The Loved One '65
- The Best Man '64
- Waltz of the Toreadors '62
- Carrington, V.C. '54
- The Elusive Pimpernel '50
- Bonnie Prince Charlie '48
- The Winslow Boy '48

Roberta Leighton (1953-)
- Covergirl '83
- Barracuda '78

Harald Leipnitz (1926-2000)
- Fight for Gold '86
- Hell Hounds of Alaska '73
- River of Evil '64

Frederick Leister (1885-1970)
- Green Grow the Rushes '51
- Spellbound '41
- O.H.M.S. '37

David Leisure (1950-)
- Elvis Has Left the Building '04
- Three Strikes '00
- Ten Things I Hate about You '99

Donovan Leitch (1968-)
- Big City Blues '99
- The '60s '99
- Love Kills '98
- One Night Stand '97
- I Shot Andy Warhol '96
- Dark Horse '92
- Gas Food Lodging '92
- Cutting Class '89
- Glory '89
- And God Created Woman '88
- The Blob '88
- The In Crowd '88

Matthew Leitch (1975-)
- The Detonator '06
- AKA '02

Virginia Leith
- The Brain that Wouldn't Die '63
- Black Widow '54

Tyron Leitso (1976-)
- Masters of Horror: Valerie on the Stairs '06
- House of the Dead '03
- Dinotopia '02
- Snow White: The Fairest of Them All '02

Jeremy Lelliott (1982-)
- Lady Jayne Killer '03
- Disappearance '02

Paul LeMat (1952-)
- Big Bad Love '02
- American History X '98
- Children of Fury '94
- Sensation '94
- Wishman '93
- Woman with a Past '92
- Blind Witness '89
- Easy Wheels '89
- Grave Secrets '89
- Puppet Master '89
- Hanoi Hilton '87
- Into the Homeland '87
- The Night They Saved Christmas '87
- P.I.: Private Investigations '87
- Private Investigations '87
- Long Time Gone '86
- On Wings of Eagles '86
- The Burning Bed '85
- P.K. and the Kid '85
- Rock & Rule '83 (V)
- Strange Invaders '83
- Jimmy the Kid '82
- Death Valley '81
- Melvin and Howard '80
- More American Graffiti '79
- Citizens Band '77
- Aloha, Bobby and Rose '74
- American Graffiti '73
- Firehouse '72

Harvey Lembeck (1923-82)
- Fireball 500 '66
- Beach Blanket Bingo '65
- How to Stuff a Wild Bikini '65
- Bikini Beach '64
- Pajama Party '64
- Beach Party '63
- Love with the Proper Stranger '63
- Stalag 17 '53

Michael Lembeck (1948-)
- Danielle Steel's Heartbeat '93
- Conspiracy: The Trial of the Chicago Eight '87
- On the Right Track '81
- Gorp '80
- The In-Laws '79
- The Boys in Company C '77

Kris Lemche (1978-)
- Final Destination 3 '06
- Ginger Snaps '01

Stephanie Lemelin
- Raising Flagg '06
- Anonymous Rex '04

Valerie Lemercier (1964-)
- Avenue Montaigne '06
- Friday Night '02
- The Visitors '95

Rachel Lemieux
- Mommy 2: Mommy's Day '96
- Mommy '95

Tutte Lemkow (1924-91)
- Inspector Clouseau '68
- The Guns of Navarone '61
- Moulin Rouge '52

Steve Lemme (1973-)
- Beerfest '06
- The Dukes of Hazzard '05
- Club Dread '04
- Super Troopers '01

Chris Lemmon (1954-)
- Best of the Best: Without Warning '98
- Just the Ticket '98
- Land of the Free '98
- Wishmaster '97
- Weekend Warriors '86
- Swing Shift '84
- C.O.D. '83
- The Happy Hooker Goes Hollywood '80
- Just Before Dawn '80

Jack Lemmon (1925-2001)
- The Legend of Bagger Vance '00
- Inherit the Wind '99
- Tuesdays with Morrie '99
- Neil Simon's The Odd Couple 2 '98
- Out to Sea '97
- Twelve Angry Men '97
- Getting Away With Murder '96
- My Fellow Americans '96
- A Weekend in the Country '96
- Hamlet '96
- The Grass Harp '95
- Grumpier Old Men '95
- Grumpy Old Men '93
- A Life in the Theater '93
- Short Cuts '93
- For Richer, for Poorer '92
- Glengarry Glen Ross '92
- The Player '92
- JFK '91
- Dad '89
- Long Day's Journey into Night '88
- The Murder of Mary Phagan '87
- That's Life! '86
- Macaroni '85
- Mass Appeal '84
- Missing '82
- Buddy Buddy '81
- Tribute '80
- The China Syndrome '79
- Airport '77 '77
- The Front Page '74
- Prisoner of Second Avenue '74
- Save the Tiger '73
- Avanti! '72
- The Out-of-Towners '70
- April Fools '69
- The Odd Couple '68
- Luv '67
- The Fortune Cookie '66
- The Great Race '65
- Good Neighbor Sam '64
- How to Murder Your Wife '64
- Irma La Douce '63
- Under the Yum-Yum Tree '63
- Days of Wine and Roses '62
- The Apartment '60
- Some Like It Hot '59
- Voyage en Balloon '59 (N)
- Bell, Book and Candle '58
- Cowboy '58
- Fire Down Below '57
- Mister Roberts '55
- My Sister Eileen '55
- Three for the Show '55
- It Should Happen to You '54
- Phffft! '54

Kasi Lemmons (1961-)
- Til There Was You '96
- DROP Squad '94
- Fear of a Black Hat '94
- Hard Target '93
- Candyman '92
- School Daze '88
- Vampire's Kiss '88

Michel Lemoine (1929-)
- The Sensuous Teenager '70
- Conquest of Mycene '63
- Planets Against Us '61

Genevieve Lemon
- Soft Fruit '99
- Moscow Parade '92
- Billy's Holiday '95
- The Piano '93
- Sweetie '89

Ute Lemper (1963-)
- Appetite '98
- A River Made to Drown In '97
- Bogus '96

Mark Lenard (1928-96)
- Star Trek 6: The Undiscovered Country '91
- Star Trek 4: The Voyage Home '86
- Star Trek 3: The Search for Spock '84
- Star Trek: The Motion Picture '79
- Noon Sunday '75

Vanessa Lengies (1985-)
- Stick It '06
- The Perfect Man '05
- Waiting... '05
- Ratz '99

Harry J. Lennix (1964-)
- Resurrecting the Champ '07
- Stomp the Yard '07
- Barbershop 2: Back in Business '04
- Ray '04
- Suspect Zero '03
- The Human Stain '03
- The Matrix Reloaded '03
- The Matrix Revolutions '03
- Collateral Damage '02
- Pumpkin '02
- Love and Basketball '00
- Titus '99
- Get On the Bus '96
- Bob Roberts '92
- Mo' Money '92
- The Five Heartbeats '91

Jarrett Lennon (1982-)
- Amityville Dollhouse '96
- Short Cuts '93
- Servants of Twilight '91

John Lennon (1940-80)
- Chuck Berry: Hail! Hail! Rock 'n' Roll '87
- Let It Be '70
- The Magic Christian '69
- Yellow Submarine '68 (V)
- How I Won the War '67
- Magical Mystery Tour '67
- Help! '65
- A Hard Day's Night '64

Julian Lennon (1963-)
- Leaving Las Vegas '95
- The Linguini Incident '92
- Chuck Berry: Hail! Hail! Rock 'n' Roll '87

Maria Lennon
- Bloom '03
- Oktober '98
- The Informant '97

Thomas Lennon (1969-)
- Balls of Fury '07
- Reno 911! Miami '07
- Conversations with Other Women '05
- Herbie: Fully Loaded '05
- The Hitchhiker's Guide to the Galaxy '05 (V)
- Heights '04
- A Guy Thing '03
- How to Lose a Guy in 10 Days '03
- Le Divorce '03

Annie Lennox (1954-)
- Edward II '92
- The Room '87
- Revolution '85

Jay Leno (1950-)
- Ice Age: The Meltdown '06 (V)
- Robots '05 (V)
- Calendar Girls '03
- Stuck On You '03
- The Flintstones '94
- Dave '93
- We're Back! A Dinosaur's Story '93 (V)
- Collision Course '89
- Americathon '79
- Silver Bears '78

Jack Lenoir (1926-81)
- Breakfast in Paris '81
- Once in Paris... '79

Rosetta LeNoire (1911-2002)
- The Father Clements Story '87
- Fritz the Cat '72 (V)

Lotte Lenya (1899-1981)
- Semi-Tough '77
- From Russia with Love '63
- Roman Spring of Mrs. Stone '61
- The Threepenny Opera '31

Kay Lenz (1953-)
- A Gun, a Car, a Blonde '97
- A Gunfighter's Moon '96
- Trapped in Space '94
- Falling from Grace '92
- Hitler's Daughter '90
- Headhunter '89
- Murder by Night '89
- Physical Evidence '89
- Fear '88
- Death Wish 4: The Crackdown '87
- Stripped to Kill '87
- House '86
- Prisoners of the Lost Universe '84
- Fast Walking '82
- Sanctuary of Fear '79
- Initiation of Sarah '78
- Mean Dog Blues '78
- Great Scout & Cathouse Thursday '76
- Moving Violation '76
- Rich Man, Poor Man '76

White Line Fever '75

Rick Lenz (1939-)
Little Dragons '80
Scandalous John '71
Cactus Flower '69

Melissa Leo (1960-)
Back Irish '07
Mr. Woodcock '07
Stephanie Daley '06
American Gun '05
Confess '05
Hide and Seek '05
The Three Burials of
Melquiades Estrada '05
From Other Worlds '04
21 Grams '03
Homicide: The Movie '00
The 24 Hour Woman '99
Last Summer in the
Hamptons '96
Scarlet '94
Carolina Skeletons '92
Venice, Venice '92
A Time of Destiny '88
Deadtime Stories '86
Always '85
Silent Witness '85
Streetwalkin' '85

Leon (1952-)
Cover '08
Little Richard '00
Friends & Lovers '99
Mean Streak '99
Mr. Rock 'n' Roll: The Alan
Freed Story '99
The Temptations '98
Pure Danger '96
Spirit Lost '96
Once Upon a Time...
When We Were Colored
'95
Waiting to Exhale '95
Above the Rim '94
Bad Attitude '93
Cliffhanger '93
Cool Runnings '93
The Five Heartbeats '91
Colors '88

David Leon
These Foolish Things '06

Loles Leon (1950-)
The Girl of Your Dreams
'99
Amor de Hombre '97
Don Juan, My Love '90
Tie Me Up! Tie Me Down!
'90

The Boys Next Door '96
Killer: A Journal of
Murder '95

Valerie Leon (1945-)
Never Say Never Again '83
The Spy Who Loved Me '77
Blood from the Mummy's
Tomb '71
Zeta One '69

Joshua Leonard (1975-)
The Shaggy Dog '06
Shooting Livien '05
Madhouse '04
Live from Baghdad '03
Two Days '03
Scorched '02
Men of Honor '00
Sacrifice '00
The Blair Witch Project '99

Tea Leoni (1966-)
You Kill Me '07
Fun with Dick and Jane '05
House of D '04
Spanglish '04
Hollywood Ending '02
People I Know '02
Jurassic Park 3 '01
Family Man '00
The Famous '99
Deep Impact '98
Bad Boys '95
Flirting with Disaster '95

Lu Leonard (1927-2004)
A Climate for Killing '91
Circuitry Man '90
Shadowzone '89
Princess Academy '87

Robert Sean Leonard (1969-)
A Painted House '03
Chelsea Walls '01
Driven '01
Tape '01
A Glimpse of Hell '01
Ground Control '98
The Last Days of Disco '98
I Love You, I Love You Not
'97
In the Gloaming '97
Standoff '97

The Age of Innocence '93
Safe Passage '94
La Balance '82
La Petite Sirene '80
Married to It '93
Much Ado about Nothing
'93
Swing Kids '93
Mr. & Mrs. Bridge '90
Dead Poets Society '89
My Best Friend Is a
Vampire '88
Bluffing It '87

Sheldon Leonard (1907-97)
The Manhattan Project '86
The Brink's Job '78
Guys and Dolls '55
Here Come the Nelsons '52
Abbott and Costello Meet
the Invisible Man '51
Shep Comes Home '49
Open Secret '48
Sinbad, the Sailor '47
Decoy '46
It's a Wonderful Life '46
Rainbow over Texas '46
Captain Kidd '45
The Falcon in Hollywood
'44
Tortilla Flat '42
Week-End in Havana '41

Marco Leonardi (1971-)
Once Upon a Time in
Mexico '03
Texas Rangers '01
The Five Senses '99
From Dusk Till Dawn 3:
The Hangman's
Daughter '99
David '97
Cinema Paradiso '88

Al Leong
Lethal Weapon '87
Die Hard '88

Stephanie Leonidas (1984-)
Dracula '06
MirrorMask '05
Yes '04

Chauncey Leopardi (1981-)
ShadowZone: The Undead
Express '96
Sticks and Stones '96
The Big Green '95
Houseguest '94
The Sandlot '93

Adrian Lester (1970-)
Doomsday '08

Les Misérables '95

Gregoire Leprince-Ringuet
Love Songs '07
Strayed '03

Michael Lerner (1941-)
The Last Time '06
When Do We Eat? '05
Poster Boy '04
Elf '03
For Richer or Poorer '97
No Way Back '96
A Pyromaniac's Love Story
'95
Girl in the Cadillac '94
No Escape '94
Radioland Murders '94
The Road to Wellville '94
Amos and Andrew '93
Blank Check '93
The Comrades of Summer
'92
Newsies '92
Barton Fink '91
The Closer '91
Omen 4: The Awakening
'91
Any Man's Death '90
Harlem Nights '89
Anguish '88
Eight Men Out '88
Hands of a Stranger '87
The Execution '85
Rita Hayworth: The Love
Goddess '83
Strange Invaders '83
National Lampoon's Class
Reunion '82
The Postman Always Rings
Twice '81
Outlaw Blues '77
F. Scott Fitzgerald in
Hollywood '76
Busting '74

Ken Lerner
Senseless '98
Mother's Boys '94
Relentless 4 '94
Fallen Angels 1 '93
Unlawful Entry '92
Fast Getaway '91
Relentless '89

Logan Lerman (1992-)
3:10 to Yuma '07
Hoot '06
The Patriot '00

Ted Leplat
Emissary '89

Robert Lepage (1957-)
Far Side of the Moon '03
Stardom '00
Jesus of Montreal '89

Philippe Leotard (1940-2001)
Les Misérables '95
La Balance '82
Swift Justice '88
The Kirlian Witness '78

Riding in Cars with Boys
'01

Joan Leslie (1925-)
Jubilee Trail '54
The Male Animal '42
Sergeant York '41
The Wagons Roll at Night
'41
Thank Your Lucky Stars '43
This is the Army '43
Yankee Doodle Dandy '42
High Sierra '41

John Leslie
Love Affair '39

Nan Leslie (1926-2000)
The Bamboo Saucer '68
Iron Mountain Trail '53
Pioneer Marshal '49
Rim of the Canyon '49
Desperate '47

Bethel Leslie (1929-99)
Message in a Bottle '98
Old Boyfriends '79
Captain Newman, M.D. '64
The Rabbit Trap '59

Ed LeSaint (1870-1940)
Thunder Mountain '35
Texas Bad Man '32
Range Feud '31

Sam Lerner (1992-)
Monster House '06 (V)
Envy '04

Maxime LeRoux (1951-)
The Son of the Shark '93
Mama, There's a Man in
Your Bed '89

Phillippe LeRoy (1930-)
Quo Vadis '85
Vate '00

Message in a Bottle '98
Saint Maybe '98
In Cold Blood '96
Long Day's Journey into
Night '88
Ironweed '87

Jalil Lespert
Le Petit Lieutenant '05
Sade '00

Lori Lethin (1955-)
Return to Horror High '87
Brotherly Love '85
Bloody Birthday '80
The Prey '80

Shelli Lether
Death Warmed Up '85
The Sender '98

David Leth
Dark of the Night '85

James Lesure
Loveless in Los Angeles
'07

Len Lesser (1922-)
Miss Potter '06
Almost Strangers '01
Charlotte Gray '01
Outlaw Blues '77

Ben Lessy (1902-92)
Baadasssss! '03
Ain't No Way Back '89
Grandma's House '89
DuBeat-E.O. '84
Joy Ride to Nowhere '78
Kelly's Heroes '70
How to Stuff a Wild Bikini
'65
Pajama Party '64
Shack Out on 101 '55

Mimi Lessos
Beyond Fear '93
Pushed to the Limit '92
Final Impact '91
The American Angels:
Baptism of Blood '89
Lady Dragon '92
Vanity Fair '91
Moses '96

Anton Lesser (1952-)
Strangers in Paradise '84
Lonely Hearts '06
Lord of War '05
Alexander '04
Panic Room '02
Highway '01
Requiem for a Dream '00
American Psycho '99
Black and White '99
Fight Club '99
Girl, Interrupted '99
Basil '98
The Thin Red Line '98
Urban Legend '98
Switchback '97
The Last of the High Kings
'96
Prefontaine '96
How to Make an American
Quilt '95
Cool and the Crazy '94
The Postman Always Rings
Twice '81

Matt Letscher (1970-)
Gods and Generals '03
Identity '03
Super Sucker '03

Bruce Lester (1912-)
Charade '53
A Married Woman '65
Golden Earrings '47
British Intelligence '40

Jeff Lester (1955-)
In the Cold of the Night '89

Kate Lester (1857-1924)
Redneck '73
What the Peeper Saw '72
Black Beauty '71
Melody '71
Who Slew Auntie Roo? '71
Eye Witness '70
Oliver! '68

Ron Lester (1975-)
Not Another Teen Movie
'01
Varsity Blues '98
Good Burger '97

Mark Lester (1958-)
Cracking Up '83
Big Mouth! '67
The Patsy '64
The Nutty Professor '63

Buddy Lester (1917-2002)
Ocean's 11 '60
Prison on Fire '87
Return to Horror High '87
Born to Run '93

David Letterman (1947-)
Beavis and Butt-Head Do
America '96 (V)

Dan Lett
Get a Clue '02

Al Lettieri (1928-75)
The Godfather 1902-1959:
The Complete Epic '81
McQ '74
Mr. Majestyk '74
The Don Is Dead '73
The Getaway '72
The Godfather '72
Pulp '72

Ken Leung (1970-)
Shanghai Kiss '07
X-Men: The Last Stand '06
Sucker Free City '05
Saw '04
Red Dragon '02

Katie Leung (1987-)
Harry Potter and the Goblet
of Fire '05

Tony Leung Chiu-Wai (1962-)
Lust, Caution '07
2046 '04
Hero '03
In the Mood for Love '00
Tokyo Raiders '00
Gorgeous '99
Flowers of Shanghai '98
Happy Together '96
Chungking Express '95
Cyclo '95
Hard-Boiled '92
A Bullet in the Head '90
The Laserman '92
The Prisoner '90
A Better Tomorrow, Part 3
'89

Tony Leung Ka-Fai (1958-)
Three... Extremes '04
Double Vision '02
The Lover '92
Kill or Be Killed '93
Hellbent '88

Oscar Levant (1906-72)
The Band Wagon '53
An American in Paris '51
The Barkleys of Broadway
'49
Humoresque '46
Rhythm on the River '40

Jared Leto (1971-)
Chapter 27 '07
Lord of War '05
Alexander '04
Panic Room '02
Highway '01
Requiem for a Dream '00
American Psycho '99

Clinton Leupp
Trick '99
Nick and Jane '95

Lynn Levand

Calvin Levels (1954-)
Hate '95
A Very Long Engagement
'48
Romance on the High Seas
'48

Francois Levantal
Dance of Life 23

King of Texas '02
Jackie, Ethel, Joan: The
Kennedy Women '01
Madison '01
John John in the Sky '00
The Mask of Zorro '98

Starting Out in the Evening
'07
As You Like It '06
Scenes of a Sexual Nature
'06
The Day After Tomorrow
'04
Born Romantic '00
Jason and the Argonauts
'00
Primary Colors '98
Maybe Baby '99
Love's Labour's Lost '00

Dust '01
Born Romantic '00
The Letter '40
Boy Meets Girl '38

The Ring 2 '05

Point of No Return '93
Johnny Suede '92
Live! From Death Row '92
Adventures in Babysitting
'87
A Christmas Without Snow
'80

Sam Levene (1905-80)
God Told Me To '76
A Dream of Kings '69
Designing Woman '57
Sweet Smell of Success '57
Babe Ruth Story '48
Boomerang '47
The Killers '46
The Purple Heart '44
Action in the North Atlantic '43
I Dood It '43
Whistling in Brooklyn '43
Shadow of the Thin Man '41
Golden Boy '39
Mad Miss Manton '38
Shopworm Angel '38
Three Men on a Horse '36

Joanna "JoJo" Levesque (1990-)
Aquamarine '06
RV '06

Marcel Levesque (1877-1962)
The Fantastic Night '42
Les Vampires '15

Mariette Levesque

Zachary Levi (1980-)
Spiral '07

John Levin
Bounce '00
Zoltan... Hound of Dracula '78

Rachel Levin (1952-)
White Palace '90
Gaby: A True Story '87
Ice '93

Floyd Levine
Watchers Reborn '98

Ilana Levine (1963-)
Tanner on Tanner '04
Anything But Love '02
Just Looking '99

Jean Levine
Hollywood in Trouble '87
The Newlydeads '87

Jerry Levine (1957-)
Ghosts of Mississippi '96
Born on the Fourth of July '89
Casual Sex? '88
Iron Eagle '86

Samm Levine (1982-)
Pulse '06
Club Dread '04
Home on the Range '04 (V)
Not Another Teen Movie '01

Ted Levine (1958-)
American Gangster '07
The Assassination of Jesse James by the Coward Robert Ford '07
The Hills Have Eyes '06
Birth '04
The Manchurian Candidate '04
Wonderland '03
The Truth About Charlie '02
Ali '01
Evolution '01
The Fast and the Furious '01
Joy Ride '01 (V)
Harlan County War '00
Wild Wild West '99
From the Earth to the Moon '98
Moby Dick '98
Ellen Foster '97
Flubber '97
Mad City '97
Switchback '97
Georgia '95
Heat '95
Bullet '94
The Mangler '94
Detonator '93
Nowhere to Run '93
The Silence of the Lambs '91

Barry Levinson (1942-)
Fulfillment '89
Love at Large '89
Ironweed '87
Bee Movie '07 (V)
Jimmy Hollywood '94
Quiz Show '94
History of the World: Part 1 '81

Emile Levisetti
Alien Terminator '95
Sexual Response '92
Bix '90

Steve Levitt
Blue Movies '88
The Incredible Hulk Returns '88
Hunk '87
Last Resort '86

Uta Levka (1942-)
Scream and Scream Again '70

Eugene Levy (1946-)
American Pie Presents: Beta House '07
American Pie Presents: The Naked Mile '06
Curious George '06 (V)
For Your Consideration '06
Over the Hedge '06 (V)
American Pie Presents Band Camp '05
Cheaper by the Dozen 2 '05
The Man '05
New York Minute '04
American Wedding '03
Bringing Down the House '03
Dumb and Dumberer: When Harry Met Lloyd '03
A Mighty Wind '03
Like Mike '02
American Pie 2 '01
Club Land '01
Down to Earth '01
Repli-Kate '01
Serendipity '01
Best in Show '00
The Ladies Man '00
American Pie '99
The Secret Life of Girls '99
Almost Heroes '97
Multiplicity '96
Waiting for Guffman '96
Father of the Bride Part 2 '95
Kurt Vonnegut's Harrison Bergeron '95
I Love Trouble '94
Stay Tuned '92
Father of the Bride '91
Speed Zone '88
Armed and Dangerous '86
Club Paradise '86
The Last Polka '84
Splash '84
Going Berserk '83
National Lampoon's Vacation '83
Heavy Metal '81 (V)
Strange Brew '83

Micky Levy
Rails & Ties '07

James Lew (1952-)
18 Fingers of Death '05
Boogie Boy '98
High Voltage '98
Balance of Power '96
Robo Warriors '96
Blood for Blood '95
Red Sun Rising '94
Private Wars '93

Jose Lewgoy (1920-2003)
Cobra Verde '88
Fitzcarraldo '82
Earth Entranced '66

Al Lewis (1923-2006)
South Beach Academy '96
Car 54, Where Are You? '94
My Grandpa Is a Vampire '92
Fright House '89
Married to the Mob '88
The Munsters' Revenge '81
Used Cars '80
Way He Was '76
The Night Strangler '72
They Shoot Horses, Don't They? '69
Munster, Go Home! '66

Ben Lewis
That Russell Girl '08
Stir of Echoes 2: The Homecoming '07

Brittney Lewis
Rubin & Ed '92

Charlotte Lewis (1968-)
Mutual Needs '97
Navajo Blues '97
The Glass Cage '96
Decoy '95
Embrace of the Vampire '95
Red Shoe Diaries 6: How I Met My Husband '95
Men of War '94
Excessive Force '92
Sketch Artist '92
Storyville '92
Bare Essentials '91
Tripwire '89
Dial Help '88
The Golden Child '86
Pirates '86

Clea Lewis (1965-)
Ice Age: The Meltdown '06 (V)
The Rich Man's Wife '96

Damian Lewis (1971-)
Alex Rider: Operation Stormbreaker '06
The Situation '06
Friends & Crocodiles '05
An Unfinished Life '05
Keane '04
Dreamcatcher '03
Band of Brothers '01
Robinson Crusoe '96

David Lewis (1916-2000)
Lake Placid '99
The Apartment '60

Dawn Lewis (1961-)
The 10th Kingdom '00
Race to Freedom: The Story of the Underground Railroad '94
I'm Gonna Git You Sucka '88

Diana Lewis (1919-97)
Somewhere I'll Find You '42
Whistling in Dixie '42
Andy Hardy Meets Debutante '40
Go West '40

Fiona Lewis (1946-)
Innerspace '87
Strange Invaders '83
Strange Behavior '81
Wanda Nevada '79
Tintorera... Tiger Shark '78
Stunts '77
Drum '76
Lisztomania '75
Blue Blood '73
Dracula '73
Doctor Phibes Rises Again '72

Forrest Lewis (1899-1977)
The Monster of Piedras Blancas '57
Escape from Fort Bravo '53

Gary Lewis (1958-)
Eragon '06
Goal! The Dream Begins '06
Joyeux Noel '05
Yes '04
Warrior Queen '03
Gangs of New York '02
Pure '02
Billy Elliot '00
My Name Is Joe '98
Postmortem '98
Carla's Song '97
Orphans '97
Hardly Working '81

Geoffrey Lewis (1935-)
The Devil's Rejects '05
Down in the Valley '05
A Painted House '03
A Light in the Darkness '02
The New Guy '02
Sunstorm '01
Way of the Gun '00
The Prophet's Game '99
Midnight in the Garden of Good and Evil '97
Rough Riders '97
An Occasional Hell '96
Trilogy of Terror 2 '96
When the Dark Man Calls '95
Army of One '94
Maverick '94
National Lampoon's Last Resort '94
White Fang 2: The Myth of the White Wolf '94
The Man Without a Face '93
Only the Strong '93
Point of No Return '93
Wishman '93
The Lawnmower Man '92
Double Impact '91
Disturbed '90
Matters of the Heart '90
Catch Me... If You Can '89
Fletch Lives '89
Pink Cadillac '89
Tango and Cash '89
Out of the Dark '88
Pancho Barnes '88
Maximum Security '87
Lust in the Dust '85
Stitches '85
Night of the Comet '84
Return of the Man from U.N.C.L.E. '83
September Gun '83
I, the Jury '82
Heaven's Gate '81
Shoot the Sun Down '81
Any Which Way You Can '80
Bronco Billy '80
Every Which Way But Loose '78
Tilt '78
When Every Day Was the Fourth of July '77
The Return of a Man Called Horse '76
The Great Waldo Pepper '75
Smile '75
The Wind and the Lion '74
Macon County Line '74
Thunderbolt & Lightfoot '74
Culpepper Cattle Co. '72
Moon of the Wolf '72

George Lewis (1903-95)
Indian Paint '64
The Sign of Zorro '60
King of the Bullwhip '51
Outlaw Fury '50
Rangeland Empire '50
The Big Sombrero '49
Outlaw Gang '49
Radar Patrol vs. Spy King '49
Federal Operator 99 '45
Perils of the Darkest Jungle '44
Zorro's Black Whip '44
Outlaws of the Desert '41

Gilbert Lewis (1941-)
Candyman '92
The Kid Who Loved Christmas '90
Touched '82

Greg Lewis
Prehysteria 2 '94
Frankie and Johnny '91

Gus Lewis (1993-)
Asylum '05
Batman Begins '05

Huey Lewis (1950-)
Duets '00
Shadow of Doubt '98
Short Cuts '93
Back to the Future '85

Jason Lewis
Sex and the City: The Movie '08
Bobby Z '07
Mr. Brooks '07
The Attic '06

Jazsmin Lewis (1976-)
Barbershop 2: Back in Business '04
Barbershop '02

Jean Ann Lewis
See Eve Brent

Jenifer Lewis (1957-)
Tyler Perry's Meet the Browns '08
Dirty Laundry '07
Who's Your Caddy? '07
Cars '06 (V)
Madea's Family Reunion '06
The Cookout '04
Nora's Hair Salon '04
Shark Tale '04 (V)
Juwanna Mann '02
The Brothers '01
Cast Away '00
Dancing in September '00
Little Richard '00
Jackie's Back '99
Mystery Men '99
Partners '99
The Mighty '98
Girl 6 '96
The Preacher's Wife '96
Corrina, Corrina '94
Deconstructing Sarah '94
Renaissance Man '94
What's Love Got to Do with It? '93

Jenny Lewis (1977-)
Little Boy Blue '97
Foxfire '96
Runaway Daughters '94
Runaway Father '91
Troop Beverly Hills '89
The Wizard '89
A Friendship in Vienna '88
Trading Hearts '87

Jerry Lewis (1926-)
Arizona Dream '94
Funny Bones '94
Mr. Saturday Night '92
Cookie '89
Slapstick of Another Kind '84
Cracking Up '83
King of Comedy '82
Hardly Working '81
Which Way to the Front? '70
Don't Raise the Bridge, Lower the River '68
Big Mouth '67
Boeing Boeing '65
Family Jewels '65
Disorderly Orderly '64
The Patsy '64
It's a Mad, Mad, Mad, Mad World '63
The Nutty Professor '63
Who's Minding the Store? '63
The Errand Boy '61
The Ladies' Man '61
The Bellboy '60
Cinderfella '60
The Geisha Boy '58
Rock-A-Bye Baby '57
The Sad Sack '57
The Delicate Delinquent '56
Hollywood or Bust '56
Pardners '56
Artists and Models '55
The Caddy '53
The Road to Bali '53
Scared Stiff '53
Jumping Jacks '52
Sailor Beware '52
The Stooge '51
At War with the Army '50
My Friend Irma '49

Jerry Lee Lewis (1935-)
Chuck Berry: Hail! Hail! Rock 'n' Roll '87
High School Confidential '58

Joe Lewis (1943-)
Force: Five '81
Jaguar Lives '79

Joe E. Lewis (1902-71)
Lady in Cement '68
Private Buckaroo '42
The Holy Terror '37

Johnny Lewis
Aliens vs. Predator: Requiem '07
Raise Your Voice '04

Juliette Lewis (1973-)
Catch and Release '07
Aurora Borealis '06
Grilled '06
Daltry Calhoun '05
Chasing Freedom '04
Starsky & Hutch '04
Cold Creek Manor '03
Old School '03
Enough '02
Hysterical Blindness '02
My Louisiana Sky '02
Gaudi Afternoon '01
Picture Claire '01
Way of the Gun '00
The 4th Floor '99
The Other Sister '98
The Evening Star '96
The Basketball Diaries '95
From Dusk Till Dawn '95
Strange Days '95
Mixed Nuts '94
Natural Born Killers '94
Kalifornia '93
Romeo Is Bleeding '93
That Night '93
What's Eating Gilbert Grape '93
Husbands and Wives '92
Cape Fear '91
Crooked Hearts '91
Too Young to Die '90
Meet the Hollowheads '89
National Lampoon's Christmas Vacation '89
My Stepmother Is an Alien '88

Leigh Lewis
Revelation '00
Tribulation '00

Louise Lewis (1914-96)
Blood of Dracula '57
I Was a Teenage Werewolf '57

Matthew Lewis (1989-)
Harry Potter and the Goblet of Fire '05
Harry Potter and the Sorcerer's Stone '01
The Legend of Wolf Mountain '92

Michael Lewis (1939-)
Signs of Life '89
Gruesome Twosome '67

Mitchell Lewis (1880-1956)
Cairo '42
Billy the Kid '41
The Wizard of Oz '39
Linda '29
Salome '22

Phill Lewis (1968-)
Elvis Has Left the Building '04
I Spy '02
Spent '00
Once Upon a Time... When We Were Colored '95 (N)
Brother Future '91

City Slickers '91

Ralph Lewis (1872-1937)
The Birth of a Nation '15

Richard Lewis (1947-)
Drunks '96
Hugo Pool '97
Leaving Las Vegas '95
Robin Hood: Men in Tights '93
Once Upon a Crime '92
The Wrong Guys '88
That's Adequate '90
Diary of a Young Comic '79

Robert Q. Lewis (1921-91)
Ski Party '65
Good Neighbor Sam '64
An Affair to Remember '57

Ronald Lewis (1928-82)
Billy Budd '62
Mr. Sardonicus '61
Conspiracy of Hearts '60
Bachelor of Hearts '58
Robbery under Arms '57
Helen of Troy '56
Blacksmith '78

Russell Scott Lewis
Green Plaid Shirt '96
Boys Life '94

Sheldon Lewis (1869-1958)
Tombstone Canyon '32
The Phantom '31
Beyond the Trail '26
With Kit Carson over the Great Divide '25

Tommy (Tom E.) Lewis (1957-)
The Proposition '05

Vera Lewis (1873-1956)
Ella Cinders '26

Vicki Lewis (1960-)
California Dreaming '07
Finding Nemo '03 (V)
Pushing Tin '99
Godzilla '98
Mouse Hunt '97

John Ley (1951-)
Out of the Body '88
BMX Bandits '83

Leo Leyden (1929-2007)
The Mask '61

Jacob Leygraf
Sunday's Children '94
The Slingshot '93

Johan Leysen (1950-)
Trahir '93
The Gambler '97
Egg '88
The Music Teacher '88
Hail Mary '85

Drue Leyton
Charlie Chan at the Circus '36
Charlie Chan in London '34

John Leyton (1939-)
Schizo '77
Seaside Swingers '65
Von Ryan's Express '65
Guns at Batasi '64
The Great Escape '63

Thierry Lhermitte (1957-)
Le Divorce '03
And Now Ladies and Gentlemen '02
The Closet '00
The Dinner Game '98
An American Werewolf in Paris '97
Augustin '95
Little Indian, Big City '95
Grosse Fatigue '94
My Best Friend's Girl '84
My New Partner '84
Until September '84
Next Year If All Goes Well '83
French Fried Vacation '79

Robert Lewis (1909-97)
Misbegotten '98
My Very Best Friend '96
Hello Again '87
Monsieur Verdoux '47

Bin Li (1982-)
Beijing Bicycle '01

Bingbing Li
The Road Home '01
The Forbidden Kingdom '08

Bruce Li (1950-)
Silver Hawk '04
Counter Attack '84

Baotian Li (1946-)
Shanghai Triad '95
Ju Dou '90

Gong Li (1965-)
The Three Avengers '80
The Young Bruce Lee '80
Return of the Tiger '78
Chinese Connection 2 '77
Sharky's Machine '81
Popeye '80
The In-Laws '79
I Wonder Who's Killing Her Now? '76
Catch-22 '70
Miami Vice '06
Memoirs of a Geisha '05
Eros '04
2046 '04
Zhou Yu's Train '02
The Emperor and the Assassin '99
Chinese Box '97
Temptress Moon '96
Shanghai Triad '95
To Live '94
Farewell My Concubine '93
Raise the Red Lantern '91
The Story of Qiu Ju '91
Ju Dou '90
Red Sorghum '87

Jet Li (1963-)
The Forbidden Kingdom '08
The Mummy: Tomb of the Dragon Emperor '08
War '07
Jet Li's Fearless '06
Unleashed '05
Cradle 2 the Grave '03
Hero '03
Kiss of the Dragon '01
The One '01
Romeo Must Die '00
Lethal Weapon 4 '98
Black Mask '96
Jet Li: The Enforcer '95
Meltdown '95
The Bodyguard from Beijing '94
Fist of Legend '94
Once Upon a Time in China II '92
Once Upon a Time in China '91
Twin Warriors '93
Once Upon a Time in China III '93
Swordsman II '92

Xuejian Li (1954-)
Happy Times '00
The Emperor and the Assassin '99
Shanghai Triad '95

Peter Paul Liapis
Fast Getaway 2 '94
Ghoulies 4 '93
For the Love of Angela '82
Starhops '78

Brian Libby
Platoon Leader '87
Silent Rage '82

Liberace (1919-87)
Sincerely Yours '56
The Loved One '65

Richard Libertini (1933-)
Grilled '06
Fletch Lives '89
Fletch '85
Big Trouble '86
All of Me '84
Unfaithfully Yours '84
Going Berserk '83
Soup for One '82
Popeye '80
Fourth Wise Man '85
The In-Laws '79
Catch-22 '70

Richard Liberty (1932-)
Day of the Dead '85
The Crazies '73

Alain Libolt (1943-)
The Lady and the Duke '01
Autumn Tale '98
Army of Shadows '69

Jeremy Licht (1971-)
Next One '84
Twilight Zone: The Movie '83
Lois Gibbs and the Love Canal '82
Father Figure '80
The Seekers '79

Mitchell Lichtenstein (1956-)
The Wedding Banquet '93
Streamers '83

Gabriella Licudi (1943-)
The Last Safari '67
The Unearthly Stranger '64

G. Gordon Liddy (1930-)
Adventures in Spying '92
Camp Cucamonga: How I Spent My Summer Vacation '90
Street Asylum '90
When Nature Calls '85

Anki Liden (1947-)
My Life As a Dog '85
Expectations '97

Matthew Lillard (1970-)
Without a Paddle '04
Scooby-Doo 2: Monsters Unleashed '04
The Perfect Score '04
Scooby-Doo '02
The Groomsmen '06
Thirteen '03
Summer Catch '01
Love's Labour's Lost '00
She's All That '99
Wing Commander '99
SLC Punk! '98
Dead Man on Campus '98
Without Limits '98
Scream 2 '97
Hackers '95
Serial Mom '94

Tina Lifford
Hostage '05
Urban Legends: Bloody Mary '05
Blood Work '02

John Light (1972-)
Partition '07
Heights '05
Benedict Arnold: A Question of Honor '03

Judith Light
Intimate Affairs '01
Stamp of a Killer '87

Cody Lightning (1986-)
Four Sheets to the Wind '07

Marilyn Lightstone (1941-)
Abraxas: Guardian of the Universe '90
Surrogate '88
Wild Pony '83
Spasms '82

Lil' Kim
See Kimberly (Lil' Kim) Jones

Tom Ligon (1945-)
Paint It Black '89
Lies My Father Told Me '75
The Woman in White '97
Gangster No. 1 '00
Boston Kickout '95
Scottsboro Boys '76
Fury on Wheels '71

Dennis (Denis) Lill (1942-)
Element of Doubt '96
Bad Blood '87
Lillie '79
Dynasty of Fear '72

Elmo Lincoln (1889-1952)
Tarzan's New York Adventure '42
Wyoming Outlaw '39
The Adventures of Tarzan '21
Tarzan of the Apes '18
Hoodoo Ann '16

Pamela Lincoln (1937-)
Anatomy of a Psycho '61
The Tingler '59

Gillian Lind (1904-83)
And Now the Screaming Starts '73

Traci Lind (1966-)
No Strings Attached '96
Red Meat '97
The End of Violence '97
Wolverine '96
The Road to Wellville '94

Pamela Lincoln
...

Abbey Lincoln (1930-)
Mo' Better Blues '90
For Love of Ivy '68
Nothing but a Man '64
The Girl Can't Help It '56

Andrew Lincoln (1973-)
These Foolish Things '06
Enduring Love '04
Love Actually '03
Scenes of a Sexual Nature '06

Aida Linares
Clueless '95
U-Turn '97

Peter Linari
The Curse of the Jade Scorpion '01

Jennifer Lien (1974-)
American History X '98

Brian Libby
...

Jennifer Lim
Hostel '06

Ching-hsai Lin
See Brigitte Lin

Kay Linaker (1914-)
Two Weeks to Live '43
Charlie Chan at Monte Carlo '37

Brigitte Lin (1954-)
Chungking Express '95
The Bride with White Hair 2 '93
The Bride with White Hair '93

Cec Linder (1921-92)
Heavenly Bodies '84
Deadly Eyes '82
The Devil's Web '74
Vengeance Is Mine '74
A Touch of Class '73
Goldfinger '64
Lolita '62
Quatermass and the Pit '58

Max Linder (1883-1925)
Seven Years Bad Luck '21
Max in the Silk Hat '15

Jennie Linden (1939-)
Charlie Muffin '79
Hedda '75
Women in Love '70
Nightmare '63

Hal Linden (1931-)
Out to Sea '97
A New Life '88
The Colony '95

Doris Linden
The Virgin Spring '59
The Seventh Seal '56

Eric Linden (1909-94)
Criminals Within '41
Gone with the Wind '39
Frolics on Ice '40
Ah, Wilderness! '35
Let 'Em Have It '35
No Other Woman '33

Viveca Lindfors (1920-95)
Last Summer in the Hamptons '96
Stargate '94
Backstreet Justice '93
The Linguini Incident '92
Child of Darkness, Child of Light '91
Zandalee '91
Exiled in America '90
The Ann Jillian Story '88
Rachel River '87
Secret Weapons '85
The Sure Thing '85
Silent Madness '84
Creepshow '82
The Hand '81
Lady Beware '87
Inside the Third Reich '82
The Best Little Girl in the World '81
For Ladies Only '81
Marilyn: The Untold Story '80

Gunnel Lindblom (1931-)
Hunger '66
October Sky '99
The Rookie '02

Rachael Lillis
Pokémon: The First Movie '99 (V)
Pokémon 3: The Movie '01 (V)

Beatrice Lillie (1898-1989)
Thoroughly Modern Millie '67
Around the World in 80 Days '56
On Approval '44

Albert Lieven (1906-71)
The Victors '63
Brainwashed '60
Frieda '47
Beware of Pity '46
The Seventh Veil '46
Sleeping Car to Trieste '45
The Life and Death of Colonel Blimp '43
Night Train to Munich '40

Anne Libert (1946-)
The Demons '74
Erotic Escape '72
Rites of Frankenstein '72
Virgin among the Living Dead '71

Chad Lindberg (1976-)
My Boyfriend's Back '93
13 Ghosts '01
Voyager '91
Class of 1999 '90
The Handmaid's Tale '90

Boguslaw Linda (1952-)
The Decalogue '88
Danton '82

Gunnel Lindblom
National Lampoon's Adam & Eve '05
Push '06

Lo Lieh (1939-2002)
The Painted Lady '97
Sex and Zen '93
The Stranger and the Gunfighter '76

Jennifer Lien
Spanish Judges '99
Wing Commander '99
Senseless '98
The Curve '97

Tarantella '95
Serial Mom '94

Michael Liebman
2 by 4 '98

Mimi Lieber
What Love Is '07
The Perfect Score '04
Ideas '06

Matthew Lillard
...

Leon Liebgold (1910-93)
Yidl Mitn Fidl '36

Michael Liebman
...

Drue Leyton
...

Mom, the Wolfman and Me '80
Natural Enemies '79
Girlfriends '78
A Question of Guilt '78
A Wedding '78
Welcome to L.A. '77
Bell from Hell '74
The Way We Were '73
Coming Apart '69
Cauldron of Blood '67
The King of Kings '61
The Story of Ruth '60
Moonfleet '55
Four in a Jeep '51
Adventures of Don Juan '49

Peter Lindgren (1915-81)
The New Land '73
I Am Curious (Yellow) '67

Carl Michael Lindner (1988-)
The Extreme Adventures of Super Dave '98
Krippendorf's Tribe '98
Slappy and the Stinkers '97

Delroy Lindo (1952-)
This Christmas '07
Wondrous Oblivion '06
Domino '05
Sahara '05
The Core '03
Heist '01
The Last Castle '01
The One '01
Gone in 60 Seconds '00
Romeo Must Die '00
The Book of Stars '99
The Cider House Rules '99
Pros & Cons '99
Strange Justice: The Clarence Thomas and Anita Hill Story '99
Glory & Honor '98
The Winner '96
Broken Arrow '95
Clockers '95
Get Shorty '95
Crooklyn '94
Blood In ... Blood Out: Bound by Honor '93
Mr. Jones '93
Malcolm X '92
Bright Angel '91
Mountains of the Moon '90
More American Graffiti '79
Find the Lady '76

Olga Lindo (1899-1968)
The Hidden Room '49
Things Happen at Night '48

Vincent Lindon (1959-)
La Moustache '05
Friday Night '02
Chaos '01
Seventh Heaven '98
A Man in Love '87
Betty Blue '86

Matt Lindquist
In Enemy Hands '04

Margaret Lindsay (1910-81)
Please Don't Eat the Daisies '60
Cass Timberlane '47
Club Havana '46
The Adventures of Rusty '45
The Spoilers '42
British Intelligence '40
The House of the Seven Gables '40
Jezebel '38
Dangerous '35
Devil Dogs of the Air '35
"G" Men '35
Baby Face '33
Cavalcade '33
Lady Killer '33

Robert Lindsay (1949-)
Friends & Crocodiles '05
Gideon's Daughter '05
Wimbledon '04
Horatio Hornblower: The Adventure Continues '01
Oliver Twist '00
Horatio Hornblower '99
Fierce Creatures '96
Genghis Cohn '93
Strike It Rich '90
Bert Rigby, You're a Fool '89
That'll Be the Day '73

Stuart Lindsell
Profile '54
Man of Evil '48

George Lindsey (1933-)
Return to Mayberry '85
Robin Hood '73 (V)

Joseph Lindsey
Caught Up '98
Public Enemies '96
Amongst Friends '93

Blake Lindsley (1973-)
Plain Dirty '04
Coastlines '02
Trial by Media '00
Starship Troopers '97
Swingers '96

Pierre Lindstedt (1943-)
The New Land '73
The Emigrants '72

Angela Lindvall (1979-)
Kiss Kiss Bang Bang '05
CQ '01

Helga Line (1932-)
Pulsebeat '85
Black Venus '83
The Mummy's Revenge '73
When the Screaming Stops '73
Horror Express '72
Horror Rises from the Tomb '72
The Saga of the Draculas '72
One Step to Hell '67
Nightmare Castle '65

Richard Lineback (1937-)
Ready to Rumble '00
Dangerous Evidence: The Lori Jackson Story '99
The Baby Dance '98
Meet the Deedles '98
Varsity Blues '98
The Jackal '97
Tin Cup '96
Twister '96
Natural Born Killers '94
Speed '94
Woman with a Past '92
Beyond the Next Mountain '87

Stephi Lineburg (1982-)
Zoe '01
Breathing Lessons '94
Richie Rich '94

Rosaleen Linehan (1937-)
About Adam '00
Mad About Mambo '00
The Hi-Lo Country '98
The Matchmaker '97
Sharpe's Gold '94

Bai Ling (1972-)
Living '07
The Beautiful Country '04
My Baby's Daddy '04
She Hate Me '04
Three ... Extremes '04
Point of Origin '02
The Breed '01
The Lost Empire '01
Anna and the King '99
Wild Wild West '99
Row Your Boat '98
Red Corner '97
Somewhere in the City '97
Dead Weekend '95
The Crow '93

Wendy Lingham
Demonstrator '71
Zeta One '69

Paul (Link) Linke (1948-)
The Fear Inside '92
Parenthood '89
Motel Hell '80

Richard Linklater (1961-)
Waking Life '01
Beavis and Butt-Head Do America '96 (V)
The Underneath '95
Slacker '91

Art Linkletter (1912-)
Champagne for Caesar '50
People Are Funny '46

Cody Linley (1989-)
Hoot '06
My Dog Skip '99

Rex Linn (1956-)
The Zodiac '05
After the Sunset '04
Cheaper by the Dozen '03
The Hunted '03
Crossfire Trail '01
Neil Simon's The Odd Couple 2 '98
Rush Hour '98
The Postman '97
Breakdown '96
Ghosts of Mississippi '96
Tin Cup '96
Children of Fury '94
Drop Zone '94
Wyatt Earp '94
Cliffhanger '93

Mark Linn-Baker (1953-)
Noises Off '92
Bare Essentials '91
Me and Him '89 (V)
Ghostwriter '84
My Favorite Year '82
Manhattan '79

Laura Linney (1964-)
John Adams '08
Breach '07
The Nanny Diaries '07
The Savages '07
Driving Lessons '06
The Hottest State '06
Jindabyne '06
Man of the Year '06
The Exorcism of Emily Rose '05
The Squid and the Whale '05
Kinsey '04
P.S. '04
The Life of David Gale '03
Love Actually '03
Mystic River '03
The Laramie Project '02
The Mothman Prophecies '02
Absolute Power '97
Armistead Maupin's More Tales of the City '97
Primal Fear '96
A Simple Twist of Fate '94
Armistead Maupin's Tales of the City '93
Blind Spot '93
Dave '93
Class of '61 '92

Richard Lintern
The Bank Job '08
The House of Eliott '92

Joanne Linville (1928-)
James Dean '01
From the Dead of Night '89
Secrets '77
Scorpio '73

Larry Linville (1939-2000)
No Dessert Dad, 'Til You Mow the Lawn '94
Body Waves '92
Rock 'n' Roll High School Forever '91
Earth Girls Are Easy '89
Blue Movies '88
School Spirit '85
Night Partners '83
The Night Stalker '71
The Stepmother '71

Alex D. Linz (1989-)
Red Dragon '02 (V)
Max Keeble's Big Move '01
Race to Space '01
Bounce '00
Titan A.E. '00 (V)
The Dress Code '99
Tarzan '99 (V)
Home Alone 3 '97
One Fine Day '96
The Cable Guy '96
Vanished '95

Lio (1962-)
Carnage '02
Love After Love '94
Window Shopping '86
Elsa, Elsa '85
The Eighties '83

Leon M. Lion (1879-1947)
Amazing Adventure '37
No. 17 '32

Alberto Lionello (1930-94)
Till Marriage Do Us Part '74
Porcile '69

Therese Liotard (1949-)
My Father's Glory '91
My Mother's Castle '91
The Disenchanted '90
Cloud Waltzing '87
One Sings, the Other Doesn't '77

Ray Liotta (1955-)
Crossing Over '08
Hero Wanted '08
In the Name of the King: A Dungeon Siege Tale '08
Bee Movie '07 (V)
Smokin' Aces '07
Wild Hogs '07
Even Money '06
Revolver '05
Slow Burn '05
The Last Shot '04
Identity '03
John Q '02
Narc '02
Point of Origin '02
Blow '01
Heartbreakers '01
A Rumor of Angels '00
Forever Mine '99
Inferno '99
Muppets from Space '99
Phoenix '98
The Rat Pack '98
Cop Land '97
Turbulence '96
Unforgettable '96
Operation Dumbo Drop '95
Corrina, Corrina '94
No Escape '94
Article 99 '92
Unlawful Entry '92
Women & Men: In Love There Are No Rules '91
Goodfellas '90
Field of Dreams '89
Dominick & Eugene '88
Something Wild '86
The Lonely Lady '83

Daniele Liotti (1971-)
Doctor Zhivago '03
Mad Love '01

Eugene Lipinski (1956-)
The Lost Angel '04
The Recruit '03
Bless the Child '00
Restless Spirits '99
Small Vices: A Spenser Mystery '99
Aldrich Ames: Traitor Within '98
Perfectly Normal '91
Riders of the Storm '88
Going Home '86
Moonlighting '82

Maureen Lipman (1946-)
The Pianist '02
Captain Jack '98
Solomon and Gaenor '98
The Little Princess '87
Educating Rita '83

Jonathan Lipnicki (1990-)
Like Mike '02
Stuart Little 2 '02
Stuart Little '99
Jerry Maguire '96

Jonathon Lippe
Blood Voyage '77
Green Eyes '76

David Lipper
Federal Protection '02
Last Run '01
Bug Buster '99

Sarah K. Lippmann
Addicted to Murder 3: Bloodlust '99
Addicted to Murder 2: Tainted Blood '97

Dennis Lipscomb (1941-)
Automatic '94
Retribution '88
Guilty of Innocence '87
Sister, Sister '87
Slow Burn '86
Eyes of Fire '84
Union City '81

Peggy Lipton (1947-)
Jackpot '01
Intern '00
Skipped Parts '00
The Postman '97
The Spider and the Fly '94
Fatal Charm '92
Twin Peaks: Fire Walk with Me '92
Kinjite: Forbidden Subjects '89
I'm Gonna Git You Sucka '88
Purple People Eater '88
Mosby's Marauders '66

Robert Lipton
A Woman, Her Men and Her Futon '92
Lethal Woman '88

LisaRaye (1967-)
Beauty Shop '05
Gang of Roses '03
Civil Brand '02
All About You '01
The Wood '99
The Players Club '98

Joe Lisi (1950-)
Kiss of Death '94
Traces of Red '92

Virna Lisi (1937-)
Balzac: A Life of Passion '99
Queen Margot '94
I Love N.Y. '87
Christopher Columbus '85
La Cicada '83
Miss Right '81
Night Flight from Moscow '73
Bluebeard '72
The Statue '71
Carbon Copy '69
The Secret of Santa Vittoria '69
When Wolves Cry '69
Assault on a Queen '66
Casanova '70 '65
How to Murder Your Wife '64
Eva '62

Leon Lissek (1927-)
Bloodmoon '90
The Unbearable Lightness of Being '88
Adventures of Eliza Fraser '76
Blockhouse '73

Moira Lister (1923-2007)
The 10th Kingdom '00
Cop-Out '67
Abandon Ship '57
John and Julie '55
The Limping Man '53
Trouble in Store '53
Uneasy Terms '48

Tommy (Tiny) Lister (1958-)
Who Made the Potatoe Salad? '05
Blast '04
My Baby's Daddy '04
Never Die Alone '04
Asylum of the Damned '03
Confidence '03
Austin Powers In Goldmember '02
The Wash '01
Circus '00
Little Nicky '00
Next Friday '00
Judgment Day '99
Supreme Sanction '99
I Got the Hook-Up '98
Never 2 Big '98
The Players Club '98
Wishmaster 2: Evil Never Dies '98
Body Count '97
The Fifth Element '97
Jackie Brown '97
Phat Beach '96
White Cargo '96
Friday '95
Hologram Man '95
Things to Do in Denver When You're Dead '95
Immortal Combat '94
Men of War '94
Posse '93
9 1/2 Ninjas '90
No Holds Barred '89
Secret Agent 00-Soul '89
Prison '88
Beverly Hills Cop 2 '87
Extreme Prejudice '87

Giorgio Listuzzi (1934-)
White Nights '57
The Roof '55

Litefoot (1969-)
Adaptation '02
Kull the Conqueror '97
Mortal Kombat 2: Annihilation '97
The Indian in the Cupboard '95

John Litel (1892-1972)
Sitting Bull '54
Montana Belle '52
The Fuller Brush Girl '50
Outpost in Morocco '49
Rusty's Birthday '49
Pitfall '48
Cass Timberane '47
Northwest Trail '46
San Antonio '45
Boss of Big Town '43
So Proudly We Hail '43
Invisible Agent '42
They Died with Their Boots On '41
The Fighting 69th '40
Nancy Drew and the Hidden Starcase '39
Nancy Drew, Reporter '39

Nancy Drew—Trouble Shooter '39
Amazing Dr. Clitterhouse '38
Blazing Saddles '74
Homecoming: A Christmas Story '71
Nancy Drew—Detective '38
A Slight Case of Murder '38
The Black Legion '37

John Lithgow (1945-)
Kinsey '04
Orange County '02
Shrek '01 (V)
Don Quixote '00
Rugrats in Paris: The Movie '00 (V)
A Civil Action '98
Homegrown '97
Johnny Skidmarks '97
Hollow Point '95
My Brother's Keeper '95
Redwood Curtain '95
The Tuskegee Airmen '95
A Good Man in Africa '94
Princess Caraboo '94
Silent Fall '94
World War II: When Lions Roared '94
Cliffhanger '93
Love, Cheat & Steal '93
The Pelican Brief '93
The Wrong Man '93
Raising Cain '92
At Play in the Fields of the Lord '91
Ricochet '91
Ivory Hunters '90
Memphis Belle '90
Out Cold '89
Traveling Man '89
Distant Thunder '88
Baby Girl Scott '87
Harry and the Hendersons '87
The Manhattan Project '86
Santa Claus: The Movie '85
The Adventures of Buckaroo Banzai Across the Eighth Dimension '84
Footloose '84
The Day After '83
Goldilocks & the Three Bears '83
Terms of Endearment '83
Twilight Zone: The Movie '83
I'm Dancing as Fast as I Can '82
The World According to Garp '82
Blow Out '81
Mom, the Wolfman and Me '80
Oldest Living Graduate '80
All That Jazz '79
Rich Kids '79
The Big Fix '78
Obsession '76
Savage Fun '70

Paulie (Litowsky) Litt
Speed Racer '08
Eternal Sunshine of the Spotless Mind '04
Jersey Girl '04

Cleavon Little (1939-92)
Perfect Harmony '91
Separate but Equal '91
Fletch Lives '89
Murder by Numbers '89
Gore Vidal's Lincoln '88
The Gig '85
Once Bitten '85
E. Nick: A Legend in His Own Mind '84
Surf 2 '84
Toy Soldiers '84
Double Exposure '82
Jimmy the Kid '82
The Salamander '82
Don't Look Back: The Story of Leroy "Satchel" Paige '81
High Risk '81
Scavenger Hunt '79
FM '78
Greased Lightning '77
Once Upon a Brothers Grimm '77
Blazing Saddles '74
Vanishing Point '71
Cotton Comes to Harlem '70

Lucien Littlefield (1895-1960)
Susanna Pass '49
Lights of Old Santa Fe '44
Treasure of Fear '45
One Body Too Many '44
Zoro's Black Whip '44
Bells of Capistrano '42
The Gladiator '38
Hollywood Stadium Mystery '38
Wide Open Faces '38
Bulldog Drummond's Revenge '37
Let's Sing Again '36
The Moon's Our Home '36
Kiss and Make Up '34
The Bitter Tea of General Yen '33
Rainbow over Broadway '33
Strangers of the Evening '32
Tom Sawyer '30
Seven Keys to Baldpate '29
The Cat and the Canary '27
Buckeye and Blue '87
Teen Witch '89
Not Quite Human 2 '89
Not Quite Human '87

Kim Little
Social Intercourse '01
Sorority House Party '92

Mark Little (1959-)
The Wacky World of Wills & Burke '85

Michelle Little
Apollo 13 '95
Heartstrings '93
Blood Clan '91
Bluffing '87
My Demon Lover '87
Radioactive Dreams '86
Appointment with Fear '85

Natasha Little (1969-)
Vanity Fair '04
Greenfingers '00
The Criminal '00

Mickey Little (1941-)
Gun Crazy '49

Rich Little (1938-)
The Late Shift '96
Happy Hour '87
Dirty Tricks '81

Little JJ (1990-)

Little Nell
See Nell Campbell

Little Richard (1935-)
Mystery, Alaska '99
Why Do Fools Fall in Love? '98

Sacheen Little Feather (1947-)
Shoot the Sun Down '81
Johnny Firecloud '75
The Trial of Billy Jack '74

Eddie Little Sky (1932-67)
Journey Through Rosebud '72

Gary Littlejohn
Angels Hard As They Come '71
Bury Me an Angel '71
Badlands '74
The Sheik '21
Leap Year '21
Tumbleweeds '25
Charley's Aunt '25

Ernest Liu
Get a Clue! '98
From Dusk Till Dawn '95

Gordon (Chia Hui) Liu (1955-)
Kill Bill Vol. 2 '04
Kill Bill Vol. 1 '03

Harrison Liu
Warriors of Heaven and Earth '03

Lucy Liu (1968-)
Kung Fu Panda '08 (V)
Code Name: The Cleaner '07
Rise: Blood Hunter '07
Lucky Number Slevin '06
Domino '05
Kill Bill Vol. 2 '04
Kill Bill Vol. 1 '03
Charlie's Angels: Full Throttle '03
Chicago '02
Cypher '02
Ballistic: Ecks vs. Sever '02
Charlie's Angels '00
Shanghai Noon '00
City of Industry '96
Molly '99
Play It to the Bone '99
Payback '98
Flypaper '97

Matty Liu
Off the Lip '04

Peiqi Liu
Shadow Magic '00
Ermo '94

Rene Liu (1970-)
Double Vision '02
Fleeing by Night '00

Boris Livanov
Baltic Deputy '37
Ten Days That Shook the World '27

Blake Lively (1981-)
Sisterhood of the Traveling Pants 2 '08
Accepted '06
Sisterhood of the Traveling Pants '05

Eric Lively (1981-)
Sex and Breakfast '07
The Butterfly Effect 2 '06
Speak '04
Crash Course '04
Uprising '01

Ernie Lively (1947-)
Sisterhood of the Traveling Pants 2 '08
The Legend of Cryin' Ryan '98

Jason Lively (1968-)
Night of the Creeps '86
National Lampoon's European Vacation '85

Robin (Robyn) Lively (1972-)
Crazy from the Heart '91
The Karate Kid: Part 3 '89
Teen Witch '89

Ron Livingston (1968-)
Music Within '07
Relative Strangers '06
Pretty Persuasion '05
Little Black Book '04
Adaptation '02
Buying the Cow '02
Band of Brothers '01
Beat '00
A Rumor of Angels '00
Two Ninas '00
The Big Brass Ring '99
Body Shots '99
Campfire Tales '98
Office Space '98
Swingers '96

Barry Livingston (1953-)
You Don't Mess with the Zohan '08
Steel Sharks '97
Invisible Mom '96
Easy Wheels '89

John Livingston (1961-)
Dopamine '03
The Mating Habits of the Earthbound Human '99
Where's Marlowe? '98
The Stickup '01
Mr. Wrong '95

Margaret Livingston (1895-1984)
The Lady Refuses '31
Seven Keys to Baldpate '29
Through the Breakers '28
Sunrise '27
The Bushel '19

Robert "Bob" Livingston (1904-88)
Blazing Stewardesses '75
I Spit on Your Corpse '74
Mysterious Desperado '49
Grand Canyon Trail '48
The Cheaters '45
Don't Fence Me In '45
Death Rides the Plains '44
Law of the Saddle '43
Raiders of Red Gap '43
Covered Wagon Days '40
Rocky Mountain Rangers '40
Cowboys from Texas '39
The Kansas Terrors '39
Heroes of the Hills '38
Outlaws of Sonora '38
Purple Vigilantes '38
Come on, Cowboys '37
Heart of the Rockies '37
Hit the Saddle '37
Larceny On the Air '37
Riders On the Whistling Skull '37
The Vigilantes Are Coming '36

Jack Livesey (1901-61)
The World Owes Me a Living '47
Never Too Late to Mend '37

Roger Livesey (1906-76)
Of Human Bondage '64
The Entertainer '60
The League of Gentlemen '60
The Master of Ballantrae '53
Green Grow the Rushes '51
Stairway to Heaven '46
I Know Where I'm Going '45
The Life and Death of Colonel Blimp '43
Drums '38
Lorna Doone '34

Desmond Llewelyn (1914-99)
The World Is Not Enough '99
Tomorrow Never Dies '97
GoldenEye '95
Licence to Kill '89
The Living Daylights '87
A View to a Kill '85
For Your Eyes Only '81
Moonraker '79
The Spy Who Loved Me '77
On Her Majesty's Secret Service '69
You Only Live Twice '67
Thunderball '65
Goldfinger '64
From Russia with Love '63

Suzette Llewellyn
Welcome II the Terrordome '95

Shelby Livingston
2000 Maniacs '64

Kari Lizer (1961-)
Private School '83
Smokey Bites the Dust '81
Private Parts '72

LL Cool J (1968-)
Edison Force '05
Mindhunters '05
Slow Burn '05
Deliver Us from Eva '03
Rugrats Go Wild! '03 (V)
S.W.A.T. '03
Deep Blue Sea '99
In Too Deep '99
Halloween: H20 '98
Caught Up '98
Woo '97
Out of Sync '95
The Right to Remain Silent

Stanley Livingston (1950-)
Nude on the Moon '61

Christopher Lloyd (1938-)
Masters of Horror: Valerie on the Stairs '06
A Perfect Day '06 (TV)
Hey Arnold! The Movie '02 (V)
Interstate 60 '02
When Good Ghouls Go Bad '01
Wit '01
Chasing Destiny '00
Wish You Were Dead '00
Alice in Wonderland '99
Baby Geniuses '98
It Came from the Sky '98
My Favorite Martian '98
Premonition '98
Anastasia '97 (V)
Quicksilver Highway '97 (TV)
The Real Blonde '97
Cadillac Ranch '96
Changing Habits '96
Rent-A-Kid '95
Things to Do in Denver When You're Dead '95
Angels in the Outfield '94
Camp Nowhere '94
The Pagemaster '94 (V)
Radioland Murders '94
Addams Family Values '93
Dennis the Menace '93
Twenty Bucks '93
Dead Ahead: The Exxon Valdez Disaster '92
T Bone N Weasel '92
The Addams Family '91
Suburban Commando '91
Back to the Future, Part 3 '90
Why Me? '90 (V)
The Dream Team '89
Back to the Future, Part 2 '89
Eight Men Out '88
Track 29 '88
Who Framed Roger Rabbit '88
Walk Like a Man '87
Miracles '86
Clue '85
Back to the Future '85
To Be or Not to Be '83
Pilgrim, Farewell '82
Legend of the Lone Ranger '81
National Lampoon Goes to the Movies '81
The Postman Always Rings Twice '81
The Black Marble '79
Goin' South '78
Three Warriors '77
One Flew Over the Cuckoo's Nest '75

Danny Lloyd (1972-)
The Shining '80

Doris Lloyd (1896-)
The Time Machine '60
The Black Doll '38
A Shot in the Dark '35
Disraeli '30
The Drake Case '29

Emily Lloyd (1971-)
Boogie Boy '98
The Real Thing '97
Welcome to Sarajevo '97
Under the Hula Moon '95
When Saturday Comes '95
A River Runs Through It '92
Scorchers '92
Chicago Joe & the Showgirl '90
Cookie '89
In Country '89
Wish You Were Here '87

Eric Lloyd (1986-)
The Santa Clause 3: The Escape Clause '06
The Santa Clause 2 '02
Luminous Motion '00
Chameleon '98
Deconstructing Harry '97
Dunston Checks In '96
The Santa Clause '94

Emily Ann Lloyd (1984-)
Annie: A Royal Adventure '95

George Lloyd (1897-)
I Accuse My Parents '45
White Pongo '45
San Quentin '37

Harold Lloyd (1893-1971)
Days of Thrills and Laughter '61
The Sin of Harold Diddlebock '47
Milky Way '36
Feet First '30
Speedy '28
The Kid Brother '27
For Heaven's Sake '26
The Freshman '25
Girl Shy '24
Safety Last '23

Harold Lloyd, Jr. (1931-71)
Married Too Young '62
Platinum High School '60
Girls' Town '59

Hugh Lloyd (1923-)
The Flaming Urge '53
Cider with Rosie '99

Jake Lloyd (1989-)
August '95
Madison '01
Race to Space '01
Star Wars: Episode 1—The Phantom Menace '99
Jingle All the Way '96
Unhook the Stars '96

Jimmy Lloyd (1918-88)
G.I. Jane '51
Miss Grant Takes Richmond '49
Riders of the Whistling Pines '49
Sea Hound '47
The Jolson Story '46
The Story of G.I. Joe '45

John Bedford Lloyd (1956-)
The Killing Floor '06
The Bourne Supremacy '04
The Manchurian Candidate '04
Super Troopers '01
Fair Game '95
Gangster Wars '81
Killer: A Journal of Murder '95
Take Down '79
It's Alive 2: It Lives Again '78
The Car '77
Skateboard '77
Missouri Breaks '76
Philadelphia '93
Waiting for the Light '90
The Abyss '89
Crossing Delancey '88
Sweet Lorraine '87
Tough Guys Don't Dance '87

Kathleen Lloyd (1949-)
Fly Boy '99
Call to Glory '84
Audrey Rose '77
The Nude Bomb '80
Jaws of Satan '81
Journey of Honor '91
Amityville 4: The Evil Escapes '89
Goldenrod '77
God Told Me To '76
Mean Frank and Crazy Tony '75
Mr. Inside, Mr. Outside '74
The Story of Jacob & Joseph '74
Escape from Death Row '75

Norman Lloyd (1914-)
In Her Shoes '05
The Song of the Lark '01
The Adventures of Rocky & Bullwinkle '00
Fall Safe '00
The Lives of a Bengal Lancer '35
Carnival Lady '33

Rollo Lloyd (1883-1938)

Sabrina Lloyd (1970-)
The Breakup Artist '04
Dopamine '03
On Edge '03
Father Hood '93

Sue Lloyd (1939-)
Bullet to Beijing '95
The Bitch '78
Number 1 of the Secret Service '77
Ned Kelly '70
The Ipcress File '65
Hysteria '64

Charles Lloyd-Pack (1905-83)
If.... '69
Bedazzled '68
The Reptile '66
Victim '61
The Horror of Dracula '58
Stranger in Town '57
River Beat '54

Roger Lloyd-Pack (1944-)
The History of Mr. Polly '07
Harry Potter and the Goblet of Fire '05
The Young Poisoner's Handbook '94
Fright '71

Carmen (Lee) Llywelyn
Cowboys and Angels '00
The Mod Squad '99
Never Been Kissed '99
Chasing Amy '97

Candy Lo (1974-)
The Eye '02
Time and Tide '00

Chi Muoi Lo
Catfish in Black Bean Sauce '00
The Relic '96

Luigi Lo Cascio (1967-)
Don't Tell '05
Best of Youth '06
Light of My Eyes '01

Enrico Lo Verso (1964-)
Hannibal '01
Moses '96
Lamerica '95
Farinelli '94
La Scorta '94

Tony LoBianco (1935-)
The Stolen Children '92
Endangered Species '02
Friends and Family '01
Rocky Marciano '99
Mafia! '98
Bomb Squad '97
Sworn to Justice '97
The Juror '96
Nixon '95
Tyson '95
The Ascent '94
Boiling Point '93
Teamster Boss: The Jackie Presser Story '92
City of Hope '91
The Ten Million Dollar Getaway '91
The Ann Jillian Story '88
Blood Ties '87
City Heat '84
Separate Ways '82
Last Cry for Help '79
Marciano '79
Bloodbrothers '78
F.I.S.T. '78
Magee and the Lady '78
Goldenrod '77
The Seven-Ups '73
The French Connection '71
Honeymoon Killers '70

Jane Lobre
The Green Room '78
A Gentle Woman '69

Amy Locane (1972-)
Secretary '02
Hell's Gate '01

Bongwater '98
Implicated '98
Route 9 '98
Bram Stoker's The Mummy '97
Ebenezer '97
End of Summer '97
Going All the Way '97
Love to Kill '97
Prefontaine '96
Carried Away '95
Criminal Hearts '95
Airheads '94
School Ties '92
Blue Sky '91
No Secrets '91
Lost Angels '89

David Lochary (1944-77)
Female Trouble '74
Pink Flamingos '72
Multiple Maniacs '70
Mondo Trasho '69

Bruce Locke
Ripper Man '96
RoboCop 3 '91

Katherine Locke (1910-95)
People Will Talk '51
Try and Get Me '50
The Seventh Cross '44

Philip Locke (1928-2004)
Othello '95
Tom & Viv '94
And the Ship Sails On '83
Fiction Makers '67

Sondra Locke (1947-)
The Prophet's Game '99
Tales of the Unexpected '91
Ratboy '86
Sudden Impact '83
Rosie: The Rosemary Clooney Story '82
Any Which Way You Can '80
Bronco Billy '80
Second Coming of Suzanne '80
Every Which Way But Loose '78
The Gauntlet '77
Seducers '77
Shadow of Chikara '77
The Outlaw Josey Wales '76
A Reflection of Fear '72
Willard '71
The Heart Is a Lonely Hunter '68

Spencer Locke (1991-)
Resident Evil: Extinction '07
Monster House '06 (V)

Anne Lockhart (1953-)
Bug Buster '99
Big Bad John '90
Dark Tower '87
Troll '86
Hambone & Hillie '84
Savage Hunger '84
Mission Galactica: The Cylon Attack '78
Joyride '77
Slashed Dreams '74

Calvin Lockhart (1934-2007)
Predator 2 '90
The Baron '88
Coming to America '88
The Beast Must Die '75
Let's Do It Again '75
Uptown Saturday Night '74
Cotton Comes to Harlem '70
Dark of the Sun '68

Gene Lockhart (1891-1957)
Carousel '56
The Man in the Gray Flannel Suit '56
Francis Covers the Big Town '53
Face to Face '52
A Girl in Every Port '52
Hoodlum Empire '52
I'd Climb the Highest Mountain '51
The Big Hangover '50
Riding High '50
The Inspector General '49
Madame Bovary '49
Her Husband's Affairs '47
Miracle on 34th Street '47
A Scandal in Paris '46
The Strange Woman '46
House on 92nd Street '45
Leave Her to Heaven '45
Action in Arabia '44
Going My Way '44
Northern Pursuit '43
Hangmen Also Die '42
Billy the Kid '41
The Devil & Daniel Webster '41
International Lady '41
Meet John Doe '41
The Sea Wolf '41
They Died with Their Boots On '41
Abe Lincoln in Illinois '40
Edison the Man '40
His Girl Friday '40
South of Pago Pago '40
The Story of Alexander Graham Bell '39
Algiers '38
Blondie '38
A Christmas Carol '38
Of Human Hearts '38
Sinners in Paradise '38
Earthworm Tractors '36
Something to Sing About '36
Wedding Present '36

June Lockhart (1925-)
Lost in Space '98
The Colony '95
Out There '95
Sleep with Me '94
Dead Women in Lingerie '90
The Gift of Love '90
The Big Picture '89
Rented Lips '88
Troll '86
Strange Invaders '83
Butterfly '82
The Capture of Grizzly Adams '82
Deadly Games '80
Just Tell Me You Love Me '80
Walking Through the Fire '80
Curse of the Black Widow '77
Lassie's Great Adventure '62
T-Men '47
Easy to Wed '46
She Wolf of London '46
The Yearling '46
Son of Lassie '45
Meet Me in St. Louis '44
The White Cliffs of Dover '44
Miss Annie Rooney '42
Adam Had Four Sons '41
Sergeant York '41
All This and Heaven Too '40

Heather Locklear (1962-)
Angels Fall '07
The Perfect Man '05
Looney Tunes: Back in Action '03
Uptown Girls '03
Double Tap '98
Money Talks '97
The First Wives Club '96
The Great American Sex Scandal '94
Fade to Black '93
Body Language '92
Illusions '91
The Big Slice '90
Lethal Charm '90
The Return of Swamp Thing '89
City Killer '87
Firestarter '84
Twirl '81

Loryn Locklin
Fortress '93
Taking Care of Business '90
Catch Me... If You Can '89

Gary Lockwood (1937-)
Night of the Scarecrow '95
Terror in Paradise '90
The Wild Pair '87
Survival Zone '84
The Incredible Journey of Dr. Meg Laurel '79
Bad Georgia Road '77
Project: Kill! '77
Manhunter '74
R.P.M.* (" Revolutions Per Minute) '70
Firecreek '68
2001: A Space Odyssey '68
It Happened at the World's Fair '63
The Magic Sword '62
Wild in the Country '61
Tall Story '60

Margaret Lockwood (1911-90)
The Slipper and the Rose '76
Cast a Dark Shadow '55
Trouble in the Glen '54
Bedelia '46
The Man in Grey '45
The Wicked Lady '45
Night Train to Munich '40
The Stars Look Down '39
Susannah of the Mounties '39
The Lady Vanishes '38
Dr. Syn '37
Lorna Doone '34

Thomas Lockyer
Dog Soldiers '01
Jesus '00
Ultraviolet '98
Incognito '97
Teenagers from Outer Space '59

Barbara Loden (1932-80)
Iron Cowboy '68
Splendor in the Grass '61

Anne Marie Loder (1969-)
Life-Size '00
Blacklight '98

John Loder (1898-1988)
Small Hotel '57
The Story of Esther Costello '57
Dishonored Lady '47
Brighton Strangler '45
The Woman Who Came Back '45
Abroad with Two Yanks '44
The Hairy Ape '44
Passage to Marseilles '44
How Green Was My Valley '41
Tin Pan Alley '40
Dr. Syn '37
King Solomon's Mines '37
Non-Stop New York '37
The Man Who Lived Again '36
River of Unrest '36
Sabotage '36
Java Head '35
The Silent Passenger '35
Lorna Doone '34
My Song Goes Round the World '34
The Private Life of Henry VIII '33
Wedding Rehearsal '32

Kathryn Loder (1940-)
Foxy Brown '74
The Big Doll House '71

David Lodge (1921-2003)
Edge of Sanity '89
Killer with Two Faces '74
The Railway Children '70
Oh! What a Lovely War '69
What's Good for the Goose '69
Trial & Error '62
The Hellfire Club '61
Two-Way Stretch '60

Jean Lodge (1927-)
Terror Ship '54
Dick Barton Strikes Back '48

John Lodge (1903-85)
The Witchmaker '69
De Mayerling à Sarajevo '40
Bulldog Drummond at Bay '37
River of Unrest '36
The Little Colonel '35
Scarlet Empress '34
Murders in the Zoo '33
Seas Beneath '31

Fiona Loewi (1975-)
Invasion! '99
Blackheart '98
Love anc Death on Long Island '97

Jeanette Loff (1906-42)
Fightin' Ranch '30
Fighting Thru '30
King of Jazz '30
Party Girls '29
Annapolis '28

Marianne Lofgren (1910-57)
Only One Night '42
June Night '40

Arthur Loft (1897-1947)
Lights of Old Santa Fe '47
Charlie Chan in the Secret Service '44
Woman in the Window '44
Blue, White and Perfect '42
Carson City Kid '40
Riders of Pasco Basin '40
Southward Ho! '39
Gang Bullets '38
I Am the Law '38
Public Cowboy No. 1 '37
Kid Courageous '35
Western Justice '35

Lenny Y. Loftin
From Dusk Till Dawn 3: The Hangman's Daughter '99
Underground Terror '88

Cecilia Loftus (1876-1943)
The Black Cat '41
Lucky Partners '40

Jacqueline Logan (1901-83)
King of the Kongo '29
Ships in the Night '28
King of Kings '27

Phyllis Logan (1956-)
All the King's Men '99
Invasion: Earth '98
Secrets and Lies '95
Freddie the Frog '92 (V)
And a Nightingale Sang '91
Goldeneye The Secret Life of Ian Fleming '89
The Inquiry '87
The Kitchen Toto '87
The Doctor and the Devils '85
The McGuffin '85
Another Time, Another Place '83

Ricky Dean Logan
Freddy's Dead: The Final Nightmare '91
Back to the Future, Part 3 '90
Back to the Future, Part 2 '89

Robert F. Logan (1941-)
Man Outside '88

Death Ray 2000 '81
Mountain Family Robinson '79
Sea Gypsies '78
Further Adventures of the Wilderness Family, Part 2 '77
Snowbeast '77
Across the Great Divide '76
The Adventures of the Wilderness Family '75

Donal Logue (1966-)
The Ex '07
Ghost Rider '07
Zodiac '07
The Groomsmen '06
Just Like Heaven '05
American Splendor '03
Confidence '03
Two Days '03
Comic Book Villains '02
The Patriot '01
The Chateau '01
Reindeer Games '00
Steal This Movie! '00
The Big Tease '99
The Million Dollar Hotel '99
Runaway Bride '99
Blade '98
A Bright Shining Lie '98
The Thin Red Line '98
Metro '96
Dear God '96
Glam '96
The Grave '95
The Crew '95
Baja '95
Gettysburg '93
Sneakers '92
And the Band Played On '93

Stanley Logan (1885-1953)
Double Crossbones '51
That Forsyte Woman '50
My Son, My Son '40

Robert Loggia (1930-)
Forget About It '06
Return to Me '00
Rain '06
The Deal '05
Bonanno: A Godfather's Story '99
Joan of Arc '99
The Suburbans '99
American Virgin '98
Holy Man '98
Flypaper '97
Joe Torre: Curveballs Along the Way '97
National Lampoon's The Don's Analyst '97
The Proposition '97
Wide Awake '97
Independence Day '96
Lost Highway '96
Mistrial '96
Smilla's Sense of Snow '96
Man with a Gun '95
Picture Windows '95
The Right to Remain Silent '95
Bad Girls '94
Coldblooded '94
I Love Trouble '94
White Mile '94
Lifepod '93
Mercy Mission '93
Wild Palms '93
Afterburn '92
Gladiator '92
Innocent Blood '92
The Marrying Man '91
Necessary Roughness '91
Code Name: Chaos '90
Intrigue '90
Opportunity Knocks '90
Relentless '89
Running Away '89
Triumph of the Spirit '89
Armed and Dangerous '86
Over the Top '86
Big '88
Oliver & Company '88 (V)
The Believers '87
Echoes in the Darkness '87
Gaby: A True Story '87
Hot Pursuit '87
Target: Favorite Son '87
That's Life! '86
The Jagged Edge '85
Prizzi's Honor '85
Curse of the Pink Panther '83
Psycho 2 '83
Scarface '83
An Officer and a Gentleman '82
A Woman Called Golda '82
S.O.B. '81
The Ninth Configuration '79
Revenge of the Pink Panther '78
Speedtrap '78
First Love '77
The Greatest Story Ever Told '65
The Three Sisters '65
The Lost Missile '58
The Nine Lives of Elfego Baca '58
Somebody Up There Likes Me '56

Lindsay Lohan (1986-)
Georgia Rule '07
I Know Who Killed Me '07
Bobby '06
Just My Luck '06
A Prairie Home Companion '06
Herbie: Fully Loaded '05
Confessions of a Teenage Drama Queen '04
Mean Girls '04
Freaky Friday '03
Get a Clue '02
Life-Size '00
The Parent Trap '98

Alison Lohman (1979-)
Beowulf '07 (V)
Things We Lost in the Fire '07
Flicka '06
The Big White '05
Where the Truth Lies '05
Big Fish '03
Matchstick Men '03
White Oleander '02
The Thirteenth Floor '99

Marie Lohr (1890-1975)
A'bandon Ship '57
Small Hotel '57
Escapade '55
Counterblast '48
The Magic Box '47
South Riding '37
Pygmalion '38

Florence Loiret-Caille
Time of the Wolf '03

Kristanna Loken (1979-)
In the Name of the King: A Dungeon Siege Tale '08
BloodRayne '06
Terminator 3: Rise of the Machines '03

Gina Lollobrigida (1927-)
Bad Man's River '72
King, Queen, Knave '72
Woman of Straw '64
Come September '61
Buona Sera, Mrs. Campbell '68
Imperial Venus '71
Private Navy of Sgt. O'Farrell '68
Hotel Paradiso '66
Strange Bedfellows '65
Solomon and Sheba '59
Never So Few '59
Where the Hot Wind Blows '59
Four Ways Out '57

Carole Lombard (1908-42)
To Be or Not to Be '42
Mr. & Mrs. Smith '41
They Knew What They Wanted '40
In Name Only '39
Made for Each Other '39
Nothing Sacred '37
Swing High, Swing Low '37
My Man Godfrey '36
The Princess Comes Across '36
Hands Across the Table '35
Now and Forever '34
Twentieth Century '34
We're Not Dressing '34
No Man of Her Own '32
No One Man '32
Sinners in the Sun '32
Man of the World '31
Supernatural '33
The Eagle and the Hawk '33

Herbert Lomas
The Ghost Train '41
The Ghost Goes West '36

Beba Loncar (1943-)
Don't Look in the Attic '81

Alexandra London
Van Gogh '92

Daniel London
Patch Adams '98
Minority Report '02
Old Joy '06
Four Dogs Playing Poker '00

Jason London (1972-)
Axe '06
Glass House: The Good Mother '06
Dracula 3: Legacy '05
Dracula 2: Ascension '03
Grind '03
Out Cold '01
The Hound of the Baskervilles '00
Jason and the Argonauts '00
The Rage: Carrie 2 '99
Broken Vessels '98
If These Walls Could Talk '96
Serial Bomber '96
My Teacher's Wife '95
To Wong Foo, Thanks for Everything, Julie Newmar '95
Dazed and Confused '93
December '91
The Man in the Moon '91

Herbert Lom (1917-)
The Devil's Daughter '91
The Pope Must Diet '91
Masque of the Red Death '90
River of Death '90
Skeleton Coast '89
Ten Little Indians '89
Going Bananas '88
King Solomon's Mines '85
Curse of the Pink Panther '83
Dead Zone '83
Whoops Apocalypse '83
Trail of the Pink Panther '82
Peter and Paul '81
The Man with Bogart's Face '80
Hopscotch '80
The Lady Vanishes '79
Revenge of the Pink Panther '78
The Pink Panther Strikes Again '76
Ten Little Indians '75
Return of the Pink Panther '74
And Now the Screaming Starts '73
Asylum '72
Count Dracula '71
Murders in the Rue Morgue '71
Dorian Gray '70
Journey to the Far Side of the Sun '69
99 Women '69
Mark of the Devil '69
Uncle Tom's Cabin '69
Villa Rides '68
Gambit '65
A Shot in the Dark '64
The Horse Without a Head '63
Tiara Tahiti '62
The Frightened City '61
Mysterious Island '61
Flame Over India '60
Spartacus '60
Third Man on the Mountain '59
Room 43 '58
Fire Down Below '57
War and Peace '57
The Ladykillers '55
Paris Express '53
The Golden Salamander '51
The Hunchback of Notre Dame '57
The Black Rose '50
Night and the City '50
Dual Alibi '47
The Seventh Veil '46
Appointment with Crime '45
Hotel Reserve '44
Secret Mission '42

Louise Lombard (1971-)
Hidalgo '04
After the Rain '99
3000 Miles to Graceland '01

Domenick Lombardozzi (1976-)
Find Me Guilty '06
Carlito's Way: Rise to Power '05
S.W.A.T. '03

Ulli Lommel (1944-)
Chinese Roulette '86
Strangers in Paradise '84
Boogey Man 2 '83
Effi Briest '74
Fanny Hill: Memoirs of a Woman of Pleasure '64
Beware of a Holy Whore '70

Tadeusz Lomnicki (1927-92)
Contract '80
Man of Marble '76
Colonel Wolodyjowski '69
Innocent Sorcerers '60
A Generation '54

Karina Lombard (1969-)
Foorsteps '06
Kull the Conqueror '97
Last Man Standing '96
Legends of the Fall '94
The Firm '93
Wide Sargasso Sea '92

Louis Lombardi (1968-)
Confidence '03
Deuces Wild '02
3000 Miles to Graceland '01
The Crew '00
Suicide Kings '97
The Immortals '95
The Usual Suspects '95
Beverly Hills Cop 3 '94
Natural Born Killers '94
Amongst Friends '93

Julie London (1926-2000)
Man of the West '58
The Girl Can't Help It '56
The Great Man '56
Drango '57
Saddle the Wind '58
A Question of Adultery '58
The Wonderful Country '59
The George Raft Story '61
Task Force '49
The Red House '47
Nabonga '44

Lisa London (1957-)
H.O.T.S. '79
Savage Beach '89

Tom London (1889-1963)
Tribute to a Bad Man '56
Blue Canadian Rockies '52
Red Desert '49
Brand of Fear '49
Under Colorado Skies '47
Homesteaders of Paradise '47
Alias Billy the Kid '46
Santa Fe Uprising '46
Rough Riders of Cheyenne '45
Sunset in El Dorado '45
Fighting Seabees '44
Zorro's Black Whip '44
Fugitive Valley '41
The Lone Rider in Frontier Fury '41
Flaming Lead '39
Phantom Rancher '39
Roll, Wagons, Roll '39
Southward Ho! '39
Prairie Moon '38
Western Gold '37
Courage of the North '35
The Miracle Rider '35
Rio Rattler '35
Toll of the Desert '35
Beyond the Rockies '32
Outlaw Justice '32
Arizona Terror '31
Two Gun Man '31

Jeremy London (1972-)
Gods and Generals '03
Journey to the Center of the Earth '99
The Defenders: Taking the First '98
White Wolves 2: Legend of the Wild '94
Mallrats '95
Dazed and Confused '93
Fall Time '94
Safe Passage '94
Alien Cargo '99
Poor White Trash '00
Spent '00

Nia Long (1970-)
Premonition '07
Are We Done Yet? '07
Big Momma's House 2 '06
Are We There Yet? '05
Alfie '04
Baadasssss! '03
Big Momma's House '00
Boiler Room '00
Held Up '00
If These Walls Could Talk 2 '00
The Best Man '99
In Too Deep '99
Stigmata '99
Soul Food '97
love jones '96
Friday '95
Made in America '93
Boyz N the Hood '91

Tom London (1889-1963)
Man of the West '58

Julie London (1926-2000)
Gods and Generals '03

Kathy Long (1965-)
Under the Gun '95
Knights '93

Justin Long (1978-)
Strange Wilderness '08
Alvin and the Chipmunks '07
Live Free or Die Hard '07
Walk Hard: The Dewey Cox Story '07 (V)
Accepted '06
Dreamland '06
Idiocracy '06
The Sasquatch Gang '06
The Break-Up '06
Herbie: Fully Loaded '05
Waiting '05
Dodgeball: A True Underdog Story '04
Raising Genius '04
Crossroads '02
Jeepers Creepers 2 '03
Jeepers Creepers '01
Happy Campers '01
Galaxy Quest '99

Jodi Long (1954-)
ATL '06
Amos and Andrew '93
Patty Hearst '88

Howie Long (1960-)
Firestorm '97
Broken Arrow '95
3000 Miles to Graceland '01
The Adventures of Galant Bess '01

Audrey Long (1924-)
Indian Uprising '51
The Adventures of Gallant Bess '48
Desperate '47

Keith Loneker
Leatherheads '08
Out of Sight '98

Jackie Long
The Comebacks '07
ATL '06

Matt Long
Ghost Rider '07
Sydney White '07

John Lone (1952-)
War '07
Rush Hour 2 '01
The Hunted '98
The Shadow '94
M. Butterfly '93
Shadow of China '91
The Moderns '88
The Last Emperor '87
Echoes of Paradise '87
Year of the Dragon '85
Iceman '84

Tony London
24 Hours in London '00
S'd & Nancy '86

Lotus Long (1909-90)
Phantom of Chinatown '40
Mr. Wong in Chinatown '39
Mystery of Mr. Wong '39
Mr. Wong, Detective '38

Shelley Long (1949-)
Dr. T & the Women '00
A Very Brady Sequel '96

Richard Long (1927-74)
Death Cruise '74
House on Haunted Hill '58
Cult of the Cobra '55
Boy on a Dolphin '57 (?)
Ma and Pa Kettle '49
Ma and Pa Kettle Back On the Farm '51
Ma and Pa Kettle Go to Town '50
Criss Cross '48
The Stranger '46
Tomorrow Is Forever '46

The Brady Bunch Movie '95
Frozen Assets '92
Don't Tell Her It's Me '90
Troop Beverly Hills '89
Hello Again '87
Outrageous Fortune '87
The Money Pit '86
Irreconcilable Differences '84
Losin' It '82
Night Shift '82
Caveman '81
A Small Circle of Friends '80
The Cracker Factory '79

Tom Long
Do or Die '01
The Dish '00
Risk '00
Strange Planet '99
Two Hands '98

Walter Long (1879-1952)
Silver Stallion '41
Flaming Lead '39
Man's Country '38
Six Shootin' Sheriff '38
The Glory Trail '36
Cornered '32
Sea Devils '31
Yankee Clipper '27
Soul-Fire '25
Little Church Around the Corner '23
Blood and Sand '22
Moran of the Lady Letty '22
The Sheik '21
The Little American '17
The Birth of a Nation '15

John Longden (1900-71)
Quatermass 2 '57
Alias John Preston '56
Tower of Terror '42
Clouds over Europe '39
Young and Innocent '37
Juno and the Paycook '30
Blackmail '29

Terence Longdon (1922-)
Another Time, Another Place '58
Murder on the Campus '52

Sue Longhurst
Auntie '73

Victoria Longley
Talk '94

Tony Longo (1962-)
The Cooler '03
Hard Luck '01
Houseguest '94
Prehysteria '93
Remote '93
Rapid Fire '92
The Last Boy Scout '91
Suburban Commando '91
Bloodhounds of Broadway '89
Worth Winning '89
Fletch '85

Ray Lonnen (1940-)
Belfast Assassin '84

Eva Longoria (1975-)
Over Her Dead Body '08
The Sentinel '06
Harsh Times '05

Emily Longstreth
Confessions of a Hit Man '94
Rising Son '90
Too Young to Die '90
The Big Picture '89
Wired to Kill '86
Private Resort '84

Michael (Michel) Lonsdale (1931-)
Goya's Ghosts '06
Munich '05
5x2 '04
Ronin '98
Nelly et Monsieur Arnaud '95

The Remains of the Day '93
Souvenir '88
The Name of the Rose '86
The Holcroft Covenant '85
Erendira '83
Enigma '82
Moonraker '79
Mr. Klein '76
Phantom of Liberty '74
The Day of the Jackal '73
Les Assassins de L'Ordre '71
Murmur of the Heart '71
The Bride Wore Black '68
Stolen Kisses '68
Is Paris Burning? '66

Leon Lontoc (1908-74)
The Gallant Hours '60
The Hunters '58

Richard Loo (1903-83)
The Man with the Golden Gun '74
The Sand Pebbles '66
Battle Hymn '57
The Clay Pigeon '49
Malaya '49
Back to Bataan '45
First Yank into Tokyo '45
God is My Co-Pilot '45
Betrayal from the East '44
China Sky '44
The Purple Heart '44
China '43
Across the Pacific '42
Mr. Wong in Chinatown '39
The Bitter Tea of General Yen '33

Theodore Loos (1883-1954)
M '31
Metropolis '26
Kriemhilde's Revenge '24

Tanya Lopert (1942-)
Changing Times '04
Tales of Ordinary Madness '83
A Very Brady Christmas '88

Nancy Loomis (1949-)
Halloween '78
Assault on Precinct 13 '76

Rod Loomis (1942-)
Bill & Ted's Excellent Adventure '89
Jack's Back '87

Michael (Mike) Lookinland (1960-)
The Brady Bunch Movie '95
Stephen King's The Stand '94

Carmen Lopez
Our Song '01
Curdled '95

George Lopez (1961-)
Swing Vote '08
The Adventures of Sharkboy and Lavagirl in 3-D '05
Real Women Have Curves '02
Bread and Roses '00

Jennifer Lopez (1970-)
Bordertown '06
El Cantante '06
Monster-in-Law '05
An Unfinished Life '05
Jersey Girl '04
Shall We Dance? '04
Gigli '03
Enough '02
Maid in Manhattan '02
Angel Eyes '01
The Wedding Planner '01
The Cell '00
Antz '98 (V)
Out of Sight '98
U-Turn '97
Anaconda '96
Blood & Wine '96

Jack '96
Selena '96
Money Train '95
My Family '94

Kamala Lopez
Erotique '94
Crazy from the Heart '91
Dollman '90
Exiled in America '90
Born in East L.A. '87

Mario Lopez (1973-)
The Street King '02
Outta Time '01
Big Brother Trouble '00
A Crack in the Floor '00
Eastside '99
Depraved '98
Killing Mr. Griffin '97
Breaking the Surface: The Greg Louganis Story '96

Perry Lopez (1931-)
Chinatown '74
McLintock! '63
Taras Bulba '62
Battle Cry '55
Mister Roberts '55

Priscilla Lopez (1948-)
Maid in Manhattan '02
Center Stage '00
Chutney Popcorn '99
Jesse '88

Sal Lopez (1954-)
Comanche Moon '08
Silver City '04
Price of Glory '00
Luminarias '99
Selena '96
The Fire Next Time '93
American Me '92
Full Metal Jacket '87

Seidy Lopez
Gabriela '01
The Stray '00
Depraved '98
Solo '96
Mi Vida Loca '94

Sergi Lopez (1965-)
Pan's Labyrinth '06
Dirty Pretty Things '03
Jet Lag '02
With a Friend Like Harry '00
An Affair of Love '99
Between Your Legs '99
Lisboa '99
The New Eve '98
Caresses '97
Western '96

Trini Lopez (1937-)
Antonio '73
The Dirty Dozen '67
The Poppy Is Also a Flower '66

Sophie Lorain (1957-)
Mambo Italiano '03
The Sign of Four '01
Home Team '98

Isabel Lorca
She's Having a Baby '88
Lightning: The White Stallion '86

Theodore Lorch (1880-1947)
The Man on the Box '25
The Last of the Mohicans '20

Jack Lord (1920-98)
The Doomsday Flight '66
Dr. No '62
God's Little Acre '58
The Court Martial of Billy Mitchell '55

Justine Lord (1937-)
Skeezer '82
He Kills Night After Night After Night '69
Night Slasher '67
Fiction Makers '67

Marjorie Lord (1922-)
Boy, Did I Get a Wrong Number! '66
Stop That Cab '51
Riding High '50

Johnny Come Lately '43
Sherlock Holmes in Washington '43

Stephen Lord (1972-)
Lethal Dose '03
Pulse '03

Traci Lords (1968-)
Crazy Eights '06
Novel Romance '06
The Killing Club '01
D.R.E.A.M. Team '99
Me & Will '99
Blade '98
Boogie Boy '98
Extramarital '98
Stir '98
Nowhere '96
As Good as Dead '95
The Nutt House '95
Dragstrip Girl '94
Serial Mom '94
Desperate Crimes '93
Ice '93
Skinner '93
Stephen King's The Tommyknockers '93
Laser Moon '92
Raw Nerve '91
A Time to Die '91
Cry-Baby '90
Shock 'Em Dead '90
Fast Food '89
Not of This Earth '88

Tony Lorea
Smokey & the Hotwire Gang '79
The Deadly and the Beautiful '73

Donna Loren (1947-)
Bikini Beach '64
Muscle Beach Party '64
Pajama Party '64

Sophia Loren (1934-)
Between Strangers '02
Grumpier Old Men '95
Ready to Wear '94
Running Away '89
Courage '86
Aurora '84
Sophia Loren: Her Own Story '80
Two Women '61
Breath of Scandal '60
Heller in Pink Tights '60
It Started in Naples '60
The Millionairess '60
Black Orchid '59
Desire Under the Elms '58
Houseboat '58
The Key '58
Legend of the Lost '57
The Pride and the Passion '57
What a Woman! '56
The Gold of Naples '54
Too Bad She's Bad '54
Two Nights with Cleopatra '54
Quo Vadis '51

Tray Loren
The American Angels: Baptism of Blood '89

Gator Bait 2: Cajun Justice '88
Rocktober Blood '85

Livio Lorenzon (1923-71)
The Good, the Bad and the Ugly '67
Last Gun '64
The Invincible Gladiator '63
Gladiators 7 '62
Pirates of the Coast '61

Susanne Loret
Atom Age Vampire '61
Uncle Was a Vampire '59

Teala Loring (1922-)
Fall Guy '47
Hard-Boiled Mahoney '47
Riding the California Trail '47
Delinquent Daughters '44

James Lorinz (1964-)
The Jerky Boys '95
Me and the Mob '94
Frankenhooker '90
Punch the Clock '90
Street Trash '87

Jean-Pierre Lorit
The White Countess '05
Jeanne la Pucelle '94
Trois Couleurs: Rouge '94

Marion Lorne (1888-1968)
The Graduate '67
Strangers on a Train '51

George Loros (1944-)
Shakedown '88
Apology '86

Louise Lorraine (1901-81)
Near the Rainbow's End '30
The Adventures of Tarzan '21

Peter Lorre (1904-64)
The Comedy of Terrors '64
Muscle Beach Party '64
The Patsy '64
The Raven '63
Five Weeks in a Balloon '62
Tales of Terror '62
Voyage to the Bottom of the Sea '61
Hell Ship Mutiny '57
The Sad Sack '57
Silk Stockings '57
Around the World in 80 Days '56
Meet Me in Las Vegas '56
Promise to Murder '56
20,000 Leagues under the Sea '54
Beat the Devil '53
The Lost One '51
Quicksand '50
Casbah '48
My Favorite Brunette '47
The Beast with Five Fingers '46
Black Angel '46
The Chase '46
Arsenic and Old Lace '44
Hollywood Canteen '44
The Mask of Dimitrios '44
Passage to Marseilles '44
Background to Danger '43
All Through the Night '42
The Boogie Man Will Get You '42
Casablanca '42
Invisible Agent '42
The Maltese Falcon '41
They Met in Bombay '41
Strange Cargo '40
Stranger on the Third Floor '40
You'll Find Out '40
Mr. Moto in Danger Island '39
Mr. Moto's Last Warning '39
Mr. Moto Takes a Vacation '39
Mr. Moto Takes a Chance '38
Mr. Moto's Gamble '38
Mysterious Mr. Moto '38
Thank you, Mr. Moto '37
Think Fast, Mr. Moto '37

The Secret Agent '36
Crime and Punishment '35
Mad Love '35
The Man Who Knew Too Much '34
F.P. 1 Doesn't Answer '33
M '31

Joan Lorring (1926-)
Good Sam '48
The Gangster '47
The Corn Is Green '45

Diana Lorys (1940-)
House of Psychotic Women '73
Fangs of the Living Dead '68
Lightning Bolt '67
The Texican '66
The Awful Dr. Orloff '62

Susanne Lothar (1960-)
The Piano Teacher '01
Funny Games '97

Eb Lottimer (1950-)
Diamondbacks '99
Terminal on Mars '97
Bloodfist 7: Manhunt '95
Dead Center '94
Beyond the Call of Duty '92
Quake '92
The Finest Hour '91
Futurekick '91
Streets '90
Lords of the Deep '89
Stripped to Kill II: Live Girls '89
Quicker Than the Eye '88

Alexander Lou
Ninja the Battalion '90
Ninja in the U.S.A. '88
Ninja Condors '87
Mafia vs. Ninja '84

Louanne (1970-)
A Night in the Life of Jimmy Reardon '88
Missing Pieces '83
The Long Days of Summer '80
Oh, God! Book 2 '80

Lance Loud (1950-2001)
Armistead Maupin's Tales of the City '93
Inside Monkey Zetterland '93

Dorothy Loudon (1933-2003)
Midnight in the Garden of Good and Evil '97
Garbo Talks '84

Jackie Loughery (1930-)
D.I. '57
Pardners '56
Abbott and Costello Go to Mars '53

Lori Loughlin (1965-)
Moondance Alexander '07
Critical Mass '00
One of Her Own '97
To Grandmother's House We Go '94
Doing Time on Maple Drive '92
The Night Before '88
Back to the Beach '87
Rad '86
The New Kids '85
Secret Admirer '85
Amityville 3: The Demon '83

Jonathan Loughran (1966-)
Death Proof '07
I Now Pronounce You Chuck and Larry '07
Grandma's Boy '06
Anger Management '03

Bill Louie
Fist of Fear, Touch of Death '80
The Bodyguard '76

Joe Louis (1914-81)
This Is the Army '43
The Spirit of Youth '37

Justin Louis (1967-)
S'nooter '07
Dawn of the Dead '04
Silierto Dance '03
Everything Put Together '00
National Lampoon's Dad's
  Week Off '97
Elood & Donuts '95
The Big Slice '96
Hello Mary Lou: Prom Night
  2 '87

Patrick Louis
Cinderella Man '35

Julia Louis-Dreyfus (1961-)
Geppeto '00
Animal Farm '99 (V)
A Bug's Life '98 (V)
Deconstructing Harry '97
Father's Day '96
North '94
Jack the Bear '93
National Lampoon's
  Christmas Vacation '89
Troll '86

Anita Louise (1915-70)
Retreat, Hell! '52
Love Letters '45
Casanova Brown '44
Hermon of Michigan '41
The Villain Still Pursued
  Her '41
Wagon's Westward '40
The Gorilla '39
The Little Princess '39
Marie Antoinette '38
The Sisters '38
That Certain Woman '37
Anthony Adverse '36
The Story of Louis Pasteur '36
Judge Priest '34
Millie '31
Square Shoulders '29

Tina Louise (1934-)
Johnny Suede '92
Dixie Lanes '88
C.C. and Stiggs '87
Evils of the Night '85
Hellfiders '84
The Happy Ending '69
How to Commit Marriage '69
The Wrecking Crew '68
Mean Dog Blues '78
Nightmare in Badnem
  County '76
Death Scream '75
The Stepford Wives '75
The Good Guys and the
  Bad Guys '69
The Trap '55
God's Little Acre '58
Armored Command '61
The Day of the Outlaw '59

Willard Louis (1882-926)
Dor Juan '26
Beau Brummel '24
Robin Hood '22

Courtney Love (1964-)
Trapped '02
Beat '00
Man on the Moon '99
200 Cigarettes '98
Basquiat '96
Feeling Minnesota '96
The People vs. Larry Flynt '96

Darlene Love (1938-)
Lethal Weapon 4 '98
Lethal Weapon 3 '92
Lethal Weapon 2 '89
Lethal Weapon '87

Darris Love
Sucker Free City '05

Faizon Love (1968-)
Shrunken Heads '94
The Perfect Holiday '07
Who's Your Caddy? '07
Idlewild '06
Just My Luck '06
Elf '03
Wonderland '03
Blue Crush '02
Made '01
Inhumanity '00
Three Strikes '00
The Replacements '00
The Players Club '98
Fear of a Black Hat '94
Bebe's Kids '92 (V)

Lucretia Love
Dr. Heckyl and Mr. Hype '80

Montagu Love (1877-1943)
Wings over the Pacific '43
Lady for a Night '42
Sherlock Holmes: The
  Voice of Terror '42
All This and Heaven Too '40
The Mark of Zorro '40
The Son of Monte Cristo '40
Gunga Din '39
The Adventures of Robin
  Hood '38
A Damsel in Distress '37
The Prince and the Pauper '37
Prisoner of Zenda '37
Lloyds of London '36
One in a Million '36
The Crusades '35
His Double Life '33
Murder on the High Seas '32

Mother Love (1953-)
Twinsisters '95
The Surgeon '94
Armistead Maupin's Tales
  of the City '93
Mr. Nanny '93

Suzanna Love
Boogey Man 2 '83
Boogey Man '93
The Poppy Is Also a Flower '66
Roman Spring of Mrs.
  Stone '61
Mora's for Women '31
Cocaine Cowboys '79
Broadway Melody '29
The King on Main Street '25
The Lost World '25
Soul-Fire '25
The Sea Lion '21
Intolerance '16

Victor Love (1957-)
A Gun, a Car, a Blonde '97
The Assassination File '96
Gang Related '96
Final Shot: The Hank
  Gathers Story '92
Guilty as Innocence '91
Heaven Is a Playground '91
Native Son '86

Alec Lovejoy (1893-)
Murder on Lenox Avenue '41

Frank Lovejoy (1914-62)
Moon over Harlem '39
The Hitch-Hiker '53
House of Wax '53
Retreat, Hell! '52
The Winning Team '52
I'll See You in My Dreams '51
In a Lonely Place '50
South Sea Sinner '50
Three Secrets '50

Jacqueline Lovell (1974-)
A Place Called Truth '98
Erotic House of Wax '97
Hideous '97
Lolita 2000 '97
Femalien '96
Head of the Family '96

Pedro Lovell (1945-)
Rocky Balboa '06
Rocky '76

Raymond Lovell (1900-53)
Appointment with Crime '45
Hotel Reserve '44
Immortal Battalion '44
Contraband '40

Ray Lovelock (1950-)
King of the Damned '36
From Hell to Victory '79
You've Got to Have Heart '77
Autopsy '74
Let Sleeping Corpses Lie '74
One Russian Summer '73
Fiddler on the Roof '71

Devonsville Terror '83
Olivia '83
Brainwaves '82
The Boogey Man '80
Acam Sandler's 8 Crazy
  Nights '02 (V)
Good Advice '01
3C00 Miles to Graceland '01
Americano '55
The Finger Man '55
Shack Out on 101 '55
Strategic Air Command '55
Men of the Fighting Lady '54

Alex Lowe (1968-)
Everybody's Famous! '00
Character '97

Victor Low (1962-)
36 Hours '64
Mobster '58
Rhapsody '54

Celia Lovsky (1897-1979)
The Strange Case of the
  End of Civilization As We
  Know It '93
Sweet William '79
The Bawdy Adventures of
  Tom Jones '76
No Sex Please—We're
  British '73
O Lucky Man! '73
Theatre of Blood '73
The Ruling Class '72
If... '69

Arthur Lowe (1915-82)
Peter's Friends '92
Haunted '95
This Sporting Life '63
Black Tide '58
Kind Hearts and Coronets '49

The Stepford Wives '04
Dickie Roberts: Former
  Child Star '03
Trapped in Paradise '94
National Lampoon's
  Loaded Weapon 1 '93
A League of Their Own '92
Mom and Dad Save the
  World '92
High School High '96
The Great White Hype '96
The Wedding Singer '97
Happiness '98
Lost and Found '99
Small Time Crooks '00
Sand '00
Little Nicky '00
Jumpin' Jack Flash '86
Big '88
My Stepmother Is an Alien '88
North '94
Wayne's World '92
The Finest Hour '91
Tommy Boy '95
Frank and Jesse '94
Stephen King's The Stand '94

Chad Lowe (1968-)
Unfaithful '02
Acceptable Risk '01
Take Me Home: The
  John Denver Story '00
Floating '97
Apartment Complex '98
In the Presence of Mine
  Enemies '97
Nobody's Perfect '90
True Blood '89
Apprentice to Murder '88
Silence of the Heart '84
Quiet Days in Hollywood '97

Dorothy Lovett (1915-98)
Call Out the Marines '42
They Meet Again '41
Courageous Dr. Christian '40
Dr. Christian Meets the
  Woman '40
Remedy for Riches '40

Ed Lover (1963-)
Gunmen '93
Who's the Man? '93

Black Christmas '06
Final Destination 3 '06
Blood Angels '05
Insomnia '02
Children of the Corn:
  Revelation '01

Crystal Lowe (1981-)
Wrong Turn 2: Dead End '07

Lyle Lovett (1959-)
The New Guy '02
Cookie's Fortune '99
Fear and Loathing in Las
  Vegas '98
The Opposite of Sex '98
Bastard out of Carolina '96
Trading Favors '97
Ready to Wear '94
The Player '92
Short Cuts '93

David Lovgren (1969-)
Something More '99
Live Bait '95

Jon Lovitz (1957-)
The Benchwarmers '06
I Could Never Be Your
  Woman '07
Bailey's Billion$ '05
The Producers '05

Edmund Lowe (1890-1971)
Heller in Pink Tights '60
Wings of Eagles '57

Rob Lowe (1964-)
Stir of Echoes 2: The
  Homecoming '07
A Perfect Day '06
Thank You for Smoking '06
The Christmas Blessing '05
Jiminy Glick in LaLa Wood '05
Salem's Lot '04
View from the Top '03
The Christmas Shoes '02
Escape under Pressure '00
Proximity '00
The Specials '00
Atomic Train '99
Austin Powers 2: The Spy
  Who Shagged Me '99
Dead Silent '99
Crazy Six '98
For Hire '98
Outrage '98
Contact '97
Hostile Intent '97
Living in Peril '97
Jack Higgins' Midnight Man '96
First Degree '95
Jack Higgins' On
  Dangerous Ground '95
Mulholland Falls '95
Stroke of Midnight '90
Bad Influence '90
Masquerade '88
Illegally Yours '87
Square Dance '87
About Last Night... '86
Youngblood '86
St. Elmo's Fire '85
The Hotel New Hampshire '84
Oxford Blues '84
Class '83
The Outsiders '83

Susan Lowe
Serial Mom '94
Hairspray '88
Polyester '81
Desperate Living '77
Female Trouble '74
Multiple Maniacs '71

Carey Lowell (1961-)
Fierce Creatures '96
Leaving Las Vegas '95
Sleepless in Seattle '93
Road to Ruin '91
The Guardian '90
Down Twisted '90
License to Kill '89
Me and Him '89
Club Paradise '86
Dangerously Close '86

Tom Lowell (1941-)
The Carpetbaggers '64

Patrick Lowe
Primal Rage '90
Slumber Party Massacre 2 '87

Harrison Lowe
Buffalo Soldiers '97
Geronimo '93
The Eyes of Youth '19
My Antonia '94
Basquiat '96
Jane Doe '96
Nadia '95
Amateur '94
Immortality '98
In the Presence of Mine
  Enemies '97
S.mple Men '92

Carolyn Lowery
Octopus '00
Vicious Circles '97

Robert Lowery (1914-71)
The Undertaker and His
  Pals '67
Johnny Reno '66
The Rise and Fall of Legs
  Diamond '60
Western Pacific Agent '51
Border Rangers '50
Gunfire '50
Shot Silly the Kid '50
Train to Tombstone '50
Call of the Forest '49
Outlaw Gang '49
Dangerous Passage '44
Dark Mountain '44
The Mummy's Ghost '44
Mystery of the Riverboat '44
Revenge of the Zombies '43
Dawn on the Great Divide '42
Lure of the Islands '42
Murder over New York '40
Drums Along the Mohawk '39

Todd Louiso (1970-)
School for Scoundrels '06
Snakes on a Plane '06
Thank You for Smoking '06
High Fidelity '00
8 Heads in a Duffel Bag '96
Jerry Maguire '96
The Rock '96
Apollo 13 '95

Tim Lounibos
Life Tastes 3ood '99
Steel Sharks '97

Alan Lowe
The Apple '80
That Sinking Feeling '79

Bessie Love (1898-1986)
Vampyres '74
Catlow '71
Sunday, Bloody Sunday '71
Isadora '68

Edmund Lowe (1890-1971)
Good Sam '48
Dillinger '45
Call Out the Marines '42
I Love You Again '40
Every Day's a Holiday '38
Get Well Soon '01
No More Women '34
Dinner at Eight '33
Women of All Nations '31
Misleading Lady '32
Chandu the Magician '32
The Squeaker '37

William E. (W.E., W.A.) Lowery (1885-1941)
Robin Hood '22
The Nut '21
Reggie Mixes In '16

Klaus Lowitsch (1936-2002)
The Lamb '15

Lynn Lowry (1947-)
The Odessa File '74
Sugar Cookies '77
Fighting Mad '76
They Came from Within '75
The Crazies '73
Score '73
Shadow of Angels '76
Cross of Iron '76
Despair '78
Braun '79
The Marriage of Maria
  Braun '79

Tom Lowell (1941-)
The Carpetbaggers '64
Dangerously Close '86

Carolyn Lowery
Operation Intercept '95
Extreme Ops '02
Gotcha! '85

Curt Lowens (1925-)
Operation Intercept '95
Invisible: The Chronicles of
  Benjamin Knight '93

Edmund Lowe (1890-1971)
The Manchurian Candidate '62
The Guardian '90

A Midnight Clear '92
Werewolf in a Girl's
  Dormitory '61

Andrew Lowry (1970-)
Conspiracy of Fear '96
Color of Night '94

Elina Lowensohn (1967-)
Fay Grim '06
Dark Water '05
Get Well Soon '01
Six Ways to Sunday '99
Quicksand '01

Robert Lowery (1914-71)
Queen of the Amazons '47
Death Valley '46
God's Country '46
House of Horrors '46
Dangerous Passage '44
Navy Way '44
Rhythm Parade '43
Highway 13 '48
Big Town '47

Sam Lowry
See Steven Soderbergh

Morton Lowry (1914-87)
Immortal Sergeant '43
Dawn Patrol '38
Mandroid '93

T.J. Lowther (1986-)
Mad Love '95
One Christmas '95
A Perfect World '93

Myrna Loy (1905-93)
Summer Solstice '81
Just Tell Me What You Want '80
The End '78
Ants '77
Airport '75 '75
From the Terrace '60
Midnight Lace '60
Lonelyhearts '58
The Ambassador's Daughter '56
Belles on Their Toes '52
Cheaper by the Dozen '50
The Red Pony '49
Mr. Blandings Builds His Dream House '48
The Bachelor and the Bobby-Soxer '47
Song of the Thin Man '47
The Best Years of Our Lives '46
The Thin Man Goes Home '44
Love Crazy '41
Shadow of the Thin Man '41
I Love You Again '40
Another Thin Man '39
The Rains Came '39
Test Pilot '38
Too Hot to Handle '38
Double Wedding '37
Evelyn Prentice '34
Manhattan Melodrama '34
The Thin Man '34
Night Flight '33
Penthouse '33
The Jazz Singer '27
Don Juan '26
So This Is Paris '26
Topaze '33
The Animal Kingdom '32
Arrowsmith '32
The Mask of Fu Manchu '32
Vanity Fair '32
A Connecticut Yankee '31
Consolation Marriage '31
Rogue of the Rio Grande '30

Ivan Lucas
Mama Africa '02
Ernest in the Army '97

Jessica Lucas
Cloverfield '08

Josh(ua) Lucas (1972-)
The Covenant '06
Glory Road '06
Poseidon '06
Empire Falls '05
An Unfinished Life '05
Stealth '05
Around the Bend '04
Undertow '04
Hulk '03
Secondhand Lions '03
Wonderland '03
Coastlines '02
A Beautiful Mind '01
Cash Crop '01
The Deep End '01
Session 9 '01
The Weight of Water '00
American Psycho '99
No Money Down '97
Class of '61 '92

Laurent Lucas (1965-)
Lemming '05
Who Killed Bambi? '03
With a Friend Like Harry '00
Pola X '99

Lisa Lucas (1961-)
Hadley's Rebellion '84
Forbidden Love '82
The Migrants '74
A House without a Christmas Tree '72

Peter J. Lucas (1962-)
Inland Empire '06
Heart of Stone '01

Wilfrid Lucas (1871-1940)
A Chump at Oxford '40
Roaring Speedboats '37
Dishonored '31
The Phantom '31
Cyclone Cavalier '25

William Lucas (1926-)
The Very Edge '63
X The Unknown '56
The Prizefighter and the Lady '33

Angela Luce (1938-)
'Tis a Pity She's a Whore '73
The Decameron '70

Enrique Lucero (1920-89)
Night Sun '90
Jean de Florette '87
Manon of the Spring '87
Half of Heaven '86
Kaos '85

Liping Lu (1961-)
Shadow Magic '00
The Blue Kite '93

Lisa Lu (1931-)
I Love Trouble '94
The Joy Luck Club '93
Demon Seed '77

Arthur Lucan (1887-1954)
My Son, the Vampire '52
Old Mother Riley's Jungle Treasure '51
Old Mother Riley, Headmistress '50
Old Mother Riley's New Venture '49
Old Mother Riley's Ghosts '41

Margarita Lozano (1931-)
Night Sun '90

Laurent Lucas (1965-)

Fabrice Luchini (1951-)
Moliere '07
Intimate Strangers '04
On Guard! '03
Beaumarchais the Scoundrel '96
Colonel Chabert '94
Uranus '91
La Discrete '90
Full Moon in Paris '84
Perceval '78

Charles (Chip) Lucia
Primary Target '89
Hospital Massacre '81

Laurence Luckinbill (1934-)
Dash and Lilly '99
Star Trek 5: The Final Frontier '89
Cocktail '88
Messenger of Death '88
To Heal a Nation '88
Not for Publication '84
Mating Season '81
Ike '79
The Promise '79
The Lindbergh Kidnapping Case '76

The Money '75
Death Sentence '74
Panic on the 5:22 '74
The Boys in the Band '70

William Lucking (1942-)
The Rundown '03
K-PAX '01
The Last Best Sunday '98
The Trigger Effect '96
Rescue Me '93
Duplicates '92
Naked Lie '89
Kung Fu: The Movie '86
Humanoid Defender '85
Coast to Coast '80
Doc Savage '75
Hell's Belles '69

Ludacris
Crash '05
Hustle & Flow '05
2 Fast 2 Furious '03

Barbara Luddy (1908-79)
Sleeping Beauty '59 (V)
Lady and the Tramp '55 (V)

Jack Luden (1902-51)
Phantom Gold '38
The Last Outlaw '27

Charles Ludlam (1943-87)
The Big Easy '87
Impostors '80

Patrick Ludlow (1903-96)
Gangway '37
Evergreen '34

Pamela Ludwig
Pale Blood '91
Race for Glory '89
Dead Man Walking '88
Rush Week '88
Death of an Angel '86
Over the Edge '79

Salem Ludwig (1915-2007)
Family Business '89
I Love You, Alice B. Toklas! '68

Laurette Luez (1928-99)
Ballad of a Gunfighter '64
Prehistoric Women '50
D.O.A. '49

Lorna Luft (1952-)
Life with Judy Garland—Me and My Shadows '01
Where the Boys Are '84 '84
Grease 2 '82

Bela Lugosi (1882-1956)
The Black Sleep '56
Plan 9 from Outer Space '56
Bride of the Monster '55
Glen or Glenda? '53
Bela Lugosi Meets a Brooklyn Gorilla '52
My Son, the Vampire '52
Abbott and Costello Meet Frankenstein '48
Scared to Death '46
The Body Snatcher '45
One Body Too Many '44
Return of the Ape Man '44
Zombies on Broadway '44
The Ape Man '43
Ghost on the Loose '43
Return of the Vampire '43
The Black Dragons '42
Bowery at Midnight '42
The Corpse Vanishes '42
Frankenstein Meets the Wolfman '42
The Ghost of Frankenstein '42
Night Monster '42
The Black Cat '41
The Devil Bat '41
The Invisible Ghost '41
Spooks Run Wild '41
The Wolf Man '41
Black Friday '40
The Saint's Double Trouble '40
You'll Find Out '40

The Gorilla '39
The Human Monster '39
Ninotchka '39
The Phantom Creeps '39
S.O.S. Coast Guard '37
Son of Frankenstein '39
The Invisible Ray '36
Postal Inspector '36
Shadow of Chinatown '36
Mark of the Vampire '35
Murder by Television '35
Mysterious Mr. Wong '35
The Mystery of the Mary Celeste '35
The Raven '35
The Black Cat '34
Chandu on the Magic Island '34
Return of Chandu '34
The Death Kiss '33
International House '33
Night of Terror '33
Whispering Shadow '33
Chandu the Magician '32
Island of Lost Souls '32
Murders in the Rue Morgue '32
The White Zombie '32
The Black Camel '31
Dracula '31
Midnight Girl '25

James Luisi (1928-2002)
Feds '88
Lethal Woman '88
Murphy's Law '86
The Dark Side '84
Fade to Black '80
One in a Million: The Ron LeFlore Story '78
Stunts '77

Paul Lukas (1887-1971)
Lord Jim '65
55 Days at Peking '63
Fun in Acapulco '63
20,000 Leagues under the Sea '54
Kim '50
Berlin Express '48
Whispering City '47
Deadline at Dawn '46
Experiment Perilous '45
Uncertain Glory '44
Watch on the Rhine '43
The Monster and the Girl '41
The Ghost Breakers '40
Strange Cargo '40
Lady in Distress '39
The Mutiny of the Elsinore '39
The Lady Vanishes '38
Dinner at the Ritz '37
Dodsworth '36
The Three Musketeers '35
Little Women '33
No One Man '32
Vice Squad '31

Paul Lukather (1936-)
Hands of a Stranger '62
Dinosaurus! '60

Benny Luke
La Cage aux Folles 3: The Wedding '86
La Cage aux Folles 2 '81
La Cage aux Folles '78

Derek Luke (1974-)
Definitely, Maybe '08
Lions for Lambs '07
Catch a Fire '06
Glory Road '06
Friday Night Lights '04
Spartan '04
Biker Boyz '03
Pieces of April '03
Antwone Fisher '02

Jorge Luke
Salvador '86

Keye Luke (1904-91)
Alice '90
Gremlins 2: The New Batch '90

The Mighty Quinn '89
Dead Heat '88
Kung Fu: The Movie '86
Blade in Hong Kong '85
Gremlins '84
The Amsterdam Kill '78
Noon Sunday '75
Kung Fu '72
Battle Hell '56
Across the Pacific '42
The Falcon's Brother '42
Bowery Blitzkrieg '41
Burma Convoy '41
Let's Go Collegiate '41
The Gang's All Here '40
No, No Nanette '40
Phantom of Chinatown '40
The Green Hornet '39
Mr. Moto's Gamble '38
Charlie Chan at Monte Carlo '37
Charlie Chan at the Olympics '37
Charlie Chan on Broadway '37
Charlie Chan at the Opera '36
Charlie Chan at the Race Track '36
Charlie Chan in Paris '35
Charlie Chan in Shanghai '35
The Good Earth '37
Mad Love '35

Wolfgang Lukschy (1905-83)
Frozen Alive '64

Folco Lulli (1912-70)
Lightning Bolt '67
The Organizer '64
The Mercenaries '62
The Great War '59
Wages of Fear '55
Variety Lights '51

Pierro Lulli (1923-91)
Fistful of Lead '70
The Triumph of Hercules '66
Samson Against the Sheik '62

Lum & Abner
See Chester Lauck; Norris Goff

Carl Lumbly (1952-)
Little Richard '00
Men of Honor '00
Buffalo Soldiers '97
Nightjohn '96
America's Dream '95
Eyes of a Witness '94
South Central '92
Brother Future '91
Pacific Heights '90
To Sleep with Anger '90
Everybody's All American '88
Judgment in Berlin '88
The Bedroom Window '87
The Adventures of Buckaroo Banzai Across the Eighth Dimension '84
Escape from Alcatraz '79

Jenny Lumet (1967-)
Q & A '90

Sidney Lumet (1924-)
Tougher Than Leather '88
Running on Empty '88
One Third of a Nation '39

Joanna Lumley (1946-)
Doogal '05 (V)
Tim Burton's Corpse Bride '05 (V)
Ella Enchanted '04
Eurotrip '04
The Cat's Meow '01
Whispers: An Elephant's Tale '00 (V)
Maybe Baby '99
Coming Home '98
Parting Shots '98
A Rather English Marriage '98

Prince Valiant '97
Absolutely Fabulous: The Last Shout '96
James and the Giant Peach '96 (V)
Innocent Lies '95
Cold Comfort Farm '94
Shirley Valentine '89
Weather in the Streets '84
Curse of the Pink Panther '83
The Satanic Rites of Dracula '73
On Her Majesty's Secret Service '69

Barbara Luna (1939-)
The Concrete Jungle '82
The Hanged Man '74
Gentle Savage '73
The Gatling Gun '72
Firecreek '68

Diego Luna (1979-)
Criminal '04
Dirty Dancing: Havana Nights '04
The Terminal '04
Open Range '03
Frida '02
Y Tu Mama Tambien '01

Art Lund (1915-90)
Bucktown '75
Black Caesar '73
The Last American Hero '73

Deanna Lund (1937-)
Red Wind '91
Elves '89
Hardly Working '81
Dr. Goldfoot and the Bikini Machine '66

Jana Lund (1933-91)
Married Too Young '62
Loving You '57

John Lund (1913-92)
Wackiest Ship in the Army '61
Dakota Incident '56
Latin Lovers '53
My Friend Irma '49
A Foreign Affair '48
The Perils of Pauline '47
To Each His Own '46

Lucille Lund (1913-2002)
Prison Shadows '36
The Black Cat '34

Nicole Lund
Grizzly Mountain '97
The Legend of Wolf Mountain '92

Zoe Lund
See Zoe Tamerlis

Christine Lunde
Masque of the Red Death '90
Hardcase and Fist '89
Dead End City '88

Dolph Lundgren (1959-)
Missionary Man '07
Detention '03
Hidden Agenda '01
Agent Red '00
Jill the Ripper '00
Bridge of Dragons '99
The Last Warrior '99
Storm Catcher '99
Sweepers '99
The Minion '98
The Peacekeeper '98
Blackjack '97
Silent Trigger '97
Johnny Mnemonic '95
Army of One '94
Hidden Assassin '94
Men of War '94
Pentathlon '94
Universal Soldier '92
Cover-Up '91
Showdown in Little Tokyo '91
I Come in Peace '90
The Punisher '90

Red Scorpion '89
Masters of the Universe '87
A View to a Kill '85
Rocky 4 '85

William Lundigan (1914-75)
Terror Ship '54
The White Orchid '54
I'd Climb the Highest Mountain '51
Love Nest '51
Follow Me Quietly '49
Pinky '49
State Department: File 649 '49
Dishonored Lady '47
Andy Hardy's Double Life '42
Three Smart Girls Grow Up '39
Danger on the Air '38

Vic Lundin
Robinson Crusoe on Mars '64

Steve Lundquist
Killer Tomatoes Eat France '91
Killer Tomatoes Strike Back '90
Return of the Killer Tomatoes! '88

Jessica Lundy (1966-)
Just a Little Harmless Sex '99
Something About Sex '98
RocketMan '97
The Stupids '96
I Love Trouble '94
Single White Female '92
Madhouse '90
Bright Lights, Big City '88
Caddyshack 2 '88
Vampire's Kiss '88

Kenneth Lundy
Sioux City Sue '46
Junior G-Men '40

Jamie Luner (1971-)
Sacrifice '00
Confessions of Sorority Girls '94
The St. Tammany Miracle '94

The Sign of Four '83
Oliver Twist '82
Excalibur '81

Kathleen Luong (1976-)
Missing Brendan '03
Two for the Seesaw '62
Ma Barker's Killer Brood '60
'78
Food of the Gods '76
Devil's Rain '75
Junior Bonner '72
While the City Sleeps '56
The Big Knife '55
Private Hell 36 '54
The Bigamist '53
Beware, My Lovely '52
On Dangerous Ground '51
Lust for Gold '49
Road House '48
The Man I Love '46
Hollywood Canteen '44
Forever and a Day '43
Thank Your Lucky Stars '43
High Sierra '41
The Sea Wolf '41
They Drive by Night '40
The Adventures of Sherlock Holmes '39
Sea Devils '37
One Rainy Afternoon '36
The Gay Desperado '36
The Ghost Camera '33

Alberto Lupo (1924-84)
Django Shoots First '74
The Agony and the Ecstasy '65
Coriolanus, Man without a Country '64

Patti LuPone (1949-)
City by the Sea '02
Monday Night Mayhem '02
Heist '01
State and Main '00
Cold Blooded '00
Bonanno: A Godfather's Story '99
Just Looking '99
Summer of Sam '99
The 24 Hour Woman '99
Song Spinner '95
The Water Engine '92
Family Prayers '91
Driving Miss Daisy '89
LBJ: The Early Years '88
Wise Guys '86
Witness '85
Fighting Back '82
1941 '79

Roldano Lupi (1909-89)
The Giant of Metropolis '61
The Mongols '60

Ida Lupino (1914-95)

Peter Lupus (1932-)
Acting on Impulse '93
Think Big '90
Pulsebeat '85
Escapist '83
Muscle Beach Party '64

John Lurie (1952-)
New Rose Hotel '98
The Bacchantes '63
The Lion of Thebes '64
Stuart Saves His Family '94
Stranger than Paradise '84
Permanent Vacation '84
Down by Law '86

Jaques Lussier (1960-)
Norman's Awesome Experience '88
Pouvoir Intime '87

Aaron Lustig (1956-)
Tuesdays with Morrie '99
Pinocchio's Revenge '96
The Shadow '94

A Mighty Wind '03
Alvin and the Chipmunks '07
For Your Consideration '06
Eye of the Dolphin '06
Ballad of Ricky Bobby '06
Bam Bam & Celeste '05
The 40 Year Old Virgin '05
Sleepover '04
Exposed '03

Jane Lynch (1960-)
Talladega Nights: The

Angel Baby '95
Nothing Personal '95
Princess Caraboo '94
The Secret of Roan Inish '94
In the Name of the Father '93

Vampires of Sorority Row:
Kickboxers From Hell '99
Bram Stoker's The Mummy '97

Eric Lutes (1962-)
Distant Justice '92
The Twelve Dogs of Christmas '05
Darkman '90
Maniac '80

William Lustig (1955-)
Army of Darkness '92

John Lynch (1961-)
Tornado '76
The Bridge of San Luis Rey '04
Dolemite 2: Human Tornado '76
H.P. Lovecraft's Necronomicon: Book of the Dead '93
Lassie '05
Conspiracy of Silence '03
Evelyn '02
The Seventh Stream '01
The Quarry '98
Sliding Doors '97
Moll Flanders '96
Some Mother's Son '96
This is the Sea '96

Jesse James Meets Frankenstein's Daughter '65
The Rebel Set '59
Battle Cry '55
Diane '55
All the Brothers Were Valiant '53

Dorothy Lyman (1947-)
I Love Trouble '94
Ruby in Paradise '93
Camp Cucamonga: How I Spent My Summer Vacation '90
Ollie Hopnoodle's Haven of Bliss '88
Summer Fantasy '84
The 300 Year Weekend '71

Evan Lurie (1954-2003)
Mortal Challenge '97
Hologram Man '95
Shadow Warriors '95
T-Force '94
American Kickboxer 2: To the Death '93
Ring of Fire 2: Blood and Steel '92
Martial Law 2: Undercover '91

Luis Luque (1956-)
Little Children '06 (V)
The Siege '98
Floating '97

David Lynch (1946-)
On the Fiddle '61
Zelly & Me '88
Twin Peaks: Fire Walk with Me '92

Helen Lynch (1900-65)
Smouldering Fires '25
The Return of Grey Wolf '22

Will Lyman
Dallas 352 '03
Summer Catch '01
Joe Somebody '01

Jimmy Lynch
Avenging Disco Godfather '76

Alfred Lynch (1931-2003)
The Krays '90
Blockhouse '73
The Hill '65

Pauline Lynch
Trainspotting '95

Richard Lynch (1940-)
Diamond Run '00
Blackout '00
Total Force '98
Under Oath '97
Warrior of Justice '96
Cyborg 3: The Recycler '95
Destination Vegas '95
Dragon Fury '95
Midnight Confessions '95
Werewolf '95
Scanner Cop '94
Terrified '94
Maximum Force '92
Merlin '92
Alligator 2: The Mutation '90
The Forbidden Dance '90
Invasion Force '90
Lockdown '90
Puppet Master 3: Toulon's Revenge '90
Trancers 2: The Return of Jack Deth '90
High Stakes '89
One Man Force '89
Aftershock '88
Bad Dreams '88
The Baron '88
Little Nikita '88
Nightforce '86
The Barbarians '87
Cut and Run '85
Invasion U.S.A. '85
Savage Dawn '84
Sword & the Sorcerer '82
Sizzle '81

Ken Lynch (1910-90)
My Pleasure Is My Business '74
Legend of Tom Dooley '59
Pork Chop Hill '59

Kate Lynch
Coast to Coast '04
Def-Con 4 '85
My Story '92
Reckless Disregard '84
Meatballs '79

Kelly Lynch (1959-)
Northern Lights '79
A Royal Scandal '97
The Secret of Roan Inish '94
Kings in Grass Castles '97

Amy Lynden
Big City Blues '99
Slaves of Hollywood '99

Jaques Lussier
Slaves of Hollywood '99

Paul Lynde (1926-82)
The Villain '79
Rabbit Test '78
Hugo the Hippo '76 (V)
Charlotte's Web '73 (V)
Journey Back to Oz '71 (V)
The Glass Bottom Boat '66
Beach Blanket Bingo '65
Send Me No Flowers '64
How Sweet It Is! '68
Bye, Bye, Birdie '63
Son of Flubber '63
Under the Yum-Yum Tree '63
New Faces of 1952 '54

Helen Lynd (1902-92)
So Proudly We Hail '43
Hats Off '37

David Copperfield '99
Drowning on Dry Land '00
Howling 6: The Freaks '90
Spirits '90
Balboa '82
Vigilante '83
Blackout '88
Dark Tower '87
Cotter '72

Carol Lynley (1942-)
Gulliver's Travels '95
Stalag Luft '93
Bad Georgia Road '77
The Cat and the Canary '79
Washington Affair '77
Fantasy Island '76
Flood! '76
Four Deuces '75
If It's a Man, Hang Up '75
The Night Stalker '71
Blood Island '68
The Cardinal '63
The Stripper '63
Beware! The Blob '72
Death Stalk '74
The Poseidon Adventure '72

Simon Lyndon (1971-)
Chopper '00

Nicholas Lyndhurst (1961-)
Gulliver's Travels '95

Ann Lynn (1939-)
Estate of Insanity '70
Baby Love '69

Betty Lynn (1926-)
Return to Mayberry '86
Texas John Slaughter: Geronimo's Revenge '60
Meet Me in Las Vegas '56
Cheaper by the Dozen '50
Father Was a Fullback '49
June Bride '48

Susan Lynch (1971-)
Casa de los Babys '03
16 Years of Alcohol '03
From Hell '01
The Mazemaker '01
Nora '00
Beautiful Creatures '00
Waking Ned Devine '98
Ivanhoe '97
The Secret of Roan Inish '94

The Formula '80
Steel '80
Death 'Sport '78
Delta Fox '77
God Told Me To '76
The Premonition '75
Scarecrow '73

Cheryl Lynn
Fate '90
Emanon '86
Thunder Run '86

Leslie Lyles
Coming Soon '99
A Thousand Acres '97
Volcano '97
Fargo '96
Face/Off '97

Steve Lundquist

TI Lung (1946-)
The Legend of Drunken Master '94
A Better Tomorrow, Part 1 '86
Duel of Fists '71

Cherie Lunghi (1953-)
Back to the Secret Garden '01

Robert LuPone (1946-)
Swindled '04
The Devil's Backbone '01
Lisboa '99
Autumn Sun '98
Hombres Armados '97
Martin (Hache) '97
Cronos '94
A Place in the World '92
Killing Grandpa '91
Mayalunta '88
Funny, Dirty Little War '83
Time for Revenge '82

John Lupton (1926-93)
Private Parts '72

Federico Luppi (1934-)

Gary Lydon (1954-)
The Last September '99
Nothing Personal '95
Amazon Warrior '97

Jimmy Lydon (1923-)
Island in the Sky '53
The Magnificent Yankee '50
Life with Father '47
Strange Illusion '45
Little Men '40
Tom Brown's School Days '40
Back Door to Heaven '39

John (Johnny Rotten) Lydon (1956-)
The Independent '00
The Filth and the Fury '99
Corrupt '84

Christine Lydon (1966-)
Merchants of Death '99

Franc Luz (1950-)
The Bad News Bears '76
Ghost Town '88
The Nest '88
Ecstasy '84

Alfred Lutter (1962-)
The Bad News Bears in Breaking Training '77
The Bad News Bears '76

Sihung Lung (1930-2002)
Crouching Tiger, Hidden Dragon '00
Eat Drink Man Woman '94
The Wedding Banquet '93
Pushing Hands '92

John Carroll Lynch (1963-)
Full of It '07
Things We Lost in the Fire '07
Zodiac '07
Looking for Comedy in the Muslim World '06
Mozart and the Whale '05
Catch That Kid '04
Confidence '03
Gothika '03
Live from Baghdad '02
The Good Girl '02
Bubb a Boy '01
Tuesdays with Morrie '99
From the Earth to the Moon '98

Reg Lye (1912-88)
Freedom '82
Walk into Hell '57
King Rat '65

Carol Lynley

Attila '01
Run Silent, Run Deep '59

Amy Lyndon

Simon Lyndon

Diana Lynn (1924-71)
An Annapolis Story '55
The Kentuckian '55
Bedtime for Bonzo '51
My Friend Irma '49
Every Girl Should Be Married '48
Miracle of Morgan's Creek '44
The Major and the Minor '42

Emmett Lynn (1897-1958)
The Fighting Redhead '50
Trail of the Mounties '47

Fonda Lynn
Ninja Brothers of Blood '89
Deadly Darling '85

George Lynn (1906-64)
Teenage Frankenstein '58
To Be or Not to Be '42

Jeffrey Lynn (1909-95)
Tony Rome '67
Home Town Story '51
A Letter to Three Wives '49
For the Love of Mary '48
Song of Old Wyoming '45
Underground '41
All This and Heaven Too '40
The Fighting 69th '40
The Roaring Twenties '39
Four Daughters '38

Jenny Lynn
The Greed of William Hart '48

Jonathan Lynn (1943-)
Greedy '94
Three Men and a Little Lady '90

Mara Lynn (1927-88)
G.I. Jane '51
Leave It to the Marines '51
Sky High '51
Prehistoric Women '50

Meredith Scott Lynn
How to Go Out on a Date in Queens '06
When Do We Eat? '05
Hollywood Homicide '03
Legally Blonde '01
Forces of Nature '99
Standing on Fishes '99
Billy's Hollywood Screen Kiss '98
I Love You, Don't Touch Me! '97

Peter George Lynn (1906-67)
Mr. Wong in Chinatown '39
Mystery Plane '39
Wolf Call '39

Theresa Lynn (1964-)
Psycho Sisters '98
Private Parts '96
Vampire Vixens from Venus '94

Melanie Lynskey (1977-)
Comanche Moon '08
Flags of Our Fathers '06
Say Uncle '05
Serial Slayer '03
Shattered Glass '03
Abandon '02
Sweet Home Alabama '02
Coyote Ugly '00
Shooters '00
Ever After: A Cinderella Story '98
Heavenly Creatures '94

Ben Lyon (1901-79)
Mad About Money '37
Crimson Romance '34
I Cover the Waterfront '33
The Crooked Circle '32
Indiscreet '31
Night Nurse '31
Hell's Angels '30

Earle Lyon (1926-)
Lonesome Trail '55
Silver Star '55
Silent Raiders '54

Richard Lyon (1934-)
The Tender Years '47
Anna and the King of Siam '46

Sue Lyon (1946-)
Alligator '80
End of the World '76
The Invisible Strangler '76
Autopsy '74
Evel Knievel '72
Four Rode Out '69
Film-Flam Man '67
Tony Rome '67
The Night of the Iguana '64
Lolita '62

Wendy Lyon
Hello Mary Lou: Prom Night 2 '87

Natasha Lyonne (1979-)
Robots '05 (V)
Blade: Trinity '04
Madhouse '04
Die Mommie Die! '03
Party Monster '03
Comic Book Villains '02
Night at the Golden Eagle '02
ZigZag '02
American Pie 2 '01
Fast Sofa '01
The Grey Zone '01
Scary Movie 2 '01
If These Walls Could Talk 2 '00
American Pie '99
But I'm a Cheerleader '99
Detroit Rock City '99
Freeway 2: Confessions of a Trickbaby '99
Krippendorf's Tribe '98
Modern Vampires '98
Slums of Beverly Hills '98
Everyone Says I Love You '96

Bruce Lyons
The Navigator '88
Model Behavior '82

Cliff Lyons (1901-74)
The Horse Soldiers '59
She Wore a Yellow Ribbon '49

Elena Lyons (1973-)
Club Dread '04
Face the Music '00

James Lyons (1960-2007)
I Shot Andy Warhol '96
Frisk '95
Postcards from America '95
Poison '91

Jennifer Lyons (1977-)
Killer Pad '06
Tequila Body Shots '99
Tiger Heart '96

Phyllis Lyons (1960-)
The Rat Pack '98
The Casualties of Love: The "Long Island Lolita" Story '93

Robert F. Lyons (1940-)
Counter Measures '99
The Omega Code '99
Ripper Man '96
American Eagle '90
Platoon Leader '87
Murphy's Law '86
Cease Fire '85
Black Oak Conspiracy '77
Shoot Out '71
The Todd Killings '71
Getting Straight '70

Susan Lyons (1957-)
Napoleon '96 (V)
Ebbtide '94
The Winds of Jarrah '83

Tom Lyons
Factotum '06
Burn! '70

Stanislav Lyubshin (1933-)
To See Paris and Die '93
The Theme '79

Monika M.
Nekromantik 2 '91
Nekromantik '87

Tzi Ma
Rush Hour 3 '07
Akeelah and the Bee '06
Red Doors '05
The Ladykillers '04
The Quiet American '02
Catfish in Black Bean Sauce '00
Rush Hour '98
Dante's Peak '97
Red Corner '97
Chain Reaction '96
Golden Gate '93
Rapid Fire '92

Hidde Maas (1944-)
The Delivery '99
Amsterdamned '88

Byron Mabe (1932-2001)
The Doberman Gang '72
The Defilers '65

Ricky Mabe (1983-)
Believe '99
Little Men '98

Kate Maberly (1982-)
Murderous Intent '06
Gulliver's Travels '95
Stephen King's The Langoliers '95
The Secret Garden '93

Eric Mabius (1971-)
Voodoo Moon '05
The Job '03
Resident Evil '02
On the Borderline '01
Tempted '01
The Crow: Salvation '00
The Minus Man '99
Splendor '99
Wirey Spindell '99
Around the Fire '98
Cruel Intentions '98
Black Circle Boys '97
I Shot Andy Warhol '96
Lawn Dogs '96
Welcome to the Dollhouse '95

Moms (Jackie) Mabley (1894-1975)
Amazing Grace '74
Boardinghouse Blues '48
Killer Diller '48

Luke Mably (1976-)
The Prince & Me 2: Royal Wedding '06
The Prince & Me '04

Sunny Mabrey (1975-)
Snakes on a Plane '06
One Last Thing... '05
XXX: State of the Union '05
The New Guy '02

Bernie Mac (1958-)
Ocean's Thirteen '07
Pride '07
Transformers '07
Guess Who '05
Inspector Gadget's Biggest Caper Ever '05 (V)
Mr. 3000 '04
Ocean's Twelve '04
Bad Santa '03
Charlie's Angels: Full Throttle '03
Head of State '03
Ocean's Eleven '01
What's the Worst That Could Happen? '01
Life '99
The Players Club '98
Def Jam's How to Be a Player '97
Don King: Only in America '97
Booty Call '96
Get On the Bus '96
Friday '95
Above the Rim '94
House Party 3 '94

Anne MacAdams (1925-2003)
Don't Look in the Basement '73
Common Law Wife '63

Cal Macaninch (1969-)
Dear Frankie '04
A Mind to Murder '96

James MacArthur (1937-)
Storm Chasers: Revenge of the Twister '98
Hang 'Em High '67
Mosby's Marauders '66
Battle of the Bulge '65
Bedford Incident '65
Cry of Battle '63
Spencer's Mountain '63
The Interns '62
Kidnapped '60
The Swiss Family Robinson '60
Third Man on the Mountain '59
The Light in the Forest '58

Charles Macaulay (1927-99)
The Big Red One '80
Blacula '72

Marc Macaulay (1948-)
Cleaner '07
The Punisher '04
Holy Man '98
Wild Things '98
Cop and a Half '93
Hidden Fears '93

Donald MacBride (1889-1957)
Meet Danny Wilson '52
Holiday Rhythm '50
Buck Privates Come Home '47
Egg and I '47
A Night to Remember '42
The Invisible Woman '40
Michael Shayne: Private Detective '40
Murder over New York '40
The Saint's Double Trouble '40
Blondie Takes a Vacation '39
Charlie Chan at Treasure Island '39
The Flying Irishman '39
The Great Man Votes '38
Room Service '38

Catriona MacCall
See Katherine (Katriona) MacColl

Ralph Macchio (1961-)
Beer League '06
Forever Together '00
Naked in New York '93
My Cousin Vinny '92
Too Much Sun '90
The Karate Kid: Part 3 '89
Distant Thunder '88
Crossroads '86
The Karate Kid: Part 2 '86
The Karate Kid '84
Teachers '84
The Outsiders '83
Up the Academy '80

Aldo Maccione (1935-)
The Chambermaid on the Titanic '97

Katherine (Katriona) MacColl (1954-)
The House by the Cemetery '83
The Beyond '82
Gates of Hell '80

Simon MacCorkindale (1952-)
The Girl Next Door '98
Family of Cops '95
Obsessive Love '84
Jaws 3 '83
Robbers of the Sacred Mountain '83
Sword & the Sorcerer '82
Cabo Blanco '81
The Manions of America '81
Visitor from the Grave '81
Quatermass Conclusion '79
The Riddle of the Sands '79
Death on the Nile '78

Aimi MacDonald (1963-)
Number 1 of the Secret Service '77
Vendetta for the Saint '68

Ann-Marie MacDonald (1958-)
Better Than Chocolate '99
I've Heard the Mermaids Singing '87

Bill MacDonald
Mercy '00
One Kill '00
The Corruptor '99

Edmund MacDonald (1908-51)
Shoot to Kill '47
Detour '46
The Lady Confesses '45
Prison Break '38

J. Farrell MacDonald (1875-1952)
Outlaw Gang '49
Shep Comes Home '49
Texas Masquerade '44
Phantom Killer '42
The Ape Man '43
In Old Cheyenne '41
Riders of the Timberline '41
I Take This Oath '40
Knights of the Range '40
Susannah of the Mounties '39
Come on Rangers '38
Gang Bullets '38
Shadows of the Orient '37
Romance in Manhattan '34
Hearts of Humanity '32
No Man of Her Own '32
Phantom Express '32
Probation '32
13th Guest '32
Touchdown '31
Sunrise '27
Sky High '22

James MacDonald (1906-)
Hollywood Homicide '03
Phone Booth '02
Sour Grapes '98
Cinderella '50 (V)

Jeanette MacDonald (1901-65)
The Sun Comes Up '49
Three Daring Daughters '48
Cairo '42
I Married an Angel '42
Smilin' Through '41
Bitter Sweet '40
New Moon '40
Broadway Serenade '39
Girl of the Golden West '38
Sweethearts '38
The Firefly '37
Maytime '37
Rose Marie '36
San Francisco '36
Naughty Marietta '35
The Cat and the Fiddle '34
The Merry Widow '34
One Hour with You '32
Lottery Bride '30
Monte Carlo '30
The Love Parade '29

Jennifer MacDonald
Campfire Tales '98
Alien Chaser '96
Headless Body in Topless Bar '96
Dead Weekend '95
Clean, Shaven '93

Kelly Macdonald (1977-)
No Country for Old Men '07
Nanny McPhee '06
The Girl in the Cafe '05
Lassie '05
Tristram Shandy: A Cock and Bull Story '05
Finding Neverland '04
Brush with Fate '03
State of Play '03
Gosford Park '01
Strictly Sinatra '01
Entropy '99
Splendor '99
Two Family House '99
The Loss of Sexual Innocence '98
My Life So Far '98
Cousin Bette '97
Stella Does Tricks '96
Trainspotting '95

Kenneth MacDonald (1950-2001)
Touching Evil '97
Storm over Wyoming '50
U-Boat Prisoner '44
Six Gun Gospel '43
Border Vengeance '35

Norm MacDonald (1963-)
Deuce Bigalow: European Gigolo '05
Dr. Dolittle 2 '01 (V)
Screwed '00
Dr. Dolittle '98 (V)
Dirty Work '97
The People vs. Larry Flynt '96
Billy Madison '94

Scott MacDonald
Jarhead '05
Straight into Darkness '04
A Rat's Tale '98 (V)

Shauna Macdonald (1963-)
The Descent '05
Saint Ralph '04

Wallace MacDonald (1891-1978)
Between Fighting Men '32
Daring Danger '32
Hello Trouble '32
The Riding Tornado '32
Texas Cyclone '32
Two-Fisted Law '32
Range Feud '31
Fightin' Ranch '30
Red Signals '27

Wendy MacDonald
Broken Trust '93

William Macdonald
White Noise 2: The Light '07
Hollow Man 2 '06

Andie MacDowell (1958-)
Barnyard '06 (V)
Beauty Shop '05
Tara Road '05
Crush '02
Harrison's Flowers '02
Dinner with Friends '01
Town and Country '01
Muppets from Space '99
The Muse '99
Just the Ticket '98
Shadrach '98
The End of Violence '97
Michael '96
Multiplicity '96
Unstrung Heroes '95
Bad Girls '94
Four Weddings and a Funeral '94
Groundhog Day '93
Short Cuts '93
Deception '92
The Player '92
Hudson Hawk '91
The Object of Beauty '91

Women & Men: In Love '91
There Are No Rules '91
Green Card '90
sex, lies and videotape '89
St. Elmo's Fire '85
Greystoke: The Legend of Tarzan, Lord of the Apes '84

Rita Macedo (1928-93)
The Criminal Life of Archibaldo de la Cruz '55
Nazarin '58

Angus MacFadyen (1964-)
Impulse '08
Redline '07
Fatwa '06
.45 '06
Saw III '06
The Pleasure Drivers '05
Divine Secrets of the Ya-Ya Sisterhood '02
Equilibrium '02
A Woman's a Helluva Thing '01
Jason and the Argonauts '00
Second Skin '00
Styx '00
Titus '99
Facade '98
The Rat Pack '98
Nevada '97
Still Breathing '97
Warriors of Virtue '97
The Brylcreem Boys '96
Braveheart '95
The Lost Language of Cranes '92

Moyna MacGill (1895-1975)
Three Daring Daughters '48

Matthew MacFadyen (1974-)
Pride and Prejudice '05
The Way We Live Now '02
Almost Strangers '01
Enigma '01

Niall MacGinnis (1913-78)
The Viking Queen '67
Island of Terror '66
The War Lord '65
A Face in the Rain '63
Jason and the Argonauts '63
Sword of Sherwood Forest '60
Curse of the Demon '57
Helen of Troy '56
Lust for Life '56
Betrayed '54
Martin Luther '53
No Highway in the Sky '51
Anna Karenina '48
Captain Boycott '47
Henry V '44
The Day Will Dawn '42
Edge of the World '37

Jack MacGowran (1918-73)
The Exorcist '73
King Lear '71
Start the Revolution without Me '70
Wonderwall: The Movie '69
The Fearless Vampire Killers '67
Cul de Sac '66
Doctor Zhivago '65
Lord Jim '65
The Brain '62
The Quiet Man '52

Tara MacGowran (1964-)
The Dawning '88
Las Vegas Serial Killer '86
Secret Places '85

Sterling Macer (1963-)
Double Take '01
The Beast '96
Dragon: The Bruce Lee Story '93

Ali MacGraw (1938-)
Glam '97
Natural Causes '94
Murder Elite '85
The Winds of War '83
Just Tell Me What You Want '80
Players '79
Convoy '78
The Getaway '72
Love Story '70
Goodbye Columbus '69

Justina Machado (1972-)
The Accidental Husband '08
Fatal Contact: Bird Flu in America '06
Torque '04
Final Destination 2 '03
Sticks '98

Ignacy Machowski (1920-2001)
Contract '80
First Spaceship on Venus '60

Gabriel Macht (1972-)
Because I Said So '07
The Good Shepherd '06
Archangel '05
A Love Song for Bobby Long '04
Grand Theft Parsons '03
The Recruit '03
Bad Company '02
American Outlaws '01
Behind Enemy Lines '01
The Audrey Hepburn Story '00
101 Ways (The Things a Girl Will Do to Keep Her Volvo) '00

Stephen Macht (1942-)
DC 9/11: Time of Crisis '04
Watchers Reborn '98
Graveyard Shift '90
Blind Witness '89
A Friendship in Vienna '88
The Monster Squad '87
Agatha Christie's A Caribbean Mystery '83
American Dream '81
Killjoy '81
Enola Gay: The Men, the Mission, the Atomic Bomb '80
Galaxina '80
Nightwing '79
The Choirboys '77

Keegan Macintosh (1984-)
Cutland '81

Angus MacInnes (1947-)
Strange Brew '83
The Sender '82

J.C. MacKenzie
The Return '06
The Aviator '04
Final '01

Jan MacKenzie
The American Angels: Baptism of Blood '89
Gator Bait 2: Cajun Justice '88

Evan MacKenzie
The Kovak Box '06
Possession '02

Georgia Mackenzie
Children of the Night '92
Ghoulies 3: Ghoulies Go to College '91

Kenneth MacKenna (1899-1962)
Judgment at Nuremberg '61
Sin Takes a Holiday '30

Janet MacLachlan (1933-)
For Us, the Living '88
Murphy's Law '86
She's in the Army Now '81
Sophisticated Gents '81
Big Mo '73
Sounder '72
Darker than Amber '70

Andrew MacLachlan
The Adventures of Baron Munchausen '89
Erik the Viking '89
A Fish Called Wanda '88
Monty Python's The Meaning of Life '83

Matthew Mackay
Rocket Attack U.S.A. '58
The Peanut Butter Solution '85

John MacKay
Niagara, Niagara '97
Simple Men '92
Trust '91
Alligator Eyes '90
The Rejuvenator '88
I Was a Teenage TV Terrorist '87
Fat Guy Goes Nutzoid '86
Krush Groove '85
Secret Life of an American Wife '68
Assault on the Rebel Girls '59

Jim MacKrell (1937-)
London Kills Me '91
Cannibal Women in the Avocado Jungle of Death '89

Helen MacKellar (1895-1966)
Sundown Kid '43
Bad Boy '39
Delinquent Parents '38

Charles Mack (1900-27)
America '24
Dream Street '21

Helen Mack (1913-86)
His Girl Friday '40
Fit for a King '37
I Promise to Pay '37
The Wrong Road '37
Milky Way '36
The Return of Peter Grimm '35
She '35
Kiss and Make Up '34
Son of Kong '33
Fargo Express '32
Melody Cruise '32
Struggle '31

Kerry Mack (1957-)
Fantasy Man '84
Savage Attraction '83
Fair Game '82

Wayne Mack (1924-93)
Isle of Secret Passion '82
Graduation Day '81
Black Eliminator '78
Goodbye, Norma Jean '75

Dorothy Mackaill (1903-90)
Bulldog Drummond at Bay '37
No Man of Her Own '32
Kept Husbands '31
Ranson's Folly '26

Fulton Mackay (1922-87)
Porridge '91
Defense of the Realm '85
Local Hero '83
A Sense of Freedom '81
Nothing But the Night '72

Barry Mackay (1906-85)
Sailing Along '38
Gangway '37
The Private Secretary '35
Evergreen '34

Steven Mackintosh (1967-)
Underworld: Evolution '05
The Mother '03
The Criminal '00
Lady Audley's Secret '00
The Land Girls '98
Our Mutual Friend '98
The Ebb-Tide '98
Different for Girls '96
Twelfth Night '96
Blue Juice '95
The Return of the Native '94
A Dark Adapted Eye '93
The Buddha of Suburbia '92

Peter M. MacKenzie
Major League 3: Back to the Minors '98
Tom and Huck '95

Philip Charles MacKenzie
EMs Has Left the Building '04

Anthony Mackie (1979-)
Crossover '06
Freedomland '06
Half Nelson '06
Heavens Fall '06
We Are Marshall '06
The Man '05
Sucker Free City '05
Brother to Brother '04
Haven '04
The Manchurian Candidate '04
Million Dollar Baby '04
She Hate Me '04
8 Mile '02

Allison Mackie
The Gymnast '06
Orginal Sin '01
Me '92

Shirley MacLaine (1934-)
Bewitched '05
In Her Shoes '05
Rumor Has It... '05
These Old Broads '01
The Dress Code '99
Joan of Arc '99
The Evening Star '96
Mrs. Winterbourne '96
A Smile Like Yours '96
Guarding Tess '94
Wrestling Ernest Hemingway '93
Used People '92
Postcards from the Edge '90
Waiting for the Light '90
Steel Magnolias '89
Madame Sousatzka '88
Out on a Limb '87
Cannonball Run 2 '84
Terms of Endearment '83
A Change of Seasons '80
Loving Couples '80
Being There '79
The Turning Point '77
The Possession of Joel Delaney '72
Desperate Characters '71
Two Mules for Sister Sara '70
Sweet Charity '69
The Bliss of Mrs. Blossom '68
Woman Times Seven '67
Gambit '66
Irma La Douce '63
My Geisha '62
Two for the Seesaw '62
All in a Night's Work '61
The Children's Hour '61
The Apartment '60
Can-Can '60
Ocean's 11 '60
Ask Any Girl '59
Career '59
Hot Spell '58
The Matchmaker '58
Some Came Running '58
Around the World in 80 Days '56
Artists and Models '55
The Trouble with Harry '55

Kyle MacLachlan (1959-)
Sisterhood of the Traveling Pants 2 '08
Touch of Pink '04
Northfork '03
Miranda '01
Perfume '01
Hamlet '00
The Spring '00
Time Code '00
Xchange '00
Route 9 '98
Jack Higgins' The Windsor Protocol '97
Jack Higgins' Thunder Point '97
One Night Stand '97
The Souler Opposite '97
Moonshine Highway '96
The Trigger Effect '96
Trigger Happy '96
Showgirls '95
Schemes '95
Against the Wall '94
The Flintstones '94
Roswell: The U.F.O. Cover-Up '94
The Trial '93
Rich in Love '93
Where the Day Takes You '92
Twin Peaks: Fire Walk with Me '92
The Doors '91
Don't Tell Her It's Me '90
The Hidden '87
Blue Velvet '86
Dune '84

Gavin MacLeod (1930-)
Scruples '80
Only with Married Men '74
Kelly's Heroes '70
The Party '68
The Sand Pebbles '66
McHale's Navy Joins the Air Force '65
McHale's Navy '64
Compulsion '59
Pork Chop Hill '59

Mary MacLaren (1896-1985)
The Duke of West Point '38
A Lawman Is Born '37
The New Frontier '35
The Three Musketeers '21

Michael MacLiammoir (1899-1978)
What's the Matter with Helen? '71
Othello '52

Ellie MacLure (1985-)
Air Hawk '84
Heat of the Flame '76
Alvin Purple '73

Aline MacMahon (1899-1991)
I Could Go on Singing '63
The Man from Laramie '55
The Flame & the Arrow '50
The Search '48
Guest in the House '44
Dragon Seed '44
The Lady Is Willing '42
Back Door to Heaven '39
Ah, Wilderness! '35
I Live My Life '35
Heroes for Sale '33
Gold Diggers of 1933 '33
One Way Passage '32

Barton MacLane (1902-69)
Buckskin '68
Arizona Bushwackers '67
The Geisha Boy '58
Naked in the Sun '57
Three Violent People '57
Jaguar '56
Wetbacks '56
Silver Star '55
Kansas Pacific '53
Bugles in the Afternoon '52
Drums in the Deep South '51
The Half-Breed '51
Let's Dance '50
Silver River '48
Treasure of the Sierra Madre '48
Unknown Island '48
Santa Fe Uprising '46
The Spanish Main '45
Treasure of Fear '45
Cry of the Werewolf '44
The Mummy's Ghost '44
Nabonga '44
Bombardier '43
Marine Raiders '43
Song of Texas '43
The Underdog '43
All Through the Night '42
Big Street '42
The Maltese Falcon '41
Dr. Jekyll and Mr. Hyde '41
Western Union '41
Melody Ranch '40
Mutiny in the Big House '39
Bullets or Ballots '38
Prison Break '38
You and Me '38
The Prince and the Pauper '37
San Quentin '37
Wine, Women and Horses '37
G-Men '35
Black Fury '35
The Case of the Lucky Legs '35

Will MacMillan (1944-)
Bad Girls '94
Aspen Extreme '93
Salvador '86
Tin Man '83
The Enforcer '76
The Sister-in-Law '74
The Crazies '73

Fred MacMurray (1908-91)
The Swarm '78
Beyond the Bermuda Triangle '75
Charley and the Angel '73
The Happiest Millionaire '67

MacMurray

Follow Me, Boys! '66
Kisses for My President '64
Son of Flubber '63
Bon Voyage! '62
The Absent-Minded Professor '61
The Apartment '60
The Shaggy Dog '59
Good Day for a Hanging '58
At Gunpoint '55
The Far Horizons '55
The Caine Mutiny '54
A Woman's World '54
Borderline '50
Never a Dull Moment '50
Father Was a Fullback '49
The Miracle of the Bells '48
On Our Merry Way '48
Egg and I '47
Singapore '47
Murder, He Says '45
Double Indemnity '44
Above Suspicion '43
The Lady Is Willing '42
Dive Bomber '41
Remember the Night '40
My Love For Yours '39
Swing High, Swing Low '37
The Princess Comes Across '36
The Texas Rangers '36
The Trail of the Lonesome Pine '36
Alice Adams '35
Hands Across the Table '35

Alan MacNaughton (1920-2002)
The Dark Angel '91
A Very British Coup '88
Frankenstein Created Woman '66
Victim '61

Patrick Macnee (1922-)
The Avengers '98
Thunder in Paradise 2 '94
Thunder in Paradise: The Luck of the Draw '93
The Gambler Returns: The Luck of the Draw '93
The Hound of London '93
Thunder in Paradise '93
Sherlock Holmes and the Incident at Victoria Falls '91
Waxwork 2: Lost in Time '91
Chill Factor '90
Super Force '90
Around the World in 80 Days '89
Lobster Man from Mars '89
Masque of the Red Death '89
Sorry, Wrong Number '89
Transformations '88
Waxwork '88
Shadey '87
Down Under '86 (N)
This Is Spinal Tap '84
A View to a Kill '85
Return of the Man from U.N.C.L.E. '83
Rehearsal for Murder '82
Young Doctors in Love '82
The Creature Wasn't Nice '81
The Howling '81
Sea Wolves '81
Spaceship '81
Sweet 16 '81

Robert MacNaughton (1966-)
I Am the Cheese '83
E.T.: The Extra-Terrestrial '82

Meredith MacNeill (1975-)
Confetti '06

Peter MacNeill
The Queen's Sister '05
A History of Violence '05
Who is Cletis Tout? '02
Angel Eyes '01
Sex & Mrs. X '00
Dangerous Evidence: The Lori Jackson Story '99
The Hanging Garden '97
Closer and Closer '96
Crash '95
A Vow to Kill '94

Tress MacNeille (1951-)
Rugrats Go Wild! '03 (V)
Hey Arnold! The Movie '02
Kiki's Delivery Service '98 (V)
The Rugrats Movie '98 (V)
Tiny Toon Adventures: How I Spent My Vacation '91 (V)

Peter MacNichol (1954-)
Breakin' All The Rules '04
The Ponder Heart '01
The Pooch and the Pauper '99 (V)
Baby Geniuses '98
Bean '97
Dracula: Dead and Loving It '95
Radioland Murders '94
Roswell: The U.F.O. Cover-Up '94
Addams Family Values '93
Hard Promises '92
Housesitter '92
American Blue Note '89
Ghostbusters 2 '89
Heat '87
Sophie's Choice '82
The Boy Who Left Home to Find Out About the Shivers '81
Dragonslayer '81

Elle Macpherson (1964-)
A Girl Thing '01
With Friends Like These '98
Batman and Robin '97
The Edge '97
Jane Eyre '96
The Mirror Has Two Faces '96
If Lucy Fell '95
Sirens '94
Alice '90

George MacQuarrie
The Idol Dancer '20
The Love Flower '20

Murdoch MacQuarrie (1875-1942)
Man from Montana '41
Ghost Town Riders '38
Pinto Rustlers '36
Stormy Trails '36
Laramie Kid '35
The New Frontier '35
Silent Valley '35
The Tonto Kid '35
Daring Danger '32
Oubliette '14

Duncan MacRae (1905-67)
Casino Royale '67
Our Man in Havana '59
The Woman in Question '50

Gordon MacRae (1921-86)
Danger in the Skies '79
Carousel '56
Oklahoma! '55
By the Light of the Silvery Moon '53
The Desert Song '53
On Moonlight Bay '51
Tea for Two '50
The West Point Story '50
Look for the Silver Lining '49

Heather MacRae (1948-)
Secrets of Three Hungry Wives '78
Bang the Drum Slowly '73
The Connection '73

Meredith MacRae (1944-2000)
Husbands, Wives, Money, and Murder '86
Vultures '84
Sketches of a Strangler '78
Bikini Beach '64

Michael MacRae (1949-)
Masterminds '96
Madhouse '87
Isle of Secret Passion '82
Dear Detective '78
Great Ride '78
Greedy Terror '78

Carol MacReady
Wondrous Oblivion '06
102 Dalmatians '00
Agatha Christie's Murder is Easy '82

George Macready (1908-73)
The Return of Count Yorga '71
Tora! Tora! Tora! '70
Night Gallery '69
The Great Race '65
Dead Ringer '64
The Human Duplicators '64
Seven Days in May '64
Where Love Has Gone '64
Taras Bulba '62
The Nevadan '50
The Doolins of Oklahoma '49
Knock on Any Door '49
The Big Clock '48
Black Arrow '48
Coroner Creek '48
Down to Earth '47
Gilda '46
The Seventh Cross '44

Tim Maculan
Inside Out '05

Bruce MacVittie
2B Perfectly Honest '04
Where the Money Is '00
Hi-Life '98
Stonewall '95
Devlin '92

Bill Macy (1922-)
Mr. Woodcock '07
The Holiday '06
Surviving Christmas '04
Analyze This '98
Me, Myself & I '92
The Doctor '91
Sibling Rivalry '90
Bad Medicine '85
Movers and Shakers '85
My Favorite Year '82
Serial '80
The Jerk '79
The Late Show '77
Oh! Calcutta! '72

William H. Macy (1950-)
He Was a Quiet Man '07
Wild Hogs '07
Bobby '06
Everyone's Hero '06 (V)
Thank You for Smoking '06
Sahara '05
Cellular '04
In Enemy Hands '04
Spartan '04
Stealing Sinatra '04
The Cooler '03
Out of Order '03
Seabiscuit '03
Welcome to Collinwood '02
Focus '01
Jurassic Park 3 '01
Panic '00
State and Main '00
Happy, Texas '99
Magnolia '99
Mystery Men '99
A Slight Case of Murder '99
A Civil Action '98
The Con '98
Jerry and Tom '98
Pleasantville '98
Psycho '98
Air Force One '97
Boogie Nights '97
Wag the Dog '97
Down Periscope '96
Fargo '96
Ghosts of Mississippi '96
Hit Me '96
Andersonville '95
Mr. Holland's Opus '95
Murder in the First '95
Being Human '94
Children of Fury '94
The Client '94
Dead on Sight '94
Evolver '94 (V)
Oleanna '94
Benny & Joon '93
Searching for Bobby Fischer '93
Twenty Bucks '93
A Private Matter '92
The Water Engine '92
Homicide '91
Things Change '88
Foolin' Around '80

Ciaran Madden (1945-)
Ivanhoe '97
Fortunes of War '87
A Married Man '84
The Beast Must Die '75

John Madden (1949-)
The Replacements '00
Little Giants '94
P.K. and the Kid '85

Peter Madden (1910-76)
Frankenstein Created Woman '66
Doctor Zhivago '65
Woman of Straw '64
Kiss of the Vampire '62
The Loneliness of the Long Distance Runner '62

Victor Maddern (1926-93)
I'm All Right Jack '59
Blood of the Vampire '58
Abandon Ship! '57
The Shadow Man '53

Rebecca Mader (1979-)
Great World of Sound '07
The Devil Wears Prada '06
Mimic 3: Sentinel '03

Amy Madigan (1957-)
Gone Baby Gone '07
Winter Passing '05
The Laramie Project '02
Shot in the Heart '01
The Sleepy Time Gal '01
Pollock '00
A Time for Dancing '00
A Bright Shining Lie '98
With Friends Like These '98
Loved '97
Female Perversions '96
Riders of the Purple Sage '96
The Dark Half '91
Field of Dreams '89
Roe vs. Wade '89
Uncle Buck '89
Prince of Pennsylvania '88
Alamo Bay '85
Twice in a Lifetime '85
Places in the Heart '84
Streets of Fire '84
Love Letters '83
Nowhere to Hide '83
The Ambush Murders '82
Love Child '82

James Madio (1975-)
The Box '07
Searching for Bobby D '05
Band of Brothers '01
The Basketball Diaries '95
Hero '92

Guy Madison (1922-96)
Computer Wizard '77
Where's Willie? '77
Hell Commandos '69
Place in Hell '69
Special Forces '68
Bang Bang Kid '67
Superago '67
Five Giants from Texas '66
The Snake Hunter Strangler '66
Cold Steel for Tortuga '65
Apache's Last Battle '64
The Conqueror & the Empress '64
Executioner of Venice '63
Jet Over the Atlantic '59
Bullwhip '58
Savage Wilderness '55
Drums in the Deep South '51
Till the End of Time '46
Since You Went Away '44

Noel Madison (1897-1975)
Footsteps in the Dark '41
The Great Plane Robbery '40
Charlie Chan in City of Darkness '39
Sailing Along '38
Gangway '37
The House of Secrets '37
A Nation Aflame '37
Cocaine Fiends '36

Philip Madoc (1934-)
A Mind to Kill '95
A Very British Coup '88
Space: 1999—Alien Attack '79

Ruth Madoc (1943-)
Very Annie Mary '00
Agatha Christie's The Pale Horse '96

Madonna (1959-)
Arthur and the Invisibles '06 (V)
Swept Away '02
The Next Best Thing '00
Evita '96
Girl 6 '96
Blue in the Face '95
Four Rooms '95
Dangerous Game '93
Body of Evidence '92
A League of Their Own '92
Shadows and Fog '92
Truth or Dare '91
Dick Tracy '90
Bloodhounds of Broadway '89
Who's That Girl? '87
Shanghai Surprise '86
Desperately Seeking Susan '85
Certain Sacrifice '80

Teresa Madruga (1953-)
Two Drifters '05
In the White City '83

Michael Madsen (1959-)
Afghan Knights '07
Living & Dying '07
The Number: 23 '07
Tooth and Nail '07
All In '06
BloodRayne '06
Scary Movie 4 '06
UKM: The Ultimate Killing Machine '06
Chasing Ghosts '05
L.A. Dicks '05
The Last Drop '05
Sin City '05
Kill Bill Vol. 2 '04
44 Minutes: The North Hollywood Shootout '03
Kill Bill Vol. 1 '03
My Boss's Daughter '03
Die Another Day '02
Extreme Honor '01
L.A.P.D.: To Protect and Serve '01
Choke '00
High Noon '00
The Inspectors 2: A Shred of Evidence '00
Luck of the Draw '00
Sacrifice '00
The Stray '00
Agent of Death '99
Detour '99
Supreme Sanction '99
Voodoo Dawn '99
Catherine's Grove '98
The Florentine '98
The Maker '98
The Sender '98
Species 2 '98
Surface to Air '98
Trail of a Serial Killer '98
Diary of a Serial Killer '97
Executive Target '97
Love to Kill '97
Donnie Brasco '96
The Last Days of Frankie the Fly '96
Red Line '96
The Winner '96
Free Willy 2: The Adventure Home '95
Man with a Gun '95
Mulholland Falls '95
Species '95
Dead Connection '94
Season of Change '94
Wyatt Earp '94
Almost Blue '93
Final Combination '93
Free Willy '93
The Getaway '93
A House in the Hills '93
Money for Nothing '93
Beyond the Law '92
Fatal Instinct '92
Inside Edge '92
Reservoir Dogs '92
Straight Talk '92
Trouble Bound '92
The Doors '91
Thelma & Louise '91
The End of Innocence '90
Iguana '89
Kill Me Again '89
Shadows in the Storm '88
The Natural '84
Racing with the Moon '84
One for the Road '82

Virginia Madsen (1963-)
The Astronaut Farmer '07
Firewall '06
A Prairie Home Companion '06
Brave New Girl '04
Sideways '04
American Gun '02
Crossfire Trail '01
Full Disclosure '00
The Florentine '98
The Haunting '99
The Prophecy '95
Bitter Vengeance '94
Blue Tiger '94
Caroline at Midnight '93
Linda '93
Becoming Colette '92
Candyman '92
Highlander 2: The Quickening '91
Love Kills '91
Victim of Love '91
The Hot Spot '90
Ironclads '90
The Heart of Dixie '89
Third Degree Burn '89
Gotham '88
Hot to Trot! '88
Mr. North '88
Slam Dance '87

Zombie High '87
Fire with Fire '86
Modern Girls '86
Creator '85
The Hearst and Davies Affair '85
Dune '84
Electric Dreams '84

Beverly (Bibari) Maeda (1948-)
Face of Another '66
Son of Godzilla '56

Christian Maelen
Remedy '05
Deepwater '05
Poseidon '06
The Box '07

Mia Maestro (1978-)
Poseidon '06
Deepwater '05
The Motorcycle Diaries '04
Frida '02
In the Time of the Butterflies '01
I Think I Do '97
Time Code '00

Roma Maffia (1958-)
Holes '03
Things You Can Tel Just by Looking at Her '00
Double Jeopardy '99
Eraser '96
Disclosure '94
Nick of Time '95

Dominic Mafham (1968-)
Our Mutual Friend '98
Shooting Fish '98

Cass Magca
Blade Boxer '97

Patrick Magee (1922-82)
The Monster Club '85
The Black Cat '81
Chariots of Fire '81
Rough Cut '80
Sleep of Death '79
Barry Lyndon '75
A Killer in Every Corner '74
Luther '74
And Now the Screaming Starts '73
The Final Programme '73
Asylum '72
Demons of the Mind '72
Young Winston '72
A Clockwork Orange '71
Trojan Women '71
King Lear '71
Cromwell '70
Teleton '77
Anzio '68
Portrait in Terror '66
Die, Monster, Die! '65
Masque of the Red Death '65
The Skull '65
Seance on a Wet Afternoon '64
Zulu '64
Dementia 13 '63
The Very Edge '63

Brandon Maggart (1933-)
Running Mates '92
The World According to Garp '82
Christmas Evil '80
Dressed to Kill '80

Jad Mager (1969-)
Big City Blues '99
Blue Flame '93

Anna Magnani (1907-73)
Fellini's Roma '72
The Secret of Santa Vittoria '69
Mamma Roma '62
The Fugitive Kind '60
Joyful Laughter '60
The Rose Tattoo '55
The Golden Coach '52
Bellissima '51
The Miracle '48
Amore '48
Open City '45
Peddlin' In Society '47
Teresa Venerdi '41

Donna Magnani
29th Street '91

Ann Magnuson (1956-)
United States of Leland '03
Panic Room '02
The Caveman's Valentine '01
Glitter '01
Love & Sex '00
From the Earth to the Moon '98
Small Soldiers '98
Levitation '97
Still Breathing '97
Before and After '95
Tank Girl '94
Cabin Boy '94
Checking Out '89
Heavy Petting '89
Love at Large '89
A Night in the Life of Jimmy Reardon '88
Sleepwalk '88
Tequila Sunrise '88
Making Mr. Right '86
Desperately Seeking Susan '85
Perfect Strangers '84
The Hunger '83
Vortex '81

Kate Magowan
Stardust '07
It's All Gone, Pete Tong '04

Pierre Maguelon (1933-)
Alice et Martin '98
Cyrano de Bergerac '90

Tobey Maguire (1975-)
Tropic Thunder '08
Spider-Man 3 '07
The Good German '06
Spider-Man 2 '04
Seabiscuit '03
Spider-Man '02
Cats & Dogs '01 (V)
Wonder Boys '00
The Cider House Rules '99
Ride with the Devil '99
Fear and Loathing in Las Vegas '98
Pleasantville '98
Deconstructing Harry '97
The Ice Storm '97
Joyride '97
Revenge of the Red Baron '93

Mary Maguire
Black Eyes '39
Mysterious Mr. Moto '38

Santiago Magill (1977-)
City of M '01
I Love You Baby '01

Benoit Magimel (1974-)
Crimson Rivers 2: Angels of the Apocalypse '05
The Piano Teacher '04
Children of the Century '01
Les Voleurs '96
A Single Girl '96
Life is a Long Quiet River '88

George Maharis (1928-)
The Sword & the Sorcerer '82
The Crash of Flight 401 '78
Return to Fantasy Island '77
Murder on Flight 502 '75
Land Raiders '69
Last Day of the War '69
Exodus '60

Bill Maher (1956-)
Pizza Man '91
Cannibal Women in the Avocado Jungle of Death '89
House 2: The Second Story '87

Joseph Maher (1934-98)
Sister Act '92
I.Q. '94
The Shadow '94
Funny Farm '88
My Stepmother Is an Alien '88
The Evil That Men Do '84
Frankenweenie '84
Under the Rainbow '81

Sean Maher (1975-)
Wedding Wars '06
Serenity '05
Brian's Song '01

Bruce Mahler (1950-)
Funland '89
Police Academy 6: City under Siege '89

Shiek Mahmud-Bey
Leprechaun 6: Back 2 Tha Hood '03
Friendly Persuasion '56

Grace Mahlaba
Being Human '94
Bopha! '93

Laurie Main (1922-)
Tarzan, the Ape Man '81
Private Parts '72

Marjorie Main (1890-1975)
The Kettles on Old MacDonald's Farm '57
The Kettles in the Ozarks '56
Ma and Pa Kettle at Waikiki '55
Ma and Pa Kettle at Home '54
Ma and Pa Kettle on Vacation '53
The Belle of New York '52
Ma and Pa Kettle at the Fair '52
Ma and Pa Kettle Back On the Farm '51
Summer Stock '50
Ma and Pa Kettle Go to Town '50
Ma and Pa Kettle '49
Egg and I '47
The Wistful Widow of Wagon Gap '47
The Harvey Girls '46
The Show-Off '46
Undercurrent '46
Murder, He Says '45
Heaven Can Wait '43
Johnny Come Lately '43
Honky Tonk '41
A Woman's Face '41
Dark Command '40
Susan and God '40
They Shall Have Music '39
The Women '39
Little Tough Guys '38
Dead End '37
Stella Dallas '37
The Wrong Road '37

Michael Mahonen (1964-)
Captured '99
By Way of the Stars '92
Giant Steps '92

Brian Mahoney
Boondock Saints '99

John Mahoney (1940-)
Dan in Real Life '07
Atlantis: The Lost Empire '01 (V)
The Broken Hearts Club '00
Iron Giant '99 (V)
Primal Fear '96
She's the One '96

Jock Mahoney (1919-89)
Bad Bunch '76
The Glory Stompers '67
The Walls of Hell '64
A Time to Love & a Time to Die '58
Battle Hymn '57
The Land Unknown '57
The Nevadan '50
Cow Town '50
Rim of the Canyon '49
The Shepherd of the Hills '41

Valerie Mahaffey (1953-)
My First Wedding '04
Seabiscuit '03
Jungle 2 Jungle '96
National Lampoon's Senior Trip '95
Witch Hunt '94
They Watch '93
Code Name: Dancer '87
The Rise & Rise of Daniel Rocket '85
Women of Valor '86
Love Hurts '91
The Ten Million Dollar Getaway '91
Unnatural Pursuits '91
The Russia House '90
The Image '89
Say Anything '89
Dinner at Eight '89
Betrayed '88
Eight Men Out '88
Frantic '88
Suspect '87
Moonstruck '87
Tin Men '87
The Manhattan Project '86
Trapped in Silence '86

Deborah Mailman (1972-)
Rabbit-Proof Fence '02
Radiance '98

Caludette Maille
Like A Bride '94
Like Water for Chocolate '93

Aissa Maiga (1975-)
Bamako '06
Paris, je t'aime '06
Russian Dolls '05

Tim Maier
Turnaround '87
Raw Courage '84

Steven Mailer (1966-)
Ride with the Devil '99
Red Meat '98
24 Nights '99
Quiet Days in Hollywood '97

Austin Majors (1995-)
The Ant Bully '06 (V)
Treasure Planet '02 (V)

Lee Majors (1940-)
The Brothers Solomon '07
Arizona Summer '03
Big Fat Liar '02
Out Cold '01
Trojan War '97
The Cover Girl Murders '93
Chinatown Connection '90
Keaton's Cop '90
Scrooged '88
A Smoky Mountain Christmas '86
The Cowboy & the Ballerina '84
Starflight One '83
The Agency '81
Last Chase '81
High Noon: Part 2 '80
Steel '80
Killer Fish '79
Norseman '78
Francis Gary Powers: The True Story of the U-2 Spy Incident '76
The Bionic Woman '75
The Ballad of Andy Crocker '69
Will Penny '67
Strait-Jacket '64

Tina Majorino (1985-)
Napoleon Dynamite '04
Alice in Wonderland '99
Waterworld '95
Andre '94
Corrina, Corrina '94
When a Man Loves a Woman '94

Marne Maitland (1920-92)
Fellini's Roma '72
The Reptile '66
The Bushbaby '70
Bhowani Junction '56

Valerie Mairesse (1955-)
One to Another '06
The Sacrifice '86
Investigation '79
One Sings, the Other Doesn't '77

Guy Mairesse (1924-)
A Reason to Live, a Reason to Die '73

Dragan Maksimovic (1949-2001)
Meetings with Remarkable Men '79

Lawrence Makoare (1968-)
Lord of the Rings: The Return of the King '03
Die Another Day '02

Mala (1906-52)
The Tuttles of Tahiti '42
Hawk of the Wilderness '38
Robinson Crusoe of Clipper Island '36
Robinson Crusoe of Mystery Island '36
Last of the Pagans '35

Heike Makatsch (1971-)
Love Actually '03
Aimee & Jaguar '98
Obsession '97

Chris Makepeace (1964-)
Aloha Summer '88
Captive Hearts '87
Vamp '86
Undergrads '85
Savage Hunger '84
The Terry Fox Story '83
Mazes and Monsters '82
The Mysterious Stranger '82
My Bodyguard '80
Meatballs '79

Wendy Makkena (1963-)
Air Bud '97
Finding North '97
Death Benefit '96
Serving in Silence: The Margarethe Cammermeyer Story '95
Camp Nowhere '94
Sister Act 2: Back in the Habit '93
Sister Act '92

Mako (1933-2006)
TMNT (Teenage Mutant Ninja Turtles) '07 (V)
Rise: Blood Hunter '07
Memoirs of a Geisha '05
Bulletproof Monk '03
Pearl Harbor '01
Rugrats in Paris: The Movie '00
Seven Years in Tibet '97
Sworn to Justice '97
Balance of Power '96
Bloodfor Blood '95
Riot in the Streets '96
A Dangerous Place '94
Highlander: The Final Dimension '94
Red Sun Rising '94
Sidekicks '93
My Samurai '92
Hiroshima: Out of the Ashes '90
Pacific Heights '90

Patrick Malahide (1945-)
Five Days '07
Murderous Intent '06
Elizabeth I '05
Friends & Crocodiles '05
Sahara '05
Eurotrip '04
Goodbye, Mr. Chips '02
Captain Corelli's Mandolin '01
Victoria & Albert '01
All the King's Men '99
Fortress 2: Re-Entry '99
Heaven '99
Ordinary Decent Criminal '00
Deacon Brodie '98
Miracle at Midnight '98
The Long Kiss Goodnight '96

Two Deaths '94
Middlemarch '93
December Bride '91
The Franchise Affair '88
A Month in the Country '87
The Singing Detective '86
Comfort and Joy '84

Christophe MaLavoy (1952-)
Madame Bovary '91
The Cry of the Owl '87
Peril '85

Paolo Malco
The House by the Cemetery '83
New York Ripper '82
Scorpion with Two Tails '82
Watch Me When I Kill '77

Romany Malco (1968-)
Baby Mama '08
The Love Guru '08
The Ex '07
The 40 Year Old Virgin '05
The Tuxedo '02
The Chateau '01
Urban Menace '99

Christopher Malcolm (1946-)
We'll Meet Again '82
The Great Riviera Bank Robbery '79

Robyn Malcolm (1965-)
Boogeyman '05
Perfect Strangers '03

Karl Malden (1914-)
Nuts '87
Billy Galvin '86
Alice in Wonderland '85
Fatal Vision '84
Urge to Kill '84
The Sting 2 '83
Miracle on Ice '81
Beyond the Poseidon Adventure '79
Meteor '79
Skag '79
Ricco '74
The Streets of San Francisco '72
The Cat o' Nine Tails '71
Wild Rovers '71
Patton '70
Blue '68
Hot Millions '68
Hotel '67
Murderers' Row '66
Nevada Smith '66
The Cincinnati Kid '65
Cheyenne Autumn '64
Dead Ringer '64
How the West Was Won '63
All Fall Down '62
Birdman of Alcatraz '62
Gypsy '62
The Great Impostor '61
One-Eyed Jacks '61
Parrish '61
Pollyanna '60
The Hanging Tree '59
Fear Strikes Out '57
Baby Doll '56
On the Waterfront '54
I Confess '53
Diplomatic Courier '52
Ruby Gentry '52
A Streetcar Named Desire '51
The Gunfighter '50
The Halls of Montezuma '50
Boomerang '47
Kiss of Death '47
13 Rue Madeleine '46
They Knew What They Wanted '40

Ruth Maleczech
The Ballad of Little Jo '93
Anna '87

Jonathan Malen (1987-)
Charlie Bartlett '07

Possessed '00

Arthur Malet (1927-)
A Little Princess '95
Beastmaster 2: Through the Portal of Time '91
Hook '91
The Black Cauldron '85 (V)
Halloween '78
Munster, Go Home! '66
King Rat '65

Laurent Malet (1955-)
The Possessed '88
Querelle '83
Invitation au Voyage '82
Jacko & Lise '82
Roads to the South '78
Blood Relatives '77

Ryan Malgarini (1992-)
Freaky Friday '03
United States of Leland '03

Wendie Malick (1950-)
Racing Stripes '05
Waiting '05
Raising Genius '04
On Edge '03
Manna from Heaven '02
Strange Frequency 2 '01
The Emperor's New Groove '00 (V)
Dead Husbands '98
Jerome '98
North Shore Fish '97
Trojan War '97
The American President '95
Madonna: Innocence Lost '94

Keram Malicki-Sanchez (1974-)
Happy Campers '01
Cherry Falls '00
Skin Deep '94

Art Malik (1952-)
Cleopatra '99
Catherine Cookson's Colour Blind '98
Path to Paradise '97
Booty Call '96
A Kid in King Arthur's Court '95
True Lies '94
Uncovered '94
City of Joy '92
The Killing Beach '92
Year of the Comet '92
The Living Daylights '87
Harem '86
Transmutations '85
The Jewel in the Crown '84

Joshua Malina (1966-)
View from the Top '03
Bulworth '98
From the Earth to the Moon '98
The American President '95

Judith Malina (1926-)
Let It Snow '99
The Deli '97
Music from Another Room '97
Household Saints '93
The Addams Family '91
Awakenings '90
Enemies, a Love Story '89
Eve of Destruction '90

Cylia Malki (1976-)
La Moustache '05
Daughter of Keltoum '01

Sam Malkin
Blood Relations '87

Caribe '87

John Malkovich (1953-)
Beowulf '07 (V)
Art School Confidential '06
Eragon '06
Klimt '06
Color Me Kubrick '05
The Hitchhiker's Guide to the Galaxy '05
The Libertine '05
Johnny English '03
Napoleon '03
Ripley's Game '02
Hotel '01
Knockaround Guys '01
I'm Going Home '00
Shadow of the Vampire '00
Being John Malkovich '99
The Messenger: The Story of Joan of Arc '99
RKO 281 '99
Time Regained '99
The Man in the Iron Mask '98
Rounders '98
Con Air '97
The Ogre '96
Portrait of a Lady '96
Beyond the Clouds '95
The Convent '95
Mary Reilly '95
Mulholland Falls '95
Alive '93 (N)
Heart of Darkness '93
In the Line of Fire '93
Jennifer 8 '92
Of Mice and Men '92
Shadows and Fog '92
The Object of Beauty '91
Queens Logic '91
The Sheltering Sky '90
Dangerous Liaisons '88
Miles from Home '88
Empire of the Sun '87
The Glass Menagerie '87
Death of a Salesman '86
Making Mr. Right '86
Rocket to the Moon '86
True West '86
Eleni '85
The Killing Fields '84
Places in the Heart '84
American Dream '81

Perry Mallette
Thou Shalt Not Kill...Except '87
Going Back '83

Brian Mallon
Gods and Generals '03
Gettysburg '93

Patricia "Boots" Mallory (1913-58)
Powdersmoke Range '35
Sing Sing Nights '35
Carnival Lady '33
Wolf Dog '33

Matt Malloy
Wedding Daze '06
Spartan '04
Tanner on Tanner '04
Elephant '03
United States of Leland '03
Changing Lanes '02
The Great Gatsby '00
Dr. T & the Women '00
Everything Put Together '00
Running Mates '00
Cookie's Fortune '99

Drop Dead Gorgeous '99
Election '99
In the Company of Men '96
Surviving Desire '91

Tom Malloy
The Attic '06
Gravesend '97

Jan Malmsjo (1932-)
Fanny and Alexander '83
Scenes from a Marriage '73

Birger Malmsten (1920-91)
The Silence '63
Summer Interlude '50
To Joy '50
Three Strange Loves '49
Night Is My Future '47

Bonz Malone
Bomb the System '05
White Boyz '99
Slam '98

Dorothy Malone (1925)
Basic Instinct '92
Rest in Pieces '87
Day Time Ended '80
Off Your Rocker '80
Winter Kills '79
Abduction '75
The Man Who Would Not Die '75
Beach Party '63
The Last Voyage '60
Warlock '59
Man of a Thousand Faces '57
Tarnished Angels '57
Sincerely Yours '56
Tension at Table Rock '56
Written on the Wind '56
Artists and Models '55
At Gunpoint '55
Battle Cry '55
The Fast and the Furious '54
Private Hell 36 '54
Young at Heart '54
Scared Stiff '53
Torpedo Alley '53
The Nevadan '50
South of St. Louis '48
The Big Sleep '46
Night and Day '46

Jena Malone (1984-)
The Ruins '08
Into the Wild '07
Four Last Songs '06
The Ballad of Jack and Rose '05
Pride and Prejudice '05
Howl's Moving Castle '04 (V)
Saved! '04
Cold Mountain '03
Hitler: The Rise of Evil '03
United States of Leland '03
The Badge '02
Corn '02
The Dangerous Lives of Altar Boys '02
Donnie Darko '01
Life as a House '01
Cheaters '00
The Book of Stars '99
For Love of the Game '99
Stepmom '98
Contact '97
Ellen Foster '97
Hope '97
Bastard out of Carolina '96
Hidden in America '96

Mollie Malone (1888-1952)
Battling Bunyon '24
Straight Shootin' '17

Nancy Malone (1935-)
Man Who Loved Cat Dancing '73
Fright '56

Patrick Malone (1969-)
Face the Music '00
Hostage Sign '97
Grand Canyon '91
Rock 'n' Roll High School Forever '91

Michael Maloney (1957-)
Pinochet's Last Stand '06
P. D. James: The Murder Room '04
Me & Mrs. Jones '02
The Painted Lady '97
Hamlet '96
A Midwinter's Tale '95
Othello '95
Truly, Madly, Deeply '91
Henry V '89
Sharma & Beyond '84

Peter Maloney
Washington Square '97
Robot in the Family '94

H.F. Maltby (1880-1963)
Pygmalion '38
Young and Innocent '37

Natassia Malthe (1974-)
BloodRayne 2: Deliverance '07
DOA: Dead or Alive '06
Bound by Lies '05
Confessions of a Sociopathic Social Climber '05
Call Me: The Rise and Fall of Heidi Fleiss '04

Leonard Maltin (1950-)
Forgotten Silver '96
Gremlins 2: The New Batch '90
The Lost Stooges '33 (N)

Eily Malyon (1879-1961)
She Wolf of London '46
Treasure of Fear '45
The Seventh Cross '44
I Married a Witch '42

Barbara Mamabolo (1986-)
Brave New Girl '04
Dangerous Evidence: The Lori Jackson Story '99

Peter Mamakos (1918-)
The Conqueror '56
Pier 23 '51

David Mamet (1947-)
The Water Engine '92
Black Widow '87

Tony Mamet
Spartan '04
Lakeboat '00

Robert Mammone
The Condemned '07
The Great Raid '05
Salem's Lot '04
Heaven's Burning '97
The Crossing '92

Biff Manard (1939-)
Trancers 2: The Return of Jack Deth '91
Zone Troopers '84

Michael Manasseri (1974-)
Sunstorm '01
When Danger Follows You Home '97
License to Drive '88

Melissa Manchester (1951-)
For the Boys '91
The Great Mouse Detective '86 (V)

Al Mancini (1932-2007)
The Ticket '97
My Summer Story '94
Mission Manila '87
The Dirty Dozen '67

Ray "Boom Boom" Mancini (1961-)
Body and Soul '98
The Search for One-Eyed Jimmy '96
Wishful Thinking '92
Timebomb '91
Backstreet Dreams '90
The Dirty Dozen: The Fatal Mission '88

Oceans of Fire '86

Nick Mancuso (1948-)
Firefight '03
Revelation '00
Tribulation '00
Captured '99
The Pact '99
Total Recall 2070: Machine Dreams '99
Against the Wall '98
Matter of Trust '98
Misbegotten '98
Past Perfect '98
Perfect Assassins '98
Twists of Terror '98
Laws of Deception '97
The Ex '96
The Invader '96
Marquis de Sade '96
Provocateur '96
Under Siege 2: Dark Territory '95
A Young Connecticut Yankee in King Arthur's Court '95
Young Ivanhoe '95
Flinch '94
Suspicious Agenda '94
The Takeover '94
Wild Palms '93
Lies Before Kisses '92
Rapid Fire '92
Fatal Exposure '91
Lena's Holiday '90
Double Identity '89
Death of an Angel '86
Half a Lifetime '86
Blame It on the Night '84
Heartbreakers '84
Maria Chapdelaine '84
Tell Me That You Love Me '84
Legend of Walks Far Woman '82
Mother Lode '82
Ticket to Heaven '81
Death Ship '80
The House on Garibaldi Street '79
Nightwing '79

Elena Mandalis
Head On '98
Only the Brave '94

Robert Mandan (1932-)
The Nutt House '95
National Lampoon's Last Resort '94
Perry Mason: The Case of the Lost Love '87
In Love with an Older Woman '82
Zapped! '82

Howie Mandel (1955-)
Tribulation '00
Kurt Vonnegut's Harrison Bergeron '95
Shake, Rattle & Rock! '94
A Fine Mess '86
Gremlins '84 (V)
Gremlins 2: The New Batch '90 (V)
Mother Goose Rock 'n' Rhyme '90
Little Monsters '89
Walk Like a Man '87
The Princess Who Never Laughed '84
Gas '81
Return of the Rebels '81

Miles Mander (1888-1946)
Brighton Strangler '45
Picture of Dorian Gray '45
Murder, My Sweet '44
The Pearl of Death '44
Scarlet Claw '44
The White Cliffs of Dover '44
Five Graves to Cairo '43
Guadalcanal Diary '43
Return of the Vampire '43
To Be or Not to Be '42
Shadows on the Stairs '41
Primrose Path '40
The Little Princess '39

Stanley and Livingstone '39
The Three Musketeers '39
The Tower of London '39
Wuthering Heights '39
Mad Miss Manton '38
Youth on Parole '37
Don Quixote '35
The Three Musketeers '35
The Private Life of Henry VIII '33
Murder '30

Barbara Mandrell (1948-)
Burning Rage '84

Neil Mandt (1969-)
The Concrete Cowboys '79
Arthur's Quest '99
Hijacking Hollywood '97

Aasif Mandvi
Music & Lyrics '07
Sorry, Haters '05
The War Within '05
Spider-Man 2 '04
The Mystic Masseur '01

Costas Mandylor (1965-)
Saw 4 '07
Saw III '06
'05
The Game of Their Lives '05
The Pledge '00
Bonanno: A Godfather's Story '99
Stealth Fighter '99
The Fury Within '98
Fist of the North Star '95
Portraits of a Killer '95
Venus Rising '95
Virtuosity '95
Shelter '98
Double Take '97
Just Write '97
Fatal Past '94
The Doors '91
Mobsters '91
Soapdish '91
Triumph of the Spirit '89

Louis Mandylor (1966-)
Redline '07
The Game of Their Lives '05
Gang of Roses '03
Lady Jayne Killer '03
My Big Fat Greek Wedding '02
Price of Glory '00
Rogue Force '99
Mafia! '98
The Quest '96

Tyler Mane (1966-)
Halloween '07
The Devil's Rejects '05
Troy '04
How to Make a Monster '01
X-Men '00

Marshall Manesh (1950-)
Pirates of the Caribbean: At World's End '07
Kazaam '95

Larry Manetti (1947-)
The Corporation '96
Subliminal Seduction '96
A Call to Remember '97
Body Chemistry 4: Full Exposure '95
Exit '95
C.I.A. 2: Target Alexa '94
The Take '90
Magnum P.I.: Don't Eat the Snow in Hawaii '80

Nino Manfredi (1921-2004)
Alberto Express '92
In the Name of the Pope-King '85
Cafe Express '85
Nudo di Donna '83
Spaghetti House '82
We All Loved Each Other So Much '77

Down & Dirty '76
Bread and Chocolate '73
Head of the Family '71

Joe Manganiello (1976-)
Spider-Man 3 '07
Spider-Man '02

Anthony Mangano
All Saint's Day '98
8 Heads in a Duffel Bag '96
Point Break '91

Silvana Mangano (1930-89)
Dark Eyes '87
Dune '84
Conversation Piece '75
Ludwig '72
Death in Venice '71
Teorema '68
Oedipus Rex '67
Barabbas '62
The Great War '59
Mambo '55
Ulysses '55
The Gold of Naples '54
Anna '51
Bitter Rice '49

Alec Mango (1911-89)
Lure of the Sila '49
The Cosmic Monsters '58
The Seventh Voyage of Sinbad '58
Race for Life '55

Camryn Manheim (1961-)
Slipstream '07
Marilyn Hotchkiss' Ballroom Dancing & Charm School '06
Dark Water '05
An Unfinished Life '05
Twisted '04
Scary Movie 3 '03
A Girl Thing '01
The Loretta Claiborne Story '00
The 10th Kingdom '00
What Planet Are You From? '00
The Tic Code '99
Happiness '98
Mercy '98
David Searching '97
Romy and Michele's High School Reunion '97
Wide Awake '97
She's the One '96
Things I Never Told You '96

Karin Mani
Avenging Angel '85
Alley Cat '84

Jim Maniaci
The Rock '96
Timebomb '91

Cindy Manion
My Twentieth Century '90

Blu Mankuma
Tin Man '07
Connor's War '06
Fierce People '05
Jasper, Texas '03
Johnson County War '02
Mermaid '00
Atomic Train '99
Premonition '98
A Call to Remember '97
Bliss '96
Dead Silence '96
Watchers '88

Paulus Manker (1958-)
Preppies '84

Margaret Mann (1868-1941)
The Law Rides '36
Kentucky Blue Streak '35
Four Sons '28

Robert Mann
Getaway '91
Critters 2: The Main Course '88

Double Edge '97
Red Corner '97
Street Fighter '94

Gabriel Mann (1972-)
A Lot Like Love '05
The Bourne Supremacy '04
The Life of David Gale '03
Abandon '02
The Bourne Identity '02
Josie and the Pussycats '01
Summer Catch '01
Things Behind the Sun '01
Cherry Falls '00
Sleep Easy, Hutch Rimes '00
No Vacancy '99
Outside Providence '99
American Virgin '98
High Art '98
Kiss of Death '98

John Mann (1962-)
Underworld: Evolution '05
8 Mile '02
crazy/beautiful '01

Hank Mann (1887-1971)
City Lights '31
Spite Marriage '29
Perfect Crime '79

Leonard Mann (1947-)
Cut and Run '85
Corrupt '84
Night School '81

Leslie Mann (1972-)
Knocked Up '07
Drillbit Taylor '08
The 40 Year Old Virgin '05
Orange County '02
Stealing Harvard '02
Time Code '00
Big Daddy '99
George of the Jungle '97
The Cable Guy '96
Last Man Standing '96
She's the One '96

Dinah Manoff (1958-)
Welcome Home, Roxy Carmichael '90
Bloodhounds of Broadway '89
Backfire '88
Child's Play '88
Table Settings '84
I Ought to Be in Pictures '82
For...adies Only '81
Ordinary People '80
Grease '78
The Possessed '77

Miki (Predrag) Manojlovic (1950-)
Criminal Lovers '99
Set Me Free '99
Cabaret Balkan '98
Artemisia '97
Portraits Chinois '96
Underground '95

Sheila (Manors) Mannors (1911-2003)
Cowboy Counselor '33
Lawless Range '35
Westward Ho '35
Prescott Kid '36
The Breed '06
Desert Phantom '36
Kelly of the Secret Service '36
Cocaine Fiends '36
Torture Ship '39
Waterfront '39
Texas Pioneers '32

Taryn Manning (1978-)
Cult '07
Weirdsville '07
A Lot Like Love '05
Hustle & Flow '05
Cold Mountain '03
Crossroads '02

Vic Manni
Trapped in Paradise '94

Marilyn Manning
29th Street '91
The Sadist '63
What's Up Front '63
Eegah! '62

The Mummy '32
They Call It Sin '32
Three Broadway Girls '32
Dracula '31
The Miracle Woman '31

Lucie Mannheim (1895-1976)
Hotel Reserve '44
The 39 Steps '35

Sheila Manners
See Sheila (Manors) Mannors

Ettore Manni (1927-79)
City of Women '81
Street People '76
Heroes in Hell '73
The Battle of El Alamein '68
Mademoiselle '66
Giants of Rome '63
Hercules and the Captive Women '63
The Battle of Austerlitz '60
Angel in a Taxi '59
Two Nights with Cleopatra '54

Leonor Manso (1948-)
Made in Argentina '86
House of Shadows '83
Far Away and Long Ago '74

Martha Mansfield (1899-1927)
Is Money Everything? '23
Dr. Jekyll and Mr. Hyde '20

Alan Manson (1920-2002)
Whiffs '75
Let's Scare Jessica to Death '71

Paul Mantee (1936-)
The Rain People '69
Memorial Day '98
Lurking Fear '94
Dead Funny '94
Sins of the Mind '97
When Hell Was in Session '82

Joe Mantegna (1947-)
Redbelt '08
Witless Protection '08
Cougar Club '07
The Simpsons Movie '07
Uncle Nino '03
(V)
The Kid and I '05
Nine Lives '05
Stateside '04
Women vs. Men '02
Lakeboat '00
More Dogs Than Bones '00
Thin Air '00
The Trumpet of the Swan '01

Gina Mantegna (1990-)
In the Land of Women '06
Unaccompanied Minors '06

A Guide for the Married Man '67
Searching for Bobby Fischer '93

The Fat Spy '66
Las Vegas Hillbillys '66
Dog Eat Dog '64
Promises! Promises! '63
Panic Button '63
The Loves of Hercules '60
It Takes a Thief '59
The Sheriff of Fractured Jaw '57
Will Success Spoil Rock Hunter? '57
The Female Jungle '56
The Girl Can't Help It '56
Hell on Frisco Bay '55
Illegal '55
Pete Kelly's Blues '55
Underwater! '55

The Manitou '78
Robinson Crusoe on Mars '64
The Kid and I '05
Eight Men Out '88
City of Hope '91
The Night We Never Met '93
When Hell Was in Session '82

Bronwen Mantel
Gothika '03
Pin... '88

Henriette Mantel
A Very Brady Sequel '96
The Brady Bunch Movie '95

Joe Mantell (1920-)
Chinatown '74
The Birds '63
Marty '55

Michael Mantell
Ocean's Thirteen '07
Secretary '02
Chain of Command '00

Randolph Mantooth (1945-)
Fire Serpent '07
Agent Red '00
Terror at London Bridge '85
Boom in the Moon '46

Fernando Soto Mantequilla (1911-80)
Invasion of the Vampires '61

Leslie Manville (1956-)
All or Nothing '02
Plain Jane '01
Topsy Turvy '99
The Secret Rapture '93
Secrets and Lies '95
High Hopes '88
Dance with a Stranger '85
Grown Ups '80

Linda Manz (1961-)
Gummo '97
The Snow Queen '83
Long Shot Kids '81
The Painted Lady '97
The Wanderers '79
Out of the Blue '80
Orphan Train '79
Days of Heaven '78

Marla Maples (1963-)
Happiness '98
Loving Annabelle '06
Black and White '99

Angela (Mao Ying) Mao (1952-)
When Taekwondo Strikes '73
Return of the Tiger '78
Enter the Dragon '73
'83

William Mapother (1965-)
The Lather Effect '06

Things Change '88
House of Games '87
Suspect '87
Weeds '87
Critical Condition '86
The Money Pit '86
Three Amigos '86
Off Beat '86
The Godfather, Part 3 '90
Alice '90
The Comrades of Summer '92
Bugsy '91
Family Prayers '91
Homicide '91
Body of Evidence '93
The Water Engine '92
Queens Logic '91
Wait until Spring, Bandini '90
Compromising Positions '85
Second Thoughts '83
Elvis: The Movie '79

The Zodiac '05, The Grudge '04, Suspect Zero '04, In the Bedroom '01

Adele Mara (1923-)
Sands of Iwo Jima '49, Night Time in Nevada '48, Robin Hood of Texas '47, The Inner Circle '46, Bells of Rosarita '45, Twilight on the Rio Grande '41

Kate Mara (1983-)
Full of It '07, Shooter '07, We Are Marshall '06, Zoom '06, Brokeback Mountain '05, Urban Legends: Bloody Mary '05, Random Hearts '99

Mary Mara (1960-)
K-PAX '01, Lloyd '00, Bound '96, Love Potion #9 '92, Mr. Saturday Night '92

Steve Marachuk
Hot Target '85, Piranha 2: The Spawning '82, Waikiki '80

Jean Marais (1913-98)
Stealing Beauty '96, Peau D'Ane '71, Donkey Skin '70, Slashdance '89, The Rape of the Sabines '61, The Battle of Austerlitz '60, The Testament of Orpheus '59, Girl in His Pocket '57, White Nights '57, Elena and Her Men '56, Orpheus '49, The Eagle Has Two Heads '48, Ruyblas '48, The Storm Within '48, Eternal Return '43

Josie Maran (1978-)
The Aviator '04, Little Black Book '04, Van Helsing '04

Cindy Maranne
Provoked '89

Dominique Marcas (1920-)
The Butterfly '02, La Vie de Bohème '93, Dr. Petiot '90

Marcel Marceau (1923-2007)
Silent Movie '76, Barbarella '68

Sophie Marceau (1966-)
Alex & Emma '03, Lost and Found '99, The World Is Not Enough '99, Firelight '97, Leo Tolstoy's Anna Karenina '96, Beyond the Clouds '95, Braveheart '95, Revenge of the Musketeers '94, Police '85, Fort Saganne '84, La Boum '81

Elspeth March (1911-99)
The Magician of Lublin '79, Goodbye, Mr. Chips '69, Woman Times Seven '67, The Three Lives of Thomasina '63 (V), Roman Spring of Mrs. Stone '61, Midnight Lace '60, Quo Vadis '51, Mr. Emmanuel '44

Fredric March (1897-1975)
The Iceman Cometh '73, Hombre '67, Seven Days in May '64, Inherit the Wind '60, The Man in the Gray Flannel Suit '56, Alexander the Great '55, The Bridges at Toko-Ri '55, Desperate Hours '55, A Christmas Carol '54, Executive Suite '54, Death of a Salesman '51, Christopher Columbus '49, The Best Years of Our Lives '46, The Adventures of Mark Twain '44, Tomorrow the World '44, I Married a Witch '42, So Ends Our Night '41, Susan and God '40, Nothing Sacred '37, A Star Is Born '37, Anthony Adverse '36, Mary of Scotland '36, Anna Karenina '36, The Dark Angel '35, Les Miserables '35, The Barretts of Wimpole Street '34, Death Takes a Holiday '34, The Eagle and the Hawk '33, The Sign of the Cross '33, Smilin' Through '33, Dr. Jekyll and Mr. Hyde '32, Strangers in Love '32

Jane March (1973-)
The Stone Merchant '06, Dracula: The Dark Prince '01, Tarzan and the Lost City '98, Circle of Passion '97, Provocateur '96, Color of Night '94, The Lover '92

Stephanie March (1974-)
Flannel Pajamas '06, Jesse Stone: Night Passage '06, The Treatment '06, Head of State '03

Georges Marchal (1920-97)
Belle de Jour '67, Death in the Garden '56, The French Way '40

Corinne Marchand (1937-)
Bandits '86, Borsalino '70, Cleo from 5 to 7 '61

Guy Marchand (1937-)
Inside Paris '06, New World '95, May Wine '90, Conseil de Famille '86, Heat of Desire '84, Petit Con '84, Entre-Nous '83, Coup de Torchon '81, Loulou '80, Dear Detective '77, Cousin, Cousine '76

Nancy Marchand (1928-2000)
Dear God '96, Sabrina '95, Brain Donors '92, Regarding Henry '91, The Naked Gun: From the Files of Police Squad '88, North and South Book 2 '86, The Bostonians '84, Agatha Christie's Sparkling Cyanide '83, Killjoy '81, The Hospital '71

Josh Marchette (1973-)
Tequila Body Shots '99, Floating '97

Ron Marchini
Karate Cop '91, Return Fire '91, Omega Cop '90, Forgotten Warrior '86, Wolf '86, Death Machines '76

David Marciano (1960-)
The Last Don 2 '98, The Last Don '97, Kiss Shot '89, Hellbent '88

Vanessa Marcil (1968-)
Nice Guys Sleep Alone '99, The Rock '96

Paul Marco (1927-2006)
Night of the Ghouls '59, Plan 9 from Outer Space '56, Bride of the Monster '55

Andre Marcon (1948-)
La Vie Promise '02, Les Destinees '00, Up/Down/Fragile '95, Jeanne la Pucelle '94

Lisa Marcos
Diary of a Mad Black Woman '05, King's Ransom '05

Ted Marcoux
Andersonville '95, Ghost in the Machine '93, The Nightman '93

Andrea Marcovicci (1948-)
Jack the Bear '93, The Water Engine '92, Someone to Love '87, The Stuff '85, Sprague '84, Kings and Desperate Men '83, Packin' It In '83, Spacehunter: Adventures in the Forbidden Zone '83, The Hand '81, The Concorde: Airport '79 '79, The Front '76, The Devil's Web '74

James A. Marcus (1867-1937)
The Lone Avenger '33, The Broken Mask '28, Sadie Thompson '28, The Eagle '25, Oliver Twist '22

Jeff Marcus (1960-)
Alien Nation: Millennium '96, Alien Nation: Dark Horizon '94

Richard Marcus
Cannibal Campout '88, Deadly Friend '86, Enemy Mine '85

Stephen Marcus (1962-)
The Greatest Game Ever Played '05, Sorted '04, Lock, Stock and 2 Smoking Barrels '98, My Beautiful Laundrette '85

Jordan Marder (1973-)
American History X '98, Lord of Illusions '95, Walking on Air '87

Tom Mardirosian (1947-)
The Dark Half '91, Presumed Innocent '90

Ivano Marescotti (1946-)
King Arthur '04, The Monster '96

Bam Margera (1979-)
Jackass Number Two '06, Jackass: The Movie '02

Arthur Margetson (1887-1951)
Sherlock Holmes Faces Death '43, Juggernaut '37, The Mystery of the Mary Celeste '35

Margo (1917-85)
Who's Got the Action? '63, I'll Cry Tomorrow '55, Viva Zapata! '52, Behind the Rising Sun '43, The Leopard Man '43, Lost Horizon '37, Winterset '36

Janet Margolin (1943-93)
The Game of Love '90, Ghostbusters 2 '89, Distant Thunder '88, Plutonium Incident '82, Last Embrace '79, The Triangle Factory Fire Scandal '79, Annie Hall '77, Planet Earth '74, Pray for the Wildcats '74, Take the Money and Run '69, Enter Laughing '67, Nevada Smith '66, Morituri '65, David and Lisa '62

Stuart Margolin (1940-)
The Student Affair '97, To Grandmother's House We Go '94, Impolite '92, Guilty by Suspicion '91, Bye Bye Blues '89, Iron Eagle 2 '88, A Fine Mess '86, The Glitter Dome '84, Class '83, Running Hot '83, S.O.B. '81, Days of Heaven '78, The Big Bus '76, Futureworld '76, Death Wish '74, Kelly's Heroes '70, Women of the Prehistoric Planet '66

Mark Margolis (1939-)
The Fountain '06, Stay '05, 2B Perfectly Honest '04, Infested: Invasion of the Killer Bugs '02, Hardball '01, Dinner Rush '00, The Tailor of Panama '00, Jakob the Liar '99, The Thomas Crown Affair '99, Pi '98, Where the Rivers Flow North '94, Descending Angel '90, Scarface '83

Miriam Margolyes (1941-)
Flushed Away '06 (V), Happy Feet '06 (V), Being Julia '04, Chasing Liberty '04, Ladies in Lavender '04, Modigliani '04, Harry Potter and the Chamber of Secrets '02, Cats & Dogs '01, Dreaming of Joseph Lees '99, End of Days '99, Sunshine '99, Vanity Fair '99, Mulan '98 (V), Different for Girls '96, James and the Giant Peach '96 (V), William Shakespeare's Romeo and Juliet '96, Babe '95 (V), Balto '95 (V), Cold Comfort Farm '94, Immortal Beloved '94, The Age of Innocence '93, Ed and His Dead Mother '93, Stalin '92, The Butcher's Wife '91, Orpheus Descending '91, I Love You to Death '90, Pacific Heights '90, Little Dorrit, Film 1: Nobody's Fault '88, Little Dorrit, Film 2: Little Dorrit's Story '88

Michael Margotta (1946-)
Can She Bake a Cherry Pie? '83, The Blue Knight '75

David Margulies (1937-)
Bought and Sold '03, Looking for an Echo '99, Last Breath '96, Out on a Limb '92, Family Prayers '91, Funny About Love '90, Ghostbusters 2 '89, Running on Empty '88, 9 1/2 Weeks '86, Ghostbusters '84, Dressed to Kill '80, All That Jazz '79

Julianna Margulies (1966-)
The Darwin Awards '06, Snakes on a Plane '06, Hitler: The Rise of Evil '03, Evelyn '02, Ghost Ship '02, The Man from Elysian Fields '01, Mists of Avalon '01, Dinosaur '00 (V), What's Cooking? '00, The Big Day '99, The Newton Boys '97, Paradise Road '97, A Price above Rubies '97, Traveller '96, If Looks Could Kill '86

A. L. Mariaux
See Jess (Jesus) Franco

Constance Marie (1965-)
Tortilla Soup '01, The Last Marshal '99, Selena '96, My Family '94

Jeanne Marie
Young Nurses in Love '89

Lisa Marie (1968-)
Sleepy Hollow '99, Tail Lights Fade '99, Frogs for Snakes '98, Breast Men '97, Mars Attacks! '96, Ed Wood '94, Roller Blade '85

Jean-Pierre Marielle (1932-)
The Da Vinci Code '06, La Petite Lili '03, L'Eleve '95, Tous les Matins du Monde '92, Uranus '91, Menage '86, Coup de Torchon '81, One Wild Moment '78, The Women '68

Eli Marienthal (1986-)
Confessions of a Teenage Drama Queen '04, The Country Bears '02, American Pie 2 '01, Jay and Silent Bob Strike Back '01, Iron Giant '99 (V), First Love, Last Rites '98, Jack Frost '98, Slums of Beverly Hills '98

Marietto (1951-)
It Started in Naples '60, Angel in a Taxi '59

Jacques Marin (1919-2001)
The Island at the Top of the World '74, Shaft in Africa '73, Darling Lili '70, The Night of the Following Day '69, How to Steal a Million '66, The Trail '65, Duke of the Derby '62, Forbidden Games '52

Richard "Cheech" Marin (1946-)
Cars '06 (V), Underclassman '05, Christmas With the Kranks '04, The Lion King 1 1/2 '04 (V), Good Boy! '03 (V), Once Upon a Time in Mexico '03, Spy Kids 3-D: Game Over '03, Pinocchio '02 (V), Spy Kids 2: The Island of Lost Dreams '02, Spy Kids '01, Luminarias '99, Picking Up the Pieces '99, Paulie '98, The Great White Hype '96, Tin Cup '96, The Courtyard '95, Desperado '95, From Dusk Till Dawn '95, Charlie's Ghost: The Secret of Coronado '94, The Cisco Kid '94, The Lion King '94 (V), A Million to Juan '94, Ring of the Musketeers '93, Ferngully: The Last Rain Forest '92 (V), Mother Goose Rock 'n' Rhyme '90, The Shrimp on the Barbie '90, Far Out Man '89, Ghostbusters 2 '89, Rude Awakening '89, Oliver & Company '88 (V), Born in East L.A. '87, Fatal Beauty '87, Echo Park '86, After Hours '85, Cheech and Chong's The Corsican Brothers '84, Cheech and Chong: Still Smokin' '83, Yellowbeard '83, Cheech and Chong: Things Are Tough All Over '82, Cheech and Chong's Nice Dreams '81, Cheech and Chong's Next Movie '80, Cheech and Chong's Up in Smoke '79

Rikki Marin
Cheech and Chong's The Corsican Brothers '84, Cheech and Chong: Things Are Tough All Over '82

Ed Marinaro (1950-)
Urban Legends: Bloody Mary '05, Deadly Game '98, Panic in the Skies '96, Dancing with Danger '93, Lethal Lolita—Amy Fisher: My Story '92, The Diamond Trap '91, Queens Logic '91, The Game of Love '90, Dead Aim '87, Policewoman Centerfold '83

Sonny Marinelli
Born Beautiful '82, Dot.Kill '05

Boss of Bosses '99

Ethier Crispin Marini
See Chris-Pin (Ethier Crispin Martini) Martin

Dan Marino (1961-)
Little Nicky '00
Ace Ventura: Pet Detective '93

Ken Marino (1968-)
The Ten '07
Diggers '06
Love for Rent '05
Joe Somebody '01
Alphabet City '84
Prince of the City '81

George F. Marion, Sr. (1860-1945)
Death from a Distance '36
Anna Christie '30
The Big House '30
Hook, Line and Sinker '30
Evangeline 29
Anna Christie 23

Howard Marion-Crawford (1914-69)
The Castle of Fu Manchu '68
The Charge of the Light Brigade '68
Kiss and Kill '68
Paid to Kill '54
Mister Drake's Duck '50
The Singing Princess '49
Man in the Run '49

Mona Maris (1903-91)
The Falcon in Mexico '44
I Married an Angel '42
Underground '41
Love on the Run '36
Kiss and Make Up '34
Seas Beneath '31

Sari Maritza (1910-87)
Crimson Romance '34
International House '33
Greek Street '30

Robert Marius
The Devil in Silk '56

Heidi Mark (1971-)
Rock Star '01
Luscious Lola '00

Jane (Jeanne) Marken
Crazy for Love 52
Dedee d'Anvers '49
A Day in the Country '46
Children of Paradise '44
Eternal Return '43

Tony Markes
Welcome to Hollywood '00
In the Aftermath: Angels Never Sleep '87

Enid Markey (1896-1981)
Tarzan of the Apes '17
Civilization '16
The Fugitive: Taking of Luke McVane '15

Kika Markham (1942-)
Longford '06
Wonderland '99
Deep Cover '88
Miss A & Miss M '86
Outland '81
Two English Girls '72

Monte Markham (1935-)
At First Sight '95
Piranha '95
Defense Play '88
Judgment Day '88
Hot Pursuit '87
Counter Measures '85
Hotline '82

Beth Marion (1912-2003)
Phantom Gold '38
The Phantom of the Range '38
Everyman's Law '36
Rip Roarin' Buckaroo '36
Between Men '35

Brian Markinson
Charlie Wilson's War '07
Bixby Boys '82
Airport '77 '77
Midway '76
Hustling '75
Ginger in the Morning '73
Guns of the Magnificent Seven '69
Illegal '55
Casanova's Big Night '54
Garden of Evil '54
Bugles in the Afternoon '52
The Day the Earth Stood Still '51

Ted Markland
American Kickboxer 2: To the Death '93
Category 6: Day of Destruction '04
Chasing Freedom '04
Angels in America '03
The Curse of the Jade Scorpion '01
Take Me Home: The John Denver Story '00
Sweet and Lowdown '99

Olivera Markovic (1925-)
Siberian Lady Macbeth '61

Karl Markovics (1963-)
All the Queen's Men '02

Alfred Marks (1921-96)
Antonia and Jane '91
Fanny Hill '83
Valentino '77
Scream and Scream Again '70

Margaret Markov (1951-)
The Arena '73
Hot Box '72
Run, Angel, Run! '69

Jennifer Marks
Naked Wishes '00
The Strangers '98

Winnie Markus (1922-2002)
The Devil in Silk '56
The Mozart Story '48

Robert Marius
The Devil in Silk '56

Arnold Marle (1888-1970)
The Snake Woman '61
Men of Two Worlds '46

Ben Marley
From the Earth to the Moon '98

John Marley (1907-84)
The Mosaic Project '95
On the Edge '86
The Glitter Dome '84
Threshold '83
Utilities '83
The Godfather 1902-1959: The Complete Epic '81
Hooper '78
It's Alive 2: It Lives Again '78
The Car '77
Framed '75
The Godfather '72
Jory '72
A Man Called Sledge '71
Love Story '70
Faces 68

Carla Marler
Spirits of the Dead '68
Any Number Can Win '63
The Avenger '62
Zazie dans le Metro '61

Lucy Marlow (1932-)
My Sister Eileen '55
Queen Bee '55

Kelli Maroney (1964-)
Face Down '97
Servants of Twilight '91
Zero Boys '86
Night of the Comet '84
Slayground '84
Fast Times at Ridgemont High '82

Michael Maronna (1977-)
40 Days and 40 Nights '02
Slackers '02

Richard Marner (1921-2004)
The Sum of All Fears '02
Race for Life '55
The African Queen '51

Percy Marmont (1883-1977)
Lisbon '56
Four Sided Triangle '53
Young and Innocent '37
The Secret Agent '36
Rich and Strange '32
Mantrap '26

Florence Marly (1919-78)
Dr. Death, Seeker of Souls '73
Games '67
Planet of Blood '66
Tokyo Joe '49

David Marriott
Monster High '89
Operation Warzone '89

Moore Marriott (1885-1949)
Oh, Mr. Porter '37
The Flying Scotsman 29

Sylvia Marriott
The Story of Adele H. '75
Two English Girls '72

Hugh Marlowe (1911-82)
Castle of Evil '66
Seven Days in May '64
Birdman of Alcatraz '62
Elmer Gantry '60
Please Not Now! '61
Earth vs. the Flying Saucers '55

Juliette Marquis
This Girl's Life '03

Margaret Marquis (1917-)

Linda Marlowe (1944-)
The Green Man '91
Mr. Love '86
Big Zapper '73
He Kills Night After Night After Night '69
Night Slasher '69

June Marlowe (1903-84)
The Lone Defender '32
Pardon Us '31
Don Juan '26

Ron Marquette (-1995)
Red Shoe Diaries 7: Burning Up '96
Deadly Past '95
Fed Shoe Diaries 5: Weekend Pass '95
Public Access '93

Marlo Marron
Funny Valentine '05
Mi Vida Loca '94

Kenneth Mars (1936-)
Citizen Ruth '96
The Secret of Saurus Rock '98 (V)
Spirited Away '01 (V)
The Land Before Time series 2–6 (V)
Thumbelina '94 (V)
We're Back! A Dinosaur's Story '93 (V)
Shadows and Fog '92
Get Smart, Again! '89
The Little Mermaid '89 (V)
For Keeps '88
Illegally Yours '87
Radio Days '87
Fletch '85
Misfits of Science '85
Yellowbeard '83
Protocol '84
Goin' Cocoanuts '78
Rabbit Test '78
Night Moves '75
The Parallax View '74
What's Up, Doc? '72
Young Frankenstein '74

Serge Marquand (1930-2004)
April Fools '69
Barbarella '68
Blood and Roses '61

Christian Marquand (1927-2000)
Victory '81
The Corrupt Ones '67
End of Desire '62
Love Play '60
And God Created Woman '57

Erika Marozsan (1972-)
Gloomy Sunday '02

Adoni Maropis (1963-)
Hidalgo '04
Bad Company '02

Carl Marotte (1959-)
One Kill '00
Prisoner of Love '99
When Justice Falls '98
The Ultimate Weapon '97
Breaking All the Rules '85
Pick-Up Summer '79

Eddie Marr (1900-87)
The Damned Don't Cry '50
Hollywood Canteen '44

Maria Elena Marques (1926-91)
Ambush at Tomahawk Gap '53
Across the Wide Missouri '51
The Pearl '48

Christopher Marquette (1984-)
The Invisible '07
American Gun '05
Just Friends '05
Come to the Stable '49

Jason Marsden (1975-)
How to Make a Monster '01 (V)
Spirited Away '01 (V)
White Squall '96
Pride '98 (V)
DOA: Dead or Alive '06
A Goofy Movie '94 (V)
The Lion King: Simba's Pride '98 (V)

Matthew Marsden (1972-)
Anacondas: The Hunt for the Blood Orchid '04
Helen of Troy '03
Black Hawk Down '01
An American Haunting '05
Rambo '08

James Marsden (1973-)
Enchanted '07
27 Dresses '08
Hairspray '07
Heights '06
Superman Returns '06
X-Men: The Last Stand '06
The Notebook '04
The 24th Day '04
X2: X-Men United '03
Interstate 60 '02
Sugar & Spice '01
X-Men '00
Gossip '00
Disturbing Behavior '98
Campfire Tales '98
Bella Mafia '97
Public Enemies '96

Carol Marsh (1926-)
The Horror of Dracula '58
A Christmas Carol '51
Alice in Wonderland '50
Brighton Rock '47

Garry Marsh (1902-81)
Who Done It? '56
Just William's Luck '47
A Girl in a Million '46
Dead of Night '45
Old Mother Riley's Jungle Treasure '51
Someone at the Door '50

Roy Marsden (1941-)
A Certain Justice '99
A Mind to Murder '96
Devices and Desires '91
Shiner '00

Eddie Marsan (1968-)
Beowulf & Grendel '06
The Illusionist '06
Mission: Impossible 3 '06
V for Vendetta '06
Friends & Crocodiles '05
Vera Drake '04
Gangs of New York '02
The Emperor's New Clothes '01

Maurice Marsac (1915-2007)
The Big Red One '80
Clarence, the Cross-eyed Lion '65
Werewolf in a Girl's Dormitory '61
Lion '65
Tarzan and the Trappers '58

Branford Marsalis (1960-)
School Daze '88
Throw Momma from the Train '87

Marjorie Mars (1903-)
Brief Encounter '46

Jean Mars (1934-)
Spy of Napoleon '36

Jamie Marsh
Beethoven's 3rd '00
Best Laid Plans '99
Brainscan '94

Jean Marsh (1934-)
Sense & Sensibility '07
Agatha Christie's The Pale Horse '04
Fatherland '94
A Connecticut Yankee in King Arthur's Court '89
Willow '88
Return to Oz '85
The Changeling '80
Frenzy '72
The Unearthly Stranger '64

Joan Marsh (1914-2000)
Follow the Leader '44
Charlie Chan on Broadway '37
Champagne for Breakfast '35
High Gear '33
Rainbow over Broadway '33

Mae Marsh (1895-1968)
From the Terrace '60
Sergeant Rutledge '60
While the City Sleeps '56
The Tall Men '55
The Quiet Man '52
The Gunfighter '50
My Blue Heaven '50
Impact '49
Fort Apache '48
Three Godfathers '48
Blue, White and Perfect '42
Hoodoo Ann '16
Intolerance '15
The Birth of a Nation '15
Home Sweet Home '14
Judith of Bethulia '13
The Battle of Elderbush Gulch '13

Marian Marsh (1913-2006)
House of Errors '42
Gentleman from Dixie '41
When's Your Birthday? '37
Youth on Parole '37
Crime and Punishment '35
Svengali '31

Matthew Marsh (1954-)
Spy Game '01
A Certain Justice '99
An Affair in Mind '89
In the Secret State '85

Michele Marsh
Evil Town '87
Deadly Alliance '78
Fiddler on the Roof '71

Alan Marshal (1909-61)
The Day of the Outlaw '59
House on Haunted Hill '58
The White Cliffs of Dover '44
Lydia '41
Tom, Dick, and Harry '41
The Howards of Virginia '40
The Hunchback of Notre Dame '39
Conquest '37
Night Must Fall '37
After the Thin Man '36
The Garden of Allah '36
Dame '37

Brenda Marshall (1915-92)
Strange Impersonation '46
Background to Danger '43
Captains of the Clouds '42

Marshall

Footsteps in the Dark '41
The Sea Hawk '40

Bryan Marshall (1938-)
Return to Snowy River '88
The Long Good Friday '80
Because of the Cats '74
Vanity Fair '67

Connie Marshall (1938-)
Kill the Umpire '50
The Green Promise '49
Daisy Kenyon '47
Mother Wore Tights '47

David Anthony Marshall
The Demolitionist '95
Another 48 Hrs. '90

Dodie Marshall
Easy Come, Easy Go '67
Spinout '66

Don Marshall (1936-)
Terminal Island '73
The Thing with Two Heads '72

E.G. Marshall (1910-98)
Absolute Power '97
The Defenders: Payback '97
Miss Evers' Boys '97
Nixon '95
Oldest Confederate Widow Tells All '95
Russian Roulette '93
Stephen King's The Tommyknockers '93
Consenting Adults '92
Ironclads '90
Two Evil Eyes '90
National Lampoon's Christmas Vacation '89
Saigon: Year of the Cat '87
My Chauffeur '86
Power '86
Kennedy '83
Creepshow '82
Eleanor: First Lady of the World '82
Superman 2 '80
The Lazarus Syndrome '79
Interiors '78
Abduction of St. Anne '75
Pursuit '72
The Pursuit of Happiness '70
Toral Toral Toral '70
The Bridge at Remagen '69
The Littlest Angel '69
The Chase '66
Is Paris Burning? '66
Town without Pity '61
Cash McCall '60
Compulsion '59
The Buccaneer '58
Twelve Angry Men '57
The Mountain '56
The Left Hand of God '55
Broken Lance '54
The Caine Mutiny '54
The Silver Chalice '54
13 Rue Madeleine '46

Garry Marshall (1934-)
Keeping Up with the Steins '06
Chicken Little '05 (V)
Orange County '02
Never Been Kissed '99
With Friends Like These '98
The Twilight of the Golds '97
Dear God '96
Hocus Pocus '93
A League of Their Own '92
Soapdish '91
Jumpin' Jack Flash '86
Lost in America '85

Herbert Marshall (1890-1966)
The Fly '58
Stage Struck '57
The Virgin Queen '55
The Black Shield of Falworth '54
Angel Face '52
Captain Blackjack '51
The Underworld Story '50
The Secret Garden '49
Crack-Up '46
Duel in the Sun '46
The Razor's Edge '46
The Enchanted Cottage '45
Forever and a Day '43
The Moon and Sixpence '43
The Little Foxes '41
When Ladies Meet '41
Foreign Correspondent '40
The Letter '40
Mad About Music '38
Angel '37
A Woman Rebels '36
The Dark Angel '35
The Good Fairy '35
The Painted Veil '34
Riptide '34
Blonde Venus '32
Trouble in Paradise '32
Murder '30

James Marshall (1967-)
Come as You Are '05
The Shaft '01
Luck of the Draw '00
Soccer Dog: The Movie '98
The Ticket '97
Don't Do It '94
A Few Good Men '92
Gladiator '92
Twin Peaks: Fire Walk with Me '92
Feds '88
Krull '83

Kris Marshall (1973-)
Death at a Funeral '07
The Merchant of Venice '04
Doctor Zhivago '03
Love Actually '03
Deathwatch '02
The Four Feathers '02

Ken Marshall (1951-)
Double Exposure: The Story of Margaret Bourke-White '89
Tilt '78

Marion Marshall (1930-)
Sailor Beware '52
The Stooge '51
I Was a Male War Bride '49

Paula Marshall (1964-)
I Know Who Killed Me '07
Cheaper by the Dozen '03
Thursday '98
Get Shorty '95
Hocus Pocus '93
The Hard Way '91

Penny Marshall (1947-)
Looking for Comedy in the Muslim World '06
Stateside '04
A Family Thing '96
That Old Feeling '96
Challenge of a Lifetime '85
Movers and Shakers '85
1941 '79
How Come Nobody's On Our Side? '73
Evil Roy Slade '71

Peter Marshall (1930-)
Americathon '79
A Guide for the Married Woman '78
Return of Jesse James '50

Sarah Marshall (1933-)
French Silk '94
The People vs. Jean Harris '81
Lord Love a Duck '66

Sean Marshall (1965-)
Pete's Dragon '77
Wonderland Cove '75

Trudy Marshall (1920-2004)
Married Too Young '62
Crash Dive '43
The Fighting Sullivans '42

Tully Marshall (1864-1943)
Behind Prison Walls '43
This Gun for Hire '42
Mr. Boggs Steps Out '38
Night of Terror '33
The Cabin in the Cotton '32
Red Dust '32
Strangers of the Evening '32
Two-Fisted Law '32
Fighting Caravans '31
Big Trail '30
Tom Sawyer '30
Queen Kelly '29
The Cat and the Canary '27
Smouldering Fires '25
He Who Gets Slapped '24
Broken Hearts of Broadway '23
Let's Go! '23
What Happened to Rosa? '21
Hawthorne of the USA '19

William Marshall (1917-94)
That Brennan Girl '46
State Fair '45

William Marshall (1924-2003)
Vasectomy: A Delicate Matter '86
The Great Skycopter Rescue '82
Twilight's Last Gleaming '77
Scream Blacula Scream '73
Blacula '72
The Boston Strangler '68
Demetrius and the Gladiators '54

Zena Marshall (1926-)
The Terronauts '67
Dr. No '62

Christina Marsillach (1963-)
Opera '88

Tony Marsina
Last Mercenary '84
Tornado '83

James Marsters
P.S. I Love You '93
Shadow Puppets '07
Strange Frequency 2 '01

Nathaniel Marston (1975-)
Ordinary Sinner '02
Love is All There Is '96

Lynn(e) Marta (1946-)
Blood Beach '81
Joe Kidd '72
Richard Petty Story '72

Judy Marte (1983-)
On the Outs '05
Raising Victor Vargas '03

Henri Marteau (1933-2005)
Indochine '92
La Femme Infidele '69

Arlene Martel (1936-)
Angels from Hell '68
Demon with a Glass Hand '64

June Martel (1909-78)
Santa Fe Stampede '38
Forlorn River '37
Wild Horse Rodeo '37
Arizona Mahoney '36

K.C. Martel (1970-)
White Water Summer '87
E.T.: The Extra-Terrestrial '82
The Munsters' Revenge '81
The Amityville Horror '79

Chris Martell
Flesh Feast '69
Scream, Baby, Scream '69
Gruesome Twosome '67

Donna (Dona Martel) Martell (1927-)
Ten Wanted Men '54
Give a Girl a Break '53
Project Moon Base '53
Abbott and Costello Meet the Killer, Boris Karloff '49

Gillian Martell
Cause Celebre '87
Oliver Twist '85

Peter Martell
See Peter Martellanza

Peter Martellanza (1938-)
Mission Phantom '79
Planet on the Prowl '65

Cynthia Martells
Paid in Full '02
The Wood '99
Broken Trust '95
Zooman '95
A Modern Affair '94
Blind Spot '93

Frank Marth (1922-)
Showdown '93
Fight '56

Francois Marthouret (1943-)
The Lady and the Duke '01
Sitcom '97

Andrea Martin (1947-)
Black Christmas '06 (V)
Brother Bear 2 '06 (V)
The Producers '05
New York Minute '04
Kurt Vonnegut's Harrison Bergeron '95
My Big Fat Greek Wedding '02
All Over the Guy '01
Jimmy Neutron: Boy Genius '01 (V)
Hedwig and the Angry Inch '00
Loser '00
Believe '99
Wag the Dog '97
Bogus '96
Guitarman '95
Gypsy '93
Ted & Venus '93
Boris and Natasha: The Movie '92
All I Want for Christmas '91
Stepping Out '91
Too Much Sun '90
Rude Awakening '89
Worth Winning '89
Club Paradise '86
Soup for One '82
Black Christmas '75

Anna Maxwell Martin
Becoming Jane '07
Bleak House '05

Barney Martin (1923-2005)
Arthur 2: On the Rocks '88
Arthur '81

Charles Martin (1910-83)
Fighting Black Kings '76
You've Ruined Me, Eddie '58

Chris-Pin (Ethier Crispin Martini) Martin (1894-1953)
Rimfire '49
Down Argentine Way '40
Lucky Cisco Kid '40
Stagecoach '39
The Texans '38
South of Santa Fe '32

Christopher Martin (1963-)
House Party 3 '94
Class Act '91
House Party 2: The Pajama Jam '91
House Party '90

Damon Martin
Amityville 1992: It's About Time '92
Ghoulies 2 '87

Dan (Daniel, Danny) Martin (1935-)
Devil's Kiss '75
The Last Tomahawk '65
Gunfight at Red Sands '63

Dean Martin (1917-95)
That's Dancing! '85
Cannonball Run 2 '84
Cannonball Run '81
Showdown '73
Airport '70
Bandolero! '68
Five Card Stud '68
The Wrecking Crew '68
The Ambushers '67
Rough Night in Jericho '67
Murderers' Row '66
The Silencers '66
Texas Across the River '66
Marriage on the Rocks '65
Sons of Katie Elder '65
Kiss Me, Stupid! '64
Robin and the 7 Hoods '64
Four for Texas '63
Toys in the Attic '63
Who's Got the Action? '63
All in a Night's Work '61
Bells Are Ringing '60
Ocean's 11 '60
Career '59
Rio Bravo '59
Some Came Running '58
The Young Lions '58
Hollywood or Bust '56
Pardners '56
Artists and Models '55
The Caddy '53
The Road to Bali '53
Scared Stiff '53
Jumping Jacks '52
Sailor Beware '52
At War with the Army '50
My Friend Irma '49

Dean Paul (Dino Martin Jr.) Martin (1951-87)
Backfire '88
Misfits of Science '85
Players '79

Dewey Martin (1923-)
Seven Alone '75
Flight to Fury '66
Savage Sam '63
Desperate Hours '55
Land of the Pharaohs '55
Men of the Fighting Lady '54
The Big Sky '52
The Thing '51

Dick Martin (1928-)
Bartleby '01
Air Bud 2: Golden Receiver '98
Carbon Copy '81
The Glass Bottom Boat '66

Duane Martin (1970s-)
Deliver Us from Eva '03
Mutiny '99
Scream 2 '97
Woo '97
Down Periscope '96
Above the Rim '94

D'Urville Martin (1938-84)
Big Score '83
Death Journey '76
Dolemite '75
Sheba, Baby '75
Boss '74
Hell Up in Harlem '73
Final Comedown '72
Watermelon Man '70

Eddy Martin (1990-)
Rebound '05
The Maldonado Miracle '03

Edie Martin (1880-1964)
The Ladykillers '55
Genevieve '53

George Martin (1926-)
Drunks '96
One Fine Day '96
Blood at Sundown '88
Crossing Delancey '88
Falling in Love '84
Psychopath '68

Gilbert Martin
Beautiful People '99
Rob Roy '95

Gregory Mars Martin
See Mars Callahan
Kalifornia '93

Helen Martin (1909-2000)
I Got the Hook-Up '98
Don't Be a Menace to South Central While Drinking Your Juice in the Hood '95
Doc Hollywood '91
House Party 2: The Pajama Jam '91
Night Angel '90
Hollywood Shuffle '87
A Hero Ain't Nothin' but a Sandwich '78

Ivan Martin
Funny Valentine '05
Prey for Rock and Roll '03

Jared Martin (1943-)
Twinsitters '95
Karate Warrior '88
Quiet Cool '86
The Sea Serpent '85
The Lonely Lady '83
The New Gladiators '83
Second Coming of Suzanne '80

Jean Martin (1922-)
Lucie Aubrac '98
The Messiah '75
The Battle of Algiers '66

John Martin
Dr. Terror's House of Horrors '65
The Tell-Tale Heart '60
Mesa of Lost Women '52

John Martin (1951-)
The Underneath '95
Dark Before Dawn '89
Black Roses '88
Fire in the Night '85

Justin Martin
A Raisin in the Sun '08
Bloody Murder '99

Kellie Martin (1975-)
Mystery Woman: Mystery Weekend '05
Christy '94
A Goofy Movie '94 (V)
Matinee '92
Troop Beverly Hills '89

Kiel Martin (1944-90)
Convicted: A Mother's Story '87
Child Bride of Short Creek '81
Panic in Needle Park '71

Lewis Martin (1894-1969)
Men of the Fighting Lady '54
The War of the Worlds '53
Ace in the Hole '51

Lock Martin (1916-59)
Invaders from Mars '53
The Day the Earth Stood Still '51

Marion Martin (1918-85)
The Great Mike '44
Mexican Spitfire at Sea '42
Big Store '41
The Man in the Iron Mask '39
Sinners in Paradise '38

Mary Martin (1913-90)
Peter Pan '60
Main Street to Broadway '53

Mel Martin (1947-)
Poldark '96
Darlings of the Gods '90
White Hunter, Black Heart '90
Love for Lydia '79
Horsemasters '61

Millicent Martin (1934-)
Shallow Hal '01
The Song of the Lark '01
Cast Away '00
Alfie '66
Those Magnificent Men in Their Flying Machines '65

Nan Martin (1927-)
Big Eden '00
Matters of the Heart '90
A Nightmare on Elm Street 3: Dream Warriors '87
Proud Men '87
The Young Nurses '73
Goodbye Columbus '69
For Love of Ivy '68
Toys in the Attic '63

Pamela Sue Martin (1953-)
Flicks '85
Torchlight '85
Lady in Red '79
Buster and Billie '74
Our Time '74
The Girls of Huntington House '75

Pepper Martin (1936-)
Evil Altar '89
Scream '83
Dead Men Don't Wear Plaid '82
Penn's from Heaven '81
The Kids Are Alright '79
Love and Bullets '79

Remi Martin (1965-)
Clean '04
The Possessed '88
Conseil de Famille '86

Richard Martin (1919-94)
Gunplay '51
Dynamite Pass '50
Rider from Tucson '50
Riders of the Range '50
Storm over Wyoming '50
Mysterious Desperado '49
Having Wonderful Crime '45
West of the Pecos '45

Ross Martin (1920-81)
More Wild, Wild West '80
Wild, Wild West Revisited '79
The Seekers '79
Wild & Wooly '78
Dying Room Only '73
Experiment in Terror '52
Conquest of Space '55
Geronimo '62
Tender Comrade '43
Nevada '44

Rudolf Martin (1967-)
Dracula: The Dark Prince '01

Sandy Martin (1950-)
Sparkler '99
Barfly '87
Vendetta '85
Scalpe '76

Sharlene Martin
Possession: Until Death Do You Part '90

Tina Martin
Kiss Me Deadly '55

Strother Martin (1919-80)
Hotwire '80
Better Late Than Never '79
The Champ '79
Cheech and Chong's Up in Smoke '79
Nightwing '79
The Villain '79
Steel Cowboy '78
Slap Shot '77
Rooster Cogburn '75
Hard Times '75
Pocket Money '72
The Brotherhood of Satan '71
Ballad of Cable Hogue '70
Butch Cassidy and the Sundance Kid '69
True Grit '69
The Wild Bunch '69
Cool Hand Luke '67
Shenandoah '65
Invitation to a Gunfighter '64
McLintock! '63
The Man Who Shot Liberty Valance '62
The Horse Soldiers '59
Attack! '56

Skip Martin (1928-84)
Horror Hospital '73
Masque of the Red Death '65

Steve Martin (1945-)
The Pink Panther '06
Cheaper by the Dozen 2 '05
Shopgirl '05
Bringing Down the House '03
Cheaper by the Dozen '03
Looney Tunes: Back in Action '03
Novocaine '01
Joe Gould's Secret '00
Bowfinger '99
The Out-of-Towners '99
Prince of Egypt '98 (V)
The Spanish Prisoner '97
Father of the Bride Part 2 '95
A Simple Twist of Fate '94
Mixed Nuts '94
Sgt. Bilko '95
Housesitter '92
Leap of Faith '92
Father of the Bride '91
Grand Canyon '91
L.A. Story '91
My Blue Heaven '90
Parenthood '89
Dirty Rotten Scoundrels '88
Planes, Trains & Automobiles '87
Roxanne '87
Little Shop of Horrors '86
Three Amigos '86
Movers and Shakers '85
All of Me '84
The Lonely Guy '84
The Man with Two Brains '83
Dead Men Don't Wear Plaid '82
Pennies from Heaven '81
The Jerk '79
The Muppet Movie '79
Sgt. Pepper's Lonely Hearts Club Band '78

Tony Martin (1912-)
Meet Me in Las Vegas '56
Hit the Deck '55
Here Come the Girls '53
Easy to Love '53
Two Tickets to Broadway '51
Casbah '48
Big Store '41
Till the Clouds Roll By '46
Ziegfeld Girl '41
Music in My Heart '40
Thanks for Everything '38
Pigskin Parade '36

Tony (Anthony) Martin (1953-)
Candy '06

Vera Martin
Loyalties '86

Vince Martin
Breaking Loose '90
Night Master '87

Vivian Martin (1893-1987)
The Belles of St. Trinian's '53

W.T. Martin
The Wishing Ring '14

Margo Martindale (1951-)
Paris, je t'aime '06
Wedding Daze '06
High Stakes '89
Hardhat & Legs '80

Elsa Martinelli (1932-)
Once Upon a Crime '92
Belle Star '79
Candy '68
Madigan's Millions '67
Maros 7 '67
Oldest Profession '67
Woman Times Seven '67
10th Victim '65
The Trial '63
The V.I.P.'s '63
Hatari! '62
Blood and Roses '61

Alessandra Martines (1963-)
And Now, Ladies and Gentlemen '02
Les Misérables '95

A. Martinez (1948-)
Once Upon a Wedding '05
Ordinary Sinner '02
What's Cooking? '00
Double Trap '98
Last Rites '88
Wind River '98
The Cherokee Kid '96
Grand Avenue '96
One Night Stand '95
Where's the Money, Noreen? '95
Deconstructing Sarah '94
The Hunt for the Night Stalker '91
Powwow Highway '89

Adrian Martinez
Mail Order Wife '04
Corn '02

Joaquin Martinez (1932-)
The Cowboy Way '94
Jeremiah Johnson '72

Nacho Martinez (1952-96)
Law of Desire '86
Matador '86

Olivier Martinez (1966-)
Blood & Chocolate '07
Taking Lives '04
S.W.A.T. '03
Unfaithful '02
Before Night Falls '00
The Chambermaid on the Titanic '97
Mon Homme '96
The Horseman on the Roof '95

Vanessa Martinez
Casa de los Babys '03

Maximillian Martini (1969-)
Saving Private Ryan '98

Steven Martini (1978-)
Smiling Fish & Goat on Fire '99
Major Payne '95

Susanna Martinkova
Ring of Death '69
Diary of a Rebel '68

Al Martino (1927-)
The Godfather, Part 3 '90
The Godfather '72

Orlando Martins (1899-1985)
Call Me Bwana '63
Simba '55
Men of Two Worlds '46

Lee Marvin (1924-87)
Delta Force '86
The Dirty Dozen: The Next Mission '85
Gorky Park '83
Death Hunt '81
The Big Red One '80
Avalanche Express '79
Great Scout & Cathouse Thursday '76
Shout at the Devil '76
The Klansman '74
Emperor of the North Pole '73
The Iceman Cometh '73
Pocket Money '72
Prime Cut '72
Monte Walsh '70
Hell in the Pacific '69
Paint Your Wagon '69
Sergeant Ryker '68
The Dirty Dozen '67
The Meanest Men in the West '67
Point Blank '67
The Professionals '66
Cat Ballou '65
Ship of Fools '65
The Killers '64
Donovan's Reef '63
The Man Who Shot Liberty Valance '62
The Comancheros '61
The Missouri Traveler '58
Raintree County '57
Attack! '56
I Died a Thousand Times '55
Pete Kelly's Blues '55
Shack Out on 101 '55
Bad Day at Black Rock '54
The Caine Mutiny '54
The Wild One '54
The Big Heat '53
Gun Fury '53
The Stranger Wore a Gun '53

Susanna Martinkova

Laia Marull (1973-)
Take My Eyes '03
Café Olé '00

Harpo Marx (1888-1964)
Love Happy '50
A Night in Casablanca '46
The Big Store '41
Room Service '38
A Day at the Races '37
A Night at the Opera '35
A Night at the Circus '39
Monkey Business '31
The Cocoanuts '29
Animal Crackers '30
Duck Soup '33
Horse Feathers '32

Zeppo Marx (1901-79)
The Marx Brothers in a Nutshell '90
Duck Soup '33
Horse Feathers '32
Monkey Business '31
The Cocoanuts '29
Animal Crackers '30

Groucho Marx (1890-1977)
The Marx Brothers in a Nutshell '90
Will Success Spoil Rock Hunter? '57
Double Dynamite '51
Love Happy '50
Mr. Music '50
Copacabana '47
A Night in Casablanca '46
Big Store '41
Go West '40
At the Circus '39
Room Service '38
A Day at the Races '37
A Night at the Opera '35
Duck Soup '33
Horse Feathers '32
Monkey Business '31
Animal Crackers '30
The Cocoanuts '29

Chico Marx (1886-1961)
The Marx Brothers in a Nutshell '90
Love Happy '50
A Night in Casablanca '46
Go West '40
At the Circus '39
Room Service '38
A Day at the Races '37
A Night at the Opera '35
Duck Soup '33
Horse Feathers '32
Monkey Business '31
Animal Crackers '30
The Cocoanuts '29

Franca Marzi (1926-89)
Nights of Cabiria '57

Ron Masak (1936-)
Island '78
Harper Valley P.T.A. '78
Tora! Tora! Tora! '70

Masasa
Team America: World Police '04 (V)
Kingdom Come '01

Pierrino Mascarino
Love Comes Softly '03

Joseph Mascolo (1935-)
Jaws 2 '78
Love Desperado '68

Marino (Martin) Mase (1939-)
The Belly of an Architect '87

Vladimir Mashkov (1963-)
Behind Enemy Lines '01
Dancing at the Blue Iguana '00
The Thief '97

Giulietta Masina (1921-94)
Ginger & Fred '86
The Madwoman of Chaillot '69
Juliet of the Spirits '65
Nights of Cabiria '57
Il Bidone '55
La Strada '54
Europa '51 '52
The White Sheik '52
Variety Lights '51

Ace Mask (1948-)
Transylvania Twist '89
Not of This Earth '88

Connie Mason (1937-)
2000 Maniacs '64
Blood Feast '63

Hilary Mason (1917-2006)
Meridian: Kiss of the Beast '90
Robot Jox '90
Dolls '87
Don't Look Now '73

Ingrid Mason (1952-)
The Thorn Birds: The Missing Years '96

Jackie Mason (1934-)
Caddyshack 2 '88
History of the World: Part 1 '81
The Jerk '79

Eric Mason (1934-)
The Ghost Goes West '36
Kiss of the Tarantula '75
Black Starlet '74

Elliot Mason (1897-1949)
On Approval '44

James Mason (1890-1954)
The Plainsman '37
A Night in Casablanca '46
Strictly G.I. '44
Stage Door Canteen '43
Big Shot '41

James Mason (1909-84)
A.D. '85
The Shooting Party '85
The Assisi Underground '84
Dangerous Summer '82
Yellowbeard '83
George Washington '84
Evil under the Sun '82
Ivanhoe '82
The Verdict '82
ffolkes '80
Murder by Decree '79
Salem's Lot '79

Mason
Sidney Sheldon's Bloodline '79
Water Babies '79
The Boys from Brazil '78
Heaven Can Wait '78
Jesus of Nazareth '77
Cross of Iron '76
Kidnap Syndicate '76
Street War '76
Voyage of the Damned '76
Autobiography of a Princess '75
Inside Out '75
Mandingo '75
The Destructors '74
11 Harrowhouse '74
The Last of Sheila '73
Mackintosh Man '73
Bad Man's River '72
Cold Sweat '70
Yin & Yang of Mr. Go '71
Mayering '68
Cop-Out '67
The Blue Max '66
Georgy Girl '66
Lord Jim '65
The Fall of the Roman Empire '64
The Pumpkin Eater '64
Lolita '62
Tiara Tahiti '62
The Trials of Oscar Wilde '60
Journey to the Center of the Earth '59
North by Northwest '59
Island in the Sun '57
Forever Darling '56
Prince Valiant '54
A Star Is Born '54
20,000 Leagues under the Sea '54
Botany Bay '53
Charade '53
The Desert Rats '53
Julius Caesar '53
Face to Face '52
Five Fingers '52
Prisoner of Zenda '52
The Desert Fox '51
Pandora and the Flying Dutchman '51
Caught '49
East Side, West Side '49
Madame Bovary '49
Reckless Moment '49
Man of Evil '48
Odd Man Out '47
The Seventh Veil '46
The Man in Grey '45
The Wicked Lady '45
Hotel Reserve '44
The Night Has Eyes '42
Secret Mission '42
I Met a Murderer '39
Fire Over England '37
High Command '37
The Mill on the Floss '37
Secret of Stamboul '36
Late Extra '35

Laurence Mason
Ali '01
Hackers '95
Parallel Sons '95
The Crow '93

Leroy Mason (1903-47)
Daughter of Don Q '46
The Phantom Rider '46
Vigilantes of Boom Town '47
California Joe '43
The Man Who Wouldn't Die '42
Western Mail '42
Silver Stallion '41
Range Busters '40
Rocky Mountain Rangers '40
Wyoming Outlaw '39
Heroes of the Hills '38
Outlaw Express '38
Santa Fe Stampede '38
Children of the Wild '37
The Painted Stallion '37
Western Gold '36
Black Gold '36
Go-Get-'Em-Haines '35
The Mystery Man '35
Texas Terror '35
Valley of Wanted Men '35
Dude Ranger '34
The Fighting Trooper '34
When a Man Sees Red '34
Phantom of the Air '33

Madison Mason
Thirteen Days '00
Glitz '88

Marsha Mason (1942-)
Bride & Prejudice '04
Life with Judy Garland—Me and My Shadows '01
Restless Spirits '99
Two Days in the Valley '96
Broken Trust '95
Nick of Time '95
I Love Trouble '94
Drop Dead Fred '91
Dinner at Eight '89
The Image '89
Stella '89
Heartbreak Ridge '86
Trapped in Silence '86
Max Dugan Returns '83
Lois Gibbs and the Love Canal '82
Only When I Laugh '81
Chapter Two '79
Promises in the Dark '79
The Cheap Detective '78
Audrey Rose '77
The Goodbye Girl '77
Blume in Love '73
Cinderella Liberty '73

Pamela Mason (1922-96)
Navy vs. the Night Monsters '66
Door to Door Maniac '61
Charade '53

Tom Mason
Brooklyn Lobster '05
Looking for an Echo '99
Runaway Bride '99
Maternal Instincts '96
My Very Best Friend '96
The Amy Fisher Story '93
Final Appeal '93
Men Don't Leave '88
Mississippi Burning '88
Kicks '85
Aliens Are Coming '80
Walking Through the Fire '80
Apocalypse Now '79

Varvara O. Massalitinova
My Apprenticeship '39
Alexander Nevsky '38
My Childhood '38

Lea Massari (1930-)
Vengeance '86
Christ Stopped at Eboli '79
Les Rendez-vous D'Anna '78
Allonsanfan '73
The Story of a Love Story '73
And Hope to Die '72
Murmur of the Heart '71
The Things of Life '70
L'Avventura '60

Michael Massee
Catwoman '04
Momentum '03
The Theory of the Leisure Class '01
The Last Don '97
Lost Highway '96
One Fine Day '96
Playing God '96
Tales from the Hood '95
The Crow '93
My Father Is Coming '91

Osa Massen (1914-2006)
Outcasts of the City '58
Rocketship X-M '50
Cry of the Werewolf '44
Master Race '44
Background to Danger '43
Iceland '42
A Woman's Face '41

Andrew Masset (1949-)
From the Earth to the Moon '98
Perfect Crime '97

Anna Massey (1937-)
Pinochet's Last Stand '06
Mrs. Palfrey at the Claremont '05
Agatha Christie: A Life in Pictures '04
The Machinist '04
The Importance of Being Earnest '02
Possession '02
Dark Blue World '01
Captain Jack '98
Deja Vu '98
A Respectable Trade '98
Grave Indiscretions '96
Angels and Insects '95
Haunted '95
Impromptu '90
Mountains of the Moon '90
The Man from the Pru '89
A Tale of Two Cities '89
The Tall Guy '89
Foreign Body '86
Hotel du Lac '86
Anna Karenina '85
Mansfield Park '85
The McGuffin '85
Another Country '84
The Little Drummer Girl '84
The Corn Is Green '79
Sweet William '79
A Doll's House '73
Vault of Horror '73
Frenzy '72
Peeping Tom '60

Athena Massey (1971-)
Harold Robbins' Body Parts '99
Shadow of a Scream '97
Star Portal '97
Termination Man, '97
Red Shoe Diaries: Strip Poker '96
Virtual Combat '95
Undercover '94

Daniel Massey (1933-98)
The Miracle Maker: The Story of Jesus '00 (V)
Samson and Delilah '96
The Vacillations of Poppy Carew '94
Catherine Cookson's The Man Who Cried '93
In the Name of the Father '93
Stalin '92
Scandal '89
Intimate Contact '87
Love with a Perfect Stranger '86
Dance with a Stranger '85
Victory '81
The Cat and the Canary '79
The Incredible Sarah '76
Vault of Horror '73
The Golden Bowl '72
Mary, Queen of Scots '71
Star! '68
The Entertainer '60

Edith Massey (1918-84)
Polyester '81
Desperate Living '77
Female Trouble '74
Pink Flamingos '72
Multiple Maniacs '70

Ilona Massey (1910-74)
Love Happy '50
Northwest Outpost '47
Holiday in Mexico '46
Frankenstein Meets the Wolfman '42
Invisible Agent '42
International Lady '41
Melody Master '41
Balalaika '39
Rosalie '38

Raymond Massey (1896-1983)
The President's Plane Is Missing '71
MacKenna's Gold '69
How the West Was Won '63
The Great Impostor '61
The Naked and the Dead '58
Omar Khayyam '57
Battle Cry '55
East of Eden '54
The Desert Song '53
David and Bathsheba '51
Chain Lightning '50
The Fountainhead '49
The Possessed '47
Stairway to Heaven '46
God Is My Co-Pilot '45
Arsenic and Old Lace '44
Woman in the Window '44
Action in the North Atlantic '43
Desperate Journey '42
Reap the Wild Wind '42
The Forty-Ninth Parallel '41
Abe Lincoln in Illinois '40
Santa Fe Trail '40
Black Limelight '38
Drums '38
Dreaming Lips '37
Fire Over England '37
The Hurricane '37
Prisoner of Zenda '37
Things to Come '36
Under the Red Robe '36
The Scarlet Pimpernel '34
The Old Dark House '32
The Speckled Band '31

Paul Massie (1932-)
The Two Faces of Dr. Jekyll '60
Sapphire '59

Master P (1967-)
Dark Blue '03
Hollywood Homicide '03
Scary Movie 3 '03
Gone in 60 Seconds '00
Lockdown '00
Foolish '99
No Tomorrow '99

Ben Masters (1947-)
Running Mates '92
Noble House '88
The Deliberate Stranger '86
Making Mr. Right '86
Celebrity '85
Dream Lover '85
Key Exchange '85
The Shadow Box '80
Mandingo '75

Chase Masterson (1963-)
Manticore '05
Comic Book: The Movie '04
Sometimes They Come Back... For More '99
In a Moment of Passion '93
Married People, Single Sex '93

Christopher K. Masterson (1980-)
MTV's Wuthering Heights '03
Scary Movie 2 '01
Dragonheart: A New Beginning '00

Danny Masterson (1976-)
Smiley Face '07
Puff, Puff, Pass '06
Comic Book Villains '02
Dracula 2000 '00
Star Kid '97
Bye Bye, Love '94

Fay Masterson (1974-)
Sorted '04
Johnson County War '02
Eyes Wide Shut '99
Apartment Complex '98
Cops and Robbersons '94
The Man Without a Face '93
The Power of One '92

Mary Stuart Masterson (1966-)
The Insurgents '06
The Sisters '05
Leo '02
The Book of Stars '99
Digging to China '98
The Florentine '98
Dogtown '97
Lily Dale '96
Bed of Roses '95
Heaven's Prisoners '95
Bad Girls '94
Radioland Murders '94
Benny & Joon '93
Married to It '93
Mad at the Moon '92
Fried Green Tomatoes '91
Funny About Love '90
Chances Are '89
Immediate Family '89
Mr. North '88
Gardens of Stone '87
My Little Girl '87
Some Kind of Wonderful '87
At Close Range '86
Heaven Help Us '85
The Stepford Wives '75

Peter Masterson (1934-)
Gardens of Stone '87
A Question of Guilt '78
The Stepford Wives '75
The Exorcist '73

Sean Masterson
Deranged '01
Fatal Games '84

Mary Elizabeth Mastrantonio (1958-)
That Russell Girl '08
The Perfect Storm '00
Limbo '99
Witness Protection '99
My Life So Far '98
Two Bits '96
Three Wishes '95
Consenting Adults '92
White Sands '92
Class Action '91
Robin Hood: Prince of Thieves '91
Fools of Fortune '90
The Abyss '89
The January Man '89
Slamdance '87
The Color of Money '86
Scarface '83

Gina Mastrogiacomo (1962-2001)
Bloodhounds '96
Tall, Dark and Deadly '95
Alien Space Avenger '91
Jungle Fever '91

Chiara Mastroianni (1972-)
Love Songs '07
Persepolis '07 (V)
Carnage '02
Time Regained '99
For Sale '98
Nowhere '96

Marcello Mastroianni (1923-96)
Three Lives and Only One Death '96
Voyage to the Beginning of the World '96
Beyond the Clouds '95
One Hundred and One Nights '95
I Don't Want to Talk About It '94
Ready to Wear '94
A Fine Romance '92
Used People '92
Everybody's Fine '90
Dark Eyes '87
Intervista '87
Ginger & Fred '86
Henry IV '85
Macaroni '85
Gabriela '84
Beyond Obsession '82
La Nuit de Varennes '82
City of Women '81
Blood Feud '79
A Slightly Pregnant Man '79
Wifemistress '79
Stay As You Are '78
A Special Day '77
We All Loved Each Other So Much '77
Lunatics & Lovers '76
Get Rita '76
Lady of the Evening '75
Salut l'Artiste '74
Allonsanfan '73
Diary of Forbidden Dreams '73
La Grande Bouffe '73
Massacre in Rome '73
Fellini's Roma '72
Divine Nymph '71
The Poppy Is Also a Flower '66
Shoot Loud, Louder, I Don't Understand! '66
Casanova '70 '65
10th Victim '65
Marriage Italian Style '64
The Organizer '64
Yesterday, Today and Tomorrow '64
8 1/2 '63
Divorce—Italian Style '62
A Very Private Affair '62
Il Bell'Antonio '60
La Dolce Vita '60
Where the Hot Wind Blows '59
Big Deal on Madonna Street '58
White Nights '57
What a Woman! '56
Too Bad She's Bad '54

Richard Masur (1948-)
Palindromes '04
61* '01
Noriega: God's Favorite '00
Play It to the Bone '99
Fire Down Below '97
Multiplicity '96
Forget Paris '95
Hiroshima '95
My Brother's Keeper '95
My Girl 2 '94
And the Band Played On '93
The Man Without a Face '93
Six Degrees of Separation '93
Encino Man '92
My Girl '91
Stephen King's It '90
Cast the First Stone '89
Far from Home '89
Flashback '89
Third Degree Burn '89
Hiroshima Maiden '88
License to Drive '88
Rent-A-Cop '88
Shoot to Kill '88
The Believers '87
Walker '87
Hard Lessons '86
Heartburn '86
When the Bough Breaks '86
The Burning Bed '85
Embassy '85
Mean Season '85
My Science Project '85
Wild Horses '84
Adam '83
Nightmares '83
Risky Business '83
Timerider '83
Under Fire '83
The Thing '82
Fallen Angel '81
Heaven's Gate '81
East of Eden '80
Walking Through the Fire '80
Betrayal '78
Who'll Stop the Rain? '78

Semi-Tough '77

Clelia Matania (1918-81)
Don't Look Now '73
The Seven Hills of Rome '58

Heather Matarazzo (1982-)
Hostel: Part 2 '07
Believe in Me '06
The Princess Diaries 2: Royal Engagement '04
Saved! '04
Sorority Boys '02
The Princess Diaries '01
Blue Moon '00
Company Man '00
Scream 3 '00
All I Wanna Do '98
54 '98
The Dell '97
The Devil's Advocate '97
Hurricane Streets '96
Welcome to the Dollhouse '95

Kari Matchett (1970-)
Civic Duty '06
Cube 2: Hypercube '02
Cypher '02
Men with Brooms '02

Julian Mateos (1938-96)
Kashmiri Run '69
Hellbenders '67
Return of the Magnificent Seven '66

Aubrey Mather (1885-1958)
That Forsyte Woman '50
Adventures of Don Juan '49
House of Fear '45
Jane Eyre '44
Hello, Frisco, Hello '43
Mrs. Miniver '42
The Undying Monster '42
Sabotage '36
The Silent Passenger '35

Marie Matheron (1940-)
Come Undone '00
Western '96

Marissa Mathes (1940-)
Track of the Vampire '65
How to Succeed with Girls '64

Marshall Mathers, III
See Eminem

Hans Matheson (1975-)
Doctor Zhivago '02
Deathwatch '02
Mists of Avalon '01
Bodywork '99
Still Crazy '98
Les Miserables '97
Poldark '96
Stella Does Tricks '96

Judy Matheson
Flesh and Blood Show '73
The House that Vanished '73
Crucible of Terror '72
Twins of Evil '71

Michelle Matheson (1971-)
Threesome '94
Test Tube Teens from the Year 2000 '93

Tim Matheson (1947-)
Redline '07
Howling 6: The Freaks '90
National Lampoon's Van Wilder '02
Don't Come Knocking '05
The Story of Us '99
Deadly Game '98
Forever Love '98

Jerry Mathers (1948-)
Larry the Cable Guy: Health Inspector '06
Down the Drain '89
Back to the Beach '87
The Trouble with Harry '55
Men of the Fighting Lady '54

Kerwin Mathews (1926-2007)
Killer Likes Candy '78
Nightmare in Blood '75
Octaman '71
Battle Beneath the Earth '68
Maniac '63
Waltz King '63
Jack the Giant Killer '62
The Devil at 4 O'Clock '61
The Three Worlds of Gulliver '59
The Seventh Voyage of Sinbad '58

George Mathews (-1984)
The Men with the Golden Arm '55
Last of the Comanches '52
Yankee Buccaneer '52

Carole Mathews (1920-)
Showdown at Boot Hill '58
Strange Awakening '58
Swamp Women '55
Shark River '53

Norman Matlock
Crooklyn '94
It's My Party '95

Marion Mathie
Dracula Has Risen from the Grave '68
Lolita '62

Samantha Mathis (1970-)
For One More Day '07
Believe in Me '06
Kids in America '05
Touched '05
The Punisher '04
Salem's Lot '04
Collected Stories '02
Mists of Avalon '01
Mermaid '00
American Psycho '01
The Simian Line '99
Sweet Jane '98

Pam Matteson (1962-)
Prehysteria 3 '95

Kayo Matsuo
Shogun Assassin '80
Gate of Flesh '64

Yusaku Matsuda (1950-89)
Black Rain '89
The Family Game '83
Murders in the Doll House '79

Keiko Matsuzaka (1952-)
Dr. Akagi '98
Fall Guy '82
The Go-Masters '82

Danilo Mattei
In the Name of the Pope-King '85

Eva Mattes (1954-)
Enemy at the Gates '00
The Promise '94
A Man Like Eva '83
Celeste '81
David '79
In a Year of 13 Moons '78
Stroszek '77
Woyzeck '78
The Bitter Tears of Petra von Kant '72

Chieko Matsubara (1945-)
Dolls '02
Black Tight Killers '66
Tokyo Drifter '66

Eiko Matsuda (1947-)
In the Realm of the Senses '76

John Matshikiza (1954-)
Dust '85
Mandela '87

Marlee Matlin (1965-)
What the #$*! Do We Know? '04
Two Shades of Blue '99
Where the Truth Lies '99
Dead Silence '96
When Justice Fails '98
Hear No Evil '93
It's My Party '95
The Linguini Incident '92
The Player '92
A New Leaf? '71?

Elisa Matilla
Km. 0 '00

Marie Matiko
Date Movie '06
The Art of War '00

Jacques Mathou
Ridicule '96
The Hairdresser's Husband '92

DeLane Matthews (1961-)
Running Red '99
From the Earth to the Moon '98
The Invaders '95

Francis Matthews (1927-)
The McGuffin '85
Dracula, Prince of Darkness '66
Corridors of Blood '58
The Hellfire Club '61
Rasputin the Mad Monk '66
Bhowani Junction '56
Small Hotel '57

Fritz Matthews
Born Killer '89
Deadly Prey '87

Jessie Matthews (1907-81)
Candles at Nine '44
Forever and a Day '43
Sailing Along '38
Gangway '37
It's Love Again '36
First a Girl '35
Evergreen '34

John Matthews
A Secret Space '88
Sleuth '72

Junius Matthews
The Many Adventures of Winnie the Pooh '77
The Sword in the Stone '63

Lester Matthews (1900-75)
The Far Horizons '55
King Richard and the Crusaders '54
Man in the Attic '53
Tales of Robin Hood '52
The Invisible Man's Revenge '44
Across the Pacific '42
The Raven '35
Werewolf of London '35

Liesl Matthews (1984-)
A Little Princess '95
Air Force One '97

Terumi Matthews
In Between '92
Take Two '87

A.E. Matthews (1869-1960)
Carry On Admiral '57
Made in Heaven '52
Mister Drake's Duck '50
Immortal Battalion '44
The Iron Duke '34

Al Matthews (1942-)
American Roulette '88
Aliens '86
The Sender '82
Red Nights '87

Brian Matthews (1953-)
The Burning '82

Dakin Matthews (1933-)
Thirteen Days '00
The Muse '99
From the Earth to the Moon '98
The Siege '98
Bean '97
Rough Riders '97
The Swan Princess '94 (V)
White Mile '94
And the Band Played On '93
The Temp '93

Walter Matthau (1920-2000)
Hanging Up '99
My Brother's Wife '89
Naked Lie '89
Permanent Record '88
Nuts '87
Out to Sea '97
I'm Not Rappaport '96
The Grass Harp '95
Grumpier Old Men '95
I.Q. '94
Dennis the Menace '93
Grumpy Old Men '93
JFK '91
Pirates '86
The Couch Trip '87
Movers and Shakers '85
Survivors '83
The Incident '89
Buddy Buddy '81
First Monday in October '81
Hopscotch '80
Little Miss Marker '80
California Suite '78
Casey's Shadow '78
House Calls '78
The Bad News Bears '76
The Sunshine Boys '75
Earthquake '74
The Front Page '74
The Taking of Pelham One Two Three '74
Charley Varrick '73
Pete 'n' Tillie '72
Kotch '71
A New Leaf '71
Plaza Suite '71
Cactus Flower '69
Hello, Dolly! '69
Candy '68
The Odd Couple '68
The Secret Life of an American Wife '68
A Guide for the Married Man '67
The Fortune Cookie '66
Mirage '66
Ensign Pulver '64
Fail-Safe '64
Goodbye Charlie '64
Charade '63
Who's Got the Action? '63
Lonely Are the Brave '62
Strangers When We Meet '60
King Creole '58
A Face in the Crowd '57
The Kentuckian '55
The Indian Fighter '55
Wilma '77

John Matuszak (1950-89)
Down the Drain '89
Ghost Writer '89
One Man Force '89
The Goonies '85
Ice Pirates '84
Caveman '81
North Dallas Forty '79
Semi-Tough '77

Johanna (Hannelr) Matz (1932-)
The Life and Loves of Mozart '59
They Were So Young '55
Party Girls for Sale '54

Tony Maudsley (1968-)
Vanity Fair '04
The Intended '02
Strange Relations '02
The Tempest '98
Power '34

Joan Maude (1908-98)
The Temptress '49
Ten Little Indians '89

Monica Maughan (1938-)
Road to Nhill '97
A Woman's Tale '92
Cactus '86

Wayne Maunder (1938-)
Crazy Horse and Custer: "The Untold Story" '90
Porky's '82

Sarah Maur-Thorp
River of Death '90
Edge of Sanity '89

Joan Maude (1908-98)
Down the Drain '39

Carmen Maura (1945-)
Free Zone '06
Vovor '06
Free Zone '05
800 Bullets '02
Valentin '02
Lisboa '99
Alice et Martin '98
Women '97
Le Bonheur Est Dans le Pre '95
Between Heaven and Earth '93
How to Be a Woman and Not Die in the Attempt '91
Ay, Carmela! '90
Baton Rouge '88
Women on the Verge of a Nervous Breakdown '88
Law of Desire '86
Matador '85
Extranuros '85
What Have I Done to Deserve This? '85
Dark Habits '84
Pepi, Luci, Bom and Other Girls on the Heap '80

Robin Mattson (1956-)
In Between '92
Captain America '79
Take Two '87
Hot Rod '79
Wolf Lake '79
Return to Macon County '75
Candy Stripe Nurses '74
Bonnie's Kids '73
Island of the Lost '68
Namu, the Killer Whale '66
Wonder Woman '76

Victor Mature (1915-99)
Head '68
After the Fox '66
The Long Haul '57
Samson and Delilah '84
Savage Wilderness '55
Betrayed '54
Dangerous Mission '54
Demetrius and the Gladiators '54
The Egyptian '54
The Robe '53
Androcles and the Lion '52
The Las Vegas Story '52
Million Dollar Mermaid '52
Samson and Delilah '50
Easy Living '49
Kiss of Death '47
My Darling Clementine '46
Footlight Serenade '42
Seven Days' Leave '42
The Shanghai Gesture '42
Song of the Islands '42
I Wake Up Screaming '41
Captain Caution '40
No, No Nanette '40
One Million B.C. '40

Nicole Maurey (1925-)
Day of the Triffids '63
The Jayhawkers '59
Me and the Colonel '58
Rogue's Yarn '56

Joshua Maurer
Taken Away '89
Tour of Duty '87

Howard Maurer
Ilsa, the Tigress of Siberia '79
Ilsa, the Wicked Warden '78

John Matuszak (1950-89)

Crazy Horse and Custer

Diary of a Country Priest '50

Claire Maurier (1929-)
Amelie '01
Un Air de Famille '96
La Cage aux Folles '78
A Very Curious Girl '69
Sweet Ecstasy '62
The 400 Blows '59
Back to the Wall '56

Gerda Maurus (1909-68)
Woman in the Moon '29
Spies '28

Gary Mavers (1964-)
The Unknown Soldier '98
Body & Soul '93

Dawn Maxey
Raising Flagg '06
The Killing Club '01
Ringmaster '98
Normal Life '96
That Thing You Do! '96

Chenoa Maxwell (1969-)
G '02
Hav Plenty '97

Edwin Maxwell (1886-1948)
Woman in Brown '48
Swamp Fire '46
Waterfront '44
Behind Prison Walls '43
Way Down South '39
Mystery Liner '34
Night of Terror '33
The Taming of the Shrew '29

Frank Maxwell (1916-2004)
Shame '61
Lonelyhearts '58

John Maxwell
Prowler '51
Boss of Big Town '43
The Payoff '43
Honky Tonk '41

Larry Maxwell (1953-96)
Public Access '93
Poison '93

Lois Maxwell (1927-2007)
The Fourth Angel '01
Eternal Evil '87
A View to a Kill '85
For Your Eyes Only '81
Moonraker '79
The Spy Who Loved Me '77
The Man with the Golden Gun '74
Live and Let Die '73
Diamonds Are Forever '71
On Her Majesty's Secret Service '69
You Only Live Twice '67
Thunderball '65
Goldfinger '64
From Russia with Love '63
The Haunting '63
Dr. No '62
Lolita '62

Marilyn Maxwell (1922-72)
Wild Women '70
Arizona Bushwackers '67
Critic's Choice '63
Rock-A-Bye Baby '57
Off Limits '53
The Lemon Drop Kid '51
Key to the City '50
Champion '49
Summer Holiday '48
The Show-Off '46
Lost in a Harem '44

Paul Maxwell (1920-91)
Cloud Waltzing '87
Going Home '86

Roberta Maxwell (1944-)
Brokeback Mountain '05
Gracie's Choice '04
Full Disclosure '00
Last Night '98
The Postman '97
Mistrial '96
Dead Man Walking '95
Philadelphia '93
Psycho 3 '86
Lois Gibbs and the Love Canal '82
The Changeling '80

Deborah May
Caged Fear '92
Johnny Be Good '88
Rage of Angels '83

Donald May (1927-)
Bogie: The Last Hero '80
Kisses for My President '64

Elaine May (1932-)
Small Time Crooks '00
In the Spirit '90
California Suite '78
A New Leaf '71
Enter Laughing '67
Luv '67

Jack May (1922-97)
He Kills Night After Night After Night '69
Night Slasher '69

Jodhi May (1975-)
Land of the Blind '06
Friends & Crocodiles '05
On a Clear Day '05
The Mayor of Casterbridge '03
The Other Boleyn Girl '03
Daniel Deronda '02
Tipping the Velvet '02
House of Mirth '00
The Aristocrats '99
The Turn of the Screw '99
The Gambler '97
Sister My Sister '94
The Last of the Mohicans '92

Herschel Mayall (1863-1941)
Kismet '20
The Bargain '15

Rik Mayall (1958-)
Valiant '05 (V)
Chilly Dogs '01
Jesus Christ Superstar '00
Drop Dead Fred '91
Little Noises '91
Whoops Apocalypse '83
An American Werewolf in London '81
Eye of the Needle '81
Shock Treatment '81

Anthony (Jose, J. Antonio, J.A.) Mayans (1939-)
Revenge in the House of Usher '82
Zombie Lake '80
Sex Is Crazy '74
Heat of the Flame '76

Eddie Mayehoff (1911-92)
How to Murder Your Wife '64
Artists and Models '55
The Stooge '51

Jose Mayens
See Anthony (Jose, J. Antonio, J.A.) Mayans

Chip (Christopher) Mayer (1955-)
Fugitive Champion '99
Liar Liar '97
Survivor '87
Our Family Business '81

Ray Mayer (1901-48)
Swing It, Sailor! '37
Special Investigator '36

Peter Mayhew (1944-)
Star Wars: Episode 3—Revenge of the Sith '05
Comic Book: The Movie '04
Return of the Jedi '83
The Empire Strikes Back '80
Star Wars '77

John Maynard (1959-)
Biohazard: The Alien Force '95
Dark Universe '93

Ken Maynard (1895-1973)
Arizona Whirlwind '44
Death Valley Rangers '44
Death Rides Again '43
Death Rides the Range '40
Lightning Strikes West '40
Flaming Lead '39
Phantom Rancher '39
Six Shootin' Sheriff '38
Whirlwind Horseman '38
Boots of Destiny '37
Western Frontier '35
Honor of the Range '34
In Old Santa Fe '34
Mystery Mountain '34
Drum Taps '33
The Fiddlin' Buckaroo '33
The Lone Avenger '33
Phantom Thunderbolt '33
Strawberry Roan '33
Trail Drive '33
Between Fighting Men '32
Come on Tarzan '32
Dynamite Ranch '32
False Faces '32
Fargo Express '32
Hell Fire Austin '32
Sunset Trail '32
Texas Gunfighter '32
Tombstone Canyon '32
Whistlin' Dan '32
Arizona Terror '31
Branded Men '31
The Pocatello Kid '31
Range Law '31
Two Gun Man '31
Fightin' Ranch '30
The Fighting Legion '30
Fighting Thru '30
Mountain Justice '30
$50,000 Reward '25

Kermit Maynard (1897-1971)
The Black Lash '52
Trail of Robin Hood '50
Ambush Trail '46
'Neath Canadian Skies '46
Gangster's Den '45
Texas Kid '43
Along the Sundown Trail '42
Arizona Stagecoach '42
The Mysterious Rider '42
Prairie Pals '42
Rock River Renegades '42
Trail Riders '42
Billy the Kid '41
Bury Me Not on the Lone Prairie '41
Man from Montana '41
Pony Post '40
Range Busters '40
Riders of Pasco Basin '40
The Showdown '40
Valley of Terror '38
Galloping Dynamite '37
Roaring Six Guns '37
Rough Ridin' Rhythm '37
Phantom Patrol '36
Song of the Trail '36
Whistling Bullets '36
His Fighting Blood '35
The Fighting Trooper '34
Drum Taps '33
Outlaw Justice '32

Mimi Maynard
Adventures in Dinosaur City '92
False Identity '90

Terence Maynard
Revolver '05
Reign of Fire '02

Belinda Mayne (1958-)
Don't Open Till Christmas '84
White Fire '84

Ferdinand "Ferdy" Mayne (1916-98)
Benefit of the Doubt '93
River of Diamonds '90
A Friendship in Vienna '88
Magdalene '88
Howling 2: Your Sister Is a Werewolf '85
Night Train to Terror '84
The Secret Diary of Sigmund Freud '84
Yellowbeard '83
Frightmare '81
Hawk the Slayer '81
Au Pair Girls '72
The Vampire Happening '71
When Eight Bells Toll '71
The Adventurers '70
The Vampire Lovers '70
The Magic Christian '69
Where Eagles Dare '68
The Fearless Vampire Killers '67
Masters of Venus '62
Our Man in Havana '59
Abandon Ship '57
Captain's Paradise '53
Roadhouse Girl '53
White Fire '53
Made in Heaven '52
The Temptress '49
Echo Murders '45

Juliette Mayniel (1935-)
The Bloodstained Shadow '78
Assassination in Rome '65
The Trojan Horse '62
The Cousins '59

Alfredo Mayo (1911-85)
Bell from Hell '74
The Hunt '65
Mission in Morocco '59

Frank Mayo (1886-1963)
Across the Pacific '42
The Fighting 69th '40
Tim Tyler's Luck '37
Hell's Headquarters '32
Doughboys '30

Virginia Mayo (1920-2005)
Midnight Witness '93
Evil Spirits '91
The Haunted '79
French Quarter '78
Runaways '75
Castle of Evil '66
Jet Over the Atlantic '59
Great Day in the Morning '56
Pearl of the South Pacific '55
King Richard and the Crusaders '54
The Silver Chalice '54
Devil's Canyon '53
South Sea Woman '53
Along the Great Divide '51
Captain Horatio Hornblower '51
The Flame & the Arrow '50
The West Point Story '50
White Heat '49
A Song Is Born '48
Out of the Blue '47
The Secret Life of Walter Mitty '47
The Best Years of Our Lives '46
Kid from Brooklyn '46
Wonder Man '45
Jack London '44
The Princess and the Pirate '44
Seven Days Ashore '44

Whitman Mayo (1930-2001)
Boycott '02
Waterproof '99
Boyz N the Hood '91
Of Mice and Men '81

Karen Mayo-Chandler (1958-2006)
Death Feud '89
Stripped to Kill II: Live Girls '89

Gale Mayron
Almost Blue '93
The Feud '90
Heart of Midnight '89

Melanie Mayron (1952-)
Range of Motion '00
Toothless '97
Ordeal in the Arctic '93
My Blue Heaven '90
Checking Out '89
Sticky Fingers '88
The Boss' Wife '86
Wanted: The Perfect Guy '86
Missing '82
The Best Little Girl in the World '81
Heartbeeps '81
Playing for Time '80
Girlfriends '78
You Light Up My Life '77
Car Wash '76
Harry and Tonto '74

Daniel Mays (1978-)
The Bank Job '08
Vera Drake '04
All or Nothing '02

Jefferson Mays (1965-)
The Notorious Bettie Page '06
Alfie '04
The Big Brass Ring '99
Some Folks Call It a Sling Blade '94

Joshua Gibran Mayweather (1981-)
Nowhere '96
Camp Nowhere '94
Candyman 2: Farewell to the Flesh '94

Bob Maza (1939-2000)
Back of Beyond '95
Reckless Kelly '93
Ground Zero '88

Debi Mazar (1964-)
Lies & Alibis '06
Be Cool '05
Collateral '04
The Tuxedo '02
Life in the Fast Lane '00
More Dogs Than Bones '00
The Insider '99
Frogs for Snakes '98
Hush '98
Witness to the Mob '98
Meet Wally Sparks '97
She's So Lovely '97
Space Truckers '97
Girl 6 '96
Nowhere '96
Things I Never Told You '96
Tree's Lounge '96
Bad Love '95
Batman Forever '95
Empire Records '95
Witch Hunt '94
Beethoven's 2nd '93
Inside Monkey Zetterland '93
Money for Nothing '93
In the Soup '92
Jungle Fever '91
Little Man Tate '91
Goodfellas '90

Monet Mazur (1976-)
Monster-in-Law '05
Stoned '05
Torque '04
Whirlygirl '04
Just Married '03
Comic Book Villains '02
40 Days and 40 Nights '02
Stark Raving Mad '02
Angel Eyes '01
The Learning Curve '01
Raging Angels '95

Mike Mazurki (1907-90)
Doin' Time '85
The Adventures of Huckleberry Finn '78
The Incredible Rocky Mountain Race '77
Challenge To Be Free '76
The McCullochs '75
Cheyenne Autumn '64
Donovan's Reef '63
The Errand Boy '61
Some Like It Hot '59
Hell Ship Mutiny '57
Blood Alley '55
Pier 23 '51
Night and the City '50
Come to the Stable '49
Neptune's Daughter '49
The Noose Hangs High '48
Killer Dill '47
Nightmare Alley '47
Sinbad, the Sailor '47
Unconquered '47
Abbott and Costello in Hollywood '45
Dick Tracy, Detective '45
The Canterville Ghost '44
Murder, My Sweet '44
Behind the Rising Sun '43
The Shanghai Gesture '42

Paul Mazursky (1930-)
Coast to Coast '04
Big Shot's Funeral '01
Crazy in Alabama '99
A Slight Case of Murder '99
Antz '98 (V)
Why Do Fools Fall in Love? '98
Weapons of Mass Distraction '97
Touch '96
Two Days in the Valley '96
Faithful '95
Miami Rhapsody '95
Love Affair '94
Man Trouble '92
Enemies, a Love Story '89
Scenes from the Class Struggle in Beverly Hills '89
Moon over Parador '88
Punchline '88
Into the Night '85
History of the World: Part 1 '81
A Man, a Woman, and a Bank '79
A Star Is Born '76
Harry and Tonto '74
Alex in Wonderland '70
Blackboard Jungle '55

Marcello Mazzarello (1965-)
Felicidades '00
Time Regained '99

Joseph Mazzello (1983-)
Simon Birch '98
The Lost World: Jurassic Park 2 '97
Star Kid '97
The Cure '95
Three Wishes '95
The River Wild '94
Jurassic Park '93
Shadowlands '93
Jersey Girl '92
Radio Flyer '92

M.C. Lyte (1971-)
Civil Brand '02

An Alan Smithee Film: Burn, Hollywood Burn '97
Fly by Night '93

Rachel McAdams (1976-)
Married Life '07
The Family Stone '05
Red Eye '05
Wedding Crashers '05
Mean Girls '04
The Notebook '04
The Hot Chick '02

Anndi McAfee (1979-)
The Land Before Time 7: The Stone of Cold Fire '00 (V)
The Land Before Time 6: The Secret of Saurus Rock '98 (V)
The Land Before Time 5: The Mysterious Island '97 (V)

Scott McAfee
Conagher '91
The Land Before Time 4: Journey Through the Mists '96 (V)
The Land Before Time 3: The Time of the Great Giving '95 (V)
The Land Before Time 2: The Great Valley Adventure '94 (V)

Ray McAnally (1926-89)
My Left Foot '89
We're No Angels '89
A Perfect Spy '88
Taffin '86
A Very British Coup '88
Empire State '87
The Fourth Protocol '87
The Mission '86
No Surrender '86
Cal '84
Danny Boy '82
Sea of Sand '58
Four Days in July '85

Marianne McAndrew (1938-)
Hello, Dolly! '74
The Bat People '74

Andrea McArdle (1963-)
Rainbow '78
Annie '99

Alex McArthur (1957-)
Stealing Candy '04
Suspended Animation '02
Kiss the Girls '97
Lady Killer '84
Urge to Kill '84

Hugh McArthur
Drug Wars 2: The Cocaine Cartel '92
Race for G ory '89
Rampage '87
Silent Witness '85

Alphonso McAuley
Pride '07
Glory Road '06
Fat Albert '04

James McAvoy (1979-)
Wanted '08
Atonement '07
Becoming Jane '07
The Last King of Scotland '05
Penelope '06
Starter for Ten '06
The Chronicles of Narnia: The Lion, the Witch and the Wardrobe '05
Rory O'Shea Was Here '04
Wimbledon '04
Bright Young Things '03
Children of Dune '03
State of Play '03

May McAvoy (1901-84)
Gun Glory '57
The Jazz Singer '27
Ben-Hur '26

Diane McBain (1941-)
Puppet Master 5: The Final Chapter '94
Flying from the Hawk '86
Donner Pass: The Road to Survival '84
Monster '78
Deathhead Virgin '74
Thunder Alley '67
Spinout '66
Parrish '61

Tom McBeath
Off Season '01
Firestorm '97

Daron McBee (1961-)
Mortal Kombat 2: Annihilation '97
T-Force '94
The Killing Zone '90

Chi McBride (1961-)
First Sunday '08
The Brothers Solomon '07
Annapolis '06
Let's Go to Prison '06
Roll Bounce '05
Waiting '05
I, Robot '04
The Terminal '04
Cradle 2 the Grave '03
Narc '02
Paid in Full '02
Undercover Brother '02
Dancing in September '00
Disney's The Kid '00
Gone in 60 Seconds '00
Mercury Rising '98
The Frighteners '96
Hoodlum '96
Cosmic Slop '94
What's Love Got to Do with It? '93

Danny McBride
Pineapple Express '08
Tropic Thunder '08
The Peacemaker '97
Rough Riders '97
The Search for One-Eyed Jimmy '96
Tecumseh: The Last Warrior '95

Jon McBride
Feeders '96
Blades '89
Woodchipper Massacre '89
Cannibal Campout '88

Michelle McBride
Masque of the Red Death '90

Simon McBurney (1957-)
Friends with Money '06
The Last King of Scotland '06
The Manchurian Candidate '04

David McCallum (1933-99)
Coming Home '98
Mortal Challenge '97
Shattered Image '93
The Haunting of Morella '91
Hear My Song '91
The Wind '87
Behind Enemy Lines '85
Terminal Choice '85
Return of the Man from U.N.C.L.E. '83
The Watcher in the Woods '81
King Solomon's Treasure '76
She Waits '71
Around the World Under the Sea '65
The Great Escape '63
Billy Budd '62
A Night to Remember '58
Robbery under Arms '57

Richard McCabe
Mesmer '94
Kafka '91

Ruth McCabe
Heat of the Sun '99
Notting Hill '99
American Women '00
An Everlasting Piece '00
Talk of Angels '96
The Snapper '93
My Left Foot '89

Tony McCabe (-1968)
Something Weird '68
Suburban Roulette '67

Joanna McCallum
Tom & Viv '94
The Franchise Affair '88

Frankie McCafferty (1967-)
The Informant '97
Fools of Fortune '90

John McCafferty (1917-)
Testament of Youth '79

James McCaffrey (1960-)
Feel the Noise '07
The Perfect Gift '95

Frances Lee McCain (1944-)
Patch Adams '98
Question of Faith '93
Gremlins '84
Broken Badge '85
Tex '82
Two of a Kind '82
Real Life '79

Catriona McCall
See Katharine (Katriona) MacColl

Ross McCall (1976-)
Green Street Hooligans '05
The Return of the Borrowers '96
Lethal Dose '03

William (Bill, Billy) McCall (1870-1938)
Lightning Bill '35
Outlaws o' the Range '36
Trailing Trouble '30
Rounding Up the Law '22

Irish McCalla (1929-2002)
Hands of a Stranger '62
She Demons '58

Holt McCallany (1964-)
Vantage Point '08
The Upside of Anger '05
Below '02
Men of Honor '00
Three Kings '99
Thrashin' '86
That's Adequate '90 (V)
Cameron's Closet '89
Alien 3 '92
Creepshow 2 '87
Tyson '95

Lon (Bud) McCallister (1923-2005)
The Big Cat '49
The Story of Seabiscuit '49
The Red House '47
Stage Door Canteen '43

Macon McCalman (1932-2005)
Doc Hollywood '91
Fleshburn '84
The Ultimate Imposter '79
Run '91

Mercedes McCambridge (1918-2004)
Echoes '83
The Concorde: Airport '79
The Sacketts '79
The Exorcist '73 (V)
The Girls of Huntington House '73
Sixteen '72
The President's Plane Is Missing '71
99 Women '69
Angel Baby '61
Cimarron '60
Suddenly, Last Summer '59
Touch of Evil '58
Giant '56
Johnny Guitar '53
All the King's Men '49

Tom McCamus (1955-)
Waking Up Wally '05
New Waterford Girl '99
Long Day's Journey Into Night '96
The Sweet Hereafter '96
First Degree '95
A Man in Uniform '93
Norman's Awesome Experience '88
I'm Losing You '98
Perfect Assassins '98
Getting In '94
Mrs. Parker and the Vicious Circle '94
Night of the Running Man '94

Chuck McCann (1936-)
Storyville '92
Duck Tales the Movie: Treasure of the Lost Lamp '90 (V)
That's Adequate '90 (V)
Cameron's Closet '89
Rosebud Beach Hotel '85
C.H.O.M.P.S. '79
If Things Were Different '79
Foul Play '78
They Went That-a-Way & That-a-Way '78
The Heart Is a Lonely Hunter '68
The Projectionist '71

Donal McCann (1943-99)
Illuminata '98
The Nephew '97
The Serpent's Kiss '97
Stealing Beauty '96
December Bride '91
The Miracle '91
The Dead '87
Rawhead Rex '87
The Reagers '04
Out of Africa '85
Cal '84
Hard Way '80
Screamer '74

Sean McCann (1935-)
Wedding Wars '06
The River King '05
Miracle '04
Dead Men Don't Wear Plaid '82

Rory McCann (1969-)
Beowulf & Grendel '06
Alexander '04

Andrew McCarthy (1963-)
The Spiderwick Chronicles '08
2B Perfectly Honest '04
Anything But Love '02
Nowhere in Sight '01
Beyond Redemption '99
New Waterford Girl '99
New World Disorder '99
I'm Losing You '98
Perfect Assassins '98
Mulholland Falls '95
Dead Funny '94
Dream Man '94
The Joy Luck Club '93
Weekend at Bernie's 2 '93
Only You '92
Year of the Gun '91
Club Extinction '89
Weekend at Bernie's '89
Fresh Horses '88
Kansas '88
Less Than Zero '87
Mannequin '87
Waiting for the Moon '87
Pretty in Pink '86
Heaven Help Us '85
St. Elmo's Fire '85
The Beniker Gang '85
Class '83

Fred McCarren (1952-)
Red Flag: The Ultimate Game '81

Brian McCardie (1965-)
Rip It Off '02
200 Cigarettes '98
Speed 2: Cruise Control '97
The Ghost and the Darkness '96
Rob Roy '95
Quiet Day in Belfast '74
Saga of Hal C. Banks '85
Canada's Sweetheart: The Saga of Hal C. Banks '85
Unnatural Causes '86
Mindfield '89
The Air Up There '94
Trapped in Paradise '94
Guilty as Sin '93
Trial and Error '92
Run '91
Just Cause '94

Kevin McCarthy (1914-)
Swann '96
Iron Eagle 4 '95
Loving Annabelle '06
The Sister-in-Law '95
Just Cause '94
The Distinguished Gentleman '92
Duplicates '92
Matinee '92
Dead on the Money '91
Final Approach '91
Ghoulies 3: Ghoulies Go to College '91
The Rose and the Jackal '90
The Sleeping Car '90
Texas Guns '90
Fast Food '89
UHF '89
For Love or Money '88
LBJ: The Early Years '88
Dark Tower '87
Hostage '87
Innerspace '87
Poor Little Rich Girl: The Barbara Hutton Story '87
The Midnight Hour '86
Invitation to Hell '84
Ratings Game '84
Twilight Zone: The Movie '83
My Tutor '82
Rosie: The Rosemary Clooney Story '82
The Howling '81
Those Lips, Those Eyes '80
Hero at Large '80
Piranha '78
Buffalo Bill & the Indians '76
The Seagull '75
Order to Kill '73
Ace High '68
Dead Right '68
Hotel '67
A Big Hand for the Little Lady '66
Mirage '66
The Three Sisters '65
The Best Man '64
A Gathering of Eagles '63
40 Pounds of Trouble '62
An Annapolis Story '55
Death of a Salesman '51
Invasion of the Body Snatchers '56

Lin McCarthy (1918-2002)
D.I. '57

Molly McCarthy
Yellowbeard '83

Nobu McCarthy (1934-2002)
Pacific Heights '90
The Wash '88
The Karate Kid: Part 2 '86
The Geisha Boy '58

Sheila McCarthy (1956-)
Being Julia '04
Confessions of a Teenage Drama Queen '04
The Day After Tomorrow '04

James McCarthy
Nightwaves '03 [?]

Jenny McCarthy (1972-)
Witless Protection '08
John Tucker Must Die '06
Santa Baby '06
Dirty Love '05
Scary Movie 3 '03
Crazy Little Thing '02
Python '00
Scream 3 '00
Diamonds '99
BASEketball '98
Oktober '98

Francis X. (Frank) McCarthy
Nightwaves '03
A Case of Deadly Force '86

Neil McCarthy (1933-85)
Where Eagles Dare '68
The Hill '65
Zulu '64

The Lotus Eaters '93
Beautiful Dreamers '92
Beethoven Lives Upstairs '92
A Private Matter '92
Bright Angel '92
George's Island '91
Paradise '91
Stepping Out '91
Die Hard 2: Die Harder '90
Pacific Heights '90
Friends, Lovers & Lunatics '89
I've Heard the Mermaids Singing '87
Really Weird Tales '86

Steven McCarthy
The Crossing '00
Locked in Silence '99

Thomas (Tom) McCarthy (1969-)
Year of the Dog '07
Flags of Our Fathers '06
The Great New Wonderful '06
Good Night, and Good Luck '05
Meet the Parents '00
Saint Maybe '98

Jesse McCartney (1987-)
Alvin and the Chipmunks '07 (V)

Linda McCartney (1941-98)
The Biggest Fan '02

Paul McCartney (1942-)
Eat the Rich '87
Give My Regards to Broad Street '84
Let It Be '70
Yellow Submarine '68 (V)
Magical Mystery Tour '67
Help! '65
A Hard Day's Night '64

Patti McCarty (1920-85)
Outlaw of the Plains '46
Devil Riders '44
Fighting Valley '43

Rod McCary (1941-)
Night of the Demons 2 '94
A Girl to Kill For '90
Rebel Storm '90
No Drums, No Bugles '71

Charles McCaughan
Impulse '90
Slaves of New York '89
Heat and Dust '82

Saundra McClain (1947-)
The Sixth Man '97
Mr. & Mrs. Bridge '90

Rue McClanahan (1935-)
Miracle Dogs '03
A Saintly Switch '99
Out to Sea '97
Starship Troopers '97
This World, Then the Fireworks '97
Dear God '96
Baby of the Bride '91
After the Shock '90
Modern Love '90
The Little Match Girl '87
Sergeant Matlovich vs. the U.S. Air Force '78
Hollywood after Dark '65
How to Succeed with Girls '64
Five Minutes to Love '63

Clyde McClary (1888-1939)
Riding Speed '35
Rawhide Romance '34
Circle Canyon '33

Gary McCleery
The Chair '87
Hard Choices '84

Michael (Mick) McCleery
Addicted to Murder 3: Bloodlust '99
Rage of the Werewolf '99
If I Die Before I Wake '98
Addicted to Murder 2: Tainted Blood '97
The Alien Agenda: Out of the Darkness '96
Addicted to Murder '95
Harry and Tonto '74

Catherine McClements (1965-)
After the Deluge '03
Better Than Sex '00
Desperate Prey '94
My Brother Tom '86

Sean McClory (1924-2003)
Fools of Fortune '90
My Chauffeur '87
Roller Boogie '79
Diane '55
The King's Thief '55
Them! '54
Charade '53
Island in the Sky '53
Man in the Attic '53
The Quiet Man '52

Leigh McCloskey (1955-)
Accidental Meeting '93
Cameron's Closet '89
Double Revenge '89
Dirty Laundry '87
Hamburger... The Motion Picture '86
Fraternity Vacation '85
Just One of the Guys '85
Hearts & Armour '83
Inferno '80
Alexander: The Other Side of Dawn '77

Doug McClure (1934-95)
Maverick '94
The Gambler Returns: The Luck of the Draw '93
Battling for Baby '92
Dark Before Dawn '89
Tapeheads '89
Prime Suspect '88
Omega Syndrome '87
52 Pick-Up '86
Fight for Gold '86
House Where Evil Dwells '82
Firebird 2015 A.D. '81
Humanoids from the Deep '80
The Rebels '79
Bananas Boat '78
Wild & Wooly '78
The People That Time Forgot '77
At the Earth's Core '76
The Land That Time Forgot '75
Hell Hounds of Alaska '73
Playmates '72
Bull of the West '71
Shenandoah '65
The Unforgiven '60
Enemy Below '57

Greg McClure (1915-)
Roaring City '51
Stop That Cab '51
Outlaw Gang '49
Sky Liner '49

Marc McClure (1957-)
That Thing You Do! '96
Apollo 13 '95
Back to the Future, Part 3 '90
After Midnight '89
Grim Prairie Tales '89
Perfect Match '88

Superman 4: The Quest for Peace '87
Back to the Future '85
Supergirl '84
Superman 3 '83
Pandemonium '82
Strange Behavior '81
Superman 2 '80
I Wanna Hold Your Hand '78
Superman: The Movie '78

Molly McClure (1919-)
Finding North '97
Pure Country '92
Daddy's Dyin'... Who's Got the Will? '90

Tane McClure (1959-)
Death and Desire '97
Night Shade '97
Scorned 2 '96
Sexual Roulette '96
Caged Hearts '96
Lap Dancing '95
Midnight Tease 2 '95
Stripshow '95
Hot Under the Collar '91

Edie McClurg (1950-)
Home on the Range '04 (V)
Air Bud 5: Buddy Spikes Back '03
Dickie Roberts: Former Child Star '03
Master of Disguise '02
A Bug's Life '98 (V)
Murder She Purred: A Mrs. Murphy Mystery '98
Flubber '97
Inhumanoid '96
The Prince '95
Under the Hula Moon '95
Natural Born Killers '94
Airborne '93
A River Runs Through It '92
Tiny Toon Adventures: How I Spent My Vacation '91 (V)
The Little Mermaid '89 (V)
Elvira, Mistress of the Dark '88
She's Having a Baby '88
Planes, Trains & Automobiles '87
Back to School '86
Ferris Bueller's Day Off '86
Cheech and Chong's The Corsican Brothers '84
Mr. Mom '83
Eating Raoul '82
Pandemonium '82
The Pee-wee Herman Show '82
The Secret of NIMH '82 (V)
Cheech and Chong's Next Movie '80
Carrie '76

Stephen McCole
The Acid House '98
Postmortem '98
Rushmore '98
Orphans '97

Philo McCollough
See Philo (Philip, P.H., P.M.) McCullough

Warren McCollum (1918-87)
The Great Commandment '41
Boy's Reformatory '39
Reefer Madness '38

Matt McColm
Cellular '04
The Matrix Reloaded '03
Acts of Betrayal '98
Subterfuge '98
Body Armor '96
Red Scorpion 2 '94

Lorissa McComas (1970-)
Mad As Nails '01
Lap Dancing '95
Stormswept '95

Heather McComb (1977-)
Steel City '06
If These Walls Could Talk 2 '00
Blowin' Smoke '99

Apt Pupil '97
God's Lonely Man '96
Stay Tuned '92
New York Stories '89

Matthew McConaughey (1969-)
Fool's Gold '08
Tropic Thunder '08
Right at Your Door '06
We Are Marshall '06
Failure to Launch '06
Sahara '05
Two for the Money '05
Paparazzi '04
How to Lose a Guy in 10 Days '03
Tiptoes '03
Reign of Fire '02
Frailty '02
Thirteen Conversations About One Thing '01
The Wedding Planner '01
U-571 '00
EDtv '99
Amistad '97
Contact '97
Larger Than Life '96
Glory Daze '96
Scorpion Spring '96
A Time to Kill '96
Lone Star '95
The Texas Chainsaw Massacre 4: The Next Generation '95
Boys on the Side '94
Dazed and Confused '93

Elias McConnell
Paris, je t'aime '06
Elephant '03

John McConnell (1958-)
The Ladykillers '04
King of the Hill '93
Delta Heat '92

Judith McConnell (1944-)
The Weather Man '05
The Thirsty Dead '74

Keith McConnell (1922-87)
Border Saddlemates '52
Five Fingers '52

Marilyn McCoo (1943-)
My Mom's a Werewolf '89
The Fantastic World of D.C. Collins '84

John McCook (1945-)
Scorned 2 '96
Codename: Foxfire '85

Kent McCord (1942-)
Renaissance '06 (V)

Catherine McCormack (1972-)
28 Weeks Later '07
A Sound of Thunder '05
Spy Game '01
Born Romantic '00
A Rumor of Angels '00
Shadow of the Vampire '00
The Tailor of Panama '01
The Weight of Water '00
Dancing at Lughnasa '98
Dangerous Beauty '98
Deacon Brodie '98
The Land Girls '98
North Star '96
Braveheart '95
Loaded '94

Eric McCormack (1963-)
The Sisters '05
The Audrey Hepburn Story '00
Free Enterprise '98
Holy Man '98
Call of the Wild '93

Gary McCormack
Sweet Sixteen '02

Mary McCormack (1969-)
1408 '07
Right at Your Door '06
Dickie Roberts: Former Child Star '03
Full Frontal '02
Cash Crop '01
High Heels and Low Lifes '01
K-PAX '01
Madison '01
World Traveler '01
The Broken Hearts Club '00
Gun Shy '00
The Big Tease '99
Mystery, Alaska '99
True Crime '99
The Alarmist '98
Deep Impact '98
Harvest '98
Private Parts '96

Patty McCormack (1945-)
Shallow Ground '04
Acceptable Risk '01
Silent Predators '99
Mommy 2: Mommy's Day '96
Mommy '95
Saturday the 14th Strikes Back '88
Invitation to Hell '84
Bug '75
The Adventures of Huckleberry Finn '60
All Mine to Give '56
The Bad Seed '56

Will McCormack
Abandon '02
American Outlaws '01

Carolyn McCormick (1959-)
You Know My Name '99
Rain Without Thunder '93
Enemy Mine '85

Gilmer McCormick (1947-)
Silent Night, Deadly Night '84

Maureen McCormick (1956-)
The Million Dollar Kid '99
Dogtown '97
Panic in the Skies '96
A Very Brady Christmas '88
Return to Horror High '87
Texas Lightning '81
Idolmaker '80
Take Down '79
Moonshine County Express '77
Pony Express Rider '76

Merrill McCormick (1892-1953)
The Kansas Terrors '39
Range Riders '35
Cowboy Counselor '33
Robin Hood '22

Michelle McCormick
Showdown '93
Fatal Pulse '88

Myron McCormick (1908-62)
A Public Affair '62
The Hustler '61
No Time for Sergeants '58
Not as a Stranger '55
Three for the Show '55
Jigsaw '49
One Third of a Nation '39

Pat McCormick (1927-2005)
Chinatown Connection '90
Rented Lips '88
Bombs Away! '86
Doin' Time '85
E. Nick: A Legend in His Own Mind '84
The Princess and the Pea '83

Smokey and the Bandit, Part 3 '83
Under the Rainbow '81
Smokey and the Bandit 2 '80
A Wedding '78
If You Don't Stop It... You'll Go Blind '77
Smokey and the Bandit '77

Grayson McCouch (1968-)
Momentum '03
Armageddon '98
Sins of the Mind '97

Emer McCourt
Boston Kickout '95
Riff Raff '92
London Kills Me '91

Malachy McCourt (1931-)
Ash Wednesday '02
The Guru '02
JFK: Reckless Youth '93
Q (The Winged Serpent) '82

Alec McCowen (1925-)
Gangs of New York '02
Longitude '00
The Age of Innocence '93
Maria's Child '93
Henry V '89
Cry Freedom '87
Personal Services '87
A Dedicated Man '86
Forever Young '85
Hanover Street '79
Stevie '78
Frenzy '72
Travels with My Aunt '72
The Witches '66
A Night to Remember '58
Time Without Pity '57

Larry McCoy
The Players Club '98
Bulletproof '96

Lisa Ray McCoy
See LisaRaye

Matt McCoy (1958-)
National Security '03
Beethoven's 4th '01
Forever Together '00
Rangers '00
Tales of the Kama Sutra 2: Monsoon '98
Buck and the Magic Bracelet '97
L.A. Confidential '97
Monsoon '97
The Apocalypse '96
Fast Money '96
Little Bigfoot '96
Rent-A-Kid '95
Synapse '95
Bigfoot: The Unforgettable Encounter '94
Hard Bounty '94
Hard Drive '94
The Soft Kill '94
Dead On '93
Samurai Cowboy '93
The Cool Surface '92
Eyes of the Beholder '92
The Hand that Rocks the Cradle '92
Archie: Return to Riverdale '90
Deepstar Six '89
Police Academy 6: City under Siege '89
Police Academy 5: Assignment Miami Beach '88
Fraternity Vacation '85

Sylvester McCoy (1943-)
Doctor Who '96
Spellbreaker: Secret of the Leprechauns '96
Leapin' Leprechauns '95

Tim McCoy (1891-1978)
Run of the Arrow '56
Below the Border '42

Dawn on the Great Divide '42
Down Texas Way '42
Ghost Town Law '42
Riders of the West '42
West of the Law '42
Arizona Bound '41
Forbidden Trails '41
Gunman from Bodie '41
Arizona Gangbusters '40
Gun Code '40
Fighting Renegade '39
Outlaw's Paradise '39
Texas Wildcats '39
Lightnin' Carson Rides Again '38
Phantom Ranger '38
Aces and Eights '36
Border Caballero '36
Ghost Patrol '36
Lion's Den '36
The Man from Gun Town '36
Roaring Guns '36
The Traitor '36
Bulldog Courage '35
Fighting Shadows '35
The Fighting Marshal '32
The Riding Tornado '32
Texas Cyclone '32
Two-Fisted Law '32

Darius McCrary (1976-)
Transformers '07 (V)
John Carpenter Presents Vampires: Los Muertos '02
15 Minutes '01
Kingdom Come '01
Don King: Only in America '97
Big Shots '87

Jody McCrea (1934-)
Cry Blood, Apache '70
Free Grass '69
The Glory Stompers '67
Beach Blanket Bingo '65
How to Stuff a Wild Bikini '65
Bikini Beach '64
Muscle Beach Party '64
Pajama Party '63
Beach Party '63
Operation Bikini '63
Force of Impulse '60

Joel McCrea (1905-90)
Ride the High Country '62
The Gunfight at Dodge City '59
The Oklahoman '56
Stars in My Crown '50
South of St. Louis '49
Four Faces West '48
Ramrod '47
The Virginian '46
Buffalo Bill '44
The Great Moment '44
The More the Merrier '43
The Great Man's Lady '42
The Palm Beach Story '42
Sullivan's Travels '41
Foreign Correspondent '40
Primrose Path '40
They Shall Have Music '39
Union Pacific '39
Dead End '37
Internes Can't Take Money '37

Paul McCrane (1961-)
The Portrait '93
RoboCop '87
Purple Hearts '84
Fame '80

Mark McCracken (1960-)
Pumpkinhead 2: Blood Wings '94
Matinee '92

Kyle McCulloch
Careful '92
Tales from the Gimli Hospital '88

Julie McCullough (1965-)
The St. Tammany Miracle '94
Round Trip to Heaven '92
Big Bad Mama 2 '87

Philo (Philip, P.H., P.M.) McCullough (1890-1981)
Ridin' Thru '35
Captured in Chinatown '35
Inside Information '34
Tarzan the Fearless '33
Sunset Trail '32

Mathew McCurley (1982-)
Little Giants '94

Natalie McCurry
Dead End Drive-In '86

Bill McCutcheon (1924-2002)
Mr. Destiny '90
Tune in Tomorrow '90
Family Business '89
Steel Magnolias '89

Hattie McDaniel (1895-1952)
Never Say Goodbye '46
Since You Went Away '44
The Great Lie '41
They Died with Their Boots On '41
In This Our Life '42
The Male Animal '42
George Washington Slept Here '42
Gone with the Wind '39
Carefree '38
Mad Miss Manton '38
Shopworn Angel '38
Saratoga '37
The Bride Walks Out '36
Show Boat '36
Alice Adams '35
China Seas '35
Harmony Lane '35
The Little Colonel '35
I'm No Angel '33
Blonde Venus '32

James McDaniel (1958-)
Sunshine State '02
Steel City '05
Taken '02
Malcolm X '92

Helen McCrory (1968-)
Becoming Jane '07
The Queen '06
Casanova '05
Enduring Love '04
Charlotte Gray '01
Anna Karenina '00
Dad Savage '97
Split Second '99
Uncovered '94

Bruce McCulloch (1961-)
Stealing Harvard '02
Dog Park '98
Kids in the Hall: Brain Candy '96
Running Blind '78? Brain Candy

Ian McCulloch (1940-)
Witching Time '84
Alien Contamination '81
Doctor Butcher M.D. '80
Zombie '80

Dean McDermott (1966-)
Open Range '03
Britain's Song '01

Dylan McDermott (1962-)
The Messengers '07
The Tenants '06
Edison Force '05
The Mistress of Spices '05
Party Monster '03
Wonderland '03
Texas Rangers '01
Three to Tango '99
Til There Was You '96
Destiny Turns on the Radio '95
Home for the Holidays '95
The Cowboy Way '94
Miracle on 34th Street '94
In the Line of Fire '93
The Fear Inside '92
Into the Badlands '92
Jersey Girl '92
Where Sleeping Dogs Lie '91
Hardware '90
The Neon Empire '89
Steel Magnolias '89
Twister '89
Blue Iguana '88
Hamburger Hill '87

Hugh McDermott (1908-72)
Devil Girl from Mars '54
The Seventh Veil '46

Ruth McDevitt (1895-1976)
Homebodies '74
Change of Habit '69
The Shakiest Gun in the West '68
The Birds '63

Ian McDiarmid (1947-)
Elizabeth I '05
Star Wars: Episode 3 — Revenge of the Sith '05
Star Wars: Episode 2 — Attack of the Clones '02
Sleepy Hollow '99
Star Wars: Episode 1 — The Phantom Menace '99
Touching Evil '97
Rasputin: Dark Servant of Destiny '96
Annie: A Royal Adventure '95
Dragonslayer '81
The Awakening '80

Francis McDonald (1891-1968)
Zachariah '70
Bad Men of the Border '45
Mystery Man '44
Texas Masquerade '44
Zorro's Black Whip '44
The Kansan '43
The Sea Wolf '41
Carson City Kid '40
The Prisoner of Shark Island '36
Terror Trail '33
Hidden Valley '32
Texas Buddies '32
The Notorious Lady '27
Battling Butler '26
The Confession '20

Country Joe McDonald (1942-)
Armistead Maupin's Tales of the City '93
Zachariah '70

Grace McDonald (1918-99)
Follow the Boys '44
Gung Ho! '43
It Ain't Hay '43

Garry McDonald (1948-)
Rabbit-Proof Fence '02
Moulin Rouge '01
Ghosts Can Do It '87
The Wacky World of Wills & Burke '85
Pirate Movie '82

Christopher McDonald (1955-)
Awake '07
Kickin' It Old Skool '07
The Naked Mile '06
Broken Flowers '05
Rumor Has It... '05
Grind '03
Children On Their Birthdays '02
61* '01
The Theory of the Leisure Class '01
The Perfect Storm '00
Requiem for a Dream '00
The Skulls '00
Iron Giant '99 (V)
S.C.Punk! '99
The Faculty '98
Dirty Work '97
The Eighteenth Angel '97
Flubber '97
Into Thin Air: Death on Everest '97
Leave It to Beaver '97
Celtic Pride '96
Happy Gilmore '96
House Arrest '96
Jaded '96
Lawn Dogs '96
The Rich Man's Wife '96
A Smile Like Yours '96
Unforgettable '96
Best of the Best 3: No Turning Back '95
Fair Game '95
My Teacher's Wife '95
The Tuskegee Airman '95
Quiz Show '94
Monkey Trouble '94
Terminal Velocity '94
Benefit of the Doubt '93
Burns '93
Cover Story '93
Fatal Instinct '93
Grumpy Old Men '93
Wild Orchid 2: Two Shades of Blue '92
Conflict of Interest '92
Fatal Exposure '91
Red Wind '91
Thelma & Louise '91
Playroom '90
Chances Are '89
Paramedics '88
The Boys Next Door '85
Breakin' '84
Where the Boys Are '84
Grease 2 '82
Chattanooga Choo Choo '84

Audra McDonald (1970-)
A Raisin in the Sun '08
It Runs in the Family '03
Wit '01
The Last Debate '00
Having Our Say: The Delany Sisters' First 100 Years '99
Annie '99

Jeff (Jeffrey) McDonald (1963-)
Sugar Town '99

Kenneth McDonald
The Coast Patrol '25
Dynamite Dan '24

Kevin McDonald (1961-)
Lilo & Stitch 2: Stitch Has a Glitch '05 (V)
Sky High '05
Lilo & Stitch '02 (V)
The Godson '98
Kids in the Hall: Brain Candy '96
National Lampoon's Senior Trip '95
Spirit of '76 '91

Marie McDonald (1923-65)
Promises! Promises! '63
The Geisha Boy '58
Tell It to the Judge '49
Getting Gertie's Garter '45
Guest in the House '44

Mary McDonnell (1952-)
Crazy Like a Fox '04
Donnie Darko '01
Behind the Mask '99
Mumford '99
Evidence of Blood '97
Twelve Angry Men '97
Independence Day '96
Woman Undone '95
Blue Chips '94
Passion Fish '92
Sneakers '92
Grand Canyon '91
Dances with Wolves '90
Matewan '87
Tiger Warsaw '87

Mary Ann McDonald
Resurrecting the Champ '07

Michael McDonald
Outing Riley '04
The Nutcracker Prince '91 (V)
Far Cry from Home '81
Love at First Sight '76

Peter McDonald (1972-)
Blow Dry '00
Nora '00
When Brendan Met Trudy '00
Felicia's Journey '99
Captain Jack '98
I Went Down '97

Ryan McDonald (1984-)
Resurrecting the Champ '07

William McDonald
Subhuman '04
Don't Look Down '98

Mary (Elizabeth) McDonough (1961-)
Mom '07
Snowballing '85
A Day for Thanks on Walton's Mountain '82
The Waltons: The Christmas Carol '80

Neal McDonough (1966-)
88 Minutes '08
Brothers Three '07
The Guardian '06
Flags of Our Fathers '06
The Last Time '06
I Know Who Killed Me '07
Tin Man '07
The Hitcher '07
Walking Tall '04
Timeline '03
Minority Report '02
Band of Brothers '01
The Killing Club '01
Ravenous '99

Frances McDormand (1958-)
Miss Pettigrew Lives for a Day '08
Friends with Money '06
Aeon Flux '05
North Country '05
Something's Gotta Give '03
City by the Sea '02
Laurel Canyon '02
The Man Who Wasn't There '01
Almost Famous '00
Wonder Boys '00
Madeline '98
Johnny Skidmarks '97
Paradise Road '97
Fargo '96
Hidden in America '96
Primal Fear '96
Lone Star '95
The Good Old Boys '95
Palookaville '95
Short Cuts '93
Passed Away '92
Crazy in Love '92
Darkman '90
Hidden Agenda '90
Chattahoochee '89
Mississippi Burning '88
Raising Arizona '87
Blood Simple '85
Crimewave '85

Jake McDorman (1986-)
Aquamarine '06
Bring It On: All or Nothing '06

Roddy McDowall (1928-98)
A Bug's Life '98 (V)
Rudyard Kipling's The Second Jungle Book: Mowgli and Baloo '97
Unlikely Angel '97
Last Summer in the Hamptons '96
The Color of Evening '95
Fatally Yours '95
The Grass Harp '95
Star Hunter '95
Unknown Origin '95
Mirror, Mirror 2: Raven Dance '94
Heads '93
Deadly Game '91
Double Trouble '91
An Inconvenient Woman '91
Around the World in 30 Days '89
The Big Picture '89
Cutting Class '89
Shakma '89
Doin' Time on Planet Earth '88
Fright Night 2 '88
Dead of Winter '87
Overboard '87
Class of 1984 '82
Evil under the Sun '82
Charlie Chan and the Curse of the Dragon Queen '81
The Return of the King '80 (V)
The Martian Chronicles: Part 3 '79
The Martian Chronicles: Part 2 '79
Scavenger Hunt '79

Betty McDowall (1933-)
Ballad in Blue '66
Dead Lucky '60
Jack the Ripper '60
Time Lock '57

The Cat from Outer Space '78
Circle of Iron '78
Laserblast '78
Rabbit Test '78
The Thief of Baghdad '78
Embryo '76
Flood! '76
Funny Lady '75
Mean Johnny Barrows '75
Dirty Mary Crazy Larry '74
Arnold '73
Battle for the Planet of the Apes '73
The Legend of Hell House '73
Conquest of the Planet of the Apes '72
Life & Times of Judge Roy Bean '72
The Poseidon Adventure '72
Bedknobs and Broomsticks '71
Escape from the Planet of the Apes '71
Night Gallery '69
Five Card Stud '68
Planet of the Apes '68
Lord Love a Duck '66
The Adventures of Bullwhip Griffin '66
Inside Daisy Clover '65
The Greatest Story Ever Told '65
The Loved One '65
That Darn Cat '65
Cleopatra '63
The Tempest '63
The Longest Day '62
Midnight Lace '60
Hill Number One '51
Macbeth '48
Holiday in Mexico '46
The White Cliffs of Dover '44
Lassie, Come Home '43
My Friend Flicka '43
On the Sunny Side '42
Son of Fury '42
How Green Was My Valley '41

Claire McDowell (1877-1966)
Ben-Hur '26
The Show Off '26
The Big Parade '25
West-Bound Limited '23

Malcolm McDowell (1943-)
Doomsday '08
Halloween '07
Mirror Wars: Reflection One '05
Bobby Jones: Stroke of Genius '04
Hidalgo '04
The Company '03
Gangster No. 1 '00
Island of the Dead '00
St. Patrick: The Irish Legend '00
Y2K '99
Where Truth Lies '96
Yesterday's Target '96
Cyborg 3: The Recycler '95
2103: Deadly Wake '97
Kids of the Round Table '96
The First 9 1/2 Weeks '98
My Life So Far '98
Asylum '97
Hugo Pool '97
Mr. Magoo '97
Tales from a Parallel Universe: Giga Shadow '97
Between Strangers '02
Firestarter 2: Rekindled '02
I Spy '02
Just Visiting '01
Princess of Thieves '01
The Void '01
Can of Worms '00

Fist of the North Star '95
Dangerous Indiscretion '94
Star Trek: Generations '94
The Surgeon '94
Tank Girl '94
Bophal '93
Chain of Desire '93
Night Train to Venice '93
The Player '92
The Light in the Jungle '91
Class of 1999 '90
Disturbed '90
Jezebel's Kiss '90
Moon 44 '90
Buy & Cell '89
Sunset '88
The Caller '87
Monte Carlo '86
Gulag '85
Merlin and the Sword '85
Blue Thunder '83
Cross Creek '83
Get Crazy '83
Little Red Riding Hood '83
Britannia Hospital '82
Cat People '82
Caligula '80
Look Back in Anger '80
Time After Time '79
Voyage of the Damned '76
Royal Flash '75
A Clockwork Orange '71
O Lucky Man! '73
Long Ago Tomorrow '71
If... '69

Nelson McDowell (1870-1947)
Roll, Wagons, Roll '39
Desert Phantom '36
Feud of the West '35
Lightning Bill '35
Texas Jack '35
Rustler's Roundup '33
Come on Tarzan '32
Mason of the Mounted '32
The Phantom Bullet '26
Oliver Twist '22
The Last of the Mohicans '20

Trevyn McDowell (1967-)
Mary Shelley's Frankenstein '94
Middlemarch '93

James McEachin (1930-)
Double Exposure '93
Honeyboy '82
He Who Walks Alone '78
The Dead Don't Die '75
The Groundstar Conspiracy '72

Ellen McElduff
Working Girls '87
Impostors '98

Rob McElhenney
Latter Days '04

Ian McElhinney (1948-)
The Front Line '06
The Mapmaker '01
Hamlet '96
Small Faces '95
A Woman's Guide to Adultery '93
The Playboys '92

Jack McElhone (1994-)
Dear Frankie '04
Young Adam '03

Natascha (Natasha) McElhone (1971-)
The Company '07
Big Nothing '06
Ladies in Lavender '04
City of Ghosts '03
The Other Boleyn Girl '03
Feardotcom '02
Laurel Canyon '02
Solaris '02
Killing Me Softly '01
Love's Labour's Lost '00
Ronin '98
The Truman Show '98

Mrs. Dalloway '97
The Devil's Own '96
Surviving Picasso '96

John McEnery (1945-)
Merlin '98
Tess of the D'Urbervilles '98
When Saturday Comes '95
Black Beauty '94
The Buddha of Suburbia '92
Codename Kyril '91
The Krays '90
A.D. '85
Gulag '85
Pope John Paul II '84
Schizo '77
The Land That Time Forgot '75
One Russian Summer '73
Bartleby '70

Peter McEnery (1940-)
Pictures '80s
The Cat and the Canary '79
Primal Impulse '74
Tales That Witness Madness '73
Negatives '68
I Killed Rasputin '67
The Fighting Prince of Donegal '66
The Game Is Over '66
The Moon-Spinners '64
Victim '61

Annie McEnroe (1955-)
Howling 2: Your Sister Is a Werewolf '85
Purple Hearts '84
Warlords of the 21st Century '82
The Hand '81
Running Scared '79
True Stories '86
Cop '88

John McEnroe (1959-)
Anger Management '03
Mr. Deeds '02

Reba McEntire (1955-)
Charlotte's Web '06 (V)
The Fox and the Hound 2 '06 (V)
One Night at McCool's '01
Forever Love '98
Buffalo Girls '95
Is There Life Out There? '94
North '94
The Gambler Returns: The Luck of the Draw '93
The Man from Left Field '93
Tremors '89

Barry McEvoy
An Everlasting Piece '00
Gloria '98

Geraldine McEwan (1932-)
Carrie's War '04
Vanity Fair '04
Food of Love '02
The Magdalene Sisters '02
Pure '02
Love's Labour's Lost '00
The Love Letter '99
Titus '99
Moses '96
Robin Hood: Prince of Thieves '91
Henry V '89
Oranges Are Not the Only Fruit '89
Foreign Body '86
Mapp & Lucia '85

Davenia McFadden (1961-)
Smokin' Aces '07
Double Jeopardy '99

Gates (Cheryl) McFadden (1949-)
Star Trek: Nemesis '02
Star Trek: Insurrection '98
Star Trek: First Contact '96

Star Trek: Generations '94
Taking Care of Business '90

Joseph McFadden (1975-)
Dad Savage '97
The Crow Road '96
Small Faces '95

George "Spanky" McFarland (1928-93)
The Aurora Encounter '85
Peck's Bad Boy with the Circus '38
General Spanky '36
The Trail of the Lonesome Pine '36
Kentucky Kernels '34

Douglas McFerran
Johnny English '03
Antitrust '00

William F. McGaha
Iron Horsemen '71
The Speed Lovers '68

Mark McGann (1961-)
Shackleton '02
Endgame '01

Paul McGann (1959-)
Kidnapped '05
Queen of the Damned '02
Horatio Hornblower: The Adventure '01
Our Mutual Friend '98
FairyTale: A True Story '97
Doctor Who '96
The One That Got Away '96
Catherine the Great '95
Afraid of the Dark '92
Alien 3 '92
Paper Mask '91
Innocent Victim '90
Dealers '89
The Rainbow '89
Withnail and I '87

Darren McGavin (1922-2006)
Billy Madison '94
Happy Hell Night '92
Mastergate '92
Perfect Harmony '91
Blood & Concrete: A Love Story '90
Child in the Night '90
Around the World in 80 Days '89
By Dawn's Early Light '89
Captain America '89
Dead Heat '88
Sunset '88
Raw Deal '86
The Natural '84
A Christmas Story '83
Power, Passion & Murder '83
Firebird 2015 A.D. '81
Hangar 18 '80
Zero to Sixty '78
Airport '77 '77
No Deposit, No Return '76
The Richard Petty Story '72
Say Goodbye, Maggie Cole '72
The Night Stalker '71
Tribes '70
Mission Mars '67
The Delicate Delinquent '56

The Court Martial of Billy Mitchell '55
The Man with the Golden Arm '55
Summertime '55
Queen for a Day '51

Patrick McGaw
Dream with the Fishes '97
Scorpion Spring '96
The Basketball Diaries '95
Malicious '95
Forbidden Choices '94
Amongst Friends '93

Jack McGee (1928-2003)
Bread and Roses '00
Treehouse Hostage '99
Chairman of the Board '97
The Last Days of Frankie the Fly '96
The Quest '96
Crash and Burn '90

Vic McGee
Alien Massacre '67
Monsters Crash the Pajama Party '65
Horrors of the Red Planet '64

Vonetta McGee (1948-)
Johnny B. '00
You Must Remember This '92
Brother Future '91
To Sleep with Anger '90
Repo Man '83
The Eiger Sanction '75
The Big Bust Out '73
The Norliss Tapes '73
Shaft in Africa '73
Blacula '72

Johnny Rae McGhee
Love Field '91
Project X '87

William (Bill) McGhee (1930-2007)
Don't Look in the Basement '73

Bruce McGill (1950-)
Vantage Point '08
The Lookout '07
Outlaw Trail '06
Cinderella Man '05
Elizabethtown '05
Slow Burn '05
Collateral '04
Legally Blonde 2: Red White & Blonde '03
Live from Baghdad '03
Matchstick Men '03
Runaway Jury '03
Path to War '02
The Sum of All Fears '02
Ali '01
Exit Wounds '01
Shallow Hal '01
61* '01
Deep Core '00
The Legend of Bagger Vance '00
Running Mates '00
A Dog of Flanders '99
The Insider '99
Everything That Rises '98
Ground Control '98
Letters from a Killer '98
Murder She Purred: A Mrs. Murphy Mystery '98
Black Sheep '96
Lawn Dogs '96
Rosewood '96
The Good Old Boys '95
Timecop '94
My Cousin Vinny '92
Play Nice '92
The Last Boy Scout '91
Little Vegas '90
Out Cold '89
Three Fugitives '89
End of the Line '88
The Last Innocent Man '87
Waiting for the Moon '87
No Mercy '86
Wildcats '86

Charlotte Forten's Mission: Experiment in Freedom '85
Into the Night '85
Ballad of Gregorio Cortez '83
Silkwood '83
Tough Enough '83
The Hand '81
Whale for the Killing '81
National Lampoon's Animal House '78
Citizens Band '77

Everett McGill (1945-)
My Fellow Americans '96
Under Siege 2: Dark Territory '95
The People under the Stairs '91
Drug Wars: The Camarena Story '90
Jezebel's Kiss '90
Iguana '89
License to Kill '89
Field of Honor '86
Heartbreak Ridge '86
Silver Bullet '85
Dune '84
Quest for Fire '82
Union City '81
Brubaker '80

Kelly McGillis (1957-)
The Monkey's Mask '00
Morgan's Ferry '99
The Settlement '99
At First Sight '98
Ground Control '98
Storm Chasers: Revenge of the Twister '98
The Wicked, Wicked West '97
North '94
The Babe '92
Grand Isle '92
Cat Chaser '90
Winter People '89
The Accused '88
The House on Carroll Street '88
Unsettled Land '88
Made in Heaven '87
Top Gun '86
Witness '85
Code of Honor '84
Reuben, Reuben '83

John C. McGinley (1959-)
Are We Done Yet? '07
Wild Hogs '07
Identity '03
Crazy as Hell '02
Stealing Harvard '02
The Animal '01
Highway '01
Get Carter '00
Any Given Sunday '99
Three to Tango '99
The Jack Bull '99
Office Space '98
The Pentagon Wars '98
Flypaper '97
Truth or Consequences, N.M. '97
Mother '96
Nothing to Lose '96
The Rock '96
Set It Off '96
Born to Be Wild '95
Seven '95
Car 54, Where Are You? '94
Mother's Boys '94
On Deadly Ground '94
Surviving the Game '94
Wagons East '94
Hear No Evil '93
The Last Outlaw '93
Watch It '93
Article 99 '92
A Midnight Clear '92
Highlander 2: The Quickening '91
Point Break '91
Little Noises '91
Suffering Bastards '90
Fat Man and Little Boy '89
Lost Angels '89
Prisoners of Inertia '89

McHugh

Talk Radio '88
Wall Street '87
Platoon '86

Sean McGinley (1956-)
On a Clear Day '05
Freeze Frame '04
Conspiracy of Silence '03
Dead Bodies '03
American Women '00
Dr. Bell and Mr. Doyle: The Dark Beginnings of Sherlock Holmes '00
The General '98
The Break '97
The Butcher Boy '97
The Informant '97
Resurrection Man '97
Michael Collins '96
Trojan Eddie '96
Braveheart '95
Family '94
The Field '90

Ted McGinley (1958-)
Daybreak '01
Pearl Harbor '01
Face the Music '00
Dick '99
Every Mother's Worst Fear '98
Major League 3: Back to the Minors '98
Revenge of the Nerds 4: Nerds in Love '94
Revenge of the Nerds 3: The Next Generation '92
Blue Tornado '90
Physical Evidence '89
Revenge of the Nerds '84

Scott McGinnis (1958-)
You Can't Hurry Love '88
Odd Jobs '85
Thunder Alley '85
Making the Grade '84
Joy Sticks '83

Boris McGiver (1962-)
Connie and Carla '04
Little Odessa '94

John McGiver (1912-75)
Mame '74
The Adventures of Tom Sawyer '73
Arnold '73
Lawman '71
Midnight Cowboy '69
The Glass Bottom Boat '66
Marriage on the Rocks '65
A Global Affair '63
Man's Favorite Sport? '63
Who's Got the Action? '63
Who's Minding the Store? '63
The Manchurian Candidate '62
Mr. Hobbs Takes a Vacation '62
Period of Adjustment '62
Breakfast at Tiffany's '61
Bachelor in Paradise '59
The Gazebo '59
Love in the Afternoon '57
The Man in the Raincoat '57
I Married a Woman '56

Mike McGlone (1972-)
Bad City '06
Fortunes '05
The War Within '05
Hardball '01
Dinner Rush '00
One Tough Cop '98
Subway Stories '97
Ed '96
She's the One '96
The Brothers McMullen '94

Frank McGlynn (1866-1951)
Rogue's Gallery '44
Western Gold '37
The Prisoner of Shark Island '36
Custer's Last Stand '36

Patrick McGoohan (1928-)
Treasure Planet '02 (V)
The Phantom '96
A Time to Kill '96
Braveheart '95
Escape from Alcatraz '79
Brass Target '78
The Man in the Iron Mask '77
Silver Streak '76
Mary, Queen of Scots '71
Ice Station Zebra '68
Koroshi '67
Dr. Syn, Alias the Scarecrow '64
The Three Lives of Thomasina '63
I Am a Camera '55

Barry McGovern (1948-)
Miracle at Midnight '98
Braveheart '95
Joe Versus the Volcano '90

Elizabeth McGovern (1961-)
Buffalo Soldiers '01
The Flamingo Rising '01
House of Mirth '00
The Scarlet Pimpernel '99
The Scarlet Pimpernel 2: Mademoiselle Guillotine '99
The Scarlet Pimpernel 3: The Kidnapped King '99
The Wings of the Dove '97
Broken Glass '96
The Summer of Ben Tyler '96
Broken Trust '95
Me & Veronica '93
King of the Hill '93
The Favor '92
Racing with the Moon '84
Once Upon a Time in America '84
Ragtime '81
Ordinary People '80

Terence McGovern (1942-)
DuckTales the Movie: Treasure of the Lost Lamp '90 (V)
Americathon '79

Charles McGowan
A Chorus Line '85
The Notorious Bettie Page '06

Matt McGrath (1969-)
Boys Don't Cry '99
The Broken Hearts Club '00
The Imposters '98
1999 '98
C.

Douglas McGrath (1958-)
Company Man '00
Pale Rider '85
Porky's '82

Derek McGrath (1951-)
Full of It '07
Stuart Bliss '98
Chameleon '95
Freaked '93
She's Out of Control '89

Debra McGrath (1954-)
DC 9/11: Time of Crisis '04
Termini Station '89

Brian McGrath
A Love Divided '01

Alethea McGrath
Alien Visitor '95
Star Wars: Episode II — Attack of the Clones '02
Star Wars: Episode III — Revenge of the Sith '05

Walter McGrail (1888-1970)
Code of the Fearless '39
The Green Hornet '39
The Shadow Strikes '37
Sunset Range '35
Night Nurse '31
The Lone Star Ranger '30

Michael McGrady
Dog Gone Love '03
As Good As It Gets '97
Operation Delta Force 2: Mayday '97
White Dwarf '95
Malevolence '95
The Babe '92

Tom McGowan (1959-)
The Doom Generation '95
The Birdcage '95
Mrs. Parker and the Vicious Circle '94

Angela Punch McGregor (1953-)
The Efficiency Expert '92
Double Deal '84
A Test of Love '84
We of the Never Never '82
The Island '80
Survivor '80
The Chant of Jimmie Blacksmith '78
Newsfront '78

Ewan McGregor (1971-)
Deception '08
Cassandra's Dream '07
Alex Rider: Operation Stormbreaker '06
Scenes of a Sexual Nature '06
Miss Potter '06
The Island '05
Robots '05 (V)
Stay '05
Valiant '05 (V)
Down With Love '03
Young Adam '03
Big Fish '03
Star Wars: Episode II — Attack of the Clones '02
Black Hawk Down '01
Moulin Rouge '01
Nora '00
Eye of the Beholder '99
Star Wars: Episode I — The Phantom Menace '99
Little Voice '98
Rogue Trader '98
Velvet Goldmine '98
A Life Less Ordinary '97
The Serpent's Kiss '97
Brassed Off '96
Emma '96
Nightwatch '96
Blue Juice '95
The Pillow Book '95
Trainspotting '95
Being Human '94
Lipstick on Your Collar '94
Shallow Grave '94

Charles McGregor (1922-96)
Superfly '72
The Baron '88

Kenneth John McGregor
The Ten Million Dollar Getaway '91
Primal Scream '87
The Navigator '24

Malcolm McGregor (1892-1945)
Lost Zeppelin '29
Midnight Faces '26
The Reckless Way '36
Smouldering Fires '25
The Untamable '23

Kim McGuire (1926-)
Acting on Impulse '93
Cry-Baby '90

Marcy McGuire (1926-)
Seven Days Ashore '44
Around the World '43
Seven Days' Leave '42

Kathryn McGuire (1903-78)
Sherlock, Jr. '24

Michael McGuire (1934-)
Bird '88

Kate McGregor-Stewart
Ma and Pa Kettle Go to Town '50
Side Street '50
Border Incident '49
The Killers '46
T-Men '47

Angela Punch McGregor — Caroline? '90

Don McGuire (1919-99)
Double Dynamite '51
Armored Car Robbery '50
The Threat '49
The Fuller Brush Man '48
The Man I Love '46

Dorothy McGuire (1918-2001)
Caroline? '90
Amos '85
The Incredible Journey of Dr. Meg Laurel '79
Little Women '78
Rich Man, Poor Man '76
The Runaways '75
Summer Magic '63
Swiss Family Robinson '60
A Summer Place '59
Old Yeller '57
Friendly Persuasion '56
Make Haste to Live '54
Three Coins in the Fountain '54
I Want You '51
Gentleman's Agreement '47
Till the End of Time '46
The Spiral Staircase '46
The Enchanted Cottage '45
A Tree Grows in Brooklyn '45

John McGuire (1910-80)
Sands of Iwo Jima '49
The Invisible Ghost '41
Stranger on the Third Floor '40

Biff McGuire (1926-)
The Deep End of the Ocean '98
Deep Impact '98
A Midsummer Night's Sex Comedy '82
Serpico '73
Child of Glass '78
The Thomas Crown Affair '68

Barry McGuire (1930-)
Werewolves on Wheels '71
The President's Analyst '67

Matthew McGrory (1973-2005)
The Devil's Rejects '05
Big Fish '03

Michael McGreevey (1948-)
The Strongest Man in the World '75
Superdad '73
Now You See Him, Now You Don't '72
The Computer Wore Tennis Shoes '69

Tim McGraw (1967-)
Flicka '06
Black Cloud '04
Friday Night Lights '04

Melinda McGraw (1963-)
The Dark Knight '08
The Shadow '94

Aislin McGuckin (1974-)
The Unknown Soldier '98
The Nephew '97

Stephen McHattie (1947-)
300 '07
All Hat '07
Jesse Stone: Death in Paradise '06
Jesse Stone: Night Passage '06
A History of Violence '05
Jesse Stone: Stone Cold '05
Secretary '02
Twist '03
The Highway Men '99
Beverly Hills Cop 3 '94
The Dark '94
Geronimo: An American Legend '93
Erik '90
Bloodhounds of Broadway '89
One Man Out '89
Call Me '88
Sticky Fingers '88
Salvation! '87
Belizaire the Cajun '86
Death Valley '81
Roughnecks '80
Mary and Joseph: A Story of Faith '79
Centennial '78
Tomorrow Never Comes '77
James Dean '76
Moving Violation '76

Frank McHugh (1898-1981)
Easy Come, Easy Go '67
A Tiger Walks '64
Last Hurrah '58
There's No Business Like Show Business '54
A Lion Is in the Streets '53
Mighty Joe Young '49
Miss Grant Takes Richmond '49
Velvet Touch '48
Carnegie Hall '47
State Fair '45
Going My Way '44
Marine Raiders '43
All Through the Night '42
Back Street '41
City for Conquest '40
I Love You Again '40
Virginia City '40
Dodge City '39
The Roaring Twenties '39
Boy Meets Girl '38
Four Daughters '38
Bullets or Ballots '36
Stage Struck '36
Three Men on a Horse '36
Devil Dogs of the Air '35
Gold Diggers of 1935 '35
Fashions of 1934 '34
Ex-Lady '33
Havana Widows '33
Telegraph Trail '33
Tomorrow at Seven '33
Mystery of the Wax Museum '33
The Strange Love of Molly Louvain '32
Corsair '31
Millie '31

Robert McHeady
Find the Lady '76
Deranged '74
The People Next Door '70
The Greatest Story Ever Told '65

Blinded by the Light '82
The Long Days of Summer '80

Cast Index 1569

McIlvaine

Julia McIlvaine
The Lost Child '00
The Summer of Ben Tyler '96

David McIlwraith
Hollow Man 2 '06
DC 9/11: Time of Crisis '04
Caracara '00
Cruel Intentions 2 '99
The Happy Face Murders '99
In the Company of Spies '99
Gunfighter's Moon '96
On My Own '95
Millennium '89
Really Weird Tales '86
The Vindicator '85

Tim (McInnerny) McInnerny (1956-)
The Line of Beauty '06
Severance '06
Casanova '05
The Emperor's New Clothes '01
Longitude '00
102 Dalmatians '00
Notting Hill '99
Rogue Trader '98
FairyTale: A True Story '97
A Very British Coup '88
Wetherby '85

William McInnes (1961-)
Irresistible '06
Look Both Ways '05
Do or Die '01

John McIntire (1907-91)
Heroes of the Heart '94
As Summers Die '86
Cloak & Dagger '84
Honkytonk Man '82
American Dream '81
The Fox and the Hound '81 (V)
Mrs. R's Daughter '79
Rooster Cogburn '75
Herbie Rides Again '74
Rough Night in Jericho '67
Summer and Smoke '61
Two Rode Together '61
Elmer Gantry '60
Flaming Star '60
Psycho '60
The Gunfight at Dodge City '59
The Light in the Forest '58
The Mark of the Hawk '57
The Tin Star '57
Far Country '55
The Kentuckian '55
Apache '54
A Lion Is in the Streets '53
War Arrow '53
Horizons West '52
The Lawless Breed '52
The World in His Arms '52
Westward the Women '51
The Asphalt Jungle '50
Walk Softly, Stranger '50
Winchester '73 '50
Francis the Talking Mule '49
Call Northside 777 '48

Tim McIntire (1943-86)
Sacred Ground '83
Fast Walking '82
The Choirboys '77
Gumball Rally '76
A Boy and His Dog '75 (V)
Aloha, Bobby and Rose '74
The Sterile Cuckoo '69
Shenandoah '65

Burr McIntosh (1862-1942)
The Adorable Cheat '28
That Certain Thing '28
The Average Woman '24
Way Down East '20

Judy McIntosh
The Chronicles of Narnia: The Lion, the Witch and the Wardrobe '05
Ebbtide '94

Neve McIntosh (1972-)
The Hound of the Baskervilles '02

Christine McIntyre (1911-84)
Breakin' Through '84
Twirl '81
Land of the Lawless '47
Gentleman from Texas '46
The Stranger from Pecos '45
Partners of the Trail '44
Rock River Renegades '42

Marvin J. McIntyre
Born to Be Wild '95
Wilder Napalm '93
Fandango '85

Susan McIver (1951-)
Smokey and the Bandit '77
I Spit on Your Corpse! '77

David McKay
My Name Is Joe '98
The Girl in the Picture '86

Scott McKay (1915-87)
Christmas Evil '80
Creature of Destruction '67
Guest in the House '44
The Black Raven '43
Corregidor '43

Wanda McKay (1916-96)
Roaring City '51
Jungle Goddess '49
There Goes Kelly '45
The Monster Maker '44
Raiders of Ghost City '44
Bowery at Midnight '42
Law and Order '42
The Pioneers '41
Twilight on the Trail '41

Michael McKean (1947-)
Joshua '07
Surf's Up '07 (V)
For Your Consideration '06
The Producers '05
And Starring Pancho Villa as Himself '03
A Mighty Wind '03
Auto Focus '02
The Guru '02
100 Mile Rule '02
My First Mister '01
Never Again '01
Beautiful '00
Best in Show '00
Little Nicky '00
Teaching Mrs. Tingle '99
True Crime '99
Final Justice '98
Highway Hitcher '98
No Strings Attached '98
Small Soldiers '98 (V)
With Friends Like These '98
Jack '96
Nothing to Lose '96
That Darn Cat '96
The Brady Bunch Movie '95
Edie & Pen '95
The Sunshine Boys '95
Across the Moon '94
Airheads '94
Radioland Murders '94
Coneheads '93
Man Trouble '92
Memoirs of an Invisible Man '92
The Return of Spinal Tap '92
Book of Love '91
Hider in the House '90
The Big Picture '89
Earth Girls Are Easy '89
Flashback '89
Portrait of a White Marriage '88
Short Circuit 2 '88
Light of Day '87
Planes, Trains and Automobiles '87
Jumpin' Jack Flash '86
Clue '85
D.A.R.Y.L. '85
This Is Spinal Tap '84
Young Doctors in Love '82
Used Cars '80
1941 '79

Donna McKechnie (1940-)
Breakin' Through '84
The Little Prince '74

Gina McKee (1964-)
Atonement '07
Scenes of a Sexual Nature '06
MirrorMask '05
The Reckoning '03
Divine Secrets of the Ya-Ya Sisterhood '02
Notting Hill '99
Wonderland '99
Croupier '97
Element of Doubt '96
Naked '93

John McKee
The Gallant Hours '60
Above and Beyond '53

Lafe (Lafayette) McKee (1872-1959)
Inside the Law '42
Covered Wagon Trails '40
Riders of Pasco Basin '40
Brothers of the West '37
Melody of the Plains '37
Mystery of the Hooded Horseman '37
The Rangers Step In '37
Santa Fe Bound '37
Last of the Warrens '36
Little Red Schoolhouse '36
Boss Cowboy '35
Ghost Rider '35
Kid Courageous '35
Lightning Bill '35
The Miracle Rider '35
The Revenge Rider '35
Ridin' Thru '35
Riding Speed '35
Rustlers of Red Dog '35
Swifty '35
Western Justice '35
Law of the Wild '34
Man from Utah '34
Rawhide Romance '34
The Silver Bullet '34
Deadwood Pass '33
The Dude Bandit '33
Fighting Champ '33
Jaws of Justice '33
Lightning Range '33
Man from Monterey '33
Telegraph Trail '33
Terror Trail '33
Trail Drive '33
The Big Stampede '32
Boiling Point '32
The Riding Tornado '32
Tombstone Canyon '32
The Pocatello Kid '31
Range Law '31
Two Gun Man '31
Near the Rainbow's End '30
Under Montana Skies '30
Little Orphan Annie '18

Lonette McKee (1954-)
ATL '06
She Hate Me '04
Honey '03
Lift '01
Men of Honor '00
Having Our Say: The Delany Sisters' First 100 Years '99
Blind Faith '98
He Got Game '98
Dangerous Passion '95
Queen '93
Malcolm X '92
Jungle Fever '91
The Women of Brewster Place '89
Gardens of Stone '87
Round Midnight '86
Brewster's Millions '85
The Cotton Club '84
Cuba '79
Which Way Is Up? '77
Sparkle '76
Detroit 9000 '73

Raymond (Ray) McKee (1892-1984)
Campus Knights '29
Free to Love '25
Down to the Sea in Ships '22

Todd McKee (1963-)
Devil in the Flesh 2 '00
Blade Boxer '97

Michael McKeever
Around the Fire '98
Junior '86
The Three Stooges Meet Hercules '61

Danica McKellar (1976-)
Hack! '07
Raising Genius '04
Sidekicks '93
Camp Cucamonga: How I Spent My Summer Vacation '90

Don McKellar (1963-)
Slings & Arrows: Season 2 '05
Clean '04
The Event '03
Sea People '00
eXistenZ '99
The Passion of Ayn Rand '99
Last Night '98
The Red Violin '98
In the Presence of Mine Enemies '97
Never Met Picasso '96
When Night Is Falling '95
Exotica '94
The Adjuster '91
Highway 61 '91
Roadkill '89

Ian McKellen (1939-)
The Golden Compass '07 (V)
Stardust '07 (N)
The Da Vinci Code '06
Flushed Away '06 (V)
X-Men: The Last Stand '06
Asylum '05
Doogal '05 (V)
Emile '03
Lord of the Rings: The Return of the King '03
X2: X-Men United '03
Lord of the Rings: The Two Towers '02
Lord of the Rings: The Fellowship of the Rings '01
X-Men '00
David Copperfield '99
Gods and Monsters '98
Apt Pupil '97
Bent '97
Swept from the Sea '97
Rasputin: Dark Servant of Destiny '96
Jack and Sarah '95
Restoration '94
The Shadow '94
And the Band Played On '93
Armistead Maupin's Tales of the City '93
The Ballad of Little Jo '93
Six Degrees of Separation '93
Scandal '89
Windmills of the Gods '88
Plenty '85
The Keep '83
The Scarlet Pimpernel '82
Priest of Love '81

Alex McKenna (1984-)
Campfire Tales '98
Joey '85
Safety Patrol '98
The Stupids '95

Siobhan McKenna (1923-86)
Doctor Zhivago '65
Of Human Bondage '64
Playboy of the Western World '62
The King of Kings '61
The Adventurers '51

T.P. McKenna (1929-)
Red Scorpion '89
Valmont '89
Bleak House '85
The Doctor and the Devils '85

Virginia McKenna (1931-)
Sliding Doors '97
The Camomile Lawn '92
Duel of Hearts '92
The First Olympics: Athens 1896 '84
Disappearance '81
The Chosen '77
Christian the Lion '76
The Gathering Storm '74
Waterloo '71
An Elephant Called Slowly '69
Ring of Bright Water '69
Born Free '66
The Wreck of the Mary Deare '59
Carve Her Name with Pride '58
The Smallest Show on Earth '57
Simba '55
The Cruel Sea '53

Dallas McKennon (1919-)
Mystery Mansion '83
Lady and the Tramp '55 (V)

Ben(jamin) McKenzie (1978-)
88 Minutes '08
Junebug '05

Fay McKenzie (1918-)
Heart of the Rio Grande '42
Down Mexico Way '41
Death Rides the Range '40
Ghost Town Riders '38
Boss Cowboy '35

Jacqueline McKenzie (1967-)
Divine Secrets of the Ya-Ya Sisterhood '02
On the Beach '00
Deep Blue Sea '99
Under the Lighthouse Dancing '97
Angel Baby '95
Mr. Reliable: A True Story '95
Talk '94
Traps '93
Romper Stomper '92

Julia McKenzie (1941-)
These Foolish Things '06
Bright Young Things '03
The Old Curiosity Shop '94
Shirley Valentine '89

Richard McKenzie (1930-)
In Love and War '91
Corvette Summer '78

Tim McKenzie
The 13th Floor '88
The Lighthorsemen '87
Gallipoli '81

Doug McKeon (1966-)
The Empty Mirror '99
From the Earth to the Moon '98
Sub Down '97
Where the Red Fern Grows: Part 2 '92
Breaking Home Ties '87
Turnaround '87
Heart of a Champion: The Ray Mancini Story '85
Mischief '85
Desperate Lives '82
Night Crossing '81
On Golden Pond '81
Centennial '78

Nancy McKeon (1966-)
Category 6: Day of Destruction '04
Just Write '97
The Wrong Woman '95
Teresa's Tattoo '94
Where the Day Takes You '92
The Lightning Incident '91
Poison Ivy '85
High School USA '84

Philip McKeon (1964-)
Red Surf '90
Return to Horror High '87

Charles McKeown
The Adventures of Baron Munchausen '89
Erik the Viking '89

Fintan McKeown
Conspiracy of Silence '03
Waking Ned Devine '98

Leo McKern (1920-2002)
Molokai: The Story of Father Damien '99
A Foreign Field '93
Monsignor Quixote '91
Travelling North '87
Agatha Christie's Murder with Mirrors '85
Ladyhawke '85
The French Lieutenant's Woman '81
The Blue Lagoon '80
The House on Garibaldi Street '79
The Adventures of Sherlock Holmes' Smarter Brother '78
Candleshoe '78
The Omen '76
Massacre in Rome '73
Ryan's Daughter '70
The Shoes of the Fisherman '68
The Amorous Adventures of Moll Flanders '65
Help! '65
King and Country '64
Doctor in Distress '63
The Horse Without a Head '63
The Day the Earth Caught Fire '61
The Mouse That Roared '59
Time Without Pity '57
X The Unknown '56

Kevin McKidd (1973-)
Made of Honor '08
Hannibal Rising '07
The Last Legion '07
Kingdom of Heaven '05
De-Lovely '04
The Purifiers '04
16 Years of Alcohol '03
Max '02
Dog Soldiers '01
Anna Karenina '00
Topsy Turvy '99
The Acid House '98
Bedrooms and Hallways '98
Behind the Lines '97
Dad Savage '97
Small Faces '95
Trainspotting '95

Robert McKim (1886-1927)
The Bat '26
Heart's Haven '22
Wagon Tracks '19
Blue Blazes Rawden '18
Hell's Hinges '16

The Disciple '15

Bill McKinney (1931-)
Undertow '04
Asylum of the Damned '03
It Came from Outer Space
2 '95
City Slickers 2: The Legend
of Curly's Gold '94
Lone Justice 2 '93
The China Lake Murders
'90
Against All Odds '84
Heart Like a Wheel '83
St. Helen's; Killer Volcano
'82
Tex '82
Bronco Billy '80
The Parallax View '74
Deliverance '72
Angel Unchained '70
She-Freak '67
Cannonball '76
The Outlaw Josey Wales
'76
The Shootist '76

Gregory McKinney (1957-98)
Recoil '97
Star Quest '94
A Brilliant Disguise '93

Mark McKinney (1959-)
Slings & Arrows: Season 2
'05
The Saddest Music in the
World '03
Jacob Two Two Meets the
Hooded Fang '99
The Out-of-Towners '99
Superstar '99
Dog Park '98
A Night at the Roxbury '98
Spice World: The Movie '97
Kids in the Hall: Brain
Candy '96

Kurt McKinney (1962-)
Cupid & Cate '00
No Retreat, No Surrender
'86

Mira McKinney (1892-1978)
Double Trouble '41
Rough Riders o' Cheyenne
'45

Nina Mae McKinney (1912-67)
Pinky '49
The Devil's Daughter '39
Hallelujah! '29

Ray McKinnon (1957-)
The Missing '03
The Badge '02
O Brother, Where Art Thou? '00
Goodbye, Lover '99
Larry McMurtry's Dead
Man's Walk '96
The Net '95
A Perfect World '93
Paris Trout '91

Craig McLachlan (1965-)

Clifford McLaglen (1892-1978)

Victor McLaglen (1886-1959)
Around the World in 80
Days '56
Prince Valiant '54
The Mystery of the Mary
Celeste '35
Late Extra '35

Trouble in the Glen '54
The Quiet Man '52
Rio Grande '50
She Wore a Yellow Ribbon
'49
Fort Apache '48
Whistle Stop '46
The Princess and the Pirate
'44
Forever and a Day '43
Call Out the Marines '42
Broadway Limited '41
South of Pago Pago '40
Gunga Din '39
Let Freedom Ring '39
Sea Devils '37
Wee Willie Winkie '37
Klondike Annie '36
The Informer '35
Murder at the Vanities '34
The Lost Patrol '34

Hollis McLaren
Atlantic City '81
Outrageous! '77

Ron McLarty (1947-)
A Girl in Every Port '28

Bill McLaughlin
Silk '86

Duane McLaughlin
Naked Vengeance '85

Ellen McLaughlin
Finding Buck McHenry '00
The Runaway '00
Just Write '97

Gibb McLaughlin (1884-1960)
Everything's Relative '96
The Bed You Sleep In '93
The Old Curiosity Shop '35
Bulldog Jack '35
Mr. Reeder in Room 13 '38
Inspector Hornleigh '39
The Scarlet Pimpernel '34
The Private Life of Henry
VIII '33

Maya McLaughlin
Milo '98

David McLean (1922-95)
Children of the Night '92
Death Sport '78
Hughes & Harlow: Angels
in Hell '77
The Strangler '64

B.J. McLellan
Summer of the Monkeys

Zoe McLellan (1974-)
Dungeons and Dragons '00
Stonebrook '98

Gordon McLellan

Catherine McLeod (1921-97)
Sword of Venus '53
I've Always Loved You '46

Cody McMains (1985-)
Not Another Teen Movie
'01
Bring It On '00

Don McManus
Premonition '07
Fantastic Four '05
Chasing Sleep '00
Magenta '96
Wet and Wild Summer '92

Julian McMahon (1968-)
Fantastic Four: Rise of the
Silver Surfer '07
Premonition '07
Fantastic Four '05
Melody Ranch '40
The Wrong Road '37

Horace McMahon (1906-71)
The Detective '68
Never Steal Anything Small
'59
The Delicate Delinquent '55
My Sister Eileen '55
Slaughter's Big Ripoff '73
The Incident '67
Detective Story '51
Birth of the Blues '41
Mars '53

Ed McMahon (1923-)
Silk '86
Angela's Ashes '99

Pauline McLynn (1962-)
An Everlasting Piece '00
When Brendan Met Trudy
'00

Kenneth McMillan (1932-89)
Three Fugitives '89
Malone '87
Armed and Dangerous '86
Cat's Eye '85
Dixie: Changing Habits '85
Runaway Train '85
Dune '84
Concrete Beat '84
Killing Hour '84
The Pope of Greenwich
Village '84
Protocol '84
Reckless '84
Blue Skies Again '83
In the Custody of Strangers
'82
Partners '82
Eyewitness '81
Heartbeeps '81
Ragtime '81
True Confessions '81
Whose Life Is It Anyway?
'81
Borderline '80
Carny '80
Hide in Plain Sight '80
Chilly Scenes of Winter '79
Salem's Lot '79
Bloodbrothers '78
Girlfriends '78
Johnny We Hardly Knew
Ye '77
The Taking of Pelham One
Two Three '74

Richard McMillan
Cube: Zero '04
A Different Loyalty '04
The Sandy Bottom
Orchestra '00
Bram Stoker's
Shadowbuilder '98
Naked City: A Killer
Christmas '98
M. Butterfly '93
Ordeal in the Arctic '93
The 6th Day '00

Roddy McMillan (1923-79)
Killer with Two Faces '74
The Battle of the Sexes '60
Ring of Spies '63

Ross McMillan
The Saddest Music in the
World '03
The Twilight of the Ice
Nymphs '97

Out for Blood '93
Showdown '93
Judgment Day '88
Insecticidal '05
Snakes on a Plane '06
Tales from a Parallel
Universe: Super Nova
'97

Allyn Ann McLerie (1926-)
Living Proof: The Hank
Williams Jr. Story '83
And Baby Makes Six '79
A Shining Season '79
Death Scream '75
Someone I Touched '75
The Way We Were '73
Jeremiah Johnson '72
They Shoot Horses, Don't
They? '69
Calamity Jane '53

John McLiam (1918-94)
Split Decisions '88
The Ambush Murders '82
The Five of Me '81
Freedom Road '79
The Iceman Cometh '73
Showdown '73
Sleeper '73
Private Lover '85
Day One '89
Gore Vidal's Lincoln '88
Roots: The Gift '88
Legal Eagles '86
Murrow '86
Native Son '86
Dream Lover '85
Sweet Charity '69
Cool Hand Luke '67
In Cold Blood '67

Rachel McLish (1955-)
Ravenhawk '95
Aces: Iron Eagle 3 '92

Marshall McLuhan (1911-80)
Annie Hall '77
Third Walker '79

Ciaran McMenamin (1975-)
The Last Minute '01
To End All Wars '01
David Copperfield '99
The Trench '99

Niles McMaster
Alice Sweet Alice '75
Bloodsucking Freaks '75

Barbara McNair (1934-2007)
They Call Me Mr. Tibbs!
'70
Venus in Furs '70
Change of Habit '69
Stiletto '69
Dead Right '68

Kevin McNally (1956-)
Pirates of the Caribbean:
At World's End '07
Dead Man's Chest '06
Pirates of the Caribbean:
The Curse of the Black
Pearl '03
Johnny English '03
De-Lovely '04
The Phantom of the Opera
'04
When the Sky Falls '99
Abraham '94
Cry Freedom '87
The Berlin Affair '85
Hi-Riders '77
Dear Detective '73
The Fiend Who Walked the
West '58

Stephen McNally (1913-94)
Tribute to a Bad Man '55
A Bullet Is Waiting '54
Make Haste to Live '54
Devil's Canyon '53
Split Second '53
The Black Castle '52
Diplomatic Courier '52
Duel at Silver Creek '52
No Way Out '50
Winchester '73 '50
Criss Cross '48
Magnificent Doll '46
Thirty Seconds Over Tokyo
'44
Air Raid Wardens '43
For Me and My Gal '42
Keeper of the Flame '42

Tales from a Parallel
Universe: Giga Shadow
'97

Sam McMurray (1952-)
Sex Through a Window '72
Shenandoah '65
Lake Placid 2 '07
Stealing Sinatra '04
Lone Star State of Mind '02
Getting Even with Dad '94
National Lampoon's Attack
of the 5 Ft. 2 Women '94
L.A. Story '91
The Mod Squad '99
Slappy and the Stinkers '98
Raising Arizona '87
C.H.U.D. '84

Pamela McMyler
Blood Beach '81
The $5.20 an Hour Dream
'80

W.G. McMillan
See Will MacMillan

James McMullan (1929-)
Sex Through a Window '72
Shenandoah '65

Mercedes McNab (1981-)
White Wolves 3: Cry of the
White Wolf '98
Escape from Atlantis '97
Savage Land '94
Addams Family Values '93

Pat McNamara
Ash Wednesday '02
Copycat '95

William McNamara (1965-)
Natural Enemy '96
Copycat '95
Storybook '95
Black Water '94
Chasers '94
Girl in the Cadillac '94
Radio Inside '94
Surviving the Game '94
Doing Time on Maple Drive
'92
Wildflower '91
Texasville '90
Stealing Home '88
Opera '88

Maggie McNamara (1928-78)
The Cardinal '63
The Moon Is Blue '53
Three Coins in the Fountain
'54

Julianne McNamara (1965-)
The Gumshoe Kid '90

Brian McNamara (1960-)
The Gunman '03
The Ghost of Spoon River
'00
Where the Truth Lies '99
Mystery Date '91
When the Party's Over '91
Arachnophobia '90
Billionaire Boys Club '87
Short Circuit '86
Detective Sadie & Son '84

James McMullan
See Will MacMillan

Gus McNaughton (1881-1969)
Clouds over Europe '39
Sidewalks of London '38

Penny McNamee
See No Evil '06
Salem's Lot '04

Howard McNear (1905-69)
The Errand Boy '61
Follow That Dream '61
Escape from Fort Bravo '53

Julia McNeal (1961-)
The Unbelievable Truth '90

Ian McNeice (1950-)
Kiss Me, Stupid '64
Fun in Acapulco '63
The Black Dahlia '06
The Hitchhiker's Guide to
the Galaxy '05 (V)
Oliver Twist '05
White Noise '05
Around the World in 80
Days '04
Freeze Frame '04
A Certain Justice '99
Children of Dune '03
The Body '01
I'll Be There '03
Dune '00
The Fourth Angel '01
Conspiracy '01
A Life Less Ordinary '97
The Beautician and the
Beast '97
Ace Ventura: When Nature
Calls '95

McNeice (continued)
The Englishman Who Went up a Hill But Came down a Mountain '95
Funny Bones '94
No Escape '94
The Blackheath Poisonings '92
Year of the Comet '92
The Russia House '90
Valmont '89
The Lonely Passion of Judith Hearne '87

Claudia McNeil (1916-93)
Roll of Thunder, Hear My Cry '78
Cry Panic '74
The Migrants '74
A Raisin in the Sun '61

Kate McNeil (1959-)
One Kill '00
Escape Clause '96
Shadow Dancer '96
Sudden Death '95
Monkey Shines '88
The House on Sorority Row '83

Jimmy (James Vincent) McNichol (1967-)
Escape from El Diablo '83
Blinded by the Light '82
Night Warning '82
Smokey Bites the Dust '81

Kristy McNichol (1962-)
Baby of the Bride '91
The Forgotten One '89
Two Moon Junction '88
You Can't Hurry Love '88
Women of Valor '86
Dream Lover '85
Just the Way You Are '84
Blinded by the Light '82
Pirate Movie '82
The Night the Lights Went Out in Georgia '81
Only When I Laugh '81
Little Darlings '80
My Old Man '79
The End '78
The Summer of My German Soldier '78

Kevin McNulty (1955-)
A Call to Remember '97
Eye on the Sparrow '91
Inside Out '91
Tricks '97
Maternal Instincts '96
Titanic '96
Live Bait '95
The NeverEnding Story 3: Escape from Fantasia '94
Timecop '94
Anything for Love '93
Impolite '92

Sandy McPeak (1935-97)
My Mother's Secret Life '84
Tarantulas: The Deadly Cargo '77
Ode to Billy Joe '76

Marnie McPhail (1966-)
Stir of Echoes 2: The Homecoming '07
The Greatest Game Ever Played '05
RFK '02

Kris McQuade (1952-)
December Boys '07
Ned Kelly '03
Better Than Sex '00
Billy's Holiday '95
Resistance '92
Strictly Ballroom '92
Two Friends '86
The Coca-Cola Kid '84

Murdock McQuarrie
See Murdock MacQuarrie

Butterfly McQueen (1911-95)
The Mosquito Coast '86
The Adventures of Huckleberry Finn '85
Amazing Grace '74
Killer Diller '48
Duel in the Sun '46
I Dood It '43
Gone with the Wind '39

Chad McQueen (1960-)
Surface to Air '98
Trail of a Serial Killer '98
Red Line '96
Indecent Behavior 2 '94
Money to Burn '94
New York Cop '94
Number One Fan '94
Death Ring '93
Firepower '93
Possessed by the Night '93
Sexual Malice '93
Where the Red Fern Grows: Part 2 '92
Martial Law '90
Nightforce '86
Fever Pitch '85
The Karate Kid '84
Skateboard '77

Justus E. McQueen
See L.Q. Jones

Steve McQueen (1930-80)
The Hunter '80
Tom Horn '80
The Towering Inferno '74
Papillon '73
The Getaway '72
Junior Bonner '72
Le Mans '71
The Reivers '69
Bullitt '68
The Thomas Crown Affair '68
Nevada Smith '66
The Sand Pebbles '66
The Cincinnati Kid '65
Baby, the Rain Must Fall '64
The Great Escape '63
Love with the Proper Stranger '63
Soldier in the Rain '63
Hell Is for Heroes '62
War Lover '62
The Honeymoon Machine '61
The Magnificent Seven '60
The Great St. Louis Bank Robbery '59
Never So Few '59
The Blob '58
Never Love a Stranger '58
Somebody Up There Likes Me '56

Alan McRae
3 Ninjas: High Noon at Mega Mountain '97
3 Ninjas '92

Elizabeth McRae
The Slayer '82
The Conversation '74
The Incredible Mr. Limpet '64

Frank McRae (1952-)
Asteroid '97
Lightning Jack '94
Last Action Hero '93
Sketch Artist '92
Farewell to the King '89
License to Kill '89
Lock Up '89
"batteries not included" '87
National Lampoon's Vacation '83
Cannery Row '82
1941 '79

Hilton McRae (1949-)
Voices from a Locked Room '95
The Secret Rapture '94

Leslie McRae
Blood Orgy of the She-Devils '74
Girl in Gold Boots '69

Gerald McRaney (1948-)
Saving Shiloh '06
Ike: Countdown to D-Day '04
Danger Beneath the Sea '02
Take Me Home: The John Denver Story '00
Murder by Moonlight '91
Blind Vengeance '90
Dynamite and Gold '88
City Killer '87
Hobo's Christmas '87
American Justice '86
The NeverEnding Story '84
The Haunting Passion '83
Mind Warp '72
Night of Bloody Horror '69

Peter McRobbie (1943-)
The Notorious Bettie Page '06
Brokeback Mountain '05
Corn '02
Kill by Inches '99
The Neon Bible '95
And the Band Played On '93

Ian McShane (1942-)
Johnny Suede '92
Kung Fu Panda '08 (V)
The Golden Compass '07 (V)
Hot Rod '07
The Seeker: The Dark Is Rising '07
Shrek the Third '07 (V)
Scoop '06
We Are Marshall '06
Nine Lives '05
Agent Cody Banks '03
Nemesis Game '03
Sexy Beast '00
D.R.E.A.M. Team '99
Grand Larceny '92
War & Remembrance: The Final Chapter '89
The Great Escape 2: The Untold Story '88
War & Remembrance '88
Young Charlie Chaplin '88
The Murders in the Rue Morgue '86
A.D. '85
Too Scared to Scream '85
Torchlight '85
Ordeal by Innocence '84
Exposed '83
The Grace Kelly Story '83
Disraeli '79
The Fifth Musketeer '79
The Great Riviera Bank Robbery '79
Yesterday's Hero '79
Code Name: Diamond Head '77
Journey into Fear '74
The Terrorists '74
The Last of Sheila '73
Freelance '71
Battle of Britain '69
If It's Tuesday, This Must Be Belgium '69

Jenny (Jennifer) McShane
Shark Attack 3: Megalodon '02
The Watcher '00
Shark Attack '00
Tales of the Kama Sutra 2: Monsoon '98
Monsoon '97
Stag '97
The Rage '96

Kitty McShane (1898-1964)
Old Mother Riley's Jungle Treasure '51
Old Mother Riley, Headmistress '50
Old Mother Riley's New Venture '49
Old Mother Riley's Ghosts '41

Michael McShane (1957-)
Happily N'Ever After '07 (V)
Keena: The Prophecy '03 (V)
Memron '04
Treasure Planet '02 (V)
Drop Dead Gorgeous '99
A Bug's Life '98 (V)
Office Space '98
Richie Rich '94
Robin Hood: Prince of Thieves '91

Gerard McSorley (1950-)
The Front Line '06
The Constant Gardener '05
Rory O'Shea Was Here '04
Dead Bodies '03
Veronica Guerin '03
Bloody Sunday '01
Felicia's Journey '99
Ordinary Decent Criminal '99
The Boxer '97
Michael Collins '96
Some Mother's Son '96
Moondance '95
Nothing Personal '95
An Awfully Big Adventure '94
Widow's Peak '94
In the Name of the Father '93

Monica McSwain
What About Your Friends: Weekend Getaway '02
The Little Match Girl '84

Virginia McSweeney
See Virginia Valli

Malcolm "Bud" McTaggart (1910-49)
Billy the Kid Trapped '42
Meet the Mob '42
Six Gun Rhythm '39

Janet McTeer (1962-)
Five Days '07
Sense & Sensibility '07
As You Like It '06
Tideland '05
The Intended '02
The King Is Alive '00
Waking the Dead '00
Songcatcher '99
Tumbleweeds '98
Carrington '95
Saint-Ex: The Life and Times of the Storyteller '95
Catherine Cookson's The Black Velvet Gown '92
Emily Bronte's Wuthering Heights '92
Hawks '89

Patrick McVey (1910-73)
Desperate Characters '71
The Detective '68

Paul McVey (1898-1973)
Phantom of Chinatown '40
Buried Alive '39

Tyler McVey (1912-2003)
The Gallant Hours '60
Attack of the Giant Leeches '59
Night of the Blood Beast '58
From Here to Eternity '53

Daniel McVicar (1958-)
Alone in the Woods '95
Guardian Angel '94
Scorned '93

Margaret McWade (1872-1956)
Mr. Deeds Goes to Town '36
Theodora Goes Wild '36
The Confession '20

Robert McWade (1872-1938)
Healer '36
Next Time We Love '36
Kept Husbands '31
Feet First '30

Jillian McWhirter
The Dentist 2: Brace Yourself '98
Progeny '98
Bloodfist 7: Manhunt '95
Last Man Standing '95
Rage '95
Stranglehold '94
Beyond the Call of Duty '92
Dune Warriors '91
After Midnight '89

Caroline McWilliams (1945-)
Switched at Birth '91
Mermaids '90
Into Thin Air '85
Rage '80

Anne Meacham (1925-)
Seizure '74
Lilith '64

Courtland Mead (1988-)
Tom and Huck '95
The Little Rascals '94
Dragonworld '94

Taylor Mead (1924-)
Coffee and Cigarettes '03
Frogs for Snakes '98
Superstar: The Life and Times of Andy Warhol '90

Jayne Meadows (1920-)
The Story of Us '99
Casino '95
The Player '92
City Slickers '91
Murder by Numbers '89
Ratings Game '84
Miss All-American Beauty '82
James Dean '76
Norman, Is That You? '76
David and Bathsheba '51
Song of the Thin Man '47
Lady in the Lake '46

Joyce Meadows
Zebra in the Kitchen '65
The Girl in Lover's Lane '60
The Brain from Planet Arous '57
Flesh and the Spur '57

Stephen Meadows
A Cry in the Wild '90
The End of Innocence '90

Tim Meadows (1961-)
Walk Hard: The Dewey Cox Story '07
The Benchwarmers '06
The Cookout '04
Mean Girls '04
The Ladies Man '00
It's Pat: The Movie '94

Stanley Meadows (1931-)
Performance '70
The Terrornauts '67

Karen Meagher
Threads '85
Experience Preferred... But Not Essential '83

Ray Meagher (1944-)
Dark Age '88

Colm Meaney (1953-)
The Hades Factor '06
Layer Cake '05
The Boys and Girl From County Clare '03
King of Texas '02
How Harry Became a Tree '01
Four Days '99
The Magical Legend of the Leprechauns '99
Mystery, Alaska '99
This Is My Father '99
Monument Ave. '98
Claire Dolan '97
Con Air '97
The Last of the High Kings '96
The Englishman Who Went up a Hill But Came down a Mountain '95
The Van '95
War of the Buttons '95
The Road to Wellville '94
Scarlett '94
The Snapper '93
Far and Away '92
Into the West '92
The Last of the Mohicans '92
The Commitments '91
Die Hard 2: Die Harder '90

Kevin Meaney
Shut Up and Kiss Me '05
Plump Fiction '97

Russell Means (1939-)
Pathfinder '07
Unearthed '07
Black Cloud '04
Cowboy Up '00
Black Cat Run '98
Wind River '98
Buffalo Girls '95
Natural Born Killers '94
The Pathfinder '94
Wagons East '94
Windrunner '94
The Last of the Mohicans '92

Anne Meara (1929-)
Night at the Museum '06
Like Mike '02
Get Well Soon '01
The Independent '00
Judy Berlin '99
Southie '98
The Daytrippers '96
The Search for One-Eyed Jimmy '96
Heavyweights '94
Kiss of Death '94
Reality Bites '94
Awakenings '90
That's Adequate '90
My Little Girl '87
The Longshot '86
Fame '80
Nasty Habits '77
Lovers and Other Strangers '70
The Out-of-Towners '70

Michael Mears (1957-)
Sylvia '03
Sharpe's Legend '97
The Old Curiosity Shop '94
Sharpe's Rifles '93

Scott Mechlowicz (1981-)
Peaceful Warrior '06
Eurotrip '04
Mean Creek '04

Julio Oscar Mechoso (1955-)
Planet Terror '07
The Legend of Zorro '05
The Lost City '05
Assassination Tango '03
Pumpkin '02
Heartbreakers '01
Jurassic Park 3 '01
All the Pretty Horses '00
Missing Pieces '00
Krippendorf's Tribe '98
Virus '98
Switchback '97
White Squall '96
Bad Boys '95

Karen Medak
Galaxies Are Colliding '92
Treacherous Crossing '92
A Girl to Kill For '90

Kay Medford (1920-80)
Windows '80
Lola '69
Funny Girl '68
A Fine Madness '66
Butterfield 8 '60
The Rat Race '60

Harriet Medin (1914-2005)
Blood Beach '81
Blood and Black Lace '64
The Ghost '63
The Whip and the Body '63
The Horrible Dr. Hichcock '62

Ofelia Medina (1950-)
Innocent Voices '04
Frida '84

Patricia Medina (1920-)
The Big Push '75
The Killing of Sister George '69
Snow White and the Three Stooges '61
Mr. Arkadin '55
Botany Bay '53
Abbott and Costello in the Foreign Legion '50
The Jackpot '50
Francis the Talking Mule '49
The Three Musketeers '48
Hotel Reserve '44
The Day Will Dawn '42
Spitfire '42
Dinner at the Ritz '37

Frank Medrano (1954-)
Shade '03
The Apostate '98
Kissing a Fool '98
The Replacement Killers '98

Michael Medwin (1923-)
Serpent's Lair '95
The Fear '94

Heather Medway
Telling You '98
Winchell '98
The Fan '96
Sleepers '96

George Meeker (1904-84)
Heart Condition '90
Night of the Cyclone '90
Winter People '89
The Invisible Monster '50
Twilight in the Sierras '50
Omoo Omoo, the Shark God '49
People's Choice '46
I Accuse My Parents '45
Seven Doors to Death '44
Michael Shayne: Private Detective '40
Danger on the Air '38
Murder by Television '35
Four Sons '28

Ralph Meeker (1920-88)
Winter Kills '79
My Boys Are Good Boys '78
Hi-Riders '77
The Alpha Incident '76
Food of the Gods '76
The Dead Don't Die '75
Johnny Firecloud '75
Birds of Prey '72
Mind Snatchers '72
The Anderson Tapes '71
I Walk the Line '70
The Night Stalker '71
The Detective '68
The Dirty Dozen '67
Gentle Giant '67
The St. Valentine's Day Massacre '67
Paths of Glory '57
Battle Shock '56
Run of the Arrow '56
Kiss Me Deadly '55
Jeopardy! '53
The Naked Spur '53
Four in a Jeep '51

Donald Meek (1880-1946)
Magic Town '47
Because of Him '45
Colonel Effingham's Raid '45
State Fair '45
Bathing Beauty '44
The Thin Man Goes Home '44
Two Girls and a Sailor '44
Air Raid Wardens '43
Du Barry Was a Lady '43
They Got Me Covered '43
Keeper of the Flame '42
Tortilla Flat '42
A Woman's Face '41
My Little Chickadee '40
Return of Frank James '40
Blondie Takes a Vacation '39
Jesse James '39
Stagecoach '39
Young Mr. Lincoln '39
The Adventures of Tom Sawyer '38
Little Miss Broadway '38
You Can't Take It with You '38
Three Legionnaires '37
Toast of New York '37
One Rainy Afternoon '36
Pennies from Heaven '36
Barbary Coast '35
The Informer '35
Mark of the Vampire '35
The Return of Peter Grimm '35
The Merry Widow '34
Mrs. Wiggs of the Cabbage Patch '34
Murder at the Vanities '34
Personal Maid '31

Jeffrey Meek (1959-)
Timelock '99

Lew Meehan (1890-1951)
Feud Maker '38
Thunder in the Desert '38
Melody of the Plains '37
Ridin' the Lone Trail '37
Feud of the West '36
Range Riders '35
Ridin' Thru '35
Texas Jack '35
The Silver Bullet '35
Whistlin' Dan '32
Road Agent '25
Backfire '22

John Megna (1953-95)
Go Tell the Spartans '78
To Kill a Mockingbird '62

Don Megowan (1922-81)
The Devil's Brigade '68
The Creation of the Humanoids '62
The Jayhawkers '59
The Creature Walks among Us '56
A Lawless Street '55

Blanche Mehaffey (1907-68)
Devil Monster '46
Silent Code '35
Mystery Trooper '32
Sunrise Trail '31
Battling Orioles '24

Wendel Meldrum (1958-)
National Lampoon's Dad's Week Off '97
Sodbusters '94
City Boy '93

Leighton Meester (1986-)
Flourish '06
Inside '06
Hangman's Curse '03

Armand Meffre
Jean de Florette '87
Manon of the Spring '87

Isabelle Mejias
Unfinished Business '89
Higher Education '88
Fall from Innocence '88

Gerardo Mejia (1965-)
Loco Love '03
A Million to Juan '94
Somebody to Love '94
Colors '88
Can't Buy Me Love '87
Winners Take All '87

Gunter Meisner (1928-94)
Magdalene '88
In a Glass Cage '86
Between Wars '74
Willy Wonka & the Chocolate Factory '71

Kathryn Meisle (1960-)
Rosewood '96
Basket Case 2 '90

Otto Melies
Minna von Barnhelm or The Soldier's Fortune '62
Intrigue and Love '59

Andree Melly (1932-)
The Belles of St. Trinian's '53
The Brides of Dracula '60

Christopher Meloni (1961-)
Harold & Kumar Escape from Guantanamo Bay '08
Harold & Kumar Go to White Castle '04
Murder in Greenwich '02
Wet Hot American Summer '01
Runaway Bride '99
The Souler Opposite '97
Bound '96

Eva Mendes (1978-)
Cleaner '07
Ghost Rider '07
We Own the Night '07
Trust the Man '06
Hitch '05
Once Upon a Time in Mexico '03
Out of Time '03
Stuck On You '03
2 Fast 2 Furious '03
All About the Benjamins '02
Exit Wounds '01
Training Day '01
Urban Legends 2: Final Cut '00
Children of the Corn 5: Fields of Terror '98

Tobias Mehler (1976-)
Carrie '02
Wishmaster 3: Beyond the Gates of Hell '01
Sabrina the Teenage Witch '96

Yan-Fang Mei
See Anita (Yim-Fong) Mui

Armin Meier (1943-78)
Mother Kusters Goes to Heaven '76
Fear of Fear '75

Christian Meier (1970-)
La Mujer de Mi Hermano '06

Thomas Meighan (1879-1936)
Peck's Bad Boy '34
Peck's Bad Boy '21
Why Change Your Wife? '20
Male and Female '19
The Forbidden City '18

John Meillon (1934-89)
Crocodile Dundee 2 '88
Frenchman's Farm '87
The Blue Lightning '86
Crocodile Dundee '86
The Dunera Boys '85
Camel Boy '84 (V)
Fourth Wish '75
Ride a Wild Pony '75
The Cars That Ate Paris '74
Inn of the Damned '74
Walkabout '71
Billy Budd '62

Mariangela Melato (1941-)
Dancers '87
Summer Night with Greek Profile, Almond Eyes & Scent of Basil '87
So Fine '81
To Forget Venice '79
Swept Away... '75
Love and Anarchy '73

Kurt Meisel (1912-94)
The Odessa File '74
A Time to Love & a Time to Die '58
Party Girls for Sale '54
Wozzeck '47

Tarcisio Meira (1935-)
Boca '94
Love Strange Love '82
I Love You '81

Randle Mell (1951-)
Cookie's Fortune '99
Wyatt Earp '94
Grand Canyon '91

John Cougar Mellencamp (1951-)
Falling from Grace '92

Marisa Mell (1939-92)
Mad Dog '84
Hostages '80
Danger: Diabolik '68
Secret Agent Super Dragon '66

Joseph Mell (1915-77)
Call Northside 777 '48

Jack Melford (1899-1972)
The Ladykillers '55
When Thief Meets Thief '37

Jill Melford (1934-)
Edge of Sanity '89
Abandon Ship! '57

George Melford (1877-1961)

Claude Melki (1939-94)
A Slightly Pregnant Man '79
Six in Paris '65

Gilbert Melki (1958-)
Angel-A '05
Cote d'Azur '05
Changing Times '04
Intimate Strangers '04
Monsieur Ibrahim '03

Nicholas Mele
Impulse '90
Capone '89

Murray Melvin (1932-)
The Emperor's New Clothes '01
The Fixer '68
Alfie '66
A Taste of Honey '61

Sam Melville (1936-89)
Start the Revolution without Me '70
The Devils '71
Machuca's Mansion '74

Sid Melton (1920-)
Hit! '72
Lady Sings the Blues '72
Leave It to the Marines '51
The Lost Continent '51
The Steel Helmet '51
Stop That Cab '51
Hi-Jacked '50
Motor Patrol '50
Tough Assignment '49
Girls in Chains '43

Frank Melton (1907-51)
The Glory Trail '36
The Traitor '36
David Harum '34
Stand Up and Cheer '34
365 Nights in Hollywood '34
Tanks a Million '41

George Memmoli (1938-85)
Twice Dead '88
Rock 'n' Roll High School '79
Phantom of the Paradise '74
Mean Streets '73

Nasser Memarzia
The Situation '06
Millions '05

Stephen Mendel
The Terminal '04
Midnight Heat '96
Scanner Cop 2: Volkin's Revenge '94
Scanners: The Showdown '94
Sirens '94
Metal Skin '94

David Mendenhall (1971-)
Streets '90
Over the Top '86
Going Bananas '88
Space Raiders '83

Ben Mendelsohn (1969-)
The New World '05
Vertical Limit '00
Amy '98
Idiot Box '97
Cosi '95
Metal Skin '94
Sirens '94
The Efficiency Expert '92
Quigley Down Under '90
The Year My Voice Broke '87

Stephen Mendillo (1942-)
Ethan Frome '92
Slap Shot '77

Maria Luisa Mendonca (1970-)
Carandiru '03
The 3 Marias '03

Mauro Mendonca (1932-)
Love Strange Love '82
Dona Flor and Her Two Husbands '78

Natalie Mendoza (1978-)
The Descent '05
The Great Raid '05
Moulin Rouge '01

Victor Manuel Mendoza (1913-95)
Cowboy '58
Garden of Evil '54
The Proud Ones '53

Gonzalo Menendez
The Descent '05

Alex Meneses (1965-)
44 Minutes: The North Hollywood Shootout '03
The Flintstones in Viva Rock Vegas '00
Living in Peril '97
Amanda and the 41 en '95
Payback '89

Bernard Menez
Dracula and Son '76
No Problem! '75

John Mengatti (1954-)
Knights of the City '85
Meatballs 2 '84

Alex Menglet (1956-)
Zone 39 '96
A Woman's Tale '92

Adolphe Menjou (1890-1963)
Pollyanna '60
Paths of Glory '57
The Ambassador's Daughter '56
Bundle of Joy '56
I Married a Woman '56
Across the Wide Missouri '51
To Please a Lady '50
My Dream Is Yours '49
State of the Union '48
The Goldwyn Follies '38
A Star Is Born '37
Stage Door '37
One in a Million '36
Gold Diggers of 1935 '35
Little Miss Marker '34
Morning Glory '33
A Farewell to Arms '32
Morocco '30
The Front Page '31
The Grand Duchess and the Waiter '26
The Sorrows of Satan '26
The Marriage Circle '24
The Sheik '21

Shepard Menken (1921-99)
The Great Caruso '51
The Red Menace '49
Peter Mensah
The Incredible Hulk '08
Hidalgo '04
Tears of the Sun '03
Jason X '01
Oleg Menshikov (1960-)
East-West '99
Prisoner of the Mountains '96
Burnt by the Sun '94
Vladimir Menshov
Day Watch '06
Night Watch '04
Vladimir Mensik (1924-88)
All My Good Countrymen '68
Murder Czech Style '66
Idina Menzel (1971-)
Enchanted '07
Ask the Dust '06
Rent '05
The Tollbooth '04
Heather Menzies (1949-)
Captain America '79
Piranha '78
Red, White & Busted '75
Sssssss '73
The Sound of Music '65
Robert Menzies (1955-)
Innocence '00
Cactus '86
Tobias Menzies (1974-)
Casino Royale '06
The Low Down '00
Christian Meoli
The Song of the Lark '01
The Low Life '95
Alive '93
Julino Mer
The Last Warrior '99
Under the Domim Tree '95
Doro Merande (1898-1975)
The Russians Are Coming, the Russians Are Coming '66
Kiss Me, Stupid! '64
The Gazebo '59
The Man with the Golden Arm '55
The Seven Year Itch '55
Hector Mercado (1949-)
Leather Jacket Love Story '98
Nomads '86
Beryl Mercer (1862-1939)
Jane Eyre '34
Cavalcade '33
Smilin' Through '33
Supernatural '33
The Miracle Woman '31
Public Enemy '31
All Quiet on the Western Front '30
On the Sunny Side '42
Mae Mercer (1932-)
Pretty Baby '78
The Swinging Cheerleaders '74
Frogs '72
Marian Mercer (1935-)
Out on a Limb '92
The Seagull '75
Vivien Merchant (1929-83)
The Offence '73

Under Milk Wood '73
Frenzy '72
Accident '67
Alfie '66
Denis Mercier
Bogus '96
Le Sexe des Etoiles '93
Michele Mercier (1939-)
Call of the Wild '72
Web of the Spider '70
Oldest Profession '67
How I Learned to Love Women '66
Casanova '70 '65
Black Sabbath '64
A Global Affair '63
Shoot the Piano Player '62
Melina Mercouri (1925-94)
A Dream of Passion '78
Nasty Habits '77
It's Not Enough '75
Topkapi '64
The Victors '63
Phaedra '61
Never on Sunday '60
Where the Hot Wind Blows '59
Stella '55
Monique Mercure (1930-)
Set Me Free '99
Conquest '98
The Red Violin '98
When Justice Fails '98
Naked Lunch '91
Tramp at the Door '87
The Odyssey of the Pacific '82
Third Walker '79
Micole Mercurio (1938-)
Bandits '01
While You Were Sleeping '95
Colors '88
Paul Mercurio (1963-)
The First 9 1/2 Weeks '98
Dark Planet '97
Back of Beyond '95
Cosi '95
Joseph '95
Exit to Eden '94
Strictly Ballroom '92
Burgess Meredith (1908-97)
Grumpier Old Men '95
Across the Moon '94
Grumpy Old Men '93
Mastergate '92
Oddball Hall '91
Mr. Corbett's Ghost '90
Rocky 5 '90
State of Grace '90
Full Moon in Blue Water '88
King Lear '87
Outrage! '86
Santa Claus: The Movie '85
Wet Gold '84
Twilight Zone: The Movie '83
Rocky 3 '82
Thumbelina '82
Clash of the Titans '81
Last Chase '81
True Confessions '81
Final Assignment '80
When Time Ran Out '80
Rocky 2 '79
Foul Play '78
Great Bank Hoax '78
Magic '78
The Manitou '78
Golden Rendezvous '77
Johnny We Hardly Knew Ye '77
Burnt Offerings '76
92 in the Shade '76
Rocky '76
The Sentinel '76
The Day of the Locust '75
The Hindenburg '75
Beware! The Blob '72
Probe '72
Yin & Yang of Mr. Go '71

There Was a Crooked Man '70
MacKenna's Gold '69
Stay Away, Joe '68
Torture Garden '67
Batman '66
A Big Hand for the Little Lady '66
Madame X '66
In Harm's Way '65
The Cardinal '63
Advise and Consent '62
Jigsaw '49
Man on the Eiffel Tower '48
On Our Merry Way '48
Mine Own Executioner '47
Diary of a Chambermaid '46
Magnificent Doll '46
The Story of G.I. Joe '45
That Uncertain Feeling '41
Tom, Dick, and Harry '41
Second Chorus '40
Idiot's Delight '39
Of Mice and Men '39
Winterset '36
Don Meredith (1938-)
Three Days of Rain '03
Three Days of Rain '02
Wyatt Earp: Return to Tombstone '94
The Night the City Screamed '80
Express to Terror '79
Banjo Hackett '76
Sky Hei$t '75
Terror on the 40th Floor '74
Ifan Meredith
Metroland '97
Iris Meredith (1916-80)
Rangers Take Over '42
Green Archer '40
A Lawman Is Born '37
Mystery of the Hooded Horseman '37
Judi Meredith (1936-)
Planet of Blood '66
Jack the Giant Killer '62
Lee Meredith (1947-)
The Sunshine Boys '75
The Producers '68
Luc Merenda (1942-)
Could It Happen Here? '77
Violent Professionals '73
Le Mans '71
Stanislas Merhar (1971-)
Merci Docteur Rey '04
Almost Peaceful '02
The Count of Monte Cristo '99
Dry Cleaning '97
Jalal Merhi
Expect No Mercy '95
Fearless Tiger '94
Operation Golden Phoenix '94
TC 2000 '93
Talons of the Eagle '92
Tiger Claws '91
Auriele Meriel
The Butterfly '02
The Delivery '99
Macha Meril (1940-)
Meeting Venus '91
Chinese Roulette '86
Vagabond '85
Beau Pere '81
Deep Red: Hatchet Murders '75
Night Train Murders '75
Torture Train '75
A Married Woman '65
Eda Reiss Merin (1913-98)
For Better or Worse '95
The Reluctant Agent '95
Don't Tell Mom the Babysitter's Dead '91
Philip Merivale (1886-1946)
Sister Kenny '46

Nothing But Trouble '44
Lady for a Night '42
Lee Meriwether (1935-)
The Ultimate Gift '07
Brothers O'Toole '73
The Undefeated '69
Batman '66
Namu, the Killer Whale '66
The 4D Man '59
Una Merkel (1903-86)
Spinout '66
A Tiger Walks '64
Summer Magic '63
The Parent Trap '61
Summer and Smoke '61
The Mating Game '59
The Girl Most Likely '57
The Kettles in the Ozarks '56
The Kentuckian '55
I Love Melvin '53
The Merry Widow '52
With a Song in My Heart '52
Rich, Young and Pretty '51
Kill the Umpire '50
My Blue Heaven '50
It's a Joke, Son! '47
Twin Beds '42
Cracked Nuts '41
The Road to Zanzibar '41
The Bank Dick '40
Destry Rides Again '39
On Borrowed Time '39
Rhythm Romance '39
Saratoga '37
Born to Dance '36
Broadway Melody of 1936 '35
Riff Raff '35
Evelyn Prentice '34
The Merry Widow '34
Bombshell '33
42nd Street '33
They Call It Sin '32
Red Headed Woman '32
The Maltese Falcon '31
Private Lives '31
Abraham Lincoln '30
The Bat Whispers '30
S. Epatha Merkerson (1952-)
Black Snake Moan '07
Slipstream '07
Jersey Girl '04
Radio '03
A Mother's Prayer '95
A Place for Annie '94
She's Gotta Have It '86
Maurizio Merli
Fearless '77
Street War '76
Jan Merlin (1925-)
Twilight People '72
Take the Money and Run '69
Joanna Merlin (1931-)
City of Angels '98
Two Bits '96
Class Action '91
Mystic Pizza '88
Baby It's You '82
Fame '80
Ethel Merman (1909-84)
Airplane! '80
Journey Back to Oz '71 (V)
It's a Mad, Mad, Mad, Mad World '63
There's No Business Like Show Business '54
Stage Door Canteen '43
Alexander's Ragtime Band '38
Happy Landing '38
Strike Me Pink '36
Kid Millions '34
We're Not Dressing '34
Mary Merrall (1890-1973)
The Belles of St. Trinian's '53
The Obsessed '51
They Made Me a Fugitive '47

Nicholas Nickleby '46
Dead of Night '45
Pink String and Sealing Wax '45
Charlotte Merriam (1906-72)
Night Nurse '31
One-Punch O'Day '26
Lynn Merrick (1919-2007)
Radar Patrol vs. Spy King '49
Down to Earth '47
California Joe '43
The Sombrero Kid '42
Sundown Fury '42
Dina Merrill (1925-)
Shade '03
The Other Sister '98
Open Season '95
Suture '93
The Player '92
True Colors '91
Fear '90
Caddyshack 2 '88
Twisted '86
Anna to the Infinite Power '84
Hot Pursuit '84
Tenth Month '79
A Wedding '78
The Greatest '77
The Meal '75
Running Wild '73
I'll Take Sweden '65
The Courtship of Eddie's Father '62
The Young Savages '61
Butterfield 8 '60
The Sundowners '60
Operation Petticoat '59
Desk Set '57
Frank Merrill (1893-1966)
Tarzan the Tiger '29
The Adventures of Tarzan '21
Gary Merrill (1915-90)
The Seekers '79
Huckleberry Finn '74
Pueblo Affair '73
Clambake '67
The Incident '67
Around the World Under the Sea '65
The Great Impostor '61
Mysterious Island '61
Missouri Traveler '58
Another Man's Poison '52
Phone Call from a Stranger '52
All About Eve '50
Twelve O'Clock High '49
Ryan Merriman (1983-)
Comanche Moon '08
Final Destination 3 '06
The Ring 2 '05
Spin '04
Halloween: Resurrection '02
Dangerous Child '01
Smart House '99
Just Looking '99
Lansky '99

Jane Merrow (1941-)
The Appointment '82
Hands of the Ripper '71
The Lion in Winter '68
Island of the Burning Doomed '67
The Girl Getters '66
John Merton (1901-59)
Radar Patrol vs. Spy King '49
Border Bandits '46
Devil Riders '44
Rustler's Hideout '44
Wild Horse Phantom '44
Cowboy Commandos '43
Fighting Valley '43
Land of Hunted Men '43
Boot Hill Bandits '42
The Mysterious Rider '42
Prairie Pals '42
Battling Outlaw '40
Billy the Kid in Texas '40
Covered Wagon Days '40
Code of the Fearless '39
Hopalong Cassidy: Renegade Trail '39
In Old Montana '39
Zorro's Fighting Legion '39
Gang Bullets '38
Gunsmoke Trail '38
Phantom Ranger '38
Valley of Terror '38
The Rangers Step In '37
Roaring Six Guns '37
Slaves in Bondage '37
Two-Gun Troubador '37
Aces and Eights '36
Crooked Trail '36
Lion's Den '36
The Gun Ranger '34
William Mervyn (1912-76)
The Ruling Class '72
The Railway Children '70
Murder Ahoy '64
The Battle of the Sexes '60
John Mese (1963-)
Red Dirt '99
Excessive Force 2: Force on Force '95
Night of the Scarecrow '95
Daniel Mesguich (1952-)
Le Divorce '03
The Musketeer '01
Hannes Messemer (1924-91)
The Odessa File '74
The Great Escape '63
Donald E. Messick (1926-97)
Tiny Toon Adventures: How I Spent My Vacation '91 (V)
Jetsons: The Movie '90 (V)
Flight of Dragons '82 (V)
The Hobbit '78 (V)
Marc Messier (1947-)
The Boys '97
A Wind from Wyoming '94
Chris Messina
Made of Honor '08
Ira & Abby '06
Francesco Messina
13 Moons '02
Everything That Rises '98
Clive Merrison (1945-)
The History Boys '06
Photographing Fairies '97
The English Patient '96
An Awfully Big Adventure '94
Heavenly Creatures '94
George Merritt (1890-1977)
I, Monster '71
Clouds over Europe '39
Young and Innocent '37
Theresa Merritt (1922-98)
Billy Madison '94
Voodoo Dawn '89
The Serpent and the Rainbow '87
Debra Messing (1968-)
Lucky You '07
The Starter Wife '06 (V)
Open Season '06 (V)
The Wedding Date '05
Garfield: The Movie '04 (V)
Along Came Polly '04
Hollywood Ending '02
The Mothman Prophecies '02
Jesus '00
McHale's Navy '97
A Walk in the Clouds '95
Gertrude Messinger (1911-95)
Miracle Kid '42
Aces Wild '37

The Adventurous Knights '35
Fighting Pilot '35
Rider of the Law '35
Roaring Roads '35
Rustler's Paradise '35
Social Error '35
Wagon Trail '35
Hidden Valley '32
Riders of the Desert '32
Tears of the Desert '32

Johnny Messner (1970-)
Loaded '08
Believers '07
Running Scared '06
Hostage '05
Anacondas: The Hunt for the Blood Orchid '04
Spartan '04
The Whole Ten Yards '04
Finding Home '03
Tears of the Sun '03

George Metaxa (1899-1950)
The Mask of Dimitrios '44
Doctor Takes a Wife '40

Laurie Metcalf (1955-)
Georgia Rule '07 (V)
Meet the Robinsons '07 (V)
Beer League '06
Steel City '06
Treasure Planet '02 (V)
Runaway Bride '99
Toy Story 2 '99 (V)
Bulworth '98
Chicago Cab '98
Balloon Farm '97
Scream 2 '97
U-Turn '97
Dear God '96
Leaving Las Vegas '95
Toy Story '95 (V)
Blink '93
A Dangerous Woman '93
JFK '91
Mistress '91
Internal Affairs '90
Pacific Heights '90
Uncle Buck '89
Miles from Home '88
Stars and Bars '88
Candy Mountain '87
Making Mr. Right '86
Desperately Seeking Susan '85
Execution of Raymond Graham '85

Mark Metcalf (1946-)
Drive Me Crazy '99
Hijacking Hollywood '97
Rage '95
The Stupids '96
Dead Ahead: The Exxon Valdez Disaster '92
Mr. North '88
One Crazy Summer '86
The Final Terror '83
National Lampoon's Animal House '78
Julia '77

Earl Metcalfe (1889-1928)
The Notorious Lady '27
With Kit Carson over the Great Divide '25

Jesse Metcalfe (1978-)
Loaded '08
John Tucker Must Die '06

Ken Metcalfe
Nam Angels '88
Savage Justice '88
Warriors of the Apocalypse '85

Aaron Michael Metchik ('75)
Milo '98
Trading Mom '94

Asher Metchik (1986-)
The Baby-Sitters' Club '95
Trading Mom '94

Saul Meth
Double Agent 73 '80

Deadly Weapons '70

Method Man (1971-)
Meet the Spartans '08
Venom '05
My Baby's Daddy '04
Soul Plane '04
How High '01
Belly '98

Mayo Methot (1904-51)
Marked Woman '37
Goodbye Love '34
Counsellor-at-Law '33
Corsair '31

Nancy Mette
Meet the Hollowheads '89
Matewan '87
Key Exchange '85

Omar Metwally
Rendition '07
Munich '05

Jim Metzler (1955-)
The Doe Boy '01
St. Patrick's Day '99
A Gun, a Car, a Blonde '97
Cadillac Ranch '96
Children of the Corn 3: Urban Harvest '95
French Silk '94
Circuitry Man 2 '94
Delusion '91
Love Kills '91
One False Move '91
Murder by Night '89
Circuitry Man '90
Tex '82
Four Friends '81
Squeeze Play '79

Paul Meurisse (1912-79)
Gypsy '75
Le Gitan '75
Army of Shadows '69
The Monocle '64
Picnic on the Grass '59
Diabolique '55

Jason Mewes (1974-)
Bottoms Up '06
Clerks 2 '06
The Tripper '06
The Pleasure Drivers '05
R.S.V.P. '02
Jay and Silent Bob Strike Back '01
Scream 3 '00
Dogma '99
Chasing Amy '97
Mallrats '95
Clerks '94

Anne-Laure Meury
Boyfriends & Girlfriends '88
The Aviator's Wife '80

Harry Meyers — See Harry C. (Henry) Myers

Hans Meyer (1925-)
Brotherhood of the Wolf '01
Mauvais Sang '86
Le Magnifique '76

Michael Meyer (1957-)
Children of the Damned '63
A Night to Remember '58

Russ Meyer (1922-2004)
Amazon Women on the Moon '87
Motor Psycho '65

Torben Meyer (1884-1975)
Judgment at Nuremberg '61
The Matchmaker '58
Sullivan's Travels '41
The Day the Sky Exploded '57

Breckin Meyer (1974-)
Blue State '07
Corporate Affairs '07
Garfield: A Tail of Two Kitties '06
Herbie: Fully Loaded '05
Rebound '05
Blast '04
Garfield: The Movie '04
Pinocchio '02 (V)
Kate & Leopold '01
Rat Race '01
Road Trip '00
Go '99
Dancer, Texas—Pop. 81 '98
54 '98
Prefontaine '96
Touch '96
Clueless '95

Emile Meyer (1910-87)
The Fiend Who Walked the West '58
Good Day for a Hanging '58
Blackboard Jungle '55
The Girl in the Red Velvet Swing '55
Riot in Cell Block 11 '54
Shane '53

Gerard Meylan
The Town Is Quiet '00
Marius and Jeannette '97
Nenette and Boni '96

Michelle Meyrink (1962-)
Permanent Record '88
Nice Girls Don't Explode '87
One Magic Christmas '85
Real Genius '85
Joy of Sex '84
Revenge of the Nerds '84

Bess Meyer
H.P. Lovecraft's Necronomicon: Book of the Dead '93
The Inner Circle '91

Myriam Mézière (1949-)
Mouth to Mouth '95

Francoise Michaud
The Butterfly '02
Eminent Domain '91

Genia Michaela
Is There 'Life Out There? '94

Russ Meyer (1922-2004)
The Biggest Fan '02
Virtual Desire '95

Dario Michaels
The Day the Sky Exploded '57

Al Michaels (1944-)
BASEketball '98

Bret Michaels (1963-)
A Letter from Death Row '98
No Code of Conduct '98

Julie Michaels
Jason Goes to Hell: The Final Friday '93
Witchboard 2: The Devil's Doorway '93

Pat Michaels
The Cut Throats '69

Joel Michaely
Cruel World '05
Cut '07

Jeff Michalski
Star Maps '97
Pet Shop '94

Ralph Michael (1907-94)
Diary of a Mad Old Man '88
The Heroes of Telemark '65
Children of the Damned '63
A Night to Remember '58

Gertrude Michael (1911-64)
Bugles in the Afternoon '52
Caged '50
Flamingo Road '49
Behind Prison Walls '43
Cleopatra '34
Murder at the Vanities '34
I'm No Angel '33

Art Metrano (1937-)
Beverly Hills Bodysnatchers '89
Police Academy 3: Back in Training '86
Police Academy 2: Their First Assignment '85
Malibu Express '85
Breathless '83
Going Ape! '81
Seven '79
Slaughter's Big Rip-Off '73
The Heartbreak Kid '72
They Only Kill Their Masters '72
Rocket Attack U.S.A. '58

Svetlana Metkina
Bobby '06

Dina Meyer (1969-)
The Second Front '05
Crazy Eights '06
Saw III '06
Saw II '05
Saw '04
Federal Protection '02
Star Trek: Nemesis '02
Unspeakable '02
Opposite Corners '96
Eye See You '01
Time Lapse '01
Bats '99
Stranger than Fiction '99
Nowhere Land '98
Poodle Springs '98
Starship Troopers '97
Dragonheart '96
Johnny Mnemonic '95

Cora Miao (1958-)
Eat a Bowl of Tea '89
Dim Sum: A Little Bit of Heart '85

Tien Miao
Goodbye, Dragon Inn '03
What Time Is It There? '01

Robert Miano (1942-)
The Still Life '07
The Stickup '01
Dungeons and Dragons '00
Loser '00
Luckytown '00
Detour '99
Thick as Thieves '99
Matter of Trust '98
State of Deception '97
Donnie Brasco '97
Taxi Dancers '93
Chained Heat '83

Michael Michele (1966-)
Dark Blue '03
How to Lose a Guy in 10 Days '03
Ali '01
Homicide: The Movie '00
New Jack City '91

Helena Michell (1963-)
Devices and Desires '91
The Deceivers '88
Piece of Cake '88

Keith Michell (1928-)
My Brother Tom '86
Grendel, Grendel, Grendel '82 (V)
Memorial Day '83
The Story of David '76
The Story of Jacob & Joseph '74
Six Wives of Henry VIII '72
The Executioner '70
Soldier in Love '67
The Helfire Club '61

Janee Michelle
The House on Skull Mountain '74
Scream Blacula Scream '73

Anne Michelle (1952-)
House of Whipcord '75
The Virgin Witch '70

Shelley Michelle
Married People, Single Sex '93
Bikini Summer '91
Sunset Strip '91

Maria Michi (1921-80)
Last Tango in Paris '73
Redneck '73
Paisan '46
Open City '45

Eric Micklewood (1911-2003)
Nine Men '43
Salute John Citizen '42

Tracy Middendorf (1970-)
The Assassination of Richard Nixon '05
Wes Craven's New Nightmare '94

Frank Middlemass (1919-2006)
One Against the Wind '91
The Magnificent Seven '98
The Brents '88
Oliver Twist '85
The Island '80

Charles Middleton (1879-1949)
Spook Busters '46
Santa Fe Uprising '46
Northwest Trail '45
Strangler of the Swamp '46
Western Union '41
Flash Gordon Conquers the Universe '40
Flash Gordon: Rocketship '40
Flash Gordon: Mars Attacks the World '39
Oklahoma Kid '39
Way Down South '39
Wyoming Outlaw '39
Dick Tracy Returns '38
Yodalin' Kid from Pine Ridge '37
Rocketship '36
Hopalong Cassidy '35
The Miracle Rider '35
David Harum '34
Mrs. Wiggs of the Cabbage Patch '34
Murder at the Vanities '34
Duck Soup '33
The Strange Love of Molly Louvain '32
Too Busy to Work '32
Palmy Days '31
The Miracle Woman '31

Vittorio Mezzogiorno (1942-94)
Cafe Express '83
L'Homme Blessé '83
Moon in the Gutter '83
Three Brothers '80
Car Crash '80

Marc Michel
The Umbrellas of Cherbourg '64
Lola '61
Le Trou '59

Marcella Michelangeli
Padre Padrone '77

Giovanna Mezzogiorno (1974-)
Love in the Time of Cholera '07
Don't Tell '05
Facing Windows '03
The Last Kiss '01

Guy Middleton (1906-73)
Oh! What a Lovely War '69
The Belles of St. Trinian's '53
The Happiest Days of Your Life '50
A Man About the House '47
The Demi-Paradise '43
Dangerous Moonlight '41

Fran Middleton
Martin '77

Ray Middleton (1908-84)
Jubilee Trail '54
I Dream of Jeannie '52
Lady for a Night '42
Lady from Louisiana '41

Noelle Middleton (1926-)
The Vicious Circle '57
John and Julie '55
Carrington, V.C. '54

Robert Middleton (1911-77)
Harrad Experiment '73
Career '59
The Law and Jake Wade '58
Tarnished Angels '57
Court Jester '56
Love Me Tender '56
Desperate Hours '55

Dale Midkiff (1959-)
Flight of the Living Dead: Outbreak on a Plane '07
Love's Unending Legacy '07
Love's Enduring Promise '04
Love Comes Softly '03
Video Voyeur: The Susan Wilson Story '02
Air Bud 3: World Pup '00
Alien Fury: Countdown to Invasion '00
Another Woman's Husband '00
Love Potion #9 '92
Blackmail '91
Pet Sematary '89
Elvis and Me '88
Nightmare Weekend '86
Streetwalkin' '85
The First Turn-On! '84

Dominique Michel (1932-)
The Barbarian Invasions '03
The Decline of the American Empire '86
Jonah Who Will Be 25 in the Year 2000 '76

Bette Midler (1945-)
Then She Found Me '07
The Stepford Wives '04
Isn't She Great '00
Drowning Mona '00
What Women Want '00
That Old Feeling '97
The First Wives Club '96
Get Shorty '95
Gypsy '93
Hocus Pocus '93
For the Boys '91
Scenes from a Mall '91
Stella '90
Beaches '88
Big Business '88
Oliver & Company '88 (V)
Outrageous Fortune '87
Ruthless People '86
Down and Out in Beverly Hills '86
Jinxed! '82
The Rose '79

Big Business '88
Oliver & Company '88 (V)
Outrageous Fortune '87
Down and Out in Beverly Hills '86
Ruthless People '86
Jinxed '82
The Rose '79
The Thorn '74
Hawaii '66

Anne-Marie Mieville (1945-)
Comment Ca Va? '76
Here and Elsewhere '76

Toshiro Mifune (1920-97)
Picture Bride '94
Shadow of the Wolf '92
Journey of Honor '91
The Challenge '82
Shogun '80
1941 '79
Winter Kills '79
Love and Faith '78
Proof of the Man '77
Midway '76
Paper Tiger '74
Red Sun '71
The Battle of the Japan Sea '70
Zatoichi vs. Yojimbo '70
Hell in the Pacific '69
Red Lion '69
Samurai Banners '69
Samurai Rebellion '67
Sword of Doom '67
Grand Prix '66
Red Beard '65
Attack Squadron '63
High & Low '62
Sanjuro '62
Yojimbo '61
The Bad Sleep Well '60
The Gambling Samurai '60
I Bombed Pearl Harbor '60
Saga of the Vagabond '59
The Hidden Fortress '58
Rikisha-Man '58
The Lower Depths '57
Throne of Blood '57
Samurai 3: Duel at Ganryu Island '56
I Live in Fear '55
Samurai 1: Musashi Miyamoto '55
Samurai 2: Duel at Ichijoji Temple '55
Seven Samurai '54
Life of Oharu '52
The Idiot '51
Rashomon '51
Scandal '50
A Quiet Duel '49
Stray Dog '49
Drunken Angel '48

Julia Migenes (1949-)
The Krays '90
Berlin Blues '89
Mack the Knife '89

R.A. Mihailoff
Pumpkinhead 2: Blood Wings '94
Leatherface: The Texas Chainsaw Massacre 3 '89

Tatsuya Mihashi (1923-2004)
Dolls '02
Tora! Tora! Tora! '70
What's Up, Tiger Lily? '66
None But the Brave '65
High & Low '62

Dash Mihok (1974-)
Firehouse Dog '07
I Am Legend '07
Loveless in Los Angeles '07
Hollywoodland '06
10th & Wolf '06
Kiss Kiss Bang Bang '05
Connie and Carla '04
The Day After Tomorrow '04
Hustle '04
Basic '03
Dark Blue '03

The Guru '02
Finder's Fee '01
The Perfect Storm '00
White Boyz '99
Telling You '98

Takashi Miike (1960-)
The Neighbor No. Thirteen '05
Last Life in the Universe '03

Nadia Mikhalkov
Burnt by the Sun '94
Anna '93

Nikita Mikhalkov (1945-)
Burnt by the Sun '94
Anna '93
Close to Eden '90
Siberiade '79
An Unfinished Piece for a Player Piano '77

Norihei Miki (1923-99)
Black Rain '88
Himatsuri '85

Mads Mikkelsen (1965-)
After the Wedding '06
Casino Royale '06
Adam's Apples '05
King Arthur '04
The Green Butchers '03
Wilbur Wants to Kill Himself '02
Flickering Lights '01
Pusher '96

Izabella Miko (1981-)
The House of Usher '06
The Forsaken '01
Coyote Ugly '00

Rentaro Mikuni (1923-)
Rikyu '90
A Taxing Woman's Return '88
The Go-Masters '82
Nomugi Pass '79
Vengeance Is Mine '79
Swords of Death '71
Kwaidan '64
Harakiri '62
The Burmese Harp '56

Lita Milan (1933-)
I, Mobster '58
The Left-Handed Gun '58
Never Love a Stranger '58
Naked in the Sun '57
Poor White Trash '57
The Ride Back '57

Alyssa Milano (1972-)
Pathology '08
Dickie Roberts: Former Child Star '03
Goldrush: A Real Life Alaskan Adventure '98
Hugo Pool '97
Fear '96
Glory Daze '96
Double Dragon '94
Casualties of Love: The "Long Island Lolita" Story '93
Conflict of Interest '92
Little Sister '92
Where the Day Takes You '92
Commando '85
Old Enough '84

Adolph Milar (1886-1950)
The Savage Girl '32
Bulldog Drummond '29
The Michigan Kid '28

David Milbern
See David Millbern

Oliver Milburn (1973-)
The Descent '05
Me Without You '01
Tess of the D'Urbervilles '98
The Choir '95
Loaded '94

Ben Miles (1967-)
V for Vendetta '06
Under the Greenwood Tree '05
Three Blind Mice '02
Catherine Cookson's The Round Tower '98

Bernard Miles (1907-91)
Sapphire '59
The Smallest Show on Earth '57
The Man Who Knew Too Much '56
Never Let Me Go '53
The Guinea Pig '48
Fame is the Spur '47
Great Expectations '46
Nicholas Nickleby '46
In Which We Serve '43

Betty Miles (1910-92)
Sonora Stagecoach '44
Law of the Saddle '43
The Law Rides Again '43
Lone Star Law Men '42
The Driftin' Kid '41
Riding the Sunset Trail '41

Elaine Miles (1960-)
The Business of Fancydancing '02
Smoke Signals '98

Joanna Miles (1940-)
Sex and Breakfast '07
Monte Walsh '03
Crossfire Trail '01
Horton Foote's Alone '97
The Avenging Angel '95
Cooperstown '93
The Water Engine '92
Rosencrantz & Guildenstern Are Dead '90
Blackout '88
Sound of Murder '82
Sophisticated Gents '81
The Orphan '79
The Dark Secret of Harvest Home '78
Bug '75
Born Innocent '74

Kate Miles
Longford '06

Kevin Miles
The Chant of Jimmie Blacksmith '78
Endplay '75
The Cars That Ate Paris '74
Reefer Madness '38

Maria Miles
Catherine Cookson's The Cinder Path '94
Cold Comfort Farm '94

Peter Miles (1938-2002)
Trigger, Jr. '50
The Red Pony '49
Who Killed Doc Robbin? '48

Rosalind Miles
The Black Six '74
I Spit on Your Corpse '74
The Manhandlers '73
Shaft's Big Score '72

Sarah Miles (1941-)
The Silent Touch '94
White Mischief '88
Hope and Glory '87
Queenie '87
Harem '86
Steaming '86
Ordeal by Innocence '84
Venom '82
The Big Sleep '78
Dynasty '76
The Sailor Who Fell from Grace with the Sea '76
Lady Caroline Lamb '73
Man Who Loved Cat Dancing '73
Ryan's Daughter '70
Blow-Up '66
Those Magnificent Men in Their Flying Machines '65
The Servant '63

Sherry Miles (1952-)
Jailbreakin' '72
The Todd Killings '71
The Velvet Vampire '71

Sylvia Miles (1932-)
Denise Calls Up '95
Superstar: The Life and Times of Andy Warhol '90
She-Devil '89
Sleeping Beauty '89
Crossing Delancey '88
Spike of Bensonhurst '88
No Big Deal '83
Evil under the Sun '82
The Funhouse '81
Deadly Thief '78
Zero to Sixty '78
The Sentinel '76
Farewell, My Lovely '75
Heat '72
The Last Movie '71
Who Killed Mary What's 'Er Name? '71
Midnight Cowboy '69
Psychomania '63
Parrish '61

Vera Miles (1929-)
Separate Lives '94
Into the Night '85
The Initiation '84
Psycho 2 '83
Brainwaves '82
Mazes and Monsters '82
Our Family Business '81
And I Alone Survived '78
Run for the Roses '78
Fire '77
Twilight's Last Gleaming '77
Judge Horton and the Scottsboro Boys '76
The Castaway Cowboy '74
A Strange and Deadly Occurrence '74
One Little Indian '73
Baffled '72
Molly & Lawless John '72
Jigsaw '71
Mission Batangas '69
Hellfighters '68
Sergeant Ryker '68
Gentle Giant '67
Follow Me, Boys! '66
Those Calloways '65
A Tiger Walks '64
The Man Who Shot Liberty Valance '62
Back Street '61
Psycho '60
The FBI Story '59
Autumn Leaves '56
The Searchers '56
The Wrong Man '56

Vicki (Allison Louise Downe) Miles
Scum of the Earth '63
Nature's Playmates '62

Kim Milford (1950-88)
Corvette Summer '78
Laserblast '78

Penelope Milford (1948-)
Henry: Portrait of a Serial Killer 2: Mask of Sanity '96
Take This Job & Shove It '81
The Last Word '80
Oldest Living Graduate '80
Seizure: The Story of Kathy Morris '80
Coming Home '78

Christina Milian (1981-)
Pulse '06
Be Cool '05
Man of the House '05
Love Don't Cost a Thing '03

Tomas Milian (1937-)
The Lost City '05
Washington Heights '02
For Love or Country: The Arturo Sandoval Story '00
Traffic '00
The Yards '00
Amistad '97
Fools Rush In '97
The Burning Season '94
The Cowboy Way '94
Nails '92
JFK '91
Cat Chaser '90
Drug Wars: The Camarena Story '90
Havana '90
Revenge '90
Salome '85
Identification of a Woman '82
Almost Human '79
Blood and Guns '79
Cop in Blue Jeans '78
Sonny and Jed '73
Don't Torture a Duckling '72
Counter Punch '71
Companeros '70
Time of Indifference '64
Boccaccio 70 '62
Il Bell'Antonio '60

Ivana Milicevic (1974-)
Witless Protection '08
Casino Royale '06
Running Scared '06
Just like Heaven '05
Head Over Heels '01

Frank Military
The Last Castle '01
Everybody Wins '90
Dead Bang '89

John Miljan (1892-1960)
Mrs. Mike '49
Queen of the Amazons '47
I Accuse My Parents '45
Wildfire '45
Boss of Big Town '43
The Fallen Sparrow '43
Motorcycle Squad '41
Riot Squad '41
Young Bill Hickok '40
Arizona Mahoney '36
Charlie Chan in Paris '35
Mississippi '35
Under the Pampas Moon '35
Belle of the Nineties '34
The Ghost Walks '34
What! No Beer? '33
Kid from Spain '32
Possessed '31
Susan Lenox: Her Fall and Rise '31
The Unholy Three '30
Yankee Clipper '27
The Unchastened Woman '25

Hugh Millais
The Dogs of War '81
Images '72
McCabe & Mrs. Miller '71

Robyn Millan
Murph the Surf '75
Murder Motel '74
The Witchmaker '69

Victor Millan (1920-)
Boulevard Nights '79
The FBI Story '59
Terror in a Texas Town '58
Touch of Evil '58

Gloria Milland
Goliath Against the Giants '63
Beauty on the Beach '61

Ray Milland (1905-86)
Game for Vultures '86
Masks of Death '86
The Sea Serpent '85
Starflight One '83
Our Family Business '81
The Attic '80
Survival Run '80
Blackout '78
Cruise into Terror '78
Oil '78
Oliver's Story '78
The Uncanny '78
Slavers '77
Swiss Conspiracy '77
The Last Tycoon '76
Rich Man, Poor Man '76
The Dead Don't Die '75
Escape to Witch Mountain '75
Night of the Laughing Dead '75
Terror in the Wax Museum '73
Embassy '72
Frogs '72
The Thing with Two Heads '72
Quick, Let's Get Married '71
Love Story '70
X: The Man with X-Ray Eyes '63
Panic in the Year Zero! '62
Premature Burial '62
Lisbon '56
The Girl in the Red Velvet Swing '55
A Man Alone '55
Dial "M" for Murder '54
Bugles in the Afternoon '52
The Thief '52
Copper Canyon '50
A Life of Her Own '50
A Woman of Distinction '50
It Happens Every Spring '49
The Big Clock '48
Golden Earrings '47
The Lost Weekend '45
Ministry of Fear '44
The Uninvited '44
Forever and a Day '43
The Major and the Minor '42
Reap the Wild Wind '42
Star Spangled Rhythm '42
Doctor Takes a Wife '40
Beau Geste '39
Everything Happens at Night '39
Bulldog Drummond Escapes '37
Easy Living '37
Next Time We Love '36
Three Smart Girls '36
Charlie Chan in London '34
We're Not Dressing '34
Ambassador Bill '31
Blonde Crazy '31
The Flying Scotsman '29

Gregory Millar
Lethal Weapon 3 '92
Uncaged '91

David Millbern (1957-)
Ice Spiders '07
Christmas Do-Over '06
Chupacabra Terror '05
Gods and Monsters '98
Amanda and the Alien '95
Bikini Summer '91
Sorceress '82

David Millburn
See David Millbern

Allan Miller (1929-)
Warlock '91
Obsessive Love '84
Pearl '78

Andrew Miller
Cube '98
The Last of the Dogmen '95

Ann Miller (1919-2004)
Mulholland Drive '01
The Opposite Sex '56
Hit the Deck '55
Deep in My Heart '54
Kiss Me Kate '53

Small Town Girl '53
Lovely to Look At '52
Texas Carnival '51
Watch the Birdie '50
On the Town '49
Easter Parade '48
Melody Ranch '40
Too Many Girls '40
Room Service '38
You Can't Take It with You '38

Annette Miller
Lift '01
The Imported Bridegroom '89

Aubree Miller (1979-)
The Ewoks: Battle for Endor '85
The Ewok Adventure '84

Barry Miller (1958-)
Flawless '99
Love Affair '94
The Pickle '93
Love at Large '89
The Last Temptation of Christ '88
Peggy Sue Got Married '86
The Chosen '81
Fame '80
Saturday Night Fever '77

Ben Miller (1966-)
The Prince & Me '04

Bodil Miller (1928-)
Reptilicus '62

Charles F. Miller (1891-1955)
Ma and Pa Kettle on Vacation '53

Cheryl Miller (1943-)
Mountain Man '77
Dr. Death, Seeker of Souls '73
Clarence, the Cross-eyed Lion '65

Christa Miller (1964-)
The Operator '01

C.T. Miller
Friend of the Family '95

David Keith Miller
Lap Dancing '95

Dax Miller
Playing Dangerous '95

Dennis Miller (1953-)
Joe Dirt '01
Murder at 1600 '97
Tales from the Crypt Presents Bordello of Blood '96
The Net '95
Never Talk to Strangers '95
Disclosure '94
Madhouse '90
The Everlasting Secret Family '88

Denny Miller (1934-)
The Quest '86
Buck and the Preacher '72
The Party '68

Dick Miller (1928-)
Small Soldiers '98
National Lampoon's Attack of the 5 Ft. 2 Women '94
Pulp Fiction '94
Runaway Daughters '94
Shake, Rattle & Rock! '94
Tales from the Crypt Presents Demon Knight '94
Batman: Mask of the Phantasm '93 (V)
Fallen Angels 1 '93
Fallen Angels 2 '93
Amityville 1992: It's About Time '92
Body Waves '92
Matinee '92
Quake '92
Unlawful Entry '92
Motorama '91
Evil Toons '90
Gremlins 2: The New Batch '90
Far from Home '89
Under the Boardwalk '89
Amazon Women on the Moon '87
Innerspace '87
Project X '87
Chopping Mall '86
Night of the Creeps '86
After Hours '85
Gremlins '84
The Terminator '84
Heart Like a Wheel '83
Get Crazy '83
Lies '83
Twilight Zone: The Movie '83
The Howling '81
Dr. Heckyl and Mr. Hype '80
Used Cars '80
Rock n' Roll High School '79
Lady in Red '79
Piranha '78
Starhops '78
New York, New York '77
Cannonball '76
Hollywood Boulevard '76
Crazy Mama '75
Big Bad Mama '74
Candy Stripe Nurses '74
Truck Turner '74
The Young Nurses '73
Night Call Nurses '72
The St. Valentine's Day Massacre '67
The Wild Angels '66
The Trip '67
The Terror '63
X: The Man with X-Ray Eyes '63
Premature Burial '62
Atlas '60
Little Shop of Horrors '60
A Bucket of Blood '59
Carnival Rock '57
Rock All Night '57
Sorority Girl '57
The Undead '57
The Gunslinger '56
It Conquered the World '56

F.E. (Flourney) Miller (1887-1971)
Yes, Sir, Mr. Bones '51
Mystery in Swing '40
Bronze Buckaroo '39
Harlem Rides the Range '39
Harlem on the Prairie '38

Gabrielle Miller (1973-)
The Silencer '99
Rupert's Land '98

Geri Miller
Trash '70
Flesh '68

Glenn Miller (1904-44)
Orchestra Wives '42
Sun Valley Serenade '41

Jason Miller (1939-2001)
Finding Home '03
Rudy '93
Small Kill '93
Exorcist 3: Legion '90
Light of Day '87
Vengeance '86
Toy Soldiers '84
Monsignor '82
That Championship Season '82
The Best Little Girl in the World '81
The Henderson Monster '80
Marilyn: The Untold Story '80
The Ninth Configuration '79
The Dain Curse '78
F. Scott Fitzgerald in Hollywood '76
A Home of Our Own '75
The Exorcist '73

Jean Miller
The Exorcist '73
Speak of the Devil '90
Silent Night, Deadly Night 2 '87

Jeremy Miller (1976-)
Emanon '90
The Willies '90

Joel McKinnon Miller
Friday After Next '02

Johnny Miller
The Flying Scotsman '06
The Swan Princess '94 (V)

Jonny Lee Miller (1972-)
Aeon Flux '05
Melinda and Melinda '05
Mindhunters '05
Byron '03
Dracula 2000 '00
Love, Honour & Obey '00
Mansfield Park '99
Plunkett & Macleane '98
Afterglow '97
Behind the Lines '97
Larry McMurtry's Dead Man's Walk '96
Hackers '95
Trainspotting '95

Joshua John Miller (1974-)
And You Thought Your Parents Were Weird! '91
Class of 1999 '90
Teen Witch '89
Near Dark '87
River's Edge '87
Nightflyers '87

Kathleen Miller (1945-)
Coming Home '78
Fighting Mad '76
Strange New World '75

Kelly Miller
Newsbreak '00
George of the Jungle '97

Kenny (Ken) Miller (1931-)
Surf Party '64

Kristen Miller (1977-)
All In '06
Single White Female 2: The Psycho '05

Kristine Miller (1929-)
High Lonesome '50
Too Late for Tears '49
Jungle Patrol '48

Larry Miller (1953-)
Bee Movie '07 (V)
The Ant Bully '06 (V)
Kiss Kiss Bang Bang '05
The Final Season '07
The Princess Diaries 2: Royal Engagement '04
A Mighty Wind '03
Max Keeble's Big Move '01
The Princess Diaries '01
What's the Worst That Could Happen? '01
Best in Show '00
The Nutty Professor 2: The Klumps '00
The Big Tease '00
10 Things I Hate about You '99
Keeping Up with the Steirs '98

Lorraine Miller (1922-78)
Ambush Trail '46
Border Badmen '45
Frontier Fugitives '45

Linda Miller (1942-)
Savannah Smiles '82
One Summer Love '76

Mark Thomas Miller (1953-)
Blue De Ville '86
Misfits of Science '85

Martin Miller (1899-1969)
Children of the Damned '63
The Phantom of the Opera '62
Peeping Tom '60
Man on the Run '49
Frenzy '45
Hotel Reserve '44

Marvin Miller (1913-85)
Kiss Daddy Goodbye '81
The Day the Earth Froze '59 (V)
Sleeping Beauty '59 (V)
Forbidden Planet '56 (V)
Red Planet Mars '52
Dead Reckoning '47

Mary Louise Miller (1924-)
Sparrows '26
The Night Cry '26

Mindi Miller (1950-)
Return Fire '91
Caged Fury '90
Nudity Required '90
Hollywood Boulevard 2 '89
The Big Turnaround '88
Deadly Embrace '88
Penitentiary 3 '87
Amazons '86
Body Double '84
Sacred Ground '83
Hell Up in Harlem '73

Mirta Miller (1948-)
Icebox Murders '82
Dracula's Great Love '72
Dr. Jekyll and the Wolfman '71

Omar Benson Miller (1978-)
Things We Lost in the Fire '07
Get Rich or Die Tryin' '05
Shall We Dance? '04
8 Mile '02

Patsy Ruth Miller (1905-95)
Lonely Wives '31
So This is Paris '26
Head Winds '25
The Hunchback of Notre Dame '23
The Sheik '21

Penelope Ann Miller (1964-)
Blonde Ambition '07
The Messengers '07
Carry Me Home '04
National Lampoon's Holiday Reunion '03
Rudy: The Rudy Giuliani Story '03
Dead in a Heartbeat '02
Along Came a Spider '01
A Woman's a Helluva Thing '01
Along for the Ride '00
Full Disclosure '00
Ruby Bridges '98
Outside Ozona '98
The Break Up '98
Little City '97
The Relic '96
The Shadow '94
Witch Hunt '94
Carlito's Way '93
Chaplin '92
Year of the Comet '92
The Gun in Betty Lou's Handbag '92
Other People's Money '91
Awakenings '90
Kindergarten Cop '90
The Freshman '90
Downtown '89
Dead Bang '89
Our Town '89
Big Top Pee-wee '88
Biloxi Blues '88
Miles from Home '88
Adventures in Babysitting '87

Percy Miller (1962-)
See Master P

Rebecca Miller
Mrs. Parker and the Vicious Circle '94
The Pick-up Artist '87
Consenting Adults '92
Wind '92
The Murder of Mary Phagan '87

Roger Miller (1936-92)
Robin Hood '73 (V)

Sarah Jane Miller
Mommy 2: Mommy's Day '97
Mommy '95

Sherry Miller
The Minus Man '99
Pros & Cons '99

Sienna Miller (1981-)
Interview '07
Stardust '07
Factory Girl '06
Casanova '05
Layer Cake '05
Alfie '04

Stephen E. Miller
Air Bud '97
Home is Where the Hart Is '88

T.J. Miller
Cloverfield '08

Tangi Miller (1974-)
Leprechaun 6: Back 2 Tha Hood '03

Ty Miller (1964-)
Trancers 4: Jack of Swords '93
Trancers 5: Sudden Deth '94

Walter Miller (1892-1940)
Wild Horse Rodeo '37
Ghost Patrol '36
The Ivory Handled Gun '35
Law for Tombstone '35
Rustlers of Red Dog '35
Stone of Silver Creek '35
The Fighting Trooper '34
The Lone Defender '32
Shadow of the Eagle '32
The Galloping Ghost '31
Rogue of the Rio Grande '30

Wentworth Miller (1972-)
Stealth '05 (V)
The Human Stain '03
Underworld '03
Dinotopia '02

Christiane Millet
Dinotopia '02

Andra Millian
Nightfall '88
Stacy's Knights '83

James Millican (1910-55)
Bugles in the Afternoon '52
The Winning Team '52
Last of the Wild Horses '49
Men from Colorado '49
Outlaw Gang '49
Rimfire '49
The Adventures of Gallant Bess '48
Return of Wildfire '48

Dustin Milligan
Extract '09
The Messengers '07

Spike Milligan (1918-2002)
Monty Python's Life of Brian '79
The Hound of the Baskervilles '77
The Great McGonagall '75
Ghost in the Noonday Sun '74
Digby, the Biggest Dog in the World '73
Rentadick '72

Deanna Milligan
Suspicious River '00
Must Be Santa '99

Alley Mills (1951-)
Goin' Berserk '83

Angie Milliken
Paperback Hero '99
Dead Heart '96
Talk '94

Barbara Mills
Chain Gang Women '72
Sweet Georgia '72
Rape and Marriage: The Rideout Case '80

Brooke Mills (1985-)
Dream No Evil '75
The Student Teachers '73
The Big Doll House '71

Donna Mills (1942-)
False Arrest '92
The Student Teachers '73
The Big Doll House '71

Murph the Surf '75
Killer with Two Faces '74
One Deadly Owner '74
Haunts of the Very Rich '72
Play Misty for Me '71
The Incident '67

Eddie Mills (1972-)
Winter Break '02
At Any Cost '00
The Tempest '99
Dancer, Texas—Pop. 81 '98
Heartwood '98

Grace Mills
Night of the Howling Beast '75
Exorcism '74

Hayley Mills (1946-)
2B Perfectly Honest '04
A Troll in Central Park '94 (V)
Back Home '90
Appointment with Death '88
Deadly Strangers '82
The Flame Trees of Thika '81
Bananas Boat '78
Kingfisher Caper '76
Cry of the Penguins '71
Endless Night '71
Africa Texas Style '67
The Trouble with Angels '66
That Darn Cat '65
The Chalk Garden '64
The Moon-Spinners '64
Summer Magic '63
In Search of the Castaways '62
The Parent Trap '61
Whistle down the Wind '61
Tiger Bay '59
Pollyanna '60

John Mills (1908-)
Hamlet '96
Martin Chuzzlewit '94
Frankenstein '93
Around the World in 80 Days '89
The Lady and the Highwayman '89
A Tale of Two Cities '89
Who's That Girl? '87
Hold the Dream '86
Masks of Death '86
When the Wind Blows '86 (V)
Agatha Christie's Murder with Mirrors '85
A Woman of Substance '84
Sahara '83
Gandhi '82
Quatermass Conclusion '79
The Thirty-Nine Steps '79
Zulu Dawn '79
Ryan's Daughter '70
Oh! What a Lovely War '69
A Black Veil for Lisa '68
Africa Texas Style '67
Chuka '67
The Wrong Box '66
King Rat '65
Operation Crossbow '65
The Chalk Garden '64
Tiara Tahiti '62
The Swiss Family Robinson '60
Tunes of Glory '60
Tiger Bay '59
The Vicious Circle '57
Above Us the Waves '56
War and Peace '56
The Colditz Story '55
End of the Affair '55
Escapade '55
Hobson's Choice '53
The October Man '48
Scott of the Antarctic '48
This Happy Breed '47
Great Expectations '46
In Which We Serve '43
We Dive at Dawn '43
Cottage to Let '41
Goodbye, Mr. Chips '39
O.H.M.S. '37
Nine Days a Queen '36
The Ghost Camera '33

Judson Mills (1969-)
Chill Factor '99

Juliet Mills (1941-)
The Other Sister '98
Waxwork 2: Lost in Time '91
The Cracker Factory '79
Alexander: The Other Side of Dawn '77
Barnaby and Me '77
Beyond the Door '75
QB VII '74
Jonathan Livingston Seagull '73
Avanti! '72
Oh! What a Lovely War '69
The Rare Breed '66

Martin Milner (1927-)
Nashville Beat '89
The Seekers '79
Flood! '76
Hurricane '74
Columbo: Murder by the Book '71
Valley of the Dolls '67
Zebra in the Kitchen '65
13 Ghosts '60
Compulsion '59
Gunfight at the O.K. Corral '57
Sweet Smell of Success '57
Francis in the Navy '55
Mister Roberts '55
Pete Kelly's Blues '55
Belles on Their Toes '52
I Want You '51
The Halls of Montezuma '50
Our Very Own '50
Sands of Iwo Jima '49
Life with Father '47

Jean-Roger Milo (1957-)
Lucie Aubrac '98
L.627 '92

Sandra Milo (1935-)
Incantato '03
Dead for a Dollar '70
Bang Bang Kid '67
Juliet of the Spirits '65
8 1/2 '63
Vanina Vanini '61
Generale Della Rovere '60
Herod the Great '60

Andy Milonakis (1976-)
Who's Your Caddy? '07
Killer Pad '06
Waiting '05

Ernest Milton (1890-1974)
Cat Girl '57
Alice in Wonderland '50
The Foreman Went to France '42
The Scarlet Pimpernel '34

Mantoyo Mimasu
47 Ronin, Part 1 '42
47 Ronin, Part 2 '42

Yvette Mimieux (1939-)
Obsessive Love '84
Circle of Power '83
Night Partners '83
Forbidden Love '82
The Black Hole '79
Devil Dog: The Hound of Hell '78
Outside Chance '78
Snowbeast '77
Jackson County Jail '76
Legend of Valentino '75
Hit Lady '74
Journey into Fear '74
Neptune Factor '73
Dark of the Sun '68
Three in the Attic '68
Caper of the Golden Bulls '67
Monkeys, Go Home! '66
Toys in the Attic '63
Diamond Head '62
The Four Horsemen of the Apocalypse '62
The Wonderful World of the Brothers Grimm '62
Platinum High School '60
The Time Machine '60
Where the Boys Are '60

Christiane Minazzoli (1931-)
Betty '92
The Story of O '75

Esther Minciotti (1883-1962)
Full of Life '56
Marty '55

Sal Mineo (1939-76)
Escape from the Planet of the Apes '71
Cheyenne Autumn '64
The Longest Day '62
Exodus '60
The Gene Krupa Story '59
Tonka '58
Dino '57
Giant '56
Rock, Pretty Baby '56
Somebody Up There Likes Me '56
The Private War of Major Benson '55
Rebel without a Cause '55

Jan Miner (1917-2004)
Mermaids '90
Willie & Phil '80
Lenny '74

Rachel Miner (1980-)
Cut '07
The Still Life '07
Tooth and Nail '07
The Black Dahlia '06
Fatwa '06
Little Athens '05
Bully '01

Max Minghella (1985-)
Art School Confidential '06
Bee Season '05
Syriana '05

Elvira Minguez (1965-)
The Reckoning '03
The Dancer Upstairs '02

Ming Na (1968-)
Final Fantasy: The Spirits Within '01 (V)
Mulan '98 (V)
One Night Stand '97
Hong Kong '97 '94
Star Quest '94
Street Fighter '94
The Joy Luck Club '93

Birgit Minichmayr (1977-)
The Crown Prince '06
Falling '06
Taking Sides '01

Claudette Mink (1975-)
Shattered '07
Children of the Corn: Revelation '01
Deadly Heroes '96

Liza Minnelli (1946-)
Jackie's Back '99
Parallel Lives '94
Stepping Out '91
Arthur 2: On the Rocks '88
Rent-A-Cop '88
That's Dancing! '85
A Time to Live '85
The Muppets Take Manhattan '84
The Princess and the Pea '83
Arthur '81
New York, New York '77
A Matter of Time '76
Silent Movie '76
Cabaret '72
Journey Back to Oz '71 (V)
The Sterile Cuckoo '69
In the Good Old Summertime '49

Kylie Minogue (1968-)
Doogal '05 (V)
Moulin Rouge '01
Cut '00
Bio-Dome '96
Street Fighter '94

Bob Minor (1942-)
Black Eliminator '78
The Swinging Cheerleaders '74

Kelly Jo Minter (1966-)
The People under the Stairs '91
A Nightmare on Elm Street 5: Dream Child '89
Miracle Mile '89
Popcorn '89
Summer School '87

Kristin Minter (1965-)
The Bread, My Sweet '01
Tick Tock '00
The Apostate '98
Savage '96
Flashfire '94
There Goes My Baby '92
Cool As Ice '91

Mary Miles Minter (1902-84)
Nurse Marjorie '20
Eyes of Julia Deep '18

Frank Minucci
Friends and Family '01
A Brother's Kiss '97
Tar '97

Fabrizio Mioni (1930-)
Hercules '58
Roland the Mighty '56

Miou-Miou (1950-)
The Science of Sleep '06
Dry Cleaning '97
Women '97
The Eighth Day '95
Little Indian, Big City '95
Germinal '93
May Fools '90
La Lectrice '88
Menage '86
My Other Husband '85
Dog Day '83
Entre-Nous '83
Josepha '82
Roads to the South '77
This Sweet Sickness '77
Jonah Who Will Be 25 in the Year 2000 '76
No Problem '75
Going Places '74
The Mad Adventures of Rabbi Jacob '73

Brigitte Mira (1910-2005)
Chinese Roulette '86
Berlin Alexanderplatz '80
Mother Kusters Goes to Heaven '76
Every Man for Himself & God Against All '75
Fear of Fear '75
Ali: Fear Eats the Soul '74

Irene Miracle (1954-)
Puppet Master '89
The Last of Philip Banter '87
In the Shadow of Kilimanjaro '86
Inferno '80
Night Train Murders '75
Torture Train '75

Evan Mirand
Megalodon '03
My Best Friend Is a Vampire '88
Weekend War '88
Brotherhood of Justice '86

Aurora Miranda (1915-2005)
The Three Caballeros '45 (V)
Phantom Lady '44

Carmen Miranda (1909-55)
Scared Stiff '53
Nancy Goes to Rio '50
A Date with Judy '48
Copacabana '47
Doll Face '46
If I'm Lucky '46
Greenwich Village '44
Something for the Boys '44
The Gang's All Here '43
Springtime in the Rockies '42
That Night in Rio '41
Week-End in Havana '41
Down Argentine Way '40

Isa Miranda (1909-82)
The Night Porter '74
Twitch of the Death Nerve '71
Dorian Gray '70
Dog Eat Dog '64
Just Another Pretty Face '58
Summertime '55
Seven Deadly Sins '53
La Ronde '51
The Walls of Malapaga '49
La Signora di Tutti '34

Robert Miranda
Blue Streak '99
Black Thunder '98
For Which He Stands '98
The Rat Pack '98
Steel Sharks '97
Gotti '96
Desire '95
Lost in Yonkers '93
What's Love Got to Do with It? '93
Sister Act '92
Chips, the War Dog '90
Sons '89

Soledad Miranda (1943-72)
Count Dracula '71
Sound of Horror '64

Helen Mirren (1946-)
National Treasure: Book of Secrets '07
The Queen '06
Shadowboxer '06
Elizabeth I '05
The Hitchhiker's Guide to the Galaxy '05 (V)
The Clearing '04
Raising Helen '04
Calendar Girls '03
The Roman Spring of Mrs. Stone '03
Gosford Park '01
Last Orders '01
No Such Thing '01
Greenfingers '00
The Pledge '00
The Passion of Ayn Rand '99
Teaching Mrs. Tingle '99
Prince of Egypt '98 (V)
Critical Care '97
The Painted Lady '97
Losing Chase '96
Some Mother's Son '96
The Madness of King George '94
Royal Deceit '94
The Hawk '93
Prime Suspect '92
The Comfort of Strangers '91
Where Angels Fear to Tread '91
The Cook, the Thief, His Wife & Her Lover '90
Dr. Bethune '90
Red King, White Knight '89
When the Whales Came '89
Pascali's Island '88
Cause Celebre '87
The Gospel According to Vic '87
The Mosquito Coast '86
Coming Through '85
White Nights '85
Cal '84
2010: The Year We Make Contact '84
Excalibur '81
Priest of Love '81
Caligula '80
The Fiendish Plot of Dr. Fu Manchu '80
Hussy '80
The Long Good Friday '80
S.O.S. Titanic '79
O Lucky Man! '73
Savage Messiah '72
A Midsummer Night's Dream '68

Masao Mishima (1906-73)
Harakiri '62
The Human Condition: No Greater Love '58

Dorian Missick (1976-)
Lucky Number Slevin '06
Two Weeks Notice '02

Karen Mistal
Cannibal Women in the Avocado Jungle of Death '89
Return of the Killer Tomatoes! '88

Mr. T (1952-)
Not Another Teen Movie '01
Freaked '93
Straight Line '88
D.C. Cab '84
Penitentiary 2 '82
Rocky 3 '82

Mr. Wiggles
See Ludacris.

Jorge Mistral (1920-72)
The Sword and the Cross '58
Wuthering Heights '53

Jimi Mistry (1973-)
Partition '07
Blood Diamond '06
Dead Fish '04
Ella Enchanted '04
The Truth About Love '04
The Guru '02

Brian Stokes Mitchell (1957-)
One Last Thing '05
Call Me Claus '01
Ruby's Bucket of Blood '01
Double Platinum '99

Cameron Mitchell (1918-94)
Jack-O '93
Trapped Alive '93
Crossing the Line '90
Terror in Beverly Hills '90
Action U.S.A. '89
Easy Kill '89
Killers '88
Memorial Valley Massacre '88
Rage to Kill '88
Space Mutiny '88
Swift Justice '88
Mission... Kill '85
Go for the Gold '84
Killpoint '84
Night Train to Terror '84
The Guns and the Fury '83
Prince Jack '83
Code of Honor '82
It's Called Murder, Baby '82
My Favorite Year '82
Cataclysm '81
The Demon '81
Frankenstein Island '81
Kill Squad '81
Raw Force '81

(Cameron Mitchell, continued)
Texas Lightning '81
The Last Reunion '80
Silent Scream '80
The Bastard '78
Enforcer from Death Row '78
Supersonic Man '78
The Swarm '78
The Toolbox Murders '78
Haunts '77
Return to Fantasy Island '77
Scalp Merchant '77
Slavers '77
Texas Detour '77
The Andersonville Trial '70
Nightmare in Wax '69
Rebel Rousers '69
Autopsy of a Ghost '67
Hombre '67
Knives in the Whirlwind '66
Minnesota Clay '65
Blood and Black Lace '64
Dog Eat Dog '64
Last Gun '64
The Invaders '63
Conquest of the Normans '62
The Unstoppable Man '59
Escapade in Japan '57
All Mine to Give '56
Carousel '56
Tension at Table Rock '56
House of Bamboo '55
Blood Alley '55
Love Me or Leave Me '55
The Tall Men '55
Desiree '54
Garden of Evil '54
How to Marry a Millionaire '53
Flight to Mars '52
Death of a Salesman '51
The Adventures of Gallant Bess '48
Homecoming '48
They Were Expendable '45

Charlotte Mitchell (1926-)
Persuasion '71
Village of the Damned '60

Chuck "Porky" Mitchell (1928-92)

Daryl (Chill) Mitchell (1965-)
Inside Man '06
The Country Bears '02
13 Moons '02
Black Knight '01
Lucky Numbers '00
Galaxy Quest '99
The Pooch and the Pauper '99
Ten Things I Hate about You '99 (V)
Home Fries '98
Toothless '97
Quiet Days in Hollywood '97
A Thin Line Between Love and Hate '96
Sgt. Bilko '96
Fly by Night '93

Donna Mitchell
Bomb the System '05
Mona Lisa Smile '03
Two Bits '96
Psycho 4: The Beginning '90

Duke Mitchell (1926-81)
The Executioner '78
Bela Lugosi Meets a Brooklyn Gorilla '52

E. Roger Mitchell (1971-)
Miracle '04
Boycott '02
How I Spent My Summer Vacation '97

Eddy Mitchell (1942-)
Le Bonheur Est Dans le Pre '95
Coup de Torchon '81

Elizabeth Mitchell (1970-)
The Santa Clause 3: The Escape Clause '06
Running Scared '06
The Santa Clause 2 '02
Double Bang '01
Frequency '00
Molly '99
Gia '98

Eric Mitchell
Underground U.S.A. '84
The Foreigner '78
Rome '78 '78

Ewing Mitchell (1910-88)
Above and Beyond '53
Cavalry Charge '51

Gene Mitchell
Flipping '95
The Takeover '94

Gordon Mitchell (1923-2003)
Commando Invasion '87
Mines of Kilimanjaro '87
Rush '84
Frankenstein '80 '79
Operation Orient '78
Slaughterday '77
The Big Bust Out '73
Fistful of Death '71
Beyond the Law '68
Erik the Viking '65
Fighting Fists of Shanghai Joe '65
Battle of Valiant '63
Vulcan God of Fire '62
The Giant of Metropolis '61

Grant Mitchell (1874-1957)
Easy to Wed '46
Conflict '45
Laura '44
The Amazing Mrs. Holiday '43
Caro '42
Footsteps in the Dark '41
The Great Lie '41
The Man Who Came to Dinner '41
The Grapes of Wrath '40
Next Time We Love '36
Gold Diggers of 1935 '35
In Person '35
365 Nights in Hollywood '34
Heroes for Sale '33
No Man of Her Own '32
Three on a Match '32

Gwen Mitchell
Black Force 2 '78
Shaft '71

Heather Mitchell
A Little Bit of Soul '97
Proof '91

Ilan Mitchell-Smith (1967-)
Identity Crisis '90
The Chocolate War '88
Journey to the Center of the Earth '88
Weird Science '85

John Cameron Mitchell (1963-)
Hedwig and the Angry Inch '00
David Searching '97
Book of Love '91
The Everlasting Secret Family '88

Julien Mitchell (1888-1954)
Bedelia '46
Echo Murders '45
Hotel Reserve '44

Kel Mitchell (1978-)
Ganked '05
Clifford's Really Big Movie '04 (V)
The Adventures of Rocky & Bullwinkle '00
Mystery Men '99
Good Burger '97

Kenneth Mitchell (1974-)
Charms for the Easy Life '02

Laurie Mitchell (1922-)
Missile to the Moon '59
Queen of Outer Space '58

Mark Mitchell (1955-)
The Outing '87

Mary Mitchell (1940-)
A Swingin' Summer '65
Spider Baby '64
Dementia 13 '63
Panic in the Year Zero! '62

Millard Mitchell (1900-53)
Here Come the Girls '53
The Naked Spur '53
Singin' in the Rain '52
The Gunfighter '50
Winchester '73 '50
Twelve o'Clock High '49
A Foreign Affair '48
A Double Life '47

Radha Mitchell (1973-)
Feast of Love '07
PU-239 '06
Silent Hill '06
Mozart and the Whale '05
Melinda and Melinda '05
Finding Neverland '04
Man on Fire '04
Visitors '03
Phone Booth '02
Dead Heat '01
Nobody's Baby '01
Uprising '01
Cowboys and Angels '00
Everything Put Together '00
Pitch Black '00
High Art '98
Love and Other Catastrophes '96

Red Mitchell (1964-94)
8 Seconds '94
Forever Evil '87

Sasha Mitchell (1967-)
Luck of the Draw '00
Kickboxer 4: The Aggressor '94
Class of 1999 II: The Substitute '93
Kickboxer 3: The Art of War '92
Kickboxer 2: The Road Back '90
Spike of Bensonhurst '88

Scoey Mitchell (1930-)
Jo Jo Dancer, Your Life Is Calling '86
The Voyage of the Yes '72

Sharon Mitchell (1956-)
Kamikaze Hearts '91
Maniac '80

Silas Weir Mitchell
The Whole Ten Yards '04
Johnson County War '02
Incident at Channel Q '86

Steve Mitchell
Diamondbacks '99
Lethal Seduction '97
Fugitive X '96
Biohazard: The Alien Force '95

Thomas Mitchell (1892-1962)
By Love Possessed '61
Pocketful of Miracles '61
While the City Sleeps '56
The Big Wheel '52
High Noon '52
Silver River '48
Dark Waters '44
The Keys of the Kingdom '44
Buffalo Bill '44
Wilson '44
Bataan '43
The Outlaw '43
Immortal Sergeant '43
The Black Swan '42
Moontide '42
Joan of Paris '42
Song of the Islands '42
The Long Voyage Home '40
Our Town '40
Angels Over Broadway '40
Swiss Family Robinson '40
The Hunchback of Notre Dame '39
Mr. Smith Goes to Washington '39
Gone with the Wind '39
Stagecoach '39
Only Angels Have Wings '39
The Hurricane '37
Lost Horizon '37
Theodora Goes Wild '36
Craig's Wife '36

Warren Mitchell (1926-)
Knights & Emeralds '87
Foreign Body '86
The Dunera Boys '85
The Incredible Sarah '76
Demons of the Mind '72
Crucible of Horror '69
The Assassination Bureau '69
Help! '65
The Unearthly Stranger '64
The Crawling Eye '58

Yvonne Mitchell (1925-79)
Jabberwocky '77
Bananas Boat '78
Norman Loves Rose '82
Johnny Nobody '61
Conspiracy of Hearts '60
The Trials of Oscar Wilde '60
Sapphire '59
Tiger Bay '59
The Queen of Spades '49

Bentley Mitchum (1970-)
Conviction '02
U.S. Navy SEALs: Dead or Alive '02
Shark Attack '99
Chained Heat 3: Hell Mountain '98
On the Border '98
Deadly Exposure '93
Ruby in Paradise '93
Teenage Bonnie & Klepto Clyde '93
Demonic Toys '90

Chris Mitchum (1943-)
Striking Point '94
Tombstone '93
Faceless '88
Aftershock '88
Angel of Death '86
American Commandos '84
The Executioner, Part 2 '84
No Time to Die '84
Frozen Scream '84
My Champion '81
Summertime Killer '72
H-Bomb '71
Big Jake '71
Rio Lobo '70
Chisum '70

Jim Mitchum (1941-)
Fatal Mission '89
Marked for Murder '89
Mercenary Fighters '88
Hollywood Cop '87
Code Name: Zebra '84
Maniac '77
The Invincible Six '68
In Harm's Way '65
Ride the Wild Surf '64
The Victors '63
Girls Town '59
Thunder Road '58

John Mitchum (1919-2001)
Escapes '86
The Enforcer '76
The Outlaw Josey Wales '76
Big Foot '72
Bloody Trail '72
The Devil's Sleep '51

Julie Mitchum (1914-2003)
House on Haunted Hill '58
The High and the Mighty '54

Robert Mitchum (1917-97)
James Dean: Live Fast, Die Young '97
A Kid in Aladdin's Palace '97
Dead Man '95
Backfire! '94
Tombstone '93 (N)
Woman of Desire '93
Midnight Ride '92
Cape Fear '91
Thompson's Last Run '90
War & Remembrance: The Final Chapter '89
The Brotherhood of the Rose '89
Scrooged '88
War & Remembrance '88
Mr. North '88
North and South Book 1 '85
Maria's Lovers '84
The Ambassador '84
The Winds of War '83
That Championship Season '82
One Shoe Makes It Murder '82
Agency '81
Nightkill '80
The Amsterdam Kill '78
The Big Sleep '78
Matilda '78
Breakthrough '78
The Last Tycoon '76
Midway '76
The Yakuza '75
Farewell, My Lovely '75
Ryan's Daughter '70
The Good Guys and the Bad Guys '69
Young Billy Young '69
Secret Ceremony '69
Anzio '68
Five Card Stud '68
Villa Rides '68
El Dorado '67
The Way West '67
The Longest Day '62
Two for the Seesaw '62
Cape Fear '62
The Grass Is Greener '61
Home from the Hill '60
The Sundowners '60
The Hunters '58
Fire Down Below '57
Heaven Knows, Mr. Allison '57
The Night of the Hunter '55
Not as a Stranger '55
River of No Return '54
Second Chance '53
Angel Face '52
The Lusty Men '52
Macao '52
The Racket '51
Where Danger Lives '50
Big Steal '49
Holiday Affair '49
The Red Pony '49
Blood on the Moon '48
Rachel and the Stranger '48
Out of the Past '47
Crossfire '47
Pursued '47
Till the End of Time '46
Undercurrent '46
The Story of G.I. Joe '45
West of the Pecos '45
Girl Rush '44
Nevada '44
Thirty Seconds Over Tokyo '44

Koji Mitsui
Day Time Ended '80
Desperate Target '80
A Rumor of War '80
One Man Jury '78
Stingray '78

Labina Mitevska (1975-)
I Want You '98
Before the Rain '94

Rhona Mitra (1976-)
Doomsday '08
The Number 23 '07
Shooter '07
Skinwalkers '07
Highwaymen '03
The Life of David Gale '03
Sweet Home Alabama '02
Get Carter '00
Beowulf '98

Ruth Mix (1907-77)
Custer's Last Stand '36
The Riding Avenger '36
The Tonto Kid '35

Art Mix (1895-1972)
Yodelin' Kid from Pine Ridge '37
Powdersmoke Range '35

Tom Mix (1880-1940)
The Miracle Rider '35
Rustler's Roundup '33
Terror Trail '33
Hidden Gold '33
Destry Rides Again '32
My Pal, the King '32
Justice Rides Again '32
Texas Bad Man '32
Riders of the Purple Sage '25
Dick Turpin '25
Sky High '22
Trailin' '21
Child of the Prairie '18
Heart of Texas Ryan '17
In the Days of the Thundering Herd & the Law & the Outlaw '14
Great K & A Train Robbery '26

Jerod Mixon (1981-)
The New Guy '02
Me, Myself, and Irene '00

Seiji Miyaguchi (1913-85) The Human Condition: No Greater Love '58 Seven Samurai '54 Early Summer '51 **Kuniko Miyake (1916-92)** Good Morning '59 Early Summer '51 **Nobuko Miyamoto (1945)** Minbo—Or the Gentle Art of Japanese Extortion '92 A Taxing Woman's Return '88 A Taxing Woman '87 Tampopo '86 The Funeral '84 **Eric Miyeni** Dangerous Ground '96 Cry, the Beloved Country '95 **Kim Miyori (1951-)** The Grudge 2 '06 Metro '96 Body Shot '93 Hiroshima: Out of the Ashes '90 The Punisher '90 The Big Picture '89 When the Bough Breaks '86 John & Yoko: A Love Story '85 **Eiko Miyoshi** The Hidden Fortress '58 Snow Country '57 I Live in Fear '55 Samurai 1: Musashi Miyamoto '55 No Regrets for Our Youth '46 **Isaac Mizrahi (1961-)** Hollywood Ending '02 Celebrity '98 For Love or Money '93 **Kumi Mizuno (1937-)** War of the Gargantuas '70 Godzilla vs. Monster Zero '68 Godzilla vs. the Sea Monster '66 What's Up, Tiger Lily? '66 Attack of the Mushroom People '63 **Genevieve Mnich (1942-)** Beau Pere '81 The Mother and the Whore '73 **Mary Ann Mobley (1939-)** Crazy Horse and Custer: "The Untold Story" '90 My Dog, the Thief '69 Girl Happy '65 Harum Scarum '65 **Roger Mobley (1949-)** Emil and the Detectives '64 Jack the Giant Killer '62 **Tony Mockus, Sr.** Charming Billy '98 Backdraft '91 **Matthew Modine (1959-)** Kettle of Fish '06 Transporter 2 '05 Hitler: The Rise of Evil '03 Hollywood North '03 Le Divorce '03 Redeemer '02 The American '01 In the Shadows '01 Jack and the Beanstalk: The Real Story '01 Nobody's Baby '01 Any Given Sunday '99 The Maker '98 What the Deaf Man Heard '98 The Blackout '97 The Real Blonde '97 Cutthroat Island '95 Fluke '95 The Browning Version '94	Bye Bye, Love '94 Jacob '94 And the Band Played On '93 Equinox '93 Short Cuts '93 Wind '92 Memphis Belle '90 Pacific Heights '90 Gross Anatomy '89 The Gamble '88 Married to the Mob '88 Full Metal Jacket '87 Orphans '87 Vision Quest '85 Birdy '84 The Hotel New Hampshire '84 Mrs. Soffel '84 Private School '83 Streamers '83 Baby It's You '82 **Gaston Modot (1887-1970)** Casque d'Or '52 Beauty and the Devil '50 Children of Paradise '44 The Rules of the Game '39 Grand Illusion '37 L'Age D'Or '30 Under the Roofs of Paris '29 **Enrica Maria Modugno (1958-)** The Story of Boys & Girls '91 Kaos '85 **Ralph (Ralf) Moeller (1959-)** Pathfinder '07 Beerfest '06 The Scorpion King '02 Gladiator '00 The Bad Pack '98 The Viking Sagas '95 Best of the Best 2 '93 **Donald Moffat (1930-)** 61* '01 Cookie's Fortune '99 The Evening Star '96 A Smile Like Yours '96 Clear and Present Danger '94 Is There Life Out There? '94 Trapped in Paradise '94 Armistead Maupin's Tales of the City '93 Love, Cheat & Steal '93 Class Action '91 Regarding Henry '91 When the Time Comes '91 The Bonfire of the Vanities '90 Danielle Steel's Kaleidoscope '90 Music Box '89 The Bourne Identity '88 Far North '88 Necessary Parties '88 The Unbearable Lightness of Being '88 The Best of Times '86 Alamo Bay '85 License to Kill '84 The Right Stuff '83 The Thing '82 Jacqueline Bouvier Kennedy '81 The Long Days of Summer '80 On the Nickel '80 Mrs. R's Daughter '79 Promises in the Dark '79 Strangers: The Story of a Mother and Daughter '79 Winter Kills '79 Mary White '77 Showdown '73 The Great Northfield Minnesota Raid '72 Rachel, Rachel '68 **D.W. Moffett (1954-)** Twisted '04	Thirteen '03 Kill Me Later '01 Traffic '00 Molly '99 Stealing Beauty '96 The Little Death '95 Rough Magic '95 Falling Down '93 In the Deep Woods '91 Danielle Steel's Fine Things '90 Lisa '90 Pacific Heights '90 Black Widow '87 The Misfit Brigade '87 An Early Frost '85 **Gregory Moffett** Robot Monster '53 Let's Dance '50 **Michelle Moffett** Indecent Behavior '93 Deathstalker 4: Match of Titans '92 **Sharyn Moffett (1936-)** The Judge Steps Out '49 The Body Snatcher '45 **Jerry Mofokeng** Tsotsi '05 **Carl Mohner (1916-2005)** A Woman at Her Window '77 Wanted: Babysitter '75 Cave of the Living Dead '65 Last Gun '64 Sink the Bismarck '60 It Takes a Thief '59 The Last Bridge '54 Rififi '54 **Gerald Mohr (1914-68)** The Angry Red Planet '59 Terror in the Haunted House '58 Duel at Silver Creek '52 Invasion U.S.A. '52 The Ring '52 Son of Ali Baba '52 Detective Story '51 Sirocco '51 Hunt the Man Down '50 King of the Cowboys '43 The Monster and the Girl '41 Charlie Chan at Treasure Island '39 Love Affair '39 **Jay Mohr (1970-)** Street Kings '08 Christmas Do-Over '06 Even Money '06 The Groomsmen '06 Are We There Yet? '05 King's Ransom '05 Seeing Other People '04 The Adventures of Pluto Nash '02 Simone '02 Dean Koontz's Black River '01 Cherry Falls '00 Pay It Forward '00 Go '99 From the Earth to the Moon '98 Mafia! '98 Paulie '98 (V) Playing by Heart '98 Small Soldiers '98 200 Cigarettes '98 Suicide Kings '97 Jerry Maguire '96 Picture Perfect '96 For Better or Worse '95 **Wotan Wilke Mohring** Antibodies '05 **Zia Mohyeddin (1933-)** The Experiment '01 We Are the Children '87 Bombay Talkie '70	**Richard Moir (1950-)** Welcome to Woop Woop '97 Wrangler '88 An Indecent Obsession '85 Remember Me '85 Heatwave '83 Panic Station '82 In Search of Anna '79 The Odd Angry Shot '79 **Marisa Moitzi** **Jose Mojica Marins (1929-)** Hallucinations of a Deranged Mind '78 Awakenings of the Beast '68 Strange World of Coffin Joe '68 At Midnight, I'll Take Your Soul '63 **Karen Mok (1970-)** Vampire Effect '03 Black Mask '96 Fallen Angels '95 **Zakes Mokae (1935-)** Krippendorf's Tribe '98 Vampire in Brooklyn '95 Waterworld '95 Dust Devil '93 Percy & Thunder '93 Body Parts '91' A Rage in Harlem '91 Dad '89 A Dry White Season '89 Gross Anatomy '89 Cry Freedom '87 The Serpent and the Rainbow '87 Master Harold and the Boys '84 Agatha Christie's A Caribbean Mystery '83 The Comedians '67 A World of Strangers '62 **Albert Mol (1917-2004)** Dear Boys '80 Business is Business '71 **Gretchen Mol (1973-)** The Ten '07 3:10 to Yuma '07 The Notorious Bettie Page '06 Puccini for Beginners '06 The Shape of Things '03 The Magnificent Ambersons '02 Get Carter '00 The Cradle Will Rock '99 Forever Mine '99 Just Looking '99 Sweet and Lowdown '99 The Thirteenth Floor '99 Celebrity '98 Finding Graceland '98 New Rose Hotel '98 Rounders '98 Music from Another Room '97 Calm at Sunset '96 The Funeral '96 The Last Time I Committed Suicide '96 **Karin Molander (1889-1978)** Thomas Graal's First Child '18 Thomas Graal's Best Film '17 **Jeff Moldovan** Trancers 5: Sudden Deth '94 Master Blaster '85 **Alfred Molina (1953-)** The Company '07 Silk '07 As You Like It '06 The Da Vinci Code '06 The Hoax '06 Steamboy '05 (V) Cronicas '04 Spider-Man 2 '04 Coffee and Cigarettes '03 Identity '03 Luther '03 My Life Without Me '03	Frida '02 Texas Rangers '01 Chocolat '00 The Miracle Maker: The Story of Jesus '00 (V) Dudley Do-Right '99 The Imposters '98 Pete's Meteor '98 Rescuers: Stories of Courage—Two Couples '98 The Treat '98 Boogie Nights '97 The Man Who Knew Too Little '97 Leo Tolstoy's Anna Karenina '96 Mojave Moon '96 Scorpion Spring '96 Before and After '95 Dead Man '95 Species '95 Maverick '94 The Perez Family '94 White Fang 2: The Myth of the White Wolf '94 The Trial '93 When Pigs Fly '93 Enchanted April '92 American Friends '91 Not Without My Daughter '90 A Night of Love '87 Prick Up Your Ears '87 Letter to Brezhnev '85 Ladyhawke '85 Meantime '81 Raiders of the Lost Ark '81 The Big Scam '79 **Angela Molina (1955-)** Carnage '02 Live Flesh '97 1492: Conquest of Paradise '92 Half of Heaven '86 Camorra: The Naples Connection '85 The Eyes, the Mouth '83 Demons in the Garden '82 That Obscure Object of Desire '77 **Jacinto (Jack) Molina** See Paul Naschy **Rolando Molina (1971-)** crazy/beautiful '01 Next Friday '00 **Charles Moll (1943-)** Combat Academy '86 Night Train to Terror '84 Cataclysm '81 **Georgia Moll (1938-)** What a Way to Die '70 Contempt '64 Thief of Baghdad '61 **Richard Moll (1943-)** The Biggest Fan '02 Evolution '01 Scary Movie 2 '01 Spiders 2: Breeding Ground '01 Boltneck '98 Dish Dogs '98 The Survivor '98 Living in Peril '97 The Glass Cage '96 The Secret Agent Club '96 Galaxis '95 Storybook '95 Beanstalk '94 The Flintstones '94 No Dessert Dad, 'Til You Mow the Lawn '94 Dream Date '93 National Lampoon's Loaded Weapon 1 '93 Sidekicks '93 Highlander: The Gathering '92	Metalstorm: The Destruction of Jared Syn '83 Savage Journey '83 Sword & the Sorcerer '82 Hard Country '81 **Jordi Molla (1968-)** Elizabeth: The Golden Age '07 The Stone Merchant '06 The Alamo '04 Bad Boys 2 '03 Blow '01 Second Skin '99 Jamon, Jamon '93 **Clothilde Mollet** The Page Turner '06 Amelie '01 **Dearbhla Molloy (1946-)** Frankie Starlight '95 Paddy '70 **Patrick Molloy** Phantom Brother '88 Plutonium Baby '87 **Tibor Molnar (1921-82)** The Red and the White '68 The Round Up '66 **Alessandro Momo** The Scent of a Woman '75 Malicious '74 **Sloane Momsen (1997-)** Daddy Day Care '03 We Were Soldiers '02 Dr. Seuss' How the Grinch Stole Christmas '00 **Taylor Momsen (1993-)** Paranoid Park '07 Underdog '07 We Were Soldiers '02 Dr. Seuss' How the Grinch Stole Christmas '00 **Dominic Monaghan (1976-)** Shooting Livien '05 The Purifiers '04 Lord of the Rings: The Return of the King '03 Lord of the Rings: The Two Towers '02 Lord of the Rings: The Fellowship of the Rings '01 **Michelle Monaghan (1976-)** Made of Honor '08 Gone Baby Gone '07 The Heartbreak Kid '07 Mission: Impossible 3 '06 Kiss Kiss Bang Bang '05 North Country '05 The Bourne Supremacy '04 Winter Solstice '04 It Runs in the Family '03 **Dan Monahan (1955-)** Stephen King's The Night Flier '96 Porky's Revenge '85 Porky's 2: The Next Day '83 Porky's '82 **Jeff Monahan** Bruiser '00 One Way Out '95 **Richard Monahan** Fixed Bayonets! '51 Pier 23 '51 The Steel Helmet '51 **Karen Moncrieff (1963-)** Xtro 3: Watch the Skies '95 Deathfight '93 Midnight Witness '93 **Merwin Mondesir** Godsend '04 Bones '01 **Jorge Mondragon (1903-97)** Spiritism '61 The New Invisible Man '58

Daniella Monet (1989-)
Nancy Drew '07

Richard Monette (1944-)
Murder by Night '89
Higher Education '88
Dancing in the Dark '86
Fat City from Home '81
Big Zapper '73

Mo'Nique (1968-)
Welcome Home Roscoe Jenkins '08
Beerfest '06
Phat Girlz '06
Shadowboxer '06
Domino '05
Hair Show '04
Soul Plane '04
Good Fences '03
Half Past Dead '02
Queens of Comedy '01
Two Can Play That Game '01
Three Strikes '00

Debra Monk (1949-)
Dark Water '05
Palindromes '04
Extreme Measures '96
Bed of Roses '95
Redwood Curtain '95

Lawrence Monoson (1965-)
Machine Gun Blues '95
And the Band Played On '93
Dangerous Love '87
Gaby: A True Story '87
Mask '85
Devilfish '84
Last American Virgin '82

Marilyn Monroe (1926-62)
The Love Goddesses '65
Let's Make Love '60
Some Like It Hot '59
The Prince and the Showgirl '57
Bus Stop '56
The Seven Year Itch '55
River of No Return '54
There's No Business Like Show Business '54
Gentlemen Prefer Blondes '53
How to Marry a Millionaire '53
Clash by Night '52
Don't Bother to Knock '52
Monkey Business '52
Niagara '52
We're Not Married '52
As Young As You Feel '51
Home Town Story '51
Let's Make It Legal '51
Love Nest '51
All About Eve '50
The Asphalt Jungle '50
Love Happy '50
Ticket to Tomahawk '50

Carlo Monni (1943-)
The Tesseract '03
Berlinguer I Love You '77

Yvonne Monlaur (1940-)
License to Kill '64
The Brides of Dracula '60
Circus of Horrors '60

Bob Monkhouse
All or Nothing at All '93
Dial Help '88
Dentist in the Chair '60

Valentine Monnier
After the Fall of New York '85

Meredith Monroe
Masters of Horror: Family '05

Mircea Monroe
New Best Friend '02

Steve Monroe
Fast Girl '07
School for Scoundrels '06
All Souls Day '05
The Santa Trap '02
Going Greek '01
Cast Away '00
Miss Congeniality '00
Inherit the Wind '99
Can't Hardly Wait '98

Renzo Montagnani (1930-77)
Voyage of Terror: The Achille Lauro Affair '90
A Joke of Destiny, Lying in Wait Around the Corner Like a Bandit '84
You've Got to Have Heart '77
The Mad Adventures of Rabbi Jacob '73
The Libertine '69

Monte Montague (1891-1959)
Radio Patrol '37
Trigger Tricks '30

Ricardo Montalban (1920-)
The Ant Bully '06 (V)
Spy Kids 3-D: Game Over '03
Spy Kids 2: The Island of Lost Dreams '02
The Naked Gun: From the Files of Police Squad! '88
Cannonball Run 2 '84
Star Trek 2: The Wrath of Khan '82
Mission to Glory '80
Return to Fantasy Island '77
Fantasy Island '76
Joe Panther '76
Train Robbers '73
Conquest of the Planet of the Apes '72
Escape from the Planet of the Apes '71
Black Water Gold '69
Sweet Charity '69
Blue '68
Iron Cowboy '68
Alice Through the Looking Glass '66
Madame X '66
The Singing Nun '66
Cheyenne Autumn '64
Let No Man Write My Epitaph '60
Sayonara '57
Latin Lovers '53
Across the Wide Missouri '51
Mystery Street '50
Two Weeks with Love '50
Border Incident '49
Neptune's Daughter '49
On an Island with You '48

Paolo Montalban
The Great Raid '05
American Adobo '02
Cinderella '97

Lee Montague (1927-)
Jekyll and Hyde '90
Madame Sousatzka '88
Mahler '74
Brother Sun, Sister Moon '73

Lisa Montell (1933-)
The Nine Lives of Elfego Baca '58
She Gods of Shark Reef '56

Yves Montand (1921-91)
Jean de Florette '87
Manon of the Spring '87
Choice of Arms '83
Roads to the South '78
Vincent, François, Paul and the Others '76
Le Cercle Rouge '70
On a Clear Day You Can See Forever '70
Z '69
Grand Prix '66
Is Paris Burning? '66
La Guerre Est Finie '66
Le Joli Mai '62 (N)
My Geisha '62
Goodbye Again '61
Let's Make Love '60
Where the Hot Wind Blows '59
The Wages of Fear '55
Napoleon '55

Liliane Montevecchi (1932-)
King Creole '58
Me and the Colonel '58
The Young Lions '58
Meet Me in Las Vegas '56

Maria Montez (1918-51)
Portrait of an Assassin '49
Cobra Woman '44
Ali Baba and the Forty Thieves '43
Arabian Nights '42
Boss of Bullion City '41

Enrico Montesano (1945-)
Sotto, Sotto '85
Lobster for Breakfast '82

Elisa Montés (1936-)
The White Orchid '54
Return of the Magnificent Seven '66
Texas, Adios '66
Seven '66

Rosenda Monteros (1935-)
Cauldron of Blood '67
Mighty Jungle '64
Tiara Tahiti '62
Battle Shock '56
The Magnificent Seven '60

Fernanda Montenegro (1929-)
House of Sand '05
Central Station '98

Julia Montgomery (1960-)
Revenge of the Nerds 4: Nerds in Love '94
Revenge of the Nerds 3: The Next Generation '92
Revenge of the Nerds 2: Nerds in Paradise '87
Savage Justice '88
The Kindred '87
Stewardess School '86
Girls Just Want to Have Fun '85
Revenge of the Nerds '84
Up the Creek '84

Lee Montgomery (1961-)
Into the Fire '88
The Midnight Hour '86
Prime Risk '84
Mutant '83
Baker's Hawk '76
Savage Is Loose '74
Ben '72
Pete 'n' Tillie '72

George Montgomery (1916-2000)
From Hell to Borneo '64
Samar '62
The Steel Claw '61
Hostile Guns '67
Satan's Harvest '65
Battle of the Bulge '65
Indian Uprising '51
Sword of Monte Cristo '51
The Texas Rangers '51
Orchestra Wives '42
Roxie Hart '42
Young People '40

Elizabeth Montgomery (1933-95)
Deadline Assault '90
Missing Pieces '83
The Court Martial of Billy Mitchell '55

Monte Montana (1910-98)
Down Dakota Way '49
Circle of Death '36

Belinda J. Montgomery (1950-)
Stone Fox '87
Silent Madness '84
Blackout '78
The Man from Atlantis '77
The Todd Killings '71

Chuck Montgomery
Fay Grim '06
Amateur '94

Dan Montgomery, Jr. (1969-)
Club Dread '04
You Stupid Man '02
On the Line '01
The Last Man '00
Red Dirt '99

Robert Montgomery (1904-81)
Eye Witness '49
June Bride '48
Lady in the Lake '46
They Were Expendable '45
Here Comes Mr. Jordan '41
Mr. & Mrs. Smith '41
The Last of Mrs. Cheyney '37
Night Must Fall '37
Forsaking All Others '35
Hide-Out '34
Riptide '34
The Divorcee '30
Free and Easy '30
The Big House '30
Private Lives '31

Poppy Montgomery (1972-)
How to Lose Your Lover '04
Blonde '01
Life '99
The Other Sister '98
Dead Man on Campus '98

Silvia Monti (1946-)
Sicilian Connection '72
A Lizard in a Woman's Skin '71
The Brain '69

Douglass Montgomery (1907-66)
Harmony Lane '35
The Mystery of Edwin Drood '35
Little Women '33

Flora Montgomery (1974-)
Basic Instinct 2 '06
When Brendan Met Trudy '00

Luigi Montini (1934-)
Mediterraneo '91
Satanik '69

Pascale Montpetit (1961-)
Savage Messiah '02
Street Heat '98
Eclipse '94

Alex Montoya (1907-70)
Escape from Fort Bravo '53
West to Glory '47

Michael Monty (1936-2006)
The 13th Mission '91
My First Wife '84
Heatwave '83

King Moody (1929-2001)
The Dark Backward '91
Get Smart, Again! '89
Sweet November '69
Slash '87

Jim Moody (1943-)
Who's the Man? '93
Bad Boys '83
Some Kind of Hero '82
Home '33

Ben Moore
She-Freak '67

Lynne Moody (1948-)
A Certain Justice '99
Eclipse '94
Who's the Man? '93
H '90
Space '85
Roots: The Next Generation '79
Nightmare in Badham County '76
Scream Blacula Scream '73

Ralph Moody (1886-1971)
The Last Hunt '56
The Road to Bali '53

Ron Moody (1924-)
A Kid in King Arthur's Court '95
The Strange Case of the End of Civilization As We Know It '82
Wrong Is Right '82
Unidentified Flying Oddball '79
Dominique Is Dead '79
Dog Pound Shuffle '75
Legend of the Werewolf '75
David Copperfield '70
The Twelve Chairs '70
Oliver! '68
Murder Most Foul '65
The Mouse on the Moon '62

Keith Moon (1946-78)
Sextette '78
The Kids Are Alright '79
Tommy '75
That'll Be the Day '73
200 Motels '71

Sheri Moon (1970-)
The Devil's Rejects '05
House of 1000 Corpses '03

Dennis Mooney
Death Row Diner '88

Laura Mooney (1976-)
Little Nemo: Adventures in Slumberland '92 (V)
She's Out of Control '89

Paul Mooney
Bamboozled '00
Dance with a Stranger '85

Anna Maria Monticelli (1952-)
Nomads '86
The Empty Beach '85

Candy Moore (1947-)
Lunch Wagon '81
Tomboy & the Champ '58

Clayton Moore (1914-99)
Justice of the West '61
Lone Ranger '56
Jungle Drums of Africa '53
Radar Men from the Moon '52

Colleen Moore (1902-88)
The Scarlet Letter '34
Ella Cinders '26
Broken Hearts of Broadway '23

Constance Moore (1920-2005)
Delightfully Dangerous '45
Argentine Nights '40
Buck Rogers Conquers the Universe '39
Charlie McCarthy, Detective '39
Destination Saturn '39
Mutiny on the Blackhawk '39
You Can't Cheat an Honest Man '39

Deborah Maria Moore (1963-)
Jack Higgins' On Dangerous Ground '95
Jack Higgins' Midnight Man '96

Archie Moore (1913-)
The Carpetbaggers '64
The Adventures of Huckleberry Finn '60

Christine Moore
Lurkers '88

Christina Moore
Delta Farce '07
Without a Paddle '04

Alvy Moore (1921-97)
Intruder '88
They're Playing with Fire '84
Scream '83
Smokey & the Hotwire Gang '79
A Boy and His Dog '75
The Specialist '75
The Brotherhood of Satan '71
The Witchmaker '69
Move Over, Darling '63
Designing Woman '57
An Annapolis Story '55
The Wild One '54
The War of the Worlds '53

Del Moore (1917-70)
The Patsy '64
The Nutty Professor '63

Demi Moore (1962-)
Flawless '07
Mr. Brooks '07
Bobby '06
Half Light '05
Charlie's Angels: Full Throttle '03
Passion of Mind '00
Deconstructing Harry '97
G.I. Jane '97
Beavis and Butt-Head Do America '96 (V)
The Hunchback of Notre Dame '96 (V)
If These Walls Could Talk '96
The Juror '96
Striptease '96
Now and Then '95
The Scarlet Letter '95
Disclosure '94
Indecent Proposal '93
A Few Good Men '92
The Butcher's Wife '91
Mortal Thoughts '91
Nothing But Trouble '91
Ghost '90
We're No Angels '89
The Seventh Sign '88
Wisdom '87
About Last Night... '86
One Crazy Summer '86
St. Elmo's Fire '85
Blame It on Rio '84
No Small Affair '84
Parasite '82
Young Doctors in Love '82
Choices '81

Dennie Moore (1907-78)
Dive Bomber '41
Sylvia Scarlett '35

Dennis Moore (1908-64)
Tribute to a Bad Man '56
King of the Bullwhip '51
Range Renegades '48
The Tioga Kid '48
Colorado Serenade '46
Driftin' River '46
D-Day on Mars '45
Land of Hunted Men '43
Texas Justice '42
Arizona Bound '41
Border Roundup '41
Spooks Run Wild '41
East Side Kids '40
Rocky Mountain Rangers '40
Across the Plains '39
Mutiny in the Big House '39
Wild Horse Canyon '39

Dickie Moore (1925-)
Out of the Past '47
Heaven Can Wait '43
Miss Annie Rooney '42
Sergeant York '41
Jive Junction '43
The Gladiator '38
Little Red Schoolhouse '36
The World Accuses '35
Gabriel Over the White House '33
Oliver Twist '33
Blonde Venus '32

Dorothy Moore (1919-2005)
Blondie Meets the Boss '39
Blondie '38
Vivacious Lady '38

Dudley Moore (1935-2002)
A Weekend in the Country '96
The Disappearance of Kevin Johnson '95
Parallel Lives '94
The Pickle '93
Blame It on the Bellboy '92
Crazy People '90
The Adventures of Milo & Otis '89 (N)
Milo & Otis '89 (N)
Arthur 2: On the Rocks '88
Like Father, Like Son '87
Santa Claus: The Movie '85
Best Defense '84
Micki & Maude '84
Unfaithfully Yours '84
Lovesick '83
Six Weeks '82
Arthur '81
Wholly Moses! '80
10 '79
Foul Play '78
The Hound of the Baskervilles '77
Those Daring Young Men in Their Jaunty Jalopies '69
Bedazzled '68
30 Is a Dangerous Age, Cynthia '68
The Wrong Box '66

Duke Moore (1913-76)
The Sinister Urge '60
Night of the Ghouls '59
Plan 9 from Outer Space '56

Frank Moore
Blood & Donuts '95
Hostage for a Day '94
Kings and Desperate Men '83
Rabid '77

Gar Moore (1920-85)
The Underworld Story '50
Abbott and Costello Meet the Killer, Boris Karloff '49
Paisan '46

Ida Moore (1882-1964)
Rock-A-Bye Baby '57
Leave It to the Marines '51
Money Madness '47

Jeanie Moore
Dream Trap '90

Joanna Moore (1934-97)
The Final Alliance '89
Vampire at Midnight '88
Countdown '68
Never a Dull Moment '68
Son of Flubber '63
Follow That Dream '61
Monster on the Campus '59
Touch of Evil '58

Joel David Moore (1977-)
The Dead One '07
Shanghai Kiss '07
Spiral '07
Art School Confidential '06
Grandma's Boy '06
Dodgeball: A True Underdog Story '04

Julianne Moore (1961-)
I'm Not There '07
Next '07
Children of Men '06
Freedomland '06
Trust the Man '06
The Prize Winner of Defiance, Ohio '05
The Forgotten '04
Laws of Attraction '04
The Hours '02
Evolution '01
Hannibal '01
The Shipping News '01
World Traveler '01
The Ladies Man '00
Cookie's Fortune '99
The End of the Affair '99
An Ideal Husband '99
Magnolia '99
A Map of the World '99
Chicago Cab '98
Psycho '98
The Big Lebowski '97
Boogie Nights '97
The Lost World: Jurassic Park 2 '97
The Myth of Fingerprints '97
Surviving Picasso '96
Assassins '95
Nine Months '95
Roommates '95
Safe '95
Vanya on 42nd Street '94
Benny & Joon '93
The Fugitive '93
Short Cuts '93
Body of Evidence '92
The Gun in Betty Lou's Handbag '92
The Hand that Rocks the Cradle '92

Kaycee Moore
Daughters of the Dust '91

Kenya Moore (1971-)
I Know Who Killed Me '07
No Turning Back '01
Senseless '98

Kieron Moore (1924-2007)
Arabesque '66
The Thin Red Line '64
Day of the Triffids '63
Doctor Blood's Coffin '62
The 300 Spartans '62
Darby O'Gill & the Little People '59
The Key '58
David and Bathsheba '51
Anna Karenina '48
A Man About the House '47
Mine Own Executioner '47

Lisa Bronwyn Moore
I'm Not There '07
The Aviator '04
Head in the Clouds '04
Mambo Italiano '03
The Reagans '03

Mandy Moore (1984-)
Because I Said So '07
Dedication '07
License to Wed '07
American Dreamz '06
Brother Bear 2 '06 (V)
Southland Tales '06
Racing Stripes '05 (V)
Romance & Cigarettes '05
Chasing Liberty '04
Saved! '04
How to Deal '03
All I Want '02
A Walk to Remember '02
The Princess Diaries '01

Mary Moore
Murder at 1600 '97
D-Day on Mars '45

Mary Tyler Moore (1937-)
Labor Pains '99
Keys to Tulsa '96
Flirting with Disaster '95
The Last Best Year '90
Gore Vidal's Lincoln '88
Just Between Friends '86
Finnegan Begin Again '84
Six Weeks '82
Ordinary People '80
Change of Habit '69
Thoroughly Modern Millie '67

Matt Moore (1888-1960)
An Affair to Remember '57
I Bury the Living '58
Deluge '33
Consolation Marriage '31
Coquette '29
The Unholy Three '25
White Tiger '23
Pride of the Clan '18
20,000 Leagues under the Sea '16
Traffic in Souls '13

Melba Moore (1945-)
The Fighting Temptations '03
All Dogs Go to Heaven '89 (V)
Charlotte Forten's Mission: Experiment in Freedom '85

Melissa Moore (1963-)
Stormswept '95
Evil Lives '92
Sorority House Massacre 2: Nighty Nightmare '92
Hard to Die '90
The Invisible Maniac '90
The Killing Zone '90
Vampire Cop '90
Scream Dream '89

Michael Moore (1954-)
The Fever '04
Lucky Numbers '00
The Insider '99
The Big One '98 (N)
Canadian Bacon '94
Roger & Me '89

Norma Moore (1935-)
Poor White Trash 2 '75
Fear Strikes Out '57

Owen Moore (1887-1939)
She Done Him Wrong '33
As You Desire Me '32
Married? '26

Pauline Moore (1914-2001)
Motorcycle Squad '41
Carson City Kid '40
Young Buffalo Bill '40
Charlie Chan at Treasure Island '39
Days of Jesse James '39
The Three Musketeers '39
Charlie Chan at the Olympics '37

Richard Moore (1925-)

R.J. (Geoffrey) Moore (1966-)
Fit to Kill '93
Hard Hunted '92

Roger Moore (1928-)
Boat Trip '03
The Enemy '01
D.R.E.A.M. Team '99
Spice World: The Movie '97
The Quest '96
Bed & Breakfast '92
Fire, Ice and Dynamite '91
Bullseye! '90
A View to a Kill '85
The Naked Face '84
Octopussy '83
Cannonball Run '81
For Your Eyes Only '81
Sea Wolves '80
ffolkes '80
Moonraker '79
Escape to Athena '79
Wild Geese '78
The Spy Who Loved Me '77
Shout at the Devil '76
Street People '76
That Lucky Touch '75
The Man with the Golden Gun '74
Live and Let Die '73
The Man Who Haunted Himself '70
The Saint '68
Vendetta for the Saint '68
Fiction Makers '67
The Rape of the Sabines '61
Diane '55
Interrupted Melody '55
The King's Thief '55
The Last Time I Saw Paris '54

Rudy Ray Moore (1937-)
Vampire Assassin '05
Devil's Son-in-Law '77
Monkey Hustle '77
Avenging Disco Godfather '76
Dolemite 2: Human Tornado '76
Dolemite '75

Sam Moore (1935-)
Night at the Golden Eagle '02

Shemar Moore (1970-)
Diary of a Mad Black Woman '05
Motives '03
The Brothers '01
Mama Flora's Family '98
Never 2 Big '98

Shiela Moore (1938-)
The Reflecting Skin '91
Bye Bye Blues '89
Overdrawn at the Memory Bank '83

Stephan Campbell Moore (1979-)
Amazing Grace '06
The History Boys '06
A Good Woman '04
Bright Young Things '03

Stephen Moore (1937-)
Clockwise '86
Under Suspicion '92

Tedde Moore
A Christmas Story '83
Second Wind '76

Terry Moore (1929-)
The Still '07
Kill Your Darlings '06
Second Chances '98
Beverly Hills Brats '89
Death Blow '87
Hellhole '85
Kill Factor '78
Platinum High School '60
Peyton Place '57
Between Heaven and Hell '56
Postmark for Danger '56
Daddy Long Legs '55
Shack Out on 101 '55
Beneath the 12-Mile Reef '53
Come Back, Little Sheba '52
The Great Rupert '50
Mighty Joe Young '49
Gaslight '44
Since You Went Away '44

Toby Moore
A Separate Peace '04
Murder in Greenwich '02

Victor Moore (1876-1962)
The Seven Year Itch '55
We're Not Married '52
On Our Merry Way '48
Ziegfeld Follies '46
The Heat's On '43
Star Spangled Rhythm '42
Louisiana Purchase '41
Swing Time '36

Agnes Moorehead (1906-74)
Charlotte's Web '73 (V)
Dear Dead Delilah '72
What's the Matter with Helen? '71
Bachelor in Paradise '69
The Ballad of Andy Crocker '69
Alice Through the Looking Glass '66
The Singing Nun '66
Hush, Hush, Sweet Charlotte '65
How the West Was Won '63
Who's Minding the Store? '63
Pollyanna '60
The Bat '59
Raintree County '57
The Conqueror '56
Meet Me in Las Vegas '56
The Opposite Sex '56
Pardners '56
All That Heaven Allows '55
The Left Hand of God '55
Magnificent Obsession '54
Main Street to Broadway '53
Adventures of Captain Fabian '51
Captain Blackjack '51
Show Boat '51
Caged '50
The Stratton Story '49
Johnny Belinda '48
Station West '48
Summer Holiday '48
Dark Passage '47
Lost Moment '47
Our Vines Have Tender Grapes '45
Dragon Seed '44
Jane Eyre '44
Mrs. Parkington '44
The Seventh Cross '44
Since You Went Away '44
Tomorrow the World '44
Big Street '42
Journey into Fear '42
The Magnificent Ambersons '42
Citizen Kane '41

Natalie Moorhead (1901-92)
The Thin Man '34
Dancing Man '33
The King Murder '32
Murder on the High Seas '32
Illicit '31
Morals for Women '31
Hook, Line and Sinker '30

Tiriel Mora (1958-)
Garage Days '03
The Castle '97

Esai Morales (1962-)
Fast Food Nation '06
How to Go Out on a Date in Queens '06
Once Upon a Wedding '05
Paid in Full '02
Atomic Train '99
The Wonderful Ice Cream Suit '98
Dogwatch '97
The Real Thing '97
The Disappearance of Garcia Lorca '96
Scorpion Spring '96
The Burning Season '94
Deadlock 2 '94
Don't Do It '94
In the Army Now '94
My Family '94
Rapa Nui '93
Freejack '92
Naked Tango '91
Ultraviolet '91
Bloodhounds of Broadway '89
La Bamba '87
The Principal '87
On Wings of Eagles '86
L.A. Bad '85
Bad Boys '83

Ines Morales
Curse of the Devil '73
House of Psychotic Women '73

Santos Morales
Hot to Trot '88
The Boys in Company C '77

Dan Moran
Rick '03
Mob Queen '98

Dolores Moran (1924-82)
The Man I Love '46
The Horn Blows at Midnight '45
To Have & Have Not '44

Dylan Moran (1971-)
Run, Fat Boy, Run '07
Tristram Shandy: A Cock and Bull Story '05
Shaun of the Dead '04

Erin Moran (1951-)
Galaxy of Terror '81
Twirl '81
Watermelon Man '70
How Sweet It Is! '68

Frank Moran (1887-1967)
Return of the Ape Man '44
Motorcycle Squad '41
Old Swimmin' Hole '40
Ships in the Night '28

Jackie Moran (1923-90)
Since You Went Away '44
Let's Go Collegiate '41
Old Swimmin' Hole '40
Tomboy '40
Buck Rogers Conquers the Universe '39
The Adventures of Tom Sawyer '38
Mad About Music '38

Lee Moran (1890-1961)
High Gear '33
Pardon My Gun '30
My Lady of Whims '25
The Tomboy '24

Nick Moran (1969-)
Silent Partner '05
Chaos & Cadavre's '03
The Musketeer '01
The Proposal '00
New Blood '99
Lock, Stock and 2 Smoking Barrels '98

Pat Moran
Desperate Living '77
Female Trouble '74
Pink Flamingos '72
Multiple Maniacs '70

Patrick Moran (1960-)
Biohazard: The Alien Force '95

Peggy Moran (1918-2002)
Argentine Nights '43
The Mummy's Hand '40
One Night in the Tropics '40

Polly Moran (1883-1952)
Adam's Rib '50
Hollywood Party '34

Rob Moran (1963-)
Shallow Hal '01
Me, Myself, and Irene '00
There's Something about Mary '98
Kingpin '96
Mary '98
Dumb & Dumber '94

Rick Moranis (1954-)
Brother Bear '03 (V)
Brother Bear 2 '06 (V)
The Flintstones '94
Little Giants '94
Splitting Heirs '93
Honey, I Blew Up the Kid '92
Big Bully '95
Honey, We Shrunk Ourselves '97
My Blue Heaven '90
Ghostbusters 2 '89
Honey, I Shrunk the Kids '89
Parenthood '89
Spaceballs '86
Club Paradise '86
Head Office '86
Little Shop of Horrors '86
Brewster's Millions '85
Ghostbusters '84
The Last Polka '84
Hockey Night '84
Streets of Fire '84
The Wild Life '84
Strange Brew '83

Richard Morant (1945-)
Scandal '89
John & Yoko: A Love Story '85
Poldark '75
Mahler '74

Laura Morante (1956-)
Molière '07
Avenue Montaigne '06
Private Fears in Public Places '06
The Dancer Upstairs '02
The Son's Room '00
The Tragedy of a Ridiculous Man '81

Milburn (Milt) Morante (1887-1964)
Ghost Rider '43
Between Men '35

Kestie Morassi
Wolf Creek '05
Dirty Deeds '02
Strange Bedfellows '04

Kenneth More (1914-82)
A Tale of Two Cities '80
Unidentified Flying Oddball '79
Leopard in the Snow '78
Where Time Began '77
The Slipper and the Rose '76
Scrooge '70
Battle of Britain '69
Oh! What a Lovely War '69
Dark of the Sun '68
The Longest Day '62
Flame Over India '60
Sink the Bismarck '60
The Sheriff of Fractured Jaw '59
A Night to Remember '58
The Admirable Crichton '57
Reach for the Sky '56
The Adventures of Sadie '55
Doctor in the House '53
Genevieve '53
Never Let Me Go '53
The Clouded Yellow '51
No Highway in the Sky '51
Morning Departure '50
Man on the Run '49
Scott of the Antarctic '48

Jeanne Moreau (1928-)
Go West '05
Time to Leave '05
Balzac: A Life of Passion '99
Ever After: A Cinderella Story '98
I Love You, I Love You Not '97
The Proprietor '96
Beyond the Clouds '95
Catherine the Great '95
The Summer House '94
A Foreign Field '93
Map of the Human Heart '93
Alberto Express '92
The Lover '92 (N)
La Femme Nikita '91
The Old Lady Who Walked in the Sea '91
Until the End of the World '91
Heat of Desire '84
Your Ticket Is No Longer Valid '84
La Truite '83
Querelle '83
The Last Tycoon '76
Lumiere '76
Mr. Klein '76
Going Places '74
The Train '65
Viva Maria! '65
Diary of a Chambermaid '64
The Fire Within '64
The Trial '63
The Victors '63
Eva '62
Jules and Jim '62
The 400 Blows '59
The Lovers '59
Back to the Wall '56
Grisbi '53

Marguerite Moreau (1977-)
Off the Lip '04
Runaway Jury '03
Two Days '03
Firestarter 2: Rekindled '02
The Locket '02
Queen of the Damned '02
Wet Hot American Summer '01

Marsha Moreau
The Last Winter '89

Nathaniel Moreau
Miracle at Moreaux '86
George's Island '91

Sylvie Moreau (1964-)
The Last Winter '89
The Widow of Saint-Pierre '00

Yolande Moreau (1953-)
Paris, je t'aime '06
Amelie '01
Vagabond '85

Mantan Moreland (1902-73)
The Young Nurses '73
Spider Baby '64
Juke Joint '47
Tall, Tan and Terrific '46
The Jade Mask '45
The Scarlet Clue '45
The Shanghai Cobra '45
Charlie Chan in the Secret Service '44
The Chinese Cat '44
Meeting at Midnight '44
Revenge of the Zombies '43
Footlight Serenade '42
Law of the Jungle '42
Phantom Killer '42
Cracked Nuts '41
The Gang's All Here '41
Let's Go Collegiate '41
King of the Zombies '41
Up in the Air '40
Frontier Scout '38
Harlem on the Prairie '38
Two-Gun Man from Harlem '38
The Spirit of Youth '37

Elizabeth Morehead
Sand Trap '92
Interceptor '92

Nanni Moretti (1953-)
The Son's Room '00
Caro Diario '93
Palombella Rossa '89

Michele Moretti (1977-)
Apres-Vous '03
Wild Reeds '94

Chloe Grace Moretz (1997-)
The Eye '08
Big Momma's House 2 '06
The Amityville Horror '05

Andre Morell (1909-78)
10 Rillington Place '71
Dark of the Sun '68
Plague of the Zombies '66
Woman of Straw '64
The Hound of the Baskervilles '59
Quatermass and the Pit '58
The Bridge on the River Kwai '57
The Man Who Never Was '55

Rina Morelli (1908-)
The Leopard '63
Il Bell'Antonio '60

Antonio Moreno (1887-1967)
The Searchers '56
Creature from the Black Lagoon '54
Captain from Castile '47
Valley of the Sun '42
Rose of Rio Grande '38

Catalina Sandino Moreno (1981-)
Love in the Time of Cholera '07
Fast Food Nation '06
The Hottest State '06
Paris, je t'aime '06
Maria Full of Grace '04

Jose Elias Moreno (1910-69)
Santa Claus '59
Night of the Bloody Apes '68

Lea Moreno (1977-)
Doom Runners '97

Rene L. Moreno (1969-)
Jungle Boy '96
Band of Brothers '01

Rita Moreno (1931-)
Tequila Body Shots '99
King of the Corner '04
Casa de los Babys '03
Blue Moon '00
Slums of Beverly Hills '98
The Spree '96
Angus '95
I Like It Like That '94
Italian Movie '93
Age Isn't Everything '91
Portrait of a Showgirl '82
The Four Seasons '81
Happy Birthday, Gemini '80
Anatomy of a Seduction '79
The Boss' Son '78
The Ritz '76
Carnal Knowledge '71
Marlowe '69
Popi '69
Cry of Battle '63
Summer and Smoke '61
West Side Story '61
The King and I '56
Seven Cities of Gold '55
Garden of Evil '54
The Ring '52
Singin' in the Rain '52
Pagan Love Song '50
The Toast of New Orleans '50

Frank Morgan (1890-1949)
Key to the City '50
Any Number Can Play '49
The Stratton Story '49
Summer Holiday '48
The Three Musketeers '48
The White Cliffs of Dover '44
Casanova Brown '44
The Human Comedy '43
Thousands Cheer '43
Tortilla Flat '42
White Cargo '42
Honky Tonk '41
Boom Town '40
Broadway Melody of 1940 '40
The Mortal Storm '40
The Shop Around the Corner '40
Balalaika '39
Broadway Serenade '39
The Wizard of Oz '39
Sweethearts '38
Rosalie '37
Saratoga '37
The Last of Mrs. Cheyney '37
Dancing Pirate '36
Dimples '36
The Great Ziegfeld '36
The Good Fairy '35
Naughty Marietta '35
The Cat and the Fiddle '34
The Half Naked Truth '32
Manhandled '24

Debbi (Deborah) Morgan (1956-)
Back in the Day '05
Coach Carter '05
Love and Basketball '00
The Runaway '00
The Hurricane '99
Asunder '99
Eve's Bayou '97
Guilty of Innocence '87
The Jesse Owens Story '84
Monkey Hustle '77

Dennis Morgan (1910-94)
Pearl of the South Pacific '55
It's a Great Feeling '49
Christmas in Connecticut '45
God Is My Co-Pilot '45
Captains of the Clouds '42
In This Our Life '42
The Fighting 69th '40
Kitty Foyle '40
Waterfront '39

Cindy Morgan (1954-)
Tron '82
Caddyshack '80

Clive Morgan (1896-1984)
Gunga Din '39
The Lives of a Bengal Lancer '35

Chesty Morgan (1928-)
Double Agent 73 '80
Deadly Weapons '70

Chad Morgan
Taken '02
Whatever '98

Boyd 'Red' Morgan (1915-88)
Dragnet '87
The Incident '89

George Morfogen (1933-)
Twenty Bucks '93
Deadly Business '86
Man '60

Gary Morgan (1950-)
The Power Within '95
Storybook '95

Harry (Henry) Morgan (1915-)
Dragnet '87
The Amazing Transparent Man '60
Buckaroo Banzai Across the Eighth Dimension '84
Agatha Christie's Sparkling Cyanide '83
M*A*S*H: Goodbye, Farewell & Amen '83
Roughnecks '80
Scout's Honor '80
The Apple Dumpling Gang Rides Again '79
Backstairs at the White House '79
Better Late Than Never '79
Roots: The Next Generation '79
Wild, Wild West Revisited '79
The Shootist '76
The Apple Dumpling Gang '75
Charley and the Angel '73
Snowball Express '72
Scandalous John '71
Support Your Local Gunfighter '71
The Barefoot Executive '71
Support Your Local Sheriff '69
Flim-Flam Man '67
What Did You Do in the War, Daddy? '66
Frankie and Johnny '65
How the West Was Won '63
The Mountain Road '60
Inherit the Wind '60
It Started with a Kiss '59
The Teahouse of the August Moon '56
Far Country '55
The Glenn Miller Story '54
Torch Song '53
Bend of the River '52
High Noon '52
The Well '51
The Showdown '50
Holiday Affair '49
All My Sons '48
The Big Clock '48
The Gangster '47
State Fair '45
A Wing and a Prayer '44
Crash Dive '43
The Ox-Bow Incident '43
Orchestra Wives '42
To the Shores of Tripoli '42
The Smallest Show on Earth '48

Helen Morgan (1900-41)
Frankie and Johnny '36
Show Boat '36
Marie Galante '34
Applause '29

Jaye P. Morgan (1931-)
Confessions of a Dangerous Mind '02
Night Patrol '85

Jeffrey Dean Morgan (1966-)
P.S. I Love You '07
Jam '06
Legal Deceit '95
Undercover '94
Uncaged '91

Melissa Morgan
See Liz Renay

Michele Morgan (1920-)
The Other Brother '02
Everybody's Fine '90
Cat and Mouse '78
The Lost Command '66
Bluebeard '63

Les Grandes Manoeuvres '55
The Proud Ones '53
The Fallen Idol '49
Fabiola '48
The Chase '46
La Symphonie Pastorale '46
Higher and Higher '44
Passage to Marseilles '44
Heart of a Nation '43
Joan of Paris '42
Stormy Waters '41

Nancy Morgan (1949-)
Lucky Luke '94
Danielle Steel's Heartbeat '93
The Nest '88
Pray TV '80
Americathon '79
Backstairs at the White House '79
Grand Theft Auto '77

Ralph Morgan (1882-1956)
Heart of the Rockies '51
The Creeper '48
Song of the Thin Man '47
Enemy of Women '44
The Monster Maker '44
Gang Busters '42
Night Monster '42
Dick Tracy vs. Crime Inc. '41
Way Down South '39
Shadows over Shanghai '38
Mannequin '37
General Spanky '36
Yellowstone '36
Condemned to Live '35
Transatlantic Merry-Go-Round '34
The Kennel Murder Case '33
Rasputin and the Empress '33
Strange Interlude '32

Richard Morgan (1958-2006)
The Wicked '89
Innocent Prey '88

Shelley Taylor Morgan
Malibu Express '85
My Tutor '82

Stafford Morgan
The Capture of Bigfoot '79
The Alpha Incident '76

Terence Morgan (1921-2005)
The Lifetaker '89
Svengali '55
The Love of Three Queens '54

Tracy Morgan (1968-)
First Sunday '08
Little Man '06
Are We There Yet? '05
The Longest Yard '05
Head of State '03
Frank McKlusky, C.I. '02
30 Years to Life '01
Half-Baked '97
A Thin Line Between Love and Hate '96

Trevor Morgan (1986-)
The Prize Winner of Defiance, Ohio '05
Mean Creek '04
Uncle Nino '03
The Rookie '02
The Glass House '01
Jurassic Park 3 '01
The Patriot '00
A Rumor of Angels '00
I'll Remember April '99
The Sixth Sense '99
Barney's Great Adventure '98
In the Doghouse '98

Wendy Morgan
Pictures '80s
The Mirror Crack'd '80

Maia Morgenstern (1962-)
The Passion of the Christ '04
Ulysses' Gaze '95
The Oak '93
Trahir '93

Stephanie Morgenstern (1965-)
Cafe Ole '00
Maelstrom '00
P.T. Barnum '99

Masayuki Mori (1911-73)
The Bad Sleep Well '60
When a Woman Ascends the Stairs '60
Princess Yang Kwei Fei '55
Ugetsu '53
The Idiot '51
Rashomon '51

Toshia Mori (1912-95)
The Bitter Tea of General Yen '33
The Secrets of Wu Sin '32

Pat Moriarity (1896-1962)
Kings Row '41
Mutiny in the Big House '39

Cathy Moriarty (1961-)
Analyze That '02
Prince of Central Park '00
But I'm a Cheerleader '99
Crazy in Alabama '99
The Crimson Code '99
New Waterford Girl '99
Digging to China '98
P.U.N.K.S. '98
A Brother's Kiss '97
Cop Land '97
Dream with the Fishes '97
Hugo Pool '97
Foxfire '96
Opposite Corners '96
Casper '95
Forget Paris '95
Pontiac Moon '94
Runaway Daughters '94
Another Stakeout '93
Me and the Kid '93
The Gun in Betty Lou's Handbag '92
The Mambo Kings '92
Matinee '92
Soapdish '91
Kindergarten Cop '90
Burndown '89
White of the Eye '88
Neighbors '81
Raging Bull '80

James Moriarty
Ten Benny '97

Michael Moriarty (1941-)
Taken '02
Along Came a Spider '01
James Dean '01
Mindstorm '01
Cold Blooded '00
The Art of Murder '99
Shiloh 2: Shiloh Season '99
Woman Wanted '98
Shiloh '97
Calm at Sunset '96
Courage Under Fire '96
Crime of the Century '96
A Good Day to Die '95
Full Fathom Five '90
Secret of the Ice Cave '89
Tailspin: Behind the Korean Airline Tragedy '89
Nitti: The Enforcer '88
Windmills of the Gods '88
Dark Tower '87
Hanoi Hilton '87
It's Alive 3: Island of the Alive '87
Return to Salem's Lot '87
Bloodlink '86
Troll '86
Odd Birds '85
Pale Rider '85
The Stuff '85
Q (The Winged Serpent) '82
Sound of Murder '82
Reborn '81
Too Far to Go '79
Holocaust '78
Who'll Stop the Rain? '78
The Winds of Kitty Hawk '78
Report to the Commissioner '74
Shoot It Black, Shoot It Blue '74
Bang the Drum Slowly '73
The Last Detail '73
My Old Man's Place '71

P. H. Moriarty (1939-)
Children of Dune '03
Dune '00
Lock, Stock and 2 Smoking Barrels '98
The Long Good Friday '80

Tara Morice (1964-)
Salem's Lot '04
Sorrento Beach '95
Metal Skin '94
Strictly Ballroom '92

Philippe Morier-Genoud
Time Regained '99
Trois Couleurs: Blanc '94
Cyrano de Bergerac '90
Au Revoir les Enfants '87
Confidentially Yours '83

Johnny Morina
Home Team '98
Kids of the Round Table '96
The Other Side of the Law '95

Patricia Morison (1914-)
Song Without End '60
The Prince of Thieves '48
Return of Wildfire '48
Queen of the Amazons '47
Song of the Thin Man '47
Dressed to Kill '46
Without Love '45
The Fallen Sparrow '43
The Roundup '41

Alanis Morissette (1974-)
Jay and Silent Bob Strike Back '01
Dogma '99

Noriyuki "Pat" Morita (1932-2005)
18 Fingers of Death '05
Elvis Has Left the Building '04
Karate Dog '04
The Biggest Fan '02
Desert Heat '99
I'll Remember April '99
King Cobra '98
Mulan '98 (V)
Bloodsport 3 '97
Bloodsport 2: The Next Kumite '95
Timemaster '95
Even Cowgirls Get the Blues '94
The Next Karate Kid '94
North '94
Auntie Lee's Meat Pies '92
Honeymoon in Vegas '92
Mastergate '92
Miracle Beach '92
Do or Die '91
Hiroshima: Out of the Ashes '90
Lena's Holiday '90
Collision Course '89
The Karate Kid: Part 3 '89
Captive Hearts '87
Babes in Toyland '86
The Karate Kid: Part 2 '86
Alice in Wonderland '85
Amos '85
Night Patrol '85
The Karate Kid '84
Slapstick of Another Kind '84
The Vegas Strip Wars '84
For the Love of It '80
When Time Ran Out '80
I Wonder Who's Killing Her Now? '76
Midway '76
Cancel My Reservation '72
Evil Roy Slade '72
The Shakiest Gun in the West '68
Thoroughly Modern Millie '67

Louisa Moritz (1946-)
Chained Heat '83
Last American Virgin '82
True Confessions '81
New Year's Evil '78
Death Race 2000 '75
One Flew Over the Cuckoo's Nest '75

Henning Moritzen (1928-)
Allegro '05
The Celebration '98
Sofie '92
Memories of a Marriage '90
Cries and Whispers '72

Yuko Moriyama (1968-)
Zeram 2 '94
Zeram '91

Karen Morley (1909-2003)
Beloved Enemy '36
Healer '36
The Littlest Rebel '35
Our Daily Bread '34
Dinner at Eight '33
Gabriel Over the White House '33
The Mask of Fu Manchu '32
Mata Hari '32
Scarface '31
The Sin of Madelon Claudet '31

Robert Morley (1908-92)
A Troll in Central Park '94 (V)
Istanbul '90
Around the World in 80 Days '89
The Lady and the Highwayman '89
War & Remembrance: The Final Chapter '89
Little Dorrit, Film 1: Nobody's Fault '88
Little Dorrit, Film 2: Little Dorrit's Story '88
War & Remembrance '88
The Trouble with Spies '87
Alice in Wonderland '85
Second Time Lucky '84
High Road to China '83
Loophole '83
Deadly Game '82
The Great Muppet Caper '81
Oh, Heavenly Dog! '80
The Human Factor '79
Scavenger Hunt '79
Who Is Killing the Great Chefs of Europe? '78
Hugo the Hippo '76 (V)
Theatre of Blood '73
When Eight Bells Toll '71
Cromwell '70
Song of Norway '70
Lola '69
Hot Millions '68
Woman Times Seven '67
A Study in Terror '66
The Alphabet Murders '65
The Loved One '65
Those Magnificent Men in Their Flying Machines '65
Of Human Bondage '64
Topkapi '64
Ladies Who Do '63
Murder at the Gallop '63
The Battle of the Sexes '60
Around the World in 80 Days '56
Beau Brummel '54
Beat the Devil '53
Curtain Up '53
The African Queen '51
The Small Back Room '49
Ghosts of Berkeley Square '47
I Live in Grosvenor Square '46
The Foreman Went to France '42
Major Barbara '41
Marie Antoinette '38

Stanley Morner
See Dennis Morgan

Alicia Moro
Hot Blood '89
Slugs '87
Exterminators in the Year 3000 '83

Mike Moroff
Three Bad Men '05
The Crew '00
My Little Assassin '99
The Wonderful Ice Cream Suit '98
Angel Town '89
The Cage '89

Michael Morra
See Rockets Redglare

Priscilla Morrill (1927-94)
Right of Way '84
The People vs. Jean Harris '81

Adrian Morris (1903-41)
Angels with Dirty Faces '38
Radio Patrol '37

Anita Morris (1944-94)
Radioland Murders '94
Home for Christmas '93
Me and the Kid '93
Martians Go Home! '90
Off and Running '90
Bloodhounds of Broadway '89
A Sinful Life '89
Aria '88
18 Again! '88
Absolute Beginners '86
Blue City '86
Ruthless People '86
A Smoky Mountain Christmas '86
The Hotel New Hampshire '84
Maria's Lovers '84

Aubrey Morris (1930-)
She Creature '01
The St. Valentine's Day Massacre '67
Lifeforce '85
Lisztomania '75
A Clockwork Orange '71
Night Caller from Outer Space '66

Barboura Morris (1932-75)
The Dunwich Horror '70
The Haunted Palace '63
X: The Man with X-Ray Eyes '63
Atlas '60
A Bucket of Blood '59
The Wasp Woman '59
Machine Gun Kelly '58
Sorority Girl '57
Teenage Doll '57

Beth Morris (1949-)
That'll Be the Day '73
Crucible of Terror '72

Chester Morris (1901-70)
The Great White Hope '70
Gambler's Choice '44
Wagon's Westward '40
Five Came Back '39
Law of the Underworld '38
Smashing the Rackets '38
Flight from Glory '37
I Promise to Pay '37
Frankie and Johnny '36
They Met in a Taxi '36
Tomorrow at Seven '33
Red Headed Woman '32
Sinners in the Sun '32
Corsair '31
The Bat Whispers '30
The Big House '30
The Divorcee '30
Playing Around '30
Alibi '29

Colleen Morris
Prehysteria '93
Crossing the Line '90

Dorothy Morris (1922-)
Club Havana '46
Thirty Seconds Over Tokyo '44
Bataan '43

Frances Morris
Boss Cowboy '35
Pals of the Range '35

Garrett Morris (1944-)
The Salon '05
Jackpot '01
Little Richard '00
Twin Falls Idaho '99
Black Scorpion 2: Ground Zero '96
Santa with Muscles '96
Black Scorpion '95
Machine Gun Blues '95
Almost Blue '93
Children of the Night '92
Severed Ties '92
Motorama '91
The Underachievers '88
Husbands, Wives, Money, and Murder '86
The Stuff '85
Cooley High '75
The Anderson Tapes '71
Where's Poppa? '70

Greg Morris (1934-96)
Vegas '78
The Doomsday Flight '66

Haviland (Haylie) Morris (1959-)
Cherry Crush '07
Rick '03
Home Alone 3 '97
Larry McMurtry's Dead Man's Walk '96
Gremlins 2: The New Batch '90
For Love or Money '88
Who's That Girl? '87
Sixteen Candles '84

Howard Morris (1919-2005)
The Wonderful Ice Cream Suit '98
It Came from Outer Space 2 '95
Tom and Jerry: The Movie '93 (V)
Life Stinks '91
End of the Line '88
Splash '84
Portrait of a Showgirl '82
History of the World: Part 1 '81
The Munsters' Revenge '81
High Anxiety '77
The Many Adventures of Winnie the Pooh '77 (V)
The Nutty Professor '63
40 Pounds of Trouble '62

Iona Morris (1957-)
Next Time '99

Jane Morris
Pet Shop '94
Frankie and Johnny '91
Pretty Woman '90
Nothing in Common '86

Jeff Morris (1934-2004)
The Crossing Guard '94
Payday '73
Kelly's Heroes '70

John Morris (1926-)
Toy Story 2 '99 (V)
Toy Story '95 (V)
Beyond Innocence '87

Jonathan Morris (1960-)
Bloodstorm: Subspecies 4 '98
Vampire Journals '96
The Fantasticks '95
Best Enemies '86
Razorback '84
In Search of Anna '79
Plumber '79
Cass '78
Between Wars '74

Judy Morris (1947-)
Phar Lap '84

Julian Morris (1983-)
CryWolf '05
Whirlygirl '04

Kathryn Morris (1969-)
Resurrecting the Champ '07
Mindhunters '05
Minority Report '02
Inferno '98
Sleepstalker: The Sandman's Last Rites '94

Lana Morris (1930-98)
The Woman in Question '50

Mary Morris (1915-88)
The Gay Lady '49
The Weaker Sex '49
Train of Events '49
Pimpernel Smith '42
The Thief of Bagdad '40

Kirk Morris (1938-)
Terror of the Steppes '64
Devil of the Desert Against the Son of Hercules '62
Maciste in Hell '62

Phil Morris (1959-)
Meet the Spartans '08
Bottoms Up '06
Comic Book: The Movie '04
Atlantis: The Lost Empire '01 (V)
Clay Pigeons '98
Devil in the Flesh '98
Legal Deceit '95
P.I. Private Investigations '87

Robert Morris (1940-)
One Deadly Owner '74
Frankenstein Created Woman '66

Wayne Morris (1914-59)
Paths of Glory '57
Plunder Road '57
Lonesome Trail '55
The Bushwackers '52
Task Force '49
Kid Galahad '37

Jenny (Jennifer) Morrison (1979-)
Flourish '06
Surviving Christmas '04
Grind '03
Big Shot: Confessions of a Campus Bookie '02
Urban Legends 2: Final Cut '00
Stir of Echoes '99
Intersection '93

Kenny Morrison (1974-)
Little Athens '05
NeverEnding Story 2: The Next Chapter '91
The Quick and the Dead '87

Sammy (Earnest) Morrison (1912-89)
Follow the Leader '44
'Neath Brooklyn Bridge '42
Flying Wild '41
Spooks Run Wild '41

Pete Morrison (1890-1973)
Trailing Trouble '30
Trigger Tricks '30

Max Morrow (1991-)
That Russell Girl '08

Shelley Morrison (1936-)
Devil Times Five '74
Castle of Evil '66

Temuera Morrison (1961-)
Star Wars: Episode III – Revenge of the Sith '05
The Beautiful Country '04
Star Wars: Episode II – Attack of the Clones '02
Vertical Limit '00
From Dusk Till Dawn 3: The Hangman's Daughter '99
Six Days, Seven Nights '98
Speed 2: Cruise Control '97
Barb Wire '96
The Island of Dr. Moreau '96
Once Were Warriors '94

Billy Morrissette
Get a Clue! '98
Severed Ties '92

David Morrissey (1963-)
The Other Boleyn Girl '08
The Reaping '07
Sense & Sensibility '08
The Water Horse: Legend of the Deep '07
Basic Instinct 2 '06
Derailed '05
Stoned '05
State of Play '03
Captain Corelli's Mandolin '01

Neil Morrissey (1962-)
Triggermen '02
The Match '99
Being Human '94

Eamon Morrissey (1943-)
The Seventh Stream '01
Eat the Peach '86

Byron Morrow (1911-2006)
Missiles of October '74
Johnny Got His Gun '71

Edwin Morrow (1980-)
We Were Soldiers '02
What About Your Friends: Weekend Getaway '02

Jeff Morrow (1913-93)
Soul of the Game '96
Octaman '71
The Giant Claw '57
Hour of Decision '57
The Creature Walks among Us '56
This Island Earth '55
The Robe '53

Jo Morrow (1940-)
Dr. Death, Seeker of Souls '73
Sunday in New York '63
13 Ghosts '60
Our Man in Havana '59
The Three Worlds of Gulliver '59

Mari Morrow
Uninvited Guest '99
Dead Man on Campus '97
Def Jam's How to Be a Player '97

David Morse (1953-)
John Adams '08
Disturbia '07
16 Blocks '06
Down in the Valley '05
Dreamer: Inspired by a True Story '05
Nearing Grace '05
Double Vision '02
Hearts in Atlantis '01
The Slaughter Rule '01
Bait '00
The Green Mile '99
Crazy in Alabama '99
Contact '97
12 Monkeys '95
The Crossing Guard '94
The Getaway '94
The Good Son '93
The Indian Runner '91
Desperate Hours '90
The Brotherhood of the Rose '89
Shattered Vows '84
Prototype '83
Inside Moves '80

Rob Morrow (1962-)
The Bucket List '07
Going Shopping '05
The Emperor's Club '02
The Guru '02
Maze '01
The Thin Blue Lie '00
Labor Pains '99
Only Love '98
Last Dance '96
Mother '96
Quiz Show '94

Patricia Morrow (1944-)
Surf Party '64
China Gate '57

Neyle Morrow
The Green Mile '99
The Negotiator '98
Contact '97
The Rock '96
Stephen King's The Langoliers '95
Tecumseh: The Last Warrior '95
Dead Ahead: The Exxon Valdez Disaster '92

Vic Morrow (1932-82)
Twilight Zone: The Movie '83
1990: The Bronx Warriors '83
B.A.D. Cats '80
Humanoids from the Deep '80
The Evictors '79
Express to Terror '79
The Seekers '79
Wild & Wooly '78
Curse of the Black Widow '77
Funeral for an Assassin '77
The Bad News Bears '76
The Treasure of Matecumbe '76
Wanted: Babysitter '75
Death Stalk '74
Dirty Mary Crazy Larry '74
The Glass House '72
Cimarron '60
God's Little Acre '58
King Creole '58
Men in War '57
Tribute to a Bad Man '56
Blackboard Jungle '55

Susan Morrow (1931-85)
Battle Cry '55
Cat Women of the Moon '53

Helen Morse (1946-)
Far East '85
A Town Like Alice '85
Agatha '79
Caddie '76
Picnic at Hanging Rock '75

Laila Morse (1945-)
Love, Honour & Obey '00
Nil by Mouth '96

Robert Morse (1931-)
Great Expectations '99
The Boatniks '70
Where Were You When the Lights Went Out? '68
A Guide for the Married Man '67
How to Succeed in Business without Really Trying '67
Oh Dad, Poor Dad (Momma's Hung You in the Closet & I'm Feeling So Sad) '67
The Loved One '65
The Matchmaker '58

Robin Morse (1915-)
Rock All Night '57
Marty '55

Glenn Morshower (1959-)
Transformers '07
All the King's Men '06
Good Night, and Good Luck '05
Hostage '05
The Last Shot '04
Black Hawk Down '01
Pearl Harbor '01
The Jack Bull '99
My Little Assassin '99
Dominion '94
84 Charlie MoPic '89
Tango and Cash '89
Drive-In '76

Viggo Mortensen (1958-)
Eastern Promises '07
A History of Violence '05
Hidalgo '04
The Lord of the Rings: The Return of the King '03
Lord of the Rings: The Two Towers '02
The Lord of the Rings: The Fellowship of the Ring '01
28 Days '00
A Walk on the Moon '99
A Perfect Murder '98
Psycho '98
G.I. Jane '97
Albino Alligator '96
Daylight '96
Portrait of a Lady '96
The Crew '95
Crimson Tide '95
The Prophecy '95
American Yakuza '94
Boiling Point '93
Carlito's Way '93
Young Americans '93
Deception '92
The Indian Runner '91
The Reflecting Skin '91
Young Guns 2 '90
Leatherface: The Texas Chainsaw Massacre 3 '89
Fresh Horses '88
Prison '88
Salvation! '87
Witness '85

Gregory Morton (1911-86)
Cop-Out '67
A Matter of WHO '62

Joe Morton (1947-)
American Gangster '07
The Night Listener '06
Back in the Day '05
Stealth '05
Paycheck '03
Jasper, Texas '03
Dragonfly '02
Ali '01
Bounce '00
What Lies Beneath '00
The Astronaut's Wife '99
Mutiny '99
Blues Brothers 2000 '98
Apt Pupil '97
Miss Evers' Boys '97
Speed 2: Cruise Control '97
Executive Decision '96
Lone Star '96
The Pest '96
The Inkwell '94
Speed '94
The Walking Dead '94
Forever Young '92
Legacy of Lies '92
Of Mice and Men '92
The Good Mother '88
Zelly & Me '88
Crossroads '86
Trouble in Mind '86
The Brother from Another Planet '84
Alone in the Neon Jungle '87

Clive Morton (1904-75)
The Saint '97
The Gırl and the Darkness '96
The Last of the High Kings '96
Catherine Cookson's The Glass Virgin '95
Sharpe's Sword '94
The First '97

Alicia Morton (1987-)
Sharpe's Journey '01
Dodson's Journey '01
Annie '99

Emily Mortimer (1971-)
Chaos Theory '08
Redbelt '08
Lars and the Real Girl '07
Paris, je t'aime '06
The Pink Panther '06
Match Point '05
Dear Frankie '04
Howl's Moving Castle '04 (V)
Bright Young Things '03
2 Brothers & a Bride '03
Young Adam '03
Lovely & Amazing '02
The Sleeping Dictionary '02
Formula 51 '01
Disney's The Kid '00
Love's Labour's Lost '00
Scream 3 '00
Cider with Rosie '99
Noah's Ark '99
Coming Home '98
Elizabeth '98
The Saint '97
The Ghost and the Darkness '96

Mos Def (1973-)
Be Kind Rewind '08
16 Blocks '06
The Woodsman '04
The Italian Job '03
Brown Sugar '02
Civil Brand '02
Showtime '02
Carmen: A Hip Hopera '01
Monster's Ball '01
Bamboozled '00
Island of the Dead '00
Where's Marlowe? '98

Samantha Morton (1977-)
Control '07
Elizabeth: The Golden Age '07
The Libertine '05
Enduring Love '04
Code 46 '03
In America '02
Minority Report '02
Morvern Callar '02
Pandaemonium '00
Dreaming of Joseph Lees '99
Jesus' Son '99
Sweet and Lowdown '99
Tom Jones '98
Emma '97
Jane Eyre '97
Under the Skin '97
This Is the Sea '97
Band of Gold '95
Cracker: The Big Crunch '94

Gastone Moschin (1929-)
A Joke of Destiny, Lying in Wait Around the Corner Like a Bandit '84
A Woman at Her Window '76

Maurice Moscovitch (Moscovich) (1871-1940)
The Great Dictator '40
The Great Commandment '41

David Moscow (1974-)
Nearing Grace '05
Honey '03
Just Married '03
Riding in Cars with Boys '01
Newsies '92
Big '88

Bill Moseley (1957-)
Thr3e '07
A Dead Calling '06
The Devil's Rejects '05
House of 1000 Corpses '03
The Convent '00
Crash and Burn '90
Night of the Living Dead '90
Fair Game '89
Silent Night, Deadly Night 3: Better Watch Out! '89

The Passion of Darkly Noon '95
City of Hope '91
Terminator 2: Judgment Day '91
Day '91
The Prophecy '95
American Yakuza '94
Boiling Point '93
Carlito's Way '93
Tap '89
Skin '89
The Good Mother '88
Zelly & Me '88

The Texas Chainsaw Massacre 2 '86
Osa '85

William Moseley
The Chronicles of Narnia: Prince Caspian '08
The Chronicles of Narnia: The Lion, the Witch and the Wardrobe '05

David Moses (1962-)
Storm Tracker '99
Scared to Death '80
Daring Dobermans '73

Harry Moses
Sweater Girls '78
The Van '77

Marian Moses (1932-2004)
Buona Sera, Mrs. Campbell '68
Dead Heat on a Merry-Go-Round '66

Mark Moses (1958-)
Big Momma's House 2 '06
Treehouse Hostage '99
One Man's Hero '98
Rough Riders '97
A Kiss Goodnight '94
Gettysburg '93
Dead Men Don't Die '91
Hollywood Heartbreak '89
The Tracker '88
Platoon '86

William R. Moses (1959-)
The Derby Stallion '05
Hangman's Curse '03
Chain of Command '00
Missing Pieces '00
The Perfect Wife '00
75 Degrees '00
Alone with a Stranger '99
Wicked '98
The Nurse '97
Evil Has a Face '96
The Fiance '96
Circumstances Unknown '95
Almost Dead '94
Fun '94
The Haunting of Seacliff Inn '94
Double Exposure '93
Mystic Pizza '88
Alien from L.A. '87

Benny Moshe
Tsotsi '05

Moni Moshonov
We Own the Night '07
Year Zero '04
Late Marriage '01

Michael Mosley
The Big Bad Swim '06
The Insurgents '06

Roger E. Mosley (1944-)
Letters from a Killer '98
A Thin Line Between Love and Hate '96
Pentathlon '94
Unlawful Entry '92
Heart Condition '90
Zora Is My Name! '90
Attica '80
Magnum P.I.: Don't Eat the Snow in Hawaii '80
Pray TV '80
Steel '80
I Know Why the Caged Bird Sings '79
The Jericho Mile '79
The Greatest '77
The River Niger '76
Darktown Strutters '74
The Mack '73

Arnold Moss (1910-89)
The Fool Killer '65
The 27th Day '57
Viva Zapata! '52
Border Incident '49
Reign of Terror '49
The Loves of Carmen '48

Bertha Moss (1919-)
The Exterminating Angel '62

Invasion of the Vampires '61

Carrie-Anne Moss (1970-)
Disturbia '07
Fido '06
Snow Cake '06
The Chumscrubber '05
Suspect Zero '04
The Matrix Reloaded '03
The Matrix Revolutions '03
Chocolat '00
The Crew '00
Memento '00
Red Planet '00
The Matrix '99
New Blood '99
Lethal Tender '96
Sabotage '96
The Soft Kill '94

Elissabeth (Elisabeth, Liz) Moss (1983-)
Day Zero '07
The Attic '06
Heart of America '03
The Missing '03
Virgin '03
Earthly Possessions '99
Girl, Interrupted '99
Mumford '99
A Thousand Acres '97
Imaginary Crimes '94
Separate Lives '94
Midnight's Child '93

Jesse Moss (1983-)
Partition '07
Final Destination 3 '06
Ginger Snaps '01

Jimmy Moss
Border Saddlemates '52
The Damned Don't Cry '50

Ron Moss (1952-)
Hard Ticket to Hawaii '87
Hearts & Armour '83

Stewart Moss (1937-)
The Bat People '74
Missiles of October '74
Dr. Death, Seeker of Souls '73

Tegan Moss (1985-)
Inspector Gadget's Biggest Caper Ever '05 (V)
Video Voyeur: The Susan Wilson Story '02
Sea People '00
Big Daddy '99
Rounders '98
Great Expectations '97
The Basketball Diaries '95
The Maddening '95
Billy Madison '94
City Slickers 2: The Legend of Curly's Gold '94
The Chase '93
City of Hope '91
City Slickers '91
Little Man Tate '91
Animal Behavior '89
Heavy Petting '89
Matewan '87
Radio Days '87
Wall Street '87
The Money Pit '86
Almost You '85
Compromising Positions '85
Stoogemania '85
Windy City '84
Star 80 '83
Sophie's Choice '82
Deadly Hero '75
Harry and Tonto '74

Jesus Christ, Superstar '73
The King of Marvin Gardens '72

Zero Mostel (1915-77)
Watership Down '78 (V)
The Front '76
Foreplay '75
Journey into Fear '74
Marco '73
Master Mind '73
Once Upon a Scoundrel '73
The Angel Levine '70
The Hot Rock '70
The Producers '68
A Funny Thing Happened on the Way to the Forum '66
The Enforcer '51
Sirocco '51
Panic in the Streets '50
Du Barry Was a Lady '43

Zeze Motta (1944-)
Orfeu '99
Tieta of Agreste '96
Quilombo '84
Xica '76

Greg Mottola (1964-)
Hollywood Ending '02
Celebrity '98

John Moulder-Brown (1953-)
Rumpelstiltskin '86
Killing Heat '84
King, Queen, Knave '72
Vampire Circus '71
Deep End '70
First Love '70

Anson Mount (1973-)
In Her Shoes '05
The Battle of Shaker Heights '03
City by the Sea '02
Crossroads '02
Poolhall Junkies '02
Tully '00
Urban Legends 2: Final Cut '00

Moustache (1929-87)
Beyond Fear '75
Zorro '74

Benjamin Mouton
All the Real Girls '03
The Whole Wide World '96

Movita (1915-)
Panic in Echo Park '77
Mysterious Desperado '49
Tower of Terror '42
Wolf Call '39
Rose of Rio Grande '38
Mutiny on the Bounty '35

Alan Mowbray (1896-1969)
The King and I '56
A Majority of One '56
The Man Who Knew Too Much '56
The King's Thief '55
Ma and Pa Kettle at Home '54
Abbott and Costello Meet the Killer, Boris Karloff '49
The Lovable Cheat '49
My Dear Secretary '49
The Prince of Thieves '48
Captain from Castile '48
Lured '47
Merton of the Movies '47
My Darling Clementine '46
Terror by Night '46
Never Say Die '39
Topper Takes a Trip '39
Way Down South '39
On the Avenue '37
Vogues of 1938 '37

Desire '36
It Happened in New Orleans '36
Mary of Scotland '36
My Man Godfrey '36
In Person '35
Charlie Chan in London '34
The Girl from Missouri '34
A Study in Scarlet '33

Jack Mower (1890-1965)
Skull & Crown '35
The Fiddlin' Buckaroo '33
Law and Lawless '33
Mystery Squadron '33
Ships in the Night '28
Cyclone Cavalier '25

Patrick Mower (1940-)
Carry On England '76
Catch Me a Spy '71
The Bloodsuckers '70
Cry of the Banshee '70
The Devil Rides Out '68

Tamera Mowry (1978-)
Twitches Too '07
Twitches '05
The Hot Chick '02
Seventeen Again '00

Tia Mowry (1978-)
Twitches Too '07
Twitches '05
The Hot Chick '02
Seventeen Again '00

Stephen Moyer (1971-)
88 Minutes '08
The Starter Wife '07
Princess of Thieves '01
Uprising '01
Catherine Cookson's The Secret '00
Comic Act '98
Ultraviolet '98
Prince Valiant '97

Bridget Moynahan (1972-)
Gray Matters '06
Lord of War '05
I, Robot '04
The Recruit '03
The Sum of All Fears '02
Serendipity '01
Coyote Ugly '00

George Mozart (1864-1947)
Song of Freedom '36
The Mummy '32

David Mucci
Unforgiven '92
Prom Night '80

Leonard Mudie (1883-1965)
British Intelligence '40
The Jury's Secret '38
Song of Freedom '36
The Mummy '32

Cookie Mueller (1949-89)
Polyester '81
Desperate Living '77
Female Trouble '74
Pink Flamingos '72
Multiple Maniacs '70

Maureen Mueller
Larger Than Life '96
Oldest Confederate Widow Tells All '95
The New Age '94
In a Shallow Grave '88

Armin Mueller-Stahl (1930-)
Eastern Promises '07
The Story of an African Farm '04
Jesus '00
Inferno '99
Jakob the Liar '99
The Third Miracle '99
The Thirteenth Floor '99
The X-Files '98
The Game '97
The Assistant '97
In the Presence of Mine Enemies '97
The Peacemaker '97

Twelve Angry Men '97
The Ogre '96
A Pyromaniac's Love Story '95
Red Hot '95
Shine '95
Theodore Rex '95
Holy Matrimony '94
The Last Good Time '94
The House of the Spirits '93
Utz '93
The Power of One '92
Kafka '91
Night on Earth '91
Avalon '90
Music Box '89
Midnight Cop '88
Lethal Obsession '87
Angry Harvest '85
Forget Mozart '85
Colonel Redl '84
A Love in Germany '84
Jacob the Liar '74
The Third '72
Five Cartridges '60

Marianne Muellerleile (1948-)
Return to Me '00
A Smile Like Yours '96
Curse 2: The Bite '88
The Trouble with Dick '88

Amanda Muggleton
Idiot Box '97

Ulrich Muhe (1953-2007)
Amen '02
Straight Shooter '97
Funny Games '97
Benny's Video '92

Anita (Yim-Fong) Mui (1963-2003)
Rumble in the Bronx '96
Jet Li's The Enforcer '95
The Legend of Drunken Master '94
The Executioners '93
The Heroic Trio '93
A Better Tomorrow, Part 3 '89
Miracles '89

Esther Muir (1903-95)
Misbehaving Husbands '41
A Day at the Races '37
Racing Luck '35
So This Is Africa '33

Gavin Muir (1900-72)
Night Tide '63
Abbott and Costello Meet the Invisible Man '51
O.S.S. '46
House of Fear '45
Sherlock Holmes Faces Death '43
Charlie Chan at the Race Track '36
Mary of Scotland '36

Oliver Muirhead
MVP (Most Valuable Primate) '00

Madhabi Mukherjee (1943-)
Charulata '64
The Big City '63

Diana Muldaur (1938-)
Return of Frank Cannon '80
Beyond Reason '77
McQ '74
Planet Earth '74
The Other '72

Patrick Muldoon (1969-)
Ice Spiders '07
Miracle Dogs Too '06
Heart of America '03
Blackwoods '02
Whacked! '02
Hell's Gate '01
Chain of Command '00
The Crimson Code '99
Stigmata '99
The Arrival 2 '98
Black Cat Run '98
Wicked '98

Starship Troopers '97
Rage and Honor 2: Hostile Takeover '93

Nancy Mulford
Act of Piracy '89
Skeleton Coast '89

Kate Mulgrew (1955-)
Star Trek: Nemesis '02
Captain Nuke and the Bomber Boys '95
Camp Nowhere '94
Danielle Steel's Daddy '91
Round Numbers '91
Roots: The Gift '88
Throw Momma from the Train '87
Remo Williams: The Adventure Begins '85
A Stranger Is Watching '82
The Manions of America '81
A Time for Miracles '80
Lovespell '79
The Word '78

Jack Mulhall (1887-1979)
'Neath Canadian Skies '46
Dawn Express '42
I Killed That Man '42
Mr. Wise Guy '42
Desperate Cargo '41
International Lady '41
Saddle Mountain Roundup '41
Outlaws of Sonora '38
100 Men and a Girl '37
Radio Patrol '37
Tim Tyler's Luck '37
The Clutching Hand '36
Custer's Last Stand '36
A Face in the Fog '36
Kelly of the Secret Service '36
Rogue's Tavern '36
Roaring Roads '35
Skull & Crown '35
Mystery Squadron '33
The Three Musketeers '33
Hell's Headquarters '32
Murder on the High Seas '32

Edward Mulhare (1923-97)
Out to Sea '97
Megaforce '82
Caprice '67
Our Man Flint '66
Von Ryan's Express '65
Hill 24 Doesn't Answer '55

Michael Mulheren
Ash Wednesday '02
The Curse of the Jade Scorpion '01
Johnny Suede '92

Matt Mulhern (1960-)
Sunchaser '96
Biloxi Blues '88
Extreme Prejudice '87

Chris Mulkey (1948-)
Broken Trail '06
Dreamland '06
Mysterious Skin '04
Radio '03
Jimmy Zip '00
Requiem for Murder '99
Sugar Town '99
Psychopath '97
Sub Down '97
Weapons of Mass Distraction '97
Behind Enemy Lines '96
Dead Cold '96
The Fan '96
Bound and Gagged: A Love Story '93
Ghost in the Machine '93
Deadbolt '92
Gas Food Lodging '92
The Silencer '92
Runaway Father '91
Write to Kill '91
Rainbow Drive '90
K-9000 '89
Roe vs. Wade '89
Heartbreak Hotel '88
In Dangerous Company '88
Patti Rocks '88

- Tricks of the Trade '88
- The Hidden '87
- Jack's Back '87

Martin Mull (1943-)
- Attention Shoppers '99
- Zack & Reba '98
- Beverly Hills Family Robinson '97
- How the West Was Fun '95
- Edie & Pen '95
- The Day My Parents Ran Away '93
- Mrs. Doubtfire '93
- Ted & Venus '93
- Miracle Beach '92
- Mr. Write '92
- The Player '92
- Think Big '90
- Cutting Class '89
- Far Out Man '89
- Ski Patrol '89
- Home Is Where the Hart Is '88
- Portrait of a White Marriage '88
- Rented Lips '88
- O.C. and Stiggs '87
- The Boss' Wife '85
- Pecos Bill '86
- Clue '85
- Flicks '85
- Lots of Luck '85
- Bad Manners '84
- Mr. Mom '83
- Take This Job & Shove It '81

Megan Mullally (1958-)
- Bee Movie '07 (V)
- Rebound '05
- Disney's Teacher's Pet '04 (V)
- Stealing Harvard '02
- Monkeybone '01
- Everything Put Together '99
- Winchell '98
- Rainbow Drive '90
- Serial '80
- FM '78

Peter Mullan (1954-)
- The Last Legion '07
- Children of Men '06
- On a Clear Day '05
- Criminal '04
- Young Adam '03
- Session 9 '01
- The Claim '00
- Ordinary Decent Criminal '99
- My Name Is Joe '98

Jack Mullaney (1932-82)
- George! '70
- Spinout '66
- Tickle Me '65
- The Honeymoon Machine '61

Greg Mullavey (1939-)
- Cock & Bull Story '03
- Deadly Conspiracy '91
- Not Quite Human 2 '89
- Body Count '87
- Husbands, Wives, Money and Murder '86
- I Dismember Mama '74
- The Love Machine '71
- C.C. & Company '70

Barbara Mullen (1914-79)
- The Very Edge '63
- It Takes a Thief '59
- Murder in the Footlights '46

Conor Mullen
- Reckless '97

Marie Mullen (1963-)
- When Brendan Met Trudy '00
- Dancing at Lughnasa '95

Patty Mullen
- Frankenhooker '90
- Doom Asylum '88

David Muller
- Spiral '07

Harrison Muller
- Ernest in the Army '97
- Miami Golem '89
- 2020 Texas Gladiators '85
- The Final Executioner '83
- She '83
- Violent Breed '83

Michel Muller (1966-)
- Wasabi '01
- Like a Fish Out of Water '99
- Train of Life '98

Paul Muller (1923-)
- The Arena '73
- Lady Frankenstein '72
- Count Dracula '71
- Virgin among the Living Dead '71
- Nightmare Castle '65
- Fangs of the Living Dead '68
- Goliath and the Sins of Babylon '64
- The Black Devils of Kali '55
- Four Ways Out '57
- Two Nights with Cleopatra '54

Carey Mulligan (1985-)
- Northanger Abbey '07
- Bleak House '05
- Pride and Prejudice '05

Richard Mulligan (1932-2000)
- Gore Vidal's Lincoln '88
- Oliver & Company '88 (V)
- Poker Alice '87
- A Fine Mess '86
- Babes in Toyland '86
- Doin' Time '85
- The Heavenly Kid '85
- Meatballs 2 '84
- Teachers '84
- Micki & Maude '84
- S.O.B. '81
- Scavenger Hunt '79
- The Big Bus '76
- The Hideaways '73
- Pueblo Affair '73
- Little Big Man '70
- The Group '66

Terry David Mulligan (1942-)
- Masters of Horror: Homecoming '05
- Can of Worms '00
- Sweetwater: A True Rock Story '99

Rod Mullinar (1942-)
- Deadly Sins '95
- Dead Calm '89
- Echoes of Paradise '86
- Breakfast in Paris '81
- Breaker Morant '80
- Patrick '78

Dermot Mulroney (1963-)
- Georgia Rule '07
- Gracie '07
- Zodiac '07
- The Family Stone '05
- Must Love Dogs '05
- The Wedding Date '05
- Undertow '04
- About Schmidt '02
- Lovely & Amazing '02
- Intimate Affairs '01
- The Safety of Objects '01
- Trixie '00
- Where the Money Is '00
- Goodbye, Lover '99
- My Best Friend's Wedding '97

- Living in Oblivion '94
- Family Pictures '93
- The Last Outlaw '93
- Point of No Return '93
- The Thing Called Love '93
- Samantha '92
- Silent Tongue '92
- There Goes My Baby '92
- Where the Day Takes You '92
- Bright Angel '91
- Career Opportunities '91
- Longtime Companion '90
- Staying Together '89
- Survival Quest '89
- Sunset '88
- Young Guns '88

Kieran Mulroney (1965-)
- Quigley '03
- Pursuit of Happiness '01
- From the Earth to the Moon '98
- God's Lonely Man '96
- The Immortals '95
- The Spitfire Grill '95
- Sensation '94
- Gettysburg '93
- Career Opportunities '91
- Nowhere to Run '88

Samantha Mumba (1983-)
- Johnny Was '05
- The Time Machine '02

Danny Mummert (1934-)
- Blondie Hits the Jackpot '49
- Blondie Knows Best '46
- Footlight Glamour '43
- It's a Great Life '43
- Blondie for Victory '43
- Blondie Goes Latin '42
- Blondie's Blessed Event '42
- Blondie in Society '41
- Blondie Has Trouble '40
- Blondie On a Budget '40
- Blondie Plays Cupid '40
- Blondie Brings Up Baby '39
- Blondie Meets the Boss '39
- Blondie Takes a Vacation '39

Billy Mumy (1954-)
- Comic Book: The Movie '04
- Twilight Zone: The Movie '83
- Bless the Beasts and Children '71
- Dear Brigitte '65
- Sammy, the Way-Out Seal '62

Liliana Mumy (1995-)
- Snow Buddies '08 (V)
- The Santa Clause 3: The Escape Clause '06
- Cheaper by the Dozen 2 '05
- Lilo & Stitch 2: Stitch Has a Glitch '05 (V)
- Howl's Moving Castle '04 (V)
- Cheaper by the Dozen '03
- The Santa Clause 2 '02

Misty Mundae (1979-)
- The Rage '07
- Masters of Horror: Sick Girl '06

Mary Munday (1926-97)
- Pressure Point '62
- Serpent Island '54

Herbert Mundin (1898-1939)
- The Adventures of Robin Hood '38
- Little Man '06
- Mutiny on the Bounty '35
- Cavalcade '33

- How to Go Out on a Date in Queens '06
- The Lost City '05
- Miss Congeniality 2: Armed and Fabulous '05
- Black Hawk Down '01
- Traffic '00
- Speed 2: Cruise Control '97

Janet Munro (1934-72)
- The Day the Earth Caught Fire '61
- Horsemasters '61
- Swiss Family Robinson '60
- Darby O'Gill & the Little People '59
- Third Man on the Mountain '59
- The Crawling Eye '58
- The Young and the Guilty '58

Lochlyn Munro (1966-)
- Daddy Day Camp '07
- Hack! '07
- The Benchwarmers '06
- Final Move '06
- The Tooth Fairy '06
- Chasing Ghosts '05
- Dirty Love '05

- Hoopla '33

Kevin Mundy (1977-)
- Jailbait! '00

Ian Mune (1941-)
- Better Than Chocolate '99
- Ike: Countdown to D-Day '04

Paul Muni (1895-1967)
- The Last Angry Man '59
- Angel on My Shoulder '46
- A Song to Remember '45
- Commandos Strike at Dawn '43
- Stage Door Canteen '43
- Juarez '39
- The Good Earth '37
- The Life of Emile Zola '37
- The Story of Louis Pasteur '36
- Black Fury '35
- I Am a Fugitive from a Chain Gang '32
- Scarface '31

Frankie Muniz (1985-)
- Walk Hard: The Dewey Cox Story '07
- Stay Alive '06
- Racing Stripes '05 (V)
- Agent Cody Banks 2: Destination London '04
- Agent Cody Banks '03
- Deuces Wild '02
- Big Fat Liar '02
- It Had to Be You '00
- Miracle in Lane Two '00
- My Dog Skip '99
- What the Deaf Man Heard '98

Pep Munne (1953-)
- Barcelona '94
- Where Time Began '77

Amparo Munoz (1954-)
- A Paradise Under the Stars '99

Caroline Munro (1950-)
- Black Cat '90
- Faceless '88
- Slaughter High '86
- Don't Open Till Christmas '84
- Fanatic '82
- Maniac '80
- Star Crash '78
- The Spy Who Loved Me '77
- At the Earth's Core '76
- I Don't Want to Be Born '75
- Captain Kronos: Vampire Hunter '74
- Golden Voyage of Sinbad '73
- Dracula A.D. 1972 '72
- The Abominable Dr. Phibes '71

Neil Munro
- Beethoven Lives Upstairs '92

- White Chicks '04
- Freddy vs. Jason '03
- A Guy Thing '03
- Heart of America '03
- Net Games '03
- Pressure '02
- Rock My World '02
- Chilly Dogs '01
- Kill Me Later '01
- Scary Movie '00
- Dracula 2000 '00
- High Voltage '98
- Dead Man on Campus '98
- Downhill Willie '96
- Trancers 5: Sudden Deth '94
- Wagons East '94
- Anything for Love '93

Ona Munson (1906-56)
- The Red House '47
- Dakota '45
- Idaho '43
- Lady from Louisiana '42
- The Shanghai Gesture '42
- Wagon's Westward '40
- Gone with the Winc '39
- The Big Guy '39

Jules Munshin (1915-70)
- On the Town '49
- Take Me Out to the Ball Game '49
- Easter Parade '48

Silvia Munt
- Secrets of the Heart '97
- Butterfly Wings '91

John Mylong Munz
See John (Jack) Mylong

Fuyuki Murakami (1911-2007)
- Godzilla, King of the Monsters '56
- Godzilla vs. Monster Zero '68

Jean Murat (1888-1968)
- Dishonorable Discharge '57
- Rich, Young and Pretty '51
- Eternal Return '43
- Carnival in Flanders '35

Takehiro Murata (1960-)
- Godzilla 2000 '99
- Godzilla '93
- Okoge '92
- Mimbo—Or the Gentle Art of Japanese Extortion '92

George Murcell (1925-98)
- Cutthroat Island '95
- Year of the Gun '91

Enrique Murciano (1973-)

Vince Murdocco
- L.A. Wars '94
- Ring of Fire 2: Blood and Steel '92
- Ring of Fire '91
- Flesh Gordon 2: Flesh Gordon Meets the Cosmic Cheerleaders '90

George Murdock (1930-)
- Serial Killing 101 '04
- Orange County '02
- Spider's Web '01
- Scorpio One '97
- Crossout '95
- Firepower '93

- Grand Tour: Disaster in Time '92
- Strange Case of Dr. Jekyll & Mr. Hyde '89
- In Love with an Older Woman '82

Christopher Murney (1943-)
- Winning Girls Through Psychic Mind Control '02
- Baron Fink '91
- The Ten Million Dollar Getaway '91
- Murder by the Book '87
- Maximum Overdrive '86
- The Last Dragon '85

Tim Murdock (1943-)
- They Were Expendable '45
- Thirty Seconds Over Tokyo '44

Jack Murdock (1922-2001)
- Mission Galactica: The Cylon Attack '78
- Breaker! Breaker! '77

Peter Murnik (1965-)
- The Texican '66
- Arizona Raiders '65
- Rowing Through '96
- Anderson ville '95
- Go-den Gate '93
- Body Parts '91

Audie Murphy (1924-71)
- The Unforgiven '60
- No Name on the Bullet '59
- Night Passage '57
- Walk the Proud Land '56
- To Hell and Back '55
- Ride Clear of Diablo '54
- Gunsmoke '53
- Duel at Silver Creek '52
- The Red Badge of Courage '51

Aaron Murphy (1992-)
- Boogeyman '05
- The World's Fastest Indian '05

Annette Murphy (1967-)
- Race '99
- Star Maps '97

Barri Murphy
- Armed for Action '92
- Action U.S.A. '89

Ben Murphy (1942-)
- The Dead Girl '06
- The Groomsmen '06
- Happy Feet '06 (V)
- Sin City '05
- Little Black Book '04
- Uptown Girls '03
- Just Married '03
- Good Boy! '03 (V)
- Don't Say a Word '01
- Riding in Cars with Boys '01

Brittany Murphy (1977-)
- Sidewalks of New York '01
- Summer Catch '01
- Cherry Falls '00
- Common Ground '00
- Trixie '00
- Drive '96
- Clueless '95
- Freeway '95

Murphy

Charlie (Charles Q.) Murphy (1959-)
The Perfect Holiday '07
Unearthed '07
King's Ransom '05
Roll Bounce '05
CB4: The Movie '93

Cillian Murphy (1974-)
The Dark Knight '08
Sunshine '07
The Wind That Shakes the Barley '06
Batman Begins '05
Red Eye '05
Girl with a Pearl Earring '03
28 Days Later '02
The Way We Live Now '02
Disco Pigs '01
How Harry Became a Tree '01
On the Edge '00

Donald Murphy (1910-95)
Lord Love a Duck '66
Frankenstein's Daughter '58

Donna Murphy (1958-)
The Nanny Diaries '07
Spider-Man 2 '04
Center Stage '00
The Last Debate '00
The Astronaut's Wife '99
Star Trek: Insurrection '98

Eddie Murphy (1961-)
Meet Dave '08
Norbit '07
Shrek the Third '07 (V)
Dreamgirls '06
Shrek 2 '04 (V)
Daddy Day Care '03
The Haunted Mansion '03
The Adventures of Pluto Nash '02
I Spy '02
Showtime '02
Dr. Dolittle 2 '01
Shrek '01 (V)
Nutty Professor 2: The Klumps '00
Bowfinger '99
Life '99
Dr. Dolittle '98
Holy Man '98
Mulan '98 (V)
Metro '96
The Nutty Professor '96
Vampire in Brooklyn '95
Beverly Hills Cop 3 '94
Boomerang '92
The Distinguished Gentleman '92
Another 48 Hrs. '90
Harlem Nights '89
Coming to America '88
Beverly Hills Cop 2 '87
The Golden Child '86
Best Defense '84
Beverly Hills Cop '84
Trading Places '83
48 Hrs. '82

George Murphy (1902-92)
Battleground '49
Border Incident '49
Having Wonderful Crime '45
Broadway Rhythm '44
Show Business '44
Step Lively '44
Bataan '43
This Is the Army '43
For Me and My Gal '42
The Navy Comes Through '42
A Girl, a Guy, and a Gob '41
Tom, Dick, and Harry '41
Broadway Melody of 1940 '40
Little Nellie Kelly '40
Letter of Introduction '38
Little Miss Broadway '38
Broadway Melody of 1938 '37
Kid Millions '34

Horace Murphy (1880-1975)
Bad Man of Deadwood '41
Down the Wyoming Trail '39
Rollin' Plains '38
Wide Open Faces '38
Boothill Brigade '37
Border Phantom '37
Come on, Cowboys '37
Paroled to Die '37
Sing, Cowboy, Sing '37
Tex Rides with the Boy Scouts '37
Last of the Warrens '36
Undercover Man '36

Jimmy Murphy (1931-)
Platinum High School '60
Curse of the Undead '59

Johnny Murphy
War of the Buttons '95
The Commitments '91

Kim Murphy (1974-)
The In Crowd '00
Campfire Tales '98
Houseguest '94

Mary Murphy (1931-)
I Love You, Goodbye '74
40 Pounds of Trouble '62
The Electronic Monster '57
Desperate Hours '55
A Man Alone '55
The Maverick Queen '55
Sitting Bull '54
The Wild One '54
Houdini '53
Main Street to Broadway '53
Carrie '52

Maurice Murphy (1913-78)
Abe Lincoln in Illinois '40
Delinquent Parents '38
Found Alive '34
Tailspin Tommy '34
Pilgrimage '33

Megan Murphy
Money Buys Happiness '99
Shredder Orpheus '89

Michael Murphy (1938-)
Away From Her '06
X-Men: The Last Stand '06
Heights '04
Silver City '04
Tanner on Tanner '04
Live from Baghdad '02
The Day Reagan Was Shot '01
Breaking the Surface: The Greg Louganis Story '96
Private Parts '96
Kansas City '95
Clean Slate '94
Batman Returns '92
Dead Ahead: The Exxon Valdez Disaster '92
Folks! '92
Shocker '89
Tailspin: Behind the Korean Airline Tragedy '89
The Caine Mutiny Court Martial '88
Salvador '86
Cloak & Dagger '84
Mesmerized '84
Talk to Me '84
The Year of Living Dangerously '82
Strange Behavior '81
Manhattan '79
The Class of Miss MacMichael '78
Great Bank Hoax '78
An Unmarried Woman '78
The Front '76
Nashville '75
The Autobiography of Miss Jane Pittman '74
I Love You, Goodbye '74
Phase 4 '74
The Thief Who Came to Dinner '73
McCabe & Mrs. Miller '71
Brewster McCloud '70
Count Yorga, Vampire '70
M*A*S*H '70
That Cold Day in the Park '69
Countdown '68
Double Trouble '67

Rosemary Murphy (1927-)
Dust '01
Message in a Bottle '98
The Tuskegee Airmen '95
For the Boys '91
A Woman Named Jackie '91
The Attic '80
Julia '77
Eleanor & Franklin '76
Walking Tall '73
Ben '72
You'll Like My Mother '72
Any Wednesday '66
To Kill a Mockingbird '62

Timothy Patrick Murphy (1959-88)
National Treasure: Book of Secrets '07
Shallow Ground '04
Doin' Time on Planet Earth '88
Sam's Son '84
The Seekers '79

William Murphy
Sands of Iwo Jima '49
The Story of G.I. Joe '45

Barbara Murray (1929-)
The Bretts '88
A Cry from the Streets '57
Death Goes to School '53
Another Man's Poison '52
Tony Draws a Horse '51

Beverly Murray
The Carpenter '89
Cathy's Curse '77

Bill Murray (1950-)
Get Smart '08
Garfield: A Tail of Two Kitties '06 (V)
Broken Flowers '05
The Lost City '05
Garfield: The Movie '04 (V)
Coffee and Cigarettes '03
Lost in Translation '03
Osmosis Jones '01
The Royal Tenenbaums '01
Charlie's Angels '00
Hamlet '00
The Cradle Will Rock '99
Rushmore '98
Wild Things '98
With Friends Like These '98
The Man Who Knew Too Little '97
Kingpin '96
Larger Than Life '96
Space Jam '96
Ed Wood '94
Groundhog Day '93
Mad Dog and Glory '93
What about Bob? '91
Quick Change '90
Ghostbusters 2 '89
Scrooged '88
Little Shop of Horrors '86
Ghostbusters '84
The Razor's Edge '84
Tootsie '82
Stripes '81
Caddyshack '80
Where the Buffalo Roam '80
Meatballs '79
Mr. Mike's Mondo Video '79
All You Need Is Cash '78
Shame of the Jungle '75 (V)

Brian Murray (1937-)
Nearing Grace '05
Treasure Planet '02 (V)
Bob Roberts '92

Chad Michael Murray (1981-)
Home of the Brave '06
House of Wax '05
A Cinderella Story '04
Freaky Friday '03

David Murray
Cowboys & Angels '04
Veronica Guerin '03

Don Murray (1929-)
Kickboxer the Champion '91
Ghosts Can't Do It '90
Made in Heaven '87
Mistress '87
Peggy Sue Got Married '86
Radioactive Dreams '86
Scorpion '86
Something in Common '85
Quarterback Princess '85
License to Kill '84
I Am the Cheese '83
Endless Love '81
Justin Morgan Had a Horse '81
Return of the Rebels '81
If Things Were Different '79
Rainbow '78
Deadly Hero '75
Confessions of Tom Harris '72
Conquest of the Planet of the Apes '72
Cotter '72
Sweet Love, Bitter '67
The Viking Queen '67
Baby, the Rain Must Fall '64
One Man's Way '63
Advise and Consent '62
The Hoodlum Priest '61
Shake Hands with the Devil '59
Bus Stop '56

James Murray (1901-36)
All the King's Men '99
Skull & Crown '35
Baby Face '33
High Gear '33
The Crowd '28

Jan Murray (1916-2006)
Banjo Hackett '76
Which Way to the Front? '70
Thunder Alley '67

Joel Murray (1963-)
The Cable Guy '96
One Crazy Summer '86
Scrooged '88

Ken Murray (1903-88)
Follow Me, Boys! '66
The Man Who Shot Liberty Valance '62

Kate Murtagh (1920-)
Doctor Detroit '83
Switchblade Sisters '75

James Murtaugh
Two Weeks '06
Private Parts '97
The Rosary Murders '87
The River Is Red '48

Mae Murray (1889-1965)
Bachelor Apartment '31
A Mormon Maid '17

Stephen Murray (1912-83)
Elizabeth R '72
Four Sided Triangle '53
Alice in Wonderland '50
Pygmalion '38

Peter Murray-Hill (1908-57)
The Ghost Train '41
Mr. Reeder in Room 13 '38

Lionel Murton (1915-2006)
Carry On Admiral '57
Meet the Navy '46

Tony Musante (1936-)
We Own the Night '07
The Yards '00
The Deep End of the Ocean '98
Collector's Item '89
The Pope of Greenwich Village '84
High Ice '80
Breaking Up Is Hard to Do '79
Fatal Chase '77
The Grissom Gang '71
The Bird with the Crystal Plumage '70
The Detective '68
The Incident '67

Clarence Muse (1889-1979)
The Black Stallion '79
A Dream for Christmas '73
Great Dan Patch '49
Watch on the Rhine '43
Gentleman from Dixie '41
The Invisible Ghost '41
Broken Strings '40
That Gang of Mine '40
Way Down South '39
Prison Train '38
The Spirit of Youth '37
The White Zombie '32

Victoria (Tory) Mussett (1978-)
The Condemned '07
Boogeyman '05

Louis Mustillo (1947-)
Dudley Do-Right '99
Just the Ticket '98

Marjorie Ann Mutchie (1939-)
Blondie Hits the Jackpot '49
Blondie Knows Best '46
Footlight Glamour '43
It's a Great Life '43

Ellen Muth (1981-)
SuperFire '02
A Gentleman's Game '01
Cora Unashamed '00
The Truth About Jane '00
The Young Girl and the Monsoon '99

Ornella Muti (1955-)
The Heart Is Deceitful Above All Things '04
Last Run '01
The Count of Monte Cristo '99
Esther '98
Somewhere in the City '97
Once Upon a Crime '92
Oscar '91
Wait until Spring, Bandini '90
Casanova '87
Swann in Love '84
Tales of Ordinary Madness '83
Flash Gordon '80
Life Is Beautiful '79
Summer Affair '79
Leonor '75

Roger Mutton
The Charge of the Light Brigade '68
The Girl on a Motorcycle '68

Mya (1979-)
Cover '08
Cursed '04
Dirty Dancing: Havana Nights '04
Shall We Dance? '04

Bruce Myers
The Mahabharata '89
The Unbearable Lightness of Being '88

Carmel Myers (1900-80)
Chinatown After Dark '31
Pleasure '31
Ben-Hur '26
Beau Brummel '24

Dwight "Heavy D" Myers (1967-)
Step Up '06
Dallas 362 '03
Big Trouble '02
The Cider House Rules '99

Harry C. (Henry) Myers (1886-1938)
Rainbow over Broadway '33
Convicted '32
The Savage Girl '32
City Lights '31
The Marriage Circle '24

Johann Myers
The Medallion '03
24-7 '97

Kim Myers (1966-)
Letters from a Killer '98
Hellraiser 3: Bloodline '95
White Palace '90
A Nightmare on Elm Street 2: Freddy's Revenge '85

Lou Myers (1945-)
All About You '01
Tin Cup '96
The Piano Lesson '94

Mike Myers (1963-)
The Love Guru '08
Shrek the Third '07 (V)
Shrek 2 '04 (V)
Dr. Seuss' The Cat in the Hat '03
View from the Top '03
Austin Powers In Goldmember '02
Shrek '01 (V)
Austin Powers 2: The Spy Who Shagged Me '99
Mystery, Alaska '99
54 '98
Pete's Meteor '98
Austin Powers: International Man of Mystery '97
So I Married an Axe Murderer '93
Wayne's World 2 '93
Wayne's World '92

Susan Myers
Desperate Women '78
The Spell '77

Peter Mygind (1963-)
The Kingdom 2 '97
The Kingdom '95

Bruce Myles (1940-)
A Woman's Tale '92
Sweet Talker '91

Sophia Myles (1980-)
Art School Confidential '06
Dracula '06
The Hades Factor '06
Tristan & Isolde '06
Underworld: Evolution '05
Thunderbirds '04
Underworld '03
Oliver Twist '00

John (Jack) Mylong (1892-1975)
The Mermaids of Tiburon '62
Robot Monster '53
For Whom the Bell Tolls '43

Jim Nabors (1932-)
Return to Mayberry '85
Cannonball Run 2 '84
Stroker Ace '83
The Best Little Whorehouse in Texas '82

Matheus Nachtergaele (1969-)
City of God '02
Mango Yellow '02

Nikolai Nademsky (1892-1937)
Earth '30
Zvenigora '28

George Nader (1921-2002)
Beyond Atlantis '73
The House of 1000 Dolls '67
The Human Duplicators '64
Away All Boats '56
Lady Godiva '55
Carnival Story '54
Sins of Jezebel '53
Robot Monster '53

Michael Nader (1945-)
The Finishing Touch '92

The Flash '90
Nick Knight '89
The Great Escape 2: The Untold Story '88
Lady, Mobster '88
The Trip '67

Lycia Naff (1962-)
Chopper Chicks in Zombietown '91
Lethal Weapon '87

Masatoshi Nagase (1966-)
The Hidden Blade '04
Cold Fever '95
Autumn Moon '92
Mystery Train '89

Anne Nagel (1912-66)
Don Winslow of the Navy '43
Dawn Express '42
The Mad Monster '42
The Secret Code '42
Man Made Monster '41
Argentine Nights '40
Black Friday '40
Winners of the West '40
Yellow Cargo '36
Dangerous Corner '34
Ann Vickers '33
The Kiss '29
Dubarry '30
The Divorcee '30
The Michigan Kid '28
The Mysterious Lady '28

Alan Naggar
Cleo/Leo '89

Parminder K. Nagra (1975-)
Ella Enchanted '04
Bend It Like Beckham '02

Philippe Nahon (1938-)
High Tension '03
Irreversible '02
Brotherhood of the Wolf '01
The Chateau '01
I Stand Alone '98

Ajay Naidu (1972-)
The Honeymooners '05
The War Within '05
K-PAX '01
You Are Here * '00
Chutney Popcorn '99
Office Space '99
Pi '98
subUrbia '96
More Dogs Than Bones '00
Touch and Go '86
Where the River Runs Black '86
Gung Ho '86

Joanne Nail (1947-)
The Visitor '80
Switchblade Sisters '75

J. Carrol Naish (1900-73)
Dracula vs. Frankenstein '71
Force of Impulse '60
This Could Be the Night '57
The Last Command '55
Rage at Dawn '55
Sitting Bull '54
Beneath the 12-Mile Reef '53
Fighter Attack '53
Clash by Night '52
Across the Wide Missouri '51
The Denver & Rio Grande '51
Annie Get Your Gun '50
Rio Grande '50
The Black Hand '50
The Toast of New Orleans '50
That Midnight Kiss '49
The Fugitive '48
The Kissing Bandit '48
The Beast with Five Fingers '46
Humoresque '46
Getting Gertie's Garter '45
The Southerner '45
Strange Confession '45
Dragon Seed '44
House of Frankenstein '44
Jungle Woman '44
The Monster Maker '44
Waterfront '44
Behind the Rising Sun '43
Sahara '43
The Corsican Brothers '42
Tales of Manhattan '42
Birth of the Blues '41
Blood and Sand '41
Down Argentine Way '40
Beau Geste '39
King of Alcatraz '38
Sea Racketeers '37
Thunder Trail '37
The Charge of the Light Brigade '36
Charlie Chan at the Circus '36
Special Investigator '36
Black Fury '35
Captain Blood '35
Confidential '35
The Lives of a Bengal Lancer '35
Under the Pampas Moon '35
Mystery Squadron '33
No Other Woman '33
The World Gone Mad '33
Kid from Spain '32
The Royal Bed '31

Laurence Naismith (1908-92)
Amazing Mr. Blunden '72
Diamonds Are Forever '71
Quest for Love '71
The Bushbaby '70
The Valley of Gwangi '69
Jason and the Argonauts '63
The Prince and the Pauper '62
Greyfriars Bobby '61
Sink the Bismarck '60
The Trials of Oscar Wilde '60
Village of the Damned '60
The World of Suzie Wong '60
Third Man on the Mountain '59
A Night to Remember '58
Abandon Ship '57
Robbery under Arms '57
The Man Who Never Was '55
Carrington, V.C. '54
Room to Let '49
Train of Events '49

Takashi Naito (1955-)
After Life '98
Maborosi '95
Merry Christmas, Mr. Lawrence '83

Taketoshi Naito (1926-)
After Life '98
The Human Condition: A Soldier's Prayer '61

Kathy Najimy (1957-)
Getting Played '05
Say Uncle '05
Rat Race '01
The Wedding Planner '01
If These Walls Could Talk 2 '00
Attention Shoppers '99
Bride of Chucky '98
Hope Floats '98
Zack & Reba '98
Nevada '97
New York Cop '94
Jeffrey '95
It's Pat: The Movie '94
Hocus Pocus '93
Sister Act 2: Back in the Habit '93
Sister Act '92
Soapdish '91
The Fisher King '91

Tatsuya Nakadai (1932-)
Wicked City '92
Ran '85
Hunter in the Dark '80
Kagemusha '80
Phoenix '78
Today We Kill, Tomorrow We Die '71
The Wolves '71
The Battle of the Japan Sea '70
Kojiro '67
Samurai Rebellion '67
Sword of Doom '67
Face of Another '66
Kwaidan '64
Harakiri '62
High & Low '62
Sanjuro '62
Yojimbo '61
The Human Condition: A Soldier's Prayer '61
The Human Condition: Road to Eternity '59
The Human Condition: No Greater Love '58
Enjo '58

Kiichi Nakai (1961-)
Riding Alone for Thousands of Miles '05
Warriors of Heaven and Earth '03

Haruo Nakajima (1929-)
War of the Gargantuas '70
King Kong vs. Godzilla '63

Ganjiro Nakamura (1902-83)
An Actor's Revenge '63
Odd Obsession '60
Drifting Weeds '59
Enjo '58
The Lower Depths '57

Katsuo Nakamura (1938-)
Steamboy '05 (V)
Samurai Banners '69
Kwaidan '64

Kinnosuke Nakamura (1932-97)
Swords of Death '71
Samurai Banners '69

Satoshi Nakamura (1908-92)
That Man Bolt '73
The Manster '59

Shido Nakamura (1972-)
Jet Li's Fearless '06
Letters from Iwo Jima '06
The Neighbor No. Thirteen '05

Tamao Nakamura (1939-)
Sleepy Eyes of Death: The Chinese Jade '63

Tadao Nakamura (1933-)
What's Up, Tiger Lily? '66
The Secret of the Telegian '61

Suzy Nakamura
Stark Raving Mad '02
Strawberry Fields '97

Alan Napier (1903-88)
The Bastard '78
Batman '66
The Loved One '65
Marnie '64
36 Hours '64
The Sword in the Stone '63
Premature Burial '62
Wild in the Country '61
Journey to the Center of the Earth '59
Until They Sail '57
The Mole People '56

Toru Nakamura (1965-)
Purple Butterfly '03
Tokyo Raiders '00
Gen-X Cops '99
Blue Tiger '94
New York Cop '94

Rodion Nakhapetov
Border Blues '03
A Slave of Love '78

Nita Naldi (1897-1961)
You Can't Fool Your Wife '40
Cobra '25
The Ten Commandments '23
Dr. Jekyll and Mr. Hyde '20
Blood and Sand '22
The Man from Beyond '22

Reggie Nalder (1911-91)
Border Blues '03
Dracula Sucks '79
Salem's Lot '79
Zoltan... Hound of Dracula '78
Mark of the Devil 2 '72
The Bird with the Crystal Plumage '70
Mark of the Devil '69

Leonardo Nam (1979-)
Vantage Point '08
The Fast and the Furious: Tokyo Drift '06
The Perfect Score '04

Joe Namath (1943-)
Chattanooga Choo Choo '84
Avalanche Express '79
C.C. & Company '70

Jack Nance (1943-96)
Little Witches '96
Lost Highway '96
The Secret Agent Club '96
The Demolitionist '95
Voodoo '95
Across the Moon '94
Meatballs 4 '92
The Hot Spot '90
Wild at Heart '90
Colors '88
Barfly '87
Blue Velvet '86
Dune '84
Ghoulies '84
Eraserhead '78
Breaker! Breaker! '77
Fury on Wheels '71

Charles Napier (1936-)
The Manchurian Candidate '04
Extreme Honor '01
Nutty Professor 2: The Klumps '00
Austin Powers 2: The Spy Who Shagged Me '99
The Big Tease '99
Cypress Edge '99
Austin Powers: International Man of Mystery '97
Hunter's Moon '97
Steel '97
The Cable Guy '96
Riot '96
Ripper Man '96
Felony '95
Hard Justice '95
Jury Duty '95
3 Ninjas Knuckle Up '95
Tyson '95
Ballistic '95
Silk Degrees '94
Mortal Danger '94
Body Shot '93
Skeeter '93
Center of the Web '92
Eyes of the Beholder '92
Indio 2: The Revolt '92
Return to Frogtown '92
Treacherous Crossing '92
The Silence of the Lambs '91
Soldier's Fortune '91
Dragon Fight '90
Ernest Goes to Jail '90
Future Zone '90
The Grifters '90
Miami Blues '90
One Man Force '89
The Hit List '88
The Incredible Hulk Returns '88
Married to the Mob '88
Deep Space '87
Kidnapped '87
Instant Justice '86
Something Wild '86
Rambo: First Blood, Part 2 '85
In Search of a Golden Sky '84

Jessica Napier (1979-)
The Alice '04
Cut '00
Love Serenade '96
Strange Planet '99
Starlight Hotel '90

Chieko Naniwa (1908-73)
Snow Country '57
A Geisha '53

Erica Nann (1962-)
Mind Twister '93

Isabelle Nanty (1962-)
Amelie '01
Tatie Danielle '91

Igal Naor
Munich '05
Rendition '07

Neriah Napaul (1972-)
The Bikini Car Wash Company 2 '92
The Bikini Car Wash Company '90

Tony Nardi (1958-)
Bonanno: A Godfather's Story '99
La Sarrasine '92

Daniela Nardini (1968-)
Reckless '02
Sirens '02

Tom Nardini (1945-)
Self-Defense '83
Africa Texas Style '67
The Young Animals? '70
Cat Ballou '65

Toni Naples (1952-)
Dinosaur Island '93
Deathstalker 2: Duel of the Titans '87

Darling Narita
Pups '99
Barq '99
Reckless '95

Kathrine Narducci (1965-)
Two Family House '99
A Bronx Tale '93

Paul Naschy (1934-)
The Craving '80
Human Beasts '80
Inquisition '76
Night of the Howling Beast '75
People Who Own the Dark '75
The Devil's Possessed '74
Exorcism '74
Curse of the Devil '73
Dracula's Great Love '72
The Hanging Woman '72
Horror Rises from the Tomb '72
Vengeance of the Zombies '72
Dr. Jekyll and the Wolfman '71
The Fury of the Wolfman '70
The Werewolf vs. the Vampire Woman '70
Dracula vs. Frankenstein '69

Arthur J. Nascarelli
The Groomsmen '06
Running Scared '06
Remedy '05
The Cooler '03
Wisegirls '02
Bringing Out the Dead '99
Cop Land '97
Belly '98

Nas (1973-)
Murda Muzik '03
Ticker '01
Belly '98

Tony Nardi (1958-)
Bonanno: A Godfather's Story '99
La Sarrasine '92

Chris Nash
Mischief '85
Silent Witness '85

Marilyn Nash (1924-)
Unknown World '51
Monsieur Verdoux '47
The Rains Came '39

Graham Nash (1942-)
Gimme Shelter '70

Niecy Nash (1970-)
Code Name: The Cleaner '07
Reno 911!: Miami '07
Guess Who '05
Cookie's Fortune '99

Mary Nash (1885-1976)
Cobra Woman '44
Last Embrace '79
The Philadelphia Story '40
Citizens Band '77
Easy Living '37
Heidi '37
Gimme Shelter '70

Marshall Napier
Strange Planet '99
Starlight Hotel '90

Noreen Nash (1924-)
Phantom from Space '53
Guess Who '05
The Devil on Wheels '47

Russell Napier (1910-75)
The Navigator '88
The Mark '61
Unholy Four '54
Across the Wide Missouri '51

The Red Stallion '47
The Tender Years '47

Deborah Ann Nassar
Dance of the Damned '88
Stripped to Kill '87

Joseph Nasser
Voyage of Terror: The Achille Lauro Affair '90
The Taking of Flight 847: The Uli Derickson Story '88

Frank Nasso
Dot.Kill '05
Prince of Central Park '00

Marie-Jose Nat (1940-)
Les Violons du Bal '74
Embassy '72
Love and the Frenchwoman '60

Anthony Natale
His Bodyguard '98
Mr. Holland's Opus '95

Adam Nathan
I Was a Teenage TV Terrorist '87
Parting Glances '86

Stephen Nathan (1948-)
You Light Up My Life '77
The First Nudie Musical '75
1776 '72
Those Glory, Glory Days '83

Francesca "Kitten" Natividad (1948-)
Suburban Girl '07
The Devil Wears Prada '06
Factory Girl '06
Fascination '04

Zoe Nathenson
One Night Stand '97
Mona Lisa '86

Mari Natsuki (1952-)
Remembering the Cosmos Flower '99
The Hunted '94

Yosuke Natsuki (1936-)
Dagora, the Space Monster '65
Ghidrah the Three Headed Monster '65
Attack Squadron '63
I Bombed Pearl Harbor '60

Masako Natsume (1958-85)
The Imperial Japanese Empire '85
MacArthur's Children '85
Antarctica '84

Mildred Natwick (1905-94)
Dangerous Liaisons '88
Kiss Me Goodbye '82
Daisy Miller '74
A House without a Christmas Tree '72
If It's Tuesday, This Must Be Belgium '69
Barefoot in the Park '67
Tammy and the Bachelor '57
Court Jester '56
The Trouble with Harry '55
Against All Flags '52
The Quiet Man '52
Cheaper by the Dozen '50
She Wore a Yellow Ribbon '49
The Kissing Bandit '48
Three Godfathers '48
The Enchanted Cottage '45
Yolanda and the Thief '45
The Long Voyage Home '40

Myron Natwick
Masters of Horror: The Washingtonians '07
DC 9/11: Time of Crisis '04

Shallow Ground '04
Project Vampire '93

David Naughton (1951-)
A Crack in the Floor '00
Mirror, Mirror 3: The Voyeur '96
Ice Cream Man '95
Beanstalk '94
Desert Steel '94
Amityville: A New Generation '93
Body Bags '93
Wild Cactus '92
Overexposed '90
The Sleeping Car '90
Steel and Lace '90
Private Affairs '89
Kidnapped '87
Boy in Blue '86
Separate Vacations '86
Getting Physical '84
Hot Dog...The Movie! '83
Separate Ways '82
An American Werewolf in London '81
Midnight Madness '80

James Naughton (1945-)
The Birds 2: Land's End '94
Blown Away '90
The Good Mother '88
The Glass Menagerie '87
Cat's Eye '85
A Stranger Is Watching '82
Second Wind '76
The Paper Chase '73

Demetrius Navarro
The Wash '01
187 '97
Soldier Boyz '95
First Kid '96

Nieves Navarro (1938-)
Blood at Sundown '88
Day of the Maniac '77
Trap Them & Kill Them '77
The Slasher '72

John P. Navin, Jr. (1968-)
Losin' It '82
Taps '81

Cliff Nazarro (1904-61)
'Neath Canadian Skies '46
Rhythm Parade '43
Hillbilly Blitzkrieg '42
Dive Bomber '41
In Old Colorado '41
Singing Buckaroo '37

Alla Nazimova (1879-1945)
The Bridge of San Luis Rey '44
Since You Went Away '44
Blood and Sand '41
Salome '22
Camille '21

Amedeo Nazzari (1907-79)
Nefertiti, Queen of the Nile '64
Journey Beneath the Desert '61
The Naked Maja '59
Nights of Cabiria '57
Lure of the Sila '49

Anna Neagle (1904-86)
Teenage Bad Girl '59
The King's Rhapsody '55
Let's Make Up '55
Maytime in Mayfair '49
Elizabeth of Ladymead '48
I Live in Grosvenor Square '46
Forever and a Day '43

Sunny '41
No, No Nanette '40
Nurse Edith Cavell '39
London Melody '37
Bitter Sweet '33

Billie Neal (1955-99)
Sweet Nothing '96
Consenting Adults '92
Mortal Thoughts '91
Down by Law '86

Diane Neal (1975-)
Dracula 3: Legacy '05
Dracula 2: Ascension '03

Dylan Neal (1969-)
Chupacabra Terror '05
40 Days and 40 Nights '02
Prom Night 3: The Last Kiss '89

Edwin Neal (1945-)
Future Kill '85
Neurotic Cabaret '90
The Texas Chainsaw Massacre '74

Elise Neal (1970-)
Hustle & Flow '05
Paid in Full '02
The Rising Place '02
Brian's Song '01
Restaurant '98
Mission to Mars '00

Ella Neal
Doctor Satan's Robot '40
Mysterious Doctor Satan '40

Patricia Neal (1926-)
Cookie's Fortune '99
Heidi '93
Caroline? '90
An Unremarkable Life '89
Love Leads the Way '84
Shattered Vows '84
Ghost Story '81
The Bastard '78
Love Affair: The Eleanor & Lou Gehrig Story '77
Widow's Nest '77
Eric '75
Things in Their Season '74
Run, Stranger, Run '73
Homecoming: A Christmas Story '71
The Subject Was Roses '68
In Harm's Way '65
Hud '63
Breakfast at Tiffany's '61
A Face in the Crowd '57
The Stranger from Venus '54
Diplomatic Courier '52
The Day the Earth Stood Still '51
Three Secrets '50

Peggy Neal (1947-)
X from Outer Space '67
Terror Beneath the Sea '66

Rome Neal
Pinero '01
Hamlet '00

Siri Neal (1972-)
Urban Ghost Story '98
The Children '90

Tom Neal (1914-72)
Danger Zone '51
Fingerprints Don't Lie '51
G.I. Jane '51
King of the Bullwhip '51
Stop That Cab '51
Apache Chief '50
I Shot Billy the Kid '50
Radar Secret Service '50
Red Desert '50
Train to Tombstone '50
Great Jesse James Raid '49
Hat Box Mystery '47
The Brute Man '46
Club Havana '46
Detour '46
My Dog Shep '46

First Yank into Tokyo '45
Behind the Rising Sun '43
Bowery at Midnight '42
Miracle Kid '42
Andy Hardy Meets Debutante '40
Courageous Dr. Christian '40

Kevin Nealon (1953-)
Grandma's Boy '06
Anger Management '03
Daddy Day Care '03
Good Boy! '03
Adam Sandler's 8 Crazy Nights '02 (V)
Bar Hopping '00
Little Nicky '00
The Principal Takes a Holiday '98
The Wedding Singer '97
Happy Gilmore '96
All I Want for Christmas '91
Roxanne '87

Christopher Neame (1947-)
The Apocalypse Watch '97
Project Shadowchaser 3000 '95
Hellbound '94
Street Knight '93
Boris and Natasha: The Movie '92
Still Not Quite Human '92
Suburban Commando '91
Bloodstone '88
D.O.A. '88
Transformations '88
Steel Dawn '87
Dracula A.D. 1972 '72

Holly Near (1949-)
Dogfight '91
Minnie and Moskowitz '71

Jesus Nebot
No Turning Back '01
Dementia '98

Claire Nebout (1964-)
On Guard! '01
Venus Beauty Institute '98
Beaumarchais the Scoundrel '96
Ponette '95
Scene of the Crime '87

Vaclav Neckar (1943-)
Larks on a String '68
Closely Watched Trains '66

Raisa Nedashkovskaya (1943-)
Commissar '68
The Tsar's Bride '66

Tracey Needham (1967-)
Backlash '99
Buried Alive 2 '97
Last Stand at Saber River '96
Sensation '94

Nique Needles (1964-)
Beverly Hills Family Robinson '97
Dogs in Space '88

Ted Neeley (1943-)
Hard Country '81
Of Mice and Men '81
Shadow of Chikara '77
Jesus Christ, Superstar '73

Cam Neely (1965-)
Me, Myself, and Irene '00
Dumb & Dumber '94

Mark Neely
The Siege of Firebase Gloria '89
Off the Mark '87
The Bastard '78

Liam Neeson (1952-)
The Chronicles of Narnia: Prince Caspian '08 (V)
Seraphim Falls '06
Batman Begins '05
The Chronicles of Narnia: The Lion, the Witch and the Wardrobe '05 (V)
Kingdom of Heaven '05

Kinsey '04
Love Actually '03
Gangs of New York '02
K-19: The Widowmaker '02
Gun Shy '00
The Haunting '99
Star Wars: Episode 1—The Phantom Menace '99
Les Miserables '98
Michael Collins '96
Before and After '95
Rob Roy '95
Nell '94
Schindler's List '93
Deception '92
Ethan Frome '92
Husbands and Wives '92
Leap of Faith '92
Shining Through '92
Under Suspicion '92
The Big Man: Crossing the Line '91
Darkman '90
Next of Kin '89
The Dead Pool '88
The Good Mother '88
High Spirits '88
Satisfaction '88
Suspect '87
Duet for One '86
Hold the Dream '86
The Mission '86
Lamb '85
The Bounty '84
A Woman of Substance '84
Krull '83
Excalibur '81

Hildegarde Neff
See Hildegarde Knef

Toshie Negishi (1954-)
Masters of Horror: Imprint '05
Okoge '93
Akira Kurosawa's Dreams '90

Natalia (Natalya) Negoda (1964-)
Back in the USSR '92
The Comrades of Summer '92
Little Vera '88

Francois Negret (1966-)
Night and Day '91
Au Revoir les Enfants '87

Pola Negri (1894-1987)
The Moon-Spinners '64
Hi Diddle Diddle '43
Hotel Imperial '27
One Arabian Night '21
Passion '19
Gypsy Blood '18

Mary Joan Negro
No Big Deal '83

Taylor Negron (1958-)
Call Me Claus '01
The Fluffer '01
Lloyd '00
Loser '00
A Kid in Aladdin's Palace '97
Mr. Stitch '95
Inevitable Grace '94
The Last Boy Scout '91
Nothing But Trouble '91
Punchline '88
Bad Medicine '85
Better Off Dead '85
Easy Money '83

David Neidorf
Rainbow Drive '90
Empire of the Sun '87
Undercover '87
Hoosiers '86
Platoon '86

Hildegard(e) Neil (1939-)
Antony and Cleopatra '73
A Touch of Class '73
The Man Who Haunted Himself '70

Richard Neil
Blondes Have More Guns '95

The Disappearance of Kevin Johnson '95

James Neill (1860-1931)
The Cheat '15
King of Kings '27

Noel Neill (1920-)
Superman Returns '06
Invasion U.S.A. '52
Atom Man vs. Superman '50
The Adventures of Frank and Jesse James '48
Here Come the Waves '45
The Stork Club '45

Sam Neill (1948-)
Irresistible '06
Merlin's Apprentice '06
The Incredible Journey of Mary Bryant '05
Little Fish '05
Wimbledon '04
Yes '04
Doctor Zhivago '03
Perfect Strangers '03
Dirty Deeds '02
Jurassic Park 3 '01
The Dish '00
Sally Hemings: An American Scandal '00
Bicentennial Man '99
Molokai: The Story of Father Damien '99
Merlin '98
Sweet Revenge '98
Event Horizon '97
The Horse Whisperer '97
Snow White: A Tale of Terror '97
Forgotten Silver '96
In Cold Blood '96
Children of the Revolution '95
Country Life '95
In the Mouth of Madness '95
Victory '95
Rainbow Warrior '94
Restoration '94
Rudyard Kipling's The Jungle Book '94
Sirens '94
Family Pictures '93
Jurassic Park '93
The Piano '93
Question of Faith '93
Hostage '92
Memoirs of an Invisible Man '92
Fever '91
One Against the Wind '91
Until the End of the World '91
Death in Brunswick '90
The Hunt for Red October '90
Dead Calm '89
A Cry in the Dark '88
Reilly: Ace of Spies '87
For Love Alone '86
The Good Wife '86
Plenty '85
Attack Force Z '84
The Blood of Others '84
Enigma '82
Ivanhoe '82
The Final Conflict '81
From a Far Country: Pope John Paul II '81
Possession '81
My Brilliant Career '79
Sleeping Dogs '77

Don Nakaya Neilsen
Blood Ring '93
Fist of Steel '93

John Neilson (1944-2000)
Terror at Red Wolf Inn '72
Honky '71

George Neise (1916-96)
The Three Stooges Meet Hercules '62
Outcasts of the City '58

Stacey Nelkin (1959-)
Everything Relative '96

Halloween 3: Season of the Witch '82
Children of Divorce '80
Up the Academy '80
The Triangle Factory Fire Scandal '79

David Nell
See David Knell

Nathalie Nell (1950-)
Echoes '83

Kate Nelligan (1951-)
Premonition '07
The Cider House Rules '99
U.S. Marshals '98
Calmat Sunset '96
Up Close and Personal '96
How to Make an American Quilt '95
Margaret's Museum '95
Wolf '94
Fatal Instinct '93
Terror Stalks the Class Reunion '93
Shadows and Fog '92
Frankie and Johnny '91
The Prince of Tides '91
Love and Hate: A Marriage Made in Hell '90
Control '87
Eleni '85
Without a Trace '83
Crossover '82
Eye of the Needle '81
Therese Raquin '80
Dracula '79
Bethune '77
Romantic Englishwoman '75
The Count of Monte Cristo '74

Nelly (1978-)
The Longest Yard '05
Snipes '01

Adam Nelson
Mystic River '03
Phantoms '97

Ann Nelson (1916-92)
My Girl '91

Barry Nelson (1920-2007)
Ghosts That Still Walk '77
'41

Bob Nelson (1956-)
Brein Donors '92
Miracles '86
Ryder P.I. '86

Bobby Nelson (1923-93)
Boothill Brigade '37
The Red Rope '37
Cowboy & the Bandit '35
Cyclone of the Saddle '35
Ghost Rider '35
Rough Riding Ranger '35
Way of the West '35
Rearing Ranch '30

Craig Richard Nelson (1947-)
My Bodyguard '80
Tank '78

Craig T. Nelson (1946-)
Blades of Glory '07
The Family Stone '05
The Incredibles '04 (V)
Dirty Pictures '00
3 Women '77
The Paper Chase '73
Greener Over the Septic Tank '78

Danny Nelson
A Good Baby '99
Blood Salvage '90

David Nelson (1936-)
Cry-Baby '90
High School USA '84
The Day of the Outlaw '59
Peyton Place '57
Here Come the Nelsons '52

Ed Nelson (1928-)
Jackie Chan's Who Am I '98
Cries of Silence '97
The Bone Yard '90
Deadly Weapon '88
Brenda Starr '86
Soldier in the Rain '63
A Bucket of Blood '59
T-Bird Gang '59
The Devil's Partner '58
Night of the Blood Beast '58
Teenage Doll '57
Invasion of the Saucer Men '57
Carnival Rock '57
Hot Rod Girl '56
Mohawk '56
Pardners '56
Day the World Ended '55
I Died a Thousand Times '55
Swamp Women '55
Airport '75 '75
Midway '76

Gene Nelson (1920-96)
The Atomic Man '56
The Way Out '56
Oklahoma! '55
Crime Wave '54
Lullaby of Broadway '51
Tea for Two '50
The West Point Story '50

Harriet Hilliard Nelson (1909-94)
The Kid with the 200 I.Q. '83
Here Come the Nelsons '52
Take It Big '44
Swingtime Johnny '43
Honeymoon Lodge '43
Follow the Fleet '36

Lloyd Nelson (1927-2007)
The Wild World of Batwoman '66
Curse of the Stone Hand '64
The Incredible Petrified World '58

Lori Nelson (1933-)
The Pied Piper of Hamelin '57
Ma and Pa Kettle at Waikiki '55
Revenge of the Creature '55
Francis Goes to West Point '52

Margaret Nelson
Picnic at Hanging Rock '75

Novella Nelson
Dear Wendy '05
Preaching to the Choir '05
Antwone Fisher '02
A Perfect Murder '98
Manny & Lo '96
Scalp Merchant '77

Tracy Nelson (1963-)
Perfect Game '00
The Perfect Nanny '00
Perfect Tenant '99
The Night Caller '97
The Game of Love '90
Down and Out in Beverly Hills '85
Maria's Lovers '84
Yours, Mine & Ours '68

Willie Nelson (1933-)
Blonde Ambition '07
The Dukes of Hazzard '05
The Big Bounce '04
Outlaw Justice '99
Austin Powers 2: The Spy Who Shagged Me '99
Gone Fishin' '97
Half-Baked '97
Starlight '97
Wag the Dog '97
Windmills of the Gods '88
Django Strikes Again '87
Sweet Country '87
Challenge to White Fang '86
Another Pair of Aces: Three of a Kind '91
Pair of Aces '90
Texas Guns '90
Dynamite and Gold '88
Baja Oklahoma '87
Red Headed Stranger '87
Amazons '86
Last Days of Frank & Jesse James '86
Stagecoach '86
Songwriter '84
Barbarosa '82
Coming Out of the Ice '82
Thief '81
Honeysuckle Rose '80
The Electric Horseman '79

Jerry Nelson (1934-)
The Muppet Christmas Carol '92 (V)
The Muppet Movie '79 (V)

Herbert Nelson (1913-90)
Mercy '96

John Allen Nelson (1959-)
Deathstalker 3 '89
Killer Klowns from Outer Space '88
Saigon Commandos '88
Hunk '87

Judd Nelson (1959-)
The Other '04
The Lost Angel '04
Cybermut '02
Dark Asylum '01
Jay and Silent Bob Strike Back '01
Lost Voyage '01
Cabin by the Lake '00
Light It Up '99
Mr. Rock 'n' Roll: The Alan Freed Story '99
Steel '97
Blackwater Trail '95
Circumstances Unknown '95
Airheads '94
The Dark Backward '91
New Jack City '91
Hiroshima: Out of the Ashes '90
Relentless '89
Far Out Man '89
Blue City '86
From the Hip '86
Fandango '85
St. Elmo's Fire '85
The Breakfast Club '85
Making the Grade '84

Ozzie Nelson (1906-75)
The Impossible Years '68
Here Come the Nelsons '52
People Are Funny '46
Take It Big '44
Big Street '42

Peter Nelson (1921-)
Eye of the Eagle 3 '91
Sounds of Silence '91
The Expendables '89
Silk 2 '89

Ricky Nelson (1940-85)
Over the Hill Gang '69
Love and Kisses '65
The Wackiest Ship in the Army '61
Rio Bravo '59
Here Come the Nelsons '52

Ruth Nelson (1905-92)
The Haunting Passion '83
A Christmas Without Snow '80
3 Women '77
Humoresque '46
Wilson '44

Sandra Nelson (1962-)
De-Lovely '04
Maternal Instincts '96
American Buffalo '95
Little Ninjas '92

Sean Nelson (1980-)
The Corner '00
The Wood '99
American History X '98
Fresh '94

Steven Nelson
Men Cry Bullets '00

Tim Blake Nelson (1965-)
The Incredible Hulk '08
The Astronaut Farmer '07
Come Early Morning '06
The Darwin Awards '06
Fido '06
Hoot '06
The Big White '05
The Mogus '05
Syriana '05
Meet the Fockers '04
Scooby-Doo 2: Monsters Unleashed '04
Holes '03
2 Brothers & a Bride '03
Wonderland '03
Cherish '02
The Good Girl '02
Minority Report '02
O Brother Where Art Thou? '00
The Thin Red Line '98

Corin "Corky" Nemec (1971-)
Mosquitoman '05
Killer Bud '02
Brother's Keeper '02
The First to Go '97
The War at Home '96
Operation Dumbo Drop '95
Drop Zone '94
Stephen King's The Stand '94
White Wolves 2: Legend of the Wild '94
Men of War '94
Solar Crisis '92
Tucker: The Man and His Dream '88

Franco Nero (1942-)
David '97
Talk of Angels '96
The Innocent Sleep '95
Young Catherine '91
Die Hard 2: Die Harder '90
Magdalene '88
Wagner: The Complete Epic '85
Wagner: The Movie '85
Day of the Cobra '84
Querelle '83
The Salamander '82
Enter the Ninja '82
The Man with Bogart's Face '80
Shark Hunter '79
Submission '77
Last Four Days '77
21 Hours at Munich '76
Sardinia Kidnapped '75
Legend of Valentino '75
Spaghetti Western '75
Force 10 from Navarone '78
The Virgin and the Gypsy '70
Tristana '70
Companeros '70
Battle of Neretva '69
Ring of Death '69
Django '68
Camelot '67
Texas, Adios '67
The Bible '87

Neil Nephew
Panic in the Year Zero! '62
The Young Savages '61

Francesca Neri (1964-)
Collateral Damage '02
Hannibal '01
Live Flesh '97
Flight of the Innocent '93
Outrage '93

Rosalba Neri (1940-)
The Arena '73
Devil's Wedding Night '73
Lady Frankenstein '72
Amuck! '71
Slaughter Hotel '71
The Seducers '70
The Castle of Fu Manchu '68

David Nerman
Nightwaves '03
The Witness Files '00
The Minion '98
Sir Arthur Conan Doyle's The Lost World '98
Witchboard 3: The Possession '95
The Scorpio Factor '90

Michael Nesmith (1942-)
Tapeheads '89
Head '68

James Nesbitt (1966-)
Jekyll '07
Match Point '05
Millions '05
Bloody Sunday '01
Lucky Break '01
Waking Ned Devine '98
Welcome to Sarajevo '97
Resurrection Man '97
Go Now '96

Caroline Neron (1973-)
Eternal '04
Strip Search '97

Toni Nero
No Dead Heroes '87
Silent Night, Deadly Night '84

Cathleen Nesbitt (1888-1982)
Family Plot '76
Promise Her Anything '66
The Parent Trap '61
Separate Tables '58
An Affair to Remember '57
Black Widow '54
Desiree '54
Men of Two Worlds '46
Nicholas Nickleby '46
The Passing of the Third Floor Back '36

Derren Nesbitt (1932-)
Funny Money '82
Horrors of Burke & Hare '71
Where Eagles Dare '68
The Blue Max '66
Victim '61

Loni Nest (1915-)
The Golem '20
Joyless Street '25

Lois Nettleton (1927-2008)
David '97
The Painted Lady '97
Brass '85
Soggy Bottom U.S.A. '84
The Best Little Whorehouse in Texas '82
Butterfly '82
Deadly Blessing '81
Centennial '78
Bull of the West '71
The Good Guys and the Bad Guys '69
Period of Adjustment '62
Mirror, Mirror 2: Raven Dance '94

Martin Neufeld
Relative Fear '95
H '90

Alex Neuberger (1992-)
Underdog '07
Running Scared '06

Dorothy Neumann (1912-94)
Private Parts '72
The Terror '63
The Undead '57

Jenny Neumann
Delos Adventure '86
Stage Fright '83
Hell Night '81
Mistress of the Apes '79
Swim Team '79

Bebe Neuwirth (1958-)
Game 6 '05
The Big Bounce '04
How to Lose a Guy in 10 Days '03
Le Divorce '03
Tadpole '02
Cupid & Cate '00
Dash and Lilly '99
Liberty Heights '99
Summer of Sam '99
Celebrity '98
The Faculty '98
The Adventures of Pinocchio '96
The Associate '96
All Dogs Go to Heaven 2 '95 (V)
Jumanji '95
Malice '93
The Paint Job '93
Wild Palms '93
Bugsy '91
Green Card '90
Say Anything '89

Chantal Neuwirth
Gabrielle '05
A Very Long Engagement '04
Rendez-Moi Ma Peau '81

Aaron Neville (1941-)
The Last Ride '94
Posse '93
Zandalee '91

John Neville (1925-)
Hollywood North '03
The Statement '03
Spider '02
The Duke '99
Goodbye, Lover '99
Sunshine '99
My Teacher Ate My Homework '98
Urban Legend '98
Behind the Lines '97
The Fifth Element '97
Sabotage '96
Swann '96
Dangerous Minds '95
Song Spinner '95
Baby's Day Out '94
Little Women '94
The Road to Wellville '94
The Adventures of Baron Munchausen '89
A Study in Terror '66
The Unearthly Stranger '64
Billy Budd '62

Brooke Nevin (1982-)
The Comebacks '07
Running Wild '99

Robyn Nevin (1942-)
The Matrix Reloaded '03
The Matrix Revolutions '03
Angel Baby '95
Resistance '92
Careful, He Might Hear You '84

Claudette Nevins
Star Trek: Insurrection '98
Sweet Evil '77
Widow's Kiss '94
Child of Darkness, Child of Light '91
Sleeping with the Enemy '91
Tuff Turf '85
Don't Go to Sleep '82
Take Your Best Shot '82
...All the Marbles '81
Jacqueline Bouvier Kennedy '81
The Possessed '77
The Mask '61

Anzhelika Nevolina (1962-)
Of Freaks and Men '98
Creation of Adam '93

Derek Newark (1933-98)
Bellman and True '88
The Offence '73
The Blue Max '66

George Newbern (1964-)
A Dennis the Menace Christmas '07
Crazy Eights '06
If These Walls Could Talk 2 '00
Friends & Lovers '99
The Simple Life of Noah Dearborn '99
The Evening Star '96
Far Harbor '96
Father of the Bride Part 2 '95
Witness to the Execution '94
Father of the Bride '91
Doppelganger: The Evil Within '90
It Takes Two '88
Paramedics '88
Switching Channels '88
Adventures in Babysitting '87
My Little Girl '87

Anthony Newcastle
Metallica '85

William "Billy" Newell (1894-1967)
Captive Planet '78
Escape from Fort Bravo '53
Doctor Satan's Robot '40
The Invisible Killer '40
Mysterious Doctor Satan '40
The Mandarin Mystery '37
Bulldog Edition '36

Bob Newhart (1929-)
Elf '03
Legally Blonde 2: Red White & Blonde '03
In and Out '97
First Family '80
Little Miss Marker '80
Marathon '80
The Rescuers Down Under '90 (V)
The Rescuers '77 (V)
Thursday's Game '74
Cold Turkey '71
Catch-22 '70
On a Clear Day You Can See Forever '70
Hot Millions '68
Hell Is for Heroes '62

James Newill (1911-75)
Boss of Rawhide '44
Guns of the Law '44
Outlaw Roundup '44
Fighting Valley '43
Rangers Take Over '42
The Great American Broadcast '41
Danger Ahead '40
Murder on the Yukon '40
Sky Bandits '40
Yukon Flight '40
Fighting Mad '39
Renfrew on the Great White Trail '38
Renfrew of the Royal Mounted '37

Anthony Newlands (1926-95)
Scream and Scream Again '70
Circus of Fear '67

Anthony Newley (1931-99)
Boris and Natasha: The Movie '92
The Garbage Pail Kids Movie '87
Outrage! '86
Stagecoach '86
Alice in Wonderland '85
Blade in Hong Kong '85
It Seemed Like a Good Idea at the Time '75
The Old Curiosity Shop '75
Sweet November '68
Doctor Dolittle '67
Let's Get Married '60
Fire Down Below '57
Above Us the Waves '56
X The Unknown '56
Oliver Twist '48
Little Ballerina '47

Alec Newman (1974-)
Children of Dune '03
Dr. Bell and Mr. Doyle: The Dark Beginnings of Sherlock Holmes '00
Dune '00

Barry Newman (1938-)
Daylight '96
Fatal Vision '84
Having It All '82
Amy '81
Deadline '81
City on Fire '78
The Salzburg Connection '72
Vanishing Point '71

Daniel Newman (1976-)
Endgame '01
The Return of the Borrowers '96
Shopping '93

Laraine Newman (1952-)
Barnyard '06 (V)
The Modern Adventures of Tom Sawyer '98
Jingle All the Way '96
Alone in the Woods '95
The Flintstones '94
Coneheads '93
Her Life as a Man '83
Wholly Moses! '80
Mr. Mike's Mondo Video '79
Tunnelvision '76

Nanette Newman (1934-)
The Mystery of Edwin Drood '93
The Stepford Wives '75
Long Ago Tomorrow '71
The Madwoman of Chaillot '69
Oh! What a Lovely War '69
The Wrong Arm of the Law '63

Paul Newman (1925-)
Cars '06 (V)
Empire Falls '05
Our Town '03
Road to Perdition '02
Where the Money Is '00
Message in a Bottle '98
Twilight '98
Nobody's Fool '94
Mr. & Mrs. Bridge '90
Blaze '89
Fat Man and Little Boy '89
The Color of Money '86
Harry & Son '84
The Verdict '82
Absence of Malice '81
Fort Apache, the Bronx '81
When Time Ran Out '80
Quintet '79
Slap Shot '77
Buffalo Bill & the Indians '76
Silent Movie '76
The Drowning Pool '75
The Towering Inferno '74
Mackintosh Man '73
The Sting '73
Life & Times of Judge Roy Bean '72
Pocket Money '72
Sometimes a Great Notion '71
Butch Cassidy and the Sundance Kid '69
Winning '69
The Secret War of Harry Frigg '68
Cool Hand Luke '67
Hombre '67
Harper '66
Tom Curtain '66
Lady L '65
Hud '63
A New Kind of Love '63
The Prize '63
Sweet Bird of Youth '62
The Hustler '61
Paris Blues '61
Exodus '60
From the Terrace '60
The Young Philadelphians '59
Cat on a Hot Tin Roof '58
The Left-Handed Gun '58
The Long, Hot Summer '58
Rally 'Round the Flag, Boys! '58
Until They Sail '57
Bang the Drum Slowly '56
Somebody Up There Likes Me '56
The Silver Chalice '54

Phyllis Newman (1933-)
The Human Stain '03
It Had to Be You '00
A Price above Rubies '97
A Secret Space '88
Follies in Concert '85
Picnic '55

Stephen D. Newman (1943-)
Yuri Nosenko, KGB '86
Sophie's Choice '82

Julie Newmar (1935-)
Oblivion 2 '95
To Wong Foo, Thanks for Everything, Julie Newmar '95
Oblivion '94
Nudity Required '90
Body Beat '88
Deep Space '87
Evils of the Night '85
Streetwalkin' '85
Ecstasy '84
Hysterical '83
Terraces '77
MacKenna's Gold '69
For Love or Money '63
Li'l Abner '59
Seven Brides for Seven Brothers '54

Lisa Marie Newmyer
A Scanner Darkly '06
Sin City '05
The House on Todville Road '95
The Texas Chainsaw Massacre 4: The Next Generation '95

John Haymes Newman (1965-)
Operation Sandman: Warriors in Hell '00
Alive '93
Desert Kickboxer '92

Margit Evelyn Newton
Hell of the Living Dead '83
The Last Hunter '80

Mary Newton
Zero Hour! '57
Tomorrow the World '44

Matt Newton (1977-)
Poster Boy '04
Dahmer '02

Robert Newton (1905-56)
Around the World in 80 Days '56
The High and the Mighty '54
Long John Silver '54
The Desert Rats '53
Androcles and the Lion '52
Blackbeard the Pirate '52
Tom Brown's School Days '51
Treasure Island '50
The Hidden Room '49
Oliver Twist '48
Odd Man Out '47
This Happy Breed '47
Henry V '44
Gaslight '40
Jamaica Inn '39
Beachcomber '38
21 Days '37

Thandie Newton (1972-)
Norbit '07
Run, Fat Boy, Run '07
The Pursuit of Happyness '06
Crash '05
The Chronicles of Riddick '04
Shade '03
The Truth About Charlie '02
Mission: Impossible 2 '00
Beloved '98
Besieged '98
Gridlock'd '96
The Leading Man '96
The Journey of August King '95
Jefferson in Paris '95
Loaded '94
The Young Americans '93
Flirting '89

Theodore Newton (1942-)
Ace of Aces '33
The Sphinx '33

Wayne Newton (1942-)
Ocean's Eleven '01
Elvis Meets Nixon '98
Vegas Vacation '96
Best of the Best 2 '93
The Dark Backward '91
The Adventures of Ford Fairlane '90
License to Kill '89

Olivia Newton-John (1948-)
Sordid Lives '00
It's My Party '95
Two of a Kind '83
Xanadu '80
Grease '78

Richard Ney (1916-2004)
Premature Burial '62
The Lovable Cheat '49
Mrs. Miniver '42

Anne Neyland
Jailhouse Rock '57
Motorcycle Gang '57

Marina Neyolova (1947-)
Autumn Marathon '79
The Errors of Youth '78

Jinpachi Nezu (1947-)
Nobody '99
Ran '85

Carrie Ng (1963-)
Sex and Zen '93
Naked Killer '92
City on Fire '87

Frances Ng
Exiled '06
The Mission '99
The Bride with White Hair '93

Lawrence Ng
Sex and Zen '93
Lethal Panther '90

David Ngoombujarra (1967-)
Kangaroo Jack '02
Kings in Grass Castles '97
Breaking Loose '90

Haing S. Ngor (1940-96)
Hit Me '96
Fortunes of War '94
Heaven and Earth '93
My Life '93
Ambition '91
In Love and War '91
Last Flight Out: A True Story '90
Vietnam, Texas '90
The Iron Triangle '89
Eastern Condors '87
The Killing Fields '84

Dustin Nguyen (1962-)
Little Fish '05
3 Ninjas Kick Back '94
Heaven and Earth '93
No Escape, No Return '93
Rapid Fire '92

Long Nguyen (1958-)
Coyote Waits '03
Green Dragon '01

Michelle Nicastro (1960-)
The Swan Princess 2: Escape from Castle Mountain '97 (V)
The Swan Princess '94 (V)
When Harry Met Sally... '89
Bad Guys '86
Body Rock '84

Maurizio Nichetti (1948-)
Luna e L'Altra '96
Stephano Quantestorie '93
Volere Volare '92
The Icicle Thief '89
Allegro Non Troppo '76

Angela Nicholas
Alien Space Avenger '91
Galactic Gigolo '87

Anna Nicholas
Bloodstone '88
Mutants in Paradise '84

Denise Nicholas (1944-)
Ghost Dad '90
Sophisticated Gents '81
Piece of the Action '77
Let's Do It Again '75
Blacula '72

Harold Nicholas (1921-2000)
The Five Heartbeats '91
Tap '89
Fass Black '77

Thomas Ian Nicholas (1980-)
Stealing Sinatra '04
American Wedding '03
Halloween: Resurrection '02
American Pie 2 '01
American Pie '99
A Kid in Aladdin's Palace '97
A Kid in King Arthur's Court '95
Rookie of the Year '93
The Fear Inside '92

Paul Nicholas (1945-)
Alice '86
Nutcracker Sweet '84
The World Is Full of Married Men '80
Yesterday's Hero '79
Lisztomania '75
Tommy '75
Invitation to the Wedding '73
French Intrigue '70
Judge & Jury '96

Allan Nicholls (1945-)
The Crew '00
Bob Roberts '92
Obsessed '88
Trouble in Mind '86
Home Free All '84
Popeye '80
A Wedding '78
Slap Shot '77
Nashville '75
Playgirl Killer '66

Anthony Nicholls (1902-77)
The Merchant of Venice '73
Say Goodbye, Maggie Cole '72
Victim '61
Othello '65
Burn Witch, Burn! '62
The Franchise Affair '52
White Gold '28
The Eagle '25

George Nicholls, Jr. (1897-1939)
Finishing School '33
The Country Kid '23
The Greatest Question '19

Paul Nicholls (1979-)
Bridget Jones: The Edge of Reason '04

Phoebe Nicholls (1958-)
The Trench '99
Heart of Darkness '93
Deep Cover '88
Maurice '87
Party Party! '83

Nichelle Nichols (1933-)
Are We There Yet? '05
Snow Dogs '02
Star Trek 6: The Undiscovered Country '91
Star Trek 5: The Final Frontier '89
Star Trek 4: The Voyage Home '86
The Supernaturals '86
Star Trek 3: The Search for Spock '84
Star Trek 2: The Wrath of Khan '82
Star Trek: The Motion Picture '79
Truck Turner '74

Rachel Nichols (1980-)
Resurrecting the Champ '07
The Amityville Horror '05
Sisterhood of the Traveling Pants 2 '08
P2 '07
Dumb and Dumberer: When Harry Met Lloyd '03

Jennifer Nicholson (1963-)
The Wild Ride '60

Taylor Nichols (1959-)
Jurassic Park 3 '01
Boiler Room '00
Gideon '99
The Sex Monster '99
Born Bad '97
Barcelona '94
Metropolitan '90

Stephen Nichols (1951-)
Second Sight '99
Fairy Tale: A True Story '97
The Glass Cage '96
Phoenix '95
Soapdish '91
Witchboard '87

Robert Nichols (1928-)
The Night They Robbed Big Bertha's '75
The Thing '51

Austin Nichols (1980-)
How She Move '08
Rude '96
Skin Deep '94

Melanie Nicholls-King
The Next Step '95
Norma Jean and Marilyn '95

Barbara Nichols (1929-76)
The Loved One '65
The Human Duplicators '64
Scarface Mob '62
Where the Boys Are '60
Pal Joey '57
Sweet Smell of Success '57
Beyond a Reasonable Doubt '56
The King and Four Queens '56

Britt Nichols
The Demons '74
Rites of Frankenstein '72
Virgin among the Living Dead '71

Conrad Nichols
Buck and the Magic Bracelet '97
Days of Hell '84
A Man Called Rage '84
Rush '84

Dandy Nichols (1907-86)
Georgy Girl '66
Ladies Who Do '63
The Leather Boys '63
The Fallen Idol '49

Marisol Nichols (1973-)
Delta Farce '07
Big Momma's House 2 '06
Vegas Vacation '96

Jack Nicholson (1937-)
The Bucket List '07
The Departed '06
Something's Gotta Give '03
Anger Management '03
About Schmidt '02
The Pledge '00
As Good as It Gets '97
Blood & Wine '96
The Evening Star '96
Mars Attacks! '96
The Crossing Guard '94
Wolf '94
A Few Good Men '92
Hoffa '92
Man Trouble '92
The Two Jakes '90
Batman '89
Broadcast News '87
Ironweed '87
The Witches of Eastwick '87
Heartburn '86
Prizzi's Honor '85
Terms of Endearment '83
The Border '82
The Postman Always Rings Twice '81
Reds '81
The Shining '80
Goin' South '78
The Last Tycoon '76
The Missouri Breaks '76
One Flew over the Cuckoo's Nest '75
The Passenger '75
Tommy '75
Chinatown '74
The Last Detail '73

Julianne Nicholson (1971-)
Flannel Pajamas '06
Puccini for Beginners '06
Two Weeks '06
Kinsey '04
Little Black Book '04
Seeing Other People '04
I'm with Lucy '02
Cash Crop '01
Dead Dog '00
Tully '00

Nick Nicholson
Long Time Since '97
Fist of Steel '93
Raiders of the Sun '92
Triple Impact '92

Grant Nickalls
Power and Beauty '02
Glitter '01

Denise Nickerson (1959-)
Zero to Sixty '78
Smile '75
Willy Wonka & the Chocolate Factory '71

Michael A. (M.A.) Nickles (1968-)
Baja '95
Desert Winds '95
Wayne's World 2 '93
Hamburger Hill '87

Julia Nickson-Soul (1959-)
Life Tastes Good '99
White Tiger '95
Double Dragon '94
Amityville: A New Generation '93
Sidekicks '93
K2: The Ultimate High '92
China Cry '91
Around the World in 80 Days '89
Rambo: First Blood, Part 2 '85

Alex Nicol (1919-2001)
A*P*E '76
A Matter of WHO '62
The Screaming Skull '58
Strangler of the Swamp... [Great Day in the Morning '56]
The Man from Laramie '55
Black Glove '54
The Gilded Cage '54
Heat Wave '54
The Redhead from Wyoming '53

Daria Nicolodi (1950-)
Scarlet Diva '00

Leslie Nielsen (1926-)
Superhero Movie '08
Scary Movie 4 '06
Scary Movie 3 '03
Men with Brooms '02
Chilly Dogs '01
2001: A Space Travesty '00
Safety Patrol '98
Wrongfully Accused '98
Mr. Magoo '97
Spy Hard '96
The Chinatown Murders: It '95
Rent-A-Kid '95
Digger '94
Naked Gun 33 1/3: The Final Insult '94
All I Want for Christmas '91
Naked Gun 2 1/2: The Smell of Fear '91
Repossessed '90
Dangerous Curves '88
Home is Where the Hart is '88
The Naked Gun: From the Files of Police Squad '88
Nightstick '87
Nuts '87
Striker's Mountain '87
The Patriot '86
Soul Man '86
Blade in Hong Kong '85
Reckless Disregard '84
Foxfire Light '82
Wrong is Right '82

Hans Nielsen (1911-65)
The Monster of London City '64
Strangler of Blackmoor Castle '63
Sherlock Holmes and the Deadly Necklace '62
The Third Sex '57

Connie Nielsen (1965-)
Brothers '05
The Great Raid '05
The Ice Harvest '05
Convicted '04
Basic '03
The Hunted '03
Demonlover '02
One Hour Photo '02
Gladiator '00
Innocents '00
Mission to Mars '00
Rushmore '98
Soldier '98
The Devil's Advocate '97
Voyage '93

Jennifer Nicholson (1963-)
The Raven '63

Michael Nicolosi
Hell's Kitchen NYC '97
Persons Unknown '96
Things to Do in Denver When You're Dead '95
Dream a Little Dream 2 '94
Murders '75

Brigitte Nielsen (1963-)
Doomsday '01
Doomsdayer '99
Snowboard Academy '96
Galaxis '95
Chained Heat 2 '92
Murder by Moonlight '91
Body Court '95
Beverly Hills Cop 2 '87
Cobra '86
Red Sonja '85
Rocky 4 '85

The King of Marvin Gardens '72
Carnal Knowledge '71
Five Easy Pieces '70
On a Clear Day You Can See Forever '70
Easy Rider '69
Head '68
Rebel Rousers '69
Psych-Out '68
Hell's Angels on Wheels '67
The St. Valentine's Day Massacre '67
Flight to Fury '66
Ride in the Whirlwind '66
The Shooting '66
Ensign Pulver '64
The Terror '63
Little Shop of Horrors '60
Studs Lonigan '60

Star Trek 6: The Undiscovered Country '91
Star Trek 5: The Final Frontier '89
Star Trek 4: The Voyage Home '86
Star Trek 3: The Search for Spock '84
Star Trek 2: The Wrath of Khan '82
Star Trek: The Motion Picture '79

Bill Nighy (1949-)
Hot Fuzz '07
Pirates of the Caribbean: At World's End '07
Stormbreaker '06
Flushed Away '06 (V)
Notes on a Scandal '06
Pirates of the Caribbean: Dead Man's Chest '06
The Constant Gardener '05
Doogal '05 (V)
Gideon's Daughter '05
The Girl in the Cafe '05
The Hitchhiker's Guide to the Galaxy '05
Shaun of the Dead '04
Underworld: Evolution '05
Love Actually '03
State of Play '03
Underworld '03
AKA '02
I Capture the Castle '02
Lawless Heart '01
Lucky Break '01
Blow Dry '00
Longitude '00
Still Crazy '98
FairyTale: A True Story '97
Alive and Kicking '96
Being Human '94
Antonia and Jane '91
The Phantom of the Opera '89
Agatha Christie's Thirteen at Dinner '85

Jane Nigh (1925-93)
Motor Patrol '50

Jose Nieto (1942-)
Super Force '90
Steel Dawn '87
Harlow '65

Lisa Niemi (1957-)
Forbidden Planet 56 [?]
Tammy and the Bachelor '57
They Call It Murder '71
Four Rode Out '69
How to Commit Marriage '69
Dayton's Devils '68
The Reluctant Astronaut '67
Resurrection of Zachary Wheeler '71
Snatched '72

Michael Nicolosi
Hell's Kitchen NYC '97

Miho Nikaido (1966-)
Flirt '95
Tokyo Decadence '91

Jan Niklas (1947-)
The Winter War '89
The Match Factory Girl '90
The House of the Spirits '93
Club Extinction '89
The Rose Garden '89
Anastasia: The Mystery of Anna '86
Colonel Redl '84

Esko Nikkari (1938-2006)
The Terminal '04
Aberration '97
The Saint '97
U-Turn '97

Anna Q. Nilsson (1888-1974)
Fighting Father Dunne '48

Najwa Nimri (1972-)
The Method '05
Sex and Lucia '01
Before Night Falls '00
Lovers of the Arctic Circle '98
Open Your Eyes '97

Annibale Ninchi (1887-1967)
Time Out for Love '61
La Dolce Vita '60

Yvette Nipar (1964-)
Black Horizon '01
Kept '01
Submerged '00
Twilight Man '96
Doctor Mordrid: Master of the Unknown '90
Ski Patrol '90

Joe Nipote
Soul's Midnight '06
Casper '95 (V)
Run if You Can '87

John Nishio
Dim Sum: A Little Bit of Heart '85

Greta Nissen (1906-88)
Melody Cruise '32
Ambassador Bill '31
Women of All Nations '31
The King on Main Street '25

Ronald Nitschke
Redline '07
Serial Killing 101 '04

Inger Nilsson (1959-)
Pippi in the South Seas '70
Pippi on the Run '70
Pippi Goes on Board '69
Pippi Longstocking '69

Maj-Britt Nilsson (1924-2006)
Secrets of Women '52
Summer Interlude '50
To Joy '50

Rob Nilsson (1940-)
Heat and Sunlight '87
Northern Lights '79

Leonard Nimoy (1931-)
Atlantis: The Lost Empire '01 (V)
David '97
The Pagemaster '94 (V)
Never Forget '91
Star Trek 6: The Undiscovered Country '91
Star Trek 5: The Final Frontier '89
Star Trek 4: The Voyage Home '86
Transformers: The Movie '86
Star Trek 3: The Search for Spock '84
Seizure: The Story of Kathy Morris '82
A Woman Called Golda '82
Star Trek 2: The Wrath of Khan '82
Star Trek: The Motion Picture '79
Invasion of the Body Snatchers '78
Catlow '71
Baffled '72
The Balcony '63
The Brain Eaters '58
Them! '54
Kid Monk Baroni '52
Zombies of the Stratosphere '52

Lisa Niemi (1957-)
The Opposite Sex '55 [?]

Barbara Niven (1953-)
Sons of Trinity '95
The Innocent '07

Alone with a Stranger '99
Depraved '98
I Married a Monster '98
Taken Alive '95
Psycho Cop '88

David Niven (1909-83)
Better Late Than Never '83
Curse of the Pink Panther '83
Trail of the Pink Panther '82
Sea Wolves '81
Rough Cut '80
The Big Scam '79
Escape to Athena '79
Candleshoe '78
Death on the Nile '78
Murder by Death '76
No Deposit, No Return '76
Paper Tiger '74
King, Queen, Knave '72
The Statue '71
The Brain '69
The Impossible Years '68
Casino Royale '67
Lady L '65
The Pink Panther '64
Bedtime Story '63
55 Days at Peking '63
The Guns of Navarone '61
Please Don't Eat the Daisies '60
Ask Any Girl '59
Separate Tables '58
Bonjour Tristesse '57
My Man Godfrey '57
Around the World in 80 Days '56
Birds & the Bees '56
The King's Thief '55
Carrington, V.C. '54
The Moon Is Blue '53
Happy Go Lovely '51
The Lady Says No '51
The Elusive Pimpernel '50
The Toast of New Orleans '50
Bonnie Prince Charlie '48
The Bishop's Wife '47
Magnificent Doll '46
The Perfect Marriage '46
Stairway to Heaven '46
Immortal Battalion '44
Spitfire '42
Bachelor Mother '39
Eternally Yours '39
The Real Glory '39
Wuthering Heights '39
Bluebeard's Eighth Wife '38
Dawn Patrol '38
Four Men and a Prayer '38
Dinner at the Ritz '37
Prisoner of Zenda '37
Beloved Enemy '36
Dodsworth '36
Rose Marie '36
Barbary Coast '35
Splendor '35

Kip Niven (1945-)
Blind Ambition '79
New Year's Evil '78
Midway '76
Magnum Force '73

Alessandro Nivola (1972-)
The Eye '08
The Company '07
Grace Is Gone '07
The Darwin Awards '06
Goal! The Dream Begins '06
Junebug '05
The Clearing '04
Laurel Canyon '02
Jurassic Park 3 '01
Love's Labour's Lost '00
Time Code '00
Best Laid Plans '99
Mansfield Park '99
I Want You '98
Reach the Rock '98
Face/Off '97

Tommy Nix
Sin City '05
Roadracers '94

Allan Nixon (1920-95)
Mesa of Lost Women '52
Prehistoric Women '50

Cynthia Nixon (1966-)
Sex and the City: The Movie '08
Little Manhattan '05
One Last Thing '05
Tanner on Tanner '04
Igby Goes Down '02
Papa's Angels '00
Marvin's Room '96
Let It Ride '89
Tanner '88 '88
The Manhattan Project '86
Amadeus '84
I Am the Cheese '83

Marion (Marian) Nixon (1904-83)
The Reckless Way '36
Tango '36
Doctor Bull '33
Pilgrimage '33
Too Busy to Work '32
Hands Up '26
Spangles '26

Marni Nixon (1930-)
Mulan '98 (V)
I Think I Do '97
The Sound of Music '65
Daughter of Horror '55 (V)

Mojo Nixon (1956-)
Super Mario Bros. '93
Rock 'n' Roll High School Forever '91

Stephanie Niznik (1967-)
Spiders 2: Breeding Ground '01
Epoch '00
Inferno '98
Memorial Day '98

Chelsea Noble (1964-)
Left Behind: The Movie '00
Instant Karma '90

Christian Noble (1961-)
Human Desires '97
Illegal Affairs '96

James Noble (1922-)
Chances Are '89
When the Bough Breaks '86
Dempsey '83
The Private Eyes '80

Bernard Noel (1926-70)
A Married Woman '65
The Fire Within '64

Chris Noel (1941-)
The Tormentors '71
The Glory Stompers '67

Magali Noel (1932-)
The Eighties '83
Les Rendez-vous D'Anna '78
Amarcord '74
Season for Assassins '71
La Dolce Vita '60

Noelia Noel (1933-)
Night of the Bloody Apes '68
Sputnik '61

Ulrich Noethen (1959-)
Downfall '04
The Harmonists '99

Yumiko Nogawa
Zatoichi: The Blind Swordsman and the Fugitives '68
Story of a Prostitute '65
Gate of Flesh '64

Natalija Nogulich (1950-)
Confessions of Sorority Girls '94
Hoffa '92
Homicide '91
The Guardian '90
Sister, Sister '87

Philippe Noiret (1930-2006)
On Guard! '03
Grosse Fatigue '94
The Postman '94
Revenge of the Musketeers '94
The Palermo Connection '91
Uranus '91
Life and Nothing But '89
The Return of the Musketeers '89
Cinema Paradiso '88
The Family '87
Aurora '84
Fort Saganne '84
My New Partner '84
Next Summer '84
Birgit Haas Must Be Killed '81
Coup de Torchon '81
Jupiter's Thigh '81
Three Brothers '80
Who Is Killing the Great Chefs of Europe? '78
Dear Detective '77
The Purple Taxi '77
A Woman at Her Window '77
The Desert of the Tartars '76
Old Gun '76
The Judge and the Assassin '75
Le Secret '74
The Clockmaker '73
La Grande Bouffe '73
Night Flight from Moscow '73
The Holes '72
Murphy's War '71
The Assassination Bureau '69
Justine '69
Topaz '69
Night of the Generals '67
Woman Times Seven '67
Lady L '65
Zazie dans le Metro '61

Bob Nolan (1908-80)
Melody Time '48 (V)
Lights of Old Santa Fe '47
Song of Arizona '46
King of the Cowboys '43
Heart of the Golden West '42
Sunset on the Desert '42

Doris Nolan (1916-98)
Follies Girl '43
Holiday '38

Jeanette Nolan (1911-98)
The Horse Whisperer '97
Street Justice '89
Cloak & Dagger '84
The Fox and the Hound '81 (V)
The Rescuers '77 (V)
The Manitou '78
Babel '75
The Reluctant Astronaut '67
The Man Who Shot Liberty Valance '62
Psycho '60 (V)
Seventh Cavalry '56
Tribute to a Bad Man '56
A Lawless Street '55
Hangman's Knot '52
Macbeth '48

John Nolan (1933-2000)
Following '99
The Terror '79
In the Steps of a Dead Man '74

Lloyd Nolan (1902-85)
Hannah and Her Sisters '86
It Came Upon a Midnight Clear '84
Prince Jack '83
My Boys Are Good Boys '78
Galyon '77
Abduction of St. Anne '75
Earthquake '74
Airport '70
Ice Station Zebra '68
Sergeant Ryker '68
Circus World '64
Girl Hunters '63
Abandon Ship '57
Portrait in Black '60
Peyton Place '57
The Last Hunt '56
Island in the Sky '53
The Lemon Drop Kid '51
Easy Living '49
The Sun Comes Up '49
The Street with No Name '48
Lady in the Lake '46
House on 92nd Street '45
A Tree Grows in Brooklyn '45
Bataan '43
Guadalcanal Diary '43
Blue, White and Perfect '42
The Man Who Wouldn't Die '42
Sleepers West '41
House Across the Bay '40
Johnny Apollo '40
Michael Shayne: Private Detective '40
Every Day's a Holiday '38
King of Alcatraz '38
Internes Can't Take Money '37
Big Brown Eyes '36
The Texas Rangers '36
"G" Men '35

Mary Nolan (1905-48)
Undertow '30
West of Zanzibar '28

Tom Nolan (1948-)
Voyage of the Rock Aliens '87
School Spirit '85

Amaury Nolasco (1970-)
Street Kings '08
The Benchwarmers '06
Transformers '07
Mr. 3000 '04

Michelle Nolden
All Hat '07
Show Me '04
Rudy: The Rudy Giuliani Story '03
Cybermutt '02
Men with Brooms '02

Claude Nollier (1919-)
Forbidden Fruit '52
Moulin Rouge '52

Jacques Nolot (1943-)
Under the Sand '00
Artemisia '97

Nick Nolte (1941-)
The Spiderwick Chronicles '08 (V)
Tropic Thunder '08
Chicago 10 '07 (V)
Over the Hedge '06 (V)
Paris, je t'aime '06
Peaceful Warrior '06
The Beautiful Country '04
Clean '04
Hotel Rwanda '04
The Good Thief '03
Hulk '03
Northfork '03
Intimate Affairs '01
The Golden Bowl '00
Trixie '00
Simpatico '99
Breakfast of Champions '98
The Thin Red Line '98
Affliction '97
Afterglow '97
U-Turn '97
Mother Night '96
Nightwatch '96
Mulholland Falls '95
Blue Chips '94
I Love Trouble '94
Jefferson in Paris '94
I'll Do Anything '93
Lorenzo's Oil '92
The Player '92
Cape Fear '91
The Prince of Tides '91
Another 48 Hrs. '90
Everybody Wins '90
Q & A '90
Farewell to the King '89
New York Stories '89
Three Fugitives '89
Extreme Prejudice '87
Weeds '87
Down and Out in Beverly Hills '86
Grace Quigley '84
Teachers '84
Under Fire '83
Cannery Row '82
48 Hrs. '82
Heart Beat '80
North Dallas Forty '79
Who'll Stop the Rain? '78
The Deep '77
Rich Man, Poor Man '76
Return to Macon County '75
The Runaway Barge '75
Death Sentence '74

Takashi Nomura
Suicide Club '02
Ran '85

Tom NonDorf
Rage of the Werewolf '99
Addicted to Murder 2: Tainted Blood '97

John Ford Noonan (1943-)
Flirting with Disaster '95
Adventures in Babysitting '87

Tom Noonan (1951-)
Snow Angels '07
Seraphim Falls '06
Eight Legged Freaks '02
Knockaround Guys '01
The Astronaut's Wife '99
Phoenix '98
Heat '95
The Wife '95
What Happened Was... '94
Last Action Hero '93
RoboCop 2 '90
Mystery Train '89
The Monster Squad '87
Manhunter '86
The Man with One Red Shoe '85
Wolfen '81

Tommy Noonan (1921-68)
Three Nuts in Search of a Bolt '64
Promises! Promises! '63
The Girl Most Likely '57
The Ambassador's Daughter '56
A Star Is Born '54
Gentlemen Prefer Blondes '53
Adam's Rib '50
Return of Jesse James '50
Jungle Patrol '48

Kathleen Noone (1945-)
Citizen Ruth '96
Serpent's Lair '95

Nora-Jane Noone (1984-)
The Descent '05
The Good Thief '03
Hulk '03
Northfork '03
The Magdalene Sisters '02

Ghita Norby (1935-)
The Inheritance '03
The Kingdom 2 '97
Hamsun '96
The Kingdom '95
Like It Never Was Before '95
The Best Intentions '92
Sofie '92
Freud Leaving Home '91
Memories of a Marriage '90
Babette's Feast '87 (N)
The Wolf at the Door '87

Christine Norden (1924-88)
Night Beat '48
Mine Own Executioner '47

Jeffrey Nordling (1962-)
Flicka '06
Turbulence 2: Fear of Flying '99
Saint Maybe '98
True Women '97
D3: The Mighty Ducks '96
A Stranger in Town '95
Holy Matrimony '94
And the Band Played On '93
Dangerous Heart '93

Carsten Norgaard (1963-)
Alien vs. Predator '04
Red Shoe Diaries 6: How I Met My Husband '95
Out of Annie's Past '94

Eduardo Noriega (1916-2007)
The Devil's Backbone '01
Burnt Money '00
The Yellow Fountain '99
Open Your Eyes '97
Thesis '96

Eduardo Noriega (1918-)
Vantage Point '08
The Method '05
The Far Horizons '55
Seven Cities of Gold '55

Felix Noriego (1930-)
Battle Cry '55
To Hell and Back '55

Maidie Norman (1913-98)
Sixteen '72
What Ever Happened to Baby Jane? '62
Charlie Chaplin ... Our Hero! '15
Tillie's Punctured Romance '14

Susan Norman
Safe '95
Poison '91

Zack Norman
Festival at Cannes '02
Crosscut '94
Babyfever '94
Venice, Venice '92
Cadillac Man '90
America '86
Romancing the Stone '84
Sitting Ducks '80
Tracks '76

Mabel Normand (1894-1930)
Extra Girl 23
What Happened to Rosa? '21
Mickey '17
Mabel & Fatty '16
Charlie Chaplin ... Our Hero! '15
Tillie's Punctured Romance '14

David Norona (1972-)
Mrs. Santa Claus '96
Twisted '96

Bruce Norris (1960-)
The Sixth Sense '99
A Civil Action '98
Reach the Rock '98

Chuck Norris (1939-)
Dodgeball: A True Underdog Story '04
Forest Warrior '95
Top Dog '95
Hellbound '94
Sidekicks '93

[Chuck Norris, continued]
Walker, Texas Ranger: One Riot, One Ranger '93
The Hitman '91
Delta Force 2: Operation Stranglehold '90
Braddock: Missing in Action 3 '88
Hero and the Terror '88
Code of Silence '85
Firewalker '86
Invasion U.S.A. '85
Missing in Action '84
Missing in Action 2: The Beginning '85
Good Guys Wear Black '78
Breaker! Breaker! '77
Enter the Dragon '73
Return of the Dragon '73
The Student Teachers '73

Dean Norris
The Cell '00
Three Strikes '00
Mysterious Desperado '49
Heartaches '47
Decoy '46
Without Limits '97
Lethal Weapon 2 '89

Edward Norris (1911-2002)
The Lawnmower Man '92
Hard to Kill '89
Slaughter in San Francisco '81
Octagon '80
Force of One '79
Game of Death '79
They Won't Forget '37
Show Them No Mercy '35
Wagon Trail '35
The Man with Two Lives '42

Mike Norris (1963-)
Delta Force 3: The Killing Game '91
Death Ring '93
Survival Game '87
Born American '86

Terry Norris (1930-)
Road to Nhill '97

Simon Norrthon (1967-)
Like It Never Was Before '95

Noelle North
Diary of a Teenage Hitchhiker '82

J.J. North
Psycho Sisters '98
Attack of the 60-Foot Centerfold '95
Vampire Vixens from Venus '94

Jay North (1952-)
Maya '66
Zebra in the Kitchen '65

Heather North (1950-)
The Barefoot Executive '71
Girl! '65
Scout's Honor '80
The Teacher '74

Alan North (1920-2000)
I'll Take You There '99
The Jerky Boys '95
Crazy People '90
Glory '89
Lean on Me '89
Rachel River '87
Billy Galvin '85
Highlander '85

Jeremy Northam (1961-)
The Invasion '07
Tristram Shandy: A Cock and Bull Story '05
Bobby Jones: Stroke of Genius '04
The Singing Detective '03
The Statement '03
Cypher '02
Possession '02
Enigma '01
Gosford Park '01
The Golden Bowl '00
Happy, Texas '99
An Ideal Husband '99
Gloria '98
The Winslow Boy '98
Mimic '97
Emma '96
Carrington '95
The Net '95
A Village Affair '95
Voices from a Locked Room '95

Ted North (1916-)
The Devil Thumbs a Ride '47

Ryan Northcott (1980-)
Ripper: Letter from Hell '01
Mystery, Alaska '99
Orphans '97
Squanto: A Warrior's Tale '94

Alex Norton (1950-)
Pirates of the Caribbean: Dead Man's Chest '06
The Count of Monte Cristo '02
Beautiful Creatures '00

Edward Norton (1969-)
The Incredible Hulk '08
The Illusionist '06
The Painted Veil '06
Down in the Valley '05
Kingdom of Heaven '05
The Italian Job '03

Edgar Norton (1868-1953)
Son of Frankenstein '39
Thirty Day Princess '34
Dr. Jekyll and Mr. Hyde '32
The Lady Refuses '31
The Love Parade '29
The King on Main Street '25

Barry Norton (1909-56)
Devil Monster '46
Dishonored '31
Dracula (Spanish Version) '31

Jack Noseworthy (1969-)
A Dennis the Menace Christmas '07
Phat Girlz '06
Poster Boy '04
Unconditional Love '03
Undercover Brother '02
Cecil B. Demented '00
U-571 '00
Idle Hands '99
Event Horizon '97
Murder at Devil's Glen '99
Cinderella '97
Barb Wire '96
Breakdown '96
The Brady Bunch Movie '95
Kiss Me, Stupid! '64

Judy Norton-Taylor (1958-)
A Day for Thanks on Walton's Mountain '82
The Waltons: The Christmas Carol '80

Brandy Norwood (1979-)
Osmosis Jones '01 (V)
Double Platinum '99
I Still Know What You Did Last Summer '98
Cinderella '97

Terry Norton
Gymkata '85
American Kickboxer 1 '91

Eva Novak (1898-1988)
Red Signals '27
Sky High '22
Trailin' '21

Jane Novak (1896-1990)
Three Word Brand '21
Wagon Tracks '19
The White Buffalo '77
Tales That Witness Madness '73
The Amorous Adventures of Moll Flanders '65
Boys' Night Out '62
Of Human Bondage '64
The Great Caruso '51

Frank Novak (1945-)
Virtual Seduction '96
Watchers 3 '94
Laughing at Danger '24

Tom Novembre (1959-)
The Ice Rink '99
An American Werewolf in Paris '97

Kim Novak (1933-)
Liebestraum '91
The Children '90
The Mirror Crack'd '80
Just a Gigolo '79
The White Buffalo '77
The Great Caruso...

John Novak (1955-)
Wishmaster 4: The Prophecy Fulfilled '02
Wishmaster 3: Beyond the Gates of Hell '01
Tierra '95

Jarmila Novotna (1908-94)
The Search '48
The Great Caruso '51

Jerzy Nowak (1923-)
The Healer '02
Trois Couleurs: Blanc '94

Tom Nowicki
Flash '98
Kiss of Fire '98
The Legend of 1900 '98
Blood Brothers '97
Ellen Foster '97
Kiss the Girls '97
Bulletproof '95
Mad City '97
Mr. & Mrs. Loving '96
Extreme Measures '96
Money Train '95
True Crime '95
Canadian Bacon '94
When You're Dead... '95

Philomena Nowlin
Ebony Dreams '80
Miss Melody Jones '73

Zachi Noy (1953-)
Young Love—Lemon Popsicle 7 '87
Private Manoeuvres '83
Baby Love '83
Hot Bubblegum '81

Christopher Noth (1956-)
Sex and the City: The Movie '08
The Perfect Man '05
Mr. 3000 '04
Searching for Paradise '02
Double Whammy '01
Cast Away '00
The Glass House '01
A Texas Funeral '99
The Confession '98
The People vs. Larry Flynt '96
Chicago Joe & the Showgirl '90

Jack Norton (1889-1958)
The Bank Dick '40
Finishing School '33
The Colt Around the Heart '97
Rough Riders '97
Burnzy's Last Call '95
Jakarta '88
Baby Boom '87
Apology '86
Off Beat '86
Smithereens '82

Ken Norton (1945-)
Drum '76
Mandingo '75

Jim Norton (1938-)
Driving Lessons '06
Conspiracy of Silence '03
Midnight's Child '93
Memoirs of an Invisible Man '92
Hidden Agenda '90

Richard Norton
Nautilus '99
Black Thunder '98
Mr. Nice Guy '98
Kiss and Be Killed '91
Oceans of Fire '86
Gangster Wars '81
Inner Sanctum 2 '94
Lady in Waiting '94
No Escape, No Return '93
Black Ice '92
DaVinci's War '92
6th ... '01
Firing Forrester '00
Overkill '96
Hologram Man '95
To the Limit '95
American Yakuza '94
Fortunes of War '94
Terminal Error '02
The Gun '96
Fugitive X '96
The Kick Fighter '91
China O'Brien 2 '89
Crossfire '89
Hyper Space '89
China O'Brien '88
Equalizer 2000 '86
Rage and Honor 2: Hostile Takeover '93
Rage and Honor '92
Lady Dragon '92
Raiders of the Sun '92
Ironheart '92

Michael Nouri (1945-)
Invincible '06
Last Holiday '06
The Boynton Beach Club '05
The Terminal '04
Finding Forrester '00
Lovely & Amazing '02
Terminal Error '02
The Hidden '87
Between Two Women '86
Imagemaker '86
Flashdance '83
Spragueville '84
Psychic '91
Total Exposure '91
Little Vegas '90
Shattered Dreams '90
Project: Alien '89
Thieves of Fortune '89
Danielle Steel's Changes '91

Jay Novello (1904-82)
What Did You Do in the War, Daddy? '66
Harum Scarum '65
The Pride and the Passion '57
Jaguar '56
Sabaka '55
The Prodigal '55
Crime Wave '54
Ma and Pa Kettle on Vacation '53
Miracle of Our Lady of Fatima '52

Tom Novembre (1959-)
The Border Legion '40
Sheriff of Tombstone '41
Robin Hood of the Pecos '41
Bad Man of Deadwood '41
Lethal Weapon 3 '92
Return of the Living Dead '85

Bill Nunn (1953-)
A Raisin in the Sun '08
Firehouse Dog '07
Spider-Man 3 '07
Spider-Man 2 '04
Runaway Jury '03
People I Know '02
Spider-Man '02
Lockdown '00
The Substitute 4: Failure is Not an Option '00
Foolish '99
Passing Glory '99
The Tic Code '99
Always Outnumbered '98
He Got Game '98
Kiss the Girls '97

Don Novello (1943-)
Atlantis: The Lost Empire '01 (V)
The Adventures of Rocky & Bullwinkle '00
Just One Night '00
Just the Ticket '98
Jack '96
Casper '95
One Night Stand '95
New York Stories '89
Tucker: The Man and His Dream '88
Gilda Live '80

Ramon Novarro (1899-1968)
Heller in Pink Tights '60
Big Steal '49
The Cat and the Fiddle '34
Mata Hari '32
The Student Prince in Old Heidelberg '27
Ben-Hur '26

Ivor Novello (1893-1951)
Phantom Fiend '35
The Lodger '26
The White Rose '23

Carole Nugent
Belles on Their Toes '52

Danny Nucci (1968-)
Night of the Cyclone '90
A Dry White Season '89
Break a Leg '03
American Cousins '02
Homage '95
Roosters '95
Book of Love '91
Friends & Lovers '99
Love Walked In '97
Titanic '97
The Big Squeeze '96
Eraser '96
The Rock '96
That Old Feeling '96
Crimson Tide '95
Firestarter 2: Rekindled '02

Eddie Nugent (1904-95)
Doughnuts & Society '36
Prison Shadows '36
Kentucky Blue Streak '35
Night Nurse '31
Vagabond Lover '29

Elliott Nugent (1900-80)
Welcome Stranger '47
Romance '30
The Unholy Three '30

Miguel A. Nunez, Jr. (1964-)
Kickin' It Old Skool '07
The Adventures of Pluto Nash '02
Juwanna Mann '02
Scooby-Doo '02
MacArthur Park '01
Life '99
For Richer or Poorer '97
If You Only Knew '00

Mel Novak
Vampire Assassin '05
Capital Punishment '91
Hit the Dutchman '92
Killer Instinct '92
Game of Death '79

Winston Ntshona (1941-)
Tarzan and the Lost City '98
A Dry White Season '89
The Wild Geese '78

Bruce Nozick
The Reaper '97
Nightwaves '03
Bleecker '97

Joanna Noyes
The French Line '54
Phffft! '54

Ralph Nossek
Citizen X '95

Nancho Novo (1958-)
Lovers of the Arctic Circle '98
The Red Squirrel '93

Jarmila Novotna (1908-94)
The Search '48
The Great Caruso '51

Pal Joey '57
Vertigo '58
Bell, Book and Candle '58
Strangers When We Meet '60
The Eddy Duchin Story '56

The Last Seduction '94
Save Me '93
Sister Act '92
New Jack City '91
Regarding Henry '91
White Lie '91
Def by Temptation '90
Mo' Better Blues '90
Do the Right Thing '89
School Daze '88

Teri Nunn (1961-)
Follow That Car '80
Thank God It's Friday '78

Rudolf Nureyev (1938-93)
Exposed '83
Valentino '77

Maila Nurmi
See Vampira

Loredana Nusciak (1942-)
Django '68
Gladiators 7 '62

Danny Nussbaum
Beautiful People '99
24-7 '97

Mike Nussbaum (1923-)
The Water Engine '92
Things Change '88
House of Games '87

Jeff Nuttall (1933-2004)
Beaumarchais the Scoundrel '96
Captives '94
Robin Hood '91

Mayf Nutter (1941-)
Hunter's Blood '87
The $5.20 an Hour Dream '80

France Nuyen (1939-)
A Smile Like Yours '96
A Passion to Kill '94
The Joy Luck Club '93
China Cry '91
Code Name: Diamond Head '77
Return to Fantasy Island '77
Black Water Gold '69
Diamond Head '62
South Pacific '58

Carrie Nye (1937-2006)
Hello Again '87
Creepshow '82
The Group '66

Carroll Nye (1901-74)
Gone with the Wind '39
Lottery Bride '30

Louis Nye (1933-2005)
O.C. and Stiggs '87
Alice in Wonderland '85
Harper Valley P.T.A. '78
Charge of the Model T's '76
A Guide for the Married Man '67

Andy Nyman
Death at a Funeral '07
Severance '06

Lena Nyman (1944-)
The Adventures of Picasso '80
Autumn Sonata '78
I Am Curious (Yellow) '67

Michael Nyquist
Mother of Mine '05
London Voodoo '04

Pascal Nzonzi
Lumumba '00
Night on Earth '91

Henry O
The Lost Empire '01
Dragonheart: A New Beginning '00
Romeo Must Die '00
Shanghai Noon '00

Jack Oakie (1903-78)
Lover Come Back '61
Around the World in 80 Days '56
Tomahawk '51
It Happened Tomorrow '44
Hello, Frisco, Hello '43
Wintertime '43
Iceland '42
Song of the Islands '42
The Great American Broadcast '41
The Great Dictator '40
Little Men '40
Tin Pan Alley '40
Young People '40
The Affairs of Annabel '38
Thanks for Everything '38
Toast of New York '37
The Texas Rangers '36
That Girl from Paris '36
Murder at the Vanities '34
College Humor '33

Simon Oakland (1922-83)
Emperor of the North Pole '73
The Night Strangler '72
Chato's Land '71
The Night Stalker '71
On a Clear Day You Can See Forever '70
Bullitt '68
Tony Rome '67
The Sand Pebbles '66
Follow That Dream '61
West Side Story '61
Psycho '60
The Rise and Fall of Legs Diamond '60
I Want to Live! '58

Wheeler Oakman (1890-1949)
Teenage '44
The Ape Man '43
Meet the Mob '42
Double Trouble '41
Wolf Call '39
Slaves in Bondage '37
Aces and Eights '36
Death from a Distance '36
Ghost Patrol '36
The Man from Gun Town '36
Roaring Guns '36
Song of the Trail '36
Frontier Days '34
In Old Santa Fe '34
The Lost Jungle '34
Man of Action '33
Boiling Point '32
The Riding Tornado '32
Texas Cyclone '32
Two-Fisted Law '32
Roaring Ranch '30
The Broken Mask '28
Outside the Law '21
Peck's Bad Boy '21
The Spoilers '14

Simon Oates
Jewels '92
Doomwatch '72
The Terrornauts '67

Warren Oates (1928-82)
Blue Thunder '83
Tough Enough '83
The Border '82
Stripes '81
East of Eden '80
And Baby Makes Six '79
My Old Man '79
1941 '79
Brink's Job '78
Gunfire '78
Prime Time '77
Sleeping Dogs '77
Dixie Dynamite '76
Drum '76
92 in the Shade '76
Race with the Devil '75
The White Dawn '75
Badlands '74
Bring Me the Head of Alfredo Garcia '74
Cockfighter '74
Dillinger '73
The Thief Who Came to Dinner '73
Tom Sawyer '73
Hired Hand '71
Two Lane Blacktop '71
There Was a Crooked Man '70
Crooks & Coronets '69
The Wild Bunch '69
In the Heat of the Night '67
Return of the Magnificent Seven '66
The Shooting '66
Shenandoah '65
Ride the High Country '62

Devin Oatway (1978-)
Galgameth '96
Camp Nowhere '94

Philip Ober (1902-82)
The Ghost and Mr. Chicken '66
The Facts of Life '60
Beloved Infidel '59
The Mating Game '59
North by Northwest '59
Escapade in Japan '57
From Here to Eternity '53
Come Back, Little Sheba '52
The Magnificent Yankee '50
Never a Dull Moment '50

Merle Oberon (1911-79)
Interval '73
Hotel '67
The Oscar '66
Deep in My Heart '54
Desiree '54
Berlin Express '48
A Song to Remember '45
Dark Waters '44
Forever and a Day '43
Stage Door Canteen '43
Lydia '41
That Uncertain Feeling '41
The Lion Has Wings '40
Wuthering Heights '39
The Cowboy and the Lady '38
The Divorce of Lady X '38
Beloved Enemy '36
These Three '36
The Dark Angel '35
Broken Melody '34
Private Life of Don Juan '34
The Scarlet Pimpernel '34
The Private Life of Henry VIII '33
Wedding Rehearsal '32

Jacqueline Obradors (1967-)
A Man Apart '03
Atlantis: The Lost Empire '01 (V)
Tortilla Soup '01
Deuce Bigalow: Male Gigolo '99
Six Days, Seven Nights '98

Anna (Ana Garcia) Obregon (1955-)
Bolero '84
Treasure of the Four Crowns '82
Car Crash '80

Claudio Obregon (1955-)
Esmeralda Comes by Night '98
Midaq Alley '95
Reed: Insurgent Mexico '73

Rodrigo Obregon
L.A. Wars '94
Enemy Gold '93
Fit to Kill '93
Hard Hunted '92
Tides of War '90
Picasso Trigger '89
Savage Beach '89
Django Strikes Again '87
Hard Ticket to Hawaii '87

Hugh O'Brian (1925-)
Wyatt Earp: Return to Tombstone '94
The Gambler Returns: The Luck of the Draw '93
Doin' Time on Planet Earth '88
Twins '88
The Seekers '79
Cruise into Terror '78
Fantasy Island '76
The Shootist '76
Killer Force '75
Murder on Flight 502 '75
Probe '72
Wild Women '70
The Wild Bunch '69
Africa Texas Style '67
Assassination in Rome '65
In Harm's Way '65
Love Has Many Faces '65
Alias Jesse James '59
The Fiend Who Walked the West '58
Broken Lance '54
There's No Business Like Show Business '54
Man from the Alamo '53
The Lawless Breed '52
Red Ball Express '52
Son of Ali Baba '52
Little Big Horn '51
Vengeance Valley '51
Return of Jesse James '50
Rocketship X-M '50

Austin O'Brien (1981-)
The Baby-Sitters' Club '95
Lawnmower Man 2: Beyond Cyberspace '95
My Girl 2 '94
Last Action Hero '93
Prehysteria '93

Clay O'Brien (1961-)
Cahill: United States Marshal '73
One Little Indian '73
The Cowboys '72

Dave O'Brien (1912-69)
Enemy of the Law '45
Flaming Bullets '45
Frontier Fugitives '45
Marked for Murder '45
The Phantom of 42nd Street '45
Three in the Saddle '45
Boss of Rawhide '44
Dead or Alive '44
Gangsters of the Frontier '44
Guns of the Law '44
Fighting Valley '43
Bowery at Midnight '42
King of the Stallions '42
Law and Order '42
Rangers Take Over '42
The Devil Bat '41
Double Trouble '41
Spooks Run Wild '41
Buzzy Rides the Range '40
Danger Ahead '40
Murder on the Yukon '40
Sky Bandits '40
That Gang of Mine '40
Yukon Flight '40
Daughter of the Tong '39
Phantom Rancher '39
The Singing Cowgirl '39
Water Rustlers '39
Law of the Texan '38
Reefer Madness '38
Brothers of the West '37
Lightning Bill Crandall '37
Lion's Den '36

Donald O'Brien (1930-2003)
Quest for the Mighty Sword '90
Doctor Butcher M.D. '80
Trap Them & Kill Them '77
The Train '65

Edmond O'Brien (1915-85)
Dream No Evil '75
Lucky Luciano '74
99 & 44/100 Dead '74
They Only Kill Their Masters '72
Jigsaw '71
The Love God? '70
The Wild Bunch '69
The Doomsday Flight '66
Fantastic Voyage '66
Rio Conchos '64
Seven Days in May '64
Birdman of Alcatraz '62
The Longest Day '62
The Man Who Shot Liberty Valance '62
Moon Pilot '62
The Great Impostor '61
The Last Voyage '60
Up Periscope '59
Stopover Tokyo '57
D-Day, the Sixth of June '56
The Girl Can't Help It '56
1984 '56
Pete Kelly's Blues '55
The Barefoot Contessa '54
The Bigamist '53
The Hitch-Hiker '53
Julius Caesar '53
The Denver & Rio Grande '51
The Admiral Was a Lady '50
D.O.A. '49
White Heat '49
For the Love of Mary '48
A Double Life '47
The Killers '46
The Amazing Mrs. Holliday '43
A Girl, a Guy and a Gob '41
The Hunchback of Notre Dame '39

George O'Brien (1900-85)
Cheyenne Autumn '64
Gold Raiders '51
She Wore a Yellow Ribbon '49
Bullet Code '40
Legion of the Lawless '40
Racketeers of the Range '39
Park Avenue Logger '37
Windjammer '37
Cowboy Millionaire '35
Thunder Mountain '35
Daniel Boone '34
Dude Ranger '34
Mystery Ranch '34
Painted Desert '31
Seas Beneath '31
The Lone Star Ranger '30
Sunrise '27
The Iron Horse '24

Joan O'Brien (1936-)
It Happened at the World's Fair '63
The Alamo '60
Operation Petticoat '59

Kieran O'Brien (1973-)
Goal! The Dream Begins '06
Bloodlines '05
Tristram Shandy: A Cook and Bull Story '05
Dungeons and Dragons '00
Dark City '97
Spice World: The Movie '97

Margaret O'Brien (1937-)
Amy '81
Heller in Pink Tights '60
Glory '56
Little Women '49
Our Vines Have Tender Grapes '45
The Canterville Ghost '44
Jane Eyre '44
Meet Me in St. Louis '44
Thousands Cheer '43
Journey for Margaret '42

Maria O'Brien (1950-)
In a Stranger's Hand '92
Promised a Miracle '88

Maureen O'Brien (1944-)
American Women '00
Falling for a Dancer '98
The Land Girls '98
The Lost Boys '78

Myles O'Brien
Scorned 2 '96
Sexual Roulette '96

Niall O'Brien
Secret of the Cave '06
Broken Harvest '94
Class of '61 '92
Rawhead Rex '87
Excalibur '81
Lovespell '79

Pat O'Brien (1899-1983)
Ragtime '81
Scout's Honor '80
The End '78
Some Like It Hot '59
Last Hurrah '58
Jubilee Trail '54
The Boy with the Green Hair '48
Fighting Father Dunne '48
Riff-Raff '47
Crack-Up '46
Having Wonderful Crime '45
His Butler's Sister '44
Bombardier '43
The Iron Major '43
Marine Raiders '43
The Navy Comes Through '42
The Fighting 69th '40
Knute Rockne: All American '40
Slightly Honorable '40
Torrid Zone '40
The Night of Nights '39
Angels with Dirty Faces '38
Boy Meets Girl '38
San Quentin '37
Ceiling Zero '35
Devil Dogs of the Air '35
Flirtation Walk '34
Bombshell '33
Bureau of Missing Persons '33
The World Gone Mad '33
American Madness '32
Hell's House '32
Consolation Marriage '31
The Front Page '31
Personal Maid '31

Pat J. O'Brien
Doomed Caravan '41
Hawaiian Buckaroo '38
Tim Tyler's Luck '37

Peter O'Brien (1960-)
The Return '06
Hotel de Love '96
Angel of Fury '93
A Kink in the Picasso '90
The Grand Duel '73

Richard O'Brien (1942-)
Elvira's Haunted Hills '02
Dungeons and Dragons '00
Dark City '97
Robin Hood... The Legend: The Time of the Wolf '85
Shock Treatment '81
The Rocky Horror Picture Show '75

Shauna O'Brien (1970-)
The Seductress '00
The Escort '97
Body Armor '96
Friend of the Family 2 '96
Fugitive Rage '96
Friend of the Family '95
Over the Wire '95

Tom O'Brien (1965-)
A Thousand Heroes '92
The Accused '88
The Big Easy '87

Virginia O'Brien (1921-2001)
Merton of the Movies '47
The Harvey Girls '46
The Show-Off '46
Two Girls and a Sailor '44
Du Barry Was a Lady '43
Thousands Cheer '43
Panama Hattie '42
Ship Ahoy '42
Big Store '41
Lady Be Good '41
Till the Clouds Roll By '46

Erin O'Brien-Moore (1902-79)
Destination Moon '50
The Black Legion '37
Our Little Girl '35
His Greatest Gamble '34

Jeffrey Obrow
The Kindred '87
The Power '80

Sean O'Bryan
The Princess Diaries 2: Royal Engagement '04
Raising Helen '04
Big Fat Liar '02
The Princess Diaries '01
Nice Guys Sleep Alone '99
I'll Be Home for Christmas '98
The Twilight of the Golds '97

Ric Ocasek (1949-)
Hairspray '88
Made in Heaven '87

Andrea Occhipinti (1957-)
Amor de Hombre '97
Running Away '89
Control '87
The Family '87
Bolero '84
El Barbaro '84
A Blade in the Dark '83
Conquest '83
New York Ripper '82

P.J. Ochlan
Quigley '03
Little Man Tate '91

Jesus Ochoa (1959-)
Innocent Voices '04
Man on Fire '04

Juan Manuel Ochoa
Alias, La Gringa '91
The City and the Dogs '85

Uwe Ochsenknecht (1956-)
Luther '03
Kaspar Hauser '93
Schtonk '92

Arthur O'Connell (1908-81)
Huckleberry Finn '74
Ben '72
They Only Kill Their Masters '72
The Last Valley '71
There Was a Crooked Man '70
The Reluctant Astronaut '67
Fantastic Voyage '66
The Silencers '66
Monkey's Uncle '65
Kissin' Cousins '64
7 Faces of Dr. Lao '63
Follow That Dream '61
The Great Impostor '61
Misty '61
Cimarron '60
Anatomy of a Murder '59
Gidget '59
Operation Petticoat '59
Man of the West '58
Bus Stop '56
Picnic '55
Solid Gold Cadillac '56
Open Secret '48
Blondie's Blessed Event '42

Pat O'Bryan
976-EVIL 2: The Astral Factor '91
Relentless '88
976-EVIL '88

Charlie O'Connell (1975-)
Kraken: Tentacles of the Deep '06
The Devil's Prey '01
Dude, Where's My Car? '00

Deirdre O'Connell
Stephanie Daley '06
Imaginary Heroes '05
Winter Passing '05
Hearts in Atlantis '01
Murder in a Small Town '99
Lifetom '96
Fearless '93
Cool World '92
Falling from Grace '92
Straight Talk '92
Pastime '91

Hugh O'Connell
Personal Maid '31

Jerry O'Connell (1974-)
Yours, Mine & Ours '05
Buying the Cow '02
Kangaroo Jack '02
Tomcats '01
Mission to Mars '00
Body Shots '99
The '60s '99
Can't Hardly Wait '98
Scream 2 '97
Jerry Maguire '96
Joe's Apartment '96
Blue River '95
Calendar Girl '93
Stand by Me '86

Patrick O'Connell (1934-)
We'll Meet Again '82
McKenzie Break '70

Raoul O'Connell
Frisk '95
Boys Life '94

Taaffe O'Connell
Galaxy of Terror '81
Caged Fury '80

Carroll O'Connor (1925-2001)
Return to Me '00
Gideon '99
36 Hours to Die '39
The Father Clements Story '87
Cleopatra '63
Lonely Are the Brave '62
Parrish '61
Johnny Frenchman '46

Derrick O'Connor (1941-)
Daredevil '03
End of Days '99
Love at Large '89
Hope and Glory '87

Donald O'Connor (1925-2003)
Out to Sea '97
Toys '92
A Time to Remember '87
Pandemonium '82
Ragtime '81
That Funny Feeling '65
The Wonders of Aladdin '61
Francis in the Navy '55
Francis Joins the WACs '54
There's No Business Like Show Business '54
Francis Covers the Big Town '53
I Love Melvin '53
Francis Goes to West Point '52
Singin' in the Rain '52
Double Crossbones '51
Francis Goes to the Races '51
Francis the Talking Mule '49

Frances O'Connor (1967-)
Book of Love '04
Timeline '03
The Importance of Being Earnest '02
Windtalkers '02
A.I.: Artificial Intelligence '01
About Adam '00
Bedazzled '00
Madame Bovary '00
Mansfield Park '99
Kiss or Kill '97
A Little Bit of Soul '97
The Wedding Party '97
Love and Other Catastrophes '96

Glynnis O'Connor (1956-)
New Best Friend '02
Saint Maybe '98
Ellen Foster '97
Past the Bleachers '95
To Heal a Nation '88
A Conspiracy of Love '87
The Deliberate Stranger '86
Johnny Dangerously '84
Melanie '82
Night Crossing '81
Those Lips, Those Eyes '80
California Dreaming '79
The Dark Side of Love '79
Our Town '77
The Boy in the Plastic Bubble '76
Ode to Billy Joe '76
Kid Vengeance '75
Someone I Touched '75

Kevin J. O'Connor (1964-)
Flight of the Living Dead: Outbreak on a Plane '07
There Will Be Blood '07
Kettle of Fish '06
Seraphim Falls '06
Van Helsing '04
Chill Factor '99
The Mummy '99
Black Cat Run '98
Deep Rising '98
Gods and Monsters '98
Virtuosity '95
Canadian Bacon '94
Color of Night '94
No Escape '94
Equinox '93
Hero '92
Signs of Life '89
Steel Magnolias '89
The Caine Mutiny Court Martial '88
The Moderns '88
Candy Mountain '87
Peggy Sue Got Married '86
Special Effects '85
Let's Scare Jessica to Death '71

Tim O'Connor (1927-)
Naked Gun 2 1/2: The Smell of Fear '91
Manhunter '74
Sssssss '73
Across 110th Street '72
The Groundstar Conspiracy '72

Una O'Connor (1880-1959)
Witness for the Prosecution '57
Something in the Wind '47
The Adventures of Robin Hood '38
Personal Property '37
Lloyds of London '36
The Bride of Frankenstein '35
David Copperfield '35
The Informer '35
The Barretts of Wimpole Street '34
Chained '34
Cavalcade '32
The Canterville Ghost '44
This Land Is Mine '43
Strawberry Blonde '41
The Sea Hawk '40
Fighting Father Dunne '48

Robert Emmett O'Connor (1885-1962)
Picture Snatcher '33
Up the River '30

Renee O'Connor (1971-)
Boogeyman 2 '07
Darkman 2: The Return of Durant '94

Sinead O'Connor (1966-)
The Butcher Boy '97
Emily Brontë's Wuthering Heights '92

Hugh O'Conor (1975-)
Bloom '03
Deathwatch '02
Chocolat '00
The Young Poisoner's Handbook '94
My Left Foot '89
Da '88
Lamb '85

Nell O'Day (1909-89)
Boss of Rawhide '44
Bury Me Not on the Lone Prairie '41
Man from Montana '41
The Masked Rider '41
Pony Post '40

Denis O'Dea (1905-78)
Esther and the King '60
The Story of Esther Costello '57
Mogambo '53
Niagara '52
Captain Horatio Hornblower '51
The Long Dark Hall '51
Treasure Island '50
The Fallen Idol '49
Under Capricorn '49

Judith O'Dea (1945-)
Serial Slayer '03
Night of the Living Dead '68

Georgia O'Dell (1892-1950)
West of Nevada '36
Big Calibre '35

Bob Odenkirk (1962-)
The Cable Guy '96
Waiting for Guffman '96
Clean Slate '94
Wayne's World 2 '93

Deborah Odell
Godsend '04
Protection '01

Jennifer O'Dell (1974-)
Slayer '06

Chris O'Donnell (1970-)
The Company '07
The Sisters '05
Kinsey '04
Vertical Limit '00
The Bachelor '99
Cookie's Fortune '99
Batman and Robin '97
The Chamber '96
In Love and War '96
Batman Forever '95
Mad Love '95
Circle of Friends '94
The Three Musketeers '93
Scent of a Woman '92
School Ties '92
Blue Sky '91
Fried Green Tomatoes '91
Men Don't Leave '89

Anthony O'Donnell
Agatha Christie: A Life in Pictures '04
The Miniver Story '50
Nuts in May '76

Cathy O'Donnell (1925-70)
Ben-Hur '59
Terror in the Haunted House '58
The Man from Laramie '55
The Best Years of Our Lives '46
Detective Story '51
Side Street '50
They Live by Night '49
The Amazing Mr. X '48

Christophe Odent
Nouvelle Vague '90
First Name: Carmen '83

Devon Odessa
Mad Cowgirl '06

Odetta (1930-)
The Omega Code '99
The Autobiography of Miss Jane Pittman '74

Rosie O'Donnell (1962-)
Tarzan '99 (V)
The Twilight of the Golds '97
Wide Awake '97
Beautiful Girls '96
Harriet the Spy '96
A Very Brady Sequel '96
Now and Then '95
Car 54, Where Are You? '94
Exit to Eden '94
The Flintstones '94
Another Stakeout '93
Sleepless in Seattle '93
A League of Their Own '92

Keir O'Donnell
Wedding Crashers '05
Pathology '08

"Spec" (Walter) O'Donnell (1911-86)
Hello Trouble '32
Sparrows '26

Martha O'Driscoll (1922-98)
Carnegie Hall '47
Criminal Court '46
Here Come the Co-Eds '45
House of Dracula '45
The Fallen Sparrow '43
Crazy House '43
Reap the Wild Wind '42
Young and Willing '42

Steve Oedekerk
Barnyard '06 (V)
Kung Pow! Enter the Fist '02
High Strung '91

Gregoire Oestermann
Look at Me '04

Bernadette O'Farrell (1924-99)
The Happiest Days of Your Life '50

Conor O'Farrell
Stir of Echoes '99
From the Earth to the Moon '98

Damian O'Flynn (1907-82)
Daniel Boone: Trail Blazer '56

Nick Offerman (1970-)
Wristcutters: A Love Story '06
Sin City '05
November '05
Groove '00
Treasure Island '99

George Offerman, Jr. (1917-63)
A Walk in the Sun '46
The Fighting Sullivans '42
The Outlaw Deputy '35

Ken Ogata (1937-)
The Hidden Blade '04
The Pillow Book '95
Mishima: A Life in Four Chapters '85
The Ballad of Narayama '83
Vengeance Is Mine '79
Zatoichi: The Blind Swordsman's Vengeance '56

Mayumi Ogawa (1939-)
The Go-Masters '82

Bulle Ogier (1939-)
The Duchess of Langeais '07
Belle Toujours '06
Merci Docteur Rey '04
Shattered Image '98
Venus Beauty Institute '98
Somewhere in the City '97
Irma Vep '96
Son of Gascogne '95
Candy Mountain '87
Maîtresse '76
Céline and Julie Go Boating '74

The Discreet Charm of the Bourgeoisie '72
La Salamandre '71
The Valley Obscured by the Clouds '70

Ian Ogilvy (1943-)
Fugitive Mind '99
The Disappearance of Kevin Johnson '95
Puppet Master 5: The Final Chapter '94
Death Becomes Her '92
Eddie Presley '92
Invasion of Privacy '92
Anna Karenina '85
And Now the Screaming Starts '73
From Beyond the Grave '73
No Sex Please—We're British '73
Waterloo '71
Wuthering Heights '70
The Conqueror Worm '68
The Invincible Six '68
Cop-Out '67
The She-Beast '65

Jorgo Ognenovski
Stalked '99
Warrior of Justice '96

Dean O'Gorman (1976-)
Beyond Justice '01
When Love Comes '98
Young Hercules '97

Gail O'Grady (1963-)
Lucky Seven '03
Hope Ranch '02
Another Woman's Husband '00
Lip Service '00
Sleep Easy, Hutch Rimes '00
Deuce Bigalow: Male Gigolo '99
The Three Lives of Karen '97
Celtic Pride '96
That Old Feeling '96
Nobody's Perfect '90
Blackout '88

Olivia Oguma
Robot Stories '03

Soon-Teck Oh (1943-)
True Blue '01
Mulan '98 (V)
Yellow '98
Beverly Hills Ninja '96
Red Sun Rising '94
A Home of Our Own '93
Missing in Action 2: The Beginning '85
East of Eden '80
Fantastic Seven '79
The Man with the Golden Gun '74

Michael O'Hagan (1941-)
Quicksand '01
For Love or Country: The Arturo Sandoval Story '00

Brian O'Halloran (1969-)
Clerks 2 '06
Jay and Silent Bob Strike Back '01
Chasing Amy '97
Mallrats '95
Clerks '94

Jack O'Halloran (1943-)
Hero and the Terror '88
Dragnet '87
The Baltimore Bullet '80
Superman 2 '80
Superman: The Movie '78
King Kong '76
Farewell, My Lovely '75

Natsuko Ohama
Skin Deep '94
Speed '94

Claudia Ohana (1962-)
Erotique '94
Priceless Beauty '90
The Fable of the Beautiful Pigeon Fancier '88
Luzia '88
Opera do Malandro '87
Erendira '83

George O'Hanlon (1917-89)
Jetsons: The Movie '90 (V)
Heading for Heaven '47

George O'Hanlon, Jr. (1953-)
The Evil '78
Our Time '74
Where Have All the People Gone? '74

Brian O'Hara
Get Rich or Die Tryin' '05
Married Too Young '02
California Joe '43

Catherine O'Hara (1954-)
Brother Bear 2 '06 (V)
For Your Consideration '06
Monster House '06 (V)
Over the Hedge '06 (V)
Penelope '06
Chicken Little '05 (V)
Game 6 '05
Lemony Snicket's A Series of Unfortunate Events '04
Surviving Christmas '04
A Mighty Wind '03
Orange County '02
Best in Show '00
Late Last Night '99
The Life Before This '99
Home Fries '98
Hope '97
There Goes the Neighborhood '92
Betsy's Wedding '90
Dick Tracy '90
Home Alone '90
Little Vegas '90
Beetlejuice '88
Heartburn '86
Really Weird Tales '86
After Hours '85
The Last Polka '84
Rock & Rule '83 (V)
Nothing Personal '80

David O'Hara (1965-)
Doomsday '08
Wanted '08
Tristan & Isolde '06
Hotel Rwanda '04
Stander '03
Crossfire Trail '01
Made '01
Jesus '00
Fever '99
Janice Beard '99
The Match '99
The Matchmaker '97
Oliver Twist '97
Some Mother's Son '96
Braveheart '95
Maria's Child '93
WarCat '88

Jenny O'Hara (1943-)
Forty Shades of Blue '05
Mystic River '03
The Truth About Jane '00
Wishmaster '97
Robin Cook's Terminal '96
A Mother's Prayer '95
Angie '94
Career Opportunities '91
Last Song '80

Maureen O'Hara (1920-)
The Christmas Box '95
Only the Lonely '91
The Red Pony '76
Big Jake '71
The Rare Breed '66
McLintock! '63
Spencer's Mountain '63
Mr. Hobbs Takes a Vacation '62
Deadly Companions '61
The Parent Trap '61
Our Man in Havana '59
Wings of Eagles '57
Lisbon '56
Lady Godiva '55
The Long Gray Line '55
The Magnificent Matador '55
The Redhead from Wyoming '53
War Arrow '53
Against All Flags '52
At Sword's Point '51
Flame of Araby '51
Rio Grande '50
Comanche Territory '50
Bagdad '49
Father Was a Fullback '49
A Woman's Secret '49
Sitting Pretty '48
Miracle on 34th Street '47
Sinbad, the Sailor '47
The Spanish Main '45
Buffalo Bill '44
The Fallen Sparrow '43
Immortal Sergeant '43
This Land Is Mine '43
The Black Swan '42
To the Shores of Tripoli '42
How Green Was My Valley '41
Dance, Girl, Dance '40
The Hunchback of Notre Dame '39
Jamaica Inn '39

Denis O'Hare (1962-)
Charlie Wilson's War '07
A Mighty Heart '07
Stephanie Daley '06
Angel Rodriguez '05
Derailed '05
Garden State '04
The Anniversary Party '01
Saint Maybe '98

Michael O'Hare (1952-)
C.H.U.D. '84
The Promise '79

Caitlin (Kathleen Heaney) O'Heaney (1953-)
He Knows You're Alone '80
Savage Weekend '80

Cornelia Hayes O'Herlihy
Mother Teresa: In the Name of God's Poor '97
Rudyard Kipling's the Second Jungle Book: Mowgli and Baloo '94
The Old Curiosity Shop '94

Dan O'Herlihy (1919-2005)
The Rat Pack '98
Love, Cheat & Steal '93
RoboCop 2 '90
RoboCop '87
The Dead '87
Two by Forsyth '86
The Last Starfighter '84
Halloween 3: Season of the Witch '82
Death Ray 2000 '81
MacArthur '77
Banjo Hackett '76
The Tamarind Seed '74
The People '71
Waterloo '71
Fail-Safe '64
The King of the Roaring '20s: The Story of Arnold Rothstein '61
The Young Land '59
The Virgin Queen '55
The Black Shield of Falworth '54
Sword of Venus '53
Actors and Sin '52
Invasion U.S.A. '52
Macbeth '48
Odd Man Out '47

Gavan O'Herlihy (1954-)
Prince Valiant '97
Hidden Assassin '94
Tailspin: Behind the Korean Airline Tragedy '89
Willow '88
Space Riders '83
A Wedding '78

Nils Ohlund
You'll Get Over It '02
Come Undone '00

Carol Ohmart (1927-)
Spider Baby '64
One Man's Way '63
Born Reckless '59
Naked Youth '59
House on Haunted Hill '58

John O'Hurley (1954-)
Firetrap '01
Race to Space '01
The Power Within '95
Mirror Images '91

Eiji Okada (1920-95)
Traffic Jam '91
X from Outer Space '67
Face of Another '66
Woman in the Dunes '64
She and He '63
The Ugly American '63
Hiroshima, Mon Amour '59
Mother '52

Mariko Okada (1933-)
An Autumn Afternoon '62
Samurai 3: Duel at Ganryu Island '56
Samurai 2: Duel at Ichijoji Temple '55

Dennis O'Keefe (1908-68)
The Naked Flame '68
Follow the Sun '51
Great Dan Patch '49
Raw Deal '48
Dishonored Lady '47
T-Men '47
Doll Face '46
Brewster's Millions '45
Getting Gertie's Garter '45
Abroad with Two Yanks '44
Fighting Seabees '44
Sensations of 1945 '44
The Story of Dr. Wassell '44
Hi Diddle Diddle '43
The Leopard Man '43
Hangmen Also Die '42
Broadway Limited '41
Lady Scarface '41
Topper Returns '41
Pop Always Pays '40
You'll Find Out '40
Libeled Lady '36
Cimarron '31

Doug O'Keefe (1966-)
The Invitation '03
Specimen '97
When the Bullet Hits the Bone '96

Jodi Lyn O'Keefe (1978-)
The Crow: Salvation '00
Devil in the Flesh 2 '00
Whatever It Takes '00
She's All That '99
Halloween: H20 '98

John E. O'Keefe
Conceiving Ada '97
Out of the Rain '90

Michael O'Keefe (1955-)
Cherry Crush '07
Michael Clayton '07
The Hot Chick '02
The Glass House '01
Prancer Returns '01
Just One Night '00
The Pledge '00
Ghosts of Mississippi '96
Edie & Pen '95
Three Wishes '95
Incident at Deception Ridge '94
Nina Takes a Lover '94
Me & Veronica '93
Fear '90
Out of the Rain '90
Too Young to Die '90
Bridge to Silence '89
Disaster at Silo 7 '88
Ironweed '87
The Whoopee Boys '86
The Slugger's Wife '85
Finders Keepers '84
Nate and Hayes '83
Split Image '82
Caddyshack '80
The Great Santini '80
A Rumor of War '80
The Dark Secret of Harvest Home '78
Gray Lady Down '77

Miles O'Keeffe (1954-)
Clawed: The Legend of Sasquatch '05
Out of the Black '01
Diamondbacks '99
Dead Tides '97
True Vengeance '97
Marked Man '96
Pocahontas: The Legend '95
King's Ransom '91
Relentless 2: Dead On '91
Cartel '90
Liberty & Bash '90
The Drifter '88
The Lone Runner '88
Waxwork '88
Campus Man '87
Iron Warrior '87
Blade Master '84
S.A.S. San Salvador '84
Ator the Fighting Eagle '83
Sword of the Valiant '83
Tarzan, the Ape Man '81

Don O'Kelly (1924-66)
The Hostage '67
Frontier Uprising '61

Donal O'Kelly
Bloom '03
I Went Down '97
The Van '95

Tim O'Kelly
The Passing of Evil '70
Targets '68

Megumi Okina
Shutter '08
Ju-On: The Grudge '03

Denjiro Okochi (1898-1962)
No Regrets for Our Youth '46
The Men Who Tread on the Tiger's Tail '45
Sanshiro Sugata '43

Sophie Okonedo (1969-)
Martian Child '07
Alex Rider: Operation Stormbreaker '06
Scenes of a Sexual Nature '06
Aeon Flux '05
Hotel Rwanda '04
Dirty Pretty Things '03
Go Now '96
Ace Ventura: When Nature Calls '95
Maria's Child '93

Yuji Okumoto (1959-)
The Crow: Wicked Prayer '05
I'll Remember April '99
Partners '99
Mean Guns '97
Hard Justice '95
Bloodfist 5: Human Target '93
Brain Smasher... A Love Story '93
Nemesis '93
Robot Wars '93
True Believer '89
Aloha Summer '88
The Karate Kid: Part 2 '86

Olafur Darri Olafsson (1973-)
Beowulf & Grendel '06
101 Reykjavik '00

Warner Oland (1880-1938)
Charlie Chan at Monte Carlo '37
Charlie Chan at the Olympics '37
Charlie Chan on Broadway '37
Charlie Chan at the Circus '36
Charlie Chan at the Opera '36
Charlie Chan at the Race Track '36
Charlie Chan in Egypt '35
Charlie Chan in Paris '35
Charlie Chan in Shanghai '35
Charlie Chan's Secret '35
Werewolf of London '35
Charlie Chan in London '34
The Painted Veil '34
Shanghai Express '32
The Black Camel '31
Daughter of the Dragon '31
Dishonored '31
Drums of Jeopardy '31
The Return of Dr. Fu Manchu '30
The Mysterious Dr. Fu Manchu '29
Stand and Deliver '28
The Jazz Singer '27
Don Juan '26
Riders of the Purple Sage '25
The Fighting American '24

Ken Olandt (1958-)
Interceptor Force '99
Velocity Trap '99
Darkdrive '98
Digital Man '94
Leprechaun '93
Super Force '90
Summer School '87
April Fool's Day '86

Daniel Olbrychski (1945-)
Ivan and Abraham '94
The Decalogue '88
The Unbearable Lightness of Being '88
Rosa Luxemburg '86
La Truite '83
Maids of Wilko '79
The Tin Drum '79
Land of Promise '74
The Deluge '73
Family Life '71
Landscape After Battle '70
Colonel Wolodyjowski '69
The Structure of Crystals '69

Eric Oldfield (1948-)
Stones of Death '88
Air Hawk '84
Gone to Ground '76

Island Trader '71

William Oldham (1970-)
Old Joy '06
Thousand Pieces of Gold '91
Matewan '87

Gary Oldman (1958-)
The Dark Knight '08
Harry Potter and the Order of the Phoenix '07
Batman Begins '05
Harry Potter and the Goblet of Fire '05
Dead Fish '04
Harry Potter and the Prisoner of Azkaban '04
Tiptoes '03
Interstate 60 '02
Sin '02
Hannibal '01
Nobody's Baby '01
The Contender '00
Jesus '00
Lost in Space '98
Quest for Camelot '98 (V)
Air Force One '97
The Fifth Element '97
Basquiat '96
Murder in the First '95
The Scarlet Letter '95
The Professional '94
Immortal Beloved '94
Fallen Angels 2 '93
Romeo Is Bleeding '93
True Romance '93
Bram Stoker's Dracula '92
JFK '91
Rosencrantz & Guildenstern Are Dead '90
State of Grace '90
Chattahoochee '89
Criminal Law '89
Track 29 '88
We Think the World of You '88
Prick Up Your Ears '87
Sid & Nancy '86
Meantime '81

Matt O'Leary (1987-)
Death Sentence '07
Brick '06
Spy Kids 3-D: Game Over '03
Frailty '02
Spy Kids 2: The Island of Lost Dreams '02
Domestic Disturbance '01
A Town Has Turned to Dust '98

William O'Leary
Candyman 2: Farewell to the Flesh '94
In the Line of Duty: Ambush in Waco '93
Flight of Black Angel '91
Hot Shots! '91
Nice Girls Don't Explode '87

Larisa Oleynik (1981-)
100 Girls '00
A Time for Dancing '00
Ten Things I Hate about You '99
The Baby-Sitters' Club '95

Gabriel Olds (1972-)
Life of the Party '05
Now & Forever '02
Urbania '00
Without Limits '97
Andersonville '95
Animal Room '95
Calendar Girl '93

Ken Olin (1954-)
Queens Logic '91
The Game of Love '90

Lena Olin (1955-)
Awake '07
Casanova '05
Hollywood Homicide '03
United States of Leland '03
Darkness '02
Queen of the Damned '02
Chocolat '01
Ignition '01
Chocolat '00
Mystery Men '99
The Ninth Gate '99
Polish Wedding '97
Night Falls on Manhattan '96
The Night and the Moment '94
Mr. Jones '93
Romeo Is Bleeding '93
Havana '90
Enemies, a Love Story '89
The Unbearable Lightness of Being '88
After the Rehearsal '84

Ingrid Oliu
Real Women Have Curves '02

Barret Oliver (1973-)
Stand and Deliver '88
Invitation to Hell '84
Frankenweenie '84
D.A.R.Y.L. '85
Cocoon '85
The Secret Garden '87
Cocoon: The Return '88
The NeverEnding Story '84

Charles Oliver
The Hooded Terror '38
The Avenging Hand '36
Midnight at the Wax Museum '36

Christian Oliver (1972-)
Speed Racer '08
The Good German '06
Subject Two '06
Kept '01
Eat Your Heart Out '96

David Oliver (1900-78)
The Invisible Killer '40
Postal Inspector '36

David Oliver (1962-92)
Miracle in the Wilderness '91
The Horror Show '89
Defense Play '88
Night of the Creeps '86

Edna May Oliver (1883-1942)
Pride and Prejudice '40
Drums Along the Mohawk '39
Nurse Edith Cavell '39
Second Fiddle '39
The Story of Vernon and Irene Castle '39
Little Miss Broadway '38
Rosalie '38
Romeo and Juliet '36
A Tale of Two Cities '36
David Copperfield '35
Ann Vickers '33
Little Women '33
Hold 'Em Jail '32
Cimarron '31
Half-Shot at Sunrise '30
Lucky Devil '25

Gordon Oliver (1911-95)
The Spiral Staircase '46
Seven Days Ashore '44
Follies Girl '43
Blondie '38
San Quentin '37
Youth on Parole '37

Stephen Oliver (1942-)
Savage Abduction '73
Cycle Psycho '72
Werewolves on Wheels '71
Angels from Hell '68
Motor Psycho '65

Susan Oliver (1937-90)
Tomorrow's Child '82
Hardly Working '81

Rochelle Oliver (1937-)
Scent of a Woman '92
An Unremarkable Life '89
On Valentine's Day '86
1918 '85

Michael Oliver (1981-)
Problem Child 2 '91
Problem Child '90

Paul Olivier (1876-1948)
A Nous la Liberte '31
Le Million '31

Silvio Oliviero
Gotti '96
Understudy: The Graveyard Shift 2 '88
Graveyard Shift '87
Psycho Girls '86

Walter Olkewicz (1948-)
The Client '94
The Good Old Boys '95
Pronto '97
Milo '98
Meeting Daddy '98

Robert Oliveri (1978-)
Honey, I Blew Up the Kid '92
Edward Scissorhands '90
Honey, I Shrunk the Kids '89

Laurence Olivier (1907-89)
Sky Captain and the World of Tomorrow '04
Ebony Tower '86
Peter the Great '86
Wagner: The Complete Epic '85
Wagner: The Movie '85
Wild Geese 2 '85
The Bounty '84
The Jigsaw Man '84
A Voyage 'Round My Father '89
Clash of the Titans '81
Brideshead Revisited '81
The Jazz Singer '80
Dracula '79
A Little Romance '79
The Betsy '78
The Boys from Brazil '78
A Bridge Too Far '77
Jesus of Nazareth '77
Marathon Man '76
The Seven-Per-Cent Solution '76
Love Among the Ruins '75
Lady Caroline Lamb '73
The Merchant of Venice '73
Sleuth '72
Nicholas and Alexandra '71
David Copperfield '70
Oh! What a Lovely War '69
Romeo and Juliet '68 (N)
The Shoes of the Fisherman '68
Khartoum '66
Othello '65
Spartacus '60
The Entertainer '60
Richard III '55
Carrie '52
Hamlet '48
This Happy Breed '47 (N)
Henry V '44
The Demi-Paradise '43
That Hamilton Woman '41
Pride and Prejudice '40
Rebecca '40
Clouds over Europe '39
Wuthering Heights '39
The Divorce of Lady X '38
Fire Over England '37
21 Days '40
As You Like It '36
I Stand Condemned '36

Gertrude (Olmstead) Olmsted (1904-75)
The Cheerful Fraud '27
Sweet Adeline '26
California Straight Ahead '25
Cobra '25
The Monster '25

Dan Olmstead
The Manchurian Candidate '04

Edward James Olmos (1949-)
Splinter '06
In the Time of the Butterflies '01
The Road to El Dorado '00 (V)
Bonanno: A Godfather's Story '99
Gossip '99
The Wall '99
Twelve Angry Men '97
Hollywood Confidential '97
Caught '96
The Disappearance of Garcia Lorca '96
Larry McMurtry's Dead Man's Walk '96
Selena '96
The Limbic Region '96
Roosters '95
My Family '95
The Burning Season '94
Mirage '94
A Million to Juan '94
American Me '92
Talent for the Game '91
Triumph of the Spirit '89
Stand and Deliver '88
Saving Grace '86
Blade Runner '82
Virus '82
Wolfen '81
Zoot Suit '81

Alex O'Loughlin (1977-)
The Invisible '07
Feed '05
The Incredible Journey of Mary Bryant '05

Gerald S. O'Loughlin (1921-)
Crimes of Passion '84
Frances '82
A Matter of Life and Death '81
Pleasure Palace '80
Blind Ambition '79
The Crash of Flight 401 '78
Quicksilver '86
In Cold Blood '67
A Fine Madness '66
Ensign Pulver '64

Richard Olsen
Stephen King's The Night Flier '96
Wildflower '91

Ole Olsen (1892-1963)
Crazy House '43
All Over Town '37
Country Gentlemen '36

James Olson (1943-)
Rachel River '87
Commando '85
Amityville II: The Possession '82
Ragtime '81
My Sister, My Love '78
The Spell '77
Someone I Touched '75
Strange New World '75
Missiles of October '74
The Groundstar Conspiracy '72
The Andromeda Strain '71

Nancy Olson (1928-)
Making Love '82
Airport 1975 '75
Snowball Express '72
Son of Flubber '63
The Absent-Minded Professor '61
Pollyanna '60
Battle Cry '55
Big Jim McLain '52
Mr. Music '50
Sunset Boulevard '50
Union Station '50

Eric Christian Olsen (1977-)
The Comebacks '07
License to Wed '07
Beerfest '06
Cellular '04
Dumb and Dumberer: When Harry Met Lloyd '03
The Hot Chick '02
Local Boys '02
Not Another Teen Movie '01

Gary Olsen (1957-2000)
24 Hours in London '00
Winter Flight '84

Mary-Kate Olsen (1986-)
New York Minute '04
Charlie's Angels: Full Throttle '03
Billboard Dad '98
How the West Was Fun '95
It Takes Two '95
Double Double Toil and Trouble '93
To Grandmother's House We Go '93

Ashley (Fuller) Olsen (1986-)
New York Minute '04
Charlie's Angels: Full Throttle '03
Billboard Dad '98
How the West Was Fun '95
It Takes Two '95
Double Double Toil and Trouble '93
To Grandmother's House We Go '93

Larry Olsen (1938-)
Curley '47
Who Killed Doc Robbin? '48

Merlin Olsen (1940-)
Mitchell '75
The Undefeated '69

Moroni Olsen (1899-1954)
The Long, Long Trailer '54
Father's Little Dividend '51
Father of the Bride '50
The Fountainhead '49
Task Force '49
Call Northside 777 '48
The Long Night '47
The Possessed '47
Notorious '46
Buffalo Bill '44
Cobra Woman '44
Air Force '43
Ali Baba and the Forty Thieves '43
The Glass Key '42
Reunion in France '42
Brigham Young: Frontiersman '40
Snow White and the Seven Dwarfs '37 (V)
Allegheny Uprising '39
Rose of Washington Square '39
Susannah of the Mounties '39
Mary of Scotland '36
Yellow Dust '36
Annie Oakley '35
The Three Musketeers '35

J. Pat O'Malley (1901-85)
A Small Killing '81
Willard '71
101 Dalmatians '61 (V)
Courage of Black Beauty '57
Lassie, Come Home '43

Michael O'Malley (1966-)
Meet Dave '08
28 Days '00

Pat O'Malley (1891-1966)
Invasion of the Body Snatchers '56
The Adventures of Ichabod and Mr. Toad '49 (V)
The Perfect Man '05
Stunt Pilot '39
The Fighting Marines '36
The Miracle Rider '35
Evelyn Prentice '34
The Perils of Pauline '34
The Fighting Marshal '32
Night Life in Reno '31
Spangles '26
The Fighting American '24
The Virginian '23

Bingo O'Malley
Bob Roberts '92
Two Evil Eyes '90

Daragh O'Malley (1954-)
Sharpe's Challenge '06
Longitude '99
Cleopatra '99
The Magnificent Seven '98
Sharpe's Justice '97
Sharpe's Revenge '97
Sharpe's Waterloo '97
Sharpe's Mission '96
Sharpe's Siege '96
Sharpe's Regiment '96
Sharpe's Battle '94
Sharpe's Enemy '94
Sharpe's Gold '94
Sharpe's Honour '94
Sharpe's Company '94
Sharpe's Eagle '93
Sharpe's Rifles '93
Sharpe's Sword '94

Rex O'Malley (1901-)
Midnight '39
Camille '36

Kate O'Mara (1939-)
Nativity '01
Whose Child Am I? '75
The Vampire Lovers '70
The Horror of Frankenstein '70

Mollie O'Mara
Escape from Safehaven '88
Girls School Screamers '86

Omarion
See Omari (Omarion)

Omari (Omarion)
(Grandberry)

Niclas Olund (1977-)
Expectations '97
The Slingshot '93

Judd Omen
Bounty Tracker '93
Dollman '90

Timothy Olyphant (1968-)
Stop-Loss '08
Hitman '07
Catch and Release '07
Live Free or Die Hard '07
The Girl Next Door '04
Dreamcatcher '03
A Man Apart '03
Coastlines '02
Rock Star '01
The Safety of Objects '01
Beyond Suspicion '00
Gone in 60 Seconds '00
The Broken Hearts Club '00
Go '99
No Vacancy '99
When Trumpets Fade '98
Ellen Foster '97
Scream 2 '97

Howling 2: Your Sister Is a Werewolf '85
Pee-wee's Big Adventure '85

Afemo Omilami (1950-)
Drumline '02
Bringing Out the Dead '99
DROP Squad '94

Pat O'Moore (1909-83)
The Two Mrs. Carrolls '47
Sahara '43

Anny Ondra (1903-87)
Blackmail '29
The Manxman '29

Anne O'Neal (1893-1971)
Gun Crazy '49
Open Secret '48

Griffin O'Neal (1964-)
Evil Lives '91
Ghoulies 3: Ghoulies Go to College '91
Night Children '89
Assault of the Killer Bimbos '88
The Wraith '87
April Fool's Day '86
The Children of Times Square '86
Hadley's Rebellion '84
The Escape Artist '82

Patrick O'Neal (1927-94)
Under Siege '92
For the Boys '91
Alice '90
Q & A '90
New York Stories '89
Perry Mason Returns '85
The Stuff '85
Spraggue '84
Make Me an Offer '80
The Stepford Wives '75
Silent Night, Bloody Night '73
The Way We Were '73
El Condor '70
Castle Keep '69
Stiletto '69
Secret Life of an American Wife '68
Where Were You When the Lights Went Out? '68
Alvarez Kelly '66
A Fine Madness '66
In Harm's Way '65
King Rat '65
From the Terrace '60
The Black Shield of Falworth '54

Ron O'Neal (1937-2004)
Original Gangstas '96
Up Against the Wall '91
Hero and the Terror '88
Mercenary Fighters '88
Trained to Kill '88
As Summers Die '86
Red Dawn '84
St. Helen's, Killer Volcano '82
Sophisticated Gents '81
Freedom Road '79
The Hitter '79
When a Stranger Calls '79
Superfly T.N.T. '73
Superfly '72

Ryan O'Neal (1941-)
Malibu's Most Wanted '03
People I Know '02
Epoch '00
Coming Soon '99
The List '99
An Alan Smithee Film: Burn, Hollywood, Burn '97
Sink or Swim '97
Zero Effect '97
Faithful '95
The Man Upstairs '93
Chances Are '89
Small Sacrifices '89
Tough Guys Don't Dance '87
Fever Pitch '85

Irreconcilable Differences '84
Partners '82
Green Ice '81
So Fine '81
The Main Event '79
The Driver '78
Oliver's Story '78
A Bridge Too Far '77
Barry Lyndon '75
Paper Moon '73
The Thief Who Came to Dinner '73
What's Up, Doc? '72
Wild Rovers '71
Love Story '70
The Big Bounce '69

Shaquille O'Neal (1972-)
Scary Movie 4 '06
Good Burger '97
Steel '97
Kazaam '96
Blue Chips '94

Tatum O'Neal (1963-)
My Brother '06
The Home Front '02
Basquiat '96
Little Noises '91
Certain Fury '85
Goldilocks & the Three Bears '83
Circle of Two '80
Little Darlings '80
International Velvet '78
The Bad News Bears '76
Paper Moon '73

Ty O'Neal (1978-)
American Outlaws '01
Bug Buster '99
D2: The Mighty Ducks '94

Barbara O'Neil (1910-80)
Flame of the Islands '55
Angel Face '52
I Remember Mama '48
Secret Beyond the Door '48
All This and Heaven Too '40
Gone with the Wind '39
The Tower of London '39
I Am the Law '38
Stella Dallas '37

Nance O'Neil (1875-1965)
Cimarron '31
The Royal Bed '31

Nancy O'Neil (1908-95)
Jack Ahoy '34
The Secret of the Loch '34

Sally O'Neil (1910-68)
Sixteen Fathoms Deep '34
Battle of the Sexes '28
Battling Butler '26

Angela O'Neill
Enemy Unseen '91
River of Diamonds '90
Sorority House Massacre '86

Chris O'Neill (1945-97)
2 by 4 '98
Backbeat '94
James Joyce's Women '85

Dick O'Neill (1928-98)
My Summer Story '94
Dark Justice '91
She's Out of Control '89
The Mosquito Coast '86
Wolfen '81
The Jerk '79
Prime Time '77
The Taking of Pelham One Two Three '74
Hail '73
Pretty Poison '68

Ed O'Neill (1946-)
Spartan '04
Nobody's Baby '01
Lucky Numbers '00
The 10th Kingdom '00
The Bone Collector '99
The Spanish Prisoner '97
Prefontaine '96

Blue Chips '94
Little Giants '94
Wayne's World 2 '93
Wayne's World '92
Dutch '91
The Adventures of Ford Fairlane '90
Sibling Rivalry '90
Disorganized Crime '89
K-9 '89
When Your Lover Leaves '83
Cruising '80
The Day the Women Got Even '80
Deliverance '72

Henry O'Neill (1891-1961)
Holiday Affair '49
The Virginian '46
Nothing But Trouble '44
Air Raid Wardens '43
Whistling in Brooklyn '43
Johnny Eager '42
White Cargo '42
Billy the Kid '41
Honky Tonk '41
Men of Boys Town '41
Shadow of the Thin Man '41
The Fighting 69th '40
Amazing Dr. Clitterhouse '38
It Happened in New Orleans '36
Black Fury '35
Massacre '34
Lady Killer '33
America '24

Jennifer O'Neill (1948-)
The Corporate Ladder '97
Bad Love '95
The Cover Girl Murders '93
Discretion Assured '93
Invasion of Privacy '92
Perfect Family '92
Committed '91
Personals '90
Full Exposure: The Sex Tape Scandals '89
I Love N.Y. '87
A.D. '85
Chase '85
Scanners '81
Cloud Dancer '80
Steel '80
Force of One '79
Love's Savage Fury '79
The Psychic '78
The Reincarnation of Peter Proud '75
Whiffs '75
Lady Ice '73
Summer of '42 '71
Rio Lobo '70

Kel O'Neill
Redacted '07
Stephanie Daley '06
Domino '05
XX/XY '02

Maggie O'Neill (1967-)
Mansfield Park '07
Invasion: Earth '98
Under Suspicion '92

Maire O'Neill (1887-1952)
Great Day '46
Sidewalks of London '38
Juno and the Paycock '30

Michael O'Neill
Transformers '07
Dreamcatcher '03
Seabiscuit '03
The Legend of Bagger Vance '00
Dancer, Texas—Pop. 81 '98
The Gun in Betty Lou's Handbag '92
Gore-Met Zombie Chef from Hell '87

Remy O'Neill
To Die For 2: Son of Darkness '91
Hollywood Hot Tubs 2: Educating Crystal '89

Terry O'Neill (1948-)
The League of Extraordinary Gentlemen '03
Kull the Conqueror '97
Dragonheart '96

Alannah Ong
New York Minute '04
Double Happiness '94

Yoko Ono (1933-)
Let It Be '70
The Magic Christian '69

Peter Onorati (1954-)
Ordinary Sinner '02
Dancing in September '00
The Art of Murder '99
Just Looking '99
Shelter '98
True Friends '98
Tycus '98
RocketMan '97
Dead Ahead '96
Not Like Us '96
Donor Unknown '95
Camp Nowhere '94
Fire Birds '90
Goodfellas '90

Lupe Ontiveros (1942-)
Mr. St. Nick '02
Gabriela '01
Storytelling '01
Chuck & Buck '00
Picking Up the Pieces '99
Candyman 3: Day of the Dead '98
As Good As It Gets '97
Selena '96
My Family '94
El Norte '83

Michael Ontkean (1950-)
A Killing Spring '02
Just a Little Harmless Sex '99
Summer of the Monkeys '98
Swann '96
Legacy of Lies '92
Postcards from the Edge '90
Bye Bye Blues '89
Cold Front '89
Street Justice '89
Clara's Heart '88
The Allnighter '87
Maid to Order '87
The Blood of Others '84
Just the Way You Are '84
Making Love '82
Willie & Phil '80
Slap Shot '77
Girls on the Road '73
Where the Eagle Flies '72
The Witching '72
Peacekillers '71

Amanda Ooms (1964-)
Wilderness '96
The Women on the Roof '89

Dhobi Oparei
Seven Seconds '05

David Opatoshu (1918-96)
Forty Days of Musa Dagh '85
Americathon '79
Who'll Stop the Rain? '78
Conspiracy of Terror '75
Romance of a Horsethief '71
Death of a Gunfighter '69
The Fixer '68
Tom Curtain '66
Exodus '60
The Light Ahead '39

Anne Openshaw
Narc '02
We'll Meet Again '02

Alan Oppenheimer (1930-)
Trancers 5: Sudden Deth '94
Invisible: The Chronicles of Benjamin Knight '93
Trancers 4: Jack of Swords '93
Child of Darkness, Child of Light '91
Blind Ambition '79
A Pleasure Doing Business '79
Helter Skelter '76
The Bionic Woman '75
The Groundstar Conspiracy '72
Star! '68

Don Opper (1949-)
Critters 3 '91
Critters 4 '91
The Forgotten '89
Critters 2: The Main Course '88
Critters '86
Android '82

Terry O'Quinn (1952-)
Old School '03
Hometown Legend '02
The Locket '02
American Outlaws '01
Winds of Terror '01
Rated X '00
Murder in a Small Town '99
The X-Files '98
Breast Men '97
Ghosts of Mississippi '96
Primal Fear '96
The Shadow Conspiracy '96
JAG '95
Shadow Warriors '95
Don't Talk to Strangers '94
Amityville: A New Generation '93
Lipstick Camera '93
Tombstone '93
The Cutting Edge '92
The Good Fight '92
My Samurai '92
Take Down '92
Wildcard '92
Company Business '91
Prisoners of the Sun '91
The Rocketeer '91
Son of the Morning Star '91
When the Time Comes '91
Blind Fury '90
The Forgotten One '89
Roe vs. Wade '89
Stepfather 2: Make Room for Daddy '89
Pin... '88
Young Guns '88
Black Widow '87
The Stepfather '87
SpaceCamp '86
Women of Valor '86
Mischief '85
Silver Bullet '85
Mrs. Soffel '84
Places in the Heart '84
Heaven's Gate '81
Mahler '74

Mr. Saturday Night '92
Straight Talk '92
Universal Soldier '92
Beauty and the Beast '91 (V)
Delirious '91
Delusion '91
Out for Justice '91
Toy Soldiers '91
Dead Women in Lingerie '90
Last Exit to Brooklyn '90
California Casanova '89
Crimes & Misdemeanors '89
Dirty Dancing '87
I Love N.Y. '87
Out on a Limb '87
Someone to Watch Over Me '87
F/X '86
Imagemaker '86
Brewster's Millions '85
Prince of the City '81
Underground Aces '80
Foreplay '75
24 Hours in a Woman's Life '61

Roy Orbison (1936-88)
Chuck Berry: Hail! Hail! Rock 'n' Roll '87
Roadie '80
Fastest Guitar Alive '68

Cyril O'Reilly (1958-)
Air Rage '01
Shadow of a Scream '97
Bloodfist 7: Manhunt '95
Philadelphia Experiment 2 '93
The Cool Surface '92
Navy SEALS '90
Dance of the Damned '88
On Wings of Eagles '86
Purple Hearts '84
Porky's 2: The Next Day '83
Porky's '82

Joan Orenstein
The Hanging Garden '97
Charlie Grant's War '80

Fereshteh Sadr Orfani
The Circle '00
The White Balloon '95

Liana Orfei (1937-)
Casanova '70 '65
Nefertiti, Queen of the Nile '64
The Avenger '64
The Giant of Metropolis '61
Pirates of the Coast '61
Mill of the Stone Women '60

Moira Orfei (1931-)
The Scent of a Woman '75
The Triumph of Hercules '66
Terror of the Steppes '64
Ursus in the Valley of the Lions '62
Mole Men Against the Son of Hercules '61

Silvio Orlando (1957-)
After Midnight '04
Light of My Eyes '01
The Son's Room '99
Not of This World '99
Children of Hannibal '98
Palombella Rossa '89

Tony Orlando (1944-)
Waking Up in Reno '02
Rosie: The Rosemary Clooney Story '82

Julia Ormond (1965-)
Prince of Central Park '00
Animal Farm '99 (V)
Smilla's Sense of Snow '96
First Knight '95
Sabrina '95
Captives '94
Legends of the Fall '94
Nostradamus '93

Stalin '92
Traffik '90
Young Catherine '91

Alan Ormsby (1944-)
Children Shouldn't Play with Dead Things '72
Deathdream '72

Ed O'Ross (1949-)
Delta Farce '07
Curious George '06 (V)
Hoodlum '96
Mindstorm '07
Y2K '99
Dark Angel '90
Miami Vice '06
Navajo Blues '97
Play Nice '92
Universal Soldier '92
Another 48 Hrs. '90
Tailspin: Behind the Korean Airline Tragedy '89
Red Heat '88
Full Metal Jacket '87
The Hidden '87
Lethal Weapon '87

Heather O'Rourke
Ruby's Dream '82
Poltergeist '82
Poltergeist 3 '88
Poltergeist 2: The Other Side '86

Ashley Rose Orr (1990-)
Carry Me Home '04
Child Star: The Shirley Temple Story '01
Poltergeist '82

Christopher Orr
Robin Cook's Invasion '97
D3: The Mighty Ducks '96

Leland Orser (1960-)
Twisted '04
The Good German '06
Confidence '03
Daredevil '03
Runaway Jury '03
Brother's Keeper '02
Pearl Harbor '01
The Bone Collector '99
Resurrection '99
Saving Private Ryan '98
Very Bad Things '98
Alien: Resurrection '97
Excess Baggage '96
Independence Day '96

Marina Orsini (1967-)
Lifeform '96
Steel Toes '06
Eddie and the Cruisers 2: Eddie Lives! '89
Battle of the Worlds '61

Umberto Orsini (1934-)
Good-bye, Emmanuelle '77
Emmanuelle, the Joys of a Woman '76
The Outside Man '73
A Woman at Her Window '77
Cesar & Rosalie '72
The Family '70

Dyana Ortelli
Mademoiselle '66
Luminarias '99
Alienator '89

Frank Orth (1880-1962)
The Great Rupert '50
Heartaches '47
I Wake Up Screaming '41
Nancy Drew and the Hidden Staircase '39

Zak Orth (1970-)
Nancy Drew—Detective '38
Prime '05
Kill the Poor '06
The Baxter '05
Wet Hot American Summer '01
Down to You '00
Loser '00
When Trumpets Fade '98
In and Out '57
Rose Hill '97
My Teacher's Wife '95

Antonio Ortiz
Illegal Tender '07
Knights of the South Bronx '05

Humberto Ortiz (1979-)
Arcade '93
Dollman '90

John Ortiz
Aliens vs. Predator: Requiem '07
American Gangster '07
El Cantante '06
Miami Vice '06
Take the Lead '06
Narc '02
The Last Marshal '99
Riot in the Streets '96

Meaghan Ory
Blonde and Blonder '07
Merlin's Apprentice '06

Romano Orzari (1964-)
Stiletto Dance '01
Wilder '00

Andrew Osborn (1912-85)
Angels One Five '54
Blackout '54
Spaceways '53
Three Stops to Murder '53

Lyn Osborn (1926-58)
The Amazing Colossal Man '57
Invasion of the Saucer Men '57

Bud Osborne (1884-1964)
Night of the Ghouls '59
Gun Glory '57
Tribute to a Bad Man '56
Bride of the Monster '55
Border Bandits '46
The Caravan Trail '46
Outlaw of the Plains '46
Wild West '46
Border Badmen '45
His Brother's Ghost '45
Dead or Alive '44
Range Law '44
Rustler's Hideout '44
Wild Horse Phantom '44
Six Gun Gospel '43
Death Rides the Range '40
West of Pinto Basin '40
Across the Plains '39
Western Gold '37
Where Trails Divide '37
The Crimson Trail '35
Lightning Bill '35
The Outlaw Deputy '35
Ridin' Thru '35
Riding Speed '35
Rustlers of Red Dog '35
Deadwood Pass '33
Diamond Trail '33
Rustler's Roundup '33
When a Man Rides Alone '33
Mark of the Spur '32
The Racing Tornado '32
Battling with Buffalo Bill '31
Apache Kid's Escape '30
The Fighting Stallion '26

Holmes Osborne (1952-)
Southland Tales '06
A Lot Like Love '05
Dreamer: Inspired by a True Story '05
Cheaper by the Dozen '03
Identity '03
Donnie Darko '01
Waking Up in Reno '02
The Quiet American '02
Election '99
Crazy in Alabama '99
Affliction '97
That Thing You Do! '96
From the Earth to the Moon '98
The Mod Squad '99
Danger in the Skies '79

John Osborne (1929-94)
The Power of One '92
Get Carter '71

Vivienne Osborne (1896-1961)
Captain Caution '40
Primrose Path '40
Let's Sing Again '36
The Phantom Broadcast '33
Supernatural '33
Tomorrow at Seven '33

Ozzy Osbourne (1948-)
Austin Powers in Goldmember '02
Little Nicky '00
The Jerky Boys '95
Decline of Western Civilization 2: The Metal Years '88
Trick or Treat '86

Henry Oscar (1891-1969)
The Brides of Dracula '60
The Spaniard's Curse '58
Postmark for Danger '56
The Greed of William Hart '48
The Four Feathers '39
Black Limelight '38
The Terror '38
The Courageous Mr. Penn '41

Per Oscarsson (1927-)
Dreaming of Rita '94
House of Angels '92
Sleep of Death '79
Blockhouse '73
The New Land '73
Endless Night '71
The Last Valley '71
Secrets '71
The Night Visitor '70
Dandy in Aspic '68
Hunger '66
The Doll '62

Brian O'Shaughnessy (1931-2001)
Alien Chaser '96
Claws '85
Mr. Kingstreet's War '71
Joe Panther '76
Sharks' Treasure '75
Invasion of the Bee Girls '73
Sweet Sugar '72
The Fortune Cookie '66
Kiss Me, Stupid '64

Michael O'Shea (1906-73)
This is the Sea '96
The Underworld Story '50
The Big Wheel '49
Parole, Inc. '49
Fixed Bayonets! '51

Marc O'Shea
I'll Sleep When I'm Dead '03

Kevin O'Shea (1915-)
The Purple Heart '44
A Wing and a Prayer '44

Donny Osmond (1957-)
Joseph and the Amazing Technicolor Dreamcoat '00
Mulan '98 (V)
The Adventures of Nellie Bly '81

Cliff Osmond (1937-)
Forrest Gump '94
In Search of a Golden Sky '84
Hangar 18 '80
Mountain Man '77

Marie Osmond (1959-)
Goin' Coconuts '78
Hugo the Hippo '76 (V)

Yelba Osorio
Shut Up and Kiss Me '05
Riot in the Streets '96

Jeffery Osterhage (1953-)
Sex Crimes '92
Big Bad John '90
Dark Before Dawn '89
Masque of the Red Death '89
Buckeye and Blue '87
South of Reno '87
The Shadow Riders '82
The Sacketts '79

Robert Osterloh (1918-2001)
I Bury the Living '58
An Annapolis Story '55
One Minute to Zero '52
Peter Lundy and the Medicine Hat Stallion '77
It's Not the Size That Counts '74
Theatre of Blood '73
Sacco & Vanzetti '71
The Angel Levine '70
Loot... Give Me Money, Honey! '70

Haley Joel Osment (1988-)
Pay It Forward '00
I'll Remember April '99
The Sixth Sense '99
Bogus '96
Last Stand at Saber River '96
Forrest Gump '94

Emily Osment (1992-)
Spy Kids 3-D: Game Over '03
Spy Kids 2: The Island of Lost Dreams '02
Sarah, Plain and Tall: Winter's End '99
A.I.: Artificial Intelligence '01

K.T. Oslin (1941-)
Murder So Sweet '93

Yukari Oshima
Immortal Battalion '44

Ren Osugi (1951-)
Fireworks '97
Sonatine '96

Tessie O'Shea (1913-95)
Dr. Jekyll and Mr. Hyde '68
The Russians Are Coming, the Russians Are Coming '66
Paddy '70
Barbarella '68
Romeo and Juliet '68
Ulysses '67

Bibi Osterwald (1918-2002)
Prowler '51
Gun Crazy '49
As Good As It Gets '97
Bank Shot '74
A Fine Madness '66

William Ostrander (1959-)
Red Heat '85
Christine '84
Mike's Murder '84
Fire and Ice '83 (V)
The World of Henry Orient '64
Parrish '61

Aisling O'Sullivan (1968-)
Me & Mrs. Jones '02
The American '01
The Wyvern Mystery '00
The Butcher Boy '97

Maureen O'Sullivan (1911-98)
The River Pirates '88
Stranded '87
Hannah and Her Sisters '86
Peggy Sue Got Married '86
Too Scared to Scream '85
The Tall T '57
All I Desire '53
Where Danger Lives '50
The Big Clock '48
Tarzan's New York Adventure '42
A Day at the Races '37
Tarzan Finds a Son '39
A Connecticut Yankee '31
Tarzan, the Ape Man '32
Devil Doll '36
Tarzan Escapes '36
Anna Karenina '35
Cardinal '35
David Copperfield '35
The Barretts of Wimpole Street '34
Hide-Out '34
Tarzan and His Mate '34
The Thin Man '34
Skyscraper Souls '32
Strange Interlude '32

Patton Oswalt (1969-)
Ratatouille '07
Failure to Launch '06
Blade: Trinity '04
Starsky & Hutch '04

Hideji Otaki (1925-)
Rikyu '90
Kagemusha '80
The Funeral '84

Cheri Oteri (1962-)
Shrek the Third '07 (V)
The Ant Bully '06 (V)
Dumb and Dumberer: When Harry Met Lloyd '03
Sol Goode '01
Love & Sex '00
Scary Movie '00

Carre Otis (1968-)
Under Heavy Fire '01
Exit in Red '97
Wild Orchid '90

Annette O'Toole (1953-)
Here on Earth '00
Final Justice '98
The Christmas Box '95
The Kennedys of Massachusetts '90
My Brother's Keeper '95
Imaginary Crimes '94
Kiss of a Killer '93
Love Matters '93
Jewels '92
White Lie '91
A Girl of the Limberlost '90
Stephen King's It '90
Love at Large '89
Cross My Heart '88
Broken Vows '87
Superman 3 '83
48 Hrs. '82
Cat People '82
Superman 2 '80
Foolin' Around '80
King of the Gypsies '78
One on One '77
War Between the Tates '76
Smile '75

Peter O'Toole (1932-)
Ratatouille '07 (V)
Venus '06
Casanova '05
Troy '04
Bright Young Things '03
Hitler: The Rise o' Evil '03
Rock My World '02
Joan of Arc '99
The Dark Angel '91
King Ralph '91
The Nutcracker Prince '91 (V)
High Spirits '88
The Last Emperor '87
Club Paradise '86
Creator '85
Kim '84
Supergirl '84
Svengali '83
My Favorite Year '82
Masada '81
Power Play '81
Caligula '80
The Stunt Man '80
Zulu Dawn '79
Foxtrot '76
Rogue Male '76
Man Friday '75
Rosebud '75
Under Milk Wood '73
Man of La Mancha '72
The Ruling Class '72
Murphy's War '71
Goodbye, Mr. Chips '69
The Lion in Winter '68
Casino Royale '67
Night of the Generals '67
How to Steal a Million '66
Lord Jim '65
What's New Pussycat? '65
Becket '64
Lawrence of Arabia '62
Kidnapped '60

Nobuko Otowa (1925-95)
Last War '68
Onibaba '64
The Island '61

James Ottaway (1908-99)
Absolution '81
Malcolm X '92

John Ottavino
Fight for Gold '86
Hell Hounds of Alaska '73

Angelica Ott
Tampopo '86

Barry Otto (1941-)
Dead Letter Office '98
Mr. Nice Guy '98
She Done Him Wrong '33
That'll Be the Day '73

Rafaela (Rafael, Raphaella) Ottiano (1888-1942)
Devil Doll '36
Curly Top '35

Cosi '95
Lilian's Story '95
Mr. Reliable: A True Story '95
The Custodian '94
Strictly Ballroom '92
Howling 3: The Marsupials '87
Bliss '85

Goetz Otto (1967-)
Downfall '04
The Girl of Your Dreams '99
Beowulf '98

Miranda Otto (1967-)
The Starter Wife '07
War of the Worlds '05
Flight of the Phoenix '04
Danny Deckchair '03
Lord of the Rings: The Return of the King '03
Close Your Eyes '02
The Healer '02
Human Nature '02
Lord of the Rings: The Two Towers '02
The Way We Live Now '02
What Lies Beneath '00
The Jack Bull '99
Dead Letter Office '98
In the Winter Dark '98
The Thin Red Line '98
Doing Time for Patsy Cline '97
The Well '97
Love Serenade '96
The Last Days of Chez Nous '92
The Nostradamus Kid '92
The 13th Floor '88

Assita Ouedraogo
La Promesse '96

Rasmane Ouedraogo
La Promesse '96
Tilai '90
Yaaba '89

Stephen Ouimette
Slings & Arrows: Season 2

Andre Oumansky (1933-)
Spy Games '99
Othello '95
Burnt by the Sun '94
Joy House '64

Gerard Oury (1919-2006)
The Prize '63
Back to the Wall '56

Maria Ouspenskaya (1876-1949)
Frankenstein Meets the Wolfman '42
The Shanghai Gesture '42
Kings Row '41
The Wolf Man '41
Beyond Tomorrow '40
Dance, Girl, Dance '40
Waterloo Bridge '40
Love Affair '39
The Rains Came '39
Conquest '37
Dodsworth '36

Levani Outchanechvili (1958-)
25th Hour '02
The Legend of Suram Fortress '85

Peter Outerbridge (1966-)
Lucky Number Slevin '06
Population 436 '06
Men with Brooms '02
The Rendering '02
Lip Service '00
Mission to Mars '00
Better Than Chocolate '99
Escape from Mars '99
Escape Velocity '99
Thrill Seekers '99
Closer and Closer '96
Kissed '96
The Android Affair '95
For the Moment '94
Paris, France '94
Cool Runnings '93
Victim of Beauty '91

Kati Outinen (1961-)
The Man Without a Past '02
The Match Factory Girl '90

Park Overall (1957-)
Sparkler '99
The Good Old Boys '95
The Gambler Returns: The Luck of the Draw '93
Undercover Blues '93
The Vanishing '93
House of Cards '92
Kindergarten Cop '90
Lost Angels '88
Biloxi Blues '88
Mississippi Burning '88
Tainted '88

Kellie Overbey (1964-)
Love Thy Neighbor '02
Sweet and Lowdown '99
EDtv '99

Lynne Overman (1887-1943)
Reap the Wild Wind '42
Roxie Hart '42
Caught in the Draft '41
Edison the Man '40
Union Pacific '39
Paris in Spring '35
Little Miss Marker '34
Midnight '34

Frank Overton (1918-67)
To Kill a Mockingbird '62
Desire Under the Elms '58

Rick Overton (1954-)
Off the Lip '04
Serial Killing 101 '04
Eight Legged Freaks '02
Heater '99
National Lampoon's Attack of the 5 Ft. 2 Women '94
The High Crusade '92
Blind Fury '90
Earth Girls Are Easy '89
A Sinful Life '89
Million Dollar Mystery '87
Traxx '87
Odd Jobs '85
Beverly Hills Cop '84

Baard Owe (1936-)
The Kingdom 2 '97
The Kingdom '95
Medea '88
Gertrud '64

Bill Owen (1914-99)
Singleton's Pluck '84
The Comeback '77
In Celebration '75
The Hellfire Club '61
The Gay Lady '49

Chris Owen (1980-)
Dear Wendy '05
National Lampoon's Gold Diggers '04
National Lampoon's Van Wilder '02
American Pie 2 '01
Ready to Rumble '00
American Pie '99
October Sky '99
Angus '95

Clive Owen (1965-)
Elizabeth: The Golden Age '07
Shoot 'Em Up '07
Children of Men '06
Inside Man '06
The Pink Panther '06
Derailed '05
Sin City '05
Closer '04
King Arthur '04
Beyond Borders '03
I'll Sleep When I'm Dead '03
The Bourne Identity '02
Gosford Park '01
Greenfingers '00
Second Sight '99
Split Second '99
Bent '97
Croupier '97
The Rich Man's Wife '96
Century '94
The Return of the Native '94
The Magician '93
Class of '61 '92
Close My Eyes '91
Lorna Doone '90

Garry Owen (1897-1951)
Dark Mirror '46
San Quentin '37

Lloyd Owen (1966-)
Miss Potter '06
Dead Gorgeous '02
Catherine Cookson's The Cinder Path '94

Michael Owen
Youth Aflame '44
Dick Tracy vs. Crime Inc. '41

Reginald Owen (1887-1972)
The Thrill of It All '63
Red Garters '54
The Miniver Story '50
Challenge to Lassie '49
National Velvet '44
Above Suspicion '43
Madame Curie '43
Cairo '42
I Married an Angel '42
Mrs. Miniver '42
Random Harvest '42
Reunion in France '42
Somewhere I'll Find You '42
White Cargo '42
Woman of the Year '42
Charley's Aunt '41
Tarzan's Secret Treasure '41
They Met in Bombay '41
A Woman's Face '41
The Real Glory '39
A Christmas Carol '38
Everybody Sing '38
Rosalie '38
The Bride Wore Red '37
Conquest '37
Madame X '37
Personal Property '37
The Great Ziegfeld '36
Love on the Run '36
Rose Marie '36
A Tale of Two Cities '36
Anna Karenina '35
The Good Fairy '35
Fashions of 1934 '34
Here is My Heart '34
Of Human Bondage '34
Queen Christina '33
A Study in Scarlet '33
Ghost City '32

Rena Owen (1962-)
Nemesis Game '03
Players '03
Soul Assassin '01
Dance Me to My Song '98
When Love Comes '98
Once Were Warriors '94

Seena Owen (1894-1966)
Queen Kelly '29
Intolerance '16
The Lamb '15

Ciaran Owens
Agnes Browne '99
Angela's Ashes '99

Eamon Owens (1983-)
The Boys and Girl From County Clare '03
St. Patrick: The Irish Legend '01
The General '98
The Butcher Boy '97

Gary Owens (1936-)
Digging Up Business '91
Killcrazy '89
I'm Gonna Git You Sucka '88

Patricia Owens (1925-2000)
Hell to Eternity '60
The Fly '58
The Law and Jake Wade '58
Sayonara '57
The Happiest Days of Your Life '50

Earl Owensby (1936-)
The Rutherford County Line '87
Dogs of Hell '83
Manhunter '83
Death Driver '78
Challenge '74

Monroe Owsley (1900-37)
Goin' to Town '35
Ex-Lady '33

Catherine Oxenberg (1961-)
The Vector File '03
Road Rage '01
Sanctimony '01
Frozen in Fear '00
The Collectors '99
The Omega Code '99
Time Served '99
Deadly Game '98
Boys Will Be Boys '97
Heaven Before I Die '96
Charles & Diana: A Palace Divided '93
Rubdown '93
Sexual Response '92
Overexposed '90
K-9000 '89
Swimsuit '89

Ben Oxenbould
Black Water '07
Fatty Finn '84

David Oxley (1920-85)
House of the Living Dead '73
Night Ambush '57

David Oyelowo
A Raisin in the Sun '08
Five Days '07
As You Like It '06

Moishe Oysher (1907-58)
The Singing Blacksmith '38
The Cantor's Son '37

Frank Oz (1944-)
Star Wars: Episode 3—Revenge of the Sith '05 (V)
A Sound of Thunder '05
Zathura '05 (V)
Star Wars: Episode 2—Attack of the Clones '02 (V)
Monsters, Inc. '01 (V)
Muppets from Space '99 (V)
Star Wars: Episode 1—The Phantom Menace '99 (V)
Blues Brothers 2000 '98
Muppet Treasure Island '96
Innocent Blood '92
The Muppet Christmas Carol '92 (V)
Sesame Street Presents: Follow That Bird '85 (V)
Spies Like Us '85
The Muppets Take Manhattan '84 (V)
Return of the Jedi '83 (V)
The Dark Crystal '82 (V)
An American Werewolf in London '81
The Great Muppet Caper '81 (V)
The Blues Brothers '80
The Empire Strikes Back '80
The Muppet Movie '79 (V)

Eitaro (Sakae, Saka Ozawa) Ozawa (1909-88)
Sandakan No. 8 '74
The Human Condition: No Greater Love '58
Princess Yang Kwei Fei '55
Ugetsu '53
Record of a Tenement Gentleman '47

Sakae (Saka) Ozawa
See Eitaro (Sakae, Saka Ozawa) Ozawa

Shoichi Ozawa (1929-)
Black Rain '88
The Ballad of Narayama '83
The Pornographers '66

Yuya Ozeki (1996-)
The Grudge '04
Ju-On: The Grudge '03

Madeleine Ozeray (1908-89)
Crime and Punishment '35
Liliom '35

Jack Paar (1918-2004)
Love Nest '51
Walk Softly, Stranger '50
Easy Living '49

Johnny Pacar
Wild Child '08
Purgatory House '04

Judy Pace (1946-)
Frogs '72
Brian's Song '71
Cotton Comes to Harlem '70
Three in the Cellar '70

Lee Pace (1979-)
Miss Pettigrew Lives for a Day '08
The Good Shepherd '06
Infamous '06
The White Countess '05
Soldier's Girl '03

Tom Pace
Blood Orgy of the She-Devils '74
Girl in Gold Boots '69
The Astro-Zombies '67

Frederico Pacifici (1955-)
Fluke '95
Flight of the Innocent '93

Al Pacino (1940-)
88 Minutes '08
Ocean's Thirteen '07
Two for the Money '05
The Merchant of Venice '04
Gigli '03
The Recruit '03
Insomnia '02
People I Know '02
Simone '02
Any Given Sunday '99
The Insider '99
The Devil's Advocate '97
Donnie Brasco '96
Looking for Richard '96
Two Bits '96
City Hall '95
Heat '95
Carlito's Way '93
Glengarry Glen Ross '92
Scent of a Woman '92
Frankie and Johnny '91
Dick Tracy '90
The Godfather, Part 3 '90
Sea of Love '89
Revolution '85
Scarface '83
Author! Author! '82
The Godfather 1902-1959: The Complete Epic '81
Cruising '80
And Justice for All '79
Bobby Deerfield '77
America at the Movies '76
Dog Day Afternoon '75
The Godfather, Part 2 '74
Scarecrow '73
Serpico '73
The Godfather '72
Panic in Needle Park '71

David Packer (1962-)
The Killing Club '01
No Strings Attached '98
Silent Motive '91
The Runnin' Kind '89
Trust Me '89
You Can't Hurry Love '88

Joanna Pacula (1957-)
Forget About It '06
The Hit '01
The Art of Murder '99
Crash & Byrnes '99
My Giant '98
Virus '98
The White Raven '98
The Haunted Sea '97
Business for Pleasure '96
Heaven Before I Die '96
Not Like Us '96
Captain Nuke and the Bomber Boys '95
Timemaster '95
Deep Red '94
The Last Gasp '94
Every Breath '93
Silence of the Hams '93
Tombstone '93
Under Investigation '93
Warlock: The Armageddon '93
Black Ice '92
Eyes of the Beholder '92
Husbands and Lovers '91
Marked for Death '90
The Kiss '88
Options '88
Sweet Lies '88
Death Before Dishonor '87
Escape from Sobibor '87
Not Quite Paradise '86
Gorky Park '83

Jared Padalecki (1982-)
CryWolf '05
House of Wax '05
New York Minute '04
A Little Inside '01

Sarah Padden (1881-1967)
My Dog Shep '46
Wild West '46
Song of Old Wyoming '45
Wildfire '45
Girl Rush '44
Range Law '44
Law and Order '42
The Mad Monster '42
Riders of the West '42
Snuffy Smith, Yard Bird '42
In Old Colorado '41
Reg'lar Fellers '41
Three Comrades '38
Exiled to Shanghai '37
Tomorrow's Children '34
Cross Examination '32

Hugh Paddick (1915-2000)
Naughty Knights '71
The Killing of Sister George '69

Pilar Padilla
In the Time of the Butterflies '01
Bread and Roses '00

Robert Padilla
Twisted Nightmare '87
The Great Gundown '75

Lea Padovani (1920-91)
The Naked Maja '59
Modigliani '58

Dira Paes (1969-)
Mango '05
Chronically Unfeasible '00
The Emerald Forest '85

David Paetkau (1978-)
Final Destination 2 '03
National Lampoon's
Holiday Reunion '03

Michael J. Pagan
See No Evil '06
The Gospel '05
How Stella Got Her Groove
Back '98

Anita Page (1910-)
After Midnight '33
Jungle Bride '33
Skyscraper Souls '32
Sidewalks of New York '31
Free and Easy '30
Broadway Melody '29
Our Modern Maidens '29
Our Dancing Daughters '28

Bradley Page (1901-85)
The Affairs of Annabel '38
Mistaken Identity '36
Champagne for Breakfast '35

Diamond Dallas Page (1956-)
Ready to Rumble '00

Dorothy Page (1904-61)
Ride 'Em Cowgirl '41
The Singing Cowgirl '39
Water Rustlers '39

Ellen Page (1987-)
Smart People '08
Juno '07
Hard Candy '06
X-Men: The Last Stand '06

Gale Page (1911-83)
Knute Rockne: All
American '40
They Drive by Night '40
Amazing Dr. Clitterhouse '38
Four Daughters '38

Geneviève Page (1930-)
Buffet Froid '79
The Private Life of Sherlock
Holmes '70
Mayerling '68
Belle de Jour '67
The Day and the Hour '63
El Cid '61
Song Without End '60
Girl in His Pocket '57
Fanfan la Tulipe '51

Geraldine Page (1924-87)
Native Son '86
The Bride '85
White Nights '85
Walls of Glass '85
The Dollmaker '84
The Pope of Greenwich
Village '84
Harry's War '84
I'm Dancing as Fast as I
Can '82
Honky Tonk Freeway '81
Interiors '78
Nasty Habits '77
The Rescuers '77 (V)
The Day of the Locust '75
Hazel's People '73
Pete 'n' Tillie '72
The Beguiled '70
Whatever Happened to
Aunt Alice? '69
The Happiest Millionaire '67
You're a Big Boy Now '66
Barefoot in Athens '66
Memory '66
ABC Stage 67: Truman
Capote's A Christmas
Memory '66
The Three Sisters '65
Toys in the Attic '63
Sweet Bird of Youth '62
Summer and Smoke '61

Grant Page (1939-)
Road Games '81
Deathcheaters '76

Harrison Page (1941-)
Carnosaur '93
Lionheart '90

Joanna Page (1978-)
Love Actually '03
Very Annie Mary '00
David Copperfield '99

Joy Page (1924-)
Conquest of Cochise '53
Fighter Attack '53
Casablanca '42

Ken Page (1954-)
The Alamo '04
The Nightmare before
Christmas '93 (V)
The Kid Who Loved
Christmas '90

LaWanda Page (1920-2002)
Friday '95
The Meteor Man '93
Shakes the Clown '92
Mausoleum '83
Zapped! '82
B.A.D. Cats '80

Patti Page (1927-2002)
Boys Night Out '62
Elmer Gantry '60

Paul Page (1903-74)
Palmy Days '31

Tony Page (1939-84)
Pleasure '31

Heidi Paige
Q (The Winged Serpent) '82

Mabel Paige (1880-1954)
The Scar '48
Nocturne '46
Murder, He Says '45

Robert Paige (1910-87)
Abbott and Costello Go to
Mars '53
The Green Promise '49
The Red Stallion '47
Can't Help Singing '45
Son of Dracula '43
Pardon My Sarong '42
The Monster and the Girl '41

Geraldine Pailhas (1971-)
5x2 '04
They Came Back '04
Don Juan DeMarco '94

Didier Pain
On Guard! '03
My Father's Glory '91
My Mother's Castle '91

Cathy Paine
Helter Skelter '76

Josh Pais (1964-)
Teeth '07
Year of the Dog '07
Phone Booth '02
Scotland, PA '02
Swimming '00
Music of the Heart '99
New York's Finest '87

Alfred Paget (1880-1925)
Intolerance '16
The Lamb '15
Battle of Elderbush Gulch '13

Debra Paget (1933-)
The Haunted Palace '63
The Mercenaries '62
Tales of Terror '62
The Indian Tomb '59
From the Earth to the Moon '58
Journey to the Lost City '58
Omar Khayyam '57
The Last Hunt '56
Love Me Tender '56
The Ten Commandments '56
Demetrius and the
Gladiators '54
Prince Valiant '54
Princess of the Nile '54
Belles on Their Toes '52
Stars and Stripes Forever '52
Broken Arrow '50
House of Strangers '49

Melinda Page Hamilton
Sleeping Dogs Lie '06

Nicola Pagett (1945-)
An Awfully Big Adventure '94
Privates on Parade '84
A Woman of Substance '84
Oliver's Story '78
The Seducer '69
The Viking Queen '67

Marcel Pagliero (1907-80)
Dedée d'Anvers '49
Open City '45

Maria Pakulnis (1956-)
The Decalogue '88
No End '84

Stratos Pahis
The Travelling Players '75

Liana Pai
Happy Accidents '00
The Siege '98
The Enchantress '85

Janis Paige (1922-)
Natural Causes '94
Love at the Top '86
Angel on My Shoulder '80

Nestor Paiva (1905-66)
Jesse James Meets
Frankenstein's Daughter '65
They Saved Hitler's Brain '64
Girls! Girls! Girls! '62
Frontier Uprising '61
The Nine Lives of Elfego
Baca '58
Outcasts of the City '58
The Mole People '56
Revenge of the Creature '55
Tarantula '55
Creature from the Black
Lagoon '54
Five Fingers '52
The Great Caruso '51
Double Dynamite '51
Follow Me Quietly '49
Shoot to Kill '47
Fear '46
The Road to Utopia '46
The Falcon in Mexico '44
The Purple Heart '44
Hold That Ghost '41
Beau Geste '39
Prison Train '38

Holly Palance (1950-)
The Best of Times '86
Tuxedo Warrior '82
The Omen '76

David Palffy (1969-)
House of the Dead '03
The Box '03
Sinners '89

Joe Palese
Panic in the Streets '50

Ron Palillo (1954-)
Committed '91
Hellgate '89

Jack Palance (1919-2006)
Prancer Returns '01
Sarah, Plain and Tall:
Winter's End '99
Treasure Island '99
Ebenezer '97
Buffalo Girls '95
City Slickers 2: The Legend
of Curly's Gold '94
The Swan Princess '94 (V)
Cops and Robbersons '94
Cyborg 2 '93
Solar Crisis '92
City Slickers '91
Batman '89
SnakeEater '89
Tango and Cash '89
Young Guns '88
Bagdad Café '88
Gor '88
Outlaw of Gor '87
Doin' Time '85
The Last Contract '85
Alone in the Dark '82
Hawk the Slayer '81
Bloody Avenger '80
Hell's Brigade: The Final
Assault '80
Unknown Powers '80
Angel's Brigade '79
Cocaine Cowboys '79
The Last Ride of the Dalton
Gang '79
One Man Jury '78
Mr. Scarface '77
Portrait of a Hitman '77
Welcome to Blood City '77
Rulers of the City '76
The Sensuous Nurse '76
Four Deuces '75
God's Gun '75
Great Adventure '75
The Hatfields & the
McCoys '75
Craze '74
Dracula '73
Oklahoma Crude '73
Chato's Land '71
Companeros '70
The Horsemen '70
The McMasters '70
Monte Walsh '70
Desperados '69
Deadly Sanctuary '68
The Professionals '66
Contempt '64
Barabbas '62
The Mongols '60
The Battle of Austerlitz '60
Lonely Man '57
Attack! '56
Requiem for a Heavyweight '56
The Big Knife '55
I Died a Thousand Times '55
The Silver Chalice '54
Arrowhead '53
Man in the Attic '53
Second Chance '53
Shane '53
Sudden Fear '52
The Halls of Montezuma '50
Panic in the Streets '50

Anna Palk (1943-90)
The Nightcomers '72
Fahrenheit 451 '66
The Skull '65

Erik Palladino (1968-)
Return to House on
Haunted Hill '07
The Thirst '06
Alchemy '05
L.A. Dicks '05
Latter Days '04
Finder's Fee '01
Life Without Dick '01
U-571 '00
Can't Hardly Wait '98

Aleksa Palladino (1980-)
Before the Devil Knows
You're Dead '07
Wrong Turn 2: Dead End '07
Storytelling '01
The Adventures of
Sebastian Cole '98
Red Dirt '99
Wrestling with Alligators '98
Manny & Lo '96

Anita Pallenberg (1944-)
Performance '70
Barbarella '68
Candy '68

Kumar Pallana (1919-)
Bomb the System '05
The Terminal '04
The Royal Tenenbaums '01
Bottle Rocket '96

Eugene Pallette (1889-1954)
The Cheaters '45
Pin-Up Girl '44
Sensations of 1945 '44
Step Lively '44
The Gang's All Here '43
Heaven Can Wait '43
It Ain't Hay '43
The Kansan '43
Big Street '42
The Male Animal '42
Silver Queen '42
The Bride Came C.O.D. '41
The Lady Eve '41
The Mark of Zorro '40
Young Tom Edison '40
First Love '39
Mr. Smith Goes to
Washington '39
The Adventures of Robin
Hood '38
Topper '37
100 Men and a Girl '37
My Man Godfrey '36
The Ghost Goes West '36
Steamboat Round the
Bend '35
The Kennel Murder Case '33
Shanghai Express '32
Strangers of the Evening '32

Michael Palin (1943-)
Fierce Creatures '96
The Wind in the Willows '96
American Friends '91
A Fish Called Wanda '88
Brazil '85
A Private Function '84
The Meaning of Life '83
The Missionary '82
Time Bandits '81
Monty Python's Life of
Brian '79
All You Need Is Cash '78
Jabberwocky '77
Monty Python and the Holy
Grail '75
And Now for Something
Completely Different '72
John Cleese on How to
Irritate People '68

Geoffrey Palmer (1927-)
Peter Pan '03
Mrs. Brown '97
Tomorrow Never Dies '97
A Question of Attribution '91
A Fish Called Wanda '88
Christabel '89

Gregg (Hunter) Palmer (1927-)
The Rebel Set '59
Zombies of Moratau '57
The Creature Walks among
Us '56
To Hell and Back '55
Francis Goes to West Point '52

Byron Palmer (1925-)
Ma and Pa Kettle at Waikiki '55

Betsy Palmer (1929-)
Still Not Quite Human '92
Friday the 13th, Part 2 '81
Friday the 13th '80
The Last Angry Man '59
The Tin Star '57
The Long Gray Line '55
Mister Roberts '55
Queen Bee '55

Ulf Palme (1920-93)
Dreams '55
Miss Julie '50

Gabriella Pallotta (1938-)
Hero of Rome '63
The Mongols '60
Il Grido '57
The Roof '56

Joseph Pallister
Broadcast Bombshells '95
Bikini Bistro '95

Mimmo Palmara (1928-81)
The Trojan Horse '62
The Last Days of Pompeii '60

Keke Palmer (1993-)
The Longshots '08
Cleaner '07
Jump In! '07
Akeelah and the Bee '06
Madea's Family Reunion '06
Knights of the South Bronx '05

Gretchen Palmer (1961-)
I Got the Hook-Up '98
Chopper Chicks in
Zombietown '91

Lilli Palmer (1914-86)
The Holcroft Covenant '85
The Boys from Brazil '78
What the Peeper Saw '72
Murders in the Rue Morgue '71
Sebastian '68
The Amorous Adventures
of Moll Flanders '65
Miracle of the White
Stallions '63
Adorable Julia '62
The Counterfeit Traitor '62
Conspiracy of Hearts '60
But Not for Me '59
Modigliani '58
The Long Dark Hall '51
My Girl Tisa '48
Body and Soul '47
Beware of Pity '46

Cloak and Dagger '46
Chamber of Horrors '40
The Secret Agent '36

Maria Palmer (1924-81)
Outcasts of the City '58
By the Light of the Silvery Moon '53
Days of Glory '43

Rebecca Palmer
Blood Trails '06
Intimacy '00

Renzo Palmer (1928-88)
Street Law '74
Sting of the West '72

Shirley Palmer (1908-2000)
Somewhere in Sonora '33
Campus Knights '29

Teresa Palmer (1986-)
December Boys '07
The Grudge 2 '06

Zoie Palmer
Godsend '04
The Reagans '04

Chazz Palminteri (1952-)
Arthur and the Invisibles '06 (V)
A Guide to Recognizing Your Saints '06
Little Man '06
Push '06
Running Scared '06
Animal '05
Hoodwinked '05 (V)
In the Mix '05
Noel '04
One Last Ride '03
Poolhall Junkies '02
Down to Earth '01
Boss of Bosses '99
Excellent Cadavers '99
Stuart Little '99 (V)
Analyze This '98
Hurlyburly '98
Scarred City '98
Diabolique '96
Faithful '95
Jade '95
The Last Word '95
Mulholland Falls '95
The Usual Suspects '95
Bullets over Broadway '94
The Perez Family '94
A Bronx Tale '93
Innocent Blood '92
There Goes the Neighborhood '92
Oscar '91

Carlos Palomino (1949-)
Die Watching '93
Geronimo: An American Legend '93
My Samurai '92
Nasty Hero '89
Strangers Kiss '83

Gwyneth Paltrow (1973-)
Iron Man '08
The Good Night '07
Infamous '06
Running with Scissors '06
Proof '05
Sky Captain and the World of Tomorrow '04
Sylvia '03
View from the Top '03
Austin Powers in Goldmember '02
Possession '02
The Anniversary Party '01
The Royal Tenenbaums '01
Shallow Hal '01
Bounce '00
Duets '00
The Talented Mr. Ripley '99
Hush '98
A Perfect Murder '98
Shakespeare in Love '98
Great Expectations '97
Sliding Doors '97
Emma '96
Hard Eight '96
Moonlight and Valentino '95
The Pallbearer '95
Seven '95
Jefferson in Paris '94
Mrs. Parker and the Vicious Circle '94
Flesh and Bone '93
Malice '93
Hook '91

Luciana Paluzzi (1931-)
The Klansman '74
Medusa '74
Hit Men '73
Manhunt '73
99 Women '69
A Black Veil for Lisa '68
The Green Slime '68
Murder for Sale '68
Chuka '67
One-Eyed Soldiers '67
Thunderball '65
Muscle Beach Party '64
Return to Peyton Place '61
Carlton Browne of the F.O. '59
Journey to the Lost City '58

Danielle Panabaker (1987-)
Mr. Brooks '07
Empire Falls '05
Sky High '05
Yours, Mine & Ours '05

Kay Panabaker (1990-)
Moondance Alexander '07
Nancy Drew '07
The Prince and the Pauper '07

Alessandra Panaro (1939-)
The Bacchantes '63
Conquest of Mycene '63
Executioner of Venice '63
Rocco and His Brothers '60

Richard Panebianco (1971-)
Dogfight '91
China Girl '87

Michael Panes (1963-)
Broken English '07
Fabled '02
The Anniversary Party '01

Hayden Panettiere (1989-)
Shanghai Kiss '07
The Architect '06
Bring It On: All or Nothing '06
Ice Princess '05
Racing Stripes '05
Raising Helen '04
Normal '03
The Affair of the Necklace '01
Joe Somebody '01
Dinosaur '00 (V)
Remember the Titans '00
A Bug's Life '98 (V)

Andrew Pang
Petty Crimes '02
The Corruptor '99

Franklin Pangborn (1889-1958)
Romance on the High Seas '48
I'll Be Yours '47
The Sin of Harold Diddlebock '47
The Great Moment '44
Hail the Conquering Hero '44
His Butler's Sister '44
Honeymoon Lodge '43
Two Weeks to Live '43
Call Out the Marines '42
The Palm Beach Story '42
The Flame of New Orleans '41
A Girl, a Guy and a Gob '41
Never Give a Sucker an Even Break '41
Sullivan's Travels '41
The Bank Dick '40
Christmas in July '40
Fifth Avenue Girl '39
Topper Takes a Trip '39
Bluebeard's Eighth Wife '38
Carefree '38
Just Around the Corner '38
Vivacious Lady '38
All Over Town '37
Dangerous Holiday '37
Easy Living '37
Hats Off '37
The Mandarin Mystery '37
A Star Is Born '37
Doughnuts & Society '36
My Man Godfrey '36
Tango '36
King Kelly of the U.S.A. '34
Flying Down to Rio '33
The Half Naked Truth '32

Corrado Pani (1936-2005)
Watch Me When I Kill '77
The Girl with a Suitcase '60

Ty Panitz (1999-)
Because I Said So '07
Yours, Mine & Ours '05

Archie Panjabi (1972-)
A Mighty Heart '07
A Good Year '06
The Constant Gardener '05
Bend It Like Beckham '02
East Is East '99

Stuart Pankin (1946-)
Miss Cast Away '04
Chasing Destiny '00
Honey, We Shrunk Ourselves '97
Down, Out and Dangerous '95
Beanstalk '94
Father and Scout '94
I Love Trouble '94
Squanto: A Warrior's Tale '94
Silence of the Hams '93
Betrayal of the Dove '92
The Vagrant '92
Life Stinks '91
Mannequin 2: On the Move '91
That's Adequate '90
Second Sight '89
Fatal Attraction '87
Love at Stake '87
Dirt Bike Kid '86
The Hollywood Knights '80

John Pankow (1954-)
The Object of My Affection '98
A Stranger Among Us '92
Mortal Thoughts '91
Year of the Gun '91
Johnny Be Good '88
Monkey Shines '88
Talk Radio '88

Joe Pantoliano (1951-)
Canvas '06
Deceit '06
Larry the Cable Guy: Health Inspector '06
Wedding Daze '06
The Moguls '05
Racing Stripes '05 (V)
Second Best '05
Bad Boys 2 '03
Daredevil '03
Cats & Dogs '01 (V)
A Better Way to Die '00
Memento '00
Tinseltown '97
Top of the World '97
Bound '96
Natural Enemy '96
Bad Boys '95
The Immortals '95
Steal Big, Steal Little '95
Baby's Day Out '94
Robot in the Family '94
The Spy Within '94
Teresa's Tattoo '94
Calendar Girl '93
Dangerous Heart '93
The Fugitive '93
Me and the Kid '93
Three of Hearts '93
Through the Eyes of a Killer '92
Used People '92
Zandalee '91
El Diablo '90
The Last of the Finest '90
Short Time '90
Downtown '89
Nightbreaker '89
Tales from the Crypt '89
In the Crowd '88
Midnight Run '88
Empire of the Sun '87
La Bamba '87
Scenes from the Goldmine '87
The Squeeze '87
Running Scared '86
Mean Season '85
The Goonies '85
Eddie and the Cruisers '83
The Final Terror '83
Risky Business '83
Idolmaker '80

Cecile Paoli
Sharpe's Revenge '97
Sharpe's Waterloo '97
Riders '88

Connor Paolo
Snow Angels '07
Alexander '04

Michael (Mike) Papajohn (1964-)
I Know Who Killed Me '07
Spider-Man 3 '07
The Last Shot '04
Spider-Man '02
Whacked! '02
The Animal '01
Rustin '01
Charlie's Angels '00
For Love of the Game '99
My Giant '98
Spawn '97
Eraser '96
The Indian in the Cupboard '95
Naked Souls '95
Dominion '94
Little Big League '94
The Babe '92
The Last Boy Scout '91
Predator 2 '90

Irene Papas (1926-)
Captain Corelli's Mandolin '01
Yerma '99
The Odyssey '97
Party '96
Jacob '94
High Season '88
Sweet Country '87
Into the Night '85
The Assisi Underground '84
Erendira '83
Lion of the Desert '81
Christ Stopped at Eboli '79
Sidney Sheldon's Bloodline '79
Iphigenia '77
The Message '77
Moses '76
Don't Torture a Duckling '72
1931: Once Upon a Time in New York '72
Trojan Women '71
Anne of the Thousand Days '69
A Dream of Kings '69
Z '69
The Brotherhood '68
The Moon-Spinners '64
Zorba the Greek '64
The Guns of Navarone '61
The Unfaithfuls '60
Tribute to a Bad Man '56

Ike Pappas (1933-)
The Package '89
Moon over Parador '88

Anna Paquin (1982-)
Blue State '07
Bury My Heart at Wounded Knee '07
X-Men: The Last Stand '06
The Squid and the Whale '05
Steamboy '05 (V)
Darkness '02
25th Hour '02
Buffalo Soldiers '01
Finding Forrester '00
X-Men '00
It's the Rage '99
She's All That '99
A Walk on the Moon '99
Hurlyburly '98
Amistad '97
The Member of the Wedding '97
Fly Away Home '96
Jane Eyre '96
The Piano '93

Vanessa Paradis (1972-)
The Girl on the Bridge '98
Elisa '94

John Paragon (1954-)
UHF '89
Elvira, Mistress of the Dark '88
Pee-wee's Big Adventure '85
Eating Raoul '82
The Pee-wee Herman Show '82

Kiri Paramore
Ned Kelly '03
Doing Time for Patsy Cline '97
The Last Days of Chez Nous '92
Flirting '89

Rawiri Paratene
The Legend of Johnny Lingo '03
Whale Rider '02

J.D. Pardo
Supercross: The Movie '05
A Cinderella Story '04
Hope Ranch '02

Michael Parducci
Hit and Runway '01
Gravesend '97

Kip Pardue (1976-)
Imaginary Heroes '05
Loggerheads '05
The Heart Is Deceitful Above All Things '04
The Iris Effect '04
Devil's Pond '03
Thirteen '03
This Girl's Life '03
The Rules of Attraction '02
Driven '01
Road to Riches '01
Remember the Titans '00

Jessica Paré (1982-)
Wicker Park '04
Posers '02
Lost and Delirious '01
Stardom '00

Michael Pare (1958-)
BloodRayne 2: Deliverance '07
BloodRayne '06
Heart of America '03
Blackwoods '02
Sanctimony '01
Peril '01
In the Dead of Space '99
Men of Means '99
The Debt '99
Hope Floats '98
Falling Fire '97
Mission of Death '97
Strip Search '97
2103: Deadly Wake '97
Bad Moon '96
Carver's Gate '96
Deadly Heroes '96
Sworn Enemies '96
The Dangerous '95
Raging Angels '95
Triplecross '95
Village of the Damned '95
Solar Force '94
Warriors '94
Point of Impact '93
Blink of an Eye '92
Into the Sun '92
Sunset Heat '92
The Closer '91
Killing Streets '91
The Last Hour '91
Dragonfight '90
Moon 44 '90
Eddie and the Cruisers 2: Eddie Lives! '89
World Gone Wild '88
Women's Club '87
Instant Justice '86
Space Rage '86
The Philadelphia Experiment '84
Streets of Fire '84
Eddie and the Cruisers '83

Marisa Paredes (1946-)
Four Last Songs '06
The Devil's Backbone '01
All About My Mother '99
Life Is Beautiful '98
Doctor Chance '97
Deep Crimson '96
Talk of Angels '96
Three Lives and Only One Death '96
The Flower of My Secret '95
High Heels '91
In a Glass Cage '86
Dark Habits '84

Mila Parely (1917-)
Three Stops to Murder '53
Beauty and the Beast '46
The Rules of the Game '39

Monique Parent (1965-)
The Pornographer '00
The Catcher '98
James Dean: Live Fast, Die Young '97
Tender Flesh '97
Illegal Affairs '96
Mirror, Mirror 3: The Voyeur '96
Play Time '94
Dark Secrets '95
Masseuse '95
Midnight Confessions '95
The Perfect Gift '95
Stripshow '95
Married People, Single Sex 2: For Better or Worse '94

Judy Parfitt (1935-)
Asylum '05
Girl with a Pearl Earring '03
Berkeley Square '98
Ever After: A Cinderella Story '98
Wilde '98
Element of Doubt '96
The Borrowers '96
Dolores Claiborne '94
Midnight's Child '93
The Blackheath Poisonings '92
Dark Obsession '90
Getting It Right '89
The Charmer '87
Maurice '87
Office Romances '86
The Jewel in the Crown '84
Hamlet '69

Woodrow Parfrey (1922-84)
Backstairs at the White House '79
The Outlaw Josey Wales '76
Oklahoma Crude '73
Sam Whiskey '69

Anne Parillaud (1960-)
Sex is Comedy '02 · The Man in the Iron Mask '98 · Shattered Image '98 · Frankie Starlight '95 · Six Days, Six Nights '94 · Map of the Human Heart '93 · Innocent Blood '92 · La Femme Nikita '91

Jerry Paris (1925-86)
Evil Roy Slade '72 · Zero Hour! '57 · D-Day, the Sixth of June '56 · Marty '55 · The Caine Mutiny '54 · The Wild One '54

Sarah Parish (1968-)
The Wedding Date '05 · The Man Who Lived Again '36

Annie Parisse (1975-)
Definitely, Maybe '08 · Monster-in-Law '05 · Prime '05 · How to Lose a Guy in 10 Days '03

Kris Park
Ordinary Sinner '02 · Drive Me Crazy '99 · I Love You, I Love You Not '97

Ray Park (1974-)
Slayer '06 · Ballistic: Ecks vs. Sever '02 · X-Men '00 · Star Wars: Episode 1—The Phantom Menace '99

Reg Park (1928-2007)
Hercules in the Haunted World '64 · Hercules, Prisoner of Evil '64 · Hercules and the Captive Women '63 · Hercules '59

Anthony Ray Parker
The Matrix '99

Lar Park-Lincoln (1961-)
Friday the 13th, Part 7: The New Blood '88 · House 2: The Second Story '87

Evan Dexter Parke (1968-)
King Kong '05 · Brother's Keeper '02 · Nightstalker '02 · Planet of the Apes '01 · The Replacements '00 · The Cider House Rules '99

MacDonald Parke (1891-1960)
The Mouse That Roared '59 · Summertime '55

Anthony Ray Parker
The Matrix '06 (?)

F. William Parker

Fess Parker (1926-)
Hell Is for Heroes '62 · Alias Jesse James '59 · The Jayhawkers! '59 · The Light in the Forest '58 · Old Yeller '57 · Westward Ho, the Wagons! '56 · The Great Locomotive Chase '56 · Davy Crockett and the River Pirates '56 · Davy Crockett, King of the Wild Frontier '55 · Battle Cry '55 · Them! '54 · Island in the Sky '53

Erica Parker
See Erica Durance

Cecil Parker (1897-1971)
Oh! What a Lovely War '69 · A Study in Terror '66 · Lady L '65 · Heavens Above '63 · The Brain '62 · On the Fiddle '61 · The Pure Hell of St. Trinian's '61 · A Tale of Two Cities '58 · Indiscreet '58 · The Wreck of the Mary Deare '59 · Court Jester '56 · The Ladykillers '55 · The Detective '54 · Tony Draws a Horse '51 · Under Capricorn '49 · Captain Boycott '47 · The Weaker Sex '47 · The Magic Bow '47

Joong-Hoon Park (1964-)
The Truth About Charlie '02 · Double Edge '97

Chris Parker
Red Nights '87

Corey Parker (1965-)
Mr. & Mrs. Loving '96 · A Mother's Prayer '95 · Broadway Bound '92 · The Lost Language of Cranes '92 · I'm Dangerous Tonight '90 · White Palace '90 · Big Man on Campus '89 · How I Got into College '89 · Biloxi Blues '88 · Friday the 13th, Part 7: The New Blood '88 · Permanent Vacation '84

Eddie (Ed, Eddy, Edwin) Parker (1900-60)
The Secret Code '42 · God's Country and the Man '37 · Ghost Rider '35

Eleanor Parker (1922-)
Dead on the Money '91 · She's Dressed to Kill '79 · The Bastard '78 · Fantasy Island '76 · Home for the Holidays '72 · Maybe I'll Be Home in the Spring '70 · Hans Brinker '69 · The Oscar '66 · The Sound of Music '65 · Panic Button '62 · Return to Peyton Place '61 · Home from the Hill '60 · A Hole in the Head '59 · The King and Four Queens '56 · Interrupted Melody '55 · The Man with the Golden Arm '55 · Naked Jungle '54 · Valley of the Kings '54 · Above and Beyond '53 · Escape from Fort Bravo '53 · Scaramouche '52 · Detective Story '51 · Caged '50 · Chain Lightning '50 · Three Secrets '50 · It's a Great Feeling '49 · Escape Me Never '47 · Never Say Goodbye '46 · Hollywood Canteen '44

Ed Parker (1931-90)
Curse of the Pink Panther '83 · Kill the Golden Goose '79

Cecilia Parker (1905-93)
Andy Hardy's Double Life '42 · Andy Hardy Meets Debutante '40 · Andy Hardy Gets Spring Fever '39 · Love Finds Andy Hardy '38 · Sweetheart of the Navy '37 · Roll Along Cowboy '37 · Ah, Wilderness! '35 · Naughty Marietta '35 · Honor of the Range '34 · The Lost Jungle '34 · Mystery Ranch '34 · Rainbow Ranch '33 · Riders of Destiny '33 · Trail Drive '33 · Tombstone Canyon '32

Kim Parker
Fiend without a Face '58 · Fire Maidens from Outer Space '56

Lara Parker (1942-)
Foxfire Light '82 · The Solitary Man '82 · The Lazarus Syndrome '79 · Race with the Devil '75 · Night of Dark Shadows '71 · Hi, Mom! '70

Lloyd "Sunshine" Parker (1928-99)
Cannery Row '82 · Spittin' Image '83

Mary-Louise Parker (1964-)
The Assassination of Jesse James by the Coward Robert Ford '07 · Romance & Cigarettes '05 · Saved! '04 · Angels in America '03 · Pipe Dream '02 · Red Dragon '02 · Cupid & Cate '00 · Goodbye, Lover '99 · The Five Senses '99 · The Maker '98 · Saint Maybe '98 · Murder in Mind '97 · The End of Violence '97 · Portrait of a Lady '96 · Boys on the Side '95 · Reckless '95 · Sugartime '95 · The Incredibly True Adventure of Two Girls in Love '95 · Bullets over Broadway '94 · The Client '94 · Naked in New York '93 · Mr. Wonderful '93 · Fried Green Tomatoes '91 · Grand Canyon '91 · Longtime Companion '90 · Signs of Life '89

Nicole Ari Parker (1970-)
Welcome Home Roscoe Jenkins '08 · King's Ransom '05 · Brown Sugar '02 · Dancing in September '00 · Remember the Titans '00 · Blue Streak '99 · Loving Jezebel '99 · Spark '98 · 200 Cigarettes '98 · Boogie Nights '97

Noelle Parker (1969-)
The Loretta Claiborne Story '00 · Newsbreak '00 · Ernest Saves Christmas '88

Norman Parker
Twisted '86 · Question of Faith '93

Jameson Parker (1947-)
Curse of the Crystal Eye '93 · Spy '89 · Prince of Darkness '87 · American Justice '86 · Callie and Son '81 · A Small Circle of Friends '80 · Anatomy of a Seduction '79 · The Gathering: Part 2 '79

Jean Parker (1915-2005)
Apache Uprising '66 · A Lawless Street '55 · The Gunfighter '50 · Rolling Home '48 · Bluebeard '44 · Lady in the Death House '44 · One Body Too Many '44 · Navy Way '44 · Flying Blind '41 · Knights of the Range '40 · Beyond Tomorrow '40 · The Flying Deuces '39 · The Texas Rangers '36 · The Ghost Goes West '36 · Two Alone '34 · Lucky Texan '34 · Little Women '33 · Lady for a Day '33 · Rasputin and the Empress '33 · Gabriel Over the White House '33

Molly Parker (1971-)
Hollywoodland '06 · The Wicker Man '06 · Nine Lives '05 · Men with Brooms '02 · Max '02 · Marion Bridge '02 · Pure '02 · The Center of the World '01 · Rare Birds '01 · The War Bride '01 · Waking the Dead '00 · Suspicious River '00 · Wonderland '99 · The Five Senses '99 · Sunshine '99

Monica Parker
Coming Out Alive '84 · Improper Channels '82

Nathaniel Parker (1963-)
The Great Debaters '07 · Stardust '07 · Bleak House '05 · The Haunted Mansion '03 · Inspector Lynley Mysteries: A Great Deliverance '01 · David '97 · Vanity Fair '99 · Far from the Madding Crowd '97 · Into Thin Air: Death on Everest '97 · Beverly Hills Ninja '96 · Othello '95 · Squanto: A Warrior's Tale '94 · The Wide Sargasso Sea '92 · Hamlet '90 · Piece of Cake '88

Michael Parker (1969-)
Kill Line '91 · My Own Private Idaho '91

Trey Parker (1969-)
Team America: World Police '04 · South Park: Bigger, Longer and Uncut '99 · BASEketball '98 · Orgazmo '98 · Cannibal! The Musical '96

Suzy Parker (1932-2003)
The Interns '62 · The Best of Everything '59 · Ten North Frederick '58 · Funny Face '57

Willard Parker (1912-96)
The Great Jesse James Raid '53

Shaun Parkes (1972-)
The Mummy Returns '01 · Human Traffic '99

Gerard Parkes
A House Divided '00 · Rescuers: Stories of Courage: "Two Women" '97

Barbara Parkins (1942-)
Calendar Girl Murders '84 · To Catch a King '84 · Breakfast in Paris '81 · Christina '74 · Puppet on a Chain '72 · Asylum '72 · The Mephisto Waltz '71 · Valley of the Dolls '67 · Shout at the Devil '76 · Law of the Land '76

Sachi (MacLaine) Parker (1956-)
Welcome Home, Roxy Carmichael '90 · Riders to the Sea '88 · Peggy Sue Got Married '86 · The Dancing Princesses '84

Sarah Jessica Parker (1965-)
Sex and the City: The Movie '08 · Smart People '08 · Failure to Launch '06 · Strangers with Candy '06 · The Family Stone '05 · Life Without Dick '01 · State and Main '00 · Dudley Do-Right '99 · The Substance of Fire '96 · 'Til There Was You '96 · If Lucy Fell '96 · Extreme Measures '96 · The First Wives Club '96 · Mars Attacks! '96 · Miami Rhapsody '95 · Ed Wood '94 · Hocus Pocus '93 · Striking Distance '93 · Honeymoon in Vegas '92 · L.A. Story '91 · Flight of the Navigator '86 · Somewhere Tomorrow '85 · Going for the Gold: The Bill Johnson Story '85 · Girls Just Want to Have Fun '85 · First Born '84 · Footloose '84

Paula Jai Parker (1969-)
Cover '08 · Animal '05 · Hustle & Flow '05 · My Baby's Daddy '04 · She Hate Me '04 · Phone Booth '02 · 30 Years to Life '01 · Woo '97 · Sprung '96

Larry Parks (1914-75)
Love Is Better Than Ever '52 · Jolson Sings Again '49 · Down to Earth '47 · The Jolson Story '46 · Destroyer '43 · You Were Never Lovelier '42 · The Boogie Man Will Get You '42 · Blondie Goes to College '42 · Harmon of Michigan '41

James Parks (1968-)
Death Proof '07 · Planet Terror '07 · The Listening '06 · Kill Bill Vol. 2 '04 · Kill Bill Vol. 1 '03 · From Dusk Till Dawn 3: The Hangman's Daughter '99

Michael Parks (1938-)
Planet Terror '07 · Death Proof '07 · Niagara, Niagara '97 · Julian Po '97 · Wicked '98 · From Dusk Till Dawn 3: The Hangman's Daughter '99 · The China Lake Murders '90 · Gore Vidal's Billy the Kid '89 · Welcome to Spring Break '88 · Arizona Heat '87 · Club Life '86 · The Return of Josey Wales '86 · Savannah Smiles '82 · Hard Country '81 · The Evictors '79 · Breakthrough '78 · Night Cries '78 · Sidewinder One '77 · The Private Files of J. Edgar Hoover '77 · The Last Hard Men '76 · The Savage Bees '76 · The Bible '66

Catherine Parks (1956-)
Body of Influence '93 · Friday the 13th, Part 3 '82

Bert Parks (1914-92)
The Freshman '90 · Shining Star '75

Trina Parks (1965-)
The Muthers '76 · Darktown Strutters '74 · Diamonds Are Forever '71

Tammy Parks (1965-)
Attack of the 60-Foot Centerfold '95 · Play Time '94

Parkyakarkus (Harry Einstein) (1904-58)
Strike Me Pink '36

Steve Parlavecchio (1970-)
The First to Go '97
Bandwagon '95
Amongst Friends '93

Dita Parlo (1906-71)
Grand Illusion '37
L'Atalante '34
Homecoming '28

Chris Parnell (1967-)
Hot Rod '07
Walk Hard: The Dewey Cox Story '07
I'm Reed Fish '06
Ira & Abby '06
Anchorman: The Legend of Ron Burgundy '04

Emory Parnell (1892-1979)
Man of the West '58
Pardners '56
Shadows of Tombstone '53
Lost in Alaska '52
Ma and Pa Kettle at the Fair '52
Ma and Pa Kettle Back On the Farm '51
Trail of Robin Hood '50
The Show-Off '46
Colonel Effingham's Raid '45
Casanova Brown '44
I Married a Witch '42
They All Kissed the Bride '42

Marriam Parris
Maryam '00
Club Vampire '98

Helen Parrish (1924-59)
Overland Mail '42
Sunset Serenade '42
They All Kissed the Bride '42

Paradise, Hawaiian Style '66

Leslie Parrish (1935-)
The Invisible Strangler '76
The Giant Spider Invasion '75
Sex and the Single Girl '64
For Love or Money '63
The Manchurian Candidate '62
Li'l Abner '59

Steve Parrish
Scanners 3: The Takeover '92
Midnight '89

David Parry (1954-)
Auntie Lee's Meat Pies '92
Dr. Caligari '89
The Lost Platoon '89

Natasha Parry (1930-)
Haunted: The Ferryman '74
Oh! What a Lovely War '69
Crow Hollow '52

Tom Parsekian
Club Life '86
Hot Resort '85

Frederick Parslow (1940-2003)
Wrangler '88
The Last Wave '77

Estelle Parsons (1927-)
Empire Falls '05
The Love Letter '98
Looking for Richard '96
That Darn Cat '96
A Private Matter '92
Dick Tracy '90
Come Along with Me '84
Gentleman Bandit '81
Backstairs at the White House '79
Foreplay '75
For Pete's Sake '74
I Never Sang for My Father '70
I Walk the Line '70
Watermelon Man '70
Don't Drink the Water '69
Rachel, Rachel '68
Bonnie & Clyde '67

Jim Parsons
The Great New Wonderful '06
Garden State '04

Karyn Parsons (1968-)
13 Moons '02
The Ladies Man '00
Mixing Nia '98
Gulliver's Travels '95
Major Payne '95
Class Act '91

Mike Parsons
The Ravagers '65
The Walls of Hell '64

Nancy Parsons (1942-2001)
Lakota Woman: Siege at Wounded Knee '94
Wishman '93
Ladybugs '92
Porky's Revenge '85
Porky's 2: The Next Day '83
Porky's '82
Motel Hell '80

Percy Parsons (1878-1944)
Dangerous Moonlight '41
Rhodes '36
Power '34
Blackmail '29

Dolly Parton (1946-)
Frank McKlusky, C.I. '02
Jackie's Back '99
Unlikely Angel '97
The Beverly Hillbillies '93
Straight Talk '92
Steel Magnolias '89
A Smoky Mountain Christmas '86
Rhinestone '84
The Best Little Whorehouse in Texas '82
9 to 5 '80

Julia Parton (1964-)
Good Girls Don't '95
Vice Academy 3 '91

Adam Pascal (1970-)
Rent '05
School of Rock '03
SLC Punk! '99

Christine Pascal (1953-96)
Le Grand Chemin '87
Sincerely Charlotte '86
Maids of Wilko '79
Spoiled Children '77
The Best Way '76
The Clockmaker '73

Mary Ann Pascal (1958-)
Lethal Lolita—Amy Fisher: My Story '92
Writer's Block '91

Olivia Pascal (1957-)
Bloody Moon '83
C.O.D. '83

Isabelle Pasco (1966-)
Invisible Circus '00
Sous Sol '96
Prospero's Books '91
High Frequency '88

Nicholas Pasco
The Undertaker's Wedding '97
Red Blooded 2 '96

Richard Pasco (1926-)
Mrs. Brown '97
The Watcher in the Woods '81
Rasputin the Mad Monk '66
The Gorgon '64
Sword of Sherwood Forest '60
Room at the Top '59

Adrian Pasdar (1965-)
Secondhand Lions '03
The Big Day '99
Mutiny '99
A Brother's Kiss '97
Wounded '97
Just Like a Woman '95
The Pompatus of Love '95
The Last Good Time '94
Carlito's Way '93
Grand Isle '92
The Lost Capone '90
Vital Signs '90
Cookie '89
Torn Apart '89
Made in USA '88
Near Dark '87
Streets of Gold '86
Top Gun '86

Pier Paolo Pasolini (1922-75)
The Canterbury Tales '71
The Decameron '70
Oedipus Rex '67

Giorgio Pasotti (1973-)
After Midnight '04
The Last Kiss '01

David Pasquesi
I Want Someone to Eat Cheese With '06
Strangers with Candy '06

Cyndi Pass
Hindsight '97
The Night Caller '97
Serial Killer '95
The Force '94
Scanner Cop '94
Bounty Tracker '93
Deadbolt '92
Desperate Motives '92
Mission of Justice '92
Bikini Island '91

George Pastell (1976-)
Vendetta for the Saint '68
The Mummy '59
The Gambler & the Lady '52

Reagan Pasternak (1977-)
Cake '05
Verdict in Blood '02
Jailbait! '00

Earl Pastko
Subhuman '04
Masterminds '96
The Sweet Hereafter '96
Eclipse '94
Highway 61 '91

Rosana Pastor (1960-)
Mad Love '01
The Break '97
Land and Freedom '95

Vincent Pastore (1946-)
Bachelor Party Vegas '05
Remedy '05
Revolver '05
Shark Tale '04 (V)
A Tale of Two Pizzas '03
This Thing of Ours '03
American Cousins '02
Deuces Wild '02
Serving Sara '02
Made '01
Blue Moon '00
Hitman's Journal '99
The Hurricane '99
Mickey Blue Eyes '99
A Slight Case of Murder '99
Under Hellgate Bridge '99
Mafia! '98
Witness to the Mob '98
Gotti '96
Walking and Talking '96
West New York '96
The Jerky Boys '95
Money Train '95
It Could Happen to You '94
Carlito's Way '93
The Ref '93
Awakenings '90
True Love '89

Robert Pastorelli (1954-2004)
Be Cool '05
Retribution '98
Modern Vampires '98
A Simple Wish '97
Eraser '96
Michael '96
The Yam Princess '94
The Paint Job '93
Sister Act 2: Back in the Habit '93
Striking Distance '93
Folks! '92
Dances with Wolves '90
Beverly Hills Cop 2 '87

Willie Pastrano (1935-97)
Alligator Alley '72
Wild Rebels '71

Patachou (1918-)
The Adventures of Felix '99
French Can-Can '55

Michael Pataki (1938-)
One More Chance '90
Death House '88
Halloween 4: The Return of Michael Myers '88
The Underachievers '88
American Anthem '86
Remo Williams: The Adventure Begins '85
Rocky 4 '85
Delinquent School Girls '84
Dead and Buried '81
The Last Word '80
Love at First Bite '79
On the Onion Field '79
When Every Day Was the Fourth of July '78
Zoltan... Hound of Dracula '78
The Amazing Spider-Man '77
The Bat People '74
The Last Porno Flick '74
The Baby '72
Grave of the Vampire '72
Dirt Gang '71

Elsa Pataky (1976-)
Snakes on a Plane '06
Beyond Re-Animator '03

Wally Patch (1888-1970)
Calling Paul Temple '48
Butler's Dilemma '43
Cottage to Let '41
Night Train to Munich '40
Inspector Hornleigh '39
Pygmalion '38
Don Quixote '35
The Private Life of Henry VIII '33

Michael Pate (1920-)
Howling 3: The Marsupials '87
Camel Boy '84 (V)
Return of Captain Invincible '83
The Singing Nun '66
McLintock! '63
Tower of London '62
Curse of the Undead '59
Green Mansions '59
The Oklahoman '56
Seventh Cavalry '56
A Lawless Street '55
King Richard and the Crusaders '54
Hondo '53
Houdini '53
Julius Caesar '53
Face to Face '52
Five Fingers '52
The Strange Door '51

Bill Paterson (1945-)
Miss Potter '06
Doctor Zhivago '03
Crush '02
Wives and Daughters '01
Heart '99
The Match '99
Hilary and Jackie '98
Spice World: The Movie '97
The Crow Road '96
Chaplin '92
Rodgers & Hammerstein's South Pacific '01
Bait '00
Truly, Madly, Deeply '91
The Object of Beauty '91
Traffik '90
The Witches '90
The Adventures of Baron Munchausen '89
The Rachel Papers '89
Coming Up Roses '87
Dutch Girls '87
Hidden City '87
Defense of the Realm '85
Comfort and Joy '84
The Killing Fields '84
A Private Function '84
The Ploughman's Lunch '83

Mandy Patinkin (1952-)
Pinero '01
Strange Justice: The Clarence Thomas and Anita Hill Story '99
Lulu on the Bridge '98
Hombres Armados '97
The Hunchback '97
Broken Glass '96
Squanto: A Warrior's Tale '94
The Music of Chance '93
The Doctor '91
True Colors '91
Dick Tracy '90
Impromptu '90
Alien Nation '88
The House on Carroll Street '88
The Princess Bride '87
Sunday in the Park with George '86
Follies in Concert '85
Maxie '85
Daniel '83
Yentl '83
Ragtime '81
Night of the Juggler '80
French Postcards '79
Last Embrace '79
The Big Fix '78

Tatjana Patitz (1966-)
Restraining Order '99
Rising Sun '93

Angela Paton
The Final Season '07
American Wedding '03
United States of Leland '03
The Con '98
Trapped in Paradise '94
Groundhog Day '93

Laurie Paton
The Amy Fisher Story '93
Norman's Awesome Experience '88

Jason Patric (1966-)
The Alamo '04
Narc '02
Your Friends & Neighbors '98
Incognito '97
Speed 2: Cruise Control '97
Sleepers '96
The Journey of August King '95
Geronimo: An American Legend '93
Denial: The Dark Side of Passion '91
Rush '91
After Dark, My Sweet '90
Frankenstein Unbound '90
The Beast '88
The Lost Boys '87
Solarbabies '86
Toughlove '85

Dennis Patrick (1918-2002)
The Air Up There '94
Heated Vengeance '87
Choices '81
Missiles of October '74
Dear Dead Delilah '72
Joe '70
The Time Travelers '64

Dorothy Patrick (1922-87)
Men of the Fighting Lady '54
Thunder Pass '54
Torch Song '53
Follow Me Quietly '49
New Orleans '47

Gail Patrick (1911-80)
Brewster's Millions '45
Love Crazy '41
Doctor Takes a Wife '40
My Favorite Wife '40
King of Alcatraz '38
Mad About Music '38
Wives under Suspicion '38
Stage Door '37
My Man Godfrey '36
Mississippi '35
Death Takes a Holiday '34
Murder at the Vanities '34
Wagon Wheels '34
Badmen of Nevada '33
Murders in the Zoo '33
The Mysterious Rider '33
The Phantom Broadcast '33
The Last Man '33

Gregory Patrick
Sexpot '88
A Woman Obsessed '88

Lee Patrick (1911-82)
Black Bird '75
7 Faces of Dr. Lao '63
Summer and Smoke '61
Pillow Talk '59
Vertigo '58
Caged '50
The Fuller Brush Girl '50
Inner Sanctum '48
Gambler's Choice '44
Mrs. Parkington '44
In This Our Life '42
Somewhere I'll Find You '42
Footsteps in the Dark '41
The Maltese Falcon '41
Fisherman's Wharf '39
Law of the Underworld '38

Nigel Patrick (1913-81)
Mackintosh Man '73
The Executioner '70
Battle of Britain '69
The Virgin Soldiers '69
Johnny Nobody '61
The League of Gentlemen '60
The Trials of Oscar Wilde '60
Sapphire '59
Raintree County '57
The Pickwick Papers '54
Encore '52
The Browning Version '51
Pandora and the Flying Dutchman '51
Morning Departure '50
Trio '50
Uneasy Terms '48

Robert Patrick (1959-)
Strange Wilderness '08
Balls of Fury '07
Bridge to Terabithia '07
Firewall '06
Flags of Our Fathers '06
The Marine '06
Walk the Line '05
Ladder 49 '04
Charlie's Angels: Full Throttle '03
Backflash '01
Eye See You '01
Spy Kids '01
Texas Rangers '01

All the Pretty Horses '00
Angels Don't Sleep Here
'00
Mexico City '00
Rogue Force '99
Tactical Assault '99
A Texas Funeral '99
The Faculty '98
Forgotten City '98
From Dusk Till Dawn 2:
Texas Blood Mcney '98
Perfect Assassins '98
Asylum '97
Cop Land '97
The Only Thrill '97
Striptease '96
Decoy '95
Double Dragon '94
Hong Kong '97 '94
The Last Gasp '94
Body Shot '93
Fire in the Sky '93
Last Action Hero '93
Zero Tolerance '93
The Cool Surface '92
Terminator 2: Judgment
Day '91
Die Hard 2: Die Harder '90
Future Hunters '88
Eye of the Eagle '87
Behind Enemy L nes '85

Luana Patten (1938-96)
Follow Me, Boys! '66
Johnny Tremain & the Sons
of Liberty '58
Rock, Pretty Baby '56
So Dear to My Heart '49

Elizabeth Patterson (1875-1966)
Tall Story '60
Pal Joey '57
Intruder in the Dust '49
Welcome Stranger '47
Colonel Effingham's Raid
'45
Lady on a Train '45
Follow the Boys '44
The Sky's the Limit '43
I Married a Witch '42
Remember the Night '40
Bulldog Drummond's Bride
'39
Bluebeard's Eighth Wife '38
Go West, Young Man '36
Hide-Out '34
Hold Your Mar '33
A Bill of Divorcement '32
No Man of Her Own '32

James Patterson (1932-72)
Castle Keep '69
Lilith '64

Jay Patterson (1954-)
Excessive Force 2: Force
on Force '95
Nobody's Fool '94
McBain '91
D.O.A. '88
Nadine '87
Street Smart '87
Heaven Help Us '85

John D. Patterson (1940-2005)
Helltown '38
Chato's Land '71
He Lives: The Search for
the Evil One '67
Jack the Ripper '60
The Spaniard's Curse '58
The Key Man '57
Costello '57
Time Lock '57
Above Us the Waves '56

Lee Patterson (1929-)
Bullseye! '90

Lorna Patterson (1956-)
The Impostor '84
Airplane! '80

Neva Patterson (1922-)
Women of Valor '86
V '83
The Runaways '75
David and Lisa '62
An Affair to Remember '57
Desk Set '57
Solid Gold Cadillac '56

Pat Patterson
The Body Shop '72
Gas-s-s-s! '70

Rocky Patterson (1945-)
Moonshine Mountain '64
Time Tracers '97
The Dark Dealer '95
Armed for Action '92
Blood on the Badge '92
Nail Gun Massacre '86

Sarah Patterson (1972-)
Do I Love You? '02
Snow White '89
The Company of Wolves
'85

Scott Patterson (1958-)
Saw 4 '07
Alien Nation: Dark Horizon
'94
Little Big League '94

Shirley Patterson (1922-95)
Black Hills '48
Driftin' River '46

Antwan Andre Patton (1975-)
Who's Your Caddy? '07
ATL '06
Idlewild '06

Bill(y) Patten (William Patten) (1894-1951)
Rustlers of Red Dog '35
Beyond the Trail '26
Fangs of Fate '25

Mark Patton (1964-)
A Nightmare on Elm Street
2: Freddy's Revenge '85
Anna to the Infinite Power
'84

Paula Patton (1975-)
Swing Vote '08
Déjà Vu '06
Idlewild '06

Will Patton (1954-)
Code Name: The Cleaner
'07
A Mighty Heart '07
Road House 2: Last Call
'06
The Punisher '04
The Mothman Prophecies
'02
Gone in 60 Seconds '00
Remember the Titans '00
Trixie '00
Entrapment '99
Jesus' Son '99
Armageddon '98
Breakfast of Champions '98
Inventing the Abbotts '97
This World, Then the
Fireworks '97
Fled '96
Copycat '95
The Spitfire Grill '95
The Client '94
The Puppet Masters '94
Natural Causes '94
Judicial Consent '94
Tollbooth '94
Midnight Edition '93
The Paint Job '93
Romeo is Bleeding '93
Cold Heaven '92
In the Soup '92
Deadly Desire '91
Dillinger '91
In the Deep Woods '91
Murder on the Bayou '91
A Shock to the System '90
Signs of Life '89
Stars and Bars '88

David Paul
Double Trouble '91
Think Big '90
Ghost Writer '89
The Barbarians '87

Don Michael Paul (1963-)
Half Past Dead '02
Robot Wars '93
Rich Girl '91
Aloha Summer '88
The Heart of Dixie '89
Alien from L.A. '87
Rolling Vengeance '87
Winners Take All '87
Brotherhood of Justice '86
Loveliness '84

Peter Paul
Twinsitters '95
Double Trouble '91
Think Big '90

Richard Paul (1940-98)
The People vs. Larry Flynt
'96

Richard Joseph Paul
Wounded '97
Vampirella '96
Oblivion '94

Alexandra Paul (1963-)
A Woman Hunted '03
Facing the Enemy '00
Fallen Angel '99
Spectre '96
Piranha '95
Cyber Bandits '94
The Paperboy '94
Detonator '93
In Between '92
Sunset Grill '92
Frey of the Chameleon '91
Millions '90
Out of the Shadows '88
Dragnet '87
American Flyers '85
8 Million Ways to Die '85
Getting Physical '84
Christine '84
Just the Way You Are '84
American Nightmare '81

Aaron Paul (1979-)
K-PAX '01
Whatever It Takes '00

Adrian Paul (1959-)
Dead Men Can't Dance '97
The Cover Girl Murders '93
Highlander: The Gathering
'92
Masque of the Red Death
'89

Tina Ona Pauksteiis (1970-)
5 Dark Souls '96
The Unearthing '93

Nemesis Game '03
The Breed '01
The Void '01
Teen Wolf '85
Fatal Vision '84
A Soldier's Story '84
The Right Stuff '83
Forbidden World '82
Weekend War '88
The Last of Philip Banter

Scott Paulin (1950-)
Emanon '86
Wildfire '88
No Way Out '87
Belizaire the Cajun '86
After Hours '85
Knights '93
Pump Up the Volume '90
Capone '89
Captain America '89
Deceit '89
From Hollywood to
Deadwood '89
Grim Prairie Tales '89
Turner and Hooch '89
To Heal a Nation '88
Tricks of the Trade '88
Doctor at Large '57
Weekend War '88
The Last of Philip Banter

Stuart Paul
Fate '90
'99

Morgan Paull (1944-)
Surf 2 '84
Fade to Black '80
The Last Hard Men '76
Patton '70

Pat Paulsen (1927-97)
Auntie Lee's Meat Pies '92
They Still Call Me Bruce '86
Night Patrol '85

Gaston Pauls (1972-)
Felicidades '00
Nine Queens '00
What Your Eyes Don't See
'99

Albert Paulsen (1929-2004)
The Arab Conspiracy '76
Millions of October '74
The Manchurian Candidate
'62

Rob Paulsen (1956-)
The Ant Bully '06 (V)
The Fox and the Hound 2
'06 (V)
Disney's Teacher's Pet '04
(V)
Jimmy Neutron: Boy
Genius '01 (V)
Land Before Time 7: The
Stone of Cold Fire '00 (V)
The Land Before Time 5:
The Mysterious Island
'97 (V)
The Land Before Time 4:
Journey Through the
Mists '96 (V)
The Land Before Time 3:
Back to Back '90 (V)
The Time of the Great
Giving '95 (V)
A Goofy Movie '94 (V)
The Land Before Time 2:
The Great Valley
Adventure '94 (V)
Perfect Match '88
Eyes of Fire '84

Jay Paulson
Imaginary Heroes '05
Go '99

Sarah Paulson (1974-)
Diggers '06
The Notorious Bettie Page
'06
Down With Love '03
Held Up '00
What Women Want '00
The Other Sister '98
Levitation '97
Aquamarine '06
Sydney White '07

Rodolphe Pauly
Before Sunset '04
A Very Long Engagement
'04
Close to Leo '02
Merci pour le Chocolat '00

Johnny Paycheck (1938-2003)
Sweet Country Road '83
Take This Job & Shove It
'81

Bill Paxton (1955-)
Club Dread '04
Haven '04
Thunderbirds '04
Spy Kids 3-D: Game Over
'03
Frailty '02
U-571 '00
Vertical Limit '00
A Bright Shining Lie '98
Mighty Joe Young '98
A Simple Plan '98
Titanic '97
Traveler '96
The Evening Star '96
The Last Supper '96
Apollo 13 '95
Frank and Jesse '94
True Lies '94
Tombstone '93
Boxing Helena '93
Future Shock '93
Indian Summer '93
Monolith '93
The Vagrant '92
Trespass '92
The Dark Backward '91
One False Move '91
Navy SEALs '90
The Last of the Finest '90
Predator 2 '90
Brain Dead '89
Next of Kin '89
Slipstream '89
Back to Back '90
Pass the Ammo '88
Near Dark '87
Aliens '86
Commando '85
Weird Science '85
Impulse '84
Streets of Fire '84
The Terminator '84
The Lords of Discipline '83
Crazy Mama '75

Sara Paxton (1988-)
Sydney White '07
Aquamarine '06
Sleepover '04

Katina Paxinou (1900-73)
Rocco and His Brothers '60
Prince of Foxes '49
Inheritance '47
For Whom the Bell Tolls '43
Mr. Saturday Night '92
City Slickers '91
Crazy People '50
No Way Out '87
Howard the Duck '87
Carpool '96
Quiz Show '94
Heart and Souls '93
Searching for Bobby
Fischer '93
City Hall '95
Get Shorty '95
Nixon '95
Crime of the Century '96
Gang Related '96
Unforgettable '96
City Slickers 2: The Legend
of Curly's Gold '94
State and Main '00
Chill Factor '99
Dash and Lilly '99
The Hurricane '99
Mumford '99
Bounce '00
Bartleby '01
Focus '01
Bait '00
Partners '99

James Pax
In Love and War '91
The Chinatown Murders:
Man against the Mob '89

Adam Pawlikowski (1925-76)
Lotna '61
Ashes and Diamonds '58

Lennox Pawle (1872-1936)
Sylvia Scarlet '35
David Copperfield '35

Muriel Pavlow (1921-)
Doctor at Large '57
Doctor in the House '53
Malta Story '53

Terele Pavez (1939-)
The Day of the Beast '95

Marisa Pavan (1932-)
A Slightly Pregnant Man '79
Solomon and Sheba '59
Diane '55
The Rose Tattoo '55
What Price Glory? '52

Allen Payne (1968-)
30 Years to Life '01
A Price above Rubies '98
The Perfect Storm '00
The Tuskegee Airmen '95
Jason's Lyric '94
The Walking Dead '94
New Jack City '91

Bruce Payne (1960-)
Paranoia 1.0 '04
Asylum of the Damned '03
Ripper: Letter from Hell '01
Britannic '00
Dungeons and Dragons '00
Highlander: Endgame '00
One Man's Justice '95
Operation Intercept '95
The Cisco Kid '94
Full Eclipse '93
Passenger 57 '92
Pyrates '91
Switch '91
Howling 6: The Freaks '90
Wonderland '88

Carl Anthony Payne, II (1969-)
The Breaks '99
Ed '96
Gridlock'd '96
She's Gotta Have It '86

Eric Payne
Redbelt '08
Ocean's Thirteen '07

David Paymer (1954-)
Resurrecting the Champ
'07
Marilyn Hotchkiss' Ballroom
Dancing & Charm School
'06
School of Life '06
In Good Company '04
Spartan '04
Alex & Emma '03
Joe and Max '02
RFK '02

John Payne (1912-89)
Bail Out at 43,000 '57

Slightly Scarlet '56
Tennessee's Partner '55
Silver Lode '54
Kansas City Confidential '52
Miracle on 34th Street '47
The Dolly Sisters '46
The Razor's Edge '46
Hello, Frisco, Hello '43
Footlight Serenade '42
Iceland '42
Springtime in the Rockies '42
To the Shores of Tripoli '42
The Great American Broadcast '41
Sun Valley Serenade '41
Week-End in Havana '41
Tin Pan Alley '40
College Swing '38
Hats Off '37
Dodsworth '36

Laurence Payne (1919-)
One Deadly Owner '74
Vampire Circus '71
The Tell-Tale Heart '60
The Crawling Eye '58
Train of Events '49

Sally Payne (1914-99)
Man from Cheyenne '42
Romance on the Range '42
Bad Man of Deadwood '41
In Old Cheyenne '41
Jesse James at Bay '41
Nevada City '41
Red River Valley '41
Sheriff of Tombstone '41
Young Bill Hickok '40

Amanda Pays (1959-)
The Santa Trap '02
Ablaze '00
Spacejacked '98
Subterfuge '98
Hollywood Confidential '97
Solitaire for 2 '94
Dead on the Money '91
Exposure '91
The Flash '90
Leviathan '89
The Kindred '87
Off Limits '87
A.D. '85
Agatha Christie's Thirteen at Dinner '85
Cold Room '84
Oxford Blues '84

Barbara Payton (1927-67)
Four Sided Triangle '53
Bride of the Gorilla '51
Drums in the Deep South '51
Kiss Tomorrow Goodbye '50
Only the Valiant '50
Great Jesse James Raid '49
Trapped '49

Pamela Payton-Wright (1941-)
In Dreams '98
Resurrection '80

Rock Peace
Killer Tomatoes Strike Back '90
Return of the Killer Tomatoes! '88
Attack of the Killer Tomatoes '77

Mary Peach (1934-)
Disraeli '79
Ballad in Blue '66
A Gathering of Eagles '63
No Love for Johnnie '60
Room at the Top '59

Trevor Peacock (1931-)
Fred Claus '07
Madame Bovary '00
A Christmas Carol '99
For Roseanna '96
Neil Gaiman's NeverWhere '96

E.J. Peaker (1942-)
The Banker '89
Hello, Dolly! '69

Adele Pearce
See Pamela Blake

Alice Pearce (1913-66)
The Glass Bottom Boat '66
Dear Brigitte '65
The Belle of New York '52

Craig Pearce
Pirates '86

Guy Pearce (1967-)
First Snow '07
Factory Girl '06
The Proposition '05
Two Brothers '04
The Count of Monte Cristo '02
The Hard Word '02
Till Human Voices Wake Us '02
The Time Machine '02
Memento '00
Rules of Engagement '00
Ravenous '99
A Slipping Down Life '99
L.A. Confidential '97
Flynn '96
Dating the Enemy '95
The Adventures of Priscilla, Queen of the Desert '94
Heaven Tonight '93
The Hunting '92

Jacqueline Pearce (1943-)
Princess Caraboo '94
White Mischief '88
Don't Raise the Bridge, Lower the River '68
Plague of the Zombies '66
The Reptile '66

Joanne Pearce
Morons from Outer Space '85

Mary Vivian Pearce
Pecker '98
Serial Mom '94
Cry-Baby '90
Hairspray '88
Polyester '81
Desperate Living '77
Female Trouble '74
Pink Flamingos '72
Multiple Maniacs '70
Mondo Trasho '69

Slade Pearce (1995-)
Air Bud 6: Air Buddies '06
Yours, Mine & Ours '05

Patricia Pearcy
Delusion '84
Squirm '76

Aaron Pearl (1972-)
Montana Sky '07
All I Want '02

Barry Pearl (1950-)
Avenging Angel '85
Grease '78

Randy Pearlstein
Dead Man on Campus '97
Revenge of the Radioactive Reporter '91

Corey Pearson (1974-)
Jiminy Glick in LaLa Wood '04
Going Greek '01
Summer Catch '01

David Pearson
Masters of Horror: Sounds Like '06
Tomb '86

Drew Pearson (1897-1969)
The Day the Earth Stood Still '51
Betrayal from the East '44

James Anthony Pearson
Control '07
Kidnapped '05

Neil Pearson (1959-)
The State Within '06
Bridget Jones: The Edge of Reason '04
Rhodes '97
Fever Pitch '96

Richard Pearson (1918-)
Pirates '86
Thirteenth Reunion '81
Therese Raquin '80
The Woman in Question '50

Virginia Pearson (1886-1958)
The Taxi Mystery '26
The Phantom of the Opera '25

Harold (Hal) Peary (1908-85)
Clambake '67
Wetbacks '56
Gildersleeve on Broadway '43
The Great Gildersleeve '43
Here We Go Again! '42
Seven Days' Leave '42
Look Who's Laughing '41

Patsy Pease (1956-)
Improper Conduct '94
He Knows You're Alone '80

Sierra Pecheur
Kalifornia '93
Bronco Billy '80
3 Women '77

Bob Peck (1945-99)
The Miracle Maker: The Story of Jesus '00 (V)
FairyTale: A True Story '97
Smilla's Sense of Snow '96
Surviving Picasso '96
Jurassic Park '93
Catherine Cookson's The Black Velvet Gown '92
Slipstream '89
After Pilkington '88
The Kitchen Toto '87
Edge of Darkness '86
Parker '84

Cecilia Peck (1958-)
Blue Flame '93
The Portrait '93
Ambition '91
Torn Apart '89
My Best Friend Is a Vampire '88
Wall Street '87

George Peck
Curse of the Puppet Master: The Human Experiment '98
Dawn of the Mummy '82

Gregory Peck (1916-2003)
Moby Dick '98
The Portrait '93
Cape Fear '91
Other People's Money '91
Old Gringo '89
Amazing Grace & Chuck '87
The Scarlet & the Black '83
The Blue and the Gray '82
Sea Wolves '81
The Boys from Brazil '78
MacArthur '77
The Omen '76
Billy Two Hats '74
Shoot Out '71
I Walk the Line '70
MacKenna's Gold '69
The Stalking Moon '69
Arabesque '66
Mirage '66
Behold a Pale Horse '64
Captain Newman, M.D. '63
How the West Was Won '63
To Kill a Mockingbird '62
Cape Fear '62
The Guns of Navarone '61
Beloved Infidel '59
On the Beach '59
Pork Chop Hill '59
The Big Country '58
The Bravados '58
Designing Woman '57
The Man in the Gray Flannel Suit '56
Moby Dick '56
Roman Holiday '53
The Snows of Kilimanjaro '52
The World in His Arms '52
Captain Horatio Hornblower '51
David and Bathsheba '51
The Gunfighter '50
Only the Valiant '50
Twelve o'Clock High '49
Gentleman's Agreement '47
The Paradine Case '47
Duel in the Sun '46
Spellbound '45
The Yearling '45
The Valley of Decision '45
The Keys of the Kingdom '44
Days of Glory '43

J. Eddie Peck (1958-)
Blind Heat '00
To Grandmother's House We Go '94
Lambada '89

Josh Peck (1986-)
Drillbit Taylor '08
Ice Age: The Meltdown '06 (V)
Mean Creek '04
Max Keeble's Big Move '01

Tony Peck (1956-)
Carnosaur 3: Primal Species '96
Die Hard: With a Vengeance '95
Fit to Kill '93

Sam Peckinpah (1925-84)
The Visitor '80
Gunfire '80
Invasion of the Body Snatchers '56
An Annapolis Story '55

Chris Pederson
Point Break '91
Platoon '86
Suburbia '83

David Peel (1920-82)
The Brides of Dracula '60
The Hands of Orlac '60

Nia Peeples (1961-)
Connor's War '06
Inside Out '05
Half Past Dead '02
Alone with a Stranger '99
Blues Brothers 2000 '98
Poodle Springs '98
Tower of Terror '97
Bloodhounds 2 '96
Robin Cook's Terminal '96
Mr. Stitch '95
Deadlock 2 '94
Improper Conduct '94
Return to Lonesome Dove '93

Joan Peers (1911-75)
The Tip-Off '31
Applause '29

Lisa Peers (1956-)
Glass '89
Solo '77

Amanda Peet (1972-)
The Ex '07
Martian Child '07
A Lot Like Love '05
Melinda and Melinda '05
Syriana '05
The Whole Ten Yards '04
Identity '03
Something's Gotta Give '03
Changing Lanes '02
High Crimes '02
Igby Goes Down '02
Saving Silverman '01
Isn't She Great '00
Two Ninas '00
Whipped '00
The Whole Nine Yards '00
Body Shots '99
1999 '98
Southie '98
Ellen Foster '97
Grind '96
One Fine Day '96
She's the One '96

Simon Pegg (1970-)
The Good Night '07
Hot Fuzz '07
Run, Fat Boy, Run '07
Big Nothing '06
Mission: Impossible 3 '06
George A. Romero's Land of the Dead '05
Shaun of the Dead '04

Luke Pegler
The Condemned '07
See No Evil '06

Edward Peil, Sr. (1883-1959)
The Lone Rider in Frontier Fury '41
Trigger Men '41
Justice Rides Again '32
Local Badman '32
$50,000 Reward '25

Mary Beth Peil (1940-)
The Reagans '04
Neil Simon's The Odd Couple 2 '98

Ashley Peldon (1984-)
Get a Clue! '98
With Friends Like These '98
Cats Don't Dance '97 (V)
Deceived '91

Courtney Peldon (1981-)
Mortuary '05
National Lampoon's Adam & Eve '05
Wild Grizzly '99

Pele (1940-)
Hot Shot '86
A Minor Miracle '83
Victory '81

Lisa Pelikan (1954-)
Color of Justice '97
Into the Badlands '92
Return to the Blue Lagoon '91
Lionheart '90
Ghoulies '84
Swing Shift '84
The Best Little Girl in the World '81
Jennifer '78
Julia '77

Valentine Pelka (1956-)
Under the Tuscan Sun '03
The Last of the Blonde Bombshells '00
Ivanhoe '97

Oana Pellea
I Really Hate My Job '07
High Tension '03

Raymond Pellegrin (1925-2007)
Street War '76
Imperial Venus '71
Taste of Death '68
Scandal Man '67
A Woman of Rome '56
Napoleon '55

Frank Pellegrino (1957-)
Friends and Family '01
Execution of Justice '99
Mickey Blue Eyes '99
Tarantella '95

Mark Pellegrino (1965-)
The Number 23 '07
Capote '05
Twisted '04
The Hunted '03
Mulholland Drive '01
Say It Isn't So '01
Drowning Mona '00
Midnight Witness '93
Prayer of the Rollerboys '91
Blood & Concrete: A Love Story '90

Clara Peller (1903-87)
Moving Violations '85
The Stuff '85

Andree Pelletier (1950-)
Third Walker '79
Outrageous! '77

Michelle-Barbara Pelletier
Twist '03
P.T. Barnum '99
La Deroute '98
The Lotus Eaters '93

Yves Pelletier (1961-)
2 Seconds '98
Karmina '96

Mark Pellington (1965-)
Almost Famous '00
Jerry Maguire '96

Matti Pellonpaa (1951-95)
La Vie de Boheme '93
Night on Earth '91
Zombie and the Ghost Train '91
Ariel '89
Leningrad Cowboys Go America '89

Meeno Peluce (1970-)
Nightstalker '81
Scout's Honor '80

Ana Luisa Peluffo (1929-)
The Living Head '59
The New Invisible Man '58

Ron Pember (1934-)
Suspicion '87
Bullshot '83

Steve Pemberton (1967-)
Mr. Bean's Holiday '07
Lassie '05
Under the Greenwood Tree '05

George Pembroke (1900-72)
The Black Dragons '42
Dawn Express '42
I Killed That Man '42
Gangs, Inc. '41
Buried Alive '39

Candela Pena (1973-)
Torremolinos 73 '03
All About My Mother '99
Running Out of Time '94

Elizabeth Pena (1959-)
Adrift in Manhattan '07
The Lost City '05
Sueno '05
Transamerica '05
The Incredibles '04 (V)
Impostor '02
ZigZag '02
On the Borderline '01
Things Behind the Sun '01
Tortilla Soup '01
Seven Girlfriends '00
Aldrich Ames: Traitor Within '98
Dee Snider's Strangeland '98
Highway Hitcher '98
Rush Hour '98
The Second Civil War '97
Contagious '96

Free Willy 2: The Adventure Home '95
It Came from Outer Space 2 '95
Lone Star '95
Across the Moon '94
Dead Funny '94
The Waterdance '91
Fugitive Among Us '92
Blue Steel '90
Drug Wars: The Camarena Story '90
Jacob's Ladder '90
Vibes '88
*batteries not included '87
La Bamba '87
Down and Out in Beverly Hills '86
Crossover Dreams '85
They All Laughed '81
Times Square '80
El Super '79

Michael Peña (1976-)
Lions for Lambs '07
Shooter '07
World Trade Center '06
Crash '05
Little Athens '05
United States of Leland '03
Buffalo Soldiers '01
Bellyfruit '99
Running Free '94

Beverly Penberthy (1949-)
Judas Kiss '98
Bloodsucking Pharoahs of Pittsburgh '90

Austin Pendleton (1940-)
Bad City '06
The Notorious Bettie Page '06
Raising Flagg '06
Christmas With the Kranks '04
Finding Nemo '03 (V)
Uptown Girls '03
A Beautiful Mind '01
The 4th Floor '99
Joe the King '99
Men of Means '99
Amistad '97
A River Made to Drown In '97
The Mirror Has Two Faces '96
The Proprietor '96
Trial and Error '96
Home for the Holidays '95
Guarding Tess '94
Four Eyes and Six Guns '93
Mr. Nanny '93
My Boyfriend's Back '93
Rain Without Thunder '93
My Cousin Vinny '92
Mr. & Mrs. Bridge '90
Hello Again '87
Short Circuit '86
Talk to Me '84
Simon '80
Starting Over '79
The Front Page '74
The Thief Who Came to Dinner '73
What's Up, Doc? '72
Catch-22 '70
Petulia '68

Cedric Pendleton
Nothin' 2 Lose '00

Nat Pendleton (1895-1967)
Buck Privates Come Home '47
Scared to Death '46
Northwest Passage '40
At the Circus '39
The Secret of Dr. Kildare '39
Shopworn Angel '38
Gangway '37
Sing Me a Love Song '37
The Great Ziegfeld '36
Reckless '35
Manhattan Melodrama '34
Sing and Like It '34
The Thin Man '34
Penthouse '33
The Sign of the Cross '33
Hell Fire Austin '32
Horse Feathers '32
Blonde Crazy '31

Steve Pendleton (1908-84)
I Married a Woman '56
Sky Liner '49
Seas Beneath '31

Thaao Penghlis
Les Patterson Saves the World '90
Altered States '80
The Lookalike '90

Matthew Penn
Delta Force 3: The Killing Game '91
Playing for Keeps '86

Susan Penhaligon (1949-)
Soldier of Orange '78
Nasty Habits '77
Bouquet of Barbed Wire '76
The Confessional '75
The Land That Time Forgot '75
No Sex Please—We're British '73

Sean Penn (1960-)
Crossing Over '08
All the King's Men '06
The Assassination of Richard Nixon '05
The Interpreter '05
It's All About Love '03
Mystic River '03
21 Grams '03
I Am Sam '01
Before Night Falls '00
Up at the Villa '00
The Weight of Water '00
Sweet and Lowdown '99
Hurlyburly '98
The Thin Red Line '98
The Game '97
Hugo Pool '97
Loved '97
She's So Lovely '97
U-Turn '97
Dead Man Walking '95
Carlito's Way '93
State of Grace '90
Casualties of War '89
Colors '88
Cool Blue '88
Judgment in Berlin '88
At Close Range '86
Shanghai Surprise '86
The Falcon and the Snowman '85
Racing with the Moon '84
Bad Boys '83
Fast Times at Ridgemont High '82
Taps '81
Killing of Randy Webster '81

Leonard Penn (1907-)
Streets of Sin '49
Girl of the Golden West '38

Bruce Penhall (1960-)
Enemy Gold '93
Fit to Kill '93
Hard Hunted '92
Do or Die '91
Picasso Trigger '89
Savage Beach '89

Christopher Penn (1965-2006)
The Darwin Awards '06
After the Sunset '04
Starsky & Hutch '04
Shelter Island '03
Murder by Numbers '02
Stealing Harvard '02
American Pie 2 '01
Corky Romano '01
Cement '99
Let the Devil Wear Black '99
The Florentine '98
One Tough Cop '98
Trail of a Serial Killer '98
Deceiver '97
The Boys Club '96
Down Periscope '96
The Funeral '96
The Last Supper '96
Wedding Bell Blues '96
Fist of the North Star '95
Mulholland Falls '95
To Wong Foo, Thanks for Everything, Julie Newmar '95
Under the Hula Moon '95
Imaginary Crimes '94
Beethoven's 2nd '93
Best of the Best 2 '93
Josh and S.A.M. '93
The Music of Chance '93
The Pickle '93
Short Cuts '93
True Romance '93
Reservoir Dogs '92
Futurekick '91
Mobsters '91
Bloodfist 7: Manhunt '95
Leather Jackets '90
Best of the Best '89
Made in USA '88
A Fool and His Money '88
At Close Range '86
Pale Rider '85
Footloose '84
The Wild Life '84
All the Right Moves '83
Rumble Fish '83

Lea Penman (1895-1962)
We're No Angels '55
Fancy Pants '50

Larry Pennell (1928-)
Bubba Ho-Tep '03
The Fear: Halloween Night '99
The FBI Story '59
The Far Horizons '55

George Peppard (1928-94)
The Tigress '93
Night of the Fox '90
Silence Like Glass '90
The Chinatown Murders: Man against the Mob '89
Target Eagle '84
Your Ticket Is No Longer Valid '84
Treasure of the Yankee Zephyr '83
Battle Beyond the Stars '80
From Hell to Victory '79
Torn Between Two Lovers '79
Damnation Alley '77
Newman's Law '74
The Groundstar Conspiracy '72
The Executioner '70
Pendulum '69
Rough Night in Jericho '67
Tobruk '66
The Blue Max '66
Operation Crossbow '65
The Carpetbaggers '64
How the West Was Won '63
The Victors '63
Breakfast at Tiffany's '61
Home from the Hill '60

Nicholas Pennell (1939-95)
Cry of the Penguins '71
Isadora '68

Jonathan Penner (1962-)
Cleopatra's Second Husband '00

Alan Penney
Around the World in 80 Ways '86
Gone to Ground '76

Del Pentacost
Coyote Ugly '00
O Brother, Where Art Thou? '00

Rupert Penry-Jones (1970-)
Persuasion '07
Casanova '05
Match Point '05
Cambridge Spies '03
The Four Feathers '02
Charlotte Gray '01
Virtual Sexuality '99
Hilary and Jackie '98

John Penrose (1914-83)
The Shadow Man '53
Kind Hearts and Coronets '49

Sydney Penny (1971-)
Hidden Places '06
Child of Darkness, Child of Light '97
The Capture of Grizzly Adams '82
Pale Rider '85
Bernadette '90
News at Eleven '86
Hyper-Sapien: People from Another Star '86

Joe Penny (1956-)
The Prophet's Game '99
Family of Cops 3 '98
Family of Cops 2: Breach of Faith '97
Danger of Love '95
Blood Vows: The Story of a Mafia Wife '87
Gangster Wars '81
Bloody Birthday '80
Lifepod '80
Deathmoon '78
The Great Texas Dynamite Chase '76

Chris Pennock (1944-)
Running Woman '98
Frances '82

Kal Penn (1977-)
Harold & Kumar Escape from Guantanamo Bay '08
Epic Movie '07
The Namesake '06
National Lampoon's Van Wilder 2: The Rise of Taj '06
Superman Returns '06
A Lot Like Love '05
Bachelor Party Vegas '05
Dancing in Twilight '05
Son of the Mask '05
Ball & Chain '04
Harold and Kumar Go to White Castle '04
Love Don't Cost a Thing '03
Malibu's Most Wanted '03
National Lampoon's Van Wilder '02

Jack Pennick (1895-1964)
The Man Who Shot Liberty Valance '62
The Alamo '60
The Horse Soldiers '59
Mister Roberts '55
Girls in Chains '43
Hollywood Stadium Mystery '38
Wide Open Faces '38
Last Outlaw '36
Rogue's Tavern '36
Our Daily Bread '34
Stagecoach '39

Barbara Pepper (1915-69)
Kiss Me, Stupid! '64
Murder, He Says '45
Our Daily Bread '34

Eileen (Elaine) Percy (1901-73)
The Phantom Bullet '26
Let's Go! '23
Down to Earth '17
The Man from Painted Post '17
Reaching for the Moon '17

Esme Percy (1887-1957)
Pygmalion '38
Dead of Night '45
21 Days '37
Accused '36
Old Spanish Custom '36
Bitter Sweet '33

Ed Peranio
Desperate Living '77
Female Trouble '74
Multiple Maniacs '70

Missy Peregrym (1982-)
Stick It '06
Call Me: The Rise and Fall of Heidi Fleiss '04

Wayne Pere
Soundman '99
An American Summer '90

Tony Perenski
Varsity Blues '98

Jose Perez (1940-)
Miami Blues '90
Courage '86
One Shoe Makes It Murder '82
Short Eyes '79
Life & Times of Judge Roy Bean '72

George Perez (1972-)
The Underneath '95
Manhattan Merengue! '95

Joe Penny (1956-83)
The Shadow Man '53
Kind Hearts and Coronets '49

Barry Pepper (1970-)
Flags of Our Fathers '06
The Three Burials of Melquiades Estrada '05
The Snow Walker '03
25th Hour '02
We Were Soldiers '02
Knockaround Guys '01
61* '01
Battlefield Earth '00
The Green Mile '99
Enemy of the State '98
Saving Private Ryan '98
Firestorm '98
Titanic '97

Marilia Pera (1943-)
Central Station '98
Tieta of Agreste '96
Mixed Blood '84
Pixote '81

Piper Perabo (1977-)
Because I Said So '07
First Snow '07
Imagine Me & You '06
The Prestige '06
10th & Wolf '06
The Cave '05
Cheaper by the Dozen 2 '05
Edison Force '05
Cheaper by the Dozen '03
Lost and Delirious '01
The Adventures of Rocky & Bullwinkle '00
Coyote Ugly '00
Whiteboyz '99

Vincent Perez (1964-)
Talk of Angels '96
Beyond the Clouds '95
Queen Margot '94
The Crow 2: City of Angels '96
Swept from the Sea '97
The Treat '98
I Dreamed of Africa '00
On Guard! '03
Time Regained '99
Queen of the Damned '02
Bride of the Wind '01
Those Who Love Me Can Take the Train '98
Shot Through the Heart '98
Indochine '92
Cyrano de Bergerac '90

Timothy Paul Perez
Trade '07

Marco Perez
Amores Perros '00

Rosie Perez (1964-)
Pineapple Express '08
The Take '07
Human Nature '01
Widows '02
King of the Jungle '01
The Road to El Dorado '00 (V)
The 24 Hour Woman '99
A Brother's Kiss '97
Subway Stories '97
Somebody to Love '94
It Could Happen to You '94
Untamed Heart '93
Fearless '93
White Men Can't Jump '92
Night on Earth '91
Criminal Justice '90
Do the Right Thing '89

Anthony Perkins (1932-92)
A Demon in My View '92
In the Deep Woods '91
Daughter of Darkness '90
Edge of Sanity '89
Destroyer '88
Psycho 3 '86
The Glory Boys '84
Crimes of Passion '84
Psycho 2 '83
The Sins of Dorian Gray '82
The Black Hole '79
Twice a Woman '79
Winter Kills '79
Les Miserables '78
Mahogany '75
Murder on the Orient Express '74
Ten Days Wonder '72
Someone Behind the Door '71
Pretty Poison '68
Catch-22 '70
Is Paris Burning? '66

George Periolat (1876-1940)
The Street King '21

Francois Perier (1919-2002)
Stavisky '74
Z '69
Le Cercle Rouge '70
Le Samourai '67
The Organizer '64
The Testament of Orpheus '59
Nights of Cabiria '57
Gervaise '56
Orpheus '49
Sylvia and the Phantom '45

Manny Perez
Illegal Tender '07
El Cantante '06
Yellow '06
Washington Heights '02

The Fool Killer '65
Ravishing Idiot '64
The Trial '63
Goodbye Again '61
Phaedra '61
Psycho '60
Tall Story '60
Green Mansions '59
On the Beach '59
Desire Under the Elms '58
The Matchmaker '58
Fear Strikes Out '57
Lonely Man '57
The Tin Star '57
Friendly Persuasion '56

Elizabeth Perkins (1960-)
Fierce People '05
Jiminy Glick in LaLa Wood '05
Kids in America '05
Must Love Dogs '05
The Ring 2 '05
The Thing About My Folks '05
Speak '04
Finding Nemo '03 (V)
All I Want '02
My Sister's Keeper '02
Cats & Dogs '01
If These Walls Could Talk 2 '00
28 Days '00
Crazy in Alabama '99
From the Earth to the Moon '98
I'm Losing You '98
Rescuers: Stories of Courage "Two Women" '97
Moonlight and Valentino '95

Emily Perkins (1977-)
She's the Man '06
Ginger Snaps Back: The Beginning '04
Ginger Snaps: Unleashed '04
Ginger Snaps '01
Prozac Nation '01
Small Sacrifices '89

Millie Perkins (1938-)
The Lost City '05
The Chamber '96
Bodily Harm '95
Pistol: The Birth of a Legend '90
Two Moon Junction '88
Wall Street '87
At Close Range '86
A.D. '85
License to Kill '84
Sweet Hearts Dance '88
About Last Night... '86
From the Hip '86
Table for Five '83
The Haunting Passion '83
Witch Who Came from the Sea '76
Cockfighter '74
Wild in the Streets '68
Ride in the Whirlwind '66
The Shooting '66
Ensign Pulver '64
Wild in the Country '61
The Diary of Anne Frank '59

Osgood Perkins (1892-1937)
Scarface '31
Love 'Em and Leave 'Em '26

Oz (Osgood) Perkins, II (1974-)
Quigley '03
Secretary '02
Legally Blonde '01

Wolf '94
Six Degrees of Separation '93
Psycho 2 '83

Orli Perl (1972-)
Pick a Card '97
Under the Domim Tree '95

Max Perlich (1968-)
Protecting the King '07
The Missing '03
Deuces Wild '02
Blow '01
Sol Goode '01
Homicide: The Movie '00
The Independent '00
Freeway 2: Confessions of a Trickbaby '99
Goodbye, Lover '99
House on Haunted Hill '99
Sometimes They Come Back... For More '99
Gummo '97
Truth or Consequences, N.M. '97
Beautiful Girls '96
The Curse of Inferno '96
Georgia '95
Dead Beat '94
Maverick '94
Shake, Rattle & Rock! '94
Terrified '94
Born Yesterday '93
Cliffhanger '93
Rush '91
The Butcher's Wife '91
Drugstore Cowboy '89
Plain Clothes '88
Can't Buy Me Love '87
Ferris Bueller's Day Off '86

Rhea Perlman (1948-)
10 Items or Less '06
Miracle on 34th Street '94
Indian Summer '93
The Doctor '91
He Said, She Said '91
Avalon '90
Enid Is Sleeping '90
Love at Large '89
Big '88
Canadian Bacon '94
Ted & Venus '93
We're Back! A Dinosaur's Story '93 (V)
There Goes the Neighborhood '92
Class Act '91
Enid Is Sleeping '90
Stamp of a Killer '87
Amazing Stories '85
Ratings Game '84
Intimate Strangers '77

Ron Perlman (1950-)
Hellboy 2: The Golden Army '08
In the Name of the King: A Dungeon Siege Tale '08
How to Go Out on a Date in Queens '06
Masters of Horror: Pro-Life '05
The Second Front '05
Tarzan 2 '05 (V)
Comic Book: The Movie '04
Hellboy '04
Hoodlum & Son '03
Blade 2 '02
Shakedown '02
Star Trek: Nemesis '02
The King's Guard '01
The Shaft '01
Enemy at the Gates '00
Operation Sandman: Warriors in Hell '00
Price of Glory '00
Titan A.E. '00 (V)
The Trial of Old Drum '00
Happy, Texas '99
Houdini '99
Supreme Sanction '99
Frogs for Snakes '98
The Magnificent Seven '98
A Town Has Turned to Dust '98
Alien: Resurrection '97
Betty '97
Prince Valiant '97
The Second Civil War '97

Tinseltown '97
Body Armor '96
The Island of Dr. Moreau '96
The Last Supper '96
The City of Lost Children '95
Fluke '95
Mr. Stitch '95
Phantom 2040 Movie: The Ghost Who Walks '95 (V)
Cronos '94
Police Academy 7: Mission to Moscow '94
Sensation '94
The Adventures of Huck Finn '93
Double Exposure '93
Romeo Is Bleeding '93
When the Bough Breaks '93
Sleepwalkers '92
Blind Man's Bluff '91
The Name of the Rose '86
Ice Pirates '84
Quest for Fire '82

Florence Pernel (1966-)
Trois Couleurs: Blanc '94
Trois Couleurs: Bleu '93

Gigi Perreau (1941-)
Hell on Wheels '67
Journey to the Center of Time '67
Girls' Town '59
Dance with Me, Henry '56
The Man in the Gray Flannel Suit '56
Never a Dull Moment '50
My Foolish Heart '49
Song of Love '47

Paul Perri (1953-)
Without Evidence '96
Hellraiser 4: Bloodline '95
Delta Force 2: Operation Stranglehold '90
Manhunter '86
Hit & Run '82

Mireille Perrier (1959-)
The Ice Rink '99
Trahir '93
Love Without Pity '91
Toto le Heros '91
Chocolat '88
Mauvais Sang '86
Boy Meets Girl '84

Olivier Perrier (1940-)
Blame It on Fidel '06
Read My Lips '01
Les Destinees '00

Pierre Perrier
One to Another '06
Cold Showers '05

Jack Perrin (1896-1967)
Sunrise at Campobello '60
When Gangland Strikes '56
The Court Martial of Billy Mitchell '55
Ten Wanted Men '54
Them! '54
Bandit Queen '51
I Shot Billy the Kid '50
The North Star '43
New Moon '40
West of Pinto Basin '40
The Story of Vernon and Irene Castle '39
Gun Grit '36
Texas Jack '35
Hell Fire Austin '32
Apache Kid's Escape '30
Midnight Faces '26

Jacques Perrin (1941-)
Le Petit Lieutenant '05
Brotherhood of the Wolf '01
Winged Migration '01 (N)
Flight of the Innocent '93
Cinema Paradiso '88
Le Crabe Tambour '77
Black and White in Color '76
The Desert of the Tartars '76

State of Siege '73
Peau D'Ane '71
Donkey Skin '70
Z '69
The 317th Platoon '65
The Young Girls of Rochefort '68
The Girl with a Suitcase '60

Valerie Perrine (1944-)
The Moguls '05
What Women Want '00
Brown's Requiem '98
A Place Called Truth '98
Shame, Shame, Shame '98
Curtain Call '97
The Break '95
Girl in the Cadillac '94
Boiling Point '93
Bright Angel '91
Sweet Bird of Youth '89
Maid to Order '87
Water '85
The Three Little Pigs '84
When Your Lover Leaves '83
The Border '82
The Agency '81
Can't Stop the Music '80
Superman 2 '80
The Electric Horseman '79
The Magician: The Movie '79
Superman: The Movie '78
Mr. Billion '77
Lenny '74
Slaughterhouse Five '72

Harold Perrineau, Jr. (1963-)
28 Weeks Later '07
The Matrix Reloaded '03
The Matrix Revolutions '03
OnLine '01
Woman on Top '00
The Best Man '99
The Tempest '99
The Edge '97
Blood & Wine '97
William Shakespeare's Romeo and Juliet '96
Smoke '95

Joe Perrino (1982-)
The Bumblebee Flies Anyway '98
The Mighty '98
Sleepers '96

Leslie Perrins (1902-62)
Man on the Run '49
Mr. Reeder in Room 13 '38
Nine Days a Queen '36
The Silent Passenger '35
The Living Dead '33

Michel Perron
Lost Junction '03
The Sign of Four '01
Battlefield Earth '00

Francois Perrot (1924-)
Life and Nothing But '89
Women's Prison Massacre '85

Felton Perry (1942-)
My Best Friend's Girl '84
Buck and the Magic Bracelet '97
Dumb & Dumber '94
RoboCop 3 '91
RoboCop 2 '90
Checking Out '89
RoboCop '87
Sudden Death '77
Walking Tall '73
Night Call Nurses '72

Jeff(rey) Perry (1955-)
Wild Things '98
Kingfish: A Story of Huey P. Long '95
Playmaker '94

Jeffrey S. (Jeff) Perry
The Chronicles of Narnia '89
Oxford Blues '84

John Bennett Perry (1941-)
Loaded '08
Protecting the King '07
Fools Rush In '97
George of the Jungle '97
The Last Fling '86
A Matter of Life and Death '81
Only When I Laugh '81

Lou Perry
The Texas Chainsaw Massacre 2 '86
Last Night at the Alamo '83

Luke Perry (1966-)
Johnson County War '02
The Enemy '01
The Triangle '01
Attention Shoppers '99
Storm Tracker '99
The Florentine '98
Indiscreet '98
The Fifth Element '97
Robin Cook's Invasion '97
American Strays '96
Last Breath '96
Normal Life '96
Riot in the Streets '96
8 Seconds '94
Buffy the Vampire Slayer '92
Terminal Bliss '91
Sweet Trash '70

Matthew Perry (1969-)
Numb '07
The Whole Ten Yards '04
Serving Sara '02
The Whole Nine Yards '00
Three to Tango '99
Almost Heroes '97
Fools Rush In '97
She's Out of Control '89
A Night in the Life of Jimmy Reardon '88

Rod Perry (1941-)
Black Gestapo '75
Black Godfather '74

Roger Perry (1933-)
Roller Boogie '79
Conspiracy of Terror '75
The Thing with Two Heads '72
The Return of Count Yorga '71
Count Yorga, Vampire '70
The Cat '66

Tyler Perry (1969-)
Tyler Perry's Meet the Browns '08
Tyler Perry's Why Did I Get Married? '07
Madea's Family Reunion '06
Diary of a Mad Black Woman '05

Maria Perschy (1938-)
People Who Own the Dark '75
Exorcism '74
Horror of the Zombies '74
House of Psychotic Women '73
The Rue Morgue Massacres '73
Last Day of the War '69
The Castle of Fu Manchu '68
A Witch Without a Broom '68
The Mad Executioners '65
633 Squadron '64
Man's Favorite Sport? '63
No Survivors, Please '63

Lisa Jane Persky
An American Rhapsody '01
My First Mister '01
Meat Loaf: To Hell and Back '00

The Last of the Finest '90
Vital Signs '90
Great Balls of Fire '89
When Harry Met Sally... '89
The Big Easy '87
Peggy Sue Got Married '86
The Sure Thing '85
The Cotton Club '84
Shattered Vows '84
Breathless '83
American Pop '81 (V)
The Great Santini '80
KISS Meets the Phantom of the Park '78

Nehemiah Persoff (1920-)
An American Tail: Fievel Goes West '91 (V)
The Last Temptation of Christ '88
Twins '88
An American Tail '86 (V)
Sadat '83
Yentl '83
The Henderson Monster '80
The Rebels '79
Killing Stone '78
Francis Gary Powers: The True Story of the U-2 Spy '76
Voyage of the Damned '76
Eric '75
Missiles of October '74
The Stranger Within '74
Deadly Harvest '72
The People Next Door '70
A Global Affair '63
The Comancheros '61
Al Capone '59
The Day of the Outlaw '59
Green Mansions '59
Never Steal Anything Small '59
Some Like It Hot '59
The Badlanders '58
Men in War '57
The Wrong Man '56
On the Waterfront '54

Essy Persson (1941-)
Cry of the Banshee '70
Mission Stardust '68
Vibration '68
Therese & Isabelle '67
I, a Woman '66

Maria Persson (1959-)
Pippi in the South Seas '70
Pippi on the Run '70
Pippi Goes on Board '69
Pippi Longstocking '69

Jon Pertwee (1919-96)
Carry On Screaming '66
Ladies Who Do '63
Mister Drake's Duck '50

Sean Pertwee (1964-)
Botched '07
Goal! The Dream Begins '06
When Evil Calls '06
The Last Drop '05
Dog Soldiers '01
Formula 51 '01
Seven Days to Live '01
Love, Honour & Obey '00
Cleopatra '99
Russell Mulcahy's Tale of the Mummy '99
Soldier '98
Event Horizon '97
Deadly Voyage '96
Stiff Upper Lips '96
Blue Juice '95
Shopping '93
Clarissa '91

Jorge Perugorria (1965-)
Life According to Muriel '97
Guantanamera '95
Strawberry and Chocolate '93

Frank Pesce
Night Vision '97
Trapped in Paradise '94
The Pamela Principle '91
29th Street '91

Joe Pesci (1943-)
Vigilante '83
The Good Shepherd '06
Daring Game '68
Lethal Weapon 4 '98
Gone Fishin' '97
8 Heads in a Duffel Bag '96
Casino '95
Jimmy Hollywood '94
With Honors '94
A Bronx Tale '93
Home Alone 2: Lost in New York '92
My Cousin Vinny '92
Lethal Weapon 3 '92
The Public Eye '92
JFK '91
The Super '91
Betsy's Wedding '90
Goodfellas '90
Home Alone '90
Backtrack '89
Lethal Weapon 2 '89
Man on Fire '87
Once Upon a Time in America '84
Easy Money '83
I'm Dancing as Fast as I Can '82
Eureka! '81
Raging Bull '80
Family Enforcer '76

Lisa Pescia
Body Chemistry 2: Voice of a Stranger '91
Body Chemistry '90

Donna Pescow (1954-)
Policewoman Centerfold '83
Saturday Night Fever '77

Bernadette Peters (1948-)
Partners '99
Dead Husbands '98
Ivory Tower '97
Glory Years '87
Impromptu '90
The Last Best Year '90
Pink Cadillac '89
Slaves of New York '89
Sunday in the Park with George '86
Sleeping Beauty '83
Annie '82
Heartbeeps '81
Pennies from Heaven '81
Tulips '81
Silent Movie '76
The Longest Yard '74
The Martian Chronicles: Part 2 '79
The Martian Chronicles: Part 3 '79
Baadasssss! '03
They Saved Hitler's Brain '64

Scott Peters (1930-94)
Girl Hunters '63

Susan Peters (1921-52)
Random Harvest '42

Werner Peters (1918-71)
The Bird with the Crystal Plumage '70
The Corrupt Ones '67
A Fine Madness '66
The Phantom of Soho '64
36 Hours '64
Curse of the Yellow Snake '63
The Counterfeit Traitor '62
The Kaiser's Lackey '51

Edward Petherbridge (1936-)
Strange Interlude '90

Brock Peters (1927-2005)
The Wild Thornberrys Movie '02
The Locket '02
To Heal a Nation '88
Star Trek 4: The Voyage Home '86
Home '86
Agatha Christie's A Caribbean Mystery '83
The Adventures of Huckleberry Finn '78
Framed '75
Slaughter's Big Rip-off '73
Soylent Green '73
The Secret '93
Star Trek 6: The Undiscovered Country '91
Alligator 2: The Mutation '90
Andy Hardy's Double Life '42
The McMasters '70
Ace High '68

Chris Petersen
Vampire Raiders—Ninja Queen '89
Ninja Masters of Death '85
Little Dragons '80

House Peters, Sr. (1880-1967)
Head Winds '25
Human Hearts '22

House Peters, Jr. (1916-)
The Leopard Woman 20

Jean Peters (1926-2000)
A Man Called Peter '55
Apache '54
Broken Lance '54
Three Coins in the Fountain '54
Pickup on South Street '53
Niagara '52
Viva Zapata! '52
As Young As You Feel '51
It Happens Every Spring '49
Captain from Castile '47

Luan Peters (1948-)
Land of the Minotaur '77
Flesh and Blood Show '73
Not Tonight Darling '72
Man of Violence '71
Twins of Evil '71

Molly Peters (1942-)
Target for Killing '66
Thunderball '65

Ralph Peters (1903-59)
Sky Liner '49
Meeting at Midnight '44
I Married a Witch '42
Death Rides the Range '40
Six Gun Rhythm '39
Man's Country '38
Rough Ridin' Rhythm '37

Rick Peters (1967-)
The Happy Face Murders '99

Cassandra Peterson (1951-)
Elvira's Haunted Hills '02
Acting on Impulse '93
Ted & Venus '93
Elvira, Mistress of the Dark '88
Echo Park '86
Pee-wee's Big Adventure '85
Balboa '82
Working Girls '75

Dorothy Peterson (1900-79)
Woman in the Window '44
Air Force '43
Peck's Bad Boy '34

Kimberlee Peterson (1980-)
Homecoming '96

Vidal Peterson
Wizards of the Lost Kingdom '85
Something Wicked This Way Comes '83

Eric Peterson (1980-)
Henry & Verlin '94
Tramp at the Door '87

Robert Peters
Night of the Demons 2 '94

Bob Peterson
Finding Nemo '03 (V)
Monsters, Inc. '01 (V)

Annika Peterson
Explorers '85

Amanda Peterson (1971-)
Windrunner '94
Fatal Charm '92
I Posed for Playboy '91
Listen to Me '89
Can't Buy Me Love '87
Explorers '85

William L. Petersen (1953-)
The Contender '00
The Skulls '00
Gunshy '98
Kiss the Sky '98
The Rat Pack '98
Twelve Angry Men '97
The Beast '96
Fear '96
The Kennedys of Massachusetts '95
Mulholland Falls '95
In the Kingdom of the Blind, the Man with One Eye is King '94
Return to Lonesome Dove '93
Hard Promises '92
Keep the Change '92
Passed Away '92
Young Guns 2 '90
Cousins '89
Amazing Grace & Chuck '87
Long Gone '87
Manhunter '86
To Live & Die in L.A. '85

Oscar Petersen
Mama Africa '02

Pat Petersen (1966-)
The Quarry '98
Cold River '81

Stewart Petersen (1960-)
Against a Crooked Sky '75
Seven Alone '75
Where the Red Fern Grows '74

Victor Petit
Street Warriors '87
Night of the Death Cult '75
Terror Beach '75

Isabelle Petit-Jacques

Gio Petre (1937-)
The Doll '62
Gorilla '56

Ian Petrella (1974-)
Crimes of Passion '84
A Christmas Story '83

Hay Petrie (1895-1948)
Great Expectations '46
A Canterbury Tale '44
Spellbound '41
Contraband '40
Clouds over Europe '39
Crimes at the Dark House '39
The Four Feathers '39
Spy in Black '39
21 Days '37
The Ghost Goes West '36
The Old Curiosity Shop '35
The Private Life of Henry VIII '33

Susan Petrie
Snapshot '77
They Came from Within '75
Vengeance is Mine '74

Joanna Pettet (1944-)
Terror in Paradise '90
Sweet Country '87
Double Exposure '82
Cry of the Innocent '80
Return of Frank Cannon '80
The Evil '78
A Killer in Every Corner '74
Pioneer Woman '73
Blue '68
Casino Royale '67
Night of the Generals '67
Robbery '67
The Group '66

Christopher Pettiet (1976-2000)
Carried Away '95
The Goodbye Bird '93
Fatal Exposure '91

Steven Petrarca
Sparkler '99

Brian Pettifer
Conspiracy '01
If.... '69

Michelle Pfeiffer (1957-)
Hairspray '07
Stardust '07
I Could Never Be Your Woman '06
Sinbad: Legend of the Seven Seas '03 (V)
White Oleander '02
I Am Sam '01
What Lies Beneath '00
The Story of Us '99
A Midsummer Night's Dream '99
The Deep End of the Ocean '99
The Prince of Egypt '98 (V)
A Thousand Acres '97
One Fine Day '96
To Gillian on Her 37th Birthday '96
Dangerous Minds '95
Up Close and Personal '96
Wolf '94
The Age of Innocence '93
Batman Returns '92
Frankie and Johnny '91
Love Field '91
The Russia House '90
The Fabulous Baker Boys '89
Married to the Mob '88
Dangerous Liaisons '88
Tequila Sunrise '88
Amazon Women on the Moon '87

Pascale Petit (1938-)
Four Times That Night '69
Eros of Desire '62

Valerie Pettiford (1960-)
Stomp the Yard '07
Glitter '01

Frank Pettingell (1891-1966)
Trial & Error '62
Gaslight '40
Butler's Dilemma '43

Lori Petty (1964-)
Prey for Rock and Roll '03
Firetrap '01
MacArthur Park '01
Route 666 '01
Blood Money '98
Relax... It's Just Sex! '98
Serial Bomber '96
The Glass Shield '95
Tank Girl '95
In the Army Now '94
Free Willy '93
A League of Their Own '92
Point Break '91

Richard Petty (1937-)
Cars '06 (V)
Cadillac Man '90
Richard Petty Story '72
Speedway '68

Ross Petty
Spenser: A Savage Place '94

Tom Petty (1950-)
The Postman '97
Made in Heaven '87

Alex Pettyfer (1990-)
Stormbreaker '06
Alex Rider: Operation Stormbreaker '06

Angelique Pettyjohn (1943-90)
The Wizard of Speed and Time '88
Bio Hazard '85
The Lost Empire '83
Repo Man '83
Confessions of Tom Harris '72

JoAnn Pflug (1940-)
The Day the Women Got Even '80
M*A*S*H '70

Liz Phair (1967-)
Cherish '02

Katija Pevec (1988-)
Air Bud 5: Buddy Spikes '03
Back '03

Joseph Pevney (1920-)
The Street with No Name '48

Penny Peyser (1951-)
In-Laws '79
The Frisco Kid '79

Dedee Pfeiffer (1965-)
The Prince and the Pauper '07
Meat Loaf: To Hell and Back '00
Up Close and Personal '96
Double Exposure '93
Falling Down '93
Running Cool '93
Shoot '92
Red Surf '90
Brothers in Arms '88
The Midnight Hour '86
Vamp '86
Toughlove '85

Linh Dan Pham (1973-)
The Beat My Heart Skipped '05

Joe Phelan
See Joe Estevez

Peter Phelan (1960-)
Indochine '92

Shawn (Michael) Phelan (1975-98)
Breaking the Rules '92
Toy Soldiers '91

Mekhi Phifer (1975-)
Puff, Puff, Pass '06
Slow Burn '05
Dawn of the Dead '04
Honey '03
8 Mile '02
Impostor '02
Paid in Full '02
The Other Brother '02
O '01
Carmen: A Hip Hopera '01
Shaft '00
A Lesson Before Dying '99
Uninvited Guest '99
I Still Know What You Did Last Summer '98
Hell's Kitchen NYC '97
High School High '96
Soul Food '97
Clockers '95

Mary Philbin (1903-93)
The Man Who Laughs '27
The Phantom of the Opera '25

John Philbin (1965-)
Martians Go Home! '90
The Four Minute Mile '88
North Shore '87
Shy People '87

Regis Philbin (1934-)
Shrek the Third '07 (V)
The Breakup Artist '04
Little Nicky '00
Dudley Do-Right '99
Night and the City '92
The Bad News Bears Go to Japan '78
Sextette '78

James Philbrook (1924-82)
Last Day of the War '69
Finger on the Trigger '65
Sound of Horror '64
The Thin Red Line '64

Dominic Philie
For Hire '98
The Boys '97

Gerard Philipe (1922-59)
Dangerous Liaisons '60
Fever Mounts at El Pao '59
Modigliani '58
The Red and the Black '57
Les Grandes Manoeuvres '55
The Proud Ones '53
Beauties of the Night '52
Fanfan la Tulipe '51
La Ronde '51
Beauty and the Devil '50
La Chartreuse de Parme '48
Devil in the Flesh '46
L'Idiot '46

Busy Phillips (1979-)
Made of Honor '08
White Chicks '04
Home Room '02
The Smokers '00

Emo Philips (1956-)
Meet the Parents '91
UHF '89

Gina Philips (1970-)
Chronicle of the Raven '04
Jeepers Creepers '01

Gina Philips (1970-)
Bella Mafia '97
Breaking Free '95

Lee Philips (1927-99)
Psychomania '63
The Hunters '58
Peyton Place '57

Mary (Phillips) Phillips (1900-75)
Leave Her to Heaven '45
A Farewell to Arms '32

Ryan Phillippe (1974-)
Stop-Loss '08
Breach '07
Flags of Our Fathers '06
Crash '05
Igby Goes Down '02
Gosford Park '01
Antitrust '00
Company Man '00
Way of the Gun '00
Cruel Intentions '98
54 '98
Playing by Heart '98
Homegrown '97
I Know What You Did Last Summer '97
Little Boy Blue '97
Lifeform '96
Nowhere '96
White Squall '96

Angie Phillips
Duets '00
Manny & Lo '96

Barney (Bernard) Phillips (1913-82)
Savage Run '70
The Sand Pebbles '66
I Was a Teenage Werewolf '57
Thirty Seconds Over Tokyo '44

Bobbie Phillips (1972-)
Chameleon 3: Dark Angel '00

Red Shoe Diaries:
Luscious Lola '00
Chameleon 2: Death Match '99
American Virgin '98
Carnival of Souls '98
Chameleon '98
Back in Action '94
Hail Caesar '94
Ring of Fire 3: Lion Strike '94
TC 2000 '93

Chris Phillips
Doug's 1st Movie '99 (V)
Felix the Cat: The Movie '91 (V)

Chynna Phillips (1968-)
Hollywood Homicide '03
Lone Hero '02
Stark Raving Mad '02
Red Water '01
Route 666 '01
A Better Way to Die '00
Hangman '00
Bats '99
Brokedown Palace '99
In a Class of His Own '99
Picking Up the Pieces '99
Supernova '99
Another Day in Paradise '98
The Big Hit '98
Courage Under Fire '96
Shadow of the Wolf '92
Extreme Justice '93
Ambition '91
The Dark Wind '91
Harley '90
A Show of Force '90
Young Guns 2 '90
Disorganized Crime '89
The First Power '89
Renegades '89
Dakota '88
Stand and Deliver '88
Young Guns '88
La Bamba '87
Trespasses '86

MacKenzie Phillips (1959-)
The Jacket '05
True Friends '98
How the West Was Fun '95
Dogfight '91

Michelle Phillips (1944-)
Kids in America '05
Harry and Max '04
Sweetwater: A True Rock Story '99
Army of One '94
Rubdown '93
Scissors '91
Let It Ride '89
Assault and Matrimony '87
American Anthem '86
Secrets of a Married Man '84
Sidney Sheldon's Bloodline '79
Valentino '77
The Death Squad '73
Dillinger '73

Nathan Phillips (1980-)
Redline '07
Snakes on a Plane '06
Wolf Creek '05

Robert Phillips (1925-)
The Car '77

The Killing of a Chinese Bookie '76
Adios Amigo '75
Mitchell '75
Detroit 9000 '73
Slaughter '72
MacKenna's Gold '69
The Dirty Dozen '67
Hour of the Gun '67
Cat Ballou '65
The Killers '64

Sally Phillips (1970-)
Bridget Jones: The Edge of Reason '04
Bridget Jones's Diary '01

Samantha (Sam) Phillips (1966-)
The Dallas Connection '94
Sexual Malice '93
Deceit '89
Phantasm 2 '88

Sian Phillips (1934-)
P.D. James: The Murder Room '04
Attila '01
The Aristocrats '99
Ivanhoe '97
Return of the Borrowers '96
The Vacillations of Poppy Carew '94
The Borrowers '93
Heidi '93
Valmont '89
The Doctor and the Devils '85
The Ewoks: Battle for Endor '85
Dune '84
Smiley's People '82
The Carpathian Eagle '81
Clash of the Titans '81
Nijinsky '80
Tinker, Tailor, Soldier, Spy '80
Murphy's War '71
Goodbye, Mr. Chips '69

Sydney Coale Phillips
Maximum Breakout '91
Cause of Death '90

Wendy Phillips (1953-)
Bugsy '91
Midnight Run '88
Death Be Not Proud '75

Max Phipps (1939-2000)
What the Moon Saw '90
Dark Age '88
Sky Pirates '87
The Blue Lightning '86
Nate and Hayes '83
Return of Captain Invincible '83
The Road Warrior '82

Nicholas Phipps (1913-80)
Captain's Paradise '53
Maytime in Mayfair '49
Elizabeth of Ladymead '48

William Phipps (1923-)
Cavalry Command '63
The War of the Worlds '53
Loan Shark '52
Cinderella '50 (V)
The Vanishing Westerner '50

Joaquin Rafael (Leaf) Phoenix (1974-)
Reservation Road '07
We Own the Night '07
Walk the Line '05
Hotel Rwanda '04
Ladder 49 '04
The Village '04
Brother Bear '03 (V)
It's All About Love '03
Signs '02
Gladiator '00
Quills '00
The Yards '00
Clay Pigeons '98

8mm '98
Return to Paradise '98
Inventing the Abbotts '97
U-Turn '97
To Die For '95
Parenthood '89
Russkies '87
SpaceCamp '86

Rain Phoenix (1973-)
Kids in America '05
Harry and Max '04
O '01
Spent '00
Even Cowgirls Get the Blues '94

River Phoenix (1970-93)
The Thing Called Love '93
Silent Tongue '92
Sneakers '92
Dogfight '91
My Own Private Idaho '91
I Love You to Death '90
Indiana Jones and the Last Crusade '89
Little Nikita '88
A Night in the Life of Jimmy Reardon '88
Running on Empty '88
The Mosquito Coast '86
Stand by Me '86
Explorers '85

Summer Phoenix (1978-)
The Believer '01
Dinner Rush '00
Esther Kahn '00
SLC Punk! '99
Girl '98

Maurice Pialat (1925-2003)
Under Satan's Sun '87
A Nos Amours '84
This Man Must Die '70

Jean Piat
Tower of Screaming Virgins '68
The Would-Be Gentleman '58

Ben Piazza (1934-91)
Guilty by Suspicion '91
Clean and Sober '88
Consenting Adult '85
Scene of the Crime '85
The Five of Me '81
The Children of An Lac '80
Nightwing '79
The Hanging Tree '59
A Dangerous Age '57

Tony Pica (1933-)
House of Psychotic Women '73
Yesterday, Today and Tomorrow '64

Robert Picardo (1953-)
Masters of Horror:
Homecoming '05
Small Soldiers '98
Menno's Mind '96
Star Trek: First Contact '96
Revenge of the Nerds 4: Nerds in Love '94
Runaway Daughters '94
Wagons East '94
White Mile '94
Matinee '92
Frame Up '91
Motorama '91
Gremlins 2: The New Batch '90
China Beach '88
976-EVIL '88
Innerspace '87
Jack's Back '87
Munchies '87
Back to School '86
Explorers '85

Michel Piccoli (1925-)
The Duchess of Langeais '07

Beaumarchais the Scoundrel '96
Party '96
Traveling Companion '96
One Hundred and One Nights '95
Martha and I '91
La Belle Noiseuse '90
May Fools '90
La Puritaine '86
Mauvais Sang '86
Peril '85
Dangerous Moves '84
Prize of Peril '84
Success Is the Best Revenge '84
La Passante '83
Beyond Obsession '82
La Nuit de Varennes '82
Passion '82
Atlantic City '81
L'Etat Sauvage '78
Spoiled Children '77
Mado '76
Vincent, Francois, Paul and the Others '76
Leonor '75
The Infernal Trio '74
Phantom of Liberty '74
Wedding in Blood '74
La Grande Bouffe '73
The Discreet Charm of the Bourgeoisie '72
Ten Days Wonder '72
The Things of Life '70
Topaz '69
Danger: Diabolik '68
The Milky Way '68
The Young Girls of Rochefort '68
Belle de Jour '67
The Game Is Over '66
La Guerre Est Finie '66
Lady L '65
Contempt '64
Diary of a Chambermaid '64
The Day and the Hour '63
Le Doulos '61
Death in the Garden '56

Paul Picerni (1922-)
Fearmaker '89
The Scalphunters '68
To Hell and Back '55
House of Wax '53

Irving Pichel (1891-1954)
How Green Was My Valley '41 (N)
Torture Ship '39
Dick Tracy '37
Dracula's Daughter '36
General Spanky '36
Badmen of Nevada '33
Oliver Twist '33

Jean-Francois Pichette
Mouvements du Desir '94
Being at Home with Claude '92

Joe Pichler (1987-)
Children On Their Birthdays '02
Beethoven's 4th '01
When Good Ghouls Go Bad '01
Beethoven's 3rd '00
Shiloh 2: Shiloh Season '99
Varsity Blues '98

John Pickard (1913-93)
Above and Beyond '53
Government Agents vs. Phantom Legion '51

Raymond Pickard (1982-)
The Borrowers '97
The Canterville Ghost '96

Sorrels Pickard (1940-2003)
Hardbodies '84
Running Hot '83

James Pickens, Jr. (1954-)
Venom '05
Home Room '02
Liberty Heights '99

Slim Pickens (1919-83) — continued
A Slight Case of Murder '99
RocketMan '97
Bloodhounds '96
Ghosts of Mississippi '96
Gridlock'd '96
Hot to Trot '88
Lily in Winter '94
Sharon's Secret '95
Sodbusters '94
Crazy Horse and Custer: "The Untold Story" '90
Charlie and the Great Balloon Chase '82
Pink Motel '82
The Howling '81
Story of a Cowboy Angel '81
The Swarm '78
Mr. Billion '77
Shadow of Chikara '77
The White Buffalo '77
Banjo Hackett '76
Hawmps! '76
Pony Express Rider '76
The Apple Dumpling Gang '75
Babe! '75
Rancho Deluxe '75
White Line Fever '75
Blazing Saddles '74
Legend of Earl Durand '74
Ginger in the Morning '73
Pat Garrett & Billy the Kid '73
Poor Pretty Eddie '73
The Cowboys '72
The Getaway '72
Iron Horsemen '71
Ride to Glory '71
Ballad of Cable Hogue '70
Never a Dull Moment '68
Rough Night in Jericho '67
Talion '66
Major Dundee '65
Dr. Strangelove, or: How I Learned to Stop Worrying and Love the Bomb '64
One-Eyed Jacks '61
The Desperate Mission '60
Phantom Stallion '54
Iron Mountain Trail '53
Shadows of Tombstone '53
Border Saddlemates '52
Colorado Sundown '52

Josh Picker
Beverly Hills Family Robinson '97
Alex '92
Flirting '89

Marc Pickering
Cashback '06
Sleepy Hollow '99

Sarah Pickering
Little Dorrit, Film 1: Nobody's Fault '88
Little Dorrit, Film 2: Little Dorrit's Story '88

Blake Pickett
Dark Universe '93
Haunted Ween '91

Bobby "Boris" Pickett (1940-)
Lobster Man from Mars '89
Frankenstein General Hospital '88
Hot Money '79

Cindy Pickett (1947-)
Hate Crime '05
The Stepdaughter '00
Atomic Dog '98
Coyote Summer '96
Painted Hero '95
Evolver '94
The Goodbye Bird '93
Sleepwalkers '92
Son-in-Law '93

Mary Pickford (1893-1979)
Coquette '29
The Taming of the Shrew '29
A Kiss for Mary Pickford '27
My Best Girl '27
Sparrows '26
Little Annie Rooney '25
Tess of the Storm Country '22
The Love Light '21
Pollyanna '20
Suds '20
Daddy Long Legs '19
Amarilly of Clothesline Alley '18
Pride of the Clan '18
Stella Maris '18
The Little American '17
A Poor Little Rich Girl '17
Rebecca of Sunnybrook Farm '17
Less in Love '94

Jim Piddock (1956-)
The Seeker: The Dark Is Rising '07
A Different Loyalty '04
For Your Consideration '06
Love for Rent '05

Christina Pickles (1938-)
The Family Holiday '07
Sol Goode '01
Angels Don't Sleep Here '00
Murder She Purred: A Mrs. Murphy Mystery '98
That Forsyte Woman '50
Distraction '05
The Wedding Singer '97
William Shakespeare's Romeo and Juliet '96
Revenge of the Nerds 4: Nerds in Love '94
Seizure '74

Vivian Pickles (1933-)
Candleshoe '78
Elizabeth R '72
Harold and Maude '71
Sunday, Bloody Sunday '71

Ronald Pickup (1941-)
The Christmas Miracle of Jonathan Toomey '07
The Attic: The Hiding of Anne Frank '88
The Mission '86
Eleni '85
Ivanhoe '82
Life of Verdi '82
Nijinsky '80
Scarlet '94
The Rector's Wife '94
My Friend Walter '93
Journey of Honor '91
Dr. Bethune '90
Jekyll and Hyde '90
A Murder of Quality '90

Jacques Pieller
Wedding in Blood '74

Adrienne Pierce
Styx '00
Warriors from Hell '90

Bradley Michael Pierce (1982-)
The Town Is Quiet '00
Three Lives and Only One Death '96
Jumanji '95
Beauty and the Beast '91

Brock Pierce (1938-)
The Christmas Miracle of Jonathan Toomey '07
This Sweet Sickness '77
The Best Way '76
Phantom of Liberty '74
First Kid '96
Legend of the Lost Tomb '97

Claude Pieplu (1956-)
The Undercover Kid '95

Charles B. Pierce (1938-)
Boggy Creek II '83
Grayeagle '77
Town That Dreaded Sundown '76
Winterhawk '76

Frederic Pierrot (1960-)
They Came Back '04
Monsieur N. '33
The Girl from Paris '02
Artemisia '97
For Ever Mozart '97
Land and Freedom '95

Sarah Pierse
Heavenly Creatures '94

Eric Pierpoint (1950-)
Liar Liar '97
Alien Nation: Millennium '96
Alien Nation: The Enemy Within '96
Little Witches '96
Where Truth Lies '96
Alien Nation: Body and Soul '95
The Stranger '95
Alien Nation: Dark Horizon '94
Sex, Love and Cold Hard Cash '93

Olivier Pierre (1953-)
The Lonely Lady '83
The Sender '82

David Hyde Pierce
Hellboy '04 (V)
Down With Love '03
Full Frontal '02
Treasure Planet '22 (V)
Osmosis Jones '01 (V)
We: Not America's Summer '01
Chain of Fools '00
Isn't She Great '00
The Winslow Boy '98
Jackie's Back '99
The Spanish Prisoner '97
Homicide '91
Shopgirl '05
Heist '01
State and Main '00
The Dawning '88
Little Man Tate '91
Wolf '94
Nixon '95
A Bug's Life '98 (V)

Rebecca Pidgeon (1963-)
Redbelt '08
Jesse Stone: Sea Change '07

Walter Pidgeon (1897-1984)
Sextette '78
The Lindbergh Kidnapping Case '76
Two Minute Warning '76
Murder on Flight 502 '75
Neptune Factor '73
Big Red '62
Voyage to the Bottom of the Sea '61
Advise and Consent '62
Cinderella '64
Funny Girl '68
The Glass Slipper '55 (N)
Forbidden Planet '56
Hit the Deck '55
Deep in My Heart '54
Executive Suite '54
The Last Time I Saw Paris '54
Blackmail '39
Men of the Fighting Lady '54
The Bad and the Beautiful '52
Million Dollar Mermaid '52
Quo Vadis '51 (N)
The Miniver Story '50
Command Decision '48
Julia Misbehaves '48
Cass Timberlane '47
Holiday in Mexico '46
If Winter Comes '47
Weekend at the Waldorf '45
Mrs. Parkington '44
Madame Curie '43
White Cargo '42
Mrs. Miniver '42
Blossoms in the Dust '41
How Green Was My Valley '41
Dark Command '40
House Across the Bay '40
It's a Date '40
Shopworn Angel '38
Too Hot to Handle '38
Saratoga '37

Norman Pierce
The Four Feathers '39

Jill Pierce
Omega Doom '96
Cyborg Soldier '94
Darkroom '90

Justin Pierce (1975-2000)
Next Friday '00
Enemy Unseen '91
A Rage in Harlem '91
Murphy's Fault '88
Night Call Nurses '72

Tony Pierce
Big Bully '95
Trancers 3: Deth Lives '92

Preston Pierce
Ticket of Leave Man '37

Stack Pierce
24 Hours to Midnight '92

Wendell Pierce (1962-)
I Think I Love My Wife '07
Life Support '07
A Hole in One '04
Ray '04
Brown Sugar '02
The 24 Hour Woman '99
Bulworth '98
Get On the Bus '96
Hackers '95
Bye Bye, Love '94
It Could Happen to You '94
Family Business '89

Tim Pigott-Smith (1946-)
V for Vendetta '06
Johnny English '03
Alexander '04
Bloody Sunday '01
The Remains of the Day '93
The Jewel in the Crown '84
The Hunchback of Notre Dame '97
The Lost Boys '73

Luciano Pigozzi
Whiskey Mountain '77
I Spit on Your Corpse '74

Rosamund Pike (1979-)
Fracture '07
Doom '05
The Libertine '05
Pride and Prejudice '05
Die Another Day '02

Mitch Pileggi (1952-)
The X-Files: I Want to Believe '08
Gun Shy '00
The X-Files '98
Shocker '89

Nova Pilbeam (1919-)
Counterblast '48
Young and Innocent '37
Nine Days a Queen '36
The Man Who Knew Too Much '34

Joe Pilato (1949-)
Fatal Passion '94
Married People, Single Sex '93
Day of the Dead '85

Chris Pine (1980-)
Smokin' Aces '07
Blind Dating '06
Just My Luck '06
The Princess Diaries 2: Royal Engagement '04

Larry Pine
True Romance '93
The Cleaning '04
2 Brothers & a Bride '03
The Shipping News '01
Let It Snow '99
A Stranger in the Kingdom '98

Lorraine Pilkington (1975-)
Human Traffic '99
The Nephew '97
The Last of the High Kings '96
The Miracle '91

Phillip Pine (1920-)
Bonnie's Pictures '78
Money to Burn '83
Pot, Parents, and Police '71
The Lost Missile '58
Men in War '57
The Phantom from 10,000 Leagues '56

Robert Pine (1941-)
Lost Voyage '01
Body Count '97
Sins of the Mind '97
Independence Day '96
Are You Lonesome Tonight '92
Mysterious Two '82
Enola Gay: The Men, the Mission, the Atomic Bomb '80
Empire of the Ants '77
Munster, Go Home! '66
The Collectors '99
Sex & Mrs. X '00
The Ultimate Weapon '99
Poltergeist: The Legacy '96

Alison Pill (1985-)
Dan in Real Life '07
Dear Wendy '05
Confessions of a Teenage Drama Queen '04
A Separate Peace '04
Pieces of April '03
Baby '00
The Pilot's Wife '01
Skipped Parts '00

Soren Pilmark (1955-)
Flickering Lights '21
The Kingdom 2 '97
The Kingdom '94

Jeffrey Pillars
Bloodmoon '97

Daniel Pilon (1940-)
Ernest Rides Again '93
The Last of the High Kings '96
The Kingdom 2 '97
Left Behind: The Movie '00
Short Eyes '79

Donald Pilon (1941-)
It's My Turn, Laura Cadieux '98
A Wind from Wyoming '94
Keeping Track '86
Left for Dead '78
The Pyx '73

Silvia Pinal (1931-)
Viridiana '61
Simon of the Desert '66
The Exterminating Angel '62

Bronson Pinchot (1959-)
Second Best '05
Winning Girls Through Psychic Mind Control '02
Out of the Cold '99
All New Adventures of Laurel and Hardy: For Love or Mummy '98
Quest for Camelot '98 (V)
Courage Under Fire '96
The First Wives Club '96
It's My Party '95
Stephen King's The Langoliers '95
Beverly Hills Cop 3 '94
The Great American Sex Scandal '94
True Romance '93
Blame It on the Bellboy '92
Second Sight '89
After Hours '85
Beverly Hills Cop '84
Hot Resort '85
Risky Business '83

Angela Pietropinto
Strapless '90
Smart Money '88
Goodfellas '90
Honeymoon in Vegas '92
It Could Happen to You '94
Shaft '00
Finding North '97
Welcome to the Dollhouse '95

Alexandra Pigg (1962-)
Bullseye! '90
Chicago Joe & the Showgirl '90

Geoffrey Pierson (1949-)
The Navigator '88
Sleeping Dogs Lie '05
Spartan '04
Snowballin' '71
The Red Half-Breed '70
In Trouble '62
Venomous '01

Miguel Pinero (1946-88)
Almost You '85
Alphabet City '84
Short Eyes '79

John Pinette (1962-)
The Punisher '04
My 5 Wives '00
Simon Sez '99

Jada Pinkett Smith (1971-)
Reign Over Me '07
Madagascar '05 (V)
Collateral '04
The Matrix Reloaded '03
The Matrix Revolutions '03
Ali '01
Kingdom Come '01
Bamboozled '00
Princess Mononoke '98 (V)
Return to Paradise '98
Scream 2 '97
Woo '97
If These Walls Could Talk '96
The Nutty Professor '96
Set It Off '96
The Inkwell '94
Jason's Lyric '94
A Low Down Dirty Shame '94
Tales from the Crypt Presents Demon Knight '94
Menace II Society '93

Rob Pinkston
The Sasquatch Gang '06
The Derby Stallion '05

Arnold Pinnock
Twitches Too '07
Twitches '05
Must Be Santa '99

Danny Pino
Flicka '06
Rx '06

Dominique Pinon (1955-)
When Evil Calls '06
A Very Long Engagement '04
Amelie '01
Like a Fish Out of Water '99
Alien: Resurrection '97
The City of Lost Children '95
Alberto Express '92
Delicatessen '92
Moon in the Gutter '83
Diva '82

Gordon Pinsent (1930-)
Away From Her '06
The Confessor '04
Saint Ralph '04
Fallen Angel '03
The Shipping News '01
Pale Saints '97
A Vow to Kill '94
Blood Clan '91
Babar: The Movie '88 (V)
John and the Missus '87
Who Has Seen the Wind? '77
Newman's Law '74
Blacula '72
Colossus: The Forbin Project '70
The Thomas Crown Affair '68

Leah K. Pinsent (1968-)
Virus '96
The Little Kidnappers '90
Brutal Glory '89
Double Identity '89
April Fool's Day '86
The Bay Boy '85

Danny Pintauro (1976-)
The Great American Sex Scandal '94
The Beniker Gang '83
Cujo '83

Harold Pinter (1930-)
Wit '01
The Tailor of Panama '00
Mansfield Park '99
Breaking the Code '95
Accident '67

Billie Piper
Mansfield Park '07
Ruby in the Smoke '06

Frederick Piper (1902-79)
The Frightened City '61

Juliet of the Spirits '65
Hue and Cry '47
San Demetrio, London '47
Johnny Frenchman '46
Pink String and Sealing Wax '45
Nine Men '43
Oh, Mr. Porter '37
Sabotage '36

Kelly Piper
Rawhead Rex '87
Maniac '80

Roddy Piper (1951-)
Kickin' It Old Skool '07
Honor '06
Cybercity '99
Shepherd '99
The Bad Pack '98
Dead Tides '97
First Encounter '97
Marked Man '96
Sci-Fighters '96
Terminal Rush '96
Jungleground '95
Back in Action '94
Immortal Combat '94
No Contest '94
Tough and Deadly '94
Buy & Cell '89
Hell Comes to Frogtown '88
They Live '88
Body Slam '87

Grant Piro
Darkness Falls '03
The Outsider '02
Mr. Accident '99

Mark Pirro (1956-)
Curse of the Queerwolf '87
A Polish Vampire in Burbank '80

Carlo Pisacane (1891-)
Joyful Laughter '60
Paisan '46

Joe Piscopo (1951-)
Dead Lenny '06
Bartleby '01
Captain Nuke and the Bomber Boys '95
Open Season '95
Two Bits & Pepper '95
Huck and the King of Hearts '93
Sidekicks '93
Dead Heat '88
Wise Guys '86
Johnny Dangerously '84
American Tickler '76
King Kong '76

Marie-France Pisier (1944-)
The Ice Rink '99
Time Regained '99
Son of Gascogne '95
Prize of Peril '84
Hot Touch '82
Chanel Solitaire '81
Miss Right '81
French Postcards '79
We Will Not Enter the Forest '79
Love on the Run '78
The Other Side of Midnight '77
Barocco '76
Cousin, Cousine '76
Celine and Julie Go Boating '74
Nous N'Irons Plus au Bois '69

Luigi Pistilli (1930-96)
Your Vice is a Closed Room and Only I Have the Key '72
The Case of the Scorpion's Tail '71
The Scorpion's Tail '71
Twitch of the Death Nerve '71
The Libertine '69
The Good, the Bad and the Ugly '67

Kimberly Pistone
WhiteForce '88
Blue De Ville '86

Mario Pisu (1910-76)
The Sensuous Nurse '76

Hedwig and the Angry Inch '00

Carl Pitti (1917-2003)
Gun Glory '57
Tribute to a Bad Man '56
Billy the Kid '41

Tom Pittman
Invasion of the Bee Girls '73
The Zodiac Killer '71

Jacob Pitts
21 '08
Eurotrip '04

Zasu Pitts (1898-1963)
It's a Mad, Mad, Mad, Mad World '63
The Thrill of It All! '63
This Could Be the Night '57
Francis Joins the WACs '54
The Denver & Rio Grande '51
Francis the Talking Mule '49
Life with Father '47
Breakfast in Hollywood '46
The Perfect Marriage '46
The Bashful Bachelor '42
Meet the Mob '42
Mexican Spitfire at Sea '42
Broadway Limited '41
No, No Nanette '40
Eternally Yours '39
Nurse Edith Cavell '39
Sing Me a Love Song '37
Way Out West '37
Hot Tip '35
Ruggles of Red Gap '35
Dames '34
Mrs. Wiggs of the Cabbage Patch '34
Sing and Like It '34
Two Alone '34
Aggie Appleby, Maker of Men '33
Mr. Skitch '33
The Crooked Circle '32
Justice Rides Again '32
Strangers of the Evening '32
The Guardsman '31
Lottery Bride '30
Monte Carlo '30
Sin Takes a Holiday '30
Risky Business '28
Sunny Side Up '28
The Wedding March '28
Greed '24

Byrne Piven (1929-2002)
Madison '01
Wavelength '96

Jeremy Piven (1965-)
The Kingdom '07
Smokin' Aces '07
Keeping Up with the Steins '06
Two for the Money '05
Chasing Liberty '04
Old School '03
Runaway Jury '03
Scary Movie 3 '03
Black Hawk Down '01
Highway '01
Rush Hour 2 '01
Serendipity '01
The Crew '00
Family Man '00
Red Letters '00
Phoenix '98
Very Bad Things '98
Don King: Only in America '97
Grosse Pointe Blank '97
Just Write '97
Kiss the Girls '97
Music from Another Room '97
The Real Thing '97
Larger Than Life '96
Wavelength '96
Heat '95
Miami Rhapsody '95
Car 54, Where Are You? '94
Floundering '94
P.C.U. '94

Twogether '94
Judgment Night '93
12:01 '93
Bob Roberts '92
Singles '92
Body Chemistry 2: Voice of a Stranger '91
The Grifters '90
Say Anything '89
Eternal '04
The Rendering '02
Swindle '02

Lou Place (1912-)
Apache Woman '55
Swamp Women '55

Mary Kay Place (1947-)
Lonesome Jim '06
Nine Lives '05
Evergreen '04
Killer Diller '04
Latter Days '04
Silver City '04
Human Nature '02
Sweet Home Alabama '02
My First Mister '01
The Safety of Objects '01
A Woman's a Helluva Thing '01
Being John Malkovich '99
Girl, Interrupted '99
Pecker '98
Eye of God '97
John Grisham's The Rainmaker '97
Citizen Ruth '96
Manny & Lo '96
My Very Best Friend '96
Teresa's Tattoo '94
Armistead Maupin's Tales of the City '93
Captain Ron '92
Samantha '92
Bright Angel '91
Crazy from the Heart '91
A New Life '88
Portrait of a White Marriage '88
The Girl Who Spelled Freedom '86
Explorers '85
Smooth Talk '85
For Love or Money '84
The Big Chill '83
Waltz across Texas '83
Modern Problems '81
Private Benjamin '80
More American Graffiti '79
Starting Over '79
New York, New York '77

Michele Placido (1946-)
Searching for Paradise '02
Lamerica '95
Drug Wars 2: The Cocaine Cartel '92
Forever Mary '89
Private Affairs '89
Big Business '88
Summer Night with Greek Profile, Almond Eyes & Scent of Basil '87
The Sicilian Connection '85
Three Brothers '80
Ernesto '79

Tony Plana (1953-)
The Dead One '07
Goal! The Dream Begins '06
The Lost City '05
Cuban Blood '03 (V)
Fidel '02
Half Past Dead '02
Noriega: God's Favorite '00
Backlash '99
My Little Assassin '99
187 '97
Santa Fe '97
Sub Down '97
Primal Fear '96
The Burning Season '94
A Million to Juan '94
JFK '91
One Good Cop '91

Drug Wars: The Camarena Story '90
Havana '90
In the Line of Duty: A Cop for the Killing '90
Sweet 15 '90
Why Me? '90
The Hillside Strangler '89
Romero '89
Break of Dawn '88
Born in East L.A. '87
Salvador '86
Latino '85

Roger Planchon (1931-)
The Return of Martin Guerre '83

Nigel Planer (1955-)
Roads to the South '78
Mr. Toad's Wild Ride '96
Supergrass '87

Scott Plank (1958-2002)
Holes '03
Frozen in Fear '00
Moonbase '97
Marshal Law '96
Without Evidence '96
Saints and Sinners '95
Dying to Remember '93
Red Shoe Diaries 4: Auto Erotica '93
Pastime '91
The In Crowd '88

Dana Plato (1964-99)
Blade Boxer '97
High School USA '84
Return to Boggy Creek '77
Beyond the Bermuda Triangle '75

Edward Platt (1916-74)
Atlantis, the Lost Continent '61
North by Northwest '59
The Rebel Set '59
Gunman's Walk '58
Designing Woman '57
Rock, Pretty Baby '56
Written on the Wind '56
Rebel without a Cause '55

Louise Platt (1915-2003)
Captain Caution '40
Stagecoach '39
Spawn of the North '38

Marc Platt (1913-)
Tonight and Every Night '45
Down to Earth '47

Oliver Platt (1960-)
The Ten '07
Casanova '05
The Ice Harvest '05
Loverboy '05
Kinsey '04
Pieces of April '03
Ash Wednesday '02
Liberty Stands Still '02
ZigZag '02
Don't Say a Word '01
Gun Shy '00
Ready to Rumble '00
Bicentennial Man '99
Martian Child '07
Lake Placid '99
Three to Tango '99
Bulworth '98
Dangerous Beauty '98
Dr. Dolittle '98
The Imposters '98
Simon Birch '98
Executive Decision '96
A Time to Kill '96
The Infiltrator '95
Tall Tale: The Unbelievable Adventures of Pecos Bill '95
Funny Bones '94
Benny & Joon '93
Indecent Proposal '93
The Temp '93
The Three Musketeers '93
Beethoven '92
Diggstown '92
Flatliners '91

Postcards from the Edge '90
Working Girl '88

Alice Playten (1947-)
Doug's 1st Movie '99 (V)
Felix the Cat: The Movie '91 (V)
Legend '86

Angela Pleasence (1941-)
the Favor, the Watch, & the Very Big Fish '92
Stealing Heaven '88
A Christmas Carol '84
The Godsend '80
Six Wives of Henry VIII '71

Donald Pleasence (1919-95)
Halloween 6: The Curse of Michael Myers '95
The Advocate '93
Shadows and Fog '92
Millions '90
River of Death '90
American Tiger '89
Buried Alive '89
Casablanca Express '89
Halloween 5: The Revenge of Michael Myers '89
Ten Little Indians '89
Django Strikes Again '87
Phantom of Death '87
Prince of Darkness '87
The Great Escape 2: The Untold Story '88
Ground Zero '88
Specters '87
Warrior Queen '87
Hanna's War '88
The House of Usher '88
Into the Darkness '86
Arch of Triumph '85
Creepers '85
The Monster Club '85
Mansfield Park '85
Operation 'Nam '85
Nothing Underneath '85
Alone in the Dark '82
Halloween 2: The Nightmare Isn't Over! '81
Warrior of the Lost World '84
Escape from New York '81
The Puma Man '80
Power Play '81
All Quiet on the Western Front '79
Better Late Than Never '79
Dracula '79
Gold of the Amazon Women '79
Jaguar Lives '79
Night Creature '79
The Bastard '78
The Dark Secret of Harvest Home '78 (N)
Halloween '78
Sgt. Pepper's Lonely Hearts Club Band '78
The Uncanny '77
Blood Relatives '77
The Eagle Has Landed '77
Goldenrod '77
Land of the Minotaur '77
Oh, God! '77
Telefon '77
Tomorrow Never Comes '77
Choice of Weapons '76
The Last Tycoon '76
Escape to Witch Mountain '75
Hearts of the West '75
I Don't Want to Be Born '75
The Passover Plot '75
Barry McKenzie Holds His Own '74
The Black Windmill '74
The Count of Monte Cristo '74
Journey into Fear '74
Dr. Jekyll and Mr. Hyde '73
The Freakmaker '73
From Beyond the Grave '73
The Rainbow Gang '73
Tales That Witness Madness '73
Wedding in White '72
House of the Damned '71
The Shaming '71
THX 1138 '71
Soldier Blue '70
The Madwoman of Chaillot '69
Night of the Generals '67
You Only Live Twice '67
Will Penny '67
Cul de Sac '66
Fantastic Voyage '66
The Greatest Story Ever Told '65
The Hallelujah Trail '65
The Great Escape '63
What a Carve-Up! '62
Horsemasters '61
The Flesh and the Fiends '60
The Hands of Orlac '60
No Love for Johnnie '60
The Battle of the Sexes '60
Circus of Horrors '60
A Tale of Two Cities '58
Look Back in Anger '58
1984 '56
The Caretaker

Suzanne Pleshette (1937-2008)
Spirited Away '01 (V)
The Lion King: Simba's Pride '98 (V)
Battling for Baby '92
The Queen of Mean '90
Alone in the Neon Jungle '87
Dixie: Changing Habits '85
Kojak: The Belarus File '85
For Love or Money '84
One Cooks, the Other Doesn't '83
Help Wanted: Male '82
Hot Stuff '80
Oh, God! Book 2 '80
If Things Were Different '79
The Shaggy D.A. '76
Legend of Valentino '75
Support Your Local Gunfighter '71
Suppose They Gave a War and Nobody Came? '70
If It's Tuesday, This Must Be Belgium '69
Blackbeard's Ghost '68
The Adventures of Bullwhip Griffin '67
Nevada Smith '66
The Ugly Dachshund '65
Mr. Wrong '95
The Birds '63
40 Pounds of Trouble '62
Rome Adventure '62
A Pyromaniac's Love Story '95
The Scarlet Letter '95
Sorento Beach '95
A Place for Annie '94
The Geisha Boy '58

John Pleshette (1942-)
Like Mike '02
The Curse of Inferno '96
Eye of the Stranger '93
Lies of the Twins '91
Burning Rage '84
The Kid with the Broken Halo '82

Jesse Plemons (1988-)
Children On Their Birthdays '02
Like Mike '02
James Dean '01

George Plimpton (1927-2003)
Just Visiting '01
Just Cause '94
Little Man Tate '91
Easy Wheels '89
A Fool and His Money '88
Volunteers '85
Stair '92
And a Nightingale Sang '91
Rio Lobo '70
The Detective '68

Martha Plimpton (1970-)
The Sleepy Time Gal '01
The Defenders: Taking the First '98
Pecker '98
200 Cigarettes '98
The Defenders: Payback '97
Eye of God '97
I Love You to Death '90
The Mosquito Coast '86
Parenthood '89
Shy People '87
Samantha '92
Silence Like Glass '90
Stanley and Iris '90
Running on Empty '88
Another Woman '88
Stars and Bars '88
Josh and S.A.M. '93

Jack Plotnick (1968-)
Down With Love '06
Sleeping Dogs Lie '06
Rollover '81
Say It Isn't So '01
Gods and Monsters '98
Chairman of the Board '97

Anna-Louise Plowman (1975-)
The Foreigner '03
Cambridge Spies '03

Joan Plowright (1929-)
The Spiderwick Chronicles '08
Curious George '06 (V)
Bringing Down the House '03
I Am David '04
Callas Forever '02
Rock My World '02
Back to the Secret Garden '01
Dinosaur '00 (V)
Tea with Mussolini '99
Alexandra '04
Aldrich Ames: Traitor Within '98
Dance with Me '98
The Assistant '97
Jane Eyre '96
101 Dalmatians '96
Surviving Picasso '96
A Pyromaniac's Love Story '95

Hilda Plowright (1890-1973)
Home Town Story '51
Mrs. Palfrey at the Claremont '05

Melinda Plowman
Billy the Kid Versus Dracula '66

Amanda Plummer (1957-)
Satan's Little Helper '04
My Life Without Me '03
Get a Clue '02
Triggermen '02
Seven Days to Live '01
3 1/2 Women '99
Forbidden Choices '96
Butterfly Kiss '94
Pulp Fiction '94
Last Light '93
Needful Things '93
Nostradamus '93
So I Married an Axe Murderer '93
Freejack '92
Miss Rose White '92
Joe Versus the Volcano '90
Prisoners of Inertia '89
Gryphon '88
Riders to the Sea '88
Courtship '87
Made in Heaven '87
Static '87
The Dollmaker '84
Daniel '83
The World According to Garp '82

Eve Plumb (1958-)
Nowhere '96
...And God Spoke '94
I'm Gonna Git You Sucka '88
Last Summer in the Hamptons '95

Christopher Plummer (1927-)
Beautiful Girls '96
Drowning by Numbers '89
Revolution '85
Brimstone & Treacle '82
Britannia Hospital '82
Eyes of Laura Mars '78
Equus '77
The Merchant of Venice '73
Time Without Pity '57
The Entertainer '60
Alexander the Other Side of Dawn '77
Force of Evil '77
The Day That Shook the World '78
International Velvet '78
The Silent Partner '78
Star Crash '78
Conduct Unbecoming '75
The Man Who Would Be King '75
Return of the Pink Panther '74
The Pyx '73
Waterloo '71
Battle of Britain '69
The Night of the Generals '67
Triple Cross '67
Inside Daisy Clover '65
The Sound of Music '65
The Fall of the Roman Empire '64
A Doll's House '59
Stage Struck '57
The Amateur '82
Eyewitness '81
Somewhere in Time '80
Hanover Street '79
Murder by Decree '79
The Assignment '78
Riel '79

Glenn Plummer (1966-)
The Longshots '08
Saw II '05
The Day After Tomorrow '04
Baadasssss! '03
Shade '03
Foolhardy Junkies '02
The Salton Sea '02
MacArthur Park '01
Rangers '00
Thursday '98
Spy Games '99
One Night Stand '97
Pronto '97
Speed 2: Cruise Control '97
The Corner '00
Love Beat the Hell Outta Me '00
Interceptor Force '99
Lucky Break '01
American Tragedy '00
A Beautiful Mind '01
Nicholas Nickleby '02
The Lake House '06
Must Love Dogs '05
The New World '05
Syriana '05

Clarence Poesy
In Bruges '08
Harry Potter and the Goblet of Fire '05

Ken Pogue
Johnson County War '02
Crossfire Trail '01
Out of Time '00
The 6th Day '00
The Jack Bull '99
National Lampoon's Dad's Week Off '97
Rhapsody '97
Ruby's Bucket of Blood '01
Bad Moon '96
In the Lake of the Woods '96

Judith Pogany
The Midas Touch '89
A Hungarian Fairy Tale '87

Kathryn Pogson
Millions '05
Over Indulgence '87
The Company of Wolves '85

Amy Poehler (1971-)
Baby Mama '08
Blades of Glory '07
Mr. Woodcock '07
Shrek the Third '07 (V)
Tenacious D in the Pick of Destiny '06
Envy '04
Mean Girls '04
Wet Hot American Summer '01

Gerard Plunkett
Convict Cowboy '95
Showgirls '95
Strange Days '95
Things to Do in Denver When You're Dead '95
Dolores Claiborne '95
Wolf '94
12 Monkeys '95
Bergeron '95
Crackerjack '94
Malcolm X '92
Rock-a-Doodle '92 (V)
Star Trek 6: The Undiscovered Country '91

Werner Pochath (1939-93)
Where the Heart Is '90
Light Years '88 (V)
Shadow Dancing '88
Souvenir '88
Dragnet '87
I Love N.Y. '87
An American Tail '86 (V)
The Boss' Wife '86
Boy in Blue '86
Many Faces of Sherlock Holmes '85
Lily in Love '85
Dreamscape '84
Ordeal by Innocence '84
Prototype '83
The Scarlet & the Black '83
The Thorn Birds '83

Rossana Podesta (1934-)
The Sensual Man '74
The Virgin of Nuremberg '65
Sodom and Gomorrah '62
Helen of Troy '56
Ulysses '55

Rick Podell (1946-)
World Gone Wild '88
Lunch Wagon '81

Denis Podalydes (1963-)
Almost Peaceful '02
Comedy of Innocence '00
Children of the Century '99
Pas Tres Catholique '93
Alone Against Rome '62

Fernando Poe, Jr. (1939-2004)
Baby Monitor: Sound of Fear '94
My Husband's Secret Life '98
Speed '94
Menace II Society '93
South Central '92
Pastime '91
Colors '88
Skeletons '96
Kurt Vonnegut's Harrison Bergeron '95
Eight Men Out '88
Two for the Money '05
A Cooler Climate '99

Eric Pohlmann (1913-79)
Second Wind '76, Tiffany Jones '75, Glass Tomb '55, Terror Street '54, The Belles of St. Trinian's '53, Mogambo '53, Three Stops to Murder '53, The Gambler & the Lady '52, Moulin Rouge '52, Blackout '50

Larry Poindexter (1959)
S.W.A.T. '03, Black Horizon '01, Poison '01, Steel Sharks '97, Body Chemistry 4: Full Exposure '95, Sorcerers '94, Blue Movies '88, American Ninja 2: The Confrontation '87

Priscilla Pointer (1924-)
Carried Away '95, Grosse Fatigue '94, A Pure Formality '94, Back in the USSR '92, The Magic Bubble '93, Disturbed '90, A Nightmare on Elm Street 3: Dream Warriors '87, Blue Velvet '86, Rumpelstiltskin '86, The Falcon and the Snowman '85, Mysterious Two '82, Archer: The Fugitive from the Empire '81, The Competition '80, Honeysuckle Rose '80, The Onion Field '79

Jean Poiret (1926-92)
The Elegant Criminal '92, The Last Metro '80

Earl C. Poitier (1974-)
Drumline '02, Remember the Titans '00

Sidney Poitier (1924-)
The Simple Life of Noah Dearborn '99, Free of Eden '98, The Jackal '97, Mandela and de Klerk '97, A Good Day to Die '95, Sneakers '92, Separate but Equal '91, Little Nikita '88, Shoot to Kill '88, Piece of the Action '77, Let's Do It Again '75, Uptown Saturday Night '74, Buck and the Preacher '72, The Organization '71, Brother John '70, They Call Me Mr. Tibbs! '70, The Lost Man '69, For Love of Ivy '68, Guess Who's Coming to Dinner '67, In the Heat of the Night '67, To Sir, with Love '67, Duel at Diablo '66, Bedford Incident '65, The Greatest Story Ever Told '65, A Patch of Blue '65, The Slender Thread '65, The Long Ships '64, Lilies of the Field '63, Pressure Point '62, Paris Blues '61, A Raisin in the Sun '61, All the Young Men '60, The Defiant Ones '58, Band of Angels '57, The Mark of the Hawk '57, Something of Value '57, Goodbye, My Lady '56, Blackboard Jungle '55, Red Ball Express '52, Cry, the Beloved Country '51, No Way Out '50

Sydney Tamiia Poitier (1973-)
Death Proof '07, Nine Lives '05, MacArthur Park '01, Noah's Ark '99, True Crime '99, Free of Eden '98

Simon Poland
Nemesis 4: Cry of Angels '97, Alien from L.A. '87

Roman Polanski (1933-)
Zemsta '02, A Pure Formality '94, Back in the USSR '92, The Tenant '76, Andy Warhol's Dracula '74, Chinatown '74, Diary of Forbidden Dreams '73, Ciao Federico! Fellini Directs Satyricon '69, The Magic Christian '69, The Fearless Vampire Killers '67, Innocent Sorcerers '60, A Generation '54

Victor Poletti
Meeting Venus '91, And the Ship Sails On '83

Maurice Poli
Gangster's Law '86, Five Dolls for an August Moon '70

Mark Polish (1972-)
The Astronaut Farmer '07, The Bridge of San Luis Rey '05, The Good Thief '03, Northfork '03, Twin Falls Idaho '99

Michael Polish (1972-)
The Bridge of San Luis Rey '05, The Good Thief '03, Northfork '03, Twin Falls Idaho '99

Jon Polito (1950-)
American Gangster '07, Cougar Club '07, Big Nothing '06, Grilled '06, The Family Plan '05, The Honeymooners '05, The Last Shot '04, The Box '03, The Singing Detective '03, Women vs. Men '02, The Man Who Wasn't There '01, Mimic 2 '01, The Adventures of Rocky & Bullwinkle '00, Homicide: The Movie '00, Angel's Dance '99, Blankman '94, Girls in Prison '94, The Crow '93, Fallen Angels 2 '93, Barton Fink '91, The Freshman '90, Leather Jackets '90, Miller's Crossing '90, Deadly Business '86, Fire with Fire '86, Highlander '86

Lina Polito (1954-)
All Screwed Up '74

Haydee Politoff (1946-)
Dracula's Great Love '72, La Collectionneuse '67

Vic Polizos
Light It Up '99, Winchell '98

Oscar Polk (1899-1949)
Gone with the Wind '39, Green Pastures '36

Stephen Polk
Cherish '02

Ben Pollack (1903-71)
The Benny Goodman Story '55

Sydney Pollack (1934-)
Made of Honor '08, Michael Clayton '07, Avenue Montaigne '06, The Interpreter '05, Changing Lanes '02, Eyes Wide Shut '99, Random Hearts '99, A Civil Action '98, Death Becomes Her '92, Husbands and Wives '92, The Player '92, Tootsie '82

Cheryl Pollak (1967-)
Art House '98, No Strings Attached '98, Betty '97, Sin and Redemption '94, Crossing the Bridge '92, Night Life '90, Pump Up the Volume '90, Swimsuit '89, The Dark Side of the Sun '88

Kevin Pollak (1958-)
My Best Friend Is a Vampire '88, Numb '07, Niagara Motel '06, The Santa Clause 3: The Escape Clause '06, Hostage '05, The Whole Ten Yards '04, Frank McKlusky, C.I. '02, Juwanna Mann '02, The Santa Clause 2 '02, Stolen Summer '02, Dr. Dolittle 2 '01, 3000 Miles to Graceland '01, The Wedding Planner '01, Deterrence '00, Steal This Movie! '00, The Whole Nine Yards '00, Deal of a Lifetime '99, End of Days '99, She's All That '99, From the Earth to the Moon '98, Hoods '98, Outside Ozona '98, Ruby Bridges '98, National Lampoon's The Don's Analyst '97, Truth or Consequences, N.M. '97, House Arrest '96, That Thing You Do! '96, Casino '95, Chameleon '95, Grumpier Old Men '95, Miami Rhapsody '95, The Usual Suspects '95, Canadian Bacon '94, Clean Slate '94, Grumpy Old Men '93, Indian Summer '93, The Opposite Sex and How to Live With Them '93, Wayne's World 2 '93, A Few Good Men '92, Another You '91, L.A. Story '91, Ricochet '91

Sarah Polley (1979-)
John Adams '08, Beowulf & Grendel '06, Don't Come Knocking '05, Dawn of the Dead '04, Siblings '04, The Event '03, My Life Without Me '03, No Such Thing '01, The Claim '00, Love Come Down '00, The Weight of Water '00, eXistenZ '99, Go '99, Guinevere '99, The Life Before This '99, Last Night '98, White Lies '98, The Hanging Garden '97, Junior's Groove '97, The Sweet Hereafter '96, Exotica '94, Lantern Hill '90, The Adventures of Baron Munchausen '89, Babar: The Movie '88 (V), Big Town '87

Tracy Pollan (1960-)
The Kennedys of Massachusetts '95, A Stranger Among Us '92, Danielle Steel's Fine Things '90, Bright Lights, Big City '88, Promised Land '88, The Abduction of Kari Swenson '87, The Tender Age '84, Baby It's You '82

Daphne Pollard (1890-1978)
Our Relations '36, Bonnie Scotland '35, The Lady Refuses '31

Michael J. Pollard (1939-)
House of 1000 Corpses '03, Out of the Black '01, Along for the Ride '00, Stir '98, Tumbleweeds '98, The Odyssey '97, Trigger Happy '96, Skeeter '93, Split Second '92, Motorama '91, The Arrival '90, The Art of Dying '90, Dick Tracy '90, I Come in Peace '90, Why Me? '90, Fast Food '89, Next of Kin '89, Night Visitor '89, Season of Fear '89, Sleepaway Camp 3: Teenage Wasteland '89, Tango and Cash '89, Legend of Frenchie King '71, Bonnie & Clyde '67, Caprice '67, Enter Laughing '67, The Wild Angels '66

Snub Pollard (1886-1962)
The Errand Boy '61, Rollin' Plains '38, A Nation Aflame '37, Arizona Days '37, Riders of the Rockies '37, Tex Rides with the Boy Scouts '37, The White Legion '36

David Pollock (1961-)
The Bad News Bears Go to Japan '78, The Bad News Bears in Breaking Training '77, The Bad News Bears '76

Dee Pollock (1937-2005)
Legend of Tom Dooley '59, Beware, My Lovely '52

Eileen Pollock (1947-)
Far and Away '92, Four Days in July '85

Ellen Pollock (1903-97)
Horror Hospital '73, Non-Stop New York '37

Teri Polo (1969-)
Full of It '07, Meet the Fockers '04, Beyond Borders '03, Domestic Disturbance '01, The Unsaid '01, Meet the Parents '00, A Prayer in the Dark '97, The Arrival '96, Aspen Extreme '93, Golden Gate '93, The House of the Spirits '93, Quick '93, Passed Away '92, Born to Ride '91, Mystery Date '91

John Polson (1965-)
Mission: Impossible 2 '00, The Boys '98, Idiot Box '97, Back of Beyond '95, Sirens '94, The Sum of Us '94, Dangerous Game '90

Max Pomeranc (1984-)
Fluke '95, Journey '95, Searching for Bobby Fischer '93

Ellen Pompeo (1969-)
Art Heist '05, Life of the Party '05, Eternal Sunshine of the Spotless Mind '04, Old School '03, Undermind '03, Moonlight Mile '02

Carlos Ponce (1972-)
Just My Luck '06, Deuce Bigalow: European Gigolo '05

Eusebio Poncela (1947-)
800 Bullets '02, Intacto '01, Martin (Hache) '97, A Shadow You Soon Will Be '94, Law of Desire '86

Merce Pons (1966-)
Caresses '97

Yvan Ponton (1945-)
The Boys '97, Scanners 2: The New Order '91, Men of Steel '88, Pouvoir Intime '87

Chris Pontius (1974-)
Jackass Number Two '06, Jackass: The Movie '02

Bray Poor
Two Ninas '00

Iggy Pop (1947-)
Coffee and Cigarettes '03, Snow Day '00, The Crow 2: City of Angels '96, Dead Man '95, Tank Girl '94, Cry-Baby '90, Hardware '90, Sid & Nancy '86

Carly Pope (1980-)
Beneath '07, Two for the Money '05, Eighteen '04, White Coats '04, Window Theory '04, Nemesis Game '03, Finder's Fee '01, A Cooler Climate '99

Marc Poppel
Separate Lives '94, Damned River '89

Anna Popplewell (1988-)
The Chronicles of Narnia: Prince Caspian '08, The Chronicles of Narnia: The Lion, the Witch and the Wardrobe '05, The Little Vampire '00

Albert "Poppy" Popwell (1926-99)
Scissors '91, Wild at Heart '90, Gloria '89, Who's That Girl? '87, Sudden Impact '83, The Buddy Holly Story '78, The Enforcer '76, Cleopatra Jones & the Casino of Gold '75, Charley Varrick '73, Cleopatra Jones '73, Magnum Force '73, Fuzz '72, Dirty Harry '71, Coogan's Bluff '68, The Harder They Fall '56, The Joe Louis Story '53

Johnny Popwell
Manhunter '83, Challenge '74

Jorge Porcel (1936-)
Carlito's Way '93, Naked Is Better '73

Marc Porel (1949-83)
The Psychic '78, The Innocent '76, Don't Torture a Duckling '72

Paulina Porizkova (1965-)
Second Best '05, Dark Asylum '01, Intern '00, Partners in Crime '99, Thursday '98, Long Time Since '97, Female Perversions '96, Wedding Bell Blues '96, Arizona Dream '94, Her Alibi '88, Portfolio '88, Anna '87

Maria Poroshina
Day Watch '06, Night Watch '04

Louise Portal (1951-)
Heading South '05, The Barbarian Invasions '03, Sous Sol '96, The Decline of the American Empire '86, The Klutz '73

Robert Portal
Mrs. Dalloway '97

Billy Porter
The Broken Hearts Club '00, Intern '00, Twisted '86

Brett Porter (1956-)
Stiletto Dance '01, Firehead '90

Don Porter (1912-96)
The Christmas Coal Mine Miracle '77, Mame '74, The Norliss Tapes '73, The Candidate '72, Bachelor in Paradise '69

Live a Little, Love a Little '68
Our Miss Brooks '56
The Racket '51
Buck Privates Come Home '47
She Wolf of London '46
Night Monster '42
Who Done It? '42

Eric Porter (1928-95)
Oliver Twist '85
Churchill and the Generals '81
The Fall of the Roman Empire '64
The Pumpkin Eater '64
The Heroes of Telemark '65
Macbeth '70
The Belstone Fox '73
Hands of the Ripper '71
Antony and Cleopatra '73
The Thirty-Nine Steps '79
Hennessy '75
Little Lord Fauntleroy '80

Jean Porter (1925-)
G.I. Jane '51
Kentucky Jubilee '51
Abbott and Costello in Hollywood '45
Bathing Beauty '44
San Fernando Valley '44

Susie Porter
Better Than Sex '00
Bootmen '00
Two Hands '98

Scott Porter
Prom Night '08
Speed Racer '08

Robert Porter
Deadly Fieldtrip '74
The Jesus Trip '71
Inside Information '34

Natalie Portman (1981-)
The Other Boleyn Girl '08
Mr. Magorium's Wonder Emporium '07
My Blueberry Nights '07
Goya's Ghosts '06
Paris, je t'aime '06
V for Vendetta '06
Free Zone '05
Star Wars: Episode 3—Revenge of the Sith '05
Star Wars: Episode 2—Attack of the Clones '02
Closer '04
Garden State '04
Cold Mountain '03
Star Wars: Episode 1—The Phantom Menace '99
Anywhere But Here '99
Where the Heart Is '00
Beautiful Girls '96
Everyone Says I Love You '96
Mars Attacks! '96
Heat '95
The Professional '94

Blanca Portillo
Goya's Ghosts '06
Volver '06

Eric Portman (1903-69)
Bedford Incident '65
The Naked Edge '61
The Colditz Story '55
The Spider and the Fly '49
Moonlight Sonata '38
Missing '41
One of Our Aircraft Is Missing '41
The Forty-Ninth Parallel '41
We Dive at Dawn '43
Men of Two Worlds '46
A Canterbury Tale '44
Great Day '46
Dear Murderer '47
Murder in the Old Red Barn '36
Hawke '36

Richard Portnow (1950-)
Triggermen '02
The Shipping News '01
Cowboy Up '00
Perfect Stranger '07
Alice in Wonderland '99
The Substitute 3: Winner Takes All '99
Witness Protection '99
Going Postal '98
Private Parts '96
Donor Unknown '95
Man of the House '95
S.F.W. '94
Trial by Jury '94
Sister Act '92
Barton Fink '91
Kindergarten Cop '90
Meet the Hollowheads '89
Say Anything '89
In Dangerous Company '88
Good Morning, Vietnam '87

Parker Posey (1968-)
The Eye '08
Broken English '07
Fay Grim '06
For Your Consideration '06
Superman Returns '06
Adam & Steve '05
Blade: Trinity '04
Laws of Attraction '04
A Mighty Wind '03
Personal Velocity: Three Portraits '02
The Sweetest Thing '02
The Anniversary Party '01
Josie and the Pussycats '01
Best in Show '00
Scream 3 '00
Henry Fool '98
You've Got Mail '98
Clockwatchers '97
The House of Yes '97
The Daytrippers '96
Drunks '96
subUrbia '96
Waiting for Guffman '96
The Doom Generation '95
Dazed and Confused '93
Frisk '95
Kicking and Screaming '95
Party Girl '95
Sleep with Me '94
Armistead Maupin's Tales of the City '93

Markie Post (1950-)
Tricks of the Trade '88
Scene of the Crime '85
Glitz '88
Mary '98
There's Something about Mary '98

William Post, Jr. (1901-89)
Call Northside 777 '48
House on 92nd Street '45
Sherlock Holmes and the Secret Weapon '42
Ship Ahoy '42

Saskia Post (1961-)
Dogs in Space '87

Pete Postlethwaite (1945-)
Ghost Son '06
The Omen '06
The Constant Gardener '05
Dark Water '05
Red Mercury '05
Strange Bedfellows '04
Aeon Flux '05
Triple Cross '85
Between Strangers '02
The Shipping News '01
Triggermen '02
Cowboy Up '00
Alice in Wonderland '99
Animal Farm '99
Butterfly Collectors '99
Lost for Words '99
When the Sky Falls '99
Among Giants '98
Brassed Off '96
Crimetime '96
Dragonheart '96
James and the Giant Peach '96
The Serpent's Kiss '97
William Shakespeare's Romeo and Juliet '96
The Usual Suspects '95
When Saturday Comes '95
Martin Chuzzlewit '94
Sharpe's Company '94
Suite 16 '94
In the Name of the Father '93
The Last of the Mohicans '92
Split Second '92
Waterland '92
The Dressmaker '89
Hamlet '90
To Kill a Priest '89
Distant Voices, Still Lives '88
A Private Function '84

Madeleine Potter (1963-)
The Golden Bowl '00
The White Countess '05
The Pacifier '05
Slaves of New York '89

Chris Potter (1960-)
The Pacifier '05
Final Justice '98

Brian Poth (1975-)
Dog Gone Love '03
Boycott '02
Venomous '01

Franka Potente (1974-)
Romulus, My Father '07
The Bourne Supremacy '04
I Love Your Work '03
All I Want '02
The Bourne Identity '02
Blow '01
Storytelling '01
The Princess and the Warrior '01
Anatomy '00

CCH Pounder (1952-)
Things Behind the Sun '01
Disappearing Acts '00
End of Days '99
Face/Off '97
Tom Clancy's Netforce '98

Georges Poujouly (1940-2000)
Forbidden Games '52

Jose Maria Pou (1944-)
The Sea Inside '04

Tom Poston (1921-2007)
The Princess Diaries 2: Royal Engagement '04
Beethoven's 5th '03
The Story of Us '99
Krippendorf's Tribe '98
A Perfect Little Murder '90
Carbon Copy '81
Up the Academy '80
Cold Turkey '71
Soldier in the Rain '63
Zotz! '62
The Old Dark House '63

Laurens C. Postma
To Live and Die in Hong Kong '89

Victor Potel (1889-1947)
Heroes Three '84

Jonathan Potts
Silent Running '71
Kong '89

Ely Pouget (1961-)
Beloved/Friend '99
Total Reality '97
Death Machine '95

Cliff (Potter) Potts (1947-)
Corvette Summer '78
King of the Gypsies '78

Charles Powell (1963-)
Counter Measures '99
Sahara '83

Annie Potts (1952-)
Saw '04
I'm with Lucy '02
Along Came a Spider '01
Toy Story 2 '99
Breaking the Rules '92
Toy Story '95
Texasville '90
Who's Harry Crumb? '89
Pass the Ammo '88
Jumpin' Jack Flash '86
Pretty in Pink '86
Crimes of Passion '84
Ghostbusters '84
King of the Gypsies '78
Corvette Summer '78
Heartaches '82
Flatbed Annie and Sweetiepie: Lady Truckers '79

Andrew Lee Potts
Dead Fish '04
Alice '09

Monica Potter (1971-)
Saw '04
Silver '93
Head Over Heels '01
A Cool, Dry Place '98
The Very Thought of You '98
Without Limits '98
Con Air '97
Patch Adams '98
Martin and Lewis '02

Martin Potter (1944-)
Gunpowder '87
Fellini Satyricon '69

Andre Pousse
Deadly Sting '82
Killer '73

Henri Poupon (1882-)
Harvest '37
Angele '34

Melvil Poupaud (1973-)
Broken English '07
Time to Leave '05
Le Divorce '03
Genealogies of a Crime '97
A Summer's Tale '96
Three Lives and Only One Death '96

Addison Powell (1921-)
The Rosary Murders '87
The Man Without a Country '73

Brittney Powell (1972-)
Dragonworld '94
Airborne '93
To Be the Best '93

Clifton Powell (1956-)
Norbit '07
The Gospel '05
Who Made the Potato Salad? '05
Never Die Alone '04
Ray '04
Woman, Thou Art Loosed '04
Civil Brand '02
Friday After Next '02
Bones '01
Lockdown '00
The Breaks '99
Caught Up '98
The Players Club '98
Phantoms '98
Dead Presidents '95

Michael Powell (1905-90)
Peeping Tom '60

Marcus Powell (1932-2000)
Father of Lies '07
Kill by Inches '99
The Rejuvenator '88

Robert Powell (1944-)
Secrets '71
Jesus of Nazareth '77
The Thirty-Nine Steps '78
The Four Feathers '78
Jane Austen in Manhattan '80
Survivor '80
The Jigsaw Man '84
Dark Forces '83
Frankenstein '82
What Waits Below '83
Shaka Zulu '83
Mahler '74
Tommy '75
The Asphyx '72
Jude the Obscure '71

Dick Powell (1904-63)
Susan Slept Here '54
The Bad and the Beautiful '52
Cry Danger '51
Mrs. Mike '49
Pitfall '48
Station West '48
Cornered '45
It Happened Tomorrow '44
Murder, My Sweet '44
Star Spangled Rhythm '42
In the Navy '41
Christmas in July '40
On the Avenue '37
Stage Struck '36
Gold Diggers of 1935 '35
A Midsummer Night's Dream '35
Dames '34

William Powell (1892-1984)
Mister Roberts '55
The Girl Who Had Everything '53
How to Marry a Millionaire '53
Dancing in the Dark '49
Life with Father '47
Mr. Peabody & the Mermaid '48

Lee Powell (1908-44)
Along the Sundown Trail '42
Fighting Devil Dogs '43
Deep in My Heart '54
Prairie Pals '42
Tumbleweed Trail '42
Trigger Pals '39
The Lone Ranger '38

Jane Powell (1929-)
The Sandy Bottom Orchestra '00
Enchanted Island '58
The Girl Most Likely '57
Hit the Deck '55
Athena '54
Deep in My Heart '54
Seven Brides for Seven Brothers '54
Small Town Girl '53
Rich, Young and Pretty '51
Royal Wedding '51
Nancy Goes to Rio '50
Two Weeks with Love '50
A Date with Judy '48
Three Daring Daughters '48
Holiday in Mexico '46
Delightfully Dangerous '45

Esteban Louis Powell (1977-)
Bunny Whipped '05
Hitman's Run '99
Powder '95

Eleanor Powell (1912-82)
The Duchess of Idaho '50
Sensations of 1945 '44
I Dood It '43
Thousands Cheer '43
Ship Ahoy '42
Lady Be Good '41
Broadway Melody of 1940 '40
Honolulu '39
Rosalie '38
Broadway Melody of 1938 '37
Born to Dance '36
Broadway Melody of 1936 '35

Tales from the Crypt Presents Demon Knight '94
Benny & Joon '93
The Disappearance of Christina '93
The Ernest Green Story '93
Lifepod '93
Psycho 4: The Beginning '90
Bagdad Cafe '88
Prizzi's Honor '85
Union City '81
Honolulu '39
Rosalie '38
Broadway Melody of 1938 '37
Flirtation Walk '34
Footlight Parade '33
42nd Street '33
Gold Diggers of 1935 '33
Blessed Event '32
Too Busy to Work '32

Powell
The Senator Was Indiscreet '47
Song of the Thin Man '47
Ziegfeld Follies '46
The Thin Man Goes Home '44
Love Crazy '41
Shadow of the Thin Man '41
I Love You Again '40
Another Thin Man '39
Double Wedding '37
The Last of Mrs. Cheyney '37
After the Thin Man '36
Ex-Mrs. Bradford '36
The Great Ziegfeld '36
Libeled Lady '36
My Man Godfrey '36
Reckless '35
Star of Midnight '35
Evelyn Prentice '34
Fashions of 1934 '34
Manhattan Melodrama '34
The Thin Man '34
The Kennel Murder Case '33
One Way Passage '32
Man of the World '31
Feel My Pulse '28
Last Command '28
Nevada '27
Romola '25

Power
Black and White '99
Belly '98

Chad Power (1984-)
3 Ninjas Knuckle Up '95
3 Ninjas '92

Hartley Power (1894-1966)
Dead of Night '45
Evergreen '34

Romina Power
Deadly Sanctuary '68
How I Learned to Love Women '66

Taryn Power (1953-)
Sinbad and the Eye of the Tiger '77
Tracks '77
The Count of Monte Cristo '74

Tyrone Power (1913-58)
Abandon Ship '57
Witness for the Prosecution '57
The Eddy Duchin Story '56
The Long Gray Line '55
Diplomatic Courier '52
The Black Rose '50
Rawhide '50
The Black Swan '42
Son of Fury '42
Blood and Sand '41
A Yank in the R.A.F. '41
Brigham Young: Frontiersman '40
Johnny Apollo '40
Jesse James '39
The Rains Came '39
Rose of Washington Square '39
Second Fiddle '39
Alexander's Ragtime Band '38
Marie Antoinette '38
In Old Chicago '37
Thin Ice '37
Lloyds of London '36
Braveheart '25

Tyrone Power, Jr. (1959-)
Evil Lives '92
California Casanova '89
Shag: The Movie '89
Cocoon '85

Tyrone Power, Sr. (1869-1931)
Big Trail '30

Test of Donald Norton '26
Red Kimono '25
Dream Street '21

Alexandra Powers (1967-)
Double Down '01
Storm Tracker '99
Last Man Standing '96
Rising Sun '93
The Seventh Coin '92
Cast a Deadly Spell '91
Dangerous Pursuit '89
Dead Poets Society '89
Plain Clothes '88
Sonny Boy '87
Mask '85

Beverly (Hills) Powers
Knights & Emeralds '87
Sixteen '72
Brides of the Beast '68
The Comedy of Terrors '64
Kissin' Cousins '64

Lucille Powers (1911-81)
Texas Bad Man '32
Two Gun Man '31

Mala Powers (1931-2007)
Daddy's Gone A-Hunting '69
Escape from Planet Earth '67
Storm Rider '57
Rage at Dawn '55
City That Never Sleeps '53
Cyrano de Bergerac '50
Outrage '50

Stefanie Powers
Scott Turow's The Burden of Proof '92
Shadow on the Sun '88
Family Secrets '84
Mistral's Daughter '84
Escape to Athena '79
Little Moon & Jud McGraw '78
The Invisible Strangler '76
The Man Inside '76
Return to Earth '76
It Seemed Like a Good Idea at the Time '75
Sky Heist '75
Herbie Rides Again '74
Manhunter '74
Gone with the West '72
No Place to Run '72
Paper Man '71
The Boatniks '70
Die! Die! My Darling! '65
Love Has Many Faces '65
McLintock! '63
Palm Springs Weekend '63
Experiment in Terror '62
The Interns '62
The Day Reagan Was Shot '01
Dirty Pictures '00
Hiroshima '95
How the West Was Fun '95
Spenser: The Judas Goat '94

Tom Powers (1890-1955)
Lucky Me '54
Destination Moon '50
The Nevadan '50
Mexican Hayride '48
Station West '48
Up in Central Park '48
Son of Rusty '47
The Blue Dahlia '46
Double Indemnity '44

Leon Pownall (1943-2006)
Love and Hell: A Marriage Made in Hell '90
Bye Bye Blues '89
Termini Station '89

Clare Powney (1963-)
The Girl '86

Jose Maria Prada (1925-78)
The Diabolical Dr. Z '65
The Hunt '65

Bruno Pradal (1949-92)
November Moon '85
Charlie Bravo '80

Lilla Prado (1928-2006)

Jerome Pradon (1964-)
Jesus Christ Superstar '00
Simon Sez '99

Michael Praed (1960-)
Darkness Falls '88
To Die For 2: Son of Darkness '91
Writer's Block '91
Riders '88
Nightflyers '87
Robin Hood... The Legend: Robin Hood and the Sorcerer '83
Robin Hood... The Legend: The Swords of Wayland '83

Stanley Prager (1917-72)
Gun Crazy '49
A Foreign Affair '48
You Gotta Stay Happy '48

Pras (1972-)
Nora's Hair Salon '04
Da Hip Hop Witch '00
Turn It Up '00
Mystery Men '99

Eric Prat
Brotherhood of the Wolf '01
Tatie Danielle '91

Joan Prather (1951-)
The Deerslayer '78
Devil's Rain '75
Smile '75
Big Bad Mama '74

Judson Pratt (1916-2002)
The Horse Soldiers '59
Monster on the Campus '59

Keri Lynn Pratt (1978-)
The Smokers '00
Cruel Intentions 2 '99

Kyla Pratt (1986-)
Dr. Dolittle 4: Tail to the Chief '08
Dr. Dolittle 3 '06
The Proud Family Movie '05 (V)
Fat Albert '04
Dr. Dolittle 2 '01
Love and Basketball '00
Barney's Great Adventure '98
Dr. Dolittle '98

Purnell Pratt (1885-1941)
Come on Rangers '38
Bachelor Apartment '31
The Silver Horde '30

Susan May Pratt (1974-)
Undermind '03
Charms for the Easy Life '02
Searching for Paradise '02
Center Stage '00
Drive Me Crazy '99
Ten Things I Hate about You '99

Victoria Pratt (1974-)
What Love Is '07
Kraken: Tentacles of the Deep '06
House of the Dead 2: Dead Aim '05

George Pravda (1918-85)
The Duchess of Duke Street '78
Frankenstein Must Be Destroyed '69

Wolfgang Preiss (1910-2002)
Club Extinction '89
A Bridge Too Far '77
Raid on Rommel '71
Cave of the Living Dead '65
The Mad Executioners '65
The Train '65
Von Ryan's Express '65
The Invisible Dr. Mabuse '62
Testament of Dr. Mabuse '62
The Return of Dr. Mabuse '61
Mill of the Stone Women '60
The Thousand Eyes of Dr. Mabuse '60
Mistress of the World '59

June Preisser (1920-84)
Strike Up the Band '40
Babes in Arms '39

Albert Prejean (1893-1979)
Princess Tam Tam '35
Under the Roofs of Paris '29
Italian Straw Hat '27
The Crazy Ray '22

Otto Preminger (1906-86)
The Hobbit '78 (V)
Stalag 17 '53
They Got Me Covered '43

Luis Prendes (1913-98)
Alien Predators '80
The Christmas Kid '68
Ursus in the Valley of the Lions '62

Jordan Prentice
In Bruges '08
Weirdsville '07

Paula Prentiss (1939-)
Mrs. Winterbourne '96
M.A.D.D.: Mothers Against Drunk Driving '83
Packin' It In '83
Buddy Buddy '81
Saturday the 14th '81
The Black Marble '79
No Room to Run '78
The Stepford Wives '75
The Parallax View '74
Last of the Red Hot Lovers '72
Born to Win '71
Catch-22 '70
Bachelor in Paradise '69
In Harm's Way '65
What's New Pussycat? '65
The World of Henry Orient '64
Man's Favorite Sport? '63
The Horizontal Lieutenant '62
The Honeymoon Machine '61
Where the Boys Are '60

Robert Prentiss
The Alamo '04
Total Exposure '91

Laura Prepon (1980-)
Come Early Morning '06
Karla '06
Slackers '02

Robert Prescott
Michael Clayton '07
Blue De Ville '86
Real Genius '85
Bachelor Party '84

Micheline Presle (1922-)
Transfixed '01
Bad Company '99
A Chef in Love '96
Diary of a Seducer '95
Pas Tres Catholique '93
I Want to Go Home '89
A Slightly Pregnant Man '79
Legend of Frenchie King '71
The King of Hearts '66

The Nun '66
The Prize '63
Time Out for Love '61
Mistress of the World '59
The Bride Is Much Too Beautiful '58
Adventures of Captain Fabian '51
Devil in the Flesh '46
The Fantastic Night '42
The French Way '40

Brian Presley
Home of the Brave '06
Guarding Eddy '04

Elvis Presley (1935-77)
This is Elvis '81
Change of Habit '69
Charro! '69
The Trouble with Girls (and How to Get into It) '69
Live a Little, Love a Little '68
Speedway '68
Stay Away, Joe '68
Clambake '67
Double Trouble '67
Easy Come, Easy Go '67
Paradise, Hawaiian Style '66
Spinout '66
Frankie and Johnny '65
Girl Happy '65
Harum Scarum '65
Tickle Me '65
Kissin' Cousins '64
Fun in Acapulco '63
It Happened at the World's Fair '63
Viva Las Vegas '63
Blue Hawaii '62
Girls! Girls! Girls! '62
Kid Galahad '62
Follow That Dream '61
Wild in the Country '61
Flaming Star '60
G.I. Blues '60
King Creole '58
Jailhouse Rock '57
Loving You '57
Love Me Tender '56

Priscilla Presley (1946-)
Naked Gun 33 1/3: The Final Insult '94
Naked Gun 2 1/2: The Smell of Fear '91
The Adventures of Ford Fairlane '90
The Naked Gun: From the Files of Police Squad '88
Jackie, Ethel, Joan: The Kennedy Women '01
Family Man '00
The Legend of Bagger Vance '00

Harve Presnell (1933-)
Flags of Our Fathers '06
Old School '03
Super Sucker '03
Mr. Deeds '02
Escanaba in da Moonlight '01
A Bright Shining Lie '98
Everything That Rises '98
Patch Adams '98
Saving Private Ryan '98
Face/Off '97
Julian Po '97
Fargo '96
Larger Than Life '96
The Whole Wide World '96
Paint Your Wagon '69
The Unsinkable Molly Brown '64

Nathalie Press
Red Road '06
My Summer of Love '05

Jaime Pressly (1977-)
Dr. Seuss' Horton Hears a Who! '08 (V)
DOA: Dead or Alive '06
Bachelor Party Vegas '05
Cruel World '05
Karate Dog '04

Torque '04
Survival Island '02
Joe Dirt '01
Not Another Teen Movie '01
Ticker '01
Tomcats '01
100 Girls '00
Poor White Trash '00
Ringmaster '98
Poison Ivy 3: The New Seduction '97

Lawrence Pressman (1939-)
American Dreamz '06
The Far Side of Jericho '06
DC 9/11: Time of Crisis '03
American Wedding '03
American Pie '99
The Maker '98
Mighty Joe Young '98
The Late Shift '96
Sunchaser '96
Trial and Error '96
Angus '95
White Hot: The Mysterious Murder of Thelma Todd '91
Fire and Rain '89
Hanoi Hilton '87
The Deliberate Stranger '86
On Wings of Eagles '86
For Love or Money '84
The Winds of War '83
Rehearsal for Murder '82
Blind Ambition '79
The Gathering: Part 2 '79
The Gathering '77
The Trial of Lee Harvey Oswald '77
Rich Man, Poor Man '76
The Man in the Glass Booth '75
The Hellstrom Chronicle '71
Shaft '71

Jason Presson (1971-)
The Lady in White '88
Saturday the 14th Strikes Back '88
Explorers '85
The Stone Boy '84

Jo Prestia (1960-)
Irreversible '02
The Dreamlife of Angels '98

Billy Preston (1946-)
Wired '89
Blame It on the Night '84
Let It Be '70

Cynthia (Cyndy, Cindy) Preston (1968-)
The Event '03
Facing the Enemy '00
The Thin Blue Lie '00
Total Recall 2070: Machine Dreams '99
Premonition '98
The Ultimate Weapon '97
Black Fox: The Price of Peace '94
Whale Music '94
Prom Night 3: The Last Kiss '89
Pin... '88
The Brain '88
The Darkside '87

J.A. Preston
Harvest of Fire '95
A Few Good Men '92
Fire Birds '90
Remo Williams: The Adventure Begins '85
Body Heat '81
The Spook Who Sat by the Door '73

Kelly Preston (1963-)
Death Sentence '07
Sky High '05
Convicted '04
Eulogy '04
Dr. Seuss' The Cat in the Hat '03
View from the Top '03
What a Girl Wants '03
Bar Hopping '00

Battlefield Earth '00
Daddy & Them '99
For Love of the Game '99
Holy Man '98
Jack Frost '98
Addicted to Love '96
Citizen Ruth '96
Jerry Maguire '96
Nothing to Lose '96
From Dusk Till Dawn '95
Cheyenne Warrior '94
Double Cross '94
Love Is a Gun '94
Only You '92
The Perfect Bride '91
Run '91
The Experts '89
The Spellbinder '88
Twins '88
Amazon Women on the Moon '87
Secret Admirer '85
Mischief '85
SpaceCamp '86
52 Pick-Up '86
A Tiger's Tale '87
Love at Stake '87
Metalstorm: The Destruction of Jared Syn '83

Mike (Michael) Preston (1938-)
The Road Warrior '82
Surabaya Conspiracy '75
Mame '74
My Father's House '75
Junior Bonner '72
How the West Was Won '63

Robert Preston (1918-87)
Outrage! '86
Finnegan Begin Again '84
The Last Starfighter '84
September Gun '83
Rehearsal for Murder '82
Victor/Victoria '82
S.O.B. '81
The Chisholms '79
Semi-Tough '77
Mame '74
Junior Bonner '72
How the West Was Won '63
Blood on the Moon '48
Reap the Wild Wind '42
Wake Island '42
This Gun for Hire '42
Night of January 16th '41
Beau Geste '39
King of Alcatraz '38
Union Pacific '39
Tulsa '49
Best of the Badmen '50

Wayde Preston (1929-92)
Smokey & the Judge '80
Today We Kill, Tomorrow We Die '71

Nancy Price (1880-1970)
The Three Weird Sisters '48
Secret Mission '42
The Speckled Band '31

Oliver Price
Dark Corners '06
Parasite '03

Richard Price (1949-)
Ransom '96
Night and the City '92
Shocker '89

Stanley Price (1892-1955)
Roaring City '51
The Invisible Monster '50
Outlaw Fury '50
Rangeland Empire '50
Sudden Death '50
Outlaw Gang '49
Rimfire '49
Son of Zorro '47
Tough Assignment '49

Giancarlo Prete (1942-2001)
Escape from the Bronx '85
Tornado '83
Warriors of the Wasteland '83

Daniel Prevost
The Dinner Game '98
Uranus '91

Francoise Prevost (1930-97)
L'Amour en Herbe '77
Spirits of the Dead '68
Time Out for Love '61
Love Play '60
Paris Belongs to Us '60

Marie Prevost (1898-1937)
Tango '36
Hands Across the Table '35
The Sin of Madelon Claudet '31
Party Girls '29
The Marriage Circle '24

Alan Price (1941-)
Oh, Alfie '75
O Lucky Man! '73

Dennis Price (1915-73)
Horror Hospital '73
Theatre of Blood '73
Pulp '72
Rites of Frankenstein '72
The Screaming Dead '72
Twins of Evil '71
The Horror of Frankenstein '70
Venus in Furs '70
Murder Most Foul '65
Cool Mikado '63
The Wrong Arm of the Law '63
What a Carve-Up! '62
The Millionairess '60
No Love for Johnnie '60
The Naked Truth '58
Tunes of Glory '60
Victim '61
The Adventurers '51
Eight Witnesses '54
Kind Hearts and Coronets '49
Dear Murderer '47
The Magic Bow '47
Echo Murders '45
A Canterbury Tale '44

Marc Price (1968-)
Killer Tomatoes Eat France '91

Lindsay Price (1976-)
Club Dread '04
No Turning Back '01

Kate Price (1872-1943)
Linda '29
Annally of Clothesline Alley '18

Hal Price (1886-1964)
Lawmen '44
Rustler's Hideout '44
Trigger Men '41
Across the Plains '39
Man from Texas '39
Melody of the Plains '37
Where Trails Divide '37
Cavalry '36
Desert Phantom '36

Molly Price (1966-)
Chasing Sleep '00
Kiss Me, Guido '97
Risk '94
Jersey Girl '92

Nancy Price (1880-1970)
The Rescue '88
Trick or Treat '86

Marc Price
Pirate Warrior '64
Tomb of Ligeia '64
Beach Party '63
Diary of a Madman '63
The Haunted Palace '63
The Raven '63
Twice-Told Tales '63
Tales of Terror '62
Tower of London '62
Master of the World '61
The Pit and the Pendulum '61
The Fall of the House of Usher '60
The Bat '59
Return of the Fly '59
The Tingler '59
The Fly '58
House on Haunted Hill '58
The Ten Commandments '56
While the City Sleeps '56
Son of Sinbad '55
Casanova's Big Night '54
Dangerous Mission '54
House of Wax '53
The Las Vegas Story '52
Baron of Arizona '51
His Kind of Woman '51
Champagne for Caesar '50
Bagdad '49
Abbott and Costello Meet Frankenstein '48 (V)

Vincent Price (1911-93)
The Thief and the Cobbler '97
Edward Scissorhands '90
Once Upon a Midnight Scary '90 (N)
Backtrack '89
Dead Heat '88
The Offspring '87
The Whales of August '87
Escapes '86
The Great Mouse Detective '86
Bloodbath at the House of Death '85
The Monster Club '85
Snow White and the Seven Dwarfs '83
House of the Long Shadows '82
Scavenger Hunt '79
The Butterfly Ball '76 (N)
It's Not the Size That Counts '74
Journey into Fear '74
Madhouse '74
Theatre of Blood '73
Doctor Phibes Rises Again '72
The Abominable Dr. Phibes '71
Cry of the Banshee '70
Scream and Scream Again '70
The Oblong Box '69
The Trouble with Girls (and How to Get Into It) '69
The Conqueror Worm '68
More Dead Than Alive '68
Spirits of the Dead '68 (N)
The House of 1000 Dolls '67
The Jackals '67
Dr. Goldfoot and the Bikini Machine '66
Masque of the Red Death '65
The Comedy of Terrors '64
The Last Man on Earth '64
Nefertiti, Queen of the Nile '64
The Oblong Box... (cont.)

Sue Price (1965-)
Nemesis 4: Cry of Angels '97
Nemesis 3: Time Lapse '96
Nemesis 2: Nebula '94

Alan Price
The Flying Fool '29

Dynamite Canyon '41
The Singing Cowgirl '39
The Long Night '47
Shock! '46
Leave Her to Heaven '45
The Keys of the Kingdom '44
Laura '44
Wilson '44
The Song of Bernadette '43
Brigham Young: Frontiersman '40
The Tower of London '39
Service De Luxe '38
The Great Mouse Detective... (cont.)

Robert Prichard
Alien Space Avenger '91
Class of Nuke 'Em High '86
The Toxic Avenger '86

Dan Priest (1924-2004)
Ratliers '76
Black Like Me '64

Martin Priest
Zebrahead '92

Pat Priest (1936-)
Some Call It Loving '73
The Incredible Two-Headed Transplant '71
Easy Come, Easy Go '67

Jason Priestley (1969-)
Luna: Spirit of the Whale '07
Hot Tamale '06
Masters of Horror: The Screwfly Solution '06
Die Mommie Die! '03
Cherish '02
Dark Side '02
Double Down '01
The Fourth Angel '01
Common Ground '00
Homicide: The Movie '00
Kiss Tomorrow Goodbye '00
Eye of the Beholder '99
The Highway Man '99
Standing on Fishes '99
Love and Death on Long Island '97
Sink or Swim '97
Coldblooded '94
Calendar Girl '93
Tombstone '93
Nowhere to Run '89

Aurore Prieto
Dr. Petiot '90

Paco Christian Prieto (1955-)
Street Law '95
Only the Strong '93

Suzy Prim (1896-1991)
Heart of a Nation '43
The Lower Depths '36

Louis Prima (1910-78)
The Jungle Book '67 (V)
Manhattan Merry-Go-Round '37

Barry Primus (1938-)
When Will I Be Loved '04
James Dean '01
Elmore Leonard's Gold Coast '97
Flipping '96
Crime of the Century '96
Trade Off '95
Guilty by Suspicion '91
Cannibal Women in the Avocado Jungle of Death '89

Andrew Prine (1936-)
Daltry Calhoun '05
Critical Mass '00
Witchouse 2: Blood Coven '00
Possums '99
Without Evidence '96
Serial Killer '95
Deadly Exposure '93
Gettysburg '93
Mission of the Shark '91
Chill Factor '90
The Eliminators '86
The Last of the Mohicans '85
Donner Pass: The Road to Survival '84
Amityville 2: The Possession '82
They're Playing with Fire '84

V '83

Callie and Son '81
A Small Killing '81

The Three Musketeers '48
Up in Central Park '48
Shooting Walls '85
Talking Walls '85
Absence of Malice '81
Heartland '81
Grizzly '76
Night Games '80
New York, New York '77
Autopsy '74
Boxcar Bertha '72

Prince (1958-)
Graffiti Bridge '90
Under the Cherry Moon '86
Purple Rain '84

Clayton Prince (1965-)
Dark Justice '91
Hairspray '88

Faith Prince (1957-)
It Had to Be You '00
A Season for Miracles '99
Picture Perfect '96
Dave '93

Bryan Pringle (1935-)
Getting It Right '89
Haunted Honeymoon '86
Morning '60

Aileen Pringle (1895-1989)
The Sons of Steel '35
Jane Eyre '34
Convicted '32
Police Court '32
Dance '31
Murder at Midnight '31

William Prince (1913-96)
The Portrait '93
The Taking of Beverly Hills '91
Second Sight '89
Spontaneous Combustion '89
Vice Versa '88
Nuts '87
Spies Like Us '85
The Soldier '82
City in Fear '80
The Promise '79
Johnny We Hardly Knew Ye '77
Family Plot '76
Network '76
The Stepford Wives '75
Missiles of October '74
Cyrano de Bergerac '50
Carnegie Hall '47
Dead Reckoning '47
Objective, Burma! '45

Steven Prince
The Alamo '04
Allie & Me '97

Jonathan Prince (1958-)
Private School '83
Pray TV '82

Joan Pringle
Original Sin '01
J.D.'s Revenge '76

Scooby-Doo '02
Head Over Heels '01
Summer Catch '01
Boys and Girls '00
Down to You '00
She's All That '99
Sparkler '99
Wing Commander '99
I Still Know What You Did Last Summer '98
The House of Yes '97
Hostage High '97
Money Kings '98
To Gillian on Her 37th Birthday '96
The P.A.C.K. '96
Brooklyn Rules '07
Mutant Species '95
Possessed by the Night '93
Center of the Web '92
Raw Nerve '91
Future Zone '90
Born Killer '89
Final Sanction '89
Hardcase and Fist '89
Jungle Assault '89
Hell on the Battleground '88
Deadly Prey '87
Killer Workout '86
Sledgehammer '83

Ted Prior (1959-)

David Pritchard
Slashed Dreams '74

Albert Priscoe
The Prairie King '27
The Love Light '21

Michael Pritchard
Lightblast '85

Sandra Prinsloo
Claws '85
The Gods Must Be Crazy '84

Freddie Prinze, Jr. (1976-)
Happily N'Ever After '07 (V)
Scooby-Doo 2: Monsters Unleashed '04
Scooby-Doo '02
Summer Catch '01

Lucien Prival (1900-94)
Panama Menace '41
Hell's Angels '30
Party Girls '29

Jurgen Prochnow (1941-)
Primeval '07

The Evil '78
The Christmas Coal Mine Miracle '77
Riding with Death '76
Town That Dreaded Sundown '76
The Centerfold Girls '74
Barn of the Naked Dead '73
Crypt of the Living Dead '73
One Little Indian '73
Simon, King of the Witches '71
Generation '69
Bandolero! '68
Texas Across the River '66
The Miracle Worker '62
The Devil's Brigade '68

Prochnow
Beerfest '06
The Celestine Prophecy '06
The Da Vinci Code '06
Heart of America '03
House of the Dead '03
Dark Asylum '01
Last Run '01
Ripper: Letter from Hell '01
Heaven's Fire '99
The Last Stop '99
Wing Commander '99
Esther '98
The Fall '98
The Replacement Killers '98
Air Force One '97
DNA '97
Human Bomb '97
The English Patient '96
In the Mouth of Madness '95
Jack Higgins' On Dangerous Ground '95
Judge Dredd '95
Lie Down with Lions '94
The Fire Next Time '93
Body of Evidence '92
Hurricane Smith '92
Interceptor '92
Jewels '92
Twin Peaks: Fire Walk with Me '92
Robin Hood '91
The Fourth War '90
Kill Cruise '90
The Man Inside '89
A Dry White Season '89
The Seventh Sign '88
Beverly Hills Cop 2 '87
The Cop & the Girl '86
Blitz '85
Forbidden '85
My Sweet Victim '85
Dune '84
The Keep '83
Das Boot '81
The Lost Honor of Katharina Blum '75
Tenderness of the Wolves '73

Emily Procter (1968-)
Big Momma's House 2 '06
Body Shots '99
Guinevere '99
Breast Men '97

Marland Proctor (1941-88)
Terrorists '88

Phil(ip) Proctor (1940-)
The Rugrats Movie '98 (V)
Lobster Man from Mars '89
J-Men Forever! '79

Tome Proculi
See Anthony (Jose, J. Antonio, J.A.) Mayans

Luigi Proietti
Revenge of the Musketeers '94

Melissa Prophet (1957-)
Invasion U.S.A. '85
Better Late Than Never '83
Van Nuys Blvd. '79

Robert Prosky (1930-)
Eye See You '01
Dudley Do-Right '99
Mad City '97
The Chamber '96
Dead Man Walking '95
Miracle on 34th Street '94
Hit Woman: The Double Edge '93
Last Action Hero '93
Mrs. Doubtfire '93
Rudy '93
Far and Away '92
Hoffa '92
Teamster Boss: The Jackie Presser Story '92
Age Isn't Everything '91
Funny About Love '90
Green Card '90
Gremlins 2: The New Batch '90
From the Dead of Night '89
The Heist '89
Things Change '88
Big Shots '87
Broadcast News '87
The Murder of Mary Phagan '87
World War III '86
Into Thin Air '85
Christine '84
The Natural '84
The Keep '83
The Lords of Discipline '83
Thief '81

Joe Prospero (1988-)
Finding Neverland '04
My Uncle Silas '01

Jed Prouty (1879-1956)
Remedy for Riches '40
The Gracie Allen Murder Case '39
Danger on the Air '38
100 Men and a Girl '37
Small Town Boy '37
Broadway Melody 29
Ella Cinders 26

David Proval (1942-)
Smokin' Aces '07
Murder Without Conviction '04
Bookies '03
13 Moons '02
Double Down '01
The Hollywood Sign '01
Mob Queen '98
The Siege '98
Flipping '96
The Phantom '96
Four Rooms '95
To the Limit '95
Being Human '94
Romeo Is Bleeding '93
Innocent Blood '92
Vice Versa '88
Wizards '77 (V)
Mean Streets '73

Dorothy Provine (1937-)
Never a Dull Moment '68
Who's Minding the Mint? '67
That Darn Cat '65
Good Neighbor Sam '64
It's a Mad, Mad, Mad, Mad World '63
Escapade in Japan '57
All Mine to Give '56
Back from Eternity '56
The 30-Foot Bride of Candy Rock '59

Jon(athan) Provost (1950-)
This Property Is Condemned '66
Lassie's Great Adventure '62

David Prowse (1935-)
Comic Book: The Movie '04
Return of the Jedi '83
The Empire Strikes Back '80
Jabberwocky '77
Star Wars '77
Frankenstein and the Monster from Hell '74
Blacksnake! '73
A Clockwork Orange '71
Vampire Circus '71
The Horror of Frankenstein '70
Casino Royale '67

Juliet Prowse (1937-96)
Dingaka '65
Can-Can '60
G.I. Blues '60

Anna Prucnal (1940-)
City of Women '81
Sweet Movie '75

Harold P. Pruett (1969-2002)
The Perfect Daughter '96
Precious Find '96
Spellcaster '91
Summer Camp Nightmare '86

Karl Pruner
Welcome to Mooseport '04
The Recruit '03
Finding Buck McHenry '00
Total Recall 2070: Machine Dreams '99
The Fixer '97

Alex Prusmack
In Enemy Hands '04

Jonathan Pryce (1947-)
Leatherheads '08
Pirates of the Caribbean: At World's End '07
Brothers of the Head '06
Pirates of the Caribbean: Dead Man's Chest '06
Renaissance '06
The Brothers Grimm '05
The New World '05
De-Lovely '04
Pirates of the Caribbean: The Curse of the Black Pearl '03
Unconditional Love '03
What a Girl Wants '03
The Affair of the Necklace '01
Bride of the Wind '01
Very Annie Mary '00
Robert Louis Stevenson's The Game of Death '99
Stigmata '99
Ronin '98
Behind the Lines '97
David '97
Tomorrow Never Dies '97
Evita '96
Carrington '95
A Troll in Central Park '94 (V)
The Age of Innocence '93
Barbarians at the Gate '93
A Business Affair '93
Deadly Advice '93
Shades of Fear '93
Shopping '93
Thicker Than Water '93
Freddie the Frog '92 (V)
Glengarry Glen Ross '92
The Adventures of Baron Munchausen '89
The Man from the Pru '89
The Rachel Papers '89
Consuming Passions '88
Man on Fire '87
Haunted Honeymoon '86
Jumpin' Jack Flash '86
Brazil '85
Breaking Glass '80
Voyage of the Damned '76
Loophole '83
The Ploughman's Lunch '83
Praying Mantis '83
Something Wicked This Way Comes '83
Agatha Christie's Murder is Easy '82

Ainslie Pryor (1921-58)
The Last Hunt '56
The Girl in the Red Velvet Swing '55

Nicholas Pryor (1935-)
American Tragedy '00
Hail Caesar '94
Hoffa '92
Pacific Heights '90
Brain Dead '89
Nightbreaker '89
Morgan Stewart's Coming Home '87
The Falcon and the Snowman '85
Into Thin Air '85
Risky Business '83
East of Eden '80
The $5.20 an Hour Dream '80
Last Song '80
The Fish that Saved Pittsburgh '79
Damien: Omen 2 '78
Gumball Rally '75
The Life and Assassination of the Kingfish '76
Night Terror '76
Force Five '75
The Happy Hooker '75
Smile '75

Richard Pryor (1940-2005)
Lost Highway '96
Trigger Happy '96
Another You '91
Harlem Nights '89
See No Evil, Hear No Evil '89
Moving '88
Critical Condition '86
Jo Jo Dancer, Your Life Is Calling '86
Brewster's Millions '85
Superman 3 '83
Some Kind of Hero '82
The Toy '82
Bustin' Loose '81
In God We Trust '80
Stir Crazy '80
Wholly Moses! '80
Blue Collar '78
California Suite '78
The Wiz '78
Greased Lightning '77
Which Way Is Up? '77
Bingo Long Traveling All-Stars & Motor Kings '76
Car Wash '76
Silver Streak '76
Adios Amigo '75
Uptown Saturday Night '74
Hit! '73
The Mack '73
Some Call It Loving '73
Lady Sings the Blues '72
Dynamite Chicken '70
Black Brigade '69
Wild in the Streets '68

Roger Pryor (1901-74)
Identity Unknown '45
Kid Sister '45
Meet the Mob '42
Flying Blind '41
Panama Menace '41
The Man They Could Not Hang '39
Headline Woman '35
Belle of the Nineties '34
Lady by Choice '34

Wojtek Psoniak
See Wojciech Pszoniak

Wojtek Pszoniak
See Wojciech Pszoniak

Wojciech Pszoniak (1942-)
Chaos '01
Korczak '90
Angry Harvest '85
Danton '82
Land of Promise '74

Lou Taylor Pucci (1985-)
The Chumscrubber '05
Empire Falls '05
Thumbsucker '05
Personal Velocity: Three Portraits '02

Vladimir Pucholt (1942-)
Loves of a Blonde '65
Black Peter '63

Jesus Puente
Hatchet for the Honeymoon '70

Tito Puente (1925-2000)
The Mambo Kings '92
Radio Days '87

Robert Pugh (1950-)
The Last Legion '07
Kinky Boots '06
Longford '06
Bloodlines '05
Master and Commander: The Far Side of the World '03
The Intended '02
Enigma '01
Sword of Honour '01
A Mind to Murder '96
Priest '94
Thicker Than Water '93
Danger UXB '81
Nighthawks '81

Willard Pugh
Puppet Master 5: The Final Chapter '94
CB4: The Movie '93
Eddie Presley '92
Ambition '91
A Rage in Harlem '91
Traxx '87
Native Son '86
The Color Purple '85

Frank Puglia (1892-1975)
Girls! Girls! Girls! '62
20 Million Miles to Earth '57
The Black Hand '50
Bagdad '49
Without Reservations '46
Ali Baba and the Forty Thieves '43
For Whom the Bell Tolls '43
Casablanca '42
Billy the Kid '41
The Fatal Hour '40
In Old Caliente '39
Bulldog Drummond's Revenge '37
Viva Villa! '34
Romola 25

Aldo Puglisi (1935-)
Marriage Italian Style '64
Seduced and Abandoned '64

Benjamin Pullen (1972-)
Intern '00
An Ideal Husband '99
Prince Valiant '97

Keisha Knight Pulliam (1979-)
Beauty Shop '05
The Gospel '05
Christmas at Water's Edge '04
Motives '03
What About Your Friends: Weekend Getaway '02
A Connecticut Yankee in King Arthur's Court '89
The Little Match Girl '87

Bill Pullman (1953-)
You Kill Me '07
Scary Movie 4 '06
Dear Wendy '05
The Grudge '05
Rick '03
Igby Goes Down '02
Ignition '01
Lucky Numbers '00
Titan A.E. '00 (V)
Brokedown Palace '99
The Guilty '99
Lake Placid '99
Spy Games '99
The Virginian '99
The End of Violence '97
Zero Effect '97
Independence Day '96
Lost Highway '96
Mistrial '96
Casper '95
Mr. Wrong '95
While You Were Sleeping '95
The Last Seduction '94
Wyatt Earp '94
Malice '93
Nervous Ticks '93
Sleepless in Seattle '93
Sommersby '93
Crazy in Love '92
The Favor '92
A League of Their Own '92
Newsies '92
Singles '92
Bright Angel '91
Going Under '91
Liebestraum '91
Sibling Rivalry '90
Brain Dead '89
Cold Feet '89
The Accidental Tourist '88
Rocket Gibraltar '88
The Serpent and the Rainbow '87
Spaceballs '87
Ruthless People '86

Lilo (Liselotte) Pulver (1929-)
The Nun '66
A Global Affair '63
A Time to Love & a Time to Die '58

Bernard Punsley (1923-2004)
Junior G-Men of the Air '42
Junior G-Men '40
Angels with Dirty Faces '38
Dead End '37

Romano Puppo
The Great Alligator '81
Spaghetti Western '75

Dick Purcell (1908-44)
Captain America '44
Timber Queen '44
Phantom Killer '42
X Marks the Spot '42
Flying Blind '41
King of the Zombies '41
The Abe Lincoln of Ninth Avenue '39
Heroes in Blue '39
Irish Luck '39
Tough Kid '39
Wine, Women and Horses '37

Dominic Purcell (1970-)
Primeval '07
Blade: Trinity '04
3-Way '04

James Purcell
Sabotage '96
Playroom '90
White Light '90

Leah Purcell (1970-)
Jindabyne '06
The Proposition '05
Somersault '04
Lantana '01

Lee Purcell (1957-)
Movies Money Murder '96
Long Road Home '91
The Incredible Hulk Returns '88
To Heal a Nation '88
Jailbait: Betrayed By Innocence '86
Space Rage '86
Eddie Macon's Run '83
Valley Girl '83
Homework '82
Killing at Hell's Gate '81
Kenny Rogers as the Gambler '80
Stir Crazy '80
Big Wednesday '78
Summer of Fear '78
The Amazing Howard Hughes '77
Mr. Majestyk '74
The Witching '72
Adam at 6 a.m. '70

Noel Purcell (1900-85)
Mutiny on the Bounty '62
The Old Curiosity Shop 35

Edmund Purdom (1924-)
After the Fall of New York '85
Don't Open Till Christmas '84
Ator the Fighting Eagle '83
Big Boss 77

Reginald Purdell (1896-1953)
Brighton Rock '47
Candles at Nine '44
Clouds over Europe '39

Mr. Scarface '77
Ruler's of the City '76
Dr. Frankenstein's Castle of Freaks '74
Nefertiti, Queen of the Nile '64
Herod the Great '60
The King's Thief '55
The Prodigal '55
Athena '54
The Egyptian '54
The Student Prince '54

Carolyn Purdy-Gordon
Dolls '87
From Beyond '86
Re-Animator '84

James Purefoy (1964-)
Vanity Fair '04
The Mayor of Casterbridge '03
Resident Evil '02
A Knight's Tale '01
Don Quixote '00
Mansfield Park '99
Maybe Baby '99
The Tenant of Wildfell Hall '96
Feast of July '95

Om Puri (1950-)
Charlie Wilson's War '07
Code 46 '03
The Mystic Masseur '01
East is East '99
My Son the Fanatic '97
The Ghost and the Darkness '96
Brothers in Trouble '95
In Custody '94
City of Joy '92
Spices '86
Gandhi '82

Linda Purl (1953-)
Fear of the Dark '02
Perfect Tenant '99
Mighty Joe Young '98
Incident at Deception Ridge '94
Natural Causes '94
Accidental Meeting '93
In Self Defense '93
Body Language '92
Spies, Lies and Naked Thighs '91
Viper '88
Outrage! '86
Visiting Hours '82
The Adventures of Nellie Bly '81
High Country '81
The Manions of America '81
The Night the City Screamed '80
The Flame Is Love '79
Last Cry for Help '79
Little Ladies of the Night '77
Eleanor & Franklin '76
Crazy Mama '75

Edna Purviance (1894-1958)
The Kid '21
A Dog's Life '18
Three Charlies and One Phoney! '18
The Immigrant '17
The Cure '17
The Vagabond '16
Pawnshop '16
The Fireman '16
Burlesque on Carmen '16
Charlie Chaplin: Night at the Show '15
Charlie Chaplin ... Our Hero! '15

Alexandra Purvis (1988-)
Now & Forever '02
Ronnie and Julie '97
Contagious '96

John Putch (1961-)
Same River Twice '97
The Souler Opposite '97
Camp Nowhere '94
Fallen Angels 2 '93
Curfew '86
Impure Thoughts '86
Jaws 3 '83

Bruno Putzulu
Monsieur N. '03
In Praise of Love '01
L'Appat '94

Hy Pyke (1935-)
Halloween Night '90
Hack O'Lantern '87
Lemora, Lady Dracula '73

Denver Pyle (1920-97)
Maverick '94
Mountain Man '77
Hawmps! '76
Winterhawk '76
The Adventures of Frontier Fremont '75
Escape to Witch Mountain '75
Life & Times of Grizzly Adams '74
Murder or Mercy '74
The Legend of Hillbilly John '73
Bonnie & Clyde '67
The Rounders '65
Shenandoah '65
Geronimo '62
The Man Who Shot Liberty Valance '62
The Alamo '60
The Horse Soldiers '59
Naked Hills '56
Seventh Cavalry '56
To Hell and Back '55
Ride Clear of Diablo '54
Johnny Guitar '53
Hills of Utah '51
Oklahoma Annie '51
Dynamite Pass '50
Rim of the Canyon '49
Too Late for Tears '49
Where the North Begins '47

Missi Pyle (1973-)
Harold & Kumar Escape from Guantanamo Bay '08
Alex Rider: Operation Stormbreaker '06
Just My Luck '06
Charlie and the Chocolate Factory '05
Along Came Polly '04
Dodgeball: A True Underdog Story '04
50 First Dates '04
Soul Plane '04
Big Fish '03
Bringing Down the House '03
Exposed '03

John Pyper-Ferguson (1964-)
Josie and the Pussycats '01
Galaxy Quest '99
I'll Take You There '99
Trick '99
As Good As It Gets '97
For Richer or Poorer '97
Drive '96
Hard Core Logo '96
Space Marines '96
Killer Image '92
Showdown at Williams Creek '91
Bird on a Wire '90

Maggie Q (1979-)
Deception '08
Live Free or Die Hard '07
Mission: Impossible 3 '06

Q-Tip
She Hate Me '04
Love Goggles '99

Gregory Qaiyum
See GQ

Shu Qi (1976-)
Three Times '05
The Transporter '02

Shaobo Qin (1982-)
Ocean's Thirteen '07
Ocean's Twelve '04
Ocean's Eleven '01

Xu Qing (1969-)
The Emperor's Shadow '96
Life on a String '90

Yun Qu
Stomp the Yard '07

John Quade (1938-)
Jet Li's Fearless '06
And You Thought Your Parents Were Weird! '91
The Tracker '88
Fury to Freedom: The Life Story of Raul Ries '85
Tightrope '84
Dirkham Detective Agency '83
Peter Lundy and the Medicine Hat Stallion '77
The Last Hard Men '76
Night Terror '76
The Outlaw Josey Wales '76

Stephen Quadros
Auntie Lee's Meat Pies '92
C.I.A.: Code Name Alexa '92

Buddy Quaid (1974-)
Psycho Beach Party '00
Shock 'Em Dead '90

Dennis Quaid (1954-)
Smart People '08
Vantage Point '08
American Dreamz '06
Yours, Mine & Ours '05
The Day After Tomorrow '04
Flight of the Phoenix '04
In Good Company '04
Cold Creek Manor '03
Far from Heaven '02
The Rookie '02
Dinner with Friends '01
Traffic '00
Any Given Sunday '99
Everything That Rises '98
The Parent Trap '98
Playing by Heart '98
Switchback '97
Dragonheart '96
Gang Related '96
Something to Talk About '95
Wyatt Earp '94
Flesh and Bone '93
Undercover Blues '93
Wilder Napalm '93
Come See the Paradise '90
Postcards from the Edge '90
Great Balls of Fire '89
Everybody's All American '88
D.O.A. '88
The Big Easy '87
Innerspace '87
Suspect '87
Enemy Mine '85
Dreamscape '84
Jaws 3 '83
The Right Stuff '83
Tough Enough '83
Johnny Belinda '82
All Night Long '81
Bill '81
Caveman '81
The Night the Lights Went Out in Georgia '81
Gorp '80
The Long Riders '80
Bound for Glory '76

Randy Quaid (1953-)
Goya's Ghosts '06
Brokeback Mountain '05
Category 7: The End of the World '05
The Ice Harvest '05
Category 6: Day of Destruction '04
Home on the Range '04 (V)
Black Cadillac '03
Grind '03
Milwaukee, Minnesota '03
National Lampoon's Christmas Vacation 2: Cousin Eddie's Big Island Adventure '03
The Adventures of Pluto Nash '02
Frank McKlusky, C.I. '02
The Day the World Ended '01
Not Another Teen Movie '01
The Adventures of Rocky & Bullwinkle '00
Mail to the Chief '00
Sand '00
The Thin Blue Lie '00
Get On the Bus '96
Independence Day '96
Kingpin '96
Last Dance '96
Moonshine Highway '96
Vegas Vacation '96
Larry McMurtry's Streets of Laredo '95
Legends of the North '95
Woman Undone '95
Bye Bye, Love '94
Curse of the Starving Class '94
Major League 2 '94
Next Door '94
The Paper '94
Frankenstein '93
Days of Thunder '90
Martians Go Home! '90
Quick Change '90
Texasville '90
Bloodhounds of Broadway '89
National Lampoon's Christmas Vacation '89
Out Cold '89
Parents '89
Caddyshack 2 '88
Dead Solid Perfect '88
Moving '88
LBJ: The Early Years '87
No Man's Land '87
Sweet Country '87
The Wraith '87
Fool for Love '86
The Slugger's Wife '85
A Streetcar Named Desire '84
The Wild Life '84
National Lampoon's Vacation '83
Heartbeeps '81
Of Mice and Men '81
Foxes '80
The Guyana Tragedy: The Story of Jim Jones '80
The Long Riders '80
To Race the Wind '80
The Last Ride of the Dalton Gang '79
Midnight Express '78
The Choirboys '77
Three Warriors '77
Bound for Glory '76
Breakout '75
Missouri Breaks '76
The Apprenticeship of Duddy Kravitz '74
The Last Detail '73
Paper Moon '73
What's Up, Doc? '72
The Last Picture Show '71
Targets '68

DJ Qualls (1978-)
Delta Farce '07
I'm Reed Fish '06
Hustle & Flow '05
Little Athens '05
The Core '03
Comic Book Villains '02
The New Guy '02
Road Trip '00

John Qualen (1899-1987)
I'll Take Sweden '65
A Patch of Blue '65
Those Calloways '65
Cheyenne Autumn '64
7 Faces of Dr. Lao '63
The Man Who Shot Liberty Valance '62
The Searchers '56
At Gunpoint '55
See Chase '55
The High and the Mighty '54
Passion '54
Big Steal '49
The Fugitive '48
The Scar '48
Song of Scheherazade '47
Adventure '45
Captain Kidd '45
Dark Waters '44
Casablanca '42
The Jungle Book '42
Tortilla Flat '42
The Devil & Daniel Webster '41
Angels Over Broadway '40
Blondie On a Budget '40
The Grapes of Wrath '40
His Girl Friday '40
Knute Rockne: All American '40
The Long Voyage Home '40
Black Fury '35
Charlie Chan in Paris '35
Our Daily Bread '34
365 Nights in Hollywood '34

Jonathan Ke Quan (1971-)
Breathing Fire '91
The Goonies '85

Robert Quarry (1924-)
Teenage Exorcist '93
Evil Spirits '91
Spirits '90
Alienator '89
Warlords '88
Commando Squad '87
Cyclone '87
Phantom Empire '87
Madhouse '74
Doctor Phibes Rises Again '72
The Return of Count Yorga '71
Count Yorga, Vampire '70
Crime of Passion '57
Soldier of Fortune '55

Hugh Quarshie (1954-)
Conspiracy of Silence '03
The Murder of Stephen Lawrence '99
Star Wars: Episode 1 — The Phantom Menace '99
To Walk with Lions '99
The Church '98
Melissa '97

Philip Quast (1957-)
Introducing the Dwights '07
Me & Mrs. Jones '02
Ultraviolet '98
Napoleon '96 (V)
Around the World in 80 Ways '86

Van Quattro
Desperate Crimes '93
Beretta's Island '92

James Quattrochi (1961-)
True Friends '98

Anna Quayle (1937-)
Mistress Pamela '74
Naughty Knights '71
Chitty Chitty Bang Bang '68
Casino Royale '67
Smashing Time '67
Arrivederci, Baby '66
A Hard Day's Night '64

Anthony Quayle (1913-89)
The Bourne Identity '88
Buster '88
Magdalene '88
Masada '81
Murder by Decree '79
The Chosen '78
The Eagle Has Landed '77
Moses '77
The Story of David '76
21 Hours at Munich '76
QB VII '74
The Tamarind Seed '74
Everything You Always Wanted to Know about Sex (But Were Afraid to Ask) '72
Anne of the Thousand Days '69
MacKenna's Gold '69
A Study in Terror '65
Operation Crossbow '65
Damn the Defiant! '62
Lawrence of Arabia '62
The Guns of Navarone '61
It Takes a Thief '59
The Wrong Man '56
Hamlet '48

Queen Kong
See Deanna (Dee) Booher

Queen Latifah (1970-)
Mad Money '08
What Happens in Vegas '08
Arctic Tale '07 (N)
Hairspray '07
Life Support '07
The Perfect Holiday '07
Ice Age: The Meltdown '06 (V)
Last Holiday '05
Stranger Than Fiction '06
Beauty Shop '05
The Muppets' Wizard of Oz '05
Barbershop 2: Back in Business '04
The Cookout '04
Taxi '04
Scary Movie 3 '03
Brown Sugar '02
Chicago '02
The Country Bears '02
The Bone Collector '99
Living Out Loud '98
Mama Flora's Family '98
Sphere '97
Hoodlum '96
Set It Off '96
My Life '93
Jungle Fever '91
House Party 2: The Pajama Jam '91

Valerie Quennessen (1957-89)
Conan the Barbarian '82
Summer Lovers '82
French Postcards '79

John Quentin
The Stendahl Syndrome '95
Wittgenstein '93
Isadora '68

Rosette Quere
See Rosette

Mae Questel (1908-98)
National Lampoon's Christmas Vacation '89
New York Stories '89
Who Framed Roger Rabbit '88 (V)
A Majority of One '56

Hugues Quester (1948-)
Trois Couleurs: Bleu '93
A Tale of Springtime '89

Diana Quick (1946-)
AKA '02
Heat of the Sun '99
The Leading Man '96
Rasputin: Dark Servant of Destiny '96
Nostradamus '93
The Misadventures of Mr. Witt '90
Ordeal by Innocence '84
Brideshead Revisited '81
The Duellists '77

Charles Quigley (1906-64)
Cyclotrode "X" '46
A Woman's Face '41
Heroes in Blue '39
Daredevils of the Red Circle '38
Lady from Nowhere '36
Charlie Chan's Secret '35
Saddle Buster '32

Linnea Quigley (1958-)
Kolobos '99
Boogie Boy '98
Death Mask '98
Assault of the Party Nerds 2: Heavy Petting Detective '95
Jack-O '95
Pumpkinhead 2: Blood Wings '94
Beach Babes from Beyond '93
Innocent Blood '92
Vice Academy 2 '90
Virgin High '90
Assault of the Party Nerds '89
WitchTrap '89
Deadly Embrace '88
Hollywood Chainsaw Hookers '88
Night of the Demons '88
Vice Academy '88
Creepozoids '87
Nightmare Sisters '87
Sorority Babes in the Slimeball Bowl-A-Rama '87
Return of the Living Dead '85
Savage Streets '83
The Black Room '82
Nightstalker '81

Rita Quigley (1923-)
Riot Squad '41
Susan and God '40

Tim Quill
Suicide Ride '97
Endangered '94
Army of Darkness '92
Listen to Me '89
Staying Together '89
Hamburger Hill '87
Hiding Out '87
Thou Shalt Not Kill...Except '87

Eddie Quillan (1907-90)
Move Over, Darling '63
Dark Mountain '44
Hi, Good Lookin'! '44
Mystery of the Riverboat '44
Slightly Terrific '44
Here Comes Kelly '43
It Ain't Hay '43
Flying Blind '41
The Grapes of Wrath '40
The Flying Irishman '39
Young Mr. Lincoln '39
The Mandarin Mystery '37
Mutiny on the Bounty '35
The Tip-Off '31

Marie Quillen (1909-98)
Saddle Buster '32
Campus Knights '29

Denis Quilley (1927-2003)
A Dangerous Man: Lawrence after Arabia '91
Mister Johnson '91
The Shell Seekers '89
A.D. '85
Privates on Parade '84
In This House of Brede '75
Murder on the Orient Express '74

Veronica Quilligan
Halfmoon '95
Danny Boy '82
Lisztomania '75

Richard Quine (1920-89)
The Clay Pigeon '49
For Me and My Gal '42
Babes on Broadway '41

Kathleen Quinlan (1952-)
Made of Honor '08
Breach '07
The Hills Have Eyes '06
The Battle of Shaker Heights '03
A Civil Action '98
My Giant '98
Event Horizon '97
Breakdown '96
In the Lake of the Woods '96
Lawn Dogs '96
Zeus and Roxanne '96
Apollo 13 '95
Perfect Alibi '94
Trial by Jury '94
Last Light '93
An American Story '92
The Doors '91
Strays '91
Trapped '89
Clara's Heart '88
Man Outside '88
Sunset '88
Dreams Lost, Dreams Found '87
Wild Thing '87
Blackout '85
Warning Sign '85
The Last Winter '84
Independence Day '83
Twilight Zone: The Movie '83
Hanky Panky '82
She's in the Army Now '81
The Promise '79
The Runner Stumbles '79
Airport '77 '77
I Never Promised You a Rose Garden '77
Lifeguard '76
American Graffiti '73

Maeve Quinlan (1964-)
Heart of America '03
Net Games '03
Totally Blonde '01

Charles Quinlivan
All the Young Men '60
Zero Hour! '57

Aidan Quinn (1959-)
Wild Child '08
Bury My Heart at Wounded Knee '07
Empire Falls '05
Nine Lives '05
Bobby Jones: Stroke of Genius '04
Convicted '04
Benedict Arnold: A Question of Honor '03
Evelyn '02
Stolen Summer '02
The Prince and the Pauper '01
Two of Us '00
Music of the Heart '99
Songcatcher '99
This Is My Father '99
In Dreams '98
Practical Magic '98
The Assignment '97
Commandments '96
Looking for Richard '96
Michael Collins '96
Haunted '95
Legends of the Fall '94
Mary Shelley's Frankenstein '94
The Stars Fell on Henrietta '94
Benny & Joon '93
Blink '93
The Playboys '92
A Private Matter '92
At Play in the Fields of the Lord '91
Lies of the Twins '91
Avalon '90
The Handmaid's Tale '90
Crusoe '89
The Lemon Sisters '90
Perfect Witness '89
Stakeout '87
All My Sons '86
The Mission '86
Desperately Seeking Susan '85
An Early Frost '85
Reckless '84

Anthony Quinn (1915-2001)
Avenging Angelo '02
Gotti '96
A Walk in the Clouds '95
Hercules the Legendary Journeys, Vol. 1: And the Amazon Women '94
Hercules the Legendary Journeys, Vol. 2: The Lost Kingdom '94
Hercules the Legendary Journeys, Vol. 3: The Circle of Fire '94
Hercules the Legendary Journeys, Vol. 4: In the Underworld '94
Somebody to Love '94
Last Action Hero '93
Jungle Fever '91
Mobsters '91
Only the Lonely '91
Ghosts Can't Do It '90
Revenge '90
A Man of Passion '88
Onassis '88
Regina '83
The Salamander '82
High Risk '81
Lion of the Desert '80
The Con Artists '80
Across 110th Street '72
R.P.M.* (*Revolutions Per Minute) '70
Walk in the Spring Rain '70
A Dream of Kings '69
The Secret of Santa Vittoria '69
The Shoes of the Fisherman '68
The Rover '67
The Lost Command '66
Behold a Pale Horse '64
Zorba the Greek '64
Barabbas '62
Lawrence of Arabia '62
Requiem for a Heavyweight '62
The Guns of Navarone '61
Heller in Pink Tights '60
Portrait in Black '60
Black Orchid '59
Last Train from Gun Hill '59
Warlock '59
Hot Spell '58
The Hunchback of Notre Dame '57
The Ride Back '57
Lust for Life '56
The Magnificent Matador '55
Seven Cities of Gold '55
Ulysses '55
Blowing Wild '54
La Strada '54
Viva Zapata! '52
Against All Flags '52
The World in His Arms '52
Sinbad, the Sailor '47
Tycoon '47
Back to Bataan '45
Buffalo Bill '44
China Sky '44
Guadalcanal Diary '43
The Ox-Bow Incident '43
The Black Swan '42
The Road to Morocco '42
Blood and Sand '41
They Died with Their Boots On '41
City for Conquest '40
The Ghost Breakers '40
The Road to Singapore '40
The Texas Rangers Ride Again '40
Union Pacific '39
The Plainsman '37
Waikiki Wedding '37

Bill Quinn (1912-94)
Twilight Zone: The Movie '83
Bustin' Loose '81
Dead and Buried '81
Backstairs at the White House '79
Big Calibre '35

Colin Quinn (1959-)
Who's the Man? '93
Crocodile Dundee 2 '88

Daniel Quinn
Raising Flagg '06
Miracle at Sage Creek '05
Spiders 2: Breeding Ground '01
Wolverine '96
A Reason to Believe '95
American Cop '94
Scanner Cop '94
Scanner Cop 2: Volkin's Revenge '94
Scanners: The Showdown '94
Conagher '91

Elizabeth Quinn
Love and Death on Long Island '97
The Sound and the Silence '93

Francesco Quinn (1962-)
Afghan Knights '07
Vlad '03
Nowhere Land '98
Rough Riders '97
Cannes Man '96
The Dark Dancer '95
Red Shoe Diaries 5: Weekend Pass '95
Top Dog '95
Dead Certain '92
Deadly Rivals '92
Indio '90
The Old Man and the Sea '90
Priceless Beauty '90
Platoon '86
Quo Vadis '85

Glenn Quinn (1970-2002)
R.S.V.P. '02
At Any Cost '00
Campfire Tales '98
Live Nude Girls '95
Dr. Giggles '92

James W. Quinn
Endangered Species '02
WitchTrap '89
Witchboard '87

J.C. Quinn (1943-)
Primary Colors '98
Hit Me '96
The Babe '92
Crisscross '92
All-American Murder '91
Megaville '91
Prayer of the Rollerboys '91
Priceless Beauty '90
The Abyss '89
Turner and Hooch '89
Barfly '87
Heartbreak Ridge '86
Twisted '86
Violated '84

Louis Quinn (1915-88)
Unholy Rollers '72
Superchick '71

Martha Quinn (1961-)
Bad Channels '92
The Return of Spinal Tap '92
Chopper Chicks in Zombietown '91
Motorama '91
Eddie and the Cruisers 2: Eddie Lives! '89
Tapeheads '89

Pat Quinn (1937-)
Clean and Sober '88
Zachariah '70

Patricia Quinn (1944-)
Alice's Restaurant '69
Witching Time '84
Monty Python's The Meaning of Life '83
Shock Treatment '81
The Rocky Horror Picture Show '75

Terry Quinn
The Witching '72
The Two Faces of Dr. Jekyll '60

Adolfo "Shabba Doo" Quinones
Deadly Dancer '90
Lambada '90
Breakin' '84
Breakin' 2: Electric Boogaloo '84

Jonathan Quint
Silicon Towers '99
Floating '97

Pauline Quirke (1959-)
Carrie's War '04
David Copperfield '99
The Sculptress '97

Oscar Quitak
Tangiers '83
The Revenge of Frankenstein '58

Beulah Quo (1923-2002)
The Children of An Lac '80
The Seventh Dawn '64
Girls! Girls! Girls! '62

Marianne Quon (1923-91)
Charlie Chan in the Secret Service '44
China '43

Ellie Raab (1977-)
The Ref '93
Eyes of an Angel '91
The Fabulous Baker Boys '89

Kurt Raab (1946-88)
Angry Harvest '85
Mussolini & I '85
Parker '84
Tricheurs '84
The Stationmaster's Wife '77
Satan's Brew '76
Fox and His Friends '75
Tenderness of the Wolves '73
The American Soldier '70
Beware of a Holy Whore '70
Why Does Herr R. Run Amok? '69

Birgitte Raaberg (1954-)
The Kingdom 2 '97
The Kingdom '95

Francesco Rabal (1925-2001)
Goya in Bordeaux '99
Talk of Angels '96
Tie Me Up! Tie Me Down! '90
A Time of Destiny '88
Camorra: The Naples Connection '85
Padre Nuestro '85
The Holy Innocents '84
The Stilts '84
Reborn '81
City of the Walking Dead '80
Hostages '80
Stay As You Are '78
Sorcerer '77
El Muerto '75
Exorcism's Daughter '74
Devil's Crude '71
Diary of a Rebel '68
Belle de Jour '67
The Eclipse '66
The Nun '66
Viridiana '61
Nazarin '58
The Wide Blue Road '57

Pamela Rabe (1959-)
Paradise Road '97
The Well '97
Cosi '95
Sirens '94

Francine Racette (1947-)
Au Revoir les Enfants '87
Lumiere '76
Mr. Klein '76

Alan Rachins (1947-)
Leave It to Beaver '97
Meet Wally Sparks '97
The Stepsister '97
Showgirls '95
Star Quest '94
Heart Condition '90
Mistress '87
L.A. Law '86
Always '85

Victoria Racimo (1945-)
White Fang 2: The Myth of the White Wolf '94
Ernest Goes to Camp '87
Roanoak '86
Prophecy '79
Green Eyes '76
Search for the Gods '75
G.I. Executioner '71

Kurt Rackelmann (1910-73)
First Spaceship on Venus '60

Damaine Radcliff
Glory Road '06
Step Up '06

Daniel Radcliffe (1989-)
December Boys '07
Harry Potter and the Order of the Phoenix '07
My Boy Jack '07
Harry Potter and the Goblet of Fire '05
Harry Potter and the Prisoner of Azkaban '04
Harry Potter and the Chamber of Secrets '02
Harry Potter and the Sorcerer's Stone '01
The Tailor of Panama '00
David Copperfield '99

Rosemary Radcliffe
Anne of Green Gables: The Continuing Story '99
Anne of Green Gables '85

Sascha Radetsky (1977-)
Center Stage '00
Home at Last '88

Basil Radford (1897-1952)
Passport to Pimlico '49
The Winslow Boy '48
Whiskey Galore '48
Captive Heart '47
Dead of Night '45
Night Train to Munich '40
The Lady Vanishes '38
Young and Innocent '37

Natalie Radford (1959-)
Last Call: The Final Chapter of F. Scott Fitzgerald '02
Agent Red '00
Killing Moon '00
P.T. Barnum '99
The Android Affair '95
Spenser: The Judas Goat '94
Sniper '92

Gilda Radner (1946-89)
Haunted Honeymoon '86
Movers and Shakers '85
The Woman in Red '84
Hanky Panky '82
First Family '80
Mr. Mike's Mondo Video '79
All You Need Is Cash '78
The Last Detail '73

Jerzy Radziwilowicz (1950-)
No End '84
Passion '82
Man of Iron '81
Man of Marble '76

Cassidy Rae (1976-)
Extremedays '01
National Lampoon's Favorite Deadly Sins '95

Charlotte Rae (1926-)
Another Woman's Husband '00
Nowhere '96
Thunder in Paradise '93
Tom and Jerry: The Movie '93 (V)
The Worst Witch '85
Words by Heart '84
The Triangle Factory Fire Scandal '79
Sidewinder One '77
Bananas '71
The Hot Rock '70
Jenny '70
Hello Down There '69

John Rae
Oh! What a Lovely War '69
Morgan: A Suitable Case for Treatment '66

Raekwon (1970-)
Scary Movie 3 '03
Black and White '99

Bob Rafelson (1933-)
Always '85
Head '68

Cyril Raffaelli (1974-)
Live Free or Die Hard '07
District B13 '04

Giuliano Raffaelli
And God Said to Cain '69
Blood and Black Lace '64

Chips Rafferty (1909-71)
Skullduggery '70
Double Trouble '67
Wackiest Ship in the Army '61
The Sundowners '60
Walk into Hell '57
The Desert Rats '53

Frances Rafferty (1922-2004)
Curley '47
Money Madness '47
Hollywood '45
Abbott and Costello in Hollywood '45
Mrs. Parkington '44
Forty Thousand Horsemen '41

Giovanni Lombardo Radice (1954-)
Cannibal Apocalypse '80
Deadly Impact '84

Ken Radley
Mr. Reliable: A True Story '95

Deborah Raffin (1953-)
Morning Glory '93
Scanners 2: The New Order '91
Night of the Fox '90
Noble House '88
Claudia '85
Death Wish 3 '85
Jungle Heat '84
Killing at Hell's Gate '81
For the Love of It '80
Touched by Love '80
Willa '79
The Dove '74
Forty Carats '73

George Raft (1895-1980)
Sextette '78
Casino Royale '67
Five Golden Dragons '67
Ocean's 11 '60
Jet Over the Atlantic '59
Some Like It Hot '59
Around the World in 80 Days '56
A Bullet for Joey '55
Black Widow '54
Man from Cairo '54
I'll Get You '53
Loan Shark '52
They Drive by Night '40
Each Dawn I Die '39
Spawn of the North '38
You and Me '38
Souls at Sea '37
The Bowery '33
Night After Night '32
Scarface '31

Rags Ragland (1905-46)
Panama Hattie '42
Whistling in Dixie '42
Whistling in the Dark '41

Joe Ragno
Day at the Beach '98
Jane Doe '96
No Way Home '96
The Base '92

William Ragsdale (1961-)
The Reaping '07
Road House 2: Last Call '06
Just a Little Harmless Sex '99

Theodore (Ted) Raimi (1965-)
Spider-Man 3 '07
The Grudge '04
Spider-Man 2 '04
The Shot '96
Players '03
Spider-Man '02
Thou Shalt Not Kill...Except '87

Sam Raimi (1959-)
Stephen King's The Stand '94
Body Bags '93
Indian Summer '93
Innocent Blood '92
Maniac Cop '88
Evil Dead 2: Dead by Dawn '87
Thou Shalt Not Kill...Except '87

Ford Rainey (1908-2005)
Bed & Breakfast '92
The Cellar '90
Backstairs at the White House '79
Strangers: The Story of a Mother and Daughter '79
Mountain Man '77
Babe! '75
Strange New World '75
Sixteen '72
My Sweet Charlie '70
The Gypsy Moths '69
The Sand Pebbles '66
Flaming Star '60
3:10 to Yuma '57

Frances Raines
Disconnected '87
Breeders '86
The Mutilator '85

Jessie Ralph (1864-1944)
They Met in Bombay '41
The Bank Dick '40
The Blue Bird '40
Drums Along the Mohawk '39
Double Wedding '37
The Last of Mrs. Cheyney '37
After the Thin Man '36
Yellow Dust '36
San Francisco '36
Little Lord Fauntleroy '36
I Live My Life '35
Les Miserables '35
Paris in Spring '35
Evelyn Prentice '34
Murder at the Vanities '34
One Night of Love '34

Giovanna Ralli (1935-)
What Did You Do in the War, Daddy? '66
Era Notte a Roma '60

Christopher Ralph (1977-)
The Skulls 2 '02

Umberto Raho (1922-)
The Blonde '92
Aladdin '86
Anuck! '71
The Night Evelyn Came Out of the Grave '71
The Bird with the Crystal Plumage '70
Satanik '69

Rah Digga (1972-)
Carmen: A Hip Hopera '01

Aishwarya Rai (1973-)
The Last Legion '07
Mistress of Spices '05
Bride & Prejudice '04

Victor Raider-Wexler (1943-)
Die Mommie Die! '03
Tom Clancy's Netforce '98

Steve Railsback (1948-)
The Devil's Rejects '05
The Box '03
Ed Gein '01
Made Men '99
Barb Wire '96
Calendar Girl '93
Final Mission '93
Nukie '93
Private Wars '93
Save Me '93
Forever: A Ghost of a Love Story '92
Scissors '91
Alligator 2: The Mutation '90
Assassin '89
The Forgotten '89
Deadly Intent '88
Blue Monkey '87
Distortions '87
Scenes from the Goldmine '87
The Survivalist '87
The Wind '87
Armed and Dangerous '86
Lifeforce '85
Torchlight '85
The Golden Seal '83
Nightmares '83
Trick or Treats '82
Escape 2000 '81
The Stunt Man '80
From Here to Eternity '79
Angela '77
Helter Skelter '76

Christina Raines (1952-)
Firewall '06
Grilled '06
North Shore '87
Silver Dream Racer '83
Touched by Love '80
Centennial '78
The Sentinel '76
The Duellists '77
Nashville '75
Russian Roulette '75
The Shrieking '73
Stacey '73

Luise Rainer (1910-)
The Gambler '97
Tiefland '44
The Great Waltz '38
The Good Earth '37
The Emperor's Candlesticks '37
The Great Ziegfeld '36

Douglas Rain (1928-)
2010: The Year We Make Contact '84 (V)
2001: A Space Odyssey '68 (V)

Jack Raine (1897-1979)
Last House on the Left '72

Jeramie Rain (1948-)
The Abductors '72

Raimu (1883-1946)
The Hammer '07
Well-Digger's Daughter '46
Heart of a Nation '43
Cesar '36
The Baker's Wife '33
Fanny '32
Marius '31

Ruggero Raimondi
Crimewave '85
Evil Dead '83

Victor... / Steve Railsback (1948-) (V)

Tommy (Thomas) Rall (1929-)
Dancers '87
My Sister Eileen '55
Seven Brides for Seven Brothers '54
Kiss Me Kate '53

Mary Lynn Rajskub (1971-)
Firewall '06
Little Miss Sunshine '06
Mysterious Skin '04
Legally Blonde 2: Red, White & Blonde '03
Punch-Drunk Love '02
Sweet Home Alabama '02
Road to Graceland '98

Pierre-Loup Rajot (1958-)
The Adventures of Felix '99
The New Eve '98

Claude Rains (1889-1967)
The Greatest Story Ever Told '65
Lawrence of Arabia '62
Battle of the Worlds '61
The Pied Piper of Hamelin '57
Lisbon '56
Paris Express '53
The White Tower '50
Where Danger Lives '50
Notorious '46
Deception '46
Angel on My Shoulder '46
Caesar and Cleopatra '46
Mr. Skeffington '44
Passage to Marseilles '44
Forever and a Day '43
Casablanca '42
Now, Voyager '42
Here Comes Mr. Jordan '41
Kings Row '41
The Wolf Man '41
The Sea Hawk '40
Juarez '39
Mr. Smith Goes to Washington '39
They Made Me a Criminal '39
Four Daughters '38
The Adventures of Robin Hood '38
The Prince and the Pauper '37
Anthony Adverse '36
The Invisible Man '33

Sheryl Lee Ralph (1956-)
Deterrence '00
Personals '00
Bogus '96
White Man's Burden '95
Witch Hunt '94
Sister Act 2: Back in the Habit '93
The Distinguished Gentleman '92
Mistress '91
To Sleep with Anger '90
The Mighty Quinn '89
Oliver & Company '88 (V)
Codename: Foxfire '85

Esther Ralston (1902-94)
Tin Pan Alley '40
The Spy Ring '38
Shadows of the Orient '37
We're in the Legion Now '37

John Ralston
Earthstorm '06
Power and Beauty '02
Oliver Twist '22

Jobyna Ralston (1900-67)
Lonely Wives '31
The Kid Brother '27
Wings '27
For Heaven's Sake '26
The Freshman '25
Girl Shy '24
Peter Pan '24

Vera Hruba Ralston (1923-2003)
Jubilee Trail '54
Hoodlum Empire '52
The Fighting Kentuckian '49
Dakota '45

Cecil Ramage (1895-1988)
Kind Hearts and Coronets '49

Marjorie Rambeau (1889-1970)
Man of a Thousand Faces '57
A Man Called Peter '55
Forever Female '53
Torch Song '53
The Rains Came '39
Santa Fe Marshal '40
Primrose Path '40
Laughing Sinners '31
Min & Bill '30

Enrique Rambal (1924-71)
The Man and the Monster '65
The Exterminating Angel '62

Dack Rambo (1942-94)
Ultra Warrior '92
River of Diamonds '90
The Spring '89
Waikiki '80
Hit Lady '74

Henry Ramer
The Big Slice '90
Hockey Night '84
Reno and the Doc '84

Carlos Ramirez (1914-86)
Wassup Rockers '06
Anchors Aweigh '45
Bathing Beauty '44
Two Girls and a Sailor '44

Dania Ramirez (1979-)
Illegal Tender '07

X-Men: The Last Stand '06
Fat Albert '04
She Hate Me '04
South Seas Massacre '74

Edgar Ramirez (1977-)
Vantage Point '08
The Bourne Ultimatum '07
Domino '05

Efren Ramirez (1973-)
Crank '06
Employee of the Month '06
Napoleon Dynamite '04

Frank Ramirez
Details of a Duel: A Question of Honor '89
Miracle in Rome '88
Code of Honor '82
Smith! '69

Harold Ramis (1944-)
Knocked Up '07
Walk Hard: The Dewey Cox Story '07
The Last Kiss '06
I'm with Lucy '02
Orange County '02
As Good As It Gets '97
Love Affair '94
Ghostbusters 2 '89
Stealing Home '88
Baby Boom '87
Ghostbusters '84
Heavy Metal '81 (V)
Stripes '81

Haley Ramm (1992-)
Walking Tall: Lone Justice '07
X-Men: The Last Stand '06
Flightplan '05
Yours, Mine & Ours '05

Rudy Ramos (1950-)
The Spy Within '94
Blindsided '93
Colors '88
Open House '86
Quicksilver '86

Eulalia Ramon (1959-)
Goya in Bordeaux '99

Charlotte Rampling (1945-)
Babylon AD '08
Deception '08
Basic Instinct 2 '06
Heading South '05
Lemming '05
I'll Sleep When I'm Dead '03
The Statement '03
Swimming Pool '03
The Fourth Angel '01
My Uncle Silas '01
Spy Game '01
Aberdeen '00
Signs & Wonders '00
Under the Sand '00
Great Expectations '99
The Wings of the Dove '97
Invasion of Privacy '96
Hammers over the Anvil '91
D.O.A. '88
Angel Heart '87
Mascara '87
Max, Mon Amour '86
The Verdict '82
Stardust Memories '80
Orca '77
Foxtrot '76
The Purple Taxi '77
Farewell, My Lovely '75
Sardinia Kidnapped '75
Ski Bum '75
Caravan to Vaccares '74
The Night Porter '74
'Tis a Pity She's a Whore '73
Zardoz '73
Asylum '72
The Damned '69
Georgy Girl '66

Anne Elizabeth Ramsay (1960-)
The Final Cut '96
A League of Their Own '92

Bruce Ramsay (1968-)
Jericho Mansions '03
Island of the Dead '00
Bonanno: A Godfather's Story '99
Hit Me '96
Curdled '95
Hellraiser 4: Bloodline '95
Dead Beat '94
Killing Zone '94
The New Age '94
Alive '93

Remak Ramsay (1937-)
Addicted to Love '96
Mr. & Mrs. Bridge '90
The Dining Room '86

Bobby Ramsen
It's Alive 2: It Lives Again '78
Hell Up in Harlem '73

Anne Ramsey (1929-88)
Perfect Alibi '94
Meet the Hollowheads '89
Another Chance '88
Dr. Hackenstein '88
The River Pirates '88
Throw Momma from the Train '87
Weeds '87
Deadly Friend '86
The Goonies '85
A Small Killing '81
Marilyn: The Untold Story '80
White Mama '80
The Black Marble '79
Goin' South '78
The Boy in the Plastic Bubble '76

David Ramsey
Fatal Contact: Bird Flu in America '06
Hair Show '04
Pay It Forward '00
Mutiny '99

Laura Ramsey (1982-)
The Ruins '08
The Covenant '06
She's the Man '06
Cruel World '05
Venom '05

Logan Ramsey (1921-2000)
Dr. Hackenstein '88
Say Yes! '86
The Beast Within '82
Conspiracy of Terror '75
Red, White & Busted '75 (Confessions of Tom Harris)
Fury on Wheels '71
Head '68
The Hoodlum Priest '61

Lois Ramsey
Road to Nhill '97
River Street '95

Marion Ramsey (1947-)
Police Academy 6: City under Siege '89
Police Academy 5: Assignment Miami Beach '88
Police Academy 3: Back in Training '86

Natalie Ramsey (1975-)
Cruel Intentions 3 '04
Children of the Corn 666: Isaac's Return '99

Stacey Linn Ramsower
The Baby-Sitters' Club '95
The Quick and the Dead '95

Nick Ramus (1952-2007)
3 Ninjas Knuckle Up '95
Geronimo '93
Journey to Spirit Island '92

Frederica Ranchi (1939-)
Son of Samson '62
The Wide Blue Road '57

Sally Rand
Sunny Side Up '28
Braveheart '25

Monica Randal
See Monica Randall

Addison "Jack" Randall (1906-45)
Covered Wagon Trails '40
Across the Plains '39
Wild Horse Canyon '39
Gun Packer '38
Gunsmoke Trail '38
Man's Country '38
Red Lights Ahead '36

Jack Randall
See Addison "Jack" Randall

Lexi (Faith) Randall (1980-)
Sarah, Plain and Tall: Winter's End '99
The Stars Fell on Henrietta '94
The War '94
Heidi '93
Sarah, Plain and Tall: Skylark '93
Sarah, Plain and Tall '91

Meg Randall (1926-)
Ma and Pa Kettle Back On the Farm '51
Ma and Pa Kettle Go to Town '50
Ma and Pa Kettle '49

Monica Randall (1942-)
Cria Cuervos '76
Inquisition '76
Witches' Mountain '71
Commando Attack '67
Five Giants from Texas '66

Tony Randall (1920-2004)
Down With Love '03
Fatal Instinct '93
Gremlins 2: The New Batch '90 (V)
That's Adequate '90
King of Comedy '82
Foolin' Around '80
Scavenger Hunt '79
Everything You Always Wanted to Know about Sex (But Were Afraid to Ask) '72
Hello Down There '69
The Littlest Angel '69
The Alphabet Murders '65
Robin and the 7 Hoods '64
Send Me No Flowers '64
The Brass Bottle '63
7 Faces of Dr. Lao '63
Boys' Night Out '62
Lover Come Back '61
The Adventures of Huckleberry Finn '60
Let's Make Love '60
The Mating Game '59
Pillow Talk '59
Will Success Spoil Rock Hunter? '57

Steven Randazzo
Mac '93
In the Soup '92
Jungle Fever '91

Monica Randel
See Monica Randall

Ron Randell (1918-2005)
Girl in Black Stockings '57
The Story of Esther Costello '57
Omoo Omoo, the Shark God '49
The Loves of Carmen '48

Theresa Randle (1967-)
The Hunt for Eagle One: Crash Point '06
Bad Boys 2 '03
Livin' for Love: The Natalie Cole Story '00
Spawn '97
Girl 6 '96
Space Jam '96
Bad Boys '95
Beverly Hills Cop 3 '94
Sugar Hill '94
CB4: The Movie '93
Malcolm X '92
Jungle Fever '91

Dan Ranger
Cop-Out '91
The Last Ride '91

Arthur (L.) Rankin (1900-47)
Terror Trail '33
Fighting Fool '32
Below the Deadline '29
Walking Back '26

Kenny Ransom
The Crocodile Hunter: Collision Course '02
Border Patrol '01
Prison for Children '93
There Goes My Baby '92

Tim Ransom (1963-)
Courage Under Fire '96
Vital Signs '90

Prunella Ransome (1943-)
Man in the Wilderness '71
Far from the Madding Crowd '67

Donald Randolph (1906-93)
The Deadly Mantis '57
Gunsmoke '53

Jane Randolph (1919-)
Abbott and Costello Meet Frankenstein '48
Open Secret '48
Railroaded '47
Curse of the Cat People '44
Cat People '42
The Falcon's Brother '42

Anders Randolf (1870-1930)
The Kiss '29
Ranson's Folly '26
The Idol Dancer '20
The Love Flower '20

John Randolph (1915-2004)
You've Got Mail '98
A Price above Rubies '97
A Foreign Field '93
Iron Maze '91
National Lampoon's Christmas Vacation '89
The Wizard of Loneliness '88
As Summers Die '86
Prizzi's Honor '85
Frances '82
Lovely... But Deadly '82
There Was a Crooked Man '70
Pretty Poison '68
Seconds '66

Lillian Randolph (1898-1980)
Magic '78
How to Seduce a Woman '74

Ty Randolph
See Mindi Miller

Windsor Taylor Randolph
See Mindi Miller

Robert Random (1943-)
Danger Zone 3: Steel Horse War '90
Danger Zone 2 '89

Salvo Randone (1906-91)
Fellini Satyricon '69
Spirits of the Dead '68
10th Victim '65
The Mercenaries '62

Joe Ranft (1960-2005)
Cars '06 (V)
Finding Nemo '03 (V)
Toy Story 2 '99 (V)
A Bug's Life '98 (V)

Michael Rapaport (1970-)
Grilled '06
Hitch '05
This Girl's Life '03
Comic Book Villains '02
Triggermen '02
Dr. Dolittle 2 '01 (V)
King of the Jungle '01
Bamboozled '00
Chain of Fools '00
Kiss Toledo Goodbye '00
Lucky Numbers '00
Men of Honor '00
Small Time Crooks '00
Deep Blue Sea '99
The Naked Man '98
Palmetto '98
A Brother's Kiss '97
Cop Land '97
Kicked in the Head '97
Subway Stories '97
Beautiful Girls '96
Illtown '96
Metro '96
The Basketball Diaries '95
Mighty Aphrodite '95
The Pallbearer '95
Higher Learning '94
Kiss of Death '94
The Scout '94
Hand Gun '93
Money for Nothing '93
True Romance '93
Zebrahead '92

Anthony Rapp (1971-)
Danny Roane: First Time Director '06
Rent '05
A Beautiful Mind '01
Road Trip '00
Man of the Century '99
David Searching '97
Dazed and Confused '93
Six Degrees of Separation '93
School Ties '92
Far from Home '89
Adventures in Babysitting '87

David Rappaport (1952-90)
Peter Gunn '89
The Bride '85
Mysteries '84

Sheri Rappaport (1977-)
Seeing Other People '04
Serial Slayer '03
United States of Leland '03
Little Witches '96

Eva Ras (1941-)
The Love Affair, or The Case of the Missing Switchboard Operator '67
Man Is Not a Bird '65

Renato Rascel (1912-91)
The Secret of Santa Vittoria '69
Uncle Was a Vampire '59
The Seven Hills of Rome '58

David Rasche (1944-)
The Sentinel '06
Final Approach '04
Off the Lip '04
Exposed '03
Just Married '03
Divine Secrets of the Ya-Ya Sisterhood '02
Hostage Hotel '00
The Big Tease '99
Friends & Lovers '99
The Settlement '99
Tourist Trap '98
That Old Feeling '96
Dead Weekend '95
Out There '95
Bigfoot: The Unforgettable Encounter '94
A Million to Juan '94
Twenty Bucks '93
Bingo '91
Delirious '91
Silhouette '91
The Masters of Menace '90
An Innocent Man '89
Wedding Band '89
Wicked Stepmother '89
Made in Heaven '87
Native Son '86
Manhattan '79
Sanctuary of Fear '79

Phylicia Rashad (1949-)
A Raisin in the Sun '08
The Old Settler '01
The Visit '00
Loving Jezebel '99
Free of Eden '98
Once Upon a Time... When We Were Colored '95
False Witness '89
Uncle Tom's Cabin '87

Sharif Rashed
Hell's Kitchen NYC '97
Blue in the Face '95
Crooklyn '94

Rie Rasmussen
Angel-A '05
Femme Fatale '02

Fritz Rasp (1891-1976)
The Threepenny Opera '31
Diary of a Lost Girl '29
Spies '28
Metropolis '26

Julien Rassam (1968-)
Queen Margot '94
The Accompanist '93

Ivan Rassimov (1938-2003)
Emerald Jungle '80
Shock '79
Man from Deep River '77
Your Vice is a Closed Room and Only I Have the Key '72
The Next Victim '71
Blade of the Ripper '70
Planet of the Vampires '65

Rada Rassimov (1938-)
Torture Chamber of Baron Blood '72
The Good, the Bad and the Ugly '67

Victor Rasuk (1984-)
Stop-Loss '08
Adrift in Manhattan '07
Feel the Noise '07

Bonneville '06
I'm Reed Fish '06
Lords of Dogtown '05
Haven '04
Raising Victor Vargas '03

Thalmus Rasulala (1939-91)
Mom and Dad Save the World '92
New Jack City '91
Blind Vengeance '90
The Package '89
Above the Law '88
Bulletproof '88
Born American '86
Sophisticated Gents '81
Adios Amigo '75
Bucktown '75
Friday Foster '75
Blacula '72

Mikhail Rasumny (1890-1956)
The Kissing Bandit '48
Anna and the King of Siam '46
For Whom the Bell Tolls '43
Wake Island '42

Jeremy Ratchford (1965-)
Angel Eyes '01
The Crew '00
Fly Away Home '96
Moonshine Highway '96
Prom Night 3: The Last Kiss '89

Sandy Ratcliff (1950-)
Yesterday's Hero '79
Family Life '71

Basil Rathbone (1892-1967)
Many Faces of Sherlock Holmes '86
Autopsy of a Ghost '67
Hillbillies in a Haunted House '67
Planet of Blood '66
Voyage to the Prehistoric Planet '65
The Comedy of Terrors '64
The Magic Sword '62
Tales of Terror '62
Victoria Regina '61
Last Hurrah '58
The Black Sleep '56
Court Jester '56
We're No Angels '55
Casanova's Big Night '54
A Christmas Carol '54
The Adventures of Ichabod and Mr. Toad '49 (V)
Dressed to Kill '46
Heartbeat '46
Terror by Night '46
Pursuit to Algiers '45
The Woman in Green '45
Bathing Beauty '44
Frenchman's Creek '44
The Pearl of Death '44
Spider Woman '44
Above Suspicion '43
Sherlock Holmes Faces Death '43
Sherlock Holmes in Washington '43
Sherlock Holmes and the Secret Weapon '42
Sherlock Holmes: The Voice of Terror '42
The Black Cat '41
International Lady '41
The Mark of Zorro '40
Rhythm on the River '40
The Hound of the Baskervilles '39
Son of Frankenstein '39
The Tower of London '39
The Adventures of Marco Polo '38
The Adventures of Robin Hood '38
Dawn Patrol '38
If I Were King '38
Love from a Stranger '37
Make a Wish '37
The Garden of Allah '36
Romeo and Juliet '36
A Tale of Two Cities '36
Anna Karenina '35
Captain Blood '35
David Copperfield '35
Last Days of Pompeii '35
Sin Takes a Holiday '30

Benjamin Ratner
Firestorm '97
Bounty Hunters '96

Gregory Ratoff (1897-1960)
Exodus '60
Abdulla the Great '56
All About Eve '50
I'm No Angel '33
Skyscraper Souls '32

Devin Ratray (1977-)
Home Alone 2: Lost in New York '92
Spy Trap '92
Home Alone '90

Peter Ratray (1941-)
Stonewall '95
Will: G. Gordon Liddy '82

Heather Rattray (1966-)
Basket Case 2 '90
Mountain Family Robinson '79
Sea Gypsies '78
Further Adventures of the Wilderness Family, Part 2 '77
Across the Great Divide '76

John Ratzenberger (1947-)
WALL-E '08 (V)
Ratatouille '07 (V)
Cars '06 (V)
Finding Nemo '03 (V)
Monsters, Inc. '01 (V)
Spirited Away '01 (V)
Tick Tock '00
Toy Story 2 '99 (V)
A Bug's Life '98 (V)
Under Pressure '98
One Night Stand '97
That Darn Cat '96
Toy Story '95 (V)
Camp Cucamonga: How I Spent My Summer Vacation '90
House 2: The Second Story '87
Timestalkers '87
Combat Academy '86
Gandhi '82
Outland '81
Ragtime '81
The Empire Strikes Back '80
Motel Hell '80
The Bitch '78
A Bridge Too Far '77
Twilight's Last Gleaming '77

Andrea Rau (1949-)
Beyond Erotica '79
Daughters of Darkness '71

Siegfried Rauch (1932-)
Sons of Trinity '95
Alien Contamination '81
The Big Red One '80
We Will Not Enter the Forest '79
The Uranium Conspiracy '78
Patton '70
Nous N'Irons Plus au Bois '69

Raven (1985-)
The Princess Diaries 2: Royal Engagement '04
Everyone's Hero '06 (V)
Dr. Dolittle 2 '01
Dr. Dolittle '98
Queen '93

Gina Ravara
See Gina Ravera

Mike Raven (1924-97)
Crucible of Terror '72
Disciple of Death '72
I, Monster '71
Lust for a Vampire '71

Raven-Symone
See Raven

Christopher Ravenscroft (1946-)
A Mind to Murder '96
Henry V '89

Kim Raver (1969-)
Night at the Museum '06
Kiss the Girls '97

Gina Ravera (1968-)
The Great Debaters '07
The Temptations '98
Showgirls '95
Soul of the Game '96

Adrian Rawlins (1958-)
Breaking the Waves '95
Woman in Black '89

Herbert Rawlinson (1885-1953)
Jail Bait '54
Nabonga '44
Shake Hands with Murder '44
Colt Comrades '43
Lost Canyon '43
I Killed That Man '42
The Panther's Claw '42
Smart Alecks '42
Bad Man of Deadwood '41
Gentleman from Dixie '41
Riot Squad '41
Blind Fools '40
Flash Gordon Conquers the Universe '40
Blake of Scotland Yard '36
Robinson Crusoe of Clipper Island '36
Mystery Island '36
Show Them No Mercy '35
Confidential '35
The Tomboy '24

Navi Rawat (1977-)
Loveless in Los Angeles '07
Feast '06
Undead or Alive '07
House of Sand and Fog '03

Lou Rawls (1936-)
Motel Blue '98
Watchers Reborn '98
Don King: Only in America '97
Still Breathing '97
Malevolence '95
Showdown '94

Aldo Ray (1926-91)
Shock 'Em Dead '90
Shooters '89
Blood Red '88
Swift Justice '88
Hollywood Cop '87
Star Slammer '87
Terror on Alcatraz '87
Bio Hazard '86
Evils of the Night '85
Bog '84
The Executioner, Part 2: Frozen Scream '84
To Kill a Stranger '84
Lite Moon & Jud McGraw '78
The Lucifer Complex '78
Haunts '77
Bad Bunch '76
Inside Out '75
The Man Who Would Not Die '75
Psychic Killer '75
Seven Alone '75
The Centerfold Girls '74
The Dynamite Brothers '74
Gone with the West '72
And Hope to Die '72
The Green Berets '68
What Did You Do in the War, Daddy? '66
City of Hope '91
The Man Who Envied Women '85
God's Little Acre '58
The Naked and the Dead '58
Men in War '57
Nightfall '56
Battle Cry '55
We're No Angels '55
Kiss Them for Me '57
Miss Sadie Thompson '53
The Marrying Kind '52
Pat and Mike '52

Anthony Ray
Shadows '60

Charles Ray (1891-1943)
The Garden of Eden '28
Sweet Adeline '26
The Busher '19
Clodhopper '17

Andrew Ray (1939-)
Tarzana, the Wild Girl '69
The Young and the Guilty '58
Escapade '55

Connie Ray (1956-)
Flourish '06

Gene Raymond (1908-98)
The Best Man '64
Plunder Road '57
Hit the Deck '55
Mr. & Mrs. Smith '41
Smilin' Through '41
The Bride Walks Out '36
That Girl from Paris '36
Sadie McKee '34
Transatlantic Merry-Go-Round '34
Ex-Lady '33
Flying Down to Rio '33
Red Dust '32
Personal Maid '31

Gary Raymond (1935-)
Scarlet '94
The Two Faces of Evil '82
Jason and the Argonauts '63
Playboy of the Western World '62
Look Back in Anger '58
The Moonraker '58

James Ray (1932-88)
She's Having a Baby '88
Mass Appeal '84
Return Engagement '78

Joey Ray
The Old Man and the Sea '58

Lisa Ray (1972-)
Water '05
Ball & Chain '04

Michel Ray (1944-)
Lawrence of Arabia '62
The Tin Star '57
The Brave One '56

Nicholas Ray (1911-79)
Hair '79
The American Friend '77

Rene Ray (1911-93)
The Vicious Circle '57
They Made Me a Fugitive '47

Leah Ray (1915-99)
The Holy Terror '37
One in a Million '36

Lina Raymond
Last Command '28

Martha Raye (1916-94)
Alice in Wonderland '85
Pippin '81
The Concorde: Airport '79
Pufnstuf '70
Billy Rose's Jumbo '62
Monsieur Verdoux '47
Pin-Up Girl '44
Keep 'Em Flying '41
Never Say Die '39
The Big Broadcast of 1938
College Swing '38
Give Me a Sailor '38
Double or Nothing '37
Waikiki Wedding '37
Rhythm on the Range '36

Candy (Candida) Raymond (1950-)
Freedom '82
Monkey Grip '82
Money Movers '78
Don's Party '76

Cyril Raymond (1897-1973)
Angels One Five '54
Brief Encounter '45
Men of Two Worlds '46
Spy in Black '39
The Shadow '36

Jack Raymond (1902-51)
Shake Hands with Murder '44

Bill Raymond
A Hole in One '04
Dogville '03
A Death in the Family '02
A Stranger in the Kingdom '98
Where the Rivers Flow North '94

Paula Raymond (1924-2003)
Blood of Dracula's Castle '69
King Richard and the Crusaders '54
The Beast from 20,000 Fathoms '53
City That Never Sleeps '53
Texas Carnival '51
Adam's Rib '50
The Duchess of Idaho '50

Robin Raymond (1916-94)
High School Confidential '58
Rogue's Gallery '44

Usher Raymond (1978-)
In the Mix '05
Texas Rangers '05
She's All That '99
Light It Up '99
The Faculty '98

Rufus Read
Gepetto '00

Barbara Read (1917-)
Behind the Mask '46
Three Smart Girls '36

James Read (1953-)
A Lot Like Love '05
Harvest of Fire '95
When the Dark Man Calls '95
Walking Thunder '94
Love Crimes '92
Web of Deceit '90
Beaches '88
North and South Book 2 '86
North and South Book 1 '85
The Initiation '84

Michael Raynor

Peggy Rea (1921-)
The Waiting Game '99
A Brother's Kiss '97
Federal Hill '94
Love Field '91
In Country '89
The Waltons: The Confessor '04

Stephen Rea (1946-)
Christmas Carol '04
The Confessor '05
Tara Road '05
V for Vendetta '06
The Reaping '07
The Musketeer '01
Feardotcom '02
Evelyn '02
Bloom '03
The Life Before This '99
This Is My Father '99
The End of the Affair '99
Guinevere '99
In Dreams '98
Still Crazy '98
The Butcher Boy '97
The Last of the High Kings '96
Fever Pitch '96
Crime of the Century '96
Michael Collins '96
Citizen X '95
Angie '94
Interview with the Vampire '94
Princess Caraboo '94
Ready to Wear '94
Bad Behavior '92
The Crying Game '92
Life Is Sweet '90
The Company of Wolves '87
Loose Connections '87
Four Days in July '85
The Doctor and the Devils '85
Danny Boy '82

Ronald Reagan (1911-2004)
The Killers '64
Hellcats of the Navy '57
Tennessee's Partner '55
Cattle Queen of Montana '54
Prisoner of War '54
Law and Order '53
The Winning Team '52
Bedtime for Bonzo '51
Storm Warning '51
Cavalry Charge '51
The Hasty Heart '50
It's a Great Feeling '49
This Is the Army '43
Desperate Journey '42
Kings Row '41
Santa Fe Trail '40
Knute Rockne: All American '40
Dark Victory '39
Boy Meets Girl '38

Marjorie Reardon
See Marjorie (Reardon) Riordan

Elizabeth Reaser (1975-)
Puccini for Beginners '06
The Family Stone '05
Stay '05
Sweet Land '05
Mind the Gap '04

Rex Reason (1928-)
Band of Angels '57
The Creature Walks among Us '56
Lady Godiva '55
This Island Earth '55

Sady Rebbot (1935-94)
Friends '71
My Life to Live '62

James Rebhorn (1948-)
Bernard and Doris '08
Comanche Moon '08
How to Eat Fried Worms '06
The Last Shot '04
Cold Mountain '03
Head of State '03
The Adventures of Pluto Nash '02
Far from Heaven '02
Scotland, PA '02
The Adventures of Rocky & Bullwinkle '00
Meet the Parents '00
Snow Falling on Cedars '99
The Talented Mr. Ripley '99
A Bright Shining Lie '98
From the Earth to the Moon '98
The Game '97
Independence Day '96
The Buccaneers '95
If Lucy Fell '95
8 Seconds '94
I Love Trouble '94
Carlito's Way '93
JFK: Reckless Youth '93
Lorenzo's Oil '92
Scent of a Woman '92
White Sands '92
Deadly Business '86
Rockabye '86
Will: G. Gordon Liddy '82
He Knows You're Alone '80

Richard Rebrere
Heavenly Bodies '84
Happy Birthday to Me '81

Donnamarie Recco
Analyze That '02
Analyze This '98

Winston Reckert
See Winston Rekert

Paco Reconti
I Am David '04
Men Men Men '95

Jeff Rector
Rapid Assault '99
Dinosaur Valley Girls '96
Friend of the Family 2 '96
The Black Gate '95
Street Soldiers '91
The Siege '98

Lois Red Elk
Skins '02
Outside Ozona '98
Three Warriors '77

Mary-Robin Redd
Mirrors '78

Lance Reddick (1956-)
Bad City '06
Don't Say a Word '01
I Dreamed of Africa '00
The Siege '98

Keith Reddin (1956-)
Eye of the Storm '97
Lolita '97

Brian Reddy
Lost Souls '00

Helen Reddy (1942-)
Pete's Dragon '77
Airport '75 '75

Quinn (K.) Redeker (1936-)
Coast to Coast '80
Spider Baby '64
The Three Stooges Meet Hercules '61

Dennis Redfield (1943-)
The Tempest '99
Pulse '88
The Annihilators '85
The McCullochs '75
Private Duty Nurses '71

William Redfield (1927-76)
One Flew Over the Cuckoo's Nest '75
Death Wish '74
For Pete's Sake '74
A New Leaf '71
The Hot Rock '70
Fantastic Voyage '66
Morituri '65
The Connection '61
I Married a Woman '56
Conquest of Space '55

Amy Redford (1970-)
The Last Confederate: The Story of Robert Adams '05
This Revolution '05
Giving It Up '99

Robert Redford (1937-)
Lions for Lambs '07
Charlotte's Web '06 (V)
An Unfinished Life '05
The Clearing '04
The Last Castle '01
Spy Game '01
The Horse Whisperer '97
All the President's Men '76
The Great Waldo Pepper '75
Three Days of the Condor '75
The Great Gatsby '74
The Sting '73
The Way We Were '73
The Candidate '72
Jeremiah Johnson '72
The Hot Rock '70
Butch Cassidy and the Sundance Kid '69
Downhill Racer '69
Tell Them Willie Boy Is Here '69
Barefoot in the Park '67
The Chase '66
This Property Is Condemned '66
Inside Daisy Clover '65

Rockets Redglare (1948-2001)
Cookie '89
In the Soup '92

Corin Redgrave (1939-)
Enduring Love '04
Close Your Eyes '02
Enigma '01
Ultraviolet '98
The Ice House '97
The Woman in White '97
Persuasion '95
Four Weddings and a Funeral '94
In the Name of the Father '93

O Brother Where Art Thou? '00
Dante's Peak '97

Jemma Redgrave (1965-)
Mansfield Park '07
Lassie '05
Like Father Like Son '05
I'll Be There '03
The Acid House '98
Mosley '98
Diana: Her True Story '93
The Buddha of Suburbia '92
Howard's End '92
Dream Demon '88

Lynn Redgrave (1943-)
The Jane Austen Book Club '07
The White Countess '05
Kinsey '04
Peter Pan '03
Unconditional Love '03
My Sister's Keeper '02
Spider '02
The Wild Thornberrys Movie '02 (V)
Varian's War '01
The Next Best Thing '00
Deeply '00
A Season for Miracles '99
The Simian Line '99
All I Wanna Do '98
Gods and Monsters '98
White Lies '97
Toothless '97
Shine '95
The Great American Sex Scandal '94
What Ever Happened To... '93
Getting It Right '89
Midnight '89
Morgan Stewart's Coming Home '87
Walking on Air '87
The Bad Seed '85
Rehearsal for Murder '82
Shooting '82
To Love Again '80
Centennial '78
Sooner or Later '78
The Big Bus '76
The Happy Hooker '75
The Turn of the Screw '74
Everything You Always Wanted to Know about Sex (But Were Afraid to Ask) '72
The Virgin Soldiers '69
Smashing Time '67
Georgy Girl '66
Girl with Green Eyes '64
Tom Jones '63

Michael Redgrave (1908-85)
Dr. Jekyll and Mr. Hyde '73
The Go-Between '71
Nicholas and Alexandra '71
Twinsanity '70
Goodbye, Mr. Chips '69
Battle of Britain '69
Heidi '67
The Heroes of Telemark '65
The Hill '65
The Loneliness of the Long Distance Runner '62
The Innocents '61
Shake Hands with the Devil '59
The Wreck of the Mary Deare '59
Time Without Pity '57
1984 '56
Dam Busters '55
Mr. Arkadin '55
The Sea Shall Not Have Them '55
The Importance of Being Earnest '52
The Browning Version '51
Secret Beyond the Door '48
Captive Heart '47
Fame Is the Spur '47
Dead of Night '45
Kipps '41
Lady in Distress '39
The Stars Look Down '39
The Lady Vanishes '38

Vanessa Redgrave (1937-)
Atonement '07
Evening '07
Venus '06
The Keeper: The Legend of Omar Khayyam '05
The White Countess '05
The Fever '04
Merci Docteur Rey '04
Byron '03
Good Boy! '03 (V)
The Gathering Storm '02
The Locket '02
Jack and the Beanstalk: The Real Story '01
If These Walls Could Talk 2 '00
A Rumor of Angels '00
The Pledge '00
The Cradle Will Rock '99
Girl, Interrupted '99
Deep Impact '98
Deja Vu '98
Lulu on the Bridge '98
Bella Mafia '97
Mrs. Dalloway '97
Wilde '97
Looking for Richard '96
Mission: Impossible '96
Smilla's Sense of Snow '96
A Month by the Lake '94
Down Came a Blackbird '94
Little Odessa '94
Mother's Boys '94
The House of the Spirits '93
Shades of Fear '93
They Watch '93
What Ever Happened To... '93
Howard's End '92
The Ballad of the Sad Cafe '91
Orpheus Descending '91
Young Catherine '91
Consuming Passions '88
A Man for All Seasons '88
Prick Up Your Ears '87
Peter the Great '86
Steaming '86
Three Sovereigns for Sarah '85
Wagner: The Complete Epic '85
Wagner: The Movie '85
Wetherby '85
The Bostonians '84
Snow White and the Seven Dwarfs '83
Bear Island '80
Playing for Time '80
Agatha '79
Yanks '79
Julia '77
The Seven-Per-Cent Solution '76
Out of Season '75
Murder on the Orient Express '74
The Devils '71
Mary, Queen of Scots '71
Trojan Women '71
Oh! What a Lovely War '69
The Charge of the Light Brigade '68
Isadora '68
Camelot '67
Blow-Up '66
A Man for All Seasons '66
Morgan: A Suitable Case for Treatment '66

Juli Reding (1935-)
Tormented '60
Mission in Morocco '59

Nick Reding (1962-)
In Love and War '01
Croupier '97
Mister Johnson '91

Christian Redl (1948-)
The Trio '97
Lea '96

Redman (1970-)
Seed of Chucky '04
Scary Movie 3 '03
How High '01

Amanda Redman (1959-)
Suspicion '03
Sexy Beast '00
King Lear '98
Body & Soul '93
Richard's Things '80

Joyce Redman (1918-)
The Rector's Wife '94
Othello '65
Tom Jones '63

Teal Redmann (1982-)
Dumb and Dumberer: When Harry Met Lloyd '03
Chameleon 3: Dark Angel '00

Eddie Redmayne
The Other Boleyn Girl '08
Elizabeth: The Golden Age '07
The Good Shepherd '06
Murderous Intent '06

Liam Redmond (1913-89)
The Last Safari '67
The Ghost and Mr. Chicken '66
Curse of the Demon '57
Devil on Horseback '54

Moira Redmond (1928-2006)
Catherine Cookson's The Wingless Bird '97
Nightmare '63

Sarah Jane Redmond
The Invitation '03
Dead in a Heartbeat '02
Suspicious River '00

Siobhan Redmond (1959-)
Beautiful People '99
Every Woman Knows a Secret '99
Captives '94
Look Back in Anger '89

Yekaterina Rednikova (1973-)
Archangel '05
Border Blues '03
The Thief '97

Manning Redwood (1929-2006)
Outland '81

Alan Reed (1936-)
Shinbone Alley '70 (V)
Tarnished Angels '57
A Woman's World '54
Actors and Sin '52
The Postman Always Rings Twice '46
Days of Glory '43

Alan Reed, Jr.
Peyton Place '57
Rock, Pretty Baby '56

Alyson Reed (1958-)
High School Musical '06
Manhattan Merenquel '95
Skin Deep '89

Bobby Reed
A Simple Promise '07

Donald Reed (1901-73)
Slaves in Bondage '37
Evangeline '29

Donna Reed (1921-86)
The Benny Goodman Story '55
The Far Horizons '55
The Last Time I Saw Paris '54
The Caddy '53
From Here to Eternity '53
Gun Fury '53
Trouble along the Way '53
Hangman's Knot '52
Green Dolphin Street '47
It's a Wonderful Life '46
Picture of Dorian Gray '45
They Were Expendable '45
The Human Comedy '43
Thousands Cheer '43
Shadow of the Thin Man '41

George Reed (1866-1952)
Strange Illusion '45
Green Pastures '36

Hal Reed
The Doberman Gang '72
The Zodiac Killer '71

Jerry Reed (1937-)
The Waterboy '98
Bat 21 '88
What Comes Around '85
Smokey and the Bandit, Part 3 '83
Survivors '83
Hot Stuff '80
Smokey and the Bandit 2 '80
Smokey and the Bandit '77
Gator '76

Lou Reed (1942-)
Blue in the Face '95
Faraway, So Close! '93
Superstar: The Life and Times of Andy Warhol '90
Get Crazy '83
One Trick Pony '80

Marshall Reed (1917-80)
The Hard Ride '71
They Saved Hitler's Brain '64
Lawmen '44

Maxwell Reed (1919-74)
Roadhouse Girl '53
Sea Devils '53
The Clouded Yellow '51
Flame of Araby '51
Blackout '50
Night Beat '48
Dear Murderer '47

Nikki Reed (1988-)
Cherry Crush '07
American Gun '05
Lords of Dogtown '05
Thirteen '03

Oliver Reed (1938-99)
Gladiator '00
Jeremiah '98
Parting Shots '98
The Bruce '96
Funny Bones '94
Return to Lonesome Dove '93
Severed Ties '92
Hired to Kill '91
The Pit & the Pendulum '91
Prisoner of Honor '91
The Revenger '90
The Adventures of Baron Munchausen '89
The Lady and the Highwayman '89
Master of Dragonard Hill '89
The Return of the Musketeers '89
Skeleton Coast '89
Treasure Island '89
Captive Rage '88
Dragonard '88
Gor '88
The House of Usher '88
Rage to Kill '88
Captive '87

Castaway '87
The Misfit Brigade '87
Christopher Columbus '85
The Black Arrow '84
Fanny Hill '83
The Sting 2 '83
Two of a Kind '83
Spasms '82
Venom '82
Condorman '81
Lion of the Desert '81
Dr. Heckyl and Mr. Hype '80
The Class of Miss MacMichael '78
The Prince and the Pauper '78
Maniac '77
Tomorrow Never Comes '77
Triple Echo '77
Burnt Offerings '76
Great Scout & Cathouse Thursday '76
The Three Musketeers '74
Blue Blood '73
One Russian Summer '73
Zero Population Growth '72
The Devils '71
Women in Love '70
The Assassination Bureau '69
The Curse of the Werewolf '61
Paranoiac '62
Trap '66
The Girl Getters '66
I'll Never Forget What's
  'isname '67
Oliver! '68
The Two Faces of Dr.
  Jekyll '60
Sword of Sherwood Forest
  '60
No Love for Johnnie '60
Beat Girl '60
The Four Musketeers '75
Royal Flash '75
Lisztomania '75
Ten Little Indians '75
Tommy '75
Sell Out '76

Pamela Reed (1949-)
Life of the Party '05
Tanner on Tanner '04
Proof of Life '00
Standing on Fishes '99
Why Do Fools Fall in Love?
  '98
Bean '97
Critical Choices '97
Santa Fe '97
Junior '94
Bob Roberts '92
Passed Away '92
Woman with a Past '92
Cadillac Man '90
Caroline? '90
Kindergarten Cop '90
Chattahoochee '89
Rachel River '87
The Best of Times '86
The Clan of the Cave Bear
  '86
Tanner '88 '88
Scandal Sheet '85
The Goodbye People '83
The Right Stuff '83
Young Doctors in Love '82
Eyewitness '81
Melvin and Howard '80
The Long Riders '80

Penelope Reed
Hired to Kill '91
Amazons '86

Philip Reed (1908-96)
The Girl in the Red Velvet
  Swing '55
Bandit Queen '51
Unknown Island '48
Big Town '47
Big Town After Dark '47

Robert Reed (1932-92)
Prime Target '91
The Big Sleep '78
The Seekers '79
Nurse '80
Casino '80
Death of a Centerfold '81
Bud and Lou '78
No Prince for My Cinderella
  '78

Richard Rees
Men with Brooms '02

Jed Rees (1970-)
Chasing Christmas '05
The Ringer '05
Dangerous Ground '95

Donough Rees
Crush '93
Iris '89

Roger Rees (1944-)
The Invasion '07
Garfield: A Tail of Two
  Kitties '06
The Pink Panther '06
The Treatment '06
Game 6 '05
Crazy Like a Fox '04
The Emperor's Club '02
Frida '02
Return to Never Land '02
(V)
The Scorpion King '02
The Crossing '00
Blackmale '99
Double Platinum '99
William Shakespeare's A
  Midsummer Night's
  Dream '99
The Bumblebee Flies
  Anyway '98
Next Stop, Wonderland '98
Sudden Manhattan '96
Mountains of the Moon '90
Ebony Tower '86
A Christmas Carol '84
Star 80 '83

Anghared Rees (1949-)
The Wolves of Kromer '98
Poldark 2 '75

George Reeves (1914-59)
Westward Ho, the Wagons!
  '56
Superman and the Mole Men
  '51
The Great Lover '49
Forever Female '53
From Here to Eternity '53
Bugles in the Afternoon '52
Rancho Notorious '52
Samson & the Mole Men
The Great Gardenia '53
Thunder in the Pines '49
Jungle Goddess '49
Border Patrol '43
Colt Comrades '43
Hoppy Serves a Writ '43
The Kansan '43
Leather Burners '43
So Proudly We Hail '43
Blue, White and Perfect '42
Blood and Sand '41
Lydia '41
Strawberry Blonde '41
The Fighting 69th '40
Argentine Nights '40
Torrid Zone '40
Gone with the Wind '39

Keanu Reeves (1964-)
Street Kings '08
The Lake House '06
A Scanner Darkly '06
Constantine '05
Ellie Parker '05
Thumbsucker '05
The Matrix Reloaded '03
The Matrix Revolutions '03
Something's Gotta Give '03
Hardball '01
Sweet November '01
The Gift '00
The Replacements '00
The Watcher '00
The Matrix '99
Feeling Minnesota '96
Chain Reaction '96
The Last Time I Committed
  Suicide '96
Johnny Mnemonic '95
A Walk in the Clouds '95
Even Cowgirls Get the
  Blues '94
Speed '94
Freaked '93
Little Buddha '93
Much Ado about Nothing
  '93
Bram Stoker's Dracula '92
Bill & Ted's Bogus Journey
  '91
My Own Private Idaho '91
Point Break '91
I Love You to Death '90
Tune in Tomorrow '90
Bill & Ted's Excellent
  Adventure '89
Parenthood '89
Dangerous Liaisons '88
The Night Before '88
Permanent Record '88
Prince of Pennsylvania '88
River's Edge '87
The Prodigal '83
Youngblood '86
Babes in Toyland '86
Act of Vengeance '86
Brotherhood of Justice '86
The Flood: Who Will Save
  Our Children? '84

Steve Reevis
The Missing '03
Wild Grizzly '99
Crazy Horse '96
Fargo '96

Joe Regalbuto (1949-)
Mr. Moto's Gamble '38
Writer's Block '91
Bodily Harm '95
Mrs. Winterbourne '96

Jayne Regan (1909-2000)
Mr. Moto's Gamble '38
Thank you, Mr. Moto '37
Texas Jack '35
The Silver Bullet '34

Laura Regan (1977-)
Dead Silence '07
Hollow Man 2 '06
They '02
Someone Like You '01

Mary Regan
Fever '88
Midnight Dancer '87
Sylvia '86

Phil Regan (1906-96)
Swing Parade of 1946 '46
Sweet Rosie O'Grady '43
Manhattan Merry-Go-
  Round '37

Vincent Regan
300 '07
Tracy '04
Black Knight '01

Lisa Reeves
Snowbird '78
The Chicken Chronicles '77
Pom Pom Girls '76

Perrey Reeves
Old School '03
Red Shoe Diaries:
  Luscious Lola '00
Child's Play 3 '91

Saskia Reeves (1962-)
Suspicion '03
The Tesseract '03
Dune '00
A Christmas Carol '99
Heart '99
Different for Girls '96
Butterfly Kiss '94
Traps '93
Antonia and Jane '91
Close My Eyes '91
December Bride '91

Phil Reeves
13 Going on 30 '04
Election '99

Duncan Regehr (1952-)
Air Bud 3: World Pup '00
Blood Surf '00
Timemaster '95
The Last Samurai '90
The Banker '89
The Monster Squad '87
My Wicked, Wicked Ways
  '84

Saskia Reeves ...

Serge Reggiani (1922-2004)
Mauvais Sang '86
Vincent, Francois, Paul and
  the Others '76
Le Doulos '61
Les Misérables '57
Casque d'Or '52
La Ronde '51

Benoit Regent (1953-94)
Trois Couleurs: Rouge '94
Trois Couleurs: Bleu '93

Regine (1929-)
My New Partner II '90
My New Partner '84
Robert et Robert '78
The Seven-Per-Cent
  Solution '76

Nadia Regin (1921-93)
Goldfinger '64
From Russia with Love '63

Paul Regina (1956-)
Prey of the Jaguar '96
It's My Party '95
Sharon's Secret '95

Carola Regnier (1946-)
Rosenstrasse '03
Seduction: The Cruel
  Woman '89

Natacha Regnier (1972-)
How I Killed My Father '03
Criminal Lovers '99
The Dreamlife of Angels '98

Meg Register
Boxing Helena '93
Demonia '90

Charles Regnier (1914-2001)
A Man Like Eva '83
A Time to Love & a Time to
  Die '58

Frank Reicher (1875-1965)
Watch on the Rhine '43
To Be or Not to Be '42
Dr. Cyclops '40
South of the Border '39
King Kong '33
Scarlet Dawn '32

Wolfgang Reichmann (1932-91)
Woyzeck '78
The Nun '66
Signs of Life '68

Alex Reid
The Descent '05
The Honeymooners '05
Arachnid '01
The Mother '03

Anne Reid (1935-)
The Mother '03
Liam '00
Catherine Cookson's The
  Wingless Bird '97

Harry (Herbert) Reems (1947-)
R.S.V.P. '84
Deadly Weapons '70

Della Reese (1932-)
Beauty Shop '05
Dinosaur '00 (V)
Harlem Nights '89
Nothing Personal '80

The Life and Adventures of
  Nicholas Nickleby '81

Tracy Reed (1941-)
Piece of the Action '77
No Way Back '74
Dr. Strangelove, or: How I
  Learned to Stop
  Worrying and Love the
  Bomb '64

Suzanne Reed
Up from the Depths '79
Beyond the Bermuda
  Triangle '75

Shanna Reed (1956-)
The Night Caller '97
Alien Avengers '96
Rattled '96

Walter Reed (1916-2001)
The Sand Pebbles '66
The Horse Soldiers '59
How to Make a Monster '58
Government Agents vs.
  Phantom Legion '51
Seven Days' Leave '42

Serena Reeder
The Architect '06
Get Rich or Die Tryin' '05

Norman Reedus (1969-)
Hero Wanted '08
The Notorious Bettie Page
  '06
Masters of Horror:
  Cigarette Burns '05
Pulse '03
Blade 2 '02
Deuces Wild '02
Bad Seed '00
Sand '00
Boondock Saints '99
Gossip '99
Let the Devil Wear Black
  '99
Six Ways to Sunday '99
Dark Harbor '98
Reach the Rock '98
Floating '97

Christopher Reeve (1952-2004)
Above Suspicion '95
Village of the Damned '95
Black Fox: Blood Horse '94
Black Fox: Good Men and
  Bad '94
Black Fox: The Price of
  Peace '94
Speechless '94
Morning Glory '93
The Remains of the Day
  '93
The Sea Wolf '93
Death Dreams '92
Mortal Sins '92
Noises Off '92
The Rose and the Jackal
  '90
The Great Escape 2: The
  Untold Story '88
Switching Channels '88
Street Smart '87
Superman 4: The Quest for
  Peace '87
Anna Karenina '85
The Aviator '85
The Bostonians '84
Superman 3 '83
Deathtrap '82
Monsignor '82
Somewhere in Time '80
Superman 2 '80
Superman: The Movie '78
Gray Lady Down '77

Kynaston Reeves (1893-1971)
Hot Millions '68
Fiend without a Face '58
Bedelia '46
Phantom Fiend '35

George Regas (1890-1940)
Beau Geste '39
Gunga Din '39

Scott Reeves (1966-)
Edge of Honor '91
Friday the 13th, Part 8:
  Jason Takes Manhattan
  '89

The Fighting Trooper '34
Sixteen Fathoms Deep '34
The Love Light 21
Lancer '35
The Last Samurai '90
The Lives of a Bengal
  Lancer '35
Gore Vidal's Billy the Kid
  '89

The Rains Came '39
Mr. Moto Takes a Chance
  '38
The Charge of the Light
  Brigade '36
Hell-Ship Morgan '36

Triangle '75
The Torch '50
Tornado '51

Lady Reeds
Avenging Disco Godfather
  '76

Dolemite 2: Human
  Tornado '76
Dolemite '75

**Jayne Regan (1909-
2000)**

Beryl Reid (1920-96)
Duel of Hearts '92
The Doctor and the Devils '85
Yellowbeard '83
Smiley's People '82
Tinker, Tailor, Soldier, Spy '80
Carry On Emmanuelle '78
Joseph Andrews '77
No Sex Please—We're British '73
Psychomania '73
Doctor Phibes Rises Again '72
Beast in the Cellar '70
Entertaining Mr. Sloane '70
The Assassination Bureau '69
The Killing of Sister George '69
Inspector Clouseau '68
Star! '68
Trial & Error '62
The Belles of St. Trinian's '53

Carl Benton Reid (1893-1973)
Pressure Point '62
The Bramble Bush '60
The Gallant Hours '60
The Trap '59
Battle Hymn '57
The Egyptian '54
Escape from Fort Bravo '53
The Great Caruso '51
Indian Uprising '51
In a Lonely Place '50
The Fuller Brush Girl '50
Inherit the Wind '60
A Woman's World '54
Gentlemen Prefer Blondes '53
The Story of Dr. Wassell '44
The Little Foxes '41

Christopher Reid (1964-)
House Party 3 '94
Class Act '91
House Party 2: The Pajama Jam '91
House Party '90

Don Reid
Rikky and Pete '88

Elliott Reid (1920-)
Blackbeard's Ghost '67
Follow Me, Boys! '66
Move Over, Darling '63
Inherit the Wind '60

Fiona Reid (1951-)
My Big Fat Greek Wedding '02
Deceived '91

Frances Reid (1914-)
The Affair '73
Seconds '66

Kate Reid (1930-93)
Teamster Boss: The Jackie Presser Story '92
The Last Best Year '90
Bye Bye Blues '89
Signs of Life '89
Control '87
Death of a Salesman '86
Fire with Fire '86
Execution of Raymond Graham '85
Heaven Help Us '85
The Blood of Others '84
Atlantic City '81
Circle of Two '80
Death Ship '80
The Double Negative '80
Highpoint '80
Crossbar '79
The Andromeda Strain '71

Michael Earl Reid
Army of Darkness '92

R.D. Reid
Dawn of the Dead '04
Dirty Pictures '00

Sheila Reid (1937-)
The Winter Guest '97
Othello '65

Tara Reid (1975-)
Alone in the Dark '05
The Crow: Wicked Prayer '05
Incubus '05
Knots '05
Silent Partner '05
Devil's Pond '03
My Boss's Daughter '03
National Lampoon's Van Wilder '02
American Pie 2 '01
Josie and the Pussycats '01
Just Visiting '01
Dr. T & the Women '00
American Pie '99
Body Shots '99
Around the Fire '98
Girl '98
Urban Legend '98

Tim Reid (1944-)
The Reading Room '05
For Real '02
Race to Freedom: The Story of the Underground Railroad '94
Mastergate '92
You Must Remember This '92
The Fourth War '90
Stephen King's It '90
Dead Bang '89

Wallace Reid (1891-1923)
Affairs of Anatol '21
Hawthorne of the USA '19
The Roaring Road '19
The Birth of a Nation '15

Timothy Reifsnyder (1986-)
Hearts in Atlantis '01
Wide Awake '97

Halina Reijn (1975-)
Black Book '06
Zus & Zo '01

Charles Nelson Reilly (1931-2007)
Boys Will Be Boys '97
A Troll in Central Park '94 (V)
Rock-a-Doodle '92 (V)
All Dogs Go to Heaven '89 (V)
Body Slam '87
Cannonball Run 2 '84
Chuka '67

John C. Reilly (1965-)
Step Brothers '08
Walk Hard: The Dewey Cox Story '07
Year of the Dog '07
A Prairie Home Companion '06
Talladega Nights: The Ballad of Ricky Bobby '06
Tenacious D in the Pick of Destiny '06
Dark Water '05
The Aviator '04
Criminal '04
Anger Management '03
Chicago '02
Gangs of New York '02
The Good Girl '02
The Hours '02
The Anniversary Party '01
The Perfect Storm '00
For Love of the Game '99
Magnolia '99
Never Been Kissed '99
The Settlement '99
Chicago Cab '98
The Thin Red Line '98
Boogie Nights '97
Hard Eight '96
Nightwatch '96
Boys '95
Georgia '95
Dolores Claiborne '94
The River Wild '94
Fallen Angels 1 '93
What's Eating Gilbert Grape '93
Hoffa '92
Out on a Limb '92
Days of Thunder '90
State of Grace '90
Casualties of War '89
We're No Angels '89
Touch and Go '86
Missing Pieces '83

Kelly Reilly (1977-)
The Libertine '05
Mrs. Henderson Presents '05
Pride and Prejudice '05
Russian Dolls '05
Dead Bodies '03
L'Auberge Espagnole '02
Last Orders '01
Poldark '96

Luke Reilly
Zebrahead '92

Robert Reilly
Frankenstein Meets the Space Monster '65
Lilith '64

Tom Reilly (1959-)
Mirror Images 2 '93
Kiss and Be Killed '91

Gary Reineke
Spider '02
The Golden Spiders: A Nero Wolfe Mystery '00
George's Island '91

Carl Reiner (1922-)
Ocean's Thirteen '07
Ocean's Twelve '04
Good Boy! '03 (V)
Ocean's Eleven '01
The Adventures of Rocky & Bullwinkle '00
Slums of Beverly Hills '98
The Right to Remain Silent '95
Spirit of '76 '91
Summer School '87
Pinocchio '83
Dead Men Don't Wear Plaid '82
The Jerk '79
The End '78
Generation '69
A Guide for the Married Man '67
The Russians Are Coming, the Russians Are Coming '66
It's a Mad, Mad, Mad, Mad World '63
The Thrill of It All! '63
Gidget Goes Hawaiian '61
The Gazebo '59

Rob Reiner (1945-)
Everyone's Hero '06 (V)
Alex & Emma '03
Dickie Roberts: Former Child Star '03
EDtv '99
The Muse '99
The Story of Us '99
Primary Colors '98
The First Wives Club '96
Trigger Happy '96
For Better or Worse '95
Bullets over Broadway '94
Bye Bye, Love '94
Mixed Nuts '94
Sleepless in Seattle '93
The Return of Spinal Tap '92
Spirit of '76 '91
Postcards from the Edge '90
Throw Momma from the Train '87
Johnny Appleseed '86
This Is Spinal Tap '84
The Jerk '79
Thursday's Game '74
How Come Nobody's On Our Side? '70
Where's Poppa? '70
Enter Laughing '67

Tracy Reiner (1964-)
Apollo 13 '95
A League of Their Own '92
Frankie and Johnny '91
Masque of the Red Death '89
New Year's Day '89
When Harry Met Sally... '89
Jumpin' Jack Flash '86
Nothing in Common '86

Judge Reinhold (1958-)
Swing Vote '08
The Santa Clause 3: The Escape Clause '06
Clifford's Really Big Movie '04 (V)
The Hollow '04
National Lampoon's Holiday Reunion '03
Dead in a Heartbeat '02
The Santa Clause 2 '02
Whacked! '02
Beethoven's 4th '01
Beethoven's 3rd '00
Enemies of Laughter '00
Newsbreak '00
Ping! '99
Boltneck '98
Last Lives '98
Tom Clancy's Netforce '98
Crackerjack 2 '97
Homegrown '97
As Good as Dead '95
The Right to Remain Silent '95
The Wharf Rat '95
Beverly Hills Cop 3 '94
The Santa Clause '94
Bank Robber '93
Four Eyes and Six Guns '93
Roadhouse 66 '84
The Lords of Discipline '83
Fast Times at Ridgemont High '82
Pandemonium '82
Stripes '81
On the Edge: The Survival of Dana '79
Running Scared '79

Ann Reinking (1949-)
Micki & Maude '84
Annie '82
All That Jazz '79

Michelle Reis (1970-)
Flowers of Shanghai '98
Fallen Angels '95

Geri Reischl (1959-)
I Dismember Mama '74

Hans Reiser (1919-92)
The Great Escape '63
Secret of the Black Trunk '62

Paul Reiser (1956-)
The Thing About My Folks '05
Purpose '02
Strange Relations '02
Women vs. Men '02
One Night at McCool's '01
The Story of Us '99
Bye Bye, Love '94
Mr. Write '92
Family Prayers '91
The Marrying Man '91
Crazy People '90
Cross My Heart '88
Beverly Hills Cop 2 '87
Aliens '86
From Here to Maternity '85
Odd Jobs '85
Beverly Hills Cop '84
Sunset Limousine '83
Diner '82

Robbie Reist
See Robbie (Reist) Rist

Jack Reitzen (1924-98)
Kentucky Jubilee '51
Mask of the Dragon '51

Winston Rekert (1949-)
Savage Island '03
A Cooler Climate '99
The World's Oldest Living Bridesmaid '92
Glory! Glory! '90
Eternal Evil '87
Toby McTeague '87
Agnes of God '85
Dead Wrong '83
Heartaches '82
Suzanne '80

Maria Therese Relin (1966-)
Quo Vadis '85
Secret Places '85

James Remar (1953-)
Pineapple Express '08
Ratatouille '07 (V)
Blade: Trinity '04
The Girl Next Door '04
Ike: Countdown to D-Day '04
Duplex '03
Fear X '03
Lady Jayne Killer '03
2 Fast 2 Furious '03
Guardian '01
The Guardian '00
Hellraiser 5: Inferno '00
What Lies Beneath '00
Blowback '99
D.R.E.A.M. Team '99
Rites of Passage '99
Psycho '98
Born Bad '97
Mortal Kombat 2: Annihilation '97
The Phantom '96
The Quest '96
Robo Warriors '96
One Good Turn '95
Across the Moon '94
Boys on the Side '94
Confessions of a Hit Man '94
Miracle on 34th Street '94
Renaissance Man '94
The Surgeon '94
Blink '93
Fatal Instinct '93
The Tigress '93
Fatal Charm '92
Indecency '92
Deadlock '91
White Fang '91
Silence Like Glass '90
Tales from the Darkside: The Movie '90
The Dream Team '89
Drugstore Cowboy '89
Rent-A-Cop '88
Windwalker '81
Cruising '80
The Warriors '79

Erika Remberg (1932-)
The Lickerish Quartet '70
Cave of the Living Dead '65
Circus of Horrors '60

Lee Remick (1935-91)
Around the World in 80 Days '89
Bridge to Silence '89
Jesse '88
The Vision '87
Follies in Concert '85
Toughlove '85
Mistral's Daughter '84
The Snow Queen '83
The Competition '80
Tribute '80
The Europeans '79
Ike '79
Torn Between Two Lovers '79
Breaking Up '78
The Medusa Touch '78
Telefon '77
The Omen '76
Hennessy '75
Hustling '75
QB VII '74
Touch Me Not '74
Sometimes a Great Notion '71
Loot... Give Me Money, Honey! '70
The Detective '68
No Way to Treat a Lady '68
The Hallelujah Trail '65
Baby, the Rain Must Fall '64
The Tempest '63
The Wheeler Dealers '63
Days of Wine and Roses '62
Experiment in Terror '62
Anatomy of a Murder '59
The Long, Hot Summer '58
A Face in the Crowd '57

Bert Remsen (1925-99)
Crime of the Century '96
Humanoids from the Deep '96
Maverick '94
Evil Spirits '91
Only the Lonely '91
Daddy's Dyin'... Who's Got the Will? '90
Payback '90
Peacemaker '90
Miss Firecracker '89
Curfew '88
South of Reno '87
Eye of the Tiger '86
Tai-Pan '86
Terrorvision '86
Code of Silence '85
Burning Rage '84
I Married a Centerfold '84
Lies '83
M.A.D.D.: Mothers Against Drunk Driving '83
Policewoman Centerfold '83
Joni '79
A Wedding '78
Tarantulas: The Deadly Cargo '77
Nashville '75
Sweet Hostage '75
Thieves Like Us '74
The Death Squad '73
McCabe & Mrs. Miller '71
Dead Ringer '64
Pork Chop Hill '59

Kerry Remsen
Pumpkinhead '88
Ghoulies 2 '89

Albert Remy (1912-67)
The Train '65
Shoot the Piano Player '62
The 400 Blows '59
Children of Paradise '44

Ronald Remy
Mad Doctor of Blood Island '68
No Man is an Island '62
The Vampire People '66

Duncan Renaldo (1904-80)
The Capture '50
Guns of Fury '49
In Old New Mexico '45
South of the Rio Grande '45
Border Patrol '43
For Whom the Bell Tolls '43
Manhunt in the African Jungles '43
Down Mexico Way '41
Outlaws of the Desert '41
Panama Menace '41
Covered Wagon Days '40
Gaucho Serenade '40
Rocky Mountain Rangers '40
Cowboys from Texas '39
The Kansas Terrors '39
Rough Riders' Roundup '39
South of the Border '39
Rose of Rio Grande '38
Spawn of the North '38
The Painted Stallion '37
Zorro Rides Again '37
Trader Horn '31

Tito Renaldo (1911-2004)
The Story of G.I. Joe '45
For Whom the Bell Tolls '43

Simone Renant (1911-2004)
Dear Detective '77
That Man from Rio '64
Dangerous Liaisons '60
Jenny Lamour '47

Renaud (1952-)
Germinal '93

Francis Renaud (1967-)
Perfect Love '96
Pigalle '95

Madeleine Renaud (1900-94)
Le Plaisir '52
Stormy Waters '41
Maria Chapdelaine '34

Isabelle Renauld (1966-)
Monsieur Ibrahim '03
eXistenZ '99

Georges Renavent (1894-1969)
Manhunt in the African Jungles '43
Whistlin' Dan '32
East of Borneo '31

Liz Renay (1926-2007)
Desperate Living '77
Blackenstein '73
Lady Godiva Rides '68
Deadwood '65
The Thrill Killers '65
Nasty Rabbit '64

Mark Rendall (1988-)
Charlie Bartlet '07
30 Days of Night '07
A Different Loyalty '04

Liz Rene
See Liz Renay

Brad Renfro (1982-2008)
10th & Wolf '06
The Jacket '05
The Job '03
Deuces Wild '02
Bully '01
Ghost World '01
Happy Campers '01
Tart '01
The Theory of the Leisure Class '01
Skipped Parts '00
Apt Pupil '97

Jeremie Renier (1981-)
In Bruges '08
Private Property '06
The Child '05
The Client '94

Yannick Renier
Love Songs '07
Private Property '06

Serge Renko
Rendezvous in Paris '95

Patrick Renna (1979-)
P.U.N.K.S. '98

Jeremy Renner (1971-)
28 Weeks Later '07
The Assassination of Jesse James by the Coward Robert Ford '07
North Country '05
12 and Holding '05
S.W.A.T. '03
Dahmer '02
The Invisible '07
Shattered '07
Tin Man '07
Whole New Thing '05
The Highway Man '99
The Last Stop '99
The Life Before This '99

Robin Renucci (1956-)
Comedy of Power '06
The Dreamers '03
Taking Sides '01
Children of the Century '99

Sophie Renoir
Boyfriends & Girlfriends '88
Le Beau Mariage '82

Michael Rennie (1909-71)
Dracula vs. Frankenstein '69
The Devil's Brigade '68
Commando Attack '67
Hotel '67
Third Man on the Mountain '59
Omar Khayyam '57
Mambo '55
Seven Cities of Gold '55
Soldier of Fortune '55
Demetrius and the Gladiators '54
Desiree '54
Dangerous Crossing '53
Five Fingers '52
Phone Call from a Stranger '52
The Day the Earth Stood Still '51

Callum Keith Rennie (1960-)
The X-Files: I Want to Believe '08
Fish in a Barrel '01
Memento '00
Suspicious River '00
eXistenZ '99
Blade: Trinity '04
Now & Forever '02
Picture Claire '01
Ice '02
Torso '01

Sleepers '96
Telling Lies in America '96
The Cure '95
Tom and Huck '95

Ginette Reno (1946-)
Mambo Italiano '03
It's My Turn, Laura Cadieux '98

Jean Reno (1948-)
Leolo '92
The Da Vinci Code '06
Flushed Away '06 (V)
Jet Lag '02
Rollerball '02
The Crimson Rivers '01
The Crimson Rivers 2: Angels of the Apocalypse '05
The Tiger and the Snow '05
Hotel Rwanda '04
The Pink Panther '06
Flyboys '06
The Big Green '95
La Femme Nikita '91
The Professional '94
The Visitors '95
French Kiss '95
Beyond the Clouds '95
Mission: Impossible '96

Deborah Rennard (1959-)
Lionheart '90
Land of Doom '84

Pierre Renoir (1885-1952)
Children of Paradise '44
La Marseillaise '37
Madame Bovary '34
The Rules of the Game '39

Jean Renoir (1894-1979)
The Little Theatre of Jean Renoir '71
The Rules of the Game '39

Kelly Reno (1966-)
The Black Stallion Returns '83
The Black Stallion '79

John Reno
Bloodspell '87
Mirror of Death '87

Paul (Pee-wee Herman) Reubens (1952-)
Blow '01
South of Heaven, West of Hell '00
Mystery Men '99
Dr. Dolittle '98 (V)
Buddy '97
Matilda '96
Dunston Checks In '95
The Nightmare before Christmas '93 (V)
Batman Returns '92
Buffy the Vampire Slayer '92
Big Top Pee-wee '88
Back to the Beach '87
Flight of the Navigator '86 (V)
Pee-wee's Big Adventure '85
Meatballs 2 '84
Pinocchio '83
Pandemonium '82
The Pee-wee Herman Show '82
Cheech and Chong's Nice Dreams '81
The Blues Brothers '80
Cheech and Chong's Next Movie '80

The Black Rose '50
Trio '50
Uneasy Terms '48
The Wicked Lady '45
Tower of Terror '42

Frank Ressel (1925-85)
Sabata '69

Dale Resteghini (1968-)
Da Hip Hop Witch '00

Tommy Rettig (1941-96)
The Cobweb '55
River of No Return '54
The 5000 Fingers of Dr. T '53

Raoul Retzer (1919-74)
2069: A Sex Odyssey '78
The Vampire Happening '71

Gloria Reuben (1964-)
Life Support '07
Little John '02
Anne Rice's The Feast of All Saints '01
Cold Blooded '00
Timecop '94

Rex
Robinson Crusoe of Clipper Island '36

Simon Rex (1974-)
Scary Movie 4 '06
Scary Movie 3 '03
Scary Movie '00

Kamar Reyes
See Kamar De Los Reyes

Dominique Reymond
Demonlover '02
Les Destinees '00
Come Undone '00
Will It Snow for Christmas? '96

Judy Reyes (1967-)
Washington Heights '02
Jack and His Friends '92

Julian Reyes (1961-)
Rush Hour 2 '01
White Wolves 2: Legend of the Wild '94
Point Break '91

Ernie Reyes, Jr. (1972-)
The Rundown '03
Surf Ninjas '93
Teenage Mutant Ninja Turtles 2: The Secret of the Ooze '91

Walter Reyer (1922-)
Journey to the Lost City '58
The Indian Tomb '59

Alejandro Rey (1930-87)
Stickfighter '89
Terrorvision '86
Moscow on the Hudson '84
The Grace Kelly Story '83
Rita Hayworth: The Love Goddess '83
The Ninth Configuration '79
The Stepmother '71
Fun in Acapulco '63
Solomon and Sheba '59

Antonia Rey (1927-)
Tarantella '95
Spike of Bensonhurst '88

Fernando Rey (1917-94)
1492: Conquest of Paradise '92
Naked Tango '91
The Tunnel '89
Moon over Parador '88
Angel of Death '86
Saving Grace '86
A.D. '85
The Hit '85
Padre Nuestro '85
Star Knight '85
Monsignor '82
Cabo Blanco '81
Honey '81
Quintet '79
The Assignment '78
Elisa, Vida Mia '77
That Obscure Object of Desire '77
The Desert of the Tartars '76
Insanity '76
Seven Beauties '76
French Connection 2 '75
Autopsy '74
La Grande Bourgeoise '74
Antony and Cleopatra '73
High Crime '73
The Discreet Charm of the Bourgeoisie '72
A Town Called Hell '72
The French Connection '71
The Adventurers '70
Companeros '70
Tristana '70
Cold Eyes of Fear '70
Guns of the Magnificent Seven '69
The Castilian '63
Goliath Against the Giants '63
Viridiana '61
Navajo Joe '67
Attack of the Robots '66
Mission in Morocco '59
Pentalions '57
The Miracle of Marcelino '55

The Girl of Your Dreams '99
How to Be a Woman and Not Die in the Attempt '91
Skyline '84

Clive Revill (1930-)
Possums '99
Dracula: Dead and Loving It '95
Chimes at Midnight '67
The Sea Wolf '93
Let Him Have It '91
Mack the Knife '89
Rumpelstiltskin '86
George Washington '84
Zorro, the Gay Blade '81
The Empire Strikes Back '80
Avanti! '72
One of Our Dinosaurs Is Missing '75
The Black Windmill '74
Ghost in the Noonday Sun '74
Escape to the Sun '72
The Private Life of Sherlock Holmes '70
The Assassination Bureau '69
A Fine Madness '66
Modesty Blaise '66
Fathom '67
The Legend of Hell House '73
The Little Prince '74

Dorothy Revier (1904-93)
Circumstantial Evidence '35
Green Eyes '34
When a Man Sees Red '34
The King Murder '32
The Black Camel '31
The Secrets of Wu Sin '32
The Dropkick '27
Dance of Life '29
Charlie Ruffin '79
Matilda '78

Mony Rey
Not Without My Daughter '90
Mademoiselle '66

Janine Reynaud (1930-)

Burt Reynolds (1936-)
In the Name of the King: A Dungeon Siege Tale '08
Castle of the Creeping Flesh '68
Forget About It '06
End Game '06
Grilled '06
The Dukes of Hazzard '05
The Longest Yard '05
Without a Paddle '04
The Crew '00
Big City Blues '99
Mystery, Alaska '99
Pups '99
Crazy Six '98
Waterproof '99
Snapshots '02
Driven '01
Tempted '01
The Hollywood Sign '01
The Final Hit '02
Johnson County War '02
Universal Soldier 3: Unfinished Business '99
Bean '97
Boogie Nights '97

Hunter's Moon '97
Meet Wally Sparks '97
Raven '97
The Cherokee Kid '96
Citizen Ruth '96
Frankenstein and Me '96
Striptease '96
Trigger Happy '96
The Maddening '95
Cop and a Half '93
The Man from Left Field '93 (V)
The Player '92
Modern Love '90
All Dogs Go to Heaven '89 (V)
Breaking In '89
Physical Evidence '89
Rent-A-Cop '88
Switching Channels '88
Heat '87
Malone '87
Sherman's March '86
Stick '85
Uphill All the Way '85
Cannonball Run 2 '84
City Heat '84
The Man Who Loved Women '83
Smokey and the Bandit, Part 3 '83
Stroker Ace '83
Best Friends '82
The Best Little Whorehouse in Texas '82
Cannonball Run '81
Paternity '81
Sharky's Machine '81
Rough Cut '80
Smokey and the Bandit 2 '80
Starting Over '79
The End '78
Hooper '78
Semi-Tough '77
Smokey and the Bandit '77
Gator '76
Silent Movie '75
The Hustle '75
The Longest Yard '74
Man Who Loved Cat Dancing '73
Shamus '73
White Lightning '73
Deliverance '72
Everything You Always Wanted to Know about Sex (But Were Afraid to Ask) '72
Fuzz '72
Hard Frame '70
Savage Run '70
Skullduggery '70
100 Rifles '69
Sam Whiskey '69
Iron Cowboy '68
Navajo Joe '67
Operation C.I.A. '65
Angel Baby '61
Armored Command '61

Craig Reynolds (1907-49)
Nevada '44
I Take This Oath '40

Debbie Reynolds (1932-)
Connie and Carla '04
These Old Broads '01
Rugrats in Paris: The Movie '00 (V)
Kiki's Delivery Service '98
Zack & Reba '98
In and Out '97
Mother '96
Wedding Bell Blues '96
Heaven and Earth '93
Battling for Baby '92
The Bodyguard '92
Detective Sadie & Son '84
Charlotte's Web '73 (V)
What's the Matter with Helen? '71
How Sweet It Is! '68
Divorce American Style '67
The Singing Nun '66
Goodbye Charlie '64

The Unsinkable Molly Brown '64
How the West Was Won '63
The Rat Race '60
The Gazebo '59
It Started with a Kiss '59
The Mating Game '59
This Happy Feeling '58
Tammy and the Bachelor '57
Bundle of Joy '56
The Catered Affair '56
Meet Me in Las Vegas '56
Hit the Deck '55
The Tender Trap '55
Athena '54
Susan Slept Here '54
The Affairs of Dobie Gillis '53
Give a Girl a Break '53
I Love Melvin '53
Singin' in the Rain '52
Skirts Ahoy! '52
Three Little Words '50
Two Weeks with Love '50

Gene Reynolds (1925)
Country Girl '54
Jungle Patrol '48
Junior G-Men of the Air '42
The Tuttles of Tahiti '42
Andy Hardy's Private Secretary '41
Life Begins for Andy Hardy '41
The Flying Irishman '39
They Shall Have Music '39
Boys Town '38
Love Finds Andy Hardy '38
In Old Chicago '37

Marjorie Reynolds (1916-97)
His Kind of Woman '51
Home Town Story '51
Monsieur Beaucaire '46
The Time of Their Lives '46
Ministry of Fear '44
Holiday Inn '42
Robin Hood of the Pecos '41
Doomed to Die '40
The Fatal Hour '40
Midnight Limited '40
Up in the Air '40
The Abe Lincoln of Ninth Avenue '39
Gone with the Wind '39
Mr. Wong in Chinatown '39
Mystery Plane '39
Stunt Pilot '39
Man's Country '38
Six Shootin' Sheriff '38
Western Trails '38
Murder in Greenwich Village '37
Tex Rides with the Boy Scouts '37

Michael J. Reynolds (1939-)
Ms. Scrooge '97
Wicked City '89 (V)
The Big Turnaround '88
War Between the Tates '76

Peter Reynolds (1926-75)
The Great Armored Car Swindle '64

Robert Reynolds
Devil Girl from Mars '54
It Takes a Thief '97
Jacob's Ladder '90
Rising Son '90
The Long Walk Home '89
Patty Hearst '88

Ryan Reynolds (1976-)
Chaos Theory '08
Definitely, Maybe '08
The Nines '07
Smokin' Aces '07
School of Life '06
The Amityville Horror '05
Just Friends '05

Waiting '05
Blade: Trinity '04
Harold and Kumar Go to White Castle '04
The In-Laws '03
Buying the Cow '02
National Lampoon's Van Wilder '02
Finder's Fee '01
Coming Soon '99
Dick '99
The Alarmist '98
Boltneck '98
Sabrina the Teenage Witch '96

Simon Reynolds
Ordinary Magic '93

Simon Reynolds (1969)
The Prize Winner of Defiance, Ohio '05
Gate 2 '92

Vera Reynolds (1900-62)
The Monster Walks '32
Tangled Destinies '32
Risky Business '28
Sunny Side Up '28
The Night Club '25
The Road to Yesterday '25

William Reynolds (1931-)
The Land Unknown '57
All That Heaven Allows '55
Cult of the Cobra '55
Gunsmoke '53
Carrie '52
Francis Goes to West Point '52
Son of Ali Baba '52

Ving Rhames (1961-)
Animal 2 '07
I Now Pronounce You Chuck and Larry '07
Idlewild '06
Mission: Impossible 3 '06
Animal '05
Back in the Day '05
Dawn of the Dead '04
Dark Blue '03
Lilo & Stitch '02 (V)
Little John '02
RFK '02
Sin '02
Undisputed '02
Baby Boy '01
Final Fantasy: The Spirits Within '01 (V)
Sins of the Father '01
American Tragedy '00
Holiday Heart '00
Mission: Impossible 2 '00
Bringing Out the Dead '99
Entrapment '99
Out of Sight '98
Body Count '97
Con Air '97
Don King: Only in America '97
Dangerous Ground '96
Mission: Impossible '96
Rosewood '96
Striptease '96
DROP Squad '94
Kiss of Death '94
Pulp Fiction '94
Dave '93
The Saint of Fort Washington '93
Homicide '91
The People under the Stairs '91
Flight of the Intruder '90

Best of the Best '89
Silent Assassins '88

Simon Rhee (1957-)
Kung Pow! Enter the Fist '02
The Substitute 4: Failure is Not an Option '00
Best of the Best 2 '93
Best of the Best '89

Ashlie Rhey (1961-)
Bikini Drive-In '94
Midnight Tease '94
Play Time '94

Julian Rhind-Tutt (1968-)
The River King '05
Lara Croft: Tomb Raider '01
Miranda '01
Heat of the Sun '99
The Trench '99
Reckless '97

Barbara Rhoades (1947-)
Sex and the Single Parent '82
The Day the Women Got Even '80
Serial '80
The Choirboys '77
The Goodbye Girl '77
Conspiracy of Terror '75
Hunter '73
Scream Blacula Scream '73
Up the Sandbox '72
The Shakiest Gun in the West '68

Bobby Rhodes (1947-)
Demons 2 '87
Endgame '85
The Last Hunter '80

Brian Rhodes (1947-)
DC 9/11: Time of Crisis '04
Nemesis Game '03

Cynthia Rhodes (1957-)
Curse of the Crystal Eye '93
Dirty Dancing '87
Runaway '84
Flashdance '83
Staying Alive '83

Donnelly Rhodes (1937-)
Pressure '02
Big and Hairy '98
Guitarman '95
Dirty Work '92
Kurt Vonnegut's Monkey House '91
Showdown at Williams Creek '91
After the Promise '87
Goldenrod '77
Hard Part Begins '73

Dusty Rhodes (1945-)
Heroes of the Heart '94
Gold Raiders '83

Erik Rhodes (1906-90)
Mysterious Mr. Moto '38
Special Investigator '36
Charlie Chan in Paris '35
Top Hat '35
The Gay Divorcee '34

Grandon Rhodes (1904-87)
Revenge of the Creature '55
Magnificent Doll '46

Hari Rhodes (1932-92)
Backstairs at the White House '79
Coma '78
A Woman Called Moses '78
Detroit 9000 '73
Conquest of the Planet of the Apes '72
The Shock Corridor '63

Marjorie Rhodes (1903-79)
Hands of the Ripper '71
Decameron Nights '53
Great Day '46
Butler's Dilemma '43

Busta Rhymes (1972-)
Halloween: Resurrection '02
Narc '02
Finding Forrester '00
Shaft '00
The Rugrats Movie '98 (V)

Matthew Rhys (1974-)
Fakers '04
Sorted '04
Deathwatch '02
The Lost World '02
Shooters '00
Very Annie Mary '00
Heart '99
Titus '99

Paul Rhys (1963-)
Hellraiser: Deader '05
Food of Love '02
King Lear '97
A Dance to the Music of Time '97
Gallowglass '95
Nina Takes a Lover '94
Becoming Colette '92
Chaplin '92
Vincent & Theo '90

John Rhys-Davies (1944-)
In the Name of the King: A Dungeon Siege Tale '08
Chupacabra Terror '05
The Game of Their Lives '05
Dragon Storm '04
The Lost Angel '04
The Princess Diaries 2: Royal Engagement '04
Helen of Troy '03
The Jungle Book 2 '03 (V)
Lord of the Rings: The Return of the King '03
The Medallion '03
Vlad '03
Endangered Species '02
Lord of the Rings: The Two Towers '02 (V)
Scorcher '02
Lord of the Rings: The Fellowship of the Rings '01
Sabretooth '01
Britannic '00
Secre of the Andes '98
Bloodsport 3 '97
Cats Don't Dance '97 (V)
Aladdin and the King of Thieves '96 (V)
Glory Daze '96
The Great White Hype '96
Marquis de Sade '96
Beyond Forgiveness '94
Catherine the Great '95
Robot in the Family '94
Cyborg Cop '93
Return to the Lost World '93
Ring of the Musketeers '93
Canvas: The Fine Art of Crime '92
The Double O Kid '92
The High Crusade '92
The Lost World '92
The Seventh Coin '92
Sunset Grill '92
The Unnamable 2: The Statement of Randolph Carter '92
Journey of Honor '91
Rebel Storm '90
Secret Weapon '90
Great Expectations '89
Indiana Jones and the Last Crusade '89
The Trial of the Incredible Hulk '89
Tusks '89
War & Remembrance: The Final Chapter '89

Nairobi Affair '88
Noble House '88
War & Remembrance '88
Waxwork '88
The Little Match Girl '87
The Living Daylights '87
In the Shadow of Kilimanjaro '86
King Solomon's Mines '85
Kim '84
Best Revenge '83
Sadat '83
Sahara '83
Sword of the Valiant '83
Ivanhoe '82
Victor/Victoria '82
Raiders of the Lost Ark '81
Sphinx '81
Shogun '80
Nativity '78

Griff Rhys Jones (1953-)
The Misadventures of Mr. Witt '90
Morons from Outer Space '85

Jonathan Rhys Meyers (1977-)
August Rush '07
Mission: Impossible 3 '06
Match Point '05
Alexander '04
Vanity Fair '04
The Lion in Winter '03
Pulse '03
The Tesseract '03
Bend It Like Beckham '02
The Magnificent Ambersons '02
Prozac Nation '01
Tangled '01
Ride with the Devil '99
Titus '99
The Governess '98
The Loss of Sexual Innocence '98
The Maker '98
Velvet Goldmine '98
B. Monkey '97
Killer Tongue '96
Michael Collins '96
Samson and Delilah '96
Telling Lies in America '96

Candice Rialson (1952-)
Moonshine County Express '77
Chatterbox '76
Hollywood Boulevard '76
Summer School Teachers '75
Candy Stripe Nurses '74
Mama's Dirty Girls '74

Renie Riano (1899-1971)
Nancy Drew and the Hidden Staircase '39
Nancy Drew—Trouble Shooter '39
Nancy Drew—Detective '38

Alfonso Ribeiro (1971-)
Ticks '93
The Mighty Pawns '87

Jacques Riberolles (1929-82)
The Young Girls of Rochefort '68
Please Not Now! '61

Giovanni Ribisi (1974-)
Perfect Stranger '07
The Dead Girl '06
The Dog Problem '06
10th & Wolf '06
The Big White '05
Flight of the Phoenix '04
Sky Captain and the World of Tomorrow '04
Basic '03
Cold Mountain '03
I Love Your Work '03
Lost in Translation '03
Heaven '01
Shot in the Heart '01
Boiler Room '00
The Gift '00

Gone in 60 Seconds '00
It's the Rage '99
The Mod Squad '99
The Virgin Suicides '99 (N)
First Love, Last Rites '98
The Other Sister '98
Saving Private Ryan '98
The Postman '97
subUrbia '96
That Thing You Do! '96
Promised a Miracle '88

Marissa Ribisi (1974-)
True Crime '99
Changing Habits '96
Armistead Maupin's Tales of the City '93
Dazed and Confused '93

Christina Ricci (1980-)
Speed Racer '08
Black Snake Moan '07
Home of the Brave '06
Penelope '06
Cursed '04
Anything Else '03
I Love Your Work '03
Monster '03
The Gathering '02
The Laramie Project '02
Pumpkin '02
All Over the Guy '01
Miranda '01
Prozac Nation '01
Bless the Child '00
The Man Who Cried '00
No Vacancy '00
Sleepy Hollow '99
Desert Blue '98
200 Cigarettes '98 (V)
Buffalo 66 '97
The Ice Storm '97
Fear and Loathing in Las Vegas '98
That Darn Cat '96
Casper '95
Gold Diggers: The Secret of Bear Mountain '95
Now and Then '95
The Cemetery Club '93
The Addams Family '91
Mermaids '90

Alex Rice
The New World '05
Coyote Waits '03
Skinwalker '02

Bill Rice (1931-2006)
Coffee and Cigarettes '03
Landlord Blues '87
Doomed Love '83
Vortex '81

Brett Rice (1954-)
Bobby Jones: Stroke of Genius '04
Final Cut '88

Florence Rice (1911-74)
Boss of Big Town '43
The Ghost and the Guest '43
At the Circus '39
Sweethearts '38
Double Wedding '37
Navy Blue and Gold '37

Frank Rice (1892-1936)
The Gore-Gore Girls '72
The Ivory Handled Gun '35
The Fiddlin' Buckaroo '33
Phantom Thunderbolt '33
Somewhere in Sonora '33
Trail Drive '33
Hello Trouble '33
Sunset Trail '32
Border Law '31
The Fighting Legion '30
Red Signals '27
Dynamite Dan '24

Joan Rice (1930-97)
The Horror of Frankenstein '70
His Majesty O'Keefe '53
The Story of Robin Hood & His Merrie Men '52

Adam Rich (1968-)
Zertigo Diamond Caper '82
Kuni Lemel in Tel Aviv '77

Allan Rich (1926-)
The Devil & Max Devlin '81
Light It Up '99
In His Father's Shoes '97
Matters of the Heart '90
Archer: The Fugitive from the Empire '81
The Seekers '79

Charlie Rich (1932-95)
Take This Job & Shove It '81

Christopher Rich (1953-)
The Joy Luck Club '93

Claude Rich (1929-)
Capitaine Conan '96
The Green House '96
La Crabe Tambour '77
The Bride Wore Black '68
Is Paris Burning? '66
The Burning Court '62
The Elusive Corporal '62

Eli Rich
Deadly Diamonds '91

Irene Rich (1891-1988)
Angel and the Badman '47
The Lady in Question '40
The Mortal Storm '40
That Certain Age '38
The Champ '32
Beau Brummel '24

Lillian Rich
Mark of the Spur '32
Braveheart '25

Addison Richards (1887-1964)
Call Northside 777 '48
A Southern Yankee '48
Criminal Court '46
Bells of Rosarita '45
Betrayal from the East '45
Since You Went Away '44
Air Force '43
The Fighting Sullivans '42
The Man with Two Lives '42
Ridin' Down the Canyon '42
Underground Agent '42
Dive Bomber '41
Sheriff of Tombstone '41
Bad Lands '39
The Black Legion '37
Our Daily Bread '34

Ann Richards (1917-2006)
Breakdown '53
Sorry, Wrong Number '48
Love from a Stranger '47
Love Letters '45

Ariana Richards (1979-)
Tremors 3: Back to Perfection '01
The Lost World: Jurassic Park 2 '97
Angus '95
Jurassic Park '93
Grand Tour: Disaster in Time '92
Switched at Birth '91
Spaced Invaders '90
Prancer '89
Tremors '89

Beah Richards (1926-2000)
Beloved '98
Inside Out '91
Drugstore Cowboy '89
As Summers Die '86
Acceptable Risks '86
Sophisticated Gents '81
A Christmas Without Snow '80
Roots: The Next Generation '79
A Dream for Christmas '73
Guess Who's Coming to Dinner '67
Gone Are the Days '63
Purlie Victorious '63
Hurry Sundown '67
Hollywood Shuffle '87

Michael Richards (1948-)
Bee Movie '07 (V)
Trial and Error '95
Unstrung Heroes '95
Airheads '94
Coneheads '93
So I Married an Axe Murderer '93
Problem Child '90
UHF '89
Transylvania 6-5000 '85
Whoops Apocalypse '83

Lisa Richards
Eating '90
Return '88

Kyle Richards (1969-)
Curfew '88
The Watcher in the Woods '81
Halloween '78
Eaten Alive '76
Assault on Precinct 13 '76
Escape to Witch Mountain '75
Tobe Hooper's...

Michele Lamar Richards (1954-)
Top Dog '95
The Bodyguard '92

Paul Richards (1934-)
Kiss Daddy Goodnight '87
Beach Girls '82

Paul (E.) Richards (1924-74)
Beneath the Planet of the Apes '70
All the Young Men '60

Tom Richards (1922-)
The Cursed Mountain '...

Denise Richards (1972-)
Blonde and Blonder '07
Undercover Brother '02
You Stupid Man '02
Good Advice '01
Valentine '01
Drop Dead Gorgeous '99
Tail Lights Fade '99
Wild Things '98
Starship Troopers '97
Nowhere '96
Tammy and the T-Rex '94

Emily Richard (1948-)
Empire of the Sun '87
The Life and Adventures of Nicholas Nickleby '81

Firmine Richard (1947-)
8 Women '02
Mama, There's a Man in Your Bed '89

Jean Richard (1921-2001)
Elena and Her Men '56
Seven Deadly Sins '53
Original Sin '01
North Shore Fish '97

Cordelia Richards
Empire '02
Scary Movie 3 '03
Love Actually '03

Derek Richardson (1976-)
Hostel '06
Dumb and Dumberer: When Harry Met Lloyd '03

Cameron Richardson
Alvin and the Chipmunks '07
Supercross: The Movie '05
The Good Humor Men '05

Pierre Richard (1934-)
A Chef in Love '96
Les Comperes '83
Too Shy to Try '82
La Chevre '81
The Daydreamer '75
Return of the Tall Blond Man with One Black Shoe '74

Jean-Louis Richard (1921-)
After Sex '97
Jeanne la Pucelle '94
La Sentinelle '92
Le Professionnel '81
The Last Metro '80

Nathalie Richard (1962-)
Le Divorce '03
Confusion of Genders '00
Irma Vep '96
Up/Down/Fragile '95

Robert Ri'chard (1983-)
The Comebacks '07
Coach Carter '05
House of Wax '05

Jeff Richards (1922-89)
Born Reckless '59
It's a Dog's Life '55
Seven Brides for Seven Brothers '54
Above and Beyond '53
Battle Circus '53
Angels in the Outfield '51
Kill the Umpire '50

Kim Richards (1964-)
Escape to Witch Mountain '07
Meatballs 2 '84
Tuff Turf '85
Devil Dog: The Hound of Hell '78
Return from Witch Mountain '78
Escape to Witch Mountain '75

Keith Richards (1915-87)
C·huck Berry: Hail! Hail! Rock 'n' Roll '87
Gimme Shelter '70

Evan Richards (1970-)
Mute Witness '95
Society '92
Dream Machine '91
Rock 'n' Roll High School Forever '91
Down and Out in Beverly Hills '86

Jay Richardson
Fugitive Rage '96
Killing for Love '95
Attack of the 60-Foot Centerfold '95
Illegal Affairs '96
Vice Academy 3 '91
Bad Girls from Mars '90
Vice Academy 2 '90
Original Intent '91
Sins of Desire '92
Alienator '89
The Channeler '89
Death Row Diner '88
Slashdance '89

Jack (H.) Richardson (1883-1957)
They Never Come Back '32
Dynamite Dan '24

Marie Richardson (1959-)
Evil '03
Faithless '00
Eyes Wide Shut '99

Miranda Richardson (1958-)
Fred Claus '07
Merlin's Apprentice '06
Paris, je t'aime '06
Southland Tales '06
Gideon's Daughter '05
Harry Potter and the Goblet of Fire '05
The Prince & Me '04
The Hours '02
Spider '02
Chicken Run '00 (V)
Get Carter '00
The Miracle Maker '00 (V)
Alice in Wonderland '99
The Big Brass Ring '99
Sleepy Hollow '99
Merlin '98
St. Ives '98
The Apostle '97
The Designated Mourner '97
The Evening Star '96
Swann '96
Kansas City '95
Saint-Ex: The Story of the Storyteller '95
Century '94
Fatherland '94
Tom & Viv '94
The Night and the Moment '94
The Crying Game '92
Damage '92
Enchanted April '92
Twisted Obsession '90
After Pilkington '87
Eat the Rich '87
Empire of the Sun '87
Dance with a Stranger '85

Lee Richardson (1926-99)
Sarah, Plain and Tall: Skylark '93
A Stranger Among Us '92
Q & A '90
The Fly 2 '89
Sweet Lorraine '87
Tiger Warsaw '87
Prizzi's Honor '85

Joely Richardson (1965-)
The Patriot '00
Return to Me '00
Maybe Baby '99
In the Shadows '98
Wrestling with Alligators '98
Event Horizon '97
Loch Ness '95
Sister My Sister '94
I'll Do Anything '93
Shining Through '92
King Ralph '91
Drowning by Numbers '87
Wetherby '85

Ian Richardson (1934-2007)
Becoming Jane '07
Joyeux Noel '05
From Hell '01
Dr. Bell and Mr. Doyle: The Dark Beginnings of Sherlock Holmes '00
102 Dalmatians '00
Dream Machine '91
M. Butterfly '93
Year of the Comet '92
A Knight in Camelot '98
B.A.P.s '97
Foreign Affairs '93
To Play the King '93
A Royal Scandal '95 (N)
Catherine the Great '95
The Final Cut '95
Incognito '97
The Woman in White '97
The Vengeance of She '68
Whisperers: An Elephant's Tale '00 (V)
Brazil '85
The Hound of the Baskervilles '83
The Sign of Four '83
Tinker, Tailor, Soldier, Spy '80
Charlie Muffin '79
A Midsummer Night's Dream '68

Kevin M. Richardson (1964-)
Queer Duck: The Movie '06

John Richardson (1936-)
Broadcast Bombshells '95
Cosmos: War of the Planets '80
Eyeball '78
Frankenstein '80 '79
War in Space '77
Torso '73
The Vengeance of She '68
One Million Years B.C. '66
She '65

A Woman of Substance '84

Natasha Richardson (1963-)
Wild Child '08
Evening '07
Asylum '05
The White Countess '05
Maid in Manhattan '02
Antwone Fisher '02
Waking Up in Reno '02
Chelsea Walls '01
Blow Dry '00
The Parent Trap '98
Nell '94
Widow's Peak '94
Hostages '93
The Favor, the Watch, & the Very Big Fish '92
Past Midnight '92
The Comfort of Strangers '91
The Handmaid's Tale '90
Fat Man and Little Boy '89
Patty Hearst '88
Gothic '87
A Month in the Country '87

Patricia Richardson (1951-)
California Dreaming '07
Blonde '01
Dead Simple '01
Ulee's Gold '97
In Country '89
Christmas Evil '80

Ralph Richardson (1902-83)
Wagner: The Complete Epic '85
Give My Regards to Broad Street '84
Greystoke: The Legend of Tarzan, Lord of the Apes '84
Dragonslayer '81
Early Days '81
Time Bandits '81
Charlie Muffin '79
Watership Down '78 (V)
Long Day's Journey into Night '62
The 300 Spartans '62
Exodus '60
Our Man in Havana '59
Richard III '55
The Fallen Idol '49
The Heiress '49
Anna Karenina '48
The Day Will Dawn '42
The Lion Has Wings '40
Clouds over Europe '39
The Four Feathers '39
The Citadel '38
The Divorce of Lady X '38
Amazing Adventure '37
South Riding '37
Thunder in the City '37
Things to Come '36
Bulldog Jack '35
Java Head '35
The Ghoul '34

Regina Richardson
Nine Deaths of the Ninja '85

Russell Richardson
The Rookie '02
Ancient Evil: Scream of the Mummy '00
Tigerland '00

Salli Richardson (1967-)
I Am Legend '07
Anacondas: The Hunt for the Blood Orchid '04
Biker Boyz '03
Antwone Fisher '02
Never 2 Big '98
True Women '97
The Great White Hype '96
Soul of the Game '96
Gargoyles, The Movie: The Heroes Awaken '94 (V)
Lily in Winter '94
A Low Down Dirty Shame '94
Sioux City '94
How U Like Me Now? '92
Up Against the Wall '91
Posse '93

Sy Richardson
Floundering '94
Ring of Fire 2: Blood and Steel '92
Street Asylum '90
Backtrack '89
Tapeheads '89
Three Fugitives '89
Bad Dreams '88
Colors '88
Dead Man Walking '88
They Live '88
Straight to Hell '87
Repo Man '83
Fairy Tales '76

LaTanya Richardson Jackson
Freedomland '06
Kill Bill Vol. 2 '04
The Fighting Temptations '03
Introducing Dorothy Dandridge '99
U.S. Marshals '98
Julian Po '97
Losing Isaiah '94
When a Man Loves a Woman '94

Carole Richert
The Night and the Moment '94
Tous les Matins du Monde '92

William Richert (1944-)
Manic '01
The Man in the Iron Mask '97
My Own Private Idaho '91

Julian Richings (1955-)
Shoot 'Em Up '07
My Life Without Me '03
Wrong Turn '03
The Claim '00
Cube '98

Charles Richman (-1940)
In Old Kentucky '35
Struggle '31

Peter Mark Richman (1927-)
Poolhall Junkies '02
Naked Gun 2 1/2: The Smell of Fear '91
Friday the 13th, Part 8: Jason Takes Manhattan '89
Judgment Day '88
City Killer '87
Dempsey '83
PSI Factor '80
Blind Ambition '79
Black Orchid '59
The Strange One '57

Anthony Richmond (1942-)
One Wish Too Many '55
Devil Girl from Mars '54

B.L. Richmond
See Branscombe Richmond

Branscombe Richmond (1955-)
Black Cloud '04
The Scorpion King '02

To the Limit '95
Vegas Vice '94
Jericho Fever '93
Christopher Columbus: The Discovery '92
DaVinci's War '92
Inside Edge '92
The Taking of Beverly Hills '91

Deon Richmond (1978-)
National Lampoon's Van Wilder '02
Not Another Teen Movie '01
Scream 3 '00
Trippin' '99

Fiona Richmond (1945-)
Eat the Rich '87
The House on Straw Hill '76

Kane Richmond (1906-73)
Behind the Mask '46
Haunted Harbor '44
Action in the North Atlantic '43
Spy Smasher '42
Spy Smasher Returns '42
Motorcycle Squad '41
Anything for a Thrill '37
Devil Diamond '37
The Reckless Way '36
Confidential '35
Silent Code '35
The Lost City '34
Cavalier of the West '31

Warner Richmond (1886-1948)
Colorado Serenade '46
Wild West '46
Wild Horse Canyon '39
Doomed at Sundown '37
A Lawman Is Born '37
Where Trails Divide '37
Headin' for the Rio Grande '36
Song of the Gringo '36
The New Frontier '35
Rainbow's End '35
The Lost Jungle '34
Big News '29
The Speed Spook '24

Andy Richter (1966-)
Semi-Pro '08
Talladega Nights: The Ballad of Ricky Bobby '06
Madagascar '05 (V)
New York Minute '04
Seeing Other People '04
Elf '03
My Boss's Daughter '03
Big Trouble '02
Frank McClusky, C.I. '02
Dr. Dolittle 2 '01
Pootie Tang '01
Scary Movie 2 '01
Dr. T & the Women '00
Cabin Boy '94

Deborah Richter (1961-)
The Banker '89
Cyborg '89
Promised Land '88
Square Dance '87
Hot Moves '84
Twirl '81
The Rebels '79
Swap Meet '79

Jason James Richter (1980-)
Laserhawk '99
Ricochet River '98
Free Willy 3: The Rescue '97
Free Willy 2: The Adventure Home '95
The Cops and Robbersons '94

The NeverEnding Story 3: Escape from Fantasia '94
Free Willy '93

Paul Richter (1896-1961)
Kriemhilde's Revenge '24
Siegfried '24
Dr. Mabuse, The Gambler '22
The Indian Tomb '21

Tony Rickards
Castaway '87
Robbery '85
Great Gold Swindle '84
Waterfront '83

Don Rickles (1926-)
Toy Story 2 '99 (V)
Dennis the Menace Strikes Again '98
Beverly Hills Cop 2 '87
Rosie: The Rosemary Clooney Story '82
Who Am I This Time? '82
Casino '95
Toy Story '95 (V)
Innocent Blood '92
Keaton's Cop '90
For the Love of It '80
Kelly's Heroes '70
Enter Laughing '67
Beach Blanket Bingo '65
Bikini Beach '64
Muscle Beach Party '64
Pajama Party '64
X: The Man with X-Ray Eyes '63
The Rat Race '60
Run Silent, Run Deep '58

Alan Rickman (1946-)
Harry Potter and the Order of the Phoenix '07
Sweeney Todd: The Demon Barber of Fleet Street '07
Perfume: The Story of a Murderer '06
Snow Cake '06
Harry Potter and the Goblet of Fire '05
The Hitchhiker's Guide to the Galaxy '05 (V)
Harry Potter and the Prisoner of Azkaban '04
Love Actually '03
Harry Potter and the Chamber of Secrets '02
Harry Potter and the Sorcerer's Stone '01
Blow Dry '00
Dogma '99
Galaxy Quest '99
Dark Harbor '98
Judas Kiss '98
Michael Collins '96
Rasputin: Dark Servant of Destiny '96
Sense and Sensibility '95
An Awfully Big Adventure '94
Mesmer '94
Fallen Angels 1 '93
Bob Roberts '92
Close My Eyes '91
Robin Hood: Prince of Thieves '91
Truly, Madly, Deeply '91
Closet Land '90
Quigley Down Under '90
Die Hard '88

Allen Rickman
I Was a Teenage Zombie '87
Shock! Shock! Shock! '87

Maria Ricossa
The In-Laws '03
Bojangles '01
Dead Man Out '89

Stephane Rideau (1976-)
Come Undone '00
Sitcom '97

John Ridgely (1909-68)
As You Were '51

Cavalry Charge '51
Border Incident '49
Task Force '49
Cry Wolf '47
The Possessed '47
The Big Sleep '46
The Man I Love '46
My Reputation '46
God Is My Co-Pilot '45
Arsenic and Old Lace '44
Air Force '43
Destination Tokyo '43

Robert Ridgely (1931-96)
Boogie Nights '97
Hard Eight '96
Philadelphia '93
The Ref '93
Beverly Hills Cop 2 '87
Rosie: The Rosemary Clooney Story '82
Prime Time '77

Stanley Ridges (1891-1951)
No Way Out '50
Task Force '49
The Possessed '47
Mr. Ace '46
Because of Him '45
God Is My Co-Pilot '45
Master Race '44
The Story of Dr. Wassell '44
Wilson '44
Air Force '43
The Lady Is Willing '42
To Be or Not to Be '42
The Sea Wolf '41
Sergeant York '41
They Died with Their Boots On '41
Black Friday '40
Each Dawn I Die '39
Union Pacific '39
If I Were King '38
Internes Can't Take Money '37

Harry Riebauer (1921-99)
The Great Escape '63
Strangler of Blackmoor Castle '63

Leni Riefenstahl (1902-2003)
Tiefland '44
The Blue Light '32

Eden Riegel (1981-)
Henry Hill '03
Prince of Egypt '98 (V)

Peter Riegert (1947-)
King of the Corner '04
Bojangles '01
How to Kill Your Neighbor's Dog '01
Passion of Mind '00
Traffic '00
The Mask '94
Barbarians at the Gate '93
Gypsy '93
Utz '93
Passed Away '92
The Object of Beauty '91
Oscar '91
A Shock to the System '90
That's Adequate '89
Crossing Delancey '88
North Shore Fish '97
Infinity '96
The Infiltrator '95
Pie in the Sky '95
Bleeding Hearts '94
Coldblooded '94
The January Man '89
A Man in Love '87
The Stranger '87
News at Eleven '86
Local Hero '83
National Lampoon Goes to the Movies '81
Americathon '79
Chilly Scenes of Winter '79
National Lampoon's Animal House '78

Richard Riehle (1948-)
The Man from Earth '07
Midnight Clear '06
The Twelve Dogs of Christmas '05
Home on the Range '04 (V)
Mysterious Skin '04
Palindromes '04
Bandits '01
The Fluffer '01
Say It Isn't So '01
Deuce Bigalow: Male Gigolo '99
Desperate Measures '98
Lethal Weapon 4 '98
Office Space '98
The Lesser Evil '97
Trading Favors '97
Ghosts of Mississippi '96
Soul of the Game '96
A Stranger in Town '95
Dominion '94
Holy Matrimony '94
Lightning Jack '94
A Dangerous Woman '93
Lone Justice 2 '93
Body of Evidence '92
Hero '92
Of Mice and Men '92
The Public Eye '92
Glory '89

Katja Riemann (1963-)
Blood & Chocolate '07
Agnes and His Brothers '04
Rosenstrasse '03
Balzac: A Life of Passion '99
Bandits '99
The Harmonists '99
Maybe... Maybe Not '94

Adam Rifkin (1966-)
Welcome to Hollywood '00
Something About Sex '98
The Dark Backward '91

Richard Rifkin
Eragon '06
Assault of the Party Nerds '89

Ron Rifkin (1939-)
Pulse '06
Dragonfly '02
The Sum of All Fears '02
Deliberate Intent '01
The Majestic '01
The Chosen '81
Mrs. R's Daughter '79
Silent Running '71

Jorge (George) Rigaud (1905-84)
The Case of the Bloody Iris '72
Horror Express '72
One Step to Hell '67
Black Box Affair '66
The Castillan '63
Quatorze Juillet '32

Cathy Rigby (1952-)
Challenge of a Lifetime '85
The Great Wallendas '78

Edward Rigby (1879-1951)
The Happiest Days of Your Life '50
Salute John Citizen '42
Convoy '40
Young and Innocent '37
Lorna Doone '34

Terence Rigby (1927-)
- Get Carter '71
- Color Me Kubrick '05
- Mona Lisa Smile '03
- Essex Boys '99
- Plunkett & Macleane '98
- The Young Americans '93
- Tinker, Tailor, Soldier, Spy '80

Diana Rigg (1938-)
- The Painted Veil '06
- The American '01
- Victoria & Albert '01
- Speedy Death '99
- Rebecca '97
- Moll Flanders '96
- Samson and Delilah '96
- A Good Man in Africa '94
- Genghis Cohn '93
- Running Delilah '93
- Mrs. 'Arris Goes to Paris '92
- Snow White '89
- Unexplained Laughter '89
- The Worst Witch '86
- Bleak House '85
- Evil under the Sun '82
- The Great Muppet Caper '81
- A Little Night Music '77
- In This House of Brede '75
- Theatre of Blood '73
- The Hospital '71
- Julius Caesar '70
- The Assassination Bureau '69
- On Her Majesty's Secret Service '69
- A Midsummer Night's Dream '68

Rebecca Rigg (1967-)
- Ellie Parker '05
- Tunnel Vision '95
- The Efficiency Expert '92
- The Hunting '92
- Fortress '85

Mitchell Riggs
- Doctors and Nurses '82

Massimo Righi
- Death Ray '67
- Black Sabbath '64

Alex(andre) Rignault (1901-85)
- Numero Deux '75
- The Horror Chamber of Dr. Faustus '59
- Eternal Return '43

Lucia Rijker (1967-)
- Million Dollar Baby '04

Elaine Riley (1923-)
- Clipped Wings '53
- Rider from Tucson '50
- The Dreamers '03

Brad Rijn
- Special Effects '85
- Perfect Strangers '84
- Smithereens '82

Robin Riker (1952-)
- Stepmonster '92
- Body Chemistry 2: Voice of a Stranger '91
- Alligator '80

Jack Riley (1935-)
- Rugrats Go Wild! '03 (V)
- Rugrats in Paris: The Movie '00 (V)
- The Rugrats Movie '98 (V)
- Portrait of a White Marriage '88
- Night Patrol '85
- Attack of the Killer Tomatoes '78
- McCabe & Mrs. Miller '71

Jeannine Riley (1939-)
- Spacehunter: Adventures in the Forbidden Zone '83
- Wackiest Wagon Train in the West '77

- Electra Glide in Blue '73
- The Comic '69
- Big Mouth '67

Larry Riley (1953-92)
- Dead Solid Perfect '88
- Long Gone '87
- Crackers '84
- A Soldier's Story '84

Michael Riley (1962-)
- Cube: Zero '04
- The Way We Live Now '02
- Pale Saints '97
- French Kiss '95
- Heck's Way Home '95
- The Prince '95
- ...And God Spoke '94
- Race to Freedom: The Story of the Underground Railroad '94
- Because Why? '93
- To Catch a Killer '92
- Perfectly Normal '91

Tom Riley
- Return to House on Haunted Hill '07
- A Few Days in September '06

Walter Rilla (1894-1980)
- Frozen Alive '64
- The Gamma People '56
- The Golden Salamander '51
- Mr. Emmanuel '44
- House of Mystery '41
- The Scarlet Pimpernel '34

Shane Rimmer
- Space Truckers '97
- Crusoe '89
- Dreamchild '85
- Out of Africa '85
- Charlie Muffin '79
- The People That Time Forgot '77
- Dr. Strangelove, or: How I Learned to Stop Worrying and Love the Bomb '64

Blanche Ring (1877-1961)
- Having Wonderful Crime '45
- It's the Old Army Game '26

Cyril Ring (1892-1967)
- I Wake Up Screaming '41
- The Cocoanuts '29

Molly Ringwald (1968-)
- Not Another Teen Movie '01
- Cowboy Up '00
- Cut '00
- The Brutal Truth '99
- Requiem for Murder '99
- Teaching Mrs. Tingle '99
- Office Killer '97
- Since You've Been Gone '97
- Baja '95
- Malicious '95
- Some Folks Call It a Sling Blade '94
- Stephen King's The Stand '94
- Face the Music '92
- Betsy's Wedding '90
- Strike It Rich '90
- Women & Men: Stories of Seduction '90
- For Keeps '88
- Fresh Horses '88
- King Lear '87
- The Pick-Up Artist '87
- Pretty in Pink '86
- P.K. and the Kid '85
- The Breakfast Club '85
- Sixteen Candles '84
- Packin' It in '83
- Tempest '82

Lisa Rinna (1963-)
- Another Woman's Husband '00

Nicole Rio
- Visitants '87
- Sorority House Massacre '86

Michael Ripper (1913-)
- No Surrender '86
- The Creeping Flesh '72
- Girly '70
- The Scars of Dracula '70
- Taste the Blood of Dracula '70
- Dracula Has Risen from the Grave '68
- Plague of the Zombies '66
- The Reptile '66
- Where the Bullets Fly '66
- The Curse of the Werewolf '61
- The Brides of Dracula '60
- Dead Lucky '60
- The Mummy '59
- Quatermass 2 '57
- Eye Witness '49

Fay Ripley (1966-)
- Dead Gorgeous '02
- For Roseanna '96

Marjorie (Reardon) Riordan (1921-84)
- The Hoodlum '51
- South of Monterey '47
- Pursuit to Algiers '45
- Stage Door Canteen '43

David Rintoul (1948-)
- Horatio Hornblower: The Adventure Continues '01
- Pride and Prejudice '85
- Legend of the Werewolf '75

Leon Rippy
- Gridiron Gang '06
- The Alamo '04
- The Life of David Gale '03
- Eight Legged Freaks '02
- The Patriot '00
- Stargate '94
- Kuffs '92
- Young Guns 2 '90
- Moon 44 '90
- The Hot Spot '90
- Eye of the Storm '91

June Ritchie (1939-)
- The Mouse on the Moon '62
- A Kind of Loving '62

Jill Ritchie (1974-)
- Herbie: Fully Loaded '05
- Little Athens '05
- Breakin' All The Rules '04
- D.E.B.S. '04
- Seeing Other People '04

Clint Ritchie (1938-)
- Peacekillers '71
- The St. Valentine's Day Massacre '67

Bob Ritchie
- See Kid Rock

Cyril Ritchard (1897-1977)
- The Hobbit '78 (V)
- Hans Brinker '69
- Half a Sixpence '67
- Peter Pan '60
- Blackmail '29

Lazar Ristovski (1952-)
- Underground '95
- Tito and Me '92

Robbie (Reist) Rist (1964-)
- Unseen Evil '99
- Teenage Mutant Ninja Turtles: The Movie '90

Jacques Rispal
- Le Chat '75

Michael Rispoli (1960-)
- Black Irish '07
- The Bronx Is Burning '07
- Invincible '06
- One Last Thing '05
- Danielle Steel's Heartbeat '93
- Household Saints '93
- Night and the City '92
- While You Were Sleeping '95
- Homeward Bound 2: Lost in San Francisco '96

Jeff Risk
- Code of Honor '82
- Kill Squad '81

Miriam Riselle
- Tevye '39
- The Singing Blacksmith '38

Elisabeth Risdon (1887-1958)
- Scaramouche '52
- Guilty of Treason '50
- Hills of Oklahoma '50
- Down Dakota Way '49
- The Amazing Mrs. Holiday '43
- The Lady Is Willing '42
- Mexican Spitfire at Sea '42
- Reap the Wild Wind '42
- Mexican Spitfire Sees a Ghost '42
- The Great Man Votes '38
- Mannequin '37
- Theodora Goes Wild '36
- Crime and Punishment '35

Maurice Risch (1943-)
- The Last Metro '81
- Beau Pere '81

Blake Ritson
- Mansfield Park '07

Martin Ritt (1914-90)
- The Slugger's Wife '85
- Conrack '74

Jason Ritter (1980-)
- Good Dick '08
- The Education of Charlie Banks '07
- The Last Winter '06
- Happy Endings '05
- Raise Your Voice '04
- Freddy vs. Jason '03
- Swimfan '02
- Mumford '99

John Ritter (1948-2003)
- Clifford's Really Big Movie '04 (V)
- Bad Santa '03
- Tadpole '02
- Panic '00
- Terror Tract '00
- TripFish '00
- The Million Dollar Kid '99
- Bride of Chucky '98
- Dead Husbands '98
- It Came from the Sky '98
- Shadow of Doubt '98
- A Gun, a Car, a Blonde '97
- Montana '97
- Nowhere '97
- Sling Blade '96
- Mercenary '96
- The Colony '95
- North '94
- Noises Off '92
- Problem Child 2 '91
- Problem Child '90
- Stephen King's It '90
- My Brother's Wife '89
- Skin Deep '89
- Tricks of the Trade '88
- Real Men '87
- The Last Fling '86
- A Smoky Mountain Christmas '86
- Unnatural Causes '86
- Letting Go '85
- Sunset Limousine '83
- In Love with an Older Woman '82
- They All Laughed '81
- Hero at Large '80
- Wholly Moses! '80
- Americathon '79
- The Other '72

Thelma Ritter (1905-69)
- Boeing Boeing '65
- For Love or Money '63
- How the West Was Won '63
- Move Over, Darling '63
- A New Kind of Love '63
- Birdman of Alcatraz '62
- The Misfits '61
- A Hole in the Head '59
- Pillow Talk '59
- Daddy Long Legs '55
- Rear Window '54
- Titanic '53
- With a Song in My Heart '52
- As Young As You Feel '51
- All About Eve '50
- Father Was a Fullback '49
- A Letter to Three Wives '49
- Miracle on 34th Street '47

Tex Ritter (1905-74)
- Down the Wyoming Trail '39
- Man from Texas '39
- Roll, Wagons, Roll '39
- Rollin' Plains '38
- Utah Trail '38
- Arizona Days '37
- Hittin' the Trail '37
- Mystery of the Hooded Horseman '37
- Riders of the Rockies '37
- Sing, Cowboy, Sing '37
- Tex Rides with the Boy Scouts '37
- Trouble in Texas '37
- Headin' for the Rio Grande '36
- Song of the Gringo '36

Jimmy Ritz (1903-85)
- Blazing Stewardesses '75
- Argentine Nights '40
- The Gorilla '39
- The Three Musketeers '39
- The Goldwyn Follies '38
- On the Avenue '37
- One in a Million '36

Harry Ritz (1906-86)
- Silent Movie '76
- Blazing Stewardesses '75
- Argentine Nights '40
- The Gorilla '39
- The Three Musketeers '39
- The Goldwyn Follies '38
- On the Avenue '37
- One in a Million '36

Al Ritz (1901-65)
- Argentine Nights '40
- The Gorilla '39
- The Three Musketeers '39
- The Goldwyn Follies '38
- On the Avenue '37
- One in a Million '36

Emmanuelle Riva (1927-)
- Trois Couleurs: Bleu '93
- Leon Morin, Priest '61
- Hiroshima, Mon Amour '59
- Kapo '59

Naike Rivelli (1974-)
- Ancient Relic '02
- The Count of Monte Cristo '99

Geoffrey Rivas
- Luminarias '99

Mabel Rivera
- The Orphanage '07
- The Sea Inside '04

Rene Rivera
- Break a Leg '03
- Rangers '00

Chita Rivera (1933-)
- Pippin '81
- Sweet Charity '69

Carlos Rivas (1928-2003)
- True Grit '69
- They Saved Hitler's Brain '64
- The Black Scorpion '57
- The King and I '56

Jorge (George) Rivero (1938-)
- Fist Fighter '88
- Counterforce '87
- Target Eagle '84
- Conquest '83
- Day of the Assassin '81
- Priest of Love '81
- Warrior of Justice '96
- Werewolf '95
- Ice '93
- Soldier Blue '70
- Rio Lobo '70

Enrique Rivero
- The Blood of a Poet '30

Julian Rivero (1890-1976)
- Underground Agent '42
- Arizona Gangbusters '40
- Death Rides the Range '40
- Heroes of the Alamo '37
- Ridin' the Lone Trail '37
- Phantom Patrol '36
- Western Justice '35
- Law and Lawless '35
- Beyond the Rockies '32
- Man from Hell's Edges '32
- Night Rider '32

Joan Rivers (1933-)
- Intern '00
- Whispers: An Elephant's Tale '00 (V)
- Napoleon '96 (V)
- Serial Mom '94
- Spaceballs '87
- The Muppets Take Manhattan '84
- Les Patterson Saves the World '90
- What's Cooking? '00
- Two for Texas '94
- A Million to Juan '94
- Blood In ... Blood Out: Bound by Honor '93

Victor Rivers
- The Weather Man '05
- Mr. 3000 '04
- Death to Smoochy '02
- Summer of Sam '99
- The Third Miracle '99
- Two Family House '00
- Rounders '98
- Scarred City '98
- Snake Eyes '98

Black Magic Woman '91

Jorge Rivier
See Jorge (George) Rivero

George Riviere (1924-)
The Virgin of Nuremberg '65
Castle of Blood '64
Journey Beneath the Desert '61

George(s) Riviere
See Jorge (George) Rivero

Julien Riviere
Ma Vie en Rose '97
Les Voleurs '96

Marie Riviere (1956-)
Time to Leave '05
The Lady and the Duke '01
Autumn Tale '98
A Tale of Winter '92
Four Adventures of Reinette and Mirabelle '89
Summer '86
The Aviator's Wife '80

George Riviya
See Jorge (George) Rivero

Gianni Rizzo (1925-92)
Sabata '69
Mission Stardust '68
Desert Commandos '67

Bert Roach (1891-1971)
San Francisco '36
The Crowd '28
Smouldering Fires '25

Daryl Roach
Gang Boys '97

Martin Roach
Cube: Zero '04
The Wall '99

Linus Roache (1964-)
Find Me Guilty '06
Batman Begins '05
12 and Holding '05
The Chronicles of Riddick '04
The Forgotten '04
Beyond Borders '03
The Gathering Storm '02
Hart's War '02
RFK '02
Pandaemonium '00
Siam Sunset '99
Shot Through the Heart '98
The Wings of the Dove '97
Priest '94

Adam Roarke (1938-96)
Sioux City '94
Trespasses '86
Beach Girls '82
The Stunt Man '80
Hughes & Harlow: Angels in Hell '77
Four Deuces '75
Dirty Mary Crazy Larry '74
How Come Nobody's On Our Side? '73
This Is a Hijack '73
Frogs '72
The Losers '70
Hell's Belles '69
The Savage Seven '68
Hell's Angels on Wheels '67
Women of the Prehistoric Planet '66

Jason Robards, Sr. (1892-1963)
Western Pacific Agent '51 (N)
Rimfire '49
Mr. Blandings Builds His Dream House '48
Return of the Bad Men '48
Desperate '47
Riff-Raff '47
Trail Street '47
Bedlam '45
Isle of the Dead '45
Mademoiselle Fifi '44 ...
The Fatal Hour '40
Stunt Pilot '39
Sweetheart of the Navy '37
Fighting Marines '36
The Miracle Rider '35
Crimson Romance '34
Carnival Lady '33
Woman Condemned '33
Wayne Murder Case '32
White Eagle 32

Jason Robards, Jr. (1922-2000)
Magnolia '99
Beloved '98
Enemy of the State '98
Heartwood '98
The Real Macaw '98
A Thousand Acres '97
Crimson Tide '95
Journey '95
The Enemy Within '94
Little Big League '94
My Antonia '94
The Paper '94
The Adventures of Huck Finn '93
Heidi '93
Philadelphia '93
The Trial '93
Storyville '92
Black Rainbow '91
An Inconvenient Woman '91
Mark Twain and Me '91
Final Warning '90
Quick Change '90
Dream a Little Dream '89
Parenthood '89
Bright Lights, Big City '88
The Christmas Wife '88
The Good Mother '88
Reunion '88
Breaking Home Ties '87
Laguna Heat '87
Square Dance '87
The Long, Hot Summer '86
Sakharov '84
You Can't Take It with You '84
The Day After '83
Max Dugan Returns '83
Something Wicked This Way Comes '83
Burden of Dreams '82
Cabo Blanco '81
Legend of the Lone Ranger '81
Melvin and Howard '80
Raise the Titanic '80
Hurricane '79
A Christmas to Remember '78
Comes a Horseman '78
Julia '77
All the President's Men '76
A Boy and His Dog '75
Mr. Sycamore '74
A House without a Christmas Tree '72
Divorce American Style '67
Hour of the Gun '67
The St. Valentine's Day Massacre '67
Any Wednesday '66
A Big Hand for the Little Lady '66
A Thousand Clowns '65
Long Day's Journey into Night '62
By Love Possessed '61
A Doll's House '59

Sam Robards (1961-)
Awake '07
Catch That Kid '04
A.I.: Artificial Intelligence '01
Hamlet '01
Life as a House '01
Bounce '00
American Beauty '99
Dinner and Driving '97
Beautiful Girls '96
The Man Who Captured Eichmann '96
Donor Unknown '95
Mrs. Parker and the Vicious Circle '94

Andrew Robb
Ready to Wear '94

AnnaSophia Robb (1993-)
Jumper '08
Sleepwalking '08
Bridge to Terabithia '07
The Reaping '07
Because of Winn-Dixie '05
Charlie and the Chocolate Factory '05

David Robb (1947-)
Behind the Lines '97
The Crow Road '96
The Flame Trees of Thika '81

R.D. Robb (1972-)
Eight Days a Week '97
A Christmas Story '83

Amy Robbins (1971-)
Strange Relations '02
All the Little Animals '98
Rudyard Kipling's Second Jungle Book: Mowgli and Baloo '97

Brian Robbins (1964-)
DaVinci's War '92
C.H.U.D. 2: Bud the Chud '89
Cellar Dweller '87

Gale Robbins (1921-80)
Parasite '82
The Girl in the Red Velvet Swing '55
The Belle of New York '52
The Fuller Brush Girl '50
Three Little Words '50
The Barkleys of Broadway '49
My Girl Tisa '48

Marty Robbins (1925-82)
Hell on Wheels '67
Road to Nashville '67
Ballad of a Gunfighter '64

Skeeter Bill Robbins (1887-1933)
Fighting Parson '35
Cowboy Counselor '33
The Dude Bandit 33
Boiling Point '32
Man's Land '32
Hard Hombre '31

Tim Robbins (1958-)
Catch a Fire '06
Tenacious D in the Pick of Destiny '06
War of the Worlds '05
Zathura '05
Anchorman: The Legend of Ron Burgundy '04
Code 46 '03
Mystic River '03
Human Nature '02
The Truth About Charlie '02
Antitrust '00
High Fidelity '00
Mission to Mars '00
Arlington Road '99
Austin Powers 2: The Spy Who Shagged Me '99
Nothing to Lose '96
I.Q. '94
Ready to Wear '94
The Shawshank Redemption '94
The Hudsucker Proxy '93
Short Cuts '93
Bob Roberts '92
The Player '92
Jungle Fever '91
Cadillac Man '90
Jacob's Ladder '90
Erik the Viking '89
Miss Firecracker '89
Tapeheads '89
Twister '89
Bull Durham '88
Five Corners '88
Howard the Duck '86
Top Gun '86
Fraternity Vacation '85
Quarterback Princess '85
The Sure Thing '85
No Small Affair '84
Toy Soldiers '84

Richard Rober (1910-52)
Jet Pilot '57
Kid Monk Baroni '52
Man in the Saddle '51
The Well '51
Task Force '49
Call Northside 777 '48

David Roberson
Steel Sharks '94

Yves Robert (1920-2002)
The Judge and the Assassin '75
Les Grandes Manoeuvres '55

Allene Roberts (1928-)
The Hoodlum '51
Union Station '50
The Red House 47

Arthur Roberts (1938-)
The Capitol Conspiracy '99
Femme Fontaine: Killer Babe for the C.I.A. '95
Illegal Entry: Formula for Fear '01
Not of This Earth '88
Revenge of the Ninja '83
Deadly Vengeance '81

Bart Roberts
See Rex Reason

Bret Roberts
Rampage: The Hillside Strangler Murders '04
Cock & Bull Story '03
Nightstalker '02

Christian Roberts (1944-)
The Adventurers '70
Desperados '69
The Anniversary '68
To Sir, with Love '67

Conrad Roberts
The Scorpion King '02
The Million Dollar Hotel '99
The Serpent and the Rainbow '87

Dallas Roberts (1970-)
Joshua '07
3:10 to Yuma '07
Flicka '06
The Notorious Bettie Page '06
Walk the Line '05
Winter Passing '05
A Home at the End of the World '04

Daniel Roberts
Valiant '05 (V)
Walking on Water '02

David Roberts
Fool's Gold '08
Me Myself I '99

Des Roberts
Black Bikers from Hell '70
The Outlaw Bikers—Gang Wars '70

Doris Roberts (1930-)
Grandma's Boy '06
Keeping Up with the Steins '06
Dickie Roberts: Former Child Star '03
A Time to Remember '03
All Over the Guy '01
My Giant '98
The Night We Never Met '93
Used People '92
Honeymoon Academy '90
National Lampoon's Christmas Vacation '89
Simple Justice '89
The Fig Tree '87
Number One with a Bullet '87
Ordinary Heroes '85
Hester Street '75
The Taking of Pelham One Two Three '74
Honeymoon Killers '70

Edith Roberts (1899-1935)
Man from Headquarters '28
The Taxi Mystery '26

Emma Roberts (1991-)
Wild Child '08
Nancy Drew '07
Aquamarine '06
Blow '01

Eric Roberts (1956-)
The Dark Knight '08
Witless Protection '08
Pandemic '07
DOA: Dead or Alive '06
A Guide to Recognizing Your Saints '06
Phat Girlz '06
Final Approach '04
Miss Cast Away '04
Border Blues '03
Break a Leg '03
National Security '03
Con Games '02
Endangered Species '02
Spun '02
Fast Sofa '01
The King's Guard '01
The Long Ride Home '01
Mindstorm '01
Sanctimony '01
Stiletto Dance '01
Cecil B. Demented '00
Frozen in Fear '00
Luck of the Draw '00
No Alibi '00
Race Against Time '00
TripFall '00
Agent of Death '99
Heaven's Fire '99
Hitman's Run '99
La Cucaracha '99
Lansky '99
Purgatory '99
Restraining Order '99
Wildflowers '99
Bitter Sweet '98
Dead End '98
Facade '98
Past Perfect '98
T.N.T. '98
Two Shades of Blue '98
Most Wanted '97
The Odyssey '97
The Prophecy 2: Ashtown '97
American Strays '96
Doctor Who '96
The Glass Cage '96
In Cold Blood '96
Power 98 '96
Public Enemies '96
The Grave '95
Heaven's Prisoners '95
The Immortals '95
It's My Party '95
Saved by the Light '95
Babyfever '94
Firefall '94
The Hard Truth '94
Love Is a Gun '94
Nature of the Beast '94
Sensation '94
The Specialist '94
Best of the Best 2 '93
By the Sword '93
Love, Cheat & Steal '93
Voyage '93
Final Analysis '92
Fugitive Among Us '92
A Family Matter '91
Lonely Hearts '91
The Ambulance '90
Descending Angel '90
The Lost Capone '90
Best of the Best '89
Rude Awakening '89
Blood Red '88
Options '88
To Heal a Nation '88
Nobody's Fool '86
Slow Burn '86
Runaway Train '85
The Coca-Cola Kid '84
The Pope of Greenwich Village '84
Star 80 '83
Raggedy Man '81
King of the Gypsies '78

Ewan Roberts (1914-83)
Day of the Triffids '63
Curse of the Demon '57

Florence Roberts (1860-1940)
Harmony Lane '35
Sons of Steel '35
Hoopla '33
Kept Husbands '31

Francesca Roberts
Prison Stories: Women on the Inside '91
The Heart of Dixie '89

Ian Roberts
Tsotsi '05
Wah-Wah '05
Tarzan and the Lost City '98
Mandela and de Klerk '97
Terminal Impact '95
The Power of One '92
Violated 53

Jay Roberts, Jr.
Warlords 3000 '93
Aftershock '88
White Phantom: Enemy of Darkness '87

Jeremy Roberts (1954-)
Herbie: Fully Loaded '05
The Thirteenth Floor '99
Jungle Boy '96

J.H. Roberts (1884-1961)
Uneasy Terms '48
Spitfire '42
The Courageous Mr. Penn '41
Young and Innocent '37
Nine Days a Queen '36

Joe Roberts
Cider with Rosie '98
Shakespeare in Love '98

Judith Anna Roberts
The Nanny Diaries '07
Eraserhead '78

Julia Roberts (1967-)
Charlie Wilson's War '07
The Ant Bully '06 (V)
Charlotte's Web '06 (V)
Closer '04
Ocean's Twelve '04
Mona Lisa Smile '03
Confessions of a Dangerous Mind '02
Full Frontal '02
America's Sweethearts '01
The Mexican '01
Ocean's Eleven '01
Erin Brockovich '00
Notting Hill '99
Runaway Bride '99
Stepmom '98
Conspiracy Theory '97
My Best Friend's Wedding '97
Everyone Says I Love You '96
Michael Collins '96
Mary Reilly '95
Something to Talk About '95
I Love Trouble '94

Ready to Wear '94
The Pelican Brief '93
The Player '92
Dying Young '91
Hook '91
Sleeping with the Enemy '91
Flatliners '90
Pretty Woman '90
Steel Magnolias '89
Blood Red '88
Mystic Pizza '88
Satisfaction '88
Baja Oklahoma '87
Firehouse '87

Kimberly Roberts
Get a Clue '02
Range of Motion '00
Vice Girls '96
Love Jones '95

Lee Roberts
Battling Marshal '48

Leonard Roberts (1972-)
Drumline '02
Joe and Max '02
The '60s '99

Lynne Roberts (1922-78)
Because of You '52
Dynamite Pass '50
Hunt the Man Down '50
Eyes of Texas '48
Robin Hood of Texas '47
Sioux City Sue '46
In Old Caliente '39
Frolics on Ice '39
Rough Riders' Roundup '39
Southward Ho! '39
Billy the Kid Returns '38
Come on Rangers! '38
Hollywood Stadium Mystery '38
Shine On, Harvest Moon '38
Heart of the Rockies '37

Mark Roberts (1921-2006)
Bulletproof '96
Posse '75

Michael D. Roberts (1947-)
Live! From Death Row '92
Rain Man '88
Ice Pirates '84
Heartbreaker '83

Pernell Roberts (1928-)
Around the World in 80 Days '89
The Night Train to Kathmandu '88
High Noon: Part 2 '80
Hot Rod '79
The Errand Boy '61
Ride Lonesome '59
Dishonorable Discharge '57
The Peking Blond '68

Pascale Roberts (1933-)
The Town Is Quiet '00
Marius and Jeannette '97
Le Grand Chemin '87
Friends '71

Theodore Roberts (1861-1928)
The Ten Commandments '23
Affairs of Anatol '21
Suds '20
The Roaring Road '19

Ken Roberts (1910-)
Fatal Pulse '88
The Great Land of Small '86

Rachel Roberts (1927-80)
Charlie Chan and the Curse of the Dragon Queen '81
The Hostage Tower '80
Yanks '79
When a Stranger Calls '79
Sorrows of Gin '79
Foul Play '78
Picnic at Hanging Rock '75
Murder on the Orient Express '74
O Lucky Man! '73
Alpha Beta '73
The Belstone Fox '73
Baffled '72
Wild Rovers '71
Doctors' Wives '71
This Sporting Life '63
Saturday Night and Sunday Morning '60
Our Man in Havana '59

Rick Roberts (1965-)
Man of the Year '06
Love and Human Remains '93

Wink Roberts (1955-)
The Day It Came to Earth '77

Roy Roberts (1900-75)
The Strongest Man in the World '75
I'll Take Sweden '65
The King and Four Queens '56
Second Chance '53
The Enforcer '51
Santa Fe '51
Borderline '50
Force of Evil '49
He Walked by Night '48
Colonel Effingham's Raid '45

Tanya Roberts (1954-)
Deep Down '94
Sins of Desire '92
Almost Pregnant '91
Inner Sanctum '91
Legal Tender '90
Night Eyes '90
Purgatory '89
Body Slam '87
A View to a Kill '85
Sheena '84
Beastmaster '82
California Dreaming '79
Racquet '79
Tourist Trap '79
Fingers '78

Teal Roberts
Fatal Games '84
Hardbodies '84

Ted Jan Roberts (1979-)
Dead Broke '99

Tony Roberts (1939-)
Popcorn '89
18 Again! '88
Radio Days '87
Hannah and Her Sisters '86
Seize the Day '86
Key Exchange '85
Amityville 3: The Demon '83
Packin' It In '83
A Midsummer Night's Sex Comedy '82
Just Tell Me What You Want '80
Stardust Memories '80
Annie Hall '77
The Lindbergh Kidnapping Case '76
Play It Again, Sam '72

Dale Robertson (1923-)
The Last Ride of the Dalton Gang '79
Melvin Purvis: G-Man '74
One-Eyed Soldiers '67
Dakota Incident '56
Son of Sinbad '55
Sitting Bull '54
Devil's Canyon '53
The Farmer Takes a Wife '53

Francoise Robertson
The Minion '98
Twists of Terror '98
Searching for Paradise '02
Oxygen '99

Iain Robertson (1981-)
Basic Instinct 2 '06
The Match '99
Plunkett & Macleane '98
Small Faces '95

Cliff Robertson (1925-)
Spider-Man 3 '07
Riding the Bullet '04
Spider-Man 2 '04
Spider-Man '02
Family Tree '00
Mach 2 '00
Escape from L.A. '96
Renaissance Man '94
Wind '92
Wild Hearts Can't Be Broken '91
Dead Reckoning '89
Dominique Is Dead '79
Obsession '76
Out of Season '75
Three Days of the Condor '75
The Man Without a Country '73
Too Late the Hero '70
The Great Northfield Minnesota Raid '72
The Devil's Brigade '68
Charly '68
The Honey Pot '67
Love Has Many Faces '65
The Best Man '64
633 Squadron '64
PT 109 '63
Sunday in New York '63
The Interns '62
All in a Night's Work '61
Underworld, U.S.A. '60
Gidget '59
The Naked and the Dead '58
Autumn Leaves '56
Picnic '55
The First Time '69

Kathleen Robertson (1973-)
Hollywoodland '06
XX/XY '02
Scary Movie 2 '01
Beautiful '00
Psycho Beach Party '00
Splendor '99
Dog Park '98
Nowhere '96
Blown Away '93

Paul Robeson (1898-1976)
Tales of Manhattan '42
Jericho '38
Big Fella '37
King Solomon's Mines '37
Show Boat '36
Song of Freedom '36
Sanders of the River '35
Emperor Jones '33
Body and Soul '24

George Robey (1869-1954)
Salute John Citizen '42
Henry V '44
Don Quixote '35

Herb Robins
The Worm Eaters '77
The Thrill Killers '65

Kim Robillard
Ali '01
Home Fries '98
The Fan '96
Breakdown '96
Chrome Soldiers '92
Rain Man '88

Michel Robin
Merci pour le Chocolat '00
La Chevre '81

Laila Robins (1959-)
The Blood Oranges '97
Female Perversions '96
Live Nude Girls '95
True Crime '99
An Innocent Man '89
Planes, Trains & Automobiles '87

Jessie Robins (1905-91)
The Fearless Vampire Killers '67
Magical Mystery Tour '67

Edward G. Robinson (1893-1973)
Soylent Green '73
Song of Norway '70
MacKenna's Gold '69
The Cincinnati Kid '65
Cheyenne Autumn '64
Good Neighbor Sam '64
Robin and the 7 Hoods '64
The Prize '63
My Geisha '62
Two Weeks in Another Town '62
Seven Thieves '60
A Hole in the Head '59
A Bullet for Joey '55
Hell on Frisco Bay '55
Illegal '55
Tight Spot '55
The Violent Men '55
Actors and Sin '52
My Daughter Joy '49
It's a Great Feeling '49
Key Largo '48
All My Sons '48
The Red House '47
The Stranger '46
Our Vines Have Tender Grapes '45
Scarlet Street '45
The Woman in the Window '44
Double Indemnity '44
Mr. Winkle Goes to War '44
Tales of Manhattan '42
Larceny, Inc. '42
The Sea Wolf '41
Brother Orchid '40
Dr. Ehrlich's Magic Bullet '40
A Dispatch from Reuter's '40
I Am the Law '38
A Slight Case of Murder '38
Amazing Dr. Clitterhouse '38
Kid Galahad '37
Thunder in the City '37
The Last Gangster '37
Barbary Coast '35
Bullets or Ballots '36
The Whole Town's Talking '35
Smart Money '31
Little Caesar '30

Jenny Robertson (1963-)
Twitches '05
The Boys Next Door '96
Danger of Love '95
The Nightman '93
Bull Durham '88
Jacob Have I Loved '88

Andrew (Andy) Robertson (1942-)
Poltergeist 2: The Other Side '86
Poltergeist '82

Mikul Robins
Witchcraft 11: Sisters in Blood '00
Witchcraft 9: Bitter Flesh '96

Steven Robertson (1980-)
Joyeux Noel '05
Rory O'Shea Was Here '04

Robbie Robertson (1943-)
The Crossing Guard '94
Carny '80

Kimmy Robertson (1954-)
Speed 2: Cruise Control '97
Leprechaun 2 '94
Beauty and the Beast '91

Ken Robertson
Nighthawks '78

Willard Robertson (1886-1948)
Remember the Night '40
Fury at Furnace Creek? '41
Two Alone '34
Supernatural '33

Bill Robertson (1878-1949)
Stormy Weather '43
War of the Worlds '05
Attack from Mars '88
Dragnet '54
The War of the Worlds '53
The Little Colonel '35
The Littlest Rebel '35
Dixiana '30

Ann (Robin) Robinson (1935-)
War of the Worlds '05
Attack from Mars '88
Dragnet '54
The War of the Worlds '53

Chris Robinson (1938-)
Shenandoah '65
Savannah Smiles '82
Women's Prison Escape '74
Stanley '72
Darker than Amber '70
The Worm Eaters '77

Charles Robinson (1945-)
Set It Off '96
Land of the Free '98
Still Crazy '98
The Story of Adele H. '75
Fatal Chase '77
Black Gestapo '75
Daring Dobermans '73
The Brotherhood of Satan '71

Bruce Robinson (1946-)
Still Crazy '98
Land of the Free '98
The Story of Adele H. '75

Claudia Robinson
Back in the USSR '92

Dar Robinson (1947-86)
Stick '85
Cyclone '87

Eartha D. Robinson (1960-)
The Old Settler '01
Daughters of the Dust '91

John Robinson (1908-79)
Stanley '72

John Robinson (1985-)
Seraphim Falls '06
Lords of Dogtown '05
The Lion Has Wings '40
Elephant '03

Karen Robinson
Lars and the Real Girl '07
Jasper, Texas '03

Oliver Robins (1971-)
Poltergeist 2: The Other Side '86
Poltergeist '82

Joe Robinson (1929-)
Diamonds Are Forever '71
The Robe '53
Demetrius and the Gladiators '54

Jay Robinson (1930-)
Transylvania Twist '89
Malibu Bikini Shop '86
Partners '82
Dragnet '87
Shampoo '75
The Robe '53
Demetrius and the Gladiators '54

Frances Robinson (1916-71)
Smilin' Through '41
Red Barry '38
Tim Tyler's Luck '37

Holly Robinson (1964-)
Howard the Duck '86

Stalked '94

Keith D. Robinson (1962-)
This Christmas '07
Dreamgirls '06
Fat Albert '04

Leon Robinson (1962)
Buffalo Soldiers '01
The Father Clements Story '87
Band of the Hand '86
Streetwalkin' '85
Sole Survivor '84

Madeleine Robinson (1916-2008)
Camille Claudel '89
I Married a Dead Man '82
Mission to Venice '63
Duke of the Derby '62

Paul Michael Robinson
Kept '01
The Capitol Conspiracy '99
Friend of the Family 2 '96

Roger Robinson (1940-)
Brother to Brother '04
Bumzy's Last Call '95
Newman's Law '74

Sherry Robinson
Hot Summer in Barefoot County '74
Gruesome Twosome '67

"Sugar Ray" Robinson (1921-89)
Candy '68
The Detective '68
Paper Lion '68

Wendy Raquel Robinson (1967-)
Something New '06
Rebound '05
Hidalgo '04
The Namesake '06

Flora Robson (1902-84)
A Tale of Two Cities '80
Les Miserables '78
Restless '72
Beast in the Cellar '70
Blood Island '68
Those Magnificent Men in Their Flying Machines '65
Guns at Batasi '64
55 Days at Peking '63
Murder at the Gallop '63
Romeo and Juliet '54
Malta Story '53
Black Narcissus '47
Frieda '47
Caesar and Cleopatra '46
Great Day '46
Saratoga Trunk '45
Bahama Passage '42
The Lion Has Wings '40
The Sea Hawk '40
Wuthering Heights '39
Fire Over England '37
Catherine the Great '34

Greer Robson (1971-)
Starlight Hotel '90
Smash Palace

May Robson (1858-1942)
Joan of Paris '42
Playmates '41
The Texas Rangers Ride Again '40
Nurse Edith Cavell '39
The Adventures of Tom Sawyer '38
Bringing Up Baby '38
Four Daughters '38
The Texans '38
A Star Is Born '37
It Happened in New Orleans '36
Wife Versus Secretary '36
Anna Karenina '35
Reckless '35
Lady by Choice '34
Dancing Lady '33
Dinner at Eight '33
Lady for a Day '33
Little Orphan Annie '32
Red Headed Woman '32
Strange Interlude '32

Wayne Robson (1946-)
Welcome to Mooseport '04
Wrong Turn '03
Harlan County War '00
Cube '98
Murder She Purred: A Mrs. Murphy Mystery '98
Affliction '97
Two If by Sea '95
Stand Off '93
Love & Murder '91
Bye Bye Blues '89
And Then You Die '88
The Grey Fox '83

Patricia Roc (1915-2003)
Captain Blackjack '51
Man on the Eiffel Tower '48
Canyon Passage '46
Johnny Frenchman '46
The Wicked Lady '45
Police '85
The Rascals '81

Daniela Rocca (1938-95)
Divorce—Italian Style '62
The Mercenaries '62
The Giant of Marathon '60
Revenge of the Barbarians '60

Stefania Rocca (1971-)
Don't Tell '05
The 4 Musketeers '05
Heaven '01
Jesus '00
Love's Labour's Lost '00
The Talented Mr. Ripley '99
Solomon '98

Alex Rocco (1936-)
Smokin' Aces '07
Find Me Guilty '06
Jam '06
The Job '03
Big Shot: Confessions of a Campus Bookie '02
The Country Bears '02
The Wedding Planner '01
Dudley Do-Right '99
Goodbye, Lover '99
A Bug's Life '98 (V)
Just Write '97
That Thing You Do! '96
The Spy Within '94
Boris and Natasha: The Movie '92
The Pope Must Diet '91
A Perfect Little Murder '90
Dream a Little Dream '89
Wired '89
The Lady in White '88
Return to Horror High '87
Scenes from the Goldmine '87
Badge of the Assassin '85
Gotcha! '85
P.K. and the Kid '85
The Entity '83

The Godfather 1902-1959: The Complete Epic '81
Herbie Goes Bananas '80
The Stunt Man '80
The Grass Is Always Greener Over the Septic Tank '78
A Question of Guilt '78
Rabbit Test '78
The Blue Knight '75
Hustling '75
Three the Hard Way '74
Bonnie's Kids '73
Detroit 9000 '73
Slither '73
The Godfather '72
Stanley '72
Wild Riders '71
Blood Mania '70
The St. Valentine's Day Massacre '67
Motor Psycho '65

Mario Roccuzzo
One Last Ride '03
Earth vs. the Spider '01

Kail Rocha (1971-)
The Family Plan '05
29th & Gay '05
Meet the Fockers '04
Gods and Generals '03
Meet the Parents '00

Eugene Roche (1928-2004)
When a Man Loves a Woman '94
Eternity '90
Oh, God! You Devil '84
Rape and Marriage: The Rideout Case '80
Corvette Summer '78
Foul Play '78
The Winds of Kitty Hawk '78
The Late Show '77
The Possessed '77
Newman's Law '74
Slaughterhouse Five '72
They Might Be Giants '71
Cotton Comes to Harlem '70

Sebastien Roche (1964-)
Crossing Delancey '88

Suzzy Roche
Crossing '00
The Hunley '99
Merlin '98
Naked City: Justice with a Bullet '98
Household Saints '93

Jean Rochefort (1930-)
Mr. Bean's Holiday '07
The Man on the Train '02
The Closet '00
The Count of Monte Cristo '99
Ridicule '96
Ready to Wear '94
The Hairdresser's Husband '92
My Wonderful Life '90
Birgitt Haas Must Be Killed '83
I Sent a Letter to My Love '81
Le Cavaleur '78
Who's Killing the Great Chefs of Europe? '78
Le Crabe Tambour '77
Pardon Mon Affaire, Too! '77
Pardon Mon Affaire '76
Innocents with Dirty Hands '76
Mean Frank and Crazy Tony '75
Return of the Tall Blond Man with One Black Shoe '74
Salut l'Artiste '74
Till Marriage Do Us Part '74
The Clockmaker '73
Escape from Death Row '73

Le Complot '73
The Tall Blond Man with One Black Shoe '72
A Coeur Joie '67

Claire Rochelle (1908-81)
Shake Hands with Murder '44
Harvest Melody '43
Texas Justice '42
Buzzy Rides the Range '40
Lightning Strikes West '40
Code of the Fearless '39
El Diablo Rides '39
Boothill Brigade '37
Guns in the Dark '37
Ridin' the Lone Trail '37
Two-Gun Troubador '37

Debbie Rochon (1968-)
Rapturious '07
Blood Relic '05
Witchouse 3: Demon Fire '01
American Nightmare '00
Rage of the Werewolf '99
The Alien Agenda: Endangered Species '97
Hellblock 13 '97
Broadcast Bombshells '95
Tromeo & Juliet '95
Abducted 2: The Reunion '94
Vampire's Kiss '88

Lela Rochon (1966-)
Any Given Sunday '99
Labor Pains '99
The Big Hit '98
Knock Off '98
Ruby Bridges '98
Why Do Fools Fall in Love? '98
The Chamber '96
Gang Related '96
Mr. & Mrs. Loving '96
Legal Deceit '95
Waiting to Exhale '95

Chris Rock (1966-)
Bee Movie '07 (V)
I Think I Love My Wife '07
The Longest Yard '05
Madagascar '05 (V)
Paparazzi '04
Head of State '03
Bad Company '02
A.I.: Artificial Intelligence '01 (V)
Down to Earth '01
Jay and Silent Bob Strike Back '01
Osmosis Jones '01 (V)
Pootie Tang '01
Nurse Betty '00
Dogma '99
Dr. Dolittle '98 (V)
Lethal Weapon 4 '98
Beverly Hills Ninja '96
The Immortals '95
CB4: The Movie '93
Coneheads '93
Boomerang '92
New Jack City '91
I'm Gonna Git You Sucka '88
Beverly Hills Cop 2 '87

Crissy Rock
Butterfly Collectors '99
Ladybird, Ladybird '93

Rock, The
See Dwayne "The Rock" Johnson

Charles Rocket (1949-2005)
The Killing Grounds '97
Shade '03
Father's Day '96
Steal Big, Steal Little '95
Dumb & Dumber '94
It's Pat: The Movie '94
Brain Smasher... A Love Story '93
Hocus Pocus '93
Wild Palms '93
Delirious '91
Dances with Wolves '90
Honeymoon Academy '90

Down Twisted '89
Earth Girls Are Easy '89
How I Got into College '89
Miracles '86
Fraternity Vacation '85

Jack Rockwell (1890-1947)
Rough Riders of Cheyenne '45
Prairie Moon '38
The Law Rides '36
The Lone Avenger '33
Trail Drive '33

Jack Rockwell (1949-)
Raiders of Sunset Pass '43
Tumbleweed Trail '42
Twilight on the Trail '41
Hopalong Cassidy: Renegade Trail '39
Renegade Trail '39
The Rangers Step in '37
Brand of the Outlaws '36
Outlaw Rule '36
The Tonto Kid '35
The Man from Hell '34
The Fiddlin' Buckaroo '33
Come on Tarzan '32

Rick Rockwell (1956-)
Killer Tomatoes Eat France '91
Killer Tomatoes Strike Back '90

Robert Rockwell (1920-2003)
Lassie: Adventures of Neeka '68
The Red Menace '49

Sam Rockwell (1968-)
The Assassination of Jesse James by the Coward Robert Ford '07
Joshua '07
Snow Angels '07
The Hitchhiker's Guide to the Galaxy '05
Matchstick Men '03
Confessions of a Dangerous Mind '02
Welcome to Collinwood '02
Heist '01
Charlie's Angels '00
Galaxy Quest '99
The Green Mile '99
William Shakespeare's A Midsummer Night's Dream '99
Jerry and Tom '98
Safe Men '98
Box of Moonlight '96
Glory Daze '96
Lawn Dogs '96
Mercy '96
The Search for One-Eyed Jimmy '96
Happy Hell Night '92
Jack and His Friends '92
Clown House '88

Jay Rodan
The Game of Their Lives '05
Monsieur N. '03
Callas Forever '02
The Caveman's Valentine '01
Lost Battalion '01
The Triumph of Love '01

Ziva Rodann (1935-)
Samar '62
The Giants of Thessaly '60
Macumba Love '60
Last Train from Gun Hill '59
Teenage Doll '57

James Roday (1976-)
Don't Come Knocking '05
The Dukes of Hazzard '05
Repli-Kate '01
Coming Soon '99

Marcia Rodd (1940-)
Keeping On '81
Citizens Band '77
How to Break Up a Happy Divorce '76
Little Murders '71

Ebbe Rode (1910-98)
Babette's Feast '87
Topsy Turvy '84
Gertrud '64

Karel Roden (1962-)
Mr. Bean's Holiday '07
The Abandoned '06
Running Scared '06
The Last Drop '05
The Bourne Supremacy '04
Dead Fish '04
Hellboy '04
Bulletproof Monk '03
Blade 2 '02
15 Minutes '01
Crackerjack 2 '97

Struan Rodger (1956-)
Sherlock: Case of Evil '02
The Waiting Time '99

Anton Rodgers (1933-2007)
Longford '06
The Merchant of Venice '04
Impromptu '90
Pictures '80s
Dirty Rotten Scoundrels '88
Agatha Christie's Murder with Mirrors '85
Disraeli '79
Lillie '79

J.J. Rodgers
Vampire Time Travelers '98
Amazon Warrior '97

Michael E. Rodgers (1969-)
Auto Focus '02
Uncorked '98

Dennis Rodman (1961-)
The Comebacks '07
Cutaway '00
Simon Sez '99
Double Team '97

Serge Rodnunsky
Lovers Lovers '94
Body Beat '88

Michael Rodrick (1970-)
Revolution #9 '01
Under Hellgate Bridge '99
Desolation Angels '95

Estelita Rodriguez (1928-66)
Sunset in the West '50
Twilight in the Sierras '50
The Golden Stallion '49
Susanna Pass '49
The Gay Ranchero '42

Freddy Rodriguez (1975-)
Planet Terror '07
Bobby '06
Lady in the Water '06
Poseidon '06
Dreamer: Inspired by a True Story '05
Harsh Times '05
Chasing Papi '03
Dallas 362 '03
Players '03
Rip It Off '02
For Love or Country: The Arturo Sandoval Story '00
The Pest '97
Dead Presidents '95
A Walk in the Clouds '95

Marco Rodriguez
Unspeakable '02
Angel Blue '97
Two for Texas '97
Serial Killer '95
... And the Earth Did Not Swallow Him '94
The Crow '93
Internal Affairs '90

Michelle Rodriguez (1978-)
BloodRayne '06
The Breed '06
S.W.A.T. '03
Blue Crush '02
Resident Evil '02
The Fast and the Furious '01
3 A.M. '01
Girlfight '99

Paul Rodriguez (1955-)
The World's Fastest Indian '05
A Cinderella Story '04
Baadasssss! '03
Blood Work '02
Ali '01
Crocodile Dundee in Los Angeles '01
Rat Race '01
Tortilla Soup '01
Mambo Café '00
Price of Glory '00
Race '99
Rough Magic '95
A Million to Juan '94
Made in America '93
Born in East L.A. '87
Miracles '86
Quicksilver '86
The Whoopee Boys '86

Valente Rodriguez
The Big Squeeze '96
Ed '96

Norman Rodway (1929-2001)
The Empty Mirror '99
The Bretts '88
Coming Through '85
Chimes at Midnight '67

Channon Roe (1969-)
Rampage: The Hillside Strangler Murders '04
Girl '98
Marshal Law '96
Persons Unknown '96
Soldier Boyz '95
Last Call '90

Matt Roe (1952-2003)
Sins of the Night '93

Paul Roebling (1934-94)
Carolina Skeletons '92
End of August '82

Daniel Roebuck (1963-)
Flourish '06
Confessions o' a Sociopathic Social Climber '05
The Devil's Rejects '05
Agent Cody Banks 2: Destination London '04
Straight into Darkness '04
Agent Cody Banks '03
We Were Soldiers '02
Double Take '01
A Glimpse of Hell '01
Final Destination '00
Stir '98
U.S. Marshals '98
Money Talks '97
The Late Shift '96
The Fugitive '93
Eddie Presley '92
The Killing Mind '90
Disorganized Crime '89
Miles from Home '88
Dudes '87
River's Edge '87
Terror Eyes '87
Cave Girl '85

Sarah Roemer
Disturbia '07
Wristcutters: A Love Story '06

Gabriela Roel
In the Middle of Nowhere '93

Maurice Roeves (1937-)
Beautiful Creatures '00
Forgive and Forget '99
The Acid House '98
David '97
Moses '96
The Last of the Mohicans '92

William Roerick (1912-95)
A Separate Peace '73
The Love Machine '71
The Wasp Woman '59

Ivan Rogers (1954-)
Slow Burn '00
Ballbuster '89
Two Wrongs Make a Right '89
Crazed Cop '88

Paul Rogers (1917-)
The Return of the Native '94
The Tenth Man '88
Edwin '84
The Big Man: Crossing the Line '91
Hidden Agenda '90
Danger UXB '81
When Eight Bells Toll '71
The Looking Glass War '69
Oh! What a Lovely War '69
Ulysses '67

Michael Rogen
Punch the Clock '90

Seth Rogen (1982-)
Dr. Seuss' Horton Hears a Who! '08 (V)
Kung Fu Panda '08 (V)
Pineapple Express '08
The Spiderwick Chronicles '08 (V)
Knocked Up '07
Shrek the Third '07 (V)
Superbad '07
You, Me and Dupree '06
The 40-Year-Old Virgin '05

Charles "Buddy" Rogers (1904-99)
Double Trouble '41
Mexican Spitfire at Sea '42

Clyde Rogers
See Rik van Nutter

Ginger Rogers (1911-95)
That's Dancing! '85
Quick, Let's Get Married '71
Cinderella '64
Tight Spot '55
Black Widow '54
Forever Female '53
Monkey Business '52
We're Not Married '52
Storm Warning '51
The Barkleys of Broadway '49
Heartbeat '46
Magnificent Doll '46
Weekend at the Waldorf '45
Tender Comrade '43
I'll Be Seeing You '44
The Major and the Minor '42
Once Upon a Honeymoon '42
Roxie Hart '42
Tales of Manhattan '42
Tom, Dick, and Harry '41
Kitty Foyle '40
Lucky Partners '40
Primrose Path '40
Bachelor Mother '39
Fifth Avenue Girl '39
The Story of Vernon and Irene Castle '39
Carefree '38
Having Wonderful Time '38
Vivacious Lady '38
Shall We Dance '37
Stage Door '37
Swing Time '36
Follow the Fleet '36
In Person '35
Roberta '35
Star of Midnight '35
Top Hat '35
The Gay Divorcee '34
Romance in Manhattan '34
Finishing School '33
Flying Down to Rio '33
Gold Diggers of 1933 '33
42nd Street '33
Shriek in the Night '33
13th Guest '32
Suicide Fleet '31
The Tip-Off '31

Mimi Rogers (1956-)
Big Nothing '06
Dancing in Twilight '05
Jesse Stone: Stone Cold '05
The Door in the Floor '04
Seeing Other People '04
Dumb and Dumberer: When Harry Met Lloyd '03
The Gunman '03
Charms for the Easy Life '02
Ginger Snaps '01
Common Ground '00
Seven Girlfriends '99
Cruel Intentions 2 '99
Lost in Space '98
The Devil's Arithmetic '99
Austin Powers: International Man of Mystery '97
Weapons of Mass Distraction '97
The Mirror Has Two Faces '96
Tree's Lounge '96
Bulletproof Heart '95
Full Body Massage '95
Far from Home: The Adventures of Yellow Dog '94
Monkey Trouble '94
Reflections in the Dark '94
Dark Horse '92
Ladykiller '92
The Player '92
Shooting Elizabeth '92
White Sands '92
Deadlock '91
The Doors '91
The Palermo Connection '91
The Rapture '91
Desperate Hours '90
Fourth Story '90
Hider in the House '90
The Mighty Quinn '89
Someone to Watch Over Me '87
Street Smart '87
Embassy '85
Blue Skies Again '83
Gung Ho '65

Bill Rogers (1930-2004)
The Girl, the Body and the Pill '67
Shanty Tramp '67
A Taste of Blood '67

Jimmy Rogers (1915-)
Texas Masquerade '44
False Colors '43
Hopalong Cassidy: Riders of the Deadline '43

Kenny Rogers (1938-)
The Gambler Returns: The Luck of the Draw '91
Rio Diablo '93
Heart of the County '81
Kenny Rogers as the Gambler, Part 3: The Legend Continues '87
Wild Horses '84
Kenny Rogers as the Gambler, Part 2: The Adventure Continues '83
Six Pack '82
Coward of the County '81
Kenny Rogers as the Gambler '80

Reg Rogers (1964-)
Analyze That '02
Attila '01
I'll Take You There '99
Runaway Bride '99

Roxanne Rogers
Punk Vacation '90

Roy Rogers (1912-98)
Alias Jesse James '59
Son of Paleface '52
Heart of the Rockies '51
Spoilers of the Plains '51
North of the Great Divide '50
Sunset in the West '50
Trail of Robin Hood '50
Trigger, Jr. '50
Twilight in the Sierras '50
Down Dakota Way '49
The Golden Stallion '49
Susanna Pass '49
Eyes of Texas '48
Far Frontier '48
Grand Canyon Trail '48
Melody Time '48
Night Time in Nevada '48
Under California Stars '48
Apache Rose '47
Bells of San Angelo '47
Home in Oklahoma '47
Lights of Old Santa Fe '47
On the Old Spanish Trail '47
Springtime in the Sierras '47
Helldorado '46
My Pal Trigger '46
Rainbow over Texas '46
Roll on Texas Moon '46
Song of Arizona '46
Under Nevada Skies '46
Along the Navajo Trail '45
Bells of Rosarita '45
Don't Fence Me In '45
Sunset in El Dorado '45
Utah '45
Cowboy & the Senorita '44
San Fernando Valley '44
Song of Nevada '44
The Yellow Rose of Texas '44
Hands Across the Border '43
Idaho '43
King of the Cowboys '43
Silver Spurs '43
Song of Texas '43
Man from Cheyenne '42
Ridin' Down the Canyon '42
Romance on the Range '42
Sons of the Pioneers '42
South of Santa Fe '42
Sunset on the Desert '42
Sunset Serenade '42
Bad Man of Deadwood '41
In Old Cheyenne '41
Jesse James at Bay '41
Nevada City '41
Red River Valley '41
Robin Hood of the Pecos '41
Sheriff of Tombstone '41
The Border Legion '40
Carson City Kid '40
Colorado '40
Dark Command '40
Ranger and the Lady '40
Young Bill Hickok '40
Young Buffalo Bill '40
Arizona Kid '39
Days of Jesse James '39
Frontier Pony Express '39
In Old Caliente '39
Jeepers Creepers '39
Rough Riders' Roundup '39
Saga of Death Valley '39
Southward Ho! '39
Wall Street Cowboy '39
Billy the Kid Returns '38
Come on Rangers '38
Old Barn Dance '38
Shine on, Harvest Moon '38
Under Western Stars '38
Wild Horse Rodeo '37

Will Rogers (1879-1935)
Doubting Thomas '35
In Old Kentucky '35
Life Begins at Forty '35
Steamboat Round the Bend '35
David Harum '34
Judge Priest '34
Doctor Bull '33
Mr. Skitch '33
Too Busy to Work '32
A Connecticut Yankee '31
Ambassador Bill '31

Wayne Rogers (1933-)
Miracle Dogs '03
Ghosts of Mississippi '96
The Goodbye Bird '93
Passion in Paradise '89
Drop-Out Mother '88
The Killing Time '87
The Girl Who Spelled Freedom '86
The Gig '85
Lady from Yesterday '85
Chiefs '83
Hot Touch '82
Once in Paris... '79
Pocket Money '72
Cool Hand Luke '67

Steve Rogers
Triple Impact '92
Trident Force '88

Tristan Rogers (1946-)
Night Eyes 3 '93
Evil Lives '92
The Rescuers Down Under '90 (V)

Jean Rogers (1916-91)
Whistling in Brooklyn '43
Brigham Young: Frontiersman '40
The Mark '51
Flash Gordon: Rocketship '40
Flash Gordon: Mars Attacks the World '39
Our Man in Havana '59
Svengali '55
Beau Brummell '54
Old Man Rhythm '38 [?]

Maria Rohm (1949-)
Dorian Gray '70
Venus in Furs '70
Kiss and Kill '68
The House of 1000 Dolls '67
Count Dracula '71
She Done Him Wrong '33

Clayton Rohner (1961-)
Border Patrol '01
The Big Day '99
Sometimes They Come Back... For More '99
Where's Marlowe? '98
The Relic '96
Naked Souls '95
Caroline at Midnight '93
I, Madman '89
Nightwish '89
Bat 21 '88
Private Investigations '87
April Fool's Day '86
Just One of the Guys '85

Gylian Roland (1941-)
Deadly Sunday '82

Eduardo Lopez Rojas (1937-99)
My Family '94

Gustavo Rojo (1926-)
The Valley of Gwangi '69
The Christmas Kid '68
A Witch Without a Broom '68
Apache's Last Battle '64
No Survivors, Please '63
It Started with a Kiss '59

Helena Rojo (1944-)
Mary, Mary, Bloody Mary '76
Aguirre, the Wrath of God '72

Maria Rojo (1943-)
Esmeralda Comes by Night '98

Ruben Rojo (1922-93)
Cauldron of Blood '67
Samson in the Wax Museum '63
The Brainiac '61

Gilbert Roland (1905-)
Barbarosa '82
Cabo Blanco '81
The Sacketts '79
Islands in the Stream '77
Running Wild '73
Between God, the Devil & a Winchester '72
The Reward '65
Cheyenne Autumn '64
Samar '62
Three Violent People '57
Around the World in 80 Days '56
The Racers '55
Treasure of Pancho Villa '55
Underwater! '55
The French Line '54
Beneath the 12-Mile Reef '53
Thunder Bay '53
The Bad and the Beautiful '52
Miracle of Our Lady of Fatima '52
Bullfighter & the Lady '50
The Torch '50
Malaya '49
Riding the California Trail '47
South of Monterey '47
Captain Kidd '45
The Sea Hawk '40

Esther Rolle (1920-98)
Down in the Delta '98
My Fellow Americans '96
Rosewood '96
How to Make an American Quilt '95
Scarlett '94
To Dance with the White Dog '93
Dog '93
House of Cards '92
The Kid Who Loved Christmas '90

Guy Rolfe (1911-2003)
Retro Puppet Master '99
Puppet Master 5: The Final Chapter '94
Puppet Master 4 '93
Dolls '87
And Now the Screaming Starts '73
The Alphabet Murders '65
Mr. Sardonicus '61
King of the Khyber Rifles '53
Young Bess '53
The Spider and the Fly '49

Tutta Rolf (1907-94)
Dollar '38
Swedenhielms '35

Kirsten Rolffes (1928-2000)
The Kingdom 2 '97
The Kingdom '95
Sofie '92

Age Old Friends '89
Driving Miss Daisy '89
The Mighty Quinn '89
A Raisin in the Sun '89
P.K. and the Kid '85
I Know Why the Caged Bird Sings '79
The Summer of My German Soldier '78

Henry Rollins (1961-)
Wrong Turn 2: Dead End '07
Feast '06
Lies & Alibis '06
Bad Boys 2 '03
The New Guy '02
Time Lapse '01
Jack Frost '97
Lost Highway '96
Heat '95
Johnny Mnemonic '95
The Chase '93

Howard E. Rollins, Jr. (1950-96)
Drunks '96
For Us, the Living '88
The House of Dies Drear '88
Johnnie Gibson F.B.I. '87
The Children of Times Square '86
A Soldier's Story '84
The Member of the Wedding '83
Ragtime '81
King '78

Rose Rollins (1978-)
13 Moons '02
Undisputed '02

Mark Rolston (1952-)
Protecting the King '07
The Departed '06
Scorcher '02
Wicked Ways '99
From the Earth to the Moon '98
Letters from a Killer '98
Rush Hour '98
George Wallace '97
Hard Rain '97
Daylight '96
Eraser '96
Humanoids from the Deep '96
Best of the Best 3: No Turning Back '95
Scanner Cop '94
The Shawshank Redemption '94
Body of Evidence '92
The Comrades of Summer '92
Lethal Weapon 2 '89
Prancer '89
A Sinful Life '89
Survival Quest '89
Weeds '87
Aliens '86

Yvonne Romain (1938-)
The Last of Sheila '73
Double Trouble '67
Devil Doll '64
The Curse of the Werewolf '61
The Frightened City '61

Candice Roman
The Big Bird Cage '72
Unholy Rollers '72

Freddie Roman (1937-)
Finding North '97
Sweet Lorraine '87

Leticia Roman (1939-)
Fanny Hill: Memoirs of a Woman of Pleasure '64
The Girl Who Knew Too Much '63
G.I. Blues '60

Ruth Roman (1924-99)
Echoes '83
The Sacketts '79
Day of the Animals '77
Impulse '74
The Killing Kind '73
The Baby '72
Love Has Many Faces '65
Great Day in the Morning '56
Far Country '55
Blowing Wild '54
Strangers on a Train '51
Three Secrets '50
Beyond the Forest '49
Champion '49
The Window '49
Good Sam '48
Since You Went Away '44

Susan (Suzan) Roman (1957-)
Rock & Rule '83 (V)
Rabid '77
Weekend with the Babysitter '70

Viviane Romance (1909-91)
Any Number Can Win '63
Panique '47
Princess Tam Tam '35

Beatrice Romand (1952-)
Autumn Tale '98
Four Adventures of Reinette and Mirabelle '89
Summer '86
House of the Yellow Carpet '84
Le Beau Mariage '82
Claire's Knee '71

Carla Romanelli
The Lonely Lady '83
Steppenwolf '74
Fighting Fists of Shanghai Joe '65

Andy Romano (1936-)
Eraser '96
Fast Money '96
Ghosts of Mississippi '96
Listen '96
Two Bits '96
Chameleon '95
Under Siege 2: Dark Territory '95
Drop Zone '94
Tryst '94
Afterburn '92
Unlawful Entry '92
Pump Up the Volume '90
Over the Edge '79
Get Christie Love! '74

Christy Carlson Romano
The Cutting Edge: Going for the Gold '05
Looking for an Echo '99

Ray Romano (1957-)
Ice Age: The Meltdown '06 (V)
Eulogy '04
Welcome to Mooseport '04
Ice Age '02 (V)

Renato Romano
Frankenstein '80 '79
The Bird with the Crystal Plumage '70
Dorian Gray '70

Rino Romano (1969-)
Rocky Marciano '99
The Club '94

Anna Romantowska (1950-)
The Interrogation '82
A Woman and a Woman '80

Richard Romanus (1943-)
Cops and Robbersons '94
Point of No Return '93
To Protect and Serve '92
Oscar '91
Hollywood Heartbreak '89
The Couch Trip '87
Murphy's Law '86
Protocol '84
Strangers Kiss '83
Heavy Metal '81 (V)
Sitting Ducks '80
Wizards '77 (V)
Night Terror '76
Mean Streets '73

Robert Romanus (1956-)
The Resurrected '91
Pulse '88
Bad Medicine '85
Fast Times at Ridgemont High '82

Lina Romay (1922-)
Love Laughs at Andy Hardy '46
Adventure '45

Lina Romay (1954-)
Tender Flesh '97
Revenge in the House of Usher '82
Sex Is Crazy '79
Ilsa, the Wicked Warden '78
Jack the Ripper '76
Female Vampire '73
The Perverse Countess '73
Rites of Frankenstein '72
Order to Kill '73

Rachel Romen
Ransom Money '88
The Girl from Tobacco Row '66

Cesar Romero (1907-94)
Mortuary Academy '91
Simple Justice '89
Judgment Day '88
Lust in the Dust '85
Mission to Glory '80
The Big Push '75
Wanted: Babysitter '75
Diary of Forbidden Dreams '73
The Strongest Man in the World '75
The Spectre of Edgar Allen Poe '73
Now You See Him, Now You Don't '72
The Proud and the Damned '72
The Computer Wore Tennis Shoes '69
Crooks & Coronets '69
Gun Crazy '69
Hot Millions '68
Madigan's Millions '67
Batman '66
Marriage on the Rocks '65
The Castilian '63
Donovan's Reef '63
Ocean's 11 '60
Around the World in 80 Days '56
Americano '55
The Racers '55
The Shadow Man '53
Vera Cruz '53
FBI Girl '52
Jungle '52
Scotland Yard Inspector '52
Happy Go Lovely '51
The Lost Continent '51
The Beautiful Blonde from Bashful Bend '49
Julia Misbehaves '48
Captain from Castile '47
The Great American Broadcast '41
Week-End in Havana '41
Tales of Manhattan '42
Dance Hall '41
Orchestra Wives '42
Springtime in the Rockies '42
Wintertime '43
The Little Princess '39
Happy Landing '38
My Lucky Star '38
Wee Willie Winkie '37
The Devil Is a Woman '35
The Good Fairy '35
Show Them No Mercy '35
The Thin Man '34

George A. Romero (1940-)
Dawn of the Dead '78
Martin '77
Night of the Living Dead '68

Joanelle Romero
Miracle in the Wilderness '91
Powwow Highway '89
Lost Legacy: A Girl Called Hatter Fox '77

Ned Romero (1925-)
The Lost Child '00
The Magnificent Seven '98
Children of the Corn 2: The Final Sacrifice '92
House 4: Home Deadly Home '91
The Last of the Mohicans '85

Cindy Rome
The Deerslayer '78
I Will Fight No More Forever '75

Sydne Rome (1947-)
The Puma Man '80
Just a Gigolo '79
Twist '76
That Lucky Touch '75

Rebecca Romijn (1972-)
Lies & Alibis '06
X-Men: The Last Stand '06
Godsend '04
The Punisher '04
Femme Fatale '02
Rollerball '02
Simone '02
X-Men '00
Austin Powers 2: The Spy Who Shagged Me '99

Tiny Ron
Alien Nation: The Enemy Within '96
Alien Nation: Body and Soul '95
The Rocketeer '91

Paul Ronan (1965-)
Bloom '03
Durango '99
The Devil's Own '96

Saoirse Ronan (1994-)
Atonement '07
The Christmas Miracle of Jonathan Toomey '07
I Could Never Be Your Woman '06

Maurice Ronet (1927-83)
Beau Pere '81
Sphinx '81
Sidney Sheldon's Bloodline '79
Don Juan (Or If Don Juan Were a Woman) '73
The Deadly Trap '71
Swimming Pool '70
La Femme Infidele '69
La Piscine '69
How Sweet It Is! '68
The Women '68
Scandal Man '67
L'Odeur des Fauves '66
The Fire Within '64
The Victors '63
Time Out for Love '61
Purple Noon '60
Carve Her Name with Pride '58
Frantic '58
Rendez-vous de Juillet '49
Without Warning '52

Fabrizio Rongione
The Child '05
Rosetta '99

Linda Ronstadt (1946-)
Chuck Berry: Hail! Hail! Rock 'n' Roll '87
Find the Lady '76
Rachel's Man '75
The Pirates of Penzance '83
FM '78

Michael Roof
The Dukes of Hazzard '05
XXX: State of the Union '05
XXX '02
Black Hawk Down '01

Michael Rooker (1956-)
Jumper '08
Whisper '07
Full Count '06
Slither '06
Chasing Ghosts '05
The Box '03
Undisputed '02
Replicant '01
Here on Earth '00
Newsbreak '00
The 6th Day '00
Table One '00
The Bone Collector '99
Rogue Force '99
Wicked Ways '99
Bram Stoker's Shadowbuilder '98
Brown's Requiem '98
The Replacement Killers '98
Deceiver '97
Back to Back '96
Bastard out of Carolina '96
Keys to Tulsa '96
Rosewood '96
The Trigger Effect '96
Mallrats '95
The Hard Truth '94
Tombstone '93
Cliffhanger '93
The Dark Half '91
Afterburn '92
JFK '91
Days of Thunder '90
Henry: Portrait of a Serial Killer '90
Music Box '89
Sea of Love '89
Above the Law '88
Eight Men Out '88
Mississippi Burning '88
Light of Day '87

Mickey Rooney (1920-)
Night at the Museum '06
The Last Confederate: The Story of Robert Adams '05
Babe: Pig in the City '98
Boys Will Be Boys '97
The Gambler Returns: The Luck of the Draw '93
The Magic Voyage '93 (V)
Revenge of the Red Baron '93
The Legend of Wolf Mountain '92
Little Nemo: Adventures in Slumberland '92 (V)
Maximum Force '92
Sweet Justice '92
My Heroes Have Always Been Cowboys '91
Silent Night, Deadly Night 5: The Toymaker '91
Home for Christmas '90
Erik the Viking '89
Lightning: The White Stallion '86
Ace of Hearts '85
It Came Upon a Midnight Clear '84
Bill: On His Own '83
The Odyssey of the Pacific '82
Bill '81
The Fox and the Hound '81 (V)
Leave 'Em Laughing '81
Senior Trip '81
The Black Stallion '79
The Dark Side of Love '79
Magic of Lassie '78
The Domino Principle '77
Pete's Dragon '77
Thunder County '74
Women's Prison Escape '74
Pulp '72
Evil Roy Slade '71 (V)
Journey Back to Oz '71 (V)
Manipulator '71
The Comic '69
The Secret Invasion '64
It's a Mad, Mad, Mad, Mad World '63
Requiem for a Heavyweight '62
Breakfast at Tiffany's '61
The King of the Roaring '20s: The Story of Arnold Rothstein '61
Platinum High School '60
Francis in the Haunted House '56
The Bridges at Toko-Ri '55
The Atomic Kid '54
Off Limits '53
My Outlaw Brother '51
Quicksand '50
The Big Wheel '49
Summer Holiday '48
Words and Music '48
Love Laughs at Andy Hardy '46
National Velvet '44
Girl Crazy '43
The Human Comedy '43
Thousands Cheer '43
Andy Hardy's Double Life '42
Andy Hardy's Private Secretary '41
Babes on Broadway '41
Life Begins for Andy Hardy '41
Men of Boys Town '41
Andy Hardy Meets Debutante '40
Strike Up the Band '40
Young Tom Edison '40
The Adventures of Huckleberry Finn '39
Andy Hardy Gets Spring Fever '39
Babes in Arms '39
Mickey the Great '39
Boys Town '38
Love Finds Andy Hardy '38
Captains Courageous '37
Thoroughbreds Don't Cry '37
Healer '36
Little Lord Fauntleroy '36
Ah, Wilderness! '35
A Midsummer Night's Dream '35
Riff Raff '35
Hide-Out '34
Manhattan Melodrama '34
My Pal, the King '32

Tim Rooney (1947-)
Storyville '74
Village of the Giants '65

Jemima Rooper (1981-)
The Black Dahlia '06
Kinky Boots '06
A Sound of Thunder '05
Snapshots '02
The Railway Children '00

Camilla Overbye Roos (1969-)
The Guilty '99
Facade '98
On the Border '98
Hotel Room '93

Buddy Roosevelt (1898-1973)
Tribute to a Bad Man '56
Boss Cowboy '35
Powdersmoke Range '35
Range Riders '35
Circle Canyon '33
Lightning Range '33

Amanda Root (1963-)
Daniel Deronda '02
Anna Karenina '00
Deep in the Heart (of Texas) '98
Jane Eyre '96
Breaking the Code '95
Persuasion '95
Catherine Cookson's The Man Who Cried '93

This Lightning Always Strikes Twice '85
Coming Soon '99
Don't Tell '05

Bonnie Root (1975-)
Ice Age: The Meltdown '06
Over Her Dead Body '08
Mad Money '08
Leatherheads '08

Stephen (Steve) Root (1951-)
Rails & Ties '07
Idiocracy '06 (V)
Just Friends '05
Anchorman: The Legend of Ron Burgundy '04
Dodgeball: A True Underdog Story '04
Jersey Girl '04
The Ladykillers '04
The Road to Galveston '96
Raising Genius '04
Surviving Christmas '04
Finding Nemo '03 (V)
The Country Bears '02
Ice Age '02 (V)
O Brother Where Art Thou? '00
Bicentennial Man '99
From the Earth to the Moon '98
Krippendorf's Tribe '98
Office Space '99
Night of the Scarecrow '95
Bye Bye, Love '94
Dave '93
Extreme Justice '93
Bed & Breakfast '92
Buffy the Vampire Slayer '92
Till Murder Do Us Part '92
Guilty by Suspicion '91
RoboCop 3 '91
Stephen King's Golden Years '91
V.I. Warshawski '91
Ghost '90
Black Rain '89
Crocodile Dundee 2 '88
Monkey Shines '88

Henry Roquemore (1886-1943)
Gunsmoke Trail '38
Inside Information '34
Apache Kid's Escape '30

Noel Roquevert (1892-1973)
Une Parisienne '58
Nana '55
Fanfan la Tulipe '51
Antoine et Antoinette '47
Le Corbeau '43

Hayden Rorke (1910-87)
The Night Walker '64
Spencer's Mountain '63
Above and Beyond '53
Project Moon Base '53
South Sea Woman '53
Double Crossbones '51
Francis Goes to the Races '51

Tom Rosales (1948-)
John Carpenter's Vampires '97
Bail Out '90

Bert Rosario
A Million in Juan '94
Cold Justice '89

Tony Rosato (1954-)
The Good Fight '92
Rent-A-Kid '95
Switching Channels '88
Busted Up '86
City of Shadows '86
Hog Wild '80

Francoise Rosay (1891-1974)
The Pedestrian '73
Me and the Colonel '58
Seven Deadly Sins '53
The Red Inn '51
September Affair '50
Bizarre Bizarre '39
Carnival in Flanders '35

Alan Roscoe
Cheyenne Kid '33
Dynamite Ranch '32

Anika Noni Rose (1972-)
The Starter Wife '07
Dreamgirls '06
From Justin to Kelly '03

Gabrielle Rose (1954-)
Beneath '07
The Five Senses '99
The Sweet Hereafter '96
Timecop '94
Devlin '92
The Adjuster '91
Speaking Parts '89
Family Viewing '87

George Rose (1920-88)
Pound Puppies and the Legend of Big Paw '88 (V)
You Can't Take it with You '84
The Pirates of Penzance '83
The Hideaways '73
A New Leaf '71
The Pink Jungle '68
The Flesh and the Fiends '60
Jack the Ripper '60
The Devil's Disciple '59
A Night to Remember '58

Jamie Rose (1960-)
Chopper Chicks in Zombietown '91
To Die Standing '91
Playroom '90
Rebel Love '85
Heartbreakers '84
Tightrope '84
In Love with an Older Woman '82
Twirl '81

Laurie Rose (1948-)
Blood Voyage '77
The Hazing '77
Working Girls '75
The Abductors '72
Hot Box '72
Woman Hunt '72

Nectar Rose
Roman '06
The Hazing '04

Robin Pearson Rose
Lucy and Desi: Before the Laughter '91

Roger Rose
Comic Book: The Movie '04
Ski Patrol '89

Sherrie Rose (1966-)
Me & Will '99
Devil in the Flesh '98
The Nurse '97
Black Scorpion 2: Ground Zero '96
New Crime City: Los Angeles 2020 '94
Double Threat '92
Maximum Force '92
Martial Law 2: Undercover '91
Distant Thunder '88

Rose Marie (1925-)
Shriek If You Know What I Did Last Friday the 13th '00
Witchboard '87
Cheaper to Keep Her '80
Memory of Us '74
Dead Heat on a Merry-Go-Round '66

Roseanne (1952-)
Home on the Range '04 (V)
Blue in the Face '95
Even Cowgirls Get the Blues '94
The Woman Who Loved Elvis '93
Backfield in Motion '91
Freddy's Dead: The Final Nightmare '91
Look Who's Talking, Too '90 (V)
She-Devil '89

John Roselius
Con Air '97
Devil in a Blue Dress '95
JAG '95

Ed Roseman (1875-1957)
America '24
Sands of Sacrifice '21

Michael Rosenbaum (1972-)
Kickin' It Old Skool '07
Sweet November '01
Urban Legend '98

Alan Rosenberg (1950-)
Crash Course '00
The Temptations '98
Witch Hunt '94
In a Stranger's Hand '92
Impulse '90
After Midnight '89
Miracle Mile '89
White of the Eye '88
Happy Birthday, Gemini '80

Michael Rosenberg (1900-72)
The Two Sisters '38
Mirele Efros '38

Maxie "Slapsie" Rosenbloom (1903-76)
The Bellboy '60
I Married a Monster from Outer Space '58
Hollywood or Bust '56
Abbott and Costello Meet the Keystone Kops '54
Trouble Chasers '45
Ghost Crazy '44
Cooking Up Trouble '44
Here Comes Kelly '43
The Boogie Man Will Get You '42
To the Shores of Tripoli '42
Louisiana Purchase '41
Each Dawn I Die '39
Amazing Dr. Clitterhouse '38
Mr. Moto's Gamble '38
Kelly the Second '36

Romy Rosemont
Shopgirl '05
Sweet November '01

Sascha Rosemann
John John in the Sky '00

Charlotte Ross (1968-)
Montana Sky '07
Kidnapped in Paradise '98
Foreign Student '94
Savage Land '94

Chelcie Ross (1942-)
Racing Stripes '05 (V)
Bringing Down the House '03
Waking Up in Reno '02
The Majestic '01
Madison '01
The Gift '00
Charming Billy '98
A Simple Plan '98
Rudy '93
Amos and Andrew '33
Basic Instinct '92
Legacy of Lies '92
Above the Law '88

David W. Ross
Quinceanera '06

David Ross (1945-)
Love the Hard Way '01
Six Ways to Sunday '99
Vanity Fair '99
Mary Really '95
Splitting Heirs '93

Diana Ross (1944-)
Double Platinum '99
The Wiz '78
Mahogany '75
Lady Sings the Blues '72

Evan Ross (1988-)
ATL '06
Pride '07
Life Support '07

Gene Ross (1930-)
Class of 1984 '82
The Lucifer Complex '78
Keep My Grave Open '80
Encounter with the Unknown '75
Poor White Trash 2 '75
Don't Open the Door! '74
Don't Look in the Basement '73

Herbert Ross (1927-2001)
Play It Again, Sam '72
Goodbye, Mr. Chips '69

Howard (Red) Ross (1934-96)
New York Ripper '82
The New Gladiators '83
The Legend of the Wolf Woman '77

Hugh Ross
She's Gotta Have It '86
Joe's Bed-Stuy Barbershop: We Cut Heads '83

Betsy King Ross (1921-89)
Fighting with Kit Carson '33
The Phantom Empire '35

Beverly Ross
S.O.S. Titanic '79
Crazed '82

Romy Rosemont
Superman 3 '83

David W. Ross
Quinceanera '06

Marion Ross (1928-)
Superhero Movie '08
The Evening Star '96

Matt Ross (1970-)
Last Holiday '06
Good Night, and Good Luck '05
American Psycho '00
Pushing Tin '99
Face/Off '97
Ed's Next Move '96

Merrie Lynn Ross
Class of 1984 '82
Way He Was '76

Michael Ross (1911-93)
Attack of the 50 Foot Woman '58
D.O.A. '49

Milton Ross (1876-1941)
False Faces '18
Narrow Trail '17

Monty Ross
She's Gotta Have It '86
Joe's Bed-Stuy Barbershop: We Cut Heads '83

Ricco Ross (1960-)
Aliens '86
The Dirty Dozen: The Next Mission '85

Ron Ross
Battle Beyond the Stars '80
Joy Ride to Nowhere '78
The House of Dies Drear '88

Shavar Ross (1971-)
Friday the 13th, Part 5: A New Beginning '85
Night Vision '87

Shirley Ross (1913-75)
San Francisco '36
Waikiki Wedding '37
Blossoms on Broadway '37
Thanks for the Memory '38
The Big Broadcast of 1938 '38
Rhythm Romance '39

Katharine Ross (1942-)
Eye of the Dolphin '06
Donnie Darko '01
A Climate for Killing '91
Conagher '91
Red Headed Stranger '87
The Shadow Riders '82
Wrong Is Right '82
Murder in Texas '81
The Final Countdown '80
Rodeo Girl '80
The Legacy '79
Murder by Natural Causes '79
The Betsy '78
The Swarm '78
Voyage of the Damned '76
The Stepford Wives '75
Pigs '73
They Only Kill Their Masters '72
Fools '70
Butch Cassidy and the Sundance Kid '69
Tell Them Willie Boy Is Here '69
Hellfighters '68
Games '67
The Graduate '67
The Singing Nun '66
Shenandoah '65

Lee Ross (1971-)
Goal! The Dream Begins '06
Secret Society '00
Dreaming of Joseph Lees '99
Metroland '97
Secrets and Lies '95
Buddy's Song '91

Kimberly Ross (1955-2006)
Pumpkinhead '88
Nightmare at Noon '87

Stanley Ralph Ross (1936-2000)
The Game of Their Lives '05
Constantine '05

Ted Ross (1934-2002)
Arthur 2: On the Rocks '88
Stealing Home '88
Arthur '81
The Wiz '78

Tracee Ellis Ross (1972-)
Daddy's Little Girls '07
Life Support '07
Far Harbor '96

Yolanda Ross
United States of Leland '03
Antwone Fisher '02

Gavin Rossdale (1965-)
Constantine '05
The Game of Their Lives '05
Little Black Book '04

Isabella Rossellini (1952-)
The Accidental Husband '08
Infamous '06
Heights '04
King of the Corner '04
Monte Walsh '03
The Saddest Music in the World '03
Napoleon '03
Roger Dodger '02
Empire '02
The Sky Is Falling '00
Don Quixote '00
Left Luggage '98
The Imposters '98
Merlin '98
The Funeral '96
Big Night '95
Immortal Beloved '94
Fallen Angels 1 '93
Wyatt Earp '94
Fearless '93
The Innocent '93
Death Becomes Her '92
Lies of the Twins '91
Ivory Hunters '90
Wild at Heart '90
Cousins '89
Red Riding Hood '88
Zelly & Me '88
Siesta '87
Tough Guys Don't Dance '87
Blue Velvet '86
White Nights '85
A Matter of Time '76

Kathryn Rossetter
Shakedown '88

Carol Rossen (1937-)
The Stepford Wives '75
The Fury '78

Leo Rossi (1959-)
The Last Letter '04
The Business of Fancydancing '02
One Night at McCool's '01
Analyze This '99
Sticks '98
True Friends '98
In Cold Blood '96
Wedding Bell Blues '96
Felony '95
Mutant Species '95
Rave Review '95
Beyond Desire '94
Fast Getaway '94
Relentless 4 '94
"Long Island Lolita" Story '93
Raw Justice '93

Giacomo "Jack" Rossi-Stuart (1931-) — continued, and adjacent entries follow in index order:

Relentless 3 '93
We're Talkin' Serious Money '92
Where the Day Takes You '92
Fast Getaway '91
Relentless 2: Dead On '91
Maniac Cop 2 '90
Relentless '89
The Accused '88
The Hit List '88
River's Edge '87
Heart Like a Wheel '83

Eleanora Rossi-Drago (1925-2007)
Dorian Gray '70
Camille 2000 '69
Uncle Tom's Cabin '69

Giacomo "Jack" Rossi-Stuart (1931-)
Reactor '85
Zorro '74
The Night Evelyn Came Out of the Grave '71
Hornet's Nest '70
Macabre '69
Diary of a Rebel '68
Kill, Baby, Kill '66
Knives of the Avenger '65
Planet on the Prowl '65
The Last Man on Earth '64
Gunfight at Red Sands '63

Kim Rossi-Stuart (1969-)
Pinocchio '02
Beyond the Clouds '95

Paul Rossilli (1948-)
Bayou Romance '86

Norman Rossington (1928-99)
The Haunting Passion '83
Luther '74
2001: A Space Odyssey '68
King Rat '65

Angelo Rossitto (1908-91)
The Offspring '87
Mad Max: Beyond Thunderdome '85
Brain of Blood '71
Dracula vs. Frankenstein '71
Invasion of the Saucer Men '57
Daughter of Horror '55
Mesa of Lost Women '52
The Corpse Vanishes '42

Ronato Rossini
See Howard (Red) Ross

Leonard Rossiter (1926-84)
Water '85
Britannia Hospital '82
The Pink Panther Strikes Again '76

Rick Rossovich (1957-)
Miracle in Lane Two '00
Telling You '98
Legend of the Lost Tomb '97
Truth or Consequences, N.M. '97
Black Scorpion '95
Cover Me '95
Fatally Yours '95
New Crime City: Los Angeles 2020 '94
The Gambler Returns: The Luck of the Draw '93
Tropical Heat '93
Secret Ingredient '92
Navy SEALS '90
Paint It Black '89
The Spellbinder '88

Carlo Rota
Boondock Saints '99
32 Short Films about Glenn Gould '93

Andrea Roth (1967-)
Chasing Christmas '05
Sasquatch '02
The Stepdaughter '00
Hidden Agenda '99
Executive Power '98
Crosswords '96
Divided by Hate '96
The Club '94
The Good Fight '92
Seedpeople '92

Cecilia (Celia) Roth (1958-)
Lucia, Lucia '03
All About My Mother '99
Second Skin '99
Martin (Hache) '97
A Place in the World '92
The Stranger '87
Labyrinth of Passion '82

Eli Roth (1972-)
Death Proof '07
Cabin Fever '03

Gene Roth (1903-76)
Attack of the Giant Leeches '59
Earth vs. the Spider '58
She Demons '58
Pirates of the High Seas '50
Homesteaders of Paradise Valley '47

Joanna Roth (1965-)
Stalin '92
The Real Charlotte '91

Lillian Roth (1910-80)
Alice Adams '35
Ladies They Talk About '33
Animal Crackers '30
Madam Satan '30
The Love Parade '29

Louis Roth (1947-94)
Ninja Connection '90
Clash of the Ninja '86

Tim Roth (1961-)
The Incredible Hulk '08
Funny Games '08
Youth Without Youth '07
Even Money '06
Dark Water '05
Don't Come Knocking '05
The Beautiful Country '04
Silver City '04
Killing Emmett Young '02
Invincible '01
The Musketeer '01
Planet of the Apes '01
Lucky Numbers '00
Vatel '00
The Million Dollar Hotel '99
The Legend of 1900 '98
Deceiver '97
Everyone Says I Love You '96
Gridlock'd '96
Hoodlum '96
No Way Home '96
Four Rooms '95
Rob Roy '95
Captives '94
Little Odessa '94

John Rothman (1949-)
Brooklyn Lobster '05
Welcome to Mooseport '04
Say It Isn't So '01
The Siege '98
Hostile Waters '97
The Boost '88

Cynthia Rothrock (1957-)
Sci-Fighter '04
Night Vision '97
Sworn to Justice '97
Fast Getaway 2 '94
Guardian Angel '94
Undefeatable '94
Angel of Fury '93
Lady Dragon 2 '93
Rage and Honor 2: Hostile Takeover '93
Honor and Glory '92
Lady Dragon '92
Rage and Honor '92
24 Hours to Midnight '90
Fast Getaway '91
Martial Law 2: Undercover '91
Tiger Claws '91
Martial Law '90
China O'Brien 2 '89
China O'Brien '88
The Millionaire's Express '86

Paolo Rotondo
Stickmen '01
The Ugly '96

Yella Rottlaender
Alice in the Cities '74
The Scarlet Letter '73

Brigitte Rouan (1965-)
Love Songs '07
Time of the Wolf '03
After Sex '97
Olivier, Olivier '92
Overseas: Three Women with Man Trouble '90

Alida Rouffe (1874-1949)
Cesar '36
Fanny '32

Richard Roundtree (1942-)
Speed Racer '08
Brick '06
Boat Trip '03
Joe and Max '02
Corky Romano '01
Antitrust '00
Shaft '00
Having Our Say: The Delany Sisters' First 100 Years '99
Any Place But Home '97
George of the Jungle '97
Steel '97
Original Gangstas '96
Once Upon a Time ... When We Were Colored '95
Seven '95
Theodore Rex '95
Ballistic '94
Gypsy Angels '94
Amityville: A New Generation '93
Body of Influence '93
Bonanza: The Return '93
Mind Twister '93
Sins of the Night '93
Bloodfist 3: Forced to Fight '92
Christmas in Connecticut '92
Deadly Rivals '92
Getting Even '92
A Time to Die '91
Bad Jim '89
The Banker '89
Crack House '89
Miami Cops '89
Night Visitor '89
Angel 3: The Final Chapter '88
Maniac Cop '88
Party Line '88
Jocks '87
Opposing Force '87
Game for Vultures '86
The Last Contract '86
A.D. '85
The Baron and the Kid '84
City Heat '84
Killpoint '84
Big Score '83
Young Warriors '83
One Down, Two to Go! '82
Q (The Winged Serpent) '82
Day of the Assassin '81
An Eye for an Eye '81
Escape to Athena '79
Portrait of a Hitman '77
Man Friday '75
Earthquake '74
Shaft in Africa '73
Diamonds '72
Embassy '72
Firehouse '72
Shaft's Big Score '72
Shaft '71

Robert Rounseville (1914-74)
Carousel '56
The Tales of Hoffmann '51

Mickey Rourke (1955-)
Stormbreaker '06
Domino '05
Sin City '05
Man on Fire '04
Once Upon a Time in Mexico '03
Spun '02
Picture Claire '01
They Crawl '01
Animal Factory '00
Get Carter '00
The Pledge '00
Out in Fifty '99
Point Blank '98
Thursday '98
Buffalo 66 '97
Double Team '97
Exit in Red '97
John Grisham's The Rainmaker '97
Another 9 1/2 Weeks '96
Bullet '94
Fall Time '94
The Last Ride '94
Francesco '93
The Last Outlaw '93
White Sands '92
Harley Davidson and the Marlboro Man '91
Desperate Hours '90
Wild Orchid '90
Johnny Handsome '89
Homeboy '88
Angel Heart '87
Barfly '87
Prayer for the Dying '87
9 1/2 Weeks '86
Year of the Dragon '85
The Pope of Greenwich Village '84
Rumble Fish '83
Diner '82
Body Heat '81
Eureka! '81
Heaven's Gate '81
City in Fear '80
Fade to Black '80
Rape and Marriage: The Rideout Case '80
1941 '79

Graham Rouse (1934-)
The Odd Angry Shot '79
Weekend of Shadows '77
Ride a Wild Pony '75

Anne Roussel
The Music Teacher '88
Trade Secrets '86

Myriem Roussel (1962-)
Sacrilege '86
Hail Mary '85
First Name: Carmen '83

Nathalie Roussel
My Father's Glory '91
My Mother's Castle '91

Jean-Paul Roussillon (1931-)
The Girl from Paris '02
Same Old Song '97
Baxter '89

Alison Routledge
The Bridge to Nowhere '86
The Quiet Earth '85

Jean-Paul Rouve
La Vie en Rose '07
A Very Long Engagement '04

Catherine Rouvel (1939-)
Va Savoir '01
Sand and Blood '87
Black and White in Color '76
Les Assassins de L'Ordre '71
Borsalino '70
La Rupture '70
Picnic on the Grass '59

Jean-Louis Roux (1923-)
The Courage to Love '00
The Third Miracle '99

Jack Rovello (1994-)
Lonesome Jim '06
The Hours '02

Dominic Rowan (1971-)
David '97
Emma '97

Kelly Rowan (1967-)
Greenmail '01
Proximity '00
The Truth About Jane '00
Three to Tango '99
187 '97
Black Fox: Good Men and Bad '94
Candyman 2: Farewell to the Flesh '94
Adrift '93
The Gate '87

Brad Rowe (1970-)
The Insatiable '06
Though None Go With Me '06
Love for Rent '05
Shut Up and Kiss Me '05
Fish Without a Bicycle '03
Lucky Seven '03
The '70s '00
Body Shots '99
Christina's House '99
Billy's Hollywood Screen Kiss '98

Douglas Rowe
Stonebrook '98
Writer's Block '91
Appointment with Fear '85

Kimberly Rowe
Knocking on Death's Door '99
Rumble in the Streets '96

Leanne Rowe
Oliver Twist '05
Warrior Queen '03

Misty Rowe (1950-)
Goodnight, Sweet Marilyn '89
Meatballs 2 '84
Double Exposure '82
The Man with Bogart's Face '80
A Pleasure Doing Business '79
Goodbye, Norma Jean '75
Hitchhikers '72

Nevan Rowe
Nutcase '83
Sleeping Dogs '77

Nicholas (Nick) Rowe (1966-)
Shackleton '02
Longitude '00
Sharpe's Enemy '94
The Lawrenceville Stories '88
Young Sherlock Holmes '85

Victoria Rowell (1960-)
Home of the Brave '06
Motives '03
Anne Rice's The Feast of All Saints '01
Barb Wire '96
Dumb & Dumber '94
The Distinguished Gentleman '92

Henry Rowland (1914-84)
Beneath the Valley of the Ultra-Vixens '79
Supervixens '75
36 Hours '64

Oscar Rowland
Bats '99
Promised Land '88

Paige Rowland (1967-)
Doomsdayer '99
Riot '96

Rodney Rowland (1964-)
I Know Who Killed Me '07
Dancing at the Blue Iguana '00
The 6th Day '00
Marshal Law '96

Steve Rowland (1932-)
Naked Youth '59
Gun Glory '57

David Rowlands
Minnie and Moskowitz '71
Husbands '70

Gena Rowlands (1934-)
Broken English '07
Paris, je t'aime '06
The Skeleton Key '05
The Notebook '04
Taking Lives '04
The Incredible Mrs. Ritchie '03
Charms for the Easy Life '02
Hysterical Blindness '02
Wild Iris '01
The Weekend '00
Grace & Glorie '98
Hope Floats '98
The Mighty '98
Paulie '98
Playing by Heart '98
She's So Lovely '97
Unhook the Stars '96
The Neon Bible '95
Something to Talk About '95
Parallel Lives '94
Ted & Venus '93
Crazy in Love '92
Night on Earth '91
Once Around '93

Montana '90
Another Woman '88
Light of Day '87
An Early Frost '85
Love Streams '84
Rapunzel '82
The Tempest '82
Gloria '80
Strangers: The Story of a Mother and Daughter '79
Brink's Job '78
A Question of Love '78
Opening Night '77
Two Minute Warning '76
A Woman under the Influence '74
Faces '68
Tony Rome '67
A Child Is Waiting '63
Lonely Are the Brave '62
Minnie and Moskowitz '71
Thirty Seconds Over Tokyo '44

Polly Rowles (1914-2001)
Power '86
Springtime in the Rockies '37

Richard Roxburgh (1962-)
Van Helsing '04
Stealth '05
Murderous Intent '06
Mission: Impossible 2 '00
The Last September '99
Passion '99
In the Winter Dark '98
Doing Time for Patsy Cline '97
Oscar and Lucinda '97
The Wedding Party '97
Billy's Holiday '95
Children of the Revolution '95

The League of Extraordinary Gentlemen '03
The Hound of the Baskervilles '02
Blonde '01
The Road from Coorain '02
Moulin Rouge '01
Factory '05
'05 (V)
Alien from L.A. '87
Starship '87
Stalker '98

Allan Royal (1944-)
DC 9/11: Time of Crisis '74
The Courage to Love '00
The Boys of St. Vincent '93
Valley '99
Men of Steel '88

Maxim Roy (1972-)
Rudy: The Rudy Giuliani Story '03
A Woman Hunted '03
Federal Protection '02
Hidden Agenda '01
Cause of Death '00

Lise Roy
The Courage to Love '00
The Boys of St. Vincent '93

Deep Roy (1957-)
Charlie and the Chocolate Factory '05
Tim Burton's Corpse Bride '05 (V)

Andrew Rubin (1946-)
From the Earth to the Moon '98

Jennifer Rubin (1964-)
Amazons and Gladiators '01
Sunnyside '79

A Date with Judy '48
My Dream Is Yours '49
The Heiress '49
The Damned Don't Cry '50
The Big Hangover '53
Robot Monster '53

Selena Royle (1904-83)

Virginia Roye
Sizzle Beach, U.S.A. '74
Pace That Kills '28
The Road to Ruin '28

Roselyn Royce
Retrievers '82

The Road to Zanzibar '41
Panama Menace '41
My Favorite Blonde '42
Jungles '43
Manhunt in the African Jungles '43
White Pongo '45

Lionel Royce (1886-1946)

Benny Rubin (1899-)
Deal of a Lifetime '99
Torch Song '53
The Nose Hangs High '48
The Bashful Bachelor '42

Beyond Justice '01
Sanctimony '01
Wall Street '87
Halt a Lifetime '86
Against All Odds '84
Soup for One '82
Young Doctors in Love '82
Mr. Wise Guy '42
Sunny '41
Zis Boom Bah '41
Sunny Skies '30

Sergio Rubini (1959-)
The Passion of the Christ '04
The Count of Monte Cristo '99
The Talented Mr. Ripley '99
Nirvana '97
A Pure Formality '94
The Blonde '92
Intervista '87

Giulia Rubini (1935-)
Adios, Hombre '68
Stranger in Paso Bravo '68

John Rubinstein (1946-)

Michael Rudder
Another Stakeout '93

The Smallest Show on Earth '48
Summer Holiday '48
Cass Timberlane '47
Courage of Lassie '46
The Harvey Girls '46
Mrs. Parkington '44
Permanent Record '88
Getting Straight '70
A Nightmare on Elm Street 3: Dream Warriors '87
The Fighting Sullivans '42

William Royle (1887-1940)
Mr. Wong in Chinatown '39
Mutiny in the Big House '39
The Rains Came '39

Gregory Rozakis (1943-89)
Five Came '88
Abduction '75

Spela Rozin (1945-)
The Secret Invasion '64
Son of Hercules in the Land of Darkness '63

Christian Rub (1887-1956)
Pinocchio '40 (V)
100 Men and a Girl '37
No Other Woman '33

Alma Rubens (1897-1931)
She Goes to War '29
The Americano '17

Jan Rubes (1920-)
Believe '99
Rescuers: Stories of Courage—Two Couples '98
The White Raven '98
Flood: A River's Rampage '97
Music from Another Room '97
Serving in Silence: The Margarethe Cammermeyer Story '95
D2: The Mighty Ducks '94
The Birds 2: Land's End '94
Mesmer '94
By Way of the Stars '92
Devlin '92
Class Action '91
Deceived '91
The Amityville Curse '90
Descending Angel '90
Blind Fear '89
Courage Mountain '89
The Kiss '88
Blood Relations '87
Dead of Winter '87
Charlie Grant's War '80

She's Dressed to Kill '79
The Car '77
Defiant '81
Deranged '01
All Over the Guy '01

A Woman, Her Men and Her Futon '92
Delusion '91
Victim of Beauty '91
Bad Dreams '88
Blueberry Hill '88

Daphne Rubin-Vega (1969-)
Flawless '99
Wild Things '99
The Wild Card '03
Virgin '03

Saul Rubinek (1949-)
Jesse Stone: Sea Change '07
Jesse Stone: Night Passage '06
And Starring Pancho Villa as Himself '03
White Coats '04
Coast to Coast '04
Call Me: The Rise and Fall of Heidi Fleiss '04
Hollywood North '03
The Singing Detective '03
Triggermen '02
The Doorbell Rang: A Nero Wolfe Mystery '01
Rush Hour 2 '01
The Contender '00
Family Man '00
The Golden Spiders: A Nero Wolfe Mystery '00
Lakeboat '00
Dick '99
36 Hours to Die '99
Bad Manners '98
Past Perfect '98
Blackjack '97
Color of Justice '97
Pale Saints '97
The Android Affair '95
Getting Even with Dad '94
I Love Trouble '94
And the Band Played On '93
The Quarrel '93
True Romance '93
Reno 9/11 Miami '07
The Ten '07
Walk Hard: The Dewey Cox Story '07
Diggers '06
I Could Never 'Be Your Woman '06
Night at the Museum '06
The Baxter '05
The 40 Year Old Virgin '05
Anchorman: The Legend of Ron Burgundy '04
P.S. '04
Two Days '03
The Shape of Things '03
The Great Gatsby '01
Wet Hot American Summer '01
The Cider House Rules '99
The Object of My Affection '98
200 Cigarettes '98
The Locusts '97
Overnight Delivery '96
William Shakespeare's Romeo and Juliet '96
Clueless '95
Halloween 6: The Curse of Michael Myers '95
Runaway Daughters '94
Beulah Land '80
Last Song '80
Johnny We Hardly Knew Ye '77
Shadow on the Sun '88
Someone to Watch Over Me '87
Happily Ever After '82
Killjoy '81

Zelda Rubinstein (1936-)
Little Witches '96
Acting on Impulse '93
Teen Witch '89
Anguish '88
Poltergeist 3 '88
Poltergeist 2: The Other Side '86
Sixteen Candles '84
Poltergeist '82
Under the Rainbow '81

Richard Ruccolo (1972-)

Alan Ruck (1960-)
Luck of the Draw '00
Cheaper by the Dozen '03
Everything Put Together '00
From the Earth to the Moon '98
Twister '96
Speed '94
Star Trek: Generations '94
Young Guns 2 '90
Three Fugitives '89
Three for the Road '87
Ferris Bueller's Day Off '86
Hard Knox '83

Lamman Rucker
Tyler Perry's Meet the Browns '08
Tyler Perry's Why Did I Get Married? '07

Paul Rudd (1969-)
Forgetting Sarah Marshall '08
Over Her Dead Body '08
The Ex '07
Knocked Up '07

Lawrence of Arabia '62
Houdini '53

The Fear Inside '92

War '07

Martin Luther '53
The Fallen Idol '49
Ride with the Devil '99
You Can Count On Me '99
Safe Men '98
Mirror, Mirror 3: The Voyeur '96

Peter's Friends '92
Decoy '45
A Walk in the Sun '46
Rhapsody in Blue '45
The Seventh Cross '44
Abe Lincoln in Illinois '40
The Inheritors '98
Shrek the Third '07 (V)
Idiocracy '06
A Prairie Home Companion '06
50 First Dates '04
Duplex '03
Chuck & Buck '00
A Slipping Down Life '99
Gypsy 83 '01
The Ring '02
Director '06

Sara Rue (1979-)
Danny Roane: First Time Director '06
The Ring '02
Gypsy 83 '01
Duplex '03
Chuck & Buck '00
A Slipping Down Life '99

Gia '96
Out of the Cold '99
The Minus Man '99
What's Cooking? '00
More Dogs Than Bones '00
The Lost Child '00
Free Ride '86
Zapped Again '89
Widows '02

Reed Rudy

Joshua Rudoy
Flatliners '90
Harry and the Hendersons '87

Belen Rueda
The Orphanage '07
The Sea Inside '04

Mercedes Ruehl (1948-)
Trial '95
Last Action Hero '93
Lost in Yonkers '93
Another You '91
The Fisher King '91
Crazy People '90
Slaves of New York '89
Big '88
Married to the Mob '88
Leader of the Band '87
Radio Days '87
84 Charing Cross Road '86
The Warriors '79
Heartburn '86

Maya Rudolph (1972-)
Shrek the Third '07 (V)
Idiocracy '06
A Prairie Home Companion '06
50 First Dates '04
The Inheritors '98
The Princess and the Warrior '00
Les Miserables '95
Erendira '83

Lars Rudolph (1966-)
The Princess and the Warrior '00
The Inheritors '98

Rita Rudner (1955-)
A Weekend in the Country '96

Herbert Rudley (1911-2006)
Beloved Infidel '59
The Jayhawkers '59
The Young Lions '58
The Black Sheep '56
Artists and Models '55
The Scar '48

Rufus (1942-)
Amelie '01
Train of Life '98
Metroland '97

Follow Me, Boys! '66
The Ugly Dachshund '66
Papa's Delicate Condition '63
Son of Flubber '63
All in a Night's Work '61
The Parent Trap '61
Look for the Silver Lining '49

The Lovable Cheat '49
Ramrod '47
The Perfect Marriage '46
A Stolen Life '46
The Invisible Woman '40
Balalaika '39
Breaking the Ice '38
Bringing Up Baby '38
Service De Luxe '38
Ruggles of Red Gap '35
Goodbye Love '34
Six of a Kind '34
The Last Gasp '34
Melody Cruise '32
One Hour with You '32
Trouble in Paradise '32
The Smiling Lieutenant '31

Heinz Ruhmann (1902-94)

Barbara Ruick (1932-74)
Carousel '56
L.A. Bad '85
Missing '82
The Word '78
3 Women '77
Gunshoe '72
Doctors' Wives '70
The Swimmer '68
The Ambushers '67
Alvarez Kelly '66
The Chase '66
The Last Castle '01
Committed '99

Janice Rule (1931-2003)
American Flyers '85

Anthony Michael Ruivivar (1970-)
Swimming '00
Speed of Life '99
Starship Troopers '97
Race the Sun '96
White Fang 2: The Myth of the White Wolf '94

Mark Ruffalo (1967-)
Zodiac '07
Reservation Road '07
All the King's Men '06
Apartment 12 '06
Just Like Heaven '05
Rumor Has It... '05
Collateral '04
Eternal Sunshine of the Spotless Mind '04
13 Going on 30 '04
We Don't Live Here Anymore '04
In the Cut '03
My Life Without Me '03
View from the Top '03
Windtalkers '02
XX/XY '02
The Last Castle '01
Committed '99

Vyto Ruginis (1956-)
Faraway, So Close! '93
Ship of Fools '65
The Captain from Koepenick '56

Gene Ruffini
Ghost Dog: The Way of the Samurai '99

Leonora Ruffo (1935-2007)
Hercules in the Haunted World '64
Goliath and the Dragon '61

Charlie Ruggles (1886-1970)
Follow Me, Boys! '66
The Ugly Dachshund '66
Papa's Delicate Condition '63

Little Odessa '94
Little Women '49
Annelie '01

Jonah Who Will Be 25 in the Year 2000 '76

Bell, Book and Candle '58

Battle Shock '56

Sig Rumann (1884-1967)
36 Hours '64
The Errand Boy '61
Wings of Eagles '57
Carolina Cannonball '55
Houdini '53
Ma and Pa Kettle on Vacation '53
Stalag 17 '53
The World in His Arms '52
Border Incident '49
Emperor Waltz '48
The Dolly Sisters '46
A Night in Casablanca '46
House of Frankenstein '44
It Happened Tomorrow '44
Sweet Rosie O'Grady '43
To Be or Not to Be '42
Love Crazy '41
That Uncertain Feeling '41
The Wagons Roll at Night '41
Bitter Sweet '40
Comrade X '40
Only Angels Have Wings '39
Never Say Die '39
Ninotchka '39
The Great Waltz '38
A Day at the Races '37
Nothing Sacred '37
On the Avenue '37
Thank you, Mr. Moto '37
Thin Ice '37
Think Fast, Mr. Moto '37
The Bold Caballero '36
The Princess Comes Across '36
A Night at the Opera '35
Marie Galante '34
The World Moves On '34

Run DMC
The Show '95
Tougher Than Leather '88

Jenny Runacre (1943-)
Hussy '80
The Passenger '75
The Final Programme '73
The Creeping Flesh '72
The Canterbury Tales '71
Husbands '70

Joseph Runningfox
Lakota Woman: Siege at Wounded Knee '94
Geronimo '93

Tygh Runyan (1976-)
Emile '03
Twist '03
Cruel and Unusual '01
Antitrust '00

Jennifer Runyon (1960-)
Carnosaur '93
A Man Called Sarge '90
18 Again! '88
In the Crowd '88
A Very Brady Christmas '88
Blue De Ville '86
The Falcon and the Snowman '85
Up the Creek '84
To All a Goodnight '80 (V)

Ying Ruocheng (1929-2003)
Little Buddha '93
The Last Emperor '87

RuPaul
See RuPaul Charles

Debra Jo Rupp (1951-)
Kickin' It Old Skool '07
Disney's Teacher's Pet '04 (V)

Al Ruscio (1924-)
Boss of Bosses '99
The Garbage-Picking, Field Goal-Kicking Philadelphia Phenomenon '98
The Cage '89
Romero '89
Deadly Force '83
The Naked Flame '68
Al Capone '59

Elizabeth Ruscio (1955-)
The Clearing '04
Letters from a Killer '98
Death Benefit '96
Glory Daze '96
The Positively True Adventures of the Alleged Texas Cheerleader-Murdering Mom '93
Hider in the House '90

Barbara Rush (1927-)
Widow's Kiss '94
Web of Deceit '90
The Seekers '79
Superdad '73
Moon of the Wolf '72
Hombre '67
Robin and the 7 Hoods '64
Come Blow Your Horn '63
The Bramble Bush '60
Strangers When We Meet '60
The Young Philadelphians '59
Harry Black and the Tiger '58
The Young Lions '58
The Black Shield of Falworth '54
Magnificent Obsession '54
It Came from Outer Space '53
First Legion '51
When Worlds Collide '51

Deborah Rush (1954-)
Half Nelson '06
Strangers with Candy '06
American Wedding '03
The Good Girl '02
Three to Tango '99
In and Out '97
Reckless '95
Unnatural Pursuits '91
Family Business '89
Parents '89
The Purple Rose of Cairo '85

Geoffrey Rush (1951-)
Elizabeth: The Golden Age '07
Pirates of the Caribbean: At World's End '07
Candy '06
Munich '05
Finding Nemo '03 (V)
Intolerable Cruelty '03
Ned Kelly '03
Pirates of the Caribbean: The Curse of the Black Pearl '03
Swimming Upstream '03
The Banger Sisters '02
Frida '02
Lantana '01
Quills '00
The Tailor of Panama '00
House on Haunted Hill '99
Mystery Men '99
Elizabeth '98
Shakespeare in Love '98
Les Miserables '97
A Little Bit of Soul '97
Oscar and Lucinda '97 (N)
Twisted '96
Children of the Revolution '95
Shine '95

Sarah Rush (1955-)
For the Love of Angela '82
The Seekers '79

Claire Rushbrook (1970-)
Close Your Eyes '02
Shiner '00
Plunkett & Macleane '98
Spice World: The Movie '97
Under the Skin '97
Secrets and Lies '95

Jared Rushton (1974-)
Pet Sematary 2 '92
A Cry in the Wild '90
Honey, I Shrunk the Kids '89
Big '88
The Lady in White '88

Joseph Ruskin (1925-)
Smokin' Aces '07
King Cobra '98
The Criminal Mind '93
Cyber-Tracker '93
Firepower '93
Saturday the 14th Strikes Back '88
Prizzi's Honor '85
Captain America '79
The Gypsy Warriors '78
Superdad '73

Morgan Rusler
Solaris '02
The Tomorrow Man '01

Robert Rusler (1965-)
The Assassination Game '92
Final Embrace '92
Sometimes They Come Back '91
The Game of Love '90
Shag: The Movie '89
Thrashin' '86
Vamp '86
A Nightmare on Elm Street 2: Freddy's Revenge '85

Tim Russ (1956-)
Live Free or Die Hard '07
Bitter Vengeance '94
Final Combination '93
Night Eyes 2 '91

William Russ (1950-92)
American History X '98
When Danger Follows You Home '97
Aspen Extreme '93
Traces of Red '92
Crazy from the Heart '91
Pastime '91
Disorganized Crime '89
The Unholy '88
Dead of Winter '87
The Long, Hot Summer '86
Wanted Dead or Alive '86
Beer '85

Andy Russell (1919-92)
Copacabana '47
The Stork Club '45

Betsy Russell (1964-)
Saw 4 '07
Saw III '06
The Break '95
Amore! '93
Delta Heat '92
The Prize Pulitzer '89
Trapper County War '89
Cheerleader Camp '88
Avenging Angel '85
Out of Control '85
Tomboy '85
Private School '83

Bing (Neil) Russell (1926-2003)
Elvis: The Movie '79
Satan's School for Girls '73
Billy the Kid Versus Dracula '66
Stakeout '62
The Horse Soldiers '59
Good Day for a Hanging '58

Bryan Russell (1952-)
The Adventures of Bullwhip Griffin '66
Emil and the Detectives '64

Clive Russell (1945-)
Ladies in Lavender '04
The Mayor of Casterbridge '03

Great Expectations '99
The 13th Warrior '99
Oscar and Lucinda '97
Neil Gaiman's NeverWhere '96
Cracker: Brotherly Love '95
Cracker: True Romance '95
Margaret's Museum '95

Elizabeth Russell (1916-2002)
Bedlam '45
Curse of the Cat People '44
Cat People '42
The Corpse Vanishes '42
Meet the Mob '42

Gail Russell (1925-61)
Great Dan Patch '49
Wake of the Red Witch '49
The Smallest Show on Earth '48
Angel and the Badman '47
The Uninvited '44

Harold Russell (1914-2002)
Dogtown '97
The Best Years of Our Lives '46

Jane Russell (1921-)
Darker than Amber '70
Born Losers '67
Johnny Reno '66
The Tall Men '55
Underwater! '55
The French Line '54
Gentlemen Prefer Blondes '53
The Road to Bali '53
The Las Vegas Story '52
Macao '52
Montana Belle '52
Son of Paleface '52
Double Dynamite '51
His Kind of Woman '51
The Paleface '48
The Outlaw '43

John Russell (1921-91)
Under the Gun '88
Pale Rider '85
The Changeling '80
The Outlaw Josey Wales '76
Noon Sunday '75
Runaways '75
Smoke in the Wind '75
Blood Legacy '73
Buckskin '68
Hostile Guns '67
Apache Uprising '66
Rio Bravo '59
Jubilee Trail '54
The Sun Shines Bright '53
Hoodlum Empire '52
Man in the Saddle '51
Oklahoma Annie '51
Forever Amber '47
The Blue Bird '40

Karen Russell
Dead Certain '92
Lethal Games '90
Shock 'Em Dead '90
Wilding '90
Easy Wheels '89
Vice Academy '89

Ken Russell (1927-)
Brothers of the Head '06
Tales of Erotica '96
The Russia House '90

Keri Russell (1976-)
August Rush '07
Waitress '07
Mission: Impossible 3 '06
The Upside of Anger '05
We Were Soldiers '02
Mad About Mambo '00
The Curve '97
Eight Days a Week '97
Honey, I Blew Up the Kid '92

Kimberly Russell (1964-)
Prison of Secrets '97
The O.J. Simpson Story '94
Sugar Hill '94
Hangin' with the Homeboys '91

Kirsten Russell
Milk and Honey '03
Virgil Bliss '01

Kurt Russell (1951-)
Death Proof '07
Poseidon '06
Dreamer: Inspired by a True Story '05
Jiminy Glick in LaLa Wood '05
Sky High '05
Miracle '04
Dark Blue '03
Interstate 60 '02
3000 Miles to Graceland '01
Vanilla Sky '01
Soldier '98
Breakdown '96
Escape from L.A. '96
Executive Decision '96
Stargate '94
Tombstone '93
Captain Ron '92
Unlawful Entry '92
Backdraft '91
Tango and Cash '89
Winter People '89
Tequila Sunrise '88
Overboard '87
The Best of Times '86
Big Trouble in Little China '86
Mean Season '85
Swing Shift '84
Silkwood '83
Amber Waves '82
The Thing '82
Escape from New York '81
The Fox and the Hound '81 (V)
Used Cars '80
Elvis: The Movie '79
The Christmas Coal Mine Miracle '77
The Captive: The Longest Drive 2 '76
The Longest Drive '76
Search for the Gods '75
Sniper '75
The Strongest Man in the World '75
Charley and the Angel '73
Superdad '73
Now You See Him, Now You Don't '72
The Barefoot Executive '71
The Computer Wore Tennis Shoes '69
The Horse in the Gray Flannel Suit '68
The One and Only, Genuine, Original Family Band '68
Follow Me, Boys! '66
Mosby's Marauders '66
Guns of Diablo '64
It Happened at the World's Fair '63

Lucy Russell (1972-)
Tristan & Isolde '06
The Lady and the Duke '01
Following '99

Monte Russell
Lily in Winter '94
Laurel Avenue '93

Nipsey Russell (1918-2005)
Car 54, Where Are You? '94
Posse '93
The Wiz '78

Reb Russell (1905-78)
Outlaw Rule '36
Border Vengeance '35
The Man from Hell '34

Robert Russell
Dune '00
Bedazzled '68
The Conqueror Worm '68

Rosalind Russell (1908-76)
Where Angels Go, Trouble Follows '68
Oh Dad, Poor Dad (Momma's Hung You in the Closet & I'm Feeling So Sad) '67
The Trouble with Angels '66
Gypsy '62
Auntie Mame '58
A Majority of One '56
Picnic '55
Never Wave at a WAC '52
A Woman of Distinction '50
Tell It to the Judge '49
Velvet Touch '48
Sister Kenny '46
They Met in Bombay '41
His Girl Friday '40
The Women '39
The Citadel '38
Night Must Fall '37
Craig's Wife '36
China Seas '35
Forsaking All Others '35
Reckless '35
Evelyn Prentice '34

T.E. Russell
30 Years to Life '01
Bellyfruit '99

Theresa Russell (1957-)
Spider-Man 3 '07
Empire Falls '05
The Box '03
Love Comes Softly '03
Now & Forever '02
The Believer '01
Earth vs. the Spider '01
The House Next Door '01
Luckytown '00
Running Woman '98
Wild Things '98
Grave Indiscretions '96
The Proposition '96
Public Enemies '96
Trade Off '95
A Young Connecticut Yankee in King Arthur's Court '95
Being Human '94
The Spy Within '94
Thicker Than Water '93
The Razor's Edge '84
Eureka! '81
Blind Ambition '79
Straight Time '78
The Last Tycoon '76

Tony Russell (1925-)
The Hard Ride '71
Wild, Wild Planet '65

Chelsea Russo (1990-)
An Unexpected Life '97
An Unexpected Family '96

Gianni Russo (1941-)
Harvard Man '01
The House Next Door '01
Deep Core '00
Lepke '75
The Godfather, Part 2 '74

James Russo (1953-)
All In '06
Broken Trail '06
The Hit '06
Come as You Are '05
The Box '03
Open Range '03
The House Next Door '01
Deep Core '00
Jimmy Zip '00
Detour '99
The Ninth Gate '99
Paper Bullets '99
Sonic Impact '99
Voodoo Dawn '98
Bitter Sweet '98
First Degree '98
My Husband's Secret Life '98

Laws of Deception '97
Love to Kill '97
The Postman '97
The Real Thing '97
Under Oath '97
American Strays '96
Donnie Brasco '96
No Way Home '96
Condition Red '95
Panther '95
The Set Up '95
Bad Girls '94
The Secretary '94
Dangerous Game '93
Dario Argento's Trauma '93
Cold Heaven '92
DaVinci's War '92

John A. Russo (1939-)
The Groomsmen '06
The Majorettes '87
Night of the Living Dead '68
Demonic Toys '96

Michael Russo
Pure Danger '96
Nitti: The Enforcer '88

Rene Russo (1954-)
Two for the Money '05
Yours, Mine & Ours '05
Outbreak '94
Get Shorty '95
Tin Cup '96
Ransom '96
Buddy '97
Lethal Weapon 4 '98
'99
Major League '89
Mr. Destiny '90
One Good Cop '91
Lethal Weapon 3 '92
Freejack '92
Big Trouble '02
Showtime '02
The Adventures of Rocky &
Bullwinkle '00
The Thomas Crown Affair
'99
Vortex '82
High '82
Once Upon a Time in
America '84
Beverly Hills Cop '84
Extremities '86

Richard Rust (1938-)
Double Revenge '89
The Great Gundown '75
The Student Nurses '70
The Naked Angels '69
Comanche Station '60
Legend of Tom Dooley '59
Silver Bullet '85

Babe Ruth (1895-1948)
The Pride of the Yankees
'42
Headin' Home '20

Mary Ruth
Gentlemen from Dixie '41
Riot Squad '41

Ann Rutherford (1917-)
They Only Kill Their
Masters '72
Operation Haylift '50
Adventures of Don Juan '49
The Secret Life of Walter
Mitty '47
Whistling in Brooklyn '43
Andy Hardy's Double Life
'42
Orchestra Wives '42
Whistling in Dixie '42

Andy Hardy's Private
Secretary '41
Life Begins for Andy Hardy
'41
Whistling in the Dark '41
Andy Hardy Meets
Debutante '40
Pride and Prejudice '40
Andy Hardy Gets Spring
Fever '39
Gone with the Wind '39
A Christmas Carol '38
Love Finds Andy Hardy '38
Of Human Hearts '38
Public Cowboy No. 1 '37
Doughnuts & Society '36
Fighting Marines '36
The Lawless Nineties '36
Melody Trail '35
Ghost City '32

Margaret Rutherford (1892-1972)
Chimes at Midnight '67
A Countess from Hong
Kong '67
The Alphabet Murders '65
Murder Most Foul '65
Murder Ahoy '64
Murder at the Gallop '63
The V.I.P.'s '63
The Mouse on the Moon
'62
Murder She Said '62
The Smallest Show on
Earth '57
Innocents in Paris '53
The Runaway Bus '54
Curtain Up '53
Trouble in Store '53
The Importance of Being
Earnest '52
The Happiest Days of Your
Life '50
Passport to Pimlico '49
Blithe Spirit '45
The Demi-Paradise '43

Susan Ruttan (1950-)
The Legend of Butch &
Sundance '04
Love Kills '98
Funny About Love '90
A Perfect Little Murder '90
Sweet 15 '90
Chances Are '89
Fire and Rain '89
Bad Dreams '88
Eye of the Demon '87
L.A. Law '86
Bad Manners '84

Barbara Rutting (1927-)
The Squeaker '65
The Phantom of Soho '64
River of Evil '64
Town without Pity '61
A Time to Love & a Time to
Die '58

Sif Ruud (1916-)
The Last Bridge '54
Like It Never Was Before
'95

Wolf Ruvinskis (1921-99)
Face to Face '76
Neutron vs. the Death
Robots '62
Neutron vs. the Maniac '62
Neutron and the Black
Mask '61
Dr. Caronte '61

Basil Ruysdael (1888-1960)
Davy Crockett, King of the
Wild Frontier '55
Carrie '52

Leon Russom (1941-)
The Big Lebowski '98
A Private Matter '92
A Thousand Heroes '92
Long Road Home '91
Eye of the Demon '87

Chaos Factor '00
I Love Trouble '94

Kelly Rutherford (1968-)
Gossip Girl '06
Angels Don't Sleep Here
'00

Camilla Rutherford (1976-)
Land of the Blind '06
Gosford Park '01

Amanda Ryan
Inspector Lynley Mysteries:
A Great Deliverance '01

Anne Ryan
Three o'Clock High '87
All the Lovin' Kinfolk '70

Blanchard Ryan (1972-)
Pistol Whipped '08
Beerfest '06
Open Water '03

Eddie Ryan (1923-)
Breakfast in Hollywood '46
The Fighting Sullivans '42

Edmon Ryan (1905-84)
Total Total Total '70
Two for the Seesaw '62
Mystery Street '50
Side Street '50

Eileen Ryan (1928-)
The Assassination of
Richard Nixon '05
Eight Legged Freaks '02
Anywhere But Here '99
The Crossing Guard '94
Benny & Joon '93
Winter People '89
At Close Range '86
Johnny Belinda '82
Story of a Cowboy Angel
'81

Fran Ryan (1926-2000)
Suture '93
Archie: Return to Riverdale
'90
Chances Are '89
Gunsmoke: Return to
Dodge '87
Quiet Cool '86
Pale Rider '85
Eyes of Fire '84
Private School '83
D.O.A. '88
The Presidio '88
Promised Land '88
Innerspace '87
Woman '94
Flesh and Bone '93
Men in War '57

Ger Ryan
Forgive and Forget '99
Moll Flanders '96
Rage to Kill '88
Space Mutiny '88
Go for the Gold '84
Kill and Kill Again '81
Kill or Be Killed '80

Jeri Ryan (1968-)
Down With Love '03
Dracula 2000 '00
The Last Man '00
Men Cry Bullets '00
New York '99
Grosse Pointe Blank '97
Liar Liar '97
The Devil's Own '96

Michelle Ryan
Jekyll '07

Mitchell Ryan (1928-)
Cashback '06
Mansfield Park '07
Aftershock: Earthquake in
New York '99

People Will Talk '51
Broken Arrow '50
High Lonesome '50
The Cocoanuts '29

David Ryall (1935-)
Around the World in 80
Days '04

Amy Ryan (1970-)
Before the Devil Knows
You're Dead '07
Dan in Real Life '07
Gone Baby Gone '07
Looking for Comedy in the
Muslim World '06
Capote '05
Keane '04

Marisa Ryan (1974-)
Brooklyn Lobster '05
Riding in Cars with Boys
'01
Wet Hot American Summer
'01
Cold Hearts '99

Max Ryan (1967-)
Thr3e '07
The League of
Extraordinary Gentlemen
'03

Meg Ryan (1961-)
In the Land of Women '06
Against the Ropes '04
In the Cut '03
Kate & Leopold '01
Proof of Life '00
Hanging Up '99
City of Angels '98
You've Got Mail '98
Hurlyburly '98
Addicted to Love '96
Courage Under Fire '96
French Kiss '95
I.Q. '94
Restoration '94
When a Man Loves a
Woman '94
Flesh and Bone '93
Sleepless in Seattle '93
Prelude to a Kiss '92
The Doors '91
When Harry Met Sally... '89
Joe Versus the Volcano '90
D.O.A. '88
The Presidio '88
Promised Land '88
Innerspace '87
Armed and Dangerous '86
Top Gun '86
Amityville 3: The Demon
'83
Rich and Famous '81

White Sands '92
Delta Force 3: The Killing
Game '91
Delta Force 2: Operation
Stranglehold '90
Eternity '90
Best of the Best '89
Paramedics '88
Death Before Dying '90
The Right Stuff '83
Breathless '83
Runaway Train '85
Metroland '97
David Copperfield '99
Britannic '00
City of Shadows '86
Avenging Force '86
Three o'Cock High '87
Death Scream '75
Cops and Robbers '73
Shamus '73
My Old Man's Place '71
Monte Walsh '70
Peter Lundy and the
Medicine Hat Stallion '77
Midway '76
Lethal Weapon '87
Fatal Vision '84
The Choice '81
Death of a Centerfold '81
Of Mice and Men '81
Angel City '80
Sergeant Matlovich vs. the
U.S. Air Force '78
The Christmas Coal Mine
Miracle '77

Kathleen Ryan (1922-85)
Try and Get Me '50
Captain Boycott '47
Odd Man Out '47

Peggy Ryan (1924-2004)
Here Come the Co-Eds '45
Miss Annie Rooney '42

Lisa Dean Ryan (1972-)
The Stepdaughter '00
Twisted Love '95
Hostile Intentions '94

Remi Ryan (1984-)
Ava's Magical Adventure
'94

R.L. Ryan (1946-91)
RoboCop 3 '91
Street Trash '87
Class of Nuke 'Em High '86
Eat and Run '86

Robert Ryan (1909-73)
Executive Action '73
The Iceman Cometh '73
The Man Without a Country
'73
And Hope to Die '72
Lawman '71
The Love Machine '71
The Wild Bunch '69
Anzio '68
The Dirty Dozen '67
Hour of the Gun '67
A Minute to Pray, a Second
to Die '67
The Professionals '66
Battle of the Bulge '65
Billy Budd '62
The Longest Day '62
The King of Kings '61
Ice Palace '60
The Day of the Outlaw '59
Odds Against Tomorrow
'59
God's Little Acre '58
Lonelyhearts '58
Men in War '57
Back from Eternity '56
Escape to Burma '55
House of Bamboo '55
The Tall Men '55
Bad Day at Black Rock '54
The Naked Spur '53
Beware, My Lovely '52
Clash by Night '52
Horizons West '52
Flying Leathernecks '51
On Dangerous Ground '51
The Racket '51
Best of the Badmen '51
Born to Be Bad '50
Caught '49
The Set-Up '49
Act of Violence '48
Berlin Express '48
The Boy with the Green
Hair '48
Return of the Bad Men '48
Crossfire '47
Trail Street '47
Behind the Rising Sun '43
Bombardier '43
The Iron Major '43
Marine Raiders '44
The Sky's the Limit '43

Hot Shots! Part Deux '93
The Opposite Sex and How
to Live With Them '93
Aces: Iron Eagle 3 '92
Dirty Work '92
Blue Sky '91
Judgment '90
Double Exposure: The
Story of Margaret
Bourke-White '89
Winter People '89
Lethal Weapon '87
Railroaded '47
Heartaches '47
Ringside '49
Mask of the Dragon '51
Western Pacific Agent '51
The Cobra Strikes '48
Getting Gertie's Garter '45
Something for the Boys '44
Great Guns '41

Tim Ryan (1899-1956)
From Here to Eternity '53
Here Come the Marines '52
Detour '46
Ghost Catchers '44

Will Ryan (1939-)
An American Tail '86 (V)
The Land Before Time '88
(V)

Derek Rydall (1968-)
Night Visitor '89
Popcorn '89
Phantom of the Mall: Eric's
Revenge '89

Georg Rydeberg (1907-83)
Hour of the Wolf '68
Walpurgis Night '41
Dollar '38

Bobby Rydell (1942-)
That Lady from Peking... no

Christopher Rydell (1963-)
By the Sword '93
Dario Argento's Trauma '93
Flesh and Bone '93
For the Boys '91
In the Deep Woods '91
Side Out '90
Blood and Sand '89
How I Got into College '89
Gotcha! '85

Mark Rydell (1934-)
Hollywood Ending '02
James Dean '01
Havana '90
Punchline '88
The Long Goodbye '73

Alfred Ryder (1919-95)
Bogie: The Last Hero '80
Probe '72
True Grit '69
T-Men '47

Winona Ryder (1971-)
The Ten '07
The Darwin Awards '06
A Scanner Darkly '06
Mr. Deeds '02
Simone '02
Autumn in New York '00
Lost Souls '00
Girl, Interrupted '99
Celebrity '98
Alien: Resurrection '97
The Crucible '96
Looking for Richard '96
Boys '95
How to Make an American
Quilt '95
Little Women '94

Thomas Ryan
The Relic '96
Body Count '97

Thomas Jay Ryan (1962-)
Fay Grim '06
Eternal Sunshine of the
Spotless Mind '04
Henry Fool '98

Tim Ryan (1958-)
The Lightning Incident '91
The Runestone '91
China Beach '88

Sheila Ryan (1921-75)
On Top of Old Smoky '53
Fingerprints Don't Lie '51
Gold Raiders '51

Bobby Rydell (1942-)
Mr. Rock 'n' Roll: The Alan
Freed Story '99
Bye, Bye, Birdie '63
Bye Bye Birdie...

Tender Comrade '43

Robert Ryan (1909-73)

Cast Index | 1643

Reality Bites '94
The Age of Innocence '93
The House of the Spirits '93
Bram Stoker's Dracula '92
Night on Earth '91
Edward Scissorhands '90
Mermaids '90
Welcome Home, Roxy Carmichael '90
Great Balls of Fire '89
Heathers '89
1969 '89
Beetlejuice '88
Square Dance '87
Lucas '86

Joseph Rye
Alien vs. Predator '04
Born to Lose '99

Patrick Ryecart (1952-)
Coming Home '98
Parting Shots '98
Heart of Darkness '93
Twenty-One '91
Goldeneye: The Secret Life of Ian Fleming '89
The Bretts '88
True Colors '87
Jenny's War '85
Silas Marner '85

Georgina Rylance (1979-)
Hellraiser: Deader '05
Seven Seconds '05

Mark Rylance (1960-)
The Other Boleyn Girl '08
Intimacy '00
Angels and Insects '95
Institue Benjamenta or This Dream People Call Human Life '95
Prospero's Books '91

Rex Ryon (1953-)
Jack's Back '87

Chishu Ryu (1904-93)
Akira Kurosawa's Dreams '90
The Battle of the Japan Sea '70
An Autumn Afternoon '62
The Human Condition: A Soldier's Prayer '61
Good Morning '59
Equinox Flower '58
Tokyo Story '53
Early Summer '51
Late Spring '49
Record of a Tenement Gentleman '47

The RZA (1966-)
Derailed '05
Coffee and Cigarettes '03
Scary Movie 3 '03

Bruno S (1932-)
Stroszek '77
Every Man for Himself & God Against All '75

Daryl Sabara (1992-)
Havoc '05
Adolescent Behavior '07
Keeping Up with the Steins '06
The Polar Express '04 (V)
Spy Kids 3-D: Game Over '03
Spy Kids 2: The Island of Lost Dreams '02
Spy Kids '01

Antonio (Tony) Sabato (1943-)
High Voltage '98
Thundersquad '85
Crimebusters '85

Antonio Sabato, Jr. (1972-)
Testosterone '03
Mindstorm '01
Chaos Factor '00
Fatal Error '99
The Big Hit '98
High Voltage '98
Wolverine '96
Jailbreakers '94

This Time I'll Make You Rich '75
New Mafia Boss '72
Black Lemons '70
Twice a Judas '69
Beyond the Law '68

Bo Sabato
L.A. Crackdown 2 '88
Neon Maniacs '86

Ernie Sabella (1949-)
The Lion King 1 1/2 '04 (V)
The Lion King: Simba's Pride '98 (V)
The Lion King '94 (V)

Kyle Sabihy (1983-)
Analyze That '02
Analyze This '98

Marcel Sabourin (1935-)
Lilies '96

Sabu (1924-63)
A Tiger Walks '64
Mistress of the World '59
Jaguar '56
Jungle Hell '55
The Treasure of Bengal '53
Pardon My Trunk '52
Savage Drums '51
Black Narcissus '47
Cobra Woman '44
Arabian Nights '42
The Jungle Book '42
The Thief of Bagdad '40
Drums '38
Elephant Boy '37

Robert Sacchi (1941-)
Cold Heat '90
The Man with Bogart's Face '80

Orlando Sacha (1929-2001)
Alias, La Gringa '91
To Die Standing '91
Crime Zone '88

Adrienne Sachs
In the Cold of the Night '89
Two to Tango '88

Robin Sachs (1951-)
Megalodon '03
Northfork '03
Galaxy Quest '99
Cold War Killers '86
Deadly Recruits '86

Salli Sachse (1943-)
Devil's Angels '67
The Trip '67

Graham Sack (1981-)
Dunston Checks In '95
A Pig's Tale '94

Katee Sackhoff
The Last Sentinel '07
White Noise 2: The Light '07
Halloween: Resurrection '02

Martin Sacks
Do or Die '01
Slate, Wyn & Me '87

Michael Sacks (1948-)
Bunco '77
The Sugarland Express '74
Slaughterhouse Five '72

Jose Sacristan (1937-)
A Place in the World '92
El Diputado '78
An Autumn Afternoon '62

Keiji Sada (1926-64)
The Human Condition: No Greater Love '58

Nicholas Sadler
Idle Hands '99
Sawbones '95
Acting on Impulse '93

William Sadler (1950-)
August Rush '07
The Mist '07
A New Wave '07
Jimmy & Judy '06
Confess '05
Devour '05
Kinsey '04

The Battle of Shaker Heights '03
The Green Mile '99
Disturbing Behavior '98
Reach the Rock '98
RocketMan '97
Poltergeist: The Legacy '96
Solo '96
Roadracers '94
The Shawshank Redemption '94
Tales from the Crypt Presents Demon Knight '94
Freaked '93
Trespass '92
Bill & Ted's Bogus Journey '91
Rush '91
Die Hard 2: Die Harder '90
The Hot Spot '90
Tagget '90
Hard to Kill '89
Tales from the Crypt '89
Project X '87

Tom Sadoski (1976-)
Happy Hour '03
Loser '00

Isabelle Sadoyan (1928-)
The Eighth Day '95
Trois Couleurs: Bleu '93

Marianne Saegebrecht (1945-)
Left Luggage '98
Dust Devil '93
Martha and I '91
Rosalie Goes Shopping '89
The War of the Roses '89
Bagdad Cafe '88
Moon over Parador '88
Sugarbaby '85

Libuse Safrankova (1953-)
All My Loved Ones '00
Kolya '96

Elizabeth Sagal (1961-)
Skinheads: The Second Coming of Hate '88
Howard the Duck '86
Flashdance '83

Katey Sagal (1957-)
I'm Reed Fish '06
Smart House '00 (V)
Mr. Headmistress '98
The Good Mother '88

Jonathan Sagalle (1962-)
Deadly Outbreak '96
Schindler's List '93

Bill Sage (1962-)
Heavens Fall '06
The Maldonado Miracle '03

William Sage
Mysterious Skin '04
Sin '02
Desert Saints '01
Double Parked '00
Urbania '00
American Psycho '99
High Art '98
Rift '96
Boys '95
Flirt '95
Two Plus One '95
Simple Men '92

Melissa Sagemiller (1974-)
Mr. Woodcock '07
The Guardian '06
Sleeper Cell '05
Standing Still '05
The Clearing '04
Sorority Boys '02
Get Over It! '01
Soul Survivors '01

Ray Sager
The Gore-Gore Girls '72
This Stuff'll Kill Ya! '71

The Wizard of Gore '70
Just for the Hell of It '68
Blast-Off Girls '67
The Girl, the Body and the Pill '67
Gruesome Twosome '67

Bob Saget (1956-)
New York Minute '04
Father and Scout '94
To Grandmother's House We Go '94

Ludivine Sagnier (1979-)
Love Songs '07
Moliere '07
Paris, je t'aime '06
La Petite Lili '03
Peter Pan '03
Swimming Pool '03
8 Women '02
My Wife is an Actress '01
Water Drops on Burning Rocks '99

Ken Sagoes (1967-)
Death by Dialogue '88
A Nightmare on Elm Street 4: Dream Master '88

Luis Saguar
Against the Wall '04
Silver City '04

Elena Sahagun
Firetrap '01

Kenji Sahara (1932-)
Teenage Exorcist '93
Uncaged '91
Yog, Monster from Space '71
War of the Gargantuas '70
Godzilla's Revenge '69
Destroy All Monsters '68
Son of Godzilla '66
Ghidrah the Three Headed Monster '65
Godzilla vs. Mothra '64
Attack of the Mushroom People '63
King Kong vs. Godzilla '63
Mothra '62
H-Man '59
The Mysterians '58
Rodan '56

Amir Ali Said (1996-)
Inside Man '06
Game 6 '05

Eva Marie Saint (1924-)
Superman Returns '06
Because of Winn-Dixie '05
Don't Come Knocking '05
I Dreamed of Africa '00
Papa's Angels '00
Titanic '96
My Antonia '94
Kiss of a Killer '93
Danielle Steel's Palomino '91
Voyage of Terror: The Achille Lauro Affair '90
Breaking Home Ties '87
The Last Days of Patton '86
Nothing in Common '86
Fatal Vision '84
Love Leads the Way '84
Jane Doe '83
When Hell Was in Session '82
The Best Little Girl in the World '81
A Christmas to Remember '78
Cancel My Reservation '72
Loving '70
The Stalking Moon '69
Grand Prix '66
The Russians Are Coming, the Russians Are Coming '66
The Sandpiper '65
36 Hours '64
All Fall Down '62
Exodus '60
North by Northwest '59
Raintree County '57
On the Waterfront '54

Michael St. Clair (1921-2001)
Our Man Flint '66
Von Ryan's Express '65

Julie St. Claire (1970-)
Stealing Candy '04
Extreme Limits '01

Lili St. Cyr (1918-99)
The Naked and the Dead '58
Son of Sinbad '55

Michael St. Gerard (1961-)
Replikator: Cloned to Kill '94
Star Time '92
Great Balls of Fire '89
Hairspray '88
Senior Week '88

Soledad St. Hilaire (1950-)
The Maldonado Miracle '03
Real Women Have Curves '02
crazy/beautiful '01

Raymond St. Jacques (1930-90)
Timebomb '91
Glory '89
Voodoo Dawn '89
They Live '88
The Wild Pair '87
The Evil That Men Do '84
Sophisticated Gents '81
Kill Castro '80
The Mercenaries '80
The Private Files of J. Edgar Hoover '77
Search for the Gods '75
Final Comedown '72
Cotton Comes to Harlem '70
Dead Right '68
The Green Berets '68
The Comedians '67

Susan St. James (1946-)
Don't Cry, It's Only Thunder '82
Sex and the Single Parent '82
Carbon Copy '81
How to Beat the High Cost of Living '80
Love at First Bite '79
S.O.S. Titanic '79
Desperate Women '78
Night Cries '78
Outlaw Blues '77
Where Angels Go, Trouble Follows '68

Al "Fuzzy" St. John (1892-1963)
The Black Lash '52
King of the Bullwhip '51
Thundering Trail '51
Outlaw Country '49
Stage to Mesa City '48
Cheyenne Takes Over '47
Fighting Vigilantes '47
Ghost Town Renegades '47
Law of the Lash '47
Return of the Lash '47
My Dog Shep '46
Outlaw of the Plains '46
Gangster's Den '45
His Brother's Ghost '45
Lightning Raiders '45
Shadows of Death '45
Death Rides the Plains '44
Devil Riders '44
Frontier Outlaws '44
Oath of Vengeance '44
Rustler's Hideout '44
Thundering Gunslingers '44
Wild Horse Phantom '44
Dead Men Walk '43
Law of the Saddle '43
Raiders of Red Gap '43
Billy the Kid Trapped '42
Law and Order '42
The Lone Rider in Cheyenne '42
The Mysterious Rider '42
Prairie Pals '42

Sundown Fury '42
Texas Justice '42
Border Roundup '41
The Lone Rider in Frontier Fury '41
The Lone Rider in Ghost Town '41
Texas Trouble '41
Trigger Men '41
Battling Outlaw '40
Billy the Kid in Texas '40
Trigger Pals '39
Gunsmoke Trail '38
Ranger's Roundup '38
Songs and Bullets '38
Melody of the Plains '37
The Roamin' Cowboy '37
Sing, Cowboy, Sing '37
A Face in the Fog '36
Pinto Rustlers '36
West of Nevada '36
His Private Secretary '33
Riders of Destiny '33
Police Court '32
Riders of the Desert '32
Oklahoma Cyclone '30
Dance of Life '29
She Goes to War '29
Mabel & Fatty '16

Betta St. John (1929-)
Horror Hotel '60
Corridors of Blood '58
Alias John Preston '56
The Student Prince '54
All the Brothers Were Valiant '53

Christopher St. John
Top of the Heap '72
Shaft '71

Howard St. John (1905-74)
Strange Bedfellows '65
Strait-Jacket '64
Lover Come Back '61
Li'l Abner '59
I Died a Thousand Times '55
Illegal '55
The Tender Trap '55
Born Yesterday '50

Jill St. John (1940-)
The Trip '02
Out There '95
The Player '92
Around the World in 80 Days '89
The Act '82
The Concrete Jungle '82
Diamonds Are Forever '71
Eight on the Lam '67
Tony Rome '67
The Oscar '66
Come Blow Your Horn '63
Who's Minding the Store? '63
Roman Spring of Mrs. Stone '61

Michelle St. John
The Business of Fancydancing '02
Smoke Signals '98
Coyote Summer '96
Pocahontas '95 (V)
Geronimo '93
Spirit Rider '93
Where the Spirit Lives '89

Trevor St. John (1971-)
The King's Guard '01
Dogtown '97

Hubert Saint Macary (1949-)
Lucie Aubrac '98
Genealogies of a Crime '97
Diary of a Seducer '95

Matthew St. Patrick
War '07
Steel Sharks '97

Irma St. Paule (1927-2007)
Where the Money Is '00
Fever '99

John St. Polis (1873-1946)
Rocky Mountain Rangers '40

Phantom Ranger '38
The Shadow Strikes '37
Death from a Distance '36
Terror Trail '33
Coquette '29
Party Girls '29
The Unknown '27
The Phantom of the Opera '25
The Untamable '23
The Four Horseman of the Apocalypse '21

Lucile Saint-Simon (1937-)
The Hands of Orlac '60
Les Bonnes Femmes '60

Marin Sais (1890-1971)
The Fighting Redhead '50
Lightning Raiders '45
Frontier Outlaws '44
Rawhide Romance '34

James Saito (1955-)
Robot Stories '03
Henry Fool '98
Master Mind '73

Frankie Sakai (1929-96)
Buckaroo Banzai Across the Eighth Dimens on '84
The Adventures of
Last War '68
Mothra '62

Sachio Sakai (1929-)
Godzilla's Revenge '69
Godzilla, King of the Monsters '56
Samurai 2: Duel at Ichijoji Temple '55

S.Z. Sakall (1884-1955)
The Student Prince '54
Small Town Girl '53
Lullaby of Broadway '51
Tea for Two '50
In the Good Old Summertime '49
Look for the Silver Lining '49
My Dream is Yours '49
Never Say Goodbye '46
Christmas in Connecticut '45
San Antonio '45
Wonder Man '45
Hollywood Canteen '44
Wintertime '43
Casablanca '42
Yankee Doodle Dandy '42
Ball of Fire '41
The Devil & Miss Jones '41
That Night in Rio '41
It's a Date '40

Ryuichi Sakamoto (1952-)
New Rose Hotel '98
The Last Emperor '87
Merry Christmas, Mr. Lawrence '83

Sumiko Sakamoto (1936-)
The Ballad of Narayama '83

Amy Sakasitz
House Arrest '96
Dennis the Menace '93
A Home of Our Own '93

Harold Sakata (1920-82)
Goin' Coconuts '78
Kill Factor '78
Black Eliminator '78
Impulse '74
Jaws of Death '76
Goldfinger '64

Nancy Sakovich (1961-)
Category 6: Day of Destruction '04
Coast to Coast '04

Yoshiko Sakuma (1939-)
Samurai Banners '69
The Makioka Sisters '83

Renato Sala
Full Metal Ninja '89
Ninja of the Magnificence '89

Abel Salazar (1917-95)
The Brainiac '61
The Curse of the Crying Woman '61
The Living Head '59
The Vampire's Coffin '58
The Vampire '57
The Man and the Monster '65

Theresa Saldana (1954-)
The Night Before '88
Double Revenge '89
Angel Town '89
Raging Bull '80
Defiance '79
I Wanna Hold Your Hand '78

Zoe Saldana (1978-)
Vantage Point '08
Guess Who '05
Haven '04
The Terminal '04
Pirates of the Caribbean: The Curse of the Black Pearl '03
Drumline '02
Crossroads '02
Get Over It! '01
Snipes '01
Center Stage '00

Charles "Chic" Sale (1885-1936)
You Only Live Once '37
The Fighting Westerner '35
Treasure Island '34
Men of America '32

Peter Sallis (1921-)
Wallace & Gromit: The Curse of the Were-Rabbit '05 (V)
Eddie '96
Bad Boys '95
Taste the Blood of Dracula '70

The Jesse Ventura Story '99

Gene Saks (1921-)
Deconstructing Harry '97
I.Q. '94
Nobody's Fool '94
A Fine Romance '92
The One and Only '78
Prisoner of Second Avenue '74
A Thousand Clowns '65
Beware of Pity '46

Soupy Sales
...And God Spoke '94
Critic's Choice '63

John Salew (1897-1961)
Black Glove '54
Kind Hearts and Coronets '49

Diane Salinger (1951-)
Eyes '99
Tomorrow Never Dies '97
Captives '96
The Kid with the X-Ray Eyes '99
Last Summer in the Hamptons '95
Creature '85
Pee-wee's Big Adventure '85

Emmanuel Salinger (1964-)
Triple Agent '04
Kill by Inches '99
My Sex Life... Or How I Got into an Argument '96
One Hundred and One Nights '95
La Sentinelle '92

Matt Salinger (1960-)
Bigger Than the Sky '05
Babyfever '94
Fortunes of War '94
Firehawk '92
Captain America '89
Options '88
Power '86

Gino Saltamerenda
La Ciacca '83

Jason Salkey (1962-)
The Turn of the Screw '99
Sharpe's Fifties '93

John Salley (1964-)
The Comebacks '07
Coast to Coast '04

Aldo Sambrel (1937-)
Hot Blood '89
Navajo Joe '67
The Texican '66
Emmanuelle in the Country '78

Frank S. Salsedo
Magic in the Water '95
Creepshow 2 '87

Andy Samberg (1978-)
Hot Rod '07
Space Chimps '08 (V)

Renato Salvatori (1933-88)
State of Siege '73
Burn! '70
The Organizer '64
RoGoPaG '62
Rocco and His Brothers '60
Era Notte a Roma '60
Big Dea on Madonna Street '58

Montserrat Salvador
Caresses '97
If They Tell You I Fell '89

Udo Samel (1953-)
Go for Zucker '05
The Piano Teacher '01
Killer Condom '95
Kaspar Hauser '93
Knife in the Head '78

Sami Samir
God's Sandbox '02

Emma Samms (1960-)
Yellow Asphalt '01
Humanoids from the Deep '96
Delirious '91
Illusions '91
Star Quest '94
Jesse '88
Born American '86
Fatal Vision '84
Hard to Hold '84
The Guns and the Fury '83
Love Child '82
St. Helen's, Killer Volcano '82
Superstition '82
Dragonslayer '81
Kill Castro '80
The Mercenaries '80
Goliath Awaits '81

Paul Sampson
Deuces Wild '02
Whacked! '02
If You Only Knew '00
Detour '99

Candy Samples (1940-)
Beneath the Valley of the Ultra-Vixens '79
Flesh Gordon '72

Mercedes Sampietro (1947-)
Broken Silence '01
Second Skin '99

Jon Sanborne
Addicted to Murder 3: Bloodlust '99
Rage of the Werewolf '99

Jaime Sanchez (1938-)
Piñero '01

Olga San Juan (1927-)
The Beautiful Blonde from Bashful Bend '49
One Touch of Venus '48
Variety Girl '47
Blue Skies '46

Hiroyuki (Henry) Sanada (1960-)
Sunshine '07
Speed Racer '08
Rush Hour 3 '07
The Twilight Samurai '02
The Last Samurai '03
Royal Warriors '86
Shogun's Ninja '83
Samurai Reincarnation '81

Robert Sampson (1932-)
The Pawnbroker '65
The Arrival '90
Netherworld '90
Robot Jox '90
Re-Animator '84
Gates of Hell '80
The Grass Is Always Greener Over the Septic Tank '78

Lucia Sanchez (1969-)
Carnage '02
Sitcom '97

Will Sampson (1935-87)
Poltergeist 2: The Other Side '86
Insignificance '85
Fish Hawk '79
From Here to Eternity '79
Standing Tall '78
Vegas '78
Orca '77
The White Buffalo '77
Buffalo Bill & the Indians '76
The Outlaw Josey Wales '76
One Flew Over the Cuckoo's Nest '75

Paul Sanchez
Navy SEALS '90
Platoon '86

Pedro Sanchez (1924-)

Marisol Padilla Sanchez (1973-)
Traffic '00
Fever '99

Lea Salonga (1971-)
Redwood Curtain '95
Mulan '98 (V)
Aladdin '92 (V)
My Neighbor Totoro '88 (V)

Sonya Salomaa
Blood Angels '05
Firelight '03

Colin Salmon (1965-)
Alien vs. Predator '04
Freeze Frame '04
Die Another Day '02
The Statement '03
Resident Evil '02
The World Is Not Enough '99

Jennifer Salt (1944-)
Out of the Darkness '85
Sisters '73
Play It Again, Sam '72
Hi, Mom! '70

Russell Sams (1977-)
The Flock '07
The Rules of Attraction '02
With Friends Like These '98

Jeffrey D. Sams (1966-)
Hope '97
Just Write '97
Soul Food '97
Waiting to Exhale '95
Fly by Night '93

Victoria Sanchez (1976-)
Eternal '04
Love Walked In '97
Codename: Jaguar '00
P.T. Barnum '99
Mouth to Mouth '95

Laura San Giacomo (1962-)
Suicide Kings '97
The Apocalypse '97
Eat Your Heart Out '96
The Fright to Remain Silent '95
Nina Takes a Lover '94
Stuart Saves His Family '94
Under Suspicion '92
Where the Day Takes You '92
Once Around '91
Pretty Woman '90
Quigley Down Under '90
sex, lies and videotape '89
Vital Signs '90

Joanne Samuel (1959-)
Gallagher's Travels '87
Queen of the Road '84
Mad Max '80
Allison's Birthday '79

Jose Sancho (1944-)
Live Flesh '97
Ay, Carmela! '90

Paul Sand (1935-)
Sweet Land '05
Chuck & Buck '00
Frozen Assets '92
Teen Wolf Too '87
Wholly Moses! '80
Second Coming of Suzanne '80
Great Bank Hoax '78
Once Upon a Brothers Grimm '77

Otto Sander
Comedian Harmonists '97
Dementia 98
Wings of Desire '88

Roselyn Sanchez (1973-)
The Game Plan '07
The Machinist '04
Rush Hour 2 '01
Held Up '00

Aitana Sanchez-Gijon (1968-)
The Machinist '04
Boat Trip '03
Basic '03
I'm Not Scared '03
Jealousy '99
Yerma '98
A Walk in the Clouds '95

Fernando (Fernan) Sancho (1916-90)
Blood at Sundown '66
Return of the Evil Dead '75
Voodoo Black Exorcist '73
Dr. Orloff and the Invisible Man '70

Dominique Sanda (1948-)
The Crimson Rivers '01
Joseph '95
Voyage of Terror: The Achille Lauro Affair '90
Cabo Blanco '81
Voyage en Douce '81
Damnation Alley '77
The Inheritance '76
1900 '76

Steppenwolf '74
Mackintosh Man '73
The Story of a Love Story '73
The Conformist '71
The Garden of the Finzi-Continis '71
First Love '70
A Gentle Woman '69

Walter Sande (1906-71)
I'll Take Sweden '65
The Gallant Hours '60
Rim of the Canyon '49
The Red House '47
Nocturne '46
Don Winslow of the Navy '43

Casey Sander (1956-)
16 Blocks '06
Mystery Woman: Mystery Weekend '05
Crosscut '95

Otto Sander (1941-)
The Promise '94
Faraway, So Close! '93
Wings of Desire '88
Rosa Luxemburg '86
The Marquise of O '76

John Sanderford
Leprechaun '93
The Alchemist '81

Christopher Sanders (1960-)
Lilo & Stitch 2: Stitch Has a Glitch '05 (V)
Lilo & Stitch '02 (V)

Dirk Sanders (1934-2002)
Pierrot le Fou '65
Black Tights '60

George Sanders (1906-72)
Psychomania '73
Doomwatch '72
Endless Night '71
Invasion of the Body Stealers '69
Good Times '67
The Jungle Book '67 (V)
One Step to Hell '67
The Quiller Memorandum '66
The Amorous Adventures of Moll Flanders '65
A Shot in the Dark '64
In Search of the Castaways '62
The Last Voyage '60
Village of the Damned '60
Solomon and Sheba '59
Voyage in Italy '53
Ivanhoe '52
Captain Blackjack '51
All About Eve '50
Samson and Delilah '50
Forever Amber '47
The Ghost and Mrs. Muir '47
Lured '47
The Private Affairs of Bel Ami '47
The Saint Strikes Back: Criminal Court '46
A Scandal in Paris '46
The Strange Woman '46
Hangover Square '45
Picture of Dorian Gray '45
The Strange Affair of Uncle Harry '45
Action in Arabia '44
The Moon and Sixpence '43
This Land Is Mine '43
The Black Swan '42
The Falcon Takes Over '42
The Falcon's Brother '42
Son of Fury '42
Tales of Manhattan '42
Sundown '41
Bitter Sweet '40
Foreign Correspondent '40
The House of the Seven Gables '40
Rebecca '40
The Saint Takes Over '40
The Saint's Double Trouble '40
The Son of Monte Cristo '40
Allegheny Uprising '39
Mr. Moto's Last Warning '39
Nurse Edith Cavell '39
The Saint in London '39
The Saint Strikes Back '39
Four Men and a Prayer '38
Lloyds of London '36

Henry Sanders (1942-)
Rocky Balboa '06
Rainbow Drive '90
Deadly Sunday '82
Boss' Son '78
Killer of Sheep '77

Hugh Sanders (1911-66)
The Finger Man '55
The Fighter '52
Pride of St. Louis '52
Storm Warning '51
The Damned Don't Cry '50
The Magnificent Yankee '50

Jay O. Sander (1953-)
Half Nelson '06
Wedding Daze '06
Shooting Livien '05
The Day After Tomorrow '04
Widows '02
Along Came a Spider '01
My Husband's Double Life '01
Dead Dog '00
Boss of Bosses '99
Earthly Possessions '99
The Jack Bull '99
Music of the Heart '99
The Confession '98
Neil Simon's The Odd Couple 2 '98
Tumbleweeds '98
Wrestling with Alligators '98
For Richer or Poorer '97
Kiss the Girls '97
The Matchmaker '97
Daylight '96
The Big Green '95
Three Wishes '95
Angels in the Outfield '94
Down Came a Blackbird '94
Kiss of Death '94
Hostages '93
My Boyfriend's Back '93
JFK '91
Meeting Venus '91
V.I. Warshawski '91
Mr. Destiny '90
Glory '89
Assault of the Killer Bimbos '88

Richard Sanders (1940-)
Forbidden Choices '94
Neon City '91

Martyn Sanderson (1938-)
An Angel at My Table '89
Beyond Reasonable Doubt '80
Solo '77

Will Sanderson (1980-)
In the Name of the King: A Dungeon Siege Tale '08
BloodRayne '06
Alone in the Dark '05
Heart of America '03
House of the Dead '03
Blackwoods '02

William Sanderson (1948-)
Beyond the Wall of Sleep '06
Disappearances '06
Gods and Generals '03
Monte Walsh '03
Crossfire Trail '01
Nice Guys Sleep Alone '99
George Wallace '97
Last Man Standing '96
Lone Justice 3: Showdown at Plum Creek '96
Andersonville '95
Forest Warrior '95
Hologram Man '95
Phoenix '95
Mirror, Mirror 2: Raven Dance '94
Wagons East '94
Return to Lonesome Dove '93
Sometimes They Come Back '91
Mirror, Mirror '90
Circle Man '87
Last Man Standing '87
Fletch '85
City Heat '84
Ballad of Gregorio Cortez '83
Blade Runner '82
Raggedy Man '81
Savage Weekend '80
The Onion Field '79
Fight for Your Life '77

Elizabeth Sandifer (1962-)
Animal Instincts 2 '94
Indecent Behavior 2 '94

Adam Sandler (1966-)
You Don't Mess with the Zohan '08
I Now Pronounce You Chuck and Larry '07
Reign Over Me '07
Click '06
Deuce Bigalow: European Gigolo '05
The Longest Yard '05
50 First Dates '04
Spanglish '04
Anger Management '03
Adam Sandler's 8 Crazy Nights '02 (V)
The Hot Chick '02
Mr. Deeds '02
Punch-Drunk Love '02
Little Nicky '00
Big Daddy '99
The Waterboy '98
Dirty Work '97
The Wedding Singer '97
Bulletproof '96
Happy Gilmore '96
Airheads '94
Billy Madison '94
Mixed Nuts '94
Coneheads '93
Shakes the Clown '92
Going Overboard '89

Debra Sandlund (1962-)
Victimless Crimes '90
Murder by Numbers '89
Tough Guys Don't Dance '87

Steve Sandor (1937-)
Stryker '83
The Only Way Home '72
Hell's Angels '69 '69

Miguel (Michael) Sandoval (1951-)
Marilyn Hotchkiss' Ballroom Dancing & Charm School '06
Nine Lives '05
Ballistic: Ecks vs. Sever '02
Collateral Damage '02
Human Nature '02
Blow '01
Wild Iris '01
The Crew '00
Thin Air '00
Things You Can Tell Just by Looking at Her '00
Apartment Complex '98
Route 9 '98
The Fixer '97
Mrs. Winterbourne '96
Scorpion Spring '96
Up Close and Personal '96
Breach of Trust '95
Fair Game '95
Clear and Present Danger '94
Girls in Prison '94
Dancing with Danger '93
Lone Justice '93
White Sands '92
Jungle Fever '91
El Diablo '90
Walker '87
Howard the Duck '86

Nick Sandow
Connie and Carla '04
Swimfan '02
Return to Paradise '98

Stefania Sandrelli (1946-)
The Last Kiss '01
Stealing Beauty '96
Of Love and Shadows '94
Jamon, Jamon '93
The Sleazy Uncle '89
The Family '87
We All Loved Each Other So Much '77
1900 '76
Alfredo, Alfredo '72
The Black Belly of the Tarantula '71
The Conformist '71
Partner '68
Seduced and Abandoned '64
Divorce—Italian Style '62

Billy (Billie) Sands (1911-84)
Harrad Experiment '73
McHale's Navy Joins the Air Force '65
McHale's Navy '64

Diana Sands (1934-73)
Honeybaby '74
Georgia, Georgia '72
Doctors' Wives '70
A Raisin in the Sun '61

Julian Sands (1958-)
Stargate: The Ark of Truth '08
Ocean's Thirteen '07
The Medallion '03
Napoleon '03
Stephen King's Rose Red '02
Hotel '01
Mercy '00
Time Code '00
Vatel '00
The Million Dollar Hotel '99
The Loss of Sexual Innocence '98
The Phantom of the Opera '98
Circle of Passion '97
End of Summer '97
Long Time Since '97
One Night Stand '97
The Great Elephant Escape '95
Leaving Las Vegas '95
The Browning Version '94
Boxing Helena '93
Warlock: The Armageddon '93
Crazy in Love '92
Grand Isle '92
Tale of a Vampire '92
The Turn of the Screw '92
Husbands and Lovers '91
Murder by Moonlight '91
Naked Lunch '91
Warlock '91
Arachnophobia '90
Impromptu '90
Night Sun '90
Vibes '88
Gothic '87
The Room '87
Siesta '87
Harem '86
A Room with a View '86
After Darkness '85
The Doctor and the Devils '85
The Killing Fields '84
Oxford Blues '84
Privates on Parade '84

Stark Sands (1978-)
Pretty Persuasion '05
Catch That Kid '04
Chasing Liberty '04
Shall We Dance? '04
Die Mommie Die! '03
11:14 '03

Tommy Sands (1937-)
None But the Brave '65
Babes in Toyland '61

Gary Sandy (1945-)
Mommy 2: Mommy's Day '96
Troll '86
Hail '73

Erskine Sanford (1885-1969)
The Lady from Shanghai '48
Crack-Up '46
Ministry of Fear '44
The Magnificent Ambersons '42
Citizen Kane '41

Garwin Sanford (1955-)
Merlin's Apprentice '06
Get Carter '00
Life-Size '00
Mr. Rice's Secret '00
Firestorm '97
Ronnie and Julie '97
Maternal Instincts '96
My Very Best Friend '96
Unforgettable '96
Heartstrings '93
Quarantine '89

Isabel Sanford (1917-2004)
Desperate Moves '86
Love at First Bite '79
Guess Who's Coming to Dinner '67

Ralph Sanford (1899-1963)
Kentucky Jubilee '51
Hi-Jacked '50
Sioux City Sue '46
There Goes Kelly '45
A Night for Crime '42

Thomas Sangster (1990-)
The Last Legion '07
Nanny McPhee '06
Tristan & Isolde '06
Love Actually '03
Bobbie's Girl '02
Station Jim '01

Shiro Sano (1955-)
Godzilla 2000 '99
Violent Cop '89

Maya Sansa
The Listening '06
Best of Youth '03

Ken Sansom
Pooh's Heffalump Movie '05 (V)
Piglet's Big Movie '03 (V)

Claudio Santamaria (1974-)
Casino Royale '06
The Last Kiss '01
Besieged '98

Ray Santiago (1984-)
Meet the Fockers '04
Girlfight '99

Renoly Santiago (1974-)
Daylight '96
Dangerous Minds '95
Hackers '95

Saundra Santiago (1957-)
Hi-Life '98
Night Sun '88
Beat Street '84
Miami Vice '84

Ruben Santiago-Hudson (1956-)
American Gangster '07
Mr. Brooks '07
Winning Girls Through Psychic Mind Control '02
Domestic Disturbance '01
The Red Sneakers '01
American Tragedy '00
Shaft '00
Rear Window '98
The Devil's Advocate '97
Which Way Home '90

Santo (1917-84)
Samson in the Wax Museum '63
Invasion of the Zombies '61
Samson vs. the Vampire Women '61

Espartaco (Spartaco) Santoni (1932-98)
Lisa and the Devil '75
Exorcism's Daughter '74
The Castilian '63

Reni Santoni (1939-)
28 Days '00
Dr. Dolittle '98 (V)
The Late Shift '96
Private Parts '96
The Package '89
Cobra '86
Bad Boys '83
Dead Men Don't Wear Plaid '82
Dirty Harry '71
The Student Nurses '70
Guns of the Magnificent Seven '69
Anzio '68
Enter Laughing '67

Michael Santoro
Three Days of Rain '03
Three Days of Rain '02

Rodrigo Santoro (1975-)
Redbelt '08
300 '07
Carandiru '03
Charlie's Angels: Full Throttle '03
Love Actually '03
The Roman Spring of Mrs. Stone '03
Behind the Sun '01

Gaston Santos
Swamp of the Lost Monster '65
The Living Coffin '58
Black Pit of Dr. M '47

Joe Santos (1931-)
Beyond Suspicion '00
The Postman '97
Tyson '95
Trial by Jury '94
Mo' Money '92
Sinatra '92
Deadly Desire '91
The Last Boy Scout '91
Revenge '91
Fear City '85
Ratings Game '84
Zandy's Bride '74
Shaft's Big Score '72

Thomas Santschi (1878-1931)
Phantom of the West '31
Ten Nights in a Bar-Room '31
Paradise Island '30
Paths to Paradise '25
Little Orphan Annie '18
The Spoilers '14

Michael Sanville
Dreams Come True '84
First Turn On '83

Carlos Sanz
The Take '07
Crank '06

Horatio Sanz (1969-)
Lucky You '07
School for Scoundrels '06
The Man '05
Rebound '05
Boat Trip '03

Jorge Sanz (1969-)
The New Guy '02
Tomcats '01
I Love You Baby '01
The Girl of Your Dreams '99
Goodbye, Miss 4th of July '88
Zafarinas '94
Belle Epoque '92
Why Do They Call It Love When They Mean Sex? '92
Lovers: A True Story '90
If They Tell You I Fell '89
Midaq Alley '95

Chris Sarandon (1942-)
Loggerheads '05
Perfume '01
Race Against Time '00
Let the Devil Wear Black '99
Little Men '98
Road Ends '98
The Reaper '97
Tales from the Crypt Presents Bordello of Blood '96
Edie & Pen '95
Temptress '95
Terminal Justice: Cybertech P.D. '95
When the Dark Man Calls '95
Just Cause '94
Dark Tide '93
The Nightmare before Christmas '93 (V)
The Resurrected '91
Forced March '90
Collision Course '89
Slaves of New York '89
The Break '97
The Princess Bride '87
Mayflower Madam '87
Child's Play '88
Protocol '84
The Osterman Weekend '83
The Sentinel '76
Cuba '79
A Tale of Two Cities '80
Lipstick '76
Dog Day Afternoon '75

Margarita Sanz (1954-)
Frida '02

Al Sapienza (1962-)
Back in the Day '05
Bomb the System '05
Megalodon '03
Endangered Species '02
The Hollywood Sign '01
Blind Heat '00
Sweet Evil '98
Animal Instincts 2 '94
The Voyeur '94

Mia Sara (1967-)
Hoodlum & Son '03
Jack and the Beanstalk: The Real Story '01
Black Day Blue Night '95
Bullet to Beijing '95
The Maddening '95
The Pompatus of Love '95
Timecop '94
Undertow '95
Blindsided '93
By the Sword '93
Call of the Wild '93
Caroline at Midnight '93
A Stranger Among Us '92
A Climate for Killing '91
Any Man's Death '90
Daughter of Darkness '89
Apprentice to Murder '88
Shadows in the Storm '88
Queenie '87
Legend '86
Ferris Bueller's Day Off '86

Alice Sapritch (1916-90)
A Slightly Pregnant Man '79
Delusions of Grandeur '76

Richard Sarafian (1935-)
Dr. Dolittle 2 '01 (V)
Bulworth '98
Bound '96
Gotti '96
Miami Hustle '95
The Crossing Guard '94
Ruby '92
Bugsy '91

Susan Sarandon (1946-)
Bernard and Doris '08
Speed Racer '08
Enchanted '07
In the Valley of Elah '07
Mr. Woodcock '07
Irresistible '06
Elizabethtown '05
Jimmy Glick in LaLa Wood '05
Romance & Cigarettes '05
Alfie '04
Noel '04
Shall We Dance? '04
Children of Dune '03
The Banger Sisters '02
Igby Goes Down '02
Moonlight Mile '02
Cats & Dogs '01 (V)
Joe Gould's Secret '00
Rugrats in Paris: The Movie '00 (V)
Anywhere But Here '99
The Cradle Will Rock '99
Earthly Possessions '99
Illuminata '98
Stepmom '98
Twilight '98
James and the Giant Peach '96 (V)
Dead Man Walking '95
The Client '94
Little Women '94
Safe Passage '94
The Player '92
Lorenzo's Oil '92
Light Sleeper '92
Bob Roberts '92
Thelma & Louise '91
White Palace '90
A Dry White Season '89
The January Man '89
Bull Durham '88
Sweet Hearts Dance '88
The Witches of Eastwick '87
Women of Valor '86
Mussolini & I '85
Compromising Positions '85
A.D. '85
The Hunger '83
The Buddy System '83
The Tempest '82
Who Am I This Time? '82
Atlantic City '81
Loving Couples '80
Something Short of Paradise '79
King of the Gypsies '78
Pretty Baby '78
The Other Side of Midnight '77
The Great Smokey Roadblock '76
One Summer Love '76
The Great Waldo Pepper '75
The Rocky Horror Picture Show '75
The Front Page '74
Joe '70

Martine Sarcey (1928-)
One Wild Moment '78
Pardon Mon Affaire '76

Rosa Maria Sarda (1941-)
Take My Eyes '03
Kinsey '04
Harakiri '62

Peter Sarsgaard (1971-)
Rendition '07
Year of the Dog '07
The Dying Gaul '05
Flightplan '05
Jarhead '05
The Skeleton Key '05
Garden State '04
The Inquiry '87
Where's Picone '84
The Doomsday Flight '66
Film-Flam Man '67
The Astro-Zombies '67
The Doll Squad '73
The Lost City '05
The Count of Monte Cristo '99

Michael Sarrazin (1940-)
Feardotcom '02
The Arrival 2 '98
The Peacekeeper '98
Crackerjack 2 '97
Jack Higgins' Thunder Point '97
Midnight in Saint Petersburg '97
Jack Higgins' Midnight Man '96
Bullet to Beijing '95
Lena's Holiday '90
Malarek '89
The Phone Call '89
Captive Hearts '87
Mascara '87
Keeping Track '86
Joshua Then and Now '85
The Train Killer '83
Fighting Back '82
The Seduction '82
Beulah Land '80
The Double Negative '80
Gumball Rally '76
Loves & Times of Scaramouche '76
The Reincarnation of Peter Proud '75
For Pete's Sake '74
The Groundstar Conspiracy '72
Sometimes a Great Notion '71
The Pursuit of Happiness '71
They Shoot Horses, Don't They? '70
The Sweet Ride '68
Gunfight in Abilene '67

Fernand Sardou (1910-76)
The Little Theatre of Jean Renoir '71

Dick Sargent (1933-94)
Acting on Impulse '93
Frame Up '91
Twenty Dollar Star '91
Murder by Numbers '89
Teen Witch '89
Body Count '87
Tanya's Island '81
The Clonus Horror '79
Hardcore '79
Fantasy Island '76
Melvin Purvis: G-Man '74
Live a Little, Love a Little '68

Lewis Sargent (1903-70)
The New Adventures of Tarzan '35

Michael Sarne (1939-)
Oliver Twist '22
A Coeur Joie '67
Head Over Heels '67
Seaside Swingers '65

Jacqueline Sassard (1940-)
Accident '67
Les Biches '68
Pirates of the Seven Seas '62

Katsuhiko Sasaki (1944-)
Godzilla vs. Megalon '76
Terror of Mechagodzilla '78

Ines Sastre (1973-)
Druids '01
Faster, Pussycat! Kill! Kill! '65

Lina Sastri (1953-)
Beyond the Clouds '95
Goodnight, Michelangelo '89

Tua Satana (1935-)
The Astro-Zombies '67
Faster, Pussycat! Kill! Kill! '65

Catya (Cat) Sassoon (1968-2002)
Bloodfist 4: Die Trying '92
Dance with Death '91
Tuff Turf '85

Will Sasso (1975-)
Drop Dead Gorgeous '99
Brown's Requiem '98

Fabio Sartor (1954-)
The Fallen '05
The Passion of the Christ '04

Gailard Sartain (1946-)
The Replacements '00
Ali '01
Elizabethtown '05
Speechless '94
The Real McCoy '93
Getting Even with Dad '94
Open Season '95
The Spitfire Grill '95
The Chase '91
Fried Green Tomatoes '91
Guilty by Suspicion '91
Ernest Goes to Jail '90
The Grifters '90
Blaze '89
Ernest Goes to Camp '87
Leader of the Band '87
Trouble in Mind '86
Hard Country '81
The Hollywood Knights '80
Roadie '80

Ann Savage (1921-)
Pier 23 '51
Renegade Girl '46
Detour '46
Apology for Murder '45
Wife of Monte Cristo '46

John Savage (1949-)
Christina's House '99
The Jack Bull '99
Summer of Sam '99
The Virginian '99
Club Vampire '98
Message in a Bottle '98
The Thin Red Line '98
Hostile Intent '97
Little Boy Blue '97
Maniaca '97
American Strays '96
Amnesia '96
Hollywood Safari '96
Where Truth Lies '96
White Squall '96
The Dangerous '95
One Good Turn '95
Carnosaur 2 '94
C.I.A. 2: Target Alexa '94
Killing Obsession '94
Red Scorpion 2 '94
The Crossing Guard '94
The Takeover '94
Daybreak '93
Shattered Image '93
The Hunting '92
Primary Motive '92
Any Man's Death '90
Do the Right Thing '89
The Beast '88
Hotel Colonial '88
Caribe '87
Salvador '86
Silent Witness '85
Brady's Escape '84
Maria's Lovers '84
Soldier's Revenge '84
The Amateur '82
Coming Out of the Ice '82
Inside Moves '80

Fred Savage (1976-)
Welcome to Mooseport '04
Austin Powers in Goldmember '02
The Rules of Attraction '02
Little Monsters '89
The Wizard '89
Vice Versa '88
Convicted: A Mother's Story '87
The Boy Who Could Fly '86

Ben Savage (1980-)
Wild Palms '93
Big Girls Don't Cry... They Get Even '92

Lori Saunders (1941-)
Wackiest Wagon Train in the West '77

Jennifer Saunders (1958-)
Shrek 2 '04 (V)
Spice World: The Movie '97
Absolutely Fabulous: The Last Shout '96
A Midwinter's Tale '95

Makoto Sato
Attack Squadron '63
I Bombed Pearl Harbor '60

Paul Satterfield
Creepshow 2 '87
Arena '89

George Savalas (1926-85)
Kojak: The Belarus File '85
Kelly's Heroes '70

Telly Savalas (1924-94)
Mind Twister '93
Alice in Wonderland '85
Kojak: The Belarus File '85
The Dirty Dozen: The Fatal Mission '87
The Dirty Dozen: The Deadly Mission '87
Cannonball Run 2 '84
Cartier Affair '84
Fake Out '82
Capricorn One '78
Beyond Reason '77
Escape to Athena '79
The Muppet Movie '79
Beyond the Poseidon Adventure '79
Lisa and the Devil '75
Killer Force '75
Inside Out '75
A Town Called Hell '72
Pancho Villa '72
Scenes from a Murder '72
A Reason to Live, a Reason to Die '73
Redneck '73
Sonny and Jed '73
Land Raiders '69
MacKenna's Gold '69
Crooks & Coronets '69
The Assassination Bureau '69
The Scalphunters '68
The Dirty Dozen '67
The Interns '62
Cape Fear '61
The Young Savages '61
Birdman of Alcatraz '62
Mad Dog Coll '61

Rick Savage (1960-)
Ex-Cop '93
Sensations '87

Dany Saval (1940-)
Boeing Boeing '65
Moon Pilot '62

John Savident (1938-)
Othello '95
War and Peace '68
Middlemarch '93
Brain Donors '92
Mrs. 'Arris Goes to Paris '92

Lyudmila Savelyeva (1942-)
The Seagull '71
War and Peace '68

Doug Savant (1964-)
A Face to Kill For '99
First Daughter '99
Godzilla '98
Robin Cook's Terminal '96
Maniac Cop 3: Badge of Silence '93
Shaking the Tree '92
Red Surf '90
Paint It Black '89
Masquerade '88
Trick or Treat '86

One Against the Wind '91
Impromptu '90
Mountains of the Moon '90
Waterloo '71

Tom Savini (1946-)
Planet Terror '07
Beyond the Wall of Sleep '06
Dawn of the Dead '04
Demon Lust '01
Children of the Living Dead '00
The Demolitionist '95
From Dusk Till Dawn '95
Mr. Stitch '95
Heartstopper '92
Innocent Blood '92
Creepshow 2 '87
Creepshow '82
Knightriders '81
Maniac '80
Dawn of the Dead '78
Martin '77

Camille Saviola (1950-)
Sunset Park '96
Stuart Saves His Family '94
Nightlife '90

Suzanne Savoy
The Man with the Perfect Swing '95
The Cellar '90

Devon Sawa (1978-)
Extreme Dating '04
Extreme Ops '02
Slackers '02
Final Destination '00
The Guilty '99
Idle Hands '99
SLC Punk! '99
Around the Fire '98
A Cool, Dry Place '98
Wild America '97
The Boys Club '96
Night of the Twisters '95
Robin of Locksley '95
Little Giants '94

Kenji Sawada
Mishima: A Life in Four Chapters '85

Julia Sawalha (1968-)
Chicken Run '00 (V)
Mr. Toad's Wild Ride '96
A Midwinter's Tale '95
Pride and Prejudice '95
Martin Chuzzlewit '94

Nadim Sawalha (1935-)
Cleopatra '99
The Awakening '80
The Wind and the Lion '75

Ikio Sawamura (1905-75)
War of the Gargantuas '70
Godzilla's Revenge '69
Yojimbo '61

Joseph (Joe) Sawyer (1906-82)
The Kettles in the Ozarks '56
The Killing '56
Mr. Walkie Talkie '52
As You Were '51
Comin' 'Round the Mountain '51
Indian Uprising '51
Operation Haylift '50
The Traveling Saleswoman '50
Coroner Creek '48
Fighting Father Dunne '48
Big Town After Dark '47
G.I. War Brides '46
The Naughty Nineties '45
Raiders of Ghost City '44
The Outlaw '43
Tanks a Million '41
They Died with Their Boots On '41
The Border Legion '40
Lucky Cisco Kid '40
Melody Ranch '40
The Roaring Twenties '39
The Black Legion '37
San Quentin '37
Petrified Forest '36
Special Investigator '36
The Informer '35
College Humor '33

John Saxon (1935-)
Masters of Horror: Pelts '06
Outta Time '01
Final Payback '99
From Dusk Till Dawn '95
Beverly Hills Cop 3 '94
Killing Obsession '94
Wes Craven's New Nightmare '94
No Escape, No Return '93
Animal Instincts '92
The Baby Doll Murders '92
Hellmaster '92
Maximum Force '92
Blackmail '91
Deadly Conspiracy '91
Payoff '91
The Arrival '90
Blood Salvage '90
Crossing the Line '90
The Last Samurai '90
The Final Alliance '89
My Mom's a Werewolf '89
Aftershock '88
Criminal Act '88
Death House '88
Welcome to Spring Break '88
A Nightmare on Elm Street 3: Dream Warriors '87
Hands of Steel '86
Fever Pitch '85
Half Slave, Half Free '85
A Nightmare on Elm Street '84
Prisoners of the Lost Universe '84
Big Score '83
Scorpion with Two Tails '82
Unsane '82
Wrong Is Right '82
Blood Beach '80
Battle Beyond the Stars '80
Beyond Evil '80
Cannibal Apocalypse '80
The Electric Horseman '79
Running Scared '79
The Bees '78
Deadly Thief '78
Fast Company '78
The Glove '78
Moonshine County Express '77
Raid on Entebbe '77
Swiss Conspiracy '77
Strange Shadows in an Empty Room '76
Mitchell '75
Strange New World '75
Planet Earth '74
Enter the Dragon '73
Joe Kidd '72
Snatched '72
Mr. Kingstreet's War '71
Death of a Gunfighter '69
The Appaloosa '66
The Doomsday Flight '66
Night Caller from Outer Space '66
Planet of Blood '66
The Ravagers '65
The Cardinal '63
The Girl Who Knew Too Much '63
My Man Adam '86
Mr. Hobbs Takes a Vacation '62
Portrait in Black '60
The Unforgiven '60
The Reluctant Debutante '58
This Happy Feeling '58
Rock, Pretty Baby '56

Diane Sayer (1938-2001)
Kitten with a Whip '64
The Strangler '64

Philip Sayer (1947-89)
A.D. '85
Slayground '84
Xtro '83
Green Horizon '80

Alexei Sayle (1952-)
The Thief Lord '06
Tipping the Velvet '02
Swing '98
Deadly Currents '93
Reckless Kelly '93
Siesta '87
Whoops Apocalypse '83

John Sayles (1950-)
Girlfight '99
Gridlock'd '96
My Life's in Turnaround '94
Matinee '92
Straight Talk '92
City of Hope '91
Little Vegas '90
Eight Men Out '88
Matewan '87
Something Wild '86
Unnatural Causes '86
The Brother from Another Planet '84
Hard Choices '84
Lianna '83
The Howling '81
Return of the Secaucus 7 '80
Piranha '78

Syd Saylor (1895-1962)
Abbott and Costello Meet the Invisible Man '51
Ambush Trail '46
Harvest Melody '43
Helltown '38
Arizona Days '37
Forlorn River '37
Sea Racketeers '37
Headin' for the Rio Grande '36
Kelly of the Secret Service '36
Kelly the Second '36
Prison Shadows '36
Sky Parade '36
Dude Ranger '34
The Lost Jungle '34
When a Man Sees Red '34
Law of the Sea '32
The Light of Western Stars '30

John Sayre
Crystal's Diary '99
Crack Up '97

Kyu Sazanka (1914-71)
Yojimbo '61
Fires on the Plain '59

Leonardo Sbaraglia (1970-)
Intacto '01
Burnt Money '00
Wild Horses '95

Raphael Sbarge (1964-)
Home Room '02
Pearl Harbor '01
Message in a Bottle '98
Quicksilver Highway '98
Independence Day '96
The Hidden 2 '94
Carnosaur '93
Prison for Children '93
Murder 101 '91
Back to Hannibal: The Return of Tom Sawyer and Huckleberry Finn '90
Billionaire Boys Club '87
My Science Project '85
Vision Quest '85
Risky Business '83

Mattia Sbragia (1952-)
The Passion of the Christ '04
Beyond the Sea '04
Daniel Deronda '02
Festival at Cannes '02
Cotton Mary '99
Love and Rage '99
The Red Violin '98
The Odyssey '97
The Serpent's Kiss '97
Emma '96
Rasputin: Dark Servant of Destiny '96
Cosi '95
Country Life '95
The Browning Version '94
Jefferson in Paris '94
Desire '93
The Killing Beach '92
The Player '92
Fires Within '91
Shattered '91
Presumed Innocent '90
White Mischief '88
Good Morning, Babylon '87
A Man in Love '87
Ebony Tower '86
Burke & Wills '85
Defense of the Realm '85
The Coca-Cola Kid '84
Waterfront '83
Heat and Dust '82

Gia Scala (1934-72)
The Guns of Navarone '61
The Tunnel of Love '58
Don't Go Near the Water '57

Prunella Scales (1932-)
Station Jim '01
Emma '96
Stiff Upper Lips '96
Breaking the Code '96
An Awfully Big Adventure '94
The Rector's Wife '94
Second Best '94
Wolf '94
My Friend Walter '93
Howard's End '92
A Question of Attribution '91
A Chorus of Disapproval '89
Consuming Passions '88
The Lonely Passion of Judith Hearne '87
Mapp & Lucia '85
The Wicked Lady '83
Room at the Top '59

Jack Scalia (1951-)
End Game '06
Kraken: Tentacles of the Deep '06
Red Eye '05
Silent Predators '99
Chained Heat 3: Hell Mountain '98
First Degree '95
Undesirable '92
Deadly Desire '91
Illicit Behavior '91
Runaway Father '91
After the Shock '90
Endless Descent '90
Fear City '85
The Amazons '84

Michelle Scarabelli (1955-)
Alien Nation: Millennium '96
Alien Nation: The Enemy Within '96
Alien Nation: Body and Soul '95
The Colony '95
The Wrong Woman '95
Alien Nation: Dark Horizon '94
Deadbolt '92
Age Old Friends '89
SnakeEater 2: The Drug Buster '89
Perfect Timing '84

Adrian Scarborough (1968-)
The History Boys '06
Vera Drake '04

Margaret Scarborough
Loco Love '03
Sunstorm '01

Don Scardino (1949-)
Cruising '80
He Knows You're Alone '80
Squirm '76

Hal Scardino (1984-)
Marvin's Room '96
The Indian in the Cupboard '95
Searching for Bobby Fischer '93

Alan Scarfe (1946-)
Sanctuary '98
Back in Business '96
Once a Thief '96
The Wrong Guy '96
Heart of Darkness '93
Jericho Fever '93
Iron Eagle 2 '88
Python Wolf '88
The Bay Boy '85
Joshua Then and Now '85
The Deserters '83
Cathy's Curse '77

Jonathan Scarfe (1975-)
Carolina Moon '07
Liberty Stands Still '02
Blood Money '99
White Lies '98
The Lesser Evil '97
Our Mother's Murder '97
Eye '96

Renato Scarpa (1939-)
For Roseanna '96
The Postman '94
Volere Volare '92
The Icicle Thief '89
St. Michael Had a Rooster '72

Carmen Scarpitta (1933-)
In the Name of the Pope-King '85
La Cage aux Folles '78

Diana Scarwid (1955-)
The Clearing '04
A Guy Thing '03
Party Monster '03
Path to War '02
Dirty Pictures '00
What Lies Beneath '00
From the Earth to the Moon '98
Ruby Bridges '98
Critical Choices '97
Bastard out of Carolina '96
If These Walls Could Talk '96
The Cure '95
Gold Diggers: The Secret of Bear Mountain '95
The Neon Bible '95
Truman '95
JFK: Reckless Youth '93
After the Promise '87
Brenda Starr '86
Extremities '86
Psycho 3 '86
A Bunny's Tale '85
Rumble Fish '83
Silkwood '83
Strange Invaders '83
Desperate Lives '82
Mommie Dearest '81
Inside Moves '80
Forever '78
Pretty Baby '78
Bunco '77
The Possessed '77

Monica Scattini (1957-)
Men Men Men '95
Priceless Beauty '90

Wendy Schaal (1954-)
Loving Annabelle '06
Small Soldiers '98
Out There '95
Going Under '91
When the Time Comes '91
Innerspace '87
Munchies '87
Creature '85
Fatal Vision '84
Where the Boys Are '84

Sam Schacht (1936-)
Heart of Midnight '89
A Secret Space '88

Doris Schade (1924-)
Rosenstrasse '03
Marianne and Juliane '82

Johnathon Schaech (1969-)
Prom Night '08
Angels Fall '07
Masters of Horror: The Washingtonians '07
Road House 2: Last Call '06
Blood Crime '02
The Forsaken '01
How to Kill Your Neighbor's Dog '01
Sol Goode '01
Caracara '00
If You Only Knew '00
The Brutal Truth '99
Houdini '99
Splendor '99
Finding Graceland '98
Hush '98
Welcome to Woop Woop '97
Invasion of Privacy '96
That Thing You Do! '96
The Doom Generation '95
How to Make an American Quilt '95
Poison Ivy 2: Lily '95

Joshua Schaefer
Eight Days a Week '97
Johns '96
No Dessert Dad, 'Til You Mow the Lawn '94

Laura Schaefer
Curse 4: The Ultimate Sacrifice '90
Catacombs '89
Ghost Town '88

Eric Schaeffer (1962-)
Mind the Gap '04
One Night at McCool's '01
Wirey Spindell '99
Gunshy '98
Fall '97
If Lucy Fell '95
My Life's in Turnaround '94

Rebecca Schaeffer (1967-89)
The End of Innocence '90
Voyage of Terror: The Achille Lauro Affair '90
Scenes from the Class Struggle in Beverly Hills '89

Natalie Schafer (1900-91)
I'm Dangerous Tonight '90
Rescue from Gilligan's Island '78
Forever Darling '56
The Girl Next Door '53
Caught '49
The Time of Your Life '48
Wonder Man '45

William Schallert (1922-)
Shake, Rattle & Rock! '94 / Matinee '92 / Held Hostage '91 / House Party 2: The Pajama Jam '91 / The Incident '89 / War & Remembrance: The Final Chapter '39 / Innerspace '87 / War & Remembrance '88 / The Grace Kelly Story '83 / Twilight Zone: The Movie '83 / Blind Ambition '79 / The Strongest Man in the World '75 / Death Sentence '74 / Trial of the Catonsville Nine '72 / Man on a String '71 / Colossus: The Forbin Project '70 / The Computer Wore Tennis Shoes '69 / Sam Whiskey '69 / Speedway '68 / Lonely Are the Brave '62 / The Gallant Hours '60 / The Incredible Shrinking Man '57 / Man in the Shadow '57 / Tarnished Angels '57 / The Gunslinger '56 / An Annapolis Story '55 / The High and the Mighty '54 / Them! '54 / Sword of Venus '53 / Invasion U.S.A. '52 / The Man from Planet X '51

Mike Schank
Storytelling '01 / American Movie '99

Heidi Schanz
Universal Soldier: The Return '99

Sabrina Scharf
Hunter '73 / Easy Rider '69 / Hell's Angels on Wheels '67

Roy Scheider (1932-2008)
Dracula 3: Legacy '05 / The Punisher '04 / Chicago 10 '07 (V) / RKO 281 '99 / The Peacekeeper '98 / Silver Wolf '98 / The White Raven '98 / Executive Target '97 / John Grisham's The Rainmaker '97 / The Myth of Fingerprints '97 / Plato's Run '96 / The Rage '96 / Covert Assassin '94 / Romeo Is Bleeding '93 / Naked Lunch '91 / The Fourth War '90 / The Russia House '90 / Somebody Has to Shoot the Picture '90 / Listen to Me '89 / Night Game '89 / Cohen and Tate '88 / 52 Pick-Up '86 / The Men's Club '86 / Mishima: A Life in Four Chapters '85 (N) / 2010: The Year We Make Contact '84 / Blue Thunder '83 / Tiger Town '83 / Still of the Night '82 / All That Jazz '79 / Last Embrace '79 / Jaws 2 '78 / Sorcerer '77 / Marathon Man '76 / Jaws '75 / The Outside Man '73 / The Seven-Ups '73 / The French Connection '71 / Klute '71 / Loving '70 / Stiletto '69 / Paper Lion '68 / Curse of the Living Corpse '64

Tom Schanley (1961-)
Footsteps '98 / Nothing Underneath '85

Catherine Schell (1946-)
On the Third Day '83 / Gulliver's Travels '77 / Return of the Pink Panther '74 / Werewolf in a Girl's Dormitory '61

Maria Schell (1926-2005)
Christmas Lilies of the Field '84 / Samson and Delilah '84 / La Passante '83 / Inside the Third Reich '82 / Just a Gigolo '79 / Twist '76 / Voyage of the Damned '76 / The Odessa File '74 / 99 Women '69 / The Hanging Tree '59 / The Brothers Karamazov '58 / White Nights '57 / Gervaise '56 / Napoleon '55 / The Last Bridge '54 / Angel with the Trumpet '50

Maximilian Schell (1930-)
Coast to Coast '04 / Festival at Cannes '02 / The Song of the Lark '01 / Deep Impact '98 / Left Luggage '98 / The Eighteenth Angel '97 / John Carpenter's Vampires '97 / Telling Lies in America '96 / The Thorn Birds: The Missing Years '96 / Abraham '94 / A Far Off Place '94 / Little Odessa '94 / Miss Rose White '92 / Stalin '92 / Young Catherine '91 / The Freshman '90 / The Rose Garden '89 / Peter the Great '86 / The Assisi Underground '84 / The Chosen '81 / Avalanche Express '79 / The Black Hole '79 / Players '79 / Together? '79 / The Day That Shook the World '78 / A Bridge Too Far '77 / Julia '77 / Cross of Iron '76 / St. Ives '76 / The Man in the Glass Booth '75 / The Pedestrian '73 / First Love '77 / Simon Bolivar '69 / The Castle '68 / Heidi '67 / Topkapi '64 / Judgment at Nuremberg '61 / The Young Lions '58

Raynor Scheine (1942-)
The Sentinel '06 / The Rookie '02 / The War '94

Carl Schell (1928-)
Heart of Glass '74

Clemens Scheitz
Stroszek '77 / Heart of Glass '76

Mary Kate Schellhardt (1978-)
Apollo 13 '95 / What's Eating Gilbert Grape '93 / Free Willy '93

Wolfgang Schenck (1934-)
Effi Briest '74 / Tenderness of the Wolves '73

Robert Schenkkan (1953-)
The Manhattan Project '86 / Act of Vengeance '86

Claudia Schiffer (1970-)
Love Actually '03 / Life Without Dick '01 / In Pursuit '00 / Black and White '99 / Friends & Lovers '99 / The Blackout '97 / Richie Rich '94

Joseph Schildkraut (1895-1964)
The Diary of Anne Frank '59 / Monsieur Beaucaire '46 / The Cheaters '45 / Flame of the Barbary Coast '45 / The Shop Around the Corner '40 / The Man in the Iron Mask '39 / Idiot's Delight '39 / Mr. Takes a Vacation '39 / The Rains Came '39 / The Three Musketeers '39 / Marie Antoinette '38 / Souls at Sea '37 / The Life of Emile Zola '37 / The Garden of Allah '36 / The Crusades '35 / Cleopatra '34 / Viva Villa! '34 / King of Kings '27 / The Road to Yesterday '25 / Orphans of the Storm '21

August Schellenberg (1936-)
Bury My Heart at Wounded Knee '07 / Missionary Man '07 / Eight Below '06 / The New World '05 / The Unsaid '01 / High Noon '00 / Out of Time '00 / Free Willy 3: The Rescue '97 / Free Willy 2: The Adventure Home '95 / Tecumseh: The Last Warrior '95 / Getting Gotti '94 / Lakota Woman: Siege at Wounded Knee '94 / Iron Will '93 / Geronimo '93 / Free Willy '93 / Black Robe '91 / Striker's Mountain '87 / Confidential '86 / Crazy Horse '96 / True Heart '97 / Grand Avenue '96

Ronnie Schell (1931-)
Jetsons: The Movie '90 (V) / Night Shift '82 (V) / The Return '80 / Gus '76

Dieter Schidor (1949-87)
Schnelles Geld '84 / Cross of Iron '76

Richard Schiff (1959-)
Civic Duty '06 / Ray '04 / People I Know '02 / I Am Sam '01 / Along for the Ride '00 / Gun Shy '00 / Lucky Numbers '00 / Whatever It Takes '00 / Crazy in Alabama '99 / Forces of Nature '99 / Heaven '99 / Deep Impact '98 / Dr. Dolittle '98 / Living Out Loud '98 / The Lost World: Jurassic Park 2 '97 / The Trigger Effect '96 / City Hall '95 / Hoffa '92

Kevin G. Schmidt (1988-)
Cheaper by the Dozen 2 '05 / The Butterfly Effect '04 / Catch That Kid '04

Marlene Schmidt (1937-)
Scorchy '76 / The Stepmother '71

Wolfgang Schmidt
See Ray Dennis Steckler

Christiane Schmidtmer (1940-2003)
The Giant Spider Invasion '75 / The Big Doll House '71 / Boeing Boeing '65

August Schmolzer (1958-)
Requiem for Dominic '91

Steve Schirripa (1958-)
The Longest Yard '05 / The Family Stone '05 / Deuce Bigalow: European Gigolo '05 / Around the World in 80 Days '04 / How to Lose Your Lover '04 / All the Real Girls '03

Vivian Schilling (1968-)
Savage Land '94 / Future Shock '93 / In a Moment of Passion '93 / The Legend of Wolf Mountain '92 / Project: Eliminator '91 / Soultaker '90 / Terror Eyes '87

Tom Schiller (1956-)
Maniac Warriors '88 / Storm '87

Charlie Schlatter (1966-)
The Curse '87 / Cocaine Wars '86 / Ed '96 / Police Academy 7: Mission to Moscow '94 / 1-900 '94 / Bright Lights, Big City '88 / 18 Again! '88 / Heartbreak Hotel '88

Sharon Schlarth
Eat and Run '86 / Dead As a Doorman '85

Walter Schmidinger (1933-)
From the Life of the Marionettes '80

Ariane Schluter (1966-)
The Dress '96

Kyle Schmid (1984-)
Sisterhood of the Traveling Pants '05 / All-American Murder '91 / Sunset Heat '92

Paul Schneider (1973-)
Lars and the Real Girl '07 / The Assassination of Jesse James by the Coward Robert Ford '07 / Elizabethtown '05 / The Family Stone '05 / All the Real Girls '03

Michael Schneider (1939-)
Wanted: Babysitter '75 / Last Tango in Paris '73

Maria Schneider (1952-)
Jane Eyre '96 / Les Nuits Fauves '92 / Crime of Honor '85 / Mama Dracula '80 / The Passenger '75 / Last Tango in Paris '73

Rob Schneider (1963-)
Big Stan '08 / You Don't Mess with the Zohan '08 / I Now Pronounce You Chuck and Larry '07 / The Benchwarmers '06 / Grandma's Boy '06 / The Longest Yard '05 / Deuce Bigalow: European Gigolo '05 / 50 First Dates '04 / Adam Sandler's 8 Crazy Nights '02 (V) / The Hot Chick '02 / Mr. Deeds '02 / The Animal '01 / Little Nicky '00 / Big Daddy '99 / Deuce Bigalow: Male Gigolo '99 / Muppets from Space '99 / Dying to Get Rich '98 / Knock Off '98 / Down Periscope '96 / Judge Dredd '95 / The Beverly Hillbillies '93 / Demolition Man '93 / Surf Ninjas '93

Gus Schilling (1908-57)
The Lady from Shanghai '48 / A Thousand and One Nights '45 / Citizen Kane '41

Tom Schilling (1982-)
Agnes and His Brothers '04 / Before the Fall '04

Helmuth Schneider (1920-72)
The Death Merchant '91 / Waxwork 2: Lost in Time '91

John Schneider (1960-)
Lake Placid 2 '07 / Sydney White '07 / Collier & Co.: Hot Pursuit '06 / Snow Day '00 / True Women '97 / Night of the Twisters '95 / Texas '94 / Ministry of Vengeance '89 / Speed Zone '88 / Christmas Comes to Willow Creek '87 / The Curse '87 / The Dukes of Hazzard '83 / Smokey and the Bandit '77

Dan Schneider (1966-)
The Big Picture '89 / Happy Together '89 / Better Off Dead '85 / Hot Resort '85

Bonnie Schneider
Murderlust '86

Home Alone 2: Lost in New York '92

Romy Schneider (1938-82)
La Passante '83
Death Watch '80
Sidney Sheldon's Bloodline '79
A Simple Story '79
A Woman at Her Window '77
Innocents with Dirty Hands '76
Mado '76
Old Gun '76
The Infernal Trio '74
The Last Train '74
Assassination of Trotsky '72
Cesar & Rosalie '72
Ludwig '72
The Hero '71
Swimming Pool '70
The Things of Life '70
La Piscine '69
Triple Cross '67
What's New Pussycat? '65
Good Neighbor Sam '64
The Trial '63
The Victors '63
Boccaccio '70 '62

Andrea Schober (1964-)
Chinese Roulette '86
The Merchant of Four Seasons '71

Michael Schoeffling (1960-)
Wild Hearts Can't Be Broken '91
Longtime Companion '90
Mermaids '90
Slaves of New York '89
Let's Get Harry '87
Belizaire the Cajun '86
Sylvester '85
Vision Quest '85
Racing with the Moon '84
Sixteen Candles '84
Hot Moves '84

Jill Schoelen (1970-)
When a Stranger Calls Back '93
Adventures in Spying '92
There Goes My Baby '92
Rich Girl '91
Cutting Class '89
The Phantom of the Opera '89
Popcorn '89
Curse 2: The Bite '88
Billionaire Boys Club '87
The Stepfather '87
Babes in Toyland '86
That Was Then... This Is Now '85
Thunder Alley '85
D.C. Cab '84

Ingrid Schoeller
They Paid with Bullets: Chicago 1929 '69
Psychophta '68

Margareta Schoen (1895-1985)
Kriemhilde's Revenge '24
Siegfried '24

Ingeborg (Inge) Schoener (1935-)
Mr. Superinvisible '73
Mark of the Devil '69
Cold Steel for Tortuga '65

Dietmar Schoenherr (1926-)
Journey of Hope '90
The Monster of London City '64

Andrew Schofield
Sid & Nancy '86

Annabel Schofield (1963-)
Exit in Red '97
Body Armor '96
Midnight Blue '96
Solar Crisis '92
Dragonard '88

David Schofield (1951-)
Pirates of the Caribbean: Dead Man's Chest '06
The Musketeer '01
Gladiator '00
Leo Tolstoy's Anna Karenina '96
Band of Gold '95
Jekyll and Hyde '90
An American Werewolf in London '81

Tom Scholte
Goldrush: A Real Life Alaskan Adventure '98
Live Bait '95

Jason Schombing (1963-)
K-9 3: P.I. '01
Asylum '97
Robin Cook's Invasion '97
3 Ninjas Kick Back '94
Timecop '94

Reiner Schone (1942-)
My Little Assassin '99
Mortal Kombat 2: Annihilation '97
Crash Dive '96
The Gunfighters '87
Return of Sabata '71

Frank Schorpion
No Alibi '00
Escape from Wildcat Canyon '99
Dead End '98

Bob Schott (1949-)
Head of the Family '96
Out for Blood '93
Future Hunters '88

Maria Schrader (1965-)
Rosenstrasse '03
Advertising Rules! '01
Aimee & Jaguar '98

Lisa Schrage
China White '91
Food of the Gods: Part 2 '88
Hello Mary Lou: Prom Night 2 '87

Bitty Schram (1968-)
Cleopatra's Second Husband '00
Silent Scream '80
Flatbed Annie and Sweetiepie: Lady Truckers '79
Caught '96
One Fine Day '96
My Family Treasure '93
A League of Their Own '92
Saturday the 14th Strikes Back '88
Hunk '87
Caveman '81
Galaxina '80

Liev Schreiber (1967-)
Kissing a Fool '98
Chicago 10 '07 (V)
Love in the Time of Cholera '07
The Omen '06
The Painted Veil '06
The Manchurian Candidate '04
Hitler: The Rise of Evil '03
The Sum of All Fears '02
Kate & Leopold '01
Hamlet '00
Scream 3 '00
Jakob the Liar '99
RKO 281 '99
Spring Forward '99
A Walk on the Moon '99
Twilight '98
Phantoms '97
Scream 2 '97
Since You've Been Gone '97
Sphere '97
The Daytrippers '96
Ransom '96
Scream '96
Walking and Talking '96
Buffalo Girls '95
Denise Calls Up '95
The Sunshine Boys '95
Mixed Nuts '94
Party Girl '94

Pablo Schreiber (1978-)
Into the Fire '05
The Manchurian Candidate '04
The Mudge Boy '03
A Painted House '03

Greta Schröder (1891-1967)
Nosferatu '22
The Golem '20

Rick Schroder (1970-)
Black Cloud '04
Poolhall Junkies '02
Lost Battalion '01
Murder at Devil's Glen '99
Ebenezer '97
Hostage High '97
Crimson Tide '95
Texas '94
Call of the Wild '93
Return to Lonesome Dove '93
There Goes My Baby '92
Across the Tracks '89
Lonesome Dove '89
Two Kinds of Love '85
Hansel and Gretel '82
Earthling '80
The Last Flight of Noah's Ark '80
Little Lord Fauntleroy '80
The Champ '79

Barbet Schroeder (1941-)
The Duchess of Langeais '07
Paris, je t'aime '06
Celine and Julie Go Boating '74
Six in Paris '68

Carly Schroeder (1990-)
Gracie '07
Eye of the Dolphin '06
Firewall '06
Mean Creek '04
The Lizzie McGuire Movie '03

Steven Schub
No Vacancy '99
The Thirteenth Floor '99
Footsteps '98

Karin Schubert (1944-)
Delusions of Grandeur '76
Till Marriage Do Us Part '74
Cold Eyes of Fear '70

John Schuck (1940-)
The Curse of the Jade Scorpion '01
The Trial of Old Drum '00
Holy Matrimony '94
Tales from the Crypt Presents Demon Knight '94
Star Trek 6: The Undiscovered Country '91
My Mom's a Werewolf '89
Second Sight '89
The New Adventures of Pippi Longstocking '88
Star Trek 4: The Voyage Home '86
Finders Keepers '84
Butch and Sundance: The Early Days '79
Thieves Like Us '74
Blade '72
Hammersmith Is Out '72
McCabe & Mrs. Miller '71
Brewster McCloud '70
M*A*S*H '70

Rudolf Schuendler (1906-88)
The American Friend '77
Suspiria '77

Al Schuerman
The Bible and Gun Club '96
Presumed Guilty '91

Rebecca Schull (1929-)
Flannel Pajamas '06
Analyze This '98
Neil Simon's The Odd Couple 2 '98
That Darn Cat '96
My Life '93

Albert Schultz
White Lies '98
Ebenezer '97
Beethoven Lives Upstairs '92

Dwight Schultz (1947-)
Star Trek: First Contact '96
The Temp '93
Woman with a Past '92
Fat Man and Little Boy '89
The Long Walk Home '89
When Your Lover Leaves '83
Alone in the Dark '82

Matt Schulze (1972-)
The Flock '07
Mr. Brooks '07
Final Move '06
Torque '04
Blade 2 '02
The Transporter '02
The Fast and the Furious '01
Dementia '98

Paul Schulze
Rambo '08
Panic Room '02
Don't Say a Word '01
Alien Fury: Countdown to Invasion '00
Drowning Mona '00
Grind '96
Illtown '96
Hand Gun '93
Laws of Gravity '92

Wendy Schumacher (1971-)
Fugitive Rage '96
Scorned 2 '96
Animal Instincts 3: The Seductress '95
Star Hunter '95

Hans Schumm (1896-1990)
Spy Smasher '42
Spy Smasher Returns '42

Reinhold Schunzel (1886-1954)
Woman in Brown '48
Golden Earrings '47
Notorious '46
Fortune's Fool '21
The Threepenny Opera '31

Maurice Schutz (1866-1955)
Vampyr '31
Passion of Joan of Arc '28
Napoleon '27

Jennifer Schwalbach Smith (1971-)
Clerks 2 '06
Jay and Silent Bob Strike Back '01

Maurice Schwartz (1891-1960)
Salome '53
Tevye '39

Scott Schwartz (1969-)
Alien 3000 '04
Bridge of Dragons '99
A Time to Live '85
A Christmas Story '83
Kidco '83
The Toy '82

Jason Schwartzman (1980-)
The Darjeeling Limited '07
Walk Hard: The Dewey Cox Story '07
Marie Antoinette '06
Bewitched '05
The Hitchhiker's Guide to the Galaxy '05
Shopgirl '05
I Heart Huckabees '04
Simone '02
Slackers '02
Spun '02
CQ '01
Rushmore '98

Arnold Schwarzenegger (1947-)
Around the World in 80 Days '04
The Rundown '03
Terminator 3: Rise of the Machines '03
Collateral Damage '02
The 6th Day '00
End of Days '99
Batman and Robin '97
Eraser '96
Jingle All the Way '96
Junior '94
True Lies '94
Dave '93
Last Action Hero '93
Beretta's Island '92
Terminator 2: Judgment Day '91
Kindergarten Cop '90
Total Recall '90
Red Heat '88
Twins '88
Predator '87
The Running Man '87
Raw Deal '86
Commando '85
Red Sonja '85
Conan the Destroyer '84
The Terminator '84
Conan the Barbarian '82
The Jayne Mansfield Story '80
The Villain '79
Stay Hungry '76
The Long Goodbye '73
Hercules in New York '70

Eric Schweig (1967-)
Bury My Heart at Wounded Knee '07
It Waits '05
The Missing '03
Mr. Barrington '03
Skins '02
Big Eden '00
Larry McMurtry's Dead Man's Walk '96
Follow the River '95
Tom and Huck '95
Pontiac Moon '94
Squanto: A Warrior's Tale '94
The Broken Chain '93
The Last of the Mohicans '92

Til Schweiger (1963-)
Already Dead '07
Deuce Bigalow: European Gigolo '05
In Enemy Hands '04
King Arthur '04
Lara Croft Tomb Raider: The Cradle of Life '03
Joe and Max '02
What to Do in Case of Fire '02
Driven '01
Intimate Affairs '01
SLC Punk! '99
Judas Kiss '98
The Replacement Killers '98
Brute '97
Maybe... Maybe Not '94

Jan Schweiterman (1972-)
Warlock 3: The End of Innocence '98
Good Burger '97

David Schwimmer (1966-)
Big Nothing '06
Duane Hopwood '05
Madagascar '05 (V)
Band of Brothers '01
Hotel '01
Uprising '01
It's the Rage '99
Picking Up the Pieces '99
Kissing a Fool '98
Six Days, Seven Nights '98
Apt Pupil '97
Breast Men '97
Since You've Been Gone '97
The Pallbearer '95
Flight of the Intruder '90

Rusty Schwimmer
Broken Trail '06
The Hawk Is Dying '06
Mozart and the Whale '05
North Country '05
Runaway Jury '03
John John in the Sky '00
The Perfect Storm '00
Los Locos Posse '97
North Shore Fish '97
Prison of Secrets '97
Lone Justice 3: Showdown at Plum Creek '96
Twister '96
A Little Princess '95
Jason Goes to Hell: The Final Friday '93
Lone Justice 2 '93
T Bone N Weasel '92

Hanna Schygulla (1943-)
The Girl of Your Dreams '99
Lea '96
Dead Again '91
The Summer of Miss Forbes '88
Casanova '87
Forever, Lulu '87
Barnum '86
Delta Force '86
A Love in Germany '84
Sheer Madness '84
La Nuit de Varennes '82
Passion '82
Berlin Alexanderplatz '80
The Marriage of Maria Braun '79
The Wrong Move '78
Effi Briest '74
The Bitter Tears of Petra von Kant '72
Why Does Herr R. Run Amok? '69

Yvonne Scio (1969-)
Sorority Boys '02
Redline '97

Steve Scionti
Megalodon '03
Mom's Outta Sight '01

Annabella Sciorra (1960-)
Find Me Guilty '06
12 and Holding '05
Chasing Liberty '04
King of the Jungle '01
Above Suspicion '00
Once in the Life '00
Mr. Jealousy '98
New Rose Hotel '98
What Dreams May Come '98
Asteroid '97
Cop Land '97
Highball '97
Little City '97
The Funeral '96
Underworld '96
The Addiction '95
The Cure '95
The Innocent Sleep '95

National Lampoon's Favorite Deadly Sins '95
Mr. Wonderful '93
The Night We Never Met '93
Romeo Is Bleeding '93
The Hand that Rocks the Cradle '92
Whispers in the Dark '92
The Hard Way '9-
Jungle Fever '91
Prison Stories: Women on the Inside '91
Cadillac Man '90
Internal Affairs '90
Reversal of Fortune '90
True Love '89

Martin Scorsese (1942-)
Shark Tale '04 (V)

Zvee Scooler (1899-1985)
Uncle Moses '32

Peter Scolari (1954-)
Trumps '04
Corporate Affairs '90
Perfect Harmony '91
The Polar Express '04
From the Earth to the Moon '98
That Thing You Do! '96
Camp Nowhere '94
Fallen Angels 2 '93
Ticks '93
Twirl '81

Edith Scob (1937-)
Comedy of Innocence '00
Time Regained '99
The Milky Way '68
The Burning Court '62
The Horror Chamber of Dr. Faustus '59

Dean Scofield (1957-)
Prehysteria 2 '94
Eden 4 '93
Eden 3 '93

Paul Scofield (1922-2008)
Animal Farm '99 (V)
The Crucible '96
Martin Chuzzlewit '94
Quiz Show '94
Utz '93
Hamlet '90
Mr. Corbett's Ghost '90
Henry V '89
When the Whales Came '89
The Attic: The Hiding of Anne Frank '88
Anna Karenina '85
The Curse of King Tut's Tomb '80 (tv)
Scorpio '73
King Lear '71
Bartleby '70
A Man for All Seasons '66
The Train '65
Carve Her Name with Pride '58

Tracy Scoggins (1959-)
Asylum of the Damned '03
A Crack in the Floor '00
The Great American Sex Scandal '54
Alien Intruder '93
Dead On '93
Dollman vs Demonic Toys '93
Play Murder for Me '91
Timebomb '91

Gangs of New York '02
Diving In '90
Making the Grade '84
With Friends Like These '98
The Muse '99

Nicolette Scorsese
Aspen Extreme '93
Boxing Helena '93

Izabela Scorupco (1970-)
Cougar Club '07
Exorcist: The Beginning '04
Reign of Fire '02
Vertical Limit '00
GoldenEye '95

Adam Scott (1973-)
Step Brothers '08
Corporate Affairs '07
The Matador '06
The Return '06
Monster-in-Law '05
The Aviator '04
Off the Lip '04
Torque '04
Two Days '03
High Crimes '02
The American '01
Nora '00

Alex Scott (1929-)
Romper Stomper '92
Next of Kin '82
The Asphyx '72
The Abominable Dr. Phibes '71

Andrew Scott
Dead Bodies '03

Ashley Scott (1977-)
Strange Wilderness '08
Into the Blue '05
Lost '05
Walking Tall '04

Bainbridge Scott
Death Chase '87

Brenda Scott (1943-)
Hell Squad '85
Simon, King of the Witches '71

Campbell Scott (1962-)
Music & Lyrics '07
Duma '05
The Dying Gaul '05
The Exorcism of Emily Rose '05
Loverboy '05
Saint Ralph '04
Roger Dodger '02
The Secret Lives of Dentists '02
Hamlet '01
The Pilot's Wife '01
The Love Letter '98
Impostors '98
Spring Forward '99
Hi-Life '98
Ultimate Desires '91
Beyond the Silhouette '90
Demonic Toys '90
The Red Raven Kiss-Off '90
Watchers 2 '90
The Gumshoe Kid '89
One Last Run '89
In Dangerous Company '88
Toy Soldiers '84

Geoffrey Scott (1942-)
The Morning After '86

George C. Scott (1927-99)
First & Ten: The Team Scores Again '85
Murder She Purred: A Mrs. Murphy Mystery '98
Gloria '98
Titanic '96
Angus '95
Twelve Angry Men '97
Rocky Marciano '99
Inherit the Wind '99
The Last Days of Patton '86
Murrow '86
The Murders in the Rue Morgue '86
Choices '86
Pals '87
The Rescuers Down Under '90 (V)
Exorcist 3: Legion '90
Descending Angel '90
Malice '93
Deadly Currents '93
Tyson '95
Oliver Twist '82
Taps '81
The Changeling '80
The Formula '80
Hardcore '79
Movie Movie '78
The Prince and the Pauper '78
Islands in the Stream '77
The Hindenburg '75
Bank Shot '74
The Day of the Dolphin '73
Oklahoma Crude '73
The New Centurions '72
Rage '72
The Hospital '71
They Might Be Giants '71
Patton '70
Petulia '68
The Bible '66
Dr. Strangelove, or: How I Learned to Stop Worrying and Love the Bomb '64
The List of Adrian Messenger '63
The Hustler '61
Anatomy of a Murder '59
The Hanging Tree '59

Carey Scott (1965-)

Debralee Scott (1953-)
Police Academy '84
Film-Flam Man '67
Just Tell Me You Love Me '80

Donovan Scott (1946-)
I Know Who Killed Me '07
Savannah Smiles '82
Sheena '84
Bears '83
Zorro, the Gay Blade '81
1941 '79

Dougray Scott (1965-)
Hitman '07
The Crow Road '96
Dark Water '05
The Truth About Love '04
Ripley's Game '02
Arabian Nights '00
Mission: Impossible 2 '00
Deep Impact '98
Ever After: A Cinderella Story '98
Twin Town '97
Another 9 1/2 Weeks '96

Fred Scott (1902-91)
The Black Six '74
Ridin' the Trail '40
Code of the Fearless '39
In Old Montana '39
Ranger's Roundup '38
Songs and Bullets '38
Melody of the Plains '37
The Roamin' Cowboy '37
Singing Buckaroo '37
Two-Gun Troubador '37

Eric Scott (1958-)
A Day for Thanks on Walton's Mountain '82
The Waltons: The Christmas Carol '80
Behind the Lines '82

Jay Scott (1931-)
Grave of the Vampire '72
All the Lovin' Kinfolk '70

Janette Scott (1938-)
Paranoiac '62
Day of the Triffids '63

John Scott (1930-)
Smoke '70
Death of a Gunfighter '69
The Cut Throats '69
Horror of Party Beach '64
The Tell-Tale Heart '60

Judith Scott
Guess Who '05
Flightplan '05

Kathryn Leigh Scott (1933-)
The Last Days of Patton '86
The Adventures of Rocky & Bullwinkle '00 (V)
Witches' Brew '81
Visitor from the Grave '81
House of Dark Shadows '70

Keith Scott (1954-)
The Adventures of Rocky & Bullwinkle '00 (V)

Kimberly Scott (1961-)
Guess Who '05
Antwone Fisher '02
They Call Me Sirr '00
Sworn to Justice '97
Showdown '93
The Abyss '89

Ken Scott (1928-86)
Fantastic Voyage '66
The Fiend Who Walked the West '58

Kenn Scott
Stopover Tokyo '57
Shootfighter: Fight to the Death '93

Kente Scott (1977-)

Larry B. Scott (1961-)
The Bad Pack '98

Gregg Scott
Savage Island '03
Ghosthouse '88

Gordon Scott (1926-2007)
Tramplers '67
Hercules and the Princess of Troy '65
Coriolanus, Man without a Country '64
Conquest of Mycene '63
Gladiator of Rome '63
Hero of Rome '63
Samson and the 7 Miracles of the World '62
Tarzan and the Trappers '58

Jacqueline Scott (1935-)
Empire of the Ants '77
Charley Varrick '73
Duel '71

Pippa Scott (1935-)
Sound of Murder '82
Bad Ronald '74
Cold Turkey '71
Petulia '68

Randolph Scott (1898-1987)
Ride the High Country '62
Comanche Station '60
The Tall T '57
Seventh Cavalry '56
A Lawless Street '55
Rage at Dawn '55
Ten Wanted Men '54
The Stranger Wore a Gun '53
Hangman's Knot '52
Man in the Saddle '51
Santa Fe '51
The Cariboo Trail '50
The Nevadan '50
Abilene Town '46
Badman's Territory '46
Captain Kidd '45
China Sky '44
Bombardier '43
Gung Ho! '43
The Desperadoes '43
Pittsburgh '42
The Spoilers '42
To the Shores of Tripoli '42
Western Union '41
My Favorite Wife '40
Virginia City '40
Jesse James '39
Frontier Marshal '39

Lizabeth Scott (1922-)
Pulp '72
Loving You '57
Silver Lode '54
Scared Stiff '53
A Stolen Face '52
The Racket '51
Easy Living '49
Too Late for Tears '49
Dead Reckoning '47
Desert Fury '47
Pitfall '48
The Strange Love of Martha Ivers '46

Margaretta Scott (1912-2005)
Calling Paul Temple '48
Counterblast '48
Things to Come '36

Martha Scott (1914-2003)
Adam '83
Father Figure '80
The Turning Point '77
Ben-Hur '59
Sayonara '57
The Ten Commandments '56
Desperate Hours '55

Susan Scott
See Nieves Navarro

Seann William Scott (1976-)
Mr. Woodcock '07
Ice Age: The Meltdown '06
The Dukes of Hazzard '05
Southland Tales '06
Dude, Where's My Car? '00
Final Destination '00
Road Trip '00
American Pie 2 '01
Evolution '01
Jay and Silent Bob Strike Back '01

Timothy Scott (1938-95)
Lone Justice '93
Return to Lonesome Dove '93

Tom Everett Scott (1970-)
Because I Said So '07
Inside Out '01
National Lampoon's Van Wilder '02
Love Me Deadly '73
Boiler Room '00
The Love Letter '99
Inherit the Wind '99
One True Thing '98
An American Werewolf in Paris '97
Dead Man on Campus '97
That Thing You Do! '96

William Lee Scott (1973-)
The Butterfly Effect '04
The Opposite of Sex '98

Zachary Scott (1914-65)
The Young One '61
Flame of the Islands '55
Shotgun '55
Appointment in Honduras '53
Let's Make It Legal '51
Born to Be Bad '50
Flamingo Road '49
South of St. Louis '48
Cass Timberlane '47
Mildred Pierce '45
The Southerner '45
The Mask of Dimitrios '44

Fear of a Black Hat '94
Revenge of the Nerds 4: Nerds in Love '94
Super Force '90
SnakeEater 2: The Drug Buster '89
Extreme Prejudice '37
Revenge of the Nerds 2: Nerds in Paradise '87
The Children of Times Square '86
Iron Eagle '86
My Man Adam '86
SpaceCamp '86
That Was Then... This Is Now '85
Revenge of the Nerds '84
A Hero Ain't Nothin' but a Sandwich '78

Susannah of the Mounties '39
Rebecca of Sunnybrook Farm '38
The Texans '38
Follow the Fleet '36
Go West, Young Man '36
The Last of the Mohicans '36
The Fighting Westerner '35
She '35
Village Tale '35
Wagon Wheels '34
Buffalo Stampede '33
Heritage of the Desert '33
Murders in the Zoo '33
Supernatural '33
To the Last Man '33
Island of Lost Souls '32
When the West Was Young '32

Kristin Scott Thomas (1960-)
The Other Boleyn Girl '08
The Golden Compass '07 (V)
The Walker '07
The Valet '07
Keeping Mum '05
Gosford Park '01
Life as a House '01
Up at the Villa '00
Random Hearts '99
Sweet Revenge '98
The Horse Whisperer '97
The English Patient '96
Angels and Insects '95
The Confessional '95
Gulliver's Travels '95
The Pompatus of Love '95
Richard III '95
Four Weddings and a Funeral '94
An Unforgettable Summer '94
The Bachelor '93
Body & Soul '93
Weep No More My Lady '93
Bitter Moon '92
Framed '90
Spymaker: The Secret Life of Ian Fleming '90
The Endless Game '89
A Handful of Dust '88
The Tenth Man '88
Under the Cherry Moon '86

Serena Scott Thomas (1961-)
The Thirst '06
Hostage '05
The World Is Not Enough '99
Relax... It's Just Sex! '98
Nostromo '96
Diana: Her True Story '93
Harnessing Peacocks '92
The Endless Game '89

Andrea Scotti (1931-)
The Legend of the Wolf Woman '77
Hercules vs. the Sons of the Sun '64

Vito Scotti (1918-96)
I Wonder Who's Killing Her Now? '76
The McCullochs '75
Caper of the Golden Bulls '67
What Did You Do in the War, Daddy? '66
Von Ryan's Express '65
Two Weeks in Another Town '62
Atom Age Vampire '61
Seven Thieves '60
Me and the Colonel '58
The Big Heat '53
The Redhead from Wyoming '53
Affair in Trinidad '52
Because of You '52

Alexander Scourby (1913-85)
The Stuff '85

Don Scribner
Rapid Assault '99
Wild Man '89

Angus Scrimm (1926-)
Phantasm 4: Oblivion '98
Vampirella '96
Phantasm 3: Lord of the Dead '94
Mindwarp '91
Subspecies '90
Transylvania Twist '89
Phantasm 2 '88
The Lost Empire '83
Phantasm '79

Linda Scruggs
Las Vegas Lady '76
Shoot It Black, Shoot It Blue '74

Sean Scully (1947-)
Sara Dane '81
The Prince and the Pauper '62

Terry Scully (1936-2001)
The Asphyx '72
He Kills Night After Night After Night '69

Matthew Scurfield (1948-)
A Different Loyalty '04
Bait '02

Sandra Seacat
A Murder of Quality '90
Crazy in Alabama '99
The Destiny of Marty Fine '96
The New Age '94
Promised Land '88

Susan Seaforth Hayes (1943-)
Dream Machine '91
Billie '65

Steven Seagal (1952-)
Pistol Whipped '08
Urban Justice '07
Attack Force '06
Shadow Man '06
Submerged '05
The Foreigner '03
Half Past Dead '02
Exit Wounds '01
Ticker '01
The Patriot '99
My Giant '98
Fire Down Below '97
Executive Decision '96
The Glimmer Man '96
Under Siege 2: Dark Territory '95
On Deadly Ground '94
Under Siege '92
Out for Justice '91
Marked for Death '90
Hard to Kill '89
Above the Law '88

Jocelyn Seagrave (1968-)
Dark Justice '00
Moonbeam '97

Jenny Seagrove (1958-)
Zoe '01
Deadly Game '91
Sherlock Holmes and the Incident at Victoria Falls '91
Bullseye! '90
The Guardian '90
A Chorus of Disapproval '89
Magic Moments '89
Appointment with Death '88
Hold the Dream '86
A Woman of Substance '84
Local Hero '83
Nate and Hayes '83

Douglas Seale (1913-99)
Aladdin '92 (V)
Mr. Destiny '90
Ernest Saves Christmas '88

Franklyn Seales (1952-90)
Southern Comfort '81
The Onion Field '79

Nick Searcy (1959-)
The Comebacks '07
Welcome to Paradise '07
The Dead Girl '06
Flicka '06
The Assassination of Richard Nixon '05
Head of State '03
Runaway Jury '03
Cast Away '00
From the Earth to the Moon '98
Perfect Crime '97
The War '94

Jackie Searl (1921-91)
That Certain Age '38
Peck's Bad Boy '34
The Return of Casey Jones '34
High Gear '33
Topaze '33
Hearts of Humanity '32

Fred F. Sears (1913-57)
Bonanza Town '51
Down to Earth '47

Heather Sears (1935-94)
Estate of Insanity '70
The Phantom of the Opera '62
Room at the Top '59
The Story of Esther Costello '57

James Seay (1914-92)
The Amazing Colossal Man '57
Beginning of the End '57
Phantom from Space '53
Heartaches '29
Ridin' Down the Canyon '42
Turf Boy '42
In Old Colorado '41

Dorothy Sebastian (1906-57)
Rough Riders' Roundup '39
They Never Come Back '32
His First Command '29
Spite Marriage '29
Our Dancing Daughters '28
A Woman of Affairs '28

Lobo Sebastian
Dirty '05

Tracy Sebastian
Running Cool '93
On the Air Live with Captain Midnight '79

Jean Seberg (1938-79)
Airport '70
Macho Callahan '70
Paint Your Wagon '69
Pendulum '69
A Fine Madness '66
Moment to Moment '66
Lilith '64
Time Out for Love '61
Let No Man Write My Epitaph '60
Love Play '60
Breathless '59
The Mouse That Roared '59
Bonjour Tristesse '57
Saint Joan '57

Harry Secombe (1921-2001)
Song of Norway '70
Down Among the Z Men '52
Goon Movie '52

Kyle Secor (1958-)
Beat '00
Homicide: The Movie '00
Children of Fury '94
Drop Zone '94
Untamed Heart '93
Silent Victim '92
City Slickers '91
Delusion '91
Sleeping with the Enemy '91
The Heart of Dixie '89

Jon Seda (1970-)
Bad Boys 2 '03
The Street King '02
Undisputed '02
Double Bang '01
Love the Hard Way '01
Price of Glory '00
Thin Air '00
Dear God '96
Mistrial '96
Primal Fear '96
Selena '96
Sunchaser '96
12 Monkeys '95
I Like It Like That '94
Carlito's Way '93
Gladiator '92

Amy Sedaris (1961-)
Shrek the Third '07 (V)
Snow Angels '07
I Want Someone to Eat Cheese With '06
Bewitched '05
Chicken Little '05 (V)
My Baby's Daddy '04
Elf '03
Maid in Manhattan '02

Margaret Seddon (1872-1968)
Mr. Deeds Goes to Town '36
The Return of Casey Jones '34

Kyra Sedgwick (1965-)
The Game Plan '07
Loverboy '05
The Woodsman '04
Secondhand Lions '03
Behind the Red Door '02
Just a Kiss '02
Personal Velocity: Three Portraits '02
What's Cooking? '00
Labor Pains '99
Critical Care '97
Montana '97
Losing Chase '96
Phenomenon '96
The Low Life '95
Murder in the First '95
Something to Talk About '95
Family Pictures '93
Heart and Souls '93
Miss Rose White '92
Singles '92
Pyrates '91
Women & Men: In Love There Are No Rules '91
Mr. & Mrs. Bridge '90
Born on the Fourth of July '89
Kansas '88
Tai-Pan '86
War & Love '84

Robert Sedgwick
Tune in Tomorrow '90
Nasty Hero '89
Morgan Stewart's Coming Home '87

Miriam Seegar
Strangers of the Evening '32
Seven Keys to Baldpate '29

George Segal (1934-)
Heights '04
Houdini '99
The Cable Guy '96
The Mirror Has Two Faces '96
November Conspiracy '96
The Feminine Touch '95
Flirting with Disaster '95
It's My Party '95
To Die For '95
Army of One '94
Deep Down '94
Direct Hit '93
Look Who's Talking Now '93
Taking the Heat '93
Me, Myself & I '92
For the Boys '91
All's Fair '89
The Endless Game '89
Look Who's Talking '89
Killing 'Em Softly '85
Not My Kid '85
Stick '85
Cold Room '84
The Zany Adventures of Robin Hood '84
Deadly Game '82
Carbon Copy '81
The Last Married Couple in America '80
Lost and Found '79
Who Is Killing the Great Chefs of Europe? '78
Fun with Dick and Jane '77
Rollercoaster '77
The Duchess and the Dirtwater Fox '76
Black Bird '75
Russian Roulette '75
The Terminal Man '74
Blume in Love '73
A Touch of Class '73
Born to Win '71
The Hot Rock '70
Loving '70
The Owl and the Pussycat '70
Where's Poppa? '70
The Bridge at Remagen '69
No Way to Treat a Lady '68
The St. Valentine's Day Massacre '67
The Lost Command '66
The Quiller Memorandum '66
Who's Afraid of Virginia Woolf? '66
King Rat '65
Ship of Fools '65
Invitation to a Gunfighter '64

Jonathan Segal
See Jonathan Sagalle

Yonathan Segal
See Jonathan Sagalle

Zohra Segal
See Zohra Sehgal

Jonathan Segall
See Jonathan Sagalle

Pamela Segall (1966-)
Disney's Teacher's Pet '04 (V)
Kiki's Delivery Service '98 (V)
Plump Fiction '97
Eat Your Heart Out '96
Bed of Roses '95
Sgt. Bilko '95
Gate 2 '92
After Midnight '89
Say Anything '89
Something Special '86
Bad Manners '84

Noah Segan (1983-)
Brick '06
Adam & Steve '05

Paolo Seganti (1966-)
Cradle 2 the Grave '03
Sex & Mrs. X '00
Tea with Mussolini '99
L.A. Confidential '97
Still Breathing '97

Jason Segel (1980-)
Forgetting Sarah Marshall '08
The Good Humor Man '05
11:14 '03
Slackers '02
SLC Punk! '99

Santiago Segura (1965-)
Agent Cody Banks 2: Destination London '04
Blade 2 '02
The Girl of Your Dreams '99
Dance with the Devil '97
The Day of the Beast '95

Zohra Sehgal (1912-)
The Mystic Masseur '01
Bhaji on the Beach '94
Masala '91
The Courtesans of Bombay '85

Emmanuelle Seigner (1966-)
The Diving Bell and the Butterfly '07
La Vie en Rose '07
Four Last Songs '06
Happily Ever After '04
Buddy Boy '99
The Ninth Gate '99
Place Vendome '98
Nirvana '97
R.P.M. '97
Bitter Moon '92
Frantic '88

Louis Seigner (1903-95)
Mr. Klein '76
This Special Friendship '67
The Eclipse '66
The Would-Be Gentleman '58
Seven Deadly Sins '53

Mathilde Seigner (1968-)
The Girl from Paris '02
Alias Betty '01
With a Friend Like Harry '00
Time Regained '99
Venus Beauty Institute '98
Dry Cleaning '97
The Man I Love '97

Jerry Seinfeld (1954-)
Bee Movie '07 (V)
Ratings Game '84

Rapulana Seiphemo
Tsotsi '05
Tarzan and the Lost City '98

John Seitz (1892-1979)
End Game '06
Forced March '90
Out of the Rain '90
Five Corners '88
Hard Choices '84
The Prowler '81

Johnny Sekka (1934-2006)
The Message '77
The Bloodsuckers '70
The Last Safari '67
Khartoum '66
Woman of Straw '64

David Selby (1941-)
End Game '06
Horton Foote's Alone '97
Soldier of Fortune Inc. '97
D3: The Mighty Ducks '96
Headless Body in Topless Bar '96
White Squall '96
Intersection '93
Grave Secrets: The Legacy of Hilltop Drive '92
Dying Young '91
Rich and Famous '81
Rich Kids '79
The Girl in Blue '74
Up the Sandbox '72
Night of Dark Shadows '71

Nicholas Selby (1925-)
House of Cards '90
Macbeth '71
A Midsummer Night's Dream '68

Sarah Selby (1905-80)
Huckleberry Finn '75
An Affair to Remember '57
Stopover Tokyo '57
Battle Cry '55
Men of the Fighting Lady '54
Battle Circus '53

Viveka Seldahl (1944-2001)
A Song for Martin '01
House of Angels '92

Marian Seldes (1928-)
Mona Lisa Smile '03
Hollywood Ending '02
Town and Country '01
Duets '00
If These Walls Could Talk 2 '00
The Haunting '99
Digging to China '98
Affliction '97
Home Alone 3 '97
Tom and Huck '95
Truman '95
Fingers '78

William (Bill) Self (1921-)
The Thing '51
Sands of Iwo Jima '49
The Story of G.I. Joe '45

Elizabeth Sellars (1923-)
A Voyage 'Round My Father '89
The Chalk Garden '64
Desiree '54
Madeleine '54
Never Let Go '60
Three Cases of Murder '55

Connie Sellecca (1955-)
The Brotherhood of the Rose '89
The Last Fling '86
Captain America 2: Death Too Soon '79
She's Dressed to Kill '79

Tom Selleck (1945-)
Christopher Columbus: The Discovery '92
Folks! '92
In and Out '97
An Innocent Man '89
Her Alibi '88
High Road to China '83
Lassiter '84
Magnum P.I.: Don't Eat the Snow in Hawaii '80
Meet the Robinsons '07 (V)
Jesse Stone: Sea Change '07
Jesse Stone: Night Passage '06
Jesse Stone: Stone Cold '05
Iker Countdown to D-Day '04
Monte Walsh '03
Crossfire Trail '01
Running Mates '00
The Love Letter '99
Last Stand at Saber River '96
Ruby Jean and Joe '96
Broken Trust '95
Open Season '95
The Concrete Cowboys '79
The Sacketts '79
Coma '78
The Gypsy Warriors '78
Bunco '77
Washington Affair '77
Midway '76
Most Wanted '76
Terminal Island '73
Daughters of Satan '72
Myra Breckinridge '70

Peter Sellers (1925-80)
Trail of the Pink Panther '82
The Fiendish Plot of Dr. Fu Manchu '80
Being There '79
Prisoner of Zenda '79
Revenge of the Pink Panther '78
America at the Movies '76
Murder by Death '76
The Pink Panther Strikes Again '76
Return of the Pink Panther '74
Great McGonagall '75
Ghost in the Noonday Sun '74
Blockhouse '73
Hoffman '70
There's a Girl in My Soup '70
The Magic Christian '69
I Love You, Alice B. Toklas! '68
The Party '68
The Bobo '67
Casino Royale '67
Woman Times Seven '67
After the Fox '66
The Wrong Box '66

Paola Senatore (1949-)
Emerald Jungle '80
Mean Machine '73

Brian Sergent
Eagle vs. Shark '07
Meet the Feebles '89 (V)

Diego Serrano (1973-)
The 24 Hour Woman '99
Mixing Nia '98

Sabrina Sellers
See Sabrina Siani

Charles Sellon (1870-1937)
In Old Kentucky '35
Life Begins at Forty '35
Bright Eyes '34
Ride Him, Cowboy '32
Behind Office Doors '31
Bulldog Drummond '29
Vagabond Lover '29
The Prairie King '27
The Monster '25

Morton Selten (1860-1939)
The Thief of Bagdad '40
The Ghost Goes West '36

David Selvas (1971-)
Beloved/Friend '99
Caresses '97

Rade Serbedzija (1946-)
The Eye '08
Shooter '07
The Fog '05
Go West '05
The Keeper: The Legend of Omar Khayyam '05
Eurotrip '04
The Fever '04
The Quiet American '02
Quicksand '01
Mission: Impossible 2 '00
Snatch '00
Space Cowboys '00
Eyes Wide Shut '99
Stigmata '99
Mighty Joe Young '98
Polish Wedding '98
The Saint '97
Before the Rain '94

Katy Silverstone (1918-2006)
Divine Secrets of the Ya-Ya Sisterhood '02
Seven Girlfriends '00
Sisterhood '02

Clarissa Selwynne (1886-1948)
Jane Eyre '34
My Pal, the King '32
The Love Trap '29

Milton Selzer (1918-)
Miss Rose White '92
Tapeheads '89
The Triangle Factory Fire Scandal '79
The Evil '78

Harry Semels (1887-1946)
Stone of Silver Creek '35
Ghost Valley '32
Texas Buddies '32
America '24

Larry Semon (1889-1928)
Underworld '27
The Wizard of Oz '25

Ivan Sergei (1972-)
Bonneville '06
The Break-Up '06
Santa Baby '06
Playing Mona Lisa '00
The Big Day '06
The Opposite of Sex '98
Once a Thief '96
Gunfighter's Moon '96

Nandana Sen (1967-)
Seducing Maarya '05
The War Within '05
Bombay Talkie '70

Aparna Sen (1945-)
Hullabaloo over Georgie & Bonnie's Pictures '78

Raymond Serra (1931-2003)
The Good Shepherd '06
Warnabees '06
Men of Means '99
Gotti '96
Marilyn & Bobby: Her Final Affair '94
Sugar Hill '94
Nasty Hero '89
A Time to Remember '87
Alphabet City '84
Splitz '84
Hardhat & Legs '80
Hooch '76
Sweet Revenge '90

John Sessions (1953-)
The Good Shepherd '06
The Merchant of Venice '04
William Shakespeare's A Midsummer Night's Dream '99
Cousin Bette '97
The Scarlet Tunic '97
A Midwinter's Tale '95
Princess Caraboo '94
Freddie the Frog '92 (V)
Henry V '89

Almira Sessions (1888-1974)
Oklahoma Annie '51
Diary of a Chambermaid '46
The Heat's On '43
Miracle of Morgan's Creek '44

Jacques Sernas (1925-)
Superfly T.N.T. '73
55 Days at Peking '63
La Dolce Vita '60
Helen of Troy '56
The Golden Salamander '51

Jean Servais (1910-76)
The Devil's Nightmare '71
Black Jesus '68
Super Brother '68
That Man from Rio '64
Fever Mounts at El Pao '59
Tamango '59
Rififi '54

Henri Serre (1931-)
The Fire Within '64
Jules and Jim '62

Pepe Serna (1944-)
The Black Dahlia '06
Hidden Assassin '94
American Me '92
The Rookie '90
Bad Jim '89
The Forgotten '89
Break of Dawn '88
Fandango '85
The Adventures of Buckaroo Banzai Across the Eighth Dimension '84
Ballad of Gregorio Cortez '83
Scarface '83
The Jerk '79

Assumpta Serna (1957-)
Stella Does Tricks '96
Sharpe's Enemy '94
Sharpe's Rifles '93
Sharpe's Eagle '93
The Fencing Master '92
Nostradamus '93
Chain of Desire '93
Wild Orchid '90
I, the Worst of All '90
Matador '86

Mack Sennett (1880-1960)
Man in the Silk Hat '83
Abbott and Costello Meet the Keystone Kops '54
Charlie Chaplin.... Our Hero! '15

Noriko Sengoku (1922-)
Okoge '93
Godzilla vs. Monster Zero '68
Snow Country '57

Joe Seneca (1914-96)
The Saint of Fort Washington '93
Mississippi Masala '92
Murder on the Bayou '91
King Kong '05
School Daze '88
The Blob '88
Crossroads '86
Samaritan: The Mitch Snyder Story '86
The Verdict '82
Half Slave, Half Free '85
Wilma '77

Koreya Senda (1904-94)
Tora! Tora! Tora! '70
Face of Another '66

Yahoo Serious (1954-)
Mr. Accident '99
Reckless Kelly '93
Young Einstein '89

Heyon-a Seong
Time '06

Massimo Serato (1916-89)
The Bloodstained Shadow '78
Don't Look Now '73
Camille 2000 '69
10th Victim '65
Wild, Wild Planet '65
The Lion of Thebes '64
Hero of Rome '63
Venus Against the Son of Hercules '62
The Naked Maja '59

Andy Serkis (1964-)
Alex Rider: Operation Stormbreaker '06
Flushed Away '06 (V)
Longford '06
King Kong '05 (V)
The Prestige '06
13 Going on 30 '04
Lord of the Rings: The Return of the King '03
Deathwatch '02
Lord of the Rings: The Two Towers '02 (V)
Lord of the Rings: The Fellowship of the Rings '01
24 Hour Party People '01
The Jolly Boys' Last Stand '00
Oliver Twist '00
Pandaemonium '00
Shiner '00
Among Giants '98
Career Girls '97

Michel Serrault (1928-2007)
Joyeux Noel '05
The Butterfly '02
The Girl from Paris '02
Artemisia '97
The Swindle '97
Beaumarchais the Scoundrel '96
Nelly et Monsieur Arnaud '95
Le Bonheur Est Dans le Pre '95
The Old Lady Who Walked in the Sea '91
Dr. Petiot '90
La Cage aux Folles 3: The Wedding '86
La Cage aux Folles 2 '81
Buffet Froid '79
The Associate '79
La Cage aux Folles '78
The Holes '72
The King of Hearts '66
Love on a Pillow '62
Diabolique '55

Nestor Serrano (1957-)
Definitely, Maybe '08
Sueno '05
The Day After Tomorrow '04
Runaway Jury '03
Undefeated '03
City by the Sea '02
Empire '02
Showtime '02
Bait '00
Bringing Out the Dead '99
The Insider '99
The Negotiator '98
Bad Boys '95
City Hall '96
Hangin' with the Homeboys '91

Bruce Seton (1909-69)
Gorgo '61
The Blue Lamp '49
Love from a Stranger '37
Demon Barber of Fleet Street '36

Gerard Sety (1922-98)
Van Gogh '91

Joan Severance (1958-)
Cause of Death '00
The Last Seduction 2 '96
Matter of Trust '98
In Dark Places '97
Black Scorpion 2: Ground Zero '96
Profile for Murder '96
Black Scorpion '95
Dangerous Indiscretion '94
Hard Evidence '94
Payback '94
Lake Consequence '92
Red Shoe Diaries 2: Double Dare '92
Almost Pregnant '91
Another Pair of Aces: Three of a Kind '91
Illicit Behavior '91
Write to Kill '91
Bird on a Wire '90
No Holds Barred '89
See No Evil, Hear No Evil '89

Julieta Serrano (1933-)
Caresses '97
Tie Me Up! Tie Me Down! '90
Women on the Verge of a Nervous Breakdown '88
Matador '86
Dark Habits '84

Chloe Sevigny (1975-)
Zodiac '07
Broken Flowers '05
Manderlay '05
Melinda and Melinda '05
Mrs. Harris '05
The Brown Bunny '03
Dogville '03
Party Monster '03
Shattered Glass '03
Demonlover '02
If These Walls Could Talk 2 '00
American Psycho '00
Boys Don't Cry '99
Julien Donkey-boy '99
A Map of the World '99
The Last Days of Disco '98
Palmetto '98

Corey Sevier (1984-)
Summer of the Monkeys '98
Edge of Madness '02

William Severn (1938-83)
The Heat's On '43
Miracle of Morgan's Creek '44

Matthew Settle (1969-)
Beneath '07
Blue Smoke '07
The Celestine Prophecy '06
U-571 '00

Ed Setrakian (1928-)
Little Dorrit, Film 1: Nobody's Fault '88
Little Dorrit, Film 2: Little Dorrit's Story '88

Roshan Seth (1942-)
Proof '05
Such a Long Journey '98
Solitaire for 2 '94
Street Fighter '94
The Buddha of Suburbia '93
Mississippi Masala '92
Stalin '92
London Kills Me '91
Not Without My Daughter '90
Mountains of the Moon '90
My Beautiful Laundrette '85
Gandhi '82

Gummo '97
Tree's Lounge '96
Kids '95

Carmen Sevilla (1930-)
The Boldest Job in the West '71
Pantaloons '57

Billie Seward (1912-82)
The Man from Gun Town '36
Branded a Coward '35
The Revenge Rider '35

George Sewell
Running Blind '78
Get Carter '71

Rufus Sewell (1967-)
John Adams '08
Amazing Grace '06
The Holiday '06
The Illusionist '06
Paris, je t'aime '06
Tristan & Isolde '05
The Legend of Zorro '05
Helen of Troy '03
Extreme Ops '01
A Knight's Tale '01
She Creature '01
Arabian Nights '00
Bless the Child '00
In a Savage Land '99
Dangerous Beauty '98
Illuminata '98
Uncorked '98
The Very Thought of You '98
Dark City '97
Hamlet '96
Carrington '95
Victory '95
Cold Comfort Farm '94
A Man of No Importance '94
Middlemarch '93
Twenty-One '91

Andrzej Seweryn (1946-)
Zemsta '02
Lucie Aubrac '97
Genealogies of a Crime '97
Schindler's List '93
The Conductor '80
Without Anesthesia '78
Land of Promise '74

Brendan Sexton, III (1980-)
Love, Ludlow '05
This Revolution '05
Black Hawk Down '01
Session 9 '01
Boys Don't Cry '99
Desert Blue '98
Pecker '98
Spark '98
Hurricane Streets '96
Welcome to the Dollhouse '95

Brent Sexton
Flightplan '05
Radio '03

Amanda Seyfried (1985-)
Mamma Mia! '08
Alpha Dog '06
American Gun '05
Nine Lives '04
Mean Girls '04

Athene Seyler (1889-1990)
Curse of the Demon '57
The Franchise Affair '52
Sailing Along '38
Non-Stop New York '37
Private Life of Don Juan '34

Anne Seymour (1909-88)
Gemini Affair '74
Good Neighbor Sam '64
All the King's Men '49

Cara Seymour
The Savages '07
The Notorious Bettie Page '06
Birth '04
Evergreen '04
Hotel Rwanda '04
Adaptation '02
Gangs of New York '02
American Psycho '00
Dancer in the Dark '99
A Good Baby '99

Carolyn Seymour (1947-)
Red Shoe Diaries: Swimming Naked '00
The Break '97
Red Shoe Diaries: Strip Poker '96

Dan Seymour (1915-93)
Return of the Fly '59
Abbott and Costello Meet the Mummy '55
Key Largo '48
Hard-Boiled Mahoney '47
A Night in Casablanca '46
To Have & Have Not '44

Jane Seymour (1951-)
Blind Dating '06
Wedding Crashers '05
Quest for Camelot '98 (V)
Heidi '93
Praying Mantis '93
Are You Lonesome Tonight '92
Sunstroke '92
Matters of the Heart '90
The Tunnel '89
War & Remembrance: The Final Chapter '89
Jack the Ripper '88
Onassis '88
War & Remembrance '88
The Woman He Loved '88
Head Office '86
Lassiter '84
The Haunting Passion '83
Jamaica Inn '82
The Scarlet Pimpernel '82
East of Eden '80
Oh, Heavenly Dog! '80
Somewhere in Time '80
Battlestar Galactica '78
The Four Feathers '78
Killer on Board '77
Sinbad and the Eye of the Tiger '77
The Story of David '76
Live and Let Die '73
The Strauss Family '73
Young Winston '72
The Only Way '70
Oh! What a Lovely War '69

Jeff Seymour
Wedding Bell Blues '96
Rave Review '95

Ralph Seymour
Rain Man '88
Empire of the Sun '87
Killer Party '86
Fletch '85
Meatballs 2 '84

Delphine Seyrig (1932-90)
Window Shopping '86
Grain of Sand '84
I Sent a Letter to My Love '81
The Black Windmill '74
A Doll's House '73
The Discreet Charm of the Bourgeoisie '72
Daughters of Darkness '71
Peau D'Ane '71
Donkey Skin '70
The Milky Way '68
Stolen Kisses '68
Accident 67
Muriel '63
Last Year at Marienbad '61

Serif Sezer (1943-)
Steam: A Turkish Bath '96
Yol '82

Ted Shackleford (1946-)
Miracle Dogs '03
The Spider and the Fly '94
Dying to Remember '93
Baby of the Bride '91
Sweet Revenge '87
Summer Fantasy '84

Glenn Shadix (1952-)
The Empty Mirror '99
Red Dirt '99
Chairman of the Board '97
Dunston Checks in '95
Dark Side of Genius '94
Love Affair '94
My Summer Story '94
Demolition Man '93
The Nightmare before Christmas '93 (V)
Sleepwalkers '92
Bingo '91
Nightlife '90
The Applegates '89
Heathers '89
Beetlejuice '88

Robert (Bobby Ray) Shafer (1958-)
Monster Man '03
Psycho Cop 2 '94
A Brilliant Disguise '93
Psycho Cop '88

Paul Shaffer (1949-)
Blues Brothers 2000 '98
Hercules '97 (V)
The Return of Spinal Tap '92
Light Years '88 (V)
This Is Spinal Tap '84
Mr. Mike's Mondo Video '79

Jamal Shah
K2: The Ultimate High '92
Traffik '90

Naseeruddin Shah (1950-)
The Great New Wonderful '06
The League of Extraordinary Gentlemen '03
Monsoon Wedding '01
Such a Long Journey '98
Spices '86

Darren Shahlavi (1972-)
Alone in the Dark '05
Bloodmoon '97

Victoria Shalet
Haunted '95
The Maid '90

Tony Shalhoub (1953-)
Cars '06 (V)
The Great New Wonderful '06
Against the Ropes '04
The Last Shot '04
Spy Kids 3-D: Game Over '03
Impostor '02
Life or Something Like It '02
Men in Black 2 '02
The Man Who Wasn't There '01
Spy Kids '01
13 Ghosts '01
Galaxy Quest '99
That Championship Season '99
The Tic Code '99
A Civil Action '98
The Imposters '98
Paulie '98
Primary Colors '98
The Siege '98
Gattaca '97
A Life Less Ordinary '97
Men in Black '97
Big Night '95
I.Q. '94
Honeymoon in Vegas '92
Barton Fink '91
Quick Change '90

Chuck Shamata
The Sentinel '06
Whitewash: The Clarence Brandley Story '02
Snap Decision '01
The Thin Blue Lie '00
Princes in Exile '90
Unfinished Business '89
Night Friend '87
Mafia Princess '86
Joshua Then and Now '85
Death Weekend '76

Jeremy Shamos
The Great New Wonderful '06
Kid Colter '85

Garry Shandling (1949-)
Over the Hedge '06 (V)
Trust the Man '06
Town and Country '01
What Planet Are You From? '00
Dr. Dolittle '98 (V)
Hurlyburly '98
Love Affair '94
Mixed Nuts '94
The Night We Never Met '93
Mother Goose Rock 'n' Rhyme '90

Michael Shaner
Traveller '96
The Expert '95
Bloodfist '89
Crime Zone '88

Amelia Shankley (1972-)
The Little Princess '87
Dreamchild '85

Don Shanks (1950-)
3 Ninjas Knuckle Up '95
The Legend of Wolf Mountain '92
Spirit of the Eagle '90
Halloween 5: The Revenge of Michael Myers '89
The Last of the Mohicans '85
Mountain Man '77
Life & Times of Grizzly Adams '74

Michael Shanks (1970-)
Stargate: The Ark of Truth '08
Megasnake '07
Suspicious River '00
Escape from Mars '99
Terror Train '80

Al Shannon
Out of the Rain '90
The Drifter '88

Fay Shannon
See Fay McKenzie

Frank Shannon (1874-1959)
Flash Gordon Conquers the Universe '40
Flash Gordon: Rocketship '40

Harry Shannon (1890-1964)
Summer and Smoke '61
Man or Gun '58
Written on the Wind '56
Phantom Stallion '54
Cow Town '50
The Jackie Robinson Story '50
The Underworld Story '50
Fighting Father Dunne '48
The Red House '47
The Yellow Rose of Texas '44
Idaho '43
Song of Texas '43
Citizen Kane '41

Michael Shannon (1974-)
Before the Devil Knows You're Dead '07
Lucky You '07
Bug '06
Let's Go to Prison '06
World Trade Center '06
Dead Birds '04
The Woodsman '04
Bad Boys 2 '03
Grand Theft Parsons '03
8 Mile '02
High Crimes '02
Kangaroo Jack '02
Pearl Harbor '01
Vanilla Sky '01
Chicago Cab '98

Michael J. Shannon (1943-)
Detonator 2: Night Watch '95
We'll Meet Again '82
Future Cop '76

Molly Shannon (1964-)
Snow Buddies '08
Evan Almighty '07
Year of the Dog '07
Gray Matters '06
Little Man '06
Marie Antoinette '06
Scary Movie 4 '06
Talladega Nights: The Ballad of Ricky Bobby '06
The Twelve Days of Christmas Eve '04
American Splendor '03
Good Boy! '03
My Boss's Daughter '03
Osmosis Jones '01
Serendipity '01
Wet Hot American Summer '01
Dr. Seuss' How the Grinch Stole Christmas '00
My 5 Wives '00
Never Been Kissed '99
Superstar '99
Analyze This '98
A Night at the Roxbury '98
Dinner and Driving '97
The Phantom of the Opera '89

Peggy Shannon (1910-41)
The Case of the Lucky Legs '35
Deluge '33
False Faces '32
Touchdown '31

Polly Shannon (1973-)
Jesse Stone: Night Passage '06
Jesse Stone: Stone Cold '05
Men with Brooms '02
The Triangle '01
The Girl Next Door '98
A Young Connecticut Yankee in King Arthur's Court '95

Vicellous Shannon (1981-)
Animal 2 '07
Annapolis '06
Hart's War '02
Dancing in September '00
Freedom Song '00
The Hurricane '99

Omar Sharif (1932-)
10,000 B.C. '08 (N)
The Crown Prince '06
Hidalgo '04
Monsieur Ibrahim '03
The 13th Warrior '99
Heaven Before I Die '96
Catherine the Great '95
Gulliver's Travels '95
Lie Down with Lions '94
Beyond Justice '92
Grand Larceny '92
Mrs. 'Arris Goes to Paris '92
The Possessed '88
Anastasia: The Mystery of Anna '86
Harem '86
Peter the Great '86
The Far Pavilions '84
Top Secret! '84
Green Ice '81
The Baltimore Bullet '80
Oh, Heavenly Dog! '80
Pleasure Palace '80
Ashanti, Land of No Mercy '79
S*H*E '79
Sidney Sheldon's Bloodline '79
Crime & Passion '75
Funny Lady '75
Juggernaut '74
The Tamarind Seed '74
The Last Valley '71
The Horsemen '70
MacKenna's Gold '69
Funny Girl '68
Mayerling '68
Night of the Generals '67
Doctor Zhivago '65
Behold a Pale Horse '64
The Fall of the Roman Empire '64
Lawrence of Arabia '62

David Shark
See David "Shark" Fralick

Ray Sharkey (1953-93)
Urban Crossfire '94
Cop and a Half '93
Caged Fear '92
Chrome Soldiers '92
Round Trip to Heaven '92
Zebrahead '92
Relentless 2: Dead On '91
The Rain Killer '90
The Take '90
Act of Piracy '89
Capone '89
The Neon Empire '89
Scenes from the Class Struggle in Beverly Hills '89
Wired '89
P.I. Private Investigations '87
Private Investigations '87
No Mercy '86
Wise Guys '86
Behind Enemy Lines '85
Hellhole '85
Body Rock '84
Dubeat-E-O '84
Regina '83
Some Kind of Hero '82
Heart Beat '80
Idolmaker '80
Willie & Phil '80
Who'll Stop the Rain? '78

John Sharp (1920-92)
Misunderstood '87
The Fiendish Plot of Dr. Fu Manchu '80

Lesley Sharp
Carrie's War '04
The Full Monty '96
Priest '94
Naked '93
The Rachel Papers '89
Rita, Sue & Bob Too '87

Lesley Sharp (1964-)
From Hell '01
Great Expectations '99
Close My Eyes '91

Thom Sharp
Heartbreak Ridge '86
Stoogemania '85

Timm Sharp
Americano '05
King of the Ants '03
Stark Raving Mad '02

Albert Sharpe (1885-1970)
Darby O'Gill & the Little People '59
Brigadoon '54
Up in Central Park '48

Cornelia Sharpe (1947-)
Venom '82
S*H*E '79

The Arab Conspiracy 76
The Reincarnation of Peter Proud 75
Bustin' 74
Serpico 73

David Sharpe (1911-79)
Colorado Serenade '46
Haunted Ranch '43
Two-Fisted Justice '43
Trail Riders '42
Silver Stallion '41
Texas to Bataan '42
Gun Girls '36
Star Rider '36
The Adventurous Knights '35
Roaring Roads '35
Social Error '35

Melanie Shatner (1964-)

William Shatner (1931-)
Over the Hedge '06 (V)
The Wild '06 (V)
Miss Congeniality 2: Armed and Fabulous '05
Dodgeball: A True Underdog Story '04
American Psycho 2: All American Girl '02
A Shot or Be Shot '02
Showtime '02
Osmosis Jones '01 (V)
Miss Congeniality '00
Free Enterprise '98
Land of the Free '98
Star Trek: Generations '94
TekWar '94
National Lampoon's Loaded Weapon 1 '93
Bill & Ted's Bogus Journey '91
Secrets of a Married Man '84
Star Trek 6: The Undiscovered Country '91
Star Trek 5: The Final Frontier '89
Broken Angel '88
Star Trek 4: The Voyage Home '86
Secrets of a Married Man '84
Star Trek 3: The Search for Spock '84
Airplane 2: The Sequel '82
Star Trek 2: The Wrath of Khan '82
Visiting Hours '82
The Babysitter '80
The Kidnapping of the President '80
Riel '79
Star Trek: The Motion Picture '79
Third Walker '79
The Bastard '78
The Crash of Flight 401 '78
Little Women '78
Kingdom of the Spiders '77
The People '77
Pioneer Woman '73
The Andersonville Trial '70
White Comanche '67
Incubus '65
Judgment at Nuremberg '61
Shane '61
The Brothers Karamazov '58

Shari Shattuck (1960-)
Body Chemistry 3: Point of Seduction '93
Dead On '93
Out for Blood '93
Mad About You '90
Arena '89
The Spring '89
Desert Warrior '88
Tainted '88
The Uninvited '88
Hot Child in the City '87
Number One with a Bullet '87

Grant Shaud (1960-)
From the Earth to the Moon '93

Charles Shaughnessy (1955-)
Soldiers of Change '06
Kids in America '05
The King of the Roaring 20s: The Story of Arnold Rothstein '61
The Adventures of Huckleberry Finn '60
Gunman's Walk '58
Designing Woman '57
Jailhouse Rock '57
Conquest of Space '55
From Here to Eternity '53
Last of the Comanches '52

Mickey Shaughnessy (1920-85)

Helen Shaver (1952-)
Numb '07
Tremors 3: Back to Perfection '01
Common Ground '00
Morning Glory '93
Murder So Sweet '93
That Night '93
Trial and Error '92
Zebrahead '92
Innocent Victim '90
Pair of Aces '90
Open Season '95
The Land Before Time '88
(V)
The Believers '87
The Color of Money '86
Desert Hearts '86
Lost '86
The Park is Mine '85
Best Defense '84
Coming Out Alive '84
Harry Tracy '83
The Osterman Weekend '83
Gas '81
Off Your Rocker '80
The Amityville Horror '79
High Ballin' '78
In Praise of Older Women '78
Outrageous! '77
Who Has Seen the Wind? '77

Anabel Shaw (1923-)
To Hell and Back '55
Gun Crazy '49
Shock! '46

Bill Shaw
Total Reality '97
Ghostriders '87

Bobbi Shaw (1942-)
Beach Blanket Bingo '65
How to Stuff a Wild Bikini '65
Ski Party '65
Pajama Party '64

C. Montague Shaw (1884-1968)
'40
The Rains Came '39
Zorro's Fighting Legion '39
Square Shoulders '29

Crystal Shaw
Laser Moon '92
Hardbodies '84

Fiona Shaw (1958-)
Catch and Release '07
Fracture '07
Harry Potter and the Order of the Phoenix '07
The Black Dahlia '06
Close Your Eyes '02
Harry Potter and the Chamber of Secrets '02
Harry Potter and the Sorcerer's Stone '01
The Seventh Stream '01
The Triumph of Love '01
The Last September '99
The Avengers '98
The Butcher Boy '97
Jane Eyre '96
Leo Tolstoy's Anna Karenina '96
Persuasion '95
Mania's Child '93
Super Mario Bros. '93
Undercover Blues '93
London Kills Me '91
Mountains of the Moon '90
Three Men and a Little Lady '90
My Left Foot '89

Martin Shaw (1945-)
P.D. James: The Murder Room '04
The Last Place on Earth '85
The Hound of the Baskervilles '83
Golden Voyage of Sinbad '73
Macbeth '71

Oscar Shaw (1887-1967)
The Cocoanuts '29

Victoria Shaw (1935-88)
Alvarez Kelly '66
The Eddy Duchin Story '56

Vinessa Shaw (1976-)
3:10 to Yuma '07
The Hills Have Eyes '06
40 Days and 40 Nights '02
Corky Romano '01
The '70s '00
The Weight of Water '00
Eyes Wide Shut '99
Coyote Summer '96
Fallen Angels 2 '93
Hocus Pocus '93
Ladybugs '92

Susan Shaw (1929-78)
Blonde Blackmailer '53
Fire Maidens from Outer Space '56
The Woman in Question '50

Sebastian Shaw (1905-94)
High Season '88
Return of the Jedi '83
Spy in Black '39

Sandie Shaw (1947-)
Absolute Beginners '86

Stan Shaw (1952-)
Daylight '96
Snake Eyes '98
Fear '90
Busted Up '86
The Gladiator '86
Tough Enough '83
Rocky '79
Roots: The Next Generation '79
The Boys in Company C '77
Bingo Long Traveling All-Stars & Motor Kings '76
TNT Jackson '75

Paula Shaw (1941-)
Chupacabra Terror '05
Prehistoric Women '50

Reta Shaw (1912-82)
The Ghost and Mr. Chicken '66

Robert Shaw (1927-78)
Avalanche Express '79
Force 10 from Navarone '78
Black Sunday '77
The Deep '77
Robin and Marian '76
Swashbuckler '76
Jaws '75
The Taking of Pelham One Two Three '74
The Sting '73
Diamonds '73
A Town Called Hell '72
Young Winston '72
Battle of Britain '69
A Man for All Seasons '66
Battle of the Bulge '65
From Russia with Love '63
The Squeaker '37

Dick Shawn (1929-87)
Rented Lips '88
Beer '85
Maid to Order '87
Angel '84
The Apartment '60
Some Like It Hot '59

Joan Shawlee (1929-87)
The Pajama Game '57
All Mine to Give '56
Picnic '55
The King on Main Street '25

Alia Shawkat (1984-)
Deck the Halls '06
Rebound '05
The Trial of Old Drum '00

Wallace Shawn (1943-)
Happily N'Ever After '07 (V)
Chicken Little '05 (V)
Melinda and Melinda '05
Disney's Teacher's Pet '04
(V)
The Incredibles '04 (V)
Duplex '03
The Haunted Mansion '03
Monte Walsh '03
Love Thy Neighbor '02
Mr. St. Nick '02
Personal Velocity: Three Portraits '02
Blonde '01
The Curse of the Jade Scorpion '01
The Prime Gig '00
Toy Story 2 '99 (V)
Noah '98
Critical Care '97
Just Write '97
House Arrest '96
Just Like Dad '95
Vegas Vacation '96
All Dogs Go to Heaven 2 '95 (V)
Clueless '95
Toy Story '95 (V)
The Wife '95
The Magic Bubble '93
The Double O Kid '92
Mom and Dad Save the World '92
Nickel & Dime '92
Shadows and Fog '92
Scenes from the Class Struggle in Beverly Hills '89
Vanya on 42nd Street '94
The Cemetery Club '93
She's Out of Control '89
We're No Angels '89
The Moderns '88
The Bedroom Window '87
Nice Girls Don't Explode '87
Prick Up Your Ears '87
The Princess Bride '87
Radio Days '87
Heaven Help Us '85
The Bostonians '84
Crackers '84
The Hotel New Hampshire '84
Micki & Maude '84
Strong Medicine '84
Deal of the Century '83
Strange Invaders '83
First Time '82
A Little Sex '82
My Dinner with Andre '81
Simon '80
Manhattan '79
Starting Over '79
All That Jazz '79

Michele Shay
Beloved '98

Lin Shaye (1944-)
Snakes on a Plane '06
A Cinderella Story '04
Drop Dead Sexy '05
The Hillside Strangler '04
Boat Trip '03
Dumb and Dumberer: When Harry Met Lloyd '03
Detroit Rock City '99
There's Something about Mary '98

Al Shearer (1977-)
San Francisco '36
Glory Road '06
How High '01
For Your Consideration '06
(V)
Chicken Little '05 (V)
A Mighty Wind '03
Dick '99
EDtv '99
Godzilla '98
Small Soldiers '98 (V)

Harry Shearer (1943-)
The Simpsons Movie '07
For Your Consideration '06
A Mighty Wind '03
Dick '99
EDtv '99
Godzilla '98
Small Soldiers '98 (V)

Katt Shea (1957-)
Barbarian Queen '85
Devastator '85
Hollywood Hot Tubs '84
Preppies '82

Al Shean (1868-1949)
Ziegfeld Girl '41
The Great Waltz '38
It Could Happen to You '37
Tim Tyler's Luck '37

Gloria Shea (1910-95)
Last Days of Pompeii '35
Demon for Trouble '34

John Shea (1948-)
Southie '98
Sebastian Cole '99
Southie '98
The Adventures of Sebastian Cole '98
A New Life '88
Light Years '88 (V)
Unsettled Land '88
Stealing Home '88
Backstreet Justice '93
Freejack '92
Honey, I Blew Up the Kid '92
Ladykiller '92
Magic Moments '89
Small Sacrifices '89
Missing '82
Hussy '80
Nativity '78

Elizabeth She
Howling 5: The Rebirth '89
The Howling: New Moon Rising '95

Robert Shayne (1900-92)
Teenage Caveman '58
The Giant Claw '57
The Indestructible Man '56
Marshal of Cedar Rock '53
The Spirit of West Point '47
Welcome Stranger '47
Behind the Mask '46
Christmas in Connecticut '45
Rhapsody in Blue '45
The Insurgents '06
The Adventures of Sebastian Cole '98
Demon for Trouble '34
The Dude Bandit '33
The Fiddlin' Buckaroo '33
Phantom of the Air '33

Skyler Shaye
Bratz '07
Superbabies: Baby Geniuses 2 '04

Konstantin Shayne (1888-1974)
Song of Love '47
The Stranger '46
The Seventh Cross '44
Five Graves to Cairo '43

Tamara Shayne (1897-1983)
The Jolson Story '46
Somewhere I'll Find You '42

Wallace Shawn (1943-)
World '63
It's a Mad, Mad, Mad, Mad World '63

Robert Shayne (1900-92)

Sebastian Shaw (1905-94)
Mysterious Doctor Satan '40
Thunder Birds '42
A Midsummer Night's Dream '68

Skyler Shaye

Robert Shayne (1900-92)
Young Warriors '83
Sigmund Freud '84
Kingpin '96
Trading Favors '97
The Stranger '46
Dumb & Dumber '94
Brain Smasher... A Love Story '93

Anabel Shaw (1923-)

The Emperor's New Clothes '84
The Secret Diary of Sigmund Freud '84
Young Warriors '83
Goodbye Cruel World '82
Love at First Bite '79
Evil Roy Slade '71
The Happy Ending '69
The Producers '68
What Did You Do in the War, Daddy? '66

- Almost Heroes '97 (V)
- Little Giants '94
- A League of Their Own '92 (V)
- The Return of Spinal Tap '92
- The Fisher King '91
- Pure Luck '91
- Blood & Concrete: A Love Story '90
- Plain Clothes '88
- Portrait of a White Marriage '88
- This Is Spinal Tap '84
- The Right Stuff '83
- One Trick Pony '80
- Prime Time '77

Moira Shearer (1926-2006)
- Black Tights '60
- Peeping Tom '60
- The Tales of Hoffmann '51
- The Red Shoes '48

Norma Shearer (1900-83)
- Idiot's Delight '39
- The Women '39
- Marie Antoinette '38
- Romeo and Juliet '36
- The Barretts of Wimpole Street '34
- Riptide '34
- Smilin' Through '33
- Strange Interlude '32
- A Free Soul '31
- Private Lives '31
- The Divorcee '30
- The Student Prince in Old Heidelberg '27
- He Who Gets Slapped '24

Alan Shearman (1940-)
- Mother Teresa: In the Name of God's Poor '97
- Stoogemania '85
- Bullshot '83

Ally Sheedy (1962-)
- Day Zero '07
- The Veteran '06
- Shooting Livien '05
- Shelter Island '03
- I'll Take You There '99
- Sugar Town '99
- The Fury Within '98
- High Art '98
- Buried Alive 2 '97
- Highball '97
- Amnesia '96
- One Night Stand '95
- The Tin Soldier '95
- The Haunting of Seacliff Inn '94
- Parallel Lives '94
- Chantilly Lace '93
- Man's Best Friend '93
- The Pickle '93
- Red Shoe Diaries 4: Auto Erotica '93
- Tattle Tale '92
- Only the Lonely '91
- Betsy's Wedding '90
- Fear '90
- The Lost Capone '90
- The Heart of Dixie '89
- Maid to Order '87
- We Are the Children '87
- Blue City '86
- Short Circuit '86
- The Breakfast Club '85
- St. Elmo's Fire '85
- Twice in a Lifetime '85
- Oxford Blues '84
- Bad Boys '83
- WarGames '83
- The Best Little Girl in the World '81

Gladys Sheehan
- Hear My Song '91
- Rawhead Rex '87

Charlie Sheen (1965-)
- Scary Movie 4 '06
- The Big Bounce '04
- Scary Movie 3 '03
- Good Advice '01
- Lisa Picard Is Famous '01
- Rated X '00
- Being John Malkovich '99
- Free Money '99
- No Code of Conduct '98
- Postmortem '98
- Under Pressure '97
- Money Talks '97
- Sisters '97 (V)
- The Arrival '96
- The Shadow Conspiracy '96
- All Dogs Go to Heaven 2 '95 (V)
- Major League 2 '94
- Terminal Velocity '94
- The Chase '94
- Deadfall '93
- Hot Shots! Part Deux '93
- National Lampoon's Loaded Weapon 1 '93
- The Three Musketeers '93
- Beyond the Law '92
- Hot Shots! '91
- Men at Work '90
- Navy SEALS '90
- The Rookie '90
- Backtrack '89
- Cadence '89
- Courage Mountain '89
- Major League '89
- Tale of Two Sisters '89 (N)
- Eight Men Out '88
- Never on Tuesday '88
- Young Guns '88
- No Man's Land '87
- Three for the Road '87
- Wall Street '87
- The Wraith '87
- Ferris Bueller's Day Off '86
- Lucas '86
- Platoon '86
- The Boys Next Door '85
- Red Dawn '84
- Silence of the Heart '84

Martin Sheen (1940-)
- Talk to Me '07
- Bobby '06
- Bordertown '06
- The Departed '06
- Catch Me If You Can '02
- O '01
- D.R.E.A.M. Team '99
- Lost and Found '99
- Storm Tracker '99
- A Texas Funeral '99
- Thrill Seekers '99
- Gunfighter '98
- Monument Ave. '98
- No Code of Conduct '98
- A Stranger in the Kingdom '98
- Hostile Waters '97
- One of Her Own '97
- Spawn '97
- Truth or Consequences, N.M. '97
- Entertaining Angels: The Dorothy Day Story '96
- The War at Home '96
- The American President '95
- Born Wild '95
- The Break '95
- Captain Nuke and the Bomber Boys '95
- Dillinger and Capone '95
- Boca '94
- Fortunes of War '94
- Gospa '94
- Roswell: The U.F.O. Cover-Up '94
- Gettysburg '93
- The Ghost Brigade '93
- Hear No Evil '93
- Hot Shots! Part Deux '93
- Queen '93
- When the Bough Breaks '93
- Hearts of Darkness: A Filmmaker's Apocalypse '91
- Original Intent '91
- The Maid '90
- Beverly Hills Brats '89
- Beyond the Stars '89
- Cadence '89
- Cold Front '89
- Nightbreaker '89
- Da '88
- Judgment in Berlin '88
- The Believers '87
- Conspiracy: The Trial of the Chicago Eight '87
- Siesta '87
- Wall Street '87
- News at Eleven '86
- Samaritan: The Mitch Snyder Story '86
- Shattered Spirits '86
- Consenting Adult '85
- Fourth Wise Man '85
- Out of the Darkness '85
- Firestarter '84
- The Guardian '84
- Dead Zone '83
- Kennedy '83
- Loophole '83
- Man, Woman & Child '83
- Enigma '82
- Gandhi '82
- In the Custody of Strangers '82
- That Championship Season '82
- The Final Countdown '80
- Apocalypse Now '79
- Blind Ambition '79
- Eagle's Wing '79
- The Cassandra Crossing '76
- The Little Girl Who Lives down the Lane '76
- Sweet Hostage '75
- Badlands '74
- The Execution of Private Slovik '74
- Legend of Earl Durand '74
- Missiles of October '74
- Catholics '73
- When the Line Goes Through '73
- Pursuit '72
- Rage '72
- Where the Eagle Flies '72
- No Drums, No Bugles '71
- The Andersonville Trial '70
- Catch-22 '70
- The Incident '67
- The Subject Was Roses '68

Michael Sheen (1969-)
- Music Within '07
- Blood Diamond '06
- The Queen '06
- Kingdom of Heaven '05
- Underworld: Evolution '05
- Laws of Attraction '04
- Bright Young Things '03
- Timeline '03
- Underworld '03
- Wilde '97

Chad Sheets (1972-)
- Lone Star Kid '88
- Dirt Bike Kid '86

Craig Sheffer (1960-)
- Love Lies Bleeding '07
- The Second Front '05
- Dracula 2: Ascension '03
- Maze '01
- Deep Core '00
- Hellraiser 5: Inferno '00
- Turbulence 3: Heavy Metal '00
- Turbulence 2: Fear of Flying '99
- Executive Power '98
- The Fall '98
- Shadow of Doubt '98
- Double Take '97
- Flypaper '97
- Bliss '96
- Head Above Water '96
- Bloodknot '95
- The Grave '95
- In Pursuit of Honor '95
- The Road Killers '95
- The Desperate Trail '94
- Sleep with Me '94
- Fire in the Sky '93
- Fire on the Amazon '93
- The Program '93
- A River Runs Through It '92
- Blue Desert '91
- Eye of the Storm '91
- Instant Karma '90
- Nightbreed '90
- Babycakes '89
- Split Decisions '88
- Some Kind of Wonderful '87
- Voyage of the Rock Aliens '87
- Fire with Fire '86
- That Was Then... This Is Now '85

Jeremy Sheffield (1966-)
- The Wedding Date '05
- Merlin '98

John(ny) Sheffield (1931-)
- Tarzan's New York Adventure '42
- Tarzan's Secret Treasure '41
- Tarzan Finds a Son '39

Maceo B. Sheffield (1897-1959)
- Look Out Sister '48
- Gang War '40
- Harlem on the Prairie '38

Reginald (Reggie, Reggy) Sheffield (1901-57)
- Second Chance '53
- Gunga Din '39
- The Lives of a Bengal Lancer '35

Gene Sheldon (1908-82)
- The Sign of Zorro '60
- Toby Tyler '59
- The Dolly Sisters '46

Tom Shell
- Dinosaur Island '93
- Teenage Exorcist '93
- Beverly Hills Vamp '88
- Surf Nazis Must Die '87

Stephen Shellen (1957-)
- Luscious '97
- Rude '96
- Dr. Jekyll and Ms. Hyde '95
- The Wrong Woman '95
- Deceptions 2: Edge of Deception '94
- Model by Day '94
- Stand Off '93

Barbara Shelley (1933-)
- The Dark Angel '91
- Madhouse Mansion '74
- Dracula, Prince of Darkness '66
- The Gorgon '64
- Village of the Damned '60
- Blood of the Vampire '58
- Cat Girl '57

Carol(e) Shelley (1939-)
- Bewitched '05
- Hercules '97 (V)
- Devlin '92
- Robin Hood '73 (V)
- The Aristocats '70 (V)
- The Odd Couple '68

Rachel Shelley (1969-)
- Gray Matters '06
- Lagaan: Once upon a Time in India '01
- B.U.S.T.E.D. '99
- Dead of Night '99
- Photographing Fairies '97

Adrienne Shelly (1966-2006)
- Waitress '07
- Factotum '06
- Revolution #9 '01
- Dead Dog '00
- I'll Take You There '99
- Wrestling with Alligators '98
- Grind '96
- Sudden Manhattan '96
- The Road Killers '95
- Sleep with Me '94
- Sleeping with Strangers '94
- Teresa's Tattoo '94
- Hexed '93
- Hold Me, Thrill Me, Kiss Me '93
- Big Girls Don't Cry... They Get Over '92
- Trust '91
- The Unbelievable Truth '90

Deborah Shelton (1948-)
- Desire '95
- Plughead Rewired: Circuitry Man 2 '94
- Silk Degrees '94
- Sins of the Night '93
- Blind Vision '91
- Hunk '87
- Perfect Victims '87
- Body Double '84

John Shelton (1917-72)
- Mysterious Island of Beautiful Women '79
- Sins of Jezebel '54
- The Time of Their Lives '46
- Ghost City '32

Joy Shelton (1922-2000)
- Impulse '55
- Norman Conquest 53
- Uneasy Terms 48

Maria Shelton
- Escape to Paradise '39
- Stand-In '37

Marley Shelton (1974-)
- Death Proof '07
- Planet Terror '07
- American Dreamz '06
- The Last Kiss '06
- Don't Come Knocking '05
- Sin City '05
- Dallas 362 '03
- Grand Theft Parsons '03
- Uptown Girls '03
- Just a Kiss '02
- Bubble Boy '01
- On the Borderline '01
- Sugar & Spice '01
- Valentine '01
- The Bachelor '99
- Never Been Kissed '99
- Pleasantville '98
- Too Smooth '98
- Lured Innocence '97
- Trojan War '97
- Warriors of Virtue '97
- The Sandlot '93
- Grand Canyon '91

Reid Shelton (1925-97)
- First & Ten: The Team Scores Again '85
- Breakin' Through '84

Sloane Shelton (1934-)
- Wrestling with Alligators '98
- Orpheus Descending '91

Parry Shen (1979-)
- The Hazing '04
- Better Luck Tomorrow '02
- The New Guy '02
- Shrieker '97

Paul Shenar (1936-89)
- The Big Blue '88
- The Bedroom Window '87
- Best Seller '87
- Man on Fire '87
- Raw Deal '86
- Brass '85
- Dream Lover '85
- Deadly Force '83
- Scarface '83

Ben Shenkman (1968-)
- Just like Heaven '05
- Must Love Dogs '05
- Angels in America '03
- Roger Dodger '02
- Chasing Sleep '00
- Table One '00
- Pi '98

Dax Shepard (1975-)
- Baby Mama '08
- The Comebacks '07
- Employee of the Month '06
- Idiocracy '06
- Let's Go to Prison '06
- Zathura '05
- Without a Paddle '04

Elaine Shepard (1913-98)
- Seven Days Ashore '44
- Darkest Africa '36

Hilary Shepard (1961-)
- Avalanche '99
- Last Exit to Earth '96
- Scanner Cop '94
- Peacemaker '90

Jan Shepard (1933-)
- Attack of the Giant Leeches '59
- King Creole '58

Jewel Shepard (1962-)
- Caged Heat 2: Stripped of Freedom '94
- Scanners: The Showdown '94
- Educating Crystal '89
- Hollywood Hot Tubs 2: Scenes from the Goldmine '87
- Return of the Living Dead '85
- Hollywood Hot Tubs '84
- My Tutor '82

Patty (Patti) Shepard (1945-)
- The Stranger and the Gunfighter '76
- Crypt of the Living Dead 73
- Curse of the Devil 73
- Witches' Mountain 71
- Surprise Attack 70
- The Werewolf vs. the Vampire Woman 70
- Dracula vs. Frankenstein 69

Sam Shepard (1943-)
- The Accidental Husband '08
- The Assassination of Jesse James by the Coward Robert Ford '07
- Charlotte's Web '06 (V)
- The Return '06
- Don't Come Knocking '05
- Stealth '05
- The Notebook '04
- Leo '02
- Black Hawk Down '01
- Shot in the Heart '01
- Swordfish '01
- All the Pretty Horses '00
- Hamlet '00
- One Kill '00
- The Pledge '00
- Lily Dale '96
- The Good Old Boys '95
- Larry McMurtry's Streets of Laredo '95
- Safe Passage '94
- The Pelican Brief '93
- Thunderheart '92
- Bright Angel '91
- Defenseless '91
- Voyager '91
- Steel Magnolias '89
- Baby Boom '87
- Crimes of the Heart '86
- Fool for Love '86
- Country '84

(continued)
- The Right Stuff '83
- Frances '82
- Raggedy Man '81
- Resurrection '80
- Days of Heaven '78

Chaz Lamar Shepherd (1977-)
- The Temptations '98
- Set It Off '96

Cybill Shepherd (1950-)
- Due East '02
- The Last Word '95
- Married to It '93
- Once Upon a Crime '92
- Memphis '91
- Alice '90
- Texasville '90
- Which Way Home '90
- Chances Are '89
- The Long, Hot Summer '86
- Moonlighting '85
- Seduced '85
- Secrets of a Married Man '84
- The Return '80
- Americathon '79
- The Lady Vanishes '79
- A Guide for the Married Woman '78
- Silver Bears '78
- Special Delivery '76
- Taxi Driver '76
- Daisy Miller '74
- The Heartbreak Kid '72
- The Last Picture Show '71

Elizabeth Shepherd (1936-)
- Invitation to the Wedding '73
- The Tomb of Ligeia '64

Jack Shepherd (1940-)
- The Other Boleyn Girl '03
- Charlotte Gray '01
- Wonderland '99
- Lorna Doone '00
- The Escape '95
- Gettysburg '93
- Twenty-One '91
- No Escape '94
- Murderers Among Us: The Simon Wiesenthal Story '89
- Escape from Sobibor '87
- The Virgin Soldiers '69

John Shepherd
- Banzai Runner '86
- Thunder Run '86
- Friday the 13th, Part 5: A New Beginning '85

Simon Shepherd (1956-)
- Mr. Toad's Wild Ride '96
- Emily Brontë's Wuthering Heights '92
- Fire, Ice and Dynamite '91
- Murder on the Line One '90
- Henry V '89

Sherri Shepherd (1970-)
- Who's Your Caddy? '07
- Beauty Shop '05
- Guess Who '05

Steve John Shepherd (1973-)
- Layer Cake '05
- Me Without You '01
- Forgive and Forget '99
- Virtual Sexuality '99

Suzanne Shepherd
- A Dirty Shame '04
- The Jerky Boys '95
- Lolita '97
- Palookaville '95

W. Morgan Shepherd
- See William Morgan Sheppard

Michael Shepley (1907-61)
- Henry V '44
- The Demi-Paradise '43
- Housemaster '38
- A Shot in the Dark '33

Della Sheppard (1961-)
- Dead Boyz Can't Fly '93
- Animal Instincts '92
- Night Rhythms '92
- Secret Games '92
- Sins of Desire '92
- Mirror Images '91
- Roots of Evil '91
- Witchcraft 2: The Temptress '90

Mark Sheppard (1964-)
- Evil Eyes '04
- Megalodon '03
- Lost Voyage '01
- Out of the Cold '99
- In the Name of the Father '93

William Morgan Sheppard (1932-)
- Over Her Dead Body '08
- Transformers '07
- The Prestige '06
- Love's Long Journey '05
- Gods and Generals '03
- Goldrush: A Real Life Alaskan Adventure '98
- Elvira, Mistress of the Dark '88
- Lassiter '84
- The Keep '83
- Hawk the Slayer '81
- Sea Wolves '81
- Shogun '80

Paula Sheppard (1957-)
- Liquid Sky '83
- Alice Sweet Alice '76

Jamey Sheridan (1951-)
- Video Voyeur: The Susan Wilson Story '02
- Desert Saints '01
- Life as a House '01
- The Lost Child '00
- Luminous Motion '00
- The Cradle Will Rock '99
- Stephen King's The Stand '94
- A Stranger Among Us '92
- Whispers in the Dark '92
- All I Want for Christmas '91
- Talent for the Game '91
- Quick Change '90
- Stanley and Iris '90
- Jumpin' Jack Flash '86

Anthony Sher (1949-)
- The Miracle Maker: The Story of Jesus '00 (V)
- Shakespeare in Love '98
- Mrs. Brown '97
- Alive and Kicking '96
- Moll Flanders '96
- The Young Poisoner's Handbook '94
- Genghis Cohn '93
- Tartuffe '90
- Shadey '87

Jean Shepherd (1921-99)
- My Summer Story '94 (N)
- A Christmas Story '83 (V)

Margaret Sheridan (1926-82)
- One Minute to Zero '52
- The Thing '51

Jim Sheridan (1949-)
- '07

Nicolette Sheridan (1963-)
- Code Name: The Cleaner '07
- Possessed '05
- Karate Dog '04 (V)
- Spy Hard '96
- Beverly Hills Ninja '96
- Raw Nerve '99
- Dead Husbands '98
- Noises Off '92
- Deceptions '90

Brooke Shields (1965-)
- Bob the Butler '05
- Widows '02
- The Weekend '00
- The Bachelor '99
- Black and White '99
- Freeway '95
- The Seventh Floor '93
- Freaked '93
- Backstreet Dreams '90
- Speed Zone '88
- Brenda Starr '86
- The Muppets Take Manhattan '84
- Sahara '83
- Wet Gold '84
- Endless Love '81
- The Blue Lagoon '80
- Wanda Nevada '79
- King of the Gypsies '78
- Pretty Baby '78
- Tilt '78
- The Prince of Central Park '77
- Alice Sweet Alice '76

Maurice Sherbanee
- The Sure Thing '85

Ann Sheridan (1915-67)
- The Opposite Sex '56
- Appointment in Honduras '53
- Silver River '48
- Good Sam '48
- I Was a Male War Bride '49
- The Man Who Came to Dinner '41
- Kings Row '42
- George Washington Slept Here '42
- Torrid Zone '40
- They Drive by Night '40
- City for Conquest '40
- They Made Me a Criminal '39
- Dodge City '39
- Angels with Dirty Faces '38
- Letter of Introduction '38
- San Quentin '37
- Wine, Women and Horses '37
- The Black Legion '37
- The Fighting Westerner '35

Rade Sherbedgia
- See Rade Serbedzija

Bobby Sherman (1943-)
- Get Crazy '83
- He Is My Brother '75

Lowell Sherman (1885-1934)
- False Faces '32
- Three Broadway Girls '32
- What Price Hollywood? '32
- Bachelor Apartment '31
- The Royal Bed '31
- The Garden of Eden '28
- Monsieur Beaucaire '24
- Way Down East '20

J. Barney Sherry (1872-1944)
- The Bargain '15

Nicholas Shields
- Lost in the Barrens '91
- Princes in Exile '90

Dave Sheridan (1969-)
- Frank McKlusky, C.I. '02
- Bubble Boy '01
- Corky Romano '01
- Ghost World '01
- Scary Movie '00

Madeline Sherwood (1922-)
- Teachers '84
- Pendulum '69
- Sweet Bird of Youth '62
- Parrish '61

David Sherwood
- Curse of the Crystal Eye '93

Dinah Sheridan (1920-)
- Thirteenth Reunion '81
- The Railway Children '70
- Genevieve '53
- Blackout '50
- No Trace '50
- Calling Paul Temple '48
- Salute John Citizen '42

Robin Sherwood
- Love Butcher '82
- Tourist Trap '79

Sheetal Sheth
- Looking for Comedy in the Muslim World '06
- Dancing in Twilight '05

Vladek Sheybal (1923-92)
- The Wind and the Lion '75
- S*P*Y*S '74
- Scorpio '73
- The Boy Friend '71
- Women in Love '70

Arthur Shields (1896-1970)
- Enchanted Island '58
- The Daughter of Dr. Jekyll '57
- The River '51
- The Quiet Man '52
- She Wore a Yellow Ribbon '49
- Fighting Father Dunne '48
- The Fabulous Dorseys '47
- The Corn Is Green '45
- The Keys of the Kingdom '44
- The White Cliffs of Dover '44
- Gentleman Jim '42
- How Green Was My Valley '41
- Drums Along the Mohawk '39

George Shevtsov
- Japanese Story '03
- Love Serenade '96

Marion Shilling (1910-2004)
- Cavalcade of the West '36
- The Clutching Hand '36
- Gun Play '36
- A Shot in the Dark '35
- Stone of Silver Creek '35
- Thunder Over Texas '34
- Inside Information '34
- Man's Land '32
- Shop Angel '32

Shihomi
- See Etsuko (Sue) Shihomi

Etsuko (Sue) Shihomi (1956-)
- Shogun's Ninja '83
- The Bodyguard '76
- Sister Street Fighter '76
- Sister Street Fighter's Last Revenge '74

Sofia Shinas (1968-)
- Dilemma '97
- Hourglass '95
- The Crow '93

Eitaro Shindo (1899-1977)
- Up to His Neck '54
- The Crucified Lovers '54
- Sansho the Bailiff '54
- A Geisha '53
- Sisters of the Gion '36

Anthony Sherwood (1933-)
- Honey '03
- Closer and Closer '96
- Eddie and the Cruiser's 2: Eddie Lives! '89
- Terror Train '80

Joseph Shiloah
- The Lion of Africa '87
- Goodbye, New York '85
- Private Manoeuvres '83
- Noa at Seventeen '82

Shmuel Shilo
- Double Edge '92

Yoko Shimada
- White Badge '97
- White Badge '92
- My Champion '84
- Shogun '80

Hye-Jin Shim (1967-)
- Eagles Attack at Dawn '72

Armin Shimerman (1949-)
- The Hunted '94
- Arena '89
- Stoogemania '85

Joanna Shimkus (1943-)
- The Virgin and the Gypsy '70
- The Lost Man '69
- Boom! '68
- Six in Paris '68
- The Last Adventure '67

Misa Shimizu (1970-)
- The Eel '99
- Okoge '93

Sab Shimono (1943-)
- Robot Stories '03
- Life Tastes Good '99
- The Big Hit '98
- Paradise Road '97
- Waterworld '95
- The Shadow '94
- Teenage Mutant Ninja Turtles 3 '93
- Come See the Paradise '90
- Presumed Innocent '90
- Ashes '90
- The Wash '88
- Blind Date '87
- Gung Ho '85
- When Hell Was in Session '82

Yumi Shirakawa (1936-)
- H-Man '59
- The Mysterians '58
- Rodan '56

Talia Shire (1946-)
- Blue Smoke '07
- The Whole Shebang '01
- The Visit '00
- The Landlady '98
- Lured Innocence '97
- A River Runs Through It '92
- Cold Heaven '92
- For Richer, for Poorer '92
- Bed & Breakfast '92
- Chantilly Lace '93
- Rocky 5 '90
- The Godfather, Part 3 '90
- New York Stories '89
- Murderer's Keep '88

Toshi Shioya
- Mr. Baseball '92
- Prisoners of the Sun '91

Masayuki Shionoya
- Pulse '01
- Okoge '93

John Wesley Shipp (1955-)
- The Flash '90

Ful-On Shing (1955-)
- The Untold Story '93
- The Killer '89

Chen Shing
- The Two Great Cavaliers '73

Ronald Shiner (1903-66)
- Up to His Neck '54
- Thursday's Child '43
- Butler's Dilemma '43
- The Amsterdam Connection

David Shiner
- Man of the House '95
- Silent Tongue '92

James Shigeta (1933-)
- Brother '00
- Mulan '98 (V)
- Drive '96
- Space Marines '96
- Blood for Blood '95
- China City '91
- The Cage '91
- Die Hard '88
- Tomorrow's Child '82
- Enola Gay: The Men, the Mission, the Atomic Bomb '80
- Midway '76
- Paradise, Hawaiian Style '66
- Flower Drum Song '61
- Bridge to the Sun '61
- The Crimson Kimono '59

Takashi Shimura (1905-82)
- Ghidrah the Three Headed Monster '64
- Attack Squadron '63
- Gorath '62
- Mothra '61
- Yojimbo '61
- The Bad Sleep Well '60
- The Hidden Fortress '58
- The Mysterians '58
- Throne of Blood '57
- Godzilla, King of the Monsters '56
- I Live in Fear '55
- Seven Samurai '54
- Godzilla '54
- Sansho the Bailiff '54
- The Idiot '51
- Rashomon '51
- Scandal '50
- Stray Dog '49
- A Quiet Duel '49
- Drunken Angel '48
- The Men Who Tread on the Tiger's Tail '45

Talia Shire (continued)
Blood Vows: The Story of a Mafia Wife '87
Lionheart '87
Hyper-Sapien: People from Another Star '86
Rad '86
Rip van Winkle '85
Rocky 4 '85
Rocky 3 '82
The Godfather 1902-1959: The Complete Epic '81
Windows '80
Old Boyfriends '79
Prophecy '79
Rocky 2 '79
Rich Man, Poor Man '76
Rocky '76
The Godfather, Part 2 '74
The Godfather '72
The Dunwich Horror '70
Gas-s-s-sl '70

Bill Shirk
Ballbuster '89
Escapist '83

Anne Shirley (1918-93)
Murder, My Sweet '44
Bombardier '43
The Devil & Daniel Webster '41
Four Jacks and a Jill '41
Law of the Underworld '38
Stella Dallas '37
Steamboat Round the Bend '35
Anne of Green Gables '34
Rasputin and the Empress '33

Bill (William) Shirley (1921-89)
Sleeping Beauty '59 (V)
Abbott and Costello Meet Captain Kidd '52
I Dream of Jeannie '52
Chapayev '34
Earth '30

Cathie Shirriff
Star Trek 3: The Search for Spock '84
Covergirl '83

Joe Shishido (1933-)
Branded to Kill '67
Gate of Flesh '64
Youth of the Beast '63

Stephan Shkurat

Samia Shoaib
Pi '98
subUrbia '96

William Shockley (1963-)
Welcome to Paradise '07
Madison '01
Girl in the Cadillac '94
Dream Lover '93
Howling 5: The Rebirth '89

Ann Shoemaker (1891-1978)
Sunrise at Campobello '60
Thirty Seconds Over Tokyo '44
My Favorite Wife '40
Alice Adams '35

Craig Shoemaker (1962-)
Safe House '99
Acting on Impulse '93

Hristo Naumov Shopov
I Am David '04
The Passion of the Christ '04
Target of Opportunity '04

Dan Shor (1961-)
Red Rock West '93
Bill & Ted's Excellent Adventure '89
Daddy's Boys '87
Mesmerized '84
Mike's Murder '84
Strangers Kiss '83
Tron '82
Strange Behavior '81
A Rumor of War '80

Miriam Shor (1971-)
Pizza '05
Bedazzled '00
Hedwig and the Angry Inch '00
Let It Snow '99

Dinah Shore (1917-94)
Oh, God! '77
Fun & Fancy Free '47 (N)
Till the Clouds Roll By '46
Up in Arms '44
Thank Your Lucky Stars '43

Pauly Shore (1968-)
The Wash '01
The Bogus Witch Project '00
Bio-Dome '96
The Curse of Inferno '96
Jury Duty '95
In the Army Now '94
Dream Date '93
Son-in-Law '92
Encino Man '92

Bobby Short (1924-2005)
For Love or Money '93
Hardhat & Legs '80

Columbus Short (1982-)
Stomp the Yard '07
This Christmas '07
Accepted '06

Dorothy Short (1915-63)
Trail of the Silver Spurs '41
Pony Post '40
Daughter of the Tong '39
Phantom Rancher '39
Wild Horse Canyon '39
Reefer Madness '38
Brothers of the West '37
Assassin of Youth '35
Savage Fury '35

Florence Short (1889-1946)
The Love Flower '20
Way Down East '20

Martin Short (1950-)
The Spiderwick Chronicles '08 (V)
The Santa Clause 3: The Escape Clause '06
Treasure Planet '02 (V)
Get Over It! '01
Jimmy Neutron: Boy Genius '01 (V)
Alice in Wonderland '99
Mumford '99
Merlin '98
Prince of Egypt '98 (V)
A Simple Wish '97
Jungle 2 Jungle '96
Mars Attacks! '96
Father of the Bride Part 2 '95
The Pebble and the Penguin '94 (V)
We're Back! A Dinosaur's Story '93 (V)
Captain Ron '92
Clifford '92
The Return of Spinal Tap '92
Father of the Bride '91
Pure Luck '91
The Big Picture '89
Three Fugitives '89
Cross My Heart '88
Innerspace '87
Johnny Appleseed '86
Really Weird Tales '86
Three Amigos '86
Sunset Limousine '83
The Family Man '79
Lost and Found '79

Ken Shorter (1945-)
Dragonheart: A New Beginning '00
Ned Kelly '70

Robin Shou (1960-)
DOA: Dead or Alive '06
18 Fingers of Death '05
Mortal Kombat 2: Annihilation '97
Beverly Hills Ninja '96
Fatal Chase '92
Honor and Glory '92
Interpol Connection '92

Grant Show (1962-)
The Alchemists '99
Texas '94
Treacherous Crossing '92
A Woman, Her Men and Her Futon '92

Max (Casey Adams) Showalter (1917-2000)
Racing with the Moon '84
Sixteen Candles '84
Lord Love a Duck '66
Move Over, Darling '63
Summer and Smoke '61
The Monster That Challenged the World '57
Bus Stop '56
The Indestructible Man '56
Dangerous Crossing '53
Niagara '52
What Price Glory? '52

Michael Showalter (1970-)
The Baxter '05
Four and a Half Women '05
Wet Hot American Summer '01

Kathy Shower (1953-)
Hindsight '97
To the Limit '95
Improper Conduct '94
Married People, Single Sex 2: For Better or Worse '94
American Kickboxer 2: To the Death '93
Sexual Malice '93
L.A. Goddess '92
Wild Cactus '92
Bedroom Eyes 2 '89
Out on Bail '89
Robo-Chic '89
Frankenstein General Hospital '88
The Further Adventures of Tennessee Buck '88
Commando Squad '87

John Shrapnel (1942-)
Elizabeth: The Golden Age '07
Troy '04
K-19: The Widowmaker '02
The Body '01
Gladiator '00
Fatherland '94
Two Deaths '94
Tragedy of Flight 103: The Inside Story '91
How to Get Ahead in Advertising '89

Kin Shriner (1953-)
Hoot '06
The Corporation '96
The Crying Child '96
Subliminal Seduction '96
Cyberzone '95
Escape '90
Angel 3: The Final Chapter '88
Manhunter '86
Vendetta '85
Obsessive Love '84

Sonny Shroyer (1935-)
A Love Song for Bobby Long '04
The Rosa Parks Story '02
The Runaway '00
The Gingerbread Man '97
John Grisham's The Rainmaker '97
Wild America '97
Bastard out of Carolina '96
Forrest Gump '94
Love Crimes '92
The Devil & Max Devlin '81
They Went That-a-Way & That-a-Way '78
Smokey and the Bandit '77
Gator '76
The Longest Yard '74
Payday '73

Karin Shubert
See Karin Schubert

Andrew Shue (1967-)
Gracie '07
John Grisham's The Rainmaker '97

Elisabeth Shue (1963-)
Gracie '07
Dreamer: Inspired by a True Story '05
Hide and Seek '05
Mysterious Skin '04
Leo '02
Tuck Everlasting '02 (N)
Hollow Man '00
Molly '99
Palmetto '98
Cousin Bette '97
Deconstructing Harry '97
The Saint '97
The Trigger Effect '96
Leaving Las Vegas '95
The Underneath '95
Blind Justice '94
Heart and Souls '93
Twenty Bucks '93
The Marrying Man '91
Soapdish '91
Back to the Future, Part 3 '90
Back to the Future, Part 2 '89
Cocktail '88
Adventures in Babysitting '87
Link '86
Call to Glory '84
The Karate Kid '84

Richard B. Shull (1929-99)
Trapped in Paradise '94
Housesitter '92
Splash '84
Unfaithfully Yours '84
Heartbeeps '81
Dreamer '79
The Pack '77
The Big Bus '76
Cockfighter '74
Hail '73
Slither '73
Sssssss '73
The Anderson Tapes '71

Constance Shulman (1958-)
Doug's 1st Movie '99 (V)
Sweet and Lowdown '99

Lee Shumway (1884-1959)
Sundown Fury '42
Go-Get-'Em-Haines '35

Iris Shunn
See Iris Meredith

Antonina Shuranova (1936-)
An Unfinished Piece for a Player Piano '77
Tchaikovsky '71
War and Peace '68

Jane Sibbett (1961-)
Throne of Fire '82
The Arrival 2 '98
Noah '98
It Takes Two '95
The Resurrected '91

Clement Sibony (1976-)
He Loves Me ... He Loves Me Not '02
Dad On the Run '00
Deep in the Woods '00

Alexander Siddig (1965-)
Doomsday '08
The Last Legion '07
The Nativity Story '06
Kingdom of Heaven '05
Syriana '05
Reign of Fire '02
Vertical Limit '00
A Dangerous Man: Lawrence after Arabia '91

Sylvia Sidney (1910-99)
Mars Attacks! '96
Used People '92
Beetlejuice '88
Pals '87
An Early Frost '85
Come Along with Me '84
Corrupt '84
Finnegan Begin Again '84
Hammett '82
Having It All '82
A Small Killing '81
The Shadow Box '80
Damien: Omen 2 '78
I Never Promised You a Rose Garden '77
Raid on Entebbe '77
Snowbeast '77
God Told Me To '76
Death at Love House '75
Summer Wishes, Winter Dreams '73
Love from a Stranger '47
Mr. Ace '46
Blood on the Sun '45
The Wagons Roll at Night '41
One Third of a Nation '39
You and Me '38
Dead End '37
You Only Live Once '37
Fury '36
Sabotage '36
The Trail of the Lonesome Pine '36
Thirty Day Princess '34
Street Scene '31

Drew Sidora (1985-)
Never Die Alone '04
White Chicks '04

Charles Siebert (1938-)
A Cry for Love '80
Blue Sunshine '78
Tarantulas: The Deadly Cargo '77

Jim Siedow (1920-2003)
The Texas Chainsaw Massacre 2 '86
The Texas Chainsaw Massacre '74

Donald Siegel (1912-91)
Into the Night '85
Invasion of the Body Snatchers '78
Play Misty for Me '71
Invasion of the Body Snatchers '56

Jake Siegel
American Pie Presents: Beta House '07
American Pie Presents: The Naked Mile '06

George Siegmann (1882-1928)
Hotel Imperial '27
The Man Who Laughs '27
Uncle Tom's Cabin '27
Anna Christie '23
Oliver Twist '22
The Three Musketeers '21
The Birth of a Nation '15

Casey Siemaszko (1961-)
The Crew '00
Chameleon 2: Death Match '99
Limbo '99
Stephen King's The Storm of the Century '99
Rose Hill '97
Bliss '96
Mistrial '96
Black Scorpion '95
Milk Money '94
My Life's in Turnaround '94
Teresa's Tattoo '94
Of Mice and Men '92
The Chase '91
Near Misses '91
The Big Slice '90
Back to the Future, Part 2 '89
Breaking In '89
Biloxi Blues '88
Young Guns '88
Gardens of Stone '87
Three o'Clock High '87
Miracle of the Heart: A Boys Town Story '86
Stand by Me '86
Amazing Stories '85
Back to the Future '85
Secret Admirer '85
Class '83

Nina Siemaszko (1970-)
Mystery Woman: Mystery Weekend '05
Sleep Easy, Hutch Rimes '00
Goodbye, Lover '99
Jakob the Liar '99
Armistead Maupin's More Tales of the City '97
The American President '95
Sawbones '95
Airheads '94
Power of Attorney '94
Red Shoe Diaries 3: Another Woman's Lipstick '93
The Saint of Fort Washington '93
Twenty Bucks '93
Bed & Breakfast '92
Sinatra '92
Wild Orchid 2: Two Shades of Blue '92
Tucker: The Man and His Dream '88

Gregory Sierra (1941-)
Blood Money '99
Mafia! '98
The Wonderful Ice Cream Suit '98
Hot Shots! Part Deux '93
Deep Cover '92
Honey, I Blew Up the Kid '92
Dynamite and Gold '88
Code Name: Dancer '87
Let's Get Harry '87
Miami Vice '84
Mean Dog Blues '78
The Clones '73
The Thief Who Came to Dinner '73
Pocket Money '72

Rocco Siffredi (1964-)
Anatomy of Hell '04
Romance '99

Jamie-Lynn Sigler (1981-)
Call Me: The Rise and Fall of Heidi Fleiss '04
Extreme Dating '04

Tom Signorelli (1939-)
Robot in the Family '94
Crossover Dreams '85
One Down, Two to Go! '82
Alice Sweet Alice '76
Big Bad Mama '74
The Last Porno Flick '74
Kelly's Heroes '70
The St. Valentine's Day Massacre '67
The Trip '67

Simone Signoret (1921-85)
I Sent a Letter to My Love '81
Madame Rosa '77
Le Chat '75

Widow Couderc '74
Army of Shadows '69
Games '67
Is Paris Burning? '66
Ship of Fools '65
The Day and the Hour '63
Le Joli Mai '62 (N)
Room at the Top '59
The Crucible '57
Diabolique '55
Death in the Garden '56
Casque d'Or '52
La Ronde '51
Dedee d'Anvers '49
Against the Wind '48

Caroline Sihol (1949-)
Tous les Matins du Monde '92
Confidentially Yours '83

Cynthia Sikes (1951-)
Going Shopping '05
Possums '98
Oceans of Fire '86
Love Hurts '91
The Man Who Loved Women '83
Goodbye Cruel World '82

James B. Sikking (1934-)
Made of Honor '08
Fever Pitch '05
Nowhere to Land '00
Mutiny '99
In Pursuit of Honor '95
Tyson '95
Dead Badge '94
Seduced by Evil '94
The Pelican Brief '93
Doing Time on Maple Drive '92
Final Approach '91
Narrow Margin '90
Around the World in 80 Days '89
The Brotherhood of the Rose '89
Ollie Hopnoodle e's Haven of Bliss '88
Dress Gray '86
Morons from Outer Space '85
Star Trek 3: The Search for Spock '84
Up the Creek '84
The Star Chamber '83
The Terminal Man '74
Scorpio '73
The New Centurions '72
The Night God Screamed '71
Charro! '69
Daddy's Gone A-Hunting '69
Point Blank '67
Von Ryan's Express '65
The Strangler '64

Joe Sikora
Normal '03
The Watcher '00

Vic Silayan
Project: Kill '77
The Company of Wolves '85

Vira (Vera) Silenti (1931-)
Son of Samson '62
Atlas in the Land of the Cyclops '61
Maciste in Hell '60

Karen Sillas (1965-)
Reach the Rock '98
Sour Grapes '98
The Beast '96
Female Perversions '96
Risk '94
What Happened Was... '94
Simple Men '92

Douglas Sills (1960-)
Deuce Bigalow: European Gigolo '05
The Swan Princess '94

Darien Sills-Evans (1974-)
Preaching to the Choir '05
The Reception '05

David Silva (1917-76)
Sisters of Satan '75
Senora Tentacion '49

Geno Silva (1948-)
A Man Apart '03
Geronimo '93
Drug Wars II: The Cocaine Cartel '92
Night Eyes 2 '91

Henry Silva (1928-)
Backlash '99
Ghost Dog: The Way of the Samurai '99
The End of Violence '97
Trigger Happy '96
The Prince '95
Possessed by the Night '93
The Harvest '92
The Colombian Connection '91
Three Days to a Kill '91
Above the Law '88
Bulletproof '88
Trained to Kill '86
Thirst '87
Code of Silence '85
Escape from the Bronx '85
Lust in the Dust '85
Shoot '85
Cannonball Run 2 '84
Chained Heat '83
Violent Breed '83
Deadly Sting '82
Megaforce '82
Wrong Is Right '82
Love and Bullets '79
Crimebusters '79
Century '79
Buck Rogers in the 25th Century '79
Cry of a Prostitute: Love Kills '72
Man & Boy '71
The Desperados '70
Never a Dull Moment '68
The Secret Invasion '64
A Gathering of Eagles '63
The Manchurian Candidate '62
Cinderfella '60
Ocean's 11 '60
Green Mansions '59
The Jayhawkers '59
The Bravados '58
The Law and Jake Wade '58
The Tall T '57

Maria Silva (1941-)
Devil's Kiss '75
Curse of the Devil '73
The Mummy's Revenge '73
Tombs of the Blind Dead '72

Simone Silva (1928-57)
Big Deadly Game '54
The Shadow Man '53

Trinidad Silva (1950-88)
UHF '89
Colors '88
The Night Before '88
Crackers '84
The Jerk '79

Aldo Silvani (1891-1964)
Nights of Cabiria '57
La Strada '54
Valley of the Kings '54
The Fighter '52
Miracle of Our Lady of Fatima '52
White Mane '52

Jay Silverheels (1919-80)
Man Who Loved Cat Dancing '73
Santee '73
True Grit '69
Indian Paint '64
Justice of the West '61
Lone Ranger '56
Walk the Proud Land '56
War Arrow '53
Broken Arrow '50
Alias Jesse James '59
Last for Gold '49

Leonor Silveira (1970-)
Party '96
I'm Going Home '00
Voyage to the Beginning of the World '96
The Convent '95
Abraham's Valley '93

Fawn Silver
Terror in the Jungle '68
Orgy of the Dead '65

Daniela Silverio
Identification of a Woman '82

Joe Silver (1922-89)
Switching Channels '88
Mr. Nice Guy '86
Almost You '85
Rabid '77
The Gig '85

Ron Silver (1946-)
Find Me Guilty '06
Red Mercury '05
Spliced '03
Festival at Cannes '02
Master Spy: The Robert Hanssen Story '02
Ali '01
American Tragedy '00
Cutaway '00
Black & White '99
In the Company of Spies '99
The Arrival '96
Deadly Outbreak '96
Girl 6 '96
Kissinger and Nixon '96
ShadowZone: The Undead Express '96
Skeletons '96
Danger Zone '95
Timecop '94
A Woman of Independent Means '94
Blind Side '93
Lifepod '93
Married to It '93
Mr. Saturday Night '92
Blue Steel '90
Reversal of Fortune '90
Forgotten Prisoners '90
Enemies, a Love Story '89
Fellow Traveler '89
A Father's Revenge '88
Billionaire Boys Club '87
Eat and Run '86
Trapped in Silence '86
Garbo Talks '84
Silkwood '83
Best Friends '82
Silent Rage '82
Betrayal '78
Semi-Tough '77
Tunnelvision '76

David Michael Silverman (1966-)
Metro '96

Jonathan Silverman (1966-)
Coffee Date '06
.am '06
The Cookout '04
Bobbie's Girl '02
The Medicine Show '01
These Old Broads '01
The Inspectors 2: A Shred of Evidence '00
Lip Service '00
Just a Little Harmless Sex '99
The Inspectors '98
Neil Simon's The Odd Couple 2 '98
Something About Sex '98
French Exit '95
At First Sight '95
Little Big League '94
Sketch Artist 2: Hands That See '94
Teresa's Tattoo '94
12:01 '93
Weekend at Bernie's 2 '93
Breaking the Rules '92
Broadway Bound '92
Death Becomes Her '92
For Richer, for Poorer '92
Little Sister '92
Age Isn't Everything '91
Class Action '91
Traveling Man '89
Weekend at Bernie's '89
Caddyshack 2 '88
Stealing Home '88
Brighton Beach Memoirs '86

Sarah Silverman (1970-)
I Want Someone to Eat Cheese With '06
School for Scoundrels '06
Sarah Silverman: Jesus Is Magic '05
School of Rock '03
What Planet Are You From? '00

Robert A. Silverman
Naked Lunch '91
Scanners '81
The Brood '79

Veronique Silver (1931-)
Life Is a Bed of Roses '83
The Woman Next Door '81
This Sweet Sickness '77

Frank Silvera (1914-70)
Valdez Is Coming '71
The St. Valentine's Day Massacre '67
Death Tide '58
Killer's Kiss '55

Mary Silvers
See Maria Silva

Phil Silvers (1912-85)
A Funny Thing Happened on the Way to the Forum '66
It's a Mad, Mad, Mad, Mad World '63
40 Pounds of Trouble '62
Lucky Me '54
Summer Stock '50
If I'm Lucky '46
A Thousand and One Nights '45
Cover Girl '44
Something for the Boys '44
Footlight Serenade '42
Roxie Hart '42
Lady Be Good '41
Tom, Dick, and Harry '41

Armando Silvestre (1926-)
Wrestling Women vs. the Aztec Mummy '59
The White Orchid '54
Night of the Bloody Apes '68
Doctor of Doom '62
Geronimo '62
Neutron vs. the Death Robots '62
Neutron and the Black Mask '61

Victoria Silvstedt (1974-)
The Happy Hooker Goes Hollywood '80
Racquet '79
The Cheap Detective '78
The Chicken Chronicles '77
The Strongest Man in the World '75
The Boatniks '70
Boat Trip '02
Out Cold '01

Andrew (Dice Clay) Silverstein (1957-)
One Night at McCool's '01
My 5 Wives '00
Foolish '99
National Lampoon's Favorite Deadly Sins '95
No Contest '94
Brain Smasher... A Love Story '93
The Adventures of Ford Fairlane '90
Casual Sex? '88
Amazon Women on the Moon '87
Pretty in Pink '86
Making the Grade '84
Private Resort '84
Wacko '83

Alicia Silverstone (1976-)
Stormbreaker '06
Beauty Shop '05
Scooby-Doo 2: Monsters Unleashed '04
Scorched '02
Love's Labour's Lost '00
Blast from the Past '98
Batman and Robin '97
Excess Baggage '96
Clueless '95
The Babysitter '95
New World '95
True Crime '95
Cool and the Crazy '94
Hideaway '94
The Crush '93

Ben Silverstone (1979-)
Get Real '99
Lolita '97
The Browning Version '94

Gerald Sim (1925-)
Born to Dance '36
Broadway Melody of 1936 '35
No Sex Please—We're British '73
Dr. Jekyll and Sister Hyde '71
Long Ago Tomorrow '71
Oh! What a Lovely War '69
King Rat '65

Sid Silvers (1904-76)
(films listed)

David Michael Silverman
(see above)

Alastair Sim (1900-76)
The Littlest Horse Thieves '76
Rogue Male '76
Royal Flash '75
The Ruling Class '72
Cold Comfort Farm '71
The Millionairess '60
Blue Murder at St. Trinian's '56
Escapade '55
The Belles of St. Trinian's '53
Innocents in Paris '53
A Christmas Carol '51
The Happiest Days of Your Life '50
Stage Fright '50
Captain Boycott '47
Green for Danger '47
Hue and Cry '47
Inspector Hornleigh '39
The Terror '38
Gangway '37
Late Extra '35
The Private Secretary '35

Sheila Sim (1922-)
Pandora and the Flying Dutchman '51
The Guinea Pig '48
A Canterbury Tale '44
Dancing With Crime

Jon Simanton
The Creeps '97
Turbo: A Power Rangers Movie '96
The Terror '38

John Simm (1970-)
24 Hour Party People '01
Human Traffic '99
Wonderland '99
Miranda '01
Boston Kickout '95

Dick Simmons (1913-2003)
Men of the Fighting Lady '54
Above and Beyond '53
Battle Circus '53

Chelan Simmons (1982-)
Good Luck Chuck '07
Final Destination 3 '06
Chupacabra Terror '05
Cracker: Best Boys '95

Gene Simmons (1949-)
The New Guy '02
Wish You Were Dead '02
Detroit Rock City '99
Red Surf '90
Trick or Treat '86
Wanted Dead or Alive '86
Runaway '84
KISS Meets the Phantom of the Park '78

Henry Simmons (1970-)
The Insurgents '06
Madea's Family Reunion '06
Taxi '04

Jean Simmons (1929-)
Howl's Moving Castle '04
How to Make an American Quilt '95
Great Expectations '89

Jaason Simmons (1970-)
Frankenstein Reborn '98
Highway Hitcher '98
Nowhere '96
A Gentleman's Game '01
Let It Snow '99

The Dawning '88
A Friendship in Vienna '88 (N)
Going Undercover '88
Perry Mason: The Case of the Lost Love '87
North and South Book 2 '86
North and South Book 1 '85
December Flower '84
The Thorn Birds '83
A Small Killing '81
Dominique Is Dead '79
Mr. Sycamore '74
Say Hello to Yesterday '71
The Happy Ending '69
Divorce American Style '67
Heidi '67
Rough Night in Jericho '67
Soldier in Love '67
The Grass Is Greener '61
Elmer Gantry '60
Spartacus '60
The Big Country '58
This Could Be the Night '57
Until They Sail '57
Guys and Dolls '55
A Bullet Is Waiting '54
Desiree '54
The Egyptian '54
The Robe '53
Young Bess '53
Androcles and the Lion '52
Angel Face '52
She Couldn't Say No '52
The Clouded Yellow '51
Trio '50
Hamlet '48
Black Narcissus '47
Inheritance '47
Great Expectations '46

J.K. Simmons (1955-)
The Astronaut Farmer '07
Bury My Heart at Wounded Knee '07
First Snow '07
Juno '07
Spider-Man 3 '07
Thank You for Smoking '06
Harsh Times '05
Hidalgo '04
The Ladykillers '04
Spider-Man 2 '04
Off the Map '03
Spider-Man '02
Hit and Runway '01
The Mexican '01
The Gift '00
The Cider House Rules '99
For Love of the Game '99
Celebrity '98
Face Down '97
The Jackal '97
Love Walked In '97
Extreme Measures '96
The Ref '93

Kimora Lee Simmons (1975-)
Waist Deep '06
Beauty Shop '05

Pat Simmons

Peter Simmons
My Science Project '85
The Giant Gila Monster '59

Joey Simrin (1981-)
Star Kid '97
Nine Months '95
Little Giants '94

Larry Simms (1934-)
Blondie Hits the Jackpot '49
Blondie Knows Best '46
Blondie for Victory '42
Blondie Goes Latin '42

Ginny Simms (1913-94)
Night and Day '46
Broadway Rhythm '44
Hit the Ice '43
Seven Days' Leave '42
Playmates '41

Jessica Simpson (1980-)
Blonde Ambition '07
Employee of the Month '06
The Dukes of Hazzard '05

Jimmi Simpson (1975-)
Stay Alive '06
D.E.B.S. '04

Blondie Goes to College '42
Blondie's Blessed Event '42

Francois Simon (1917-82)
Christ Stopped at Eboli '79
Lumiere '76
Charles: Dead or Alive '69

Michel Simon (1895-1975)
The Two of Us '68
The Train '65
The Head '59
Femmes de Paris '53
Beauty and the Devil '50
Fabiola '48
Panique '47
Bizarre Bizarre '39
Circonstances Attenuantes '36
L'Atalante '34
Boudu Saved from Drowning '32
La Chienne '31

Paul Simon (1941-)
Mother Goose Rock 'n' Rhyme '90
One Trick Pony '80
All You Need Is Cash '78
Annie Hall '77

Robert F. Simon (1908-92)
Chinese Web '78
Spiderman: The Deadly Dust '78
The Man Who Shot Liberty Valance '62
Compulsion '59
Gunman's Walk '58
The Nine Lives of Elfego Baca '58
The Catered Affair '56
The Court Martial of Billy Mitchell '55

Simone Simon (1911-2005)
Le Plaisir '52
La Ronde '51
Women in Prison '49
Curse of the Cat People '44
Mademoiselle Fifi '44
Cat People '42
The Devil & Daniel Webster '41
La Bete Humaine '38

David Simonds
Amateur '94
The Refrigerator '91

Martine Simonet
The Last Metro '80
Simone Barbes '80

Mathieu Simonet (1975-)

Ivan Simpson (1875-1951)
Disraeli '30
Inside the Lines '30
The Sea God '30

Stephen King's Rose Red '02
Loser '00

O.J. Simpson (1947-)
Naked Gun 33 1/3: The Final Insult '94
No Place to Hide '93
C.I.A.: Code Name Alexa '92
Naked Gun 2 1/2: The Smell of Fear '91
The Naked Gun: From the Files of Police Squad '88
Hambone & Hillie '84
Firepower '79
Capricorn One '78
Roots '77
The Cassandra Crossing '76
The Klansman '74
The Towering Inferno '74

Russell Simpson (1880-1959)
The Horse Soldiers '59
The Sun Shines Bright '53
Ma and Pa Kettle at the Fair '52
Coroner Creek '48
My Dog Shep '46
They Were Expendable '45
Texas Masquerade '44
Border Patrol '43
The Grapes of Wrath '40
Three Faces West '40
San Francisco '36
Sixteen Fathoms Deep '34
The Riding Tornado '32
Abraham Lincoln '30
The Lone Star Ranger '30
The Virginian '23
Human Hearts '22
Peg o' My Heart '22

Joan Sims (1930-2001)
The Last of the Blonde Bombshells '00
The Canterville Ghost '96
Carry On Behind '75
Carry On Dick '75
Carry On Cowboy '66
Carry On Screaming '66
Carry On Cleo '65
Carry On Admiral '57
The Belles of St. Trinian's '53

Molly Sims (1973-)
The Benchwarmers '06
Starsky & Hutch '04

Robin Sims
The Channeler '89
Shooters '89

Frank Sinatra (1915-98)
Who Framed Roger Rabbit '88 (C)
Cannonball Run 2 '84
The First Deadly Sin '80
That's Entertainment '74
The Detective '68
Lady in Cement '68
Tony Rome '67
Assault on a Queen '66
Cast a Giant Shadow '66
The Oscar '66
Marriage on the Rocks '65
None But the Brave '65
Von Ryan's Express '65
Paris When It Sizzles '64
Robin and the 7 Hoods '64
Come Blow Your Horn '63
Four for Texas '63
The List of Adrian Messenger '63
The Manchurian Candidate '62
The Devil at 4 O'Clock '61
Can-Can '60
Ocean's 11 '60
A Hole in the Head '59
Never So Few '59
Kings Go Forth '58

Some Came Running '58
Pal Joey '57
The Pride and the Passion '57
Around the World in 80 Days '56
High Society '56
Meet Me in Las Vegas '56
Guys and Dolls '55
The Man with the Golden Arm '55
Not as a Stranger '55
The Tender Trap '55
Suddenly '54
Young at Heart '54
From Here to Eternity '53
Meet Danny Wilson '52
Double Dynamite '51
On the Town '49
Take Me Out to the Ball Game '49
The Kissing Bandit '48
The Miracle of the Bells '48
It Happened in Brooklyn '47
Till the Clouds Roll By '46
Anchors Aweigh '45
Higher and Higher '44
Step Lively '44
Strictly G.I. '44

Frank Sinatra, Jr. (1944-)
Hollywood Homicide '03
Cool World '92
Code Name: Zebra '84
Pepper and His Wacky Taxi '72
A Man Called Adam '66

Nancy Sinatra (1940-)
Speedway '68
The Wild Angels '66
Marriage on the Rocks '65

Richard Sinatra
The Beast from Haunted Cave '60
Ski Troop Attack '60

Sinbad (1956-)
Crazy as Hell '02
Good Burger '97
The Cherokee Kid '96
First Kid '96
Homeward Bound 2: Lost in San Francisco '96 (V)
Jingle All the Way '96
Houseguest '94
Coneheads '93
The Meteor Man '93
Necessary Roughness '91

Gordon John Sinclair (1962-)
The Brylcreem Boys '96
Erik the Viking '89
Gregory's Girl '80

Hugh Sinclair (1903-62)
No Trace '50
The Rocking Horse Winner '49
The Secret Four '40

Madge Sinclair (1938-95)
The Lion King '94 (V)
Queen '93
Coming to America '88
Convoy '78
One in a Million: The Ron LeFlore Story '78
Combread, Earl & Me '75
Conrack '74

Donald Sinden (1923-)
The Canterville Ghost '96
The Children '90
The Island at the Top of the World '74
Rentadick '72
The Captain's Table '60
Doctor at Large '57
Above Us the Waves '56
Simba '55
Doctor in the House '53
Mogambo '53

Jeremy Sinden (1950-96)
The Innocent '93
Fortunes of War '87

Danger UXB '81

Ngai Sing
See Collin Chou

Campbell Singer (1909-76)
The Hands of Orlac '60
The Young and the Guilty '58
Scotland Yard Inspector '52

Linda Singer
Junior '86
Zombie Nightmare '86

Lori Singer (1962-)
The Last Ride '94
Equinox '93
Short Cuts '93
Sunset Grill '92
Warlock '91
Storm and Sorrow '90
Made in USA '88
Summer Heat '87
Trouble in Mind '86
The Falcon and the Snowman '85
The Man with One Red Shoe '85
Footloose '84
Born Beautiful '82

Marc Singer (1948-)
L.A.P.D.: To Protect and Serve '01
Street Corner Justice '96
Beastmaster 3: The Eye of Braxus '95
Cyberzone '95
The Fighter '95
Silk Degrees '94
Victim of Desire '94
Sweet Justice '92
Beastmaster 2: Through the Portal of Time '91
Deadly Game '91
Ultimate Desires '91
Beyond the Silhouette '90
Body Chemistry '90
Dead Space '90
High Desert Kill '90
A Man Called Sarge '90
The Red Raven Kiss-Off '90
Watchers 2 '90
In the Cold of the Night '89
Born to Race '88
V: The Final Battle '84
Her Life as a Man '83
V '83
Beastmaster '82
If You Could See What I Hear '82
For Ladies Only '81
Roots: The Next Generation '79
The Two Worlds of Jenny Logan '79
Go Tell the Spartans '78
Sergeant Matlovich vs. the U.S. Air Force '78
Things in Their Season '74

Richard Singer
American Pop '81 (V)
Girls Next Door '79

Steve Singer
Palindromes '04

Joseph Singleton (1879-1946)
The Mad Whirl '25
The Toll Gate '20

Penny Singleton (1908-2003)
Jetsons: The Movie '90 (V)
Blondie Hits the Jackpot '49
Blondie Knows Best '46
Footlight Glamour '43
It's a Great Life '43
Blondie for Victory '42
Blondie Goes Latin '42
Blondie Goes to College '42
Blondie's Blessed Event '42
Blondie in Society '41
Blondie Has Trouble '40
Blondie On a Budget '40

Blondie Plays Cupid '40
Blondie Brings Up Baby '39
Blondie Meets the Boss '39
Blondie Takes a Vacation '39
Blondie '38
Boy Meets Girl '38
Vogues of 1938 '37

Linda Sini (1926-)
Sartana's Here... Trade Your Pistol for a Coffin '70
Venus Against the Son of Hercules '62

Gary Sinise (1955-)
Open Season '06 (V)
The Big Bounce '04
The Forgotten '04
Fallen Angel '03
The Human Stain '03
Impostor '02
Path to War '02
A Gentleman's Game '01
Mission to Mars '00
Reindeer Games '00
The Dress Code '99
The Green Mile '99
It's the Rage '99
That Championship Season '99
Snake Eyes '98
George Wallace '97
Albino Alligator '96
Ransom '96
Apollo 13 '95
The Quick and the Dead '95
Truman '95
Forrest Gump '94
Stephen King's The Stand '94
Jack the Bear '93
A Midnight Clear '92
Of Mice and Men '92
My Name Is Bill W. '89
True West '86

Sir Lancelot (1903-2001)
Zombies On Broadway '44
I Walked with a Zombie '43

Joseph Siravo
Wisegirls '02
Walking and Talking '96
Carlito's Way '93

G. Anthony "Tony" Sirico (1942-)
Mob Queen '98
Gotti '96
Backtrack '89
Cookie '89

Joseph Sirola (1929-)
Seizure '74
Hail '73

Marina Sirtis (1960-)
Net Games '03
Star Trek: Nemesis '02
Terminal Error '02
Star Trek: Insurrection '98
Star Trek: First Contact '96
Gargoyles, The Movie: The Heroes Awaken '94 (V)
Star Trek: Generations '94
Waxwork 2: Lost in Time '91
Death Wish 3 '85
Blind Date '84

Sisqo (1978-)
Pieces of April '03
Snow Dogs '02
Get Over It! '01

Noble Sissle (1889-1975)
Junction 88 '47
Murder with Music '45
Mistaken Identity '41

Jeremy Sisto (1974-)
Waitress '07
The Thirst '06
A Lot Like Love '05
In Enemy Hands '04
Paranoia 1.0 '04
Thirteen '03
Wrong Turn '03
May '02
Now You Know '02
Angel Eyes '01

Dead Dog '00
Jesus '00
The '60s '99
Bongwater '98
Playing by Heart '98
Suicide Kings '97
Without Limits '97
White Squall '96
Clueless '95
The Crew '95
Moonlight and Valentino '95
Hideaway '94
Grand Canyon '91

Rocco Sisto (1953-)
Innocent Blood '92
Red Riding Hood '88
Truth or Die '86
After Hours '85

Tim Sitarz
Axe '06
Outta Time '01

Emil Sitka (1915-98)
Frogs '72
The Incredible Petrified World '58
The Outlaws Is Coming! '65
Three Stooges in Orbit '62
Carolina Cannonball '55

Frank Sivero (1952-)
Foolish '99
Cop and a Half '93
Fist of Honor '92
Goodfellas '90
Ratings Game '84
The Godfather, Part 2 '74

Jamie Sives (1973-)
On a Clear Day '05
Wilbur Wants to Kill Himself '02

Eva Six
Beach Party '63
Operation Bikini '63

Sean Six
Alien Nation: Millennium '96
Alien Nation: The Enemy Within '96
Alien Nation: Body and Soul '95
Alien Nation: Dark Horizon '94

Tom Sizemore (1964-)
Protecting the King '07
Splinter '06
Hustle '04
Paparazzi '04
Dreamcatcher '03
Big Trouble '02
Swindle '02
Black Hawk Down '01
Pearl Harbor '01
Sins of the Father '01
Ticker '01
Red Planet '00
Bringing Out the Dead '99
Play It to the Bone '99
Witness Protection '99
Enemy of the State '98
The Florentine '98
Saving Private Ryan '98
Witness to the Mob '98
The Relic '96
Bad Love '95
Devil in a Blue Dress '95
Heat '95
Strange Days '95
Natural Born Killers '94
Wyatt Earp '94
Heart and Souls '93
Striking Distance '93
True Romance '93
Watch It '93
An American Story '92
Passenger 57 '92
Guilty by Suspicion '91
Harley Davidson and the Marlboro Man '91
Point Break '91
Flight of the Intruder '90
A Matter of Degrees '90
Born on the Fourth of July '89
Blue Steel '90
Where Sleeping Dogs Lie '91

Gunnar Sjoberg (1909-71)
Brink of Life '57

Victor Sjostrom (1879-1960)
Wild Strawberries '57
To Joy '50
Walpurgis Night '41

George Skaff (1930-95)
Tecumseh: The Last Warrior '95
Thousand Pieces of Gold '91
The Lost Capone '90
Man Beast '55

Jimmie F. Skaggs (1944-2004)
Puppet Master '89
Ghost Town '88

Norman Skaggs
Getting Out '94
Chrome Soldiers '92

Lilia Skala (1900-94)
House of Games '87
Flashdance '83
Testament '83
Heartland '81
Deadly Hero '75
Probe '72
Charly '68
Caprice '67
Lilies of the Field '63

Stellan Skarsgard (1951-)
Mamma Mia! '08
Pirates of the Caribbean: At World's End '07
Beowulf & Grendel '06
Goya's Ghosts '06
Pirates of the Caribbean: Dead Man's Chest '06
Dominion: Prequel to the Exorcist '05
King Arthur '04
City of Ghosts '03
Dogville '03
Helen of Troy '03
No Good Deed '02
Taking Sides '01
Aberdeen '00
Signs & Wonders '00
Passion of Mind '00
Time Code '00
Deep Blue Sea '99
Ronin '98
Savior '98
Amistad '97
Good Will Hunting '97
Insomnia '97
My Son the Fanatic '97
Breaking the Waves '95
Zero Degrees Kelvin '95
Good Evening, Mr. Wallenberg '93
The Slingshot '93
Wind '92
The Ox '91
The Women on the Roof '89
The Unbearable Lightness of Being '88
Hip Hip Hurrah! '87
Noon Wine '84

Alexander Skarsgard
Kill Your Darlings '06

Jackie Skarvellis
The Rats Are Coming! The Werewolves Are Here! '72

Brigitte Skay
Four Times That Night '72

Hal Skelly (1891-1934)
Struggle '31
Dance of Life '29

Carole Skinner
Napoleon '96 (V)
Adventures of Eliza Fraser '76

Red Skelton (1913-97)
Those Magnificent Men in Their Flying Machines '65
Ocean's 11 '60
Around the World in 80 Days '56
Lovely to Look At '52
Texas Carnival '51
The Fuller Brush Girl '50
Three Little Words '50
Watch the Birdie '50
The Yellow Cab Man '50
Neptune's Daughter '49
The Fuller Brush Man '48
A Southern Yankee '48
Merton of the Movies '47
The Show-Off '46
Ziegfeld Follies '46
Bathing Beauty '44
Du Barry Was a Lady '43
I Dood It '43
Thousands Cheer '43
Whistling in Brooklyn '43
Panama Hattie '42
Ship Ahoy '42
Whistling in Dixie '42
Lady Be Good '41
Whistling in the Dark '41
Having Wonderful Time '38

Tom Skerritt (1933-)
Bonneville '06
Mammoth '06
The Grand '06
Tears of the Sun '03
Path to War '02
Greenmail '01
Texas Rangers '01
High Noon '00
Trial by Media '00
Aftershock: Earthquake in New York '99
The Other Sister '99
Smoke Signals '98
What the Deaf Man Heard '98
Contact '97
Two for Texas '97
Divided by Hate '97
Singles '92
A River Runs Through It '92
Wild Orchid 2: Two Shades of Blue '92
Poison Ivy '92
Steel Magnolias '89
Big Man on Campus '89
The Heist '89
Red King, White Knight '89
Big Town '87
Opposing Force '87
Poker Alice '87
Wisdom '87
SpaceCamp '86
Top Gun '86
Calendar Girl Murders '84
Dead Zone '83
Fighting Back '82
Silence of the North '81
Alien '79
Ice Castles '79
The Turning Point '77
Devil's Rain '75
Big Bad Mama '74
Thieves Like Us '74
Fuzz '72
Wild Rovers '71
M*A*S*H '70

Claire Skinner (1965-)
Sense & Sensibility '07
Almost Strangers '01
Second Sight '99
Sleepy Hollow '99
Naked '93
Life Is Sweet '90

Cornelia Otis Skinner (1899-1979)
The Girl in the Red Velvet Swing '55
The Uninvited '44

Keith Skinner (1949-)
Goodnight, Sweet Marilyn '89
The Slipper and the Rose '76

Pat Skipper
Ed Gein '01

Alison Skipworth (1863-1952)
Wide Open Faces '38
The Princess Comes Across '36
Satan Met a Lady '36
Dangerous '35
The Devil Is a Woman '35
Here Is My Heart '34
Six of a Kind '34
The Song of Songs '33
Tonight or Never '31
Dubarry '30
Raffles '30

Espen Skjonberg (1924-)
The Last Lieutenant '94
One Day in the Life of Ivan Denisovich '71

Jerzy Skolimowski (1938-)
Eastern Promises '07
Big Shots '87

Helgi Skulason (1938-96)
Pathfinder '87
Revenge of the Barbarians '85

Azura Skye (1981-)
One Missed Call '08
Heavens Fall '06
Wristcutters: A Love Story '06
The Lather Effect '06
Fever Pitch '05
Red Dragon '02
The Salton Sea '02
Bandits '01
28 Days '00
Dementia '98

Ione Skye (1971-)
One Night Stand '97
Dream for an Insomniac '96
The Color of Evening '95
Four Rooms '95
Girls in Prison '94
Gas Food Lodging '92
Samantha '92
Guncrazy '92
Mindwalk: A Film for Passionate Thinkers '91
The Rachel Papers '89
Say Anything '89
A Night in the Life of Jimmy Reardon '88
River's Edge '87

Anita Skinner
Sole Survivor '84
Girlfriends '78

Max Elliott Slade (1980)
Apollo 13 '95
3 Ninjas Knuckle Up '95
3 Ninjas Kick Back '94
3 Ninjas '92

Jeremy Slate (1926-2006)
Dream Machine '91
Dead Pit '89
G.I. Blues '60

Demian Slade (1972-)
Cadillac Man '90
Kidco '83

Tristen Skylar (1971-)
Book of Shadows: Blair Witch 2 '00
A House in the Hills '93

Ryan Slater (1983-)
Home Team '98
Hell's Kitchen NYC '97

Christian Slater (1969-)
He Was a Quiet Man '07
Bobby '06
Hollow Man 2 '06
Alone in the Dark '05
The Deal '05
Mindhunters '05
Who Is Cletis Tout? '02
Windtalkers '02
Hard Cash '01
3000 Miles to Graceland '01
The Contender '00
Very Bad Things '98
Hard Rain '97
Julian Po '97
Bed of Roses '96
Broken Arrow '95
Murder in the First '95
Interview with the Vampire '94
Jimmy Hollywood '94
True Romance '93
Untamed Heart '93
Ferngully: The Last Rain Forest '92 (V)
Kuffs '92
Where the Day Takes You '92
Mobsters '91
Robin Hood: Prince of Thieves '91
Star Trek VI: The Undiscovered Country '91
Pump Up the Volume '90
Tales from the Darkside: The Movie '90
Young Guns 2 '90
Beyond the Stars '89
Gleaming the Cube '89
Heathers '89
The Wizard '89
Tucker: The Man and His Dream '88
The Name of the Rose '86
Twisted '86
Legend of Billie Jean '85

Richard X. Slattery (1925-97)
Zebra Force '76
I'll Take Sweden '65
Girls! Girls! Girls! '62

John Slattery (1963-)
Reservation Road '07
Underdog '07
Flags of Our Fathers '06
The Situation '06
Mona Lisa Smile '03
Bad Company '02
A Death in the Family '02
Cash Crop '01
From the Earth to the Moon '98

Tony Slattery (1959-)
Peter's Friends '92
How to Get Ahead in Advertising '89

Tod Slaughter (1885-1956)
Crimes at the Dark House '40
The Face at the Window '40
Sexton Blake and the Hooded Terror '38
Never Too Late to Mend '37
Ticket of Leave Man '37
The Crimes of Stephen Hawke '36
Demon Barber of Fleet Street '36
Murder in the Old Red Barn '36

Darla Slavens
See Darla Haun

Jonathan Slavin
Hard Pill '05

Millie Slavin
Free Enterprise '98

Bobby Slayton (1955-)
The Third Wheel '02
Bandits '01
The Rat Pack '98
Get Shorty '95

Tommy Sledge
Movie...In Your Face '90
Lobster Man from Mars '89

Helen Slater (1963-)
Seeing Other People '04
Nowhere in Sight '01
Toothless '97
No Way Back '96
Parallel Lives '94
Lassie '94
City Slickers '91
Happy Together '89
Sticky Fingers '88
The Secret of My Success '87
Ruthless People '86
Legend of Billie Jean '85
Supergirl '84

Victor Slezak (1957-)
The Notorious Bettie Page '06
The Cat's Meow '01
Lost Souls '00
One Tough Cop '98
The Siege '98
Beyond Rangoon '95
The Bridges of Madison County '95

Slezak

Bed & Breakfast '92

Walter Slezak (1902-83)
Treasure Island '72
Black Beauty '71
Caper of the Golden Bulls '67
Emil and the Detectives '64
The Wonderful World of the Brothers Grimm '62
Come September '61
Bedtime for Bonzo '51
People Will Talk '51
Abbott and Costello in the Foreign Legion '50
The Yellow Cab Man '50
The Inspector General '49
The Pirate '48
Born to Kill '47
Riff-Raff '47
Sinbad, the Sailor '47
Step Lively '44
Cornered '45
Salome, Where She Danced '45
The Spanish Main '45
Lifeboat '44
The Princess and the Pirate '44
The Fallen Sparrow '43
This Land Is Mine '43
Once Upon a Honeymoon '42

Grace Slick (1939-)
Jackie's Back '99
Gimme Shelter '70

Everett Sloane (1909-65)
Hercules and the Princess of Troy '65
Disorderly Orderly '64
The Patsy '64
Home from the Hill '60
Marjorie Morningstar '58
Lust for Life '56
Patterns '56
Somebody Up There Likes Me '56
The Big Knife '55
The Enforcer '51
Sirocco '51
The Men '50
Prince of Foxes '49
The Lady from Shanghai '48
Citizen Kane '41

Lindsay Sloane (1977-)
The Accidental Husband '08
Over Her Dead Body '08
The TV Set '06
Dog Gone Love '03
The In-Laws '03
Bring It On '00

Olive Sloane (1896-1963)
Curtain Up '53
Seven Days to Noon '50
Since You've Been Gone '97

Joey Slotnick (1968-)
I Want Someone to Eat Cheese With '06
Hollow Man '00
The Pirates of Silicon Valley '99
Blast from the Past '98
Dinner and Driving '97
The Black Arrow '84

James Sloyan (1941-)
Danielle Steel's Changes '91
Twister '96

Georgia Slowe (1966-)
The Company of Wolves '85
Deadline Assault '90
Billionaire Boys Club '87
Code Name: Dancer '87
Amos '85
Prime Suspect '82
Callie and Son '81
The Disappearance of Aimee '76

Errol Slue
Baby on Board '92
Murder One '88

Marya Small
Zapped! '82
American Pop '81 (V)

Sharon Small (1967-)
Dear Frankie '04
Inspector Lynley Mysteries: A Great Deliverance '01

Phillips Smalley (1865-1939)
The Taxi Mystery '26
Charley's Aunt '25

Jimmy Smallhorne
When the Sky Falls '99
2 by 4 '98

Amy Smart (1976-)
Crank '06
Peaceful Warrior '06
Bigger Than the Sky '05
Just Friends '05
Blind Horizon '04
The Butterfly Effect '04
Starsky & Hutch '04
Win a Date with Tad Hamilton! '04
The Battle of Shaker Heights '03
Interstate 60 '02
Scotland, PA '02
Rat Race '01
Road Trip '00
The '70s '00
Outside Providence '99
Campfire Tales '98
Dee Snider's Strangeland '98
High Voltage '98
Varsity Blues '98
Starship Troopers '97

Dee Smart
Welcome to Woop Woop '98
Back of Beyond '95
Blackwater Trail '95

Jean Smart (1959-)
Hero Wanted '08
Lucky You '07
Garden State '04
Audrey's Rain '03
Bringing Down the House '03
Sweet Home Alabama '02
Disney's The Kid '00
Snow Day '00
Guinevere '99
A Fight for Jenny '90
Maximum Security '87
Project X '87
Fire with Fire '86
Piaf '81

Rebecca Smart (1976-)
Blackrock '97
Celia: Child of Terror '89

Richard Smedley
The Abductors '72
A Place Called Today '72
Brain of Blood '71

Hana Smekalova
See Florence Marly

Ron Smerczak
Queen's Messenger II '01
Jackie Chan's Who Am I '98
Return of the Family Man '89
Hunted '88

Robert Smigel (1960-)
Little Nicky '00 (V)
Happy Gilmore '96

Tava Smiley (1971-)
Timecop 2: The Berlin Decision '03
A Girl, 3 Guys and a Gun '01
Outta Time '01

Yakov Smirnoff (1951-)
Up Your Alley '89
Heartburn '86
The Money Pit '86
The Adventures of Buckaroo Banzai Across the Eighth Dimension '84

Alexis Smith (1921-93)
The Age of Innocence '93
Dress Gray '86
Tough Guys '86
La Truite '83
Casey's Shadow '78
The Little Girl Who Lives down the Lane '76
Once Is Not Enough '75
The Young Philadelphians '59
This Happy Feeling '58
The Sleeping Tiger '54
Split Second '53
Here Comes the Groom '51
Any Number Can Play '49
South of St. Louis '48
The Two Mrs. Carrolls '47
Night and Day '46
Conflict '45
The Horn Blows at Midnight '45
Rhapsody in Blue '45
San Antonio '45
The Adventures of Mark Twain '44
Hollywood Canteen '44
Gentleman Jim '42
Dive Bomber '41

Allison Smith (1969-)
Terror Tract '00
At First Sight '95
A Reason to Believe '95
Jason Goes to Hell: The Final Friday '93
Wildflower '91

Amber Smith (1972-)
Def Jam's How to Be a Player '97
L.A. Confidential '97
Laws of Deception '97
Mars '96
Private Parts '96
Red Shoe Diaries 7: Burning Up '96

Anna Deavere Smith (1950-)
Life Support '07
CryWolf '05
The Human Stain '03
The American President '95
Dave '93
Philadelphia '93

Art Smith (1899-1973)
The Painted Hills '51
In a Lonely Place '50
The Next Voice You Hear '50
Caught '49
Letter from an Unknown Woman '48
Mr. Peabody & the Mermaid '48

Benjamin Smith (1995-)
Bob the Butler '05
Second Sight '99

Brandon Smith (1952-)
Paradise, Texas '05
The Alamo '04
Jeepers Creepers '01
Powder '95

Britta Smith
Bloom '03
The Magdalene Sisters '02
American Women '00
A Certain Justice '99
Moll Flanders '96
The Summer House '94
In the Name of the Father '93

Brooke Smith (1967-)
In Her Shoes '05
Bad Company '02
Series 7: The Contenders '01
Last Summer In the Hamptons '96
Kansas City '95
Vanya on 42nd Street '94
The Night We Never Met '93
The Silence of the Lambs '91

Bubba Smith (1945-)
Silence of the Hams '93
Fist of Honor '92
My Samurai '92
Police Academy 6: City under Siege '89
Police Academy 5: Assignment Miami Beach '88
Police Academy 4: Citizens on Patrol '87
The Wild Pair '87
Police Academy 3: Back in Training '86
More American Graffiti '79
Police Academy 2: Their First Assignment '85
Police Academy '84
Stroker Ace '83
Escape from DS-3 '81

Sir C. Aubrey Smith (1863-1948)
Unconquered '47
And Then There Were None '45
The Adventures of Mark Twain '44
Sensations of 1945 '44
The White Cliffs of Dover '44
Forever and a Day '43
Madame Curie '43
Beyond Tomorrow '40
Rebecca '40
Waterloo Bridge '40
Another Thin Man '39
Balalaika '39
East Side of Heaven '39
Five Came Back '39
The Four Feathers '39
The Hurricane '37
Prisoner of Zenda '37
Thoroughbreds Don't Cry '37
Wee Willie Winkie '37
The Garden of Allah '36
Little Lord Fauntleroy '36
Lloyds of London '36
China Seas '35
The Crusades '35
The Lives of a Bengal Lancer '35
Transatlantic Tunnel '35
Cleopatra '34
Scarlet Empress '34
Bombshell '33
Queen Christina '33
Trouble in Paradise '32
Trader Horn '31

Carolyn Smith
Perfect Time '97
Small Time '91
Something Weird '68

Cedric Smith (1943-)
The Gospel of John '03
Sea People '00
Jack Higgins' Thunder Point '97
Witchboard 3: The Possession '95
JFK: Reckless Youth '93
The Penthouse '92
Love and Hate: A Marriage Made in Hell '90
Anne of Green Gables '85
Who Has Seen the Wind? '77

Chad Smith
Hostage '05
Tears of the Sun '03

Charles Martin Smith (1953-)
Lucky You '07
P. T. Barnum '99
Apartment Complex '98
Deep Impact '98
The Beast '96
Dead Silence '96
The Final Cut '96
Wedding Bell Blues '96
Larry McMurtry's Streets of Laredo '95
The Road Home '95
I Love Trouble '94
Roswell: The U.F.O. Cover-Up '94
Speechless '94
And the Band Played On '93
Boris and Natasha: The Movie '92
Deep Cover '92
The Hot Spot '90
The Experts '89
The Untouchables '87
Starman '84
Never Cry Wolf '83
Cotton Candy '82
Herbie Goes Bananas '80
The Buddy Holly Story '78
The Campus Corpse '77
Law of the Land '76
No Deposit, No Return '76
Rafferty & the Gold Dust Twins '75
American Graffiti '73
Pat Garrett & Billy the Kid '73
Culpepper Cattle Co. '72
Fuzz '72

Cheryl "Rainbeaux" Smith (1955-2002)
Independence Day '83
Parasite '82
Vice Squad '82
Melvin and Howard '80
Cheech and Chong's Up in Smoke '79
Laserblast '78
Incredible Melting Man '77
Drum '76
Massacre at Central High '76
Pom Pom Girls '76
Revenge of the Cheerleaders '76
Slumber Party '57 '76
Farewell, My Lovely '75
Caged Heat '74
The Swinging Cheerleaders '74
Lemora, Lady Dracula '73

Connie Smith (1941-)
Hell on Wheels '67
Road to Nashville '67

Constance Smith (1928-2003)
Impulse '55
Man in the Attic '53

Cotter Smith (1949-)
X2: X-Men United '03
Ride the Wild Fields '00
Lifeform '96
Midnight's Child '93
The Last Prostitute '91
Cameron's Closet '89
K-9 '89
Lady Beware '87
Broken Badge '85
A Bunny's Tale '85

Cynthia Smith
For the Love of Benji '77
Benji '74

Cyril Smith (1892-1963)
John and Julie '55
A Stolen Face '52
Old Mother Riley, Headmistress '50
Appointment with Crime '45
Sidewalks of London '38

Daniel E. Smith
John Q '02
Heimat 2 '92

David Anthony Smith
Terror in Paradise '90
Judgment Day '88

David Lee Smith
The Man from Earth '07
Divine Secrets of the Ya-Ya Sisterhood '02
The Courage to Love '00

Ebbe Roe Smith
Tapeheads '89
Big Bad Mama 2 '87
The Big Easy '87

Eddie Bo Smith, Jr.
Stir of Echoes '99

Ethel Smith (1910-96)
Melody Time '48 (V)
Bathing Beauty '44

Geraldine Smith (1949-)
Spike of Bensonhurst '88
Mixed Blood '84
Flesh '68

Gregory Edward Smith (1983-)
The Seeker: The Dark is Rising '07
Kids in America '05
Nearing Grace '05
Book of Love '04
American Outlaws '01
The Patriot '00
Krippendorf's Tribe '98
My Teacher Ate My Homework '98
Small Soldiers '98
The Climb '97
Harriet the Spy '96
Spellbreaker: Secret of the Leprechauns '96
Leapin' Leprechauns '95

Hillary Bailey Smith (1957-)
Last Breath '96
Love Potion #9 '92

Howard Smith (1893-1968)
The Brass Bottle '63
I Bury the Living '58
No Time for Sergeants '58
Call Northside 777 '48
State of the Union '48

Howard K. Smith (1914-2002)
Dawn of the Dead '78
Nasty Habits '77

J. Augustus Smith (1891-1964)
Junction 88 '47
Drums O'Voodoo '34

Jaclyn Smith (1947-)
Charlie's Angels: Full Throttle '03
My Very Best Friend '96
Lies Before Kisses '92
Danielle Steel's Kaleidoscope '90
The Bourne Identity '88
Windmills of the Gods '88
The Night They Saved Christmas '87
Rage of Angels: The Story Continues '86
Deja Vu '84
George Washington '84
Rage of Angels '83
Jacqueline Bouvier Kennedy '81
Nightkill '80
Users '78
Probe '72
The Adventurers '70
Goodbye Columbus '69

Jacob Smith (1990-)
- Cheaper by the Dozen '03
- Cheaper by the Dozen 2 '05
- Dragonfly '02

James Todd Smith
See LL Cool J

Jamie Renee Smith (1987-)
- MVP (Most Valuable Primate) '00
- Dante's Peak '97
- Children of the Corn 4: The Gathering '96
- Magic in the Mirror: Fowl Play '96

John Smith (1932-95)
- MacDonald's Farm '57

Julie K. Smith (1967-)
- Return to Savage Beach '97
- The Dallas Connection '94

Kavan Smith (1970-)
- Stark Raving Mad '02
- Mission to Mars '00

Kellita Smith (1969-)
- Feel the Noise '07
- King's Ransom '05
- Roll Bounce '05
- Hair Show '04

Kent Smith (1907-85)
- Die Sister, Die! '74
- Pete 'n' Tillie '72
- Probe '72
- The Badlanders '58
- Party Girl '58
- Sayonara '57
- Strangers When We Meet '60
- The Balcony '63
- The Damned Don't Cry '50
- The Fountainhead '49
- My Foolish Heart '49
- Magic Town '47
- The Spiral Staircase '46
- Curse of the Cat People '44
- Cat People '42
- Back Door to Heaven '39

Kerr Smith (1972-)
- Cruel Intentions 3 '04
- The Forsaken '01
- Final Destination '00
- Pressure '02

Kevin Smith (1963-2002)
- Beyond Justice '01
- Dead Evidence '00
- Young Hercules '97
- Desperate Remedies '93

Kevin Smith (1970-)
- Catch and Release '07
- Live Free or Die Hard '07
- Clerks 2 '06
- Daredevil '03
- Jay and Silent Bob Strike Back '01
- Scream 3 '00
- Dogma '99
- Chasing Amy '97
- Mallrats '95
- Clerks '94

Kim Smith (1983-)
- Catwoman '04
- National Lampoon's Van Wilder '02

Kurtwood Smith (1943-)
- A Bright Shining Lie '98
- The Magnificent Seven '98
- Safety Patrol '98
- Shelter '98
- Citizen Ruth '96
- Prefontaine '96
- A Time to Kill '96
- To Die For '95
- The Last of the Dogmen '95
- Dead on Sight '94
- Boxing Helena '93
- The Crush '93
- Fortress '93
- Quick Change '90
- Dead Poets Society '89
- The Heart of Dixie '89
- The Nightmare Years '89
- True Believer '89
- RoboCop '87

Lane Smith (1936-2005)
- Winds of Terror '01
- The Legend of Bagger Vance '00
- Inherit the Wind '99
- The Hi-Lo Country '98
- Why Do Fools Fall in Love? '98
- From the Earth to the Moon '98
- The Distinguished Gentleman '92
- Duplicates '92
- False Arrest '92
- The Mighty Ducks '92
- My Cousin Vinny '92
- Air America '90
- Blind Vengeance '90
- The Final Days '89
- Night Game '89
- Prison '88
- Weeds '87
- Frances '82
- Prime Suspect '82
- A Rumor of War '80
- Blue Collar '78
- Network '76

Lauren Lee Smith
- Pathology '08
- The Last Kiss '06

Lewis Smith (1958-)
- Wyatt Earp '94
- Diary of a Hitman '91
- Fulfillment '89
- North and South Book 2 '86
- The Heavenly Kid '85
- The Adventures of Buckaroo Banzai Across the Eighth Dimension '84
- The Final Terror '83
- Southern Comfort '81

Linda Smith
- Taken '99
- The Phone Call '89

Lionel Mark Smith (1946-2008)
- Spartan '04
- King of the Ants '03

Liz Smith (1925-)
- Keeping Mum '05
- Oliver Twist '05
- Charlie and the Chocolate Factory '05
- Wallace & Gromit: The Curse of the Were-Rabbit '05
- A Christmas Carol '99
- Sweet Revenge '98
- A Merry War '97
- Apartment Zero '88
- We Think the World of You '88
- The Lonely Passion of Judith Hearne '87
- A Room with a View '86
- Lily in Love '85
- Mrs. Silly '85
- A Private Function '84

Lois Smith (1930-)
- Hollywoodland '06
- Sweet Land '05
- P.S. '04
- 2 Brothers & a Bride '03
- Minority Report '02
- The Pledge '00
- The Eternal '99
- Tumbleweeds '98
- Larger Than Life '96
- Twister '96
- Dead Man Walking '95
- How to Make an American Quilt '95
- Truman '95
- Holy Matrimony '94
- Falling Down '93
- Skylark '93
- Hard Promises '92
- Keep the Change '92
- Fried Green Tomatoes '91
- Switched at Birth '91
- Green Card '90
- Black Widow '87
- Twisted '86
- Morons from Outer Space '85
- Reckless '84
- Reuben, Reuben '83
- Five Easy Pieces '70

Loring Smith (1895-1981)
- Shadow of the Thin Man '41
- Ma and Pa Kettle at Waikiki '55

Madeleine Smith (1952-)
- Frankenstein and the Monster from Hell '74
- Live and Let Die '73
- The Vampire Lovers '70

Madolyn Smith (1957-)
- Funny Farm '88
- The Caller '87
- All of Me '84
- 2010: The Year We Make Contact '84
- Urban Cowboy '80

Maggie Smith (1934-)
- Harry Potter and the Order of the Phoenix '07
- Becoming Jane '07
- Keeping Mum '05
- Harry Potter and the Goblet of Fire '05
- Harry Potter and the Prisoner of Azkaban '04
- Ladies in Lavender '04
- Harry Potter and the Chamber of Secrets '02
- Divine Secrets of the Ya-Ya Sisterhood '02
- Gosford Park '01
- Harry Potter and the Sorcerer's Stone '01
- All the King's Men '99
- David Copperfield '99
- Tea with Mussolini '99
- The Last September '99
- Washington Square '97
- Curtain Call '97
- The First Wives Club '96
- Richard III '95
- The Secret Garden '93
- Sister Act 2: Back in the Habit '93
- Sister Act '92
- Hook '91
- The Lonely Passion of Judith Hearne '87
- A Room with a View '86
- Quartet '81
- Clash of the Titans '81
- California Suite '78
- Death on the Nile '78
- Murder by Death '76
- Travels with My Aunt '72
- Oh! What a Lovely War '69
- The Prime of Miss Jean Brodie '69
- Hot Millions '68
- The Honey Pot '67
- Othello '65
- The Pumpkin Eater '64
- The V.I.P.'s '63

Mamie Smith
- Murder on Lenox Avenue '41
- Paradise in Harlem '40

Maurice Smith
- Double Whammy '01
- Fist of Glory '95
- Bloodfist 2 '90

Mel Smith (1952-)
- Twelfth Night '96
- Brain Donors '92
- The Misadventures of Mr. Wilt '90
- The Princess Bride '87

Melanie Smith (1962-)
- Night Hunter '95
- The Baby Doll Murders '92
- Trancers 3: Deth Lives '92

Michael Bailey Smith (1957-)
- The Hills Have Eyes 2 '07
- The Hills Have Eyes '06
- In Hell '03
- Monster Man '03
- Ice '93

Oliver Smith
- Hellbound: Hellraiser 2 '88
- Hellraiser '87

Patricia Smith (1930-)
- Save the Tiger '73
- I Love You, Goodbye '74
- Spirit of St. Louis '57

Paul Smith (1939-)
- Maverick '94
- Desert Kickboxer '92
- Crossing the Line '90
- Gor '88
- Death Chase '87
- Outlaw Force '87
- Sonny Boy '87
- Haunted Honeymoon '86
- Platypus Cove '86
- Crimewave '85
- The Fire in the Store '85
- Red Sonja '85
- Sno-Line '85
- Dune '84
- Jungle Warriors '84
- Pieces '83
- The Salamander '82
- Mortuary '81
- Popeye '80
- Midnight Express '78
- Return of the Tiger '78
- Madron '70
- Loving You '57
- Men of the Fighting Lady '54

Pete Smith
- The Boys '98

Queenie Smith
- Once Were Warriors '94
- The Great Rupert '50
- Mississippi '35

Quinn Smith
- The Bad News Bears '76

Rebekah Louise Smith
- The Bad News Bears in Breaking Training '77
- The Bad News Bears '76

Rex Smith (1956-)
- No Sleep 'Til Madison '02
- The Watcher '00
- A Passion to Kill '94
- The Pirates of Penzance '83
- Transformations '88

Riley Smith (1978-)
- New York Minute '04
- Radio '03
- Eight Legged Freaks '02
- Not Another Teen Movie '01

Robin Smith
- Voodoo Academy '00
- Wild Grizzly '99
- Never Say Die '94
- Bophal '93
- Lights! Camera! Murder! '89

Roger Guenveur Smith (1959-)
- Cover '08
- The Take '07
- Shade '03
- All About the Benjamins '02
- Final Destination '00
- Hamlet '00
- The Color of Courage '98
- Get on the Bus '96
- Deep Cover '92

Roger Smith (1932-)
- Never Steal Anything Small '59
- Auntie Mame '58
- Man of a Thousand Faces '57

Russell Smith
- The King and I '99
- Deep Cover '92

Sam Smith
- Bloom '03
- Botched '07

Savannah Smith
- Wondrous Oblivion '06
- Oliver Twist '05

Sean Smith (1987-)
- Children of the Corn: Revelation '01
- Atomic Train '99

Seth Smith (1982-)
- The Climb '97
- Home Alone 3 '97

Shawn Smith (1922-95)
- It! The Terror from Beyond Space '58
- The Land Unknown '57

Shawnee Smith (1970-)
- Saw V '08
- Saw IV '07
- Saw III '06
- The Island '05
- Saw II '05
- Saw '04
- A Slipping Down Life '99
- Breakfast of Champions '99
- Carnival of Souls '98
- Bombshell '97
- Dogtown '97
- The Low Life '95
- Stephen King's The Stand '94
- Desperate Hours '90
- Who's Harry Crumb? '89
- The Blob '88
- Summer School '87

Shelley Smith (1952-)
- The Fantastic World of D.C. Collins '84
- National Lampoon's Class Reunion '82

Stuart Smith
- The Night the City Screamed '80

Sydney Smith (1909-78)
- No Time for Sergeants '58

Tasha Smith (1971-)
- The Longshots '08
- Daddy's Little Girls '07
- Tyler Perry's Why Did I Get Married? '07

Will Smith (1968-)
- Hancock '08
- I Am Legend '07
- The Pursuit of Happyness '06
- Hitch '05
- I, Robot '04
- Jersey Girl '04 (V)
- Shark Tale '04 (V)
- Bad Boys 2 '03
- Men in Black 2 '02
- Ali '01
- The Legend of Bagger Vance '00
- Wild Wild West '99
- Enemy of the State '98
- Men in Black '97
- Independence Day '96
- Bad Boys '95
- Made in America '93
- Six Degrees of Separation '93
- Where the Day Takes You '92

William (Bill) Smith (1934-)
- Broken Vessels '98
- The Shooter '97
- Taken Alive '95
- The Last Riders '90
- Cartel '90
- Slow Burn '90
- Spirit of the Eagle '90
- Terror in Beverly Hills '90
- Action U.S.A. '89
- Deadly Breed '89
- Evil Altar '89
- Jungle Assault '89
- Emperor of the Bronx '89
- East L.A. Warriors '89
- Memorial Valley Massacre '88
- Maniac Cop '88
- Hell on the Battleground '88
- B.O.R.N. '88
- L.A. Vice '89
- Commando Squad '87
- Platoon Leader '87
- Eye of the Tiger '86
- Moon in Scorpio '86
- Fever Pitch '85
- Mean Season '85
- Angels Die Hard '84
- Red Dawn '84
- Conan the Barbarian '82
- Any Which Way You Can '80
- The Frisco Kid '79
- The Rebels '79
- Seven '79
- Blackjack '78
- Fast Company '78
- Twilight's Last Gleaming '77
- Hollywood Man '76
- Scorchy '76
- The Ultimate Warrior '75
- Boss '74
- The Deadly Trackers '73
- Gentle Savage '73
- A Taste of Hell '73
- Invasion of the Bee Girls '73
- Grave of the Vampire '72
- Chrome and Hot Leather '71
- C.C. & Company '70
- Darker than Amber '70
- The Losers '70
- Run, Angel, Run! '69
- Atlantis, the Lost Continent '61

Yeardley Smith (1964-)
- The Simpsons Movie '07 (V)
- As Good As It Gets '97
- Just Write '97
- We're Back! A Dinosaur's Story '93 (V)
- City Slickers '91
- Ginger Ale Afternoon '89

Smith

Maximum Overdrive '86
Heaven Help Us '85
Legend of Billie Jean '85

J. Smith-Cameron
The Rage: Carrie 2 '99
In and Out '97
Harriet the Spy '96

Jamie Smith-Jackson
Bug '75
Satan's School for Girls '73

Jan Smithers (1949-)
Mr. Nice Guy '86
Where the Lilies Bloom '74

William (Bill) Smithers (1927-)
Death Sport '78
Scorpio '73
Attack! '56

Bill Smitrovich (1947-)
Iron Man '08
The Contract '07
Heavens Fall '06
The Game of Their Lives '05
Mrs. Harris '05
The Reagans '04
The Golden Spiders: A Nero Wolfe Mystery '00
Kiss Toledo Goodbye '00
Thirteen Days '00
The '60s '99
Around the Fire '98
Dean Koontz's Mr. Murder '98
Futuresport '98
Air Force One '97
Ghosts of Mississippi '96
Independence Day '96
The Trigger Effect '96
Bodily Harm '95
Nick of Time '95
Crazy People '90
Renegades '89
Manhunter '86
A Killing Affair '85
Silver Bullet '85
Overdrawn at the Memory Bank '83

Jimmy Smits (1956-)
The Jane Austen Book Club '07
Star Wars: Episode 3—Revenge of the Sith '05
Star Wars: Episode 2—Attack of the Clones '02
Bless the Child '00
Price of Glory '00
The Million Dollar Hotel '99
Murder in Mind '97
Marshal Law '96
The Last Word '95
The Cisco Kid '94
My Family '94
Gross Misconduct '93
Stephen King's The Tommyknockers '93
Fires Within '91
Switch '91
Vital Signs '90
Old Gringo '89
Glitz '88
The Believers '87
Stamp of a Killer '87
L.A. Law '86
Running Scared '86

Sonja Smits (1958-)
A Different Loyalty '04
Siblings '04
How to Deal '03
Owning Mahowny '03
Life with Judy Garland—Me and My Shadows '01
That's My Baby! '88
Videodrome '83
The Pit '81

Jurnee Smollett (1986-)
The Great Debaters '07
Roll Bounce '05
Ruby's Bucket of Blood '01
Selma, Lord, Selma '99
Eve's Bayou '97

JB Smoove
Mr. Deeds '02
Pootie Tang '01

Dick Smothers (1939-)
Casino '95
Tales of the Unexpected '91
Speed Zone '88

Tom Smothers (1937-)
Speed Zone '88
Pandemonium '82
Serial '80
The Kids Are Alright '79
A Pleasure Doing Business '79
Silver Bears '78
Alice Through the Looking Glass '66

Victoria Smurfit (1974-)
Bulletproof Monk '03
About a Boy '02
Berkeley Square '98
Ivanhoe '97
Romance and Rejection '96
The Run of the Country '95

Ann Smyrner (1934-)
Beyond the Law '68
The House of 1000 Dolls '67
Reptilicus '62

Sam Snead
The Caddy '53
Follow the Sun '51

David Snedeker
If You Only Knew '00
Detour '99

Wesley Snipes (1962-)
The Contractor '07
The Detonator '06
Seven Seconds '05
Blade: Trinity '04
Blade 2 '02
Liberty Stands Still '02
Undisputed '02
ZigZag '02
The Art of War '00
Disappearing Acts '00
Blade '98
Down in the Delta '98
Futuresport '98
U.S. Marshals '98
Murder at 1600 '97
One Night Stand '97
The Fan '96
America's Dream '95
Money Train '95
To Wong Foo, Thanks for Everything, Julie Newmar '95
Waiting to Exhale '95
Drop Zone '94
Sugar Hill '94
Boiling Point '93
Demolition Man '93
Rising Sun '93
Passenger 57 '92
White Men Can't Jump '92
Jungle Fever '91
New Jack City '91
The Waterdance '91
King of New York '90
Mo' Better Blues '90
Major League '89
Streets of Gold '86
Wildcats '86
Across the Tracks '89
Blueberry Hill '89
Murphy's Law '86
L.A. Bad '85
Pale Rider '85
Nadia '84
A Night in Heaven '83
The Solitary Man '82
Trick or Treats '82
The Attic '80
The Fury '78
Diary of a Mad Housewife '70
Silent Night, Lonely Night '69

Snoop Dogg (1971-)
The Tenants '06
Racing Stripes '05 (V)
Soul Plane '04
Starsky & Hutch '04
Malibu's Most Wanted '03 (V)
Old School '03
Baby Boy '01
Bones '01
Training Day '01
The Wash '01
Urban Menace '99
The Wrecking Crew '99
Caught Up '98
Ride '98
Half-Baked '97

Brittany Snow (1986-)
Prom Night '08
Hairspray '07
John Tucker Must Die '06
The Pacifier '05

Raven Snow
Delta of Venus '95
Red Shoe Diaries 6: How I Met My Husband '95

Victoria Snow
Waking Life '01
Waking Up Wally '05
My Husband's Double Life '01
Buffalo Jump '90
Love and Hate: A Marriage Made in Hell '90

Arlen Dean Snyder (1933-)
Cora Unashamed '00
Mommy 2: Mommy's Day '96
Running Cool '93
Internal Affairs '90
Marked for Death '90
Wheels of Terror '90
Heartbreak Ridge '86
Deadly Force '83
Night Partners '83
No Place to Hide '81
Red Flag: The Ultimate Game '81
Yanks '79
Young Love, First Love '79
Dear Detective '79
Scalpel '76

Drew Snyder (1946-)
Blindfold: Acts of Obsession '94
Separate Lives '94
Dance with Death '91
Project: Eliminator '91
Izzy & Moe '85
Firestarter '84
Night School '81

Suzanne Snyder (1962-)
Killer Klowns from Outer Space '88
The Night Before '88
Retribution '88
Prettykill '87

Michele (Michael) Soavi (1957-)
Demons '86
Creepers '85
A Blade in the Dark '83
Gates of Hell '80

Barry Sobel (1959-)
That Thing You Do! '96
I Love Trouble '94
L.A. Rules: The Pros and Cons of Breathing '94
Doc Hollywood '91
Martians Go Home! '90
Punchline '88

Leelee Sobieski (1982-)
88 Minutes '08
In the Name of the King: A Dungeon Siege Tale '08
Heavens Fall '06
The Wicker Man '06
Dangerous Liaisons '03
Max '02
The Glass House '01
Joy Ride '01
My First Mister '01
Uprising '01
Here on Earth '00
Eyes Wide Shut '99
Joan of Arc '99
Never Been Kissed '99
Deep Impact '98
A Soldier's Daughter Never Cries '98
Jungle 2 Jungle '96
A Horse for Danny '95

Maria Socas
Deathstalker 2: Duel of the Titans '87
Soldier's Revenge '84
The Warrior & the Sorceress '84

Kristina Soderbaum (1912-2001)
Night Train to Venice '93
Kolberg '45
Jud Suess '40

Steven Soderbergh (1963-)
Waking Life '01
Schizopolis '97

Camilla Soeberg (1966-)
The Empty Mirror '99
Mouse Hunt '97
Erotique '94
A Night of Love '87
Twist & Shout '84

Abraham Sofaer (1896-1988)
Demon with a Glass Hand '64
Captain Sinbad '63
Bhowani Junction '56
Elephant Walk '54
Naked Jungle '54
Quo Vadis '51
Calling Paul Temple '48
Dual Alibi '47

Sojin (1884-1954)
Seven Samurai '54

Rena Sofer (1968-)
Carrie '02
Keeping the Faith '00
Traffic '00
The Stepsister '97
Twinsitters '95

Hans Sohnker (1903-81)
The Phantom of Soho '64
Sherlock Holmes and the Deadly Necklace '62
For the First Time '59
Die Grosse Freiheit Nr. 7 '45
I Was a Teenage Werewolf '57
Baron of Arizona '51
Cloak and Dagger '46
A Scandal in Paris '46
For Whom the Bell Tolls '43
The Road to Morocco '42
Comrade X '40
The Real Glory '39
Conquest '37
The Lower Depths '36

Miguel Angel Sola (1950-)
Tango '98
A Shadow You Soon Will Be '94
Mayalunta '86
Funny, Dirty Little War '83

Silvia Solar (1940-)
Devil's Kiss '75
Night of the Howling Beast '75
The Gentleman Killer '69
Finger on the Trigger '65
As If It Were Raining '63

Domingo Soler
The Monster Demolisher '60

Fernando Soler (1896-1979)
The Great Madcap '49
Susana '51

Paul Soles (1930-)
The Score '01
The Lotus Eaters '93
Beethoven Lives Upstairs '92
The Gunrunner '84
Ticket to Heaven '81

P. J. Soles (1955-)
The Tooth Fairy '06
The Devil's Rejects '05
Jawbreaker '98
Little Bigfoot '96
Soldier's Fortune '91
Alienator '89
B.O.R.N. '88
Innocent Prey '88
Saigon Commandos '88
Sweet Dreams '85
Stripes '81
Rock 'n' Roll High School '79
Halloween '78
The Possessed '77
The Boy in the Plastic Bubble '76
Carrie '76

Marilyn Sokol
Something Short of Paradise '79
Foul Play '78
The Goodbye Girl '77

Marla Sokoloff (1980-)
Crazylove '05
Love on the Side '04
The Tollbooth '04
Sugar & Spice '01
Dude, Where's My Car? '00
Whatever It Takes '00

Vladimir Sokoloff (1889-1962)
Taras Bulba '62
Mr. Sardonicus '61
Beyond the Time Barrier '60

Yulia Solntseva (1901-89)
Earth '30
Aelita: Queen of Mars '24
The Cigarette Girl of Mosselprom '24

Bruce Solomon (1944-)
Auto Focus '02
Night of the Creeps '86
Foul Play '78
Children Shouldn't Play with Dead Things '72

Charles Solomon
Witchcraft 4: Virgin Heart '92
Witchcraft 2: The Temptress '90
Witchcraft 3: The Kiss of Death '90
The Channeler '89

Todd Solondz (1960-)
As Good As It Gets '97
Fear, Anxiety and Depression '89

Anatoli (Otto) Solonitzin (1934-82)
Stalker '79
Solaris '72
Andrei Rublev '66

Elena Solovei (1947-)
Oblomov '81
A Slave of Love '78
An Unfinished Piece for a Player Piano '77

Yanti Somer
Reactor '85
Cosmos: War of the Planets '80

Ian Somerhalder (1978-)
Marco Polo '07
Pulse '06
In Enemy Hands '04
The Rules of Attraction '02
Life as a House '01

Kristi Somers (1962-)
Tomboy '85
Hardbodies '84

Suzanne Somers (1946-)
Say It Isn't So '01
No Laughing Matter '97
Seduced by Evil '94
Serial Mom '94
Happily Ever After '82
Nothing Personal '80
Yesterday's Hero '79
Ants '77
Sky Heist '75
American Graffiti '73

Bonnie Somerville (1974-)
Wedding Wars '06
Without a Paddle '04
Sleep Easy, Hutch Rimes '00

Geraldine Somerville (1967-)
Gosford Park '01
The Aristocrats '99
Cracker: Best Boys '95
Cracker: Brotherly Love '95
Cracker: True Romance '95
Haunted '95
Cracker: Men Should Weep '94
Cracker: To Be a Somebody '94
Catherine Cookson's The Black Velvet Gown '92

Phyllis Somerville
Little Children '06
Swimfan '02

Julie Sommars (1941-)
Sex and the Single Parent '82
Herbie Goes to Monte Carlo '77
I'm the Girl He Wants to Kill '74

Elke Sommer (1940-)
Severed Ties '92
Adventures Beyond Belief '87
Anastasia: The Mystery of Anna '86
Jenny's War '85
Lily in Love '85
No One Cries Forever '85
Inside the Third Reich '82
The Big Scam '79
The Double McGuffin '79
Fantastic Seven '79
Prisoner of Zenda '79
The Treasure Seekers '79
Left for Dead '78
Swiss Conspiracy '77
The Invisible Strangler '76
One Away '76
Carry On Behind '75
Lisa and the Devil '75
Ten Little Indians '75
It's Not the Size That Counts '74
Probe '72
Torture Chamber of Baron Blood '72
Zeppelin '71
The Invincible Six '68
The Wrecking Crew '68
The Corrupt Ones '67
Deadlier Than the Male '67
Boy, Did I Get a Wrong Number! '66
The Oscar '66
A Shot in the Dark '64
The Prize '63
The Victors '63
Sweet Ecstasy '62
Daniella by Night '61

Josef Sommer (1934-)
- Stop-Loss '08
- The Invasion '07
- X-Men: The Last Stand '06
- Surf Nazis Must Die '87
- Searching for Paradise '02
- The Sum of All Fears '02
- Family Man '00
- The Next Best Thing '00
- Shaft '00
- Patch Adams '98
- Hidden in America '96
- Mistrial '96
- The Proposition '97
- Moonlight and Valentino '95
- Strange Days '95
- The Enemy Within '94
- Nobody's Fool '94
- Hostages '93
- The Mighty Ducks '92
- An American Story '92
- Yuri Nosenko, KGB '86
- Dracula's Widow '88
- Malice '93
- Absence of Malice '81
- The Rosary Murders '87
- Execution of Raymond Graham '85
- Reds '81
- Rollover '81
- Hide in Plain Sight '80
- The Scarlet Letter '79
- Iceman '84
- Witness '85
- Target '85
- Bloodhounds of Broadway '89
- Forced March '90
- Cyanide '83
- Independence Day '83
- Chances Are '89
- Silkwood '83
- Still of the Night '82

Jennifer Sommerfield
- Megalodon '03

Helga Sommerfeld (1941-91)
- Code Name Alpha '67
- The Phantom of Soho '64

Sommore (1966-)
- Friday After Next '02

Gale Sondergaard (1899-1985)
- Echoes '83
- The Return of a Man Called Horse '76
- Savage Intruder '68
- East Side, West Side '49
- The Road to Rio '47
- Anna and the King of Siam '46
- The Time of Their Lives '46
- The Climax '44
- The Invisible Man's Revenge '44
- Spider Woman '44
- Isle of Forgotten Sins '43
- A Night to Remember '42
- The Black Cat '41
- The Blue Bird '40
- The Letter '40
- The Mark of Zorro '40
- Juarez '39
- Never Say Die '39
- The Life of Emile Zola '37
- Anthony Adverse '36

Paul Sonkkila
- Mr. Reliable: A True Story '95
- The Interview '98
- The Hard Word '02

Brenda Song (1988-)
- Get a Clue '02
- Like Mike '02

Ricky Sorenson (1946-94)
- The Sword in the Stone '63 (V)
- Tarzan and the Trappers '58

Linda Sorensen
- Kavik the Wolf Dog '80
- Stone Cold Dead '80
- Family Reunion '88
- Joshua Then and Now '85
- Relative Fear '95

Michael Sonye (1928-)
- Sorority Babes in the Slimeball Bowl-A-Rama '87 (V)
- Surf Nazis Must Die '87

Jack Soo (1916-79)
- Return from Witch Mountain '78
- The Green Berets '68
- Flower Drum Song '61

Michael Sopkiw (1954-)
- After the Fall of New York '85
- Blastfighter '85
- Massacre in Dinosaur Valley '85
- Devilfish '85

Agnes Soral (1960-)
- Window to Paris '95

Kevin Sorbo (1958-)
- Meet the Spartans '08
- Walking Tall: Lone Justice '07
- Kull the Conqueror '97
- Hercules the Legendary Journeys, Vol. 1: And the Amazon Women '94
- Hercules the Legendary Journeys, Vol. 2: The Lost Kingdom '94
- Hercules the Legendary Journeys, Vol. 3: The Circle of Fire '94
- Hercules the Legendary Journeys, Vol. 4: In the Underworld '94

Alberto Sordi (1920-2003)
- Those Magnificent Men in Their Flying Machines '65

Guy Sorel (1914-94)
- MayFlower: The Pilgrims' Adventure '79

Jean Sorel (1934-)
- A Lizard in a Woman's Skin '71
- Short Night of Glass Dolls '77
- Belle de Jour '67
- Sandra of a Thousand Delights '65
- I Vitelloni '53
- The White Sheik '52

Louise Sorel (1940-)
- Mazes and Monsters '82
- When Every Day Was the Fourth of July '78
- Get Christie Love! '74
- Plaza Suite '71
- The President's Plane Is Missing '71

Nancy Sorel (1964-)
- I Love You, Don't Touch Me! '97
- In the Lake of the Woods '96

Ted (Theodore) Sorel (1936-)
- Me and the Mob '94
- Basket Case 2 '90
- From Beyond '86
- Network '76

Charo Soriano (1928-)
- Orgy of the Vampires '73
- Dracula's Great Love '72
- The Garden of Delights '70

Arleen (Arlene) Sorkin (1956-)
- Comic Book: The Movie '04
- It's Pat: The Movie '94
- I Don't Buy Kisses Anymore '92

Lodovico Sorret
- See Tom Noonan

Mira Sorvino (1967-)
- The Hades Factor '06
- Human Trafficking '05
- The Final Cut '04
- Gods and Generals '03
- Angel of Death '02
- Between Strangers '02
- Wisegirls '02
- The Great Gatsby '01
- The Grey Zone '01
- The Triumph of Love '01
- Free Money '99
- Summer of Sam '99
- At First Sight '98
- Lulu on the Bridge '98
- The Replacement Killers '98
- Mimic '97
- Romy and Michele's High School Reunion '97
- Beautiful Girls '96
- Sweet Nothing '96
- Blue in the Face '95
- The Buccaneers '95
- Mighty Aphrodite '95
- Norma Jean and Marilyn '96
- Tarantella '95
- Barcelona '94
- New York Cop '94
- Parallel Lives '94
- Quiz Show '94
- Amongst Friends '93
- Tales of Erotica '93

Paul Sorvino (1939-)
- Mr. Fix It '06
- The Cooler '03
- Mambo Italiano '03
- Hey Arnold! The Movie '02 (V)
- Perfume '01
- See Spot Run '01
- Cheaters '00
- The Thin Blue Lie '00
- Dead Broke '99
- Houdini '99
- That Championship Season '99
- Bulworth '98
- Knock Off '98
- Dogwatch '97
- Joe Torre: Curveballs Along the Way '97
- Money Talks '97
- Most Wanted '97
- Escape Clause '96
- Love is All There is '96
- William Shakespeare's Romeo and Juliet '96
- Cover Me '95
- Nixon '95
- Backstreet Justice '94
- The Firm '93
- Age Isn't Everything '91
- Nightmare '91
- The Rocketeer '91
- Dick Tracy '90
- Goodfellas '90
- Almost Partners '87
- A Fine Mess '86
- My Mother's Secret Life '84
- Very Close Quarters '84
- Chiefs '83
- I, the Jury '82
- Melanie '82
- Off the Wall '82
- That Championship Season '82
- Reds '81
- Cruising '80
- Question of Honor '80
- Lost and Found '79
- Bloodbrothers '78
- Oh, God! '77
- I Will, I Will for Now '76
- The Gambler '74
- Shoot It Black, Shoot It Blue '74
- A Touch of Class '73
- The Day of the Dolphin '73
- Cry Uncle! '71
- The Panic in Needle Park '71
- Where's Poppa? '70

Roberto Sosa (1970-)
- Hombres Armados '97
- Cabeza de Vaca '90
- Highway Patrolman '91

Nina Sosanya
- Casanova '05
- Manderlay '05

Shannyn Sossamon (1979-)
- One Missed Call '08
- Catacombs '07
- The Holiday '06
- Wristcutters: A Love Story '06
- Chasing Ghosts '05
- Devour '05
- Kiss Kiss Bang Bang '05
- The Order '03
- 40 Days and 40 Nights '02
- The Rules of Attraction '02
- A Knight's Tale '01

Paul Soter (1972-)
- Beerfest '06
- Club Dread '04
- Super Troopers '01

Ann Sothern (1909-2001)
- The Whales of August '87
- Little Dragons '80
- The Manitou '78
- Crazy Mama '75
- The Killing Kind '73
- The Best Man '64
- Lady in a Cage '64
- The Blue Gardenia '53
- Nancy Goes to Rio '50
- The Judge Steps Out '49
- A Letter to Three Wives '49
- Words and Music '48
- Panama Hattie '42
- Lady Be Good '41
- Brother Orchid '40
- Hell-Ship Morgan '36
- Kid Millions '34

Talisa Soto (1967-)
- Ballistic: Ecks vs. Sever '02
- Pinero '01
- Island of the Dead '00
- The Corporate Ladder '97
- Flypaper '97
- Mortal Kombat 2: Annihilation '97
- Sunchaser '96
- Vampirella '96
- Mortal Kombat 1: The Movie '95
- Don Juan DeMarco '94
- The Mambo Kings '92
- Hostage '92
- License to Kill '89
- Spike of Bensonhurst '88

Hugo Soto (1954-94)
- Man Facing Southeast '86
- Times to Come '81

Fernando Soto
- See Fernando Soto "Mantequilla"

Kath Soucie (1967-)
- Space Chimps '08
- Happily N'Ever After '07 (V)
- Pooh's Heffalump Movie '05 (V)
- Clifford's Really Big Movie '04 (V)
- Piglet's Big Movie '03 (V)
- Rugrats Go Wild! '03 (V)
- Return to Never Land '02
- Rugrats in Paris: The Movie '00 (V)

Sissy Spacek (1949-)
- Hot Rod '07
- Pictures of Hollis Woods '07
- An American Haunting '06
- Nine Lives '05
- North Country '05
- The Ring 2 '05
- A Home at the End of the World '04
- Last Call: The Final Chapter of F. Scott Fitzgerald '02
- Tuck Everlasting '02
- In the Bedroom '01
- The Straight Story '99
- Blast from the Past '98
- Affliction '97
- Beyond the Call '96
- If These Walls Could Talk '96
- The Good Old Boys '95
- The Grass Harp '95
- Trading Mom '94
- A Place for Annie '94
- A Private Matter '92
- JFK '91
- Hard Promises '92
- The Long Walk Home '90
- Crimes of the Heart '86
- 'night, Mother '86
- Violets Are Blue '86
- Marie '85
- The River '84
- The Man with Two Brains '83 (V)
- Missing '82
- Raggedy Man '81
- Coal Miner's Daughter '80
- Heart Beat '80
- 3 Women '77
- Welcome to L.A. '77
- Carrie '76
- Katherine '75
- Badlands '74
- Ginger in the Morning '73
- Prime Cut '72

David Soul (1943-)
- The Rugrats Movie '98 (V)
- Starsky & Hutch '04
- Pentathon '94
- Grave Secrets: The Legacy '92
- Tides of War '90
- In the Cold of the Night '89
- Appointment with Death '88
- In the Line of Duty: The FBI Murders '88
- Hanoi Hilton '87
- Through Naked Eyes '87
- World War III '86
- The Key to Rebecca '85
- The Manions of America '81
- Homeward Bound '80
- Rage '80
- Salem's Lot '79
- Little Ladies of the Night '77
- Dog Pound Shuffle '75
- Magnum Force '73

Renee Soutendijk (1957-)
- Keeper of the City '92
- Eve of Destruction '90
- Forced March '90
- Grave Secrets '89
- Murderers Among Us: The Simon Wiesenthal Story '89
- The 4th Man '79
- Spetters '80

Eve Southern (1898-)
- Morocco '30
- Law of the Sea '32

Charles Southwood
- Guns for Dollars '73
- Fistful of Lead '70

Ben Soutten
- The Mutiny of the Elsinore '39

Charles Southwood (1898-)
- Second Victory '87
- Cold Room '84
- Out of Order '84
- Johnny Got His Gun '71
- Inside the Third Reich '82

Catherine Spaak (1945-)
- Honey '81
- The Cat o' Nine Tails '71
- Counter Punch '71
- The Libertine '69
- Hotel '67
- Circle of Love '64
- Empty Canvas '64
- The Easy Life '63
- Le Trou '59

Arthur Space (1908-)
- Terror at Red Wolf Inn '72
- Night Riders of Montana '51
- The Vanishing Westerner '50
- Miss Grant Takes Richmond '49
- A Southern Yankee '48
- The Red House '47
- Magnificent Doll '46
- Riot Squad '41

Kevin Spacey (1959-)
- 21 '08
- Fred Claus '07
- Superman Returns '06
- Edison Force '05
- Beyond the Sea '04
- The Life of David Gale '03
- United States of Leland '03
- Austin Powers in Goldmember '02
- K-PAX '01
- The Shipping News '01
- The Big Kahuna '00
- Pay It Forward '00
- American Beauty '99
- Ordinary Decent Criminal '99
- A Bug's Life '98 (V)
- Hurlyburly '98
- The Negotiator '98
- L.A. Confidential '97
- Midnight in the Garden of Good and Evil '97
- A Time to Kill '96
- Looking for Richard '96
- Seven '95
- The Usual Suspects '95
- Doomsday Gun '94
- Outbreak '94
- Swimming with Sharks '94
- Iron Will '93
- Consenting Adults '92
- Glengarry Glen Ross '92
- Henry & June '90
- Dad '89
- See No Evil, Hear No Evil '89
- Long Day's Journey into Night '88
- Rocket Gibraltar '88
- Working Girl '88
- The Murder of Mary Phagan '87

David Spade (1964-)
- The Benchwarmers '06
- Grandma's Boy '06
- Racing Stripes '05 (V)
- Dickie Roberts: Former Child Star '03
- Joe Dirt '01
- The Emperor's New Groove '00 (V)
- Loser '00

Lost and Found '99
The Rugrats Movie '98 (V)
Senseless '98
Beavis and Butt-Head Do America '96 (V)
Black Sheep '96
8 Heads in a Duffel Bag '96
A Very Brady Sequel '96
Tommy Boy '95
P.C.U. '94
Coneheads '93

James Spader (1961-)
I Witness '03
Secretary '02
The Stickup '01
Slow Burn '00
The Watcher '00
Supernova '99
Critical Care '97
Curtain Call '97
Keys to Tulsa '96
Two Days in the Valley '96
Crash '95
Stargate '94
Wolf '94
Dream Lover '93
The Music of Chance '93
Bob Roberts '92
Storyville '92
True Colors '91
Bad Influence '90
White Palace '90
The Rachel Papers '89
sex, lies and videotape '89
Baby Boom '87
Jack's Back '87
Less Than Zero '87
Mannequin '87
Wall Street '87
Pretty in Pink '86
The New Kids '85
Tuff Turf '85
Family Secrets '84
Endless Love '81

Joshua Spafford (1972-)
Robot Stories '03
XX/XY '02

Douglas Spain (1974-)
Pandemic '07
The Reading Room '05
44 Minutes: The North Hollywood Shootout '03
Nightstalker '02
What's Cooking? '00
The Last Best Sunday '98
Star Maps '97
Twelve Angry Men '97
Riot in the Streets '96

Fay Spain (1932-83)
The Godfather, Part 2 '74
Flight to Fury '66
Hercules and the Captive Women '63
Al Capone '59
God's Little Acre '58
Dragstrip Girl '57
Teenage Doll '57

Rafe Spall (1983-)
Hot Fuzz '07
The Chatterley Affair '06
Dracula '06
Green Street Hooligans '05

Timothy Spall (1957-)
Enchanted '07
Sweeney Todd: The Demon Barber of Fleet Street '07
Harry Potter and the Goblet of Fire '05
Harry Potter and the Prisoner of Azkaban '04
Lemony Snicket's A Series of Unfortunate Events '04
The Last Samurai '03
My House in Umbria '03
All or Nothing '02
Nicholas Nickleby '02
Lucky Break '01
Rock Star '01
Vacuuming Completely Nude in Paradise '01 (V)
Vanilla Sky '01
Chicken Run '00 (V)
Intimacy '00
Love's Labour's Lost '00

Sweet Adeline '35
Imitation of Life '34
Marie Galante '34
Sing and Like It '34
42nd Street '33
Going Hollywood '33
Gold Diggers of 1933 '33
Lady for a Day '33
Corsair '31
Kept Husbands '31

Camilla Sparv (1943-)
Survival Zone '84
Downhill Racer '69
Dead Heat on a Merry-Go-Round '66
Murderers' Row '66

Tracy Spaulding
Stormy Nights '97
The Deadly Secret '94
Striking Point '94

Dan Speaker
Wizards of the Demon Sword '94
Glitch! '88

Jeff Speakman (1958-)
The Gunman '03
Running Red '99
Timelock '99
Land of the Free '98
Memorial Day '98
Escape from Atlantis '97
Scorpio One '97
Deadly Outbreak '96
Plato's Run '96
The Expert '95
Street Knight '93
The Perfect Weapon '91

Bernard Spear (1919-2003)
Yentl '83
Bedazzled '68

Hannah Spearritt (1981-)
Agent Cody Banks 2: Destination London '04
Seed of Chucky '04

Aries Spears (1975-)
Jiminy Glick in LaLa Wood '05

Britney Spears (1981-)
Austin Powers In Goldmember '02
Crossroads '02

Eddie Spears (1982-)
Black Cloud '04
The Slaughter Rule '01

David Speck
Crazy in Alabama '99
My Life Without Me '03
Underworld '03

Carol Speed (1945-)
Avenging Disco Godfather '76
Bummer '73
The Mack '73
Savage! '73
The Big Bird Cage '72

Scott Speedman (1975-)
Weirdsville '07
Underworld: Evolution '05
XXX: State of the Union '05
The 24th Day '04
Dark Blue '03
Duets '00

Hermann Speelmanns (1904-60)
Baron Munchausen '43
F.P. 1 Doesn't Answer '33

Hugo Speer (1969-)
The Interpreter '05
The Debt '03
Deathwatch '02
Do or Die '01
Mainline Run '98

Swing '98
The Full Monty '96

Martin Speer
The Dark Ride '84
The Hills Have Eyes '77

Richard Speight, Jr. (1970-)
Love for Rent '05
Band of Brothers '01
Speed 2: Cruise Control '97
Independence Day '96
Menno's Mind '97
Amanda and the Alien '95
Dead Weekend '95
Out There '95
Demonic Toys '92
Goodbye, Miss 4th of July '88
Ernest Goes to Camp '87
Love Leads the Way '84

Dona Speir (1964-)
Fit to Kill '93
Hard Hunted '92
Do or Die '91
Guns '90
Picasso Trigger '89
Savage Beach '89
Hard Ticket to Hawaii '87
All God's Children '80
A Dream for Christmas '73
Man & Boy '71

Tori Spelling (1973-)
The Family Plan '05
How to Lose Your Lover '04
Scary Movie 2 '01
Sol Goode '01
Trick '99
Perpetrators of the Crime '98
The House of Yes '97
Scream 2 '97
Last Action Hero '93

Peter Spellos
Men in Black 2 '02
Bound '96
Dinosaur Island '93

Georgina Spelvin (1936-)
Next Year in Jerusalem '84
Police Academy '84
Honkytonk Nights '78
I Spit on Your Corpse '74

Bruce Spence (1945-)
Aquamarine '06
Star Wars: Episode 3— Revenge of the Sith '05
Finding Nemo '03 (V)
The Matrix Revolutions '03
Inspector Gadget 2 '03
Queen of the Damned '02
Moby Dick '98
Dark City '97
Sweet Talker '91
...Almost '90
The Shrimp on the Barbie '90
Rikky and Pete '88
The Year My Voice Broke '87
Mad Max: Beyond Thunderdome '85
Midnite Spares '85
Where the Green Ants Dream '84
The Road Warrior '82

Peter Spence (1963-)
Unfinished Business '89
Crazy Moon '87

Sebastian Spence (1969-)
Shock to the System '06
Category 7: The End of the World '05
Third Man Out: A Donald Strachey Mystery '05'
Family of Cops 3 '98
Family of Cops 2: Breach of Faith '97
Firestorm '97
Family of Cops '95
The Boys of St. Vincent '93

Bud Spencer (1929-)
Troublemakers '94
Aladdin '86
Miami Supercops '85

Go for It '83
Crime Busters '78
Flatfoot '78
Odds and Evens '78
Trinity Is Still My Name '73
All the Way, Boys '73
A Reason to Live, a Reason to Die '73
They Call Me Trinity '72
Today We Kill, Tomorrow We Die '71
Boot Hill '69
Ace High '68
Beyond the Law '68

Chris Spencer (1968-)
Sin '02
All About You '01
The Sixth Man '97
Don't Be a Menace to South Central While Drinking Your Juice in the Hood '95

Danielle Spencer
The Crossing '92
What the Moon Saw '90

Douglas Spencer (1910-60)
River of No Return '54
Trouble along the Way '53
The Thing '51

Jesse Spencer (1979-)
Flourish '06
P.D. James: Death in Holy Orders '03
Swimming Upstream '03
Uptown Girls '03

John Spencer (1946-)
Ravenous '99
The Negotiator '98
Twilight '98
Cafe Society '97
Cold Around the Heart '97
Cop Land '97
Albino Alligator '96
The Rock '96
Forget Paris '95
Presumed Innocent '90
Black Rain '89
Simple Justice '89
Echoes '83

Tara Spencer-Nairn (1978-)
Waking Up Wally '05
Wishmaster 4: The Prophecy Fulfilled '02
New Waterford Girl '99
Don't Look Down '98

Volker Spengler (1939-)
The Ogre '96
Chinese Roulette '86
Veronika Voss '82
In a Year of 13 Moons '78
The Stationmaster's Wife '77
Satan's Brew '76

Jeremy Spenser (1937-)
The Prince and the Showgirl '57
Escapade '55
Summertime '55
Devil on Horseback '54
Kind Hearts and Coronets '49

Tony Sperandeo (1953-)
La Scorta '94
Acla's Descent into Floristella '87

Wendie Jo Sperber (1958-2005)
Back to the Future, Part 3
Stewardess School '86
Back to the Future '85
Moving Violations '85
Bachelor Party '84
First Time '82
Used Cars '80
1941 '79
I Wanna Hold Your Hand '78

Alessandro Sperduti
I Am David '04
Heaven '01

Scott Spiegel (1957-)
Red '91
Darkman '90
The Dead Next Door '89
Skinned Alive '89
Evil Dead 2: Dead by Dawn '87
Thou Shalt Not Kill...Except '87
Evil Dead '83

David Spielberg (1939-)
Silent Predators '99
Alice '90
The Stranger '87
Christine '84
Policewoman Centerfold '83
The Best Little Girl in the World '81
The Henderson Monster '80
Sergeant Matlovich vs. the U.S. Air Force '78
Prime Time '77
Force Five '75

Steven Spielberg (1947-)
Austin Powers In Goldmember '02
The Blues Brothers '80

Laurent Spielvogel (1955-)
The Monster '96
French Kiss '95

Riva Spier
Syngenor '90
Ghost Keeper '80

Jacques Spiesser (1947-)
Baxter '89
La Truite '83
Black and White in Color '76

Mickey Spillane (1918-2006)
Mommy 2: Mommy's Day '96
Mommy '95
Girl Hunters '63

Maria Grazia Spina (1936-)
Revolt of the Barbarians '64
Tiger of the Seven Seas '62

Joe Spinell (1938-89)
Operation Warzone '89
Rapid Fire '89
The Pick-Up Artist '87
The Children of Times Square '86
Big Score '83
Vigilante '83
Walking the Edge '83
Fanatic '82
The Last Fight '82
Night Shift '82
One Down, Two to Go! '82
The Godfather 1902-1959: The Complete Epic '81
Nighthawks '81
Cruising '80
Forbidden Zone '80
Little Dragons '80
Maniac '80
Winter Kills '79
One Man Jury '78
Star Crash '78
Rocky '76
Taxi Driver '76
The Godfather, Part 2 '74
Cops and Robbers '73

Stephen Spinella (1956-)
And Then Came Love '07
Connie and Carla '04
Our Town '03
Bubble Boy '01
Ravenous '99
What the Deaf Man Heard '98
David Searching '97
Great Expectations '97

The Jackal '97
Love! Valour! Compassion! '96
Virtuosity '95
And the Band Played On '93

Brent Spiner (1949-)
Material Girls '06
The Aviator '04
Master of Disguise '02
Star Trek: Nemesis '02
A Girl Thing '01
Gepetto '00
Introducing Dorothy Dandridge '99
South Park: Bigger, Longer and Uncut '99 (V)
Star Trek: Insurrection '98
Out to Sea '97
Phenomenon '96
Independence Day '96
Star Trek: First Contact '96
Star Trek: Generations '94
Crazy from the Heart '91
Family Sins '87

Victor Spinetti (1932-)
The Krays '90
A Hard Day's Night '64
Help! '65
Voyage of the Damned '76
Return of the Pink Panther '74
Start the Revolution without Me '70
Magical Mystery Tour '67

Jordana Spiro (1977-)
Alone With Her '07
Living & Dying '07
Must Love Dogs '05
Thirteenth Day of Christmas '00
Fruit '89
Ringmaster '98

Rick Springfield (1949-)
Legion '98
Silent Motive '91
Nick Knight '89
Hard to Hold '84

Bruce Springsteen (1949-)
High Fidelity '00
Chuck Berry: Hail! Hail! Rock 'n' Roll '87

Pamela Springsteen (1962-)
The Gumshoe Kid '89
Sleepaway Camp 3: Teenage Wasteland '89
Sleepaway Camp 2: Unhappy Campers '88
Dixie Lanes '88
My Science Project '85
Reckless '84
Fast Times at Ridgemont High '82

Ove Sprogoe (1919-2004)
Famous Five Get into Trouble '87

Cole Sprouse (1992-)
You Are Not Alone '78
The Prince and the Pauper '07

Dylan Sprouse (1992-)
Big Daddy '99
The Prince and the Pauper '07

Dina Spybey (1965-)
Just like Heaven '05
Freaky Friday '03
The Haunted Mansion '03
Isn't She Great '00
An Alan Smithee Film: Burn, Hollywood, Burn '97

June Squibb (1935-)
Welcome to Mooseport '04
About Schmidt '02

Katherine Squire (1903-95)
Ride in the Whirlwind '66
Studs Lonigan '60

Charlie Spradling (1968-)
Spent '00
A Christmas Carol '99
Paradise Road '97
The Secret Agent '96
Sense and Sensibility '95
Impromptu '90
Oranges Are Not the Only Fruit '89

Elizabeth Spriggs (1929-)
Parker '87

Jerry Springer (1944-)
Austin Powers 2: The Spy Who Shagged Me '99

G.D. Spradlin (1920-)
Dick '99
The Long Kiss Goodnight '96
Riders of the Purple Sage '96
Nick of Time '95
Canadian Bacon '94
Ed Wood '94
Carolina Skeletons '92
Tank '83
The Lords of Discipline '83
Call to Glory '84
The Formula '80
The War of the Roses '89
Wrong Is Right '82
The Godfather 1902-1959: The Complete Epic '81
Apocalypse Now '79
North Dallas Forty '79
And I Alone Survived '78
One on One '77
The Godfather, Part 2 '74
The Only Way Home '72
Zabriskie Point '70
Hell's Angels '69 '69

Ann Stafford
Keep My Grave Open '80
Poor White Trash 2 '75

Michael Stadvec
The Chosen One: Legend of the Raven '98
The Dentist '96

Sage Stallone (1976-)
Chaos '05
Daylight '96
Fatally Yours '95
Rocky 5 '90

Lewis J. Stadlen (1947-)
The Imposters '98
In and Out '97
Windy City '84
Between the Lines '77
Savages '72

William Stack (1882-1949)
Mary of Scotland '36
Pennies from Heaven '36

James Stacy (1936-)
Matters of the Heart '90
Something Wicked This Way Comes '83
Double Exposure '82
Posse '75
Paper Man '71
A Swingin' Summer '65
Fear '88

Joan Staley (1940-)
The Ghost and Mr. Chicken '66
Roustabout '64

Frank Stallone (1950-)
Total Force '96
Public Enemies '96
Taken Alive '95
Hudson Hawk '91
Lethal Games '90
Terror in Beverly Hills '90
The Dark Side of Love '79
Easy Kill '89
Heart of Midnight '89
Midnight Cop '88
Prime Suspect '88
Barfly '87
Outlaw Force '87
Take Two '87
The Pink Chiquitas '87

Ronald Squire (1886-1958)
Encore '52
No Highway in the Sky '51
Woman Hater '49

Jon Stafford
Crossing the Line '90
Full Metal Jacket '87

Jim Stafford (1944-)
Spy Kids 3-D: Game Over '03
Avenging Angelo '02
Driven '01
Eye See You '01
Get Carter '00
Antz '98 (V)
An Alan Smithee Film: Burn, Hollywood, Burn '97

Rebecca Staab (1961-)
Safe Harbour '07
The Substitute 3: Winner Takes All '99
Stray Bullet '98
T.N.T. '98
Action for Slander '38
E.S.P. '83

Robert Stack (1919-2003)
Killer Bud '00
Mumford '99
BASEketball '98
Beavis and Butt-Head Do America '96 (V)
The Return of Eliot Ness '91
Joe Versus the Volcano '90
Caddyshack 2 '88
Dangerous Curves '88
Plain Clothes '86
Big Trouble '86
Transformers: The Movie '86 (V)
George Washington '84
Uncommon Valor '83
Airplane! '80
1941 '79
Murder on Flight 502 '75
A Strange and Deadly Occurrence '74
The Corrupt Ones '67
Is Paris Burning? '66
Scarface Mob '62
The Last Voyage '60
John Paul Jones '59
Tarnished Angels '57
Great Day in the Morning '56
Written on the Wind '56
House of Bamboo '55
The High and the Mighty '54
Conquest of Cochise '53
Sabre Jet '53
My Outlaw Brother '51
Bullfighter & the Lady '50
Mr. Music '50
A Date with Judy '48
To Be or Not to Be '42
Nice Girl? '41
The Mortal Storm '40
First Love '39

Nick Stahl (1979-)
Sleepwalking '08
Sin City '05
Bookies '03
Terminator 3: Rise of the Machines '03
Twist '03
Taboo '02
Bully '01
In the Bedroom '01
The Sleepy Time Gal '01
Lover's Prayer '99
Disturbing Behavior '98
The Thin Red Line '98
Eye of God '97
Blue River '95
Safe Passage '94
The Man Without a Face '93

Chris Stack
SS Girls '77
Gunslinger '70

Ivano Staccioli (1927-)
SS Girls '77

Carola Stagnaro (1957-)
Cop Land '97

Frederick Stafford (1928-79)
The Legend of the Wolf Woman '77
Topaz '69

Philip Stainton (1908-61)
Who Done It? '56
Mogambo '53

Marion Stalens
Trois Couleurs: Rouge '94
The Lovers on the Bridge '91

Brent Stait (1959-)
Born to Run '93

Richard Stahl (1932-2006)
Private School '83
Beware! The Blob '72
Five Easy Pieces '70
The Student Nurses '70

Anne Stallybrass (1940-)
Diana: Her True Story '93
The Strauss Family '73
Six Wives of Henry VIII '71

Lynn Stalmaster
Flying Leathernecks '51

David Stambaugh
The Steel Helmet '51

John Stamos (1963-)
A Raisin in the Sun '08
Wedding Wars '06
Knots '05
The Reagans '04
The Disappearance of Christina '93
Born to Ride '91
Never Too Young to Die '86
Alice in Wonderland '85

Terence Stamp (1940-)
Get Smart '08
Wanted '08
September Dawn '07
These Foolish Things '06
Elektra '05
Dead Fish '04
Fellini: I'm a Born Liar '03
The Haunted Mansion '03
My Boss's Daughter '03
My Wife is an Actress '01
Red Planet '00
Bowfinger '99
Star Wars: Episode 1—The Phantom Menace '99
Kiss the Sky '98
Love Walked In '97
Bliss '96
The Adventures of Priscilla, Queen of the Desert '94
The Real McCoy '93
Genuine Risk '89
Alien Nation '88
Young Guns '88
The Sicilian '87
Wall Street '87
Alamut Ambush '86
Cold War Killers '86
Deadly Recruits '86
Legal Eagles '86
Link '86
The Hit '86
Vatican Conspiracy '81
Superman 2 '80
Meetings with Remarkable Men '79
Together? '79
Superman: The Movie '78
The Thief of Baghdad '78
Far from the Madding Crowd '67
Modesty Blaise '66
The Collector '65
Billy Budd '62
Divine Nymph '71
Insanity '76

Sylvester Stallone (1946-)
Rambo '08
Rocky Balboa '06
Shade '03
Spy Kids 3-D: Game Over '03
Driven '01
Get Carter '00
Antz '98 (V)
Cop Land '97
Daylight '96
Assassins '95
Judge Dredd '95
The Specialist '94
Cliffhanger '93
Demolition Man '93
Stop! or My Mom Will Shoot '92
Oscar '91
Rocky 5 '90
Lock Up '89
Tango and Cash '89
Rambo 3 '88
Over the Top '86
Cobra '86
Rambo: First Blood, Part 2 '85
Rocky 4 '85
Rhinestone '84
First Blood '82
Rocky 3 '82
Nighthawks '81
Victory '81
Rocky 2 '79
F.I.S.T. '78
Paradise Alley '78
Cannonball '76
Rocky '76
Death Race 2000 '75
Farewell, My Lovely '75
The Lords of Flatbush '74
Prisoner of Second Avenue '74
The Italian Stallion '73
Bananas '71
Rebel '70

Lionel Stander (1908-94)
The Last Good Time '94
Cookie '89
Wicked Stepmother '89
The Squeeze '80
New York, New York '77
1931: Once Upon a Time in New York '72
Pulp '72
Sting of the West '72
Treasure Island '72
Once Upon a Time in the West '68
Cul de Sac '66
Promise Her Anything '66
The Loved One '65
Blast of Silence '61 (N)
St. Benny the Dip '51
Specter of the Rose '46
Guadalcanal Diary '43
A Star is Born '37
The Gay Deception '35
Mr. Deeds Goes to Town '36

Wadeck Stanczak
Scene of the Crime '87
Rendez-vous '85

Sebastian Stan (1983-)
The Architect '06
The Covenant '06

Guy Standing (1873-1937)
Bulldog Drummond Comes Back '37
Bulldog Drummond Escapes '37
The Lives of a Bengal Lancer '35
Lloyds of London '36
I'd Give My Life '36
I Live My Life '35
Death Takes a Holiday '34
Now and Forever '34
The Eagle and the Hawk '33

Standing

Joan Standing (1903-79)
Cricket on the Hearth '23
Oliver Twist '22

John Standing (1934-)
Lassie '05
A Good Woman '04
Longitude '00
8 1/2 Women '99
Rogue Trader '98
The Man Who Knew Too Little '97
Mrs. Dalloway '97
The Woman in White '97
The Choir '95
Gulliver's Travels '95
Chaplin '92
The Endless Game '89
Riders '88
Nightflyers '87
To Catch a King '84
The Legacy '79
Rogue Male '76
Walk, Don't Run '66
King Rat '65

Aaron Stanford (1976-)
The Hills Have Eyes '06
X-Men: The Last Stand '06
Standing Still '05
Spartan '04
Winter Solstice '04
Rick '03
X2: X-Men United '03
Tadpole '02

Arnold Stang (1925-)
Dennis the Menace '93
Ghost Dad '90
Alpha Dog '06
Marco Polo, Jr. '72 (V)
Hercules in New York '70
The Wonderful World of the Brothers Grimm '62
The Man with the Golden Arm '55
Seven Days' Leave '42

Maya Stange
Garage Days '03
XX/XY '02
In a Savage Land '99
A Perfect Little Murder '90

Forrest Stanley (1889-1969)
Outlaws of the Desert '41
Bare Knees '28

Helene Stanley (1929-90)
Down With Love '03
Atlantis: The Lost Empire '01 (V)
Neil Simon's The Odd Couple 2 '98
A Goofy Movie '94 (V)
Trapped in Paradise '94
Carrie's War '04

Kim Stanley (1925-2001)
Cat on a Hot Tin Roof '84
The Right Stuff '83
Frances '82
The Three Sisters '65
Seance on a Wet Afternoon '64
To Kill a Mockingbird '62
The Goddess '58

Louise Stanley (1915-82)
Pinto Canyon '40
Sky Bandits '40
Yukon Flight '40
Danger on the Air '38
Gun Packer '38
Gunsmoke Trail '38
Thunder in the Desert '38
Gun Lords of Stirrup Basin '37

Riders of the Rockies '37
Sing, Cowboy, Sing '37

Paul Stanley (1952-)
Detroit Rock City '99
KISS Meets the Phantom of the Park '78
I Heard the Owl Call My Name '73

Rebecca Stanley
Body Double '84
Eyes of Fire '84

Don Stannard (1916-49)
The Temptress '49
Dick Barton, Special Agent '48
Dick Barton Strikes Back '48
Pink String and Sealing Wax '45

Claire Stansfield (1964-)
Sweepers '99
Darkdrive '98
Red Shoe Diaries 5: Weekend Pass '95
Wes Craven Presents Mind Ripper '95
Drop Zone '94
Sensation '94
Best of the Best 2 '93
The Swordsman '92

Finding Nemo '03 (V)
Toy Story 2 '99 (V)

Andrew Stanton (1965-)

Harry Dean Stanton (1926-)
Inland Empire '06
You, Me and Dupree '06
The Wendell Baker Story '05
The Big Bounce '04
Anger Management '03
Sonny '02
The Man Who Cried '00
The Pledge '00
Sand '00
The Green Mile '99
The Straight Story '99
Fear and Loathing in Las Vegas '98
The Mighty '98
Fire Down Below '97
She's So Lovely '97
Down Periscope '96
Larry McMurtry's Dead Man's Walk '96
Midnight Blue '96
Never Talk to Strangers '95
Playback '95
Against the Wall '94
Blue Tiger '94
Hostages '93
Hotel Room '93
Man Trouble '92
Twin Peaks: Fire Walk with Me '92
Payoff '91
The Fourth War '90
Wild at Heart '90
Dream a Little Dream '89
Twister '89
Mr. North '88
Stars and Bars '88
Slamdance '87
Fool for Love '86
Pretty in Pink '86
One Magic Christmas '85
Rip van Winkle '85
Red Dawn '84
Christine '84
Paris, Texas '83
Repo Man '83
One from the Heart '82
Young Doctors in Love '82
Escape from New York '81
The Godfather 1902-1959: The Complete Epic '81
Uforia '80
Death Watch '80
Oldest Living Graduate '80
Private Benjamin '80
Alien '79

The Black Marble '79
Flatbed Annie and Sweetiepie: Lady Truckers '79
The Rose '79
Wise Blood '79
Straight Time '78
The Missouri Breaks '76
92 in the Shade '76
Farewell, My Lovely '75
Rafferty & the Gold Dust Twins '75
Rancho Deluxe '75
Cockfighter '74
The Godfather, Part 2 '74
Where the Lilies Bloom '74
Zandy's Bride '74
Dillinger '73
Pat Garrett & Billy the Kid '73
Two Lane Blacktop '71
Kelly's Heroes '70
Rebel Rousers '69
Cool Hand Luke '67
The Hostage '67
Ride in the Whirlwind '66
The Adventures of Huckleberry Finn '60
Proud Rebel '58

John Stanton (1944-)
Day of the Panther '88
Rent-A-Cop '88
Great Expectations: The Untold Story '87
Tai-Pan '86
Dusty '85
The Naked Country '85
Bellamy '80

Paul Stanton (1884-1955)
Across the Pacific '42
The Night of January 16th '41
Whistling in the Dark '41
Stanley and Livingstone '39

Find Me Guilty '06
Head of State '03
The Quiet American '02
Mercury Rising '98
Next Stop, Wonderland '98
Red Corner '97
Washington Square '97
Dennis the Menace '93
Bob Roberts '92
I Eat Your Skin '64
Abbott and Costello in Hollywood '45

Barbara Stanwyck (1907-90)
The Thorn Birds '83
The Night Walker '64
Roustabout '64
Walk on the Wild Side '62
Crime of Passion '57
Forty Guns '57
Escape to Burma '55
The Maverick Queen '55
The Violent Men '55
Blowing Wild '54
Cattle Queen of Montana '54
Executive Suite '54
All I Desire '53
Jeopardy '53
Titanic '53
Clash by Night '52
To Please a Lady '50
East Side, West Side '49
Sorry, Wrong Number '48
Cry Wolf '47
The Two Mrs. Carrolls '47
My Reputation '46
The Strange Love of Martha Ivers '46
Christmas in Connecticut '45
Double Indemnity '44
Hollywood Canteen '44
Lady of Burlesque '43
The Great Man's Lady '42
Ball of Fire '41
The Lady Eve '41
Meet John Doe '41
Remember the Night '40
Golden Boy '39
Union Pacific '39

Mad Miss Manton '38
Internes Can't Take Money '37
Stella Dallas '37
The Bride Walks Out '36
Annie Oakley '35
Red Salute '35
Baby Face '33
The Bitter Tea of General Yen '33
Ladies They Talk About '33
The Purchase Price '32
Illicit '31
The Miracle Woman '31
Night Nurse '31

Huub Stapel (1954-)
Amsterdamned '88
The Attic: The Hiding of Anne Frank '88
The Lift '85

Jean Stapleton (1923-)
Pursuit of Happiness '01
Baby '00
You've Got Mail '98
Lily Dale '96
Michael '96
The Habitation of Dragons '91
Mother Goose Rock 'n' Rhyme '90
Grown Ups '86
Cinderella '84
The Buddy System '83
Jack & the Beanstalk '83
Eleanor: First Lady of the World '82
Cold Turkey '71
Klute '71
Up the Down Staircase '67
Bells Are Ringing '60
Damn Yankees '58

Maureen Stapleton (1925-2006)
Dead Silence '98
Addicted to Love '96
The Last Good Time '94
Trading Mom '94
Miss Rose White '92
Passed Away '92
Cocoon: The Return '88
Doin' Time on Planet Earth '88
Made in Heaven '87
Nuts '87
Sweet Lorraine '87
Heartburn '86
The Money Pit '86
Cocoon '85
Family Secrets '84
Johnny Dangerously '84
Little Gloria... Happy at Last '84
The Fan '81
On the Right Track '81
Reds '81
The Gathering: Part 2 '79
Lost and Found '79
The Runner Stumbles '79
Interiors '78
The Gathering '77
Queen of the Stardust Ballroom '75
Plaza Suite '71
Airport '70
Bye, Bye, Birdie '63
The Fugitive Kind '60
Lonelyhearts '58

Nicola Stapleton (1974-)
Urban Ghost Story '98
Courage Mountain '89

Sullivan Stapleton
December Boys '07
Darkness Falls '03
River Street '95

Richard Stapley (1934-)
D-Day, the Sixth of June '56
The Strange Door '51

Don Stark (1954-)
Double Edge '97
Santa with Muscles '96

Bloodfist 5: Human Target '93
Evilspeak '82
Switchblade Sisters '75

Graham Stark (1922-)
Adventures Beyond Belief '87
Blind Date '87
Bloodbath at the House of Death '85
Alfie '66

Jonathan Stark (1952-)
House 2: The Second Story '87
Project X '87
Fright Night '85

Koo Stark (1956-)
Eat the Rich '87
Electric Dreams '84
Emily '77
The Rocky Horror Picture Show '75

Anthony Starke (1963-)
Inferno '98
The Magnificent Seven '98
Repossessed '90
18 Again! '88
Return of the Killer Tomatoes! '88

Pauline Starke (1901-77)
Dante's Inferno '24
Little Church Around the Corner '23

Beau Starr (1944-)
Masters of Horror: Jenifer '05
Where the Truth Lies '05
The Golden Spiders: A Nero Wolfe Mystery '00
Mercy '00
The Thin Blue Lie '00
Mean Streak '99
Prisoner of Love '99
Hoodlum '96
Devil in a Blue Dress '95
Never Talk to Strangers '95
Dead Air '94
Trial by Jury '94
Goodfellas '90
Halloween 5: The Revenge of Michael Myers '89
Halloween 4: The Return of Michael Myers '88
Summer School '87

Fredro Starr (1970-)
My Brother '06
Torque '04
Save the Last Dance '01
Light It Up '99
Ride '98
Sunset Park '96

Mike Starr (1950-)
The Addiction '95
The Black Dahlia '06
Hot Tamale '06
Elvis Has Left the Building '04
Jersey Girl '04
The Next Big Thing '02
Tempted '01
3 A.M. '01
The Lady in Question '99
Murder in a Small Town '99
Frogs for Snakes '98
Gloria '98
The Deli '97
Path to Paradise '97
A River Made to Drown In '97
Flipping '96
Hoodlum '96
Just Your Luck '96
Two If by Sea '95
Dumb & Dumber '94
Ed Wood '94
Trial by Jury '94
Mad Dog and Glory '93
Mardi Gras for the Devil '93
The Bodyguard '92
Billy Bathgate '91

Goodfellas '90
Nasty Hero '89
The Money Pit '86
Cruising '80

Ringo Starr (1940-)
Alice in Wonderland '85
Water '85
Give My Regards to Broad Street '84
Princess Daisy '83
Caveman '81
The Kids Are Alright '79
Sextette '78
Lisztomania '75
That'll Be the Day '73
Born to Boogie '72
The Point '71 (N)
200 Motels '71
Let It Be '70
The Magic Christian '69
Candy '68
Yellow Submarine '68 (V)
Magical Mystery Tour '67
Help! '65
A Hard Day's Night '64

Charles Starrett (1903-86)
Bonanza Town '51
Blazing Across the Pecos '48
Make a Million '35
A Shot in the Dark '35
Sons of Steel '35
Dangerous Appointment '34
Green Eyes '34
The Return of Casey Jones '34
The Silver Streak '34
Jungle Bride '33
Mr. Skitch '33
The Mask of Fu Manchu '32

Jack Starrett (1936-89)
Nightwish '89
Brothers in Arms '88
Death Chase '87
First Blood '82
Mr. Horn '79
The Losers '70
Angels from Hell '68

Jason Statham (1972-)
The Bank Job '08
In the Name of the King: A Dungeon Siege Tale '08
War '07
Crank '06
London '05
Revolver '05
Transporter 2 '05
Cellular '04
The Italian Job '03
The Transporter '02
John Carpenter's Ghosts of Mars '01
Mean Machine '01
The One '01
Snatch '00
Turn It Up '00
Lock, Stock and 2 Smoking Barrels '98

Liz Stauber (1979-)
The Tollbooth '04
The Village '04
Almost Famous '00
Teaching Mrs. Tingle '99
Three Kings '99

Imelda Staunton (1956-)
Freedom Writers '07
Harry Potter and the Order of the Phoenix '07
Nanny McPhee '06
Shadow Man '06
Vera Drake '04
Cambridge Spies '03
I'll Be There '03
Crush '02
Chicken Run '00 (V)
David Copperfield '99
Shakespeare in Love '98
Twelfth Night '96
Citizen X '95
Sense and Sensibility '95
Deadly Advice '93

Much Ado about Nothing '93
Peter's Friends '92
Antonia and Jane '91

Mary Stavin (1957-)
The Opponent '85
House '86
Open House '86

Eddie Stazak
Day of the Panther '88
Fists of Blood '87

Alison Steadman (1946-)
Pride and Prejudice '95
Secrets and Lies '95
Clockwise '86
Coming Through '85
Champions '84
A Private Function '84
Kipperbang '82
Abigail's Party '77
Nuts in May '76
Hard Labour '73
Life Is Sweet '90
Shirley Valentine '89
Wilt '90

John Steadman (1909-93)
Battle for the Planet of the Apes '73

Rick Stear (1972-)
Astoria '00
Went to Coney Island on a Mission from God... Be Back by Five '98

Michael Stearns (1940-)
Benji the Hunted '87

Red Steagall (1937-)
Big Bad John '90
Dark Before Dawn '89

Ken Steadman (1969-96)
Hindsight '97
I Like to Play Games '95

Ray Dennis Steckler (1939-)
Las Vegas Weekend '85
The Thrill Killers '65
Incredibly Strange Creatures Who Stopped Living and Became Mixed-Up Zombies '63
Eegah! '62
Wild Guitar '62
Wild Ones on Wheels '62
Chain Gang Women '72
Chrome and Hot Leather '71

Myrtle Stedman (1885-1938)
The Mad Whirl '25
Sex '20
In the Days of the Thundering Herd & the Law & the Outlaw '14
Law & the Outlaw '14

Alan Steel
Hercules against the Moon Men '64
Samson and His Mighty Challenge '64
The Fury of Hercules '61
Samson '61

Amy Steel (1963-)
What Ever Happened To... '93
Walk Like a Man '87
April Fool's Day '86
Friday the 13th, Part 2 '81

Anthony Steel (1920-2001)
The Story of O '75
I'm the Girl He Wants to Kill '74
Massacre in Rome '73
Tiger of the Seven Seas '62
48 Hours to Live '60

Bob Steele (1907-88)
Galloping Romeo '33
Mystery Squadron '33
Young Blood '33
The Atomic Submarine '59
Rio Bravo '59
Pork Chop Hill '59
Giant from the Unknown '58
Pardners '56
Ambush '51
The Enforcer '51
The Big Sleep '46
Northwest Trail '46
Rio Grande Raiders '46
Wildfire '45
Arizona Whirlwind '44
Death Valley Rangers '44
Marked Trails '44
Outlaw Trail '44
Sonora Stagecoach '44
Texas Trouble '41
Trigger Men '41
Twilight on the Rio Grande '41
Billy the Kid in Texas '40
Batting Outlaw '40
Carson City Kid '40
City for Conquest '40
Pinto Canyon '40
El Diablo Rides '39
Mesquite Buckaroo '39
Of Mice and Men '39
Durango Valley Raiders '38
Feud Maker '38
Thunder in the Desert '38
Arizona Gunfighter '37
Border Phantom '37
Doomed at Sundown '37
Gun Lords of Stirrup Basin '37
Lightning Bill Crandall '37
Paroled to Die '37
The Red Rope '37
Ridin' the Lone Trail '37
Brand o' the Outlaws '36
Cavalry '36
Kid Ranger '36
Last of the Warrens '36
The Law Rides '36
Sundown Saunders '36
Smokey Smith '36
Alias John Law '35
Big Calibre '35
Kid Courageous '35
No Man's Range '35
Powdersmoke Range '35
Rider of the Law '35
Trail of Terror '35
Western Justice '35
Brand of Hate '34
Demon for Trouble '34
The Gun Ranger '34
Tombstone Terror '34
Breed of the Border '33
Fighting Champ '33
The Gallant Fool '33

Barbara Steele (1937-)
The Capitol Conspiracy '99
The Winds of War '83
Silent Scream '80
Piranha '78
Pretty Baby '78
The Monocle '64
Castle of Blood '64
The Ghost '63
8 1/2 '63
The Horrible Dr. Hichcock '62
An Angel for Satan '66
The Crimson Cult '68
Caged Heat '74
They Came from Within '75
The Pit and the Pendulum '61
Terror Creatures from the Grave '66
The She-Beast '65
Nightmare Castle '65
Black Sunday '60
La Dolce Vita '60

Brian Steele
Hellboy 2: The Golden Army '08
Doom '05
Underworld: Evolution '05

Don Steele (1936-97)
Death Race 2000 '75
Eating Raoul '82
Rock 'n' Roll High School '79

Fred Steele
Nevil Shute's The Far Country '85

Freddie (Fred) Steele (1912-84)
Call Northside 777 '48
A Foreign Affair '48
Black Angel '46
The Story of G.I. Joe '45
Hail the Conquering Hero '44

Jadrien Steele (1974-)
The Secret Garden '87
The Mosquito Coast '86

Karen Steele (1931-)
Trap on Cougar Mountain '72
The Rise and Fall of Legs Diamond '60
Ride Lonesome '59
Bail Out at 43,000 '57
Marty '55

Marjorie Steele (1930-)
Face to Face '52
Tough Assignment '49

Pippa Steele (1948-92)
Lust for a Vampire '71
The Vampire Lovers '70

Tommy Steele (1936-)
Oh! What a Lovely War '69
Finian's Rainbow '68
Half a Sixpence '67
The Happiest Millionaire '67

Jessica Steen (1965-)
Armageddon '98
Smart House '00
The Principal Takes a Holiday '98
Trial and Error '96
Sing '89

Anthony Steffen (1929-2006)
Garringo '69
The Gentleman Killer '69
Stranger in Paso Bravo '68
An Angel for Satan '66
The Last Tomahawk '65

Berrice Stegers
Little Lord Fauntleroy '95
A Dark Adapted Eye '95
To Play the King '93
The Girl '86
Xtro '83
City of Women '81
Macabre '80
Still Life '92

Edgar Stehli (1884-1973)

Paprika Steen (1964-)
Adam's Apples '05
The Celebration '98
Dream to Believe '85

Eddie Steeples
I Know Who Killed Me '07
Wristcutters: A Love Story '06

Leslie Stefanson (1971-)
The Hunted '03
Desert Saints '01
The Kennedy Women '01
The Stickup '01
Beautiful '00
Unbreakable '00
The General's Daughter '99
Delivered '98
An Alan Smithee Film: Burn, Hollywood, Burn '97

Mary Steenburgen (1952-)
The Trumpet of the Swan '01 (V)
Wish You Were Dead? '00
Noah's Ark '99
The Grass Harp '95
Gulliver's Travels '95
Out There '95
Powder '95
Nixon '95
Black Water '94
The Specialist '94
Armistead Maupin's Tales of the City '93
My Family '94
Pontiac Moon '94
Philadelphia '93
What's Eating Gilbert Grape '93
Parenthood '89
Miss Firecracker '89
The January Man '89
Passion in Paradise '89
The Long Walk Home '90
The Butcher's Wife '91
Back to the Future, Part 3 '90
End of the Line '88
Dead of Winter '87
The Whales of August '87
One Magic Christmas '85
Cross Creek '83
Little Red Riding Hood '83
Romantic Comedy '83
A Midsummer Night's Sex Comedy '82
Ragtime '81
Melvin and Howard '80
Time After Time '79
Goin' South '78

Rod Steiger (1925-2002)
Poolhall Junkies '02
The Hollywood Sign '01
Crazy in Alabama '99
End of Days '99
The Hurricane '99
Cypress Edge '99
Frozen in Fear '00
Body and Soul '98
Modern Vampires '98
Incognito '97
The Kid '00
Shiloh 2: Shiloh Season '99
Truth or Consequences, N.M. '97
Carpool '96
Shiloh '97
The Real Thing '97
Mars Attacks! '96
Captain Nuke and the Bomber Boys '95
The Neighbor '93
Guilty as Charged '92
The Player '92
Sinatra '92
The Ballad of the Sad Cafe '91
That Summer of White Roses '89
American Gothic '88
Catch the Heat '87
The Kindred '87
The Last Contract '86
The Naked Face '84
The Chosen '81
Lion of the Desert '81
The Amityville Horror '79
Love and Bullets '79
Wolf Lake '79
Breakthrough '78
F.I.S.T. '78
Last Four Days '77
Portrait of a Hitman '77
Innocents with Dirty Hands '76
Hennessy '75
Lucky Luciano '74
A Fistful of Dynamite '72
Waterloo '71
The Illustrated Man '69
No Way to Treat a Lady '68
In the Heat of the Night '67
The Loved One '65
Doctor Zhivago '65
The Pawnbroker '65
Time of Indifference '64
The Longest Day '62
The Mark '61
Seven Thieves '60
Al Capone '59
Across the Bridge '57
Unholy Wife '57
Back from Eternity '56
The Harder They Fall '56
The Big Knife '55
The Court Martial of Billy Mitchell '55
Jubal '56
Run of the Arrow '56
Oklahoma! '55
On the Waterfront '54

Margaret Sophie Stein (1956-)
Sarah, Plain and Tall: Skylark '93
Sarah, Plain and Tall '91
Enemies, a Love Story '89

June Stein
High Stakes '89
Bob Roberts '92

Saul Stein
Open Water '03
Grind '96
Illtown '96
New Jersey Drive '95

Ben Stein (1944-)
Ferris Bueller's Day Off '86
Planes, Trains & Automobiles '87
Ghostbusters 2 '89
Mr. Write '92
Honeymoon in Vegas '92
Mastergate '92
Dave '93
North '94
My Girl 2 '94
The Mask '94
Casper '95
Miami Rhapsody '95

David Steinberg (1942-)
The Marx Brothers in a Nutshell '82
Something Short of Paradise '79
The End '78
The Lost Man '69

John Steiner (1941-)
Sinbad of the Seven Seas '89
The Lone Runner '88
Operation 'Nam' '85
Dagger Eyes '83
Yor, the Hunter from the Future '83
Ark of the Sun God '82
Hunters of the Golden Cobra '82
Cobra '82
Caligula '80
Shock '79
Massacre in Rome '73

Jake Steinfeld (1958-)
Home Sweet Home '80
Tough Guys '86

Sherry Steiner (1948-)
Heaven Help Us '85
Asylum of Satan '72

Richard Steinmetz
The One '01
Skyscraper '95
Liquid Dreams '92

Robert J. Steinmiller, Jr. (1978-)
Jack the Bear '93
The Ref '93
Rudy '93
Bingo '91

William (Bill) Steis (1945-95)
Raiders of the Sun '92
Demon of Paradise '87
Eye of the Eagle '87
Equalizer 2000 '86

Anna Sten (1908-93)
Soldier of Fortune '55
So Ends Our Night '41
The Girl with the Hat Box '27

Karel Stepanek (1899-1981)
Devil Doll '64
Brainwashed '60
Sink the Bismarck! '60
Never Let Me Go '53
The Fallen Idol '49
Counterblast '48
Secret Mission '42

Yutte Stensgaard (1946-)
Lust for a Vampire '71
Scream and Scream Again '70
Zeta One '69

Nicole Stephane (1923-2007)
Les Enfants Terribles '50
La Silence de la Mer '47

Idwig Stephane (1944-)
The Butterfly '02
Pauline and Paulette '01
Daens '92

Daniel Stephen
2020 Texas Gladiators '85
Warbus '86

Susan Stephen (1931-2000)
Carve Her Name with Pride '58
White Huntress '54
Heat Wave '54
A Stolen Face '52

Harvey Stephens (1901-86)
The Girl in the Red Velvet Swing '55
The Lady Is Willing '42
Sergeant York '41
Abe Lincoln in Illinois '40
The Fighting 69th '40
The Texas Rangers Ride Again '40
Beau Geste '39
Oklahoma Kid '39
The Texans '38
Forlorn River '37
Let 'Em Have It '35
Evelyn Prentice '34

Heather Stephens
Tomcats '01
Blue Ridge Fall '99
Forever Love '98
With Friends Like These '98

James Stephens (1951-)
Pancho Barnes '88
Mysterious Two '82
First Monday in October '81

Martin Stephens (1949-)
The Innocents '61
Village of the Damned '60

Nancy Stephens (1945-)
Halloween: H20 '98
Halloween '78

Perry Stephens (1958-2005)
Grizzly Mountain '97
Norma Jean and Marilyn '95
Two Bits & Pepper '95

Robert Stephens (1931-95)
Century '94
The Secret Rapture '94
Searching for Bobby Fischer '93
Afraid of the Dark '92
Chaplin '92
The Bonfire of the Vanities '90
The Children '90
Henry V '89
American Roulette '88
High Season '88
Wonderland '88
Empire of the Sun '87
Fortunes of War '87
Luther '74
The Asphyx '72
Travels with My Aunt '72
The Private Life of Sherlock Holmes '70
The Prime of Miss Jean Brodie '69
Morgan: A Suitable Case for Treatment '66
A Taste of Honey '61

Toby Stephens (1969-)
Dark Corners '06
Jane Eyre '06
Severance '06
Sharpe's Challenge '06
The Queen's Sister '05
Cambridge Spies '03
Napoleon '03
Die Another Day '02
Possession '02
Almost Strangers '01
The Great Gatsby '01
Onegin '99
Cousin Bette '97
Photographing Fairies '97
Twelfth Night '96
The Camomile Lawn '92

Bob Stephenson
The Ex '07
Friends with Money '06

Henry Stephenson (1871-1956)
Challenge to Lassie '49

Oliver Twist '48
Song of Love '47
Heartbeat '46
Mr. Lucky '43
Lady from Louisiana '42
Down Argentine Way '40
It's a Date '40
The Old Maid '39
Tarzan Finds a Son '39
Marie Antoinette '38
Conquest '37
The Prince and the Pauper '37
The Charge of the Light Brigade '36
Mutiny on the Bounty '35
Thirty Day Princess '34
Tomorrow at Seven '33
The Animal Kingdom '32
A Bill of Divorcement '32
Red Headed Woman '32

James Stephenson (1889-1941)
The Letter '40
The Sea Hawk '40
Beau Geste '39
Boy Meets Girl '38
Nancy Drew—Detective '38

Mark Kinsey Stephenson
The Unnamable 2: The Statement of Randolph Carter '92
The Unnamable '88

Michael Stephenson (1978-)
Beyond Darkness '92
Troll 2 '92

Pamela Stephenson (1950-)
Les Patterson Saves the World '90
Ghosts Can Do It '87
Bloodbath at the House of Death '85
Finders Keepers '84
Scandalous '84
History of the World: Part 1 '81
The Comeback '77

Craig Stepp
Indecent Behavior 2 '94
Married People, Single Sex 2: For Better or Worse '94

Ilse Steppat (1917-69)
On Her Majesty's Secret Service '69
Naked in the Night '58

Ford Sterling (1883-1939)
Headline Woman '35
The Show Off '26
He Who Gets Slapped '24
Yankee Doodle in Berlin '19

Jan Sterling (1923-2004)
First Monday in October '81
Backstairs at the White House '79
The Dark Side of Love '79
The Incident '67
High School Confidential '58
1984 '56
Pony Express '53
Split Second '53
Ace in the Hole '51
Caged '50
Gunfire '50
Mystery Street '50
Union Station '50
Johnny Belinda '48
Tycoon '47

Maury Sterling
Smokin' Aces '07
Come as You Are '05

Mindy Sterling (1954-)
Ice Age: The Meltdown '06 (V)

The Twelve Dogs of Christmas '05
Austin Powers In Goldmember '02
Totally Blonde '01
Austin Powers 2: The Spy Who Shagged Me '99
Drop Dead Gorgeous '99
Austin Powers: International Man of Mystery '97

Philip Sterling (1922-98)
My Giant '98
Death of the Incredible Hulk '90

Robert Sterling (1917-2006)
A Global Affair '63
Return to Peyton Place '61
Voyage to the Bottom of the Sea '61
Johnny Eager '42
Somewhere I'll Find You '42
Two-Faced Woman '41

Tisha Sterling (1944-)
The Whales of August '87
The Killer Inside Me '76
Betrayal '74
Snatched '73
Defiant '70
Powder Keg '70
Coogan's Bluff '68
Village of the Giants '65

Daniel Stern (1957-)
The Last Time '06
Dead Simple '01
Tourist Trap '98
Very Bad Things '98
Celtic Pride '96
Bushwhacked '95
City Slickers 2: The Legend of Curly's Gold '94
Rookie of the Year '93
Home Alone 2: Lost in New York '92
City Slickers '91
Coupe de Ville '90
The Court Martial of Jackie Robinson '90
Home Alone '90
My Blue Heaven '90
Friends, Lovers & Lunatics '89
Leviathan '89
Little Monsters '89
D.O.A. '88
The Milagro Beanfield War '88
Weekend War '88
Born in East L.A. '87
The Boss' Wife '86
Hannah and Her Sisters '86
Key Exchange '85
C.H.U.D. '84
Frankenweenie '84
Ratings Game '84
Blue Thunder '83
Get Crazy '83
Diner '82
I'm Dancing as Fast as I Can '82
It's My Turn '80
One Trick Pony '80
Stardust Memories '80
Breaking Away '79
Starting Over '79

Howard Stern (1954-)
Private Parts '96
Ryder P.I. '86

Tom Stern (1965-)
Freaked '93
Hell's Angels '69 '69
Angels from Hell '68
The Devil's Brigade '68

Wes Stern (1947-)
Three in the Cellar '70
The First Time '69

Frances Sternhagen (1930-)
The Con '98
Curtain Call '97
Raising Cain '92
Doc Hollywood '91
Stephen King's Golden Years '91

Misery '90
Sibling Rivalry '90
See You in the Morning '89
Communion '89
Bright Lights, Big City '88
The Dining Room '86
Independence Day '83
Prototype '83
Romantic Comedy '83
Who'll Save Our Children? '82
Outland '81
Mother & Daughter: A Loving War '80
Starting Over '79

Robyn Stevan
Stepping Out '91
Bye Bye Blues '89

Jean-Francois Stevenin (1944-)
On Guard! '03
The Man on the Train '02
Brotherhood of the Wolf '01
For Sale '98
Olivier, Olivier '92
Small Change '76

Robinson Stevenin (1981-)
La Petite Lili '03
Transfixed '01
Bad Company '99

Salome Stevenin (1985-)
Cold Showers '05
The Green House '96

Andrew Stevens (1955-)
Black Horizon '01
The Shooter '97
The Corporation '96
Scorned 2 '96
Subliminal Seduction '96: Full Exposure '95
Night Eyes 4: Fatal Passion '95
Illicit Dreams '94
The Skateboard Kid 2 '94
Body Chemistry 3: Point of Seduction '93
Eyewitness to Murder '93
Night Eyes 3 '93
Scorned '92
Deadly Rivals '92
Double Threat '92
Munchie '92
Night Eyes 2 '91
The Terror Within 2 '91
Night Eyes '90
Red Blooded American Girl '90
Down the Drain '89
Tusks '89
Deadly Innocence '88
Fine Gold '88
The Ranch '88
The Terror Within '88
Counterforce '87
Scared Stiff '87
Ten to Midnight '83
Forbidden Love '82
The Seduction '82
Death Hunt '81
Miracle on Ice '81
The Rebels '79
The Bastard '78
The Fury '78
The Boys in Company C '77
Day of the Animals '77
Secrets '77
Las Vegas Lady '76
Massacre at Central High '76

Brinke Stevens (1954-)
Demon Lust '01
Mom's Outta Sight '01
Witchouse 3: Demon Fire '01
American Nightmare '00
The Kid with the X-Ray Eyes '99
Hybrid '97
Mommy 2: Mommy's Day '96
Cyberzone '95

Jack-O '95
Masseuse '95
Mommy '95
Acting on Impulse '93
Teenage Exorcist '93
Haunting Fear '91
Bad Girls from Mars '90
Spirits '90
Phantom of the Mall: Eric's Revenge '89
Transylvania Twist '89
Grandma's House '88
Warlords '88
Nightmare Sisters '87
Slave Girls from Beyond Infinity '87
Sorority Babes in the Slimeball Bowl-A-Rama '87
Sole Survivor '84
Slumber Party Massacre '82

Charles Stevens (1893-1964)
Buffalo Bill Rides Again '47
Border Bandits '46
Overland Mail '42
The Lives of a Bengal Lancer '35
The Three Musketeers '21
Mark of Zorro '20

Connie Stevens (1938-)
James Dean: Live Fast, Die Young '97
Love Is All There Is '96
Tapeheads '89
Back to the Beach '87
Side Show '84
Scruples '80
Love's Savage Fury '79
Scorchy '76
Playmates '72
The Grissom Gang '71
The Littlest Angel '69
Palm Springs Weekend '63
Parrish '61
Rock-A-Bye Baby '57

Craig Stevens (1918-2000)
La Truite '83
S.O.B. '81
Secrets of Three Hungry Wives '78
The Deadly Mantis '57
The French Line '54
Abbott and Costello Meet Dr. Jekyll and Mr. Hyde '52
Phone Call from a Stranger '52
Drums in the Deep South '51
Blues Busters '50
Humoresque '46
The Man I Love '46
God Is My Co-Pilot '45
Since You Went Away '44
Dive Bomber '41

Dan Stevens (1982-)
Sense & Sensibility '07

Fisher Stevens (1963-)
Awake '07
Factotum '06
Kettle of Fish '06
Undisputed '02
The Tic Code '99
Cold Fever '95
Hackers '95
The Right to Remain Silent '95
When the Party's Over '91
Reversal of Fortune '90
Short Circuit 2 '88
Short Circuit '86
My Science Project '85
The Flamingo Kid '84
The Burning '82

Inger Stevens (1934-70)
Savage Run '70
A Dream of Kings '69
Firecreek '68
Five Card Stud '68
Madigan '68
A Guide for the Married Man '67
Hang 'Em High '67
The Buccaneer '58

Joe Stevens
The Alamo '04
American Outlaws '01

K.T. Stevens (1919-94)
They're Playing with Fire '84
Missile to the Moon '59
Jungle Hell '55
Harriet Craig '50
Port of New York '49

Mark Stevens (1915-94)
The Fury of the Wolfman '70
Frozen Alive '64
Cry Vengeance '54
Torpedo Alley '53
Mutiny '52
The Snake Pit '48
The Street with No Name '48
Dark Corner '46
Objective, Burma! '45

Morgan Stevens (1951-)
Survival Zone '84
Up River '79

Onslow Stevens (1902-77)
Tribute to a Bad Man '56
Fangs of the Wild '54
Them! '54
A Lion Is in the Streets '53
One Too Many '51
Motor Patrol '50
The Creeper '48
Angel on My Shoulder '46
O.S.S. '46
House of Dracula '45
Hands Across the Border '43
The Monster and the Girl '41
Flight from Glory '37
Three on the Trail '36
Yellow Dust '36
The Three Musketeers '35
I Can't Escape '34
Counsellor-at-Law '33

Paul Stevens (1921-86)
Get Christie Love! '74
Patton '70
Hercules and the Princess of Troy '65
The Mask '61
Exodus '60

Rise Stevens (1913-)
Going My Way '44
The Chocolate Soldier '41

Ronnie Stevens (1925-2002)
The Parent Trap '98
Dentist in the Chair '60

Shadoe Stevens (1947-)
The Death Artist '95
Traxx '87

Stella Stevens (1936-)
The Glass Trap '04
The Long Ride Home '01
By Dawn's Early Light '00
The Corporation '96
In Cold Blood '96
Invisible Mom '96
Subliminal Seduction '96
Body Chemistry 4: Full Exposure '95
The Nutt House '95
Star Hunter '95
Virtual Combat '95
The Granny '94
Hard Drive '94
Illicit Dreams '94

Molly and Gina '94
National Lampoon's Attack of the 5 Ft. 2 Women '94
Eye of the Stranger '93
The Terror Within 2 '91
Exiled in America '90
Last Call '90
Not o' This Earth '96
Official Denial '93
Are You Lonesome Tonight '92
Adventures Beyond Belief '87
The Longshot '86
Monster in the Closet '86
The Amazons '84
Chained Heat '83
Power, Passion & Murder '83
Mom '89
Down the Drain '89
Cruise into Terror '78
The Manitou '78
Las Vegas Lady '76
Cleopatra Jones & the Casino of Gold '75
Arnold '73
Slaughter '72
A Town Called Hell '72
Ballad of Cable Hogue '70
Where Angels Go, Trouble Follows '68
The Silencers '66
The Nutty Professor '63
The Courtship of Eddie's Father '63
Girls! Girls! Girls! '62
Lil' Abner '59

Warren Stevens (1919-)
No Name on the Bullet '59
Man or Gun '58
Forbidden Planet '56
Shark River '53
The Barefoot Contessa '54

Cynthia Stevenson (1963-)
Snow Buddies '08
Full of It '07
Agent Cody Banks 2: Destination London '04
Agent Cody Banks '03
Air Bud 5: Buddy Spikes '03
Air Bud 4: Seventh Inning Fetch '02
Air Bud 2: Golden Receiver '98
Happiness '98
Forget Paris '95
Home for the Holidays '95
Live Nude Girls '95
The Player '92

Jessica Stevenson (1972-)
Confetti '06
Four Last Songs '06
Pinocchio's Last Stand '06
Bridget Jones: The Edge of Reason '04
Shaun of the Dead '04

Juliet Stevenson (1956-)
Breaking and Entering '06
Infamous '06
Red Mercury '05
Being Julia '04
Mona Lisa Smile '03
Bend It Like Beckham '02
Food of Love '02
Nicholas Nickleby '02
The Road from Coorain '02
Cider with Rosie '99
Emma '96
The Secret Rapture '94
The Trial '93
Truly, Madly, Deeply '91
Drowning by Numbers '87

McLean Stevenson (1929-96)
The Cat from Outer Space '78
Win, Place, or Steal '72

Parker Stevenson (1952-)
Legion '98
Not o' This Earth '96
Official Denial '93
Are You Lonesome Tonight '92
North and South Book 2 '86
Shooting Stars '85
Stitches '85
Stroker Ace '83
Lifeguard '76
Our Time '74
A Separate Peace '73

Ray Stevenson (1964-)
King Arthur '04
The Theory of Flight '98
Catherine Cookson's The Tide of Life '96
The Return of the Native '94

Robert Stevenson (1905-86)
One of Our Dinosaurs Is Missing '75

Tom Stevenson (1910-)
Gaslight '44

Venetia Stevenson (1938-)
Horror Hotel '60
The Day of the Outlaw '59
Darby's Rangers '58

Joe Stewardson
Son of Gasconge '95
Sans Soleil '82 (N)
The Agency '81
City of Blood '88
Flatfoot '78
Follow That Rainbow '66

Alexandra Stewart (1939-)
Under the Sand '00
Last Chase '81
In Praise of Older Women '78
Because of the Cats '74
The Destructors '74
Day for Night '73
Zeppelin '71
Kemek '70
Mickey One '65
The Fire Within '64
Exodus '60
RoGoPaG '62
Magic Island '95

Athole Stewart (1879-1940)
Accused '36
The Speckled Band '31

Amy Stewart
Trucks '97

Byron Stewart (1956-)
Grambling's White Tiger '81

James Stewart (1908-97)
An American Tail: Fievel Goes West '91 (V)
North and South Book 2 '86
Green Horizon '80
The Big Sleep '78
Right of Way '84
Magic of Lassie '78
Airport '77 '77
The Shootist '76
The Cheyenne Social Club '70
Bandolero! '68
Firecreek '68
Dear Brigitte '65
The Flight of the Phoenix '65
Shenandoah '65
Cheyenne Autumn '64
How the West Was Won '63
The Man Who Shot Liberty Valance '62
Mr. Hobbs Takes a Vacation '62
Two Rode Together '61
The Mountain Road '60
Anatomy of a Murder '59
The FBI Story '59
Bell, Book and Candle '58
Vertigo '58
Night Passage '57
Spirit of St. Louis '57
The Man Who Knew Too Much '56
The Man from Laramie '55
Strategic Air Command '55
The Far Country '55
Rear Window '54
The Glenn Miller Story '54
The Naked Spur '53
Thunder Bay '53
The Jackpot '50
Winchester '73 '50
Harvey '50
Broken Arrow '50
Malaya '49
The Stratton Story '49
Call Northside 777 '48
On Our Merry Way '48
Rope '48
Magic Town '47
It's a Wonderful Life '46
Made for Each Other '39
Mr. Smith Goes to Washington '39
Destry Rides Again '39
The Shop Around the Corner '40
The Philadelphia Story '40
The Mortal Storm '40
Navy Blue and Gold '37
Born to Dance '36
After the Thin Man '36
The Gorgeous Hussy '36
Next Time We Love '36
Rose Marie '36
Of Human Hearts '38
Shopworn Angel '38
Vivacious Lady '38
You Can't Take It with You '38
Ziegfeld Girl '41
Pot o' Gold '41
No Highway in the Sky '51
The Greatest Show on Earth '52
Bend of the River '52

Catherine Mary Stewart (1959-)
The Attic '06
Dead Silent '99
The Reaper '97
Number One Fan '94
Out of Annie's Past '94
Ordeal in the Arctic '93
Samurai Cowboy '93
Cafe Romeo '91
Perfect Harmony '91
Passion in Paradise '89
Weekend at Bernie's '89
World Gone Wild '88
Dudes '87
Murder by the Book '87
Nightflyers '87
Scenes from the Goldmine '87
Mischief '85
Sins '85
Night of the Comet '84
The Last Starfighter '84
Nighthawks '81
The Apple '80

Charlotte Stewart (1941-)
Tremors 3: Back to Perfection '01
Dark Angel: The Ascent '94
Tremors '89
Eraserhead '78

Don Stewart (1935-2006)
The Doomsday Flight '66

Elaine Stewart (1929-)
The Rise and Fall of Legs Diamond '60
Night Passage '57
Meet Me in Las Vegas '56
Brigadoon '54
The Gun Ranger '34

Eleanor Stewart (1913-2007)
Riders of the Timberline '41
The Rangers Step In '37
Where Trails Divide '37
Headin' for the Rio Grande '36

Evelyn Stewart (1942-)
Django Shoots First '74
The Psychic '78
The Scorpion's Tail '71
Murder Mansion '70
Blood for a Silver Dollar '66

Ewan Stewart (1957-)
American Women '00
Conspiracy '01
The Big Brass Ring '99
Stella Does Tricks '96
Rob Roy '95

Frank Stewart
Cemetery High '89
Sexpot '88
Galactic Gigolo '87
Psychos in Love '87
Sensations '87

French Stewart (1964-)
The Flock '07
Pandemic '07
Clockstoppers '02
Inspector Gadget 2 '02
Love Stinks '99
McHale's Navy '97
Glory Daze '96
Magic Island '95

John Stewart (1934-)
Last of the Comanches '52
Boots Malone '52

Jon Stewart (1962-)
Death to Smoochy '02
Jay and Silent Bob Strike Back '01
Big Daddy '99
The Faculty '98
Playing by Heart '98
Half-Baked '97
Since You've Been Gone '97
Wishful Thinking '96

Johna Stewart (1979-)
Young Hercules '97
Address Unknown '96
Galgameth '96

Kate McGregor Stewart
See Kate McGregor-Stewart

Kristen Stewart (1990-)
Into the Wild '07
In the Land of Women '06
Fierce People '05
Zathura '05
Catch That Kid '04
Speak '04
Cold Creek Manor '03
Panic Room '02
The Safety of Objects '01

Malcolm Stewart
Dr. Dolittle 4: Tail to the Chief '08
Deadlocked '00
Screwed '00
Fatal Error '99
Timecop '94
Titanic '96

Martha Stewart (1947-)
Men in Black 2 '02
Daisy Kenyon '47

Mel Stewart (1928-2002)
Bride of Re-Animator '89
The Kid with the 200 I.Q. '83

Paul Stewart (1908-86)
Seduced '85
The Tempest '82
Opening Night '77
Bite the Bullet '75
Murph the Surf '75
How to Commit Marriage '69
In Cold Blood '67
King Creole '58
The Cobweb '55
Kiss Me Deadly '55
The Joe Louis Story '53
Loan Shark '52
Champion '49
Easy Living '49
Twelve O'Clock High '49
Mr. Lucky '43
Citizen Kane '41

Peggy Stewart (1923-)
The Black Lash '52
The Fighting Redhead '50
Son of Zorro '47
Trail to San Antone '47
Alias Billy the Kid '46
The Phantom Rider '45
Stagecoach to Denver '46
Vigilantes of Boom Town '46
Rough Riders of Cheyenne '45
Silver City Kid '45
The Vampire's Ghost '45
Girls in Chains '43

Penelope Stewart
Boulevard of Broken Dreams '88
Vigil '84

The Man Who Knew Too Much '56
Fat Country '55
The Man from Laramie '55

Patrick Stewart (1940-)
TMNT (Teenage Mutant Ninja Turtles) '07 (V)
The Reception '05
100 Proof '96
Amateur '94

Chicken Little '05 (V)
The Game of Their Lives '05
Steamboy '05 (V)
The Lion in Winter '03
X2: X-Men United '03
King of Texas '02
Star Trek: Nemesis '02
Jimmy Neutron: Boy Genius '01 (V)
X-Men '00
Animal Farm '99 (V)
A Christmas Carol '99
Safe House '99
Moby Dick '98
Prince of Egypt '98 (V)
Star Trek: Insurrection '98
Conspiracy Theory '97
Dad Savage '97
The Canterville Ghost '96
Masterminds '96
Star Trek: First Contact '96
Jeffrey '95
The Pagemaster '94 (V)
Star Trek: Generations '94
Gunmen '93
L.A. Story '91
Code Name: Emerald '85
Excalibur '81
The Doctor and the Devils '85

Pamela Stewart
The Reception '05
100 Proof '96
Amateur '94

Nils Allen Stewart (1961-)
Undisputed '02
The Jesse Ventura Story '99

Robert Stewart (1961-)
Devour '05
Someone to Die For '95
Annie O '98

Robin Stewart
The Legend of the 7 Golden Vampires '73

Roy Stewart (1883-1933)
Masters of Venus '62
With Kit Carson over the Great Divide '25
Sparrows '26

Sara Stewart (1966-)
London Voodoo '04
Ruster's Roundup '33
Come on Tarzan '32

Sophie Stewart (1908-77)
Devil Girl from Mars '54
Made in Heaven '52
My Son, My Son '40
Nicholas Nickleby '47

Trish Stewart (1946-)
Breaking Up Is Hard to Do '79

Tonea Stewart
The Rosa Parks Story '02
A Time to Kill '96
Murder in the Old Red Barn '36

David Ogden Stiers (1942-)
TMNT '07
Lady in the Water '06 (N)
Hoodwinked '05 (V)
Lilo & Stitch 2: Stitch Has a Glitch '05 (V)
Disney's Teacher's Pet '04
Jungle Fever '91
The Majestic '01
Atlantis: The Lost Empire '01 (V)
Lilo & Stitch '02 (V)
The Curse of the Jade Scorpion '01
Spirited Away '01 (V)
Tomcats '01
Krippendorf's Tribe '98
Meet Wally Sparks '97
Everyone Says I Love You '96
Steal Big, Steal Little '95
Bad Company '95
Pocahontas '95 (V)
Mighty Aphrodite '95
Jungle 2 Jungle '96
Doc Hollywood '91
The Accidental Tourist '88
Another Woman '88
J. Edgar Hoover '87
Beauty and the Beast '91 (V)
Shadows and Fog '92
Mastergate '92
The Last of His Tribe '92
Iron Will '93
Past Tense '94
Final Notice '89
The Final Days '89
Day One '89
The Kissing Place '90
Doc Hollywood '91

Phyllis Stickney
What's Love Got to Do with It? '93
The Inkwell '94
The Uninvited '44
Murder at the Vanities '34

Dorothy Stickney (1900-98)
I Never Sang for My Father '70

North and South Book 1 '85
The First Olympics: Athens 1896 '84
Harry's War '84
The Innocents Abroad '84
M*A*S*H: Goodbye, Farewell & Amen '83
Damien: The Leper Priest '80
Oldest Living Graduate '80
Breaking Up Is Hard to Do '79
Magic '78
Sergeant Matlovich vs. the U.S. Air Force '78
Oh, God! '77

Hugo Stiglitz (1940-)
Naked Lies '98
Counterforce '87
City of the Walking Dead '80
Hostages '80
Fantastic Balloon Voyage '76
Night of a Thousand Cats '72
Robinson Crusoe & the Tiger '72

Julia Stiles (1981-)
The Bourne Ultimatum '07
The Omen '06
The Bourne Supremacy '04
The Prince & Me '04
A Guy Thing '03
Mona Lisa Smile '03
The Business of Strangers '01
O '01
Save the Last Dance '01
Down to You '00
Hamlet '00
State and Main '00
The '60s '99
Ten Things I Hate about You '99
Wicked '98

Robin Stille (1961-96)
American Ninja 4: The Annihilation '91
Slumber Party Massacre '82

Amy Stiller (1961-)
The Visit '00

Ben Stiller (1965-)
Tropic Thunder '08
The Heartbreak Kid '07
Danny Roane: First Time Director '06
Night at the Museum '06
School for Scoundrels '06
Tenacious D in the Pick of Destiny '06
Madagascar '05 (V)
Along Came Polly '04
Anchorman: The Legend of Ron Burgundy '04
Dodgeball: A True Underdog Story '04
Envy '04
Meet the Fockers '04
Starsky & Hutch '04
Duplex '03
The Royal Tenenbaums '01
Zoolander '01
The Independent '00
Keeping the Faith '00
Meet the Parents '00
Black and White '99
Mystery Men '99
The Suburbans '99
Permanent Midnight '98
There's Something about Mary '98
Your Friends & Neighbors '98
Zero Effect '97
The Cable Guy '96
Happy Gilmore '96
Flirting with Disaster '95
If Lucy Fell '95
Heavyweights '94
Reality Bites '94
Next of Kin '89
Stella '89
Fresh Horses '88
Empire of the Sun '87

Hot Pursuit '87

Brett Stiller
The Alice '04

Jerry Stiller (1927-)
Hairspray '07
The Heartbreak Kid '07
Disney's Teacher's Pet '04 (V)
The Lion King 1 1/2 '04 (V)
Serving Sara '02
On the Line '01
Zoolander '01
The Independent '00
My 5 Wives '00
The Suburbans '99
A Rat's Tale '98
Secret of the Andes '98
Stag '97
The Deli '97
Subway Stories '97
Heavyweights '94
The Pickle '93
Women & Men: In Love There Are No Rules '91
Little Vegas '90
That's Adequate '90
Hairspray '88
Hot Pursuit '87
Nadine '87
Seize the Day '86
The McGuffin '85
Those Lips, Those Eyes '80
Nasty Habits '77
The Ritz '76
The Taking of Pelham One Two Three '74

Diane Stilwell
Earth Girls Are Easy '89
Perfect Match '88

Brett Stimely
Cannibal Women in the Avocado Jungle of Death '89
Bloodstone '88

Sting (1951-)
Bee Movie '07 (V)
Lock, Stock and 2 Smoking Barrels '98
Grave Indiscretions '96
The Adventures of Baron Munchausen '89
Stormy Monday '88
Julia and Julia '87
The Bride '85
Plenty '85
Dune '84
Brimstone & Treacle '82
The Secret Policeman's Other Ball '82
Quadrophenia '79

Colin Stinton (1947-)
The Bourne Ultimatum '07
The Winslow Boy '98
In Love and War '96

Linda Stirling (1921-97)
Jesse James Rides Again '47
Cyclotrode "X" '46
Rio Grande Raiders '46
D-Day on Mars '45
Manhunt of Mystery Island '45
The Purple Monster Strikes '45
The Topeka Terror '45
Perils of the Darkest Jungle '44
Zorro's Black Whip '44

Rachael Stirling (1977-)
Freeze Frame '04
Bait '02
Tipping the Velvet '02
The Triumph of Love '01
Maybe Baby '00
Retribution '98
Still Crazy '98

Brian Stirner
Poldark 2 '75
All Creatures Great and Small '74

Barbara Stock (1956-)
Verne Miller '88
Long Time Gone '86

Nigel Stock (1919-86)
The Lion in Winter '68
The Great Escape '63
Victim '61
The Silent Enemy '58
Brighton Rock '47

Amy Stock-Poynton (1958-)
Beanstalk '94
Bill & Ted's Bogus Journey '91
Bill & Ted's Excellent Adventure '89

Sara Stockbridge (1966-)
Spider '02
24 Hours in London '00

Carl Stockdale (1874-1953)
Condemned to Live '35
The Crimson Trail '35
The Ivory Handled Gun '35
Law for Tombstone '35
Get That Girl '32
Oliver Twist '22
The Greatest Question '19
The Americano '17
Hoodoo Ann '16

Werner Stocker (1955-93)
November Moon '85
A Man Like Eva '83
The White Rose '83

Bill Stockton
Three Days of Rain '03

Dean Stockwell (1936-)
Three Days of Rain '02
The Manchurian Candidate '04
Buffalo Soldiers '01
CQ '01
Inferno '01
The Quickie '01
In Pursuit '00
Restraining Order '99
Rites of Passage '99
Air Force One '97
John Grisham's The Rainmaker '97
Living in Peril '97
McHale's Navy '97
Midnight Blue '96
Twilight Man '96
Madonna: Innocence Lost '95
Mr. Wrong '95
Naked Souls '95
Stephen King's The Langoliers '95
Chasers '94
Bonanza: The Return '93
The Player '92
Shame '92
Son of the Morning Star '91
Smokescreen '90
Backtrack '89
Banzai Runner '86
Blue Velvet '86
Legend of Billie Jean '85
To Live & Die in L.A. '85
Dune '84
To Kill a Stranger '84
Paris, Texas '83
Alsino and the Condor '82
Wrong Is Right '82
She Came to the Valley '77
One Away '76
Tracks '76
Werewolf of Washington '73
Loners '72
Win, Place, or Steal '72

Paper Man '71
The Dunwich Horror '70
Psych-Out '68
Long Day's Journey into Night '62
Compulsion '59
Kim '50
Stars in My Crown '50
The Secret Garden '49
The Boy with the Green Hair '48
Gentleman's Agreement '47
Song of the Thin Man '47
Anchors Aweigh '45

Guy Stockwell (1934-2002)
Santa Sangre '90
Grotesque '87
It's Alive '74
The Gatling Gun '72
And Now Miguel '66
Tobruk '66
The War Lord '65

John Stockwell (1961-)
Breast Men '97
The Nurse '97
Stag '97
I Shot a Man in Vegas '96
Legal Deceit '95
Operation Intercept '95
Born to Ride '91
Eyes of the Panther '90
Billionaire Boys Club '87
Dangerously Close '86
Radioactive Dreams '86
Top Gun '86
City Limits '85
My Science Project '85
Quarterback Princess '85
Christine '84
Eddie and the Cruisers '83
Losin' It '82

Malcolm Stoddard (1948-)
Coming Home '98
Catherine Cookson's The Girl '96
The Assassination Run '84
The Godsend '79
Luther '74

Austin Stoker (1934-)
Time Walker '82
Assault on Precinct 13 '76
Sheba, Baby '75
Twisted Brain '74
Battle for the Planet of the Apes '73

Barry Stokes
Allen Prey '83
Spaced Out '80

Susan Stokey
Phantom Empire '87

Oliver Stokowski (1962-)
The Experiment '01

Mink Stole (1947-)
Regular Guys '96
Eating Out 2: Sloppy Seconds '06
A Dirty Shame '04
Girl Play '04
Ring of Darkness '04
Cecil B. Demented '00
Shriek If You Know What I Did Last Friday the 13th '00
But I'm a Cheerleader '99
Leather Jacket Love Story '98
Pecker '98
The Death Artist '95
Serial Mom '94
Liquid Dreams '92
Cry-Baby '90
Hairspray '88
Polyester '81
Desperate Living '77
Female Trouble '74
Pink Flamingos '72
Multiple Maniacs '70
Mondo Trasho '69

Shirley Stoler (1929-99)
Malcolm X '92
Frankenhooker '90
Miami Blues '90
Sons '89
Shakedown '88
Sticky Fingers '88
Splitz '84
The Deer Hunter '78
Seven Beauties '76
A Real Young Girl '75
Honeymoon Killers '70

Erik Stolhanske (1968-)
Beerfest '06
Club Dread '04
Super Troopers '01

Gunther Stoll (1924-77)
Cold Blood '75
Double Face '70
The Castle of Fu Manchu '68

Fred Stoller
Rebound '05
Chairman of the Board '97
Downhill Willie '96
Dumb & Dumber '94

Eric Stoltz (1961-)
The Lather Effect '06
The Honeymooners '05
The Butterfly Effect '04
Happy Hour '03
Out of Order '03
The Rules of Attraction '02
Harvard Man '01
Things Behind the Sun '01
Common Ground '00
House of Mirth '00
One Kill '00
A Murder of Crows '99
The Passion of Ayn Rand '99
The Simian Line '99
Hi-Life '98
Mr. Jealousy '98
Highball '97
Anaconda '96
Don't Look Back '96
Grace of My Heart '96
Inside '96
Jerry Maguire '96
Keys to Tulsa '96
Two Days in the Valley '96
Fluke '95
Kicking and Screaming '95
The Prophecy '95
Rob Roy '95
Killing Zoe '94
Little Women '94
Pulp Fiction '94
A Woman at War '94
Bodies, Rest & Motion '93
Foreign Affairs '93
Naked in New York '93
Singles '92
The Waterdance '91
Memphis Belle '90
The Discovery Program '89
The Fly 2 '89
Our Town '89
Say Anything '89
Haunted Summer '88
Lionheart '87
A Night of Love '87
Sister, Sister '87
Some Kind of Wonderful '87
Code Name: Emerald '85
Mask '85
The New Kids '85
Surf 2 '84
The Wild Life '84
Running Hot '83
Fast Times at Ridgemont High '82
The Seekers '79
The Grass Is Always Greener Over the Septic Tank '78

Lena Stolze (1956-)
Rosenstrasse '03
The Nasty Girl '90
The White Rose '83
The Last Five Days '82

Adam Stone
Great World of Sound '07
Glass '90

Christopher Stone (1940-95)
Dying to Remember '93
Blue Movies '88
The Annihilators '85
Cujo '83
The Junkman '78
The Howling '81
Prisoner in the Middle '74
Love Me Deadly '73
The Passing of Evil '70

Danton Stone
Series 7: The Contenders '01
McHale's Navy '97
He Said, She Said '91
Once Around '91
Crazy People '90

Fred Stone (1873-1959)
The Westerner '40
The Trail of the Lonesome Pine '36
Alice Adams '35

George E. Stone (1903-67)
Jungle Hell '55
Treasure of Fear '45
Timber Queen '44
Broadway Limited '41
Road Show '41
A Slight Case of Murder '38
You and Me '38
Make a Million '35
Viva Villa! '34
42nd Street '33
The Last Mile '32
The Vampire Bat '32
Cimarron '31
Medicine Man '30

Harold J. Stone (1911-2005)
Legend of Valentino '75
The McCullochs '75
Mitchell '75
Big Mouth '67
The St. Valentine's Day Massacre '67
Girl Happy '65
X: The Man with X-Ray Eyes '63
The Invisible Boy '57

Leonard Stone (1923-)
Blood Money '99
Willy Wonka & the Chocolate Factory '71

Lewis Stone (1879-1953)
All the Brothers Were Valiant '53
Prisoner of Zenda '52
Scaramouche '52
Angels in the Outfield '51
Key to the City '50
Stars in My Crown '50
Any Number Can Play '49
The Sun Comes Up '49
State of the Union '48
Love Laughs at Andy Hardy '46
Andy Hardy's Double Life '42
Andy Hardy's Private Secretary '41
Life Begins for Andy Hardy '41
Andy Hardy Meets Debutante '40
Andy Hardy Gets Spring Fever '39
Love Finds Andy Hardy '38
Suzy '36
China Seas '35
David Copperfield '35
The Girl from Missouri '34
Treasure Island '34
Bureau of Missing Persons '33
Queen Christina '33
Grand Hotel '32
The Mask of Fu Manchu '32
Mata Hari '32

Red Headed Woman '32
Claudet '31
The Sin of Madelcn
Lolita '62
Terror Street '54

Marianne Stone (1922-)
The Quick and the Dead '95
Nomads of the North '20
Casino '95
Last Dance '96
Diabolique '96
Sphere '98
The Mighty '98
Antz '98 (V)
Gloria '98
Simpatico '99
Romance '30
The Big House '30
Wild Orchids '28
A Woman of Affair's '28
The Notorious Lady '27
The Lost World '25
Beau Revel '21

Michael Stone
Orgazmo '98
BASEketball '98
Cannibal! The Musical '96
Bloody Murder '99
The Quick and the Dead '95

Matt Stone (1971-)
Team America: World
Police '04 (V)
South Park: Bigger, Longer
and Uncut '99 (V)
BASEketball '98
Orgazmo '98
Cannibal! The Musical '96

Milburn Stone (1904-80)
The Private War of Major
Benson '55
Arrowhead '53
Pickup on South Street '53
The Sun Shines Bright '53
The Atomic City '52
Branded '50
The Green Promise '49
Heading for Heaven '47
Killer Dill '47
Strange Confession '45
Hi, Good Lookin'! '44
Jungle Woman '44
Master Key '44
Phantom Lady '44
Captive Wild Woman '43
The Mad Ghoul '43
Sherlock Holmes Faces
Death '43
Colorado '40
The Great Plane Robbery
'40
Fighting Mad '39
Mystery Plane '39
Stunt Pilot '39
Mr. Boggs Steps Out '38
Sinners in Paradise '38
Swing It, Professor '37
The Thirteenth Man '37
Youth on Parole '37
The Port of Missing Girls
'38

Oliver Stone (1946-)
Dave '93
Wild Palms '93
Born on the Fourth of July
'89
Wall Street '87
Platoon '86
Scarface '83
The Hand '81
Midnight Express '78

Paula Stone (1913-97)
Convicts at Large '38
Swing It, Professor '37
Red Lights Ahead '36
Hopalong Cassidy '35

Philip Stone (1924-2003)
A Certain Justice '99
Monsignor Quixote '91
The Shining '80
The Unearthly Stranger '64
Forest '07

Sharon Stone (1958-)
When a Man Falls in the

Sinners in Paradise '38

The Specialist '94
Intersection '93
Last Action Hero '93
Silver '93
Basic Instinct '92
Diary of a Hitman '91
He Said, She Said '91
Scissors '91
Where Sleeping Dogs Lie
'91
Year of the Gun '91
Total Recall '90
Beyond the Stars '89
Blood and Sand '89
War & Remembrance '88
Above the Law '88
Action Jackson '88
Tears in the Rain '88
Cold Steel '87
Police Academy 4: Citizens
on Patrol '87
Allan Quatermain and the
Lost City of Gold '86
King Solomon's Mines '85
Calendar Girl Murders '84
Irreconcilable Differences
'84
The Vegas Strip Wars '84
Deadly Blessing '81

Stuart Stone
Donnie Darko '01
Joy Ride '01
The Boys Club '96

Sherri Stoner (1965-)
Reform School Girls '86
Impulse '84
Heavenly Bodies '84

Alyson Stoner (1993-)
All the King's Men '99
Cheaper by the Dozen 2
'05
Cheaper by the Dozen '03

Jo Stone-Fewings
Wondrous Oblivion '06

Paolo Stoppa (1906-88)
The Leopard '63
Where the Hot Wind Blows
'59
The Gold of Naples '54
Seven Deadly Sins '53
Beauties of the Night '52
Miracle in Milan '51
Beauty and the Devil '50

Larry Storch (1923-)
Funny Valentine '05
Silence of the Hams '93
I Don't Buy Kisses
Anymore '92
Adventures Beyond Belief
'97
Flight of Dragons '82 (V)
S.O.B. '81
Sweet 16 '81
Better Late Than Never '79
The Adventures of
Huckleberry Finn '78
Sex and the Single Girl '64
Captain Newman, M.D. '63
40 Pounds of Trouble '62
The Miracle Maker: The
Story of Jesus '00 (V)
Plunkett & Macleane '98
Rhodes '97
Fever Pitch '96

Raymond Storti
Decay '98

Ken Stott (1955-)
Casanova '05
King Arthur '04
The Girl in the Cafe '05
I'll Sleep When I'm Dead
'03
Casablanca 42
Pittsburgh '42
House of Dracula '45
Cloak and Dagger '46
Song of Love '47
G.I. Blues '60

Ludwig Stossel (1883-1973)

If These Walls Could Talk 2
'00
The Muse '99
Picking Up the Pieces '99
Johnson County War '02
Rough Riders '97
National Lampoon's Attack
of the 5 Ft. 2 Women '94
Stephen King's The Stand
'94
Lifepod '93
Death Becomes Her '92
Highway to Hell '92
The Phantom of the Opera
'90
Mystic Pizza '88

Dirk Storm
See Kevin Nealon

Gale Storm (1922-)
The Texas Rangers '51
The Underworld Story '50
Swing Parade of 1946 '46
Revenge of the Zombies
'43
Rhythm Parade '43
Lure of the Islands '42
Man from Cheyenne '42
Smart Alecks '42
Let's Go Collegiate '41
Nacho Libre '06
Premonition '07
Witness Protection '08
Night of Dark Shadows '71
Scream of the Wolf '74
Trilogy of Terror '75
Ants '77
Firetrap '01

Peter Stormare (1953-)
Doomsdayer '99
Urban Menace '99
Constantine '05
The Brothers Grimm '05
Minority Report '02
Spun '02
13 Moons '02
The Tuxedo '02
Windtalkers '02
Happy Campers '01
Bruiser '00
Circus '00
Chocolat '00
Dancer in the Dark '99
The Million Dollar Hotel '99
Purgatory '99
Armageddon '98
Mercury Rising '98
The Big Lebowski '97
The Lost World: Jurassic
Park 2 '97
Somewhere in the City '97
Fargo '96
Le Polygraphe '96
Playing God '96
Pattems '56
Awakenings '90

Julie Strain (1962-)
Blood Gnome '02
Heavy Metal 2000 '00 (V)
The Rowdy Girls '00
Battle Queen 2020 '99
Sweet 16 '81
St. Patrick's Day '99
Lethal Seduction '97
Return to Savage Beach
'97
Day of the Warrior '96
Red Line '96
Dark Secrets '95
Midnight Confessions '95
The Mosaic Project '95
Virtual Desire '95
Play Time '94
Money to Burn '94
The Dallas Connection '94
Psycho Cop 2 '94
Sorceress '94
Victim of Desire '94
Enemy Gold '93
Fit to Kill '93
Night Rhythms '92

Susan Strasberg (1938-99)
In Praise of Older Women
'78
The Manitou '78
Rollercoaster '77
Frankenstein '73
The Brotherhood '68
Psych-Out '68
The Trip '67
The Sibling '72

Lee Strasberg (1901-82)
The Godfather 1902-1959:
The Complete Epic '81
And Justice for All '79
Going in Style '79
The Cassandra Crossing
'76
The Godfather, Part 2 '74

Adam Storke (1962-)
South of the Border '39
First Love '39
Saint-Ex: The Story of the
Storyteller '95
Sier Hunter '95
Shallow Grave '94
Witchcraft 4: Virgin Heart
'92
Mirror Images '91
Out for Justice '91
Psycho Cop '88

George Stover
Attack of the 60-'oot
Centerfold '95
Deadly Neighbor '91
Dracula's Widow '88
Fiend '83

Madeleine Stowe (1958-)
Phantom Ranger '38
Desperate Living '77
Female Trouble '74
Pulse '03
Avenging Angel's '02
Impostor '02
The Magnificent
Ambersons '02
We Were Soldiers '02
China M.con '91
Revenge '90
Stakeout '87
The Two Jakes '90
Worth Winning '89
T-ropical Snow '87
The Amazons '84
Gangster Wars '81
China Moon '91
U-nlawful Entry '92
Short Cuts '93
Blink '93
Another Stakeout '93
Bad Girls '94
12 Monkeys '95
The Proposition '97
Playing by Heart '98
The General's Daughter '99
Tre

Michael Stoyanov (1970-)
Freaked '93
Restaurant '98
Nativity '78

Anthony Strachan
Sylvia '03

Beatrice Straight (1918-2001)
The Trench '99
Deceived '91
Robert Kennedy and His
Times '90
Power '86
The Princess and the Pea
'83
Two of a Kind '83
Poltergeist '82
Endless Love '81
The Promise '79
The Formula '80
.45 '06
White Noise '05

Sarah Strange
Stargate: The Ark of Truth
'08

Robert Strange (1882-1952)
Far Frontier '48
The Saint Strikes Back '39
Dead Men Walk '43
Misleading Lady '32

Steven Strait (1986-)
10,000 B.C. '08
The Covenant '06
Sky High '05

Harry Strang (1983-72)
The Fighting Sullivans '42
Jailhouse Rock '57
The Lawless Breed '52
Comin' Round the
Mountain '51
Master Minds '49
Abbott and Costello Meet
Frankenstein '46
The Wistful Widow of
Wagon Gap '47
House of Dracula '45
House of Frankenstein '44
The Mad Monster '42
The Drift'n Kid '41
Silver City Kid '44
Boot Hill Bandits '42
Billy the Kid Trapped '42
The Black Raven '43
Action in the North Atlantic
'43
The Last of the Mohicans
'92

Glenn Strange (1899-1973)

David Strathairn (1949-)
The Spiderwick Chronicles
'08
The Bourne Ultimatum '07
Fracture '07
My Blueberry Nights '07
Heavens Fall '06
The Notorious Bettie Page
'06
We Are Marshall '06
Soup for One '82
Changes '69
The Aviator '85
Mastergate '92
And You Thought Your
Parents Were Weird! '91
Fast Getaway '91
Honey, I Shrunk the Kids
'89
The Notorious Bettie Page
Master Spy: The Robert
Hanssen Story '02
In the Gloaming '97
Evidence of Blood '97
The Climb '97
L.A. Confidential '97
Losing Isaiah '94
Dolores Claiborne '94
Home for the Holidays '95
Mother Night '96
Beyond the Call '96
Lost in Yonkers '93
S:mon Birch '98
A Good Baby '99
A Map of the Wo-ld '99
Limbo '99
With Friends Like These
'98
Bad Manners '98
Dream '99
A Dangerous Woman '93
A League of Their Own '92
Passion Fish '92
Sneakers '92
O Pioneers! '91
Son of the Morning Star '91
Without Warning: The
James Brady Story '91
The Feud '90
Heat Wave '90
Judgment '90
Memphis Belle '90
Day One '89
Dominick & Eugene '88
Eight Men Out '88
Broken Vows '87
Matewan '87
At Close Range '36
Iceman '84
Silkwood '83
Enormous Changes '83
Trumps '83
Stage Struck '57
The Cobweb '55
Picnic '55

Marcia Strassman (1948-)
Another Stakeout '93
Honey, I Blew Up the Kid
'92
The Unnamable 2: The
Statement of Randolph
Carter '92
A Different Loyalty '04
Cold Creek Manor '03
Beautiful Joe '00

Charles Stratton (1960-80)
They All Laughed '81
Galaxina '80
Americathon '79
Autumn Born '80
The Brother from Another
Planet '84
Return of the Secaucus 7
'80
Notes from Underground
'95
Munchies '87

Dorothy Stratten (1960-80)
The Lathe of Heaven '02
The Miracle Worke '00
Freedom Song '00
Twisted '04
Luck '05
Get Even '92
Bob Roberts '92
Big Girls Don't Cry... They
Get Even '92
Stand Off '93

Steven Strait
Honey, I Shrunk the Kids

Blue Car '03
The Miracle Worker '00
Harrison's Flowers '02
Midsummer Night's A
William Shakespeare's A

Summer Camp Nightmare '86

John Stratton (1925-91)
Frankenstein and the Monster from Hell '74
Abandon Ship! '57

Peter Strauss (1947-)
License to Wed '07
XXX: State of the Union '05
Strange Frequency 2 '01
Joan of Arc '99
In the Lake of the Woods '96
Keys to Tulsa '96
Nick of Time '95
The Yearling '94
Fugitive Among Us '92
Flight of Black Angel '91
The Brotherhood of the Rose '89
Peter Gunn '89
Proud Men '86
Penalty Phase '86
Spacehunter: Adventures in the Forbidden Zone '83
Masada '81
Whale for the Killing '81
Angel on My Shoulder '80
The Jericho Mile '79
The Last Tycoon '76
Rich Man, Poor Man '76
The Man Without a Country '73
Trial of the Catonsville Nine '72
Man of Legend '71
Soldier Blue '70
Hail, Hero! '69

Robert Strauss (1913-75)
The Noah '75
Family Jewels '65
Frankie and Johnny '65
That Funny Feeling '65
Girls! Girls! Girls! '62
The 4D Man '59
I, Mobster '58
Attack! '56
The Bridges at Toko-Ri '55
The Man with the Golden Arm '55
The Seven Year Itch '55
The Atomic Kid '54
Here Come the Girls '53
The Redhead from Wyoming '53
Stalag 17 '53
Jumping Jacks '52
Sailor Beware '52

Meryl Streep (1949-)
Mamma Mia! '08
Evening '07
Lions for Lambs '07
Rendition '07
The Ant Bully '06 (V)
The Devil Wears Prada '06
A Prairie Home Companion '06
Prime '05
Lemony Snicket's A Series of Unfortunate Events '04
The Manchurian Candidate '04
Angels in America '03
Adaptation '02
The Hours '02
A. I.: Artificial Intelligence '01 (V)
Music of the Heart '99
Dancing at Lughnasa '98
One True Thing '98
First Do No Harm '97
Marvin's Room '96
Before and After '95
The Bridges of Madison County '95
The River Wild '94
The House of the Spirits '93
Death Becomes Her '92
Defending Your Life '91
Postcards from the Edge '90
She-Devil '89
A Cry in the Dark '88
Ironweed '87
Heartburn '86
Out of Africa '85
Plenty '85
Falling in Love '84
Silkwood '83
Sophie's Choice '82
Still of the Night '82
The French Lieutenant's Woman '81
Kramer vs. Kramer '79
Manhattan '79
The Seduction of Joe Tynan '79
The Deer Hunter '78
Holocaust '78
Julia '77

Elliot Street (1943-)
Melvin Purvis: G-Man '74
Harrad Experiment '73
Paper Man '71

Russell Streiner (1940-)
The Majorettes '87
Night of the Living Dead '68

Barbra Streisand (1942-)
Meet the Fockers '04
The Mirror Has Two Faces '96
The Prince of Tides '91
Nuts '87
Yentl '83
All Night Long '81
The Main Event '79
A Star Is Born '76
Funny Lady '75
For Pete's Sake '74
The Way We Were '73
Up the Sandbox '72
What's Up, Doc? '72
On a Clear Day You Can See Forever '70
The Owl and the Pussycat '70
Hello, Dolly! '69
Funny Girl '68

Gary Stretch (1968-)
Afghan Knights '07
Alexander '04
Dead Man's Shoes '04
Business for Pleasure '96
Dead Connection '94
Final Combination '93

Melissa Stribling (1927-92)
Crucible of Terror '72
The Horror of Dracula '58
Crow Hollow '52

Connie Strickland
Act of Vengeance '74
Bummer! '73

David Strickland (1971-99)
Forces of Nature '99
Delivered '98

Gail Strickland (1947-)
The American President '95
Last Time Out '94
Three of Hearts '93
Scott Turow's The Burden of Proof '92
The Man in the Moon '91
Hyper-Sapien: People from Another Star '86
Oxford Blues '84
Protocol '84
Lies '83
Eleanor: First Lady of the World '82
A Matter of Life and Death '81
Rape and Marriage: The Rideout Case '80
The Gathering: Part 2 '79
Snowball '78
Who'll Stop the Rain? '78
The Gathering '77
One on One '77

KaDee Strickland (1975-)
American Gangster '07
The Flock '07
Fever Pitch '05
Knots '05
Anacondas: The Hunt for the Blood Orchid '04
The Grudge '04
Anything Else '03
Something's Gotta Give '03

Anita Strindberg (1944-)
Women in Cell Block 7 '77
The Tempter '74
Who Saw Her Die? '72
Your Vice is a Closed Room and Only I Have the Key '72
The Case of the Scorpion's Tail '71
A Lizard in a Woman's Skin '71
The Scorpion's Tail '71

Sherry Stringfield (1967-)
Dead Simple '01
Autumn in New York '00
54 '98
An Unexpected Life '97
September '88

Elaine Stritch (1925-)
Monster-in-Law '05
Romance & Cigarettes '05
Autumn in New York '00
Screwed '00
Small Time Crooks '00
Krippendorf's Tribe '98
Out to Sea '97
Providence '77
The Perfect Furlough '59
Three Violent People '57

Woody Strode (1914-94)
Posse '93
Storyville '92
Murder on the Bayou '91
Lust in the Dust '85
Jungle Warriors '84
Winterhawk '76
Kingdom of the Spiders '77
Loaded Guns '75
Hired to Kill '73
Hit Men '73
Manhunt '73
The Gatling Gun '72
Ride to Glory '71
Boot Hill '69
Black Jesus '68
Shalako '68
Super Brother '68
The Professionals '66
The Last Voyage '60
Sergeant Rutledge '60
Spartacus '60
Pork Chop Hill '59
Three Stooges in Orbit '62
Snow White and the Three Stooges '61

Brenda Strong (1960-)
The Kid and I '05
Exposed '03
Missing Brendan '03
Terror Tract '00
Undercurrent '99
Black Dog '98
The Deep End of the Ocean '98

Danny Strong (1974-)
Shriek If You Know What I Did Last Friday the 13th '00

Johnny Strong
Black Hawk Down '01
The Fast and the Furious '01
Get Carter '00
The Glimmer Man '96

Mark Strong (1963-)
Babylon AD '08
The Hills Have Eyes 2 '07
Thirteen Days '00
The Curve '97

Henry Strozier
Miss Pettigrew Lives for a Day '08
Stardust '07
Sunshine '07
Scenes of a Sexual Nature '06
Tristan & Isolde '06
Oliver Twist '05
Revolver '05
Syriana '05
It's All About Love '03
To End All Wars '01
Anna Karenina '00
Sunshine '99
Twice upon a Yesterday '98
Emma '97
Fever Pitch '96
Sharpe's Mission '96

Michael Strong (1924-80)
Queen of the Stardust Ballroom '75
Patton '70
Point Blank '67

Natalie Strong
Mrs. Parker and the Vicious Circle '94
Short Cuts '93
Bob Roberts '92
The Player '92

Rider Strong (1979-)
Tooth and Nail '07
Paradise, Texas '05
Cabin Fever '03
The Pact '99
My Giant '98
Benefit of the Doubt '93

Tara Strong (1973-)
Rugrats Go Wild! '03 (V)
Ice Age '02 (V)
The Powerpuff Girls Movie '02 (V)
Spirited Away '01 (V)
Rugrats in Paris: The Movie '00 (V)
The Rugrats Movie '98 (V)
Family Pictures '93

Don Stroud (1937-)
Dance with the Devil '97
The Haunted Sea '97
Wild America '97
Little Bigfoot '96
Criminal Hearts '95
Dillinger and Capone '95
Sawbones '95
Unknown Origin '95
Return to Frogtown '92
The King of the Kickboxers '91
Prime Target '91
Cartel '90
Down the Drain '89
Hyper Space '89
Twisted Justice '89
Two to Tango '88
Armed and Dangerous '86
The Night the Lights Went Out in Georgia '81
Search and Destroy '81
Sweet 16 '81
The Amityville Horror '79
Express to Terror '79
The Buddy Holly Story '78
The Choirboys '77
Sudden Death '77
Death Weekend '76
Hollywood Man '76
The Killer Inside Me '76
Murph the Surf '75
Slaughter's Big Rip-off '73
Joe Kidd '72
Angel Unchained '70
Bloody Mama '70
Explosion '69
Coogan's Bluff '68
Madigan '68
Games '67

Duke Stroud
Human Desires '97
Children of the Corn 3: Urban Harvest '95

Jessica Stroup
Prom Night '08
The Hills Have Eyes 2 '07

Shepperd Strudwick (1907-83)
Cops and Robbers '73
The Man Without a Country '73
Psychomania '63
Beyond a Reasonable Doubt '56
A Place in the Sun '51
Let's Dance '50
Three Husbands '50
All the King's Men '49
The Red Pony '49
I Was a Male War Bride '49
Sitting Pretty '48
The Loves of Edgar Allen Poe '42

Joe Strummer (1952-2002)
Doctor Chance '97
Mystery Train '89
Candy Mountain '87
Straight to Hell '87

Sally Struthers (1948-)
Baadasssss! '03
Out of the Black '01
Alice in Wonderland '85
A Gun in the House '81
Intimate Strangers '77
The Getaway '72
Five Easy Pieces '70

Carel Struycken (1949-)
Men in Black '97
Backlash: Oblivion 2 '95
Out There '95
Under the Hula Moon '95
Oblivion '94
The Addams Family Values '93
The Addams Family '91
Servants of Twilight '91
The Witches of Eastwick '87
The Ewoks: Battle for Endor '85

Cassie Stuart
Dolls '87
Hidden City '87

Eric Stuart (1967-)
Yu-Gi-Oh! The Movie: Pyramid of Light '04 (V)
Pokemon 3: The Movie '01 (V)
Pokemon: The First Movie '99 (V)

Gloria Stuart (1910-)
Land of Plenty '04
The Love Letter '99
Titanic '97
My Favorite Year '82
The Two Worlds of Jenny Logan '79
Enemy of Women '44
It Could Happen to You '39
The Three Musketeers '39
Rebecca of Sunnybrook Farm '38
The Poor Little Rich Girl '36
The Prisoner of Shark Island '36
Gold Diggers of 1935 '35
The Invisible Man '33
Roman Scandals '33
The Old Dark House '32

James R. Stuart
See Giacomo "Jack" Rossi-Stuart

John Stuart (1898-1979)
Sink the Bismarck! '60
Village of the Damned '60
The Mummy '59
Alias John Preston '56
John and Julie '55
The Gilded Cage '54
Man on the Run '49
The Temptress '49
Candles at Nine '44
Old Mother Riley's Ghosts '41
No. 17 '32

Katie Stuart (1985-)
Wild Things 2 '04
X2: X-Men United '03
Atomic Dog '98
Frog and Wombat '98
Summer of the Monkeys '98
Masterminds '96

Maxine Stuart (1918-)
The Haunting of Seacliff Inn '94
The Rousters '90
Coast to Coast '80

Randy Stuart (1924-96)
The Incredible Shrinking Man '57
I Was a Male War Bride '49
Sitting Pretty '48

Imogen Stubbs (1961-)
Twelfth Night '96
Jack and Sarah '95
Sense and Sensibility '95
True Colors '91
Erik the Viking '89
Fellow Traveler '89
A Summer Story '88

Stephen Stucker (1947-86)
Delinquent School Girls '84
Trading Places '83
Airplane 2: The Sequel '82
Airplane! '80

Wes Studi (1947-)
Comanche Moon '08
Bury My Heart at Wounded Knee '07
Animal '05
Miracle at Sage Creek '05
The New World '05
A Thief of Time '04
Coyote Waits '03
Skinwalker '02
SuperFire '02
Undisputed '02
Mystery Men '99
Deep Rising '98
Soundman '99
Wind River '98
Crazy Horse '96
The Killing Jar '96
Lone Justice 3: Showdown at Plum Creek '96
Heat '95
Larry McMurtry's Streets of Laredo '95
Street Fighter '94
Dances with Wolves '90
The Broken Chain '93
Geronimo: An American Legend '93
Lone Justice 2 '93
The Last of the Mohicans '92
The Doors '91

Jerzy Stuhr (1947-)
Trois Couleurs: Blanc '94
Deja Vu '89
The Decalogue '88
Hero of the Year '85
Camera Buff '79
Provincial Actors '79

Geoff Stults (1977-)
In the Mix '05
Wedding Crashers '05
D.E.B.S. '04

Johnny Stumper
Covert Action '88
Mob War '88

Malcolm Stumpf
Wild Tigers I Have Known '06
The Next Best Thing '00

Wolfgang Stumpf (1909-83)
Signs of Life '68

Preston Sturges (1898-1959)
The Bridge '59
Paris Holiday '57
Star Spangled Rhythm '42

Shannon Sturges (1968-)
The Perfect Wife '00
Silent Predators '99
Convict 762 '98
Tornado! '96
Pre-Madonnas: Rebels Without a Clue '95

Jim Sturgess
Crossing Over '08
The Other Boleyn Girl '08
21 '08
Across the Universe '07
Gulliver's Travels '04

Gary Sturgis (1966-)
Daddy's Little Girls '07
Pride '07

Thomas Sturridge (1986-)
Brothers of the Head '06
Being Julia '04

Trudie Styler (1955-)
Me Without You '01
Grave Indiscretions '96
Fair Game '89
Poldark 2 '75

Krystyna Stypulkowska (1939-)
Trace of Stones '66
Innocent Sorcerers '60

Emma Suarez (1964-)
Tierra '95
The Red Squirrel '93
Vacas '91
Against the Wind '90

Jeremy Suarez (1990-)

Jose Suarez (1919-81)
Texas, Adios '66
Carthage in Flames '60

Tara Subkoff (1973-)
The Notorious Bettie Page '06
Anchorman: The Legend of Ron Burgundy '04
Undermind '03
Teenage Caveman '01
The Cell '00

Michel Subor (1935-)
The Intruder '04
Beau Travail '98
Please Not Now! '61
Le Petit Soldat '60

David Suchet (1946-)
The Bank Job '08
Dracula '06
Flushed Away '06 (V)
The In-Laws '03
Live from Baghdad '03
Pinocchio '02 (V)
The Way We Live Now '02
Victoria & Albert '01
RKO 281 '99
Wing Commander '99
A Perfect Murder '98
Solomon '98
Deadly Voyage '96
Executive Decision '96
Moses '96
Sunday '96
Don't Hang Up '90
To Kill a Priest '89
When the Whales Came '89
A World Apart '88
Cause Celebre '87
Harry and the Hendersons '87
The Last Innocent Man '87
Iron Eagle '86
Murrow '86
Agatha Christie's Thirteen at Dinner '85
Crime of Honor '85
The Falcon and the Snowman '85
Gulag '85

Maria Suchareta
Pipe Dream '02
Whore 2 '94

Marla Sucharetza

Ania Suli
Stuart Bliss '98
Fun '94
Hold Me, Thrill Me, Kiss Me '93

Ali Sullivan
The Kingdom '07
Paradise Now '05

Margaret Sullavan (1911-60)
Back Street '41
So Ends Our Night '41
The Mortal Storm '40
The Shop Around the Corner '40
The Shining Hour '38
Shopworn Angel '38
Three Comrades '38
The Good Fairy '35
Next Time We Love '36
The Moon's Our Home '36

Kohl Sudduth (1974-)
Jesse Stone: Sea Change '07
Jesse Stone: Death in Paradise '06
Jesse Stone: Night Passage '06
Jesse Stone: Stone Cold '05

Skipp (Robert L.) Sudduth (1956-)
Flawless '99
54 '98
Ronin '98
George Wallace '97
Money Train '95

Shun Sugata (1955-)
Marebito '04
The Last Samurai '03
Pulse '01

Lam Suet
Kung Fu Hustle '04
Tsui Hark's Vampire Hunters '02
The Mission '99

Ichiro Sugai (1907-73)
Early Summer '51
Late Spring '49
No Regrets for Our Youth '46

Haruko Sugimura (1905-97)
Drifting Weeds '59
Late Chrysanthemums '54
Tokyo Story '53
Early Summer '51

Barbara Sukowa (1950-)
Thirteen Conversations About One Thing '01
Urbania '00
The Cradle Will Rock '99
The Lady in Question '99
The Third Miracle '99
Office Killer '97
Johnny Mnemonic '95
M. Butterfly '93
Zentropa '92
Voyager '91
The Sicilian '87
Rosa Luxemburg '86
Deadly Game '83
Marianne and Juliane '82
Berlin Alexanderplatz '80

Viktor Sukhorukov (1951-)
Of Freaks and Men '98
Brother '97
Sideburns '91

Elliott Sullivan (1907-74)

Diane Summerfield

Roy Summerset
Cold Heat '90

Francis L. Sullivan (1903-56)
The Prodigal '55
Behave Yourself! '52
Night and the City '50
Christopher Columbus '49
Oliver Twist '48
Caesar and Cleopatra '46
Great Expectations '46
The Day Will Dawn '42
Pimpernel Smith '42
The Citadel '38
Action for Slander '38
Non-Stop New York '37

Erik Per Sullivan (1991-)
Christmas With the Kranks '04
Finding Nemo '03 (V)
Unfaithful '02
Joe Dirt '01
Wendigo '01
The Cider House Rules '99

Slim Summerville (1892-1946)
Captain January '36
Rebecca of Sunnybrook Farm '38
Jesse James '38
Western Union '41
I'm from Arkansas '44
Under Montana Skies '30
All Quiet on the Western Front '30
The Farmer Takes a Wife '35
Life Begins at Forty '35

Barry Sullivan (1912-94)
Casino '80
The Bastard '78
No Room to Run '78
Oh, God! '77
Earthquake '74
The Human Factor '75
Take a Hard Ride '75
Washington Affair '77
Hurricane '74
Kung Fu '72
Yuma '70
Night Gallery '69
Tell Them Willie Boy Is Here '69
Buckskin '68
Shark! '68
Planet of the Vampires '65
A Gathering of Eagles '63
Another Time, Another Place '58
Forty Guns '57
Texas Lady '56
The Maverick Queen '55
Queen Bee '55
Strategic Air Command '55
Jeopardy '53
The Bad and the Beautiful '52
Skirts Ahoy! '52
Cause for Alarm! '51
Three Guys Named Mike '51
A Life of Her Own '50
Nancy Goes to Rio '50
Tension '50
Any Number Can Play '49
The Great Gatsby '49
The Gangster '47
Getting Gertie's Garter '45
The Woman of the Town '44

Jean Sullivan (1923-2003)
Uncertain Glory '44

Jenny Sullivan (1947-)
Squirm '76

Matthew Sullivan
Dementia '98

Michael Sullivan (1945-)
Max Is Missing '95
The Third Wheel '02

Sean Gregory Sullivan

Susan Sullivan (1942-)
My Best Friend's Wedding '97
Deadman's Curve '78
The Incredible Hulk '77
The Ordeal of Dr. Mudd '80
City in Fear '80
Marriage Is Alive and Well '80

Nicole Sullivan (1970-)
Meet the Robinsons '07 (V)
The Ant Bully '06 (V)
Here '69
Guess Who '05
The Third Wheel '02
Bar Hopping '00

Billy L. Sullivan (1980-)
The Big Green '95
Little Big League '94

Brad Sullivan (1931-)
Bushwhacked '95
The Jerky Boys '95
Sister Act 2: Back in the Habit '93
Guilty by Suspicion '91
Orpheus Descending '91
The Prince of Tides '91
True Colors '91
Funny Farm '88
Cold River '81

Cree Summer (1969-)
Rugrats Go Wild! '03 (V)
Atlantis: The Lost Empire '01 (V)
The Rugrats Movie '98 (V)
Clifford's Really Big Movie '04 (V)

Frank Sully (1903-75)
Midway '76

Diane Summerfield
Blackjack '78
Black Belt Jones '74
Overkill '86

Eleanor Summerfield (1921-2001)
Don't Open Till Christmas '84

Gerry Sundquist (1955-)
Don't Open Till Christmas '84
Great Expectations '81
Alexandra... Why? '78
The Dive '89

Bjorn Sundquist (1948-)
Zero Degrees Kelvin '95
The Last Lieutenant '94
Shipwrecked '90
The Dive '89

Par Sundberg (1957-)
Pippi in the South Seas '70
Pippi on the Run '70
Pippi Goes on Board '69
Pippi Longstocking '69

Ethan Suplee (1976-)
Art School Confidential '06
Clerks 2 '06
The Butterfly Effect '04
Without a Paddle '04
Cold Mountain '03
American History X '98
Chasing Amy '97
Desert Blue '98
Blow '01
Evolution '01
Remember the Titans '00
Road Trip '00
John Q '02
Mallrats '95

Daniel Sunjata (1971-)
The Bronx Is Burning '07
The Devil Wears Prada '06
Brother to Brother '04
Anne Rice's The Feast of All Saints '01

Donald (Don) Sumpter (1943-)
Eastern Promises '07
The Constant Gardener '05
K-19: The Widowmaker '02
Enigma '01
The Black-neath Poisonings '92

Hongjei Sun (1970-)
Zhou Yu's Train '02
The Road Home '01

Daolin Sun (1921-2007)
The Go-Masters '82
Crows and Sparrows '49

Clinton Sundberg (1906-87)
The Belle of New York '52
As Young As You Feel '51
Annie Get Your Gun '50
Two Weeks with Love '50
In the Good Old Summertime '49
Main Street to Broadway '53
Undercurrent '46
Mr. Peabody & the Mermaid '48
The Harvey Girls '46

Jeremy Sumpter (1989-)
The Sasquatch Gang '06
Peter Pan '03
Frailty '02
Local Boys '02

Kevin Sussman (1970-)
Star Spangled Girl '71

Catherine Sutherland (1974-)

David Sutcliffe (1969-)
Cake '05
Testosterone '03
Under the Tuscan Sun '03

Matthew Sussman
13 Moons '02
Illuminata '98

Paul Sutera (1979-)
A Very Brady Sequel '96
The Brady Bunch Movie '95
Problem Child 2 '91

Todd Susman (1947-)
Stark '85
The Act '82

Nicolas Surovy (1944-)
All Over the Guy '01
When Danger Follows You Home '97
The Man Who Captured Eichmann '96
Forever Young '92
Anastasia: The Mystery of Anna '86

Cristina Suriani
My Life on Ice '02
Intimate Strangers '04

Peter Sumner (1942-)
The Chant of Jimmie Blacksmith '78
Ned Kelly '70

Bart Sumner (1964-)
Video Violence '87
Video Violence Part 2... '87
The Exploitation! '87

Helene Surgere (1928-)

Sutherland

Shadow of the Wolf '92
Backdraft '91
Eminent Domain '91
JFK '91
Long Road Home '91
Quicksand: No Escape '91
Dr. Bethune '90
A Dry White Season '89
Lock Up '89
Lost Angels '89
Apprentice to Murder '88
The Rosary Murders '87
The Trouble with Spies '87
The Wolf at the Door '87
Heaven Help Us '85
Revolution '85
Crackers '84
Ordeal by Innocence '84
Max Dugan Returns '83
Threshold '83
Disappearance '81
Eye of the Needle '81
Gas '81
Bear Island '80
Nothing Personal '80
Ordinary People '80
The Great Train Robbery '79
A Man, a Woman, and a Bank '79
Murder by Decree '79
Invasion of the Body Snatchers '78
Bethune '77
Blood Relatives '77
The Eagle Has Landed '77
Kentucky Fried Movie '77
1900 '76
The Day of the Locust '75
S*P*Y*S '74
Dan Candy's Law '73
Don't Look Now '73
Lady Ice '73
Steelyard Blues '73
Johnny Got His Gun '71
Klute '71
Little Murders '71
Alex in Wonderland '70
Kelly's Heroes '70
M*A*S*H '70
Start the Revolution without Me '70
Sebastian '68
The Dirty Dozen '67
Bedford Incident '65
Die! Die! My Darling! '65
Dr. Terror's House of Horrors '65
Castle of the Living Dead '64

Grant Sutherland
Nine Men '43

Kiefer Sutherland (1966-)
The Sentinel '06
The Wild '06 (V)
Jiminy Glick in LaLa Wood '05
Taking Lives '04
Behind the Red Door '02
Phone Booth '02
Dead Heat '01
Desert Saints '01
To End All Wars '01
Beat '00
Cowboy Up '00
The Right Temptation '00
Eye of the Killer '99
Picking Up the Pieces '99
The Break Up '98
Ground Control '98
A Soldier's Sweetheart '98
Woman Wanted '98
Dark City '97
Truth or Consequences, N.M. '97
The Last Days of Frankie the Fly '96
A Time to Kill '96
An Eye for an Eye '95
Freeway '95
The Cowboy Way '94
Teresa's Tattoo '94
Last Light '93
The Three Musketeers '93
The Vanishing '93
Article 99 '92
A Few Good Men '92
Twin Peaks: Fire Walk with Me '92
The Nutcracker Prince '91 (V)
Chicago Joe & the Showgirl '90
Flatliners '90
Young Guns 2 '90
Flashback '89
1969 '89
Renegades '89
Bright Lights, Big City '88
Promised Land '88
Young Guns '88
Crazy Moon '87
The Killing Time '87
The Lost Boys '87
At Close Range '86
Brotherhood of Justice '86
Stand by Me '86
Trapped in Silence '86
Amazing Stories '85
The Bay Boy '85
Max Dugan Returns '83

Rossif Sutherland
Poor Man's Game '06
Red Doors '05

James Sutorius (1944-)
On Wings of Eagles '86
My Mother's Secret Life '84
Windy City '84
Prototype '83
A Question of Love '78

Dolores Sutton (1927-)
F. Scott Fitzgerald in Hollywood '76
Where Angels Go, Trouble Follows '68

Dudley Sutton (1933-)
Edward II '92
Orlando '92
Cry of the Penguins '71
The Devils '71
The Leather Boys '63

Frank Sutton (1923-74)
Hurricane '74
Town without Pity '61
Marty '55

Grady Sutton (1908-95)
Paradise, Hawaiian Style '66
Last of the Wild Horses '49
My Dog Shep '46
Goin' to Town '44
The More the Merrier '43
The Bashful Bachelor '42
Flying Blind '41
The Bank Dick '40
Dangerous Holiday '37
Waikiki Wedding '37
Alice Adams '35
Bachelor Bait '34
Pharmacist '33

John Sutton (1908-63)
The Bat '59
Beloved Infidel '59
Return of the Fly '59
Five Fingers '52 (N)
David and Bathsheba '51
The Second Woman '51
Bagdad '49
Mickey '48
Captain from Castile '47
Jane Eyre '44
Thunder Birds '42
A Yank in the R.A.F. '41
The Invisible Man Returns '40
Bulldog Drummond's Bride '39
Charlie McCarthy, Detective '39
The Tower of London '39
Arrest Bulldog Drummond '38

Kay Sutton (1915-88)
Sergeant York '41
The Saint in New York '38

Michael Sutton (1970-)
Dracula: The Dark Prince '01
Wanted '98

Mena Suvari (1979-)
Brooklyn Rules '07
The Dog Problem '06
Factory Girl '06
Beauty Shop '05
Domino '05
Rumor Has It.... '05
Standing Still '05
Sonny '02
Spun '02
American Pie 2 '01
The Musketeer '01
Loser '00
American Beauty '99
American Pie '99
Atomic Train '99
The Rage: Carrie 2 '99
American Virgin '98
Nowhere '96

Janet Suzman (1939-)
Max '02
Leon the Pig Farmer '93
Nuns on the Run '90
A Dry White Season '89
Mountbatten: The Last Viceroy '86
The Singing Detective '86
The Zany Adventures of Robin Hood '84
And the Ship Sails On '83
The Draughtsman's Contract '82
Priest of Love '81
Nijinsky '80
The House on Garibaldi Street '79
Voyage of the Damned '76
The Black Windmill '74
A Day in the Death of Joe Egg '71
Nicholas and Alexandra '71
Macbeth '70

Semyon Svashenko (1904-69)
Earth '30
Arsenal '29
Zvenigora '28

Tore Svennberg
A Woman's Face '38

Bo Svenson (1941-)
The Phantom Chariot '20
Crackerjack 3 '00
Speed 2: Cruise Control '97
Private Obsession '94
Savage Land '94
Steel Frontier '94
Steele's Law '91
Three Days to a Kill '91
Primal Rage '90
Tides of War '90
Andy and the Airwave Rangers '89
The Kill Reflex '89
Curse 2: The Bite '88
Deep Space '87
Delta Force Commando '87
The Dirty Dozen: The Deadly Mission '87
White Phantom: Enemy of Darkness '87
Choke Canyon '86
Delta Force '86
Heartbreak Ridge '86
The Last Contract '86
The Manhunt '86
Thunder Warrior '85
Thunder Warrior 2 '85
Wizards of the Lost Kingdom '85
Deadly Impact '84
Jealousy '84
Night Warning '82
Virus '82
Gold of the Amazon Women '79
North Dallas Forty '79
Deadly Mission '78
Portrait of a Hitman '77
Snowbeast '77
Walking Tall: The Final Chapter '77
Special Delivery '76
The Great Waldo Pepper '75
Big Mo '73
Frankenstein '73

Zdenek Sverak (1936-)
Kolya '96

Bob Swaim (1943-)
The Elementary School '91
Spies Like Us '85
La Balance '82

Dominique Swain (1980-)
All In '06
Alpha Dog '06
Devour '05
Plain Dirty '04
The Job '03
New Best Friend '02
Pumpkin '02
Dead in the Water '01
Happy Campers '01
Tart '01
Intern '00
The Smokers '00
Girl '98
Face/Off '97
Lolita '97

Howard Swain
Night of the Scarecrow '95
Jon Jost's Frameup '93

Mack Swain (1876-1935)
The Chaplin Revue '58
The Beloved Rogue '27
Hands Up '26
The Nervous Wreck '26
The Gold Rush '25
Three Charlies and One Phoney! '18
Tillie's Punctured Romance '14

Darwyn Swalve (1946-99)
Deadly Reactor '89
Take Two '87

Hilary Swank (1974-)
Freedom Writers '07
P.S. I Love You '07
The Reaping '07
The Black Dahlia '06
Million Dollar Baby '04
The Core '03
11:14 '04
Insomnia '02
The Affair of the Necklace '01
The Gift '00
Boys Don't Cry '99
Heartwood '98
Quiet Days in Hollywood '97
Kounterfeit '96
Sometimes They Come Back... Again '96
The Next Karate Kid '94
Buffy the Vampire Slayer '92

Brenda Swanson
Scanners: The Showdown '94

Gary Swanson
Coldfire '90
The Guardian '90
Witchfire '86
Vice Squad '82

Gloria Swanson (1897-1983)
Airport 75 '75
Three for Bedroom C '52
Sunset Boulevard '50
Indiscreet '31
Tonight or Never '31
Queen Kelly '29
Sadie Thompson '28
Manhandled '24
Beyond the Rocks '22
Affairs of Anatol '21
Why Change Your Wife? '20
Male and Female '19
Shifting Sands '18
Teddy at the Throttle '16

Jackie Swanson (1963-)
Oblivion '94
Lethal Weapon '87

Kristy Swanson (1969-)
Bound by Lies '05
Red Water '01
Soul Assassin '01
Zebra Lounge '01
Dude, Where's My Car? '00
Big Daddy '99
Supreme Sanction '99
Ground Control '98
Meeting Daddy '98
Lover Girl '97
Tinseltown '97
8 Heads in a Duffel Bag '96
Marshal Law '96
The Phantom '96
Getting In '94
Higher Learning '94
The Chase '93
The Program '93
Buffy the Vampire Slayer '92
Highway to Hell '92
Hot Shots! '91
Mannequin 2: On the Move '91
Diving In '90
Dream Trap '90
Flowers in the Attic '87
Deadly Friend '86
Ferris Bueller's Day Off '86
Pretty in Pink '86

Maureen Swanson (1932-)
Robbery under Arms '57
The Spanish Gardener '57
Moulin Rouge '52

Rochelle Swanson
On the Border '98
Mutual Needs '97
Deadly Outbreak '96
Cyberzone '95
Hard Bounty '94
Indecent Behavior 2 '94
Night Fire '94
Secret Games 3 '94

Nick Swardson (1976-)
You Don't Mess with the Zohan '08
Blades of Glory '07
I Now Pronounce You Chuck and Larry '07
Reno 911! Miami '07
Art School Confidential '06
The Benchwarmers '06
Grandma's Boy '06

Rufus Swart (1959-94)
Dust Devil '93
The House of Usher '88

Don Swayze (1958-)
Lady, Jayne Killer '03
The Prophet's Game '99
Money to Burn '94
Beach Babes from Beyond '93
Body of Influence '93
Broken Trust '93
Death Ring '93
Eye of the Stranger '93
Forced to Kill '93
Sexual Malice '93
Edge of Honor '91
Payback '90
Trapper County War '89
Driving Force '88
The Tracker '88
Death Blow '87
Shy People '87

Patrick Swayze (1952-)
The Fox and the Hound 2 '06 (V)
Frederick Forsyth's Icon '05
Keeping Mum '05
Dirty Dancing: Havana Nights '04
11:14 '03
Waking Up in Reno '02
Donnie Darko '01
Green Dragon '01
Along for the Ride '00
Black Dog '98
Letters from a Killer '98
Tall Tale: The Unbelievable Adventures of Pecos Bill '95
Three Wishes '95
To Wong Foo, Thanks for Everything, Julie Newmar '95
Father Hood '93
City of Joy '92
Point Break '91
Ghost '90
Next of Kin '89
Road House '89
Dirty Dancing '87
Steel Dawn '87
Tiger Warsaw '87
North and South Book 2 '86
Youngblood '86
North and South Book 1 '85
Grandview U.S.A. '84
Red Dawn '84
The Outsiders '83
Uncommon Valor '83
Return of the Rebels '81

Heidi Swedberg (1964-)
75 Degrees '00
The Ticket '97
Father and Scout '94
Hot Shots! '91

Bob Sweeney (1918-92)
Toby Tyler '59
A Christmas Carol '54
South Sea Woman '53

D.B. Sweeney (1961-)
Yellow '06
Speak '04
Brother Bear '03 (V)
SuperFire '02
Greenmail '01
Hardball '01
Dinosaur '00 (V)
The Weekend '00
The Book of Stars '99
Introducing Dorothy Dandridge '99
Spawn '97
Roommates '95
Fire in the Sky '93
Hear No Evil '93
The Cutting Edge '92
A Day in October '92
Miss Rose White '92
Blue Desert '91
Eight Men Out '88
Gardens of Stone '87
No Man's Land '87
Fire with Fire '86

Dominic Sweeney
In Too Deep '90

Garry Sweeney
The Acid House '98
Small Faces '95

Joseph Sweeney (1884-1963)
Twelve Angry Men '57
The Man in the Gray Flannel Suit '56

Julia Sweeney (1961-)
Don't Come Knocking '05
Clockstoppers '02
Beethoven's 4th '01
Beethoven's 3rd '00
Whatever It Takes '00
God Said "Ha!" '99
Stuart Little '99
Thick as Thieves '99
Vegas Vacation '96
It's Pat: The Movie '94
Pulp Fiction '94
Stuart Saves His Family '94
Coneheads '93
Honey, I Blew Up the Kid '92

Steve Sweeney
Beautiful People '99
Lock, Stock and 2 Smoking Barrels '98
Nil by Mouth '96

Blanche Sweet (1895-1986)
Anna Christie '30
Avenging Conscience '14
Home Sweet Home '14
Judith of Bethulia '14

Dolph Sweet (1920-85)
Jacqueline Bouvier Kennedy '81
Reds '81
Cops and Robbers '73
Sisters '73

Gary Sweet (1957-)
Macbeth '06
What the Moon Saw '90
Fever '88
The Lighthorsemen '87
An Indecent Obsession '85
Stage Fright '83

Jeep Swenson (1957-97)
Batman and Robin '97

Karl Swenson (1908-78)
Brighly of the Grand Canyon '67
Seconds '66
The Sword in the Stone '63
Lonely Are the Brave '62
Judgment at Nuremberg '61
Flaming Star '60
The Gallant Hours '60
The Hanging Tree '59
No Name on the Bullet '59

Tommy Swerdlow (1962-)
Child's Play '88

William Swetland (1913-2003)
Mirrors '78

Joel Swetow
The Seagull '75

Josef Swickard (1866-1940)
Custer's Last Stand '36
The Lone Defender '32
The Night Patrol '26
The Wizard of Oz '25
Dante's Inferno '24
The Four Horsemen of the Apocalypse '21

Clive Swift (1936-)
The Aristocrats '99
Frenzy '72

Vonte Sweet
Restaurant '98
American Strays '96
Marshal Law '96
The Walking Dead '94
Menace II Society '93

Inga Swenson (1932-)
North and South Book 1 '85
The Miracle Worker '62

Rod Sweitzer
The Malibu Beach Vampires '91
The Invisible Maniac '90
Psycho Cop '88

Ken Swofford (1932-)
Black Roses '88
All God's Children '80
Bless the Beasts and Children '71
The Taking of Beverly Hills '91 (V)

David Swift (1919-2001)
No Sex Please—We're British '73
Good Neighbor Sam '64

Francie Swift

Jeremy Swift
The Great Gatsby '01
Fall '97

Paul Swift (1934-94)
Female Trouble '74
Pink Flamingos '72
Multiple Maniacs '70

Nora Swinburne (1902-2000)
Quo Vadis '51
Betrayed '54
The River '51
Man of Evil '48

Tilda Swinton (1961-)
Michael Clayton '07
Stephanie Daley '06
Broken Flowers '05
The Chronicles of Narnia: The Lion, the Witch and the Wardrobe '05
Constantine '05
Thumbsucker '05
The Statement '03
Young Adam '03
Adaptation '02
The Deep End '01
Vanilla Sky '01
The Beach '00
Love Is the Devil '98
The War Zone '98
The Garden '90
Orlando '92
Edward II '92
Wittgenstein '93
Blue '93 (N)
Female Perversions '96
Conceiving Ada '97
Caravaggio '86

Loretta Swit (1937-)
Beer '85
The Execution '85
First Affair '83
M*A*S*H: Goodbye, Farewell & Amen '83
S.O.B. '81
Race with the Devil '75
Freebie & the Bean '74

Amanda Swisten (1978-)
The Girl Next Door '04
American Wedding '03

Harold Sylvester (1949-)
Missing Brendan '03
Trippin' '59
The Sixth Man '97
The Reluctant Agent '95
In the Deep Woods '91
In the Line of Duty: A Cop for the Killing '90
Innerspace '87
Vision Quest '85
Uncommon Valor '83
Fast Break '79

William Sylvester (1923-95)
2001: A Space Odyssey '68
Beast of Morocco '66
Devil Doll '64
Gorgo '61
Postmark for Danger '56
Unholy Four '54
Devi '60

Carl "Alfalfa" Switzer (1926-59)
Motorcycle Gang '57
Between Heaven and Hell '56
The High and the Mighty '54
Island in the Sky '53
Pat and Mike '52
Cause for Alarm '51
Redwood Forest Trail '50
Underwood Scandal '47
It's a Wonderful Life '46
The Great Mike '44
Reg'lar Fellers '41
General Spanky '36

Bill Switzer
Mail to the Chief '00
Mr. Rice's Secret '00

Kari Sylwan (1940-)
Face to Face '76
Cries and Whispers '72

Peter Symonds
Sharpe's Challenge '06
Lawless Heart '01
Last Summer in the Hamptons '96
Marilyn & Bobby: Her Final Affair '94

Robert Symonds (1926-2007)
Rumpelstiltskin '86
Mandroid '93
Girlfriends '78
The Glass House '72

Kristopher Tabori (1952-)
Bandits '99
Unveiled '05

Sylvia Syms (1934-)
I'll Sleep When I'm Dead '03
What a Girl Wants '03
Catherine Cookson's The Glass Virgin '95
Shining Through '92
A Chorus of Disapproval
Shirley Valentine '89
Intimate Contact '87

Topo Swope (1948-)
Murders at Lynch Cross '85
The Tamarind Seed '74
The Hot Rock '70

Tracy Brooks Swope (1952-)
Asylum '72
Counter Measures '99
White Wolves 3: Cry of the White Wolf '98
Inner Sanctum 2 '94
The Power of One '92

Meera Syal (1961-)
Jekyll '07
Forgive and Forget '99
Sammy & Rosie Get Laid '87

Sabrina Syan
See Sabrina Siani

Clancy Syrko
Princess of Thieves '01
The Unbearable Lightness of Being '88

Del Synnott
Othello '01

Laszlo Szabo (1936-)
Passion '82
The Last Metro '80
Nice Neighbor '79
Adoption '75
Alphaville '65
Le Petit Soldat '60

Wanda Sykes (1964-)
Evan Almighty '07
Barnyard '06 (V)
Brother Bear 2 '06 (V)
Clerks 2 '06
My Super Ex-Girlfriend '06
Over the Hedge '06 (V)
Monster-in-Law '05
Pootie Tang '01

Eric Sykes (1923-)
The Others '01
Heavens Above '63
Those Daring Young Men in Their Jaunty Jalopies '69

Brenda Sykes (1949-)
Mandingo '75
Cleopatra Jones '73
Honky '71

Keith Szarabajka (1952-)
We Were Soldiers '02
Andre '94
A Perfect World '93
Stephen King's Golden Years '91
Jnnatural Pursuits '91
Nightlife '90
The Misfit Brigade '87
Billy Galvin '86
Marie '85
Protocol '84

Magda Szubanski (1961-)
Happy Feet '06 (V)
The Crocodile Hunter: Collision Course '02
Babe: Pig in the City '98
Babe '95

Adam Szirtes
The Girl '68
Cold Days '66

Grazyna Szapolowska (1953-)
No End '84
Another Way '82

Pawel Szajda (1982-)
Venom '05
Under the Tuscan Sun '03

Said Taghmaoui (1973-)
Vantage Point '08
Hidalgo '04
Spartan '04
Crime Spree '03
The Good Thief '03
Hideous Kinky '99
Three Kings '99
Hate '95

George Takei (1940-)
Taboo '99
DC 9/11: Time of Crisis '04
Bug Buster '99
Mulan '98 (V)
Kissinger and Nixon '96
Backlash: Oblivion 2 '95
Oblivion '94
Prisoners of the Sun '91
The Undiscovered Country '91
Star Trek V: The Final Frontier '89
Star Trek IV: The Voyage Home '86
Star Trek III: The Search for Spock '84
Star Trek II: The Wrath of Khan '82
Star Trek: The Motion Picture '79
The Green Berets '68
Red Line 7000 '65
Ice Palace '60

Rita Taggart (1949-)
Limbo '99
At Home with the Webbers '94
Coupe de Ville '90
The Horror Show '89
Weeds '87
Torchlight '85
Used Cars '80
Coming Home '78

Ben Taggart
Before I Hang '40
Smart Money '31

Sharon Taggart (1947-)
The Last Picture Show '71

Sydney Tafler (1916-79)
The Adventurers '70
Alfie '66
Sink the Bismarck! '50
Carve Her Name with Pride '58
The World of Suzie Wong '60
Fire Maidens from Outer Space '56
The Way Out '56
Uneasy Terms '48

Basil Sydney (1894-1968)
The Hands of Orlac '60
The Three Worlds of Gulliver '59
John Paul Jones '59
Sea Wife '57
Dam Busters '55
Salome '53
Angel with the Trumpet '50
Treasure Island '50
Hamlet '48
The Secret Four '40
Accused '36
Rhodes '36

Cary-Hiroyuki Tagawa (1950-)
Elektra '05
Memoirs of a Geisha '05
Planet of the Apes '01
The Art of War '00
Bridge of Dragons '99
Tom Clancy's Netforce '99
Double Edge '97
John Carpenter's Vampires '97
Top of the World '97
The Phantom '96
Provocateur '96
Danger Zone '95
White Tiger '95
Natural Causes '94
Picture Bride '94
Nemesis '93
Rising Sun '93
American Me '92
Showdown in Little Tokyo '91
The Last Warrior '89
Movin '95
Soldier Boyz '95
Mortal Kombat '95

Koji Takahashi
The Mystery of Rampo '94

Ken Takakura (1931-)
Riding Alone for Thousands of Miles '05
The Yakuza '75
Too Late the Hero '70
Black Rain '89
Antarctica '84
Station '81

Hideko Takamine (1924-)
When a Woman Ascends the Stairs '60
Twenty-Four Eyes '54
Mistress '53

Nicko Takamine (1918-90)
Phoenix '78
47 Ronin, Part 1 '42

Akira Takarada (1934-)
Last War '68
Half Human '58
Godzilla, King of the Monsters '56
Godzilla vs. Mothra '64
Godzilla vs. Monster Zero '68

Masahiro Takashima
Godzilla vs. Mechagodzilla II '93
Godzilla vs. Biollante '89

Tadao Takashima (1930-)
Son of Godzilla '66
King Kong vs. Godzilla '63

Naoto Takenaka (1956-)
Shall We Dance? '96
The Mystery of Rampo '94

Beat Takeshi
See Takeshi "Beat" Kitano

Shinji Takeda (1972-)
Pulse '01

Yusuke Takita
The Mystery of Rampo '94

Osamu Takizawa (1906-2000)
Zatoichi vs. Yojimbo '70

Miiko Taka (1932-)
Walk, Don't Run '66
A Global Affair '63
Sayonara '57

Yoshifumi Tajima (1918-)
War of the Gargantuas '70
Godzilla's Revenge '69
Destroy All Monsters '68
Godzilla vs. Mothra '64

Jasmin Tabatabai (1967-)

Oleg Tabakov (1935-)
Taking Sides '01
Oblomov '81
An Unfinished Piece for a Player Piano '77
The Eel '96

Tomoroh Taguchi
Tetsuo: The Iron Man '92
Tetsuo 2: Body Hammer '97

Sharmila Tagore (1936-)
Mississippi Masala '92
Days and Nights in the Forest '70
The World of Apu '59
Devi '60

Taj Mahal (1942-)
Songcatcher '99
Outside Ozona '98

Yutaka Tadokoro
Lost in Translation '03
Tokyo Pop '88

Marissa Tait (1979-)
The Biggest Fan '02
Witchouse '99

Tristan Tait (1971-)
The Courage to Love '00

Paul-Antoine Taillefer
Maricore '05

Faran Tahir
Iron Man '08
Tetsuo: The Iron Man '92

Hiroshi Tachikawa
Attack of the Mushroom People '63
Yojimbo '61

Ljuba Tadic
Black and White As Day '78
Ward Six '78
Siberian Lady Macbeth '61

Yutaka Takita
Double Suicide '69
Irezumi '83

Bill & Ted's Bogus Journey '91
Sounder '72

Fires on the Plain '59
Oleg Taktarov (1967-)
44 Minutes: The North Hollywood Shootout '03
Rollerball '02
15 Minutes '01
Ana Claudia Talancon (1980-)
One Missed Call '08
Alone With Her '07
Love in the Time of Cholera '07
Sueno '05
The Crime of Father Amaro '02
Charlie Talbert (1978-)
Bachelor Party Vegas '05
Angus '95
Helen Talbot (1924-)
King of the Forest Rangers '46
Federal Operator 99 '45
California Joe '43
Lyle Talbot (1902-96)
Sunrise at Campobello '60
High School Confidential '58
Guns Don't Argue '57
Plan 9 from Outer Space '56
Jail Bait '54
Trader Tom of the China Seas '54
Clipped Wings '53
Glen or Glenda? '53
Mesa of Lost Women '52
Gold Raiders '51
Mask of the Dragon '51
One Too Many '51
Atom Man vs. Superman '50
Border Rangers '50
Parole, Inc. '49
Pirate Ship '49
Ringside '49
She Shoulda Said No '49
Shep Comes Home '49
Thunder in the Pines '49
The Devil's Cargo '48
Highway 13 '48
Song of Arizona '46
Strange Impersonation '46
Gambler's Choice '44
Mystery of the Riverboat '44
One Body Too Many '44
Sensations of 1945 '44
Up in Arms '44
A Night for Crime '42
Second Fiddle '39
Torture Ship '39
Three Legionnaires '37
Vengeance '37
Go West, Young Man '36
The Case of the Lucky Legs '35
Our Little Girl '35
One Night of Love '34
Havana Widows '33
Ladies They Talk About '33
Shriek in the Night '33
The Purchase Price '32
13th Guest '32
Three on a Match '32
Nita Talbot (1930-)
Amityville 1992: It's About Time '92
Puppet Master 2 '90
Take Two '87
Fraternity Vacation '85
Chained Heat '83
The Concrete Jungle '82
Night Shift '82
Frightmare '81
Sweet Creek County War '79
They Call It Murder '71
Girl Happy '65
That Funny Feeling '65
Who's Got the Action? '63
I Married a Woman '56
Gloria Talbott (1931-2000)
Arizona Raiders '65
Alias Jesse James '59
Girls' Town '59

The Leech Woman '59
I Married a Monster from Outer Space '58
The Daughter of Dr. Jekyll '57
The Kettles on Old MacDonald's Farm '57
Cyclops '56
The Oklahoman '56
All That Heaven Allows '55
Crashout '55
We're No Angels '55
Michael Talbott (1955-)
Manhunter '86
Miami Vice '84
Racing with the Moon '84
Foolin' Around '80
Vera Talchi (1934-)
Little World of Don Camillo '51
The Walls of Malapaga '49
Alberto Talegalli
Beauty on the Beach '61
Two Nights with Cleopatra '54
Hal Taliaferro (1895-1980)
Frontier Law '43
Hoppy Serves a Writ '43
Leather Burners '43
Border Vigilantes '41
Riders of the Timberline '41
Phantom Gold '38
The Rangers Step In '37
The Unknown Ranger '36
Michael "Bear" Taliferro (1961-2006)
You Got Served '04
Rude Boy: The Jamaican Don '03
Half Past Dead '02
The Replacements '00
Life '99
Night of the Living Dead '90
Steven Talley
American Pie Presents: Beta House '07
American Pie Presents: The Naked Mile '06
Margaret Tallichet (1914-91)
It Started with Eve '41
Stranger on the Third Floor '40
Patricia Tallman (1957-)
Army of Darkness '92
Constance Talmadge (1900-73)
Intolerance '16
Matrimaniac '16
Norma Talmadge (1895-1957)
Dubarry '30
The Forbidden City '18
The Social Secretary '16
Richard Talmadge (1892-1981)
Speed Reporter '36
Fighting Pilot '35
The Live Wire '34
Get That Girl '32
The Night Patrol '26
Laughing at Danger '24
Let's Go! '23
William Talman (1915-68)
Crashout '55
The Hitch-Hiker '53
One Minute to Zero '52
Armored Car Robbery '50
Isao Tamagawa
Branded to Kill '67
Story of a Prostitute '65
Tetsuro Tamba (1922-2006)
A Taxing Woman's Return '88
Tokyo Pop '88
The Imperial Japanese Empire '85
Zero '84
Hunter in the Dark '80

Last Days of Planet Earth '74
Under the Flag of the Rising Sun '72
You Only Live Twice '67
The Seventh Dawn '64
One-Eyed Swordsman '63
Harakiri '62
Carlo Tamberlani (1899-1980)
The Trojan Horse '62
The Fury of Hercules '61
Nando Tamberlani (1896-1967)
Hercules against the Moon Men '64
The Trojan Horse '62
Amber Tamblyn (1983-)
Sisterhood of the Traveling Pants 2 '08
That Russell Girl '08
Havoc 2: Normal Adolescent Behavior '07
Spiral '07
The Grudge 2 '06
Stephanie Daley '06
Sisterhood of the Traveling Pants '05
The Ring '02
Russ Tamblyn (1934-)
Inherit the Wind '99
My Magic Dog '97
Invisible Mom '96
Attack of the 60-Foot Centerfold '95
Cabin Boy '94
Desert Steel '94
Wizards of the Demon Sword '94
Running Mates '92
Aftershock '88
Blood Screams '88
B.O.R.N. '88
Necromancer: Satan's Servant '88
Commando Squad '87
Cyclone '87
Phantom Empire '87
Dracula vs. Frankenstein '71
The Last Movie '71
War of the Gargantuas '70
The Female Bunch '69
Free Grass '69
Satan's Sadists '69
The Long Ships '64
How the West Was Won '63
The Wonderful World of the Brothers Grimm '62
West Side Story '61
Cimarron '60
High School Confidential '58
Tom Thumb '58
Don't Go Near the Water '57
Peyton Place '57
Fastest Gun Alive '56
The Last Hunt '56
Hit the Deck '55
Seven Brides for Seven Brothers '54
Retreat, Hell! '52
The Winning Team '52
Father's Little Dividend '51
Father of the Bride '50
Gun Crazy '49
Jeffrey Tambor (1944-)
Hellboy 2: The Golden Army '08
Slipstream '07
The Muppets' Wizard of Oz '05
Eurotrip '04
Hellboy '04
The SpongeBob SquarePants Movie '04
Eloise at the Plaza '03
Malibu's Most Wanted '03
My Boss's Daughter '03
Get Well Soon '01
Never Again '01

Dr. Seuss' How the Grinch Stole Christmas '00
Pollock '00
Girl, Interrupted '99
Muppets from Space '99
Teaching Mrs. Tingle '99
Dr. Dolittle '98
Meet Joe Black '98
There's Something about Mary '98
Weapons of Mass Distraction '97
The Man Who Captured Eichmann '96
Big Bully '95
My Teacher's Wife '95
At Home with the Webbers '94
Heavyweights '94
Radioland Murders '94
A House in the Hills '93
Article 99 '92
Crossing the Bridge '92
Scott Turow's The Burden of Proof '92
City Slickers '91
Life Stinks '91
Pastime '91
Lisa '90
A Perfect Little Murder '90
Three O'Clock High '87
Brenda Starr '86
Desert Hearts '86
The Man Who Wasn't There '83
Mr. Mom '83
Sadat '83
Take Your Best Shot '82
Awakening of Candra '81
A Gun in the House '81
Saturday the 14th '81
And Justice for All '79
Jenny Tamburi (1952-2006)
Bloody Avenger '80
Women in Cell Block 7 '77
Zoe Tamerlis (1962-99)
Exquisite Corpses '88
Special Effects '85
Ms. 45 '81
Akim Tamiroff (1899-1972)
Deadly Sanctuary '68
Vulture '67
Hotel Paradiso '66
Lt. Robin Crusoe, U.S.N. '66
Alphaville '65
Lord Jim '65
Topkapi '64
The Bacchantes '63
The Trial '63
Panic Button '62
Ocean's 11 '60
Me and the Colonel '58
Touch of Evil '58
Anastasia '56
Battle Hell '56
The Black Sleep '56
Mr. Arkadin '55
Black Magic '49
Outpost in Morocco '49
My Girl Tisa '48
The Gangster '47
A Scandal in Paris '46
Can't Help Singing '45
The Bridge of San Luis Rey '44
Dragon Seed '44
His Butler's Sister '44
Miracle of Morgan's Creek '44
Five Graves to Cairo '43
For Whom the Bell Tolls '43
The Corsican Brothers '42
Tortilla Flat '42
The Great McGinty '40
Desire '36
The General Died at Dawn '36
The Story of Louis Pasteur '36
China Seas '35

The Lives of a Bengal Lancer '35
The Merry Widow '34
Mary Tamm (1950-)
The Assassination Run '84
The Odessa File '74
Tales That Witness Madness '73
Takahiro Tamura (1928-2006)
The Silk Road '92
Forest of Little Bear '87
The Empire of Passion '76
Tora! Tora! Tora! '70
Haruo Tanaka
The Pornographers '66
Snow Country '57
Ken Tanaka (1951-)
Godzilla 1985 '85
Phoenix '78
Kinuyo Tanaka (1910-77)
Sandakan No. 8 '74
Equinox Flower '58
Sansho the Bailiff '54
Ugetsu '53
Life of Oharu '52
Mother '52
Utamaro and His Five Women '46
Min Tanaka (1945-)
The Hidden Blade '04
The Twilight Samurai '02
Sara Tanaka (1978-)
Rushmore '98
Race the Sun '96
Toru Tanaka (1930-2000)
3 Ninjas '92
Tax Season '90
Yoshiko Tanaka (1956-)
Godzilla vs. Biollante '89
Black Rain '88
Jessica Tandy (1909-94)
Camilla '94
Nobody's Fool '94
The Story Lady '93
To Dance with the White Dog '93
Used People '92
Fried Green Tomatoes '91
Driving Miss Daisy '89
Cocoon: The Return '88
The House on Carroll Street '88
*batteries not included '87
Foxfire '87
Cocoon '85
The Bostonians '84
Gin Game '84
Best Friends '82
Still of the Night '82
The World According to Garp '82
The Birds '63
The Light in the Forest '58
The Desert Fox '51
September Affair '50
Forever Amber '47
The Valley of Decision '45
The Seventh Cross '44
Mark Tandy (1957-)
The Buccaneers '95
The Railway Station Man '92
Maurice '87
Yoko Tani (1932-99)
Koroshi '67
Invasion '65
Samson and the 7 Miracles of the World '62
First Spaceship on Venus '60
William Tannen (1911-76)
Jupiter's Darling '55
Roaring City '51
Riders of the Range '50
Mysterious Desperado '49
Whistling in the Dark '41
Antwon Tanner (1975-)
Coach Carter '05
Ganked '05

Never Die Alone '04
Sunset Park '96
Gordon Tanner (1918-83)
Dr. Strangelove, or: How I Learned to Stop Worrying and Love the Bomb '64
Time Lock '57
Warhawk Tanzania
Black Force '75
Gang Wars '75
Guo Tao
So Close to Paradise '98
To Live '94
Zoe Tapper
These Foolish Things '06
Mrs. Palfrey at the Claremont '05
Stage Beauty '04
Amanda Tapping (1965-)
The Void '01
Terror Train '80
Brian Tarantina (1959-)
City by the Sea '02
Personal Velocity: Three Portraits '02
Quentin Tarantino (1963-)
Death Proof '07
Planet Terror '07
The Muppets' Wizard of Oz '05
Little Nicky '00
Kisses in the Dark '97
Girl 6 '96
Desperado '95
Destiny Turns on the Radio '95
Four Rooms '95
From Dusk Till Dawn '95
Pulp Fiction '94
Sleep with Me '94
Somebody to Love '94
Eddie Presley '92
Reservoir Dogs '92
Andrew Tarbet (1971-)
Between Strangers '02
Cafe Ole '00
Mikhail Tarkanov
Peter the First: Part 2 '38
Peter the First: Part 1 '37
Rockne Tarkington (1932-)
Zebra Force '76
Trained to Kill, U.S.A. '75
Black Starlet '74
Clarence, the Cross-eyed Lion '65
Lilyan Tashman (1899-1934)
Riptide '34
Scarlet Dawn '32
Millie '31
Bulldog Drummond '29
So This Is Paris '26
Manhandled '24
Coralina Cataldi Tassoni
See Coralina Cataldi-Tassoni
Jun Tatara
The Human Condition: Road to Eternity '59
Seven Samurai '54
Catherine Tate
Scenes of a Sexual Nature '06
Starter for Ten '06
Lahmard Tate (1970-)
Rocky Balboa '06
Back in the Day '05
Barbershop '02
Sabretooth '01
Don't Be a Menace to South Central While Drinking Your Juice in the Hood '95
Larenz Tate (1975-)
Waist Deep '06
Crash '05
Ray '04

- Biker Boyz '03
- A Man Apart '03
- Love Come Down '00
- Why Do Fools Fall in Love? '98
- The Postman '97
- Love Jones '96
- Dead Presidents '95
- The Inkwell '94
- Menace II Society '93

Laura Tate
- Dead Space '90
- Subspecies '90
- Alpha '75

Reginald Tate (1896-1955)
- Immortal Battalion '44

Sharon Tate (1943-69)
- 12 Plus 1 '70
- Ciao Federico! Fellini Directs Satyricon '69
- The Wrecking Crew '68
- The Fearless Vampire Killers '67
- Valley of the Dolls '67

Jacques Tati (1908-82)
- Parade '74
- Traffic '71
- Playtime '67
- Mon Oncle '58
- Mr. Hulot's Holiday '53
- Jour de Fête '48
- Sylvia and the Phantom '45

Bradford Tatum (1965)
- Standing on Fishes '99
- Not in This Town '97
- Pronto '97
- Down Periscope '96
- Within the Rock '96
- Powder '95
- Cool and the Crazy '94

Channing Tatum (1980)
- Stop-Loss '08
- A Guide to Recognizing Your Saints '06
- Supercross: The Movie '05
- Coach Carter '05
- Step Up '06
- She's the Man '06

Sven-Bertil Taube (1934)
- London Voodoo '04
- Jerusalem '96
- Codename Kyril '91
- Puppet on a Chain '72

Audrey Tautou (1978-)
- The Da Vinci Code '06
- Priceless '05
- Russian Dolls '05
- A Very Long Engagement '04
- Dirty Pretty Things '03
- He Loves Me... He Loves Me Not '02
- L'Auberge Espagnole '02
- Amelie '01
- Venus Beauty Institute '00
- Happenstance '00

Jay Tavare
- Pathfinder '07
- The Missing '03
- Adaptation '02

Dino Tavarone (1942)
- Cafe Ole '00
- 2 Seconds '98

Nils (Niels) Tavernier (1965)
- After Sex '00
- Revenge of the Musketeers '94
- Mina Tannenbaum '93

Arthur Taxier
- Home Room '02
- Donnie Darko '01
- Open Fire '94

Vic Tayback (1930-90)
- The Horseplayer '91
- All Dogs Go to Heaven '89 (V)
- Beverly Hills Bodysnatchers '89
- Criminal Act '88
- The Underachievers '88
- Murderer's Keep '88
- Weekend Warriors '86
- Mysterious Two '82
- Tut & Tuttle '81
- Great American Traffic Jam '80
- The Night the City Screamed '80
- Rage '80
- Portrait of a Stripper '79
- The Cheap Detective '78
- The Choirboys '77
- The Big Bus '76
- Special Delivery '76
- The Black Bird '75
- Lepke '75
- Alice Doesn't Live Here Anymore '74
- Emperor of the North Pole '73
- They Call It Murder '71
- With Six You Get Eggroll '68
- Dead Heat on a Merry-Go-Round '66

Buck Taylor (1938-)
- The Wendell Baker Story '05
- Jericho '01
- Tombstone '93
- Conagher '91
- Gunsmoke: Return to Dodge '87
- Pony Express Rider '76

Benedict Taylor (1960)
- Duel of Hearts '92
- A Perfect Spy '88
- Every Time We Say Goodbye '86
- The Far Pavilions '84

Christine Taylor (1971-)
- Dedication '07
- License to Wed '07
- Dodgeball: A True Underdog Story '04
- Zoolander '01
- Kiss Toledo Goodbye '00
- Campfire Tales '98
- Something About Sex '98
- The Wedding Singer '97
- The Craft '96
- Night of the Demons 2 '94
- Overnight Delivery '96
- A Very Brady Sequel '96
- The Brady Bunch Movie '95
- Breaking Free '95

Courtney Taylor
- Cover Me '95
- Prom Night 3: The Last Kiss '89

Delores Taylor
- The Trial of Billy Jack '74
- Billy Jack '71

Don Taylor (1920-98)
- Men of Sherwood Forest '57
- I'll Cry Tomorrow '55
- Stalag 17 '53
- A Place in the Sun '51
- Flying Leathernecks '51
- Father's Little Dividend '51
- Father of the Bride '50
- The Naked City '48
- Battleground '49
- L.627 '92
- Beatrice '88
- The Story of Women '88

Dub Taylor (1908-94)
- Maverick '94
- Falling from Grace '92
- Conagher '91
- My Heroes Have Always Been Cowboys '91
- Back to the Future, Part 3 '90
- Texas Guns '90
- Soggy Bottom U.S.A. '84
- 1941 '79
- Moonshine County Express '77
- Creature from Black Lake '76
- Gator '76
- Pony Express Rider '76
- Flash & Firecat '75
- On the Run '73
- Poor Pretty Eddie '73
- This Is a Hijack '73
- The Getaway '72
- Support Your Local Gunfighter '71
- A Man Called Horse '70
- Death of a Gunfighter '69
- The Wild Bunch '69
- The Shakiest Gun in the West '68
- Bonnie & Clyde '67
- Spencer's Mountain '63
- Parrish '61
- Them! '54

Elayne J. Taylor
- Rules of Engagement '00

Elizabeth Taylor (1932-)
- The Wood '99
- These Old Broads '01
- The Flintstones '94
- Sweet Bird of Youth '89
- Poker Alice '87
- The Rumor Mill '86
- North and South Book 1 '85
- Between Friends '83
- The Mirror Crack'd '80
- Winter Kills '79
- Return Engagement '78
- A Little Night Music '77
- Victory at Entebbe '76
- Ash Wednesday '73
- Under Milk Wood '73
- Divorce His, Divorce Hers '72
- Hammersmith Is Out '72
- X, Y & Zee '72
- Secret Ceremony '69
- Boom! '68
- Doctor Faustus '68
- The Comedians '67
- Reflections in a Golden Eye '67
- The Taming of the Shrew '67
- Who's Afraid of Virginia Woolf? '66
- The Sandpiper '65
- Cleopatra '63
- The V.I.P.'s '63
- Butterfield 8 '60
- Suddenly, Last Summer '59
- Cat on a Hot Tin Roof '58
- Raintree County '57
- Giant '56
- Beau Brummel '54
- Elephant Walk '54
- The Last Time I Saw Paris '54
- Rhapsody '54
- Ivanhoe '52
- Love Is Better Than Ever '52
- A Place in the Sun '51
- Father's Little Dividend '51
- Father of the Bride '50
- The Big Hangover '50
- Quo Vadis '51
- Conspirator '49
- Little Women '49
- A Date with Judy '48
- Julia Misbehaves '48
- Life with Father '47
- Courage of Lassie '46
- Jane Eyre '44
- National Velvet '44
- The White Cliffs of Dover '44
- Lassie, Come Home '43

Estelle Taylor (1899-1958)
- Cimarron '31
- Street Scene '31
- Where East Is East '29
- Don Juan '26

Forrest Taylor (1883-1965)
- Shake Hands with Murder '44
- Mystery Man '44
- Driftin' River '46
- Trail Riders '42
- Trigger Men '42
- Arizona Gangbusters '40
- Outlaw's Parade '39
- Texas Wildcats '39
- Ghost Town Riders '38
- Lightnin' Carson Rides Again '38
- The Phantom of the Range '36
- The Red Rope '37
- The Roamin' Cowboy '37
- Tex Rides with the Boy Scouts '37
- A Face in the Fog '36
- Kelly of the Secret Service '36
- Prison Shadows '36
- West of Nevada '36
- Trail of Terror '35
- Riders of Destiny '33
- Sons of the Pioneers '42
- Colorado Serenade '46
- Border Saddlemates '52

Frank Hoyt Taylor
- Junebug '05
- A Lesson Before Dying '99
- Matewan '87

Grant Taylor (1917-71)
- Long John Silver '54
- His Majesty O'Keefe '53
- The Fighting Rats of Tobruk '44
- Forty Thousand Horsemen '41

Holland Taylor (1943-)
- Baby Mama '08
- The Wedding Date '08
- D.E.B.S. '04
- Spy Kids 3-D: Game Over '03
- Legally Blonde '01
- Happy Accidents '00
- Keeping the Faith '00
- Next Stop, Wonderland '98
- The Truman Show '98
- George of the Jungle '97
- Just Write '97
- Last Summer in the Hamptons '96
- One Fine Day '96
- Steal Big, Steal Little '95
- Cop and a Half '93
- The Favor '92
- Alice '90
- She's Having a Baby '88
- Romancing the Stone '84

Jack Taylor (1936-)
- The Ninth Gate '99
- Pieces '83
- Kicked in the Head '97
- Subway Stories '97
- Casa de los Babys '03
- The Notorious Bettie Page '06
- Factotum '06
- Horror of the Zombies '74
- The Mummy's Revenge '73
- Orgy of the Vampires '73
- Dr. Jekyll and the Wolfman '71
- Night of the Sorcerers '70
- Female Vampire '73

Jana Taylor
- Hell's Angels on Wheels '67

James Taylor (1948-)
- TMNT (Teenage Mutant Ninja Turtles) '07 (V)
- Two Lane Blacktop '71

Jayceon Taylor
- See The Game

Joan Taylor (1925-)
- Omar Khayyam '57
- 20 Million Miles to Earth '57
- Earth vs. the Flying Saucers '56
- Girls in Prison '56
- Apache Woman '55
- Rose Marie '54
- The Seventh Sign '88

John Taylor (1960-)
- Sugar Town '99
- The Ringer '05
- Four Dogs Playing Poker '00
- Foxstyle '73

Joseph Lyle Taylor (1964-)
- The Breakup Artist '04
- Borough of Kings '98

Joyce Taylor (1932-)
- Atlantis, the Lost Continent '61

Kent Taylor (1906-87)
- The FBI Story '59
- I Spit on Your Corpse '74
- Angels' Wild Women '72
- Brain of Blood '71
- Blood of Ghastly Horror '72
- Satan's Sadists '69
- Slightly Scarlet '56
- Western Pacific Agent '51
- Gang Busters '42
- Escape to Paradise '39
- Five Came Back '39
- The Gracie Allen Murder Case '39
- Mrs. Wiggs of the Cabbage Patch '34
- Death Takes a Holiday '34
- David Harum '34
- Badmen of Nevada '33

Kimberly Taylor
- The Jury's Secret '38
- Sky Parade '36
- Patch '34
- I'm No Angel '33
- The Mysterious Rider '33

Kit Taylor (1942-)
- Innocent Prey '88
- Long John Silver '54
- Cassandra '87
- Smiley '56

Lawrence Taylor (1959-)
- The Comebacks '07
- In Hell '03
- Any Given Sunday '99

Lili Taylor (1967-)
- Starting Out in the Evening '07
- Factotum '06
- The Notorious Bettie Page '06
- Casa de los Babys '03
- Live from Baghdad '03
- Gaudi Afternoon '01
- High Fidelity '00
- The Haunting '99
- A Slipping Down Life '99
- The Imposters '98
- Pecker '98
- The Addiction '95
- Four Rooms '95
- Girls Town '95
- Arizona Dream '94
- Mrs. Parker and the Vicious Circle '94
- Ready to Wear '94
- Household Saints '93
- Rudy '93
- Watch It '93
- Short Cuts '93
- Bright Angel '91
- Dogfight '91
- Say Anything '89
- Mystic Pizza '88

Marjorie Taylor
- The Face at the Window '39
- Ticket of Leave Man '37
- Never Too Late to Mend '37
- The Crimes of Stephen Hawke '36

Mark L. Taylor (1954-)
- Ransom '96
- Color of Justice '97
- Eight Days a Week '97
- Arachnophobia '90

Meshach Taylor (1947-)
- Friends and Family '01
- Virtual Seduction '96
- Double Double Toil and Trouble '94
- Trouble '94
- Class Act '92
- Ultra Warrior '92
- Inside Out '91
- Mannequin 2: On the Move '91
- Hard to Die '90
- Mannequin '87
- House of Games '87
- Explorers '85
- The Beast Within '82
- The Howling '81
- Damien: Omen 2 '78
- Hellraiser 5: Inferno '00

Natascha Taylor
- See Natascha (Natasha) McElhone

Noah Taylor (1969-)
- Charlie and the Chocolate Factory '05
- The New World '05
- The Proposition '05
- Lara Croft Tomb Raider: The Cradle of Life '03
- Max '02
- The Sleeping Dictionary '02
- He Died With a Felafel in His Hand '01
- Lara Croft: Tomb Raider '01
- Vanilla Sky '01
- Almost Famous '00
- Life in the Fast Lane '00
- One Crazy Night '93
- Shine '96
- Flirting '89
- The Year My Voice Broke '87

Rachael Taylor (1984-)
- Deception '08
- Shutter '08
- Transformers '07
- See No Evil '06

Regina Taylor (1960-)
- Cora Unashamed '00
- Strange Justice '99
- Clarence Thomas and Anita Hill Story '99
- The Negotiator '98
- Hostile Waters '97
- Courage Under Fire '96
- A Family Thing '96
- The Keeper '96
- Spirit Lost '96
- Lean on Me '89

- I Shot Andy Warhol '96
- Illtown '96
- Things I Never Told You '96
- Cold Fever '95
- Four Rooms '95
- Rudy '93
- Short Cuts '93
- Watch It '93
- Bright Angel '91
- Dogfight '91
- Say Anything '89
- Mystic Pizza '88
- Icebox Murders '82
- Black Tide '58

Renee Taylor (1935-)
Pandemic '07
Ice Age: The Meltdown '06 (V)
The Boynton Beach Club '05
Alfie '04
National Lampoon's Gold Diggers '04
61* '01
Love Is All There Is '96
Forever: A Ghost of a Love Story '92
Delirious '91
The End of Innocence '90
That's Adequate '90
White Palace '90
Last of the Red Hot Lovers '72
The Detective '68
The Errand Boy '61

Rip Taylor (1934-)
Alex & Emma '03
Private Obsession '94
Indecent Proposal '93
Silence of the Hams '93
Tom and Jerry: The Movie '93 (V)
Wayne's World 2 '93
DuckTales the Movie: Treasure of the Lost Lamp '90 (V)
Cheech and Chong: Things Are Tough All Over '82

Robert Taylor
The Hard Word '02
Vertical Limit '00
The Matrix '99

Robert Taylor (1911-69)
The Hot Line '69
Where Angels Go, Trouble Follows '69
Johnny Tiger '66
The Night Walker '64
The Miracle of the White Stallions '63
The Law and Jake Wade '58
Party Girl '58
D-Day, the Sixth of June '56
The Last Hunt '56
Valley of the Kings '54
All the Brothers Were Valiant '53
I Love Melvin '53
Knights of the Round Table '53
Ivanhoe '52
Quo Vadis '51
Westward the Women '51
Conspirator '49
Undercurrent '46
Bataan '43
Johnny Eager '42
Billy the Kid '41
When Ladies Meet '41
Waterloo Bridge '40
Three Comrades '38
Broadway Melody of 1938 '37
Personal Property '37
Camille '36
The Gorgeous Hussy '36
Broadway Melody of 1936 '35

Rod Taylor (1929-)
Welcome to Woop Woop '97
Open Season '95
Danielle Steel's Palomino '91
Marbella '85
On the Run '83
Time to Die '83
Jacqueline Bouvier Kennedy '81
Cry of the Innocent '80
The Treasure Seekers '79
Hell River '75
Germicide '74
The Deadly Trackers '73
Train Robbers '73
Darker than Amber '70
Man Who Had Power Over Women '70
Powder Keg '70
Zabriskie Point '70
Dark of the Sun '68
Chuka '67
Hotel '67
The Glass Bottom Boat '66
Do Not Disturb '65
Colossus and the Amazon Queen '64
36 Hours '64
The Birds '63
A Gathering of Eagles '63
Sunday in New York '63
The V.I.P.'s '63
101 Dalmatians '61 (V)
The Time Machine '60
Ask Any Girl '59
Separate Tables '58
Raintree County '57
The Catered Affair '56
Giant '56
Long John Silver '54

Russi Taylor (1944-)
Babe: Pig in the City '98 (V)
DuckTales the Movie: Treasure of the Lost Lamp '90 (V)
Jetsons: The Movie '90 (V)

Sandra Taylor (1966-)
Keeping Up with the Steins '06
The Student Affair '97

Tamara Taylor (1970-)
Diary of a Mad Black Woman '05
Introducing Dorothy Dandridge '99
Senseless '98

Tammy Taylor
Lovelines '84
Meatballs 2 '84
Nightstalker '81

Vaughn Taylor (1910-83)
The Gallant Hours '60
Jailhouse Rock '57
Meet Danny Wilson '52
Francis Goes to the Races '51

Veronica Taylor
Pokemon 3: The Movie '01 (V)
Pokemon: The First Movie '99 (V)

Wally Taylor (1930-)
Hidden Fears '93
Night of the Creeps '86
Shaft's Big Score '72

Zack Taylor
Ivanhoe '52

Scout Taylor-Compton (1989-)
Halloween '07
Sleepover '04

Leigh Taylor-Young (1944-)
Coffee Date '06
Klepto '03
Slackers '02
Bliss '96
Honeymoon Academy '90
Accidents '89
The Jagged Edge '85
Secret Admirer '85
Looker '81
Marathon '80
Soylent Green '73
The Adventurers '70
The Horsemen '70
The Big Bounce '69
I Love You, Alice B. Toklas! '68

Jun Tazaki (1910-85)
Ran '85
War of the Gargantuas '70
Destroy All Monsters '68
Godzilla vs. Monster Zero '65
King Kong vs. Godzilla '63
Seven Samurai '54

Ludmilla Tcherina (1924-2004)
Sins of Rome '54
The Red Shoes '48

Kiri Te Kanawa (1944-)
Meeting Venus '91 (V)
The Ring '52

Phil Tead (1893-1974)
Fangs of the Wild '54
Music in My Heart '40

Anthony Teague (1940-89)
The Trouble with Girls (and How to Get into It) '69
How to Succeed in Business without Really Trying '67

Marshall Teague
U.S. Seals 2 '01
Across the Line '00
Crime and Punishment in Suburbia '00
The Colony '95
Fists of Iron '94
Guardian Angel '94
Super Force '90
Road House '89
Trained to Kill '88
The Shadow Riders '82

Ray Teal (1902-76)
Judgment at Nuremberg '61
Band of Angels '57
Lucky Me '54
Ambush at Tomahawk Gap '53
Carrie '52
Jumping Jacks '52
Montana Belle '52
Ace in the Hole '51
Distant Drums '51
Rusty's Birthday '49
The Best Years of Our Lives '46
Hollywood Canteen '44

Owen Teale (1961-)
The Last Legion '07
Conspiracy '01
Cleopatra '99
The Hawk '93
Robin Hood '91

Conway Tearle (1878-1938)
Catherine Cookson's The Fifteen Streets '90
Klondike Annie '36
Headline Woman '35
Sing Sing Nights '35
Held for Murder '32
Hurricane Express '32
The King Murder '32
Vanity Fair '32
Morals for Women '31
Pleasure '31
Lost Zeppelin '29
Dancing Mothers '26
Stella Maris '18

Godfrey Tearle (1884-1953)
One of Our Aircraft Is Missing '41
The 39 Steps '35

Verree Teasdale (1904-87)
Milky Way '36
Goodbye Love '34
Skyscraper Souls '32

Sandor Tecsy (1946-)
Fever '99
Angel Blue '97
'68 '87

Paola Tedesco
Watch Me When I Kill '77
New Mafia Boss '72

Travis Tedford (1988-)
Slappy and the Stinkers '97
The Little Rascals '94

Irene Tedrow (1908-95)
The Two Worlds of Jenny Logan '79
Special Olympics '78

Jill Teed
X2: X-Men United '03
Mission to Mars '00
Impolite '92

Maureen Teefy (1954-)
Star Time '92
Supergirl '84
Legs '83
Fame '80

Blair Tefkin (1959-)
Dream Lover '93
A Sinful Life '89

Aaron Teich (1961-)
Darkroom '90
Bloodspell '87

Virgilio Teixeira (1917-)
Tricheurs '84
Saul and David '64

April Telek
Man in the Mirror: The Michael Jackson Story '04
The Immortal '01

Rut Tellefsen (1930-)
Kristin Lavransdatter '95
The Last Lieutenant '94

Teller (1948-)
Penn and Teller Get Killed '90
Light Years '88 (V)
Long Gone '87

Sybil Temchen (1970-)
Lip Service '00
Body Shots '99
Nice Guys Sleep Alone '99
The Passion of Ayn Rand '99
Restaurant '98
Ten Benny '98
Floating '97

Hedi Temessy (1925-2001)
Almanac of Fall '85
The Revolt of Job '84

Juno Temple
The Other Boleyn Girl '08
Wild Child '08
Atonement '07
Notes on a Scandal '06

Lew Temple
Waitress '07
The Texas Chainsaw Massacre: The Beginning '06
The Devil's Rejects '05
Domino '05

Shirley Temple (1928-)
The Story of Seabiscuit '49
Fort Apache '48
The Bachelor and the Bobby-Soxer '47
Since You Went Away '44
Miss Annie Rooney '42
The Blue Bird '40
Young People '40
The Little Princess '39
Just Around the Corner '38
Little Miss Broadway '38
Rebecca of Sunnybrook Farm '38
Heidi '37
Wee Willie Winkie '37
Captain January '36
Dimples '36
The Poor Little Rich Girl '36
Stowaway '36
Curly Top '35
Little Colonel '35
The Littlest Rebel '35
Our Little Girl '35
Baby, Take a Bow '34
Bright Eyes '34
Little Miss Marker '34
Stand Up and Cheer '34
Kid 'n' Hollywood and Polly Tix in Washington '33
To the Last Man '33

Harry Tenbrook (1887-1960)
They Were Expendable '45
A Slight Case of Murder '38

John Tench
The Ticket '97
Dead Ahead '96

David Tennant (1971-)
Casanova '05
Harry Potter and the Goblet of Fire '05
Bright Young Things '03
The Last September '99

Victoria Tennant (1953-)
Bram Stoker's The Mummy '97
Edie & Pen '95
L.A. Story '91
The Handmaid's Tale '90
War & Remembrance: The Final Chapter '89
Whispers '89
War & Remembrance '88
Best Seller '87
Flowers in the Attic '87
The Holcroft Covenant '85
All of Me '84
Chiefs '83
Strangers Kiss '83
The Winds of War '83
The Dogs of War '81
Inseminoid '80
Little Lord Fauntleroy '80

Anne Tenney
The Castle '97
Dead Heart '96

Jon Tenney (1961-)
Looking for Comedy in the Muslim World '06
Homecoming '05
Entropy '99
You Can Count On Me '99
With Friends Like These '98
Fools Rush In '97
Homegrown '97
Lovelife '97
Music from Another Room '97
The Twilight of the Golds '97
The Phantom '96
Free Willy 2: The Adventure Home '95
Lassie '94
Tombstone '93
Watch It '93
Guilty by Suspicion '91
Nasty Hero '89

Julius Tennon
Lone Justice 2 '93
Riverbend '90
Ran '85

Judy Tenuta (1956-)
Material Girls '06
White Hot '88

William Tepper (1948-)
Bachelor Party '84
Miss Right '81

Johanna Ter Steege (1961-)
Paradise Road '97
Immortal Beloved '94
Meeting Venus '91
Vincent & Theo '90
The Vanishing '88

Susumu Terajima (1963-)
Steamboy '05 (V)
Brother '00
After Life '98
Fireworks '97

Akira Terao (1947-)
Akira Kurosawa's Dreams '90
Ran '85

Lee Tergesen (1965-)
The Texas Chainsaw Massacre: The Beginning '06
Extreme Dating '04
A Thief of Time '04
Monster '03
Bark! '02
Shot in the Heart '01
Wild Iris '01
Shaft '00
Point Break '91

Max Terhune (1891-1973)
Black Market Rustlers '43
Cowboy Commandos '43
Haunted Ranch '43
Land of Hunted Men '43
Two-Fisted Justice '43
Arizona Stagecoach '42
Boot Hill Bandits '42
Rock River Renegades '42
Texas to Bataan '42
Thunder River Feud '42
Trail Riders '42
Fugitive Valley '41
Kid's Last Ride '41
Saddle Mountain Roundup '41
Tonto Basin Outlaws '41
Trail of the Silver Spurs '41
Tumbledown Ranch in Arizona '41
Underground Rustlers '41
Range Busters '40
Trailing Double Trouble '40
West of Pinto Basin '40
Three Texas Steers '39
Heroes of the Hills '38
Outlaws of Sonora '38
Overland Stage Raiders '38
Pals of the Saddle '38
Purple Vigilantes '38
Santa Fe Stampede '38
Come on, Cowboys '37
Heart of the Rockies '37
Hit the Saddle '37
Riders of the Whistling Skull '37
Roarin' Lead '37
The Trigger Trio '37
Wild Horse Rodeo '37
Ghost Town Gold '36
Ride, Ranger, Ride '36

Studs Terkel (1912-)
Eight Men Out '88
Long Shadows '86

John Terlesky (1961-)
Battling for Baby '92
Damned River '89
When He's Not a Stranger '89
The Allnighter '87
Deathstalker 2: Duel of the Titans '87
Chopping Mall '86

Leonard Termo
Midnight Cabaret '90
Year of the Dragon '85

Scott Terra (1987-)
Daredevil '03
Eight Legged Freaks '02
Shadrach '98

John Canada Terrell
The Five Heartbeats '91
Def by Temptation '90
She's Gotta Have It '86

Ken Terrell (1907-66)
Attack of the 50 Foot Woman '58
The Brain from Planet Arous '57
The Indestructible Man '56
Son of Zorro '47
In Old New Mexico '45
Outlaw's Paradise '39
Brothers of the West '37
Stormy Trails '36

Bob Terry
Danger Ahead '40
Lightning Strikes West '40
Down the Wyoming Trail '39

Don Terry (1902-88)
Don Winslow of the Coast Guard '43
Don Winslow of the Navy '43
Overland Mail '42
Border Romance '30

Harry Terry
The Face at the Window '39
Broken Melody '34

John Terry (1944-)
Zodiac '07
Change of Heart '98
The Big Green '95
Reflections in the Dark '94
'62
Iron Will '93
Of Mice and Men '92
The Resurrected '91
Silhouette '91
A Killing in a Small Town '90
In Country '89
Full Metal Jacket '87
Hawk the Slayer '81

Kim Terry
Rushmore '98
Slugs '87

Nigel Terry (1945-)
Feardotcom '02
Red Mercury '05
The Emperor's New Clothes '01
The Ebb-Tide '97
Far from the Madding Crowd '98
Blue '93 (N)
Christopher Columbus: The Discovery '92
Edward II '92
Caravaggio '86
Sylvia '86
Deja Vu '84
Excalibur '81

Phillip Terry (1909-93)
The Leech Woman '59
To Each His Own '46
The Monster and the Girl '41
The Lost Weekend '45
Bataan '43
Wake Island '42
'45
George White's Scandals '45

Ruth Terry (1920-)
Hands Across the Border '43
Texas Legionnaires '43
Blondie Goes Latin '42
Heart of the Golden West '42
'42
Alexander's Ragtime Band '38
The Sphinx '33
Haunted Gold '32
'Neath the Arizona Skies '34

Sheila Terry (1910-57)
Go-Get-'Em-Haines '35
Lawless Frontier '35
Social Error '35

Terry-Thomas (1911-89)
The Bawdy Adventures of Tom Jones '76
Robin Hood '73 (V)
Vault of Horror '73
Doctor Phibes Rises Again '72
The Abominable Dr. Phibes '71
12 Plus 1 '70
Those Daring Young Men in Their Jaunty Jalopies '69
Danger: Diabolik '68
Don't Raise the Bridge, Lower the River '68
How Sweet It Is! '68
Where Were You When the Lights Went Out? '68
A Guide for the Married Man '67
Those Fantastic Flying Fools '67
La Grande Vadrouille '66
Munster, Go Home! '66
Strange Bedfellows '65
Those Magnificent Men in Their Flying Machines '65
How to Murder Your Wife '64
It's a Mad, Mad, Mad, Mad World '63
A Matter of WHO '62
The Mouse on the Moon '62
The Wonderful World of the Brothers Grimm '62
Make Mine Mink '60
Carlton-Browne of the F.O. '59
I'm All Right Jack '59
Too Many Crooks '59
Lucky Jim '58
The Naked Truth '58
Tom Thumb '58
Blue Murder at St. Trinian's '56

Laurent Terzieff (1935-)
Fiesta '95
Germinal '93
Detective '85
A Coeur Joie '67
Medea '70
Kapo '59
Vanina Vanini '61

Venus Terzo
Heac Over Heels '67

Ingrid Tesch
Masters of Horror: The Washingtonians '07
Meltdown '06

Robert Tessier (1934-2000)
Future Force '89
Nightwish '89
No Safe Haven '87
Avenging Angel '85
The Last of the Mohicans '85

Desmond Tester (1919-2002)
Non-Stop New York '37
Nine Days a Queen '36
Sabotage '36

Sylvie Testud (1971-)
La Vie en Rose '07
A Loving Father '02
The Chateau '01
Beyond Silence '96

Lauren Tewes (1954-)
Nowhere '96
The Doom Generation '95
It Came from Outer Space 2 '95

John Thaw (1942-2002)
The Ninth Day '04
Goodnight, Mr. Tom '99
The Waiting Time '99
Into the Blue '97
Chaplin '92
A Year in Provence '89

Hilmar Thate (1931-)
Veronika Voss '82

Phyllis Thaxter (1921-)
Three Sovereigns for Sarah '85
Superman: The Movie '78
The World of Henry Orient '64
Springfield Rifle '52
Jim Thorpe: All American '51
Act of Violence '48
Weekend at the Waldorf '45
Thirty Seconds Over Tokyo '44

Tia Texada (1971-)
Spartan '04
Crazy as Hell '02
Phone Booth '02
Glitter '01
Thirteen Conversations About One Thing '01
Bait '00
Nurse Betty '00
The Thirteenth Floor '99
Paulie '98
From Dusk Till Dawn '96
Word '63

Eric Thal (1965-)
The Shaft '01
The Puppet Masters '94
Six Degrees of Separation '93
A Stranger Among Us '92

Gilda Texter (1946-)
Angels Hard As They Come '71
Vanishing Point '71

Katharina Thalbach (1954-)
Kaspar Hauser '93
The Tin Drum '79
The Second Awakening of Christa Klages '78

Byron Thames (1969-)
84 Charlie MoPic '89
Seven Minutes in Heaven '86

Torin Thatcher (1905-81)
The Sword and the Sorcerer '82
The 7th Voyage of Sinbad '58
Helen of Troy '56
The Black Shield of Falworth '54
Houdini '53
The Robe '53
The Desert Rats '53
Blackbeard the Pirate '52
Affair in Trinidad '52
The Snows of Kilimanjaro '52
Great Expectations '46

Heather Thatcher (1896-1987)
The Moon and Sixpence '43
Blame It on the Night '84

Charlize Theron (1975-)
Head in the Clouds '04
Monster '03
The Italian Job '03
Trapped '02
Waking Up in Reno '02
The Curse of the Jade Scorpion '01
15 Minutes '01
Sweet November '01
The Legend of Bagger Vance '00
Men of Honor '00
Reindeer Games '00
The Yards '00
The Cider House Rules '99
The Astronaut's Wife '99
Celebrity '98
Mighty Joe Young '98
The Devil's Advocate '97
That Thing You Do! '96
Trial and Error '96
Two Days in the Valley '96

Justin Theroux (1971-)
Tropic Thunder '08
Broken English '07
The Ten '07
Inland Empire '06
Miami Vice '06
The Legend of Lucy Keyes '06

Brynn Thayer (1949-)
The Game of Love '90
Hero and the Terror '88
The Tracker '88

Maria Thayer (1975-)
Forgetting Sarah Marshall '08
Accepted '06
Strangers with Candy '06

Max (Michael) Thayer (1946-)
No Retreat, No Surrender 2 '89

Tina Thayer
Jive Junction '43

Marcello Thedford
Freedom Song '00

Darryl Theirse (1967-)
Crocodile 2: Death Swamp '01

Ulrich Thein (1930-95)
Anton, the Magician '78

Brooke Theiss (1969-)
Quicksand '01
A Nightmare on Elm Street 4: The Dream Master '88

Brother Theodore (1906-2001)
That's Adequate '90
The 'Burbs '89
Nocturna '79

Jack Thibeau
Lethal Weapon '87

Debi Thibeault
Psychos in Love '87

Sean Thibodeau
The Ladies Man '00

Alan Thicke (1947-)
Hollywood North '03
Any Place But Home '97

Roy Thinnes (1936-)
In the Valley of Elah '07
Sleepwalking '08
Aeon Flux '05
North Country '05
Galactic Gigolo '87
Cemetery High '89
Rush Week '88
Airport 1975 '75
The Hindenburg '75
The Norliss Tapes '73
Satan's School for Girls '73
Journey to the Far Side of the Sun '69
Secrets '77

Ernest Thesiger (1879-1961)
The Battle of the Sexes '60
Who Done It? '56
The Robe '53
Beau Brummell '54
A Christmas Carol '51
Beware of Pity '46
Henry V '44
The Ghoul '34
The Old Dark House '32
The Bride of Frankenstein '35

David Thewlis (1963-)
Harry Potter and the Order of the Phoenix '07
Basic Instinct 2 '06
The Omen '06
The New World '05
Kingdom of Heaven '05
Harry Potter and the Prisoner of Azkaban '04
Timeline '03
Dinotopia '02
Gangster No. 1 '00
The Miracle Maker '00 (V)
Besieged '98
The Big Lebowski '98
Seven Years in Tibet '97
Dragonheart '96
The Island of Dr. Moreau '96
James and the Giant Peach '96 (V)
Restoration '95
Total Eclipse '95
Black Beauty '94
Naked '93

Lynne Thigpen (1948-2003)
Anger Management '03
Novocaine '01
Shaft '00
The Insider '99
Random Hearts '99
Just Cause '95
The Paper '94
Naked in New York '93
Article 99 '92
Bob Roberts '92
Lean on Me '89
Streets of Fire '84
Godspell '73
Tar '97

Kevin Thigpen
Tar '97
Just Another Girl on the I.R.T. '93

Chief Ted Thin Elk (1919-97)
Thunderheart '92

Tiffani-Amber Thiessen (1974-)
Pandemic '07
Hollywood Ending '02
The Ladies Man '00
Shriek If You Know What I Did Last Friday the 13th '00

Melanie Thierry
Babylon A.D. '08
The Legend of 1900 '98

Max Thieriot (1988-)
Jumper '08
The Astronaut Farmer '07
Nancy Drew '07
The Pacifier '05
Catch That Kid '04

Victoria Thivisol (1991-)
Chocolat '00
Ponette '95

Olivia Thirlby
Snow Angels '07
Juno '07

Alex Thomas
The Wash '01
The Players Club '98

Betty Thomas (1949-)
Troop Beverly Hills '89
When Your Lover Leaves '83
Homework '82

Damien Thomas (1942-)
Pirates '86
Shogun '80
The Message '77
Twins of Evil '71

Danny Thomas (1914-91)
Side by Side '88
Journey Back to Oz '71 (V)
I'll See You in My Dreams '51

Dave Thomas (1949-)
Brother Bear 2 '06 (V)
Love on the Side '04
White Coats '04
Beethoven's 5th '03
Brother Bear '03 (V)
Cold Sweat '95

Coneheads '93
Boris and Natasha: The Movie '92
Moving '88
Love at Stake '87
My Man Adam '86
Sesame Street Presents: Follow That Bird '85
Strange Brew '83
Stripes '81

Eddie Kaye Thomas (1980-)
Harold & Kumar Escape from Guantanamo Bay '08
Blind Dating '06
Dirty Love '05
Harold and Kumar Go to White Castle '04
American Wedding '03
Stolen Summer '02
Taboo '02
Winter Break '02
American Pie 2 '01
Freddy Got Fingered '01
More Dogs Than Bones '00
American Pie '99
Black and White '99
The Rage: Carrie 2 '99

Frank M. Thomas, Sr. (1889-1989)
Sunset on the Desert '42
Law of the Underworld '38
Charlie Chan in Egypt '35

Frankie Thomas, Jr. (1921-2006)
The Major and the Minor '42
Nancy Drew and the Hidden Staircase '39
Nancy Drew, Reporter '39
Nancy Drew—Trouble Shooter '39
Boys Town '38
Nancy Drew—Detective '38
Tim Tyler's Luck '37

Heather Thomas (1957-)
My Giant '98
Hidden Obsession '92
Red Blooded American Girl '90

Henry Thomas (1971-)
Dead Birds '04
Plain Dirty '04
11:14 '03
Gangs of New York '02
I Capture the Castle '02
I'm with Lucy '02
Dead in the Water '01
The Quickie '01
All the Pretty Horses '00
Fever '99
A Good Baby '99
The Happy Face Murders '99
Moby Dick '98
Bombshell '97
Hijacking Hollywood '97
Niagara, Niagara '97
Suicide Kings '97
Riders of the Purple Sage '96
Indictment: The McMartin Trial '95
Curse of the Starving Class '94
Legends of the Fall '94
Fire in the Sky '93
A Taste for Killing '92
Psycho 4: The Beginning '90
Valmont '89
Murder One '88
The Quest '86
Cloak & Dagger '84
Misunderstood '84
E.T.: The Extra-Terrestrial '82
Raggedy Man '81

Jake Thomas (1990-)
The Lizzie McGuire Movie '03
National Lampoon's Christmas Vacation 2: Cousin Eddie's Big Island Adventure '03
A.I.: Artificial Intelligence '01

James Thomas
Ice Men '04

Jameson Thomas (1888-1939)
Charlie Chan in Egypt '35
Sing Sing Nights '35
Beggars in Ermine '34
Jane Eyre '34
Convicted '32
Night Birds '31
Night Life in Reno '31
The Farmer's Wife '28

Jay Thomas (1948-)
The Santa Clause 3: The Escape Clause '06
Disney's Teacher's Pet '04 (V)
Dragonfly '02
The Santa Clause 2 '02
Trial by Media '00
Killing Mr. Griffin '97
A Smile Like Yours '96
Mr. Holland's Opus '95
Straight Talk '92
Little Vegas '90
The Gig '85
C.H.U.D. '84

Jonathan Taylor Thomas (1981-)
Common Ground '00
Speedway Junky '99
I'll Be Home for Christmas '98
Wild America '97
The Adventures of Pinocchio '96
Man of the House '95
Tom and Huck '95
The Lion King '94 (V)

Khleo Thomas (1989-)
Dirty '05
Roll Bounce '05
Walking Tall '04
Baadasssss! '03
Holes '03

Larry Thomas
Surface to Air '98
Night Ripper '86

Marcus Thomas
You Kill Me '07
Bigger Than the Sky '05
Noel '04

Marlo Thomas (1938-)
Playing Mona Lisa '00
The Real Blonde '97
Held Hostage '91
In the Spirit '90
Consenting Adult '85
Act of Passion: The Lost Honor of Kathryn Beck '83
Jenny '70

Melissa Thomas
Swimming Upstream '03
Brides of Christ '91

Michelle Rene Thomas (1970-)
National Lampoon's Van Wilder '02
The Last Don 2 '98
The Last Don '97
Midnight in Saint Petersburg '97

Patrick Thomas
The Witness '99
Eddie Presley '92

Philip Michael Thomas (1949-)
A Fight for Jenny '90
False Witness '89
The Wizard of Speed and Time '88
Miami Vice '84
Death Drug '83
Fist '76
Sparkle '76
Homeboy '75
Streetfight '75
Stigma '73

Richard Thomas (1951-)
Wonder Boys '00
The Million Dollar Kid '99
Big and Hairy '98
Flood: A River's Rampage '97
The Christmas Box '95
Down, Out and Dangerous '95
The Invaders '95
Linda '93
Stalking Laura '93
A Thousand Heroes '92
Mission of the Shark '91
Glory! Glory! '90
Stephen King's It '90
Andy and the Airwave Rangers '89
Hobson's Choice '83
Living Proof: The Hank Williams Jr. Story '83
Johnny Belinda '82
Berlin Tunnel 21 '81
Battle Beyond the Stars '80
All Quiet on the Western Front '79
Roots: The Next Generation '79
September 30, 1955 '77
Cactus in the Snow '72
You'll Like My Mother '72
Homecoming: A Christmas Story '71
The Todd Killings '71
Last Summer '69
Winning '69

Robin Thomas (1953-)
Missing Brendan '03
The Banger Sisters '02
Clockstoppers '02
Star Maps '97
Amityville Dollhouse '96
Chameleon '95
Memories of Murder '90
Personals '90
From the Dead of Night '89
Summer School '87
About Last Night... '86

Ron Thomas
Night Screams '87
The Big Bet '85

Ross Thomas
American Pie Presents: The Naked Mile '06
The Cutting Edge: Going for the Gold '06

Rufus Thomas (1917-2001)
Cookie's Fortune '99
Mystery Train '89

Sean Patrick Thomas (1970-)
A Raisin in the Sun '08
Barbershop 2: Back in Business '04
Barbershop '02
Halloween: Resurrection '02
Save the Last Dance '01
Dracula 2000 '00
Cruel Intentions '98

Sian Thomas (1953-)
A Mind to Murder '96
The Wedding Gift '93

William Thomas
Solomon and Gaenor '99
Twin Town '97

Marsha Thomason (1976-)
My Baby's Daddy '04
The Haunted Mansion '03
Pure '02
Black Knight '01

William Thomason
The Devil's Sleep '51
Test Tube Babies '48

Florence Thomassin (1966-)
Cold Showers '05
Beaumarchais the Scoundrel '96
Elisa '94
Mina Tannenbaum '93

Tim Thomerson (1945-)
Bottoms Up '06
Christmas Do-Over '06
Forget About It '06
Left in Darkness '06
Final Approach '04
Shoot or Be Shot '02
The Devil's Prey '01
Gale Force '01
They Crawl '01
Submerged '00
The Crimson Code '99
Detour '99
Unseen Evil '99
Crossfire '98
Fear and Loathing in Las Vegas '98
Escape from Atlantis '97
When Time Expires '97
Blast '96
Nemesis 3: Time Lapse '96
The Cisco Kid '94
Dominion '94
Fleshtone '94
Hong Kong '97 '94
Natural Causes '94
Spitfire '94
Trancers 5: Sudden Deth '94
Brain Smasher... A Love Story '93
Dollman vs Demonic Toys '93
Nemesis '93
Trancers 4: Jack of Swords '93
Bad Channels '92
Eddie Presley '92
The Harvest '92
Prime Time Murder '92
Trancers 3: Death Lives '92
Intimate Stranger '91
Air America '90
Dollman '90
Trancers 2: The Return of Jack Deth '90
Vietnam, Texas '90
Who's Harry Crumb? '89
Cherry 2000 '88
The Wrong Guys '88
Glory Years '87
Near Dark '87
A Tiger's Tale '87
Iron Eagle '86
Fade to Black '80
A Wedding '78
Terraces '77
Doin' Time on Planet Earth '88

Vendela Thommessen (1967-)
Model Behavior '00
Batman and Robin '97

Al Thompson
Love Don't Cost a Thing '03
A Season on the Brink '02

Alina Thompson
Dead Cold '00

Andrea Thompson (1962-)
The Fiance '96
Marked Man '96
Seduce Me: Pamela Principle 2 '94
A Gun, a Car, a Blonde '97

Anna Thompson
See Anna Thomson

Bill Thompson (1913-71)
The Aristocats '70 (V)
Lady and the Tramp '55 (V)
Peter Pan '53 (V)

Brian Thompson (1959-)
Epoch: Evolution '03
Epoch '00
Jason and the Argonauts '00
Perfect Target '98
Mortal Kombat 2: Annihilation '97
Dragonheart '96
Rage and Honor '92
Hired to Kill '91
Doctor Mordrid: Master of the Unknown '90
Lionheart '90
Moon 44 '90
Nightwish '89
Fright Night 2 '88
Commando Squad '87

Christopher Thompson (1969-)
La Buche '00
The Luzhin Defence '00
The Count of Monte Cristo '02

Derek Thompson (1948-)
Resurrection Man '97
Belfast Assassins '84
The Long Good Friday '80

Edward Thompson
Double Deal '39
The Duke Is Tops '38

Elizabeth Thompson
Metropolitan '90
The Car '77
Free Grass '69

Emma Thompson (1959-)
Harry Potter and the Order of the Phoenix '07
Nanny McPhee '06
Stranger Than Fiction '06
Harry Potter and the Prisoner of Azkaban '04
Imagining Argentina '04
Angels in America '03
Love Actually '03
Treasure Planet '02 (V)
Wit '01
Maybe Baby '00
Judas Kiss '98
Primary Colors '98
The Winter Guest '97
Carrington '95
Sense and Sensibility '95
Junior '94
In the Name of the Father '93
Much Ado about Nothing '93
My Father the Hero '93
The Remains of the Day '93
Howard's End '92
Peter's Friends '92
Dead Again '91
Impromptu '90
Henry V '89
Look Back in Anger '89
The Tall Guy '89
Fortunes of War '87

Fred Dalton Thompson (1942-)
Bury My Heart at Wounded Knee '07
Looking for Comedy in the Muslim World '06
Racing Stripes '05 (V)
Baby's Day Out '94
Barbarians at the Gate '93
Born Yesterday '93
In the Line of Fire '93
Aces: Iron Eagle 3 '92
Keep the Change '92
Thunderheart '92
White Sands '92
Cape Fear '91
Class Action '91
Curly Sue '91
Days of Thunder '90
Die Hard 2: Die Harder '90
The Hunt for Red October '90
Feds '88
No Way Out '87
Marie '85

Greg Thompson
Dark Remains '05

Hal Thompson
Ghost of the Needle '03
Animal Crackers '30

Hugh Thompson
Lassie from Lancashire '38
The Christmas Blessing '05
The Christmas Shoes '02
What Happened to Rosa? '21
Feed '05

Jack Thompson (1940-)
Leatherheads '08
December Boys '07
The Good German '06
The Assassination of Richard Nixon '05
Star Wars: Episode 2—Attack of the Clones '02
Original Sin '01
Rodgers & Hammerstein's South Pacific '01
Midnight in the Garden of Good and Evil '97
Under the Lighthouse Dancing '97
Excess Baggage '96
Last Dance '96
The Thorn Birds: The Missing Years '96
The Sum of Us '94
A Far Off Place '93
Deception '92
The Killing Beach '92
Resistance '92
Wind '92
Ground Zero '88
Shadow on the Sun '88
Trouble in Paradise '88
Bad Blood '87
Burke & Wills '85
Flesh and Blood '85
Merry Christmas, Mr. Lawrence '83
Waterfront '83
The Man from Snowy River '82
The Club '81
Breaker Morant '80
Earthling '80
The Chant of Jimmie Blacksmith '78
Love Under Pressure '78
Caddie '76
Jock Petersen '74
Sunday Too Far Away '74

Kay Thompson (1903-98)
Funny Face '57

Kenan Thompson (1978-)
Space Chimps '08 (V)
Snakes on a Plane '06
Barbershop 2: Back in Business '04
Fat Albert '04
Love Don't Cost a Thing '03
My Boss's Daughter '03
The Adventures of Rocky & Bullwinkle '00
Good Burger '97
D2: The Mighty Ducks '94
Heavyweights '94

Larry Thompson
Bobby Jones: Stroke of Genius '04
King of the Forest Rangers '46

Lea Thompson (1962-)
California Dreaming '07
The Right to Remain Silent '95
The Substitute Wife '94

The Beverly Hillbillies '93
Dennis the Menace '93
Article 99 '92
Going Undercover '88
The Wizard of Loneliness '88
Some Kind of Wonderful '87
Back to the Future, Part 3 '90
Montana '90
Back to the Future, Part 2 '89
Nightbreaker '89
Casual Sex? '88
Howard the Duck '86
SpaceCamp '86
Back to the Future '85
Red Dawn '84
The Wild Life '84
All the Right Moves '83
Jaws 3 '83

Marshall Thompson (1925-92)
Bog '84
The Turning Point '77
George! '70
Clarence, the Cross-eyed Lion '65
To the Shores of Hell '65
Mighty Jungle '64
No Man Is an Island '62
First Man into Space '59
Fiend without a Face '58
It! The Terror from Beyond Space '58
East of Kilimanjaro '57
Crashout '55
Cult of the Cobra '55
To Hell and Back '55
The Caddy '53
Mystery Street '50
Stars in My Crown '50 (N)
Battleground '49
Words and Music '48
The Show-Off '46
The Clock '45
They Were Expendable '45
The Purple Heart '44

Peter Thompson (1920-2001)
Santa Fe '51
The Wistful Widow of Wagon Gap '47

Reece Thompson (1988-)
Rocket Science '07

Rex Thompson (1942-)
All Mine to Give '56
The King and I '56
Young Bess '53

Sada Thompson (1929-)
Indictment: The McMartin Trial '95

Scott Thompson (1959-)
The Pacifier '05
My Baby's Daddy '04
Tart '01
Loser '00
Mickey Blue Eyes '99
Armistead Maupin's More Tales of the City '97
Hijacking Hollywood '97
Kids in the Hall: Brain Candy '96

Shawn Thompson
Bram Stoker's Shadowbuilder '98
Future Fear '97
Sleeping with Strangers '94
Hairspray '88

Shelley Thompson
Just Like a Woman '95
Labyrinth '86

Sophie Thompson (1962-)
Gosford Park '01
Relative Values '99
Dancing at Lughnasa '98
Emma '96
Four Weddings and a Funeral '94
Twenty-One '91

Susanna Thompson (1958-)
The Ballad of Jack and Rose '05
Dragonfly '02
High Noon '00
Random Hearts '99
Ghosts of Mississippi '96
America's Dream '95
Little Giants '94

Teri Thompson
Breakaway '95
Married People, Single Sex '93

Tessa Thompson (1983-)
When a Stranger Calls '06
Cracker: Brotherly Love '95

Victoria Thompson
Harrad Summer '74
Harrad Experiment '73

Tracie Thoms (1975-)
Death Proof '07
Sex and Breakfast '07
The Devil Wears Prada '06
Rent '05

Ulrich Thomsen (1963-)
The Company '07
Hitman '07
Adam's Apples '05
Allegro '05
Brothers '05
Kingdom of Heaven '05
The Inheritance '03
Max '02
Flickering Lights '01
Killing Me Softly '01
Mostly Martha '01
The Weight of Water '00
The World Is Not Enough '99
Angel of the Night '98
The Celebration '98

Sally Thomsett (1950-)
Straw Dogs '72
The Railway Children '70

Anna Thomson (1957-)
Intern '00
Six Ways to Sunday '99
Water Drops on Burning Rocks '99
Fiona '98
Cafe Society '97
Drunks '96
I Shot Andy Warhol '96
Jaded '96
Angus '95
Other Voices, Other Rooms '95
Outside the Law '95
Angela '94
The Crow '93
Unforgiven '92

Frankie Thorn (1964-)
Bad Blood '94
Bad Lieutenant '92
Liquid Dreams '92

Bill Thornbury (1952-)
Phantasm 4: Oblivion '98
Phantasm 3: Lord of the Dead '94
Phantasm '79

Russell Thorndike (1885-1972)
Henry V '44

Sybil Thorndike (1882-1976)
Shake Hands with the Devil '59
The Prince and the Showgirl '57
Stage Fright '50
Nicholas Nickleby '46
Major Barbara '41

Angela Thorne (1939-)
The Lady's Not for Burning '87

Callie (Calliope) Thorne (1969-)
Analyze That '02
Washington Heights '02
Revolution #9 '01
Sidewalks of New York '01

Kim Thomson (1960-)
The Princess Diaries 2: Royal Engagement '04
Murder 101 '91
Hands of a Murderer '90
Jekyll and Hyde '90
The Tall Guy '89
Stealing Heaven '88

R.H. Thomson (1947-)
Population 436 '06
P.T. Barnum '99
Bone Daddy '97
The Twilight of the Ice Nymphs '97
The Lotus Eaters '93
The Quarrel '93
Glory Enough for All: The Discovery of Insulin '92
Mark Twain and Me '91
Love and Hate: A Marriage Made in Hell '90
Heaven on Earth '89
And Then You Die '88
Ford: The Man & the Machine '87
Canada's Sweetheart: The Saga of Hal C. Banks '85
Surfacing '84
If You Could See What I Hear '82
Ticket to Heaven '81
Charlie Grant's War '80

Scott Thomson
Ghoulies '84
Fast Times at Ridgemont High '82

Jon Mikl Thor
Zombie Nightmare '86
Rock 'n' Roll Nightmare '85

Kelly Thordsen (1917-78)
Bad Charleston Charlie '73
Charley and the Angel '73
Now You See Him, Now You Don't '72
The Boatniks '70
Smoke '70
Blackbeard's Ghost '68
Good Times '67
Number! '66
Texas Across the River '66
Shenandoah '65
The Ugly Dachshund '65
The Misadventures of Merlin Jones '63
A Simple Plan '98
An Alan Smithee Film: Burn, Hollywood, Burn '97

Billy Bob Thornton (1955-)
Mr. Woodcock '07
The Astronaut Farmer '07
School for Scoundrels '06
The Bad News Bears '05
The Alamo '04
Friday Night Lights '04
Intolerable Cruelty '03
Bad Santa '03
Levity '03
The Badge '02
Waking Up in Reno '02
Bandits '01
The Man Who Wasn't There '01
Monster's Ball '01
South of Heaven, West of Hell '00
Pushing Tin '99
Daddy & Them '99
Armageddon '98
Primary Colors '98
A Simple Plan '98
U-Turn '97
Homegrown '97
A Gun, a Car, a Blonde '97
The Apostle '97
Sling Blade '96
The Winner '96
Dead Man '95
Floundering '94
On Deadly Ground '94
Some Folks Call It a Sling Blade '94
The Ghost Brigade '93
Indecent Proposal '93
Tombstone '93
Chopper Chicks in Zombietown '91
One False Move '91

David Thornton (1953-)
Dangerous Liaisons '03
Confusion of Genders '00
Mary, Mother of Jesus '99
The Summer House '94
Diana: Her True Story '93
A Casualty of War '90
A Murder of Quality '90
Conspiracy '01

William Thourlby (1924-)
Castle of Evil '66
Creeping Terror '64

Cyrille Thouvenin (1976-)
Dogs '96

Courtney Thorne-Smith (1967-)
Chairman of the Board '97
Breach of Conduct '94
Side Out '90
Revenge of the Nerds 2: Nerds in Paradise '87
Summer School '87
Welcome to 18 '87
Lucas '86

Dyanne Thorne (1932-)
Hellhole '85
Ilsa, the Tigress of Siberia '79
Ilsa, the Wicked Warden '78
Ilsa, Harem Keeper of the Oil Sheiks '76
Wham-Bam, Thank You Spaceman '75
Ilsa, She-Wolf of the SS '74
Point of Terror '71

Noley Thornton (1983-)
Heidi '93
Danielle Steel's Fine Things '90

Sigrid Thornton (1959-)
Inspector Gadget 2 '02
Trapped in Space '94
Over the Hill '93
Return to Snowy River '88
The Lighthorsemen '87
Slate, Wyn & Me '87
The Man from Snowy River '82
1915 '82
The Night After Halloween '79

Billy Bob Thornton *(cont.)*

Jim Thorpe (1888-1953)
My Pal, the King '32

Sven-Ole Thorsen (1944-)
Gladiator '00
Foolish '99
Kull the Conqueror '97
Fatal Combat '96
Mallrats '95
The Viking Sagas '95
Dragon: The Bruce Lee Story '93

Linda Thorson (1947-)
Straight into Darkness '04
Half Past Dead '02
The Other Sister '98
Walls of Glass '85

William Thourlby (1924-)

Frank Thornton (1921-)
Auntie '73
Tomb of Ligeia '64

Frank Thring, Jr. (1926-94)
Howling III: The Marsupials '87
Mad Max: Beyond Thunderdome '85
Alvin Rides Again '74
The Adventures of Barry McKenzie '72 [?]

Luc Thuillier
The Old Lady Who Walked in the Sea '91
Monsieur Hire '89

Michelle Thrush
Skins '02

Sophie Thursfield
Sister My Sister '94
Oranges Are Not the Only Fruit '89

Carol Thurston (1923-69)
Apache Chief '50
Swamp Fire '46
China Sky '44

David Threlfall (1953-)
Elizabeth: The Golden Age '07
The Queen's Sister '05
Master and Commander: The Far Side of the World '03

Uma Thurman (1970-)
The Accidental Husband '08
My Super Ex-Girlfriend '06
Be Cool '05
Prime '05
The Producers '05
Kill Bill Vol. 2 '04
Paycheck '03
Kill Bill Vol. 1 '03
Hysterical Blindness '02
Chelsea Walls '01
Tape '01
The Golden Bowl '00
Vatel '00
Sweet and Lowdown '99
The Avengers '98
Les Misérables '98
Gattaca '97
Batman and Robin '97
Beautiful Girls '96
A Month by the Lake '95
Even Cowgirls Get the Blues '94
Pulp Fiction '94
Mad Dog and Glory '93
Jennifer 8 '92
Final Analysis '92
Robin Hood '91
Henry & June '90
Where the Heart Is '90
Dangerous Liaisons '88
Johnny Be Good '88
Kiss Daddy Goodnight '87
The Adventures of Baron Munchausen '89

Dechen Thurman (1973-)
Hamlet '00
I Think I Do '97

Chief Thundercloud (1899-1955)
The Phantom Rider '46
Blazing Across the Pecos '48
Call of the Forest '49
Renegade Girl '46
Outlaw Trail '44
Sonora Stagecoach '44
King of the Stallions '42
Annie Oakley '35
Ride, Ranger, Ride '36
Rustlers of Red Dog '35

Bill (Billy) Thurman (1920-95)
Mountaintop Motel Massacre '86
Creature from Black Lake '76

Ingrid Thulin (1926-2003)
Control '87
After the Rehearsal '84
The Cassandra Crossing '76
Moses '76
Cries and Whispers '72
Short Night of Glass Dolls '71

Kenneth Thomson (1899-1967)
In Old Santa Fe '34
Jungle Bride '33
Held for Murder '32
Broadway Melody '29
White Gold '28

Helen Thomson
Nowhere to Land '00
Bloodmoon '90

Gordon Thomson (1945-)
The Fiance '96
The Donor '94
Explosion '69

Erik Thomson
The Alice '04
Somersault '04

The Story of Dr. Wassell '44

Ben Tibber (1990-)
I Am David '04
A Christmas Carol '99

Gerard Tichy (1920-92)
Ricco '74
The Hanging Woman '72
Hatchet for the Honeymoon '70
The Hot Line '69
Doctor Zhivago '65
Gladiators 7 '62

Nancy Ticotin
The Tavern '00
Ransom '96

Rachel Ticotin (1959-)
The Eye '08
Sisterhood of the Traveling Pants '05
Man on Fire '04
Something's Gotta Give '03
Desert Saints '01
Warden of Red Rock '01
Forever Together '00
Full Disclosure '01
Aftershock: Earthquake in New York '99
Malicious Intent '99
Con Air '97
First Time Felon '97
Turbulence '96
Steal Big, Steal Little '95
The Wharf Rat '95
Deconstructing Sarah '94
Don Juan DeMarco '94
Natural Born Killers '94
Falling Down '93
Keep the Change '92
Where the Day Takes You '92
F/X 2: The Deadly Art of Illusion '91
One Good Cop '91
Prison Stories; Women on the Inside '91
Spies, Lies and Naked Thighs '91
Total Recall '90
Critical Condition '86
Rockabye '86
When the Bough Breaks '86
Fort Apache, the Bronx '81

Andrea Tidona
The Listening '06
Best of Youth '03

Dov Tiefenbach (1981-)
Detention '03
Jason X '01

James Tien
Half a Loaf of Kung Fu '78
Chinese Connection '73

Andrew Tiernan (1965-)
300 '07
The Criminal '00
Horatio Hornblower '99
Face '97
The Scarlet Tunic '97
Edward II '91

Patricia Tiernan
Zero Hour! '57
Battle Circus '53

Brigid Tierney
Twist '03
Affliction '97
The Paperboy '94

Gene Tierney (1920-91)
Scruples '80
Toys in the Attic '63
Advise and Consent '62
The Left Hand of God '55
Black Widow '54
The Egyptian '54
Never Let Me Go '53
Night and the City '50
The Ghost and Mrs. Muir '47
The Razor's Edge '46
Leave Her to Heaven '45
Laura '44
Heaven Can Wait '43
The Shanghai Gesture '42
Son of Fury '42
Thunder Birds '42
Sundown '41
Return of Frank James '40

Jacob Tierney (1979-)
Poor White Trash '00
The Life Before This '99
This Is My Father '99
Dead End '98
The Neon Bible '95
Josh and S.A.M. '93
Pin... '88

Lawrence Tierney (1919-2002)
Southie '98
A Kiss Goodnight '94
Wizards of the Demon Sword '94
Casualties of Love: The "Long Island Lolita" Story '93
Eddie Presley '92
Reservoir Dogs '92
City of Hope '91
The Death Merchant '91
Red '91
Why Me? '90
The Offspring '87
Tough Guys Don't Dance '87
Murphy's Law '86
Prizzi's Honor '85
Silver Bullet '85
Midnight '81
The Prowler '81
Never Pick Up a Stranger '79
Andy Warhol's Bad '77
Abduction '75
The Female Jungle '56
The Bushwackers '52
The Greatest Show on Earth '52
The Hoodlum '51
Best of the Badmen '50
Born to Kill '47
The Devil Thumbs a Ride '47
Back to Bataan '45
Dillinger '45
Those Endearing Young Charms '45
The Ghost Ship '43

Malcolm Tierney
The Apocalypse Watch '97
House of Cards '90

Maura Tierney (1965-)
Semi-Pro '08
Danny Roane: First Time Director '06
Diggers '06
Welcome to Mooseport '04
Melvin Goes to Dinner '03
Insomnia '02
Scotland, PA '02
Forces of Nature '99
Instinct '99
Oxygen '99
Primary Colors '98
Liar Liar '97
Primal Fear '96
Fly by Night '93
The Temp '93
White Sands '92
Dead Women in Lingerie '90

Angelo Tiffe
Sword of Honor '94
3 Ninjas Kick Back '94

Jerry Tiffe
Sword of Honor '94
Hollywood in Trouble '87

Pamela Tiffin (1942-)
Viva Max '69
Harper '66
The Hallelujah Trail '65
State Fair '62
One, Two, Three '61
Summer and Smoke '61

Marie Tifo (1949-)
Pouvoir Intime '87
Les Bons Debarras '81

Ken Tigar (1942-)
The Underground '97
Hollywood Safari '96
Little Bigfoot '96
Rage '95
Phantasm 2 '88

Kevin Tighe (1944-)
The Deal '05
Stephen King's Rose Red '02
The Big Day '99
The Darwin Conspiracy '99
Mumford '99
Winchell '98
In Cold Blood '96
Race the Sun '96
The Avenging Angel '95
Better Off Dead '94
Double Cross '94
Men of War '94
Caught in the Act '93
Geronimo: An American Legend '93
A Man in Uniform '93
What's Eating Gilbert Grape '93
Newsies '92
School Ties '92
Bright Angel '91
City of Hope '91
Another 48 Hrs. '90
K-9 '89
Lost Angels '89
Road House '89
Eight Men Out '88
Matewan '87

Ramon Tikaram
Ruby in the Smoke '06
Kama Sutra: A Tale of Love '96

Zeffie Tilbury (1863-1950)
Sheriff of Tombstone '41
The Grapes of Wrath '40
Werewolf of London '35
The Single Standard '29

Nadja Tiller (1929-)
Wanted: Babysitter '75
Dead Are Alive '72
How I Learned to Love Women '66
Tonio Kroger '65
The Burning Court '62

Mel Tillis (1932-)
Uphill All the Way '85
Smokey and the Bandit 2 '80
The Villain '79

Grant Tilly (1937-)
Brilliant Lies '96
Treasure of the Yankee Zephyr '83
Carry Me Back '82
Beyond Reasonable Doubt '80

Jennifer Tilly (1963-)
Bailey's Billion$ '05
Second Best '05
Tideland '05
Home on the Range '04 (V)
Love on the Side '04
Saint Ralph '04
Seed of Chucky '04 (V)
The Haunted Mansion '03
Hollywood North '03
Jericho Mansions '03
The Magnificent Ambersons '02
The Cat's Meow '01
Fast Sofa '01
Monsters, Inc. '01 (V)
The Crew '00
Dancing at the Blue Iguana '00
Hide and Seek '00
The Dress Code '99
The Muse '99
Silent Witness '99
Stuart Little '99 (V)
Bride of Chucky '98
Hoods '98
Relax... It's Just Sex! '98
Bella Mafia '97
Liar Liar '97
Music from Another Room '97
American Strays '96
Bound '96
House Arrest '96
The Wrong Guy '96
Bird of Prey '95
Edie & Pen '95
Embrace of the Vampire '95
Man with a Gun '95
The Pompatus of Love '95
At Home with the Webbers '94
Bullets over Broadway '94
Double Cross '94
The Getaway '93
Heads '93
Made in America '93
Scorchers '92
Shadow of the Wolf '92
Inside Out '91
The Fabulous Baker Boys '89
Far from Home '89
Let It Ride '89
High Spirits '88
Remote Control '88
Rented Lips '88
He's My Girl '87
Moving Violations '85
No Small Affair '84

Meg Tilly (1960-)
Journey '95
Primal Secrets '94
Sleep with Me '94
Body Snatchers '93
Fallen Angels 2 '93
Leaving Normal '92
The Two Jakes '90
The Girl in a Swing '89
Valmont '89
Masquerade '88
Off Beat '86
Agnes of God '85
Impulse '84
The Big Chill '83
Psycho 2 '83
One Dark Night '82
Tex '82

Charlene Tilton (1958-)
Totally Blonde '01
Safety Patrol '98
Silence of the Hams '93
Center of the Web '92
Deadly Bet '91
Problem Child 2 '91
Border Shootout '90
Ragin' Cajun '90
Diary of a Teenage Hitchhiker '82
The Fall of the House of Usher '80
Sweater Girls '78
Freaky Friday '76

Martha Tilton (1915-2006)
The Benny Goodman Story '55
Sunny '41

Justin Timberlake (1981-)
The Love Guru '08
Black Snake Moan '07
Shrek the Third '07 (V)
Alpha Dog '06
Southland Tales '06
Edison Force '05
Model Behavior '00
Alien 3000 '04
Forbidden Sins '99

Cali Timmins (1963-)
Heaven's Fire '99
Hard Evidence '94
The Takeover '94

Patrick Timsit (1959-)
Pedale Douce '96
Little Indian, Big City '95

Charles "Bud" Tingwell (1923-)
Irresistible '06
Ned Kelly '03
Innocence '00
The Castle '97
A Cry in the Dark '88
Miracle Down Under '87
Malcolm '86
Windrider '86
All the Rivers Run '84
Freedom '82
Breaker Morant '80
Money Movers '78
Gone to Ground '76
Endplay '75
Dracula, Prince of Darkness '66
Murder Most Foul '65
Murder Ahoy '64
Murder at the Gallop '63
Murder She Said '62
The Desert Rats '53

Gabriele Tinti (1932-91)
Women's Prison Massacre '85
Caged Women '84
Love Camp '81
Emmanuelle, the Queen '79
Emmanuelle's Daughter '79
Emmanuelle in the Country '78
Naked Paradise '78
Trap Them & Kill Them '77
Delusions of Grandeur '76
Lisa and the Devil '75
M'Lady's Court '73
Web of Deception '71
Journey Beneath the Desert '61

Jamie Tirelli (1945-)
The Groomsmen '06
Yellow '06
Girlfight '99
Lotto Land '95
Sudden Death '85

Jennifer Tisdale
Bring It On: In It to Win It '07
Rollin' Plains '38

Jean Tissier (1896-1973)
Please Not Now! '61
The Hunchback of Notre Dame '57

James Toback (1944-)
Never Down '06
When Will I Be Loved '04
Black and White '99
Giving It Up '99
Fingers '78

Joel Tobeck (1971-)
Eagle vs. Shark '07
Little Fish '05
Perfect Strangers '03

Kenneth Tobey (1919-2002)
Body Shot '93
Desire and Hell at Sunset Motel '92
Honey, I Blew Up the Kid '92
Single White Female '92
Gremlins 2: The New Batch '90
Freeway '88
Innerspace '87
Night of the Creeps '86
The Lost Empire '83
Strange Invaders '83
The Howling '81
Missiles of October '74
Ben '72
Gunfight at the O.K. Corral '57
Wings of Eagles '57
The Great Locomotive Chase '56
The Man in the Gray Flannel Suit '56
The Search for Bridey Murphy '56
Davy Crockett, King of the Wild Frontier '55
It Came from Beneath the Sea '55
The Beast from 20,000 Fathoms '53
The Bigamist '53
Angel Face '52
The Thing '51
I Was a Male War Bride '49

George Tobias (1901-80)
A New Kind of Love '63
Silk Stockings '57
The Seven Little Foys '55
Rawhide '50
The Judge Steps Out '49
The Set-Up '49
Sinbad, the Sailor '47
Objective, Burma! '45
The Mask of Dimitrios '44
Passage to Marseilles '44
Air Force '43
This Is the Army '43
Captains of the Clouds '42
Yankee Doodle Dandy '42
The Bride Came C.O.D. '41
Sergeant York '41
Strawberry Blonde '41
City for Conquest '40
Music in My Heart '40
Torrid Zone '40
The Hunchback of Notre Dame '39

Heather Tobias (1953-)
Beautiful People '99
High Hopes '88

Oliver Tobias (1947-)
Grizzly Falls '99
Darkness Falls '98
Breeders '97
The Brylcreem Boys '96
Mata Hari '85
Operation 'Nam '85
The Wicked Lady '83
The Big Scam '79
The Stud '78
King Arthur, the Young Warlord '75
Young Warlord '75
'Tis a Pity She's a Whore '73
Romance of a Horsethief '71

Dan Tobin (1910-82)
The Last Angry Man '59
The Big Clock '48
Velvet Touch '48
Undercurrent '46
Woman of the Year '42
Black Limelight '38

Genevieve Tobin (1901-95)
Petrified Forest '36
The Case of the Lucky Legs '35
Kiss and Make Up '34
One Hour with You '32

Jason J. Tobin
The Fast and the Furious: Tokyo Drift '06
Better Luck Tomorrow '02
Yellow '98

Lawrence Tobin
Shanty Tramp '67
A Taste of Blood '67

Stephen Tobolowsky (1951-)
Loveless in Los Angeles '07
Wild Hogs '07
Failure to Launch '06
The Sasquatch Gang '06
Robots '05 (V)
Garfield: The Movie '04
Little Black Book '04
Win a Date with Tad Hamilton! '04
Freaky Friday '03
National Security '03
Adaptation '02
The Country Bears '02
Love Liza '02
The Day the World Ended '01
Dean Koontz's Black River '01
The Operator '01
Alien Fury: Countdown to Invasion '00
Memento '00
The Prime Gig '00
Sleep Easy, Hutch Rimes '00
Bossa Nova '99
The Insider '99
Black Dog '98
One Man's Hero '98

An Alan Smithee Film: Burn, Hollywood, Burn '97
Mr. Magoo '97
The Curse of Inferno '96
The Glimmer Man '96
Number 1 of the Secret Service '77
Bloodbath '76
Asylum '72
Dorian Gray '70
Subterfuge '68
The Very Edge '63
Never Let Go '60
Saint Joan '57
Battle Hell '56
D-Day, the Sixth of June '56
Dam Busters '55
A Man Called Peter '55
The Virgin Queen '55
Rob Roy—The Highland Rogue '53
The Sword & the Rose '53
The Story of Robin Hood & His Merrie Men '52
Interrupted Journey '49

Richard Todd (1919-)
House of the Long Shadows '82
The Big Sleep '78

Ann Todd (1909-93)
The Human Factor '79
Son of Captain Blood '62
Scream of Fear '61
The Seventh Veil '46
Action for Slander '38
South Riding '37

Ann E. Todd (1931-)
Three Daring Daughters '48
Homesteaders of Paradise Valley '47
How Green Was My Valley '41
Intermezzo '39

Beverly Todd (1946-)
The Bucket List '07
Animal '05
Crash '05
Class of '61 '92
Lean on Me '89
Clara's Heart '88
The Ladies Club '86
Don't Look Back: The Story of Leroy "Satchel" Paige '81
Brother John '70

Brian Tochi (1959-)
The Player '92
Teenage Mutant Ninja Turtles: The Movie '90 (V)
Stitches '85
Revenge of the Nerds '84

Hallie Todd (1962-)
The Lizzie McGuire Movie '03
Sam's Son '84

James Todd (1908-58)
High School Confidential '58

Harry Todd (1863-1935)
Sucker Money '34

Lisa Todd (1954-)
Blood Hook '86
The Doll Squad '73
Woman Hunt '72

Mabel Todd (1907-77)
The Ghost and the Guest '43
The Cowboy and the Lady '38

Thelma Todd (1905-35)
The Bohemian Girl '36
Cockeyed Cavaliers '34
Hips, Hips, Hooray! '34
Palooka '34
Counsellor-at-Law '33
The Devil's Brother '33
Horse Feathers '32
Speak Easily '32
Corsair '31
The Maltese Falcon '31
Monkey Business '31
Nevada '27

Tony Todd (1954-)
The Man from Earth '07
Shadow Puppets '07
Final Destination 2 '03
Final Destination '00
Candyman 3: Day of the Dead '98
Bram Stoker's Shadowbuilder '98
Caught Up '98
Stir '98
True Women '97
Wishmaster '97
The Rock '96
Sabotage '96
Beastmaster 3: The Eye of Braxus '95
Bunzy's Last Call '95
Black Fox: Blood Horse '94
Black Fox: Good Men and Bad '94
Black Fox: The Price of Peace '94
Candyman 2: Farewell to the Flesh '94
The Crow '94
Candyman '92
Night of the Living Dead '90
Voodoo Dawn '90
Colors '88
Platoon '86

Russell Todd (1958-)
Sweet Murder '93
Border Shootout '90
One Last Run '89
Chopping Mall '86

Saira Todd (1964-)
Bad Behavior '92
A Fatal Inversion '92

Marilyn Tokuda
Strawberry Fields '97
Farewell to the King '89
The Jitters '88
My Tutor '82

Chotaro Togin
Godzilla's Revenge '69
Godzilla vs. the Sea Monster '65

Ugo Tognazzi (1922-90)
La Cage aux Folles 3: The Wedding '86
A Joke of Destiny, Lying in Wait Around the Corner Like a Bandit '84
La Cage aux Folles 2 '81
The Tragedy of a Ridiculous Man '81
La Cage aux Folles '78
La Grande Bouffe '73
Head of the Family '71
L'Udienza '71
Porcile '69
Barbarella '68
RoGoPaG '62
Love in the City '53

Ricky Tognazzi (1955-)
Aurora '84
The Tragedy of a Ridiculous Man '81

James Tolkan (1931-)
K-PAX '01
Extreme Measures '96
Waterworld '95
Sketch Artist 2: Hands That See '94
Boiling Point '93
Sketch Artist '92
Leap of Faith '92
A Rage in Harlem '91
Problem Child 2 '91
Back to the Future, Part 3 '90
Dick Tracy '90
Opportunity Knocks '90
The Hillside Strangler '89
Family Business '89
Ministry of Vengeance '89
Second Sight '89
Split Decisions '88
Weekend War '88
Viper '88
Rawhead Rex '87
Weeds '87
In Love and War '87
Off Beat '86
Back to the Future '85

Niall Toibin (1929-)
Frankie Starlight '95
Far and Away '92
The Playboys '92
Rawhead Rex '87
Eat the Peach '86
Ryan's Daughter '70

Henriette Tol (1953-)
Broken Mirrors '85
Question of Silence '83

Michael (Lawrence) Tolan (1925-)
All That Jazz '79
Night Terror '77
The 300 Year Weekend '71
The Lost Man '69
The Enforcer '51

Fabiola Toledo
Demons '86
A Blade in the Dark '83

Goya Toledo (1969-)
Amores Perros '00

Sidney Toler (1874-1947)
The Jade Mask '45
The Scarlet Clue '45
The Shanghai Cobra '45
Charlie Chan in the Secret Service '44
The Chinese Cat '44
Meeting at Midnight '44
Adventures of Smilin' Jack '43
Castle in the Desert '42
A Night to Remember '42
Charlie Chan in Rio '41
Murder over New York '40
Charlie Chan at Treasure Island '39
Charlie Chan in City of Darkness '39
Charlie Chan in Honolulu '38
If I Were King '38
The Mysterious Rider '38
Wide Open Faces '38
Double Wedding '37
Our Relations '36
Champagne for Breakfast '35
Massacre '34
Spitfire '34
King of the Jungle '33
Blonde Venus '32
Speak Easily '32
Strangers in Love '32

Marilú Tolo (1944-)
Scorpion with Two Tails '82
Sleep of Death '79
Killer Likes Candy '78
Beyond Fear '75
Commandos '73
Confessions of a Police Captain '72
The Triumph of Hercules '64
Marriage Italian Style '64
Messalina vs. the Son of Hercules '64
Terror of Rome Against the Son of Hercules '64

Yuri Tolubeyev (1905-79)
The Overcoat '59
Don Quixote '57
The Inspector General '52

Lauren Tom (1961-)
Bad Santa '03
Catfish in Black Bean Sauce '00
When a Man Loves a Woman '94
The Joy Luck Club '93
Mr. Jones '93

David Tom (1978-)
The Hazing '04
Walking Thunder '94
Swing Kids '93
Stay Tuned '92

Layne Tom, Jr.
Charlie Chan at the Olympics '37
Charlie Chan in Honolulu '38

Nichelle Tom (1978-)
Pandemic '07
Beethoven's 2nd '93
Beethoven '92

Akihiro Tomikawa (1968-)
Lone Wolf and Cub 4 '72
Lone Wolf and Cub: Baby Cart at the River Styx '72
Lone Wolf and Cub: Baby Cart to Hades '72
Lone Wolf and Cub: Baby Cart: Baby '72

John Toles-Bey
Joe and Max '02
K-PAX '01

Joseph Tomelty (1911-95)
A Night to Remember '58
The Atomic Man '56
John and Julie '55
Devil Girl from Mars '54

Frances Tomelty (1948-)
Bellman and True '88
A Perfect Spy '88
Lamb '85
Blue Money '84
Bullshot '83

Angel Tompkins (1943-)
Relentless '89
A Tiger's Tale '87
Murphy's Law '86
Naked Cage '86
Alligator '80
The Bees '78
I Love My... Wife '70
Prime Cut '72
Probe '72

Lily Tomlin (1939-)
The Walker '07
The Ant Bully '06 (V)
A Prairie Home Companion '06
I Heart Huckabees '04
Orange County '02
Disney's The Kid '00
Tea with Mussolini '99
Krippendorf's Tribe '98
The Player '92
Shadows and Fog '92
Getting Away With Murder '96
Flirting with Disaster '96
Blue in the Face '95
The Celluloid Closet '95 (N)
The Beverly Hillbillies '93
Short Cuts '93
And the Band Played On '93
The Search for Signs of Intelligent Life in the Universe '91
Big Business '88
All of Me '84
The Incredible Shrinking Woman '81
9 to 5 '80
The Late Show '77
Nashville '75

Tamlyn Tomita (1966-)
The Day After Tomorrow '04
Robot Stories '03
Life Tastes Good '99
Soundman '99
Four Rooms '95
Picture Bride '94
The Joy Luck Club '93
Vietnam, Texas '90
The Karate Kid: Part 2 '86
Come See the Paradise '90
Hiroshima: Out of the Ashes '90

Jeana Tomasina (1955-)
Up the Creek '84
Beach Girls '82

Dara Tomanovich
Perfect Target '98
Amnesia '96
Back in Business '96
Bio-Dome '96

Andrew Tombes (1889-1976)
The Go-Getter '54
Phantom Lady '44
San Fernando Valley '44

Nichelle Tom (1978-)
The Killing Jar '96
Picture Bride '94

Dara Tomanovich
Season of Change '94

Stephen Tompkinson (1965-)
Brassed Off '96

Matthew Tompkins
Missionary Man '07
G. Whilliker! '93

Franchot Tone (1905-68)
In Harm's Way '65
Advise and Consent '62
Here Comes the Groom '51
Every Girl Should Be Married '48
Married '48
The Man on the Eiffel Tower '48
Her Husband's Affairs '47
Because of Him '45
Dark Waters '44
His Butler's Sister '43
Jigsaw '49

Kate Toncray (1867-)
The Country Kid '23
The Lamb '15

Concetta Tomei (1945-)
The Muse '99
Sin and Redemption '94
The Goodbye Bird '93
Twenty Bucks '93
Scott Turow's The Burden of Proof '92
Don't Tell Mom the Babysitter's Dead '91
In Love and War '91
China Beach '88

Marisa Tomei (1964-)
Before the Devil Knows You're Dead '07
Wild Hogs '07
Factotum '06
Marilyn Hotchkiss' Ballroom Dancing & Charm School '06
Loverboy '05
Alfie '04
Anger Management '03
The Guru '02
Just a Kiss '02
The Wild Thornberrys Movie '02 (V)
In the Bedroom '01
King of the Jungle '01
Someone Like You '01
Happy Accidents '00
The Watcher '00
What Women Want '00
My Own Country '98
Only Love '98
Slums of Beverly Hills '98
A Brother's Kiss '97
Since You've Been Gone '97
Welcome to Sarajevo '97
Unhook the Stars '96
The Perez Family '94
Four Rooms '95
Only You '94
The Paper '94
Untamed Heart '93
Equinox '93
Chaplin '92
My Cousin Vinny '92
Oscar '91
Zandalee '91

Ricky Tomlinson (1939-)
Once Upon a Time in the Midlands '02
Formula 51 '01
Preaching to the Perverted '97
Cracker: Best Boys '95
Cracker: Brotherly Love '95
Cracker: True Romance '95
Butterfly Kiss '94
Raining Stones '93
Riff-Raff '92

*David Tomlinson (1917-2000)
The Fiendish Plot of Dr. Fu Manchu '80
The Water Babies '79
Wombling Free '77
Bedknobs and Broomsticks '71
Mary Poppins '64
Tom Jones '63
Up the Creek '58
Carry On Admiral '57
Made in Heaven '52
The Wooden Horse '50
Fame is the Spur '47
Sleeping Car to Trieste '45
Pimpernel Smith '42

Phantom Lady '44
Five Graves to Cairo '43
Nice Girl? '41
Three Comrades '38
The Bride Wore Red '37
Quality Street '37
The Gorgeous Hussy '36
Love on the Run '36
Suzy '36
Dangerous '35
The Lives of a Bengal Lancer '35
Mutiny on the Bounty '35
Reckless '35
The Girl from Missouri '34
Sadie McKee '34
The World Moves On '34
Bombshell '33
Dancing Lady '33
Gabriel Over the White House '33
Today We Live '33
Tone Loc (1966-)
Rhapsody '01
They Crawl '01
Titan A.E. '00 (V)
Freedom Strike '98
Heat '95
Ace Ventura: Pet Detective '93
Blank Check '93
Posse '93
Surf Ninjas '93
Bebe's Kids '92 (V)
Ferngully: The Last Rain Forest '92 (V)
The Adventures of Ford Fairlane '90
Philip Tonge (1897-1959)
Invisible Invaders '59
Love from a Stranger '47
Eijiro Tono (1907-94)
Toral Toral Toral '70
Yojimbo '61
The Human Condition: No Greater Love '58
Taiji Tonoyama (1915-89)
Tokyo Pop '88
The Island '61
Regis Toomey (1902-91)
Change of Habit '69
Warlock '59
The Curfew Breakers '57
Great Day in the Morning '56
Guys and Dolls '55
The High and the Mighty '54
Island in the Sky '53
Never Wave at a WAC '52
Dynamite Pass '50
Beyond the Forest '49
Come to the Stable '49
The Bishop's Wife '47
Magic Town '47
The Big Sleep '46
Spellbound '45
Strange Illusion '45
Betrayal from the East '44
Dark Mountain '44
Phantom Lady '44
Raiders of Ghost City '44
Destroyer '43
Dive Bomber '41
Meet John Doe '41
They Died with Their Boots On '41
Arizona '40
The Phantom Creeps '39
Union Pacific '39
Shadows of the Orient '37
Bulldog Edition '36
"G" Men '35
Skull & Crown '35
Laughing at Life '33
Wayne Murder Case '32
Touchdown '31
The Light of Western Stars '30
Alibi '29
Gordon Tootoosis
Bury My Heart at Wounded Knee '07

Open Season '06 (V)
That Beautiful Somewhere '06
Now & Forever '02
Black Point '01
The Doe Boy '01
Nobody's Baby '01
Zoe '01
Big Bear '98
Coyote Summer '96
Crazy Horse '96
Pocahontas '95 (V)
Pocahontas: The Legend '95
Legends of the Fall '94
Call of the Wild '93
Spirit Rider '93
Stone Fox '87
Dan Candy's Law '73
Shawn Toovey
Flash '98
The Fire Next Time '93
Chaim Topol (1935-)
Left Luggage '98
War & Remembrance: The Final Chapter '89
War & Remembrance '88
Queenie '87
The Winds of War '83
For Your Eyes Only '81
Flash Gordon '80
The House on Garibaldi Street '79
Fiddler on the Roof '71
Gun Crazy '69
Cast a Giant Shadow '66
Sallah '63
Peta Toppano (1952-)
Which Way Home '90
Echoes of Paradise '86
Dan Toren
Year Zero '04
Atalia '85
Marta Toren (1926-57)
Paris Express '53
Casbah '48
Hal Torey (1915-89)
Invisible Invaders '59
Earth vs. the Spider '58
Sarah Torgov
American Gothic '88
If You Could See What I Hear '82
Drying Up the Streets '76
Peter Tork (1942-)
Ruby's Bucket of Blood '01
Wrestling with Alligators '98
The Brady Bunch Movie '95
Head '68
Mel Torme (1925-99)
The Return of Spinal Tap '92
Naked Gun 2 1/2: The Smell of Fear '91
A Man Called Adam '66
Girls' Town '59
Words and Music '48
Good News '47
John Tormey (1937-)
Impulse '08
Joe Gould's Secret '00
Ghost Dog: The Way of the Samurai '99
Angelica Torn (1964-)
Domestic Disturbance '01
Rip Torn (1931-)
Bee Movie '07 (V)
Marie Antoinette '06
Zoom '06
Forty Shades of Blue '05
The Sisters '05
Yours, Mine & Ours '05
Dodgeball: A True Underdog Story '04
Eulogy '04
Welcome to Mooseport '04
Men in Black 2 '02
Freddy Got Fingered '01
Wonder Boys '00
The Insider '99
Passing Glory '99
Senseless '98
Balloon Farm '97
Hercules '97 (V)
Men in Black '97
Down Periscope '96

Trial and Error '96
For Better or Worse '95
How to Make an American Quilt '95
Letter to My Killer '95
Canadian Bacon '94
Where the Rivers Flow North '94
Beautiful Dreamers '92
Beyond the Law '92
Dead Ahead: The Exxon Valdez Disaster '92
Dolly Dearest '92
Hard Promises '92
T Bone N Weasel '92
Another Pair of Aces: Three of a Kind '91
Defending Your Life '91
RoboCop 3 '91
Pair of Aces '90
Silence Like Glass '90
By Dawn's Early Light '89
Cold Feet '89
Sweet Bird of Youth '89
The Hit List '88
Extreme Prejudice '87
J. Edgar Hoover '87
Laguna Heat '87
Nadine '87
Manhunt for Claude Dallas '86
Beer '85
The Execution '85
Summer Rental '85
Cat on a Hot Tin Roof '84
City Heat '84
Flashpoint '84
Misunderstood '84
Songwriter '84
Cross Creek '83
Airplane 2: The Sequel '82
Beastmaster '82
Jinxed '82
A Stranger Is Watching '82
Heartland '81
One Trick Pony '80
Rape and Marriage: The Rideout Case '80
Blind Ambition '79
The Seduction of Joe Tynan '79
A Shining Season '79
Betrayal '78
The Birch Interval '78
Coma '78
Steel Cowboy '78
Nasty Habits '77
The Private Files of J. Edgar Hoover '77
The Man Who Fell to Earth '76
Payday '73
Cotter '72
Slaughter '72
The President's Plane Is Missing '71
Tropic of Cancer '70
Coming Apart '69
You're a Big Boy Now '66
The Cincinnati Kid '65
Critic's Choice '63
The King of Kings '61
24 Hours in a Woman's Life '61
Pork Chop Hill '59
Baby Doll '56
Mari Torocsik (1935-)
The Bachelor '93
Daniel Takes a Train '83
Love '71
Ingrid Torrance
Impulse '08
Act of War '96
David Torrence (1864-1951)
Jane Eyre '34
The Mask of Fu Manchu '32
Disraeli '30
Raffles '30
Tess of the Storm Country '22
Ernest Torrence (1878-1933)
I Cover the Waterfront '33
Fighting Caravans '31
Steamboat Bill, Jr. '28

King of Kings '27
Mantrap '26
The Pony Express '25
Peter Pan '24
The Covered Wagon '23
The Hunchback of Notre Dame '23
Tol'able David '21
Pip Torrens (1960-)
Beautiful Dreamers '92
Miss Austen Regrets '07
Pinochet's Last Stand '06
Valiant '05 (V)
Shackleton '02
To End All Wars '01
Incognito '97
A Dark Adapted Eye '93
A Handful of Dust '88
Ana Torrent (1966-)
The Other Boleyn Girl '08
Thesis '96
Vacas '91
Blood and Sand '89
The Nest '80
Cria '76
Cria Cuervos '76
Spirit of the Beehive '73
Fernanda Torres (1965)
House of Sand '05
Four Days in September '97
Foreign Land '95
Savage Capitalism '93
One Man's War '90
Gina Torres (1969-)
I Think I Love My Wife '07
Jam '06
Serenity '05
Hair Show '04
The Matrix Reloaded '03
The Matrix Revolutions '03
Storm Chasers: Revenge of the Twister '98
The Wonderful Ice Cream Suit '98
A Million to Juan '94
National Lampoon's Attack of the 5 Ft. 2 Women '94
Bloodfist 4: Die Trying '92
Lena's Holiday '90
Raquel Torres (1908-87)
Duck Soup '33
So This Is Africa '33
White Shadows in the South Seas '29
Philippe Torreton (1965)
Monsieur N. '03
Capitaine Conan '96
L.627 '92
Guy Torry (1969-)
Runaway Jury '03
The Animal '01
Don't Say a Word '01
Pearl Harbor '01
The '70s '00
Life '99
Trippin' '99
American History X '98
Ride '98
Joe Torry (1965-)
Getting Played '05
Hair Show '04
Motives '03
The Flamingo Rising '01
Lockdown '00
Back in Business '96
Sprung '96
Tales from the Hood '95
Poetic Justice '93
Silvia Tortosa (1947-)
When the Screaming Stops '73
Horror Express '72
Jose Torvay (1910-73)
The Hitch-Hiker '53
My Outlaw Brother '51
Borderline '50
Border Incident '49
Luis Tosar (1971-)
Miami Vice '06

Take My Eyes '03
Angel of Death '02
Mondays in the Sun '02
Jealousy '99
Luigi Tosi
The Black Devils of Kali '55
The Treasure of Bengal '53
Leslie Toth
Buying Time '89
Unfinished Business '89
Toto (1898-1967)
The Hawks & the Sparrows '67
Passionate Thief '60
Big Deal on Madonna Street '58
Merle Tottenham (1901-59)
Room to Let '49
This Happy Breed '47
Night Must Fall '37
Cavalcade '33
Audrey Totter (1918-)
The Carpetbaggers '64
Man or Gun '58
FBI Girl '52
Tension '50
Any Number Can Play '49
The Set-Up '49
Lady in the Lake '46
The Postman Always Rings Twice '46
Shaun Toub
Iron Man '08
The Kite Runner '07
The Nativity Story '06
Crash '05
Land of Plenty '04
Maryam '00
George Touliatos
36 Hours to Die '99
Tracks of a Killer '95
Red Scorpion 2 '94
Robbers of the Sacred Mountain '83
Firebird 2015 A.D. '81
Tamara Toumanova (1919-96)
The Private Life of Sherlock Holmes '70
Invitation to the Dance '56
Days of Glory '43
Sheila Tousey
Coyote Waits '03
Skinwalker '02
Christmas in the Clouds '01
Grand Avenue '96
Medicine River '94
Slaughter of the Innocents '93
Silent Tongue '92
Thunderheart '92
Beth Toussaint (1962-)
Breach of Conduct '94
Night Siege Project: Shadowchaser 2 '94
Blackmail '91
Lorraine Toussaint (1960)
If These Walls Could Talk '96
Jaded '96
Nightjohn '96
America's Dream '95
Dangerous Minds '95
Bleeding Hearts '94
Mother's Boys '94
Point of No Return '93
Breaking In '89
Roland Toutain (1905-77)
Eternal Return '43
The Rules of the Game '39
Liliom '35
Lupita Tovar (1911-)
The Westerner '40
South of the Border '39
Old Spanish Custom '36
Border Law '31
Dracula (Spanish Version) '31
Harry Towb (1925-)
Pictures '80s
The Blue Max '66

Constance Towers (1933)
A Perfect Murder '98
On Wings of Eagles '86
Sylvester '85
Naked Kiss '64
Shock Corridor '63
Sergeant Rutledge '60
The Horse Soldiers '59
Tom Towles (1950-)
The Devil's Rejects '05
House of 1000 Corpses '03
Mercenary 2: Thick and Thin '97
Gridlock'd '96
Normal Life '96
Girls in Prison '94
Blood in ... Blood Out: Bound by Honor '93
Mad Dog and Glory '93
The Pit & the Pendulum '91
Henry: Portrait of a Serial Killer '90
Night of the Living Dead '90
The Borrower '89
Aline Towne (1929-96)
Trader Tom of the China Seas '54
Radar Men from the Moon '52
Zombies of the Stratosphere '52
Don Daredevil Rides Again '51
The Invisible Monster '50
The Vanishing Westerner '50
Katharine Towne (1978-)
Something New '06
Lethal Dose '03
Evolution '01
Mulholland Drive '01
Sol Goode '01
Town and Country '01
What Lies Beneath '00
Robert Towne (1936-)
The Pick-Up Artist '87
Villa Rides '68
Jill Townsend (1945-)
The Awakening '80
Oh, Alfie '75
Poldark 2 '75
Poldark '86
The Golden Bowl '72
Patrice Townsend
Always '85
Sitting Ducks '80
Robert Kevin Townsend (1957-)
Love Songs '99
The Taxman '98
Mercenary 2: Thick and Thin '97
The Meteor Man '93
The Five Heartbeats '91
That's Adequate '90
The Mighty Quinn '89
I'm Gonna Git You Sucka '88
Hollywood Shuffle '87
Ratboy '86
American Flyers '85
Odd Jobs '85
A Soldier's Story '84
Streets of Fire '84
Stanley Townsend
The Nativity Story '06
Wondrous Oblivion '06
Stuart Townsend (1972-)
Chaos Theory '08
Head in the Clouds '04
The League of Extraordinary Gentlemen '03
Shade '03
Queen of the Damned '02
Trapped '02
About Adam '00
Wonderland '99
Shooting Fish '98
Resurrection Man '97
Under the Skin '97
Trojan Eddie '96

Pete Townshend (1945-)
The Secret Policeman's Other Ball '82
Secret Policeman's Private Parts '81
Tommy '75
The Kids Are Alright '79

Etsushi Toyokawa (1962-)
No Way Back '96
When I Close My Eyes '95

Fausto Tozzi (1921-78)
Street War '76
Escape from Death Row '73
Sicilian Connection '72
Knives of the Avenger '65
The Return of Dr. Mabuse '61
East of Kilimanjaro '57

Giorgio Tozzi (1923-)
Torn Between Two Lovers '79
South Pacific '58 (V)
The Comrades of Summer '92

Ian Tracey (1964-)
Civic Duty '06
Call Me: The Rise and Fall of Heidi Fleiss '04
Ice Men '04
Emile '03
Owning Mahowny '03
Liberty Stands Still '02
Rupert's Land '98
Bloodhounds 2 '96
Man with a Gun '95
Incident at Deception Ridge '94
Timecop '94
The Comrades of Summer '92

Jeff Trachta (1960-)
Poison '01
Interlocked '98
Night Eyes 4: Fatal Passion '95

Michelle Trachtenberg (1985-)
Kickin' It Old Skool '07
Black Christmas '06
Ice Princess '05
Eurotrip '04
Mysterious Skin '04
Forever Together '00
Inspector Gadget '99
Harriet the Spy '96

Keegan Connor Tracy (1971-)
The Net 2.0 '06
Final Destination 2 '03
Blackwoods '02
Beat '00
Wrestling with Alligators '98

Lee Tracy (1898-1968)
The Best Man '64
Betrayal from the East '44
The Payoff '43
Bombshell '33
Dinner at Eight '33
Blessed Event '32
Doctor X '32
The Half Naked Truth '32
The Strange Love of Molly Louvain '32

Spencer Tracy (1900-67)
Guess Who's Coming to Dinner '67
How the West Was Won '63
It's a Mad, Mad, Mad, Mad World '63
The Devil at 4 O'Clock '61
Judgment at Nuremberg '61
Inherit the Wind '60
Last Hurrah '58
The Old Man and the Sea '58
Desk Set '57
Bad Day at Black Rock '54
Broken Lance '54
Pat and Mike '52
Father's Little Dividend '51
Adam's Rib '50
Father of the Bride '50
Malaya '49
State of the Union '48
Cass Timberlane '47
Without Love '45
A Guy Named Joe '44
Woman of the Year '42
Tortilla Flat '42
Keeper of the Flame '42
Boom Town '40
Northwest Passage '40
Edison the Man '40
Stanley and Livingstone '39
Boys Town '38
Test Pilot '38
Captains Courageous '37
Mannequin '37
Fury '36
Libeled Lady '36
San Francisco '36
Riff Raff '35
Marie Galante '34
Up the River '30

William Tracy (1917-67)
Mr. Walkie Talkie '52
As You Were '51
George Washington Slept Here '42
To the Shores of Tripoli '42
Tanks a Million '41
Strike Up the Band '40

Mary Ellen Trainor (1950-)
Amy's O '02
Anywhere But Here '99
Lethal Weapon 4 '98
Hope '97
Executive Decision '96
Congo '95
Forrest Gump '94
Greedy '94
Little Giants '94
Death Becomes Her '92
Lethal Weapon 3 '92
Grand Canyon '91
Ricochet '91
Die Hard '88
Scrooged '88
Action Jackson '88
The Monster Squad '87
Fire Birds '90
Ghostbusters 2 '89
Tales from the Crypt '89
Lethal Weapon 2 '89
The Goonies '85
Romancing the Stone '84
The Stone Boy '84

Sam Trammell (1971-)
Aliens vs. Predator: Requiem '07
Anonymous Rex '04
Undermind '03

Steve Tracy (1952-86)
Desperate Moves '86
Beneath the Valley of the Ultra-Vixens '79

Henry Travers (1874-1965)
It's a Wonderful Life '46
The Yearling '46
The Bells of St. Mary's '45
The Naughty Nineties '45
Thrill of a Romance '45
Dragon Seed '44
Madame Curie '43
Shadow of a Doubt '43
Mrs. Miniver '42
Random Harvest '42
Ball of Fire '41
High Sierra '41
A Girl, a Guy and a Gob '41
Edison the Man '40
Primrose Path '40
Dark Victory '39
Dodge City '39
On Borrowed Time '39
Stanley and Livingstone '39
The Rains Came '39
The Sisters '38
The Invisible Man '33

Linden Travers (1913-2001)
Beware of Pity '46
The Lady Vanishes '38

Susan Travers
The Terror '38

June Travis (1914-)
The Snake Woman '51
Monster a Go-Go! '65

Nancy Travis (1961-)
The Jane Austen Book Club '07
Sisterhood of the Traveling Pants '05
Stephen King's Rose Red '02
Eyes of the Beholder '92

Bill Travers (1922-94)
The First Olympics: Athens 1896 '84
Christian the Lion '76
The Million Dollar Duck '71
An Elephant Called Slowly '69
Ring of Bright Water '69
Born Free '66
Duel at Diablo '66
Gorgo '61
The Smallest Show on Earth '57
Bhowani Junction '56
Romeo and Juliet '54
The Browning Version '51

Randy Travis (1959-)
The Long Ride Home '01
Texas Rangers '01
John John in the Sky '00
Three Men and a Little Dream '00
White River '99
Black Dog '98
T.N.T. '98
Boys Will Be Boys '97
Fire Down Below '97
John Grisham's The Rainmaker '97
The Shooter '97
Frank and Jesse '94
Texas '94
Dead Man's Revenge '93

Richard Travis (1913-89)
Missile to the Moon '59
The Girl in the Red Velvet Swing '55
Mesa of Lost Women '52
Danger Zone '51
Sky Liner '49
Big Town After Dark '47
Dive Bomber '41
The Man Who Came to Dinner '41

Stacey Travis
Venom '05
Soul Plane '04
Intolerable Cruelty '03
Two Days '03
Bandits '01
Ghost World '01
Heartbreakers '01
Sleep Easy, Hutch Rimes '00
Submerged '00
Traffic '00
What Planet Are You From? '00
The Muse '99
Mystery Men '99
Playing God '96
Suspect Device '95
National Lampoon's Attack of the 5 Ft. 2 Women '94
Caroline at Midnight '93
Dracula Rising '93
Only the Strong '93
The Super '91
Hardware '90

Susan Traylor
Broken Vessels '98
She's So Lovely '97
Bastard out of Carolina '96
To Die For '95
The New Age '94
Sleep with Me '94

Joel Thomas Traywick
Nightown '96
Conversation '02
Empire '02

Tony Travis
Flesh Gordon 2: Flesh Gordon Meets the Cosmic Cheerleaders '90
The Beatniks '60

Joey Travolta (1952-)
The Basket '99
Detour '99
DaVinci's War '92
Wilding '90
American Born '89
Ghost Writer '89
Sinners '89

Ellen Travolta (1940-)
Chaplin '92
Pressed Away '92
Air America '90
Infernal Affairs '90

Arthur Treacher (1894-1975)
Delightfully Dangerous '45
National Velvet '44
The Amazing Mrs. Holliday '43
Star Spangled Rhythm '42
The Little Princess '39
Mad About Music '38
My Lucky Star '38
Heidi '37
Thin Ice '37
Satan Met a Lady '36
Stowaway '36
Curly Top '35
David Copperfield '35
I Live My Life '35
A Midsummer Night's Dream '35
Splendor '35
Hollywood Party '34

Emerson Treacy (1900-67)
A Star Is Born '54

John Travolta (1954-)
Hairspray '07
Wild Hogs '07
Lonely Hearts '06
Be Cool '05
A Love Song for Bobby Long '04
The Punisher '04
Basic '03
Austin Powers in Goldmember '02
Domestic Disturbance '01
Swordfish '01
Battlefield Earth '00
Lucky Numbers '00
The General's Daughter '99
A Civil Action '98
Primary Colors '98
Mad City '97
She's So Lovely '97
Face/Off '97
Michael '96
Phenomenon '96
Broken Arrow '95
Get Shorty '95
White Man's Burden '95
Pulp Fiction '94
Look Who's Talking Now '93
Boris and Natasha: The Movie '92
Chains of Gold '92
Eyes of an Angel '91
Shout '91
Look Who's Talking Too '90
The Experts '89
Look Who's Talking '89
Dumb Waiter '87
Perfect '85
Staying Alive '83
Two of a Kind '83
Blow Out '81
Urban Cowboy '80
Grease '78
Saturday Night Fever '77
Carrie '76
The Boy in the Plastic Bubble '76
Devil's Rain '75

Treach (1970-)
Sub Down '97
Nighttown '96
The New Age '94

Traywick

Joel Thomas Traywick

Yann Trégouet (1975-)
Artemisia '97
Trois Couleurs: Bleu '93

Guy Tréjan (1921-2001)
I Married a Dead Man '82
The Beast '75

Danny Trejo (1944-)
Delta Farce '07
Halloween '07
Urban Justice '07
Danny Roane: First Time Director '06
Sherrybaby '05
Slayer '05
All Souls Day '05
Chasing Ghosts '05
The Crow: Wicked Prayer '05
The Devil's Rejects '05
Lost '05
Anchorman: The Legend of Ron Burgundy '04
Once Upon a Time in Mexico '03
Spy Kids 3-D: Game Over '03
Nightstalker '02
The Salton Sea '02

Michael Treanor
Brothers of the Head '06
3 Ninjas Knuckle Up '95
3 Ninjas '92

Harry Treadway
Control '07
Brothers of the Head '06

John Travolta (1954-) (cont.)
Prowler '51
Give Me a Sailor '38
Champagne for Breakfast '35

Terri Treas (1959-)
Lady Killer '97
Alien Nation: Millennium '96
Alien Nation: The Enemy Within '96
Alien Nation: Body and Soul '95
Yankee Zulu '95
Alien Nation: Dark Horizon '94
Alien Nation '89
House 4: Home Deadly Home '91
Deathstalker 3 '89
The Nest '88
The Terror Within '88
Frankenstein Unbound '90

Robert Trebor (1953-)
Jiminy Glick in LaLa Wood '05
Raise Your Voice '04
Hercules the Legendary Journeys, Vol. 2: The Lost Kingdom '94
52 Pick-Up '86
Out of the Darkness '85

David Tree (1915-)
Home for Christmas '93
Pygmalion '38
Drums '38

Mary Treen (1907-89)
Mystery of Mr. Wong '39

Dorothy Tree (1906-92)
Paradise, Hawaiian Style '66
I Married a Monster from Outer Space '58
The Sad Sack '57
Clipped Wings '53
It's a Wonderful Life '46
Casanova Brown '44
Hands Across the Border '43
Charlie Chan in City of Darkness '39
Abe Lincoln in Illinois '40
Hitler: Dead or Alive '43

Helen Traubel (1899-1972)
Deep in My Heart '54
The Ladies Man '61

Daniel J. Travanti (1940-)
Weep No More My Lady '93
Megaville '91
Tagget '90
Fellow Traveler '89
Millennium '89
Murrow '86
Aurora '84
Adam '83
A Case of Libel '83
Midnight Crossing '87
St. Ives '76
Eight Men Out '88
Married to the Mob '88
Three Men and a Baby '87
Harem '86
Lady '90
Long '04

Cordula Trantow
The Castle '68
Hitler '62

Silvano Tranquilli (1925-97)
Castle of Blood '64
The Horrible Dr. Hichcock '62

Billinger C. Tran
We Were Soldiers '02
Green Dragon '01

Kylie Travis (1970-)
Gia '98
Sanctuary '98
Retroactive '97

Rosie: The Rosemary Clooney Story '82
Car Crash '80
Sunnyside '79

Trejo

Trejo *(continued)*

Spy Kids 2: The Island of Lost Dreams '02
13 Moons '02
XXX '02
Bubble Boy '01
Spy Kids '01
Animal Factory '00
Reindeer Games '00
Desert Heat '99
From Dusk Till Dawn 3: The Hangman's Daughter '99
Soundman '99
From Dusk Till Dawn 2: Texas Blood Money '98
Point Blank '98
The Replacement Killers '98
Six Days, Seven Nights '98
Con Air '97
Dilemma '97
Los Locos Posse '97
Anaconda '96
From Dusk Till Dawn '95
Undercover Cop '94

Christine Tremarco (1977-)
Five Days '07
Under the Skin '97
Priest '94

Les Tremayne (1913-2003)
Fangs '75
Creature of Destruction '67
King Kong vs. Godzilla '63 (N)
The Slime People '63
The Gallant Hours '60
The Angry Red Planet '59
The Monolith Monsters '57
The Monster of Piedras Blancas '57
Forbidden Planet '56 (N)
A Man Called Peter '55
I Love Melvin '53
The War of the Worlds '53
Francis Goes to West Point '52

Johanne-Marie Tremblay (1950-)
The Barbarian Invasions '03

Ivan Triesault (1898-1980)
Jesus of Montreal '89
Straight from the Heart '88

Ken Tremblett (1965-)
The Guilty '99
Tourist Trap '99

Anne Tremko
The Member of the Wedding '97
My Antonia '94

Adam Trese (1969-)
2B Perfectly Honest '04
40 Days and 40 Nights '02
Cowboys and Angels '00
Polish Wedding '97
Illtown '96
The Underneath '95
The Good Fight '92
Laws of Gravity '92

Frederick Treves (1925-)
A Certain Justice '99
Shameless '94
Paper Mask '91
Flame to the Phoenix '85
Charlie Muffin '79

Leonardo Treviglio
Stealing Beauty '96
Sebastiane '79

Roger Treville (1902-2005)
Mr. Peek-A-Boo '50

Vic Trevino
Firehawk '92
Born in East L.A. '87

Austin Trevor (1897-1978)
Abandon Ship '57
Night Train to Munich '40

Jerry Trimble (1963-)
Stranglehold '94
Full Contact '93
One Man Army '93
Breathing Fire '91

Jasmine Trinca (1981-)
Best of Youth '03
The Son's Room '00

Jean-Louis Trintignant (1930-)
Those Who Love Me Can Take the Train '98
The City of Lost Children '95 (V)
Fiesta '95
A Self-Made Hero '95
Trois Couleurs: Rouge '94
A Man and a Woman: 20 Years Later '86
Rendez-vous '85
Next Summer '84
Confidentially Yours '83
I Love All of You '83
Under Fire '83
La Nuit de Varennes '82
Passion of Love '82
Il Sorpasso '63
Journey Beneath the Desert '61
Dangerous Liaisons '60
And God Created Woman '57

Marie Trintignant (1962-2003)
Harrison's Flowers '02
Portraits Chinois '96
Ponette '95
Alberto Express '92
Betty '92
The Story of Women '88
Next Summer '84

Louis Tripp (1974-)
Gate 2 '92
The Gate '87

Jeanne Tripplehorn (1963-)
The Moguls '05
Brother's Keeper '02
Swept Away '02
Steal This Movie! '00
Time Code '00
Mickey Blue Eyes '99
Relative Values '99
Monument Ave. '98
Very Bad Things '98
Sliding Doors '97
William Faulkner's Old Man '97
Til There Was You '96
Waterworld '95
Reality Bites '94
The Firm '93
The Night We Never Met '93
Basic Instinct '92

Jan Triska (1936-)
Up and Down '04
The Omega Code '99
Ronin '98
Apt Pupil '97
The People vs. Larry Flynt '96
Andersonville '95
My Antonia '94
World War II: When Lions Roared '94
The Elementary School '91

Elisabeth Trissenaar (1944-)
Angry Harvest '85
A Love in Germany '84
Berlin Alexanderplatz '80
In a Year of 13 Moons '78
The Stationmaster's Wife '77

Dorothy Tristan (1942-)
Down and Out in Beverly Hills '86
Griffin and Phoenix: A Love Story '76
Scarecrow '73
End of the Road '70

Travis Tritt (1963-)
Outlaw Justice '98
The Cowboy Way '94
Rio Diablo '93

Massimo Troisi (1953-94)
The Postman '94
Hotel Colonial '88

Margot Trooger
Pippi Goes on Board '69
Pippi Longstocking '69

Kate Trotter
Beyond Borders '03
Clarence '90

Laura Trotter (1950-)
Miami Horror '87
Rush '84
City of the Walking Dead '80

David Droughton (1950-)
All the King's Men '99
Cider with Rosie '99
Sharpe's Eagle '93
Sharpe's Rifles '93
Dance with a Stranger '85
The Norman Conquests, Part 1: Table Manners '78
The Norman Conquests, Part 2: Living Together '78
The Norman Conquests, Part 3: Round and Round the Garden '78

Michael Troughton (1955-)
Speedy Death '99
Testament of Youth '79

Patrick Troughton (1920-87)
The Omen '76
Frankenstein and the Monster from Hell '74
The Scars of Dracula '70
The Viking Queen '67
The Gorgon '64
The Moonraker '58
The Franchise Affair '52

Sam Troughton (1977-)
Alien vs. Predator '04
Sylvia '03

Tom Troupe (1928-)
My Own Private Idaho '91
Kelly's Heroes '70
The Devil's Brigade '68

Charles Trowbridge (1882-1967)
Shoot to Kill '47
Tycoon '47
Colonel Effingham's Raid '45
They Were Expendable '45
Fighting Seabees '44
Wake Island '42
Sergeant York '41
The Fatal Hour '40
The Fighting 69th '40
Johnny Apollo '40
The Mummy's Hand '40
Mysterious Doctor Satan '40
Gang Bullets '38
Sea Racketeers '37
Libeled Lady '36

Phillip Troy (1964-)
Ice '93
To Be the Best '93

Verne Troyer (1969-)
The Love Guru '08
Austin Powers in Goldmember '02
Bubble Boy '01
Hard Cash '01
Austin Powers 2: The Spy Who Shagged Me '99

Michael Trubshawe (1905-85)
Bedazzled '68
The Guns of Navarone '61

Michael Trucco (1970-)
Next '07
Wishmaster 4: The Prophecy Fulfilled '02
A Girl, 3 Guys and a Gun '01

Isabelle Truchon
Deadbolt '92
Backstab '90

John Trudell (1946-)
Smoke Signals '98
Thunderheart '92

Rachel True (1966-)
The Perfect Holiday '07
New Best Friend '02
Groove '00
Love Song '00
Half-Baked '97
The Craft '96
Nowhere '96
Embrace of the Vampire '95

Jim True-Frost (1966-)
Off the Map '03
Affliction '97
Far Harbor '96
Normal Life '96
Singles '92

Ernest Truex (1890-1973)
All Mine to Give '56
Club Havana '46
Twin Beds '42
His Girl Friday '40

Francois Truffaut (1932-84)
The Adventures of Marco Polo '38
The Green Room '78
Close Encounters of the Third Kind '77
Small Change '76
Day for Night '73
The Wild Child '70
The 400 Blows '59

Raoul Trujillo (1955-)
Tin Man '07
Apocalypto '06
The New World '05
Frankenfish '04
The Invaders '95
Black Fox: Blood Horse '94
Black Fox: The Price of Peace '94
Medicine River '94
Paris, France '94
The Adjuster '91
Scanners 2: The New Order '91

Ralph Truman (1900-77)
The Spaniard's Curse '58
The Man Who Knew Too Much '56
Treasure Island '50
Beware of Pity '46
Henry V '44
Butler's Dilemma '43
The Challenge '38
The Silent Passenger '35

Donald Trump (1946-)
Celebrity '98
Home Alone 2: Lost in New York '92

Natalie Trundy (1940-)
Huckleberry Finn '74
Battle for the Planet of the Apes '73
Conquest of the Planet of the Apes '72
Escape from the Planet of the Apes '71
Beneath the Planet of the Apes '70

Glenn Tryon (1894-1970)
Tangled Destinies '32
Dames Ahoy '30
Battling Orioles '24

Tom Tryon (1926-91)
Color Me Dead '69
In Harm's Way '65
The Cardinal '63
The Longest Day '62
Moon Pilot '62
Texas John Slaughter: Stampede at Bitter Creek '62
Geronimo's Revenge '60
The Story of Ruth '60
Texas John Slaughter: Geronimo's Revenge '60
I Married a Monster from Outer Space '58
Three Violent People '57
Unholy Wife '57

Eric Tsang (1953-)
Infernal Affairs '02
The Accidental Spy '01
Supercop 2 '93

Kenneth Tsang (1938-)
Memoirs of a Geisha '05
Die Another Day '02
Rush Hour 2 '01
The Replacement Killers '98
Supercop '92
The Killer '90
Once a Thief '90

Nicholas Tse (1980-)
The Promise '05
New Police Story '04
Time and Tide '00
Gen-X Cops '99

Lyudmila Tselikovskaya (1919-92)
Ivan the Terrible, Part 2 '46
Ivan the Terrible, Part 1 '44

Nikolai Tseretelli
Aelita: Queen of Mars '24
The Cigarette Girl of Mosselprom '24

Yee Jee Tso
Antitrust '00
Doctor Who '96

Irene Tsu (1910-89)
The Green Berets '68
Island of the Lost '68
Caprice '67
Paradise, Hawaiian Style '66
Women of the Prehistoric Planet '66
How to Stuff a Wild Bikini '65

Yoshio Tsuchiya (1927-)
Destroy All Monsters '68
Godzilla vs. Monster Zero '68
Red Beard '65
Attack of the Mushroom People '63
Yojimbo '61
Seven Samurai '54

Masahiko Tsugawa (1940-)
Heaven & Earth '90
A Taxing Woman's Return '88
The Sun's Burial '60

Shinya Tsukamoto (1960-)
Marebito '04
Tetsuo: The Iron Man '92

Gotaro Tsunashima (1973-)
The Great Raid '05
Japanese Story '03

Koji Tsurata (1924-87)
Sympathy for the Underdog '71
The Secret of the Telegian '61
Samurai 3: Duel at Ganryu Island '56

Barry Tubb (1963-)
Return to Lonesome Dove '93
Warm Summer Rain '89
Valentino Returns '88
Top Gun '86
Consenting Adult '85
Mask '85

William Tubbs (1907-53)
Wages of Fear '55
Paisan '46

Christine Tucci (1967-)
Big Fat Liar '02
K-911 '99

Maria Tucci (1941-)
To Die For '95
Touch and Go '86
Enormous Changes '83
Trumps '83

Michael Tucci (1950-)
The Man Who Captured Eichmann '96
Sunnyside '79
Grease '78

Stanley Tucci (1960-)
Space Chimps '08 (V)
Swing Vote '08
The Devil Wears Prada '06
Four Last Songs '06
The Hoax '06
Lucky Number Slevin '06
Robots '05 (V)
Shall We Dance? '04
Spin '04
The Terminal '04
Big Trouble '02
Maid in Manhattan '02
Road to Perdition '02
America's Sweethearts '01
Conspiracy '01
Sidewalks of New York '01
The Whole Shebang '01
Joe Gould's Secret '00
In Too Deep '99
William Shakespeare's A Midsummer Night's Dream '99
The Alarmist '98
The Imposters '98
Winchell '98
Deconstructing Harry '97
The Eighteenth Angel '97
A Life Less Ordinary '97
Montana '97
The Daytrippers '96
Big Night '95
Jury Duty '95
Sex and the Other Man '95
It Could Happen to You '94
Kiss of Death '94
A Modern Affair '94
Somebody to Love '94
The Pelican Brief '93
Undercover Blues '93
Beethoven '92
In the Soup '92
Prelude to a Kiss '92
The Public Eye '92
Billy Bathgate '91
Men of Respect '91
Quick Change '90
Fear, Anxiety and Depression '89
Slaves of New York '89
Monkey Shines '88

Jessica Tuck (1963-)
Secretary '02
Billboard Dad '98
The Garbage-Picking, Field Goal-Kicking Philadelphia Phenomenon '98
Batman Forever '95
The O.J. Simpson Story '94

Revenge of the Nerds 4: Nerds in Love '94
Lifepod '93
Mr. Write '92

Chris Tucker (1972-)
Rush Hour 3 '07
Rush Hour 2 '01
The Fifth Element '97
Jackie Brown '97
Money Talks '97
Friday '95
Dead Presidents '95
House Party 3 '94

Forrest Tucker (1919-86)
Timestalkers '87
Thunder Run '86
A Real American Hero '78
The Incredible Rocky Mountain Race '77
Wackiest Wagon Train in the West '77
Final Chapter: Walking Tall '77
The Rebels '79
The Abominable Snowman '57
Chisum '70
Auntie Mame '58
The Cosmic Monsters '58
The Crawling Eye '58
Three Violent People '57
The Finger Man '55
Rage at Dawn '55
Jubilee Trail '54
Trouble in the Glen '54
Pony Express '53
Bugles in the Afternoon '52
Montana Belle '52
The Nevadan '50
The Big Cat '49
Hellfire '49
Sands of Iwo Jima '49
Coroner Creek '48
Never Say Goodbye '46
The Yearling '46
Keeper of the Flame '42
Robot Pilot '41
The Westerner '40

Jonathan Tucker (1982-)
The Ruins '08
Cherry Crush '07
In the Valley of Elah '07
Pulse '06
Hostage '05
Criminal '04
Stateside '04
The Texas Chainsaw Massacre '03
The Deep End '01
100 Girls '00
The Virgin Suicides '99
Sleepers '96

Larry Tucker (1933-2001)

Michael Tucker (1944-)
D2: The Mighty Ducks '94
For Love or Money '93
Checking Out '89
Day One '89
Spy '89
Assault and Matrimony '87
Radio Days '87
Tin Men '87
L.A. Law '86
Diner '82

The Purple Rose of Cairo '85

Martin Tucker
Death Screams '83
House of Death '82

Tommy Tune (1939-)
The Boy Friend '71
Hello, Dolly! '69

Bill Tung (1933-2006)
Jackie Chan's First Strike '96
Rumble in the Bronx '95
Police Story '85

Tamara Tunie (1959-)
The Caveman's Valentine '01
Deep Cover '92

Richard Tucker (1884-1942)
Convicted '32
Delinquent Parents '38
Rebound: The Legend of Earl "The Goat" Manigault '96
The Bat Whispers '30
King of the Kongo '29
Captain Swagger '25
The Worldly Madonna '22

Rocky Tucker
The Craft '96
Steps from Hell '92
Lunatic '91

Sophie Tucker (1884-1966)
Sensations of 1945 '44
Broadway Melody of 1938 '37
Thoroughbreds Don't Cry '37

Tanya Tucker (1958-)
Hard Country '81
Follow That Car '80
The Rebels '79

Alan Tudyk (1971-)
Death at a Funeral '07
Knocked Up '07
3:10 to Yuma '07
Ice Age: The Meltdown '06 (V)
Serenity '05
Dodgeball: A True Underdog Story '04
Ice Age '02 (V)
Hearts in Atlantis '01
A Knight's Tale '01
28 Days '00
Patch Adams '98

Sonny Tufts (1911-70)
Easy Come, Easy Go '67
The Seven Year Itch '55
Serpent Island '54
So Proudly We Hail '43
Here Come the Waves '45
Cat Women of the Moon '53
The Gift Horse '52
Easy Living '49
The Virginian '46

Ulrich Tukur (1957-)
The Lives of Others '06
Amen '02
Taking Sides '01
My Mother's Courage '95

Patricia Tulasne (1959-)
The Savage Woman '91

Tom Tully (1908-82)
Coogan's Bluff '68
McHale's Navy Joins the Air Force '65
Ten North Frederick '58
Love Me or Leave Me '55
Soldier of Fortune '55
The Caine Mutiny '54
The Moon Is Blue '53
Trouble along the Way '53
Love Is Better Than Ever '52
Texas Carnival '51
Tomahawk '51
June Bride '48
Lady in the Lake '46
Till the End of Time '46
The Virginian '46
Destination Tokyo '43
Northern Pursuit '43

Frans Tumbuan
Without Mercy '95
Rage and Honor 2: Hostile Takeover '93

Glynn Turman (1946-)
Sahara '05
Freedom Song '00
Men of Honor '00
The Visit '00
Light It Up '99
Subterfuge '98
Buffalo Soldiers '97
Rebound: The Legend of Earl "The Goat" Manigault '96
Race to Freedom: The Story of the Underground Railroad '94

Eyes of Laura Mars '78

Robin Tunney (1972-)
Hollywoodland '06
The Zodiac '05
Paparazzi '04
The In-Laws '03
Cherish '02
The Secret Lives of Dentists '02
Intimate Affairs '01
Vertical Limit '00
End of Days '99
Supernova '99
Naked City: Justice with a Bullet '98

James Tupper
Love's Long Journey '05

Robert Turano
Federal Hill '94
The Pompatus of Love '95

Paige Turco (1965-)
Invincible '06
Astoria '00
Dead Dog '00
Urbania '00
November Conspiracy '96
The Feminine Touch '95
Dead Funny '94
Vibrations '94
Teenage Mutant Ninja Turtles 3 '93
Teenage Mutant Ninja Turtles 2: The Secret of the Ooze '91

Paolo Turco
Bread and Chocolate '73

Ann Turkel (1942-)
The Lickerish Quartet '70
The Fear '94
Deep Space '87
The Last Contract '86
Death Ray '80
Humanoids from the Deep '80
99 & 44/100 Dead '74
Paper Lion '69

Joe Turkel (1927-)
Blade Runner '82
The Shining '80
Cycle Psycho '70
The Sand Pebbles '66
King Rat '65
Village of the Giants '65
Paths of Glory '57
The Killing '56

John Turner (1932-)
The Slipper and the Rose '76

Kathleen Turner (1954-)
Monster House '06 (V)
Beautiful '00
Prince of Central Park '00
Love and Action in Chicago '99
The Virgin Suicides '99
Baby Geniuses '98
Legalese '98
The Real Blonde '97
A Simple Wish '97
Moonlight and Valentino '95
Serial Mom '94
Naked in New York '94
Undercover Blues '93
House of Cards '92
V.I. Warshawski '91

Snake Eyes '98
The Devil's Advocate '97
Eve's Bayou '97 (V)

John Turturro (...)
Charlotte Forten's Mission '85
Experiment in Freedom '85

Robert Turano

Florence Turner (1885-1946)
Walking Back '26

George Turner (1902-68)
Son of Zorro '47
Vigilantes of Boom Town '46

Guinevere Turner (1968-)
Go Fish '94

Janine Turner (1963-)
Miracle Dogs Too '06
Dr. T & the Women '00
Fatal Error '99
Leave It to Beaver '97
Cliffhanger '93
The Ambulance '90
Monkey Shines '88
Steel Magnolias '89
Knights of the City '85
Young Doctors in Love '82

Jim Turner
Bewitched '05
Off the Lip '04
Joe's Apartment '96
The Ref '93
My Samurai '92
Kid Colter '85

Elizabeth Turner
Cannibal Apocalypse '80

Tina Turner (1939-)
Mad Max: Beyond Thunderdome '85
Tommy '75
Gimme Shelter '70

Tyrin Turner (1971-)
Belly '98
Menace II Society '93

Zara Turner (1968-)
Resurrection Man '97
Sliding Doors '97
The Waiting Time '99

Ben Turpin (1874-1940)
Saps at Sea '40
Law of the Wild '34
Yankee Doodle in Berlin '19
Burlesque on Carmen '16

Kett Turton (1982-)
Firewall '06
Show Me '04
Heart of America '03
Gypsy 83 '01

Aida Turturro (1962-)
Romance & Cigarettes '05
2B Perfectly Honest '04
Crocodile Dundee in Los Angeles '01
Sidewalks of New York '01
Bringing Out the Dead '99
Deep Blue Sea '99
Hitman's Journal '99
The 24 Hour Woman '99
24 Nights '99
Celebrity '98
Illuminata '98
Sleepers '96

Honey, I Shrunk the Kids '89 (V)
The War of the Roses '89
The Accidental Tourist '88
Switching Channels '88
Who Framed Roger Rabbit '88 (V)
Crimes of Passion '84
A Breed Apart '84
Romancing the Stone '84
The Man with Two Brains '83
Body Heat '81

Lana Turner (1920-95)
Witches' Brew '79
Bittersweet Love '75
The Graveyard '74
Bachelor in Paradise '69
Love Has Many Faces '65
Who's Got the Action? '63
By Love Possessed '61
Portrait in Black '60
Imitation of Life '59
Another Time, Another Place '58
Peyton Place '57
Diane '55
The Prodigal '55
Sea Chase '55
The Bad and the Beautiful '52

John Turnbull (1880-1956)
The Happiest Days of Your Life '50
Nine Days a Queen '36
The Passing of the Third Floor Back '36
The 39 Steps '35
Man of Evil '48
Make-Up '37

Bree Turner (1977-)
Firehouse Dog '06
Just My Luck '06
Bring It On Again '03
The Private Life of Henry VIII '33

Florence Turner
Truck Stop

Ted Turner (1938-)
Gods and Generals '03
Gettysburg '93

Tyrin Turner

Zara Turner

Ben Turpin

Penitentiary 2 '82
Centennial '78
A Hero Ain't Nothin' but a Sandwich '78
Prizzi's Honor '85
The Blue Knight '75
Cooley High '75
Romancing the Stone '84

The Merry Widow '52
A Life of Her Own '50
Homecoming '48
The Three Musketeers '48
Cass Timberlane '47
Green Dolphin Street '47
The Postman Always Rings Twice '46
Weekend at the Waldorf '45
Ziegfeld Girl '41
Honky Tonk '41
Johnny Eager '42
Somewhere I'll Find You '42
Dr. Jekyll and Mr. Hyde '41
They Won't Forget '37
Love Finds Andy Hardy '38
Latin Lovers '53
Betrayed '54
The Three Musketeers '48

[John Turturro cont.]
Denise Calls Up '95
Money Train '95
Angie '94
Junior '94
Tales of Erotica '93
Jersey Girl '92
True Love '89

John Turturro (1957-)
You Don't Mess with the Zohan '08
The Bronx Is Burning '07
Margot at the Wedding '07
Slipstream '07
Transformers '07
A Few Days in September '06
The Good Shepherd '06
Secret Window '04
She Hate Me '04
2B Perfectly Honest '04
Anger Management '03
Fear X '03
Collateral Damage '02
Mr. Deeds '02
Monday Night Mayhem '02
Monkeybone '01 (V)
Thirteen Conversations About One Thing '01
Company Man '00
The Luzhin Defence '00
The Man Who Cried '00
O Brother Where Art Thou? '00
The Cradle Will Rock '99
He Got Game '98
Rounders '98
The Big Lebowski '97
Box of Moonlight '96
Girl 6 '96
Grace of My Heart '96
The Search for One-Eyed Jimmy '96
The Truce '96
Clockers '95
Sugartime '95
Unstrung Heroes '95
Being Human '94
Quiz Show '94
Search and Destroy '94
Fearless '93
Mac '93
Brain Donors '92
Barton Fink '91
Jungle Fever '91
Men of Respect '91
Miller's Crossing '90
Mo' Better Blues '90
State of Grace '90
Backtrack '89
Do the Right Thing '89
Five Corners '88
The Sicilian '87
The Color of Money '86
Hannah and Her Sisters '86
Off Beat '86
Desperately Seeking Susan '85
To Live & Die in L.A. '85
Gung Ho '85

Nicholas Turturro (1962-)
I Now Pronounce You Chuck and Larry '05
The Longest Yard '05
The Hillside Strangler '04
The Hollow '04
Big Shot: Confessions of a Campus Bookie '02
Monday Night Mayhem '02
Hellraiser 5: Inferno '00
Witness to the Mob '98
Mercenary 2: Thick and Thin '97
Excess Baggage '96
The Search for One-Eyed Jimmy '96
The Shadow Conspiracy '96
Cosmic Slop '94
Federal Hill '94
Mac '93
Jungle Fever '91
Mo' Better Blues '90

Rita Tushingham (1942-)
Being Julia '04
Swing '98
Under the Skin '97
An Awfully Big Adventure '94
Paper Marriage '93
The Housekeeper '86
Dream to Believe '85
Mysteries '84
Spaghetti House '82
Slaughterday '77
Green Eyes '76
The Human Factor '75
Rachel's Man '75
Dressed for Death '74
Loose in New York '74
Smashing Time '67
Trap '66
Doctor Zhivago '65
The Knack '65
Girl with Green Eyes '64
The Leather Boys '63
A Taste of Honey '61

Dorothy Tutin (1930-2001)
Alive and Kicking '96
Scarlett '94
Body & Soul '93
Shades of Fear '93
Agatha Christie's Murder with Mirrors '85
The Shooting Party '85
Sister Dora '77
Savage Messiah '72
Six Wives of Henry VIII '71
A Tale of Two Cities '58
The Importance of Being Earnest '52

Tracy Tutor
No Vacancy '99
Expose '97

Lurene Tuttle (1906-86)
Testament '83
White Mama '80
The Manitou '78
The Fortune Cookie '66
The Ghost and Mr. Chicken '66
Ma Barker's Killer Brood '60
The Glass Slipper '55
The Affairs of Dobie Gillis '53
Don't Bother to Knock '52
Niagara '52
Homecoming '48

Shannon Tweed (1957-)
Dead Sexy '01
The Rowdy Girls '00
Wish You Were Dead '00
Forbidden Sins '99
Naked Lies '98
Face the Evil '97
Human Desires '97
Indecent Dreams '94
Indecent Behavior 2 '94
Model by Day '94
Night Fire '94
No Contest '94
Vegas Vice '94
Victim of Desire '94
Cold Sweat '93
Indecent Behavior '93
Night Eyes 3 '93
Possessed by the Night '93
Scorned '93
Liar's Edge '92
Sexual Response '92
The Firing Line '91
Jungle Fever '91
Night Eyes 2 '91
Mo' Better Blues '90
Night Call '90
Cannibal Women in the Avocado Jungle of Death '89
In the Cold of the Night '89
Night Visitor '89
Twisted Justice '89
Lethal Woman '88
Surrogate '88
Codename: Vengeance '87
Meatballs 3 '87
The Last Fling '86
Hot Dog... The Movie! '83
Of Unknown Origin '83

Terry Tweed
Night Rhythms '92
The Reincarnate '71

Helen Twelvetrees (1907-58)
Panama Flo '32
Millie '31
Painted Desert '31
State's Attorney '31

Twiggy (1949-)
The Diamond Trap '91
Body Bags '93
Istanbul '90
Madame Sousatzka '88
Young Charlie Chaplin '88
Club Paradise '86
The Doctor and the Devils '85
The Blues Brothers '80
Butterfly Ball '76
W '74
The Boy Friend '71

Archie Twitchell (1906-57)
Kentucky Jubilee '51
Thundering Trail '51
Young Bill Hickok '40

Anne Twomey (1951-)
The Confession '98
Rear Window '98
Picture Perfect '96
The Scout '94
Orpheus Descending '91
Last Rites '88
Deadly Friend '86
Behind Enemy Lines '85

Alexandra Tydings (1972-)
Red Shoe Diaries 7: Burning Up '96
Sunchaser '96

Aisha Tyler (1970-)
Balls of Fury '07
Death Sentence '07
.45 '06
The Santa Clause 3: The Escape Clause '06
Never Die Alone '04
The Santa Clause 2 '02

Harry Tyler (1888-1961)
Bedtime for Bonzo '51
I Married a Witch '42
Pennies from Heaven '36

Liv Tyler (1977-)
The Incredible Hulk '08
Reign Over Me '07
Lonesome Jim '06
Jersey Girl '04
Lord of the Rings: The Return of the King '03
Lord of the Rings: The Two Towers '02
Lord of the Rings: The Fellowship of the Rings '01
One Night at McCool's '01
Dr. T & the Women '00
Cookie's Fortune '99
Onegin '99
Armageddon '98
Plunkett & Macleane '98
Inventing the Abbotts '97
U-Turn '97
Stealing Beauty '96
That Thing You Do! '96
Empire Records '95
Heavy '94
Silent Fall '94

Tom Tyler (1903-54)
Guns of Justice '50
Last Bullet '50
Outlaw Fury '50
Rangeland Empire '50
Riders of the Range '50
Sudden Death '50
Outlaw Gang '49
She Wore a Yellow Ribbon '49
Valley of the Sun '42
The Adventures of Captain Marvel '41
Riders of the Timberline '41
The Mummy's Hand '40
The Westerner '40
Stagecoach '39
Cheyenne Rides Again '38
The Phantom of the Range '38
Brothers of the West '37
Feud of the Trail '37
Riding On '37
Santa Fe Bound '37
Fast Bullets '36
Last Outlaw '36
Pinto Rustlers '36
Rip Roarin' Buckaroo '36
Roamin' Wild '36
Coyote Trails '35
Laramie Kid '35
Powdersmoke Range '35
Ridin' Thru '35
Rio Rattler '35
Silent Code '35
Silent Valley '35
The Silver Bullet '34
Deadwood Pass '33
Phantom of the Air '33
When a Man Rides Alone '33
The Forty-Niners '32
Battling with Buffalo Bill '31
Phantom of the West '31
Two Fisted Justice '31

Judy Tylor
What Love Is '07
My 5 Wives '00

George Tyne (1911-)
Sands of Iwo Jima '49
Call Northside 777 '48
Open Secret '48
A Walk in the Sun '46
Objective, Burma! '45

Charles Tyner (1925-)
Pulse '88
Planes, Trains & Automobiles '87
The Longest Yard '74
Emperor of the North Pole '73
Jeremiah Johnson '72
Harold and Maude '71
The Cheyenne Social Club '70
Cool Hand Luke '67

Tyrese
See Tyrese Gibson

Susan Tyrrell (1946-)
Buddy Boy '99
Relax... It's Just Sex! '98
The Demolitionist '95
Powder '95
Motorama '91
Cry-Baby '90
Rockula '90
Thompson's Last Run '90
Far from Home '89
Big Top Pee-wee '88
The Underachievers '88
Windmills of the Gods '88
The Offspring '87
Poker Alice '87
Avenging Angel '85
Flesh and Blood '85
Angel '84
Fire and Ice '83 (V)
Tales of Ordinary Madness '83
Fast Walking '82
Liar's Moon '82
Night Warning '82
Forbidden Zone '80
Lady of the House '78
Andy Warhol's Bad '77
Another Man, Another Chance '77
Islands in the Stream '77
September 30, 1955 '77
The Killer inside Me '76
Zandy's Bride '74
Fat City '72
Shoot Out '71

Fabiana Udenio (1964-)
The Godson '98
Austin Powers: International Man of Mystery '97
Bride of Re-Animator '89
Summer School '87
Hardbodies 2 '86

Claudia Udy (1960-)
Captive Rage '88
The Pink Chiquitas '86
Out of Control '85

Helene Udy (1962-)
Sweet Murder '93
The Hollywood Detective '89

Barbara Tyson (1964-)
K-9 3: P.I. '01
Beautiful Joe '00
Ratz '99
Resurrection '99
Baby Monitor: Sound of Fear '97

Cathy Tyson (1965-)
Band of Gold '95
Priest '94
The Lost Language of Cranes '92
Business As Usual '88
The Serpent and the Rainbow '87
Mona Lisa '86

Cicely Tyson (1933-)
Madea's Family Reunion '06
Because of Winn-Dixie '05
Diary of a Mad Black Woman '05
The Rosa Parks Story '02
Aftershock: Earthquake in New York '99
A Lesson Before Dying '99
Life '99
Always Outnumbered '98
Mama Flora's Family '98
Ms. Scrooge '97
Hoodlum '96
Riot in the Streets '96
The Road to Galveston '96
Oldest Confederate Widow Tells All '95
Duplicates '92
Fried Green Tomatoes '91
Heat Wave '90
The Kid Who Loved Christmas '90
The Women of Brewster Place '89
Acceptable Risks '86
Samaritan: The Mitch Snyder Story '86
Bustin' Loose '81
The Concorde: Airport '79 '79
A Hero Ain't Nothin' but a Sandwich '78
King '78
A Woman Called Moses '78
Roots '77
Wilma '77
The River Niger '76
The Autobiography of Miss Jane Pittman '74
Sounder '72
A Man Called Adam '66

Mike Tyson (1966-)
Crocodile Dundee in Los Angeles '01
Black and White '99

Pamela Tyson
Last Dance '96
What's Love Got to Do with It? '93
Jungle Fever '91

Richard Tyson (1961-)
Flight of the Living Dead: Outbreak on a Plane '07
Black Hawk Down '01
Firetrap '01
Battlefield Earth '00
Lethal Force '00
Operation Sandman: Warriors in Hell '00
Desert Thunder '99
Liar's Poker '99
Beneath the Bermuda Triangle '98
Tales of the Kama Sutra 2: Monsoon '98
There's Something about Mary '98
Monsoon '97
The Glass Cage '96
Kingpin '96
Pharoah's Army '93
Dark Tide '93
Red Shoe Diaries 3: Another Woman's Lipstick '93
The Babe '92
Kindergarten Cop '90
Two Moon Junction '88
Three o'Clock High '87

Galina Tyunina
Day Watch '06
Night Watch '04

Margaret Tyzack (1933-)
Match Point '05
Our Mutual Friend '98
Mrs. Dalloway '97
The King's Whore '90
Mr. Love '86
Quatermass Conclusion '79
2001: A Space Odyssey '68

Asher Tzarfati
Secret of Yolanda '82
Shell Shock '63

Alanna Ubach (1977-)
Waiting '05
Meet the Fockers '04
Legally Blonde 2: Red White & Blonde '03
Crazy Little Thing '02
Legally Blonde '01
Blue Moon '00
Clockwatchers '97
Trading Favors '97
Johns '96
Just Your Luck '96
Denise Calls Up '95
Freeway '95
Airborne '93
Pin... '88

Bob Uecker (1935-)
Major League 3: Back to the Minors '98
Homeward Bound 2: Lost in San Francisco '96 (V)
Major League 2 '94
Major League '89

Kichijiro Ueda (1904-72)
Gamera vs. Gaos '67
The Hidden Fortress '58
Seven Samurai '54
Rashomon '51

Misa(ko) Uehara (1937-)
Ju-On: The Grudge '03
I Bombed Pearl Harbor '60
Saga of the Vagabond '59
The Hidden Fortress '58

Kenjiro Uemura (1914-79)
The Human Condition: Road to Eternity '59
A Quiet Duel '49

Leslie Uggams (1943-)
Sugar Hill '94
Sizzle '81
Backstairs at the White House '79
Roots '77
Poor Pretty Eddie '73
Two Weeks in Another Town '62

Nadja Uhl (1972-)
What to Do in Case of Fire '02
The Legend of Rita '99

Gisela Uhlen (1919-2007)
Toto le Heros '91

The Marriage of Maria Braun '79
The Indian Scarf '53

Gaspard Ulliel (1984-)
Hannibal Rising '07
Paris, je t'aime '06
A Very Long Engagement '04
Strayed '03

Ricky Ullman
Adolescent Behavior '07
Havoc '05

Tracey Ullman (1961-)
I Could Never Be Your Woman '06
The Big Bad Swim '06
Tim Burton's Corpse Bride '05
A Dirty Shame '04
Panic '00
Small Time Crooks '00
Bullets over Broadway '94
Ready to Wear '94
I'll Do Anything '93
Robin Hood: Men in Tights '93
Give My Regards to Broad Street '84
Plenty '85

Liv Ullmann (1939-)
Saraband '03
Mindwalk: A Film for Passionate Thinkers '91
The Ox '91
The Rose Garden '89
Gaby: A True Story '87
The Bay Boy '85
Dangerous Moves '84
The Wild Duck '84
Richard's Things '80
Autumn Sonata '78
The Serpent's Egg '78
A Bridge Too Far '77
Face to Face '76
Leonor '75
Zandy's Bride '74
Forty Carats '73
The New Land '73
Scenes from a Marriage '73
Cries and Whispers '72
The Emigrants '72
Cold Sweat '71
The Night Visitor '70
The Passion of Anna '70
Hour of the Wolf '68
The Shame '68
Persona '66

Tristan Ulloa (1974-)
The 4 Musketeers '05
Sex and Lucia '01
Km. 0 '00

Lenore Ulric (1892-1970)
Northwest Outpost '47
Camille '36

Skeet Ulrich (1969-)
Chilly Dogs '01
Nobody's Baby '01
Soul Assassin '01
Chill Factor '99
A Soldier's Sweetheart '98
As Good As It Gets '97
The Newton Boys '97
Albino Alligator '96
The Craft '96
Last Dance '96
Touch '96
Ride with the Devil '95
Scream '95
Boys '95

Mikhail Ulyanov (1927-2007)
Private Life '82
The Theme '79

Margaret Umbers
Death Warmed Up '85
The Bridge to Nowhere '86

Mark Umbers (1973-)
These Foolish Things '06
A Good Woman '04

Miyoshi Umeki (1929-2007)
The Horizontal Lieutenant '62
Flower Drum Song '61
Sayonara '57

Yoko Umemura
The Story of the Late Chrysanthemum '39
Sisters of the Gion '36

Claudio Undari (1935-)
Bronson's Revenge '72
Fighting Fists of Shanghai Joe '73

Joe Unger
Leatherface: The Texas Chainsaw Massacre 3 '89

Edward Underdown (1908-89)
Go Tell the Spartans '78
Pattern for Plunder '62
Beat the Devil '53
The Shadow Man '53
Man on the Run '49

Blair Underwood (1964-)
The Hades Factor '06
Madea's Family Reunion '06
Something New '06
Malibu's Most Wanted '03
G '02
Rules of Engagement '00
Asunder '99
Deep Impact '98
Mama Flora's Family '98
Mistral '96
Set It Off '96
Soul of the Game '96
Just Cause '94
Dangerous Relations '93
Posse '93
Heat Wave '90
Krush Groove '85

Jay Underwood (1968-)
Dancing in September '00
Possums '99
The Nurse '97
The Sticky Fingers of Time '97
Sleepstalker: The Sandman's Last Rites '95
A Reason to Believe '95
The Raffle '94
Stalked '94
Wyatt Earp: Return to Tombstone '94
Where Eagles Dare '68
Not Quite Human 2 '89
Uncle Buck '89
The Gumshoe Kid '89
Kid Sister '89
Not Quite Human '87
Prom '88
The Invisible Kid '88
The Boy Who Could Fly '86
Desert Bloom '86

James Urbaniak (1963-)
Fay Grim '06
Fortunes '05
American Splendor '03
Henry Fool '98
The Sticky Fingers of Time '97
Stiff Upper Lips '96

Mary Ure (1933-75)
Where Eagles Dare '68
Custer of the West '67
The Luck of Ginger Coffey '64
Sons and Lovers '60
Look Back in Anger '58
Windom's Way '57

Minerva Urecal (1894-1966)
Niagara '52
Mr. Muggs Rides Again '45
Kid Sister '45
The Ape Man '43

Deborah Kara Unger (1966-)
88 Minutes '08
Lies & Alibis '06
Silent Hill '06
White Noise '05
A Love Song for Bobby Long '04
Between Strangers '02
Leo '02
Stander '03
Thirteen '03
Emile '03
Hollywood North '03
Fear X '03
The Salton Sea '02
Luminous Motion '00
Signs & Wonders '00
The Weekend '00
Sunshine '99
Payback '99
The Hurricane '99
The Game '97
Crash '96
No Way Home '96
Keys to Tulsa '96
Highlander: The Final Dimension '94
Hotel Room '93

Justin Urich
The Bronx War '90
Serial Killing 101 '04
Monster Man '03
Winter Break '02
The Rage: Carrie 2 '99

Fabio Urena
Return of the Living Dead 3 '93

Robert Urich (1946-2002)
The Lazarus Man '96
Captains Courageous '95
A Horse for Danny '95
Revolver '92
In a Stranger's Hand '92
Blind Man's Bluff '91
Hit Woman: The Double Edge '93
Spenser: Ceremony '93
Spenser: Pale Kings & Princes '94
Spenser: The Judas Goat '94
Spenser: A Savage Place '95
Turk 182! '85
Scandal Sheet '85
Ice Pirates '84
Invitation to Hell '84
Endangered Species '82
Take Your Best Shot '82
Killing at Hell's Gate '81
The Shadow Box '80
Vegas '78
Magnum Force '73

Karl Urban (1972-)
Comanche Moon '08
Pathfinder '07
Doom '05
The Bourne Supremacy '04
The Chronicles of Riddick '04
Lord of the Rings: The Return of the King '03
Ghost Ship '02
Lord of the Rings: The Two Towers '02
The Price of Milk '00

Gabrielle Union (1973-)
Meet Dave '08
The Box '07
Daddy's Little Girls '07
The Perfect Holiday '07
Running with Scissors '06
The Honeymooners '05
Say Uncle '05
Breakin' All the Rules '04
Bad Boys 2 '03
Cradle 2 tha Grave '03
Deliver Us from Eva '03
Abandon '02
Welcome to Collinwood '02
The Brothers '01
Two Can Play That Game '01
Bring It On '00
She's All That '99
Ten Things I Hate about You '99

Robert Urquhart (1922-95)
The Kitchen Toto '87
Playing Away '87
Children of the Full Moon '84
The Curse of Frankenstein '57

Benny "The Jet" Urquidez (1952-)
Grosse Pointe Blank '97
Bloodmatch '91
The Kick Fighter '91
Down the Drain '89

Peter Ustinov (1921-2004)
Luther '03
Victoria & Albert '01
Animal Farm '99
Alice in Wonderland '99
The Phoenix and the Magic Carpet '95
The Old Curiosity Shop '94
Lorenzo's Oil '92
Appointment with Death '88
Agatha Christie's Thirteen at Dinner '85
Evil under the Sun '82
Grendel, Grendel, Grendel '82
Charlie Chan and the Curse of the Dragon Queen '81
Death on the Nile '78
The Thief of Baghdad '78
The Last Remake of Beau Geste '77
The Purple Taxi '77
Logan's Run '76
Treasure of Matecumbe '76
One of Our Dinosaurs Is Missing '75
Robin Hood '73
Hammersmith Is Out '72
Viva Max! '69
Blackbeard's Ghost '67
The Comedians '67
Barefoot in Athens '66
Lady L '65
Topkapi '64
Billy Budd '62
Spartacus '60
The Sundowners '60
The Man Who Wagged His Tail '57
Lola Montès '55

Jun Usami (1911-81)
Late Spring '49
Total Total Total '70

Susan Ursitti
Teen Wolf '85
Defense Play '88

Guy Usher
Danger Ahead '40
Prison Break '38
Make a Million '35

Usher
See Usher Raymond

David Vadim (1972-)
Exit Wounds '01
Air Force One '97
Little Odessa '94

Roger Vadim (1928-2000)
Into the Night '85

Annette (Stroyberg) Vadim (1936-2005)
Blood and Roses '61
Dangerous Liaisons '60

Dan Vadis (1938-87)
Bronco Billy '80
Seven Magnificent Gladiators '84
The Gauntlet '77
Gladiators Seven '62
The Triumph of Hercules '64
Son of Hercules in the Land of Darkness '63

Brenda Vaccaro (1939-)
The Boynton Beach Club '05
Sonny '02
The Mirror Has Two Faces '96
Love Affair '94
Lethal Games '90
Masque of the Red Death '90
Ten Little Indians '89
Heart of Midnight '89
Supergirl '84
Water '85
Capricorn One '78
Death Weekend '76
Once Is Not Enough '75
Airport '77 '77
A Long Way Home '81
Honor Thy Father '73
Summertree '71
I Love My... Wife '70
Midnight Cowboy '69

Kari Vaananen (1953-)
Ambush '99
La Vie de Bohème '93
Night on Earth '91
Amazon '90
Leningrad Cowboys Go America '89

Jerry Vale (1932-)
Casino '95
Goodfellas '90

Virginia Vale (1920-2006)
Legion of the Lawless '40
Bullet Code '40

Nancy Valen (1965-)
Black Thunder '98
Final Embrace '92

Vladimir Valenta (1923-2001)
The Unbearable Lightness of Being '88
Closely Watched Trains '66

Anthony Valentine (1939-)
The Power Within '95
Children in the Crossfire '84

Barbara Valentin (1940-2002)
The Unbearable Lightness of Being '88
Horrors of Spider Island '59

Karen Valentine (1947-)
Children in the Crossfire '84
Jane Doe '83
Skeezer '82
The North Avenue Irregulars '79
Hot Lead & Cold Feet '78
Return to Fantasy Island '78

Scott Valentine (1958-)
Paranoia '98
Carnosaur 3: Primal Species '96
Mars '96
To Sleep with a Vampire '92
Write to Kill '91
After the Shock '90
Dangerous Pursuit '89
My Demon Lover '87

Rudolph Valentino (1895-1926)
Son of the Sheik '26
Cobra '25
The Eagle '25
Monsieur Beaucaire '24
Blood and Sand '22
Beyond the Rocks '22
Moran of the Lady Letty '22
Camille '21
The Four Horsemen of the Apocalypse '21
The Sheik '21
The Eyes of Youth '19
The Married Virgin '18

Charlotte Valandrey (1968-)
My Life and Times with Antonin Artaud '93
Orlando '92
Red Kiss '85

Serge-Henri Valcke (1946-)
No Man's Land '01
Soul Assassin '01
The Quarry '98
Amsterdamned '88

Birgitta Valberg (1916-)
The Shame '68
The Virgin Spring '59

Myrtle Vail (1886-1978)
The Little Shop of Horrors '60

Vera Vague
See Barbara Jo Allen

Lester Vail (1900-59)
Consolation Marriage '31
Dance Fools Dance '31

Wilmer Valderrama (1980-)
Fast Food Nation '06
Unaccompanied Minors '06
Clifford's Really Big Movie '04
The Dead One '07
The Darwin Awards '06

Tasia Valenza (1968-)
The Hillside Strangler '89
Rappin' '85
Crackers '84

Jeanne Valerie (1941-)
Dangerous Liaisons '60

Joan Valerie (1911-83)
Roaring City '51

Valerie

Charlie Chan at the Wax Museum '40
Michael Shayne: Private Detective '40
Children of the Wild '37
Rosa Valetti (1878-1937)
M '31
The Blue Angel '30
Frederick Valk (1895-1956)
Frenzy '46
Dead of Night '45
Hotel Reserve 44
Dangerous Moonlight '41
Night Train to Munich '40
Kitty Vallacher
The Legend of Frank Woods '77
Grave of the Vampire '72
Riccardo Valle
Hercules vs. the Sons of the Sun 64
The Awful Dr. Orloff 62
Marcel Vallee (1880-1957)
Topaze '33
The Crazy Ray '22
Rudy Vallee (1901-86)
Slashed Dreams '74
Live a Little, Love a Little '68
How to Succeed in Business without Really Trying '67
The Admiral Was a Lady '50
The Beautiful Blonde from Bashful Bend '49
Father Was a Fullback '49
My Dear Secretary '49
I Remember Mama '48
Unfaithfully Yours '48
The Bachelor and the Bobby-Soxer '47
The Sin of Harold Diddlebock '47
People Are Funny 46
The Palm Beach Story 42
Second Fiddle '39
International House '33
Glorifying the American Girl '30
Vagabond Lover 29
Nick Vallelonga (1959)
The Prince and the Pauper '07
In the Kingdom of the Blind the Man with One Eye Is King '94
Amber Valletta (1974-)
Dead Silence '07
Premonition '07
The Last Time '06
Hitch '05
Transporter 2 '05
Duplex '03
Max Keeble's Big Move '01
Family Man '00
What Lies Beneath '00
Mark Valley (1964-)
Jericho '01
The Next Best Thing '00
The Siege 98
George Wallace '97
Alida Valli (1921-2006)
Angel of Death '02
A Month by the Lake '95
Le Jupon Rouge '87
Beyond Erotica '79
Perfect Crime '79
Berlinguer I Love You '77
Suspiria 77
The Cassandra Crossing '76
1900 '76
Lisa and the Devil '75
The Tempter 74
The Spider's Stratagem 70
Oedipus Rex '67
The Castilian '63
The Horror Chamber of Dr. Faustus 59
Il Grido '57

The Night Heaven Fell '57
The Wide Blue Road '57
Senso '54
Walk Softly, Stranger '50
The Third Man '49
The Miracle of the Bells '48
The Paradine Case 47
We the Living 42
Frankie Valli (1937-)
Witness to the Mob 98
Eternity '90
Modern Love 90
Dirty Laundry 87
Romolo Valli (1925-80)
Bobby Deerfield '77
A Fistful of Dynamite '72
The Garden of the Finzi-Continis '71
Boom! '68
The Leopard '63
The Girl with a Suitcase '60
Virginia Valli (1898-1968)
Night Life in Reno '31
Lost Zeppelin 29
The Shock '23
Rick Vallin (1919-77)
The Last of the Redmen '47
Corregidor '43
King of the Stallions '42
The Panther's Claw '42
Raf Vallone (1917-2002)
The Godfather, Part 3 '90
Christopher Columbus '85
The Scarlet & the Black '83
Time to Die '83
Lion of the Desert '81
An Almost Perfect Affair 79
The Greek Tycoon '78
The Other Side of Midnight '77
The Girl in Room 2A '76
The Human Factor '75
Rosebud 75
That Lucky Touch '75
Ricco 74
Honor Thy Father 73
A Gunfight '71
The Italian Job '69
Nevada Smith '66
Harlow 65
El Cid '61
Phaedra '61
Two Women '61
Anna '51

Lewis Van Bergen
Pinocchio's Revenge '96
The Relic '96
Street Knight '93
False Arrest '92
Bugsy '91
Rage of Honor '87
South of Reno '87
Mabel van Buren (1878-47)
Beyond the Rocks '22
The Four Horsemen of the Apocalypse '21
Emily Van Camp (1986-)
Black Irish '07
The Ring 2 '05
A Different Loyalty '04
Lee Van Cleef (1925-89)
Thieves of Fortune '89
Speed Zone 88
Armed Response '86
Jungle Raiders '85
Codename: Wildgeese '84
Escape from New York '81
Hard Way '80
Octagon '80
The Squeeze '80
The Rip Off 78
Fatal Chase 77
Perfect Killer 77
The Stranger and the Gunfighter '76
God's Gun 75
Kid Vengeance '75
Mean Frank and Crazy Tony 75
Take a Hard Ride '75
Commandos 73
Escape from Death Row '73
The Grand Duel '73
Bad Man's River 72
New Mafia Boss 72
Captain Apache '71
Return of Sabata '71
El Condor 70
Sabata 69
Beyond the Law '68
The Good, the Bad and the Ugly 67
For a Few Dollars More '65
The Man Who Shot Liberty Valance 62
Ride Lonesome '59
The Bravados '58
The Young Lions '58
China Gate '57
Gunfight at the O.K. Corral '57
The Tin Star '57
The Conqueror '56
It Conquered the World '56
Pardners '56
Tribute to a Bad Man '56
Big Combo '55
A Man Alone '55
Gypsy Colt '54
The Beast from 20,000 Fathoms '52
High Noon 52
Kansas City Confidential '52

Timecop '94
Hard Target '93
Last Action Hero '93
Nowhere to Run '93
Universal Soldier '92
Double Impact '91
Death Warrant '90
Lionheart '90
Cyborg '89
Kickboxer 89
Black Eagle '88
Bloodsport '88
No Retreat, No Surrender 86
Monaco Forever '83
Monique Van De Ven (1952-)
The Man Inside '90
Paint It Black '89
Amsterdamned '88
The Assault '86
Katie Tippel 75
Turkish Delight '73
Sylvie van den Elsen
La Vie de Boheme '93
L'Argent '83
James Van Der Beek (1977-)
Danny Roane: First Time Director '06
Standing Still '05
The Rules of Attraction '02
Jay and Silent Bob Strike Back '01
Texas Rangers '01
Harvest 98
Varsity Blues '98
I Love You, I Love You Not '97
Angus '95
Nadine Van Der Velde (1962-)
After Midnight '89
Shadow Dancing '88
Munchies '87
Critters '86
Diana Van Der Vlis (1935-2001)
Lovespell '79
The Incident '67
X: The Man with X-Ray Eyes '63
Girl in Black Stockings '57
Frederique van der Wal (1967-)
Wild Wild West '99
Two Girls and a Guy '98
Trish Van Devere (1945-)
Deadly Currents '93
Messenger of Death '88
Hollywood Vice Squad '86
Uphill All the Way '85
All God's Children '80
The Changeling '80
The Hearse '80
Mayflower: The Pilgrims' Adventure '79
Movie, Movie '78
Stalk the Wild Child 76
Savage Is Loose 74
The Day of the Dolphin '73
Where's Poppa? '70
Casper Van Dien (1968-)
Meltdown '06
Slayer 06
The Vector File '03
Danger Beneath the Sea '02
Road Rage '01
Sanctimony '01
Under Heavy Fire '01
Chasing Destiny '00
Cutaway '00
Python '00
The Collectors '99
The Omega Code 99
Partners '99
Shark Attack 99
Sleepy Hollow 99
Thrill Seekers 99
Modern Vampires 98
The Quest 96
On the Border 98
Tarzan and the Lost City 98

James Dean: Live Fast, Die Young 97
NightScreams '97
Starship Troopers '97
Beastmaster 3: The Eye of Braxus '95
Night Eyes 4: Fatal Passion 95
Mamie Van Doren (1931-)
Slackers 02
Voyage to the Planet of Prehistoric Women '68
Las Vegas Hillbillys '66
Navy vs. the Night Monsters '66
Three Nuts in Search of a Bolt '64
Born Reckless 59
Girls' Town '59
High School Confidential '58
Teacher's Pet '58
Girl in Black Stockings '57
Francis Joins the WACs '54
John van Dreelen (1922-92)
Becoming Colette '92
Too Hot to Handle 76
Von Ryan's Express '65
13 Ghosts '60
A Time to Love & a Time to Die '58
Granville Van Dusen (1944-)
The Rose and the Jackal '90
Hotline 82
The Wild and the Free '80
Breaking Up '78
Dynasty '76
War Between the Tates 76
Jennifer Van Dyck (1962-)
Michael Clayton '07
Series 7: The Contenders '01
States of Control '98
Barry Van Dyke (1951-)
Foxfire Light '82
Ants '77
Conny Van Dyke (1945-)
Framed '75
Hell's Angels 69 69
Dick Van Dyke (1925-)
Curious George '06 (V)
Night at the Museum '06
Dick Tracy 90
Country Girl '82
The Runner Stumbles '79
Cold Turkey 71
The Comic 69
Chitty Chitty Bang Bang '68
Never a Dull Moment '68
Divorce American Style '67
Lt. Robin Crusoe, U.S.N. '66
Mary Poppins '64
Bye, Bye, Birdie '63
The Brain 62
The Thousand Eyes of Dr. Mabuse '60
A Bullet for Joey '55
Wages of Fear '55
Five Graves to Cairo '43
John Van Eyssen (1922-95)
The Horror of Dracula '58
Men of Sherwood Forest '57
Quatermass 2 '57

Four Sided Triangle '53
Jo Van Fleet (1919-96)
The Tenant '76
Satan's School for Girls '73
I Love You, Alice B. Toklas! '68
Cool Hand Luke '67
Gunfight at the O.K. Corral '57
The King and Four Queens '56
I'll Cry Tomorrow '55
The Rose Tattoo '55
East of Eden '54
Harry Van Gorkum
The Foreigner '03
Avenging Angelo '02
Dragonheart: A New Beginning '00
Escape under Pressure '00
Face the Music '00
Kevin Van Hentenryck
Basket Case 3: The Progeny '92
Basket Case 2 90
Brain Damage 88
Basket Case '82
Brian Van Holt (1969-)
House of Wax '05
Man of the House '05
Basic '03
Confidence '03
S.W.A.T. '03
Windtalkers '02
Black Hawk Down '01
Whipped '00
Patrick Van Horn (1969-)
Pursuit of Happiness '01
Three to Tango '99
Free Enterprise '98
Ivory Tower '97
Swingers '96
Fedja Van Huet (1973-)
Rosenstrasse '03
The Delivery '99
Character '97
Merete Van Kamp (1962-)
Lethal Woman 88
Princess Daisy '83
Jon Van Ness
Hospital Massacre '81
Tourist Trap 79
Peter Van Norden (1950-)
Casualties of Love: The "Long Island Lolita" Story '93
The Accused '88
Scandal in a Small Town '88
Rik van Nutter (1929-2005)
Tharus Son of Attila '87
Thunderball '65
Assignment Outer Space '61
Nina Van Pallandt (1932-)
Jungle Warriors '84
Sword & the Sorcerer '82
Cutter's Way '81
American Gigolo 79
Diary of a Young Comic '79
Quintet '79
A Wedding '78
Assault on Agathon '75
The Long Goodbye '73
Dick Van Patten (1928-)
The Santa Trap '02
Big Brother Trouble '00
Love Is All There Is '96
Demolition High '95
A Dangerous Place '94
Robin Hood: Men in Tights '93
Body Trouble '92
Final Embrace '92
The New Adventures of Pippi Longstocking '88
Spaceballs '87
The Midnight Hour '86

Diary of a Teenage
Hitchhiker '82
High Anxiety '77
Freaky Friday '77
Gang in Blue '96
Gus '76
Riot in the Streets '96
The Strongest Man in the
World '75
Soylent Green '73
Westworld '73
Beware! The Blob '72
Joe Kidd '72
Zachariah '70
Charly '68
Psychomania '63
New Jack City '91
Identity Crisis '90
Posse '93
Gunmen '93
Sophisticated Gents '81
Sweet Sweetback's
Baadasssss Song '71
Freaky Friday '76
How to Get into It) '69
I Love You, Alice B. Toklas!
'68

James Van Patten
(1956-)
Hyper Space '89
Twisted Justice '89
The Dirty Dozen: The
Deadly Mission '87
Nightforce '86
Young Warriors '83
Roller Boogie '79
Tennessee Stallion '78

Joyce Van Patten
(1934-)
Breathing Lessons '94
Trust Me '89
Monkey Shines '88
Billy Galvin '86
Crawlspace '86
The Rumor Mill '86
Housewife '72
The Stranger Within '74
Mame '74
The Bad News Bears '76
St. Elmo's Fire '85
Eleanor: First Lady of the
World '82
Thumb Tripping '72
The Trouble with Girls (and

Nels Van Patten
(1955-)
Mirror Images '91
One Last Run '89
Grotesque '87
Summer School '87

Timothy Van Patten
(1959-)
Curse 4: The Ultimate
Sacrifice '90
Catacombs '89
Dracula's Daughter '36
The Mummy '32
Dracula '31
Frankenstein '31

Vincent Van Patten
(1957-)
The Break '95
Payback '90
The Wrong Guys '88
Dress Gray '86
Zone Troopers '84
Escape from El Diablo '83
Class of 1984 '82
Rooster: Spurs of Death!
'83
Hell Night '81
Survival Run '80
Rock 'n' Roll High School
'79

Mario Van Peebles
(1958-)
Carlito's Way: Rise to
Power '05
Baadasssss! '03
44 Minutes: The North
Hollywood Shootout '03
Ali '01
The Guardian '01
American Scandal '00
Blowback '99
Judgment Day '99
Raw Nerve '99
Crazy Six '98
Love Kills '98
Mama Flora's Family '92

**Deborah Van
Valkenburgh** (1952-)
The Devil's Rejects '05
Mystery Woman: Mystery
Weekend '05
The Gospel of John '03
Narc '02
Steal This Movie! '00
Hamburger Hill '87
Percy & Thunder '93
Beyond the Law '92
The Hunt for Red October
'90
The Adventures of Huck
Finn '93

Alan Van Sprang
(1971-)

Joe Vance
Deadly Breed '89
L.A. Crackdown 2 '88

Jim Vance
Blood Cult '85
How to Make a Doll '68

Danitra Vance (1959-
94)
Jumpin' at the Boneyard
'92
Little Man Tate '91
Limit Up '89
The War of the Roses '89
Sticky Fingers '88
Rampage '87
A Bunny's Tale '85
Going for the Gold: The Bill
Johnson Story '85
Streets of Fire '84
King of the Mountain '81
The Warriors '79

**Yorick Van
Wageningen** (1964-)
The New World '05

Monique Van Vooren
(1933-)
Sugar Cookies '77
Andy Warhol's
Frankenstein '74
Ash Wednesday '73
There Goes Barder '54

Musetta Vander
(1969-)
Kicking & Screaming '05
Mosquitoman '05
O Brother Where Art Thou?
'00
Wild Wild West '99
Gunshy '98
Mortal Kombat 2:
Annihilation '97

Evelyn Varden (1895-
1958)
The Bad Seed '56
The Night of the Hunter '55
Athena '54
When Willie Comes
Marching Home '50

Norma Varden (1898-
1989)
The Sound of Music '65
Jupiter's Darling '55
Fancy Pants '50

Megan Van Peebles
(1958-2006)
South Bronx Heroes '85
Sweet Sweetback's
Baadasssss Song '71

Melvin Van Peebles
(1932-)
Love Kills '98
Calm at Sunset '96
Gang in Blue '96
Riot in the Streets '96
Terminal Velocity '94
Posse '93
Boomerang '92
O.C. and Stiggs '87
Sophisticated Gents '81
Sweet Sweetback's
Baadasssss Song '71

Karine Vanasse
(1983-)
A Soldier's Sweetheart '98

Louis Vanaria
Searching for Bobby D '05
This Thing of Ours '03

Courtney B. Vance
(1960-)
Blind Faith '98
Naked City: A Killer
Christmas '98
Naked City: Justice with a
Bullet '98
Twelve Angry Men '97
The Boys Next Door '96
The Last Supper '96
The Preacher's Wife '96
The Affair '95
Panther '95
Dangerous Minds '95
The Tuskegee Airmen '95
Holy Matrimony '94
The Piano Lesson '94
Race to Freedom: The
Story of the Underground
Railroad '94
Percy & Thunder '93
Beyond the Law '92
The Hunt for Red October
'90

Renata Vanni (1909-
2004)
Wait until Spring, Bandini
'90
South Beach '92
Neon City '91
Memories of Murder '90
Action Jackson '88
Deadly Illusion '87
52 Pick-Up '86
Never Too Young to Die '86
The Last Dragon '85
Tanya's Island '81
Terror Train '80

Edward Van Sloan
(1881-1964)
The Mask of Dijon '46
Before I Hang '40
Danger on the Air '38

Travis Van Winkle
(1982-)
Meet the Spartans '08
Transformers '07
Accepted '06
Dimension '94

Steve Van Wormer
Groove '00
Urban Crossfire '94
Full Eclipse '93
Gunmen '93

Philip Van Zandt
(1904-58)
The Pride and the Passion
'57
Clipped Wings '53
Ghost Chasers '51
Where Danger Lives '50
Woman in Brown '48
Decoy '46
A Thousand and One
Nights '45
Sherlock Holmes and the
Secret Weapon '42
Wake Island '42
Citizen Kane '41

Jean Vander Pyl
(1919-99)
The Flintstones '94
The Jetsons: The Movie '90 (V)

**Alexandra
Vandernoot** (1965-)
Once Upon a Scoundrel '73

Pierre Vaneck (1931-)
Never or Sunday '60

Antonio Vargas
Whore '91

Charles Vanel (1892-
1989)
Three Brothers '80
Death in the Garden '56
Diabolique '55
To Catch a Thief '55
Wages of Fear '55

Titos Vandis (1917-
2003)
Piece of the Action '77
Smile '75
The Crown Prince '06
The Closet '00
The Dinner Game '98
Cleopatra '99

Daniele Vargas
Jungle Inferno '72
Terror of the Steppes '64

Vanity (1959-)
DaVinci's War '92
Highlander: The Gathering
'92

Vanilla Ice (1967-)
Cool As Ice '91
Teenage Mutant Ninja
Turtles 2: The Secret of
the Ooze '91

Valentina Vargas
(1964-)
Hellraiser 4: Bloodline '95
The Tigress '93
Dirty Games '89

John Vargas (1958-)
Primary Colors '98
In Dark Places '97
Seduced by Evil '94
Unnatural Causes '86

Luigi Vannucchi
(1930-78)
The Lady in White '88
Westward the Women '51

Joanne Vannicola
(1968-)
Common Ground '00
Iron Eagle 4 '95
Love and Human Remains
'93

Victor Varconi (1891-
1976)
Unconquered '47
For Whom the Bell Tolls '43
My Favorite Blonde '42
Mr. Takes a Vacation '39
Dancing Pirate '36
The Black Camel '31
King of Kings '27

Indira Varma (1973-)
Basic Instinct 2 '06
Bride & Prejudice '04
Kama Sutra: A Tale of Love
'96

John Varley (1915-)
Meet Sexton Blake '44
In Which We Serve '43

Jim Varney (1949-
2000)
Atlantis: The Lost Empire
'01 (V)
Daddy & Them '99
Toy Story 2 '99 (V)
Treehouse Hostage '99
Ernest Goes to Africa '97
Ernest in the Army '97
3 Ninjas: High Noon at
Mega Mountain '97
100 Proof '97
Snowboard Academy '96
Toy Story '95
Slam Dunk Ernest '95
Ernest Goes to School '94
The Beverly Hillbillies '93
Ernest Rides Again '93
Ernest Scared Stupid '91
Ernest Goes to Jail '90
The Rousters '90
Fast Food '89
Ernest Saves Christmas
'88

Robert Vattier (1906-
82)
Letters from My Windmill
'54

Sofia Vassilieva
(1992-)
Day Zero '07
Eloise at the Plaza '03

Yolanda Vasquez
Pinocchio's Last Stand '06
Maria's Child '93

Leonor Varela (1972-)
Americano '05
Innocent Voices '04
Blade 2 '02
Texas Rangers '01
The Tailor of Panama '01
Cleopatra '99

Jacob Vargas (1971-)
Bobby Z '07
The Hills Have Eyes 2 '07
Love Lies Bleeding '07
Bobby '06
Jarhead '05
Mi Vida Loca '94
My Family '94
Selena '96
Gas Food Lodging '92
The Principal '87
The Children of Times
Square '86

Antonio Vargas
Whore '91

Michael Vartan
(1968-)
Monster-in-Law '05
One Hour Photo '02
Mists of Avalon '01
It Had to Be You '00
The Next Best Thing '00
Never Been Kissed '99
The Curve '97
The Myth of Fingerprints
'97

Diane Varsi (1937-92)
I Never Promised You a
Rose Garden '77
Johnny Got His Gun '71
The People '71
Bloody Mama '70
Wild in the Streets '68
Sweet Love, Bitter '67
Compulsion '59
Ten North Frederick '58
Peyton Place '57

Greg Vaughan (1973-)
Children of the Corn 5:
Fields of Terror '98
Poison Ivy 3: The New
Seduction '97

Paris Vaughan (1961-)
Buffy the Vampire Slayer
'92

Peter Vaughan (1923-)
Death at a Funeral '07
The Mother '03
Lorna Doone '01
Longitude '00
An Ideal Husband '99

Frankie Vaughan
(1928-99)
Let's Make Love '60
Dangerous Youth '58

Liz Vassey (1972-)
Fit to Kill '93
Hard Hunted '92
Do or Die '91

Beatrice Varley
(1896-1964)
Room at the Top '59
Death Goes to School '53
Bedelia '46
Great Day '46
Young and Innocent '37

Roberta Vasquez
(1963-)
The Hi-Lo Country '98
Romy and Michele's High
School Reunion '97
Bobby '06
Airborne '93

Nelson Vasquez
El Cantante '06
Pinero '01

Razvan Vasilescu
(1954-)
The Oak '93
Trahir '93

**Luiz Carlos
Vasconcelos** (1954-)
Carandiru '03
Behind the Sun '01

Vagelis Vartan
Emmanuelle, the Queen
'79
Fiorile '93
The Pallbearer '95
The Wendell Baker Story
'05
Flight of the Phoenix '04
RFK '02
Dr. Dolittle 2 '01 (V)
Next Friday '00
Traffic '00

Roland Varno (1908-
96)
Return of the Vampire '43
To Be or Not to Be '42
Gunga Din '39
The Fighting 69th '40

Dr. Otto & the Riddle of the
Gloom Beam '86
The White Cliffs of Dover
'44
National Velvet '44
Under the Hula Moon '95
Forever Amber '47
Project Shadowchaser
3000 '95

Jetsons: The Movie '90 (V)

Meet the Deedles '98

Emmanuelle's Daughter '79

Ernest Goes to Camp '87
'85

Our Mutual Friend '98
Face '97
The Crucible '96
The Secret Agent '96
The Choir '95
Circle of Deceit '94
Fatherland '93
Heart of Darkness '93
The Remains of the Day '93
Codename Kyril '91
Porridge '91
Prisoner of Honor '91
Mountains of the Moon '90
Haunted Honeymoon '86
Bleak House '85
Brazil '85
Forbidden '85
The Razor's Edge '84
Coming Out of the Ice '82
Time Bandits '81
Valentino '77
Blockhouse '73
Mackintosh Man '73
Savage Messiah '72
Straw Dogs '72
The Man Outside '68
Die! Die! My Darling! '65
The Victors '63

Vanessa Vaughn
His Bodyguard '98
Dead Silence '96
Crazy Moon '87

Alberta Vaughn (1904-92)
Laramie Kid '35
The Live Wire '34
Randy Rides Alone '34
Daring Danger '32
Wild Horse '31
The Dropkick '27

Ned Vaughn (1964-)
Life '99
Courage Under Fire '96
Wind '92
Chips, the War Dog '90

Robert Vaughn (1932-)
2B Perfectly Honest '04
Happy Hour '03
Hoodlum & Son '03
Pootie Tang '01
Lethal Force '00
An American Affair '99
BASEketball '98
Motel Blue '98
The Sender '98
Joe's Apartment '96
Menno's Mind '96
Blind Vision '91
Going Under '91
Nobody's Perfect '90
River of Death '90
That's Adequate '90
Brutal Glory '89
Buried Alive '89
C.H.U.D. 2: Bud the Chud '89
Delta Force '86
Black Moon Rising '86
Hour of the Assassin '86
Emissary '89
Skeleton Coast '89
Transylvania Twist '89
Captive Rage '88
Nightstick '87
Prince of Bel Air '87
The Mercenaries '80
Question of Honor '80
Backstairs at the White House '79
The Rebels '79
Brass Target '78
Centennial '78
Demon Seed '77 (V)

Starship Invasions '77
Blue Jeans and Dynamite '76
Wanted: Babysitter '75
The Towering Inferno '74
The Woman Hunter '72
The Shaming '71
The Statue '71
Julius Caesar '70
The Bridge at Remagen '69
Bullitt '68
The Glass Bottom Boat '66
The Magnificent Seven '60
The Young Philadelphians '59
Good Day for a Hanging '58
Teenage Caveman '58

Vince Vaughn (1970-)
Fred Claus '07
Into the Wild '07
The Break-Up '06
Vince Vaughn's Wild West Comedy Show '06
Be Cool '05
Mr. & Mrs. Smith '05
Thumbsucker '05
Wedding Crashers '05
Anchorman: The Legend of Ron Burgundy '04
Dodgeball: A True Underdog Story '04
Paparazzi '04
Starsky & Hutch '04
I Love Your Work '03
Old School '03
Domestic Disturbance '01
Made '01
The Cell '00
The Prime Gig '00
South of Heaven, West of Hell '00
Clay Pigeons '98
A Cool, Dry Place '98
Psycho '98
Return to Paradise '98
The Locusts '97
The Lost World: Jurassic Park 2 '97
Swingers '96
Rudy '93

Emmanuelle Vaugier (1976-)
Bachelor Party 2: The Last Temptation '08
Blonde and Blonder '07
Unearthed '07
House of the Dead 2: Dead Aim '05
Masters of Horror: Pro-Life '05
Saw II '05
Call Me: The Rise and Fall of Heidi Fleiss '04
Secondhand Lions '03
Water's Edge '03
40 Days and 40 Nights '02
Mindstorm '01
Return to Cabin by the Lake '01
Ripper: Letter from Hell '01
My 5 Wives '00
The Fear: Halloween Night '99
The Halfback of Notre Dame '96

Sophie Vavasseur (1992-)
Mindhunters '05
Northanger Abbey '07
Resident Evil: Apocalypse '04
Evelyn '02

Dana Vavrova (1967-)
Brother of Sleep '95

Ron Vawter (1949-94)
Ace of Hearts '85
Fury '78
Philadelphia '93
Mastergate '92
The Silence of the Lambs '91
Swoon '91
Internal Affairs '90
sex, lies and videotape '89
Sudden Death '77

Yul Vazquez
The Box '07

Music Within '07
The Take '07
War of the Worlds '05
Bad Boys 2 '03
Runaway Bride '99
Fresh '94
Fly by Night '93

Alex Veadov
We Own the Night '07
Black Horizon '01

Alexa Vega (1988-)
Sleepover '04
Spy Kids 3-D: Game Over '03
Spy Kids 2: The Island of Lost Dreams '02
Follow the Stars Home '01
Spy Kids '01
Ride the Wild Fields '00
The Deep End of the Ocean '98
Twister '96
Nine Months '95
Little Giants '94

Isela Vega (1940-)
Blood Screams '88
Barbarosa '82
Bordello '79
Drum '76
Joshua '76
Bring Me the Head of Alfredo Garcia '74
The Fear Chamber '68

Makenzie Vega (1994-)
In the Land of Women '06
Just My Luck '06
X-Men: The Last Stand '06
Sin City '05
Saw '04

Paz Vega (1976-)
10 Items or Less '06
Spanglish '04
Sex and Lucia '01

Conrad Veidt (1893-1943)
Above Suspicion '43
All Through the Night '42
Casablanca '42
A Woman's Face '41
Contraband '40
The Thief of Bagdad '40
Spy in Black '39
Dark Journey '37
King of the Damned '36
The Passing of the Third Floor Back '36
Under the Red Robe '36
Power '34
F.P. 1 '33
Congress Dances '31
The Beloved Rogue '27
The Man Who Laughs '27
Napoleon '27
Waxworks '24
Cesare Borgia '23
The Indian Tomb '21
The Hands of Orlac '25
The Cabinet of Dr. Caligari '19

Patricia Velasquez (1971-)
The Twelve Days of Christmas Eve '04
Fidel '02
The Mummy Returns '01
Committed '99
The Mummy '99
No Vacancy '99
Beowulf '98

Pilar Velasquez

Teresa Velazquez (1942-98)
The Killer Must Kill Again '75
Night of a Thousand Cats '72

Eddie Velez (1958-)
White Chicks '04
The Hunted '03

Running Woman '98
Under Oath '97
Bitter Vengeance '94
Drug Wars: The Camarena Story '90
Romero '89
Rooftops '89
Split Decisions '88
Women's Club '87
Doin' Time '85

Lauren Velez (1964-)
Prince of Central Park '00
I Think I Do '97
I Like It Like That '94

Lupe Velez (1908-44)
Mexican Spitfire at Sea '42
Playmates '41
Mexican Spitfire '40
Mad About Money '37
Hollywood Party '34
Palooka '34
The Half Naked Truth '32
Hell Harbor '30
Where East Is East '29
Stand and Deliver '28
The Gaucho '27

Reginald VelJohnson (1952-)
The Great American Sex Scandal '04
Posse '93
Die Hard 2: Die Harder '90
Die Hard '88
Plain Clothes '88
Remo Williams: The Adventure Begins '85
Ghostbusters '84

Evelyn Venable (1913-93)
Lucky Cisco Kid '40
Pinocchio '40 (V)
The Frontiersmen '38
Hollywood Stadium Mystery '38
Alice Adams '35
Harmony Lane '35
The Little Colonel '35
David Harum '34
Death Takes a Holiday '34
Mrs. Wiggs of the Cabbage Patch '34

Veronique Vendell (1942-)
Cross of Iron '76
Barbarella '68

Amy Veness (1876-1960)
Madeleine '50
Man of Evil '48
This Happy Breed '47

Ingrid Veninger
Hush Little Baby '93
Hide and Seek '77

Lenny Venito
The Brave One '07
The Wild '06 (V)
Duane Hopwood '05
War of the Worlds '05
Shark Tale '04 (V)
Gigli '03
Men in Black 2 '02
Just the Ticket '98
Rounders '98
Witness to the Mob '98
Money for Nothing '93

Chick Vennera (1952-)
The Glass Trap '04
Active Stealth '99
Tycus '98

Diane Venora (1952-)
Touched '05

Stateside '04
Hamlet '00
The Insider '99
Looking for an Echo '99
The 13th Warrior '99
True Crime '99
The Young Girl and the Monsoon '99
The Jackal '97
The Substitute '96
Surviving Picasso '96
William Shakespeare's Romeo and Juliet '96
Heat '95
Three Wishes '95
Bird '88
Ironweed '87
F/X '86
A.D. '85
Terminal Choice '85
The Cotton Club '84
Wolfen '81

Wanda Ventham (1939-)
Asylum '05
Out of the Shadows '88
Captain Kronos: Vampire Hunter '74
Blood Beast Terror '67

John Ventimiglia (1963-)
The War Within '05
Personal Velocity: Three Portraits '02 (N)
Mickey Blue Eyes '99
Row Your Boat '98
The Funeral '96
Girls Town '95
Angela '94

Milo Ventimiglia (1977-)
Pathology '08
Rocky Balboa '06
Cursed '04
Winter Break '03

Vincent Ventresca (1965-)
Mammoth '06
The Learning Curve '01
Madison '01
Love & Sex '00

Clyde Ventura (1936-90)
Gator Bait '73
Bury Me an Angel '71

Jesse Ventura (1951-)
Demolition Man '93
Ricochet '91
Abraxas: Guardian of the Universe '90
Boxcar Blues '90
Repossessed '90
Thunderground '89
Predator '87
The Running Man '87

Lino Ventura (1919-87)
Sword of Gideon '86
The Medusa Touch '78
Pain in the A— '77
The Slap '76
The French Detective '75
Happy New Year '73
Army of Shadows '69
The Last Adventure '67
Jailbird's Vacation '65
The Three Penny Opera '62
Mistress of the World '59
Modigliani '58
Grisbi '53

Richard Venture (1923-)
Series 7: The Contenders '01
Red Corner '97
Truman '95
Scent of a Woman '92
Heartbreak Ridge '86
Missing '82
The Onion Field '79
Kidnapped '87
High Risk '81
Yanks '79
Thank God It's Friday '78

Silvana Venturelli (1952-)
The Lickerish Quartet '70

Camille 2000 '69

Massimo Venturiello
My Wonderful Life '90
Rorret '87

Billy Vera (1944-)
The Doors '91
Finish Line '89
The Adventures of Buckaroo Banzai Across the Eighth Dimension '84

Victoria Vera (1953-)
A Man of Passion '88
Monster Dog '82

Vera-Ellen (1920-81)
White Christmas '54
The Belle of New York '52
Happy Go Lovely '51
Love Happy '50
Three Little Words '50
On the Town '49
Words and Music '48
Wonder Man '45

Natalia Verbeke (1975-)
The Method '05
Dot the I '03
The Son of the Bride '01

Gwen Verdon (1925-2000)
The Dress Code '99
In Cold Blood '96
Marvin's Room '96
Oldest Confederate Widow Tells All '95
Alice '90
Cocoon: The Return '88
Nadine '87
Cocoon '85
The Cotton Club '84
Legs '83
Damn Yankees '58
The Farmer Takes a Wife '53

Carlo Verdone (1950-)
Iris Blond '98
Acqua e Sapone '83

Maribel Verdu (1970-)
Pan's Labyrinth '06
Jericho Mansions '03
Y Tu Mama Tambien '01
Goya in Bordeaux '99
Belle Epoque '92

Peter Vere-Jones
Meet the Feebles '89 (V)
Bad Taste '88

Ben Vereen (1946-)
And Then Came Love '07
Idlewild '06
Anne Rice's The Feast of All Saints '01
I'll Take You There '99
Why Do Fools Fall in Love? '98
Once Upon a Forest '93 (V)
Intruders '92
The Kid Who Loved Christmas '90
Mother Goose Rock 'n' Rhyme '90
Buy & Cell '89
A.D. '85
The Zoo Gang '85
Breakin' Through '84
The Jesse Owens Story '84
Puss 'n Boots '84
Pippin '81
All That Jazz '79
Roots '77
Funny Lady '75
Gas-s-s-s! '70

Sofia Vergara (1972-)
Tyler Perry's Meet the Browns '08
Grilled '06
Four Brothers '05

The 24th Day '04
Chasing Papi '03
Big Trouble '02

Tom Verica (1964-)
Red Dragon '02
From the Earth to the Moon '98
Lost in the Bermuda Triangle '98
The Assassination File '96
Breach of Conduct '94
800 Leagues Down the Amazon '93
Die Hard 2: Die Harder '90

Bernard Verley (1939-)
Lucie Aubrac '96
Helas pour Moi '94
Pas Tres Catholique '93
Phantom of Liberty '74
Chloe in the Afternoon '72
The Milky Way '68

Francoise Verley
Chloe in the Afternoon '72

Harold Vermilyea (1889-1958)
Emperor Waltz '48
Sorry, Wrong Number '48

Denise Vernac (1916-84)
Unnatural '52

Karen Verne (1918-67)
The Seventh Cross '44
All Through the Night '42
Sherlock Holmes and the Secret Weapon '42
Kings Row '41
Underground '41

Guy Verney (1915-70)
Martin Luther '53

Adam Vernier (1972-)
Bring It On: In It to Win It '07
Black Cadillac '03

Pierre Vernier (1931-)
Under the Sand '00
Betty '92

Anne Vernon (1925-)
Therese & Isabelle '67
Umbrellas of Cherbourg '64

Conrad Vernon (1968-)
Shrek the Third '07 (V)
Shrek 2 '04 (V)
Shrek '01 (V)

Glenn Vernon (1923-99)
I Bury the Living '58
Bedlam '45

Howard Vernon (1914-96)
Faceless '88
Zombie Lake '80
Revenge in the House of Usher '82

Wally Vernon (1905-70)
Bloodhounds of Broadway '52

Bob le Flambour '55
La Silence de la Mer '47

John Vernon (1932-2005)
Malicious '95
Hostage for a Day '94
Sodbusters '94
Bail Out '90
Mob Story '90
Terminal Exposure '89
War Bus Commando '89
Deadly Stranger '88
Dixie Lanes '88
I'm Gonna Git You Sucka '88
Killer Klowns from Outer Space '88
Blue Monkey '87
Ernest Goes to Camp '87
Nightstick '87
Doin' Time '85
Fraternity Vacation '85
The Blood of Others '84
Jungle Warriors '84
Chained Heat '83
Curtains '83
Savage Streets '83
Herbie Goes Bananas '80
National Lampoon's Animal House '78
Angela '77
Golden Rendezvous '77
Journey '77
A Special Day '77
The Outlaw Josey Wales '76
The Virginia Hill Story '76
Brannigan '75
Sweet Movie '75
The Black Windmill '74
The Barbary Coast '74
Charley Varrick '73
Dirty Harry '71
Justine '69
Tell Them Willie Boy Is Here '69

Kate Vernon (1961-)
School of Life '06
Downdraft '96
Bloodknot '95
Probable Cause '95
The Sister-in-Law '95
Dangerous Touch '94
Soft Deceit '94
Malcolm X '92
Mob Story '90
Hostile Takeover '88
The Last of Philip Banter '87
Alphabet City '84
Roadhouse 66 '84

Richard Vernon (1925-97)
The Return of the Borrowers '96
The Human Factor '79
The Duchess of Duke Street '78
The Satanic Rites of Dracula '73
A Hard Day's Night '64
Tomb of Ligeia '64
The Servant '63

Hell Comes to Frogtown '88
Eye of the Eagle '87
Beach Party '63
Attack of the Giant Leeches '59

Odile Versois (1930-80)
Le Crabe Tambour '77
Cartouche '62
To Paris with Love '55

Veruschka (1939-)
The Bride '85
Blow-Up '66

Arie Verveen (1966-)
Sin City '05
Plain Dirty '04
Cabin Fever '03
Sin '02
Running Free '00
The Thin Red Line '98
Caught '96

Charlotte Very
Trois Couleurs: Bleu '93

John Vickery (1950-)
Reform School Girl '57
The Mummy '32

Viktor Verzhbitsky
Day Watch '06
Night Watch '04

Bruno VeSota (1922-76)
Hell's Angels on Wheels '67
The Wild World of Batwoman '66
The Haunted Palace '63
Night Tide '63
The Choppers '61
A Bucket of Blood '59
The Wasp Woman '59
Carnival Rock '57
Rock All Night '57
The Undead '57
Teenage Doll '57
The Female Jungle '56
The Gunslinger '56
Daughter of Horror '55
The Wild One '54

Katherine Victor (1923-2004)
SuperGuy: Behind the Cape '02
The Wild World of Batwoman '66
Teenage Zombies '58
Mesa of Lost Women '52
Creature of the Walking Dead '60
Curse of the Stone Hard '65
House of the Black Death '65

Henry Victor (1892-1945)
Blue, White and Perfect '42
Sherlock Holmes and the Secret Weapon '42
"To Be or Not to Be" '42
Underground Agent '42
King of the Zombies '41
Freaks '32
Seas Beneath '31
The Mummy '32
The Beloved Rogue '27
Beau Geste '26

Charles Victor (1896-1965)
The Pit and the Perdulum '91
Made in Heaven '52
Motor Patrol '50
The Woman in Question '50

Asia Vieira (1982-)
The Good Mother '88
Omen 4: The Awakening '91

Florence Vidor (1895-1977)
Doomsday '28
The Grand Duchess and the Waiter '26
Are Parents People? '25
The Marriage Circle '24
The Virginian '23
Beau Revel '21

Vince Vieluf (1970-)
Firewall '06
Grind '03
Rat Race '01
Clay Pigeons '98
An American Werewolf in Paris '97

Vesa Vierikko (1953-)
The Match Factory Girl '90
The Winter War '89

Abe Vigoda (1921-)
Crime Spree '03
Just the Ticket '98
Witness to the Mob '98
A Brooklyn State of Mind '97
Good Burger '97
Love Is All There Is '96
Underworld '96
Home of Angels '94
Jury Duty '95
North '94
Sugar Hill '94
Batman: Mask of the Phantasm '93 (V)
Fist of Honor '92
Joe Versus the Volcano '90
Keaton's Cop '90
Look Who's Talking '89
Prancer '89
Plain Clothes '88
Vasectomy: A Delicate Matter '86
The Stuff '85

The Godfather 1902-1959: The Complete Epic '81
The Godfather, Part 2 '74
The Godfather '72

Yvette Vickers (1936-)
Evil Spirits '91
Beach Party '63
Attack of the Giant Leeches '59
Attack of the 50 Foot Woman '58

John Vickery (1950-)
Deconstructing Sarah '94
Rapid Fire '92

Charles Victor (1896-1965)
The Foreman Went to France '42
Seven Days' Leave '42

Susan Vidler
The Woman in White '97
Naked '93

Sid Vidler (1960-)

Napoleon '96 (V)
Encounter at Raven's Gate '88

Frank Villard
Duke of the Derby '62
Seven Deadly Sins '53

Tom Villard (1954-94)
My Girl '91
Popcorn '89
Swimsuit '89
The Trouble with Dick '88
Heartbreak Ridge '86
One Crazy Summer '86
Weekend Warriors '86

J.R. Villarreal (1992-)
Akeelah and the Bee '06

Astrid Villaume (1923-95)
Wilbur Wants to Kill Himself '02

Daniel Villarreal (1960-)
Speed '94
American Me '92

Herve Villechaize (1943-93)
Two Moon Junction '88
Rumpelstiltskin '82
Forbidden Zone '80
Seizure '74

Jacques Villeret (1951-)
The Dinner Game '98
The Favor, the Watch, & the Very Big Fish '92
Edith & Marcel '83
Bolero '82

James Villemaire (1943-)
Matinee '92
Dead Silence '96
Gate 2 '92

James Villiers (1933-98)
Wavelength '96
Uncovered '94
Let Him Have It '91
Mountains of the Moon '90
Fortunes of War '87
Death by Prescription '86
Mrs. Silly '85
The Scarlet Pimpernel '82
Asylum '72
The Ruling Class '72
Blood from the Mummy's Tomb '77
Nice Girl Like Me '69
The Nanny '65
Repulsion '65
King and Country '64
Eva '62

Christopher Villiers (1960-)
First Knight '95
Top Secret! '84

Jay Villiers (1961-)
Henry V '89

Pruitt Taylor Vince (1960-)
Captivity '07
When a Man Falls in the Forest '07
Constantine '05
Drop Dead Sexy '05
Identity '03
Monster '03
Simone '02
13 Moons '02
Trapped '02
The Cell '00
Nurse Betty '00
Mumford '99
The Legend of 1900 '98
The Break '98
The End of Violence '97
Beautiful Girls '96
Under the Hula Moon '95
City Slickers 2: The Legend of Curly's Gold '94

Henri Vilbert (1904-)
The Crocodile Hunter: Collision Course '02
Child Star: The Shirley Temple Story '01
Two Hands '99

Steven Vidler (1960-)
Happy Hell Night '92
Hey, Babu Riba '88

Gala Videnovic (1969-)

Lisa Vidal (1965-)
Chasing Papi '03
Active Stealth '99
Naked City: A Killer Christmas '98
See No Evil '06
Salem's Lot '04

Karin Viard (1966-)
Time Out '01
Children of the Century '99
La Separation '98
The New Eve '98
The Separation '94
Delicatessen '92

Ronan Vibert (1964-)
Tristan & Isolde '06
The Cat's Meow '01
Shadow of the Vampire '00
Fall '97
Suit '98
The Wonderful Ice Cream '98

Herb Vigran (1910-86)
Bedtime for Bonzo '51
The Star '52

Robert Viharo (1939-)
Coldfire '90
Romero '89
Night Stalker '87
Happy Birthday, Gemini '80
Hide in Plain Sight '80
Kid from Not-So-Big '78
Bare Knuckles '77
Valley of the Dolls '67

Herb Vigran (1910-86)

Gore Vidal (1925-)
Gattaca '97
The Shadow Conspiracy '96
With Honors '94
Bob Roberts '92
Fellini's Roma '72

Henri Vidal (1919-59)
Voulez-Vous Danser avec Moi? '59
Just Another Pretty Face '58
Sois Belle et Tais-To '58
Une Parisienne '58
Fabiola '48

Lisa Vidal (1965-)

Christina Vidal (1981-)
Freaky Friday '03
Brink '98
Life with Mikey '93

Gil Vidal (1931-)
Rape '76
Night of the Howling Beast '75

Tricia Vessey (1972-)
Town and Country '01
On the Edge '00
Coming Soon '99
Ghost Dog: The Way of the Samurai '99
The Alarmist '98
Bean '97
Standoff '97

Edy Vessel (1940-)
The Trojan Horse '62
Passionate Thief '60

Ondrej Vetchy (1962-)
Dark Blue World '01
Martha and I '91

Victoria Vetri (1944-)
Invasion of the Bee Girls '73
Group Marriage '72
When Dinosaurs Ruled the Earth '70

Marthe Villalonga (1932-)
Ma Saison Preferee '93
Three Men and a Cradle '85

Jordi Vilches (1979-)
Two Tough Guys '03
Nico and Dani '00

Marthe Villalonga (1932-)

Henri Vilbert (1904-97)

Heavy '94
Natural Born Killers '94
Nobody's Fool '94
Come See the Paradise '90
Jacob's Ladder '90
Mississippi Burning '88
Barfly '87
Shy People '87

Alex Vincent (1982-)
My Family Treasure '93
Child's Play 2 '90
Wait until Spring, Bandini '90
Child's Play '88

Allen Vincent (1903-79)
After Midnight '33
Carnival Lady '33
Mystery of the Wax Museum '33

Brian Vincent (1970-)
Blue Moon '00
Under Hellgate Bridge '99
Black Dog '98
Animal Room '95

Cerina Vincent (1979-)
Return to House on Haunted Hill '07
It Waits '05
Cabin Fever '03
Not Another Teen Movie '01

Frank Vincent (1940-)
A Tale of Two Pizzas '03
This Thing of Ours '03
Snipes '01
The Crew '00
Gun Shy '00
If You Only Knew '00
Entropy '99
Under Hellgate Bridge '99
Undercurrent '99
Ten Benny '98
Tom Clancy's Netforce '98
Witness to the Mob '98
Cop Land '97
The Deli '97
Gotti '96
Grind '96
She's the One '96
West New York '96
Federal Hill '94
Jungle Fever '91
Goodfellas '90
Street Hunter '90
Raging Bull '80

Helene Vincent (1940-)
The Count of Monte Cristo '99
Ma Vie en Rose '97
Trois Couleurs: Bleu '93
Life Is a Long Quiet River '88

Jan-Michael Vincent (1944-)
Buffalo 66 '97
Deadly Heroes '96
Red Line '96
Body Count '95
Ice Cream Man '95
Abducted 2: The Reunion '94
Indecent Behavior '93
Midnight Witness '93
Animal Instincts '92
Beyond the Call of Duty '92
Hidden Obsession '92
Sins of Desire '92
The Divine Enforcer '91
Hangfire '91
Haunting Fear '91
In Gold We Trust '91
Raw Nerve '91
Xtro 2: The Second Encounter '91
Alienator '89
Demonstone '89
Dirty Games '89
Deadly Embrace '88
The Hit List '88
Born in East L.A. '87
Enemy Territory '87
Last Plane Out '83
The Winds of War '83
Hard Country '81

The Return '80
Defiance '79
Big Wednesday '78
Hooper '78
Damnation Alley '77
Bite the Bullet '75
White Line Fever '75
Buster and Billie '74
The World's Greatest Athlete '73
The Mechanic '72
Tribes '70
The Undefeated '69
The Bandits '67

June Vincent (1924-)
Clipped Wings '53
Colorado Sundown '52
The Creeper '48
Black Angel '46
Can't Help Singing '45
Here Come the Co-Eds '45
The Climax '44
Honeymoon Lodge '43

Russ Vincent
Twilight in the Sierras '50
Heading for Heaven '47

Virginia Vincent (1924-)
The Hills Have Eyes '77
The Baby '72
Sweet November '68
Love with the Proper Stranger '63

Steve Vinovich (1945-)
The Swan Princess '94 (V)
Hollywood Boulevard 2 '89

Helen Vinson (1907-99)
The Thin Man Goes Home '44
Torrid Zone '40
Vogues of 1938 '37
King of the Damned '36
Reunion '36
Transatlantic Tunnel '35
Broadway Bill '34
I Am a Fugitive from a Chain Gang '32
They Call It Sin '32

Alan Vint (1944-)
Ballad of Gregorio Cortez '83
Sniper '75
Badlands '74
Macon County Line '74
Unholy Rollers '72
Panic in Needle Park '71
The McMasters '70

Bill Vint (1942-)
Marilyn: The Untold Story '80
Summertree '71

Jesse Vint (1940-)
I Come in Peace '90
Merchants of War '90
Dempsey '83
On the Line '83
Forbidden World '82
Death Sport '78
Black Oak Conspiracy '77
Bobbie Jo and the Outlaw '76
Bug '75
Macon County Line '74
Pigs '73

Gustav Vintas
Zero Tolerance '94

Drug Wars 2: The Cocaine Cartel '92
And You Thought Your Parents Were Weird! '91
Midnight '89
Tales from the Crypt '89
Vampire at Midnight '88
Lethal Weapon '87
Welcome Back Mr. Fox '83

Arthur Vinton (1889-1963)
Circumstantial Evidence '35
Gambling Ship '33

Bobby Vinton (1935-)
Train Robbers '73
Big Jake '71
Surf Party '64

Ultra Violet (1935-)
Superstar: The Life and Times of Andy Warhol '90
Simon, King of the Witches '71

Ian Virgo (1981-)
Extreme Dating '04
Band of Brothers '01
Black Hawk Down '01

Michael Visaroff (1892-1951)
Charlie Chan at the Wax Museum '40
Arizona Terror '31
Last Command '28

Sal Viscuso (1948-)
Spaceballs '87
The Taking of Pelham One Two Three '74
M*A*S*H '70 (V)

Goran Visnjic (1972-)
Elektra '05
Close Your Eyes '02
Ice Age '02 (V)
The Deep End '01
Committed '00
Practical Magic '98
Rounders '98
Welcome to Sarajevo '97

Angela Visser (1966-)
Hot Under the Collar '91
Killer Tomatoes Eat France '91

Alex Vitale
Beyond the Door 3 '91
Urban Warriors '75

Antonella Vitale
The Church '98
Opera '88

Joseph (Joe) Vitale (1901-94)
Alias Jesse James '59
A Bullet for Joey '55
The Stranger Wore a Gun '53
Zombies on Broadway '44

Milly Vitale (1932-2006)
War and Peace '56
The Seven Little Foys '55

Keith Vitali
American Kickboxer 1 '91
No Retreat, No Surrender 3: Blood Brothers '91
Revenge of the Ninja '83

Vitamin C
See Colleen (Ann) Fitzpatrick

Joe (Johnny) Viterelli (1941-2004)
Analyze That '02
Serving Sara '02
See Spot Run '01
Shallow Hal '01
Wannabes '01
Mickey Blue Eyes '99
Analyze This '98
Facade '98
Mafia! '98
Out to Sea '97
American Strays '96
Eraser '96
Heaven's Prisoners '95
Machine Gun Blues '95
Bullets over Broadway '94
The Crossing Guard '94
The Firm '93

Ruby '92
Mobsters '91
State of Grace '90

Antoine Vitez (1930-90)
Lisbon Story '94
Faraway, So Close! '93
Until the End of the World '91
Night Sun '90
Marianne and Juliane '82
The Wrong Move '78
Kings of the Road—In the Course of Time '76
Alice in the Cities '74

Ray Vitte (1949-83)
Grambling's White Tiger '81
Sky Hei$t '75

Monica Vitti (1931-)
Immortal Bachelor '80
Tigers in Lipstick '80
An Almost Perfect Affair '79
Blonde in Black Leather '77
Phantom of Liberty '74
The Eclipse '66
Modesty Blaise '66
The Red Desert '64
L'Avventura '60

Viva (1942-)
Superstar: The Life and Times of Andy Warhol '90
State of Things '82
Forbidden Zone '80
Edie in Ciao! Manhattan '72
Play It Again, Sam '72

Floyd Vivino (1951-)
Crazy People '90
Good Morning, Vietnam '87

Marina Vlady (1938-)
Son of Gascogne '95
Chimes at Midnight '67
Two or Three Things I Know about Her '66
The Unfaithfuls '60
Double Agents '59

Sam Vlahos
Christmas in the Clouds '01
The Big Squeeze '96
Powwow Highway '89

Sandra Voe (1936-)
Janice Beard '99
The Winter Guest '97
Breaking the Waves '95
Body & Soul '93

Emmett Vogan (1893-1969)
Down Dakota Way '49
The Lady Confesses '45
Robot Pilot '41
San Quentin '37

Frederick Vogeding
Mr. Moto Takes a Chance '38
Mysterious Mr. Moto '38

Darlene Vogel (1962-)
Decoy '95
Ring of Steel '94
Back to the Future, Part 2 '89

Jack Vogel
Presumed Guilty '91
Lock 'n' Load '90

Mike Vogel (1979-)
Cloverfield '08
Poseidon '06
Sisterhood of the Traveling Pants '05
Supercross: The Movie '05
Grind '03
MTV's Wuthering Heights '03

Mitch Vogel (1956-)
Texas Detour '77
Born Innocent '74

Karl Michael Vogler (1928-)
Deep End '70
The Blue Max '66

Ruediger Vogler (1942-)
Lisbon Story '94
Faraway, So Close! '93
Until the End of the World '91
Night Sun '90
Marianne and Juliane '82
The Wrong Move '78
Kings of the Road—In the Course of Time '76
Alice in the Cities '74

Giannis Voglis (1937-)
Hero Bunker '71
The Brave Bunch '70

Joan Vohs (1931-2001)
Cry Vengeance '54
As You Were '51

Jon Voight (1938-)
Bratz '07
National Treasure: Book of Secrets '07
September Dawn '07
Transformers '07
Glory Road '06
Karate Dog '04
The Manchurian Candidate '04
National Treasure '04
Superbabies: Baby Geniuses 2 '04
Holes '03
Jasper, Texas '03
Ali '01
Jack and the Beanstalk: The Real Story '01
Lara Croft: Tomb Raider '01
Pearl Harbor '01
Uprising '01
Zoolander '01
A Dog of Flanders '99
Noah's Ark '99
Enemy of the State '98
The General '98
Varsity Blues '98
Boys Will Be Boys '97
The Fixer '97
John Grisham's The Rainmaker '97
Most Wanted '97
U-Turn '97
Anaconda '96
Mission: Impossible '96
Rosewood '96
Convict Cowboy '95
Heat '95
The Tin Soldier '95
Rainbow Warrior '94
Return to Lonesome Dove '93
The Last of His Tribe '92
Eternity '90
Final Warning '90
Desert Bloom '86
Runaway Train '85
Table for Five '83
Lookin' to Get Out '82
The Champ '79
Coming Home '78
Conrack '74
The Odessa File '74
Deliverance '72
Catch-22 '70
Midnight Cowboy '69
Hour of the Gun '67

Vicki Volante
Angels' Wild Women '72
Brain of Blood '71
Horror of the Blood Monsters '70
Blood of Dracula's Castle '69

Gian Marie Volonte (1933-94)
Open Doors '89
Christ Stopped at Eboli '79
Lucky Luciano '74
Sacco & Vanzetti '71
Le Cercle Rouge '70
A Bullet for the General '68
The Witch '66
For a Few Dollars More '65
A Fistful of Dollars '64

Journey Beneath the Desert '61
The Girl with a Suitcase '60

Philippe Volter (1959-2005)
The Five Senses '99
Trois Couleurs: Bleu '93
The Double Life of Veronique '91
Cyrano de Bergerac '90
The Music Teacher '88

Daniel von Bargen (1950-)
Coastlines '02
Simone '02
The Majestic '01
Super Troopers '01
Disney's The Kid '00
O Brother, Where Art Thou? '00
Shaft '00
The General's Daughter '99
Universal Soldier: The Return '99
Inferno '98
The Postman '97
Stephen King's Thinner '96
Before and After '95
Lord of Illusions '95
Truman '95
Philadelphia '93
Rising Sun '93
The Silence of the Lambs '91

Wilhelm von Brinken (1881-1946)
Hidden Enemy '40
International Crime '37
King Kelly of the U.S.A. '34
Inside the Lines '30

Tomas von Bromssen (1943-)
All Things Fair '95
My Life As a Dog '85
Man from Mallorca '84

Erik von Detten (1982-)
The Princess Diaries '01
Brink '98
Leave It to Beaver '97
Top Dog '95
Toy Story '95 (V)

Lenny Von Dohlen (1958-)
Teeth '07
Home Alone 3 '97
Entertaining Angels: The Dorothy Day Story '96
Bird of Prey '95
One Good Turn '95
Tollbooth '94
Eyes of the Beholder '92
Leaving Normal '92
Blind Vision '91
Love Kills '91
Dracula's Widow '88
Billy Galvin '86
Under the Biltmore Clock '85
Electric Dreams '84
Tender Mercies '83

Theodore von Eltz (1894-1964)
Confidential '35
High Gear '33
Drifting Souls '32
Strangers of the Evening '32
No Man's Law '27

Loni von Friedl (1943-)
Journey to the Far Side of the Sun '69
The Blue Max '66

Wilhelm von Homburg (1940-2004)
In the Mouth of Madness '95
Silence of the Hams '93
Diggstown '92
Eye of the Storm '91
Night of the Warrior '91
Midnight Cabaret '90
Ghostbusters 2 '89
The Package '89
Die Hard '88

Stroszek '77
The Devil's Brigade '68
The Wrecking Crew '68

Joel von Ornsteiner
Slashdance '89
Robot Holocaust '87

Heidi von Palleske
Cybercity '99
Shepherd '99
Falling Fire '97
Strip Search '97
2103: Deadly Wake '97
White Light '90
Blind Fear '89
Dead Ringers '88

Stefanie von Pfetten
Meltdown '06
The Twelve Days of Christmas Eve '04
The Invitation '03
Posers '02

Gustav von Seyffertitz (1863-1943)
She '35
Mystery Liner '34
Rasputin and the Empress '33
Ambassador Bill '31
Dishonored '31
The Mysterious Lady '28
The Gaucho '27
The Bells '26
Don Juan '26
Sparrows '26
Down to Earth '17

Erich von Stroheim (1885-1957)
Napoleon '55
Unnatural '52
Sunset Boulevard '50
Portrait of an Assassin '49
The Mask of Diijon '46
Great Flamarion '45
Five Graves to Cairo '43
The North Star '43
So Ends Our Night '41
Grand Illusion '37
The Crime of Dr. Crespi '35
Crimson Romance '34
Fugitive Road '34
As You Desire Me '32
Lost Squadron '32
The Great Gabbo '29
The Wedding March '28
Foolish Wives '22
Blind Husbands '19
Heart of Humanity '18
Hearts of the World '18
Intolerance '16
The Birth of a Nation '15

Max von Sydow (1929-)
The Diving Bell and the Butterfly '07
Rush Hour 3 '07
Minority Report '02
Druids '01
Intacto '01
Sleepless '01
Nuremberg '00
Private Confessions '98
Snow Falling on Cedars '59
Solomon '98
What Dreams May Come '98
Hostile Waters '97
Hansun '96
Jerusalem '96
Citizen X '95
Judge Dredd '95
The Bachelor '93
Needful Things '93
The Best Intentions '92
The Silent Touch '92
Zentropa '92 (N)
A Kiss Before Dying '91
The Ox '91
Until the End of the World '91
Father '90
Awakenings '90
Hiroshima: Out of the Ashes '90
Red King, White Knight '89
Pelle the Conqueror '88
Second Victory '87
The Wolf at the Door '87
Dust for One '86
Hannah and Her Sisters '86
Christopher Columbus '85
Code Name: Emerald '85
Kojak: The Belarus File '85
The Last Place on Earth '85
Never Say Never Again '83
Strange Brew '83
Conan the Barbarian '82
Flight of the Eagle '82
Victory '81
Death Watch '80
Flash Gordon '80
Hurricane '79
Brass Target '78
The Exorcist 2: The Heretic '77
March or Die '77
The Desert of the Tartars '76
Foxtrot '76
Voyage of the Damned '76
Three Days of the Condor '75
The Ultimate Warrior '75
Steppenwolf '74
The Exorcist '73
The New Land '73
The Emigrants '72
Embassy '72
The Touch '71
The Night Visitor '70
The Passion of Anna '70
Hour of the Wolf '68
The Shame '68
Hawaii '66
'66
The Greatest Story Ever Told '65
The Winter Light '62
Through a Glass Darkly '61
The Virgin Spring '59
The Magician '58
Brink of Life '57
Wild Strawberries '57
The Seventh Seal '56
Miss Julie '50

Hans von Twardowski (1898-1958)
Dawn Express '42
Hangmen Also Die '42
The Cabinet of Dr. Caligari '19

Margarethe von Trotta (1942-)
Coup de Grace '78
Beware of a Holy Whore '70
'19

Frank Vosper (1899-1937)
Secret of Stamboul '36
Spy of Napoleon '36
The Man Who Knew Too Much '34

Gustav von Wagenheim (1895-1975)
Woman in the Moon '29
Nosferatu '22

Florence Marly von Wurmbrand
See Florence Marly

Harry von Zell (1906-81)
The Strange Affair of Uncle Harry '45
Son of Paleface '52

Danielle von Zerneck (1966-)
Acceptable Risk '01
Living in Oblivion '94
Under the Boardwalk '89
Dangerous Curves '88
La Bamba '87
My Science Project '85

Gila von Weitershausen (1944-)
Schnelles Geld '84
Black and White As Day and Night '78

Vlasta Vrana
Human Trafficking '05
Secret Window '04
Protection '01
Variant's War '01
Escape from Wildcat Canyon '98
Fallen Angel '99
Grey Owl '99
The Assignment '97
Night of the Demons 3 '97
The Reaper '97
Stranger in the House '97
Hawk's Vengeance '96
Deadly Surveillance '91
Scanners 2: The New Order '91
Keeping Track '86
Order '91

Ron Vreeken
Deathfight '93
Rage and Honor 2: Hostile Takeover '93

Jan Vostrcil (1903-85)
Intimate Lighting '65
Black Peter '63

Yorgo Voyagis (1945-)
Swept Away '02
Courage Mountain '89
The Bourne Identity '88
Frantic '88
The Little Drummer Girl '84
1492: Conquest of Paradise '92
The One That Got Away '96
Carrington '95
Royal Deceit '94
Edward II '92
Ivanhoe '97
Face '97
The Hole '01
Sleepy Hollow '99
Tarzan and the Lost City '99
Warrior Queen '03

Julian Wadham (1958-)
My Boy Jack '07
Dominion: Prequel to the Exorcist '05
Wah-Wah '05
Floor '54
Monster from the Ocean '57
Teenage Monster '58
Feast '06
No Reservations '07
Shoot to Kill '47
Sundown Riders '48
Renegade Girl '46
The Body Snatcher '45
The Ghost Ship '43
The Iron Major '43

Russell Wade (1917-)

Stuart Wade

Jenny Wade (1980-)

Arnold Vosloo (1962-)
Blood Diamond '06
Agent Cody Banks '03
Endangered Species '02
The Mummy Returns '01
Progeny '98
Diary of a Serial Killer '97
Zeus and Roxanne '96
Darkman 3: Die Darkman Die '95
Darkman 2: The Return of Durant '94
Hard Target '93
The Finishing Touch '92
Red Shoe Diaries 2: Double Dare '92
Living to Die '91
Reason to Die '90
The Rutanga Tapes '90
Act of Piracy '89
Steel Dawn '87

George Voskovec (1905-81)
The Iceman Cometh '73
The Boston Strangler '68
The Bravados '58
Twelve Angry Men '57
27th Day '57

Anthony (Tony) Vorno
Sweet Trash '70
Help Wanted Female '68
Hollywood after Dark '65

Zandor Vorkov
Brain of Blood '71
Dracula vs. Frankenstein '71

Lark Voorhies (1974-)
Civil Brand '02
How High '01
Widows '02
Strange Brew '83
Der Jam's How to Be a Player '97

Kurt Vonnegut, Jr. (1922-2007)
Breakfast of Champions '98
Back to School '86
Mother Night '96

Caitlin Wachs (1989-)
Kids in America '05
A Connecticut Yankee in King Arthur's Court '49

Justine Waddell (1976-)
Thr3e '07
Wives and Daughter's '01
Dracula 2000 '00
Great Expectations '99
Mansfield Park '99
Tess of the D'Urbervilles '98
The Woman in White '97

Garry Waddell (1952-)
Chopper '00
Mad Bomber in Love '92
Mull '96

Steven Waddington (1968-)
Catherine Cookson's The Secret '00
The Hole '01
Sleepy Hollow '99
Tarzan and the Lost City '99
Warrior Queen '03
Swimsuit '89
Nightmares at Bittercreek '91
Ricochet '91
Shattered Dreams '90
The Flight '89

Jenny Wade (1980-)
Feast '06
No Reservations '07

Spencer Vrooman
The Navigator '24

Peter Von Zerneck (1908-92)
A Foreign Affair '48
13 Rue Madeleine '46

Frederick Vroom (1857-1942)
The General '26
Eyes Right! '26

Michel Vuillermoz (1963-)
My Sex Life... Or How I Got Into an Argument '96

Milena Vukotic (1930-)
A Good Woman '04
Andy Warhol's Dracula '74
Phantom of Liberty '74
The Discreet Charm of the Bourgeoisie '72

Muryyn Vye (1913-76)
Al Capone '59
Green Fire '55
River of No Return '54
Pickup on South Street '53
The Road to Bali '53
Casanova's Big Night '54
Green Grass of Wyoming '48
Whistle Stop '46

Michel Vuillermoz

Lyle Waggoner (1935-)
Wizards of the Demon Sword '94
Mind Trap '91
Dead Women in Lingerie '90
Surf 2 '84

Fernando Wagner
The Pearl '48

Jack Wagner (1959-)
Nowhere to Land '00
Dirty Little Secret '98
Trapped in Space '94
Play Murder for Me '91

Lindsay Wagner (1949-)
Frog and Wombat '98
Contagious '96
Treacherous Crossing '92
Nightmares at Bittercreek '91
Ricochet '91
Shattered Dreams '90
The Flight '89
From the Dead of Night '89
The Taking of Flight 847: The Uli Derickson Story '88
Convicted '86
Martin's Day '85
Two Kinds of Love '85
Princess Daisy '83
Callie and Son '81
High Risk '81
Nighthawks '81
Scruples '80
The Incredible Journey of Dr. Meg Laurel '79
The Two Worlds of Jenny Logan '79
Second Wind '76
The Bionic Woman '75
The Paper Chase '73

Chuck Wagner (1958-)
America 3000 '86

Stuart Wade
The Monster That Challenged the World '57
Monster from the Ocean Floor '54

Lou Wagner (1940-)
Conquest of the Planet of the Apes '72
Beneath the Planet of the Apes '70

Natasha Gregson Wagner (1970-)
Wonderland '03
John Carpenter Presents Vampires: Los Muertos '02
Two Girls and a Guy '98
First Love, Last Rites '98
Modern Vampires '98
Urban Legend '98
Dogtown '97
Glam '97
Quiet Days in Hollywood '97
Lost Highway '96
Wes Craven Presents Mind Ripper '95
Dead Beat '94
Dragstrip Girl '94
Molly and Gina '94
Tainted Blood '93
Buffy the Vampire Slayer '92
Fathers and Sons '92

Robert Wagner (1930-)
A Dennis the Menace Christmas '07
Everyone's Hero '07
Category 7: The End of the World '05
Hoot '06
Hollywood Homicide '03
Austin Powers in Goldmember '02
Sol Goode '01
The Medicine Show '01
Austin Powers 2: The Spy Who Shagged Me '99
Crazy in Alabama '99
No Vacancy '99
Wild Things '98
Play It to the Bone '99
Fatal Error '99
This Gun for Hire '90
Delirious '91
The Player '92
Jewels '92
False Arrest '92
Parallel Lives '94
Dragon: The Bruce Lee Story '93
Midway '76
Peari '78
I Am the Cheese '83
Trail of the Pink Panther '82
Curse of the Pink Panther '83
The Concorde: Airport '79 '79
The Towering Inferno '74
Death at Love House '75
The Affair '73
The Streets of San Francisco '72
Madame Sin '71
Winning '69
Harper '66
The Pink Panther '64
The Longest Day '62
War Lover '62
The Hunters '58
Stopover Tokyo '57
Between Heaven and Hell '56
The Mountain '56
Broken Lance '54
Prince Valiant '54
Beneath the 12-Mile Reef '53
Titanic '53
Stars '53
Stars and Stripes Forever '52
What Price Glory? '52
With a Song in My Heart '52
Let's Make It Legal '51
The Halls of Montezuma '50

Tabitha Wady (1976-)
Ripper '95

Henry Wadsworth (1974-)
Dead Beat '94
The Madness of King George '94
Middlemarch '93
Mountbatten: The Last Viceroy '86

Michael Wager (1925-)
Exodus '60
Hill 24 Doesn't Answer '55

Tabitha Wady
Kevin & Perry Go Large '00
Berkeley Square '98
Jane Austen in Manhattan '80

A Different Loyalty '04
Exorcist: The Beginning '04
High Heels and Low Lifes '01
Wingless Bird '97
Catherine Cookson's The English Patient '96
The Secret Agent '96
A Merry War '97
Preaching to the Perverted '97
The Madness of King George '94
Celling Zero '35
Evelyn Prentice '34
Applause '29

Robert Wagner
Stranger than Fiction '99
Another Day in Paradise '98

Thomas Wagner
Marilyn & Bobby: Her Final Affair '94
Dead On '93
The Drifter '88
Gregory Wagrowski
Asylum of the Damned '03
The Omega Code '99
Elsie Wagstaff (1899-1985)
Whistle down the Wind '61
Saturday Night and Sunday Morning '60
Yuen Wah
Kung Fu Hustle '04
Supercop '92
Dragons Forever '88
Ken Wahl (1957-)
The Favor '91
The Taking of Beverly Hills '91
Omega Syndrome '87
The Gladiator '86
The Dirty Dozen: The Next Mission '85
Purple Hearts '84
Treasure of the Yankee Zephyr '83
Jinxed '82
The Soldier '82
Fort Apache, the Bronx '81
Running Scared '79
Wanderers '79
Donnie Wahlberg (1969-)
Dead Silence '07
Annapolis '06
Marilyn Hotchkiss' Ballroom Dancing & Charm School '06
Saw III '06
Saw II '05
Dreamcatcher '03
Triggermen '02
Band of Brothers '01
Diamond Men '01
Purgatory '99
The Sixth Sense '99
Never 2 Big '98
Southie '98
Black Circle Boys '97
Body Count '97
Ransom '96
Mark Wahlberg (1971-)
The Happening '08
Shooter '07
We Own the Night '07
The Departed '06
Invincible '06
Four Brothers '05
I Heart Huckabees '04
The Italian Job '03
The Truth About Charlie '02
Planet of the Apes '01
Rock Star '01
The Perfect Storm '00
The Yards '00
The Corruptor '99
Three Kings '99
The Big Hit '98
Boogie Nights '97
Fear '96
Traveller '96
The Basketball Diaries '95
Renaissance Man '94
The Substitute '93
Edward (Robert Towne) Wain (1934-)
The Last Woman on Earth '61
James Wainwright (1938-99)
Creature from the Haunted Sea '60
Mission Manila '87
Survivors '83
Warlords of the 21st Century '82
A Woman Called Moses '78
Joe Kidd '72
Jigsaw '71
The President's Plane Is Missing '71

Loudon Wainwright III (1946-)
Elizabethtown '05
The 40 Year Old Virgin '05
Big Fish '03
Jacknife '89
The Slugger's Wife '85
Liam Waite (1971-)
King of Texas '02
John Carpenter's Ghosts of Mars '01
Second Skin '00
Malicious Intent '99
Simpatico '99
Ralph Waite (1928-)
Silver City '04
Sunshine State '02
Homeward Bound 2: Lost in San Francisco '96 (V)
Sin and Redemption '94
Sioux City '94
Cliffhanger '93
The Bodyguard '92
Crash and Burn '90
A Day for Thanks on Walton's Mountain '82
Gentleman Bandit '81
Angel City '80
On the Nickel '80
Red Alert '77
Girls on the Road '73
The Stone Killer '73
The Sporting Club '72
Chato's Land '71
The Grissom Gang '71
Lawman '71
Five Easy Pieces '70
Cool Hand Luke '67
Thomas G. Waites
McBain '91
Verne Miller '88
The Clan of the Cave Bear '86
The Thing '82
And Justice for All '79
On the Yard '79
The Warriors '79
Tom Waits (1949-)
Wristcutters: A Love Story '06
Domino '05
The Tiger and the Snow '05
Coffee and Cigarettes '03
Mystery Men '99
Short Cuts '93
Bram Stoker's Dracula '92
At Play in the Fields of the Lord '91
Queens Logic '91
Cold Feet '89
Mystery Train '89 (V)
Shakedown '88
Candy Mountain '87
Ironweed '87
Down by Law '86
The Cotton Club '84
The Outsiders '83
Rumble Fish '83
Akiko Wakabayashi (1941-)
You Only Live Twice '67
What's Up, Tiger Lily? '66
Dagora, the Space Monster '65
Ghidrah the Three Headed Monster '65
King Kong vs. Godzilla '63
Ayako Wakao (1933-)
An Actor's Revenge '63
Drifting Weeds '59
A Geisha '53
Tomisaburo Wakayama (1929-92)
Irezumi '83
Shogun Assassin '80
The Bad News Bears Go to Japan '78
Phoenix '78
Lone Wolf and Cub '72
Lone Wolf and Cub 4 '72
Lone Wolf and Cub: Baby Cart at the River Styx '72
Lone Wolf and Cub: Baby Cart to Hades '72
Sympathy for the Underdog '71

Zatoichi: Master Ichi and a Chest of Gold '64
Hugh Wakefield (1971-)
Blithe Spirit '45
The Man Who Knew Too Much '34
Deborah Wakeham (1955-)
Starlight '97
House of the Rising Sun '87
Covergirl '83
Middle Age Crazy '80
Jimmy Wakely (1914-82)
Brand of Fear '49
Range Renegades '48
Anton Walbrook (1900-67)
Saint Joan '57
Lola Montes '55
La Ronde '51
The Queen of Spades '49
The Red Shoes '48
The Life and Death of Colonel Blimp '43
Dangerous Moonlight '41
The Forty-Ninth Parallel '41
Gaslight '40
Raymond Walburn (1887-1969)
Key to the City '50
Riding High '50
Hail the Conquering Hero '44
The Desperadoes '43
Louisiana Purchase '41
Christmas in July '40
It Could Happen to You '39
Let Freedom Ring '39
Murder in Greenwich Village '37
Thin Ice '37
They Met in a Taxi '36
Mr. Deeds Goes to Town '36
Lady by Choice '34
Gregory Walcott (1928-)
Ed Wood '94
Midway '76
The Last American Hero '73
Joe Kidd '72
Prime Cut '72
Plan 9 from Outer Space '56
Texas Lady '56
Battle Cry '55
Above and Beyond '53
John Walcutt
Roseanne: An Unauthorized Biography '94
Return '88
Lynette Walden
Saved by the Light '95
Almost Blue '93
Robert Walden (1943-)
The Silencer '92
Murderer's Keep '88
Perry Mason: The Case of the Lost Love '87
Memorial Day '83
Enola Gay: The Men, the Mission, the Atomic Bomb '80
Blue Sunshine '78
Larry '74
Our Time '74
Everything You Always Wanted to Know about Sex (But Were Afraid to Ask) '72
Bloody Mama '70
Shawna Waldron (1982-)
Change of Heart '98
Mr. Headmistress '98
The American President '95

Little Giants '94
Ethel Wales (1898-1952)
Border Vigilantes '41
The Gladiator '38
Under Montana Skies '30
Made for Love '26
Wally Wales (1895-1980)
Fighting Seabees '44
Bad Man of Deadwood '41
In Old Cheyenne '41
Sheriff of Tombstone '41
Adventures of Red Ryder '40
Carson City Kid '40
The Trigger Trio '37
Gun Play '36
Danger Trails '35
The Miracle Rider '35
Pecos Kid '35
Powdersmoke Range '35
Rustlers of Red Dog '35
Silent Valley '35
Swifty '35
Way of the West '35
The Fighting Rookie '34
Deadwood Pass '33
Law and Lawless '33
Sagebrush Trail '33
Desert of the Lost '27
Sonya Walger (1974-)
All the King's Men '99
Heat of the Sun '99
Noah's Ark '99
Christopher Walken (1943-)
Balls of Fury '07
Hairspray '07
Click '06
Man of the Year '06
Domino '05
Romance & Cigarettes '05
Wedding Crashers '05
Around the Bend '04
Envy '04
Man on Fire '04
The Stepford Wives '04
Gigli '03
The Rundown '03
Catch Me If You Can '02
The Country Bears '02
Kangaroo Jack '02
Poolhall Junkies '02
Scotland, PA '02
America's Sweethearts '01
Joe Dirt '01
Kiss Toledo Goodbye '00
The Eternal '99
The Prophecy 3: The Ascent '99
Sarah, Plain and Tall: Winter's End '99
Sleepy Hollow '99
Vendetta '99
Antz '98 (V)
Blast from the Past '98
Illuminata '98
New Rose Hotel '98
Mouse Hunt '97
The Prophecy 2: Ashtown '97
Suicide Kings '97
Basquiat '96
Excess Baggage '96
The Funeral '96
Last Man Standing '96
Touch '96
The Addiction '95
Nick of Time '95
The Prophecy '95
Things to Do in Denver When You're Dead '95
Wild Side '95
Pulp Fiction '94
Search and Destroy '94
A Business Affair '93
Day of Atonement '93
Sarah, Plain and Tall: Skylark '93
Scam '93
True Romance '93

Wayne's World 2 '93
Batman Returns '92
All-American Murder '91
The Comfort of Strangers '91
McBain '91
Mistress '91
Sarah, Plain and Tall '91
King of New York '90
Communion '89
Biloxi Blues '88
Homeboy '88
The Milagro Beanfield War '88
Deadline '87
At Close Range '86
A View to a Kill '85
Brainstorm '83
Dead Zone '83
Who Am I This Time? '82
The Dogs of War '81
Heaven's Gate '81
Pennies from Heaven '81
Shoot the Sun Down '81
Last Embrace '79
The Deer Hunter '78
Annie Hall '77
Roseland '77
Next Stop, Greenwich Village '76
The Sentinel '76
Mind Snatchers '72
The Anderson Tapes '71
Ally Walker (1961-)
Happy, Texas '99
Kazaam '96
Bed of Roses '95
Someone to Die For '95
While You Were Sleeping '95
When the Bough Breaks '93
The Seventh Coin '92
Singles '92
Universal Soldier '92
Amanda Walker
Charles & Diana: A Palace Divided '93
Heat and Dust '82
Arnetia Walker (1961-)
Love Crimes '92
Scenes from the Class Struggle in Beverly Hills '89
The Wizard of Speed and Time '88
Bill Walker (1896-1992)
The Mask '61
No Time for Romance '48
Catherine Walker
Northanger Abbey '07
Conspiracy of Silence '03
Charlotte Walker (1918-71)
Annapolis '28
Midnight Girl '25
Cheryl Walker (1918-71)
Identity Unknown '45
Stage Door Canteen '43
Clint Walker (1927-)
Small Soldiers '98 (V)
The Gambler Returns: The Luck of the Draw '91
Mysterious Island of Beautiful Women '79
Snowbeast '77
The White Buffalo '77
Baker's Hawk '76
Scream of the Wolf '74
The Bounty Man '72
Deadly Harvest '72
Pancho Villa '72
Yuma '70
Sam Whiskey '69
More Dead Than Alive '68
The Dirty Dozen '67
Maya '66
Night of the Grizzly '66
None But the Brave '65
Eamonn Walker (1959-)
Duma '05
Lord of War '05
Tears of the Sun '03

Whitewash: The Clarence Brandley Story '02
Othello '01
Once in the Life '00
Unbreakable '00
Eric Walker (1970-)
Kicking & Screaming '05
And You Thought Your Parents Were Weird! '91
The Ewoks: Battle for Endor '85
The Ewok Adventure '84
Fiona Walker (1944-)
The Norman Conquests, Part 1: Table Manners '78
The Norman Conquests, Part 2: Living Together '78
The Norman Conquests, Part 3: Round and Round the Garden '78
The Asphyx '72
Jude the Obscure '71
Helen Walker (1920-68)
Big Combo '55
Impact '49
Call Northside 777 '48
Nightmare Alley '47
People Are Funny '46
Brewster's Millions '45
Murder, He Says '45
Abroad with Two Yanks '44
Jimmie Walker (1947-)
Frankenstein Sings... The Movie '95
Open Season '95
Invasion of the Space Preachers '90
Going Bananas '88
My African Adventure '87
Doin' Time '85
Water '85
Airplane! '80
B.A.D. Cats '80
The Concorde: Airport '79 '79
Let's Do It Again '75
Johnnie Walker (1894-1949)
Bare Knees '28
Broken Hearts of Broadway '23
Jonathan Walker (1967-)
Finding North '97 (V)
American Blue Note '89
Justin Walker
Boltneck '98
Born Bad '97
Kathryn Walker (1943-)
Dangerous Game '90
The Murder of Mary Phagan '87
Uncle Tom's Cabin '87
Private Contentment '83
Special Bulletin '83
Neighbors '81
Whale for the Killing '81
Rich Kids '79
Girlfriends '78
The Winds of Kitty Hawk '78
Slap Shot '77
Blade '72
Kerry Walker (1948-)
A Little Bit of Soul '97
Road to Nhill '97
Cosi '95
The Piano '93
Kim Walker (1968-2001)
Heathers '89
Deadly Weapon '88
Liza Walker (1972-)
Wavelength '96
Buddy's Song '91
Twisted Obsession '90
Maggie Walker
Three Days of Rain '03
Three Days of Rain '02
The House that Vanished '73

Marcy Walker (1961-)
Talking about Sex '94
Midnight's Child '93

Mark Walker
Disconnected '87
Random Encounter '98

Matthew (Matt) Walker (1942-)
Alone in the Dark '05
Ginger Snaps Back: The Beginning '04

Michael Walker (1941-)
Hell's Belles '69
Daring Game '68

Nancy Walker (1921-92)
Murder by Death '76
Death Scream '75
Thursday's Game '74
Forty Carats '73
Lucky Me '54
Broadway Rhythm '44
Best Foot Forward '43
Girl Crazy '43

Paul Walker (1973-)
Bobby Z '07
Eight Below '06
Flags of Our Fathers '06
Running Scared '06
Into the Blue '05
Noel '04
Timeline '03
2 Fast 2 Furious '03
The Fast and the Furious '01
Joy Ride '01
The Skulls '00
She's All That '99
8 1/2 Women '99
Meet the Deedles '98
Pleasantville '98
Varsity Blues '98

Polly Walker (1966-)
Scenes of a Sexual Nature '06
The Mayor of Casterbridge '03
State of Play '03
Savage Messiah '02
Emma '96
For Roseanna '96
Robinson Crusoe '96
Talk of Angels '96
Restoration '94
The Trial '93
Silver '93
Enchanted April '92
Patriot Games '92
A Dangerous Man: Lawrence after Arabia '91
Lorna Doone '90

Ray Walker (1904-80)
The Blue Gardenia '53
Rogue's Gallery '44
House of Errors '42
Bulldog Edition '36
Goodbye Love '34

Robert Walker (1888-1954)
El Diablo Rides '36
Fast Bullets '36

Robert Walker (1918-51)
Strangers on a Train '51
Vengeance Valley '51
One Touch of Venus '48
Song of Love '47
Till the Clouds Roll By '46
The Clock '45
Since You Went Away '44
Thirty Seconds Over Tokyo '44
Bataan '43
Madame Curie '43
The Crimson Trail '35

Robert Walker, Jr. (1940-)
Evil Town '87
Hambone & Hillie '84
Devonsville Terror '83
Oliva '83
Angkor: Cambodia Express '81
The Shrieking '73
The Spectre of Edgar Allen Poe '73
Beware! The Blob '72
Easy Rider '69
Road to Salina '69
The Savage Seven '68
The War Wagon '67
Ensign Pulver '64

Sarah Walker
Housekeeping '87
Man of Flowers '84

Terry Walker
Battling Outlaw '40
Take Me Back to Oklahoma '40

Tippy Walker (1947-)
23 1/2 Hours Leave '37
The Jesus Trip '71
The World of Henry Orient '64

Walter Walker (1901-75)
Sons of Steel '35
American Madness '32
No Man of Her Own '32
White Trail '38

Max Wall (1894-1990)
Strike It Rich '90
Little Dorrit, Film 1: Nobody's Fault '88
Little Dorrit, Film 2: Little Dorrit's Story '88
Jabberwocky '77

Basil Wallace
A Killer in Every Corner '74
Blood Diamond '06
Joy Ride '01
Caught Up '98
Return of the Living Dead 3 '93
Marked for Death '90

Beryl Wallace (1910-43)
The Kansan '43
Sunset on the Desert '42

Bill Wallace (1949-)
Rough Ridin' Rhythm '37

David Wallace (1957-)
Humongous '82
Mazes and Monsters '82

George D. Wallace (1917-2005)
Bicentennial Man '99
Forces of Nature '99
Diggstown '92
Defending Your Life '91

George Wallace (1952-)
The Ladykillers '04
The Wash '01
Three Strikes '00
Batman Forever '95

Dee Wallace Stone (1948-)
Voodoo Moon '05
Headspace '05
Out of the Black '01
Killer Instinct '00
Invisible Mom 2 '99
Invisible Mom '96
The Frighteners '96
The Skateboard Kid 2 '94
Discretion Assured '93
Huck and the King of Hearts '93
My Family Treasure '93
Rescue Me '93
Alligator 2: The Mutation '90
Popcorn '89
Miracle Down Under '87
Club Life '86
Critters '86
Shadow Play '86
Secret Admirer '85
Cujo '83
E.T.: The Extra-Terrestrial '82
The Howling '81
The Hills Have Eyes '77

Jean Wallace (1923-90)
Sword of Lancelot '63
Big Combo '55
Native Son '51
Jigsaw '49

Marcia Wallace (1942-)
The Simpsons Movie '07
My Mom's a Werewolf '89
Pray TV '80

Morgan Wallace (1881-1953)
The Vector File '03
Cover Story '93
Halloween '07
Honky Tonk '41
In Old Colorado '41
Star Reporter '39
Delinquent Parents '38
Gang Bullets '38
The House of Secrets '37
Confidential '35

William Wallace (1971-)
Nevada '97

Roberta Wallach (1955-)
The Hollywood Knights '80
The Effect of Gamma Rays on Man-in-the-Moon Marigolds '73

Sigurd Wallen (1884-1947)
Swedenhielms '35

Eli Wallach (1915-)
The Holiday '06
The Severed Arm '73
Skeezer '82
Jimmy the Kid '82
Winter Kills '79
Circle of Iron '78
Girlfriends '78
Movie, Movie '78
The Deep '77
The Domino Principle '77
Nasty Habits '77
The Sentinel '76
Stateline Motel '75
Cinderella Liberty '73
Romance of a Horsethief '71
The Angel Levine '70
The People Next Door '70
The Brain '69
MacKenna's Gold '69
Ace High '68
The Good, the Bad and the Ugly '67
How to Steal a Million '66
The Poppy Is Also a Flower '66
Lord Jim '65
Kisses for My President '64
The Moon-Spinners '64
The Victors '63
The Misfits '61
The Magnificent Seven '60
Seven Thieves '60
Baby Doll '56

Deborah Walley (1943-2001)
Benji '74
Dr. Goldfoot and the Bikini Machine '66
Spinout '66
Beach Blanket Bingo '65
Ski Party '65
Summer Magic '63
Bon Voyage! '62
Gidget Goes Hawaiian '61

David Walliams
Stardust '07
Tristram Shandy: A Cock and Bull Story '05

Eddy (Eddie, Ed) Waller (1889-1977)
El Paso Stampede '53
Marshal of Cedar Rock '53
Bandit King of Texas '49
Wild Frontier '47
Rough Riders of Cheyenne '45
Legion of the Lawless '40

George Walsh (1889-1981)
Pinto Rustlers '36
The Live Wire '34
The Count of the Old Town '34

Gwynyth Walsh
2103: Deadly Wake '97
The Limbic Region '96
Soft Deceit '94
The Crush '93
The Challengers '89
Blue Monkey '87

J.T. Walsh (1943-98)
The Negotiator '98
Pleasantville '98
Hope '97
Breakdown '97
The Big White?
Executive Decision '96
Persons Unknown '96

Jack Walsh (1935-)
Naked City: Justice with a Bullet '98

M. Emmet Walsh (1935-)
Snow Dogs '02
Christmas in the Clouds '01
Poor White Trash '00
Me & Will '99
Wild Wild West '99
Twilight '98
Chairman of the Board '97
My Best Friend's Wedding '97
Retroactive '97
Albino Alligator '96
The Killing Jar '96
A Time to Kill '96
Iron Giant '99 (V)
Romeo and Juliet '96
Criminal Hearts '96
The Glass Shield '95
Panther '95
Probable Cause '95
Relative Fear '95
Camp Nowhere '94

Kate Walsh (1967-)
The Family Man '00

Ken Walsh
Conspiracy of Fear '96
Straight Line '89

Eileen Walsh (1977-)
The Magdalene Sisters '02
Janice Beard '99

Dylan Walsh (1963-)
Power Play '02
We Were Soldiers '02
Final Voyage '99
Eden '98
Men '97
Changing Habits '96
Nobody's Fool '94
Radio Inside '94
Arctic Blue '93
Betsy's Wedding '90
Where the Heart Is '90
Congo '95
Divided by Hate '96

Dermot Walsh (1924-2002)
The Great Armored Car Swindle '64

Angela Walsh
Distant Voices, Still Lives '88

Amanda Walsh (1981-)
These Girls '05

Arthur Walsh (1923-95)
Mystic Pizza '88
Last Hurrah '58

Kay Walsh (1914-2005)
The Witches '66
Greyfriars Bobby '61
Tunes of Glory '60
The Horse's Mouth '58
Cast a Dark Shadow '55
Young Bess '53
Encore '52
Last Holiday '50
Stage Fright '50
The October Man '48
Oliver Twist '48
This Happy Breed '47
In Which We Serve '43
Secret of Stamboul '36

Jon Walmsley (1956-)
A Day for Thanks on Walton's Mountain '82
The Waltons: A Christmas Carol '80

Shani Wallis (1941-)
Arnold '73
Oliver! '68

Tom Walls (1883-1949)
Maytime in Mayfair '49
While I Live '47
Johnny Frenchman '46

William Walling (1842-1932)
Range Feud '31
Two Fisted Justice '31

Angela Walsh (1924-2002)
Catherine Cookson's The Man Who Cried '93

Dermot Walsh (1924-2002)
They Were Expendable '45
Courage of Lassie '46
You Gotta Stay Happy '48
The Fiesh and the Fiends '60
The Tell-Tale Heart '60
It Takes a Thief '59
Ghost Ship '53
Murder on the Campus '52

Tom Walls
Sam's Son '84
My Sweet Victim '65
Embassy '85
Tough Guys '86
Something in Common '66
Rocket to the Moon '86
Nuts '87
The Impossible Spy '90
The Two Jakes '90
The Godfather, Part 3 '90
The Executioner's Scng '82
The Salamander '82
Pride of Jesse Hallam '81
The Hunter '80

Jack Wallace (1933-)
Lakeboat '00
The Fixer '97
The Bear '89
Things Change '88
Assignment Outer Space '61 (V)

Shani Wallis
Round Numbers '91
Penguin '94 (IV)
Nixon '95

Dead Badge '94
Bitter Harvest '93
Equinox '93
Four Eyes and Six Guns '93
The Music of Chance '93
Wilder Napalm '93
Killer Image '92
White Sands '92
Wildcard '92
Boxcar Blues '90
Fourth Story '90
Narrow Margin '90
The Brotherhood of the Rose '89
Chattahoochee '89
The Mighty Quinn '89
Red Scorpion '89
Thunderground '89
War Party '89
Clean and Sober '88
The Milagro Beanfield War '88
Sunset '88
The Abduction of Kari Swenson '87
Broken Vows '87
Harry and the Hendersons '87
Murder Ordained '87
Raising Arizona '87
Back to School '86
The Best of Times '86
Critters '86
The Deliberate Stranger '86
Wildcats '86
Blood Simple '85
Fletch '85
Grandview U.S.A. '84
Missing in Action '84
The Pope of Greenwich Village '84
Raw Courage '84
Scandalous '84
Night Partners '83
Blade Runner '82
Cannery Row '82
Fast Walking '82
Reds '81
Brubaker '80
East of Eden '80
Ordinary People '80
The Jerk '79
Dear Detective '78
Straight Time '78
Slap Shot '77
The Gambler '74
Escape from the Planet of the Apes '71
They Might Be Giants '71
Alice's Restaurant '69
Stiletto '69

Mary Walsh (1952-)
Mambo Italiano '03
New Waterford Girl '99

Percy Walsh (1888-1952)
The Golden Salamander '51

Raoul Walsh (1887-1981)
Sadie Thompson '28
The Birth of a Nation '15

Susan Walsh
Female Trouble '74

Sydney Walsh (1961-)
MacArthur Park '01
Danger of Love '95
A Kiss Goodnight '94
Homewrecker '92
Point Break '91
Three Men and a Little Lady '90
To Die For '89
A Nightmare on Elm Street 2: Freddy's Revenge '85

Ray Walston (1918-2001)
Get a Clue! '98
My Favorite Martian '98
Tricks '97

House Arrest '96
Stephen King's The Stand '94
Of Mice and Men '92
The Player '92
Blood Salvage '90
Popcorn '89
Ski Patrol '89
Fine Gold '88
A Man of Passion '88
Paramedics '88
Saturday the 14th Strikes Back '88
Blood Relations '87
O.C. and Stiggs '87
From the Hip '86
Amos '85
For Love or Money '84
Johnny Dangerously '84
Private School '83
Fast Times at Ridgemont High '82
O'Hara's Wife '82
Galaxy of Terror '81
The Fall of the House of Usher '80
Popeye '80
The Happy Hooker Goes to Washington '77
Silver Streak '76
The Sting '73
Caprice '67
Kiss Me, Stupid! '64
Who's Minding the Store? '63
The Apartment '60
Portrait in Black '60
Tall Story '60
Damn Yankees '58
South Pacific '58

Harriet Walter (1951-)
Atonement '07
Onegin '99
Bedrooms and Hallways '98
The Governess '98
A Merry War '97
Sense and Sensibility '95
The Advocate '93
May Fools '90
The Good Father '87

Jessica Walter (1940-)
Unaccompanied Minors '06
Dummy '02
Slums of Beverly Hills '98
Temptress '95
P.C.U. '94
Ghost in the Machine '93
Tapeheads '89
The Flamingo Kid '84
Going Ape! '81
Miracle on Ice '81
Spring Fever '81
Goldengirl '79
She's Dressed to Kill '79
Dr. Strange '78
Secrets of Three Hungry Wives '78
Wild & Wooly '78
Victory at Entebbe '76
Hurricane '74
Home for the Holidays '72
Play Misty for Me '71
They Call It Murder '71
The Group '66
Lilith '64

Lisa Ann Walter (1963-)
War of the Worlds '05
Shall We Dance? '04
Bruce Almighty '03
The Parent Trap '98
Eddie '96

Tracey Walter (1942-)
How High '01
Drowning Mona '00
Erin Brockovich '00
Wild America '97
Drive '96
Larger Than Life '96
Matilda '96
Buffalo Girls '95
Destiny Turns on the Radio '95

Philadelphia '93
Liquid Dreams '92
City Slickers '91
Delusion '91
Mortuary Academy '91
The Silence of the Lambs '91
Pacific Heights '90
The Two Jakes '90
Young Guns 2 '90
Batman '89
Under the Boardwalk '89
Married to the Mob '88
Out of the Dark '88
At Close Range '86
Something Wild '86
Conan the Destroyer '84
Repo Man '83
Timerider '83
Raggedy Man '81
Mad Bull '77

Desmond Walter-Ellis (1914-94)
The Great St. Trinian's Train Robbery '66
The Hellfire Club '61

Ashley Walters (1982-)
Goal! The Dream Begins '06
Get Rich or Die Tryin' '05
House of 9 '05

Hal Walters (1891-1941)
The Four Feathers '39
Sabotage '36

Julie Walters (1950-)
Mamma Mia! '08
Becoming Jane '07
Harry Potter and the Order of the Phoenix '07
Driving Lessons '06
Ruby in the Smoke '06
Wah-Wah '05
Harry Potter and the Prisoner of Azkaban '04
Calendar Girls '03
Harry Potter and the Chamber of Secrets '02
Harry Potter and the Sorcerer's Stone '01
Billy Elliot '00
Oliver Twist '00
Lover's Prayer '99
Girls' Night '97
Melissa '97
Intimate Relations '95
Just Like a Woman '95
Sister My Sister '94
The Summer House '94
The Wedding Gift '93
Stepping Out '91
Happy Since I Met You '89
Mack the Knife '89
Buster '88
Personal Services '87
Prick Up Your Ears '87
Car Trouble '86
She'll Be Wearing Pink Pajamas '84
Educating Rita '83

Laurie Walters (1950-)
The Taking of Flight 847: The Uli Derickson Story '88
Harrad Summer '74
Harrad Experiment '73
Warlock Moon '73

Luana Walters (1912-63)
Shoot to Kill '47
The Corpse Vanishes '42
Inside the Law '42
Arizona Bound '41
Kid's Last Ride '41
Misbehaving Husbands '41
Blondie Plays Cupid '40
Range Busters '40
Aces and Eights '36
Shadow of Chinatown '36
Speed Reporter '36
Assassin of Youth '35
Fighting Texans '33

Melora Walters (1968-)
Brothers Three '07
The Big Empty '04
The Butterfly Effect '04
Cold Mountain '03
Wisegirls '02
Desert Saints '01
Magnolia '99
Boogie Nights '97
Los Locos Posse '97
American Strays '96
Hard Eight '96
Twenty Bucks '93
America's Deadliest Home Video '91

Susan Walters (1963-)
Where the Truth Lies '99
I Married a Monster '98
Galaxies Are Colliding '92
Defending Your Life '91
Elvis and Me '88
Russkies '87

Thorley Walters (1913-91)
In the Secret State '85
The Little Drummer Girl '84
The Sign of Four '83
The Adventures of Sherlock Holmes' Smarter Brother '78
The People That Time Forgot '77
Cry of the Penguins '71
Vampire Circus '71
Bartleby '70
Frankenstein Must Be Destroyed '69
Oh! What a Lovely War '69
Dracula, Prince of Darkness '66
Frankenstein Created Woman '66
Murder She Said '62
The Phantom of the Opera '62
Sherlock Holmes and the Deadly Necklace '62
The Pure Hell of St. Trinian's '61
Blue Murder at St. Trinian's '56
Who Done It? '56

Henry B. Walthall (1878-1936)
Devil Doll '36
Last Outlaw '36
A Tale of Two Cities '36
Beggars in Ermine '34
Judge Priest '34
The Scarlet Letter '34
Viva Villa! '34
Flaming Signal '33
Laughing at Life '33
Somewhere in Sonora '33
The Cabin in the Cotton '32
Chandu the Magician '32
Police Court '32
Ride Him, Cowboy '32
Strange Interlude '32
Abraham Lincoln '30
The Phantom in the House '29
Wings '27
The Plastic Age '25
Wild Carson over the Great Divide '25
The Confession '20
False Faces '18
The Birth of a Nation '15
The Raven '15
Avenging Conscience '14
Home Sweet Home '14
Judith of Bethulia '14

Bill Walton (1952-)
Little Nicky '00
Celtic Pride '96

Douglas Walton (1910-61)
Murder, My Sweet '44
Sundown Fury '42
Bad Lands '39
Wallaby Jim of the Islands '37
I Conquer the Sea '36
Mary of Scotland '36

The Bride of Frankenstein '35
Charlie Chan in London '34
The Lost Patrol '34

John Walton (1953-)
The Lighthorsemen '87
Kangaroo '86

Lisa Waltz
Starry Night '99
Neil Simon's The Odd Couple 2 '98
Brighton Beach Memoirs '86

Lau Ching Wan (1964-)
Running out of Time '99
Black Mask '96

Sam Wanamaker (1919-93)
Covert Assassin '94
City of Joy '92
Secret Ingredient '92
Guilty by Suspicion '91
Pure Luck '91
Running Against Time '90
The Shell Seekers '89
Judgment in Berlin '88
Baby Boom '87
Superman 4: The Quest for Peace '87
Raw Deal '86
The Aviator '85
Embassy '85
Detective Sadie & Son '84
Ghostwriter '84
Irreconcilable Differences '84
Our Family Business '81
The Competition '80
Private Benjamin '80
Charlie Muffin '79
From Hell to Victory '79
Sell Out '76
Voyage of the Damned '76
Spiral Staircase '75
The Spy Who Came in from the Cold '65
Those Magnificent Men in Their Flying Machines '65
Taras Bulba '62
The Battle of the Sexes '60 (N)
My Girl Tisa '48

Zoe Wanamaker (1949-)
Harry Potter and the Sorcerer's Stone '01
David Copperfield '99
The Raggedy Legend of the Leprechauns '99
A Dance to the Music of Time '97
Swept from the Sea '97
Wilde '97
The Blackheath Poisonings '92
Prime Suspect '92
Tales of the Unexpected '91
The Raggedy Rawney '90
Poor Little Rich Girl: The Barbara Hutton Story '87

Carter Wang (1947-)
Hardcase and Fist '89
Way of the Black Dragon '81

Faye Wang
See Faye Wong

Hongwei Wang
The World '04

Peter Wang
A Great Wall '86

Zhiwen Wang (1966-)
Together '02
The Emperor and the Assassin '99
Blush '95

Percy Waram (1881-1961)
The Big Hangover '50

Ministry of Fear '44

David Warbeck (1941-97)
Razor Blade Smile '98
Miami Horror '87
Formula for a Murder '85
Tiger Joe '85
Ark of the Sun God '82
The Beyond '82
Hunters of the Golden Cobra '82
The Black Cat '81
The Last Hunter '80
Panic '76
Blacksnake! '73
Twins of Evil '71

John Warburton (1887-1981)
King Rat '65
Secret File of Hollywood '62
Saratoga Trunk '45
Nothing But Trouble '44
The White Cliffs of Dover '44
Cavalcade '33

Patrick Warburton (1964-)
Space Chimps '08 (V)
Bee Movie '07 (V)
Happily N'Ever After '07 (V)
Underdog '07
Open Season '06 (V)
The Wild '06 (V)
Chicken Little '05 (V)
Hoodwinked '05 (V)
Rebound '05
Sky High '05 (V)
Home on the Range '04 (V)
Big Trouble '02
Men in Black 2 '02
Joe Somebody '01
Angels in the Infield '00
The Dish '00
The Emperor's New Groove '00 (V)
Scream 3 '00
Apartment Complex '98
Dragonard '88
Batman '66

Amelita Ward
Jungle Captive '45
Seven Days Ashore '44
Clancy Street Boys '43

B.J. Ward
The Opposite Sex and How to Live With Them '93
Pound Puppies and the Legend of Big Paw '88 (V)

Brendan Ward
South Bronx Heroes '85
Taps '81

Burt Ward (1945-)
Assault of the Party Nerds 2: Heavy Petting Detective '95
Beach Babes from Beyond '93
Smooth Talker '90
Virgin High '90
Killcrazy '89
Robo-Chic '89
Batman '66

Donal Lardner Ward (1964-)
The Suburbans '99
My Life's in Turnaround '94

Fred Ward (1943-)
Feast of Love '07
Coast to Coast '04
Abandon '02
Enough '02
Sweet Home Alabama '02
Corky Romano '01
Joe Dirt '01
Summer Catch '01
Wild Iris '01
Chaos Factor '00
Circus '00
The Crow: Salvation '00
Full Disclosure '00
Road Trip '00
The Crimson Code '99
Best Men '98
Dangerous Beauty '98
Forgotten City '98
Invasion: Earth '98

Fred Ward *(continued)*
First Do No Harm '97
Chain Reaction '96
Tremors 2: Aftershocks '96
Naked Gun 33 1/3: The Final Insult '94
Equinox '93
Four Eyes and Six Guns '93
Short Cuts '93
Two Small Bodies '93
Bob Roberts '92
The Player '92
Thunderheart '92
Henry & June '90
Miami Blues '90
Backtrack '89
Tremors '89
Big Business '88
Prince of Pennsylvania '88
Off Limits '88
Cast a Deadly Spell '91
Remo Williams: The Adventure Begins '85
Secret Admirer '85
Noon Wine '84
Swing Shift '84
The Right Stuff '83
Silkwood '83
Timerider '83
Uncommon Valor '83
Southern Comfort '81
Uforia '81
Escape from Alcatraz '79

Penelope Dudley Ward (1915-82)
The Demi-Paradise '43

Paddy Ward
Casanova '05
Waking Ned Devine '98

Megan Ward (1969-)
Murder Without Conviction '04
Rated X '00
Tick Tock '00
Don't Look Down '98
Glory Daze '96
Joe's Apartment '96
P.C.U. '94
Arcade '93
Freaked '93
Amityville 1992: It's About Time '92
Encino Man '92
Trancers 3: Death Lives '92
Trancers 2: The Return of... '91
Jack Deth '90

Mary B. Ward
Surviving Desire '91
Hangin' with the Homeboys '91

Maitland Ward (1977-)
White Chicks '04
Dish Dogs '98

Kelly Ward (1956-)
The Big Red One '80
Grease '78

Larry Ward (1915-85)
Deathhead Virgin '74
Macabre '69

Lyman Ward (1941-)
Independence Day '96
The Secret Agent Club '95
Sleepwalkers '92
Mikey '92
The Taking of Beverly Hills '91
Perfect Victims '87
Planes, Trains & Automobiles '87
Ferris Bueller's Day Off '85
Creature '85

John Ward (1924-95)
Robinson Crusoe of Clipper Island '36
Holt of the Secret Service '42

Jonathan Ward (1970-)
Ferngully: The Last Rain Forest '92 (V)
Mac and Me '88
White Water Summer '87

Rachel Ward (1957-)
The Big Fall '96
A Village Affair '95
A Dark Adapted Eye '93
Class of '61 '92
A Demon in My View '92
Christopher Columbus: The Discovery '92
Black Magic '92
The Ascent '94
Twisted '96
On the Beach '00
Johnson County War '02
Bobbie's Girl '02
How to Get Ahead in Advertising '89
After Dark, My Sweet '90
Hotel Colonial '88
The Good Wife '86
Fortress '85
The Final Terror '85
Against All Odds '84
The Thorn Birds '83
Dead Men Don't Wear Plaid '82
Night School '81
Sharky's Machine '81

Rich Ward
Vampires of Sorority Row: Kickboxers From Hell '99

Richard Ward (1915-79)
Mandingo '75
Across 110th Street '72

Robin Ward (1944-)
The Chinatown Murders: Man against the Mob '89

Roger Ward (1936-)
Quigley Down Under '90
Mad Max '80

Roy Ward
The Ugly '96

Sandy Ward (1926-2005)
Blue Desert '91
Delta Force 3: The Killing Game '91
Thrillkill '84
The Jerk '79

Sela Ward (1957-)
The Day After Tomorrow '04
The Guardian '06
Dirty Dancing: Havana Nights '04
The Badge '02
Runaway Bride '99
54 '98
Rescuers: Stories of Courage: "Two Women" '97
My Fellow Americans '96
The Fugitive '93
Double Jeopardy '93
Child of Darkness, Child of Light '91
Rainbow Drive '90
Nothing in Common '86
Steele Justice '87
Hello Again '87

Simon Ward (1941-)
The Monster Club '85
Supergirl '84
Deadly Strangers '82
Dominique Is Dead '79
Zulu Dawn '79
The Four Feathers '78
The Chosen '77
Children of Rage '75
The Four Musketeers '75
All Creatures Great and Small '74
The Three Musketeers '74
Dracula '73
Hitler: The Last Ten Days '73
Young Winston '72

Sophie Ward (1965-)
The Big Fall '96
A Village Affair '95
A Dark Adapted Eye '93
Class of '61 '92
A Demon in My View '92
A Summer Story '88
Young Sherlock Holmes '85

Susan Ward (1976-)
Wild Things 2 '04
Cruel World '05
Shallow Hal '01
The In Crowd '00

Tom Ward (1971-)
The Lost World '02
Moll Flanders '96

Vincent Ward (1956-)
One Night Stand '97
The Shot '96

Wally Ward
See Wallace (Wally) Langham

Warwick Ward (1891-1967)
The Informer '29
Variety '25

Zack (Zach) Ward (1973-)
Transformers '07
BloodRayne 2: Deliverance '07
Resident Evil: Apocalypse '04
April's Shower '03
Almost Famous '00
Brotherhood of Murder '99
Malicious Intent '99
A Christmas Story '83

Jennifer Ward-Lealand
Desperate Remedies '93
Dangerous Orphans '86

Herta Ware (1917-2005)
The Ugly '96
Top Dog '95
Crazy in Love '92
Dakota '88
Cocoon '85

Irene Ware (1910-93)
Wild Palms '93
The Lost World '92
The Unnamable 2: The Statement of Randolph Carter '92
Cast a Deadly Spell '91
Star Trek VI: The Undiscovered Country '91
Teenage Mutant Ninja Turtles 2: The Secret of the Ooze '91
Blue Tornado '90
The Raven '35
Chandu the Magician '32

Anthony Warde (1908-75)
The Challenge '38
St. Patrick's Day '39
Radar Patrol vs. Spy King '49
Roaring City '51
The Black Widow '47
Federal Agent '36
The Dark Hour '36
The Raven '35
King Kelly of the U.S.A. '34
Chandu the Magician '32

Harlan Warde (1917-80)
Diary of a Madmen '63
Above and Beyond '53
Loan Shark '52
Flying Leathernecks '51
Money Madness '47

Chris Warfield (1927-96)
Cocaine Cowboys '79

Emily Warfield (1972-)
Bonanza: The Return '93
Calendar Girl '93
The Man in the Moon '91
Pair of Aces '90

Marsha Warfield (1954-)
D.C. Cab '84
Mask '85

William Warfield (1920-2002)
Show Boat '51

Andy Warhol (1928-87)
Cocaine Cowboys '79
Driver's Seat '73

Raymond Waring (1977-)
Yes '04
Lucky Break '01

Geoffrey Wardwell (1900-55)
The Challenge '38
Crimes at the Dark House '39

David Warner (1941-)
Straight into Darkness '04
Ladies in Lavender '04
Back to the Secret Garden '01
Horatio Hornblower: The Adventure Continues '01
Planet of the Apes '01
Wing Commander '99
Houdini '99
Money Talks '97
Titanic '97
Scream 2 '97
The Leading Man '96
Rasputin: Dark Servant of Destiny '96
Beastmaster 3: The Eye of Braxus '95
Final Equinox '95
The Choir '95
Naked Souls '95
Ice Cream Man '95
In the Mouth of Madness '95
H.P. Lovecraft's Necronomicon: Book of the Dead '93
Quest of the Delta Knights '93
Wild Palms '93
The Lost World '92
The Unnamable 2: The Statement of Randolph Carter '92
Cast a Deadly Spell '91
Star Trek VI: The Undiscovered Country '91
Teenage Mutant Ninja Turtles 2: The Secret of the Ooze '91
Blue Tornado '90
Tripwire '89
Hanna's War '88
Hostile Takeover '88
Magdalene '88
Mr. North '88
My Best Friend Is a Vampire '88
Waxwork '88
A Christmas Carol '84
The Company of Wolves '85
The Man with Two Brains '83
Frankenstein '82
Mr. Saturday Night '92
Time Bandits '81
Time After Time '79
The Thirty-Nine Steps '79
S.O.S. Titanic '79
Nighthawks '79
The Concorde: Airport '79
Silver Bears '78
Providence '77
Cross of Iron '77
The Omen '76
The Old Curiosity Shop '75
A Doll's House '73
From Beyond the Grave '73
Straw Dogs '71
The Ballad of Cable Hogue '70
The Fixer '68
A Midsummer Night's Dream '68
Morgan: A Suitable Case for Treatment '66
Tom Jones '63

Amelia Warner (1982-)
Alpha Male '06
Aeon Flux '05
Stoned '05
Winter Passing '05
Lorna Doone '01
London Kills Me '91

Gordon Warnecke (1963-)
Wild West '92
My Beautiful Laundrette '85

Kimberly Warnat
Papa's Angels '00
Silver Wolf '98

Billy Warlock (1961-)
Steel Sharks '97
Opposite Corners '96
Panic in the Skies '96
Society '92
Swimsuit '89
Hot Shot '86

H.B. Warner (1876-1958)
Savage Drums '51
The Judge Steps Out '49
It's a Wonderful Life '46
Strange Impersonation '46
Action in Arabia '44
Enemy of Women '44
Rogue's Gallery '44
Boss of Big Town '43
Hitler's Children '43
Yank in Libya '42
The Corsican Brothers '41
Topper Returns '41
The Devil & Daniel Webster '41
The Ten Commandments '56

Jack Warner (1894-1981)
Dominique '79
The Quatermass Experiment '56
The Ladykillers '55
A Christmas Carol '51
Valley of the Eagles '51
The Blue Lamp '49
Train of Events '49
Against the Wind '48
Captive Heart '47
Dear Murderer '47
Hue and Cry '47
It Always Rains on Sunday '47

Julie Warner (1965-)
The Dummy Talks '43
The Puppet Masters '94
Tommy Boy '95
Stick It '06
Dean Koontz's Mr. Murder '98
Indian Summer '93
Mr. Saturday Night '92
Doc Hollywood '91

Todd Waring (1955-)
Sinatra '92
Love & Murder '91

Tron '82
The Boy Who Left Home to Find Out About the Shivers '81
Disappearance '81

Malcolm Jamal Warner (1970-)
Fool's Gold '08
Restaurant '98
The Tuskegee Airmen '95
Tyson '95
Drop Zone '94
The Father Clements Story '87

Barry Warren (1933-)
Frankenstein Created Woman '66
Kiss of the Vampire '62

C. Denier Warren (1889-1971)
Lolita '62
The Body Vanished '39

E. Alyn (Fred) Warren (1874-1940)
Get That Man '35
Mysterious Mr. Wong '35
Tarzan the Fearless '33
Abraham Lincoln '30
Medicine Man '30

Estella Warren (1978-)
The Cooler '03
Kangaroo Jack '02
Driven '01
Planet of the Apes '01
Tangled '01

Jennifer Warren (1941-)
The Amazons '84
Mutant '83
The Choice '81
Intruder Within '81
Angel City '80
Ice Castles '79
Steel Cowboy '78
Another Man, Another Chance '77
Slap Shot '77
Banjo Hackett '76
Night Moves '75
The Swap '71

Jennifer Leigh Warren (1965-)
Matter of Trust '98
Sour Grapes '98
Grace of My Heart '96
The Crossing Guard '94

Katherine Warren (1905-65)
Prowler '51

Kenneth J. Warren (1929-73)
The Creeping Flesh '72
Demons of the Mind '72
I, Monster '71
Fiction Makers '67

Kiersten Warren (1965-)
Hoot '06
Black Cadillac '03
The Snow Walker '03
Circuit '02
Divine Secrets of the Ya-Ya Sisterhood '02
Duets '00
Bicentennial Man '99
Liberty Heights '99
Independence Day '96

Lesley Ann Warren (1946-)
Cop '88
Baja Oklahoma '87
Burglar '87
Apology '86
Clue '85
Choose Me '84
The Dancing Princesses '84
Songwriter '84
A Night in Heaven '83
Treasure of the Yankee Zephyr '83
Portrait of a Showgirl '82
Victor/Victoria '82
Beulah Land '80
Portrait of a Stripper '79
Betrayal '78
Pearl '78
Harry & Walter Go to New York '76
Legend of Valentino '75
Where the Eagle Flies '72
The One and Only, Genuine, Original Family Band '68
The Happiest Millionaire '67
Cinderella '64

Marc Warren (1967-)
Wanted '08
Dracula '06
Green Street Hooligans '05
Hellraiser: Deader '05
State of Play '03
Band of Brothers '01
Dad Savage '97
Boston Kickout '95

Michael Warren (1946-)
Trippin' '99
Buffalo Soldiers '97
A Passion to Kill '94
Storyville '92
Heaven Is a Playground '91
The Kid Who Loved Christmas '90
Norman, Is That You? '76

Harold Warrender (1903-53)
Pandora and the Flying Dutchman '51
Conspirator '49
Contraband '40
Mimi '35

Ruth Warrick (1915-2005)
Deathmask '69
One Too Many '51
Let's Dance '50
Three Husbands '50
Great Dan Patch '49
Arch of Triumph '48
China Sky '44
Guest in the House '44
Mr. Winkle Goes to War '44
The Iron Major '43
The Corsican Brothers '42
Citizen Kane '41

David Warrilow (1934-95)
Barton Fink '91
Bright Lights, Big City '88
Strong Medicine '84

Dan Warry-Smith (1982-)
My Teacher Ate My Homework '98
The Legend of Gator Face '96

David Warshofsky (1959-)
Running Scared '06
Personal Velocity: Three Portraits '02
Suffering Bastards '90

John Warwick (1905-72)
While I Live '47
The Face at the Window '39
Ticket of Leave Man '37

Richard Warwick (1945-97)
Sebastiane '79
If... '69

Robert Warwick (1878-1964)
It Started with a Kiss '59
The Star '52
I Married a Witch '42
Sullivan's Travels '41
A Woman's Face '41
The Spy Ring '38
The Awful Truth '37
The Trigger Trio '37
The Bold Caballero '36
Bulldog Edition '36
Hopalong Cassidy '35
A Shot in the Dark '35
Whispering Shadow '33
The Secrets of Wu Sin '32
The Royal Bed '31
A Girl's Folly '17

Mona Washbourne (1903-88)
December Flower '84
Brideshead Revisited '81
Therese Raquin '80
Stevie '78
Driver's Seat '73
O Lucky Man! '73
If... '69
Mrs. Brown, You've Got a Lovely Daughter '68
The Collector '65
My Fair Lady '64
The Brides of Dracula '60
Stranger in Town '57
Cast a Dark Shadow '55
The Wizard of Oz '25

Beverly Washburn (1943-)
When the Line Goes Through '73
Pit Stop '67
Spider Baby '64
Old Yeller '57

Bryant Washburn (1889-1963)
Savage Fury '35
The Throwback '35
Drifting Souls '32
Kept Husbands '31

Rick Washburne (1946-)
The Outfit '93
Comrades in Arms '91
Covert Action '88
Hangmen '87

Denzel Washington (1954-)
American Gangster '07
The Great Debaters '07
Deja Vu '06
Inside Man '06
Man on Fire '04
The Manchurian Candidate '04
Out of Time '03
Antwone Fisher '02
John Q '02
Training Day '01
Remember the Titans '00
The Bone Collector '99
The Hurricane '99
He Got Game '98
The Siege '98
Fallen '97
Courage Under Fire '96
The Preacher's Wife '96
Crimson Tide '95
Devil in a Blue Dress '95
Virtuosity '95
Much Ado about Nothing '93
The Pelican Brief '93
Philadelphia '93
Malcolm X '92
Mississippi Masala '92
Ricochet '91
Heart Condition '90
Mo' Better Blues '90
Glory '89
Cry Freedom '87
Hard Lessons '86
Power '86
License to Kill '84
A Soldier's Story '84
Carbon Copy '81
Wilma '77

Fredi Washington (1903-94)
Imitation of Life '34
Emperor Jones '33

Gene Washington (1947-)
Lady Cocoa '75
The Black Six '74

Isaiah Washington, IV (1963-)
The Moguls '05
Dead Birds '04
Wild Things 2 '04
Hollywood Homicide '03
This Girl's Life '03
Ghost Ship '02
Welcome to Collinwood '02
Exit Wounds '01
Dancing in September '00
Romeo Must Die '00
A Texas Funeral '99
True Crime '99
Always Outnumbered, Always Outgunned '98
Bulworth '98
Mixing Nia '98
Out of Sight '98
Guinevere '99
Joe Torre: Curveballs Along the Way '97
Get On the Bus '96
Girl 6 '96
Love Jones '96
Mr. & Mrs. Loving '96
Clockers '95
Crooklyn '94

Jascha Washington (1989-)
Last Holiday '06
My Sister's Keeper '02
Big Momma's House '00

Ken Washington (1959-)
Laboratory '80
She Devils in Chains '76

Kerry Washington (1977-)
Fantastic Four: Rise of the Silver Surfer '07
I Think I Love My Wife '07
The Dead Girl '06
The Last King of Scotland '06
Little Man '06
Fantastic Four '05
Mr. & Mrs. Smith '05
Ray '04
She Hate Me '04
The Human Stain '03
United States of Leland '03
Bad Company '02
Sin '02
Lift '01
Our Song '01
Save the Last Dance '01

Shirley Washington
Darktown Strutters '74

Ted Wass (1952-)
Danielle Steel's Star '93
Fine Gold '88
Pancho Barnes '88
The Longshot '86
TripleCross '86
Oh, God! You Devil '84
Sheena '84
Curse of the Pink Panther '83
The Triangle Factory Fire Scandal '79

Rebecca Wassem
See Sheila Darcy

Jerry Wasserman (1945-)
A Cooler Climate '99
Quarantine '89

Craig Wasson (1954-)
Puerto Vallarta Squeeze '04
Boa '02
Epoch '00
Escape under Pressure '00
The Pornographer '99
Velocity Trap '99
The Last Best Sunday '98
Harvest of Fire '95
The Sister-in-Law '95
Trapped in Space '94
Strapped '93
Malcolm X '92
Midnight Fear '90
A Nightmare on Elm Street 3: Dream Warriors '87
The Men's Club '86
Body Double '84
The Innocents Abroad '84
Second Thoughts '83
Four Friends '81
Ghost Story '81
Carny '80
Schizoid '80
Skag '79
Go Tell the Spartans '78
The Boys in Company C '77
Rollercoaster '77

Gedde Watanabe (1955-)
Forgetting Sarah Marshall '08
Two for the Money '05
Alfie '04
EDtv '99
Guinevere '99
Mulan '98 (V)
Booty Call '96
Nick and Jane '96
That Thing You Do! '96
The Spring '89
UHF '89
Vamp '86
Gung Ho '85
Volunteers '85
Sixteen Candles '84

Ken(saku) Watanabe (1959-)
Letters from Iwo Jima '06
Batman Begins '05
Memoirs of a Geisha '05
The Last Samurai '03
Karate Warrior '88
Commando Invasion '87
Tampopo '86
MacArthur's Children '85

Tetsu Watanabe (1951-)
Fireworks '97
Sonatine '96

Tsunehiko Watase (1944-)
The Silk Road '92
Heaven & Earth '90
Sympathy for the Underdog '71

Dennis Waterman (1948-)
Circle of Deceit '94
Cold Justice '89
Fright '71
Man in the Wilderness '71
The Scars of Dracula '70

Felicity Waterman
Freedom Strike '98
Titanic '96
Hard Bounty '94
Unlawful Passage '94
Miracle Beach '92
Lena's Holiday '90

Ida Waterman (1852-1941)
Amarilly of Clothesline Alley '18
Stella Maris '18

Willard Waterman (1915-95)
Hail '73
Hollywood or Bust '56

Cheryl Waters
Didn't You Hear? '83
Image of Death '77
Macon County Line '74

Dina Waters
See Dina Spybey

Ethel Waters (1896-1977)
The Member of the Wedding '52
Pinky '49
Cabin in the Sky '43
Stage Door Canteen '43
Cairo '42
Tales of Manhattan '42

Harry Waters, Jr.
Back to the Future, Part 2 '89
Back to the Future '85

John Waters (1946-)
Seed of Chucky '04
Sweet and Lowdown '99
Pecker '98 (V)
Serial Mom '94 (V)
Hairspray '88
Something Wild '86
Pink Flamingos '72 (N)

John Waters (1948-)
Ebbtide '94
Heaven Tonight '93
Which Way Home '90
Grievous Bodily Harm '89
Boulevard of Broken Dreams '88
Miracle Down Under '87
True Colors '87
Alice to Nowhere '86
Three's Trouble '85
All the Rivers Run '84
Attack Force Z '84
Breaker Morant '80
Cass '78
Demolition '77
The Getting of Wisdom '77
Scalp Merchant '77
Weekend of Shadows '77
Endplay '75

Nick Waters (1951-)
The Big Hurt '87
The Lighthorsemen '87

Sam Waterston (1940-)
Le Divorce '03
A House Divided '00
Miracle at Midnight '98
The Proprietor '96
The Shadow Conspiracy '96
The Journey of August King '95
Assault at West Point: The Court-Martial of Johnson Whittaker '94
The Enemy Within '94
Serial Mom '94
A Captive in the Land '91
The Man in the Moon '91
Mindwalk: A Film for Passionate Thinkers '91
Lantern Hill '90
Crimes & Misdemeanors '89
The Nightmare Years '89
Welcome Home '89
Gore Vidal's Lincoln '88
September '88
Hannah and Her Sisters '86
Just Between Friends '86
Trade Secrets '86
Warning Sign '85
The Boy Who Loved Trolls '84
Finnegan Begin Again '84
The Killing Fields '84
Dempsey '83
Heaven's Gate '81
Hopscotch '80
Eagle's Wing '79
Friendly Fire '79
Sweet William '79
Capricorn One '78
Interiors '78
Rancho Deluxe '75
The Great Gatsby '74
Journey into Fear '74
Reflections of Murder '74
Savages '72
Who Killed Mary What's 'Er Name? '71
Generation '69

Gwen Watford (1927-94)
The Body in the Library '84
In This House of Brede '75
Taste the Blood of Dracula '70
The Very Edge '63
The Fall of the House of Usher '49

Ian Watkin (1940-)
Dead Alive '93
Nutcase '83

Beyond Reasonable Doubt '80

Pierre Watkin (1889-1960)
The Stranger Wore a Gun '53
Atom Man vs. Superman '50
Redwood Forest Trail '50
Wild Frontier '47
Little Giant '46
Sioux City Sue '46
Swamp Fire '46
The Great Mike '44
Nevada City '41
The Magnificent Dope '42
The Road to Singapore '40
Wall Street Cowboy '39
Country Gentlemen '36

Joanne Watkins
The Big Sweat '90

Royale Watkins (1969-)
Deliver Us from Eva '03
Speed 2: Cruise Control '97

Tuc Watkins (1966-)
Miracle in Lane Two '00
The Mummy '99
I Think I Do '97

Deborah Watling
Danger UXB '81
That'll Be the Day '73

Jack Watling (1923-2001)
The Nanny '65
Sink the Bismarck! '60
A Night to Remember '58
The Admirable Crichton '57
Under Capricorn '49
The Courtney Affair '47
Immortal Battalion '44

Leonor Watling (1975-)
Paris, je t'aime '06
Crónicas '04
My Life Without Me '03
My Mother Likes Women '02
Talk to Her '02

Alberta Watson (1955-)
The Lookout '07
Away From Her '06
Boogeyman '05
Love on the Side '04
The Prince & Me '04
Sorority Boys '02
Hedwig and the Angry Inch '00
Deeply '99
Teaching Mrs. Tingle '99
The Sweet Hereafter '96
Seeds of Doubt '96
Hackers '95
Spanking the Monkey '94
The Hitman '91
White of the Eye '88
Women of Valor '86
Best Revenge '83
The Keep '83
The Soldier '82

Barry Watson (1974-)
Boogeyman '05
Sorority Boys '02
Teaching Mrs. Tingle '99

Bob Watson
Tough Enough '83
In Hot Pursuit '77

Bobby Watson (1888-1965)
The Band Wagon '53
Hitler: Dead or Alive '43
Frolics on Ice '39
Captains Courageous '37

Bobs Watson (1930-99)
Dreaming Out Loud '40
On Borrowed Time '39
The Story of Alexander Graham Bell '39
In Old Chicago '37
Show Boat '36

Emily Watson (1967-)
The Water Horse: Legend of the Deep '07
Miss Potter '06
The Proposition '05
Tim Burton's Corpse Bride '05 (V)
Wah-Wah '05
Equilibrium '02
Punch-Drunk Love '02
Red Dragon '02
Gosford Park '01
Trixie '00
Angela's Ashes '99
The Cradle Will Rock '99
Hilary and Jackie '98
The Boxer '97
The Mill on the Floss '97
Metroland '97
Breaking the Waves '95

Emma Watson (1990-)
Harry Potter and the Order of the Phoenix '07
Harry Potter and the Goblet of Fire '05
Harry Potter and the Prisoner of Azkaban '04
Harry Potter and the Chamber of Secrets '02
Harry Potter and the Sorcerer's Stone '01

Jack Watson (1915-99)
Schizo '77
King Arthur, the Young Warlord '75
Tower of Evil '72
McKenzie Break '70
The Devil's Brigade '68
The Hill '65
The Gorgon '64
Peeping Tom '60

James A. Watson, Jr. (1949-)
Killings at Outpost Zeta '80
Backstairs at the White House '79
Sex Through a Window '72

Lucile Watson (1879-1962)
Harriet Craig '50
Let's Dance '50
The Emperor Waltz '48
Julia Misbehaves '48
Never Say Goodbye '46
My Reputation '46
The Razor's Edge '46
Tomorrow Is Forever '46
The Thin Man Goes Home '44
Uncertain Glory '44
Footsteps in the Dark '41
The Great Lie '41
Mr. & Mrs. Smith '41
Waterloo Bridge '40
The Women '39
Made for Each Other '39

Mills Watson (1940-)
Cujo '83
The Migrants '74

Minor Watson (1889-1965)
Beyond the Forest '49
A Southern Yankee '48
Action in the North Atlantic '43
Guadalcanal Diary '43
To the Shores of Tripoli '42
Woman of the Year '42
They Died with Their Boots On '41
Western Union '41
Abe Lincoln in Illinois '40
Dead End '37
Navy Blue and Gold '37
That Certain Woman '37
Charlie Chan in Paris '35

Muse Watson (1948-)
Down in the Valley '05
A Day Without a Mexican '04
Dead Birds '04
Frankenfish '04
From Dusk Till Dawn 2: Texas Blood Money '99
I Still Know What You Did Last Summer '98
If I Die Before I Wake '98
I Know What You Did Last Summer '97
Rosewood '97
Something to Talk About '95

Roy Watson (1876-1937)
Kentucky Blue Streak '35
Wolf Blood '25

Shari Watson (1971-)
All '01
The Wash '01

Tom Watson (1932-2001)
The Winter Guest '97
Go Now '96
Another Time, Another Place '83

William Watson (1938-97)
Force of Evil '77
Girl on a Chain Gang '65

Woody Watson (1949-)
The Thin Blue Lie '00
A Saintly Switch '99
In the Company of Spies '99
Naked City: A Killer Christmas '98
The Assignment '97
Critical Care '97
Rescuers: Stories of Courage: "Two Women" '97

Wylie Watson (1906-1966)
The Sundowners '60
Things Happen at Night '48
Brighton Rock '47
A Girl in a Million '46
The 39 Steps '35

Vernee Watson-Johnson (1954-)
The Ant Bully '06 (V)
Antwone Fisher '02
Home Room '02
No Turning Back '01
Death Drug '83
The Boy in the Plastic Bubble '76
Norman, Is That You? '76

George Watts (1879-1942)
Hurry, Charlie, Hurry '41
Angels Over Broadway '40

Naomi Watts (1968-)
Eastern Promises '07
Funny Games '07
Inland Empire '06 (V)
The Painted Veil '06
The Ring 2 '05
The Assassination of Richard Nixon '05
Ellie Parker '05
King Kong '05
Stay '05
I Heart Huckabees '04
We Don't Live Here Anymore '04
Ned Kelly '03
Le Divorce '03
21 Grams '03
The Ring '02
The Outsider '02
Mulholland Drive '01
The Shaft '01
The Wyvern Mystery '00
Strange Planet '99
Dangerous Beauty '98
Under the Lighthouse Dancing '97
Children of the Corn 4: The Gathering '96
Persons Unknown '96
Tank Girl '95
The Custodian '94
Gross Misconduct '93
Brides of Christ '91

Richard Watts (1912-75)
The Abominable Snowman '57
The Prince and the Showgirl '57
The Belles of St. Trinian's '53
Doctor in the House '53
Three Stops to Murder '53
Norman Conquest '53
My Son, the Vampire '52
The Star '52
Face to Face '52
The Happiest Days of Your Life '50

Twinkle Watts (1937-)
Silver City Kid '44
California Joe '43

Victoria Wauchope
Love and Hate: A Marriage Made in Hell '90

Ruby Wax (1953-)
The Borrowers '97
Shock Treatment '81

Al Waxman (1935-2001)
Bogus '96
Gotti '96
Iron Eagle IV '95
Operation Golden Phoenix '94
Teamster Boss: The Jackie Presser Story '92
The Hitman '91
Mob Story '90
Millennium '89
Collision Course '89
Cop '88
Switching Channels '88
Meatballs III '87
Clown Murders '83
Class of 1984 '82
Spasms '82
Atlantic City '81

Eileen Way (1911-94)
Queen of Hearts '89
Sea Wife '57
Three Stops to Murder '53

Damon Wayans (1960-)
Marci X '03
Bamboozled '00
Bulletproof '96
Celtic Pride '96
The Great White Hype '96
Major Payne '95
Blankman '94
Last Action Hero '93
Mo' Money '92
The Last Boy Scout '91
Look Who's Talking, Too '90
Earth Girls Are Easy '89
Colors '88
I'm Gonna Git You Sucka '88
Punchline '88
Hollywood Shuffle '87
Roxanne '87
Beverly Hills Cop '84

Keenen Ivory Wayans (1958-)
Scary Movie '00
Most Wanted '97
The Glimmer Man '96
Don't Be a Menace to South Central While Drinking Your Juice in the Hood '96
A Low Down Dirty Shame '94
I'm Gonna Git You Sucka '88
Hollywood Shuffle '87
Star 80 '83

Kim Wayans (1961-)
Juwanna Mann '02
Talking about Sex '94
I'm Gonna Git You Sucka '88

Marlon Wayans (1972-)
Norbit '07
Little Man '06
The Ladykillers '04
White Chicks '04
Scary Movie 2 '01
Dungeons and Dragons '00
Requiem for a Dream '00
Scary Movie '00
Senseless '98
The Sixth Man '97
Don't Be a Menace to South Central While Drinking Your Juice in the Hood '96
Above the Rim '94
Mo' Money '92
I'm Gonna Git You Sucka '88

Shawn Wayans (1971-)
Little Man '06
White Chicks '04
Scary Movie 2 '01
Scary Movie '00
The Sixth Man '97
Don't Be a Menace to South Central While Drinking Your Juice in the Hood '96
Above the Rim '94
Mo' Money '92
I'm Gonna Git You Sucka '88

Carol Wayne (1941-85)
Heartbreakers '84
Surf 2 '84
The Party '68

David Wayne (1914-95)
The Gift of Love '90
Poker Alice '87
Finders Keepers '84
An American Christmas Carol '79
The Apple Dumpling Gang '75
Huckleberry Finn '74
The Andromeda Strain '71
The Last Angry Man '59
The Three Faces of Eve '57
The Naked Hills '56
The Tender Trap '55
How to Marry a Millionaire '53
We're Not Married '52
With a Song in My Heart '52
As Young As You Feel '51
My Blue Heaven '50
Adam's Rib '49
Portrait of Jennie '48

John Wayne (1907-79)
The Green Berets '68
Hellfighters '68
El Dorado '67
The War Wagon '67
Cast a Giant Shadow '66
The Greatest Story Ever Told '65
In Harm's Way '65
Sons of Katie Elder '65
Circus World '64
Donovan's Reef '63
How the West Was Won '63
McLintock! '63
Hatari! '62
The Longest Day '62
The Man Who Shot Liberty Valance '62
The Comancheros '61
The Alamo '60
North to Alaska '60
The Horse Soldiers '59
Rio Bravo '59
The Barbarian and the Geisha '58
Jet Pilot '57
Legend of the Lost '57
Wings of Eagles '57
The Searchers '56
The Conqueror '55
Blood Alley '55
The Sea Chase '55
The High and the Mighty '54
Hondo '53
Island in the Sky '53
Trouble along the Way '53
Big Jim McLain '52
The Quiet Man '52
Flying Leathernecks '51
Rio Grande '50
The Fighting Kentuckian '49
Sands of Iwo Jima '49
She Wore a Yellow Ribbon '49
Wake of the Red Witch '49
Fort Apache '48
Red River '48
Three Godfathers '48
Angel and the Badman '47
Tycoon '47
Without Reservations '46
Back to Bataan '45
Dakota '45
Flame of the Barbary Coast '45
They Were Expendable '45
Fighting Seabees '44
Tall in the Saddle '44
Lady Takes a Chance '43
War of the Wildcats '43
Flying Tigers '42
In Old California '42
Lady for a Night '42
Pittsburgh '42
Reap the Wild Wind '42
Reunion in France '42
The Spoilers '42
The Shepherd of the Hills '41
The Wheel of Fortune '41
The Long Voyage Home '40
Dark Command '40
Seven Sinners '40
Three Faces West '40
Allegheny Uprising '39
Frontier Horizon '39
New Frontier '39
Stagecoach '39
Three Texas Steers '39
Wyoming Outlaw '39
Overland Stage Raiders '38
Pals of the Saddle '38
Santa Fe Stampede '38
Red River Range '38
Helltown '38
King of the Pecos '36
The Lawless Nineties '36
Winds of the Wasteland '36
The Lonely Trail '36
Dawn Rider '35
Desert Trail '35
The Lawless Frontier '35
Lawless Range '35
The New Frontier '35
Paradise Canyon '35
Texas Terror '35

Westward Ho '35
Blue Steel '34
Lucky Texan '34
Man from Utah '34
'Neath the Arizona Skies '34
Randy Rides Alone '34
The Star Packer '34
Trail Beyond '34
Baby Face '33
His Private Secretary '33
Man from Monterey '33
Riders of Destiny '33
Sagebrush Trail '33
Somewhere in Sonora '33
Telegraph Trail '33
The Big Stampede '32
Haunted Gold '32
Hurricane Express '32
Ride Him, Cowboy '32
Shadow of the Eagle '32
Texas Cyclone '32
Two-Fisted Law '32
Maker of Men '31
Range Feud '31
Big Trail '30
The Dropkick '27

John Ethan Wayne (1961-)
The Manhunt '86
Escape from El Diablo '83
Scream '83

Michael Wayne (1934-2003)
Rapid Fire '89
Alley Cat '84

Naunton Wayne (1901-70)
The Hidden Room '49
Passport to Pimlico '49
A Girl in a Million '46
Dead of Night '45
Night Train to Munich '40
The Lady Vanishes '38

Nina Wayne (1943-)
The Comic '69
Dead Heat on a Merry-Go-Round '66

Patricia Wayne (1926-74)
Texas Detour '77
The Bears & I '74
Beyond Atlantis '73
The Gatling Gun '72
Big Jake '71
Ride to Glory '71
The Green Berets '68
Talion '66
Shenandoah '65
McLintock! '63
The Young Land '59
The Alamo '60
The Searchers '56
Mister Roberts '55

Michael Weatherly (1968-)
Cabin by the Lake '00
The Substitute 4: Failure is Not an Option '00
The Colony '98
The Last Days of Disco '98
Asteroid '97

Shawn Weatherly (1960-)
Rustin '01
Amityville 1992: It's About Time '92
Mind Games '89
Shadowzone '89
Thieves of Fortune '89
Party Line '88
Police Academy 3: Back in Training '86

Carl Weathers (1948-)
The Comebacks '07
The Sasquatch Gang '06
Alien Siege '05
Little Nicky '00
Shadow Warriors '97
Shadow Warriors 2: Hunt for the Death Merchant '97
Happy Gilmore '96
Dangerous Passion '95
Hurricane Smith '92
Action Jackson '88
Predator '87
Fortune Dane '86
Rocky 4 '85
Rocky 3 '82
Death Hunt '81
Rocky 2 '79
Force 10 from Navarone '78
Semi-Tough '77
Rocky '76
Bucktown '75
Friday Foster '75

Blayne Weaver (1976-)
Return to Never Land '02 (V)
Manic '01

Dennis Weaver (1924-2006)
Home on the Range '04 (V)
High Noon '00
Submerged '00
Escape from Wildcat Canyon '99
The Virginian '99
Two Bits & Pepper '95
Mastergate '92
Disaster at Silo 7 '88
Bluffing It '87
A Winner Never Quits '86
Going for the Gold: The Bill Johnson Story '85
Cocaine: One Man's Seduction '83
Amber Waves '82
Don't Go to Sleep '82
The Ordeal of Dr. Mudd '80
Centennial '78
Pearl '78
Intimate Strangers '77
Duel '71
A Man Called Sledge '71
What's the Matter with Helen? '71
Mission Batangas '69
Gentle Giant '67
Duel at Diablo '66
The Gallant Hours '60
The Errand Boy '61
Touch of Evil '58
The Redhead from Wyoming '53
War Arrow '53
Horizons West '52
The Lawless Breed '52

Doodles Weaver (1911-83)
Way He Was '76
Runaways '75
Cancel My Reservation '72
Road to Nashville '67

Demon Seed '77
Marathon Man '76
The Day of the Dolphin '73
Hunter '73
Walk in the Spring Rain '70
Fail-Safe '64

Jacki Weaver (1947-)
Cosi '95
Three's Trouble '85
Squizzy Taylor '84
Caddie '76
Picnic at Hanging Rock '75

Jason Weaver (1979-)
ATL '06
The Ladykillers '04
Drumline '02
Freedom Song '00
The Jacksons: An American Dream '92

Lee Weaver (1930-)
The Box '03
O Brother Where Art Thou? '00

Marjorie Weaver (1913-94)
My Brother's Wife '89

Michael Weaver (1971-)
The Man Who Wouldn't Die '42
Michael Shayne: Private Detective '40
Murder over New York '40
Young Mr. Lincoln '39
The Gentleman from California '37

Sigourney Weaver (1949-)
Baby Mama '08
Be Kind Rewind '08
Vantage Point '08
WALL-E '08 (V)
Happily N'Ever After '07 (V)
Infamous '06
Snow Cake '06
The TV Set '06
Imaginary Heroes '05
The Village '04
Holes '03
Big Bad Love '02 (V)
The Guys '02
Tadpole '02
Heartbreakers '01
Company Man '00
Galaxy Quest '99
A Map of the World '99
Alien: Resurrection '97
The Ice Storm '97
Snow White: A Tale of Terror '97
Copycat '95
Jeffrey '95
Death and the Maiden '94
Dave '93
Alien 3 '92
1492: Conquest of Paradise '92
Ghostbusters 2 '89
Gorillas in the Mist '88
Working Girl '88
Aliens '86
Half Moon Street '86
Ghostbusters '84
Deal of the Century '83
The Year of Living Dangerously '82
Eyewitness '81
Alien '79
Madman '79
Sorrows of Gin '79

Hugo Weaving (1959-)
Transformers '07 (V)
Happy Feet '06 (V)
Little Fish '05
After the Deluge '03
Lord of the Rings: The Return of the King '03
The Matrix Reloaded '03
The Matrix Revolutions '03
Lord of the Rings: The Two Towers '02
Lord of the Rings: The Fellowship of the Rings '01
The Matrix '99
Strange Planet '99
Bedrooms and Hallways '98
The Interview '98
Babe '95 (V)

Rita Webb (1904-81)
Frenzy '72
Zeta One '69

Veronica Webb (1965-)
In Too Deep '99
Jungle Fever '91

Diane Webber (1932-)
Sinthia: The Devil's Doll '70
The Mermaids of Tiburon '62

Mark Webber (1980-)
The Hottest State '06
Bomb the System '05
Broken Flowers '05
Dear Wendy '05
Winter Solstice '04
Hollywood Ending '02
The Laramie Project '02
People I Know '02
The Rising Place '02
Chelsea Walls '01
Storytelling '01
Snow Day '00
Drive Me Crazy '99
White Boyz '99

Alan Webb (1906-82)
Deadly Game '82
The Great Train Robbery '79
King Lear '71
Entertaining Mr. Sloane '70
The Pumpkin Eater '64
King Rat '65
Challenge to Lassie '49

Chloe Webb (1960-)
The Newton Boys '97
She's So Lovely '97
Love Affair '94

Clifton Webb (1889-1966)
Three Coins in the Fountain '54
The Man Who Never Was '55
A Woman's World '54
Titanic '53
Stars and Stripes Forever '52
Cheaper by the Dozen '50
Sitting Pretty '48
Dark Corner '46
The Razor's Edge '46
Laura '44

Danny (Daniel) Webb (1958-)
Attack Force '06
The Hound of the Baskervilles '02
Take Me '00
Shiner '00
Frenchmen's Creek '98
Love and Death on Long Island '97
A Woman's Guide to Adultery '93
Alien 3 '92
Henry V '89
Death Wish 4: The Crackdown '87

Greg Webb
Puppet Master 2 '90
Running Mates '85

Jack Webb (1920-82)
The Commies Are Coming, the Commies Are Coming '57
D.I. '57
Pete Kelly's Blues '55
Dragnet '54
The Men '50
Sunset Boulevard '50
He Walked by Night '48

Richard Webb (1915-93)
Beware! The Blob '72
Hell Raiders '68
Girl! '65
Attack of the Mayan Mummy '63
Distant Drums '51

The Invisible Monster '50
Sands of Iwo Jima '49
Out of the Past '47
O.S.S. '46

Robert Webber (1924-89)
Nuts '87
Assassin '86
Wild Geese 2 '85
Starflight One '83
Don't Go to Sleep '82
The Final Option '82
Wrong Is Right '82
S.O.B. '81
Private Benjamin '80
The Streets of L.A. '79
10 '79
Casey's Shadow '78
Revenge of the Pink Panther '78
The Choirboys '77
Midway '76
Soldat Duroc... Ca Va Etre Ta Fete! '75
Bring Me the Head of Alfredo Garcia '74
Death Stalk '74
Dollars '71
Thief '71
The Great White Hope '70
The Big Bounce '69
The Dirty Dozen '67
The Silencers '66
The Sandpiper '65
Hysteria '64
The Stripper '63
Twelve Angry Men '57

Timothy Webber
Cypher '02
The Boys of St. Vincent '93
That's My Baby! '88
Toby McTeague '87
The Grey Fox '83
Terror Train '80

Amy Weber (1970-)
Crackerjack 3 '00
Kolobos '99
Art House '98
Forbidden Games '95

Dewey Weber (1971-)
Ulee's Gold '97
Chain of Desire '93

Jacques Weber (1949-)
Beaumarchais the Scoundrel '96
Northern Passage '95
The Elegant Criminal '92
Cyrano de Bergerac '90

Jake Weber (1964-)
Dawn of the Dead '04
Leo '02
Love Thy Neighbor '02
100 Mile Rule '02
Wendigo '01
The Cell '00
U-571 '00
Pushing Tin '99
Dangerous Beauty '98

Meet Joe Black '98
What the Deaf Man Heard '98
Skin Art '93

Steven Weber (1961-)
Inside Out '05
Masters of Horror: Jenifer '05
The Twelve Days of Christmas Eve '04
Club Land '01
Common Ground '00
Sleep Easy, Hutch Rimes '00
Time Code '00
Late Last Night '99
Love Letters '99
At First Sight '98
The Break Up '98
Sour Grapes '98
Dracula: Dead and Loving It '95
Jeffrey '95
The Kennedys of Massachusetts '95
Leaving Las Vegas '95
The Temp '93
Single White Female '92
In the Line of Duty: A Cop for the Killing '90
Hamburger Hill '87
Puddn'head Wilson '84

Derek Webster
Flight of the Living Dead: Outbreak on a Plane '07
Josh Kirby... Time Warrior: Chapter 5, Journey to the Magic Cavem '96
Josh Kirby... Time Warrior: Chapter 6, Last Battle for the Universe '96
Josh Kirby... Time Warrior: Chapter 1, Planet of the Dino-Knights '95
Josh Kirby... Time Warrior: Chapter 3, Trapped on Toyworld '95
Josh Kirby... Time Warrior: Chapter 4, Eggs from 70 Million B.C. '95

Victor Webster (1973-)
Dirty Love '05
Wishmaster 4: The Prophecy Fulfilled '02

Ann Wedgeworth (1935-)
The Hawk Is Dying '06
Hunter's Moon '97
The Whole Wide World '96
Love and a .45 '94
Cooperstown '93
Hard Promises '92
Green Card '90
Miss Firecracker '89
Steel Magnolias '89
Far North '88
Made in Heaven '87
A Tiger's Tale '87
My Science Project '85
Sweet Dreams '85
No Small Affair '84
Soggy Bottom U.S.A. '84
Killjoy '81
Bogie: The Last Hero '80
The Birch Interval '78
Citizens Band '77
One Summer Love '76
War Between the Tates '76
The Catamount Killing '74
Law and Disorder '74
Bang the Drum Slowly '73
Scarecrow '73

Barbara Weeks (1913-2003)
The Violent Years '56
Hell's Headquarters '32
White Eagle '32
Palmy Days '31
Two Fisted Justice '31

Honeysuckle Weeks
Red Mercury '05
Catherine Cookson's The Rag Nymph '96

Jimmie Ray Weeks (1942-)
Buffalo Soldiers '01

Humanoids from the Deep '80
The Prowler '81

Cindy Weintraub (1946-)
Oliver & Company '88 (V)
Sorry, Wrong Number '89

Carl Weintraub

Josh Weinstein (1966-)
Personal Velocity: Three Portraits '02
Boys Life '94

Aladdin '92 (V)
The Return of Jafar '94 (V)
Thieves '96 (V)
Aladdin and the King of Thieves '96 (V)
Scott Weinger (1975-)

'97
The Mother and the Whore
State of Things '82
Isabelle Weingarten

Life as a House '01
Stolen Summer '02
Mike Weinberg (1993-)

Android '82
Sweet Lies '88
Secret of the Ice Cave '89
Savage Beach '89
The Banker '89
Predator 2 '90
Marked for Death '90
Auntie Lee's Meat Pies '92
Free Enterprise '98
Rated X '00
Liza Weil (1977-)
Loggerheads '05
The Good German '06

Analyze This '98
The Siege '98
Dead Man '95
The Abyss '89
Frantic '88
Apology '86
The Manhattan Project '86
Kim Weeks (1962-)
Family of Cops 3 '98
Family of Cops 2: Breach of Faith '97
Perdita Weeks (1985-)
Catherine Cookson's The
Rollo Weeks (1987-)
The Thief Lord '06
The Little Vampire '00
Cold Light of Day '95
Rag Nymph '96
Paul Wegener (1874-1948)
Kolberg '45
One Arabian Night '21
The Golem '20
Student of Prague '13
'40
Tang Wei
Lust, Caution '07
Virginia Weidler (1926-68)
Best Foot Forward '43
Babes on Broadway '41
All This and Heaven Too '40
Young Tom Edison '40
The Philadelphia Story '40
The Great Man Votes '38
Too Hot to Handle '38
Glitch! '88
Return of the Killer Tomatoes! '88

Robin Weigert (1969-)
Things We Lost in the Fire '07
Rafer Weigel (1969-)
For Heaven's Sake '26
Paul Weigel (1867-1951)
The Great Dictator '40
Teri Weigel (1962-)
Predator 2 '90
Savage Beach '89
Cheerleader Camp '88
Jeffrey Weissman (1958-)
Back to the Future, Part 3 '90
Back to the Future, Part 2 '89
Robin Weigert (1969-)
Children of Fury '94
My Antonia '94
Heatseeker '95
Murder Without Conviction '04
Mother '94
Long Road Home '91
Prayer of the Roleboys '91
Shaun Weiss (1978-)
D3: The Mighty Ducks '96
D2: The Mighty Ducks '94
Heavyweights '94
The Mighty Ducks '92
Roberta Weiss (1958-)
Abducted '86
Autumn Born '79
Norbert Weisser (1946-)
Nemesis '93
Nemesis 3: Time Lapse '96
Nemesis 4: Cry of Angels '96
Adrenalin: Fear the Rush '96
Omega Doom '96
Song of Freedom '36
Morgan Weisser (1971-)

Heidelinde Weis (1940-)
Something for Everyone '70
Kevin Weisman (1970-)
The Man Outside '68
Sunshine '99
The Mummy '99
I Want You '98
Beautiful Creatures '00
The Mummy Returns '01
Enemy at the Gates '00
I Shot Andy Warhol '96
Improper Conduct '94
The Criminal Mind '94
Night Train to Venice '93
Sleeping Beauty '89
Cocoon: The Return '88
Cocoon '85
Florence Weiss
Overture to Glory '40
Joe and Max '02
Shot '01
Mach 2 '00
Facing the Enemy '00
Mistress '91
Velocity Trap '99
Deep Impact '98
The O.J. Simpson Story '94
Windrunner '94
Molly and Gina '94
Prehysteria 3 '95
Coyote Summer '96
Breaking the Surface: The Greg Louganis Story '96
The Liar's Club '93
No Place to Hide '93
The Queen of Mean '90
Rainbow Drive '90
Death of a Centerfold '81
Bruce Weitz (1943-)
Half Past Dead '02
Chris Weitz (1970-)
Chuck & Buck '00
Mr. & Mrs. Smith '05
Michael T. Weiss (1962-)
Jeffrey '95
Freeway '96
Freeway 2: Confessions of a Trickbaby '99
Howling 4: The Original Nightmare '88
Zoe Weizenbaum (1991-)
Memoirs of a Geisha '05
12 and Holding '05
Elisabeth Welch (1904-2003)
Dead of Night '45
Big Fella '37
Jess Weixler
Teeth '07
The Big Bad Swim '06
Niles Welch (1888-1976)
Stone of Silver Creek '35
Badmen of Nevada '33
The Lone Avenger '33
Come on Tarzan '32
Cornered '32

Raquel Welch (1940-)
Forget About It '06
Legally Blonde '01
Tortilla Soup '01
Chairman of the Board '97
Naked Gun 33 1/3: The Final Insult '94
Tainted Blood '93
Scandal in a Small Town '88
Trouble in Paradise '88
Legend of Walks Far Woman '82
Stuntwoman '81
The Prince and the Pauper '78
Mother, Jugs and Speed '76
The Four Musketeers '75
The Three Musketeers '74
Wild Party '74
The Last of Sheila '73
Bluebeard '72
Fuzz '72
Hannie Caulder '72
Restless '72
Myra Breckinridge '70
The Magic Christian '69
100 Rifles '69
Bandolero! '68
Lady in Cement '68
Bedazzled '68
Fathom '67
Oldest Profession '67
Fantastic Voyage '66
One Million Years B.C. '66
Shoot Loud, Louder, I Don't Understand '66
A Swingin' Summer '65
Johnny Weissmuller (1904-84)
Swamp Fire '46
Stage Door Canteen '43
Tarzan's New York Adventure '42
Tarzan's Secret Treasure '41
Tarzan Finds a Son '39
Tarzan Escapes '36
Tarzan and His Mate '34
Tarzan, the Ape Man '32
Lucinda Weist (1963-)
The Silencers '95
The Haunting of Seacliff Inn '94
'90
'89
Frank Welker (1945-)
Curious George '06 (V)
The Ant Bully '06 (V)
Doug's 1st Movie '99 (V)
Mulan '98 (V)
Aladdin and the King of Thieves '96 (V)
Pocahontas '95 (V)
Gargoyles, The Movie: The Heroes Awaken '94 (V)
The Pagemaster '94 (V)
Aladdin '92 (V)
The Rescuers Down Under '90 (V)
My Neighbor Totoro '68 (V)

Confidence '03
Constantine '05
Envy '04
Understand! '66
A Swingin' Summer '65
Rachel Weisz (1971-)
Definitely, Maybe '08
My Blueberry Nights '07
Fred Claus '07
Eragon '06 (V)
The Fountain '06
The Constant Gardener '05
The Silencers '95
Southern Belles '05
When Will I Be Loved '04
The Shape of Things '03
The Business of Strangers '01
Cash Crop '01
Aftershock: Earthquake in New York '99
My Neighbor Totoro '68 (V)
How to Frame a Figg '71
Frederick Weller (1966-)
The Shape of Things '03
Stonewall '95
Harvest '98
Fathom '67
Forced Vengeance '82
Q (The Winged Serpent) '82
Mary Louise Weller (1946-)
Blood and Guns '79
The Double McGuffin '79
Battletruck '72 (N)
The Muppet Movie '79
Hot Money '79
America at the Movies '76
Voyage of the Damned '76
Ten Little Indians '75
Ten Days' Wonder '72
The Evil '78
National Lampoon's Animal House '78

Runaway Jury '03
The Shape of Things '03
About a Boy '02
I Want You '98
Sunshine '99
The Mummy '99
Beautiful Creatures '00
The Mummy Returns '01
Body and Soul '98
I Shot Andy Warhol '96
Improper Conduct '94
The Land Girls '98
Going All the Way '97
Swept from the Sea '97
Chain Reaction '96
Stealing Beauty '96
Tuesday Weld (1943-)
Chelsea Walls '01
Intimate Affairs '01
Feeling Minnesota '96
Falling Down '93
Heartbreak Hotel '88
Something in Common '86
Once Upon a Time in America '84
When Angels Fly '84
Author! Author! '82
Thief '81
Mother & Daughter: A Loving War '80
Serial '80
A Question of Guilt '78
Who'll Stop the Rain? '78
Looking for Mr. Goodbar '77
F. Scott Fitzgerald in Hollywood '76
Reflections of Murder '74
I Walk the Line '70
Pretty Poison '68
Lord Love a Duck '66
The Cincinnati Kid '65
I'll Take Sweden '65
Return to Peyton Place '61
Wild in the Country '61
Soldier in the Rain '63
The Five Pennies '59
Rally 'Round the Flag, Boys! '58
Rock, Rock, Rock '56
Ben Welden (1901-97)
Tales of Robin Hood '52
Tough Assignment '49
Fighting Seabees '44
Smashing the Rackets '38
The Mystery of the Mary Celeste '35
Joan Weldon (1933-)
Them! '54
The Stranger Wore a Gun '53

Tahnee Welch (1961-)
Tales of the Klondike: In a Far Country '87 (N)
Tales of the Klondike: Race for Number One '87 (N)
Tales of the Klondike: The Scorn of Women '87 (N)
Tales of the Klondike: The Unexpected '87 (N)
'84
Scene of the Crime '85 (N)
Orson Welles (1915-85)
Someone to Love '87
The Transformers: The Movie '86 (V)
Slapstick of Another Kind '84
Butterfly '82
History of the World: Part 1 '81
Shogun '80 (M)
Battletruck '72 (N)
The Muppet Movie '79
Voyage of the Damned '76
Ten Days' Wonder '72
Treasure Island '72
The Witching '72
Waterloo '71
Catch-22 '70
Start the Revolution without Me '70
12 Plus 1 '70
Battle of Neretva '69
Casino Royale '67
Chimes at Midnight '67
I'll Never Forget What's 'Isname '67
A Man for All Seasons '66
Is Paris Burning? '66
The Trial '63
The V.I.P.s '63
RoGoPaG '62
The King of Kings '61 (N)
Ferry to Hong Kong '59
The Long, Hot Summer '58
The Vikings '58 (N)
Man in the Shadow '57
Moby Dick '56
Touch of Evil '58
Othello '52
Little World of Don Camillo '51 (N)
Three Cases of Murder '55
Trouble in the Glen '54
Napoleon '55
Mr. Arkadin '55
The Third Man '49
Prince of Foxes '49
Black Magic '49
The Lady from Shanghai '48
Macbeth '48
The Stranger '46
Tomorrow Is Forever '46
Jane Eyre '44
Journey into Fear '42
Citizen Kane '41

Roustabout '64
Gwen Welles (1949-93)
Boys Life '94
Eating '90
New Year's Day '89
Sticky Fingers '89
Desert Hearts '86
The Men's Club '86
Nobody's Fool '86
Nashville '75
Hit! '73
Mel Welles (1924-2005)
Wizards of the Lost Kingdom 2 '89
Rented Lips '88
Commando Squad '87
Chopping Mall '86
Dr. Heckyl and Mr. Hype '80
The She-Beast '65
Little Shop of Horrors '60
Rock All Night '57
The Undead '57
Abbott and Costello Meet the Mummy '55
Orson Welles (1915-85)
William Wellman, Jr. (1937-)
Someone to Love '87

Peter Weller (1947-)
The Order '03

Titus Welliver (1961-)
Gone Baby Gone '07
Assault on Precinct 13 '05
Twisted '04
Biker Boyz '03
Blorde '01
Once in the Life '00
Rough Riders '97
The Big Fall '96
Zero Tolerance '93
The Lost Capone '90
Tom Welling (1977-)
Cheaper by the Dozen 2 '05
The Fog '05
Cheaper by the Dozen '03
Virginia Welles (1925-)
Francis in the Haunted House '56
Dynamite '49
David Wells
Inherit the Wind '99
Wild Cactus '92
Dawn Wells (1938-)
Super Sucker '03
Evil Lives '92
Return to Boggy Creek '77
Town That Dreaded Sundown '76
Winterhawk '75
Island '78
Carole Wells (1942-)
Funny Lady '75
The House of Seven Corpses '73

Peter Weller (1947-)
The Order '03
Blacklight '98
Styx '00
Diplomatic Siege '99
End of Summer '97
Top of the World '97
Screamers '96
Beyond the Clouds '95
Decoy '95
Mighty Aphrodite '95
The New Age '94
The Substitute Wife '94
Sunset Grill '92
Naked Lunch '91
Road to Ruin '91
Cat Chaser '90
Rainbow Drive '90
RoboCop 2 '90
Leviathan '89
Shakedown '88
RoboCop '87
A Killing Affair '85
Two Kinds of Love '85
Of Unknown Origin '83
Shoot the Moon '82
Butch and Sundance: The Early Days '79
The Man Without a Country '73
Gwen Welles (1949-93)
Titus Welliver (1961-)
The Contaminated Man '01
Dracula: The Dark Prince '01
Dolores Wells (1937-)
Bikini Beach '64

John Wells (1936-98)
Muscle Beach Party '64
The Time Travelers '64
Beach Party '63

Jacqueline Wells
See Julie Bishop

John Wells (1936-98)
Princess Caraboo '94
Consuming Passions '88
Rentadick '72

Stuart Wells (1982-)
The Reckoning '03
Billy Elliot '00

Tico Wells
All About You '01
The Five Heartbeats '91

Tracy Wells (1971-)
Mirror, Mirror 2: Raven Dance '94
After Midnight '89

Vernon Wells (1945-)
King of the Ants '03
Beneath Loch Ness '01
Space Truckers '97
Hard Justice '95
Bounty Hunter 2002 '94
Plughead Rewired: Circuitry Man 2 '94
Stranglehold '94
Sexual Response '92
Enemy Unseen '91
Undeclared War '91
American Eagle '90
Circuitry Man '90
Crossing the Line '90
The Shrimp on the Barbie '90
Circle of Fear '89
Nam Angels '88
Circle Man '87
Innerspace '87
Last Man Standing '87
Commando '85

John Welsh (1904-85)
The Duchess of Duke Street '78
The Moonstone '72
Lucky Jim '58
The Revenge of Frankenstein '58

Kenneth Welsh (1942-)
Silk '07
The Hades Factor '06
The Exorcism of Emily Rose '05
The Fog '05
Four Brothers '05
Escape Clause '96
Eloise at the Plaza '03
The Aviator '04
The Day After Tomorrow '04
Miracle '04
Deliberate Intent '01
Focus '01
The Sign of Four '01
The Hound of the Baskervilles '00
Love Come Down '00
Vendetta '99
Habitat '97
Jack Higgins' Thunder Point '97
Joe Torre: Curveballs Along the Way '97
Dead Silence '96
Kissinger and Nixon '96
Rowing Through '96
The Wrong Guy '96
Hiroshima '95
Margaret's Museum '95
Portraits of a Killer '95
Death Wish 5: The Face of Death '94
Getting Gotti '94
Legends of the Fall '94
The Spider and the Fly '94
Timecop '94
Whale Music '94
Adrift '93
Dead Ahead: The Exxon Valdez Disaster '92
The Good Fight '92
Love, Lies and Murder '91
Perfectly Normal '91
The Big Slice '90
The Last Best Year '90
Love and Hate: A Marriage Made in Hell '90
And Then You Die '88
Another Woman '88
Crocodile Dundee 2 '88
The Climb '87
Lost '86
Loyalties '86
Screwball Academy '86
The War Boy '85
Reno and the Doc '84
Of Unknown Origin '83

Margaret Welsh
American Heart '92
Mr. & Mrs. Bridge '90
Smooth Talk '85

William Welsh (1870-1946)
20,000 Leagues under the Sea '16
Traffic in Souls '13

Ariadne Welter (1931-99)
The Brainiac '61
The Devil's Hand '61
The Vampire's Coffin '58
The Vampire '57
The Criminal Life of Archibaldo de la Cruz '55

Jiang Wen
Warriors of Heaven and Earth '03
Devils on the Doorstep '00
The Emperor's Shadow '96
Red Sorghum '87

Lara Wendel (1965-)
Ghosthouse '88
Intervista '87
Unsane '82

Alan J. Wendl
Serial Mom '94
Hairspray '88

George Wendt (1948-)
Santa Baby '06
Kids in America '05
Masters of Horror: Family '05
King of the Ants '03
Strange Relations '02
Lakeboat '00
The Prime Gig '00
Alice in Wonderland '99
Outside Providence '99
The Pooch and the Pauper '99
Rupert's Land '98
Space Truckers '97
Spice World: The Movie '97
Alien Avengers '96
Bye Bye Birdie '95
Man of the House '95
Hostage for a Day '94
Forever Young '92
Guilty by Suspicion '91
The Masters of Menace '90
Never Say Die '90
Plain Clothes '88
House '86
Fletch '85
Gung Ho '85
Dreamscape '84
No Small Affair '84
Ratings Game '84
Thief of Hearts '84
Sahara '83

David Wenham (1965-)
The Proposition '05
Van Helsing '04
After the Deluge '03
Lord of the Rings: The Return of the King '03
The Crocodile Hunter: Collision Course '02
Lord of the Rings: The Two Towers '02
Pure '02
The Bank '01
Dust '01
Moulin Rouge '01
Better Than Sex '00
Molokai: The Story of Father Damien '99
The Boys '98
A Little Bit of Soul '97
Cosi '95

Jann Wenner
Almost Famous '00
Perfect '85

Alexandra Wentworth (1965-)
American Virgin '00
Meeting Daddy '98
Office Space '98
The Love Bug '97
Trial and Error '96

Martha Wentworth (1889-1974)
The Sword in the Stone '63 (V)
Jupiter's Darling '55
Homesteaders of Paradise Valley '47
Santa Fe Uprising '46
Stagecoach to Denver '46
The Stranger '46
Vigilantes of Boom Town '46
Clancy Street Boys '43

Fritz Wepper (1941-)
Le Dernier Combat '84
Cabaret '72
The Bridge '59

Jan Werich (1905-80)
Fabulous Adventures of Baron Munchausen '61
The Original Fabulous Adventures of Baron Munchausen '61

Barbara Werle
Charro! '69
Battle of the Bulge '65

Oskar Werner (1922-84)
Voyage of the Damned '76
The Shoes of the Fisherman '68
Fahrenheit 451 '66
Ship of Fools '65
The Spy Who Came in from the Cold '65
Jules and Jim '62
The Life and Loves of Mozart '59
Lola Montes '55
Angel with the Trumpet '50

Roy Werner (1957-)
In Enemy Hands '04
Loco Love '03

Otto Wernicke (1893-1965)
Crimes of Dr. Mabuse '32
M '31

Gary Werntz
Pay It Forward '00
Deep Impact '98
The Peacemaker '97
The Art of Dying '90

Doug Wert (1961-)
Baby Face Nelson '97
The Wasp Woman '96
Haunted Symphony '94

Massimo Wertmuller (1956-)
Summer Night with Greek Profile, Almond Eyes & Scent of Basil '87
Sotto, Sotto '85

Paul Wesley (1982-)
That Russell Girl '08
Full Count '06
Peaceful Warrior '06
Roll Bounce '05

Dick Wessel (1913-65)
Flying Leathernecks '51
Pitfall '48
Dick Tracy vs. Cueball '46
X Marks the Spot '42
Tanks a Million '41
They Died with Their Boots On '41

Dick Wesson (1919-79)
The Errand Boy '61
Calamity Jane '53
The Desert Song '53
Jim Thorpe: All American '51
Destination Moon '50

Adam West (1928-)
Meet the Robinsons '07 (V)
Chicken Little '05 (V)
Baadasssss! '03
Drop Dead Gorgeous '99
American Vampire '97
Joyride '97
The New Age '94
Maxim Xul '91
Night of the Kickfighters '91
Return Fire '91
Mad About You '90
Omega Cop '90
Doin' Time on Planet Earth '88
Zombie Nightmare '86
Young Lady Chatterly 2 '85
Hellriders '84
One Dark Night '82
For the Love of It '80
The Happy Hooker Goes Hollywood '80
Hooper '78
Hell River '75
The Specialist '75
Batman '66
Geronimo '62

Billy West (1950-)
Queer Duck: The Movie '06 (V)
Comic Book: The Movie '04
Popeye's Voyage: The Quest for Pappy '04
Looney Tunes: Back in Action '03
Joe's Apartment '96 (V)

Chandra West (1970-)
I Now Pronounce You Chuck and Larry '07
The Long Weekend '05
White Noise '05
Category 6: Day of Destruction '04
Water's Edge '03
The Salton Sea '02
The Perfect Son '00
The '70s '00
Something More '99
Universal Soldier 2: Brothers in Arms '98
Universal Soldier 3: Unfinished Business '98
Puppet Master 5: The Final Chapter '94
Puppet Master 4 '93

Dominic West (1969-)
Hannibal Rising '07
300 '07
The Forgotten '04
Mona Lisa Smile '03
Chicago '02
Rock Star '01
28 Days '00
A Christmas Carol '99
William Shakespeare's A Midsummer Night's Dream '99
The Gambler '97
Wavelength '96
Class of 1999 2: The Substitute '93

Gregory West
The Surgeon '94

Jeremy West
Curse 4: The Ultimate Sacrifice '90
Catacombs '89

Joel West (1975-)
Blood Surf '00
The Smokers '00

Kevin West (1965-)
Bio-Dome '96
Killer Tomatoes Eat France '91
Killer Tomatoes Strike Back '90

Lockwood West (1905-89)
Bedazzled '68
The Leather Boys '63

Mae West (1893-1980)
Sextette '78
Myra Breckinridge '70
The Love Goddesses '65
The Heat's On '43
My Little Chickadee '40
Every Day's a Holiday '38
Go West, Young Man '36
Klondike Annie '36
Goin' to Town '35
Belle of the Nineties '34
I'm No Angel '33
She Done Him Wrong '33
Night After Night '32

Martin West
Assault on Precinct 13 '76
Sweet November '68
Lord Love a Duck '66
A Swingin' Summer '65

Nathan West (1978-)
Miracle '04
Home Room '02
The Skulls 2 '02

Norma West (1943-)
The Outlaws Is Coming! '65
Robinson Crusoe on Mars '64

Red West (1936-)
Forty Shades of Blue '05
John Grisham's The Rainmaker '97
The P.A.C.K. '96
The Expert '95

Samuel West (1966-)
And the Ship Sails On '83
Cause Celebre '87
Grizzly Adams: The Legend Continues '90
Proud Men '87
Hard Knox '83
Will: G. Gordon Liddy '82
Van Helsing '04
Cambridge Spies '03
Iris '01
Longitude '00
Pandaemonium '00
Horatio Hornblower '99
Retribution '98
Rupert's Land '98
The Ripper '97
Stiff Upper Lips '96
Carrington '95
Persuasion '95
Howard's End '92
Reunion '88

Shane West (1978-)
The League of Extraordinary Gentlemen '03
A Walk to Remember '02
Get Over It! '01
A Time for Dancing '00
Whatever It Takes '00
Get a Clue! '98

Tegan West
Hi-Life '98
Sleep with Me '94
Hamburger Hill '87

Timothy West (1934-)
Bleak House '05
Beyond Borders '03
Sinbad: Legend of the Seven Seas '03 (V)
The Fourth Angel '01
Iris '01
Station Jim '01
102 Dalmatians '00
Ever After: A Cinderella Story '98
King Lear '98
Hiroshima '95
Framed '93
Tragedy of Flight 103: The Inside Story '91
Consuming Passions '88
Cry Freedom '87
Death by Prescription '86
The Last Bastion '84
Oliver Twist '82
Churchill and the Generals '81
Rough Cut '80
Agatha '79
Edward the King '75
Hedda '75

Simon Westaway (1958-)
Alien Cargo '99
Chameleon 2: Death Match '99
When Love Comes '98
The Thorn Birds: The Missing Years '96

John Westbrook (1922-89)
Masque of the Red Death '65
Tomb of Ligeia '64
Room at the Top '59

Helen Westcott (1927-98)
The Invisible Avenger '58
Abbott and Costello Meet Dr. Jekyll and Mr. Hyde '52
With a Song in My Heart '52
The Gunfighter '50
Thunder Over Texas '34

Travis Wester (1977-)
All Souls Day '05
Eurotrip '04
The Paper Brigade '96

James Westerfield (1913-71)
Born in America '90
True Grit '69
That Funny Feeling '65
Homicidal '61
The Gunfight at Dodge City '59

Hakan Westergren (1899-1981)
Dollar '38
Swedenhielms '35

Carlie Westerman
Me and You and Everyone We Know '05
King of the Ants '03

Floyd "Red Crow" Westerman (1936-2007)
Comanche Moon '08
Hidalgo '04
The Last Assassins '96
Buffalo Girls '95
Lakota Woman: Siege at Wounded Knee '94
The Broken Chain '93
Walker, Texas Ranger: One Riot, One Ranger '94
Clearcut '92
Dances with Wolves '90

Jennifer Westfeldt (1970-)
Ira & Abby '06
How to Lose Your Lover '04
Kissing Jessica Stein '02

Dr. Ruth Westheimer (1928-)
Forever, Lulu '87
One Woman or Two '85

Helen Westley (1875-1942)
Lady from Louisiana '42
Sunny '41
All This and Heaven Too '40
Lillian Russell '40
Alexander's Ragtime Band '38
Rebecca of Sunnybrook Farm '38
Heidi '37
Dimples '36
Stowaway '36
Splendor '35
Anne of Green Gables '34
Death Takes a Holiday '34

Nydia Westman (1902-70)
Velvet Touch '48
The Chocolate Soldier '41
Bulldog Drummond's Revenge '37
One Night of Love '34
King of the Jungle '33

Matt Westmore
Charlotte Sometimes '02
Shakedown '02
Hard As Nails '01

James Westmoreland (1935-)
Don't Answer the Phone '80

Cecil Weston
Belles on Their Toes '52
Money Madness '47

Celia Weston (1951-)
The Invasion '07
Joshua '07
No Reservations '07
Junebug '05
The Village '04
Hulk '03
Undermind '03
Far from Heaven '02
Hearts in Atlantis '01
In the Bedroom '01
K-PAX '01
Joe Gould's Secret '00
Snow Falling on Cedars '99
Dead Man Walking '95
Flirting with Disaster '95
Little Man Tate '91
Lost Angels '89

David Weston (1938-)
The Heroes of Telemark '65
Masque of the Red Death '65

Doris Weston (1917-60)
Born to Be Wild '38

Jack Weston (1924-96)
Short Circuit 2 '88
Dirty Dancing '87
Ishtar '87
Gator '76
The Ritz '76
Marco '73
Fuzz '72
A New Leaf '71
Cactus Flower '69
The Thomas Crown Affair '68
Wait until Dark '67
Mirage '66
The Incredible Mr. Limpet '64
Palm Springs Weekend '63
The Honeymoon Machine '61
Please Don't Eat the Daisies '60

Jeff Weston (1960-)
Demonic Toys '90
Puppet Master 2 '90

Michael Weston (1973-)
Pathology '08
The Last Kiss '06
The Dukes of Hazzard '05
Garden State '04
Hart's War '02
Coyote Ugly '00
Lucky Numbers '00

Jack Wetherall
Third Man Out: A Donald Strachey Mystery '05

Virginia Wetherell (1943-)
The Victory '88
Dracula '73
Demons of the Mind '72
Disciple of Death '72
The Big Switch '70
The Crimson Cult '68

Patricia Wettig (1951-)
Bongwater '98
Dancer, Texas—Pop. 81 '98
Stephen King's The Langoliers '95
City Slickers 2: The Legend of Curly's Gold '94
Parallel Lives '94
Me & Veronica '93
City Slickers '91
Guilty by Suspicion '91
Silent Motive '91

Marius Weyers (1945-)
Stander '03
Bopha! '93
The Power of One '92
Deepstar Six '89
Farewell to the King '89
Happy Together '89
The Gods Must Be Crazy '84
African Rage '78

Ruth Weyher
Secrets of a Soul '25
Warning Shadows 23

Michael Whalen (1902-74)
Missile to the Moon '59
The Phantom from 10,000 Leagues '56
G.I. Jane '51
Kentucky Jubilee '51
King of the Bullwhip '51
Mask of the Dragon '51
Omoo Omoo, the Shark God '49
Sky Liner '49
Highway 13 '48
Dawn Express '42
Wee Willie Winkie '37
The Poor Little Rich Girl '36

Sean M. Whalen (1965-)
Employee of the Month '06
Chasing Ghosts '05
The Last Shot '04
Charlie's Angels '00
Perfect Murder, Perfect Town '00
Town '00
Idle Hands '99
Never Been Kissed '99
The Cable Guy '96
That Thing You Do! '96
Twister '96
Waterworld '95
The People under the Stairs '91

Frank Whaley (1963-)
Cherry Crush '07
Vacancy '07
Crazy Eights '06
Mrs. Harris '05
Chelsea Walls '01
The Jimmy Show '01
Pursuit of Happiness '01
The Wall '99
Went to Coney Island on a Mission from God... Be Back by Five '98
When Trumpets Fade '98
Retroactive '97
Café Society '97
Curtain Call '97
Glam '97
Homage '95
The Desperate Trail '94
I.Q. '94
Pulp Fiction '94
Swimming with Sharks '94
A Midnight Clear '92
Back in the USSR '92
Career Opportunities '91
The Doors '91
JFK '91
Dog '93
Born on the Fourth of July '89
Field of Dreams '89
Little Monsters '89
Ironweed '87

Kevin Whately (1951-)
The English Patient '96
Pink Floyd: The Wall '82

Alan Wheatley (1907-91)
Robin Hood: The Movie '55
The Limping Man '53
Calling Paul Temple '48
Counterblast '48
Brighton Rock '47
Appointment with Crime '45

Thomas Wheatley (1951-)
Piglet's Big Movie '03 (V)
The Living Daylights '87
Where Angels Fear to Tread '91

Wil Wheaton (1972-)
Star Trek: Nemesis '02
Deep Core '00
Python '00
Flubber '97
Mr. Stitch '95
Pie in the Sky '95
The Liar's Club '93
December '91
Toy Soldiers '91
The Curse '87
Stand by Me '86
The Last Starfighter '84
The Buddy System '84
The Secret of NIMH '82 (V)

Shannon Whirry (1964-)
Mach 2 '00
Me, Myself, and Irene '00
The Prophet's Game '99
Retroactive '97
Omega Doom '96
Dangerous Prey '95
Exit '95
Playback '95
The Granny '94
Animal Instincts 2 '94
Private Obsession '94
Body Count '94
Body of Influence '93
Mirror Images 2 '93
Animal Instincts '92

Barbara Whinnery
Hot to Trot '88

Liem Whatley
Heaven and Earth '93
The Iron Triangle '89

Manning Whiley (1915-75)
Meet Sexton Blake '44
The Dummy Talks '43

Shea Whigham (1969-)
First Snow '07
'06
All the Real Girls '03
Tigerland '00

Joseph Whipp (1941-)
Red Shoe Diaries: Luscious Lola '00
A Place Called Truth '98
Amazons '86
Crawlspace '85

Sam Whipple (1961-2002)
Ghost Night '81

Justin Whalin (1974-)
Dungeons and Dragons '00
Serial Mom '94
White Wolves 2: Legend of the Wild '94
The Fire Next Time '93
Perfect Harmony '91
Child's Play 3 '91

Joanne Whalley (1964-)
Played '06
Breathtaking '00
Ride the Wild Fields '00
A Texas Funeral '99
The Guilty '99
The Man Who Knew Too Little '97
A Good Man in Africa '94
Mother's Boys '94
Scarlett '94
The Secret Rapture '94
Trial by Jury '94
Storyville '92
The Big Man: Crossing the Line '91
Shattered '91
Navy SEALS '90
Kill Me Again '89
Scandal '89
To Kill a Priest '89
Willow '88
The Good Father '87
Edge of Darkness '86
No Surrender '86
The Singing Detective '86
Dance with a Stranger '85

Dana Wheeler-Nicholson (1960-)
Living in Peril '97
Nick and Jane '96
Denise Calls Up '95
The Pompatus of Love '95
Bye Bye, Love '95
My Life's in Turnaround '94
The Night We Never Met '93
Tombstone '93
Circuitry Man '90
Fletch '85

John Wheeler
Mrs. Soffel '84

Jane Wheeler
The Kid '97
Marked Man '96
The Neighbor '93

Arleen Whelan (1916-93)
The Sun Shines Bright '53
Never Wave at a WAC '52
Ramrod '47
Castle in the Desert '42
Charley's Aunt '41
Young People '40
Young Mr. Lincoln '39

Lisa Whelchel (1963-)
Where the Red Fern Grows: Part 2 '92
Twirl '81
The Double McGuffin '79
The Magician of Lublin '79

Bert Wheeler (1895-1968)
Cockeyed Cavaliers '34
Hips, Hips, Hooray '34
Kentucky Kernels '34
Diplomaniacs '33
So This Is Africa '33
Hold 'Em Jail '32
Dixiana '30
Half-Shot at Sunrise '30
Hook, Line and Sinker '30
The Cuckoos '30

Forest Whitaker (1961-)
Street Kings '08
Vantage Point '08
The Air I Breathe '07
The Great Debaters '07
Even Money '06
Everyone's Hero '06 (V)
The Last King of Scotland '06
American Gun '05
Jiminy Glick in LaLa Wood '05
First Daughter '04 (V)
Panic Room '02
Phone Booth '02
Anne Rice's The Feast of All Saints '01
The Fourth Angel '01
Green Dragon '01
Battlefield Earth '00
Four Dogs Playing Poker '00
Ghost Dog: The Way of the Samurai '99
Light It Up '99
Witness Protection '99
Phenomenon '96
Species '95
Smoke '95
Blown Away '94
The Enemy Within '94
Jason's Lyric '94
Lush Life '94
Ready to Wear '94
Bank Robber '93
Body Snatchers '93
The Crying Game '92
Consenting Adults '92
Article 99 '92
Diary of a Hitman '91
A Rage in Harlem '91
Downtown '89
Johnny Handsome '89
Bird '88
Bloodsport '88
Good Morning, Vietnam '87
Stakeout '87
Platoon '86
The Color of Money '86
Vision Quest '85
Fast Times at Ridgemont High '82

Duane Whitaker (1959-)
Feast '06
The Devil's Rejects '05
From Dusk Till Dawn 2: Texas Blood Money '99
Eddie Presley '92
Pulp Fiction '94

Damon Whitaker (1970-)
Bird '88

Christina Whitaker
Assault of the Killer Bimbos '88
Vampire at Midnight '88
Naked Cage '86
Body Count '87

Charles "Slim" Whitaker (1893-1960)
Outlaw of the Plains '46
Raiders of Red Gap '46
Pistol Packin' Mama '43
The Mysterious Rider '42
Saddle Buster '32

Johnny Whitaker (1959-)
Tom Sawyer '73
Napoleon and Samantha '72

Alice White (1904-83)
The Littlest Angel '69
Flamingo Road '49
Employees' Entrance '33
Picture Snatcher '33
Murder at Midnight '31
Playing Around '30

Bernie (Bernard) White (1959-)
Spoiler '98
Tales from the Hood '95
Pulp Fiction '94

Betty White (1922-)
Bringing Down the House '03
Whispers: An Elephant's Tale '00 (V)
Lake Placid '99
The Story of Us '99
Dennis the Menace Strikes Again '98
Hard Rain '97
A Weekend in the Country '96
Advise and Consent '62

Brian White (1973-)
Street Kings '08
In the Name of the King: A Dungeon Siege Tale '08
The Game Plan '07
Stomp the Yard '07
Brick '06
The Family Stone '05
Mr. 3000 '04

Carol White (1942-91)
The Squeeze '77
Some Call It Loving '73
Man Who Had Power Over Women '70
Daddy's Gone A-Hunting '69

Dan(iel) White (1908-80)
Attack of the Giant Leeches '59

De'voreaux White
Die Hard '88
The Children of Times Square '86

David White (1916-90)
The Amazing Spider-Man '77

Diz White
Stoogemania '85
Bullshot '83

Earl White
Omega Doom '96
Nemesis 2: Nebula '94

Harriet White (1914-2005)
The Ghost '63
Paisan '46

Harrison White (1980-)
I Got the Hook-Up '98
Doom Asylum '88

White

Jack White (1975-)
Walk Hard: The Dewey Cox Story '07
Coffee and Cigarettes '03
Cold Mountain '03

Jacqueline White (1922-)
The Narrow Margin '52
The Capture '50
Riders of the Bad Men '48
Return of the Bad Men '48
The Show-Off '46
Thirty Seconds Over Tokyo '44
Air Raid Wardens '43

Jaleel White (1976-)
Miracle Dogs Too '06
Who Made the Potatoe Salad? '05
Quest for Camelot '98 (V)

Jesse White (1919-97)
Matinee '92
Monster in the Closet '86
Bless the Beasts and Children '71
Togetherness '70
The Reluctant Astronaut '67
Pajama Party '64
The Rise and Fall of Legs Diamond '60
Beware, My Lovely '52
Tomboy & the Champ '58
Designing Woman '57
The Bad Seed '56
Forever Female '53
Gunsmoke '53
Million Dollar Mermaid '52
Bedtime for Bonzo '51
Francis Goes to the Races '51
Harvey '50

John White (1981-)
American Pie Presents: Beta House '07
American Pie Presents: The Naked Mile '06
The Legend of Gator Face '96

Julie White
Transformers '07

Lee White (1888-1949)
Red Rock Outlaw '47
In Old New Mexico '45

Lillias White
Game 6 '05
Pieces of April '03

Marjorie White
Diplomaniacs 33
The Black Camel '31

Michael Jai White (1967-)
The Dark Knight '08
Tyler Perry's Why Did I Get Married? '07
Undisputed II: Last Man Standing '06
Silver Hawk '04
Exit Wounds '01
Freedom Song '00
Mutiny '99
Thick as Thieves '99
Universal Soldier: The Return '99
Ringmaster '98
Spawn '97
City of Industry '96
Tyson '95
The Wall '99
Blood Brothers '97
Kissinger and Nixon '96
Screamers '96

Patricia White
See Patricia Barry

Peter White (1937-)
Thirteen Days '00
Mother '96

Ron White
Jasper, Texas '03
A House Divided '00
Locked in Silence '99

ShadowZone: The Undead Express '96
Frame by Frame '95
Johnny's Girl '95
Race to Freedom: The Story of the Underground Railroad '94
Guilty as Sin '93
Love & Murder '91
Cowboys Don't Cry '88

Slappy (Melvin) White (1920-95)
Mr. Saturday Night '92
Amazing Grace '74

Steve White (1961-)
Get On the Bus '96
Just for the Hell of It '68
She-Devils on Wheels '68

Vanna White (1957-)
Gypsy Angels '94
Graduation Day '81

Charles White Eagle
Altered States '80
Three Warriors '77

O.Z. Whitehead (1911-98)
The Man Who Shot Liberty Valance '62
The Horse Soldiers '59
Rally 'Round the Flag, Boys! '58
Road House 48
The Grapes of Wrath 40

Paxton Whitehead (1937-)
Kate & Leopold '01
The Adventures of Huck Finn '93
My Boyfriend's Back '93
Boris and Natasha: The Movie '92
Child of Darkness, Child of Light '91
Chips, the War Dog '90
Baby Boom '87
Back to School '86
Jumpin' Jack Flash '86

Billie Whitelaw (1932-)
Hot Fuzz '07
The Last of the Blonde Bombshells '00
The Lost Son '98
Merlin '98
Jane Eyre '96
Duel of Hearts '92
Freddie the Frog '92 (V)
Catherine Cookson's The Fifteen Streets '90
The Krays '90
Lorna Doone '90
A Murder of Quality '91
The Dressmaker 89
Maurice '87
The Secret Garden '87
Shadey 87
Murder Elite '86
Slayground '84
Tangiers 83
Make Mine Mink 60
No Love for Johnnie '60
Small Hotel '55

Arkie Whiteley (1965-2001)
The Last Musketeer '00
Gallowglass '95
Princess Caraboo '94
Razorback 83

Jon Whiteley (1945-)
The Spanish Gardener '57
Moonfleet '55

Paul Whiteman (1890-1967)
Lady Frankenstein '72
The Fabulous Dorseys 47
Strike Up the Band '40
King of Jazz '30

Charles Malik Whitfield
Bound by Lies '05
Behind Enemy Lines '01
The Temptations '98

Dondre T. Whitfield (1969-)
The Salon '05
Mr. 3000 '04
Two Can Play That Game '01

June Whitfield (1925-)
Catherine Cookson's The Secret '00
The Last of the Blonde Bombshells '00

Lynn Whitfield (1953-)
Madea's Family Reunion '06
Head of State '03
A Girl Thing '01
A Time for Dancing '00
Dangerous Evidence: The Lori Jackson Story '99
Love Songs '99
The Color of Courage '98
Stepmom '98
Eve's Bayou '97
Gone Fishin' '97
Junior's Groove '97
A Thin Line Between Love and Hate '96
State of Emergency '94
Taking the Heat '93
The Josephine Baker Story '90
Jaws: The Revenge '87
Johnnie Gibson F.B.I. '87
Hard Lessons '86
The Slugger's Wife '85
Doctor Detroit 83

Mitchell Whitfield (1968-)
TMNT (Teenage Mutant Ninja Turtles) '07 (V)
Amy's O '02
Lost and Found '99
Best Men '98
I Love You, Don't Touch Me! '97
My Cousin Vinny '92
Dogfight '91

Bradley Whitford (1959-)
Little Manhattan '05
Sisterhood of the Traveling Pants '05
Kate & Leopold '01
Behind the Mask '99
Bicentennial Man '99
The Muse '99
Red Corner '97
Masterminds '96
My Fellow Americans '96
Billy Madison '94
The Client '94
My Life '93
A Perfect World '93
Philadelphia '93
Scent of a Woman '92
Awakenings '90
Vital Signs '90
Young Guns 2 '90
Dead As a Doorman '85

Peter Whitford (1939-)
Strictly Ballroom '92
Warm Nights on a Slow-Moving Train '87
Dead End Drive-In '86
My Brilliant Career '79

Jack Whiting (1901-61)
Give Me a Sailor '38
Sailing Along '38

Leonard Whiting (1950-)
Rachel's Man '75
Say Hello to Yesterday '71
Romeo and Juliet '68

Margaret Whiting (1924-)
Trespasser '81
Disraeli '79
Sinbad and the Eye of the Tiger '77

Kym E. Whitley (1961-)
L.A. Dicks '05
The Perfect Man '05
The Salon '05
Along Came Polly '04
Up Against the Eight Ball '04
Deliver Us from Eva '03
What About Your Friends: Weekend Getaway '02
Next Friday '00

Ray Whitley (1901-79)
Racketeers of the Range '39

Isaiah Whitlock, Jr. (1954-)
Kettle of Fish '06
She Hate Me '04
Pieces of April '03
25th Hour '02

Lloyd Whitlock (1891-1966)
Lucky Texan '34
Diamond Trail '33
West of the Divide '33
Tangled Destinies '32
Man from Headquarters '28
The Michigan Kid 28
The Prairie Pirate 25

Jill Whitlow
Ghost Chase '88
Twice Dead '88
Adventures Beyond Belief 87
Night of the Creeps '86
Thunder Run 86

Kari Whitman (1969-)
Forced to Kill 93
Chained Heat 2 '92
Phantom of the Mall: Eric's Revenge 89

Mae Whitman (1988-)
Jesse Stone: Death in Paradise '06
Going Shopping '05
Disney's Teacher's Pet '04 (V)
The Jungle Book 2 '03 (V)
An American Rhapsody '01
Invisible Child '99
A Season for Miracles '99
Hope Floats '98
The Gingerbread Man '97
Independence Day '96
One Fine Day '96
Bye Bye, Love '94
When a Man Loves a Woman '94

Stuart Whitman (1926-)
The Treasure of the Amazon '84
Vultures '84
Butterfly '82
Demonoid, Messenger of Death '81
Hostages '80
Kill Castro '80
The Mercenaries '80
The Seekers '79
The Treasure Seekers '79

Fury '78
Oil '78
Run for the Roses '78
Delta Fox 77
Maniac '77
Ruby 77
The White Buffalo '77
Eaten Alive '76
Las Vegas Lady 76
Strange Shadows in an Empty Room 76
Crazy Mama '75
Mean Johnny Barrows '75
Call Him Mr. Shatter '74
Night of the Lepus '72
The Woman Hunter '72
Captain Apache '71
The Invincible Six '68
Those Magnificent Men in Their Flying Machines '65
Rio Conchos 64
The Day and the Hour '63
The Longest Day '62
The Comancheros '61
The Mark '61
The Story of Ruth '37
Darby's Rangers '58
Ten North Frederick '58
Crime of Passion '57
Silver Lode '54

Nigel Whitney (1963-)
Helen of Troy '03
Pulse '03

Steve Whitmire (1959-)
The Muppets' Wizard of Oz '05 (V)
Muppets from Space '99
Muppet Treasure Island '96 (V)
The Muppet Christmas Carol '92 (V)
Labyrinth '86

James Whitmore (1921-)
The Majestic '01
The Relic '96
The Shawshank Redemption '94
Glory! Glory! '90
Old Explorers '90
Nuts '87
Target: Favorite Son '87
All My Sons '86
The Adventures of Mark Twain '85 (V)
Don't Cry, It's Only Thunder '82
The First Deadly Sin '80
Rage '80
The Serpent's Egg '78
The Word '78
Give 'Em Hell, Harry! '75
I Will Fight No More Forever '75
Where the Red Fern Grows '74
Harrad Experiment '73
High Crime '73
Chato's Land '71
Tora! Tora! Tora! '70
Guns of the Magnificent Seven 69
Madigan 68
Planet of the Apes 68
Chuka 67
Waterhole Number 3 '67
Black Like Me '64
Deep Six '58
The Eddy Duchin Story '56
Battle Cry '55
The McConnell Story '55
Oklahoma! '55
Savage Wilderness '55
Them! 54
Above and Beyond '53
All the Brothers Were Valiant '53
The Girl Who Had Everything '53
Kiss Me Kate '53
Because You're Mine '52
The Asphalt Jungle '50

The Next Voice You Hear '50
Battleground 49

James Whitmore, Jr. (1948-)
Tricks of the Trade '88
The Five of Me '81
The Long Riders 80
The Bastard '78
The Gypsy Warriors '78
The Boys in Company C 77

Daniel Lawrence Whitney
See Larry the Cable Guy

Grace Lee Whitney (1930-)
Star Trek 6: The Undiscovered Country '91
Star Trek 3: The Search for Spock 84
Star Trek: The Motion Picture 79

Peter Whitney (1916-72)
Savage Wilderness '55
All the Brothers Were Valiant '53
The Brute Man '46
Murder, He Says '45
Action in the North Atlantic '43
Destination Tokyo '43
Rio Rita '42
Valley of the Sun '42
Whistling in Dixie '42
Underground '41

Benjamin Whitrow (1937-)
Scenes of a Sexual Nature '06
Chicken Run '00 (V)
Tom Jones '98
Pride and Prejudice '95
Belfast Assassin '84

Frank Whitson (1877-1946)
$50,000 Reward '25
The Adventures of Tarzan '21
Son of a Gun '19

Garland Whitt
Save the Last Dance '01
Blind Faith '98

Marguerite Whitten (1913-90)
Mystery in Swing '40
Two-Gun Man from Harlem '38

Margaret Whitton (1950-)
Major League 2 '94
Trial by Jury '94
The Man Without a Face '93
Big Girls Don't Cry... They Get Even '92
Little Monsters '89
Major League '89
Ironweed '87
The Secret of My Success '87
The Best of Times '86
9 1/2 Weeks '86

May Whitty (1865-1948)
Gaslight '44
The White Cliffs of Dover '44
Crash Dive '43
Lassie, Come Home '43
Madame Curie '43
Mrs. Miniver '42
Thunder Birds '42
Suspicion 41
The Lady Vanishes '38
Conquest 37
Night Must Fall '37

James Whitworth
Planet of the Dinosaurs '80
357 Magnum '79
The Hills Have Eyes '77
Black Bikers from Hell '70

Johnny Whitworth (1975-)
Pathology '08
3:10 to Yuma '07
MTV's Wuthering Heights '03
Valentine '01
Hell's Kitchen NYC '97
John Grisham's The Rainmaker '97
Somebody Is Waiting '96
Empire Records '95
Bye Bye, Love '94

Richard Whorf (1906-66)
Chain Lightning '50
Keeper of the Flame '42
Yankee Doodle Dandy '42
Midnight '34

Patrick Whyte (1907-84)
Kitten with a Whip '64
Hideous Sun Demon '59

Anna Wiazemsky (1947-)
Teorema '68

Mary Wickes (1916-95)
Dame '96 (V)
Little Women '94
Sister Act 2: Back in the Habit '93
Sister Act '92
The Canterville Ghost '91
Postcards from the Edge '90
Almost Partners '87
Where Angels Go, Trouble Follows '68
How to Murder Your Wife '64
Dance with Me, Henry '56
Ma and Pa Kettle at Home '54
By the Light of the Silvery Moon '53
I'll See You in My Dreams '51
On Moonlight Bay '51
June Bride '48
Who Done It? '42
Blondie's Blessed Event '42
The Man Who Came to Dinner '41

Jeffrey Wickham (1933-)
Clarissa '91
Another Country '84
Waterloo '71

Saskia Wickham (1967-)

Bernhard Wicki (1919-2000)
Crime & Passion '75
The Eternal Waltz '54
The Last Bridge '54

Kathleen Widdoes (1939-)
Courage Under Fire '96
Mafia Princess '86
The Group '66
Petulia '68
Savages '72

Connor Widdows (1992-)
X-Men: The Last Stand '06
Agent Cody Banks 2: Destination London '04

Johan Widerberg (1974-)
Under the Sun '98
All Things Fair '95

Richard Widmark (1914-2008)
True Colors '91
Texas Guns '90
Cold Sassy Tree '89
Blackout '85
Against All Odds '84
The Final Option '82
Hanky Panky '82
National Lampoon Goes to the Movies '81
Whale for the Killing '81
All God's Children '80
Bear Island '80
Mr. Horn '79
The Swarm '78
Coma '78
The Domino Principle '77
Rollercoaster '77
Twilight's Last Gleaming '77
Murder on the Orient Express '74
When the Legends Die '72
Death of a Gunfighter '69
Gun Crazy '69
Madigan '68
The Way West '67
Alvarez Kelly '66
Bedford Incident '65
Cheyenne Autumn '64
The Long Ships '64
How the West Was Won '63
Judgment at Nuremberg '61
Two Rode Together '61
The Alamo '60
The Trap '59
Warlock '59
The Law and Jake Wade '58
The Tunnel of Love '58
Saint Joan '57
The Cobweb '55
Broken Lance '54
Garden of Evil '54
Pickup on South Street '53
Don't Bother to Knock '52
The Halls of Montezuma '50
Night and the City '50
No Way Out '50
Panic in the Streets '50
Road House '48
The Street with No Name '48
Kiss of Death '47

Dorothea Wieck (1908-86)
A Time to Love & a Time to Die '58
Maedchen in Uniform '31

Danielle Wiener
Beethoven's 3rd '00

Kai Wiesinger (1966-)
Dresden '06
The Harmonists '99
Backbeat '94

Lynda Wiesmeier (1963-)
R.S.V.P. '84

Dianne Wiest (1948-)
Dan in Real Life '07
Robots '05 (V)
Category 6: Day of Destruction '04
Merci Docteur Rey '04
I Am Sam '01
The 10th Kingdom '00
The Simple Life of Noah Dearborn '99
Practical Magic '98
The Horse Whisperer '98
The Associate '96
Drunks '96
The Birdcage '96
The Scout '94
Bullets over Broadway '94
Cops and Robbersons '94
Little Man Tate '91
Edward Scissorhands '90
Cookie '89
Parenthood '89
Bright Lights, Big City '88
September '88
The Lost Boys '87
Radio Days '87
Hannah and Her Sisters '86
The Purple Rose of Cairo '85
Falling in Love '84
Footloose '84
Independence Day '83
It's My Turn '80
Zalmen or the Madness of God '75

Naima Wifstrand (1890-1969)
Hour of the Wolf '68
The Magician '58
Night Is My Future '48

Geoff Wigdor (1982-)
Levity '03
Sleepers '96

Chris Wiggins (1931-)
Babar: The Movie '88 (V)
Mark Twain and Me '91
Ford: The Man & the Machine '87
The Bay Boy '85
Rock & Rule '83 (V)
Kavik the Wolf Dog '80
King of the Grizzlies '79
Why Shoot the Teacher? '79

Wiley Wiggins (1976-)
Waking Life '01
Dazed and Confused '93

Peter Wight (1950-)
Pride and Prejudice '05
The Statement '03
Naked '93

Robert Wightman
Living in Oblivion '94
Stepfather 3: Father's Day '92
Opposing Force '87
A Day for Thanks on Walton's Mountain '82

Kristen Wiig (1973-)
The Brothers Solomon '07
Knocked Up '07
Walk Hard: The Dewey Cox Story '07

Carlton Wilborn (1964-)
Dance '90

George P. Wilbur
Halloween 6: The Curse of Michael Myers '95
Halloween 4: The Return of Michael Myers '88

James Wilby (1958-)
De-Lovely '04
Gosford Park '01
Cotton Mary '99
The Woman in White '97
Howard's End '92
Lady Chatterley '92
Conspiracy '89
A Tale of Two Cities '89
A Handful of Dust '88
A Summer Story '88
Maurice '87
Dreamchild '85

Frank Wilcox (1907-74)
Beginning of the End '57
A Majority of One '56
Seventh Cavalry '56
Carolina Cannonball '55
Abbott and Costello Meet the Keystone Kops '54
The Clay Pigeon '49
Infamous Crimes '47
Across the Pacific '42
They Died with Their Boots On '41
The Wagons Roll at Night '41

Collin Wilcox-Paxton (1937-)
Fluke '95
Wildflower '91
Jaws 2 '78
Fury on Wheels '71
The Baby Maker '70
Catch-22 '70
To Kill a Mockingbird '62

Larry Wilcox (1947-)
National Lampoon's Loaded Weapon 1 '93
Mission Manila '87
The Dirty Dozen: The Next Mission '85
The Last Ride of the Dalton Gang '79

Lisa Wilcox (1964-)
Watchers Reborn '98
A Nightmare on Elm Street 5: The Dream Child '89
A Nightmare on Elm Street 4: The Dream Master '88

Mary Wilcox (1944-)

Robert Wilcox (1910-55)
Doctor Satan's Robot '40
Dreaming Out Loud '40
Mysterious Doctor Satan '40
Buried Alive '39
The Man They Could Not Hang '39

Shannon Wilcox
Hollywood Harry '86
When Your Lover Leaves '83
Love Me Deadly '73
Beast of the Yellow Night '70

Henry Wilcoxon (1905-84)
Caddyshack '80
Enola Gay: The Men, the Mission, the Atomic Bomb '80
The Two Worlds of Jenny Logan '79
When Every Day Was the Fourth of July '78
Pony Express Rider '76
Against a Crooked Sky '75
Man in the Wilderness '71
Escape from Planet Earth '67
The War Lord '65
The Ten Commandments '56
Scaramouche '52
Samson and Delilah '50
A Connecticut Yankee in King Arthur's Court '49
Unconquered '47
The Corsican Brothers '42
The Man Who Wouldn't Die '42
Mrs. Miniver '42
That Hamilton Woman '41
Tarzan Finds a Son '39
If I Were King '38
The Last of the Mohicans '36
The President's Mystery '36
The Crusades '35
Cleopatra '34

Jack Wild (1952-2006)
Robin Hood: Prince of Thieves '91
Melody '71
Pufnstuf '70
Oliver! '68

Andrew Wilde
Murder on Line One '90

Cornel Wilde (1915-89)
1984 '84
The Fifth Musketeer '79
Norseman '78
Sharks' Treasure '75
The Comic '69
The Naked Prey '66
Sword of Lancelot '63
Omar Khayyam '57
Big Combo '55
Passion '54
A Woman's World '54
Main Street to Broadway '53
Treasure of the Golden Condor '53
The Greatest Show on Earth '52
At Sword's Point '51
Road House '48
Forever Amber '47
Leave Her to Heaven '45
A Song to Remember '45
A Thousand and One Nights '45
Wintertime '43
High Sierra '41
The Lady in Question '40

Lois Wilde (1907-95)
Undersea Kingdom '36
Stormy Trails '36

Olivia Wilde (1984-)
Bobby Z '07
Alpha Dog '06
Bickford Shmeckler's Cool Ideas '06
Turistas '06
Conversations with Other Women '05

Gene Wilder (1935-)
Alice in Wonderland '99
The Lady in Question '99
Murder in a Small Town '99
Another You '91
Funny About Love '90
See No Evil, Hear No Evil '89
Haunted Honeymoon '86
The Woman in Red '84
Hanky Panky '82
Stir Crazy '80
The Frisco Kid '79
The Adventures of Sherlock Holmes' Smarter Brother '78
World's Greatest Lover '77
Silver Streak '76
The Little Prince '74
Blazing Saddles '74
Thursday's Game '74
Young Frankenstein '74
Everything You Always Wanted to Know about Sex (But Were Afraid to Ask) '72
Willy Wonka & the Chocolate Factory '71
Quackser Fortune Has a Cousin in the Bronx '70
Start the Revolution without Me '70
The Producers '68
Bonnie & Clyde '67

Glenn Wilder (1933-)
Zebra Force '76
The Sand Pebbles '66

James Wilder (1963-)
Burning Down the House '01
Heart of Stone '01
First Degree '98
The Last Don 2 '98
Scorchers '92

Jan Wiley (1916-93)
She Wolf of London '46
There Goes Kelly '45
Lawmen '44
Master Key '44
Jive Junction '43
Rhythm Parade '43
So Proudly We Hail '43
The Underdog '43
Zis Boom Bah '41

Ed Wiley
Terror at Tenkiller '86

Mike Wiles
Held Up '00
Cole Justice '89

Jason Wiles (1970-)
Kicking and Screaming '95
Higher Learning '94
Roadracers '94
Windrunner '94

Dawn Wildsmith
Jack-O '95
Wizards of the Demon Sword '94
Alienator '89
Hollywood Chainsaw Hookers '88
Evil Spawn '87
Phantom Empire '87
Surf Nazis Must Die '87
Cyclone '87
Warlords '88
Terminal Force '88

Yvonne Wilder (1937-)
Honeyboy '82

Michael Wilding (1912-79)
Waterloo '71
The Naked Edge '61
The World of Suzie Wong '60
Under Capricorn '49
Maytime in Mayfair '49
The Courtney Affair '47
In Which We Serve '43
Secret Mission '42
Cottage to Let '41
Kipps '41
Convoy '40
Late Extra '35

Michael Wilding, Jr. (1953-)
Neon City '91
Inner Sanctum '91
Sweet Bird of Youth '89

John Wildman (1961-)
American Boyfriends '89
My American Cousin '85

Valerie Wildman (1953-)
Salvador '86

John Wilford
Dawn on the Great Divide '42
Thunder River Feud '42
Tonto Basin Outlaws '41

Jan Wiley (1916-93)
Zis Boom Bah '41

Ed Wiley
Class of '61 '92

Webb Wilder
Zombie High '87

Dianne Wilhite
Flesh Feast '69
Gruesome Twosome '67

Kathleen Wilhoite (1964-)
Audrey's Rain '03
My Sister's Keeper '02
Quicksand '01
Drowning Mona '00
Nurse Betty '00
Breast Men '97
Color of Night '94

Wilhoite
Getting Even with Dad '94
Lorenzo's Oil '92
Bad Influence '90
Everybody Wins '90
Dream Demon '88
Angel Heart '87
Campus Man '87
Undercover '87
Witchboard '87
The Morning After '86
Murphy's Law '86
Quarterback Princess '85
Private School '83
Xica '76

Robert J. Wilke (1915-89)
The Cheyenne Social Club '70
Never Steal Anything Small '59
Night Passage '57
Tarnished Angels '57
20,000 Leagues under the Sea '54
From Here to Eternity '53
High Noon '52
Kill the Umpire '50

Jose Wilker (1945-)
Medicine Man '92
Bye Bye Brazil '79
Dona Flor and Her Two Husbands '78
Xica '76

Guy Wilkerson (1899-1971)
Man of the West '58
Comin' Round the Mountain '51
Flaming Bullets '45
Frontier Fugitives '45
Marked for Murder '45
Boss of Rawhide '44
Dead or Alive '44
Guns of the Law '44
Outlaw Roundup '44
Fighting Valley '43
Rangers Take Over '42
Sergeant York '41

Elaine Wilkes (1965-)
Killer Party '86
Roommate '84

Barbara Wilkin
Six in Paris '68

Elizabeth Wilkinson
Suburban Roulette '67
A Taste of Blood '67
Fyre '78

June Wilkinson (1940-)
Vasectomy: A Delicate Matter '86
Sno-Line '85
Frankenstein's Great Aunt Tillie '83
The Florida Connection '74
The Bellboy and the Playgirls '62
Macumba Love '60

Linden Wilkinson
The Monkey's Mask '00
The Wedding Party '97

Scott Wilkinson
Benji: Off the Leash! '04
Wish upon a Star '96

Tom Wilkinson (1948-)
John Adams '08
Cassandra's Dream '07
Dedication '07
Michael Clayton '07
The Last Kiss '06
Batman Begins '05
The Exorcism of Emily Rose '05
Eternal Sunshine of the Spotless Mind '04
A Good Woman '04
If Only '04
Stage Beauty '04
Girl with a Pearl Earring '03
Normal '03
The Gathering Storm '02
The Importance of Being Earnest '02
Black Knight '01
In the Bedroom '01
Chain of Fools '00
The Patriot '00
David Copperfield '99 (N)
Essex Boys '99
Molokai: The Story of Father Damien '99
Ride with the Devil '99
The Governess '98
Rush Hour '98
Shakespeare in Love '98
Oscar and Lucinda '97
Wilde '97
The Full Monty '96
The Ghost and the Darkness '96
Smilla's Sense of Snow '96
Martin Chuzzlewit '94
Priest '94
Royal Deceit '94
Prime Suspect '92
Paper Mask '91
Sylvia '86

Lee Wilkof (1951-)
Private Parts '96
Chattahoochee '89

Fred Willard (1939-)
WALL-E '08 (V)
Epic Movie '07
Date Movie '06
For Your Consideration '06
I Could Never Be Your Woman '06
Ira & Abby '06
Monster House '06 (V)
Chicken Little '05 (V)
Anchorman: The Legend of Ron Burgundy '04
Harold and Kumar Go to White Castle '04
How to Lose Your Lover '04
Killer Diller '04
American Wedding '03
A Mighty Wind '03
National Lampoon's Christmas Vacation 2: Cousin Eddie's Big Island Adventure '03
How High '01
The Wedding Planner '01
Best in Show '00
Austin Powers 2: The Spy Who Shagged Me '99
Idle Hands '99
The Pooch and the Pauper '99
Permanent Midnight '98
Waiting for Guffman '96
Prehysteria 3 '95
Sodbusters '94
The Return of Spinal Tap '92
High Strung '91
Portrait of a White Marriage '88
Roxanne '87
Lots of Luck '85
Moving Violations '85
This Is Spinal Tap '84
How to Beat the High Cost of Living '80
Americathon '79
Salem's Lot '79
Chesty Anderson USN '76
So Proudly We Hail '43

Chad Willet
Carolina Moon '07
The Locket '02
Outlaw Justice '98
Annie O '95

Toyah Willcox (1958-)
Ebony Tower '86
Murder: Ultimate Grounds for Divorce '84
Quadrophenia '79

Jean Willes (1923-89)
The FBI Story '59
Invasion of the Body Snatchers '56
Abbott and Costello Go to Mars '53

Warren William (1895-1948)
Black Tower '50
The Private Affairs of Bel Ami '47
Fear '46
Strange Illusion '45
The Wolf Man '41
Arizona '40
Lillian Russell '40
The Gracie Allen Murder Case '39
The Man in the Iron Mask '39
Wives under Suspicion '38
The Firefly '37
Madame X '37
Go West, Young Man '36
Satan Met a Lady '36
The Case of the Lucky Legs '35
Cleopatra '34
Imitation of Life '34
Employees' Entrance '33
Gold Diggers of 1933 '33
Lady for a Day '33
Skyscraper Souls '32
Three on a Match '32

Adam Williams (1922-2006)
North by Northwest '59
The Badlanders '58
Fear Strikes Out '57
Crashout '55
Without Warning '52
Flying Leathernecks '51
Queen for a Day '51

Allen Williams
Scorpion '86
The Two Worlds of Jenny Logan '79

Barbara Williams (1953-)
Love Come Down '00
Family of Cops 3 '98
Krippendorf's Tribe '98
Naked City: A Killer Christmas '98
Naked City: Justice with a Bullet '98
Bone Daddy '97
Family of Cops 2: Breach of Faith '97
Inventing the Abbotts '97
Joe Torre: Curveballs Along the Way '97
Family of Cops '95
Digger '94
Spenser: Pale Kings & Princes '94
Spenser: Ceremony '93
Indecency '92
Oh, What a Night '92
City of Hope '91
Peter Gunn '89
Watchers '88
Tiger Warsaw '87
Jo Jo Dancer, Your Life Is Calling '86
Tell Me That You Love Me '84
Thief of Hearts '84

Barry Williams (1954-)
The Brady Bunch Movie '95
A Very Brady Christmas '88
Wild in the Streets '68

Bill Williams (1916-92)
Flight of the Grey Wolf '76
The Giant Spider Invasion '75
Buckskin '68
Storm Rider '57
Torpedo Alley '53
Son of Paleface '52
Cavalry Scout '51
The Cariboo Trail '50
Operation Haylift '50
The Clay Pigeon '49
The Stratton Story '49
A Woman's Secret '49
Deadline at Dawn '46
Till the End of Time '46

Billy Dee Williams (1937-)
Epoch: Evolution '03
Undercover Brother '02
The Ladies Man '00
The Visit '00
Fear Runs Silent '99
The Contract '98
Mask of Death '97
Steel Sharks '97
Moving Target '96
Dangerous Passion '95
The Prince '95
Triplecross '95
Alien Intruder '93
Percy & Thunder '93
Giant Steps '92
The Jacksons: An American Dream '92
Driving Me Crazy '91
Batman '89
Deadly Illusion '87
Number One with a Bullet '87
Courage '86
Oceans of Fire '86
Fear City '85
Shooting Stars '85
Christmas Lilies of the Field '84
The Impostor '84
Marvin & Tige '84
Chiefs '83
Return of the Jedi '83
Nighthawks '81
Children of Divorce '80
The Empire Strikes Back '80
The Hostage Tower '80
Bingo Long Traveling All-Stars & Motor Kings '76
Mahogany '75
Hit! '73
Final Comedown '72
The Glass House '72
Lady Sings the Blues '72
Brian's Song '71
The Out-of-Towners '70
Black Brigade '69

Billy "Sly" Williams (1968-)
Mission of Justice '92
Voodoo Dawn '89

Brook Williams (1938-)
Absolution '81
Where Eagles Dare '68
Plague of the Zombies '66

Cara Williams (1925-)
The White Buffalo '77
Never Steal Anything Small '59
The Defiant Ones '58
Meet Me in Las Vegas '56
The Girl Next Door '53
Boomerang '47

Caroline Williams (1957-)
Leprechaun 3 '95
Stepfather 2: Make Room for Daddy '89
The Texas Chainsaw Massacre 2 '86

Charles Williams (1909-75)
Born to Be Wild '38
Hollywood Stadium Mystery '38

Chris(topher) Williams
The World's Fastest Indian '05
Dodgeball: A True Underdog Story '04
The Courage to Love '00
Cremans '00

Chuck Williams
Dark Rider '91
Soultaker '90

Cindy Williams (1947-)
The Biggest Fan '02
Meet Wally Sparks '97
Bingo '91
Big Man on Campus '89
Rude Awakening '89
Tricks of the Trade '88
The Creature Wasn't Nice '81
Spaceship '81
Uforia '81
More American Graffiti '79
The First Nudie Musical '75
The Conversation '74
The Migrants '74
American Graffiti '73
The Killing Kind '73
Beware! The Blob '72
Travels with My Aunt '72
Gas-s-s-s! '70

Clara Williams (1888-1928)
Hell's Hinges '16
The Bargain '15
The Italian '15

Clarence Williams, III (1939-)
American Gangster '07
Mystery Woman: Mystery Weekend '05
Mindstorm '01
Reindeer Games '00
The General's Daughter '99
Life '99
Malicious Intent '99
Frogs for Snakes '98
The Legend of 1900 '98
George Wallace '97
Half-Baked '97
The Love Bug '97
Hoodlum '96
Rebound: The Legend of Earl "The Goat" Manigault '96
The Road to Galveston '96
Sprung '96
The Immortals '95
The Silencers '95
Tales from the Hood '95
Against the Wall '94
Sugar Hill '94
Dangerous Relations '93
Deep Cover '92
My Heroes Have Always Been Cowboys '91
Maniac Cop 2 '90
The House of Dies Drear '88
I'm Gonna Git You Sucka '88
The Last Innocent Man '87
Perfect Victims '87
Tough Guys Don't Dance '87
52 Pick-Up '86
Purple Rain '84

Cole Williams
Mammoth '06
North Country '05
Harry and Max '04

Cynda Williams (1966-)
When Do We Eat? '05
MacArthur Park '01
The Courage to Love '00
Introducing Dorothy Dandridge '99
Caught Up '98
Relax... It's Just Sex! '98
Gang in Blue '96
Spirit Lost '96
Condition Red '95
Machine Gun Blues '95
The Sweeper '95
The Tie That Binds '95
Armistead Maupin's Tales of the City '93
The Ghost Brigade '93
Tales of Erotica '93
One False Move '91
Mo' Better Blues '90

Darnell Williams (1955-)
Firestarter 2: Rekindled '02
Detour '99
How U Like Me Now? '92

Dick Anthony Williams (1938-)
The Players Club '98
Edward Scissorhands '90
Mo' Better Blues '90
Tap '89
For Us, the Living '88
Gardens of Stone '87
Keeping On '81
Sophisticated Gents '81
The Night the City Screamed '80
An Almost Perfect Affair '79
A Woman Called Moses '78
Dog Day Afternoon '75
The Anderson Tapes '71

D.J. Williams (1868-1949)
The Courageous Mr. Penn '41
Mr. Reeder in Room 13 '38
The Crimes of Stephen Hawke '36
Murder in the Old Red Barn '36

Edy Williams (1942-)
Bad Girls from Mars '90
Rented Lips '88
Mankillers '87
Hellhole '85
Bad Manners '84
Hollywood Hot Tubs '84
Beyond the Valley of the Dolls '70
Secret Life of an American Wife '68
Good Times '67
Naked Kiss '64

Emlyn Williams (1905-87)
Deadly Game '82
The L-Shaped Room '62
The Wreck of the Mary Deare '59
Another Man's Poison '52
The Last Days of Dolwyn '49
This England '42
The Stars Look Down '39
The Citadel '38
The Iron Duke '34

Esther Williams (1923-)
That's Entertainment '74
Jupiter's Darling '55
Dangerous When Wet '53
Easy to Love '53
Million Dollar Mermaid '52
Skirts Ahoy! '52
Texas Carnival '51
The Duchess of Idaho '50
Pagan Love Song '50
Neptune's Daughter '49
Take Me Out to the Ball Game '49
On an Island with You '48
Easy to Wed '46
Ziegfeld Follies '46
Thrill of a Romance '45
Bathing Beauty '44
A Guy Named Joe '44
Andy Hardy's Double Life '42

Finty Williams (1972-)
The Importance of Being Earnest '02

Gareth Williams
13 Moons '02
Hard Luck '01
The Cell '00
From the Earth to the Moon '98
Palookaville '95
Blessing '94

Gary Anthony Williams (1966-)
Jiminy Glick in LaLa Wood '04
Undercover Brother '02

Grant Williams (1930-85)
Brain of Blood '71
Escape from Planet Earth '67
The Leech Woman '59
The Incredible Shrinking Man '57
The Monolith Monsters '57
Written on the Wind '56

Gregory Alan Williams
Be Cool '05
Acts of Betrayal '98
In the Line of Fire '93

Guinn "Big Boy" Williams (1899-1962)
The Alamo '60
Hidden Guns '56
Springfield Rifle '52
Nevada '44
The Desperadoes '43
Hands Across the Border '43
Lure of the Islands '42
Mr. Wise Guy '42
Billy the Kid '41
The Fighting 69th '40
Virginia City '40
Wagon's Westward '40
Bad Lands '39
Mutiny on the Blackhawk '39
Dangerous Holiday '37
Feud of the Trail '37
You Only Live Once '37
Gun Play '36
Kelly the Second '36
The Vigilantes Are Coming '36
Powdersmoke Range '35
Village Tale '35
Dangerous Appointment '34
Heritage of the Desert '33
Mystery Squadron '33
The Phantom Broadcast '33
When the West Was Young '32
Burning Daylight '28
Wolfheart's Revenge '25
Rounding Up the Law '22

Guy Williams (1924-89)
Captain Sinbad '63
The Prince and the Pauper '62
The Sign of Zorro '60
I Was a Teenage Werewolf '57
The Secret of El Zorro '57
Savage Wilderness '55

Hal Williams (1938-)
Guess Who '05
Don't Look Back: The Story of Leroy "Satchel" Paige '81
On the Nickel '80

Harcourt Williams (1880-1957)
The Obsessed '51
Henry V '44

Harland Williams (1967-)
Bachelor Party 2: The Last Temptation '08
Meet the Robinsons '07 (V)
Employee of the Month '06
Robots '05 (V)
Sorority Boys '02
Freddy Got Fingered '01
The Whole Nine Yards '00
Superstar '99
Dog Park '98
Mr. Headmistress '98
There's Something about Mary '98
Half-Baked '97
RocketMan '97
Down Periscope '96
Dumb & Dumber '94

Heathcote Williams (1941-)
Basic Instinct 2 '06
The Odyssey '97
The Tango Lesson '97
Blue Juice '95
Cold Light of Day '95
Orlando '92

Hugh Williams (1904-69)
Khartoum '66
Elizabeth of Ladymead '48
A Girl in a Million '46
The Day Will Dawn '42
Secret Mission '42
One of Our Aircraft is Missing '41
The Human Monster '39
Inspector Hornleigh '39
Wuthering Heights '39
Bitter Sweet '33

Ian Patrick Williams

Jason Williams (1952-)
Danger Zone 3: Steel Horse War '90
Danger Zone 2 '89
Danger Zone '87
Vampire at Midnight '88
Cheerleaders' Wild Weekend '85
Cop Killers '73
Flesh Gordon '72

Jermaine Williams
The Comebacks '07
Fat Albert '04

Jim Williams
Ex-Cop '93

JoBeth Williams (1953-)
In the Land of Women '06
CrazyLove '05
Fever Pitch '05
Into the Fire '05
The Ponder Heart '01
Just Write '97
Little City '97
It Came from the Sky '98
When Danger Follows You Home '97
Jackie's Back '99
Parallel Lives '94
Ruby Jean and Joe '96
Welcome Home '89
My Name is Bill W. '89
Child in the Night '90
Victim of Love '91
Switch '91
Dutch '91
Memories of Me '88
Desert Bloom '86
Teachers '84
American Dreamer '84
Adam '83
Side '86
Poltergeist II: The Other Side '86
Poltergeist '82
Endangered Species '82
The Day After '83
The Big Chill '83
The Dogs of War '81
Stir Crazy '80
Kramer vs. Kramer '79
Murder Ordained '87

John Williams (1903-83)
The Secret War of Harry Frigg '68
Double Trouble '67
Dear Brigitte '65
24 Hours in a Woman's Life '61
The Young Philadelphians '59
Island in the Sun '57
Will Success Spoil Rock Hunter? '57
Witness for the Prosecution '57
D-Day, the Sixth of June '56
To Catch a Thief '55
Dial "M" for Murder '54
Sabrina '54

Katt Micah Williams (1973-)
First Sunday '08
Norbit '07
The Perfect Holiday '07
Ganked '05

Kelli Williams (1970-)
Sweetwater: A True Rock Story '99
Deception '08
Wavelength '96

Kenneth Williams (1926-88)
The Thief and the Cobbler '95 (V)
Carry On Emmanuelle '78
Carry On Behind '75
Carry On at Your Convenience '71
Carry On Camping '71
Carry On Henry VIII '71
Carry On Doctor '68
Follow That Camel '67
Carry On Cowboy '67
Carry On Screaming '66
Carry On Cleo '65
Carry On Cruising '62

Kimberly Williams (1971-)
How to Eat Fried Worms '06
How to Go Out on a Date in Queens '06
We Are Marshall '06
The Christmas Shoes '02
Lucky Seven '03
Follow the Stars Home '01
The 10th Kingdom '00
Just a Little Harmless Sex '99
Safe House '99
Simpatico '99
The War at Home '96
Father of the Bride Part 2 '95
Coldblooded '94
Indian Summer '93
Father of the Bride '91

Lee Williams (1974-)
The Deep '03
In His Life: The John Lennon Story '00

Lia Williams (1964-)
The Wolves of Kromer '98
Dancing in September '00
Shot Through the Heart '98
Firelight '97
The King is Alive '00

Malinda Williams (1975-)
First Sunday '08
Daddy's Little Girls '07
Idlewild '06
Uninvited Guest '99
The Wood '99
High School High '96
A Thin Line Between Love and Hate '96
Laurel Avenue '93

Mark Williams (1959-)
Harry Potter and the Order of the Phoenix '07
Harry Potter and the Goblet of Fire '05
Tristram Shandy: A Cock and Bull Story '05
Harry Potter and the Chamber of Secrets '02
The Borrowers '97
101 Dalmatians '96

Mary Parker Williams
Kill Line '91

Michael Williams (1935-2001)
Sarah's Child '96
Wish upon a Star '96
The Blair Witch Project '99

Michael K. Williams
Gone Baby Gone '07
I Think I Love My Wife '07

Michelle Williams (1980-)
Deception '08
I'm Not There '07
The Hawk is Dying '06
The Hottest State '06
The Baxter '05
Brokeback Mountain '05
Imaginary Heroes '05
A Hole in One '04
Land of Plenty '04
The Station Agent '03
United States of Leland '03
Me Without You '01
Prozac Nation '01
Perfume '01
Dick '99
Halloween: H20 '98
Killing Mr. Griffin '97
A Thousand Acres '97
Species '95
Timemaster '95
Lassie '94

Olivia Williams (1969-)
Miss Austen Regrets '07
X-Men: The Last Stand '06
Valiant '05 (V)
Agatha Christie: A Life in Pictures '04
Peter Pan '03
The Body '01
The Heart of Me '02
Below '02
Born Romantic '00
Lucky Break '01
The Man from Elysian Fields '01
Four Dogs Playing Poker '00
Jason and the Argonauts '00
The Sixth Sense '99
Rushmore '98
Emma '97
The Postman '97

Oren Williams (1992-)
Rebound '05
Clifford's Really Big Movie '04 (V)

Paul Williams (1940-)
The Devil's Mistress '68
The Princess Diaries 2: Royal Engagement '04
Headless Body in Topless Bar '96
A Million to Juan '94
Chill Factor '90
The Doors '91
The Night They Saved Christmas '87
Zombie High '87
Smokey and the Bandit, Part 3 '83
Smokey and the Bandit 2 '80
Stone Cold Dead '80
The Muppet Movie '79
The Cheap Detective '78
Smokey and the Bandit '77
Phantom of the Paradise '74
Battle for the Planet of the Apes '73
Watermelon Man '70
The Loved One '65

Paul W. Williams (1943-)
The November Men '93
Mirage '94
Love Come Down '00

Peter Williams (1933-)
Jungleground '95
Soul Survivor '95

Rhys Williams (1897-1969)
Skullduggery '70
The Restless Breed '58
Fastest Gun Alive '56
Battle Cry '55
The Black Shield of Falworth '54
Man in the Attic '53
Kiss Tomorrow Goodbye '50
The Showdown '50
The Corn is Green '45
Mrs. Miniver '42
Underground Agent '42
How Green Was My Valley '41

Robert Williams (1897-1931)
Devotion '31
Platinum Blonde '31

Robert B. Williams (1904-78)
Revenge of the Creature '55

Robin Williams (1952-)
August Rush '07
License to Wed '07
Everyone's Hero '06 (V)
Happy Feet '06 (V)
Man of the Year '06
Night at the Museum '06
The Night Listener '06
RV '06
The Big White '05
Robots '05 (V)
The Final Cut '04
House of D '04
Noel '04
Death to Smoochy '02
Insomnia '02
One Hour Photo '02
A.I.: Artificial Intelligence '01 (V)
Bicentennial Man '99
Jakob the Liar '99
Patch Adams '98
What Dreams May Come '98

Roger Williams (1889-1939)
Code of the Fearless '39
Cheyenne Rides Again '37
Valley of Terror '38
Aces Wild '37
Brothers of the West '37
Heroes of the Alamo '37
The Roamin' Cowboy '37
Gun Girl '36
Phantom Patrol '36
Pinto Rustlers '36
Stormy Trails '36
Pecos Kid '35
Social Error '35
Toll of the Desert '35
Wagon Trail '35

Samm-Art Williams (1946-)
A Rage in Harlem '91

Saul Williams (1972-)
K-PAX '01
Slam '98

Scot Williams (1972-)
In His Life: The John Lennon Story '00
Swing '98
Backbeat '94

Simon Williams (1946-)
The Fiendish Plot of Dr. Fu Manchu '80
The Blood on Satan's Claw '71

Spencer Williams, Jr. (1893-1969)
Juke Joint '47
Dirty Gertie from Harlem U.S.A. '46
Blood of Jesus '41
Go Down Death '41
Son of Ingagi '40
Bronze Buckaroo '39
Harlem Rides the Range '39

Steven Williams (1949-)
Darkwolf '03
Firetrap '03
Route 666 '01
Crash & Byrnes '99
The Sender '98
Jason Goes to Hell: The Final Friday '93
Better Off Dead '85
Missing in Action 2: The Beginning '85
Silent Witness '85
Twilight Zone: The Movie '83
The Blues Brothers '80

Treat Williams (1952-)
What Happens in Vegas '08
Miss Congeniality 2: Armed and Fabulous '05
Hollywood Ending '02
Extreme Limits '01
The Fraternity '01
Gale Force '01
Venomous '01
Critical Mass '00
Skeletons in the Closet '00
Journey to the Center of the Earth '99
36 Hours to Die '99
The Substitute 3: Winner Takes All '99
The Substitute 4: Failure is Not an Option '01
Deep Rising '98
Escape: Human Cargo '98
The Deep End of the Ocean '98
The Devil's Own '96
The Substitute 2: School's Out '97
The Late Shift '96

A Dance to the Music of Time '97
Murder by Night '89
Destroy All Planets '68
The Bridge on the River Kwai '57

Popeye '80
Can I Do It... Till I Need Glasses? '77

The Phantom '96
Johnny's Girl '95
Mulholland Falls '95
Things to Do in Denver When You're Dead '95
Parallel Lives '94
Where the Rivers Flow North '94
Hand Gun '93
Till Death Do Us Part '92
The Water Engine '92
Final Verdict '91
Drug Wars: The Camarena Story '90
Max and Helen '90
The Heart of Dixie '89
Third Degree Burn '89
Third Solution '89
Dead Heat '88
Sweet Lies '88
Echoes in the Darkness '87
J. Edgar Hoover '87
Night of the Sharks '87
The Men's Club '86
Smooth Talk '85
Flashpoint '84
Once Upon a Time in America '84
A Streetcar Named Desire '84
When Angels Fly '84
Dempsey '83
Prince of the City '81
The Pursuit of D.B. Cooper '81
Hair '79
1941 '79
The Eagle Has Landed '77
The Ritz '76
Deadly Hero '75

Vanessa Williams (1963-)
And Then Came Love '07
Ice Spiders '07
My Brother '06
DROP Squad '94
Candyman '92
Another You '91
New Jack City '91

Vanessa L(ynne) Williams (1963-)
Johnson Family Vacation '04
Winds of Terror '01
The Courage to Love '00
Don Quixote '00
Shaft '00
Light It Up '99
Dance with Me '98
Futuresport '98
The Odyssey '97
Soul Food '97
Eraser '96
Hoodlum '97
Bye Bye Birdie '95
The Jacksons: An American Dream '92
Harley Davidson and the Marlboro Man '91
The Kid Who Loved Christmas '90
Full Exposure: The Sex Tape Scandals '89
Under the Gun '88
The Pick-Up Artist '87

Wade Andrew Williams (1961-)
I Witness '03
Bark! '02
Terror Tract '00
K-911 '99
Route 9 '98

Kimberly Williams-Paisley
See Kimberly Williams

Alister Williamson (1918-99)
Murder on the Midnight Express '74
The Oblong Box '69

Clayton Williamson
Clowning Around 2 '93
Clowning Around '92

Felix Williamson
Dirty Deeds '02
Strange Planet '99

Fred Williamson (1938-)
Starsky & Hutch '04
Rhapsody '01
The Independent '00
Submerged '00
Active Stealth '99
Children of the Corn 5: Fields of Terror '98
Blackjack '97
Night Vision '97
Original Gangstas '96
From Dusk Till Dawn '95
Silent Hunter '94
South Beach '92
Steele's Law '91
Three Days to a Kill '91
Black Cobra 3: The Manila Connection '90
Delta Force Commando 2 '90
Black Cobra 2 '89
The Kill Reflex '89
Deadly Intent '88
The Black Cobra '87
Delta Force Commando '87
The Messenger '87
Foxtrap '85
Deadly Impact '84
White Fire '84
Big Score '83
The New Gladiators '83
1990: The Bronx Warriors '83
Vigilante '83
Warriors of the Wasteland '83
The Last Fight '82
One Down, Two to Go! '82
Fear in the City '81
Fist of Fear, Touch of Death '80
Express to Terror '79
Blind Rage '78
Deadly Mission '78
Mister Mean '77
Death Journey '76
Joshua '76
Adios Amigo '75
Bucktown '75
Mean Johnny Barrows '75
Take a Hard Ride '75
Boss '74
No Way Back '74
Three the Hard Way '74
Black Caesar '73
Hell Up in Harlem '73
That Man Bolt '73
M*A*S*H '70

Mykelti Williamson (1960-)
ATL '06
Fatwa '06
Lucky Number Slevin '06
The Assassination of Richard Nixon '05
After the Sunset '04
Ali '01
Holiday Heart '00
Gideon '99
Having Our Say: The Delany Sisters' First 100 Years '99
Three Kings '99
Double Tap '98
Primary Colors '98
Species 2 '98
Buffalo Soldiers '97
Con Air '97
Truth or Consequences, N.M. '97
Twelve Angry Men '97
Soul of the Game '96
Heat '95
How to Make an American Quilt '95
Waiting to Exhale '95
Forrest Gump '94
The First Power '89
Miracle Mile '89
Number One with a Bullet '87
Streets of Fire '84

Nicol Williamson (1938-)
Spawn '97
Mr. Toad's Wild Ride '96
The Advocate '93
Exorcist 3: Legion '90
Black Widow '87
Mountbatten: The Last Viceroy '86
Passion Flower '86
Christopher Columbus '85
Return to Oz '85
I'm Dancing as Fast as I Can '82
Venom '82
Excalibur '81
The Human Factor '79
The Cheap Detective '78
The Word '78
Robin and Marian '76
The Seven-Per-Cent Solution '76
The Wilby Conspiracy '75
Hamlet '69

Noble Willingham (1930-2004)
Up Close and Personal '96
City Slickers 2: The Legend of Curly's Gold '94
Ace Ventura: Pet Detective '93
Article 99 '92
Career Opportunities '91
City Slickers '91
The Last Boy Scout '91
Pastime '91
Blind Fury '90
The Heist '89
Good Morning, Vietnam '87
Coward of the County '81
First Monday in October '81
Kenny Rogers as the Gambler '80
Backstairs at the White House '79
The Boys in Company C '77
Aloha, Bobby and Rose '74
Big Bad Mama '74
My Sweet Charlie '70

Bruce Willis (1955-)
The Astronaut Farmer '07
Live Free or Die Hard '07
Perfect Stranger '07
Planet Terror '07
Alpha Dog '06
Fast Food Nation '06
Lucky Number Slevin '06
Over the Hedge '06 (V)
16 Blocks '06
Hostage '05
Sin City '05
The Whole Ten Yards '04
Rugrats Go Wild! '03 (V)
Tears of the Sun '03
Hart's War '02
Bandits '01
Disney's The Kid '00
Unbreakable '00
The Whole Nine Yards '00
The Sixth Sense '99
The Story of Us '99
Armageddon '98
Breakfast of Champions '98
Mercury Rising '98
The Siege '98
The Fifth Element '97
The Jackal '97
Beavis and Butt-Head Do America '96 (V)
Last Man Standing '96
The Player '92
Billy Bathgate '91
Hudson Hawk '91
The Last Boy Scout '91
Mortal Thoughts '91
The Bonfire of the Vanities '90
Die Hard 2: Die Harder '90
Look Who's Talking, Too '90
That's Adequate '90
In Country '89
Look Who's Talking '89 (V)
Die Hard '88
Sunset '88
Blind Date '87
Moonlighting '85

Dave Willis
Aqua Teen Hunger Force Colon Movie Film for Theaters '07 (V)
There Will Be Blood '07

Matt Willis (1913-89)
Shep Comes Home '49
The Noose Hangs High '48
Blonde Savage '47
A Walk in the Sun '46
Behind Prison Walls '43
Return of the Vampire '43

Norman Willis (1903-88)
In Old New Mexico '45
Legion of the Lawless '40
Tim Tyler's Luck '37

Rumer Willis (1988-)
Hostage '05
Striptease '96

Susan Willis
The Majestic '01
What about Bob? '91

Noel Willman (1917-88)
21 Hours at Munich '76
The Odessa File '74
The Reptile '66
Doctor Zhivago '65
Kiss of the Vampire '62
Abandon Ship '57
Across the Bridge '57
The Warriors '55
Beau Brummel '54

Chill Wills (1903-78)
Mr. Billion '77
Poco '77
Pat Garrett & Billy the Kid '73
Over the Hill Gang '69
Fireball 500 '66
The Rounders '65
McLintock! '63
The Wheeler Dealers '63
Deadly Companions '61
The Alamo '60
Where the Boys Are '60
Gun Glory '57
Giant '56
Kentucky Rifle '55
Francis Joins the WACs '54
City That Never Sleeps '53
Francis Covers the Big Town '53 (V)
Man from the Alamo '53
Ride the Man Down '53
Small Town Girl '53
Francis Goes to West Point '52 (V)
Francis Goes to the Races '51 (V)
High Lonesome '50
Rio Grande '50
Boom Town '40
The Westerner '40
Allegheny Uprising '39
Racketeers of the Range '39

Douglas Wilmer (1920-)
The Adventures of Sherlock Holmes' Smarter Brother '78
The Incredible Sarah '76
Golden Voyage of Sinbad '73
The Vampire Lovers '70
Woman of Straw '64
Jason and the Argonauts '63
Men of Sherwood Forest '57

Andre Wilms (1947-)
La Vie de Bohème '93
L'Enfer '93
Monsieur Hire '89
Life Is a Long Quiet River '88

Channing Wilroy
Desperate Living '77
Female Trouble '74
Pink Flamingos '72

Jay Wilsey
See Buffalo Bill Jr.

Shannon Wilsey (1971-94)
Sorority House Massacre 2: Nighty Nightmare '92
The Invisible Maniac '90

Ajita Wilson (1950-87)
Savage Island '85
Escape from Hell '79

Andreas Wilson
Kill Your Darlings '06
Evil '03

Andrew Wilson (1964-)
The Big Bounce '04
Bottle Rocket '95

Anthony H. Wilson
Tristram Shandy: A Cock and Bull Story '05
The Outcast '84

Barbara Wilson
Invasion of the Animal People '62
Lost, Lonely, and Vicious '59
Teenage Doll '57

Brad Wilson
Pterodactyl Woman from Beverly Hills '97
Grotesque '87

Brian Wilson (1942-)
Beach Blanket Bingo '65
Beach Party '63

Charles C. Wilson (1894-1948)
Blazing Across the Pecos '48
Pennies from Heaven '36

Clarence Wilson (1876-1941)
Bachelor Bait '34
Badmen of Nevada '33
Night Life in Reno '31

Claude Wilson (1900-82)
Combat Killers '71
The Boys in Company C '77

Daniel Wilson
Things to Do '06
Wait until Spring, Bandini '90

David Wilson (1949-)
The Inside Man '84
Eddie and the Cruisers '83
Hometown U.S.A. '79

Don Wilson (1900-82)
The Last Sentinel '07
Niagara '52
The Chase '46
The Roundup '41

Don "The Dragon" Wilson (1955-)
18 Fingers of Death '05
Sci-Fighter '04
Moving Target '00
The Capitol Conspiracy '99
Office Space '98
My Best Friend Is a Vampire '88
Devonsville Terror '83
Batman Forever '95
Bloodfist 7: Manhunt '95
Cyber-Tracker 2 '95
Night Hunter '95
Virtual Combat '95
Bloodfist 6: Ground Zero '94
Red Sun Rising '94
Ring of Fire 3: Lion Strike '94
Bloodfist 5: Human Target '93
Cyber-Tracker '93
Out for Blood '93
Black Belt '92
Bloodfist 3: Forced to Fight '92
Bloodfist 4: Die Trying '92
Magic Kid '92
Ring of Fire 2: Blood and Steel '92
Futurekick '91
Ring of Fire '91
Bloodfist 2 '90
Bloodfist '89
Born on the Fourth of July '89
Say Anything '89
Sailor Beware '52

Dooley Wilson (1894-1953)
Seven Days Ashore '44
Stormy Weather '43
Casablanca '42

Dorothy Wilson (1909-98)
In Old Kentucky '35
Last Days of Pompeii '35
Dangerous Appointment '34
His Greatest Gamble '34
Lucky Devils 33
Men of America '32

Earl Wilson (1907-87)
Beach Blanket Bingo '65
Night of Evil '62 (N)
Copacabana '47

Elizabeth Wilson (1921-)
The Boys Next Door '96
Quiz Show '94
Scarlett '94
Queen '93
Sarah, Plain and Tall: Skylark '93
The Addams Family '91
Regarding Henry '91
The Believers '87
A Conspiracy of Love '87
Where Are the Children? '85
Grace Quigley '84
You Can't Take It with You '84
Sanctuary of Fear '79
Miles to Go Before I Sleep '74
The Fish that Saved Pittsburgh '79
Uptown Saturday Night '74
Cancel My Reservation '72

Frank Wilson (1885-1956)
Beware '46
Paradise in Harlem '40
Green Pastures '36
Emperor Jones '33
Girl from Chicago '32

Georges Wilson (1921-)
Nudo di Donna '83
Make Room for Tomorrow '81
Attack of the Killer Tomatoes '77

Kristen Wilson (1969-)
- Twitches Too '07
- Crossover '06
- Dr. Dolittle 3 '06
- Dr. Dolittle 3 '06
- Twitches '05
- Walking Tall '04
- Confessions of a Dangerous Mind '02
- Dr. Dolittle 2 '01
- Bulletproof '96
- Girl 6 '96
- Tyson '95
- The Pompatus of Love '95

Lambert Wilson (1959-)
- Babylon AD '08
- Flawless '07
- Private Fears in Public Places '06
- Sahara '05
- Catwoman '04
- The Matrix Reloaded '03
- The Matrix Revolutions '03
- Timeline '03
- Don Quixote '00
- The Possessed '88
- The Last September '99
- Same Old Song '97
- The Leading Man '96
- Frankenstein '93
- The Belly of an Architect '91
- Five Days One Summer '82
- Sahara '83
- The Blood of Others '84
- Rendez-vous '85
- Red Kiss '85
- Julia '77

Lois Wilson (1896-1983)
- Bright Eyes '34
- In the Money '34
- Female '33
- Laughing at Life '33
- Drifting Souls '32
- The Secrets of Wu Sin '32
- The Show Off '26
- The Vanishing American '25
- Monsieur Beaucaire '24
- The Covered Wagon '23

Luke Wilson (1971-)
- Blonde Ambition '07
- Vacancy '07
- You Kill Me '07
- Hoot '06
- Idiocracy '06
- My Super Ex-Girlfriend '06
- The Family Stone '05
- The Wendell Baker Story '05
- Anchorman: The Legend of Ron Burgundy '04
- Around the World in 80 Days '04
- Alex & Emma '03
- Charlie's Angels: Full Throttle '03
- Legally Blonde 2: Red White & Blonde '03
- Masked and Anonymous '03
- Old School '03
- The Third Wheel '02
- Legally Blonde '01
- The Royal Tenenbaums '01
- Soul Survivors '01
- Bad Seed '00
- Charlie's Angels '00
- Committed '99
- My Dog Skip '99
- Best Men '98
- Bongwater '98
- Dog Park '98
- Home Fries '98
- Telling Lies in America '96
- Bottle Rocket '95

Mara Wilson (1987-)
- Thomas and the Magic Railroad '00
- A Simple Wish '97
- Balloon Farm '99
- Matilda '96

- Miracle on 34th Street '94
- Mrs. Doubtfire '93

Marie Wilson (1916-72)
- Mr. Hobbs Takes a Vacation '62
- A Girl in Every Port '52
- Never Wave at a WAC '52
- My Friend Irma '49
- Fabulous Joe '47
- The Private Affairs of Bel Ami '47
- Flying Blind '41
- Waterfront '39
- Boy Meets Girl '38
- Satan Met a Lady '36
- March of the Wooden Soldiers '34

Mary Louise Wilson (1932-)
- Searching for Paradise '02
- A Season for Miracles '99
- 24 Nights '99
- Stepmom '98
- Green Card '90
- Cheap Shots '91

Owen Wilson (1968-)
- Drillbit Taylor '08
- The Darjeeling Limited '07
- Cars '06 (V)
- Night at the Museum '06
- You, Me and Dupree '06
- Wedding Crashers '05
- The Wendell Baker Story '05
- The Big Bounce '04
- The Life Aquatic with Steve Zissou '04
- Around the World in 80 '04
- Starsky & Hutch '04
- Meet the Fockers '04
- Shanghai Knights '03
- I Spy '02
- Behind Enemy Lines '01
- The Royal Tenenbaums '01
- Zoolander '01
- Meet the Parents '00
- Shanghai Noon '00
- The Haunting '99
- The Minus Man '99
- Armageddon '98
- Permanent Midnight '98
- Breakfast of Champions '98
- Anaconda '96
- The Cable Guy '96
- Bottle Rocket '95

Patrick Wilson (1973-)
- Brothers Three '07
- Evening '07
- Hard Candy '06
- Little Children '06
- Running with Scissors '06
- The Alamo '04
- The Phantom of the Opera '04
- Angels in America '03

Perry Wilson
- The Matchmaker '58
- Fear Strikes Out '57

Peta Wilson (1970-)
- The League of Extraordinary Gentlemen '03
- Mercy '02

Rachel Wilson
- Joe and Max '02
- Loser '97

Rainn Wilson (1968-)
- The Last Mimzy '07
- My Super Ex-Girlfriend '06
- Sahara '05
- Baadasssss! '03
- Winter Break '03
- Mystery, Alaska '99

Reno Wilson (1970-)
- Transformers '07 (V)

Richard Wilson (1936-)
- The Proposition '05

- The Man Who Knew Too Little '97
- Unnatural Pursuits '91
- How to Get Ahead in Advertising '89

Rita Wilson (1958-)
- The Chumscrubber '05
- Raise Your Voice '04
- Auto Focus '02
- The Glass House '01
- Perfume '01
- Invisible Child '99
- Runaway Bride '99
- The Story of Us '99
- From the Earth to the Moon '98
- Psycho '98
- If These Walls Could Talk '96
- Jingle All the Way '96
- That Thing You Do! '96
- Now and Then '95
- Mixed Nuts '94
- Sleepless in Seattle '93
- Volunteers '85

Robert Wilson
- Day of Triumph '54
- I Beheld His Glory '53

Rod Wilson
- Widows '22

Roger Wilson (1958-)
- Power of Attorney '94
- The Ghost Brigade '93
- Thunder Alley '85
- Second Time Lucky '84
- Porky's 2: The Next Day '83
- Porky's '82

Scott Wilson (1942-)
- The Heartbreak Kid '07
- Come Early Morning '06
- Saving Shiloh '06
- Junebug '05
- The Last Samurai '03
- Monster '03
- Bark! '02
- Coastlines '02
- Pearl Harbor '01
- Way of the Gun '00
- The Jack Bull '99
- Shiloh 2: Shiloh Season '99
- Clay Pigeons '98
- G.I. Jane '97
- Shiloh '97
- Dead Man Walking '95
- Flesh and Bone '93
- Pure Luck '91
- Exorcist 3: Legion '90
- Femme Fatale '90
- Young Guns 2 '90
- Johnny Handsome '89
- Jesse '88
- The Tracker '88
- Malone '87
- Blue City '86
- The Aviator '85
- Year of the Quiet Sun '84
- On the Line '83
- The Right Stuff '83
- The Ninth Configuration '79
- The Passover Plot '75
- The New Centurions '72
- The Grissom Gang '71
- The Gypsy Moths '69
- Castle Keep '69
- In Cold Blood '67

Sheree J. Wilson (1958-)
- Hellbound '94
- Past Tense '94
- The Wedding Planner...
- Just Visiting '01
- Crimewave '85
- Walker: Texas Ranger: One Riot, One Ranger '93
- News at Eleven '86
- Fraternity Vacation '85

Stuart Wilson (1946-)
- Hot Fuzz '07
- Fascination '04
- The Rundown '03
- Dinotopia '02
- Princess of Thieves '01
- Here on Earth '00
- The Luzhin Defence '00
- Slow Burn '00
- Vertical Limit '00
- Second Sight '99
- Enemy of the State '98
- The Mask of Zorro '98
- Crossworlds '96
- The Rock '96
- Edie & Pen '96
- Death and the Maiden '94
- Exit to Eden '94
- No Escape '94
- The Age of Innocence '93
- Teenage Mutant Ninja Turtles 3 '93
- Lethal Weapon 3 '92
- Lethal Charm '90
- Secret Weapon '90
- Romance on the Orient Express '89
- The Highest Honor '84
- Running Blind '78
- The Strauss Family '73

Teddy Wilson (1943-91)
- Life Stinks '91
- Kiss Shot '89
- The Mighty Pawns '87
- The Ambush Murders '82

Thick Wilson
- The Thief and the Cobbler '96 (V)

Thomas F. Wilson (1959-)
- Zoom '06
- Larry the Cable Guy: Health Inspector '06
- That Darn Cat '95
- Andersonville '95
- Born to Be Wild '95
- Camp Nowhere '94
- Blood In ... Blood Out: Bound by Honor '93
- Caroline at Midnight '93
- Mr. Write '92
- High Strung '91
- Back to the Future, Part 3 '90
- Back to the Future, Part 2 '89
- Action Jackson '88
- Let's Get Harry '87
- April Fool's Day '86
- Back to the Future '85
- Adventures Beyond Belief '87

Tom Wilson (1880-1965)
- Battling Butler '26
- California Straight Ahead '25

Trey Wilson (1948-89)
- The Americano '?'
- Great Balls of Fire '89
- Miss Firecracker '89
- Welcome Home '89
- Bull Durham '88
- End of the Line '88
- Married to the Mob '88
- Twins '88
- Raising Arizona '87
- The Vampire Hookers '78
- Three Warriors '77

Troy Winbush
- Sniper 3 '04
- The Last Shot '04
- United States of Leland '03
- A Light in the Darkness '02
- What About Your Friends: Weekend Getaway '02
- Carmen: A Hip Hopera '01
- Gabriela '01
- The Replacements '00
- Mutiny '99
- The Principal '87

Brian Wimmer (1959-)
- Outlaw Trail '06
- Attack of the Sabretooth '05
- Beneath Loch Ness '01
- Final Justice '98
- Bitter Sweet '98
- Blue Flame '93
- Kiss of a Killer '93
- Lipstick Camera '93
- The World's Oldest Living Bridesmaid '92
- Late for Dinner '91
- Dangerous Pursuit '89
- China Beach '88

Mary Wimbush (1923-)
- Poldark '75
- Oh! What a Lovely War '69

William Windom (1923-)
- Children of the Corn 4: The Gathering '96
- Sommersby '93
- Dennis the Menace: Dinosaur Hunter '93
- Committed '91
- Funland '89
- She's Having a Baby '88
- Planes, Trains & Automobiles '87
- Grandview U.S.A. '84
- Last Plane Out '83
- Desperate Lives '82
- Leave 'Em Laughing '81
- Blind Ambition '79
- Mean Dog Blues '78
- Brewster McCloud '70
- The Gypsy Moths '69
- The Detective '68
- Columbo: Prescription Murder '67
- The Americanization of Emily '64
- For Love or Money '63
- One Man's Way '63
- To Kill a Mockingbird '62

Paul Winchell (1922-2005)
- The Fox and the Hound '81
- The Many Adventures of Winnie the Pooh '77 (V)
- The Aristocats '70 (V)

Walter Winchell (1897-1972)
- The Bellboy '60
- Scarface Mob '62 (V)

Jeff Wincott (1957-)
- The Invasion '07
- Battle Queen 2020 '99
- Paper Bullets '99
- Universal Soldier 2: Brothers in Arms '98
- Universal Soldier 3: Unfinished Business '98
- Future Fear '97
- The Undertaker's Wedding '97
- Fatal Combat '96
- Profile for Murder '96
- When the Bullet Hits the Bone '96
- Last Man Standing '95
- The Killing Man '94
- Open Fire '94
- Martial Outlaw '93
- Mission of Justice '92
- Martial Law 2: Undercover '91
- Deadly Bet '91

Philip Winchester (1981-)
- Flyboys '06
- Thunderbirds '04
- Lethal Dose '03

Penelope Wilton (1946-)
- Five Days '07
- The History Boys '06
- Match Point '05
- Pride and Prejudice '05
- Shaun of the Dead '04
- Calendar Girls '03
- Iris '01
- Victoria & Albert '01
- Wives and Daughters '01
- The Return of the Borrowers '96
- The Borrowers '97
- Carrington '95
- The Secret Rapture '94
- Blame It on the Bellboy '92
- Cry Freedom '87
- Clockwise '86
- Singleton's Pluck '84
- The Norman Conquests, Part 2: Living Together '78
- The Norman Conquests, Part 1: Table Manners '78
- The Norman Conquests '78

Michael Wincott (1959-)
- Seraphim Falls '06
- The Assassination of Richard Nixon '05
- The Count of Monte Cristo '02
- Along Came a Spider '01
- Before Night Falls '00
- Hidden Agenda '99
- Gunshy '98
- Alien: Resurrection '97
- Metro '96
- Basquiat '96
- Dead Man '95
- Strange Days '95
- The Crow '94
- Romeo Is Bleeding '93
- The Three Musketeers '93
- 1492: Conquest of Paradise '92
- The Doors '91
- Robin Hood: Prince of Thieves '91
- Talk Radio '88

Marie Windsor (1922-2000)
- Commando Squad '87
- Salem's Lot '79
- Cahill: United States Marshal '73
- Wild Women '70
- Bedtime Story '63

Barbara Windsor (1937-)
- Carry On Camping '71
- Carry On Henry VIII '71
- Carry On Doctor '68
- Carry On Dick
- Too Wise Wives '21
- The Blot '21
- The Claw '27

Claire Windsor (1897-1972)

Critic's Choice '63
Girl in Black Stockings '57
Unholy Wife '57
The Killing '56
Abbott and Costello Meet the Mummy '55
Silver Star '55
Swamp Women '55
Cat Women of the Moon '53
City That Never Sleeps '53
Tall Texan '53
Trouble along the Way '53
Jungle '52
The Narrow Margin '52
Outlaw Women '52
Little Big Horn '51
Double Deal '50
The Showdown '50
The Fighting Kentuckian '49
Force of Evil '49
Outpost in Morocco '49
Hellfire '48
Smart Alecks '42

Romy Windsor
The Howling: New Moon Rising '95
Big Bad John '90
The House of Usher '88
Howling 4: The Original Nightmare '88

Paul Winfield (1940-2004)
Catfish in Black Bean Sauce '00
Strange Justice: The Clarence Thomas and Anita Hill Story '99
Relax... It's Just Sex! '98
The Assassination File '96
The Legend of Gator Face '96
Mars Attacks! '96
Original Gangstas '96
Tyson '95
White Dwarf '95
Breathing Lessons '94
In the Kingdom of the Blind the Man with One Eye Is King '94
Scarlett '94
Cliffhanger '93
Dennis the Menace '93
Queen '93
Back to Hannibal: The Return of Tom Sawyer and Huckleberry Finn '90
Presumed Innocent '90
The Women of Brewster Place '89
For Us, the Living '88
Big Shots '87
Death Before Dishonor '87
Guilty of Innocence '87
The Mighty Pawns '87
The Serpent and the Rainbow '87
Blue City '86
Go Tell It on the Mountain '84
Mike's Murder '84
The Terminator '84
On the Run '83
Star Trek 2: The Wrath of Khan '82
Carbon Copy '81
Sophisticated Gents '81
Angel City '80
Backstairs at the White House '79
Roots: The Next Generation '79
A Hero Ain't Nothin' but a Sandwich '78
King '78
Damnation Alley '77
The Greatest '77
Twilight's Last Gleaming '77
Green Eyes '76
High Velocity '76
Huckleberry Finn '74
It's Good to Be Alive '74
Gordon's War '73
Sounder '72
Brother John '70

R.P.M.* (* Revolutions Per Minute) '70
The Lost Man '69

Oprah Winfrey (1954-)
Bee Movie '07 (V)
Charlotte's Web '06 (V)
Beloved '98
The Women of Brewster Place '89
Native Son '86
The Color Purple '85

Leslie Wing
Retribution '88
The Cowboy & the Ballerina '84

Toby Wing (1915-2001)
Mr. Boggs Steps Out '38
Murder at the Vanities '34

Mark Wing-Davey (1948-)
One Against the Wind '91
The Hitchhiker's Guide to the Galaxy '81

Debra Winger (1955-)
Sometimes in April '05
Eulogy '04
Radio '03
Big Bad Love '02
Forget Paris '95
A Dangerous Woman '93
Shadowlands '93
Wilder Napalm '93
Leap of Faith '92
Everybody Wins '90
The Sheltering Sky '90
Betrayed '88
Black Widow '87
Made in Heaven '87
Legal Eagles '86
Mike's Murder '84
Terms of Endearment '83
Cannery Row '82
E.T.: The Extra-Terrestrial '82 (V)
An Officer and a Gentleman '82
Urban Cowboy '80
French Postcards '79
Special Olympics '78
Thank God It's Friday '78
Slumber Party '57 '76

Peter Wingfield (1962-)
Catwoman '04
Superbabies: Baby Geniuses 2 '04
X2: X-Men United '03
Edge of Madness '02
Highlander: Endgame '00
Uncovered '94

Angela Winkler (1944-)
Benny's Video '92
Sheer Madness '84
Danton '82
The Tin Drum '79
Knife in the Head '78
The Lost Honor of Katharina Blum '75

Henry Winkler (1945-)
Click '06
I Could Never Be Your Woman '06
The Kid and I '05
Holes '03
Down to You '00
Little Nicky '00
Ground Control '98
P.U.N.K.S. '98
The Waterboy '98
Hostage High '97
National Lampoon's Dad's Week Off '97
Scream '96
One Christmas '95
Night Shift '82
An American Christmas Carol '79
The One and Only '78
Heroes '77
Katherine '75
The Lords of Flatbush '74

Mel Winkler
City Hall '95

Devil in a Blue Dress '95
Laurel Avenue '93

Kitty Winn (1944-)
Mirrors '78
The Exorcist 2: The Heretic '77
Miles to Go Before I Sleep '74
The Exorcist '73
Man on a String '71
Panic in Needle Park '71
They Might Be Giants '71

Vic Winner
The Rue Morgue Massacres '73
Horror Rises from the Tomb '72

Olof Winnerstrand (1875-1956)
Night Is My Future '47
Torment '44

Katheryn Winnick (1978-)
Failure to Launch '06
Hellraiser: Hellworld '05
Satan's Little Helper '04
Fabled '02

Lucyna Winnicka (1928-)
25 Fireman's Street '73
First Spaceship on Venus '60
Mother Joan of the Angels '60

Charles Winninger (1884-1969)
The Sun Shines Bright '53
Torpedo Alley '53
Something in the Wind '47
State Fair '45
Broadway Rhythm '44
Lady Takes a Chance '43
Pot o' Gold '41
Ziegfeld Girl '41
Beyond Tomorrow '40
If I Had My Way '40
Little Nellie Kelly '40
Babes in Arms '39
Destry Rides Again '39
Three Smart Girls Grow Up '39
Every Day's a Holiday '38
Nothing Sacred '37
Show Boat '36
Three Smart Girls '36
Gun Smoke '31
Night Nurse '31
The Sin of Madelon Claudet '31

Mare Winningham (1959-)
Swing Vote '08
The Maldonado Miracle '03
Snap Decision '01
Sally Hemings: An American Scandal '00
Everything That Rises '98
Under Pressure '98
George Wallace '97
The Boys Next Door '96
Georgia '95
Letter to My Killer '95
Better Off Dead '94
Teresa's Tattoo '94
The War '94
Wyatt Earp '94
Hard Promises '92
Intruders '92
Eye on the Sparrow '91
Fatal Exposure '91
Miracle Mile '89
Turner and Hooch '89
God Bless the Child '88
Made in Heaven '87
Shy People '87
Nobody's Fool '86
A Winner Never Quits '86
St. Elmo's Fire '85
Single Bars, Single Women '84
The Thorn Birds '83
Threshold '83
Amber Waves '82
One Trick Pony '80
Special Olympics '78
The Young Pioneers '76

Marissa Jaret Winokur (1973-)
Fever Pitch '05
On Edge '03

Kate Winslet (1975-)
All the King's Men '06
Flushed Away '06 (V)
The Holiday '06
Little Children '06
Romance & Cigarettes '05
Eternal Sunshine of the Spotless Mind '04
Finding Neverland '04
The Life of David Gale '03
Enigma '01
Iris '01
Quills '00
Hideous Kinky '99
Holy Smoke '99
Titanic '97
Hamlet '96
Jude '96
A Kid in King Arthur's Court '95
Sense and Sensibility '95
Heavenly Creatures '94

George Winslow (1946-)
Artists and Models '55
Gentlemen Prefer Blondes '53
Monkey Business '52

Michael Winslow (1960-)
Police Academy 7: Mission to Moscow '94
Going Under '91
Buy & Cell '89
Far Out Man '89
Police Academy 6: City under Siege '89
Police Academy 5: Assignment Miami Beach '88
Police Academy 4: Citizens on Patrol '87
Spaceballs '87
Police Academy 3: Back in Training '86
Police Academy 2: Their First Assignment '85
Alphabet City '84
Lovelines '84
Police Academy '84
Tag: The Assassination Game '82
Cheech and Chong's Nice Dreams '81

Mary Elizabeth Winstead (1984-)
Death Proof '07
Live Free or Die Hard '07
Black Christmas '06
Bobby '06
Final Destination 3 '06
Sky High '05

Hattie Winston (1945-)
True Crime '99
Jackie Brown '97
Clara's Heart '88

Helen Winston (1925-72)
Tobor the Great '54
Battle Circus '53
I Love Melvin '53

Helene Winston (1922-2004)
Utilities '83
The Devil & Max Devlin '81
Killjoy '00
Return from Witch Mountain '78
The Shaggy D.A. '76
A Boy and His Dog '75
Our Time '74

Ray Winstone (1957-)
Fool's Gold '08

Indiana Jones and the Kingdom of the Crystal Skull '08
Beowulf '07 (V)
Breaking and Entering '06
The Departed '06
The Chronicles of Narnia: The Lion, the Witch and the Wardrobe '05 (V)
Doogal '05 (V)
The Proposition '05
King Arthur '04
Cold Mountain '03
Ripley's Game '02
Last Orders '01
Love, Honour & Obey '00
Sexy Beast '00
Agnes Browne '99
Darkness Falls '98
Final Cut '98
The Very Thought of You '98
The War Zone '98
Face '97
Nil by Mouth '96
Ladybird, Ladybird '93
Quadrophenia '79
Scum '79

Maurice Dean Wint
Hedwig and the Angry Inch '00
Cube '98
Curtis's Charm '96
Rude '96

Alex Winter (1965-)
Freaked '93
Bill & Ted's Bogus Journey '91
Bill & Ted's Excellent Adventure '89
Rosalie Goes Shopping '89
Haunted Summer '88
The Lost Boys '87
Death Wish 3 '85

Edward Winter (1938-2001)
Held Hostage '91
The Buddy System '83
Mother & Daughter: A Loving War '80

Vincent Winter (1947-98)
The Horse Without a Head '63
Almost Angels '62
Gorgo '61
Time Lock '57

Dean Winters (1964-)
Hellraiser: Hellseeker '02
Snipes '01
Undercover Angel '99

Deborah Winters (1955-)
The Outing '87
Blue Sunshine '78
Tarantulas: The Deadly Cargo '77
Class of 44 '73
Kotch '71

Jonathan Winters (1925-)
Comic Book: The Movie '04
The Adventures of Rocky & Bullwinkle '00
The Thief and the Cobbler '96 (V)
The Flintstones '94
The Shadow '94
Tiny Toon Adventures: How I Spent My Vacation '91 (V)
Moon over Parador '88
The Longshot '86
Say Yes! '86
Alice in Wonderland '85
More Wild, Wild West '80
The Fish that Saved Pittsburgh '79
Viva Max '69
Eight on the Lam '67
Oh Dad, Poor Dad (Momma's Hung You in the Closet & I'm Feeling So Sad) '67

The Russians Are Coming, the Russians Are Coming '66
The Loved One '65
It's a Mad, Mad, Mad, Mad World '63

Kristoffer Ryan Winters (1978-)
Hot Blooded '98
Saint Maybe '98
Red Blooded 2 '96

Roland Winters (1904-89)
Loving '70
Blue Hawaii '62
Cash McCall '60
Jet Pilot '57
Follow the Sun '51
Guilty of Treason '50
To Please a Lady '50
The Underworld Story '50
The West Point Story '50
Abbott and Costello Meet the Killer, Boris Karloff '49
Malaya '49
Riders of the Whistling Skull '37

Shelley Winters (1922-2006)
Gideon '99
Portrait of a Lady '96
Jury Duty '95
Mrs. Munck '95
Raging Angels '95
Backfire! '94
Heavy '94
The Pickle '93
Silence of the Hams '93
Weep No More My Lady '93
Stepping Out '91
Superstar: The Life and Times of Andy Warhol '90
An Unremarkable Life '89
Purple People Eater '88
Delta Force '86
Witchfire '86
Alice in Wonderland '85
Deja Vu '84
Ellie '84
Very Close Quarters '84
Fanny Hill '83
That Lucky Touch '75
Journey into Fear '74
Blume in Love '73
Cleopatra Jones '73
Poor Pretty Eddie '73
Diamonds '72
The Poseidon Adventure '72
Shattered '72
What's the Matter with Helen? '71
Who Slew Auntie Roo? '71
Bloody Mama '70
Buona Sera, Mrs. Campbell '68
The Scalphunters '68
Wild in the Streets '68
Enter Laughing '67
Alfie '66
Harper '66
The Greatest Story Ever Told '65
A Patch of Blue '65
The Three Sisters '65
Time of Indifference '64
The Balcony '63
Lolita '62
The Young Savages '61
Let No Man Write My Epitaph '60

The Diary of Anne Frank '59
Odds Against Tomorrow '59

Tom Wisdom (1973-)
Sisterhood of the Traveling Pants 2 '08
300 '07

Robert Wisdom (1953-)
Dancing at the Blue Iguana '00
Storytelling '01
Coastlines '02
Duplex '03
Ray '04
Killer Diller '04
Haven '04
The Forgotten '04
Crazy Like a Fox '04
Business '04
Barbershop 2: Back in
Live from Baghdad '03
The Hawk Is Dying '06
Mozart and the Whale '05

Norman Wisdom (1920-)
The Night They Raided
Minsky's '69
What's Good for the Goose '69

Robert Wisden
The Snow Queen '02
Every Mother's Worst Fear
'98

Billy Wirth (1962-)
Me & Will '99
Last Lives '98
Relax... It's Just Sex! '98
Starlight '97
Space Marines '96
A Good Day to Die '95
Venus Rising '95
The Fence '94
Judicial Consent '94
Body Snatchers '93
Final Mission '93
Red Shoe Diaries '92
War Party '89
The Lost Boys '87

Estelle Winwood (1883-1984)
Murder by Death '76
The Producers '68
Games '67
Dead Ringer '64
The Magic Sword '62
The Misfits '61
Darby O'Gill & the Little
People '59
This Happy Feeling '58
The Swan '56
The Glass Slipper '55
Quality Street '37

Jane Winton (1905- 59)
The Gangster '47
A Double Life '47
The Great Gatsby '49
Winchester '73 '50
South Sea Sinner '50
A Place in the Sun '51
Executive Suite '54
Behave Yourself! '52
Meet Danny Wilson '52
Phone Call from a Stranger
'52
I Died a Thousand Times
'55
The Big Knife '55
I Am a Camera '55
Mambo '55
Treasure of Pancho Villa
'55

Greg Wise (1966-)
Johnny English '03
Sirens '02
Judas Kiss '98
The Moonstone '97
The Buccaneers '95
Madame Bovary '00
Feast of July '95
Sense and Sensibility '95

Ray Wise (1947-)
One Missed Call '08
The Flock '07
Peaceful Warrior '06
Good Night, and Good
Luck '05
The Battle of Shaker
Heights '03
Jeepers Creepers 2 '03
Two Can Play That Game
'01
The Garbage-Picking, Field
Goal-Kicking
Philadelphia
Phenomenon '98
Powder '95
Body Shot '93
The Chase '93
The Ghost Brigade '93
Rising Sun '93
Bob Roberts '92
Sunstroke '92
Twin Peaks: Fire Walk with
Me '92
Write to Kill '91
Endless Descent '90
Season of Fear '89
The Taking of Flight 847:
The Uli Derickson Story
'88
RoboCop '87
The Journey of Natty Gann
'85
Swamp Thing '82

William Wise (1962-)
In the Bedroom '01
Thirteen Conversations
About One Thing '01
Georgia '95

Jimmy Witherspoon (1921-97)
Black Godfather '74
Boomerang '92

Andreas Wisniewski (1959-)
Urban Ghost Story '98
The Living Daylights '87

Joseph Wiseman (1918-)
Farewell to the King '89
The Apprenticeship of
Duddy Kravitz '74
The Prodigal '55
The Silver Chalice '54
Viva Zapata! '52
Detective Story '51

Googie Withers (1917-)
Country Life '95
Shine '95
Northanger Abbey '87
Hotel du Lac '86
Devil on Horseback '54
Night and the City '50
Dead of Night '45
Pink String and Sealing
Wax '45
On Approval '44
One of Our Aircraft Is
Missing '41
Action for Slander '38
The Lady Vanishes '38
Accused '36

Grant Withers (1904- 59)
Iron Mountain Trail '53
Hoodlum Empire '52
Oklahoma Annie '51
Bells of Coronado '50
Trigger, Jr. '50
The Fighting Kentuckian
'49
Night Time in Nevada '48
Tycoon '47

Glenn Withrow (1953-)
Naked Lie '89

My Darling Clementine '46
Bells of Rosarita '45
Fighting Seabees '44

Reese Witherspoon (1976-)
Rendition '07
Penelope '06
Just Like Heaven '05
Walk the Line '05
Vanity Fair '04
Legally Blonde 2: Red
White & Blonde '03
The Importance of Being
Earnest '02
Sweet Home Alabama '02
Legally Blonde '01
The Trumpet of the Swan
'01 (V)
Little Nicky '00
American Psycho '00
Best Laid Plans '99
Election '99
Cruel Intentions '98
Pleasantville '98
Twilight '98
Fear '96
Overnight Delivery '96
Freeway '95
S.F.W. '94
A Far Off Place '93
Jack the Bear '93
Diary of a Madman '63
Games '67
Man with the City '50
Return to Lonesome Dove
'93

John Witherspoon (1942-)
Little Man '06
Friday After Next '02
The Ladies Man '00
Next Friday '00
I Got the Hook-Up '98
Ride '98
Sprung '96
Friday '95
Vampire in Brooklyn '95
Killer Tomatoes Strike Back
'90

Jane Withers (1926-)
Captain Newman, M.D. '63
Giant '56
The Right Approach '61
The Holy Terror '37
The Farmer Takes a Wife
'35
Bright Eyes '34

Cora Witherspoon (1890-1957)
Just for You '52
Colonel Effingham's Raid
'45
The Bank Dick '40
Just Around the Corner '38
Marie Antoinette '38
On the Avenue '37
Personal Property '37
Quality Street '37
Libeled Lady '36

David Wohl (1953-)
90 Days '86

Hilary Wolf (1977-)
Big Girls Don't Cry... They
Get Even '92
Home Alone 2: Lost in New
York '92

Kelly Wolf
A Day in October '92
Graveyard Shift '90
Triumph of the Spirit '89

Scott Wolf (1968-)
Killing Emmett Young '02
Go '99
The Evening Star '96
White Squall '96
Double Dragon '94
Teenage Bonnie & Klepto
Clyde '93

David Wolfe (1915-94)
Crazy Horse '96
Salt of the Earth '54

Sheldon Peters Wolfchild
Five Fingers '52
The Great Caruso '51
The Magnificent Yankee
'50
Houdini '53
Moonfleet '55
The Judge Steps Out '49
The White Cliffs of Dover
'44

Fred Wolf (1964-)
Chillers '88

Ian Wolfe (1896-1992)
Man on the Roof '76
The 13th Warrior '99
A Song for Martin '01
House of Angels '92
The Sacrifice '86
Man from Mallorca '84
Beethoven Lives Upstairs
'92

Ilya Woloshyn (1981-)
Zombies on Broadway '44
Mrs. Miniver '42

Louis Wolheim (1880-1931)
All Quiet on the Western
Front '30
Danger Lights '30
The Silver Horde '30
Condemned '29
Square Shoulders '29
The Tempest '28
America '24
Dr. Jekyll and Mr. Hyde '20

Kirk B.R. Woller (1962-)
Urban Justice '07
Midnight Clear '06
Hometown Legend '02

Sven Wollter (1934-)
Kira's Reason—A Love
Story '01

Stefan Wodoslowsky
Mindfield '89

Karen Witter (1961-)
Buried Alive '89
Popcorn '89
Perfect Match '88

Kathryn Witt (1950-)
Mickey Blue Eyes '99
Los Locos Posse '97
Demon of Paradise '87
Cocaine Wars '86
Saving Private Ryan '98
Two Weeks Notice '02
Vanilla Sky '01
Mr. Wong in Chinatown '39
Mr. Wong, Detective '38
Fighting Marines '36
Let's Sing Again '36
Radio Patrol '37
The Fatal Hour '40
Phantom of Chinatown '40
Tomboy '40
Boy's Reformatory '39
Daughter of the Tong '39
Irish Luck '39
Last Holiday '06
Blue Smoke '07
88 Minutes '08

Alicia Witt (1975-)
The Way West '67
Dr. Hackly and Mr. Hype
'80
Smokey Bites the Dust '81

Michael Witney (1931-83)
Lacy in Red '79
The Hollywood Knights '80
Dudes '87
Pass the Ammo '88

Donald Wolfit (1902- 68)
The Charge of the Light
Brigade '68
Becket '64
Lawrence of Arabia '62
The Mark '61
The Hands of Orlac '60
Room at the Top '59
Blood of the Vampire '58
Svengali '55
Late Extra '35

Frank Wolff (1928-71)
A Death in the Family '02
Master of Disguise '02
13 Moons '02
Four Rooms '95
Citizen Ruth '96
Mr. Holland's Opus '95

Austin Wolff
Bongwater '98
Urban Legend '98

Kedrick Wolfe
Preachers '90
Chillers '88

Traci Wolfe (1961-)
Lethal Weapon 4 '98
Lethal Weapon 3 '92
Lethal Weapon 2 '89
Lethal Weapon '87

Michael Wong (1965-)
Mulan '98 (V)
Seven Years in Tibet '97
Slappy and the Stinkers '97
The Substitute 2: School's
Out '97
Organized Crime & Triad
Bureau '93

Benedict Wong (1970-)
Sunshine '07
On a Clear Day '05
Dirty Pretty Things '03
State of Play '03

Russell Wong (1963-)
Romeo Must Die '00
The Prophecy 2: Ashtown
'97
The Joy Luck Club '93
China Moon '91
New Jack City '91
Eat a Bowl of Tea '89
China Girl '87

Victor Wong (1927- 2001)
Tremors '89
The Last Emperor '87
Prince of Darkness '87
Big Trouble in Little China
'86
The Golden Child '86
Dim Sum: A Little Bit of
Heart '85

Stevie Wonder (1950-)
Bikini Beach '64
Muscle Beach Party '64

Anna May Wong (1905-61)
Portrait in Black '60
Impact '49
Java Head '35
A Study in Scarlet '33
Shanghai Express '32
Daughter of the Dragon '31

B.D. Wong (1962-)
Father of the Bride Part 2
'95
Father of the Bride '91
Mystery Date '91
The Freshman '90

Faye Wong (1969-)
Chungking Express '95

Anthony Wong (1961-)
The Mummy: Tomb of the
Dragon Emperor '08
Infernal Affairs '02
Time and Tide '07
The Heroic Trio '93
The Mission '99

Jim Wolfe
Invasion of the Space
Preachers '90

Carter Wong
See Carter Wang

Wolfman Jack (1938- 95)
Mortuary Academy '91
Motel Hell '80
Midnight '89
Deadman's Curve '78
Hanging on a Star '78
American Graffiti '73
A Session with The
Committee '68

Arthur Wontner (1875-1960)
Genevieve '53

Mutiny on the Bounty '35
The Barretts of Wimpole
Street '34
Peter Pan '24
The Thief of Baghdad '24

The Terror '38
Murder at the Baskervilles '37
The Triumph of Sherlock Holmes '35

John Woo (1948-)
Hard-Boiled '92
Twin Dragons '92
A Bullet in the Head '90
A Better Tomorrow, Part 1 '86

Andy Wood
Brain Dead '89
Eye of the Eagle 2 '89
Ghostwarrior '86
The Annihilators '85

Britt Wood (1885-1965)
Detour to Danger '45
Knights of the Range '40
The Showdown '40

Clive Wood
The Lion in Winter '03
P.D. James: Death in Holy Orders '03
The Crucifer of Blood '91
Treasure Island '89

Cynthia Wood (1950-)
Apocalypse Now '79
Van Nuys Blvd. '79

David Wood (1944-)
Tales That Witness Madness '73
If.... '69

Edward D. Wood, Jr. (1924-78)
Plan 9 from Outer Space '56
Glen or Glenda? '53
Day Zero '07

Elijah Wood (1981-)
Bobby '06
Happy Feet '06 (V)
Paris, je t'aime '06
Everything is Illuminated '05
All I Want '02
Ash Wednesday '02
Lord of the Rings: The Two Towers '02
Lord of the Rings: The Fellowship of the Rings '01
Green Street Hooligans '05
Sin City '05
Eternal Sunshine of the Spotless Mind '04
Chain of Fools '00
Black and White '99
The Bumblebee Files
Anyway '98
Deep Impact '98
The Faculty '98
The Ice Storm '97
Oliver Twist '97
Flipper '96
North '94
The War '94
The Good Son '93
Forever Young '92
Radio Flyer '92
Paradise '91
Avalon '90
Child in the Night '90
Internal Affairs '90

Evan Rachel Wood (1987-)
Across the Universe '07
King of California '07
Running with Scissors '06
Down in the Valley '05
Pretty Persuasion '05
The Upside of Anger '05
The Missing '03
Little Secrets '02
Simone '02
Detour '99
Digging to China '98

Frank Wood
King of the Corner '04
Thirteen Days '00

Gary Wood
Martial Outlaw '93
Hardbodies '84

G(eorge) Wood (1920-2000)
Bank Shot '74
Harold and Maude '71
M*A*S*H '70

Gordon Wood
The Forty-Niners '32
Mother and Son '31

Harley Wood
Valley of Terror '38
Border Phantom '37
Marihuana '36

Helen Wood
Give a Girl a Break '53
Charlie Chan at the Race Track '36

Janet Wood (1949-)
Slumber Party '57 '76
Fangs '75
Terror at Red Wolf Inn '72
Angels Hard As They Come '71
G.I. Executioner '71

John Wood (1930-)
The White Countess '05
Imagining Argentina '04
Napoleon '03
Goodbye, Mr. Chips '02
The Body '01
Chocolat '00
The Little Vampire '00
Longitude '00
An Ideal Husband '99
The Avengers '98
Sweet Revenge '98
The Gambler '97
Jane Eyre '96
Ladyhawke '85
The Purple Rose of Cairo '85
WarGames '83
Sabrina '95
The Madness of King George '94
The Summer House '94
Uncovered '94
Shadowlands '93
The Young Americans '93
Orlando '92
Jumpin' Jack Flash '86
Citizen X '95
Richard III '95

Karen Wood
Loose Screws '85
Scalps '83

Lana Wood (1946-)
Demon Rage '82
Justin Morgan Had a Horse '81
Captain America 2: Death Too Soon '79
A Question of Guilt '78
Grayeagle '77
A Place Called Today '72
Diamonds Are Forever '71
Black Water Gold '69
Free Grass '69
The Searchers '56

Lawrence Wood
Something Weird '68
Scum of the Earth '63

Mary Laura Wood
Hour of Decision '57
Stranger in Town '57

Natalie Wood (1938-81)
Brainstorm '83
The Last Married Couple in America '80
Willie & Phil '80
The Cracker Factory '79
From Here to Eternity '79
Meteor '79
The Affair '73
Bob & Carol & Ted & Alice '69
This Property Is Condemned '66
The Great Race '65
Inside Daisy Clover '65
Sex and the Single Girl '64
Love with the Proper Stranger '63
Gypsy '62
Splendor in the Grass '61
West Side Story '61
Cash McCall '60
Kings Go Forth '58
Marjorie Morningstar '58
The Burning Hills '56
The Searchers '56
Rebel without a Cause '55
The Silver Chalice '54
Just for You '52
The Star '52
The Jackpot '50
Never a Dull Moment '50
Our Very Own '50
Father Was a Fullback '49
The Green Promise '49
The Ghost and Mrs. Muir '47
Miracle on 34th Street '47
Tomorrow Is Forever '46

Peggy Wood (1894-1978)
Flickers '80
The Sound of Music '65
The Story of Ruth '60
Magnificent Doll '46

Thomas Wood
See William Kerwin

Tom Wood (1963-)
U.S. Marshals '98
Tinseltown '97
Ulee's Gold '97
Bushwhacked '95

Alfre Woodard (1953-)
Pictures of Hollis Woods '07
Something New '06
Take the Lead '06
Beauty Shop '05
The Forgotten '04
The Core '03
Radio '03
The Singing Detective '03
The Wild Thornberrys Movie '02 (V)
K-PAX '01
Dinosaur '00 (V)
Holiday Heart '00
Love and Basketball '00
What's Cooking? '00
Mumford '99
Down in the Delta '98
The Member of the Wedding '97
Miss Evers' Boys '97
Primal Fear '96
Run for the Dream: The Gail Devers Story '96
Star Trek: First Contact '96
How to Make an American Quilt '95
Malcolm X: Make It Plain '95 (N)
Blue Chips '94
Crooklyn '94
The Piano Lesson '94
Race to Freedom: The Story of the Underground Railroad '94
Bophal '93
Heart and Souls '93
Rich in Love '93
The Gun in Betty Lou's Handbag '92
Passion Fish '92
Grand Canyon '91
Miss Firecracker '89
Mandela '87
Scrooged '88
Extremities '86
Unnatural Causes '86
Killing Floor '85
Code of Honor '84
Go Tell It on the Mountain '84
Words by Heart '84
Cross Creek '83
The Ambush Murders '82
Sophisticated Gents '81
Freedom Road '79

Charlaine Woodard (1955-)
Sunshine State '02
Unbreakable '00
The Million Dollar Hotel '99
Around the Fire '98
The Crucible '96
Buffalo Girls '95
He Said, She Said '91
One Good Cop '91
God Bless the Child '88
Crackers '84

Bokeem Woodbine (1970-)
The Last Sentinel '07
18 Fingers of Death '05
Ray '04
Jasper, Texas '03
Sniper 2 '02
The Breed '01
Hard Cash '01
3000 Miles to Graceland '01
Sacrifice '00
Blackmale '99
It's the Rage '99
Life '99
The Runner '99
The Big Hit '98
Caught Up '98
Wishmaster 2: Evil Never Dies '98
Almost Heroes '97
The Rock '96
Dead Presidents '95
Freeway '95
Panther '95
Jason's Lyric '94
Strapped '93

George Woodbridge (1907-73)
The Reptile '66
The Fallen Idol '49
Tower of Terror '42

Danny Woodburn (1964-)
Employee of the Month '06
Death to Smoochy '02
Things You Can Tell Just by Looking at Her '00

Eric Woodburn
Trial & Error '62
The Innocents '61

Joan Woodbury (1915-89)
The Time Travelers '64
Northwest Trail '46
The Chinese Cat '44
Here Comes Kelly '43
I Killed That Man '42
Phantom Killer '42
Yank in Libya '42
In Old Cheyenne '41
King of the Zombies '41
Charlie Chan on Broadway '37
Lion's Den '36
Rogue's Tavern '36
Song of the Gringo '36
Bulldog Courage '35

Margo Woode
Iron Angel '64

Pat(ricia) Woodell (1944-)
Twilight People '72
The Big Doll House '71
The Commies Are Coming, the Commies Are Coming '57

Nicholas Woodeson
Conspiracy '01
Dreaming of Joseph Lees '99
Great Expectations '99
The Man Who Knew Too Little '97
Maria's Child '93
The Blackheath Poisonings '92
A Fatal Inversion '92

Albie Woodington
The Hitchhiker's Guide to the Galaxy '05
The Count of Monte Cristo '02
The 13th Warrior '99

Lauren Woodland (1977-)
The Doorway '00
Alien Nation: Millennium '96
Alien Nation: The Enemy Within '96
Alien Nation: Body and Soul '95
Alien Nation: Dark Horizon '94

Holly Woodlawn (1947-)
Milwaukee, Minnesota '03
Twin Falls Idaho '99
Superstar: The Life and Times of Andy Warhol '90
Is There Sex After Death? '71
Trash '70

Bert Woodruff (1856-1934)
Marked Money '28
Speedy '28
Paths to Paradise '25

Blake Woodruff
Whisper '07
Cheaper by the Dozen '03

Kurt Woodruff
Moving Target '89
Party Incorporated '89

Largo Woodruff
Bill: On His Own '83
Bill '81
The Choice '81
Coward of the County '81
The Funhouse '81

Barbara Alyn Woods (1962-)
The Wild Card '03
Dead Weekend '95
Eden '93
Eden 2 '93
Eden 3 '93
Eden 4 '93
Ghoulies 4 '93
Circuitry Man '90

Carol Woods
The Honeymooners '05
Stepping Out '91

Donald Woods (1909-98)
True Grit '69
Kissin' Cousins '64
Door to Door Maniac '61
13 Ghosts '60
The Beast from 20,000 Fathoms '53
Mr. Music '50
Bells of San Fernando '47
Never Say Goodbye '46
The Bridge of San Luis Rey '44
Enemy of Women '44
Corregidor '43
Watch on the Rhine '43
If I Had My Way '40
Mexican Spitfire '40
Beauty for the Asking '39
The Black Doll '38
Danger on the Air '38
Sea Devils '37
The Story of Louis Pasteur '36
A Tale of Two Cities '36
Sweet Adeline '35

Edward (Eddie) Woods (1903-89)
Shadows over Shanghai '38
Tarzan the Fearless '33
They Never Come Back '32
Public Enemy '31

She Wore a Yellow Ribbon '49
Silver City Kid '45
West of the Pecos '45
Nevada '44
Bordertown Gunfighters '43
Dawn on the Great Divide '42
Riders of the West '42
Romance on the Range '42
Today I Hang '42
Boss of Bullion City '41
Sheriff of Tombstone '41
Bullet Code '40
Winners of the West '40
Beau Geste '39
Days of Jesse James '39
In Old Caliente '39
Come on Rangers '38
Hawaiian Buckaroo '38
Last Outlaw '36
The Lawless Nineties '36
The Phantom Rider '36
The Unknown Ranger '36
Rustlers of Red Dog '35
Savage Fury '35
Belle of the Nineties '34
Haunted Gold '32
Texas Gunfighter '32
Monkey Business '31
Palmy Days '31
Range Feud '31
Pardon My Gun '30
Dynamite Dan '24

James Woods (1947-)
Surf's Up '07 (V)
End Game '06
Be Cool '05
Pretty Persuasion '05
Northfork '03
Dirty Pictures '00
Any Given Sunday '99
The General's Daughter '99
True Crime '99
The Virgin Suicides '99
Another Day in Paradise '98
Contact '97
Hercules '97 (V)
John Carpenter's Vampires '97
Kicked in the Head '97
Ghosts of Mississippi '96
The Summer of Ben Tyler '96
Casino '95
For Better or Worse '95
Indictment: The McMartin Trial '95
Killer: A Journal of Murder '95
Nixon '95
Curse of the Starving Class '94
Next Door '94
The Specialist '94
Fallen Angels 1 '93
The Getaway '93
Chaplin '92
Citizen Cohn '92
Diggstown '92
Straight Talk '92
The Hard Way '91
In Love and War '91
The Gift of Love '90
Women & Men: Stories of Seduction '90
Immediate Family '89
My Name Is Bill W. '89
True Believer '89
The Boost '88
Cop '88
Best Seller '87
Salvador '86
Badge of the Assassin '85

Cat's Eye '85, Joshua Then and Now '85, Against All Odds '84, Once Upon a Time in America '84, When Angels Fly '84, Videodrome '83, Fast Walking '82, Split Image '82, Eyewitness '81, The Black Marble '80, The Onion Field '79, Holocaust '78, The Choirboys '77, The Disappearance of Aimee '76, F. Scott Fitzgerald in Hollywood '76, Dr. Meg Laurel '79, Night Moves '75, The Gambler '74, The Way We Were '73

Michael Woods (1957-)
Shock to the System '06, Rudy: The Rudy Giuliani Story '03, Red Shoe Diaries: Swimming Naked '00, Blindfold: Acts of Obsession '94, Hit Woman: The Double Edge '93, Omen 4: The Awakening '91, Haunting of Sarah Hardy '89

Nan Woods (1966-)
China Beach '88, One More Saturday Night '86

Ren Woods (1958-)
Hostage High '97, The Brother from Another Planet '84

Robert Woods (1936-)
Chase '85, White Fang and the Hunter '85, The Perverse Countess '73, Challenge of McKenna '70

Simon Woods (1980-)
Penelope '06, Pride and Prejudice '05, The Queen's Sister '05

DB Woodside (1969-)
More Dogs Than Bones '00, Romeo Must Die '00

Peter Woodthorpe (1931-2004)
Charge of the Light Brigade '68, The Blue Max '66, The Evil of Frankenstein '64

John Woodvine (1929-)
The Life and Adventures of Nicholas Nickleby '01, An American Werewolf in London '81, Assault on Agathon '75

Kate Woodville (1938-)
Computer Wizard '77, Where's Willie? '77, Posse '75, Sex Through a Window '72

Edward Woodward (1930-)
Five Days '07, Hot Fuzz '07, A Christmas Reunion '93, Codename Kyril '91, Mister Johnson '91, Hands of a Murderer '90, Uncle Tom's Cabin '87, King David '85, Merlin and the Sword '85, Champions '84, The Appointment '82, The Final Option '82, Breaker Morant '80, The Wicker Man '75, Young Winston '72

Joanne Woodward (1930-)
Empire Falls '05, Breathing Lessons '94, The Age of Innocence '93 (N), Blind Spot '93, Foreign Affairs '93, Philadelphia '93, Mr. & Mrs. Bridge '90, The Glass Menagerie '87, Harry & Son '84, Crisis at Central High '80, The Shadow Box '80, The Streets of L.A. '79, A Christmas to Remember '78, The End '78, See How She Runs '78, Sybil '76, The Drowning Pool '75, The Effect of Gamma Rays on Man-in-the-Moon Marigolds '73, Summer Wishes, Winter Dreams '73, They Might Be Giants '71, Winning '69, Rachel, Rachel '68, A Big Hand for the Little Lady '66, A New Kind of Love '63, The Stripper '63, Paris Blues '61, From the Terrace '60, The Fugitive Kind '60, The Long, Hot Summer '58, Rally 'Round the Flag, Boys! '58, The Three Faces of Eve '57

Jonathan M. Woodward (1973-)
The Notorious Bettie Page '06

Morgan Woodward (1925-)
Dark Before Dawn '89, Girls Just Want to Have Fun '85, Battle Beyond the Stars '80, Speedtrap '78, Moonshine County Express '77

Peter Woodward (1956-)
Hard Cash '01, Testament of Youth '79

Tim Woodward (1953-)
K-19: The Widowmaker '02, Heat of the Sun '99, RKO 281 '99, B. Monkey '97, Some Mother's Son '96, The Scarlet Letter '95, The Dark Angel '91, Piece of Cake '88, Personal Services '87, The Europeans '79

Marjorie Woodworth (1919-2000)
Broadway Limited '41

Emily Woof (1970-)
Wondrous Oblivion '06, Oliver Twist '00, Pandaemonium '00, Passion '99, Velvet Goldmine '98, Photographing Fairies '97, The Full Monty '96

Norman Wooland (1910-89)
Saul and David '64, Master of Venus '62, Teenage Bad Girl '59, Time Without Pity '57, The Quatermass Experiment '56, Madeleine '50, Angel with the Trumpet '50

Susan Wooldridge (1952-)
Just Like a Woman '95, Twenty-One '91, How to Get Ahead in Advertising '89, Hope and Glory '87, Loyalties '86, The Last Place on Earth '85, The Jewel in the Crown '84

Fenella Woolgar
Jekyll '07, Scoop '06, Bright Young Things '03

Monty Woolley (1888-1963)
As Young As You Feel '51, The Bishop's Wife '47, Night and Day '46, Since You Went Away '44, The Man Who Came to Dinner '41, Man About Town '39, Never Say Die '39, Everybody Sing '38, Three Comrades '38

Sheb Wooley (1921-2003)
Hoosiers '86, Bugles in the Afternoon '52, High Noon '52

Charles Woolf (1927-94)
No Way Back '74, Private Parts '72

Robert Woolsey (1889-1938)
Cockeyed Cavaliers '34, Hips, Hips, Hooray! '34, Kentucky Kernels '34, Diplomaniacs '33, So This Is Africa '33, Hold 'Em Jail '32, Dixiana '30, Half-Shot at Sunrise '30, Hook, Line and Sinker '30

Gordon Michael Woolvett (1970-)
Everything's Gone Green '06

Jaimz Woolvett (1967-)
The Highway Man '99, Bride of Chucky '98, The Legend of Gator Face '96, Unforgiven '92

Barbara Worth (1906-55)
Racing Luck '35, The Fighting Trooper '34

Mary Woronov (1943-)
The Devil's Rejects '05, Sweet Jane '98, Good Girls Don't '95, Grief '94, Shake, Rattle & Rock! '94, Acting on Impulse '93, Motorama '91, Rock 'n' Roll High School Forever '91, Warlock '91, Club Fed '90, Let It Ride '89, Scenes from the Class Struggle in Beverly Hills '89, Black Widow '87, Chopping Mall '86, Nomads '86, Terrorvision '86, Night of the Comet '84, The Movie House Massacre '84, Get Crazy '83, Angel of H.E.A.T. '82, Eating Raoul '82, Heartbeeps '81, Lady in Red '79, Rock 'n' Roll High School '79, Cannonball '76, Hollywood Boulevard '76, Hollywood Man '76, Jackson County Jail '76, Cover Girl Models '75, Death Race 2000 '75, Sugar Cookies '73, Seizure '74, Silent Night, Bloody Night '73, Kemek '70

Frederick Worlock (1886-1973)
101 Dalmatians '61 (V), The Last of the Redmen '47, Love from a Stranger '47, She Wolf of London '46, The Woman in Green '45

Jo Anne Worley (1937-)
A Goofy Movie '94 (V), Beauty and the Beast '91

Jimmy Workman (1980-)
As Good As It Gets '97, Addams Family Values '93, The Addams Family '91

Tom Wopat (1951-)
Bonneville '06, Contagious '96, Christmas Comes to Willow Creek '87, Burning Rage '84

Constance Worth (1912-63)
Kid Sister '45, G-Men vs. the Black Dragon '43, Dawn Express '42, Criminals Within '41, Windjammer '37

Hank Worden (1901-92)
Scream '83, Uforia '81, True Grit '69, The Alamo '60, The Horse Soldiers '59, The Searchers '56, Red River '48, Ghost Town Riders '38

Richard Wordsworth (1915-93)
Forbidden '85, Separate Tables '83, Deathtrap '82, Eyewitness '81, King Lear '71

Lilian Worth
The Fighting Sheriff '31, Tarzan the Tiger '29, The Adventures of Tarzan '21

Mike Worth (1969-)
U.S. Seals 2 '01, Fists of Iron '94, To Be the Best '93, Street Crimes '92, Final Impact '92

Nicholas Worth (1942-)
Slaves of Hollywood '99, Something About Sex '98, Dark Angel: The Ascent '94, Plughead Rewired: Circuitry Man 2 '94, Fist of Honor '92, Blood & Concrete: A Love Story '90, Darkman '90, The Red Raven Kiss-Off '90, Dirty Laundry '87, Don't Time '85

Sam Worthington (1976-)
Macbeth '06, Somersault '04, Dirty Deeds '02, Hart's War '02, Bootmen '00

Greg Wrangler
The Mummy Lives '93, Barbarian Queen 2: The Empress Strikes Back '89

Fay Wray (1907-2004)
Gideon's Trumpet '80, Crime of Passion '57, Tammy and the Bachelor '57, Rock, Pretty Baby '56, The Cobweb '55, Hell on Frisco Bay '55, Queen Bee '55, Small Town Girl '53, Treasure of the Golden Condor '53, Adam Had Four Sons '41, Melody for Three '41, The Jury's Secret '38, Murder in Greenwich Village '37, They Met in a Taxi '36, When Knights Were Bold '36, Bulldog Jack '35, The Evil Mind '34, Viva Villa! '34, Woman in the Shadows '34, The Bowery '33, King Kong '33, Mystery of the Wax Museum '33, Doctor X '32, The Most Dangerous Game '32, The Vampire Bat '32, The Sea God '30

Constance Worth (1912-63)
The Wedding March '28, The Coast Patrol '25, Blind Husbands '19

Tom Wopat (1951-)
Below the Deadline '29, The Prairie King '27

John Wray (1887-1940)
You Only Live Once '37, Green Eyes '34, All Quiet on the Western Front '30

Janet Wright (1945-)
Emile '03, Blackwoods '01

Carl Wright (1931-)
Barbershop 2: Back in Business '04, Big Momma's House '00, Soul Food '97

Cobina Wright, Jr. (1921-)
Charlie Chan in Rio '41, Week-End in Havana '41

Jeffrey Wright (1965-)
The Invasion '07, Broken Flowers '05, Lady in the Water '06, Casino Royale '06, Syriana '05, The Manchurian Candidate '04, Angels in America '03, Boycott '02, Ali '01, Eye See You '01, Crime and Punishment in Suburbia '00, Hamlet '00, Shaft '00, Cement '99, Ride with the Devil '99, Celebrity '98, Critical Care '97

Harry Worth (1903-75)
Tough to Handle '37, Adventures of Red Ryder '40

Irene Worth (1916-2002)
Onegin '99, Just the Ticket '98, Lost in Yonkers '93, The Shell Seekers '89

Clare Wren
Midnight Edition '93, Steel and Lace '90, Season of Fear '89

Aloma Wright (1950-)
Johnson Family Vacation '04

Amy Wright (1950-)
Trippin' '99, Hard Promises '92, Deceived '91, Final Verdict '91, Love Hurts '90, Daddy's Dyin'... Who's Got the Will? '90, Miss Firecracker '89, The Accidental Tourist '88, Crossing Delancey '88, The Telephone '87, Off Beat '86, Stardust Memories '80, The Amityville Horror '79, Breaking Away '79, Wise Blood '79, The Deer Hunter '78, Girlfriends '78

Bonnie Wright (1991-)
Harry Potter and the Order of the Phoenix '07, Harry Potter and the Goblet of Fire '05, Harry Potter and the Chamber of Secrets '02

Jenny Wright (1962-)
The Lawnmower Man '92, A Shock to the System '90, Young Guns 2 '90, I, Madman '89, Twister '89, The Chocolate War '88, Valentino Returns '88

Near Dark '87
Out of Bounds '86
St. Elmo's Fire '85
The Wild Life '84
The Executioner's Song '82
Pink Floyd: The Wall '82

Katie Wright (1981-)
Idle Hands '99
Too Smooth '98
Hostage High '97

Ken Wright
Eye of the Eagle 3 '91
Hollywood Boulevard 2 '89
Opposing Force '87
Prince of Darkness '87

Marie Wright (1862-)
Gaslight '40
Black Eyes '39

Max Wright (1943-)
Snow Falling on Cedars '99
Fraternity Vacation '85
Konrad '85
All That Jazz '79

From the Earth to the Moon '98
The Shadow '94
White Mile '94
Touch and Go '86
Confessions of a Hit Man '94
Sugar Hill '94
The Five Heartbeats '91
The Principal '87
Streamers '83

N'Bushe Wright (1970-)
The Abductors '72
Civil Brand '02
Widows '02
Three Strikes '00
Blade '98
Dead Presidents '95
Fresh '94
Zebrahead '92

Patrick Wright (1939-)
If You Don't Stop It... You'll Go Blind '77

Samuel E. Wright (1948-)
Dinosaur '00 (V)
The Little Mermaid '89 (V)
Bird '88

Steven Wright (1955-)
Son of the Mask '05
Coffee and Cigarettes '03
Loser '00
The Muse '99
Babe: Pig in the City '98 (V)
1999 '98
Half-Baked '97
Canadian Bacon '94
Natural Born Killers '94
So I Married an Axe Murderer '93
Reservoir Dogs '92 (V)
Men of Respect '91
Desperately Seeking Susan '85
Sledgehammer '83

Teresa Wright (1918-2005)
John Grisham's The Rainmaker '97
The Good Mother '88
The Fig Tree '87
Bill: On His Own '83
Somewhere in Time '80
Roseland '77
Flood! '76
Hail, Hero! '69
The Happy Ending '69
Escapade in Japan '57
The Search for Bridey Murphy '56
The Capture '50
The Men '50
Pursued '47

The Best Years of Our Lives '46
Casanova Brown '44
Shadow of a Doubt '43
Mrs. Miniver '42
The Pride of the Yankees '42
The Little Foxes '41

Tom Wright (1952-)
The Gunman '03
Barbershop '02
P.S. Your Cat is Dead! '02
Sunshine State '02
Palmetto '98
The Pentagon Wars '98
Tales from the Hood '95
Creepshow 2 '87

Tony Wright (1925-86)
The House in Marsh Road '60
Broth of a Boy '59

Tracy Wright
Last Night '98
When Night Is Falling '95

Trevor Wright
Air Bud 6: Air Buddies '06
MXP: Most Xtreme Primate '03

Whittni Wright (1987-)
Sudden Death '95
I'll Do Anything '93

Will Wright (1891-1962)
Alias Jesse James '59
Miss Grant Takes Richmond '49

William Wright (1911-49)
Infamous Crimes '47
The Mask of Dijon '46
A Night to Remember '42

Robin Wright Penn (1966-)
Beowulf '07 (V)
Breaking and Entering '06
Empire Falls '05
Nine Lives '05
Sorry, Haters '05
A Home at the End of the World '04
The Singing Detective '03
Virgin '03
White Oleander '02
Moll Flanders '96
The Crossing Guard '94
Forrest Gump '94
The Playboys '92
Toys '92

Highway 13 '48
White Pongo '45
Waterfront '44
Sons of the Pioneers '42
Footsteps in the Dark '41
The Ape '40
British Intelligence '40

Chien-Lien Wu (1968)
Eat Drink Man Woman '94

Daniel Wu (1974-)
Around the World in 80 Days '04
New Police Story '04

Jiang Wu
Shower '00
To Live '94

Kristy Wu (1982-)
CryWolf '05

What's Cooking? '00

Vivian Wu (1966-)
Dinner Rush '00
8 1/2 Women '99
A Bright Shining Lie '98
The Pillow Book '95
The Joy Luck Club '93
Teenage Mutant Ninja Turtles 3 '93
The Guyver '91
Iron & Silk '91
Shadow of China '91

Robert Wuhl (1951-)
The Last Don 2 '98
The Last Don '97
Open Season '95
Cobb '94
A Kiss Goodnight '94
Percy & Thunder '93
The Bodyguard '92
Missing Pieces '91
Mistress '91
Batman '89
Blaze '89
Tales from the Crypt '89
Bull Durham '88
Good Morning, Vietnam '87
Flashdance '83

Kari Wuhrer (1967-)
Hellraiser: Deader '05
The Hitcher 2: I've Been Waiting '03
King of the Ants '03
Eight Legged Freaks '02
The Medicine Show '01
Poison '01
Spider's Web '01
Kiss Tomorrow Goodbye '00
Lip Service '00
Sand '00
Kate's Addiction '99
Hot Blooded '98
Kissing a Fool '98
Phoenix '98
Ivory Tower '97
Luscious '97
The Undertaker's Wedding '97
Anaconda '96
An Occasional Hell '96
Stephen King's Thinner '96
Beastmaster 2: Through the Portal of Time '91
The Disappearance of Kevin Johnson '95
Sex and the Other Man '95
Terminal Justice: Cybertech P.D. '95
Beyond Desire '94
Boulevard '94
The Crossing Guard '94
Sensation '94
The Adventures of Ford Fairlane '90

Kai Wulff
Top Dog '95
Jungle Warriors '84
Firefox '82

Martin Wuttke (1962-)
Rosenstrasse '04
The Legend of Rita '99

Shelley Wyant
Home Free All '84
Pilgrim, Farewell '82

B. Wyatt
Luster '02

Jane Wyatt (1911-2006)
The Natural History of Parking Lots '90
Amityville 4: The Evil Escapes '89
Star Trek 4: The Voyage Home '86
Nativity '78
Katherine '75
The Adventures of Tom Sawyer '73
My Blue Heaven '50
Our Very Own '50
Task Force '49
Pitfall '48
Boomerang '47
Gentleman's Agreement '47

None But the Lonely Heart '44
Buckskin Frontier '43
The Kansan '43
The Navy Comes Through '42
Lost Horizon '37
Great Expectations '34

Don Wycherley (1967-)
Veronica Guerin '03
When Brendan Met Trudy '00

Margaret Wycherly (1881-1956)
White Heat '49
Forever Amber '47
Something in the Wind '47
The Yearling '46
Hangmen Also Die '42
Keeper of the Flame '42
Random Harvest '42
Sergeant York '41
Midnight '34

Katya Wyeth (1949-)
Dressed for Death '74
Twins of Evil '71

Michael Wyle
God's Lonely Man '96
Appointment with Fear '85

Noah Wyle (1971-)
Enough '02
White Oleander '02
Donnie Darko '01
Fail Safe '00
The Pirates of Silicon Valley '99
The Myth of Fingerprints '97
Swing Kids '93
A Few Good Men '92
There Goes My Baby '92
Crooked Hearts '91

Gretchen Wyler (1932-2007)
The Marrying Man '91
The Devil's Brigade '68

Adam Wylie (1984-)
Daybreak '01
Can of Worms '00
The King and I '99 (V)
Children of the Corn 5: Fields of Terror '98
Balloon Farm '97
Santa with Muscles '96
All Dogs Go to Heaven 2 '95 (V)
Breaking Free '95

John Wylie (1925-2004)
Robot in the Family '94
An Empty Bed '90

Daniel Wyllie
Unconditional Love '03
Chopper '00
Holy Smoke '99
Romper Stomper '92

Bill Wyman (1936-)
Eat the Rich '87
Gimme Shelter '70

Jane Wyman (1917-2007)
The Incredible Journey of Dr. Meg Laurel '79
How to Commit Marriage '69
Bon Voyage! '62
Pollyanna '60
All That Heaven Allows '55
Magnificent Obsession '54
Just for You '52
Here Comes the Groom '51
Three Guys Named Mike '51
Stage Fright '50
It's a Great Feeling '49
Johnny Belinda '48
Magic Town '47
Night and Day '46
The Yearling '46
The Lost Weekend '45
Footlight Serenade '42
The Spy Ring '38
Wide Open Faces '38
My Man Godfrey '36

John Wyman
Tuxedo Warrior '82
For Your Eyes Only '81

Patrick Wymark (1926-70)
The Blood on Satan's Claw '71
Battle of Britain '69
Journey to the Far Side of the Sun '69
The Conqueror Worm '68
Where Eagles Dare '68
Woman Times Seven '67
Repulsion '65
The Skull '65

Patrice Wymore (1926-)
The King's Rhapsody '55
Big Trees '52
I'll See You in My Dreams '51
Tea for Two '50

Geraint Wyn Davies (1957-)
American Psycho 2: All American Girl '02
Cube 2: Hypercube '02
Trilogy of Terror 2 '96
Hush Little Baby '93
Terror Stalks the Class Reunion '93

H.M. Wynant (1927-)
The Big Empty '98
Conquest of the Planet of the Apes '72
Run Silent, Run Deep '58
Run of the Arrow '56

George Wyner (1945-)
For Richer, for Poorer '92
The Taking of Beverly Hills '91
Fletch Lives '89
Spaceballs '87
Fletch '85

Joel Wyner (1969-)
Missiles of October '74

Peter Wyngarde (1923-)
Double Cross '92
Burn Witch, Burn! '62
The Innocents '61

Mick Wynhoff
5 Dark Souls '96
America's Deadliest Home Video '91

Joel D. Wynkoop (1960-)
Addicted to Murder 2: Tainted Blood '97
The Alien Agenda: Endangered Species '97

Ed Wynn (1886-1966)
The Gnome-Mobile '67
Dear Brigitte '65
The Greatest Story Ever Told '65
Those Calloways '65
Mary Poppins '64
The Absent-Minded Professor '61
Babes in Toyland '61
Cinderella '60
The Diary of Anne Frank '59
Marjorie Morningstar '58
Requiem for a Heavyweight '56
Alice in Wonderland '51 (V)

Keenan Wynn (1916-86)
Hyper-Sapien: People from Another Star '86
Call to Glory '84
Wavelength '83
Best Friends '82
The Capture of Grizzly Adams '82
The Last Unicorn '82 (V)
A Piano for Mrs. Cimino '82
Just Tell Me What You Want '80

Mission to Glory '80
Mom, the Wolfman and Me '80
The Clonus Horror '79
The Dark '79
Hard Knocks '79
Mid Knight Rider '79
The Treasure Seekers '79
The Bastard '78
Coach '78
Laserblast '78
The Lucifer Complex '78
Monster '78
Piranha '78
Orca '77
High Velocity '76
The Killer Inside Me '76
The Longest Drive '76
The Shaggy D.A. '76
Devil's Rain '75
He Is My Brother '75
The Man Who Would Not Die '75
Nashville '75
Herbie Rides Again '74
Hit Lady '74
Legend of Earl Durand '74
Internecine Project '73
Cancel My Reservation '72
The Mechanic '72
Snowball Express '72
Manipulator '71
The Desperados '70
Loving '70
MacKenna's Gold '69
Smith! '69
Viva Max '69
Finian's Rainbow '68
Once Upon a Time in the West '68
Point Blank '67
The War Wagon '67
Promise Her Anything '66
Around the World Under the Sea '65
The Great Race '65
The Americanization of Emily '64
Bikini Beach '64
Dr. Strangelove, or: How I Learned to Stop Worrying and Love the Bomb '64
The Patsy '64
Son of Flubber '63
Pattern for Plunder '62
The Absent-Minded Professor '61
The King of the Roaring '20s: The Story of Arnold Rothstein '61
A Hole in the Head '59
The Perfect Furlough '59
Deep Six '58
A Time to Love & a Time to Die '58
Don't Go Near the Water '57
The Man in the Gray Flannel Suit '56
Naked Hills '56
Requiem for a Heavyweight '56
The Glass Slipper '55
Shack Out on 101 '55
The Long, Long Trailer '54
Men of the Fighting Lady '54
All the Brothers Were Valiant '53
Battle Circus '53
Kiss Me Kate '53
The Belle of New York '52
Phone Call from a Stranger '52
Angels in the Outfield '51
Royal Wedding '51
Texas Carnival '51
Annie Get Your Gun '50
Three Little Words '54
My Dear Secretary '49
Neptune's Daughter '49
That Midnight Kiss '49
The Three Musketeers '48
The Hucksters '47
Song of the Thin Man '47
Easy to Wed '46
The Clock '45

Weekend at the Waldorf '45
Without Love '45
Since You Went Away '44
For Me and My Gal '42
Somewhere I'll Find You '42

May Wynn (1931-)
The Violent Men '55
The Caine Mutiny '54
The Farmer Takes a Wife '53

Christopher Wynne
1969 '89

Gilbert Wynne
Remote Control '88

Dana Wynter (1930-)
Backstairs at the White House '79
Lovers Like Us '75
The Connection '73
Santee '73
Airport '70
Dead Right '68
The List of Adrian Messenger '63
Sink the Bismarck '60
Shake Hands with the Devil '59
Something of Value '57
D-Day, the Sixth of June '56
Invasion of the Body Snatchers '56

Sarah Wynter (1973-)
L.A. Dicks '05
Coastlines '02
Shooting Livien '05
Bride of the Wind '01
Lost Souls '00
Race Against Time '00

Charlotte Wynters (1899-1991)
Harvest Melody '43
Tomboy '40
Hopalong Cassidy: Renegade Trail '39
Nancy Drew—Trouble Shooter '39
Panama Patrol '39
Renegade Trail '39
Sinners in Paradise '38
The Ivory Handled Gun '35
Struggle '31

Diana Wynyard (1906-64)
Gaslight '40
Cavalcade '33
Rasputin and the Empress '33

Amanda Wyss (1960-)
Desert Steel '94
Bloodfist 4: Die Trying '92
Black Magic Woman '91
To Die For 2: Son of Darkness '91
Powwow Highway '89
Shakma '89
To Die For '89
Deadly Innocence '88
Better Off Dead '85
My Mother's Secret Life '84
A Nightmare on Elm Street '84
Fast Times at Ridgemont High '82

Nelson Xavier (1941-)
At Play in the Fields of the Lord '91
Gabriela '84

Xin-Xin Xiong (1965-)
Once Upon a Time in China III '93
Once Upon a Time in China II '92

Zhu Xu
Shower '00
The King of Masks '99

Wang Xueqi
Warriors of Heaven and Earth '03
Yellow Earth '89

Salvator Xuereb (1965-)
Bloodhounds 2 '96
Dracula: Dead and Loving It '95
The Nutt House '95
The Mask '94

Xzibit (1974-)
The X-Files: I Want to Believe '08
XXX: State of the Union '05 (V)
Gridiron Gang '06
Derailed '05
Hoodwinked '05 (V)

Kaoru Yachigusa (1931-)
Snow Country '57
Samurai 3: Duel at Ganryu Island '56
Samurai 1: Musashi Miyamoto '55
Samurai 2: Duel at Ichijoji Temple '55

Frank Yaconelli (1898-1965)
Riding the California Trail '47
South of Monterey '47
Lone Star Law Men '42
Western Mail '42
Riding the Sunset Trail '41
Dr. Cyclops '40
Across the Plains '39
Escape to Paradise '39
Wild Horse Canyon '39

Raghuvir Yadav
Water '05
Lagaan: Once upon a Time in India '01
Salaam Bombay! '88
Bandit Queen '94

Jeff Yagher (1962-)
My Fellow Americans '96
Madonna: Innocence Lost '94
The Horseman on the Roof '95
Lower Level '91
Shag: The Movie '89
Big Bad Mama 2 '87

Simon Yam (1955-)
Exiled '06
Lara Croft Tomb Raider: The Cradle of Life '03
The Mission '99
Full Contact '92
Naked Killer '92
A Bullet in the Head '90
Tongs: An American Nightmare '88

Isuzu Yamada (1917-)
Yojimbo '61
The Lower Depths '57
Throne of Blood '57
Osaka Elegy '36
Sisters of the Gion '36

Isao Yamagata (1915-96)
Gate of Hell '54

Sayaka Yamaguchi
Rebirth of Mothra 2 '97
Rebirth of Mothra '96

Yoshiko (Shirley) Yamaguchi (1920-)
House of Bamboo '55
Scandal '50

Fujiko Yamamoto (1931-)
An Actor's Revenge '63
Being Two Isn't Easy '62
Golden Demon '53

So Yamamura (1910-2000)
Gung Ho '86
Something About Sex '98

Koji Yakusho (1956-)
Silk '07
Babel '06
Memoirs of a Geisha '05
Pulse '01
The Eel '96
Shall We Dance? '96
Cure '97
Tampopo '86

Hal Yamanouchi (1946-)
The Lone Runner '88
2020 Texas Gladiators '85

Tsutomu Yamazaki (1936-)
Rikyu '90
A Taxing Woman '87
Tampopo '86
The Funeral '84
Kagemusha '80

Emily Yancy (1939-)
Blacula '72
Cotton Comes to Harlem '70

Eduardo Yanez (1960-)
The Punisher '04
Held Up '00

Edward Yankie
The Sign of Four '01
Deadline '00

Weird Al Yankovic (1959-)
Naked Gun 33 1/3: The Final Insult '94
Naked Gun 2 1/2: The Smell of Fear '91
Tapeheads '89
UHF '89

Jean Yanne (1933-2003)
Brotherhood of the Wolf '01
Beaumarchais the Scoundrel '96
The Horseman on the Roof '95
A la Mode '94
Indochine '92
Madame Bovary '91
Quicker Than the Eye '88
Bandits '86
Hanna K. '83
Cobra '71
This Man Must Die '70
Le Boucher '69
Weekend '67
Victory '95

Rossana Yanni (1938-)
The Rue Morgue Massacres '73
Dracula's Great Love '72
Fangs of the Living Dead '68
White Comanche '67

Lillian Yarbo
Way Down South '39
You Can't Take It with You '38

Margaret Yarde (1878-1944)
Thursday's Child '43
The Deputy Drummer '35

Claire Yarlett (1965-)
Black Out '96

Celeste Yarnall (1944-)
Born Yesterday '93
Midnight Kiss '93
Scorpio '73
The Velvet Vampire '71

Michael Yarmush (1982-)
Crown Heights '02
Little Men '98
First Do No Harm '97

Amy Yasbeck (1963-)
Dead Husbands '98

Rikiya Yasuoka (1947-)
The Toxic Avenger, Part 2 '89
Tampopo '86

Marjorie Yates (1941-)
The Long Day Closes '92

Cassie Yates (1951-)
Perry Mason Returns '85
Unfaithfully Yours '84
Agatha Christie's A Caribbean Mystery '83
St. Helen's '80
Who'll Save Our Children? '82
Of Mice and Men '81
Father Figure '80
Convoy '78
The Evil '78
F.I.S.T. '78
FM '78

Chingmy Yau
Naked Killer '92
Meltdown '95

Jose Maria Yazpik (1970-)
Cronicas '04
Innocent Voices '04
Sueno '05

Liu Ye (1978-)
Balzac and the Little Chinese Seamstress '02
Lan Yu '01
'06

Biff Yeager
Headless Body in Topless Bar '95
Bar '96
Straight to Hell '87
Girls Just Want to Have Fun '85
Repo Man '83
Black Samurai '83

Steve Yeager (1948-)
Polyester '81

Richard Yearwood
Dangerous Evidence: The Lori Jackson Story '99
Blood Brothers '97
Pink Flamingos '72

Kelvin Han Yee
Life Tastes Good '99
A Great Wall '86

Sally Yeh (1961-)
The Killer '90

Peter Yellen
Ms. 45 '81
Driller Killer '79

Anton Yelchin (1989-)
Charlie Bartlett '07
Alpha Dog '06
Fierce People '05
House of D '04
Along Came a Spider '01
Hearts in Atlantis '01
A Time for Dancing '00

Hannah Yelland (1976-)
Dinotopia '02
Catherine Cookson's The Secret '00

Donnie Yen (1963-)
Hero '03
Shanghai Knights '03
Blade 2 '02
Highlander: Endgame '00
Wing Chun '94
Iron Monkey '93

Michelle Yeoh (1962-)
The Mummy: Tomb of the Dragon Emperor '08
Sunshine '07
Memoirs of a Geisha '05
Silver Hawk '04
Crouching Tiger, Hidden Dragon '00
Tomorrow Never Dies '97
Wing Chun '94
The Heroic Trio '93
Supercop 2 '93
Twin Warriors '93
Supercop '92
Royal Warriors '86

Don Yesso (1954-)
Out of Sync '95
The Hard Truth '94
Hero '92

Bolo Yeung (1938-)
Shootfighter: Fight to the Death '93
Death '93
TC 2000 '93
Breathing Fire '91
Tiger Claws '91
Bloodsport '88
Legacy of Rage '86

Charlie Yeung
Bangkok Dangerous '08
New Police Story '04
The White Countess '05
Big Shot's Funeral '01
Farewell My Concubine '93

Serra Yilmaz (1954-)
Facing Windows '03

Da(niel) Ying
His Secret Life '01

Cecilia Yip (1962-)
What Time Is It There? '01

Francoise Yip (1972-)
Crank '06
The Deal '05
Blade: Trinity '04
Romeo Must Die '00
Futuresport '98
Rumble in the Bronx '96
Black Mask '96

Richard Yniguez (1946-)
Stalking Laura '93
World War III '86
Boulevard Nights '79

Dwight Yoakam (1956-)
The Three Burials of Melquiades Estrada '05
Wedding Crashers '05
3-Way '04
Hollywood Homicide '03
Panic Room '02
South of Heaven, West of Hell '00
The Minus Man '99
When Trumpets Fade '98
The Newton Boys '97
Don't Look Back '96
Sling Blade '96
The Little Death '95
Painted Hero '95
Red Rock West '93

Malik Yoba (1967-)
Cop Land '97
Blue in the Face '95
Smoke '95
Up '94
Cool Runnings '93

Erica Yohn
Corrina, Corrina '94
An American Tail: Fievel Goes West '91 (V)
A Streetcar Named Desire '84

Aaron Yoo
21 '08
Disturbia '07

Tran Nu Yen-Khe (1968-)
The Vertical Ray of the Sun '00
Cyclo '95
The Scent of Green Papaya '93

Wladimir Yordanoff
The Taste of Others '00
Un Air de Famille '96
Vincent & Theo '90

Francine York (1938-)
Flood! '76
The Centerfold Girls '74
The Doll Squad '73
Curse of the Swamp Creature '66
Space Monster '64
Secret File of Hollywood '62

Jeff York (1912-95)
Savage Sam '63
Wild Ones on Wheels '62
Old Yeller '57
Davy Crockett and the River Pirates '56
Westward Ho, the Wagons! '56
The Lady Says No '51
Kill the Umpire '50
The Yearling '46

Dick York (1929-92)
Inherit the Wind '60
They Came to Cordura '59
Cowboy '58
My Sister Eileen '55

Michael York (1942-)
Wrongfully Accused '98
Austin Powers: International Man of Mystery '97
Austin Powers in Goldmember '02
Austin Powers: The Spy Who Shagged Me '99
The Omega Code '99
54 '98
Dark Planet '97
The Ripper '97
True Women '97
Not of This Earth '96
A Young Connecticut Yankee in King Arthur's Court '95
Fall from Grace '94
Gospa '94
Discretion Assured '93
Duel of Hearts '92
Wide Sargasso Sea '92
The Heat of the Day '91
Night of the Fox '90
The Lady and the Highwayman '89
The Return of the Musketeers '89
The Four Minute Mile '88
Midnight Cop '88
Lethal Obsession '87
Phantom of Death '87
Sword of Gideon '86

Kathleen York
Sublime '07
Shelter Island '03
The Big Day '99
Dead Men Can't Dance '97
Cries of Silence '97
Nightlong '96
Dream Lover '93
Thompson's Last Run '90
Checking Out '89
Cold Feet '89
Winners Take All '87

York

Nevil Shute's The Far Country '85
Success Is the Best Revenge '84
Weather in the Streets '84
Final Assignment '80
The Riddle of the Sands '79
The Island of Dr. Moreau '77
The Last Remake of Beau Geste '77
Logan's Run '76
Conduct Unbecoming '75
The Four Musketeers '75
Murder on the Orient Express '74
The Three Musketeers '74
Cabaret '72
Zeppelin '71
Justine '69
Romeo and Juliet '68
Accident '67
Smashing Time '67
The Taming of the Shrew '67

Morgan York (1993-)
Cheaper by the Dozen 2 '05
Cheaper by the Dozen '03

Rachel York (1971-)
Terror Tract '00
One Fine Day '96
Dead Center '92
Killer Instinct '92

Susannah York (1941-)
Visitors '03
St. Patrick: The Irish Legend '00
Romance and Rejection '96
Devices and Desires '91
Fate '90
The Man from the Pru '89
American Roulette '88
Diamond's Edge '88
A Summer Story '88
The Land of Faraway '87
Prettykill '87
Superman 4: The Quest for Peace '87 (V)
Alice '86
A Christmas Carol '84
Loophole '83
Yellowbeard '83
We'll Meet Again '82
The Awakening '80
Falling in Love Again '80
Second Chance '80
Superman 2 '80
Superman '78
The Silent Partner '78
The Shout '78
The Killing of Sister George '69
Battle of Britain '69
Oh! What a Lovely War '69
They Shoot Horses, Don't They? '69
Sebastian '68
A Man for All Seasons '66
The Seventh Dawn '64
Tom Jones '63
Tunes of Glory '60

Bud Yorkin (1926-)
For the Boys '91
Inspector Clouseau '68

Jitsuko Yoshimura (1943-)
Onibaba '64
The Insect Woman '63

Ge You (1957-)
Big Shot's Funeral '01
The Emperor's Shadow '96
To Live '94
Farewell My Concubine '93

Aden Young (1972-)
The Starter Wife '07
After the Deluge '03
The Crocodile Hunter: Collision Course '02
The War Bride '01
In the Shadows '98
Cousin Bette '97
Hotel de Love '96
Cosi '95
River Street '95
Metal Skin '94
Sniper '92
Black Robe '91

Alan Young (1919-)
The Time Machine '02
Beverly Hills Cop 3 '94
DuckTales the Movie: Treasure of the Lost Lamp '90 (V)
The Great Mouse Detective '86 (V)
Baker's Hawk '76
The Time Machine '60
Androcles and the Lion '52

Artie Young
Bronze Buckaroo '39
Harlem Rides the Range '39

Bill Young (1950-)
Japanese Story '03
Chopper '00
The Pacifier '05
Road to Nhill '97

Bruce A. Young (1956-)
Jurassic Park 3 '01
Normal Life '96
The War '94
Blink '93
What Ever Happened To... '93

Burt Young (1940-)
Basic Instinct '92
Deep Down '94
P.C.U. '94
Hack! '07
Rocky Balboa '06
Carlito's Way: Rise to Power '05
Shut Up and Kiss Me '05
Transamerica '05
Land of Plenty '04
The Adventures of Pluto Nash '02
Blue Moon '00
Table One '00
Mickey Blue Eyes '99
Hot Blooded '98
Kicked in the Head '97
She's So Lovely '97
The Undertaker's Wedding '97
Heaven Before I Die '96
North Star '96
Red Blooded 2 '96
Excessive Force '93
Bright Angel '91
A Family Matter '91
Backstreet Dreams '90
Betsy's Wedding '90
Club Fed '90
Diving In '90
Last Exit to Brooklyn '90
Rocky 5 '90
Wait until Spring, Bandini '90
Beverly Hills Brats '89
Going Overboard '89
Blood Red '88
Back to School '86
Rocky 4 '85
Once Upon a Time in America '84
The Pope of Greenwich Village '84
A Summer to Remember '84
When Angels Fly '84
Over the Brooklyn Bridge '83
Amityville 2: The Possession '82
Lookin' to Get Out '82
Rocky 3 '82
Blood Beach '81
Rocky 2 '79
Convoy '78
The Choirboys '77
Twilight's Last Gleaming '77
Harry & Walter Go to New York '76
Rocky '76
The Killer Elite '75
Chinatown '74
The Gambler '74
Cinderella Liberty '73
Carnival of Blood '71

Carleton Young (1907-71)
The Man Who Shot Liberty Valance '62
Armored Command '61
The Gallant Hours '60
Sergeant Rutledge '60
The Horse Soldiers '59
Battle Cry '55
20,000 Leagues under the Sea '54
From Here to Eternity '53
Kansas City Confidential '52
Flying Leathernecks '51
People Will Talk '51
Thunder River Feud '42
Texas Trouble '41
Trigger Men '41
Adventures of Red Ryder '40
Battling Outlaw '40
Billy the Kid in Texas '40
Up in the Air '40
El Diablo Rides '39
Zorro's Fighting Legion '39
Heroes of the Hills '38
Outlaw Express '38
Reefer Madness '38

Chris Young (1971-)
Killing Mr. Griffin '97
Deep Down '94
Runaway Daughters '94
Warlock: The Armageddon '93
Book of Love '91
December '91
The Runestone '91
The Great Outdoors '88

Clara Kimball Young (1890-1960)
The Frontiersmen '38
Oh Susannah! '38
Rogue's Tavern '36
Chandu on the Magic Island '34
I Can't Escape '34
Return of Chandu '34
Murder on the High Seas '32
Probation '32
Kept Husbands '31
Mother and Son '31

Damian Young
Kill the Poor '06

David Young
Double Exposure '82
Banjo Hackett '76
Mary, Mary, Bloody Mary '76

Dey Young (1955-)
Protecting the King '07
The Mod Squad '99
True Heart '97
The Shadow Conspiracy '96
Letter to My Killer '95
Pie in the Sky '95
No Place to Hide '93
Back in the USSR '92
Conflict of Interest '92
Frankie and Johnny '91
Murder 101 '91
Spontaneous Combustion '89
Doin' Time '85
Strange Invaders '83
Strange Behavior '81
Rock 'n' Roll High School '79

Faron Young (1932-96)
Daniel Boone: Trail Blazer '56
Hidden Guns '56

Gig Young (1913-78)
The Hindenburg '75
The Killer Elite '75
Bring Me the Head of Alfredo Garcia '74
Lovers and Other Strangers '70
They Shoot Horses, Don't They? '69
Blood Island '68
Strange Bedfellows '65
For Love or Money '63
Kid Galahad '62
That Touch of Mink '62
Ask Any Girl '59
Teacher's Pet '58
The Tunnel of Love '58
Desk Set '57
Desperate Hours '55
Young at Heart '54
City That Never Sleeps '53
The Girl Who Had Everything '53
Torch Song '53
Slaughter Trail '51
Hunt the Man Down '50
Only the Valiant '50
Lust for Gold '49
Tell It to the Judge '49
Wake of the Red Witch '49
The Three Musketeers '48
Escape Me Never '47
Air Force '43
Sergeant York '41
They Died with Their Boots On '41

Harrison Young (1930-2005)
The Pleasure Drivers '05
House of 1000 Corpses '03
The Adventures of Rocky & Bullwinkle '00
Reptilian '99
Saving Private Ryan '98
Factotum '05
Heading South '05
Mercy '00
Joe the King '99
Daylight '96
The Wife '95
Drug Wars 2: The Cocaine Cartel '92
Hoffa '92
The Ten Million Dollar Getaway '91
Little Sweetheart '90
Criminal Law '89
Night Game '89
Torch Song Trilogy '88
Heat '87
Jaws: The Revenge '87
9 1/2 Weeks '86
Almost You '85
Birdy '84
Maria's Lovers '84
Deep in the Heart '83

Keone Young (1947-)
Uncorked '98
Beverly Hills Bodysnatchers '89

Lee Thompson Young (1984-)
The Hills Have Eyes 2 '07
Akeelah and the Bee '06
Friday Night Lights '04

Loretta Young (1913-2000)
Because of You '52
Cause for Alarm! '51
Key to the City '50
Come to the Stable '49
The Accused '48
Rachel and the Stranger '48
The Bishop's Wife '47
The Farmer's Daughter '47
The Perfect Marriage '46
The Stranger '46
Along Came Jones '45
China '43
A Night to Remember '42
Doctor Takes a Wife '40
Eternally Yours '39
The Story of Alexander Graham Bell '39
Four Men and a Prayer '38
The Crusades '35
Employees' Entrance '33
Heroes for Sale '33
They Call It Sin '32
Big Business Girl '31
Platinum Blonde '31

Mary (Marsden) Young (1880-1971)
Alias Jesse James '59
The Lost Weekend '45
Watch on the Rhine '43

Nedrick Young (1913-68)
Terror in a Texas Town '58
Crime Wave '54
Captain Scarlett '53
Gun Crazy '49
Dead Men Walk '43

Neil Young (1945-)
Love at Large '89
Made in Heaven '87
'68 '87

Noah Young (1887-1958)
For Heaven's Sake '26
Battling Orioles '24
Safety Last '23

Otis Young (1932-2001)
Blood Beach '81
The Capture of Bigfoot '79
The Last Detail '73

Paul Young (1944-)
The Girl in the Picture '86
Another Time, Another Place '83

Polly Ann Young (1908-97)
The Invisible Ghost '41
Road Show '41
Murder on the Yukon '40
Mystery Plane '39
The Story of Alexander Graham Bell '39
The Crimson Trail '35
His Fighting Blood '35
Sons of Steel '35
Man from Utah '34

Ray Young (1940-99)
The Return of the Beverly Hillbillies '81
Blue Sunshine '78
Blood of Dracula's Castle '69

Ric Young
Voodoo Moon '05
The Transporter '02
The Lost Empire '01
Chain of Command '00
The Corruptor '99
Dragon: The Bruce Lee Story '93
Drachenfutter '87
The Last Emperor '87
Ping Pong '87

Richard Young (1951-)
An Innocent Man '89
Inferno in Paradise '88
Saigon Commandos '88
Assassin '86
Love at the Top '86
Friday the 13th, Part 5: A New Beginning '85
Ninja Masters of Death '85
Final Mission '84
Cocaine Cowboys '79
Banjo Hackett '76
Night Call Nurses '72

Robert Young (1907-98)
A Conspiracy of Love '87
Little Women '78
The Second Woman '51
That Forsyte Woman '50
Sitting Pretty '48
Crossfire '47
They Won't Believe Me '47
The Enchanted Cottage '45
Those Endearing Young Charms '45
The Canterville Ghost '44
Sweet Rosie O'Grady '43
Cairo '42
Journey for Margaret '42
Lady Be Good '41
Western Union '41
The Mortal Storm '40
Northwest Passage '40
Honolulu '39
The Shining Hour '38
Three Comrades '38
The Bride Wore Red '37
Navy Blue and Gold '37
The Bride Walks Out '36
It's Love Again '36
The Secret Agent '36
Stowaway '36
Red Salute '35
Hollywood Party '34
Spitfire '34
Today We Live '33
Kid from Spain '32
Strange Interlude '32
The Black Camel '31
The Sin of Madelon Claudet '31

Roland Young (1887-1953)
St. Benny the Dip '51
Let's Dance '49
The Great Lover '49
You Gotta Stay Happy '48
And Then There Were None '45
Forever and a Day '43
They All Kissed the Bride '42
The Flame of New Orleans '41
Topper Returns '41
Two-Faced Woman '41
No, No Nanette '40
The Philadelphia Story '40
The Night of Nights '39
Topper Takes a Trip '39
Sailing Along '38
The Young in Heart '38
King Solomon's Mines '37
The Man Who Could Work Miracles '37
Topper '37
One Rainy Afternoon '36
David Copperfield '35
Ruggles of Red Gap '35
Here is My Heart '34
His Double Life '33
One Hour with You '32
Wedding Rehearsal '32
The Guardsman '31
Madam Satan '30

Sean Young (1959-)
Jesse Stone: Sea Change '07
The Drop '06
Ghosts Never Sleep '05
Third Man Out: A Donald Strachey Mystery '05
Before I Say Goodbye '03
Even Cowgirls Get the Blues '94
Headspace '02
Threat of Exposure '02
The House Next Door '01
Mockingbird Don't Sing '01
Sugar & Spice '01
Poor White Trash '00
Motel Blue '98
Men '97
Evil Has a Face '96
The Invader '96
The Proprietor '96
Dr. Jekyll and Ms. Hyde '95
Mirage '94
Model by Day '94
Rebel Run '94
Witness to the Execution '94
Ace Ventura: Pet Detective '93
Fatal Instinct '93
Hold Me, Thrill Me, Kiss Me '93
Blue Ice '92
Forever: A Ghost of a Love Story '92
Love Crimes '92

[Sean Young]
Once Upon a Crime '92
Sketch Artist '92
A Kiss Before Dying '91
Fire Birds '90
Cousins '89
The Boost '88
No Way Out '87
Wall Street '87
Baby... Secret of the Lost Legend '85
Dune '84
Blade Runner '82
Young Doctors in Love '82
Stripes '81
Jane Austen in Manhattan '80

Stephen Young (1931-2002)
Soylent Green '73
Patton '70

Tony Young (1932-2002)
Policewomen '73
Chrome and Hot Leather '71

Victor Young (1901-66)
Charlie Chan at Treasure Island '39
Charlie Chan in Honolulu '38

William Allen Young (1953-)
Fear X '03
Serving in Silence: The Margarethe Cammermeyer Story '95
Stalking Laura '93
Johnnie Gibson F.B.I. '87
Outrage! '86

Jack Youngblood (1950-)
Python Wolf '88

Barrie Youngfellow (1950-)
Lady from Yesterday '85
It Came Upon a Midnight Clear '84

Henny Youngman (1906-98)
Goodfellas '90
Amazon Women on the Moon '87
History of the World: Part 1 '81
National Lampoon Goes to the Movies '81
The Gore-Gore Girls '72
The Unkissed Bride '66
Nightmare in Blood '75

Chief Yowlachie (1891-1966)
Rose Marie '54
Red River '48
Bowery Buckaroos '47
Wild West '46
King of the Stallions '42

Gail Youngs (1953-)
Nobody's Fool '86
Belizaire the Cajun '86
Last Days of Frank & Jesse James '86
Wanderers '79

Jim Youngs (1956-)
Skeeter '93
You Talkin' to Me? '87
Hot Shot '86
Nobody's Fool '86
Hockey Night '84
A Rumor of War '84

Rongguang Yu (1958-)
Jet Li's The Enforcer '95
Iron Monkey '93
Supercop 2 '93

Chow Yun-Fat (1955-)
Pirates of the Caribbean: At World's End '07
Curse of the Golden Flower '06
Bulletproof Monk '03
Crouching Tiger, Hidden Dragon '00
Anna and the King '99
The Corruptor '99
The Replacement Killers '98
Full Contact '92
Hard-Boiled '92
Prison on Fire 2 '91
The Killer '89
Once a Thief '90
A Better Tomorrow, Part 3 '89
A Better Tomorrow, Part 2 '88
City on Fire '87
Prison on Fire '87
A Better Tomorrow, Part 1 '86
Dream Lovers '86
Hong Kong 1941 '84

Jung-ah Yum
A Tale of Two Sisters '03
Three... Extremes '04
A Texas Funeral '99

Eugenia Yuan
Mail Order Wife '04
Charlotte Sometimes '02

Roger Yuan
Bulletproof Monk '03
Shanghai Noon '00

Masayuki Yui (1947-)
To End All Wars '01
Ran '85

Jimmy Yuill
Strictly Sinatra '01
Love's Labour's Lost '00
Much Ado about Nothing '93

Johnny Yune
They Still Call Me Bruce '86
They Call Me Bruce '82

Harris Yulin (1937-)
Fur: An Imaginary Portrait of Diane Arbus '06
The Treatment '06
Game 6 '05
King of the Corner '04
The Emperor's Club '02
American Outlaws '01
Perfume '01
Rush Hour 2 '01
Training Day '01
The Million Dollar Hotel '99
The Hurricane '99
Stuart Saves His Family '94
Clear and Present Danger '94
The Last Hit '93
Final Analysis '92
There Goes the Neighborhood '92
Ghostbusters 2 '89
Another Woman '88
Bad Dreams '88
Short Fuse '88
The Believers '87
Candy Mountain '87
Fatal Beauty '87
Scarface '83
Steel '80
When Every Day Was the Fourth of July '78
Prime Time '77
Dynasty '76
St. Ives '76
Victory at Entebbe '76
Night Moves '75
Judgment in Berlin '88
Melvin Purvis: G-Man '74
Missiles of October '74
Doc '71
End of the Road '70

Ian Yule
City of Blood '88
Chain Gang Killings '85

Joe Yule (1894-1950)
Billy the Kid '41
New Moon '40

William Zabka (1965-)
Python 2 '02
High Voltage '98
The Power Within '95
Unlawful Passage '94
Shootfighter: Fight to the Death '93
Shootfighter 2: Kill or Be Killed '96
A Tiger's Tale '87
Back to School '86
The Karate Kid: Part 2 '86
Just One of the Guys '85
The Karate Kid '84
National Lampoon's European Vacation '85

Blanche Yurka (1887-1974)
At Sword's Point '51
13 Rue Madeleine '46
Men in War '57
The Southerner '45
The Bridge of San Luis Rey '44
Cry of the Werewolf '44
One Body Too Many '44
Lady for a Night '42
A Night to Remember '42
City for Conquest '40
A Tale of Two Cities '36

Rick Yune (1971-)
Die Another Day '02
The Fast and the Furious '01

Victor Sen Yung (1915-80)
Snow Falling on Cedars '99
The Letter '40
Murder over New York '40
Charlie Chan at the Wax Museum '40
Charlie Chan in Rio '41
Castle in the Desert '42
Across the Pacific '42
China '43
Betrayal from the East '44
The Hunters '58
She Demons '58

Zabou (1959-)
One Woman or Two '85
The Perils of Gwendoline '84

Grace Zabriskie (1938-)
Inland Empire '06
The Grudge '04
The Last Letter '04
No Good Deed '02
R.S.V.P. '02
They Crawl '01
Gone in 60 Seconds '00
Houdini '98
Night Siege Project: Shadowchaser 2 '94
Blood Warriors '93
Project: Shadowchaser '92
The Passion of Darkly Noon '95
Drop Zone '94
Chain of Desire '93
Hometown Boy Makes Good '93
Desert Winds '95
The Crew '95
Blood Ties '92
My Own Private Idaho '91
Wild at Heart '90
Twin Peaks: Fire Walk with Me '92
Good '93
Ambition '91

Frank Zagarino (1959-)
Lethal '04
The Stray '04
Convict 762 '98
Airboss '97
Operation: Delta Force '97
Alien Chaser '96
The Apocalypse '96
Warhead '96
Project Shadowchaser 3000 '95
Terminal Impact '95
Without Mercy '95
Never Say Die '94
Night Siege Project: Shadowchaser 2 '94
Blood Warriors '93
Project: Shadowchaser '92
Striker '88
Trained to Kill '88
Barbarian Queen '85

Pia Zadora (1954-)
Naked Gun 33 1/3: The Final Insult '94
Hairspray '88
Voyage of the Rock Aliens '87
The Lonely Lady '83
Pajama Tops '83
Butterfly '82
Fake Out '82
Santa Claus Conquers the Martians '64

Anita Zagaria
A Matter of Dignity '57
Girl in a Swing '56
Queen of Hearts '89
Maria's Child '93

Eleni Zafirou (1916-2004)

Arnon Zadok (1949-)
Torn Apart '89
Unsettled Land '88
Beyond the Walls '84

Steve Zahn (1968-)
Money Buys Happiness '99
The Last Drop '05
The Pleasure Drivers '05
Dead Fish '04
Silver City '04
Sahara '05
Speak '04
Chicken Little '05 (V)
Rescue Dawn '06
Strange Wilderness '08
A Little Stiff '91
The Mozart Brothers '86
Comanche Moon '08

Caveh Zahedi (1960-)
A Little Stiff '91

Krystyna Zachwatowicz (1930-)
Maids of Wilko '79
Man of Marble '76

Jonathan Zaccai (1970-)
The Beat My Heart Skipped '05

Ramy Zada (1958-)
Out of Sync '95
The Judas Project: The Ultimate Encounter '94
Two Evil Eyes '90
After Midnight '89
Dark Justice '91

John Zacherle (1918-)
Frankenhooker '90
Brain Damage '88 (V)
Geek Maggot Bingo '83

Del Zamora
Heat Street '87
RoboCop 2 '90
Maria's Child '93
Son of Samson '62

Dominic Zamprogna (1979-)

Gema Zamprogna (1976-)
The Pirates of Silicon Valley '99
By Way of the Stars '92
The Challengers '89

Carmen Zapata (1927-)
The Sleepy Time Gal '01
Gang Boys '92
Boulevard Nights '79
A Home of Our Own '75
Bad Charleston Charlie '73
The Last Porno Flick '74

Monica Zanchi
Zombie '80

Billy Zane (1966-)
Alien Agent '07
BloodRayne '06
Memory '06
The Last Drop '05
The Pleasure Drivers '05
Dead Fish '04
Silver City '04
Vlad '03
CQ '01
The Believer '01
Trapped '02
Zoolander '01
Titanic '97
Head Above Water '96
The Phantom '96
Danger Zone '95
The Set Up '95
Reflections in the Dark '94
Tales from the Crypt Presents Demon Knight '94
Flashfire '94
Only You '94
Tombstone '93
Running Delilah '93
Silence of the Hams '94
Betrayal of the Dove '92
Lake Consequence '92
Sniper '92
Orlando '92
Megaville '91
Blood & Concrete: A Love Story '91
Femme Fatale '90
Memphis Belle '90
Millions '90
Back to the Future, Part 2 '89
Dead Calm '89
Going Overboard '89
Brotherhood of Justice '86
Critters '86
Back to the Future '85

Philip Zanden (1954-)
Faithless '00
Like It Never Was Before '95

Fried Green Tomatoes '91
National Security '03
Shattered Glass '03
Stuart Little 2 '02 (V)
Chelsea Walls '01
Dr. Dolittle 2 '01 (V)
Joy Ride '01
Riding in Cars with Boys '01
Saving Silverman '01
Chain of Fools '00
Hamlet '00
Stuart Little '99 (V)
Happy, Texas '99
Forces of Nature '99
Out of Sight '98
Safe Men '98
You've Got Mail '98
SubUrbia '96
That Thing You Do '96
Race the Sun '96
Crimson Tide '95
Reality Bites '94

Angelo Zanolli
Son of Samson '62
Maciste in Hell '60

Bruno Zanin
Amarcord '74

Zbigniew Zamachowski (1961-)
Trois Couleurs: Blanc '94
Trois Couleurs: Rouge '94
The Decalogue '88

Roxana Zal (1969-)
Shattered Spirits '86
River's Edge '87
Table for Five '83
Testament '83

Jerry Zaks (1946-)
Crimes & Misdemeanors '89

Esti Zakheim (1965-)
Bonjour Monsieur Shlomi '03

Lisa Zane (1967-)
Monkeybone '01
The Nurse '97
The Hillside Strangler '89
Freddy's Dead: The Final Nightmare '91
Bad Influence '90
Femme Fatale '90
Wicked Ways '99
Baby Face Nelson '95
Floundering '94
Terrified '94
Unveiled '94
Nightmare '91

Lenore Zann (1959-)
The Boss Is Served '76
One Night Only '84
American Nightmare '81
Happy Birthday to Me '81

Malgorzata Zajaczkowska
Without Love '80

Zbigniew Zapasiewicz (1934-)
Without Anesthesia '78
Stand Off '89
Bartone '85

Dweezil Zappa (1969-)
The Running Man '87
Pretty in Pink '86
Jack Frost '98
The Boy Who Left Home to Find Out About the Shivers '81
Head '68

Frank Zappa (1940-93)
The Brutal Truth '99
Pretty in Pink '86
Head '68

Maya Zapata
Under the Same Moon '07
Bordertown '06
Santitos '99

Carmen Zapata (1927-)
Mother of Kings '82
Without Anesthesia '78

Moon Zappa (1967-93)

Gema Zamprogna (1976-)

William Zappa (1948-)
Heartstopper '92
Spirit of 76 '91
The Boys Next Door '85
Nightmares '83
Bootmen '00
Zone 39 '96
Crush '93
The Road Warrior '82

Dominique Zardi (1930-)
La Femme Infidele '69
Le Trou '59

John Zaremba (1908-86)
Sophisticated Gents '81
The Gallant Hours '60
20 Million Miles to Earth '57

Asher Zarfati
See Asher Tzarfati

Tony Zarindast
Werewolf '95
Hardcase and Fist '89
Kill Alex Kill '76
Danny '79

Joe Zaso (1970-)
Addicted to Murder 3: Bloodlust '99
The Alien Agenda: Endangered Species '97

David Zayas
16 Blocks '06
Angel Rodriguez '05
The Interpreter '05
Washington Heights '02

Edmund Zayenda
A Brivele der Mamen '38
Mamele '38

Robert Z'Dar (1950-)
Decay '98
American Chinatown '96
Equal Impact '96
Fugitive X '96
Red Line '96
The Mosaic Project '95
In a Moment of Passion '93
Maniac Cop 3: Badge of Silence '93
Grotesque '87
Night Stalker '87
Code Name: Zebra '84

Rosel Zech (1942-)
Salmonberries '91
The Oppermann Family '82
Veronika Voss '82

Kevin Zegers (1984-)
The Jane Austen Book Club '07
Zoom '06
Transamerica '05
Dawn of the Dead '04
The Hollow '04
The Incredible Mrs. Ritchie '03
Wrong Turn '03
Air Bud 4: Seventh Inning Fetch '02
Fear of the Dark '02
Air Bud 3: World Pup '00
MVP (Most Valuable Primate) '00
Four Days '99
Komodo '99
Treasure Island '99
Air Bud 2: Golden Receiver '98
Air Bud '97

Nora Zehetner
Beneath '07
Brick '06
Conversations with Other Women '05

Renee Zellweger (1969-)
Leatherheads '08
Bee Movie '07 (V)
Miss Potter '06
Cinderella Man '05
Bridget Jones: The Edge of Reason '04
Shark Tale '04 (V)
Cold Mountain '03
Down With Love '03
Chicago '02
White Oleander '02
Bridget Jones's Diary '01
Me, Myself, and Irene '00
Nurse Betty '00
The Bachelor '99
One True Thing '98
Deceiver '97
A Price above Rubies '97
Jerry Maguire '96
The Whole Wide World '96
Empire Records '95
The Low Life '95
The Texas Chainsaw Massacre 4: The Next Generation '95
Love and a .45 '94
Shake, Rattle & Rock! '94

Michael Zelniker
Stuar Bliss '98
Glory Enough for All: The Discovery of Insulin '92
Naked Lunch '91
Bird '88
The Terry Fox Story '83
Pick-Up Summer '79

Roschdy Zem (1965-)
Days of Glory '06
Le Petit Lieutenant '05
Monsieur N. '03

Eracio Zepeda
El Norte '83

Anthony Zerbe (1936-)
The Matrix Reloaded '03
The Matrix Revolutions '03
True Crime '99
Star Trek: Insurrection '98
Touch '96
License to Kill '89
See No Evil, Hear No Evil '89
Onassis '88
Opposing Force '87
Private Investigations '87
Steel Dawn '87
A.D. '85
Soggy Bottom U.S.A. '84
Dead Zone '83
Attica '80
Centennial '78
Child of Glass '78
KISS Meets the Phantom of the Park '78
Who'll Stop the Rain? '78
Farewell, My Lovely '75
Rooster Cogburn '75
The Parallax View '74
Papillon '73
Omega Man '71
The Liberation of L.B. Jones '70
They Call Me Mr. Tibbs! '70
Cool Hand Luke '67
Will Penny '67

Catherine Zeta-Jones (1969-)
No Reservations '07
The Legend of Zorro '05
Ocean's Twelve '04
The Terminal '04
Intolerable Cruelty '03
Sinbad: Legend of the Seven Seas '03 (V)
Chicago '02
America's Sweethearts '01
High Fidelity '00
Traffic '00
Entrapment '99
The Haunting '99
The Mask of Zorro '98
The Phantom '96
Titanic '96
Blue Juice '95
Catherine the Great '95
Catherine Cookson's The Cinder Path '94
The Return of the Native '94
Splitting Heirs '93
Christopher Columbus: The Discovery '92

Mai Zetterling (1925-94)
Hidden Agenda '90
The Witches '90
Only Two Can Play '62
Pattern for Plunder '62
Truth about Women '58
Abandon Ship '57
Frieda '47
Night Is My Future '47
Torment '44

Monica Zetterlund (1937-2005)
The New Land '73
The Emigrants '72

Fengyi Zhang (1956-)
The Emperor and the Assassin '95
Temptation of a Monk '94
Farewell My Concubine '93

Mikhail Zharov
Peter the First: Part 2 '38
Peter the First: Part 1 '37

Malik Zidi (1975-)
Changing Times '04
Almost Peaceful '02
Water Drops on Burning Rocks '99

Joseph Ziegler
Whitewash: The Clarence Brandley Story '02
Focus '01

Sonja Ziemann (1926-)
A Matter of WHO '62
Made in Heaven '52
The Merry Wives of Windsor '50

Chip Zien (1947-)
Breakfast of Champions '98
The Siege '98
Howard the Duck '86 (V)
Grace Quigley '84

Ian Ziering (1966-)
Domino '05
The Corporation '96
No Way Back '96
Subliminal Seduction '96
The Fighter '95

Madeline Zima (1985-)
A Cinderella Story '04
The Sandy Bottom Orchestra '00
Second Chances '98
Mr. Nanny '93
The Hand that Rocks the Cradle '92

Vanessa Zima (1986-)
Zoe '01
Ulee's Gold '97

Yvonne Zima (1989-)
Storm Catcher '99
The Long Kiss Goodnight '96

Efrem Zimbalist, Jr. (1923-)
Batman: Mask of the Phantasm '93 (V)
The Avenging '92
Hot Shots! '91
Shooting Stars '85
Scruples '80
The Gathering: Part 2 '79
Family Upside Down '78
Terror Out of the Sky '78
Airport '75 '75
Who Is the Black Dahlia? '75
Wait until Dark '67
By Love Possessed '61
Deep Six '58
Band of Angels '57
House of Strangers '49

Stephanie Zimbalist (1956-)
The Prophet's Game '99
Prison of Secrets '97
Dead Ahead '96
The Great Elephant Escape '95
Jericho Fever '93
The Story Lady '93
Caroline? '90
The Killing Mind '90
Personals '90
Love on the Run '85
Tomorrow's Child '82
The Awakening '80
The Babysitter '80
The Triangle Factory Fire Scandal '79
Centennial '78
Forever '78
Long Journey Back '78
Magic of Lassie '78
The Gathering '77

Constance Zimmer (1970-)
Chaos Theory '08
Home Room '02

Joey Zimmerman (1986-)
Treehouse Hostage '99
Very Bad Things '98
Mother's Boys '94

Luca Zingaretti (1961-)
Jesus '00
Artemisia '97

Victoria Zinny
Beyond the Door 3 '91
Shoot the Living, Pray for the Dead '70
Viridiana '61

William Zipp
Future Force '89
Jungle Assault '89
Operation Warzone '89
Death Chase '87
Mankillers '87

August Zirner (1956-)
The Counterfeiters '07
A Sound of Thunder '05
Mostly Martha '01
Taking Sides '01
The Promise '94
Voyager '91

Hanns Zischler (1947-)
Munich '05
Taking Sides '01
The Cement Garden '93
Francesco '93
Club Extinction '89
A Woman in Flames '84
Les Rendez-vous D'Anna '78
Kings of the Road—In the Course of Time '76

Dan Ziskie
Satan's Little Helper '04
Dangerous Passion '95
Zebrahead '92
Twisted '86

Zhang Ziyi
Memoirs of a Geisha '05
House of Flying Daggers '04
2046 '04
Hero '03
Rush Hour 2 '01
Crouching Tiger, Hidden Dragon '00

Adrian Zmed (1954-)
Storm Chasers: Revenge of the Twister '98
Improper Conduct '94
Eyewitness to Murder '93
The Other Woman '92
Bachelor Party '84
The Final Terror '83
Grease 2 '82
For the Love of It '80

Moses Znaimer (1942-)
Abraxas: Guardian of the Universe '90
Best Revenge '83

Jean-Pierre Zola (1916-79)
The Train '65
Mon Oncle '58

Michael Zorek (1960-)
Hot Moves '84
Private School '83

Louis Zorich (1924-)
Commandments '96
Cheap Shots '91
City of Hope '91
Death of a Salesman '86
The Seagull '75
Newman's Law '74
Vengeance Is Mine '74

Vera Zorina (1917-2003)
Follow the Boys '44
Louisiana Purchase '41
The Goldwyn Follies '38

Zouzou (1943-)
S*P*Y*S '74
Chloe in the Afternoon '72

Rod Zuanic (1968-)
Danny Deckchair '03
Fast Talking '86
Mad Max: Beyond Thunderdome '85

George Zucco (1886-1960)
David and Bathsheba '51
Madame Bovary '49
The Pirate '48
Who Killed Doc Robbin? '48
Lured '47
Where There's Life '47
Scared to Death '46
Fog Island '45
Having Wonderful Crime '45
House of Frankenstein '44
The Mummy's Ghost '44
Return of the Ape Man '44
The Seventh Cross '44
The Black Raven '43
Dead Men Walk '43
The Mad Ghoul '43
Sherlock Holmes in Washington '43
The Black Swan '42
The Mad Monster '42
The Mummy's Tomb '42
My Favorite Blonde '42
International Lady '41
The Monster and the Girl '41
A Woman's Face '41
The Adventures of Sherlock Holmes '39
The Hunchback of Notre Dame '39
Arrest Bulldog Drummond '38
Charlie Chan in Honolulu '38
Marie Antoinette '38
Three Comrades '38
The Bride Wore Red '37
The Firefly '37
Saratoga '37
Souls at Sea '37

David Zucker (1947-)
Airplane! '80
Kentucky Fried Movie '77

Jerry Zucker (1950-)
Airplane! '80
Kentucky Fried Movie '77

Alex Zuckerman
Freaked '93
Me and the Kid '93

Mark Zuelzke
I Got the Hook-Up '98
Sinful Intrigue '95

Daphne Zuniga (1963-)
Christmas Do-Over '06
Enemies of Laughter '00
Stand-Ins '97
Degree of Guilt '95
Charlie's Ghost: The Secret of Coronado '94
800 Leagues Down the Amazon '93
Prey of the Chameleon '91
Eyes of the Panther '90
The Fly 2 '89
Gross Anatomy '89
Staying Together '89
Last Rites '88
Spaceballs '87
Modern Girls '86
Quarterback Princess '85
The Sure Thing '85
Vision Quest '85
The Initiation '84

Jose Zuniga
Next '07
Mission: Impossible 3 '06
Constantine '05
The Hunted '03
The Crew '00
For Love or Country: The Arturo Sandoval Story '00
Gun Shy '00
Happy Accidents '00
For Which He Stands '98
Next Stop, Wonderland '98
Con Air '97
Hurricane Streets '96
Ransom '96
Blue in the Face '95
Money Train '95
Smoke '95
Crooklyn '94

Dianik Zurakowska
Orgy of the Vampires '73
The Hanging Woman '72
Cauldron of Blood '67

Ayelet Zurer
Vantage Point '08
Munich '05

Jahi JJ Zuri
Omega Doom '96
Nemesis 2: Nebula '94

Yoshitaka Zushi (1955-)
Akira Kurosawa's Dreams '90
Dodes 'ka-den '70

Brad Zutaut (1961-)
Knock Outs '92
Nudity Required '90
Hardbodies 2 '86

Noam Zylberman
Love and Hate: A Marriage Made in Hell '90
Made in Hell '90
Outside Chance of Maximillian Glick '88

Elsa Zylberstein (1969-)
Modigliani '04
Monsieur N. '03
Three Blind Mice '03
Time Regained '99
Metroland '97
Portraits Chinois '96
Farinelli '94
Mina Tannenbaum '93

The Director Index provides a complete videography for any director with more than one video credit. The listings for the director names follow an alphabetical sort by last name (although the names appear in a first name-last name format). The videographies are listed chronologically, from most recent film to directorial debut. If a director helmed more than one film in the same year, these movies are listed alphabetically within the year. Use this index in conjunction with the **Cast** (immediately preceding this index), **Writer**, and **Cinematographer** indexes (immediately following) to see where some of today's hottest directors got their starts.

Paul Aaron
In Love and War '91
Maxie '85
Deadly Force '83
Force of One '79
The Miracle Worker '79
Different Story '78

George Abbott (1887-1995)
Damn Yankees '58
The Pajama Game '57
Too Many Girls '40
The Sea God '30

Derwin Abrahams (1903-74)
Northwest Trail '46
Border Vigilantes '41

Jim Abrahams (1944-)
Mafia! '98
First Do No Harm '97
Hot Shots! Part Deux '93
Hot Shots! '91
Welcome Home, Roxy Carmichael '90
Big Business '88
Ruthless People '86
Top Secret! '84
Airplane! '80

Robert Allen Ackerman
The Reagans '04
The Roman Spring of Mrs. Stone '03
Life with Judy Garland—Me and My Shadows '01
Baby '00
Double Platinum '99
Outrage '98
Safe Passage '94

David Acomba
Night Life '90
Slipstream '73

Daniel Adams
Primary Motive '92
A Fool and His Money '89

Al Adamson (1929-95)
Lost '83
Black Eliminator '78
Cinderella 2000 '78
Hospital of Terror '78
Kill Factor '78
Black Samurai '77
Blazing Stewardesses '75
Jessi's Girls '75
The Dynamite Brothers '74
I Spit on Your Corpse '74
Angels' Wild Women '72
Blood of Ghastly Horror '72
Brain of Blood '71
Dracula vs. Frankenstein '71
Horror of the Blood Monsters '70
Blood of Dracula's Castle '69
The Female Bunch '69
Gun Riders '69
Satan's Sadists '69

Andrew Adamson (1966-)
The Chronicles of Narnia: Prince Caspian '08
The Chronicles of Narnia: The Lion, the Witch and the Wardrobe '05
Shrek 2 '04
Shrek '01

Victor Adamson (1890-1972)
Boss Cowboy '35
Lightning Bill '35
Rawhide Romance '34
Circle Canyon '33
Fighting Cowboy '33
Lightning Range '33

Joseph Adler (1950-)
Scream, Baby, Scream '69
Sex and the College Girl '64

Percy Adlon (1935-)
Younger & Younger '94
Salmonberries '91
Rosalie Goes Shopping '89
Bagdad Cafe '88
Sugarbaby '85
The Last Five Days '82
Celeste '81

Alejandro Agresti (1961-)
The Lake House '06
Valentin '02

Javier Aguirre (1935-)
The Rue Morgue Massacres '73
Dracula's Great Love '72

Mac Ahlberg (1931-)
Gangsters '79
I, a Woman '66

Alexandre Aja (1978-)
The Hills Have Eyes '06
High Tension '03

Chantal Akerman (1950-)
A Couch in New York '95
Night and Day '91
Window Shopping '86
The Eighties '83
Toute Une Nuit '82
Les Rendez-vous D'Anna '78
News from Home '76
Je Tu Il Elle '74

Moustapha Akkad (1933-2005)
Lion of the Desert '81
The Message '77

Jordan Alan (1967-)
Kiss & Tell '99
Terminal Bliss '91

Benito Alazraki (1923-)
Invasion of the Zombies '61
Spiritism '61

Bitto Albertini
Escape from Galaxy Three '81
Jungle Inferno '72

Felix Alcala (1951-)
Taken '02
Fire Down Below '97

Jason Alexander (1959-)
Just Looking '99
For Better or Worse '95

Grigori Alexandrov (1903-83)
Ten Days That Shook the World '27
The Battleship Potemkin '25

Alan Alda (1936-)
Betsy's Wedding '90
A New Life '88
Sweet Liberty '86
The Four Seasons '81

Robert Aldrich (1918-83)
...All the Marbles '81
The Frisco Kid '79
The Choirboys '77
Twilight's Last Gleaming '77
The Hustle '75
The Longest Yard '74
Emperor of the North Pole '73
Ulzana's Raid '72
The Grissom Gang '71
Too Late the Hero '70
The Killing of Sister George '69
The Dirty Dozen '67
The Flight of the Phoenix '65
Hush, Hush, Sweet Charlotte '65
Four for Texas '63
Sodom and Gomorrah '62
What Ever Happened to Baby Jane? '62
Attack! '56
Autumn Leaves '56
The Big Knife '55
Kiss Me Deadly '55
Apache '54
Vera Cruz '54

Dan Algrant (1959-)
People I Know '02
Naked in New York '93

Marcello Aliprandi
Vatican Conspiracy '81

Marc Allegret (1900-73)
Sois Belle et Tais-Toi '58
Plucking the Daisy '56
Lady Chatterley's Lover '55
The Love of Three Queens '54
Blanche Fury '48
Zou Zou '34
Fanny '32

Yves Allegret (1907-87)
The Proud Ones '53
Seven Deadly Sins '53
Dedee d'Anvers '49

Lewis Allen (1905-2000)
Another Time, Another Place '58
A Bullet for Joey '55
Illegal '55
Suddenly '54
At Sword's Point '51
The Perfect Marriage '46
Those Endearing Young Charms '45
The Uninvited '44

Kevin Allen (1962-)
Agent Cody Banks 2: Destination London '04
The Big Tease '99
Twin Town '97

Woody Allen (1935-)
Cassandra's Dream '07
Scoop '06
Match Point '05
Melinda and Melinda '05
Anything Else '03
Hollywood Ending '02
The Curse of the Jade Scorpion '01
Small Time Crooks '00
Sweet and Lowdown '99
Celebrity '98
Deconstructing Harry '97

James Nelson Algar (1913-98)
Fantasia/2000 '00
Legend of Lobo '62
The Adventures of Ichabod and Mr. Toad '49
The Legend of Sleepy Hollow '49
Fantasia '40

Debbie Allen (1950-)
The Old Settler '01
Out of Sync '95

Fred Allen (1894-1956)
The Mysterious Rider '33
Beyond the Rockies '32
Ghost Valley '32
Ride Him, Cowboy '32
Saddle Buster '32

Irwin Allen (1916-91)
Beyond the Poseidon Adventure '79
The Swarm '78
The Towering Inferno '74
Five Weeks in a Balloon '62
Voyage to the Bottom of the Sea '61

Corey Allen (1934-)
Avalanche '78
Thunder and Lightning '77

Billy Allen
See William Allen

Dave Allen (1944-99)
Puppet Master 2 '90
Dungeonmaster '83

Everyone Says I Love You '96
Mighty Aphrodite '95
Bullets over Broadway '94
Manhattan Murder Mystery '93
Husbands and Wives '92
Shadows and Fog '92
Alice '90
Crimes & Misdemeanors '89
New York Stories '89
Another Woman '88
September '88
Radio Days '87
Hannah and Her Sisters '86
The Purple Rose of Cairo '85
Broadway Danny Rose '84
Zelig '83
A Midsummer Night's Sex Comedy '82
Stardust Memories '80
Manhattan '79
Interiors '78
Annie Hall '77
Love and Death '75
Sleeper '73
Bananas '71
Take the Money and Run '69
What's Up, Tiger Lily? '66

Roger Allers
Open Season '06
The Lion King '94

Michael Almereyda (1960-)
Hamlet '00
The Eternal '99
The Eternal '99
Nadja '95
Twister '89

Pedro Almodovar (1951-)
Volver '06
Bad Education '04
Talk to Her '02
All About My Mother '99
Live Flesh '97
The Flower of My Secret '95
Kika '94
High Heels '91
Tie Me Up! Tie Me Down! '90
Women on the Verge of a Nervous Breakdown '88
Law of Desire '86
Matador '86
What Have I Done to Deserve This? '85
Dark Habits '84
Labyrinth of Passion '82
Pepi, Luci, Bom and Other Girls on the Heap '80

Paul Almond (1931-)
The Dance Goes On '92
Captive Hearts '87
Final Assignment '80
Journey '77

John A. Alonzo (1934-2001)
Blinded by the Light '82
Portrait of a Stripper '79
FM '78

Emmett Alston
Little Ninjas '92
Force of the Ninja '88
Demonwarp '87
Tigershark '87
Nine Deaths of the Ninja '85
Three Way Weekend '81
New Year's Evil '78

Robert Altman (1925-2006)
A Prairie Home Companion '06
Tanner on Tanner '04
The Company '03
Gosford Park '01
Dr. T & the Women '00
Cookie's Fortune '99
The Gingerbread Man '97
Kansas City '95
Ready to Wear '94
Short Cuts '93
The Player '92
Vincent & Theo '90
Aria '88
The Caine Mutiny Court Martial '88
Tanner '88 '88
Dumb Waiter '87
O.C. and Stiggs '87
The Room '87
Beyond Therapy '86
Fool for Love '86
Secret Honor '85
Streamers '83
Come Back to the Five & Dime Jimmy Dean, Jimmy Dean '82
Popeye '80
Quintet '79
A Wedding '78
3 Women '77
Buffalo Bill & the Indians '76
Nashville '75
Thieves Like Us '74
The Long Goodbye '73
Images '72
McCabe & Mrs. Miller '71
Brewster McCloud '70
M*A*S*H '70
That Cold Day in the Park '69
Countdown '68

Robert Alton (1906-57)
Pagan Love Song '50
Merton of the Movies '47

Keito Amamiya (1959-)
Moon over Tao '97
Cyber Ninja '94
Zeram 2 '94

Rod Amateau (1923-2003)
The Garbage Pail Kids Movie '87
High School USA '84
Lovelines '84
The Seniors '78
Drive-In '76
The Statue '71
The Bushwackers '52

Gianni Amelio (1945-)
Lamerica '95
The Stolen Children '92
Open Doors '89

Alejandro Amenabar (1972-)
The Others '01
The Sea Inside '04
Open Your Eyes '97
Thesis '96

Pino Amenta (1952-)
Heaven Tonight '93
What the Moon Saw '90
Boulevard of Broken Dreams '88
True Colors '87
My Brother Tom '86
All the Rivers Run '84
Bellamy '80

Gideon Amir
Accidents '89

Franco Amurri (1958-)
Monkey Trouble '94
Flashback '89

Julian Amyes (1917-92)
The Lady's Not for Burning '87
Jane Eyre '83
Great Expectations '81

Dominic Anciano (1959-)
Love, Honour & Obey '00
Final Cut '98

Allison Anders (1954-)
Things Behind the Sun '01
Sugar Town '99
Grace of My Heart '96
Four Rooms '95
Mi Vida Loca '94
Gas Food Lodging '92
Border Radio '88

Andy Anderson (1947-)
Positive I.D. '87
Interface '84

Bill Anderson
Warrior Queen '03
Sword of Honour '01
Melissa '97

Brad Anderson (1964-)
Masters of Horror: Sounds Like '06
The Machinist '04
Session 9 '01
Happy Accidents '00
Next Stop, Wonderland '98

Clyde (Claudio Fragasso) Anderson (1951-)
Beyond Darkness '92
Monster Dog '82

Jane Anderson (1954-)
The Prize Winner of Defiance, Ohio '05
Normal '03
If These Walls Could Talk 2 '00
The Baby Dance '98

Kurt Anderson
The Killing Grounds '97
Dead Cold '96
Open Fire '94
Bounty Tracker '93
Martial Outlaw '93
Martial Law 2: Undercover '91

Lindsay Anderson (1923-94)
Glory! Glory! '90
The Whales of August '87
Britannia Hospital '82
Look Back in Anger '80
In Celebration '75
O Lucky Man! '73
If... '69
This Sporting Life '63

Michael Anderson, Sr. (1920-)
Summer of the Monkeys '98
20,000 Leagues Under the Sea '97
The Sea Wolf '93
Young Catherine '91
The Jeweller's Shop '90
Millennium '89
Separate Vacations '86
Sword of Gideon '86
Second Time Lucky '84
Murder by Phone '82
Dominique Is Dead '79
The Martian Chronicles: Part 1 '79
The Martian Chronicles: Part 2 '79
The Martian Chronicles: Part 3 '79
Orca '77
Logan's Run '76
Conduct Unbecoming '75
Doc Savage '75
The Shoes of the Fisherman '68
The Quiller Memorandum '66
Operation Crossbow '65
The Naked Edge '61
Shake Hands with the Devil '59
The Wreck of the Mary Deare '59
Around the World in 80 Days '56
Battle Hell '56
1984 '56
Dam Busters '55

Paul Thomas Anderson (1970-)
There Will Be Blood '07
Punch-Drunk Love '02
Magnolia '99
Boogie Nights '97
Hard Eight '96

Paul W.S. Anderson (1965-)
Alien vs. Predator '04
Resident Evil '02
Soldier '98
Event Horizon '97
Mortal Kombat 1: The Movie '95
Shopping '93

Steve (Stephen M.) Anderson
Dead Men Can't Dance '97
South Central '92

Wes Anderson (1970-)
The Darjeeling Limited '07
The Life Aquatic with Steve Zissou '04
The Royal Tenenbaums '01
Rushmore '98
Bottle Rocket '95

Mario Andreacchio (1955-)
The Real Macaw '98
Napoleon '96
Fair Game '85

Jay Andrews
See Jim Wynorski

Peter Andrews
See Steven Soderbergh

Roger Andrieux (1940-)
La Petite Sirene '80
L'Amour en Herbe '77

Chris Angel (1972-)
Wishmaster 4: The Prophecy Fulfilled '02
Wishmaster 3: Beyond the Gates of Hell '01

Robert Angelo
Dead Sexy '01
Forbidden Sins '99
Mutual Needs '97

Theo Angelopoulos (1935-)
Eternity and a Day '97
Ulysses' Gaze '95
Landscape in the Mist '88
The Travelling Players '75

Ken Annakin (1914-)
The New Adventures of Pippi Longstocking '88
Pirate Movie '82
Cheaper to Keep Her '80
The Fifth Musketeer '79
Paper Tiger '74
Call of the Wild '72
Those Daring Young Men in Their Jaunty Jalopies '69
Battle of the Bulge '65
Those Magnificent Men in Their Flying Machines '65
The Longest Day '62
The Swiss Family Robinson '60
Third Man on the Mountain '59
Across the Bridge '57
Land of Fury '55
The Sword & the Rose '53
The Story of Robin Hood & His Merrie Men '52
Trio '50

Jean-Jacques Annaud (1943-)
Two Brothers '04
Enemy at the Gates '00
Seven Years in Tibet '97
The Lover '92
The Bear '89
The Name of the Rose '86
Quest for Fire '82
Hothead '78
Black and White in Color '76

Paul Annett
The Witching of Ben Wagner '95

Reverge Anselmo (1962-)
Stateside '04

David Anspaugh (1946-)
The Game of Their Lives '05
Wiseguys '02
Moonlight and Valentino '95
Rudy '93
Fresh Horses '88
Hoosiers '86

Nimrod Antal (1973-)
Vacancy '07
Kontroll '03

Franz Antel
M'Lady's Court '73
Tower of Screaming Virgins '68

Joseph Anthony (1912-93)
Tomorrow '72
All in a Night's Work '61
Career '59
The Matchmaker '58
The Rainmaker '56

Manuel Antin (1926-)
Far Away and Long Ago '74
Don Segundo Sombra '69

Pedrag (Peter) Antonijevic (1959-)
Savior '98

Lou Antonio (1934-)
Lies Before Kisses '92
A Taste for Killing '92
The Last Prostitute '91
This Gun for Hire '90
Mayflower Madam '87
Pals '87
Agatha Christie's Thirteen at Dinner '85
Between Friends '83
Breaking Up Is Hard to Do '79

Michelangelo Antonioni (1912-2007)
Eros '04
Beyond the Clouds '95
Identification of a Woman '82
The Passenger '75
Zabriskie Point '70
Blow-Up '66
The Eclipse '66
The Red Desert '64
L'Avventura '60
Il Grido '57

Judd Apatow (1968-)
Knocked Up '07
The 40 Year Old Virgin '05

Michael Apted (1941-)
Amazing Grace '06
Enough '02
Enigma '01
The World Is Not Enough '99
Always Outnumbered '98
Extreme Measures '96
Nell '94
Blink '94
Incident at Oglala: The Leonard Peltier Story '92
Thunderheart '92
Class Action '91
Gorillas in the Mist '88
Critical Condition '86
First Born '84
Gorky Park '83
Kipperbang '82
Continental Divide '81
Coal Miner's Daughter '80
Agatha '79
The Squeeze '77
Triple Echo '77

Manuel Gutierrez Aragon (1942-)
Half of Heaven '86
Demons in the Garden '82

Gregg Araki (1959-)
Smiley Face '07
Mysterious Skin '04
Splendor '99
Nowhere '96
The Doom Generation '95
Totally F***ed Up '94
The Living End '92

Vicente Aranda (1926-)
Mad Love '01
Jealousy '99
Intruso '93
Lovers: A True Story '90
If They Tell You I Fell '89
The Blood Spattered Bride '72

Alfonso Arau (1932-)
A Painted House '03
The Magnificent Ambersons '02
Picking Up the Pieces '99
A Walk in the Clouds '95
Like Water for Chocolate '93

Denys Arcand (1941-)
The Barbarian Invasions '03
Stardom '00
Love and Human Remains '93
Jesus of Montreal '89
The Decline of the American Empire '86

George Archainbaud (1890-1959)
Last of the Pony Riders '53
On Top of Old Smoky '53
Winning of the West '53
Blue Canadian Rockies '52
Night Stage to Galveston '52
Hunt the Man Down '50
Hopalong Cassidy: Silent Conflict '48
Hopalong Cassidy: Borrowed Trouble '48
Hopalong Cassidy: Dangerous Venture '48
Hopalong Cassidy: False Paradise '48
Hopalong Cassidy: Hoppy's Holiday '47
Hopalong Cassidy: The Marauders '47
Hopalong Cassidy: Unexpected Guest '47
Hopalong Cassidy: The Devil's Playground '46
Mystery Man '44
Texas Masquerade '44
The Woman of the Town '44
False Colors '43
Hoppy Serves a Writ '43
The Kansan '43
Rhythm Romance '39
Campus Confessions '38
Thanks for the Memory '38
Lost Squadron '32
The Lady Refuses '31
State's Attorney '31
The Silver Horde '30

Emile Ardolino (1943-93)
George Balanchine's The Nutcracker '93
Gypsy '93
Sister Act '92
Three Men and a Little Lady '90
Chances Are '89
Dirty Dancing '87

The Rise & Rise of Daniel Rocket '86
Rumpelstiltskin '82

Mats Arehn (1946-)
Istanbul '90
The Assignment '78

Asia Argento (1975-)
The Heart is Deceitful Above All Things '04
Scarlet Diva '00
Masters of Horror: Pelts '06

Dario Argento (1940-)
Masters of Horror: Jenifer '05
Sleepless '01
The Phantom of the Opera '98
The Stendahl Syndrome '95
Trauma '93
Two Evil Eyes '90
Opera '88
Creepers '85
Unsane '82
Inferno '80
Suspiria '77
Deep Red: Hatchet Murders '75
The Cat o' Nine Tails '71
The Bird with the Crystal Plumage '70

Allan Arkush (1948-)
Elvis Meets Nixon '98
The Temptations '98
Shake, Rattle & Rock! '94
Caddyshack 2 '88
Get Crazy '83
Heartbeeps '81
Rock 'n' Roll High School '79
Hollywood Boulevard '76
Death Sport '78

Leslie Arliss (1901-87)
A Man About the House '47
The Man in Grey '45
The Wicked Lady '45
The Night Has Eyes '42

Karen Arthur (1941-)
Lady Beware '87
A Bunny's Tale '85
Bridge to Silence '89
Dream '92

Miguel Arteta (1965-)
The Good Girl '02
Chuck & Buck '00
Star Maps '97

Newton Arnold (1928-2000)
Hands of a Stranger '62

Adolfo Aristarain (1943-)
Martin (Hache) '97
A Place in the World '92
The Stranger '87
Time for Revenge '82
The Lion's Share '79

George Armitage (1942-)
The Big Bounce '04
Grosse Pointe Blank '97
Miami Blues '90
Hot Rod '79
Private Duty Nurses '71

Gillian Armstrong (1950-)
Death Defying Acts '07
Charlotte Gray '01
Oscar and Lucinda '97
Little Women '94
The Last Days of Chez Nous '92
Fires Within '91
High Tide '87
Mrs. Soffel '84
Starstruck '82
My Brilliant Career '79

Montxo Armendariz (1949-)
Secrets of the Heart '97
Letters from Alou '90

Moira Armstrong (1930-)
A Village Affair '95
Body & Soul '93

Gwen Arner
Necessary Parties '88

Frank Arnold (1938-)
A Matter of Principle '83
My Champion '81

Jack Arnold (1916-92)
A Waltz Through the Hills '88
The 27th Day '57
Swiss Conspiracy '77
Games Girls Play '75
Boss '74
Bachelor in Paradise '63
A Global Affair '63
Monster on the Campus '59
The Mouse That Roared '59
No Name on the Bullet '59
High School Confidential '58
The Incredible Shrinking Man '57
Man in the Shadow '57
Revenge of the Creature '55
Tarantula '55
Creature from the Black Lagoon '54
It Came from Outer Space '53

Anthony Asquith (1902-68)
The Yellow Rolls-Royce '64
The V.I.P.'s '63
The Millionairess '60
Carrington, V.C. '54
The Importance of Being Earnest '52
The Browning Version '51
The Winslow Boy '48
The Demi-Paradise '43
We Dive at Dawn '43
Cottage to Let '41
Pygmalion '38

Darren Aronofsky (1969-)
The Fountain '06
Requiem for a Dream '00
Pi '98

Dorothy Arzner (1897-1979)
First Comes Courage '43
Dance, Girl, Dance '40
The Bride Wore Red '37
Craig's Wife '36
Christopher Strong '33
Merrily We Go to Hell '32

Anthony Ascot
See Giuliano Carnimeo

Ash (1964-)
Pups '99
Bang '95

Kelly Asbury (1960-)
Shrek 2 '04
Spirit: Stallion of the Cimarron '02

David Attwood (1952-)
Fidel '02
The Hound of the Baskervilles '02
Shot Through the Heart '98
Moll Flanders '96
Wild Rose '86

Jacques Audiard (1952-)
The Beat My Heart Skipped '05
Read My Lips '01
A Self-Made Hero '95
See How They Fall '94

Richard Attenborough (1923-)
Closing the Ring '07
Grey Owl '99
In Love and War '96
Shadowlands '93
Chaplin '92
Cry Freedom '87
A Chorus Line '85
Gandhi '82
Magic '78
A Bridge Too Far '77
Young Winston '72
Oh! What a Lovely War '69

Yvan Attal (1965-)
Happily Ever After '04
My Wife is an Actress '01

Mark Atkins
Evil Eyes '04

Francisco Athié (1956-)
Optic Fiber '97
Lolo '92

Doug Atchison
Akeelah and the Bee '06

Ovidio G. Assonitis (1943-)
Madhouse '87
Desperate Moves '86
Tentacles '77
Beyond the Door '75
Forever Emmanuelle '75

Olivier Assayas (1955-)
Clean '04
Demonlover '02
Les Destinées '00
Late August, Early September '98
Irma Vep '95

Steve Austin
The Stranger '10

Igor Auzins (1949-)
Night Orchid '97
We of the Never Never '82
High Rolling in a Hot Corvette '77

Roger Avary (1965-)
The Rules of Attraction '02
Killing Zoe '94

Pupi Avati (1938-)
Incantato '03
The Best Man '97
The Story of Boys & Girls '91
Bix '90
Revenge of the Dead '84
Zeder '83

Aram Avakian (1926-87)
11 Harrowhouse '74
Cops and Robbers '73
End of the Road '70

Sam Auster
Screen Test '85

Paul Auster (1947-)
Lulu on the Bridge '98
Blue in the Face '95

Ray Austin (1932-)
Highlander: The Gathering '92
The Virgin Witch '70
Night Nurse '77
The Red Inn '51

Claude Autant-Lara (1901-2000)
Sylvia and the Phantom '45
The Red and the Black '57
Four Bags Full '56
Seven Deadly Sins '53
Devil in the Flesh '46

Jon Avnet (1949-)
88 Minutes '08
Up Close and Personal '96
The War '94
Fried Green Tomatoes '91

Gabriel Axel (1918-)
Babette's Feast '87
Royal Deceit '94

David Ayer (1972-)
Street Kings '08
Harsh Times '05

George Axelrod (1922-2003)
The Secret Life of an American Wife '68
Lord Love a Duck '66

Mario Azzopardi (1950-)
Savage Messiah '02
Stiletto Dance '01
Thrill Seekers '99
Total Recall 2070: Machine Dreams '99
Bone Daddy '97
Nowhere to Hide '83
Deadline '82

Jamie Babbit (1970-)
The Quiet '05
But I'm a Cheerleader '99

Hector Babenco (1946-)
Carandiru '03
At Play in the Fields of the Lord '91
Ironweed '87
Kiss of the Spider Woman '85
Pixote '81

Beth B (1955-)
Two Small Bodies '93
Salvation! '87
Vortex '81

Lloyd Bacon (1890-1955)
Action in the North Atlantic '43
The Fighting Sullivans '42
Silver Queen '42
She Couldn't Say No '52
The Fuller Brush Girl '50
Kill the Umpire '50
It Happens Every Spring '49
Miss Grant Takes Richmond '49
Knute Rockne: All American '40
Oklahoma Kid '39
Boy Meets Girl '38
A Slight Case of Murder '38
Marked Woman '37
42nd Street '33
Footlight Parade '33
Picture Snatcher '33

Kevin Bacon (1958-)
Loverboy '05

Graham Baker
Beowulf '98
Born to Ride '91
Alien Nation '88
Impulse '84
The Final Conflict '81

King Baggot (1879-1948)
Tumbleweeds '25

Reza Badiyi (1936-)
Policewoman Centerfold '83
Of Mice and Men '81

Max Baer, Jr. (1937-)
Hometown U.S.A. '79
Ode to Billy Joe '76
The McCullochs '75

John Bailey (1942-)
China Moon '91
Search for Signs of Intelligent Life in the Universe '91

Fenton Bailey
Inside Deep Throat '05
Party Monster '03

Stuart Baird (1947-)
Star Trek: Nemesis '02
U.S. Marshals '98
Executive Decision '96

David Baker (1931-)
Dead Enemies '36
Air Hawk '84

Charles "Chuck" Bail
Street Corner Justice '96
Choke Canyon '86
Gumball Rally '76
Cleopatra Jones & the Casino of Gold '75

Roy Ward Baker (1916-)
The Monster Club '85
The Vampire Lovers '70
The Scars of Dracula '70
The Legend of the 7 Golden Vampires '73
Asylum '72
Dr. Jekyll and Sister Hyde '71
And Now the Screaming Starts '73
Vault of Horror '73
The Anniversary '67
A Night to Remember '58
Don't Bother to Knock '52
Morning Departure '50
One That Got Away '57
The Weaker Sex '49
The October Man '48

Robert S. Baker (1916-)
The Flame Trees of Thika '81
Danger UXB '81
The Hellfire Club '61
Jack the Ripper '60
Blackout '50

Clarence Badger (1880-1964)
It '27
Hands Up '26
Paths to Paradise '25

John Badham (1939-)
Teddy at the Throttle '16
Brother's Keeper '22
The Jack Bull '99
The Last Debate '00
Incognito '97
Nick of Time '95
Drop Zone '94
Another Stakeout '93
The Hard Way '91
Bird on a Wire '90
Stakeout '87
Short Circuit '86
American Flyers '85
Blue Thunder '83
WarGames '83
Whose Life Is It Anyway? '81
Dracula '79
Saturday Night Fever '77
Bingo Long Traveling All-Stars & Motor Kings '76
Reflections of Murder '74
The Notorious Lady '27
Human Hearts '25

John Mallory Asher (1971-)
Diamonds '99
Dirty Love '05

William Asher (1921-)
Movers and Shakers '85
Night Warning '82
Fireball 500 '66
Beach Blanket Bingo '65
How to Stuff a Wild Bikini '65
Bikini Beach '64

Hal Ashby (1930-88)
8 Million Ways to Die '85
The Slugger's Wife '85
Lookin' to Get Out '82
Being There '79
Coming Home '78
Bound for Glory '76
Shampoo '75
The Last Detail '73
Harold and Maude '71
The Landlord '70

John H. Auer (1906-75)
City That Never Sleeps '53
Seven Days Ashore '44

Hy Averback (1925-97)
Where the Boys Are '84
She's in the Army Now '81
A Guide for the Married Woman '73
Suppose They Gave a War and Nobody Came? '70
I Love You, Alice B. Toklas! '68
Chamber of Horrors '66

Brian Avenet-Bradley
Dark Remains '05
Ghost of the Needle '03

Rick Avery
Deadly Outbreak '96
The Expert '95
The Power of One '92
Rocky 5 '90
The Karate Kid: Part 3 '89

John G. Avildsen (1935-)
8 Seconds '94
The Karate Kid: Part 2 '86
The Karate Kid '84
A Night in Heaven '83
Neighbors '81
Rocky '76
Save the Tiger '73
Joe '70
Cry Uncle '71
Guess What We Learned in School Today? '70
The Zany Adventures of Robin Hood '84
Return of the Man from U.N.C.L.E. '83
House of the Living Dead '73
The Mummy's Revenge '73
Horror Rises from the Tomb '72

Howard (Hikmet) Avedis
Mortuary '81
Separate Ways '82
They're Playing with Fire '84
Scorchy '76
Texas Detour '77
The Specialist '75
The Teacher '74
The Stepmother '71
The Fifth Floor '80

Joe Mari Avellana
Fist of Glory '95
Blackbelt 2: Fatal Force '93

Carlos Aured (1937-)
House of Psychotic Women '73
Curse of the Devil '73

Frank Arner
(see entries above)

Josh Kirby... Time Warrior, Chapter 3, Trapped on Toyworld '95
Beach Party '63
Muscle Beach Party '64

Ralph Bakshi (1938-)
Cool and the Crazy '94
Cool World '92
Fire and Ice '83
Hey Good Lookin' '82
American Pop '81
The Lord of the Rings '78
Wizards '77
Streetfight '75
Heavy Traffic '73
Fritz the Cat '72
Bob Balaban (1945-)
Bernard and Doris '08
Subway Stories '97
The Last Good Time '94
My Boyfriend's Back '93
Parents '89
The Stranger from Venus '54
Alexsei Balabanov (1959-)
Of Freaks and Men '98
Brother '97
Gianfranco Baldanello (1928-)
The Uranium Conspiracy '78
Great Adventure '75
Death Ray '67
Ferdinando Baldi (1917-2007)
Treasure of the Four Crowns '82
Sicilian Connection '72
Texas, Adios '66
Duel of Champions '61
Marcello Baldi
Saul and David '64
Venus Against the Son of Hercules '62
Richard Ballard (1929-)
Too Pretty to Be Honest '72
Scandal Man '67
L'Odeur des Fauves '66
Peter Baldwin (1929-)
Meet Wally Sparks '97
A Very Brady Christmas '88
Lots of Luck '85
Rafael Baledon, Sr. (1919-95)
The Man and the Monster '65
Swamp of the Lost Monster '65
The Curse of the Crying Woman '61
Carroll Ballard (1937-)
Duma '05
Fly Away Home '96
Wind '92
Nutcracker: The Motion Picture '86
Never Cry Wolf '83
The Black Stallion '79
I Bury the Living '58
Charles Band (1952-)
The Creeps '97
Hideous '97
Dollman vs Demonic Toys '93
Prehysteria '93
Robot Wars '93
Doctor Mordrid: Master of the Unknown '90
Crash and Burn '90
Doctor Mordrid: Master of the Unknown '90
Meridian: Kiss of the Beast '90
Trancers 2: The Return of Jack Deth '90
Trancers '84
Dungeonmaster '83

Metalstorm: The Destruction of Jared Syn '83
Parasite '82
The Alchemist '81
Mirra Bank
Enormous Changes '83
Trumps '83
Norberto Barba (1963-)
Lost in the Bermuda Triangle '98
Solo '96
Blue Tiger '94
Ernie Barbarash
Stir of Echoes 2: The Homecoming '07
Cube: Zero '04
Uri Barbash
Unsettled Land '88
Beyond the Walls '84
Randy Barbato
Inside Deep Throat '05
Party Monster '03
Joseph Barbera (1911-)
Jetsons: The Movie '90
Hey There, It's Yogi Bear '64
Paris Barclay (1956-)
The Cherokee Kid '96
America's Dream '95
Don't Be a Menace to South Central While Drinking Your Juice in the Hood '95
Clive Barker (1952-)
Lord of Illusions '95
Nightbreed '90
Hellraiser '87
Mike Barker (1966-)
Shattered '07
A Good Woman '04
Lorna Doone '01
Best Laid Plans '99
The Tenant of Wildfell Hall '96
Reginald Barker (1886-1945)
Healer '36
Seven Keys to Baldpate '29
Civilization '16
The Bargain '15
The Italian '15
On the Night Stage '15
The Wrath of the Gods '14
Boris Barnet (1902-65)
The Patriots '33
Steve Barnett (1955-)
Scanner Cop 2: Volkin's Revenge '94
Scanners: The Showdown '94
Mission of Justice '92
Mindwarp '91
Hollywood Boulevard 2 '89
Emmanuelle 5 '87
Neema Barnette (1949-)
Civil Brand '02
Run for the Dream: The Gail Devers Story '96
Spirit Lost '96
Better Off Dead '94
Sin and Redemption '94
Zora Is My Name! '90
Allen Baron (1935-)
Foxfire Light '82
Red, White & Busted '75
Blast of Silence '61
Douglas Barr (1949-)
Dead Badge '94
Bruno Barreto (1955-)
View from the Top '03
Bossa Nova '99
One Tough Cop '98
Four Days in September '97
Carried Away '95
A Show of Force '90
The Story of Fausta '88
Happily Ever After '86
Gabriela '84
Amor Bandido '79

Dona Flor and Her Two Husbands '78
Fabio Barreto (1957-)
O Quatrilho '95
Luzia '88
Steven Barron (1956-)
Arabian Nights '00
Merlin '98
The Adventures of Pinocchio '96
Coneheads '93
Teenage Mutant Ninja Turtles: The Movie '90
Electric Dreams '84
Zelda Barron (1929-2006)
Forbidden Sun '89
Shag: The Movie '89
Bulldance '88
Ian Barry
The Diamond of Jeru '01
Joey '98
Robo Warriors '96
Blackwater Trail '95
Crime Broker '94
Crimebroker '94
Wrangler '88
Paul Bartel (1938-2000)
Scenes from the Class Struggle in Beverly Hills '89
The Longshot '86
Lust in the Dust '85
Not for Publication '84
Eating Raoul '82
Cannonball '76
Death Race 2000 '75
Private Parts '72
Paul Bartel's The Secret Cinema '69
Andrzej Bartkowiak (1950-)
Doom '05
Cradle 2 the Grave '03
Exit Wounds '01
Romeo Must Die '00
Hall Bartlett (1922-93)
Children of Sanchez '79
Jonathan Livingston Seagull '73
Changes '69
All the Young Men '60
Zero Hour! '57
Richard Bartlett (1922-94)
Ollie Hopnoodle's Haven of Bliss '88
Rock, Pretty Baby '56
Lonesome Trail '55
Silver Star '55
Charles T. Barton (1902-81)
The Shaggy Dog '59
Toby Tyler '59
Dance with Me, Henry '56
Ma and Pa Kettle at the Fair '52
Double Crossbones '51
Abbott and Costello Meet the Killer, Boris Karloff '49
Africa Screams '49
Abbott and Costello Meet Frankenstein '48
Mexican Hayride '48
The Noose Hangs High '48
Buck Privates Come Home '47
The Wistful Widow of Wagon Gap '47
The Time of Their Lives '46
Louisiana Hayride '44
Harmon of Michigan '41
Helltown '38
Forlorn River '37
Thunder Pass '37
Thunder Trail '37
Desert Gold '36
Wagon Wheels '34
K.C. Bascombe
Fear of the Dark '02
Swindle '02

The Contract '98
Harry Basil
Soul's Midnight '06
The 4th Tenor '02
Jules Bass (1935-)
Flight of Dragons '82
The Last Unicorn '82
The Return of the King '80
The Hobbit '78
Mad Monster Party '68
Lawrence Bassoff
Hunk '87
Weekend Pass '84
Bradley Battersby (1953-)
Red Letters '00
Blue Desert '91
Roy Battersby
Red Mercury '05
Catherine Cookson's The Moth '96
Cracker: Brotherly Love '95
Catherine Cookson's The Black Candle '92
Mr. Love '86
Winter Flight '84
Giacomo Battiato (1943-)
Blood Ties '87
Hearts & Armour '83
Noah Baumbach (1969-)
Margot at the Wedding '07
The Squid and the Whale '05
Mr. Jealousy '98
Highball '97
Kicking and Screaming '95
Lamberto Bava (1944-)
Ghost Son '06
Demons 2 '87
Demons '86
Blastfighter '85
Devilfish '84
A Blade in the Dark '83
Macabre '80
Mario Bava (1914-80)
Shock '79
Lisa and the Devil '75
Torture Chamber of Baron Blood '72
Twitch of the Death Nerve '71
Five Dolls for an August Moon '70
Hatchet for the Honeymoon '70
Four Times That Night '69
Danger: Diabolik '68
Kill, Baby, Kill '66
Knives of the Vampires '65
Planet of the Vampires '65
Black Sabbath '64
Blood and Black Lace '64
Hercules in the Haunted World '64
Much '63
The Invaders '63
The Whip and the Body '63
The Wonders of Aladdin '61
Black Sunday '60
Craig R. Baxley (1949-)
The Diary of Ellen Rimbauer '03
Sniper 2 '02
Stephen King's Rose Red '02
Stephen King's The Storm of the Century '99
Under Pressure '98
Twilight Man '96
The Avenging Angel '95
Deconstructing Sarah '94
Deep Red '94
Stone Cold '91
I Come in Peace '90
Action Jackson '88
John Baxter (1896-1975)
Love on the Dole '41
Old Mother Riley's Ghosts '41

Michael Bay (1965-)
Transformers '07
The Island '05
Bad Boys 2 '03
Pearl Harbor '01
Armageddon '98
The Rock '96
Bad Boys '95
Rolf Bayer
Pacific Inferno '85
The Kill '73
Stephen Bayly (1942-)
Diamond's Edge '88
Coming Up Roses '87
David Beaird (1952-)
Scorchers '92
It Takes Two '88
Pass the Ammo '88
My Chauffeur '86
Party Animal '83
Octavia '82
Alan Beattie
Stand Alone '85
Delusion '84
Warren Beatty (1937-)
Bulworth '98
Dick Tracy '90
Reds '81
Heaven Can Wait '78
William Beaudine (1892-1970)
Billy the Kid Versus Dracula '66
Jesse James Meets Frankenstein's Daughter '65
Lassie's Great Adventure '62
Ten Who Dared '60
Westward Ho, the Wagons! '56
Bela Lugosi Meets a Brooklyn Gorilla '52
Here Come the Marines '52
Ghost Chasers '51
Blues Busters '50
Smugglers' Cove '48
Spook Busters '48
Bowery Buckaroos '47
Hard-Boiled Mahoney '47
Infamous Crimes '47
Mom & Dad '44
Follow the Leader '44
Ghost Crazy '44
The Ape Man '43
Clancy Street Boys '43
Ghost on the Loose '43
Here Comes Kelly '43
Spotlight Scandals '43
Spotlight Scandals '43
Miracle Kid '42
The Panther's Claw '42
Phantom Killer '42
Turf Boy '42
Desperate Cargo '41
Misbehaving Husbands '41
Robot Pilot '41
Sparrows '26
Little Annie Rooney '25
The Country Kid '23
Gabrielle Beaumont (1942-)
Beastmaster 3: The Eye of Braxus '95
Riders '88
He's My Girl '87
Gone Are the Days '84
Death of a Centerfold '81
The Godsend '79
Harry Beaumont (1888-1966)
The Show-Off '46
When's Your Birthday? '37
Dance Fools Dance '31
Laughing Sinners '31
Broadway Melody '29
Our Dancing Daughters '28
Beau Brummel '24
Gorman Bechard (1959-)
Cemetery High '89
Disconnected '87
Galactic Gigolo '87
Psychos in Love '87

Martin Beck
Last Game '80
Challenge '74
Steve Beck
Ghost Ship '02
13 Ghosts '01
Harold Becker (1950-)
Domestic Disturbance '01
Mercury Rising '98
City Hall '95
Malice '93
Sea of Love '89
The Boost '88
Big Town '87
Vision Quest '85
Taps '81
The Black Marble '79
The Onion Field '79
Jacques Becker (1906-60)
Le Trou '59
Modigliani '58
Ali Baba and the 40 Thieves '54
Grisbi '53
Casque d'Or '52
Rendez-vous de Juillet '49
Antoine et Antoinette '47
Jean Becker (1938-)
Elisa '94
One Deadly Summer '83
Josh Becker (1958-)
Lunatics: A Love Story '92
Thou Shalt Not Kill...Except '87
Walt Becker (1968-)
Wild Hogs '07
Buying the Cow '02
National Lampoon's Van Wilder '02
James Becket (1936-)
Final Approach '04
Plato's Run '96
Natural Causes '94
Ulterior Motives '92
James Gavin Bedford
The Street King '02
Red Shoe Diaries 8: Night of Abandon '97
Ford Beebe (1888-1978)
Red Desert '50
Outlaw Gang '49
Shep Comes Home '49
My Dog Shep '46
The Invisible Man's Revenge '44
Don Winslow of the Coast Guard '43
Don Winslow of the Navy '43
Night Monster '42
Overland Mail '42
The Masked Rider '41
Riders of Death Valley '41
Fantasia '40
Flash Gordon Conquers the Universe '40
Junior G-Men '40
Space Soldiers Conquer the Universe '40
Winners of the West '40
Buck Rogers Conquers the Universe '39
Destination Saturn '39
Flash Gordon: Mars Attacks the World '39
The Green Hornet '39
The Phantom Creeps '39
Red Barry '38
Radio Patrol '37
Tim Tyler's Luck '37
Ace Drummond '36
The Man from Gun Town '36
Greg Beeman (1962-)
Miracle in Lane Two '00
Brink '98
Bushwhacked '95
Mom and Dad Save the World '92
License to Drive '88

Charles Beeson
Cider with Rosie '99
Second Sight '99
Agatha Christie's The Pale Horse '06

Jean-Jacques Beineix (1946-)
Betty Blue '86
Moon in the Gutter '83
Diva '82

Timur Bekmambetov
Day Watch '06
Night Watch '04
Wanted '08

Arnold Belgard (1907-67)

Martin Bell
Brotherhood of Murder '99
Hidden in America '96
American Heart '92
Streetwise '84

Monta Bell (1891-1958)
Personal Maid '31
The King on Main Street '25

Earl Bellamy (1917-2003)
Desperate Women '78
Speedtrap '78
Fire '77
Sidewinder One '77
Flood! '76
Against a Crooked Sky '75
Seven Alone '75
Walking Tall: Part 2 '75
The Trackers '71
Munster, Go Home! '66
Justice of the West '61

Donald P. Bellisario (1935-)
JAG '95
Last Rites '88

Marco Bellocchio (1939-)
Devil in the Flesh '87
Henry IV '85
The Eyes, the Mouth '83

Jerry Belson (1938-2006)
Surrender '87
Jekyll & Hyde... Together Again '82

Laszlo Benedek (1907-92)
Assault on Agathon '75
The Night Visitor '70
Daring Game '68
Namu, the Killer Whale '66

Joel Bender
Karla '06
Midnight Kiss '93
Rich Girl '91
The Immortalizer '89
Gas Pump Girls '79

Jack Bender
My Little Assassin '99
It Came from the Sky '98
A Call to Remember '97
Killing Mr. Griffin '97

Roberto Benigni (1952-)
The Tiger and the Snow '05
Pinocchio '02
Life Is Beautiful '98
The Monster '96
Johnny Stecchino '92

Richard Benjamin (1938-)
Marci X '03
The Pentagon Wars '98
Tourist Trap '98
Mrs. Winterbourne '96
Milk Money '94
Made in America '93
Mermaids '90
Downtown '89
Little Nikita '88
My Stepmother Is an Alien '88
City Heat '84
Racing with the Moon '84
My Favorite Year '82

Richard Benner (1943-90)
Happy Birthday, Gemini '80
Outrageous! '77

Compton Bennett (1900-74)
King Solomon's Mines '50
The Seventh Veil '46

Rodney Bennett
Monsignor Quixote '91

Edward Bennett (1950-)
The Scarlet Pimpernel '99
A Woman at War '94

Bill Bennett (1953-)
The Nugget '02
Tempted '01
In a Savage Land '99
Kiss or Kill '97
Two If by Sea '95
Backlash '86

Spencer Gordon Bennett (1893-1987)
Atomic Submarine '59
Submarine Seahawk '59
King of the Congo '52
Atom Man vs. Superman '50
Pirates of the High Seas '50
The Black Widow '47
Son of Zorro '47
Daughter of Don Q '46
King of the Forest Rangers '46
The Phantom Rider '46
D-Day on Mars '45
Manhunt of Mystery Island '45
The Purple Monster Strikes '45
Perils of the Darkest Jungle '44
Zorro's Black Whip '44
California Joe '43
Calling Wild Bill Elliott '43
Manhunt in the African Jungles '43
The Masked Marvel '43
The Secret Code '42
Arizona Bound '41
Gunman from Bodie '41
Across the Plains '39
Zorro Rides Again '37
The Unknown Ranger '36
Get That Man '35
The Fighting Rookie '34
Last Frontier '32
Midnight Warning '32
Rogue of the Rio Grande '30
Markac Money '28

Richard Benson (1924-)
Werewolf in a Girl's Dormitory '61
The Day the Sky Exploded '57

Robby Benson (1956-)
Modern Love '90
White Hot '88

Thomas Bentley (1880-1950)
Murder at the Baskervilles '37
The Old Curiosity Shop '35
The Living Dead '33

Robert Benton (1932-)
Feast of Love '07
The Human Stain '03
Twilight '98
Nobody's Fool '94
Billy Bathgate '91
Nadine '87
Places in the Heart '84
Still of the Night '82
Kramer vs. Kramer '79
The Late Show '77
Bad Company '72

Luca Bercovici (1957-)
Luck of the Draw '00
Bitter Sweet '98
Convict 762 '98
The Granny '94
Dark Tide '93
Rockula '90
Ghoulies '85

Bruce Beresford (1940-)
The Contract '07
And Starring Pancho Villa as Himself '03
Evelyn '02
Bride of the Wind '01
Double Jeopardy '99
Paradise Road '97
Last Dance '96
A Good Man in Africa '94
Silent Fall '94
Rich in Love '93
Black Robe '91
Mister Johnson '91
Driving Miss Daisy '89
Her Alibi '88
Aria '88
Crimes of the Heart '86
The Fringe Dwellers '86
King David '85
Tender Mercies '83
The Club '81
Puberty Blues '81
Breaker Morant '80
Money Movers '78
The Getting of Wisdom '78
Don's Party '76
Barry McKenzie Holds His Own '74

William Berke (1903-58)
The Lost Missile '58
The Marshal's Daughter '53
FBI Girl '52
Jungle Jim '52
Bandit Queen '51
Pier 23 '51
Roaring City '51
Savage Drums '51
Border Rangers '50
Deputy Marshal '50
Gunfire '50
I Shot Billy the Kid '50
Operation Haylift '50
Treasure of Monte Cristo '50
Sky Liner '49
Highway 13 '48
Rolling Home '48
Shoot to Kill '47
Renegade Girl '46
Dick Tracy, Detective '45
Betrayal from the East '45
Dangerous Passage '44
Dark Mountain '44
The Falcon in Mexico '44
Navy Way '44
Gun Girl '36
Toll of the Desert '35

Peter Berg (1964-)
Hancock '08
The Kingdom '07
Friday Night Lights '04
The Rundown '03
Very Bad Things '98

Pamela Berger
The Imported Bridegroom '89
The Magic Stone '95

Andrew Bergman (1945-)
Isn't She Great '00
Striptease '96
It Could Happen to You '94
Honeymoon in Vegas '92
The Freshman '90
So Fine '81

Daniel Bergman (1962-)
Expectations '97
Sunday's Children '94

Ingmar Bergman (1918-2007)
Saraband '03
After the Rehearsal '84
Fanny and Alexander '83
From the Life of the Marionettes '80
Autumn Sonata '78
The Serpent's Egg '78
Face to Face '76
The Magic Flute '73
Scenes from a Marriage '73
Cries and Whispers '72
The Touch '71
The Passion of Anna '70
The Rite '69
The Shame '68
Hour of the Wolf '68
Persona '66
The Silence '63
Winter Light '62
Through a Glass Darkly '61
The Devil's Eye '60
The Virgin Spring '59
The Magician '58
Brink of Life '57
Wild Strawberries '57
The Seventh Seal '56
Dreams '55
Smiles of a Summer Night '55
Lesson in Love '54
Sawdust & Tinsel '53
Monika '52
Secrets of Women '52
Summer Interlude '50
To Joy '50
Devil's Wanton '49
Three Strange Loves '49
Fort of Call '48
Night Is My Future '47

Shari Springer Berman
American Splendor '03
The Nanny Diaries '07

Ted Berman (1920-2001)
The Black Cauldron '85
The Fox and the Hound '81

Monty Berman (1912-2006)
The Hellfire Club '61
Jack the Ripper '60

Edward L. Bernds (1905-2000)
The Three Stooges Meet Hercules '61
The Three Stooges in Orbit '62
Return of the Fly '59
Queen of Outer Space '58
Storm Rider '57
Bowery Boys Meet the Monsters '54
Clipped Wings '53
Gold Raiders '51
Blondie Hits the Jackpot '49

Jack Bernhard (1920-)
Unknown Island '48
Decoy '46

Curtis Bernhardt (1899-1981)
Kisses for My President '64
Interrupted Melody '55
Beau Brummell '54
Miss Sadie Thompson '53
The Merry Widow '52
Sirocco '51
The Possessed '47
My Reputation '46
A Stolen Life '46
Conflict '45

Adam Bernstein (1960-)
Six Ways to Sunday '99
It's Pat: The Movie '94

Armyan Bernstein
Cross My Heart '88
Windy City '84

Walter Bernstein (1919-)
Women & Men: In Love '91
Little Miss Marker '80

Claude Berri (1934-)
The House-keeper '02
Lucie Aubrac '98
Germinal '93
Uranus '91
Jean de Florette '87
Manon of the Spring '87
Tchao Pantin '84
I Love All of You '83
One Wild Moment '78
Le Sex Shop '73
Marry Me, Marry Me '69
The Two of Us '68

Busby Berkeley (1895-1976)
Take Me Out to the Ball Game '49
The Gang's All Here '43
For Me and My Gal '42
Babes on Broadway '41
Strike Up the Band '40
Babes in Arms '39
They Made Me a Criminal '39
Gold Diggers of 1935 '35
Stage Struck '35

Abby Berlin (1907-65)
Double Deal '50
Blondie Knows Best '46

Alain Berliner (1963-)
Passion of Mind '00
Ma Vie en Rose '97

Joe Berlinger (1961-)
Metallica: Some Kind of Monster '04
Book of Shadows: Blair Witch 2 '00
Brother's Keeper '92

Edward Bianchi (1942-)
Off and Running '90
The Fan '81

Bill Berry
Off the Mark '87

John Berry (1917-99)
Boesman & Lena '00
A Captive in the Land '91
Honeyboy '82
Angel on My Shoulder '80
The Bad News Bears Go to Japan '78
Maya '66
Tamango '59
Pantaloons '57
There Goes Barder '54
Tension '50
Casbah '48

Tom Berry
Twin Sisters '91
The Amityville Curse '90
Blind Fear '89

Bernardo Bertolucci (1940-)
The Dreamers '03
Besieged '98
Stealing Beauty '96
Little Buddha '93
The Sheltering Sky '90
The Last Emperor '87
The Tragedy of a Ridiculous Man '81
Luna '79
1900 '76
Last Tango in Paris '73
The Conformist '71
The Spider's Stratagem '70
Partner '68
Before the Revolution '65
The Grim Reaper '62

Irvin Berwick (1914-)
Malibu High '79
The 7th Commandment '61
The Monster of Piedras Blancas '57

Luc Besson (1959-)
Angel-A '05
Arthur and the Invisibles '06
The Messenger: The Story of Joan of Arc '99
The Fifth Element '97
The Professional '94
La Femme Nikita '91
The Big Blue '88
Subway '85
Le Dernier Combat '84

Gil Bettman
Night Vision '97
Crystal Heart '87
Never Too Young to Die '86

Jonathan Betuel (1949-)
Theodore Rex '95
My Science Project '85

Troy Beyer (1965-)
Love Don't Cost a Thing '03
Let's Talk About Sex '98

Frank Beyer (1932-2006)
Jacob the Liar '74
Trace of Stones '66
Carbide and Sorrel '63
Five Cartridges '60

Thomas Bezucha
The Family Stone '05
Big Eden '00

Radha Bharadwaj
Basil '98
Closet Land '90

Andrea Bianchi (1925-)
Burial Ground '85
Cry of a Prostitute: Love Kills '72

Roberto Bianchi
See Roberto Bianchi Montero

Herbert Biberman (1900-71)
Slaves '69
Salt of the Earth '54
Master Race '44

Marc Bienstock
Indiscreet '98
The Beneficiary '97

Antonio Bido (1949-)
The Bloodstained Shadow '78
Watch Me When I Kill '77

Fabian Bielinsky (1959-2006)
The Aura '05
Nine Queens '00

Suzanne Bier (1960-)
Things We Lost in the Fire '07
After the Wedding '06
Brothers '05
Like It Never Was Before '95
Freud Leaving Home '91

Robert Bierman
A Merry War '97
Clarissa '91
Vampire's Kiss '88
Apology '86

Kathryn Bigelow (1952-)
K-19: The Widowmaker '02
The Weight of Water '00
Strange Days '95
Wild Palms '93
Point Break '91
Blue Steel '90
Near Dark '87
Loveless '83

Tony Bill (1940-)
Pictures on Hollis Woods '07
Flyboys '06
Whitewash: The Clarence Brandley Story '02
Harlan County War '00
Oliver Twist '97
Beyond the Call '96
One Christmas '95
Next Door '94
A Home of Our Own '93
Untamed Heart '93
Crazy People '88
Five Corners '88
The Princess and the Pea '83
Six Weeks '82
My Bodyguard '80

Bruce Bilson (1928-)
Chattanooga Choo Choo '84
The North Avenue Irregulars '79

Danny Bilson (1956-)
The Wrong Guys '88
Zone Troopers '84

Mike Binder (1958-)
Reign Over Me '07
The Upside of Anger '05
The Sex Monster '99
Blankman '94
Indian Summer '93
Crossing the Bridge '92

William Bindley
Madison '01
The Eighteenth Angel '97
Judicial Consent '94
Freeze Frame '92

Josh Binney (1889-1956)
Boardinghouse Blues '48
Killer Diller '48
Hi-De-Ho '35

Andrew Birkin (1945-)
The Cement Garden '93
Burning Secret '89

Alan Birkinshaw
Masque of the Red Death '90
Ten Little Indians '89
The Hamburg Cell '04
Ravenous '99
Face '97
Mad Love '95
Priest '94

Brad Bird (1957-)
Ratatouille '07
The Incredibles '04
Iron Giant '99

Richard Bird (1895-1986)
Men of Ireland '38
The Terror '38

Bill Bixby (1934-93)
The Woman Who Loved Elvis '93
Another Pair of Aces: Three of a Kind '91
Baby of the Bride '91
Death of the Incredible Hulk '90
The Trial of the Incredible Hulk '89
The Barbary Coast '74

Herbert Blache (1882-1953)
Head Winds '25
The Untamable '23

The Saphead '21

Noel Black (1937-)
Eyes of the Panther '89
A Conspiracy of Love '87
Quarterback Princess '85
Private School '83
Prime Suspect '82
A Man, a Woman, and a Bank '79
Mirrors '78
Pretty Poison '68

David Blair
Anna Karenina '00
Split Second '99

George Blair (1905-70)
Jaguar '56
Silver City Bonanza '51
Thunder in God's Country '51
Missourians '50
G.I. War Brides '46

Alfonso Corona Blake (1919-99)
Samson in the Wax Museum '63
Samson vs. the Vampire Women '61

Michael Blakemore (1928-)
Country Life '95
Privates on Parade '84

John Blanchard
Shriek If You Know What I Did Last Friday the 13th '00
Really Weird Tales '86
The Last Polka '84

Jamie Blanks
Valentine '01
Urban Legend '98

Alessandro Blasetti (1900-87)
Simon Bolivar '69
What a Woman! '56
Too Bad She's Bad '54
Fabiola '48
The Iron Crown '41
1860 '33

William Peter Blatty (1928-)
Exorcist 3: Legion '90
The Ninth Configuration '79

Jeff Bleckner (1943-)
That Russell Girl '08
Have No Fear: The Life of Pope John Paul II '05
Dean Koontz's Black River '01
Rear Window '98
The Beast '96
Serving in Silence: The Margarethe Cammermeyer Story '95
Target: Favorite Son '87
White Water Summer '87
Brotherly Love '85
When Your Lover Leaves '83

Bernard Blier (1916-89)
How Much Do You Love Me? '05
Notre Histoire '84

Bertrand Blier (1939-)
Mon Homme '96
Too Beautiful for You '88
Menage '86
My Best Friend's Girl '84
Beau Pere '81
Buffet Froid '79
Get Out Your Handkerchiefs '78
Going Places '74

Jeffrey Blitz (1969-)
Rocket Science '07
Spellbound '02

Jason Bloom
Dead Simple '01
Bio-Dome '96
Overnight Delivery '96

Jeffrey Bloom
Flowers in the Attic '87
Jealousy '84
Blood Beach '81
The Stick-Up '77

Dog Pound Shuffle '75

George Bloomfield (1930-)
Jacob Two Two Meets the Hooded Fang '99
The Double Negative '80
Nothing Personal '80
Riel '79
To Kill a Clown '72
Jenny '70

Philippe Blot
Running Wild '94
Hot Blood '89

Ralph Bluemke
Kid and the Killers '74
Robby '68

Don Bluth (1938-)
Titan A.E. '00
Anastasia '97
Thumbelina '94
A Troll in Central Park '94
Rock-a-Doodle '92
All Dogs Go to Heaven '89
The Land Before Time '88
An American Tail '86
The Secret of NIMH '82

John Blystone (1892-1938)
Block-heads '38
Swiss Miss '38
23 1/2 Hours Leave '37
Great Guy '36
Too Busy to Work '32
Dick Turpin '25
Our Hospitality '23

David Blyth (1956-)
Hot Blooded '98
Red Blooded 2 '96
My Grandpa Is a Vampire '92
Red Blooded American Girl '90
Death Warmed Up '85

Hart Bochner (1956-)
High School High '96
P.C.U. '94

Sergei Bodrov (1948-)
The Quickie '01
Running Free '00
Prisoner of the Mountains '96
Freedom Is Paradise '89

Christoffer Boe
Allegro '05
Reconstruction '03

Budd Boetticher (1916-2001)
Comanche Station '60
The Rise and Fall of Legs Diamond '60
Ride Lonesome '59
The Tall T '57
The Magnificent Matador '55
Man from the Alamo '53
Horizons West '52
Red Ball Express '52
Bullfighter & the Lady '50
Behind Locked Doors '48
Human Gorilla '48

Paul Bogart (1919-)
The Heidi Chronicles '95
Broadway Bound '92
Torch Song Trilogy '88
Oh, God! You Devil '84
Power, Passion & Murder '83
Tell Me Where It Hurts '74
Class of '44 '73
Cancel My Reservation '72
A House without a Christmas Tree '72
Skin Game '71
Marlowe '69
The Three Sisters '65

Yurek Bogayevicz (1948-)
Exit in Red '97
Anna '87

Peter Bogdanovich (1939-)
Hustle '04
The Cat's Meow '01

A Saintly Switch '99
Naked City: A Killer Christmas '98
Rescuers: Stories of Courage "Two Women" '97
The Thing Called Love '93
Noises Off '92
Texasville '90
Illegally Yours '87
Mask '85
They All Laughed '81
Saint Jack '79
Daisy Miller '74
Paper Moon '73
What's Up, Doc? '72
The Last Picture Show '71
Targets '68
Voyage to the Planet of Prehistoric Women '68

Willy Bogner (1942-)
Fire, Ice and Dynamite '91
Fire and Ice '87

Michel Boisrond (1921-2002)
Catherine & Co. '76
Voulez-Vous Danser avec Moi? '59
Mam'zelle Pigalle '58
That Naughty Girl '58
Une Parisienne '58

Yves Boisset (1939-)
Double Identity '89
Prize of Peril '84
Dog Day '83
The Purple Taxi '77
Dupont Lajoie '74
Cobra '71

Jerome Boivin (1954-)
Barjo '93
Baxter '89

Richard Boleslawski (1889-1937)
The Last of Mrs. Cheyney '37
The Garden of Allah '36
Theodora Goes Wild '36
Les Miserables '35
Hollywood Party '34
The Painted Veil '34
Rasputin and the Empress '33

Uwe Boll (1965-)
In the Name of the King: A Dungeon Siege Tale '08
BloodRayne 2: Deliverance '07
BloodRayne '06
Alone in the Dark '05
Heart of America '03
House of the Dead '03
Blackwoods '02
Sanctimony '01

Mauro Bolognini (1922-2001)
Husbands and Lovers '91
The Inheritance '76
La Grande Bourgeoise '74
Oldest Profession '67
Il Bell'Antonio '60

Craig Bolotin (1954-)
Light It Up '99
That Night '93

Ben Bolt (1952-)
The Turn of the Screw '99
Wilderness '96
Big Town '87

James Bolton
The Graffiti Artist '04
Eban and Charley '01

Timothy Bond (1942-)
Running Wild '99
Night of the Twisters '95
Return to the Lost World '93
The Lost World '92
One Night Only '84
Deadly Harvest '72

Sergei Bondarchuk (1920-94)
Waterloo '71
War and Peace '68

Peter Bonerz (1938-)
Police Academy 6: City under Siege '89
Nobody's Perfekt '79

Mario Bonnard (1889-1965)
The Mercenaries '62
The Last Days of Pompeii '60

Rene Bonniere (1928-)
The Halfback of Notre Dame '96
Dream Man '94
Islands '87

J.R. Bookwalter (1966-)
Witchouse 3: Demon Fire '01
Witchouse 2: Blood Coven '00
The Dead Next Door '89

John Boorman (1933-)
In My Country '04
The Tailor of Panama '00
The General '98
Beyond Rangoon '95
Picture Windows '95
Where the Heart Is '90
Hope and Glory '87
The Emerald Forest '85
Excalibur '81
Zardoz '73
Deliverance '72
Hell in the Pacific '69
Point Blank '67

H. Gordon Boos (1958-2004)
Forgotten City '98
Perfect Assassins '98
Red Surf '90

Lizzie Borden (1958-)
Erotique '94
Love Crimes '92
Working Girls '87

Michael Borden
No Way Back '90
Ain't No Way Back '89

Bernard Borderie (1924-78)
Your Turn Darling '63
Dishonorable Discharge '57

Robert Boris (1945-)
Frank and Jesse '94
Buy & Cell '89
Steele Justice '87
Oxford Blues '84

Walerian Borowczyk (1923-2006)
Emmanuelle 5 '87
The Beast '75

Clay Borris (1950-)
Someone to Die For '95
Suspicious Agenda '95
Prom Night 4: Deliver Us from Evil '91
The Gunfighters '87
Quiet Cool '86

Phillip Borsos (1954-95)
Far from Home: The Adventures of Yellow Dog '94
Dr. Bethune '90
Mean Season '85
One Magic Christmas '85
The Grey Fox '83

Frank Borzage (1893-1962)
Journey Beneath the Desert '61
I've Always Loved You '46
The Spanish Main '45
His Butler's Sister '44
Stage Door Canteen '43
Smilin' Through '41
The Mortal Storm '40
Strange Cargo '40
Three Comrades '38
History Is Made at Night '37
Mannequin '37
Desire '36
Flirtation Walk '34
A Farewell to Arms '32
Song o' My Heart '29
Until They Get Me '18

Rick Bota
Hellraiser: Deader '05
Hellraiser: Hellworld '05
Hellraiser: Hellseeker '02

John Boulting (1913-85)
Heavens Above '63
I'm All Right Jack '59
Lucky Jim '58
Seven Days to Noon '50
Brighton Rock '47

Roy Boulting (1913-2001)
There's a Girl in My Soup '70
Heavens Above '63
Carlton Browne of the F.O. '59
Lucky Jim '58
Brothers in Law '57
Seven Days to Noon '50
The Guinea Pig '48
Fame is the Spur '47

Serge Bourguignon (1928-)
A Coeur Joie '67
Head Over Heels '67
Sundays & Cybele '62

Darren Lynn Bousman (1979-)
Saw 4 '07
Saw III '06
Saw II '05

Jenny (H. Anne Riley) Bowen
Animal Behavior '89
The Wizard of Loneliness '88

John Bowen (1948-)
Hindsight '97
Dark Secrets '95
Knock Outs '92
Lethal Games '90

George Bowers (1944-)
Private Resort '84
My Tutor '82
Body & Soul '81
The Hearse '80

Rob Bowman (1960-)
Elektra '05
Reign of Fire '02
The X-Files '98
Airborne '93

Muriel Box (1905-91)
Rattle of a Simple Man '64
Truth about Women '58

Tim Boxell
Chasing Destiny '00
Aberration '97

Daniel Boyd (1956-)
Heroes of the Heart '94
Invasion of the Space Preachers '90
Chillers '88

Don Boyd (1948-)
Kleptomania '94
Twenty-One '91
Goldeneye: The Secret Life of Ian Fleming '89
East of Elephant Rock '76

Jean Boyer (1901-65)
Fernandel the Dressmaker '57
Dressmaker '56
The French Touch '54
Femmes de Paris '53
Crazy for Love '52
Mr. Peek-A-Boo '50
Circonstances Attenuantes '36

Danny Boyle (1956-)
Sunshine '07
Millions '05
28 Days Later... '02
Vacuuming Completely Nude in Paradise '01
The Beach '00
A Life Less Ordinary '97
Trainspotting '95

Steve Boyum (1952-)
Supercross: The Movie '05
Timecop 2: The Berlin Decision '03
Slap Shot 2: Breaking the Ice '02
Meet the Deedles '98
Shallow Grave '94

Bruno Bozzetto (1938-)
VIP: My Brother Superman '90
Allegro Non Troppo '76

Charles Brabin (1883-1957)
The Mask of Fu Manchu '32
The Raven '15

Robert North Bradbury (1886-1949)
God's Country and the Man '37
Forbidden Trails '41
Riders of the Rockies '37
Sing, Cowboy, Sing '37
Trouble in Texas '37
Where Trails Divide '37
Brand of the Outlaws '36
Cavalry '36
Desert Trail '35
Kid Courageous '35
Alias John Law '35
Big Calibre '35
Courageous Avenger '35
Sundown Saunders '35
Texas Terror '35
Trail of Terror '35
Valley of the Lawless '36
Westward Ho '35
Blue Steel '34
The Gun Ranger '34
Lucky Texan '34
Man from Utah '34
The Star Packer '34
Lawless Frontier '35
No Man's Range '35
Rider of the Law '35
Lawless Range '35
Riders of the Desert '32
Tombstone Terror '34
Texas Buddies '32

Randy Bradshaw (1952-)
Cold Blooded '00
Song Spinner '95
Blades of Courage '88

John Bradshaw
Triggermen '02
Full Disclosure '00
Killing Moon '00
Breakout '98
The Reaper '97
Specimen '97
The Undertaker's Wedding '97

Al (Alfonso Brescia) Bradley (1930-2001)
Cross Mission '89
Miami Cops '89
Iron Warrior '87
Metallica '85
White Fang and the Hunter '85
Bloody Avenger '80
Cosmos: War of the Planets '80
Captive Planet '78

Michel Brault (1928-)
Mon Amie Max '94
A Paper Wedding '89
'45
D-Day on Mars '45
The Purple Monster Strikes '46
The Phantom Rider '46
Federal Agents vs. Underworld, Inc. '49
King of the Rocketmen '49
Lost Planet Airmen '49
Radar Patrol vs. Spy King '49
G-Men Never Forget '48
Jesse James Rides Again '47
Son of Zorro '47
Cyclotrode "X" '46
Daughter of Don Q '46
King of the Forest Rangers '46

Eugene Brady (1952-)
Missing Brendan '03
The Nephew '97

Carlo L. Bragaglia (1894-1998)
The Loves of Hercules '60
The Sword and the Cross '58

John Brahm (1893-1982)
Hangover Square '45
Guest in the House '44
The Undying Monster '42
Wintertime '43
Singapore '47
Face to Face '52
Miracle of Our Lady of Fatima '52

Marco Brambilla (1960-)
Dinotopia '02
Excess Baggage '96
Demolition Man '93

Bill Brame (1928-)
Ebony Dreams '80
Miss Melody Jones '73
Free Grass '69

Kenneth Branagh (1960-)
Sleuth '07
As You Like It '06
Love's Labour's Lost '00
Hamlet '96
A Midwinter's Tale '95
Mary Shelley's Frankenstein '94
Much Ado about Nothing '93
Peter's Friends '92
Dead Again '91
Henry V '89

Larry Brand
Paranoia '98
Overexposed '90
Masque of the Red Death '89
The Drifter '88

Charlotte Brandstrom (1959-)
A Business Affair '93
Road to Ruin '91
Sweet Revenge '50

Fred Brannon (1901-53)
Zombies of the Stratosphere '52
Radar Men from the Moon '52
The Invisible Monster '51
Government Agents vs. Phantom Legion '51
Night Riders of Montana '50
Bandit King of Texas '49
Don Daredevil Rides Again '51

Joseph (Jose Ramon Larraz) Braunstein (1929-)
Edge of the Axe '89
Rest in Pieces '87

Charles Braverman (1944-)
Final Shot: The Hank Gathers Story '92
Hit & Run '82

Kevin Bray '82
The Manster '59

William Wayne (1941-)
The Manhattan Project '86

George Breakston (1920-73)
The Manster '59
Scarlet Spear '54
Geisha Girl '52
36 Fillete '88
Perfect Love '96
Romance '99
Sex Is Comedy '02
Anatomy of Hell '04

Catherine Breillat (1948-)
Table One '00
Sex Is Comedy '02
Romance '99
Perfect Love '96
36 Fillete '88

Valerie Breiman
Love & Sex '00

Michael Scott Bregman
Carlito's Way: Rise to Power '05

Herbert Brenon (1880-1958)
Beau Geste '39
Dancing Mothers '26
Peter Pan '24

Alfonso Brescia
War in Space '77

Martin Brest (1951-)
Gigli '03
Meet Joe Black '98
Scent of a Woman '92
Midnight Run '88
Beverly Hills Cop '84
Going in Style '79

Howard Bretherton (1896-1969)
The Prince of Thieves '48
Trail of the Mounties '47
Where the North Begins '47
The Topeka Terror '45
Bordertown Gunfighters '43
Rhythm Parade '43
A Dog of Flanders '35
Below the Border '42
Down Texas Way '42
Ghost Town Law '42
In Old Colorado '41
West of the Law '42
Riders of the West '42

A. (Alfonso Brescia)

Steven Brill (1962-)
Without a Paddle '04
Mr. Deeds '02
Little Nicky '00
Late Last Night '99
Heavyweights '94

Burt Brinckerhoff (1936-)
Trickbaby '72
Freeway '95
Freeway 2: Confessions of a Trickbaby '99

Richard Brooks (1912-92)
Fever Pitch '85
Wrong Is Right '82
Looking for Mr. Goodbar '77
Bite the Bullet '75
Dollars '71
The Happy Ending '69
In Cold Blood '67
The Professionals '66
Lord Jim '65
Sweet Bird of Youth '62
Elmer Gantry '60
The Brothers Karamazov '58
Cat on a Hot Tin Roof '58
Something of Value '57
The Catered Affair '56
The Last Hunt '56
Blackboard Jungle '55
The Last Time I Saw Paris '54
Battle Circus '53

Deborah Brock
Rock 'n' Roll High School Forever '91
Andy and the Airwave Rangers '89
Slumber Party Massacre 2 '87

John Broderick (1942-2001)
The Warrior & the Sorceress '84

Sue Brooks (1953-)
Japanese Story '03
Road to Nhill '97

Nick Broomfield (1948-)
Aileen: Life and Death of a Serial Killer '03
Monster in a Box '92
Dark Obsession '90

Eric Bross (1964-)
On the Line '01
Ten Benny '98
Restaurant '98
Stranger than Fiction '02
Panic '02

Hilary Brougher
Stephanie Daley '06
The Sticky Fingers of Time '97

Harry Bromley-Davenport (1950-1946)
Mockingbird Don't Sing '01
Xtro 3: Watch the Skies '95
Xtro 2: The Second Encounter '91
Xtro '83

Craig Brewer (1971-)
Black Snake Moan '07
Hustle & Flow '05

Salome Breziner
Fast Sofa '01
Tollbooth '94

Paul Brickman (1949-)
Men Don't Leave '89
Risky Business '83

Marshall Brickman (1941-)
The Manhattan Project '86
Lovesick '83
Simon '80

Adam Brooks (1956-)
Definitely, Maybe '08
Invisible Circus '00
Almost You '85

Albert Brooks (1947-)
Looking for Comedy in the Muslim World '06
The Muse '99
Mother '96
Defending Your Life '91
Lost in America '85
Modern Romance '81
Real Life '79

James L. Brooks (1940-)
Spanglish '04
As Good As It Gets '97
I'll Do Anything '93
Broadcast News '87
Terms of Endearment '83

Joseph Brooks (1938-)
If Ever I See You Again '78
You Light Up My Life '77
Invitation to the Wedding '73

Mel Brooks (1926-)
Dracula: Dead and Loving It '95
Life Stinks '91
Spaceballs '87
History of the World: Part 1 '81
High Anxiety '77
Silent Movie '76
Young Frankenstein '74
Blazing Saddles '74
The Twelve Chairs '70
The Producers '68

Peter Brook (1925-)
The Mahabharata '89
Meetings with Remarkable Men '79
King Lear '71
Lord of the Flies '63

Otto Brower (1895-1946)
Postal Inspector '35
The Phantom Empire '35
The Light of Western Stars '30

Arvin Brown (1940-)
Change of Heart '98
Diary of the Dead '80

Bruce Brown (1938-)
The Endless Summer 2 '94
The Endless Summer '66

Barry Alexander Brown (1960-)
Lonely in America '91

Clarence Brown (1890-1987)
The White Cliffs of Dover '44
The Human Comedy '43
They Met in Bombay '41
Edison, the Man '40
Idiot's Delight '39
The Rains Came '39
Of Human Hearts '38
Conquest '37
The Gorgeous Hussy '36
Wife Versus Secretary '36
Ah, Wilderness! '35
Anna Karenina '35
Chained '34
Night Flight '33
Sadie McKee '34
The Son-Daughter '32
Possessed '31
A Free Soul '31
Romance '30
A Woman of Affairs '28
The Flesh and the Devil '27
The Eagle '25
Smouldering Fires '25
The Light of Faith '22
The Last of the Mohicans

Dana Brown
Dust to Glory '05
Step Into Liquid '03

Ewing Miles Brown
Killers '88
Whale of a Tale '76

Georg Stanford Brown (1943-)
The Reading Room '05
Dangerous Relations '93
Stranger in the Neon Jungle '87
Miracle of the Heart: A Boys Town Story '86
Grambling's White Tiger '81

Gregory Brown (1954-)
See No Evil '06

Harry Joe Brown (1890-1972)
The Fighting Legion '30
Dead Man Walking '88
Mountain Justice '30
One-Punch O'Day '26

Karl Brown (1896-1990)
The Port of Missing Girls '38
Fire Alarm '32
White Legion '36

Larry G. Brown
Final Cut '88

Psychopath '73

Mark Brown
The Salon '05
Two Can Play That Game '01

Melville Brown (1887-1938)
Mad About Money '37
Champagne for Breakfast '35
Behind Office Doors '31
Check & Double Check '30

Mende Brown
Nowhere to Hide '83
On the Run '83

Christopher Browne
League of Ordinary Gentlemen '04
Third World Cop '99

Ricou Browning (1930-)
Salty '73
Island of the Lost '68

Tod Browning (1882-1962)
Devil Doll '36
Mark of the Vampire '35
Freaks '32
Dracula '31
West of Zanzibar '28
The Unknown '27
The Unholy Three '25
White Tiger '23
Outside the Law '21

S.F. Brownrigg (1937-96)
Thinkin' Big '87
Keep My Grave Open '80
Poor White Trash 2 '75
Don't Open the Door! '74
Don't Look in the Basement '73

James Bruce
Whacked! '02
Love to Kill '93
Headless Body in Topless Bar '96

Clyde Bruckman (1894-1955)
Feet First '30
The General '26

Franco Brusati (1922-93)
The Sleazy Uncle '89
To Forget Venice '79
Bread and Chocolate '73

James Bryan
Lady Street Fighter '86
Hellriders '84
Mistress of the Apes '79
Hughes & Harlow: Angels in Hell '77
Goodbye, Norma Jean '75
Hell Raiders '68
It's Alive! '68
Creature of Destruction '67
Curse of the Swamp Creature '66
Mars Needs Women '66
Zontar, the Thing from Venus '66
The Eye Creatures '65
The Naked Witch '64
Free, White, and 21 '62

Amnon Buchbinder
Whole New Thing '05
The Fishing Trip '98

Dimitri Buchowetzki (1885-1932)
The Swan '25
Othello '22

Chris Buck
Surf's Up '07

Tarzan '99

Bethel Buckalew
My Boys Are Good Boys '78
Summer School '77
Dirty Mind of Young Sally '72

Allan A. Buckhantz
The Last Contract '86
Portrait of a Hitman '77

Colin Bucksey (1946-)
Midnight's Child '93
Curiosity Kills '90
Dealers '89
The McGuffin '85
Blue Money '84

Harold Bucquet (1891-1946)
Without Love '45
The Adventures of Tartu '43
Dr. Kildare's Strange Case '40
The Secret of Dr. Kildare '39
On Borrowed Time '39

Colin Budds
Dr. Jekyll & Mr. Hyde '99
Hurricane Smith '92

John Carl Buechler
Watchers Reborn '98
Ghoulies 3: Ghoulies Go to College '91
Friday the 13th, Part 7: The New Blood '88
Cellar Dweller '87
Troll '86
Dungeonmaster '83

Richard Bugajski (1943-)
Clearcut '92
The Interrogation '82
A Woman and a Woman '80

Veljko Bulajic (1928-)
The Day That Shook the World '78
Battle of Neretva '69

Luis Bunuel (1900-83)
That Obscure Object of Desire '77
Phantom of Liberty '74
The Discreet Charm of the Bourgeoisie '72
Tristana '70
The Milky Way '68
Belle de Jour '67
Simon of the Desert '66
Diary of a Chambermaid '64
The Exterminating Angel '62
Viridiana '61
The Young One '61
Fever Mounts at El Pao '59
Nazarin '58
Death in the Garden '56
The Criminal Life of Archibaldo de la Cruz '55
The Illusion Travels by Streetcar '53
Wuthering Heights '53
El '52
El Bruto '52
Mexican Bus Ride '51
Susana '51
A Woman Without Love '51
Los Olvidados '50
The Great Madcap '49
L'Age D'Or '30
Un Chien Andalou '28

Ray Burdis (1958-)
Love, Honour & Obey '00
Final Cut '98

Robert Burge
The Dark Dancer '95
The House on Todville Road '95
Keaton's Cop '90
Vasectomy: A Delicate Matter '86

Stuart Burge (1918-2002)
Julius Caesar '70
Othello '65

Neil Burger
The Illusionist '06
Interview with the Assassin '02

David J. Burke (1948-)
Animal '05

Edison Force '05

Martyn Burke (1952-)
Avenging Angelo '02
The Pirates of Silicon Valley '99
Clown Murders '83
Last Chase '81
Power Play '81

Stuart Burkin
Cash Crop '01
Harvest '98

Charles Burnett (1944-)
Finding Buck McHenry '00
Selma, Lord, Selma '99
Nightjohn '96
The Glass Shield '95
To Sleep with Anger '90
Killer of Sheep '77

Edward Burns (1968-)
The Groomsmen '06
Looking for Kitty '04
Ash Wednesday '02
Sidewalks of New York '01
No Looking Back '98
She's the One '96
The Brothers McMullen '94

Jeff Burr (1963-)
Straight into Darkness '04
Night of the Scarecrow '95
Pumpkinhead 2: Blood Wings '94
Puppet Master 5: The Final Chapter '94
Puppet Master 4 '93
Eddie Presley '92
Leatherface: The Texas Chainsaw Massacre 3 '89
Stepfather 2: Make Room for Daddy '89
The Offspring '87

Geoff Burrowes (1945-)
Run '91
Return to Snowy River '88

Tim Burstall (1929-2004)
Nightmare at Bittercreek '91
Great Expectations: The Untold Story '87
Kangaroo '86
The Naked Country '85
Attack Force Z '84
Adventures of Eliza Fraser '76
Endplay '75
Jock Petersen '74
Alvin Purple '73

David Burton (1877-1963)
Lady by Choice '34
Fighting Caravans '31

LeVar Burton (1957-)
Smart House '99
The Tiger Woods Story '98

Tim Burton (1960-)
Sweeney Todd: The Demon Barber of Fleet Street '07
Charlie and the Chocolate Factory '05
Tim Burton's Corpse Bride '05
Big Fish '03
Planet of the Apes '01
Sleepy Hollow '99
Mars Attacks! '96
Ed Wood '94
Batman Returns '92
Edward Scissorhands '90
Batman '89
Beetlejuice '88
Pee-wee's Big Adventure '85

Steve Buscemi (1957-)
Interview '07
Lonesome Jim '06
Animal Factory '00
Tree's Lounge '96

Anthony Bushell (1904-97)
The Long Dark Hall '51
Angel with the Trumpet '50

John Bushelman
L.A. Gangs Rising '89
Cruisin' High '75

David Butler (1927-2006)
Glory '56
King Richard and the Crusaders '54
By the Light of the Silvery Moon '53
Calamity Jane '53
April in Paris '52
Lullaby of Broadway '51
Tea for Two '50
It's a Great Feeling '49
Look for the Silver Lining '49
The Story of Seabiscuit '49
San Antonio '45
The Princess and the Pirate '44
Thank Your Lucky Stars '43
They Got Me Covered '43
The Road to Morocco '42
Caught in the Draft '41
Playmates '41
If I Had My Way '40
You'll Find Out '40
East Side of Heaven '39
Captain January '36
Pigskin Parade '36
Doubting Thomas '35
The Littlest Rebel '35
The Little Colonel '35
Bright Eyes '34
A Connecticut Yankee '31

Robert Butler (1927-)
Turbulence '96
White Mile '94
Out on a Limb '87
Long Time Gone '86
Moonlighting '85
Concrete Beat '84
Up the Creek '84
Night of the Juggler '80
Underground Aces '80
Hot Lead & Cold Feet '78
A Question of Guilt '78
James Dean '76
Strange New World '75
The Ultimate Thrill '74
Now You See Him, Now You Don't '72
The Barefoot Executive '71
Scandalous John '71
The Computer Wore Tennis Shoes '69

Hendel Butoy
Fantasia/2000 '00
The Rescuers Down Under '90

Jorg Buttgereit (1963-)
Nekromantik 2 '91
Der Todesking '89
Nekromantik '87

Edward Buzzell (1900-85)
A Woman of Distinction '50
Neptune's Daughter '49
Song of the Thin Man '47
Easy to Wed '46
Best Foot Forward '43
Ship Ahoy '42
Go West '40
At the Circus '39
Honolulu '39

Mark Byers
Digging Up Business '91
Criminal Act '88

Jeff Byrd
King's Ransom '05
Jasper, Texas '03
Seventeen Again '00

John Byrum (1947-)
The Whoopee Boys '86
The Razor's Edge '84
Heart Beat '80
Inserts '76

Reggie Rock Bythewood (1965-)
Biker Boyz '03
Dancing in September '00

Scott Caan (1976-)
The Dog Problem '06
Dallas 362 '03

Christy Cabanne (1888-1950)
Scared to Death '46
Dixie Jamboree '44
The Mummy's Hand '40
Mutiny on the Blackhawk '39
Last Outlaw '36
One Frightened Night '35
Jane Eyre '34
The World Gone Mad '33
Convicted '32
Hearts of Humanity '32
Annapolis '28
The Average Woman '24
Flirting with Fate '16
Reggie Mixes In '16
The Lamb '15

Michael Cacoyannis (1927-)
Sweet Country '87
Iphigenia '77
The Story of Jacob & Joseph '74
Trojan Women '71
Zorba the Greek '64
A Matter of Dignity '57
Girl in Black '56
Stella '55

Andy Cadiff
Chasing Liberty '04
Leave It to Beaver '97

David Caesar
Dirty Deeds '02
Idiot Box '97

David Caffrey (1969-)
The Aristocrats '99
Grand Theft Parsons '03

Edward L. Cahn (1899-1963)
Frontier Uprising '61
Invisible Invaders '59
It! The Terror from Beyond Space '58
Dragstrip Girl '57
Flesh and the Spur '57
Invasion of the Saucer Men '57
Motorcycle Gang '57
Shake, Rattle and Rock '57
Voodoo Woman '57
Zombies of Moratau '57
Girls in Prison '56
Confidential '35

Mario Caiano (1933-)
Adios, Hombre '68
Erik, the Viking '65
Fighting Fists of Shanghai Joe '65
Terror of Rome Against the Son of Hercules '64

Christopher Cain (1943-)
September Dawn '07
Gone Fishin' '97
Rose Hill '97
The Amazing Panda Adventure '95
The Next Karate Kid '94
Pure Country '92
Wheels of Terror '90
Young Guns '88
The Principal '87
Where the River Runs Black '86
That Was Then... This Is Now '85
The Stone Boy '84
Elmer '76

Mars Callahan (1972-)
What Love Is '07
Poolhall Junkies '02
Double Down '01

Art Camacho
Sci-Fighter '04
Final Payback '99
Recoil '97
Little Bigfoot '96
The Power Within '95

James Cameron (1954-)
Titanic '97
True Lies '94
Terminator 2: Judgment Day '91
The Abyss '89
Aliens '86
The Terminator '84
Piranha 2: The Spawning '82

Ken Cameron (1946-)
Miracle at Midnight '98
Dalva '95
Oldest Confederate Widow Tells All '95
Brides of Christ '91
Wild Thing '87
Fast Talking '86
The Good Wife '86
Monkey Grip '82

Douglas Camfield
Ivanhoe '82
Danger UXB '81

Donald Cammell (1939-96)
White of the Eye '88
Demon Seed '77
Performance '70

Joe Camp (1939-)
Benji: Off the Leash! '04
Benji the Hunted '87
Oh, Heavenly Dog! '80
The Double McGuffin '79
For the Love of Benji '77
Hawmps! '76
Benji '74

Juan J. Campanella (1959-)
The Son of the Bride '01
Love Walked In '97

Pasquale Festa Campanile (1927-86)
The Sex Machine '75
When Women Lost Their Tails '75
When Women Had Tails '70
The Libertine '69

Colin Campbell (1859-1928)
Little Orphan Annie '18
In the Days of the Thundering Herd & the Law & the Outlaw '14
The Spoilers '14

Doug Campbell
The Tomorrow Man '01
Perfect Tenant '99
Cupid '96
Season of Fear '89
Zapped Again '89

Graeme Campbell (1954-)
Casino Royale '06
Dangerous Child '01
Lip Service '00
Dream House '98
Volcano: Fire on the Mountain '97
Deadlock 2 '94
The Man in the Attic '94
Still Life '92
Into the Fire '88
Murder One '88
Blood Relations '87

Martin Campbell (1940-)
Casino Royale '06
The Legend of Zorro '05
Beyond Borders '03
Vertical Limit '00
The Mask of Zorro '98
Goldeneye '95
No Escape '94
Cast a Deadly Spell '91
Defenseless '91
Criminal Law '89
Edge of Darkness '86

Jane Campion (1954-)
In the Cut '03
Holy Smoke '99
Portrait of a Lady '96
The Piano '93
An Angel at My Table '89
Sweetie '89
Two Friends '86

Carlo Campogalliani (1885-1974)
Son of Samson '62
Ursus in the Valley of the Lions '62
Goliath and the Barbarians '60
Musica Proibita '43

Michael Campus
The Passover Plot '75
The Education of Sonny Carson '74
The Mack '73

Danny Cannon (1968-)
Goal! The Dream Begins '06
I Still Know What You Did Last Summer '98
Judge Dredd '95
Phoenix '98
The Young Americans '93

Raymond Cannon (1892-1977)
Swing It, Sailor '37
Night Life in Reno '31

Laurent Cantet (1961-)
Heading South '05
Time Out '01

Luigi Capuano
Samson and His Mighty Challenge '64
Robinson Crusoe & the Tiger '72
Cold Steel for Tortuga '65
Marauder '65
The Conqueror & the Empress '64
Tiger of the Seven Seas '62

Leos Carax (1960-)
Mauvais Sang '86
Boy Meets Girl '84
The Lovers on the Bridge '91
Pola X '99

Jack Cardiff (1914-)
The Girl on a Motorcycle '68
Dark of the Sun '68
The Freakmaker '73

Lamar Card (1942-)
The Clones '73
Shadow Warriors '95

Costa Carayiannis (1932-93)
Land of the Minotaur '77
The Brave Bunch '70

Yakima Canutt (1895-1986)
The Adventures of Frank and Jesse James '48
G-Men Never Forget '48
Oklahoma Badlands '48
Federal Operator 99 '45
Manhunt of Mystery Island '45

Giorgio Capitani (1927-)
I Hate Blondes '83
Lobster for Breakfast '82

Frank Cappello
American Yakuza '94
No Way Back '96

Frank Capra (1897-1991)
Pocketful of Miracles '61
A Hole in the Head '59
Here Comes the Groom '51
Riding High '50
State of the Union '48
It's a Wonderful Life '46
Arsenic and Old Lace '44
Prelude to War '42
Meet John Doe '41
Mr. Smith Goes to Washington '39
You Can't Take It with You '38
Lost Horizon '37
Mr. Deeds Goes to Town '36
Broadway Bill '34
It Happened One Night '34
The Bitter Tea of General Yen '33
Lady for a Day '33
American Madness '32
The Miracle Woman '31
Platinum Blonde '31
That Certain Thing '28
Long Pants '27
Strong Man '26

Roger Cardinal
The Long Ships '64
My Geisha '62
Dead Silent '99
Snowwalkin' '71
Malarek '89

Rene Cardona, Sr. (1906-88)
Doctor of Doom '62
Santa Claus '59
Wrestling Women vs. the Aztec Mummy '59

Rene Cardona, Jr. (1939-97)
Beaks: The Movie '87
The Treasure of the Amazon '84
Hostages '80
Tintorera... Tiger Shark '78
Fantastic Balloon Voyage '76
Night of a Thousand Cats '72
The Night of the Bloody Apes '68
Tiger '72

J.S. Cardone (1946-)
The Forsaken '01
True Blue '91
Outside Ozona '98
Black Day Blue Night '95
Shadowhunter '93
A Climate for Killing '91
Shadowzone '89
Thunder Alley '85
The Slayer '82

John Cardos (1928-)
Act of Piracy '89
Skeleton Coast '89
Outlaw of Gor '87
Mutant '83
The Dark '79
Day Time Ended '80
Kingdom of the Spiders '77
The Female Bunch '69

Giuliano Carnimeo (1932-)
Guns for Dollars '73
The Case of the Bloody Iris '72

Christian Carion (1963-)
Joyeux Noel '05
The Girl from Paris '02
The Other Side of the Law '95

Gilles Carle (1929-)
Blood of the Hunter '94
Maria Chapdelaine '84
The Red Half-Breed '70
In Trouble '67

Carlo Carlei (1960-)
Fluke '95
Flight of the Innocent '93

Lewis John Carlino (1932-)
Class '83
The Great Santini '80
The Sailor Who Fell from Grace with the Sea '76

Henning Carlsen (1927-)
The Wolf at the Door '87
Hunger '66
A World of Strangers '62

Joe Carnahan (1969-)
Smokin' Aces '07
Narc '02
Blood, Guts, Bullets and Octane '99

Marcel Carne (1906-96)
La Merveilleuse Visite '74
Les Assassins de L'Ordre '71
Children of Paradise '44
Les Visiteurs du Soir '42
Bizarre Bizarre '39
Le Jour Se Leve '39

Charles Robert Carner (1957-)
Witless Protection '08
Red Water '01
Echo of Murder '00
The Fixer '97

John Carney
Once '06
On the Edge '86

Marc Caro (1956-)
Dante 01 '02
In His Life: The John Lennon Story '00
Delicatessen '92
The City of Lost Children '95

Niki Caro (1967-)
North Country '05
Whale Rider '02

Glenn Gordon Caron (1954-)
Picture Perfect '96
Love Affair '94
Wilder Napalm '93
Clean and Sober '88

John Carpenter (1948-)
Masters of Horror: Cigarette Burns '05
John Carpenter's Ghosts of Mars '01
Escape from L.A. '96
In the Mouth of Madness '95
Village of the Damned '95
Body Bags '93
Memoirs of an Invisible Man '92
They Live '88
Prince of Darkness '87
Big Trouble in Little China '86
Christine '84
Starman '84
The Thing '82
Escape from New York '81
Elvis: The Movie '79
Halloween '78
The Fog '78
Assault on Precinct 13 '76
Dark Star '74

Heiner Carow (1929-97)
Coming Out '89
The Legend of Paul and Paula '73

Stephen Carpenter
Soul Survivors '01
The Kindred '87
Dorm That Dripped Blood '82
The Power '80

Bernard Carr (1911-2005)
Who Killed Doc Robbin? '48
Curley '47

John Carr
Death Wish Club '83
Runaways '75

Steve Carr
Are We Done Yet? '07
Rebound '05
Daddy Day Care '03
Dr. Dolittle 2 '01
Next Friday '00

Thomas Carr (1907-97)
Dino '57
Captain Scarlett '53
Blazing Guns '50
Guns of Justice '50
Last Bullet '50
Marshal of Heldorado '50
Outlaw Fury '50
Pirates of the High Seas '50
Rangeland Empire '50
Sudden Death '50
Jesse James Rides Again '47
Alias Billy the Kid '46
Rio Grande Raiders '46
Rough Riders of Cheyenne '45

Anthony Carras
Fearmaker '89
Operation Bikini '63

Michael Carreras (1927-94)
Call Him Mr. Shatter '74
Prehistoric Women '67
Maniac '63

David S. Cass, Sr. (1929-89)
Terror in the Swamp '85

Henry Cass (1902-89)
The Family Plan '05
Johnson County War '02
The Hard '60
Blood of the Vampire '58
Last Holiday '50

Jon Cassar (1958-)
Danger Beneath the Sea '02
Shadow Warriors 2: Hunt for the Death Merchant '97
Shadow Warriors '97
The Ultimate Weapon '97
The Final Goal '94

John Cassavetes (1929-89)
Big Trouble '86
Love Streams '84
Gloria '80
Opening Night '77
The Killing of a Chinese Bookie '76
A Woman under the Influence '74
Husbands '70
Minnie and Moskowitz '71
Faces '68
A Child is Waiting '63

Richard Casey
Hellbent '88
Horror house on Highway 5 '86

Kimberly Casey
Deadly Dancer '90
Born Killer '89

Robert Cary
Ira & Abby '06
Anything But Love '02

Steve Carver (1945-)
The Wolves '95
Dead Center '94
River of Death '90
Bulletproof '88
Jocks '87
Oceans of Fire '86
Lone Wolf McQuade '83
An Eye for an Eye '81
Steel '80
Drum '76
Big Bad Mama '74
The Arena '73

D.J. Caruso (1965-)
Disturbia '07
Two for the Money '05
Taking Lives '04
The Salton Sea '02
Black Cat Run '98

Thomas Carter (1953-)
Coach Carter '05
Save the Last Dance '01
Metro '96
Swing Kids '93
Call to Glory '84
Miami Vice '84
High Ballin' '78

Peter Carter (1933-82)
Intruder Within '81
High-point '80
Kavik the Wolf Dog '80
Klondike Fever '79
Rituals '79

Nick Castle (1947-)
Major Payne '95
Mr. Wrong '95
Dennis the Menace '93
The Last Starfighter '84
The Boy Who Could Fly '86
Tag: The Assassination Game '82
Connor's War '06

Jack Paddy Carstairs (1910-70)
Strikes Twice '85
Made in Heaven '52
Tony Draws a Horse '51
Sleeping Car to Trieste '45
The Saint in London '39
Lassie from Lancashire '38

Willard Carroll (1955-)
Playing by Heart '98
The Runestone '91

David Carson
Blue Smoke '07
Carrie '02
The 10th Kingdom '00
From the Earth to the Moon '98
Letters from a Killer '98
Star Trek: Generations '94

Renato Castellani (1913-85)
Life of Verdi '82
Romeo and Juliet '54

Enzo G. Castellari (1938-)
Escape from the Bronx '85
Lightblast '85
Day of the Cobra '84
1990: The Bronx Warriors '82
Warriors of the Wasteland '83
The Shark Hunter '79
Deadly Mission '78
Loves & Times of Scaramouche '76
Street Law '74
High Crime '73
Sting of the West '72
Cold Eyes of Fear '70
Go Kill and Come Back '68
Any Gun Can Play '67

William Castle (1914-)
Shanks '74
Zotz! '62
13 Ghosts '60
The Tingler '59
House on Haunted Hill '58
Americano '55
Conquest of Cochise '53
The Law Rides Again '43
Game '82
The Night Walker '64
Strait-Jacket '64
Homicidal '61
Mr. Sardonicus '61

Joe Catalanotto
French Quarter Undercover '85

Gilbert Cates (1934-)
Collected Stories '02
A Death in the Family '02
Backfire '88
Consenting Adult '85
Burning Rage '84
The Last Married Couple in America '80
Oh, God! Book 2 '80
The Promise '79
Johnny, We Hardly Knew Ye '77
One Summer Love '76
The Affair '73
Summer Wishes, Winter Dreams '73
To All My Friends on Shore '77
I Never Sang for My Father '70

William Allen Castleman (1922-2006)
Johnny Firecloud '75
Bummer '73

Alberto Cavalcanti (1897-1982)
Nicholas Nickleby '46
They Made Me a Fugitive '47
Dead of Night '45

Peter Cattaneo (1964-)
Lucky Break '01
The Full Monty '96

Nick Cassavetes (1959-)
Alpha Dog '06
The Notebook '04
John Q '02
She's So Lovely '97
Unhook the Stars '96

Jeff Celentano
Gunshy '98
Under the Hula Moon '95

Liliana Cavani (1937-)
Francesco '89
Ripley's Game '02
The Berlin Affair '85
Beyond Obsession '82
The Night Porter '74
The Cannibals '70

Michael Caton-Jones (1958-)
Basic Instinct 2 '06
Shooting Dogs '05
City by the Sea '02
The Jackal '97
Rob Roy '95
This Boy's Life '93
Doc Hollywood '91
Memphis Belle '90
Scandal '89

Claude Chabrol (1930-)
Comedy of Power '06
The Bridesmaid '04
Merci pour le Chocolat '00
The Swindle '97
La Ceremonie '95
L'Enfer '93
Betty '92
Madame Bovary '91
Story of Women '88
Club Extinction '89
The Cry of the Owl '87
The Blood of Others '84
The Horse of Pride '80
Violette '78
Blood Relatives '77
Innocents with Dirty Hands '77
Twist '76
A Piece of Pleasure '74
Wedding in Blood '74
High Heels '72
Ten Days Wonder '72
La Rupture '70
This Man Must Die '70
La Femme Infidele '69
Les Biches '68
Les Cousins '59
Le Beau Serge '58
Le Boucher '69
Six in Paris '68
Bluebeard '63
Les Bonnes Femmes '60

Gurinder Chadha (1960-)
Paris, je t'aime '06
Bride & Prejudice '04
Bend It Like Beckham '02
What's Cooking? '00
Bhaji on the Beach '94

Justin Chadwick
The Other Boleyn Girl '08

Don Chaffey (1917-90)
Casino '80
C.H.O.M.P.S. '79
Magic of Lassie '78
Pete's Dragon '77
The Fourth Wish '75
Ride a Wild Pony '75
The Three Lives of Thomasina '63
Jason and the Argonauts '63
A Matter of WHO '62
Greyfriars Bobby '61
Dentist in the Chair '60
The Prince and the Pauper '62
The Horse Without a Head '63
The Viking Queen '67
One Million Years B.C. '66
Creatures the World Forgot '70

Youssef Chahine (1926-)
Destiny '97

Alexandria Again and Forever '90
An Egyptian Story '82
Alexandria... Why? '78

P. (Philip) Chalong
In Gold We Trust '91
Gold Raiders '83
H-Bomb '71

Gregg Champion (1956-)
Dodson's Journey '01
The Simple Life of Noah Dearborn '99
The Cowboy Way '94
Short Time '90

Benny Chan
Robin-B-Hood '06
New Police Story '04
Gen-X Cops '99
Jackie Chan's Who Am I '98

Gordon Chan (1960-)
The Medallion '03
Fist of Legend '94

Jackie Chan (1954-)
Jackie Chan's Who Am I '98
Downdraft '96
Operation Condor '91
Miracles '89
Project A: Part 2 '87
Operation Condor 2: The Armour of the Gods '86
Police Story '85
Project A '83
Young Master '80

Jay Chandrasekhar (1968-)
Beerfest '06
The Dukes of Hazzard '05
Club Dread '04
Super Troopers '01

Charlie Chaplin (1889-1977)
A Countess from Hong Kong '67
The Chaplin Revue '58
A King in New York '57
Limelight '52
Monsieur Verdoux '47
Modern Times '36
City Lights '31
The Gold Rush '25
The Kid '21
The Circus '19
Three Charlies and One Phoney! '18
The Rink '16
The Vagabond '16
The Adventurer '17
The Cure '17
The Floorwalker '17
The Immigrant '17
Burlesque on Carmen '16
Easy Street '16
The Fireman '16
One A.M. '16
The Count '16
The Pawnshop '16
Charlie Chaplin: Night at the Show '15
Charlie Chaplin... Our Hero! '15

Joe Chappelle
The Skulls 2 '02
Dracula: The Dark Prince '01
Phantoms '97
Halloween 6: The Curse of Michael Myers '95

Michael Chapman (1935-)
The Viking Sagas '95
The Clan of the Cave Bear '86
All the Right Moves '83

Matthew Chapman (1950-)
Heart of Midnight '89
Slow Burn '86
Strangers Kiss '83
Hussy '80

Larry Charles (1956-)
Borat: Cultural Learnings of America for Make Benefit Glorious Nation of Kazakhstan '06

Henri Charr
Hollywood Safari '96
My Uncle: The Alien '96
Caged Hearts '95
Cellblock Sisters: Banished Behind Bars '95
Illegal Entry: Formula for Fear '93

Etienne Chatiliez (1952-)
Le Bonheur Est Dans le Pre '95
Tatie Danielle '91
Life Is a Long Quiet River '88

Louis Chaudet (1884-1965)
Eyes Right! '26
Fighting Jack '26

Amin Qamar Chaudhri (1942-)
An Unremarkable Life '89
Tiger Warsaw '87
Deadly Vengeance '81

Charles Chauvel
The Fighting Rats of Tobruk '44
Forty Thousand Horsemen '41

Jeremiah S. Chechik (1955-)
The Bronx Is Burning '07
The Avengers '98
Diabolique '96
Benny & Joon '93
National Lampoon's Christmas Vacation '89

Peter Chelsom (1956-)
Shall We Dance? '04
Serendipity '01
Town and Country '01
The Mighty '98
Funny Bones '94
Hear My Song '91

Joan Chen (1961-)
Autumn in New York '00
Xiu Xiu: The Sent Down Girl '97

Kuo-fu Chen (1958-)
Double Vision '02
The Personals '98

Patrice Chereau (1944-)
Gabrielle '05
Intimacy '00
Those Who Love Me Can Take the Train '98
Queen Margot '94
L'Homme Blesse '83

Christopher Scott Cherot (1967-)
G '02

John R. Cherry, III
All New Adventures of Laurel and Hardy: For Love or Mummy '98
Ernest Goes to Africa '97
Ernest in the Army '97
Slam Dunk Ernest '95
Ernest Rides Again '93
Ernest Scared Stupid '91
Ernest Goes to Jail '90
Ernest Saves Christmas '88
Ernest Goes to Camp '87

Roger Christian (1944-)
Battlefield Earth '00
Masterminds '96
Underworld '96
Nostradamus '93
Starship '87
The Sender '82

Christian-Jaque (1904-94)
Legend of Frenchie King '71
Nana '55
Fanfan la Tulipe '51
La Chartreuse de Parme '48

Lionel Chetwynd (1940-)
Varian's War '01
Hanoi Hilton '87

Alton Cheung
See Godfrey Ho

Tommy Cheung
See Godfrey Ho

Pierre Chevalier (1915-)
Dr. Orloff and the Invisible Man '70

Stephen Chiau
See Stephen (Chiau) Chow

Lisa Cholodenko (1964-)
Laurel Canyon '02
High Art '98

Sylvain Chomet (1963-)
Paris, je t'aime '06
The Triplets of Belleville '02

Marvin J. Chomsky (1929-)
Catherine the Great '95
Robert Kennedy and His Times '90
The Brotherhood of the Rose '89
Nairobi Affair '88
Billionaire Boys Club '87
Anastasia: The Mystery of Anna '86
The Deliberate Stranger '86
Peter the Great '86
Tank '83
Inside the Third Reich '82
Attica '80
Holocaust '78
Little Ladies of the Night '77
Roots '77
Victory at Entebbe '76
Murph the Surf '75
Evel Knievel '72
Fireball Forward '72
The Shaming '71

Thomas Chong (1938-)
Far Out Man '89
Cheech and Chong's The Corsican Brothers '84
Cheech and Chong: Still Smokin' '83
Cheech and Chong's Nice Dreams '81
Cheech and Chong's Next Movie '80

Joyce Chopra (1938-)
Blonde '01
The Lady in Question '99
Murder in a Small Town '99
My Very Best Friend '96
Danger of Love '95
High Stakes '93
Murder in New Hampshire: The Pamela Smart Story '91
The Lemon Sisters '90
Smooth Talk '85

Elie Chouraqui (1953-)
Harrison's Flowers '02
Man on Fire '87
Love Songs '85

Stephen (Chiau) Chow (1962-)
Kung Fu Hustle '04
Shaolin Soccer '01

Nathaniel Christian
Club Fed '90
California Casanova '89

Benjamin Christiansen (1879-1959)
Mockery '27
Haxan: Witchcraft through the Ages '22

Mark Christopher
Pizza '05
54 '98

Yen Ping Chu
The Prisoner '90
Fantasy Mission Force '84

Lyndon Chubbuck
The War Bride '01
The Right Temptation '00
Naked Souls '95

Byron Ross Chudnow (1926-)
The Amazing Dobermans '76
Daring Dobermans '73
The Doberman Gang '72

Grigori Chukhraj (1921-2001)
Life Is Beautiful '79
Ballad of a Soldier '60

Ji-Yong Chung
White Badge '97
White Badge '92

Gerard Ciccoritti (1956-)
The Life Before This '99
Paris, France '94
Understudy: The Graveyard Shift 2 '88
Graveyard Shift '87
Psycho Girls '86

Matt Cimber (1936-)
Hundra '85
Yellow Hair & the Fortress of Gold '84
Time to Die '83
Butterfly '82
Fake Out '82
Witch Who Came from the Sea '76
Candy Tangerine Man '75
Lady Cocoa '75
The Black Six '74
Gemini Affair '74
Single Room Furnished '68

Michael Cimino (1943-)
Sunchaser '96
Desperate Hours '90
The Sicilian '87
Year of the Dragon '85
Heaven's Gate '81
The Deer Hunter '78
Thunderbolt & Lightfoot '74

Osvaldo Civirani (1917-)
Dead for a Dollar '70
Hercules vs. the Sons of the Sun '64

Rene Clair (1898-1981)
Les Grandes Manoeuvres '55
Beauties of the Night '52
Beauty and the Devil '50
And Then There Were None '45
It Happened Tomorrow '44
Forever and a Day '43
I Married a Witch '42
The Flame of New Orleans '41
The Ghost Goes West '36
Quatorze Juillet '32
A Nous la Liberte '31
Le Million '31
Under the Roofs of Paris '29
Italian Straw Hat '27
The Crazy Ray '22

Bob (Benjamin) Clark (1941-2007)
Karate Dog '04
Superbabies: Baby Geniuses 2 '04
Now & Forever '02
I'll Remember April '99
Baby Geniuses '98
My Summer Story '94
Loose Cannons '90
From the Hip '86
Turk 182! '85
Rhinestone '84
A Christmas Story '83
Porky's 2: The Next Day '83
Porky's '82
Tribute '80
Murder by Decree '79
Black Christmas '75
Children Shouldn't Play with Dead Things '72
Deathdream '72

Bruce (B.D.) Clark (1945-)
Galaxy of Terror '81
Ski Bum '75

Colbert Clark (1898-1960)
Fighting with Kit Carson '33
Mystery Squadron '33
The Three Musketeers '33
Whispering Shadow '33
Wolf Dog '33

Duane Clark
Family Tree '00
Protector '97

Greydon Clark (1943-)
Bitter Harvest '93
Shaking the Tree '92
Russian Roulette '93
Killer Instinct '92
Dance Macabre '91
The Forbidden Dance '90
Out of Sight, Out of Her Mind '89
Skinheads: The Second Coming of Hate '88
The Uninvited '88
Final Justice '84
Joy Sticks '83
Wacko '83
The Return '80
Angel's Brigade '79
Hi-Riders '77
Satan's Cheerleaders '77
Bad Bunch '76
Black Shampoo '76

James B. Clark (1908-2000)
Lassie: Well of Love '70
My Side of the Mountain '69
And Now Miguel '66
Island of the Blue Dolphins '64
Flipper '63
Misty '61
A Dog of Flanders '59

Jim Clark (1931-)
Madhouse '74
Rentadick '72
Think Dirty '70

Larry Clark (1943-)
Wassup Rockers '06
Bully '01
Teenage Caveman '01
Another Day in Paradise '98
Kids '95

William Clark
Windrunner '94

Alan Clarke (1935-90)
Rita, Sue & Bob Too '87
Scum '79

James Kenelm Clarke (1941-)
Going Undercover '88
Funny Money '82
The House on Straw Hill '76

Malcolm Clarke
Prisoner of Paradise '02
Chasing Holden '01
Voices from a Locked Room '95

Shirley Clarke (1919-97)
The Cool World '63
The Connection '61

Zoe Clarke-Williams (1974-)
New Best Friend '02
Men '97

James Clavell (1925-94)
The Last Valley '71
To Sir, with Love '67

William Claxton (1914-96)
The Canterville Ghost '91
Night of the Lepus '72
Fangs of the Wild '54

Jack Clayton (1921-95)
The Lonely Passion of Judith Hearne '87
Something Wicked This Way Comes '83
The Great Gatsby '74
The Pumpkin Eater '64
The Innocents '61
Room at the Top '59

Tom Clegg (1927-)
Sharpe's Challenge '06
Sharpe's Justice '97
Sharpe's Revenge '97
Sharpe's Waterloo '97
Sharpe's Mission '96
Sharpe's Regiment '96
Sharpe's Siege '96
Sharpe's Battle '94
Sharpe's Company '94
Sharpe's Enemy '94
Sharpe's Gold '94
Sharpe's Honour '94
Sharpe's Sword '94
Sharpe's Eagle '93
Sharpe's Rifles '93
Any Man's Death '90
A Casualty of War '90
Stroke of Midnight '90
Mountbatten: The Last Viceroy '86
Children of the Full Moon '84
The Inside Man '84
The House that Bled to Death '81
McVicar '80
Destination Moonbase Alpha '75

Brian Clemens (1931-)
Anatomy of Terror '74
Captain Kronos: Vampire Hunter '74

William Clemens (1905-80)
Night of January 16th '41
Nancy Drew and the Hidden Staircase '39
Nancy Drew, Reporter '39
Nancy Drew—Trouble Shooter '39
Nancy Drew—Detective '38

Dick Clement (1937-)
Porridge '91
Water '85
Bullshot '83
Catch Me a Spy '71

Rene Clement (1913-96)
Wanted: Babysitter '75
And Hope to Die '72
The Deadly Trap '71
Rider on the Rain '70
Is Paris Burning? '66
Purple Noon '60
Joy House '64
Gervaise '56
Forbidden Games '52
The Walls of Malapaga '49
Battle of the Rails '46

Ron Clements (1953-)
Treasure Planet '02
Hercules '97
Aladdin '92
The Little Mermaid '89
The Great Mouse Detective '86

Graeme Clifford (1942-)
Redeemer '00
Caracara '00
The Last Don 2 '98
My Husband's Secret Life '98
The Last Don '97
Past Tense '94
Deception '92
Gleaming the Cube '89
The Turn of the Screw '89
Burke & Wills '85

Little Red Riding Hood '83
Frances '82
The Boy Who Left Home to Find Out About the Shivers '81

Elmer Clifton (1892-1949)
Silver Bandit '50
The Judge '49
Streets of Sin '49
Red Rock Outlaw '47
Marked for Murder '45
Boss of Rawhide '44
Dead or Alive '44
Gangsters of the Frontier '44
Guns of the Law '44
Seven Doors to Death '44
Youth Aflame '44
Frontier Law '43
Sundown Kid '43
Law of the Texan '38
Roaring Speedboats '37
Slaves in Bondage '37
Custer's Last Stand '36
Assassin of Youth '35
Captured in Chinatown '35
Cyclone of the Saddle '35
Fighting Caballero '35
Pals of the Range '35
Rough Riding Ranger '35
Skull & Crown '35
Let 'er Go Gallegher '28
Down to the Sea in Ships '22

Edward F. (Eddie) Cline (1892-1961)
Slightly Terrific '44
Crazy House '43
Swingtime Johnny '43
Private Buckaroo '42
Snuffy Smith, Yard Bird '42
Cracked Nuts '41
Never Give a Sucker an Even Break '41
The Villain Still Pursued Her '41
The Bank Dick '40
My Little Chickadee '40
Breaking the Ice '38
Hawaii Calls '38
Peck's Bad Boy with the Circus '38
Cowboy Millionaire '35
Dude Ranger '34
Peck's Bad Boy '34
So This Is Africa '33
Hook, Line and Sinker '30
Three Ages '23

Robert Clouse (1929-97)
Ironheart '92
China O'Brien 2 '89
China O'Brien '88
Gymkata '85
Deadly Eyes '82
Force: Five '81
The Big Brawl '80
Game of Death '79
The Amsterdam Kill '78
The Pack '77
The Ultimate Warrior '75
Black Belt Jones '74
Enter the Dragon '73
Darker than Amber '70

Henri-Georges Clouzot (1907-77)
Diabolique '55
Wages of Fear '55
Manon '50
Jenny Lamour '47
Le Corbeau '43

E.B. (Enzo Barboni) Clucher (1922-2002)
Sons of Trinity '95
The Odd Squad '86
Go for It '83
Crime Busters '78
Trinity Is Still My Name '75
They Call Me Trinity '72

George Clooney (1961-)
Good Night, and Good Luck '05
Confessions of a Dangerous Mind '02

Craig Clyde
The Derby Stallion '05
Miracle Dogs '03
Walking Thunder '94
The Legend of Wolf Mountain '92
Little Heroes '91

Lewis (Luigi Cozzi) Coates (1947-)
Hercules 2 '85
Hercules '83
Alien Contamination '81
Star Crash '78

Stacy Cochran
My New Gun '92
Boys '95

Jean Cocteau (1889-1963)
The Testament of Orpheus '59
Orpheus '49
The Eagle Has Two Heads '48
Beauty and the Beast '46
The Blood of a Poet '30

Ethan Coen (1957-)
The Ladykillers '04
The Man Who Wasn't There '01
O Brother, Where Art Thou? '00
The Big Lebowski '97
Fargo '96
The Hudsucker Proxy '93
Barton Fink '91
Miller's Crossing '90
Raising Arizona '87
Blood Simple '85

Joel Coen (1954-)
No Country for Old Men '07
Paris, je t'aime '06
The Ladykillers '04
The Man Who Wasn't There '01
O Brother, Where Art Thou? '00
The Big Lebowski '97
Fargo '96
The Hudsucker Proxy '93
Barton Fink '91
Miller's Crossing '90
Raising Arizona '87
Blood Simple '85

Dan Cohen
Corporate Affairs '07

Larry Cohen (1947-)
Original Gangstas '96
As Good as Dead '95
Wicked Stepmother '89
Deadly Illusion '87
It's Alive 3: Island of the Alive '87
Return to Salem's Lot '87
The Stuff '85
Special Effects '85
Perfect Strangers '84
Q (The Winged Serpent) '82
It's Alive 2: It Lives Again '78
The Private Files of J. Edgar Hoover '77
God Told Me To '76
It's Alive '74
Black Caesar '73
Hell Up in Harlem '73
Bone '72

Eli Cohen (1940-)
Under the Domim Tree '95
The Quarrel '93
The Summer of Aviya '88

Gary P. Cohen
Video Violence Part 2... The Exploitation! '87
Video Violence '87

Howard R. Cohen (1942-99)
Deathstalker 4: Match of Titans '92
Saturday the 14th Strikes Back '88
Time Trackers '88
Space Raiders '83
Saturday the 14th '81

Michael Cohn
Snow White: A Tale of Terror '97
When the Bough Breaks '93
Interceptor '92

Steve Cohen
Bar Hopping '00
Devil in the Flesh '98
Tough and Deadly '94

Rob Cohen (1949-)
The Mummy: Tomb of the Dragon Emperor '08
Stealth '05
XXX '02
The Fast and the Furious '01
The Skulls '00
The Rat Pack '98
Daylight '96
Dragonheart '96
Dragon: The Bruce Lee Story '93
A Small Circle of Friends '80
Scandalous '84

Isabel Coixet (1960-)
My Life Without Me '03
Things I Never Told You '96

Cyril Coke (1914-93)
Pride and Prejudice '85
The Duchess of Duke Street '78

Harley Cokliss (1945-)
Inferno '99
Hercules the Legendary Journeys, Vol. 2: The Lost Kingdom '94
Dream Demon '88
Malone '87
Black Moon Rising '86
Warlords of the 21st Century '82

Marcus Cole
The Christmas Box '95
From the Mixed-Up Files of Mrs. Basil E. Frankweiler '95
Century '82

Nigel Cole
A Lot Like Love '05
Calendar Girls '03
Saving Grace '00

John David Coles
The Good Fight '92
Rising Son '90
Signs of Life '89

Carl Colpaert (1963-)
Drowning on Dry Land '00
Fécade '98
The Crew '95
Delusion '91
In the Aftermath: Angels Never Sleep '87

Walter Colmes
Accomplice '46
Identity Unknown '45
The Woman Who Came Back '45

Peter Collinson (1936-80)
The Earthling '80
The House on Garibaldi Street '79
Tomorrow Never Comes '77
The Sell Out '76
Spiral Staircase '75
Ten Little Indians '75
Fright '71
The Italian Job '69

Max Allan Collins (1948-)
Real Time: Siege at Lucas Street Market '00
Mommy 2: Mommy's Day '96
Mommy '95

Bill Condon (1955-)
Dreamgirls '06
Kinsey '04
Gods and Monsters '98
Candyman 2: Farewell to the Flesh '94
Dead in the Water '91
White Lie '91
Murder 101 '91
Sister, Sister '87

Kevin Connor (1940-)
Murder Without Conviction '04
Many, Mother of Jesus '99
The Hollywood Detective '89
The Old Curiosity Shop '94
Diana: Her True Story '93
Sunset Grill '92
Iran: Days of Crisis '91
House Where Evil Dwells '82
Goliath Awaits '81
Motel Hell '80
The People That Time Forgot '77
At the Earth's Core '76
Choice of Weapons '76
The Land That Time Forgot '75
From Beyond the Grave '73

W. Merle Connell (1905-63)
The Devil's Sleep '51
Test Tube Babies '48

Giuseppe Colizzi (1925-78)
All the Way, Boys '73
Boot Hill '69
Ace High '68

Duilio Coletti (1906-99)
Submarine Attack '54
Lure of the Sila '49

Richard A. Colla (1936-)
Blind Witness '89
Naked Lie '89
The Prize Pulitzer '89
Don't Look Back: The Story of Leroy "Satchel" Paige '81
Battlestar Galactica '78
Olly Olly Oxen Free '78
Fuzz '72

Chris Columbus (1958-)
Rent '05
Harry Potter and the Chamber of Secrets '02
Harry Potter and the Sorcerer's Stone '01
Bicentennial Man '99
Stepmom '98
Nine Months '95
Mrs. Doubtfire '93
Home Alone 2: Lost in New York '92
Only the Lonely '91
Home Alone '90
Heartbreak Hotel '88
Adventures in Babysitting '87

Robert Collector
Believe in Me '06
Red Heat '85

James F. Collier (1929-91)
China Cry '91
Joni '79
The Hiding Place '75

Boon Collins
Abducted 2: The Reunion '94
Spirit of the Eagle '90
Abducted '86

Lewis D. Collins (1899-1954)
The Fighting Redhead '49
Jungle Goddess '49
Heading for Heaven '47
Killer Dill '47
Lost City of the Jungle '45
Master Key '44
Raiders of Ghost City '44
Mystery of the Riverboat '44
Junior G-Men of the Air '42
The Great Plane Robbery '40
Doughnuts & Society '35
Make a Million '35
Sing Sing Nights '35
Brand of Hate '34
The Man from Hell '34
Gun Law '33
Trouble Busters '33

Robert E. Collins
J. Edgar Hoover '87
Mafia Princess '86
Our Family Business '81
Gideon's Trumpet '80
The Life and Assassination of the Kingfish '76

Ryan Combs (1974-)
Animal 2 '07
The Hit '06
A Cry from the Mountain '85
Straight out of Compton '99
Son '04

Lance Comfort (1908-66)
The Great Armored Car Swindle '64
Great Day '46
Hotel Reserve '44
The Courageous Mr. Penn '41

Luigi Comencini (1916-2007)
Misunderstood '87
Till Marriage Do Us Part '74
Heidi '52

Don Como
Unknown Powers '80
Aliens from Spaceship Earth '77

Fernando Colomo (1942-)
Star Knight '85
Skyline '84

Richard Compton (1938-2007)
Super Force '90
Angels Die Hard '84
Wild Times '79
Deadman's Curve '78
Return to Macon County '75
Macon County Line '74

James A. Contner
The Cover Girl Murders '93
The Return of Eliot Ness '91
The Fire in the Stone '85
Sara Dare '81

Gary Conway (1936-)
The People That Time Forgot '77

Jack Conway (1887-1952)
Julia Misbehaves '48
The Hucksters '47
Dragon Seed '44
Honky Tonk '41
Love Crazy '41
Boom Town '40
Let Freedom Ring '39
Too Hot to Handle '38
Saratoga '37
Libeled Lady '36
A Tale of Two Cities '36
The Girl from Missouri '34
Tarzan and His Mate '34
Viva Villa! '34

Merian C. Cooper (1893-1973)
King Kong '33
Chang: A Drama of the Wilderness '27
The Last of the Mohicans '36
Grass '25

Phillip Cook
Invader '91

Troy Cook
Star Quest '89
Phoenix '95

Bruce Cook, Jr.
The Incredible Rocky Mountain Race '77
Nightwish '89

Fielder Cook (1923-2003)
The Member of the Wedding '97
Seize the Day '86
I Know Why the Caged Bird Sings '79
Love Affair: The Eleanor & Lou Gehrig Story '77
Judge Horton and the Scottsboro Boys '76
Miles to Go Before I Sleep '74
The Hideaways '73
Homecoming: A Christmas Story '71
A Big Hand for the Little Lady '66
Patterns '56

Martha Coolidge (1946-)
Material Girls '06
The Prince & Me '04
The Flamingo Rising '01
If These Walls Could Talk 2 '00
Introducing Dorothy Dandridge '99
Out to Sea '97
Three Wishes '95
Angie '94
Lost in Yonkers '93
Crazy in Love '92
Rambling Rose '91
Bare Essentials '91
Plain Clothes '88
Real Genius '85
Joy of Sex '84
Valley Girl '83
The City Girl '84

Michael Cooney (1967-)
Jack Frost 2: Revenge of the Mutant Killer Snowman '00
Jack Frost '97

Jackie Cooper (1921-)
Leave 'Em Laughing '81
Marathon '80
Rodeo Girl '80
White Mama '80
Rainbow '78

Stuart Cooper (1942-)
Chameleon '98
The Hunted '98
The Ticket '97
Bloodhounds 2 '96
Dead Ahead '96
Bitter Vengeance '94
Out of Annie's Past '94
Dancing with Danger '93
Rubdown '93
Payoff '91
The Long, Hot Summer '86
A.D. '85
Disappearance '81

Christopher Coppola
Gunfighter '98
Deadfall '93
Dracula's Widow '88

Francis Ford Coppola (1939-)
Youth Without Youth '07
John Grisham's The Rainmaker '97
Jack '96
Bram Stoker's Dracula '92
The Godfather, Part 3 '90
New York Stories '89

Coppola (continued)
Tucker: The Man and His Dream '88
Gardens of Stone '87
Peggy Sue Got Married '86
Rip van Winkle '85
The Cotton Club '84
The Outsiders '83
Rumble Fish '83
One from the Heart '82
The Godfather 1902-1958: The Complete Epic '81
Apocalypse Now '79
The Conversation '74
The Godfather, Part 2 '74
The Godfather '72
The Rain People '69
Finian's Rainbow '68
You're a Big Boy Now '66
Battle Beyond the Sun '63
Dementia 13 '63
The Terror '63
The Bellboy and the Playgirls '62
Tonight for Sure '61

Sofia Coppola (1971-)
Marie Antoinette '06
Lost in Translation '03
The Virgin Suicides '99

Frank Coraci (1965-)
Click '06
Around the World in 80 Days '04
The Waterboy '98
The Wedding Singer '97
Murdered Innocence '94

Gregory Corarito
Delinquent School Girls '84
Wanda, the Sadistic Hypnotist '67

Gerard Corbiau (1941-)
Farinelli '94
The Music Teacher '88

Bruno Corbucci (1931-96)
Aladdin '86
Miami Supercops '85
Cop on Blue Jeans '78

Sergio Corbucci (1927-90)
Super Fuzz '81
The Con Artists '80
Odds and Evens '78
The Switch '76
Sonny and Jed '73
Compañeros '70
Django '68
Hellbenders '67
Navajo Joe '67
Minnesota Clay '65

Bill Corcoran
Outlaw Justice '98
Portraits of a Killer '95
Sherlock Holmes and the Incident at Victoria Falls '91

Sebastian Cordero (1972-)
Cronicas '04
Ratas, Ratones, Rateros '99

Nicholas J. Corea (1943-99)
The Incredible Hulk Returns '88
Archer: The Fugitive from the Empire '81

David Corley
Angel's Dance '99
Executive Power '98

Roger Corman (1926-)
Frankenstein Unbound '90
Bloody Mama '70
Gas-s-s-s! '70
The St. Valentine's Day Massacre '67
The Trip '67
The Wild Angels '66
Masque of the Red Death '65
The Secret Invasion '64
Tomb of Ligeia '64
The Haunted Palace '63
The Raven '63
The Terror '63
X: The Man with X-Ray Eyes '63
Premature Burial '62
Tales of Terror '62
Tower of London '62
The Last Woman on Earth '61
The Pit and the Pendulum '61
Shame '61
Atlas '60
The Fall of the House of Usher '60
Little Shop of Horrors '60
Ski Troop Attack '60
A Bucket of Blood '59
The Wasp Woman '59
I, Mobster '58
Machine Gun Kelly '58
Teenage Caveman '58
Carnival Rock '57
Rock All Night '57
Sorority Girl '57
Teenage Doll '57
The Undead '57
The Gunslinger '56
It Conquered the World '56
She Gods of Shark Reef '56
Apache Woman '55
Day the World Ended '55
Swamp Women '55

Gerald Cormier
See Alan Rudolph

Alain Corneau (1943-)
Tous les Matins du Monde '92
Fort Saganne '84
Choice of Arms '83

Henry Cornelius (1913-58)
I Am a Camera '55
Genevieve '53
Passport to Pimlico '49

John Cornell (1941-)
Almost an Angel '90
Crocodile Dundee 2 '88

Hubert Cornfield (1929-2006)
The Night of the Following Day '69

Stephen Cornwell
Marshal Law '96
Killing Streets '91

Charles Correll
Philadelphia Experiment 2 '93

Michael Corrente (1960-)
Brooklyn Rules '07
Outside Providence '99
American Buffalo '95
Federal Hill '94

Lloyd Corrigan (1900-69)
Dancing Pirate '36
No One Man '32
Daughter of the Dragon '31

Don A. Coscarelli (1954-)
Bubba Ho-Tep '03
Phantasm 4: Oblivion '98
Phantasm 3: Lord of the Dead '94
Survival Quest '89
Phantasm 2 '88
Beastmaster '82
Phantasm '79

George P. Cosmatos (1941-2005)
The Shadow Conspiracy '96
Tombstone '93
Leviathan '89
Cobra '86
Rambo: First Blood, Part 2 '85
Of Unknown Origin '83
Escape to Athena '79
The Cassandra Crossing '76
Massacre in Rome '73
Restless '72

Mario Costa (1904-95)
Rough Justice '87
Gladiator of Rome '63

Constantin Costa-Gavras (1933-)
Amen '02
Mad City '97
Music Box '89
Betrayed '88
Conseil de Famille '86
Hanna K. '83
Missing '82
State of Siege '73
Z '69

Kevin Costner (1955-)
Open Range '03
The Postman '97
Dances with Wolves '90

Manny Coto
Star Kid '97
Dr. Giggles '92
Cover-Up '91
Playroom '90

Vittorio Cottafavi (1914-98)
Hercules and the Captive Women '63
Goliath and the Dragon '61

Jack Couffer (1924-)
Living Free '72
Ring of Bright Water '69
Nikki, the Wild Dog of the North '61

Allen Coulter
Hollywoodland '06

Alex Cox (1954-)
The Winner '96
Highway Patrolman '91
Straight to Hell '87
Walker '87
Sid & Nancy '86
Repo Man '83

Nell Cox
Konrad '85

Paul Cox (1940-)
Innocence '00
Molokai: The Story of Father Damien '99
Lust and Revenge '95
A Woman's Tale '92
Vincent: The Life and Death of Vincent van Gogh '87
Cactus '86
Man of Flowers '84
My First Wife '84
Lonely Hearts '82
Kostas '79

Arthur Crabtree (1900-75)
Fiend without a Face '58
Dear Murderer '47

William Crain (1949-)
Midnight Fear '90
Kid from Not-So-Big '78
Dr. Black, Mr. Hyde '76
Blacula '72

Kenneth Crane
The Manster '59
Monster from Green Hell '58
When Hell Broke Loose '58

Jay Craven
Disappearances '06
A Stranger in the Kingdom '98
Where the Rivers Flow North '94

Wes Craven (1939-)
Paris, je t'aime '06
Red Eye '05
Cursed '04
Scream 3 '00
Music of the Heart '99
Scream 2 '97
Scream '96
Vampire in Brooklyn '95
Wes Craven's New Nightmare '94
The People under the Stairs '91
Shocker '89
The Serpent and the Rainbow '87
Deadly Friend '86
The Hills Have Eyes, Part 2 '84
Invitation to Hell '84
A Nightmare on Elm Street '84
Swamp Thing '82
Deadly Blessing '81
Summer of Fear '78
The Hills Have Eyes '77
Last House on the Left '72

Guy Crawford
Autopsy: A Love Story '02
The Catcher '98
Starved '97

Wayne Crawford
American Gothic '94
Crime Lords '91

Alfredo B. Crevenna (1914-96)
Neutron vs. the Maniac '62
The New Invisible Man '58

Charles Crichton (1910-99)
A Fish Called Wanda '88
The Battle of the Sexes '60
The Lavender Hill Mob '51
Train of Events '49
Against the Wind '48
Hue and Cry '47
Dead of Night '45

Michael Crichton (1942-)
The 13th Warrior '99
Physical Evidence '89
Runaway '84
Looker '81
The Great Train Robbery '79
Coma '78
Westworld '73
Pursuit '72

Donald Crisp (1880-1974)
Stand and Deliver '28
Sunny Side Up '28
Don Q., Son of Zorro '25
The Navigator '24

Armando Crispino (1925-)
Autopsy '74
Commandos '73
Dead Are Alive '72

Michael Cristofer (1945-)
Original Sin '01
Body Shots '99
Gia '98

Emma-Kate Croghan (1972-)
Strange Planet '99
Love and Other Catastrophes '95

Donald Crombie (1942-)
Kitty and the Bagman '82
Killing of Angel Street '81
The Irishman '78
Caddie '76

John Cromwell (1888-1979)
The Goddess '58
The Racket '51
Caged '50
Dead Reckoning '47
Anna and the King of Siam '46
The Enchanted Cottage '45
Since You Went Away '44
So Ends Our Night '41
Abe Lincoln in Illinois '40
In Name Only '39
Made for Each Other '39
Algiers '38
Prisoner of Zenda '37
Little Lord Fauntleroy '36
I Dream Too Much '35
Village Tale '35
Of Human Bondage '34
Spitfire '34
Ann Vickers '33
Vice Squad '31
Tom Sawyer '30
Dance of Life '29

David Cronenberg (1943-)
Eastern Promises '07
A History of Violence '05
Spider '02
eXistenZ '99
Crash '95
M. Butterfly '93
Naked Lunch '91
Dead Ringers '88
The Fly '86
Dead Zone '83
Videodrome '83
Scanners '81
The Brood '79
Fast Company '78
Rabid '77
They Came from Within '75

Alan Crosland (1894-1936)
Massacre '34
The Beloved Rogue '27
The Jazz Singer '27
Don Juan '26

Avery Crounse (1946-)
Cries of Silence '97
The Invisible Kid '88
Eyes of Fire '84

Cameron Crowe (1957-)
Elizabethtown '05
Vanilla Sky '01
Almost Famous '00
Jerry Maguire '96
Singles '92
Say Anything '89

Christopher Crowe (1948-)
Whispers in the Dark '92
Off Limits '87

James Cruze (1884-1942)
The Wrong Road '37
David Harum '34
I Cover the Waterfront '33
Mr. Skitch '33
The Great Gabbo '29
Old Ironsides '26
The Pony Express '25
The Covered Wagon '23
Leap Year '21
Hawthorne of the USA '19
The Roaring Road '19

Billy Crystal (1947-)
61* '01
Forget Paris '95
Mr. Saturday Night '92

Alfonso Cuaron (1961-)
Children of Men '06
Paris, je t'aime '06
Harry Potter and the Prisoner of Azkaban '04
Y Tu Mama Tambien '01
Great Expectations '97
A Little Princess '95
Fallen Angels 1 '93

Michael Cuesta (1963-)
12 and Holding '05
L.I.E. '01

George Cukor (1899-1983)
Rich and Famous '81
The Corn is Green '79
Love Among the Ruins '75
Travels with My Aunt '72
Justine '69
My Fair Lady '64
Heller in Pink Tights '60
Let's Make Love '60
Song Without End '60
Les Girls '57
Bhowani Junction '56
It Should Happen to You '54
A Star is Born '54
The Marrying Kind '52
Pat and Mike '52
Adam's Rib '50
Born Yesterday '50
A Life of Her Own '50
A Double Life '47
Gaslight '44
Keeper of the Flame '42
Two-Faced Woman '41
A Woman's Face '41
The Philadelphia Story '40
Susan and God '40
The Women '39
Holiday '38
Camille '36
Romeo and Juliet '36
David Copperfield '35
Sylvia Scarlett '35
Dinner at Eight '33
Little Women '33
A Bill of Divorcement '32
One Hour with You '32
What Price Hollywood? '32

Jeremiah Cullinane
Dangerous Curves '99
Spacejacked '98

Mark Cullingham (1942-95)
Dead on the Money '91
Gryphon '88
Cinderella '84

Irving Cummings (1888-1959)
Double Dynamite '51
The Dolly Sisters '46
Sweet Rosie O'Grady '43
Springtime in the Rockies '42
Louisiana Purchase '41
That Night in Rio '41
Down Argentine Way '40
Everything Happens at Night '39
The Story of Alexander Graham Bell '39
Just Around the Corner '38
Little Miss Broadway '38
Vogues of 1938 '37
The Poor Little Rich Girl '36
Curly Top '35
Broken Hearts of Broadway '23
Flesh and Blood '22

Rusty Cundieff (1965-)
Sprung '96
Tales from the Hood '95
Fear of a Black Hat '94

Richard Cunha (1922-2005)
Missile to the Moon '59
Frankenstein's Daughter '58
Giant from the Unknown '58
She Demons '58

Sean S. Cunningham (1941-)
Deepstar Six '89
The New Kids '85
Spring Break '83
A Stranger is Watching '82
Friday the 13th '80
Manny's Orphans '78

Terry Cunningham
Earthstorm '06
Chaos Factor '00

Frederick Curiel (1917-85)
Genie of Darkness '62
Neutron vs. the Death Robots '62
Neutron vs. the Amazing Dr. Caronte '61
Neutron vs. the Black Mask '61
Curse of Nostradamus '60
The Monster Demolisher '60

John Curran
The Painted Veil '06
We Don't Live Here Anymore '04
Praise '98

Dan Curtis (1928-2006)
The Love Letter '98
Trilogy of Terror 2 '96
Me and the Kid '93
Intruders '92

War & Remembrance: The Final Chapter '89
The War & Remembrance '88
The Winds of War '83
The Long Days of Summer '80
Express to Terror '79
The Last Ride of the Dalton Gang '79
Mrs. R's Daughter '79
When Every Day Was the Fourth of July '78
Curse of the Black Widow '77
Dead of Night '77
Burnt Offerings '76
Trilogy of Terror '75
Melvin Purvis: G-Man '74
Nightmare at 43 Hillcrest '74
Scream of the Wolf '74
The Turn of the Screw '74
Dracula '73
The Norliss Tapes '73
The Night Stranger '72
House of Dark Shadows '71
Night of Dark Shadows '70

Douglas Curtis

Simon Curtis
Five Days '07
David Copperfield '99

Vondie Curtis-Hall (1956-)
Waist Deep '06
Glitter '01
Gridlock'd '96

Michael Curtiz (1888-1962)
The Comancheros '61
The Adventures of Huckleberry Finn '60
Breath of Scandal '60
King Creole '58
Proud Rebel '58
We're No Angels '55
The Egyptian '54
White Christmas '54
Trouble along the Way '53
I'll See You in My Dreams '51
Jim Thorpe: All American '51
Young Man with a Horn '50
Flamingo Road '49
My Dream Is Yours '49
Romance on the High Seas '48
Life with Father '47
Night and Day '46
Mildred Pierce '45
Passage to Marseilles '44
This Is the Army '43
The Sea Wolf '41
Santa Fe Trail '40
The Sea Hawk '40
Virginia City '40
Dodge City '39
The Private Lives of Elizabeth & Essex '39
The Adventures of Robin Hood '38
Angels with Dirty Faces '38
Four Daughters '38
Kid Galahad '37
The Charge of the Light Brigade '36
Black Fury '35
Captain Blood '35
Female '33
Mystery of the Wax Museum '33
Doctor X '32
The Cabin in the Cotton '32
The Strange Love of Molly Louvain '32

Catherine Cyran
Christmas Do-Over '06
The Prince & Me 2: Royal Wedding '06

Paul Czinner (1890-1972)
Dreaming Lips '37
As You Like It '36

Morton DaCosta (1914-89)
The Music Man '62
Auntie Mame '58

Olivier Dahan (1967-)
La Vie en Rose '07
Crimson Rivers 2: Angels of the Apocalypse '05

Renee Daalder (1944-)
Habitat '97
Massacre at Central High '76

John Dahl (1956-)
You Kill Me '07
The Great Raid '05
Joy Ride '01
Rounders '98
Unforgettable '96
The Last Seduction '94
Red Rock West '93
Kill Me Again '89

Stephen Daldry (1960-)
The Hours '02
Billy Elliot '00

Zale Dalen (1947-)
Expect No Mercy '95
Deadly Business '77

Massimo Dallamano (1917-76)
Super Bitch '73
Dorian Gray '70
A Black Veil for Lisa '68

Joe D'Amato (1936-99)
Passion '32
Quest for the Mighty Sword '90
Blade Master '84
Ator the Fighting Eagle '83
Black Cobra '83
Buried Alive '81
Grim Reaper '81
Heroes in Hell '73

Michael Damian
Moondance Alexander '07
Hot Tamale '06

Damiano Damiani (1922-)
The Inquiry '87
The Sicilian Connection '85
Arrityville 2: The Possession '82
The Warning '80
Confessions of a Police Captain '72
A Bullet for the General '68
The Witch '66
Empty Canvas '64
The Hit Man '60

Jean-Pierre Dardenne (1951-)
The Child '05
The Son '02
Rosetta '99
La Promesse '96

Jonathan Darby
Hush '98
The Enemy Within '94

Gregory Dark
See Gregory Brown

Joan Darling (1935-)
First Love '77
Willa '79

Eric Darnell
Madagascar '05
Antz '98

Mel Damski (1946-)
Wildcard '92
A Connecticut Yankee in King Arthur's Court '89
Happy Together '89
Murder by the Book '87
A Winner Never Quits '86
Badge of the Assassin '85
Mischief '85
Yellowbeard '83
Legend of Walks Far Woman '82
American Dream '81
For Ladies Only '81
Long Journey Back '78

Rod Daniel (1942-)
Beethoven's 2nd '93
The Super '91
K-9 '89
Like Father, Like Son '87
Teen Wolf '85

Harold Daniels (1903-71)
House of the Black Death '65
Terror in the Haunted House '58
Poor White Trash '57
Sword of Venus '53

Jeff Daniels (1955-)
Super Sucker '03
Escanaba in da Moonlight '01

Marc Daniels (1912-89)
Vengeance '89
Planet Earth '74

Joe Dante (1946-)
Masters of Horror: Screwfly Solution '06
Looney Tunes: Back in Action '03
Small Soldiers '98
The Second Civil War '97
Runaway Daughters '94
Matinee '92
Gremlins 2: The New Batch '90
The 'Burbs '89
Amazon Women on the Moon '87
Innerspace '87
Explorers '85
Gremlins '84
Twilight Zone: The Movie '83
The Howling '81
Piranha '78
Hollywood Boulevard '76

Ray Danton (1931-92)
Tales of the Unexpected '91
Psychic Killer '75
Crypt of the Living Dead '73

Frank Darabont (1959-)
The Mist '07
The Majestic '01
The Green Mile '99
The Shawshank Redemption '94
Buried Alive '90

Gordon Davidson (1933-)
The Trial of the Catonsville Nine '72

Martin Davidson (1939-)
Looking for an Echo '99
Follow the River '95
Hard Promises '92
The Heart of Dixie '89
Long Gone '87
Eddie and the Cruisers '83
Hero at Large '80
The Lords of Flatbush '74

Gareth Davies
A Mind to Murder '96
Unexplained Laughter '89
Oliver Twist '85
Check Is in the Mail '85

John Davies (1953-)
Devices and Desires '91
Kim '84
A Married Man '84

Terence Davies (1945-)
House of Mirth '00
The Neon Bible '95
The Long Day Closes '92
Distant Voices, Still Lives '88

Andrew Davis (1946-)
The Guardian '06
Holes '03
Collateral Damage '02
A Perfect Murder '98
Chain Reaction '96
Steal Big, Steal Little '95
Under Siege '92
The Fugitive '93
The Package '89
Above the Law '88
Code of Silence '85
The Final Terror '83

B.J. Davis
Forget About It '06

Harry D'Abbadie D'Arrast (1897-1968)
Topaze '33
Raffles '30

Julie Dash (1952-)
The Rosa Parks Story '02
Love Song '00
Subway Stories '97
Daughters of the Dust '91

Jules Dassin (1911-2008)
Circle of Two '80
A Dream of Passion '78
Topkapi '64
Phaedra '61
Never on Sunday '60
Where the Hot Wind Blows '59
Rififi '54
Night and the City '50

Dorothy Davenport
See Dorothy Davenport Reid

Delmer Daves (1904-77)
Spencer's Mountain '63
Rome Adventure '62
Parrish '61
The Hanging Tree '59
A Summer Place '59
The Badlanders '58
Cowboy '58
Kings Go Forth '58
3:10 to Yuma '57
Jubal '56
Demetrius and the Gladiators '54
Drum Beat '54
Never Let Me Go '53
Treasure of the Golden Condor '53
Broken Arrow '50
Task Force '49
The Red House '47
Hollywood Canteen '44
Destination Tokyo '43

Lorena David
Extreme Dating '04
Outta Time '01

Pierre David (1944-)
Scanner Cop '94

Boaz Davidson (1943-)
Outside the Law '95
American Cyborg: Steel Warrior '94
Solar Force '94
Going Bananas '88
Salsa '88
Dutch Treat '86
Last American Virgin '82
Hospital Massacre '81
Hot Bubblegum '81

Desmond Davis
Ordeal by Innocence '84
The Sign of Four '83
Clash of the Titans '81
Nice Girl Like Me '69
Smashing Time '67
Girl with Green Eyes '64

John A. Davis
The Ant Bully '06
Jimmy Neutron: Boy Genius '01

Julie Davis (1969-)
Amy's O '02
All Over the Guy '01
I Love You, I Love You, Don't Touch Me! '97

Lee Davis
Christmas at Water's Edge '04

Mick Davis (1961-)
Modigliani '04
The Match '99

Nick Davis
The Survivor '98

Michael Davis (1961-)
Shoot 'Em Up '07
Monster Man '03
100 Girls '00
3 A.M. '01

Ossie Davis (1917-2005)
Gordon's War '73
Cotton Comes to Harlem '70

Tamra Davis (1962-)
Crossroads '02
Skipped Parts '00
Best Men '98
Half-Baked '97
Billy Madison '94
CB4: The Movie '93
Guncrazy '92

Charles Davis
Die Watching '93
White Ghost '88

Norman Dawn (1884-)

Anthony M. Dawson (1930-2002)
Tornado '83
Codename: Wildgeese '84
Yor, the Hunter from the Future '83
Tiger Joe '85
Jungle Raiders '85
Indio '90
Ark of the Sun God '82
Hunters of the Golden Cobra '82
Cannibal Apocalypse '80
The Last Hunter '80
The Squeeze '80
Killer Fish '79
The Rip Off '78
Death Rage '77
The Stranger and the Gunfighter '76
Take a Hard Ride '75
Mr. Superinvisible '73
Andy Warhol's Dracula '74
Seven Deaths in the Cat's Eye '72
Web of the Spider '70
And God Said to Cain '70
Lightning Bolt '67
Planet on the Prowl '65
The Virgin of Nuremberg '65
Castle of Blood '64
Hercules, Prisoner of Evil '64
Battle of the Worlds '61
Assignment Outer Space '61

Ernest Day (1927-2006)
Waltz across Texas '83
Green Ice '81

Robert Day (1922-)
The Quick and the Dead '87
Lady from Yesterday '85
Your Place or Mine '83
Peter and Paul '81
The Man with Bogart's Face '80
Walking Through the Fire '79
Murder by Natural Causes '79
The Grass Is Always Greener Over the Septic Tank '78
Initiation of Sarah '78
A Home of Our Own '75
Death Stalk '74
Two-Way Stretch '60
First Man into Space '60
Corridors of Blood '58
The Haunted Strangler '58
The Count of Monte Cristo '99

Josee Dayan (1943-)
Dangerous Liaisons '03
Balzac: A Life of Passion '99

Lyman Dayton
Hot Chocolate '92
The Avenging '82
Dream Machine '9*
The Red Fury '84
Baker's Hawk '76

Jan De Bont (1943-)
Lara Croft Tomb Raider: The Cradle of Life '03
The Haunting '99
Speed 2: Cruise Control '97
Twister '96
Speed '94

Philippe de Broca (1933-2004)
On Guard! '03
Dear Detective '77
Le Magnifique '76
Le Cavalier '7*
Jupiter's Thigh '8*
Louisiana '87
King of Hearts '66
That Man from Rio '64
Cartouche '62

Fred de Cordova (1910-2001)
Frankie and Johnny '65
I'll Take Sweden '65
Here Come the Nelsons '52
Yankee Buccaneer '52
Bedtime for Bonzo '51
Buccaneer's Girl '50
For the Love of Mary '48

Frank De Felitta (1921-)
Scissors '91
Dark Night of the Scarecrow '81

Fabrizio de Angelis (1940-)
Karate Warrior '88
Thunder Warrior 3 '88
Thunder Warrior '86
Operation 'Nam '85
Thunder Warrior 2 '85

Raymond De Felitta (1964-)
Two Family House '99
Cafe Society '97
'05

Eduardo de Filippo (1900-84)
Seven Deadly Sins '53

Michael de Gaetano
The Haunted '73
UFO: Target Earth '74

Rolf de Heer (1951-)
Dance Me to My Song '98
The Quiet Room '96
Alien Visitor '95
Bad Boy Bubby '93
Dingo '90
Encounter at Raven's Gate '88

Ate De Jong (1953-)
Highway to Hell '92
Drop Dead Fred '91
A Flight of Rainbirds '81

Hubert de la Bouillerie (1951-)
The Apocalypse '96
The Right to Remain Silent '95

Alex de la Iglesia (1965-)
El Crimen Perfecto '04
Dance with the Devil '97
The Day of the Beast '95

Eloy De La Iglesia (1944-)
El Diputado '78
Cannibal Man '71

Jose Antonio De La Loma (1924-2004)
Fine Gold '88
A Man of Passion '88
Counterfeit '87
Street Warriors '87
Target Eagle '84
The Barcelona Kill '77
The Boldest Job in the West '71
Surprise Attack '70

Gerardo (Gerry) De Leon (1913-81)
Brides of the Beast '68
Mad Doctor of Blood Island '68
The Vampire People '66
The Walls of Hell '64
Terror is a Man '59

Marcus De Leon
The Big Squeeze '96
Kiss Me a Killer '91

Paul de Lussanet
Mysteries '84
Dear Boys '80

Alberto De Martino (1929-)
Hellhole '85
Miami Horror '87
Bloodlink '86
Formula for a Murder '85
The Puma Man '80
The Chosen '77
Strange Shadows in an Empty Room '76
Django Shoots First '74
The Tempter '74
New Mafia Boss '72
Scenes from a Murder '72
Dirty Heroes '71
Secret Agent 00 '67
The Triumph of Hercules '66
Medusa Against the Son of Hercules '62

Pierre De Moro
Hellhole '85
Savannah Smiles '82
Story of a Cowboy Angel '81

Robert De Niro (1943-)
The Good Shepherd '06
A Bronx Tale '93

Manoel de Oliveira (1908-)
Belle Toujours '06
I'm Going Home '00
Party '96
Voyage to the Beginning of the World '96
The Convent '95
Abraham's Valley '93

Armando de Ossorio (1926-2001)
Night of the Death Cult '75
People Who Own the Dark '75
Return of the Evil Dead '75
Terror Beach '75
Horror of the Zombies '74

Brian De Palma (1941-)
Redacted '07
The Black Dahlia '06
Femme Fatale '02
Mission to Mars '00
Snake Eyes '98
Mission: Impossible '96
Carlito's Way '93
Raising Cain '92
The Bonfire of the Vanities '90
Casualties of War '89
The Untouchables '87
Wise Guys '86
Body Double '84
Scarface '83
Blow Out '81
Home Movies '79
The Fury '78
Carrie '76
Obsession '76
Phantom of the Paradise '74
Sisters '73
Hi, Mom! '70
The Wedding Party '69
Greetings '68

Jean De Segonzac
Mimic 2 '01
Homicide: The Movie '00

Vittorio De Sica (1902-74)
The Garden of the Finzi-Continis '71
Woman Times Seven '67
Marriage Italian Style '64
Yesterday, Today and Tomorrow '64
Boccaccio '70 '62
Two Women '61
It Happened in the Park '56
The Roof '56
Umberto D '55
The Gold of Naples '54
Indiscretion of an American Wife '54
Miracle in Milan '51
The Bicycle Thief '48
Shoeshine '47
The Children Are Watching Us '44
Teresa Venerdi '41

Tom De Simone (1939-)
Angel 3: The Final Chapter '88
Reform School Girls '86
The Concrete Jungle '82
Hell Night '81
Chatterbox '76
Terror in the Jungle '68

Steven E. de Souza (1947-)
Possessed '00
Street Fighter '94

Andre de Toth (1912-2002)
The Mongols '60
Morgan the Pirate '60
The Day of the Outlaw '59
The Indian Fighter '55
Crime Wave '54
House of Wax '53
The Stranger Wore a Gun '53
Last of the Comanches '52
Springfield Rifle '52
Man in the Saddle '51
Pitfall '48
Ramrod '47
Dark Waters '44

Geoffrey De Vallois
Vampire Centerfolds '98
Sorority House Vampires '95

Alfredo de Villa
Adrift in Manhattan '07
Yellow '06
Washington Heights '02

Basil Dean (1888-1978)
21 Days '37
Lorna Doone '34

William Dear (1944-)
The Foursome '06
School of Life '05
Balloon Farm '97
Wild America '97
Angels in the Outfield '94
If Looks Could Kill '91
Harry and the Hendersons '87
Timerider '83
Northville Cemetery Massacre '76

Basil Dearden (1911-71)
The Man Who Haunted Himself '70
The Assassination Bureau '69
Woman of Straw '64
Victim '61
Sapphire '59
The Smallest Show on Earth '57
Who Done It? '56
The Blue Lamp '49
Train of Events '49
Captive Heart '47
Frieda '47
Dead of Night '45

James Dearden (1949-)
Rogue Trader '98
A Kiss Before Dying '91
Pascali's Island '88
Cold Room '84

John DeBello (1952-)
Killer Tomatoes Eat France '91
Killer Tomatoes Strike Back '90
Return of the Killer Tomatoes! '88
Happy Hour '87
Attack of the Killer Tomatoes '77

James D. Deck (1964-)
Silent Partner '05
Two Shades of Blue '98

David DeCoteau (1962-)
Witches of the Caribbean '05
Ring of Darkness '04
The Brotherhood 3: The Young Demons '02
Brotherhood 2: The Young Warlocks '01
Ancient Evil: Scream of the Mummy '00
Voodoo Academy '00
Curse of the Puppet Master: The Human Experiment '98
Frankenstein Reborn '98
Leather Jacket Love Story '98
Talisman '98
Femalien '98
Prey of the Jaguar '96
Skeletons '96
Beach Babes 2: Cave Girl Island '95
Prehysteria 3 '95
Beach Babes from Beyond '93
Test Tube Teens from the Year 2000 '93
Puppet Master 3: Toulon's Revenge '90
Lady Avenger '89
Deadly Embrace '88
Dr. Alien '88
Creepozoids '87
Nightmare Sisters '87
Sorority Babes in the Slimeball Bowl-A-Rama '87

Allessandro DeGaetano
Project Metalbeast: DNA Overload '94
Bloodbath in Psycho Town '89

Philip DeGuere (1944-2005)
Misfits of Science '85
Dr. Strange '78

Edward Dein (1907-84)
Curse of the Undead '59
The Leech Woman '59
Shack Out on 101 '55

Donna Deitch (1945-)
Common Ground '00
The Devil's Arithmetic '99
Prison Stories: Women on the Inside '91
The Women of Brewster Place '89
Desert Hearts '86

Steve DeJarnatt
Miracle Mile '89
Cherry 2000 '88

Fred Dekker (1959-)
RoboCop 3 '91
The Monster Squad '87
Night of the Creeps '86

Peter Del Monte (1943-)
Traveling Companion '96
Julia and Julia '87
Invitation au Voyage '82

Deborah Del Prete
Ricochet River '98
Simple Justice '89

Roy Del Ruth (1895-1961)
On Moonlight Bay '51
The West Point Story '50
Babe Ruth Story '48
Broadway Rhythm '44
Du Barry Was a Lady '43
The Chocolate Soldier '41
Topper Returns '41
Happy Landing '38
My Lucky Star '38
Broadway Melody of 1938 '37
On the Avenue '37
Born to Dance '36
Broadway Melody of 1936 '35
Kid Millions '34
Bureau of Missing Persons '33
Employees' Entrance '33
Lady Killer '33
Blessed Event '32
Blonde Crazy '31
The Maltese Falcon '31

Guillermo del Toro (1964-)
Hellboy 2: The Golden Army '08
Pan's Labyrinth '06
Hellboy '04
Blade 2 '02
Mimic '97
Cronos '94

Jean Delannoy (1908-)
Bernadette '90
Imperial Venus '71
This Special Friendship '67
Love and the Frenchwoman '60
The Hunchback of Notre Dame '57
La Symphonie Pastorale '46
Eternal Return '43

Dom DeLuise (1933-)
Boys Will Be Boys '97
Hot Stuff '80

Tulio Demicheli (1915-92)
Mean Machine '73
Dracula vs. Frankenstein '69
Son of Captain Blood '62

Cecil B. DeMille (1881-1959)
The Ten Commandments '56
The Greatest Show on Earth '52
Samson and Delilah '50
Unconquered '47
The Story of Dr. Wassell '44
Reap the Wild Wind '42
Union Pacific '39
The Plainsman '37
The Crusades '35
Cleopatra '34
The Sign of the Cross '33
Madam Satan '30
King of Kings '27
The Road to Yesterday '25
The Ten Commandments '23
Affairs of Anatol '21
Why Change Your Wife? '20
Male and Female '19
The Little American '17
The Cheat '15

Jonathan Demme (1944-)
Neil Young: Heart of Gold '06
The Manchurian Candidate '04
The Truth About Charlie '02
Beloved '98
Subway Stories '97
Philadelphia '93
The Silence of the Lambs '91
Married to the Mob '88
Swimming to Cambodia '87
Something Wild '86
Stop Making Sense '84
Swing Shift '84
Who Am I This Time? '82
Melvin and Howard '80
Last Embrace '79
Citizens Band '77
Fighting Mad '76
Crazy Mama '75
Caged Heat '74

Ted (Edward) Demme (1964-2002)
A Decade Under the Influence '02
Blow '01
Life '99
Monument Ave. '98
Subway Stories '96
Beautiful Girls '96
The Ref '93
Who's the Man? '93

Jacques Demy (1931-90)
A Slightly Pregnant Man '79
Peau D'Ane '71
Donkey Skin '70
The Young Girls of Rochefort '68
Umbrellas of Cherbourg '64
Lola '61

Claire Denis (1948-)
The Intruder '04
Friday Night '02
Beau Travail '98
Nenette and Boni '96
I Can't Sleep '93
No Fear, No Die '90
Chocolat '88

Pen Densham (1947-)
Houdini '99
Moll Flanders '96
The Kiss '88
The Zoo Gang '85

Ruggero Deodato (1939-)
Dial Help '88
The Lone Runner '88
The Barbarians '87
Phantom of Death '87
Cut and Run '85
House on the Edge of the Park '84

Gerard Depardieu (1948-)
Paris, je t'aime '06
The Bridge '00
Tartuffe '84

Jacques Deray (1929-2003)
The Outside Man '73
Borsalino '70
Swimming Pool '70
La Piscine '69

John Derek (1926-98)
Ghosts Can't Do It '90
Bolero '84
Tarzan, the Ape Man '81
Fantasies '73
Confessions of Tom Harris '72
Once Before I Die '65

Scott Derrickson
The Exorcism of Emily Rose '05
Hellraiser 5: Inferno '00

Dominique Deruddere (1957-)
Everybody's Famous! '00
Hombres Complicados '97
Suite 16 '94
Wait until Spring, Bandini '90

Caleb Deschanel (1941-)
Crusoe '89
The Escape Artist '82

Arnaud Desplechin (1960-)
Kings and Queen '04
Esther Kahn '00
My Sex Life... Or How I Got into an Argument '96
La Sentinelle '92

Howard Deutch (1950-)
The Whole Ten Yards '04
The Replacements '00
Neil Simon's The Odd Couple 2 '98
Grumpier Old Men '95
Getting Even with Dad '94
Article 99 '92
The Great Outdoors '88
Some Kind of Wonderful '87
Pretty in Pink '86

Geoffrey DeVallois
See Geoffrey De Vallois

Ross Devenish (1939-)
A Certain Justice '99
Over Indulgence '87
Bleak House '85

Michel DeVille (1931-)
Almost Peaceful '02
La Lectrice '88
Peril '85
Voyage en Douce '81

David Devine
Bailey's Billion$ '05
Beethoven Lives Upstairs '92

Dennis Devine
Bloodstream '00
Merchants of Death '99
Vampires of Sorority Row: Kickboxers From Hell '99
Haunted '98
Amazon Warrior '97
Things 2 '97
Things '93
Dead Girls '90
Fatal Images '89

Danny DeVito (1944-)
Duplex '03
Death to Smoochy '02
Matilda '96
Hoffa '92
The War of the Roses '89
Throw Momma from the Train '87
Amazing Grace '84
Ratings Game '84

John Dexter (1925-90)
I Want What I Want '72
The Virgin Soldiers '69

Maury Dexter (1927-)
Hell's Belles '69
Surf Party '64

Tom Dey
Failure to Launch '06
Showtime '02
Shanghai Noon '00

Fernando Di Leo (1932-2003)
- Violent Breed '83
- Big Boss '77
- Mr. Scarface '77
- Kidnap Syndicate '76
- Loaded Guns '75
- Rulers of the City '76
- Hired to Kill '73
- Hit Men '73
- Manhunt '73
- Slaughter Hotel '71

Rino Di Silvestro (1932-)
- The Legend of the Wolf Woman '77
- Women in Cell Block 7 '77

Jose Diaz Morales (1908-)
- Senora Tentacion '49

Tom DiCillo (1954-)
- Double Whammy '01
- The Real Blonde '97
- Box of Moonlight '96
- Living in Oblivion '94
- Johnny Suede '92

Nigel Dick (1953-)
- Dead Connection '94
- Final Combination '93
- Deadly Intent '88
- P.I. Private Investigations '87

Ernest R. Dickerson (1952-)
- Masters of Horror: The V Word '05
- Never Die Alone '04
- Good Fences '03
- Big Shot: Confessions of a Campus Bookie '02
- Monday Night Mayhem '02
- Bones '01
- Strange Justice: The Clarence Thomas and Anita Hill Story '99
- Blind Faith '98
- Bulletproof '96
- Surviving the Game '94
- Tales from the Crypt Presents Demon Knight '94
- Juice '92

Thorold Dickinson (1903-84)
- Hill 24 Doesn't Answer '55
- The Queen of Spades '49
- Men of Two Worlds '46
- Gaslight '40
- The Arsenal Stadium Mystery '39
- High Command '37

Katherine Dieckmann
- Diggers '06
- A Good Baby '99

Samuel Diege (1902-39)
- Ride 'Em Cowgirl '41
- The Singing Cowgirl '39
- Water Rustlers '39
- King of the Sierras '38

Carlos Diegues (1940-)
- Orfeu '99
- Tieta of Agreste '96
- Subway to the Stars '87
- Quilombo '84
- Bye Bye Brazil '79
- Xica '76

William Dieterle (1893-1972)
- Quick, Let's Get Married '71
- Mistress of the World '59
- Omar Khayyam '57
- Elephant Walk '54
- Salome '53
- Boots Malone '52
- September Affair '50
- The Accused '48
- Portrait of Jennie '48
- Love Letters '45
- The Devil & Daniel Webster '41
- The Hunchback of Notre Dame '39
- Juarez '39
- The Life of Emile Zola '37
- Satan Met a Lady '36
- The Story of Louis Pasteur '36
- A Midsummer Night's Dream '35
- Fashions of 1934 '34
- Female '33
- Scarlet Dawn '32

Erwin C. Dietrich
- Inn of Temptation '73
- Sex Adventures of the Three Musketeers '71

Erin Dignam
- Loved '97
- Denial: The Dark Side of Passion '91

John Francis Dillon (1887-1934)
- Millie '31
- Suds '20

Mark Dindal (1944-)
- Chicken Little '05
- Cats Don't Dance '97
- The Emperor's New Groove '00

Michael Dinner
- The Crew '00
- Hot to Trot '88
- Off Beat '86
- Heaven Help Us '85

Mark Dippe (1958-)
- Frankenfish '04
- Spawn '97

Mark DiSalle
- The Perfect Weapon '91
- Kickboxer '89

Denver Dixon
- See Victor Adamson

Ivan Dixon (1931-2008)
- Percy & Thunder '93
- The Spook Who Sat by the Door '73

Edward Dmytryk (1908-99)
- He Is My Brother '75
- The Human Factor '75
- Bluebeard '72
- Anzio '68
- Shalako '68
- Alvarez Kelly '66
- Mirage '66
- The Carpetbaggers '64
- Where Love Has Gone '64
- Walk on the Wild Side '62
- Warlock '59
- The Young Lions '58
- Raintree County '57
- The Mountain '56
- End of the Affair '55
- Soldier of Fortune '55
- Broken Lance '54
- The Caine Mutiny '54
- Mutiny '52
- The Hidden Room '49
- Crossfire '47
- Till the End of Time '46
- Back to Bataan '45
- Cornered '45
- Murder, My Sweet '44
- Behind the Rising Sun '43
- Hitler's Children '43
- Captive Wild Woman '43
- Tender Comrade '43
- Her First Romance '40
- Trail of the Hawk '37

Frank Q. Dobbs (1939-2006)
- Uphill All the Way '85
- Hotwire '80

David Dobkin (1969-)
- Fred Claus '07
- Wedding Crashers '05
- Shanghai Knights '03
- Clay Pigeons '98

Lawrence (Larry) Dobkin (1919-2002)
- The Waltons: The Christmas Carol '80
- Sixteen '72

Kevin James Dobson (1952-)
- The Thorn Birds: The Missing Years '96

James Dodson
- Gold Diggers: The Secret of Bear Mountain '95

Donald M. Dohler (1946-2006)
- Deadly Neighbor '91
- Galaxy Invader '85
- Fiend '83
- Night Beast '83
- The Alien Factor '78
- Blue Fire Lady '78

Jacques Doillon (1944-)
- Petits Freres '00
- Ponette '95
- La Vengeance d'une Femme '89

Bob Dolman
- How to Eat Fried Worms '06
- The Banger Sisters '02

Andrew Dominik
- The Assassination of Jesse James by the Coward Robert Ford '07
- Chopper '00

Patrick G. Donahue
- Savage Instinct '89
- Code of Honor '82
- Kill Squad '81

Roger Donaldson (1945-)
- The Bank Job '08
- The World's Fastest Indian '05
- The Recruit '03
- Thirteen Days '00
- Dante's Peak '97
- Species '95
- The Getaway '94
- White Sands '92
- Cadillac Man '90
- Cocktail '88
- No Way Out '87
- Marie '85
- The Bounty '84
- Smash Palace '82
- Sleeping Dogs '77

Harris Done (1963-)
- Firetrap '01
- Storm Tracker '99
- Sand Trap '97

Jack Donohue (1908-84)
- Assault on a Queen '66
- Marriage on the Rocks '65
- Babes in Toyland '61
- Lucky Me '54
- The Yellow Cab Man '50

Vincent J. Donohue (1915-66)
- Peter Pan '60
- Sunrise at Campobello '60
- Lonelyhearts '60

Martin Donovan (1950-)
- Somebody Is Waiting '96
- The Substitute '93
- Death Dreams '92
- Mad at the Moon '92
- Apartment Zero '88

Paul Donovan (1954-)
- Tales from a Parallel Universe: I Worship His Shadow '97
- Northern Extremes '93
- Norman's Awesome Experience '88
- George's Island '91
- Def-Con 4 '85
- Self-Defense '83

Mark Donskoi (1901-81)
- My Universities '40
- My Apprenticeship '39
- My Childhood '38

Daniel D'or
- Battle Queen 2020 '99

Jacques Dorfmann (1945-)
- Shadow of the Wolf '92

Robert Dornhelm (1947-)
- The Crown Prince '06
- Rudy: The Rudy Giuliani Story '03
- RFK '02
- Sins of the Father '01
- The Break '97
- Requiem for Dominic '91
- Cold Feet '89
- Echo Park '86
- The Children of Theatre Street '77

Stanley Donen (1924-)
- Love Letters '99
- Blame It on Rio '84
- Saturn 3 '80
- Movie Movie '78
- Lucky Lady '75
- The Little Prince '74
- Staircase '69
- Bedazzled '68
- Two for the Road '67
- Arabesque '66
- Charade '63
- The Grass Is Greener '61
- Damn Yankees '58
- Indiscreet '58
- Funny Face '57
- The Pajama Game '57
- It's Always Fair Weather '54
- Deep in My Heart '54
- Seven Brides for Seven Brothers '54
- Give a Girl a Break '53
- Love Is Better Than Ever '52
- Singin' in the Rain '52
- Royal Wedding '51
- On the Town '49

Thomas Michael Donnelly
- A Soldier's Sweetheart '98

Clive Donner (1926-)
- Charlemagne '95
- Stealing Heaven '88
- Babes in Toyland '86
- Merlin and the Sword '85
- A Christmas Carol '84
- To Catch a King '84
- Oliver Twist '82
- The Nude Bomb '80
- Charlie Chan and the Curse of the Dragon Queen '81
- The Thief of Baghdad '78
- Luv '67
- What's New Pussycat? '65

Richard Donner (1939-)
- 16 Blocks '06
- Timeline '03
- Lethal Weapon 4 '98
- Conspiracy Theory '97
- Assassins '95
- Maverick '94
- Radio Flyer '92
- Lethal Weapon 3 '92
- Lethal Weapon 2 '89
- Scrooged '88
- The Goonies '85
- Ladyhawke '85
- The Toy '82
- Inside Moves '80
- Superman: The Movie '78
- The Omen '76

Ziad Doueiri
- Lila Says '04
- West Beirut '98

Russell S. Doughten, Jr.
- The Hostage '67

Shimon Dotan (1949-)
- The Finest Hour '91
- Sworn Enemies '96
- Warriors '94

Doris Dorrie (1955-)
- Me and Him '89
- Men... '85

Gordon Douglas (1907-93)
- Viva Knievel! '77
- Slaughter's Big Ripoff '73
- Skullduggery '70
- They Call Me Mr. Tibbs! '70
- The Detective '68
- Lady in Cement '68
- Chuka '67
- In Like Flint '67
- Tony Rome '67
- Harlow '65
- Rio Conchos '64
- Robin and the 7 Hoods '64
- Call Me Bwana '63
- Follow That Dream '61
- The Fiend Who Walked the West '58
- Sincerely Yours '56
- The McConnell Story '55
- Them! '54
- Young at Heart '54
- Great Missouri Raid '51
- Kiss Tomorrow Goodbye '50
- The Nevadan '50
- Only the Valiant '50
- The Doolins of Oklahoma '49
- Black Arrow '48
- If You Knew Susie '48
- Dick Tracy vs. Cueball '46
- First Yank into Tokyo '45
- The Falcon in Hollywood '44
- Girl Rush '44
- Zombies on Broadway '43
- The Great Gildersleeve '43
- Gildersleeve on Broadway '43
- Broadway Limited '41
- Saps at Sea '40

Alexander Dovzhenko (1894-1956)
- Earth '30
- Arsenal '29
- Zvenigora '28

Lorenzo Doumani (1962-)
- Bug Buster '99
- Storybook '95
- Intrigue '90

Kevin Dowling
- Mojave Moon '96
- The Sum of Us '94

Robert Downey (1936-)
- Hugo Pool '97
- Too Much Sun '90
- Rented Lips '88
- America '86
- Up the Academy '80
- Greaser's Palace '72
- Putney Swope '69

Charles S. Dubin (1919-)
- Moving Violation '76
- Murder Once Removed '71
- The Gathering: Part 2 '79
- The Manions of America '81
- Silent Rebellion '82
- Drop-Out Mother '88

Frederick Du Chau
- Underdog '07
- Racing Stripes '05
- Quest for Camelot '98

Bert L. Dragin
- Twice Dead '88
- Summer Camp Nightmare '86

Srdjan Dragojevic (1963-)
- The Wounds '98
- Pretty Village, Pretty Flame '96

Karim Dridi (1961-)
- Bye-Bye '96
- Pigalle '95

Carl Theodor Dreyer (1889-1968)
- Gertrud '64
- Ordet '55
- Day of Wrath '43
- Vampyr '31
- Passion of Joan of Arc '28
- Master of the House '25
- Leaves from Satan's Book '19

Jean Dreville (1906-97)
- Seven Deadly Sins '53

Di Drew (1948-)
- The Right Hand Man '87

Arthur Dreifuss (1908-93)
- Reg'lar Fellers '41
- Mystery in Swing '40
- Double Deal '39

Oliver Drake (1903-91)
- Mummy & Curse of the Jackal '67
- Kid from Gower Gulch '50
- Brand of Fear '49
- Battling Marshal '48
- Fighting Valley '43

Tony Drazan (1955-)
- Hurlyburly '98
- Imaginary Crimes '94
- Zebrahead '92

Sara Driver (1955-)
- When Pigs Fly '93
- Sleepwalk '88

David Drury
- The Unknown Soldier '98
- Hostile Waters '97
- Forever Young '85
- Defense of the Realm '85

Olivier Ducastel (1962-)
- Cote d'Azur '05
- My Life on Ice '02
- The Adventures of Felix '99
- Jeanne and the Perfect Guy '98

Stan Dragoti (1932-)
- Necessary Roughness '91
- She's Out of Control '89
- The Man with One Red Shoe '85
- Mr. Mom '83
- Love at First Bite '79
- Dirty Little Billy '72

Jim Drake
- Based on an Untrue Story '93
- Speed Zone '88
- Police Academy 4: Citizens on Patrol '87

Peter Duffell
- The Far Pavilions '84

Letters to an Unknown Lover '84
Experience Preferred... But Not Essential '83
Flambards '78
Inside Out '75
The House that Dripped Blood '71

Dennis Dugan (1946-)
You Don't Mess with the Zohan '08
I Now Pronounce You Chuck and Larry '07
The Benchwarmers '06
National Security '03
Saving Silverman '01
Big Daddy '99
Beverly Hills Ninja '96
Happy Gilmore '96
Brain Donors '92
Problem Child '90

Michael Dugan
Mausoleum '83
Super Seal '77

George Dugdale
Living Doll '86
Slaughter High '86

Martine Dugowson (1958-)
Portraits Chinois '96
Mina Tannenbaum '93

Christian Duguay (1957-)
Human Trafficking '05
Hitler: The Rise of Evil '03
Extreme Ops '02
The Art of War '00
Joan of Arc '99
The Assignment '97
Screamers '96
Model by Day '94
Snowbound: The Jim and Jennifer Stolpa Story '94
Adrift '93
Live Wire '92
Scanners 3: The Takeover '92
Scanners 2: The New Order '91

John Duigan (1949-)
Head in the Clouds '04
Molly '99
Lawn Dogs '96
The Leading Man '96
The Journey of August King '95
Sirens '94
Wide Sargasso Sea '92
Flirting '89
Romero '89
The Year My Voice Broke '87
Far East '85
One Night Stand '84
The Winter of Our Dreams '82

Bill Duke (1943-)
Cover '08
The Golden Spiders: A Nero Wolfe Mystery '00
Hoodlum '96
America's Dream '95
The Cemetery Club '93
Sister Act 2: Back in the Habit '93
Deep Cover '92
A Rage in Harlem '91
A Raisin in the Sun '89
Johnnie Gibson F.B.I. '87
Maximum Security '87
Killing Floor '85

Daryl Duke (1929-2006)
Tai-Pan '86
The Thorn Birds '83
The Silent Partner '78
Griffin and Phoenix: A Love Story '76
I Heard the Owl Call My Name '73
Payday '73
The President's Plane Is Missing '71

Bruno Dumont (1958-)
Flanders '06
Twentynine Palms '03
Humanity '99
The Life of Jesus '96

Georges Dumoulin
We Will Not Enter the Forest '79
Nous N'Irons Plus au Bois '69

Patrick Sheane Duncan (1947-)
Live! From Death Row '92
84 Charlie MoPic '89

Peter Duncan (1954-)
Passion '99
A Little Bit of Soul '97
Children of the Revolution '95

Duwayne Dunham
Little Giants '94
Homeward Bound: The Incredible Journey '93

Griffin Dunne (1955-)
The Accidental Husband '08
Fierce People '05
Lisa Picard Is Famous '01
Practical Magic '98
Addicted to Love '96

Philip Dunne (1908-92)
Wild in the Country '61
Ten North Frederick '58

Cheryl Dunye (1966-)
My Baby's Daddy '04
The Watermelon Woman '97

Francois Dupeyron (1950-)
Monsieur Ibrahim '03
The Machine '96

David E. Durston (1921-)
Stigma '73
I Drink Your Blood '71

Charles S. Dutton (1951-)
Against the Ropes '04
The Corner '00
First Time Felon '97

Robert Duvall (1931-)
Assassination Tango '03
The Apostle '97
Angelo My Love '83

Julien Duvivier (1896-1967)
Diabolically Yours '67
The Burning Court '62
The Man in the Raincoat '57
Captain Blackjack '51
Little World of Don Camillo '51
Anna Karenina '48
Panique '47
Heart of a Nation '43
Tales of Manhattan '42
Lydia '41
The Great Waltz '38
Pepe Le Moko '37
Maria Chapdelaine '34
Poil de Carotte '31

Allan Dwan (1885-1981)
Enchanted Island '58
The Restless Breed '58
Slightly Scarlet '56
Escape to Burma '55
Pearl of the South Pacific '55
Tennessee's Partner '55
Cattle Queen of Montana '54
Passion '54
Silver Lode '54
I Dream of Jeanie '52
Montana Belle '52
Sands of Iwo Jima '49
Northwest Outpost '47
Brewster's Millions '45
Getting Gertie's Garter '45
Abroad with Two Yanks '44
Around the World '43
Here We Go Again! '42
Look Who's Laughing '41
Young People '40
The Gorilla '39
The Three Musketeers '39
Rebecca of Sunnybrook Farm '38
Heidi '37
Hollywood Party '34
The Iron Mask '29
Manhandled '24
Robin Hood '22

H. Kaye Dyal
Project: Eliminator '91
Trained to Kill '88
Memory of Us '74

Jesse Dylan (1966-)
Kicking & Screaming '05
American Wedding '03
How High '01

Bill Eagles
Dracula '06
Beautiful Creatures '00

B. Reeves Eason (1886-1956)
Rimfire '49
'Neath Canadian Skies '46
Darkest Africa '36
Fighting Marines '36
Red River Valley '36
Undersea Kingdom '36
The Miracle Rider '35
The Phantom Empire '35
Hollywood Mystery '34
Law of the Wild '34
Mystery Mountain '34
Cornered '32
The Last of the Mohicans '32
Sunset Trail '32
The Galloping Ghost '31
Vanishing Legion '31
Roaring Ranch '30
Spurs '30
Trigger Tricks '30
The Prairie King '27
Test of Donald Norton '26

Allan Eastman (1950-)
Danger Zone '95
Crazy Moon '87
Ford: The Man & the Machine '87
The War Boy '85
Snapshot '77

Clint Eastwood (1930-)
Flags of Our Fathers '06
Letters from Iwo Jima '06
Million Dollar Baby '04
Mystic River '03
Blood Work '02
Space Cowboys '00
True Crime '99
Absolute Power '97
Midnight in the Garden of Good and Evil '97
The Bridges of Madison County '95
A Perfect World '93
Unforgiven '92
The Rookie '90
White Hunter, Black Heart '90
Bird '88
Heartbreak Ridge '86
Pale Rider '85
Sudden Impact '83
Firefox '82
Honkytonk Man '82
Bronco Billy '80
The Gauntlet '77
The Outlaw Josey Wales '75
The Eiger Sanction '75
High Plains Drifter '73
Play Misty for Me '71

Thom Eberhardt (1947-)
Ratz '99
Face Down '97
Captain Ron '92
Gross Anatomy '89
The Night Before '88
Without a Clue '88
Night of the Comet '84
Sole Survivor '84

Uli Edel (1947-)
King of Texas '02
Mists of Avalon '01
The Little Vampire '00
Purgatory '96
Rasputin: Dark Servant of Destiny '96
Tyson '95
Confessions of Sorority Girls '94
Body of Evidence '92
Last Exit to Brooklyn '90
Christiane F. '82

Don Edmonds (1937-)
Terror on Tour '83
Bare Knuckles '77
Ilsa, Harem Keeper of the 'Oil Sheiks '76
Ilsa, She-Wolf of the SS '74
Tender Loving Care '73

Blake Edwards (1922-)
Son of the Pink Panther '93
Switch '91
Peter Gunn '89
Skin Deep '89
Sunset '88
Blind Date '87
A Fine Mess '86
That's Life! '86
Micki & Maude '84
Curse of the Pink Panther '83
The Man Who Loved Women '83
Trail of the Pink Panther '82
Victor/Victoria '82
S.O.B. '81
10 '79
Revenge of the Pink Panther '78
The Pink Panther Strikes Again '76
Return of the Pink Panther '74
The Tamarind Seed '74
Wild Rovers '71
Darling Lili '70
The Party '68
What Did You Do in the War, Daddy? '66
The Great Race '65
The Pink Panther '64
A Shot in the Dark '64
Days of Wine and Roses '62
Experiment in Terror '62
Breakfast at Tiffany's '61
Operation Petticoat '59
The Perfect Furlough '59
This Happy Feeling '58

Henry Edwards (1882-1952)
Juggernaut '37
The Private Secretary '35
Scrooge '35

Robert Edwards
Land of the Blind '06
Thunder in the Pines '49

Christine Edzard (1945-)
Little Dorrit, Film 1: Nobody's Fault '88
Little Dorrit, Film 2: Little Dorrit's Story '88

Colin Eggleston (1941-2002)
The Wicked '89
Innocent Prey '88
Cassandra '87
Sky Pirates '87
Bellamy '80

Jan Egleson (1946-)
Coyote Wails '03
The Last Hit '93
A Shock to the System '90
Roanoak '86
The Tender Age '84

Atom Egoyan (1960-)
Where the Truth Lies '05
Ararat '02
Felicia's Journey '99
The Sweet Hereafter '96
Exotica '94
Calendar '93
The Adjuster '91
Speaking Parts '89
Family Viewing '87
Next of Kin '84

Franz Eichhorn
River of Evil '64
The Violent Years '56

Rafael Eisenman
Red Shoe Diaries: Swimming Naked '00
A Place Called Truth '98
Red Shoe Diaries 8: Night of Abandon '97
Business for Pleasure '96
Red Shoe Diaries 7: Burning Up '96
Red Shoe Diaries: Four on the Floor '96
Red Shoe Diaries: Strip Poker '96
Red Shoe Diaries 3: Another Woman's Lipstick '93
Lake Consequence '92

Sergei Eisenstein (1898-1948)
Ivan the Terrible, Part 2 '46
Ivan the Terrible, Part 1 '44
Alexander Nevsky '38
Que Viva Mexico '32
The General Line '29
Ten Days That Shook the World '27
The Battleship Potemkin '25
Strike '24

Breck Eisner (1970-)
Sahara '05
Taken '02

Clifford S. Elfelt
$50,000 Reward '25
Big Stakes '22

Richard Elfman (1942-)
Modern Vampires '98
Shrunken Heads '94
Forbidden Zone '80

Harry Elfont (1968-)
Josie and the Pussycats '01
Can't Hardly Wait '98

Michael Elias (1940-)
No Laughing Matter '97
Lush Life '94

Larry Elikann (1923-2004)
Robin Cook's Terminal '96
An Unexpected Family '96
Blue River '95
A Mother's Prayer '95
Tecumseh: The Last Warrior '95
Kiss of a Killer '93
The Story Lady '93
Fever '91
The Great Los Angeles Earthquake '91
An Inconvenient Woman '91
One Against the Wind '91
Last Flight Out: A True Story '90
Disaster at Silo 7 '88
God Bless the Child '88
Hands of a Stranger '87
Stamp of a Killer '87
Poison Ivy '85
Sprague '84
Charlie and the Great Balloon Chase '82
The Great Wallendas '78

Ellory Elkayem (1972-)
Return of the Living Dead: Rave to the Grave '05
Eight Legged Freaks '02

Doug Ellin (1968-)
Kissing a Fool '98
Phat Beach '96

Lang Elliott (1950-)
Cage 2: The Arena of Death '94
The Private Eyes '80

Stephan Elliott (1963-)
Eye of the Beholder '99
Welcome to Woop Woop '97
The Adventures of Priscilla, Queen of the Desert '94
Frauds '93

Bob Ellis (1942-)
The Nostradamus Kid '92
Warm Nights on a Slow-Moving Train '87

David R. Ellis (1952-)
Snakes on a Plane '06
Cellular '04
Final Destination 2 '03
Homeward Bound 2: Lost in San Francisco '96

Joseph Ellison (1948-)
Joey '85
Don't Go in the House '80

Maurice Elvey (1887-1967)
The Obsessed '51
Beware of Pity '46
Salute John Citizen! '42
Spy of Napoleon '36
Phantom Fiend '35
Transatlantic Tunnel '35
The Evil Mind '34
Lily of Killarney '34

Bob Emenegger
Escape from DS-3 '81
Killings at Outpost Zeta '80
Laboratory '80

John Emerson (1874-1956)
The Americano '17
Down to Earth '17
Reaching for the Moon '17
His Picture in the Papers '16
The Social Secretary '16

Robert Emery
The Florida Connection '74
Ride in a Pink Car '74
My Brother Has Bad Dreams '72
Scream Bloody Murder '72

Roland Emmerich (1955-)
10,000 B.C. '08
The Day After Tomorrow '04
The Patriot '00
Godzilla '98
Independence Day '96
Stargate '94
Universal Soldier '92
Moon 44 '90
Ghost Chase '88
Making Contact '86

Cy Endfield (1914-95)
Zulu '64
Mysterious Island '61
Impulse '55
Try and Get Me '50
The Underworld Story '50

John English (1903-69)
Hills of Utah '51
Valley of Fire '51
Cow Town '50
Riders of the Whistling Pines '49
Rim of the Canyon '49
Loaded Pistols '48
Trail to San Antone '47
Don't Fence Me In '45
Silver City Kid '45
Utah '45
Captain America '44
San Fernando Valley '44
Death Valley Manhunt '43
Fighting Devil Dogs '43
Man from Thunder River '43
Raiders of Sunset Pass '43
King of the Texas Rangers '41
Adventures of Red Ryder '40
Doctor Satan's Robot '40
Drums of Fu Manchu '40
Mysterious Doctor Satan '40
Zorro's Fighting Legion '39
Daredevils of the Red Circle '38
The Lone Ranger '38
Arizona Days '37
Dick Tracy '37
Zorro Rides Again '37
Whistling Bullets '36
His Fighting Blood '35

George Englund (1926-)
Dixie: Changing Habits '85
The Vegas Strip Wars '84
A Christmas to Remember '78
Zachariah '70
The Ugly American '63

Robert Englund (1947-)
Killer-Pad '06
976-EVIL '88

Robert Enrico (1931-2001)
Old Gun '76
Le Secret '74
The Last Adventure '67
Jailbird's Vacation '65
An Occurrence at Owl Creek Bridge/Coup de Grace '62

Ray Enright (1896-1965)
Man from Cairo '54
Coroner Creek '48
Return of the Bad Men '48
South of St. Louis '48
Trail Street '47
China Sky '44
Gung Ho! '43
The Iron Major '43
The Spoilers '42
The Wagons Roll at Night '41
Sing Me a Love Song '37
Earthworm Tractors '36
Alibi Ike '35
Dames '34

Nora Ephron (1941-)
Bewitched '05
Lucky Numbers '00
You've Got Mail '98
Michael '96
Mixed Nuts '94
Sleepless in Seattle '93
This Is My Life '92

John Erman (1935-)
The Celluloid Closet '95
Breathing Lessons '94
Scarlett '94
Queen '93
Carolina Skeletons '92
Our Sons '91
When the Time Comes '91
The Last Best Year '90
Stella '89
The Attic: The Hiding of Anne Frank '88
An Early Frost '85
A Streetcar Named Desire '84
Eleanor: First Lady of the World '82
My Old Man '79
Roots: The Next Generation '79
Alexander: The Other Side of Dawn '77
Roots '77
Green Eyes '76

George Erschbamer (1954-)
Bounty Hunters 2: Hardball '97
Bounty Hunters '96
Flinch '94
Final Round '93
SnakeEater 3: His Law '92
SnakeEater 2: The Drug Buster '89
SnakeEater '89

Joakim (Jack) Ersgard
Backlash '99
Acts of Betrayal '98
Living in Peril '97
Invisible: The Chronicles of Benjamin Knight '93
Mandroid '93
The Visitors '89

Chester Erskine (1905-86)
Androcles and the Lion '52
A Girl in Every Port '52
Egg and I '47
Frankie and Johnny '36

Harry Essex (1910-97)
The Cremators '72
Octaman '71

Emilio Estevez (1962-)
Bobby '06
Rated X '00
The War at Home '96
Men at Work '90
Wisdom '87

Corey Michael Eubanks
Two Bits & Pepper '95

Bruce A. Evans
Mr. Brooks '07
Kuffs '92

David Mickey Evans (1962-)
The Final Season '07
Beethoven's 4th '01
Beethoven's 3rd '00
First Kid '96
The Sandlot '93

John Evans (1934-)
Blackjack '78
Black Godfather '74
Speeding Up Time '74

Marc Evans
Snow Cake '06
Resurrection Man '97
Thicker Than Water '93

Rene Eram
Sweet Evil '95

Rainer Erler
Voodoo '95

Roger Evans
Forever Evil '87

Tim Everitt
Jet Benny Show '86

Valie Export (1940-)
Invisible Adversaries '77
The Practice of Love '84

Chris Eyre (1969-)
A Thief of Time '04
Skins '02
Skinwalker '02
Smoke Signals '98

Richard Eyre (1943-)
Notes on a Scandal '06
Stage Beauty '04
Iris '01

Leonard Farlinger
All Hat '07
The Perfect Son '00

Donald Farmer (1954-)
Vampire Cop '90
Scream Dream '89
Demon Queen '80

Bobby Farrelly (1958-)
The Heartbreak Kid '07
Fever Pitch '05
Stuck On You '03
Osmosis Jones '01
Me, Myself, and Irene '00
There's Something about Mary '98
Kingpin '96
Dumb & Dumber '94

Peter Farrelly (1957-)
The Heartbreak Kid '07
Fever Pitch '05
Stuck On You '03
Osmosis Jones '01
Me, Myself, and Irene '00
There's Something about Mary '98
Kingpin '96
Dumb & Dumber '94

John Farrow (1904-63)
John Paul Jones '59
Unholy Wife '57
Back from Eternity '56
Sea Chase '55
A Bullet Is Waiting '54
Botany Bay '53
Hondo '53
The Devil Thumbs a Ride '47
Alligator Eyes '90
Dead Funny '94

Ferdinand Fairfax (1944-)
Frenchman's Creek '98
The Choir '95
The Last Place on Earth '85
Nate and Hayes '83
Sophisticated Gents '81
Danger UXB '81
Beulah Land '80
The Night the City Screamed '80

Harry Falk (1933-)
High Desert Kill '90
Centennial '78
Abduction of St. Anne '75
Men of the Dragon '74
The Death Squad '73

Rick Famuyiwa (1973-)
Talk to Me '07
Brown Sugar '02
The Wood '99

Jamaa Fanaka (1942-)
Street Wars '91
Penitentiary 3 '87
Penitentiary 2 '82
Penitentiary '79
Black Sister's Revenge '76
Soul Vengeance '75

Jim Fall (1962-)
The Lizzie McGuire Movie '03
Trick '99

Ernest Farino
Josh Kirby... Time Warrior: Chapter 5, Journey to the Magic Cavern '96
Josh Kirby... Time Warrior: Chapter... Planet of the Dino-Knights '95
Steel and Lace '90

Julian Farino
Our Mutual Friend '98
Byron '03
Elf '03
Zathura '05
Iron Man '08

John Fawcett (1968-)
The Dark '04
Ginger Snaps '01
Taken '02

Xie Fei (1942-)
A Mongolian Tale '94
Women from the Lake of Scented Souls '94
Girl from Hunan '86

Neill Fearnley
Escape from Mars '99
Johnny 2.0 '99
Black Ice '92

Paul Feig (1962-)
I Am David '04
Unaccompanied Minors '06

Beda Docampo Feijoo (1948-)
Deluge '33

John Feldman (1954-)
Dead Funny '94
Alligator Eyes '90

James Fargo (1938-)
Born to Race '88
Voyage of the Rock Aliens '87
Game for Vultures '86
Forced Vengeance '82
Every Which Way But Loose '78
Caravans '78
The Enforcer '76

Don E. Fauntleroy
Urban Justice '07

Jon Favreau (1966-)
Iron Man '08
Zathura '05
Elf '03
Made '01

Rainer Werner Fassbinder (1946-82)
Querelle '83
Veronika Voss '82
Berlin Alexanderplatz '80
The Marriage of Maria Braun '79
Despair '78
Germany in Autumn '78
In a Year of 13 Moons '78
The Bitter Tears of Petra von Kant '72
The Merchant of Four Seasons '71
The American Soldier '70
Beware of a Holy Whore '70
Gods of the Plague '69
Why Does Herr R. Run Amok? '69
Love is Colder Than Death '69
Fox and His Friends '75
Ali: Fear Eats the Soul '74
Effi Briest '74
The Stationmaster's Wife '77

John Fasano
Black Roses '88
The Jitters '88
Rock 'n' Roll Nightmare '85

Leslie Fenton (1902-78)
On Our Merry Way '48
Tomorrow the World '44

Abel Ferrara (1952-)
'R Xmas '01
New Rose Hotel '98
The Blackout '97
The Funeral '96
Subway Stories '97
The Addiction '95
Body Snatchers '93
Dangerous Game '93
Bad Lieutenant '92
Cat Chaser '90
King of New York '90
China Girl '87
The Gladiator '86
Fear City '85
Ms. 45 '81
Driller Killer '79

Emilio Fernandez (1904-86)
The Torch '50
Maria Candelaria '46
The Pearl '48

Larry Ferguson (1940-)
Beyond the Law '92

Guy Ferland (1966-)
Telling Lies in America '96
The Babysitter '95

Georg Fenady (1930-)
Arnold '73
Terror in the Wax Museum '73

His Kind of Woman '51 *(John Farrow, cont.)*
Copper Canyon '50
Where Danger Lives '50
The Big Clock '48
Two Years before the Mast '46
China '43
Commandos Strike at Dawn '43
Wake Island '42
Five Came Back '39
The Saint Strikes Back '39

Federico Fellini (1920-93)
Intervista '87
Ginger & Fred '86
And the Ship Sails On '83
City of Women '81
Orchestra Rehearsal '78
Amarcord '74
Fellini's Roma '72
The Clowns '71
Fellini Satyricon '69
Spirits of the Dead '68
Juliet of the Spirits '65
8 1/2 '63
Boccaccio '70 '62
La Dolce Vita '60
Nights of Cabiria '57
Il Bidone '55
La Strada '54
I Vitelloni '53
Love in the City '53
The White Sheik '52
Variety Lights '51

Davide Ferrario
After Midnight '04

Jose Ferrer (1909-92)
State Fair '62
Return to Peyton Place '61

Marco Ferreri (1928-97)
Tales of Ordinary Madness '83
The Perfect Husband '92
Under the Earth '86
The Last Woman '76

Marty Feldman (1933-82)
In God We Trust '80
The Last Remake of Beau Geste '77

Jacques Feyder (1885-1948)
Knight Without Armour '37
Carnival in Flanders '35
The Kiss '29
Crainquebille '23

Larry Fessenden (1963-)
Wendigo '01
Habit '97

Mike Figgis (1948-)
Cold Creek Manor '03
Hotel '01
Time Code '00
Miss Julie '99
The Loss of Sexual Innocence '98
One Night Stand '97
Leaving Las Vegas '95
The Browning Version '94
Mr. Jones '93
Liebestraum '91
Women & Men: In Love, There Are No Rules '91
Internal Affairs '90
Stormy Monday '88

David Fincher (1963-)
Zodiac '07
Panic Room '02
Fight Club '99
The Game '97
Se7en '95
Alien 3 '92

Charles Finch (1962-)
Where Sleeping Dogs Lie '91
Priceless Beauty '90
Skorpy, Monday '88

Nigel Finch (1950-95)
Stonewall '95
The Vampyr '92
The Lost Language of Cranes '92

Ivan Fila (1956-)
King of Thieves '04
Lea '96

Andy Fickman
She's the Man '06
The Game Plan '07

Michael Fields
Noon Wine '84
Bright Angel '91

Sally Field (1946-)
Beautiful '00
From the Earth to the Moon '98

Todd Field (1964-)
Little Children '06
In the Bedroom '01

Roberta Findlay
Lurkers '88
Prime Evil '88
Blood Sisters '85
The Oracle '85

Kenneth Fink
Tricks '97

Ken Finkleman (1946-)
Airplane 2: The Sequel '82

Laurent Firode
Happenstance '00
My First Wedding '04

Sam Firstenberg (1950-)
The Battle of El Alamein '68
Blood for a Silver Dollar '66
American Samurai '92
Operation: Delta Force '97

John Eyres
Ripper: Letter from Hell '01
Octopus '00
Judge & Jury '96
Monolith '93
Project: Shadowchaser 2 '94
Project: Shadowchaser '92
Night Siege Project: Shadowchaser 3000 '95

Peter Faiman
Dutch '91
Crocodile Dundee '86

Christian Faber
The Next Step '95
Bail Jumper '89

Roberto Faenza (1943-)
The Bachelor '90
Corrupt '84

William Fairchild (1919-2000)
The Silent Enemy '58
John and Julie '55
The Horsemasters '61

Darin Ferriola (1970-)
Mr. Fix It '06
Ivory Tower '97

Felix Feist (1906-65)
Donovan's Brain '53
Big Trees '52
Guilty of Treason '50
The Threat '49
The Devil Thumbs a Ride '47

Giorgio Ferroni (1908-81)
The Battle of El Alamein '68
Blood for a Silver Dollar '66
Secret Agent Super Dragon '66
Coriolanus, Man without a Country '64
The Lion of Thebes '64
Mill of the Stone Women '60

Edward Finney (1903-83)
Queen of the Amazons '47
King of the Stallions '42
Riot Squad '41
Silver Stallion '41

Firstenberg
Cyborg Soldier '94
Blood Warriors '93
Cyborg Cop '93
American Samurai '92
Delta Force 3: The Killing Game '91
One More Chance '90
Riverbend '89
American Ninja 2: The Confrontation '87
My African Adventure '87
Avenging Force '86
American Ninja '85
Breakin' 2: Electric Boogaloo '84
Ninja 3: The Domination '84
Revenge of the Ninja '83

Michael Firth
Sylvia '86
Heart of the Stag '84
The Lazarus Syndrome '79

Michael Fischa (1952-)
Delta Heat '92
Crack House '89
My Mom's a Werewolf '89
Death Spa '87

Max Fischer (1929-)
Taken '99

Chris Fisher (1973-)
Psychopath '97
Entangled '93
Killing 'Em Softly '85
Dirty '05
Rampage: The Hillside Strangler Murders '04
Nightstalker '02

David Fisher (1948-)
Toy Soldiers '84
Liar's Moon '82

Terence Fisher (1904-80)
Frankenstein and the Monster from Hell '74
Frankenstein Must Be Destroyed '69
The Devil Rides Out '68
Island of the Burning Doomed '67
Dracula, Prince of Darkness '66
Frankenstein Created Woman '66
Island of Terror '66
The Gorgon '64
The Phantom of the Opera '62
Sherlock Holmes and the Deadly Necklace '62
The Brides of Dracula '60
The Curse of the Werewolf '61
Sword of Sherwood Forest '60
The Two Faces of Dr. Jekyll '60
The Hound of the Baskervilles '59
The Mummy '59
The Horror of Dracula '58
The Revenge of Frankenstein '58
The Curse of Frankenstein '57
Race for Life '55
Robin Hood: The Movie '55
Black Glove '54
Blackout '54
Unholy Four '54
Four Sided Triangle '53
Spaceways '53
Three Stops to Murder '53
Man Bait '52
A Stolen Face '52

Bill Fishman
Car 54, Where Are You? '94
Tapeheads '89

Jack Fisk (1945-)
Daddy's Dyin'... Who's Got the Will? '90
Violets Are Blue '86
Raggedy Man '81

Christopher Fitchett (1951-)
Fair Game '82
Blood Money '80

Thom Fitzgerald (1968-)
The Event '03
Beefcake '99
The Hanging Garden '97

George Fitzmaurice (1885-1940)
The Last of Mrs. Cheyney '37
Suzy '36
As You Desire Me '32
Mata Hari '32
Raffles '30
Son of the Sheik '26

Cash Flagg
See Ray Dennis Steckler

Robert Flaherty (1884-1951)
Louisiana Story '48
Elephant Boy '37
Man of Aran '34
Tabu: A Story of the South Seas '31
Moana, a Romance of the Golden Age '26

Gary Fleder (1963-)
Runaway Jury '03
Impostor '02
Don't Say a Word '01
Kiss the Girls '97
Things to Do in Denver When You're Dead '95
The Companion '94

Dave Fleischer (1894-1979)
Hoppity Goes to Town '41
Gulliver's Travels '39

Richard Fleischer (1916-2006)
Million Dollar Mystery '87
Red Sonja '85
Conan the Destroyer '84
Amityville 3: The Demon '83
Tough Enough '83
The Jazz Singer '80
Ashanti, Land of No Mercy '79
The New Centurions '72
See No Evil '71
10 Rillington Place '71
Tora! Tora! Tora! '70
Soylent Green '73
The Boston Strangler '68
Doctor Dolittle '67
Fantastic Voyage '66
Barabbas '62
Compulsion '59
The Vikings '58
Between Heaven and Hell '56
20,000 Leagues under the Sea '54
The Narrow Margin '52
Armored Car Robbery '50
The Clay Pigeon '49
Follow Me Quietly '49
Trapped '49

Andrew Fleming (1964-)
Nancy Drew '07
The In-Laws '03
Dick '99
The Craft '96
Threesome '94
Bad Dreams '88

Victor Fleming (1883-1949)
Joan of Arc '48
Adventure '45
A Guy Named Joe '44
Tortilla Flat '42
Dr. Jekyll and Mr. Hyde '41
Gone with the Wind '39
The Wizard of Oz '39
Test Pilot '38
Captains Courageous '37
The Farmer Takes a Wife '35
Reckless '35
Treasure Island '34
Bombshell '33
Red Dust '32
The Virginian '29
Hula '28
Mantrap '26

Gordon Flemyng (1934-95)
Cloud Waltzing '87
Philby, Burgess and MacLean: Spy Scandal of the Century '84
Daleks—Invasion Earth 2150 A.D. '66

Rodman Flender (1964-)
Idle Hands '99
Leprechaun 2 '94
In the Heat of Passion '91
The Unborn '91

Anne Fletcher
27 Dresses '08
Step Up '06

Clive Fleury
Big City Blues '99
Tunnel Vision '95
Fatal Past '94

Theodore J. Flicker (1930-)
Soggy Bottom U.S.A. '84
Playmates '72
Three in the Cellar '70
The President's Analyst '67

James T. Flocker
Ground Zero '88
Ghosts That Still Walk '77
The Secret of Navajo Cave '76

John Florea (1916-2000)
Hot Child in the City '87
Computer Wizard '77
Where's Willie? '77
The Invisible Strangler '76
Where the Eagle Flies '72
Island of the Lost '68

Isaac Florentine
Undisputed II: Last Man Standing '06
U.S. Seals 2 '01
Bridge of Dragons '99
Cold Harvest '98
High Voltage '98
The Fighter '95
Desert Kickboxer '92

Robert Florey (1900-79)
Outpost in Morocco '49
The Beast with Five Fingers '46
God Is My Co-Pilot '45
King of Alcatraz '38
Ex-Lady '38
The Cocoanuts '29
Murders in the Rue Morgue '32

Lawrence Foldes (1959-)
Finding Home '03
Pre-Madonnas: Rebels Without a Clue '95

Nightforce '86
Young Warriors '83
The Great Skycopter Rescue '82
Nightstalker '81

Peter Foldy
Seeds of Doubt '96
Tryst '94
Widow's Kiss '94
Midnight Witness '93

James Foley (1953-)
Perfect Stranger '07
Confidence '03
The Corruptor '99
The Chamber '96
Fear '96
Two Bits '96
Glengarry Glen Ross '92
After Dark, My Sweet '90
Who's That Girl? '87
At Close Range '86
Reckless '84

Sheree Folkson
Casanova '05
A Royal Scandal '96

Peter Fonda (1939-)
Wanda Nevada '79
Idaho Transfer '73
Hired Hand '71

Leo Fong (1928-)
Showdown '93
24 Hours to Midnight '92
Hawkeye '88

Jorge Fons (1939-)
Midaq Alley '95
Jory '72

Anne Fontaine (1959-)
How I Killed My Father '03
Nathalie '03
Dry Cleaning '97
Augustin '95

Bryan Forbes (1926-)
The Endless Game '89
The Naked Face '84
Better Late Than Never '83
International Velvet '78
The Slipper and the Rose '76
The Stepford Wives '75
Long Ago Tomorrow '71
The Madwoman of Chaillot '69
The Wrong Box '66
King Rat '65
Seance on a Wet Afternoon '64
The L-Shaped Room '62
Whistle down the Wind '61

John Ford (1895-1973)
December 7th: The Movie '91
Cheyenne Autumn '64
Donovan's Reef '63
How the West Was Won '63
The Man Who Shot Liberty Valance '62
Two Rode Together '61
Sergeant Rutledge '60
The Horse Soldiers '59
Last Hurrah '58
Wings of Eagles '57
The Searchers '56
The Long Gray Line '55
Mister Roberts '55
Mogambo '53
The Sun Shines Bright '53
The Quiet Man '52
What Price Glory? '52
Rio Grande '50
Wagon Master '50
When Willie Comes Marching Home '50
She Wore a Yellow Ribbon '49
Fort Apache '48
Three Godfathers '48
The Fugitive '48
My Darling Clementine '46
They Were Expendable '45
How Green Was My Valley '41
The Grapes of Wrath '40
The Long Voyage Home '40
Drums Along the Mohawk '39
Stagecoach '39
Young Mr. Lincoln '39
Four Men and a Prayer '38
The Hurricane '37
Wee Willie Winkie '37
Mary of Scotland '36
The Prisoner of Shark Island '36
The Informer '35
Steamboat Round the Bend '35
The Whole Town's Talking '35
Judge Priest '34
The Lost Patrol '34
The World Moves On '34
Doctor Bull '33
Pilgrimage '33
Arrowsmith '32
Seas Beneath '31
Up the River '30
Four Sons '28
Hangman's House '28
The Iron Horse '24
Straight Shootin' '17

Philip Ford (1900-76)
Rodeo King and the Senorita '51
Redwood Forest Trail '50
The Vanishing Westerner '50

Ron Ford (1958-)
Witchcraft 11: Sisters in Blood '00
The Alien Agenda: Endangered Species '97

Eugene Forde
Sleepers West '41
Michael Shayne: Private Detective '40
Inspector Hornleigh '39
Charlie Chan at Monte Carlo '37
Charlie Chan on Broadway '37
Charlie Chan in London '34

Walter Forde (1896-1984)
The Ghost Train '41
The Secret Four '40
King of the Damned '36
Bulldog Jack '35

Milos Forman (1932-)
Goya's Ghosts '06
Man on the Moon '99
The People vs. Larry Flynt '96
Valmont '89
Amadeus '84
Ragtime '81
Hair '79
One Flew Over the Cuckoo's Nest '75
The Firemen's Ball '68
Loves of a Blonde '65
Black Peter '63

Tom Forman (1893-1926)
The Fighting American '24
The Virginian '23
Shadows '22

Jose Maria Forque
Beyond Erotica '79
Autopsy '74

Marc Forster (1969-)
Stay '05
Finding Neverland '04
Monster's Ball '01
Everything Put Together '00

Bill Forsyth (1948-)
Being Human '94
Breaking In '89
Housekeeping '87
Comfort and Joy '84
Local Hero '83
Gregory's Girl '80

Ed Forsyth (1920-2004)
Inferno in Paradise '88
Chesty Anderson USN '76
Superchick '71

John Fortenberry
A Night at the Roxbury '98
Jury Duty '95

Bob Fosse (1927-87)
Star 80 '83
All That Jazz '79
Lenny '74
Cabaret '72
Sweet Charity '69

Giles Foster
The Prince and the Pauper '01
Coming Home '98
The Rector's Wife '94
Innocent Victim '90
Consuming Passions '88
Dutch Girls '87
Northanger Abbey '87
Hotel du Lac '86
Silas Marner '85

Jodie Foster (1963-)
Home for the Holidays '95
Little Man Tate '91

Lewis R. Foster (1898-1974)
The Sign of Zorro '60
Tonka '58
Dakota Incident '56
Crashout '55
Cavalry Charge '51
Laurel & Hardy: Blotto '30
Laurel & Hardy: Berth Marks '29
Laurel & Hardy: Men O'War '29

Marc Foster
The Kite Runner '07

Norman Foster (1900-76)
Crazy Horse and Custer: "The Untold Story" '90
Deathhead Virgin '74
Brighty of the Grand Canyon '67
Indian Paint '64
The Sign of Zorro '60
The Nine Lives of Elfego Baca '58
Davy Crockett and the River Pirates '56
Davy Crockett, King of the Wild Frontier '55
Tell It to the Judge '49
Rachel and the Stranger '48
Journey into Fear '42
Charlie Chan at Treasure Island '39
Mr. Moto's Last Warning '39
Mr. Takes a Vacation '39
Mr. Moto Takes a Chance '38
Mysterious Mr. Moto '38
Thank you, Mr. Moto '37
Think Fast, Mr. Moto '37

Claude Fournier (1931-)
Tales of the Klondike: The Scorn of Women '87
Dan Candy's Law '73

Gene Fowler, Jr. (1917-98)
The Rebel Set '59
I Married a Monster from Outer Space '58
Showdown at Boot Hill '58
I Was a Teenage Werewolf '57

Eytan Fox (1964-)
The Bubble '06
Yossi & Jagger '02

Wallace Fox (1895-1958)
Guns of Fury '49
Bad Men of the Border '45
Mr. Muggs Rides Again '45
The Great Mike '44
Million Dollar Kid '44
Ghost Rider '43
Kid Dynamite '43
Bowery at Midnight '42
The Corpse Vanishes '42
Let's Get Tough '42
'Neath Brooklyn Bridge '42
Smart Alecks '42
Bowery Blitzkrieg '41

William A. Fraker (1923-)
Legend of the Lone Ranger '81
Monte Walsh '70
A Reflection of Fear '72

Jonathan Frakes (1952-)
Thunderbirds '04
Clockstoppers '02
Star Trek: Insurrection '98
Star Trek: First Contact '96

Freddie Francis (1917-2007)
Dark Tower '87
The Doctor and the Devils '85
The Ghoul '75
Legend of the Werewolf '75
Craze '74
Tales That Witness Madness '73
The Creeping Flesh '72
Tales from the Crypt '72
The Vampire Happening '71
Girly '70
The Evil of Frankenstein '64
The Skull '65
Hysteria '64
Nightmare '63
The Brain '62
Paranoiac '63
Dr. Terror's House of Horrors '65
Torture Garden '67
Space '67
They Came from Beyond the Grave '68
Dracula Has Risen from the Grave '68
Devil on Horseback '55
Make Me an Offer '55

Pietro Francisci (1906-77)
Hercules Unchained '59
Hercules '58
Roland the Mighty '56
Reindeer Games '00

Jess (Jesus) Franco (1930-)
Faceless '88
Bloody Moon '83
Oasis of the Zombies '82
Revenge in the House of Usher '82
Sex Is Crazy '79
Ilsa, the Wicked Warden '78
Jack the Ripper '76
The Demons '74
Female Vampire '74
The Perverse Countess '73
Rites of Frankenstein '72
The Screaming Dead '72
Count Dracula '71
Venus in Furs '70
99 Women '69
The Castle of Fu Manchu '68
Dead '77
Virgin among the Living

Carl Franklin (1949-)
Out of Time '03
High Crimes '02
One False Move '91
Full Fathom Five '90
Eye of the Eagle 2 '89
Nowhere to Run '88
One True Thing '98
Devil in a Blue Dress '95
Laurel Avenue '93

Jeff Franklin (1955-)
Love Stinks '99

Howard Franklin
The Public Eye '92
Quick Change '90
Larger Than Life '96

Ricardo Franco (1949-98)
Berlin Blues '89
In 'n Out '86

Georges Franju (1912-87)
Judex '64
L'Année des Meduses '86
Faustus '55
The Shadow Man '53

Christopher Frank (1943-93)
Josepha '82

Hubert Frank (1925-)
The Dolls '83
Melody in Love '78

Melvin Frank (1913-88)
Walk Like a Man '87
Lost and Found '79
The Duchess and the Dirtwater Fox '76
Prisoner of Second Avenue '74
A Touch of Class '73
Buona Sera, Mrs. Campbell '68
Strange Bedfellows '65
The Facts of Life '60
The Jayhawkers '59
Li'l Abner '59
Above and Beyond '53

David Frankel (1960-)
The Devil Wears Prada '06
Band of Brothers '01
Miami Rhapsody '95

John Frankenheimer (1930-2002)
Path to War '02
Reindeer Games '00
Ronin '98
George Wallace '97
The Island of Dr. Moreau '96
Andersonville '95
The Burning Season '94
Year of the Gun '91
Dead Bang '89
The Fourth War '90
52 Pick-Up '86
The Holcroft Covenant '85
The Challenge '82
Prophecy '79
Black Sunday '77
French Connection 2 '75
The Gypsy Moths '69
The Fixer '68
Grand Prix '66
Seconds '66
The Train '65
Seven Days in May '64
All Fall Down '62
Birdman of Alcatraz '62
The Manchurian Candidate '62
The Young Savages '61
Days of Wine and Roses '58
The Horsemen '70
I Walk the Line '70
The Iceman Cometh '73
The Story of a Love Story '73

Cyril Frankel (1921-)
Permission To Kill '75
The Witches '66
The Very Edge '63
On the Fiddle '61

Sidney Franklin (1893-1972)
The Good Earth '37
Wild Orchids '31
The Barretts of Wimpole Street '34
Smilin' Through '33
The Guardsman '31
The Forbidden City '18
The Dark Angel '35

Stephen Frears (1941-)
Mrs. Henderson Presents '05
The Queen '06
Dirty Pretty Things '03
Fail Safe '00
High Fidelity '00
Liam '00
The Hi-Lo Country '98
Mary Reilly '95
The Van '95
The Snapper '93
Hero '92
The Grifters '90
Dangerous Liaisons '88
Prick Up Your Ears '87
Sammy & Rosie Get Laid '87
The Hit '85
My Beautiful Laundrette '85
Saigon: Year of the Cat '87
Walter '82
The Burning '81

James Frawley (1937-)
Mr. Headmistress '98
Spies, Lies and Naked Thighs '91
The Muppet Movie '79
The Big Bus '76
Assault and Matrimony '87
Fraternity Vacation '85
Hansel and Gretel '82
Great American Traffic Jam '80
Out of Control '85

Harold French (1900-)
Rob Roy—The Highland Rogue '53
Encore '51
Trio '50
Mr. Emmanuel '44
The Day Will Dawn '42
Secret Mission '42

Charles Frend (1909-77)
The Third Key '57
The Cruel Sea '53
Scott of the Antarctic '48
San Demetrio, London '47
Johnny Frenchman '46
The Foreman Went to France '42

Robert M. Fresco (1928-)
Dirty Little Secret '98
Evil Has a Face '96
Small Kill '93

Juan Carlos Fresnadillo (1967-)
28 Weeks Later '07
Intacto '02

Karl Freund (1890-1969)
Mad Love '35
The Mummy '32

Bart Freundlich (1970-)
Catch That Kid '04
World Traveler '01
The Myth of Fingerprints '97

Fridrik Thor Fridriksson (1953-)
Devil's Island '96

Harry Fraser (1889-1974)
Chained for Life '51
Ambush Trail '46
People's Choice '46
Private Lives '31
The Riding Avenger '36
Enemy of the Law '45
Feud of the West '35
Fighting Parson '35
Three in the Saddle '45
Pecos Kid '35
Outlaw Roundup '44
Rustler's Paradise '35
'Neath the Arizona Skies '34
Wild Mustang '35
Wagon Trail '35
Social Error '35
The Tonto Kid '35
Randy Rides Alone '34
Diamond Trail '33
Rainbow Ranch '33
Wolf Dog '33
Broadway to Cheyenne '32
Ghost City '32
Mason of the Mounted '32
The Savage Girl '32
Texas Pioneers '32
The Wildcat '26

Herb Freed (1927-)
Survival Game '86
Tomboy '85
Graduation Day '81
Beyond Evil '80

Jerrold Freedman
Thompson's Last Run '90
Best Kept Secrets '86
Native Son '87
Legs '83
Borderline '80
The Streets of L.A. '79

Joan Freeman (1941-)
Streetwalkin' '85
Satisfaction '88

Morgan J. Freeman (1969-)
American Psycho 2: All American Girl '02
Desert Blue '98
Hurricane Streets '96

Hugo Fregonese (1908-87)
Dracula vs. Frankenstein '69
Apache's Last Battle '64
Harry Black and the Tiger '58
Blowing Wild '54
Decameron Nights '53
Man in the Attic '53

Thornton Freeland (1898-1987)
Jericho '38
Accused '36
Flying Down to Rio '33
They Call It Sin '32
Be Yourself '30
Whoopee! '30

Richard Friedberg
Snow in August '01

Richard Friedenberg
The Education of Little Tree '97

William Friedkin (1939-)
Bug '06
The Hunted '03
Rules of Engagement '00
Twelve Angry Men '97
Jade '95
Blue Chips '94
Jailbreakers '94
The Guardian '90
Rampage '87
To Live & Die in L.A. '85
Deal of the Century '83
Cruising '80
Brink's Job '78
Sorcerer '77
The Exorcist '73
The French Connection '71
The Boys in the Band '70
The Night They Raided Minsky's '69
Good Times '67
Python Wolf '88
Stalking Danger '86

Rick Friedberg
Spy Hard '96
Off the Wall '82
Pray TV '80

Jason Friedberg
Meet the Spartans '08
Epic Movie '07

Seymour Friedman (1917-)
I'll Get You '53
Loan Shark '52
China Gate '57
Forty Guns '57
Run of the Arrow '56
House of Bamboo '55
Baron of Arizona '51
Fixed Bayonets! '51
The Steel Helmet '51
I Shot Jesse James '49
Shock Corridor '63
Underworld, U.S.A. '60
Verboten! '59
Naked Kiss '64

Lee Frost (1935-2007)
Private Obsession '94
Dixie Dynamite '76
Black Gestapo '75
Policewomen '73
Chain Gang Women '72
The Thing with Two Heads '72
Chrome and Hot Leather '71
Rebel Vixens '69
Love Desperados '68

Harvey Frost (1917-)
Recipe for Disaster '03
National Lampoon's Go! Punks '99
Midnight Heat '95
Tracks of a Killer '95

Louis Friedlander
See Lew Landers

Richard Friedman
Darkwolf '03
Forever Together '00
Phantom of the Mall: Eric's Revenge '89
Doom Asylum '88
Scared Stiff '87
Deathmask '84

Robert Fuest (1927-)
Revenge of the Stepford Wives '80
Devil's Rain '75
The Final Programme '73
Doctor Phibes Rises Again '72
The Abominable Dr. Phibes '71
And Soon the Darkness '70
Wuthering Heights '70

Samuel Fuller (1911-97)
The Big Red One '80
Dead Pigeon on Beethoven Street '72
Shark! '68
The Meanest Men in the West '67

Lucio Fulci (1927-96)
Demonia '90
Voices from Beyond '90
Dangerous Obsession '88
Challenge to White Fang '86
The New Gladiators '83
The Black Cat '81
Conquest '83
Zombie '80
The House by the Cemetery '83
The Psychic '78
Don't Torture a Duckling '72
A Lizard in a Woman's Skin '71
The Beyond '82
New York Ripper '82
Manhattan Baby '82
Gates of Hell '80
El Barbaro '84
Contraband '86

Antoine Fuqua (1966-)
Shooter '07
King Arthur '04
American Soldiers '05
Lighting in a Bottle '04
Tears of the Sun '03
Training Day '01
Bait '00
Road Rage '99
Under Heavy Fire '01
Hide and Seek '00
My 5 Wives '00
The Collectors '99
Rock My World '02
Top of the World '97
Iron Eagle 4 '95

Keith Fulton (1965-)
Brothers of the Head '06
Lost in La Mancha '03
The Replacement Killers '98

William Fruet (1933-)
Blue Monkey '87
Bedroom Eyes '86
Killer Party '86
Funeral Home '82
Spasms '82
Search and Destroy '81
Death Weekend '76
Wedding in White '72

Kinji Fukasaku (1930-2003)
Battle Royale '00
Fall Guy '82
Virus '82
Samurai Reincarnation '81
Under the Flag of the Rising Sun '72
Sympathy for the Underdog '71
Black Lizard '68
The Green Slime '68
The Secret of the Telegian '61

Jun Fukuda (1924-2000)
Godzilla '90
Godzilla vs. Megalon '76
Godzilla vs. the Cosmic Monster '74
Son of Godzilla '66
Godzilla on Monster Island '72

Sidney J. Furie (1933-)
The Veteran '06
Hollow Point '95
The Rage '97
The Taking of Beverly Hills '91
Ladybugs '92

Herb Fried (1927-)
Life & Times of Grizzly Adams '74

Rick Friedberg
The Adventures of Frontier Fremont '75

Hu Freeland
The Horrible Dr. Hichcock '62
Samson and the 7 Miracles of the World '62
The Giants of Thessaly '60
Maciste in Hell '60
The Mongols '60
I, Vampiri '56
Giants of Rome '54

Kei Fukuda
Cold Fever '95
Children of Nature '91

Jerrold Freedman
Mr. & Mrs. Loving '96
The Deerslayer '78

Psycho 2 '83
Road Games '81
Patrick '78

Iron Eagle 2 '88
Superman 4: The Quest for Peace '87
Iron Eagle '86
Purple Hearts '84
The Entity '83
The Boys in Company C '77
Hit! '73
Lady Sings the Blues '72
The Appaloosa '66
The Ipcress File '65
The Leather Boys '63
Doctor Blood's Coffin '62
The Snake Woman '61
A Dangerous Age '57

Stephen Furst (1955-)
Dragon Storm '04
Magic Kid 2 '94

Tim Fywell (1951-)
Ice Princess '05
Cambridge Spies '03
I Capture the Castle '02
Madame Bovary '00
The Ice House '97
The Woman in White '97
Cracker: Best Boys '95
Cracker: True Romance '95
Gallowglass '95
Norma Jean and Marilyn '95
Cracker: To Be a Somebody '94
A Dark Adapted Eye '93
A Fatal Inversion '92

Richard Gabai (1964-)
Miracle Dogs Too '06
Virtual Girl '96
Vice Girls '96
Assault of the Party Nerds 2: Heavy Petting Detective '95
Hot Under the Collar '91
Virgin High '90
Assault of the Party Nerds '89

Pal Gabor (1932-87)
Brady's Escape '84
Angi Vera '78

Radu Gabrea (1937-)
Secret of the Ice Cave '89
A Man Like Eva '83

Mike Gabriel
Pocahontas '95
The Rescuers Down Under '90

Stephen Gaghan (1965-)
Syriana '05
Abandon '02

Rene Gainville (1941-)
The Associate '79
Le Complot '73

John Gale
The Firing Line '91
Commando Invasion '87
Slash '87

Richard Gale
Pressure '02
The Proposal '00
Dead Space '90

Timothy Galfas
Sunnyside '79
Fist '76
Homeboy '75

John A. Gallagher
Blue Moon '00
The Deli '97
Street Hunter '90
Beach House '82

Fred Gallo (1965-)
Termination Man '97
Machine Gun Blues '95
Lady in Waiting '94
Dracula Rising '93
The Finishing Touch '92

George Gallo (1956-)
Double Take '01
Trapped in Paradise '94
29th Street '91

Vincent Gallo (1961-)
The Brown Bunny '03
Buffalo 66 '97

Samuel Gallu (1918-91)
The Man Outside '68
Theatre of Death '67

Nisha Ganatra
Cake '05
Chutney Popcorn '99

Abel Gance (1889-1981)
The Battle of Austerlitz '60
J'Accuse '37
Beethoven '36
Napoleon 27
The Torture of Silence '17

Pierre Gang
Armistead Maupin's More Tales of the City '97
Sous Sol '96

Albert C. Gannaway (1920-)
Man or Gun '58
Daniel Boone: Trail Blazer '56
Hidden Guns '56

Christophe Gans (1960-)
Silent Hill '06
Brotherhood of the Wolf '01
H.P. Lovecraft's Necronomicon: Book of the Dead '93

Robert Ben Garant (1970-)
Balls of Fury '07
Reno 911!: Miami '07

Nicole Garcia (1946-)
Place Vendome '98
The Favorite Son '94
Every Other Weekend '91

Yolanda Garcia Serrano (1958-)
Km. 0 '00

Herb Gardner (1934-2003)
Amor de Hombre '97

Richard Harding Gardner (1949-)
Sherlock: Undercover Dog '94

Tay Garnett (1898-1977)
Challenge To Be Free '76
The Big Push '75
Main Street to Broadway '53
One Minute to Zero '52
Cause for Alarm '51
A Connecticut Yankee in King Arthur's Court '49
The Postman Always Rings Twice '46
The Valley of Decision '45
Mrs. Parkington '44
Bataan '43
Cheers for Miss Bishop '41
Seven Sinners '40
Slightly Honorable '40
Eternally Yours '39
Joy of Living '38
Stand-In '37
China Seas '35
One Way Passage '32
The Flying Fool '29

Mario Gariazzo (1930-2002)
White Slave '86
Eyes Behind the Stars '72

Lee Garmes (1898-1978)
Actors and Sin '52
Angels Over Broadway '40
Dreaming Lips '37

Roy Garrett
See Mario Gariazzo

Mick Garris (1951-)
Masters of Horror: Valerie on the Stairs '06
Riding the Bullet '04
Quicksilver Highway '98
Stephen King's The Stand '94

Otis Garrett (1893-1941)
The Black Doll '38
Danger on the Air '38

Psycho 4: The Beginning '90
Critters 2: The Main Course '88

Harry Garson (1882-1938)
The Worldly Madonna '22
Mid-Channel 20

Jerome Gary
Traxx '87
Stripper '86

Louis Gasnier (1875-1963)
Murder on the Yukon '40
Reefer Madness 38
Gambling Ship '33
Topaze '33
Parisian Love '25
Kismet 20

Leon Gast
Sweet Jane '98
When We Were Kings '96
Hell's Angels Forever '83

Tony Gatlif (1948-)
The Crazy Stranger '98
Mondo '96

Nils Gaup (1955-)
North Star '96
Shipwrecked '90
Pathfinder 87

Joe Gayton
Warm Summer Rain 89

Armand Gazarian
Prison Planet '92
Game of Survival '89

Gyula Gazdag (1947-)
Stand Off '89
A Hungarian Fairy Tale '87

Glenn Gebhard
Desert Steel '94

Augusto Genina (1892-1957)
Prix de Beaute '30

Giacomo Gentilomo (1909-2001)
Hercules against the Moon Men '64
Young Caruso 51

Terry George (1952-)
Reservation Road '07
Hotel Rwanda '04
A Bright Shining Lie '98
Some Mother's Son '96

Fred Gerber
Prison of Secrets '97
Closer and Closer '96
Rent-A-Kid '95

Marion Gering
Thunder in the City '37
Thirty Day Princess '34

Pietro Germi (1904-74)
Alfredo, Alfredo '72
Seduced and Abandoned '64
Divorce—Italian Style '62
Four Ways Out '57

Clyde Geronimi (1901-89)
101 Dalmatians '61
Sleeping Beauty 59
Lady and the Tramp 55
Alice in Wonderland '51
The Adventures of Ichabod and Mr. Toad '49
The Legend of Sleepy Hollow '49
Melody Time '48

Peter Gerretsen
Kidnapping of Baby John Doe 88

Theodore Gershuny
Silent Night, Bloody Night '73
Kemek '70

Nicolas Gessner (1931-)
Black Water '94
Quicker Than the Eye '88

It Rained All Night the Day I Left '78
The Little Girl Who Lives down the Lane '76
Someone Behind the Door '71
12 Plus 1 '70
The Peking Blond 68

Steven Gethers (1922-89)
The Hillside Strangler '89
Jenny's War '85
Kennedy '81
Damien: The Leper Priest '80
Billy: Portrait of a Street Kid '77

Bahman Ghobadi (1968-)
Turtles Can Fly '04
Marooned in Iraq '02

Francis Giacobetti
Emmanuelle 4 '84
Emmanuelle, the Joys of a Woman 76

David Giancola (1969-)
Diamond Run '00
Peril '00
Time Chasers '95

Duncan Gibbins (1952-93)
A Case for Murder '93
Eve of Destruction '90
Fire with Fire '86

Rodney Gibbons
The Sign of Four '01
The Hound of the Baskervilles '00
Wilder '00
The Pact '99

Gwyneth Gibby
Little Men '98
Captive '97
Stranger in the House '97
The Neighbor '93

Alex Gibney
Isaac Asimov's Nightfall '00
Marquis de Sade '96
Taxi to the Dark Side '07
Enron: The Smartest Guys in the Room '05

Alan Gibson (1938-87)
The Charmer '87
Martin's Day '85
Silent Scream '84
The Two Faces of Evil '82
A Woman Called Golda '82
Churchill and the Generals '81
The Satanic Rites of Dracula '73
Dracula A.D. 1972 '72
Twinsanity '70

Brian Gibson (1944-2004)
Still Crazy '98
The Juror '96
What's Love Got to Do with It? '93
Drug Wars: The Camarena Story '90
The Josephine Baker Story '90
Murderers Among Us: The Simon Wiesenthal Story '89
Poltergeist 2: The Other Side '86
Breaking Glass '80

Mel Gibson (1956-)
Apocalypto '06
Braveheart '95
The Man Without a Face '93
The Passion of the Christ '04

Coky Giedroyc
Carrie's War '04
Stella Does Tricks '96

Gregory Gieras
Centipede '05
Dark Asylum '01
The Prince and the Surfer '99
The Whispering '94

Tony Giglio (1971-)
In Enemy Hands '04
Soccer Dog: The Movie '98

Brian Gilbert (1960-)
The Gathering '02
Wilde '97
Tom & Viv '94
Not Without My Daughter '90
Vice Versa 88
The French Lesson '86
Sharma & Beyond '84

Lewis Gilbert (1920-)
Haunted '95
Stepping Out '91
Shirley Valentine '89
Not Quite Paradise '86
Educating Rita '83
Moonraker '79
The Spy Who Loved Me 77
Paul and Michelle '74
Friends '71
The Adventurers '70
You Only Live Twice '67
Alfie '66
The Seventh Dawn '64
Damn the Defiant 62
Cosh Boy 61
Sink the Bismarck '60
Ferry to Hong Kong '59
Carve Her Name with Pride '58
The Admirable Crichton '57
A Cry from the Streets '57
Reach for the Sky '56
Cast a Dark Shadow '55
The Sea Shall Not Have Them '55
Tough Guy 53
Little Ballerina 47

David Giles
A Murder Is Announced '87
Mansfield Park 85
The Strauss Family '73
Vanity Fair '67

Stuart Gillard (1950-)
Twitches Too '07
Twitches '05
RocketMan '97
Poltergeist: The Legacy '96
The Escape '95
The Outer Limits: Sandkings '95

Jim Gillespie
Venom '05
Eye See You '01
I Know What You Did Last Summer '97

Terry Gilliam (1940-)
The Brothers Grimm '05
Tideland '05
Fear and Loathing in Las Vegas '98
12 Monkeys '95
The Fisher King '91
The Adventures of Baron Munchausen 89
Brazil '85
Monty Python's The Meaning of Life '83
Time Bandits '81
Jabberwocky 77
Monty Python and the Holy Grail 75
And Now for Something Completely Different '72

Sidney Gilliat (1908-94)
Endless Night '71
The Great St. Trinian's Train Robbery '66
Only Two Can Play 62
Green for Danger 47

John Gilling (1912-85)
The Mummy's Shroud '67
Night Caller from Outer Space 66
Plague of the Zombies '66
The Reptile '66
Where the Bullets Fly 66
The Flesh and the Fiends '60
It Takes a Thief '59

The Gamma People '56
The Gilded Cage 54
White Fire '53
My Son, the Vampire '52
No Trace '50

Stuart Gilmore (1909-71)
The Half-Breed '51
Hot Lead '51
The Virginian 46

Frank D. Gilroy (1925-)
The Gig '85
Once in Paris... '79
From Noon Till Three 76
Desperate Characters '71

Milton Moses Ginsberg (1943-)
Werewolf of Washington '73
Coming Apart '69

Robert Ginty (1948-)
Woman of Desire '93
Vietnam, Texas 90
Bounty Hunters 89

Jose Giovanni (1923-2004)
Boomerang '76
Gypsy 75
Le Gitan 75
La Scoumoune 72

Buddy Giovinazzo (1957-)
No Way Home 96
Combat Shock '84

Bob Giraldi (1939-)
Dinner Rush '00
Hiding Out '83
Club Med 83

Bernard Girard (1918-97)
Little Moon & Jud McGraw '78
Mind Snatchers '72
Hard Frame 70
A Name for Evil '70
Dead Heat on a Merry-Go-Round '66
A Public Affair 62
As You Were '51

Francois Girard (1963-)
Silk '07
The Red Violin '98
32 Short Films about Glenn Gould 93

Michael Paul Girard (1954-)
Bikini Med School '98
Sweet Evil '98
Bikini House Calls 96
Illegal Affairs '96
Witchcraft 9: Bitter Flesh '96
The Perfect Gift 95
Witchcraft 7: Judgement Hour '95
Body Parts '94

Jean Girault (1924-82)
L'Annee Sainte 76
The Gendarme of Saint-Tropez '64

William Girdler (1947-78)
The Manitou '78
Day of the Animals '77
Project: Kill! '77
Grizzly 76
Sheba, Baby '75
Asylum of Satan '72
Three on a Meathook '72

Francis Girod (1944-)
Transfixed '01
The Elegant Criminal '92
L'Etat Sauvage 78
The Infernal Trio '74

Marino Girolami
You've Got to Have Heart '77

Amos Gitai (1950-)
Girl Under the Sheet '61
Free Zone '05
Kippur '00
Kadosh '99

Paul Michael Glaser (1943-)
Kazaam '96

Jean-Luc Godard (1930-)
Our Music '04
In Praise of Love '01
For Ever Mozart '96
Helas pour Moi '94
Nouvelle Vague '90
Aria '88
King Lear '87
Detective '86
Hail Mary '85
Soft and Hard '85
First Name: Carmen '82
Passion '82
Scenario du Film Passion '82
Comment Ca Va? '76
Here and Elsewhere '76
Numero Deux '75
Sympathy for the Devil '70
Six in Paris '68
Oldest Profession '67
Weekend '67
Masculine Feminine '66
Two or Three Things I Know about Her '66
Alphaville '65
A Married Woman '65
Pierrot le Fou '65
Band of Outsiders '64
Contempt '64
Les Carabiniers '63
My Life to Live '62
RoGoPaG '62
Le Petit Soldat '60
A Woman is a Woman '60
Breathless '59

Leslie Linka Glatter (1965-)
Now and Then '95
State of Emergency '94
Into the Homeland '87

David Gleeson
The Front Line '06

Richard Glatzer
Quinceanera '06
Grief '94
The Fluffer '01

Jonathan Glazer (1965-)
Birth '04
Sexy Beast '00

Francis Glebas
Piglet's Big Movie '03
Fantasia/2000 '00

John Glen (1932-)
Cowboys & Angels '04
Aces: Iron Eagle 3 '92
Christopher Columbus: The Discovery '92
License to Kill '89
The Living Daylights '87
A View to a Kill '85
Octopussy '83
For Your Eyes Only '81

John Glenister (1932-)
Love for Lydia '79
After Julius '78
Six Wives of Henry VIII '71

Bert Glennon (1893-1967)
South of Santa Fe '32
Paradise Island '30

Peter Glenville (1913-96)
The Comedians '67
Hotel Paradiso '66
Becket '64
Summer and Smoke '61
Me and the Colonel '58
The Prisoner '55

James Glickenhaus (1950-)
Timemaster '95
Slaughter of the Innocents '93
McBain '91
Shakedown '89
Protector '85
The Soldier '82
Exterminator '80

Greg Glienna (1963-)
Relative Strangers '06
Meet the Parents '91

Arne Glimcher
Just Cause '94
The Mambo Kings '92

Paul Glickler
The Cheerleaders '72

Sergio Gobbi (1938-)
Germicide '74

Menahem Golan (1929-)
Deadly Heroes '96
Hit the Dutchman '92
Silent Victim '92
Mack the Knife '89
Hanna's War '88
Delta Force '86
Over the Top '86
Enter the Ninja '81
The Apple '80
The Magician of Lublin '79
The Uranium Conspiracy '78
Operation Thunderbolt '77
Lepke '75
Diamonds '75
Escape to the Sun '72
Swashbuckler? ...

Jack Gold (1930-)
Goodnight, Mr. Tom '99
Into the Blue '97
The Return of the Native '94
The Tenth Man '88
Murrow '86
Sakharov '84
Praying Mantis '83
Little Lord Fauntleroy '80
Charlie Muffin '79
The Medusa Touch '78
The Naked Civil Servant '75
Man Friday '75
Catholics '73

Peter Godfrey (1899-1970)
Cry Wolf '47
Escape Me Never '47
The Two Mrs. Carrolls '47
Christmas in Connecticut '45

Jim Goddard (1936-)
Lie Down with Lions '94
The Four Minute Mile '88
The Impossible Spy '87
Shanghai Surprise '86
Parker '84
Reilly: Ace of Spies '83
The Life and Adventures of Nicholas Nickleby '81
A Tale of Two Cities '80

Sandra Goldbacher (1960-)
Me Without You '01
The Governess '98

Eric Goldberg (1955-)
Fantasia/2000 '00
Pocahontas '95

Gary David Goldberg (1944-)
Must Love Dogs '05
Dad '89

Willis Goldbeck (1898-1979)
Johnny Holiday '49
Love Laughs at Andy Hardy '46

Mark Goldblatt
The Punisher '90
Dead Heat '88

Dan Golden
The Haunted Sea '97
Terminal Virus '96

Gary Goldman (1944-)
Titan A.E. '00
Anastasia '97
Thumbelina '94
A Troll in Central Park '94

John Goldschmidt (1943-)
Crime of Honor '85
She'll Be Wearing Pink Pajamas '84

Scott Goldstein
Levitation '97
Ambition '91
Walls of Glass '85

James Goldstone (1931-91)
Rita Hayworth: The Love Goddess '83
Calamity Jane '82
Kent State '81
When Time Ran Out '80
Rollercoaster '77
Swashbuckler '76
Eric '75
Cry Panic '74
Things in Their Season '74
They Only Kill Their Masters '72
Brother John '70
Winning '69

Bob(cat) Goldthwait (1962-)
Sleeping Dogs Lie '06
Shakes the Clown '92

Tony Goldwyn (1960-)
The Last Kiss '06
Someone Like You '01
A Walk on the Moon '99

Steve Gomer
Sunset Park '96
Fly by Night '93
Sweet Lorraine '87
Barney's Great Adventure '98

Nick Gomez (1963-)
Drowning Mona '00
Illtown '96
New Jersey Drive '95
Laws of Gravity '92

Manuel Gomez Pereira (1958-)
Between Your Legs '99
Love Can Seriously Damage Your Health '96
Mouth to Mouth '95
Why Do They Call It Love When They Mean Sex? '92

Michel Gondry (1963-)
Be Kind Rewind '08
Dave Chappelle's Block Party '06
The Science of Sleep '06
Eternal Sunshine of the Spotless Mind '04
Human Nature '02

Sidney Goldin (1880-1937)
Uncle Moses '32
His Wife's Lover '31
East and West '24

Allan Goldstein
Snakeman '05
When Justice Falls '98
Jungle Boy '96
Virus '96
Synapse '96
Death Wish 5: The Face of Death '94

Noam Gonick (1973-)
Stryker '04
Hey, Happy! '01

Servando Gonzalez (1923-)
Yanco '64
The Fool Killer '65

Saul Goodkind (1896-1962)
Buck Rogers Conquers the Universe '39

Leslie Goodwins (1899-1969)
The Go-Getter '54
The Phantom Creeps '39

Bert I. Gordon (1922-)
Satan's Princess '90
The Big Bet '85
Empire of the Ants '77
Food of the Gods '76
The Mad Bomber '72
The Witching '72
Village of the Giants '65
Picture Mommy Dead '66
The Magic Sword '62
Tormented '60
Attack of the Puppet People '58
The Spider '58
War of the Colossal Beast '58
The Amazing Colossal Man '57
Beginning of the End '57
Cyclops '56
King Dinosaur '55

Bryan Gordon
Pie in the Sky '95
Career Opportunities '91

Bette Gordon (1950-)
Luminous Motion '00
Variety '83

Dennie Gordon
New York Minute '04
What a Girl Wants '03
Joe Dirt '01

Keith Gordon (1961-)
The Singing Detective '03
Waking the Dead '00
Mother Night '96
A Midnight Clear '92
The Chocolate War '88

Michael Gordon (1911-93)
The Impossible Years '68
Texas Across the River '66
For Love or Money '63
Move Over, Darling '63
Boys' Night Out '62
Portrait in Black '60
Pillow Talk '59
Cyrano de Bergerac '50
Underground Agent '42

Robert Gordon (1895-)
The Joe Louis Story '53
It Came from Beneath the Sea '55
The Gatling Gun '72

Stuart Gordon (1947-)
Masters of Horror: Dreams in the Witch House '05
King of the Ants '03
Dagon '01
Space Truckers '97
Castle Freak '95
Fortress '93
The Pit & the Pendulum '91
Robot Jox '90
Daughter of Darkness '89
Dolls '87
From Beyond '86
Re-Animator '84

John Gorrie (1932-)
Like A Bride '94
Cause Celebre '87
Edward the King '75

Marleen Gorris (1948-)
The Luzhin Defence '00
Mrs. Dalloway '97
Antonia's Line '95

Hideo Gosha (1929-92)
Hunter in the Dark '80
The Wolves '71

Raja Gosnell (1968-)
Yours, Mine & Ours '05
Scooby-Doo 2: Monsters Unleashed '04
Scooby-Doo '02
Big Momma's House '00
Never Been Kissed '99
Home Alone 3 '97

Jurgen Goslar (1927-)
Slavers '77
Albino '76

Andrew Goth
Cold and Dark '05
B.U.S.T.E.D. '99

Carl Gottlieb (1938-)
Amazon Women on the Moon '87
Caveman '81

Franz Gottlieb (1930-2006)
The Phantom of Soho '64
The Black Abbot '63
Curse of the Yellow Snake '63

Lisa Gottlieb
Cadillac Ranch '96
Across the Moon '94
Just One of the Guys '85

Michael Gottlieb
A Kid in King Arthur's Court '95
Mr. Nanny '93
Mannequin 2 '91
Mannequin '87

Heywood Gould
Double Bang '01
Mistrial '96
Trial by Jury '94
One Good Cop '91

Edmund Goulding (1891-1959)
Mr. 880 '50
We're Not Married '52
Nightmare Alley '47
The Razor's Edge '46
Forever and a Day '43
The Great Lie '41
Dark Victory '39
The Old Maid '39
Dawn Patrol '38
That Certain Woman '37
Riptide '34
Grand Hotel '32
Reaching for the Moon '31
The Trespasser '29

Alfred Goulding (1896-1972)
Dick Barton, Special Agent '48
A Yank in Australia '43
A Chump at Oxford '40

Anne Goursaud
Poison Ivy 2: Lily '95
Red Shoe Diaries 6: How I Met My Husband '95
Embrace of the Vampire '95
Another 9 1/2 Weeks '96

David S. Goyer (1965-)
The Invisible '07
Blade: Trinity '04
ZigZag '02

Marc Gracie
Jigsaw '90
A Kink in the Picasso '90

Gustavo Graef-Marino
Diplomatic Siege '99
Johnny 100 Pesos '93

William A. Graham (1930-)
Blood Crime '02
Acceptable Risk '01
The Man Who Captured Eichmann '96
Return to the Blue Lagoon '91
Montana '90
Gore Vidal's Billy the Kid '89
Proud Men '87
George Washington: The Forging of a Nation '86
The Guyana Tragedy: The Story of Jim Jones '80
Rage '80
Orphan Train '79
And I Alone Survived '78
One in a Million: The Ron LeFlore Story '78
Deadly Encounter '72
Birds of Prey '72
Where the Lilies Bloom '74
Harry Tracy '83
M.A.D.D.: Mothers Against Drunk Driving '83
Honky '71
Thief '71
Change of Habit '69

Pierre Granier-Deferre (1927-2007)
A Woman at Her Window '76
The French Detective '75
Le Chat '75
The Last Train '74
The Widow Couderc '74
The Doomsday Flight '65

Brian Grant
The Immortals '95
Sensation '94
Love Kills '91
Sweet Poison '91

Julian Grant
Airborne '98
Electra '96

Lee Grant (1927-)
The Loretta Claiborne Story '00
Staying Together '89

Alex Grasshof (1930-)
Tell Me a Riddle '80
A Billion for Boris '90
Pepper and His Wacky Taxi '72

Jorge Grau (1930-)
Let Sleeping Corpses Lie '74
The Legend of Blood Castle '72

Walter Grauman (1922-)
Nightmare on the 13th Floor '90
Outrage! '86

Scene of the Crime '85
Pleasure Palace '80
To Race the Wind '80
Are You in the House Alone? '78
Most Wanted '76
Force Five '75
Manhunter '74
The Streets of San Francisco '72
Paper Man '71
They Call It Murder '71
Lady in a Cage '64
633 Squadron '64

Gary Graver (1938-2006)
Sexual Roulette '96
Evil Spirits '91
Roots of Evil '91
Crossing the Line '90
Party Camp '87
Moon in Scorpio '86
Trick or Treats '82
Texas Lightning '81

Alex Graves
Casualties '97
The Crude Oasis '95

F. Gary Gray (1970-)
Be Cool '05
The Italian Job '03
A Man Apart '03
The Negotiator '98
Set It Off '96
Friday '95

James Gray (1969-)
We Own the Night '07
The Yards '00
Little Odessa '94

John Gray
Brian's Song '01
The Seventh Stream '01
The Hunley '99
The Glimmer Man '96
Born to Be Wild '95
A Place for Annie '94
An American Story '92
The Last Capone '90
When He's Not a Stranger '89
Billy Galvin '86

Godfrey Grayson (1913-98)
Room to Let '49
Dick Barton Strikes Back '48

Kjell Grede (1936-)
Good Evening, Mr. Wallenberg '93
Hip Hip Hurrah! '87

Alfred E. Green (1889-1960)
Invasion U.S.A. '52
The Jackie Robinson Story '50
Four Faces West '48
Copacabana '47
The Fabulous Dorseys '47
The Jolson Story '46
A Thousand and One Nights '45
Mr. Winkle Goes to War '44
South of Pago Pago '40
The Gracie Allen Murder Case '39
The Duke of West Point '38
Thoroughbreds Don't Cry '37
They Met in a Taxi '36
Dangerous '35
Baby Face '33
Smart Money '31
Disraeli '30
Ella Cinders '26

Bruce Seth Green
In Self Defense '93
The Hunt for the Night Stalker '91
Running Against Time '90
Rags to Riches '87

David Green (1948-)
Fire Birds '90
Buster '88
Car Trouble '86
Code of Honor '84

David Gordon Green (1975-)
Pineapple Express '08
Snow Angels '07
Undertow '04
All the Real Girls '03

Guy Green (1913-2005)
Strong Medicine '84
The Incredible Journey of Dr. Meg Laurel '79
Once Is Not Enough '75
Luther '74
Walk in the Spring Rain '70
A Patch of Blue '65
Diamond Head '62
The Mark '61
S.O.S. Pacific '60
Sea of Sand '58
River Beat '54

Jack N. Green (1946-)
Seduced: Pretty When You Cry '01
Traveller '96

Joseph Green (1900-96)
The Brain that Wouldn't Die '63

Terry Green
Heavens Fall '06
Cold Justice '89

Peter Greenaway (1942-)
8 1/2 Women '99
The Pillow Book '95
The Belly of an Architect '91
Prospero's Books '91
The Cook, the Thief, His Wife & Her Lover '90
A Zed & Two Noughts '88
Drowning by Numbers '87
The Draughtsman's Contract '82

David Greene (1921-2003)
Family of Cops 2: Breach of Faith '97
A Good Day to Die '95
What Ever Happened To... '93
In a Stranger's Hand '92
The Penthouse '92
Small Sacrifices '89
Vanishing Act '88
After the Promise '87
Miles to Go '86
World War III '86
Guilty Conscience '85
TripleCross '85
Fatal Vision '84
The Guardian '84
Prototype '83
Rehearsal for Murder '82
Take Your Best Shot '82
The Choice '81
Hard Country '81
Friendly Fire '79
Gray Lady Down '77
Roots '77
The Count of Monte Cristo '74
Godspell '73
Madame Sin '71
The People Next Door '70
Blood Island '68
Sebastian '68

Martin Greene
Undercover Cop '94
Dark Sanity '82

Luke Greenfield (1972-)
The Girl Next Door '04
The Animal '01

Paul Greengrass (1955-)
The Bourne Ultimatum '07
United 93 '06
The Bourne Supremacy '04
Bloody Sunday '01

The Murder of Stephen Lawrence '99
The Theory of Flight '98
The One That Got Away '96

Maggie Greenwald (1955-)
Get a Clue '02
Songcatcher '99
The Ballad of Little Jo '93
The Kill-Off '90
Home Remedy '88

Robert Greenwald (1948-)
Wal-Mart: The High Cost of Low Price '05
Outfoxed: Rupert Murdoch's War on Journalism '04
Uncovered: The War on Iraq '04
Steal This Movie! '00
Breaking Up '97
A Woman of Independent Means '94
Hear No Evil '93
Forgotten Prisoners '90
Sweet Hearts Dance '88
Shattered Spirits '86
The Burning Bed '85
In the Custody of Strangers '82
Xanadu '80
Flatbed Annie and Sweetiepie: Lady Truckers '79

David Greenwalt (1949-)
Rude Awakening '89
Secret Admirer '85

William Grefe (1930-)
Whiskey Mountain '77
Jaws of Death '76
Impulse '74
Alligator Alley '72
Stanley '72
Wild Rebels '71
The Hooked Generation '69
The Death Curse of Tartu '66
The Checkered Flag '63

Colin Gregg (1947-)
We Think the World of You '88
Lamb '85
To the Lighthouse '83
Trespasser '81

Ezio Greggio (1954-)
Screw Loose '99

Jean Gremillon (1901-59)
Pattes Blanches '49
Stormy Waters '41

Marc S. Grenier
Hidden Agenda '01
Cause of Death '00
Fallen Angel '99
Stalker '98

Edmond T. Greville (1906-66)
The Liars '64
Beat Girl '60
The Hands of Orlac '60
Princess Tam Tam '35

John Greyson (1960-)
Lilies '96
Zero Patience '94

Sergio Grieco (1917-82)
Mad Dog '84
Man of Legend '71

Tom Gries (1922-77)
The Greatest '77
Breakheart Pass '76
Helter Skelter '76
Hunter '76
Breakout '75
The Migrants '74
QB VII '74
The Connection '73
Lady Ice '73
The Glass House '72
Fools '70
100 Rifles '69
Will Penny '67
Serpent Island '54

Andrew Grieve (1939-)
The Adventure Continues '01
Horatio Hornblower '99
All or Nothing at All '93
Lorna Doone '90
Suspicion '87

Charles B. Griffith (1930-2007)
Wizards of the Lost Kingdom 2 '89
Smokey Bites the Dust '81
Dr. Heckyl and Mr. Hype '80
Up from the Depths '79
Eat My Dust '76

D.W. Griffith (1875-1948)
Struggle '31
Abraham Lincoln '30
Battle of the Sexes '28
The Sorrows of Satan '26
Sally of the Sawdust '25
America '24
Isn't Life Wonderful '24
The White Rose '23
Dream Street '21
Orphans of the Storm '21
The Love Flower '20
Way Down East '20
Broken Blossoms '19
The Greatest Question '19
True Heart Susie '19
Hearts of the World '18
Intolerance '16
The Birth of a Nation '15
Avenging Conscience '14
Home Sweet Home '14
Judith of Bethulia '14
Battle of Elderbush Gulch '13

Edward H. Griffith (1894-1975)
The Sky's the Limit '43
Bahama Passage '42
Young and Willing '42
My Love For Yours '39
Next Time We Love '36
The Animal Kingdom '32
Captain Swagger '25

Mark Griffiths
Love's Unending Legacy '07
Mystery Woman: Mystery Weekend '05
Beethoven's 5th '03
Tactical Assault '99
Behind Enemy Lines '96
Max Is Missing '95
Cheyenne Warrior '94
Ultraviolet '91
A Cry in the Wild '90
Heroes Stand Alone '89
Hardbodies 2 '86
Hardbodies '84
Running Hot '83

Aurelio Grimaldi (1957-)
Nerolio '96

Alan Grint
Catherine Cookson's The Secret '00
Catherine Cookson's Tilly Trotter '99
Catherine Cookson's Colour Blind '98
Catherine Cookson's The Round Tower '98
The Secret Garden '87

Brad Grinter
Blood Freak '72

Wallace Grissell (1904-54)
King of the Congo '52

Federal Operator 99 '45
Manhunt of Mystery Island '45

John Grissmer
Blood Rage '87
Scalpel '76

Ferde Grofe, Jr.
Judgment Day '88
The Proud and the Damned '72
Satan's Harvest '65
Warkill '65

Ulu Grosbard (1929-)
The Deep End of the Ocean '98
Georgia '95
Falling in Love '84
True Confessions '81
Straight Time '78
Who Is Harry Kellerman and Why Is He Saying Those Terrible Things About Me? '71
The Subject Was Roses '68

Jerry Gross (1940-2002)
Teenage Mother '67
Girl on a Chain Gang '65

Adam Grossman
Carnival of Souls '98
Sometimes They Come Back... Again '96

Charles Grosvenor
Land Before Time 7: The Stone of Cold Fire '00
The Land Before Time 6: The Secret of Saurus Rock '98
The Land Before Time 5: The Mysterious Island '97
Once Upon a Forest '93

Robert Guediguian (1953-)
The Town Is Quiet '00
Marius and Jeannette '97

Ruy Guerra (1931-)
The Fable of the Beautiful Pigeon Fancier '88
Opera do Malandro '87
Erendira '83

Romolo Guerrieri (1931-)
The Final Executioner '83
Ring of Death '69
Beauty on the Beach '61

Christopher Guest (1948-)
For Your Consideration '06
A Mighty Wind '03
Best in Show '00
Almost Heroes '97
Waiting for Guffman '96
Attack of the 50 Ft. Woman '93
The Big Picture '89

Val Guest (1911-2006)
Killer Force '75
Au Pair Girls '72
When Dinosaurs Ruled the Earth '70
Casino Royale '67
The Day the Earth Caught Fire '61
Expresso Bongo '59
Up the Creek '58
The Abominable Snowman '57
Carry On Admiral '57
Men of Sherwood Forest '57
Quatermass 2 '57
The Quatermass Experiment '56
The Runaway Bus '54
Mister Drake's Duck '50
Just William's Luck '47
Stone of Silver Creek '35

Davis Guggenheim (1964-)
Gracie '07
An Inconvenient Truth '06
Gossip '99

John Guillermin (1925-)
The Tracker '88
King Kong Lives '86
Sheena '84
Crossover '82

Death on the Nile '78
King Kong '76
The Towering Inferno '74
Shaft in Africa '73
El Condor '70
The Bridge at Remagen '69
The Blue Max '66
Guns at Batasi '64
Waltz of the Toreadors '62
Never Let Go '60

Fred Guiol (1898-1964)
Mr. Walkie Talkie '52
Tanks a Million '41
Battling Orioles '24

Sacha Guitry (1885-1957)
Napoleon '55
The Story of a Cheat '36

Yilmaz Guney (1937-84)
The Wall '83
Yol '82
Baba '73

Sturla Gunnarsson (1952-)
Beowulf & Grendel '06
Rare Birds '01
Dangerous Evidence: The Lori Jackson Story '99
Such a Long Journey '98
Joe Torre: Curveballs Along the Way '97

Lawrence (Larry) Guterman
Son of the Mask '05
Cats & Dogs '01

Sebastian Gutierrez
Rise: Blood Hunter '07
She Creature '01
Judas Kiss '98

Tomas Gutierrez Alea (1926-96)
Guantanamera '95
Strawberry and Chocolate '93

Amos Guttman (1954-93)
Amazing Grace '92
Drifting '82

Claudio Guzman (1927-)
The Hostage Tower '80
Willa '79
Antonio '73

Stephen Gyllenhaal (1949-)
Warden of Red Rock '01
Homegrown '97
Losing Isaiah '94
A Dangerous Woman '93
Question of Faith '93
Waterland '92
Paris Trout '91
A Killing in a Small Town '90
Promised a Miracle '88
The Abduction of Kari Swenson '87
Certain Fury '85

Charles F. Haas (1913-)
Platinum High School '60
Girls' Town '59
Tarzan and the Trappers '58

Philip Haas (1927-)
The Situation '06
The Lathe of Heaven '02
Up at the Villa '00
The Blood Oranges '97
Angels and Insects '95
The Music of Chance '93

Mark Haber
Border Patrol '01
Alien Cargo '99

Taylor Hackford (1944-)
Ray '04
Proof of Life '00
The Devil's Advocate '97
Dolores Claiborne '94
Blood In ... Blood Out '93
Everybody's All American '88
Bound by Honor '93
An Officer and a Gentleman '82
Chuck Berry: Hail! Hail! Rock 'n' Roll '87
White Nights '85
Against All Odds '84
Idolmaker '80

Mikael Hafstrom (1960-)
1408 '07
Derailed '05
Evil '03

Jeremy Haft
The Glove '78
B.O.R.N. '88
Back Home '90
A Summer Story '88
Venom '82

Ross Hagen (1938-)
Grizzly Mountain '97
The Crimson Code '99

Paul Haggis (1953-)
In the Valley of Elah '07
Crash '05

Stuart Hagmann (1942-)
Tarantulas: The Deadly Cargo '77
The Strawberry Statement '70

Charles Haid (1943-)
Children of Fury '94
Cooperstown '93
Iron Will '93
The Nightman '93

Randa Haines (1945-)
Dance with Me '98
The Outsider '02
Children of a Lesser God '86
The Doctor '91

Michael Haigney
Pokemon 3: The Movie '01
Pokemon: The First Movie '99
Pokemon: The Power of One '00

Richard W. Haines (1957-)
Alien Space Avenger '91
Class of Nuke 'Em High '86
Splatter University '84

Don Haldane (1914-)
The Reincarnate '71
Nikki, the Wild Dog of the North '61

Alan Hale (1892-1950)
Risky Business '28
Braveheart '25

Sonnie Hale (1902-59)
Gangway '37
Sailing Along '38

William (Billy) Hale
Harem '86
The Murder of Mary Phagan '87
One Shoe Makes It Murder '82
Murder in Texas '81

Jack Haley, Jr. (1933-2001)
That's Dancing! '85
That's Entertainment '74
The Love Machine '71

H.B. Halicki (1941-89)
Deadline Auto Theft '83
The Junkman '82
Gone in 60 Seconds '74

Alexander Hall (1894-1968)
Forever Darling '56
Because You're Mine '52
The Great Lover '49
Down to Earth '47
Goin' to Town '35
Here Comes Mr. Jordan '41
Doctor Takes a Wife '40
I Am the Law '38
Little Miss Marker '34
Sinners in the Sun '32

Kenneth J. Hall (1958-)
Ghost Writer '89
Evil Spawn '87

Peter Hall (1930-)
Never Talk to Strangers '95
Jacob '94
The Camomile Lawn '92
Orpheus Descending '91
A Midsummer Night's Dream '68

Daniel Haller (1926-)
Margin for Murder '81
Follow That Car '80
Buck Rogers in the 25th Century '79
The Dunwich Horror '70
Paddy '70
Devil's Angels '67
Die, Monster, Die! '65

Godfrey Hall
See Godfrey Ho

Ivan Hall
Kill and Kill Again '81
Kill or Be Killed '80
Funeral for an Assassin '77

Victor Halperin (1895-1983)
Buried Alive '39
Torture Ship '39
A Nation Aflame '37
Revolt of the Zombies '36
I Conquer the Sea '36
Supernatural '33
The White Zombie '32
Party Girls '29

John Hamburg (1970-)
Along Came Polly '04
Safe Men '98

Robert Hamer (1911-63)
To Paris with Love '55
The Detective '54
Kind Hearts and Coronets '49
Pink String and Sealing Wax '45
Dead of Night '45

Bent Hamer (1956-)
Factotum '06
Kitchen Stories '03

Lasse Hallstrom (1946-)
The Hoax '06
Casanova '05
An Unfinished Life '05
The Shipping News '01
Chocolat '00
The Cider House Rules '99
Something to Talk About '95
What's Eating Gilbert Grape '93
Once Around '91
More about the Children of Noisy Village '87
The Children of Noisy Village '86
My Life As a Dog '85

John Hancock (1939-)
Suspended Animation '02
Prancer '89
Weeds '87
California Dreaming '79
Bang the Drum Slowly '73
Let's Scare Jessica to Death '71

John Lee Hancock (1957-)
The Alamo '04
The Rookie '02

David Hand (1900-86)
Bambi '42
Snow White and the Seven Dwarfs '37

Michael Haneke (1942-)
Funny Games '07
Hidden '05
Time of the Wolf '03
The Piano Teacher '01
Code Unknown '00
Funny Games '97
Benny's Video '92

Susumu Hani
Green Horizon '80
She and He '63

Tom Hanks (1956-)
Band of Brothers '01
That Thing You Do! '96

Dean Hamilton (1961-)
Blonde and Blonder '07
D.R.E.A.M. Team '99

Guy Hamilton (1922-)
Remo Williams: The Adventure Begins '85
Evil under the Sun '82
The Mirror Crack'd '80
Force 10 from Navarone '78
The Man with the Golden Gun '74
Live and Let Die '73
Diamonds Are Forever '71
Battle of Britain '69
Funeral in Berlin '66
Goldfinger '64
The Devil's Disciple '59
The Colditz Story '55

John Hamilton (1894-)
Codename: Jaguar '00

Strathford Hamilton (1952-)
The Kid '97
Escape from Atlantis '97
The Proposition '96
The Set Up '95
Cold Comfort Farm '71
Betrayal of the Dove '92
Temptation '94
Diving In '90
Blueberry Hill '88

Nick Hamm (1957-)
Godsend '04
The Hole '01
The Very Thought of You '98

Peter Hammond (1923-)
Talk of Angels '96
The Dark Angel '91
The Maze '85

Christopher Hampton (1946-)
Imagining Argentina '04
The Secret Agent '96
Carrington '95

Robert Hampton
See Riccardo Freda

Victor Hanbury (1954-)
The Avenging Hand '36

Sanaa Hamri
Something New '06

Joseph Hardy (1929-90)
Users '78
Return Engagement '78
Love's Savage Fury '79
To Love Again '80

Gary Hardwick
Deliver Us from Eva '03
The Brothers '01

Catherine Hardwicke (1955-)
The Nativity Story '06
Lords of Dogtown '05
Thirteen '03

Sarah Harding
Dead Gorgeous '02

John Hanson (1922-)
Wildrose '85
Northern Lights '79

Ed Hansen (1937-)
Hell's Belles '95
The Bikini Car Wash Company '96
Party Plane '90
Party Favors '89
Robo-Chic '89

Marion Hansel (1949-)
The Quarry '98
Between Heaven and Earth '93
Dust '85

Ken Hannam (1929-2004)
The Assassination Run '84
Sunday Too Far Away '74

William Hanna (1910-2001)
Jetsons: The Movie '90
Hey There, It's Yogi Bear '64

Renny Harlin (1959-)
Cleaner '07
The Covenant '06
Mindhunters '05
Exorcist: The Beginning '04
Driven '01
Deep Blue Sea '99
The Long Kiss Goodnight '96
Cutthroat Island '95
Cliffhanger '93
The Adventures of Ford Fairlane '90
Die Hard 2: Die Harder '90
A Nightmare on Elm Street 4: Dream Master '88
Prison '89

Curtis Hanson (1945-)
Lucky You '07
In Her Shoes '05
8 Mile '02
Wonder Boys '00
L.A. Confidential '97
The River Wild '94
The Hand that Rocks the Cradle '92
Bad Influence '90
The Bedroom Window '87
The Children of Times Square '86
Losin' It '82
Little Dragons '80
The Arousers '70

John Harlow (1896-1977)
Old Mother Riley, Headmistress '50
Old Mother Riley's New Venture '49
While I Live '47
Appointment with Crime '45
Echo Murders '45
Candles at Nine '44
Meet Sexton Blake '44
Spellbound '41

Robert Harmon
Nowhere to Run '93
Eyes of an Angel '91
The Hitcher '86

Jesse Stone: Sea Change '07
Jesse Stone: Death in Paradise '06
Jesse Stone: Night Passage '06
Jesse Stone: Stone Cold '05
Ike: Countdown to D-Day '04
Highwaymen '03
Wes Craven Presents: They '02
The Crossing '00
Gotti '96
Born American '86

Curtis Harrington (1928-2007)
Usher '00

Veit Harlan (1899-1964)
Kolberg '45
Jud Suess '40

William S. Hart (1864-1946)

Harry Harris (1922-)
Alice in Wonderland '85
The Runaways '75
Killpoint '84
The Patriot '86
After/shock '88
Lockdown '90
Blue Blazes Rawden '18
Narrow Trail '17
Hell's Hinges '16
Return of Draw Egan '15
The Disciple '15
The Fugitive: Taking of Luke McVane '15

Frank Harris
The Rachel Papers '89

Damian Harris (1958-)
Mercy '00
Bad Company '94
Deceived '91
The Discovery Program '91

James B. Harris (1928-)
Boiling Point '93
Cop '88
Fast Walking '82
Some Call It Loving '73
The Bedford Incident '65

Karl Hartl (1898-1978)
The Life and Loves of Mozart '59
F.P. 1 Doesn't Answer '33

Robert Hartford-Davis (1923-77)
The Fiend '71
The Bloodsuckers '70
Black Box Affair '66

Kenneth Hartford
Hell Squad '85
The Lucifer Complex '78

Hal Hartley (1959-)
Fay Grim '06
No Such Thing '01
Henry Fool '98
Flirt '95
Amateur '94
Simple Men '92
Surviving Desire '91
Trust '91
The Unbelievable Truth '90

Greg Harrison (1969-)
November '05
Groove '00

John Harrison
Dune '00

Harvey Hart (1928-89)
Passion in Paradise '89
Stone Fox '87
Beverly Hills Madam '86
Reckless Disregard '84
Utilities '83

Mary Harron (1953-)
The Notorious Bettie Page '06
American Psycho '99
I Shot Andy Warhol '96

Lee Harry
Street Soldiers '91
Silent Night, Deadly Night 2 '87

Matthew Harrison (1960-)
Kicked in the Head '97
Rhythm Thief '94
Spare Me '92

John Kent Harrison
Helen of Troy '03
In Love and War '01
A House Divided '00
You Know My Name '99
What the Deaf Man Heard '97
Beautiful Dreamers '92
Tales from the Darkside: The Movie '90

Ken Harrison (1942-)
On Valentine's Day '86
1918 '85

Don Hartman (1900-58)
Holiday Affair '49
Every Girl Should Be Married '48
Anthony Harvey (1931-)
Grace Quigley '84
Svengali '83
Richard's Things '80
Eagle's Wing '79
Players '79
The Disappearance of Aimee '76
They Might Be Giants '71
The Lion in Winter '68
Dutchman '67
Byron Haskin (1899-1984)
Demon with a Glass Hand '64
Robinson Crusoe on Mars '64
Captain Sinbad '63
Armored Command '61
Jet Over the Atlantic '59
From the Earth to the Moon '58
Conquest of Space '55
Long John Silver '54
Naked Jungle '54
His Majesty O'Keefe '53
The War of the Worlds '53
The Denver & Rio Grande '51
Treasure Island '50
Too Late for Tears '49
Masanori Hata
The Adventures of Milo & Otis '89
Milo & Otis '89
Henry Hathaway (1898-1985)
Raid on Rommel '71
Shoot Out '71
True Grit '69
Five Card Stud '68
The Last Safari '67
Nevada Smith '66
Sons of Katie Elder '65
Circus World '64
Of Human Bondage '64
How the West Was Won '63
North to Alaska '60
Seven Thieves '60
Legend of the Lost '57
The Racers '55
Garden of Evil '54
Prince Valiant '54
Diplomatic Courier '52
Niagara '52
The Desert Fox '51
The Black Rose '50
Rawhide '50
Call Northside 777 '48
Kiss of Death '47
Dark Corner '46
13 Rue Madeleine '46
House on 92nd Street '45
A Wing and a Prayer '44
The Shepherd of the Hills '41
Sundown '41
Brigham Young: Frontiersman '40
The Real Glory '39
Spawn of the North '38
Souls at Sea '37
Go West, Young Man '36
The Trail of the Lonesome Pine '36
The Lives of a Bengal Lancer '35
Now and Forever '34
Buffalo Stampede '33
Heritage of the Desert '33
Man of the Forest '33
To the Last Man '33
When the West Was Young '32
Jeff Hathcock
Three Bad Men '05
Night Ripper '86
Wings Hauser (1948-)
Gang Boys '97
Living to Die '91
The Art of Dying '90

David Heavener (1958-)
Fugitive X '96
Dragon Fury '95
Eye of the Stranger '93
Prime Target '91
Deadly Reactor '89
Killcrazy '89
Twisted Justice '89
Outlaw Force '87
Ben Hecht (1894-1964)
Actors and Sin '52
Spectre of the Rose '46
Angels Over Broadway '40
Amy Heckerling (1954-)
I Could Never Be Your Woman '06
Loser '00
Clueless '95
Look Who's Talking, Too '90
Look Who's Talking '89
National Lampoon's European Vacation '85
Johnny Dangerously '84
Fast Times at Ridgemont High '82
Rob Hedden (1954-)
Alien Fury: Countdown to Invasion '00
Kidnapped in Paradise '98
Any Place But Home '97
The Colony '95
Friday the 13th, Part 8: Jason Takes Manhattan '89
Peter Hedges (1962-)
Dan in Real Life '07
Pieces of April '03
Richard T. Heffron (1930-2007)
Tagget '90
Broken Angel '88
Pancho Barnes '88
Convicted: A Mother's Story '87
Guilty of Innocence '87
The Mitch Snyder Story '86
V: The Final Battle '84
I, the Jury '82
Whale for the Killing '81
Foolin' Around '80
A Rumor of War '80
See How She Runs '78
Outlaw Blues '77
Futureworld '76
Death Scream '75
Newman's Law '74
Chris Hegedus (1952-)
Only the Strong Survive '03
Moon over Broadway '98
The War Room '93
Yosif Heifitz (1905-95)
The Lady with the Dog '59
Stuart Heisler (1894-1979)
Hitler '62
The Burning Hills '56
Lone Ranger '56
I Died a Thousand Times '55
Island of Desire '52
Storm Warning '51
Chain Lightning '50
Tokyo Joe '49
Tulsa '49
Smash-Up: The Story of a Woman '47
Blue Skies '46
Along Came Jones '45
The Glass Key '42
Mats Helge
The Russian Terminator '90
Ninja Mission '84
Brian Helgeland (1961-)
The Order '03
A Knight's Tale '01
Payback '98

Martin Hellberg (1905-99)
Minna von Barnhelm or The Soldier's Fortune '62
Intrigue and Love '59
Olle Hellbom (1925-82)
Brothers Lionheart '77
Pippi in the South Seas '70
Pippi on the Run '70
Pippi Goes on Board '69
Pippi Longstocking '69
Monte Hellman (1932-)
Iguana '89
Silent Night, Deadly Night 3: Better Watch Out! '89
Gunfire '78
Cockfighter '74
Two Lane Blacktop '71
Flight to Fury '66
Ride in the Whirlwind '66
The Shooting '66
The Terror '63
The Beast from Haunted Cave '60
Creature from the Haunted Sea '60
Oliver Hellman
See Ovidio G. Assonitis
Ralph Hemecker
Double Edge '97
Dead On '93
David Hemmings (1941-2003)
Lone Justice 3: Showdown at Plum Creek '96
A Christmas Reunion '93
Dark Horse '92
The Key to Rebecca '85
Treasure of the Yankee Zephyr '83
Survivor '83
Just a Gigolo '79
Joseph Henabery (1888-1976)
Leather Burners '43
Cobra '25
His Majesty, the American '19
The Man from Painted Post '17
Eric Hendershot
The Robin Hood Gang '98
Clubhouse Detectives '96
Clark Henderson (1951-)
Circle of Fear '89
Primary Target '89
Saigon Commandos '88
Warlords from Hell '87
Don Henderson (1931-97)
The Touch of Satan '70
Weekend with the Babysitter '70
John Henderson (1949-)
Two Men Went to War '02
The Magical Legend of the Leprechauns '99
The Return of the Borrowers '96
Loch Ness '95
The Borrowers '93
Frank Henenlotter (1950-)
Basket Case 3: The Progeny '92
Basket Case 2 '90
Frankenhooker '90
Brain Damage '88
Basket Case '82
Paul Henreid (1908-92)
Ballad in Blue '66
Dead Ringer '64
Battle Shock '56
Tall Lie '53
Buck Henry (1930-)
First Family '80
Heaven Can Wait '78
Brian Henson (1963-)
Jack and the Beanstalk: The Real Story '01

Muppet Treasure Island '96
The Muppet Christmas Carol '92
Jim Henson (1936-90)
Labyrinth '86
The Dark Crystal '82
The Great Muppet Caper '81
Robby Henson
Thr3e '07
The Badge '02
Pharoah's Army '95
Henry Herbert (1939-2003)
Forbidden Passion: The Oscar Wilde Movie '85
Danger UXB '81
Emily '77
Stephen Herek (1958-)
Man of the House '05
Life or Something Like It '02
Rock Star '01
Holy Man '98
101 Dalmatians '96
Mr. Holland's Opus '95
The Three Musketeers '93
The Mighty Ducks '92
Don't Tell Mom the Babysitter's Dead '91
Bill & Ted's Excellent Adventure '89
Critters '86
Al(bert) Herman (1887-1967)
The Missing Corpse '45
The Phantom of 42nd Street '45
Delinquent Daughters '44
Rogue's Gallery '44
Shake Hands with Murder '44
Dawn Express '42
Rangers Take Over '42
Yank in Libya '42
Gentleman from Dixie '41
The Pioneers '41
Take Me Back to Oklahoma '40
Down the Wyoming Trail '39
Man from Texas '39
Roll, Wagons, Roll '39
Renfrew on the Great White Trail '38
Rollin' Plains '38
Utah Trail '38
Valley of Terror '38
Renfrew of the Royal Mounted '37
The Clutching Hand '36
Gun Play '36
Outlaws of the Range '36
Cowboy & the Bandit '35
Western Frontier '35
Whispering Shadow '33
Beyond the Trail '26
Jean Herman (1933-)
Butterfly Affair '71
Queen of Diamonds '70
Honor Among Thieves '68
Mark Herman (1954-)
Little Voice '98
Brassed Off '96
Blame It on the Bellboy '92
Charles Herman-Wurmfeld (1966-)
The Hammer '07
Legally Blonde 2: Red White & Blonde '03
Kissing Jessica Stein '02
Fanci's Persuasion '95
Jaime Humberto Hermosillo (1942-)
Esmeralda Comes by Night '98
Forbidden Homework '92
Homework '90
The Summer of Miss Forbes '88
Dona Herlinda & Her Son '86
Denis Heroux (1940-)
The Uncanny '78
Born for Hell '76

Rowdy Herrington (1951-)
Bobby Jones: Stroke of Genius '04
I Witness '03
The Stickup '01
A Murder of Crows '99
Striking Distance '93
Gladiator '92
Road House '89
Jack's Back '87
W(illiam) Blake Herron
A Texas Funeral '99
Skin Art '93
Joel Hershman (1958-)
Greenfingers '00
Hold Me, Thrill Me, Kiss Me '93
Marshall Herskovitz (1952-)
Dangerous Beauty '98
Jack the Bear '93
Michael Herz (1949-)
Sgt. Kabukiman N.Y.P.D. '94
The Toxic Avenger, Part 2 '89
The Toxic Avenger, Part 3: The Last Temptation of Toxie '89
Troma's War '88
The Toxic Avenger '86
Stuck on You '84
First Turn On '83
Sugar Cookies '77
John Herzfeld
Bobby Z '07
15 Minutes '01
Don King: Only in America '97
Two Days in the Valley '96
Casualties of Love: The "Long Island Lolita" Story '93
The Preppie Murder '89
A Father's Revenge '88
Two of a Kind '83
Werner Herzog (1942-)
Rescue Dawn '06
Grizzly Man '05
The White Diamond '04
Invincible '01
Cobra Verde '88
Where the Green Ants Dream '84
Fitzcarraldo '82
Nosferatu the Vampyre '79
Woyzeck '78
Stroszek '77
Every Man for Himself & God Against All '75
Heart of Glass '74
Aguirre, the Wrath of God '72
Signs of Life '68
Jared Hess (1979-)
Nacho Libre '06
Napoleon Dynamite '04
Jon Hess
Crash & Byrnes '99
Legion '98
Mars '96
Excessive Force '93
Alligator 2: The Mutation '90
Assassin '89
The Lawless Land '88
Watchers '88
Gordon Hessler (1930-)
Journey of Honor '91
Tales of the Unexpected '91
The Girl in a Swing '89
Out on Bail '89
The Misfit Brigade '87
Rage of Honor '87
Pray for Death '85
Escape from El Diablo '83
KISS Meets the Phantom of the Park '78
Puzzle '78
Secrets of Three Hungry Wives '78

Blue Jeans and Dynamite '76
Betrayal '74
Medusa '74
Golden Voyage of Sinbad '73
Embassy '72
Murders in the Rue Morgue '71
Cry of the Banshee '70
Scream and Scream Again '70
The Oblong Box '69

Charlton Heston (1924-2008)
Alaska '96
Needful Things '93
Treasure Island '89

David L. Hewitt (1939-)
The Lucifer Complex '78
Alien Massacre '67
Journey to the Center of Time '67
Monsters Crash the Pajama Party '65
Horrors of the Red Planet '64

Peter Hewitt (1952-)
Zoom '06
The Dangerous '95
Verne Miller '88

Douglas Heyes (1919-93)
Powder Keg '77
Kitten with a Whip '64

No One Sleeps '01
Via Appia '92
Laurent Heynemann (1948-)
Birgitt Haas Must Be Killed '83

Full Eclipse '93
Warlock: The Armageddon '93
Hellraiser 3: Hell on Earth '92
Sundown '91
Waxwork 2: Lost in Time '91
Waxwork '88
Blackout '85
Sins '85
Mistral's Daughter '84
The Hound of the Baskervilles '83
Zulu Dawn '79
Sky Riders '76
Brannigan '75
Theatre of Blood '73
Entertaining Mr. Sloane '70
James D.R. Hickox
Sabretooth '01
Blood Surf '00
Children of the Corn 3: Urban Harvest '95
Scott Hicks (1953-)
No Reservations '07
Snow Falling on Cedars '99
Shine '95
Freedom '82
Howard Higgin (1891-1938)
Carnival Lady '33
Hell's House '32
Painted Desert '31
High Voltage '29
The Racketeer '29
The Leatherneck '28
Power '28
Colin Higgins (1941-88)
The Best Little Whorehouse in Texas '82
9 to 5 '80
Foul Play '78
George Hill (1895-1934)
The Big House '30
Min & Bill '30
George Roy Hill (1922-2002)
Funny Farm '88
The Little Drummer Girl '84
The World According to Garp '82
A Little Romance '79
Slap Shot '77
The Great Waldo Pepper '75
The Sting '73
Slaughterhouse Five '72
Butch Cassidy and the Sundance Kid '69
Thoroughly Modern Millie '67
Hawaii '66
The World of Henry Orient '64
Toys in the Attic '63
Period of Adjustment '62

Jack Hill (1933-)
Switchblade Sisters '75
Foxy Brown '74
Coffy '73
The Big Bird Cage '72
The Big Doll House '71
The Swinging Cheerleaders '74

Arthur Hiller (1923-)
An Alan Smithee Film: Burn, Hollywood, Burn '97
Carpool '96
Married to It '93
The Babe '92
Taking Care of Business '90
See No Evil, Hear No Evil '89
Outrageous Fortune '87
The Lonely Guy '84
Teachers '84
Romantic Comedy '83
Author! Author! '82
Making Love '82
The In-Laws '79
Nightwing '79
Silver Streak '76
The Man in the Glass Booth '75
Man of La Mancha '72
Plaza Suite '71

Scott Hillenbrand
Gamebox 1.0 '04
Survival Island '02

David Hillenbrand
Gamebox 1.0 '04
Survival Island '02

King Cobra '98

Terence Hill (1941-)
Lucky Luke '94
Troublemakers '94

Tim Hill
Alvin and the Chipmunks '07
Garfield: A Tail of Two Kitties '06
Max Keeble's Big Move '01
Muppets from Space '99

Walter Hill (1942-)
Broken Trail '06
Undisputed '02
Supernova '99
Last Man Standing '96
Wild Bill '95
Geronimo: An American Legend '93
Trespass '92
Another 48 Hrs. '90
Johnny Handsome '89
Red Heat '88
Extreme Prejudice '87
Crossroads '86
Brewster's Millions '85
Streets of Fire '84
48 Hrs. '82
Southern Comfort '81
The Long Riders '80
The Warriors '79
The Driver '78
Hard Times '75

David Hillenbrand

Alexander Gregory Hippolyte (Gregory Dark) (1954-)
Animal Instincts '92
Secret Games '91
Carnal Crimes '91
Mirror Images '91
Mirror Images 2 '93
Secret Games 2: The Escort '93
Animal Instincts 2 '94
Secret Games 3 '94
Undercover '94
Mirror Images 3: The Seductress '95
Object of Obsession '95

Bill (William) Heinzman) Hinzman (1936-)
Revenge of the Living Zombies '88
The Majorettes '87

Arthur Hilton (1897-1979)
Big Chase '54
Cat Women of the Moon '53
Return of Jesse James '50

Gregory Hines (1946-2003)
Bleeding Hearts '94
The Red Sneakers '01

Jack B. Hively (1910-95)
California Gold Rush '81
The Adventures of Huckleberry Finn '78
Starbird and Sweet William '73
Lassie: Well of Love '70
Lassie: Adventures of Neeka '68
Four Jacks and a Jill '41
The Saint Takes Over '40
The Saint's Double Trouble '40

Love Story '70
Pepi '69
East Side Kids '40
Flash Gordon: Mars Attacks the World '39
Flash Gordon '36
Robert F. "Bob" Hill (1886-1966)

The Out-of-Towners '70
The Lonely Sex '59
William B. Hillman
Quigley '03
Ragin' Cajun '90
Double Exposure '82
Photographer '75

Lambert Hillyer (1889-1969)
Range Renegades '48
Sundown Riders '48
West of Nevada '36
Danger Trails '35
Queen of the Jungle '35
Hat Box Mystery '47
Land of the Lawless '46
Border Bandits '46
Gentleman from Texas '46
South of the Rio Grande '45
The Stranger from Pecos '45
Lawmen '44
Partners of the Trail '44
Range Law '44
Three Word Brand '21
The Toll Gate '20
Wagon Tracks '19

Richard Hilliard
Psychomania '63

The Roamin' Cowboy '37
A Face in the Fog '36
Kelly of the Secret Service '36
Prison Shadows '36
Rip Roarin' Buckaroo '36
Rogue's Tavern '36
Shadow of Chinatown '36
The Wheeler Dealers '63
Cheyenne Rides Again '37
Cheyenne Kid '33
Demon for Trouble '34
Inside Information '34

Texas Kid '43
Six Gun Gospel '43
Gang Bullets '38
Dracula's Daughter '36
The Invisible Ray '36
Fighting Fool '32
Hello Trouble '32
White Eagle '32
The Shock '23

Jack Hofsiss (1950-)
Cat on a Hot Tin Roof '84

Gray Hofmeyr
Yankee Zulu '95
Dirty Games '69

Yvette Hoffman
The Catcher '99
Starved '97

Godfrey Ho (1948-)
Undefeatable '94
Honor and Glory '92
Lethal Panther '90
Ninja: American Warrior '89
Full Metal Ninja '89
Ninja of the Magnificence '89
Vampire Raiders—Ninja Queen '89
Ninja Death Squad '87
Ninja Phantom Heroes '87
Ninja Fantasy '86
Ninja, the Violent Sorcerer '86
Ninja Champion '80
Ninja Destroyer '70
The Experiment '01
The Invasion '07
Downfall '04

Oliver Hirschbiegel (1957-)

Leslie Hiscott (1894-1968)
Butler's Dilemma '43
She Shall Have Music '36
Department Store '35
The Triumph of Sherlock Holmes '35

Alfred Hitchcock (1899-1980)
Family Plot '76
Frenzy '72
Topaz '69
Torn Curtain '66
Marnie '64
The Birds '63

Psycho '60
North by Northwest '59
Vertigo '58
The Man Who Knew Too Much '56
The Wrong Man '56
To Catch a Thief '55
The Trouble with Harry '55
Dial "M" for Murder '54
Rear Window '54
I Confess '53
Strangers on a Train '51
Stage Fright '50
Under Capricorn '49
Rope '48
The Paradine Case '47
Notorious '46
Spellbound '45
Lifeboat '44
Shadow of a Doubt '43
Saboteur '42
Mr. & Mrs. Smith '41
Suspicion '41
Foreign Correspondent '40
Rebecca '40
Jamaica Inn '39
The Lady Vanishes '38
Young and Innocent '37
Sabotage '36
The Secret Agent '36
The 39 Steps '35
The Man Who Knew Too Much '34
No. 17 '32
Rich and Strange '32
Number Seventeen '32
Skin Game '31
Juno and the Paycock '30
Blackmail '29
The Manxman '29
Champagne '28
The Farmer's Wife '28
Three by Hitchcock '28
Easy Virtue '27
The Ring '27
The Lodger '26

Rupert Hitzig (1942-)
Nowhere Land '98
Backstreet Dreams '90
Night Visitor '89

Jerzy Hoffman (1932-)
With Fire and Sword '99
Promised Land '88
Some Girls '88
Restoration '94
Dream '99
One Fine Day '96
Soapdish '91

Michael Hoffman (1956-)
Game 6 '05
Restoration '94
A Midsummer Night's Dream '99
Promised Land '88
Some Girls '88
Soapdish '91

Herman Hoffman (1909-89)
The Invisible Boy '57
It's a Dog's Life '55
Before Morning '33
Drums O'Voodoo '34

Jeno Hodi
Triplecross '95
American Kickboxer 2: To the Death '93

Christopher Hodson
Code Name Alpha '67
Like a Bride '94

Arthur Hoerl (1891-1968)
Drums O'Voodoo '34
Before Morning '33

Ernest Hofbauer
Secrets of Sweet Sixteen '74

John Hodson
Good Boy! '03
Strange Confession '45

James Hogan (1891-1943)
The Mad Ghoul '43
The Texas Rangers Ride Again '40
The Texans '38
Arizona Mahoney '36
The Broken Mask '28

David Hogan
Most Wanted '97
Barb Wire '96

P.J. Hogan (1962-)
Peter Pan '03
Unconditional Love '03
My Best Friend's Wedding '97
Muriel's Wedding '94

Mike Hodges (1932-)
I'll Sleep When I'm Dead '03
Croupier '97
The Terminal Man '74
Pulp '72
Get Carter '71

Jacob Have I Loved '88

Much '56
The Man Who Knew Too Much '34
Missing Pieces '83
Flash Gordon '80
Black Rainbow '91
Florida Straits '87
Prayer from the Dying '87
Morons from Outer Space '85
The Emperor's Club '02
William Shakespeare's A Midsummer Night's

Steve Hickner
Bee Movie '07
Prince of Egypt '98
Anthony Hickox (1959-)
Blast '04
Submerged '05
Federal Protection '02
The Contaminated Man '01
Last Run '01
Jill the Ripper '00
Storm Catcher '99
Prince Valiant '97
Invasion of Privacy '96
Payback '94

George Roy Hill ...

Douglas Hickox (1929-88)

Fraser Heston (1955-)

Jochen Hick (1960-)
Via Appia '92

Rod Hewitt
The Debt '98
Strip Search '97

Timothy Hill
The Adventures of Tarzan '21

Victoria Hochberg
Sweet 15 '90

Gregory Hoblit (1944-)
Untraceable '08
Fracture '07
Hart's War '02
Frequency '00
Fallen '97
Primal Fear '96
Class of '61 '92
Roe vs. Wade '89
L.A. Law '86

Rod Holcomb (1924-)
Convict Cowboy '95
Dead to Rights '93
Royce '93
Chains of Gold '92
China Beach '88
Blind Justice '86
Chase '85
Two Fathers' Justice '85
Cartier Affair '84
The Red Light Sting '84
Captain America '79

Agnieszka Holland (1948-)
The Healer '02
Shot in the Heart '01
The Third Miracle '99
Washington Square '97
Total Eclipse '95
The Secret Garden '93
Olivier, Olivier '92
Europa, Europa '91
To Kill a Priest '89
Angry Harvest '85
Fever '81
Provincial Actors '79

Savage Steve Holland (1960-)
Safety Patrol '98
How I Got into College '89
One Crazy Summer '86
Better Off Dead '85

Todd Holland (1961-)
Firehouse Dog '07
Krippendorf's Tribe '98
The Wizard '89

Tom Holland (1943-)
Masters of Horror: We All
Scream for Ice Cream '07
Stephen King's Thinner '96
Stephen King's The
Langoliers '95
The Temp '93
Child's Play '88
Fatal Beauty '87
Fright Night '85

Allan Holleb
School Spirit '85
Candy Stripe Nurses '74

Seth Holt (1923-71)
Blood from the Mummy's
Tomb '71
The Nanny '65
Scream of Fear '61

Allan Holzman (1946-)
Intimate Stranger '91
Programmed to Kill '86
Grunt! The Wrestling Movie '85
Out of Control '85
Forbidden World '82

Edward Holzman
Body Strokes '95
Forbidden Games '95
Friend of the Family '95
Sinful Intrigue '95
Seduce Me: Pamela
Principle 2 '94

Inoshiro Honda (1911-93)
Terror of Mechagodzilla '78
Yog, Monster from Space '71
War of the Gargantuas '70
Godzilla's Revenge '69
Destroy All Monsters '68
Godzilla vs. Monster Zero '68
Dagora, the Space Monster '65
Ghidrah the Three Headed
Monster '65
Godzilla vs. Mothra '64
Attack of the Mushroom
People '63
King Kong vs. Godzilla '63
Gorath '62
Mothra '62
Varan the Unbelievable '61
H-Man '59
Half Human '58
The Mysterians '58
Godzilla, King of the
Monsters '56
Rodan '56

Elliot Hong
Retrievers '82
They Call Me Bruce? '82
Kill the Golden Goose '79

James Hong (1929-)
The Vineyard '89
Girls Next Door '79

Christophe Honore (1970-)
Love Songs '07
Inside Paris '06
Close to Leo '02

Gavin Hood (1963-)
Rendition '07
Tsotsi '05
In Desert and Wilderness '01

Harry Hook (1960-)
St. Ives '98
The Last of His Tribe '92
Lord of the Flies '90

Kevin Hooks (1958-)
Mutiny '99
Black Dog '98
Glory & Honor '98
Fled '96

Lance Hool (1948-)
One Man's Hero '98
Steel Dawn '87
Missing in Action 2: The
Beginning '85

Tobe Hooper (1946-)
Mortuary '05
Taken '02
Crocodile '00
Apartment Complex '98
The Mangler '94
Body Bags '93
I'm Dangerous Tonight '90
Spontaneous Combustion '89

Tom Hooper
John Adams '08
Longford '06
Elizabeth I '05
Daniel Deronda '02

Claudia Hoover
Gideon '99

Anthony Hopkins (1937-)
Double Exposure '93

Stephen Hopkins (1958-)
The Reaping '07
Under Suspicion '00
Lost in Space '98
The Ghost and the
Darkness '96
Blown Away '94
Judgment Night '93
Dangerous Game '90
Predator 2 '90
A Nightmare on Elm Street
5: Dream Child '89

Dennis Hopper (1936-)
Chasers '94
The Hot Spot '90
Backtrack '89
Colors '88
Out of the Blue '80
The Last Movie '71
Easy Rider '69

E. Mason Hopper (1885-1967)
Hong Kong Nights '35
Held for Murder '32
Shop Angel '32
Square Shoulders '29

Jerry Hopper (1907-88)
Bull of the West '71
Madron '70
Missouri Traveler '58
The Private War of Major
Benson '55
Pony Express '53
The Atomic City '52

Russell Hopton (1900-45)
Black Gold '36
Song of the Trail '36

James W. Horne (1880-1942)
Holt of the Secret Service '42
Green Archer '40
All Over Town '37
Way Out West '37
Bohemian Girl '36
Bonnie Scotland '35
Laurel & Hardy: Chickens
Come Home '31
Laurel & Hardy: Brats '30
College '27
Laughing at Danger '24

Harry Horner (1910-94)
New Faces of 1952 '54
Beware, My Lovely '52
Red Planet Mars '52

Robert J. Horner
Apache Kid's Escape '30
The Walloping Kid '26

Peter Horton (1953-)
The Cure '95
Amazon Women on the
Moon '87

Joy Houck, Jr. (1942-2003)
The St. Tammany Miracle '94
Creature from Black Lake '76
Night of the Strangler '73
Mind Warp '72

John Hough (1941-)
Hell's Gate '01
Duel of Hearts '92
The Dying Truth '91
The Lady and the
Highwayman '89
American Gothic '88
Howling 4: The Original
Nightmare '88
Biggles '85
The Black Arrow '84
Triumphs of a Man Called
Horse '83
Incubus '82
The Watcher in the Woods '81
Brass Target '78
Return from Witch Mountain '78
Escape to Witch Mountain '75
Dirty Mary Crazy Larry '74
The Legend of Hell House '73
Treasure Island '72
Twins of Evil '71
Eye Witness '70

Bobby Houston
Caged Fear '92
Trust Me '89
Bad Manners '84

Adrian Hoven (1922-81)
Mark of the Devil 2 '72

David Howard (1896-1941)
Bullet Code '40
Legion of the Lawless '40
Hollywood Stadium Mystery '38
Park Avenue Logger '37
Thunder Mountain '35
Crimson Romance '34
Daniel Boone '34
In Old Santa Fe '34
The Lost Jungle '34
Mystery Ranch '34

Leslie Howard (1893-1943)
Pimpernel Smith '42
Spitfire '42
Pygmalion '38

Ron Howard (1954-)
The Da Vinci Code '06
Cinderella Man '05
The Missing '03
A Beautiful Mind '01
Dr. Seuss' How the Grinch
Stole Christmas '00
EDtv '99
Ransom '96
Apollo 13 '95
The Paper '94
Far and Away '92
Backdraft '91
Parenthood '89
Willow '88
Cocoon '85
Gung Ho '85
Splash '84
Cotton Candy '82
Night Shift '82
Grand Theft Auto '77

Sandy Howard
One Step to Hell '67

William K. Howard (1899-1954)
Tarzan and the Trappers '58
Johnny Come Lately '43
Back Door to Heaven '39
Fire Over England '37
The Princess Comes Across '36
The Cat and the Fiddle '34
Evelyn Prentice '34
White Gold '28
Let's Go! '23

C. Thomas Howell (1966-)
The Big Fall '96
Pure Danger '96
Hourglass '95

Peter Howitt (1957-)
Laws of Attraction '04
Johnny English '03
Antitrust '00
Sliding Doors '97

Frank Howson (1952-)
Flynn '96
The Hunting '92

Harry Hoyt (1885-1961)
Jungle Bride '33
The Return of Boston
Blackie '27
The Lost World '25

Jan Hrebejk (1967-)
Up and Down '04
Divided We Fall '00

Hou Hsiao-Hsien (1947-)
Flight of the Red Balloon '08
Cafe Lumiere '05
Three Times '05
Flowers of Shanghai '98
Goodbye South, Goodbye '96

Talun Hsu
Body Count '95
Witchcraft 5: Dance with the
Devil '92

George Huang
How to Make a Monster '01
Trojan War '97
Swimming with Sharks '94

Jean-Loup Hubert (1949-)
Le Grand Chemin '87
Next Year If All Goes Well '83

John Huddles
Uncorked '98
Far Harbor '96

Reginald (Reggie) Hudlin (1961-)
Serving Sara '02
The Ladies Man '00
The Great White Hype '96
Cosmic Slop '94
Boomerang '92
House Party '90

Hugh Hudson (1936-)
I Dreamed of Africa '00
My Life So Far '99
Lost Angels '89
Revolution '85
Greystoke: The Legend of
Tarzan, Lord of the Apes '84
Chariots of Fire '81

Brent Huff (1961-)
Welcome to Paradise '07
100 Mile Rule '02
The Bad Pack '98
Final Justice '94

R. John Hugh (1924-85)
The Meal '75
You've Ruined Me, Eddie '58
Naked in the Sun '57
Yellowneck '55

Albert Hughes (1972-)
From Hell '01
Dead Presidents '95
Menace II Society '93

Allen Hughes (1972-)
Knights of the South Bronx '05
From Hell '01
Dead Presidents '95
Menace II Society '93

Bronwen Hughes
Stander '03
Forces of Nature '99
Harriet the Spy '96

Howard Hughes (1905-76)
The Outlaw '43
Hell's Angels '30

John Hughes (1950-)
Curly Sue '91
Uncle Buck '89
She's Having a Baby '88
Planes, Trains &
Automobiles '87
Ferris Bueller's Day Off '86
The Breakfast Club '85
Weird Science '85
Sixteen Candles '84

Ken Hughes (1922-2001)
Night School '81
Sextette '78
Oh, Alfie '75
Internecine Project '73
Cromwell '70
Chitty Chitty Bang Bang '68
Casino Royale '67
Arrivederci, Baby! '66
Of Human Bondage '64

Robert C. Hughes
St. Patrick: The Irish Legend '00
Down the Drain '89
Memorial Valley Massacre '88
Hunter's Blood '87

Terry Hughes
Mrs. Santa Claus '96
The Butcher's Wife '91
For Love or Money '84
Sunset Limousine '83

Ann Hui (1947-)
Summer Snow '94
Song of the Exile '90

Don Hulette (1937-)
Great Ride '78
Greedy Terror '78
Tennessee Stallion '78
Breaker! Breaker! '77

Steven A. Hull
Devil Wears White '86
Ten Speed '76

H. Bruce Humberstone (1903-84)
Tarzan and the Trappers '58
Ten Wanted Men '54
The Desert Song '53
Happy Go Lovely '51
South Sea Sinner '50
Wonder Man '45
Pin-Up Girl '44
Hello, Frisco, Hello '43
Iceland '42
To the Shores of Tripoli '42
I Wake Up Screaming '41
Sun Valley Serenade '41
Lucky Cisco Kid '40
Charlie Chan in Honolulu '38
Charlie Chan at the Opera '36
Charlie Chan at the Race
Track '36
King of the Jungle '33
The Crooked Circle '32
Strangers of the Evening '32

Sammo Hung (1952-)
Mr. Nice Guy '98
Dragons Forever '87
Eastern Condors '87
The Millionaire's Express '86
Heart of Dragon '85
The Prodigal Son '82
Spooky Encounters '80

Tran Anh Hung (1963-)
The Vertical Ray of the Sun '00
Cyclo '95
The Scent of Green Papaya '93

Tom Hunsinger (1952-)
Lawless Heart '01
Boyfriends '96

Ed(ward) Hunt
The Brain '88
Alien Warrior '85
Bloody Birthday '80
Starship Invasions '77

Paul Hunt (1943-)
Merlin '92
Twisted Nightmare '87
The Great Gundown '75
The Clones '73

Peter Hunt (1925-2002)
Assassination '87
Hyper-Sapien: People from
Another Star '86
Wild Geese 2 '85
Death Hunt '81
The Private History of a
Campaign That Failed '81
Gulliver's Travels '77
Shout at the Devil '76
On Her Majesty's Secret
Service '69

Peter H. Hunt (1938-)
The Adventures of
Huckleberry Finn '85
It Came Upon a Midnight
Clear '84
The Long Haul '57
The Atomic Man '56
Heat Wave '54

1776 '72
Skeezer '82
The Mysterious Stranger '82

Neil Hunter
Boyfriends '96
Lawless Heart '01

Tim Hunter (1947-)
Tex '82
Sylvester '85
River's Edge '87
Paint It Black '89
Lies of the Twins '91
The Saint of Fort Washington '93
The Maker '98
Mean Streak '99
Video Voyeur: The Susan Wilson Story '02
The Far Side of Jericho '06

Lawrence Huntington (1900-68)
Tower of Terror '42
Man on the Run '49
The Franchise Affair '52
Eight Witnesses '54
Vulture '67

Nick Hurran (1959-)
Girls' Night '97
Virtual Sexuality '99
Little Black Book '04

Michael Hurst (1973-)
House of the Dead 2: Dead Aim '05
Pumpkinhead 4: Blood Feud '07

Brian Desmond Hurst (1900-86)
River of Unrest '36
The Lion Has Wings '40
Dangerous Moonlight '41
The Gay Lady '49
A Christmas Carol '51
Malta Story '53
Simba '55
Playboy of the Western World '62

Paul Hurst (1888-1953)
The Projectionist '71
Safari 3000 '82
New Blood '99

Harry Hurwitz (1938-95)
Rosebud Beach Hotel '85
That's Adequate '90
Fleshtone '94

Waris Hussein (1938-)
Quackser Fortune Has a Cousin in the Bronx '70
Melody '71
Divorce His, Divorce Hers '72
And Baby Makes Six '79
The Henderson Monster '80
Edward and Mrs. Simpson '80
Callie and Son '81
Coming Out of the Ice '82
Princess Daisy '83
Little Gloria... Happy at Last '84
Arch of Triumph '85
When the Bough Breaks '86
Intimate Contact '87
Onassis '88
The Shell Seekers '89
Switched at Birth '91
The Summer House '94
Fall from Grace '94

Anjelica Huston (1951-)
Bastard out of Carolina '95
Agnes Browne '99

Danny Huston (1962-)
Mr. North '88
Mr. Corbett's Ghost '92
Becoming Colette '92

Jimmy Huston
Death Driver '78
Final Exam '81
My Best Friend Is a Vampire '88
The Wharf Rat '95

John Huston (1906-87)
The Maltese Falcon '41
In This Our Life '42
Across the Pacific '42
Treasure of the Sierra Madre '48
Key Largo '48
The Asphalt Jungle '50
The Red Badge of Courage '51
The African Queen '51
Moulin Rouge '52
Beat the Devil '53
Moby Dick '56
Heaven Knows, Mr. Allison '57
Barbarian and the Geisha '58
The Unforgiven '60
The Misfits '61
Freud '62
The List of Adrian Messenger '63
The Night of the Iguana '64
The Bible '66
Casino Royale '67
Reflections in a Golden Eye '67
Fat City '72
The Life & Times of Judge Roy Bean '72
The Mackintosh Man '73
The Man Who Would Be King '75
Wise Blood '79
Phobia '80
Victory '81
Annie '82
Under the Volcano '84
Prizzi's Honor '85
The Dead '87

Charles (Hutchison) Hutchison (1879-1949)
Found Alive '34
Phantom Patrol '36
Children of the Wild '37

Brian G. Hutton (1935-)
Sol Madrid '68
Where Eagles Dare '68
Kelly's Heroes '70
X, Y & Zee '72
Night Watch '72
The First Deadly Sin '80
High Road to China '83

Willard Huyck (1945-)
Messiah of Evil '74
French Postcards '79
Best Defense '84
Howard the Duck '86

Peter Hyams (1943-)
Our Time '74
Busting '74
Capricorn One '78
Hanover Street '79
Outland '81
The Star Chamber '83
Death Target '83
2010: The Year We Make Contact '84
Running Scared '86
The Presidio '88
Narrow Margin '90
Stay Tuned '92
Timecop '94
Sudden Death '95
The Relic '96
End of Days '99
The Musketeer '01
A Sound of Thunder '05

Nicholas Hytner (1957-)
The Madness of King George '94
The Crucible '96
The Object of My Affection '98
Center Stage '00
The History Boys '06

Juan Ibanez (1938-2000)
Dance of Death '68
The Fear Chamber '68
The Sinister Invasion '68

Juan Luis Iborra (1959-)
Amor de Hombre '97
Km. 0 '00

Leon Ichaso (1948-)
Crossover Dreams '85
The Fear Inside '92
Sugar Hill '94
Bitter Sugar '96
Free of Eden '98
Execution of Justice '99
Hendrix '00
Piñero '01
El Cantante '06

Kon Ichikawa (1915-2008)
The Burmese Harp '56
Enjo '58
Fires on the Plain '59
Odd Obsession '60
Being Two Isn't Easy '62
An Actor's Revenge '63
Tokyo Olympiad '66
Phoenix '78
The Makioka Sisters '83

Eric Idle (1943-)
All You Need Is Cash '78
The Tale of the Frog Prince '83

Miguel Iglesias
Green Inferno '72
Kilma, Queen of the Amazons '75
Rape '76

Toshiharu Ikeda
Evil Dead Trap '88
Beautiful Beast '95

Kazuo Ikehiro (1928-)
Zatoichi: Master Ichi and a Chest of Gold '64
Zatoichi: Zatoichi's Flashing Sword '64

Mark Illsley (1958-)
Happy, Texas '99
Bookies '03

Shohei Imamura (1926-2006)
The Insect Woman '63
The Pornographers '66
Vengeance Is Mine '79
Eijanaika '81
The Ballad of Narayama '83
Black Rain '88
The Eel '96
Dr. Akagi '98

Hiroshi Inagaki (1905-80)
Samurai 1: Musashi Miyamoto '55
Samurai 2: Duel at Ichijoji Temple '55
Samurai 3: Duel at Ganryu Island '56
Rikisha-Man '58
Kojiro '67

Alejandro Gonzalez Inarritu (1963-)
Amores Perros '00
21 Grams '03
Babel '06

Ralph Ince (1887-1937)
Men of America '32
Lucky Devils '33

Franco Indovina (1932-72)

Lloyd Ingraham (1885-1956)
American Aristocracy '16
Hoodoo Ann '16

Boris Ingster (1904-78)
Stranger on the Third Floor '40
The Judge Steps Out '49

J. Christian Ingvordsen (1957-)
Hangmen '87
Covert Action '88
Search and Destroy '88
Mob War '88
Comrades in Arms '91
The Outfit '93
Airboss '97
Blood Relic '05

Dan Ireland (1958-)
The Whole Wide World '96
The Velocity of Gary '98
Mrs. Palfrey at the Claremont '05

O'Dale Ireland (1928-)
Date Bait '60
High School Caesar '60

Matthew Irmas
When the Party's Over '91
Edie & Pen '95
Sleep Easy, Hutch Rimes '00

John Irvin (1940-)
Haunted: The Ferryman '74
Tinker, Tailor, Soldier, Spy '80
Ghost Story '81
The Dogs of War '81
Champions '84
Raw Deal '86
Turtle Diary '86
Hamburger Hill '87
The Fourth Protocol '87
Next of Kin '89
Eminent Domain '91
Robin Hood '91
Widow's Peak '94
A Month by the Lake '95
City of Industry '96
When Trumpets Fade '98
Shiner '00
The Fourth Angel '01
The Boys and Girl from County Clare '03

Sam Irvin (1956-)
Guilty as Charged '92
Acting on Impulse '93
Oblivion '94
Magic Island '95
Backlash: Oblivion 2 '96
Elvira's Haunted Hills '02

David Irving (1949-)
Goodbye Cruel World '82
Rumpelstiltskin '87
C.H.U.D. II: Bud the Chud '89
Night of the Cyclone '90

Richard Irving (1917-90)
Columbo: Prescription Murder '67
The Art of Crime '75
The Jesse Owens Story '84

James Isaac (1960-)
The Horror Show '89
Jason X '01
Skinwalkers '07

Antonio (Isasi) Isasmendi) Isasi (1927-)
Vengeance '86

Robert Iscove (1947-)
The Jesse Owens Story '84
She's All That '99
Boys and Girls '00
Firestarter 2: Rekindled '02
From Justin to Kelly '03

Neal Israel (1945-)
Americathon '79
Bachelor Party '84
Moving Violations '85
Breaking the Rules '92
Surf Ninjas '93
National Lampoon's Dad's Week Off '97
National Lampoon's Holiday Reunion '03

Juzo Itami (1933-97)
The Funeral '84
Tampopo '86
A Taxing Woman '87
A Taxing Woman's Return '88
Minbo—Or the Gentle Art of Japanese Extortion '92

James Ivory (1928-)
The Householder '63
Shakespeare Wallah '65
Bombay Talkie '70
Savages '72
The Wild Party '74
Autobiography of a Princess '75
Roseland '77
Hullabaloo over Georgie & Bonnie's Pictures '78
The Europeans '79
Jane Austen in Manhattan '80
Quartet '81
Heat and Dust '82
The Bostonians '84
A Room with a View '86
Maurice '87
Slaves of New York '89
Mr. & Mrs. Bridge '90
Howards End '92
The Remains of the Day '93
Jefferson in Paris '94
Surviving Picasso '96
A Soldier's Daughter Never Cries '98
The Golden Bowl '00
Le Divorce '03
The White Countess '05

David Jablin
National Lampoon's Favorite Deadly Sins '95
National Lampoon's The Don's Analyst '97

Fred W. Jackman (1881-1959)
King of the Wild Horses '24
No Man's Law '27

David S. Jackson
Mystery Mansion '83
Detonator '93
Detonator 2: Night Watch '95

Donald G. Jackson (1943-2003)
The Demon Lover '77
Roller Blade '85
Hell Comes to Frogtown '88
Roller Blade Warriors: Taken By Force '90
The Roller Blade Seven '92
Return to Frogtown '92
Rollergator '96

Douglas Jackson (1938-)
Deadbolt '92
The Paperboy '94
The Wrong Woman '95
Natural Enemy '96
Twists of Terror '98
Random Encounter '98
Dead End '98
Requiem for Murder '99
The Witness Files '00
Nowhere in Sight '01

G. Philip Jackson
Whispers '89
Deadbolt '92
Stalked '94

Mick Jackson (1943-)
Threads '85
Chattahoochee '89
L.A. Story '91
The Bodyguard '92
Clean Slate '94
Indictment: The McMartin Trial '95
Volcano '97
Tuesday's with Morrie '99
The First $20 Million Is Always the Hardest '02
Live from Baghdad '02
The Hades Factor '06

Pat Jackson (1916-)
Encore '52
What a Carve-Up! '62

Peter Jackson (1961-)
Bad Taste '89
Meet the Feebles '89
Dead Alive '93
Heavenly Creatures '94
Forgotten Silver '96
The Frighteners '96
Lord of the Rings: The Fellowship of the Rings '01
Lord of the Rings: The Two Towers '02
Lord of the Rings: The Return of the King '03
King Kong '05

Wilfred Jackson (1906-88)
Fantasia '40
Melody Time '48
Cinderella '50
Alice in Wonderland '51
Lady and the Tramp '55

Alan Jacobs
Nina Takes a Lover '94
A Dangerous Place '94
Just One Night '00
American Gun '02

David Jacobson
Dahmer '02
Down in the Valley '05

Rick Jacobson
Full Contact '93
Star Quest '94
The Unborn 2 '94
Bloodfist 6: Ground Zero '94
Ring of Fire 3: Lion Strike '94
Night Hunter '95
Suspect Device '95
Black Thunder '98
Interlocked '98

Gregory Jacobs
Criminal '04
Wind Chill '07

Jerry P. Jacobs
Angels of the City '89
Quiet Fire '91
Freedom Strike '98
Running Red '99

John Jacobs (1924-)
Rocket to the Moon '86
The First to Go '97

Lawrence-Hilton Jacobs (1953-)

Joseph Jacoby (1942-)
Hurry Up or I'll Be Thirty '73
The Great Bank Hoax '78

Guatiero Jacopetti (1919-)
Mondo Cane '63
Mondo Cane 2 '64

Benoit Jacquot
The Disenchanted '90
A Single Girl '96
Seventh Heaven '98
Sade '00

Just Jaeckin (1940-)
Emmanuelle '74
The Story of O '75
The French Woman '79
Lady Chatterley's Lover '81
The Perils of Gwendoline '84

Henry Jaglom (1943-)
Going Shopping '05
Festival at Cannes '02
Deja Vu '97
Last Summer In the Hamptons '96
Babyfever '94
Venice, Venice '92
Eating '90
New Year's Day '89
Someone to Love '87
Always '85
Can She Bake a Cherry Pie? '83
National Lampoon Goes to the Movies '81
Sitting Ducks '80
Tracks '76

Alan James (1890-1952)
Red Barry '38
Dick Tracy '37
Dick Tracy: The Spider Strikes '37
S.O.S. Coast Guard '37
Lucky Terror '36
Swifty '35
Valley of Wanted Men '35
When a Man Sees Red '34
The Lone Avenger '33
Phantom Thunderbolt '33
Trail Drive '33
Come on Tarzan '32
Fargo Express '32
Justice Rides Again '32
Tombstone Canyon '32
The Phantom '31
Backfire '22

Steve James
Reel Paradise '05
Joe and Max '02
Passing Glory '99
Prefontaine '96
Hoop Dreams '94

Jerry Jameson
Land of the Free '98
Bonanza: The Return '93
Fire and Rain '89
The Cowboy & the Ballerina '84
Starflight One '83
Hotline '82
Killing at Hell's Gate '81
High Noon: Part 2 '80
Raise the Titanic '80
Sniper '75
The Bat People '74
Hurricane '74
Terror on the 40th Floor '74
Dirt Gang '71

Miklos Jancso (1921-)
Hungarian Rhapsody '78
The Red and the White '68
The Round Up '66

Conrad Janis (1928-)
November Conspiracy '96

Annabel Jankel (1955-)
Super Mario Bros. '93
D.O.A. '88

Agnes Jaoui (1964-)
Look at Me '04
The Taste of Others '00

Derek Jarman (1942-94)
Blue '93
Wittgenstein '93
Edward II '92
Aria '88
The Garden '90
The Last of England '87
Caravaggio '86
Sebastiane '79

Jim Jarmusch (1953-)
Broken Flowers '05
Coffee and Cigarettes '03
Ghost Dog: The Way of the Samurai '99
Year of the Horse '97
Dead Man '95
Night on Earth '91
Mystery Train '89
Down by Law '86
Permanent Vacation '84
Stranger than Paradise '84

Julian Jarrold
Becoming Jane '07
Kinky Boots '06
Anonymous Rex '04
All the King's Men '99
Great Expectations '99
The Painted Lady '97
Touching Evil '97
Cracker: The Big Crunch '94

Charles Jarrott (1927-)
Danielle Steel's Changes '91
Lucy and Desi: Before the Laughter '91
Night of the Fox '90
The Woman He Loved '88
Poor Little Rich Girl: The Barbara Hutton Story '87
Boy in Blue '86
The Amateur '82
Condorman '81
The Last Flight of Noah's Ark '80
The Other Side of Midnight '77
The Littlest Horse Thieves '76
The Dove '74
Mary, Queen of Scots '71
Anne of the Thousand Days '69

Ilkka Jarvilaturi (1961-)
Spy Games '99
City Unplugged '95

Steve Jarvis
Bloodstream '00
Chain of Souls '00
Things 2 '97

Vojtech Jasny (1925-)
The Great Land of Small '86
All My Good Countrymen '68

Leigh Jason (1904-79)
The Choppers '61
The Go-Getter '54
Lost Honeymoon '47
Out of the Blue '47
Lady for a Night '42
The Flying Irishman '39
Mad Miss Manton '38
The Bride Walks Out '36
That Girl from Paris '36
High Gear '33

Vadim Jean (1963-)
Jiminy Glick in LaLa Wood '05
One More Kiss '99
The Real Howard Spitz '98
Leon the Pig Farmer '93
Nightscare '93

Tom Jeffrey (1938-)
The Odd Angry Shot '79
Weekend of Shadows '77

Lionel Jeffries (1926-)
Water Babies '79
Wombling Free '77
Amazing Mr. Blunden '72
The Railway Children '70

Christine Jeffs (1963-)
Sylvia '03
Rain '01

Michael Jenkins (1946-)
Sweet Talker '91
Rebel '85

Tamara Jenkins
The Savages '07
Slums of Beverly Hills '98

Anders Thomas Jensen (1972-)
Adam's Apples '05

Victoria Jenson
Shark Tale '04
Shrek '01

Alain Jessua (1932-)
The Killing Game '67
Life Upside Down '64

Jean-Pierre Jeunet (1955-)
A Very Long Engagement '04
Amelie '01
Alien: Resurrection '97
The City of Lost Children '95
Delicatessen '91

Norman Jewison (1926-)
The Statement '03
Dinner with Friends '01
The Hurricane '99
Bogus '96
Only You '94
Other People's Money '91
In Country '89
Moonstruck '87
Agnes of God '85
A Soldier's Story '84
Best Friends '82
And Justice for All '79
F.I.S.T. '78
Rollerball '75
Jesus Christ, Superstar '73
Fiddler on the Roof '71
The Thomas Crown Affair '68
In the Heat of the Night '67
The Russians Are Coming, the Russians Are Coming '66
The Cincinnati Kid '65
Send Me No Flowers '64
The Thrill of It All! '63
40 Pounds of Trouble '62

Sut Jhally (1955-)
Hijacking Catastrophe: 9/11, Fear and the Selling of America '04
Peace, Propaganda & the Promised Land '04

Phil Joanou (1961-)
Gridiron Gang '06
Entropy '99
Heaven's Prisoners '95
Fallen Angels 2 '93
Wild Palms '93
Final Analysis '92
State of Grace '90
U2: Rattle and Hum '88
Three O'Clock High '87

Richard Jobson (1960-)
The Purifiers '04
16 Years of Alcohol '03

Arthur Joffe (1953-)
Alberto Express '92
Harem '85

Mark Joffe (1956-)
The Matchmaker '97
Cosi '95
The Efficiency Expert '92
Grievous Bodily Harm '89
Night Master '87

Roland Joffe (1945-)
Captivity '07
Vatel '00
Goodbye, Lover '99
The Scarlet Letter '95
City of Joy '92
Fat Man and Little Boy '89
The Mission '86
The Killing Fields '84

Sande N. Johnsen
Teenage Gang Debs '66
The Beautiful, the Bloody and the Bare '64

Alan Johnson
Solarbabies '86
To Be or Not to Be '83

Clark Johnson (1954-)
The Sentinel '06
Sleeper Cell '05
S.W.A.T. '03
Boycott '02

Emory Johnson (1894-1960)
Phantom Express '32
West-Bound Limited '23

Irvin Johnson
Blood Ring '93
Fist of Steel '95

Jesse Johnson (1982-)
The Last Sentinel '07
Pit Fighter '05

Kenneth Johnson (1942-)
Steel '97
Alien Nation: Millennium '96
Alien Nation: The Enemy Within '96
Alien Nation: Body and Soul '95
Alien Nation: Dark Horizon '94
Short Circuit 2 '88
Hot Pursuit '84
V '83
Senior Trip '81
The Incredible Hulk '77

Lamont Johnson (1922-)
The Kennedys of Massachusetts '95
The Broken Chain '93
A Thousand Heroes '92
Escape '90
Gore Vidal's Lincoln '88
Unnatural Causes '86
Ernie Kovacs: Between the Laughter '84
Jack & the Beanstalk '83
Spacehunter: Adventures in the Forbidden Zone '83
Crisis at Central High '80
One on One '77
Lipstick '76
The Execution of Private Slovik '74
The Last American Hero '73
The Groundstar Conspiracy '72
You'll Like My Mother '72
A Gunfight '71
McKenzie Break '70
My Sweet Charlie '70

Mark Steven Johnson (1964-)
Ghost Rider '07
Daredevil '03
Simon Birch '98

Nunnally Johnson (1897-1977)
The Three Faces of Eve '57
The Man in the Gray Flannel Suit '56
Black Widow '54

Patrick Read Johnson (1964-)
When Good Ghouls Go Bad '01
Angus '95
Baby's Day Out '94
Spaced Invaders '90

Raymond K. Johnson
See Bernard B. Ray

Tim Johnson
Over the Hedge '06
Sinbad: Legend of the Seven Seas '03
Antz '98

Aaron Kim Johnston
For the Moment '94

Joe Johnston (1950-)
The Last Winter '89
Hidalgo '04
Jurassic Park 3 '01
October Sky '99
Jumanji '95
The Pagemaster '94
The Rocketeer '91
Honey, I Shrunk the Kids '89

Amy Holden Jones (1953-)
The Rich Man's Wife '96
Maid to Order '87
Love Letters '83
Slumber Party Massacre '82

Brian Thomas Jones
Posed for Murder '88
Escape from Safehaven '88
The Rejuvenator '88
Ocean Drive Weekend '85

Chuck Jones (1912-2002)
Looney Looney Looney Bugs Bunny Movie '81
Phantom Tollbooth '69

David Hugh Jones (1934-)
A Christmas Carol '99
The Confession '98
An Unexpected Life '97
Is There Life Out There? '94
The Trial '93
Jacknife '89
Look Back in Anger '89
The Christmas Wife '88
84 Charing Cross Road '86
Betrayal '83

Donald M. Jones (1953-)
Lethal Pursuit '88
Murderlust '86
Project: Nightmare '85
Deadly Sunday '82
Love Butcher '82
Sweater Girls '78

F. Richard Jones (1894-1930)
Bulldog Drummond '29
The Gaucho '27
Extra Girl '23
Yankee Doodle in Berlin '19

Gary Jones
Crocodile 2: Death Swamp '01
Spiders '00
Mosquito '95
Stay Tuned for Murder '88

Harmon Jones (1911-72)
Bullwhip '58
The Legend of the Sea Wolf '58
Bloodhounds of Broadway '52
Pride of St. Louis '52
As Young As You Feel '51

James Cellan Jones (1931-)
The Vacillations of Poppy Carew '94
Fortunes of War '87
The Golden Bowl '72
Portrait of a Lady '67

Jon Jones
Northanger Abbey '07
The Secret Life of Mrs. Beeton '06
Archangel '05
The Debt '03

Kirk Jones (1963-)
Nanny McPhee '06
Waking Ned Devine '98

Mark Jones (1953-)
Rumpelstiltskin '96
Leprechaun '93

Pete Jones
Outing Riley '04
Stolen Summer '02

Philip Jones (1963-2003)
Asylum of the Damned '03
Backflash '01
Wish Me Luck '95
Cause of Death '90

Terry Jones (1942-)
Mr. Toad's Wild Ride '96
Erik the Viking '89
Personal Services '87
Monty Python's The Meaning of Life '83
Monty Python's Life of Brian '79
Monty Python and the Holy Grail '75

Tommy Lee Jones (1946-)
The Three Burials of Melquiades Estrada '05
The Good Old Boys '95

Spike Jonze (1969-)
Adaptation '02
Being John Malkovich '99

Glenn Jordan (1936-)
Night Ride Home '99

Gregor Jordan (1967-)
Ned Kelly '03
Buffalo Soldiers '01
Two Hands '98
Twisted '96

Kevin Jordan (1974-)
Brooklyn Lobster '05
Smiling Fish & Goat on Fire '99

Neil Jordan (1950-)
The Brave One '07
The Good Thief '03
The End of the Affair '99
In Dreams '98
The Butcher Boy '97
Michael Collins '96
Interview with the Vampire '94
The Crying Game '92
The Miracle '91
We're No Angels '89
High Spirits '88
Mona Lisa '86
The Company of Wolves '85
Danny Boy '82

Jon Jost (1943-)
The Bed You Sleep In '93
Jon Jost's Frameup '93
All the Vermeers in New York '91
Sure Fire '90
Slow Moves '84

C. Courtney Joyner
Lurking Fear '94
Trancers 3: Deth Lives '92

Mike Judge (1962-)
Idiocracy '06
Office Space '98
Beavis and Butt-Head Do America '96

Rupert Julian (1889-1943)
Yankee Clipper '27
Walking Back '26
The Phantom of the Opera '25
Merry-Go-Round '23
Land Raiders '69

Gil Junger (1954-)
If Only '04
Black Knight '01
Ten Things I Hate about You '99

Nathan "Jerry" Juran (1907-2002)
First Men in the Moon '64
Jack the Giant Killer '62
Attack of the 50 Foot Woman '58
Good Day for a Hanging '58
The Seventh Voyage of Sinbad '58
The Brain from Planet Arous '57
The Deadly Mantis '57
Hellcats of the Navy '57
20 Million Miles to Earth '57
Gunsmoke '53
The Black Castle '52

Sarah, Plain and Tall: Winter's End '99
Legalese '98
My Brother's Keeper '95
A Streetcar Named Desire '95
Barbarians at the Gate '93
To Dance with the White Dog '93
O Pioneers! '91
Sarah, Plain and Tall '91
Jesse '88
Echoes in the Darkness '87
Dress Gray '86
Something in Common '86
Toughlove '85
Mass Appeal '84
The Buddy System '83
Lois Gibbs and the Love Canal '82
Only When I Laugh '81
The Family Man '79
Les Miserables '78
One of My Wives Is Missing '76
Picture of Dorian Gray '74
Frankenstein '73

Paul Justman
Standing in the Shadows of
Motown '02

Claude Jutra (1930-86)
Gimme an F '85
My Father, My Rival '85
Surfacing '84
By Design '82
Mon Oncle Antoine '71

Karel Kachyna (1924-2004)
The Cow '93
The Last Butterfly '92

George Kaczender (1933-)
Maternal Instincts '96
Vanished '95
Pretty Kill '87
Your Ticket Is No Longer
Valid '84
The Agency '81
Chanel Solitaire '81
In Praise of Older Women
'78
The Girl in Blue '74

Jan Kadar (1918-79)
Freedom Road '79
Lies My Father Told Me '75
The Angel Levine '70
The Song on Main Street
'65
Death is Called Engelchen
'63

Ellis Kadison (1928-98)
The Cat '66
Gitl '65

Jeremy Paul Kagan (1945)
Crown Heights '02
Taken '02
Color of Justice '97
Roswell: The U.F.O. Cover-
Up '94
By the Sword '93
Descending Angel '90
Big Man on Campus '89
Conspiracy: The Trial of the
Chicago Eight '87
Courage '86
The Journey of Natty Gann
'85
The Sting 2 '83
The Chosen '81
The Big Fix '78
Heroes '77

Cedric Kahn (1966-)
Red Lights '04
L'Ennui '98

Harvey Kahn
The Deal '05

Richard C. Kahn (1897-1960)
Guns Don't Argue '57
Son of Ingagi '40
Bronze Buckaroo '39
Harlem Rides the Range '39
Two-Gun Man from Harlem
'38

Chen Kaige (1952-)
The Promise '05
Together '02
Killing Me Softly '01
The Emperor and the
Assassin '99
Temptress Moon '96
Farewell My Concubine '93
Life on a String '90
Yellow Earth '89

Mikhail Kalatozov (1903-73)
Red Tent '69
I Am Cuba '64
The Cranes Are Flying '57

Max Kalmanowicz
Dreams Come True '84
The Children '80

Scott Kalvert
Deuces Wild '02
The Basketball Diaries '95

Joseph Kane (1897-1975)
Smoke in the Wind '75
He Lives: The Search for
the Evil One '67
The Maverick Queen '55
Jubilee Trail '54
Ride the Man Down '53
Hoodlum Empire '52
The Cheaters '45
Dakota '45
Flame of the Barbary Coast
'45
Cowboy & the Senorita '44
Song of Nevada '44
The Yellow Rose of Texas
'44
Hands Across the Border
'43
Idaho '43
King of the Cowboys '43
Silver Spurs '43
Song of Texas '43
Texas Legionnaires '43
Sunset Serenade '42
Sunset on the Desert '42
South of Santa Fe '42
Sons of the Pioneers '42
Romance on the Range '42
Ridin' Down the Canyon '42
Man from Cheyenne '42
Bad Man of Deadwood '41
In Old Cheyenne '41
Jesse James at Bay '41
Nevada City '41
Red River Valley '41
Robin Hood of the Pecos
'41
Sheriff of Tombstone '41
The Border Legion '40
Carson City Kid '40
Colorado '40
Ranger and the Lady '40
Young Bill Hickok '40
Young Buffalo Bill '40
Arizona Kid '39
Days of Jesse James '39
Frontier Pony Express '39
In Old Caliente '39
Rough Riders' Roundup '39
Saga of Death Valley '39
Southward Ho! '39
Wall Street Cowboy '39
Billy the Kid Returns '38
Born to Be Wild '38
Come on Rangers '38
Oh Susannah '38
Old Barn Dance '38
Shine on, Harvest Moon '38
Boots & Saddles '37
Come on, Cowboys '37
Git Along Little Dogies '37
Heart of the Rockies '37
Public Cowboy No. 1 '37
Round-Up Time in Texas
'37
Springtime in the Rockies
'37
Yodelin' Kid from Pine
Ridge '37
The Lawless Nineties '36
King of the Pecos '36
The Big Show '36
Darkest Africa '36
Fighting Marines '36
Ghost Town Gold '36
Old Corral '36
Ride, Ranger, Ride '36
Melody Trail '35
In Old Santa Fe '34

Rolfe Kanefsky (1969-)
The Hazing '04
My Family Treasure '93
There's Nothing out There
'90

Jeff Kanew (1944-)
V.I. Warshawski '91
Summer Vacation: 1999
'88
National Lampoon's Adam
& Eve '05
Troop Beverly Hills '89
Tough Guys '86
Gotcha! '85
Revenge of the Nerds '84
Eddie Macon's Run '83
Natural Enemies '79

Charles Kanganis (1952-)
Impulse '08
K-911 '99
Dennis the Menace Strikes
Again '98
3 Ninjas Kick Back '94
No Escape, No Return '93
A Time to Die '91
Chance '89
Deadly Breed '89
Sinners '89

Marek Kanievska (1952-)
A Different Loyalty '04
Where the Money Is '00
Less Than Zero '87
Another Country '84

Garson Kanin (1912-99)
A Double Life '47
Tom, Dick, and Harry '41
My Favorite Wife '40
They Knew What They
Wanted '40
Bachelor Mother '39
The Great Man Votes '38
Next Time I Marry '38

Asif Kapadia (1972-)
The Return '06
The Warrior '01

Hal Kanter (1918-99)
For the Love of It '80
Loving You '57

Ed Kaplan
Primal Secrets '94
Chips, the War Dog '90

Deborah Kaplan
Josie and the Pussycats
'01

Jonathan Kaplan (1947-)
Brokedown Palace '99
In Cold Blood '96
Bad Girls '94
Fallen Angels 1 '93
Unlawful Entry '92
Love Field '91
Immediate Family '89
The Accused '88
Project X '87
Heart Like a Wheel '83
Girls of the White Orchid
'85
Over the Edge '79
Mr. Billion '77
White Line Fever '75
Truck Turner '74
The Student Teachers '73
Night Call Nurses '72

Nelly Kaplan (1934-)
Charles et Lucie '79
Nea '78
A Very Curious Girl '69

Shekhar Kapur (1945-)
Elizabeth: The Golden Age
The Four Feathers '02
Elizabeth '98
Bandit Queen '94

Wong Kar-Wai (1958-)
My Blueberry Nights '07
2046 '04
In the Mood for Love '00
Happy Together '96
Chungking Express '95
Fallen Angels '95
Eros '04
The Grandmaster?

Lee H. Katzin (1935-2002)
Restraining Order '99
The Break '95
The Dirty Dozen: The Fatal
Mission '88
World Gone Wild '88
The Dirty Dozen: The
Deadly Mission '87
Death Ray 2000 '81
The Man from Atlantis '77
The Longest Drive '76
Savages '75
Sky Heist '75
The Salzburg Connection
'72
The Bastard '78
Terror Out of the Sky '78
Space: 1999—Alien Attack
'79

Jake Kasdan (1975-)
Walk Hard: The Dewey Cox
Story '07
The TV Set '06
Orange County '02
Zero Effect '97

Lawrence Kasdan (1949-)
Dreamcatcher '03
Mumford '99
French Kiss '95
Wyatt Earp '94
Grand Canyon '91
I Love You to Death '90
The Accidental Tourist '88
Silverado '85
The Big Chill '83
Body Heat '81

Sam Henry Kass
Body and Soul '98

Peter Kassovitz (1938-)
Jakob the Liar '99

Mathieu Kassovitz (1967-)
Babylon AD '08
Gothika '03
The Crimson Rivers '01
Hate '95
Cafe au Lait '94

Jeremy Kasten
The Thirst '06
All Souls Day '05

Brian Katkin
Shakedown '02
Hard As Nails '01
If I Die Before I Wake '98

Michael Katleman
Primeval '07
Bloodrounds '96

Milton Katselas (1933-)
Strangers: The Story of a
Mother and Daughter '79
Report to the Commissioner
'74
Forty Carats '73
Butterflies Are Free '72

Phil Karlson (1908-85)
Framed '75
Walking Tall '73
Ben '72
Hornet's Nest '70
The Wrecking Crew '68
The Silencers '66
Kid Galahad '62
Scarface Mob '62
Hell to Eternity '60
Gunman's Walk '58
Tight Spot '55
Kansas City Confidential '52
The Texas Rangers '51
The Big Cat '49
Ladies of the Chorus '49
Swing Parade of 1946 '46

Bill Karn (1913-66)
Door to Door Maniac '61
Ma Barker's Killer Brood '60
Guns Don't Argue '57
Gang Busters '55

Eric Karson
Angel Town '89
Opposing Force '87
Black Eagle '88
The Octagon '80

Matia Karrell
Once Upon a Wedding '05

Jim Kaufman
Nightwaves '03
Time at the Top '99
Night of the Demons 3 '97
Whiskers '96

Lloyd Kaufman (1945-)
Citizen Toxie: The Toxic
Avenger 4 '01
Tromeo & Juliet '96
Troma's War '88
Class of Nuke 'Em High '86
The Toxic Avenger, Part 3:
The Last Temptation of
Toxie '89
The Toxic Avenger, Part 2
'89
Sgt. Kabukiman N.Y.P.D.
'90
Stuck on You '84
Waitress '81
The First Turn On '83

Philip Kaufman (1936-)
Twisted '04
Quills '00
Rising Sun '93
Henry & June '90
The Unbearable Lightness
of Being '88
The Right Stuff '83
The Wanderers '79
Invasion of the Body
Snatchers '78
The White Dawn '75
The Great Northfield
Minnesota Raid '72
Goldstein '64

Jonathan Kaufer (1955-)
Bad Manners '98
Soup for One '82

Charles Kaufman
Jakarta '88
When Nature Calls '85
Mother's Day '80

Stephen Kay
Boogeyman '05
Get Carter '00
The Last Time I Committed
Suicide '96

Richard Kaye
Fist '76
Homeboy '88

Robert Kaylor (1934-)
Nobody's Perfect '90
Carny '80
Derby '71

Ella Kazan (1909-2003)
The Last Tycoon '76
The Arrangement '69
America America '63
Splendor in the Grass '61
A Face in the Crowd '57
Baby Doll '56
East of Eden '54
On the Waterfront '54
A Streetcar Named Desire
'51
Viva Zapata! '52
Pinky '49
Gentleman's Agreement '47
Boomerang '47
A Tree Grows in Brooklyn
'45
Panic in the Streets '50

James Keach (1948-)
Blind Dating '06
Camouflage '00
The Stars Fell on Henrietta
'94

Buster Keaton (1895-1966)
Battling Butler '26
The General '26
Seven Chances '25
The Navigator '24
Three Ages '23
Our Hospitality '23
Go West '25

Kevin Keating
Giuliani Time '05

Diane Keaton (1946-)
Hanging Up '99
Unstrung Heroes '95
Wildflower '91
Heaven '87

Bob Keen (1960-)
Proteus '95
To Catch a Yeti '95

Don Keeslar
Bog '84

Jon Keeyes
Living & Dying '07
American Nightmare '00

Worth Keeter
Snapdragon '93
L.A. Bounty '89
Illicit Behavior '91
Memorial Day '98
Lady Grey '82
Trapper County War '89
Order of the Black Eagle '87
Dogs of Hell '83
Unmasking the Idol '86
The Capture of Grizzly
Adams '82

Peter Keglevic (1950-)
Kill Cruise '90
The Cop & the Girl '86

Aki Kaurismäki (1957-)
Lights in the Dusk '06
The Man Without a Past '02
La Vie de Boheme '93
Leningrad Cowboys Go
America '89
Ariel '89

Mika Kaurismäki (1955-)
Condition Red '95
Zombie and the Ghost Train
'91
Amazon '90

Anwar Kawadri (1953-)
Nutcracker Sweet '84
Claudia '85

Denis Kavanagh (1906-84)
Flight from Vienna '56
The Ghost of Rashmon Hall
'47

Helmut Käutner (1908-80)
The Captain from
Koepenick '56
The Last Bridge '54
Die Grosse Freiheit Nr. 7 '45

Yoshiaki Kawajiri (1950-)
Wicked City '89
Lensman '84

Jerzy Kawalerowicz (1922-2007)
Pharaoh '66
Mother Joan of the Angels
'60

Kikuo Kawasaki

William Keighley (1889-1972)
The Master of Ballantrae '53
The Street with No Name
'48
George Washington Slept
Here '42

The Bride Came C.O.D. '41
The Man Who Came to Dinner '41
The Fighting 69th '40
Torrid Zone '40
Each Dawn I Die '39
Bullets or Ballots '36
The Prince and the Pauper '37
Green Pastures '36
"G" Men '35
Ladies They Talk About '33

David Keith (1954-)
The Further Adventures of Tennessee Buck '88
The Curse '87

Harvey Keith
Stand-Ins '97

Frederick King Keller
Vamping '84
The Eyes of the Amaryllis '82

Harry Keller (1913-87)
The Brass Bottle '63
Tammy and the Doctor '63
Texas John Slaughter: Stampede at Bitter Creek '62

Albert Kelley (1894-1989)
Motorcycle Squad '41
Jungle Bride 33
Campus Knights 29

Roy Kellino (1912-56)
Charade 53
I Met a Murderer '39

Nick Kellis
Endangered '94
Uncivilized '94

Bob Kelljan (1930-82)
Black Oak Conspiracy '77
Act of Vengeance '74
Scream Blacula Scream 73
The Return of Count Yorga '71
Count Yorga, Vampire '70

Barnet Kellman (1947-)
Slappy and the Stinkers '97
Straight Talk '92
Key Exchange '85

David Kellogg (1952-)
Inspector Gadget '99
Cool As Ice '91

Ray Kellogg (1905-76)
The Giant Gila Monster '59
The Killer Shrews '59

Gene Kelly (1912-96)
That's Entertainment, Part 2 '76
The Cheyenne Social Club '70
Hello, Dolly! '69
A Guide for the Married Man '67
The Tunnel of Love '58
Invitation to the Dance '56
Singin' in the Rain '52
On the Town 49

Richard Kelly (1975-)
Southland Tales '06
Donnie Darko '01

Sarah Kelly
The Lather Effect '06
Full Tilt Boogie '97

Nicholas (Nick) Kendall (1949-)
Mr. Rice's Secret '00
Cadillac Girls '93

Burt Kennedy (1922-2001)
Suburban Commando 91
Big Bad John '90
Texas Guns '90
Dynamite and Gold '88
The Trouble with Spies '87
More Wild, Wild West '80
The Concrete Cowboys 79

Alek Keshishian (1964-)
With Honors '94
Truth or Dare '91

Wild, Wild West Revisited '79
Wolf Lake 79
The Killer Inside Me '76
All the Kind Strangers 74
Train Robbers 73
Hannie Caulder 72
Ride to Glory 71
Support Your Local Gunfighter 71
The Good Guys and the Bad Guys 69
Support Your Local Sheriff '69
The War Wagon '67
Return of the Magnificent Seven '66
The Rounders 65

Chris Kennedy
Doing Time for Patsy Cline '97

Ken Kennedy
Grizzly Adams: The Legend Continues '90
Mission to Glory 80
Iron Angel 64

Michael Kennedy (1954-)
The Heist '96
Robin of Locksley '95
Hard Evidence '94
Red Scorpion 2 '94
The Swordsman '92
Talons of the Eagle '92
Erik '90
One Man Out 89
Caribe '87

Chris Kentis (1962-)
Open Water '03
Grind 97

Erle C. Kenton (1896-1980)
One Too Many '51
House of Dracula '45
House of Frankenstein '44
It Ain't Hay '43
The Ghost of Frankenstein '42
Pardon My Sarong '42
Who Done It? 42
Melody for Three '41
They Meet Again '41
Remedy for Riches 40
Escape to Paradise 39
Frolics on Ice '39
Island of Lost Souls 32
Bare Knees 28

James V. Kern (1909-66)
The Second Woman '51
Two Tickets to Broadway '51
Never Say Goodbye '46

Sarah Kernochan (1947-)
All I Wanna Do '98
Marjoe 72

Lodge Kerrigan (1964-)
Keane '04
Claire Dolan '97
Clean, Shaven '93

Irvin Kershner (1923-)
RoboCop 2 '90
Traveling Man 89
Never Say Never Again 83
The Empire Strikes Back '80
Eyes of Laura Mars 78
Raid on Entebbe '77
The Return of a Man Called Horse 76
S*P*Y*S 74
Up the Sandbox 72
Loving '70
Flim-Flam Madness '66
A Face in the Rain 63
The Hoodlum Priest 61

Harry Kerwin (1930-79)
Barracuda 78
God's Bloody Acre '75
Cheering Section 73

Bruce Kessler (1936-)
Cruise into Terror 78
Deathmoon 78
Simon, King of the Witches 71
The Gay Deceivers 69
Angels from Hell '68

Stephen Kessler
The Independent '00
Vegas Vacation '96

Michael Keusch (1955-)
Attack Force '06
Shadow Man '06
Double Cross '94
Anything for Love '93
Huck and the King of Hearts 93
Just One of the Girls '93
Samurai Cowboy '93
Lena's Holiday '91

Callie Khouri (1957-)
Mad Money '08
Divine Secrets of the Ya-Ya Sisterhood 02

Abbas Kiarostami (1940-)
The Taste of Cherry '96
Through the Olive Trees '94
Life and Nothing More... '92
Where Is My Friend's House? '87

Dylan Kidd (1969-)
P.S. '04
Roger Dodger '02

Beeban Kidron (1961-)
Bridget Jones: The Edge of Reason '04
Swept from the Sea '97
To Wong Foo, Thanks for Everything, Julie Newmar 95
Used People 92
Antonia and Jane '91
Oranges Are Not the Only Fruit 89

Fritz Kiersch (1951-)
The Stranger '95
Shattered Image 93
Into the Sun '92
Under the Boardwalk 89
Gor '88
Tuff Turf '85
Children of the Corn '84

Krzysztof Kieslowski (1941-96)
Trois Couleurs: Blanc '94
Trois Couleurs: Rouge '94
Trois Couleurs: Bleu '93
The Double Life of Veronique '91
The Decalogue '88
No End 84

Gerard Kikoine (1946-)
Buried Alive '89
Edge of Sanity '89
Dragonard 88

Edward Killy
West of the Pecos '45
Nevada '44

Clare Kilner
The Wedding Date '05
How to Deal '03
Janice Beard '99

Ki-Duk Kim
Time '06
The Isle '01

Bruce Kimmel (1947-)
The Creature Wasn't Nice '81
Spaceship '81
The First Nudie Musical 75

Anthony Kimmins (1910-62)
Captain's Paradise 53
Bonnie Prince Charlie '48
Mine Own Executioner '47

John Kincade
Back to Back '90
Terminal Entry '87

Tim Kincaid (1952-)
The Occultist '89
Maximum Thrust '88
She's Back '88
Mutant Hunt 87
Necropolis '87
Robot Holocaust '87
Breeders '86
Bad Girls Dormitory '84

Burton King (1877-1944)
When Lightning Strikes '34
The Adorable Cheat 28
The Man from Beyond '22

George King (1899-1966)
The Case of the Frightened Lady '39
Crimes at the Dark House '39
The Face at the Window '39
The Hooded Terror '38
Sexton Blake and the Hooded Terror '38
Ticket of Leave Man 37
The Crimes of Stephen Hawke '36
Demon Barber of Fleet Street '36

Henry King (1888-1982)
Beloved Infidel '59
The Bravados 58
Carousel '56
Love Is a Many-Splendored Thing '55
The Snows of Kilimanjaro '52
David and Bathsheba '51
I'd Climb the Highest Mountain '51
The Gunfighter '50
Prince of Foxes '49
Twelve O'Clock High 49
Captain from Castile 47
Wilson 44
The Song of Bernadette 43
The Black Swan 42
A Yank in the R.A.F. 41
Jesse James 39
Stanley and Livingstone 39
Alexander's Ragtime Band '38
In Old Chicago '37
Lloyds of London '36
Marie Galante '34
Hell Harbor '30
She Goes to War 29
The Winning of Barbara Worth 26
Romola 25
The White Sister 23
Tol'able David 21

Louis King (1898-1962)
Dangerous Mission '54
Sabre Jet '53
Mrs. Mike '49
Bulldog Drummond Comes Back '37
Bulldog Drummond's Revenge '37
Wine, Women and Horses '37
Special Investigator '36
Charlie Chan in Egypt '35
Drifting Souls '32
Police Court '32
Border Law '31
The Fighting Sheriff '31

Rick King
Catherine's Grove '98
Road Ends '98
Terminal Justice: Cybertech P.D. '95
A Passion to Kill '94
Quick '93

Kickboxer 3: The Art of War '92
Prayer of the Rollerboys '91
Forced March '90
The Killing Time '87
Hot Shot '86
Hard Choices '84

Robert King
Angels in the Infield '00
The Principal Takes a Holiday '98

Robert Lee King
Psycho Beach Party '00
Boys Life 94

Zalman King (1941-)
Red Shoe Diaries: Luscious Lola '04
Red Shoe Diaries: Swimming Naked '00
In God's Hands 98
Shame, Shame, Shame '98
Red Shoe Diaries: Four on the Floor '96
Red Shoe Diaries: Strip Poker 96
Delta of Venus '95
Red Shoe Diaries 3: Another Woman's Lipstick '93
Red Shoe Diaries 4: Auto Erotica 93
Red Shoe Diaries '92
Red Shoe Diaries 2: Double Dare '92
Wild Orchid 2: Two Shades of Blue '92
Wild Orchid '90
Two Moon Junction '88
Wildfire '88

Jack Kinney (1909-92)
1001 Arabian Nights '59
The Legend of Sleepy Hollow '49
Melody Time '48
Fun & Fancy Free '47

Ralf Kirsten (1930-)
Under the Pear Tree '73
On the Sunny Side '62

Takeshi "Beat" Kitano (1948-)
Zatoichi '03
Dolls '02
Brother '00
Kikujiro 99
Fireworks '97
Sonatine '96
Boiling Point '90
Violent Cop 89

Martin Kitrosser
Daddy's Girl '96
The Fiance 96
Silent Night, Deadly Night 5: The Toymaker '91

Robert J. Kizer (1952-)
Death Ring '93
Hell Comes to Frogtown '88
Godzilla 1985 '85

Alf Kjellin (1920-88)
The Girls of Huntington House 73
The McMasters 70

Robert Klane (1941-)
Weekend at Bernie's 2 '93
Thank God It's Friday 78

Cedric Klapisch (1961-)
Russian Dolls '05
L'Auberge Espagnole '02
Un Air de Famille '96
When the Cat's Away '96

Randal Kleiser (1946-)
Shadow of Doubt '98
It's My Party '95
Honey, I Blew Up the Kid '92
White Fang '91
Getting It Right '89
Big Top Pee-wee '88
Flight of the Navigator '86
Grandview U.S.A. '84
The Blue Lagoon '80
Grease 78
The Gathering '77

The Boy in the Plastic Bubble 76

Walter Klenhard
Disappearance 02
The Haunting of Seacliff Inn '94

Richard Kletter
The Android Affair '95
Dangerous Indiscretion '94

Max Kleven (1933-)
Fugitive Champion '99
Bail Out '90
Deadly Stranger '88
Ruckus '81

Elem Klimov (1933-2003)
Come and See 85
Rasputin 85

Leon Klimovsky (1907-96)
The Devil's Possessed '74
Orgy of the Vampires 73
The Saga of the Draculas 72
Vengeance of the Zombies '72
Dr. Jekyll and the Wolfman '71
Challenge of McKenna '70
The Werewolf vs. the Vampire Woman '70
Rattler Kid '68
Commando Attack '67

Werner Klingler (1903-72)
Secret of the Black Trunk '62
Testament of Dr. Mabuse '62

Dan Klores
Crazy Love '07
The Boys of 2nd Street Park '03

Elmar Klos (1910-93)
The Shop on Main Street '65
Death Is Called Engelchen '63

Steven Kloves (1960-)
Flesh and Bone '93
The Fabulous Baker Boys '89

Robert Knights (1942-)
The Man Who Made Husbands Jealous '98
Mosley '98
Double Vision '92
And a Nightingale Sang '91
The Dawning '88
A Dedicated Man '86
Ebony Tower 86
Miss A & Miss M 86
Lovers of Their Time '85

Bernard Knowles (1900-75)
Frozen Alive '64
A Soldier's Prayer '61
The Human Condition: Road to Eternity '59
The Human Condition: No Greater Love '58

Chris Koch
A Guy Thing '03
Snow Day '00

Howard W. Koch (1916-2001)
Badge 373 73
Born Reckless 59
Girl in Black Stockings '57

David Koepp (1964-)
Secret Window '04
Stir of Echoes '99

The Trigger Effect '96

Ana Kokkinos (1959-)
Head On '98
Only the Brave '94

Amos Kollek (1947-)
Fiona '98
Whore 2 '94
Double Edge '92
High Stakes '89
Goodbye, New York '85
Forever, Lulu '87

Xavier Koller (1944-)
Cowboy Up '00
Squanto: A Warrior's Tale '94
Journey of Hope '90

Andrei Konchalovsky (1937-)
House of Fools '02
The Odyssey '97
The Inner Circle '91
Homer and Eddie '89
Tango and Cash '89
Shy People '87
Duet for One '86
Runaway Train '85
Maria's Lovers '84
Siberiade '79

Jackie Kong (1954-)
The Underachievers '88
Blood Diner '87
Night Patrol '85
The Being '83

Barbara Kopple (1946-)
Fallen Champ: The Untold Story of Mike Tyson '92
Keeping On '81
Harlan County, U.S.A. '76

Alexander Korda (1893-1956)
That Hamilton Woman '41
The Thief of Bagdad '40
Rembrandt '36
Private Life of Don Juan '34
Elephant Boy '37
The Private Life of Henry VIII '33
Wedding Rehearsal '32
Marius '31

Zoltan Korda (1895-1961)
Cry, the Beloved Country '51
Sahara '43
The Jungle Book '42
The Thief of Bagdad '40
The Four Feathers '39
Drums '38

Hirokazu Kore-eda (1962-)
Nobody Knows '04
After Life '98
Maborosi '95

Harmony Korine (1974-)
Julien Donkey-boy '99
Gummo '97

Baltasar Kormakur (1966-)
The Sea '02
101 Reykjavik '00

John Korty (1936-)
Ms. Scrooge '97
Getting Out '94
They Watch '93
Eye on the Sparrow '91
Long Road Home '91
Cast the First Stone '89
Baby Girl Scott '87
Deadly Business '86
The Ewok Adventure '84
The Haunting Passion '83
A Christmas Without Snow '80
Forever '78
Oliver's Story '78
The Autobiography of Miss Jane Pittman '74

Peter Kosminsky (1956-)
White Oleander '02
Emily Bronte's Wuthering Heights '92

Henry Koster (1905-88)
The Singing Nun '66
Dear Brigitte '65
Mr. Hobbs Takes a Vacation '62
Flower Drum Song '61
The Story of Ruth '60
The Naked Maja '59
My Man Godfrey '57
D-Day, the Sixth of June '56
A Man Called Peter '55
The Virgin Queen '55
Desiree '54
The Robe '53
Stars and Stripes Forever '52
No Highway in the Sky '51
My Blue Heaven '50
Harvey '50
Come to the Stable '49
The Inspector General '49
The Bishop's Wife '47
It Started with Eve '41
First Love '39
Three Smart Girls Grow Up '39
The Rage of Paris '38
100 Men and a Girl '37
Three Smart Girls '36

Ted Kotcheff (1931-)
Family of Cops '95
Red Shoe Diaries 5: Weekend Pass '95
Hidden Assassin '94
Red Shoe Diaries 3: Another Woman's Lipstick '93
Folks! '92
Weekend at Bernie's '89
Winter People '89
Switching Channels '88
Joshua Then and Now '85
Uncommon Valor '83
First Blood '82
Split Image '82
North Dallas Forty '79
Who Is Killing the Great Chefs of Europe? '78
Fun with Dick and Jane '77
The Apprenticeship of Duddy Kravitz '74
Billy Two Hats '74
Tiara Tahiti '62

Jim Kouf (1951-)
Gang Related '96
Disorganized Crime '89
Miracles '86

Bernard L. Kowalski (1929-2007)
Nashville Beat '89
B.A.D. Cats '80
Marciano '79
Nativity '78
Sssssss '73
The Woman Hunter '72
Macho Callahan '70
Stiletto '69
Attack of the Giant Leeches '59
Night of the Blood Beast '58

Karl Kozak (1964-)
Clawed: The Legend of Sasquatch '05
Out of the Black '01

Soeren Kragh-Jacobsen (1947-)
Mifune '99
Emma's Shadow '88

Stanley Kramer (1913-2001)
The Runner Stumbles '79
The Domino Principle '77
Oklahoma Crude '73
Bless the Beasts and Children '71
R.P.M.* (*Revolutions Per Minute) '70
The Secret of Santa Vittoria '69
Guess Who's Coming to Dinner '67
Ship of Fools '65
It's a Mad, Mad, Mad, Mad World '63
Judgment at Nuremberg '61
On the Beach '59
The Defiant Ones '58
The Pride and the Passion '57
Not as a Stranger '55

Wayne Kramer (1965-)
Crossing Over '08
Running Scared '06
The Cooler '03

Norman Krasna (1909-84)
The Ambassador's Daughter '56
The Big Hangover '50

Paul Krasny (1935-2001)
Drug Wars 2: The Cocaine Cartel '92
Back to Hannibal: The Return of Tom Sawyer and Huckleberry Finn '90
When Hell Was in Session '82
Centennial '78
Joe Panther '76
Christina '74

John Krish (1923-)
The Unearthly Stranger '64
The Man Who Had Power Over Women '70

Suri Krishnamma (1961-)
A Respectable Trade '98
MTV's Wuthering Heights '03

Allen Kroeker
Showdown at Williams Creek '91
Age Old Friends '89
Heaven on Earth '89
Tramp at the Door '87

Jon Kroll
Menno's Mind '96
Amanda and the Alien '95

Steve Kroschel
Avalanche '99
Running Free '94

Lisa Krueger (1961-)
Committed '99
Manny & Lo '96

Michael Krueger (1951-90)
Mindkiller '87
Night Vision '87

Stanley Kubrick (1928-99)
Eyes Wide Shut '99
Full Metal Jacket '87
The Shining '80
Barry Lyndon '75
A Clockwork Orange '71
2001: A Space Odyssey '68
Dr. Strangelove, or: How I Learned to Stop Worrying and Love the Bomb '64
Lolita '62
Spartacus '60
Paths of Glory '57
The Killing '56
Killer's Kiss '55

Buzz Kulik (1923-99)
Around the World in 80 Days '89
Women of Valor '86
Rage of Angels '83
The Hunter '80
From Here to Eternity '79
The Lindbergh Kidnapping Case '76
Babe '75
Bad Ronald '74
Pioneer Woman '73
Shamus '73
Brian's Song '71
Riot '69
Sergeant Ryker '68
Vila Rides '67

Edward Kull (1886-)
Tarzan and the Green Goddess '38
The New Adventures of Tarzan '35

Kei Kumai (1929-2007)
Love and Faith '78
Sandakan No. 8 '74

Roger Kumble (1966-)
Just Friends '05
The Sweetest Thing '02
Cruel Intentions 2 '99
Cruel Intentions '99

Joachim Kunert
The Adventures of Werner Holt '65

Koreyoshi Kurahara
Antarctica '84

Akira Kurosawa (1910-98)
Rhapsody in August '91
Akira Kurosawa's Dreams '90
Ran '85
Kagemusha '80
Dersu Uzala '75
Dodes 'ka-den '70
Red Beard '65
High & Low '63
Sanjuro '62
Yojimbo '61
The Bad Sleep Well '60
The Hidden Fortress '58
The Lower Depths '57
Throne of Blood '57
I Live in Fear '55
Seven Samurai '54
Ikiru '52
The Idiot '51
Rashomon '51
Scandal '50
A Quiet Duel '49
Stray Dog '49
Drunken Angel '48
One Wonderful Sunday '47
No Regrets for Our Youth '46
The Men Who Tread on the Tiger's Tail '45
Sanshiro Sugata '43

Kiyoshi Kurosawa
Bright Future '03
Pulse '01

Robert Kurtzman
Wishmaster '97
The Demolitionist '95

Diane Kurys (1948-)
Children of the Century '99
Love After Love '94
A Man in Love '87
Entre-Nous '83
Peppermint Soda '77

Emir Kusturica (1954-)
Underground '95
Arizona Dream '94
Time of the Gypsies '90
When Father Was Away on Business '85

Karyn Kusama (1968-)
Aeon Flux '05
Girlfight '00

Fran Rubel Kuzui
Buffy the Vampire Slayer '92
Tokyo Pop '88

Ken Kwapis (1957-)
License to Wed '07
Sisterhood of the Traveling Pants '05
The Beautician and the Beast '97
He Said, She Said '91
Vibes '88
Sesame Street Presents: Follow That Bird '85

Jeff Kwitny (1951-)
Beyond the Door 3 '91
Iced '88

Richard Kwietniowski (1957-)
Owning Mahowny '03
Love and Death on Long Island '97

Paul Kyriazi
Omega Cop '90
Crazed Cop '88
Death Machines '76

Gregory La Cava (1892-1952)
Primrose Path '40
Fifth Avenue Girl '39
Stage Door '37
My Man Godfrey '36
Gabriel Over the White House '33
Running Wild '27
Feel My Pulse '28
The Half Naked Truth '32
Smart Woman '31
Big News '29
His First Command '29

Neil LaBute (1963-)
The Wicker Man '06
The Shape of Things '03
Possession '02
Nurse Betty '00
Your Friends & Neighbors '98
In the Company of Men '96

Gregory LaCava
See Gregory La Cava

Harry Lachman (1886-1975)
Castle in the Desert '42
The Loves of Edgar Allen Poe '42
Charlie Chan in Rio '41
Murder over New York '40
Charlie Chan at the Circus '36
Our Relations '36
Baby, Take a Bow '34

Aldo Lado (1934-)
Night Train Murders '75
Who Saw Her Die? '72
Short Night of Glass Dolls '71

John Lafia
The Rats '01
Man's Best Friend '93
Child's Play 2 '90
Blue Iguana '88

Edward Laemmle
Arizona Bad Man '32

Jean LaFleur
Ilsa, the Tigress of Siberia '79

Richard LaGravenese
Freedom Writers '07
P.S. I Love You '07
Paris, je t'aime '06
A Decade Under the Influence '02
Living Out Loud '98

Ron Lagomarsino
Mystery of the Million Dollar Hockey Puck '75
My Sister's Keeper '02
Running Mates '00
Dinner at Eight '89

Craig Lahiff
Heaven's Burning '97
Ebbtide '94
Strangers '90
Deadly Possession '88
Fever '88

Joseph Lai
Ninja Commandments '87
Ninja Operation: ...Licensed to Terminate '87
Ninja Showdown '90
Ninja Hunt '80s
Ninja Strike Force '88
The Power of the Ninjitsu '88
Ninja Terminator '84

Harvey Laidman (1942-)
Steel Cowboy '78
The Boy Who Loved Trolls '84

John Laing
Absent Without Leave '95
The Lost Tribe '89
Dangerous Orphans '86
Beyond Reasonable Doubt '80

Frank Laloggia (1954-)
Mother '94
The Lady in White '88
Fear No Evil '80

Ringo Lam (1954-)
Replicant '01
Maximum Risk '96
Full Contact '92
Twin Dragons '92
Prison on Fire 2 '91
Undeclared War '91
City on Fire '87
Prison on Fire '87

Bruce Lambert
See Godfrey Ho

Mary Lambert (1951-)
Urban Legends: Bloody Mary '05
The In Crowd '00
Dragstrip Girl '94
Grand Isle '92
Pet Sematary 2 '92
Pet Sematary '89
Siesta '87

Charles Lamont (1895-1993)
Francis in the Haunted House '56
The Kettles in the Ozarks '56
Abbott and Costello Meet the Mummy '55
Abbott and Costello Meet the Keystone Kops '55
Carolina Cannonball '55
Ma and Pa Kettle at Home '54
Abbott and Costello Go to Mars '53
Ma and Pa Kettle on Vacation '53
Abbott and Costello Meet Captain Kidd '52
Abbott and Costello Meet Dr. Jekyll and Mr. Hyde '53
Comin' Round the Mountain '51
Ma and Pa Kettle Back on the Farm '51
Abbott and Costello in the Foreign Legion '50
Ma and Pa Kettle Go to Town '50
Bagdad '49
Ma and Pa Kettle '49
Salome, Where She Danced '45
Hit the Ice '43

Steven La Rocque
Above Suspicion '00
Samantha '92

Eriq La Salle (1962-)
Crazy as Hell '02
Rebound: The Legend of Earl "The Goat" Manigault '96

Lamont

The Dark Hour '36
Little Red Schoolhouse '36
Circumstantial Evidence '35
A Shot in the Dark '35
Sons of Steel '35
The World Accuses '35
Kid 'n' Hollywood and Polly Tix in Washington '33

Albert Lamorisse (1922-70)
Circus Angel '65
Voyage en Balloon '59
The Red Balloon '56
White Mane '52

Lew Landers (1901-62)
Torpedo Alley '53
Dynamite Pass '50
The Adventures of Gallant Bess '48
Inner Sanctum '48
Son of Rusty '47
Death Valley '46
The Mask of Dijon '46
The Enchanted Forest '45
Flight from Glory '37
Without Orders '36
The Raven '35
Return of the Vampire '43
Rustlers of Red Dog '35
Savage Fury '35
Tailspin Tommy '34
Junior Army '42
Back in the Saddle '41
Ridin' on a Rainbow '41
Wagon's Westward '40
Bad Lands '39
Law of the Underworld '38
Smashing the Rackets '38

James Landis (1926-91)
Deadwood '65
Nasty Rabbit '64
The Sadist '63
Stakeout '62

John Landis (1950-)
Masters of Horror: Deer Woman '05
Masters of Horror: Family '05
An American Werewolf in London '81
The Blues Brothers '80
Blues Brothers 2000 '98
Dying to Get Rich '98
The Stupids '95
Beverly Hills Cop 3 '94
Innocent Blood '92
Oscar '91
Three Amigos '86
Coming to America '88
Amazon Women on the Moon '87
Into the Night '85
Spies Like Us '85
Trading Places '83
Twilight Zone: The Movie '83

Michael Landon (1936-91)
Sam's Son '84
Killing Stone '78
The Loneliest Runner '76
It's Good to Be Alive '74
Little House on the Prairie '74

Michael Landon, Jr. (1964-)
Saving Sarah Cain '07
Love's Long Journey '05
Love's Enduring Promise '04
Love Comes Softly '03

Jeffrey Scott Lando (1969-)
Insecticidal '05

Paul Landres (1912-2001)
Flipper's Odyssey '66
Go, Johnny Go! '59
Return of Dracula '58
Square Dance Jubilee '51

Andrew Lane (1951-)
Trade Off '95
The Secretary '94
Desperate Motives '92
Mortal Passions '90
Jake Speed '86

Eric Laneuville (1952-)
The Ernest Green Story '93
The Mighty Pawns '87
Hard Lessons '86

Sidney Lanfield (1898-1972)
Skirts Ahoy! '52
Follow the Sun '51
The Lemon Drop Kid '51
Sorrowful Jones '49
Station West '48
Where There's Life '47
My Favorite Blonde '42
You'll Never Get Rich '41
The Hound of the Baskervilles '39
Second Fiddle '39
Thin Ice '37
One in a Million '36
Red Salute '35

Fritz Lang (1890-1976)
The Thousand Eyes of Dr. Mabuse '60
The Indian Tomb '59
Journey to the Lost City '58
Beyond a Reasonable Doubt '56
While the City Sleeps '56
Moonfleet '55
Human Desire '54
The Big Heat '53
The Blue Gardenia '53
Clash by Night '52
Rancho Notorious '52
Secret Beyond the Door '48
Cloak and Dagger '46
Scarlet Street '45
Ministry of Fear '44
Woman in the Window '44
Hangmen Also Die '42
Western Union '41
Return of Frank James '40
You and Me '38
You Only Live Once '37
Fury '36
Liliom '35
Crimes of Dr. Mabuse '32
M '31
Woman in the Moon '29
Spies '28
Metropolis '26
Kriemhilde's Revenge '24
Siegfried '24
Dr. Mabuse, The Gambler '22
Destiny '21
Spiders '18

Michael (Michel) Lang (1939-)
The Gift '82
Holiday Hotel '77

Perry Lang (1959-)
Men of War '94
Little Vegas '90

Richard Lang
Texas '94

Rocky Lang
Nervous Ticks '93
Race for Glory '89

Samantha Lang (1967-)
The Monkey's Mask '00
The Well '97
Twisted '96

Walter Lang (1898-1972)
Snow White and the Three Stooges '61
Can-Can '60
But Not for Me '59
Desk Set '57
The King and I '56
There's No Business Like Show Business '54
With a Song in My Heart '52
Cheaper by the Dozen '50
The Jackpot '50
Sitting Pretty '48
Mother Wore Tights '47
State Fair '45
Greenwich Village '44
The Magnificent Dope '42
Song of the Islands '42
Moon over Miami '41
Week-End in Havana '41
The Blue Bird '40
Tin Pan Alley '40
The Little Princess '39
Red Kimono '25

Noel Langley (1911-80)
The Search for Bridey Murphy '56
Svengali '55
The Adventures of Sadie '55
The Pickwick Papers '54

Simon Langton (1941-)
Pride and Prejudice '95
Catherine Cookson's The Cinder Path '94
Casanova '87
Laguna Heat '87
The Whistle Blower '87
Act of Passion: The Lost Honor of Kathryn Beck '83
Smiley's People '82
Danger UXB '81
Therese Raquin '80
Love for Lydia '79
The Duchess of Duke Street '78

Lawrence Lanoff
The Chosen One: Legend of the Raven '98
Miami Hustle '95
Playing Dangerous '95
Temptress '95
Indecent Behavior '93
Sunday in the Park with George '86

Joseph (Jose Ramon) Larraz (1929-)
Golden Lady '79
Vampyres '74
The House that Vanished '73

Anthony M. Lanza
The Incredible Two-Headed Transplant '71
The Glory Stompers '67

James Lapine (1949-)
Earthly Possessions '99
Life with Mikey '93
Impromptu '91

Sheldon Larry (1949-)
Trial by Media '00
Family of Cops 3 '98
Behind Enemy Lines '85
Terminal Choice '85

Keith Larsen (1924-2006)
Whitewater Sam '78
Trap on Cougar Mountain '72
Mission Batangas '69

John Lasseter (1957-)
Cars '06
Toy Story 2 '99
A Bug's Life '98
Toy Story '95

Stan Lathan (1945-)
Uncle Tom's Cabin '87
Beat Street '84
Go Tell It on the Mountain '84
Amazing Grace '74

Steve Latshaw (1959-)
Death Mask '98
Biohazard: The Alien Force '95
Jack-O '95
Dark Universe '93

Alberto Lattuada (1913-2005)
Christopher Columbus '85
La Cicada '83
Stay As You Are '78
Mafioso '62
Love in the City '53
Anna '51
Variety Lights '51

Patrick Lau
The Scarlet Pimpernel '99
The Scarlet Pimpernel 2: Mademoiselle Guillotine '99

Nicholas Laughland
Like Father Like Son '05
Under the Greenwood Tree '05
Sirens '02

Michael Laughlin
Mesmerized '84
Strange Invaders '83
Strange Behavior '81

Tom Laughlin (1939-)
The Trial of Billy Jack '74
Billy Jack '71
Born Losers '67

Frank Launder (1907-97)
The Great St. Trinian's Train Robbery '66
The Pure Hell of St. Trinian's '61
Blue Murder at St. Trinian's '56
The Belles of St. Trinian's '53
The Happiest Days of Your Life '50
Captain Boycott '47
I See a Dark Stranger '46

Fabrizio Laurenti (1956-)
The Crawlers '93
Witchery '88

Georges Lautner (1926-)
La Cage aux Folles 3: The Wedding '85
My Other Husband '85
Le Professionnel '81
Icy Breasts '75
No Problem '75
Road to Salina '68
The Monocle '64

Jean-Claude Lauzon (1953-97)
Leolo '92
Night Zoo '87

Arnold Laven (1922-)
Sam Whiskey '69
Rough Night in Jericho '67
Geronimo '62
The Monster That Challenged the World '57
Without Warning '52

Martin Lavut (1939-)
Smokescreen '90
Palais Royale '88
Charlie Grant's War '80
War Brides '80

Clara Law (1957-)
Floating Life '95
Erotique '94
Temptation of a Monk '94
Autumn Moon '92
The Reincarnation of Golden Lotus '89

Diarmuid Lawrence
P.D. James: The Murder Room '04
Heat of the Sun '99
Emma '97

Francis Lawrence
I Am Legend '07
Constantine '05

John Lawrence (1931-92)
Savage Abduction '73
Cycle Psycho '72

Marc Lawrence (1959-)
Music & Lyrics '07
Two Weeks Notice '02

Ray Lawrence (1948-)
Jindabyne '06
Lantana '01
Bliss '85

J.F. Lawton (1960-)
The Hunted '94
Pizza Man '91
Cannibal Women in the Avocado Jungle of Death '89

Richard Laxton
Inspector Lynley Mysteries: A Great Deliverance '01
Invasion: Earth '98
Poldark '96
Band of Gold '95

Wilford Leach (1929-88)
The Pirates of Penzance '83
The Wedding Party '69

Philip Leacock (1917-90)
Three Sovereigns for Sarah '85
Angel City '80
The Curse of King Tut's Tomb '80
Killer on Board '77
Dying Room Only '73
Baffled '72
Shattered Silence '71
War Lover '62
Let No Man Write My Epitaph '60
The Spanish Gardener '57
Escapade '55

David Lean (1908-91)
A Passage to India '84
Ryan's Daughter '70
Doctor Zhivago '65
Lawrence of Arabia '62
The Bridge on the River Kwai '57
Summertime '55
Hobson's Choice '53
Madeleine '50
Oliver Twist '48
This Happy Breed '47
Brief Encounter '46
Great Expectations '46
Blithe Spirit '45
In Which We Serve '43

Reginald LeBorg (1902-89)
The Sibling '72
House of the Black Death '65
Diary of a Madman '63
The Black Sleep '56
Sins of Jezebel '54
The White Orchid '54
G.I. Jane '51

Jean-Paul LeChanois (1909-85)
Les Cas du Dr. Laurent '57
Les Miserables '57
Passion for Life '48

Patrice Leconte (1947-)
My Best Friend '06
Intimate Strangers '04
The Man on the Train '02
The Widow of Saint-Pierre '00
The Girl on the Bridge '98
Ridicule '96
The Hairdresser's Husband '92
Monsieur Hire '89
French Fried Vacation '79

Jacques LeCotier
See Jerry Warren

Mimi Leder (1952-)
Pay It Forward '00
Deep Impact '98
The Peacemaker '97
Woman with a Past '92

Paul Leder (1926-96)
Killing Obsession '94
Molly and Gina '94
The Abduction of Allison Tate '92
The Baby Doll Murders '92
Deadly Conspiracy '91
Frame Up '91
Twenty Dollar Star '91
Exiled in America '90
Murder by Numbers '89
Body Count '87
Vultures '84
Sketches of a Strangler '78
A*P*E* '76
I Dismember Mama '74

David Ross Lederman (1895-1972)
Cooking Up Trouble '44
Shadows on the Stairs '41
Racketeers of the Range '39
Tarzan's Revenge '38
I Promise to Pay '37
Hell-Ship Morgan '36
Daring Danger '32
The Fighting Marshal '32
The Riding Tornado '32
Texas Cyclone '32
Two-Fisted Law '32
Phantom of the West '31
Range Feud '31

Paul Leduc (1942-)
Frida '84

Ang Lee (1954-)
Lust, Caution '07
Brokeback Mountain '05
Hulk '03
Crouching Tiger, Hidden Dragon '00
Ride with the Devil '99
The Ice Storm '97
Sense and Sensibility '95
Eat Drink Man Woman '94
The Wedding Banquet '93
Pushing Hands '92

Damian Lee
Agent Red '00
Trail of a Serial Killer '98
Fatal Combat '96
Moving Target '96
Terminal Rush '96
When the Bullet Hits the Bone '96
Street Law '95
The Donor '94
Ski School '91
Abraxas: Guardian of the Universe '90
Boxcar Blues '90
Food of the Gods: Part 2 '88
Circle Man '87
Last Man Standing '87

Daniel Lee
The Kumite '03
Black Mask '96

DeWitt Lee
Ransom Money '88
The Legend of Jedediah Carver '76

Jack Lee (1913-2002)
The Captain's Table '60
Robbery under Arms '57
Wooden Horse '50

Malcolm Lee (1970-)
Welcome Home Roscoe Jenkins '08
Roll Bounce '05
Undercover Brother '02
The Best Man '99

Norman Lee (1898-1964)
Chamber of Horrors '40
Mr. Reeder in Room 13 '38

Bulldog Drummond at Bay '37

Robert Lee
The Silencer '99
Dead Fire '98
Crackerjack 2 '97
Act of War '96
Virtual Assassin '95

Rowland V. Lee (1891-1975)
Captain Kidd '45
The Bridge of San Luis Rey '44
The Son of Monte Cristo '40
Son of Frankenstein '39
The Tower of London '39
Service De Luxe '38
Love from a Stranger '37
Toast of New York '37
One Rainy Afternoon '36
The Three Musketeers '35
The Count of Monte Cristo '34
The Return of Dr. Fu Manchu '30
The Mysterious Dr. Fu Manchu '29
Doomsday '28
The Sea Lion '21

Spike Lee (1957-)
Inside Man '06
Sucker Free City '05
She Hate Me '04
25th Hour '02
Bamboozled '00
Summer of Sam '99
He Got Game '98
Get On the Bus '96
Girl 6 '96
Clockers '95
Crooklyn '94
Malcolm X '92
Jungle Fever '91
Mo' Better Blues '90
School Daze '88
Do the Right Thing '89
Joe's Bed-Stuy Barbershop: We Cut Heads '83

Herbert I. Leeds
Blue, White and Perfect '42
The Man Who Wouldn't Die '42
Charlie Chan in City of Darkness '39

Doug Lefler
Dragonheart: A New Beginning '00
Hercules the Legendary Journeys, Vol. 3: The Circle of Fire '94

Michael Lehmann (1957-)
Because I Said So '07
40 Days and 40 Nights '02
My Giant '98
Airheads '94
Hudson Hawk '91
The Applegates '89
Heathers '89

Neil Leifer
Yesterday's Hero '87

Mike Leigh (1943-)
Vera Drake '04
All or Nothing '02
Topsy Turvy '99
Career Girls '97
Secrets and Lies '95
Naked '93
Life is Sweet '90
High Hopes '88
Four Days in July '85
Home Sweet Home '82
Meantime '81
Grown Ups '80
Abigail's Party '77
Who's Who '78
Kiss of Death '77
Nuts in May '76
Hard Labour '73
Bleak Moments '71

Danny Leiner
The Great New Wonderful '06
Harold and Kumar Go to White Castle '04
Dude, Where's My Car? '00

David Leland (1947-)
Band of Brothers '01
The Big Man: Crossing the Line '91
The Land Girls '98
Checking Out '89
Courage Mountain '89
Teen Wolf Too '87
The Hitter '79

Christopher Leitch
I've Been Waiting for You '98

Claude Lelouch (1937-)
And Now Ladies and Gentlemen '02
Les Misérables '95
Bandits '86
A Man and a Woman: 20 Years Later '86
Bolero '82
Cat and Mouse '78
Robert et Robert '78
Edith & Marcel '83
Another Man, Another Chance '77
And Now My Love '74
Happy New Year '73
A Man and a Woman '66

Michael Lembeck (1948-)
The Santa Clause 3: The Escape Clause '06
Connie and Carla '04
The Santa Clause 2 '02

James (Mome) Lemmo (1949-)
Bodily Harm '95
Dream a Little Dream 2 '94
Relentless 3 '93
We're Talkin' Serious Money '92
T'jpwire '89
Heart '87

Kasi Lemmons (1961-)
Talk to Me '07
The Caveman's Valentine '01
Eve's Bayou '97

Rusty Lemorande
The Turn of the Screw '92
Journey to the Center of the Earth '88

Paul Leni (1885-1929)
The Cat and the Canary '27
The Man Who Laughs '27
Waxworks '24

Umberto Lenzi (1931-)
Bridge to Hell '87
Battle of the Commandos '71
Paranoia '69
Messalina vs. the Son of Hercules '64
Pirates of the Seven Seas '62

Bruce Lee Fights Back from the Grave '76

Jeff Leroy
Alien 3000 '04
Crystal's Diary '99
Crack Up '97

Mervyn LeRoy (1900-87)
Moment to Moment '66
Gypsy '62
The Devil at 4 O'Clock '61
The FBI Story '59
No Time for Sergeants '58
The Bad Seed '56
A Majority of One '56
Mister Roberts '55
Rose Marie '54
Latin Lovers '53
Lovely to Look At '52
Million Dollar Mermaid '52
Quo Vadis '51
Any Number Can Play '49
East Side, West Side '49
Little Women '49
Homecoming '48
Without Reservations '46
Thirty Seconds Over Tokyo '44
Madame Curie '43
Johnny Eager '42
Random Harvest '42
Blossoms in the Dust '41
Waterloo Bridge '40
They Won't Forget '37
Anthony Adverse '36
Three Men on a Horse '36
Sweet Adeline '35
Gold Diggers of 1933 '33
I Am a Fugitive from a Chain Gang '32
Three on a Match '32
Tonight or Never '31
Little Caesar '30

Mitchell Leisen (1898-1972)
The Girl Most Likely '57
To Each His Own '46
Frenchman's Creek '44
The Lady is Willing '42
Remember the Night '40
Midnight '39
The Big Broadcast of 1938 '38
Easy Living '37
Swing High, Swing Low '37
Hands Across the Table '35
Death Takes a Holiday '34
Murder at the Vanities '34

Arthur Leonard
Sepia Cinderella '47
Boy! What a Girl '45

Brett Leonard
Feed '05
Virtuosity '95
Hideaway '95
The Lawnmower Man '92
Dead Pit '89

Robert Z. Leonard (1889-1968)
The King's Thief '55
Clown '53
The Duchess of Idaho '50
Nancy Goes to Rio '50
In the Good Old Summertime '49
Weekend at the Waldorf '45
When Ladies Meet '41
Ziegfeld Girl '41
New Moon '40
Pride and Prejudice '40
Broadway Serenade '39
Girl of the Golden West '38
The Firefly '37
Maytime '37
The Great Ziegfeld '36
Dancing Lady '33
Strange Interlude '32
Susan Lenox: Her Fall and Rise '31
The Divorcee '30
A Mormon Maid '17

Sergio Leone (1929-89)
Once Upon a Time in America '84
When Angels Fly '84
A Fistful of Dynamite '72
Once Upon a Time in the West '68
The Good, the Bad and the Ugly '67
For a Few Dollars More '65
A Fistful of Dollars '64

John R. Leonetti
The Butterfly Effect 2 '06
Mortal Kombat 2: Annihilation '97

Antonio Leonviola
Tor '64
Atlas in the Land of the Cyclops '61
Mole Men Against the Son of Hercules '61

Po Chih Leong
See Po-Chih Leung

Robert Lepage (1957-)
Far Side of the Moon '03
Nô '98
Le Polygraphe '96
The Confessional '95

Dan Lerner
Target of Opportunity '04
Lone Justice 3: Showdown at Plum Creek '96

Irving Lerner (1909-76)
Cry of Battle '63
Studs Lonigan '60

Louis Leterrier (1973-)
The Incredible Hulk '08
Transporter 2 '05
Unleashed '05

Mark L. Lester (1949-)
Stealing Candy '04
Lady Jayne Killer '03
Sacrifice '00
The Base '99
Blowback '99
Misbegotten '98
Double Take '97
The Ex '96
Public Enemies '96
Night of the Running Man '94
Extreme Justice '93
Showdown in Little Tokyo '91
Class of 1999 '90
Armed and Dangerous '86
Firestarter '84
Class of 1984 '82
Gold of the Amazon Women '79
Roller Boogie '79
Stunts '77
Bobbie Jo and the Outlaw '76
Truck Stop Women '74
Steel Arena '72
The Way He Was '76

Richard Lester (1932-)
The Return of the Musketeers '89
Finders Keepers '84
Superman 3 '83
Superman 2 '80
Butch and Sundance: The Early Days '79
Cuba '79
The Ritz '76
Robin and Marian '76
The Four Musketeers '75
Royal Flash '75
Juggernaut '74
The Three Musketeers '74
Petulia '68
How I Won the War '67
A Funny Thing Happened on the Way to the Forum '66
Help! '65
The Knack '65
A Hard Day's Night '64
The Mouse on the Moon '62

Sheldon Lettich (1962-)
The Last Warrior '99
Perfect Target '98
Only the Strong '93
Double Impact '91
Lionheart '90

Po-Chih Leung (1957-)
Return to Cabin by the Lake '01
Cabin by the Lake '00
Immortality '98
Hong Kong 1941 '84

Brian Levant (1952-)
Are We There Yet? '05
Snow Dogs '02
The Flintstones in Viva Rock Vegas '00
Jingle All the Way '96
The Flintstones '94
Beethoven '92
Problem Child 2 '91

Joseph Levering
Defenders of the Law '31

Michel Levesque
Sweet Sugar '72
Werewolves on Wheels '71

William A. Levey (1943-)
Committed '91
Hellgate '89
Lightning: The White Stallion '86
Monaco Forever '83
The Happy Hooker Goes to Washington '77
Slumber Party '57 '76
Wham-Bam, Thank You Spaceman '75
Blackenstein '73

Alan J. Levi
Dead Man's Revenge '93
Blood Song '82
Riding with Death '76

Henry Levin (1901-80)
Scout's Honor '80
The Treasure Seekers '79
Run for the Roses '78
That Man Bolt '73
Desperados '69
The Ambushers '67
Murderers' Row '66
The Wonderful World of the Brothers Grimm '62
The Wonders of Aladdin '61
Where the Boys Are '60
Journey to the Center of the Earth '59
The Warriors '55
The Farmer Takes a Wife '53
Belles on Their Toes '52
Jolson Sings Again '49
Man from Colorado '49
Cry of the Werewolf '44

Marc Levin
Little Manhattan '05
Protocols of Zion '05
White Boyz '99
Slam '98

Peter Levin
A Perfect Day '06

Paul Levine
Spider's Web '01
Dea of a Lifetime '99
Operation Intercept '95

Barry Levinson (1942-)
Disclosure '94
Jimmy Hollywood '94
Toys '92
Avalon '90
Rain Man '88
Good Morning, Vietnam '87
Tin Men '87
Young Sherlock Holmes '85
The Natural '84
Diner '82

Israel Nadav Levitan (1945-)
The Seventeenth Bride '84
Intimate Story '81

Kristian Levring (1957-)
The Intended '02
The King is Alive '00

Eugene Levy (1946-)
Once Upon a Crime '92

I. Robert Levy
Can I Do It... Till I Need Glasses? '77
If You Don't Stop It... You'll Go Blind '77

Jefery Levy (1958-)
S.F.W. '94
Inside Monkey Zetterland '93

Ralph Levy (1919-2001)
Do Not Disturb '65
Bedtime Story '63
A Christmas Carol '54

Scott Levy
Unknown Origin '95
Midnight Tease '94

Shuki Levy
Turbo: A Power Rangers Movie '96
Blind Vision '91
Perfect Victims '87

Shawn Levy
Night at the Museum '06
The Pink Panther '06
Cheaper by the Dozen '03
Just Married '03
Big Fat Liar '02

Albert Lewin (1916-96)
Pandora and the Flying Dutchman '51
The Private Affairs of Bel Ami '47
Picture of Dorian Gray '45
The Moon and Sixpence '43

Ben Lewin (1946-)
Paperback Romance '96
The Favor, the Watch, & the Very Big Fish '92
Georgia '87

Christopher Lewis (1944-)
The Ripper '86
Blood Cult '85

Everett Lewis
Luster '02
The Natural History of Parking Lots '90

Herschell Gordon Lewis (1926-)
The Gore-Gore Girls '72
This Stuff'll Kill Ya! '71
The Wizard of Gore '70
How to Make a Doll '68
Just for the Hell of It '68
The Psychic '68
She-Devils on Wheels '68
Something Weird '68
Blast-Off Girls '67
The Girl, the Body and the Pill '67
Gruesome Twosome '67
Suburban Roulette '67
A Taste of Blood '67
Jimmy, the Boy Wonder '66

Monster a Go-Go! '65
Color Me Blood Red '64
Moonshine Mountain '64
2000 Maniacs '64
Blood Feast '63
Scum of the Earth '63
Nature's Playmates '62
The Prime Time '60

Jerry Lewis (1926-)
Cracking Up '83
Hardly Working '81
Which Way to the Front? '70
Big Mouth '67
Family Jewels '65
The Patsy '64
The Nutty Professor '63
The Errand Boy '61
The Ladies' Man '61
The Bellboy '60

Joseph H. Lewis (1907-2000)
Terror in a Texas Town '58
Seventh Cavalry '56
Big Combo '55
A Lawless Street '55
That Gang of Mine '40
The Spy Ring '38

Richard J. Lewis
K-9 3: P.I. '01
Whale Music '94

Robert Lewis (1909-97)
The Crying Child '96
Circumstances Unknown '95
Don't Talk to Strangers '94
Memories of Murder '90
Dead Reckoning '89
Ladykillers '88
City Killer '87
Embassy '85
A Summer to Remember '84
Agatha Christie's A Caribbean Mystery '83
Agatha Christie's Sparkling Cyanide '83
Desperate Lives '82
Child Bride of Short Creek '81
Fallen Angel '81
If Things Were Different '79
S*H*E '79
No Room to Run '78
Pray for the Wildcats '74

Jeff Lieberman (1947-)
Satan's Little Helper '04
Remote Control '88
Just Before Dawn '80
Blue Sunshine '78
Squirm '76

Robert Lieberman (1941-)
The Stepdaughter '00
Alone with a Stranger '99
Captured '99
The Dead Zone '02
Tom Clancy's Netforce '98
D3: The Mighty Ducks '96
Titanic '96
Fire in the Sky '93
Table for Five '83
Will: G. Gordon Liddy '82

Jonathan Liebesman (1976-)
The Texas Chainsaw Massacre: The Beginning '06
Darkness Falls '03

Peter Lilienthal (1929-)
Ruby's Dream '82
The Uprising '81
David '79

Edward Lilley (1896-1974)
Hi, Good Lookin'! '44
Honeymoon Lodge '43

Kevin Lima (1962-)
Enchanted '07
Eloise at the Plaza '03
102 Dalmatians '00
Tarzan '99
A Goofy Movie '94

Justin Lin (1973-)
Annapolis '06
The Fast and the Furious: Tokyo Drift '06
Better Luck Tomorrow '02

Kevin J. Lindenmuth
Addicted to Murder 3: Bloodlust '99
Rage of the Werewolf '99
Addicted to Murder 2: Tainted Blood '97
The Alien Agenda: Endangered Species '97
The Alien Agenda: Under the Skin '97
The Alien Agenda: Out of the Darkness '96
Addicted to Murder '95

Maud Linder
Man in the Silk Hat '83
Man in the Silk Hat '15

Lance Lindsay
Real Bullets '90
Star Crystal '85

Michael Lindsay-Hogg (1940-)
Two of Us '00
Horton Foote's Alone '97
Frankie Starlight '95
Running Mates '92
The Habitation of Dragons '91
Murder by Moonlight '91
The Object of Beauty '91
Strange Case of Dr. Jekyll & Mr. Hyde '89
The Little Match Girl '87
As Is '85
Master Harold and the Boys '84
Sound of Murder '82
Brideshead Revisited '81
Nasty Habits '77
Let It Be '70

Leopold Lindtberg (1902-84)
Four in a Jeep '51
The Last Chance '45

Caroline Link (1964-)
Nowhere in Africa '02
Beyond Silence '96

John F. Link
Call of the Forest '49
The Devil's Cargo '48

Richard Linklater (1961-)
Fast Food Nation '06
A Scanner Darkly '06
The Bad News Bears '05
Before Sunset '04
School of Rock '03
Tape '01
Waking Life '01
The Newton Boys '97
subUrbia '96
Before Sunrise '94
Dazed and Confused '93
Slacker '91

Art Linson (1942-)
The Wild Life '84
Where the Buffalo Roam '80

Aaron Lipstadt (1952-)
Blood Money '99
Pair of Aces '90
City Limits '85
Android '82

Steven Lisberger (1951-)
Slipstream '89
Hot Pursuit '87
Tron '82

David Lister
The Story of an African Farm '04
The Rutanga Tapes '90
Hunted '88

Peter MacKenzie Litten
Heaven's a Drag '94
Living Doll '90

Dwight Little (1947-)
Anacondas: The Hunt for the Blood Orchid '04
Murder at 1600 '97
Free Willy 2: The Adventure Home '95
Rapid Fire '92
Marked for Death '90
The Phantom of the Opera '89
Bloodstone '88
Halloween 4: The Return of Michael Myers '88
Getting Even '86

Ryan Little
Outlaw Trail '06
Saints and Soldiers '03

Lynne Littman (1941-)
Having Our Say: The Delany Sisters' First 100 Years '99
Rescuers: Stories of Courage—Two Couples '98
Testament '83

Anatole Litvak (1902-74)
Night of the Generals '67
Goodbye Again '61
Anastasia '56
The Snake Pit '48
Sorry, Wrong Number '48
The Long Night '47
All This and Heaven Too '40
City for Conquest '40
Amazing Dr. Clitterhouse '38
The Sisters '38
Mayerling '36

Gerry Lively
Darkness Falls '98
Body Moves '90

Carlo Lizzani (1922-)
House of the Yellow Carpet '84
Last Four Days '77
Love in the City '53

Luis Llosa (1951-)
Anaconda '96
The Specialist '94
800 Leagues Down the Amazon '93
Fire on the Amazon '93
Sniper '92
Crime Zone '88
Hour of the Assassin '86

Frank Lloyd (1886-1960)
The Last Command '55
Blood on the Sun '45
Forever and a Day '43
The Howards of Virginia '40
If I Were King '38
Mutiny on the Bounty '35
Cavalcade '33
Hoopla '33
Oliver Twist '22

Ken Loach (1936-)
The Wind That Shakes the Barley '06
A Fond Kiss '04
Sweet Sixteen '02
The Navigators '01
Bread and Roses '00
My Name is Joe '98
Carla's Song '97
Land and Freedom '95
Ladybird, Ladybird '93
Raining Stones '93
Riff Raff '92
Hidden Agenda '90
Singing the Blues in Red '87
Family Life '77

Victor Lobl
Eden '93

Sondra Locke (1947-)
Trading Favors '97
Impulse '90
Ratboy '86

Bob Logan
Meatballs 4 '92
Repossessed '90
Up Your Alley '89

Joshua Logan (1908-88)
Paint Your Wagon '69
Camelot '67
Ensign Pulver '64
Fanny '61
Tall Story '60
South Pacific '58
Sayonara '57
Bus Stop '56
Picnic '55

Tom Logan (1954-)
Dream Trap '90
The Night Brings Charlie '90

Dimitri Logothetis
The Lost Angel '04
Body Shot '93
The Closer '91
Slaughterhouse Rock '88
Pretty Smart '87

J. Anthony Loma
See Jose Antonio De La Loma

Lou Lombardo (1932-2002)
P.K. and the Kid '84
Russian Roulette '75

Ulli Lommel (1944-)
BTK Killer '05
The Big Sweat '90
Cold Heat '90
Warbirds '89
Overkill '86
Strangers in Paradise '84
Devonsville Terror '83
Olivia '83
Brainwaves '82
The Boogey Man '80
Cocaine Cowboys '79
Tenderness of the Wolves '73

Richard Loncraine (1946-)
Firewall '06
Wimbledon '04
My House in Umbria '03
The Gathering Storm '02
Band of Brothers '01
Richard III '95
The Wedding Gift '93
Bellman and True '88
Deep Cover '88
Brimstone & Treacle '82
The Missionary '82
Full Circle '77

Jerry London (1937-)
Counterstrike '03
Take Me Home: The John Denver Story '00
Victim of Love '91
Haunting of Sarah Hardy '89
Kiss Shot '89
Rent-A-Cop '88
Manhunt for Claude Dallas '86
Chiefs '83
The Scarlet & the Black '83
Father Figure '80
Shogun '80

Stanley Long (1933-)
Adventures of a Private Eye '87
Adventures of a Taxi Driver '76

Harry S. Longstreet
The Perfect Daughter '96
A Vow to Kill '94
Sex, Love and Cold Hard Cash '93

Temistocles Lopez (1947-)
Bird of Prey '95
Chain of Desire '93
Exquisite Corpses '88

Del Lord (1894-1970)
I Love a Bandleader '45
Vengeance '37

Jean-Claude Lord (1943-)
Landslide '92
Eddie and the Cruisers 2: Eddie Lives! '89
Mindfield '89
Toby McTeague '87
The Vindicator '85
Covergirl '83
Visiting Hours '82

Joseph Losey (1909-84)
Steaming '86
La Truite '83
Roads to the South '78
Mr. Klein '76
Romantic Englishwoman '75
A Doll's House '73
Assassination of Trotsky '72
The Go-Between '71
Secret Ceremony '69
Boom! '68
Accident '67
Modesty Blaise '66
King and Country '64
The Servant '63
Eva '62
Time Without Pity '57
The Sleeping Tiger '54
Prowler '51
The Boy with the Green Hair '48

Eb Lottimer (1950-)
Twisted Love '95
Love Matters '93

Ye Lou
Summer Palace '06
Purple Butterfly '03

Pavel (Lungin) Lounguine (1949-)
Luna Park '91
Taxi Blues '90

John Lounsbery
The Many Adventures of Winnie the Pooh '77
The Rescuers '77

Eugene Lourie (1903-91)
Gorgo '61
The Beast from 20,000 Fathoms '53

Eric Louzil (1951-)
Class of Nuke 'Em High 3: The Good, the Bad and the Subhumanoid '94
Class of Nuke 'Em High 2: Subhumanoid Meltdown '91
Wilding '90
Fortress of Amerikka '89
Lust for Freedom '87

Charles Loventhal
Mr. Write '92
My Demon Lover '87
First Time '82

Otho Lovering (1892-1968)
Drift Fence '36
Sky Parade '36

Steven Lovy
Plughead Rewired: Circuitry Man 2 '94
Circuitry Man '90

Lucas Lowe
American Shaolin: King of the Kickboxers 2 '91
The King of the Kickboxers '91
No Retreat, No Surrender 3: Blood Brothers '91

Richard Lowenstein (1959-)
He Died With a Felafel in His Hand '01
Dogs in Space '87

Dick Lowry (1944-)
Category 7 : The End of the World '05
Category 6 : Day of Destruction '04
Little John '02
Attila '01
The Diamond of Jeru '01
Follow the Stars Home '01
Atomic Train '99
Dean Koontz's Mr. Murder '98
Last Stand at Saber River '96
A Horse for Danny '95
Urban Crossfire '94
The Gambler Returns: The Luck of the Draw '93
In the Line of Duty: Ambush in Waco '93
Till Murder Do Us Part '92
Midnight Murders '91
Archie: Return to Riverdale '90
In the Line of Duty: A Cop for the Killing '90
In the Line of Duty: The FBI Murders '88
Kenny Rogers as the Gambler, Part 3: The Legend Continues '87
Agatha Christie's Murder with Mirrors '85
Wet Gold '84
Wild Horses '84
Kenny Rogers as the Gambler, Part 2: The Adventure Continues '83
Living Proof: The Hank Williams Jr. Story '83
Smokey and the Bandit, Part 3 '83
Coward of the County '81
The Jayne Mansfield Story '80
Kenny Rogers as the Gambler '80

Sam Lowry
See Steven Soderbergh

Nanni Loy (1925-95)
Where's Picone '84
Cafe Express '83
Head of the Family '71

Arthur Lubin (1899-1995)
The Incredible Mr. Limpet '64
Thief of Baghdad '61
Escapade in Japan '57
Francis in the Navy '55
Lady Godiva '55
Francis Joins the WACs '54
Francis Covers the Big Town '53
South Sea Woman '53
Francis Goes to West Point '52
Francis Goes to the Races '51
Queen for a Day '51
Francis the Talking Mule '49
Impact '49
New Orleans '47
Delightfully Dangerous '45
Ali Baba and the Forty Thieves '43
The Phantom of the Opera '43
Ride 'Em Cowboy '42
Buck Privates '41
Hold That Ghost '41
In the Navy '41
Keep 'Em Flying '41
Black Friday '40
Prison Break '38
Yellowstone '36

Ernst Lubitsch (1892-1947)
Heaven Can Wait '43
To Be or Not to Be '42
That Uncertain Feeling '41
The Shop Around the Corner '40
Ninotchka '39
Bluebeard's Eighth Wife '38
Angel '37
The Merry Widow '34
One Hour with You '32
Trouble in Paradise '32
The Smiling Lieutenant '31
Monte Carlo '30
The Love Parade '29
The Student Prince in Old Heidelberg '27

So This Is Paris '26
The Marriage Circle '24
One Arabian Night '21
Passion '19
Gypsy Blood '18

S. Roy Luby (1904-76)
Black Market Rustlers '43
Cowboy Commandos '43
Land of Hunted Men '43
Arizona Stagecoach '42
Boot Hill Bandits '42
Thunder River Renegades '42
Fugitive Valley '41
Kid's Last Ride '41
Saddle Mountain Roundup '41
Tonto Basin Outlaws '41
Trail of the Silver Spurs '41
Tumbledown Ranch in Arizona '41
Underground Rustlers '41
Range Busters '40
Trailing Double Trouble '40
West of Pinto Basin '40
Border Phantom '37
The Red Rope '37
Tough to Handle '37
Crooked Trail '36
Desert Phantom '36
Outlaw Rule '36
Rogue of the Range '36

George Lucas (1944-)
American Graffiti '73
THX 1138 '71
Star Wars '77
Star Wars: Episode 1—The Phantom Menace '99
Star Wars: Episode 2—Attack of the Clones '02
Star Wars: Episode 3—Revenge of the Sith '05

Maurizio Lucidi (1932-)
Street People '76
Stateline Motel '75

Edward Ludwig (1898-1982)
The Black Scorpion '57
Flame of the Islands '55
Big Jim McLain '52
The Big Wheel '49
Wake of the Red Witch '49
Fighting Seabees '44
That Certain Age '38

Baz Luhrmann (1962-)
Moulin Rouge '01
William Shakespeare's Romeo and Juliet '96
Strictly Ballroom '92

Eric Luke
Not Quite Human 2 '89
Still Not Quite Human '92

Robert Luketic (1973-)
21 '08
Monster-in-Law '05
Win a Date with Tad Hamilton! '04
Legally Blonde '01

Sidney Lumet (1924-)
Before the Devil Knows You're Dead '07
Find Me Guilty '06
Gloria '98
Critical Care '97
Night Falls on Manhattan '96
Guilty as Sin '93
A Stranger Among Us '92
Q & A '90
Family Business '89
Running on Empty '88
The Morning After '86
Power '86
The Verdict '82
Deathtrap '82
Daniel '83
Garbo Talks '84
Prince of the City '81
Just Tell Me What You Want '80
The Wiz '78
Equus '77
Network '76
Dog Day Afternoon '75
Murder on the Orient Express '74
Serpico '73
The Offence '73
The Anderson Tapes '71
The Group '66
The Hill '65
The Pawnbroker '65
Fail-Safe '64
Long Day's Journey into Night '62
The Fugitive Kind '60
Stage Struck '57
Twelve Angry Men '57

Ida Lupino (1914-95)
The Trouble with Angels '66
The Bigamist '53
The Hitch-Hiker '53

Michele Lupo (1932-89)
Mean Frank and Crazy Tony '75
Master Touch '74

Rod Lurie (1962-)
Resurrecting the Champ '07
The Last Castle '01
The Contender '00
Deterrence '00

Hamilton Luske (1903-68)
101 Dalmatians '61
Lady and the Tramp '55
Peter Pan '53
Alice in Wonderland '51
Melody Time '48
Fun & Fancy Free '47
Fantasia '40
Pinocchio '40

Patrick Lussier
White Noise 2: The Light '07
Prince Brat and the Whipping Boy '95
Dracula 2000 '00
Dracula 2: Ascension '03
Dracula 3: Legacy '05

Dana Lustig (1963-)
Confessions of a Sociopathic Social Climber '05
Kill Me Later '01
Wedding Bell Blues '96

David Lynch (1946-)
Inland Empire '06
Mulholland Drive '01
The Straight Story '99
Lost Highway '96
Twin Peaks: Fire Walk with Me '92
Wild at Heart '90
Blue Velvet '86
Dune '84
The Elephant Man '80
Eraserhead '78

Liam Lynch (1970-)
Tenacious D in the Pick of Destiny '06
Sarah Silverman: Jesus Is Magic '05

Paul Lynch (1946-)
Face the Evil '97
The Reluctant Agent '95
No Contest '95
Victim of Beauty '94
Murder by Night '89
Blindside '88
Bullies '86
Really Weird Tales '86
Dream to Believe '85
Cross Country '83
Humongous '82
Prom Night '80

Adrian Lyne (1941-)
Unfaithful '02
Lolita '97
Indecent Proposal '93
Jacob's Ladder '90
9 1/2 Weeks '86
Fatal Attraction '87
Flashdance '83
Foxes '80

Jonathan Lynn (1943-)
The Fighting Temptations '03
The Whole Nine Yards '00
Trial and Error '96
Sgt. Bilko '96
The Distinguished Gentleman '92
My Cousin Vinny '92
Nuns on the Run '90
Clue '85

Francis D. Lyon (1905-96)
Castle of Evil '66
Tomboy & the Champ '58
Bail Out at 43,000 '57
The Great Locomotive Chase '56
The Oklahoman '56
Cult of the Cobra '55

Jingle Ma
Silver Hawk '04
Tokyo Raiders '00

Dick Maas (1951-)
The Shaft '01
Amsterdamned '88
The Lift '85

Syd Macartney
A Love Divided '01
The Canterville Ghost '96

Kurt MacCarley
Sexual Intent '94

David MacDonald (1904-83)
The Moonraker '58
Small Hotel '57
Alias John Preston '56
Devil Girl from Mars '54
The Adventurers '51
Christopher Columbus '49
This England '42
Never Too Late to Mend '37

Kevin Macdonald
The Last King of Scotland '06
Touching the Void '03

Peter Macdonald
The Extreme Adventures of Super Dave '00
Legionnaire '98
The NeverEnding Story 3: Escape from Fantasia '94
Mo' Money '92

Hamilton MacFadden (1901-77)
Inside the Law '42
Legion of Missing Men '37
Sea Racketeers '37
Three Legionnaires '37
Stand Up and Cheer '34
Charlie Chan Carries On '31

Mike MacFarland
Pink Motel '82
Hanging on a Star '78

Brice Mack (1915-2008)
Rooster: Spurs of Death! '83
Swap Meet '79
Jennifer '78

David Mackay
Black Point '01

Alexander MacKendrick (1912-93)
Sweet Smell of Success '57
The Ladykillers '55
Mandy '53
The Man in the White Suit '51

David MacKenzie (1966-)
Asylum '05
Young Adam '03

John MacKenzie (1932-)
Quicksand '01
When the Sky Falls '00
The Infiltrator '95
Voyage '93
Ruby '92
The Fourth Protocol '87
Act of Vengeance '86
Beyond the Limit '83
The Long Good Friday '80
A Sense of Freedom '78
One Brief Summer '70

Peter N. MacKenzie
Merchants of War '90
Mission Manila '87

Will MacKenzie (1938-)
Perfect Harmony '91
Worth Winning '89
Hobo's Christmas '87

Douglas Mackinnon
The Flying Scotsman '06

Gilles Mackinnon
Gentleman's Relish '01
Hideous Kinky '99
Regeneration '97
Trojan Eddie '96
Small Faces '96
A Simple Twist of Fate '94
The Playboys '92

Alison Maclean (1958-)
Jesus' Son '99
Crush '93

Henry MacRae (1876-1944)
Rustler's Roundup '33
Tarzan the Tiger '29

John Madden (1949-)
Proof '05
Captain Corelli's Mandolin '01
Shakespeare in Love '98
Mrs. Brown '97
Golden Gate '93
Ethan Frome '92
Grown Ups '86

Lee Madden
Night Creature '79
The Manhandlers '73
The Night God Screamed '71
Angel Unchained '70
Hell's Angels '69

Guy Maddin (1956-)
Brand Upon the Brain '06
The Saddest Music in the World '03
The Twilight of the Ice Nymphs '97
Careful '92
Tales from the Gimli Hospital '88

Guy Magar (1948-)
Children of the Corn: Revelation '01
Stepfather 3: Father's Day '92
Retribution '88

Maria Maggenti (1962-)
Puccini for Beginners '06
The Incredibly True Adventure of Two Girls in Love '95

Joe Maggio
Milk and Honey '03
Virgil Bliss '01

Albert Magnoli
Dark Planet '97
Born to Run '93
Street Knight '93
American Anthem '86
Purple Rain '84

Dezso Magyar (1938-)
No Secrets '91
King of America '80

Anthony Maharaj
Life 101 '95

Redge Mahaffey
First Encounter '97

Brendan Maher
Kidnapped '05
The Road from Coorain '02
Doom Runners '97

Barry Mahon (1921-99)
The Beast That Killed Women '65
Pagan Island '60
Assault of the Rebel Girls '59
Violent Women '59
Rocket Attack U.S.A. '55

Stewart Main
One of Them '99
First Love and Other Pains
Desperate Remedies '93

Majid Majidi (1959-)
Baran '01
The Color of Paradise '99
Children of Heaven '98
Baran '01

Dusan Makavejev (1932-)
Gorilla Bathes at Noon '93
Manifesto '88
Montenegro '81
Sweet Movie '75
WR: Mysteries of the Organism '71
Innocence Unprotected '68
The Love Affair, or The Case of the Missing Switchboard Operator '67
Man Is Not a Bird '65

Mohsen Makhmalbaf (1957-)
Kandahar '01
Gabbeh '96
Silk Stockings

Karoly Makk (1925-)
The Gambler '97
Lily in Love '85
Another Way '82
Cat's Play '74
Love '71

Kelly Makin
Mickey Blue Eyes '99
Kids in the Hall: Brain Candy '96
National Lampoon's Senior Trip '95

Guido Malatesta (1919-70)
Revolt of the Barbarians '64
Goliath Against the Giants '63
Fire Monsters Against the Son of Hercules '62

Rob Malenfant
Facing the Enemy '00
The Perfect Nanny '00
The Landlady '98
The Night Caller '97

Terrence Malick (1943-)
The New World '05
The Thin Red Line '98
Days of Heaven '78
Badlands '74

Louis Malle (1932-95)
Vanya on 42nd Street '94
Damage '92
May Fools '90
Au Revoir les Enfants '87
Alamo Bay '85
Crackers '84
Atlantic City '81
My Dinner with André '81
Pretty Baby '78
Murmur of the Heart '71
Spirits of the Dead '68
Viva Maria! '65
The Fire Within '64
A Very Private Affair '62
The Lovers '59
Frantic '58

James Mallon
Mystery Science Theater 3000: The Movie '96

Bruce Malmuth
Pentathlon '94
Hard to Kill '89
Where Are the Children? '85
The Man Who Wasn't There '83
Nighthawks '81
Foreplay '75

Mark Malone
Dead Heat '01
The Last Stop '99
Hoods '98
Bulletproof Heart '95

William Malone (1953-)
Masters of Horror: Fair Haired Child '06
Feardotcom '02
House on Haunted Hill '99
Creature '85
Scared to Death '80

David Mamet (1947-)
Redbelt '08
Spartan '04
Heist '01
State and Main '00
The Winslow Boy '99
The Spanish Prisoner '97
Oleanna '94
Homicide '91
Things Change '88
House of Games '87

Yuri Mamin (1946-)
Window to Paris '95
Sideburns '91

Rouben Mamoulian (1897-1987)
Silk Stockings '57
Summer Holiday '48
Blood and Sand '41
The Mark of Zorro '40
Golden Boy '39
The Gay Desperado '36
Becky Sharp '35
Queen Christina '33
The Song of Songs '33
Dr. Jekyll and Mr. Hyde '32
Love Me Tonight '32
City Streets '31
Applause '29

Mitcho Manchevski (1959-)
Dust '01
Before the Rain '94

Jeffrey Mandel
Robo-Chic '89

Robert Mandel
School Ties '92
Perfect Witness '89
Big Shots '87
Touch and Go '86
F/X '86
Independence Day '83

Artie Mandelberg
His Bodyguard '98
Where's the Money, Noreen? '95
Luis Mandoki (1954-)
Innocent Voices '04
Trapped '02
Angel Eyes '01
Message in a Bottle '98
When a Man Loves a Woman '94
Born Yesterday '93
White Palace '90
Gaby: A True Story '87
Arthur's Quest '99
The Million Dollar Kid '99
Hijacking Hollywood '97
Joseph Manduke
The Gumshoe Kid '89
Omega Syndrome '87
Beatlemania! The Movie '81
Cornbread, Earl & Me '75
Kid Vengeance '75
Fury on Wheels '71
James Mangold (1964-)
3:10 to Yuma '07
Walk the Line '05
Identity '03
Kate & Leopold '01
Girl, Interrupted '99
Cop Land '97
Heavy '94
Francis Mankiewicz (1944-93)
Love and Hate: A Marriage Made in Hell '90
And Then You Die '88
Les Bons Debarras '81
Joseph L. Mankiewicz (1909-93)
Sleuth '72
There Was a Crooked Man '70
The Honey Pot '67
Cleopatra '63
Suddenly, Last Summer '59
Guys and Dolls '55
The Barefoot Contessa '54
Julius Caesar '53
Five Fingers '52
People Will Talk '51
All About Eve '50
No Way Out '50
House of Strangers '49
A Letter to Three Wives '49
The Ghost and Mrs. Muir '47
Tom Mankiewicz (1942-)
Taking the Heat '93
Delirious '91
Dragnet '87
Anthony Mann (1906-67)
Dandy in Aspic '68
The Heroes of Telemark '65
The Fall of the Roman Empire '64
El Cid '61
Cimarron '60
God's Little Acre '58
Man of the West '58
Men in War '57
The Tin Star '57
Far Country '55
The Man from Laramie '55
Strategic Air Command '55
The Glenn Miller Story '54
The Naked Spur '53
Thunder Bay '53
Bend of the River '52
Side Street '50
Winchester 73 '50
Border Incident '49
Reign of Terror '49
He Walked by Night '48
Raw Deal '48
Desperate '47
Railroaded '47
T-Men '47
Strange Impersonation '46
Great Flamarion '45
Daniel Mann (1912-91)
The Man Who Broke 1,000 Chains '87

Playing for Time '80
Matilda '78
Journey into Fear '74
Big Mo '73
Interval '73
Willard '71
A Dream of Kings '69
For Love of Ivy '68
Our Man Flint '66
Who's Got the Action? '63
Butterfield 8 '60
The Mountain Road '60
The Last Angry Man '59
Hot Spell '58
The Teahouse of the August Moon '56
I'll Cry Tomorrow '55
The Rose Tattoo '55
Come Back, Little Sheba '52
Delbert Mann (1920-2007)
Lily in Winter '94
Ironclads '90
The Last Days of Patton '86
Love Leads the Way '84
The Member of the Wedding '83
Night Crossing '81
All Quiet on the Western Front '79
Home to Stay '79
Tom Between Two Lovers '79
The Birch Interval '78
Breaking Up '78
Francis Gary Powers: The True Story of the U-2 Spy '76
The Man Without a Country '73
No Place to Run '72
She Waits '72
David Copperfield '70
The Pink Jungle '68
Heidi '68
A Gathering of Eagles '63
That Touch of Mink '62
Lover Come Back '61
Desire Under the Elms '58
Separate Tables '58
Marty '55
Edward Andrew (Santos Alcocer) Mann (1923-95)
Hooch '76
Cauldron of Blood '67
Hallucination '67
Farhad Mann
'Lawnmower Man 2: Beyond Cyberspace '95
Return to Two Moon Junction '93
Nick Knight '89
Michael Mann (1943-)
Miami Vice '06
Collateral '04
Ali '01
The Insider '99
Heat '95
The Last of the Mohicans '92
Manhunter '86
The Keep '83
Thief '81
The Jericho Mile '79
Peter Manoogian
Soldiers of Change '06
Seedpeople '92
Demonic Toys '90
Arena '89
Enemy Territory '87
The Eliminators '86
Dungeonmaster '83
Mark Manos
Josh Kirby... Time Warrior: Chapter 4, Eggs from 70 Million B.C. '95
Liquid Dreams '92
Rene Manzor (1959-)
Red Shoe Diaries 8: Night of Abandon '97
Legends of the North '95
Warrior Spirit '94
Robert Marcarelli
The Long Ride Home '01
The Omega Code '99

I Don't Buy Kisses Anymore '92
Original Intent '91
Terry Marcel (1942-)
The Last Seduction 2 '98
Jane & the Lost City '87
Prisoners of the Lost Universe '84
Hawk the Slayer '81
Alex March (1921-89)
Master Mind '73
Firehouse '72
The Big Bounce '69
Paper Lion '68
Max Marcin (1879-1948)
Gambling Ship '33
King of the Jungle '33
Adam Marcus (1968-)
Let It Snow '99
Jason Goes to Hell: The Final Friday '93
Mitch Marcus
The Haunting of Hell House '99
Knocking on Death's Door '99
Boltneck '98
A Boy Called Hate '95
Paul Marcus (1955-)
Eye of the Killer '99
The Break Up '98
Andreas Marfori
Desperate Crimes '93
Evil Clutch '89
Antonio Margheriti
See Anthony M. Dawson
Car Crash '80
Giants of Rome '63
Stuart Margolin (1940-)
The Sweetest Gift '98
How the West Was Fun '95
Medicine River '94
Paramedics '88
A Shining Season '79
A. L. Mariaux
See Jess (Jesus) Franco
Edwin L. Marin (1899-1951)
The Cariboo Trail '50
Christmas Eve '47
Abilene Town '46
Mr. Ace '46
Nocturne '46
Johnny Angel '45
Show Business '44
Tall in the Saddle '44
Invisible Agent '42
Miss Annie Rooney '42
A Christmas Carol '38
Everybody Sing '38
Listen, Darling '38
I'd Give My Life '36
The Death Kiss '33
A Study in Scarlet '33
Lex Marinos (1949-)
An Indecent Obsession '85
Remember Me '85
Peter Maris
Diplomatic Immunity '91
Hangfire '91
Ministry of Vengeance '89
True Blood '89
Viper '88
Terror Squad '87
Land of Doom '84
Delirium '77
Monte Markham (1935-)
Neon City '91
Defense Play '88
Fletcher Markle (1921-91)
The Incredible Journey '63
Jigsaw '49

Peter Markle (1946-)
The Last Days of Frankie the Fly '96
White Dwarf '95
Wagons East '94
Through the Eyes of a Killer '92
El Diablo '90
Nightbreaker '89
Bat 21 '88
Youngblood '86
Hot Dog... The Movie! '83
The Personals '83
Robert Markowitz (1935-)
The Great Gatsby '01
The Pilot's Wife '01
Small Vices: A Spenser Mystery '99
David '97
Into Thin Air: Death on Everest '97
The Tuskegee Airmen '95
Afterburn '92
Love, Lies and Murder '91
Decoration Day '90
Too Young to Die '90
Dangerous Life '89
Kojak: The Belarus File '85
My Mother's Secret Life '84
Pray TV '82
A Long Way Home '81
Arthur Marks (1927-)
Monkey Hustle '77
J.D.'s Revenge '76
Friday Foster '75
Bucktown '75
Bonnie's Kids '73
Detroit 9000 '73
Togetherness '70
Ross Kagen Marks
The Twilight of the Golds '97
Homage '95
Richard Rarquand (1938-87)
Hearts of Fire '87
The Jagged Edge '85
Until September '84
Return of the Jedi '83
Eye of the Needle '81
The Legacy '79
David Marsh
Stormswept '95
Philip Marshak
Cataclysm '81
Dracula Sucks '79
Frank Marshall (1954-)
Eight Below '06
From the Earth to the Moon '98
Congo '95
Alive '93
Garry Marshall (1934-)
Georgia Rule '07
The Princess Diaries 2: Royal Engagement '04
Raising Helen '04
The Princess Diaries '01
Runaway Bride '99
The Other Sister '98
Dear God '96
Exit to Eden '94
Frankie and Johnny '91
Pretty Woman '90
Beaches '88
Overboard '87
Nothing in Common '86
The Flamingo Kid '84
Young Doctors in Love '82

Off Limits '53
Scared Stiff '53
Fancy Pants '50
Never a Dull Moment '50
My Friend Irma '49
The Perils of Pauline '47
Variety Girl '47
The Blue Dahlia '46
Monsieur Beaucaire '46
Murder, He Says '45
Star Spangled Rhythm '42
Valley of the Sun '42
Pot o' Gold '41
Texas '41
The Ghost Breakers '40
Destry Rides Again '39
You Can't Cheat an Honest Man '39
The Goldwyn Follies '38
In Old Kentucky '35
Life Begins at Forty '35
Show Them No Mercy '35
365 Nights in Hollywood '34
Pack Up Your Troubles '32
Neil Marshall (1970-)
Doomsday '08
The Descent '05
Dog Soldiers '01
Penny Marshall (1947-)
Riding in Cars with Boys '01
The Preacher's Wife '96
Renaissance Man '94
A League of Their Own '92
Awakenings '90
Big '88
Jumpin' Jack Flash '86
Rob Marshall (1960-)
Memoirs of a Geisha '05
Chicago '02
Annie '99
Scott Marshall
Blonde Ambition '07
Keeping Up with the Steins '06
Tonie Marshall
Venus Beauty Institute '98
Pas Tres Catholique '93
William Marshall (1924-2003)
The Phantom Planet '61
Adventures of Captain Fabian '51
Charles Martin (1910-83)
One Man Jury '78
How to Seduce a Woman '74
Dead Right '68
Death of a Scoundrel '56
My Dear Secretary '49
D'Urville Martin (1938-84)
Fass Black '77
Dolemite '75
Eugenio (Gene) Martin (1935-)
Bad Man's River '72
Horror Express '72
Pancho Villa '72
It Happened at Nightmare Inn '70
Frank Martin
Elvis in Hollywood '93
Doctor Butcher M.D. '80
Gregory Mars Martin
See Mars Callahan
Richard Martin (1956-)
Air Bud 2: Golden Receiver '98
Wounded '97
White Tiger '95
Elizabeth R '72
Jacques Martineau (1963-)
Cote d'Azur '05
My Life on Ice '02
The Adventures of Felix '99
Jeanne and the Perfect Guy '98
Richard Martini (1955-)
Cannes Man '96
Limit '89
You Can't Hurry Love '88

Raymond Martino
Skyscraper '95
To the Limit '95
DaVinci's War '92
American Born '89
Sergio Martino (1938-)
American Tiger '89
Casablanca Express '89
The Opponent '89
Hands of Steel '86
After the Fall of New York '85
Scorpion with Two Tails '82
The Great Alligator '81
Screamers '80
Mountain of the Cannibal God '79
Day of the Maniac '77
The Cheaters '76
Sex with a Smile '76
Torso '73
Violent Professionals '73
Your Vice is a Closed Room and Only I Have the Key '72
The Case of the Scorpion's Tail '71
The Next Victim '71
The Scorpion's Tail '71
Blade of the Ripper '70
Leslie Martinson (1915-)
Return to Africa '89
The Fantastic World of D.C. Collins '84
The Kid with the 200 I.Q. '83
The Kid with the Broken Halo '82
Rescue from Gilligan's Island '78
Fathom '67
Batman '66
PT 109 '63
Hot Rod Girl '56
The Atomic Kid '54
Andrew Marton (1904-92)
Africa Texas Style '67
Around the World Under the Sea '65
Clarence, the Cross-eyed Lion '65
The Longest Day '62
The Thin Red Line '64
Green Fire '55
Gypsy Colt '54
Men of the Fighting Lady '54
Secret of Stamboul '36
Mike Marvin
Sunstorm '01
Wishman '93
The Wraith '87
Hamburger... The Motion Picture '86
Francesco Maselli (1930-)
Time of Indifference '64
Love in the City '53
Noel Mason Smith (1895-1955)
Fighting Pilot '35
The Night Patrol '26
Stelvio Massi (1929-2004)
Black Cobra 2 '89
The Black Cobra '87
Fearless '77
Joe Massot
Space Riders '83
Wonderwall: The Movie '69
Quentin Masters (1946-)
Dangerous Summer '82
The Stud '78
Thumb Tripping '72
Peter Masterson (1934-)
Lost Junction '03
Mermaid '00
The Only Thrill '97
Lily Dale '96
Arctic Blue '93
Night Game '89
Blood Red '88
Full Moon in Blue Water '88

The Trip to Bountiful '85

Nico Mastorakis (1941-)
Hired to Kill '91
Ninja Academy '90
In the Cold of the Night '89
Glitch! '88
Nightmare at Noon '87
The Wind '87
Zero Boys '86
Blind Date '84
Next One '84
Sky High '84

Camillo Mastrocinque (1901-69)
An Angel for Satan '66
Full Hearts & Empty Pockets '63

Armand Mastroianni (1948-)
Pandemic '07
The Celestine Prophecy '06
Though None Go With Me '06
Nowhere to Land '00
Fatal Error '99
First Daughter '99
One of Her Own '97
Robin Cook's Invasion '97
Cameron's Closet '89
Double Revenge '89
Distortions '87
The Supernaturals '86
Killing Hour '84
He Knows You're Alone '80

Toshio Masuda (1927-)
Zero '84
Last Days of Planet Earth '74

Eddy Matalon
Sweet Killing '93
Blackout '78
Cathy's Curse '77

Rudolph Maté (1898-1964)
For the First Time '59
Deep Six '58
Three Violent People '57
The Far Horizons '55
The Violent Men '55
The Black Shield of Falworth '54
Second Chance '53
The Green Glove '52
When Worlds Collide '51
Branded '50
Union Station '50
The Dark Past '49
D.O.A. '49

Ted Mather
Faith '90
Body Beat '88

Tim Matheson (1947-)
In the Company of Spies '99
Buried Alive 2 '97
Tails You Live, Heads You're Dead '95
Breach of Conduct '94

Shue Matsubayashi (1920-)
Last War '63
Attack Squadron '63
I Bombed Pearl Harbor '60

Bruno Mattei (1931-2007)
Strike Commando '87
Caged Women '84
Seven Magnificent Gladiators '84
Hell of the Living Dead '83
Rats '83
SS Girls '77

Charles Matthau (1964-)
The Grass Harp '95
Doin' Time on Planet Earth '88

Paul Matthews
Hooded Angels '00
Breeders '97
Grim '95

Arne Mattson (1920-95)
The Girl '86
The Doll '62

Norman Maurer (1926-86)
The Outlaws Is Coming! '65
Around the World in a Daze '63

Robert (Roberto) Mauri (1924-)
Animal Called Man '87
Invincible Gladiators '64
The Slaughter of the Vampires '62

Garth Maxwell (1963-)
When Love Comes '98
Jack Be Nimble '94

Ronald F. Maxwell (1947-)
Gods and Generals '03
Gettysburg '93
Kidco '83
Little Darlings '80

Bradford May
Darkman 2: The Return of Durant '94
Marilyn & Bobby: Her Final Affair '94
Lethal Lolita—Amy Fisher: My Story '92
Mortal Sins '92

Elaine May (1932-)
Ishtar '87
Mikey & Nicky '76
The Heartbreak Kid '72
A New Leaf '71

Joe May (1880-1954)
The House of the Seven Gables '40
The Invisible Man Returns '40
Music in the Air '34

Russ Mayberry
The Indian Tomb '21
Probe '72
The Jesus Trip '71

John Maybury (1958-)
The Jacket '05
Love Is the Devil '98

Daisy von Scherler Mayer (1965-)
The Guru '02
Madeline '98
Woo '97
Party Girl '94

Michael Mayer (1960-)
Flicka '06
A Home at the End of the World '04

Paul Mayersberg (1941-)
Nightfall '88
Captive '87

Les Mayfield
Code Name: The Cleaner '07
The Man '05
American Outlaws '01
Blue Streak '99
Flubber '97
Miracle on 34th Street '94
Encino Man '92

Tony Maylam (1943-)
Split Second '92
The Burning '82
The Riddle of the Sands '79

Ken Maynard (1895-1973)
Honor of the Range '34
The Fiddlin' Buckaroo '33
Strawberry Roan '33

Archie Mayo (1891-1968)
Angel on My Shoulder '46
A Night in Casablanca '46
Crash Dive '43
Orchestra Wives '42
Charley's Aunt '41
The Great American Broadcast '41
House Across the Bay '40
They Shall Have Music '39
The Adventures of Marco Polo '38
The Black Legion '37
Petrified Forest '36
The Case of the Lucky Legs '35
The Mayor of Hell '33
Night After Night '32
Illicit '31
Svengali '31

Michael Mazo
Crackerjack '94
Time Runner '92

Paul Mazursky (1930-)
Coast to Coast '04
Winchell '98
Faithful '96
The Pickle '93
Scenes from a Mall '91
Enemies, a Love Story '89
Moon over Parador '88
Down and Out in Beverly Hills '86
Moscow on the Hudson '84
The Tempest '82
Willie & Phil '80
An Unmarried Woman '78
Next Stop, Greenwich Village '76
Harry and Tonto '74
Blume in Love '73
Alex in Wonderland '70
Bob & Carol & Ted & Alice '69

Des McAnuff
The Adventures of Rocky & Bullwinkle '00
Cousin Bette '98

Don McBrearty
Luna: Spirit of the Whale '07
Chasing Freedom '04
Race to Freedom: The Story of the Underground Railroad '94
Really Weird Tales '86
Coming Out Alive '84
American Nightmare '81

Jim McBride (1941-)
Meat Loaf: To Hell and Back '00
The Informant '97
Pronto '97
Uncovered '94
The Wrong Man '93
Blood Ties '92
Great Balls of Fire '89
The Big Easy '87
Breathless '83
Hot Times '74
Glen and Randa '71
David Holzman's Diary '67

Jon McBride
Terror House '97
Cannibal Campout '88
Woodchipper Massacre '89

Howard McCain
Shadow of a Scream '97
No Dessert Dad, Till You Mow the Lawn '94

Rod McCall
Lewis and Clark and George '97

James McCalmont
Escape from Safehaven '88
Underground Terror '88

Tim McCanlies (1953-)
Secondhand Lions '03
Dancer, Texas—Pop. 81 '98

Tim McCann (1968-)
Revolution #9 '01
Desolation Angels '95

Leo McCarey (1898-1969)
Rally 'Round the Flag, Boys! '58
An Affair to Remember '57
Good Sam '48
Going My Way '44
Once Upon a Honeymoon '42
Love Affair '39
The Awful Truth '37
Make Way for Tomorrow '37
Ruggles of Red Gap '35
Belle of the Nineties '34
Six of a Kind '34
Duck Soup '33
The Kid from Spain '32

Ray McCarey (1898-1948)
So This Is Washington '43
You Can't Fool Your Wife '40

John P. McCarthy (1884-1962)
Marked Trails '44
Raiders of the Border '44
The Lion Man '36
Song of the Gringo '36
The Return of Casey Jones '34

Michael McCarthy (1917-59)
Operation Amsterdam '60
Crow Hollow '52

Thomas (Tom) McCarthy (1969-)
The Visitor '07
The Station Agent '03

John McCauley
Rattlers '76
Deadly Intruder '84

Michael McClary
Annie O '95

Michael (Mick) McCleery
Curse of the Starving Class '94

Bret McCormick (1958-)
Time Tracers '97
Rumble in the Streets '96
Blood on the Badge '92
Tabloid! '88

Nelson McCormick
Prom Night '08
Operation Sandman: Warriors in Hell '00

George McCowan (1927-95)
July Group '81
Return to Fantasy Island '77
Murder on Flight 502 '75
Frogs '72
Savage Run '70
The Ballad of Andy Crocker '69
Black Brigade '69

Ian McCrudden
Trailer, the Movie '99

Bruce McCulloch (1961-)
Stealing Harvard '02
Superstar '99
Dog Park '98

Jim McCullough
The Aurora Encounter '85
Charge of the Model T's '76
Where the Red Fern Grows: Part 2 '92
Mountaintop Motel Massacre '86

Frank McDonald (1899-1980)
Wyatt Earp: Return to Tombstone '94
Thunder Pass '54
Sioux City Sue '46
Song of Arizona '46
Under Nevada Skies '45
Along the Navaho Trail '45
Bells of Rosarita '45
Sunset in El Dorado '45
Apache Chief '50
The Big Sombrero '49
Lights of Old Santa Fe '47
My Pal Trigger '46
Treasure of Fear '45
Gambler's Choice '44
One Body Too Many '44
Take It Big '44
Timber Queen '44
Wildcat '42
Flying Wild '41

Bruce McDonald (1959-)
Picture Claire '01
Hard Core Logo '96
Dance Me Outside '95

Michael James McDonald (1964-)
The Crazysitter '94

Rodney McDonald
Nautilus '99
Sonic Impact '99
Surface to Air '98
Steel Sharks '97
Scorned 2 '96
Desire '95
Night Eyes 4: Fatal Passion '95
Night Eyes 2 '91

Charles McDougall
Call Me: The Rise and Fall of Heidi Fleiss '04

Edward T. McDougal
The Prodigy '98
One for the Road '82

Ross McElwee (1947-)
Time Indefinite '93
Sherman's March '86

Bernard McEveety (1924-2004)
Roughnecks '80
Centennial '78
The Bears & I '74
One Little Indian '73
Napoleon and Samantha '72
The Brotherhood of Satan '71

Vincent McEveety
Gunsmoke: Return to Dodge '87
Amy '81
Herbie Goes Bananas '80
The Apple Dumpling Gang Rides Again '79
Herbie Goes to Monte Carlo '77
Gus '76
The Treasure of Matecumbe '76
The Castaway Cowboy '74
Charley and the Angel '73
Superdad '73
Menace on the Mountain '70
Smoke '70
The Million Dollar Duck '71
Firecreek '68

McG (1968-)
We Are Marshall '06
Charlie's Angels: Full Throttle '03
Charlie's Angels '00

William F. McGaha
Iron Horsemen '71
The Speed Lovers '68

William McGann (1893-1977)
American Empire '42
In Old California '42
Dr. Christian Meets the Women '40

Scott McGehee
Bee Season '05
The Deep End '01
Suture '93

Robert McGinley
Shredder Orpheus '89

Scott McGinnis (1958-)
Caroline at Midnight '93

John (Jim) Paterson McGowan (1880-1952)
Roaring Six Guns '37
Rough Ridin' Rhythm '37
Deadwood Pass '33
Drum Taps '33
Lone Bandit '33
The Outlaw Tamer '33
Red Signals '27
Blood and Steel '25

Robert McGowan (1882-1955)
Tomboy '40
Frontier Justice '35

Stuart E. McGowan (1904-99)
The Billion Dollar Hobo '78
The Showdown '50

Tom McGowan
Savage Journey '83

Joseph McGrath (1930-)
The Strange Case of the End of Civilization as We Know It '77
Digby, the Biggest Dog in the World '73
The Magic Christian '69

Douglas McGrath (1958-)
Infamous '06
Nicholas Nickleby '02
Company Man '00
Emma '96

Sean McGregor
Devil Times Five '74
Gentle Savage '73
Gunsmoke: Return to Dodge '87

Mary McGuckian (1963-)
The Bridge of San Luis Rey '05
This Is the Sea '96

Paul McGuigan (1963-)
Lucky Number Slevin '06
Wicker Park '04
The Reckoning '03
Gangster No. 1 '00
The Acid House '98

Doug McHenry
Kingdom Come '01
Jason's Lyric '94
House Party 2: The Pajama Jam '91

Christian McIntire (1964-)
Antibody '02
Lost Voyage '01

Chris T. McIntyre
Backstreet Justice '93
Border Shootout '90

David McNally
Kangaroo Jack '02
Coyote Ugly '00

Sean McNamara (1963-)
Bratz '07

Adam McKay (1968-)
Step Brothers '08
Talladega Nights: The Ballad of Ricky Bobby '06
Anchorman: The Legend of Ron Burgundy '04

Cole McKay
The Underground '97
Star Hunter '95
The Double O Kid '92
Scavengers '87

Jim McKay
Angel Rodriguez '05
Our Song '01
Girls Town '95

Andrew V. McLaglen (1920-)
On Wings of Eagles '86
The Dirty Dozen: The Next Mission '85
Sahara '83
The Blue and the Gray '82
The Shadow Riders '82
Sea Wolves '81
ffolkes '80
Breakthrough '78
Wild Geese '78
Banjo Hackett '76
The Last Hard Men '76
Mitchell '75
Cahill: United States Marshal '73
Chisum '70
The Undefeated '69
Bandolero! '68
The Devil's Brigade '68
Hellfighters '68
The Way West '67
Monkeys, Go Home! '66
The Rare Breed '66
Shenandoah '65
McLintock! '63

Lucky McKee (1975-)
Masters of Horror: Sick Girl '06
The Woods '03
May '02

Duncan McLachlan
Rudyard Kipling's the Second Jungle Book: Mowgli and Baloo '97
Born Wild '95

Norman Z. McLeod (1898-1964)
Alias Jesse James '59
Casanova's Big Night '54
Never Wave at a WAC '52
Let's Dance '50
The Paleface '48
The Road to Rio '47
The Secret Life of Walter Mitty '47
Kid from Brooklyn '46
Panama Hattie '42
Lady Be Good '41
Little Men '40
Topper Takes a Trip '39
Topper '37
Pennies from Heaven '36
Here Comes Cookie '35
It's a Gift '34
Horse Feathers '32
Monkey Business '31
Touchdown '31

Tom McLoughlin (1950-)
Murder in Greenwich '02
The Unsaid '01
Behind the Mask '99
Journey '95
The Yarn Princess '94
The Fire Next Time '93
Sometimes They Come Back '91
Date with an Angel '87
Friday the 13th, Part 6: Jason Lives '86
One Dark Night '82

David McNally
Kangaroo Jack '02
Coyote Ugly '00

Sean McNamara (1963-)
Bratz '07

Don McLennan (1949-)
Slate, Wyn & Me '87
Hard Knocks '80

John McNaughton (1950-)
Lansky '99
Wild Things '98
Normal Life '96
Girls in Prison '94
Mad Dog and Glory '93
Sex, Drugs, Rock & Roll: Eric Bogosian '91
Henry: Portrait of a Serial Killer '90
The Borrower '89

John McPherson (1941-2007)
Incident at Deception Ridge '94
Fade to Black '93
Dirty Work '92
Strays '91

John McTiernan (1951-)
Basic '03
Rollerball '02
The 13th Warrior '99
The Thomas Crown Affair '99
Die Hard: With a Vengeance '95
Last Action Hero '93
Medicine Man '92
The Hunt for Red October '90
Die Hard '88
Predator '87
Nomads '86

Nancy Meckler
Alive and Kicking '96
Sister My Sister '94

Shane Meadows (1972-)
This Is England '06
Dead Man's Shoes '04
Once Upon a Time in the Midlands '02
24-7 '97

Nick Mead
Swing '98
Bank Robber '93

Peter Medak (1940-)
Masters of Horror: The Washingtonians '07
Species 2 '98
The Hunchback '97
Pontiac Moon '94
Romeo Is Bleeding '93
Let Him Have It '91
The Krays '90
The Men's Club '86
Breakin' Through '84
The Emperor's New Clothes '84
Pinocchio '83
The Snow Queen '83
Snow White and the Seven Dwarfs '83
Zorro, the Gay Blade '81
The Babysitter '80
The Changeling '80
The Odd Job '78
Ghost in the Noonday Sun '74
The Ruling Class '72
A Day in the Death of Joe Egg '71
Negatives '68

Don Medford (1917-)
The Organization '71

Julio Medem (1958-)
Sex and Lucia '01
Lovers of the Arctic Circle '98
Tierra '95
The Red Squirrel '93
Vacas '91

Cary Medoway (1949-)
The Heavenly Kid '85
Paradise Motel '84

Alexander Medvedkin
Happiness '32

Francis Megahy (1937-)
The Disappearance of Kevin Johnson '95
Red Sun Rising '94
Taffin '88
Freelance '71

Alan Mehrez
Bloodsport 3 '97
Bloodsport 2: The Next Kumite '95

Deepa Mehta (1950-)
Water '05
Earth '98
Fire '96
Camilla '94

Gus Meins (1893-1940)
The Gentleman from California '37
March of the Wooden Soldiers '34

Fernando Meirelles (1955-)
The Constant Gardener '05
City of God '02

Norbert Meisel (1930-)
Night Children '89
Walking the Edge '83
The Adultress '77

Ib Melchior (1917-)
The Time Travelers '64
The Angry Red Planet '59

George Melford (1877-1961)
Cowboy Counselor '33
The Dude Bandit '33
Man of Action '33
Boiling Point '32
Dracula (Spanish Version) '31
East of Borneo '31
Moran of the Lady Letty '22
The Sheik '21

James Melkonian
The Jerky Boys '95
The Stoned Age '94

Jean-Pierre Melville (1917-73)
Le Cercle Rouge '70
Army of Shadows '69
Le Samourai '67
Le Doulos '61
Leon Morin, Priest '61
Bob le Flambeur '55
Les Enfants Terrible '50
La Silence de la Mer '47

Christopher Menaul
One Kill '00
The Passion of Ayn Rand '99
Feast of July '95
Fatherland '94
Prime Suspect '92
A Dangerous Man: Lawrence after Arabia '91

George Mendeluk (1948-)
Men of Means '99
Meatballs 3 '87
Doin' Time '85
The Kidnapping of the President '80
Stone Cold Dead '80

Lothar Mendes (1894-1974)
Moonlight Sonata '38
The Man Who Could Work Miracles '37
Power '34
Strangers in Love '32
Personal Maid '31

Sam Mendes (1965-)
Jarhead '05
Road to Perdition '02
American Beauty '99

Fernando Mendez (1908-66)
The Living Coffin '58
The Vampire's Coffin '58
The Vampire '57
Black Pit of Dr. M '47

Ramon Menendez
Money for Nothing '93
Stand and Deliver '88

Chris Menges (1940-)
The Lost Son '98
Second Best '94
Crisscross '92
A World Apart '88

Jiri Menzel (1938-)
My Sweet Little Village '86
Larks on a String '68
Closely Watched Trains '66

William Cameron Menzies (1896-1957)
Invaders from Mars '53
The Thief of Bagdad '40
Things to Come '36
Chandu the Magician '32

Ismail Merchant (1936-2005)
The Mystic Masseur '01
Cotton Mary '99
The Proprietor '96
In Custody '94
The Courtesans of Bombay '85

Burgess Meredith (1908-97)
Yin & Yang of Mr. Go '71
Man on the Eiffel Tower '48

Michael Meredith
Three Days of Rain '03

James Merendino (1967-)
SLC Punk! '99
The Real Thing '97
A River Made to Drown In '97
Hard Drive '94
Terrified '94
Witchcraft 4: Virgin Heart '92

Joseph Merhi (1953-)
Executive Target '97
Riot '96
Last Man Standing '95
Rage '95
The Sweeper '95
Direct Hit '93
To Be the Best '93
Zero Tolerance '93
C.I.A.: Code Name Alexa '92
Magic Kid '92
Maximum Force '92
Final Impact '91
The Last Riders '90
Night of the Wilding '90
Repo Jake '90
Emperor of the Bronx '89
L.A. Vice '89
Midnight Warrior '89
The Glass Jungle '88
L.A. Crackdown 2 '88
L.A. Crackdown '87
L.A. Heat '88
Fresh Kill '87
Heat Street '87
Hollywood in Trouble '87
The Killing Game '87
Mayhem '87
The Newlydeads '87

Edmund Elias Merhige (1964-)
Suspect Zero '04
Shadow of the Vampire '00

Jose Luis Merino (1927-)
The Hanging Woman '72
Scream of the Demon Lover '71
Hell Commandos '69

Agnes Merlet (1959-)
Artemisia '97
The Son of the Shark '93

Laurence Merrick (1926-77)
Black Bikers from Hell '70
The Outlaw Bikers—Gang Wars '70

Keith Merrill (1940-)
The Twelve Dogs of Christmas '05
Windwalker '81
Take Down '79
Three Warriors '77

William Mesa (1940-)
DNA '97
The Black Gate '95
Galaxis '95

Marta Meszaros (1931-)
Adoption '75
The Girl '68
The Girl '68

Alan Metter
Billboard Dad '98
Police Academy 7: Mission to Moscow '94
Moving '88
Back to School '86
Girls Just Want to Have Fun '85

Alan Metzger
My Husband's Double Life '01
Snap Decision '01
New Eden '94
Fatal Exposure '91
Red Wind '91

Radley Metzger (1929-)
The Princess & the Call Girl '84
The Cat and the Canary '79
Score '72
The Lickerish Quartet '70
Camille 2000 '69
Therese & Isabelle '67
Carmen, Baby '66
The Alley Cats '65
The Dirty Girls '64
Dark Odyssey '57

Andrew Meyer (1943-87)
Tidal Wave '75
Night of the Cobra Woman '72

Kevin Meyer
Perfect Alibi '94
Under Investigation '93
Invasion of Privacy '92
Civil War Diary '90

Nicholas Meyer (1945-)
Vendetta '99
Company Business '91
Star Trek 6: The Undiscovered Country '91
The Deceivers '88
Volunteers '85
The Day After '83
Star Trek 2: The Wrath of Khan '82
Time After Time '79

Russ Meyer (1922-2004)
Beneath the Valley of the Ultra-Vixens '79
Supervixens '75
Blacksnake! '73
Beyond the Valley of the Dolls '70
Faster, Pussycat! Kill! Kill! '65
Motor Psycho '65
Fanny Hill: Memoirs of a Woman of Pleasure '64

Turi Meyer (1964-)
Candyman 3: Day of the Dead '98
Sleepstalker: The Sandman's Last Rites '94

Janet Meyers
The Ripper '97

Nancy Meyers (1949-)
The Holiday '06
Something's Gotta Give '03
What Women Want '00
The Parent Trap '98

Menno Meyjes (1954-)
Martian Child '07
Max '02

Eric Meza
The Breaks '99
House Party 3 '94

Richard Michaels (1936-)
Father and Scout '94
Backfield in Motion '91
Lethal Charm '90
Indiscreet '88
Rockabye '86

Oscar Micheaux (1884-1951)
Lying Lips '39
Girl from Chicago '32
Body and Soul '24

Roger Michell (1957-)
Venus '06
Enduring Love '04
The Mother '03
Changing Lanes '02
Notting Hill '99
The Buddha of Suburbia '92

Anne-Marie Mieville (1945-)
Soft and Hard '85
Scenario du Film Passion '82

Radu Mihaileanu (1958-)
Train of Life '98
Trahir '93

George Mihalka (1952-)
Cruel and Unusual '01
Jack Higgins' The Windsor Protocol '97
Jack Higgins' Thunder Point '97
Bullet to Beijing '95

(continued)
- Relative Fear '95
- Deceptions 2: Edge of Deception '94
- Psychic '91
- Hostile Takeover '88
- Straight Line '88
- Eternal Evil '87
- My Bloody Valentine '81
- Pick-Up Summer '79

Takashi Miike (1960-)
- Masters of Horror: Imprint '05
- Three ... Extremes '04
- Gozu '03
- Graveyard of Honor '02
- Audition '99

Ted V. Mikels (1929-)
- WarCat '88
- Aftermath '85
- 10 Violent Women '79
- Girl in Gold Boots '69
- The Astro-Zombies '67
- The Black Klansman '66

Nikita Mikhalkov (1945-)
- Burnt by the Sun '94
- Anna '93
- Close to Eden '90
- Dark Eyes '87
- Oblomov '81
- A Slave of Love '78
- An Unfinished Piece for a Player Piano '77
- The Virgin and the Gypsy '70

Christopher Miles (1939-)
- Priest of Love '81
- That Lucky Touch '75

Lewis Milestone (1895-1980)
- Mutiny on the Bounty '62
- Ocean's 11 '60
- Pork Chop Hill '59
- The Halls of Montezuma '50
- The Red Pony '49
- The North Star '43
- The Purple Heart '44
- Edge of Darkness '43
- The North Star '43
- A Walk in the Sun '46
- Arch of Triumph '48
- The Strange Love of Martha Ivers '46
- The Front Page '31
- Rain '32
- Hallelujah, I'm a Bum '33
- The Night of Nights '39
- Of Mice and Men '39
- The General Died at Dawn '36
- Paris in Spring '35
- The Garden of Eden '28
- All Quiet on the Western Front '30

John Milius (1944-)
- Rough Riders '97
- Flight of the Intruder '90
- Farewell to the King '89
- Conan the Barbarian '82
- Big Wednesday '78
- The Wind and the Lion '75
- Dillinger '73

Gerry Mill
- Second Chance '80
- The Duchess of Duke Street '78

Ray Milland (1905-86)
- Panic in the Year Zero! '62
- Lisbon '56
- A Man Alone '55

Catherine Millar
- Twisted '96
- Darlings of the Gods '90

Gavin Millar (1938-)
- Reunion '88
- The Crow Road '96
- Catherine Cookson's The Dwelling Place '94
- My Friend Walter '93
- A Murder of Quality '90
- Tidy Endings '88
- Dreamchild '85
- Secrets '82

Stuart Millar (1929-)
- Rooster Cogburn '75
- When the Legends Die '72

Nick Millard
- Gunbast '74
- Terrorists '88

Claude Miller (1942-)
- Alias Betty '01
- The Accompanist '93
- Class Act '91
- This Sweet Sickness '77
- The Best Way '76

David Miller (1909-92)
- Bittersweet Love '76
- Executive Action '73
- Hail, Hero! '69
- Captain Newman, M.D. '63
- Back Street '61
- Midnight Lace '60
- The Story of Esther Costello '57
- The Opposite Sex '56
- Diane '55
- Love Happy '52
- Our Very Own '50
- Flying Tigers '42
- Billy the Kid '41

George Miller (1943-)
- Andre '94
- Gross Misconduct '93
- The Aviator '85
- Nevil Shute's The Far Country '85

George Miller (1945-)
- Happy Feet '06
- Over the Hill '93
- Frozen Assets '92
- NeverEnding Story 2: The Next Chapter '91
- Les Patterson Saves the World '90
- Goodbye, Miss 4th of July '88
- The Man from Snowy River '84
- All the Rivers Run '84

Tom Milo
- Cybermutt '02
- Babe: Pig in the City '98
- Robinson Crusoe '96
- Silver Strand '95
- Lorenzo's Oil '92
- Miracle Down Under '87
- The Witches of Eastwick '87
- Mad Max: Beyond Thunderdome '85
- Twilight Zone: The Movie '83
- The Road Warrior '82
- Mad Max '80

Harvey Miller (1936-99)
- Getting Away With Murder '96

Michael Miner
- Deadly Weapon '88

Steve Miner (1951-)
- Texas Rangers '01
- Lake Placid '99
- Halloween: H20 '98
- Big Bully '95
- My Father the Hero '93
- Forever Young '92
- Warlock '91
- Wild Hearts Can't Be Broken '91
- House '86
- Soul Man '86
- Friday the 13th, Part 3 '82
- Friday the 13th, Part 2 '81

David Mitchell
- UKM: The Ultimate Killing Machine '06
- Downhill Willie '96
- Mask of Death '97
- A Woman's Face '38
- Intermezzo '36
- Swedenhielms '35

Michael Miller
- Bad Medicine '85
- Dangerous Passion '95
- Silent Rage '82
- National Lampoon's Class Reunion '82
- Silent Witness '85
- Outside Chance '78

Anthony Minghella (1954-2008)
- Breaking and Entering '06

Wu Ming
- See Xiaoshuai Wang

Sergio Mimica-Gezzan
- Sundance '04

Ilias Milonakos (1941-)
- Operation Orient '78
- Emmanuelle, the Queen '79

Alec Mills (1932-)
- Dead Sleep '91
- Bloodmoon '90

Bill Milling
- Body Trouble '92
- Caged Fury '90
- Smooth Talker '90
- Lauderdale '89

Andy Milligan (1929-91)
- The Weirdo '89
- Carnage '84
- Legacy of Horror '78
- The Rats Are Coming! The Werewolves Are Here! '72
- Fleshpot on 42nd Street '71
- Torture Dungeon '70
- The Body Beneath '70
- The Ghastly Ones '68

Troy Miller
- Dumb and Dumberer: When Harry Met Lloyd '03
- Jack Frost '98

Sharron Miller
- The Woman Who Willed a Miracle '83

Robert Ellis Miller (1932-)
- House of the Dead '78
- Bed & Breakfast '92
- Brenda Starr '86
- Her Life as a Man '83
- Reuben, Reuben '83
- The Baltimore Bullet '80
- The Girl from Petrovka '74
- The Heart Is a Lonely Hunter '68
- Sweet November '68
- Any Wednesday '66

Randall Miller
- Marilyn Hotchkiss' Ballroom Dancing & Charm School '06
- The Sixth Man '97
- Houseguest '94
- Class Act '91

Rebecca Miller (1962-)
- The Ballad of Jack and Rose '05
- Personal Velocity: Three Portraits '02
- Angela '94

Neal Miller
- Raising Flagg '06
- Mr. Wonderful '93

Rob Minkoff
- The Forbidden Kingdom '09
- The Haunted Mansion '03
- Stuart Little 2 '02
- Stuart Little '99
- The Lion King '94

David Mirkin (1955-)
- Heartbreakers '01
- Romy and Michele's High School Reunion '97

Emilio P. Miraglio (1924-)
- The Night Evelyn Came Out of the Grave '71

Kenji Misumi (1921-75)
- Halloween Night '90
- Night Eyes '90
- School Reunion '97

Bob Misiorowski
- Derailed '02
- Shark Attack '99
- On the Border '98
- Beyond Forgiveness '94
- Point of Impact '93
- Blink of an Eye '92

Bruce Mitchell (1880-1952)
- The Phantom Flyer '28
- Dynamite Dan '24

Vincente Minnelli (1903-86)
- A Matter of Time '76
- On a Clear Day You Can See Forever '70
- Goodbye Charlie '64
- Two Weeks in Another Town '62
- Bells Are Ringing '60
- Home from the Hill '60
- Gigi '58
- Some Came Running '58
- Designing Woman '57
- Lust for Life '56
- Tea and Sympathy '56
- The Cobweb '55
- Kismet '55
- Brigadoon '54
- The Long, Long Trailer '54
- The Bad and the Beautiful '52
- An American in Paris '51
- Father's Little Dividend '51
- Father of the Bride '50
- Madame Bovary '49
- The Pirate '48
- Undercurrent '46
- Ziegfeld Follies '46
- The Clock '45
- Yolanda and the Thief '45
- Meet Me in St. Louis '44
- Cabin in the Sky '43
- I Dood It '43

Hayao Miyazaki (1941-)
- Howl's Moving Castle '04
- Spirited Away '01
- Princess Mononoke '98
- My Neighbor Totoro '88
- Kiki's Delivery Service '89

Kenji Mizoguchi (1898-1956)
- Street of Shame '56
- Princess Yang Kwei Fei '55
- Shin Heike Monogatari '55
- The Crucified Lovers '54
- Sansho the Bailiff '54
- A Geisha '53
- Ugetsu '53
- Life of Oharu '52
- Utamaro and His Five Women '46
- 47 Ronin, Part 1 '42
- 47 Ronin, Part 2 '42

Moshe Mizrahi (1931-)
- Every Time We Say Goodbye '86
- War & Love '84
- La Vie Continue '82
- I Sent a Letter to My Love '81
- Madame Rosa '77
- Rachel's Man '75
- The House on Chelouche Street '73

David Mitchell
- Dr. T and the Women '?'

Juan Lopez Moctezuma (1932-95)
- To Kill a Stranger '84
- I Love You Rosa '72

Jose Mojica Marins (1929-)
- Hallucinations of a Deranged Mind '76
- Awakenings of the Beast '68
- Strange World of Coffin Joe '72
- At Midnight, I'll Take Your Soul '63
- This Night I'll Possess Your Corpse '67

Hans Petter Moland (1955-)
- The Beautiful Country '04
- Aberdeen '00
- Zero Degrees Kelvin '95
- The Last Lieutenant '94

Gustaf Molander (1888-1973)
- Dollar '38
- Only One Night '42

Jacinto (Jack) Molina
- The Runner '99
- Club Med '83

Mike Mitchell
- See Paul Naschy
- Sky High '05
- Surviving Christmas '04
- Deuce Bigalow: Male Gigolo '99

William H. Molina
- The Last Assassins '96
- Where Truth Lies '96

Edouard Molinaro (1928-)
- Beaumarchais the Scoundrel '96
- Just the Way You Are '84
- La Cage aux Folles 3 '81
- La Cage aux Folles II '78
- Pain in the A— '77
- Dracula and Son '76

Dominik Moll (1962-)
- Lemming '05
- With a Friend Like Harry '00

Karen Moncrieff (1963-)
- The Dead Girl '06
- Blue Car '03

Paul Mones (1955-)
- Lovers and Liars '81
- Casanova '70 '65

Christopher Monger (1950-)
- The Englishman Who Went Up a Hill But Came Down a Mountain '95
- Just Like a Woman '95
- Waiting for the Light '90

Stephen R. Monroe
- House of 9 '05
- It Waits '05

Carl Monson (1932-88)
- Death Feud '89
- Blood Legacy '73
- Please Don't Eat My Mother '72

Edward Montagne (1912-2003)
- They Went That-a-Way & That-a-Way '78
- The Reluctant Astronaut '67
- McHale's Navy Joins the Air Force '65
- McHale's Navy '64

Leonide Moguy (1899-1976)
- Action in Arabia '44

Guiliano Montaldo
- Sacco & Vanzetti '71

Robert Bianchi Montero (1907-86)
- Tharus Son of Attila '67
- The Slasher '72
- Mondo Balordo '64

George Montgomery (1916-2000)
- From Hell to Borneo '64
- Samar '62
- The Steel Claw '61

Robert Montgomery (1904-81)
- The Gallant Hours '60
- Eye Witness '49

Jorge Montesi
- Bloodknot '95
- Soft Deceit '94
- Hush Little Baby '93
- Omen 4: The Awakening '91
- The Killing Man '94
- Ski School 2 '94
- Thunderground '89

Ron Moler
- Local Boys '02

Mario Monicelli (1915-)
- The Organizer '64
- Joyful Laughter '60
- Passionate Thief '60
- The Unfaithfuls '60
- The Great War '59
- Big Deal on Madonna Street '58

Andrew Mondshein (1962-)
- An Unfinished Life '05
- Evidence of Blood '97

Oswald Mitchell (1890-1949)
- The Dummy Talks '43
- The Temptress '49
- The Greed of William Hart '48

Sollace Mitchell
- Row Your Boat '98
- Call Me '88

Ron Moler
- Local Boys '02

Montgomery

Lady in the Lake '46

Vincent Monton (1949-)
The Hit '01
Fatal Bond '91
Windrider '86

Charles Philip Moore
Angel of Destruction '94
Black Belt '92
Dance with Death '90
Demon Wind '90

John Moore (1970-)
The Omen '06
Flight of the Phoenix '04
Behind Enemy Lines '01

Michael Moore (1954-)
Sicko '07
Fahrenheit 9/11 '04
Bowling for Columbine '02
The Big One '98
Canadian Bacon '94
Roger & Me '89

Michael D. Moore (1914-)
Buckskin '68
Fastest Guitar Alive '68
Paradise, Hawaiian Style '66
Talion '66

Robert Moore (1927-84)
Chapter Two '79
The Cheap Detective '78
Murder by Death '76

Tom (Thomas R.) Moore
Gepetto '00
Danielle Steel's Fine Things '91
'night, Mother '86
Return to Boggy Creek '77

Jocelyn Moorhouse (1960-)
A Thousand Acres '97
How to Make an American Quilt '95
Proof '91

Philippe Mora (1949-)
Burning Down the House '01
Mercenary 2: Thick and Thin '97
Pterodactyl Woman from Beverly Hills '97
Back in Business '96
Precious Find '96
Communion '89
Howling 3: The Marsupials '87
Death of a Soldier '85
Howling 2: Your Sister Is a Werewolf '85
A Breed Apart '84
Return of Captain Invincible '83
The Beast Within '82
Screams of a Winter Night '79
Mad Dog Morgan '76

Andrew Morahan
Murder in Mind '97
Highlander: The Final Dimension '94

Christopher Morahan (1929-)
Element of Doubt '96
Paper Mask '91
After Pilkington '88
Troubles '88
Clockwise '86
In the Secret State '85
The Jewel in the Crown '84

David Moreton
Testosterone '03
Edge of Seventeen '99

Nanni Moretti (1953-)
The Son's Room '00
Caro Diario '93
Palombella Rossa '89

Glen Morgan
Black Christmas '06
Willard '03

William M. Morgan (1899-1964)
The Violent Years '56
Fun & Fancy Free '47
Bells of Capistrano '42
Heart of the Rio Grande '42

Brett Morgen
Chicago 10 '07
The Kid Stays in the Picture '02

Louis Morneau
The Hitcher 2: I've Been Waiting '03
Bats '99
Made Men '99
Retroactive '97
Soldier Boyz '95
Carnosaur 2 '94
Final Judgment '92
Quake '92
To Die Standing '91

David Burton Morris (1948-)
The Three Lives of Karen '97
Hometown Boy Makes Good '93
Jersey Girl '92
Patti Rocks '88

Ernest Morris
Masters of Venus '62
The Tell-Tale Heart '60

Errol Morris (1948-)
The Fog of War: Eleven Lessons from the Life of Robert S. McNamara '03
Fast, Cheap & Out of Control '97
A Brief History of Time '92
The Dark Wind '91
The Thin Blue Line '88

Howard Morris (1919-2005)
Goin' Coconuts '78
Don't Drink the Water '69
With Six You Get Eggroll '68
Who's Minding the Mint? '67

Betsan Morris-Evans
Lady Audley's Secret '00
Dad Savage '97

Bruce Morrison
Tearaway '87
Shaker Run '85

Paul Morrison
Wondrous Oblivion '06
Solomon and Gaenor '98

Paul Morrissey (1939-)
Beethoven's Nephew '88
Spike of Bensonhurst '88
Mixed Blood '84
The Hound of the Baskervilles '77
Andy Warhol's Dracula '74
Andy Warhol's Frankenstein '74
Heat '72
Trash '70
Flesh '68

Hollingsworth Morse (1910-88)
Justin Morgan Had a Horse '81
Daughters of Satan '72
Pufnstuf '70
Rocky Jones, Space Ranger: Renegade Satellite '54

Terry Morse (1906-84)
Godzilla, King of the Monsters '56
Unknown World '51
Bells of San Fernando '47
Danny Boy '46
Fog Island '45
British Intelligence '40
Waterfront '39

Catherine Morshead
Me & Mrs. Jones '02

Edmund Mortimer (1874-1944)
The Prairie Pirate '25
County Fair '20

Rocky Morton (1955-)
Super Mario Bros. '93
D.O.A. '88

Gilbert Moses (1943-95)
A Fight for Jenny '90
The Fish that Saved Pittsburgh '79
Roots '77

Gregory Mosher
The Prime Gig '00
A Life in the Theater '93
Our Town '89

Elijah Moshinsky (1946-)
Genghis Cohn '93
The Green Man '91

Jonathan Mostow (1961-)
Terminator 3: Rise of the Machines '03
U-571 '00
From the Earth to the Moon '98
Breakdown '96
Flight of Black Angel '91
Beverly Hills Bodysnatchers '89

Greg Mottola (1964-)
Superbad '07

Malcolm Mowbray (1961-)
Sweet Revenge '98
Don't Tell Her It's Me '90
Out Cold '89
A Private Function '84

John Llewellyn Moxey (1925-)
Lady Mobster '88
Through Naked Eyes '87
Detective Sadie & Son '84
The Cradle Will Fall '83
The Solitary Man '82
Killjoy '81
Mating Season '81
No Place to Hide '81
The Children of An Lac '80
The Power Within '79
Sanctuary of Fear '79
President's Mistress '78
Intimate Strangers '77
Nightmare in Badham County '76
Conspiracy of Terror '75
A Strange and Deadly Occurrence '74
Where Have All the People Gone? '74
The Bounty Man '72
Home for the Holidays '72
The Night Stalker '71
Circus of Fear '67
Horror Hotel '60

Allan Moyle (1947-)
Weirdsville '07
Man in the Mirror: The Michael Jackson Story '04
Say Nothing '01
Jailbait? '00
Xchange '00
New Waterford Girl '99
Empire Records '95
The Gun in Betty Lou's Handbag '92
Pump Up the Volume '90
Times Square '80

Gabriele Muccino (1967-)
The Pursuit of Happyness '06
The Last Kiss '01

Russell Mulcahy (1953-)
Resident Evil: Extinction '07
Swimming Upstream '03
Lost Battalion '01
On the Beach '00
Resurrection '99
Russell Mulcahy's Tale of the Mummy '99
Silent Trigger '97
The Shadow '94
The Real McCoy '93
Blue Ice '92
Highlander 2: The Quickening '91
Ricochet '91
Highlander '86
Razorback '84

Peter Mullan (1954-)
The Magdalene Sisters '02
Orphans '97

Edward (Edoardo Mulargia) Muller (1925-)
Savage Island '85
Escape from Hell '79

Robert Mulligan (1925-)
The Man in the Moon '91
Clara's Heart '88
Kiss Me Goodbye '82
Bloodbrothers '78
Same Time, Next Year '78
The Other '72
Summer of '42 '71
The Pursuit of Happiness '70
The Stalking Moon '69
Up the Down Staircase '67
Inside Daisy Clover '65
Baby, the Rain Must Fall '64
Love with the Proper Stranger '63
To Kill a Mockingbird '62
Come September '61
The Great Impostor '61
The Rat Race '60
Fear Strikes Out '57

Claude Mulot (-1986)
Black Venus '83
The Immoral One '80

Christopher Munch (1962-)
Harry and Max '04
The Sleepy Time Gal '01
Color of a Brisk and Leaping Day '95
The Hours and Times '92

Richard W. Munchkin
Evil Obsession '96
Texas Payback '95
Fists of Iron '94
Guardian Angel '94
Out for Blood '93
Ring of Fire 2: Blood and Steel '92
Deadly Bet '91
Ring of Fire '91

Marc Munden
Miranda '02
Vanity Fair '99
Touching Evil '97

Jag Mundhra (1946-)
Tales of the Kama Sutra 2: Monsoon '98
Tales of the Kama Sutra: The Perfumed Garden '98
Monsoon '97
Irresistible Impulse '95
Improper Conduct '94
Eyewitness to Murder '93
Sexual Malice '93
Tropical Heat '93
L.A. Goddess '92
The Other Woman '92
Wild Cactus '92
Last Call '90
Legal Tender '90
Jigsaw Murders '89
Hack O'Lantern '87
Open House '86

Ian Mune (1941-)
The Bridge to Nowhere '86
Came a Hot Friday '85

Chris Munger
Kiss of the Tarantula '75
Black Starlet '74

Lance Mungia (1972-)
The Crow: Wicked Prayer '05
Six-String Samurai '98

Robert Munic (1968-)
They Call Me Sirr '00
In a Class of His Own '99
Timelock '99
L.A. Rules: The Pros and Cons of Breathing '94

Jimmy T. Murakami (1933-)
When the Wind Blows '86
Battle Beyond the Stars '80

Ryu Murakami (1952-)
Because of You '95
Tokyo Decadence '91

Toru Murakawa
New York Cop '94
Distant Justice '92

John Murlowski
Black Cadillac '03
Terminal Error '02
Santa with Muscles '96
The Secret Agent Club '96
Automatic '94
Amityville: A New Generation '93
Return of the Family Man '89

F.W. Murnau (1888-1931)
Tabu: A Story of the South Seas '31
City Girl '30
Sunrise '27
Faust '26
The Last Laugh '24
Nosferatu '22
Phantom '22
The Haunted Castle '21

Dudley Murphy (1897-1968)
One Third of a Nation '39
Emperor Jones '33

Edward Murphy
Heated Vengeance '87
Raw Force '81

Geoff Murphy (1938-)
Race Against Time '00
Fortress 2: Re-Entry '99
The Magnificent Seven '98
Don't Look Back '96
Under Siege 2: Dark Territory '95
Blind Side '93
The Last Outlaw '93
Freejack '92
Never Say Die '90
Young Guns 2 '90
Red King, White Knight '89
The Quiet Earth '85
Utu '83
Goodbye Pork Pie '81

Maurice Murphy (1939-)
15 Amore '98
Wet and Wild Summer '92
Fatty Finn '84
Doctors and Nurses '82

Ralph Murphy (1895-1967)
The Black Devils of Kali '55
Mickey '48
The Spirit of West Point '47
Panama Flo '32

Robin Murray
Season of Change '94
Dance '90

John Musker (1953-)
Treasure Planet '02
Hercules '97
Aladdin '92
The Little Mermaid '89
The Great Mouse Detective '86

Victoria Muspratt
White Wolves 3: Cry of the White Wolf '98
Inhumanoid '96

Floyd Mutrux (1941-)
There Goes My Baby '92
The Hollywood Knights '80
Aloha, Bobby and Rose '74

Alan Myerson
Holiday Affair '96
Police Academy 5: Assignment Miami Beach '88
Bayou Romance '86
Private Lessons '75
Steelyard Blues '73

Daniel Myrick
Believers '07
The Blair Witch Project '99

Petter Naess (1960-)
Mozart and the Whale '05
Elling '01

Ivan Nagy (1938-)
Skinner '93
Jane Doe '83
A Gun in the House '81
Captain America 2: Death Too Soon '79
Deadly Hero '75
Bad Charleston Charlie '73

Mira Nair (1957-)
The Namesake '06
Vanity Fair '04
Hysterical Blindness '02
Monsoon Wedding '01
My Own Country '98
Kama Sutra: A Tale of Love '96
The Perez Family '94
Mississippi Masala '92
Salaam Bombay! '88

Rodion Nakhapetov
Border Blues '03
Stir '98

Bharat Nalluri (1965-)
Miss Pettigrew Lives for a Day '08
The Crow: Salvation '00
Killing Time '97

Silvio Narizzano (1927-)
The Body in the Library '84
Why Shoot the Teacher '79
The Class of Miss MacMichael '78
Bloodbath '76
Redneck '73
Loot... Give Me Money, Honey! '70
Blue '68
Georgy Girl '66
Die! Die! My Darling! '65
24 Hours in a Woman's Life '61

Mikio Naruse (1905-69)
When a Woman Ascends the Stairs '60
Late Chrysanthemums '54
Mother '52

Paul Naschy (1934-)
The Craving '80
Human Beasts '80
Inquisition '76

Vincenzo Natali (1969-)
Paris, Je t'aime '06
Cypher '02
Cube '98

Mort Nathan
National Lampoon's Van Wilder 2: The Rise of Taj '06
Boat Trip '03

Bill Naud
Ricky 1 '88
Whodunit '82

Gregory Nava (1949-)
Bordertown '06
Why Do Fools Fall in Love? '98
Selena '96
My Family '94
A Time of Destiny '88
El Norte '83

Ray Nazarro (1902-86)
Dog Eat Dog '64
Kansas Pacific '53
Indian Uprising '51
Blazing Across the Pecos '48

Ronald Neame (1911-)
Foreign Body '86
First Monday in October '81
Hopscotch '80
Meteor '79
The Odessa File '74
The Poseidon Adventure '72
Scrooge '70
The Prime of Miss Jean Brodie '69
Gambit '66
The Chalk Garden '64
I Could Go on Singing '63
Tunes of Glory '60
The Horse's Mouth '58
Windom's Way '57

'55
The Man Who Never Was '55
The Promoter '52

Hal Needham (1931-)
Hostage Hotel '00
Body Slam '87
Rad '86
Cannonball Run 2 '84
Stroker Ace '83
Megaforce '82
Cannonball Run '81
Smokey and the Bandit 2 '80
The Villain '79
Hooper '78
Smokey and the Bandit '77

The Golden Salamander '51

Jean Negulesco (1900-93)
The Invincible Six '68
The Best of Everything '59
Daddy Long Legs '55
Three Coins in the Fountain '54
A Woman's World '54
How to Marry a Millionaire '53
Titanic '53
Phone Call from a Stranger '52
Three Came Home '50
Johnny Belinda '48
Road House '48
Humoresque '46
The Mask of Dimitrios '44

Marshall Neilan (1891-1958)
Swing It, Professor '37
Vagabond Lover '29
Daddy Long Legs '19
Amarilly of Clothesline Alley '18
Stella Maris '18
Rebecca of Sunnybrook Farm '17

Alberto Negrin (1940-)
Voyage of Terror: The Achille Lauro Affair '90
Mussolini & I '85

Gary Nelson
Melanie Darrow '97
Revolver '92
The Lookalike '90
Get Smart, Again! '89
Noble House '88
White Phantom: Enemy of Darkness '87
Jimmy the Kid '82
The Black Hole '79
Freaky Friday '76
Santee '73
Molly & Lawless John '72

Gene Nelson (1920-96)
Harum Scarum '65
Kissin' Cousins '64

Jessie Nelson
I Am Sam '01
Corrina, Corrina '94

Ralph Nelson (1916-87)
Christmas Lilies of the Field '84
A Hero Ain't Nothin' but a Sandwich '78
The Lady Confesses '78
Embryo '75
Soldier Blue '70
Charly '68
Duel at Diablo '66
Father Goose '64
Lilies of the Field '63
Soldier in the Rain '63
Requiem for a Heavyweight '62

Dusty Nelson
Inferno '01
Necromancer: Satan's Servant '88

Tim Blake Nelson (1965-)
The Grey Zone '01
O '01
Eye of God '97

Jan Nemec (1936-)
The Report on the Party and the Guests '66
Diamonds of the Night '64

Avi Nesher (1953-)
Raw Nerve '99
The Taxman '98
Mercenary '96
Savage '96
Timebomb '91
Doppelganger: The Evil Within '90
She '83

Confessions of Tom Harris '72

David Nelson (1936-)
Last Plane Out '83
House of Death '82
A Rare Breed '81

Frans Nel
Lights! Camera! Murder! '91
American Kickboxer 1 '91

Night Passage '57
Mooncussers '52
Moon Pilot '62
Bon Voyage! '62
Summer Magic '63
Johnny Shiloh '63
The Moon-Spinners '64
Scarecrow '64
Dr. Syn, Alias the Scarecrow '64
Dr. Syn '37
The Black Room '35

James Neilson (1910-79)
The Adventures of Tom Sawyer '73
The First Time '69
Where Angels Go, Trouble Follows '68
Gentle Giant '67
The Adventures of Bullwhip Griffin '66

Roy William Neill (1886-1946)
Black Angel '46
Dressed to Kill '46
Terror by Night '46
House of Fear '45
Pursuit to Algiers '45
The Woman in Green '45
The Pearl of Death '44
Scarlet Claw '44
Spider Woman '44
Sherlock Holmes Faces Death '43
Sherlock Holmes in Washington '43
Frankenstein Meets the Wolfman '42
Sherlock Holmes and the Secret Weapon '42

Sam Newfield (1899-1964)
Adventure Island '47
Money Madness '47
Outlaw of the Plains '46
Border Badmen '45
Gangster's Den '45
His Brother's Ghost '45
Frontier Outlaws '45
The Monster Maker '44
Nabonga '44
Death Rides the Plains '44
Devil Riders '44
Oath of Vengeance '44
Rustler's Hideout '44
Thundering Gunslingers '44
Wild Horse Phantom '44
The Black Raven '43
Dead Men Walk '43
Harvest Melody '43
Raiders of Red Gap '43
Tiger Fangs '43
Along the Sundown Trail '42
Billy the Kid Trapped '42
Law and Order '42
The Lone Rider in Cheyenne '42
The Mad Monster '42
The Mysterious Rider '42
Prairie Pals '42
Texas Justice '42
Tumbleweed Trail '42
Border Roundup '41
The Lone Rider in Frontier Fury '41
The Lone Rider in Ghost Town '41
Texas Trouble '41
Trigger Men '41
Arizona Gangbusters '40
Billy the Kid in Texas '40
Death Rides the Range '40
Gun Code '40
I Take This Oath '40
The Invisible Killer '40
Fighting Mad '39
Flaming Lead '39
Flaming Renegade '39
Outlaw's Paradise '39
Six Gun Rhythm '39
Texas Wildcats '39
Trigger Pals '39
Durango Valley Raiders '38
Feud Maker '38
Frontier Scout '38
Gunsmoke Trail '38
Harlem on the Prairie '38
Lightnin' Carson Rides Again '38
Phantom Ranger '38
Songs and Bullets '38
Six Gun Trail '38
Thunder in the Desert '38
Arizona Gunfighter '37
Terror of Tiny Town '38
Guns in the Dark '37
A Lawman is Born '37
Lightning Bill Crandall '37
Melody of the Plains '37
Roarin' Lead '37
Sky High '51
Western Pacific Agent '51
Hi-Jacked '50
Motor Patrol '50
Radar Secret Service '50
Three Desperate Men '50
She Shoulda Said No '49
State Department File 649 '49
The Gambler & the Lady '52
Aces and Eights '36
Border Caballero '36
Federal Agent '36
Ghost Patrol '36
Lion's Den '51
Roaring Guns '36
Stormy Trails '36
The Traitor '36
Branded a Coward '35
Bulldog Courage '35
Go-Get-'Em Haines '35
Racing Luck '35
Reckless Roads '35
Frontier Justice '35
Windjammer '37

Four Weddings and a Funeral '94
Enchanted April '92
Into the West '92
Amazing Grace & Chuck '87
Bad Blood '87
The Good Father '87
Dance with a Stranger '85
The Awakening '80
The Man in the Iron Mask '77

Doomed at Sundown '37
The Gambling Terror '37
Gun Lords of Stirrup Basin '37
Boothill Brigade '37

Joseph M. Newman (1909-2006)
The Legend of Hillbilly John '73

John Newland (1917-2000)
Don't Be Afraid of the Dark '73

Paul Newman (1925-)
The Glass Menagerie '87
Harry & Son '84
The Shadow Box '80
The Effect of Gamma Rays on Man-in-the-Moon Marigolds '73
Sometimes a Great Notion '71
Rachel, Rachel '68

Fred Newmeyer (1888-1967)
General Spanky '36
They Never Come Back '32
The Freshman '25
Girl Shy '24
Safety Last '23

The King of the Roaring '20s: The Story of Arnold Rothstein '61
The Gunfight at Dodge City '59
This Island Earth '55
Dangerous Crossing '53
Love Nest '51
Great Dan Patch '49
Jungle Patrol '48

Fred Niblo (1874-1948)
Blood and Sand '22
Camille '21
The Three Musketeers '21
Mark of Zorro '20
Sex '20

Andrew Niccol (1964-)
Lord of War '05
S1m0ne '02
Gattaca '97

Maurizio Nichetti (1948-)
Luna e L'Altra '96
Stefano Quantestorie '93
Volere Volare '92
The Icicle Thief '89

Paul Nicholas (1945-)
Luckytown '00
Naked Cage '86
Chained Heat '83

George Nicholls, Jr. (1897-1939)
Anne of Green Gables '34
The Return of Peter Grimm '35

Jack Nicholson (1937-)
The Two Jakes '90
Goin' South '78
Drive, He Said '71

Arch Nicholson (1941-90)
Dark Age '88
Fortress '85

Ted Nicolaou
Bloodstorm: Subspecies 4 '98
Magic in the Mirror: Fowl Play '96
Spellbreaker: Secret of the Leprechauns '96
Vampire Journals '96
Leapin' Leprechauns '95
Dragonworld '94
Bloodlust: Subspecies 3 '93
Remote '93
Bad Channels '92
Bloodstone: Subspecies 2 '92
Subspecies '90
Terrorvision '86
Dungeonmaster '83

Mike Nichols (1931-)
Charlie Wilson's War '07
Closer '04
Angels in America '03
Wit '01
What Planet Are You From? '00
Primary Colors '98
The Birdcage '95
Wolf '94
Regarding Henry '91
Postcards from the Edge '90
Working Girl '88
Biloxi Blues '88
Heartburn '86
Silkwood '83
The Day of the Dolphin '73
Carnal Knowledge '71
Catch-22 '70
The Graduate '67
Who's Afraid of Virginia Woolf? '66

Alex Nicol (1919-2001)
Point of Terror '71
The Screaming Skull '58

John Nicolella (1946-98)
Kull the Conqueror '97
Sunset Heat '92
Runaway Father '91
Finish Line '89

Sebastian Niemann (1968-)
Ancient Relic '02

William Nigh (1881-1955)
Riding the California Trail '47
South of Monterey '47
Corregidor '43
The Ghost and the Guest '43
Mr. Wong in Chinatown '39
Mutiny in the Big House '39
Mr. Wong, Detective '38
Mr. Wise Guy '42
Mr. Wong in the Scarlet Clue
Rose of Rio Grande '38
The Underdog '43
The Black Dragons '42
Zis Boom Bah '41
The Ape '40
Doomed to Die '40
The Fatal Hour '40
The Ape Man '43
The Hoosier Schoolboy '37
The Lincoln of Ninth Avenue '39
The Thirteenth Man '37
Headline Woman '35
Mysterious Mr. Wong '35
House of Mystery '34
Monte Carlo Nights '34
Mystery Liner '34
Border Devils '32
Night Rider '32
Without Honors '32
Fightin' Ranch '30

Finishing School '33
Fighting Thru '30

Rob Nilsson (1940-)
Heat and Sunlight '87
On the Edge '86
Signal 7 '83
Northern Lights '79

Gaspar Noe (1963-)
Irreversible '02
I Stand Alone '98

Christopher Nolan (1970-)
The Dark Knight '08
The Prestige '06
Batman Begins '05
Insomnia '02
Memento '00
Following '99

Chris Noonan (1952-)
Miss Potter '06
Babe '95

Tom Noonan (1951-)
The Wife '95
What Happened Was... '94

Stephen Norrington (1965-)
The League of Extraordinary Gentlemen '03
The Last Minute '01
Blade '98
Death Machine '95

Aaron Norris (1951-)
Forest Warrior '95
Top Dog '95
Sidekicks '93
Hellbound '94
The Hitman '91
Delta Force 2: Operation Stranglehold '90
Braddock: Missing in Action 3 '88
Platoon Leader '87

Bill W.L. Norton (1943-)
Every Mother's Worst Fear '98
Our Mother's Murder '97
Hercules and the Legendary Journeys '94
Hercules, Vol. 1: And the Amazon Women '94
Seven Days to Live '01

Leonard Nimoy (1931-)
Holy Matrimony '94
Funny About Love '90
Three Men and a Baby '87
The Good Mother '88
Star Trek 4: The Voyage Home '86
Star Trek 3: The Search for Spock '84

Marcus Nispel (1964-)
Pathfinder '07
The Texas Chainsaw Massacre '03

Noel Nosseck (1943-)
Another Woman's Husband '00
Tour of Duty '87
Baby... Secret of the Lost Legend '85
More American Graffiti '79

Max Nosseck (1902-72)
Silent Predators '99
The Fury Within '98
NightScreams '97
Tornado! '96
Down, Out and Dangerous '95
The Sister-in-Law '95
French Silk '94
Full Exposure: The Sex Tape Scandal '89
Summer Fantasy '84
Night Partners '83
The Hoodlum '51
Black Beauty '46
Brighton Strangler '45
Dillinger '45

Nosseck

King of the Mountain '81
Return of the Rebels '81
Dreamer '79
Las Vegas Lady '76
Jonathan Nossiter (1961-)
Mondovino '04
Signs & Wonders '00
Sunday '96
Thierry Notz
Fortunes of War '94
Watchers 2 '90
The Terror Within '88
Cherie Nowlan
Introducing the Dwights '07
The Wedding Party '97
Phillip Noyce (1950-)
Catch a Fire '06
The Quiet American '02
Rabbit-Proof Fence '02
The Bone Collector '99
The Saint '97
Clear and Present Danger '94
Silver '93
Patriot Games '92
Blind Fury '90
Dead Calm '89
Echoes of Paradise '86
Heatwave '83
Newsfront '78
Simon Nuchtern
Savage Dawn '84
Silent Madness '84
Elliott Nugent (1900-80)
Just for You '52
My Outlaw Brother '51
The Great Gatsby '49
My Girl Tisa '48
My Favorite Brunette '47
Welcome Stranger '47
Up in Arms '44
The Male Animal '42
Never Say Die '39
Give Me a Sailor '38
Love in Bloom '35
Splendor '35
Two Alone '34
Victor Nunez (1945-)
Coastlines '02
Ulee's Gold '97
Ruby in Paradise '93
A Flash of Green '85
Gal Young 'Un '79
Trevor Nunn (1940-)
Twelfth Night '96
Lady Jane '85
Hedda '75
Joe Nussbaum (1973-)
Sydney White '07
American Pie Presents: The Naked Mile '06
Sleepover '04
Raphael Nussbaum (1932-93)
Trespassing '87
Sinai Commandos '68
The Invisible Terror '63
Colin Nutley (1944-)
Under the Sun '98
The Last Dance '93
House of Angels '92
David Nutter (1960-)
Band of Brothers '01
Disturbing Behavior '98
Trancers 5: Sudden Deth '94
Cease Fire '85
Christian Nyby (1913-93)
Mission Galactica: The Cylon Attack '78
Operation C.I.A. '65
The Thing '51
Roger Nygard
Back to Back '96
High Strung '91
Sven Nykvist (1922-2006)
The Ox '91

Gorilla '56
Dan O'Bannon (1946-)
The Resurrected '91
Return of the Living Dead '85
Michael Oblowitz
The Foreigner '03
The Breed '01
On the Borderline '01
This World, Then the Fireworks '97
Jim O'Brien (1947-)
Rebecca '97
Foreign Affairs '93
The Dressmaker '89
The Jewel in the Crown '84
John O'Brien (1962-)
Vermont Is for Lovers '92
The Big Dis '89
Jeffrey Obrow
Bram Stoker's The Mummy '97
Servants of Twilight '91
The Kindred '87
Dorm That Dripped Blood '82
The Power '80
Masayuki Ochiai
Shutter '08
Parasite Eve '97
James O'Connolly (1924-87)
Tower of Evil '72
Crooks & Coronets '69
The Valley of Gwangi '69
Vendetta for the Saint '68
Berserk! '67
Frank O'Connor (1882-1959)
Mystic Circle Murder '39
Spangles '26
Free to Love '25
Gavin O'Connor
Miracle '04
Tumbleweeds '98
Pat O'Connor (1943-)
Sweet November '01
Dancing at Lughnasa '98
Inventing the Abbotts '97
Circle of Friends '94
Fools of Fortune '90
The January Man '89
Stars and Bars '88
A Month in the Country '87
Cal '84
W.A. O'Connor
See William A. O'Connor
William A. O'Connor (1900-)
Cocaine Fiends '36
The Drifter '32
Ten Nights in a Bar-Room '31
Pace That Kills '28
Bob Odenkirk (1962-)
The Brothers Solomon '07
Let's Go to Prison '06
Melvin Goes to Dinner '03
Damien O'Donnell (1967-)
Rory O'Shea Was Here '04
East Is East '99
Steve Oedekerk (1961-)
Barnyard '06
Kung Pow! Enter the Fist '02
Nothing to Lose '96
Ace Ventura: When Nature Calls '95
Peter O'Fallon
A Rumor of Angels '00
Suicide Kings '97
George More O'Ferrall (1907-82)
Three Cases of Murder '55
Angels One Five '54
George Ogilvie (1931-)
The Crossing '92
Mad Max: Beyond Thunderdome '85
Jorgo Ognenovski
Stalked '99
Warrior of Justice '96

Rockin' Road Trip '85
Gerry O'Hara (1924-)
The Mummy Lives '93
Fanny Hill '83
The Bitch '78
Leopard in the Snow '78
Maroc 7 '67
Terrence O'Hara
The Perfect Bride '91
Darkroom '90
Tommy O'Haver (1968-2005)
Ella Enchanted '04
Get Over It! '01
Billy's Hollywood Screen Kiss '98
Michael O'Herlihy (1919-97)
Two by Forsyth '86
Cry of the Innocent '80
A Time for Miracles '80
Backstairs at the White House '79
The Flame Is Love '79
Peter Lundy and the Medicine Hat Stallion '77
The Young Pioneers '76
Smith! '69
The One and Only, Genuine, Original Family Band '68
The Fighting Prince of Donegal '66
Mosby's Marauders '66
Kihachi Okamoto (1923-2005)
Zatoichi vs. Yojimbo '70
Red Lion '69
Sword of Doom '67
Takao Okawara
Godzilla 2000 '99
Godzilla vs. Mechagodzilla II '93
Godzilla vs. King Ghidora '91
Godzilla vs. Biollante '89
Sidney Olcott (1873-1949)
The Claw '27
Ranson's Folly '26
Monsieur Beaucaire '24
From the Manger to the Cross '15
Pedro Olea (1938-)
Zafarinas '94
The Fencing Master '92
Ken Olin (1954-)
In Pursuit of Honor '95
White Fang 2: The Myth of the White Wolf '94
Doing Time on Maple Drive '92
Ron Oliver
A Dennis the Menace Christmas '07
Shock to the System '06
Chasing Christmas '05
Blood Angels '05
Third Man Out: A Donald Strachey Mystery '05
Tales from a Parallel Universe: Super Nova '97
Prom Night 3: The Last Kiss '89
Hector Olivera (1931-)
A Shadow You Soon Will Be '94
Play Murder for Me '91
Two to Tango '88
Cocaine Wars '86
Barbarian Queen '85
Wizards of the Lost Kingdom '85
Funny, Dirty Little War '83
Fridays of Eternity '81
El Muerto '75
Laurence Olivier (1907-89)
The Prince and the Showgirl '57
Richard III '55
Hamlet '48
Henry V '44
Ermanno Olmi (1931-)
The Tree of Wooden Clogs '78
William Olsen (1950-)
Return to Eden '89

David O'Malley (1944-)
Easy Wheels '89
Kid Colter '85
Robert Vincent O'Neil
Avenging Angel '85
Angel '84
Paco '75
Ron O'Neal (1937-2004)
Up Against the Wall '91
Superfly T.N.T. '73
Marcel Ophuls (1927-)
The Troubles We've Seen '94
The Sorrow and the Pity '71
Max Ophuls (1902-57)
Lola Montes '55
The Earrings of Madame De... '54
Le Plaisir '52
La Ronde '51
Caught '49
Reckless Moment '49
Letter from an Unknown Woman '48
De Mayerling a Sarajevo '40
La Signora di Tutti '34
Liebelei '32
Charlie Ordonez
Forgotten Warrior '86
Wolf '86
Shaun O'Riordan
If It's a Man, Hang Up '75
The Devil's Web '74
I'm the Girl He Wants to Kill '74
In the Steps of a Dead Man '74
Screamer '74
Stuart Orme
Goodbye, Mr. Chips '02
The Lost World '02
The Waiting Time '99
Ivanhoe '97
The Sculptress '97
The Puppet Masters '94
The Blackheath Poisonings '92
The Heist '89
James Ormerod
Hands of a Murderer '90
Ron Ormond (1911-81)
The Girl from Tobacco Row '66
The Black Lash '52
Mesa of Lost Women '52
Kentucky Jubilee '51
King of the Bullwhip '51
Thundering Trail '51
Yes, Sir, Mr. Bones '51
Alan Ormsby (1944-)
Popcorn '89
Deranged '74
Gary Orona (1964-)
Stripshow '95
James Orr (1953-)
Man of the House '95
Mr. Destiny '90
Breaking All the Rules '85
Kenny Ortega (1950-)
High School Musical 2 '07
High School Musical '06
Hocus Pocus '93
Newsies '92

Ken Osborne
Escape from Cell Block 3 '74
Jailbreakin' '72
Wild Wheels '69
Kent Osborne
Women Unchained '72
Cain's Cutthroats '71
Mountain Man '77
Nagisa Oshima (1932-)
Taboo '99
Max, Mon Amour '86
Merry Christmas, Mr. Lawrence '83
The Empire of Passion '76
In the Realm of the Senses '76
Suzanne Osten (1944-)
Speak Up! It's So Dark '93
The Mozart Brothers '86
Sam O'Steen (1923-2000)
The Best Little Girl in the World '81
Sparkle '76
I Love You, Goodbye '74
Brand New Life '72
Thaddeus O'Sullivan (1948-)
The Heart of Me '02
Ordinary Decent Criminal '99
Witness to the Mob '98
Nothing Personal '95
December Bride '91
Gerd Oswald (1919-89)
Brainwashed '60
Crime of Passion '57
Paris Holiday '57
Richard Oswald (1880-1963)
The Lovable Cheat '49
My Song Goes Round the World '34
Cesare Borgia '23
Dominique Othenin-Girard (1958-)
Beyond Desire '94
Private Lessons, Another Story '94
Omen 4: The Awakening '91
Night Angel '90
Halloween 5: The Revenge of Michael Myers '89
After Darkness '85
Katsuhiro Otomo (1954-)
Steamboy '05
Akira '89
Idrissa Ouedraogo (1954-)
Tilai '90
Yaaba '89
Jean-Paul Ouellette
The Unnamable 2: The Statement of Randolph Carter '92
The Unnamable '88
Gerard Oury (1919-2006)
Delusions of Grandeur '76
The Brain '69
La Grande Vadrouille '66
The Sucker '65
Cliff Owen (1919-93)
The Bawdy Adventures of Tom Jones '76
No Sex Please—We're British '73
The Vengeance of She '68
The Wrong Arm of the Law '63
Frank Oz (1944-)
Death at a Funeral '07
The Stepford Wives '04
The Score '01
Bowfinger '99
In and Out '97

The Indian in the Cupboard '95
Housesitter '92
What about Bob? '91
Dirty Rotten Scoundrels '88
Little Shop of Horrors '86
The Muppets Take Manhattan '84
The Dark Crystal '82
Sakae Ozawa
See Shigehiro (Sakae) Ozawa
Shigehiro (Sakae) Ozawa
Return of the Street Fighter '74
The Street Fighter '74
Francois Ozon (1967-)
Time to Leave '05
5x2 '04
Swimming Pool '03
8 Women '02
Under the Sand '00
Criminal Lovers '99
Water Drops on Burning Rocks '99
Sitcom '97
Ferzan Ozpetek (1959-)
Facing Windows '03
His Secret Life '01
Harem '99
Steam: A Turkish Bath '96
Yasujiro Ozu (1903-63)
An Autumn Afternoon '62
Drifting Weeds '59
Good Morning '59
Equinox Flower '58
Tokyo Story '53
Early Summer '51
Late Spring '49
Record of a Tenement Gentleman '47
I Was Born But... '32
G.W. Pabst (1885-1967)
Don Quixote '35
Kameradschaft '31
The Threepenny Opera '31
Westfront 1918 '30
Diary of a Lost Girl '29
Pandora's Box '28
The Love of Jeanne Ney '27
Joyless Street '25
Secrets of a Soul '25
Anthony Page (1935-)
Human Bomb '97
Middlemarch '93
Final Warning '90
The Nightmare Years '89
Scandal in a Small Town '88
Pack of Lies '87
Heartbreak House '86
Monte Carlo '86
Forbidden '85
My Sweet Victim '85
Bill: On His Own '83
The Grace Kelly Story '83
Johnny Belinda '82
Absolution '81
Bill '81
The Lady Vanishes '79
I Never Promised You a Rose Garden '77
F. Scott Fitzgerald in Hollywood '76
Missiles of October '74
Alpha Beta '73
Pueblo Affair '73
Teddy Page
Blood Debts '83
Fireback '78
Marcel Pagnol (1895-1974)
Letters from My Windmill '54
Topaze '51
Well-Digger's Daughter '46
Le Schpountz '38
Harvest '37
Cesar '36
Angele '34
The Baker's Wife '33
John Paizs
Invasion! '99

Alan J. Pakula (1928-98)
The Big Crimewave '86
The Devil's Own '93
The Pelican Brief '93
Consenting Adults '92
Presumed Innocent '90
See You in the Morning '89
Orphans '87
Dream Lover '85
Sophie's Choice '82
Rollover '81
Starting Over '79
Comes a Horseman '78
All the President's Men '76
The Parallax View '74
Klute '71
The Sterile Cuckoo '69

George Pal (1908-80)
7 Faces of Dr. Lao '63
The Wonderful World of the Brothers Grimm '62
Atlantis, the Lost Continent '61
The Time Machine '60
Tom Thumb '58

Euzhan Palcy (1957-)
The Killing Yard '01
Ruby Bridges '98
A Dry White Season '89
Sugar Cane Alley '83

Jean Marie Pallardy (1940-)
White Fire '84
Truck Stop

Anders Palm (1949-)
Dead Certain '90
Unmasked Part 25 '88

Tony Palmer
Women vs. Men '02
Noel '04
The Children '90
Wagner: The Movie '85
Wagner: The Complete Epic '85

Bruce Paltrow (1943-2002)
Duets '00

Jafar Panahi (1960-)
Crimson Gold '03
The Circle '00

Chazz Palminteri (1952-)
A Little Sex '82

Conrad Palmisano (1948-)
Busted Up '86
Space Rage '86

Norman Panama (1914-2003)
Barnaby and Me '77
I Will, I Will... for Now '76
How to Commit Marriage '69
The Road to Hong Kong '62
The Trap '59
Above and Beyond '53
Court Jester '56

Danny Pang (1965-)
Bangkok Dangerous '08
Bangkok Dangerous '03
The White Balloon '95
The Messengers '07
The Eye '02

Oxide Pang (1965-)
Bangkok Dangerous '08
The Messengers '07
The Eye '02

Chan-wook Park (1963-)
Lady Vengeance '05
Three... Extremes '04

Nick Park (1958-)
Wallace & Gromit: The Curse of the Were-Rabbit '05
Chicken Run '00

Dean Parisot
Fun With Dick and Jane '05
Galaxy Quest '99
Home Fries '98
Framed '90

Richard W. Park
Gang Justice '94
American Chinatown '96

Alan Parker (1944-)
Angela's Ashes '99
Evita '96
The Road to Wellville '94
The Commitments '91
Come See the Paradise '90
Mississippi Burning '88
Angel Heart '87
Birdy '84
Pink Floyd: The Wall '82
Shoot the Moon '82
Fame '80
Midnight Express '78
Bugsy Malone '76

Albert Parker (1887-1974)
The Black Pirate '26

Trey Parker (1969-)
Team America: World Police '04
South Park: Bigger, Longer and Uncut '99
Orgazmo '98
Cannibal! The Musical '96

Oliver Parker (1960-)
Fade to Black '06
The Eyes of Youth '19
Shifting Sands '18

Norton S. Parker
Race That Kills '28
The Road to Ruin '28

Eric Parkinson
Futura Shock '93
Terror Eyes '87

John Parkinson
An Ideal Husband '99
Othello '95
Late Extra '35

John Paragon (1954-)
Twinsitters '95
Shaft's Big Score '72

Paul S. Parco (1934-79)
Pucker Up and Bark Like a Dog '89

Chuck Parello
The Hillside Strangler '04
Ed Gein '01
Henry: Portrait of a Serial Killer 2: Mask of Sanity '96

Hugh Parks
Fatal Passion '94
Shoot '92

Jerry Paris (1925-86)
Police Academy 4: Citizens on Patrol '87
Police Academy 3: Back in Training '86
Police Academy 2: Their First Assignment '85
Make Me an Offer '80
How to Break Up a Happy Divorce '76
Only with Married Men '74
Star Spangled Girl '71
The Grass Is Greener
Never a Dull Moment '68
How Sweet It Is! '68
Don't Raise the Bridge, Lower the River '68
Viva Max! '69

Domonic Paris
Splitz '84
Dracula's Last Rites '79

Gianfranco Parolini (1930-)
Adios, Sabata '71
Return of Sabata '71
Sabata '69
Five for Hell '67
The Fury of Hercules '61
Samson '61

Robert Parrish (1916-95)
The Destructors '74
A Town Called Hell '72
Journey to the Far Side of the Sun '69
The Bobo '67
Casino Royale '67
Fire Down Below '57
Cry Danger '51

John H. Parr
Prey for the Hunter '92
Pursuit '90

James Parrott
Laurel & Hardy: Be Big '31
Pardon Us '31
Laurel & Hardy: Another Fine Mess '30
Laurel & Hardy: Below Zero '30
Laurel & Hardy: Night Owls '30
Laurel & Hardy: Hog Wild '30
Laurel & Hardy: Perfect Day '29
Laurel & Hardy: The Hoose-Gow '29

Richard Patterson
The Marx Brothers in a Nutshell '90

Willi Patterson
J-Men Forever! '79

Michael Pattinson (1957-)
The Limbic Region '96
Ground Zero '88
Street Hero '84
Moving Out '83

Gordon Parry (1908-81)
Innocents in Paris '53
Tom Brown's School Days '51

Gabriel Pascal (1894-1954)
Caesar and Cleopatra '46
Major Barbara '41

Goran Paskaljevic (1947-)
Gow '29

Pier Paolo Pasolini (1922-75)
Saló, or the 120 Days of Sodom '75
Arabian Nights '74
The Canterbury Tales '71
The Decameron '70
Medea '70
Porcile '69
Teorema '68
The Hawks & the Sparrows '67
Oedipus Rex '67
The Gospel According to St. Matthew '64

David Paulsen
Savage Weekend '80
Schizoid '80

George Pavlou (1953-)
Rawhead Rex '87
Transmutations '85

Bill Paxton (1955-)
The Greatest Game Ever Played '05
Frailty '02

Don Michael Paul (1963-)
Who's Your Caddy? '07
Half Past Dead '02
Slaughter/day '77

Steven Paul (1954-)
Eternity '90
Slapstick of Another Kind '84

Stuart Paul
Emanon '86
Fate '90
Falling in Love Again '80

John D. Patterson (1940-2005)
Grave Secrets: The Legacy of Hilltop Drive '92
The Spring '89
Taken Away '89
Deadly Innocence '88

Stuart Paton (1883-1944)
Silent Code '35
Mystery Trooper '32
Chinatown After Dark '31
20,000 Leagues under the Sea '16

Jonas Pate (1970-)
Deceiver '97
The Grave '96

Robert Patton-Spruill
Body Count '97
Squeeze '97

Peter Patzak (1945-)
Midnight Cop '98
Lethal Obsession '87
The Uppe crust '91

Giovanni Pastrone (1883-1959)
Cabiria '14

Giuseppe Patroni-Griffi (1921-2005)
Divine Nymph '71
'Tis a Pity She's a Whore '73
Driver's Seat '73

Gordon Parks (1912-2006)
Leadbelly '76
The Super Cops '74
Shaft's Big Score '72
Shaft '71
The Learning Tree '69

Gordon Parks, Jr. (1934-79)
Aaron Loves Angela '75
Three the Hard Way '74
Superfly '72

John Pasquin
Miss Congeniality 2: Armed and Fabulous '05
Joe Somebody '01

Ivan Passer (1933-)
Kidnapped '95
About Schmidt '02
Stalin '92
Haunted Summer '88

Sam Peckinpah (1925-84)
The Osterman Weekend '83
Convoy '78
Cross of Iron '76
The Killer Elite '75
Bring Me the Head of Alfredo Garcia '74
Pat Garrett & Billy the Kid '73
The Getaway '72
Junior Bonner '72
Straw Dogs '71
Ballad of Cable Hogue '70
The Wild Bunch '69
Major Dundee '65
Ride the High Country '62
Deadly Companions '61

Ron Peck (1948-)
Empire State '87
Nighthawks '78

Raoul Peck (1953-)
Sometimes in April '05
Lumumba '01

Max Pecas (1925-2003)
Sweet Ecstasy '62
Daniella by Night '61

Peter Pearson (1938-)
The Sensuous Teenager '70

Larry Peerce (1935-)
Deadly Companions '61 [?]
A Woman Named Jackie '91
Prison for Children '93
Murder So Sweet '93
The Abduction '96
The Other Side of the Mountain, Part 2 '78
The Other Side of the Mountain '75

Giuliano Paparella [uncertain]

Steven Pearl
Heartland '81

Richard Pearce (1943-)
South Pacific '01
A Family Thing '96
Leap of Faith '92
The Long Walk Home '89
Country '84
No Mercy '86
Threshold '83
Heartland '81

Dave Payne
Not Like Us '96
Alien Terminator '95

Alexander Payne (1961-)
Sideways '04
Election '99
Citizen Ruth '96

Jean Pellerin
Daybreak '01
Escape under Pressure '00

Kimberly Peirce
Stop-Loss '08
Boys Don't Cry '99

Anthony Pelissier (1912-88)
The Rocking Horse Winner '49

Mark Pellington (1965-)
Henry Poole Is Here '08
The Mothman Prophecies '02
Arlington Road '99
Going All the Way '97

Arthur Penn (1922-)
Inside '96
The Portrait '93
Penn and Teller Get Killed '90
Dead of Winter '87
Target '85
Four Friends '81
The Missouri Breaks '76
Night Moves '75
Little Big Man '70
Alice's Restaurant '69
Bonnie & Clyde '67
The Chase '66
Mickey One '65
The Miracle Worker '62
The Left-Handed Gun '58

Sean Penn (1960-)
Into the Wild '07
The Pledge '00
The Crossing Guard '94
The Indian Runner '91

Leo Penn (1921-98)
Judgment in Berlin '88

Eagle Pennell (1952-2002)
Ice House '89
Last Night at the Alamo '83
The Whole Shootin' Match '79

D.A. Pennebaker (1925-)
Only the Strong Survive '03
Moon over Broadway '98
The War Room '93
Monterey Pop '68
Don't Look Back '67

C.M. Pennington-Richards (1911-2005)
A Challenge for Robin Hood '68

Louis Pepe (1966-)
Lost in La Mancha '03
Brothers of the Head '06

Richard Pepin
The Box '03
Mindstorm '01
Y2K '99
The Sender '98
Dark Breed '96
Cyber-Tracker 2 '95
Cyber-Tracker '94
T-Force '94
The Silencers '95
Hologram Man '95
Firepower '93
Cyber-Tracker '93
Fist of Honor '93

Clare Peploe (1942-)
The Triumph of Love '01
Rough Magic '95

Barbara Peeters
Humanoids from the Deep '80
Starhops '78
Summer School Teachers '75

High Season '88
Mark Peploe (1943-)
Victory '95
Afraid of the Dark '92
Hope Perello
St. Patrick's Day '99
Pet Shop '94
Jesse Peretz (1968-)
The Ex '07
The Chateau '01
First Love, Last Rites '98
Jack Perez
Wild Things 2 '04
La Cucaracha '99
The Big Empty '98
America's Deadliest Home Video '91
Etienne Perier (1931-)
Investigation '79
When Eight Bells Toll '71
Zeppelin '71
The Hot Line '69
Murder at 45 R.P.M. '65
Anthony Perkins (1932-92)
Lucky Stiff '88
Psycho 3 '86
Frank Perry (1930-95)
Hello Again '87
Compromising Positions '85
Monsignor '82
Mommie Dearest '81
Skag '79
Rancho Deluxe '75
Diary of a Mad Housewife '70
Last Summer '69
The Swimmer '68
ABC Stage 67: Truman Capote's A Christmas Memory '66
David and Lisa '62
Nickolas Perry (1967-)
The Hunting of the President '04
Speedway Junky '99
Tyler Perry (1969-)
Tyler Perry's Meet the Browns '08
Daddy's Little Girls '07
Tyler Perry's Why Did I Get Married? '07
Madea's Family Reunion '06
Body Waves '92
Brooke L. Peters
See Boris L. Petroff
Charlie Peters
Music from Another Room '97
Passed Away '92
Wolfgang Petersen (1941-)
Poseidon '06
Troy '04
Sniper 3 '04
The Perfect Storm '00
Air Force One '97
Outbreak '94
In the Line of Fire '93
Shattered '91
Enemy Mine '85
The NeverEnding Story '84
Das Boot '81
For Your Love Only '79
Black and White As Day and Night '78
Kristine Peterson
Slaves to the Underground '96
Redemption: Kickboxer 5 '95
The Hard Truth '94
Eden 2 '93
Eden 4 '93
Critters 3 '91

Lower Level '91
Body Chemistry '90
Deadly Dreams '88
Christopher Petit (1949-)
Chinese Boxes '84
Unsuitable Job for a Woman '82
Daniel Petrie (1920-2004)
Walter and Henry '01
Wild Iris '01
Inherit the Wind '99
The Assistant '97
Calm at Sunset '96
Kissinger and Nixon '96
Lassie '94
Mark Twain and Me '91
My Name Is Bill W. '89
Cocoon: The Return '88
Square Dance '88
Rocket Gibraltar '88
Half a Lifetime '86
The Bay Boy '85
Execution of Raymond Graham '85
The Dollmaker '84
Six Pack '82
Fort Apache, the Bronx '81
Resurrection '80
The Betsy '78
Eleanor & Franklin '76
Lifeguard '76
Sybil '76
Buster and Billie '74
Neptune Factor '73
Moon of the Wolf '72
Silent Night, Lonely Night '69
Spy with a Cold Nose '66
Stolen Hours '63
A Raisin in the Sun '61
The Bramble Bush '60
Bang the Drum Slowly '56
Daniel Petrie, Jr. (1952-)
Dead Silence '96
In the Army Now '94
Toy Soldiers '91
J.T. Petty
Mimic 3: Sentinel '03
Soft for Digging '01
Joseph Pevney (1920-)
Anatomy of a Psycho '61
Outcasts of the City '58
The Unearthly '57
Hats Off '37
Man of a Thousand Faces '57
Tammy and the Bachelor '57
Away All Boats '56
Because of You '52
Meet Danny Wilson '52
The Strange Door '51

John Peyser (1916-2002)
Fantastic, Seven '75
The Centerfold Girls '74
Four Rode Out '69
Kashmiri Run '69
Lee Phillips (1927-99)
Silent Motive '91
Blind Vengeance '90
Windmills of the Gods '88
Barnum '86
The Blue Lightning '86
Mae West '84
Samson and Delilah '84
On the Right Track '81
Special Olympics '78
The Spell '77
Dynasty '76
War Between the Tates '76
Sweet Hostage '75
The Stranger Within '74
Lou Diamond Phillips (1962-)
Dangerous Touch '94
Sioux City '94
Maurice Phillips
Another You '91
Enid Is Sleeping '90
Riders of the Storm '88
Nick (Steve Millard) Phillips (1941-)
Death Nurse '87
Crazy Fat Ethel II '85
Criminally Insane '75
Toby Phillips
See Paul Thomas
Todd Phillips (1970-)
School for Scoundrels '06
Starsky & Hutch '04
Old School '03
Road Trip '00
Maurice Pialat (1925-2003)
Van Gogh '92
Under Satan's Sun '87
Police '85
A Nos Amours '84
Loulou '80
Giuseppe Piccioni (1953-)
Light of My Eyes '01
Not of This World '99
Irving Pichel (1891-1954)
Day of Triumph '54
Martin Luther '53
Santa Fe '51
Destination Moon '50
The Great Rupert '50
Quicksand '50
The Miracle of the Bells '48
Mr. Peabody & the Mermaid '48
Something in the Wind '47
They Won't Believe Me '47
O.S.S. '46
Tomorrow Is Forever '46
Colonel Effingham's Raid '45
Dance Hall '41
The Great Commandment '41
Larceny On the Air '37
She '35
The Most Dangerous Game '32
Andrew Piddington
The Killing of John Lennon '07
The Fall '98
Arthur C. Pierce (1923-87)
Las Vegas Hillbillys '66
Women of the Prehistoric Planet '66
Charles B. Pierce (1938-)
Hawken's Breed '87
Boggy Creek II '83
Sacred Ground '83
The Evictors '79
Norseman '78
Grayeagle '77
Town That Dreaded Sundown '76

Winterhawk '76
Legend of Boggy Creek '75
Carl Pierson (1891-1977)
The New Frontier '35
Paradise Canyon '35
Frank Pierson (1925-)
Soldier's Girl '03
Conspiracy '01
Dirty Pictures '00
Truman '95
Lakota Woman: Siege at Wounded Knee '94
Citizen Cohn '92
Somebody Has to Shoot the Picture '90
King of the Gypsies '78
A Star Is Born '76
Alex Pillai
Take Me '01
The Wyvern Mystery '00
Sam Pillsbury
Audrey's Rain '03
Morgan's Ferry '99
Free Willy 3: The Rescue '97
Into the Badlands '92
Zandalee '91
Starlight Hotel '90
William H. Pine (1896-1955)
Dynamite '49
Swamp Fire '46
Marcelo Pineyro (1953-)
The Method '05
Burnt Money '00
Wild Horses '95
He Ping (1957-)
Warriors of Heaven and Earth '03
Red Firecracker, Green Firecracker '93
Yuen Woo Ping (1945-)
Wing Chun '94
Eagle's Shadow '84
Sidney W. Pink (1916-2002)
The Christmas Kid '68
Finger on the Trigger '65
Reptilicus '62
Efren C. Pinon
Blind Rage '78
Enforcer from Death Row '78
Claude Pinoteau (1925-)
La Boum '81
The Slap '76
Gordon Pinsent (1930-)
John and the Missus '87
Far Cry from Home '81
Lucian Pintilie (1933-)
An Unforgettable Summer '94
The Oak '93
Ward Six '78
Ernest Pintoff (1931-2002)
St. Helen's, Killer Volcano '82
Lunch Wagon '81
Jaguar Lives '79
Blade '72
Who Killed Mary What's 'Er Name? '71
Dynamite Chicken '70
Bret Piper
Screaming Dead '03
They Bite '95
A Nymphoid Barbarian in Dinosaur Hell '94
Robert Pirosh (1910-89)
Valley of the Kings '54
Go for Broke! '51
Massimo Pirri (1945-)
Fatal Fix '80
Mark Pirro (1956-)
Could It Happen Here? '77
Buford's Beach Bunnies '92
Deathrow Gameshow '88

Curse of the Queerwolf '87
A Polish Vampire in Burbank '80
Peter Pistor
In Pursuit '00
The Fence '94
Glen Pitre
The Home Front '02
Time Served '99
Belzaire the Cajun '86
Bruce Pittman (1950-)
No Alibi '00
Locked in Silence '99
Blood Brothers '97
Flood: A River's Rampage '97
Kurt Vonnegut's Harrison Bergeron '95
Where the Spirit Lives '89
Hello Mary Lou: Prom Night 2 '87
Confidential '86
Mark of Cain '84
Mark Piznarski
Here on Earth '00
The '60s '99
Death Benefit '96
Lucas Platt
Subway Stories '97
Girl in the Cadillac '94
Allen Plone
Sweet Justice '92
Phantom of the Ritz '88
Night Screams '87
Jeremy Podeswa (1962-)
The Five Senses '99
Eclipse '94
Amos Poe
Frogs for Snakes '98
Dead Weekend '95
Alphabet City '84
The Foreigner '78
Jean-Marie Poire (1945-)
Just Visiting '01
The Visitors '95
Sidney Poitier (1924-)
Ghost Dad '90
Fast Forward '84
Hanky Panky '82
Stir Crazy '80
Piece of the Action '77
Let's Do It Again '75
Uptown Saturday Night '74
Buck and the Preacher '72
James Polakof
The Vals '85
Balboa '82
Demon Rage '82
Swim Team '79
Roman Polanski (1933-)
Oliver Twist '05
The Pianist '02
The Ninth Gate '99
Death and the Maiden '94
Bitter Moon '92
Frantic '88
Pirates '86
Tess '79
The Tenant '76
Chinatown '74
Diary of Forbidden Dreams '73
Macbeth '71
Rosemary's Baby '68
The Fearless Vampire Killers '67
Repulsion '65
Knife in the Water '62
Two Men & a Wardrobe '58
Stephen Poliakoff (1952-)
Friends & Crocodiles '05
Gideon's Daughter '05
Almost Strangers '01
Shooting the Past '99
Century '94
Close My Eyes '91
Hidden City '87

Michael Polish (1972-)
The Astronaut Farmer '07
Northfork '03
Jackpot '01
Twin Falls Idaho '99
Jon Poll
Charlie Bartlett '07
Charlie Bartlett '07
Jeff Pollack (1959-)
Lost and Found '99
Booty Call '96
Above the Rim '94
Sydney Pollack (1934-)
The Interpreter '05
Random Hearts '99
Sabrina '95
The Firm '93
Havana '90
Out of Africa '85
Tootsie '82
Absence of Malice '81
The Electric Horseman '79
Bobby Deerfield '77
Three Days of the Condor '75
The Yakuza '75
The Way We Were '73
Jeremiah Johnson '72
Castle Keep '69
They Shoot Horses, Don't They? '69
The Scalphunters '68
This Property Is Condemned '66
The Slender Thread '65
Bud Pollard (1886-1952)
Look Out Sister '48
Beware '46
Tall, Tan and Terrific '46
The Black King '32
Harry A. Pollard (1883-1934)
Uncle Tom's Cabin '27
California Straight Ahead '25
George Pollock (1907-79)
Murder Most Foul '65
Murder Ahoy '64
Murder at the Gallop '63
Murder She Said '62
Broth of a Boy '59
Stranger in Town '57
John Polonia
Razorteeth '05
Terror House '97
Feeders '96
Mark Alan Polonia
Terror House '97
Feeders '96
Abraham Polonsky (1910-99)
Romance of a Horsethief '71
Tell Them Willie Boy Is Here '69
Force of Evil '49
John Polson (1965-)
Hide and Seek '05
Swimfan '02
Siam Sunset '99
Ventura Pons (1945-)
Food of Love '02
Beloved/Friend '99
Caresses '97
Gillo Pontecorvo (1919-2006)
Burn! '70
The Battle of Algiers '66
Kapo '59
Maurizio Ponzi (1939-)
Aurora '84
DJ Pooh
The Wash '01
Three Strikes '00
Lea Pool (1950-)
The Blue Butterfly '04
Lost and Delirious '01
Set Me Free '99

Angela Pope (1945-)
Hollow Reed '95
Captives '94
Leo Popkin (1914-)
Gang War '40
All I Want '02
Jeffrey Porter
Straight for the Heart '88
The Savage Woman '91
Mouvements du Desir '94

Rafael Portillo (1916-95)
The Curse of the Aztec Mummy '59
The Robot vs. the Aztec Mummy '59
Ralph Portillo
Hollywood Dreams '94
Stolen Hearts '95
Naked Lies '98
Bloody Murder '00
Big Brother Trouble '00
One of Them '03
P.J. Posner
Last Breath '96
Ted Post (1918-)
Stagecoach '86
Diary of a Teenage Hitchhiker '82
Nightkill '80
Go Tell the Spartans '78
Good Guys Wear Black '73
Whiffs '75
Harrad Experiment '73
Magnum Force '73
The Baby '72
Beneath the Planet of the Apes '70
Yuma '70
Hang 'Em High '67
Legend of Tom Dooley '59
H.C. Potter (1904-77)
Three for the Show '55
The Miniver Story '50
Mr. Blandings Builds His Dream House '48
The Time of Your Life '48
You Gotta Stay Happy '48
The Farmer's Daughter '47
Mr. Lucky '43
Second Chorus '40
The Story of Vernon and Irene Castle '39
Shopworn Angel '38
Beloved Enemy '36
'38
The Cowboy and the Lady '38

Gerald Potterton (1931-)
Heavy Metal '81
The Rainbow Gang '73
Railroader '65
Michel Poulette
Bonanno: A Godfather's Story '99
Orlando '92
The Man Who Cried '00
Yes '04
Sally Potter (1947-)
Forever Amber '47
Laura '44

Dick Powell (1904-63)
The Hunters '58
Enemy Below '57
The Conqueror '56
Split Second '53
Michael Powell (1905-90)
Peeping Tom '60
Night Ambush '57
The Tales of Hoffmann '51
The Small Back Room '49
The Red Shoes '48
Black Narcissus '47
Stairway to Heaven '46
I Know Where I'm Going '45
A Canterbury Tale '44
The Life and Death of Colonel Blimp '43

Paul Powell (1881-1944)
Pollyanna 20
The Liar's Club '33
Matrimaniac '16

John Power (1930-)
Father '90
Alice to Nowhere '86
Goicrush: A Real Life
Alaskan Adventure '98
Spy in Black '39
The Thief of Bagdad '40
The Lion Has Wings '40
Contraband '40
Missing 41
One of Our Aircraft Is
The Forty-Ninth Parallel '41

Tristam Powell (1940-)
American Friends '91
Ghostwriter '84

Wayne Powers
Out of Order '03
Sound of Love '78
Great God Swindle '84
All My Sons '86
Stanley Prager (1917-72)
Skeletons in the Closet '00
Michael Preece
Beretta's Island '92
Brothers in Trouble '95
My Son the Fanatic '97
Udayan Prasad (1953-)
Prize Fighter '79
Bang Bang Kid '67
Madigan's Millions '67
H.C. Potter

Otto Preminger (1906-86)
Rosebud '75
The Human Factor '79
In Harm's Way '65
The Cardinal '63
Advise and Consent '62
Exodus '60
Anatomy of a Murder '59
Bonjour Tristesse '57
Saint Joan '57
The Court Martial of Billy Mitchell '55
The Man with the Golden Arm '55
Carmen Jones '54
River of No Return '54
The Moon is Blue '53
Angel Face '52

Michael Pressman (1950-)
Saint Maybe '98
A Season for Miracles '99
To Gillian on Her 37th Birthday '96
Teenage Mutant Ninja Turtles 2: The Secret of the Ooze '91
Dark River: A Father's Revenge '90
Man against the Mob: The Chinatown Murders '89
The Imposter '84
To Heal a Nation '88

Emeric Pressburger (1902-88)
Night Ambush '57
The Tales of Hoffmann '51
The Small Back Room '49
The Red Shoes '48
Black Narcissus '47
Stairway to Heaven '46
I Know Where I'm Going '45
A Canterbury Tale '44
The Life and Death of Colonel Blimp '43
One of Our Aircraft is Missing '41
The Contender '44

Alex Proyas (1965-)
I, Robot '04
Garage Days '03
Dark City '97
The Crow '93
Craig Pryce
The Dark '94
Revenge of the Radioactive Reporter '91
Alexander Ptushko (1900-73)
Sword & the Dragon '56
The Magic Voyage of Sinbad '52
Storm over Asia '28
Vsevolod Pudovkin (1893-1953)

Franco Prosperi (1928-)
The Wild Beasts '85
Invincible Barbarian '83
Throne of Fire '82
Counter Punch '71
Mondo Cane 2 '64
Alex Proyas

David A. Prior
Felony '95
Mutant Species '95
Mardi Gras for the Devil '93
Raw Justice '93
Center of the Web '92
Double Threat '92
Future Zone '90
Invasion Force '90
Lock 'n' Load '90
White Fury '90
Future Force '89
Final Sanction '88
Jungle Assault '89
The Lost Platoon '89
Operation Warzone '89
Rapid Fire '89
Night Wars '88
Deadly Prey '87
Killer Workout '86
Mankillers '87
Sledgehammer '83

Gina Prince-Bythewood (1969-)
Disappearing Acts '00
Love and Basketball '00
Prince (1958-)
Graffiti Bridge '90
Under the Cherry Moon '86
Harold Prince (1928-)
Something for Everyone '70
A Little Night Music '77
Joseph Prieto
To Die For 2: Son of Darkness '91
Final Sacrifice '92
Children of the Corn 2: The
Dr. Jekyll and Ms. Hyde '95
David F. Price (1961-)
Love in Florence '62
Escapade in Florence '62
Almost Angels '62
Waltz King '63
Steve Previn (1925-93)
Divided '93
Charles & Diana: A Palace Divided '93
Stephen King's The
Tommyknockers '93
Father '90

Gaylene Preston
Perfect Strangers '03
Dark of the Night '85
Ruben Preuss
The Art of Murder '99
Almost Dead '94
Dead on Sight '94
Write to Kill '91
Deceptions '90
In Dangerous Company '88
Evelyn Purcell
Nobody's Fool '86
Joe Pytka (1938-)
Space Jam '96
Left it Rice '89
Albert Pyun (1954-)
Ticker '01
Corrupt '99
Urban Menace '99
Ravenhawk '95
Heatseeker '95
Hong Kong '97, '94
Nemesis '93
Knights '93
Brain Smasher... A Love Story '93
Arcade '93
Spitfire '94
Nemesis 2: Nebula '94
Kickboxer 4: The Aggressor '94
Dollman '91
Bloodmatch '91
Captain America '89
Cyborg '89
Deceit '89
Down Twisted '89
Alien from L.A. '87
Dangerously Close '86
Radioactive Dreams '86
Sword & the Sorcerer '82

Joseph Prieto
Savages from Hell '68
Shanty Tramp '67
Adrenalin: Fear the Rush
Blast '96
Omega Door '96
Nemesis 3: Time Lapse '96
Sweeney Todd: The Demon Barber of Fleet Street '84

Jon Purdy
Joshua '02
Reflections in the Dark '94
John Quinn
Cheerleader Camp '88
Total Exposure '91
Gene Quintano (1946-)
National Lampoon's Loaded Weapon 1 '93
Honeymoon Academy '90
Why Me? '90
Eduardo Quiroz
I Got Five on It '05
Jose Quiroz
San Franpsycho '06
I Got Five on It '05
John Putch (1961-)
Tycus '98
My Magic Dog '97
Alone in the Woods '97
A Time to Remember '03
Dillinger and Capone '95
Pursuit of Happiness '01

Gene Quintano
Luis Puenzo (1946-)
Old Gringo '89
The Plague '92
The Official Story '85
The Great Texas Dynamite Chase '76
Robert Radler
The Substitute 4: Failure is Not an Option '00
The Substitute 3: Winner Takes All '99
The Substitute '96
Eric Radomski
Batman: Mask of the Phantasm '93
Michael Raeburn (1943-)
Killing Heat '84
Bob Rafelson (1933-)
No Good Deed '02
Poodle Springs '98
Blood & Wine '96
Man Trouble '92
Mountains of the Moon '90
Black Widow '87
The Postman Always Rings Twice '81
Stay Hungry '76
Five Easy Pieces '70
Head '68

Fons Rademakers (1920-2007)
The Assault '86
Because of the Cats '74
The Rose Garden '89
Peter Rader
Grandma's House '88
Hired to Kill '93
Michael Radford (1946-)
Flawless '07
The Merchant of Venice '04
Dancing at the Blue Iguana '00
B. Monkey '97
The Postman '94
White Mischief '88
1984 '84
Another Time, Another Place '83
Harold Ramis (1944-)
The Ice Harvest '05
Analyze That '02
Bedazzled '00
Analyze This '98
Multiplicity '96
Stuart Saves His Family '94
Groundhog Day '93
Club Paradise '86
National Lampoon's Vacation '82
Caddyshack '80

Lynne Ramsay (1969-)
Morvern Callar '02
Ratcatcher '99
Addison Randall (1949-)
The Killing Zone '90
Chance '89
East L.A. Warriors '89
Payback '89
Tony Randel (1956-)
Rattled '96
Fist of the North Star '95
One Good Turn '95
Ticks '93
Amityville 1992: It's About Time '92
Children of the Night '92
Hellbound: Hellraiser 2 '88
Arthur Rankin, Jr. (1924-)
Flight of Dragons '82
The Return of the King '80
The Hobbit '78

Mark Rappaport (1932-)
From the Journals of Jean Seberg '95
Rock Hudson's Home Movies '92
Impostors '80
Jean-Paul Rappeneau (1932-)
Bon Voyage '03
Cyrano de Bergerac '90
Swashbuckler '84
Lovers Like Us '75
The Horseman on the Roof '95

Alan Rafkin (1928-)
The Tender Warrior '71
Ski Party '65
How to Frame a Figg '71
Sam Raimi (1959-)
Spider-Man 3 '07
Spider-Man 2 '04
Spider-Man '02
The Gift '00
For Love of the Game '99
A Simple Plan '98
The Quick and the Dead '95
Army of Darkness '92
Darkman '90
Evil Dead 2: Dead by Dawn '87
Crimewave '85
Evil Dead '83
The First Olympics: Athens 1896 '84
Alvin Rakoff (1927-)
A Voyage 'Round My Father '82
A Dance to the Music of Time '97
A Brooklyn State of Mind '97
Frank Rainone
King Solomon's Treasure '78
Death Ship '80
Dirty Tricks '81
Lynne Ramsay

Irving Rapper (1898-1999)
Born Again '73

Alan Rafkin
When the North Wind Blows '74
Sex and the Single Girl '64
Paris When It Sizzles '64
Stranger's When We Meet '60
The World of Suzie Wong '60
Bell, Book and Candle '58
Full of Life '56
Solid Gold Cadillac '56
My Sister Eileen '55

Marjorie Morningstar '58
The Brave One '56
Forever Female '53
Another Man's Poison '52
Deception '46
The Corn Is Green '45
Rhapsody in Blue '45
The Adventures of Mark Twain '44
Now, Voyager '42

Steve Rash
Bring It On: In It to Win It '07
Bring It On: All or Nothing '06
American Pie Presents Band Camp '05
Good Advice '01
Held Up '00
Eddie '96
Son-in-Law '93
Queens Logic '91
Can't Buy Me Love '87
Under the Rainbow '81
The Buddy Holly Story '78

Ian Iqbal Rashid
How She Move '08
Touch of Pink '04

Daniel Raskov
A Kiss Goodnight '94
The Masters of Menace '90
Wedding Band '89

Brett Ratner (1970-)
Rush Hour 3 '07
X-Men: The Last Stand '06
After the Sunset '04
Red Dragon '02
Rush Hour 2 '01
Family Man '00
Rush Hour '98
Money Talks '97

Gregory Ratoff (1897-1960)
Abdulla the Great '56
Black Magic '49
Abrabian Nights '42
Overland Mail '42
Sherlock Holmes: The Voice of Terror '42
Junior G-Men '40

Albert Ray (1897-1944)
Everyman's Law '36
Undercover Man '36
Dancing Man '33
Shriek in the Night '33
13th Guest '32

Bernard B. Ray (1895-1964)
Movie Stuntmen '53
Buffalo Bill Rides Again '47
House of Errors '42
Broken Strings '40
Covered Wagon Trails '40
Pinto Canyon '40
Roamin' Wild '36
Speed Reporter '36
Coyote Trails '35
Kentucky Blue Streak '35
The Midnight Phantom '35
Silent Valley '35
Texas Jack '34
The Silver Bullet '34

Billy Ray
Breach '07
Shattered Glass '03

Fred Olen Ray (1954-)
The Glass Trap '04

Air Rage '01
Black Horizon '01
Venomous '01
Kept '01
Critical Mass '00
Mach 2 '00
Submerged '00
Active Stealth '99
The Capitol Conspiracy '99
Fugitive Mind '99
The Kid with the X-Ray Eyes '99
Rapid Assault '99
Mom, Can I Keep Her? '98
Death and Desire '97
Hybrid '97
Invisible Dad '97
Night Shade '97
The Shooter '97
Friend of the Family 2 '96
Fugitive Rage '96
Invisible Mom '96
Attack of the 60-Foot Centerfold '95
Cyberzone '95
Over the Wire '95
Bikini Drive-In '94
Inner Sanctum 2 '94
Wizards of the Demon Sword '94
Dinosaur Island '93
Mind Twister '93
Possessed by the Night '93
Haunting Fear '91
Inner Sanctum '91
Bad Girls from Mars '90
Evil Toons '90
Mob Boss '90
Spirits '90
Alienator '89
Beverly Hills Vamp '88
Hollywood Chainsaw Hookers '88
Terminal Force '88
Warlords '88
Commando Squad '87
Cyclone '87
Deep Space '87
Phantom Empire '87
Star Slammer '87
Armed Response '86
Tomb '86
Bio Hazard '85
Alien Dead '79

Nicholas Ray (1911-79)
55 Days at Peking '63
The King of Kings '61
Party Girl '58
Rebel without a Cause '55
Johnny Guitar '53
The Lusty Men '52
Flying Leathernecks '51
On Dangerous Ground '51
Born to Be Bad '50
In a Lonely Place '50
Knock on Any Door '49
They Live by Night '49
A Woman's Secret '49

Satyajit Ray (1921-92)
The Stranger '92
The Home and the World '84
The Middleman '76
Distant Thunder '73
The Adversary '71
Days and Nights in the Forest '70
Charulata '64
The Big City '63
Two Daughters '61
Devi '60
The World of Apu '59
Aparajito '58
Jalsaghar '58
Pather Panchali '54

Ed Raymond
See Fred Olen Ray

David Raynr
Whatever It Takes '00
Trippin' '99

Spiro Razatos (1960-)
Class of 1999 2: The Substitute '93
Fast Getaway '91

Bill Rebane (1937-)
The Capture of Bigfoot '79

The Alpha Incident '76
The Giant Spider Invasion '75
Rana: The Legend of Shadow Lake '75
Monster a Go-Go! '65

Eric Red (1961-)
Bad Moon '96
Undertow '95
Body Parts '91
Cohen and Tate '88

Robert Redford (1937-)
Lions for Lambs '07
The Legend of Bagger Vance '00
The Horse Whisperer '97
Quiz Show '94
A River Runs Through It '92
The Milagro Beanfield War '88
Ordinary People '80

Carol Reed (1906-76)
Oliver! '68
The Agony and the Ecstasy '65
Our Man in Havana '59
The Key '58
Trapeze '56
A Kid for Two Farthings '55
The Fallen Idol '49
The Third Man '49
Odd Man Out '47
Immortal Battalion '44
Kipps '41
Night Train to Munich '40
The Stars Look Down '39

Theodore Reed
Double or Nothing '37

Tripp Reed
Walking Tall: Lone Justice '07
Manticore '05

Clive Rees
When the Whales Came '89
Blockhouse '73

Christopher Reeve (1952-2004)
Everyone's Hero '06
In the Gloaming '97

Geoffrey Reeve (1932-)
Souvenir '88
Caravan to Vaccares '74
Puppet on a Chain '72

Matt Reeves (1966-)
Cloverfield '08
Fear X '03
Pusher '96
The Nut 21

Joel M. Reed (1933-)
Night of the Zombies '81
Bloodsucking Freaks '75
G.I. Executioner '71

Peyton Reed (1964-)
The Break-Up '06
Down With Love '03
Bring It On '00
The Love Bug '97

Roland D. Reed (1894-1974)
The House of Secrets '37
Red Lights Ahead '36

Michael Reeves (1944-69)
The Conqueror Worm '68
The She-Beast '65

Nicolas Winding Refn (1970-)
River of Grass '94

Alastair Reid (1939-)
Nostromo '96
Armistead Maupin's Tales of the City '93
Teamster Boss: The Jackie Presser Story '92

Traffik '90
Shattered '72
Baby Love '69

Dorothy Reid
See Dorothy Davenport Reid

Dorothy Davenport Reid (1895-1977)
Sucker Money '34
Woman Condemned '33
Linda '29

Tim Reid (1944-)
For Real '02
Asunder '99
Once Upon a Time... When We Were Colored '95

Roel Reine
Pistol Whipped '08
The Delivery '99

Carl Reiner (1922-)
That Old Feeling '96
Fatal Instinct '93
Bert Rigby, You're a Fool '89
Summer School '87
Summer Rental '85
All of Me '84
The Man with Two Brains '83
The Jerk '79
The One and Only '78
Oh, God! '77
Where's Poppa? '70
The Comic '69
Enter Laughing '67

Jeff Reiner
Deadly Game '98
Smalltime '96
Serpent's Lair '95
Trouble Bound '92
Blood & Concrete: A Love Story '90

Rob Reiner (1945-)
The Bucket List '07
Rumor Has It... '05
Alex & Emma '03
The Story of Us '99
Ghosts of Mississippi '96
The American President '95
North '94
Misery '90
When Harry Met Sally... '89
The Princess Bride '87
Stand by Me '86
The Sure Thing '85
This Is Spinal Tap '84

Gottfried Reinhardt (1911-94)
Town without Pity '61
Betrayed '54

Harald Reinl (1908-86)
Fight for Gold '86
Hell Hounds of Alaska '73
The Torture Chamber of Dr. Sadism '69
The Last Tomahawk '65
Carpet of Horror '64
Strangler of Blackmoor Castle '63
The Invisible Dr. Mabuse '62
Forger of London '61
The Return of Dr. Mabuse '61

Irving Reis (1906-53)
Three Husbands '50
All My Sons '48
The Bachelor and the Bobby-Soxer '47
Crack-Up '46
Big Street '42
The Falcon Takes Over '42

Walter Reisch (1903-83)
Song of Scheherazade '47
Men Are Not Gods '37

Charles Reisner (1887-1962)
Train to Tombstone '50
The Traveling Saleswoman '50
The Cobra Strikes '48

Lost in a Harem '44
Big Store '41
Manhattan Merry-Go-Round '37
Steamboat Bill, Jr. '28
The Man on the Box '25

Karel Reisz (1926-2002)
Everybody Wins '90
Sweet Dreams '85
The French Lieutenant's Woman '81
Who'll Stop the Rain? '78
The Gambler '74
Isadora '68
Morgan: A Suitable Case for Treatment '66
Saturday Night and Sunday Morning '60

Wolfgang Reitherman (1909-85)
The Many Adventures of Winnie the Pooh '77
The Rescuers '77
Robin Hood '73
The Aristocats '70
The Jungle Book '67
The Sword in the Stone '63
101 Dalmatians '61
Sleeping Beauty '59

Ivan Reitman (1946-)
My Super Ex-Girlfriend '06
Evolution '01
Six Days, Seven Nights '98
Father's Day '96
Junior '94
Dave '93
Kindergarten Cop '90
Ghostbusters 2 '89
Twins '88
Legal Eagles '86
Ghostbusters '84
Stripes '81
Meatballs '79

Jason Reitman
Juno '07
Thank You for Smoking '06

Edgar Reitz (1932-)
Heimat 2 '92
Heimat 1 '84

Norman Rene (1951-96)
Reckless '95
Prelude to a Kiss '92
Longtime Companion '90

Jeff Renfroe
Civic Duty '06
Paranoia 1.0 '04

Jean Renoir (1894-1979)
The Little Theatre of Jean Renoir '71
The Elusive Corporal '62
Picnic on the Grass '59
The Testament of Dr. Cordelier '59
Elena and Her Men '56
French Can-Can '55
The Golden Coach '52
The River '51
A Day in the Country '46
Diary of a Chambermaid '46
The Southerner '45
This Land Is Mine '43
The Rules of the Game '39
La Bete Humaine '38
Grand Illusion '37
La Marseillaise '37
The Crime of Monsieur Lange '36
The Lower Depths '36
Madame Bovary '34
Toni '34
Boudu Saved from Drowning '32
La Chienne '31
Tournament '29
Renoir Shorts '27
Charleston '26

Nicholas Renton (1946-)
Bait '02
Wives and Daughters '01
Far from the Madding Crowd '97

Alain Resnais (1922-)
Private Fears in Public Places '06
Same Old Song '97
Smoking/No Smoking '94
I Want to Go Home '89
Melo '86
Life Is a Bed of Roses '83
Mon Oncle d'Amerique '80
Providence '77
Stavisky '74
La Guerre Est Finie '66
Muriel '63
Last Year at Marienbad '61
Hiroshima, Mon Amour '59

Dale Resteghini (1968-)
Da Hip Hop Witch '00
Colorz of Rage '97

Harry Revier (1889-1957)
The Lost City '34
When Lightning Strikes '34
Stick '85
Sharky's Machine '81
The End '78
Gator '76
Empire '02

Franc Reyes
Illegal Tender '07

Burt Reynolds (1936-)
The Final Hit '02
The Man from Left Field '93

Kevin Reynolds (1950-)
Tristan & Isolde '06
The Count of Monte Cristo '02
187 '97
Waterworld '95
Rapa Nui '93
Robin Hood: Prince of Thieves '91
The Beast '88
Fandango '85

Lynn F. Reynolds (1889-1927)
Riders of the Purple Sage '25
Sky High '22
Trailin' '21

Scott Reynolds (1968-)
Heaven '99
The Ugly '96

Phillip Rhee (1960-)
Best of the Best: Without Warning '98
Best of the Best 3: No Turning Back '95

Michael Rhodes (1935-)
Christy '94
Heidi '93
The Killing Mind '90
Matters of the Heart '90

Michael Ray Rhodes
Entertaining Angels: The Dorothy Day Story '96
Fourth Wise Man '85
Shooting '82

Tonino Ricci (1927-)
Buck and the Magic Bracelet '97
Rush '84
Great Treasure Hunt '72
Liberators '69

David Lowell Rich (1923-)
Choices '86
Convicted '86
The Hearst and Davies Affair '85
Scandal Sheet '85
Chu Chu & the Philly Flash '81
Enola Gay: The Men, the Mission, the Atomic Bomb '80
Nurse '80
The Concorde: Airport '79 '79
Family Upside Down '78
Little Women '78
Satan's School for Girls '73
That Man Bolt '73

The Tunnel '01
Roland Suso Richter
Dresden '06
A Man Called Rage '84
Deja Vu '84
Days of Hell
Night of the Sharks '87
Anthony Richmond (1942)
Winter Kills '79
Reardon '88
A Night in the Life of Jim'ny Reardon '88
The Man in the Iron Mask '97
William Richert (1944)
Hamlet '69
Ned Kelly '70
Joseph Andrews '77
The Phantom of the Opera '90
Blue Sky '91
Tony Richardson (1928-91)
The Border '82
The Hotel New Hampshire '84
Penalty Phase '86
Shadow on the Sun '88
The Piano Lesson '94
Peter Richardson (1951-)
Paul Robeson '77
The Pope Must Diet '91
Eat the Rich '87
Supergrass '87
Lloyd Richards (1919-2006)
Twins '75
Dick Richards (1934-)
Culpepper Cattle Co. '72
Rafferty & the Gold Dust Twins '75
Farewell, My Lovely '75
March or Die '77
Death Valley '81
Kiss and Tell '96
Man, Woman & Child '83
David Richards
Reckless: The Sequel '98
Virtual Encounters '96
Femalien '96
Lolita 2000 '97
Erotic House of Wax '97
Cybil (Sybil) Richards
See Hal Hartley
Ned Rifle

Pierre Richard (1934-)
Too Shy to Try '82
The Daydreamer '75
Richard (Jeff) Jefferson (1946-)
Berserker '87
In Search of a Golden Sky '84
Matty Rich (1971-)
The Inkwell '94
Straight out of Brooklyn '91
Richard Rich
The Trumpet of the Swan '01
The King and I '99
The Swan Princess 2: Escape from Castle Mountain '97
The Black Cauldron '85
The Fox and the Hound '81
The Swan Princess '94
John Rich (1925-)
Have Rocket Will Travel '59
Easy Come, Easy Go '67
Boeing Boeing '65
Roustabout '64
Northeast of Seoul '72
Madame X '66

W.D. Richter (1945-)
Late for Dinner '91
The Adventures of Buckaroo Banzai Across the Eighth Dimension '84
Thomas (Tom) Rickman
Crash Course '00
The River Rat '84
Philip Ridley
The Passion of Darkly Noon '95
The Reflecting Skin '91
Leni Riefenstahl (1902-2003)
Tiefland '44
Triumph of the Will '34
The Blue Light '32
Adam Rifkin (1966-)
The Dark Backward '91
The Invisible Maniac '90
Never on Tuesday '88
The Chase '93
The Nutt House '95
Psycho Cop 2 '94
Tale of Two Sisters '89
Night at the Golden Eagle '02
Arthur Ripley (1895-1961)
Thunder Road '58
The Chase '46
Maria Ripoli
Tortilla Soup '01
Twice upon a Yesterday '98
Arturo Ripstein (1943-)
Deep Crimson '96
Foxtrot '76
Dino Risi (1916-)
Scent of a Woman '75
Il Sorpasso '63
Love in the City '53
Michael Rissi
Soultaker '90
Terror Eyes '87
Guy Ritchie (1968-)
Revolver '05
Swept Away '02
Snatch '00
Lock, Stock and 2 Smoking Barrels '98
Michael Ritchie (1938-2001)
A Simple Wish '97
The Fantasticks '95
Cops and Robbersons '94
The Positively True Adventures of the Alleged Texas Cheerleader-Murdering Mom '93
Diggstown '92
Fletch Lives '89
The Couch Trip '87
The Golden Child '86
Wildcats '86
Fletch '85
Survivors '83
The Island '80
An Almost Perfect Affair '79
Semi-Tough '77
The Bad News Bears '76
Smile '75
The Candidate '72
Prime Cut '72
Downhill Racer '69
Tim Robbins (1958-)
The Cradle Will Rock '99
Dead Man Walking '95
Bob Roberts '92
Matthew Robbins (1945-)
Bingo '91
batteries not included '87
The Legend of Billie Jean '85
Dragonslayer '81
Corvette Summer '78
Arthur Robison (1883-1935)
The Informer '29
Mark Robson (1913-)
Earthquake '74
Avalanche Express '79
Happy Birthday Wanda June '71
Valley of the Dolls '67
Von Ryan's Express '65
The Prize '63
Nine Hours to Rama '63
From the Terrace '60
The Inn of the Sixth Happiness '58
Peyton Place '57
The Harder They Fall '56
The Bridges at Toko-Ri '55
Return to Paradise '53
Phffft! '54
I Want You '51
Champion '49
Home of the Brave '49
My Foolish Heart '49

Jacques Rivette (1928-)
The Duchess of Langeais '07
Va Savoir '01
Up/Down/Fragile '95
Jeanne la Pucelle '94
La Belle Noiseuse '90
Céline and Julie Go Boating '74
Paris Belongs to Us '60
Lance Rivera
The Cookout '04
The Perfect Holiday '07
Daryl Roberts
How U Like Me Now? '92
Alan Roberts
Save Me '93
Round Trip to Heaven '92
Karate Cop '91
The Happy Hooker Goes Hollywood '80
Young Lady Chatterly 2 '85
Charles E. Roberts (1894-1951)
Mexican Hayride '48
Stephen Roberts (1917-99)
Star of Midnight '35
Romance in Manhattan '34
The Ex-Mrs. Bradford '36
John S. Robertson (1878-1964)
Our Little Girl '35
Little Orphan Annie '32
Captain Salvation '27
Tess of the Storm Country '22
Dr. Jekyll and Mr. Hyde '20
Jay Roach (1957-)
Meet the Fockers '04
Austin Powers in Goldmember '02
Meet the Parents '00
Austin Powers 2: The Spy Who Shagged Me '99
Mystery, Alaska '99
Austin Powers: International Man of Mystery '97
Hal Roach (1892-1992)
One Million B.C. '40
The Devil's Brother '33
Bruce Robinson (1946-)
Jennifer 8 '92
How to Get Ahead in Advertising '89
Withnail and I '87
Chris Robinson (1938-)
Sunshine Run '79
Thunder County '74
Women's Prison Escape '74
Angela Robinson (1971-)
Herbie: Fully Loaded '05
D.E.B.S. '04
Phil Alden Robinson (1950-)
The Sum of All Fears '02
Sneakers '92
Field of Dreams '89
In the Mood '87
Richard Robinson
Poor Pretty Eddie '73
Bloody Trail '72
John Mark Robinson
Roadhouse 66 '84
All Tied Up '92
Kid '90
Seymour Robbie (1928-2004)
Marco '73
C.C. & Company '70
Norbit '07
Brian Robbins (1964-)
Meet Dave '08
The Shaggy Dog '06
The Perfect Score '04
Hardball '01
Ready to Rumble '00
Varsity Blues '98
Good Burger '97
The Show '95
Mike Robe
Montana Sky '07
The Junction Boys '02
Degree of Guilt '95
Return to Lonesome Dove '93
Murder Ordained '87
News at Eleven '86
Urge to Kill '84
Yves Robert (1920-2002)
My Father's Glory '91
My Mother's Castle '91
Pardon Mon Affaire, Too! '77
Pardon Mon Affaire '76

Martin Ritt (1914-90)
Stanley and Iris '90
Nuts '87
Murphy's Romance '85
Cross Creek '83
Back Roads '81
Norma Rae '79
Casey's Shadow '78
The Front '75
Conrack '74
Pete 'n' Tillie '72
Sounder '72
The Great White Hope '70
The Molly Maguires '70
The Brotherhood '68
Hombre '67
The Spy Who Came in from the Cold '65
Hud '63
Paris Blues '61
The Long, Hot Summer '58
John Roberts
Welcome to Hollywood '00
Detroit Rock City '99
Something About Sex '98
Eric Rochant (1961-)
Love without Pity '91
Chris Rock (1966-)
I Think I Love My Wife '07
Head of State '03
Charles R. Rogers (1887-1956)
March of the Wooden Soldiers '34
Alexandre Rockwell (1957-)
13 Moons '02
Four Rooms '95
Somebody to Love '94
In the Soup '92
Sons '89
Franc Roddam (1946-)
Cleopatra '99
Moby Dick '98
K2: The Ultimate High '92
War Party '89
Aria '88
The Bride '85
The Lords of Discipline '83
Quadrophenia '79
Serge Rodnunsky
Newsbreak '00
TripFall '00
Cypress Edge '99
Fear Runs Silent '99
Paper Bullets '99
Silicon Towers '99
Bomb Squad '97
Dead Cert '96
Powder Burn '96
Final Equinox '96
Lovers' Lovers '94

Marc Rocco (1965-)
Murder in the First '95
Where the Day Takes You '92
Dream a Little Dream '89
Scenes from the Goldmine '87
Glauce Rocha (1930-73)
Antonio Das Mortes '68
Earth Entranced '66
Black God, White Devil '64
Albert Rogell (1901-88)
The Admiral Was a Lady '50
War of the Wildcats '43
The Black Cat '41
Argentine Nights '40
Li'l Abner '40
Murder in Greenwich Village '37
No More Women '34
Suicide Fleet '31
The Tip-Off '31
Michael Roemer (1928-)
The Plot Against Harry '69
Pilgrim, Farewell '82
Nothing but a Man '64
Maclean Rogers (1899-1962)
Down Among the Z Men '52
Goon Movie '52
Old Mother Riley's Jungle Treasure '51
James B. Rogers (19??-)
The Devil's Brother '33
American Pie 2 '01
Say It Isn't So '01
Eric Rohmer (1920-)
Triple Agent '04
The Lady and the Duke '01
Autumn Tale '98
A Summer's Tale '96
Rendezvous in Paris '95
A Tale of Winter '92
Four Adventures of Reinette and Mirabelle '89
A Tale of Springtime '89
Boyfriends & Girlfriends '88
Summer '86
Full Moon in Paris '84
Pauline at the Beach '83
Le Beau Mariage '82
The Aviator's Wife '80
Six in Paris '68
La Collectionneuse '67
Perceval '78
Chloe in the Afternoon '72
Claire's Knee '71
The Marquise of O '76
Nicolas Roeg (1928-)
Puffball '07
Samson and Delilah '96
Full Body Massage '95
Two Deaths '94
Cold Heaven '92
The Witches '90
Track 29 '88
Aria '88
Castaway '87
Insignificance '85
Eureka '81
Bad Timing '80
The Man Who Fell to Earth '76
Don't Look Now '73
Walkabout '71
Performance '70
Phil Roman (1930-)
Tom and Jerry: The Movie '93
Jean Rollin (1938-)
Two Orphan Vampires '97
Lost in New York '89
Emmanuelle 6 '88
The Living Dead Girl '82
Zombie Lake '80
Lips of Blood '75
The Iron Rose '73
Mark Romanek (1959-)
One Hour Photo '02
Static '87
Eddie Romero (1924-)
Beast of the Yellow Night '70
Brides of the Beast '68
Mad Doctor of Blood Island '68
The Ravagers '65
The Walls of Hell '64
Cavalry Command '63
Raiders of Leyte Gulf '63
George A. Romero (1940-)
Diary of the Dead '07
Land of the Dead '05
Bruiser '00
The Dark Half '93
Two Evil Eyes '90
Monkey Shines '88
Day of the Dead '85
Knightriders '81
Dawn of the Dead '79
Martin '78
The Crazies '73
Season of the Witch '72
Night of the Living Dead '68
Robert Rodriguez (1968-)
Planet Terror '07
Grindhouse '07
The Adventures of Sharkboy and Lavagirl in 3-D '05
Sin City '05
Once Upon a Time in Mexico '03
Spy Kids 3-D: Game Over '03
Spy Kids 2: The Island of Lost Dreams '02
Spy Kids '01
The Faculty '98
Desperado '95
Four Rooms '95
From Dusk Till Dawn '95
Roadracers '94
El Mariachi '93
Joao Pedro Rodrigues (1966-)
Two Drifters '05
O Fantasma '00
Ismael Rodriguez (1917-2004)
Autopsy of a Ghost '67
Daniel Boone: Trail Blazer '56
Sutton Roley (1922-2007)
Snatched '72
Loners '72
Chosen Survivors '74
Satan's Triangle '75

George A. Romero
Romero's Land of the Dead '05
Bruiser '00
The Dark Half '91
Two Evil Eyes '90
Monkey Shines '88
Day of the Dead '85
Creepshow '82
Knightriders '81
Dawn of the Dead '78
Martin '77
The Crazies '73
Season of the Witch '73
Night of the Living Dead '68

Charles R. Rondeau (1917-96)
The Girl in Lover's Lane '60
The Devil's Partner '58

Darrell Roodt (1963-)
Queen's Messenger II '01
Second Skin '00
Dangerous Ground '96
Cry, the Beloved Country '95
Father Hood '93
To the Death '93
Sarafina! '92
City of Blood '88
Place of Weeping '86

Don Roos (1959-)
Happy Endings '05
Bounce '00
The Opposite of Sex '98

Tom Ropelewski
Look Who's Talking Now '93
Madhouse '90

Mark Roper (1958-)
Queen's Messenger II '01
Operation Delta Force 3: Clear Target '98
Alien Chaser '96
Warhead '96
Live Wire: Human Timebomb '95

Cliff Roquemore (1948-2002)
Devil's Son-in-Law '77
Dolemite 2: Human Tornado '76

Giuseppe Rosati
Perfect Crime '79
Street War '76

Bernard Rose (1960-)
Leo Tolstoy's Anna Karenina '96
Immortal Beloved '94
Candyman '92
Chicago Joe & the Showgirl '90
Paperhouse '89
Smart Money '88

Lee Rose
A Girl Thing '01
The Truth About Jane '00
The Color of Courage '98

Les Rose
Gas '81
Title Shot '81
Hog Wild '80

Barry Rosen
The Yum-Yum Girls '78
Gang Wars '75

Martin Rosen
Stacking '87
The Plague Dogs '82
Watership Down '78

Phil Rosen (1888-1951)
In Old New Mexico '45
The Jade Mask '45
The Scarlet Clue '45
Charlie Chan in the Secret Service '44
The Chinese Cat '44
Meeting at Midnight '44
Return of the Ape Man '44
Wings over the Pacific '43
I Killed That Man '42
The Man with Two Lives '42
Gangs, Inc. '41
Spooks Run Wild '41
Phantom of Chinatown '40
It Could Happen to You '37
Youth on Parole '37
Mistaken Identity '36
The President's Mystery '36
Tango '36
Beggars in Ermine '34
Dangerous Corner '34
Woman in the Dark '34
The Phantom Broadcast '33
The Sphinx '33
Young Blood '33
Man's Land '32
Texas Gunfighter '32
Whistlin' Dan '32
Arizona Terror '31
Branded Men '31
The Pocatello Kid '31
Range Law '31
Two Gun Man '31
The Peacock Fan '29
The Phantom in the House '29

Craig Rosenberg (1965-)
Half Light '05
Hotel de Love '96

Rick Rosenberg
Southern Man '99

Stuart Rosenberg (1927-2007)
Distant Thunder '88
My Heroes Have Always Been Cowboys '91
The Pope of Greenwich Village '84
Brubaker '80
The Amityville Horror '79
Love and Bullets '79
Voyage of the Damned '76
The Drowning Pool '76
The Laughing Policeman '74
Pocket Money '72
April Fools '69
Cool Hand Luke '67

Seth Zvi Rosenfeld
King of the Jungle '01
A Brother's Kiss '97
Subway Stories '97

Rick Rosenthal (1949-)
Nearing Grace '05
Halloween: Resurrection '02
Just a Little Harmless Sex '99
The Birds 2: Land's End '94
Devlin '92
Russkies '87
American Dreamer '84
Bad Boys '83
Halloween 2: The Nightmare Isn't Over! '81

Robert J. Rosenthal
Zapped! '82
Malibu Beach '78

Francesco Rosi (1922-)
The Truce '96
The Palermo Connection '91
Three Brothers '80
Christ Stopped at Eboli '79
Lucky Luciano '74

Mark Rosman (1959-)
The Perfect Man '05
A Cinderella Story '04
Life-Size '00
Model Behavior '00
The Invader '96
Evolver '94
The Force '94
The Blue Yonder '86
The House on Sorority Row '83

Milton Rosmer (1881-1971)
The Challenge '38
Murder in the Old Red Barn '36
The Secret of the Loch '34

Gary Ross (1956-)
Seabiscuit '03
Pleasantville '98

Herbert Ross (1927-2001)
Boys on the Side '94
Undercover Blues '93
True Colors '91
My Blue Heaven '90
Steel Magnolias '89
Dancers '87
The Secret of My Success '87
Footloose '84
Protocol '84
Max Dugan Returns '83
I Ought to Be in Pictures '82
Pennies from Heaven '81
Nijinsky '80
California Suite '78
The Goodbye Girl '77
The Turning Point '77
The Seven-Per-Cent Solution '76
Funny Lady '75
The Sunshine Boys '75
The Last of Sheila '73
Play It Again, Sam '72
The Owl and the Pussycat '70
Goodbye, Mr. Chips '69
Goodbye Love '34

Roberto Rossellini (1906-77)
The Messiah '75
Augustine of Hippo '72
Blaise Pascal '71
The Rise of Louis XIV '66
RoGoPaG '62
Vanina Vanini '61
Era Notte a Roma '60
Generale Della Rovere '60
Seven Deadly Sins '53
Voyage in Italy '53
Europa '51 '52
The Flowers of St. Francis '50
Stromboli '50
Amore '48
Machine to Kill Bad People '48
The Miracle '48
Deutschland im Jahre Null '47
Paisan '46
Open City '45
Man with a Cross '43

Robert Rossen (1908-66)
Lilith '64
The Hustler '61
They Came to Cordura '59
Island in the Sun '57
Alexander the Great '55
Mambo '55
Body and Soul '47

Arthur Rosson (1886-1960)
Boots of Destiny '37
Hidden Gold '33
The Concentratin' Kid '30
Trailing Trouble '30
The Last Outlaw '27

Bobby Roth (1950-)
Brave New Girl '04
Keeper of the City '92
The Game of Love '90
The Man Inside '90
Rainbow Drive '90
Dead Solid Perfect '88
Baja Oklahoma '87
Heartbreakers '84
Circle of Power '83
Boss' Son '78

Eli Roth (1972-)
Hostel: Part 2 '07
Hostel '06
Cabin Fever '03

Joe Roth (1948-)
Freedomland '06
Christmas With the Kranks '04
America's Sweethearts '01
Coupe de Ville '90
Revenge of the Nerds 2: Nerds in Paradise '87
Streets of Gold '86

Phillip J. Roth (1959-)
Boa '02
Interceptor Force '99
Velocity Trap '99
Darkdrive '98
Total Reality '97
A.P.E.X. '94
Digital Man '94
Prototype X29A '92
Red Snow '91

Stephanie Rothman (1936-)
Working Girls '75
Terminal Island '73
Group Marriage '72
The Velvet Vampire '71
The Student Nurses '70
Track of the Vampire '66

William Rotsler (1926-97)
Mantis in Lace '68
Agony of Love '66

Nick Rotundo
G2: Mortal Conquest '99
Gladiator Cop: The Swordsman 2 '95

Brigitte Rouan (1965-)
After Sex '97
Overseas: Three Women with Man Trouble '90

Russell Rouse (1913-87)
Caper of the Golden Bulls '67
The Oscar '66
Fastest Gun Alive '56
The Thief '52
The Well '51

Peter Rowe (1947-)
Treasure Island '99
Personal Exemptions '88
Take Two '87
Lost '86

Roy Rowland (1902-95)
Girl Hunters '63
The Seven Hills of Rome '58
Gun Glory '57
Meet Me in Las Vegas '56
Hit the Deck '55
The 5000 Fingers of Dr. T '53
Bugles in the Afternoon '52
Two Weeks with Love '50
Our Vines Have Tender Grapes '45

William Rowland (1898-)
Flight to Nowhere '46
Follies Girl '43

Christopher Rowley
Bonneville '06
Soul Patrol '80

Jean-Claude Roy
Deadly Sting '82
Killer '73

Patricia Rozema (1958-)
Mansfield Park '99
When Night Is Falling '95
I've Heard the Mermaids Singing '87

John Ruane (1952-)
Dead Letter Office '98
That Eye, the Sky '94
Death in Brunswick '90

Andy Ruben
Club Vampire '98
Streets '90

J. Walter Ruben (1899-1942)
Java Head '35
Riff Raff '35
Ace of Aces '33
No Marriage Ties '33
No Other Woman '33

Joseph Ruben (1951-)
The Forgotten '04
Return to Paradise '98
Money Train '95
The Good Son '93
Sleeping with the Enemy '91
True Believer '89
The Stepfather '87
Dreamscape '84
Gorp '80
Joyride '77
Pom Pom Girls '76

Percival Rubens
Sweet Murder '93
Wild Zone '89
Survival Zone '84
The Demon '81
Mr. Kingstreet's War '71

Saul Rubinek (1949-)
Club Land '01
Jerry and Tom '98

Sergio Rubini (1959-)
The Blonde '92
The Station '92

Alan Rudolph (1943-)
The Secret Lives of Dentists '02
Intimate Affairs '01
Trixie '00
Breakfast of Champions '98
Afterglow '97
Mrs. Parker and the Vicious Circle '94
Equinox '93
Mortal Thoughts '91
Love at Large '89
The Moderns '88
Made in Heaven '87
Trouble in Mind '86
Choose Me '84
Songwriter '84
Endangered Species '82
Roadie '80
Welcome to L.A. '77
Barn of the Naked Dead '73
Premonition '71

Wesley Ruggles (1889-1972)
Somewhere I'll Find You '42
Arizona '40
College Humor '33
I'm No Angel '33
No Man of Her Own '32
Cimarron '31
Condemned '29
The Plastic Age '25
The Leopard Woman '20

Raul Ruiz (1941-)
Klimt '06
Comedy of Innocence '00
Time Regained '99
Shattered Image '98
Genealogies of a Crime '97
Three Lives and Only One Death '96
On Top of the Whale '82
The Hypothesis of the Stolen Painting '78

Richard Rush (1930-)
Color of Night '94
The Stunt Man '80
Freebie & the Bean '74
Getting Straight '70
Psych-Out '68
The Savage Seven '68
Hell's Angels on Wheels '67
Thunder Alley '67

Josef Rusnak
The Contractor '07
The Thirteenth Floor '99
No Strings Attached '98
Quiet Days in Hollywood '97

Chuck Russell (1952-)
The Scorpion King '02
Bless the Child '00
Eraser '96
The Mask '94
The Blob '88
A Nightmare on Elm Street 3: Dream Warriors '87

David O. Russell (1959-)
I Heart Huckabees '04
Three Kings '99
Flirting with Disaster '95
Spanking the Monkey '94

Jay Russell (1960-)
The Water Horse: Legend of the Deep '07
Ladder 49 '04
Tuck Everlasting '02
My Dog Skip '99
End of the Line '88

Ken Russell (1927-)
Tales of Erotica '93
Lady Chatterley '92
Prisoner of Honor '91
Whore '91
Women & Men: Stories of Seduction '90
The Rainbow '89
Aria '88
The Lair of the White Worm '88
Salome's Last Dance '88
Gothic '87
Crimes of Passion '84
Altered States '80
Valentino '77
Lisztomania '75
Tommy '75
Mahler '74
Savage Messiah '72
The Boy Friend '71
The Devils '71
The Music Lovers '71
Women in Love '70
Dante's Inferno: Life of Dante Gabriel Rossetti '69

William D. Russell (1908-68)
Best of the Badmen '50
The Green Promise '49

Anthony Russo
You, Me and Dupree '06
Welcome to Collinwood '02

Joe Russo
You, Me and Dupree '06
Welcome to Collinwood '02

John A. Russo (1939-)
Midnight 2: Sex, Death, and Videotape '93
Heartstopper '92
Midnight '81

Marti Rustam
James Dean: Live Fast, Die Young '97
Evils of the Night '85

Stefan Ruzowitzky (1961-)
The Counterfeiters '07
All the Queen's Men '02
Anatomy '00
The Inheritors '98

Frank Ryan (1947-)
Can't Help Singing '45
Call Out the Marines '42

James Ryan
Bachelor Party 2: The Last Temptation '08
Private Life '82

Mark Rydell (1934-)
Even Money '06
James Dean '01
Crime of the Century '96
Intersection '93
For the Boys '91
The River '84
On Golden Pond '81
The Rose '79
Harry & Walter Go to New York '76
Cinderella Liberty '73
The Cowboys '72
The Reivers '69

Renny Rye (1947-)
Oliver Twist '00
Lipstick on Your Collar '93

Michael Rymer (1963-)
Queen of the Damned '02
Perfume '01
In Too Deep '99
Allie & Me '97
Angel Baby '95

Ira Sachs (1965-)
Married Life '88
Forty Shades of Blue '05
The Delta '97

William Sachs
The Last Hour '91
Hitz '89
Galaxina '80
Van Nuys Blvd. '79
Incredible Melting Man '77

South of Hell Mountain '70

Daniel Sackheim — The Glass House '01, Grand Avenue '96

James Sadwith (1952-) — Sinatra '92, Bluffing It '87

Henri Safran (1932-) — Prince and the Great Race '83, Norman Loves Rose '82

Boris Sagal (1917-81) — Masada '81, Angela '77, The Runaway Barge '75, Omega Man '71, Night Gallery '69, Girl Happy '65, Guns of Diablo '64

Malcolm St. Clair (1897-1952) — Bullfighters '45, Two Weeks to Live '43, The Bashful Bachelor '42, The Grand Duchess and the Waiter '26, The Show Off '26, Are Parents People? '25

Gene Saks (1921-) — Bye Bye Birdie '95, Brighton Beach Memoirs '86, Mame '74, Last of the Red Hot Lovers '72, Cactus Flower '69, The Odd Couple '68, Barefoot in the Park '67

Luciano Salce — The Innocents Abroad '84, How I Learned to Love Women '66

Richard Sale (1911-93) — Abandon Ship '57, The Girl Next Door '53, Let's Make It Legal '51, Ticket to Tomahawk '51

Sidney Salkow (1909-2000) — The Last Man on Earth '64, Twice-Told Tales '63, Sitting Bull '54, City Without Men '43

Walter Salles (1956-) — Paris, je t'aime '06, Dark Water '05, The Motorcycle Diaries '04, Behind the Sun '01, Central Station '98, Foreign Land '95

Mikael Salomon (1945-) — The Company '07, Salem's Lot '04, Benedict Arnold: A Question of Honor '03, Band of Brothers '01, A Glimpse of Hell '01, Aftershock: Earthquake in New York '99, Hard Rain '97, A Far Off Place '93

Victor Salva (1958-) — Peaceful Warrior '06, Jeepers Creepers 2 '03, Jeepers Creepers '01, Rites of Passage '99, Powder '95, Nature of the Beast '94, Clown House '88

Pierre Salvadori (1964-) — Priceless '06, Apres-Vous '03, Les Apprentis '95

Gabriele Salvatores (1950-) — Nirvana '97, Mediterraneo '91

Salvatore Samperi (1944) — Ernesto '79, Submission '77

Keith Samples — Love Lies Bleeding '07, Single White Female 2: The Psycho '05

Barry Samson — Bloodfist 8: Hard Way Out '96

Rachel Samuels — Robert Louis Stevenson's The Game of Death '99

Denis Sanders (1929-87) — Invasion of the Bee Girls '73, One Man's Way '63

Allan Sandler — Killers at Outpost Zeta '80

Jay Sandrich (1932-) — Seems Like Old Times '80, For Richer, for Poorer '92

Mark Sandrich (1900-45) — Here Come the Waves '45, So Proudly We Hail '43, Holiday Inn '42, Man About Town '39, Carefree '38, Shall We Dance '37, Follow the Fleet '36, A Woman Rebels '36, Top Hat '35, Cockeyed Cavaliers '34, The Gay Divorcee '34, Hips, Hips, Hooray '34, Aggie Appleby, Maker of Men '33

Arlene Sanford — I'll Be Home for Christmas '98

Jonathan Sanger — A Very Brady Sequel '96

Jimmy Sangster (1924-) — Dynasty of Fear '72, Lust for a Vampire '71, The Horror of Frankenstein '70

Alfred Santell (1895-1981) — That Brennan Girl '46, The Hairy Ape '44, Jack London '44, Having Wonderful Time '38, Internes Can't Take Money '37, Winterset '36, Melody Cruise '32

Cirio H. Santiago (1936-) — Caged Heat 3000 '95, Caged Heat 2: Stripped of Freedom '94, Stranglehold '94, Fast Gun '93, One Man Army '93, Beyond the Call of Duty '92, Field of Fire '92, Firehawk '92, Raiders of the Sun '92, Dune Warriors '91, Eye of the Eagle 3 '91, The Expendables '89, Silk 2 '89, Future Hunters '88, Nam Angels '88, The Sisterhood '88, Demon of Paradise '87, Eye of the Eagle '87, Equalizer 2000 '86, Silk '86, Devastator '85, Naked Vengeance '85, Final Mission '84, Wheels of Fire '84, Stryker '83, Death Force '78

Joseph Santley (1889-1971) — Call of the Canyon '42, Down Mexico Way '41, Melody Ranch '40, Music in My Heart '40, Harmony Lane '35

Damon Santostefano — Bring It On Again '03, Three to Tango '99, Severed Ties '92

Ken Sanzel — Lone Hero '02, Scarred City '98

David Saperstein (1937-) — Beyond the Stars '89, A Killing Affair '85

Deran Sarafian (1968-) — Gunmen '93, Terminal Velocity '94, The Road Killers '95, Back in the USSR '92, Death Warrant '90, To Die For '89, Interzone '88, Alien Predators '80

Richard Sarafian (1935-) — Solar Crisis '92, Street Justice '89, Eye of the Tiger '86, Gangster Wars '81, Sunburn '79, The Man Who Loved Cat Dancing '73, Man in the Wilderness '71, Vanishing Point '71

Ron Satlof — Perry Mason: The Case of the Lone Star '87, Perry Mason Returns '85, Spider-Man: The Deadly Dust '78

Peter Sasdy (1935-) — The Lonely Lady '83, The Two Faces of Evil '82, Rude Awakening '81, Thirteenth Reunion '81, Welcome to Blood City '77, The Devil's Undead '75, King Arthur, the Young Warlord '75, Doomwatch '72, Nothing But the Night '72, Hands of the Ripper '71, Taste the Blood of Dracula '70

Joseph Sargent (1925-) — For Love or Country: The Arturo Sandoval Story '00, A Lesson Before Dying '99, The Wall '98, Mandela and de Klerk '97, Miss Evers' Boys '97, Larry McMurtry's Streets of Laredo '95, Abraham '94, My Antonia '94, World War II: When Lions Roared '94, Caroline? '90, Day One '89, The Incident '89, Jaws: The Revenge '87, Passion Flower '86, Memorial Day '83, Nightmares '83, Tomorrow's Child '82, The Manions of America '81, Amber Waves '80, Coast to Coast '80, Goldengirl '79, MacArthur '77, Hustling '75, The Taking of Pelham One Two Three '74, White Lightning '73

Marina Sargenti — Child of Darkness, Child of Light '97, Mirror, Mirror '90

Vic Sarin (1945-) — Partition '07, Love on the Side '04, Sea People '00, In His Father's Shoes '97, The Legend of Gator Face '96, Cold Comfort '90

Michael J. Sarna — Doomsday '99

Hajime Sato (1929-95) — Body Snatcher from Hell '69, Terror Beneath the Sea '66

Junya Sato (1932-) — The Silk Road '92, The Go-Masters '82, Proof of the Man '77

Ernest G. Sauer — Broadcast Bombshells '95, Bikini Bistro '94, Beauty School '93

Carlos Saura (1932-) — Goya in Bordeaux '99, Tango '98, Outrage '93, El Amor Brujo '86, Carmen '83, Antonieta '82, Blood Wedding '81

Claude Sautet (1924-2000) — Nelly et Monsieur Arnaud '95, Un Coeur en Hiver '93, A Simple Story '79, Vincent, Francois, Paul and the Others '76, Cesar & Rosalie '72, The Things of Life '70

Oley Sassone — Playback '95, Fast Getaway 2 '94, Relentless 4 '94, Final Embrace '92

Stefan Scaini — Anne of Green Gables: The Continuing Story '99, Double Play '96

Joseph L. Scanlan (1927-) — Spenser: Pale Kings & Princes '94, Spenser: A Savage Place '94, Spenser: The Judas Goat '94, Nightstick '87, Spring Fever '81

Steven Schachter — A Slight Case of Murder '99, The Con '98, Above Suspicion '95, Getting Up and Going Home '92, The Water Engine '92

Don Schain — Too Hot to Handle '76, Girls Are for Loving '73, The Abductors '72, Ginger '72

Armand Schaefer (1898-1967) — The Miracle Rider '35, Law of the Wild '34, The Lost Jungle '34, Sixteen Fathoms Deep '34, Fighting Texans '33, Fighting with Kit Carson '33, Law and Lawless '33, Sagebrush Trail '33, Terror Trail '33, The Three Musketeers '33

George Schaefer (1920-97) — Who'll Save Our Children? '82, The People vs. Jean Harris '81, Blind Ambition '79, Mayflower: The Pilgrims' Adventure '79, Lost Legacy: A Girl Called Hatter Fox '77, The Last of Mrs. Lincoln '76, In This House of Brede '75, Once Upon a Scoundrel '73, Doctors' Wives '71, Generation '69, Pendulum '69, Soldier in Love '67, Barefoot in Athens '66, Lamp at Midnight '66, Holy Terror '65, Invincible Mr. Disraeli '63, The Tempest '63, A Doll's House '59, Victoria Regina '61, Elizabeth, the Queen '68, Children in the Crossfire '84, Right of Way '84, Deadly Game '82, A Piano for Mrs. Cimino '82

Eric Schaeffer (1962-) — Never Again '01, Fall '97, If Lucy Fell '95, My Life's in Turnaround '94

Francis Schaeffer (1920-89) — Baby on Board '92, Headhunter '89, Wired to Kill '86, Rebel Storm '90

Franklin J. Schaffner (1920-89) — Welcome Home '89, Lionheart '87, Yes, Giorgio '82, Sphinx '81, The Boys from Brazil '78, Islands in the Stream '77, Papillon '73, Nicholas and Alexandra '71, Patton '70, Planet of the Apes '68, The War Lord '65, The Best Man '64, The Stripper '63

Jerry Schatzberg (1927-) — Blood Money: The Story of Clinton and Nadine '88, Reunion '88, Street Smart '87, Misunderstood '84, No Small Affair '84, Honeysuckle Rose '80, The Seduction of Joe Tynan '79, Scarecrow '73, A Place Called Today '72, Panic in Needle Park '71, Puzzle of a Downfall Child '70

Robert Scheerer (1929-) — Happily Ever After '82, How to Beat the High Cost of Living '80, The World's Greatest Athlete '73, Adam at 6 a.m. '70, Hans Brinker '69

Maximilian Schell (1930-) — Marlene '84, The Pedestrian '73, First Love '70

Henning Schellerup — Time Machine '78, The Legend of Sleepy Hollow '81, The Adventures of Nellie Bly '81

Carl Schenkel (1948-2003) — Missing Pieces '00, Tarzan and the Lost City '98, In the Lake of the Woods '96, The Surgeon '94

Victor Saville (1897-1979) — The Silver Chalice '54, Kim '50, Conspirator '49, Green Dolphin Street '47, Tonight and Every Night '45, Forever and a Day '43, Dark Journey '37, Storm in a Teacup '37, South Riding '38, First a Girl '35, Evergreen '34, The Iron Duke '34

Nancy Savoca (1960-) — The 24 Hour Woman '99, If These Walls Could Talk '96, Household Saints '93, Dogfight '91, True Love '89

Geoffrey Sax — White Noise '05, Tipping the Velvet '02, Stormbreaker '06, Doctor Who '96, Othello '01

John Sayles (1950-) — Honeydripper '07, Silver City '04, Casa de los Babys '03, Sunshine State '02, Limbo '99, Men with Guns '98, Lone Star '95, The Secret of Roan Inish '94, Passion Fish '92, City of Hope '91, Eight Men Out '88, Matewan '87, The Brother from Another Planet '84, Lianna '83, Baby, It's You '82, The Return of the Secaucus 7 '80

Knight Moves '93
Silhouette '91
The Mighty Quinn '89
Eye of the Demon '87
Out of Order '84
Strike Back '80

Richard Schenkman (1958-)
And Then Came Love '07
The Man from Earth '07
Went to Coney Island on a Mission from God... Be Back by Five '98

Fred Schepisi (1939-)
Empire Falls '05
It Runs in the Family '03
Last Orders '01
Fierce Creatures '96
I.Q. '94
Six Degrees of Separation '93
Mr. Baseball '92
The Russia House '90
A Cry in the Dark '88
Roxanne '87
Plenty '85
Iceman '84
Barbarosa '82
The Chant of Jimmie Blacksmith '78
The Devil's Playground '76

Lone Scherfig (1959-)
Wilbur Wants to Kill Himself '02
Italian for Beginners '01

Victor Schertzinger (1890-1941)
Birth of the Blues '41
The Road to Zanzibar '41
Rhythm on the River '40
The Road to Singapore '40
Something to Sing About '36
One Night of Love '34
Uptown New York '32
What Happened to Rosa? '21
Clodhopper '17

Lawrence Schiller (1936-)
Master Spy: The Robert Hanssen Story '02
American Tragedy '00
Perfect Murder, Perfect Town '00
Double Jeopardy '92
Double Exposure: The Story of Margaret Bourke-White '89
Spalding Gray: Terrors of Pleasure '88

Thomas Schlamme (1950-)
Kingfish: A Story of Huey P. Long '95
You So Crazy '94
So I Married an Axe Murderer '93
The Innocent '93

John Schlesinger (1926-2003)
The Next Best Thing '00
An Eye for an Eye '95
Cold Comfort Farm '94
The Innocent '93
A Question of Attribution '91
Pacific Heights '90
Madame Sousatzka '88
The Believers '87
The Falcon and the Snowman '85
An Englishman Abroad '83
Separate Tables '83
Honky Tonk Freeway '81
Yanks '79
Marathon Man '76
The Day of the Locust '75
Sunday, Bloody Sunday '71
Midnight Cowboy '69
Far from the Madding Crowd '67
Darling '65

Billy Liar '63
A Kind of Loving '62

Volker Schlöndorff (1939-)
The Ninth Day '04
The Legend of Rita '99
Palmetto '98
The Ogre '96
Voyager '91
The Handmaid's Tale '90
Death of a Salesman '86
Swann in Love '84
The Tin Drum '79
Coup de Grace '78
Germany in Autumn '78
The Lost Honor of Katharina Blum '75
An Occurrence at Owl Creek Bridge/Coup de Grace '62

Rob Schmidt (1965-)
Masters of Horror: Right to Die '07
Wrong Turn '03
Crime and punishment in Suburbia '00
Speed of Life '99

Wolfgang Schmidt
See Ray Dennis Steckler

David Schmoeller (1947-)
The Arrival '90
Curse 4: The Ultimate Sacrifice '90
Netherworld '90
Catacombs '89
Puppet Master '89
Crawlspace '86
The Seduction '82
Tourist Trap '79

Julian Schnabel (1951-)
The Diving Bell and the Butterfly '07
Before Night Falls '00
Basquiat '96

Paul Schneider (1973-)
Can of Worms '00
Honor Thy Father and Mother: The True Story of the Menendez Brothers '94
Roseanne: An Unauthorized Biography '94
Babycakes '89
Something Special '86

Robert Allen Schnitzer
Kandyland '87
The Premonition '75
Rebel '70

Ernest B. Schoedsack (1893-1979)
Mighty Joe Young '49
Dr. Cyclops '40
Last Days of Pompeii '35
King Kong '33
Son of Kong '33
The Most Dangerous Game '32
Chang: A Drama of the Wilderness '27

Pierre Schoendoerffer (1928-)
Le Crabe Tambour '77

Paul Schrader (1946-)
The Walker '07
Dominion: Prequel to the Exorcist '05
Auto Focus '02
Forever Mine '99
Affliction '97
Touch '96
Witch Hunt '94
Light Sleeper '92
The Comfort of Strangers '91
Patty Hearst '88
Light of Day '87
Mishima: A Life in Four Chapters '85

Reinhold Schunzel (1886-1954)
Balalaika '39

Cat People '82
American Gigolo '79
Hardcore '79
Blue Collar '78

Myrl A. Schreibman (1945-)
Liberty & Bash '90
Angel of H.E.A.T. '82

Barbet Schroeder (1941-)
Murder by Numbers '02
Our Lady of the Assassins '01
Desperate Measures '98
Before and After '95
Single White Female '92
Reversal of Fortune '90
Barfly '87
Tricheurs '84
Maitresse '76
The Valley Obscured by the Clouds '70
More '69

Michael Schroeder (1952-)
The Glass Cage '96
Cover Me '95
Cyborg 3: The Recycler '95
Cyborg 2 '93
Mortuary Academy '91
Relentless 2: Dead On '91
Damned River '89
Out of the Dark '88

Carl Schultz (1939-)
To Walk with Lions '99
Deadly Currents '93
Which Way Home '90
The Seventh Sign '88
Travelling North '87
Careful, He Might Hear You '84
Blue Fin '78

John Schultz
The Honeymooners '05
Like Mike '02
Drive Me Crazy '99
Bandwagon '95

Michael A. Schultz (1938-)
Woman, Thou Art Loosed '04
The Great American Sex Scandal '04
Livin' Large '91
For Us, the Living '88
Disorderlies '87
Timestalkers '87
Krush Groove '85
The Last Dragon '85
Scavenger Hunt '79
Sgt. Pepper's Lonely Hearts Club Band '78
Greased Lightning '77
Which Way Is Up? '77
Car Wash '76
Cooley High '75
Honeybaby '74

Joel Schumacher (1942-)
The Number 23 '07
The Phantom of the Opera '04
Veronica Guerin '03
Bad Company '02
Phone Booth '02
Tigerland '00
Flawless '99
8mm '98
Batman and Robin '97
A Time to Kill '96
Batman Forever '95
The Client '94
Falling Down '93
Dying Young '91
Flatliners '90
Cousins '89
The Lost Boys '87
St. Elmo's Fire '85
D.C. Cab '84
The Incredible Shrinking Woman '81
The Virginia Hill Story '76

Fortune's Fool '21

Harold Schuster (1902-86)
Courage of Black Beauty '57
The Finger Man '55
Kid Monk Baroni '52
So Dear to My Heart '49
The Tender Years '47
Breakfast in Hollywood '46
Marine Raiders '43
My Friend Flicka '43
On the Sunny Side '42
Dinner at the Ritz '37
Wings of the Morning '37

Douglas Schwartz
Baywatch the Movie: Forbidden Paradise '95
Thunder in Paradise 2 '94
Thunder in Paradise 3 '94
Thunder in Paradise '93
Peacekillers '71

David Schwimmer (1966-)
Run, Fat Boy, Run '07
Since You've Been Gone '97

Alberto Sciamma
Jericho Mansions '03
Killer Tongue '96

Ettore Scola (1931-)
The Family '87
Macaroni '85
La Nuit de Varennes '82
Le Bal '82
Passion of Love '82
A Special Day '77
We All Loved Each Other So Much '77
Down & Dirty '76

Martin Scorsese (1942-)
The Departed '06
The Aviator '04
Gangs of New York '02
Bringing Out the Dead '99
Kundun '97
Casino '95
The Age of Innocence '93
Cape Fear '91
Goodfellas '90
New York Stories '89
The Last Temptation of Christ '88
The Color of Money '86
After Hours '85
King of Comedy '82
Raging Bull '80
The Last Waltz '78
New York, New York '77
Taxi Driver '76
Alice Doesn't Live Here Anymore '74
Mean Streets '73
Boxcar Bertha '72
Who's That Knocking at My Door? '68

Campbell Scott (1962-)
Off the Map '03
Final '01
Hamlet '01
Big Night '95

George C. Scott (1927-99)
Descending Angel '90
Don't Look Back: The Story of Leroy "Satchel" Paige '81
Savage Is Loose '74
Rage '72

Michael Scott
Possessed '05
Heck's Way Home '95
Sharon's Secret '95
Dangerous Heart '93
Spirit Rider '93
Ladykiller '92

Oz Scott (1950-)
Spanish Judges '99
Bustin' Loose '81

Peter Graham Scott
Subterfuge '68
Let's Get Married '60

Ridley Scott (1939-)
American Gangster '07
A Good Year '06
Kingdom of Heaven '05
Matchstick Men '03
Black Hawk Down '01
Hannibal '01
Gladiator '00
RKO 281 '99
G.I. Jane '97
White Squall '96
1492: Conquest of Paradise '92
Thelma & Louise '91
Black Rain '89
Someone to Watch Over Me '87
Legend '86
Blade Runner '82
Alien '79
The Duellists '77

Sherman Scott
See Fred Olen Ray

T.J. Scott
Young Hercules '97
TC 2000 '93

Tony Scott (1944-)
Deja Vu '06
Domino '05
Man on Fire '04
Spy Game '01
Enemy of the State '98
The Fan '96
Crimson Tide '95
True Romance '93
The Last Boy Scout '91
Days of Thunder '90
Revenge '90
Beverly Hills Cop 2 '87
Top Gun '86

James Seale
Momentum '03
Scorcher '02
Asylum '97

Francis Searle (1909-2002)
Profile '54
Someone at the Door '50
Things Happen at Night '48
A Girl in a Million '46

Fred F. Sears (1913-57)
The Giant Claw '57
Earth vs. the Flying Saucers '56
Teenage Crime Wave '55
Ambush at Tomahawk Gap '53
Bonanza Town '51

George Seaton (1911-79)
Showdown '73
Airport '70
36 Hours '64
The Counterfeit Traitor '62
Teacher's Pet '58
Country Girl '54
The Big Lift '50
Miracle on 34th Street '47

Beverly Sebastian
Running Cool '93
The American Angels: Baptism of Blood '89
Gator Bait 2: Cajun Justice '88

Ferd Sebastian
Running Cool '93
The American Angels: Baptism of Blood '89
Gator Bait 2: Cajun Justice '88
On the Air Live with Captain Midnight '79
Delta Fox '77
Flash & Firecat '75
Gator Bait '73
Hitchhikers '72

Mike Sedan
Naked Wishes '00
Lap Dancing '95
Married People, Single Sex 2: For Better or Worse '94
Night Fire '94

Married People, Single Sex '93

Edward Sedgwick (1892-1953)
Ma and Pa Kettle Back On the Farm '51
A Southern Yankee '48
Air Raid Wardens '43
The Gladiator '38
Fit for a King '37
Pick a Star '37
Riding on Air '37
What! No Beer? '33
Speak Easily '32
Maker of Men '31
Parlor, Bedroom and Bath '31
Doughboys '30
Free and Easy '30
Spite Marriage '29
The Cameraman '28
The Phantom of the Opera '25

Paul Seed (1947-)
Strange Relations '02
Dr. Bell and Mr. Doyle: The Dark Beginnings of Sherlock Holmes '00
Every Woman Knows a Secret '99
Heat of the Sun '99
A Rather English Marriage '98
The Affair '95
To Play the King '93
Dead Ahead: The Exxon Valdez Disaster '92
House of Cards '90

Charles Seeling
Wolfheart's Revenge '25
Rounding Up the Law '22

Alex Segal (1915-77)
The Story of David '76
My Father's House '75

Peter Segal (1962-)
Get Smart '08
The Longest Yard '05
50 First Dates '04
Anger Management '03
Nutty Professor 2: The Klumps '00
My Fellow Americans '96
Tommy Boy '95
Naked Gun 33 1/3: The Final Insult '94

Stu Segall
Illegal in Blue '95
Drive-In Massacre '74

Peter Sehr (1951-)
Love the Hard Way '01
Obsession '97
Kaspar Hauser '93

Arthur Allan Seidelman
The Sisters '05
Puerto Vallarta Squeeze '04
By Dawn's Early Light '00
The Runaway '00
Sex & Mrs. X '00
Grace & Glorie '98
The Summer of Ben Tyler '96
Harvest of Fire '95
Trapped in Space '94
Dying to Remember '93
Rescue Me '93
Body Language '92
The Kid Who Loved Christmas '90
False Witness '89
A Friendship in Vienna '88
The Caller '87
Glory Years '87
Poker Alice '87
Echoes '83
Children of Rage '75
Hercules in New York '70

Susan Seidelman (1952-)
The Boynton Beach Club '05
Power and Beauty '02
Gaudi Afternoon '01
A Cooler Climate '99
Tales of Erotica '93
Cookie '89

Smithereens '82
She-Devil '89
Making Mr. Right '86
Desperately Seeking Susan '85

Joseph Seiden (1892-1974)
God, Man and Devil '49
Eli Eli '40
Paradise in Harlem '40

Lewis Seiler (1890-1964)
The Winning Team '52
Doll Face '46
If I'm Lucky '46
Something for the Boys '44
Guadalcanal Diary '43
Pittsburgh '42
Charlie Chan in Paris '35
Lady Takes a Chance '43
You Were Never Lovelier '42
Great K & A Train Robbery '26

William A. Seiter (1890-1964)
Make Haste to Live '54
Borderline '50
One Touch of Venus '48
I'll Be Yours '47
Up in Central Park '48
Little Giant '46
Destroyer '43
Nice Girl? '41
It's a Date '40
Susannah of the Mounties '39
Allegheny Uprising '39
The Moon's Our Home '36
Thanks for Everything '38
Room Service '38
Dimples '36
Stowaway '36
In Person '35
Roberta '35
Sing and Like It '34
Diplomaniacs '33
Sons of the Desert '33
Way Back Home '32
Big Business Girl '31
The Cheerful Fraud '27
Skinner's Dress Suit '26
The White Sin '24
Little Church Around the Corner '23

George B. Seitz (1888-1944)
Andy Hardy's Double Life '42
Kit Carson '40
Love Finds Andy Hardy '38
Life Begins for Andy Hardy '41
Andy Hardy's Private Secretary '41
Andy Hardy Meets Debutante '40
Drums of Jeopardy '31
Danger Lights '30
The Ice Flood '26
The Vanishing American '25

Steve Sekely (1899-1979)
Day of the Triffids '63
The Scar '48
Blonde Savage '47
Lady in the Death House '44
Waterfront '44
Behind Prison Walls '43
Revenge of the Zombies '43

Andrzej Sekula (1954-)
Cube 2: Hypercube '02
Vacuums '03

Lesley Selander (1900-79)
Arizona Bushwackers '67
Shotgun '55
Dragonfly Squadron '54
Fighter Attack '53
Flat Top '52
Flight to Mars '52
Gunplay '51
Rider from Tucson '50
Riders of the Range '50
Storm over Wyoming '50
Mysterious Desperado '49
The Red Stallion '47
The Vampire's Ghost '45
Call of the Rockies '44
Border Patrol '43
Buckskin Frontier '43
Colt Comrades '43
Hopalong Cassidy; Riders of the Deadline '43
Lost Canyon '43
Doomed Caravan '41
The Roundup '41
Riders of the Timberline '41
Knights of the Range '40
The Light of Western Stars '40
Santa Fe Marshal '40
Hopalong Cassidy: Renegade Trail '39
The Frontiersmen '38
The Mysterious Rider '38

Henry Selick (1952-)
Monkeybone '01
James and the Giant Peach '96
The Nightmare before Christmas '93

Jack M. Sell (1954-)
The Psychotronic Man '91
Deadly Spygames '89

Michael D. Sellers
Eye of the Dolphin '06

Charles E. Sellier
The Annihilators '85
Snowballing '85
Silent Night, Deadly Night '84

David Selman
Prescott Kid '36
Fighting Shadows '35
The Revenge Rider '35

Edgar Selwyn (1875-1944)
Skyscraper Souls '32
The Sin of Madelon Claudet '31

David Semel
Let's Kill All the Lawyers '93

Dean Semler (1943-)
Firestorm '97
The Patriot '99

Aaron Seltzer
Meet the Spartans '08
Date Movie '06

David Seltzer (1940-)
Nobody's Baby '01
Shining Through '92
Punchline '88
Lucas '86

Dominic Sena (1949-)
Swordfish '01
Gone in 60 Seconds '00
Kalifornia '93

Lorraine Senna
Sweetwater: A True Rock Story '99
Paradise, Texas '05

Ralph Senensky (1923-)
Death Cruise '74
A Dream for Christmas '73

Ron Senkowski
Wicked Ways '99

Mario Sequi (1954-)
Tramplers '66

Yahoo Serious
Reckless Kelly '93
Young Einstein '89
Mr. Accident '99

Mack Sennett (1880-1960)
Mickey '17
Tillie's Punctured Romance '14

Coline Serreau (1947-)
Chaos '01
Mama, There's a Man in Your Bed '89
Three Men and a Cradle '85

Alex Sessa (1928-98)
Stormquest '87
Amazons '86

Javier Seto
Macabre '69

Vernon Sewell (1903-2001)
Horrors of Burke & Hare '71
The Crimson Cult '68
Blood Beast Terror '67

Ben Sharpsteen (1895-1980)
Dumbo '41
Pinocchio '40
Fantasia '40

Nicholas Sgarro
Fortune Dane '86
The Happy Hooker '75

Tom Shadyac (1960-)
Evan Almighty '07
Bruce Almighty '03
Dragonfly '02
Patch Adams '98
Liar Liar '97
Ace Ventura: Pet Detective '93

Krishna Shah (1938-)
Hard Rock Zombies '85
Deadly Thief '78
The River Niger '76
Rivals '72

Steven Shainberg (1963-)
Fur: An Imaginary Portrait of Diane Arbus '06
Secretary '02
Hit Me '96

Adam Shankman (1964-)
Hairspray '07
Cheaper by the Dozen 2 '05
The Pacifier '05
Bringing Down the House '03
A Walk to Remember '02
The Wedding Planner '01

Bashar Shbib
Lana in Love '92

Larry Shaw
Julia Has Two Lovers '91

Kat Shea (1957-)
The Rage: Carrie 2 '99
Poison Ivy '92
Streets '90
Stripped to Kill II: Live Girls '89
Dance of the Damned '88
Stripped to Kill '87

Robert Shaye (1939-)
Book of Love '90

Melville Shavelson (1917-2007)
Ike '79
The War Between Men and Women '72
Yours, Mine & Ours '68
A New Kind of Love '63
It Started in Naples '60
The Five Pennies '59
Houseboat '58
The Seven Little Foys '55

Alfred Shaughnessy (1916-2005)
Cat Girl '57
Suspended Alibi '56

William Shatner (1931-)
TekWar '94
Star Trek V: The Final Frontier '89

Alan Shapiro (1957-)
Flipper '96
The Crush '93
Tiger Town '83

Ken Shapiro (1943-)
Modern Problems '81
The Groove Tube '72

Paul Shapiro (1955-)
Murder at Devil's Glen '99
Dead Husbands '98
The Invaders '95
Heads '93
Miracle at Moreaux '86
Hockey Night '84

Jim Sharman (1945-)
Shock Treatment '81
The Rocky Horror Picture Show '75

Don Sharp (1922-)
Tears in the Rain '88
Hold the Dream '86
A Woman of Substance '84
What Waits Below '83
The Thirty-Nine Steps '79
Bear Island '80
The Four Feathers '78
Hennessy '75
Psychomania '73
Dark Places '73
Rasputin the Mad Monk '66
Those Fantastic Flying Fools '67
Kiss of the Vampire '62

Barry Shear (1923-79)
Strike Force '75
The Deadly Trackers '73
Across 110th Street '72
The Todd Killings '71
Wild in the Streets '68

Ian Sharp (1946-)
Tass of the D'Urbervilles '98
R.P.M. '97
Codename Kyril '91
Secret Weapon '90
Robin Hood... The Legend: Robin Hood and the Sorcerer '83
The Final Option '82

Linda Shayne
The Undercover Kid '95
Purple People Eater '88

Helen Shaver (1952-)
Summer's End '99

Donald Shebib (1938-)
Goblin '93
The Ascent '94
The Pathfinder '94
The Little Kidnappers '90
Men of Steel '88
Heartaches '82
The Climb '87
Fish Hawk '79
Second Wind '76

Todd Sheets
Prehistoric Bimbos in Armageddon City '93

Riki Shelach
Mercenary Fighters '88
The Last Winter '84

Forrest Sheldon
Between Fighting Men '32
Dynamite Ranch '32

Adrienne Shelly (1966-2006)
Waitress '07
I'll Take You There '99

Ron Shelton (1945-)
Hollywood Homicide '03
Dark Blue '03
Play It to the Bone '99
Tin Cup '96
Cobb '94
White Men Can't Jump '92
Blaze '89
Bull Durham '88

Jon Sherman
I'm with Lucy '02
Breathing Room '96

Lowell Sherman (1885-1934)
Morning Glory '33
She Done Him Wrong '33
False Faces '32
Three Broadway Girls '32
Bachelor Apartment '31
The Royal Bed '31

Vincent Sherman (1906-2006)
Bogie: The Last Hero '80
Ice Palace '60
The Young Philadelphians '59
Affair in Trinidad '52
Lone Star '52
The Damned Don't Cry '50
Harriet Craig '50
Adventures of Don Juan '49
Mr. Skeffington '44
All Through the Night '42
Underground '41

Sam Shepard (1943-)
Far North '88
Silent Tongue '92

John Shepphird
Chupacabra Terror '05
The Santa Trap '02

Richard Shepard
The Hunting Party '07
The Matador '06
Mexico City '00
Oxygen '99
Mercy '00

Brent Shields (1963-)
Brush with Fate '03
Cupid & Cate '00

Frank Shields (1908-)
Project: Alien '89
Savage Attraction '83
The Island '61

Jim Sheridan (1949-)
Get Rich or Die Tryin' '05
In America '02
The Boxer '97
In the Name of the Father '93

Kristen Sheridan
Disco Pigs '01
August Rush '07

Edwin Sherin (1930-)
My Old Man's Place '71
Valdez is Coming '71

Adrian Shergold
Persuasion '07
Heat of the Sun '99

Gary Sherman (1945-)
Murderous Vision '91
After the Shock '90
Lisa '90
Poltergeist 3 '88
Wanted Dead or Alive '86
Vice Squad '82
Dead and Buried '81

George Sherman (1908-91)
Big Jake '71
Panic Button '62
Treasure of Pancho Villa '55
War Arrow '53
Against All Flags '52
Tomahawk '51
Comanche Territory '50
The Last of the Redmen '47
The Sombrero Kid '42
Sundown Fury '42
X Marks the Spot '42
Covered Wagon Days '40
Rocky Mountain Rangers '40
Cowboys from Texas '39
Frontier Horizon '39
The Kansas Terrors '39
South of the Border '39
Three Texas Steers '39
Wyoming Outlaw '39
Heroes of the Hills '38
Outlaws of Sonora '38
Overland Stage Raiders '38
Pals of the Saddle '38
Purple Vigilantes '38
Santa Fe Stampede '38
Wild Horse Rodeo '37

John Sherwood (1959-)
The Monolith Monsters '57
The Creature Walks among Us '56

Masahiro Shinoda (1931-)
Gonza the Spearman '86
MacArthur's Children '85
Double Suicide '69

Dominic Shiach
Dark Side '02
Blackheart '98

Barry Shils
Wigstock: The Movie '95
Motorama '91

Takashi Shimizu (1972-)
Marebito '04
The Grudge 2 '05
The Grudge '04
Ju-On: The Grudge '03
Ju-On: The Grudge 2 '03

Kaneto Shindo (1912-)
Onibaba '64

Koji Shima (1901-86)
Warning from Space '56
Golden Demon '53

Jack Sholder (1945-)
Arachnid '01
Wishmaster 2: Evil Never Dies '98
Sketch Artist 2: Hands That See '94
12:01 '93
By Dawn's Early Light '89
Renegades '89
The Hidden '87
A Nightmare on Elm Street 2: Freddy's Revenge '85
Alone in the Dark '82

Lee Sholem (1913-2000)
Escape from Planet Earth
Tobor the Great '54
Superman and the Mole Men '51

Lindsay Shonteff (1935-2006)
The Killing Edge '86
Number 1 of the Secret Service '77
Big Zapper '73
Night Slasher '69

Sig Shore (1919-2006)
The Survivalist '87
Sudden Death '85
The Act '82
Shining Star '75

Lynn Shores (1893-1949)
Charlie Chan at the Wax Museum '40

A Million to One '37
The Shadow Strikes '37
The Glory Trail '36

M. Night Shyamalan (1970-)
The Happening '08
Lady in the Water '06
The Village '04
Signs '02
Unbreakable '00
The Sixth Sense '99
Wide Awake '97

Charles Shyer (1941-)
Alfie '04
The Affair of the Necklace '01
Father of the Bride Part 2 '95
I Love Trouble '94
Father of the Bride '91
Baby Boom '87
Irreconcilable Differences '84

Melville Shyer (1895-1968)
Mad Youth '40
Sucker Money '34

James Shyman
Slashdance '89
Hollywood's New Blood '88

Alex Sichel (1963-)
All Over Me '96

Andy Sidaris (1933-)
Return to Savage Beach '97
Day of the Warrior '96
The Dallas Connection '94
Fit to Kill '93
Hard Hunted '92
Do or Die '91
Guns '90
Picasso Trigger '89
Savage Beach '89
Hard Ticket to Hawaii '87
Malibu Express '85
Seven '79
Stacey '73

George Sidney (1916-2002)
Half a Sixpence '67
Bye, Bye, Birdie '63
Viva Las Vegas '63
Pal Joey '57
The Eddy Duchin Story '56
Jupiter's Darling '55
Kiss Me Kate '53
Young Bess '53
Scaramouche '52
Show Boat '51
Annie Get Your Gun '50
Key to the City '50
The Three Musketeers '48
Cass Timberlane '47
The Harvey Girls '46
Holiday in Mexico '46
Anchors Aweigh '45
Bathing Beauty '44
Thousands Cheer '43

Scott Sidney (1872-1928)
The Nervous Wreck '26
Charley's Aunt '25
Tarzan of the Apes '17

Marcos Siega (1969-)
Chaos Theory '08
Pretty Persuasion '05
Underclassman '05

David Siegel
Bee Season '05
The Deep End '01
Suture '93

Donald Siegel (1912-91)
Jinxed '82
Rough Cut '80
Escape from Alcatraz '79
Telefon '77
The Shootist '76
The Black Windmill '74
Charley Varrick '73
Dirty Harry '71
The Beguiled '70
Two Mules for Sister Sara '70
Death of a Gunfighter '69
Coogan's Bluff '68
Madigan '68
The Killers '64
Hell Is for Heroes '62
Flaming Star '60
Invasion of the Body Snatchers '56
An Annapolis Story '55
Private Hell 36 '54
Riot in Cell Block 11 '54
Duel at Silver Creek '52
Big Steal '49

Robert Siegel
Swimming '00

Robert Sigl (1964-)
School's Out '99
Tales from a Parallel Universe: Giga Shadow '97

James Signorelli
Hotel Room '93
Elvira, Mistress of the Dark '88

Dai Sijie (1954-)
Easy Money '83
Balzac and the Little Chinese Seamstress '02
China, My Sorrow '89

Joel Silberg (1927-)
Lambada '89
Catch the Heat '87
Bad Guys '86
Rappin' '85
Breakin' '84

Brad Silberling (1962-)
10 Items or Less '06
Lemony Snicket's A Series of Unfortunate Events '04
Moonlight Mile '02
City of Angels '98
Casper '95

Joan Micklin Silver (1935-)
Charms for the Easy Life '02
Invisible Child '99
In the Presence of Mine Enemies '97
Big Girls Don't Cry... They Get Even '92
A Private Matter '92
Prison Stories: Women on the Inside '91
Loverboy '89
Crossing Delancey '88
Finnegan Begin Again '84
Chilly Scenes of Winter '79
Between the Lines '77
Hester Street '75

Marisa Silver (1960-)
Indecency '92
He Said, She Said '91
Vital Signs '90
Permanent Record '88
Old Enough '84

Scott Silver
The Mod Squad '99
Johns '96

Elliot Silverstein (1937-)
Flashfire '94
Jailbait: Betrayed By Innocence '86
The Car '77
A Man Called Horse '70
Cat Ballou '65

Lloyd A. Simandl (1948-)
Crackerjack 3 '00
Escape Velocity '99
Dangerous Prey '95
Chained Heat 2 '92
Ultimate Desires '91
Beyond the Silhouette '90
Possession: Until Death Do You Part '90
Maniac Warriors '88
Ladies of the Lotus '87
Autumn Born '87

Lawrence L. Simeone (1954-2002)
Blindfold: Acts of Obsession '94
Eyes of the Beholder '92
Cop-Out '91
Presumed Guilty '91

Adam Simon (1962-)
Carnosaur '93
Body Chemistry 2: Voice of a Stranger '91
Brain Dead '89

J(uan) Piquer Simon (1934-)
Cthulhu Mansion '91
Endless Descent '90
Slugs '87
Pieces '83
Supersonic Man '78
Where Time Began '77

Roger L. Simon
Lies and Whispers '98

S. Sylvan Simon (1910-51)
Lust for Gold '49
Her Husband's Affairs '47
Abbott and Costello in Hollywood '45
Son of Lassie '45
Whistling in Brooklyn '43
Rio Rita '42
Whistling in Dixie '42
Whistling in the Dark '41

Yves Simoneau (1955-)
Bury My Heart at Wounded Knee '07
44 Minutes: The North Hollywood Shootout '03
Napoleon '03
Ignition '01
Nuremberg '00
Free Money '99
36 Hours to Die '99
Larry McMurtry's Dead Man's Walk '96
Amelia Earhart: The Final Flight '94
Mother's Boys '94
Till Death Do Us Part '92
Memphis '91
Perfectly Normal '91
Pouvoir intime '87

Jane Simpson
Little Witches '96

Megan Simpson
Number One Fan '94
Dating the Enemy '95
Alex '92

Michael A. Simpson
Fast Food '89
Funland '89
Sleepaway Camp 3: Teenage Wasteland '89
Sleepaway Camp 2: Unhappy Campers '88
Impure Thoughts '86

Andrew Sinclair (1935-)
Tuxedo Warrior '82
Blue Blood '73
Under Milk Wood '73

Gerald Seth Sindell (1944-)
H.O.T.S. '79
Teenager '74

Alexander Singer (1932-)
Pearl '78
Bunco '77
Captain Apache '71
Love Has Many Faces '65

Bryan Singer (1966-)
Superman Returns '06
X2: X-Men United '03
X-Men '00
Apt Pupil '97
The Usual Suspects '95
Public Access '93

John Singleton (1968-)
Four Brothers '05
2 Fast 2 Furious '03
Baby Boy '01
Shaft '00
Rosewood '96
Higher Learning '94
Poetic Justice '93
Boyz N the Hood '91

Gary Sinise (1955-)
Of Mice and Men '92
Miles from Home '88

Bruce Sinofsky (1956-)
Metallica: Some Kind of Monster '04

Gary Sinyor (1962-)
Bob the Butler '05
The Bachelor '99
Stiff Upper Lips '96
Solitaire for 2 '94
Leon the Pig Farmer '93

Robert Siodmak (1900-73)
Crimson Pirate '52
Criss Cross '48
Dark Mirror '46
The Killers '46
The Spiral Staircase '46
The Strange Affair of Uncle Harry '45
Cobra Woman '44
Phantom Lady '44
Son of Dracula '43

Douglas Sirk (1900-87)
Imitation of Life '59
A Time to Love & a Time to Die '58
Battle Hymn '57
Tarnished Angels '57
Written on the Wind '56
All That Heaven Allows '55
Magnificent Obsession '54
All I Desire '53
First Legion '51
Lured '47
A Scandal in Paris '46

Rob Sitch (1962-)
The Dish '00
The Castle '97

Alf Sjoberg (1903-80)
Miss Julie '50
Torment '44

John Sjogren (1966-)
Choke '00
Red Line '96

Victor Sjostrom (1879-1960)
Under the Red Robe '36
The Wind '28
He Who Gets Slapped '24
The Phantom Chariot '20
The Outlaw and His Wife '17

Erik Skjoldbjaerg (1964-)
Prozac Nation '01
Insomnia '97

Keri Skogland
Liberty Stands Still '02
Zebra Lounge '01
The Courage to Love '00

Jerzy Skolimowski (1938-)
Torrents of Spring '90
The Lightship '86
Success Is the Best Revenge '84
Moonlighting '82
Hands Up '81
The Shout '78
King, Queen, Knave '72
Deep End '70

David Slade
30 Days of Night '07
Hard Candy '06

Bob Slatzer (1927-2005)
Big Foot '72
Hellcats '68

John Sledge
The Invisible Avenger '58
New Orleans After Dark '58

Brian Sloan
I Think I Do '97
Boys Life '94

Holly Goldberg Sloan (1958-)
The Secret Life of Girls '99
The Big Green '95

Paul Sloane (1893-1963)
Consolation Marriage '31
Half-Shot at Sunrise '30
Made for Love '26
The Coming of Amos '25

Rick Sloane (1961-)
Good Girls Don't '95
Mind, Body & Soul '92
Vice Academy 4
Vice Academy 2 '90
Marked for Murder '89
Vice Academy '88
Hobgoblins '87
Visitants '87
The Movie House Massacre '78

Edward Sloman (1886-1972)
The Jury's Secret '38
Gun Smoke '31
Lost Zeppelin '29

Karl Slovin
On Edge '03
Sex and the Other Man '95

George Sluizer (1932-)
Crimetime '96
Utz '93
The Vanishing '93
The Vanishing '88
Red Desert Penitentiary '83
Twice a Woman '79

Ralph Smart (1908-2001)
Robin Hood: The Movie '55
Curtain Up '53

Robert J. Smawley
American Eagle '90
River of Diamonds '90
Murphy's Fault '88

Jack Smight (1926-2003)
Intimate Power '89
Number One with a Bullet '87
Holocaust Survivors... Remembrance of Love '83
Loving Couples '80
Fast Break '79
Roll of Thunder, Hear My Cry '78
Airport '77 '77
Damnation Alley '77
Midway '76
Airport '75 '75
The Illustrated Man '69
No Way to Treat a Lady '68
The Secret War of Harry Frigg '68
Harper '66

Brian J. Smith
Tarzan 2 '05

Bruce Smith
Body of Influence 2 '96
The Proud Family Movie '05
Bebe's Kids '92

Charles Martin Smith (1953-)
Frederick Forsyth's Icon '05
The Snow Walker '03
Air Bud '97
Boris and Natasha: The Movie '92
Trick or Treat '86

Chris Smith (1970-)
Severance '06
The Yes Men '03
American Movie '99

Cliff(ord) Smith (1894-1937)
Radio Patrol '37
The Phantom Bullet '26
The Fugitive: Taking of Luke McVane '15

John N. Smith (1943-)
A Cool, Dry Place '98
Dangerous Minds '95
Sugartime '95
The Boys of St. Vincent '93

Kevin Smith (1970-)
Clerks 2 '06
Jersey Girl '04
Jay and Silent Bob Strike Back '01
Dogma '99
Chasing Amy '97
Mallrats '95
Clerks '94

Mark Smith
Seance '06
Overnight '03

Mel Smith (1952-)
High Heels and Low Lifes '01
Bean '97
Radioland Murders '94
The Tall Guy '89

Noel Mason Smith (1895-1955)
Gang Busters '42
Burma Convoy '41

Peter Smith
The Alchemists '99
No Surrender '86

Richard Smith
Pinochet's Last Stand '06
Agatha Christie: A Life in Pictures '04

Roy Allen Smith (1954-)
The Land Before Time 4: Journey Through the Mists '96
The Land Before Time 3: The Time of the Great Giving '95
The Land Before Time 2: The Great Valley Adventure '94

Alan Smithee
Sub Down '97
Hellraiser 4: Bloodline '95
Raging Angels '95
Gypsy Angels '94
The O.J. Simpson Story '94
Call of the Wild '93
Fatal Charm '92
Solar Crisis '92
Bloodsucking Pharoahs of Pittsburgh '90
The Shrimp on the Barbie '90
Ghost Fever '87
I Love N.Y. '87
Let's Get Harry '87
Appointment with Fear '85
Morgan Stewart's Coming Home '87
Stitches '85
City in Fear '80
Iron Cowboy '68

Stephen Smoke
Street Crimes '92
Final Impact '91

Skott Snider
Midnight Blue '96
Miracle Beach '92

Zack Snyder (1966-)
300 '07
Dawn of the Dead '04

Michele (Michael) Soavi (1957-)
The Church '98
Cemetery Man '95
The Devil's Daughter '91
Stagefright '87

Mark Sobel (1956-)
Storm Chasers: Revenge of the Twister '98
Ordeal in the Arctic '93
Trial and Error '92
Sweet Revenge '87
Access Code '84

Steven Soderbergh (1963-)
Ocean's Thirteen '07
Bubble '06
The Good German '06
Eros '04
Ocean's Twelve '04
Full Frontal '02
Ocean's Eleven '01
Solaris '02
Erin Brockovich '00
Traffic '00

The Limey '99
Out of Sight '98
Schizopolis '97
Gray's Anatomy '96
The Underneath '95
Fallen Angels 2 '93
King of the Hill '93
Kafka '91
sex, lies and videotape '89

Iain Softley (1951-)
The Skeleton Key '05
K-PAX '01
The Wings of the Dove '97
Hackers '95
Backbeat '94

Russell Solberg
Prison Stories: Women on the Inside '91
Thunder & Mud '89

Alexander Sokurov (1951-)
Father and Son '03
Russian Ark '02
Mother and Son '97

Alfred Sole (1943-)
Pandemonium '82
Tanya's Island '81
Alice Sweet Alice '76

Courtney Solomon (1971-)
An American Haunting '05
Dungeons and Dragons '00

Todd Solondz (1960-)
Palindromes '04
Storytelling '01
Happiness '98
Welcome to the Dollhouse '95
Fear, Anxiety and Depression '89

Ola Solum (1943-96)
The Polar Bear King '94
Turnaround '87

Stephen Sommers (1962-)
Van Helsing '04
The Mummy Returns '01
The Mummy '99
Deep Rising '98
Rudyard Kipling's The Jungle Book '94
The Adventures of Huck Finn '93

Barry Sonnenfeld (1953-)
RV '06
Big Trouble '02
Men in Black 2 '02
Wild Wild West '99
Men in Black '97
Get Shorty '95
Addams Family Values '93
For Love or Money '93
The Addams Family '91

Lodovico Sorret
See Tom Noonan

Jim Sotos (1935-)
Hot Moves '84
Sweet 16 '81
Forced Entry '75

Kevin Spacey (1959-)
Albino Alligator '96

Robert Sparr (1915-69)
More Dead Than Alive '68
A Swingin' Summer '65

Greg Spence
The Prophecy 2: Ashtown '97
Children of the Corn 4: The Gathering '96

Richard Spence (1957-)
New World Disorder '99
Different for Girls '96
Blind Justice '94

Brenton Spencer
The Club '94

Robert Spera
Bloody Murder 2 '03
Blown Away '94
Leprechaun 5: In the Hood '99

Penelope Spheeris (1945-)
The Kid and I '05
Senseless '98
Black Sheep '96
The Little Rascals '94
The Beverly Hillbillies '93
Wayne's World '92
Hollywood Vice Squad '86
The Boys Next Door '85
Suburbia '83
Decline of Western Civilization 1 '81

Steven Spielberg (1947-)
Munich '05
War of the Worlds '05
The Terminal '04
Catch Me If You Can '02
Minority Report '02
A.I.: Artificial Intelligence '01
Saving Private Ryan '98
Amistad '97
The Lost World: Jurassic Park 2 '97
Schindler's List '93
Jurassic Park '93
Hook '91
Always '89
Indiana Jones and the Last Crusade '89
Empire of the Sun '87
The Color Purple '85
Indiana Jones and the Temple of Doom '84
E.T.: The Extra-Terrestrial '82
Raiders of the Lost Ark '81
1941 '79
Close Encounters of the Third Kind '77
Jaws '75
The Sugarland Express '74
Duel '71
Night Gallery '69

Bob Spiers
Spice World: The Movie '97
That Darn Cat '96

Philip Spink
The Duke '99

Tony Spiridakis (1959-)
Tinseltown '96
The Last Word '95

Roger Spottiswoode (1945-)
Stop! or My Mom Will Shoot '92
Air America '90
Third Degree Burn '89
Turner and Hooch '89
Shoot to Kill '88
The Best of Times '86
Under Fire '83
The Pursuit of D.B. Cooper '81
Terror Train '80
The Only Way Home '72

Marcus Spiegel
Rangers: The Movie '95

Scott Spiegel (1957-)
From Dusk Till Dawn 2: Texas Blood Money '98
Intruder '88

Bryan Spicer
Taken '02
For Richer or Poorer '97
McHale's Navy '97
Mighty Morphin Power Rangers: The Movie '95

Jill Sprecher
Thirteen Conversations About One Thing '01
Clockwatchers '97

G.D. Spradlin (1920-)
Red, White & Busted '75

Tim Spring
Raw Target '95
Reason to Die '90

R.G. Springsteen (1904-89)
Hostile Guns '67
Apache Uprising '66
Johnny Reno '66
When Gangland Strikes '56
Oklahoma Annie '51
Hills of Oklahoma '50
Arizona Cowboy '49
The Red Menace '49
Hellfire '49
Son of God's Country '48
Homesteaders of Paradise Valley '47
Under Colorado Skies '47
Santa Fe Uprising '46
Stagecoach to Denver '46
Vigilantes of Boom Town '46

Robin Spry (1939-)
Obsessed '88
Keeping Track '86
Suzanne '80
Drying Up the Streets '76

Stephen Stafford
Blood Brothers '74

Pasquale Squitieri (1938-)
Third Solution '89
Corleone '79
The Sniper '78

Nick Stagliano
The Florentine '98
Home of Angels '94

C. Ray Stahl (1921-59)
Scarlet Spear '54
Geisha Girl '52

Eric Steven Stahl (1959-)
Safe House '99
Final Approach '91

John M. Stahl (1886-1950)
Father Was a Fullback '49
Leave Her to Heaven '45
The Keys of the Kingdom '44
Immortal Sergeant '43
Letter of Introduction '38
Imitation of Life '34

Sylvester Stallone (1946-)
Rocky Balboa '06
Rambo '08
Rocky 4 '85
Staying Alive '83
Rocky 3 '82
Rocky 2 '79
Paradise Alley '78

Herbert Stein
Escape to Love '82
Isle of Secret Passion '82

Paul Stein (1892-1951)
The Rain Killer '90
Counterblast '48
Black Limelight '38
Heart's Desire '37
Mimi '35
Lottery Bride '30
Sin Takes a Holiday '30

Darren Stein (1973-)
Sparkler '99
Jawbreaker '98

Ken Stein
Killer Instinct '92

David Steinberg
The Wrong Guy '96
Going Berserk '83
Paternity '81

Danny Steinmann
Friday the 13th, Part 5: A New Beginning '85
Savage Streets '83

Paul Stanley
The Ultimate Imposter '79

Jeremy Stanford (1952-)
A Crack in the Floor '00

Richard Stanley (1966-)
Dust Devil '93
Hardware '90

Ringo Starr (1940-)
Born to Boogie '72

Jeff Stanzler
Sorry, Haters '05
Jumpin' at the Boneyard '92

Jack Starrett (1936-89)
Hollywood Man '76
A Small Town in Texas '76
Race with the Devil '75
The Gravy Train '74
Cleopatra Jones '73
Slaughter '72
The Losers '70
Run, Angel, Run! '69

Andrew Stanton (1965-)
WALL-E '08
Finding Nemo '03

Frederick Stephani
Flash Gordon: Rocketship '40

Steno (1915-88)
Flatfoot '78
How to Kill 400 Duponts '65
The Unfaithful... '60
Uncle Was a Vampire '59

Jos Stelling (1945-)
The Pointsman '86
Rembrandt—1669 '77

Noah Stern
Pyrates '91

A.C. (Stephen Apostolof) Stephen (-2005)
Lady Godiva Rides '68
Orgy of the Dead '65

Jason Robert Stephens
Merchants of Death '99
Decay '98

Sandor Stern (1936-)
Jericho Fever '93
Duplicates '92
Web of Deceit '90
Amityville 4: The Evil Escapes '89

Steven Hilliard Stern (1937-)
Breaking the Surface: The Greg Louganis Story '96
Black Fox: Blood Horse '94
Black Fox: Good Men and Bad '94
Morning Glory '93
Love & Murder '91
Personals '90
Final Notice '89
Weekend War '88
Not Quite Human '87
Rolling Vengeance '87
The Park is Mine '85
Undergrads '85
Getting Physical '84
Obsessive Love '84
The Ambush Murders '82
Forbidden Love '82
Mazes and Monsters '82
Portrait of a Showgirl '82
The Devil & Max Devlin '81
Miracle on Ice '81
A Small Killing '81
Anatomy of a Seduction '79
Young Love, First Love '79
I Wonder Who's Killing Her Now? '76
Harrad Summer '74

Patrick Stettner
The Night Listener '06
The Business of Strangers '01

Andrew Stevens (1955-)
The White Raven '98
The Corporation '96
Crash Dive '96
Subliminal Seduction '96
Virtual Combat '96
Illicit Dreams '94
The Skateboard Kid 2 '94
Night Eyes 3 '93
Scorned '93
The Terror Within 2 '91

David Stevens (1940-)
Kansas '88
A Town Like Alice '85
Roses Bloom Twice '77

Wolfgang Staudte (1906-84)
The Three Penny Opera '62
The Kaiser's Lackey '51
The Murderers Are Among Us '45

Ralph Staub (1899-1969)
Danger Ahead '40
Sky Bandits '40
Yukon Flight '40
Prairie Moon '38
The Mandarin Mystery '37

Ray Dennis Steckler (1939-)
Las Vegas Serial Killer '86
The Hollywood Strangler Meets the Skid Row Slasher '79
Sinthia: The Devil's Doll '70
Rat Pfink a Boo-Boo '66
The Thrill Killers '65
The Incredibly Strange Creatures Who Stopped Living and Became Mixed-Up Zombies '63
Wild Guitar '62

Giorgio Stegani (1928-)
Beyond the Law '68
The Gentleman Killer '69

Michael Steinberg (1959-)
Bodies, Rest & Motion '93
The Waterdance '91

Jeremy Stanford
Stepmonster '92
Watchers 3 '94
Played '06

George Stevens (1904-75)
The Greatest Story Ever Told '65
The Diary of Anne Frank '59
Giant '56
Shane '53
A Place in the Sun '51
I Remember Mama '48
A Damsel in Distress '37
Quality Street '37
Woman of the Year '42
The More the Merrier '43
Talk of the Town '42
Penny Serenade '41
Vivacious Lady '38
Swing Time '36
Annie Oakley '35
Alice Adams '35
Bachelor Bait '34
Kentucky Kernels '34

Robert Stevenson (1905-86)
The Shaggy D.A. '76
One of Our Dinosaurs Is Missing '75
Herbie Rides Again '74
The Island at the Top of the World '74
Bedknobs and Broomsticks '71
The Love Bug '69
Blackbeard's Ghost '67
The Gnome-Mobile '67
Monkeys, Go Home! '67
That Darn Cat! '65
The Misadventures of Merlin Jones '64
Mary Poppins '64
Son of Flubber '63
In Search of the Castaways '62
The Absent-Minded Professor '61
Kidnapped '60
Darby O'Gill & the Little People '59
Johnny Tremain & the Sons of Liberty '58
Old Yeller '57
Jane Eyre '44
Forever and a Day '43
Back Street '41
Tom Brown's School Days '40
King Solomon's Mines '37
Non-Stop New York '37
Nine Days a Queen '36
The Man Who Lived Again '36

Leslie Stevens (1924-98)
Three Kinds of Heat '87
Incubus '65

Robert Stewart (1961-)
Rock & Roll Cowboys '92
Mark of the Beast '87
Action U.S.A. '89

John Stewart (1934-)
Hidden Obsession '92
Cartel '90

Jean Stewart
Ghetto Blaster '89
Ghostriders '87

Alan L. Stewart (1951-)
Butterfly Collectors '99
Thief of Hearts '84

Douglas Day Stewart
Listen to Me '89
Thief of Hearts '84

Alex Steyermark (1961-)
Prey for Rock and Roll '03
One Last Thing '05

Ben Stiller (1965-)
Tropic Thunder '08
Zoolander '01
The Cable Guy '96

Reality Bites '94

Mauritz Stiller (1883-1928)
Hotel Imperial '27
The Atonement of Gosta Berling '24
Treasure of Arne '19
Thomas Graal's First Child '18
Thomas Graal's Best Film '17

Whit Stillman (1952-)
The Last Days of Disco '98
Barcelona '94
Metropolitan '90

John Stockwell (1961-)
Turistas '06
Into the Blue '05
Blue Crush '02
crazy/beautiful '01
Cheaters '00
Undercover '87

Bryan Michael Stoller (1960-)
Miss Cast Away '04
Undercover Angel '99
Turn of the Blade '97
Dragon Fury 2 '96

Ben Stoloff (1895-1960)
It's a Joke, Son! '47
The Affairs of Annabel '38
Sea Devils '37
Palooka '34
Transatlantic Merry-Go-Round '34
Night of Terror '33
Justice Rides Again '32

Victor Stoloff (1913-)
Washington Affair '77
The 300 Year Weekend '71

Andrew L. Stone (1902-99)
Song of Norway '70
The Last Voyage '60
Sensations of 1945 '44
Hi Diddle Diddle '43
Stormy Weather '43
The Girl Said No '37
Hell's Headquarters '32

Charles Stone, III (1966-)
Mr. 3000 '04
Drumline '02
Paid in Full '02

Norman Stone
Catherine Cookson's The Gambling Man '98
Catherine Cookson's The Black Velvet Gown '92
The Vision '87
Shadowlands '85

Oliver Stone (1946-)
World Trade Center '06
Alexander '04
Any Given Sunday '99
U-Turn '97
Nixon '95
Natural Born Killers '94
Heaven and Earth '93
The Doors '91
JFK '91
Born on the Fourth of July '89
Talk Radio '88
Wall Street '87
Platoon '86
Salvador '86
The Hand '81
Seizure '74

Virginia Lively Stone (1964-)

Lynne Stopkewich (1964-)
Suspicious River '00
Kissed '96

Michael Storey
Before I Say Goodbye '03
We'll Meet Again '02
Blacklight '98

Esben Storm (1950-)
Subterano '01
In Search of Anna '79

Howard Storm (1939-)
Once Bitten '85
The Three Little Pigs '84

Jerome Storm (1890-1958)
Courtin' Wildcats '29
Sweet Adeline '26
The Busher '19

Tim Story (1970-)
Fantastic Four: Rise of the Silver Surfer '07
Fantastic Four '05
Taxi '04
Barbershop '02

Frank Strayer (1891-1964)
Footlight Glamour '43
It's a Great Life '43
Blondie for Victory '42
Blondie Goes Latin '42
Blondie Goes to College '42
Blondie's Blessed Event '42
Blondie in Society '41
Blondie Has Trouble '40
Blondie On a Budget '40
Blondie Plays Cupid '40
Blondie Brings Up Baby '39
Blondie Meets the Boss '39
Blondie Takes a Vacation '39
Blondie '38
Death from a Distance '36
Condemned to Live '35
Dangerous Appointment '34
Fugitive Road '34
The Ghost Walks '34
In the Money '34
The Monster Walks '32
Tangled Destinies '32
The Vampire Bat '32
Murder at Midnight '31

Mel Stuart (1928-)
Sophia Loren: Her Own Story '80
The Chisholms '79
The Triangle Factory Fire Scandal '79
Mean Dog Blues '78
Willy Wonka & the Chocolate Factory '71
I Love My... Wife '70
If It's Tuesday, This Must Be Belgium '69

John Sturges (1910-92)
The Eagle Has Landed '77
Chino '75
McQ '74
Joe Kidd '72
Marooned '69
Ice Station Zebra '68
Hour of the Gun '67
The Hallelujah Trail '65
The Great Escape '63
By Love Possessed '61
The Magnificent Seven '60
Last Train from Gun Hill '59
Never So Few '59
The Law and Jake Wade '58
The Old Man and the Sea '58
Gunfight at the O.K. Corral '57
Underwater! '55
Bad Day at Black Rock '54
Escape from Fort Bravo '53
Jeopardy '53
The Capture '50
The Magnificent Yankee '50
Mystery Street '50

Preston Sturges (1898-1959)
The Beautiful Blonde from Bashful Bend '49
Unfaithfully Yours '48
The Sin of Harold Diddlebock '47
The Great Moment '44
Hail the Conquering Hero '44
Miracle of Morgan's Creek '44
The Palm Beach Story '42
The Lady Eve '41
Sullivan's Travels '41
Christmas in July '40
The Great McGinty '40

Charles Sturridge (1951-)
Lassie '05
Shackleton '02
Longitude '00
FairyTale: A True Story '97
Gulliver's Travels '95
A Foreign Field '93
Where Angels Fear to Tread '91
Aria '88
A Handful of Dust '88
Brideshead Revisited '81

Eric Styles (1967-)
Dreaming of Joseph Lees '99
Relative Values '99

Richard Styles
Midnight Tease 2 '95
Escape '90
Shallow Grave '87

Bobby Suarez
Warriors of the Apocalypse '85
American Commandos '84
Pay or Die '83

Gonzalo Suarez (1934-)
Rowing with the Wind '88
House of the Damned '71

Eliseo Subiela (1944-)
The Dark Side of the Heart '92
Man Facing Southeast '86

Sara Sugarman (1962-)
Confessions of a Teenage Drama Queen '04
Very Annie Mary '00

Kevin Sullivan (1955-)
Cosmic Slop '94
Lantern Hill '90
Looking for Miracles '90
Anne of Avonlea '87
Anne of Green Gables '85
Wild Pony '83

Kevin Rodney Sullivan (1958-)
Guess Who '05
Barbershop 2: Back in Business '04
Conviction '02
How Stella Got Her Groove Back '98
Soul of the Game '96
America's Dream '95

Jeremy Summers (1931-)
Danger UXB '81
Five Golden Dragons '67
The House of 1000 Dolls '67

Walter Summers (1896-1973)
House of Mystery '41
The Human Monster '39

Cedric Sundstrom
American Ninja 4: The Annihilation '91
The Revenger '90
American Ninja 3: Blood Hunt '89
Captive Rage '88

Stephen Surjik
Weapons of Mass Distraction '97
Wayne's World 2 '93

Edward Sutherland (1895-1974)
Having Wonderful Crime '45
Follow the Boys '44
The Navy Comes Through '42
Sing Your Worries Away '42
Beyond Tomorrow '40
The Invisible Woman '40
One Night in the Tropics '40
The Flying Deuces '39
Every Day's a Holiday '38
Mississippi '35
International House '33
Murders in the Zoo '33
Mr. Robinson Crusoe '32
Palmy Days '31
Behind the Front '26
It's the Old Army Game '26

Kiefer Sutherland (1966-)
Woman Wanted '98
Truth or Consequences, N.M. '97
Last Light '93

Junichi Suzuki
Haunted Highway '05
Remembering the Cosmos Flower '99

Seijun Suzuki (1923-)
Branded to Kill '67
Fighting Elegy '66
Tokyo Drifter '66
Story of a Prostitute '65
Gate of Flesh '64
Youth of the Beast '63

Peter Svatek
The Rendering '02
Silver Wolf '98
Bleeders '97
Jack London's The Call of the Wild '97
Witchboard 3: The Possession '95

Jan Sverak (1965-)
Dark Blue World '01
Kolya '96
The Elementary School '91

E.W. Swackhamer (1927-94)
Are You Lonesome Tonight '92
Perfect Family '92
The Secret Passion of Robert Clayton '92
Death at Love House '75
Death Sentence '74
Man & Boy '71

Bob Swaim (1943-)
The Climb '97
Masquerade '88
Half Moon Street '86

David Swift (1919-2001)
How to Succeed in Business without Really Trying '67
Good Neighbor Sam '64
Under the Yum-Yum Tree '63
The Interns '62
The Parent Trap '61
Pollyanna '60

Saul Swimmer (1936-2007)
Mrs. Brown, You've Got a Lovely Daughter '68
Force of Impulse '60

Michael Switzer
Fallen Angel '03
Forever Love '98
Unlikely Angel '97
Past the Bleachers '95
Fergie & Andrew: Behind Palace Doors '93
Stalking Laura '93
Undesirable '92
The Lightning Incident '91
Nitti: The Enforcer '88

Peter Sykes (1939-)
Jesus '79
To the Devil, a Daughter '76
Night of the Laughing Dead '75
Demons of the Mind '72

Istvan Szabo (1938-)
Being Julia '04
Taking Sides '01
Sunshine '99
Meeting Venus '91
Hanussen '88
Mephisto '81
25 Fireman's Street '73
Love Film '70
Father '67

William Szarka
Phantom Brother '88
South Bronx Heroes '85

Boris Szulzinger
Mama Dracula '80
Shame of the Jungle '75

Jeannot Szwarc (1937-)
Grand Larceny '92
The Murders in the Rue Morgue '86
Santa Claus: The Movie '85
Supergirl '84
Enigma '82
Somewhere in Time '80
Jaws 2 '78
Code Name: Diamond Head '77
Bug '75
Sex Through a Window '72

Juan Carlos Tabio
Guantanamera '95
Strawberry and Chocolate '93

Jean-Charles Tacchella (1925-)
Blue Country '77
Cousin, Cousine '76

Kidlat Tahimik (1942-)
Perfumed Nightmare '89
Turumba '84

Tibor Takacs (1954-)
Ice Spiders '07
Megasnake '07
Kraken: Tentacles of the Deep '06
Sanctuary '98
Redline '97
Sabotage '96
Sabrina the Teenage Witch '96
Deadly Past '95
Bad Blood '94
Gate 2 '92
Red Shoe Diaries 2: Double Dare '92
I, Madman '89
The Gate '87

Beat Takeshi
See Takeshi "Beat" Kitano

Rachel Talalay
Tank Girl '94
Ghost in the Machine '93
Freddy's Dead: The Final Nightmare '91

Igor Talankin
Tchaikovsky '71
A Summer to Remember '61

Paul Talbot
Hellblock 13 '97
Freakshow '95

Gregg Tallas (1915-)
Cataclysm '81
Espionage in Tangiers '65
Prehistoric Women '50

Richard Talmadge (1892-1981)
Project Moon Base '53
Detour to Danger '45
Devil Horse '32

Lee Tamahori (1950-)
Next '07
XXX: State of the Union '05
Die Another Day '02
Along Came a Spider '01
The Edge '97
Mulholland Falls '95
Once Were Warriors '94

Harry (Hurwitz) Tampa (1938-95)
Nocturna '79
Fairy Tales '76

Tokuzo Tanaka (1925-2007)
Zatoichi: The Blind Swordsman's Vengeance '66
Sleepy Eyes of Death: The Chinese Jade '63

Senkichi Taniguchi (1912-2007)
What's Up, Tiger Lily? '66
The Gambling Samurai '60

Terrell Tannen
Shadows in the Storm '88
A Mirror Miracle '83

William (Bill) Tannen
Hero and the Terror '88
Deadly Illusion '87
Flashpoint '84

Alain Tanner (1929-)
In the White City '83
Messidor '77
Jonah Who Will Be 25 in the Year 2000 '76
La Salamandre '71
Charles: Dead or Alive '69

Robert Emmett Tansey (1897-1951)
The Caravan Trail '46
Colorado Serenade '46
Driftin' River '46
God's Country '46
Wild West '46
Song of Old Wyoming '45
Wildfire '45
Arizona Whirlwind '44
Death Valley Rangers '44
Outlaw Trail '44
Western Mail '42
Where Trails End '42
The Driftin' Kid '41
Dynamite Canyon '41
Riding the Sunset Trail '41
Courage of the North '35
Way of the West '35

Daniel Taplitz
Breakin' All The Rules '04
Commandments '96
Black Magic '92
Nightlife '90

Michael Tarantini
Massacre in Dinosaur Valley '85

Quentin Tarantino (1963-)
Crimebusters '79
Death Proof '07
Kill Bill Vol. 2 '04
Kill Bill Vol. 1 '03
Jackie Brown '97
Four Rooms '95
Pulp Fiction '94
Reservoir Dogs '92

Andrei Tarkovsky (1932-86)
The Sacrifice '86
Nostalghia '83
Stalker '79
The Mirror '75
Solaris '72
Andrei Rublev '66
My Name Is Ivan '62

Frank Tashlin (1913-72)
Private Navy of Sgt. O'Farrell '68

Caprice '67
The Glass Bottom Boat '66
The Alphabet Murders '65
Disorderly Orderly '64
Will Success Spoil Rock Hunter? '57
The Girl Can't Help It '56
Hollywood or Bust '56
Artists and Models '55
Susan Slept Here '54
Son of Paleface '52
The Fuller Brush Man '48
Cinderfella '60
The Geisha Boy '58
Rock-A-Bye Baby '57
Who's Minding the Store? '63

Nadia Tass (1956-)
Child Star: The Shirley Temple Story '01
The Miracle Worker '00
Amy '98
Mr. Reliable: A True Story '95
Pure Luck '91
Rikky and Pete '88
Malcolm '86

John Tatoulis
Zone 39 '96
The Silver Stallion: King of the Wild Brumbies '93

Norman Taurog (1899-1981)
Live a Little, Love a Little '68
Speedway '68
Double Trouble '67
Dr. Goldfoot and the Bikini Machine '66
Spinout '66
Tickle Me '65
It Happened at the World's Fair '63
Palm Springs Weekend '63
Blue Hawaii '62
Girls! Girls! Girls! '62
G.I. Blues '60
Birds & the Bees '56
Bundle of Joy '56
Pardners '56
The Caddy '53
Jumping Jacks '52
Rich, Young and Pretty '51
The Stooge '51
The Toast of New Orleans '50
That Midnight Kiss '49
Words and Music '48
Girl Crazy '43
Presenting Lily Mars '43
Men of Boys Town '41
Broadway Melody of 1940 '40
Little Nellie Kelly '40
Young Tom Edison '40
The Adventures of Tom Sawyer '38
Boys Town '38
Mad About Music '38
Rhythm on the Range '36
Strike Me Pink '36
Mrs. Wiggs of the Cabbage Patch '34
We're Not Dressing '34
Hold 'Em Jail '32
Sunny Skies '30

David Tausik
Haunted Symphony '94
Homicidal Impulse '92

Bertrand Tavernier (1941-)
Capitaine Conan '96
L'Appat '94
Revenge of the Musketeers '94
L.627 '92
Daddy Nostalgia '90
Life and Nothing But '89
Beatrice '88
Round Midnight '86
A Sunday in the Country '84
Coup de Torchon '81
Death Watch '80
Spoiled Children '77
The Judge and the Assassin '75

Jacques Tati (1908-82)
Parade '74
Traffic '71
Playtime '67
Mon Oncle '58
Mr. Hulot's Holiday '53
Jour de Fete '48

Vittorio Taviani (1929-)
Paolo Taviani (1931-)
Elective Affinities '96
Fiorile '93
Night Sun '90
Good Morning, Babylon '87
Kaos '85
The Night of the Shooting Stars '82
Padre Padrone '77
Allonsanfan '73
St. Michael Had a Rooster '72

Alan Taylor (1965-)
Kill the Poor '06
Palookaville '95

Baz Taylor (1944-)
Shooting Elizabeth '92

Don Taylor (1920-98)
The Diamond Trap '91
Going for the Gold: The Bill Johnson Story '85
Secret Weapons '85
My Wicked, Wicked Ways '84
Listen to Your Heart '83
September Gun '83
Red Flag: The Ultimate Game '81
The Final Countdown '80
Damien: Omen 2 '78
The Island of Dr. Moreau '77
Great Scout & Cathouse Thursday '76
Tom Sawyer '73
Escape from the Planet of the Apes '71
Wild Women '70
Ride the Wild Surf '64

Finn Taylor (1958-)
The Darwin Awards '06
Cherish '02
Dream with the Fishes '97

Jud Taylor (1940-)
Secrets '94
Danielle Steel's Kaleidoscope '90
The Old Man and the Sea '90
Question of Honor '80
The Christmas Coal Mine Miracle '77
Future Cop '76
Search for the Gods '75
Say Goodbye, Maggie Cole '72

Malcolm Taylor
A Killer in Every Corner '74
Murder Motel '74

Ray Taylor (1888-1952)
Outlaw Country '49
Navy SEALS '90
Deadlock '91
Black Hills '48
Check Your Guns '48
Return of Wildfire '48
Stage to Mesa City '48
The Tioga Kid '48
Border Feud '47
Cheyenne Takes Over '47
Fighting Vigilantes '47
Ghost Town Renegades '47
Law of the Lash '47
West to Glory '47
Wild Country '47
The Hawk of Powder River '48
Don Winslow of the Coast Guard '43
Don Winslow of the Navy '43
Adventures of Smilin' Jack '43
Gang Busters '42
Junior G-Men of the Air '42
Boss of Bullion City '41
Riders of Death Valley '41
Man from Montana '41
Bury Me Not on the Lone Prairie '41
Flash Gordon Conquers the Universe '40
Riders of Pasco Basin '40
Winners of the West '40
The Green Hornet '39
Flaming Frontiers '38
Panamint's Bad Man '38
Rawhide '38
The Painted Stallion '37
Tex Rides with the Boy Scouts '37
Mystery of the Hooded Horseman '37
Law for Tombstone '37
The Phantom Rider '36
The Vigilantes Are Coming '36
The Throwback '35
Stone of Silver Creek '35
The Ivory Handled Gun '35
Chandu on the Magic Island '34
The Fighting Trooper '34
The Perils of Pauline '34
Return of Chandu '34
Phantom of the Air '33
Battling with Buffalo Bill '31

Sam Taylor (1895-1958)
The Tempest '28
The Taming of the Shrew '29
Coquette '29
My Best Girl '27
For Heaven's Sake '26
The Freshman '25
Safety Last '23

S. Lee Taylor
See Steve Taylor

Steve Taylor (1957-)
The Second Chance '06
Social Intercourse '01

Julie Taymor (1952-)
Across the Universe '07
Frida '02
Titus '99

Colin Teague (1970-)
The Last Drop '05
Shooters '00

Lewis Teague (1941-)
The Triangle '01
Saved by the Light '95
T Bone N Weasel '92
Deadlock '91
Collision Course '89
Cat's Eye '85
The Jewel of the Nile '85
Cujo '83
Fighting Back '82
Alligator '80
Lady in Red '79

Andre Techine (1943-)
Changing Times '04
Strayed '03
Alice et Martin '98
Les Voleurs '96
Wild Reeds '94
Ma Saison Preferee '93
Scene of the Crime '87
Rendez-vous '85
Barocco '76

Julien Temple (1953-)
Pandaemonium '01
The Filth and the Fury '99
Bullet '94
Earth Girls Are Easy '89
Aria '88
Absolute Beginners '86
Running out of Luck '86
The Secret Policeman's Other Ball '82
The Secret Policeman's Private Parts '81

Andy Tennant (1955-)
Fool's Gold '08
Hitch '05
Sweet Home Alabama '02
Anna and the King '99
Ever After: A Cinderella Story '98
Fools Rush In '97
It Takes Two '95
The Amy Fisher Story '93
Keep the Change '92

Kevin S. Tenney
Endangered Species '02
Tick Tock '00
The Arrival 2 '98
Pinocchio's Revenge '96
Witchboard 2: The Devil's Doorway '93
Peacemaker '90
Witchtrap '89
Night of the Demons '88
Witchboard '87

Del Tenney (1930-)
Horror of Party Beach '64
I Eat Your Skin '64
Curse of the Living Corpse '64

John Terlesky (1961-)
Fire Serpent '07
Guardian '01
Chain of Command '00
Judgment Day '99
Supreme Sanction '99

Hiroshi Teshigahara (1927-2001)
Rikyu '90
Face of Another '66
Woman in the Dunes '64

Duccio Tessari (1926-94)
Beyond Justice '92
Blood at Sundown '88
Zoro '74

Ted Tetzlaff (1903-95)
The Young Land '59
Son of Sinbad '55
The White Tower '50
The Window '49
Fighting Father Dunne '48
Riff-Raff '47

Joan Tewkesbury (1936-)
Strangers '91
Sudie & Simpson '90
Cold Sassy Tree '89
Acorn People '82
Old Boyfriends '79

Peter Tewkesbury (1923-2003)
The Trouble with Girls (and How to Get into It) '69
Stay Away, Joe '68
Emil and the Detectives '64

Andre Techine (1943-)
'03

Graham Theakston
Sherlock: Case of Evil '02

Daniele Thompson (1942-)
Avenue Montaigne '06
Jet Lag '02
La Buche '00

Donald W. Thompson
Blood on the Mountain '88
The Prodigal Planet '88

Ernest Thompson (1949-)
Out of Time '00
1969 '89

J. Lee Thompson (1914-2002)
Kinjite: Forbidden Subjects '89
Messenger of Death '88
Death Wish 4: The Crackdown '87
Firewalker '86
Murphy's Law '86
King Solomon's Mines '85
The Ambassador '84
The Evil That Men Do '84
Ten to Midnight '83
Happy Birthday to Me '81
The Greek Tycoon '78
The White Buffalo '77
St. Ives '76
The Reincarnation of Peter Proud '75
Huckleberry Finn '74
Battle for the Planet of the Apes '73
Conquest of the Planet of the Apes '72
MacKenna's Gold '69
Kings of the Sun '63
Taras Bulba '62
Cape Fear '62
The Guns of Navarone '61
Tiger Bay '59

Betty Thomas (1949-)
John Tucker Must Die '06
I Spy '02
28 Days '00
Dr. Dolittle '98
The Late Shift '96
Private Parts '97
The Brady Bunch Movie '95

Dave Thomas (1949-)
The Experts '89
Strange Brew '83

Gerald Thomas (1920-93)
Carry On Columbus '92
Carry On Emmanuelle '78
Carry On England '76
Carry On Behind '75
Carry On Dick '75
Carry On Girls '73
Carry On at Your Convenience '71
Carry On Henry VIII '71
Carry On Camping '71
Carry On Doctor '68
Carry On Screaming '66
Carry On Cowboy '66
Carry On Cleo '65
Carry On Cruising '62
Carry On Nurse '59

John G. Thomas (1948-)
Arizona Heat '87
Banzai Runner '86
Tin Man '83

Paul Thomas (1947-)
Killer Looks '94
The Pamela Principle '91

Ralph Thomas (1915-2001)
Quest for Love '71
Deadlier Than the Male '67
Doctor in Distress '63
Conspiracy of Hearts '60
No Love for Johnnie '60
A Tale of Two Cities '58
Doctor at Large '57
Above Us the Waves '56
Doctor at Sea '55
Doctor in the House '53
The Clouded Yellow '51

Ralph L. (R.L.) Thomas (1939-)
A Young Connecticut Yankee in King Arthur's Court '95
Young Ivanhoe '95
Apprentice to Murder '88
The Terry Fox Story '83
Ticket to Heaven '81

Scott Thomas
Flight of the Living Dead: Outbreak on a Plane '07
Latin Dragon '03
Deranged '01
Silent Assassins '88

William C. Thomas (1903-84)
Big Town After Dark '47
Big Town '47

Harry Z. Thomason (1940-)
The Hunting of the President '04
The Day It Came to Earth '77
Encounter with the Unknown '75

David Thacker
The Mayor of Casterbridge '03

Caroline Thompson (1956-)
Snow White: The Fairest of Them All '02
Buddy '97
Black Beauty '94

Chris Thomson (1945-)
Trucks '97
Swimsuit '89
The Empty Beach '85
Three's Trouble '85
The Last Bastion '84
Waterfront '83
Robbery '88
Family '88
Between Wars '74

Rich Thorne
Dr. Dolittle 3 '06

Michael Thornhill (1941-)
The Everlasting Secret Family '88

Billy Bob Thornton (1955-)
All the Pretty Horses '00
Daddy & Them '99
Sling Blade '96

Jerry Thorpe (1930-)
All God's Children '80
For Heaven's Sake '79
A Question of Love '78
The Possessed '77
Wonderland Cove '75
Smile, Jenny, You're Dead '74
Kung Fu '72

Richard Thorpe (1896-1986)
That Funny Feeling '65
Fun in Acapulco '63
The Horizontal Lieutenant '62
The Honeymoon Machine '61
Jailhouse Rock '57

The Prodigal '55
Athena '54
The Student Prince '54
All the Brothers Were Valiant '53
The Girl Who Had Everything '53
Knights of the Round Table '53
Ivanhoe '52
Prisoner of Zenda '52
The Great Caruso '51
Vengeance Valley '51
The Black Hand '50
Three Little Words '50
Challenge to Lassie '49
Malaya '49
The Sun Comes Up '49
A Date with Judy '48
On an Island with You '48
Thrill of a Romance '45
The Thin Man Goes Home '44
Two Girls and a Sailor '44
Above Suspicion '43
Tarzan's New York Adventure '42
White Cargo '42
Tarzan's Secret Treasure '41
The Adventures of Huckleberry Finn '39
Tarzan Finds a Son '39
Double Wedding '37
Night Must Fall '37
Tarzan Escapes '36
Green Eyes '34
After Midnight '33
Rainbow over Broadway '33
Cross Examination '32
The King Murder '32
The Lone Defender '32
Probation '32
The Secrets of Wu Sin '32
Wild Horse '31
Border Romance '30
Under Montana Skies '30
King of the Kongo '29
Desert of the Pampas Moon '35

Antonio Tibaldi
Kiss of Fire '98
Little Boy Blue '97
On My Own '92

Eric Till (1929-)
Luther '03
The Girl Next Door '98
Glory Enough for All: The Discovery of Insulin '92
Oh, What a Night '92
To Catch a Killer '92
Clarence '91
Buffalo Jump '90
A Case of Libel '83
If You Could See What I Hear '82
Improper Channels '82
An American Christmas Carol '79
Mary and Joseph: A Story of Faith '79
Wild Horse Hank '79
Bethune '77
Hot Millions '68

George Tillman, Jr. (1969-)
Men of Honor '00
Soul Food '97

James Tinling (1889-1967)

Robert Tinnell (1961-)
Believe '99
Frankenstein and Me '96
Kids of the Round Table '96

Stacy Title
Let the Devil Wear Black '99
The Last Supper '96

Johnny To (1955-)
Exiled '06
The Mission '99
Running out of Time '99

The Heroic Trio '93

James Toback (1944-)
When Will I Be Loved '04
Harvard Man '01
Black and White '99
Two Girls and a Guy '98
The Pick-Up Artist '87
Exposed '83
Fingers '78

Ricky Tognazzi (1955-)
Excellent Cadavers '99
La Scorta '94

Norman Tokar (1920-79)
Candleshoe '78
The Cat from Outer Space '78
No Deposit, No Return '76
The Apple Dumpling Gang '75
Where the Red Fern Grows '74
Snowball Express '72
The Boatniks '70
The Horse in the Gray Flannel Suit '68
The Happiest Millionaire '67
Follow Me, Boys! '66
Those Calloways '65
The Ugly Dachshund '65
A Tiger Walks '64
Savage Sam '63
Big Red '62
Sammy, the Way-Out Seal '62

Michael Tolkin (1950-)
The New Age '94
The Rapture '91

Stephen Tolkin
Carolina Moon '07
Daybreak '93
Stephen King's Golden Years '91

Mike Tollin (1956-)
Radio '03
Summer Catch '01
Hank Aaron: Chasing the Dream '95

Stanley Tong (1960-)
Mr. Magoo '97
Jackie Chan's First Strike '96
Rumble in the Bronx '96
Supercop 2 '93
Supercop '92

Burt Topper (1928-2007)
Soul Hustler '76
The Hard Ride '71
The Strangler '64
Tank Commando '59
Hell Squad '58

Giuseppe Tornatore (1956-)
The Legend of 1900 '98
The Star Maker '95
A Pure Formality '94
Everybody's Fine '90
Cinema Paradiso '88

Joe Tornatore
Curse of the Crystal Eye '93
Grotesque '87
Code Name: Zebra '84
Zebra Force '76

Fina Torres (1951-)
Woman on Top '00
Oriana '85

Ivan Tors (1916-83)
Galyon '77
Zebra in the Kitchen '65

Robert Totten (1938-95)
Dark Before Dawn '89
The Sacketts '79
Pony Express Rider '76
The Red Pony '76
Huckleberry Finn '75
The Wild Country '71
Death of a Gunfighter '69

Jacques Tourneur (1904-77)
The Comedy of Terrors '64
The Giant of Marathon '60
Curse of the Demon '57
Great Day in the Morning '56
Nightfall '56
Appointment in Honduras '53
The Flame & the Arrow '50
Stars in My Crown '50
Easy Living '49
Berlin Express '48
Out of the Past '47
Canyon Passage '46
Experiment Perilous '45
Days of Glory '43
I Walked with a Zombie '43
The Leopard Man '43
Cat People '42

Maurice Tourneur (1876-1961)
Volpone '39
Lorna Doone '22
County Fair '20
The Last of the Mohicans '20
Pride of the Clan '18
A Girl's Folly '17
Trilby '17
The Wishing Ring '14

Robert Towne (1936-)
Ask the Dust '06
Without Limits '97
Tequila Sunrise '88
Personal Best '82

Bud Townsend (1921-97)
Ecstasy '84
Coach '78
Terror at Red Wolf Inn '72
Nightmare in Wax '69

Robert Kevin Townsend (1957-)
Carmen: A Hip Hopera '01
Holiday Heart '00
Little Richard '00
Livin' for Love: The Natalie Cole Story '00
Jackie's Back '99
Love Songs '99
B.A.P.'s '97
The Meteor Man '93
The Five Heartbeats '91
Hollywood Shuffle '87

Ian Toynton
Annie: A Royal Adventure '95
The Maid '90

Shiro Toyoda (1906-77)
Snow Country '57
Mistress '53

Jean-Claude Tramont (1930-96)
As Summers Die '86
All Night Long '81

Alfred Travers
Dual Alibi '46
Meet the Navy '46

Joey Travolta (1952-)
Final Move '06
Arizona Summer '03
The House Next Door '01
Enemies of Laughter '00
Detour '99
Partners '99
Matter of Trust '98
Laws of Deception '97
Navajo Blues '97
Hard Vice '94
Vegas Vice '94

Jeff Tremaine
Jackass Number Two '06
Jackass: The Movie '02

Brian Trenchard-Smith (1946-)
DC 9/11: Time of Crisis '04
Britannic '00
Britannia '99
The Happy Face Murders '99
Atomic Dog '98

Escape Clause '96
Leprechaun 4: In Space '96
Leprechaun 3 '95
Night of the Demons 2 '94
Official Denial '93
The Siege of Firebase Gloria '89
Day of the Panther '88
Out of the Body '88
Dead End Drive-In '86
The Quest '86
BMX Bandits '83
Day of the Assassin '81
Escape 2000 '81
Deathcheaters '76

John Trent (-1983)
Best Revenge '83
Middle Age Crazy '80
Crossbar '79
Find the Lady '76
It Seemed Like a Good Idea at the Time '75
Vengeance Is Mine '74
The Bushbaby '70

Blair Treu
Little Secrets '02
Just Like Dad '96
The Paper Brigade '96
Wish upon a Star '96

Monika Treut (1954-)
Erotique '94
My Father Is Coming '91
Seduction: The Cruel Woman '89
Virgin Machine '88

Dale Trevillion
'Heart of Stone' '01
Play Time '94
One Man Force '89
Las Vegas Weekend '85

Gus Trikonis (1938-)
The Rumor Mill '86
Love on the Run '85
Jungle Heat '84
Dempsey '83
First Affair '83
Miss All-American Beauty '82
Take This Job & Shove It '81
Twirl '81
Touched by Love '80
She's Dressed to Kill '79
The Evil '78
Moonshine County Express '77
Nashville Girl '76
Fowl Play '75

Rose Troche
The Safety of Objects '01
Bedrooms and Hallways '98
Go Fish '94

Jan Troell (1931-)
Hamsun '96
Flight of the Eagle '82
Hurricane '79
Zandy's Bride '74
The New Land '73
The Emigrants '72

Gary Trousdale (1960-)
Atlantis: The Lost Empire '01
The Hunchback of Notre Dame '96
Beauty and the Beast '91

Fernando Trueba (1955-)
The Girl of Your Dreams '99
Two Much '96
Belle Epoque '92
Twisted Obsession '90

Francois Truffaut (1932-84)
Confidentially Yours '83
The Woman Next Door '81
The Last Metro '80
The Green Room '78
Love on the Run '78
The Man Who Loved Women '77
Small Change '76
The Story of Adele H. '75
Day for Night '73
Two English Girls '72
Bed and Board '70

The Wild Child '70
Mississippi Mermaid '69
The Bride Wore Black '68
Stolen Kisses '68
Fahrenheit 451 '66
The Soft Skin '64
Jules and Jim '62
Shoot the Piano Player '62
The 400 Blows '59
Les Mistons '57

Douglas Trumbull (1942-)
Brainstorm '83
Silent Running '71

Glenn Tryon (1894-1970)
Beauty for the Asking '39
Law West of Tombstone '38
Small Town Boy '37

Ming-liang Tsai
Goodbye, Dragon Inn '03
What Time Is It There? '01

Shinya Tsukamoto (1960-)
Tetsuo 2: Body Hammer '97
Tetsuo: The Iron Man '92

Stanley Tucci (1960-)
Joe Gould's Secret '00
The Imposters '98
Big Night '95

Michael Tuchner (1954-)
Back to the Secret Garden '01
Rainbow Warrior '94
Firestorm: 72 Hours in Oakland '93
The Misadventures of Mr. Wilt '90
Mistress '87
Trapped in Silence '86
Amos '85
Not My Kid '85
Adam '83
Trenchcoat '83
The Hunchback of Notre Dame '82
The Summer of My German Soldier '78
The Old Curiosity Shop '75

Anand Tucker (1963-)
Shopgirl '05
Hilary and Jackie '98
Saint-Ex: The Story of the Storyteller '95

James Tucker
Steps from Hell '92
Lunatic '91

Phil Tucker (1927-85)
Dance Hall Racket '58
Robot Monster '53

Richard Tuggle (1948-)
Out of Bounds '86
Tightrope '84

Montgomery Tully (1904-88)
Battle Beneath the Earth '68
The Terrornauts '67
Dead Lucky '60
The House in Marsh Road '60
Strange Awakening '58
The Electronic Monster '57
The Key Man '57
The Way Out '56
Glass Tomb '55
Paid to Kill '54
Terror Street '54

Ching Siu Tung (1953-)
The Executioners '93
The Heroic Trio '93

Sandy Tung (1950-)
Saving Shiloh '06
Shiloh 2: Shiloh Season '99
Across the Tracks '89

Gary J. Tunnicliffe (1968-)
Guardian '01
Within the Rock '96

Rosemarie Turko (1951-)
Scarred '84
Dungeonmaster '83

Ann Turner (1960-)
Irresistible '06
Hammers over the Anvil '91
Celia: Child of Terror '89

Brad Turner
The Inspectors 2: A Shred of Evidence '00
Must Be Santa '99
The Inspectors '98
Goof Balls '87

Jon Turteltaub (1963-)
National Treasure: Book of Secrets '07
National Treasure '04
Disney's The Kid '00
Instinct '99
From the Earth to the Moon '98
Phenomenon '96
While You Were Sleeping '95
Cool Runnings '93
3 Ninjas '92
Driving Me Crazy '91

John Turturro (1957-)
Romance & Cigarettes '05
Illuminata '98
Mac '93

Frank Tuttle (1892-1963)
Hell on Frisco Bay '55
This Gun for Hire '42
Charlie McCarthy, Detective '39
Waikiki Wedding '37
Here is My Heart '34
Roman Scandals '33
Love 'Em and Leave 'Em '26
Lucky Devil '25

David N. Twohy (1955-)
The Chronicles of Riddick '04
Below '02
Pitch Black '00
The Arrival '96
Grand Tour: Disaster in Time '92

Tom Tykwer (1965-)
Paris, je t'aime '06
Perfume: The Story of a Murderer '06
Heaven '01
The Princess and the Warrior '00
Run Lola Run '98
Winter Sleepers '97

Liv Ullmann (1939-)
Faithless '00
Private Confessions '98
Sofie '92

Edgar G. Ulmer (1904-72)
Journey Beneath the Desert '61
The Amazing Transparent Man '60
Beyond the Time Barrier '60
Naked Venus '58
The Daughter of Dr. Jekyll '57
The Man from Planet X '51
St. Benny the Dip '51
Carnegie Hall '47
Club Havana '46
Detour '46
The Strange Woman '46
Strange Illusion '45
Bluebeard '44
Girls in Chains '43
Isle of Forgotten Sins '43
Jive Junction '43
American Matchmaker '40
The Light Ahead '39
Moon over Harlem '39
The Singing Blacksmith '38
The Black Cat '34
Thunder Over Texas '34

Ron Underwood (1953-)
Santa Baby '06
In the Mix '05
Stealing Sinatra '04
The Adventures of Pluto Nash '02

Mighty Joe Young '98
Speechless '94
Heart and Souls '93
City Slickers '91
Tremors '89

Michael Toshiyuki Uno
A Face to Kill For '99
The Road to Galveston '96
Blind Spot '93
Call of the Wild '93
Without Warning: The James Brady Story '91
The Wash '88

Chano Urueta (1895-1979)
The Brainiac '61
The Witch's Mirror '61
The Living Head '59

Peter Ustinov (1921-2004)
Hammersmith Is Out '72
Lady L '65
Billy Budd '62

Jamie Uys (1921-96)
The Gods Must Be Crazy 2 '89
The Gods Must Be Crazy '84
Dingaka '65

Roger Vadim (1928-2000)
And God Created Woman '88
Game of Seduction '86
Beauty and the Beast '83
Hot Touch '82
Night Games '80
Blood and Roses '61
Please Not Now! '61
Dangerous Liaisons '60
And God Created Woman '57
Barbarella '68
Spirits of the Dead '68
The Game Is Over '66
Circle of Love '64
Le Repos du Guerrier '62
Love on a Pillow '62

Ladislao Vajda (1906-65)
The Man Who Wagged His Tail '57
The Miracle of Marcelino '55

Luis Valdez (1940-)
The Cisco Kid '94
La Bamba '87
Zoot Suit '81

Tonino Valerii (1934-)
My Name Is Nobody '74
A Reason to Live, a Reason to Die '73

Nick Vallelonga (1959-)
All In '06

Rudolf Van Den Berg (1949-)
The Corporate Ladder '97
In the Kingdom of the Blind the Man with One Eye Is King '94
A Brilliant Disguise '93

Frank (Pierluigi Ciriaci) Valenti
Delta Force Commando 2 '90
War Bus Commando '89
Delta Force Commando '87

Jaco Van Dormael (1957-)
The Eighth Day '95
Toto le Heros '91

Woodbridge S. Van Dyke (1889-1943)
Cairo '42
I Married an Angel '42
Journey for Margaret '42
Shadow of the Thin Man '41
I Love You Again '40
Bitter Sweet '40
Andy Hardy Gets Spring Fever '39
Another Thin Man '39
Marie Antoinette '38
Rosalie '38
Sweethearts '38
Personal Property '37
After the Thin Man '36
San Francisco '36
Rose Marie '36
Love on the Run '36
I Live My Life '35
Forsaking All Others '35
Naughty Marietta '35
Hide-Out '34
The Thin Man '34
Penthouse '33
Manhattan Melodrama '34
The Prizefighter and the Lady '33
Tarzan, the Ape Man '32
Trader Horn '31
White Shadows in the South Seas '29

Buddy Van Horn (1929-)
Pink Cadillac '89
The Dead Pool '88
Any Which Way You Can '80

Andre Van Heerden (1971-)
Revelation '00
Tribulation '00

Melvin Van Peebles (1932-)
Gang in Blue '96
Identity Crisis '90
Sweet Sweetback's Baadasssss Song '71
Watermelon Man '70
The Story of a Three Day Pass '68

Mario Van Peebles (1958-)
Baadasssss! '03
Love Kills '98
Gang in Blue '96
Panther '95
Posse '93
New Jack City '91

Gus Van Sant (1952-)
Paranoid Park '07
Paris, je t'aime '06
Last Days '05
Elephant '03
Gerry '02
Finding Forrester '00
Psycho '98
Good Will Hunting '97
To Die For '95
Even Cowgirls Get the Blues '94
My Own Private Idaho '91
Drugstore Cowboy '89

Andrew Van Slee (1965-)
Net Games '03

Norman Thaddeus Vane
Taxi Dancers '93
Midnight '89
Club Life '86
The Black Room '82
Frightmare '81

Carlo Vanzina (1952-)
Nights '95
Jacquot '91

Agnes Varda (1928-)
One Hundred and One Nights '95
Jacquot '91
Le Petit Amour '87
Vagabond '85
One Sings, the Other Doesn't '77
Le Bonheur '65
Cleo from 5 to 7 '61

Giuseppe Vari (1916-93)
The Legend of Sea Wolf '75
Shoot the Living, Pray for the Dead '70
Place in Hell '69
Conquest of the Normans '62
Revenge of the Barbarians '60

Marco Vicario (1925-)
Wifemistress '79

Bruno VeSota (1922-76)
The Female Jungle '56
The Brain Eaters '58

Todd Verow (1966-)
Little Shots of Happiness '97
Frisk '95

The Sheep Has Five Legs '54

Stephen Verona (1940-)
Talking Walls '85
Pipe Dreams '76
The Lords of Flatbush '74

Christian Vincent (1955-)
La Separation '94
La Discrete '90

Chuck Vincent (1940-91)
Enrapture '90
Wildest Dreams '90
Bedroom Eyes 2 '89
Cleo/Leo '89
Party Incorporated '89
Young Nurses in Love '89
Sexpot '88
Student Affairs '88
A Woman Obsessed '88
Deranged '87
New York's Finest '87
Sensations '87
Slammer Girls '87
Warrior Queen '87
Wimps '87
If Looks Could Kill '86
Hollywood Hot Tubs '84
Preppies '82
C.O.D. '83
Hot T-Shirts '79
A Matter of Love '78
American Tickler '77

Marcel Varnel (1894-1947)
Oh, Mr. Porter '37
Chandu the Magician '32

Joseph B. Vasquez (1962-95)
Manhattan Merengue! '95
Street Hitz '92
Hangin' with the Homeboys '91
The Bronx War '90

Tom Vaughan
What Happens in Vegas '08
Starter for Ten '06

Matthew Vaughn
Stardust '07
Layer Cake '05

Francis Veber (1937-)
The Valet '06
The Closet '00
The Dinner Game '98

Gore Verbinski (1964-)
Pirates of the Caribbean: At World's End '07
Pirates of the Caribbean: Dead Man's Chest '06
The Weather Man '05
Pirates of the Caribbean: The Curse of the Black Pearl '03
The Ring '02
The Mexican '01
Mouse Hunt '97

Carlo Verdone (1950-)
Iris Blond '98
Acqua e Sapone '83

Michael Verhoeven (1929-)
My Mother's Courage '95
The Nasty Girl '90

Paul Verhoeven (1938-)
Black Book '06
Hollow Man '00
Starship Troopers '97
Showgirls '95
Basic Instinct '92
Total Recall '90
RoboCop '87
Flesh and Blood '85
Spetters '80
The 4th Man '79
Soldier of Orange '78
Katie Tippel '75
Turkish Delight '73
Business Is Business '71
The Eternal Waltz '54

Reynaldo Villalobos (1940-)
Hollywood Confidential '97

Robert Vince
Snow Buddies '08
Air Bud 6: Air Buddies '06
MXP: Most Xtreme Primate '03
Air Bud 4: Seventh Inning Fetch '02
MVP2: Most Vertical Primate '01
MVP (Most Valuable Primate) '00

Alfred Vohrer (1918-86)
Creature with the Blue Hand '70
The Mysterious Magician '65
The Squeaker '65
The Indian Scarf '63
Inn on the River '62
Dead Eyes of London '61
Door with the Seven Locks '62

Daniel Vigne (1942-)
One Woman or Two '85
The Return of Martin Guerre '83

Jean Vigo (1905-34)
Killing in the Sun '73
L'Atalante '34
Zero for Conduct '33
A Propos de Nice '29

Berthold Viertel (1885-1954)
The Passing of the Third Floor Back '36
Rhodes '36

King Vidor (1894-1982)
Solomon and Sheba '59
War and Peace '56
Man Without a Star '55
Ruby Gentry '52
Beyond the Forest '49
The Fountainhead '49
Duel in the Sun '46
On Our Merry Way '48
Comrade X '40
Northwest Passage '40
The Citadel '38
Stella Dallas '37
The Texas Rangers '36
Our Daily Bread '34
Bird of Paradise '32
The Champ '32
Street Scene '31
Hallelujah! '29
The Crowd '28
Show People '28
The Big Parade '25
Peg o' My Heart '22
The Sky Pilot '21
The Jack-Knife Man '20

Charles Vidor (1900-59)
The Swan '56
Love Me or Leave Me '55
Rhapsody '54
Hans Christian Andersen '52
Gilda '46
The Loves of Carmen '48
A Song to Remember '45
Cover Girl '44
The Desperadoes '43
The Tuttles of Tahiti '42
The Lady in Question '40
My Son, My Son! '40

Joseph Vilsmaier (1939-)
The Harmonists '99
Brother of Sleep '95
Stalingrad '94

The Sensual Man '74

Thomas Vinterberg (1969-)
Dear Wendy '05
It's All About Love '03
The Celebration '98

Albert T. Viola
Preacherman '83

Joe Viola
Cry of the Penguins '71
Hot Box '72
Angels Hard As They Come '71

Norton Virgien
Rugrats Go Wild '03
The Rugrats Movie '98

Clement Virgo (1966-)
Love Come Down '00
Junior's Groove '97
Rude '96

Luchino Visconti (1906-76)
The Innocent '76
Conversation Piece '75
Ludwig '72
Death in Venice '71
The Damned '69
The Stranger '67
Sandra of a Thousand Delights '65
The Leopard '63
Boccaccio '70 '62
Rocco and His Brothers '60
White Nights '57
Senso '54
Bellissima '51
La Terra Trema '48
Ossessione '42

Tony Vitale
One Last Ride '03
Kiss Me, Guido '97

Virgil W. Vogel (1920-96)
Walker: Texas Ranger: One Riot, One Ranger '95
Portrait of a Rebel: Margaret Sanger '82
Beulah Land '80
Centennial '78
Law of the Land '76
Invasion of the Animal People '62
The Kettles on Old MacDonald's Farm '57
The Land Unknown '57
The Mole People '56

Linda Voorhees
California Dreaming '07

Bernard Vorhaus (1904-2000)
The Amazing Mr. X '48
Lady from Louisiana '42
Courageous Dr. Christian '40

Thrilled to Death '88

Charles Vidor (1900-59)

Marc Voizard
Escape from Wildcat Canyon '99

Paul G. Volk
Steel Frontier '94
Sunset Strip '91

Andy Wachowski (1967-)
Speed Racer '08
The Matrix Revolutions '03
The Matrix Reloaded '03
The Matrix '99
Bound '96

Larry Wachowski (1965-)
Speed Racer '08
The Matrix Revolutions '03
The Matrix Reloaded '03
The Matrix '99
Bound '96

Margarethe von Trotta (1942-)
Rosenstrasse '03
The Promise '94
Sheer Madness '84
Marianne and Juliane '82
The Second Awakening of Christa Klages '78
The Lost Honor of Katharina Blum '75

Lars von Trier (1956-)
The Boss of It All '06
Manderlay '05
Dogville '03
The Idiots '99
The Kingdom 2 '97
Breaking the Waves '95
The Kingdom '95
Zentropa '92
Medea '88
The Element of Crime '84

Erich von Stroheim (1885-1957)
Queen Kelly '29
Greed '24
Merry-Go-Round '23
Foolish Wives '22
The Wedding March '28
Blind Husbands '19

Ernst R. von Theumer
Hell Hunters '87
Jungle Warriors '84

Josef von Sternberg (1894-1969)
Jet Pilot '57
Macao '52
The Shanghai Gesture '42
Crime and Punishment '35
The Devil Is a Woman '35
The Scarlet Empress '34
Blonde Venus '32
Shanghai Express '32
Dishonored '31
Morocco '30
The Blue Angel '30
Docks of New York '28
The Last Command '28
Underworld '27
It '27

Josef von Baky (1902-66)
Baron Munchausen '43
The Strange Countess '61

Katja von Garnier (1966-)
Blood & Chocolate '07
Bandits '99

Kurt Voss (1963-)
Sugar Town '99
Highway Hitcher '98
Body Count '97
Baja '95
The Horseplayer '91
Genuine Risk '89
Border Radio '88

Wacks

Jonathan Wacks
Ed and His Dead Mother '93
Mystery Date '91
Powwow Highway '89

Andrucha Waddington (1970-)
House of Sand '05
Me You Them '00

Michael Wadleigh (1941-)
Wolfen '81
Woodstock '70

Jeff Wadlow
Never Back Down '08
CryWolf '05

George Waggner (1894-1984)
The Commies Are Coming, the Commies Are Coming '57
The Fighting Kentuckian '49
The Climax '44
Man Made Monster '41
The Wolf Man '41
Mystery Plane '39
Stunt Pilot '39
Wolf Call '39
Ghost Town Riders '38
Outlaw Express '38
Western Trails '38

Andrew Wagner
Starting Out in the Evening '07
The Talent Given Us '04

David Wain
The Ten '07
Wet Hot American Summer '01

Rupert Wainwright (1961-)
The Fog '05
Stigmata '99
Blank Check '93
Dillinger '91

Andrzej Wajda (1927-)
Zemsta '02
Korczak '90
The Possessed '88
A Love in Germany '84
Danton '82
Man of Iron '81
The Conductor '80
Maids of Wilko '79
Without Anesthesia '78
Man of Marble '76
Land of Promise '74
Landscape After Battle '70
Everything for Sale '68
Lotna '64
Siberian Lady Macbeth '61
Innocent Sorcerers '60
Ashes and Diamonds '58
Kanal '56
A Generation '54

Chris Walas (1953-)
The Vagrant '92
The Fly 2 '89

Grant Austin Waldman
Teenage Exorcist '93
Gator King '70

Dorian Walker
Teen Witch '89
Making the Grade '84

Giles Walker (1946-)
Ordinary Magic '93
Princes in Exile '90
90 Days '86

Hal Walker (1896-1972)
The Road to Bali '53
Sailor Beware '52
At War with the Army '50
The Road to Utopia '46
The Stork Club '45

Pete Walker (1939-)
Home Before Midnight '84
House of the Long Shadows '82
The Comeback '77
Schizo '77
The Confessional '75
House of Whipcord '75
Tiffany Jones '75
Frightmare '74
Die Screaming, Marianne '73
Flesh and Blood Show '73
Man of Violence '71
The Big Switch '70

Stuart Walker (1887-1941)
The Mystery of Edwin Drood '35
Werewolf of London '35
Great Expectations '34
The Eagle and the Hawk '33
Misleading Lady '32

Gary Walkow
Beat '00
Notes from Underground '95
The Trouble with Dick '88

Randall Wallace (1949-)
We Were Soldiers '02
The Man in the Iron Mask '98

Richard Wallace (1894-1951)
Sinbad, the Sailor '47
Tycoon '47
Because of Him '45
It's in the Bag '45
Bombardier '43
The Fallen Sparrow '43
A Night to Remember '42
A Girl, a Guy and a Gob '41
Captain Caution '40
The Young in Heart '38
Blossoms on Broadway '37
Wedding Present '36
Little Minister '34
Man of the World '31

Rick Wallace
Acceptable Risks '86
A Time to Live '85
California Girls '84

Stephen Wallace (1943-)
The Killing Beach '92
Prisoners of the Sun '91
For Love Alone '86
Winner Takes All '84

Tommy Lee Wallace (1949-)
John Carpenter Presents Vampires: Los Muertos '02
Final Justice '98
The Spree '96
Witness to the Execution '94
The Comrades of Summer '92
Stephen King's It '90
Aloha Summer '88
Fright Night 2 '88
Halloween 3: Season of the Witch '82

Anthony Waller (1959-)
The Guilty '99
An American Werewolf in Paris '97
Mute Witness '95

Raoul Walsh (1887-1981)
Esther and the King '60
The Sheriff of Fractured Jaw '59
The Naked and the Dead '58
Band of Angels '57
The King and Four Queens '56
Battle Cry '55
The Tall Men '55
Gun Fury '53
A Lion Is in the Streets '53
Sea Devils '53
Blackbeard the Pirate '52
The Lawless Breed '52
The World in His Arms '52
Along the Great Divide '51
Captain Horatio Hornblower '51
Distant Drums '51
The Enforcer '51
White Heat '49
Silver River '48
Pursued '47
The Man I Love '46
The Horn Blows at Midnight '45
Objective, Burma! '45
Uncertain Glory '44
Background to Danger '43
Northern Pursuit '43
Desperate Journey '42
Gentleman Jim '42
High Sierra '41
Strawberry Blonde '41
They Died with Their Boots On '41
Dark Command '40
They Drive by Night '40
The Roaring Twenties '39
College Swing '38
O.H.M.S. '37
When Thief Meets Thief '37
Big Brown Eyes '36
Klondike Annie '36
The Bowery '33
Going Hollywood '33
Women of All Nations '31
Big Trail '30
Sadie Thompson '28
The Thief of Baghdad '24
Regeneration '15

Charles Walters (1911-82)
Walk, Don't Run '66
The Unsinkable Molly Brown '64
Billy Rose's Jumbo '62
Please Don't Eat the Daisies '60
Ask Any Girl '59
Don't Go Near the Water '57
High Society '56
The Glass Slipper '55
The Tender Trap '55
Dangerous When Wet '53
Easy to Love '53
Lili '53
Torch Song '53
Texas Carnival '51
Three Guys Named Mike '51
Summer Stock '50
The Barkleys of Broadway '49
Easter Parade '48
Good News '47

Fred Walton
The Courtyard '95
Dead Air '94
When a Stranger Calls Back '93
Homewrecker '92
Trapped '89
The Rosary Murders '87
April Fool's Day '86
Hadley's Rebellion '84
When a Stranger Calls '79
The Executioner '70

Peter Wang
Laserman '90
A Great Wall '86

Steve Wang
Drive '96
Guyver 2: Dark Hero '94
The Guyver '91

Wayne Wang (1949-)
Last Holiday '06
Because of Winn-Dixie '05
Maid in Manhattan '02
The Center of the World '01
Anywhere But Here '99
Chinese Box '97
Blue in the Face '95
Smoke '95
The Joy Luck Club '93
Eat a Bowl of Tea '89
Slamdance '87
Dim Sum: A Little Bit of Heart '85
Chan Is Missing '82

Xiaoshuai Wang (1966-)
Beijing Bicycle '01
Frozen '98
So Close to Paradise '98

David S. Ward (1947-)
Down Periscope '96
Major League 2 '94
The Program '93
King Ralph '91
Major League '89
Cannery Row '82

Donal Lardner Ward (1964-)
My Life's in Turnaround '94

Vincent Ward (1956-)
What Dreams May Come '98
Map of the Human Heart '93
The Navigator '88
Vigil '84

Clyde Ware (1936-)
Bad Jim '89
The Hatfields & the McCoys '75
When the Line Goes Through '73
No Drums, No Bugles '71

Regis Wargnier (1948-)
East-West '99
Indochine '92

Charles Marquis Warren (1912-90)
Charro! '69
Tension at Table Rock '56
Arrowhead '53
Little Big Horn '51
Red Desert '50

Deryn Warren
Black Magic Woman '91
Bloodspell '87
Mirror of Death '87

Jennifer Warren (1941-)
Partners in Crime '99
Forbidden Choices '94

Jerry Warren (1921-88)
The Wild World of Batwoman '66
Curse of the Stone Hand '64
Attack of the Mayan Mummy '63
Invasion of the Animal People '62
Terror of the Bloodhunters '62
Creature of the Walking Dead '60
Face of the Screaming Werewolf '59
Teenage Zombies '58
Man Beast '55

John Warren (1953-)
Major League 3: Back to the Minors '98

Norman J. Warren (1942-)
Bloody New Year '87
Gunpowder '87
Alien Prey '83
Inseminoid '80
Spaced Out '80
The Terror '79

Denzel Washington (1954-)
The Great Debaters '07
Antwone Fisher '02

John Waters (1946-)
A Dirty Shame '04
Cecil B. Demented '00
Pecker '98
Serial Mom '94
Cry-Baby '90
Divine '90
Hairspray '88
Polyester '81
Desperate Living '77
Female Trouble '74
Pink Flamingos '72
Multiple Maniacs '70
Mondo Trasho '69

Mark S. Waters (1964-)
The Spiderwick Chronicles '08
Just like Heaven '05
Mean Girls '04
Freaky Friday '03
Head Over Heels '01
The House of Yes '97

Frederick P. Watkins
Lethal Seduction '97
A Matter of Honor '95
Brutal Fury '92

Peter Watkins (1935-)
Edvard Munch '74
The Gladiators '70

John Watson
The Zoo Gang '85
Deathstalker '83

Harry Watt (1906-87)
Eureka Stockade '49
Overlanders '46

Nate Watt (1889-1968)
Frontier Vengeance '40
Law of the Pampas '39
Rustler's Valley '37
Hopalong Cassidy Returns '36

Ric Roman Waugh (1968-)
In the Shadows '01
Exit '95

Al Waxman (1935-2001)
Diamond Fleece '92
White Light '90
My Pleasure Is My Business '74

Keoni Waxman (1968-)
The Highway Man '99
I Shot a Man in Vegas '96
Serial Bomber '96
Almost Blue '93

Keenen Ivory Wayans (1958-)
A Low Down Dirty Shame '94
I'm Gonna Git You Sucka '88

John Wayne (1907-79)
The Green Berets '68
The Alamo '60

Harry S. Webb (1896-1959)
Mesquite Buckaroo '39
Riding On '37
Santa Fe Bound '37
Fast Bullets '36
Pinto Rustlers '36
Laramie Kid '35
Ridin' Thru '35
The Live Wire '34

Jack Webb (1920-82)
D.I. '57
Pete Kelly's Blues '55
Dragnet '54

Lewin Webb
The Confessor '04
Gone Dark '03

Millard Webb (1893-1935)
Glorifying the American Girl '30

Robert D. Webb (1903-90)
The Jackals '67
Love Me Tender '56
Seven Cities of Gold '55
Beneath the 12-Mile Reef '53

William Webb
The Hit List '93
The Banker '89
Party Line '88
Dirty Laundry '87
Sunset Strip '85

Peter Webber (1968-)
Hannibal Rising '07
Girl with a Pearl Earring '03

Lois Weber (1881-1939)
The Blot '21
Too Wise Wives '21
Discontent '16

Nicholas Webster (1912-2006)
Mission Mars '67
Santa Claus Conquers the Martians '64
Gone Are the Days '63
Purlie Victorious '63

David Wechter (1956-)
Malibu Bikini Shop '86
Midnight Madness '80

Chris Wedge (1957-)
Robots '05
Ice Age '02

Stephen Weeks (1948-)
Sword of the Valiant '83
Madhouse Mansion '74
I, Monster '71

Paul Wegener (1874-1948)
The Golem '20
Student of Prague '13

Lo Wei (1918-96)
New Fist of Fury '76
Chinese Connection '73
Fists of Fury '73

John Weidner
Space Marines '96
Blood for Blood '95
Private Wars '93

Samuel Weil
See Lloyd Kaufman

Paul Welland (1953-)
Made of Honor '08
For Roseanna '96
City Slickers 2: The Legend of Curly's Gold '94
Bernard and the Genie '91
Leonard Part 6 '87

Claudia Weill (1947-)
Critical Choices '97
Once a Hero '88
It's My Turn '80
Girlfriends '78

Yossi Wein
Octopus 2: River of Fear '02
Shark Attack 2 '00
U.S. Seals '98
Mission of Death '97
Operation Delta Force 2: Mayday '97
Terminal Impact '95
Never Say Die '94
Lethal Ninja '93

Peter Weir (1944-)
Master and Commander: The Far Side of the World '03
The Truman Show '98
Fearless '93
Green Card '90
Dead Poets Society '89
The Mosquito Coast '86
Witness '85
The Year of Living Dangerously '82
Gallipoli '81
Plumber '79
The Last Wave '77
Picnic at Hanging Rock '75
The Cars That Ate Paris '74

Don Weis (1922-2000)
The Munsters' Revenge '81
Zero to Sixty '78
Billie '65
Pajama Party '64
Critic's Choice '63
The Gene Krupa Story '59
The Affairs of Dobie Gillis '53
I Love Melvin '53

Gary Weis
Wholly Moses! '80
Diary of a Young Comic '79

All You Need Is Cash '78

Jack Wells
Mardi Gras Massacre '78
Crypt of Dark Secrets '76
Storyville '74

Sam Weisman
Dickie Roberts: Former Child Star '03
What's the Worst That Could Happen? '01
The Out-of-Towners '99
George of the Jungle '97
Bye Bye, Love '94
D2: The Mighty Ducks '94

Jirí Weiss (1913-2004)
Martha and I '91
Murder Czech Style '66
The Coward '62
Sweet Light in a Dark Room '63

Michael Cole Weiss
Wolf Trap '57

Chris Weitz (1970-)
Decoit '06
Star ding St'll '05

Paul Weitz (1966-)
The Golden Compass '07
American Pie '99
Down to Earth '01
About a Boy '02
American Dreamz '06
In Good Company '04
Down to Earth '01
American Pie 2 '99

Mel Weiss (1924-2005)
Joy Ride to Nowhere '78

Orson Welles (1915-85)
It's All True '93
Chimes at Midnight '67
The Trial '63
Touch of Evil '53
Mr. Arkadin '55
Othello '52
The Lady from Shanghai '48
Macbeth '48
The Stranger '46
The Magnificent Ambersons '42
Citzen Kane '41

David Wellington (1963-)
Long Day's Journey Into Night '95
The Carpenter '89

William A. Wellman (1896-1975)
Lafayette Escadrille '58
Darby's Rangers '58
Goodbye, My Lady '56
Blood Alley '55
The High and the Mighty '54
Island in the Sky '53
Across the Wide Missouri '51
Westward the Women '51
The Next Voice You Hear '50
Battleground '49
Magic Town '47
The Story of G.I. Joe '45
Buffalo Bill '44
Roxie Hart '42
The Great Man's Lady '42
The Ox-Bow Incident '43
Lady of Burlesque '43
Thunder Birds '42
Beau Geste '39
Nothing Sacred '37
A Star Is Born '37
Heroes for Sale '33
The Purchase Price '32
Night Nurse '31
Public Enemy '31
Beggars of Life '28
Wings '27

Audrey Wells (1960-)
Under the Tuscan Sun '03
Guinevere '99

Byron Werner
Boca '94

Sandra Werneck (1951-)
Possible Loves '00

Alfred Werker (1896-1975)
At Gunpoint '55
Devil's Canyon '53
Lost Boundaries '49
He Walked by Night '48
Shock! '46
The Adventures of Sherlock Holmes '39
It Could Happen to You '39

Richard Wenk (1956-)
Just the Ticket '98
National Lampoon's Attack of the 5 Ft. 2 Women '94
Vamp '86

James Whale (1896-1957)
The Man in the Iron Mask '39
Sinners in Paradise '38
Wives under Suspicion '38
Show Boat '36
The Bride of Frankenstein '35
The Invisible Man '33
The Old Dark House '32
Frankenstein '31

Frank Whaley (1963-)
The Jimmy Show '01
Joe the King '99

Haskell Wexler (1926-)
Latino '85
Medium Cool '69

Tony Wharmby
Covert Assassin '92
Like A Bride '94

Eric Weston
To Protect and Serve '92
Marvin & Tige '84
Evilspeak '82

William West
Flying Wild '41
Double Trouble '41

Roland West (1885-1952)
Corsair '31
The Bat Whispers '30
Alibi '29
The Monster '25
The Bat '25

Jake West
Pumpkinhead 3: Ashes to Ashes '06
Razor Blade Smile '98

Simon West (1961-)
When a Stranger Calls '06
Lara Croft: Tomb Raider '01
The General's Daughter '99
Con Air '97

Forest Whitaker (1961-)
First Daughter '04
Hope Floats '98
Waiting to Exhale '95
Strapped '93

Alan White
Risk '00
Erskineville Kings '99

Andrew White
See Andrea Bianchi

Susanna White
Jane Eyre '06
Bleak House '05

John Whitesell
Big Mcmma's House 2 '06
Deck the Halls '06
Malibu's Most Wanted '03
See Spot Run '01
Calendar Girl '93

Philip H. (Phil, P.H.) Whitman (1893-1935)
His Private Secretary '33
Girl from Calgary '32
Wayne Murder Case '32

Preston A. Whitmore, II (1962-)
This Christmas '07

Simon Wells (1961-)
The Time Machine '02
Prince of Egypt '98
Balto '95
We're Back! A Dinosaur's Story '93
An American Tail: Fievel Goes West '91

Wim Wenders (1945-)
Don't Come Knocking '05
Land of Plenty '04
Buena Vista Social Club '99
The Million Dollar Hotel '99
The End of Violence '97
Beyond the Clouds '95
Faraway, So Close! '93
Until the End of the World '91
Wings of Desire '88
Tokyo-Ga '85
Paris, Texas '83
Hammett '82
State of Things '82
The Wrong Move '78
The American Friend '77
Kings of the Road—In the Course of Time '76
Alice in the Cities '74
The Scarlet Letter '73
The Goalie's Anxiety at the Penalty Kick '71

Paul Wendkos (1922-)
The Chase '91
Blood Vows: The Story of a Mafia Wife '87
Rage of Angels: The Story Continues '86
Secrets '77
The Bad Seed '85
Celebrity '85
The Execution '85
Cocaine: One Man's Seduction '83
Awakening of Candra '81
The Five of Me '81
A Cry for Love '80
The Ordeal of Dr. Mudd '80
Betrayal '78
The Death of Richie '76
Special Delivery '76
Honor Thy Father '73
Haunts of the Very Rich '72
The Mephisto Waltz '71
The Tattered Web '71
Guns of the Magnificent Seven '69
Johnny Tiger '66
Gidget Goes to Rome '63
Gidget Goes Hawaiian '61
Angel Baby '61
Gidget '59

Jeff Werner
Cheerleaders' Wild Weekend '85

Peter Werner (1947-)
Die Laughing '80
Gracie's Choice '04
Call Me Claus '01
Ruby's Bucket of Blood '01
The '70s '00
Mena Flora's Family '98
The Substitute Wife '94
Lone Justice '93
Hiroshima: Out of the Ashes '90
The Image '89
BJ: The Early Years '88
The Alamo: Thirteen Days to Glory '87
No Man's Land '87
I Married a Centerfold '84
Hard Knox '83
Don't Cry, It's Only Thunder '82
In the Region of Ice '76

Lina Wertmuller (1928-)
The Worker and the Hairdresser '96
Ciao, Professore! '94
Summer Night with Greek Profile, Almond Eyes & Scent of Basil '87
Camorra: The Naples Connection '85
Sotto, Sotto '85
A Joke of Destiny, Lying in Wait Around the Corner Like a Bandit '84
Blood Feud '79
A Night Full of Rain '78
Seven Beauties '76
Swept Away... '75
All Screwed Up '74
Love and Anarchy '73
The Seduction of Mimi '72

David Wheatley (1950-)
Catherine Cookson's The Wingless Bird '97
Catherine Cookson's The Girl '96
Catherine Cookson's The Rag Nymph '96
Catherine Cookson's The Tide of Life '96
Catherine Cookson's The Gambling Man '95
Catherine Cookson's The '85

Claude Whatham (1927-2008)
Buddy's Song '91
Murder Elite '86
Agatha Christie's Murder Is Easy '82
Disraeli '79
Sweet William '79
All Creatures Great and Small '74
That'll Be the Day '73
Elizabeth R '72

Ken Wheat (1950-)
Pitch Black '00
After Midnight '89
The Ewoks: Battle for Endor '85

Jim Wheat (1952-)
Pitch Black '00
After Midnight '89
The Ewoks: Battle for Endor '85

David Wickes
Jekyll and Hyde '90
Jack the Ripper '88
Silver Dream Racer '83

Bernhard Wicki (1919-2000)
Morituri '65
The Longest Day '62
The Bridge '59

Bo Widerberg (1930-97)
All Things Fair '95
Man on the Roof '76
Elvira Madigan '67

Robert Wiemer (1938-)
The Night Train to Kathmandu '88
Somewhere Tomorrow '85
Anna to the Infinite Power '84

Anne Wheeler (1946-)
Edge of Madness '02
Better Than Chocolate '99
Angel Square '92
Bye Bye Blues '89
Cowboys Don't Cry '88
Loyalties '86

Tim Whelan (1893-1957)
Texas Lady '56
Rage at Dawn '55
Badman's Territory '46
Higher and Higher '44
Step Lively '44
Seven Days' Leave '42
Twin Beds '42
International Lady '41
The Thief of Bagdad '40
Clouds over Europe '39
Sidewalks of London '38
The Divorce of Lady X '38
Action for Slander '38

Robert Wiene (1881-1938)
The Hands of Orlac '25
The Cabinet of Dr. Caligari '19

Ken Wiederhorn (1938-)
Dark Tower '87
Meatballs 2 '84
Eyes of a Stranger '81
Shock Waves '77

Georg Wildhagen (1920-)
The Merry Wives of Windsor '50

Crane Wilbur (1886-1973)
The Bat '59
The Devil on Wheels '47
We're in the Legion Now '37
Yellow Cargo '36
Tomorrow's Children '34

Fred M. Wilcox (1905-64)
Forbidden Planet '56
The Secret Garden '49
The Hills of Home '48
Three Daring Daughters '48
Courage of Lassie '46
Lassie, Come Home '43

Herbert Wilcox (1892-1977)
Teenage Bad Girl '59
Dangerous Youth '58
The King's Rhapsody '55
Let's Make Up '55
Trouble in the Glen '54
Elizabeth of Ladymead '48
The Courtney Affair '47
Maytime in Mayfair '49
I Live in Grosvenor Square '46
Nurse Edith Cavell '39
London Melody '37
Bitter Sweet '33

Charles Wilkinson
Breach of Trust '95
Quarantine '89

Robert Wiener (1938-)
All Things Fair '95
Man from Mallorca '84

Ethan Wiley
Children of the Corn 5: Fields of Terror '98
House 2: The Second Story '87

Richard Whorf (1906-66)
It Happened in Brooklyn '47
Champagne for Caesar '50
Love from a Stranger '47
Till the Clouds Roll By '46

Tom Whitus
The Wild Card '03
Threat of Exposure '02

Billy Wilder (1906-2002)
Buddy Buddy '81
The Front Page '74
Avanti! '72
The Private Life of Sherlock Holmes '70
The Fortune Cookie '66
Kiss Me, Stupid '64
Irma La Douce '63
One, Two, Three '61
The Apartment '60
Some Like It Hot '59
Spirit of St. Louis '57
Love in the Afternoon '57
Witness for the Prosecution '57
The Seven Year Itch '55
Sabrina '54
Stalag 17 '53
Ace in the Hole '51
Sunset Boulevard '50
A Foreign Affair '48
The Emperor Waltz '48
The Lost Weekend '45
Double Indemnity '44
Five Graves to Cairo '43
The Major and the Minor '42

Oscar Williams (1944-)
Death Drug '83
Hot Potato '76

Lester Williams
See William Berke

Elmo Williams (1913-)
Hell Ship Mutiny '57
Tall Texan '53

Anson Williams (1949-)
All-American Murder '91
A Perfect Little Murder '90
Little White Lies '89

Irvin Willat (1890-1976)
The Michigan Kid '28

Ted Wilde (1893-1929)
Speedy '28
The Kid Brother '27
Battling Orioles '24

Michael Whyte
Catherine Cookson's The Man Who Cried '93
The Railway Station Man '92

William Wiard (1928-)
Help Wanted: Male '82
Tom Horn '80
Snowbird '78

Gene Wilder (1935-)
Haunted Honeymoon '86
The Woman in Red '84
The Adventures of Sherlock Holmes' Smarter Brother '78
The World's Greatest Lover '77

W. Lee Wilder (1904-82)
Fright '56
Manfish '56
Big Bluff '55
Killers from Space '54
The Snow Creature '54
Phantom from Space '53

Gordon Wiles (1902-50)
The Gangster '47
Mr. Boggs Steps Out '38
Prison Train '38
Charlie Chan's Secret '35

Gavin Wilding
Spliced '03
Christina's House '99
Premonition '95

Georg Wildhagen (1920-)
The Marriage of Figaro '49

Cornel Wilde (1915-89)
Sharks' Treasure '75
The Naked Prey '66
Sword of Lancelot '63

Charles Wilkinson
Crossover '06
The Walking Dead '94
Seduced by Evil '94
Treacherous Crossing '92
Sorry, Wrong Number '89
Love for Lydia '79

Williams

Final Comedown '72
Paul W. Williams (1943-)
Mirage '94
The November Men '93
Spencer Williams, Jr. (1893-1969)
Juke Joint '47
Dirty Gertie from Harlem U.S.A. '46
Blood of Jesus '41
Go Down Death '41
Stephen Williams
A Killing Spring '02
Verdict in Blood '02
My Teacher Ate My Homework '98
ShadowZone: The Undead Express '96
Soul Survivor '95
Tod Williams (1968-)
The Door in the Floor '04
The Adventures of Sebastian Cole '99
Tony Williams (1942-)
Next of Kin '82
Solo '77
Fred Williamson (1938-)
Silent Hunter '94
South Beach '92
Steele's Law '91
Three Days to a Kill '91
The Kill Reflex '89
The Messenger '87
Foxtrap '85
Big Score '83
The Last Fight '82
One Down, Two to Go! '82
Mister Mean '77
Death Journey '76
Adios Amigo '75
Mean Johnny Barrows '75
No Way Back '74
Nick Willing (1961-)
The River King '05
Close Your Eyes '02
Jason and the Argonauts '00
Alice in Wonderland '99
Photographing Fairies '97
J. Elder Wills (1900-70)
Big Fella '37
Song of Freedom '36
Ben F. Wilson
The Fighting Stallion '26
Wild Horse Canyon '25
Dean Wilson
Blind Faith '89
Free Amerika Broadcasting '89
Clayton County Line '78
Hugh Wilson (1943-)
Dudley Do-Right '99
Blast from the Past '98
The First Wives Club '96
Guarding Tess '94
Burglar '87
Rustler's Rhapsody '85
Police Academy '84
Jim Wilson
Whirlygirl '04
Head Above Water '96
Movie Maker '86
Stacy's Knights '83
Richard Wilson (1915-91)
It's All True '93
Three in the Attic '68
Invitation to a Gunfighter '64
Al Capone '59
Sandy Wilson (1947-)
American Boyfriends '89
My American Cousin '85
Kurt Wimmer (1964-)
Ultraviolet '06
Equilibrium '02
One Man's Justice '95
James R. Winburn
Miami Beach Cops '93
The Death Merchant '91
Evil Altar '89
Simon Wincer (1943-)
Comanche Moon '08

Monte Walsh '03
Crocodile Dundee in Los Angeles '01
Crossfire Trail '01
P.T. Barnum '99
The Echo of Thunder '98
Escape: Human Cargo '98
Flash '98
Murder She Purred: A Mrs. Murphy Mystery '98
The Phantom '96
Operation Dumbo Drop '95
Lightning Jack '94
Free Willy '93
Harley Davidson and the Marlboro Man '91
Quigley Down Under '90
Lonesome Dove '89
The Lighthorsemen '87
The Girl Who Spelled Freedom '86
D.A.R.Y.L. '85
Phar Lap '84
Dark Forces '83
The Night After Halloween '79
Bretaigne Windust (1906-60)
The Pied Piper of Hamelin '57
The Enforcer '51
June Bride '48
Winter Meeting '48
Harry Winer (1947-)
Lucky Seven '03
Jeremiah '98
House Arrest '96
JFK: Reckless Youth '93
SpaceCamp '86
Mirrors '85
Single Bars, Single Women '84
Jonathan Winfrey
Legend of the Lost Tomb '97
Black Scorpion 2: Ground Zero '96
Carnosaur 3: Primal Species '96
Black Scorpion '95
Bloodfist 7: Manhunt '95
Excessive Force 2: Force on Force '95
The Assassination Game
Gary Winick (1961-)
Charlotte's Web '06
13 Going on 30 '04
Tadpole '02
The Tic Code '99
Sweet Nothing '96
Out of the Rain '90
Curfew '88
Charles Winkler
The Net 2.0 '06
At Any Cost '00
Rocky Marciano '99
Disturbed '90
You Talkin' to Me? '87
David Winkler
Devour '05
Finding Graceland '98
Henry Winkler (1945-)
Cop and a Half '93
Memories of Me '88
A Smoky Mountain Christmas '86
Irwin Winkler (1934-)
De-Lovely '04
Life as a House '01
At First Sight '98
The Net '95
Night and the City '92
Guilty by Suspicion '91
Terence H. Winkless
Get a Clue! '98
Lady Killer '97
Not of This Earth '96
White Wolves 2: Legend of the Wild '94
Rage and Honor '92
The Berlin Conspiracy '91
Corporate Affairs '90
Bloodfist '89
The Nest '88

Michael Winner (1935-)
Parting Shots '98
Bullseye! '90
A Chorus of Disapproval '89
Appointment with Death '88
Scream for Help '86
Death Wish 3 '85
The Wicked Lady '83
Death Wish 2 '82
Firepower '79
The Big Sleep '78
The Sentinel '76
Death Wish '74
Scorpio '73
The Stone Killer '73
The Mechanic '72
The Nightcomers '72
Chato's Land '71
Lawman '71
I'll Never Forget What's 'Isname '67
The Girl Getters '66
Cool Mikado '63
Murder on the Campus '52
David Winning (1961-)
He Sees You When You're Sleeping '02
Profile for Murder '96
Turbo: A Power Rangers Movie '96
Killer Image '92
Storm '87
Peter Winograd
One Last Run '89
Flicks '85
Terry Winsor
Essex Boys '99
The Magician '93
Fool's Gold: The Story of the Brink's-Mat Robbery '92
Party! Party! '83
Stan Winston (1946-)
The Adventures of a Gnome Named Gnorm '90
Pumpkinhead '88
Alex Winter (1965-)
Fever '99
Freaked '93
Michael Winterbottom (1961-)
A Mighty Heart '07
The Road to Guantanamo '06
Tristram Shandy: A Cock and Bull Story '05
Code 46 '03
In This World '03
24 Hour Party People '01
The Claim '00
Wonderland '99
I Want You '98
Welcome to Sarajevo '97
Go Now '96
Jude '96
Butterfly Kiss '94
Family '94
David Winters (1939-)
Rage to Kill '88
Space Mutiny '88
Codename: Vengeance '87
Thrashin' '86
Mission... Kill '85
Fanatic '82
Racquet '79
Scott Wiper (1970-)
The Condemned '07
A Better Way to Die '00
Frank Wisbar (1899-1967)
The Devil Bat's Daughter '46
Strangler of the Swamp '46
Herbert Wise (1924-)
The 10th Kingdom '00
Breaking the Code '95
Strange Interlude '90
Woman in Black '89
Pope John Paul II '84
The Norman Conquests, Part 1: Table Manners '78

The Norman Conquests, Part 2: Living Together '78
The Norman Conquests, Part 3: Round and Round the Garden '78
The Gathering Storm '74
Elizabeth R '72
Castle of the Living Dead '64
Alone Against Rome '62
Kirk Wise (1963-)
Atlantis: The Lost Empire '01
The Hunchback of Notre Dame '96
Beauty and the Beast '91
Robert Wise (1914-2005)
Rooftops '89
Star Trek: The Motion Picture '79
Audrey Rose '77
The Hindenburg '75
The Andromeda Strain '71
Star! '68
The Sand Pebbles '66
The Sound of Music '65
The Haunting '63
Two for the Seesaw '62
West Side Story '61
Odds Against Tomorrow '59
I Want to Live! '58
Run Silent, Run Deep '58
This Could Be the Night '57
Until They Sail '57
Helen of Troy '56
Somebody Up There Likes Me '56
Tribute to a Bad Man '56
Executive Suite '54
The Desert Rats '53
The Day the Earth Stood Still '51
Three Secrets '50
The Set-Up '49
Blood on the Moon '48
Born to Kill '47
Criminal Court '46
The Body Snatcher '45
Curse of the Cat People '44
Mademoiselle Fifi '44
The Magnificent Ambersons '42
Carol Wiseman
Face the Music '92
Does This Mean We're Married? '90
May Wine '90
The Little Princess '87
Len Wiseman (1973-)
Live Free or Die Hard '07
Underworld: Evolution '05
Underworld '03
Doris Wishman (1920-2002)
Double Agent 73 '80
The Amazing Transplant '70
Deadly Weapons '70
Bad Girls Go to Hell '65
Nude on the Moon '61
William Witney (1915-2002)
Darktown Strutters '74
Arizona Raiders '65
Master of the World '61
The Outcast '54
Iron Mountain Trail '53
Shadows of Tombstone '53
Border Saddlemates '52
Colorado Sundown '52
Heart of the Rockies '51
Bells of Coronado '50
North of the Great Divide '50
Sunset in the West '50
Trail of Robin Hood '50
Trigger, Jr. '50
Twilight in the Sierras '50
Down Dakota Way '49
The Golden Stallion '49
Susanna Pass '49
Eyes of Texas '48
Far Frontier '48
Grand Canyon Trail '48
Night Time in Nevada '48
Under California Stars '48
Apache Rose '47

Bells of San Angelo '47
Home in Oklahoma '47
On the Old Spanish Trail '47
Springtime in the Sierras '47
Cyclotrode "X" '46
Helldorado '46
Roll on Texas Moon '46
Fighting Devil Dogs '43
G-Men vs. the Black Dragon '43
The Gay Ranchero '42
Nyoka and the Tigermen '42
Spy Smasher '42
Spy Smasher Returns '42
The Adventures of Captain Marvel '41
Dick Tracy vs. Crime Inc. '41
King of the Texas Rangers '41
Adventures of Red Ryder '40
Doctor Satan's Robot '40
Drums of Fu Manchu '40
Mysterious Doctor Satan '40
Zorro's Fighting Legion '39
Daredevils of the Red Circle '38
Dick Tracy Returns '38
Hawk of the Wilderness '38
The Lone Ranger '38
The Painted Stallion '37
The Trigger Trio '37
Zorro Rides Again '37
Peter Wittman
Ellie '84
Play Dead '81
Jay Woelfel (1962-)
Unseen Evil '99
Things '93
Beyond Dream's Door '88
Fred Wolf (1915-2004)
Mouse and His Child '77
The Point '71
Konrad Wolf (1925-82)
Solo Sunny '80
I Was Nineteen '68
Andy Wolk
The Christmas Shoes '02
Deliberate Intent '01
Mr. Rock 'n' Roll: The Alan Freed Story '99
The Defenders: Taking the First '98
The Defenders: Payback '97
Traces of Red '92
Criminal Justice '90
Dan Wolman (1941-)
Soldier of the Night '84
Baby Love '83
Nana '82
Hide and Seek '80
My Michael '75
M. Wallace Wolodarsky
Seeing Other People '04
Sorority Boys '02
Coldblooded '94
James Wong (1940-2004)
Final Destination 3 '06
The One '01
Final Destination '00
Kirk Wong (1949-)
The Big Hit '98
Crime Story '93
Organized Crime & Triad Bureau '93
John Woo (1948-)
Paycheck '03
Windtalkers '02
Mission: Impossible 2 '00
Blackjack '97
Face/Off '97
Once a Thief '96
Broken Arrow '95
Hard Target '93
A Bullet in the Head '90
The Killer '90
Once a Thief '88
A Better Tomorrow, Part 2 '88
A Better Tomorrow, Part 1 '86
Heroes Shed No Tears '86

Last Hurrah for Chivalry '78
Edward D. Wood, Jr. (1924-78)
The Sinister Urge '60
Night of the Ghouls '59
Plan 9 from Outer Space '56
The Violent Years '56
Bride of the Monster '55
Jail Bait '54
Glen or Glenda? '53
Sam Wood (1883-1949)
The Stratton Story '49
Command Decision '48
Heartbeat '46
Guest Wife '45
Saratoga Trunk '45
Casanova Brown '44
For Whom the Bell Tolls '43
The Pride of the Yankees '42
The Devil & Miss Jones '41
Kings Row '41
Kitty Foyle '40
Our Town '40
Goodbye, Mr. Chips '39
A Day at the Races '37
Madame X '37
Navy Blue and Gold '37
Let 'Em Have It '35
A Night at the Opera '35
Hold Your Man '33
Beyond the Rocks '22
Peck's Bad Boy '21
Bille Woodruff
Beauty Shop '05
Honey '03
John Woods
Plain Jane '01
Kings in Grass Castles '97
Rowan Woods (1959-)
Little Fish '05
Do or Die '01
The Boys '98
Skip Woods
Hitman '07
Thursday '98
Jeff Woolnough
Taken '02
Strange Frequency 2 '01
Universal Soldier 2: Brothers in Arms '98
Universal Soldier 3: Unfinished Business '98
First Degree '95
Chuck Workman
Superstar: The Life and Times of Andy Warhol '90
Stoogemania '85
Kill Castro '80
The Mercenaries '80
The Money '75
Duke Worne (1888-1933)
Man from Headquarters '28
Ships in the Night '28
Wallace Worsley, II (1878-1944)
The Hunchback of Notre Dame '23
The Penalty '20
David Worth
Honor '06
Shark Attack 3: Megalodon '02
Time Lapse '01
Shark Attack 2 '00
The Prophet's Game '99
True Vengeance '97
Chain of Command '95
Lady Dragon 2 '93
Lady Dragon '92
Soldier's Revenge '84
Warrior of the Lost World '84
Mid Knight Rider '79
William Worthington
The Dragon Painter '19
The Tong Man '19
Soenke Wortmann (1959-)
The Hollywood Sign '01
Maybe... Maybe Not '94

John Griffith Wray (1896-1929)
- Anna Christie '23
- One Day in the Life of Ivan Denisovich '71

Alexander Wright
- Fast Money '96

Edgar Wright (1974-)
- Hot Fuzz '07
- Shaun of the Dead '04

Geoffrey Wright (1959-)
- Macbeth '06
- Cherry Falls '00
- Romper Stomper '92

Joe Wright
- Atonement '07
- Pride and Prejudice '05

Mack V. Wright (1895-1965)
- Sea Hound '47
- Rootin' Tootin' Rhythm '38
- Big Show '37
- Hit the Saddle '37
- Riders of the Whistling Skull '37
- Roarin' Lead '37
- Robinson Crusoe of Clipper Island '36
- Robinson Crusoe of Mystery Island '36
- The Vigilantes Are Coming '36
- Winds of the Wasteland '36
- Man from Monterey '33
- Somewhere in Sonora '33
- Haunted Gold '32

Tenny Wright (1885-1971)
- Telegraph Trail '33
- The Big Stampede '32

Thomas J. Wright
- Taken '02
- Unspeakable '02
- Chrome Soldiers '92
- Highlander: The Gathering '92
- Deadly Game '91
- The Fatal Image '90
- Snow Kill '90
- No Holds Barred '89
- Torchlight '85

Donald Wrye
- Range of Motion '00
- Not in This Town '97
- Ice Castles '79
- Death Be Not Proud '75
- Born Innocent '74

David Wu
- Merlin's Apprentice '06
- The Snow Queen '02
- Formula 51 '01
- The Bride with White Hair 2 '93

William Wyler (1902-81)
- The Liberation of L.B. Jones '70
- Funny Girl '68
- How to Steal a Million '66
- The Collector '65
- The Children's Hour '61
- Ben-Hur '59
- The Big Country '58
- Friendly Persuasion '56
- Desperate Hours '55
- Roman Holiday '53
- Carrie '52
- Detective Story '51
- The Heiress '49
- The Best Years of Our Lives '46
- Mrs. Miniver '42
- The Little Foxes '41
- The Letter '40
- The Westerner '40

Casper Wrede (1929-98)
- The Terrorists '74
- The Love Trap '66

Paul Wynne
- Barrio Wars '02
- Makin' Baby '02
- Bombshell '97
- Destination Vegas '95

Jim Wynorski (1950-)
- Extreme Limits '01
- Gate Force '01
- Poison '01
- Ablaze '00
- Rangers '00
- Final Voyage '99
- Militia '98
- Against the Law '98
- Storm Trooper '98
- Vampirella '96
- The Wasp Woman '96
- Body Chemistry 4: Full Exposure '95
- Demolition High '95
- Hard Bounty '94
- Sorceress '94
- Victim of Desire '94
- Body Chemistry 3: Point of Seduction '93
- Dinosaur Island '93
- Ghoulies 4 '93
- Home for Christmas '93
- Munchie '92
- Sins of Desire '92
- Sorority House Massacre 2: Nighty Nightmare '92
- The Haunting of Morella '91
- 976-EVIL 2: The Astral Factor '91
- Hard to Die '90
- The Return of Swamp Thing '89
- Transylvania Twist '89
- Not of This Earth '88
- Big Bad Mama 2 '87
- Deathstalker 2: Duel of the Titans '87
- Chopping Mall '86
- The Lost Empire '83

Greg Yaitanes (1970-)
- Children of Dune '03
- Double Tap '98
- Hard Justice '95

Boaz Yakin (1944-)
- Uptown Girls '03
- Remember the Titans '00
- A Price above Rubies '97
- Fresh '94

Yoji Yamada (1931-)
- Twilight of the Cockroaches '90

Harold Young (1897-1970)
- Jungle Captive '45
- The Mummy's Tomb '42
- Dreaming Out Loud '40
- Little Tough Guys '38
- The Scarlet Pimpernel '34

Mitsuo Yanagimachi (1944-)
- Himatsuri '85

Jean Yarbrough (1900-75)
- Over the Hill Gang '69
- Hillbillies in a Haunted House '67
- Jack & the Beanstalk '52
- Lost in Alaska '52
- Holiday in Havana '49
- Master Minds '49
- Pirate Ship '49
- The Creeper '48
- The Brute Man '46
- House of Horrors '46
- She Wolf of London '46
- The Naughty Nineties '45
- Here Come the Co-Eds '45
- In Society '44
- Law of the Jungle '42
- Lure of the Islands '42
- The Devil Bat '41
- King of the Zombies '41
- Let's Go Collegiate '41
- Panama Menace '41
- The Gang's All Here '40

James L. Young (1872-1948)
- The Bells '26
- The Unchastened Woman '25

John G. Young
- The Reception '05
- Parallel Sons '95

Robert M. Young (1924-)
- One Special Night '99
- Captain Jack '98
- Jane Eyre '97
- Caught '96
- Roosters '95
- Doomsday Gun '94
- Splitting Heirs '93
- Talent for the Game '91
- Triumph of the Spirit '89
- Dominick & Eugene '88
- We Are the Children '87
- Extremities '86
- Saving Grace '86
- The Worst Witch '86

Peter Yates (1929-)
- A Separate Peace '04
- Don Quixote '00
- Curtain Call '97
- Roommates '95
- The Run of the Country '95
- Year of the Comet '92
- An Innocent Man '89
- The House on Carroll Street '88
- Suspect '87
- Eleni '85
- The Dresser '83
- Krull '83
- Eyewitness '81
- Breaking Away '79
- The Deep '77
- Mother, Jugs and Speed '76
- For Pete's Sake '74
- Murphy's War '71
- Bullitt '68
- Robbery '67

Irvin S. Yeaworth, Jr. (1926-2004)
- Dinosaurus! '60
- The 4D Man '59
- The Blob '58

Linda Yellen (1949-)
- The Simian Line '99
- The Flaming Teen-Age '56

Jeff Yonis
- Chantilly Lace '93
- Parallel Lives '94

Yaky Yosha (1951-)
- Sexual Response '92
- Dead End Street '83

Hiroaki Yoshida
- Iron Maze '91
- Twilight of the Cockroaches '90

Bud Yorkin (1926-)
- Love Hurts '91
- Arthur 2: On the Rocks '88
- Twice in a Lifetime '85
- The Thief Who Came to Dinner '73
- Start the Revolution without Me '70
- Divorce American Style '67
- Come Blow Your Horn '63

Terence Young (1915-94)
- The Jigsaw Man '84
- Bloodline '79
- The Klansman '74
- Cold Sweat '71
- Red Sun '71
- When Wolves Cry '69
- Mayerling '68
- The River '67
- Triple Cross '67
- Wait until Dark '67
- The Poppy Is Also a Flower '66
- The Amorous Adventures of Moll Flanders '65
- Thunderball '65
- From Russia with Love '63
- Dr. No '62
- Black Tights '60
- Valley of the Eagles '51
- Woman Hater '49

Ben Younger (1972-)
- Prime '05
- Boiler Room '00

Henry Younger
- See Michael Carreras

Gary Youngman
- Dead As a Doorman '85

Ronny Yu (1950-)
- Jet Li's Fearless '06
- Freddy vs. Jason '03
- Formula 51 '01
- Bride of Chucky '98
- Warriors of Virtue '97
- The Phantom Lover '95
- The Bride with White Hair 2 '93
- The Bride with White Hair '93
- China White '91
- Legacy of Rage '86

Noriaki Yuasa (1933-)
- Gamera vs. Zigra '71
- Gamera vs. Guiron '69
- Destroy All Planets '68
- Gamera vs. Gaos '67
- Gamera, the Invincible '66

Corey Yuen (1951-)
- DOA: Dead or Alive '06
- The Transporter '02
- Jet Li's The Enforcer '95

David Yates
- Harry Potter and the Order of the Phoenix '07
- The Girl in the Café '05
- State of Play '03
- The Way We Live Now '02

Robin Hood.... The Legend: The Swords of Wayland '83
Robin Hood.... The Legend: The Legend of Gregorio Cortez '83

Under Western Stars '38

Robert W. Young
- Hostage '92
- Homebodies '74
- Scandalous '88

The World Is Full of Married Men '80

Charlie Boy '81
One Trick Pony '80
Rich Kids '79
Short Eyes '79
Romance with a Double Bass '74
Trauma '83
Bass '74

Roger Young (1942-)
- Jesus '00
- The Thin Blue Lie '00
- Kiss the Sky '98
- A Knight in Camelot '98
- Into Thin Air '85
- Lassiter '84
- Bitter Harvest '81
- Magnum P.I.: Don't Eat the Snow in Hawaii '80
- Held Hostage '91
- Jewels '92
- The Squeeze '87
- Gulag '85
- Geronimo '93
- Getting Gotti '94
- Gotti '96
- Joseph '95
- Moses '95
- Mercy Mission '93
- Solomon '98

Brian Yuzna (1951-)
- Beyond Re-Animator '03
- Faust: Love of the Damned '00
- The Dentist 2: Brace Yourself '98
- Progeny '98
- The Dentist '96
- H.P. Lovecraft's Necronomicon: Book of the Dead '93
- Return of the Living Dead 3 '93
- Silent Night, Deadly Night 4: Initiation '90
- Bride of Re-Animator '89
- Society '92

Alfredo Zacharias
- Demonoid, Messenger of Death '81
- The Bees '78
- The Bandits '67

Raja Zahr
- Extreme Vengeance '90

Steven Zaillian (1951-)
- A Civil Action '98
- Searching for Bobby Fischer '93

Alain Zaloum (1961-)
- Suspicious Minds '96
- Canvas: The Fine Art of Crime '92

Alex Zamm
- Inspector Gadget 2 '02
- The Pooch and the Pauper '99
- My Date with the President's Daughter '98
- Chairman of the Board '97

Luigi Zampa (1905-91)
- Tigers in Lipstick '80
- A Woman of Rome '56

Mario Zampi (1903-63)
- Too Many Crooks '58
- The Naked Truth '58

Will Zens (1920-)
- The Fix '84
- Truck'er's Woman '83
- Hot Summer in Barefoot County '74
- Hell on Wheels '67

Krzysztof Zanussi (1939-)
- The Silent Touch '94
- Year of the Quiet Sun '84
- The Unapproachable '82
- From a Far Country: Pope John Paul II '81
- Contract '80
- The Catamount Killing '74
- Illumination '73
- Family Life '71
- The Structure of Crystals '69

Lili Fini Zanuck (1954-)
- From the Earth to the Moon '98
- Rush '91

Janusz Zaorski
- Baritone '85
- Mother of Kings '82

Woo-ping Yuen (1945-)
- Fist of Legend '94
- Iron Monkey '93
- Twin Warriors '93
- Dragons Forever '88
- No Retreat, No Surrender 2 '89
- The Bodyguard from Beijing '94

Larry Yust (1930-)
- Say Yes! '86
- Homebodies '74

Peter Yuval
- Firehead '90
- Dead End '98
- Shooters '89

Kunihiko Yuyama (1952-)
- Pokémon 3: The Movie '01
- Pokémon the Movie 2000: The Power of One '00
- Pokémon: The First Movie '99

Yuri Zeltser (1962-)
- Playmaker '94
- Eye of the Storm '91

Karel Zeman (1910-89)
- On the Comet '68
- The Original Fabulous Adventures of Baron Munchausen '61

Robert Zemeckis (1952-)
- Beowulf '07
- The Polar Express '04
- Cast Away '00
- What Lies Beneath '00
- Contact '97
- Forrest Gump '94
- Death Becomes Her '92
- Back to the Future, Part 3 '90
- Back to the Future, Part 2 '89
- Who Framed Roger Rabbit '88
- Romancing the Stone '84
- Used Cars '80
- I Wanna Hold Your Hand '78

Mier Zarchi (1937-)
- Don't Mess with My Sister! '85
- I Spit on Your Grave '77

Tony Zarindast
- Werewolf '95
- Hardcase and Fist '89

Edwin Zbonek (1928-2006)
- The Mad Executioners '65
- The Monster of London City '64

Franco Zeffirelli (1923-)
- Callas Forever '02
- Tea with Mussolini '99
- Jane Eyre '96
- Hamlet '90
- Otello '86
- Endless Love '81
- The Champ '79
- Jesus of Nazareth '77
- Brother Sun, Sister Moon '73
- Romeo and Juliet '68
- The Taming of the Shrew '67

Alfred Zeisler (1897-1985)
- Parole, Inc. '49
- Fear '46

Yimou Zhang (1951-)
- Curse of the Golden Flower '06
- Riding Alone for Thousands of Miles '05
- House of Flying Daggers '04
- Hero '03
- The Road Home '01
- Happy Times '01
- Not One Less '99
- To Live '94
- Raise the Red Lantern '91
- The Story of Qiu Ju '91
- Shanghai Triad '95
- Ju Dou '90
- Red Sorghum '87

Xiaowen Zhou (1954-)
The Emperor's Shadow '96
Ermo '94
Tian Zhuangzhuang (1952-)
The Blue Kite '93
The Horse Thief '87
Claude Zidi (1934-)
My New Partner '84
Stuntwoman '81
Howard Zieff (1943-)
My Girl 2 '94
My Girl '91
The Dream Team '89
Unfaithfully Yours '84
Private Benjamin '80
The Main Event '79
House Calls '78
Hearts of the West '75
Slither '73
Scott Ziehl
Road House 2: Last Call '06
Cruel Intentions 3 '04
3-Way '04
Earth vs. the Spider '01
Proximity '00
Broken Vessels '98
Howard Ziehm (1940-)
Flesh Gordon 2: Flesh Gordon Meets the Cosmic Cheerleaders '90
Flesh Gordon '72
Rafal Zielinski (1954-)
Fun '94
National Lampoon's Last Resort '94
Jailbait '93
Night of the Warrior '91
Spellcaster '91
Ginger Ale Afternoon '89
Recruits '86
Loose Screws '85
Screwballs '83
Paul Ziller
Firefight '03
Moving Target '00
Ms. Bear '97
Panic in the Skies '96
Shootfighter 2: Kill or Be Killed '96
Virtual Seduction '96
Probable Cause '95
Back in Action '94
Breaking Point '94
Bloodfist 4: Die Trying '92
Deadly Surveillance '91
Pledge Night '90
Vernon Zimmerman
Fade to Black '80
Unholy Rollers '72
Fred Zinnemann (1907-97)
Five Days One Summer '82
Julia '77
The Day of the Jackal '73
A Man for All Seasons '66
Behold a Pale Horse '64
The Sundowners '60
The Nun's Story '59
Oklahoma! '55
From Here to Eternity '53
High Noon '52
The Member of the Wedding '52
The Men '50
Act of Violence '48
The Search '48
The Seventh Cross '44
Daniel Zirilli
Fast Girl '07
Winner Takes All '98
Joseph Zito (1949-)
Power Play '02
Red Scorpion '89
Invasion U.S.A. '85
Friday the 13th, Part 4: The Final Chapter '84
Missing in Action '84
The Prowler '81
Abduction '75
Rob Zombie (1966-)
Halloween '07
The Devil's Rejects '05
House of 1000 Corpses '03

Ralph Zondag
Dinosaur '00
We're Back! A Dinosaur's Story '93
Tom Zuber
Little Athens '05
Lansdown '01
David Zucker (1947-)
Scary Movie 4 '06
My Boss's Daughter '03
BASEketball '98
Naked Gun 2 1/2: The Smell of Fear '91
The Naked Gun: From the Files of Police Squad '88
Ruthless People '86
Top Secret! '84
Airplane! '80
Jerry Zucker (1950-)
Scary Movie 3 '03
Rat Race '01
First Knight '95
Ghost '90
Ruthless People '86
Top Secret! '84
Airplane! '80
Frank Zuniga (1936-)
Fist Fighter '88
The Golden Seal '83
Heartbreaker '83
Further Adventures of the Wilderness Family, Part 2 '77
Flight of the Grey Wolf '76
Marcos Zurinaga (1952-)
The Disappearance of Garcia Lorca '96
Tango Bar '88
Guido Zurli
The Mad Butcher '72
Psychopath '68
Valerio Zurlini (1926-82)
The Desert of the Tartars '76
Black Jesus '68
Super Brother '68
The Girl with a Suitcase '60
Harald Zwart (1965-)
Agent Cody Banks '03
One Night at McCool's '01
Edward Zwick (1952-)
Blood Diamond '06
The Last Samurai '03
The Siege '98
Courage Under Fire '96
Legends of the Fall '94
Leaving Normal '92
Glory '89
About Last Night... '86
Special Bulletin '83
Having It All '82
Joel Zwick (1942-)
Elvis Has Left the Building '04
Fat Albert '04
My Big Fat Greek Wedding '02
Second Sight '89
Karl Zwicky (1958-)
Vicious '88
Contagion '87
Terry Zwigoff (1948-)
Art School Confidential '06
Bad Santa '03
Ghost World '01
Crumb '94

Writer Index

The **Writer Index** provides a videography for any writer with more than one video credit. The listings for the writer names follow an alphabetical sort by last name (although the names appear in a first name-last name format). The videographies are listed chronologically, from most recent film to their first. If a writer wrote more than one film in the same year, these movies are listed alphabetically within the year. Used in conjunction with the **Cast** index, this index will let you find actors and actresses who wrote themselves juicy parts (with varying degrees of success). Directors also tend to show up here, either before their directorial ambitions surfaced, or after they'd gained enough clout to get one of their scripts to the screen.

Douglas Aarniokoski
Puppet Master 5: The Final Chapter '94
Puppet Master 4 '93

Paul Aaron
In Too Deep '99
Laurel Avenue '93
Octagon '80

George Abbott (1887-1995)
The Pajama Game '57
All Quiet on the Western Front '30
The Sea God '30

Paul Abbott (1960-)
State of Play '03
Butterfly Collectors '99
Reckless: The Sequel '98
Reckless '97
Touching Evil '97
Cracker: Best Boys '95
Cracker: True Romance '95

Scott Abbott
Introducing Dorothy Dandridge '99
Tha Wall '99
Winchell '98
Run for the Dream: The Gail Devers Story '96
Breach of Conduct '94
A Fool and His Money '88

Dustin Lee Abraham (1966-)
How High '01
The Runner '99

Jim Abrahams (1944-)
Scary Movie 4 '06
Mafia! '98
Hot Shots! Part Deux '93
Hot Shots! '91
The Naked Gun: From the Files of Police Squad! '88
Top Secret! '84
Airplane! '80
Kentucky Fried Movie '77

Keith Aberdein (1943-)
Utu '83

Kobe Abe (1924-93)
Woman in the Dunes '64

J.J. (Jeffrey) Abrams (1966-)
Mission: Impossible 3 '06
Joy Ride '01
Armageddon '98
Gone Fishin' '97
Forever Young '92
Regarding Henry '91
Taking Care of Business '90

Rodney Ackland (1908-91)
Thursday's Child '43
Dangerous Moonlight '41

Allen Actor
Dungeonmaster '83
Terror at Red Wolf Inn '72

Daniel Adams
Primary Motive '92

Douglas Adams (1952-2001)
The Hitchhiker's Guide to the Galaxy '05

Andrew Adamson (1966-)
The Chronicles of Narnia: Prince Caspian '08
The Chronicles of Narnia: The Lion, the Witch and the Wardrobe '05
Shrek 2 '04
Shrek '01

Ewart Adamson (1882-1945)

Lisa Addario (1968-)
Surf's Up '07
Lover Girl '97

Milo Addica
Birth '04
Monster's Ball '01

Robert Adetuyi
Code Name: The Cleaner '07
Stomp the Yard '07
Turn It Up '00

Alan J. Adler
Metalstorm: The Destruction of Jared Syn '83
The Concrete Jungle '82
Parasite '82
The Alchemist '81

Duane Adler
Step Up '05
Save the Last Dance '01

Gilbert Adler
Tales from the Crypt Presents Bordello of Blood '95
Children of the Corn 2: The Final Sacrifice '92

Eleonore Adlon
A Couch in New York '95
Salmonberries '91

Felix Adlon
Eat Your Heart Out '96
Younger & Younger '94
Salmonberries '91

Percy Adlon (1935-)
Younger & Younger '94
Rosalie Goes Shopping '89
Bagdad Cafe '88
Sugarbaby '85
Celeste '81

Ed Adlum (1944-)
Shriek of the Mutilated '74
Invasion of the Blood Farmers '72

Frank (Franklyn) Adreon (1902-79)
Son of Zorro '47
Adventures of Red Ryder '40
Drums of Fu Manchu '40
Mysterious Doctor Satan '40
Zorro's Fighting Legion '39
S.O.S. Coast Guard '37

Gilles Adrien
The City of Lost Children '95
Delicatessen '92

Ben Affleck (1972-)
Gone Baby Gone '07
Good Will Hunting '97

James Agee (1909-55)
The Night of the Hunter '55
The African Queen '51

Kamal Ahmed
Rapturous '07
The Jerky Boys '95

Karim Ainouz (1966-)
Madame Sata '02
Behind the Sun '01

Alexandre Aja (1978-)
P2 '07
High Tension '03

Chantal Akerman (1950-)
A Couch in New York '95
Night and Day '91
Window Shopping '86
The Eighties '83
Les Rendez-vous D'Anna '78
News from Home '76

Luis Alcoriza (1918-92)
The Exterminating Angel '62
Death in the Garden '56
El '52

Todd Alcott (1961-)
Antz '98

Alan Alda (1936-)
Betsy's Wedding '90
A New Life '88
Sweet Liberty '86
The Four Seasons '81

Robert Alden
Uncaged '91
Streetwalkin' '85

Will Aldis
Black Cadillac '03
Avenging Angelo '02
Clifford '92
Stealing Home '88
The Couch Trip '87
Back to School '85

Robert Aldrich (1918-83)
Too Late the Hero '70
Four for Texas '63

David Alexander
The Ticket '97
Dead Ahead '96

J. Grubb Alexander (1887-1932)
Svengali '31
County Fair '20

Scott M. Alexander (1963-)
1408 '07
Agent Cody Banks '03
Screwed '00
Man on the Moon '99
The People vs. Larry Flynt '96
That Darn Cat '96
Ed Wood '94
Never Say Die '94
Problem Child 2 '91
Problem Child '90

Grigori Alexandrov (1903-83)
Que Viva Mexico '32
Ten Days That Shook the World '27

Sherman Alexie (1966-)
The Business of Fancydancing '02
Smoke Signals '98

Richard Alfieri (1952-)
The Sisters '05
Puerto Vallarta Squeeze '04
Harvest of Fire '95
A Friendship in Vienna '88
Echoes '83

Ted Allan (1916-95)
Dr. Bethune '90
Love Streams '84
Falling in Love Again '80
Lies My Father Told Me '75

Chris Allen
In God We Trust '00

Curt Allen
Alligator 2: The Mutation '90
Blind Vengeance '90
Bloodstone '88
Hollywood Harry '86
Walking the Edge '83

Irwin Allen (1916-91)
The Last Remake of Beau Geste '77
Five Weeks in a Balloon '62
Voyage to the Bottom of the Sea '61

Janis Allen
The Double Negative '80
Meatballs '79

Jay Presson Allen (1922-2006)
Year of the Gun '91
Deathtrap '82

Prince of the City '81
Just Tell Me What You Want '80
Funny Lady '75
Forty Carats '73
Cabaret '72
Travels with My Aunt '72
The Prime of Miss Jean Brodie '69
Mamie '64

Jim Allen (1926-99)
Land and Freedom '95
Raining Stones '93
Hidden Agenda '90

J.T. Allen
Jesse Stone: Death in Paradise '06

Woody Allen (1935-)
Cassandra's Dream '07
Scoop '06
Match Point '05
Melinda and Melinda '05
Anything Else '03
Hollywood Ending '02
The Curse of the Jade Scorpion '01
Small Time Crooks '00
Sweet and Lowdown '99
Celebrity '98
Deconstructing Harry '97
Everyone Says I Love You '96
Mighty Aphrodite '95
Bullets over Broadway '94
Manhattan Murder Mystery '93
Husbands and Wives '92
Shadows and Fog '92
Alice '90
Crimes & Misdemeanors '89
New York Stories '89
Another Woman '88
September '88
Radio Days '87
Hannah and Her Sisters '86
The Purple Rose of Cairo '85
Broadway Danny Rose '84
Zelig '83
A Midsummer Night's Sex Comedy '82
Stardust Memories '80
Manhattan '79
Interiors '78
Annie Hall '77
Love and Death '75
Sleeper '73
Everything You Always Wanted to Know about Sex (But Were Afraid to Ask) '72
Play It Again, Sam '72
Bananas '71
Take the Money and Run '69
What's Up, Tiger Lily? '66
What's New Pussycat? '65

Bradley Allenstein
Who's Your Caddy? '07

Gila Almagor (1939-)
Under the Domim Tree '95
The Summer of Aviya '88

Michael Almereyda (1960-)
Hamlet '00
The Eternal '99
Nadja '95
Search and Destroy '94
Twister '89

Pedro Almodovar (1951-)
Volver '06
Bad Education '04
Talk to Her '02
All About My Mother '99
Live Flesh '97
The Flower of My Secret '95
Kika '94
High Heels '91
Tie Me Up! Tie Me Down! '90
Women on the Verge of a Nervous Breakdown '88
Law of Desire '86
Matador '86
What Have I Done to Deserve This? '85
Dark Habits '84
Labyrinth of Passion '82
Pepi, Luci, Bom and Other Girls on the Heap '80

Arthur Alsberg (1917-2004)
Hot Lead & Cold Feet '78
Herbie Goes to Monte Carlo '77
Gus '76
No Deposit, No Return '76

Emmett Alston
Hunter's Blood '87
Nine Deaths of the Ninja '85
New Year's Evil '78

Eric Alter
The Experts '89

Sergio D. Altieri (1952-)
Silent Trigger '97
Little Sister '92
Blind Fear '89

Mark Altman
All Souls Day '05
House of the Dead '03
Free Enterprise '98
Hardbodies 2 '86
Hardbodies '84

Robert Altman (1925-2006)
Kansas City '95
Ready to Wear '94
Short Cuts '93
Aria '88
Beyond Therapy '86
A Wedding '78
3 Women '77
Buffalo Bill & the Indians '76
Thieves Like Us '74
Images '72
McCabe & Mrs. Miller '71

D. Alvelo (1965-2004)
Bound by Lies '05
Spider's Web '01

David Amann
The Rendering '02
Dead Air '94

Rod Amateau (1923-2003)
Sunset '88
The Garbage Pail Kids Movie '87
The Wilby Conspiracy '75
Hook, Line and Sinker '30

Dail Ambler (1925-)
He Kills Night After Night / Night Slasher '69
Beat Girl '60

Eric Ambler (1909-98)
The Wreck of the Mary Deare '59
A Night to Remember '58
Battle Hell '56
The Cruel Sea '53
The Promoter '52
The Clouded Yellow '51
The October Man '48
Immortal Battalion '44

David Ambrose (1943-)
Year of the Gun '91
Taffin '88
Blackout '85
D.A.R.Y.L. '85
Amityville 3: The Demon '83
Dangerous Summer '82
The Final Countdown '80
Survivor '80
The Fifth Musketeer '79

Gianni Amelio (1945-)
Lamerica '95
The Stolen Children '92
Open Doors '89

Deborah Amelon (1955-)
Tricks '97
Exit to Eden '94

Alejandro Amenabar (1972-)
The Sea Inside '04
The Others '01
Open Your Eyes '97
Thesis '96

Sergio Amidei (1904-81)
Generale Della Rovere '60
Shoeshine '47
Open City '45

Jack Amiel
The Shaggy Dog '06
The Prince & Me '04
Raising Helen '04

Cesar Amigo
The Ravagers '65
The Walls of Hell '64

Santiago Amigorena
A Few Days in September '06

Mark Amin
After Sex '07

Hossein Amini (1966-)
The Four Feathers '02
The Wings of the Dove '97
Jude '96

Dominic Anciano (1959-)
Love, Honour & Obey '00
Final Cut '98

Allison Anders (1954-)
Things Behind the Sun '01
Sugar Town '99
Grace of My Heart '96
Four Rooms '95
Mi Vida Loca '94
Gas Food Lodging '92
Border Radio '88

Brad Anderson (1964-)
Session 9 '01
Happy Accidents '00
Next Stop, Wonderland '98

Elizabeth Anderson
Three Wishes '95
Lassie '94

Gerry Anderson
Blonde and Blonder '07
Journey to the Far Side of the Sun '69

Hesper Anderson (1934-)
Grand Isle '92
Children of a Lesser God '86

Jane Anderson (1954-)
The Prize Winner of Defiance, Ohio '05
Normal '03
If These Walls Could Talk 2 '00
The Baby Dance '98
How to Make an American Quilt '95
It Could Happen to You '94
The Positively True Adventures of the Alleged Texas Cheerleader-Murdering Mom '93

Josef Anderson
Stephen King's Golden Years '91
Shooting '82

Maxwell Anderson (1888-1959)
A Christmas Carol '54
Death Takes a Holiday '34
Rain '32
Women of All Nations '31
All Quiet on the Western Front '30

Paul Thomas Anderson (1970-)
There Will Be Blood '07
Punch-Drunk Love '02
Magnolia '99
Boogie Nights '97
Hard Eight '96

Paul W.S. Anderson (1965-)
Resident Evil: Extinction '07
Alien vs. Predator '04
Resident Evil: Apocalypse '04
Resident Evil '02
Shopping '93

Robert Anderson (1923-)
I Never Sang for My Father '70
The Sand Pebbles '66
The Nun's Story '59
Until They Sail '57
Tea and Sympathy '56

Wes Anderson (1970-)
The Darjeeling Limited '07
The Life Aquatic with Steve Zissou '04
The Royal Tenenbaums '01
Rushmore '98
Bottle Rocket '95

Guy Andrews
The Infiltrator '95
Lie Down with Lions '94

Jay Andrews
See Jim Wynorski

Peter Andrews
See Steven Soderbergh

Robert D. (Robert Hardy) Andrews (1903-76)
Girls' Town '59
Bataan '43
Before I Hang '40

Tina Andrews (1951-)
Sally Hemings: An American Scandal '00
Why Do Fools Fall in Love? '98

Roger Andrieux (1940-)
La Petite Sirene '80
L'Amour en Herbe '77

James Andronica (1945-)
Mirage '94

Mark Andrus
Georgia Rule '07
Divine Secrets of the Ya-Ya Sisterhood '02
Life as a House '01
As Good As It Gets '97
Late for Dinner '91

Mikel Angel
Evil Spirits '91
Grotesque '87
Psychic Killer '75

Michael Angeli
Killing Mr. Griffin '97
Sketch Artist 2: Hands That See '94
Conflict of Interest '92
Sketch Artist '92

Theo Angelopoulos (1935-)
Eternity and a Day '97
Ulysses' Gaze '95
Landscape in the Mist '88
The Travelling Players '75

Edward Anhalt (1914-2000)
The Take '90
Peter the Great '86
The Holcroft Covenant '85
Green Ice '81
Escape to Athena '79
Fatal Chase '72
The Man in the Glass Booth '75
Luther '74
QB VII '74
Jeremiah Johnson '72
The Madwoman of Chaillot '69
The Boston Strangler '68
Hour of the Gun '67
Boeing Boeing '65
Becket '64
Girls! Girls! Girls! '62
The Young Savages '61
The Young Lions '58
The Pride and the Passion '57
Not as a Stranger '55
The Member of the Wedding '52
Panic in the Streets '50

Erik Anjou (1961-)
The Cool Surface '02
976-EVIL 2: The Astral Factor '91

Ken Annakin (1914-)
The New Adventures of Pippi Longstocking '88
Those Daring Young Men in Their Jaunty Jalopies '69
Those Magnificent Men in Their Flying Machines '65
The Road to Ruin '28

Jean-Jacques Annaud (1943-)
Two Brothers '04
Enemy at the Gates '00
The Lover '92
Black and White in Color '76

Jean Anouilh (1910-87)
Circle of Love '64
Monsieur Vincent '47

Reverge Anselmo (1962-)
Stateside '04

Joseph Anthony (1912-93)
Lovers' Prayer '99

Stuart Anthony (1891-1942)
The Monster and the Girl '41
The Shepherd of the Hills '41
Helltown '38
Arizona Mahoney '36
Drift Fence '36
Police Court '32
Border Law '31

Steve Antin (1956-)
Chasing Papi '03
Gloria '98
Inside Monkey Zetterland '93

Michelangelo Antonioni (1912-2007)
Eros '04
Beyond the Clouds '95
Identification of a Woman '82
The Passenger '75
Zabriskie Point '70
Blow-Up '66
The Eclipse '66
The Red Desert '64
L'Avventura '60
Il Grido '57
The Lady Without Camelias '53
Story of a Love Affair '50

Judd Apatow (1968-)
You Don't Mess with the Zohan '08
Knocked Up '07
Walk Hard: The Dewey Cox Story '07
The 40 Year Old Virgin '05
Fun With Dick and Jane '05
The Cable Guy '96
Celtic Pride '96
Heavyweights '94

Max Apple
Roommates '95
The Air Up There '94
Smokey Bites the Dust '81

William Applegate, Jr. (1972-)
The Big Fall '96
Pure Danger '96
Riot '96
Tiger Heart '96
Skyscraper '95
The Sweeper '95

Gregg Araki (1959-)
Mysterious Skin '04
Splendor '99
Nowhere '96
The Doom Generation '95
Totally F***ed Up '94
The Living End '92

Shimon Arama (1941-)
Triumph of the Spirit '89
Black Eagle '88

Vicente Aranda (1926-)
Mad Love '01
Jealousy '99
Intruso '93
Lovers: A True Story '90
If They Tell You I Fell '89
The Blood Spattered Bride '72

David Arata
Spy Game '01
Brokedown Palace '99

Denys Arcand (1941-)
The Barbarian Invasions '03
Stardom '00
Jesus of Montreal '89
The Decline of the American Empire '86

Manuel Arce
Crossover Dreams '85
El Super '79

Jeffrey Arch
Iron Will '93
Sleepless in Seattle '93

William Archibald (1917-70)
The Innocents '61
I Confess '53

Robert Ardrey (1908-80)
Khartoum '66
Song of Love '47

Asia Argento (1975-)
The Heart Is Deceitful Above All Things '04
Scarlet Diva '00

Dario Argento (1940-)
Sleepless '01
The Church '98
The Phantom of the Opera '98
Dario Argento's Trauma '93
The Devil's Daughter '91
Two Evil Eyes '90
Opera '88
Demons 2 '87
Demons '86
Creepers '85
Unsane '82
Inferno '80
Suspiria '77
Deep Red: Hatchet Murders '75
Commandos '73
The Cat o' Nine Tails '71
The Bird with the Crystal Plumage '70
Once Upon a Time in the West '68

Adolfo Aristarain (1943-)
Martin (Hache) '97
A Place in the World '92
The Lion's Share '79

Alice Arlen
The Weight of Water '00
Cookie '89
Alamo Bay '85
Silkwood '83

Giorgio Arlorio (1929-)
Zorro '74
Burn! '70

Montxo Armendáriz (1949)
Secrets of the Heart '97
Letters from Alou '90

George Armitage (1942)
The Late Shift '96
The Last of the Finest '90
Miami Blues '90
Private Duty Nurses '71
Gas-s-s-s! '70

Steve Armogida
Masseuse '95

Michael Armstrong (1944-)
House of the Long Shadows '82
Black Panther '77

Mike Armstrong
Monument Ave. '98
Two If by Sea '95

Scot Armstrong (1970-)
Semi-Pro '08
The Heartbreak Kid '07
School for Scoundrels '06
Starsky & Hutch '04
Road Trip '00
Old School '03

Elliott Arnold
The Sum of All Fears '02

Jack Arnold (1916-92)
Kings of the Sun '63
The Monolith Monsters '57
Tarantula '55

David Arnott (1976-)
The Adventures of Ford Fairlane '90

Darren Aronofsky (1969-)
The Fountain '06
Below '02
Requiem for a Dream '00
Pi '98

Brooks Arthur (1932-)
Good-bye, Emmanuelle '77

Emmanuelle Arsan (1932-)
Emmanuelle '75

Guillermo Arriaga (1958-)
Babel '06
The Three Burials of Melquiades Estrada '05
21 Grams '03
Amores Perros '00

John August (1970-)
The Nines '07

Ash (1964-)
This Girl's Life '03
Peps '99
Bang '95

William Asher (1921-)
Fireball 500 '65
Beach Blanket Bingo '65
How to Stuff a Wild Bikini '65
Bikini Beach '64
Muscle Beach Party '64

Fiers Ashworth
Nosferatu '93

Peter Askin
Company Man '00
Smithereens '82

Olivier Assayas (1955-)
Paris, je t'aime '06
Clean '04
Demonlover '02
Les Destinées '00
Alice et Martin '98
Late August, Early September '98
Irma Vep '96
Scene of the Crime '87
Rendez-vous '85

Ovidio G. Assonitis (1943)

Tom J. Astle
Get Smart '08
Failure to Launch '06

Doug Atchison
The Longshots '08
Akeelah and the Bee '06

Francisco Athié (1956-)
Optic Fiber '97
Lolo '92

David Atkins
Novocaine '01

Peter Atkins (1955-)
Wishmaster '97
Hellraiser 4: Bloodline '95
Hellraiser 3: Hell on Earth '92

Paul Attanasio
The Good German '06
Sphere '97
Donnie Brasco '96
Disclosure '94
Quiz Show '94

David Auburn (1970-)
The Lake House '06
Proof '05

Yvan Attal (1965-)
Happily Ever After '04
My Wife is an Actress '01

Leopold Atlas (1907-54)
Raw Deal '48
The Story of G.I. Joe '45
Tomorrow the World '44

Michel Audiard (1920-85)

Jacques Audiard (1952-)
The Beat My Heart Skipped '05
Read My Lips '01
A Self-Made Hero '95

Bille August (1948-)
A Song for Martin '01
Jerusalem '96
The House of the Spirits '93
Pelle the Conqueror '88
Twist & Shout '84

Joe Augustyn
Exit '95
Night of the Demons 2 '94
Night Angel '90
Night of the Demons '88

Jean Aurel (1925-96)
Confidentially Yours '83
The Women '69

Jean Aurenche (1904-92)
The Judge and the Assassin '75
The Clockmaker '73
The Hunchback of Notre Dame '57
Forbidden Games '52
The Red Inn '51
The Walls of Malapaga '49

Alan Ayckbourn (1939-)
Private Fears in Public Places '06
A Chorus of Disapproval '89
The Norman Conquests, Part 1: Table Manners '78

George Axelrod (1922-2003)
The Fourth Protocol '87
The Holcroft Covenant '85
The Lady Vanishes '79
Secret Life of an American Wife '69
Lord Love a Duck '66
How to Murder Your Wife '64
Paris When It Sizzles '64
The Manchurian Candidate '62
Breakfast at Tiffany's '61
Phffft! '54

Howard (Hikmet) Avedis
Kidnapped '87
Mortuary '81
The Fifth Floor '80
Scorchy '75

Belle Avery

Brian Avenet-Bradley
Dark Remains '05
Ghost of the Needle '05

Robert J. Avrech
Body Double '84

Jean-Pierre Bacri (1951-)
Look at Me '04
Same Old Song '97
Un Air de Famille '96

Tom Badal
Vietnam, Texas '90
Out on Bail '89

Nicola Badalucco
Escape from Death Row '73

Michael Bafaro
Act of War '96
Listen '96
Crackerjack '94

Fax Bahr

Phillip Badger
Retroactive '97
The Forgotten One '89

Geoffrey Baere
Corporate Affairs '90
Campus Man '87
School Spirit '85

Randall Badat
Born to Run '93
Hear No Evil '93
Surf 2 '84

Jaime Jesus Balcazar

Robert Alan Aurthur (1922-78)
All That Jazz '79
Warlock '59

Paul Auster (1947-)
The Inner Life of Martin Frost '07
Lulu on the Bridge '98
Blue in the Face '95
Smoke '95

Sam Auster
Screen Test '85

Carl Austin (1968-)
Improper Conduct '94

Michael Austin
Princess Caraboo '94

Roger Avary (1965-)
Beowulf '07
Silent Hill '06
The Rules of Attraction '02
Killing Zoe '94
Pulp Fiction '94

Antonio Avati
Bix '90
Zeder '83
Macabre '80

Pupi Avati (1938-)
Incantato '03
The Best Man '97
The Story of Boys & Girls '91
Bix '90
Zeder '83

Phillip Avalon (1955-)
Fatal Bond '91
Summer City '77

Gerald Ayres
Rich and Famous '81
Foxes '80

David Ayer (1972-)
Harsh Times '05
Dark Blue '03
S.W.A.T. '03
The Fast and the Furious '01
Training Day '01
U-571 '00

Dan Aykroyd (1952-)
Blues Brothers 2000 '98
Coneheads '93
Nothing But Trouble '91
Ghostbusters 2 '89
Dragnet '87
Spies Like Us '85
The Blues Brothers '80

Rafael Azcona (1926-)
Crazy in Love '92
The Girl of Your Dreams '99
Belle Epoque '92
Ay, Carmela! '90
Blood and Sand '89
Autopsy '74
La Grande Bouffe '73
El Cochecito '60
Vortex '87

Thom Babbes (1958-)
Body Chemistry '90
Deadly Dreams '88

Hector Babenco (1946-)
Carandiru '03
At Play in the Fields of the Lord '91
Ironweed '87
Kiss of the Spider Woman '85
Pixote '81

Michael Bacall
Manic '01

Danilo Bach
Escape Clause '96
Bookies '03
April Fool's Day '86
Beverly Hills Cop '84

The Norman Conquests, Part 2: Living Together '78
Part 3: Round and Round '78

Alexsei Balabanov (1959-)

Fenton Bailey
Inside Deep Throat '05
Party Monster '03

Frederick Bailey
Terminal Justice: Cybertech P.D. '95

Sandra K. Bailey
False Identity '90

John Baines (1909-)
The KGB: The Secret War '86

Jon Robin Baitz (1961-)
People I Know '02
The Substance of Fire '96

Bart Baker
Supercross: The Movie '05
Any Place But Home '97
Live Wire '92
Baby of the Bride '91

Elliott Baker (1922-2007)
Fire and Ice '83

Herbert Baker (1920-83)
The Jazz Singer '80
Sextette '78
Oh Dad, Poor Dad... '67
Murderers' Row '66
King Creole '58

David Barenbaum
Elf '02

Ralph Bakshi (1938-)
Cool and the Crazy '94
Fire and Ice '83
Hey Good Lookin' '82
Wizards '77
Coonskin '75
Heavy Traffic '73
Fritt the Cat '72

Bela Balazs (1884-1949)
The Blue Light '32
The Threepenny Opera '31

John Lloyd Balderston (1889-1954)
Red Planet Mars '52
Gaslight '44
Prisoner of Zenda '37
The Lives of a Bengal Lancer '35
Mad Love '35
The Mystery of Edwin Drood '35
The Mummy '32
Frankenstein '31
The Bride of Frankenstein '35

Ferdinando Baldi (1917-2007)
Texas, Adios '66
Sicilian Connection '72

Richard Balducci (1929-)
Scandal Man '67
The Gendarme of Saint-Tropez '64

Steven Baigelman
Brother's Keeper '02
Feeling Minnesota '96

Earl Baldwin
The Go-Getter '54
South Sea Woman '53
Africa Screams '49

Jack Baran
Uncovered '94
Great Balls of Fire '89

Steve Barancik (1961-)
The Last Seduction '94

Ernie Barbarash
Stir of Echoes 2: The Homecoming '07
Cube: Zero '04

Randy Barbato
Inside Deep Throat '05
Party Monster '03

Neal Barbera
Quicksand: No Escape '92

Peter Baloff
No Misses '91

Albert Band (1924-2002)
She Came to the Valley '77
Gunfight at Red Sands '63
The Red Badge of Courage '51

Alexander Baron (1917-99)
Oliver Twist '85
Poldark 2 '75

Allen Baron (1935-)
Red, White & Busted '75
Blast of Silence '61

Clive Barker (1952-)
The Haunted Mansion '03
Lord of Illusions '95
Nightbreed '90
Hellraiser '87
Rawhead Rex '87
Transmutations '85

Frank Barhydt
Kansas City '96
Short Cuts '93
Quintet '79

Leora Barish
Basic Instinct 2 '06
Venus Rising '95
Desperately Seeking Susan '85

Jeff Barmash (1957-)
Bounty Hunters 2: Hardball '97

Joseph John Barmettler, Jr.
Timelock '99
Pure Danger '96
Riot '96
Rage '95
Witchcraft 8: Salem's Ghost '95

Peter Barnes (1931-2004)
Arabian Nights '00
Alice in Wonderland '99
A Christmas Carol '99
A Midsummer Night's Dream '68 ... The Ruling Class '72
The Mummy '32

Malcolm Barbour
Deadly Sins '95
No Good Deed '02

Ann Louise Bardach
Cuba: Zero '74

Jessica Barondes
Lucky Seven '03
Little Secrets '02

Wish upon a Star '96

Douglas Barr (1949-)
Frame by Frame '95
Dead Badge '94
The Cover Girl Murders '93
Fade to Black '93

Jackson Barr
Body Chemistry 3: Point of Seduction '93
800 Leagues Down the Amazon '93
Mandroid '93
Bad Channels '92
Seedpeople '92
Body Chemistry 2: Voice of a Stranger '91
Body Chemistry '90

Bruno Barreto (1955-)
Gabriela '84
Dona Flor and Her Two Husbands '78

James Lee Barrett (1929-89)
Warden of Red Rock '01
Ruby Jean and Joe '96
Poker Alice '87
Angel City '80
Mayflower: The Pilgrims' Adventure '79
The Green Berets '68
The Greatest Story Ever Told '65
Shenandoah '65

Simon Barrett
Dead Birds '04
Frankenfish '04

H.E. Barrie
Missile to the Moon '59
She Demons '58

J.M. Barrie (1860-1937)
Quality Street '37
As You Like It '36

Michael Barrie
Bad Boys '95
National Lampoon's Favorite Deadly Sins '95
Oscar '91
Amazon Women on the Moon '87
Ratings Game '84

Michael Barringer
Butler's Dilemma '43
The Dummy Talks '43

Barry Barrington
Valley of Wanted Men '35
Dynamite Ranch '32

Fred Barron
Something Short of Paradise '79
Between the Lines '77

Janet Barron
The Tenant of Wildfell Hall '96
Clarissa '91

Julian Barry (1931-)
Me, Myself & I '92
The River '84
Lenny '74

Odile Barski
Comedy of Power '06
The Cry of the Owl '87
Violette '78

Peter Barsocchini
High School Musical 2 '07
Drop Zone '94

Paul Bartel (1938-2000)
Not for Publication '84
Eating Raoul '82
Cannonball '76
Paul Bartel's The Secret Cinema '69

Hall Bartlett (1922-93)
Children of Sanchez '79
All the Young Men '60
Zero Hour! '57

Richard Bartlett (1922-94)
Lonesome Trail '55
Silver Star '55

Sy Bartlett (1900-78)
Beloved Infidel '59
The Big Country '58
Twelve O'Clock High '49
13 Rue Madeleine '46

Hal Barwood
Warning Sign '85
Dragonslayer '81
Corvette Summer '78
MacArthur '77
Bingo Long Traveling All-Stars & Motor Kings '76
The Sugarland Express '74

Ben Barzman (1911-89)
The Blue Max '66
The Heroes of Telemark '65
Time Without Pity '57
The Lady in Question '40

K.C. Bascombe
Fear of the Dark '02
Swindle '02

Ron Base
Deadline '00
First Degree '95

Harry Basil
The 4th Tenor '02
My 5 Wives '00
Meet Wally Sparks '97

Ronald Bass (1942-)
Mozart and the Whale '05
Passion of Mind '00
Entrapment '99
Snow Falling on Cedars '99
How Stella Got Her Groove Back '98
Stepmom '98
What Dreams May Come '98
My Best Friend's Wedding '97
Dangerous Minds '95
Waiting to Exhale '95
The Enemy Within '94
When a Man Loves a Woman '94
The Joy Luck Club '93
Sleeping with the Enemy '91
Rain Man '88
Black Widow '87
Gardens of Stone '87
Code Name: Emerald '85

Seth Bass
Martian Child '07

Lawrence Bassoff
Hunk '87
Weekend Pass '84

Bradley Battersby (1953-)
Red Letters '00
Blue Desert '91

Lucio Battistrada
Autopsy '74
Commandos '73
Dead Are Alive '72
Stranger in Paso Bravo '68

Hans Bauer
The Flock '07
Highwaymen '03
Anaconda '99

Thomas Baum
Dracula: The Dark Prince
Journey to the Center of the Earth '99
Witness to the Execution '94
The Manhattan Project '86
The Sender '82
Carny '80
Simon '80
Hugo the Hippo '76

Noah Baumbach (1969-)
Margot at the Wedding '07
The Squid and the Whale '05
The Life Aquatic with Steve Zissou '04
Mr. Jealousy '98
Highball '97
Kicking and Screaming '95

Lamberto Bava (1944-)
Ghost Son '06
Demons 2 '87
Demons '86
Macabre '80
Shock '79

Mario Bava (1914-80)
Lisa and the Devil '75
Twitch of the Death Nerve '71
Hatchet for the Honeymoon '70
Danger: Diabolik '68
Kill, Baby, Kill '66
Knives of the Avenger '65
Planet of the Vampires '65
Black Sabbath '64
Blood and Black Lace '64
The Girl Who Knew Too Much '63
Black Sunday '60

George L. Baxt (1923-2003)
Burn Witch, Burn! '62
Circus of Horrors '60
Horror Hotel '60

Sergio Bazzini
Husbands and Lovers '91

Wayne Beach
Slow Burn '05
The Art of War '00
Murder at 1600 '97
The Shadow Conspiracy '96

Peter S. Beagle (1939-)
The Last Unicorn '82
The Lord of the Rings '78
The Dove '74

David Beaird (1952-)
Scorchers '92
My Chauffeur '86
Party Animal '83
Octavia '82

John Beaird (1953-93)
Happy Birthday to Me '81
My Bloody Valentine '81

Henry Bean (1945-)
The Believer '01
Basic Instinct 2 '06
Desperate Measures '98
Deep Cover '92
Internal Affairs '90
Running Brave '83

Richard Beattie
The Highway Man '99
Face the Evil '97
Cold Sweat '93

Stuart Beattie
30 Days of Night '07
Derailed '05
Collateral '04
Joey '98

Warren Beatty (1937-)
Bulworth '98
Love Affair '94
Reds '81
Heaven Can Wait '78
Shampoo '75

D.D. Beauchamp (1908-69)
Alias Jesse James '59
Tennessee's Partner '55
Ride Clear of Diablo '54
Abbott and Costello Go to Mars '53
Gunsmoke '53

Simon Beaufoy (1967-)
Miss Pettigrew Lives for a Day '08
This Is Not a Love Song '02
Blow Dry '00
Among Giants '98
The Full Monty '96

Jerome Beaujour
La Moustache '05
Seventh Heaven '98
A Single Girl '96

Phil Beauman
Not Another Teen Movie '01
Don't Be a Menace to South Central While Drinking Your Juice in the Hood '95

Charles Beaumont (1929-67)
Brain Dead '89
Masque of the Red Death '65
The Haunted Palace '63
7 Faces of Dr. Lao '63
Premature Burial '62
Shame '61
Queen of Outer Space '58

Gorman Bechard (1959-)
Cemetery High '89
Disconnected '87

Jacques Becker (1906-60)
Le Trou '59
Modigliani '58
Ali Baba and the 40 Thieves '54
Grisbi '53
Casque d'Or '52
Rendez-vous de Juillet '49
Antoine et Antoinette '47

Josh Becker (1958-)
Lunatics: A Love Story '92
Thou Shalt Not Kill...Except '87

Barry Beckerman (1943-96)
St. Ives '76
Shamus '73

James Becket (1936-)
Final Approach '04
Plato's Run '96

Michael Frost Beckner (1963-)
Spy Game '01
Sniper '92

Dick Beebe
Book of Shadows: Blair Witch 2 '00
House on Haunted Hill '99
The Lazarus Man '96
Into the Badlands '92
Prison Stories: Women on the Inside '91

Ford Beebe (1888-1978)
Red Desert '50
Outlaw Gang '49
Shep Comes Home '49
My Dog Shep '46
Riders of Pasco Basin '40
Prescott Kid '36
Fighting Shadows '35

Elizabeth Beecher (1898-1973)
Rough Riders of Cheyenne '45
Land of Hunted Men '43

Michael Begler
The Shaggy Dog '06
The Prince & Me '04
Raising Helen '04

Marc Behm (1925-2007)
Nana '82
Hospital Massacre '81
Someone Behind the Door '71
The Peking Blond '68
Help! '65

Harry Behn (1898-1973)
Hell's Angels '30
The Big Parade '25

S.N. Behrman (1893-1973)
Me and the Colonel '58
Waterloo Bridge '40
A Tale of Two Cities '36
Anna Karenina '35
Hallelujah, I'm a Bum '33

Albert Beich (1918-96)
Dead Ringer '64
Girls in Chains '43

Jean-Jacques Beineix (1946-)
Betty Blue '86
Moon in the Gutter '83
Diva '82

Timur Bekmambetov
Day Watch '06
Night Watch '04

Charles Belden
Charlie Chan in Honolulu '38
Mr. Moto's Gamble '38
Charlie Chan at Monte Carlo '37
Charlie Chan on Broadway '37

Elisa Bell
Little Black Book '04
Sleepover '04
Sex & Mrs. X '00
Vegas Vacation '96
Dancing with Danger '93
Treacherous Crossing '92
Writer's Block '91

Neal Bell
Two Small Bodies '93
Terminal Choice '85

James Warner Bellah (1899-1976)
The Man Who Shot Liberty Valance '62
Sergeant Rutledge '60

Donald P. Bellisario (1935-)
JAG '95
Last Rites '88
Magnum P.I.: Don't Eat the Snow in Hawaii '80

Marco Bellocchio (1939-)
My Mother's Smile '02
Devil in the Flesh '87
Henry IV '85
The Eyes, the Mouth '83

Peter Bellwood
Highlander 2: The Quickening '91
Highlander '86
Phobia '80

Edmund Beloin (1910-92)
Paris Holiday '57
The Great Lover '49
My Favorite Brunette '47
Because of Him '45
Lady on a Train '45

Jerry Belson (1938-2006)
Always '89
Surrender '87
Jekyll & Hyde... Together Again '82
Smokey and the Bandit 2 '80
The End '78
Fun with Dick and Jane '77
Smile '75
Evil Roy Slade '71
How Sweet It Is! '68

James Belushi (1954-)
Number One with a Bullet '87
Birthday Boy '85

Maria-Luisa Bemberg (1922-95)
I Don't Want to Talk About It '94
I, the Worst of All '90
Miss Mary '86

Peter Benchley (1940-)
The Island '80
The Deep '77
Jaws '75

Jessica Bendinger (1966-)
Aquamarine '06
Stick It '06
First Daughter '04
The Truth About Charlie '02
Bring It On '00

Barbara Benedek (1952-)
Sabrina '95
Immediate Family '89
Men Don't Leave '89
The Big Chill '83

Tom Benedek
The Adventures of Pinocchio '96
Zeus and Roxanne '96
Cocoon '85

Roberto Benigni (1952-)
The Tiger and the Snow '05
Pinocchio '02
Life Is Beautiful '98
The Monster '96
Johnny Stecchino '92
Berlinguer I Love You '77

David Benioff (1970-)
The Kite Runner '07
Stay '05
Troy '04
25th Hour '02

Richard Benner (1943-90)
Happy Birthday, Gemini '80
Outrageous! '77

Alan Bennett (1934-)
The History Boys '06
The Madness of King George '94
A Question of Attribution '91
Prick Up Your Ears '87
A Private Function '84
An Englishman Abroad '83

Bill Bennett (1953-)
The Nugget '01
Tempted '01
In a Savage Land '99
Kiss or Kill '97
Backlash '86

Charles Bennett (1899-1995)
Five Weeks in a Balloon '62
Voyage to the Bottom of the Sea '61
Curse of the Demon '57
Dangerous Mission '54
The Green Glove '52
Where Danger Lives '50
Black Magic '49
Unconquered '47
The Story of Dr. Wassell '44
Forever and a Day '43
Joan of Paris '42
Reap the Wild Wind '42
Foreign Correspondent '40
Balalaika '39
The Young in Heart '38
Young and Innocent '37
King of the Damned '36
Sabotage '36
The Secret Agent '36
The 39 Steps '35
The Evil Mind '34
The Man Who Knew Too Much '34
Blackmail '29

Harve Bennett (1930-)
A Thousand Heroes '92
Star Trek 4: The Voyage Home '86
Star Trek 3: The Search for Spock '84

Parker Bennett
Super Mario Bros. '93
Mystery Date '91

Ronan Bennett
The Hamburg Cell '04
Lucky Break '01
Face '97

Wallace C. Bennett
Rage of Honor '87
Silent Scream '80
George! '70

John Robert Bensink
Every Mother's Worst Fear '98

Robby Benson (1956-)
Betrayal of the Dove '92
Modern Love '90
Die Laughing '80
One on One '77

Sally Benson (1897-1972)
The Farmer Takes a Wife '53
Come to the Stable '49
Conspirator '49
Anna and the King of Siam '46
Shadow of a Doubt '43

Robert Benton (1932-)
The Ice Harvest '05
Twilight '98
Nobody's Fool '94
Nadine '87
Places in the Heart '84
Still of the Night '82
Kramer vs. Kramer '79
The Late Show '77
Superman: The Movie '78
Bad Company '72
Oh! Calcutta! '72
What's Up, Doc? '72
There Was a Crooked Man '70

David Benullo
Around the World in 80 Days '04
Cupid '96

Leo Benvenuti
Kicking & Screaming '05
The Santa Clause 2 '02
Space Jam '96

Leonardo Benvenuti (1923-2000)
The Worker and the Hairdresser '96
Ciao, Professore! '94
The Sleazy Uncle '89
Once Upon a Time in America '84
Alfredo, Alfredo '72

Eric Bercovici (1933-)
Hell in the Pacific '69

Luc Beraud (1945-)
The Accompanist '93
This Sweet Sickness '77
The Best Way '76

Luca Bercovici (1957-)
The Granny '94
Rockula '90
Ghoulies '84

Leonardo Bercovici (1908-95)
Portrait of Jennie '48
The Bishop's Wife '47

Daniel Berendsen (1964-)
Twitches Too '07
The Cutting Edge: Going for the Gold '05
Twitches '05

Bruce Beresford (1940-)
Paradise Road '97
Curse of the Starving Class '94
Mister Johnson '91
Aria '88
The Fringe Dwellers '86
Breaker Morant '80
Money Movers '78
Barry McKenzie Holds His Own '74

David Berenbaum
The Spiderwick Chronicles '08
Zoom '06
Elf '03

Pamela Berger
The Imported Bridegroom '89

Andrew Bergman (1945-)
Sorceress '88
Striptease '96
It Could Happen to You '94
Honeymoon in Vegas '92
The Freshman '90
Soapdish '91
Fletch '85
Big Trouble '86
Oh, God! You Devil '84
So Fine '81
The In-Laws '79
Blazing Saddles '74

Ingmar Bergman (1918-2007)
Saraband '03
Faithless '00
Private Confessions '98
Sunday's Children '92
The Best Intentions '92
Scenes from a Marriage '73
Cries and Whispers '72
Face to Face '76
The Serpent's Egg '78
After the Rehearsal '84
Fanny and Alexander '83
From the Life of the Marionettes '80
Autumn Sonata '78
The Magician '58
The Devil's Eye '60
Through a Glass Darkly '61
The Silence '63
The Winter Light '62
Persona '66
The Shame '68
Hour of the Wolf '68
The Passion of Anna '70
The Touch '71
The Rite '69
Wild Strawberries '57
The Seventh Seal '56
Dreams '55
Smiles of a Summer Night '55
Lesson in Love '54
Sawdust & Tinsel '53
Monika '52
Secrets of Women '52
Summer Interlude '50
To Joy '50
Devil's Wanton '49
Torment '44

Robert Bergman
Fail Safe '00

Eric Bergren
Skull: A Night of Terror '88
A Whisper to a Scream '88
The Dark Wind '91
Frances '82
The Elephant Man '80

Linda J. Bergman
The Lookalike '90
Matters of the Heart '90

Sarah Bernstein
Call Me Claus '01
Trial and Error '96

Walter Bernstein
Durango '99
Miss Evers' Boys '97
Doomsday Gun '94
The House on Carroll Street '88
Little Miss Marker '80
An Almost Perfect Affair '79
Yanks '79
The Front '76
Fail-Safe '64
Paris Blues '61
Heller in Pink Tights '60
The Train '65
Molly Maguires '70
The Betsy '78
Sem-Tough '77
Semi-Tough '77

Eleanor Bergstein
Let's Talk About Sex '98
Love Don't Cost a Thing '03
B.A.P.'s '97

Martin Berkeley (1904-79)
The Deadly Mantis '57
Revenge of the Creature '55
Tarantula '55
A Stolen Face '52

Eric Bergren
The Hitcher '07

Shari Springer Berman
The Nanny Diaries '07
American Splendor '03

Jon Bernstein
Meet the Robinsons '07
Larry the Cable Guy: Health Inspector '06
Max Keeble's Big Move '01
Beautiful '00
Ringmaster '98

Armyan Bernstein
Cross My Heart '88
The Hurricane '99
Windy City '84
One from the Heart '82
Thank God It's Friday '78

Marcos Bernstein (1970-)
Central Station '98
Foreign Land '95

Jonathan Betuel (1949-)
Theodore Rex '95
My Science Project '85
The Last Starfighter '84

Alberto Bevilacqua (1934-)
Planet of the Vampires '65
Black Sabbath '64
Atom Age Vampire '61

Emmanuele Bernheim
5x2 '04
Swimming Pool '03
Friday Night '02
Under the Sand '00

Gisella Bernice
The Simian Line '99
Parallel Lives '94

Kevin Bernhardt (1961-)
Crimson Rivers 2: Angels of the Apocalypse '05
District B13 '04
Transporter 2 '05
Unleashed '05
The Transporter '02
Kiss of the Dragon '01
Wasabi '01
The Messenger: The Story of Joan of Arc '99
The Fifth Element '97
The Professional '94
La Femme Nikita '91
The Big Blue '88
Subway '85
Le Dernier Combat '84

Patrick Bermel
Surviving the Game '94
The Invitation '03

Peter Berneis (1910-)
My Man Godfrey '48
Portrait of Jennie '48

Edward L. Bernds (1905-2000)
Return of the Fly '59
Reform School Girl '57
Storm Rider '57
Blondie Knows Best '46

Bernardo Bertolucci (1940-)
The Luzhin Defence '00
Besieged '98
Stealing Beauty '96
The Sheltering Sky '90
The Last Emperor '87
The Tragedy of a Ridiculous Man '81
Luna '79
1900 '76
Last Tango in Paris '73
The Conformist '71
The Spider's Stratagem '70
Before the Revolution '65

Luc Besson (1959-)
Angel-A '05
Arthur and the Invisibles '06
Beowulf & Grendel '06
Blood & Donuts '95
Rampants of Clay '68

Andrew Rai Berzins
Judicial Consent '94
Madison '01

Giuseppe Bertolucci (1947-)
Berlinguer I Love You '77

Jean-Louis Bertucelli
1900 '76
The Desert of the Tartars '76

William Bindley
Judicial Consent '94
Madison '01

Paul Bernbaum (1957-)
Next '07
Hollywoodland '06

Sam Bernard
The Destructors '74

Peter Berry
The Incredible Journey of Mary Bryant '05

Michael Berry
Blue Streak '99
Short Time '90

John Berry (1917-99)
Boesman & Lena '00
There Goes Barder '54
Payback '94
Diplomatic Siege '99
Blood Surf '00

Claude Berri (1934-)
Lucie Aubrac '97
Germinal '93
Uranus '91
Jean de Florette '87
Manon of the Spring '87
Tchao Pantin '83

Claude Binyon (1905-78)
A Woman's World '54
My Blue Heaven '50
Arizona '40
Mississippi '35

Charlotte Bingham
Riders '88

Brad Bird (1957-)
Ratatouille '07
The Incredibles '04

Steve Bing (1965-)
Kangaroo Jack '02
Every Breath '93

Mike Binder (1958-)
Reign Over Me '07
The Upside of Anger '05
The Sex Monster '99
Indian Summer '93
Crossing the Bridge '92
Coupe de Ville '90

John Binder (1940-)
Uforia '81
Honeysuckle Rose '80

Carl Binder
The Eliminators '86
Trancers '84

Danny Bilson (1956-)
The Rocketeer '91
Arena '89
Zone Troopers '84
Future Cop '76

Kathryn Bigelow (1952-)
Blue Steel '90
Near Dark '87
Loveless '83

Fabian Bielinsky (1959-2006)
Nine Queens '00
The Aura '05

James Biederman
Cash City '01

Shem Bitterman
Off the Lip '04
Peephole '93

Jerome Bixby (1923-98)
It! The Terror from Beyond Space '58
Curse of the Faceless Man '58

Emerson Bixby (1963-)
Bikini Island '91
Disturbed '91

David Black (1945-)
The Confession '98
Legacy of Lies '92

Michael Ian Black (1971-)
Run, Fat Boy, Run '07
Wedding Daze '06

Stephen Black
Eden 2 '93
Eden '93

Shane Black (1961-)
Kiss Kiss Bang Bang '05
The Long Kiss Goodnight '96
The Last Boy Scout '91
Lethal Weapon '87
The Monster Squad '87
The Last Action Hero '93

Kenneth G. Blackwell
Dark Tower '87

Richard Blackburn
Eating Raoul '82
Lemora, Lady Dracula '73

Michael Blake (1945-)
Dances with Wolves '90
Stacy's Knights '83

Joel Blasberg
College Humor '33

Michael Blankfort (1907-82)
Tribute to a Bad Man '56
The Caine Mutiny '54
The Halls of Montezuma '50
Broken Arrow '50

Philippe Blasband (1964-)
Thomas in Love '01
An Affair at Love '99

William Peter Blatty (1928-)
Exorcist 3: Legion '90
The Ninth Configuration '79
The Exorcist '73
Darling Lili '70
Promise Her Anything '66
What Did You Do in the War, Daddy? '66
A Shot in the Dark '64

Brian Bird
Saving Sarah Cain '07
Bophal '93

Vera Blasi
Woman on Top '00
Tortilla Soup '01

Barry W. Blaustein
The Honeymooners '05
Nutty Professor 2: The Klumps '00
The Nutty Professor '96
Boomerang '92
Coming to America '88
Police Academy 2: Their First Assignment '85

Lajos Biro (1880-)
The Thief of Bagdad '40
The Four Feathers '35
The Scarlet Pimpernel '34
The Private Life of Henry VIII '33

Andrew Birkin (1945-)
Perfume: The Story of a Murderer '06
The Cement Garden '93
The Name of the Rose '86
King David '85
Burning Secret '89

Thomas Bezucha
The Family Stone '05
Big Eden '00

A(lbert) I(saac) Bezzerides (1908-2007)
A Bullet for Joey '55
Kiss Me Deadly '55
Beneath the 12-Mile Reef '53
Action in the North Atlantic '43

Troy Beyer (1965-)
Love Don't Cost a Thing '03
B.A.P.'s '97

John Bishop (1929-2006)
Drop Zone '94
The Package '89

Larry Bishop (1947-)
Trigger Happy '96
Underworld '96

Antonio Bido (1949-)
The Bloodstained Shadow '78

Wes Bishop (1933-93)
Dixie Dynamite '76

Ann Biderman
Primal Fear '96
Smilla's Sense of Snow '96

Alan Bleasdale (1946-)
Oliver Twist '20
Melissa '97
No Surrender '86

Corey Blechman
Free Willy 2: The Adventure Home '95

Free Willy '93
Max and Helen '90
Dominick & Eugene '88

Robert Blees (1925-)
Doctor Phibes Rises Again '72
Frogs '72
Who Slew Auntie Roo? '71
From the Earth to the Moon '58
High School Confidential '58
The Black Scorpion '57
Autumn Leaves '56
Slightly Scarlet '56
Cattle Queen of Montana '54
Magnificent Obsession '54
All I Desire '53

Lee Blessing
Steal Big, Steal Little '95
Cooperstown '93

Bernard Blier (1916-89)
How Much Do You Love Me? '05
Notre Histoire '84

Bertrand Blier (1939-)
Mon Homme '96
Too Beautiful for You '88
Menage '86
My Best Friend's Girl '84
Beau Pere '81
Buffet Froid '79
Get Out Your Handkerchiefs '78
Going Places '74

William Blinn (1938-)
Brian's Song '01
The Boys Next Door '96
Purple Rain '84
For Heaven's Sake '79
The Lazarus Syndrome '79
Roots '77
Brian's Song '71

Robert Bloch (1917-94)
Asylum '72
The House that Dripped Blood '71
Torture Garden '67
The Night Walker '64
Strait-Jacket '64

Larry Block (1943-)
My Blueberry Nights '07
The Funhouse '81

Michael Blodgett (1940-2007)
The White Raven '98
Run '91
Turner and Hooch '89
Hero and the Terror '88
Rent-A-Cop '88

George Arthur Bloom
The Man Who Guards the Greenhouse '88
The Last Flight of Noah's Ark '80

Harold Jack Bloom (1925-99)
A Gunfight '71
Land of the Pharaohs '55
The Naked Spur '53

Jeffrey Bloom
Flowers in the Attic '87
Nightmares '83
Blood Beach '81
The Stick-Up '77
Dog Pound Shuffle '75
11 Harrowhouse '74

Steven L. Bloom
Jack Frost '98
Overnight Delivery '96
Tall Tale: The Unbelievable Adventures of Pecos Bill '95
Like Father, Like Son '87
The Sure Thing '85

Edwin Blum (1906-95)
Pearl of the South Pacific '55
South Sea Woman '53
Stalag 17 '53
Down to Earth '47
The Canterville Ghost '44
The Boogie Man Will Get You '42
Young People '40
The Adventures of Sherlock Holmes '39

Len Blum
Over the Hedge '06
The Pink Panther '06
Private Parts '96
Beethoven's 2nd '93
Feds '88
Spacehunter: Adventures in the Forbidden Zone '83
Heavy Metal '81
Stripes '81
Meatballs '79

Stuart Blumberg (1969-)
The Girl Next Door '04
Keeping the Faith '00

John Blumenthal
Blue Streak '99
Short Time '90

Don Bluth (1938-)
Thumbelina '94
All Dogs Go to Heaven '89
The Secret of NIMH '82

Jeffrey Boam (1949-2000)
The Phantom '96
Lethal Weapon 3 '92
Indiana Jones and the Last Crusade '89
Lethal Weapon 2 '89
Funny Farm '88
Innerspace '87
The Lost Boys '87
Dead Zone '83
Straight Time '78

Paul Harris Boardman
The Exorcism of Emily Rose '05
Hellraiser 5: Inferno '00
Urban Legends 2: Final Cut '00

Al Boasberg (1892-1937)
A Night at the Opera '35
Myrt and Marge '33
Freaks '32
Battling Butler '26
The General '26

Sam Bobrick (1932-)
Jimmy the Kid '82
Norman, Is That You? '76

Steven Bochco (1943-)
Columbo: Murder by the Book '71
Silent Running '71

DeWitt Bodeen (1908-88)
Mrs. Mike '49
I Remember Mama '48
Cat People '42

Sergei Bodrov (1948-)
Schizo '04
The Quickie '01
East-West '99
Prisoner of the Mountains '96
Somebody to Love '94
Freedom's Paradise '89

Christoffer Boe
Allegro '05
Reconstruction '03

Sydney (Sidney) Boehm (1908-90)
Seven Thieves '60
The Tall Men '55
The Big Heat '53
Second Chance '53
When Worlds Collide '51
Mystery Street '50
Side Street '50

Peter Bogdanovich (1939-)
Texasville '90
They All Laughed '81
Saint Jack '79
The Last Picture Show '71
Targets '68
The Wild Angels '66

Nicholas Bogner
No Strings Attached '98
The Little Death '95

Eric Bogosian (1953-)
subUrbia '96
Sex, Drugs, Rock & Roll '91
Talk Radio '88

Roger Bohbot
Lady Chatterley '06
Kings and Queen '04
Since Otar Left... '03
The Dreamlife of Angels '98

Endre Bohem (1900-90)
Twenty Bucks '93
Monster from Green Hell '58

Leslie Bohem (1952-)
The Alamo '04
Taken '02
Dante's Peak '97
Daylight '96
Twenty Bucks '93
The Horror Show '89
A Nightmare on Elm Street 5: Dream Child '89

Charles F. Bohl
Swimfan '02

Don Bohlinger
The Experiment '01
Women '97
The Killing Time '87

Tewd A. Bohus
This Thing of Ours '03
Vampire Vixens from Venus '94

Jerome Boivin (1954-)
Barjo '93
Baxter '89

Jon Bokenkamp
Taking Lives '04
Bad Seed '00

Bridget Boland (1913-88)
Anne of the Thousand Days '69
War and Peace '56
Gaslight '40

Uwe Boll (1965-)
Heart of America '03
Blackwoods '02
Sanctimony '01

Joseph Bologna (1938-)
Love Is All There Is '96
Lovers and Other Strangers '70

Craig Bolotin (1954-)
Light It Up '99
That Night '92
Straight Talk '92
Black Rain '89

Troy Bolotnick
Cyborg 3: The Recycler '95
Red Scorpion 2 '94

Robert Bolt (1924-95)
Without Warning: The James Brady Story '91
The Mission '86
The Bounty '84
Lady Caroline Lamb '73
Ryan's Daughter '70
A Man for All Seasons '66
Lawrence of Arabia '62
Doctor Zhivago '65

Guy Bolton (1884-1979)
Weekend at the Waldorf '45
Angel '37
The Love Parade '29

James Bolton
The Graffiti Artist '04
Eban and Charley '01

Adriano Bolzoni
Your Vice is a Closed Room and Only I Have the Key '72
Place in Hell '69
Diary of a Rebel '68

Mark Bomback
Deception '08
Live Free or Die Hard '07
Godsend '04

Julian Bond (1930-)
Lie Down with Lions '94
The Whistle Blower '87
The Shooting Party '85
Love for Lydia '79
The Duchess of Duke Street '78
Choice of Weapons '76

Vittorio Bonicelli (1919-94)
Moses '76
Waterloo '71
Barbarella '68
The Bible '66

Pascal Bonitzer (1946-)
Lantana '01
Head On '98
Changing Times '04
The Duchess of Langeais '07
Lumumba '01
Va Savoir '01
Genealogies of a Crime '97
Three Lives and Only One Death '96
Jeanne la Pucelle '94
Night and Day '91
La Belle Noiseuse '90

John Boorman (1933-)
The General '98
Where the Heart Is '90
Hope and Glory '87
Excalibur '81
Zardoz '73

Telsche Boorman (1957-97)
French Twist '95
Where the Heart Is '90

James Booth (1927-2005)
American Ninja 2: The Confrontation '87
Avenging Force '86
Pray for Death '85
Sunburn '79

Lizzie Borden (1958-)
Erotique '94
Working Girls '87

Bernard Borderie (1924-78)
Your Turn Darling '63
Dishonorable Discharge '57

Allen Boretz (1900-86)
Copacabana '47
Where There's Life '47
It Ain't Hay '43

Robert Boris (1945-)
Diplomatic Siege '99
Frank and Jesse '94
Extreme Justice '93
Steele Justice '87
Oxford Blues '84
Doctor Detroit '83
Electra Glide in Blue '73
Some Kind of Hero '82

Michael Bortman
Resurrecting the Champ '07
Chain Reaction '96
Crooked Hearts '91

Aida Bortnik (1938-)
The Good Mother '88
Old Gringo '89
Wild Horses '85
The Official Story '85

Pierre Bost (1901-75)
The Judge and the Assassin '75
The Clockmaker '73
Forbidden Games '52
The Walls of Malapaga '49
Devil in the Flesh '46

Daniel Boulanger (1922-)
Spirits of the Dead '68
The King of Hearts '66
Love Play '60

Roy Boulting (1913-2001)
Carlton Browne of the F.O. '59
Brothers in Law '57
Seven Days to Noon '50
The Guinea Pig '48

Emmanuel Bourdieu
Esther Kahn '00
My Sex Life... Or How I Got into an Argument '96

Kate Boutilier
Rugrats Go Wild! '03
The Wild Thornberrys Movie '02
Rugrats in Paris: The Movie '00

Nouri Bouzid (1945-)
The Silences of the Palace '94
Man of Ashes '86

Andrew Bovell (1962-)
Lantana '01

Susan Bowen
The Power Within '95
Storybook '95

T.R. Bowen (1942-)
Catherine Cookson's The Secret '00
Catherine Cookson's The Gambling Man '98
Catherine Cookson's The Round Tower '98
Catherine Cookson's The Rag Nymph '96
The Body in the Library '84

William Bowers (1916-87)
Support Your Local Sheriff '69
Alias Jesse James '59
My Man Godfrey '57
Tight Spot '55
Split Second '53
Something in the Wind '47

Douglas Bowie
Must Be Santa '99
Boy in Blue '86

Mike Bowler
Things 2 '97
Things '93

Brandon Boyce
Venom '05
Wicker Park '04
Apt Pupil '97

Daniel Boyd (1956-)
Heroes of the Heart '94
Invasion of the Space Preachers '90
Chillers '88

Don Boyd (1948-)
Kleptomania '94
Twenty-One '91
East of Elephant Rock '76

William Boyd (1952-)
Sword of Honour '01
The Trench '99
A Good Man in Africa '94
Chaplin '92
Mister Johnson '91
Tune in Tomorrow '90
Stars and Bars '88

Philippa Boyens
King Kong '05
Lord of the Rings: The Return of the King '03
Lord of the Rings: The Two Towers '02
Lord of the Rings: The Fellowship of the Rings '01

Malcolm Stuart Boylan (1897-1967)
One Too Many '51
Son of Rusty '47
Red River Valley '41
Hangman's House '28

Bruno Bozzetto (1933-)
VIP, My Brother Superman '90
Allegro Non Troppo '76

Bill Bozzone
Ivory Hunters '90

Gerard Brach (1927-2006)
The Phantom of the Opera '98
Bitter Moon '92
The Lover '92
The Bear '89
Frantic '88
Jean de Florette '87
Manon of the Spring '87
Shy People '87
The Name of the Rose '86
Pirates '86
Maria's Lovers '84
My Best Friend's Girl '84
Identification of a Woman '82
Quest for Fire '82
I Sent a Letter to My Love '81
Tess '79
The Tenant '76
Diary of Forbidden Dreams '73
The Fearless Vampire Killers '67
Cul de Sac '66
Repulsion '65

Charles Brackett (1892-1969)
Journey to the Center of the Earth '59
The Girl in the Red Velvet Swing '55
Titanic '53
Niagara '52
Sunset Boulevard '50
Emperor Waltz '48
A Foreign Affair '48
To Each His Own '46
The Lost Weekend '45
Five Graves to Cairo '43
The Major and the Minor '42
Ball of Fire '41
Midnight '39
Bluebeard's Eighth Wife '38

Leigh Brackett (1915-78)
The Empire Strikes Back '80
The Long Goodbye '73
Hatari! '62
Rio Bravo '59
The Big Sleep '46

Jacob Brackman (1943-)
Times Square '80
The King of Marvin Gardens '72

Malcolm Bradbury (1932-2000)
Cold Comfort Farm '94
The Green Man '91

Ray Bradbury (1920-)
The Wonderful Ice Cream Suit '98
Something Wicked This Way Comes '83
Moby Dick '56
It Came from Outer Space '53

Robert North Bradbury (1886-1949)
Rangeland Empire '50
Valley of the Lawless '36
Kid Courageous '35
Texas Terror '35
Western Justice '35
Lucky Texan '34
The Star Packer '34
Tombstone Terror '34
The Gallant Fool '33
Riders of Destiny '33
West of the Divide '33
Texas Buddies '32

Sue Bradford
The Atomic Brain '64
The Indestructible Man '56

John Bradshaw (1952-)
The Undertaker's Wedding '97
The Big Slice '90

Pam Brady
Hot Rod '07
Team America: World Police '04
South Park: Bigger, Longer and Uncut '99

Tom Brady
The Hot Chick '02

Brannon Braga (1965-)
Star Trek: First Contact '96
Star Trek: Generations '94

Melvyn Bragg (1939-)
Jesus Christ, Superstar '73
The Music Lovers '71
Isadora '68

Kenneth Branagh (1960-)
As You Like It '06
Love's Labour's Lost '00
Hamlet '96
A Midwinter's Tale '95
Henry V '89

Chris Brancato
Species 2 '98

John Brancato
Primeval '07
Catwoman '04
Terminator 3: Rise of the Machines '03
The Game '97
The Net '95
Interceptor '92

Richard Brandes
Halloween: Resurrection '02
Paranoia '98

Larry Brand
Femme Fatale '90
The Unborn '91

David Brandes
The Quarrel '93

Michael Brandman
Party_ine '88

Gary Brandner (1933-)
Cameron's Closet '89
Howling 2: Your Sister is a Werewolf '85

Clark Brandon (1958-)
Skeeter '93

Michael Brandt (1963-)
Wanted '08
3:10 to Yuma '07
Catch That Kid '04
2 Fast 2 Furious '03

Calope Brattlestreet
Murder So Sweet '93

Irving Brecher (1914-)
Bye, Bye, Birdie '63
Best Foot Forward '43
Du Barry Was a Lady '43
Ship Ahoy '42
Go West '40
At the Circus '39

Andy Breckman (1955-)
Rat Race '01
Sgt. Bilko '95
I.Q. '94
True Identity '91
Arthur 2: On the Rocks '88
Moving '88

Don Bredes
A Stranger in the Kingdom '98

Richard L. Breen (1918-67)
Tony Rome '67
Do Not Disturb '65
The FBI Story '59
A Foreign Affair '48

Catherine Breillat (1948-)
The Last Mistress '07
Anatomy of Hell '04
Sex is Comedy '02
Romance '99
Perfect Love '96
36 Fillette '88
Police '85

Martin Bregman (1931-)
Peter's Friends '92
A Weekend in the Country '96

Michael Scott Bregman
Carlito's Way: Rise to Power '05

Paul Brickman (1949-)
Uprising '01
True Crime '99
Men Don't Leave '89
Deal of the Century '83
Risky Business '83
The Bad News Bears in Breaking Training '77
Citizens Band '77

J. Robert Bren (1903-81)
Underground Agent '42
Without Orders '36

Frederick Hazlitt Brennan (1901-62)
Follow the Sun '51

Alfonso Brescia
Adventure '45
War in Space '77
Reactor '85

Lou Breslow (1900-87)
Bedtime for Bonzo '51
On Our Merry Way '48
Merton of the Movies '47
Murder, He Says '45
Blondie Goes to College '42
Sleepers West '41
Mr. Moto Takes a Chance '38
The Holy Terror '37
No More Women '34

Robert Bresson (1907-99)
L'Argent '83
The Devil, Probably '77
Lancelot of the Lake '74
A Gentle Woman '69
Pickpocket '59
A Man Escaped '57
Diary of a Country Priest '50
The Ladies of the Bois de Bologne '44

Eric Bress
The Butterfly Effect '04
Final Destination 2 '03

Jonathan Brett
Turbulence '96

Matthew Bright (1952-)
Tiptoes '03
Going in Style '79
Freeway 2: Confessions of a Trickbaby '99
Modern Vampires '98
Freeway '95
Dark Angel: The Ascent '94
Shrunken Heads '94
Wildfire '88
Forbidden Zone '80
Guncrazy '92

John Briley (1925-)
Molokai: The Story of Father Damien '99
Christopher Columbus: The Discovery '92
Cry Freedom '87
Marie '86
Enigma '82
Eagle's Wing '79
The Medusa Touch '78
That Lucky Touch '75
Children of the Damned '63

Steven Brill (1962-)
Little Nicky '00
Ready to Rumble '00
D3: The Mighty Ducks '96
D2: The Mighty Ducks '94
Heavyweights '94
The Mighty Ducks '92

Ralph Brooke (1920-63)
Bloodlust '59
Giant from the Unknown '58

Albert Brooks (1947-)
Looking for Comedy in the Muslim World '06
The Muse '99
Mother '96
Defending Your Life '91
Lost in America '85
Modern Romance '81
Real Life '79

George Bricker (1898-1955)
The Brute Man '46
House of Horrors '46
I'm Lucky '46
She Wolf of London '46

Marshall Brickman (1941-)
Intersection '93
For the Boys '91
The Manhattan Project '86
Lovesick '83
Simon '80
Manhattan '79
Annie Hall '77
Sleeper '73

G. Allan Brocka
Boy Culture '06
Eating Out 2: Sloppy Seconds '06

Kevin Brodbin (1964-)
Constantine '05
The Glimmer Man '96
Mindhunters '05

Oscar Brodney (1906-)
Ghost Fever '87
Bullseye! '90
Spacejacked '98
Spectre '96

James Bridges (1936-93)
White Hunter, Black Heart '90
Perfect '85
Mike's Murder '84
Urban Cowboy '80
The China Syndrome '79
September 30, 1955 '77
The Paper Chase '73
The Baby Maker '70
Colossus: The Forbin Project '70
The Appaloosa '66

Leslie Bricusse (1931-)
Scrooge '70
Doctor Dolittle '67
Bachelor of Hearts '58

Henry Bromell (1947-)
Last Call: The Final Chapter of F. Scott Fitzgerald '02
Panic '00

Dan Bronson
A Taste for Killing '92

Peter Brook (1925-)
The Last Innocent Man '87
Swann in Love '84
Lord of the Flies '63

Hilary Brougher
Stephanie Daley '06
The Sticky Fingers of Time '97

Bruce Brown (1938-)
The Endless Summer 2 '94
The Endless Summer '66

Dana Brown
Dust to Glory '05
Step Into Liquid '03

Larry Brothers
Two for Texas '97

Stephen Brooks
Spiders 2: Breeding Ground '01

Adam Brooks (1956-)
Definitely, Maybe '08
Wimbledon '04
Invisible Circus '00
Beloved '98
Practical Magic '98
Subway Stories '97
French Kiss '95
Heads '93

William Brookfield
Close Your Eyes '02
Rough Magic '95

Brendan Broderick
Turbulence 2: Fear of Flying '99
Bloodfist 6: Ground Zero '94

James L. Brooks (1940-)
The Simpsons Movie '07
Spanglish '04
As Good As It Gets '97
I'll Do Anything '93
Broadcast News '87
Terms of Endearment '83
Starting Over '79

Mel Brooks (1926-)
Dracula: Dead and Loving It '95
The Producers '05
Robin Hood: Men in Tights '93
Life Stinks '91
Spaceballs '87
History of the World: Part 1 '81
High Anxiety '77
Silent Movie '76
Blazing Saddles '74
Young Frankenstein '74
The Twelve Chairs '70
The Producers '68

Richard Brooks (1912-92)
Fever Pitch '85
Wrong Is Right '82
Looking for Mr. Goodbar '77
Bite the Bullet '75
Dollars '71
The Happy Ending '69
In Cold Blood '67
The Professionals '66
Lord Jim '65
Sweet Bird of Youth '62
Elmer Gantry '60
The Brothers Karamazov '58
Cat on a Hot Tin Roof '58
Something of Value '57
The Last Hunt '56
Blackboard Jungle '55
The Last Time I Saw Paris '54

George Bricker

Eduardo Brochero (1919-)
The Case of the Scorpion's Tail '71

Deborah Brock
Rock 'n' Roll High School Forever '91
Slumber Party Massacre 2 '87

Jeremy Brock (1959-)
Driving Lessons '06
The Last King of Scotland '06
Charlotte Gray '01
Mrs. Brown '97

Tricia Brock
Killer Diller '04
Due East '02

Joseph Brooks
If Ever I See You Again '79
You Light Up My Life '77

Mark Brown
The Salon '05
Barbershop '02
Two Can Play That Game '01

Leigh Brown (1939-98)
My Summer Story '94
A Christmas Story '83

Karl Brown (1896-1990)
Dangerous Appointment '34
Fire Alarm '32

Michael Henry Brown
Dead Presidents '95
Laurel Avenue '93

Riwia Brown
Once Were Warriors '94

Rowland Brown (1897-1963)
The Nevadan '50
Nocturne '46
Johnny Apollo '40
Angels with Dirty Faces '38
What Price Hollywood? '32
State's Attorney '31

Janet Brownell
Angels Fall '07
Eloise at the Plaza '03
Eloise at Christmastime '03
The Amy Fisher Story '93
Christmas in Connecticut '92

Michael Browning
Sweet Revenge '90
Bad Company '02
More Dogs Than Bones '00
Six Days, Seven Nights '98
Mark of the Vampire '35
Intolerance '16

Tod Browning (1882-1962)
Devil Doll '36
Dracula '31
The Unknown '27

John Brownjohn
The Ninth Gate '99
Bitter Moon '92

William Broyles, Jr. (1944-)
Flags of Our Fathers '06
Jarhead '05
Unfaithful '02
Planet of the Apes '01
Entrapment '99
Cast Away '00
Apollo 13 '95
JFK: Reckless Youth '93

George Carleton Brown
McHale's Navy '64
Mr. Walkie Talkie '52

Harry Brown (1917-86)
Ocean's 11 '60
The Corsican Brothers '42
A Gentleman After Dark '42
The Son of Monte Cristo '40
The Man in the Iron Mask '39
Two Years before the Mast '46
Bugles in the Afternoon '52
Kansas City Confidential '52

George Bruce (1898-1974)
All the Brothers Were Valiant '53
Navy Blue and Gold '37
A Place in the Sun '51
Sands of Iwo Jima '49
Arch o' Triumph '46

Rod Browning (1942-)
Cruel and Unusual '01

Glenn A. Bruce
Undercover Cop '94
Cyborg Cop '93
Kickboxer 2 '91

Jamie Brown (1945-98)
A Walk in the Sun '46

Julie Brown (1958-)
The Brykcreem Boys '96
Toby McTeague '87

George Bricker
Defending Your Life '91

James L. Brooks (1940-)
National Lampoon's Attack of the 5 Ft. 2 Women '94
Earth Girls Are Easy '89

Clyde Bruckman (1894-1955)
Honeymoon Lodge '43
Swingtime Johnny '43
The General '26
Seven Chances '25
The Navigator '24
Sherlock, Jr. '24
Our Hospitality '23

Claude Brule
Barbarella '68
Blood and Roses '61
Please Not Now! '61

James Bruner
Braddock: Missing in Action 3 '88
Delta Force '86
The P.O.W. Escape '86
Invasion U.S.A. '85
Missing in Action '84
An Eye for an Eye '81

Bob Brunner
The Other Sister '98
Exit to Eden '94

Franco Brusati (1922-93)
The Sleazy Uncle '89
Bread and Chocolate '73
Romeo and Juliet '68
The Unfaithfuls '60

Peter Bryan
A Challenge for Robin Hood '68
Blood Beast Terror '67
Plague of the Zombies '66
The Brides of Dracula '60
The Hound of the Baskervilles '59

Chris Bryant (1936-)
Miracle at Midnight '98
Foreign Affairs '93
One Against the Wind '91
Young Catherine '91
Stealing Heaven '88
Sword of Gideon '86
Martin's Day '85

John Bryant
Scanner Cop '94
Martial Outlaw '93

Bill Bryden (1942-)
Aria '88
The Long Riders '80

Zbynek Brynych (1927-95)
Transport from Paradise '65
The Fifth Horseman Is Fear '64

James David Buchanan
Deadly Currents '93
Brenda Starr '86

Larry Buchanan (1923-2004)
Mistress of the Apes '79
It's Alive! '68
Mars Needs Women '66
Zontar, the Thing from Venus '66
The Naked Witch '64

Harold Buchman (1912-90)
On the Fiddle '61
The Sleeping Tiger '54
Boots Malone '52

Peter Buchman (1967-)
Eragon '06
Jurassic Park 3 '01

Sidney Buchman (1902-75)
The Mark '61
Here Comes Mr. Jordan '41
Mr. Smith Goes to Washington '39
Holiday '38
Theodora Goes Wild '36
His Greatest Gamble '34
The Sign of the Cross '33
No One Man '32

Andrea Buck
Born Wild '95
The Double O Kid '92

Kristen Buckley
How to Lose a Guy in 10 Days '03
102 Dalmatians '00

Robert Buckner (1906-89)
Love Me Tender '56
Yankee Doodle Dandy '42
Dive Bomber '41
Santa Fe Trail '40
Jezebel '38

Albert (Don) Buday (1939-2001)
KISS Meets the Phantom of the Park '78
Too Hot to Handle '76

Adele Buffington (1900-73)
Bad Men of the Border '45
Raiders of the Border '44
Haunted Gold '32

Takashi Bufford (1952-)
The Tiger Woods Story '98
Booty Call '96
Set It Off '96
House Party 3 '94

Ray Buffum (1904-80)
The Brain from Planet Arous '57
Teenage Monster '57

Jeff Buhai
Eddie '96
Revenge of the Nerds 3: The Next Generation '92
Johnny Be Good '88
Jocks '87
Last Resort '86
Revenge of the Nerds '84

Timothy Linh Bui (1969-)
Green Dragon '01
Three Seasons '98

Tony Bui (1973-)
Green Dragon '01
Three Seasons '98

Walter Bullock (1907-53)
The Farmer Takes a Wife '53
Greenwich Village '44
Springtime in the Rockies '42

Edward (Eddie) Bunker (1933-2005)
Animal Factory '00
Runaway Train '85
Straight Time '79

Luis Bunuel (1900-83)
That Obscure Object of Desire '77
Phantom of Liberty '74
The Discreet Charm of the Bourgeoisie '72
Tristana '70
Belle de Jour '67
Simon of the Desert '66
Diary of a Chambermaid '64
The Exterminating Angel '62
Viridiana '61
The Young One '61
Death in the Garden '56
The Criminal Life of Archibaldo de la Cruz '55
L'Age D'Or '30
Un Chien Andalou '28

Betty Burbridge (1895-1987)
Guns of Fury '49
Return of Wildfire '48
Trail of the Mounties '47
Where the North Begins '47
In Old New Mexico '45
Texas Legionnaires '43
South of the Border '39
Heroes of the Hills '38
Prairie Moon '38
Purple Vigilantes '38
Come on, Cowboys '37
Wild Horse Rodeo '37
The Lone Avenger '33

Ron Burch
Yours, Mine & Ours '05
Head Over Heels '01

Ray Burdis (1958-)
Love, Honour & Obey '00
Final Cut '98

Andy Burg
Trojan War '97
Alaska '96

Robert Burge
The Dark Dancer '95
The House on Todville Road '95

Neil Burger
The Illusionist '06
Interview with the Assassin '02

Anthony Burgess (1917-93)
A.D. '85
Cyrano de Bergerac '85
Jesus of Nazareth '77
Moses '76

David J. Burke (1948-)
Edison Force '05
Women vs. Men '02

Martyn Burke (1952-)
Animal Farm '99
The Pirates of Silicon Valley '99
The Pentagon Wars '98
The Second Civil War '97
Sugartime '95
Top Secret! '84
Last Chase '81
Power Play '81

Simon Burke (1961-)
Persuasion '07
Tom Jones '98
Faith '94

Stuart Burkin
Cash Crop '01
Harvest '98

Alan Burnett (1949-)
Batman: Mask of the Phantasm '93
DuckTales the Movie: Treasure of the Lost Lamp '90

Allison Burnett
Untraceable '08
Feast of Love '07
Resurrecting the Champ '07
Autumn in New York '00
Red Meat '98
Bloodfist 3: Forced to Fight '92

Charles Burnett (1944-)
The Glass Shield '95
To Sleep with Anger '90
Killer of Sheep '77

W.R. Burnett (1899-1982)
The Great Escape '63
I Died a Thousand Times '55
Dangerous Mission '54
Action in the North Atlantic '43
This Gun for Hire '42
Wake Island '42
High Sierra '41

Allan Burnett (1935-)
Just Between Friends '86
Just the Way You Are '84
Butch and Sundance: The Early Days '79
A Little Romance '79

Edward Burns (1968-)
The Groomsmen '06
Flight of the Phoenix '04
Looking for Kitty '04
Ash Wednesday '02
Sidewalks of New York '01
No Looking Back '98
She's the One '96

Mark Burns (1936-)
She-Devil '89
Married to the Mob '88

Rich Burns
Brother Bear 2 '06
The Fox and the Hound 2 '06

Scott Burns
The Bourne Ultimatum '07
PU-239 '06

Tim Burns (1953-)
Jacob Two Two Meets the Hooded Fang '99
An American Werewolf in Paris '97
Freaked '93

Jim Burnstein
D3: The Mighty Ducks '96
Renaissance Man '94

Jeff Burr (1963-)
Straight into Darkness '04
The Offspring '87

Maryedith Burrell (1952-)
Mr. St. Nick '02
Hot Chocolate '92

Richard Burridge (1951-)
The Little Match Girl '87

Abe Burrows (1910-85)
The Fourth Protocol '87
Absolute Beginners '86
How to Succeed in Business without Really Trying '67
Solid Gold Cadillac '56

Tim Burstall (1929-2004)
Alvin Rides Again '74
Alvin Purple '73

Mark Burton
Madagascar '05
Wallace & Gromit: The Curse of the Were-Rabbit '05

Michael Burton
Aldrich Ames: Traitor Within '98
Shoot to Kill '88
Flight of the Navigator '86

Tim Burton (1960-)
The Nightmare before Christmas '93
Edward Scissorhands '90
Frankenweenie '84

Scott Busby
Texas Rangers '01
The Escape '95

Steve Buscemi (1957-)
Interview '07
Tree's Lounge '96

Charles Busch (1954-)
A Very Serious Person '06
Die Mommie Die! '03
Psycho Beach Party '00

Niven Busch (1903-91)
The Postman Always Rings Twice '46
The Westerner '40
Scarlet Dawn '32

John Bushelman
The Iron Triangle '89
Violent Zone '89

Adrian Butchart
Goal! The Dream Begins '06
I Love Your Work '03

David Butler
Like a Brother '94
Mountbatten: The Last Viceroy '86
Disraeli '79
Voyage of the Damned '76
The Strauss Family '73

Frank Butler (1890-1967)
The Road to Bali '53
Golden Earrings '47
Going My Way '44
China '43
My Favorite Blonde '42
Wake Island '42
The Road to Morocco '42
The Road to Zanzibar '41
The Road to Singapore '40
Never Say Die '39
Give Me a Sailor '38
Waikiki Wedding '37
The Princess Comes Across '36
Strike Me Pink '36
March of the Wooden Soldiers '34
College Humor '33

Hugo Butler (1914-68)
A Face in the Rain '63
Eva '62
The Young One '61
Autumn Leaves '56
Torero '56
Prowler '51
The Southerner '45
Young Tom Edison '40

John K. Butler (1908-64)
Rodeo King and the Senorita '51
G.I. War Brides '46

Michael Butler
Execution of Justice '99
Pronto '97
White Mile '94
Code of Silence '85
Pale Rider '85
Flashpoint '84
Murder by Phone '82
The Car '77
The Gauntlet '77
Brannigan '75
The Don Is Dead '73

William Butler
Return of the Living Dead: Rave to the Grave '05
Madhouse '04

Jez Butterworth (1969-)
The Last Legion '07
Birthday Girl '02

Tom Butterworth (1967-)
The Last Legion '07
Birthday Girl '02

Jorg Buttgereit (1963-)
Nekromantik 2 '91
Der Todesking '89
Nekromantik '87

Floyd Byars
Masterminds '96
Mindwalk: A Film for Passionate Thinkers '91
Making Mr. Right '86
Inserts '76

Jim Byrnes (1948-)
Dead Man's Revenge '93
Miracle in the Wilderness '91
The Shadow Riders '82

John Byrum (1947-)
Duets '00
Dancing in September '00
Get On the Bus '96
Harry & Walter Go to New York '76

Scott Caan (1976-)
The Dog Problem '06
Dallas 362 '03

Michael Cacoyannis (1927-)
Iphigenia '77
A Matter of Dignity '57
Stella '55

Jerome Cady (1903-48)
Call Northside 777 '48
A Wing and a Prayer '44
Guadalcanal Diary '43
Mr. Moto's Gamble '38
Charlie Chan at Monte Carlo '37

David Caesar
Dirty Deeds '02
Idiot Box '97

Mario Caiano (1933-)
Erik, the Viking '65
Medusa Against the Son of Hercules '62

Alan Caillou (1914-2006)
Kingdom of the Spiders '77
The Losers '70
Clarence, the Cross-eyed Lion '65

Bill Cain
Papa's Angels '00
Nightjohn '96

Jeffrey Caine
The Constant Gardener '05
Rory O'Shea Was Here '04
Goldeneye '95
Way Past Cool '00
Free of Eden '98

Yule Caise (1964-)

Joseph M. Cala (1932-)
Avenging Angel '85
Angel '84

Mars Callahan (1972-)
What Love Is '07
Poolhall Junkies '02
Double Down '01

Gian Paolo Callegari (1912-)
Samson Against the Sheik '62
The Treasure of Bengal '53

Dayton Callie
Executive Target '97
The Last Days of Frankie the Fly '96

Paul Callisi
Josh Kirby...Time Warrior: Chapter 1, Planet of the Dino-Knights '95
Josh Kirby...Time Warrior: Chapter 2, The Human Pets '95

James Cameron (1954-)
Titanic '97
Strange Days '95
True Lies '94
Terminator 2: Judgment Day '91
The Abyss '89
Aliens '86
Rambo: First Blood, Part 2 '85
The Terminator '84

Ken Cameron (1946-)
Fast Talking '86
Monkey Grip '82

Lorne Cameron
Over the Hedge '06
Brother Bear '03
Deadly Game '98
The Extreme Adventures of Super Dave '98
Clarence '91
Like Father, Like Son '87

China Cammell
Wild Side '95

Donald Cammell (1939-96)
Wild Side '95
White of the Eye '88
Performance '70

Joe Camp (1939-)
Benji: Off the Leash! '04
Benji the Hunted '87
Oh, Heavenly Dog! '80
For the Love of Benji '77
Benji '74

Juan J. Campanella (1959-)
The Son of the Bride '01
Love Walked In '97

Pasquale Festa Campanile (1927-86)
The Sex Machine '75
Rocco and His Brothers '60

Alan Campbell (1904-63)
Tales of Manhattan '42
The Moon's Our Home '36

Robert W(right) Campbell (1927-2000)
Hell's Angels on Wheels '67
Masque of the Red Death '65

Jane Campion (1954-)
Holy Smoke '99
In the Cut '03
Holy Smoke '99
The Piano '93
Sweetie '89

Robin Campillo
Heading South '05
They Came Back '04
Time Out '01

Anna Campion (1952-)
Loaded '94

Christopher Canaan
No Good Deed '02
The Apocalypse Watch '97
Robinson Crusoe '96
The Great Elephant Escape '95

Cuca Canals
The Chambermaid on the Titanic '97

Stephen J. Cannell (1942-)
It Waits '05
The Tooth Fairy '06
The Rousers '90

Laurent Cantet (1961-)
Heading South '05
Time Out '01

Leon Capetanos
Fetch Lives '89
Moon over Parador '88
Moscow on the Hudson '84
Down and Out in Beverly Hills '86

Truman Capote (1924-84)
ABC Stage 67: Truman Capote's A Christmas Memory '67
The Innocents '61
Indiscretion of an American Wife '54
Beat the Devil '53

Frank Cappello
Constantine '05
No Way Back '96
Suburban Commando '91

James (Jim) Carabatsos
Lost Battalion '01
Hamburger Hill '87
Heartbreak Ridge '86
Heroes '77

Steven W. Carabatsos
Hot Pursuit '87

John Carney
Once '06
On the Edge '00

Matthew Carnahan
The Kingdom '07
Lions for Lambs '07

Charles Robert Carner (1957-)
Witless Protection '08
Crossfire Trail '01
Echo of Murder '00
Head of the Family '96
The Fixer '97
Eyes of a Witness '94
Blind Fury '90
Let's Get Harry '87
Gymkata '85

A.J. Carothers (1931-2007)
Condorman '81
The Secret of My Success '87

Glenn Gordon Caron (1954-)
Picture Perfect '95
Moonlighting '85

Marc Caro (1956-)
The City of Lost Children '95
Delicatessen '92

Rene Cardona, Jr. (1939-2003)
Hostages '80
Night of the Bloody Apes '68

J.S. Cardone (1946-)
Prom Night '08
The Covenant '06
Sniper 3 '04

The Forsaken '01
True Blue '01
Outside Ozona '98
Black Day Blue Night '95
Shadowhunter '93
A Climate for Killing '91
Crash and Burn '90
Shadowzone '89
Thunder Alley '85
The Slayer '82

Mark Patrick Carducci (1955-97)
Buried Alive '90
Pumpkinhead '88

Topper Carew (1943-)
Talkin' Dirty after Dark '91
D.C. Cab '84

Peter Carey (1943-)
Until the End of the World '91
Bliss '85

Christian Carion (1963-)
Joyeux Noel '05

Richard Carpenter (1933-)
The Scarlet Pimpernel '99
The Scarlet Pimpernel 2: Mademoiselle Guillotine '99

Carlo Carlei (1960-)
Fluke '95
Flight of the Innocent '93

John Carlen
Sonny '02
Blind Side '93

Lewis John Carlino (1932-2007)
Haunted Summer '88
The Great Santini '80
Resurrection '80
I Never Promised You a Rose Garden '77
The Sailor Who Fell from Grace with the Sea '76
The Mechanic '72
A Reflection of Fear '72
Seconds '66

Jim Carlson (1932-2007)
Pound Puppies and the Legend of Big Paw '88

Roy Carlson
China Moon '91
Stand Alone '85

Don Carmody
Whispers '89
Junior '86

Joe Carnahan (1969-)
Smokin' Aces '07
Narc '02
Blood, Guts, Bullets and Octane '99

Allan Carr (1937-99)
Can't Stop the Music '80

Benjamin Carr
Retro Puppet Master '99
Curse of the Puppet Master: The Human Experiment '98

Tito Carpi
Shark Hunter '79
Tentacles '77

Fabio Carpi
Basileus Quartet '82

Caleb Carr (1955-)
Zarkorr! The Invader '96
The X-Files: I Want to Believe '08
The X-Files '98

Carroll Cartwright
Where the Money Is '00

Richard Carr (1929-88)
Americana '81
Hell Is for Heroes '62

Joan Carr-Wiggin
My First Wedding '04
Sleeping with Strangers '94

Michael Carreras (1927-94)
Creatures the World Forgot '70
Unholy Four '54

Jean-Claude Carriere (1931-)
Goya's Ghosts '06
Birth '04
Chinese Box '97
The Ogre '96
The Horseman on the Roof '95
Circle of Deceit '94

Richard Casey
Hellbent '88
Horror House on Highway 5 '86

John Carpenter (1948-)
John Carpenter's Ghosts of Mars '01
Silent Predators '99
John Carpenter's Vampires '97
Escape from L.A. '96
Village of the Damned '95
El Diablo '90
They Live '88
Prince of Darkness '87
Black Moon Rising '86
Escape from New York '81
Halloween 2: The Nightmare isn't Over! '81
Eyes of Laura Mars '78
The Fog '78
Halloween '78
The Return of the Borrowers '96
The Scarlet Pimpernel '99
The Scarlet Pimpernel 2: Mademoiselle Guillotine '99
Dark Star '74
Assault on Precinct 13 '76

Stephen Carpenter
The Borrowers '93

Robert B. Carrington
The Man '05
Soul Survivors '01
Blue Streak '99
Servants of Twilight '91
The Kindred '87
Dorm That Dripped Blood '82
The Power '80
Buck and the Magic Bracelet '97

L.M. Kit Carson (1947-)
Perfume '01
The Texas Chainsaw Massacre 2 '86
Breathless '83
Paris, Texas '83
The Last Word '80
David Holzman's Diary '67
Sting of the West '72
Cold Eyes of Fear '70
Fistful of Lead '70
Sartana's Here... Trade Your Pistol for a Coffin '70
Beauty on the Beach '61

Robert Carson (1913-83)
Just for You '52
The Desperadoes '43
Beau Geste '39

Sidney Carroll (1913-88)
Dynasty '76
The Man Without a Country '73

James Carrington
Fluke '55

Willard Carroll (1955-)
Three Cases of Murder '55
Playing by Heart '98
The Runestone '91

Johnny Stecchino '92

Bill Carter (1918-95)
Monday Night Mayhem '02
The Late Shift '96

Chris Carter
The X-Files: I Want to Believe '08
The X-Files '98

William Carson
Judgment Day '99
Militia '99

Jim Cash (1940-2000)
The Flintstones in Viva Rock Vegas '00
Anaconda '96
Dick Tracy '90
Turner and Hooch '89
The Secret of My Success '87
Legal Eagles '86
Top Gun '86

The Miracle of the White Stallions '63
The Night and the Moment '94
At Play in the Fields of the Lord '91
Cyrano de Bergerac '90
Mars '01
The Mahabharata '89
Valmont '89
The Possessed '88
The Unbearable Lightness of Being '88
Max, Mon Amour '86
Swann in Love '84
The Return of Martin Guerre '83
Danton '82
La Piscine '69
The Milky Way '68
Belle de Jour '67
Attack of the Robots '66
The Diabolical Dr. Z '65
Viva Maria! '65
Diary of a Chambermaid '64
The Discreet Charm of the Bourgeoisie '72
Borsalino '70

James Carrington
Fluke '55

Robert B. Carrington
Joseph '95
Venom '82

Renato Castellani (1913-85)
Life of Verdi '82

Nick Castle (1947-)
August Rush '07
Hook '91
The Boy Who Could Fly '86
Tap '89
The Last Starfighter '84
The Iron Crown '41
Dennis the Menace '93

Robert Caswell (1946-2006)
Escape from New York '31
A Cry in the Dark '88
The Doctor '91

Jean Cau (1925-93)
A Fistful of Dollars '64
Don Juan (Or If Don Juan Were a Woman) '73

Jackie Chan (1954-)
Robin-B-Hood '06
Gen-X Cops '99
Jackie Chan's Who Am I '98
The Executioners '93

Benny Chan
Robin-B-Hood '06

Liliana Cavani (1937-)
Ripley's Game '02
Francesco '93
Beyond Obsession '82
The Night Porter '74

Vincenzo Cerami (1940-)
Pinocchio '02
Life is Beautiful '98
The Monster '96

Ginny Cerrella
Tainted Blood '93
Hot Chocolate '92
Sister, Sister '87

Robert Caswell
Operation Concor '91
Operation Condor 2: The Armour of the Gods '86

Jack e Chan's Who Am I '98

Victor Andres Catena
Panic '76

Susan Chan
Silver Hawk '04
Tokyo Raiders '00

Harry Chandlee (1882-1956)
The Adventures of Mark Twain '44
Our Town '40
It Happened in New Orleans '36

Project A '83
Young Master '80

Claude Chabrol (1930-)
Comedy of Power '06
The Bridesmaid '04
Merci pour le Chocolat '00
The Swindle '97
La Ceremonie '95
L'Enfer '93
Betty '92
Madame Bovary '91
The Story of Women '88
The Cry of the Owl '87
Blood Relatives '74
Wedding in Blood '74
La Rupture '70
La Femme Infidele '69
Le Boucher '69
Les Biches '68
Les Cousins '59
Six in Paris '65
Le Beau Serge '58

Gurinder Chadha (1960-)
Paris, je t'aime '06
The Mistress of Spices '05
Bride & Prejudice '04
What's Cooking? '00
Bend It Like Beckham '02

Tom Chaney
Mosquito '95

Roy Chanslor (1899-1964)
Black Angel '46
Burma Convoy '41

Charlie Chaplin (1889-1977)
A King in New York '57
A Countess from Hong Kong '67
Limelight '52
Monsieur Verdoux '47
The Great Dictator '40
Modern Times '36
City Lights '31
The Gold Rush '25
The Kid '21
The Circus '28
Three Charlies and One Phoney! '18
The Immigrant '17
Burlesque on Carmen '16

John Cassavetes (1929-89)
She's So Lovely '97
Opening Night '77
The Killing of a Chinese Bookie '76
A Woman under the Influence '74
Minnie and Moskowitz '71
Husbands '70
Faces '68
Shadows '59

Nick Cassavetes (1959-)
Alpha Dog '06
Blow '01
Unhook the Stars '96
She's So Lovely '97
The Bodyguard from Beijing '94

Gordon Chan (1960-)
The Medallion '03
Gen-X Cops '99

Terry Chambers
The Dark Dancer '95
Breakset Breaker '77

Eric Champrella
Mr. 3000 '04
Mail to the Chief '00
Eddie '96

John C. Champion (1923-)
Zero Hour! '57
The Texican '66

Kitty Chalmers
Cyborg '89
Deceit '89
Journey to the Center of the Earth '88

Ilene Chaiken (1929-)
Dirty Pictures '00
Barb Wire '96

Elizabeth Chandler
Sisterhood of the Traveling Pants 2 '08
Sisterhood of the Traveling Pants '05
What a Girl Wants '03
Someone Like You '01
A Little Princess '95

Raymond Chandler (1888-1959)
Strangers on a Train '51
The Blue Dahlia '46
Double Indemnity '44

Jay Chandrasekhar (1968-)
Beerfest '06
The Dukes of Hazzard '05
Club Dread '04
Super Troopers '01

Youssef Chahine (1926-)
Destiny '97
Alexandria Again and Forever '90
An Egyptian Story '82
Alexandria... Why? '78

Chaplin

One A.M. '16
Pawnshop '16
Charlie Chaplin: Night at the Show '15

Graham Chapman (1941-89)
Monty Python's The Meaning of Life '83
Yellowbeard '83
Monty Python's Life of Brian '79
Monty Python and the Holy Grail '75
And Now for Something Completely Different '72
Rentadick '72
The Magic Christian '69

Leigh Chapman (1940-)
Impulse '90
Storm and Sorrow '90
Octagon '80
Steel '80
Dirty Mary Crazy Larry '74
Truck Turner '74
How Come Nobody's On Our Side? '73
A Swingin' Summer '65

Matthew Chapman (1950-)
Runaway Jury '03
What's the Worst That Could Happen? '01
Color of Night '94
Consenting Adults '92
Heart of Midnight '89
Slow Burn '86
Strangers Kiss '83
Hussy '80

Richard Chapman
Live from Baghdad '03
My Fellow Americans '96

Robin Chapman
Force 10 from Navarone '78
Triple Echo '77

Borden Chase (1900-71)
Night Passage '57
Lone Star '52
The World in His Arms '52
Red River '48
Tycoon '47
Fighting Seabees '44

Peter Chase
Fast Sofa '01
Portraits Chinois '96

David Chaskin
Midnight's Child '93
I, Madman '89
The Curse '87
A Nightmare on Elm Street 2: Freddy's Revenge '85

Etienne Chatiliez (1952-)
Tatie Danielle '91
Life Is a Long Quiet River '88

Paddy Chayefsky (1923-81)
Altered States '80
Network '76
The Hospital '71
Paint Your Wagon '69
The Americanization of Emily '64
The Goddess '58
Marty '55
As Young As You Feel '51

Semi Chellas
Picture Claire '01
The Life Before This '99
Restless Spirits '99

Peter Chelsom (1956-)
Funny Bones '94
Hear My Song '91

Kuo-fu Chen (1958-)
Double Vision '02
The Personals '98

J. Benton Cheney
King of the Cowboys '43
Romance on the Range '42
Twilight on the Trail '41

Patrice Chereau (1944-)
Gabrielle '05
Intimacy '00
Those Who Love Me Can Take the Train '98
Queen Margot '94

Cy Chermack (1929-)
Rescuers: Stories of Courage—Two Couples '98

John R. Cherry, III
Ernest Goes to Africa '97
Slam Dunk Ernest '95
Ernest Rides Again '93
Ernest Scared Stupid '91
Ernest Goes to Camp '87

Hal E. Chester (1921-)
Curse of the Demon '57
Crashout '55

Lionel Chetwynd (1940-)
DC 9/11: Time of Crisis '04
Ike: Countdown to D-Day '04
Varian's War '01
P.T. Barnum '99
Tom Clancy's Netforce '98
Color of Justice '97
Kissinger and Nixon '96
The Man Who Captured Eichmann '96
Moses '96
Joseph '95
Doomsday Gun '94
Jacob '94
The Heroes of Desert Storm '91
To Heal a Nation '88
Hanoi Hilton '87
Quintet '79
The Apprenticeship of Duddy Kravitz '74

Alton Cheung
See Godfrey Ho

Tommy Cheung
See Godfrey Ho

Stephen Chiau
See Stephen (Chiau) Chow

David Chisholm
Kidnapped in Paradise '98
The Three Lives of Karen '97
Dead Man's Revenge '93
The Wizard '89

Tina Gordon Chism
ATL '06
Drumline '02

Edward Chodorov (1904-88)
Road House '48
The Hucksters '47
Undercurrent '46
The Mayor of Hell '33

Jerome Chodorov (1911-2004)
The Tunnel of Love '58
Louisiana Purchase '41
All Over Town '37

Lisa Cholodenko (1964-)
Laurel Canyon '02
High Art '98

Sylvain Chomet (1963-)
Paris, je t'aime '06
The Triplets of Belleville '02

Felix Chong (1968-)
Infernal Affairs '02
Tokyo Raiders '00

Thomas Chong (1938-)
Far Out Man '89
Cheech and Chong's The Corsican Brothers '84
Cheech and Chong: Still Smokin' '83
Cheech and Chong: Things Are Tough All Over '82
Cheech and Chong's Nice Dreams '81
Cheech and Chong's Next Movie '80
Cheech and Chong's Up in Smoke '79

Stephen (Chiau) Chow (1962-)
Kung Fu Hustle '04
Shaolin Soccer '01

Christian-Jaque (1904-94)
Nana '55
Fanfan la Tulipe '51
La Chartreuse de Parme '48

Mark Christopher
Pizza '05
54 '98

Tien-wen Chu (1956-)
Flowers of Shanghai '98
Goodbye South, Goodbye '96

Gerard Ciccoritti (1956-)
Skull: A Night of Terror '88
A Whisper to a Scream '88
Psycho Girls '86

Cynthia Cidre
The Mambo Kings '92
Fires Within '91
In Country '89

Santo Cilauro (1962-)
The Dish '00
The Castle '00

Matt Cimber (1936-)
Yellow Hair & the Fortress of Gold '84
Butterfly '82

Michael Cimino (1943-)
Year of the Dragon '85
Heaven's Gate '81
The Deer Hunter '78
Thunderbolt & Lightfoot '74
Magnum Force '73
Silent Running '71

Tony Cinciripini
Hell's Kitchen NYC '97
Confessions of a Hit Man '94

Patrick Cirillo
Tears of the Sun '03
The Surgeon '94
Dangerous Heart '93
Homer and Eddie '89

Louis CK (1967-)
I Think I Love My Wife '07
Down to Earth '01
Pootie Tang '01

John Claflin
Fool's Gold '08
Anacondas: The Hunt for the Blood Orchid '04

Rene Clair (1898-1981)
Les Grandes Manoeuvres '55
Beauties of the Night '52
Beauty and the Devil '50
And Then There Were None '45
It Happened Tomorrow '44
A Nous la Liberté '31
Under the Roofs of Paris '29

Bob (Benjamin) Clark (1941-2007)
Baby Geniuses '98
My Summer Story '94
Loose Cannons '90
From the Hip '86
A Christmas Story '83
Porky's 2: The Next Day '83
Porky's '82
Children Shouldn't Play with Dead Things '72

Bruce (B.D.) Clark (1945-)
Galaxy of Terror '81
The Naked Angels '69

Dennis Lynton Clark
In Pursuit of Honor '95

Frank Howard Clark (1888-1962)
The Prairie King '27
$50,000 Reward '25
Big Stakes '22

Greydon Clark (1943-)
Dance Macabre '91
Skinheads: The Second Coming of Hate '88
Final Justice '84
Angel's Brigade '79
Satan's Cheerleaders '77
Psychic Killer '75

Richard Clark
Double Play '96
The Halfback of Notre Dame '96

Ron Clark (1933-)
The Funny Farm '82
Revenge of the Pink Panther '78
High Anxiety '77
Norman, Is That You? '76
Silent Movie '76

Arthur C. Clarke (1917-2008)
2010: The Year We Make Contact '84
2001: A Space Odyssey '68

Frank Clarke (1956-)
Wonderland '88
Letter to Brezhnev '86

John Clarke (1948-96)
Lust and Revenge '95
Lonely Hearts '82

Roy Clarke (1930-)
A Foreign Field '93
Pictures '80s
Flickers '80
Hawks '89

T.E.B. Clarke (1907-89)
Who Done It? '56
The Lavender Hill Mob '51
Johnny Frenchman '46
Dead of Night '45

James Clavell (1925-94)
The Last Valley '71
To Sir, with Love '67
King Rat '65
633 Squadron '64
The Great Escape '63
The Fly '58

Christian Clavier (1952-)
Just Visiting '01
The Visitors '95

Elliot J. Clawson
The Leatherneck '28
The Phantom of the Opera '25

Thomas McKelvey Cleaver
Field of Fire '92
Raiders of the Sun '92
Immortal Sins '91
Heroes Stand Alone '89
The Terror Within '88

John Cleese (1939-)
Fierce Creatures '96
The Strange Case of the End of Civilization As We Know It '93
A Fish Called Wanda '88
Monty Python's The Meaning of Life '83
Monty Python's Life of Brian '79
And Now for Something Completely Different '72
Rentadick '72
The Magic Christian '69

Brian Clemens (1931-)
The Watcher in the Woods '81
The Naked Angels '69
Cry Terror '76
If It's a Man, Hang Up '75
Captain Kronos: Vampire Hunter '74
Death in Deep Water '74
The Devil's Web '74
I'm the Girl He Wants to Kill '74
In the Steps of a Dead Man '74
A Killer in Every Corner '74
Killer with Two Faces '74
Murder Motel '74
Murder on the Midnight Express '74
One Deadly Owner '74
Screamer '74
Golden Voyage of Sinbad '73
Dr. Jekyll and Sister Hyde '71
See No Evil '71
And Soon the Darkness '70
The Corrupt Ones '67
The Tell-Tale Heart '60

Dick Clement (1937-)
The Bank Job '08
Across the Universe '07
Flushed Away '06
Goal! The Dream Begins '06
Archangel '05
Still Crazy '98
Excess Baggage '96
The Commitments '91
Vice Versa '88
Water '85

Rene Clement (1913-96)
Joy House '64
Purple Noon '60
Forbidden Games '52
Battle of the Rails '46

Ron Clements (1953-)
Treasure Planet '02
Hercules '97
Aladdin '92
The Little Mermaid '89
The Great Mouse Detective '86

Gianfranco Clerici
Devilfish '84
New York Ripper '82

Rick Cleveland
Runaway Jury '03
Jerry and Tom '98

Elmer Clifton (1892-1949)
Kid from Gower Gulch '50
Silver Bandit '50
Red Rock Outlaw '47
Lightning Raiders '45
Marked for Murder '45
Boss of Rawhide '44
Captain America '44
Gangsters of the Frontier '44
Guns of the Law '44
Teenage '44
Youth Aflame '44
Frontier Law '43
Rangers Take Over '42
Fighting Caballero '35
Pals of the Range '35
Rough Riding Ranger '35

Harry Clork (1888-1978)
Ma and Pa Kettle at Waikiki '55
Broadway Rhythm '44
Ship Ahoy '42
Whistling in the Dark '41

Robert Clouse (1929-97)
China O'Brien '88
Force: Five '81
The Big Brawl '80
The Amsterdam Kill '78
The Pack '77
The Ultimate Warrior '75

Henri-Georges Clouzot (1907-77)
L'Enfer '93
Diabolique '55
Wages of Fear '55

Daniel Clowes (1961-)
Art School Confidential '06
Ghost World '01

Craig Clyde
Miracle Dogs '03
Walking Thunder '94
The Legend of Wolf Mountain '92
Little Heroes '91

Lewis (Luigi Cozzi) Coates (1947-)
Black Cat '90
Hercules '83
Alien Contamination '81
Star Crash '78

Stacy Cochran
Boys '95
My New Gun '92

Jay Cocks (1944-)
De-Lovely '04
Gangs of New York '02
Strange Days '95
The Age of Innocence '93

Jean Cocteau (1889-1963)
The Testament of Orpheus '59
Les Enfants Terrible '50
Orpheus '49
The Eagle Has Two Heads '48
Ruyblas '48
The Storm Within '48
Beauty and the Beast '46
The Ladies of the Bois de Bologne '44
Eternal Return '43
The Blood of a Poet '30

Ethan Coen (1957-)
No Country for Old Men '07
Paris, je t'aime '06
The Ladykillers '04
Intolerable Cruelty '03
The Man Who Wasn't There '01
O Brother Where Art Thou? '00
The Naked Man '98
The Big Lebowski '97
Fargo '96
The Hudsucker Proxy '93
Barton Fink '91
Miller's Crossing '90
Raising Arizona '87
Blood Simple '85
Crimewave '85

Franklin Coen (1912-90)
Alvarez Kelly '66
The Train '65

Joel Coen (1954-)
No Country for Old Men '07
Paris, je t'aime '06
The Ladykillers '04
Intolerable Cruelty '03
The Man Who Wasn't There '01
O Brother Where Art Thou? '00
The Big Lebowski '97
Fargo '96
The Hudsucker Proxy '93
Barton Fink '91
Miller's Crossing '90
Raising Arizona '87
Blood Simple '85

Lenore Coffee (1896-1984)
Cash McCall '60
End of the Affair '55
Sudden Fear '52
My Son, My Son '40
Four Daughters '38
Evelyn Prentice '34

Charlie Coffey
National Lampoon's Attack of the 5 Ft. 2 Women '94
Earth Girls Are Easy '89

Barney Cohen
Doom Runners '97
Sabrina the Teenage Witch '96
Next Door '94
Killer Party '86
Friday the 13th, Part 4: The Final Chapter '84

Bennett Cohen
Chameleon 2: Death Match '99
The Hunted '98
Rainbow Drive '90

Bennett Cohen (1890-1964)
Sagebrush Law 43

Man from Montana '41
Frontier Vengeance '40
Melody of the Plains '37
Skull & Crown '35
The Three Musketeers '33
Come on Danger! '32
Sunset Trail '32
Texas Gunfighter '32

Charles Cohen (1948-)
The Gambler '97

Charles Zev Cohen
Beyond Forgiveness '94

David Aaron Cohen
Eddie and the Cruisers 2: Eddie Lives! '89
Lady Beware '87

David M. Cohen
Friday Night Lights '04
The Devil's Own '96
V.I. Warshawski '91
Hollywood Zap '86
Midnight Faces '26

Etan Cohen
Idiocracy '06
Tropic Thunder '08

Howard R. Cohen (1942-99)
Barbarian Queen 2: The Empress Strikes Back '89
Deathstalker 3 '89
Deathstalker '83
Space Raiders '83
Stryker '83
Saturday the 14th Strikes Back '88
Saturday the 14th '81
Sister, Sister '87
The Young Nurses '73
Time Trackers '88

Joel Cohen
Garfield: A Tail of Two Kitties '06
Garfield: The Movie '04
Cheaper by the Dozen '03
Goodbye, Lover '99
Money Talks '97
Toy Story '95
Pass the Ammo '88

Larry Cohen (1947-)
Captivity '07
Cellular '04
Phone Booth '02
Misbegotten '98
The Ex '96
Invasion of Privacy '96
Uncle Sam '96
As Good as Dead '95
Guilty as Sin '93
Maniac Cop 3: Badge of Silence '93
The Ambulance '90
Maniac Cop 2 '90
Wicked Stepmother '89
Maniac Cop '88
Best Seller '87
Deadly Illusion '87
It's Alive 3: Island of the Alive '87
Return to Salem's Lot '87
Special Effects '85
The Stuff '85
Perfect Strangers '84
Scandalous '84
I, the Jury '82
Q (The Winged Serpent) '82
It's Alive 2: It Lives Again '78
The Private Files of J. Edgar Hoover '77
God Told Me To '76
It's Alive '74
Black Caesar '73
Hell Up in Harlem '73
Housewife '72
El Condor '70
Daddy's Gone A-Hunting '69
Return of the Magnificent Seven '66

Lawrence D. Cohen
Rodgers & Hammerstein's South Pacific '01
Stephen King's The Tommyknockers '93
Ghost Story '81
Carrie '76

Lawrence J. Cohen
Delirious '91
The Big Bus '76
S*P*Y*S '74
Start the Revolution without Me '70

Martin B. Cohen
Humanoids from the Deep '80
Rebel Rousers '69

Neil Cohen
Radioactive Dreams '86

Rob Cohen (1949-)
Dragon: The Bruce Lee Story '93

Ronald M. Cohen (1939-98)
Scandalous '84
Blue '68

Steve Cohen
Tough and Deadly '95

Art Cohn (1909-58)
The Set-Up '49
Men of the Fighting Lady '54

Isabel Coixet (1960-)
Paris, je t'aime '06
My Life Without Me '03
Things I Never Told You '96

Brandon Cole
Illuminata '98
Mac '93
Sons '89

Lester Cole (1904-85)
Born Free '66
Blood on the Sun '45
Objective, Burma! '45
Footsteps in the Dark '41
The Invisible Man Returns '40

Tom Cole
High Stakes '89
Streets of Gold '86
Smooth Talk '85

Duilio Coletti (1906-99)
Sicilian Connection '72
Operation Crossbow '65

Lewis Colick
Ladder 49 '04
Beyond the Sea '04
October Sky '99
Bulletproof '96
Ghosts of Mississippi '96
Domestic Disturbance '01
Judgment Night '93
Unlawful Entry '92
Dirt Bike Kid '86

Ryan Combs (1974-)
The Hit '06
I Accidentally Domed Your Son '04

Adele Comandini (1898-1987)
Beyond Tomorrow '40
Her First Romance '40
Three Smart Girls '36

Betty Comden (1915-2006)
Bells Are Ringing '60
Auntie Mame '58
It's Always Fair Weather '55
The Band Wagon '53
Singin' in the Rain '52
The Barkleys of Broadway '49
On the Town '49
Good News '47

Bill Collage
Accepted '06
Out of Time '03

Dave Collard
Annapolis '06

Bob Comfort
Good Luck '96
Dogfight '91

Michael Colleary
Firehouse Dog '07
Face/Off '97

Jacques Companeez (1906-56)
Casque d'Or '52
Forbidden Fruit '52

Georges Conchon
The Elegant Criminal '92
Black and White in Color '76

Greg Coolidge
Employee of the Month '06
Sorority Boys '02

Robert Collector
Die '95
Darkman 3: Die Darkman! '96
Memoirs of an Invisible Man '92
Believe in Me '06

Bill Condon (1955-)
Dreamgirls '06
Kinsey '04
Chicago '02

John Collee (1955-)
Happy Feet '06
Master and Commander: The Far Side of the World '03
Paper Mask '91

Gene L. Coon (1924-73)
The Killers '64
No Name on the Bullet '59

Peter Colley
Illusions '91
Mark of Cain '84

John Collier
Murder 101 '91
Sister, Sister '87
Strange Invaders '83
Sylvia Scarlett '35
The War Lord '65

Boon Collins
Abducted 2: The Reunion '94
Spirit of the Eagle '90

Jackie Collins (1941-)
The World Is Full of Married Men '90
Yesterday's Hero '79
The Stud '78

Max Allan Collins (1948-)
Real Time: Siege at Lucas Street Market '00
Mommy 2: Mommy's Day '96
Mommy '95
The Expert '95

Monte (Monty) Collins, Jr. (1898-1951)
Utopia '51
The Green Promise '49
Heartaches '47

Nina Colman
Johnny Dangerously '84

Harry Colomby
Touch and Go '86

John Colton (1891-1946)
The Invisible Ray '36
Werewolf of London '35

Chris Columbus (1958-)
Christmas With the Kranks '04
Nine Months '95
Little Nemo: Adventures in Slumberland '92
Only the Lonely '91
Heartbreak Hotel '88
Young Sherlock Holmes '85
Reckless '84
Gremlins '84
The Goonies '85

Carl Colpaert (1963-)
Facade '98
The Crew '95

William Conselman
The Perfect Nanny '00
East Side of Heaven '39
Bright Eyes '34
365 Nights in Hollywood '34

Robert Conte
The Breed '06
Who's Harry Crumb? '89
Odd Jobs '85

Alessandro Continenza (1920-96)
Deadly Mission '78
Let Sleeping Corpses Lie '74
The Loves of Hercules '60
What a Woman! '56
Too Bad She's Bad '54

Ernie Contreras
Fairy Tale: A True Story '97
The Pagemaster '94

Gary Conway (1936-)
American Ninja 3: Blood Hunt '89
American Ninja 2: The Confrontation '87
Over the Top '86

Tim Conway (1933-)
The Longshot '86
The Private Eyes '80
The Prize Fighter '79
They Went That-a-Way & That-a-Way '78

Douglas S. Cook
Double Jeopardy '99
Holy Matrimony '94
Payoff '91

Peter Cook (1938-95)
Yellowbeard '83
Bedazzled '68

T.S. Cook (1947-)
Murder 101 '91
High Noon '00
High Desert Kill '90
Nightbreaker '89
Out of the Darkness '85
The China Syndrome '79

Gods and Monsters '98
F/X 2: The Deadly Art of Illusion '91

Michael Cooney (1967-)
Identity '03
Jack Frost 2: Revenge of the Mutant Killer Snowman '00
Jack Frost '97
Murder in Mind '97

Shane Connaughton (1947-)
Tara Road '05
The Run of the Country '95
The Playboys '92
My Left Foot '89

Jon Connolly
The Dream Team '89

Ray Connolly
Forever Young '85
That'll Be the Day '73

Barry Connors
Pilgrimage '33
Too Busy to Work '32

Jean Conover
Jesus of Nazareth '28

Steve Conrad (1968-)
The Weather Man '05
Wrestling Ernest Hemingway '93
The Pursuit of Happyness '06

Christine Conradt (1973-)
Ghetto Dawg 2: Out of the Pits '05

Barry Connors
Pilgrimage '33

Heather Conkie
Bailey's Billions '05

Jon Connolly
The Dream Team '89

Barry Michael Cooper
Above the Rim '94
Sugar Hill '94
New Jack City '91

David Corley
Second in Command '05
Companeros '70

Adam Cooper
Accepted '06
New York Minute '04

John C. Cooper (1907-94)
The First Man into Space '59

Olive Cooper (1892-1987)
The Haunted Strangler '58

Paul Cooper
The Maldonado Miracle '03
Once Upon a Time... When We Were Colored '95

Robert Cooper (1968-)
Stargate: The Ark of Truth '08

Willis Cooper
Son of Frankenstein '39

Susan Cooper
George Balanchine's The Nutcracker '93
To Dance with the White Dog '93

Martin Copeland
Texas Rangers '01

Alec Coppel (1972-)
The Heavenly Kid '85

Francis Ford Coppola (1939-)
Youth Without Youth '07
John Grisham's The Rainmaker '97
The Godfather, Part 3 '90
New York Stories '89
The Cotton Club '84
Rumble Fish '83
The Outsiders '83
One from the Heart '82
The Godfather 1902-1959: The Complete Epic '81
Apocalypse Now '79
The Godfather, Part 2 '74
The Conversation '74
The Great Gatsby '74
The Godfather '72
Patton '70
The Rain People '69
Is Paris Burning? '66
You're a Big Boy Now '66
Dementia 13 '63
The Bellboy and the Playgirls '62
Tonight for Sure '61
The Magic Voyage of Sinbad '62

Don A. Coscarelli (1954-)
Bubba Ho-Tep '03
Phantasm 4: Oblivion '98
Phantasm 3: Lord of the Dead '94
Survival Quest '89
Phantasm 2 '88
Beastmaster '82
Phantasm '79

George P. Cosmatos (1941-2005)
Shadow Conspiracy '97
Tombstone '93
Leviathan '89
Rambo: First Blood Part 2 '85
Cobra '86
Of Unknown Origin '83
Escape to Athena '79
The Cassandra Crossing '76
Massacre in Rome '73

Jean Cosmos (1923-)
On Guard! '03
Capitaine Conan '96
Colonel Chabert '94

Roman Coppola
CQ '01

Sofia Coppola (1971-)
Marie Antoinette '06
Lost in Translation '03
The Virgin Suicides '99

Constantin Costa-Gavras (1933-)
Amen '02
Conseil de Famille '86
Missing '82
Z '69

Willis Cooper
Son of Frankenstein '39

Robert Cooper
Outside Providence '99
Federal Hill '94
Wildrose '85

Michael Corrente (1960-)
Brooklyn Rules '07
A Shot at Glory '00
Outside Providence '99
Federal Hill '94

Eugene Corr
Prefontaine '96
Getting Out '94
Desert Bloom '86

Gerald Cormier
See Alan Rudolph

Alain Corneau (1943-)
Tous les Matins du Monde '92
Fort Saganne '84

Laurence Corfat
A Mighty Heart '07
Me Without You '01
Wonderland '99
The Terror '63

David Corley
Second in Command '05

Roger Corman (1926-)
The Scateboard Kid 2 '93
Frankenstein Unbound '90

Sebastian Cordero (1972-)
Cronicas '04
Rats, Ratones, Rateros '99

Sergio Corbucci (1927-90)
Super Fuzz '81
Companeros '70
Django '68

Stephen Cornwell
Killing Streets '91

Lloyd Corrigan (1900-69)
The Return of Dr. Fu Manchu 3C
The Mysterious Dr. Fu Manchu 29

John W. Corrington (1932-88)
Omega Man '71
Boxcar Bertha '72
The Arena '73
Battle for the Planet of the Apes '73
The Omega Man '71

Joyce H. Corrington
Battle for the Planet of the Apes '73
The Omega Man '71

Catherine Corsini
The New Eve '98
Full Speed '96

Bill Cosby (1937-)
Leonard Part 6 '87

Michael Cooney
Super Fuzz

Maurizio Costanzo (1938-)
Zeder '83
A Special Day '77
James Costigan (1926-2007)
Mr. North '88
King David '85
S.O.S. Titanic '79
Manny Coto
Hostile Intent '97
Star Kid '97
Dr. Giggles '92
William Cottrell (1906-95)
Peter Pan '53
Pinocchio '40
Frank Cottrell-Boyce (1961-)
Code 46 '03
24 Hour Party People '01
The Claim '00
Pandaemonium '00
Hilary and Jackie '98
Welcome to Sarajevo '97
Saint-Ex: The Story of the Storyteller '95
Butterfly Kiss '94
A Woman's Guide to Adultery '93
Bob Couttie
Doomsdayer '01
Doomsdayer '99
Suzette Couture
Jesus '00
Love and Hate: A Marriage Made in Hell '90
Allen Covert (1964-)
The Benchwarmers '06
Grandma's Boy '06
Adam Sandler's 8 Crazy Nights '02
Alex Cox (1954-)
Fear and Loathing in Las Vegas '98
Straight to Hell '87
Sid & Nancy '86
Repo Man '83
Brian Cox (1946-)
Scorpion Spring '96
Deadly Obsession '88
C. Jay Cox (1962-)
Latter Days '04
Sweet Home Alabama '02
Deb Cox
After the Deluge '03
Dead Letter Office '98
Jim Cox
Murder She Purred: A Mrs. Murphy Mystery '98
Ferngully: The Last Rain Forest '92
The Rescuers Down Under '90
Oliver & Company '88
Morgan Cox (1900-68)
Raiders of Ghost City '44
Gang Busters '42
Desperate Cargo '41
Zorro's Fighting Legion '39
Paul Cox (1940-)
Innocence '00
Lust and Revenge '95
A Woman's Tale '92
Vincent: The Life and Death of Vincent van Gogh '87
Cactus '86
Man of Flowers '84
My First Wife '84
Lonely Hearts '82
Kerry Crabbe
Innocent Lies '95
The Playboys '92
Peter Crabbe
McHale's Navy '97
Car 54, Where Are You? '94

H.A.L. Craig (1921-78)
Lion of the Desert '81
The Message '77
Anzio '68
Laurie Craig
Ella Enchanted '04
Paulie '98
Modern Girls '86
Frank Craven (1875-1945)
Our Town '40
Sons of the Desert '33
Jay Craven
Disappearances '06
A Stranger in the Kingdom '98
Where the Rivers Flow North '94
Jonathan Craven (1965-)
The Hills Have Eyes 2 '07
Wes Craven Presents Mind Ripper '95
Wes Craven (1939-)
The Hills Have Eyes 2 '07
Paris, je t'aime '06
Pulse '06
Wes Craven's New Nightmare '94
The People under the Stairs '91
Shocker '89
A Nightmare on Elm Street 3: Dream Warriors '87
The Hills Have Eyes, Part 2 '84
A Nightmare on Elm Street '84
Swamp Thing '82
Deadly Blessing '81
The Hills Have Eyes '77
Last House on the Left '72
Joanna Crawford
Sophia Loren: Her Own Story '80
Wayne Crawford
Jake Speed '86
Valley Girl '83
James A. Creelman (1901-41)
King Kong '33
The Most Dangerous Game '32
James Cresson (1934-2004)
Defenseless '91
Chattahoochee '89
The Morning After '86
John Cresswell
Cast a Dark Shadow '55
The Woman in Question '50
Michael Crichton (1942-)
Twister '96
The 13th Warrior '99
Jurassic Park '93
Rising Sun '93
Runaway '84
Looker '81
The Great Train Robbery '79
Coma '78
Westworld '73
Sex Through a Window '72
Armando Crispino (1925-)
Autopsy '74
Commandos '73
Dead Are Alive '72
Autopsy of a Ghost '67
Michael Cristofer (1945-)
Original Sin '01
Gia '98
Breaking Up '97
Mr. Jones '93
The Bonfire of the Vanities '90
Keith Critchlow
New Jack City '91
Night Life '89

Emma-Kate Croghan (1972-)
Strange Planet '99
Love and Other Catastrophes '95
David Cronenberg (1943-)
eXistenZ '99
Crash '95
Naked Lunch '91
Dead Ringers '88
The Fly '86
Videodrome '83
Scanners '81
The Brood '79
Fast Company '78
Rabid '77
They Came from Within '75
Allison Cross
Blood & Wine '96
Serving in Silence: The Margarethe Cammermeyer Story '95
Beverley Cross (1932-98)
Clash of the Titans '81
Sinbad and the Eye of the Tiger '77
Half a Sixpence '67
The Long Ships '64
Jason and the Argonauts '63
Avery Crounse (1946-)
Cries of Silence '97
The Invisible Kid '88
Eyes of Fire '84
Bill Crounse
American Cyborg: Steel Warrior '94
9 1/2 Ninjas '90
Say Anything '89
The Wild Life '84
Fast Times at Ridgemont High '82
Cameron Crowe (1957-)
Elizabethtown '05
Vanilla Sky '01
Almost Famous '00
Jerry Maguire '96
Singles '92
Christopher Crowe (1948-)
Fear '96
The Last of the Mohicans '92
Whispers in the Dark '92
Off Limits '87
Mean Season '85
Nightmares '83
Last Chase '81
John Crowther
Damned River '89
The Evil That Men Do '84
Kill and Kill Again '81
Jim Cruickshank
Man of the House '95
Sister Act 2: Back in the Habit '93
Mr. Destiny '90
Three Men and a Baby '87
Tough Guys '86
Breaking All the Rules '85
Jon Cryer (1965-)
Went to Coney Island on a Mission from God... Be Back by Five '98
The Pompatus of Love '95
Billy Crystal (1947-)
America's Sweethearts '01
Forget Paris '95
City Slickers 2: The Legend of Curly's Gold '94
Memories of Me '88
Alfonso Cuaron (1961-)
Children of Men '06
Paris, je t'aime '06
Y Tu Mama Tambien '01
Allan Cubitt
The Hound of the Baskervilles '02
Anna Karenina '00
St. Ives '98

Milo G. Cuccia
Count Dracula '71
Venus in Furs '70
Tom Cudworth
Restaurant '98
Ten Benny '98
Alma Cullen
All the King's Men '99
A Village Affair '95
Intimate Contact '87
Mike Cullen
Bloodlines '05
Horatio Hornblower '99
Carmen Culver
The Last Prostitute '91
Agatha Christie's Murder is Easy '82
David Cummings
Kevin & Perry Go Large '00
The Last Seduction 2 '98
Hugh Cummings
Hot Tip '35
Pardon My Gun '30
Rusty Cundieff (1965-)
Sprung '96
Tales from the Hood '95
Fear of a Black Hat '94
House Party 2: The Pajama Jam '91
Jack Cunningham (1882-1941)
Mississippi '35
It's a Gift '34
The Black Pirate '26
Don Q., Son of Zorro '25
Beyond the Rocks '22
Jere P. Cunningham
The Last of the Finest '90
Michael Cunningham (1952-)
Evening '07
A Home at the End of the World '04
Splatter University '84
Terry Cunningham
The Stray '00
Y2K '99
Land of the Free '98
Pat Cupo
One Last Ride '03
Tim Curnen
Ghostwarrior '86
Forbidden World '82
Ian Curteis (1935-)
The Choir '95
Philby, Burgess and MacLean: Spy Scandal of the Century '84
Valerie Curtin (1945-)
Toys '92
Unfaithfully Yours '84
Best Friends '82
Inside Moves '80
Dan Curtis (1928-2006)
Trilogy of Terror 2 '96
Burnt Offerings '76
Nathaniel Curtis (1909-83)
Jack & the Beanstalk '52
Blood on the Sun '45
Richard Curtis (1956-)
The Girl in the Cafe '05
Bridget Jones: The Edge of Reason '04
Love Actually '03
Bridget Jones's Diary '01
Notting Hill '99
Bean '97
Four Weddings and a Funeral '94
The Tall Guy '89
Vondie Curtis-Hall (1956-)
Waist Deep '06
Gridlock'd '96
Stephen J. Curwick (1960-)
Police Academy 6: City under Siege '89

Police Academy 5: Assignment Miami Beach '88
John Cusack (1966-)
High Fidelity '00
Grosse Pointe Blank '97
Neil Cuthbert
The Adventures of Pluto Nash '02
Mystery Men '99
Hocus Pocus '93.
Ron Cutler
Article 99 '92
Blood Red '88
Catherine Cyran
True Heart '97
Hostile Intentions '94
Fire on the Amazon '93
Uncaged '91
Bloodfist 2 '90
A Cry in the Wild '90
Slumber Party Massacre 3 '90
Renee Daalder (1944-)
Habitat '97
Massacre at Central High '76
Jean-Loup Dabadie (1938-)
Vincent, Francois, Paul and the Others '76
Cesar & Rosalie '72
Ingram D'Abbes
Big Fella '37
Song of Freedom '36
Don DaGradi
Bedknobs and Broomsticks '71
Blackbeard's Ghost '67
Lady and the Tramp '55
John Dahl (1956-)
Red Rock West '93
Kill Me Again '89
P.I. Private Investigations '87
Private Investigations '87
Roald Dahl (1916-90)
Willy Wonka & the Chocolate Factory '71
Chitty Chitty Bang Bang '68
You Only Live Twice '67
36 Hours '64
Salvador Dali (1904-89)
L'Age D'Or '30
Un Chien Andalou '28
Walter Dallenbach
Greedy Terror '78
Las Vegas Lady '76
Ian Dalrymple (1903-89)
Three Cases of Murder '55
Clouds over Europe '39
Pygmalion '38
South Riding '37
Joe D'Amato (1936-99)
Trap Them & Kill Them '77
Heroes in Hell '73
Janeen Damian
Moondance Alexander '07
Hot Tamale '06
Michael Damian
Moondance Alexander '07
Hot Tamale '06
Damiano Damiani (1922-)
The Sicilian Connection '85
Confessions of a Police Captain '72
The Hit Man '60
Suso Cecchi D'Amico (1914-)
The Sky Is Falling '00
Jesus of Nazareth '77
The Innocent '76
Conversation Piece '75
Sandra of a Thousand Delights '65
The Leopard '63
Joyful Laughter '60
Rocco and His Brothers '60

Big Deal on Madonna Street '58
White Nights '57
What a Woman! '56
Too Bad She's Bad '54
The Lady Without Camelias '53
Bellissima '51
Matt Damon (1970-)
Gerry 02
Good Will Hunting '97
Clemence Dane (1888-1965)
Salute John Citizen '42
Sidewalks of London '38
Fire Over England '37
Anna Karenina '35
Rodney Dangerfield (1921-2004)
The 4th Tenor '02
My 5 Wives '00
Meet Wally Sparks '97
Easy Money '83
Damon "Coke" Daniels
Who Made the Potatoe Salad? '05
My Baby's Daddy '04
Jeff Daniels (1955-)
Super Sucker '03
Escanaba in da Moonlight '01
Stan Daniels (1934-2007)
The Substitute Wife '94
For Richer, for Poorer '92
Kurt Vonnegut's Monkey House '91
Glory! Glory! '90
The Lonely Guy '84
Monja Danischewsky (1911-94)
Topkapi '64
The Battle of the Sexes '60
Max Dann
Siam Sunset '99
Marcello Danon (-1997)
The Efficiency Expert '92
La Cage aux Folles '78
The Black Belly of the Tarantula '71
Richard Danus
No Place to Hide '93
Xanadu '80
Frank Darabont (1959-)
The Mist '07
The Green Mile '99
Black Cat Run '98
Saving Private Ryan '98
Mary Shelley's Frankenstein '94
The Shawshank Redemption '94
The Fly 2 '89
The Blob '88
A Nightmare on Elm Street 3: Dream Warriors '87
Jack Darcus (1941-)
The Portrait '93
The Deserters '83
Jean-Pierre Dardenne (1951-)
The Child '05
Rosetta 99
La Promesse '96
Luc Dardenne (1954-)
The Child '05
Rosetta 99
La Promesse '96
Scott Darling (1898-1951)
Bush Pilot '47
The Ghost of Frankenstein '42
Sherlock Holmes and the Secret Weapon 42
Cracked Nuts 41
The Fatal Hour '40
Stunt Pilot '39
King of the Sierras '38
W. Scott Darling
See Scott Darling

William Scott Darling
See Scott Darling

Christian Darren
Surf's Up '07

Julie Dash (1952-)
Hustle '04
Subway Stories '97
Daughters of the Dust '91

Sean Dash
Watchers Reborn '98
Breakaway '95
Fists of Iron '94
Ice '93
Emperor of the Bronx '89

Jules Dassin (1911-2008)
A Dream of Passion '78
Phaedra '61
Never on Sunday '60
Where the Hot Wind Blows '59
Riff '54

Ken Daurio
Bubble Boy '01

Dorothy Davenport
See Dorothy Davenport Reid

Delmer Daves (1904-77)
Spencer's Mountain '63
Rome Adventure '62
Parrish '61
A Summer Place '59
An Affair to Remember '57
Task Force '49
The Red House '47
Hollywood Canteen '44
Stage Door Canteen '43
Night of January 16th '41
Love Affair '39
Petrified Forest '36
Dames '34
Flirtation Walk '34
No More Women '34

Marjorie David
Into the Badlands '92
Shy People '87
Maria's Lovers '84

Peter David (1956-)
Backlash: Oblivion 2 '95
Oblivion '94
Trancers 5: Sudden Deth '94
Trancers 4: Jack of Swords '93

Paul Davids
Starry Night '99
Roswell: The U.F.O. Cover-Up '94

Boaz Davidson (1943-)
Delta Force 3: The Killing Game '91
Salsa '88
Hot Resort '85
Private Manoeuvres '83
Last American Virgin '82
Hot Bubblegum '81

Martin Davidson (1939-)
Looking for an Echo '99
Eddie and the Cruisers '83
The Lords of Flatbush '74

Ronald Davidson (1899-1965)
Trader Tom of the China Seas '54
Government Agents vs. Phantom Legion '51
King of the Forest Rangers '46
Manhunt in the African Jungles '43

Andrew Davies
The Way We Live Now '02
Othello '01
Bridget Jones's Diary '01
Wives and Daughters '01
Vanity Fair '99
A Rather English Marriage '98
Moll Flanders '96
Wilderness '96
The Final Cut '95
Pride and Prejudice '95
Circle of Friends '95
Middlemarch '93
To Play the King '93
House of Cards '90
Consuming Passions '88
Private Life '82

Jack Davies (1911-92)
Paper Tiger '74
Those Daring Young Men in Their Jaunty Jalopies '69
Gambit '66
Those Magnificent Men in Their Flying Machines '65
Doctor at Sea '56
Curtain Up '53

Russell T. Davies (1963-)
Casanova '05
Touching Evil '97
The Neon Bible '95
The Long Day Closes '92
Distant Voices, Still Lives '88

Valentine Davies (1905-61)
Bachelor in Paradise '69
The Bridges at Toko-Ri '55
The Glenn Miller Story '54
It Happens Every Spring '49

William Davies
Flushed Away '06
Johnny English '03
Ignition '01
The Guilty '99
Dr. Jekyll and Ms. Hyde '95
Ghost in the Machine '93
Stop! or My Mom Will Shoot '92

Twins '98

Andrew Davis (1946-)
Steal Big, Steal Little '95
Above the Law '88
Beat Street '84

Charles Davis
Thunder Run '86

Bart Davis
Full Fathom Five '90
For Love or Money '88

Frank Davis
The Train '65
Hazel's People '73

Ivan Davis
Dance, Girl, Dance '40

John A. Davis
The Ant Bully '06
Jimmy Neutron: Boy Genius '01

Julie Davis (1969-)
Amy's O '02
I Love You, Don't Touch Me! '97

Luther Davis (1921-)
Across 110th Street '72
Lady in a Cage '64
Kismet '55
The Hucksters '47

Jerry Davis (1917-91)
L.A. Goddess '92
Pardners '56

Nick Davis
1999 '98
The Other Side of Heaven '02

Mitch Davis
The Match '99
Another 9 1/2 Weeks '96

Mick Davis (1961-)
The Invisible '07
Modigliani '04

Randolph Davis
Police Academy 7: Mission to Moscow '94

Tom Davis (1952-)
Coneheads '93
One More Saturday Night '86

Walter Halsey Davis
Dangerous Relations '93
Last Flight Out: A True Story '90

Michael Davis (1965-)
In the Mouth of Madness '95
Kiss Me a Killer '91

Marcus De Leon
The Big Squeeze '96
Kiss Me a Killer '91

Robert De Laurentiis
Dance with the Devil '97
The Day of the Beast '95
Seven Hours to Judgment '88

Anthony M. Dawson (1930-2002)
Deadline '81
Yor, the Hunter from the Future '83
Cannibal Apocalypse '80
And God Said to Cain '69

Gordon Dawson
Purgatory '99
Into the Badlands '92
Bring Me the Head of Alfredo Garcia '74

Peter Dawson
Killings at Outpost Zeta '80
Escape from DS-3 '81

Ossie Davis (1917-2005)
Cotton Comes to Harlem '70
Gone Are the Days '63
Purlie Victorious '63

Alex de la Iglesia (1965-)
El Crimen Perfecto '04

Rolf de Heer (1951-)
Dance Me to My Song '98
The Quiet Room '96
Alien Visitor '95
Bad Boy Bubby '93

Anatole de Grunwald (1910-67)
Pygmalion '38

Claude de Givray (1933-)
Bed and Board '70

Raymond De Felitta (1964-)
Two Family House '99
Café Society '97

Vittorio De Sica (1901-74)
Umberto D '55
The Bicycle Thief '48
The Children Are Watching Us '44

Steven E. de Souza (1947-)
Knock Off '98
Beverly Hills Cop 3 '94
Street Fighter '94
The Flintstones '94
Hudson Hawk '91
Ricochet '91
Die Hard 2: Die Harder '90
Die Hard '88
Bad Dreams '88
Commando '85
Return of Captain Invincible '83
48 Hrs. '82

Michael De Luca (1965-)
In the Mouth of Madness '95

Alberto De Martino (1929-)
Formula for a Murder '85
Django Shoots First '74

Kirk De Micco
Space Chimps '08
Quest for Camelot '98

Albert De Mond
See Albert DeMond

Manoel de Oliveira (1908-)
Belle Toujours '06
I'm Going Home '00
Party '95
Voyage to the Beginning of the World '96
The Convent '95
Abraham's Valley '93

Alfredo de Villa
Adrift in Manhattan '07
Washington Heights '02

Marina de Van (1971-)
8 Women '02
Under the Sand '00

Gary De Vore (1941-97)
Timecop '94
Raw Deal '86
Running Scared '86
Back Roads '81

Karen De Wolf (1909-89)
Footlight Glamour '43
It's a Great Life '43
Blondie for Victory '42
Blondie Goes Latin '42
Blondie's Blessed Event '42
Blondie in Society '41
Blondie Plays Cupid '40

Annie de Young
MTV's Wuthering Heights '03
The Day the World Ended '01
Earth vs. the Spider '01

Brian De Palma (1941-)
Redacted '07
Femme Fatale '02
Raising Cain '92
Blow Out '81
Dressed to Kill '80
Home Movies '79
Phantom of the Paradise '74
Sisters '73
Hi, Mom! '70
Greetings '68

Philippe de Broca (1933-2004)
On Guard '03
The Green House '96
Jupiter's Thigh '81
Dear Detective '77
Le Magnifique '76
That Man from Rio '64
Cartouche '62

Frank Deasy
Prozac Nation '01
Captives '94

Nick Dear (1955-)
The Turn of the Screw '99
Byron '03
Persuasion '95

Frank Deasy
A Kiss Before Dying '91
Fatal Attraction '87

William Dear (1944-)
Harry and the Hendersons '87

James Dearden (1949-)
Rogue Trader '98

Ennio de Concini (1923-)
The Bachelor '93
Devil in the Flesh '87
Corrupt '84
Bluebeard '72
The Girl Who Knew Too Much '63
Divorce—Italian Style '62
Black Sunday '60
That Long Night in '43 '60
Il Grido '57

Arpad De Riso
Hercules against the Moon Men '64
Fire Monsters Against the Son of Hercules '62

Massimo De Rita
Car Crash '80
The Switch '76
Chino '75
Street Law '74

Brian Degas (1935-)
Barbarella '68
Danger: Diabolik '68

Paul Denn (1912-76)
Murder on the Orient Express '74
The Dogs of War '81
The Spy Who Came in from the Cold '65
Goldfinger '64
Seven Days to Noon '50

Edward Dein (1907-84)
Curse of the Undead '59
Shack Out on 101 '55

Mildred Dein
Curse of the Undead '59
Shack Out on 101 '55

Alvaro del Amo
Jealousy '99

John DeBello (1952-)
Killer Tomatoes Eat France '91
Killer Tomatoes Strike Back '90
Return of the Killer Tomatoes! '88
Attack of the Killer Tomatoes! '77

Steve DeJarnatt
Miracle Mile '89
Strange Brew '83

Fred Dekker (1959-)
RoboCop 3 '91
Night of the Creeps '86
The Monster Squad '87

Michael deGuzman
Hidden in America '96

Michael DeForrest
The Lickerish Quartet '70

Frank De Felice
Angel Square '92
Out of the Dark '88
Why Shoot the Teacher '79

Christopher DeFaria (1959-)
Danger: Diabolik '68

James DeFelice
Why Shoot the Teacher '79

Everett De Roche
Visitors '03
Razorback '84

James D. Deck (1964-)
The Night After Halloween '79

Guiseppe de Santis (1917-97)
Bitter Rice '49

Denise DeClue
The Cherokee Kid '96
For Keeps '88
About Last Night... '86

Edward Decter
The Santa Clause 3: The Escape Clause '06
The Lizzie McGuire Movie '03
The Santa Clause 2 '02
There's Something about Mary '98

Didier Decoin (1945-)
The Crown Prince '06
Napoleon '03
Balzac: A Life of Passion '99
The Count of Monte Cristo '99

Frank Deese
Options '88

Remigio del Grosso (1912-)
Coriolanus, Man without a Country '64
Conquest of Mycene '63
Mill of the Stone Women '60

Peter Del Monte (1943-)
Traveling Companion '96
Julia and Julia '87

Guillermo del Toro (1964-)
Hellboy 2: The Golden Army '08
Pan's Labyrinth '06
Hellboy '04
The Devil's Backbone '01
Cronos '94

Shelagh Delaney (1939-)
The Railway Station Man '92
Dance with a Stranger '85
A Taste of Honey '61

Walter DeLeon (1884-1947)
Little Giant '46
Birth of the Blues '41
Pot o' Gold '41
The Ghost Breakers '40
Union Pacific '39
Lonely Wives '31

Francis Delia
Trouble Bound '92
Freeway '88

William F. Delligan (1944-95)
A Passion to Kill '94
Praying Mantis '93

Jeffrey Delman
Double Obsession '93
Voodoo Dawn '89

Julie Delpy (1969-)
2 Days in Paris '07
Before Sunset '04

Rudy DeLuca
Screw Loose '99
Dracula: Dead and Loving It '95
Life Stinks '91
The Eliminators '86
Zone Troopers '84
Future Cop '76

Paul DeMeo
The Rocketeer '91
Arena '89
The Wrong Guys '88

William DeMeo (1968-)
Searching for Bobby D '05
Wannabes '01

Jonathan Demme (1944-)
The Truth About Charlie '02
Fighting Mad '76
Caged Heat '74
Hot Box '72

James DeMonaco (1968-)
Skinwalkers '07
Assault on Precinct 13 '05
The Negotiator '98

Albert DeMond (1901-73)
Marshal of Cedar Rock '53
Border Saddlemates '52
Wild Frontier '47
Cyclotrode "X" '46
Daughter of Don Q '46
King of the Forest Rangers '46
Federal Operator 99 '45
Manhunt of Mystery Island '45
The Purple Monster Strikes '45
Ridin' Down the Canyon '42
The Great Plane Robbery '40
The Love Trap '29

Jacques Demy (1931-90)
A Slightly Pregnant Man '79
The Young Girls of Rochefort '68
Umbrellas of Cherbourg '64

Claire Denis (1948-)
The Intruder '04
Friday Night '02
Beau Travail '98
Nenette and Boni '96
I Can't Sleep '93
No Fear, No Die '90
Chocolat '88

Wilton Denmark
Johnny Firecloud '75

Gill Dennis
Walk the Line '05
Riders of the Purple Sage '96
Without Evidence '96
Return to Oz '85

Pen Densham (1947-)
Houdini '98
Moll Flanders '96
Lifepod '93
Robin Hood: Prince of Thieves '91
The Zoo Gang '85

Alan Dent (1905-78)
Hamlet '48
Henry V '44

Greg DePaul
Saving Silverman '01
Killer Bud '00

Jacques Deray (1929-2003)
Borsalino '70
La Piscine '69

Everett DeRoche
See Everett De Roche
Link '86
Razorback '84
Road Games '81

Scott Derrickson
The Exorcism of Emily Rose '05
Hellraiser 5: Inferno '00
Urban Legends 2: Final Cut '00

Dominique Deruddere (1957-)
Everybody's Famous! '00
Hombres Complicados '97
Wait until Spring, Bandini '90

Georges des Esseintes
Animal Instincts '92
Secret Games '92

Arnaud Desplechin (1960-)
Kings and Queen '04
Esther Kahn '00
My Sex Life... Or How I Got into an Argument '96
La Sentinelle '92

Helen Deutsch (1906-92)
Valley of the Dolls '67
King Solomon's Mines '50
The Loves of Carmen '48
Golden Earrings '47
National Velvet '44
The Seventh Cross '44

Michel DeVille (1931-)
La Lectrice '88
Peril '85

D.V. DeVincentis
High Fidelity '00
Grosse Pointe Blank '97

Dennis Devine
Bloodstream '00
Chain of Souls '00
Vampires of Sorority Row: Kickboxers From Hell '99
Things 2 '97
Things '89
Fatal Images '89

Scott Devine (1969-)
Shark Attack 3: Megalodon '02
Shark Attack 2 '00
Shark Attack '99

Dean Devlin (1962-)
Godzilla '98
Independence Day '96
Stargate '94
Universal Soldier '92

Christopher DeVore
Hamlet '90
Frances '82

Jack DeWitt (1900-81)
Triumphs of a Man Called Horse '83
The Return of a Man Called Horse '76
Sky Riders '76
Neptune Factor '73
Man in the Wilderness '71
A Man Called Horse '70
The Legend of the Sea Wolf '58
Sitting Bull '54
Bells of San Fernando '47

Pete Dexter
Michael '96
Mulholland Falls '95
Paris Trout '91
Rush '91

Elize D'Haene
Red Shoe Diaries: Luscious Lola '00
Red Shoe Diaries: Strip Poker '96

Fernando Di Leo (1932-2003)
Rulers of the City '76
Hired to Kill '73
Hit Men '73

Edward Di Lorenzo
Lady Frankenstein '72
A Place Called Glory '66

Mario di Nardo
Mean Machine '73
Five Dolls for an August Moon '70

Gerald Di Pego (1941-)
The Forgotten '04
Angel Eyes '01
Instinct '99
Message in a Bottle '98
Phenomenon '96
Keeper of the City '92
Sharky's Machine '81

David Diamond
The Tenants '06
Evolution '01
Family Man '00
Body Count '97

I.A.L. Diamond (1920-88)
Buddy Buddy '81
The Front Page '74
Avanti! '72
The Private Life of Sherlock Holmes '70
Cactus Flower '69
The Fortune Cookie '66
Kiss Me, Stupid! '64
Irma La Douce '63
One, Two, Three '61
The Apartment '60
Some Like It Hot '59
Love in the Afternoon '57
Monkey Business '52
Let's Make It Legal '51
Love Nest '51
Never Say Goodbye '46

Agustin Diaz Yanes (1950-)
No News from God '01
Baton Rouge '88

Tom DiCillo (1954-)
Double Whammy '01
The Real Blonde '97
Box of Moonlight '96
Living in Oblivion '94
Johnny Suede '92

Basil Dickey (1880-1958)
Brand of Fear '49
Son of Zorro '47
Daughter of Don Q '46
King of the Forest Rangers '46
The Phantom Rider '46
Federal Operator 99 '45
Manhunt of Mystery Island '45
The Purple Monster Strikes '45
Manhunt in the African Jungles '43
Flash Gordon Conquers the Universe '40
Junior G-Men '40
Space Soldiers Conquer the Universe '40
The Green Hornet '39
Brothers of the West '37
The Phantom Rider '36

Joan Didion (1934-)
Up Close and Personal '96
Broken Trust '95
True Confessions '81
A Star Is Born '76
Panic in Needle Park '71

Carlos Diegues (1940-)
Orfeu '99
Tieta of Agreste '96
Quilombo '84
Bye Bye Brazil '79

Anton Diether
Cleopatra '99
Moby Dick '98

Erwin C. Dietrich
Ilsa, the Wicked Warden '78
Inn of Temptation '73
Sex Adventures of the Three Musketeers '71

Frank Dietz
Cold Harvest '98
Magic in the Mirror: Fowl Play '96
Naked Souls '95

John Dighton (1909-89)
The Devil's Disciple '59
The Happiest Days of Your Life '50
Kind Hearts and Coronets '49
The Foreman Went to France '42

Erin Dignam
Loved '97
Denial: The Dark Side of Passion '91

Richard Dilello
Riot in the Streets '96
Bad Boys '83

Flint Dille (1955-)
Venom '05
An American Tail: Fievel Goes West '91

Constantine Dillon (1953-)
Killer Tomatoes Eat France '91
Killer Tomatoes Strike Back '90
Return of the Killer Tomatoes! '88

Robert Dillon (1889-1944)
Waking the Dead '00
Deception '92
Flight of the Intruder '90
The Survivalist '87
Revolution '85
The River '84
French Connection 2 '75
99 & 44/100 Dead '74
Prime Cut '72
Bikini Beach '64
Muscle Beach Party '64
X: The Man with X-Ray Eyes '63

Robert A.(R.A.) Dillon (1889-1944)
Slaves in Bondage '37
The Last of the Mohicans '20

Howard Dimsdale (1914-44)
The Sheriff of Fractured Jaw '59
Abbott and Costello Meet Dr. Jekyll and Mr. Hyde '52
The Traveling Saleswoman '50

Dennis Dimster-Denk (1965-)
Outside the Law '95
Terminal Impact '95

Brian DiMuccio
Moonbase '97
Little Witches '96
The Demolitionist '95
Voodoo '95

Mel Dinelli
Jeopardy '53
The Spiral Staircase '46

Leslie Dixon
Hairspray '07
The Heartbreak Kid '07
Just like Heaven '05
Freaky Friday '03
Pay It Forward '00
The Thomas Crown Affair '99
That Old Feeling '96
Look Who's Talking Now '93
Mrs. Doubtfire '93
Loverboy '89
Outrageous Fortune '87
Overboard '87

Peter Dixon
Unlawful Passage '94
Down the Wyoming Trail '39

Peter Dobai (1944-)
Hanussen '88
Colonel Redl '84
Mephisto '81

Frank Q. Dobbs (1939-2006)
The Magnificent Seven '98
Hotwire '80

Lem Dobbs (1961-)
The Score '01
The Limey '99
Dark City '97
The Hard Way '91
Kafka '91

Donald M. Dohler (1946-2006)
Galaxy Invader '85
The Alien Factor '78

Jacques Dolillon (1944-)
Petits Freres '00
Ponette '95
La Vengeance d'une Femme '89

Bob Dolman
How to Eat Fried Worms '06
The Banger Sisters '02
Far and Away '92
Willow '88

Henry Dominic
See John Brancato

Andrew Dominik
The Assassination of Jesse James by the Coward Robert Ford '07
Chopper '00

Patrick G. Donahue
Savage Instinct '89
Code of Honor '82
Kill Squad '81

Simon Donald
Beautiful Creatures '00
Deacon Brodie '98
My Life So Far '98
The Ebb-Tide '97

Sergio Donati (1933-)
North Star '96
Beyond Justice '92
Orca '77
Spaghetti Western '75
Escape from Death Row '73
The Good, the Bad and the Ugly '67

Thomas Dean Donnelly
Sahara '05
A Sound of Thunder '05

Thomas Michael Donnelly
Bonanno: A Godfather's Story '99
A Soldier's Sweetheart '98
The Garden of Redemption '97
Talent for the Game '91
Quicksilver '86
Defiance '79

Mary Agnes Donoghue
Veronica Guerin '03
White Oleander '02
Deceived '91
Paradise '91
Beaches '88
The Buddy System '83

Martin Donovan (1950-)
Somebody Is Waiting '96
Death Becomes Her '92
Mad at the Moon '92
Apartment Zero '88

Paul Donovan (1954-)
Tales from a Parallel Universe: Eating Pattern '97
Tales from a Parallel Universe: Giga Shadow '97
Tales from a Parallel Universe: I Worship His Shadow '97
Tales from a Parallel Universe: Super Nova '97
Tomcat: Dangerous Desires '93
Self-Defense '83

Mark Donskoi (1901-81)
My Universities '40
My Apprenticeship '39

Anita Doohan
Whispers '89
Embryo '76

Matt Dorff
Category 6 : Day of Destruction '04
Mr. Rock 'n' Roll: The Alan Freed Story '99
Requiem for Murder '99
Silent Predators '99
Random Encounter '98
The Reaper '97
The Stepsister '97
Closer and Closer '96

David Dorfman (1993-)
Anger Management '03
My Boss's Daughter '03

Gil Doud (1914-57)
Walk the Proud Land '56
To Hell and Back '55

Ziad Doueiri
Lila Says '04
West Beirut '98

Joseph Dougherty
Witch Hunt '94
Attack of the 50 Ft. Woman '93
Cast a Deadly Spell '91
Steel and Lace '90

Michael Dougherty
Superman Returns '06
Urban Legends: Bloody Mary '05
X2: X-Men United '03

Lorenzo Doumani (1962-)
Storybook '95
Amore! '93

Richard D'Ovidio
Exit Wounds '01
13 Ghosts '01

Alexander Dovzhenko (1849-1956)
Earth '30
Arsenal '29

Nancy Dowd (1945-)
Let It Ride '89
Slap Shot '77

Allison Louise Downe
Just for the Hell of It '68
She-Devils on Wheels '68
The Girl, the Body and the Pill '67
Gruesome Twosome '67
Blood Feast '63

Robert Downey (1935-)
Greaser's Palace '72
Putney Swope '69

Carol Doyle
Human Trafficking '05
Veronica Guerin '03
Washington Square '97

Larry Doyle
Duplex '03
Looney Tunes: Back in Action '03

Brian Doyle-Murray (1945-)
Family '94
The Snapper '93
The Van '95

Roddy Doyle (1958-)
When Brendan Met Trudy '00
The Commitments '91

Srdjan Dragojevic (1963-)
The Wounds '98
Pretty Village, Pretty Flame '96

Oliver Drake (1903-91)
Fighting Valley '43
Trailing Double Trouble '40
Cowboys from Texas '39
Purple Vigilantes '38
Public Cowboy No. 1 '37
Roarin Lead '37
Law and Lawless '33
The Drifter '32
Rogue of the Rio Grande '30

Pete Draper
Poldark '75
I'll Never Forget What's 'Isname '67
The Girl Getters '66

Jay Dratler (1911-68)
Impact '49
Call Northside 777 '48
Dark Corner '46

Hal Dresner
Sssssss '73
The Eiger Sanction '75

Carl Theodor Dreyer (1889-1968)
Gertrud '64
Ordet '55
Day of Wrath '43
Vampyr '31
Passion of Joan of Arc '28
Master of the House '25

Karim Dridi (1961-)
Bye-Bye '96
Pigalle '95

Robin Driscoll
Mr. Bean's Holiday '07
Bean '97

Kevin Droney (1948-)
Wing Commander '99
Mortal Kombat 1: The Movie '95

Michael B. Druxman (1941-)
Down Came a Blackbird '94

Olivier Ducastel (1962-)
Cote d'Azur '05
My Life on Ice '02

Lee Drysdale
Leather Jackets '90

James Duff (1955-)
The War at Home '96

Warren Duff (1904-73)
Step Lively '44

Jesse Duffy (1894-1952)
Son of Zorro '47
Daughter of Don Q '46
King of the Forest Rangers '46
The Phantom Rider '46
Federal Operator 99 '45
Manhunt of Mystery Island '45
Manhunt in the African Jungles '43

Jo Duffy
Puppet Master 5: The Final Chapter '94
Puppet Master 4 '93

Martine Dugowson (1958-)
Portraits Chinois '96
Mina Tannenbaum '93

John Duigan (1949-)
Head in the Clouds '04
The Leading Man '96
Sirens '94
Wide Sargasso Sea '92
Flirting '89
The Year My Voice Broke '87

Bruno Dumont (1958-)
Flanders '06
Twentynine Palms '03
Humanity '99
The Life of Jesus '96

Don Carlos Dunaway
Cujo '83

David Duncan (1913-99)
The Time Machine '60
The Leech Woman '59
Monster on the Campus '59

Patrick Duncan
A Painted House '03

Patrick Sheane Duncan (1947-)
Courage Under Fire '96
Mr. Holland's Opus '95
Live! From Death Row '92
84 Charlie MoPic '89

Peter Duncan (1954-)
Children of the Revolution '95

Dave Edison
Driving Force '88
BMX Bandits '83

Philip Dunne (1908-92)
Nick of Time '95

Phil Dunham (1885-1972)
The Duke Is Tops '38
Two-Gun Troubacor '37
Stormy Trails '36

John Gregory Dunne (1932-2003)
The Dropkick '27
Sparrows '26

Winifred Dunn
Been '07

Thom Eberhardt (1947-)
Ratz '99
Face Down '97
Captain Ron '92
Honey, I Blew Up the Kid '92
All I Want for Christmas '91
The Night Before '88
Night of the Comet '84

Roger Ebert (1942-)
Beneath the Valley of the Ultra-Vixens '79
Beyond the Valley of the Dolls '70

Patrick Edgeworth (1942-)
Switch '91
Skin Deep '89
Sunset '88
A Fine Mess '86
That's Life! '86
City Heat '84
Curse of the Pink Panther '83
The Man Who Loved Women '83
Trail of the Pink Panther '82
Victor/Victoria '82
S.O.B. '81
10 '79
Revenge of the Pink Panther '78
Return of the Pink Panther '74
The Tamarind Seed '74
Wild Rovers '71
Darling Lili '70
The Party '68
What Did You Do in the War, Daddy? '66
The Great Race '65
The Pink Panther '64
A Shot in the Dark '64
Soldier in the Rain '63
Operation Petticoat '59
Mister Cory '57
Bring Your Smile Along '55
My Sister Eileen '55

Blake Edwards (1922-)
Son of the Pink Panther '93

Cheryl Edwards
Save the Last Dance '01

Marcus Dunstan
Saw 4 '07
Feast '06

François Dupeyron (1950-)
Monsieur Ibrahim '03

Carl DuPre
Hellraiser: Hellworld '05
Hellraiser: Hellseeker '02
Detroit Rock City '99

Arnaud d'Usseau (1916-90)
Psychomania '73
Horror Express '72
The Man Who Wouldn't Die '42

Robert Duvall (1931-)
Assassination Tango '03
The Apostle '97

Julien Duvivier (1896-1967)
Anna Karenina '48
Pepe Le Moko '37

Jim Dwyer (1970-)
Little Shots of Happiness '97
Frisk '95

H. Kaye Dyal
Trained to Kill '88

Robert Easter (1945-2002)
Kiss Toledo Goodbye '00
Sworn to Justice '97
The Toolbox Murders '78

Christine Edzard (1945-)
Little Dorrit, Film 1: Nobody's Fault '88
Little Dorrit, Film 2: Little Dorrit's Story '88

Atom Egoyan (1960-)
Where the Truth Lies '05
Ararat '02
Felicia's Journey '99
The Sweet Hereafter '96
Exotica '94
Calendar '93
Speaking Parts '89
Family Viewing '87
Next of Kin '84

Kerry Ehrin
Inspector Gadget '99

Max Ehrlich (1909-83)
The Reincarnation of Peter Proud '75

Robert Eisele
The Great Debaters '07

Jo Eisinger (1909-91)
Strike '24
The Rover '67
Crime of Passion '57
Night and the City '50
Gilda '46

Sergei Eisenstein (1898-1948)
Ivan the Terrible, Part 2 '46
Ivan the Terrible, Part 1 '44
Alexander Nevsky '38
Que Viva Mexico '32
Ten Days That Shook the World '27
The Battleship Potemkin '25

Philip Eisner
Firestarter 2: Rekindled '02
Event Horizon '97

Bob Ellis (1942-)
The Wedding Planner '01
Bounty Hunters 2: Hardball '97

Michael Ellis
The Puppet Masters '94
Little Monsters '89

Robert Ellis (1892-)
If I'm Lucky '46
Something for the Boys '44
Hello, Frisco, Hello '43
Iceland '42
Lucky Cisco Kid '40
Tin Pan Alley '40
Charlie Chan in City of Darkness '39
Charlie Chan at the Olympics '37
Charlie Chan at the Circus '36
Charlie Chan at the Race Track '36
Charlie Chan in Egypt '35
Dangerous Appointment '34
A Woman Called Moses '78

Lonnie Elder, III (1926-96)
Bustin' Loose '81

Kevin Elders
Scunder '72
Ravenhawk '95
Iron Eagle 4 '88
Iron Eagle II '88
Iron Eagle '86

Trey Ellis (1962-)
Good Fences '03
The Tuskegee Airmen '95
Cosmic Slop '94
The Inkwell '94

Harlan Ellison
The Oscar '66
Demon with a Glass Hand '64

Paul F. Edwards
Tecumseh: The Last Warrior '55

Harry Elfont (1968-)
Made of Honor '08
Surviving Christmas '04
Josie and the Pussycats '01
The Flintstones in Viva Rock Vegas '00
Can't Hardly Wait '98
A Very Brady Sequel '96

Caroline Ellacheff
Merci pour le Chocolat '00
La Ceremonie '95

Joyce Eliason (1934-)
A Perfect Day '06
Gracie's Choice '04
Blonde '01

Michael Elias (1940-)
No Laughing Matter '97
Lush Life '94
Young Doctors in Love '82
Serial '80
The Jerk '79

Ted Elliott (1961-)
Pirates of the Caribbean: At World's End '07
Pirates of the Caribbean: Dead Man's Chest '06
Pirates of the Caribbean: The Curse of the Black Pearl '03
Shrek '01
The Road to El Dorado '00
The Mask of Zorro '96
Small Soldiers '98
Aladdin '92

Michael Elliot
Brown Sugar '02

Doug Ellin (1968-)
Kissing a Fool '98
Phat Beach '96

Stephan Elliott (1963-)
Eye of the Beholder '99
The Adventures of Priscilla, Queen of the Desert '94
Frauds '93

Samuel G. Engel (1904-84)
My Darling Clementine '46

Richard English (1910-57)
A Thousand and One Nights '45

Don Enright
Spasms '82

Max Enscoe
Blackrock '97
Lorenzo's Oil '92

Nick Enright (1950-2003)
Blackrock '97

Ken Englund (1914-93)
The Secret Life of Walter Mitty '47
Springtime in the Rockies '42

Otto Englander (1906-69)
Fantasia '40
Pinocchio '40
Snow White and the Seven Dwarfs '37

Guy Endore (1900-70)
Captain Sinbad '63
The Story of G. I. Joe '45
Devil Doll '36
Mad Love '36
Mark of the Vampire '35

Cy Endfield (1914-95)
Zulu '64

Roland Emmerich (1955-)
10,000 B.C. '08
Godzilla '98
Independence Day '96
Stargate '94
Ghost Chase '85

Robert Emery
His Picture in the Papers '16

Matt Ember
Get Smart '08
Red Eye '05

Carl Ellsworth
Disturbia '07
Red Eye '05

John Emerson (1874-1956)
Riding the Sunset Trail '41
His Picture in the Papers '16

Toby Emmerich (1963-)
The Last Mimzy '07
Frequency '00

Robert Emmett (1921-)
Gun Packer '38

E.V.H. Emmett (1902-71)
Non-Stop New York '37
Sabotage '36

Frank Encarnacao
A Young Connecticut Yankee in King Arthur's Court '95

Joseph Ellison (1948-)
Joey '85

Ildiko Enyedi (1955-)
Simon the Magician '99
My Twentieth Century '90

Delia Ephron
Bewitched '05
Sisterhood of the Traveling Pants '05
Hanging Up '99
Michael '96
Mixed Nuts '94
This Is My Life '92

Henry Ephron (1911-92)
Desk Set '57
Carousel '56
There's No Business Like Show Business '54
Belles on Their Toes '52
Look for the Silver Lining '49

Nora Ephron (1941-)
Bewitched '05
Hanging Up '99
You've Got Mail '98
Michael '96
Mixed Nuts '94
Sleepless in Seattle '93
This Is My Life '92
My Blue Heaven '90
Cookie '89
When Harry Met Sally... '89
Heartburn '86
Silkwood '83

Phoebe Ephron (1914-71)
Desk Set '57
Carousel '56
There's No Business Like Show Business '54
Belles on Their Toes '52
Look for the Silver Lining '49

Tom Epperson
Jesse Stone: Night Passage '06
Camouflage '00
The Gift '00
A Gun, a Car, a Blonde '97
Don't Look Back '96
A Family Thing '96
One False Move '91

Jack Epps, Jr. (1949-)
The Flintstones in Viva Rock Vegas '00
Anaconda '96
Dick Tracy '90
Turner and Hooch '89
The Secret of My Success '87
Legal Eagles '86
Top Gun '86

Julius J. Epstein (1909-2000)
Reuben, Reuben '83
Cross of Iron '76
Once Is Not Enough '75
Pete 'n' Tillie '72
Any Wednesday '66
Send Me No Flowers '64 •
Fanny '61
Tall Story '60
The Tender Trap '55
Young at Heart '54
Forever Female '53
My Foolish Heart '49
Arsenic and Old Lace '44
Casablanca '42
The Male Animal '42
The Bride Came C.O.D. '41
The Man Who Came to Dinner '41
Strawberry Blonde '41
Four Daughters '38

Philip G. Epstein (1909-52)
The Last Time I Saw Paris '54
Forever Female '53
My Foolish Heart '49
Arsenic and Old Lace '44
Casablanca '42
The Male Animal '42
The Bride Came C.O.D. '41
The Man Who Came to Dinner '41
Strawberry Blonde '41

Greg Erb
Senseless '98
RocketMan '97

Dave Erickson
Murder in Greenwich '02
Power and Beauty '02

Rainer Erler
Nuclear Conspiracy '85
Spare Parts '79

George Erschbamer (1954-)
Bounty Hunters 2: Hardball '97
Bounty Hunters '96
Power of Attorney '94

Patrick Ersgard
Backlash '99
Living in Peril '97

Chester Erskine (1905-86)
All My Sons '48
Midnight '34

John Eskow
The Mask of Zorro '98
Pink Cadillac '89

John Esposito
Russell Mulcahy's Tale of the Mummy '99
Graveyard Shift '90

Harry Essex (1910-97)
Octaman '71
Sons of Katie Elder '65
Creature from the Black Lagoon '54
It Came from Outer Space '53
Kansas City Confidential '52

Howard Estabrook (1884-1978)
Lone Star '52
The Bridge of San Luis Rey '44
International Lady '41
David Copperfield '35
The Bowery '33
Hell's Angels '30

Jacob Aaron Estes
Nearing Grace '05
Mean Creek '04

Emilio Estevez (1962-)
Bobby '06
Men at Work '90
That Was Then... This Is Now '85

Jonathan Estrin
Jasper, Texas '03
Jewels '92

Joe Eszterhas (1944-)
An Alan Smithee Film: Burn, Hollywood, Burn '97
Telling Lies in America '96
Jade '95
Showgirls '95
Nowhere to Run '93
Silver '93
Basic Instinct '92
Checking Out '89
Music Box '89
Betrayed '88
Big Shots '87
Hearts of Fire '87
The Jagged Edge '85
Flashdance '83

Corey Michael Eubanks
Two Bits & Pepper '95
Bigfoot: The Unforgettable Encounter '94
Forced to Kill '93

Rich Eustis
Young Doctors in Love '82
Serial '80

Bruce A. Evans
Mr. Brooks '07
Jungle 2 Jungle '96
Kuffs '92
Made in Heaven '87
Starman '84
A Man, a Woman, and a Bank '79

David Mickey Evans (1962-)
Ed '96
The Sandlot '93

John Evans (1934-)
Black Godfather '74
Speeding Up Time '71

Shelley Evans
Ladykiller '92

Vincent B. Evans
Battle Hymn '57
Chain Lightning '50

Clive Exton (1930-2007)
The Awakening '80
Doomwatch '72
10 Rillington Place '71
Entertaining Mr. Sloane '70
Isadora '68

David Eyre
Pastime '91
Wolfen '81

Richard Eyre (1943-)
Iris '01
King Lear '98

John Eyres
Irish Jam '05
Judge & Jury '96

Diego Fabbri (1911-80)
Generale Della Rovere '60

Nicholas Factor
Hostage Hotel '00
Sabrina the Teenage Witch '96

Roberto Faenza (1943-)
The Bachelor '93
Corrupt '84

Douglas Fairbanks, Sr. (1883-1939)
Mr. Robinson Crusoe '32
The Iron Mask '29
The Black Pirate '26
Robin Hood '22
The Three Musketeers '21
Mark of Zorro '20
The Mollycoddle '20

William Fairchild (1919-2000)
Sound of Murder '82
Star! '68
John and Julie '55
The Gift Horse '52
Morning Departure '50

John Fairley
Premonition '98

Gerald Fairlie (1899-1983)
Conspirator '49
Charlie Chan in Shanghai '35
Jack Ahoy '34

Aleksey Fajko
Aelita: Queen of Mars '24
The Cigarette Girl of Mosselprom '24

David Fallon
White Fang 2: The Myth of the White Wolf '94
White Fang '91

Kevin Falls
Split Decisions '88
Summer Catch '01

Rick Famuyiwa (1973-)
Talk to Me '07
Brown Sugar '02
The Wood '99

Jamaa Fanaka (1942-)
Street Wars '91
Penitentiary 3 '87
Penitentiary 2 '82
Penitentiary '79
Black Sister's Revenge '76
Soul Vengeance '75

Barry Fanaro
I Now Pronounce You Chuck and Larry '07
Men in Black 2 '02
The Crew '00

Hampton Fancher (1938-)
The Minus Man '99
The Mighty Quinn '89
Blade Runner '82

John Fante (1909-83)
Maya '66
Walk on the Wild Side '62
Full of Life '56

Claude Faraldo (1936-)
The Widow of Saint-Pierre '00

Jean-Pol Fargeau
The Intruder '04
Pola X '99

Ernest Farino
Wizards of the Demon Sword '94

Bobby Farrelly (1958-)
The Heartbreak Kid '07
Stuck On You '03
Shallow Hal '01
Me, Myself, and Irene '00
Outside Providence '99
There's Something about Mary '98
Kingpin '96
Dumb & Dumber '94

Peter Farrelly (1957-)
The Heartbreak Kid '07
Stuck On You '03
Shallow Hal '01
Me, Myself, and Irene '00
Outside Providence '99
There's Something about Mary '98
Dumb & Dumber '94

John Farrow (1904-63)
John Paul Jones '59
Around the World in 80 Days '56

John Fasano
Jesse Stone: Stone Cold '05
The Legend of Butch & Sundance '04
Darkness Falls '03
Mean Streak '99
Universal Soldier: The Return '99
The Hunchback '97

Rainer Werner Fassbinder (1946-82)
Chinese Roulette '86
Querelle '83
Berlin Alexanderplatz '80
The Marriage of Maria Braun '79
In a Year of 13 Moons '78
The Stationmaster's Wife '77
Satan's Brew '76
Shadow of Angels '76
Fear of Fear '75
Ali: Fear Eats the Soul '74
Effi Briest '74
Bummer '73
The Bitter Tears of Petra von Kant '72
The Merchant of Four Seasons '71
Beware of a Holy Whore '70
Whity '70
Love Is Colder Than Death '69
Why Does Herr R. Run Amok? '69

Alvin L. Fast
Satan's Cheerleaders '77
Eaten Alive '76

Matthew Faulk
Vanity Fair '04
Jason and the Argonauts '00

William Faulkner (1897-1962)
The Big Sleep '46
The Southerner '45
To Have & Have Not '44
Air Force '43
Gunga Din '39
Today We Live '33

Jon Favreau (1966-)
The First $20 Million Is Always the Hardest '02
Made '01
Swingers '96

Jacqueline Feather
By Dawn's Early Light '00
The King and I '99
Goldrush: A Real Life Alaskan Adventure '98
The Rumor Mill '86

Terence Feely (1928-2000)
The Lady and the Highwayman '89
Destination Moonbase Alpha '75

F.X. Feeney (1953-)
The Big Brass Ring '99
Frankenstein Unbound '90

Jules Feiffer (1929-)
I Want to Go Home '89
Popeye '80
Oh! Calcutta! '72
Carnal Knowledge '71
Little Murders '71

Beda Docampo Feijoo (1948-)
What Your Eyes Don't See '99
The Perfect Husband '92

Steve Feinberg
Fortress 2: Re-Entry '99
Fortress '93
Prime Time '77

Bruce Feirstein (1956-)
The World Is Not Enough '99
Tomorrow Never Dies '97

Dennis Feldman
Virus '98
Species '95
The Golden Child '86

John Feldman (1954-)
Dead Funny '94
Alligator Eyes '90

Jonathan Marc Feldman
From the Earth to the Moon '98
Swing Kids '93

Marty Feldman (1933-82)
In God We Trust '80
The Last Remake of Beau Geste '77

Randy Feldman
The Reading Room '05
Metro '96
Nowhere to Run '93
Tango and Cash '89
Hell Night '81

Federico Fellini (1920-93)
Intervista '87
Ginger & Fred '86
And the Ship Sails On '83
City of Women '81
Orchestra Rehearsal '78
Amarcord '74
Fellini's Roma '72
The Clowns '71
Fellini Satyricon '69
Spirits of the Dead '68
Juliet of the Spirits '65
8 1/2 '63
Boccaccio '70 '62
La Dolce Vita '60
Nights of Cabiria '57
Il Bidone '55
La Strada '54
I Vitelloni '53
The White Sheik '52
Variety Lights '51
The Miracle '48
Paisan '46
Open City '45

Julian Fellowes (1950-)
Vanity Fair '04
Gosford Park '01

Earl Felton (1909-72)
20,000 Leagues under the Sea '54
Armored Car Robbery '50

Andrew J. Fenady (1928-)
The Sea Wolf '93
The Man with Bogart's Face '80
Chisum '70

Pablo F. Fenjves (1956-)
One of Her Own '97
Bloodhounds '96
Bloodhounds 2 '96
Twilight Man '96
The Affair '95
When the Dark Man Calls '94
Bitter Vengeance '94
Out of Annie's Past '94
A Case for Murder '93

Frank Fenton (1906-57)
Garden of Evil '54
River of No Return '54
Escape from Fort Bravo '53
His Kind of Woman '51
Malaya '49

Mark Fergus
Iron Man '08
First Snow '07

Craig Ferguson (1962-)
I'll Be There '03
Saving Grace '00
The Big Tease '99

Larry Ferguson (1940-)
Rollerball '02
Gunfighter's Moon '96
Maximum Risk '96
Beyond the Game '91
Talent for the Game '91
The Hunt for Red October '90
The Presidio '88
Beverly Hills Cop 2 '87
Highlander '86

Abel Ferrara (1952-)
'R Xmas '01
New Rose Hotel '98
The Blackout '97
Bad Lieutenant '92

Davide Ferrario (1956-)
After Midnight '04
Children of Hannibal '98

Will Ferrell (1968-)
Step Brothers '08
Talladega Nights: The Ballad of Ricky Bobby '06
Anchorman: The Legend of Ron Burgundy '04
A Night at the Roxbury '98

Marco Ferreri (1928-97)
Tales of Ordinary Madness '83
La Grande Bouffe '73
Mafioso '62
El Cochecito '60

Linda Ferri
Light of My Eyes '01
The Son's Room '00

Franco Ferrini (1944-)
Sleepless '01
The Church '98
Two Evil Eyes '90
Opera '86
Demons '86
Creepers '85
Once Upon a Time in America '84

Darin Ferriola (1970-)
Mr. Fix It '06
Ivory Tower '97

Michael Ferris (1961-)
Primeval '07
Catwoman '04

Terminator 3: Rise of the Machines '03
The Game '97
Interceptor '92
Into the Sun '92
Mindwarp '91
Femme Fatale '90

Walter Ferris (1882-1965)
At Sword's Point '51
The Little Princess '39
Four Men and a Prayer '38
Heidi '37
Lloyds of London '36
Death Takes a Holiday '34

Giorgio Ferroni (1908-81)
The Lion of Thebes '64
Conquest of Mycene '63
Mill of the Stone Women '60

Jean Ferry (1906-75)
Daughters of Darkness '71
Nana '55

Larry Fessenden (1963-)
Wendigo '01
Habit '97

Michael Fessler
Red Garters '54
Greenwich Village '44

Darrell Fetty
Trouble Bound '92

David Field
Invisible Child '99

Todd Field (1964-)
Little Children '06
In the Bedroom '01

Pat Fielder
Return of Dracula '58
The Monster That Challenged the World '57

Helen Fielding (1958-)
Bridget Jones: The Edge of Reason '04
Bridget Jones's Diary '01

Herbert Fields (1897-1958)
Up in Central Park '48
Honolulu '39
Hands Across the Table '35

Joseph Fields (1895-1966)
The Farmer Takes a Wife '53
A Night in Casablanca '46
Louisiana Purchase '41
Mexican Spitfire '40

W.C. Fields (1879-1946)
Never Give a Sucker an Even Break '41
The Bank Dick '40
My Little Chickadee '40
The Dentist '32
Pool Sharks '15

Harvey Fierstein (1954-)
Common Ground '00
Tidy Endings '88
Torch Song Trilogy '68

Jacques Fieschi
How I Killed My Father '03
Nathalie '03
Les Destinees '00
Sade '00
Place Vendome '98
Nelly et Monsieur Arnaud '95
Un Coeur en Hiver '93
Every Other Weekend '91

Mike Figgis (1948-)
Hotel '01
Time Code '00
The Loss of Sexual Innocence '98
One Night Stand '98
Leaving Las Vegas '95
Lebestraum '91
Stormy Monday '88

Ivan Fila (1956-)
King of Thieves '04
Lea '96

Peter Filardi (1962-)
The Craft '96
Salem's Lot '04

Hal Fimberg (1907-74)
In Like Flint '67
Our Man Flint '66
Big Store '41

Brian Finch (1936-2007)
Goodbye, Mr. Chips '02
Goodnight, Mr. Tom '99

Scot (Scott) Finch
Catlow '71
Shalako '68

Diane Fine
Art Heist '05
Firerap '01

Anthony Fingleton
Swimming Upstream '03
Drop Dead Fred '91

Abem Finkel (1889-1948)
God Is My Co-Pilot '45
Sergeant York '41
Jezebel '38
The Black Legion '37

Fred Finkelhoffe (1910-77)
The Stooge '51
At War with the Army '50
Mr. Ace '46

Melanie Finn
Red Shoe Diaries: Swimming Naked '00

Alan Finney
Lake Consequence '92
Alvin Rides Again '74
Alvin Purple '73

Augusto Finocchi
Hit Men '73
Count Dracula '71
They Paid with Bullets: Chicago 1929 '69
Rattler Kid '68

Odoardo Fiory
Count Dracula '71

Tim Firth (1964-)
Kinky Boots '06
Calendar Girls '03
Blackball '03

Antwone Fisher (1959-)
ATL '06
Antwone Fisher '02

Bob Fisher
Wedding Crashers '05
Eight on the Lam '67
I'll Take Sweden '65
A Global Affair '63

Carrie Fisher (1956-)
These Old Broads '01
Postcards from the Edge '90

Chris Fisher (1973-)
Dirty '05
Rampage: The Hillside Strangler Murders '04
Nightstalker '02

Michael Fisher
The Woman Inside '83
Profile for Murder '96
Brothers in Arms '88

Steve Fisher (1912-80)
On the Run '83
Nowhere to Hide '83
The Hitch-Hiker '53
Sorry, Wrong Number '48

Steve(n) Fisher
Hostile Guns '67
Johnny Reno '66
Terror Street '54
Dead Reckoning '47
I Wake Up Screaming '41
Strangler Murders '04
Taboo '02

Jeffrey Alladin Fiskin
The '60s '99
From the Earth to the Moon '98
Cutter's Way '81
Angel Unchained '70

Benedict Fitzgerald (1949-)
The Passion of the Christ '04

Ed Fitzgerald
Dead Silent '99

F. Scott Fitzgerald (1896-1940)
Three Comrades '38

Thom Fitzgerald (1968-)
The Event '03
Beefcake '99
The Hanging Garden '97

Peter Fitzpatrick
Brilliant Lies '96

Jennifer Flackett
Little Manhattan '05
Madeline '98
Wimbledon '04

Cash Flagg
See Ray Dennis Steckler

Ennio Flaiano (1910-72)
Juliet of the Spirits '65
10th Victim '65
8 1/2 '63
La Dolce Vita '60
Nights of Cabiria '57
Il Bidone '55
La Strada '54
Too Bad She's Bad '54
I Vitelloni '53
The White Sheik '52
Variety Lights '51

Sara Flanigan (1931-2006)
Other Voices, Other Rooms '95
Wildflower '91

Harvey Flaxman (1939-)
Grizzly '76

Hugh Fleetwood
The Bachelor '93

Andrew Fleming (1964-)
The Craft '96
Threesome '94
Bad Dreams '88

R. Lee Fleming, Jr. (1970-)
Get Over It '01
She's All That '99

Lucille Fletcher (1912-2000)
The Hitch-Hiker '53
Sorry, Wrong Number '48

Charlie Fletcher
Mean Machine '01
Fair Game '95

Clive Fleury
Big City Blues '99
Tunnel Vision '95

Richard Flournoy
Chaplin '92
Blondie Goes Latin '42
Blondie's Blessed Event '42
Blondie Has Trouble '40
Blondie On a Budget '40
Blondie Plays Cupid '40
Blondie Brings Up Baby '39
Blondie Meets the Boss '39
Blondie Takes a Vacation '39
Blondie '38

Bryan Forbes (1926-)
The Endless Game '89
The Slipper and the Rose '76
The Chase '66
King Rat '65
The L-Shaped Room '62

George "Buck" Flower (1936-)
Hell's Belles '95

Christian Ford
Merlin's Apprentice '06
Category 7: The End of the World '05
Slow Burn '00

Ladislas Fodor (1899-78)
Apache's Last Battle '64
Strangler of Blackmoor Castle '63
Testament of Dr. Mabuse '62

Dan Fogelman
Cars '06

Lawrence Foldes
Young Warriors '83
Nightstalker '81

Peter Foldy
Nightstalker '81

James Foley (1953-)
Confidence '03
The Chamber '96
Fear '96
Glengarry Glen Ross '92
After Dark, My Sweet '90
Who's That Girl '87
At Close Range '86
Reckless '84

Marcello Fondato (1924-)
Blood and Black Lace '64

Naomi Foner (1946-)
Bee Season '05
Losing Isaiah '94
A Dangerous Woman '93
Running on Empty '88
Violets Are Blue '86

Eddie Ling-Ching Fong (1954-)
Floating Life '95
Erotique '94

Leo Fong (1928-)
Showdown '93
Enforcer from Death Row '78

Tom Fontana
Homicide: The Movie '00

Dennis Foon
Torso '01

Anne Fontaine (1959-)
Nathalie '03
How I Killed My Father '03
Dry Cleaning '97
Augustin '95

Bradbury Foote (1894-1995)
Young Tom Edison '40
Of Human Hearts '38

Horton Foote (1916-)
Of Mice and Men '92
The Habitation of Dragons '91
On Valentine's Day '86
1918 '85
The Trip to Bountiful '85
Tender Mercies '83
Tomorrow '72
The Chase '66
Baby, the Rain Must Fall '64
To Kill a Mockingbird '62

John Taintor Foote (1881-1950)
Great Dan Patch '49
The Mark of Zorro '40

Alyson Fouse
Bring It On: In It to Win It '07
Bring It On: All or Nothing '06

Vincent Fotre
Scary Movie 2 '01
Missile to the Moon '59
Torture Chamber of Baron Blood '72

Dana Fox
What Happens in Vegas '08
The Wedding Date '05

Victoria Foyt
Going Shopping '05
Deja Vu '98
Last Summer in the Hamptons '96
BabyFever '94

Gene Fowler, Sr. (1890-1960)
Billy the Kid '41
Rhythm Romance '39
What Price Hollywood? '32
State's Attorney '31

Bob Fosse (1927-87)
Star 80 '83
All That Jazz '79

Lewis R. Foster (1898-1974)
Never Say Goodbye '46
Can't Help Singing '45
Rhythm Romance '39

Norman Foster (1900-76)
Mr. Moto Takes a Vacation '39
Mysterious Mr. Moto '38
Thank You, Mr. Moto '37
Think Fast, Mr. Moto '37
The Commies Are Coming, the Commies Are Coming '57

Carl Foreman (1914-84)
High Noon '52
MacKenna's Gold '69
The Victors '63
The Guns of Navarone '61
The Key '58
The Bridge on the River Kwai '57
The Clay Pigeon '49
Home of the Brave '49
Champion '49
Cyrano de Bergerac '50
Young Winston '72

Larry Forrester
Tora! Tora! Tora! '70
Hercules and the Princess of Troy '65

Bengt Forslund
The New Land '73
The Emigrants '71

Bill Forsyth (1948-)
Being Human '94
Housekeeping '87
Comfort and Joy '84
Local Hero '83
Gregory's Girl '80
That Sinking Feeling '79

Frederick Forsyth (1938-)
A Casualty of War '90
The Fourth Protocol '87
The Dogs of War '80

Milos Forman (1932-)
Goya's Ghosts '06
The Firemen's Ball '68
Loves of a Blonde '65
Black Peter '63

Garrett Fort (1900-45)
Dracula '31
Frankenstein '31
Dracula's Daughter '36
The Lost Patrol '34
Dracula (Spanish Version) '31

Frederic M. Frank (1911-77)
The Ten Commandments '56

Melvin Frank (1913-88)
A Funny Thing Happened on the Way to the Forum '66
The Facts of Life '60
Strange Bedfellows '65
Above and Beyond '53
Mr. Blandings Builds His Dream House '48
Monsieur Beaucaire '46
The Road to Utopia '46
The Court Jester '56

Scott Frank (1960-)
The Lookout '07
The Interpreter '05
Flight of the Phoenix '04
Minority Report '02
Out of Sight '98
Get Shorty '95
Heaven's Prisoners '95
Dead Again '93
Malice '93
Little Man Tate '91
Plain Clothes '88

Harriet Frank, Jr. (1917-)
Stanley and Iris '90
Murphy's Romance '85
Norma Rae '79
Conrack '74
The Cowboys '72
The Reivers '69
Hombre '67
Hud '63
Home from the Hill '60
The Long, Hot Summer '58
Ten Wanted Men '54
Silver River '48

Debra Frank
The Muppets' Wizard of Oz '05
Mr. St. Nick '02

Dan Franck
La Separation '94

Laurie Frank
Love Crimes '92
Making Mr. Right '86

David Frankel (1960-)
Miami Rhapsody '95

Jess (Jesus) Franco (1930-)
The Separation '93
Ilsa, the Wicked Warden '78
The Demons '74
Zombie Lake '80
Oasis of the Zombies '82
Jack the Ripper '76
Rites of Frankenstein '72
Count Dracula '71
Venus in Furs '70
The Diabolical Dr. Z '65
The Awful Dr. Orloff '62
In 'n' Out '86

Ricardo Franco (1949-98)

Michael France (1962-)
The Punisher '04
Hulk '03
Fantastic Four '05
Goldeneye '95
Cliffhanger '93

Randall Frakes
Instinct to Kill '01
The Force '94
Blowback '99
Roller Blade Warriors: Taken By Force '90

Ron Ford (1958-)
Witchcraft 11: Sisters in Blood '00

Claudio Fragasso (1951-)
Hell of the Living Dead '83
Rats '82

Al Franken (1951-)
Stuart Saves His Family '94
When a Man Loves a Woman '94
One More Saturday Night '86

Carl Franklin (1949-)
Devil in a Blue Dress '95
Eye of the Eagle 3 '91

Howard Franklin
Antitrust '00
The Man Who Knew Too Little '97
The Public Eye '92
Quick Change '90
Someone to Watch Over Me '87
The Name of the Rose '86

Jeff Franklin (1955-)
Love Stinks '99

Richard Franklin (1948-)
Brilliant Lies '96
Sorrento Beach '95

David Franzoni
King Arthur '04
Gladiator '00
Amistad '97
Citizen Cohn '92
Jumpin' Jack Flash '86

Brad Fraser (1959-)
Leaving Metropolis '02
Love and Human Remains '93

George MacDonald Fraser (1925-2008)
The Return of the Musketeers '89
Casanova '87
The Prince and the Pauper '78
The Four Musketeers '75
Royal Flash '75
The Three Musketeers '74

Harry Fraser (1889-1974)
Flaming Bullets '45
Wagon Trail '35
Galloping Romeo '33
Night Rider '32
Texas Pioneers '32

Paul Fraser (1973-)
Once Upon a Time in the Midlands '02
24-7 '97

Riccardo Freda (1909-99)
Double Face '70
The Ghost '63
I, Vampiri '56

Donald Freed
Secret Honor '85

Robert Freedman
Bad Girls '94
Cadillac Man '90

Everett Freeman (1911-91)
The Glass Bottom Boat '66
My Man Godfrey '57
The Secret Life of Walter Mitty '47
The Princess and the Pirate '44

Fred Freeman
The Big Bus '76
Start the Revolution without Me '70

Gillian Freeman (1929-)
The Girl on a Motorcycle '68
The Leather Boys '63

Joan Freeman (1941-)
Uncaged '91

Morgan J. Freeman (1969-)
Desert Blue '98
Hurricane Streets '96

Fred Freiberger (1915-2003)
Beginning of the End '57
Big Chase '54
The Beast from 20,000 Fathoms '53

Jeff Freilich
Naked City: A Killer Christmas '98
Naked City: Justice with a Bullet '89

Robert M. Fresco (1928-)
Dirty Little Secret '98
Evil Has a Face '96
The Monolith Monsters '57
Tarantula '55

Juan Carlos Fresnadillo (1967-)
28 Weeks Later '07
Intacto '01

Bart Freundlich (1970-)
Trust the Man '06
World Traveler '01
The Myth of Fingerprints '97

Ron Fricke
Baraka '93
Koyaanisqatsi '83

Fridrik Thor Fridriksson (1953-)
Children of Nature '91

Jason Friedberg
Meet the Spartans '08
Epic Movie '07
Date Movie '06
Spy Hard '96

Richard Friedenberg
Snow in August '01
The Education of Little Tree '97
Mr. & Mrs. Loving '95
A River Runs Through It '92
Dying Young '91

William Friedkin (1939-)
The Guardian '90
Rampage '87
To Live & Die in L.A. '85
Cruising '80

Brent Friedman (1962-)
H.P. Lovecraft's Necronomicon: Book of the Dead '93

Josh Friedman
The Black Dahlia '06

Ken Friedman
Made in USA '88
Heart Like a Wheel '83
White Line Fever '75

Ron J. Friedman
Chicken Little '05
Brother Bear '03

Ketti Frings (1909-81)
Because of You '52
Guest in the House '44

James Fritzell (1920-79)
The Shakiest Gun in the West '68
The Reluctant Astronaut '67
The Ghost and Mr. Chicken '66
Good Neighbor Sam '64

George Froeschel (1891-1979)
Me and the Colonel '58
Never Let Me Go '53
The Miniver Story '50
Command Decision '48
The White Cliffs of Dover '44
Mrs. Miniver '42
Random Harvest '42
The Mortal Storm '40
Waterloo Bridge '40

Pea Frolich
Veronika Voss '82
The Marriage of Maria Braun '79

Lee Frost (1935-2007)
Private Obsession '94
Dixie Dynamite '76
Black Gestapo '75
Race with the Devil '75
Love Desperados '68

Mark Frost (1953-)
Fantastic Four: Rise of the Silver Surfer '07
Fantastic Four '05

Roy Frumkes
The Substitute 3: Winner Takes All '99
The Substitute 2: School's Out '97
The Substitute '96
Street Trash '87

Christopher Fry (1907-2005)
The Lady's Not for Burning '87
The Brontës of Haworth '73
The Bible '66
Barabbas '62

E. Max Frye
Band of Brothers '01
Where the Money Is '00
Palmetto '98
Amos and Andrew '93
Something Wild '86

Carol Fuchs
No Reservations '07

Daniel Fuchs (1909-93)
The Underneath '95
Storm Warning '51
Criss Cross '48

Robert Fuest (1927-)
The Final Programme '73
Doctor Phibes Rises Again '72

Kinji Fukasaku (1930-2003)
Samurai Reincarnation '81
Under the Flag of the Rising Sun '72
Sympathy for the Underdog '71

Lucio Fulci (1927-96)
Wax Mask '97
Demonia '90
The Beyond '82
New York Ripper '82
The Black Cat '81
Gates of Hell '80
Don't Torture a Duckling '72
A Lizard in a Woman's Skin '71
The House by the Cemetery '83

Charles Fuller (1939-)
Love Songs '99
Zooman '95
A Soldier's Story '84

David Fuller
Gang in Blue '96
Necessary Roughness '91

Kim Fuller
From Justin to Kelly '03
High Heels and Low Lifes '01
Spice World: The Movie '97

Samuel Fuller (1911-97)
Girls in Prison '94
Let's Get Harry '87
The Big Red One '80
The Klansman '74
Dead Pigeon on Beethoven Street '72
Shark! '68
Naked Kiss '64
Shock Corridor '63
Merrill's Marauders '62
Underworld, U.S.A. '60
Verboten! '59
China Gate '57
Forty Guns '57
Run of the Arrow '56
Pickup on South Street '53
Baron of Arizona '51
Fixed Bayonets! '51
The Steel Helmet '51
I Shot Jesse James '49

Jules Furthman (1888-1966)
Rio Bravo '59
Nightmare Alley '47
The Big Sleep '46
To Have & Have Not '44
The Outlaw '43
Only Angels Have Wings '39
Spawn of the North '38
Come and Get It '36
China Seas '35
Mutiny on the Bounty '35
Shanghai Express '32

Sidney J. Furie (1933-)
The Taking of Beverly Hills '91
Iron Eagle 2 '88
Iron Eagle '86
Purple Hearts '84
The Boys in Company C '77
A Dangerous Age '57

John Fusco
Hidalgo '04
Spirit: Stallion of the Cimarron '02
Loch Ness '95
Young Guns 2 '90
Young Guns '88
Crossroads '86

Richard Gabai (1964-)
Assault of the Party Nerds 2: Heavy Petting '95
Virgin High '90

Frank Gabrielson
Something for the Boys '44

Antonio Gades (1936-2004)
Carmen '83
Blood Wedding '81

Reg Gadney
The Sculptress '97
Goldeneye: The Secret Life of Ian Fleming '89

Christos N. Gage
The Breed '01
Teenage Caveman '01

Stephen Gaghan (1965-)
Syriana '05
The Alamo '04
Abandon '02
Rules of Engagement '00
Traffic '00

Neil Gaiman (1960-)
Beowulf '07
MirrorMask '05
Princess Mononoke '98
Neil Gaiman's NeverWhere '96

Bob Gale (1951-)
Interstate 60 '02
Trespass '92
Back to the Future, Part 3 '90
Back to the Future, Part 2 '89
Back to the Future '85
Used Cars '80
1941 '79

Henrik Galeen (1881-1949)
Waxworks '24
Nosferatu '22
The Golem '20

John A. Gallagher
Blue Moon '00
The Deli '97
Beach House '82

George Gallo (1956-)
Code Name: The Cleaner '07
The Whole Ten Yards '04
Double Take '01
See Spot Run '01
Trapped in Paradise '94
29th Street '91
Midnight Run '88

Vincent Gallo (1961-)
The Brown Bunny '03
Buffalo 66 '97

Kenneth Gamet (1903-71)
A Lawless Street '55
Flying Leathernecks '51
Man in the Saddle '51
Santa Fe '51
Coroner Creek '48
Pittsburgh '42

Abel Gance (1889-1981)
Beethoven '36
Napoleon '27
The Torture of Silence '17

Paul Gangelin (1898-1961)
Son of God's Country '48
The Mad Ghoul '43
Junior Army '42

Brad Gann
Black Irish '07
Invincible '06

Ernest K. Gann (1910-91)
Soldier of Fortune '55
The High and the Mighty '54
Island in the Sky '53

Christophe Gans (1960-)
Brotherhood of the Wolf '01
H.P. Lovecraft's Necronomicon: Book of the Dead '93

Lowell Ganz (1948-)
Fever Pitch '05
Robots '05
Where the Heart Is '00
EDtv '99
Father's Day '96
Multiplicity '96
Forget Paris '95
City Slickers 2: The Legend of Curly's Gold '94
Greedy '94
A League of Their Own '92
Mr. Saturday Night '92
City Slickers '91
Parenthood '89
Vibes '88
Gung Ho '85
Spies Like Us '85
Splash '84
Night Shift '82

Robert Ben Garant (1970-)
Balls of Fury '07
Reno 911!: Miami '07
Let's Go to Prison '06
Night at the Museum '06
Herbie: Fully Loaded '05
The Pacifier '05

Nicole Garcia (1946-)
Place Vendome '98
The Favorite Son '94
Every Other Weekend '91

Rodrigo Garcia (1959-)
Nine Lives '05
Things You Can Tell Just by Looking at Her '00

Gabriel Garcia Marquez (1927-)
The Fable of the Beautiful Pigeon Fancier '88
Letters from the Park '88
Miracle in Rome '88
Erendira '83
Mary, My Dearest '83

Yolanda Garcia Serrano (1958-)
Km. 0 '00
Between Your Legs '99
Amor de Hombre '97

Louis Gardel
East-West '99
Indochine '92
Fort Saganne '84

Eric Gardner
Race to Space '01
Breakaway '95

Herb Gardner (1934-2003)
I'm Not Rappaport '96
The Goodbye People '83
A Thousand Clowns '65

Pierce Gardner
Dan in Real Life '07
Lost Souls '00

Richard Harding Gardner (1949-)
Sherlock: Undercover Dog '94
Deadly Daphne's Revenge '93

Louis Garfinkle (1928-2005)
The Deer Hunter '78
I Bury the Living '58

Alex Garland (1970-)
Sunshine '07
The Tesseract '03
28 Days Later '02

Robert Garland
No Way Out '87
The Electric Horseman '79

Helen Garner (1942-)
The Last Days of Chez Nous '92
Two Friends '86

Tony Garnett (1936-)
Fat Man and Little Boy '89
Deep in the Heart '83

David Garrett
Deuce Bigalow: European Gigolo '05
Corky Romano '01

Oliver H.P. Garrett (1894-1952)
Dead Reckoning '47
Duel in the Sun '46
The Hurricane '37
Manhattan Melodrama '34
Night Flight '33
A Farewell to Arms '32

Mick Garris (1951-)
Riding the Bullet '04
Quicksilver Highway '98
Hocus Pocus '93
The Fly 2 '89
Critters 2: The Main Course '88

Harold Gast (1918-2003)
The Jesse Owens Story '84
A Woman Called Golda '82
From Here to Eternity '79

Ernesto Gastaldi (1934-)
The Sicilian Connection '85
Scorpion with Two Tails '82
The Great Alligator '81
Lady of the Evening '75
The Grand Duel '73
Torso '73
The Case of the Bloody Iris '72
Your Vice is a Closed Room and Only I Have the Key '72
The Scorpion's Tail '71
Blade of the Ripper '70
Giants of Rome '63
The Whip and the Body '63

Venus Against the Son of Hercules '62

Harvey Gates (1894-1948)
Mr. Muggs Rides Again '45
Clancy Street Boys '43
Zis Boom Bah '41
Badmen of Nevada '33

Tudor Gates (1930-2007)
Fright '71
Lust for a Vampire '71
Twins of Evil '71
The Vampire Lovers '70
Barbarella '68
Danger: Diabolik '68

John Gatins
Coach Carter '05
Dreamer: Inspired by a True Story '05
Hardball '01
Summer Catch '01

Tony Gatlif (1948-)
The Crazy Stranger '98
Mondo '96

Nate Gatzert (1890-1959)
The Fiddlin' Buckaroo '33
Trail Drive '33

Emile Gaudreault (1964-)
Mambo Italiano '03

Peter Gaulke
King of the Airwaves '94

John Gay (1924-)
Luther '03
Final Notice '89
'86
Fatal Vision '84
A Tale of Two Cities '80
Run Silent, Run Deep '58
Sometimes a Great Notion '71
Soldier Blue '70
No Way to Treat a Lady '68
The Last Safari '67
The Hallelujah Trail '65
The Courtship of Eddie's Father '62
The Four Horsemen of the Apocalypse '62

Cabo Blanco '81

Erwin Gelsey (1900-88)
Double or Nothing '37
Scarlet Dawn '32

Pierre Gendron (1896-1956)
Fog Island '45
Bluebeard '44
The Monster Maker '44
Louvain '32

Jonathan Gems
The Treat '98
Mars Attacks! '96

Michael Genet (1958-)
Talk to Me '07
She Hate Me '04

Robert Geoffrion
The Peacekeeper '98

Dean Georgaris
Tristan & Isolde '06
Lara Croft Tomb Raider: The Cradle of Life '03
Paycheck '03

Nelson George
Life Support '07
CB4: The Movie '93

Terry George (1952-)
Hart's War '02
A Bright Shining Lie '98
The Boxer '97
Some Mother's Son '96
In the Name of the Father '93

Gerald Geraghty (1906-54)
Phantom Stallion '54
Iron Mountain Trail '53
Shadows of Tombstone '53
Sunset in the West '50
Trigger, Jr. '50
Rainbow over Texas '46
Along the Navaho Trail '45
Carson City Kid '40
In Old Caliente '39
South of the Border '39
Southward Ho! '39
Wall Street Cowboy '39
Come on Rangers '38

Bart Gavigan
End of the Spear '06

Gary Gerani
Vampirella '96
Pumpkinhead '88

Pietro Germi (1904-74)
Alfredo, Alfredo '72
Seduced and Abandoned '64

Eleanor Gaver
Dead in the Water '91
Slipping into Darkness '88

Maurice Geraghty (1908-87)
Mohawk '56
Tomahawk '51
Who Killed Doc Robbin? '48

Gregory Gieras
Centipede '05
Dark Asylum '01

Adam Gierasch
Crocodile '00
Crocodile 2: Death Swamp '01

Lewis Gilbert (1920-)
The Sea Inside '04
Open Your Eyes '97
Thesis '96

Mateo Gil (1972-)
Panic '89
Iguana '89

Jaime Comas Gil
Hotel Room '93
Lost Highway '96

Barry Gifford (1946-)
Dance with the Devil '97
City of Ghosts '03
Mad Money '08
Fracture '07
Brother's Keeper '02
Off Season '01

Glen Gers
Mississippi Burning '88
Miles from Home '88

Chris Gerolmo
Citizen X '95

A lice Doesn't Live Here Anymore '74

Steven Gethers (1922-89)
Jenny's War '85
A Woman Called Golda '82

Bahman Ghobadi (1968-)
Turtles Can Fly '04
Marooned in Iraq '02

Robert Gianviti
Don't Torture a Duckling '72
A Lizard in a Woman's Skin '71

Duncan Gibbins
Eve of Destruction '90

Rodney Gibbons
Captive '97

Alex Gibney
Taxi to the Dark Side '07
Enron: The Smartest Guys in the Room '05

Stuart Gibbs (1969-)
Repli-Kate '01

Mel Gibson (1956-)
The Passion of the Christ '04

Channing Gibson
Walking Tall '04
Lethal Weapon 4 '98

Mark Gibson
The Wild '06
Snow Dogs '02

John Gilling (1912-85)
The Mummy's Shroud '67
The Gorgon '64
The Flesh and the Fiends '60

Rob Gilmer
Out of Time '00

Dan Gilroy (1959-)
Two for the Money '05
Chasers '94
Freejack '92

Tom Gilroy
Spring Forward '99

Tony Gilroy (1956-)
The Bourne Ultimatum '07
Michael Clayton '07
The Bourne Supremacy '04
Proof of Life '00
The Devil's Advocate '97
Dolores Claiborne '95
The Cutting Edge '92
For Better and for Worse '92

Frank D. Gilroy (1925-)
The Gig '85
Once in Paris... '79
From Noon Till Three '76
Desperate Characters '71
The Subject Was Roses '68
The Gallant Hours '60
Fastest Gun Alive '56

Milton Moses Ginsberg (1943-)
Werewolf of Washington '73
Coming Apart '69

Mario Giordano
The Experiment '01

Buddy Giovinazzo (1957-)
No Way Home '96
Combat Shock '84

The Parallax View '74
Myra Breckinridge '70

David Giles
Paradise Road '97
Under the Lighthouse Dancing '97

Terry Gilliam (1940-)
Tideland '05
Fear and Loathing in Las Vegas '98
The Adventures of Baron Munchausen '89
Brazil '85
Monty Python's The Meaning of Life '83
Time Bandits '81
Monty Python's Life of Brian '79
Jabberwocky '77
Monty Python and the Holy Grail '75
And Now for Something Completely Different '72

Sidney Gilliat (1908-94)
Endless Night '71
The Belles of St. Trinian's '53
Night Train to Munich '40
The Lady Vanishes '38

Stuart Gilliard (1950-)
Gould '93

Vince Gilligan (1967-)
Hancock '08
Home Fries '98
Wilder Napalm '93

Amos Gitai (1950-)
Free Zone '05
Kippur '00
Kadosh '99

Richard Glatzer
Quinceanera '06
Grief '94

Benjamin Glazer (1887-1956)
A Farewell to Arms '32
Beggars of Life '28

Mitch Glazer
Running Against Time '90
The Day My Parents Ran Away '93
The Recruit '03
Great Expectations '97
Scrooged '88
Mr. Mike's Mondo Video '79

David Gleeson
The Front Line '06
Cowboys & Angels '04

Tom Gleisner
The Dish '00
The Castle '97

James Glickenhaus (1950-)
McBain '91
Shakedown '88
Exterminator '80

Greg Glienna (1963-)
Relative Strangers '06

Jean-Luc Godard (1930-)
Our Music '04
In Praise of Love '01
For Ever Mozart '96
Helas pour Moi '94
Nouvelle Vague '90
Aria '88
Hail Mary '85
Passion '82

Francois Girard (1954-)
Silk '07
The Red Violin '98
32 Short Films about Glenn Gould '93

Michael Paul Girard
Bikini Med School '98
Sweet Evil '98
Bikini House Calls '96
Illegal Affairs '96
The Perfect Gift '95
Body Parts '94

William Girdler (1947-78)
The Manitou '78
Sheba, Baby '75
Grizzly '76
Asylum of Satan '72
Three on a Meathook '72

Marino Girolami (1914-94)
White Heat '49

Francis Girod (1944-)
Transfixed '01
The Elegant Criminal '92
You've Got to Have Heart '77

Menahem Golan (1929-)
Hanna's War '88
The Apple '80
Lepke '75

Michael Goldberg
Harry Potter and the Order of the Phoenix '07
Snow Dogs '02
Bushwhacked '95
Little Giants '94
Cool Runnings '93

Kenny Golde
The Job '03

Dan Golden
The Smokers '00
Venomous '01

Bernard Girard (1918-97)
Dead Heat on a Merry-Go-Round '66
A Public Affair '62
The Rebel Set '59

Francois Giroud
Where the Hot Wind Blows '59

Sandra Goldbacher
The Governess '98
Me Without You '01

Dan Goldberg
Feds '88
Heavy Metal '81

Evan Goldberg (1972-)
Superbad '07
Pineapple Express '08

Brent Goldberg
Deuce Bigalow: Male Gigolo '99

Gary David Goldberg (1944-)
Must Love Dogs '05
Bye Bye, Love '94
Dad '89

Howard Goldberg
Eden '98

Marshall Goldberg
Where the Truth Lies '99

Numero Deux '75
Six in Paris '68
Oldest Profession '67
Weekend '67
Two or Three Things I Know about Her '66
Alphaville '65
The Joy of Knowledge '65
A Married Woman '65
Band of Outsiders '64
Contempt '64
Les Carabiniers '63
RoGoPaG '62
My Life to Live '62
Le Petit Soldat '61
A Woman Is a Woman '60
Breathless '59
Legend of the Lone Ranger '81

Golden

Wizards of the Demon Sword '94

Ray Golden (1906-87)
Big Store '41
Argentine Nights '40

Jeffrey Goldenberg
Blowback '99
Looking for an Echo '99

Jorge Goldenberg
I Don't Want to Talk About It '94
Eversmile New Jersey '89
Miss Mary '86

Michael Goldenberg (1965-)
Peter Pan '03
Contact '97
Bed of Roses '95

Marilyn Goldin
The Triumph of Love '01
Camille Claudel '89
Barocco '76

Bo Goldman (1932-)
Meet Joe Black '98
City Hall '95
Scent of a Woman '92
Little Nikita '88
Swing Shift '84
Shoot the Moon '82
Melvin and Howard '80
One Flew Over the Cuckoo's Nest '75

Gary Goldman (1944-)
Next '07
Navy SEALS '90
Total Recall '90
Big Trouble in Little China '86

James Goldman (1927-98)
The Lion in Winter '03
Anastasia: The Mystery of Anna '86
Oliver Twist '82
Nicholas and Alexandra '71
They Might Be Giants '71
The Lion in Winter '68

William Goldman (1931-)
Dreamcatcher '03
Hearts in Atlantis '01
The General's Daughter '99
Absolute Power '97
The Chamber '96
The Ghost and the Darkness '96
Maverick '94
Chaplin '92
Year of the Comet '92
Misery '90
Casual Sex? '88
Heat '87
The Princess Bride '87
Mr. Horn '79
Magic '78
A Bridge Too Far '77
All the President's Men '76
Marathon Man '76
The Great Waldo Pepper '75
The Stepford Wives '75
Butch Cassidy and the Sundance Kid '69
Harper '66

Akiva Goldsman (1963-)
I Am Legend '07
The Da Vinci Code '06
Cinderella Man '05
I, Robot '04
A Beautiful Mind '01
Lost in Space '98
Batman and Robin '97
A Time to Kill '96
Batman Forever '95
The Client '94
Silent Fall '94

John Goldsmith
The Gospel of John '03
Victoria & Albert '01
Agnes Browne '99
Coming Home '98
The Apocalypse Watch '97
The Island on Bird Street '97
Catherine the Great '95
Kidnapped '95
The Old Curiosity Shop '94

Josh Goldsmith (1970-)
13 Going on 30 '04
What Women Want '00

Martin Goldsmith
The Gunfight at Dodge City '59
Detour '46

Allan Goldstein
Snakeman '05
Jungle Boy '96
Death Wish 5: The Face of Death '94
Rooftops '89

Mark Goldstein
Pet Shop '94
Prehistory '93

Bob(cat) Goldthwait (1962-)
Sleeping Dogs Lie '06
Shakes the Clown '92

Larry Golin
Rocky Marciano '99
Hostage High '97
Love Walked In '97
Rebound: The Legend of Earl "The Goat" Manigault '96
Final Combination '93

Bryan Goluboff
The Affair '95
The Basketball Diaries '95

Sy Gomberg (1918-2001)
Three Warriors '77
Bloodhounds of Broadway '52

Michel Gondry (1963-)
Be Kind Rewind '08
The Science of Sleep '06
Eternal Sunshine of the Spotless Mind '04

Nick Gomez (1963-)
Illtown '96
New Jersey Drive '95
Laws of Gravity '92

Manuel Gomez Pereira (1958-)
Between Your Legs '99
Love Can Seriously Damage Your Health '96
Mouth to Mouth '95
Why Do They Call It Love When They Mean Sex? '92

Noam Gonick (1973-)
Stryker '04
Hey, Happy! '01

Reuben Gonzalez
Once Upon a Wedding '05
Mambo Cafe '00

Gregory Goodell
Don't Look Down '98
My Brother's Keeper '95
Shattered Spirits '86

William Goodhart (1925-99)
Cloud Dancer '80
The Exorcist 2: The Heretic '77
Generation '69

J. Mills Goodloe
Pride '07

David Zelag Goodman
Monte Walsh '03
Fighting Back '82
Eyes of Laura Mars '78
March or Die '77
Logan's Run '76
Farewell, My Lovely '75
Straw Dogs '72
Lovers and Other Strangers '70
Monte Walsh '70

Frances Goodrich (1890-1984)
The Long, Long Trailer '54
Seven Brides for Seven Brothers '54
Father's Little Dividend '51
Father of the Bride '50
Easter Parade '48
It's a Wonderful Life '46
The Virginian '46
The Thin Man '34

Alex Gordon (1922-2003)
Bride of the Monster '55
Jail Bait '54

Bernard Gordon (1918-2007)
The Thin Red Line '64
Day of the Triffids '63
Hellcats of the Navy '57
Earth vs. the Flying Saucers '56
Crime Wave '54
The Lawless Breed '52

Bert I. Gordon (1922-)
Empire of the Ants '77
The Witching '72
Tormented '60
The Amazing Colossal Man '57
King Dinosaur '55

Bryan Gordon
Pie in the Sky '95
The Discovery Program '89

Dan Gordon
The Celestine Prophecy '06
The Hurricane '99
Murder in the First '95
New Eden '94
Wyatt Earp '94
Surf Ninjas '93
Taking the Heat '93
Highlander: The Gathering '93
Passenger 57 '92
Gotcha! '85
Tank '83

Keith Gordon (1961-)
A Midnight Clear '92
The Chocolate War '88
Static '87

Leo Gordon (1922-2000)
The Terror '63
Tower of London '62
Attack of the Giant Leeches '59
The Wasp Woman '59

Leon Gordon (1894-1960)
White Cargo '42
They Met in Bombay '41
Balalaika '39
Gulliver's Travels '39
Tarzan and His Mate '34
Freaks '32

Richard Gordon
Death by Prescription '86
The Lion Man '36

Robert Gordon
Lemony Snicket's A Series of Unfortunate Events '04
Men in Black 2 '02
Galaxy Quest '99
Addicted to Love '96

Rose Gordon
Coyote Trails '35
Kentucky Blue Streak '35
Silent Valley '35

Ruth Gordon (1896-1985)
Hardhat & Legs '80
It Should Happen to You '54
The Marrying Kind '52
Pat and Mike '52
Adam's Rib '50
A Double Life '47

Stuart Gordon (1947-)
The Dentist '96
Body Snatchers '93
Honey, I Shrunk the Kids '89
Re-Animator '84

Laszlo Gorog (1903-97)
Earth vs. the Spider '58
The Land Unknown '57
The Mole People '56

Marleen Gorris (1948-)
Antonia's Line '95
Broken Mirrors '85

Rene Goscinny
Lucky Luke '94
The Holes '72

Carl Gottlieb (1938-)
Doctor Detroit '83
Jaws 3 '83
Caveman '81
The Jerk '79
Jaws 2 '78
Which Way Is Up? '77
Jaws '75

Alfred Gough (1967-)
The Mummy: Tomb of the Dragon Emperor '08
Herbie: Fully Loaded '05
Spider-Man 2 '04
Shanghai Knights '03
Showtime '02
Shanghai Noon '00

Heywood Gould
Double Bang '01
Mistrial '96
Trial by Jury '94
One Good Cop '91
Cocktail '88
Streets of Gold '86
Fort Apache, the Bronx '81
The Boys from Brazil '78
Rolling Thunder '77

Peter Gould
Meeting Daddy '98
Double Dragon '94

Edmund Goulding (1891-1959)
That Certain Woman '37
Riptide '34
No Man of Her Own '32
Tol'able David '21

David S. Goyer (1965-)
Jumper '08
Batman Begins '05
Blade: Trinity '04
Blade 2 '02
ZigZag '02
Blade '98
The Crow 2: City of Angels '96
The Puppet Masters '94
Arcade '93

Jean-Francois Goyet
Western '96
La Vengeance d'une Femme '89

Todd Graff (1959-)
Camp '03
Coyote Ugly '00
The Beautician and the Beast '97
Angie '94
Fly by Night '93
The Vanishing '93
Used People '92

Benoit Graffin
Priceless '06
Apres-Vous '03

Sue Grafton (1940-)
Agatha Christie's A Caribbean Mystery '83
Agatha Christie's Sparkling Cyanide '83

Bruce Graham
Steal This Movie! '00
Anastasia '97
Dunston Checks In '95

Ronny Graham (1919-99)
Spaceballs '87
Finders Keepers '84
To Be or Not to Be '83

Michael Grais
Cool World '92
Marked for Death '90
Poltergeist 2: The Other Side '86
Poltergeist '82
Death Hunt '81

Jean-Christophe Grange (1961-)
Crimson Rivers 2: Angels of the Apocalypse '05
The Crimson Rivers '01

Derek Granger
Where Angels Fear to Tread '91
A Handful of Dust '88

Pierre Granier-Deferre (1927-2007)
A Woman at Her Window '77
The Last Train '74

James Edward Grant (1905-66)
Support Your Local Gunfighter '71
Circus World '64
Donovan's Reef '63
McLintock! '63
The Alamo '60
Three Violent People '57
Hondo '53
Flying Leathernecks '51
Sands of Iwo Jima '49
Angel and the Badman '47
Gambler's Choice '44
Johnny Eager '42
The Lady is Willing '42

John Grant (1891-1955)
Abbott and Costello Meet the Mummy '55
Abbott and Costello Meet the Keystone Kops '54
Abbott and Costello Go to Mars '53
Abbott and Costello Meet Dr. Jekyll and Mr. Hyde '52
Ma and Pa Kettle at the Fair '52
Abbott and Costello Meet the Invisible Man '51
Comin' 'Round the Mountain '51
Abbott and Costello in the Foreign Legion '50
Abbott and Costello Meet the Killer, Boris Karloff '49
Abbott and Costello Meet Frankenstein '48
Buck Privates Come Home '47
Here Come the Co-Eds '45
In Society '44
It Ain't Hay '43
Buck Privates '41
Hold That Ghost '41
In the Navy '41

Susannah Grant (1963-)
Catch and Release '07
Charlotte's Web '06
In Her Shoes '05
Erin Brockovich '00
28 Days '00
Ever After: A Cinderella Story '98
Pocahontas '95

Robert Grasmere
Baby Geniuses '98
A Million to Juan '94

Alex Graves
Casualties '97
The Crude Oasis '95

Beverly Gray
Haunted Symphony '94
Full Contact '93

James Gray (1969-)
We Own the Night '07
The Yards '00
Little Odessa '94

John Gray
Brian's Song '01
The Seventh Stream '01
The Hunley '99
An American Story '92
Showdown at Williams Creek '91
The Lost Capone '90
Billy Galvin '86

Mike Gray
Code of Silence '85
Wavelength '83
The China Syndrome '79

Pamela Gray
Music of the Heart '99
A Walk on the Moon '99
Calm at Sunset '96

Simon Gray (1936-)
Unnatural Pursuits '91
A Month in the Country '87

William Gray
Humongous '82
The Changeling '80
Prom Night '80

Charles Grayson (1903-73)
Battle Hymn '57
Outpost in Morocco '49
Underground '41
One Night in the Tropics '40

Brian Grazer (1951-)
Housesitter '92
Armed and Dangerous '86

Claudio Grazioso
Are We There Yet? '05
Bring It On Again '03

Kjell Grede (1936-)
Good Evening, Mr. Wallenberg '93
Hip Hip Hurrah! '87

Adolph Green (1915-2002)
Bells Are Ringing '60
Auntie Mame '58
It's Always Fair Weather '55
Singin' in the Rain '52
The Barkleys of Broadway '49
On the Town '49

Clifford Green
Bless the Child '00
Mystery Island '81
Picnic at Hanging Rock '75

David Gordon Green (1975-)
Snow Angels '07
Undertow '04
All the Real Girls '03

Howard J. Green (1893-1965)
Having Wonderful Crime '45
Take It Big '44
Harmon of Michigan '41
They Met in a Taxi '36
Blessed Event '32
I Am a Fugitive from a Chain Gang '32
They Call It Sin '32
Maker of Men '31

Lewis Green
Never Talk to Strangers '95
Dead on Sight '94
The Spy Within '94

Paul Green
Doctor Bull '33

Terry Green
Heavens Fall '06
Cold Justice '89

Walon Green (1936-)
The Hi-Lo Country '98
Eraser '96
RoboCop2 '90
Crusoe '89
Solarbabies '86
The Border '82
Brink's Job '78
The Wild Bunch '69
Sorcerer '77

Peter Greenaway (1942-)
8 1/2 Women '99
The Pillow Book '95
The Belly of an Architect '91
Prospero's Books '91
The Cook, the Thief, His Wife & Her Lover '90
A Zed & Two Noughts '88
Drowning by Numbers '87
The Draughtsman's Contract '82

Everett Greenbaum (1920-99)
The Shakiest Gun in the West '68
Good Neighbor Sam '64

Dan Greenberg
The Guardian '90
Oh! Calcutta! '72

Matt Greenberg
1408 '07
Reign of Fire '02
Halloween: H20 '98
The Prophecy 2: Ashtown '97

Stanley R. Greenberg (1928-2002)
Soylent Green '73

Anthony Laurence Greene
Dead Sexy '01
Number One Fan '94

Graham Greene (1904-91)
The Comedians '67
Our Man in Havana '59
Saint Joan '57
The Fallen Idol '49
The Third Man '49
Brighton Rock '47
21 Days '37

Clarence Greene (1913-95)
The Oscar '66
D.O.A. '49

Harold Greene (1915-2000)
Texas Across the River '66
Kansas City Confidential '52
The House of the Seven Gables '40

Paul Greengrass (1955-)
United 93 '06
Bloody Sunday '01
The Murder of Stephen Lawrence '99
The One That Got Away '96

Seth Greenland
My Teacher's Wife '95
Who's the Man? '93

Maggie Greenwald (1955-)
Songcatcher '99
The Ballad of Little Jo '93

Edwin Greenwood (1895-1939)
Young and Innocent '37
The Man Who Knew Too Much '34

James Greer
Larry the Cable Guy: Health Inspector '05
Max Keeble's Big Move '01

William Grefe (1930-)
The Hooked Generation '69
The Death Curse of Tartu '66

Andre Gregory (1934-)
Vanya on 42nd Street '94
My Dinner with Andre '81

Nick Gregory
DOA: Dead or Alive '06
Devour '05

Jerry Gross (1940-2002)
Teenage Mother '67
Girl on a Chain Gang '65

Tom Gries (1922-77)
Will Penny '67

Maurice Griffe
King Dinosaur '55

Ted Griffin (1970-)
Matchstick Men '03
Ocean's Eleven '01
Best Laid Plans '99
Ravenous '99

Charles B. Griffith (1930-2007)
Not of This Earth '88
Dr. Heckyl and Mr. Hype '80
Death Race 2000 '75
Eat My Dust '76
Devil's Angels '67
The Wild Angels '66
Atlas '60
The Beast from Haunted Cave '60
Creature from the Haunted Sea '60
Little Shop of Horrors '60
Ski Troop Attack '60
A Bucket of Blood '59
Rock All Night '57
Teenage Doll '57
The Undead '57
The Gunslinger '56
It Conquered the World '56

D.W. Griffith (1875-1948)
Struggle '31
Isn't Life Wonderful '24
Orphans of the Storm '21
The Love Flower '20
Way Down East '20
Broken Blossoms '19
Hoodoo Ann '16
Intolerance '16
The Birth of a Nation '15
Judith of Bethulia '14

Thomas Ian Griffith (1962-)
Excessive Force '93

David Griffiths (1952-)
The Hunted '03

Leon Griffiths (1928-92)
Piece of Cake '88

Peter Griffiths (1950-)
The Hunted '03
The Grissom Gang '71
The Flesh and the Fiends '60

Trevor Griffiths (1935-)
Singing the Blues in Red '87
The Last Place on Earth '85

Aurelio Grimaldi (1957-)
Nerolio '96
Acla's Descent into Floristella '92

Maria Grimm
November Conspiracy '96
The Feminine Touch '95

Christopher Grimm
Heartbreakers '01

Tony Grisoni
Tideland '05
Brothers of the Head '06
In This World '03
Fear and Loathing in Las Vegas '98

Adam Gross
DOA: Dead or Alive '06

Joel Gross
No Escape '94

Larry Gross (1953-)
The Beautiful Country '04
We Don't Live Here Anymore '04
Crime and Punishment in Suburbia '00
True Crime '99
The Virginian '99
Gunshy '99
Rear Window '98
Chinese Box '97
David '97
This World, Then the Fireworks '97
Geronimo: An American Legend '93

Jean Gruault (1924-)
The Mystery of Alexina '86
Love Unto Death '84
The Eighties '83
Life is a Bed of Roses '83
Mon Oncle d'Amérique '80
The Green Room '78
The Story of Adele H. '75
The Wild Child '70
Jules and Jim '62
Paris Belongs to Us '60

Frank Gruber (1904-1969)
Dressed to Kill '46
Terror by Night '46

J. Mackye Gruber
The Butterfly Effect '04
Final Destination 2 '03

Jean-Claude Grumberg (1939-)
Amen '02

Ilya Gruzdev
The Last Metro '80
My Universities '40
My Childhood '38

Robert Gunter
The Sandlot '93

James Gunn (1970-)
Slither '06
Dawn of the Dead '04
Scooby-Doo 2: Monsters Unleashed '04
Scooby-Doo '02
The Specials '00

Robert Guenette
The Town Is Quiet '00
Marius and Jeannette '97

Paul Guay
Liar Liar '97
The Little Rascals '94

Richard Guay
The 24 Hour Woman '99
Household Saints '93
True Love '89

Bill Gucwa
Storm Catcher '99
No Code of Conduct '98

John Guare (1938-)
Subway Stories '97
Six Degrees of Separation '93
Atlantic City '81

Robert Guediguian (1953-)
The Town Is Quiet '00
Marius and Jeannette '97

Annette Goliti Gutierrez
Kill Me Later '01

Sebastian Gutierrez
Wedding Bell Blues '96
The Eye '08
Rise: Blood Hunter '07
Snakes on a Plane '06
The Big Bounce '04
Gothika '03
She Creature '01
Judas Kiss '98

Tomas Gutierrez Alea (1926-96)
Guantanamera '95
Strawberry and Chocolate '93
Letters from the Park '88
Up to a Certain Point '83
Memories of Underdevelopment '68
Death of a Bureaucrat '66

Ferde Grofe, Jr.
Warkill '65

Christopher Grimm
Rhythm Thief '94
Spare Me '92

Dan Gurskis
The Substitute 4: Failure is Not an Option '00
Nerds in Paradise '87

Dan Guntzelman
Perfect Game '00
Revenge of the Nerds 2: Nerds in Paradise '87

Tonino Guerra (1920-)
Weeping Meadow '04
The Truce '96
And the Ship Sails On '83
Nostalghia '83
The Night of the Shooting Stars '82
Zabriskie Point '70
Blow-Up '66
The Eclipse '66
Casanova '74
The Red Desert '64
L'Avventura '60

Jorge Guerricaechevarria (1949-)
Homegrown '97
El Crimen Perfecto '04
Dance with the Devil '97
Live Flesh '97

Lynn Grossman
Subway Stories '97

Adam Grossman
Carnival of Souls '98

Norman Grossfeld (1963-)
Yu-Gi-Oh! The Movie: Pyramid of Light '04
Pokemon 3: The Movie '01
Pokemon 4Ever '02
Pokemon: The First Movie '99
Pokemon: The Power of One '00
Pokemon: The Movie 2000: The Power of One '00

Seth Gross
DOA: Dead or Alive '06
Devour '05

Val Guest (1911-2006)
Au Pair Girls '72
When Dinosaurs Ruled the Earth '70
The Day the Earth Caught Fire '61

Christopher Guest (1948-)
For Your Consideration '06
A Mighty Wind '03
Best in Show '00
Waiting for Guffman '96
The Big Picture '89
This is Spinal Tap '84
The Return of Spinal Tap '92

Leonard Gross
Divided by Hate '96

Jonathan Hales
Star Wars: Episode 2 — Attack of the Clones '02
Northern Passage '95

John Hale (1926-)
Nostromo '96
Mary, Queen of Scots '71
Anne of the Thousand Days '69

William Wisher
Command Decision '43

Richard W. Haines (1957-)
Alien Space Avenger '91
Class of Nuke 'Em High '86
Splatter University '84

Fred Haines (1936-)
Steppenwolf '74
Ulysses '67

Paul Haggis (1953-)
In the Valley of Elah '07
Casino Royale '06
Flags of Our Fathers '06
The Last Kiss '06
Letters from Iwo Jima '06
Crash '05
Million Dollar Baby '04
Red Hot '95

Michael Haigney
Pokemon 3: The Movie '01
Pokemon: The Movie 2000 '00
Pokemon: The First Movie '99

Ross Hagen (1938-)
Bad Charleston Charlie '73

Albert Hackett (1900-95)
The Long, Long Trailer '54
Seven Brides for Seven Brothers '54
Father's Little Dividend '51
Father of the Bride '50
Easter Parade '48
It's a Wonderful Life '46
The Thin Man '46
The Virginian '46

Steve Haberman
The Music of Chance '93
Dracula: Dead and Loving It '95

Philip Haas
The Blood Oranges '97
Angels and Insects '95

Charles S. Haas (1952-)
The Blood Oranges '97
The Music of Chance '93
Runaway Daughters '94
Matinee '92
Gremlins 2: The New Batch '90
Tex '82

Derek Haas (1970-)
Wanted '08
3:10 to Yuma '07
Catch That Kid '04
2 Fast 2 Furious '03

Belinda Haas
Up at the Villa '00
The Blood Oranges '97
Angels and Insects '95

Willis Hall (1929-2005)
Billy Liar '63
A Kind of Loving '62
Whistle down the Wind '61

Edward Halperin (1898-1981)
White Zombie '32

Joc Halpin
Sky Bandits '40
Yukon Flight '40

Forrest Halsey (1877-1949)
Dancing Mothers '26
Sally of the Sawdust '25

Philip Halprin
The Wild '06
Snow Dogs '02
The It Crowd '07

Craig Hamann
Boogie Boy '98

John Hamburg (1970-)
Along Came Polly '04
Meet the Fockers '04
Zoolander '01
Meet the Parents '00
Safe Men '98

Dean Hamilton
Pink String and Sealing Wax '45

Sam Hamm
Masters of Horror: The Screwfly Solution '06
Monkeybone '01
Never Cry Wolf '83
Batman '89

Oscar Hammerstein (1895-1960)
The Quiet American '02
Imagining Argentina '04
The Secret Agent '96
Carrington '95
Mary Reilly '96
Dangerous Liaisons '88
The Good Father '87
The Wolf at the Door '87
Beyond the Limit '83

Bert Hamer (1956-)
Factotum '06
Kitchen Stories '03

Robert Hamer (1911-63)
Kind Hearts and Coronets '49

Christopher Hampton (1946-)
Atonement '07
The Quiet American '02

Earl Hamner (1923-)
Charlotte's Web '73
Heidi '67

Stephen Gyllenhaal (1949-)
Homegrown '97

Norman S. Hall (1896-1964)
The Young Land '55
Missouri Traveler '53
The Topeka Terror '45
Borderton Gunfighters '43
California Joe '43
Sundown Kid '43
Adventures of Red Ryder '40

Sam Hall
Night of Dark Shadows '71
House of Dark Shadows '70

Joc Halpin
Drums of Fu Manchu '40
Wall Street Cowboy '39
The Three Musketeers '33

Godfrey Ho
See Godfrey Ho

James Andrew Hall
The Franchise Affair '88
Great Expectations '81

Kenneth J. Hall (1958-)
Die Watching '93

Arch (Archie) Hall, Sr. (1908-78)
Wild Guitar '62
The Choppers '61

Ellen Hammrill
Joey '85

Orville H. Hampton (1917-97)
Friday Foster '75
Detroit 9000 '73
Jack the Giant Killer '62
Atomic Submarine '59
Scotland Yard Inspector '52
Leave It to the Marines '51
Mask of the Dragon '51
Sky High '51
Hi-Jacked '50
Motor Patrol '50

Robert Hampton
See Riccardo Freda

Blanche Hanalis
The Secret Garden '87
A Home of Our Own '75
Where Angels Go, Trouble Follows '68

John Lee Hancock (1957-)
The Alamo '04
Midnight in the Garden of Good and Evil '97
A Perfect World '93

Peter Handke (1942-)
Wings of Desire '88
The Goalie's Anxiety at the Penalty Kick '71

Daniel Handler (1970-)
Kill the Poor '06
Rick '03

Michael Haneke (1942-)
Funny Games '07
Hidden '05
Time of the Wolf '03
The Piano Teacher '01
Code Unknown '00
Funny Games '97
Benny's Video '92

Daryl Haney (1963-)
Mockingbird Don't Sing '01
Forbidden Sins '99
Xtro 3: Watch the Skies '95
Stranger by Night '94
To Die Standing '91
Lords of the Deep '89
Masque of the Red Death '89
Crime Zone '88
Friday the 13th, Part 7: The New Blood '88
Daddy's Video '87

Tom Hanks (1956-)
Band of Brothers '01
From the Earth to the Moon '98
That Thing You Do! '96

Brent Hanley
Masters of Horror: Family '05
Frailty '02

William Hanley (1931-)
Ellen Foster '97
The Kennedys of Massachusetts '95
Scarlett '94
Our Sons '91
The Attic: The Hiding of Anne Frank '88
Too Far to Go '79
The Gypsy Moths '69

Mark Hanlon
Ghost Ship '02
Buddy Boy '99

Gordon Hann
Catherine Cookson's The Colour Blind '98
Catherine Cookson's The Girl '96
Catherine Cookson's The Moth '96
Catherine Cookson's The Tide of Life '96
Catherine Cookson's The Dwelling Place '94
Catherine Cookson's The Man Who Cried '93
Catherine Cookson's The Black Candle '92
Catherine Cookson's The Black Velvet Gown '92

Mark Hanna (1917-2003)
Not of This Earth '88
Attack of the 50 Foot Woman '58
The Amazing Colossal Man '57
The Undead '57
The Gunslinger '56

Marion Hansel (1949-)
The Quarry '98
Between Heaven and Earth '93
Dust '85

Curtis Hanson (1945-)
Lucky You '07
L.A. Confidential '97
The Bedroom Window '87
The Children of Times Square '86
Never Cry Wolf '83
The Silent Partner '78
The Arousers '70
The Dunwich Horror '70

Marla Hanson
The Blackout '97
Subway Stories '97

Kenchiro Hara
47 Ronin, Part 1 '42
47 Ronin, Part 2 '42

Carl Harbaugh (1886-1960)
Three Legionnaires '37
Steamboat Bill, Jr. '28
College '27
Regeneration '15

Patrick Harbinson
Horatio Hornblower '99
The Waiting Time '99
Frenchman's Creek '98

Gary Hardwick
Deliver Us from Eva '03
The Brothers '01
Trippin' '99
Todd McFarlane's Spawn '97

David Hare (1947-)
The Hours '02
The Secret Rapture '94
Damage '92
Strapless '90
Saigon: Year of the Cat '87
Plenty '85
Wetherby '85

Lance Z. Hargreaves
First Man into Space '59

Marion Hargrove (1919-2003)
40 Pounds of Trouble '62
The Music Man '62
Cash McCall '60

Tsui Hark (1951-)
Tsui Hark's Vampire Hunters '02
Time and Tide '00
Black Mask '96
Iron Monkey '93
Once Upon a Time in China III '93
Once Upon a Time in China II '92
Twin Dragons '92
Wicked City '92
Once Upon a Time in China '91

Eric Harlacher
Murder at Devil's Glen '99
Homewrecker '92

Robert Harling (1951-)
Laws of Attraction '04
The Evening Star '96
The First Wives Club '96
Soapdish '91
Steel Magnolias '89

John Harlow (1896-1977)
Appointment with Crime '45
Echo Murders '45
Meet Sexton Blake '44

Julian Harmon (1908-66)
Danger Zone '51
Pier 23 '51
Roaring City '51

Phil Harnage
Inspector Gadget's Biggest Caper Ever '05
Banzai Runner '86

Sam Harper
Cheaper by the Dozen 2 '05
Cheaper by the Dozen '03
Just Married '03
Rookie of the Year '93

Stephen Harrigan
King of Texas '02
Take Me Home: The John Denver Story '00
Cleopatra '99
Lone Justice 3: Showdown at Plum Creek '96
The O.J. Simpson Story '94

Curtis Harrington (1928-2007)
Planet of Blood '66
Night Tide '63

Damian Harris (1958-)
Mercy '00
The Rachel Papers '89

Daniel P. "Dan" Harris (1979-)
Superman Returns '06
Imaginary Heroes '05
X2: X-Men United '03

Elmer Harris (1878-1966)
Red Salute '35
Tess of the Storm Country '22

Eoghan Harris
Sharpe's Revenge '97
Sharpe's Mission '96
Sharpe's Regiment '96
Sharpe's Siege '96
Sharpe's Enemy '94
Sharpe's Sword '94
Sharpe's Eagle '93
Sharpe's Rifles '93

James B. Harris (1928-)
Boiling Point '93
Cop '88

Joe Harris
The Tripper '06
Darkness Falls '03

Kirk Harris
Hard Luck '01
Loser '01

Timothy Harris (1946-)
Pure Luck '91
Kindergarten Cop '90
My Stepmother Is an Alien '88
Twins '88
Brewster's Millions '85
Trading Places '83
Cheaper to Keep Her '80

Trent Harris (1952-)
Plan 10 from Outer Space '95
Rubin & Ed '92
Cold Feet '89

Vernon Harris (1905-99)
Oliver! '68
Carve Her Name with Pride '58
The Admirable Crichton '57

Jim Harrison (1937-)
Dalva '95
Wolf '94
Revenge '90

John Harrison
Children of Dune '03
Dinosaur '00
Donor Unknown '95

John Kent Harrison
You Know My Name '99
Calm at Sunset '96
City Boy '93
The Sound and the Silence '93
Beautiful Dreamers '92
Memories of Murder '90
Murder by Phone '82
Shock Waves '77

Matthew Harrison (1960-)
Kicked in the Head '97
Rhythm Thief '94

Mary Harron (1953-)
The Notorious Bettie Page '06
American Psycho '99
I Shot Andy Warhol '96

Jacobsen Hart
Raven '97
The Power Within '95
Rage '95

James V. Hart
August Rush '07
Sahara '05
Tuck Everlasting '02
Jack and the Beanstalk: The Real Story '01
Muppet Treasure Island '96
Bram Stoker's Dracula '92

Moss Hart (1904-61)
A Star Is Born '54
Hans Christian Andersen '52
Gentleman's Agreement '47

Hal Hartley (1959-)
Fay Grim '06
No Such Thing '01
Henry Fool '98
Flirt '95
Amateur '94
Simple Men '92
Trust '91
The Unbelievable Truth '90

Don Hartman (1900-58)
Wonder Man '45
The Princess and the Pirate '44
My Favorite Blonde '42
The Road to Morocco '42
The Road to Zanzibar '41
The Road to Singapore '40
Never Say Die '39
Waikiki Wedding '37
The Princess Comes Across '36
Here Comes Cookie '35

Edmund Hartmann (1911-2003)
Casanova's Big Night '54
The Lemon Drop Kid '51
Variety Girl '47
In Society '44
Ali Baba and the Forty Thieves '43

Steven Hartov
Mars '96

Jack Harvey (1881-1954)
Last of the Wild Horses '49
Unknown Island '48

Johanna Harwood
Call Me Bwana '63
From Russia with Love '63
Dr. No '62

Ronald Harwood (1934-)
The Diving Bell and the Butterfly '07
Love in the Time of Cholera '07
Oliver Twist '05
Being Julia '04
The Statement '03
The Pianist '02
Taking Sides '01
The Browning Version '94
A Fine Romance '92
The Doctor and the Devils '85
The Dresser '83
One Day in the Life of Ivan Denisovich '71

Claude Harz
Find the Lady '76
It Seemed Like a Good Idea at the Time '75

Shinobu Hashimoto (1918-)
Dodes 'ka-den '70
Samurai Rebellion '67
Attack Squadron '63
Harakiri '62
The Bad Sleep Well '60
I Bombed Pearl Harbor '60
The Hidden Fortress '58
Throne of Blood '57
I Live in Fear '55
Seven Samurai '54
Ikiru '52
Rashomon '51

Michael Hastings (1938-)
The American '01
Tom & Viv '94
The Nightcomers '72

Jeffrey Hatcher
Casanova '05
Stage Beauty '04

Richard Hatem (1966-)
The Mothman Prophecies '02
Under Siege 2: Dark Territory '95

Wings Hauser (1948-)
Gang Boys '97
No Safe Haven '87

Chris Hauty
Never Back Down '08
Homeward Bound 2: Lost in San Francisco '96

Anthony Havelock-Allan (1904-2003)
Brief Encounter '46
Blithe Spirit '45

Jean C. Havez (1870-1925)
Seven Chances '25
The Navigator '24
Sherlock, Jr. '24
Our Hospitality '23
Safety Last '23

Ethan Hawke (1971-)
The Hottest State '06
Before Sunset '04

John Hawkesworth (1920-2003)
Forbidden Passion: The Oscar Wilde Movie '85
The Flame Trees of Thika '81
The Duchess of Duke Street '78

Christopher Hawthorne
Whiskers '96
The Courtyard '95
Parents '89

Ian Hay (1876-1952)
Sabotage '36
The 39 Steps '35

Phil Hay
Aeon Flux '05
crazy/beautiful '01

Carey Hayes (1961-)
The Reaping '07

Chad Hayes (1961-)
The Reaping '07
House of Wax '05
First Daughter '99
Down, Out and Dangerous '95

John Hayes (1930-2000)
All the Lovin' Kinfolk '70
Corruption '70
The Cut Throats '69

John Michael Hayes (1919-)
Iron Will '93
Pancho Barnes '88
Nevada Smith '66
Harlow '65
The Carpetbaggers '64
The Chalk Garden '64
Where Love Has Gone '64
The Children's Hour '61
Butterfield 8 '60
But Not for Me '59
The Matchmaker '58
Peyton Place '57
The Man Who Knew Too Much '56
It's a Dog's Life '55
To Catch a Thief '55
The Trouble with Harry '55
Rear Window '54
Thunder Bay '53
War Arrow '53
Red Ball Express '52

Joseph Hayes (1918-2006)
Desperate Hours '90
Stolen Hours '63

Steve Hayes
The Muppets' Wizard of Oz '05
Mr. St. Nick '02
Fantastic Planet '73

Terry Hayes (1951-)
From Hell '01
Vertical Limit '00
Payback '98
Mr. Reliable: A True Story '95
Dead Calm '89
Mad Max: Beyond Thunderdome '85
The Road Warrior '82

Gregory C. Haynes (1968-)
Cowboys and Angels '00
Heaven or Vegas '98
Magenta '96

Todd Haynes (1961-)
I'm Not There '07
Far from Heaven '02
Velvet Goldmine '98
Office Killer '97
Safe '95
Poison '91

David Hayter (1969-)
The Scorpion King '02
X-Men '00

Lillie Hayward (1891-1977)
Proud Rebel '58
On the Sunny Side '42
The Undying Monster '42
Lady Killer '33
They Call It Sin '32

Ping He (1957-)

Percy Heath (1884-1933)
Dr. Jekyll and Mr. Hyde '32
No One Man '32

David Heavener (1958-)
Fugitive X '96
Eye of the Stranger '93
Prime Target '91
Killcrazy '89
Twisted Justice '89

Julie Hebert
Ruby's Bucket of Blood '01
Female Perversions '96

Ben Hecht (1894-1964)
Circus World '64
Walk on the Wild Side '62
The Indian Fighter '55
Actors and Sin '52
Monkey Business '52
The Thing '51
Notorious '46
Spectre of the Rose '46
Spellbound '45
The Black Swan '42
Tales of Manhattan '42
Angels Over Broadway '40
Comrade X '40
Gunga Din '39
Let Freedom Ring '39
Wuthering Heights '39

Nothing Sacred '37
Twentieth Century '34
Viva Villa! '34
Hallelujah, I'm a Bum '33
The Great Gabbo '29

Amy Heckerling (1954-)
Clueless '95
Look Who's Talking, Too '90
Loser '00
I Could Never Be Your
Woman '06

Rob Hedden (1954-)
The Condemned '07
Clockstoppers '02
Alien Fury: Countdown to
Invasion '00
Friday the 13th, Part 8:
Jason Takes Manhattan
'89

Roger Hedden
Hi-Life '98
Sleep with Me '94
Bodies, Rest & Motion '92

Peter Hedges (1962-)
Pieces of April '03
Dan in Real Life '07
About a Boy '02
A Map of the World '99
What's Eating Gilbert Grape
'93

Victor Heerman (1893-1977)
Golden Boy '39
Stella Dallas '37
Break of Hearts '35
Little Minister '34
My Boy '21

Kevin Heffernan (1968-)
Beerfest '06
Club Dread '04
Super Troopers '01

Carol Heikkinen (1966-)
Center Stage '00
Empire Records '95
The Thing Called Love '93

Adelaide Heilbron (1892-1974)
Misleading Lady '32
Personal Maid '31

Jo Heims (1930-78)
Play Misty for Me '71
Double Trouble '67

Robert Heinlein (1907-88)
Project Moon Base '53
Destination Moon '50

Ross Helford
Single White Female 2: The
Psycho '05
Sniper 3 '04
Wild Things 2 '04

Brian Helgeland (1961-)
Man on Fire '04
Mystic River '03
The Order '03
Blood Work '02
A Knight's Tale '01
Payback '98
Conspiracy Theory '97
The Postman '97
L.A. Confidential '97
Assassins '95
A Nightmare on Elm Street
4: Dream Master '88
976-EVIL '89

Lukas Heller (1930-88)
Monte Walsh '03
Blue City '86
Damnation Alley '77
The Killing of Sister George
'69
The Dirty Dozen '67
Hush, Hush, Sweet
Charlotte '65
What Ever Happened to
Baby Jane? '62

Lillian Hellman (1905-84)
The Chase '66
The North Star '43
Watch on the Rhine '43
The Little Foxes '41
Dead End '37
These Three '36
The Dark Angel '35

Oliver Hellman
See Ovidio G. Assonitis

Sam Hellman (1885-1950)
My Darling Clementine '46
The Three Musketeers '39
In Old Kentucky '35
Little Miss Marker '34
Murder at the Vanities '34
Thirty Day Princess '34

Axel Hellstenius
Elling '01

Zach Helm
Mr. Magorium's Wonder
Emporium '07
Stranger Than Fiction '06

James Henerson
Mutiny '99

Paul Hengge
The Rose Garden '89
Double Face '70

Kim Henkel
The Texas Chainsaw
Massacre 4: The Next
Generation '95
Eaten Alive '76
The Texas Chainsaw
Massacre '74

Hilary Henkin (1962-)
Wag the Dog '97
Romeo Is Bleeding '93
Fatal Beauty '87

Beth Henley (1952-)
Miss Firecracker '89
Crimes of the Heart '86
Nobody's Fool '86
True Stories '86

Jack Henley (1896-1958)
Ma and Pa Kettle at Waikiki
'55
Ma and Pa Kettle on
Vacation '53
Ma and Pa Kettle Back On
the Farm '51
Blondie Hits the Jackpot '49
A Thousand and One Nights
'45
Zis Boom Bah '41

Paul Henning (1911-2005)

Todd Henschell '67
Puppet Master 5: The Final
Chapter '94
Puppet Master 4 '93

John Henschell
Puppet Master 4 '93

Buck Henry (1930-)
To Die For '95
Protocol '84
First Family '80
The Day of the Dolphin '73
What's Up, Doc? '72
Catch-22 '70
The Owl and the Pussycat
'70
Candy '68
The Graduate '67

Marshall Herskovitz (1952-)
The Last Samurai '03
Glory '89

Adam Herz (1973-)
American Wedding '03
American Pie 2 '01
American Pie '99

Michael Herz (1949-)
Stuck on You '84

Jim Herzfeld
Meet the Fockers '04
Meet the Parents '00
Meet the Deedles '98

John Herzfeld
15 Minutes '01
Two Days in the Valley '96
Casualties of Love: The
"Long Island Lolita" Story
'93

Joel Hershman (1958-)
Greenfingers '00
Hold Me, Thrill Me, Kiss Me
'93

Rowdy Herrington (1951-)
Bobby Jones: Stroke of
Genius '04
The Stickup '01
A Murder of Crows '99
Striking Distance '93
Jack's Back '87

W(illiam) Blake Herron
The Bourne Identity '02
A Texas Funeral '99
Skin Art '93

Anthony Hickox (1959-)
Submerged '05
Last Run '01
Prince Valiant '97
Waxwork 2: Lost in Time '91
Waxwork '88

Julie Hickson
Snow White: The Fairest of
Them All '02
Homeward Bound 2: Lost in
San Francisco '96

Adam Herz (1973-)
Special Bulletin '83
American Wedding '03
American Pie 2 '01
American Pie '99

Michael Herr (1940-)
Full Meta Jacket '87
Apocalypse Now '79

Gyula Hernadi (1926-2005)
Adoption '75
The Red and the White '68
The Round Up '66

**Jaime Humberto
Hermosillo (1942-)**
Esmeralda Comes by Night
'98
Homework '90
Dona Herlinda & Her Son
'86

Pee-wee Herman
See Paul (Pee-wee)
Reubens

Mark Herman (1954-)
Little Voice '98
Brassed Off '96
Blame It on the Bellboy '92

Tim Herlihy (1966-)
Mr. Deeds '02
Little Nicky '00
Big Daddy '99
The Waterboy '98
The Wedding Singer '98
Happy Gilmore '96

Robby Henson
The Badge '02
Pharoah's Army '95

F. Hugh Herbert (1897-1958)
Let's Make It Legal '51
Our Very Own '50
Sitting Pretty '48

Ron Herbst
Warlords 3000 '93

Jonathan Hensleigh
Next '07
The Punisher '04
Armageddon '98
The Saint '97
The Rock '96
Die Hard: With a Vengeance
'95

Werner Herzog (1942-)
Rescue Dawn '06
Invincible '01
Cobra Verde '88
Fitzcarraldo '82
Woyzeck '78
Nosferatu the Vampyre '79
Stroszek '77
Every Man for Himself &
God Against All '75
Heart of Glass '74
Aguirre, the Wrath of God
'72
Signs of Life '68

Eugene Hess
Cruel World '05
Don't Do It '94

Jared Hess (1979-)
Nacho Libre '06
Napoleon Dynamite '04

Jerusha Hess (1980-)
Nacho Libre '06
Napoleon Dynamite '04

Fraser Heston (1955-)
Treasure Island '89
The Mountain Men '80

Rod Hewitt
The Debt '98

Douglas Heyes (1919-93)
Ice Station Zebra '68
Kitten with a Whip '64
Battle Shock '56

Louis M. Heyward (1920-2002)
The Conqueror Worm '68
Planet of the Vampires '65
Pajama Party '64

Winston Hibler (1910-76)
Nikki, the Wild Dog of the
North '61
Perri '57
The Adventures of Ichabod
and Mr. Toad '49

Jochen Hick (1960-)
No One Sleeps '01
Via Appia '92

George Hickenlooper (1964-)
Mayor of the Sunset Strip
'03
The Big Brass Ring '99
Dogtown '97
The Low Life '95
Hearts of Darkness: A
Filmmaker's Apocalypse
'91

Sid Herzig (1897-1985)
They Made Me a Criminal
'39
Sing Me a Love Song '37

Robert J. Hill
Fanny Hill: Memoirs of a
Woman of Pleasure '64

David Hillenbrand
Scott Hillenbrand
Survival Island '02
King Cobra '99

David Hilton
The Delivery '99

Richard Hilliard
Horror of Party Beach '64
The Lonely Sex '59

James Hilton (1900-54)
Mrs. Miniver '42
Foreign Correspondent '40
Camille '36

David Hilton

Walter Hill (1942-)
Undisputed '02
Last Man Standing '96
Wild Bill '95
Trespass '92
Aliens '86
Blue City '86
Streets of Fire '84
48 Hrs. '82
Southern Comfort '81
The Warriors '79
The Driver '78
Hard Times '75
The Drowning Pool '75
The Thief Who Came to
Dinner '73
The Getaway '72
The Mackintosh Man '73

Jack Hill (1933-)
Switchblade Sisters '75
Foxy Brown '74
Coffy '73
The Big Bird Cage '72
Pit Stop '67
Spider Baby '64

John Hill (1964-)
Quigley Down Under '90
Little Nikita '88
Heartbeeps '81

Robert F. "Bob" Hill (1886-1966)
West of Nevada '36
Murder on the High Seas '32
The Cat and the Canary '27
The Adventures of Tarzan
'21

Debra Hill (1950-2005)
Escape from L.A. '96
Halloween II: The
Nightmare Isn't Over! '81
The Fog '80
Halloween '78

Charles Higson (1958-)
King of the Arts '03
Suite 16 '94

David Hill

John C. Higgins (1908-95)
Robinson Crusoe on Mars
'64
The Black Sleep '56
Border Incident '49
He Walked by Night '48
Raw Deal '48
T-Men '47
Railroaded! '47

Colin Higgins (1941-88)
Foul Play '78
Silver Streak '76
Harold and Maude '71

Patrick Highsmith
Acts of Betrayal '98

Roger O. Hirson (1926-)
A Christmas Carol '84
Pippin '81
Demon Seed '77

Alan Hines
My Husband's Double Life
'01
Breaking the Surface: The
Greg Louganis Story '96
Square Dance '87

David Himmelstein
Soul of the Game '96
Village of the Damned '95
Talent for the Game '91
Power '86

James Hilton (1900-54)

Arthur Hoerl (1891-1968)
Blind Fools '40
The Singing Cowgirl '39
Reefer Madness '38

Mike Hodges (1932-)
Black Rainbow '91
Damien: Omen II '78
The Terminal Man '74
Pulp '72
Get Carter '71

Adrian Hodges
The History of Mr. Polly '07
Ruby in the Smoke '06
The Lost World '01
Lorna Doone '01
David Copperfield '99
Metroland '97
Tom & Viv '94

John Hodge (1964-)
The Beach '00
A Life Less Ordinary '97
Trainspotting '96
Shallow Grave '94

Danny Hoch (1970-)
White Boyz '99
Subway Stories '97
Rising '07

Godfrey Ho (1948-)
Ninja Champion '80
Ninja Destroyer '70

Ken Hixon
Tough Assignment '49
City by the Sea '02
Inventing the Abbotts '97
Incident at Deception Ridge
'94

Carl K. Hittleman (1907-99)
Jesse James Meets
Frankenstein's Daughter
'66
Billy the Kid Versus Dracula
'66

Michael Hitchcock (1958-)
House Arrest '96

Alfred Hitchcock (1899-1980)
Saboteur '42
No. 17 '32
Rich and Strange '32
Skin Game '31
Murder '30
Juno and the Paycock '30
Blackmail '29
Champagne '28
The Farmer's Wife '28
The Ring '26
The Lodger '26

Michael Hitchcock (1958-)

Michael Hirst (1952-)
Elizabeth: The Golden Age
'07
Elizabeth '98
Fools of Fortune '90

Samuel Hoffenstein (1890-1947)
Laura '44
His Butler's Sister '44
The Phantom of the Opera
'43
Tales of Manhattan '42
The Song of Songs '33
Dr. Jekyll and Mr. Hyde '32
Sinners in the Sun '32

Charles Hoffman
The Blue Gardenia '53
The West Point Story '50

Joseph Hoffman (1909-97)
At Sword's Point '51
Buccaneer's Girl '50
The Man with Two Lives '42

Michael Hoffman (1956-)
William Shakespeare's A Midsummer Night's Dream '99
Promised Land '88

Gray Hofmeyr
Yankee Zulu '95
The Outcast '84

Michael Hogan
Forever and a Day '43
Arabian Nights '42
King Solomon's Mines '37

Paul Hogan (1939-)
Lightning Jack '94
Almost an Angel '90
Crocodile Dundee 2 '88
Crocodile Dundee '86

P.J. Hogan (1962-)
Peter Pan '03
Unconditional Love '03
Muriel's Wedding '94

Brian Hohlfield
Without Anesthesia '78

Savage Steve Holland (1960-)
One Crazy Summer '86
Better Off Dead '85

Michael Holden
No Strings Attached '98
The Little Death '95

Jeremy Hole
A Killing Spring '02
Verdict in Blood '02

Agnieszka Holland (1948-)
The Healer '02
Trois Couleurs: Bleu '93
Olivier, Olivier '92
Europa, Europa '91
Korczak '90
To Kill a Priest '89
Psycho 2 '83
The Beast Within '82
Anna '87
Angry Harvest '85
A Love in Germany '84
Danton '82

Cliff Hollingsworth
Cinderella Man '05
Too Good to Be True '98

Jean Holloway (1917-89)
Madame X '66
Till the Clouds Roll By '46

Geoffrey Holmes
See Daniel Mainwaring

Nicole Holofcener (1960-)
Friends with Money '06
Lovely & Amazing '02
Walking and Talking '96

Edward Holzman
Forbidden Games '95
Friend of the Family '95

Geoffrey Homes
See Daniel Mainwaring

Inoshiro Honda (1911-93)
War of the Gargantuas '70
Destroy All Monsters '68
Godzilla, King of the Monsters '56

Christophe Honore (1970-)
Love Songs '07
Inside Paris '06
Close to Leo '02
Girls Can't Swim '99

Gavin Hood (1963-)
Tsotsi '05
In Desert and Wilderness '01

Sean Hood (1966-)
The Crow: Wicked Prayer '05
Halloween: Resurrection '02

William Hooke
Shark Attack 3: Megalodon '02
Shark Attack 2 '00
Shark Attack '99

Tobe Hooper (1946-)
The Mangler '94
Spontaneous Combustion '89
The Texas Chainsaw Massacre '74

Arthur Hopcraft (1932-2004)
Rebecca '97
A Tale of Two Cities '89
A Perfect Spy '88
Tinker, Tailor, Soldier, Spy '80

Edward Hope (1986-58)
The Long Gray Line '55
Three for the Show '55

Alan Hopgood (1934-)
Alvin Rides Again '74
Alvin Purple '73

John Hopkins
Dunston Checks In '95
Hiroshima '95
Codename Kyril '91
The Holcroft Covenant '85
Torment '85
Smiley's People '82
Murder by Decree '79
The Offence '73
The Virgin Soldiers '69
Thunderball '65

Karen Leigh Hopkins
Because I Said So '07
The Strawberry Statement '70

Anthony Horowitz (1955-)
Alex Rider: Operation Stormbreaker '06
The Gathering '02
Diamond's Edge '88

Ed Horowitz
Exit Wounds '01
K-9: P.I. '01
On Deadly Ground '94

Israel Horovitz (1939-)
James Dean '01
Sunshine '99
North Shore Fish '97
A Man in Love '87
Author! Author! '82

Jason Horwitch
Joe and Max '02
Finding Graceland '98

David Hoselton
Over the Hedge '06
Brother Bear '03
Deadly Game '98

Coleman Hough
Bubble '06
Full Frontal '01

Don Houghton (1930-91)
The Legend of the 7 Golden Vampires '73
The Satanic Rites of Dracula '73
Dracula A.D. 1972 '72

Lionel Houser (1908-49)
First Love '39
Smashing the Rackets '38
I Promise to Pay '37

Dianne Houston
Take the Lead '06
Knights of the South Bronx '05
Run for the Dream: The Gail Devers Story '96

Norman Houston (1887-1958)
Riders of the Range '50
Mysterious Desperado '49
In Old Caliente '39

Cy Howard (1915-93)
Marriage on the Rocks '65
My Friend Irma '49

Elizabeth Jane Howard (1923-)
Getting It Right '89
The Very Edge '63

Karin Howard
The Tigress '93
NeverEnding Story 2: The Next Chapter '91

Rance Howard (1929-)
Tut & Tuttle '81
Grand Theft Auto '77

Ron Howard (1954-)
Parenthood '89
Cotton Candy '82
Grand Theft Auto '77

Sidney Howard (1891-1939)
Gone with the Wind '39
Dodsworth '36
Raffles '30
Bulldog Drummond '29
Condemned '29

C. Thomas Howell (1966-)
Hope Ranch '02
Hourglass '95

Dorothy Howell (1899-1971)
The Miracle Woman '31
Platinum Blonde '31

Frank Howson (1952-)
Flynn '96
The Hunting '92
What the Moon Saw '90

Perry Howze
Chances Are '89
Mystic Pizza '88
Maid to Order '87

Rita Hsiao
Toy Story 2 '99
Mulan '98

George Huang
How to Make a Monster '01
Swimming with Sharks '94

Lucien Hubbard
Smart Money '31
The Vanishing American '25
Outside the Law '21

Tom Hubbard (1919-74)
Daniel Boone: Trail Blazer '56
Thunder Pass '54
Two Lost Worlds '50

Tom Huckabee
Deep in the Heart (of Texas) '98
Deathfight '93

John Huddles
Uncorked '98
Far Harbor '96

Reginald (Reggie) Hudlin (1961-)
Bebe's Kids '92
House Party '90

Brent Huff (1961-)
Welcome to Paradise '07
Power Play '02
Final Justice '94

Clair Huffaker (1926-90)
Chino '75
Hellfighters '68
Flaming Star '60

Gwyneth Hughes
Five Days '07

John Hughes (1950-)
Just Visiting '01
Reach the Rock '98
Flubber '97
Home Alone 3 '97
101 Dalmatians '96
Baby's Day Out '94
Miracle on 34th Street '94
Dennis the Menace '93
Beethoven '92
Home Alone 2: Lost in New York '92
Career Opportunities '91
Curly Sue '91
Dutch '91
Home Alone '90
National Lampoon's Christmas Vacation '89
Uncle Buck '89
The Great Outdoors '88
She's Having a Baby '88
Planes, Trains & Automobiles '87
Some Kind of Wonderful '87
Ferris Bueller's Day Off '86
Pretty in Pink '86
The Breakfast Club '85
National Lampoon's European Vacation '85
Weird Science '85
Sixteen Candles '84
Mr. Mom '83
National Lampoon's Vacation '83
National Lampoon's Class Reunion '82

Ken Hughes (1922-2001)
Oh, Alfie '75
Cromwell '70
Chitty Chitty Bang Bang '68
Arrivederci, Baby! '66
The Trials of Oscar Wilde '60
Heat Wave '54

Tom Hughes
Red Letters '00
Breathing Room '96

William Humble
Every Woman Knows a Secret '99

Cyril Hume (1900-66)
The Invisible Boy '57
Forbidden Planet '56
The Great Gatsby '49
Trader Horn '31

Steve Humphrey
Agatha Christie's A Caribbean Mystery '83
Agatha Christie's Sparkling Cyanide '83

Sammo Hung (1952-)
The Millionaire's Express '86

Tran Anh Hung (1963-)
The Vertical Ray of the Sun '00
Cyclo '95
The Scent of Green Papaya '93

Tom Hunsinger (1952-)
Lawless Heart '01
Boyfriends '96

Ed(ward) Hunt
Bloody Birthday '80
Starship Invasions '77

Evan Hunter (1926-2005)
The Birds '63
High & Low '62

Ian McLellan Hunter (1915-91)
Captain Sinbad '63
The Amazing Mr. X '48

John Hunter (1911-)
Hollywood North '03
The Grey Fox '83
Hard Part Begins '73

Neil Hunter
Lawless Heart '01
Boyfriends '96

Tim Hunter (1947-)
Tex '82
Over the Edge '79

Lawrence Huntington (1900-68)
The Oblong Box '69
Man on the Run '49

William Hurlbut (1878-1957)
It Happened in New Orleans '36
The Bride of Frankenstein '35
Imitation of Life '34

Andy Hurst
Are You Scared? '06
Single White Female 2: The Psycho '05
Wild Things 2 '04

Michael Hurst (1973-)
Pumpkinhead 4: Blood Feud '07
Mosquitoman '05
New Blood '99

Harry Hurwitz (1938-95)
Fleshtone '94
That's Adequate '90
Under the Rainbow '81
The Projectionist '71

Jon Hurwitz
Harold & Kumar Escape from Guantanamo Bay '08
Harold and Kumar Go to White Castle '04

Rich Husky
Children of Fury '94
Nightmare '91

John Huston (1906-87)
Mr. North '88
The Man Who Would Be King '75
The Night of the Iguana '64
Heaven Knows, Mr. Allison '57
Moby Dick '56
Beat the Devil '53
Moulin Rouge '52
The African Queen '51
Key Largo '48
Treasure of the Sierra Madre '48
The Killers '46
High Sierra '41
The Maltese Falcon '41
Sergeant York '41
Amazing Dr. Clitterhouse '38
Jezebel '38
Murders in the Rue Morgue '32

Paul Huston
Junior G-Men of the Air '42
Overland Mail '42

Ron Hutchinson
Marco Polo '07
The Island of Dr. Moreau '96
The Tuskegee Airmen '95
Against the Wall '94
The Burning Season '94
Fatherland '94
Blue Ice '92

Willard Huyck (1945-)
Radioland Murders '94
Howard the Duck '86
Best Defense '84
Indiana Jones and the Temple of Doom '84
French Postcards '79
More American Graffiti '79
Messiah of Evil '74
American Graffiti '73

David Henry Hwang (1957-)
Possession '02
The Lost Empire '01
Golden Gate '93
M. Butterfly '93

Peter Hyams (1943-)
Narrow Margin '90
2010: The Year We Make Contact '84
The Star Chamber '83
Outland '81
The Hunter '80
Hanover Street '79
Capricorn One '78
Telefon '77
Busting '74

Chris Hyde
Chained Heat 3: Hell Mountain '98
Crackerjack 2 '97
Crackerjack '94
Chained Heat 2 '92

Marc Hyman
The Perfect Score '04
Osmosis Jones '01

Jeremy Iacone
The Bone Collector '99
One Tough Cop '98
Blood In... Blood Out: Bound by Honor '93

Juan Luis Iborra (1959-)
Km. 0 '00
Between Your Legs '99
Amor de Hombre '97
Mouth to Mouth '95

Rustam Ibragimbekov (1939-)
East-West '99
Burnt by the Sun '94
Close to Eden '90

Ice Cube (1969-)
All About the Benjamins '02
Friday After Next '02
Next Friday '00
The Players Club '98
Friday '95

Leon Ichaso (1948-)
El Cantante '06
Pinero '01
Bitter Sugar '96
Crossover Dreams '85
El Super '79

Masato Ide (1922-)
Ran '85
Kagemusha '80

Eric Idle (1943-)
Splitting Heirs '93
National Lampoon's European Vacation '85
Monty Python's The Meaning of Life '83
The Tale of the Frog Prince '83
Monty Python's Life of Brian '79
All You Need Is Cash '78
Monty Python and the Holy Grail '75
And Now for Something Completely Different '72

Miguel Iglesias
Rape '76
Kilma, Queen of the Amazons '75

W. Peter Iliff
Under Suspicion '00
Varsity Blues '98
Patriot Games '92
Point Break '91
Prayer of the Rollerboys '91

Shohei Imamura (1926-2006)
Dr. Akagi '98
The Eel '96
Black Rain '88
The Ballad of Narayama '83

Hiroshi Inagaki (1905-80)
Samurai 3: Duel at Ganryu Island '56
Samurai 1: Musashi Miyamoto '55

Samurai 2: Duel at Ichijoji Temple '55

Thomas Ince (1882-1924)
The Bargain '15
The Disciple '15
The Italian '15
The Wrath of the Gods '14

Agenore Incrocci (1919-2005)
Ugly '67
Mafioso '62
Joyful Laughter '60

Don Ingalls
Airport '75 '75
Bull of the West '71

William Inge (1913-73)
All Fall Down '62
Splendor in the Grass '61
Breach of Trust '95

Boris Ingster (1904-78)
Happy Landing '38
Thin Ice '37

J. Christian Ingvordsen (1957-)
Blood Relic '05
The Outfit '93
Comrades in Arms '91
Mob War '88
Search and Destroy '88
Firehouse '87
Hangmen '87

Sheldon Inkol
Dark Side '02
Specimen '97
Carver's Gate '96

Christopher Isherwood (1904-86)
Diane '55
Forever and a Day '43

Toshiro Ishido (1932-)
Hiroshima '95
Black Rain '88

Kazuo Ishiguro (1954-)
The White Countess '05

Ira Israel (1966-)
American Virgin '98
Dilemma '97

Neal Israel (1945-)
Week Off '97
All I Want for Christmas '91
Look Who's Talking, Too '90
Real Genius '85
Police Academy '84
Americathon '79

Juzo Itami (1933-97)
Minbo--Or the Gentle Art of Japanese Extortion '92
A Taxing Woman's Return
A Taxing Woman '87
Tampopo '86

Kazunori Ito (1954-)
Ghost in the Shell '95

Daisuke Ito (1898-1981)
Zatoichi: The Blind Swordsman and the Chess Expert '65
An Actor's Revenge '63

James Ivory (1928-)
H.P. Lovecraft's Necronomicon: Book of the Dead '93
A Soldier's Daughter Never Cries '98
Maurice '87
Shakespeare Wallah '65

Renato Izzo
Night Train Murders '75
Adios, Sabata '71
Return of Sabata '71
Sabata '69

David S. Jackson
Detonator 2: Night Watch '95
Detonator '93
Mystery Mansion '83

Felix Jackson (1902-92)
Back Street '41
Destry Rides Again '39
Three Smart Girls Grow Up '39
Mad About Music '38

Horace Jackson (1898-1952)
We're Not Dressing '34

Peter Jackson (1961-)
King Kong '05
Lord of the Rings: The Return of the King '03
Lord of the Rings: The Two Towers '02
Lord of the Rings: The Fellowship of the Rings '01
The Frighteners '96
Heavenly Creatures '94
Dead Alive '93
Meet the Feebles '89
Bad Taste '88

Alan Jacobs
American Gun '02
Just One Night '00
Nina Takes a Lover '94

Harrison Jacobs (1892-1968)
Renegade Trail '39
Three on the Trail '36
Lassie '94
Lorna Doone '90
Paperhouse '88
Smart Money '88

Robert Nelson Jacobs
The Water Horse: Legend of the Deep '07
The Shipping News '01
Chocolat '00
Dinosaur '00
Out to Sea '97

Danny Jacobson
The Honeymooners '05

Michael Jacoby
Dahmer '02

David Jacobson
Down in the Valley '05

Michael Jacobs (1956-)
The Matchmaker '97
The Heist '96

Matthew Jacobs
The Girl with the Hungry Eyes '94
The Loved One '65
The Saddest Music in the World '03
The Shipping News '01

Jon Jacobs (1966-)
Welcome Says the Angel '01

Benoit Jacquot (1947-)
Seventh Heaven '98
A Single Girl '96
The Disenchanted '90

Robert Jaffe
Motel Hell '80
Demon Seed '77

Rick Jaffa
The Relic '96

Henry Jaglom (1943-)
Going Shopping '05
Festival at Cannes '02
Deja Vu '98
Last Summer in the Hamptons '96
Babyfever '94
Venice, Venice '92
Eating '90
New Year's Day '89
Someone to Love '87
Always '85
Can She Bake a Cherry Pie? '83
Sitting Ducks '80

Derek Jarman (1942-94)
Blue '93
Wittgenstein '93
Edward II '92
The Garden '90
Caravaggio '86
Sebastiane '79
The Last of England '87
Aria '88

Jim Jarmusch (1953-)
Broken Flowers '05
Coffee and Cigarettes '03
Ghost Dog: The Way of the Samurai '99
Dead Man '95
Night on Earth '91
Mystery Train '89
Down by Law '86
Permanent Vacation '84
Stranger than Paradise '84

Kevin Jarre
The Devil's Own '96
Tombstone '93
Glory '89

John Jarrell
Romeo Must Die '00
Mr. & Mrs. Bridge '90

Rollin Jarrett
American Vampire '97
Laws of Deception '97

Don Jakoby
Evolution '01
Double Team '97
Arachnophobia '90
Invaders from Mars '86
Lifeforce '85
The Philadelphia Experiment '84
Blue Thunder '83

Alan James (1890-)
On the Edge '00

Daniel James
Come on Tarzan '33
Things '93

Rian James (1899-1953)
The Lone Avenger '33
Trail Drive '33

Polly James
The Redhead from Wyoming '53
Mrs. Parkington '44

Steve Jankowski
42nd Street '33

Karen Janszen
Duma '05
C.I.A. 2: Target Alexa '94
Deadly Target '94
Firepower '93
To Be the Best '93

Michael January
The Savages '07
Slums of Beverly Hills '98

Tamara Jenkins
The Break '95

Dan Jenkins
Dead Solid Perfect '88

Talbot Jennings (1894-1985)
The Black Rose '50
Anna and the King of Siam '46

Susan Estelle Jansen
Bratz '07

Agnes Jaoui (1964-)
Look at Me '04
The Taste of Others '00
Same Old Song '97
Un Air de Famille '96
Smoking/No Smoking '94

Petr Jarchovsky (1966-)
Zelary '03
Divided We Fall '00

Sebastien Japrisot (1931-2003)
The Story of O '75
Honor Among Thieves '68

Anders Thomas Jensen (1972-)
After the Wedding '06
Adam's Apples '05
Brothers '05
The Green Butchers '03
Wilbur Wants to Kill Himself '02
Flickering Lights '01
The King is Alive '00
Mifune '99
Wonder Man '45
Wintertime '43

Jim Jennewein
Getting Even with Dad '94
The Flintstones '94

Erik Jendresen
Sublime '07

Griffin Jay (1905-54)
Crazy as Hell '02
Band of Brothers '01
Deadlocked '00
Lightning Bill '35
Rawhide Romance '34
Lightning Range '33

Steve Jarvis
The Mask of Dijon '46
The Mummy's Ghost '44
Captive Wild Woman '43
Return of the Vampire '43
The Mummy's Tomb '42
The Mummy's Hand '40

Henri Jeanson (1900-70)
16 Years of Alcohol '03
Modigliani '04
Nana '55
Pepe Le Moko '37

L.V. Jefferson (1873-1959)

Don Jakoby
Tracks '76

Paul Jarrico (1915-97)
Messenger of Death '88
The Girl Most Likely '57
Pars Express '53
The Las Vegas Story '52
The White Tower '50
The Search '48
Tom, Dick, and Harry '41
Thousands Cheer '43
Experiment '84

Steve Jarvis
Blue Thunder '83
Bloodstream '00
Haunted '98
Amazon Warrior '97
Things 2 '97

Wong Jing (1955-)
Her Name is Cat '99

Neal Jimenez (1960-)
Hideaway '95
The Waterdance '91
River's Edge '87

Peter Jobin (1944-)
Meltdown '95
Desperate Measures '98

Richard Jobson
16 Years of Alcohol '03

Bayard Johnson
Tarzan and the Lost City '98
Mowgli and Baloo '97

Charles Johnson
Beyond Atlantis '73

Charles Eric Johnson
The Last Sentinel '07

David C(lark) Johnson (1962-)
Steele's Law '91
Hard Lessons '86

Kenneth Johnson (1942-)
Steel '97
Alien Nation: Millennium '96
Hot Pursuit '84
V '83

Mark Steven Johnson (1964-)
Ghost Rider '07
Daredevil '03
Simon Birch '98
Big Bully '95
Grumpier Old Men '95
Grumpy Old Men '93

Niall Johnson
The Scout '94
Mother '96
The Muse '99

Monica Johnson (1956-)
Americathon '79
Modern Romance '81
Torque '04
Real Life '79

Nunnally Johnson (1897-1977)
The Dirty Dozen '67
The World of Henry Orient '64
Jekyll & Hyde... Together Again '82

Matt Johnson
Into the Blue '05

Kristine Johnson
I Am Sam '01

Jesse Johnson (1982-)
DROP Squad '94
Woo '97
Pit Fighter '05

Tony Johnston (1960-)
Hollywood North '03
Triggermen '02
Full Disclosure '00
Killing Moon '03

Stephen Johnston
Starkweather '04
Ed Gein '01

Rory Johnston
Prey of the Jaguar '96

Ed Jones
Carried Away '95
Ninja in the U.S.A. '88

Evan Jones (1927-)
Shadow of the Wolf '92
A Show of Force '90
Kangaroo '86
Modesty Blaise '66
King and Country '64

Grover Jones (1893-1940)
Souls at Sea '37
The Trail of the Lonesome Pine '36
The Lives of a Bengal Lancer '35
Strangers in Love '32
Trouble in Paradise '32
Gun Smoke '31
Touchdown '31

Amy Holden Jones (1953-)
The Relic '96
The Rich Man's Wife '96
The Getaway '93
Indecent Proposal '93
Beethoven '92
Indecency '92
Mystic Pizza '88
Love Letters '83

Toni Johnson
Crown Heights '02
Ruby Bridges '98
The Courage to Love '00

Robert P. Johnson
The Prisoner of Shark Island '36

Becky Johnston
Seven Years in Tibet '97
The Prince of Tides '91

Agnes Christine Johnston (1896-1978)
Lucky Devils '33
The Last Winter '89

Aaron Kim Johnston
For the Moment '96

Kurt Johnstad
300 '07

Bojangles '01
The Temptations '98
Tyson '95

Ian Jones (1931-)
The Lighthorsemen '87
Ned Kelly '70
Dolemite 2: Human Tornado '76

Jerry Jones
The Three Faces of Eve '57
Black Widow '54
The Bostonians '84
Mr. Hobbs Takes a Vacation '62
Heat and Dust '83
Quartet '81

Ruth Prawer Jhabvala (1927-)
Le Divorce '03
The Golden Bowl '00
The City of Lost Children '95
Delicatessen '92
A Room with a View '86
Madame Sousatzka '88
Howard's End '92
The Remains of the Day '93
Jefferson in Paris '94
Surviving Picasso '96
A Soldier's Daughter Never Cries '98

Jean-Pierre Jeunet
Amelie '01
Alien: Resurrection '97

Jack Jevne (1892-1972)

Peter Jobin
Autobiography of a Princess '75
Bombay Talkie '70
Shakespeare Wallah '65

Wong Jing
The Europeans '79
Hullabaloo over Georgie & Bonnie's Pictures '78
Roseland '77

Jane Austen in Manhattan '80
How to Marry a Millionaire '53
Phone Call from a Stranger '52
We're Not Married '52
Three Came Home '50
Mr. Peabody & the Mermaid '48
Along Came Jones '45
Casanova Brown '44
The Keys of the Kingdom '44
Woman in the Window '44
Roxie Hart '42
The Grapes of Wrath '40
Jesse James '39
Rose of Washington Square '39
The Prisoner of Shark Island '36

Dolemite '75
Laura Jones (1951-)
Possession '02
Angela's Ashes '99
Oscar and Lucinda '97
A Thousand Acres '97
The Well '97
Portrait of a Lady '96
An Angel at My Table '89
High Tide '87
Cass '78
Mark Jones (1953-)
Rumpelstiltskin '96
Leprechaun '93
Pete Jones
Outing Riley '04
Stolen Summer '02
Robert C. Jones
P.D. James: The Murder Room '04
P.D. James: Death in Holy Orders '03
Coming Home '78
Terry Jones (1942-)
Mr. Toad's Wild Ride '96
Erik the Viking '89
Labyrinth '86
Monty Python's The Meaning of Life '83
Monty Python's Life of Brian '79
Monty Python and the Holy Grail '75
And Now for Something Completely Different '72
Gregor Jordan (1967-)
Buffalo Soldiers '01
Two Hands '99
Neil Jordan (1950-)
The Good Thief '03
The End of the Affair '99
In Dreams '98
The Butcher Boy '97
Michael Collins '96
The Crying Game '92
The Miracle '91
High Spirits '88
Mona Lisa '86
The Company of Wolves '85
Danny Boy '82
Robert L. Joseph (1923-2002)
World War III '86
The Hitch-Hiker '53
Jon Jost (1943-)
The Bed You Sleep In '93
Jon Jost's Frameup '93
All the Vermeers in New York '91
Sure Fire '90
Slow Moves '84
Adrien (Carole Eastman) Joyce (1934-2004)
Man Trouble '92
Five Easy Pieces '70
The Shooting '66
Odette Joyeux (1917-2000)
The Bride Is Much Too Beautiful '58
Sois Belle et Tais-Toi '58
C. Courtney Joyner
Stealing Candy '04
Lady Jayne Killer '03
Nautilus '99
Public Enemies '96
Lurking Fear '94
Desperate Motives '92
Trancers 3: Death Lives '92
Class of 1999 '90
Puppet Master 3: Toulon's Revenge '90
Vietnam, Texas '90
Catacombs '89
Prison '88
Mike Judge (1962-)
Idiocracy '06
Office Space '98

Beavis and Butt-Head Do America '96
Jerry Juhl (1938-2005)
Muppets from Space '99
Muppet Treasure Island '96
The Muppet Movie '79
Lenny Juliano
Desert Thunder '99
Stealth Fighter '99
Harry Junkin
Vendetta for the Saint '68
Fiction Makers '67
Karel Kachyna (1924-2004)
The Cow '93
The Last Butterfly '92
Cedric Kahn (1966-)
Red Lights '04
L'Ennui '98
Gordon Kahn (1902-62)
Lights of Old Santa Fe '47
Cowboy & the Senorita '44
Chen Kaige (1952-)
The Promise '05
Together '02
The Emperor and the Assassin '99
Life on a String '90
Michael Kalesniko (1961-)
How to Kill Your Neighbor's Dog '01
Spoiler '98
Private Parts '96
Tom Kalin
Office Killer '97
Swoon '91
Bert Kalmar (1884-1947)
A Night at the Opera '35
Duck Soup '33
Horse Feathers '32
Kid from Spain '32
Laeta Kalogridis (1965-)
Pathfinder '07
Alexander '04
Steven Kaman
The Outfit '93
Firehouse '87
Hangmen '87
Karl Kamb (1903-88)
Pitfall '48
Robert Mark Kamen
Transporter 2 '05
The Transporter '02
Kiss of the Dragon '01
A Walk in the Clouds '95
Gladiator '92
Lethal Weapon 3 '92
The Karate Kid: Part 3 '89
The Karate Kid: Part 2 '86
The Karate Kid '84
Taps '81
Steven Kampmann (1947-)
Clifford '92
Stealing Home '88
The Couch Trip '87
Back to School '86
John Kamps
Zathura '05
David Kane
The River King '05
Born Romantic '00
Michael Kane
The Cisco Kid '94
The Bear '89
All the Right Moves '83
Hard Country '81

Legend of the Lone Ranger '81
Southern Comfort '81
Foolin' Around '80
Hot Stuff '80
Smokey and the Bandit 2 '80
Rolfe Kanefsky (1969-)
Blonde and Blonder '07
The Hazing '04
Red Line '96
There's Nothing out There '90
Charles Kanganis
Impulse '08
No Escape, No Return '93
Fist of Honor '92
A Time to Die '91
Fay Kanin (1917-)
Teacher's Pet '58
The Opposite Sex '56
Rhapsody '54
Garson Kanin (1912-99)
It Should Happen to You '54
The Marrying Kind '52
Pat and Mike '52
Adam's Rib '49
A Double Life '47
Michael Kanin (1910-93)
How to Commit Marriage '69
Teacher's Pet '58
The Opposite Sex '56
Rhapsody '54
Woman of the Year '42
Panama Lady '39
Hal Kanter (1918-)
Bachelor in Paradise '69
Dear Brigitte '65
Move Over, Darling '63
Blue Hawaii '62
Pocketful of Miracles '61
Loving You '57
Artists and Models '55
The Rose Tattoo '55
Casanova's Big Night '54
Here Come the Girls '53
The Road to Bali '53
Deborah Kaplan
Made of Honor '08
Surviving Christmas '04
Josie and the Pussycats '01
The Flintstones in Viva Rock Vegas '00
Can't Hardly Wait '98
A Very Brady Sequel '96
Jonathan Kaplan (1947-)
In the Mood for Love '00
Happy Together '96
Chungking Express '95
Fallen Angels '95
Wong Kar-Wai (1958-)
My Blueberry Nights '07
2046 '04
Eros '04
Marty Kaplan
Mr. Billion '77
White Line Fever '75
Larry Karaszewski (1961-)
1408 '07
Agent Cody Banks '03
Screwed '00
Man on the Moon '99
The People vs. Larry Flynt '96
Luca Karall
Maria's Day '84
25 Fireman's Street '73
The Distinguished Gentleman '92
Noises Off '92
Mitchell Kapner
The Whole Ten Yards '04
The Whole Nine Yards '00
Jake Kasdan (1975-)
Walk Hard: The Dewey Cox Story '07

The TV Set '06
Zero Effect '97
Lawrence Kasdan (1949-)
Dreamcatcher '03
Mumford '99
Wyatt Earp '94
The Bodyguard '92
Grand Canyon '91
The Accidental Tourist '88
Silverado '85
The Big Chill '83
Return of the Jedi '83
Body Heat '81
Continental Divide '81
The Empire Strikes Back '80
Sam Henry Kass
Body and Soul '98
The Search for One-Eyed Jimmy '96
Mathieu Kassovitz (1967-)
Babylon AD '08
The Crimson Rivers '01
Hate '95
Cafe au Lait '94
Brian Katkin
Shakedown '02
Hard As Nails '01
If I Die Before I Wake '98
A.L. Katz
Tales from the Crypt Presents Bordello of Blood '96
Children of the Corn 2: The Final Sacrifice '92
Gloria Katz
Radioland Murders '94
Howard the Duck '86
Best Defense '84
Indiana Jones and the Temple of Doom '84
French Postcards '79
More American Graffiti '79
Messiah of Evil '74
American Graffiti '73
Jordan Katz (1960-)
Valiant '05
Incognito '97
Stephen Katz (1946-2005)
From the Earth to the Moon '98
Satan's Princess '90
Steven Katz
Wind Chill '07
Shadow of the Vampire '00
Fallen Angels 1 '93
Charles Kaufman
Ferocious Female Freedom Fighters '88
Waitress '81
Mother's Day '80
Squeeze Play '79
Charles A. Kaufman (1904-91)
The Story of Esther Costello '57
Return to Paradise '53
Charlie Kaufman (1958-)
Eternal Sunshine of the Spotless Mind '04
Adaptation '02
Confessions of a Dangerous Mind '02
Human Nature '02
Being John Malkovich '99
George S. Kaufman (1889-1961)
Star Spangled Rhythm '42
A Night at the Opera '35
The Cocoanuts '29
Ken Kaufman (1963-)
Curious George '06
The Missing '03
Space Cowboys '00
In the Army Now '94
Lloyd Kaufman (1945-)
Citizen Toxie: The Toxic Avenger 4 '01

Class of Nuke 'Em High 3: The Good, the Bad and the Subhumanoid '94
Sgt. Kabukiman N.Y.P.D. '94
Class of Nuke 'Em High 2: Subhumanoid Meltdown '91
The Toxic Avenger, Part 2 '89
The Toxic Avenger, Part 3: The Last Temptation of Toxie '89
Troma's War '88
Class of Nuke 'Em High '86
Stuck on You '83
First Turn On '83
Millard Kaufman (1917-)
Living Free '72
The War Lord '65
Philip Kaufman (1936-)
Rising Sun '93
Henry & June '90
The Unbearable Lightness of Being '88
The Right Stuff '83
Raiders of the Lost Ark '81
Wanderers '79
The Outlaw Josey Wales '76
The Great Northfield Minnesota Raid '72
Goldstein '64
Robert Kaufman
Love at First Bite '79
Ski Party '65
Aki Kaurismaki (1957-)
Lights in the Dusk '06
The Man Without a Past '02
La Vie de Boheme '93
The Match Factory Girl '90
Ariel '89
Leningrad Cowboys Go America '89
Helmut Kautner (1908-80)
The Last Bridge '54
Die Grosse Freiheit Nr. 7 '45
Frances Kavanaugh
Driftin' River '46
Wild West '46
Trail Riders '42
Jerzy Kawalerowicz (1922-2007)
Pharaoh '66
Mother Joan of the Angels '60
Kikuo Kawasaki
Lured Innocence '97
Private Passions '85
Stephen Kay
The Mod Squad '99
Tony Kayden
When Justice Falls '98
Slipstream '89
John Kaye
Along for the Ride '00
Where the Buffalo Roam '80
Nicholas Kazan (1950-)
Enough '02
Bicentennial Man '99
Fallen '97
Homegrown '97
Matilda '96
Dream Lover '93
Mobsters '91
Reversal of Fortune '90
Patty Hearst '88
At Close Range '86
Impulse '84
Frances '82
Tim Kazurinsky (1950-)
Strange Relations '02
The Cherokee Kid '96
For Keeps '88
About Last Night... '86

James Keach (1948-)
The Forgotten '89
Armed and Dangerous '86
The Long Riders '80
Slashed Dreams '74
Gene R. Kearney
The Invasion of Carol Enders '74
Night of the Lepus '72
Games '67
Joe Keenan (1958-)
Flushed Away '06
Sleep with Me '94
Jon Keeyes
Living & Dying '07
American Nightmare '00
Harvey Keith
Stand-Ins '97
Jezebel's Kiss '90
Woody Keith
Dementia '98
Bride of Re-Animator '89
Ed Kelleher (1944-2005)
Stand-Ins '97
Lurkers '88
Shriek of the Mutilated '74
Invasion of the Blood Farmers '72
Sean Keller
Kraken: Tentacles of the Deep '06
Mammoth '06
Cindy Kelley
Saving Sarah Cain '07
Love's Enduring Promise '04
David E. Kelley (1956-)
Lake Placid '99
Mystery, Alaska '99
To Gillian on Her 37th Birthday '96
Nick Kellis
Endangered '94
Uncivilized '94
Bob Kelljan (1930-82)
The Return of Count Yorga '71
Count Yorga, Vampire '70
Bill Kelly
Enchanted '07
Premonition '07
Blast from the Past '98
Karen Kelly
The Last Best Sunday '98
Poison Ivy 3: The New Seduction '97
The Corporation '96
Body Chemistry 4: Full Exposure '95
Hard Bounty '94
Illicit Dreams '94
Patrick Smith Kelly
Don't Say a Word '01
A Perfect Murder '98
Richard Kelly (1975-)
Southland Tales '06
Domino '05
Donnie Darko '01
Tim Kelly (1931-98)
Fist '76
Homeboy '75
Cry of the Banshee '70
Edmond Kelso (1910-69)
King of the Zombies '41
Up in the Air '40
Roll, Wagons, Roll '39
Tex Rides with the Boy Scouts '37
Kurt Kempler
Telegraph Trail '33
The Big Stampede '32
Two-Fisted Law '32
Anne Kennedy (1959-)
The Monkey's Mask '00
Crush '93
Burt Kennedy (1922-2001)
Texas Guns '90
White Hunter, Black Heart '90

Dyna nite and Gold '88
The Trouble with Spies '87
Train Robbers '73
Hannie Caulder '72
The Rounders '65
Comanche Station '60
Ride Lonesome '59
The "all T" '57

Chris Kennedy
Doing Time for Patsy Cline '97

Jane Kennedy (1964-)
The Dish '00
The Castle '97

Kerry Kennedy
Baby '00
Hope '97

Michael Kennedy (1954-)
The Swordsman '92
Erik '90

William Kennedy (1928-)
Ironweed '87
The Cotton Club '84

Doug Kenney
Caddyshack '80
National Lampoon's Animal House '78

Gary Kent (1933-)
Street Corner Justice '96
L.A. Bad '85

Robert E. Kent
Diary of a Madman '63
Twice-Told Tales '63
Dick Tracy vs. Cueball '46
Zombies on Broadway '44
Gildersleeve on Broadway '43

Willis Kent (1878-1966)
Mad Youth '40
Sucker Money '34

Earl Kenton
Invisible: The Chronicles of Benjamin Knight '93
Mandroid '93

Charles Kenyon (1880-1961)
103 Men and a Girl '37
The Penalty '20

Curtis Kenyon (1914-)
Think Fast, Mr. Moto '37
Wounded Knee '94

Rob Kercher
Twin Beds '42

Bill Kerby
On the Beach '00
Dead Men Can't Dance '97
Hooper '78

Rob Kerchner
Heaven's Fire '99
Turbulence 2: Fear of Flying '99
Route 9 '98
Boodfist 7: Manhunt '95
Boodfist 6: Ground Zerc '94
Boodfist: Blue Smoke '07

Fonni Kern
Jesse Stone: Sea Change '07

Sarah Kernochan (1947-)
All I Wanna Do '98
Sommersby '93
Impromptu '90

Lodge Kerrigan (1964-)
Keane '04
Claire Dolan '97
Clean, Shaven '93

Wendy Kesselman
A Separate Peace '04
I Love You, I Love You Not '97

Lyle Kessler
The Saint of Fort Washington '93
Gladiator '92
Orphans '87

Michael Keusch (1955-)
Samurai Cowboy '93
Lena's Holiday '90

Edward Khmara
Merlin '98
Dragon: The Bruce Lee Story '93
Enemy Mine '85
Ladyhawke '85

Callie Khouri (1957-)
Divine Secrets of the Ya-Ya Sisterhood '02
Something to Talk About '95
Thelma & Louise '91

Abbas Kiarostami (1940-)
Crimson Gold '03
The Taste of Cherry '96
The White Balloon '95
Through the Olive Trees '94
Life and Nothing More... '92
Where Is My Friend's House? '87

David Kidd
Yours, Mine & Ours '05
Head Over Heels '01

Dylan Kidd (1969-)
P.S. '04
Roger Dodger '02

Krzysztof Kieslowski (1941-96)
Heaven '01
Trois Couleurs: Blanc '94
Trois Couleurs: Rouge '94
Trois Couleurs: Bleu '93
The Double Life of Veronique '91
The Decalogue '88
No End '84

Ryuzo Kikushima
High & Low '62
Sanjuro '62
Yojimbo '61
Throne of Blood '57
Scandal '50

Ki-Duk Kim
Time '06
The Isle '01

Lawrence Kimble (1904-77)
Seven Days Ashore '44
Zombies on Broadway '44
Bells of Capistrano '42

Bruce Kimmel (1947-)
The Creature Wasn't Nice '81
The First Nudie Musical '75

Simon Kinberg (1973-)
Jumper '08
X-Men: The Last Stand '06
Mr. & Mrs. Smith '05
XXX: State of the Union '05
Fantastic Four '05

Tim Kincaid (1952-)
The Occultist '89
Mutant Hunt '87
Robot Holocaust '87
Breeders '86

Bradley King
Under the Pampas Moon '35

Chloe King
Red Shoe Diaries: Luscious Lola '00
Swimming Naked '00

I. Marlene King
Just My Luck '06
Now and Then '95
If These Walls Could Talk '96

Robert King
Vertical Limit '00
Red Corner '97
Cutthroat Island '95
Clean Slate '94
Speechless '94

Stephen King (1947-)
Stephen King's Rose Red '02
The Nest '88
Stephen King's The Storm of the Century '99
Stephen King's The Stand '94
Sleepwalkers '92
Stephen King's Golden Years '91
Graveyard Shift '90
Stephen King's It '90
Pet Sematary '89
Maximum Overdrive '86
Cat's Eye '85
Silver Bullet '85
Creepshow '82

Zalman King (1941-)
Red Shoe Diaries: Swimming Naked '00
In God's Hands '98
Business for Pleasure '96
Red Shoe Diaries: Strip Poker '96
Two Moon Junction '88
Wild Orchid '90
Wild Orchid 2: Two Shades of Blue '92
Lake Consequence '92
Wildfire '88

Dorothy Kingsley (1909-97)
Valley of the Dolls '67
Green Mansions '59
Don't Go Near the Water '57
Pal Joey '57
Seven Brides for Seven Brothers '54
Angels in the Outfield '51
Easy to Wed '46
Broadway Rhythm '44

Ernest Kinoy (1925-)
Rescuers: Stories of Courage "Two Women" '97
Gore Vidal's Lincoln '88
Murrow '86
Roots '77
The Story of David '76
Victory at Entebbe '76

Ralf Kirsten (1930-)
'90

Takeshi "Beat" Kitano (1948-)
Zatoichi '03
Dolls '02
Brother '00
Kikujiro '99
Fireworks '97
Sonatine '96

Martin Kitrosser
Facing the Enemy '00
The Toymaker '91
Friday the 13th, Part 5: A New Beginning '85
Friday the 13th, Part 3 '82

Cedric Klapisch (1961-)
Russian Dolls '05
L'Auberge Espagnole '02
Un Air de Famille '96
When the Cat's Away '96

David Klass
Walking Tall '04
Kiss the Girls '97
Desperate Measures '96
In the Time of the Butterflies '01

Marc Klein
A Good Year '06
Serendipity '01
Suburban Girl '07

Andrew Klavan
One Missed Call '08
Don't Say a Word '01
A Shock to the System '90

Philip Klein
Too Busy to Work '32
The Black Camel '31
Four Sons '28

Nicholas Klein
The End of Violence '97
The Million Dollar Hotel '99

Robert Dean Klein
Heart of America '03

Harry Kleiner (1916-2007)
Le Mans '71
Fantastic Voyage '66
House of Bamboo '55
Carmen Jones '54

Walter Klenhard
Disappearance '02
Buried Alive 2 '97
The Haunting of Seacliff Inn '94
The Last Hit '93
Blackwoods '02

Richard Kletter
Missing Pieces '00
The Android Affair '95
Dangerous Indiscretion '94
The Colony '96

Claude Klotz (1932-)
The Man on the Train '02

The Story of Jacob & Joseph '74

Teinosuke Kinugasa (1896-1982)
Gate of Hell '54

Jack Kirkland
The Golden Coach '52

Karey Kirkpatrick
The Spiderwick Chronicles '08
Charlotte's Web '06
Over the Hedge '06
Chicken Run '00
The Little Vampire '00
Honey, We Shrunk Ourselves '97

Robert Klane (1941-)
Weekend at Bernie's 2 '93
Weekend at Bernie's '89
National Lampoon's European Vacation '85
Unfaithfully Yours '84
Where's Poppa? '70

Patricia Louisianna Knop
Red Shoe Diaries: Strip Poker '96
Delta of Venus '95
Siesta '87
9 1/2 Weeks '86

Masaki Kobayashi (1916-96)
The Human Condition: Road to Eternity '59
The Human Condition: No Greater Love '58

Christopher Knopf
Not My Kid '85
Emperor of the North Pole '73
20 Million Miles to Earth '57

Andrew Knight
The Efficiency Expert '92

Steven Knight (1959-)
Eastern Promises '07
Amazing Grace '06
Dirty Pretty Things '03

Howard Koch (1901-95)
War Lover '62
Rhapsody in Blue '45
Casablanca '42
Sergeant York '41
The Letter '40
The Sea Hawk '40

Laird Koenig
Black Water '94
The Little Girl Who Lives down the Lane '76

David Koepp (1964-)
Indiana Jones and the Kingdom of the Crystal Skull '08
War of the Worlds '05
Zathura '05
Secret Window '04
Panic Room '02
Spider-Man '02
Stir of Echoes '99
Snake Eyes '98
The Lost World: Jurassic Park 2 '97
Mission: Impossible '96
The Trigger Effect '96
The Paper '94
The Shadow '94
Carlito's Way '93
Jurassic Park '93
Death Becomes Her '92
Apartment Zero '88

The Hairdresser's Husband '92

Steven Kloves (1960-)
Harry Potter and the Goblet of Fire '05
Harry Potter and the Prisoner of Azkaban '04
Harry Potter and the Chamber of Secrets '02
Harry Potter and the Sorcerer's Stone '01
Wonder Boys '00
Flesh and Bone '93
The Fabulous Baker Boys '89
Racing with the Moon '84

Nigel Kneale (1922-2006)
Sharpe's Gold '94
Woman in Black '89
The Witches '66
First Men in the Moon '64
Damn the Defiant! '62
The Entertainer '60
Look Back in Anger '58
Quatermass and the Pit '58
The Abominable Snowman '57
Quatermass 2 '57

Ana Kokkinos (1959-)

Amos Kollek (1947-)
Fiona '98
Whore 2 '94
Double Edge '92
High Stakes '89

Andrei Konchalovsky (1937-)
House of Fools '02
The Odyssey '97
The Inner Circle '91
Runaway Train '85
Maria's Lovers '84
Shy People '87
Siberiade '79

Kate Kondell (1973-)
First Daughter '04
Legally Blonde 2: Red White & Blonde '03

Larry Konner
Flicka '06
Mona Lisa Smile '03
Planet of the Apes '01
Mighty Joe Young '98
The Beverly Hillbillies '93
For Love or Money '93
Sometimes They Come Back '91

Brian Koppelman
Ocean's Thirteen '07
The Insatiable '06
Knockaround Guys '01
Rounders '98

Peter Koper
Island of the Dead '00
Headless Body in Topless Bar '96

Chuck Konzelman
The Jewel of the Nile '85

Howard Korder
Stealing Sinatra '04
Walking Tall '04
My Little Assassin '99

Steve Koren
Click '06
Bruce Almighty '03
Superstar '99
A Night at the Roxbury '98

Hirokazu Kore-eda (1962-)
Nobody Knows '04
After Life '98

Arthur Kopit (1937-)
Roswell: The U.F.O. Cover-Up '94
The Phantom of the Opera '90
Hands of a Stranger '87

Abby Kohn
He's Just Not That Into You '08
Never Been Kissed '99

Emil Kolbe
Only the Brave '94

Wolfgang Kohlhaase (1931-)
The Legend of Rita '99
Solo Sunny '80

Randy Kornfield
Jingle All the Way '96

David A. Korn
Cash Crop '01

Harmony Korine (1974-)
Julien Donkey-boy '99
Gummo '97
Kids '95

Balsazar Kormakur (1966-)
The Sea '02
101 Reykjavik '00

Mari Kornhauser
The Last Ride '94
Zardalee '91

Scott Kosar
The Machinist '04
The Texas Chainsaw Massacre '03
Ron Koslow
Last Dance '96
Running Delilah '93
Into the Night '85
Lifeguard '76
Jim Kouf (1951-)
National Treasure '04
Taxi '04
Snow Dogs '02
Rush Hour '98
Gang Related '96
Operation Dumbo Drop '95
Another Stakeout '93
Disorganized Crime '89
The Hidden '87
Stakeout '87
Class '83
Edward Kovach
Blink of an Eye '92
Jailbird Rock '88
Paul Koval
Dead Silent '99
Psychic '91
Blue Movies '88
Janet Kovalcik
My Girl 2 '94
Married to It '93
Karl Kozak (1964-)
Clawed: The Legend of Sasquatch '05
Out of the Black '01
Soeren Kragh-Jacobsen (1947-)
Mifune '99
Andrzej Krakowski (1946-)
Eminent Domain '91
Triumph of the Spirit '89
Mindhunters '05
The Cooler '03
Norman Krasna (1909-84)
Sunday in New York '63
Let's Make Love '60
Indiscreet '58
The Ambassador's Daughter '56
The Big Hangover '50
The Flame of New Orleans '41
It Started with Eve '41
Mr. & Mrs. Smith '41
It's a Date '40
Wife Versus Secretary '36
Hands Across the Table '35
So This is Africa '33
Stu Krieger (1952-)
In the Army Now '94
Monkey Trouble '94
A Troll in Central Park '94
The Land Before Time '88
Peter Krikes
Star Trek 4: The Voyage Home '86
Milton Krims (1904-88)
Mohawk '56
Tennessee's Partner '55
Prince of Foxes '49
Henry Krinkle
Night Eyes 4: Fatal Passion '95
Sandy Kroopf
Contagious '96
Birdy '84

Lisa Krueger (1961-)
Committed '99
Manny & Lo '96
Ehren Kruger (1972-)
Blood & Chocolate '07
The Brothers Grimm '05
The Ring 2 '05
The Skeleton Key '05
Impostor '02
The Ring '02
Reindeer Games '00
Scream 3 '00
Arlington Road '99
New World Disorder '99
Carl Krusada (1879-1951)
El Diablo Rides '39
Fast Bullets '36
Silent Valley '35
Skull & Crown '35
Mystery Trooper '32
John Kruse
Vendetta for the Saint '68
Fiction Makers '67
Stanley Kubrick (1928-99)
Eyes Wide Shut '99
Full Metal Jacket '87
The Shining '80
Barry Lyndon '75
A Clockwork Orange '71
2001: A Space Odyssey '68
Dr. Strangelove, or: How I Learned to Stop Worrying and Love the Bomb '64
Paths of Glory '57
The Killing '56
Killer's Kiss '55
Robert Kuhn
Mickey Blue Eyes '99
The Cure '95
High Strung '91
Sid Kuller (1910-93)
Big Store '41
Argentine Nights '40
Roger Kumble (1966-)
Cruel Intentions 2 '99
Cruel Intentions '98
National Lampoon's Senior Trip '95
Hanif Kureishi (1954-)
Venus '06
The Mother '03
My Son the Fanatic '97
The Buddha of Suburbia '92
London Kills Me '91
Sammy & Rosie Get Laid '87
My Beautiful Laundrette '85
Harry Kurnitz (1908-68)
How to Steal a Million '66
Goodbye Charlie '64
Witness for the Prosecution '57
The Inspector General '49
One Touch of Venus '48
Something in the Wind '47
They Got Me Covered '43
Ship Ahoy '42
Akira Kurosawa (1910-98)
Rhapsody in August '91
Akira Kurosawa's Dreams '90
Ran '85
Kagemusha '80
Dersu Uzala '75
Dodes 'ka-den '70
High & Low '62
Sanjuro '62
Yojimbo '61
The Bad Sleep Well '60
The Hidden Fortress '58
Throne of Blood '57
The Lower Depths '57
I Live in Fear '55
Seven Samurai '54
Ikiru '52
Rashomon '51
Scandal '50
A Quiet Duel '49
One Wonderful Sunday '47
No Regrets for Our Youth '46

The Men Who Tread on the Tiger's Tail '45
Kiyoshi Kurosawa (1955-)
Bright Future '03
Pulse '01
Alex Kurtzman (1973-)
Transformers '07
Mission: Impossible 3 '06
The Island '05
The Legend of Zorro '05
Andrew Kurtzman
Down Periscope '96
Camp Nowhere '94
See No Evil, Hear No Evil '89
Number One with a Bullet '87
Diane Kurys (1948-)
Children of the Century '99
Love After Love '94
Six Days, Six Nights '94
A Man in Love '87
Entre-Nous '83
Peppermint Soda '77
Tony Kushner (1956-)
Munich '05
Alex Kustanovich
Angels in America '03
Mirror Wars: Reflection One '05
Emir Kusturica (1954-)
Underground '95
Arizona Dream '94
Richard Kwietniowski (1957-)
Owning Mahowny '03
Love and Death on Long Island '97
Christopher Kyle
Alexander '04
K-19: The Widowmaker '02
The Weight of Water '00
Gregory La Cava (1892-1952)
My Man Godfrey '36
The Half Naked Truth '32
Ian La Frenais (1937-)
The Bank Job '08
Across the Universe '07
Flushed Away '06
Goal! The Dream Begins '06
Archangel '05
Still Crazy '98
Excess Baggage '96
The Commitments '91
Vice Versa '88
Water '85
Prisoner of Zenda '79
It's Not the Size That Counts '74
Catch Me a Spy '71
Lynda La Plante (1946-)
Widows '02
Bella Mafia '97
Framed '93
Prime Suspect '92
Michael LaBash
Lilo & Stitch 2: Stitch Has a Glitch '05
Jeanne Labrune (1950-)
Vatel '00
Neil LaBute (1963-)
The Wicker Man '06
The Shape of Things '03
Possession '02
Your Friends & Neighbors '98
In the Company of Men '96
Gregory LaCava
See Gregory La Cava
Kathleen Laccinole
Dr. Dolittle 4: Tail to the Chief '08
A Dennis the Menace Christmas '07
Antoine Lacomblez
Love After Love '94

Six Days, Six Nights '94
Aldo Lado (1934-)
Night Train Murders '75
Torture Train '75
Short Night of Glass Dolls '71
John Lafia
Man's Best Friend '93
Child's Play '88
Ian LaFrenais
See Ian La Frenais
Jacques Lagrange
Traffic '71
Mon Oncle '58
Mr. Hulot's Holiday '53
Richard LaGravenese (1959-)
Freedom Writers '07
P.S. I Love You '07
Paris, je t'aime '06
Beloved '98
Living Out Loud '98
The Horse Whisperer '97
The Mirror Has Two Faces '96
The Bridges of Madison County '95
A Little Princess '95
Unstrung Heroes '95
The Ref '93
The Fisher King '91
Rude Awakening '89
Don Lake (1956-)
Return to Me '00
The Extreme Adventures of Super Dave '98
Frank Laloggia (1954-)
The Lady in White '88
Fear No Evil '80
Paul LaLonde
Revelation '00
Tribulation '00
Peter LaLonde (1960-)
Revelation '00
Tribulation '00
Ross LaManna
Rush Hour '98
John Lamb
Postmortem '98
The Mermaids of Tiburon '62
Bruce Lambert
See Godfrey Ho
Gavin Lambert (1924-2005)
Dead on the Money '91
Sweet Bird of Youth '89
I Never Promised You a Rose Garden '77
Inside Daisy Clover '65
Roman Spring of Mrs. Stone '61
Ken Lamplugh
Midnight Kiss '93
Private Wars '93
Bill Lancaster (1947-97)
The Bad News Bears '05
The Thing '82
The Bad News Bears Go to Japan '78
The Bad News Bears '76
Richard H. Landau (1914-93)
Race for Life '55
Blackout '54
Sins of Jezebel '54
A Stolen Face '52
The Lost Continent '51
James Landis (1926-91)
The Sadist '63
Stakeout '62
John Landis (1950-)
Blues Brothers 2000 '98
Dying to Get Rich '98
Clue '85

Twilight Zone: The Movie '83
An American Werewolf in London '81
The Blues Brothers '80
Schlock '73
Christopher Landon (1975-)
Blood & Chocolate '07
Disturbia '07
Another Day in Paradise '98
Joseph Landon
Von Ryan's Express '65
The Hoodlum Priest '61
Michael Landon (1936-91)
Sam's Son '84
Killing Stone '78
Michael Landon, Jr. (1964-)
Love's Long Journey '05
Love's Enduring Promise '04
Love Comes Softly '03
Fritz Lang (1890-1976)
The Thousand Eyes of Dr. Mabuse '60
M '31
Metropolis '26
Dr. Mabuse, The Gambler '22
The Indian Tomb '21
Harry Langdon (1884-1944)
Road Show '41
The Flying Deuces '39
John Langley
Deadly Sins '95
Noel Langley (1911-80)
Snow White and the Three Stooges '61
The Search for Bridey Murphy '56
The Adventures of Sadie '55
Svengali '55
Ivanhoe '52
A Christmas Carol '51
They Made Me a Fugitive '47
The Wizard of Oz '39
Maytime '37
King of the Damned '36
Arlette Langmann
Germinal '93
A Nos Amours '84
Kate Lanier
Beauty Shop '05
Glitter '01
The Mod Squad '99
Set It Off '96
What's Love Got to Do with It? '93
T.L. Lankford
Storm Trooper '98
Hollywood Chainsaw Hookers '88
Phantom Empire '87
Ring Lardner, Jr. (1915-2000)
The Greatest '77
M*A*S*H '70
The Cincinnati Kid '65
Forever Amber '47
Cloak and Dagger '46
Laura '44
Tomorrow the World '44
Woman of the Year '42
John Larkin
The Dolly Sisters '46
Charlie Chan in Honolulu '39
Glen Larson (1937-)
The Darwin Conspiracy '99
Magnum P.I.: Don't Eat the Snow in Hawaii '80
Battlestar Galactica: The Cylon Attack '78
Mission Galactica: The...
Louis LaRusso, II (1935-2003)
The Closer '91
Hell Hunters '87

James Lasdun (1958-)
Signs & Wonders '00
Sunday '96
Alex Lasker
Tears of the Sun '03
Beyond Rangoon '95
Lawrence Lasker (1949-)
Sneakers '92
Project X '87
WarGames '83
Andrew Laskos
A Face to Kill For '99
A Prayer in the Dark '97
Jesse Lasky, Jr. (1910-88)
John Paul Jones '59
The Ten Commandments '56
Unconquered '47
Reap the Wild Wind '42
Back in the Saddle '41
Union Pacific '39
Louise Lasser (1939-)
Just Me & You '78
What's Up, Tiger Lily? '66
Aaron Latham
The Program '93
Perfect '85
Urban Cowboy '80
Jonathan Latimer (1906-83)
The Big Clock '48
Nocturne '46
The Glass Key '42
Topper Returns '41
Steve Latshaw (1959-)
Scorcher '02
U.S. Navy SEALS: Dead or Alive '02
Black Horizon '01
Ablaze '00
Mach 2 '00
Rangers '00
Submerged '00
Counter Measures '99
Militia '99
Invisible Dad '97
Scorpio One '97
Greg Latter
The Color of Freedom '07
Dangerous Ground '96
Cyborg Cop '93
Michael Laughlin
Town and Country '01
Strange Behavior '81
Tom Laughlin (1939-)
The Trial of Billy Jack '74
Billy Jack '71
Born Losers '67
Frank Launder (1907-97)
The Belles of St. Trinian's '53
The Happiest Days of Your Life '50
Captain Boycott '47
Night Train to Munich '40
The Lady Vanishes '38
Dale Launer (1952-)
Love Potion #9 '92
My Cousin Vinny '92
Dirty Rotten Scoundrels '88
Blind Date '87
Salvatore Laurani (1924-)
Confessions of a Police Captain '72
A Bullet for the General '68
S.K. Lauren (1893-1979)
When Ladies Meet '41
Crime and Punishment '35
Christine Laurent (1948-)
Va Savoir '01
Jeanne la Pucelle '94
La Belle Noiseuse '90
Arthur Laurents (1918-)
Gypsy '93
The Turning Point '77

The Way We Were '73
Gypsy '62
Bonjour Tristesse '57
Anastasia '56
Rope '48

Russell Lavalle
Secret Games 2: The Escort '93

Paul Laverty (1957-)
Sins of the Night '93
Bartley '06
Sweet Sixteen '02
Bread and Roses '00
My Name Is Joe '98
Carla's Song '96

George LaVoo
Real Women Have Curves '02
Frisk '95

Evan Law
Hero Wanted '09

William Lawlor
Hero Wanted '09
Mexican Blow '02
The Underground '97

Bruno Lawrence (1941-95)
The Quiet Earth '85

John Lawrence (1931-92)
Cycle Psycho '72

Marc Lawrence (1959-)
Music & Lyrics '07
Miss Congeniality 2: Armed and Fabulous '05
Two Weeks Notice '02
Miss Congeniality '00
Forces of Nature '99
The Out-of-Towners '99
Life with Mikey '93

Martin Lawrence (1965-)
A Thin Line Between Love and Hate '96
You So Crazy '94

Vincent Lawrence (1890-1946)
Adventure '45
Hands Across the Table 35
Now and Forever '34
Night After Night '32

John Lawson
Sinners in the Sun '32
Sahara 43
Action in the North Atlantic '43
Bachelor Apartment '31

John Howard Lawson (1894-1977)
Cry, the Beloved Country '51
Smash-Up: The Story of a Woman '47

J.F. Lawton (1960-)
DOA: Dead or Alive '06
Chain Reaction '96
Blankman '94
The Hunted '94
Under Siege '92
Mistress '91
Pizza Man '91
Pretty Woman '90
Cannibal Women in the Avocado Jungle of Death '89

Beirne Lay, Jr. (1509-82)
The Gallant Hours '60
Above and Beyond '53
Twelve o'Clock High '49

Cooper Layne
The Fog '05
The Core '03

Michael Lazarou
Possessed '00
Heat Wave '90

Martin Lazarus
Deep Core '00

Interceptor Force '99

Philip LaZebnik
Mulan '98
Pocahontas '95

Alain Le Henry
A Self-Made Hero '95

Didier Le Pecheur (1959-)
Three ... Extremes '04
Harrison's Flowers '02
Don't Let Me Die on a Sunday '98

Paul Leadon
Back of Beyond '95
Around the World in 80 Ways '86

Larry Leahy
Confessions of a Hit Man '94

David Lean (1908-91)
A Passage to India '84
Summertime '55
Oliver Twist '48
This Happy Breed '47
Brief Encounter '46
Great Expectations '45

Norman Lear (1922-)
Cold Turkey '71
The Night They Raided Minsky's '69
Divorce American Style '67
Come Blow Your Horn '63

Keith Ross Leckie
To Walk with Lions '99
Lost in the Barrens '91
Where the Spirit Lives '89

Charles Leavitt
Blood Diamond '06
K-PAX '01
The Mighty '98
Sunchaser '96

Patrice Leconte (1947-)
My Best Friend '06
Intimate Strangers '04
The Hairdresser's Husband '92
Monsieur Hire '89

Jacques LeCotier
See Jerry Warren

Paul Leder (1926-96)
Killing Obsession '94
The Baby Doll Murders '92
Exiled in America '90
Murder by Numbers '89

Reuben Leder (1950-)
Molly and Gina '94
A*P*E* '76

Charles Lederer (1911-76)
A Global Affair '63
Mutiny on the Bounty '62
Follow That Dream '61
Ocean's 11 '60
Kismet '55
Gentlemen Prefer Blondes '53
Monkey Business '52
The Thing '51
I Was a Male War Bride '49
His Girl Friday '40
Broadway Serenade '39
Double or Nothing '37

Ang Lee (1954-)
Eat Drink Man Woman '94
The Wedding Banquet '93
Pushing Hands '92

Bruce Lee (1940-73)
Circle of Iron '78
Fists of Fury '73
Return of the Dragon '73

Connie Lee
Nice Girl? '41

Damian Lee
Agent Red '00
Deadly Heroes '97
Fatal Combat '96
Jungle Boy '96

May Wine '90

Ernest Lehman (1915-2005)
Black Sunday '77
Family Plot '76
Portnoy's Complaint '72
Hello, Dolly! '69
Who's Afraid of Virginia Woolf? '66
The Prize '63
The Sound of Music '65
West Side Story '61
From the Terrace '60
North by Northwest '59
Sweet Smell of Success '57
The King and I '56
Somebody Up There Likes Me '56
Executive Suite '54
Sabrina '54

Gladys Lehman (1892-1993)
Blondie Brings Up Baby '39
Death Takes a Holiday '34
Little Miss Marker '34

When the Bullet Hits the Bone '96
Electra '95
Street Law '95
The Killing Man '95
Abraxas: Guardian of the Universe '90
Circle Man '87

Lillian Lee
Farewell My Concubine '93

Malcolm Lee (1970-)
Welcome Home Roscoe Jenkins '08
The Best Man '99

Mark Lee (1958-)
Grown Ups '80
Who's Who '78
Kiss of Death '77

Spike Lee (1957-)
She Hate Me '04
Bamboozled '00
Summer of Sam '99
He Got Game '98
Clockers '95
Malcolm X '92
Jungle Fever '91
Mo' Better Blues '90
Do the Right Thing '89
School Daze '88
She's Gotta Have It '86
Joe's Bed-Stuy Barbershop: We Cut Heads '83

Timothy Lee
2103: Deadly Wake '97

William Lee
The Pact '99

Robert Lees (1912-2004)
Abbott and Costello Meet the Invisible Man '51
Comin' Round the Mountain '51
Abbott and Costello Meet Frankenstein '48
Buck Privates Come Home '47
Crazy House '43
The Black Cat '41
Hold That Ghost '41
The Invisible Woman '40

Alan LeMay (1899-1964)
High Lonesome '50
The Adventures of Mark Twain '44
The Story of Dr. Wassell '44
Reap the Wild Wind '42

Michael Leeson
The Tuxedo '02
What Planet Are You From? '00
I.Q. '94
The War of the Roses '89

Peter Lefcourt
Danielle Steel's Fine Things '90

Vicente Lenero (1933-)
The Crime of Father Amaro '02
Midac Alley '95

Peter M. Lenkov
Dr. Jekyll & Mr. Hyde '99

Isobel Lennart (1915-71)
Funny Girl '68
Period of Adjustment '62
Two for the Seesaw '62
Please Don't Eat the Daisies '60
Meet Me in Las Vegas '56
The Girl Next Door '53
Latin Lovers '53
A Life of Her Own '50
The Kissing Bandit '48

Jonathan Lemkin
Shooter '07
Red Planet '00
The Devil's Advocate '97

Steve Lemme (1973-)
Beerfest '06
Club Dread '04
Super Troopers '01

James (Mome) Lemmo (1949-)
Nowhere in Sight '01
Bodily Harm '95
Relentless 3 '93
We're Talkin' Serious Money '92

Kay Lenard (1911-97)
The Kettles in the Ozarks '56
Ma and Pa Kettle at Home '54

Robert Lepage (1957-)
Far Side of the Moon '03
No '98
Le Polygraphe '96
The Confessional '95

Alan Jay Lerner (1918-86)
The Little Prince '74
Camelot '67
My Fair Lady '64
Gigi '58
Brigadoon '54
Royal Wedding '51
An American in Paris '51

Ali LeRoi
Head of State '03
Down to Earth '01

Jeff Le'roy
Crystal's Diary '99
Crack U.F. '97

Mimi Lesseos
Beyond Fear '93
Pushed to the Limit '92

Elana Lesser
Beethoven's 5th '03
Cats Don't Dance '97
Balto '95

Sheldon Lettich (1962-)
Legionnaire '98
The Misadventures of Merlin Jones '64

Jerry Leichtling (1948-)
Blue Sky '91
Peggy Sue Got Married '86

Mike Leigh (1943-)
Vera Drake '04
All or Nothing '02
Topsy Turvy '99
Career Girls '97
Secrets and Lies '95
Naked '93
Life Is Sweet '90
High Hopes '88
Home Sweet Home '82

Warren Leight (1957-)
Dear God '96
The Night We Never Met '93
Mother's Day '80

David Leland (1947-)
White River '99
The Land Girls '99
Personal Services '87
Wish You Were Here '87
Mona Lisa '86

Claude Lelouch (1937-)
And Now Ladies and Gentlemen '02
Les Miserables '95
Bandits '86
Bolero '82
Cat and Mouse '73
And Now My Love '74
Happy New Year '73
A Man and a Woman: 20 Years Later '86
Another Man, Another Chance '77
A Man and a Woman '66

Sergio Leone (1929-89)
Once Upon a Time in America '84
Once Upon a Time in the West '68
The Good, the Bad and the Ugly '67
For a Few Dollars More '65
A Fistful of Dollars '64
The Last Days of Pompeii '60

Robert Leoni
Santa Sangre '90
Thundersquad '85

Richard Levinson (1934-87)
Guilty Conscience '85
Rehearsal for Murder '82
The Hindenburg '75
The Executor of Private S ovik '74
And Justice for All '79
High Anxiety '77
Silent Movie '76
Internecine Project '73
Columbo: Prescription Murder '67 '

Gary Lennon
.45 '06
Drunks '96

Thomas Lennon (1969-)
Balls of Fury '07
Reno 911!: Miami '07
Let's Go to Prison '06
Night at the Museum '06
Herbie: Fully Loaded '05
Taxi '04

Robert W. Lenski (1927-2002)
Ironmaster '82
Emerald Jungle '80
Desert Commandos '67
Hoe in the Sky '95
Breathing Lessons '94
The Return of the Native '94
Decoration Day '90
Who Is the Black Dahlia? '75

Umberto Lenzi (1931-)
Welcome to Spring Break '88

Hugh Leonard (1926-)
Widow's Peak '94

Elmore Leonard (1925-)
Cat Chaser '90
The Rosary Murders '87
52 Pick-Up '86
Stick '85
Mr. Majestyk '74
Joe Kidd '72

Barry Levinson (1942-)
Man of the Year '06
Liberty Heights '99
Sleepers '96
Jimmy Hollywood '94
Toys '92
Avalon '90
Bugsy '91
Tin Men '87
Good Morning, Vietnam '87
The Natural '84
Diner '82

Holiday in Mexico '46

Robert W. Lenski (1927-2002)
Mutual Needs '97
Urban Harvest '95

David Levien
Ocean's Thirteen '07
Runaway Jury '03
Knockaround Guys '01
Rounders '98

Dode Levenson
Urban Harvest '95

Sonya Levien (1888-1960)
Oklahoma! '55
The Merry Widow '52
Three Daring Daughters '48
The Valley of Decision '45
The Hunchback of Notre Dame '39
Four Men and a Prayer '38
In Old Chicago '37
State Fair '33

Jeremy Leven (1941-)
The Notebook '04
Alex & Emma '03
Crazy as Hell '02
The Legend of Bagger Vance '00
Don Juan DeMarco '94
Creator '85

Larry Levin
Dr. Dolittle 2 '01
Dr. Dolittle '98

Marc Levin
Journey to the Center of the Earth 3D '08
Nim's Island '08
Tin Man '07
Wimbledon '04
White Boyz '99
Madeline '98
Slam '98

Eugene Levy (1946-)
For Your Consideration '06
A Mighty Wind '03
Waiting for Guffman '96
Sodbusters '94
Best in Show '00

Benn W. Levy (1900-73)
The Old Dark House '32
Blackmail '29
The Informer '29
Mrs. Mike '49
Jones '63

Helen Levitt (1916-93)
The Misadventures of Merlin Jones '64

Kristian Levring (1957-)
The Intended '02
The King Is Alive '00

Alfred Lewis Levitt (1915-2002)
Monkey's Uncle '65
The Misadventures of Merlin Jones '64

Gregory Levasseur
P2 '07
The Hills Have Eyes '06

Robert L. Levy
Blood Surf '00

A Kid in King Arthur's Court '95

Scott Lew
Bickford Shmeckler's Cool Ideas '06
Aberration '97

Albert Lewin (1916-96)
Eight on the Lam '67
Boy, Did I Get a Wrong Number! '66
Pandora and the Flying Dutchman '51
The Private Affairs of Bel Ami '47
Picture of Dorian Gray '45

Ben Lewin (1946-)
Paperback Romance '96
The Favor, the Watch, & the Very Big Fish '92

David Lewis
Rock Haven '07

Everet Lewis
Luster '02
The Natural History of Parking Lots '90

Herschell Gordon Lewis (1926-)
This Stuff'll Kill Ya! '71
How to Make a Doll '68
Blast-Off Girls '67
Suburban Roulette '67
Monster a Go-Go! '65
Color Me Blood Red '64
Moonshine Mountain '64
2000 Maniacs '64
Scum of the Earth '63

Jefferson Lewis
Mon Amie Max '94
Ordinary Magic '93

Jerry Lewis (1926-)
Hardly Working '81
Big Mouth '67
The Patsy '64
Family Jewels '65
The Nutty Professor '63
The Errand Boy '61
The Ladies' Man '61
The Bellboy '60

Joyce Renee Lewis
Civil Brand '02
Spirit Lost '96

Russell Lewis (1963-)
Sharpe's Challenge '06
Heat of the Sun '99
Horatio Hornblower '99
Sharpe's Battle '94

Val Lewton (1904-51)
Bedlam '45
The Body Snatcher '45

Feng Li
House of Flying Daggers '04
Hero '03

Peter Paul Liapis
Alone with a Stranger '99
Stranger in the House '97
Sins of Desire '92

Ugo Liberatore (1927-)
The Trojan Horse '62
Mill of the Stone Women '60

Jimmy Lifton (1955-)
Phoenix '95
Mirror, Mirror 2: Raven Dance '94

Jeffrey Lieberman
Tangled '01

Jeff Lieberman (1947-)
Satan's Little Helper '04
Blue Sunshine '78
Squirm '76

Leo Lieberman
Carnival Rock '57
Sorority Girl '57

Louis D. Lighton (1895-1963)
It '27
Wings '27

Topper Lilien
Dungeons and Dragons '00
Where the Money Is '00

Livia Linden
Tropix '02
The Spree '96

Kevin J. Lindenmuth
Addicted to Murder 3: Bloodlust '99
Rage of the Werewolf '99
Addicted to Murder 2: Tainted Blood '97
The Alien Agenda: Endangered Species '97
The Alien Agenda: Under the Skin '97
The Alien Agenda: Out of the Darkness '96
Addicted to Murder '95

Astrid Lindgren (1907-2002)
Pippi on the Run '70
Pippi Goes on Board '69
Pippi Longstocking '69

Erik Lindsay
American Pie Presents: Beta House '07
American Pie Presents: The Naked Mile '06

Kara Lindstrom
Killing Me Softly '01
A Time for Dancing '00

Eugene Ling (1915-95)
Loan Shark '52
Lost Boundaries '49
Behind Locked Doors '48
Human Gorilla '48

Caroline Link (1964-)
Nowhere in Africa '02
Beyond Silence '96

William Link
Vanishing Act '88
Guilty Conscience '85
Rehearsal for Murder '82
Rollercoaster '77
The Hindenburg '75
The Execution of Private Slovik '74
Columbo: Prescription Murder '67

Richard Linklater (1961-)
Fast Food Nation '06
A Scanner Darkly '06
Before Sunset '04
Waking Life '01
Before Sunrise '94
Dazed and Confused '93
Slacker '91

William R. Lipman (1894-1951)
Les Miserables '35

Shelley List (1930-96)
Jewels '92
And Baby Makes Six '79

Stephen Lister
Monolith '93
Slow Burn '90

William Lively (1907-73)
Radar Patrol vs. Spy King '49
Range Renegades '48
Texas Trouble '41
Fighting Renegade '39
Phantom Rancher '39

Andrew Lloyd Webber (1948-)
Jesus Christ Superstar '00

Robert Locash
BASEketball '98
High School High '96
Naked Gun 33 1/3: The Final Insult '94
CB4: The Movie '93

Allan Loeb
21 '08
Things We Lost in the Fire '07

Helen Logan (1906-)
If I'm Lucky '46
Something for the Boys '44
Hello, Frisco, Hello '43
Iceland '42
Lucky Cisco Kid '40
Tin Pan Alley '40
Charlie Chan in City of Darkness '39
Charlie Chan at the Olympics '37
Charlie Chan at the Circus '36
Charlie Chan at the Race Track '36
Charlie Chan in Egypt '35

John Logan (1961-)
Sweeney Todd: The Demon Barber of Fleet Street '07
The Aviator '04
The Last Samurai '03
Sinbad: Legend of the Seven Seas '03
Star Trek: Nemesis '02
The Time Machine '02
Gladiator '00
Any Given Sunday '99
Bats '99
RKO 281 '99
Tornado! '96

Charles Logue (1889-1938)
Make a Million '35
The Drake Case '29

Christopher Logue (1926-)
Crusoe '89
Savage Messiah '72

Ulli Lommel (1944-)
BTK Killer '06
Warbirds '88
Strangers in Paradise '84
Devonsville Terror '83
Brainwaves '82
The Boogey Man '80
Cocaine Cowboys '79

Kenneth Lonergan (1963-)
Gangs of New York '02
The Adventures of Rocky & Bullwinkle '00
You Can Count On Me '99
Analyze This '98

Nathan Long
The Sender '98

Sheryl Longin
Dick '99

Harry S. Longstreet
Wounded '97
A Vow to Kill '94
Sex, Love and Cold Hard Cash '93

Renee Longstreet
Double Platinum '99
A Vow to Kill '94
Undesirable '92

Anita Loos (1888-1981)
I Married an Angel '42
They Met in Bombay '41
When Ladies Meet '41
Susan and God '40
The Women '39
Saratoga '37
San Francisco '36
The Girl from Missouri '34
Hold Your Man '33
Red Headed Woman '32
Struggle '31
His Picture in the Papers '16
Matrimaniac '16

Mary Loos (1910-2004)
A Woman's World '54
Ticket to Tomahawk '50
When Willie Comes Marching Home '50
Father Was a Fullback '49

Phillips Lord (1902-75)
Guns Don't Argue '57
Gang Busters '42

Robert Lord (1900-76)
Stage Struck '36
Heroes for Sale '33
One Way Passage '32
The Purchase Price '32
Big Business Girl '31

Dean Lorey (1967-)
Major Payne '95
Jason Goes to Hell: The Final Friday '93
My Boyfriend's Back '93

Hope Loring (1894-1959)
Reckless '95
Prelude to a Kiss '92
Longtime Companion '90
It '27
My Best Girl '27
Wings '27
Shadows '22

Ye Lou
Summer Palace '06
Purple Butterfly '03

David Loucka
Borderline '02
Eddie '96
The Dream Team '89

David Loughery
Money Train '95
Tom and Huck '95
The Three Musketeers '93
Passenger 57 '92
Star Trek 5: The Final Frontier '89

Pavel (Lungin) Lounguine (1949-)
Luna Park '91
Taxi Blues '90

Eric Louzil (1951-)
Class of Nuke 'Em High 2: Subhumanoid Meltdown '91

Robert Lovy
Plughead Rewired: Circuitry Man 2 '94
Circuitry Man '90

Steven Lovy
Plughead Rewired: Circuitry Man 2 '94
Circuitry Man '90

Edward T. Lowe (1890-1973)
House of Dracula '45
House of Frankenstein '44
Bulldog Drummond Escapes '37

Sherman Lowe (1894-1968)
Yank in Libya '42
Bury Me Not on the Lone Prairie '41
The Masked Rider '41
Pony Post '40
Undertow '30

Jeff Lowell
Over Her Dead Body '08
John Tucker Must Die '06

Richard Lowenstein (1959-)
He Died With a Felafel in His Hand '01
Dogs in Space '87

Andrew Lowery (1970-)
Boys and Girls '00

Sam Lowry
See Steven Soderbergh

John Loy
Beethoven's 4th '01

The Land Before Time 6: The Secret of Saurus Rock '98
The Land Before Time 5: The Mysterious Island '97
The Land Before Time 3: The Time of the Great Giving '95

Ernst Lubitsch (1892-1947)
To Be or Not to Be '42
The Smiling Lieutenant '31

Craig Lucas (1950-)
The Dying Gaul '05
The Secret Lives of Dentists '02
Reckless '95
Prelude to a Kiss '92
Longtime Companion '90

George Lucas (1944-)
Star Wars: Episode 3—Revenge of the Sith '05
Star Wars: Episode 2—Attack of the Clones '02
Star Wars: Episode 1—The Phantom Menace '99
Return of the Jedi '83
Raiders of the Lost Ark '81
Star Wars '77
American Graffiti '73
THX 1138 '71

Jon Lucas
Full of It '07
Rebound '05
Rustin '01

Ralph Lucas
Planet of the Dinosaurs '80
The Child '76

John Ludin
The Land Before Time 3: The Time of the Great Giving '95
The Land Before Time 2: The Great Valley Adventure '94

William Ludwig (1912-99)
Gun Glory '57
Interrupted Melody '55
Oklahoma! '55
Athena '54
The Sun Comes Up '49
The Hills of Home '48

Kurt Luedtke
Random Hearts '99
Out of Africa '85
Absence of Malice '81

Baz Luhrmann (1962-)
Moulin Rouge '01
Night Watch '04

Sergei Lukyanenko
Day Watch '06
Night Watch '04

Sidney Lumet (1924-)
Find Me Guilty '06
Night Falls on Manhattan '96
Q & A '90
Prince of the City '81

Bigas Luna (1946-)
The Chambermaid on the Titanic '97
Jamon, Jamon '93
Anguish '88

Ida Lupino (1914-95)
Reborn '81
Private Hell 36 '54
The Hitch-Hiker '53
Streets of Sin '49

Rod Lurie (1962-)
The Contender '00
Deterrence '00

Patrick Lussier
Dracula 3: Legacy '05
Dracula 2: Ascension '03

Arnost Lustig
A Prayer for Katarina Horovitzova '69
Diamonds of the Night '64

Jan Lustig (1902-79)
Young Bess '53
Homecoming '48
The White Cliffs of Dover '44

Karen McCullah Lutz
She's the Man '06
Ella Enchanted '04
Legally Blonde '01
Ten Things I Hate about You '99

David Lynch (1946-)
Inland Empire '06
Mulholland Drive '01
Lost Highway '96
Twin Peaks: Fire Walk with Me '92
Wild at Heart '90
Blue Velvet '86
Dune '84
The Elephant Man '80
Eraserhead '78

Barre Lyndon (1896-1972)
Man in the Attic '53
The War of the Worlds '53
To Please a Lady '50
Hangover Square '45
House on 92nd Street '45

Jonathan Lynn (1943-)
Nuns on the Run '90
Clue '85

Fibe Ma
Mr. Nice Guy '98
Rumble in the Bronx '96
Supercop '92

Dick Maas (1951-)
The Shaft '01
Amsterdamned '88

John Maass (1960-)
The Last Debate '00
Curdled '95

Charles MacArthur (1895-1956)
Wuthering Heights '39
Twentieth Century '34
Rasputin and the Empress '33

Richard Macaulay
Across the Pacific '42
Torrid Zone '40
The Roaring Twenties '39

Ruggero Maccari
The Family '87
A Special Day '77
Down & Dirty '76
The Scent of a Woman '75

Nora MacCoby
Buffalo Soldiers '01
Bongwater '98

Philip MacDonald (1901-80)
Love from a Stranger '47
The Body Snatcher '45
Mr. Takes a Vacation '39
Mysterious Mr. Moto '38
River of Unrest '36

Ranald MacDougall (1915-73)
Queen Bee '55
We're No Angels '55
June Bride '48
Mildred Pierce '45
Objective, Burma! '45

Aeneas MacKenzie (1889-1962)
The Ten Commandments '56
Fighting Seabees '44
They Died with Their Boots On '41

Billy Mackinnon
Hideous Kinky '99
Small Faces '95

Patricia MacLachlan (1938-)
Baby '00
Journey '95

Writer Index

Sarah, Plain and Tall:
Skylark '93

Bernard MacLaverty (1942-)
Hostages '93
The Real Charlotte '91
When Eight Bells Toll '71
Cal '84

Alistair MacLean (1922-87)
Breakheart Pass '76
When Eight Bells Toll '71
Where Eagles Dare '68

Andrew Maclear
The Man Who Made Husbands Jealous '98

Angus MacPhail (1903-62)
Dead of Night '45
No Time for Sergeants '58
The Foreman Went to France '42

Don MacPherson
The Avengers '98

Jeanie Macpherson
Male and Female '19
The Little American '17

Earl MacRauch
Wired '89
The Adventures of Buckaroo Banzai Across the Eighth Dimension '84

William H. Macy (1950-)
A Slight Case of Murder '99
The Con '98

Guy Maddin (1956-)
Brand Upon the Brain! '06
The Saddest Music in the World '03
Careful '92
Tales from the Gimli Hospital '88

Brent Maddock
Wild Wild West '99
Tremors 2: Aftershocks '96
Heart and Souls '93
Ghost Dad '90
Tremors '89
Short Circuit 2 '88
"batteries not included" '87
Short Circuit '86

Ben Maddow (1909-92)
The Secret of Santa Vittoria '69
The Balcony '63
Men in War '57
The Asphalt Jungle '50

David Magee
Finding Neverland '04

Doug Magee
Beyond the Call '96

David Magee (1962-)
Miss Pettigrew Lives for a Day '08

Joe Maggio
Milk and Honey '03

Jeff Maguire
Gridiron Gang '06
In the Line of Fire '93

Redge Mahaffey
First Encounter '97

John Lee Mahin (1902-84)
Moment to Moment '66
The Horse Soldiers '59
Boom Town '40
Dr. Jekyll and Mr. Hyde '41
Johnny Eager '42
Mogambo '53
The Bad Seed '56
Red Dust '32
Wife Versus Secretary '36
Love on the Run '36

Richard Maibaum (1909-91)
License to Kill '89
The Living Daylights '87
The Spy Who Loved Me '77
On Her Majesty's Secret Service '69
S*P*E '79
Thunderball '65
Goldfinger '64
From Russia with Love '63
Dr. No '62
The Great Gatsby '49
O.S.S. '46

Wilkie Mahoney (1897-1976)
Whistling in Brooklyn '43
Whistling in Dixie '42

Mark Malone
Dead Heat '01
Bulletproof Heart '95

Miles Malleson (1888-1969)
The Thief of Bagdad '40
Nine Days a Queen '36
Night Birds '31

David Mamet (1947-)
Redbelt '08
Spartan '04
Heist '01
Hannibal '01
Lakeboat '00
State and Main '00
Lansky '99
Ronin '98
The Winslow Boy '98
The Edge '97
The Spanish Prisoner '97
Wag the Dog '97
American Buffalo '95
Oleanna '94
Vanya on 42nd Street '94
A Life in the Theater '93
Glengarry Glen Ross '92
Hoffa '92
The Water Engine '92
Homicide '91
We're No Angels '89
Things Change '88
House of Games '87
The Untouchables '87
The Verdict '82
The Postman Always Rings Twice '81

Terrence Malick (1943-)
The New World '05
The Thin Red Line '98
Badlands '74
Days of Heaven '78

Louis Malle (1932-95)
Pocket Money '72
May Fools '90
Au Revoir les Enfants '87
c'razy/beautiful '01
Murmur of the Heart '71
Spirits of the Dead '68
Viva Maria! '65
Zazie dans le Metro '61
The Lovers '59

Matt Manfredi
Aeon Flux '05

Dr. Seuss' The Cat in the Hat '03

David Main
Find the Lady '76
It Seemed Like a Good Idea at the Time '75

Daniel Mainwaring (1902-77)
Atlantis, the Lost Continent '61
Invasion of the Body Snatchers '56
An Annapolis Story '55
A Bullet for Joey '55
The Hitch-Hiker '53
Bugles in the Afternoon '52
Cavalry Charge '51
Big Steal '49
Big Town '47
Out of the Past '47
Swamp Fire '46
Treasure of Fear '45
Dangerous Passage '44

Norman Mailer (1923-2007)
Master Spy: The Robert Hanssen Story '02
American Tragedy '00
Tough Guys Don't Dance '87
King Lear '87

James Mangold (1964-)
Walk the Line '05
Kate & Leopold '01
Girl, Interrupted '99
Cop Land '97
Heavy '94

The Robe '53
Broken Arrow '50
The Naked City '48
Cloak and Dagger '46
This Gun for Hire '42

Herman J. Mankiewicz (1897-1953)
Pride of St. Louis '52
Citizen Kane '41
Dinner at Eight '33
Lost Squadron '32

Joseph L. Mankiewicz (1909-93)
The Honey Pot '67
Cleopatra '63
Guys and Dolls '55
The Barefoot Contessa '54
Julius Caesar '53
People Will Talk '51
All About Eve '50
No Way Out '50
A Letter to Three Wives '49
The Keys of the Kingdom '44

Tom Mankiewicz (1942-)
Dragnet '87
Ladyhawke '85
The Cassandra Crossing '77
The Eagle Has Landed '77
Mother, Jugs and Speed '76
The Man with the Golden Gun '74
Live and Let Die '73
Diamonds Are Forever '71

Chan Man-keung
Kung Fu Hustle '04
Summer Snow '94

Micho Manchevski (1959-)
Dust '01
Before the Rain '94

Don Mancini (1963-)
Seed of Chucky '04
Bride of Chucky '98
Child's Play 3 '91
Child's Play 2 '90
Child's Play '88

Babaloo Mandel (1949-)
Fever Pitch '05
Robots '05
Where the Heart Is '00
Father's Day '96
Multiplicity '96
Forget Paris '95
City Slickers 2: The Legend of Curly's Gold '94
Greedy '94
A League of Their Own '92
Mr. Saturday Night '92
City Slickers '91
Parenthood '89
Vibes '88
Gung Ho '85
Spies Like Us '85
Splash '84

David Mandel (1971-)
Eurotrip '04

Max Marcin (1879-1948)
Gambling Ship '33
King of the Jungle '33
I'm Not Scared '03
Iris Blond '98

Francesca Marciano (1955-)
Don't Tell '05

Abby Mann (1927-2008)
Indictment: The McMartin Trial '95
A Kid for Two Farthings '55
A Child Is Waiting '63
Judgment at Nuremberg '61
Report to the Commissioner '74

Edward Andrew (Santos Alcocer) Mann (1923-95)
The Detective '68
Ship of Fools '65

Antonio Margheriti
Evil Clutch '89

Andreas Marfori
Desperate Crimes '93

Mitch Marcus
The Haunting of Hell House '99

Lawrence B. Marcus (1917-2001)
The Harvest '92
Enemy of the State '98
A Boy Called Hate '95
The Force '94
Petulia '68
Justin '69
The Stunt Man '80

David Marconi
Enemy of the State '98

James Mangold
The Keep '83

David Mandel (1971-)
Thief '81
Vegas '78
Night Shift '82

Max Marcin
The Two Faces of Dr. Jekyll '60
A Kid for Two Farthings '55
Expresso Bongo '59
Casino Royale '67
Waltz of the Toreadors '62
The Day the Earth Caught Fire '61

Wolf Mankowitz (1925-98)
...

Joseph Moncure March (1899-1977)
Two Alone '34
Hoopla '33
Allegro Non Troppo '76
Trapper County War '89
Rush Week '88
Long Shot Kids '81

Bruce Manning (1902-65)
Back Street '41
First Love '39
Three Smart Girls Grow Up '39
Whistling in the Dark '41

Albert Mannheimer (1913-72)
Born Yesterday '50

Gilles Marchand (1963-)
Lemming '05
Bon Voyage '03
With a Friend Like Harry '00

Patrick Marber (1964-)
Notes on a Scandal '06
Closer '04

Rene Manzor (1959-)
The Winning of Barbara Worth '26

Gene Markey (1895-1980)
On the Avenue '37
Baby Face '33
Female '33

Clarence Marks (1893-1972)
Terror of Tiny Town '38
The Love Trap '29
Venture '49

Christopher Markus
The Chronicles of Narnia: Prince Caspian '08
The Chronicles of Narnia: The Lion, the Witch and the Wardrobe '05

Andrew Marlowe
Hollow Man '00
Air Force One '97
End of Days '99

Graeme Manson
Cube '98

Guido Manuli '98
Volere Volare '92

Russell V. Manzatt (1937-)
Weeping Meadow '04
Ulysses' Gaze '95

Petros Markaris (1937-)
Weeping Meadow '04

Frances Marion (1888-1973)
Camille '36
Dinner at Eight '33
The Champ '32
The Big House '30
The Wind '28
Son of the Sheik '26
Stella Maris '18
Tillie Wakes Up '17

Stanley Mann (1928-)
Conan the Destroyer '84
Firestarter '84
Eye of the Needle '81
Meteor '79
The Collector '65
Woman of Straw '64
The Mouse That Roared '59

Ben Markson (1892-)
Crazy People '90
Good Morning, Vietnam '87

Mitch Markowitz
Crazy People '90
Good Morning, Vietnam '87

Jack Marks (1895-1987)
Lady Killer '33
Lucky Devils '33
What Price Hollywood? '32
You Kill Me '07

Malcolm Marmorstein
Pete's Dragon '77
Return from Witch Mountain '78
At Home with the Webbers '94

Brad (Sean) Marlowe
Object of Obsession '95

Henri Marquet
Mr. Hulot's Holiday '53
Jour de Fete '48

Franco Marotta
The Sicilian Connection '85
Deadly Mission '91

Garry Marshall (1934-)
The Other Sister '99
The Flamingo Kid '84

Herbert Margolis
The Kettles on Old MacDonald's Farm '57
Francis in the Haunted House '56
The Freakmaker '73
Cauldron of Blood '67
Hallucination '67
Seizure '74

Donald Marguties
Collected Stories '02
Dinner with Friends '01

A. L. Mariaux
See Jess (Jesus) Franco

Richard "Cheech" Marin (1946-)
Born in East L.A. '87
Cheech and Chong's The Corsican Brothers '84
Cheech and Chong: Still Smokin' '83
Cheech and Chong; Things Are Tough All Over '82
Cheech and Chong's Nice Dreams '81
Cheech and Chong's Next Movie '80
Cheech and Chong's Up in Smoke '79

Marshall

Neil Marshall (1970-)
Doomsday '08
The Descent '05
Dog Soldiers '01
Killing Time '97

Roger Marshall (1934-)
The Flamingo Kid '84
And Now the Screaming Starts '73
Theatre of Death '67

Steve Marshall
Revenge of the Nerds 2: Nerds in Paradise '87
Laboratory '80

Tonie Marshall
Venus Beauty Institute '98
Pas Tres Catholique '93

William Martell
The Base '99
Black Thunder '98
Steel Sharks '97
Crash Dive '96
Invisible Mom '96
Cyberzone '95
Virtual Combat '95
Hard Evidence '94
Victim of Desire '94

Peter Marthesheimer
Veronika Voss '82
The Marriage of Maria Braun '79

Al Martin (1897-1971)
Invasion of the Saucer Men '57
Money Madness '47
Blondie Knows Best '46
Flying Wild '41
The Invisible Ghost '41
The Shadow Strikes '37
Kelly of the Secret Service '36
The Law Rides '36
Prison Shadows '36

Charles Martin (1910-83)
How to Seduce a Woman '74
Dead Right '68
My Dear Secretary '49

Gregory Mars Martin
See Mars Callahan

Helen Martin (1909-2000)

Donald Martin
Ebenezer '97
Spenser: A Savage Place '94

Francis Martin
One Night in the Tropics '40
The Big Broadcast of 1938 '38
College Swing '38
Waikiki Wedding '37
The Princess Comes Across '36

John Benjamin Martin
Before I Say Goodbye '03
We'll Meet Again '02
Wishmaster 4: The Prophecy Fulfilled '02
The House Next Door '01

Mardik Martin (1937-)
Raging Bull '80
New York, New York '77
Valentino '77
Mean Streets '73

Robert Martin (1948-)
Basket Case 3: The Progeny '92
Frankenhooker '90

Steve Martin (1945-)
The Pink Panther '06
Shopgirl '05
Bowfinger '99
A Simple Twist of Fate '94
L.A. Story '91
Roxanne '87
Three Amigos '86
The Man with Two Brains '83
Dead Men Don't Wear Plaid '82
The Jerk '79

Jacques Martineau (1963-)
Cote d'Azur '05
My Life on Ice '02
The Adventures of Felix '99
Jeanne and the Perfect Guy '98

Luciano Martino (1933-)
Your Vice is a Closed Room and Only I Have the Key '72
Giants of Rome '63
The Whip and the Body '63

Raymond Martino
To the Limit '95
DaVinci's War '92
American Born '89
Angels of the City '89

Sergio Martino (1938-)
The Great Alligator '81
Torso '73

Mike Marvin
Wishman '93
The Wraith '87

Arthur Marx (1921-)
Cancel My Reservation '72
Eight on the Lam '67
I'll Take Sweden '65

Rick Marx (1955-)
Firehouse '87
Warrior Queen '87

R.J. Marx
Double Obsession '93
Master of Dragonard Hill '89
Dead Man Walking '88
Dragonard '88
Gor '88
Outlaw of Gor '87
Platoon Leader '87
C.O.D. '83

Sarah Y. Mason (1896-1980)
Golden Boy '39
Stella Dallas '37
Little Women '33

Elan Mastai
Alone in the Dark '05
MVP2: Most Vertical Primate '01

Ed Masterson
Storm Catcher '99
No Code of Conduct '98

Nico Mastorakis (1941-)
Hired to Kill '91
In the Cold of the Night '89
Bloodstone '88
Glitch! '88
The Wind '87
Zero Boys '86
Blind Date '84
Blood Tide '82

William Mastrosimone
Benedict Arnold: A Question of Honor '03
The Burning Season '94
With Honors '94
Sinatra '92
The Beast '88
Extremities '86

Berkely Mather (1909-96)
The Long Ships '64
Dr. No '62

Ted Mather
Faith '90
Body Beat '88

Chris Matheson
Mr. Wrong '95
A Goofy Movie '94
Bill & Ted's Bogus Journey '91
Bill & Ted's Excellent Adventure '89

Richard Matheson (1926-)
Trilogy of Terror 2 '96
Jaws 3 '83
Twilight Zone: The Movie '83
Young Warriors '83
Somewhere in Time '80
Trilogy of Terror '75
Scream of the Wolf '74
Dracula '73
Dying Room Only '73
The Legend of Hell House '73
The Night Strangler '72
Duel '71
The Night Stalker '71
The Devil Rides Out '68
Die! Die! My Darling! '65
The Comedy of Terrors '64
The Last Man on Earth '64
The Raven '63
Burn Witch, Burn! '62
Tales of Terror '62
Master of the World '61
The Pit and the Pendulum '61
The Fall of the House of Usher '60
The Incredible Shrinking Man '57

Richard Christian Matheson (1953-)
It Waits '05
Full Eclipse '93
Loose Cannons '90
It Takes Two '88
Three O'Clock High '87

June Mathis (1892-1927)
Blood and Sand '22
The Four Horsemen of the Apocalypse '21
The Saphead '21

Melissa Mathison (1950-)
Kundun '97
The Indian in the Cupboard '95
The Escape Artist '82
E.T.: The Extra-Terrestrial '82
The Black Stallion '79

Francisca Matos
Baby Geniuses '98

Zenzo Matsuyama
A Million to Juan '94
The Human Condition: Road to Eternity '59
The Human Condition: No Greater Love '58

Paul Matthews
Hooded Angels '00
Breeders '97
The Proposition '96
Grim '95

John Mattson
Free Willy 3: The Rescue '97
Free Willy 2: The Adventure Home '95
Milk Money '94

Nat Mauldin
The Perfect Holiday '07
The In-Laws '03
Dr. Dolittle '98

J. Stephen Maunder
The Veteran '06
Expect No Mercy '95
Talons of the Eagle '92
Tiger Claws '91

Armistead Maupin (1944-)
The Night Listener '06
The Celluloid Closet '95

Joseph Maurer
The Song of the Lark '01
The Sandy Bottom Orchestra '00

Captain Mauzner
Factory Girl '06
Wonderland '03

Garth Maxwell (1963-)
When Love Comes '98
Jack Be Nimble '94

Richard Maxwell
Shadow of China '91
The Serpent and the Rainbow '87
The Challenge '82

Ronald F. Maxwell (1947-)
Gods and Generals '03
Gettysburg '93

Elaine May (1932-)
Primary Colors '98
The Birdcage '95
Ishtar '87
Heaven Can Wait '78
Mikey & Nicky '76
A New Leaf '71

Carl Mayer (1894-1944)
The Last Laugh '24
Shattered '21
The Cabinet of Dr. Caligari '19

Edwin Justus Mayer (1896-1960)
To Be or Not to Be '42
They Met in Bombay '41
Desire '36
Thirty Day Princess '34

Paul Mayersberg (1941-)
Croupier '97
Merry Christmas, Mr. Lawrence '83
The Man Who Fell to Earth '76

Wendell Mayes (1918-92)
Monsignor '82
Love and Bullets '79
Go Tell the Spartans '78
Bank Shot '74
Death Wish '74
The Poseidon Adventure '72
Hotel '67
In Harm's Way '65
Von Ryan's Express '65
Advise and Consent '62
Anatomy of a Murder '59
The Hanging Tree '59
The Hunters '58
Spirit of St. Louis '57

Craig Mazin (1971-)
Scary Movie 4 '06
Scary Movie 3 '03
Senseless '98

Stephen Mazur
Wedding Wars '06
Heartbreakers '01
Liar Liar '97
The Little Rascals '94

Paul Mazursky (1930-)
The Pickle '93
Scenes from a Mall '91
Enemies, a Love Story '89
Moon over Parador '88
Down and Out in Beverly Hills '86
Moscow on the Hudson '84
The Tempest '82
Willie & Phil '80
An Unmarried Woman '78
Next Stop, Greenwich Village '76
Harry and Tonto '74
Blume in Love '73
Alex in Wonderland '70
Bob & Carol & Ted & Alice '69
I Love You, Alice B. Toklas! '68

Danny McBride
Underworld: Evolution '05
Underworld '03

Jim McBride (1941-)
Uncovered '94
Great Balls of Fire '89
Breathless '83
Hot Times '74
Glen and Randa '71
David Holzman's Diary '67

Mary C. McCall (1904-86)
The Fighting Sullivans '42
Breaking the Ice '38
I Promise to Pay '37
A Midsummer Night's Dream '35

Tim McCanlies (1953-)
Secondhand Lions '03
Iron Giant '99
Dancer, Texas—Pop. 81 '98

Tim McCann (1968-)
Revolution #9 '01
Desolation Angels '95

Leo McCarey (1898-1969)
An Affair to Remember '57
Going My Way '44
My Favorite Wife '40
Love Affair '39
Laurel & Hardy: Blotto '30
Laurel & Hardy: Brats '30
Laurel & Hardy: Berth Marks '29
Laurel & Hardy: Men O'War '29

John P. McCarthy (1884-1962)
Marked Trails '44
Beyond the Rockies '32

Peter McCarthy (1953-)
Car 54, Where Are You? '94
Floundering '94
Tapeheads '89

Thomas (Tom) McCarthy (1969-)
The Visitor '07
The Station Agent '03

Michael (Mick) McCleery
Track 16 '02
The Alien Agenda: Out of the Darkness '96

Jonas McCord (1952-)
The Body '01
Class of '61 '52

Mark McCorkle
Sky High '05

Pete McCormack
The Blue Butterfly '04
Whirlygirl '04

John McCormick
Living on Tokyo Time '87

Nelson McCormick
Operation Sandman: Warriors in Hell '00
For Which He Stands '98

Pat McCormick (1927-2005)
Under the Rainbow '81
Oh Dad, Poor Dad (Momma's Hung You in the Closet & I'm Feeling So Sad) '67

Horace McCoy (1897-1955)
Rage at Dawn '55
The Texas Rangers Ride Again '40
Postal Inspector '36
The Trail of the Lonesome Pine '36

Michael McCullers
Baby Mama '08
Thunderbirds '04
Austin Powers in Goldmember '02
Undercover Brother '02
Austin Powers 2: The Spy Who Shagged Me '99

Bruce McCulloch (1961-)
Dog Park '98
Kids in the Hall: Brain Candy '96

Jim McCullough, Jr.
The St. Tammany Miracle '94
Mountaintop Motel Massacre '86

Michael James McDonald (1964-)
Alien Avengers '96
The Death Artist '95
The Crazysitter '94
Revenge of the Red Baron '93

Rodney McDonald
Steel Sharks '97
Desire '95

Michael McDowell (1950-99)
Stephen King's Thinner '96
The Nightmare before Christmas '93
Tales from the Darkside: The Movie '90
Beetlejuice '88

Alan B. McElroy
Thr3e '07
The Marine '06
Wrong Turn '03
Ballistic: Ecks vs. Sever '02
Left Behind: The Movie '00
Spawn '97
Todd McFarlane's Spawn '97

Ross McElwee (1947-)
Time Indefinite '93
Sherman's March '86

Donald McEnery
A Bug's Life '98
Hercules '97

Ian McEwan (1948-)
The Innocent '93

Stephen McFeely
The Chronicles of Narnia: Prince Caspian '08
You Kill Me '07
The Chronicles of Narnia: The Lion, the Witch and the Wardrobe '05

Mark Thomas McGee
Sorceress '94
Sins of Desire '92
Bad Girls from Mars '90

Ron McGee
Fatal Contact: Bird Flu in America '06
Shock to the System '06
Meat Loaf: To Hell and Back '00

Scott McGehee
The Deep End '01
Suture '93

Kathleen McGhee-Anderson
The Color of Courage '98
Sunset Park '96

Josann McGibbon
The Starter Wife '07
Runaway Bride '99
The Favor '92
Three Men and a Little Lady '90
Worth Winning '89

David McGillivray (1947-)
The Terror '79
House of Whipcord '75
Frightmare '74

Jimmy McGovern (1949-)
Liam '00
Heart '99
Go Now '96
Cracker: Brotherly Love '95
Cracker: Men Should Weep '94
Cracker: The Big Crunch '94

Cracker: To Be a Somebody '94

Dorrell McGowan (1899-1997)
Priest '94
The Showdown '50
Don't Fence Me In '45
Jeepers Creepers '39
San Fernando Valley '44
King of the Pecos '36

Douglas McGrath (1958-)
Infamous '06
Nicholas Nickleby '02
Company Man '00
Emma '96
Born Yesterday '93

Patrick McGrath (1950-)
Spider '02
Grave Indiscretions '96

John McGreevey
Ms. Scrooge '97
Captains Courageous '95
Consenting Adult '85
Night Crossing '81
The Disappearance of Aimee '76
Hello Down There '69
Hot Rod Girl '56

Thomas McGuane (1939-)
Cold Feet '89
Tom Horn '80
Missouri Breaks '76
92 in the Shade '75
Rancho Deluxe '75

Frank McGuinness (1959-)
Dancing at Lughnasa '98
Talk of Angels '96

James Kevin McGuinness (1893-1950)
Rio Grande '50
China Seas '35
Tarzan and His Mate '34

Don McGuire (1919-99)
Tootsie '82
Suppose They Gave a War and Nobody Came? '70
The Delicate Delinquent '56
Meet Danny Wilson '52

William Anthony McGuire (1881-1640)
Lillian Russell '40
The Great Ziegfeld '36
Kid from Spain '32

Jay McInerney (1955-)
Gia '98
Hotel Room '93

Adam McKay (1968-)
Step Brothers '08
Talladega Nights: The Ballad of Ricky Bobby '06
Anchorman: The Legend of Ron Burgundy '04

Jim McKay
Life Support '07
Angel Rodriguez '05
Our Song '01
Girls Town '96

Steven McKay
Darkman 2: The Return of Durant '94
Diggstown '92
Hard to Kill '89

Stuart E. McGowan (1904-99)
The Showdown '50
Don't Fence Me In '45
Jeepers Creepers '39
San Fernando Valley '44
King of the Pecos '36

Grace McKeaney
The Loretta Claiborne Story '00

Lucky McKee (1975-)
Roman '06
May '02

Don McKellar (1963-)
The Devil Wears Prada '06
Last Night '98
The Red Violin '98
Dance Me Outside '95
32 Short Films about Glenn Gould '93
Highway 61 '91
Roadkill '89

David McKenna
S.W.A.T. '03
Blow '01
Get Carter '00
American History X '98
Body Shots '99

Aline Brosh McKenna (1967-)
27 Dresses '08
The Devil Wears Prada '06
Laws of Attraction '04
Three to Tango '99

Charles McKeown
Ripley's Game '02
Plunkett & Macleane '98
The Adventures of Baron Munchausen '89
Brazil '85

Mark McKinney (1959-)
Slings & Arrows: Season 2 '05

Vince McKewin
The Replacements '00
The Climb '97
Fly Away Home '96

John McLaughlin
The Double O Kid '92
Man of the House '05
The Great Gatsby '01
The Masked Rider '41

Duncan McLachlan
Born Wild '95

Victor McLeod
Gang Busters '42
Boss of Bullion City '41
Bury Me Not on the Lone Prairie '41

Tom McLoughlin (1950-)
Date with an Angel '87
Friday the 13th, Part 6: Jason Lives '86

John McMahon
Rip It Off '02
Broken Vessels '98
Good Guys Wear Black '78

James McManus
La Cucaracha '99
The Big Empty '98

John Meehan (1890-1954)
Three Daring Daughters '48
The Valley of Decision '45
Seven Sinners '40
Madame X '37
Off Beat '86

Larry McMurtry (1936-)
Comanche Moon '06
Brokeback Mountain '05
Johnson County War '02
Larry McMurtry's Dead Man's Walk '56
Larry McMurtry's Streets of Laredo '95
Falling from Grace '92
Memphis '91
Montana '90
The Last Picture Show '71

Terrance McNally (1939-)
Common Ground '00
Love! Valour! Compassion! '96
Frankie and Johnny '91
Earth Girls Are Easy '89

Steve Meerson
Anna and the King '99
Star Trek 4: The Voyage Home '86

Thomas Meehan
Hairspray '07
The Producers '05
Spaceballs '87

Michael Meredith
Three Days of Rain '03

Anne Meredith
Rated X '00
Bastard out of Carolina '96
Losing Chase '96
Homage '95
Morgan: A Suitable Case for Treatment '66

Bess Meredyth
That Night in Rio '41
Don Juan '26

Joseph Merhi (1953-)
SLC Punk! '99
The Real Thing '97
Hard Drive '94
Terrified '94

James Merendino (1967-)
I Love Trouble '94

Agnes Merlet (1959-)
Artemisia '97

Monte Merrick
The Son of the Shark '93
The Miracle Worker '00

Robert T. Megginson
Wolverine '96
F/X '86

Deepa Mehta (1950-)
Earth '98
Fire '96

Michael McKean (1947-)
The Return of Spiral Tap '92
The Big Picture '89
This Is Spinal Tap '84

Eoin McNamee
I Want You '98
Resurrection Man '97

William Slavens McNutt (1885-1938)
The Lives of a Bengal Lancer '35
Strangers in Love '32
Touchdown '31

Christopher McQuarrie (1968-)
Way of the Gun '00
Public Access '93
The Usual Suspects '95

Kay Mellor (1950-)
Girls' Night '97
Jane Eyre '97
Band of Gold '95

Greg Mellott
American Soldiers '05

Will McRobb
Alvin and the Chipmunks '07
Snow Day '00

Anna McRoberts
Snow Buddies '08
Air Bud 6: Air Buddies '06

Nick Mead
Parting Shots '98
Swing '98
Bank Robber '93
Lone Ranger '56
The Redhead from Wyoming '53

Patrick Melton
Saw 4 '07
Feast '06

Herb Meadow (1912-95)
The Strange Woman '46

Shane Meadows (1972-)
This Is England '06
Dead Man's Shoes '04
Once Upon a Time in the Midlands '02
24-7 '97
The Lion King '94

Lewis Meltzer (1911-95)
High School Confidential '58
Autumn Leaves '56
The Man with the Golden Arm '55

Julio Medem (1958-)
Sex and Lucia '01
Lovers of the Arctic Circle '98
Tierra '95
The Red Squirrel '93
Vacas '91

Irene Mecchi
Annie '99
Hercules '97
The Hunchback of Notre Dame '96

Aaron Mendelsohn (1966-)
Air Bud 2: Golden Receiver '98
Air Bud '97

George Mendeluk (1948-)
Doin' Time '85
Stone Cold Dead '80

Enrico Medioli (1925-)
Once Upon a Time in America '84
Conversation Piece '75
The Leopard '63
Rocco and His Brothers '60

Harold Medford (1911-77)
Brainwashed '60
The Damned Don't Cry '50

Mark Medoff (1940-)
Santa Fe '97
Homage '95
City of Joy '92
Clara's Heart '88
Apology '86
Children of a Lesser God '86

David Mercer (1928-80)
Providence '77
Morgan: A Suitable Case for Treatment '66

Joe Menosky
Anonymous Rex '04

Jiri Menzel (1938-)
Closely Watched Trains '66

Ramon Menendez
Money for Nothing '93
Stand and Deliver '88

Jean-Pierre Melville (1917-73)
Le Cercle Rouge '70
Army of Shadows '69
Le Samourai '67
Bob le Flambeur '55
Les Enfants Terrible '50
La Silence de la Mer '47

Gordon Melbourne
Bulletproof Heart '95
White Tiger '95

Roger Merton
Queen of the Amazons '47
Down the Wyoming Trail '39

Stephen Metcalfe
Beautiful Joe '00
Roommates '95
Cousins '89
Jacknife '89

Kevin Meyer
A Smile Like Yours '96
Under Investigation '93
Civil War Diary '90

Radley Metzger (1929-)
The Cat and the Canary '79
The Alley Cats '65
Dark Odyssey '57

Tim Metcalfe (1956-)
44 Minutes: The North Hollywood Shootout '03
Killer: A Journal of Murder '95
Kalifornia '93
Iron Maze '91
Fright Night 2 '88
Million Dollar Mystery '87
Three for the Road '87
Revenge of the Nerds '84

Nicholas Meyer (1945-)
The Human Stain '03
The Informant '97
Sommersby '93
Company Business '91
Star Trek 6: The Undiscovered Country '91
Star Trek 4: The Voyage Home '86
Time After Time '79
The Seven-Per-Cent Solution '76
Invasion of the Bee Girls '73

Russ Meyer (1922-2004)
Beneath the Valley of the Ultra-Vixens '79
Supervixens '75
Blacksnake! '73
Faster, Pussycat! Kill! Kill! '65
Motor Psycho '65

Turi Meyer (1964-)
Leprechaun 2 '94

Nancy Meyers (1949-)
The Holiday '06
Something's Gotta Give '03
What Women Want '00
The Parent Trap '98
Father of the Bride Part 2 '95
I Love Trouble '94
Father of the Bride '91
Baby Boom '87
Irreconcilable Differences '84
Protocol '84
Private Benjamin '80

Menno Meyjes (1954-)
Max '02
The Siege '98
Foreign Student '94
Empire of the Sun '87
The Color Purple '85

Ronald Millar (1919-98)
Never Let Me Go '53
The Miniver Story '50

Nick Millard
Terrorists '88
Gunblast '74
Dead Ringer '64

Miles Millar (1970-)
The Mummy: Tomb of the Dragon Emperor '08
The Wind and the Lion '75

John Milius (1944-)
Farewell to the King '89
Red Dawn '84
Conan the Barbarian '82
Apocalypse Now '79
Big Wednesday '78
Dillinger '73
Magnum Force '73
Evel Knievel '72
Jeremiah Johnson '72
Life & Times of Judge Roy Bean '72

Frank Military
Blind Faith '98
Buffalo Soldiers '97

Lewis Milestone (1895-1980)
Arch of Triumph '48
Lucky Partners '40
Anna '93

Nikita Mikhalkov (1945-)
The Barber of Siberia '98
Burnt by the Sun '94

Ted V. Mikels (1929-)
10 Violent Women '79
The Doll Squad '73
The Corpse Grinders '71
The Astro-Zombies '67

Gordan Mihic (1938-)
Black Cat, White Cat '98

Anne-Marie Mieville (1945-)
First Name: Carmen '83
Comment Ca Va? '76
Numero Deux '75

William Mickelberry
The Fox and the Hound '81

Elizabeth (Lizzie) Mickery
The State Within '06
Inspector Lynley Mysteries: A Great Deliverance '01
Love or Money '01
The Ice House '97

Romano Migliorini
The Bloody Pit of Horror '65

Radu Mihaileanu (1958-)
Train of Life '98
Trahir '93

Jean-Louis Milesi
Marius and Jeannette '97
Toby McTeague '87

Djordje Milicevic (1942-)
Iron Will '93
Runaway Train '85
Victory '81

Boleslaw Michalek (1925-97)
Danton '82

Oscar Millard (1908-90)
A Love in Germany '84

Dave Michener
The Great Mouse Detective '86

Marta Meszaros (1931-)
Adoption '75

Kay Mellor — see above

Michael Meredith — see above

[Winston Miller, cont.]
The Conqueror '56
Second Chance '53
Angel Face '52
No Highway in the Sky '51
Come to the Stable '49

Alice Duer Miller (1874-1942)
Wife Versus Secretary '36
Are Parents People? '25

Andrew Miller
Boys and Girls '00
Simon Sez '99

Arthur Miller (1915-2005)
The Crucible '96
Everybody Wins '90
The Misfits '61

Chris Miller (1942-)
Multiplicity '96
National Lampoon's Animal House '78

Claude Miller (1942-)
Alias Betty '01
The Accompanist '93
The Little Thief '89
This Sweet Sickness '77
The Best Way '76

David Keith Miller
The Glass Cage '96
I Like to Play Games '95

Frank Miller
RoboCop 3 '91
The Living Dead '33
Trapped by the Mormons '22

George Miller (1945-)
Babe '95
Lorenzo's Oil '92
Mad Max: Beyond Thunderdome '85
The Road Warrior '82
Mad Max '80

Harvey Miller (1936-99)
Getting Away With Murder '96
Bad Medicine '85
Cannonball Run 2 '84
Protocol '84

Jeff Miller
Eye of the Killer '99
Hellblock 13 '97

Jennifer Miller
Cupid & Cate '00
Family Pictures '93

J(ames) P(inckney) Miller (1919-2001)
Helter Skelter '76
The Lindbergh Kidnapping Case '76
The People Next Door '70
Behold a Pale Horse '64
Days of Wine and Roses '62

Rebecca Miller (1962-)
The Ballad of Jack and Rose '05
Personal Velocity: Three Portraits '02
Angela '94

Seton I. Miller (1902-74)
Istanbul '57
Singapore '47
Two Years before the Mast '46
Ministry of Fear '44
The Black Swan '42
Here Comes Mr. Jordan '41
The Adventures of Robin Hood '38
Bullets or Ballots '38
Dawn Patrol '38
Kid Galahad '37
"G" Men '35
The Eagle and the Hawk '33
A Girl in Every Port '28

Winston Miller (1910-94)
The Far Horizons '55
Cavalry Charge '51
My Darling Clementine '46
One Body Too Many '44
Man from Cheyenne '42
Dick Tracy: The Spider Strikes '37
S.O.S. Coast Guard '37

Bertram Millhauser (1892-1958)
The Woman in Green '45
The Invisible Man's Revenge '44
The Texans '38

Andy Milligan (1929-91)
Man with Two Heads '72
The Rats Are Coming! The Werewolves Are Here! '72
The Ghastly Ones '68

Bill Milling
Body Trouble '92
Lauderdale '89

Hugh Mills (1913-71)
Blanche Fury '48
Personal Property '37

Mark Mills
The Reckoning '03
Rock My World '02
The Lost Son '98

Paula Milne
I Dreamed of Africa '00
Second Sight '99
Hollow Reed '95
Mad Love '95

Peter Milne (1896-1968)
God Is My Co-Pilot '45
Step Lively '44
San Quentin '37
The Kennel Murder Case '33

Daniel Minahan
Series 7: The Contenders '01

Seishi Minakimi
Paprika '06
Paprika 2 '06

Michael Miner
Anacondas: The Hunt for the Blood Orchid '04
Deadly Weapon '88
RoboCop '87

Anthony Minghella (1954-2008)
Breaking and Entering '06
Cold Mountain '03
The Talented Mr. Ripley '99
The English Patient '96
Truly, Madly, Deeply '91

Joe Minion (1957-)
After Hours '85
Motorama '91
Vampire's Kiss '88

Susan Minot (1956-)
Evening '07
Stealing Beauty '96

Wu Ming
See Xiaoshuai Wang

Pang Ming
Frozen '96
So Close to Paradise '98

Sam Mintz (1897-1957)
Here Comes Cookie '35
No Marriage Ties '33

Brad Mirman (1953-)
Crime Spree '04
Joshua '02

Craig Mitchell
The Flock '07
Highwaymen '03
Komodo '98
Milo '98

David Mitchell
Dead Fish '04
The Killing Man '94
Circle Man '87

Gene Mitchell
Flipping '96
The Takeover '94

Joseph A. Mitchell
Seven Chances '25
The Navigator '24
Sherlock, Jr. '24
Our Hospitality '23

Julian Mitchell (1935-)
Wilde '97
August '95
Vincent & Theo '90
Another Country '84
Elizabeth R '72
Persuasion '71

Keith Mitchell (1967-)
Mr. 3000 '04
Eddie '96

Steve Mitchell
Tin Man '07
Against the Law '98
Chopping Mall '86

Hayao Miyazaki (1941-)
Howl's Moving Castle '04
Spirited Away '01
Kiki's Delivery Service '98
My Neighbor Totoro '88

Wilson Mizner (1876-1933)
Heroes for Sale '33
One Way Passage '32

Moshe Mizrahi (1931-)
Every Time We Say Goodbye '86
La Vie Continue '82
I Sent a Letter to My Love '81
Madame Rosa '77
I Love You Rosa '72

Patrick Modiano (1945-)
Bon Voyage '03
Son of Gascogne '95

Ivan Moffat (1918-2002)
They Came to Cordura '59
Bhowani Junction '56
Giant '56

Jordan Moffet
Like Mike '02
Whispers: An Elephant's Tale '00

John Moffitt
Double or Nothing '37
Rhythm on the Range '36

Jose Mojica Marins (1929-)
Hallucinations of a Deranged Mind '78
Awakenings of the Beast '68
Strange World of Coffin Joe '68
At Midnight, I'll Take Your Soul '63

Hans Petter Moland (1955-)
Aberdeen '00
Zero Degrees Kelvin '95
The Last Lieutenant '94

Gustaf Molander (1888-1973)
Intermezzo '36

Jacinto (Jack) Molina
See Paul Naschy

Edouard Molinaro (1928-)
Beaumarchais the Scoundrel '96
La Cage aux Folles '78
Pain in the A— '77
Dracula and Son '76

Dominik Moll (1962-)
Lemming '05
With a Friend Like Harry '00

William Monahan (1960-)
The Departed '06
Kingdom of Heaven '05

Paul Monash (1917-2003)
The Golden Spiders: A Nero Wolfe Mystery '00
Rescuers: Stories of Courage—Two Couples '98
George Wallace '97
Kingfish: A Story of Huey P. Long '95
Stalin '92
All Quiet on the Western Front '79
Salem's Lot '79
Scarface Mob '62
Bail Out at 43,000 '57

Nate Monaster (1911-90)
Call Me Bwana '63
That Touch of Mink '62

Santiago Moncada
Mean Machine '73
Voodoo Black Exorcist '73
Hatchet for the Honeymoon '70

Karen Moncrieff (1963-)
The Dead Girl '06
Blue Car '03

Paul Mones (1955-)
Double Team '97
The Quest '96
Saints and Sinners '95
Fathers and Sons '92

Christopher Monger (1950-)
Seeing Red '99
The Englishman Who Went up a Hill But Came down a Mountain '95
Waiting for the Light '90

Vincent Mongol
Hellhole '85
Chained Heat '83

Mario Monicelli (1915-)
Lovers and Liars '81
The Organizer '64
The Unfaithfuls '60
Big Deal on Madonna Street '58

John Monks, Jr. (1910-2004)
No Man Is an Island '62
The West Point Story '50
Knock on Any Door '49
13 Rue Madeleine '46
House on 92nd Street '45

Eric Monte (1944-)
Cooley High '75
Nine Lives of Fritz the Cat '74

Luigi Montefiore (1942-)
Beyond Justice '92

Art Monterastelli (1955-)
Rambo '08
The Hunted '03

Doreen Montgomery (1916-92)
Lassie from Lancashire '38
Mr. Reeder in Room 13 '38

Michael Thomas Montgomery
Night Vision '97

Martin Mooney (1896-1967)
The Monster Maker '44
Gangs, Inc. '41

Brian Moore (1921-99)
Black Robe '91
The Blood of Others '84
Torn Curtain '66

Charles Philip Moore (1962-)
Heaven's Fire '99
Termination Man '97
The Last Assassins '96
Not of This Earth '96
Black Belt '92

Dudley Moore (1935-2002)
The Hound of the Baskervilles '77
Bedazzled '68
30 Is a Dangerous Age, Cynthia '68

Michael Moore (1954-)
Sicko '07
Fahrenheit 9/11 '04
Bowling for Columbine '02
Canadian Bacon '94
Roger & Me '89

Ronald D. Moore (1964-)
Star Trek: First Contact '96
Star Trek: Generations '94

Scott Moore
Full of It '07
Rebound '05

Simon Moore (1958-)
Dinotopia '02
The Snow Queen '02
Gulliver's Travels '95
Under Suspicion '92
Traffik '90

Wesley Moore (1955-)
Are You Lonesome Tonight '92
Apprentice to Murder '88

Jocelyn Moorhouse (1960-)
Unconditional Love '03
Proof '91

Philippe Mora (1949-)
Pterodactyl Woman from Beverly Hills '97
Howling 3: The Marsupials '87

Eddie Moran
Wonder Man '45
Twin Beds '42

Patrick Moran (1960-)
Jack-O '95
Dark Universe '93

Julian More (1928-)
The Bloodsuckers '70
The Valley of Gwangi '69

Rob Moreland
Space Chimps '08
Happily N'Ever After '07

Robert Moresco (1960-)
10th & Wolf '06
Crash '05

Nanni Moretti (1953-)
The Son's Room '00
Caro Diario '93
Palombella Rossa '89

Rafael Moreu
The Rage: Carrie 2 '99
Hackers '95

Chris Morgan
Wanted '08
The Fast and the Furious: Tokyo Drift '06
Cellular '04

George Morgan
Silent Code '35
The Fighting Rookie '34

Glen Morgan
Black Christmas '06
Final Destination 3 '06
Willard '03

Peter Morgan (1963-)
The Other Boleyn Girl '08
The Last King of Scotland '06
Longford '06
The Queen '06
The Very Thought of You '98

Brett Morgen
Chicago 10 '07

Louis Morheim
The Beast from 20,000 Fathoms '53
Pier 23 '51
Roaring City '51
Ma and Pa Kettle '49

Tony Morphett (1938-)
Kings in Grass Castles '97
Crime Broker '94
Crimebroker '93
Sweet Talker '91
The Last Wave '77
Alternative '76

Judy Morris (1947-)
Happy Feet '06
Babe: Pig in the City '98

Richard Morris (1924-96)
Thoroughly Modern Millie '67
Ma and Pa Kettle at the Fair '52

Wendell Morris
Eye of the Dolphin '06
The Medicine Show '01

Paul Morrison
Wondrous Oblivion '06
Solomon and Gaenor '98

Rebecca Morrison
Scorcher '02
Legionnaire '98

Paul Morrissey (1939-)
Beethoven's Nephew '88
Spike of Bensonhurst '88
Mixed Blood '84
The Hound of the Baskervilles '77
Andy Warhol's Dracula '74
Andy Warhol's Frankenstein '74
Heat '72
Trash '70
Flesh '68

Barry Morrow
Race the Sun '96
Rain Man '88

Douglas S. Morrow (1913-94)
Beyond a Reasonable Doubt '56
Jim Thorpe: All American '51
The Stratton Story '49

Lisa Morton
Blood Angels '05

John Mortimer (1923-)
In Love and War '01
Don Quixote '00
Cider with Rosie '99
Tea with Mussolini '99
Edwin '84
No Sex Please—We're British '73
The Innocents '61
24 Hours in a Woman's Life '61

April Moskowitz
Body Strokes '95
Friend of the Family '95

Nat Moss
Adrift in Manhattan '07
Washington Heights '02

Jonathan Mostow (1961-)
U-571 '00
Breakdown '96

Greg Mottola (1964-)
Superbad '07
The Daytrippers '96

Marcel Moussey (1924-95)
Shoot the Piano Player '62
The 400 Blows '59

Oren Moverman
I'm Not There '07
Married Life '07

Allan Moyle (1947-)
The Thing Called Love '93

Love Crimes '92
Pump Up the Volume '90

Niels Mueller (1961-)
The Assassination of Richard Nixon '05
Tadpole '02

Jim Mulholland
Bad Boys '95
National Lampoon's Favorite Deadly Sins '95
Amazon Women on the Moon '87
Oscar '91
Ratings Game '84

Peter Mullan (1954-)
The Magdalene Sisters '02
Orphans '97

Christopher Munch (1952-)
The Hours and Times '92

Lance Mungia (1972-)
The Crow: Wicked Prayer '05
Six-String Samurai '98

Robert Munic (1968-)
They Call Me Sir '00
In a Class of His Own '99
L.A. Blues: The Pros and Cons of Breathing '05

John Murlowski
Possessed '05
Black Cadillac '03

Charles Murphy
Norbit '07

Geoff Murphy (1938-)
Spitfire '34
Dark of the Night '85
Uru '83

Tab Murphy
Brother Bear '03
Atlantis: The Lost Empire '01
Tarzan '99

Richard Murphy (1912-93)
Compulsion '59
Boomerang '47
Sundown Fury '42
Back in the Saddle '41
Flying Blind '41

Daniel Myrick
The Blair Witch Project '99
Believers '07

Richard D. (R.D.) Murphy (1956-)
Milwaukee, Minnesota '03
Betty '07

Warren B. Murphy (1933-)
Remo Williams: The Adventure Begins '85
The Eiger Sanction '75
Confessions of Tom Harris '72

Don Murray (1929-)
The Hoodlum Priest '61

John Fenton Murray ('1917-96)
McHale's Navy Joins the Air Force '65
Robin and the 7 Hoods '64

Michael J. Murray
Acceptable Risk '01

Madonna: Innocence Lost '95
Honor Thy Father and Mother: The True Story of the Menendez Brothers '94

Tom Musca
Tortilla Soup '01
Race '99
Money for Nothing '93
Stand and Deliver '88

John Musker (1953-)
Treasure Planet '02
Hercules '97
Aladdin '92
The Little Mermaid '89

Floyd Mutrux (1941-)
Blood In ... Blood Out: Bound by Honor '93
American Me '92
There Goes My Baby '92
The Hollywood Knights '80
Aloha, Bobby and Rose '74

Henry Myers (1893-1975)
Destry Rides Again '39
The Black Room '35
Diplomaniacs '33

Mike Myers (1963-)
The Love Guru '08
Austin Powers in Goldmember '02
Austin Powers 2: The Spy Who Shagged Me '99
Austin Powers: International Man of Mystery '97
So I Married an Axe Murderer '93

Rona Munro
Aimee & Jaguar '98
Ladybird, Ladybird '93

Jane Murfin (1892-1955)
Come and Get It '36

Ryu Murakami (1952-)
Because of You '95
Tokyo Decadence '91

Scott Myers
Trojan War '97
K-9 '89

Fred Myton (1885-1955)
Here Come the Waves '45
April Fool '26

John Myhers (1921-92)
Terror in Beverly Hills '90
The Longshot '86
The Private Eyes '80
Bait '00

Zion Myers (1898-1948)
Murder in the Doll House '79

Yuri Nagibin (1920-94)
Dersu Uzala '75

Takehiro Nakajima (1935-)
Okoge '93

Desmond Nakano (1953-)
White Man's Burden '95

Shuichi Nagahara (1940-2001)
Godzilla 1985 '85
Gunsmoke Trail '38

Ed Naha (1950-)
Omega Doom '96
Honey, I Shrunk the Kids '89
Dolls '87
Troll '86

Tchaikovsky '71

Kurt Nachmann
Tower of Screaming Virgins '73

Christopher Neame
Feast of July '95
Zeta One '69

David Newman (1954-)
Santa Claus: The Movie '85
Sheena '84

Rodion Nakhapetov (1911-)
American Me '92
Border Blues '03
Stir '98

Yin Nam
Full Contact '92
Prison on Fire '87

Michael Nankin (1955-)
Gate 2 '92
The Gate '87

Paul Naschy (1934-)
Human Beasts '80
Inquisition '76
Night of the Howling Beast '75
Exorcism '74
Curse of the Devil '73
House of Psychotic Women '73
The Mummy's Revenge '73
Dracula's Great Love '72
Horror Rises from the Tomb '72
Dr. Jekyll and the Wolfman '71
The Fury of the Wolfman '70
The Werewolf vs. the Vampire Woman '70

N. Richard Nash (1913-2000)
Helen of Troy '56
The Rainmaker '56

Gustin Nash
Charlie Bartlett '07

Vincenzo Natali (1969-)
Paris, je t'aime '07
Cube '98

Jeff Nathanson
Rush Hour 3 '07
The Last Shot '04
The Terminal '04
Catch Me If You Can '02
Rush Hour 2 '01
Speed 2: Cruise Control '97
For Better or Worse '95

Mort Nathan
Boat Trip '03
Kingpin '96

Maria Nation
A Season for Miracles '99

Rick Natkin
Blue River '95
Gang in Blue '96

Jack Natteford (1894-1970)
The Crimson Trail '35
Rider of the Law '35
Thundering Gunslingers '44
Necessary Roughness '91
The Boys in Company C '77
Demon for Trouble '34
Cowboy Counselor '33
The Dude Bandit '33
My Pal, the King '32
Arizona Terror '31
Border Romance '30

William T. Naud
Necromancer: Satan's Servant '88
Island of Blood '82

Gregory Nava (1949-)
Bordertown '06
Frida '02
Selena '96
My Family '94
A Time of Destiny '88
El Norte '83

Craig J. Nevius

Edward Neumeier
Anacondas: The Hunt for the Blood Orchid '04
Starship Troopers '97
RoboCop '87

Kurt Neumann (1906-58)
Party Girls for Sale '54
Rocketship X-M '50
The Midnight Phantom '35
Trader Horn '31

Ronald Neame (1911-)
This Happy Breed '47
Brief Encounter '46
Great Expectations '46

Hal Needham (1931-)
Smokey and the Bandit '77

Troy Neighbors
Fortress 2: Re-Entry '99
Fortress '93

B.J. Nelson
Stroker Ace '83
Alien Chaser '96
Scanners 2: The New Order '91

Brian Nelson
30 Days of Night '07
Hard Candy '06

Hank Nelken
Are We Done Yet? '07
Saving Silverman '01
Killer Bud '00

Jessie Nelson
Because I Said So '07
Stepmom '98
Corrina, Corrina '94

Tim Blake Nelson (1965-)
The Grey Zone '01
Eye of God '94

John Allen Nelson (1959-)
American Yakuza '94
Best of the Best 2 '93

Peter Nelson
Getting Up and Going Home '92
The Lonely Passion of Judith Hearne '87

Dennis Nemec
The Avenging Angel '95
God Bless the Child '88
Murder in Coweta County '83

Jan Nemec (1936-)
The Report on the Party and the Guests '66
Diamonds of the Night '64

Vladimir Nemirovsky
Hangman '00
Indiscreet '98
Timebomb '91

Claude Neron (1927-91)
Vincent, Francois, Paul and the Others '76
Cesar & Rosalie '72

Avi Nesher (1953-)
The Taxman '98
Mercenary '96
Doppelganger: The Evil Within '90

Ted Nicolaou
Bloodstorm: Subspecies 4 '98
Leprechauns '96
Vampire Journals '96
Leapin' Leprechauns '95
Dragonworld '94
Bloodlust: Subspecies 3 '93
Bloodstone: Subspecies 2 '92

David Nichols
Starter for Ten '06
Simpatico '99

Dudley Nichols (1895-1960)
Prince Valiant '54
Pinky '49
The Fugitive '48
And Then There Were None '45
The Bells of St. Mary's '45
It Happened Tomorrow '44
Air Force '43
For Whom the Bell Tolls '43
Stagecoach '39
Bringing Up Baby '38
The Hurricane '37
The Crusades '35
The Informer '35
She '35
The Lost Patrol '34

Jack Nicholson (1937-)
Head '68
The Trip '67
Flight to Fury '66
Ride in the Whirlwind '65

William Nicholson (1948-)
Gladiator '00
Grey Owl '99
Firelight '97
Nell '94
Shadowlands '93
A Private Matter '92
Sarafina! '92

Nicholas Niciphor (1948-)
Fatal Charm '92
Death Sport '78

Ted Nicolaou

Stephen Norrington (1965-)
The Last Minute '01
Death Machine '95

Marsha Norman (1947-)
'night, Mother '86

Edmund H. North (1911-90)
Damn the Defiant! '62
Sink the Bismarck '60
The Fat Horizons '55
The Day the Earth Stood Still '51

Bill W.L. Norton (1943-)
Gator '76
Day of the Animals '77
Back to the Beach '87
Losin' It '82

William W. Norton, Sr. (1925-)
Dirty Tricks '81
Night of the Juggler '80
Day of the Animals '77
Moving Violation '76
A Small Town in Texas '76

On the Edge '86
Signal 7 '83
Northern Lights '79

Brian Nissen
The Swan Princess 2: Escape from Castle Mountain '97
The Swan Princess '94

David Nokes
The Tenant of Wildfell Hall '96
Clarissa '91

Gaspar Noe (1963-)
Irreversible '02
I Stand Alone '96

Marie Noelle
Love the Hard Way '01

Kuang Ni
Infra-Man '76
Duel of Fists '71

Sloan Nibley (1908-90)
Hostile Guns '67
Fat Frontier '48

Andrew Niccol (1964-)
Lord of War '05
The Terminal '04
Simone '02
The Truman Show '98
Gattaca '97

Maurizio Nichetti
Luna e L'Altra '96
Stefano Quantestorie '93
Volere Volare '92
Allegro Non Troppo '76

Ken Nolan
Black Hawk Down '01

Jonathan Nolan
The Dark Knight '08
The Prestige '06
Following '99

Christopher Nolan (1970-)
The Dark Knight '08
The Prestige '06
Batman Begins '05
Memento '00
Following '99

William F. Nolan (1928-)
Trilogy of Terror 2 '96
The Norliss Tapes '73

Tom Noonan (1951-)
The Wife '95
What Happened Was... '94

Eric Norden
Blood Legacy '73
Please Don't Eat My Mother '72

William Nolte (1889-1965)
Square Dance Jubilee '51
Two-Fisted Justice '43

George Nolfi
The Bourne Ultimatum '07
Ocean's Twelve '04
Timeline '03

Marc Norman (1941-)
Shakespeare in Love '98
Cutthroat Island '95
Waterworld '95
The Aviator '85
Breakout '75
Zandy's Bride '74
Oklahoma Crude '73

Brannigan '75
Big Bad Mama '74
I Dismember Mama '74
White Lightning '73
McKenzie Break '70
Sam Whiskey '69
The Scalphunters '68
Frank Norwood
Past Midnight '92
Driven to Kill '90
Jonathan Nossiter (1961-)
Signs & Wonders '00
Sunday '96
Louis Nowra (1950-)
Radiance '98
Heaven's Burning '97
The Matchmaker '97
Cosi '95
Map of the Human Heart '93
Frank Nugent (1908-66)
Donovan's Reef '63
Gunman's Walk '58
Last Hurrah '58
The Searchers '56
Mister Roberts '55
The Tall Men '55
Angel Face '52
The Quiet Man '52
She Wore a Yellow Ribbon '49
Fort Apache '48
Victor Nunez (1945-)
Coastlines '02
Ulee's Gold '97
Ruby in Paradise '93
A Flash of Green '85
Gal Young 'Un '79
Tom Nursall
Without a Paddle '04
I'll Be Home for Christmas '98
Raphael Nussbaum (1932-93)
Speak of the Devil '90
The Invisible Terror '63
Colin Nutley (1944-)
Under the Sun '98
The Last Dance '93
Ron Nyswaner (1956-)
The Painted Veil '06
Soldier's Girl '03
Philadelphia '93
Love Hurts '91
Gross Anatomy '89
Prince of Pennsylvania '88
Mrs. Soffel '84
Purple Hearts '84
Swing Shift '84
Smithereens '82
Dan O'Bannon (1946-)
Alien vs. Predator '04
Bleeders '97
Screamers '96
Total Recall '90
Invaders from Mars '86
Lifeforce '85
Return of the Living Dead '85
Blue Thunder '83
Dead and Buried '81
Alien '79
Dark Star '74
Rockne S. O'Bannon (1955-)
Fatal Error '99
Robin Cook's Invasion '97
Alien Nation '88
Sean O'Bannon
Air Rage '01
Mom's Outta Sight '01
Poison '01
Margaret Grieco Oberman
The Man '05
Night Shade '97
Invisible Mom '96
Troop Beverly Hills '89

Edna O'Brien (1930-)
X, Y & Zee '72
Girl with Green Eyes '64
Jeff O'Brien (1965-)
Insecticidal '05
Blind Heat '00
John O'Brien (1962-)
Starsky & Hutch '04
Cradle 2 the Grave '03
The Big Dis '89
Liam O'Brien (1913-96)
Young at Heart '54
Chain Lightning '50
Richard O'Brien (1942-)
Shock Treatment '81
The Rocky Horror Picture Show '75
Robert O'Brien (1918-2005)
By the Light of the Silvery Moon '53
The Lemon Drop Kid '51
Lady on a Train '45
Jeffrey Obrow
Bram Stoker's The Mummy '97
The Kindred '87
The Power '80
James O'Connolly (1924-87)
Tower of Evil '72
Night Caller from Outer Space '66
David Odell
Masters of the Universe '87
Supergirl '84
The Dark Crystal '82
Cry Uncle '71
Clifford Odets (1906-63)
Wild in the Country '61
Sweet Smell of Success '57
Deadline at Dawn '46
Humoresque '46
None But the Lonely Heart '44
The General Died at Dawn '36
Joseph O'Donnell (1891-1963)
Manhunt in the African Jungles '43
Raiders of Red Gap '43
Battling Outlaw '40
Billy the Kid in Texas '40
Border Caballero '36
The Traitor '36
His Fighting Blood '35
Michael O'Donoghue (1940-94)
Scrooged '88
Steve Oedekerk (1961-)
Evan Almighty '07
Barnyard '06
Bruce Almighty '03
Kung Pow! Enter the Fist '02
Jimmy Neutron: Boy Genius '01
Nutty Professor 2: The Klumps '00
Patch Adams '98
Nothing to Lose '96
The Nutty Professor '96
Ace Ventura: When Nature Calls '95
High Strung '91
Mo Ogrodnik (1966-)
Uptown Girls '03
Ripe '97
Hideo Oguni (1904-96)
Ran '85
Dodes 'ka-den '70
Toral Toral Toral '70
High & Low '62
Sanjuro '62
Yojimbo '61
The Bad Sleep Well '60
The Hidden Fortress '58
The Lower Depths '57

Throne of Blood '57
I Live in Fear '55
Seven Samurai '54
Ikiru '52
Colo Tavernier O'Hagan
L'Appat '94
Daddy Nostalgia '90
Beatrice '88
The Story of Women '88
A Sunday in the Country '84
James O'Hanlon (1910-69)
Calamity Jane '53
Destination Moon '50
Sahara '43
Paul Ohl
North Star '96
Highlander: The Final Dimension '94
Mark O'Keefe
Click '06
Bruce Almighty '03
Pedro Olea (1938-)
Zafarinas '94
Joel Oliansky (1935-2002)
Bird '88
The Todd Killings '71
Deanna Oliver
My Favorite Martian '98
Casper '95
Ron Oliver
Liar's Edge '92
Prom Night 3: The Last Kiss '89
Hello Mary Lou: Prom Night 2 '87
Hector Olivera (1931-)
The Road '00
A Shadow You Soon Will Be '94
Funny, Dirty Little War '83
Ermanno Olmi (1931-)
The Tree of Wooden Clogs '78
Fiances '63
Arne Olsen
Escape from Atlantis '97
All Dogs Go to Heaven 2 '95
Mighty Morphin Power Rangers: The Movie '95
Cop and a Half '93
Final Round '93
Red Scorpion '89
Dana Olsen
George of the Jungle '97
The 'Burbs '89
Josh Olson
A History of Violence '05
Infested: Invasion of the Killer Bugs '02
On the Border '98
David O'Malley (1944-)
Fatal Instinct '93
Edge of Honor '91
Easy Wheels '89
Kid Colter '85
Hangar 18 '80
House of the Dead '78
Mountain Man '77
Kazuki Omori (1952-)
Godzilla vs. King Ghidora '91
Godzilla vs. Biollante '89
Charles "Blackie" O'Neal (1904-96)
Lassie's Great Adventure '62
Return of the Bad Men '48
Cry of the Werewolf '44
The Seventh Victim '43
Robert Vincent O'Neil
Jailbait '93
Deadly Force '83
Vice Squad '82
The Baltimore Bullet '80
Ella O'Neill
The Phantom Rider '36
Battling with Buffalo Bill '31
Max Ophuls (1902-57)
Modigliani '58

Lola Montes '55
The Earrings of Madame De... '54
George Oppenheimer (1900-77)
Undercurrent '46
A Day at the Races '37
Libeled Lady '36
Joshua Oppenheimer
Sahara '05
A Sound of Thunder '05
Timothy O'Rawe
Midnight Confessions '95
Ghoul School '90
Roberto Orci
Transformers '07
Mission: Impossible 3 '06
The Legend of Zorro '05
The Island '05
Joaquin Oristrell
Between Your Legs '99
Mouth to Mouth '95
Arthur Orloff
Thunder in God's Country '51
Missourians '50
John Orloff
A Mighty Heart '07
Band of Brothers '01
Ron Ormond (1911-81)
Kentucky Jubilee '51
Yes, Sir, Mr. Bones '51
Last Bullet '50
Outlaw Fury '50
Rangeland Empire '50
Red Desert '50
Sudden Death '50
Rimfire '49
Ringside '49
Alan Ormsby (1944-)
The Substitute '96
High Stakes '93
Indecency '92
Popcorn '89
Porky's 2: The Next Day '83
Cat People '82
Little Dragons '80
My Bodyguard '80
Touch & Go '80
Deranged '74
Children Shouldn't Play with Dead Things '72
Deathdream '72
James Orr (1953-)
Man of the House '95
Sister Act 2: Back in the Habit '93
Mr. Destiny '90
Three Men and a Baby '87
Tough Guys '86
J.O.C. Orton (1889-1962)
The Ghost Train '41
Non-Stop New York '37
Paul Osborn (1901-88)
South Pacific '58
Sayonara '57
East of Eden '54
Homecoming '48
Portrait of Jennie '48
The Young in Heart '38
Ron Osborn
Meet Joe Black '98
Andrew Osborne
OnLine '01
Behind Enemy Lines '96
John Osborne (1929-94)
Look Back in Anger '80
Look Back in Anger '58
Luther '74
Tom Jones '63
The Entertainer '60
Ken Osborne
Escape from Cell Block 3 '74
Wild Wheels '69

William Osborne
Thunderbirds '04
The Scorpion King '02
Chilly Dogs '01
Dr. Jekyll and Ms. Hyde '95
Ghost in the Machine '93
The Real McCoy '93
Stop! or My Mom Will Shoot '92
Twins '88
Nagisa Oshima (1932-)
Taboo '99
Max, Mon Amour '86
Merry Christmas, Mr. Lawrence '83
In the Realm of the Senses '76
The Cruel Story of Youth '60
Diana Ossana
Comanche Moon '08
Brokeback Mountain '05
Johnson County War '02
Larry McMurtry's Dead Man's Walk '96
Larry McMurtry's Streets of Laredo '95
Hawk Ostby
Iron Man '08
First Snow '07
Katsuhiro Otomo (1954-)
Steamboy '05
Akira '89
Idrissa Ouedraogo (1954-)
Tilai '90
Yaaba '89
Jean-Paul Ouellette
The Unnamable 2: The Statement of Randolph Carter '92
The Unnamable '88
Richard Outten
Last Rites '98
Little Nemo: Adventures in Slumberland '92
Pet Sematary 2 '92
Lionheart '87
Eric Overmyer (1951-)
Homicide: The Movie '00
Rear Window '98
Alun Owen
Unexplained Laughter '89
A Hard Day's Night '64
Francois Ozon (1967-)
Time to Leave '05
5x2 '04
Swimming Pool '03
8 Women '02
Under the Sand '00
Criminal Lovers '99
Water Drops on Burning Rocks '99
Sitcom '97
Ferzan Ozpetek (1959-)
Facing Windows '03
His Secret Life '01
Harem '99
Steam: A Turkish Bath '96
Yasujiro Ozu (1903-63)
An Autumn Afternoon '62
Good Morning '59
Tokyo Story '53
William R. Pace (1958-)
Charming Billy '98
Blades '89
Ernesto Pagano
Greenwich Village '44
The Flying Irishman '39
Jo Pagano (1906-82)
Try and Get Me '50
The Man I Love '46
Marcel Pagnol (1895-1974)
Nais '45
Le Schpountz '38
Harvest '37
Cesar '36
The Baker's Wife '33
Topaze '33

Fanny '32
Marius '31
Nick Paine
Josh Kirby... Time Warrior: Chapter 3. Trapped on Toyworld '95
Philadelphia Experiment 2 '93
Alan J. Pakula (1928-98)
The Pelican Brief '93
Presumed Innocent '90
See You in the Morning '89
Sophie's Choice '82
Euzhan Palcy (1957-)
A Dry White Season '89
Sugar Cane Alley '83
Michael Palin (1943-)
American Friends '91
Consuming Passions '88
Monty Python's The Meaning of Life '83
The Missionary '82
The Secret Policeman's Other Ball '82
Time Bandits '81
Monty Python's Life of Brian '79
Monty Python and the Holy Grail '75
And Now for Something Completely Different '72
Rospo Pallenberg
Druids '01
The Emerald Forest '85
Excalibur '81
Anders Palm (1949-)
Dead Certain '92
Murder on Line One '90
Chazz Palminteri (1952-)
Faithful '95
A Bronx Tale '93
Norman Panama (1914-2003)
I Will, I Will for Now '76
The Road to Hong Kong '62
The Facts of Life '60
Li'l Abner '59
The Trap '59
Court Jester '56
White Christmas '54
Above and Beyond '53
Mr. Blandings Builds His Dream House '48
Monsieur Beaucaire '46
The Road to Utopia '46
Thank Your Lucky Stars '43
Star Spangled Rhythm '42
Alan Pao
Loaded '08
Chasing Ghosts '05
Dennis Paoli
The Dentist '96
Castle Freak '95
Body Snatchers '93
Mortal Sins '92
The Pit & the Pendulum '91
Meridian: Kiss of the Beast '90
From Beyond '86
Re-Animator '84
Jaroslav Papousek (1929-95)
The Fireman's Ball '68
Intimate Lighting '65
Loves of a Blonde '65
Black Peter '63
John Paragon (1954-)
Elvira's Haunted Hills '02
Twinsitters '95
Elvira, Mistress of the Dark '88
Edward Paramore (1895-1956)
Three Comrades '38
The Bitter Tea of General Yen '33
Gail Parent
Confessions of a Teenage Drama Queen '04
All I Want for Christmas '91
Chan-wook Park (1963-)
Lady Vengeance '05
Three...Extremes '04

Alan Parker (1944-)
Evita '96
The Road to Wellville '94
Come See the Paradise '90
Angel Heart '87
Bugsy Malone '76
Melody '71

Amy '98
Rikky and Pete '88
Malcolm '86

David Parker (1947-)
House of the Dead '03

Dorothy Parker (1893-1967)
A Star is Born '37
The Moon's Our Home '36

Jean H. Parker
Spenser: Pale Kings & Princes '94
Spenser: Ceremony '93

Norton S. Parker
Rio Grande Raiders '46
Young Bill Hickok '40

Oliver Parker (1960-)
The Importance of Being Earnest '02
Othello '95
An Ideal Husband '99

Robert B. Parker (1932-)
Thin Air '00
Small Vices: A Spenser Mystery '99
Stay Tuned '92

Ronald Parker
Joan of Arc '99
Gargantua '96

Scott Parker
De Laughing '80
He Knows You're Alone '80

Tom S. Parker
The Flintstones '94
Getting Even with Dad '94
Richie Rich '94

Trey Parker (1969-)
Team America: World Police '04
South Park: Bigger, Longer and Uncut '99
Orgazmo '98
Cannibal! The Musical '96

William Parker (1886-1941)
The Nut '21

Lindsley Parsons (1905-92)
Rollin' Plains '38
Desert Trail '35
Paradise Canyon '35
Man from Utah '34
Randy Rides Alone '34
Trail Beyond '34
Sagebrush Trail '33

Walter F. Parkes
Sneakers '92
WarGames '83

Gianfranco Parolini (1930-)
Adios, Sabata '71
Return of Sabata '71
Sabata '69
Island of Lost Girls '68

Sara Parriott
The Starter Wife '07
Runaway Bride '99
The Favor '92
Three Men and a Little Lady '90
Worth Winning '89

Michael Part (1949-)
A Kid in King Arthur's Court '95

Frank Partos (1901-56)
The Snake Pit '48
The Uninvited '44
Honolulu '39
Wings in the Dark '35
Thirty Day Princess '34

John Paxton (1911-85)
On the Beach '59
The Wild One '54
Murder, My Sweet '44

Alexander Payne (1961-)
I Now Pronounce You Chuck and Larry '07
Sideways '04
About Schmidt '02

Goran Paskaljevic (1947-)
How Harry Became a Tree '01

Pier Paolo Pasolini (1922-75)
Salo, or the 120 Days of Sodom '75
Arabian Nights '74
The Canterbury Tales '71
The Decameron '70
The Hawks & the Sparrows '67
The Gospel According to St. Matthew '64
Mamma Roma '62
Accatone! '61

Ivan Passer (1933-)
Law and Disorder '74
Born to Win '71
The Fireman's Ball '68
Intimate Lighting '65
Loves of a Blonde '65

Jonas Pate (1970-)
The Take '07
Deceiver '97

Josh Pate (1970-)
The Take '07
The Grave '95
Deceiver '97

David Paterson
Bridge to Terabithia '07

John Patrick (1905-95)
Love, Ludlow '05
Love is a Many-Splendored Thing '55

Vincent Patrick
The Devil's Own '96
Family Business '89
The Pope of Greenwich Village '84

Don Michael Paul (1963-)
Who's Your Caddy? '07
Half Past Deac '02
Harley Davidson and the Marlboro Man '91

David Paulsen
Savage Weekend '80
The Uranium Conspiracy '78

Steven Paul (1954-)
Karate Dog '04
Baby Geniuses '98

Sean Penn (1960-)
Into the Wild '07
The Crossing Guard '94
A Woman's Face '41
New Orleans '47

Elliot Paul (1891-1958)
A Woman's Face '41
New Orleans '47

Cinco Paul
Dr. Seuss' Horton Hears a Who! '08
The Santa Clause 2 '02
Bubble Boy '01

Simon Pegg (1970-)
Hot Fuzz '07
Shaun of the Dead '04

Kimberly Peirce
Stop-Loss '08
Boys Don't Cry '99

Louis Pelletier (1907-2000)
Smith! '69
The Horse in the Gray Flannel Suit '68
Follow Me, Boys! '66
Those Calloways '65
Big Rec '62

Lynn Perkins
The Gracie Allen Murder Case '39
Dimples '36

Bill Peet (1915-2002)
101 Dalmatians '61
Peter Pan '53
Fantasia '40

Zak Penn (1968-)
X-Men: The Last Stand '06
The Incredible Hulk '08
Elektra '05
Suspect Zero '04
Behind Enemy Lines '01
Inspector Gadget '99
P.C.U. '94

Erdman Penner (1905-56)
Lady and the Tramp '55
Peter Pan '53
The Adventures of Ichabod and Mr. Toad '49
Pinocchio '40

John Penney
The Contaminated Man '01

Sam Peckinpah (1925-84)
Bring Me the Head of Alfredo Garcia '74
Straw Dogs '72
The Wild Bunch '69
Villa Rides '68
Invasion of the Body Snatchers '56

David Peckinpah (1951-2006)
The Paperboy '94

Craig Pearce
Romeo and Juliet '96
Strictly Ballroom '92
Moulin Rouge '01
William Shakespeare's Romeo and Juliet '96

Ann Peacock
Pictures of Hollis Woods '07
In My Country '04
A Lesson Before Dying '99
Cora Unashamed '00

Humphrey Pearson (1894-1937)
Red Salute '35
Lost Squadron '32
Men of America '32

Mark Peploe (1943-)
Victory '95
Afraid of the Dark '92
High Season '88
The Last Emperor '87
The Passenger '75

Stacy Peralta (1957-)
Riding Giants '04
Lords of Dogtown '05
Dogtown and Z-Boys '01

Mark Perez
Accepted '06
The Country Bears '02

Jesse Peretz (1968-)
The Chateau '01
First Love, Last Rites '98

Frank Ray Perilli
Alligator '80
Laserblast '78
Zoltan... Hound of Dracula '78
The Doberman Gang '72

S.J. Perelman (1904-79)
Around the World in 80 Days '56
Horse Feathers '32
Monkey Business '31

Ivo Perilli (1902-94)
The Sword in the Stone '63
Barabbas '62
The Unfaithfuls '60
War and Peace '56

Ernest Pascal (1896-1966)
Jurassic Park 3 '01
In Pursuit '00
Matter of Trust '98
Past Perfect '98
Perfect Assassins '98
Return of the Living Dead 3 '93
The Kindred '87

Keith Payson
My Super Ex-Girlfriend '06

Dave Payne
Boltneck '98
Criminal Hearts '95

Senel Paz
A Paradise Under the Stars
Strawberry and Chocolate '93

Don Payne
Fantastic Four: Rise of the Silver Surfer '07

Phil Penningroth
In the Line of Duty: Ambush in Waco '93
The Power '80

David Peoples (1940-)
Soldier '98
12 Monkeys '95
Unforgiven '92
Hero '92
The Blood of Heroes '89
Leviathan '89
Blade Runner '82

Steve Peace (1953-)
Killer Tomatoes Eat France '91
Return of the Killer Tomatoes! '88
Strawberry and Chocolate '93

Clare Peploe (1942-)
The Triumph of Love '01

Charlie Peters
Krippendorf's Tribe '98
Music from Another Room '97
My Father the Hero '93
Passed Away '92
Three Men and a Little Lady '90
Her Alibi '88
Blame It on Rio '84
Kiss Me Goodbye '82
Paternity '81

Nat Perrin (1905-98)
I'll Take Sweden '65
The Big Store '41
Whistling in Brooklyn '43
Whistling in Dixie '42
Dimples '36
Duck Soup '33
Case '39

Eleanor Perry (1914-81)
The Man Who Loved Cat Dancing '73
David and Lisa '62

Fred C. Perry
The Wind '87
Zero Boys '86

Nickolas Perry (1967-)
Speedway Junky '99

J.T. Petty
Mimic 3: Sentinel '03
Soft for Digging '01

Harley Peyton
Bandits '01
Keys to Tulsa '96
Heaven's Prisoners '95
Less Than Zero '87

Pamela Pettler
Monster House '06

Vladimir Petrov (1896-1966)
The Inspector General '52
Peter the First: Part 1 '37

Michael Petroni
The Dangerous Lives of Altar Boys '02
Till Human Voices Wake Us '02

Daniel Petrie, Jr. (1952-)
In the Army Now '94
Toy Soldiers '91
Shoot to Kill '88
Beverly Hills Cop '84
The Big Easy '87
Forever Mary '89
Julia and Julia '87

Sandro Petraglia (1947-)
Best of Youth '03
The Truce '96
Fiorile '93

Cassandra Peterson (1951-)
Elvira's Haunted Hills '02
Elvira, Mistress of the Dark '88

Wolfgang Petersen (1941-)
Shattered '91
Das Boot '81
The NeverEnding Story '84
Madeleine '50

Stephen Peters (1947-)
Wild Things '98
The Wolves '95

John Pielmeier
Hitler: The Rise of Evil '03
Dodson's Journey '01
Sins of the Father '01
The Happy Face Murders '99
Agnes of God '85
An Inconvenient Woman '91
Through the Eyes of a Killer '92
The Shell Seekers '89

Arthur C. Pierce (1923-87)
The Invisible Strangler '76
Invasion of the Animal People '62

Charles B. Pierce (1938-)
The Cosmic Man '59
The Town That Dreaded Sundown '76
Grayeagle '77
Winterhawk '76
Boggy Creek II '83
Sacred Ground '83
The Evictors '79
Norseman '78

Frank Pierson (1925-)
Presumed Innocent '90
In Country '89
A Star is Born '76
Dog Day Afternoon '75
King of the Gypsies '78
The Anderson Tapes '71
The Looking Glass War '69
Cool Hand Luke '67
Cat Ballou '65

Michael Pertwee (1916-91)
A Funny Thing Happened on the Way to the Forum '66
Strange Bedfellows '65
Ladies Who Do '63
The Mouse on the Moon '92

Roland Pertwee (1885-1963)
The Magic Bow '47
King Solomon's Mines '37
Non-Stop New York '37
The Ghoul '34

Steve Pesce (1960-)
Strangler in the House '07

Jeff Phillips
Treehouse Hostage '99
3 Ninjas: High Noon at Mega Mountain '97

Giuseppe Piccioni (1953-)
Light of My Eyes '01
Not of This World '99

Jim Piddock (1956-)
The Man '05
One Good Turn '95
Traces of Red '92

Maurice Pialat (1925-2003)
Van Gogh '92
A Nos Amours '84
Under Satan's Sun '87
Loulou '80

Anna Hamilton Phelan
Madea's Family Reunion '06
Diary of a Mad Black Woman '05
Girl, Interrupted '99
In Love and War '96
Gorillas in the Mist '88
Mask '85

Brian Phelan
In the Secret State '85

Bill Phillips (1908-57)
Little Mother '71
Forbidden Choices '94

Todd Phillips (1970-)
School for Scoundrels '06
Starsky & Hutch '04
Old School '03
Road Trip '00
Christine '84

Lou Diamond Phillips (1962-)
Ambition '91
Trespasses '86

Robert Phippeny
Simon, King of the Witches '71

Nicholas Phipps (1913-80)
Day '69

Chuck Pfarrer
Virus '98
The Jackal '97
Barb Wire '96
Darkman '90
Red Planet '00

Krzysztof Piesiewicz (1945-)
Heaven '01
Trois Couleurs: Blanc '94
Trois Couleurs: Rouge '94
Trois Couleurs: Bleu '93

[Krzysztof Piesiewicz]
The Double Life of Veronique '91
The Decalogue '88
No End '84

Tseng Pik-Yin
The Bride with White Hair '93
Iron Monkey '93

Jeremy Pikser
Bulworth '98
The Lemon Sisters '90

Nicholas Pileggi (1933-)
Casino '95
City Hall '95
Goodfellas '90

Michael Piller (1948-2005)
The Dead Zone '02
Star Trek: Insurrection '98

Tullio Pinelli (1908-)
Ginger & Fred '86
Juliet of the Spirits '65
8 1/2 '63
Boccaccio 70 '62
La Dolce Vita '60
Nights of Cabiria '57
Il Bidone '55
La Strada '54
Love in the City '53
The White Sheik '52
Variety Lights '51

Marcelo Pineyro (1953-)
The Method '05
Wild Horses '95

Sidney W. Pink (1916-2002)
The Castilian '63
Reptilicus '62
The Angry Red Planet '59

Steve Pink (1966-)
High Fidelity '00
Grosse Pointe Blank '97

Harold Pinter (1930-)
Sleuth '07
The Trial '93
The Go-Between '71
Accident '67
The Quiller Memorandum '66
The Pumpkin Eater '64
The Servant '63

[Lucian Pintilie (1933-)]
An Unforgettable Summer '94
The Oak '93
Ward Six '78

Bret Piper
Screaming Dead '03
They Bite '95
A Nymphoid Barbarian in Dinosaur Hell '94

David Pirie (1953-)
Dr. Bell and Mr. Doyle: The Dark Beginnings of Sherlock Holmes '00
The Wyvern Mystery '00
The Woman in White '97

Robert Pirosh (1910-89)
Hell Is for Heroes '62
Valley of the Kings '54
Go for Broke! '51
Battleground '49
I Married a Witch '41
Night of January 16th '41
A Day at the Races '37

Mark Pirro (1956-)
Buford's Beach Bunnies '92
My Mom's a Werewolf '92
Deathrow Gameshow '88
Curse of the Queerwolf '87

Glen Pitre
The Home Front '02
Belizaire the Cajun '86

Angelo Pizzo
The Game of Their Lives '05
Rudy '93
Hoosiers '86

Alan Plater (1935-)
The Last of the Blonde Bombshells '00
A Merry War '97
A Very British Coup '88
Fortunes of War '87
Coming Through '85
The Inside Man '84
Priest of Love '81
The Virgin and the Gypsy '70

Jonathan Platnick
End of Summer '97
Silent Victim '92

Polly Platt (1939-)
A Map of the World '99
Pretty Baby '78

George Plympton (1889-1972)
Trouble Chasers '45
Gang Busters '42
Junior G-Men of the Air '42
Flash Gordon Conquers the Universe '40
Junior G-Men '40
The Green Hornet '39
Texas Wildcats '39
Feud Maker '38
Doomed at Sundown '37
Paroled to Die '37
The Red Rope '37
Crooked Trail '36
The Phantom Rider '36
Range Riders '35
Murder on the High Seas '32
Battling with Buffalo Bill '31
Blood and Steel '25

Jeremy Podeswa (1962-)
The Five Senses '99
Eclipse '94

Amos Poe
Frogs for Snakes '98
Rocket Gibraltar '88
Alphabet City '84
The Foreigner '78

James Poe (1921-80)
The Nightman '93
Riot '69
They Shoot Horses, Don't They? '69
Lilies of the Field '63
Toys in the Attic '63
Cat on a Hot Tin Roof '58
Around the World in 80 Days '56
Attack! '56

Charles Edward Pogue
Kull the Conqueror '97
Dragonheart '96
Hands of a Murderer '90
D.O.A. '88
The Fly '86
Psycho 3 '86
The Hound of the Baskervilles '83
The Sign of Four '83

John Pogue
Ghost Ship '02
Rollerball '02
The Skulls '00
U.S. Marshals '98

Jean-Marie Poire (1945-)
Just Visiting '01
The Visitors '95
No Problem '75

Gregory Poirier
A Sound of Thunder '05
Tomcats '01
Gossip '99
Rosewood '96
The Stranger '95

Joseph Poland (1892-1962)
Federal Operator 99 '45
Manhunt of Mystery Island '45
The Purple Monster Strikes '45
Manhunt in the African Jungles '43
Mysterious Doctor Satan '40
Winds of the Wasteland '36
The Sea Lion 21

Roman Polanski (1933-)
The Ninth Gate '99
Bitter Moon '92
Frantic '88
Pirates '86
Tess '79
The Tenant '76
Diary of Forbidden Dreams '73
Macbeth '71
Rosemary's Baby '68
The Fearless Vampire Killers '67
Cul de Sac '66
Repulsion '65
Knife in the Water '62

Stephen Poliakoff (1952-)
Gideon's Daughter '05
Friends & Crocodiles '05
Almost Strangers '01
Shooting the Past '99
Century '94
Close My Eyes '91

Mark Polish (1972-)
The Astronaut Farmer '07
Northfork '03
Jackpot '01
Twin Falls Idaho '99

Michael Polish (1972-)
The Astronaut Farmer '07
Northfork '03
Jackpot '01
Twin Falls Idaho '99

Jack Pollexfen (1908-2003)
The Atomic Brain '64
The Daughter of Dr. Jekyll '57
The Man from Planet X '51

Gene Pollock
The Thrill Killers '65
Incredibly Strange Creatures Who Stopped Living and Became Mixed-Up Zombies '63

Vicki Polon
Mr. Wonderful '93
Girlfriends '78

Mark Alan Polonia
Terror House '97
Feeders '96

Abraham Polonsky (1910-99)
Monsignor '82
Avalanche Express '79
Tell Them Willie Boy Is Here '69
Madigan '68
Odds Against Tomorrow '59
Force of Evil '49
Body and Soul '47
Golden Earrings '47

Abe Polsky
The Baby '72
Rebel Rousers '69

Darryl Ponicsan
The Enemy Within '94
School Ties '92
The Boost '88
Nuts '87
Vision Quest '85
Taps '81
Cinderella Liberty '73

Ventura Pons (1945-)
Food of Love '02
Caresses '97

Gillo Pontecorvo (1919-2006)
The Battle of Algiers '66
Kapo '59
The Wide Blue Road '57

One in a Million '36
Three Strikes '00

DJ Pooh
The Wash '01
Three Strikes '00
Friday '95

Lea Pool (1950-)
Set Me Free '99
Mouvements du Desir '94

Robert Roy Pool
Outbreak '94
Dead to Rights '93
Big Town '87

Duane Poole
I Married a Monster '98
I've Been Waiting for You '98
Shattered Image '98
One Christmas '95
The Man in the Attic '94
Praying Mantis '93
Sunstroke '92

Marty Poole
Diamond Run '00
Reptilian '99

Elaine Pope
Alfie '04
These Old Broads '01

Jeff Pope
Essex Boys '99
The Magician '93
Fool's Gold: The Story of the Brink's-Mat Robbery '92

Tom Pope
The Manitou '78
Don't Look in the Basement '73

Joel Posner
The Next Big Thing '02

P.J. Posner
The Next Big Thing '02
Last Breath '96
Getting In '94

Dennis Potter (1935-94)
The Singing Detective '03
Lipstick on Your Collar '94
Mesmer '94
Christabel '89
Track 29 '88
Dreamchild '85
Gorky Park '83
Brimstone & Treacle '82
Pennies from Heaven '81

Sally Potter (1947-)
The Man Who Cried '00
The Tango Lesson '97
Orlando '92

Gerald Potterton (1931-)
The Rainbow Gang '73
Railroader '65

Michel W. Potts (1946-)
Night Eyes 3 '93
Tropical Heat '93

Michael Powell (1905-90)
The Elusive Pimpernel '50
The Red Shoes '48
Black Narcissus '47
I Know Where I'm Going '45
Contraband '40
Edge of the World '37

Donna Powers
The Italian Job '03
Out of Order '03
Valentine '01

Wayne Powers
The Italian Job '03
Out of Order '03
Valentine '01

Tim Prager
Quicksand '01
Heat of the Sun '99
Vendetta '99
Haunted '95

Leonard Praskins
So This Is Washington '43

John Prebble (1915-2001)
Elizabeth R '72
Zulu '64
Mysterious Island '61

Robert Presnell, Jr. (1914-86)
Conspiracy of Hearts '60
Let No Man Write My Epitaph '60
Man in the Attic '53

Robert Presnell, Sr. (1894-1969)
Second Chance '53
Meet John Doe '41
The Real Glory '39
They Shall Have Music '39
Postal Inspector '36
Bureau of Missing Persons '33
Employees' Entrance '33
The Kennel Murder Case '33

Emeric Pressburger (1902-88)
The Elusive Pimpernel '50
The Red Shoes '48
Black Narcissus '47
Stairway to Heaven '46
I Know Where I'm Going '45
The Forty-Ninth Parallel '41

Steven Pressfield (1943-)
Army of One '94
Separate Lives '94
Freejack '92
Above the Law '88
King Kong Lives '86

Gaylene Preston
Perfect Strangers '03
Dark of the Night '85

Richard Preston, Jr.
Parker '84

Trevor Preston
I'll Sleep When I'm Dead '03
Thicker Than Water '93

Jacques Prevert (1900-77)
The Hunchback of Notre Dame '57

Jeffrey Price (1949-)
Shrek the Third '07
Last Holiday '06
Dr. Seuss' How the Grinch Stole Christmas '00
Wild Wild West '99
Doc Hollywood '91
Who Framed Roger Rabbit '88
Trenchcoat '83

Richard Price (1949-)
Freedomland '06
Shaft '00
Ransom '96
Clockers '95
Kiss of Death '94
Mad Dog and Glory '93
Night and the City '92
New York Stories '89
Sea of Love '89
The Color of Money '86
Streets of Gold '86

Stanley Price (1892-1955)
A Royal Scandal '96
Genghis Cohn '93

Tim Rose Price
The Serpent's Kiss '97
Rapa Nui '93
A Dangerous Man: Lawrence after Arabia '91
Dark Obsession '90

J.B. Priestley (1894-1984)
Last Holiday '50
Dangerous Corner '34

Peter Prince
Waterland '92
The Hit '85

David A. Prior
Final Move '06
The Sender '98
Recoil '97
Little Bigfoot '96
Cyber-Tracker 2 '95
Felony '95
Mutant Species '95
Mardi Gras for the Devil '93
Raw Justice '93
Raw Nerve '91
Deadly Dancer '90
Lock 'n' Load '90
Final Sanction '89
Future Force '89
Operation Warzone '89
Hell on the Battleground '88
Deadly Prey '87
Sledgehammer '83

Ted Prior (1959-)
The Last Ride '91
Operation Warzone '89

David Pritchard
Violent Zone '89
Slashed Dreams '74

Pat Proft (1947-)
Scary Movie 3 '03
Wrongfully Accused '98
Mr. Magoo '97
High School High '96
Naked Gun 33 1/3: The Final Insult '94
Hot Shots! Part Deux '93
Brain Donors '92
Hot Shots! '91
Naked Gun 2 1/2: The Smell of Fear '91
Lucky Stiff '88
The Naked Gun: From the Files of Police Squad '88
Moving Violations '85
Real Genius '85
Bachelor Party '84
Police Academy '84

Biagio Proietti
The Black Cat '81
Taste of Death '68

Chip Proser
Innerspace '87
Iceman '84

Giorgio Prosperi
The Naked Maja '59
The Seven Hills of Rome '58

Mark Protosevich (1961-)
I Am Legend '07
Poseidon '06
The Cell '00

Monique Proulx (1952-)
Street Heart '98
Le Sexe des Etoiles '93

Alex Proyas (1965-)
Garage Days '03
Dark City '97

Richard Pryor (1940-2005)
Jo Jo Dancer, Your Life Is Calling '86
Bustin' Loose '81
Blazing Saddles '74

Robert Pucci
The Corruptor '99
The Spider and the Fly '94

Luis Puenzo (1946-)
Old Gringo '89
The Official Story '85

Frank Pugliese
Undefeated '03
Shot in the Heart '01

Jack Pulman (1925-79)
Poldark '75
War and Peace '73
The Golden Bowl '72
Portrait of a Lady '67

Daniella Purcell
Spacejacked '98
Not Like Us '96
The Wasp Woman '96
Midnight Tease '94

Timothy Quay (1947-)
Piano Tuner of Earthquakes '05

Stephen Quay (1947-)
Piano Tuner of Earthquakes '05
Institute Benjamenta or This Dream People Call Human Life '95

Jonas Quastel
Sasquatch '02

Paul Quarrington (1953-)
Camilla '94
Whale Music '94
Giant Steps '92
Perfectly Normal '91

Paris Qualles
A Raisin in the Sun '08
The Rosa Parks Story '02
A House Divided '00
Blood Brothers '97
The Tuskegee Airmen '95
The Inkwell '94

Darryl Quarles (1954-)
Black Knight '01
Big Momma's House '00
Soldier Boyz '95

John Quaintance
Aquamarine '06
Material Girls '06
Spitfire '94

Gertrude Purcell (1855-1963)
Follow the Boys '44
The Invisible Woman '44
One Night in the Tropics '40
Destry Rides Again '39
Service De Luxe '38
The Longest Day '62

David Pursall
Heaven Help Us '85
The Blue Max '66

Neal Purvis (1961-)
Casino Royale '06
Stoned '05
Corrected '04
Johnny English '03
Die Another Day '02
The World Is Not Enough '99
Plunkett & Macleane '98
Let Him Have It '91

Charles Purpura (1945-2005)
Satisfaction '88

Mario Puzo (1920-99)
Christopher Columbus: The Discovery '92
The Cotton Club '84
The Godfather, Part 3 '90
The Godfather 1902-1959: The Complete Epic '81
Superman 2 '80
Superman: The Movie '78
Earthquake '74
The Godfather, Part 2 '74
The Godfather '72

Daniel Pyne
Fracture '07
The Manchurian Candidate '04
The Sum of All Fears '02
Where's Marlowe? '98
White Sands '92
Doc Hollywood '91
The Hard Way '91
Pacific Heights '90
Alien from L.A. '87

Albert Pyun (1954-)
Radioactive Dreams '86
Sword & the Sorcerer '82
Adrenalin: Fear the Rush '96
Nemesis 3: Time Lapse '95
Nemesis 4: Cry of Angels '97
Knights '93
Down Twisted '89

Pascal Quignard (1946-)
Tous les Matins du Monde '94
A Pure Formality '94
Le Bonheur Est Dans le Pre '98
Life Is a Long Quiet River '88

Florence Quentin (1946-)
Evil Dead 2: Dead by Dawn '87
Army of Darkness '92
Darkman '90

Gene Quintano (1946-)
The Musketeer '01
Operation Dumbo Drop '95
Sudden Death '95
National Lampoon's Loaded Weapon 1 '93
Honeymoon Academy '90
Police Academy 4: Citizens on Patrol '87
Lost City of Gold '86
Police Academy 3: Back in Training '86
King Solomon's Mines '85
Making the Grade '84

Jose Quiroz
San Franspsycho '06

Eduardo Quiroz
San Franspsycho '06

David Rabe (1940-)
I Got Five on It '05
Hurlyburly '98
Casualties of War '89
Streamers '83
I'm Dancing as Fast as I Can '82

Michael Radford (1946-)
Dancing at the Blue Iguana '00
The Merchant of Venice '04
A Loving Father '02
The Dream Catcher '99
Another Time, Another Place '83
White Mischief '88
The Postman '94

Edward A. Radtke
The Dream Catcher '99

Martin Rackin (1918-76)
The Horse Soldiers '59
Long John Silver '54
Loan Shark '52
Sailor Beware '52
The Enforcer '51
The Stooge '51

Robert Ramsey (1962-)
Man of the House '05
Intolerable Cruelty '03
Big Trouble '02
Life '99
Destiny Turns on the Radio '95

Lynne Ramsay (1969-)
Morvern Callar '02
Ratcatcher '99

Charles Randolph
The Interpreter '05

Joe Ranft (1960-2005)
Cars '06
A Bug's Life '98
The Rescuers Down Under '90

Whitney Ransick
Hand Gun '93

Caleb Ranson
The Outfit '93

A.R. Rawlinson (1894-1984)
Gaslight '40

Billy Ray
Breach '07
Flightplan '05
Suspect Zero '04
Shattered Glass '03
Hart's War '02
Legalese '98
Volcano '97

Rand Ravich
The Astronaut's Wife '99
The Maker '98
Candyman 2: Farewell to the Flesh '94

Irving Ravetch (1920-)
Stanley and Iris '90
Murphy's Romance '85
Norma Rae '79
Conrack '74
The Cowboys '72
The Reivers '69
Hombre '67
Hud '63
Home from the Hill '60
The Long, Hot Summer '58
Ten Wanted Men '54
Vengeance Valley '51

Frederic Raphael (1931-)
Coast to Coast '04
The King's Whore '90
Richard's Things '80
Rogue Male '76
Daisy Miller '74
Far from the Madding Crowd '67
Two for the Road '67
Darling '65
Bachelor of Hearts '58

Sam Raimi (1959-)
Spider-Man 3 '07
The Hudsucker Proxy '93
Army of Darkness '92
Darkman '90
Evil Dead 2: Dead by Dawn '87
Crimewave '85
Evil Dead '83
The Nutt House '95

Norman Reilly Raine (1894-1971)
Captain Kidd '45
The Fighting 69th '40
Each Dawn I Die '39
The Adventures of Robin Hood '38
The Life of Emile Zola '37

Frank Rainone
A Brooklyn State of Mind '97
Me and the Mob '94

Ron Raley
The Locket '02

Milton Raison (1930-82)
Motorcycle Squad '41
Underworld Scandal '47

Harold Ramis (1944-)
Analyze That '02
Analyze This '99
Bedazzled '00
Multiplicity '96
Groundhog Day '93
Rover Dangerfield '91
Ghostbusters 2 '89
Caddyshack 2 '88
Armed and Dangerous '86
Back to School '86
Club Paradise '86
Ghostbusters '84
National Lampoon's Vacation '83
Stripes '81
Caddyshack '80
Meatballs '79
National Lampoon's Animal House '78

Rick Ramage
The Proposition '97
Stigmata '99

Gilbert Ralston (1912-99)
Ben '72
Willard '71

Judith Rascoe (1941-)
Havana '90
Eat a Bowl of Tea '89
Endless Love '81
Who'll Stop the Rain? '78
Road Movie '72

John Rathmell
Range Busters '40
Renegade Trail '39

Terence Rattigan (1911-77)
The V.I.P.'s '63
The Prince and the Showgirl '57
The Winslow Boy '48
The Day Will Dawn '42

Herman Raucher (1928-)
Summer of '42 '71
Watermelon Man '70
Sweet November '68

Stanley Rauh
Sleepers West '41
Michael Shayne: Private Detective '41

I.C. Rapoport
Jericho Fever '93
Living Proof: The Hank Williams Jr. Story '83

Anne Rapp
D: T. & the Women '00
One Hour with You '32

Philip Rapp (1907-96)
Cookie's Fortune '99
Trouble in Paradise '32
The Smiling Lieutenant '31

Mark Rappaport
From the Journals of Jean Seberg '95
Rock Hudson's Home Movies '92
Impostors '80

Ezra D. Rappaport
Wonder Man '45
Mitty '47
The Secret Life of Walter Mitty '47

Jean-Paul Rappeneau (1932-)
Cyrano de Bergerac '90
Lovers Like Us '75
That Man from Rio '64
The Horseman on the Roof '95

David Rayfiel (1923-)
Deja Vu '84
The Firm '93
Intersection '93
Havana '90
Round Midnight '86
Death Watch '80
Lipstick '76
Three Days of the Condor '75
Valdez Is Coming '71
Castle Keep '69

William Raynor (1920-94)
The Kettles on Old MacDonald's Farm '57
Francis in the Haunted House '56

Ed Raymond
See Fred Olen Ray

Jan Read (1917-)
First Men in the Moon '64
Jason and the Argonauts '63

Michael Reaves (1950-)
Gargoyles, The Movie: The Heroes Awaken '94
Batman: Mask of the Phantasm '93

Theresa Rebeck
Gossip '99
Harriet the Spy '96

Paulo Rebelo
Two Drifters '05
O Fantasma '00

Eric Red (1961-)
Bad Moon '96
Undertow '95
Body Parts '91
Blue Steel '90
Cohen and Tate '88
Near Dark '87
The Hitcher '86

Jeffrey Reddick
Final Destination '00
Return to Cabin by the Lake '01
Tales from the Crypt Presents Demon Knight '94

Samson Raphaelson
The Shop Around the Corner '40
Angel '37
Hollywood Cavalcade '39

Fred Olen Ray (1954-)
Hidden Assassin '94
Hollywood Chainsaw Hookers '88
Phantom Empire '87
Alien Dead '79

Satyajit Ray (1921-92)
The Stranger '92
The Middleman '76
Distant Thunder '73
The Adversary '71
Days and Nights in the Forest '70
The World of Apu '59
Devi '60
Two Daughters '61
Aparajito '58
Jalsaghar '58
Charulata '64
The Big City '63
Pather Panchali '54

Nicolas Winding Refn (1970-)
Fear X '03
Pusher '96

Brian Regan
How to Lose a Guy in 10 Days '03
102 Dalmatians '00

Frank Rehwaldt
The Perfect Wife '00
The Landlady '95
The Night Caller '97
The Fiance '96

Kelly Reichardt
Old Joy '06
River of Grass '94

Piero Regnoli (1921-2001)
Demonia '90
Voices from Beyond '90
Invincible Barbarian '83
City of the Walking Dead '80
Nightmare City '80

Garfield Reeves-Stevens
Fire Serpent '07

Judith Reeves-Stevens
Fire Serpent '07
My Teacher Ate My Homework '98
Internes Can't Take Money '37

Theodore Reeves (1910-73)
National Velvet '44
Blossoms on Broadway '37

Dorothy Davenport Reid (1895-1977)
Impact '49

Dorothy Reid
See Dorothy Davenport Reid

J. Reifel
Convict 762 '98

Ethan Reiff (1965-)
Sleeper Cell '05
Bulletproof Monk '03
Josh Kirby... Time Warrior: Chapter 6, Last Battle for the Universe '96
Josh Kirby... Time Warrior: Chapter 1, Planet of the Dino-Knights '95
Josh Kirby... Time Warrior: Chapter 2, The Human Pets '95

William Reilly
Men of War '94
Men of Respect '91
Mortal Thoughts '91

Al Reinert
Final Fantasy: The Spirits Within '01
Blood & Concrete: A Love Story '91
Apollo 13 '95
From the Earth to the Moon '98

Jeff Reiner
Smalltime '96

Carl Reiner (1922-)
The Comic '69
Enter Laughing '67
The Thrill of It All! '63

Joel M. Reed (1933-)
Bloodsucking Freaks '75
Night of the Zombies '81

Tom Reed (1901-61)
Murders in the Rue Morgue '32

Rhett Reese
Clifford's Really Big Movie '04
Cruel Intentions 3 '04

Matt Reeves (1966-)
The Pallbearer '95
The Yards '00

Michael Reeves (1944-69)
The Conqueror Worm '68
The She-Beast '65

Color of Night '94

Irving Reis (1906-53)
Gambler's Choice '44
King of Alcatraz '38

Walter Reisch (1903-83)
Journey to the Center of the Earth '59
Stopover Tokyo '57
The Girl in the Red Velvet Swing '55
Titanic '53
Niagara '52
Song of Scheherazade '47
Gaslight '44
Somewhere I'll Find You '42
That Uncertain Feeling '41

Paul Reiser (1956-)
The Thing About My Folks '05
Popeye's Voyage: The Quest for Pappy '04

Philip Reisman, Jr.
Pudd'nhead Wilson '84
The Private History of a Campaign That Failed '81

Mike Reiss (1960-)
The Simpsons Movie '07
Queer Duck: The Movie '06

Edgar Reitz (1932-)
Heimat 2 '92
Heimat 1 '84

Robert Reneau
Demolition Man '93
Action Jackson '88

Jeff Reno
Meet Joe Black '98
Radioland Murders '94

Jean Renoir (1894-1979)
The Little Theatre of Jean Renoir '71
The Testament of Dr. Cordelier '59
The Golden Coach '52
The River '51
The Southerner '45
The Rules of the Game '39
La Bete Humaine '38
Grand Illusion '37
La Marseillaise '37
The Crime of Monsieur Lange '36
Toni '34
The Lower Depths '36
Boudu Saved from Drowning '32
La Chienne '31
Tournament '29

Ed Earl Repp (1901-79)
Gunplay '51
Storm over Wyoming '50
The Tioga Kid '48

John Requa
The Bad News Bears '05
Bad Santa '03
Cats & Dogs '01

David Reskin
Hidden Obsession '92
Action U.S.A. '89

Alain Resnais (1922-)
Private Fears in Public Places '06
Melo '86
Last Year at Marienbad '61

Adam Resnick
Death to Smoochy '02
Lucky Numbers '00
Cabin Boy '94

Patricia Resnick
Straight Talk '92
Second Sight '89
Maxie '85
9 to 5 '80
Quintet '79
A Wedding '78
3 Women '77

Dale Resteghini (1968-)
Da Hip Hop Witch '00
Colorz of Rage '97

Paul (Pee-wee Herman) Reubens (1952-)
Big Top Pee-wee '88
Pee-wee's Big Adventure '85

Alma Reville (1899-1982)
Shadow of a Doubt '43
Young and Innocent '37
Sabotage '36
The 39 Steps '35
Rich and Strange '32

Bernard Revon
The Rascals '81
Bed and Board '70

Franc Reyes
Illegal Tender '07
Empire '02

Clarke Reynolds (1917-94)
Shalako '68
The Viking Queen '67

Dave Reynolds
Finding Nemo '03
The Emperor's New Groove '00

Jonathan Reynolds
My Stepmother Is an Alien '88
Switching Channels '88
Leonard Part 6 '87
Micki & Maude '84

Kevin Reynolds (1950-)
Rapa Nui '93
Fandango '85
Red Dawn '84

Lee Reynolds
Jackie Chan's Who Am I '98
Storyville '92
Delta Force 2: Operation Stranglehold '90
Allan Quatermain and the Lost City of Gold '86

Scott Reynolds (1968-)
Heaven '99
The Ugly '96

Don Rhymer
Surf's Up '07
Big Momma's House 2 '06
Deck the Halls '06
The Honeymooners '05
Agent Cody Banks 2: Destination London '04
The Santa Clause 2 '02
Big Momma's House '00
Carpool '96

Shonda Rhimes (1970-)
The Princess Diaries 2: Royal Engagement '04
Crossroads '02
Introducing Dorothy Dandridge '99

Susan Rhinehart
Glory & Honor '98
Buffalo Soldiers '97

Richard Rich
The Swan Princess '94
The Black Cauldron '85

Jean-Louis Richard (1921-)
After Sex '97
Emmanuelle '74
Day for Night '73
The Bride Wore Black '68
Fahrenheit 451 '66
The Soft Skin '64

John C. Richards (1957-)
Sahara '05
Nurse Betty '00

Robert L. Richards
Gorgo '61
The Indian Fighter '55
Act of Violence '48

Doug Richardson
Hostage '05
Welcome to Mooseport '04
Money Train '95
Die Hard 2: Die Harder '90

Tony Richardson (1928-91)
The Hotel New Hampshire '84
Ned Kelly '70
A Taste of Honey '61

William Richert (1944-)
The Man in the Iron Mask '97
A Night in the Life of Jimmy Reardon '88
Winter Kills '79
Law and Disorder '74

Mordecai Richler (1931-2001)
Joshua Then and Now '85
Fun with Dick and Jane '77
The Apprenticeship of Duddy Kravitz '74
No Love for Johnnie '60

Maurice Richlin (1930-90)
For Pete's Sake '74
Come September '61
Operation Petticoat '59
Pillow Talk '59

Jason Richman
Bangkok Dangerous '08
Swing Vote '08
Bad Company '02

W.D. Richter (1945-)
Stealth '05
Home for the Holidays '95
Needful Things '93
Big Trouble in Little China '86
All Night Long '81
Brubaker '80
Dracula '79
Invasion of the Body Snatchers '78
Slither '73

Thomas (Tom) Rickman
The Reagans '04
Bless the Child '00
Tuesdays with Morrie '99
Truman '95
Hooper '78

Tom Ricostronza
See Trey Ellis

John Ridley (1965-)
Undercover Brother '02
Cold Around the Heart '97
U-Turn '97

Phillip Ridley
The Passion of Darkly Noon '95
The Reflecting Skin '91
The Krays '90

Leni Riefenstahl (1902-2003)
Triumph of the Will '34
The Blue Light '32

August Rieger (1914-84)
The Uranium Conspiracy '78
The Vampire Happening '71

Dean Riesner (1918-2002)
Fatal Beauty '87
Charley Varrick '73
High Plains Drifter '73
Dirty Harry '71
Play Misty for Me '71
Coogan's Bluff '68
Operation Haylift '50

Adam Rifkin (1966-)
Underdog '07
Zoom '06
Night at the Golden Eagle '02
Small Soldiers '98
Something About Sex '98
Mouse Hunt '97
The Chase '94
The Dark Backward '91
The Invisible Maniac '90
Never on Tuesday '88

Ned Rifle
See Hal Hartley

Ray Rigby
The Hill '65
Operation Crossbow '65

Lawrence Riggins
Replicant '01
Ironheart '92

Sharon Riis
Savage Messiah '02
Loyalties '86

Wolf Rilla (1920-2005)
Village of the Damned '60
Roadhouse Girl '53

Joe Rinaldi (1914-74)
Peter Pan '53
The Adventures of Ichabod and Mr. Toad '49

Frederic Rinaldo (1913-92)
Abbott and Costello Meet the Invisible Man '51
Comin' 'Round the Mountain '51
Abbott and Costello Meet Frankenstein '48
Buck Privates Come Home '47
The Black Cat '41
Hold That Ghost '41
The Invisible Woman '40

David W. Rintels (1938-)
A Season on the Brink '02
Nuremberg '00
The Member of the Wedding '97
Andersonville '95
World War II: When Lions Roared '94
The Last Best Year '90
Not Without My Daughter '90
Day One '89
Scorpio '73

Robert Riskin (1897-1955)
Riding High '50
Meet John Doe '41
You Can't Take It with You '38
Lost Horizon '37
Mr. Deeds Goes to Town '36
It Happened One Night '34
Lady for a Day '33
American Madness '32

Guy Ritchie (1968-)
Revolver '05
Swept Away '02
Snatch '00
Lock, Stock and 2 Smoking Barrels '98

Thomas Ritz
The Killing Grounds '97
Marked Man '96
Open Fire '94
Martial Outlaw '93

Stephen J. Rivele (1949-)
Ali '01
Nixon '95

Jose Rivera
Trade '07
The Motorcycle Diaries '04

Jacques Rivette (1928-)
The Duchess of Langeais '07
Va Savoir '01
La Belle Noiseuse '90
Celine and Julie Go Boating '74
Paris Belongs to Us '60

Allen Rivkin (1903-90)
Tension '50
Dead Reckoning '47
Dancing Lady '33
Picture Snatcher '33
What Price Hollywood? '32

Janet Roach
Mr. North '88
Pizzi's Honor '85

Matthew Robbins (1945-)
Mimic '97
*batteries not included '87
Warning Sign '85
Dragonslayer '81
Corvette Summer '78
MacArthur '77

Tim Robbins (1958-)
The Cradle Will Rock '99
Dead Man Walking '95
Bob Roberts '92

Ben Roberts (1916-84)
Portrait in Black '60
Green Fire '55
White Heat '49

Charles E. Roberts (1894-1951)
Goin' to Town '44
Mexican Spitfire '40
Roaring Roads '35
Social Error '35
Flaming Signal '33

Jonathan Roberts
Jack Frost '98
The Hunchback of Notre Dame '96
The Lion King '94
Once Bitten '85
The Sure Thing '85

Jordan Roberts
March of the Penguins '05
Around the Bend '04

June Roberts
Mermaids '90
Experience Preferred... But Not Essential '83

Marguerite Roberts (1905-89)
Shoot Out '71
True Grit '69
Five Card Stud '68
Ivanhoe '52
Undercurrent '46
Somewhere I'll Find You '42

Scott Roberts
The Hard Word '02
K2: The Ultimate High '92

Stanley Roberts (1916-82)
The Caine Mutiny '54
Death of a Salesman '51
Prairie Moon '38

William Roberts (1913-97)
Legend of the Lone Ranger '81
Posse '75
The Last American Hero '73
Red Sun '71
The Bridge at Remagen '69
The Devil's Brigade '68
The Wonderful World of the Brothers Grimm '62
The Magnificent Seven '60
The Mating Game '59
The Private War of Major Benson '55
Easy to Love '53

Mira Robertson
Head On '98
Only the Brave '94

R.J. Robertson
Home for Christmas '93
Final Embrace '92
The Haunting of Morella '91
Think Big '90
Transylvania Twist '89
Not of This Earth '88
Big Bad Mama 2 '87
Forbidden World '82

John Robins
Hot Resort '85
Death Ship '80

Bruce Robinson (1946-)
In Dreams '98
Return to Paradise '98
Jennifer 8 '92
Fat Man and Little Boy '89
How to Get Ahead in Advertising '89
Withnail and I '87
The Killing Fields '84

Butch Robinson
Crazy as Hell '02
DROP Squad '94

Casey Robinson (1903-79)
The Egyptian '54
The Snows of Kilimanjaro '52
Father Was a Fullback '49
Saratoga Trunk '45
Now, Voyager '42
Dark Victory '39
Captain Blood '35

James Robinson
The League of Extraordinary Gentlemen '03
Cyber Bandits '94

Matt Robinson
Nanny McPhee '06
Amazing Grace '74

Phil Alden Robinson (1950-)
Freedom Song '00
The Chamber '96
Sneakers '92
Field of Dreams '89
In the Mood '87
All of Me '84
Rhinestone '84

Sally Robinson
Follow the Stars Home '01
Princess of Thieves '01
The Lost Child '00
A Far Off Place '93

Todd Robinson
Lonely Hearts '06
Mermaid '00
White Squall '96

Marc Rocco (1965-)
Where the Day Takes You '92
Dream a Little Dream '89

Glauce Rocha (1930-73)
Antonio das Mortes '68
Earth Entranced '66
Black God, White Devil '64

Eric Rochant (1961-)
Love Without Pity '91
The Fifth Monkey '90

Chris Rock (1966-)
I Think I Love My Wife '07
Head of State '03
Down to Earth '01
CB4: The Movie '93

Kevin Rock
Raging Angels '95
Suspicious Agenda '94
Philadelphia Experiment 2 '93
Warlock: The Armageddon '93

Alexandre Rockwell (1957-)
13 Moons '02
Four Rooms '95
Somebody to Love '94
In the Soup '92
Sons '89

Robert Rodat (1953-)
The Patriot '00
36 Hours to Die '99
Saving Private Ryan '98
The Ripper '97
Fly Away Home '96
Tall Tale: The Unbelievable Adventures of Pecos Bill '95

Franc Roddam (1946-)
The Comrades of Summer '92
Moby Dick '98
Aria '88
Quatrophenia '79

Geoff Rodkey
Daddy Day Camp '07
RV '06
The Shaggy Dog '06
Daddy Day Care '03

Hans Rodionoff
The Hollow '04
The Skulls 3 '02

Franz Rodenkirchen (1963-)
Nekromantik 2 '91
Der Todesking '89
Nekromantik '87

Howard Rodman (1920-85)
Scandal Sheet '85
Winning '69

Serge Rodnunsky (1959-)
Dead Lenny '06
Newsbreak '00
TripFall '00
Cypress Edge '99
Fear Runs Silent '99
Paper Bullets '99
Silicon Towers '99
Bomb Squad '97
Dead Titles '97

Robert Rodriguez (1968-)
Planet Terror '07
The Adventures of Sharkboy and Lavagirl in 3-D '05
Once Upon a Time in Mexico '03
Spy Kids 3-D: Game Over '03
Spy Kids 2: The Island of Lost Dreams '02
Desperado '95
Four Rooms '95
Roadracers '94
El Mariachi '93

Michael Roemer (1928-)
The Plot Against Harry '69
Nothing but a Man '64

Michael Roesch (1974-)
Alone in the Dark '05
House of the Dead 2: Dead Aim '05

Seth Rogen (1982-)
Dellbit Taylor '08
Superbad '07

Howard Emmett Rogers (1890-1971)
Gambler's Choice '44
Libeled Lady '36
Tarzan and His Mate '34
Hold Your Man '33

Ivan Rogers (1954-)
Two Wrongs Make a Right '89

John Rogers
Catwoman '04
The Core '03
American Outlaws '01

Foswell Rogers
So This Is Washington '43
Two Weeks to Live '43

Steven Rogers
P.S. I Love You '07
Kate & Leopold '01
Hope Floats '98
Stepmom '98

Eric Rohmer (1920-)
The Lady and the Duke '01
Autumn Tale '98
A Summer's Tale '96
Rendezvous in Paris '95
A Tale of Winter '92
Four Adventures of Reinette and Mirabelle '89
A Tale of Springtime '89
Boyfriends & Girlfriends '88
Summer '86
Full Moon in Paris '84
Le Beau Mariage '82
Pauline at the Beach '83
Perceval '78
The Aviator's Wife '80
The Marquise of O '76
Claire's Knee '71
Chloe in the Afternoon '72
My Night at Maud's '69
Six in Paris '68
La Collectionneuse '67

Joao Pedro Rodrigues (1966-)
Two Drifters '05
O Fantasma '00

Mark Romanek (1959-)
One Hour Photo '02
Static '87

Sam Rolfe (1920-85)
They Call It Murder '71
The Naked Spur '53

Eddie Romero (1924-)
Brides of the Beast '68
The Ravagers '65
The Walls of Hell '64
Cavalry Command '63

George A. Romero (1940-)
Diary of the Dead '07
George A. Romero's Land of the Dead '05
Bruiser '00
Creepshow 2 '87
Day of the Dead '85
Knightriders '81
Dawn of the Dead '78
Martin '77
The Crazies '73
Season of the Witch '73
Night of the Living Dead '68

Gianni Romoli (1948-)
Facing Windows '03
His Secret Life '01
Harem '99

Brunello Rondi (1924-89)
Cemetery Man '95
She '35

David Ronn
Norbit '07
Guess Who '05
National Security '03
I Spy '02
Serving Sara '02

Don Roos (1959-)
Happy Endings '05
Bounce '00
The Opposite of Sex '98
Diabolique '96
Boys on the Side '94
Single White Female '92
Love Field '91

Gary Rosen
The Last Supper '96

Arthur Ross
Brubaker '80
Satan's School for Girls '73
The Three Worlds of Gulliver '59
The Creature Walks among Us '56
Creature from the Black Lagoon '54

Brian Ross
Dying to Remember '93
Body Language '92
The Secret Passion of Robert Clayton '92

Bradford Ropes (1905-66)
Redwood Forest Trail '50
Gaucho Serenade '40

Tom Ropelewski
Look Who's Talking Now '93
Madhouse '90
Loverboy '88
The Kiss '88

Wells Root (1900-93)
Texas Across the River '66
Prisoner of Zenda '37

Martin Rosen
The Plague Dogs '82
Watership Down '78

Henry Rosenbaum
Get Crazy '83
The Dunwich Horror '70

Craig Rosenberg (1965-)
Half Light '05
After the Sunset '04
Hotel de Love '96

Gualtiero Rosella
The Ladykillers '55
Genevieve '53

Dan Rosen (1963-)
The Curve '97
Flight of the Innocent '93
Not of This World '99

William Rose (1914-87)
Dr. Frankenstein's Castle of Freaks '74
The Secret of Santa Vittoria '69
Guess Who's Coming to Dinner '67
It's a Mad, Mad, Mad, Mad World '63
The Smallest Show on Earth '57
The Ladykillers '55

Ruth Rose (1896-1978)
King Kong '33

Reginald Rose (1920-2002)
Twelve Angry Men '97
Wild Geese 2 '85
The Final Option '82
Somebody Killed Her Husband '78
Whose Life Is It Anyway? '81
Sea Wolves '81
Wild Geese '78
Man of the West '58
Twelve Angry Men '57
The Wrong Man '56

Jack Rosenthal (1931-2004)
Captain Jack '98
The Wedding Gift '93

Mark Rosenthal
Flicka '06
Mona Lisa Smile '03
Planet of the Apes '01
Mercury Rising '98
Mighty Joe Young '98
The Beverly Hillbillies '93
For Love or Money '33
Desperate Hours '90
The In Crowd '88
Superman 4: The Quest for Peace '87
The Jewel of the Nile '85
Legend of Billie Jean '85

Francesco Rosi (1922-)
The Truce '96
The Palermo Connection '91
Three Brothers '80
Christ Stopped at Eboli '79
Illustrious Corpses '76

Leo Rosten (1908-97)
Dark Corner '46
Lured '47
Velvet Touch '48

Giuseppe Rosati
Running Free '00
Street War '76
Heidi '93
White Fang '91
The Journey of Natty Gann '85

Bernard Rose (1960-)
Perfect Crime '97
Leo Tolstoy's Anna Karenina '96
Immortal Beloved '94
Candyman '92
Paperhouse '88

Jack Rose (1911-95)
The Great Muppet Caper '81
Lost and Found '79
A Touch of Class '73
Papa's Delicate Condition '63
Who's Got the Action? '63
It Started in Naples '60
The Five Pennies '59
Houseboat '58
The Seven Little Foys '55
Trouble along the Way '53
April in Paris '52
I'll See You in My Dreams '51
On Moonlight Bay '51
Riding High '50
The Great Lover '49
Sorrowful Jones '49
My Favorite Brunette '47
The Road to Rio '47

Lee Rose
The Truth About Jane '00
An Unexpected Life '97
An Unexpected Family '96
A Mother's Prayer '95
Deconstructing Sarah '94

Louisa Rose
Sisters '73

Mickey Rose (1935-)
Student Bodies '81
I Wonder Who's Killing Her Now? '76
Bananas '71
What's Up, Tiger Lily? '66
Take the Money and Run '69

Dale Rosenbloom (1964-)
Saving Shiloh '06
Shiloh 2: Shiloh Season '99
Shiloh '97

Jeanne Rosenberg
Running Free '00
The Land Before Time 4 '96
White Fang '91
The Journey of Natty Gann '85

Marc Rosenberg
December Boys '07
Serpent's Lair '95
Dingo '90

Philip Rosenberg (1942-)
Missing Pieces '00
Joe Torre: Curveballs Along the Way '97
Death Benefit '96
In the Lake of the Woods '96
In the Line of Duty: A Cop for the Killing '90

Gary Ross (1956-)
Seabiscuit '03
Pleasantville '98
Lassie '94
Dave '93
Big '88

Scott Rosenberg (1963-)
Kangaroo Jack '02
Highway '01
Gone in 60 Seconds '00
High Fidelity '00
Disturbing Behavior '98
Con Air '97
Beautiful Girls '96
Things to Do in Denver When You're Dead '95

Roberto Rossellini (1906-77)
The Messiah '75
Blaise Pascal '71
RoGoPaG '63
Era Notte a Roma '60
Generale Della Rovere '60
Voyage in Italy '53
The Flowers of St. Francis '50
Paisan '46
Man with a Cross '43
Open City '45

Robert Rossen (1908-66)
Lilith '64
Billy Budd '62
The Hustler '61
All the King's Men '49
The Strange Love of Martha Ivers '46
A Walk in the Sun '46
Edge of Darkness '43
The Sea Wolf '41
The Roaring Twenties '39
They Won't Forget '37

Seth Zvi Rosenfeld
King of the Jungle '01
A Brother's Kiss '97
Subway Stories '97
Sunset Park '96

Terry Rossio (1960-)
Pirates of the Caribbean: At World's End '07
Deja Vu '06
Pirates of the Caribbean: Dead Man's Chest '06
Pirates of the Caribbean: The Curse of the Black Pearl '03
Shrek '01
The Road to El Dorado '00
Small Soldiers '98
The Puppet Masters '94
Aladdin '92
Little Monsters '89

Charles Francis Royal (1880-1955)
The Jewel '36
The Oregon Trail '37
The Outsiders '83
Royal '83

Patricia Rozema (1958-)
Mansfield Park '99
When Night Is Falling '95
I've Heard the Mermaids Singing '87

Dev Ross
The Land Before Time 4: Journey Through the Mists '96

Bobby Roth (1950-)
The Man Inside '90
Dead Solid Perfect '88
Baja Oklahoma '87
Heartbreakers '84
Boss' Son '78

Eli Roth (1972-)
Hostel: Part 2 '07
Hostel '06
Cabin Fever '03

Eric Roth (1945-)
Lucky You '07
The Good Shepherd '05
Munich '05
Ali '01
The Insider '99
The Horse Whisperer '97
The Postman '97
Forrest Gump '94
Mr. Jones '93
Memories of Me '88
Suspect '87
The Concorde: Airport '79 '79
The Onion Field '79

Phillip J. Roth (1959-)
Boa '02
Interceptor Force '99
Velocity Trap '99

J. Walter Ruben (1899-1942)
Bachelor Apartment '31
The Royal Bed '31

Bruce Joel Rubin (1943-)
The Last Mimzy '07
Stuart Little 2 '02
Deep Impact '98
My Life '93
Ghost '90
Jacob's Ladder '90
Deadly Friend '86
Brainstorm '83

Mann Rubin (1927-)
The First Deadly Sin '80
The Best of Everything '59

Sergio Rubini (1959-)

Cliff Ruby
Beethoven's 5th '03
Cats Don't Dance '97
Balto '95

Andy Ruben
Club Vampire '98
Poison Ivy '92

John Ruane (1952-)
That Eye, the Sky '94
Death in Brunswick '90

Kenneth Ross (1941-)
Out of the Blue '88
The Odessa File '74
The Day of the Jackal '73

Nick Rotundo
G2: Mortal Conquest '99
Gladiator Cop: The Swordsman 2 '95

Kathleen Rowell
Video Voyeur: The Susan Wilson Story '02
Killing Mr. Griffin '97
Courageous Avenger '35

Russell Rouse (1913-87)
The Oscar '66
Fastest Gun Alive '56
The Thief '52
D.O.A. '49

Jeff Rothberg
The Whole Shebang '01
A Simple Wish '97
The Amazing Panda Adventure '95

Stephanie Rothman (1936-)
Starhops '78
The Velvet Vampire '71
Group Marriage '72

Talbot Rothwell (1916-81)
Carry On Camping '71
Carry On Henry VIII '71
Carry On Cowboy '66

Brigitte Rouan (1965-)
After Sex '97
Overseas: Three Women with Man Trouble '90

Jean Rouveral (1916-)
A Face in the Rain '63
Autumn Leaves '56

Pierre Rouve (1915-98)
Cop-Out '67
Trial & Error '62

Mark Rosman (1959-)
The Perfect Man '05
A Cinderella Story '04
Life-Size '00
The Invader '96
Evolver '94
The House on Sorority Row '83

Harry Ruby (1895-1974)
A Night at the Opera '35
Duck Soup '33
Horse Feathers '32
Kid from Spain '32
David Rudkin (1936-)
December Bride '91
Fahrenheit 451 '66
Rita Rudner (1955-)
A Weekend in the Country '96
Peter's Friends '92
Paul Rudnick (1957-)
The Stepford Wives '04
Marci X '03
Isn't She Great '00
In and Out '97
Jeffrey '95
Addams Family Values '93
Steve Rudnick
Kicking & Screaming '05
The Santa Clause '94
Alan Rudolph (1943-)
Intimate Affairs '01
Trixie '00
Breakfast of Champions '98
Afterglow '97
Equinox '93
Love at Large '89
The Moderns '88
Trouble in Mind '86
Choose Me '84
Endangered Species '82
Roadie '80
Welcome to L.A. '77
Buffalo Bill & the Indians '76
Barn of the Naked Dead '73
Premonition '71
Ed Rugoff
Double Take '97
Mr. Nanny '93
Mannequin 2: On the Move '91
Mannequin '87
Raul Ruiz (1941-)
Comedy of Innocence '00
Time Regained '99
Genealogies of a Crime '97
Three Lives and Only One Death '96
On Top of the Whale '82
The Hypothesis of the Stolen Painting '78
Mogens Rukov (1943-)
Reconstruction '03
The Celebration '98
Stefano Rulli (1949-)
Best of Youth '03
The Truce '96
The Stolen Children '92
Terry Runte (1960-94)
Super Mario Bros. '93
Mystery Date '91
Richard Rush (1930-)
Color of Night '94
Air America '90
The Stunt Man '80
Psych-Out '68
Harry Ruskin (1894-1969)
Lady Godiva '55
The Postman Always Rings Twice '46
The Secret of Dr. Kildare '39
Six of a Kind '34
Josef Rusnak
The Thirteenth Floor '99
Quiet Days in Hollywood '97
Lou Rusoff (1911-63)
Beach Party '63
Cat Girl '57
Motorcycle Gang '57
Shake, Rattle and Rock '57
It Conquered the World '56
The Phantom from 10,000 Leagues '56
Day the World Ended '55
Chuck Russell (1952-)
The Blob '88
A Nightmare on Elm Street 3: Dream Warriors '87
Dreamscape '84

David O. Russell (1959-)
I Heart Huckabees '04
Three Kings '99
Flirting with Disaster '95
Spanking the Monkey '94
Ken Russell (1927-)
Lady Chatterley '92
Whore '91
The Rainbow '89
Aria '88
The Lair of the White Worm '88
Salome's Last Dance '88
Valentino '77
Lisztomania '75
Tommy '75
Mahler '74
The Boy Friend '71
The Devils '71
Michael Russell
A Certain Justice '99
Tangiers '83
Ray Russell (1924-99)
X: The Man with X-Ray Eyes '63
Premature Burial '62
Zotz! '62
Mr. Sardonicus '61
Vivian Russell
The Rainbow '89
Willy Russell (1947-)
Shirley Valentine '89
Educating Rita '83
John A. Russo (1939-)
Heartstopper '92
Night of the Living Dead '90
Voodoo Dawn '89
The Majorettes '87
Return of the Living Dead '85
Night of the Living Dead '68
Richard Russo (1949-)
Empire Falls '05
The Ice Harvest '05
Keeping Mum '05
Brush with Fate '03
The Flamingo Rising '01
Twilight '98
Marti Rustam
Evils of the Night '85
Eaten Alive '76
Neil Ruttenberg
Magic Island '95
Prehysteria 3 '95
Bad Blood '94
Morrie Ruvinsky
A Woman Hunted '03
Jack Higgins' Thunder Point '97
Stefan Ruzowitzky (1961-)
The Counterfeiters '07
Anatomy '00
The Inheritors '98
David Ryan (1964-)
Mean Streak '99
Frank Ryan (1947-)
First Love, Last Rites '98
Can't Help Singing '45
The Amazing Mrs. Holiday '43
Call Out the Marines '42
Tim Ryan (1899-1956)
Bela Lugosi Meets a Brooklyn Gorilla '52
Ghost Crazy '44
Florence Ryerson (1892-1965)
The Return of Dr. Fu Manchu '30
The Mysterious Dr. Fu Manchu '29
Michael Rymer (1963-)
Perfume '01
Allie & Me '97
Angel Baby '95
Morrie Ryskind (1895-1985)
Penny Serenade '41
Room Service '38

My Man Godfrey '36
A Night at the Opera '35
Palmy Days '31
Animal Crackers '30
The Cocoanuts '29
Joseph Sabo
Fantasia '40
Pinocchio '40
Dardano Sacchetti (1944-)
Specters '87
Demons '86
Devilfish '84
A Blade in the Dark '83
The House by the Cemetery '83
The New Gladiators '83
The Beyond '82
Manhattan Baby '82
New York Ripper '82
Cannibal Apocalypse '80
Gates of Hell '80
Zombie '80
Shock '79
Ira Sachs (1965-)
Married Life '07
Forty Shades of Blue '05
The Delta '97
William Sachs
Hitz '89
Galaxina '80
Peter Sagal
Dirty Dancing: Havana Nights '04
Savage '96
Arthur St. Claire (1899-1950)
Rimfire '49
The Mask of Diijon '46
Yank in Libya '42
Nicholas St. John
The Funeral '96
The Addiction '95
Body Snatchers '93
Dangerous Game '93
King of New York '90
China Girl '87
Fear City '85
Ms. 45 '81
Driller Killer '79
Alfredo Salazar (1922-)
Doctor of Doom '62
The Robot vs. the Aztec Mummy '59
Wrestling Women vs. the Aztec Mummy '59
Richard Sale (1911-93)
Assassination '87
Abandon Ship '57
Suddenly '54
A Woman's World '54
Ticket to Tomahawk '50
When Willie Comes Marching Home '50
Father Was a Fullback '49
Kario Salem
The Score '01
The Rat Pack '98
Don King: Only in America '97
Claudia Salter
Man in the Mirror: The Michael Jackson Story '04
Mark Saltzman
Third Man Out: A Donald Strachey Mystery '05
The Red Sneakers '01
Mrs. Santa Claus '96
Napoleon '96

3 Ninjas Kick Back '94
Iron & Silk '91
The Adventures of Milo & Otis '89
Milo & Otis '89
Victor Salva (1958-)
Peaceful Warrior '06
Jeepers Creepers 2 '03
Jeepers Creepers '01
Rites of Passage '99
Powder '95
Nature of the Beast '94
Pierre Salvadori (1964-)
Priceless '06
Apres-Vous '03
Les Apprentis '95
Hal Salwen
Denise Calls Up '95
Probable Cause '94
Jon Robert Samsel
Animal Instincts '92
Carnal Crimes '91
Lesser Samuels (1894-1980)
Ace in the Hole '51
No Way Out '50
Bitter Sweet '40
Strange Cargo '40
Gangway '37
Duke Sandefur
The Phantom of the Opera '89
Ghost Town '88
Christopher Sanders (1960-)
Lilo & Stitch '02
Mulan '98
Adam Sandler (1966-)
You Don't Mess with the Zohan '08
Adam Sandler's 8 Crazy Nights '02
Little Nicky '00
Big Daddy '99
The Waterboy '98
Happy Gilmore '96
Billy Madison '94
Barry Sandler
All-American Murder '91
Crimes of Passion '84
Making Love '82
The Mirror Crack'd '80
The Duchess and the Dirtwater Fox '76
Loners '72
Anna Sandor
My Louisiana Sky '02
Amelia Earhart: The Final Flight '94
Jimmy Sangster (1924-)
The Devil & Max Devlin '81
Phobia '80
Dynasty of Fear '72
The Horror of Frankenstein '70
The Anniversary '68
Deadlier Than the Male '67
The Nanny '65
Hysteria '64
Maniac '63
Nightmare '63
Paranoiac '62
The Hellfire Club '61
Scream of Fear '61
The Brides of Dracula '60
The Mummy '59
Blood of the Vampire '58
The Crawling Eye '58
The Horror of Dracula '58
The Revenge of Frankenstein '58
The Curse of Frankenstein '57
X The Unknown '56
Marie-Jose Sanselme
Free Zone '05
Kippur '00
Ken Sanzel
Lone Hero '02
The Replacement Killers '98
Scarred City '98

Alvin Sapinsley (1922-2002)
The Scarlet Letter '79
Moon of the Wolf '72
Tedi Sarafian (1966-)
The Road Killers '95
Tank Girl '94
Solar Crisis '92
Jan Sardi
The Notebook '04
Shine '95
Barney A. Sarecky (1895-1968)
Buffalo Bill Rides Again '47
The Phantom Rider '46
The Purple Monster Strikes '45
The Ape Man '43
Adventures of Red Ryder '40
Drums of Fu Manchu '40
Mysterious Doctor Satan '40
Zorro's Fighting Legion '39
Darkest Africa '36
Fighting Marines '36
Alvin Sargent (1931-)
Spider-Man 3 '07
Spider-Man 2 '04
Unfaithful '02
Anywhere But Here '99
Bogus '96
Other People's Money '91
What about Bob? '91
White Palace '90
Nuts '87
Ordinary People '80
Straight Time '78
Bobby Deerfield '77
Julia '77
Paper Moon '73
I Walk the Line '70
The Stalking Moon '69
The Sterile Cuckoo '69
Gambit '66
Arlene Sarner
The Healer '02
Blue Sky '91
Peggy Sue Got Married '86
Robert Sarno
Decoy '95
Oley Sassone
Playback '95
Wild Hearts Can't Be Broken '91
Oscar Saul (1912-94)
The Silencers '66
Road House '48
George Saunders (1959-)
The Perfect Wife '00
Bloodsport 4: The Dark Kumite '98
The Landlady '98
Intimate Deception '96
Malicious '95
Scanner Cop '94
Carlos Saura (1932-)
Goya in Bordeaux '99
Tango '98
Outrage '93
Carmen '83
Blood Wedding '81
Elisa, Vida Mia '77
Cria '76
Cria Cuervos '76
Claude Sautet (1924-2000)
Nelly et Monsieur Arnaud '95
Vincent, Francois, Paul and the Others '76
Cesar & Rosalie '72
Borsalino '70

Jody Savin
Marilyn Hotchkiss' Ballroom Dancing & Charm School '06
Witchcraft '88
Nancy Savoca (1960-)
The 24 Hour Woman '99
If These Walls Could Talk '96
Household Saints '93
True Love '89
Gerald Savory
Mapp & Lucia '85
Young and Innocent '37
John Sayles (1950-)
The Spiderwick Chronicles '08
Honeydripper '07
Silver City '04
Casa de los Babys '03
Sunshine State '02
Limbo '99
Hombres Armados '97
Mimic '97
Lone Star '95
Men of War '94
The Secret of Roan Inish '94
Passion Fish '92
City of Hope '91
Breaking In '89
Eight Men Out '88
Matewan '87
Wild Thing '87
The Clan of the Cave Bear '86
Unnatural Causes '86
The Brother from Another Planet '84
Enormous Changes '83
Lianna '83
Trumps '83
Baby It's You '82
The Challenge '82
The Howling '81
Alligator '80
Battle Beyond the Stars '80
Return of the Secaucus 7 '80
Lady in Red '79
Piranha '78
Furio Scarpelli (1919-)
The Postman '94
Time to Kill '89
The Family '87
The Good, the Bad and the Ugly '67
Mafioso '62
Big Deal on Madonna Street '58
Sauro Scavolini (1934-)
Your Vice is a Closed Room and Only I Have the Key '72
The Case of the Scorpion's Tail '71
The Scorpion's Tail '71
Steven Schachter
A Slight Case of Murder '99
The Con '98
Eric Schaeffer (1962-)
Mind the Gap '04
Never Again '01
Wirey Spindell '99
Fall '97
If Lucy Fell '95
My Life's in Turnaround '94
Jeff Schaffer
Eurotrip '04
Dr. Seuss' The Cat in the Hat '03
Don Schain
Girls Are for Loving '73
The Abductors '72
Ginger '71
James Schamus (1959-)
Lust, Caution '07
Hulk '03
Crouching Tiger, Hidden Dragon '00
Ride with the Devil '99
The Ice Storm '97
Eat Drink Man Woman '94
The Wedding Banquet '93

Dore Schary (1905-80)
Sunrise at Campobello '60
(1939)

Olivier Schatzky
(1949)
L'Eleve '95
A Man in Love '87

Richard Schayer
(1880-1956)
Justice Rides Again '32
Private Lives '31
The Dragon Painter '19
Trader Horn '31

Adam Scheinman
Bait '00
Mickey Blue Eyes '99

Andrew Scheinman
Little Big League '94

David Schmoeller
(1947-)
The Arrival '90
Crawlspace '86

George Schenck
Dying to Remember '93
Escape 2000 '81
Futureworld '76
More Dead Than Alive '68

Robert Schenkkan
(1953-)
Crazy Horse '02

Richard Schenkman
(1958-)
Went to Coney Island on a
Mission from God... Be
Back by Five '98
The Pompatus of Love '95

Fred Schepisi (1939-)
Last Orders '01
A Cry in the Dark '88
The Chant of Jimmie
Blacksmith '78
The Devil's Playground '76

Shawn Schepps
Drumline '02
Serving Sara '02
Son-in-Law '93
Encino Man '92

Stephen Schiff
True Crime '99

Karl Schiffman
'98

Michael Schiffer
Lolita '97
The Four Feathers '02
The Peacemaker '97
Crimson Tide '95

Jay Scherick
Norbit '07
Guess Who '05
I Spy '02
Serving Sara '02
Colors '88

Lone Scherfig (1959-)
Italian for Beginners '01
Wilbur Wants to Kill Himself
'02

George Schlatter
(1932)
Fire and Ice '87
Norman, Is That You? '76

Murray Schisgal
(1926-)
Tootsie '82
Luv '67

Vivian Schilling
(1968-)
Future Shock '93
Soultaker '90
Terror Eyes '87
Sorceress '88

Suzanne Schiffman
(1930-2001)
Confidentially Yours '83
The Woman Next Door '81
The Last Metro '80
The Man Who Loved
Women '77
Small Change '76
The Story of Adele H. '75
Day for Night '73

**Bernard C.
Schoenfeld (1907-90)**
Dark Corner '46
Phantom Lady '44

Robert Schooley
Sky High '05

David J. Schow
The Crow '93
Critters 4 '91
Critters 3 '91
Leatherface: The Texas
Chainsaw Massacre 3 '89

Leonard Schrader
(1943-2006)
Naked Tango '91
Kiss of the Spider Woman
'85
Mishima: A Life in Four
Chapters '85

**Roger S.H.
Schulman**
The Fox and the Hound 2
'06
Shrek '01
Balto '95

Tom Schulman
(1951-)
Welcome to Mooseport '04
Holy Man '98
8 Heads in a Duffel Bag '96
Medicine Man '92
What about Bob? '91
Dead Poets Society '89

**Volker Schlondorff
(1939-)**
The Legend of Rita '99
The Ogre '96
Voyager '91
The Tin Drum '79

**Hayden
Schlossberg**
Harold & Kumar Escape
from Guantanamo Bay
'08
Harold and Kumar Go to
White Castle '04

Wolfgang Schmidt
A.P.E.X. '94

Ronald Schmidt
See Ray; Dennis Steckler

**Stephen Schneck
(1933-96)**
Welcome to Blood City '77

**Charles Schnee
(1916-63)**
Butterfield 8 '60
The Bad and the Beautiful
'52
Westward the Women '51
They Live by Night '49
Red River '48

Barry Schneider
Mother's Boys '94
Deadly Force '83
Take This Job & Shove It
'81

**Dan Schneider
(1966-)**
Big Fat Liar '02
Good Burger '97

**David Schneider
(1963-)**
All the Queen's Men '02

**Peter Schneider
(1940-)**
The Promise '94
Knife in the Head '78

**Rob Schneider
(1963-)**
Deuce Bigalow: European
Gigolo '05
Deuce Bigalow: Male Gigolo
'99

**Julian Schnabel
(1951-)**
Before Night Falls '00
Basquiat '96

Stephen Schneck
Hi-Jacked '50

**Doris Schroeder
(1893-1981)**
Hopalong Cassidy:
Dangerous Venture '48
Sundown Fury '42
Bullet Code '40
Hopalong Cassidy Returns
'36
Three on the Trail '36

**Bernard Schubert
(1895-1988)**
Jungle Woman '44
The Mummy's Curse '44
Breaking the Ice '38
Mark of the Vampire '35
No Other Woman '33

**Budd Schulberg
(1914-)**
Question of Honor '80
A Face in the Crowd '57
On the Waterfront '54

**Martin Scorsese
(1942-)**
Casino '95
The Age of Innocence '93
Goodfellas '90
Mean Streets '73

**Arnold Schulman
(1925-)**
Tucker: The Man and His
Dream '88
A Chorus Line '85
Players '79
Funny Lady '75
The Night They Raided
Minsky's '69
Love with the Proper
Stranger '63
Cimarron '60
A Hole in the Head '59

Allan Scott (1907-95)
Behind the Lines '97
In Love and War '97
The Preacher's Wife '95
Two Deaths '94
Cold Heaven '92
The Witches '90
Castaway '87
D.A.R.Y.L. '85
Martin's Day '85
The Awakening '80
Joseph Andrews '77
Spiral Staircase '75
The Girl from Petrovka '74
Don't Look Now '73
Man Who Had Power Over
Women '70
The 5000 Fingers of Dr. T
'53
So Proudly We Hail '43
Lucky Partners '40
Top Hat '35

**Raymond L. Schrock
(1892-1950)**
Danny Boy '46
White Pongo '45
The Phantom of the Opera
'25

Peter Schreck
Cinderella '64
A Slight Case of Murder '38
Love Under Pressure '78

Carol Schreder
Mama Flora's Family '98
In Love and War '91

Nevin Schreiner
Don't Talk to Strangers '94
Linda '93
The China Lake Murders '90
Memories of Murder '90

**Joseph Schrank
(1900-84)**
Sex and the Single Girl '64

Kathryn Scola
One Night in the Tropics '40
Alexander's Ragtime Band
'38
Baby Face '33
Female '33
Night After Night '32

Ettore Scola (1931-)
The Family '87
Macaroni '85
La Nuit de Varennes '82
Passion of Love '82
A Special Day '77
Down & Dirty '76
Two Nights with Cleopatra
'54

**Aleksander Scibor-
Rylski (1928-83)**
Man of Iron '81
Man of Marble '76

Alberto Sciamma
Jericho Mansions '03
Killer Tongue '96

Beverly Sebastian
Running Cool '93
Gator Bait 2: Cajun Justice
'88
Gator Bait '73

Ferd Sebastian
Running Cool '93
Gator Bait 2: Cajun Justice
'88
Gator Bait '73

Eliroy Schwartz
Rescue from Gilligan's
Island '78
Rescue from Gilligan's
Island: The Second Girl '64

Wackiest Wagon Train in
the West '77

**Sherwood Schwartz
(1916-)**
Rescue from Gilligan's
Island '78

Mark Evan Schwartz
Little Men '98
Wanted '98

**David R. Schwartz
(1911-2003)**
That Funny Feeling '65
The Bobo '67
Robin and the 7 Hoods '64

**Mark Schwahn
(1966-)**
Coach Carter '05
The Perfect Score '04
Whatever It Takes '00

Sherman Scott
See Fred Olen Ray

Gavin Scott (1950-)
Mists of Avalon '01
Small Soldiers '98
The Borrowers '97

**Peter S. Seaman
(1951-)**
Shrek the Third '07
Last Holiday '06
Dr. Seuss' How the Grinch
Stole Christmas '00
Who Framed Roger Rabbit
'88

Edward E. Seabrook
Road to Perdition '02

Darin Scott
West Deep '06
Caught Up '98

Don D. Scott
Barbershop 2: Back in
Business '04
Barbershop '02
Tales from the Hood '95

**Joel Schumacher
(1942-)**
The Phantom of the Opera
'04

**Shinichi Sekizawa
(1921-92)**
Godzilla vs. Megalon '76
Godzilla's Revenge '69
Godzilla vs. Monster Zero
'68
Godzilla vs. the Sea
Monster '66
Son of Godzilla '66
Ghidrah the Three Headed
Monster '65
Godzilla vs. Mothra '64
King Kong vs. Godzilla '63
Mothra '62

**Michael Seitzman
(1967-)**
North Country '05
Here on Earth '00
Farmer & Chase '96

Michael D. Sellers
Eye of the Dolphin '06

Peter Sehr (1951-)
Love the Hard Way '01
Obsession '97
Kaspar Hauser '93

**Susan Seidelman
(1952-)**
The Boynton Beach Club
'05
Tales of Erotica '93

David Seidler
By Dawn's Early Light '00
The King and I '99

Erich Segal (1937-)
Man, Woman & Child '83
A Change of Seasons '80
Oliver's Story '78
Love Story '70
R.P.M.* (*Revolutions Per
Minute) '70
Yellow Submarine '68

**Manuel Seff (1895-
1969)**
Louisiana Hayride '44
Breaking the Ice '38
Love on the Run '36
Red Salute '35

**Jack Seddon (1924-
2001)**
The Blue Max '66
The Longest Day '62

**David O. Selznick
(1902-65)**
The Paradine Case '47
Duel in the Sun '46
Since You Went Away '44
A Star Is Born '37

**Lorenzo Semple, Jr.
(1923-)**
Never Say Never Again '83
Flash Gordon '80
King Kong '76
The Parallax View '74
Papillon '73
Pretty Poison '68
Batman '66

**Jorge Semprun
(1923-)**
Roads to the South '78
A Woman at Her Window
'77
Stavisky '74
La Guerre Est Finie '66

Ted Sears (1900-58)
Peter Pan '53
The Adventures of Ichabod
and Mr. Toad '49
Pinocchio '40
Snow White and the Seven
Dwarfs '37

**George Seaton (1911-
79)**
Miracle on 34th Street '94
Airport '70
36 Hours '64
The Counterfeit Traitor '62
Country Girl '54
Miracle on 34th Street '47
That Night in Rio '41
Doctor Takes a Wife '40
Charley's Aunt '41

Phil Sears
Flyboys '06
Ripper Man '96

David Self
Road to Perdition '02
Thirteen Days '00
The Haunting '99

Michael D. Sellers
The Omen '06
Dragonfly '02
Nobody's Baby '01
My Giant '98
The Eighteenth Angel '97
Shining Through '92
Bird on a Wire '90
Punchline '88
Lucas '86
Table for Five '33
Prophecy '79
My Father's House '75
The Other Side of the
Mountain '75
King, Queen, Knave '72
The Hellstrom Chronicle '71

**Hubert Selby, Jr.
(1928-2004)**
Fear X '03
Requiem for a Dream '00

Michael Seitzman
The Rumor Mill '86

Aaron Seltzer
Meet the Spartans '08
Date Movie '06
Spy Hard '96

Terrel Seltzer
One Fine Day '96
How I Got into College '89
Dim Sum: A Little Bit of
Heart '85
Chan Is Missing '82

David Seltzer (1940-)
The Omen '06
Dragonfly '02
Nobody's Baby '01
My Giant '98
The Eighteenth Angel '97
Shining Through '92
Bird on a Wire '90
Punchline '88
Lucas '86
Table for Five '33
Prophecy '79
My Father's House '75
The Other Side of the
Mountain '75
King, Queen, Knave '72
The Hellstrom Chronicle '71

**Mack Sennett (1880-
1960)**
Extra Girl '23

Ron Senkowski
Wicked Ways '59
Let's Kill All the Lawyers '93

Al Septien (1966-)
Yankee Doodle in Berlin '19
Wrong Turn 2: Dead End '07
Candyman 3: Day of the Dead '98
Chairman of the Board '97
Leprechaun 2 '94

Yahoo Serious (1954)
Mr. Accident '99
Reckless Kelly '93
Young Einstein '89

Rod Serling (1924-75)
A Town Has Turned to Dust '98
In the Presence of Mine Enemies '97
Night Gallery '69
Planet of the Apes '68
Assault on a Queen '66
The Doomsday Flight '66
Seven Days in May '64
Requiem for a Heavyweight '62
Patterns '56
Requiem for a Heavyweight '56

Alexandra Seros
The Specialist '94
Point of No Return '93

Leopoldo Serran
Four Days in September '97
O Quatrilho '95

Coline Serreau (1947-)
Chaos '01
Mama, There's a Man in Your Bed '89

Mark Sevi
Arachnid '01
Dead Men Can't Dance '97
Moving Target '96
Sci-Fighters '96
Excessive Force 2: Force on Force '95
Serial Killer '95
Fast Getaway 2 '94
Relentless 4 '94
Scanner Cop 2: Volkin's Revenge '94
Scanners: The Showdown '94
Class of 1999 2: The Substitute '93
Ghoulies 4 '93

Vernon Sewell (1903-2001)
Mr. Frost '89
Honeymoon '87
Detective '85

Timothy J. Sexton
The World Owes Me a Living '47
Frenzy '46

Tom Shadyac (1960-)
The Nutty Professor '96
Ace Ventura: Pet Detective '93

Anthony Shaffer (1926-2001)
Appointment with Death '88
Evil under the Sun '82
Whodunit '82
Absolution '81
Death on the Nile '78
The Wicker Man '75
Frenzy '72
Sleuth '72
Cry of the Penguins '71

Peter Shaffer (1926-)
Amadeus '84
Equus '77

Steve Shagan (1927-)
Gotti '96
Primal Fear '96
The Sicilian '87
Nightwing '79
Voyage of the Damned '76

Robert Shallcross
Uncle Nino '03
Little Giants '94

Maxwell Shane (1905-83)
Big Town '47
Fear in the Night '47
Treasure of Fear '45
Dark Mountain '44
Gambler's Choice '44
Navy Way '44
One Body Too Many '44
Wildcat '42
Flying Blind '41
The Mummy's Hand '40

Peter Shaner
Lover's Knot '96
Shootfighter 2: Kill or Be Killed! '96
Shootfighter: Fight to the Death '93

John Patrick Shanley (1950-)
Live from Baghdad '03
Congo '95
Alive '93
We're Back! A Dinosaur's Story '93
Joe Versus the Volcano '90
The January Man '89
Five Corners '88
Moonstruck '87

Alan Shapiro (1957-)
Flipper '96
The Crush '93

J. David Shapiro (1969-)
Battlefield Earth '00
Robin Hood: Men in Tights '93

Paul Shapiro (1955-)
Calendar Girl '93
Breaking the Rules '92

Stanley Shapiro (1925-90)
Dirty Rotten Scoundrels '88
Carbon Copy '81
For Pete's Sake '74
That Touch of Mink '62
Come September '61
Operation Petticoat '59
The Perfect Furlough '59
Pillow Talk '59

Jim Sharman (1945-)
Shock Treatment '81
The Rocky Horror Picture Show '75

Alan Sharp (1934-)
The Lathe of Heaven '02
Rob Roy '95
The Last Hit '93
Little Treasure '85
Damnation Alley '77
Night Moves '75
Billy Two Hats '74
Ulzana's Raid '72
Hired Hand '71

Melville Shavelson (1917-2007)
Shadow Play '86
The Adventures of Mark Twain '85
Double Dynamite '51
I'll See You in My Dreams '51
On Moonlight Bay '51
Riding High '50
The Great Lover '49
Sorrowful Jones '49
Where There's Life '47
Wonder Man '45
The Princess and the Pirate '44

Bob Shaw
A Bug's Life '98
Hercules '97

Irwin Shaw (1913-84)
Fire Down Below '57
War and Peace '56
I Want You '51

Wallace Shawn (1943-)
The Fever '04
The Designated Mourner '97
My Dinner with Andre '81

Katt Shea (1957-)
Last Exit to Earth '96
Poison Ivy '92
Stripped to Kill II: Live Girls '89
Dance of the Damned '88
Stripped to Kill '87

Harry Shearer (1943-)
The Patriot '86
The Return of Spinal Tap '92
This Is Spinal Tap '84
Real Life '79

Arthur Sheekman (1901-78)
Blue Skies '46
Welcome Stranger '47
Dimples '36
Duck Soup '33
Monkey Business '31

Charlie Sheen (1965-)
No Code of Conduct '98
Tale of Two Sisters '89

David Sheffield
The Honeymooners '05
Nutty Professor 2: The Klumps '00
Boomerang '92
Coming to America '88

Forrest Sheldon
The Fighting Trooper '34
The Lone Avenger '33

Sidney Sheldon (1917-2007)
Billy Rose's Jumbo '62
All in a Night's Work '61
Birds & the Bees '56
Pardners '56
Rich, Young and Pretty '51
Three Guys Named Mike '51
Annie Get Your Gun '50
Nancy Goes to Rio '50
Easter Parade '48
The Bachelor and the Bobby-Soxer '47

Adrienne Shelly (1966-2006)
Waitress '07

Angela Shelton (1972-)
Tumbleweeds '98

Ron Shelton (1945-)
Bad Boys 2 '03
Hollywood Homicide '03
Play It to the Bone '99
The Great White Hype '96
Tin Cup '96
Blue Chips '94
Cobb '94
Blaze '89
Bull Durham '88
The Best of Times '86
Under Fire '83

Nina Shengold
Double Platinum '99
Blind Spot '93

Richard Shepard
The Hunting Party '07
The Matador '05
Mexico City '00
Oxygen '99
Mercy '96
The Linguini Incident '92

Sam Shepard (1943-)
Don't Come Knocking '05
Silent Tongue '92
Far North '88
Fool for Love '86
Paris, Texas '83
Oh! Calcutta! '72
Zabriskie Point '70

Jean Shepherd (1921-99)
My Summer Story '94
A Christmas Story '83

John Scott Shepherd (1964)
Life or Something Like It '02
Joe Somebody '01

John Shepphird
Chupacabra Terror '05
The Santa Trap '02
Teenage Bonnie & Klepto Clyde '93

Eyal Sher
Axe '06

Jack Sher (1913-88)
Under the Domim Tree '95
Critic's Choice '63
Move Over, Darling '63
Paris Blues '61
The Three Worlds of Gulliver '59
Walk the Proud Land '56
Shane '53

Ted Sherdeman (1909-87)
Island of the Blue Dolphins '64
Misty '61
Away All Boats '56
Them! '54

Bob Sheridan
Against the Law '98
Dinosaur Island '93

Jim Sheridan (1949-)
Sorority House Massacre 2: Nighty Nightmare '92
In America '02
The Boxer '97
The Field '90
My Left Foot '89

Michael J. Sheridan
Some Mother's Son '96
In the Name of the Father '93

Fenn Sherie (1896-1953)
Big Fella '37

David Sherman
Song of Freedom '36

Gary Sherman (1945-)
After the Shock '90
Poltergeist 3 '88
Phobia '80

J. Michael Sherman
KISS Meets the Phantom of the Park '78

Martin Sherman (1938-)
Mrs. Henderson Presents '05
The Roman Spring of Mrs. Stone '03
Callas Forever '02
Bent '97
Alive and Kicking '96

Teddi Sherman
The Summer House '94
Four for Texas '63
Tennessee's Partner '55

R.C. Sherriff (1896-1975)
No Highway in the Sky '51
Odd Man Out '47
The Four Feathers '39
Goodbye, Mr. Chips '39
The Invisible Man '33
The Old Dark House '32

David Sherwin (1942-)
Britannia Hospital '82
If... '69

Robert Sherwood (1896-1955)
The Bishop's Wife '47
The Best Years of Our Lives '46
Abe Lincoln in Illinois '40
Rebecca '40
The Ghost Goes West '36
The Scarlet Pimpernel '34

Susan Shilliday
I Dreamed of Africa '00
Legends of the Fall '94

Takashi Shimizu (1972-)
The Grudge '04
Ju-On: The Grudge '03

Barry Shipman (1912-94)
Carolina Cannonball '55
Flash Gordon Conquers the Universe '40
Frontier Vengeance '40
Space Soldiers Conquer the Universe '40
Dick Tracy: The Spider Strikes '37
S.O.S. Coast Guard '37

Jack Sholder (1945-)
Wishmaster 2: Evil Never Dies '98
Alone in the Dark '82

Del Shores (1957-)
Sordid Lives '00
Daddy's Dyin'... Who's Got the Will? '90

Michael Showalter (1970-)
The Baxter '05
Wet Hot American Summer '01

Dennis Shryack (1936-)
Pale Rider '85
The Car '77

Takeshi Shudo
Pokemon 3: The Movie '01
Pokemon the Movie 2000: The Power of One '00
Pokemon: The First Movie '99

Harold Shumate (1893-1983)
Buccaneer's Girl '50
Abilene Town '46
The Kansan '43
The Roundup '41
Charlie McCarthy, Detective '39
Through the Breakers '28

Ronald Shusett (1945-)
Bleeders '97
Freejack '92
King Kong Lives '86
Dead and Buried '81

M. Night Shyamalan (1970-)
The Happening '08
Lady in the Water '06
The Village '04
Signs '02
Unbreakable '00
The Sixth Sense '99
Stuart Little '99
Wide Awake '97

Charles Shyer (1941-)
Alfie '04
The Parent Trap '98
Father of the Bride Part 2 '95
I Love Trouble '94
Father of the Bride '91
Baby Boom '87
Irreconcilable Differences '84
Protocol '84
Private Benjamin '80
Goin' South '78
House Calls '78
Smokey and the Bandit '77

Sylvia Sichel
If These Walls Could Talk 2 '00
All Over Me '96

Andy Sidaris (1933-)
Return to Savage Beach '97
Day of the Warrior '96
Fit to Kill '93
Hard Hunted '92
Do or Die '91
Guns '90
Picasso Trigger '89
Hard Ticket to Hawaii '87

Lynn Siefert
Cousin Bette '97
Cool Runnings '93

David Siegel
The Deep End '01
Suture '93

Dai Sijie (1954-)
Balzac and the Little Chinese Seamstress '02
China, My Sorrow '89

Sean Silas (1970-)
The Perfect Daughter '96
A Vow to Kill '94

Brad Silberling (1962)
10 Items or Less '06
Moonlight Mile '02

James R. Silke
Ninja 3: The Domination '84
Revenge of the Ninja '83
Sahara '83

Robert Silliphant (1937-99)
Creeping Terror '64
Incredibly Strange Creatures Who Stopped Living and Became Mixed-Up Zombies '63

Stirling Silliphant (1918-96)
The Grass Harp '95
Catch the Heat '87
Over the Top '86
When Time Ran Out '80
Circle of Iron '78
Pearl '78
The Swarm '78
Telefon '77
The Enforcer '76
Death Scream '75
The Killer Elite '75
The Towering Inferno '74
Shaft in Africa '73
The New Centurions '72
The Poseidon Adventure '72
Murphy's War '71
The Liberation of L.B. Jones '70
Walk in the Spring Rain '70
Marlowe '69
Charly '68
In the Heat of the Night '67
The Slender Thread '65
Village of the Damned '60
Nightfall '56

Amanda Silver
The Relic '96
An Eye for an Eye '95
Fallen Angels 1 '93
The Hand that Rocks the Cradle '92

Joan Micklin Silver (1935-)
Chilly Scenes of Winter '79
Hester Street '75

Scott Silver
8 Mile '02
The Mod Squad '99
johns '96

Peter Silverman
Harlan County War '00
Hidden in America '96
American Heart '92

Nancy Silvers
One Special Night '99
Battling for Baby '92

Marc Silverstein
He's Just Not That Into You '03
Never Been Kissed '99

Lawrence L. Simeone (1954-2002)
Blindfold: Acts of Obsession '94
Eyes of the Beholder '92
Cop-Out '91
Presumed Guilty '92

Michael L. Simmons
Two Weeks to Live '43
Murder in Greenwich Village '37

Gary Sinyor (1962-)
Bob the Butler '05
Stiff Upper Lips '96
Solitaire for 2 '94
Leon the Pig Farmer '93

Stephen Sinclair
Lord of the Rings: The Two Towers '02
Meet the Feebles '89

Bryan Singer (1966-)
Superman Returns '06
Public Access '93

Theodore Simonson
The 4D Man '59
The Blob '58

Albert Simonin (1905-80)
Cold Sweat '71
Any Number Can Win '63

Rocco Simonelli
Assassination in Rome '65

Giovanni Simonelli
Gunslinger '70

Jay Simms
Panic in the Year Zero! '62
The Giant Gila Monster '59
The Killer Shrews '59

Adam Simon (1962-)
Bones '01
Carnosaur '93
Brain Dead '89

Alex Simon (1967-)
My Brother's War '97
Bigfoot!: Hard Way Out '96
Piranha '95
Suspect Device '95
Urknown Origin '95

Ellen Simon
One Fine Day '96
Moonlight and Valentino '55

J(uan) Piquer Simon (1934-)
Cthulhu Mansion '91
Slugs '87

Neil Simon (1927-)
Couple 2 '98
The Sunshine Boys '95
Lost in Yonkers '93
Broadway Bound '92
The Marrying Man '91
Bloxi Blues '88
Brighton Beach Memoirs '86
The Slugger's Wife '85
Max Dugan Returns '83
I Ought to Be in Pictures '82
Only When I Laugh '81
Seems Like Old Times '80
Chapter Two '79
California Suite '78
The Cheap Detective '78
The Goodbye Girl '77
Murder by Death '76
The Sunshine Boys '75
Prisoner of Second Avenue '74
The Heartbreak Kid '72
Last of the Red Hot Lovers '72
Plaza Suite '71
Star Spangled Girl '71
The Out-of-Towners '70
The Odd Couple '68
Barefoot in the Park '67
After the Fox '66

Raymond Singer
Mulan '98
NightScreams '97

John Singleton (1968-)
Baby Boy '01
Higher Learning '94
Poetic Justice '93
Boyz N the Hood '91

Curt Siodmak (1902-2000)
Bride of the Gorilla '51
The Beast with Five Fingers '46
Son of Dracula '43
The Wolf Man '41
Black Friday '40
The Invisible Man Returns '40
Non-Stop New York '37
The Invisible Agent '42

Victor Sjostrom (1879-1960)
He Who Gets Slapped '24
The Phantom Chariot '20

John Sjogren (1966-)
The Mosaic Project '95
Money to Burn '94
Red Line '96

Rob Sitch (1962-)
The Castle '97
The Dish '00

Rosemary Anne Sisson (1923-)
The Littlest Horse Thieves '76
Candleshoe '78
The Duchess of Duke Street '78
Elizabeth R '72

Warren Skaaren (1946-90)
Batman '89
Beetlejuice '88
Beverly Hills Cop 2 '87

Kerl Skogland
Liberty Stands Still '02
John John in the Sky '00

Jerzy Skolimowski (1938-)
Hands Up '81
Deep End '70
Knife in the Water '62

Vance Skarstedt (1922-84)
The Slime People '63
Man or Gun '58

Mark Skeet
Vanity Fair '04
Jason and the Argonauts '00

Brian Sloan
I Think I Do '97

Holly Goldberg Sloan (1958-)
The Crocodile Hunter: Collision Course '02
Whispers: An Elephant's Tale '00
The Big Green '95
Angels in the Outfield '94
Made in America '93
Indecency '92

Douglas J. Sloan
Children On Their Birthdays '02

Scott B. Smith (1965-)
The Ruins '08
A Simple Plan '98

Rick Sloane (1961-)
Good Girls Don't '95
Mind, Body & Soul '92
Vice Academy 3 '91
The Movie House Massacre '78

Trace Slobotkin
Kickin' It Old Skool '07
Serial Killing 101 '04

Karl Slovin
On Edge '03
Sex and the Other Man '95

Shawn Slovo (1950-)
Captain Corelli's Mandolin '01
Catch a Fire '06
A World Apart '88

George Sluizer (1932-)
The Vanishing '93
Twice a Woman '79

Adam Small
Malibu's Most Wanted '03
In the Army Now '94
Son-in-Law '93

Craig Smith
Santa Fe Uprising '46
Caracara '00
Persons Unknown '96

Charles Henry Smith (1866-1942)
The General '26
Battling Butler '26

Earl E. Smith
West of Pinto Basin '40
Days of Jesse James '39
Rogue of the Range '36
Everyman's Law '36
Thunder River Feud '42
Tombstone Canyon '32
Saddle Mountain Roundup '41
Range Law '31

Webb Smith
Fantasia '40
Pinocchio '40
Bulldog Drummond '29

Ebbe Roe Smith
Car 54, Where Are You? '94
Falling Down '93

Harold Jacob Smith (1912-70)
Inherit the Wind '99
Inherit the Wind '60
The Defiant Ones '58

Kevin Smith (1970-)
Clerks 2 '06
Jersey Girl '04
Jay and Silent Bob Strike Back '01
Dogma '99
Chasing Amy '97
Mallrats '95
Clerks '94

Kirsten Smith (1970-)
She's the Man '06
Ella Enchanted '04
Legally Blonde '01
Ten Things I Hate about You '99

Lance Smith
Facade '98
Munchies '87
Rescue Me '93

Mark Smith
Seance '07
Vacancy '07

Martin Smith
Under the Rainbow '81
Coyote Ugly '00

Murray Smith
The Art of Crime '75

Robert Smith
Hi, Good Lookin'! '44
Hurry, Charlie, Hurry '41
Battling Butler '26

Richard Smith
Pinochet's Last Stand '06
Agatha Christie: A Life in Pictures '04

Paul Girard Smith (1894-1968)
Girls' Town '59
The Beast from 20,000 Fathoms '53
Invasion U.S.A. '52
Sudden Fear '52
The Second Woman '51
Quicksand '50

Steven Soderbergh (1963-)
Criminal '04
Eros '04
Solaris '02
Schizopolis '97
Nightwatch '96
The Underneath '95
King of the Hill '93
sex, lies and videotape '89

Gerard Soeteman
Black Book '06
Flesh and Blood '85
Soldier of Orange '79
Katie Tippel '75
Turkish Delight '73
Business is Business '71

Carol Sobieski (1939-90)
Money for Nothing '93
Fried Green Tomatoes '91
Sarah, Plain and Tall '91
Winter People '89
The Bourne Identity '88
The Toy '82
Honeysuckle Rose '80

Michael Snyder
D.R.E.A.M. Team '99

Blake Snyder
Blank Check '93
Stop! or My Mom Will Shoot '92

Michael Anthony Snowden
White Chicks '04
Scary Movie 2 '01

Melinda M. Snodgrass
The Outer Limits: Sandkings '95

Norman Snider
Call Me: The Rise and Fall of Heidi Fleiss '04
Rated X '00
Body Parts '91
Dead Ringers '88

Roger Soffer
Merlin's Apprentice '06
Category 7: The End of the World '05

Elena Soarez
City of Men '07
House of Sand '05

Edith Sommer
This Property Is Condemned '66

Stephen Sommers (1962-)
Van Helsing '04
The Scorpion King '02
The Mummy Returns '01
The Mummy '99
Deep Rising '98
Tom and Huck '95
Rudyard Kipling's The Jungle Book '94
The Adventures of Huck Finn '93
Gunmen '93

Michael Sonye
Blood Diner '87
Star Slammer '87

Trish Soodik
Annie: A Royal Adventure '95

Aaron Sorkin (1961-)
Charlie Wilson's War '07
Malice '93
A Few Good Men '92

Lodovico Sorret
See Tom Noonan

Scott Marshall Smith
The Score '01
Men of Honor '00

Sue Smith
The Road from Coorain '02
Brides of Christ '91

Wallace Smith (1888-1937)
The Gay Desperado '36
Lost Squadron '32
The Lady Refuses '31
The Silver Horde '30

Stephen Smoke
Magic Kid '92

Alec Sokolow
Garfield: A Tail of Two Kitties '06
Garfield: The Movie '04
Cheaper by the Dozen '03
Goodbye, Lover '99
Money Talks '97
Toy Story '95

Earle Snell (1886-1965)
Street Crimes '92

Cary Solomon
The Insatiable '06
Earth vs. the Spider '01

Edward Solomon (1961-)
Levity '03
What Planet Are You From? '00
Men in Black '97
Super Mario Bros. '93
Bill & Ted's Bogus Journey '91
Bill & Ted's Excellent Adventure '89

Todd Solondz (1960-)
Palindromes '04
Storytelling '01
Happiness '98

Franco Solinas (1927-82)
Mr. Klein '76
Burn! '70
A Bullet for the General '68
The Battle of Algiers '66
The Wide Blue Road '57

Ken Solarz (1953-)
Supercross: The Movie '05
City of Industry '96

Andrew Solt (1916-90)
This Is Elvis '81
For the First Time '59
In a Lonely Place '50
Little Women '49
They All Kissed the Bride '42

Don Spencer
The Big Doll House '71
The Student Nurses '70

Scott Spencer (1945-)
Father Hood '93
Act of Vengeance '86

Milton Sperling (1912-88)
Merrill's Marauders '62
Happy Landing '38
Thin Ice '37

David Spade (1964-)
The Benchwarmers '06
Joe Dirt '01
Lost and Found '99
Dickie Roberts: Former Child Star '03

David Sparling
Operation Delta Force 3: Clear Target '98
Mission of Death '97
Operation Delta Force 2: Mayday '97

Greg Spence
The Prophecy 2: Ashtown '97
Children of the Corn 4: The Gathering '95

Charles Spaak (1903-75)
L'Idiot '46
Grand Illusion '37
The Lower Depths '36

Ralph Spence (1890-1949)
Down Argentine Way '40
The Flying Deuces '39
Stand Up and Cheer '34

Jack Speirs (1916-2002)
The Bears & I '74

Samuel Spewack (1899-1971)
The Cat and the Fiddle '34
Boy Meets Girl '38
My Favorite Wife '40
Weekend at the Waldorf '45

Bella Spewack (1899-1990)
Weekend at the Waldorf '45
My Favorite Wife '40
Boy Meets Girl '38
The Cat and the Fiddle '34

Penelope Spheeris (1945-)
The Little Rascals '94
The Beverly Hillbillies '93
Wayne's World '92
Suburbia '83
The Decline of Western Civilization '81

Scott Spiegel (1957-)
From Dusk Till Dawn 2: Texas Blood Money '98
Intruder '89
Evil Dead 2: Dead by Dawn '87

Steven Spielberg (1947-)
The Goonies '85
Poltergeist '82
Close Encounters of the Third Kind '77
The Sugarland Express '74
A.I.: Artificial Intelligence '01

Leonard Spigelgass (1908-85)
Gypsy '62
A Majority of One '62

Paul Soter (1972-)
Beerfest '06
Club Dread '04

Joel Soisson
Slow Burn '00
Kazaam '96
Hollow Man 2 '06
Super Troopers '01

Terry Southern (1926-95)
The Telephone '87
End of the Road '70
Easy Rider '69
The Magic Christian '69
Barbarella '68
The Cincinnati Kid '65
The Loved One '65
Dr. Strangelove, or: How I Learned to Stop Worrying and Love the Bomb '64

Spigelgass
A Majority of One '56
Athena '54
I Was a Male War Bride '49
The Perfect Marriage '46
Service De Luxe '38

Evan Spiliotopolos
Art Heist '05

Tony Spiridakis (1959-)
Tinseltown '97
If Lucy Fell '95
The Last Word '95
Queens Logic '91

Marian Spitzer (1899-1983)
Look for the Silver Lining '49
The Dolly Sisters '46

Frank Spotnitz
The X-Files: I Want to Believe '08
The X-Files '98

Mark Spragg
An Unfinished Life '05
Everything That Rises '98

Jill Sprecher
Thirteen Conversations About One Thing '01
Clockwatchers '97

Karen Sprecher
Thirteen Conversations About One Thing '01
Clockwatchers '97

Robin Spry (1939-)
A Cry in the Night '93
Suzanne '80

Hildegarde Stadie
Marihuana '36
Maniac '34

Bima Stagg
Stander '03
Inside '03

C. Ray Stahl (1921-59)
Geisha Girl '52
Scarlet Spear '54

Jerry Stahl (1953-)
Bad Boys 2 '03
Dr. Caligari '89

Laurence Stallings (1894-1968)
She Wore a Yellow Ribbon '49
On Our Merry Way '48
Christmas Eve '47
The Jungle Book '42

Sylvester Stallone (1946-)
Rambo '08
Rocky Balboa '06
Driven '01
Cliffhanger '93
Rocky 5 '90
Rambo 3 '88
Cobra '86
Over the Top '86
Rambo: First Blood, Part 2 '85
Rocky 4 '85
Rhinestone '84
Staying Alive '83
First Blood '82
Rocky 3 '82
Rocky 2 '79
F.I.S.T. '78
Paradise Alley '78
Rocky '76
The Lords of Flatbush '74

Sean Stanek
Played '06

Zac Stanford
Sleepwalking '08
The Chumscrubber '05
A Crack in the Floor '00

Justin Stanley (1973-)
Beneath Loch Ness '01
The Last Assassins '96

Richard Stanley (1966-)
The Island of Dr. Moreau '96
Dust Devil '93

Eliot Stannard (1888-1944)
The Manxman '29
The Lodger '26

Andrew Stanton (1965-)
WALL-E '08
Finding Nemo '03
Monsters, Inc. '01
Toy Story 2 '99
A Bug's Life '98

Jeff Stanzler
Sorry, Haters '05
Jumpin' at the Boneyard '92

Anthony Stark
The Art of Murder '99
The Dogfighters '95

Jim Stark
Factotum '06
Cold Fever '95

Lynn Starling (1888-1955)
The Climax '44
Wintertime '43
Thanks for the Memory '38

Ben Starr
How to Commit Marriage '69
Our Man Flint '66
Texas Across the River '66
The Murderers Are Among Us '46

Jean Stawarz
Spirit Rider '93
Powwow Highway '89

Ray Dennis Steckler (1939-)
Las Vegas Serial Killer '86
The Thrill Killers '65

Burr Steers (1966-)
How to Lose a Guy in 10 Days '03
Igby Goes Down '02

Joseph Stefano (1922-2006)
Psycho '98
Two Bits '96
Psycho 4: The Beginning '90
The Kindred '87
Blackout '78
A Perfect Little Murder '90
The Naked Edge '61
Psycho '60
Black Orchid '59

Darren Stein (1973-)
Sparkler '99
Jawbreaker '98

Jeff Stein
The Perfect Holiday '07
The Kids Are Alright '79

Mark Stein
Housesitter '92

Hank Steinberg (1969-)
RFK '02
61* '01

Michael Steinberg (1959-)
The Cave '05
Sleep with Me '94

Norman Steinberg (1939-)
Funny About Love '90
Johnny Dangerously '84
My Favorite Year '82
Yes, Giorgio '82
Blazing Saddles '74

Reed Steiner
Night of the Scarecrow '95

Peter Steinfeld
21 '08
Be Cool '05
Analyze That '02
Drowning Mona '00

Bill Steinkellner
Disney's Teacher's Pet '04
The Pee-wee Herman Show '82

J. David Stem
Are We There Yet? '05
Shrek 2 '04
Clockstoppers '02
Jimmy Neutron: Boy Genius '01
The Rugrats Movie '98

Gerard Stembridge (1958-)
About Adam '00
Nora '00
Ordinary Decent Criminal '99

Robert A. Stemmle (1903-73)
Apache's Last Battle '64
Testament of Dr. Mabuse '62

Jason Robert Stephens
Merchants of Death '99
Decay '98

Todd Stephens
Gypsy 83 '01
Edge of Seventeen '99

John Steppling
Animal Factory '00
52 Pick-Up '86

David Stern (1909-2003)
Gepetto '00
Swamp Women '55

Henry Stern
Eden '93
Eden 2 '93

Joshua Michael Stern
Swing Vote '08
The Contractor '07

Leonard Stern (1923-)
Missing Pieces '91
Three for the Show '55
Lost in Alaska '52
Abbott and Costello in the Foreign Legion '50
Ma and Pa Kettle Go to Town '50

Noah Stern
The Invisibles '99
The Opposite Sex and How to Live With Them '93

Sandor Stern (1936-)
Web of Deceit '90
Amityville 4: The Evil Escapes '89
Pin... '88

Stewart Stern (1922-)
Summer Wishes, Winter Dreams '73
The Last Movie '71
Rachel, Rachel '68
The Ugly American '63
Rebel without a Cause '55

Patrick Stettner
The Night Listener '06
The Business of Strangers '01

Dana Stevens
Life or Something Like It '02
For Love of the Game '99
City of Angels '98
Blink '93

David Stevens
Jackie, Ethel, Joan: The Kennedy Women '01
Aftershock: Earthquake in New York '99
Dostoevsky's Crime and Punishment '99
Mama Flora's Family '98
Merlin '98
The Thorn Birds: The Missing Years '96
The Sum of Us '94

Gosta Stevens (1897-1964)
Intermezzo '36
The Count of the Old Town '34

Leslie Stevens (1924-98)
Gordy '95
Jungleground '95
Probe '72
Incubus '65

Louis Stevens (1899-1963)
The Border Legion '40
The Texas Rangers '36
Hot Tip '35

Neal Marshall Stevens
Hellraiser: Deader '05
13 Ghosts '01

Robert Stevenson (1905-86)
Jane Eyre '44
Nine Days a Queen '36

Donald Stewart (1930-99)
Dead Silence '96
Clear and Present Danger '94
Patriot Games '92
The Hunt for Red October '90
Missing '82
Death Sport '78
Cannonball '76
Jackson County Jail '76

Donald Ogden Stewart (1894-1980)
An Affair to Remember '57
Escapade '55
Cass Timberlane '47
Life with Father '47
Without Love '45
Forever and a Day '43
Keeper of the Flame '42
Tales of Manhattan '42
That Uncertain Feeling '41
A Woman's Face '41
Love Affair '39
The Night of Nights '39
Holiday '38
Prisoner of Zenda '37
Dinner at Eight '33
Going Hollywood '33

Douglas Day Stewart
The Scarlet Letter '95
Silver Strand '95
Thief of Hearts '84
An Officer and a Gentleman '82
The Blue Lagoon '80
The Boy in the Plastic Bubble '76
Where the Red Fern Grows '74

R.J. Stewart
The Rundown '03
Major League 2 '94

Nicolas Stiliadis
Hot Blooded '98
Red Blooded 2 '96

Ben Stiller (1965-)
Tropic Thunder '08
Zoolander '01

Joe Stillman
Shrek 2 '04
Shrek '01
Beavis and Butt-Head Do America '96

Whit Stillman (1952-)
The Last Days of Disco '98
Barcelona '94
Metropolitan '90

Jeff Stockwell
Bridge to Terabithia '07
The Dangerous Lives of Altar Boys '02

John Stockwell (1961-)
Blue Crush '02
Rock Star '01
Cheaters '00
Breast Men '97

Hugh Stoddart
The Mill on the Floss '97
Trespasser '97

Michael Stokes
Deadline '00
Bram Stoker's Shadowbuilder '98
Sanctuary '98
Sabotage '96
Iron Eagle 4 '95

Josh Stolberg (1971-)
Evan Almighty '07
Good Luck Chuck '07
Kids in America '05

Erik Stolhanske (1968-)
Beerfest '06
Club Dread '04
Super Troopers '01

Bryan Michael Stoller (1960-)
Miss Cast Away '04
Undercover Angel '99

Andrew L. Stone (1902-99)
The Last Voyage '60
The Girl Said No '37

Jerico Stone
Matinee '92
My Stepmother Is an Alien '88

Matt Stone (1971-)
Team America: World Police '04
South Park: Bigger, Longer and Uncut '99

Matthew Stone (1963-)
Man of the House '05
Intolerable Cruelty '03
Big Trouble '02
Life '99
Destiny Turns on the Radio '95

Oliver Stone (1946-)
Alexander '04
Any Given Sunday '99
Evita '96
Nixon '95
Natural Born Killers '94
Heaven and Earth '93
The Doors '91
JFK '91
Born on the Fourth of July '89
Talk Radio '88
Wall Street '87
Platoon '86
Salvador '86
8 Million Ways to Die '85
Year of the Dragon '85
Scarface '83
Conan the Barbarian '82
The Hand '81
Midnight Express '78
Seizure '74

Peter Stone (1930-2003)
The Taking of Pelham One Two Three '74
Father Goose '64
Charade '63

Sherri Stoner (1965-)
My Favorite Martian '98
Casper '95

Lynne Stopkewich (1964-)
Suspicious River '00
Kissed '96

Tom Stoppard (1937-)
Enigma '01
Vatel '00
Shakespeare in Love '98
Billy Bathgate '91
Rosencrantz & Guildenstern Are Dead '90
The Russia House '90
Empire of the Sun '87
Brazil '85

David Storey (1933-)
Early Days '81
In Celebration '75
This Sporting Life '63

Jim Strain
Summer of the Monkeys '98
Bingo '91

Keith W. Strandberg
Bloodmoon '97
No Retreat, No Surrender 3: Blood Brothers '91

Richard Stratton (1946-)
White Boyz '99
Slam '98

John J. Strauss (1957-)
The Santa Clause 3: The Escape Clause '06
The Wild '06
The Lizzie McGuire Movie '03
The Santa Clause 2 '02
There's Something about Mary '98

Robert Strauss
Retroactive '97
Body Shot '93

Gavin Strawhan
Beyond Justice '01
Dead Evidence '00

Arthur Strawn (1900-89)
Flight to Mars '52
The Black Room '35

Wesley Strick (1954-)
Doom '05
The Glass House '01
Hitched '01
Return to Paradise '98
The Saint '97
Wolf '94
Final Analysis '92
Cape Fear '91
Arachnophobia '90
True Believer '89

Max Strom
Shelter '98
American Yakuza '94
Best of the Best 2 '93

Aaron Strongoni
Return of the Living Dead: Rave to the Grave '05
Madhouse '04

Fred Stroppel
A Brooklyn State of Mind '97
Dark Side of Genius '94
Almost Pregnant '91

James C. Strouse
Grace Is Gone '07
Lonesome Jim '06

Barry Strugatz
From Other Worlds '04
She-Devil '89
Married to the Mob '88

Stuart Strutin
Class of Nuke 'Em High '86
First Turn On '83

Jeb Stuart (1961-)
Fire Down Below '97
Switchback '97
Just Cause '94
Another 48 Hrs. '90
Vital Signs '90
Leviathan '89
Lock Up '89
Die Hard '88

Preston Sturges (1898-1959)
I'll Be Yours '47
Miracle of Morgan's Creek '44
The Lady Eve '41
Sullivan's Travels '41
The Great McGinty '40
Remember the Night '40
Never Say Die '39
If I Were King '38
Easy Living '37
The Good Fairy '35
Imitation of Life '34
Thirty Day Princess '34

Charles Sturridge (1951-)
Lassie '05
Shackleton '02
Longitude '00
Where Angels Fear to Tread '91
Aria '88

Burt Styler
Eight on the Lam '67

Boy, Did I Get a Wrong Number! '66

Hel Styverson
Forbidden Sins '99
Indecent Behavior 3 '95

Milton Subotsky (1921-91)
At the Earth's Core '76
Vault of Horror '73
I, Monster '71
Dr. Terror's House of Horrors '65

Greg Suddeth
Pet Shop '94

Henry Sucher (1894-1983)
Jungle Woman '44
The Mummy's Ghost '44
Captive Wild Woman '43
The Mummy's Tomb '42

C. Gardner Sullivan (1884-1965)
Prehysteria '93
Union Pacific '39
Alibi '29
Sparrows '26

Kevin Sullivan (1955-)
Anne of Green Gables: The Continuing Story '99
Looking for Miracles '90
Anne of Avonlea '87
Anne of Green Gables '85

Tim Sullivan
Jack and Sarah '95

Lasse Summanen
Where Angels Fear to Tread '91
A Handful of Dust '88

Walter Summers (1896-1973)
The Human Monster '39
Black Limelight '38

Shirley Sun
Iron & Silk '91
A Great Wall '86

Masayuki Suo (1956-)
Shall We Dance? '04
Shall We Dance? '96

Phoel Sutton
The Fan '96
Mrs. Winterbourne '96

J. Unichi Suzuki
Haunted Highway '05
Remembering the Cosmos Flower '99

Zdenek Sverak (1936-)
Dark Blue World '01
Kolya '96
The Elementary School '91
My Sweet Little Village '86

Garry Swallow
Ice Age: The Meltdown '06
Black Knight '01

Ron Swanson
Say It Isn't So '01

Nick Swardson (1976-)
The Benchwarmers '06
Grandma's Boy '06
Malibu's Most Wanted '03

Roger E. Swaybill (1943-91)
Porky's 2: The Next Day '83

Julia Sweeney (196?-)
It's Pat: The Movie '94

John Sweet
The Affair of the Necklace '01

Tommy Swerdlow (196?-)
Snow Dogs '02
Bushwhacked '95

Michael Swerdlick
Love Don't Cost a Thing '03
Can't Buy Me Love '87

Jo Swerling (1893-1964)
It's a Wonderful Life '46
Leave Her to Heaven '45
Lifeboat '44
Crash Dive '43
The Pride of the Yankees '42
Blood and Sand '41
The Westerner '40
Made for Each Other '39
I Am the Law '38
Double Wedding '37
Pennies from Heaven '36
The Whole Town's Talking '35
Lady by Choice '34
The Mirace Woman '31
Platinum Blonde '31

David Swift (1919-2001)
The Parent Trap '98
Candleshoe '78
How to Succeed in Business without Really Trying '67
Good Neighbor Sam '64
Under the Yum-Yum Tree '63
The Interns '62
The Parent Trap '61
Pollyanna '60

Joe Syracuse (1967-)
Surf's Up '07
Lover Girl '97

Istvan Szabo (1938-)
Sunshine '99
Meeting Venus '91
Mephisto '81
25 Fireman's Street '73
Love Film '70
Father '67

Roy Szeto
The Phantom Lover '95
Wicked City '92
Dragons Forever '88
Mr. Vampire '86

Kam-yuen Szeto
Dog Bite Dog '06
Black Magic '92

Thomas Szollosi
It Waits '05
Bone Daddy '97
Snow White: A Tale of Terror '97

Matthew Tabak
Beyond Suspicion '00
Point of Origin '02
Three O'Clock High '87

Paul Tabori (1908-74)
Paid to Kill '54
Four Sided Triangle '53
Spaceways '53

Jean-Charles Tacchella (1925-)
Blue Country '77
Cousin, Cousine '76

Massy Tadjedin
The Jacket '05
Leo '02

Brian Taggert
Trucks '97
Dangerous Passion '95
What Ever Happened To... '93

Don Tait
The North Avenue Irregulars '79
Unidentified Flying Oddball '79

Koji Takada (1934-)
Return of the Street Fighter '74
The Street Fighter '74

Beat Takeshi
See Takeshi "Beat" Kitano

Igor Talankin
Tchaikovsky '71

Ted Tally (1952-)
Red Dragon '02
All the Pretty Horses '00
The Juror '96
Before and After '95
The Silence of the Lambs '91

Paul Tamasy
Air Bud 2: Golden Receiver '98
Air Bud '97

Nat Tanchuck (1912-78)
Married Too Young '62
Chained for Life '51

Edward Tang (1946-)
Mr. Nice Guy '98
Rumble in the Bronx '96
The Legend of Drunken Master '94
Supercop '92
Operation Condor '91
Operation Condor 2: The Armour of the Gods '86
Project A: Part 2 '87
Project A '83

Alain Tanner (1929-)
In the White City '83
Messidor '77
Jonah Who Will Be 25 in the Year 2000 '76
La Salamandre '71
Charles, Dead or Alive '69

Robert Emmett Tansey (1897-1951)
The Drrftin' Kid '41
Dynamite Canyon '41
Sing, Cowboy, Sing '37
Pinto Rustlers '36
Courage of the North '35
Paradise Canyon '35

Daniel Taplitz
Chaos Theory '08
Breakin' All The Rules '04
Dean Koontz's Black River '01

Daniel Taradash (1913-2003)
The Other Side of Midnight '77
Doctors' Wives '70
Castle Keep '69
Hawaii '66
Bell, Book and Candle '58
Picnic '55
Desiree '54
From Here to Eternity '53
Don't Bother to Knock '52
Rancho Notorious '52
Knock on Any Door '49
Golden Boy '39

Sooni Taraporevala
Mississippi Masala '92
Salaam Bombay! '88

Paul Tarantino
Headhunter '05
News2reak '00

Quentin Tarantino (1963-)
Death Proof '07
Kill Bill Vol. 2 '04
Kill Bill Vol. 1 '03
Jackie Brown '97
Four Rooms '95
From Dusk Till Dawn '95
Pulp Fiction '94
True Romance '93

Andrei Tarkovsky (1932-86)
The Sacrifice '86
Nostalgia '83
The Mirror '75
Solaris '72
Andrei Rublev '66

Frank Tarloff (1916-99)
A Guide for the Married Man '67
Father Goose '64

Susan Tarr
My Sister's Keeper '02
Cousin Bette '97
Get Crazy '83

Robert Tasker (1898-1944)
San Quentin '37
Doctor X '32

Frank Tashlin (1913-72)
Private Navy of Sgt. O'Farrel '68
Caprice '67
Who's Minding the Store? '63
Cinderfella '60
Rock-A-Bye Baby '57
Will Success Spoil Rock Hunter? '57
The Girl Can't Help It '56
Artists and Models '55
Son of Paleface '52
The Lemon Drop Kid '51
The Fuller Brush Girl '50
Kill the Umpire '50
Love Happy '50
One Touch of Venus '48
The Variety Girl '47
A Night in Casablanca '46

Jacques Tati (1908-82)
Parade '74
Traffic '71
Mon Oncle '58
Mr. Hulot's Holiday '53
Jour de Fête '48

Eli Tavor
Dead End Street '83
Secret of Yolanda '82
Hot Bubblegum '81

Gilles Taurand (1943-)
Strayed '03
Time Regained '99
Alice et Martin '98
Dry Cleaning '97
Les Voleurs '96
Wild Reeds '94

Catherine Tavel (1959-)
Night Fire '94
Married People, Single Sex '93

Bertrand Tavernier (1941-)
Holy Lola '04
Safe Conduct '02
Capitaine Conan '96
L'Appat '94
L.627 '92
Life and Nothing But '89
Round Midnight '86
A Sunday in the Country '84
Coup de Torchon '81
Spoiled Children '77
The Judge and the Assassin '75
The Clockmaker '73

Paolo Taviani (1931-)
See Vittorio Taviani

Vittorio Taviani (1929-)
Elective Affinities '96
Fiorile '93
Good Morning, Babylon '87
The Night of the Shooting Stars '82
Kaos '85
Padre Padrone '77
Allonsanfan '73
St. Michael Had a Rooster '72

David Taylor
At Any Cost '00
Inferno '98

Bruce Taylor
The Brave One '07

Delores Taylor
The Trial of Billy Jack '74
Billy Jack '71

Doug Taylor
In the Name of the King: A Dungeon Siege Tale '08

Dwight Taylor (1902-86)
We're Not Married '52
I Wake Up Screaming '41
Rhythm on the River '40
Top Hat '35

Eric Taylor (1897-1952)
Dick Tracy Meets Gruesome '47
Son of Dracula '43
The Phantom of the Opera '43
The Black Cat '41
Black Friday '40

Finn Taylor (1958-)
The Darwin Awards '06
Cherish '02
Dream with the Fishes '97

Greg Taylor
Prancer Returns '01
Summer of the Monkeys '98
The Christmas Box '95
Prancer '89

Jim Taylor (1962-)
I Now Pronounce You Chuck and Larry '07
About Schmidt '02
Jurassic Park 3 '01
Election '99
Citizen Ruth '96

Kenneth Taylor (1922-)
The Camomile Lawn '92
Cause Célèbre '87

Renee Taylor (1935-)
Love Is All There Is '96
Lovers and Other Strangers '70

Roderick Taylor
The Brave One '07

Sam Taylor (1895-1958)
The Freshman '25
Girl Shy '24
Safety Last '23

Samuel A. Taylor (1912-2000)
Topaz '69
Goodbye Again '61
Vertigo '58
The Love Machine '71

S. Lee Taylor
See Steve Taylor

Steve Taylor (1957-)
The Second Chance '06

Pierre Tchernia
The Hades '72
Belle Americaine '61

Andre Techine (1943-)
Changing Times '04
Strayed '03
Alice et Martin '98
Les Voleurs '96
Wild Reeds '94
Ma Saison Preferee '93
Barocco '76

Miguel Tejada-Flores
Screamers '96
Revenge of the Nerds '84

William Templeton
Fright Night 2 '88

Daisuke Tengan (1959-)
Audition '99
Dr. Akagi '98
The Eel '98

Kevin S. Tenney
Endangered Species '02
Witchboard 3: The Possession '95
Witchboard 2: The Devil's Doorway '93
Peacemaker '90
Witchboard '86

Gay Partington Terry
The Toxic Avenger, Part 3: The Last Temptation of Toxie '89
The Toxic Avenger, Part 2 '89

Andy Tennant (1955-)
Fool's Gold '08
Hitch '05
Sweet Home Alabama '02
Anna and the King '99
Ever After: A Cinderella Story '98
It Takes Two '95

John Terlesky (1961-)
The Guardian '00
Supreme Sanction '99

Steve Tesich (1942-96)
American Flyers '85
Eleni '85
The World According to Garp '82
Eyewitness '81
Four Friends '81
Breaking Away '79

Joan Tewkesbury (1936-)
Cold Sassy Tree '89
Nashville '75

Harvey Thew (1883-1946)
She Done Him Wrong '33
The Public Enemy '31

Daniel Therriault (1953-)
Witness Protection '99
First Time Felon '97

Nick Thiel
The Associate '96
V.I. Warshawski '91
White Fang '91
Fire Birds '90
The Experts '89

Robert Thoeren (1903-57)
Singapore '47
Mrs. Parkington '44

Robert Thom (1929-79)
Third Walker '79
Crazy Mama '75
Death Race 2000 '75
Bloody Mama '70
Wild in the Streets '68

Michael Thoma
We'll Meet Again '02
The Set Up '95

Anna Thomas (1948-)
Frida '02
My Family '94
A Time of Destiny '88
El Norte '83
End of August '82

Daniela Thomas
Paris, je t'aime '06
Foreign Land '95

Heidi Thomas
I Capture the Castle '02
Madame Bovary '00
Kiss and Tell '96

Jim Thomas
Mission to Mars '00
Executive Decision '96
Predator 2 '90
The Rescue '88
Predator '87

John Thomas
Mission to Mars '00
Executive Decision '96
Predator 2 '90
The Rescue '88
Predator '87
Escape from Galaxy Three '81

Michael Thomas
The Night We Called It a Day '03
B. Monkey '97
Welcome to Woop Woop '97
Backbeat '94
Deception '92
Scandal '89
Burke & Wills '85
Ladyhawke '85
The Hunger '83

Ralph L. (R.L.) Thomas (1939-)
A Young Connecticut Yankee in King Arthur's Court '95
Young Ivanhoe '95

Scott Thomas
Flight of the Living Dead: Outbreak on a Plane '07
Deranged '01

Camille Thomasson
Luther '03
The Disappearance of Christina '93

Brett Thompson
Blood Angels '05
The Glass Trap '04
Britanic '99

Caroline Thompson (1956-)
Tim Burton's Corpse Bride '05
Snow White: The Fairest of Them All '02
Buddy '97
Black Beauty '94
Homeward Bound: The Incredible Journey '93
The Nightmare before Christmas '93
The Secret Garden '93
The Addams Family '91
Edward Scissorhands '90

Christopher Thompson (1969-)
Jet Lag '02
La Buche '00

Daniele Thompson (1942-)
Avenue Montaigne '06
Jet Lag '02
La Buche '00
Those Who Love Me Can Take the Train '98
Queen Margot '94

Donald G. Thompson (1938-)
The Evil '78
Project: Kill! '77

Emma Thompson (1959-)
Nanny McPhee '06
Wit '01
Sense and Sensibility '95

Ernest Thompson (1949-)
Out of Time '00
1969 '89
Sweet Hearts Dance '88
On Golden Pond '81

Galen Thompson
See Donald G. Thompson

Gary Scott Thompson (1959-)
88 Minutes '08
Timecop 2: The Berlin Decision '03
The Fast and the Furious '01
K-9: P.I. '01
K-911 '99

Keene Thompson (1886-1937)
Love in Bloom '35
Palmy Days '31

Peggy Thompson
Better Than Chocolate '99
The Lotus Eaters '93

Rob Thompson
The Cowboy Way '94
Ratboy '86
Hearts of the West '75

Billy Bob Thornton (1955-)
Camouflage '00
The Gift '00
Daddy & Them '99
Don't Look Back '96
A Family Thing '96
Sling Blade '96
Some Folks Call It a Sling Blade '94
One False Move '91

Ralph Thornton
See Aben Kandel

George Tibbles (1913-87)
How to Frame a Figg '71
Munster, Go Home! '66

Ernest Tidyman (1928-84)
Stark '85
High Plains Drifter '73
Shaft's Big Score '72
The French Connection '71
Shaft '71

Gary Tieche
The First $20 Million is Always the Hardest '02
Nevada '97
Just like Heaven '05
Analyze That '02
Stealing Harvard '02
America's Sweethearts '01
Bedazzled '00
What Planet Are You From? '00
Analyze This '98
My Fellow Americans '96

George Toles (1948-)
Brand Upon the Brain! '06
The Saddest Music in the World '03
Careful '92

Jonathan Tolins
Martian Child '07
The Twilight of the Golds '97

Michael Tolkin (1950-)
Changing Lanes '02
Deep Impact '98
The Burning Season '94
The New Age '94
Deep Cover '92
The Player '92
The Rapture '91
Gleaming the Cube '89

Neil Tolkin
The Emperor's Club '02
Sticks and Stones '96

Stephen Tolkin
Carolina Moon '07
Fidel '02
Dean Koontz's Mr. Murder '98
Daybreak '93
Captain America '89

Maurice Tombragel (1913-2000)
Kentucky Jubilee '51
Last Bullet '50
Motor Patrol '50
Outlaw Fury '50
Rangeland Empire '50
Sudden Death '50
Sky Liner '49
The Prince of Thieves '48

Stanley Tong (1960-)
Jackie Chan's First Strike '96
Supercop 2 '93

Jerome Tonnerre
My Best Friend '06
Intimate Strangers '04
On Guard! '93
Un Coeur en Hiver '93

Rhet Topham
976-EVIL '88
Trick or Treat '86

Roland Topor
Marquis '90
Fantastic Planet '73

Tom Topor
Perfect Murder, Perfect Town '00
Judgment '90
The Accused '88
Nuts '87

Burt Topper (1928-2007)
The Hard Ride '71
Tank Commando '59

Tracy Torme (1959-)
Fire in the Sky '93
The Spellbinder '88

Giuseppe Tornatore (1956-)
Malena '00
The Legend of 1900 '98
The Star Maker '95
A Pure Formality '94
Everybody's Fine '90
Cinema Paradiso '88

Antonio Toro
Amityville: A New Generation '93
Amityville 1992: It's About Time '92

Peter Torokvei
Guarding Tess '94
Hostage for a Day '94
Caddyshack 2 '88
Armed and Dangerous '86
Back to School '86
Real Genius '85

Fina Torres (1951-)
Celestial Clockwork '94
Oriana '85

Ivan Tors (1916-83)
Island of the Lost '68
Song of Love '68

Laura Toscano
The Sicilian Connection '85
Deadly Mission '78

Wellyn Totman (1903-77)
Fighting Champ '33
Riders of the Desert '32
Texas Pioneers '32

Harry Alan Towers (1920-)
Queen's Messenger II '01
Bullet to Beijing '95
The Mangler '94
Black Venus '83
Call of the Wild '72
Count Dracula '71
The Castle of Fu Manchu '68

Gene Towne (1904-79)
Joy of Living '38
You Only Live Once '37

Robert Towne (1936-)
Ask the Dust '06
Mission: Impossible 2 '00
Without Limits '97
Mission: Impossible '96
Love Affair '94
Days of Thunder '90
The Two Jakes '90
Tequila Sunrise '88
Personal Best '82
Shampoo '75
The Yakuza '75
Chinatown '74
The Last Detail '73
Villa Rides '68
Tomb of Ligeia '64
The Last Woman on Earth '61

Roger Towne
The Recruit '03
In the Company of Spies '99
The Natural '84

Leo Townsend (1908-87)
Fireball 500 '66
Beach Blanket Bingo '65
How to Stuff a Wild Bikini '65
Bikini Beach '64
Dangerous Crossing '53
It Started with Eve '41

Robert Kevin Townsend (1957-)
The Meteor Man '93
The Five Heartbeats '91
Hollywood Shuffle '87

Michael Traeger
The Moguls '05

Bill Travers (1922-94)
An Elephant Called Slowly '69
Ring of Bright Water '69

Joey Travolta (1952-)
To the Limit '95
Hard Vice '94
Vegas Vice '94

Caspian Tredwell-Owen
The Island '05
Beyond Borders '03

Monika Treut (1954-)
Erotique '94
My Father Is Coming '91
Virgin Machine '88

Dale Trevillion
Beyond Desire '94
One Man Force '89
Las Vegas Weekend '85

Lawrence Trilling
Delivered '98
Dinner and Driving '97

Dorothy Tristan (1942-)
Suspended Animation '02
Weeds '87

Victor Trivas (1896-1970)
The Head '59
The Stranger '46

Anne-Louise Trividic
Gabrielle '05
Intimacy '00

Pierre Trividic
Lady Chatterley '06
Those Who Love Me Can Take the Train '98

Rose Troche
The Safety of Objects '01
Go Fish '94

Jan Troell (1931-)
The New Land '73
The Emigrants '72

Guy Trosper (1911-63)
The Spy Who Came in from the Cold '65
Birdman of Alcatraz '62
Darby's Rangers '58
The Stratton Story '49
Jailhouse Rock '57

Lamar Trotti (1900-52)
With a Song in My Heart '52
I'd Climb the Highest Mountain '51
Cheaper by the Dozen '50
My Blue Heaven '50
Captain from Castile '47
Mother Wore Tights '47
The Razor's Edge '46
Wilson '44
Guadalcanal Diary '43
Immortal Sergeant '43
The Ox-Bow Incident '43
Thunder Birds '42
Brigham Young: Frontiersman '40
The Story of Alexander Graham Bell '39
Young Mr. Lincoln '39
Alexander's Ragtime Band '38
In Old Chicago '37
Life Begins at Forty '35
Steamboat Round the Bend '35

David Trueba
The Girl of Your Dreams '99
Dance with the Devil '97
Two Much '96

Guerdon (Gordon) Trueblood
The Chase '91
The Bastard '78
Terror Out of the Sky '78

Francois Truffaut (1932-84)
Confidentially Yours '83
The Last Metro '80
The Man Who Loved Women '77
Small Change '76
Day for Night '73
Two English Girls '72
Bed and Board '70
The Wild Child '70
Mississippi Mermaid '69
The Bride Wore Black '68
Stolen Kisses '68
Fahrenheit 451 '66
The Soft Skin '64
Jules and Jim '62
Shoot the Piano Player '62
The 400 Blows '59
Les Mistons '57

Dalton Trumbo (1905-76)
Papillon '73
Johnny Got His Gun '71
The Horsemen '70
The Fixer '68
Hawaii '66
Lonely Are the Brave '62
Exodus '60
Spartacus '60
Terror in a Texas Town '58
The Brave One '56
Roman Holiday '53
Prowler '51
Rocketship X-M '50
Gun Crazy '49
Our Vines Have Tender Grapes '45
A Guy Named Joe '44
Thirty Seconds Over Tokyo '44
The Flying Irishman '39

Alan R. Trustman (1930-)
The Arab Conspiracy '76
Hit! '73
Lady Ice '73
They Call Me Mr. Tibbs! '70
Bullitt '68
The Thomas Crown Affair '68

Glenn Tryon (1894-1970)
Lawmen '44
Small Town Boy '37
Bachelor Bait '34

Ming-liang Tsai
Goodbye, Dragon Inn '03
What Time Is It There? '01

Kan-Cheung (Sammy) Tsang
Kung Fu Hustle '04
Shaolin Soccer '01

Shinya Tsukamoto (1960-)
Tetsuo 2: Body Hammer '97
Tetsuo: The Iron Man '92

Stanley Tucci (1960-)
Joe Gould's Secret '00
The Imposters '98
Big Night '95

James Tucker
Steps from Hell '92
Lunatic '91

Larry Tucker (1933-2001)
Alex in Wonderland '70
Bob & Carol & Ted & Alice '69
I Love You, Alice B. Toklas! '68

Harry Tugend (1897-1989)
Who's Minding the Store? '63
Pocketful of Miracles '61
Take Me Out to the Ball Game '49
Star Spangled Rhythm '42
Birth of the Blues '41
Caught in the Draft '41
Seven Sinners '40
Second Fiddle '39
My Lucky Star '38
Thanks for Everything '38
Pigskin Parade '36

Jim Tully (1891-1947)
The Raven '35
Beggars of Life '28

Karl Tunberg (1909-92)
The Seventh Dawn '64
Ben-Hur '59
Beau Brummel '54
Valley of the Kings '54
Up in Central Park '48
You Gotta Stay Happy '48
Week-End in Havana '41
Down Argentine Way '40

Gary J. Tunnicliffe (1968)
Megalodon '03
The Guardian '00
Within the Rock '96

Ann Turner (1960-)
Irresistible '06
The Killing Beach '92
Hammers over the Anvil '91

Barbara Turner
The Company '03
Pollock '00
Georgia '95
War Between the Tates '76

Bonnie Turner (1968-)
The Brady Bunch Movie '95
Tommy Boy '95
Coneheads '93
Wayne's World 2 '93
Wayne's World '92

Guinevere Turner (1968-)
BloodRayne '06
The Notorious Bettie Page '06
American Psycho '00
Go Fish '94

Sheldon Turner
The Texas Chainsaw Massacre: The Beginning '06

Terry Turner
The Longest Yard '05
The Brady Bunch Movie '95
Tommy Boy '95
Coneheads '93
Wayne's World 2 '93
Wayne's World '92

Catherine Turney (1906-98)
Cry Wolf '47
The Man I Love '46
My Reputation '46

John Turturro (1957-)
Romance & Cigarettes '05
Illuminata '98
Mac '93

Derek Twist (1905-79)
Angels One Five '54

John Twist (1898-1976)
The FBI Story '59
Band of Angels '57
Helen of Troy '56
King Richard and the Crusaders '54
Pittsburgh '42

David N. Twohy (1955-)
The Chronicles of Riddick '04
Below '02
Impostor '02
Pitch Black '00
G.I. Jane '97
The Arrival '96
Waterworld '95
Terminal Velocity '94
The Fugitive '93
Grand Tour: Disaster in Time '92
Warlock '91
Critters 2: The Main Course '88

Jonathan Tydor
The King's Guard '01
The Hard Truth '94

Tom Tykwer (1965-)
Paris, je t'aime '06
Perfume: The Story of a Murderer '05
The Princess and the Warrior '00
Run Lola Run '98
Winter Sleepers '97

Steve Tymon (1956-)
Hindsight '97
Mirror, Mirror 3: The Voyeur '96
Dark Secrets '95

Jim Uhls
Fight Club '99
Jumper '08

Bob Tzudiker
Anastasia '97
Tarzan 2 '05
102 Dalmatians '00
Tarzan '99
The Hunchback of Notre Dame '96
Newsies '92

Keinosuke Uegusa
Drunken Angel '48
One Wonderful Sunday '47

Alfred Uhry (1936-)
Rich in Love '93
Driving Miss Daisy '89
Mystic Pizza '88

Daniel Ullman (1918-79)
Wyatt Earp: Return to Tombstone '94
Mysterious Island '61
The Gunfight at Dodge City '59
Good Day for a Hanging '58
An Annapolis Story '55
Square Dance Jubilee '51
Red Desert '50
Ringside '49

Elwood Ullman (1903-85)
Snow White and the Three Stooges '61
The Three Stooges Meet Hercules '61
Ma and Pa Kettle at Waikiki '55
The Stooge '51

Liv Ullmann (1939-)
Kristin Lavransdatter '95
Sofie '92

John Van Druten (1901-57)
Gaslight '44
Night Must Fall '37

Gladys Unger (1885-1940)
The Mystery of Edwin Drood '35
Sylvia Scarlett '35
Great Expectations '34

Eve Unsell (1887-1937)
The Plastic Age '25
Shadows '22

Leon Uris (1924-2003)
Gunfight at the O.K. Corral '57
Battle Cry '55

Peter Ustinov (1921-2004)
Hot Millions '68
Lady L '65
Billy Budd '62

Pierre Uytterhoeven (1921-)
And Now Ladies and Gentlemen '02
Bandits '86
Happy New Year '73
A Man and a Woman '66

Roger Vadim (1928-2000)
Barbarella '68
Spirits of the Dead '68
The Game Is Over '66
Love on a Pillow '62
Blood and Roses '61
Please Not Now! '61
Dangerous Liaisons '60
Sois Belle et Tais-Toi '58
And God Created Woman '57

Laszlo Vadnay (1904-67)
The Great Rupert '50
Copacabana '47
Uncertain Glory '44

Ernest Vajda (1886-1954)
The Smiling Lieutenant '31
Tonight or Never '31
Monte Carlo '30
The Love Parade '29

Agnes Varda (1928-)
One Hundred and One Nights '95
Vagabond '85
Le Bonheur '65
Cleo from 5 to 7 '61

Michael Varhol
The Big Picture '89
Pee-wee's Big Adventure '85
The Last Word '80

Nia Vardalos (1962-)
Connie and Carla '04
My Big Fat Greek Wedding '02

Ladislao Vajda (1906-65)
The Miracle of Marcelino '55
The Threepenny Opera '31

Luis Valdez (1940-)
The Cisco Kid '94
La Bamba '87
Zoot Suit '81

Val Valentine (1895-1971)
The Belles of St. Trinian's '53
My Son, the Vampire '52

Vincent Valentini
Sepia Cinderella '47
Murder on Lenox Avenue '41

Nick Vallelonga (1959-)
The Corporate Ladder '97
In the Land of the Blind
the Man with One Eye is King '94

Jean-Claude Van Damme (1961-)
Double Impact '91

Jaco Van Dormael (1957-)
The Eighth Day '95
Toto le Heros '91

Dale Van Every (1896-1976)
Souls at Sea '37
Wings in the Dark '35
Murders in the Rue Morgue '32

Mario Van Peebles (1958-)
Panther '95
Love Kills '98
Baadasssss! '03

Melvin Van Peebles (1932-)
Panther '95
Sophisticated Gents '81
Greased Lightning '77
Sweet Sweetback's Baadasssss Song '71
The Story of a Three Day Pass '68

Gus Van Sant (1952-)
Paranoid Park '07
Last Days '05
Elephant '03
Gerry '02
Even Cowgirls Get the Blues '94
My Own Private Idaho '91
Drugstore Cowboy '89

Andrew Van Slee (1965-)
Net Games '03

Virginia Van Upp (1902-70)
Bahama Passage '42
Young and Willing '42
You and Me '38

Norman Vance, Jr.
Roll Bounce '05
Pride '07

James Vanderbilt
The Rundown '03
Darkness Falls '03
Basic '03
Zodiac '07

Michael Vickerman
SuperFire '02
Warriors of Virtue '97

Joseph B. Vasquez (1962-95)
Manhattan Merengue! '95
Hangin' with the Homeboys '91
Bronx War '91

Francis Veber (1937-)
The Valet '06
The Dinner Game '98
The Closet '00
My Father the Hero '93
Three Fugitives '89
Les Comperes '83
Partners '82
La Cage aux Folles 2 '81
Hothead '78
La Cage aux Folles '78
Le Magnifique '76

Anthony Veiller (1903-65)
The Night of the Iguana '64
Moulin Rouge '52
Red Planet Mars '52
The Killers '46
The Stranger '46

David Veloz
Behind Enemy Lines '01
Permanent Midnight '98

Louis Venosta
Kisses in the Dark '97
The Last Dragon '85

Jeffrey Ventimiglia
Paper Clips '04

Michael Ventura
Echo Park '86
Roadie '80

Luis Enrique Vergara
The Fear Chamber '68
The Sinister Invasion '68

Michael Verhoeven
My Mother's Courage '95
The Nasty Girl '90
The White Rose '83

Paul Verhoeven (1938-)
Black Book '06
Flesh and Blood '85
The 4th Man '83
Soldier of Orange '78

Henri Verneuil (1920-2002)
Any Number Can Win '63
Forbidden Fruit '52

Todd Verow (1966-)
Little Shots of Happiness '97
Frisk '95

Richard Vetere
How to Go Out on a Date in Queens '06

Daniel Ullman — (see above)

John Varley (1947-)
Millennium '89

Peter Viertel (1920-2007)
White Hunter, Black Heart '90
The Old Man and the Sea '58
Saboteur '42

Daniel Vigne (1942-)
The King's Whore '90
One Woman or Two '85
The Return of Martin Guerre '83

Jean Vigo (1905-34)
L'Atalante '34
Zero for Conduct '33
A Propos de Nice '29

Anne Vince
MXP: Most Xtreme Primate '03
MVP2: Most Vertical Primate '01
MVP (Most Valuable Primate) '00

Robert Vince
Snow Buddies '08
Air Bud 6: Air Buddies '06
MXP: Most Xtreme Primate '03
MVP2: Most Vertical Primate '01
MVP (Most Valuable Primate) '00
The Duke '99

Christian Vincent (1955-)
La Separation '98
La Discrete '90

Luciano Vincenzoni
Orca '77
The Rover '67
For a Few Dollars More '65
The Good, the Bad and the Ugly '67
Escape from Death Row '73
Spaghetti Western '75

Dino Vindeni
Moonbase '97
Little Witches '96
Voodoo '95
The Demolitionist '95
Bertha's '75
Coup de Grace '78
The Second Awakening of Christa Klages '78

Dan Vining
Black Dog '98

Joe Viola
Subway Stories '97
Mondo Balordo '64
Hot Box '72
Angels Hard As They Come '71

Jeff Vintar (1964-)
I, Robot '04
Final Fantasy: The Spirits Within '01

Albert T. Viola
Preacherman '83

Dino Vindeni — (see above)

Clement Virgo (1966-)
Love Come Down '00
Junior's Groove '97
Rude '96

Chris Viscardi
Snow Day '00

Mark Victor
Cool World '92
Marked for Death '90
Poltergeist III '88
Poltergeist II: The Other Side '86
Poltergeist '82
Side '86

Barry Victor
Cyborg 3: The Recycler '95
Red Scorpion 2 '94

Luchino Visconti (1906-76)
The Innocent '76
Conversation Piece '76
Ludwig '72
Death in Venice '71
Sandra of a Thousand Delights '65
The Leopard '63
Boccaccio '70 '62
Rocco and His Brothers '60
White Nights '57
Bellissima '51

Gore Vidal (1925-)
The Palermo Connection '90
Caligula '80
Dress Gray '86
Is Paris Burning? '66
The Best Man '64
Suddenly, Last Summer '59
The Catered Affair '56

King Vidor (1894-1982)
War and Peace '56
Our Daily Bread '34

Peter Viertel (1920-2007) — (see above)

Jon Vitti
Alvin and the Chipmunks '07
The Simpsons Movie '07

John Vlahos (1916-2004)
Rock River Renegades '42
Thunder River Feud '42
Saddle Mountain Roundup '41
Tonto Basin Outlaws '41

Jesse Vogel
Therese & Isabelle '67
Carmen, Baby '66

Stephen Volk (1954-)
The Guardian '90
Gothic '87
Fulse '03

Karl Vollmoller (1878-1948)
The Blue Angel '30

Thea von Harbou (1886-1954)
Metropolis '26
M '31

Lars von Trier (1956-)
The Boss of It All '06
Dear Wendy '05
Manderlay '05
Dogville '03
Dancer in the Dark '00
The Idiots '99
Breaking the Waves '95
The Kingdom 2 '97
The Kingdom '95
Zentropa '92
Medea '88
The Element of Crime '84

Josef von Sternberg (1894-1969)
The Shanghai Gesture '42
Dishonored '31

Erich von Stroheim (1885-1957)
The Wedding March '28
Greed '24
Foolish Wives '22
Queen Kelly '29
Devil Doll '36
Blind Husbands '19

Margarethe von Trotta (1942-)
Rosenstrasse '03
The Promise '94
Rosa Luxemburg '86
Sheer Madness '84
Marianne and Juliane '82
Sisters, Or the Balance of Happiness '79

Linda Voorhees
California Dreaming '07
Raising Genius '04

Cyrus Voris
Bulletproof Monk '03
Sleeper Cell '05

Louis Vittes (1911-69)
I Married a Monster from Outer Space '58
Monster from Green Hell '58
Showdown at Boot Hill '58
The Rebel Set '59

Niels Vorsel (1953-)
The Kingdom 2 '97
The Kingdom '95
Zentropa '92
The Element of Crime '84

Kurt Voss (1963-)
Things Behind the Sun '01
Sugar Town '99
Highway Hitcher '98
Baja '95
Where the Day Takes You '92
Delusion '91
Genuine Risk '89
Border Radio '88

William W. Vought
Stricken '98

Andy Wachowski (1967-)
Speed Racer '08
V for Vendetta '06
The Matrix Reloaded '03
The Matrix Revolutions '03
The Matrix '99
Bound '96
Assassins '95

Larry Wachowski (1965-)
Speed Racer '08
V for Vendetta '06
The Matrix Reloaded '03
The Matrix Revolutions '03
The Matrix '99
Bound '96
Assassins '95

Natto Wada (1920-83)
An Actor's Revenge '63
Fires on the Plain '59
Enjo '58
The Burmese Harp '56

Kevin Wade (1954-)
Maid in Manhattan '02
Meet Joe Black '98
Junior '94
Mr. Baseball '92
Working Girl '88

Robert Wade (1962-)
Casino Royale '06
Stoned '05
Convicted '04
Johnny English '03
Die Another Day '02
The World Is Not Enough '99
Plunkett & Macleane '98
Let Him Have It '91

Annette Wademant (1928-)
Voulez-Vous Danser avec Moi? '59
Une Parisienne '58
The Earrings of Madame De... '54

Maggie Wadey
Mansfield Park '07
The Buccaneers '95
Northanger Abbey '87
The Duchess of Duke Street '78

George Waggner (1894-1984)
The Fatal Hour '40
Phantom of Chinatown '40
Stunt Pilot '39
Wolf Call '39
The Spy Ring '38
Three Legionnaires '37

Andrew Wagner
Starting Out in the Evening '07

David T. Wagner
Underclassman '05
The Girl Next Door '04
My Baby's Daddy '04
National Lampoon's Van Wilder '02

Jane Wagner (1935-)
Search for Signs of Intelligent Life in the Universe '91
The Incredible Shrinking Woman '81

David Wain
The Ten '07
Wet Hot American Summer '01

Andrzej Wajda (1927-)
Zemsta '02
A Love in Germany '84
Danton '82
Without Anesthesia '78
Land of Promise '74
Landscape After Battle '70
Everything for Sale '68
Lotna '64
Innocent Sorcerers '60
Ashes and Diamonds '58

Tokuhei Wakao (1918-)
Samurai 3: Duel at Ganryu Island '56
Samurai 1: Musashi Miyamoto '55

Eliot Wald (1946-2003)
Down Periscope '96
Camp Nowhere '94
See No Evil, Hear No Evil '89

Jerry Wald
Torrid Zone '40
Sing Me a Love Song '37

Malvin Wald (1917-2008)
The Legend of Sleepy Hollow '79
Venus in Furs '70
Behind Locked Doors '48
Human Gorilla '48

Frank Waldman (1919-90)
Trail of the Pink Panther '82
Revenge of the Pink Panther '78
The Pink Panther Strikes Again '76
Return of the Pink Panther '74
Inspector Clouseau '68

Andrew Kevin Walker (1964-)
Sleepy Hollow '99
8mm '98
Seven '95
Brainscan '94
Hideaway '94

H.M. Walker
Laurel & Hardy: Be Big '31
Laurel & Hardy: Chickens Come Home '31
Laurel & Hardy: Another Fine Mess '30
Laurel & Hardy: Below Zero '30
Laurel & Hardy: Blotto '30
Laurel & Hardy: Brats '30
Laurel & Hardy: Hog Wild '30
Laurel & Hardy: Night Owls '30
Laurel & Hardy: Berth Marks '29
Laurel & Hardy: Men O'War '29
Laurel & Hardy: Perfect Day '29
Laurel & Hardy: The Hoose-Gow '29

Michael Walker
Chasing Sleep '00
Relative Values '99

Gary Walkow
Beat '00
Notes from Underground '95
The Trouble with Dick '88

Jake Wade Wall
The Hitcher '07
When a Stranger Calls '06

Earl W. Wallace
Rose Hill '97
The Broken Chain '93
Witness '85

Irving Wallace (1916-90)
Sincerely Yours '56
Split Second '53
The West Point Story '50

Pamela Wallace
Love's Unending Legacy '07
Though None Go With Me '06

Randall Wallace (1949-)
We Were Soldiers '02
Pearl Harbor '01
The Man in the Iron Mask '98
Braveheart '95

Tommy Lee Wallace (1949-)
John Carpenter Presents Vampires: Los Muertos '02
Fright Night 2 '88
Amityville 2: The Possession '82
Halloween 3: Season of the Witch '82

Ira Wallach (1913-95)
Hot Millions '68
Boys' Night Out '62

Anthony Waller (1959-)
An American Werewolf in Paris '97
Mute Witness '95

Hugh Walpole (1884-1941)
Little Lord Fauntleroy '36
David Copperfield '35

Bill Walsh (1913-75)
Bedknobs and Broomsticks '71
Blackbeard's Ghost '67
Mary Poppins '64
The Absent-Minded Professor '61

Fran Walsh (1959-)
King Kong '05
Lord of the Rings: The Return of the King '03
Lord of the Rings: The Two Towers '02
Lord of the Rings: The Fellowship of the Rings '01
The Frighteners '96
Heavenly Creatures '94
Dead Alive '93
Meet the Feebles '89

Matthew Jason Walsh (1970-)
Ring of Darkness '04
Witchouse '99

Raoul Walsh (1887-1981)
Esther and the King '60
Big Brown Eyes '36
Sadie Thompson '28

Fred Walton
When a Stranger Calls Back '93
Trapped '89
The Rosary Murders '87
Hadley's Rebellion '84
When a Stranger Calls '79

Bin Wang
House of Flying Daggers '04
Hero '03

Hui-Ling Wang
Fleeing by Night '00
Eat Drink Man Woman '94

Peter Wang
The Laserman '90
A Great Wall '86

Wayne Wang (1949-)
The Center of the World '01
The Chinese Box '97
Blue in the Face '95
Chan Is Missing '82

Xiaoshuai Wang (1966-)
Beijing Bicycle '01
Frozen '98
So Close to Paradise '98

David S. Ward (1947-)
Flyboys '06
The Program '93
Sleepless in Seattle '93
King Ralph '91
Major League '89
The Milagro Beanfield War '88
Saving Grace '86
The Sting '83
Cannery Row '82
Steelyard Blues '73
The Sting '73

Donal Lardner Ward (1964-)
My Life's in Turnaround '94
The Suburbans '99

Edmund Ward (1928-93)
Prayer for the Dying '87
Twinsanity '70

Jason Ward
Deuce Bigalow: European Gigolo '05
Corky Romano '01

Kelly Ward (1956-)
All Dogs Go to Heaven 2 '95
Once Upon a Forest '93

Morgan Ward
Riding in Cars with Boys '01
A Pyromaniac's Love Story '95

Vincent Ward (1956-)
Map of the Human Heart '93
The Navigator '88
Vigil '84

David Warfield
Kiss of a Killer '93
Kill Me Again '89
P.I. Private Investigations '87

Regis Wargnier (1948-)
East-West '99
Indochine '92

Dave Warner (1953-)
Garage Days '03
Cut '00

Jerry Warren (1921-88)
The Wild World of Batwoman '66
Terror of the Bloodhunters '62
Teenage Zombies '58

John Warren (1953-)
Major League 3: Back to the Minors '98
The Curse of Inferno '96
Flashfire '94
Girl in the Cadillac '94
Naked in New York '93

Deric Washburn
Extreme Prejudice '87
The Border '82
The Deer Hunter '78
Silent Running '71

Art Washington
Hendrix '00
Percy & Thunder '93

Wendy Wasserstein (1950-2006)
Trial by Media '00
The Object of My Affection '98
The Heidi Chronicles '95
Sorrows of Gin '79

Keith Waterhouse (1929-)
Charlie Muffin '79
Billy Liar '63

John Waters (1946-)
A Dirty Shame '04
Cecil B. Demented '00
Pecker '98
Serial Mom '94
Cry-Baby '90
Hairspray '88
Polyester '81
Desperate Living '77
Female Trouble '74
Pink Flamingos '72
Multiple Maniacs '70
Mondo Trasho '69

Lawrence Edward Watkin (1901-81)
Darby O'Gill & the Little People '59
The Great Locomotive Chase '56

Maurine Watkins (1896-1969)
Libeled Lady '36
No Man of Her Own '32
Up the River '30

Carol Watson
Crazylove '05
Friday the 13th, Part 3 '82

John Watson
Robin Hood: Prince of Thieves '91
The Zoo Gang '85

Kim Watson
Honey '03
What About Your Friends: Weekend Getaway '02

Damon Wayans (1960-)
Major Payne '95
Blankman '94
Mo' Money '92

Keenen Ivory Wayans (1958-)
Little Man '06
White Chicks '04
Most Wanted '97
A Low Down Dirty Shame '94
The Five Heartbeats '91
I'm Gonna Git You Sucka '88
Hollywood Shuffle '87

Marlon Wayans (1972-)
Little Man '06
White Chicks '04
Scary Movie 2 '01
Scary Movie '00
Don't Be a Menace to South Central While Drinking Your Juice in the Hood '95

Shawn Wayans (1971-)
Little Man '06
White Chicks '04
Scary Movie 2 '01
Scary Movie '00
Don't Be a Menace to South Central While Drinking Your Juice in the Hood '95

Frank Wead (1895-1947)
They Were Expendable '45
Dive Bomber '41
Ceiling Zero '35

James R. Webb (1910-74)
The Organization '71
How the West Was Won '63
Kings of the Sun '63
Pork Chop Hill '59
The Big Country '58
Vera Cruz '53
Bad Man of Deadwood '41
Nevada City '41

Steven Weber (1961-)
Masters of Horror: Jenifer '05
Club Land '01

M. Coates Webster (1903-55)
Night Riders of Montana '50
The Brute Man '46
Jungle Captive '45
Strange Confession '45

David Wechter (1956-)
Malibu Bikini Shop '86
Midnight Madness '80

Bob Wehling (1919-83)
Eegah! '62
Wild Guitar '62

Lo Wei (1918-96)
New Fist of Fury '76
Chinese Connection '73
Fists of Fury '73

Lu Wei
To Live '94
Farewell My Concubine '93

John Weidner
Midnight Kiss '93
Private Wars '93

Samuel Weil
See Lloyd Kaufman

Herschel Weingrod (1947-)
Pure Luck '91
Kindergarten Cop '90
My Stepmother Is an Alien '88
Twins '88
Brewster's Millions '85
Trading Places '83
Cheaper to Keep Her '80

Peter Weir (1944-)
Master and Commander: The Far Side of the World '03
Green Card '90
The Year of Living Dangerously '82
Gallipoli '81
Plumber '79
The Last Wave '77
The Cars That Ate Paris '74

Brenda Weisberg
Rusty's Birthday '49
The Mummy's Ghost '44
The Mad Ghoul '43

David Weisberg
Double Jeopardy '99
Holy Matrimony '94

Stanley Weiser
Rudy: The Rudy Giuliani Story '03
Freedom Song '00
Witness to the Mob '98
Fatherland '94
Project X '87
Wall Street '87

David Weisman (1942-)
Shogun Assassin '80
Edie in Ciao! Manhattan '72

Straw Weisman
Fight for Your Life '77
Toga Party '77

Allan Weiss
Paradise, Hawaiian Style '66
Sons of Katie Elder '65

David N. Weiss
Daddy Day Camp '07
Are We There Yet? '05
Shrek 2 '04
Clockstoppers '02
Jimmy Neutron: Boy Genius '01
Rugrats in Paris: The Movie '00
The Rugrats Movie '98
Rock-a-Doodle '92
All Dogs Go to Heaven '89

Eric Weiss
Buffalo Soldiers '01
Bongwater '98
Wicked '98

Jiri Weiss (1913-2004)
Martha and I '91
Murder Czech Style '66
The Coward '62
Wolf Trap '57

Michael D. Weiss
Journey to the Center of the Earth 3D '08
The Butterfly Effect 2 '06
Octopus 2: River of Fear '02
U.S. Seals 2 '01
Crocodile '00
Octopus '00

David Weissman
Evolution '01
Family Man '00
Dream a Little Dream 2 '94

Chris Weitz (1970-)
The Golden Compass '07
About a Boy '02

Nutty Professor 2: The Klumps '00
Antz '98
Madeline '98

Paul Weitz (1966-)
American Dreamz '06
In Good Company '04
About a Boy '02
Nutty Professor 2: The Klumps '00
Antz '98
Madeline '98

Peter Welbeck
See Harry Alan Towers

Robert L. Welch (1910-64)
Son of Paleface '52
Variety Girl '47

Sandy Welch
Jane Eyre '06

William Welch
The Brotherhood of Satan '71

Les Weldon
Target of Opportunity '05
Hidden Agenda '01
Replicant '01
Cause of Death '00

Colin Welland (1934-)
War of the Buttons '95
A Dry White Season '89
Twice in a Lifetime '85
Chariots of Fire '81
Yanks '79

Michael Weller (1943-)
Lost Angels '89
Ragtime '81
Hair '79

Halsted Welles
3:10 to Yuma '07
The Hanging Tree '59
3:10 to Yuma '57
Mr. Arkadin '55
Othello '52

Orson Welles (1915-85)
Treasure Island '72
Chimes at Midnight '67
The Trial '63
Touch of Evil '58
The Lady from Shanghai '48
The Magnificent Ambersons '42
Citizen Kane '41

Audrey Wells (1960-)
Under the Tuscan Sun '03
Disney's The Kid '00
Guinevere '99
George of the Jungle '97
The Truth about Cats and Dogs '96

George Wells (1909-2000)
The Impossible Years '68
The Horizontal Lieutenant '62
The Honeymoon Machine '61
Where the Boys Are '60
The Gazebo '59
Designing Woman '57
Don't Go Near the Water '57
Angels in the Outfield '51
Show Boat '51
Summer Stock '50
Take Me Out to the Ball Game '49
The Hucksters '47
Merton of the Movies '47
The Show-Off '46

John Wells (1936-98)
Entertaining Angels: The Dorothy Day Story '96
Princess Caraboo '94

Peter Wells
First Love and Other Pains / When Love Comes '98
One of Them '99
Desperate Remedies '93

Wim Wenders (1945-)
Don't Come Knocking '05
Land of Plenty '04
Beyond the Clouds '95
Lisbon Story '94
Faraway, So Close! '93
Until the End of the World '91
Wings of Desire '88
Tokyo-Ga '85
The American Friend '77
Kings of the Road—In the Course of Time '76
Alice in the Cities '74
The Goalie's Anxiety at the Penalty Kick '71

Gina Wendkos
The Perfect Man '05
The Princess Diaries '01
Coyote Ugly '00
Jersey Girl '92

Richard Wenk (1956-)
16 Blocks '06
Just the Ticket '98
Vamp '86

Mike Werb
Firehouse Dog '07
Face/Off '97
Darkman 3: Die Darkman Die '95
The Mask '94

Snag Werris
If I'm Lucky '46

Lina Wertmuller (1928-)
The Worker and the Hairdresser '96
Ciao, Professore! '94
Summer Night with Greek Profile, Almond Eyes & Scent of Basil '87
Camorra: The Naples Connection '85
Sotto, Sotto '85
A Joke of Destiny, Lying in Wait Around the Corner Like a Bandit '84
Blood Feud '79
A Night Full of Rain '78
Seven Beauties '76
Swept Away... '75
All Screwed Up '74
Love and Anarchy '73
Seduction of Mimi '72
The Lizards '63

Con West
Bojangles '01

Mae West (1893-1980)
My Little Chickadee '40
Every Day's a Holiday '38
Go West, Young Man '36
Klondike Annie '36
Goin' to Town '35

Jessamyn West (1902-84)
Stolen Hours '63
The Big Country '58

Jake West
Pumpkinhead 3: Ashes to Ashes '06
Razor Blade Smile '98

Claudine West (1890-1943)
Mrs. Miniver '42
Random Harvest '42
The Mortal Storm '40
Goodbye, Mr. Chips '39

Quentin Werty
That Man Bolt '73

Richard Wesley
Dark of the Sun '68
The White Cliffs of Dover '44

Hannah Weyer
Life Support '07
Angel Rodriquez '05
Mandela and de Klerk '97
Native Son '86

Frank Whaley (1963-)
The Jimmy Show '99
Joe the King '99

Leigh Whannell (1977-)
Dead Silence '07
Saw III '06
Saw II '05
Saw '04

Jim Wheat (1952-)
Rattled '96
The Birds 2: Land's End '94
After Midnight '89
The Fly 2 '89
Silent Scream '80

Ken Wheat (1950-)
Rattled '96
The Birds 2: Land's End '94
After Midnight '89
The Fly 2 '89
Silent Scream '80

John Whedon (1905-91)
The Fly '58

Joss Whedon (1964-)
Serenity '05

Roland West (1885-1952)
The Bat Whispers '30
Alibi '29
The Bat '26

Robert Westerby (1909-68)
Sea of Sand '58
War and Peace '56
The Spider and the Fly '49

Jennifer Westfeldt (1970-)
Ira & Abby '06
Kissing Jessica Stein '01

Donald E. Westlake (1933-)
Why Me? '90
The Grifters '90
The Stepfather '87
Cops and Robbers '73

Ellen Weston
Outrage '98
Sin and Redemption '94

Garnett Weston (1890-1980)
Bulldog Drummond's Bride '39
Bulldog Drummond's Secret Police '39
The White Zombie '32
Blackmail '29

Edwin Westrate (1894-1955)
Rolling Home '48
Shoot to Kill '47
Renegade Girl '46

Haskell Wexler (1926-)
Latino '85
Medium Cool '69

Norman Wexler (1926-99)
Saturday Night Fever '77
Mandingo '75
Serpico '73
Joe '70

John Wexley (1907-85)
The Long Night '47
Hangmen Also Die '42
Footsteps in the Dark '41
City for Conquest '40
Amazing Dr. Clitterhouse '38
Angels with Dirty Faces '38

James Gordon White
The Thing with Two Heads '72
The Incredible Two-Headed Transplant '71
The Tormentors '71
Free Grass '69
Hell's Belles '69

J.B. White
The Twelve Days of Christmas Eve '04
Countersnike '03

Mike White (1970-)
Year of the Dog '07
Nacho Libre '06
School of Rock '03
The Good Girl '02
Orange County '02
Chuck & Buck '00

Noni White
Anastasia '97
Tarzan '99
102 Dalmatians '00
Tarzan 2 '05

Robb White (1909-)
The Tingler '59
13 Ghosts '60
Homicidal '61

Ted Whitehead
The Mayor of Casterbridge '03
Tess of the D'Urbervilles '98
Cracker: The Big Crunch '94

Hugh Whitemore (1936-)
A Dance to the Music of Time '97
Jane Eyre '96
Breaking the Code '95
The Rector's Wife '94
My House in Umbria '03
The Gathering Storm '02

David White (1916-90)
Undisputed II: Last Man Standing '06
Great Gold Swindle '84

Garry Michael White
The Promise '79
Sky Riders '76
Scarecrow '73

Cynthia Whitcomb
From Dusk Till Dawn 2: Texas Blood Money '98
Eddie Presley '92
The Last Bastion '84
Degree of Guilt '95

Duane Whitaker
Sunny Boy '87
Hot Stuff '80

Denis Whitburn (1944-)
Billy's Holiday '95
The Cursed Mountain Mystery '93

Graeme Whifler
Dr. Giggles '92

Anne Wheeler (1946-)
Edge of Madness '22
Bye Bye Blues '89

Rene Wheeler (1912-2000)
Fanfan la Tulipe '51
Utopia '51

William Wheeler
The Hoax '06
The Prime Gig '00

Tim Whelan (1893-1957)
My Best Girl '27
Safely Last '23

Cormac Wibberley (1959-)
National Treasure: Book of Secrets '07
The Shaggy Dog '06
National Treasure '04
Charlie's Angels: Full Throttle '03
I Spy '02
The 6th Day '00
Motel Blue '98
The Walking Dead '94
Flubber '96
Lockdown '00

Marianne S. Wibberley (1965-)
National Treasure: Book of Secrets '07
The Shaggy Dog '06
National Treasure '04
Charlie's Angels: Full Throttle '03
I Spy '02
The 6th Day '00
Motel Blue '98

Preston A. Whitmore, II (1962-)
This Christmas '07
Crossover '06
Blood Crime '02
Civil Brand '02
Lockdown '00

Gregory Widen
The Prophecy '95
Backdraft '91
Highlander '86

Bo Widerberg (1930-97)
All Things Fair '95
Man from Mallorca '84
Man on the Roof '76
Elvira Madigan '67

Christopher Wicking (1943-)
To the Devil, a Daughter '76
Demons of the Mind '72
Blood from the Mummy's Tomb '71
Cry of the Banshee '70
Scream and Scream Again '70

David Wickes
Frankenstein '93
Jekyll and Hyde '90
Jack the Ripper '88

Thornton Wilder (1897-1975)
Our Town '03
Shadow of a Doubt '43

Georg Wildhagen (1920-)
The Merry Wives of Windsor '50

Ethan Wiley
Children of the Corn 5: Fields of Terror '98
House 2: The Second Story '87
House '86

Ken Wiederhorn
Return of the Living Dead 2 '88
Shock Waves '77

Joe Wiesenfeld
The Marriage of Figaro '49
A Killing Spring '02
Back to the Secret Garden '01
Child Star: The Shirley Temple Story '01
The Sign of Four '01
The Hound of the Baskervilles '00
A Knight in Camelot '98
20,000 Leagues Under the Sea '97

Rich Wilkes (1966-)
XXX '02
Glory Daze '96
The Jerky Boys '95
Airheads '94

Christopher Wilkinson (1950-)
Ali '01
Nixon '95

Bob Williams
20 Million Miles to Earth '57

Charles Williams (1909-75)
The Hot Spot '90
The Pink Jungle '68
Yellow Cargo '36

Crane Wilbur (1886-1973)
Mysterious Island '61
House on Haunted Hill '58
Crime Wave '54
The Bat '59
The Devil on Wheels '47
The Man Who Knew Too Much '34
House of Wax '53

Billy Wilder (1906-2002)
Buddy Buddy '81
The Front Page '74
Avanti! '72
The Private Life of Sherlock Holmes '70
The Fortune Cookie '66
Kiss Me, Stupid! '64
Irma La Douce '63
One, Two, Three '61
The Apartment '60
Some Like It Hot '59
Love in the Afternoon '57
Witness for the Prosecution '57
The Seven Year Itch '55
Sabrina '54
Stalag 17 '53
Ace in the Hole '51
Sunset Boulevard '50
A Foreign Affair '48
The Emperor Waltz '48
The Lost Weekend '45
Double Indemnity '44
Five Graves to Cairo '43
Ball of Fire '41
The Major and the Minor '42
Midnight '39
Ninotchka '39
Bluebeard's Eighth Wife '38
Mauvaise Graine '33

Gene Wilder (1935-)
The Woman in Red '84
Haunted Honeymoon '86
The World's Greatest Lover '77
The Adventures of Sherlock Holmes' Smarter Brother '78
Young Frankenstein '74

John Wilder
Murder in a Small Town '99
See No Evil, Hear No Evil '89

Robert Wilder (1901-74)
The Big Country '58
Flamingo Road '49

Emlyn Williams (1905-87)
The Last Days of Dolwyn '49
Evergreen '34

Sarah Williams
Becoming Jane '07

Spencer Williams, Jr. (1893-1969)
Blood of Jesus '41
Son of Ingagi '40
Harlem Rides the Range '39

Tennessee Williams (1911-83)
The Roman Spring of Mrs. Stone '03
Orpheus Descending '91
The Glass Menagerie '87
Cat on a Hot Tin Roof '84
Boom! '68
Baby Doll '56
The Rose Tattoo '55
A Streetcar Named Desire '51

Tod Williams (1968-)
The Door in the Floor '04
The Adventures of Sebastian Cole '99

David Williamson (1942-)
On the Beach '00
Dangerous Life '89
The Four Minute Mile '88
Travelling North '87
The Last Bastion '84
Phar Lap '84
The Year of Living Dangerously '82
The Club '81
Gallipoli '81
Don's Party '76

Fred Williamson (1938-)
Adios Amigo '75
Boss '74

Kevin Williamson (1965-)
Cursed '04
Teaching Mrs. Tingle '99
The Faculty '98
I Know What You Did Last Summer '97
Scream 2 '97
Scream '96

Nick Willing (1961-)
Close Your Eyes '02
Photographing Fairies '97

Calder Willingham (1922-95)
Rambling Rose '91
Thieves Like Us '74
Little Big Man '70
The Graduate '67
One-Eyed Jacks '61
The Vikings '58
Paths of Glory '57
The Strange One '57

Tim Willocks
Sin '02
Swept from the Sea '97

Carey Wilson (1889-1962)
Mutiny on the Bounty '35
Gabriel Over the White House '33
Behind Office Doors '31

David Wilson (1949-)
The Perfect Weapon '91
Strangers in Good Company '91

Erin Cressida Wilson (1964-)
Fur: An Imaginary Portrait of Diane Arbus '06
Secretary '02

Gerald Wilson
Scorpio '73
Chato's Land '71
Lawman '71
Free Grass '69

Hugh Wilson (1943-)
Dudley Do-Right '99
Blast from the Past '98
Rough Riders '97
Down Periscope '96
Guarding Tess '94
Burglar '87
Rustler's Rhapsody '85
Police Academy '84
Stroker Ace '83

Michael Wilson (1914-78)
Planet of the Apes '68
Lawrence of Arabia '62
The Bridge on the River Kwai '57
Friendly Persuasion '56
Salt of the Earth '54
Five Fingers '52
A Place in the Sun '51

Michael G. Wilson (1943-)
License to Kill '89
The Living Daylights '87
A View to a Kill '85
Octopussy '83
For Your Eyes Only '81

Michael J. Wilson (1920-2002)
Shark Tale '04
Ice Age '02

Owen Wilson (1968-)
The Tuxedo '02
The Royal Tenenbaums '01
Rushmore '98
Bottle Rocket '95

Sandy Wilson (1947-)
American Boyfriends '89
My American Cousin '85

S.S. Wilson
Wild Wild West '99
Tremors 2: Aftershocks '96
Heart and Souls '93
Ghost Dad '90
Tremors '89
Short Circuit 2 '88
*batteries not included '87
Short Circuit '86

Kurt Wimmer (1964-)
Street Kings '08
Ultraviolet '06
The Recruit '03
Equilibrium '02
The Thomas Crown Affair '99
Relative Fear '95
The Neighbor '93

Arthur Wimperis (1874-1953)
Young Bess '53
Mrs. Miniver '42
Random Harvest '42
The Four Feathers '39
The Scarlet Pimpernel '34
The Private Life of Henry VIII '33

Michael Winder
Welcome to Blood City '77
The Beast Must Die '75

Charles Winkler
Rocky Marciano '99
Disturbed '90
You Talkin' to Me? '87

Terence H. Winkless
Rage and Honor '92
Corporate Affairs '90
He's My Girl '87
The Howling II '87

Michael Winner (1935-)
Parting Shots '98
Bullseye! '90
A Chorus of Disapproval '89
Appointment with Death '88
The Wicked Lady '83
Firepower '79
The Big Sleep '78
The Sentinel '76
Murder on the Campus '52

Terry Winsor
Essex Boys '99
Fool's Gold: The Story of the Brink's-Mat Robbery '92

Alex Winter (1965-)
Fever '99
Freaked '93

Terence Winter
Brooklyn Rules '07
Get Rich or Die Tryin' '05

Scott Wiper (1970-)
The Condemned '07
A Better Way to Die '00

Mildred Wirt Benson
Staircase '39
Nancy Drew and the Hidden Staircase '39
Nancy Drew—Trouble Shooter '39
Nancy Drew—Detective '38

Frank Wisbar (1899-1967)
Rimfire '49
Strangler of the Swamp '46

Aubrey Wisberg
Hercules in New York '70
The Man from Planet X '51
The Adventures of Rusty '45

William Wisher
Dominion: Prequel to the Exorcist '05
Exorcist: The Beginning '04

Theodore Witcher
Body Count '97
Love Jones '97

William D. Wittliff
The Perfect Storm '00
The Cowboy Way '94
Legends of the Fall '94
Lone Justice '93
Lone Justice 2 '93
Lonesome Dove '89
Red Headed Stranger '87
Country '84
Raggedy Man '81
Honeysuckle Rose '80
The Black Stallion '79

Dick Wolf (1946-)
Masquerade '88
No Man's Land '87
Gas '81
Skateboard '77

Fred Wolf (1964-)
Strange Wilderness '08
Without a Paddle '04
Dickie Roberts: Former Child Star '03
Joe Dirt '01
Dirty Work '97
Black Sheep '96

Jurgen Wolff (1948-)
The Real Howard Spitz '98
Jack Higgins' Midnight Man '95

P.J. Wolfson (1903-79)
They All Kissed the Bride '42
Mad Love '35
Dancing Lady '33
Picture Snatcher '33

Andy Wolk
The Defenders: Taking the First '98
From the Earth to the Moon '98
The Defenders: Payback '97
Criminal Justice '90

Peter Wolk
The Defenders: Taking the First '98

Dave Wollert
Near Misses '91
Quicksand: No Escape '91

M. Wallace Wolodarsky
Seeing Other People '04
Coldblooded '94

Barry Wong (1946-92)
Hard-Boiled '92
Twin Dragons '92

James Wong (1940-2004)
Final Destination 3 '06
The One '01
Final Destination '00
The Boys Next Door '85

Jing Wong
Naked Killer '92
The Prodigal Son '82

Raymond Wong (1948-)
The Phantom Lover '95
Mad Mission '83

John Woo (1948-)
Hard-Boiled '92
A Bullet in the Head '90
The Killer '90
Once a Thief '90
A Better Tomorrow, Part 2 '88
A Better Tomorrow, Part 1 '86
Heroes Shed No Tears '86
Last Hurrah for Chivalry '78

Charles Wood (1932-)
Iris '01
An Awfully Big Adventure '94
Sharpe's Company '94
Cuba '79
The Charge of the Light Brigade '68
How I Won the War '67
Help! '65
The Knack '65

Christopher Wood (1935-)
Dangerous Curves '99
Stray Bullet '98
Remo Williams: The Adventure Begins '85
Moonraker '79
The Spy Who Loved Me '77

Edward D. Wood, Jr. (1924-78)
Class Reunion '72
Orgy of the Dead '65
The Sinister Urge '60
Night of the Ghouls '59
The Bride & the Beast '58
Plan 9 from Outer Space '56
The Violent Years '56
Bride of the Monster '55
Jail Bait '54
Glen or Glenda? '53

Christopher Wooden
The Showgirl Murders '95
Dinosaur Island '93
Body Chemistry 2: Voice of a Stranger '91

Jack Woods
Beware! The Blob '72
Equinox '71

Lotta Woods (1869-1957)
The Gaucho '27
The Three Musketeers '21

Skip Woods
Swordfish '01
Thursday '98

Walter Woods
David Harum '34
The Pony Express '25
Leap Year '21

Abbe Wool
Roadside Prophets '92
Sid & Nancy '86

Linda Woolverton (1959-)
Homeward Bound: The Incredible Journey '93
Beauty and the Beast '91

Chuck Workman
Superstar: The Life and Times of Andy Warhol '90
Stoogemania '85

David Worth
Lady Dragon '92
Soldier's Revenge '84

Ardel Wray (1907-83)
Isle of the Dead '45
I Walked with a Zombie '43
The Leopard Man '43

Alexander Wright
Wishmaster 3: Beyond the Gates of Hell '01
The First 9 1/2 Weeks '98
Fast Money '96

Edgar Wright (1974-)
Hot Fuzz '07
Shaun of the Dead '04

Geoffrey Wright (1959-)
Macbeth '06
Metal Skin '94
Romper Stomper '92

Lawrence Wright
Noriega: God's Favorite '00
The Siege '98

Ralph Wright (1908-88)
Nikki, the Wild Dog of the North '61
Lady and the Tramp '55
Peter Pan '53

David Wu
The Bride with White Hair '93
The Bride with White Hair 2 '93

Rudy Wurlitzer (1936-)
Little Buddha '93
Shadow of the Wolf '92
Wind '92
Voyager '91
Candy Mountain '87
Walker '87
Pat Garrett & Billy the Kid '73
Glen and Randa '71
Two Lane Blacktop '71

Robert Wyler (1900-71)
The Big Country '58
Detective Story '51

Philip Wylie (1902-71)
Murders in the Zoo '33
Island of Lost Souls '32

J.H. Wyman (1967-)
The Mexican '01
Mr. Rice's Secret '00

Tracy Keenan Wynn (1945-)
Robinson Crusoe '96
Carolina Skeletons '92
Capone '89
In the Line of Duty: The FBI Murders '88
The Deep '77
The Drowning Pool '75
The Autobiography of Miss Jane Pittman '74
The Longest Yard '74

Paul Wynne
Barrio Wars '02
Bombshell '97
Destination Vegas '95

Jim Wynorski (1950-)
Final Voyage '99
Home for Christmas '93
The Haunting of Morella '91
Final Embrace '92
Think Big '90
Not of This Earth '88
Big Bad Mama 2 '87
Deathstalker 2: Duel of the Titans '87
Chopping Mall '86
The Lost Empire '83
Screwballs '83
Sorceress '82

Frank Yablans (1935-)
Mommie Dearest '81
North Dallas Forty '79

Jeff Yagher (1962-)
Guardian '01

Boaz Yakin (1944-)
Dirty Dancing: Havana Nights '04
A Price above Rubies '97
Fresh '94
The Punisher '90

Kazuo Yamada
Godzilla vs. the Sea Monster '66

Yoji Yamada (1931-)
The Hidden Blade '04
The Twilight Samurai '02

Brock Yates
Cannonball Run '81
Smokey and the Bandit 2 '80

George Worthing Yates (1901-75)
Tormented '60

Jack Yellen (1892-1991)
My Lucky Star '38
Pigskin Parade '36

Linda Yellen (1949-)
End of Summer '97
Chantilly Lace '93

Bennett Yellin
The Pooch and the Pauper '99
Dumb & Dumber '94

Yevgeny Yevtushenko
Kindergarten '84

Valentin Yezhov (1921-2004)
I Am Cuba '64

Rafael Yglesias
Dark Water '05
From Hell '01
Les Miserables '97
Death and the Maiden '94
Fearless '93

Yoshikata Yoda (1909-)
Sansho the Bailiff '54
A Geisha '53
Ugetsu '53
Utamaro and His Five Women '46
47 Ronin, Part 1 '42
47 Ronin, Part 2 '42
Sisters of the Gion '36

Jeff Yonis
Humanoids from the Deep '96
Bloodfist 5: Human Target '93
Firehawk '92

Philip Yordan (1914-2003)
The Unholy '88
Bloody Wednesday '87
Night Train to Terror '84
Bad Man's River '72
Captain Apache '71
Battle of the Bulge '65
The Fall of the Roman Empire '64
Day of the Triffids '63
55 Days at Peking '63
El Cid '61
The King of Kings '61
The Bramble Bush '60
Studs Lonigan '60
The Day of the Outlaw '59
The Bravados '58
The Fiend Who Walked the West '58
God's Little Acre '58
Men in War '57
The Harder They Fall '56
Big Combo '55
The Man from Laramie '55
Savage Wilderness '55
Blowing Wild '54
Broken Lance '54
Naked Jungle '54
Houdini '53
Johnny Guitar '53
Mutiny '52
Detective Story '51
Drums in the Deep South '51
House of Strangers '49
Reign of Terror '49
The Chase '46
Whistle Stop '46
Dillinger '45

Graham Yost
Band of Brothers '01
The Last Castle '01
Mission to Mars '00
From the Earth to the Moon '98
Hard Rain '97
Broken Arrow '95
Speed '94

Robert Yost (1886-1967)
Carson City Kid '40
Helltown '38
Arizona Mahoney '36
Drift Fence '36

Clarence Upson Young
Riding the California Trail '47
Night Monster '42

Dalene Young (1939-)
Locked in Silence '99
Evidence of Blood '97
The Baby-Sitters Club '95
Is There Life Out There? '94
Cross Creek '83

David Young
Calm at Sunset '96
Swann '96

John G. Young
The Reception '05

John Sacret Young
Parallel Sons '95
Sirens '99
Romero '89
China Beach '88
Testament '83
A Rumor of War '80

Mark Young
Tooth and Nail '07
All Dogs Go to Heaven 2 '95
Once Upon a Forest '93

Nedrick Young (1913-68)
Inherit the Wind '99
Inherit the Wind '60
The Defiant Ones '58
Decoy '46

Robert M. Young (1924-)
Triumph of the Spirit '89
Agatha Christie's Sparkling Cyanide '83
Ballad of Gregorio Cortez '83
Nothing but a Man '64

Terence Young (1915-94)
Mayerling '68
On Approval '44
Dangerous Moonlight '41

Waldemar Young (1878-1938)
Desire '36
The Crusades '35
The Lives of a Bengal Lancer '35
The Sign of the Cross '33
Island of Lost Souls '32

Ben Younger (1972-)
Prime '05
Boiler Room '00

Henry Younger
See Michael Carreras
Prehistoric Women '67

Cathy Yuspa (1971-)
13 Going on 30 '04
What Women Want '00

Brian Yuzna (1951-)
The Dentist 2: Brace Yourself '98
H.P. Lovecraft's Necronomicon: Book of the Dead '93
Silent Night, Deadly Night 5: The Toymaker '91
Bride of Re-Animator '89

Bruce Zabel
Pandemic '07
Mortal Kombat 2: Annihilation '97
Official Denial '93

Steve Zacharias
Eddie '96
Revenge of the Nerds 4: Nerds in Love '94
Revenge of the Nerds 3: The Next Generation '92

Jon Zack
Out Cold '01
The Perfect Score '04
Shrek the Third '07

Justin Zackham
Going Greek '01
The Bucket List '07

Steven Zaillian (1951-)
American Gangster '07
All the King's Men '06
The Interpreter '05
Gangs of New York '02
Hannibal '01
A Civil Action '98
Clear and Present Danger '94
Jack the Bear '93
Schindler's List '93
Searching for Bobby Fischer '93
Awakenings '90
The Falcon and the Snowman '85

Alex Zamm
Inspector Gadget 2 '02
Chairman of the Board '97

Krzysztof Zanussi (1939-)
From a Far Country: Pope John Paul II '81
Contract '80
Illumination '73
Family Life '71
The Structure of Crystals '69

Barnardino Zapponi (1927-2000)
Deep Red: Hatchet Murders '75
The Clowns '71
Fellini Satyricon '69
Spirits of the Dead '68

Tony Zarindast
Werewolf '95
Hardcase and Fist '89

Cesare Zavattini (1902-89)
The Garden of the Finzi-Continis '71
After the Fox '66
Boccaccio '70 '62
Two Women '61
The Hit Man '60
Umberto D '55
Bellissima '51
Miracle in Milan '51
The Bicycle Thief '48
Shoeshine '47
The Children Are Watching Us '44

Edward Zebrowski (1935-)
Trois Couleurs: Bleu '93
The Structure of Crystals '69

Franco Zeffirelli (1923-)
Callas Forever '02
Tea with Mussolini '99
Jane Eyre '96
Hamlet '90
Jesus of Nazareth '77
Romeo and Juliet '68
The Taming of the Shrew '67

J.D. Zeik
Pistol Whipped '08
Ronin '98

Daniel Zelman (1967-)
Fool's Gold '08
Anacondas: The Hunt for the Blood Orchid '04

Yuri Zeltser (1962-)
High Crimes '02
Black & White '99
'89

Robert Zemeckis (1952-)
Back to the Future, Part 3 '90
Back to the Future, Part 2 '89
Back to the Future '85
Used Cars '80
1941 '79
I Wanna Hold Your Hand '78

Will Zens (1920-)
To the Shores of Hell '65
The Starfighters '63

Edward Zwick (1952-)
The Siege '98
Special Bulletin '83

Alan Zweibel (1950-)
Dragnet '87
North '94
The Story of Us '99

Valerio Zurlini (1926-82)

George Zuckerman (1916-96)
Tarnished Angels '57
Written on the Wind '56
Ride Clear of Diablo '54
Border Incident '49

Jerry Zucker (1950-)
The Naked Gun: From the Files of Police Squad! '88
Top Secret! '84
Kentucky Fried Movie '77
Airplane! '80

David Zucker (1947-)
Scary Movie 4 '06
BASEketball '98
High School High '96
Naked Gun 33 1/3: The Final Insult '94
Naked Gun 2 1/2: The Smell of Fear '91
The Naked Gun: From the Files of Police Squad! '88
Top Secret! '84
Airplane! '80

Tom Zuber
Little Athens '05
Lansdown '01

Stephen Zito
Diana: Her True Story '93
Full Exposure: The Sex Tape Scandals '89

Chris Zois
New Rose Hotel '98
The Blackout '97

Rob Zombie (1966-)
Halloween '07
The Devil's Rejects '05
House of 1000 Corpses '03

Yimou Zhang (1951-)
Curse of the Golden Flower '06
House of Flying Daggers '04
Hero '03

Scott Ziehl
Broken Vessels '98
Red Line '96
Money to Burn '94

Paul Ziller
Firefight '03
Moving Target '00

Julian Zimet
Caged Heat 3000 '95
Horror Express '72
Circus World '64

Harv Zimmel
Snow Kill '90
Shoot to Kill '88

Bruce Zimmerman
The Inspectors 2: A Shred of Evidence '00
The Inspectors '98

Paul Zimmerman
A Modern Affair '94
Consuming Passions '88
King of Comedy '82
Lovers and Liars '81

Paul Zindel (1936-2003)
A Connecticut Yankee in King Arthur's Court '89
Babes in Toyland '86
Alice in Wonderland '85
Runaway Train '85
Maria's Lovers '84
Mame '74
The Effect of Gamma Rays on Man-in-the-Moon Marigolds '73
Up the Sandbox '72

cinematographer Index

The **Cinematographer Index** provides a videography for any cinematographer, or Director of Photography, as they are also known, with a video credit. The listings for the cinematographer names follow an alphabetical sort by last name (although the names appear in a first name last name format). The videographies are listed chronologically, from oldest film to the most recent. If a cinematographer lensed more than one film in the same year, these movies are listed alphabetically within the year. Many of today's top directors started as cinematographers, the people responsible for the "look" of a movie.

Bernie Abramson
Ants '77

Thomas Ackerman
Baker's Hawk '76
Superhero Movie '08
Balls of Fury '07
The Benchwarmers '06
Looking for Comedy in the Muslim World '06
Scary Movie 4 '06
Are We There Yet? '05
Anchorman: The Legend of Ron Burgundy '04
The Battle of Shaker Heights '03
Dickie Roberts: Former Child Star '03
Snow Dogs '02
Rat Race '01
The Adventures of Rocky & Bullwinkle '00
Beautiful Joe '00
The Muse '99
My Favorite Martian '98
The Eighteenth Angel '97
George of the Jungle '97
Jumanji '95
Baby's Day Out '94
Dennis the Menace '93
National Lampoon's Christmas Vacation '89
Beetlejuice '88
Back to School '86
Girls Just Want to Have Fun '85
Frankenweenie '84
Roadhouse 66 '84
Foxfire Light '82

Barry Ackroyd (1954-)
United 93 '06
Battey '06
The Wind That Shakes the Barley '06
Friends & Crocodiles '05
Gideon's Daughter '05
A Fond Kiss '04
Sweet Sixteen '02
Dust '01
The Navigators '01
Bread and Roses '00
Very Annie Mary '00
Beautiful People '99
The Lost Son '98
My Name Is Joe '98
Carla's Song '97
Under the Skin '97
Stella Does Tricks '96
Land and Freedom '95
Ladybird, Ladybird '93
Raining Stones '93

Remi Adefarasin (1948-)
Christabel '89
Truly, Madly, Deeply '91
The Lost Language of Cranes '92
Bitter Harvest '93
The Wedding Gift '93
Captives '94
Hollow Reed '95
Sliding Doors '97
Elizabeth '99
Onegin '99
House of Mirth '00
Arabian Nights '00
Band of Brothers '01
About a Boy '02
Johnny English '03
Unconditional Love '03
in Good Company '04
Match Point '05
Scoop '06
Amazing Grace '06
Fred Claus '07
Elizabeth: The Golden Age '07

Steve Adcock
Facing the Enemy '00
Speedway Junky '99
Timelock '99
L.A. Rules: The Pros and Cons of Breathing '94

Witold Adamek (1945-)
The Decalogue '86
The Possessed '88
Train to Hollywood '86
Hero of the Year '85

Lance Acord (1964-)
Marie Antoinette '06
Lost in Translation '03
The Dangerous Lives of Altar Boys '02
Adaptation '02
Being John Malkovich '99
Buffalo 66 '97

Javier Aguirresarobe (1948-)
Goya's Ghosts '06
The Bridge of San Luis Rey '05
The Sea Inside '04
Talk to Her '02
The Others '01
The Girl of Your Dreams '99
Secrets of the Heart '97
Fiesta '95
Tierra '95
Running Out of Time '94
Outrage '93

Lloyd Ahern (1905-83)
Father Was a Fullback '49
Miracle on 34th Street '47

Lloyd Ahern, II (1942-)
Broken Trail '06
Kicking & Screaming '05
American Wedding '03
My Sister's Keeper '02
Undisputed '02
The Unsaid '01
Supernova '99
Can't Hardly Wait '98
Last Man Standing '96
Turbulence '96
Wild Bill '95
Geronimo: An American Legend '93
Trespass '92
Danielle Steel's Palomino '91

Tom Agnello
Rapturous '07
Fresh Cut Grass '04

Jose F. Aguayo (1911-99)
Tristana '70
Viridiana '61

Mac Ahlberg (1931-)
King of the Ants '03
Air Rage '01
The Wonderful Ice Cream Suit '98
Good Burger '97
The Second Civil War '97
Space Truckers '97
The Late Shift '96
A Very Brady Sequel '96
The Brady Bunch Movie '95
Beverly Hills Cop 3 '94
My Boyfriend's Back '93
Striking Distance '93
Innocent Blood '92
Oscar '91
Robot Jox '90
Deepstar Six '89
The Horror Show '89
Prison '88
House 2: The Second Story '87
From Beyond '86
Ghostwarrior '86
House '86
Ghoulies '84
Re-Animator '84
Zone Troopers '84
Chained Heat '83
Metalstorm: The Destruction of Jared Syn '83
Young Warriors '83
My Tutor '82
Parasite '82
The Seduction '82
Hell Night '81
Nocturna '79
I, a Woman '66

Pierre Aïm
Paris, je t'aime '06
Wah-Wah '05
Monsieur N. '03
He Loves Me ... He Loves Me Not '02
Madeline '98
Resurrection Man '97
Hate '95
Cafe au Lait '94

Yuzuru Aizawa
Godzilla vs. Megalon '76
The Bad Sleep Well '60

Robert Alazraki
American Women '00
Born Romantic '00
St. Ives '98
Another 9 1/2 Weeks '96
My Father's Glory '91
The Old Lady Who Walked in the Sea '91
Conseil de Famille '86
Love Songs '85
Zorro '74

Maryse Alberti
Taxi to the Dark Side '07
We Don't Live Here Anymore '04
The Guys '02
Get Over It! '01
Tape '01
Joe Gould's Secret '00
Happiness '98
Velvet Goldmine '98
I Love You, I Love You Not '97
Stag '97
Crumb '94
Deadfall '93
Tales of Erotica '93
Zebra head '92
Poison '91

Romano Albani (1945-)
The Sleazy Uncle '89
Troll '86
Creepers '85
Inferno '80

Giulio Albonico
Demons in the Garden '82

Jose Luis Alcaine (1938-)
Volver '06
Bad Education '04
The Dancer Upstairs '02
Jealousy '99
Blast from the Past '98
Two Much '96
Jamon, Jamon '93
Belle Epoque '92
Ay, Carmela! '90
Lovers: A True Story '90
Tie Me Up! Tie Me Down! '90
Twisted Obsession '90
Women on the Verge of a Nervous Breakdown '88
Rustler's Rhapsody '85

John Alcott (1931-86)
No Way Out '87
Under Fire '83
Beastmaster '82
Fort Apache, the Bronx '81
The Shining '80
Terror Train '80
Barry Lyndon '75

Arthur Albert (1946-)
Puff, Puff, Pass '06
Max Keeble's Big Move '01
Saving Silverman '01
Behind the Mask '99
Dirty Work '97
Beverly Hills Ninja '96
Happy Gilmore '96
One Night Stand '95
You So Crazy '94
By the Sword '93
Surf Ninjas '93
Passed Away '92
Heart Condition '90
The Principal '87
The Squeeze '87
Streets of Gold '86
The Boys Next Door '85
Night of the Comet '84
Prime Risk '84

A Clockwork Orange '71
2001: A Space Odyssey '68

Robert Alcott
It's Alive! '68
Zontar, the Thing from Venus '66

Henri Alekan (1909-2001)
Wings of Desire '88
On Top of the Whale '82
Mayerling '68
Topkapi '64
The Would-Be Gentleman '58
Forbidden Fruit '52
Anna Karenina '48
Beauty and the Beast '46

Maxime Alexandre (1971-)
Catacombs '07
P2 '07
The Hills Have Eyes '06
The Last Drop '05
High Tension '03

Sepp Allgeier (1895-1968)
Triumph of the Will '34
Diary of a Lost Girl '29

Nestor Almendros (1930-92)
Billy Bathgate '91
New York Stories '89
Nadine '87
Heartburn '86
Places in the Heart '84
Confidentially Yours '83
Pauline at the Beach '83
Sophie's Choice '82
Still of the Night '82
The Blue Lagoon '80
The Last Metro '80
Kramer vs. Kramer '79
Days of Heaven '78
The Green Room '78
Love on the Run '78
Perceval '78
Madame Rosa '77
The Man Who Loved Women '77
Maitresse '76
The Marquise of O '76
The Story of Adele H. '75
Cockfighter '74
Chloe in the Afternoon '72
Two English Girls '72
Claire's Knee '71
Bed and Board '70
The Valley Obscured by the Clouds '70
The Wild Child '70
More '69
My Night at Maud's '69
Six in Paris '68
La Collectionneuse '67

Alan Almond
Kevin & Perry Go Large '00
Get Real '99
My Son the Fanatic '97
Kiss and Tell '96
Brothers in Trouble '95
Loaded '94

John A. Alonzo (1934-2001)
Deuces Wild '02
The Prime Gig '00
Lansky '99
Letters from a Killer '98
The Grass Harp '95
Star Trek: Generations '94
World War II: When Lions Roared '94
The Meteor Man '93
Clifford '92
Cool World '92
Housesitter '92
The Guardian '90
Internal Affairs '90
Navy SEALS '90
Physical Evidence '89
Steel Magnolias '89
Roots: The Gift '88
Overboard '87
Real Men '87
Jo Jo Dancer, Your Life Is Calling '86
Nothing in Common '86
The Hit '85
Out of Control '85
No Small Affair '84
Runaway '84
Blue Thunder '83
Cross Creek '83
Scarface '83
Back Roads '81
Zorro, the Gay Blade '81
Tom Horn '80
Norma Rae '79
Casey's Shadow '78
The Cheap Detective '78
Beyond Reason '77
Black Sunday '77
Which Way Is Up? '77
The Bad News Bears '76
I Will, I Will for Now '76
Farewell, My Lovely '75
Once Is Not Enough '75
Chinatown '74
Conrack '74
Lady Sings the Blues '72
Pete 'n' Tillie '72
Sounder '72
Harold and Maude '71
Vanishing Point '71
Bloody Mama '70

Herbert S. Alpert (1918-)
The Mask '61
A Dangerous Age '57

Russ T. Alsobrook (1946-)
Forgetting Sarah Marshall '08
Reign Over Me '07
Superbad '07

John Alton (1901-96)
Elmer Gantry '60
The Brothers Karamazov '58
Designing Woman '57
The Catered Affair '56
Slightly Scarlet '56
Tea and Sympathy '56
The Teahouse of the August Moon '56
Big Combo '55
Pearl of the South Pacific '55
Tennessee's Partner '55
Battle Circus '53
An American in Paris '51
Father's Little Dividend '51
Father of the Bride '50
Mystery Street '50
Border Incident '49
Reign of Terror '49
The Amazing Mr. X '48
He Walked by Night '48
Raw Deal '48
T-Men '47
Courageous Dr. Christian '40

Michel Amathieu
The Man of My Life '06
Paris, je t'aime '06
Spy Games '99

Samuel Ameen
Zoe '01
Spark '98

Alex Ameri (1937-86)
The Gore-Gore Girls '72
This Stuff'll Kill Ya! '71
The Wizard of Gore '70

Juan Amoros (1936-)
Between Your Legs '99
Love Can Seriously Damage Your Health '96
Mouth to Mouth '95
Sons of Trinity '95
How to Be a Woman and Not Die in the Attempt '91
If They Tell You I Fell '89

Mitchell Amundsen (1958-)
Wanted '08
Transformers '07
Transformers 2 '05

Juan Ruiz Anchia
See Juan Ruiz-Anchia
Sleepwalking '08
In 'n Out '86

Jamie Anderson
Art School Confidential '06
The Girl Next Door '04
Bad Santa '03
Jay and Silent Bob Strike Back '01
The Flintstones in Viva Rock Vegas '00
The Gift '00
Neil Simon's The Odd Couple 2 '98
Small Soldiers '98
The Temptations '98
Grosse Pointe Blank '97
The Juror '96
Man of the House '95
What's Love Got to Do with It? '93
Unlawful Entry '92
Malibu Beach '78
Piranha '78
Hollywood Boulevard '76

M.A. Anderson
Little Red Schoolhouse '36
Dangerous Appointment '34
Cross Examination '32
Night Life in Reno '31
The Peacock Fan '29

Michael Anderson
Our Brand Is Crisis '05
Take It to the Limit '00

Peter Andrews
See Steven Soderbergh

Stephen F. Andrich
The Junction Boys '02
Killer Tomatoes Strike Back '90

Lucien N. Andriot (1892-1979)
Borderline '50
Outpost in Morocco '49
New Orleans '47
The Strange Woman '46
And Then There Were None '45
The Southerner '45
The Fighting Sullivans '42
On the Sunny Side '42
Lucky Cisco Kid '40
Mr. Moto in Danger Island '39
Mr. Moto's Gamble '38
Thanks for Everything '38
The Gay Desperado '36
Two Alone '34

Theo Angell (1962-)
Black Horizon '01
Kept '01
Mom's Outta Sight '01
Critical Mass '00
Fugitive Mind '00
The Kid with the X-Ray Eyes '99

Yves Angelo (1956-)
The Accompanist '93
Germinal '93
Un Coeur en Hiver '93
Tous les Matins du Monde '92
Baxter '89

Gregg Araki (1959-)
Totally F***ed Up '94
The Living End '92

Thierry Arbogast
Babylon AD '08
Arthur and the Invisibles '06
Angel-A '05
Catwoman '04
Swindled '04
Bon Voyage '03
Femme Fatale '02
The Crimson Rivers '01
Kiss of the Dragon '01
Woman on Top '00
The Messenger: The Story of Joan of Arc '99
Wing Commander '99
Black Cat, White Cat '98
The Fifth Element '97
She's So Lovely '97
Ridicule '96
The Horseman on the Roof '95
The Professional '94
Ma Saison Preferee '93
La Femme Nikita '91

Arch Archambault
Little Men '98
Count Yorga, Vampire '70

Georges Archambault
Nightwaves '03
Fallen Angel '99
The Witness '99
Dead End '98
Random Encounter '98
Stalker '98

Simon Archer
The Bachelor '99
Stiff Upper Lips '96

Fernando Arguelles
Bloodhounds '96
Wes Craven Presents Mind Ripper '95
Hidden Assassin '94
Star Time '92

Arthur E. Arling (1906-91)
Ski Party '65
Strait-Jacket '64
Pillow Talk '59
Man in the Shadow '57
Three for the Show '55
The Farmer Takes a Wife '53
Belles on Their Toes '52
My Blue Heaven '50
Captain from Castile '47

Arledge Armenaki
Auntie Lee's Meat Pies '92
Club Fed '90
Crack House '89
Howling 5: The Rebirth '89
Blackout '88
Off the Mark '87
Crime Killer '85
Grad Night '81
Avenging Disco Godfather '76

Chuck (Charles G.) Arnold
The Chase '91
Assassin '86
The Lazarus Syndrome '79

John Arnold (1889-1964)
The Garden of Eden '28
The Big Parade '25

Steve Arnold
Mr. Accident '99
Doom Runners '97
Dating the Enemy '95

Ricardo Aronovich (1930-)
Klimt '06
Time Regained '99
Celestial Clockwork '94
Christmas Evil '80
Providence '77
Lumiere '76
Murmur of the Heart '71

John Aronson
In Hell '03
Beethoven's 4th '01
Beethoven's 3rd '00
Trippin' '99
Gunshy '98
In God's Hands '98
The Haunted Sea '97
Murder in Mind '97
Bloodfist 8: Hard Way Out '96
The Glass Cage '96
Inhumanoid '96
Dillinger and Capone '95
Machine Gun Blues '95
Suspect Device '95
Carnosaur 2 '94
White Wolves 2: Legend of the Wild '94
Class of Fear '91

Fernando Arribas (1940-)
Cannibal Apocalypse '80
The Blood Spattered Bride '72

Yorgos Arvanitis (1941-)
Anatomy of Hell '04
Signs & Wonders '00
Romance '99
Train of Life '98
Bent '97
Eternity and a Day '97
Someone Else's America '96
Total Eclipse '95
Ulysses' Gaze '95
Landscape in the Mist '88
A Dream of Passion '78
Iphigenia '77
The Travelling Players '75

Jerome Ash (1892-1953)
Hi, Good Lookin'! '44
Swingtime Johnny '43
Flash Gordon Conquers the Universe '40
Junior G-Men '40
Space Soldiers Conquer the Universe '40
The Green Hornet '39
Rocketship '36
Undertow '30
The Drake Case '29

Jack Asher (1916-91)
The Brides of Dracula '60
The Two Faces of Dr. Jekyll '60
The Hound of the Baskervilles '59
The Mummy '59
The Horror of Dracula '58
The Curse of Frankenstein '57
The Magic Bow '47

Monroe Askins (1915-2001)
Napoleon and Samantha '72
Thunder Alley '67
Blood of Dracula '57
Sorority Girl '57

William Asman
Sheba, Baby '75
Three on a Meathook '72

Jacques Assuerus
Black Venus '82
Dark Justice '00
The Doorway '00
Moving Target '00
Plan B '97

Howard Atherton
Color Me Kubrick '05
Lassie '05
Hanging Up '99
Deep Rising '98
Lolita '97
Bad Boys '95
Gulliver's Travels '95
Indecent Proposal '93
Mermaids '90
The Boost '88
Fatal Attraction '87

Yuuharu Atsuta (1905-93)
An Autumn Afternoon '62
Good Morning '59
Tokyo Story '53

Giorgio Attili
Awakenings of the Beast '68
At Midnight, I'll Take Your Soul '63

Joseph August (1890-1947)
Portrait of Jennie '48
They Were Expendable '45
Gunga Din '39
The Whole Town's Talking '35
The Black Camel '31
Seas Beneath '31
Up the River '30
The Toll Gate '20
The Bargain '15

Laurence Avenet-Bradley
Dark Remains '05
Ghost of the Needle '03

Gordon Avil (-1970)
Zotz! '62
The Black Sleep '55
King Dinosaur '55
On Our Merry Way '48

John G. Avildsen (1935-)
Cry Uncle '71
Joe '70

Joaquin Baca-Asay
We Own the Night '07
Thumbsucker '05
P.S. '04
Roger Dodger '02
Super Troopers '01
Two Ninas '00
Coming Soon '99
Dead Broke '99

Jean Bachelet (1894-1977)
The Crime of Monsieur Lange '36
The Lower Depths '36

Jean Badal (1927-)
Good-bye, Emmanuelle '77
Germicide '74
A Very Curious Girl '69

Hanania Baer (1943-)
Going Shopping '05
Festival at Cannes '02
Bug Buster '99
Deja Vu '98
Last Summer in the Hamptons '96
The Prince '95
Babyfever '94
Rescue Me '93
Body Language '92
Venice, Venice '92
Ernest Scared Stupid '91
Diving In '90
Eating '90
The Kid Who Loved Christmas '90
The Queen of Mean '90
Elvira, Mistress of the Dark '88
Seven Hours to Judgment '88
Assassination '87
Masters of the Universe '87
Someone to Love '87
Bad Guys '86
Always '85
American Ninja '85
Night Patrol '85
Breakin' '84
Breakin' 2: Electric Boogaloo '84
Cartier Affair '84
Ninja 3: The Domination '84
Echoes '83
Choices '81

Christopher Baffa
Running with Scissors '06
Unaccompanied Minors '06
Beethoven's 5th '03
Next Friday '00
Idle Hands '99
Baby Face Nelson '97
Lady Killer '97
Suicide Kings '97
True Heart '97
Alien Avengers '96
Humanoids from the Deep '96
Sometimes They Come Back... Again '96
Spectre '96
Criminal Hearts '95
The Death Artist '95
Piranha '95
Sawbones '95
The Crazysitter '94

James R. Bagdonas (1951-)
National Lampoon's Van Wilder '02
Slackers '02
Brotherhood of Murder '99

Cruel Intentions 2 '99
Love Songs '99
Hidden in America '96
American Heart '92

King Baggot
Boiling Point '93
The .ast Starfighter '84
Revenge of the Nerds '34
The .land '81

John Bailey (1942-)
He's Just Not That Into You '03
MadMoney '08
Over Her Dead Body '08
License to Wed '07
The Architect '06
Must Love Dogs '05
The 'roducers '05
Sisterhood of the Traveling Pants '05
Incident at Loch Ness '04
How to Lose a Guy in 10 Days '03
Divine Secrets of the Ya-Ya Sisterhood '02
The Kid Stays in the Picture '02
The Anniversary Party '01
Antitrust '00
For Love of the Game '99
Forever Mine '99
The Out-of-Towners '99
Always Outnumbered '98
Living Out Loud '98
As Good As It Gets '97
Extreme Measures '95
Nobody's Fool '94
Groundhog Day '93
In the Line of Fire '93
A Brief History of Time '92
My Blue Heaven '90
Vibes '88
Light of Day '87
Swimming to Cambodia '87
Tough Guys Don't Dance '87
'87
Brighton Beach Memoirs '86
Crossroads '86
The Pope of Greenwich Village '84
The Big Chill '83
Racing with the Moon '84
Silverado '85
Chapters '85
The Accidental Tourist '88
Cat People '82
That Championship Season '82
Continental Divide '81
Honky Tonk Freeway '81
Ordinary People '80
American Gigolo '79
Boulevard Nights '79
Prerronition '77
Vance '00

Bob Bailin
Family Enforcer '76
Shoot It Black, Shoot It Blue '74

The Groove Tube '72

Bryan Baker (1898-1973)
Ballad of a Gunfighter '64
The Phantom from 10,000 Leagues '56
Wetbacks '56

Lubomir Bakchev
2 Days in Paris '07
Games of Love and Chance '03

Ian Baker
Evan Almighty '07
Empire Falls '05
It Runs in the Family '03
Japanese Story '03
Queen of the Damned '02
The Chamber '96
Fierce Creatures '96
I.Q. '94
Six Degrees of Separation '93
Mr. Baseball '92

Walter Bal (1939-)
Say Nothing '01
Pterodactyl Woman from Beverly Hills '97
Back in Business '96
Precious Find '96
The Chant of Jimmie Blacksmith '78
The Devil's Playground '76

Robert M. "Bob" Baldwin, Jr. (1933-)
Basket Case 2 '90
Frankenhooker '90
Exterminator '80

Lucien Ballard (1908-88)
Breakheart Pass '76
Drum '76
From Noon Till Three '76
Breakout '75
The Getaway '72
Junior Bonner '72
Ballad of Cable Hogue '70
True Grit '69
The Wild Bunch '69
How Sweet It Is! '68
The Party '68
Will Penny '67
Nevada Smith '66
Sons of Katie Elder '65
Ride the High Country '52
The Killing '56
The Parent Trap '61
I Married a Woman '56
Diplomatic Courier '52
Don't Bother to Knock '52
Fixed Bayonets! '51
Let's Make It Legal '51
The Undying Monster '42
I Promise to Pay '37
The Devil Is a Woman '35

Antonio Ballesteros
Insanity '76
Cold Eyes of Fear '70

Florian Ballhaus (1965-)
Definitely, Maybe '08
The Devil Wears Prada '06
Gangs of New York '02
The Legend of Bagger Vance '00
'00

Michael Ballhaus (1935-)
The Departed '06
Something's Gotta Give '03
Uptown Girls '03
Gangs of New York '02
The Legend of Bagger Vance '00
What Planet Are You From? '00
Wild Wild West '99
Primary Colors '98
Air Force One '97
Sleepers '96
Outbreak '94
Quiz Show '94
The Age of Innocence '93
I'll Do Anything '93
Bram Stoker's Dracula '92
The Mambo Kings '92
Guilty by Suspicion '91
What about Bob? '91
Postcards from the Edge '90
Goodfellas '90
The Fabulous Baker Boys '89
'89
Big '89
Dirty Rotten Scoundrels '88
The House on Carroll Street '88
The Last Temptation of Christ '88
Working Girl '88
Baja Oklahoma '87
Broadcast News '87
The Glass Menagerie '87
Chinese Roulette '86

Leonida Barboni
After the Fox '66
Divorce—Italian Style '62
Joyful Laughter '60
Passionate Thief '60

Enzo Barboni (1922-2002)
Kemek '70
Django '68
Texas, Adios '66
Erik the Viking '65
Hercules and the Princess of Troy '65

Charles L. Barbee
The Trip '67
Warm Blooded Killers '01
Free Enterprise '98
The Devil's Advocate '97
The Mirror Has Two Faces '96

Diane Baratier
Triple Agent '04
Satin Rouge '02
Autumn Tale '98
A Summer's Tale '96
Rendezvous in Paris '95

Larry Banks
The Substitute 2: School's Out '97
The Show '95
Juice '92

Lionel Banes (1904-96)
Fiend without a Face '58
The Haunted Strangler '58
Crazy Little Thing '02

Michael Barrow
On the Borderline '01
A Slipping Down Life '99
Row Your Boat '98
Whatever '98

Carl F. Bartels
Acani & Steve '05
Later Days '04
Bool '05
A Light in the Darkness '02
Deranged '01

Andrzej Bartkowiak (1950-)
Doom '05
Cradle 2 the Grave '03
Exit Wounds '01
Romeo Must Die '00
Gossip '99
Thirteen Days '00
Lethal Weapon 4 '98
U.S. Marshals '98
Dante's Peak '97
Speed '94
Guilty as Sin '93
Falling Down '93
Off and Running '90
A Stranger Among Us '92
Q & A '90
Family Business '89
Twins '88
Beyond Innocence '87
Nuts '87
The Morning After '86
Power '86
Prizzi's Honor '85
Gerbo Taks '84
Daniel '83
Terms of Endearment '83
The Verdict '82
Prince of the City '81
Deadly Hero '75

Mario Barroso
The Convent '95
Abraham's Valley '93

Michael Barrett
You Don't Mess with the Zohan '08
Bobby '06
Goal! The Dream Begins '06
Kiss Kiss Bang Bang '05
Lone Star State of Mind '02
75 Degrees '00
Skeletons in the Closet '00
Trie Suburbans '99
Safe Men '98
Finding North '97
Out '97

J.E. Bash
Stealth Fighter '99
Storm Trooper '98

Miroslaw Baszak
George A. Romero's Land of the Dead '05
The Gospel of John '03
Picture Claire '01
Two of Us '00
Four Days '99
Naked City: Justice with a Bullet '98
Rescuers: Stories of Courage—Two Couples '98
Rescuers: Stories of Courage "Two Women" '97

Joe Batac
Eclipse '94
Raiders of the Sun '92
The Siege of Firebase Gloria '89

Edson Batista
Massacre in Dinosaur Valley '85
Women in Fury '84

Gianlorenzo Battaglia
Men Men Men '95
Interzone '88
Demons 2 '87
Demons '86
Warrior Queen '87
Formula for a Murder '85
A Blade in the Dark '83

Jurgen Baum
What About Your Friends: Weekend Getaway '02
The Dentist 2: Braca Yourself '98
American Vampire '97
Flypaper '97
The Big Fall '96
Phat Beach '96
One Man's Justice '95
Open Fire '94
Slumber Party Massacre 3 '90

James Bartle
California Dreaming '07
Inherit the Wind '99
Dead Heart '96
Twisted '96
Hammers over the Anvil '91
Iris '89
My Best Friend Is a Vampire '88

Peter Baumgartner
Jack the Ripper '76
Inn of Temptation '73
Sex Adventures of the Three Musketeers '71

Adolfo Bartoli
Antibody '02
Queen's Messenger II '01
Final Encounter '00
The Horrible Dr. Bcnes '00
Octopus '00
Bloodstorm: Subspecies 4 '98
The Creeps '97
Rudyard Kipling's the Second Jungle Book: Mowgli and Baloo '97
Forbidden Zone: Alien Abduction '96
Head of the Family '96
Magic in the Mirror: Fowl Play '96
Spellbreaker: Secret of the Leprechauns '96
Vampire Journals '96
Puppet Master 5: The Final Chapter '94
Netherworld '90
Bad Channels '92
Puppet Master 3: Toulon's Revenge '90

Jeff Baynes
Pinocchio's Last Stand '06
Agatha Christie: A Life in Pictures '04
The Rapture '91
Curiosity Kills '90
King of New York '90
Somebody Has to Shoot the Picture '90
Deep Cover '92
The Fear Inside '92
Fever '91

Bojan Bazelli
Hairspray '07
Mr. & Mrs. Smith '05
The Ring '02
Dangerous Beauty '98
Sugar Hill '94
Surviving the Game '94
Body Snatchers '33
Boxing Helena '93
Kalifornia '93

Jeff Beesley
Bloodsuckers '05
I, Vampiri '61
Roland the Mighty '56

Jack Beckett
Desperate Target '60
Blood Legacy '73
Please Don't Eat My Mother '72

Terry Bedford (1943-)
Jabberwocky '77
Monty Python and the Holy Grail '75

Jeff Baustert
The Prince and the Pauper '07

John Bartley
The Good Wife '86
The Quiet Earth '85

Mario Bava (1914-80)
True Friends '98
Mockingbird Don't Sing '01
All In '06
Gray Matters '06
Wrong Turn '03
Eight Legged Freaks '02
Dean Koontz's Black River '01
See Spot Run '01
A Cooler Climate '99
Disturbing Behavior '98
Tricks '97
Hatchet for the Honeymoon '70
The Girl Who Knew Too Much '63
Black Sunday '60
The Giant of Marathon '60
Candleshoe '78

Dion Beebe
Rendition '06
Miami Vice '06
Memoirs of a Geisha '05
Collateral '04
In the Cut '03
Chicago '02
Equilibrium '02
Charlotte Gray '01
Cougar '07
Holy Smoke '00
Praise '98
Floating Life '95
Crush '93

Lloyd Beebe
Charlie, the Lonesome Cougar '67

Alfonso Beato
Love in the Time of Cholera '07
The Queen '06
Dark Water '05
Dot the I '03

Frank Beasoechea
In the Line of Duty: A Cop for the Killing '92

The Flower of My Secret '95
The Wrong Man '33
Ed Is Sleeping '90
Great Balls of Fire '89
The Big Easy '87
Happily Ever After '86
Circle of Power '83
Boss' Son '78
Antonio Das Mortes '68
The Informant '97
Live Flesh '97
The Fighting Temptations '03

Jack Beckett

Gloria '89
South Seas Massacre '74

Big Man on Campus '89
Haunting of Sarah Hardy '89
Tapeheads '88
Patty Hearst '88
Pumpkinhead '88
China Girl '87
Deep Cover '92

Nick Knight '89
Orfeu '99
All About My Mother '99

View from the Top '03
Ghost World '01
Price of Glory '00
Uncovered '94
Pronto '97

Paul Beeson (1921-2001)
Jane & the Lost City '87
Unidentified Flying Oddball '79

Hercules '58
The Day the Sky Exploded '57

The Littlest Horse Thieves '76
The Freakmaker '73
To Sir, with Love '67
Die, Monster, Die! '65
The Prince and the Pauper '62

Yves Belanger (1960)
Cause of Death '00
The List '99

Peter Belcher
Octopus 2: River of Fear '02
Spiders 2: Breeding Ground '01
U.S. Seals 2 '01
Mission of Death '97
Operation Delta Force 2: Mayday '97

Andreas Bellis
In the Cold of the Night '89
The Wind '87

Ted C. Bemiller (1924-2003)
Heavy Traffic '73
Fritz the Cat '72

Youssef Ben Youssef
The Silences of the Palace '94
Man of Ashes '86

Richard Benda
Sworn to Justice '97
Slaughterhouse '87

Henning Bendtsen (1925-)
Gertrud '64
Ordet '55

Peter Benison
Memory '06
Cruel and Unusual '01
Big and Hairy '98
Jack Higgins' The Windsor Protocol '97
Jack Higgins' Thunder Point '97
Nowhere to Run '93
Conspiracy of Fear '96
The Wrong Woman '95

Albert Benitz (1904-79)
Testament of Dr. Mabuse '62
The Challenge '38

Mark Benjamin
Protocols of Zion '05
White Boyz '99
Slam '98

David Bennett
Endgame '01
Human Traffic '99

Georges Benoit (1883-1942)
Regeneration '15

Michael A. Benson
Universal Soldier: The Return '99

Roberto Benvenuti
Have No Fear: The Life of Pope John Paul II '05
Red Riding Hood '03

Andres Berenguer
The Story of O, Part 2 '87
Satan's Blood '77

Manuel Berenguer
Flying from the Hawk '86
Simon Bolivar '69
The Thin Red Line '64

Giovanni Bergamini
Buck and the Magic Bracelet '97
Panic '76

Carl Berger
One Too Many '51
Stop That Cab '51
Sky Liner '49

Christian Berger (1945-)
Hidden '05
The Piano Teacher '01

Kalle Bergholm
Pippi in the South Seas '70
Pippi on the Run '70
Pippi Goes on Board '69
Pippi Longstocking '69

Gabriel Beristain (1955-)
Street Kings '08
The Invisible '06
The Sentinel '06
The Shaggy Dog '06
The Ring 2 '05
Blade: Trinity '04
S.W.A.T. '03
Blade 2 '02
Molly '99
Russell Mulcahy's Tale of the Mummy '99
The Spanish Prisoner '97
Trial and Error '96
Dolores Claiborne '94
Greedy '94
Blood In ... Blood Out: Bound by Honor '93
The Distinguished Gentleman '92
Caravaggio '86

Michael Bernard
Haven '04
On the Line '01

Kristian Bernier (1968-)
April's Shower '03
Dog Gone Love '03
Net Games '03
MacArthur Park '01
Enemies of Laughter '00
Partners '99
Sugar Town '99
Six-String Samurai '98

Steven Bernstein
Little Man '06
White Chicks '04
Monster '03
Big Shot: Confessions of a Campus Bookie '02
Christmas in the Clouds '01
Corky Romano '01
Scary Movie 2 '01
The Wood '99
Mr. Jealousy '98
The Waterboy '98
Half-Baked '97
Highball '97
Murder at 1600 '97
Bulletproof '96
Underworld '96
Curdled '95
Kicking and Screaming '95
Moondance '95
The Secretary '94
Like Water for Chocolate '93

Gonzalo F. Berridi
Two Tough Guys '03
Lovers of the Arctic Circle '98
The Red Squirrel '93

John Berrie
The Christmas Shoes '02
The Red Sneakers '01
The Peacekeeper '98
Hawk's Vengeance '96
A Young Connecticut Yankee in King Arthur's Court '95
Young Ivanhoe '95

Ross Berryman (1954-)
Pursuit of Happiness '01
Tycus '98
Living in Peril '97
The Thom Birds: The Missing Years '96
Chameleon '95
Gold Diggers: The Secret of Bear Mountain '95
The Hard Truth '94
Playmaker '94

Renato Berta (1945-)
Kippur '00
Merci pour le Chocolat '00
Same Old Song '97
Party '96
Voyage to the Beginning of the World '96
May Fools '90

Twister '89
Au Revoir les Enfants '87
Full Moon in Paris '84
L'Homme Blesse '83
Messidor '77
Jonah Who Will Be 25 in the Year 2000 '76
Charles: Dead or Alive '69

Jacques Besse
Bamako '06

Thom Best
Hollow City '04
Men with Brooms '02
Ginger Snaps '01
Ride the Wild Fields '00
Grizzly Falls '99
Hidden Agenda '99
The Boys Club '96

Amit Bhattacharya
Pandemic '07
Though None Go With Me '06
The Souler Opposite '97

Pete Biagi
Green Plaid Shirt '96
I Want Someone to Eat Cheese With '06
Outing Riley '04
Stolen Summer '02

Giulio Biccari
The Breed '06
Blast '04
Queen's Messenger II '01

Adrian Biddle (1952-2005)
V for Vendetta '06
An American Haunting '05
Bridget Jones: The Edge of Reason '04
Laws of Attraction '04
Shanghai Knights '03
Reign of Fire '02
The Mummy Returns '01
102 Dalmatians '00
The Mummy '99
The World Is Not Enough '99
Holy Man '98
The Butcher Boy '97
Event Horizon '97
Fierce Creatures '96
101 Dalmatians '96
Judge Dredd '95
Lamerica '95
Thelma & Louise '91
The Tall Guy '89
Willow '88
The Princess Bride '87
Aliens '86

Luca Bigazzi (1958-)
Bread and Tulips '01
Not of This World '99
Kiss of Fire '98
Luna e L'Altra '96

Ray Binger (1888-1970)
Stagecoach '39
Private Lives '31

Joseph Biroc (1903-96)
Airplane 2: The Sequel '82
Hammett '82
...All the Marbles '81
Airplane! '80
Beyond the Poseidon Adventure '79
The Choirboys '77
The Duchess and the Dirtwater Fox '76
The Hustle '75
Blazing Saddles '74
The Longest Yard '74
The Towering Inferno '74
Emperor of the North Pole '73
Ulzana's Raid '72
Brian's Song '71
Escape from the Planet of the Apes '71
The Grissom Gang '71
The Organization '71
Too Late the Hero '70
The Killing of Sister George '69
Whatever Happened to Aunt Alice? '69
The Detective '68
Lady in Cement '68
Enter Laughing '67
Tony Rome '67
Who's Minding the Mint? '67
The Russians Are Coming, the Russians Are Coming '66
The Flight of the Phoenix '65
Hush, Hush, Sweet Charlotte '65
Kitten with a Whip '64
Bye, Bye, Birdie '63
Promises! Promises! '63
Toys in the Attic '63
Under the Yum-Yum Tree '63
Viva Las Vegas '63
The Devil at 4 O'Clock '61
Ice Palace '60
13 Ghosts '60
The Bat '59
The FBI Story '59
Verboten! '59
The Amazing Colossal Man '57
China Gate '57
Forty Guns '57
Attack! '56
Run of the Arrow '56
Donovan's Brain '53
Tall Texan '53
Loan Shark '52
Cry Danger '51
Mrs. Mike '49
On Our Merry Way '48
Magic Town '47
It's a Wonderful Life '46

Billy (G.W.) Bitzer (1872-1944)
Battle of the Sexes '28
America '24
Orphans of the Storm '21
Way Down East '20
Broken Blossoms '19
Intolerance '16
The Birth of a Nation '15
Battle of Elderbush Gulch '13

Peter Biziou (1944-)
Ladies in Lavender '04
Festival Express '03
Unfaithful '02
The Truman Show '98
Richard III '95
The Road to Wellville '94
In the Name of the Father '93
City of Joy '92
Damage '92
Rosencrantz & Guildenstern Are Dead '90
Mississippi Burning '88
A World Apart '88
9 1/2 Weeks '86
Another Country '84
Pink Floyd: The Wall '82
Time Bandits '81
Monty Python's Life of Brian '79
Bugsy Malone '76

Stephen Blackman
Strictly Sinatra '01
The Cement Garden '93

Hilding Bladh (1906-82)
Invasion of the Animal People '62
Dreams '55

Rudolf Blahacek (1942-)
Crown Heights '02
The Pilot's Wife '01

Stephen Blake
Final Shot: The Hank Gathers Story '92
Beverly Hills Vamp '88
Hack O'Lantem '87
Sorority Babes in the Slimeball Bowl-A-Rama '87

Ken Blakey (1947-)
Christmas Do-Over '06
The 4th Tenor '02
Extreme Honor '01
Agent Red '00
Rangers '00
The Stray '00
Terror Tract '00
Final Voyage '99
Running Red '99
Land of the Free '98
Executive Target '97
Recoil '97
The Underground '97
Little Bigfoot '96
Pure Danger '96
Riot '96
Rage '95
The Sweeper '95
Cyber-Tracker '93
Firepower '93

Larry Blanford
Hero Wanted '08
Fantastic Four: Rise of the Silver Surfer '07
Operation Sandman: Warriors in Hell '00
For Which He Stands '98

Sebastian Blenkov
Adam's Apples '05
The Green Butchers '03

David Blood
Bad City '06
Steele's Law '91

Patrick Blossier (1949-)
Days of Glory '06
La Moustache '05
Red Lights '04
Amen '02
Jet Lag '02
The Chambermaid on the Titanic '97
Mad City '97
Innocent Lies '95
Revenge of the Musketeers '94
Jacquot '91
Dr. Petiot '90
Music Box '89
Betrayed '88
Sorceress '88
Vagabond '85

Nigel Bluck
Murderous Intent '06
Stickmen '01

Sydney Blythe
Juggernaut '37
She Shall Have Music '36
Scrooge '35

Sean Bobbitt
Sense & Sensibility '07
The Situation '06
Lawless Heart '01
Wonderland '99

Ralf Bode (1942-2001)
Boys and Girls '00
Annie '99
Sarah, Plain and Tall: Winter's End '99
A Simple Wish '97
Sink or Swim '97
The Big Green '95
A Streetcar Named Desire '95
Don Juan DeMarco '94
Safe Passage '94
George Balanchine's The Nutcracker '93
Gypsy '93
Made in America '93
Leaving Normal '92
Love Field '91
One Good Cop '91
Cousins '89
Uncle Buck '89
The Accused '88
Distant Thunder '88
Big Town '87
Critical Condition '86
Violets Are Blue '86
The Whoopee Boys '86
First Born '84
Gorky Park '83
A Little Sex '82
A Long Way Home '81
Raggedy Man '81
Coal Miner's Daughter '80
Dressed to Kill '80
Rich Kids '79
Saturday Night Fever '77
Foreplay '75

Jean Boffety (1925-88)
Vincent, Francois, Paul and the Others '76
Cesar & Rosalie '72
The Last Adventure '67

Kip Bogdahn
Bought and Sold '03
Camp '03

Hagen Bogdanski
The Lives of Others '06
Antibodies '05

Haskell Boggs (1909-2003)
Bonanza: The Return '93
The Bellboy '60
I Married a Monster from Outer Space '58
Teacher's Pet '58
Rock-A-Bye Baby '57

Ludek Bogner
Psychic '91
Erik '90

Oliver Bokelberg (1964)
The Visitor '07
Strangers with Candy '06
Loggerheads '05
The Station Agent '03
The Next Big Thing '02
Cash Crop '01
Harvest '98
Last Breath '96

Alun Bollinger
Perfect Strangers '03
Forgotten Silver '96
The Frighteners '96
Heavenly Creatures '94
A Soldier's Tale '91
Came a Hot Friday '85
Goodbye Pork Pie '81

Balasz Bolygo
Fakers '04
It's All Gone, Pete Tong '04

Jean-Louis Bompoint
Grace Is Gone '07
The Science of Sleep '06

Michael Bonvillain
Cloverfield '08
Sniper 3 '04
A Texas Funeral '99
Saints and Sinners '95
The Desperate Trail '94
Amongst Friends '93
When the Bough Breaks '93

Lamar Boren (1917-86)
The Spy Who Loved Me '77
Brewster McCloud '70

Harlan Bosmajian
Havoc: Normal Adolescent Behavior '07
Starting Out in the Evening '07
The Great New Wonderful '06
Ira & Abby '06
Kill the Poor '05
Shooting Livien '05
Brother to Brother '04
Saving Face '04
Winter Solstice '04
Lovely & Amazing '02
Virgil Bliss '01
Maryam '00
Spin the Bottle '97

Rick Bota
Valentine '06
House on Haunted Hill '99
Barb Wire '96
The Glimmer Man '96
The Companion '94
Tales from the Crypt Presents Demon Knight '94
Article 99 '92
Bloodfist 3: Forced to Fight '92
Pure Country '92
Wheels of Terror '90

Davis Boulton (1911-89)
The Haunting '63

Jacques Bouquin
War '04

Jean (Yves) Georges) Bourgoin (1913-91)
Children of the Damned '63
The Man I Love '97
Comedy of Innocence '00
The Counterfeit Traitor '62
The Longest Day '62
Black Orpheus '58
Mon Oncle '58
Mr. Arkadin '55
Decee d'Anvers '49
Voyage Suprise '46
La Marseillaise '37

Richard Bowen
Head Above Water '96
A Smile Like Yours '96
Fair Game '95
Major Payne '95
The Little Rascals '94
Runaway Daughters '94
Animal Behavior '89
The Wizard of Loneliness '88

David Boyd
Street Music '81

Russell Boyd (1944-)
Master and Commander: The Far Side of the World '03
Ghost Rider '07
Firestarter 2: Rekindled '02
Full Count '06
Tin Cup '96
Operation Dumbo Drop '95
The Rescue '88
Crocodile Dundee 2 '88
High Tide '87
Crocodile Dundee '86
Cobb '94
Forever Young '92
The Killing Beach '92
White Men Can't Jump '92
Sweet Talker '91
Almost an Angel '90
In Country '89
A Paper Wedding '89
Burke & Wills '85
Mrs. Soffel '84
Phar Lap '84
A Soldier's Story '84
Dawn! '83
Tender Mercies '83
Starstruck '82
The Year of Living Dangerously '82
Gallipoli '81
Chain Reaction '80
The Last Wave '77
Alternative '76
Gone to Ground '76
Picnic at Hanging Rock '75

Charles P. Boyle (1892-1968)
Old Yeller '57
The Great Locomotive Chase '56
Gunsmoke '53
Tomahawk '51
She Wore a Yellow Ribbon '49

John Boyle (1891-1959)
Fur & Fancy Free '47
We're in the Navy Now '27

Kurt Brabbee
The Crow: Wicked Prayer '05
Dead Silence '99
Get a Clue! '98

American Outlaws '01
Company Man '00
200 : A Space Travesty '00
The Boys '97
Dr. Dolittle '98
Liar Liar '97
Jack London's The Call of the Wild '97
Rowing Through '96
Deal of a Lifetime '99
St. Patrick's Day '99
Sworn Enemies '56
The Amazing Mrs. Holiday '43

Ulf Brantas
Show Me Love '99
The Woman on the Roof '89

Denise Brassard
Seamless '00

Sylvain Brault (1958-)
One Way Out '02
Hidden Agenda '01
The Boys '97
The Female Jungle '56
The Inspector General '49
The Killers '46
His Butler's Sister '44
Lady on a Train '45
Can't Help Singing '45
Phantom Lady '44

Julio Bragado
Jungles '43
Slugs '87
Blue Jeans and Dynamite '76

Russ Brandt
The Haunting of Hell House '99

Don't Be a Menace to South Central While Drinking Your Juice in the Hood '95
Excessive Force 2: Force on Force '95

Henry Braham (1965-)
The Golden Compass '07
Flyboys '06
Nanny McPhee '05
Bright Young Things '03
Crush '02
Shackleton '02
Invisible Circus '00
The Land Girls '98
Shooting Fish '98
Waking Ned Devine '98
For Roseanna '96
Solitaire for 2 '94

Jochen Breitenstein
The Boogey Man '80
Cocaine Cowboys '79

Jules Brenne
1969 '89
Return of the Living Dead '85
Combread, Earl & Me '75

Jonathan Brown
The Pink Panther '06
School for Scoundrels '06
The Family Stone '05
Without a Paddle '04
Cheaper by the Dozen '03

William Bradford (1905-59)
Trail to San Antone '47
Along the Navaho Trail '47
Don't Fence Me In '45
Rough Riders of Cheyenne '45
Fighting Seabees '44
San Fernando Valley '44
Manhunt in the African
Jungles '43

David Bridges
Catastrophes '95

Justin Brickle
Strange Planet '99
Love and Other
Catastrophes '95
What tha #$*! Do We Know? '04
Rip It Off '02
Big City Blues '99
The Simian Line '99
The Joe Louis Story '53
Crosscut '95
End of Summer '97

Uta Briesewitz
Life Support '07
Walk Hard: The Dewey Cox Story '07
The TV Set '06
The Home Front '02
Session 9 '01
Love Stinks '99
Next Stop, Wonderland '98

Robert Brinkmann (1962-)
Tenacious D in the Pick of Destiny '06
Standing Still '05
The Rules of Attraction '02
Serving Sara '02
Sugar & Spice '01
Screwed '00
Dogs '96
The Beverly Hillbillies '93
Encino Man '92
Snout '91
Mirror, Mirror '90
U2: Rattle and Hum '88

Anchise Brizzi
Othello '52
1860 '33

Norbert Brodine (1896-1970)
Sitting Pretty '48
Boomerang '47
13 Rue Madeleine '46
House on 92nd Street '45
Topper Returns '41
Of Mice and Men '39
Libeled Lady '36
The Good Fairy '36
Counsellor-at-Law '33
House of '05

Robert J. Bronner (1907-69)
Dot.Kill '05
7 Faces of Dr. Lao '63
Pockets of Miracles '61
Please Don't Eat the Daisies '60

Damian Bromley
Anna '87
Kiss Daddy Goodnight '87

Leonce-Henri Burel (1892-1977)
Pickpocket '59
A Man Escaped '57
Diary of a Country Priest '50
Napoleon '27

Edward R. Brown
Blind Ambition '79
Shadows of the Orient '37
The Fighting Rookie '34

Robert Brooks
Jailhouse Rock '57
Where the Boys Are '60

James S. Brown, Jr. (1892-1949)
Amazing Grace '74
The Great Plane Robbery '40
Land of Hunted Men '43
Terminator 3: Rise of the Machines '03
Spider-Man '02
Cast Away '00
What Lies Beneath '00
Eight Below '06
Enchanted '07
My Super Ex-Girlfriend '06
Christmas With the K'ranks '04

Don Burgess (1956-)
The Torture of Silence '17
Fool's Gold '08

Brian J. Breheny
Aquamarine '06
The Adventures of Priscilla, Queen of the Desert '94
The Other Side of Heaven '02
When Good Ghouls Go Bad '01
Siam Sunset '99
That's the Way I Like It '99
Heaven's Burning '97
The Hard Word '02
The Mummy's Hand '40
The Invisible Woman '40
Boom Town '40
Black Friday '40
Argentine Nights '40
Man Made Monster '41
Holic That Ghost '41

Thomas Burstyn
Marco Polo '07
Tin Man '07
Population 436 '06
The Boys and Girl From County Clare '03
Lost Junction '03
Deadlocked '00
Where the Money Is '00
When Trumpets Fade '98
City of Industry '96
Crazy Horse '96
Dead Silence '96
Magic in the Water '95
Andre '94
The Surgeon '94
Arctic Blue '93
Toy Soldiers '91
Cheetah '89
Promised a Miracle '88
Forget Paris '95
Forrest Gump '94
Richie Rich '94
Josh and S.A.M. '93

Dillinger '73
Johnny Got His Gun '71
Big Fat Liar '02
Renegade Girl '46
Strangler of the Swamp '46
Kid Sister '45
Radio '03
The Polar Express '04
13 Going on 30 '04
The Evening Star '96
Contact '97
The Night '87

Dan Burstall (1951-)
Under the Gun '95

David Burr
Father and Son '03

Alexander Burov
The Italian '05

Alexander Buono
Crime and Punishment in Suburbia '00
Arlington Road '99
The Minus Man '99

Bobby Bukowski
Glass House: The Good Mother '06
The Hawk Is Dying '05
The Tripper '06
Boogeyman '05
The Dying Gaul '05
Tangled '01
Saved! '04

Eigil Bryld
In Bruges '08
Becoming Jane '07
Kinky Boots '05
PU-239 '06

Laurent Brunet
Free Zone '05
C.r (My Treasure) '04

Neal Brown
Submerged '05
Miracle Dogs '03
Leap Year '21

Karl Brown (1896-1990)
Death Before Dishonor '87
Night Stalker '87
Summer Camp Nightmare '86
World Gone Wild '88
Under the Boardwalk '89
Intolerance '16

Joseph Brun (1907-98)
The 300 Year Weekend '71
Teenage Bonnie & Klepto Clyde '93
The Joe Louis Story '53
Martin Luther '53

Michael Bucher
The Mating Habits of the Earthbound Human '99
My Brother's War '97

Hans Burman (1937-)
Open Your Eyes '97
Thesis '96
Guantanamera '95
Why Do They Call It Love When They Mean Sex? '92

Robert Burks (1910-68)
Fury to Freedom: The Life Story of Raul Ries '85
Ruckus '81
The Music Man '62
The Birds '63
Marnie '64
The Great Impostor '61
The Enforcer '51
I Confess '53
Strangers on a Train '51
The Rat Race '60
The Black Orchid '59
But Not for Me '59
Vertigo '58
Spirit of St. Louis '57
The Man Who Knew Too Much '56
The Wrong Man '56
To Catch a Thief '55
The Trouble with Harry '55
Dial "M" for Murder '54
Rear Window '54
The Desert Song '53
Hondo '53
Car Crash '80
City of the Walking Dead '80
Why Don't They Call It Love '83
Joey '98
Wild America '97
The Phantom '96
Ghosts Can Do It '87
Green Street Hooligans '05
Snipes '01

Stephen Burum (1940-)
Confessions of a Teenage Drama Queen '04
Life or Something Like It '02
Mission to Mars '00
Mystery Men '99
Snake Eyes '98
Father's Day '96
Mission: Impossible '96
The Shadow '94
Carlito's Way '93
Hoffa '92
Raising Cain '92
He Said, She Said '91
Casualties of War '89
The War of the Roses '89
Arthur 2: On the Rocks '88
The Untouchables '87
8 Million Ways to Die '85
St. Elmo's Fire '85
Body Double '84
The Outsiders '83
Rumble Fish '83

Geoff Burton (1946-)
After the Deluge '03
Heavenly Bodies '84
The Beast '96
Brilliant Lies '96
Sirens '94
The Sum of Us '94
Wide Sargasso Sea '92
Romero '89

Dick Bush (1931-97)
The Man in the Attic '94
Shadowhunter '93
Son of the Pink Panther '93
Switch '91
Little Monsters '89
Staying Together '89
The Lair of the White Worm '88
Uncommon Valor '83
The Escape Artist '82
Death Valley '81
Wild Gypsies '69
Crocodile Dundee in Los Angeles '01
Paperback Hero '99
Escape: Human Cargo '98

Bill Butler (1931-)
Foxfire '87
Native Son '86
Blind Fury '90
The Court Martial of Jackie Robinson '90
Pros & Cons '99
Tommy '75
Mahler '75
One Trick Pony '80
Victor/Victoria '82
The Fan '81
The Legacy '79
Yanks '79
Capricorn One '78
Grease '78
The Deep '77
Jaws '75
The Conversation '74

Passing Glory '99
Deceiver '97
Don King: Only in America '97

Anaconda '96
Flipper '96
Beethoven's 2nd '93
Cop and a Half '93
Sniper '91
Hot Shots! '91
Graffiti Bridge '90
Biloxi Blues '88
Child's Play '88
Wildfire '88
Big Trouble '86
Beer '85
Rocky 4 '85
A Streetcar Named Desire '84
The Sting 2 '83
The Thorn Birds '83
Rocky 3 '82
The Night the Lights Went Out in Georgia '81
Stripes '81
Can't Stop the Music '80
It's My Turn '80
Ice Castles '79
Rocky 2 '79
Capricorn One '78
Damien: Omen 2 '78
Grease '78
Demon Seed '77
Mary White '77
Raid on Entebbe '77
Bingo Long Traveling All-Stars & Motor Kings '76
Lipstick '76
Jaws '75
One Flew Over the Cuckoo's Nest '75
The Conversation '74
The Execution of Private Slovik '74
The Return of Count Yorga '71
The Rain People '69

Michael C. Butler
Cannonball Run '81
Smokey and the Bandit 2 '80
Jaws 2 '78
Harry and Tonto '74

Taylor Byars
Shame '61
Teenage Monster '57

Frank Byers
Illegal Tender '07
Jackie, Ethel, Joan: The Kennedy Women '01
Kiss Toledo Goodbye '00
Having Our Say: The Delany Sisters' First 100 Years '99
Ride '98
Shiloh '97
Trigger Happy '96
Archie: Return to Riverdale '90

Bobby Byrne
The Lemon Sisters '90
Bull Durham '88
Stealing Home '88
Sixteen Candles '84
The Villain '79
Blue Collar '78
The End '78
Hooper '78
Smokey and the Bandit '77

Patrick Cady
The Far Side of Jericho '06
Sunshine State '02
Girlfight '99

Sharon Calahan
Ratatouille '07
Finding Nemo '03
A Bug's Life '98

Duke Callaghan
Conan the Barbarian '82
The Last Hard Men '76
Jeremiah Johnson '72

Thomas Callaway
Undead or Alive '07

Who's Your Caddy? '07
Feast '06
Drop Dead Sexy '05
Cruel Intentions 3 '04
National Lampoon's Gold Diggers '04
Earth vs. the Spider '01
She Creature '01
Mach 2 '00
Submerged '00
Counter Measures '99
Caught Up '98
A River Made to Drown In '97
Amityville Dollhouse '96
Night of the Scarecrow '95
Eddie Presley '92
Cartel '90
Steel and Lace '90
Action U.S.A. '89
Lady Avenger '89
Assault of the Killer Bimbos '88
Slave Girls from Beyond Infinity '87
Slumber Party Massacre 2 '87

Antonio Calvache
Little Children '06
3-Way '04
Prey for Rock and Roll '03
Unspeakable '02
In the Bedroom '01
Broken Vessels '98
I Got the Hook-Up '98

Maurizio Calvesi (1954-)
Up at the Villa '00
Nerolio '96
Acla's Descent into Floristella '87

Alistair Cameron
Surveillance 24/7 '07
Like It Is '98
Autumn Sun '98

John Campbell
Just One Night '00
Change of Heart '98
Reach the Rock '98
Rough Magic '95
Even Cowgirls Get the Blues '94
Imaginary Crimes '94
My Own Private Idaho '91

Gary Capo
Cellular '04

Michael Caporale
Final Destination 2 '03

Yves Cape (1960-)
Flanders '06
Buffalo Boy '04
Humanity '99
Ma Vie en Rose '97

Marco Cappetta (1963-)
Now You Know '02
Hard As Nails '01

Robert Caramico (1932-97)
KISS Meets the Phantom of the Park '78
Slithis '78
Eaten Alive '76
Blackenstein '73
Lemora, Lady Dracula '73
Octaman '71
Orgy of the Dead '65

Jack Cardiff (1914-)
Million Dollar Mystery '87
Tai-Pan '86
Cat's Eye '85
Rambo: First Blood, Part 2 '85

Conan the Destroyer '84
The Far Pavilions '84
Scandalous '84
The Wicked Lady '83
The Dogs of War '81
Ghost Story '81
The Awakening '80
Avalanche Express '79
The Fifth Musketeer '79
A Man, a Woman, and a Bank '79
Death on the Nile '78
The Prince and the Pauper '78
Ride a Wild Pony '75
The Girl on a Motorcycle '68
War and Peace '68
Fanny '61
The Vikings '58
Legend of the Lost '57
The Prince and the Showgirl '57
The Brave One '56
War and Peace '56
The Barefoot Contessa '54
The African Queen '51
Pandora and the Flying Dutchman '51
The Black Rose '50
Under Capricorn '49
The Red Shoes '48
Black Narcissus '47
Stairway to Heaven '46
The Four Feathers '39
Wings of the Morning '37
As You Like It '36
Last Days of Pompeii '35

Carlo Carlini (1929-)
Autopsy '74
Street Law '74
Era Notte a Roma '60
Generale Della Rovere '60
I Vitelloni '53

Paolo Camera (1957-)
Ginger and Cinnamon '03
Pizzicata '96

Russell Carpenter (1950-)
21 '08
Awake '07
Monster-in-Law '05
Noel '04
Charlie's Angels: Full Throttle '03
Shallow Hal '01
The Negotiator '98
Money Talks '97
Titanic '97
The Indian in the Cupboard '95
True Lies '94
Hard Target '93
Pet Sematary 2 '92
Solar Crisis '92
Death Warrant '90
Cameron's Closet '89
Critters 2: The Main Course '88
The Lady in White '88
The Wizard of Speed and Time '88
Sole Survivor '84

Ezequiel Carrasco (1900-78)
Wrestling Women vs. the Aztec Mummy '59
Senora Tentacion '49

Ellis W. Carter (1906-64)
Diary of a Madman '63
Twice-Told Tales '63
Curse of the Undead '59
The Incredible Shrinking Man '57
Radar Patrol vs. Spy King '49
Big Town After Dark '47
Underworld Scandal '47

James L. Carter (1914-)
Believe in Me '06
Ladder 49 '04
Sleepover '04
The Shape of Things '03

Evil under the Sun '82
The Mirror Crack'd '80
S.O.S. Titanic '79
Force 10 from Navarone '78
The Deep '77
The Little Prince '74
Mary, Queen of Scots '71
The Private Life of Sherlock Holmes '70
Chitty Chitty Bang Bang '68
Two for the Road '67
The Long Ships '64
A Shot in the Dark '64
The Victors '63
Damn the Defiant '62
The Grass Is Greener '61
Sink the Bismarck '60
Angels One Five '54
Genevieve '53

Douglas Chamberlain
Moving McAllister '07
I'm Reed Fish '06

Caroline Champetier (1954-)
Le Petit Lieutenant '05
Lush '01
Alice et Martin '98
Dry Cleaning '97
A Single Girl '96
Ponette '95
Helas pour Moi '94
La Sentinelle '92
The Disenchanted '90
Aria '88

Marc Champion
Out of the Blue '80
Vengeance Is Mine '74
Slipstream '73

Chi Ying Chan
DOA: Dead or Alive '06
Silver Hawk '04

Joe Chan
Tsui Hark's Vampire Hunters '02
Wicked City '92

Tom Chaney
Mosquito '95
Frostbiter: Wrath of the Wendigo '94

Gu Changwei (1957-)
Devils on the Doorstep '00
Hurlyburly '98
The Gingerbread Man '97
Farewell My Concubine '93
Ju Dou '90
Red Sorghum '87

Michael Chapman (1935-)
Bridge to Terabithia '07
Hoot '06
Eulogy '04
House of D '04
Suspect Zero '04
Evolution '01
The Watcher '00
The Story of Us '99
White River '99
Six Days, Seven Nights '98
Primal Fear '96
Space Jam '96
Rising Sun '93
Whispers in the Dark '92
Doc Hollywood '91
Kindergarten Cop '90
Quick Change '90
Ghostbusters 2 '89
Gotham '88
Scrooged '88
Shoot to Kill '88
The Lost Boys '87
The Man with Two Brains '83
Dead Men Don't Wear Plaid '82
Personal Best '82
Raging Bull '80
Hardcore '79
Wanderers '79
Fingers '78
Invasion of the Body Snatchers '78
The Last Waltz '78
The Front '76

Taxi Driver '76
The White Dawn '75
The Last Detail '73

Ron Chapman
Class of Nuke 'Em High 3: The Good, the Bad and the Subhumanoid '94
Class of Nuke 'Em High 2: Subhumanoid Meltdown '91
Shock 'Em Dead '90
Fortress of Amerikka '89

Robert Chappell
The Fog of War: Eleven Lessons from the Life of Robert S. McNamara '03
The Thin Blue Line '88

Dominique Chapuis (1948-2001)
Mina Tannenbaum '93
Pas Tres Catholique '93
The Little Thief '89
Sugar Cane Alley '83

Marc Charlebois
Fear of the Dark '02
Protection '01
Treasure Island '99

Cesar Charlone (1958-)
The Constant Gardener '05
City of God '02

Rodney Charters (1948-)
Intern '00
Blind Faith '98
Kull the Conqueror '97
Frame by Frame '95
Sleepwalkers '92
Psycho 4: The Beginning '90

Chuy Chavez
Me and You and Everyone We Know '05
The Sisters '05
Puerto Vallarta Squeeze '04
Chuck & Buck '00
Star Maps '97

Claudio Chea
El Cantante '06
Yellow '06

Enrique Chediak
The Flock '07
28 Weeks Later '07
Lies & Alibis '06
Turistas '06
Down in the Valley '05
Cronicas '04
A Home at the End of the World '04
Undefeated '03
Brown Sugar '02
The Good Girl '02
The Safety of Objects '01
3 A.M. '01
Boiler Room '00
Songcatcher '99
Desert Blue '98
The Faculty '98
Frogs for Snakes '98
Hurricane Streets '96

Pierre Chemaly
Fear Runs Silent '99
Powder Burn '96

Carolyn Chen
The Crow: Salvation '00
Entropy '99

Chin-Kui Chen
Downdraft '96

Man Po Cheung
Half a Loaf of Kung Fu '78
Vampire Effect '03

Yiu-tsou Cheung
Gorgeous '99
The Legend of Drunken Master '94
Police Story '85

Remy Chevrin
Love Songs '07
Happily Ever After '04
Monsieur Ibrahim '03
Close to Leo '02
My Wife is an Actress '01
Doctor Chance '97

Michael G. Chin
Life Tastes Good '99
Chan is Missing '82

Roger Chingirian
Hack! '07
Loaded '08

Steven Chivers
High Heels and Low Lifes '01
Highlander: The Final Dimension '94

Chris Chomyn
Dust Devil '93

Tempted '00
Innocence '00
Dance Me to My Song '98

Gordon Chou
Milk and Horey '03

Alain Chocquart
Lockdown '00

James Chressanthis
The Reagans '04
Margarita Happy Hour '01

Chen Ching Chu
Chinese Connection '73
Fists of Fury '73

Bruce Chun (1963-)
Swindle '02
The Reaper '97

Fabio Cianchetti
The Tiger and the Snow '05
The Dreamers '03
The Triumph of Love '01
Besieged '98

Richard Ciupka (1950-)
Atlantic City '81

David Claessen
Love Song '00
Diary of a Mad Black Woman '05

Curtis Clark (1947-)
Dominick & Eugene '88
Extremities '86
Agatha Christie's Thirteen at Dinner '85
Sesame Street Presents: Follow That Bird '85

Daniel B. Clark (1890-1961)
Charlie Chan at Monte Carlo '37
Charlie Chan at the Olympics '37
Charlie Chan at the Circus '36
Charlie Chan in Egypt '35
Justice Rides Again '32
My Pal, the King '32
The Black Camel '31

Matthew Clark
Day Zero '07
Bam Bam & Celeste '05
Evergreen '04

Charles Clarke
Flaming Star '60
The Hunters '58
Carousel '56
Black Widow '54
Suddenly '54
Captain from Castile '47
Miracle on 34th Street '47
Guadalcanal Diary '43
Mr. Takes a Vacation '39
Charlie Chan in Honolulu '38
The Cat and the Fiddle '34
Tarzan and His Mate '34
Toc Busy to Work '32

Ross Clarkson (1963-)
Undisputed II: Last Man Standing '06
Derailed '02

Manuel Alberto Claro
Allegro '05
Reconstruction '03
Erendira '83

Dominic Clemence
Sirens '02
Like Father Like Son '05

Danny Cohen
Longford '06
This is England '06
Dead Man's Shoes '04

Chuck Cohen
Phantom from Space '53

Ted Cohen
Red Dirt '99
Yellow '98

Dominique Colin
Russian Dolls '05
L'Auberge Espagnole '02
I Stand Alone '98

Andy Collins (1961-)
David Copperfield '99
Little Voice '98
Erased Off '96

Peter Lyons Collister (1956-)
Alvin and the Chipmunks '07
Garfield: A Tail of Two Kitties '06
Buffalo Girls '95
Stephen King's The Night Flier '96
Twilight Men '96
Zeus and Roxanne '96
Mozy Dick '98
Two for Texas '97
Robinson Crusoe '97
Heaven Tonight '93
Over the Hill '92
NeverEnding Story 2: The Next Chapter '91
Les Patterson Saves the World '90

Ghislan Cloquet (1925-82)
Four Friends '81
You Can't Hurry Love '88
Can't Buy Me Love '87
He's My Girl '87
Getting Even '86
Tess '79
Love and Death '75
Donkey Skin '70
A Gentle Woman '69
Marry Me, Marry Me '69
The Young Girls of Rochefort '68
Mouchette '67
Mickey One '65
The Fire Within '64
Belle Americaine '61
Le Trou '59

William Clothier (1903-96)
Train Robbers '73
Big Jake '71
The Cheyenne Social Club '70
Chisum '70
Rio Lobo '70
The Undefeated '69
The Devil's Brigade '68
Bandolero! '68
The War Wagon '67
The Way West '67
The Rare Breed '66
Shenandoah '65
Cheyenne Autumn '64
Donovan's Reef '63
McLintock! '63
The Man Who Shot Liberty Valance '62
Merrill's Marauders '62
The Comancheros '61
The Alamo '60
The Horse Soldiers '59

Edward Colman (1905-95)
The Love Bug '68
The Ambushers '67
Blackbeard's Ghost '67
The Gnome-Mobile '67
The Happiest Millionaire '67
The Adventures of Bullwhip Griffin '66
Monkey's Uncle '65
That Darn Cat '65
Those Calloways '65
The Ugly Dachshund '65
Mary Poppins '64
Ths Misadventures of Merlin Jones '63
Savage Sam '63
Son of Flubber '63
Big Red '62
The Absent-Minded Professor '61
Babes in Toyland '61

Ben Colman (1907-88)
Suburban Roulette '67
Gruesome Twosome '67
Sre-Devils on Wheels '68
The Girl, the Body and the Dic '67

Roy Collodi
Just for the Hell of It '69
Two by Forsyth '86
The Fire Within '64

Alfio Contini (1927-)
Ripley's Game '02
The Flamingo Kid '84
Beyond the Clouds '95
The Night Porter '74
The Libertine '69

James A. Contner
Monkey Shines '88

Giovanni Fiore Coltellacci
Hostage '05
Love and War '01

Fred Conde
Do emite 2: Human Tornado '76
Too Hot to Handle '76
Deathhead Virgin '74
A Taste of Hell '73
The Big Doll House '71

Denys Coop (1920-81)
And Now the Screaming Starts '73
Asylum '72
10 Rillington Place '71
King and Country '64
Billy Liar '63
This Sporting Life '63
Bunny Lake is Missing '65

Wilkie Cooper (1911-2001)
First Men in the Moon '64
Jason and the Argonauts '63
The Mouse on the Moon '62
Mysterious Island '61
The Three Worlds of Gulliver '59
Sea of Sand '58
The Seventh Voyage of Sinbad '58
Abandon Ship '57
The Admirable Crichton '57
End of the Affair '55
Captain Boycott '47
The Foreman Went to France '42

David Connell
December Boys '07
The Snow Walker '03
Disappearance '02
Sniper 2 '02
Stephen King's Rose Red '02

John Coquillon (1933-87)
Clockwise '86
Hold the Dream '86
The Last Place on Earth '85
Absolution '81
The Changeling '80
All Quiet on the Western Front '79
The Big Scam '79
Cross of Iron '76
Pat Garrett and Billy the Kid '73
Straw Dogs '72
Cry of the Banshee '70
Scream and Scream Again '70
Witchfinder General '68
The Oblong Box '69
The Conqueror Worm '68

Raoul Coutard (1924-)
Dr. Bethune '90
Max, Mon Amour '86
Dangerous Moves '84
First Name: Carmen '83
Passion '82
Le Crabe Tambour '77
The Bride Wore Black '68
Two or Three Things I Know '66
Alphaville '65
A Married Woman '65
Pierrot le Fou '65
The 317th Platoon '65
Band of Outsiders '64
Contempt '64
The Soft Skin '64
Les Carabiniers '63
Jules and Jim '62

Jack Conroy
Tick Tock '00
Halloween 4: The Return of Michael Myers '88
Pulse '88
Everything That Rises '98
The Magnificent Seven '99
The Nephew '97
Homeward Bound 2: Lost in San Francisco '96
Blind Justice '94
Broken Harvest '94
The Hunted '94
The Playboys '92
Silent Tongue '92
The Field '90
My Left Foot '89
The Girl with the Red Hair '81

Michael Coulter
Love Actually '03
Killing Me Softly '01
Mansfield Park '99
Notting Hill '99
My Giant '98
FairyTale: A True Story '97
The Neon Bible '95
Sense and Sensibility '95
Being Human '94
Four Weddings and a Funeral '94
The Bank Job '08
The Long Day Closes '92
Where Angels Fear to Tread '91
Monster in a Box '92
The Gospel According to Vic '87
Housekeeping '87
No Surrender '86
Gregory's Girl '80
That Sinking Feeling '79
The Man Who Knew Too Much '87
Much '24

Peter Coombs
The Norman Conquests, Part 1: Table Manners '78
The Norman Conquests, Part 2: Living Together '78

Fabio Conversi
Pédale Douce '96
Love After Love '94

James A. Contner

Paul Cotteret
The Twilight Girls '57
Mauvaise Graine '33

Andrew M. Costikyan
Bananas '71
The Beast from Haunted Cave '60

Stanley Cortez (1905-97)
The Bridge at Remagen '69
Naked Kiss '64
The Three Faces of Eve '57
The Night of the Hunter '55
Since You Went Away '44
The Black Cat '41
Shock Corridor '63
Dinosaurus! '60
The Angry Red Planet '59
The Magnificent Ambersons '42

Charles Correll (1944-)
Revenge of the Nerds 2: Nerds in Paradise '87
Star Trek 3: The Search for Spock '84
Cheech and Chong's Nice Dreams '81
In God We Trust '80
National Lampoon's Animal House '78

My Life to Live '62
Shoot the Piano Player '62
Le Petit Soldat '60
A Woman Is a Woman '60
Breathless '59

Graeme Cowley
Utu '83

Jack Cox (1896-1960)
Carry Me Back '82
Devil Girl from Mars '54
Mister Drake's Duck '50
The Magic Bow '47
We Dive at Dawn '43
The Ghost Train '41
The Lady Vanishes '38
No. 17 '32
Rich and Strange '32
The Ring '27
Blackmail '29
The Manxman '29
The Farmer's Wife '28

Vincent Cox
Hooded Angels '00
Act of Piracy '89
Lethal Woman '88
The Demon '81
Chain Gang Killings '80

James A. Crabe (1931-89)
The Karate Kid: Part 2 '86
Night Shift '82
The China Syndrome '79
Sextette '78
The Disappearance of Aimee '76
Rocky '76
The Autobiography of Miss Jane Pittman '74

Jeff Cronenweth (1962-)
Down With Love '03
K-19: The Widowmaker '02
One Hour Photo '02
Fight Club '99

Jordan Cronenweth (1935-96)
Final Analysis '92
State of Grace '90
U2: Rattle and Hum '88
Gardens of Stone '87
Just Between Friends '86
Peggy Sue Got Married '86
Stop Making Sense '84
Best Friends '82
Blade Runner '82
Cutter's Way '81
Altered States '80
And I Alone Survived '78
One in a Million: The Ron LeFlore Story '78
Citizens Band '77
Rolling Thunder '77
The Front Page '74
Zandy's Bride '74
Birds of Prey '72
Brewster McCloud '70

Edward Cronjager (1904-60)
Beneath the 12-Mile Reef '53
Bloodhounds of Broadway '52
On Our Merry Way '48
Canyon Passage '46
Colonel Effingham's Raid '45
I Wake Up Screaming '41
Everything Happens at Night '39
No Other Woman '33
Lost Squadron '32

Henry Cronjager (1877-1967)
Ace of Aces '33
No Marriage Ties '33
The Love Light '21
To Fable David '21
Daddy Long Legs '19

Henry Cronjager, Jr. (1906-91)
The Ballad of Andy Crocker '69
Over the Hill Gang '69
Hands of a Stranger '62

Krippendorf's Tribe '98
The Parent Trap '98
Flubber '97
Apollo 13 '95
Casper '95
The Flintstones '94
Jurassic Park '93
Death Becomes Her '92
Hook '91
Nothing But Trouble '91
Back to the Future, Part 3 '90
Back to the Future, Part 2 '89
Road House '89
Big Business '88
Who Framed Roger Rabbit '88
Project X '87
Big Trouble in Little China '86
Back to the Future '85
Warning Sign '85
D.C. Cab '84
The Fall of the House of Usher '60
It Came Upon a Midnight Clear '84
Romancing the Stone '84
M.A.D.D.: Mothers Against Drunk Driving '83
Psycho 2 '83
Teenage Caveman '58
Carnival Rock '57
Reform School Girl '57
Rock All Night '57
Teenage Doll '57
Shack Out on 101 '55
The Fast and the Furious '54
Monster from the Ocean Floor '54
The Fighter '52
High Noon '52
Tabu: A Story of the South Seas '31

Nat Crosby
Paper Mask '91
Northanger Abbey '87
In the Secret State '85

Eric Cross
Mr. Reeder in Room 13 '38
Song of Freedom '36
The Mystery of the Mary Celeste '35

Denis Crossan
Agent Cody Banks 2: Destination London '04
Agent Cody Banks '03
The Hole '01
Me Without You '01
I Know What You Did Last Summer '97
Incognito '97
Killer Tongue '96
The Real McCoy '93
A Murder of Quality '90

Richard Crudo
Pistol Whipped '08
Brooklyn Rules '07
Bring It On Again '03
Grind '03
Down to Earth '01
In Pursuit '00
Out Cold '01
American Pie '99
Outside Providence '99
Bongwater '99
Music from Another Room '97
Persons Unknown '96
American Buffalo '95
The Low Life '95
Federal Hill '94

Luis Cuadrado (1934-80)
Spirit of the Beehive '73
Bronson's Revenge '72
What the Peeper Saw '72

R(aul) P. Cubero
The Grandfather '98

Dean Cundey (1946-)
Whisper '07
The Holiday '06
Garfield: The Movie '04
Looney Tunes: Back in Action '03
What Women Want '00

Ake Dahlqvist
June Night '40
Intermezzo '36

Laurent Dailland (1956-)
The Taste of Others '00
East-West '99
Place Vendome '98
Perfect Love '96
36 Fillete '88

Massimo Dallamano (1917-76)
For a Few Dollars More '65
A Fistful of Dollars '64
Gunfight at Red Sands '63

John Daly
Lila Says '04
Me & Mrs. Jones '02
Greenfingers '00
The Railway Children '00
Essex Boys '99
A Royal Scandal '96
Persuasion '95

Arch R. Dalzell (1911-92)
The Boy in the Plastic Bubble '76
The Trip '67
Tower of London '62
Little Shop of Horrors '60

Joe D'Amato (1936-99)
Trap Them & Kill Them '77
The Arena '73
Escape from Death Row '73
Heroes in Hell '73
Fistful of Death '71
Jaws of Satan '81
Galaxina '80
Angel's Brigade '79
Rock 'n' Roll High School '79
Roller Boogie '79
The Fog '78
Halloween '78
Bare Knuckles '77
Satan's Cheerleaders '77
Ilsa, Harem Keeper of the Oil Sheiks '76
Trained to Kill, U.S.A. '75
Where the Red Fern Grows '74

Jan Curik
Transport from Paradise '65
The Gleiwitz Case '61

Alec Curtis
Horatio Hornblower '99
Hostile Waters '97
Rhodes '97

Oliver Curtis
Death at a Funeral '07
The Wedding Date '05
Owning Mahowny '03
Bait '02
Vanity Fair '99
Immortality '98
Love and Death on Long Island '97
Madagascar Skin '95
To the Limit '95

Henryk Cymerman
Brothers Three '07

Stefan Czapsky
Blades of Glory '07
Bulletproof Monk '03
Matilda '96
Ed Wood '94
Batman Returns '92
Prelude to a Kiss '92
Child's Play 2 '90
Edward Scissorhands '90
Last Exit to Brooklyn '90
Sons '89
The Thin Blue Line '88
Vampire's Kiss '88

Stephen Dade (1909-)
The Viking Queen '67
Night Caller from Outer Space '66
Zulu '64
The Obsessed '51

Francois Dagenais
Stir of Echoes 2: The Homecoming '07
Cube: Zero '04
The Rendering '02

Camille '36
Romeo and Juliet '36
Rose Marie '36
Anna Karenina '35
Naughty Marietta '35
The Barretts of Wimpole Street '34
The Painted Veil '34
Dinner at Eight '33
Queen Christina '33
Rasputin and the Empress '33
Grand Hotel '32
Mata Hari '32
A Free Soul '31
Susan Lenox: Her Fall and Rise '31
Anna Christie '30
Romance '30
The Kiss '29
The Mysterious Lady '28
Wild Orchids '28
The Flesh and the Devil '27
Foolish Wives '22

Jeff Darling
The Crossing '92
Young Einstein '89

Allen Daviau (1942-)
Van Helsing '04
The Astronaut's Wife '99
Congo '95
Fearless '93
Bugsy '91
Defending Your Life '91
Avalon '90
Empire of the Sun '87
Harry and the Hendersons '87
The Color Purple '85
The Falcon and the Snowman '85
Harry Tracy '83
Legs '83
Twilight Zone: The Movie '83
E.T.: The Extra-Terrestrial '82
Rage '80
The Streets of L.A. '79

Zoltan David (1955-)
Hitman's Run '99
The Colony '98
Row Your Boat '98
Redline '97
Donor Unknown '95
The Last Word '95
My Teacher's Wife '95

Andrew Davis (1946-)
Over the Edge '79
Private Parts '72

Benjamin Davis
Hannibal Rising '07
Stardust '07
Imagine Me & You '06
Layer Cake '05
Miranda '01
Sleepaway Camp '83

Elliot Davis
The Nativity Story '06
Lords of Dogtown '05
A Love Song for Bobby Long '04
Legally Blonde 2: Red White & Blonde '03
Thirteen '03
40 Days and 40 Nights '02
White Oleander '02
Happy Campers '01
I Am Sam '01
The Next Best Thing '00
Forces of Nature '99
Light It Up '99
Breakfast of Champions '98
Finding Graceland '98
Out of Sight '98
Get On the Bus '96
Larger Than Life '96
Lawn Dogs '96
Nightjohn '96
The Glass Shield '94
Things to Do in Denver When You're Dead '95
The Underneath '95
The Air Up There '94
Mother's Boys '94
Equinox '93

Mr. Write '92
Shakes the Clown '92
Mortal Thoughts '91
Bloodhounds of Broadway '89
Love at Large '89
Signs of Life '89
Miles from Home '88
Summer Heat '87
Vamp '86

Michael J. Davis
A Woman, Her Men and Her Futon '92
Riders '88

Mohammad Davudi
Baran '01
The Color of Paradise '99

Ernest Day (1927-2006)
Parents '89
A Passage to India '84
Revenge of the Pink Panther '78

Acacio De Almeida (1938-)
Yerma '99
In the White City '83

Ricardo De Angelis (1948-)
A Place in the World '92
Man Facing Southeast '86

Gerard de Battista
La Petite Lili '03
Venus Beauty Institute '98
French Twist '95
The Rascals '81

Jan De Bont (1943-)
Basic Instinct '92
Lethal Weapon 3 '92
Shining Through '92
Flatliners '90
The Hunt for Red October '90
Total Recall '90
Bert Rigby, You're a Fool '89
Black Rain '89
Die Hard '88
Leonard Part 6 '87
RoboCop '87
Who's That Girl? '87
The Clan of the Cave Bear '86
Jumpin' Jack Flash '86
Ruthless People '86
Flesh and Blood '85
The Jewel of the Nile '85
Bad Manners '84
All the Right Moves '83
Cujo '83
I'm Dancing as Fast as I Can '82
Spetters '80
The 4th Man '79
Soldier of Orange '78
Katie Tippel '75
Private Lessons '75
Turkish Delight '73
Business is Business '71

John de Borman (1954-)
Miss Pettigrew Lives for a Day '08
A Lot Like Love '05
Tara Road '05
Ella Enchanted '04
Shall We Dance? '04
The Guru '02
Pure '02
Serendipity '01
Hamlet '00
Saving Grace '00
Hideous Kinky '99
The Mighty '98
Photographing Fairies '97
The Full Monty '96
Trojan Eddie '96
Death Machine '95
The Passion of Darkly Noon '95
Small Faces '95

Cian de Buitlear
Blow Dry '00
I Went Down '97

Robert De Grasse (1900-71)
The Clay Pigeon '49
Home of the Brave '49
The Body Snatcher '45
Step Lively '44
Forever and a Day '43
The Leopard Man '43
Lucky Partners '40

Bruno De Keyzer (1949-)
About Adam '00
North Star '96
The Ogre '96
Victory '95
War of the Buttons '95
Afraid of the Dark '92
December Bride '91
Impromptu '90
Life and Nothing But '89
Beatrice '88
Little Dorrit, Film 1: Nobody's Fault '88
Little Dorrit, Film 2: Little Dorrit's Story '88
Reunion '88
The Murders in the Rue Morgue '86
Round Midnight '86
Sincerely Charlotte '86
A Sunday in the Country '84

Kiko de la Rica
Sex and Lucia '01

Axel de Roche
The Nasty Girl '90
The White Rose '83

Pasqualino De Santis (1927-96)
The Truce '96
A Month by the Lake '95
The Palermo Connection '91
Salome '85
Misunderstood '84
Sheena '84
L'Argent '83
Immortal Bachelor '80
Three Brothers '80
Christ Stopped at Eboli '79
The Devil, Probably '77
A Special Day '77
Conversation Piece '75
The Innocent '76
Lancelot of the Lake '74
Lucky Luciano '74
Assassination of Trotsky '72
Death in Venice '71
Romeo and Juliet '68

Jean De Segonzac
Homicide: The Movie '00
Normal Life '96
Path to Paradise '97
Confessions of Sorority Girls '94
Girls in Prison '94
Shake, Rattle & Rock! '94
Laws of Gravity '92

Clyde De Vinna (1892-1953)
Jungle '52
Immortal Sergeant '43
Whistling in Dixie '42
Of Human Hearts '38
Ah, Wilderness! '35
Tarzan and His Mate '34
Treasure Island '34
Tarzan, the Ape Man '32
Trader Horn '31
White Shadows in the South Seas '29
Ben-Hur '26

Roger Deakins (1949-)
The Assassination of Jesse James by the Coward Robert Ford '07
No Country for Old Men '07
In the Valley of Elah '07
Jarhead '05
The Village '04
The Ladykillers '04
House of Sand and Fog '03
Intolerable Cruelty '03
Levity '03
A Beautiful Mind '01
The Man Who Wasn't There '01
O Brother, Where Art Thou? '00
Anywhere But Here '99
The Hurricane '99
The Siege '98
The Big Lebowski '97
Kundun '97
Courage Under Fire '96
Fargo '96
Dead Man Walking '95
Rob Roy '95
The Shawshank Redemption '94
The Hudsucker Proxy '93
The Secret Garden '93
Passion Fish '92
Thunderheart '92
Barton Fink '91
Homicide '91
Air America '90
Mountains of the Moon '90
The Long Walk Home '89
Pascali's Island '88
Stormy Monday '88
White Mischief '88
Personal Services '87
Shadey '87
The Kitchen Toto '87
Defense of the Realm '86
Sid & Nancy '86
Return to Waterloo '85
1984 '84
Another Time, Another Place '83

Faxon M. Dean (1890-1965)
Texas Pioneers '32
Braveheart '25

Seamus Deasy
In My Country '04
Benedict Arnold: A Question of Honor '03
The Seventh Stream '01
An Everlasting Piece '00
When the Sky Falls '99
The General '98

Benoit Debie
Joshua '07
Day Night Day Night '06

Henri Decae (1915-87)
Exposed '83
Le Professionnel '81
The Island '80
The Boys from Brazil '78
Bobby Deerfield '77
Don Juan (Or if Don Juan Were a Woman) '73
Light at the Edge of the World '71
Joe '70
Le Cercle Rouge '70
Castle Keep '69
Le Samourai '67
Viva Maria! '65
Les Bonnes Femmes '60
Purple Noon '60
The 400 Blows '59
Bob le Flambeur '55
La Silence de la Mer '47

Jackson Deerson
When the Line Goes Through '73

Frank DeMarco
Bee Season '06
Hedwig and the Angry Inch '01
Joe the King '99
Habit '97

Peter Deming (1957-)
The Love Guru '08
Lucky You '07
Married Life '07
The Jacket '05
I Heart Huckabees '04
Twisted '04
Austin Powers in Goldmember '02
People I Know '02
From Hell '01
Mulholland Drive '01
If These Walls Could Talk 2 '00
Scream 3 '00
Music of the Heart '99
Mystery, Alaska '99
Austin Powers: International Man of Mystery '97
Scream 2 '97
Lost Highway '97
Joe's Apartment '96
Cosmic Slop '94
National Lampoon's Loaded Weapon 1 '93
Son-in-Law '93
My Cousin Vinny '92
Get Crazy '83
Hysterical '83
Motel Hell '80

Caleb Deschanel (1941-)
The Spiderwick Chronicles '08
Ask the Dust '06
National Treasure '04
The Passion of the Christ '04
The Hunted '03
Timeline '03
The Patriot '00
Anna and the King '99
The Haunting '99
Message in a Bottle '99
Hope Floats '98
Fly Away Home '96
It Could Happen to You '94
The Slugger's Wife '85
The Natural '84
Being There '79
The Black Stallion '79
More American Graffiti '79

Paul Desatoff
Carnal Crimes '91

Joe DeSalvo
Sexus '64
Fever '99
Fall '97
All Over Me '96
What Happened Was... '94
Joey Breaker '93

Alain Derobe
We Will Not Enter the Forest '79

Hap Depew (1887-1940)
Man from Headquarters '26
Ships in the Night '28

Thomas Denove
Secret Games '92
Puppet Master 2 '90
Fanatic '82

Jim Denault (1960-2004)
The Believer '01
Our Song '01
Chasing Sleep '00
Double Parked '00
Boys Don't Cry '99
The Eternal '99
A Good Baby '99
The Taxman '98
Clockwatchers '97
Breathing Room '96
Illtown '96
Sudden Manhattan '96
Nadja '95
River of Grass '94

Dario Di Palma
Down & Dirty '76
Divorce—Italian Style '62

Carlo Di Palma (1925-2004)
Deconstructing Harry '97
Everyone Says I Love You '96
Mighty Aphrodite '95
Bullets over Broadway '94
Manhattan Murder Mystery '93
Husbands and Wives '92
Shadows and Fog '92
Alice '90
September '88
Radio Days '87
Hannah and Her Sisters '86
Off Beat '86
Gabriela '84
The Black Stallion Returns '83
The Appointment '82
The Secret of My Success '87
Blow-Up '66
The Red Desert '64

Franco Delli Colli (1929-2004)
Macabre '80

Tonino Delli Colli (1922-2005)
Life Is Beautiful '98
Bitter Moon '92
Intervista '87
Ginger & Fred '86
The Name of the Rose '86
Once Upon a Time in America '84
When Angels Fly '84
Tales of Ordinary Madness '83
Lovers and Liars '81
Seven Beauties '76
Salo, or the 120 Days of Sodom '75
The Decameron '70
Porcile '69
Murder for Sale '69
Once Upon a Time in the West '68
The Good, the Bad and the Ugly '67
The Gospel According to St. Matthew '64
Mamma Roma '62
Accattone! '61

Austin Dempster (1921-75)
A Touch of Class '73
Bedazzled '68

Daniil Demutsky (1893-1954)
Earth '30
Arsenal '29

Mario Di Leo '75
See Mario DiLeo

Benoit Delhomme (1961-)
Breaking and Entering '06
The Proposition '05
The Merchant of Venice '04
What Time Is It There? '01
Sade '00
Miss Julie '99
The Loss of Sexual Innocence '98
The Winslow Boy '98
Artemisia '97
Un Air de Famille '97
When the Cat's Away '96
Cyclo '95
The Scent of Green Papaya '93

Bruno Delbonnel
Across the Universe '07
Infamous '06
Paris, je t'aime '06
A Very Long Engagement '04
Amelie '01
The Cat's Meow '01

John L. (Ndiaga) Demps, Jr.
Hollywood Shuffle '87

Dennis Devine
Bloodstream '00
Chain of Souls '00
Vampire Night '00
Merchants of Death '99
Decay '98
Dark Eyes '87

Franco Di Giacomo (1932-)
The Sky Is Falling '00
Foreign Student '94
The Postman '94
The Show '95
The Night of the Shooting Stars '82
The Sex Machine '75

Mario DiLeo
Sudie & Simpson '90
Hell Hunters '85
Nightmares '83

Billy Dickson
Halloween 6: The Curse of Michael Myers '95
Tainted Blood '93
Chrome Soldiers '92

Bill Dill
Dancing in September '00
B.A.P.'s '97
The Five Heartbeats '91
Breaker! Breaker! '77

Iri Dixon

George E. Diskant (1907-65)
They Live by Night '49
Dick Tracy vs. Cueball '46
Kansas City Confidential '52
The Traveling Saleswoman '50

Mark Doering-Powell
One Last Ride '03
The Trial of Old Drum '00
Treehouse Hostage '99
Telling You '98

Mike Dolgetta
The Bone Yard '90
Trapper County War '89
The Squeeze '80

Phillip W. Dingeldein (1954-)
Dancer, Texas—Pop. 81 '98
Cowboy Up '00

Andrew Dintenfass

Desmond Dickinson (1902-86)
Tower of Evil '72
The Bloodsuckers '70
The Frightened City '61
The Hands of Orlac '60
Horror Hotel '60
Fire Down Below '57
The Importance of Being Earnest '52
Morning Departure '50
The Woman in Question '50
Hamlet '48

James Desmond
A Woman under the Influence '74

Roxanne Di Santo
Frankenstein and Me '96
Kids of the Round Table '96

Gianni Di Venanzo (1920-66)
The Eclipse '66
Juliet of the Spirits '65
10th Victim '65
8 1/2 '63
Eva '62
Big Deal on Madonna Street '58
Il Grido '57
Love in the City '53

Sergio d'Offizi (1934-)
Don't Torture a Duckling '72

Ernest R. Dickerson (1952-)
Jungle Fever '91
Def by Temptation '90
Mo' Better Blues '90
Do the Right Thing '89
School Daze '88
She's Gotta Have It '86
Joe's Bed-Stuy Barbershop: We Cut Heads '83

Tom DiCillo (1954-)
Coffee and Cigarettes '03
Stranger than Paradise '84
Variety '83

James Diamond (1894-1936)
Relative Values '99

Peter Donahue
Junebug '05
Lessons from the Life of Robert S. McNamara '03
The Fog of War: Eleven

Jimmy Dibling
Night Rider '32
They Never Come Back '32
Woman Condemned '33
Sucker Money '34
Circle of Death '36

Raul Dominguez
The Road to Ruin '28
The Fear Chamber '68
The Sinister Invasion '68

Bruce Dorfman
Raw Target '95
An American Summer '90
Bloodfist 2 '90

Harris Done (1963-)
Forbidden Games '95
Sinful Intrigue '95

Alan Dostie (1943-)
Silk '07
Nuremberg '00
The Red Violin '98
The Confessional '95
32 Short Films about Glenn Gould '93
Jungle Fever '91
Iron Eagle 2 '88

Dermott Downs
Sublime '07
Dracula: The Dark Prince '01

Christopher Doyle (1952-)
Paranoid Park '07
Lady in the Water '06
Paris, je t'aime '06
The White Countess '05
Eros '04
Three ... Extremes '04
2046 '04
Hero '03
Last Life in the Universe '03
The Quiet American '02
Rabbit-Proof Fence '02
Made '01
In the Mood for Love '00
Liberty Heights '99
Psycho '98
Happy Together '96
Temptress Moon '96
Chungking Express '95
Fallen Angels '95

Rob Draper
Trucks '97
The Assassination File '96
The Spitfire Grill '95
Sex, Love and Cold Hard Cash '93
Stalking Laura '93
Dr. Giggles '92
Undesirable '92
Tales from the Darkside: The Movie '90
Halloween 5: The Revenge of Michael Myers '89

Jean-Marie Dreujou
My Best Friend '06
Two Brothers '04
Balzac and the Little Chinese Seamstress '02
The Man on the Train '02
The Girl on the Bridge '98
Augustin '95

Randy Drummond
Series 7: The Contenders '01
Anima '98
Welcome to the Dollhouse '95

Stuart Dryburgh (1952-)
Nim's Island '08
No Reservations '07
The Painted Veil '06
Aeon Flux '05
The Recruit '03
Bridget Jones's Diary '01
Kate & Leopold '01
Shaft '00
Runaway Bride '99
Analyze This '98
Poodle Springs '98
Portrait of a Lady '96
Lone Star '95
Once Were Warriors '94
The Perez Family '94
The Piano '93

Georges Dufaux (1927-)
Le Polygraphe '96
A Wind from Wyoming '94
Jesus of Montreal '89

Guy Dufaux (1943-)
The Barbarian Invasions '03
Napoleon '03
The Great Gatsby '01
Love the Hard Way '01
Stardom '00
Eye of the Beholder '99
One Special Night '99
Polish Wedding '97
Jesus of Montreal '89

Bryan Duggan
T.N.T. '98
Rubin & Ed '92
Cold Feet '89
P.I.: Private Investigations '87

Simon Duggan (1959-)
The Mummy: Tomb of the Dragon Emperor '08
Live Free or Die Hard '07
Underworld: Evolution '05
I, Robot '04
Garage Days '03
Risk '00
The Interview '98

Albert J. Dunk
Anonymous Rex '04
The Inspectors 2: A Shred of Evidence '00
Mail to the Chief '00
Trial by Media '99
The Happy Face Murders '99
Must Be Santa '99
The Inspectors '98
Flashfire '94
Class of 1984 '82
Incubus '82

David M. Dunlap
Game 6 '05
Shaun of the Dead '04

Andrew Dunn
Hot Rod '07
The History Boys '06
Miss Potter '06
Hitch '05
Mrs. Henderson Presents '05
Stage Beauty '04
The Company '03
What a Girl Wants '03
Ever After: A Cinderella Story '98
Hush '98
Addicted to Love '96
The Crucible '96
Grave Indiscretions '96
George '94
The Bodyguard '92
L.A. Story '90
Strapless '90

Elmer Dyer (1892-1970)
Air Force '43
Lightning Strikes West '40
The Flying Deuces '39
Night Flight '33
Hell's Angels '30

Paul Eagler (1890-1961)
All the King's Men '06
Oliver Twist '05
Ray '04
Zemsta '02

Arthur Edeson (1891-1970)
The Mask of Dimitrios '44
Across the Pacific '42
Casablanca '42
The Male Animal '42
The Maltese Falcon '41
Each Dawn I Die '39
The Invisible Man '33
The Old Dark House '32
Frankenstein '31
All Quiet on the Western Front '30
The Lost World '25
Robin Hood '22
The Three Musketeers '21
The Eyes of Youth '19

Eric Alan Edwards (1953-)
First Snow '07
Knocked Up '07
The Break-Up '06
The Heart Is Deceitful Above All Things '04
Crossroads '02
The Slaughter Rule '01
On the Edge '00
Another Day in Paradise '98
Clay Pigeons '98
Cop Land '97
Kids '95
To Die For '95
Even Cowgirls Get the Blues '94
My Own Private Idaho '91

David Eggby (1950-)
Underdog '07
The Marine '06
Racing Stripes '05
Eurotrip '04
Monte Walsh '03
Scooby-Doo '02
Crossfire Trail '01
Pitch Black '00
Blue Streak '99
Daylight '96
Dragonheart '96
Lightning Jack '94
Dragon: The Bruce Lee Story '93
Fortress '93
Harley Davidson and the Marlboro Man '91
Warlock '91
Quigley Down Under '90
The Blood of Heroes '89
Kansas '88
The Naked Country '85
Mad Max '80

Edgar Egger
Breakout '98
Hot Blooded '98
The Undertaker's Wedding '97
Red Blooded 2 '96
Gladiator Cop: The Swordsman 2 '95

Eagle Egilsson (1966-)
Red Shoe Diaries: Luscious Lola '00
Red Shoe Diaries: Swimming Naked '00
Sirens '99
American Virgin '98
Business for Pleasure '96
Red Shoe Diaries: Strip Poker '96
Delta of Venus '95

Mike Eley
Jane Eyre '06
Touching the Void '03
The Navigators '01

Ian Elkin
The Crimson Code '99
For the Moment '94
The Last Winter '89
Outside Chance of Maximillian Glick '88

Paul Elliott
Elvis Has Left the Building '04
Fat Albert '04
King of Texas '02
The Broken Hearts Club '00
If These Walls Could Talk 2 '00
Diamonds '99
Lost and Found '99
'Santa Fe '97
Soul Food '97
Riot in the Streets '96
Truman '95
My Girl 2 '94
And the Band Played On '93
Citizen Cohn '92
And You Thought Your Parents Were Weird! '91
Final Verdict '91

Frederick Elmes (1946-)
The Namesake '06
Broken Flowers '05
Coffee and Cigarettes '03
Hulk '03
Trapped '02
The Empty Mirror '99
Ride with the Devil '99
The Ice Storm '97
In the Gloaming '97
Reckless '95
Trial by Jury '94
The Saint of Fort Washington '93
Night on Earth '91
Wild at Heart '90
Permanent Record '88
River's Edge '87
Allan Quatermain and the Lost City of Gold '86
Blue Velvet '86
Valley Girl '83
Eraserhead '78
Opening Night '77
The Killing of a Chinese Bookie '76

John Else
The Crow Road '99
A Village Affair '95

Danny Elsen
The Memory of a Killer '03
The Red Dwarf '99

Robert Elswit (1950-)
Redbelt '08
Michael Clayton '07
There Will Be Blood '07
American Dreamz '06
Good Night, and Good Luck '05
Syriana '05
Gigli '03
Runaway Jury '03
Behind the Red Door '02
Impostor '02
Punch-Drunk Love '02
Heist '01
Bounce '00
Magnolia '99
8mm '98
Boogie Nights '97
Tomorrow Never Dies '97
Hard Eight '96
Boys '95
The Pallbearer '95
The River Wild '94
A Dangerous Woman '93
The Hand that Rocks the Cradle '92
Waterland '92
Paris Trout '91
Bad Influence '90
A Killing in a Small Town '89
How I Got into College '89
Return of the Living Dead 2 '88
The Heart of Dixie '89
Double Exposure: The Story of Margaret Bourke-White '89
Amazing Grace & Chuck '87
Desert Hearts '86
Trick or Treat '86
Moving Violations '85
The Sure Thing '85
Tiger Town '85
Waltz across Texas '83
End of August '82

Dimitry Elyashkavich (1975-)
Jackass Number Two '06
Jackass: The Movie '02

Susan Emerson
First Degree '98
Men '97

Bryan England
Robin Cook's Invasion '97
Raging Angels '95
The Judas Project: The Ultimate Encounter '94
Conflict of Interest '92
Gate 2 '92
The Water Engine '92
Sometimes They Come Back '91
Friday the 13th, Part 8: Jason Takes Manhattan '89
I, Madman '89
My Mom's a Werewolf '89
Wicked Stepmother '89
Cheerleader Camp '88
Hunk '87
Weekend Pass '84
Party Animal '84

Michael Epp
Beaumarchais the Scoundrel '96
My Mother's Courage '95

Nils Erickson
Sticks '98
Mirror, Mirror 3: The Voyeur '96

Tom Erisman
Shooters '00
1-900 '94

Teodoro Escamilla (1940-97)
Carmen '83
Blood Wedding '81
The Nest '80
Cria Cuervos '76

Jean-Yves Escoffier (1951-2003)
The Human Stain '03
Possession '02
15 Minutes '01
Nurse Betty '00
The Cradle Will Rock '99
Rounders '98
Good Will Hunting '97
Gummo '97
The Crow 2: City of Angels '96
Excess Baggage '96
Grace of My Heart '96
Jack and Sarah '95
Dream Lover '93
The Lovers on the Bridge '91

Jesus Escosa (1959-)
Caresses '97

Lukas Ettlin
Never Back Down '08
The Take '07

Blake T. Evans
The Prince & Me 2: Royal Wedding '06
All I Want '02

Kelly Evans
Die Mommie Die! '03
Let's Talk About Sex '98

R. Kent Evans
The Abductors '72
Ginger '72

Nikos Evdemon
Blue Smoke '07
Dangerous Child '01
Torso '01
Lip Service '00

Jean-Marc Fabre (1964-)
Avenue Montaigne '06
Lemming '05
How I Killed My Father '03
Nathalie '03
A Soldier's Daughter Never Cries '98
A Self-Made Hero '95
Ivan and Abraham '94

Geoffrey Faithfull (1893-1979)
Village of the Damned '60
First Man into Space '59
Black Tide '58
Corridors of Blood '58
Goon Movie '52
The Mystery of the Mary Celeste '35

Christopher Faloona
Beowulf '98
Dennis the Menace Strikes Again '98
Breaking Free '95
3 Ninjas Kick Back '94

Pasquale Fanetti
Invincible Barbarian '83
The Boss Is Served '76

George Fanto (1911-)
It's All True '93
Othello '52

Daniel F. Fapp (1901-86)
Marooned '69
Five Card Stud '68
Ice Station Zebra '68
Sweet November '68
Lord Love a Duck '66
Our Man Flint '66
I'll Take Sweden '65
Send Me No Flowers '64
The Unsinkable Molly Brown '64
Fun in Acapulco '63
The Great Escape '63
Move Over, Darling '63
A New Kind of Love '63
One, Two, Three '61
West Side Story '61
All the Young Men '60
Let's Make Love '60
The Five Pennies '59
Li'l Abner '59
On the Beach '59
Desire Under the Elms '58
Kings Go Forth '58
Artists and Models '55
The Far Horizons '55
Jumping Jacks '52
Sailor Beware '52
The Lemon Drop Kid '51
The Stooge '51
Union Station '50
Sorrowful Jones '49
Golden Earrings '47
To Each His Own '46

Mike Fash
The Golden Spiders: A Nero Wolfe Mystery '00
Take Me Home: The John Denver Story '00
Love Letters '99
The Confession '98
Grace & Glorie '98
The Dorothy Day Story '96
Sarah, Plain and Tall: Skylark '93
Sarah, Plain and Tall '91
The Whales of August '87
Women of Valor '86
King of America '80

Etienne Fauduet
Red Shoe Diaries: Four on the Floor '96
Marquis '96

Don E. Fauntleroy
Urban Justice '07
Jeepers Creepers 2 '03
U.S. Navy SEALS: Dead or Alive '07
Jeepers Creepers '01
The Perfect Nanny '00
Seven Girlfriends '00
Sex & Mrs. X '00
Rites of Passage '99
The Only Thrill '97
Lily Dale '96
Body Chemistry 3: Point of Seduction '93

Jim Fealy
Splendor '99

Gerald Feil
The Doom Generation '95
Friday the 13th, Part 3 '82
He Knows You're Alone '80

Jockey A. Feindel (1895-1971)
Day the World Ended '55
Revolt of the Zombies '36

Buzz Feitshans, IV
Dragonheart: A New Beginning '00
Black Dog '98
For Richer or Poorer '97
McHale's Navy '97
The Shadow Conspiracy '96

Maurice Fellous
Sweet Young Thing '79
The Monocle '64

Marc Felperlaan
Deuce Bigalow: European Gigolo '05
Amor de Hombre '97
Zafarinas '94
Amsterdamned '88
Teenage Mutant Ninja Turtles: The Movie '90
Carol '92

John Fenner
Valiant '05

Paco Femenia
Mad Love '01
No News from God '01
When Father Was Away on Business '85

Roger Fellous (1919-)
Faceless '88
White Fire '84
No Problem! '75
Erotic Escape '72
Diary of a Chambermaid '64
The Three Penny Opera '62
El '52

David Ferrara
Harvard Man '01
Kill Me Later '01
Black and White '99

Michael Ferris
Bar Girls '95

Giancarlo Ferrando
The Messenger '87
Thundersquad '85
Dark Habits '84
Devil '84
Ironmaster '82
Scorpion with Two Tails '82
The Great Alligator '81
Inhibition '76
Torso '73
Your Vice is a Closed Room and Only I Have the Key '72

Angel Luis Fernandez (1947-)
Baton Rouge '88
Law of Desire '86
Matador '86
Dark Habits '83
'88

Joao Fernandes
The Diary of Ellen Rimbauer '03
Lady Jayne: Killer '03
Gideon '99
One Man's Hero '98
Sprung '96
Forest Warrior '95
Top Dog '95
Deconstructing Sarah '94
Sidekicks '93
The Hitman '91
Delta Force 2: Operation Stranglehold '90
Red Scorpion '89
Braddock: Missing in Action 3 '88
Pretty Kill '87
Invasion U.S.A. '85
Rosebud Beach Hotel '85
Friday the 13th, Part 4: The Final Chapter '84
Missing in Action '84
Big Score '83
The Nesting '80

Gerald Perry Finnerman (1931-)
Nightmares '83
Devil Dog: The Hound of Hell '78
Sssssss '73
That Man Bolt '73
Hard Frame '70
They Call Me Mr. Tibbs! '70
The Lost Man '69

Gavin Finney
The Flying Scotsman '06
These Foolish Things '05
Bailey's Billions '05
Keeping Mum '05

Mauro Fiore
Smokin' Aces '07
The Kingdom '07
The Island '05
Get Carter '00
Driven '01
Training Day '01
Highway '01
The Center of the World '01
Tears of the Sun '03

Steven Fierberg
Suburban Girl '07
Secretary '02
A Horse for Danny '95
Atomic Train '99
Now and Forever '34
Aspen Extreme '92
29th Street '91
Criminal Justice '90
Scenes from the Class Struggle in Beverly Hills '89
A Nightmare on Elm Street 4: Dream Master '88
Spike of Bensonhurst '88
Seven Minutes in Heaven '86
Streetwalkin' '85
Vortex '81

Gabriel Figueroa (1907-97)
Kelly's Heroes '70
Simon of the Desert '64
The Night of the Iguana '64
The Exterminating Angel '62
El '52

Vilko Filac (1950-)
Novocaine '01
Children of the Century '99
Chinese Box '97
Underground '95
Arizona Dream '94
Business '85

Michael Fimognari
Black Irish '07
Think Tank '06
Knots '05
The Twelve Dogs of Christmas '05

Roberta Findlay
Lurkers '88
Shriek of the Mutilated '74

Russell Fine
Sherrybaby '06
Office Killer '97
Ash Wednesday '02
The Grey Zone '01
Girls Town '95
O '01
Eye of God '97

Steven Finestone
Once Upon a Wedding '05
Dawg '02
How to Make a Monster '01
I Shot a Man in Vegas '95
Swimming with Sharks '94
That's Entertainment, Part 2 '76

Harry Fischbeck (1879-1968)
I Don't Buy Kisses Anymore '92
Bulldog Drummond's Bride '39
The Big Broadcast of 1938 '38
The Last of Mrs. Cheyney '37

Pili Flores-Guerra
Evelyn '02
And Starring Pancho Villa as Himself '03

Brendan Flynt
Remedy '05
Citizen Toxie: The Toxic Avenger 4 '01
Tromeo & Juliet '95
The Pink Panther '06

George Folsey, Jr.
Housewife '72

George J. Folsey (1898-1988)
That's Entertainment, Part 2 '76
The Balcony '63
Cash McCall '60
Torpedo Run '58
Fastest Gun Alive '56
Forbidden Planet '56
The Cobweb '55
Hit the Deck '55
Deep in My Heart '54
Executive Suite '54
Seven Brides for Seven Brothers '54
All the Brothers Were Valiant '53
Lovely to Look At '52
Million Dollar Mermaid '52
Adam's Rib '49
Malaya '49
Take Me Out to the Ball Game '49
State of the Union '48
Green Dolphin Street '47
The Harvey Girls '46
The Clock '45
Meet Me in St. Louis '44
The White Cliffs of Dover '44
Thousands Cheer '43
A Life of Her Own '50
The Big Hangover '50

Andre Fleuren
See Ray Dennis Steckler

Cash Flagg
See Ray Dennis Steckler

Gunnar Fischer
The Devil's Eye '60
Wild Strawberries '57
The Seventh Seal '56
To Joy '50
Under the Sun '58

Jens Fischer (1946-)
Under the Sun '98
The Last Dance '93
More about the Children of Noisy May '87
The Children of Noisy Village '86

Now and Forever '34
The Eagle and the Hawk '33
The Mysterious Dr. Fu Manchu '29
Sally of the Sawdust '25

The Cocoanuts '29
Animal Crackers '30
Applause '29
The Smiling Lieutenant '31
Going Hollywood '33
The Animal Kingdom '32
Chained '34
Reckless '35
I Live My Life '35
Forsaking All Others '35
The Gorgeous Hussy '36
Woman '76
The Story of O '75

Gerry Fisher (1926-)
When Saturday Comes '95
Cops and Robbersons '94
Exorcist III: Legion '90
Dead Bang '89
Running on Empty '88
Highlander '86
Lovesick '83
Yellowbeard '83
Victory '81
Wolfen '81
The Go-Between '71
Accident '67

David Foreman
Chameleon 3: Dark Angel '00
Look at Me '04

Stephane Fontaine
The Beat My Heart Skipped '05

Larry Fong
300 '07

Cinders Forshaw
Looking for Mr. Goodbar '77
The Killer Inside Me '76
One Flew Over the Cuckoo's Nest '75

Joey Forsyte
Tipping the Velvet '02
Almost Strangers '01
Butterfly Collectors '99

John Foster
Beethoven '36
Tropez '64

Ian Fox
Urban Legends: Bloody Mary '05
No Turning Back '01
Do It! '94

Mike J. Fox
Jimmy Glick in LaLa Wood '04
Dr. Jekyll and the Wolfman '71

Marc Fossard (1912-)
The Gendarme of Saint-Tropez '64

Ron Fortunato
Before the Devil Knows You're Dead '07
Catch a Fire '06
Find Me Guilty '06
The Weekend '00
One Tough Cop '98
Basquiat '96
Night Falls on Manhattan '97

Emilio Foriscot
The Case of the Scorpion's Tail '71
They Paid with Bullets: Chicago 1929 '69

Tony Forsberg (1933-)
The White Lioness '96
Revenge of the Barbarians '85

Robert Fraisse
Call Me: The Rise and Fall of Heidi Fleiss '04
44 Minutes: The North Hollywood Shootout '03
Mr. St. Nick '02
3000 Miles to Graceland '01
The Whole Nine Yards '00
Earthly Possessions '99
Free Money '99
The Last Don 2 '98
The Assignment '97
Silent Trigger '97
Vendetta '95
The Notebook '04

Francisco Fraile
The Color of Freedom '07
Alpha Dog '06
The Valet '06
Mean Machine '73

David Franco (1963-)
Bury My Heart at Wounded Knee '07
Code Name: The Cleaner '07
One More Kiss '99
Night '96
Long Day's Journey Into Night '96
Hollow Point '95
Soul Survivor '95
A Man in Uniform '93
The Carpenter '89

Freddie Francis (1917-2007)
The Straight Story '99
Princess Caraboo '94
School Ties '92
Cape Fear '91
Glory '89
Her Alibi '88
Brenda Starr '86
Dune '84
The French Lieutenant's Woman '81
The Elephant Man '80
The Innocents '61
The Battle of the Sexes '60
Saturday Night and Sunday Morning '60
Room at the Top '59
Time Without Pity '57

William A. Fraker (1923-)
Waking Up in Reno '02
Town and Country '01
Rules of Engagement '00
The Island of Dr. Moreau '96
A Woman's Guide to Adultery '93
Father of the Bride Part 2 '95
Street Fighter '94
Tombstone '93
Honeymoon in Vegas '92
The Freshman '90
Chances Are '89
Baby Boom '87
Burglar '87
Protocol '84
WarGames '83
Sharky's Machine '81
The Hollywood Knights '80
1941 '79
Heaven Can Wait '78
The Exorcist II: The Heretic '77
Looking for Mr. Goodbar '77
Rancho Deluxe '75
Aloha, Bobby and Rose '75
Bullitt '68
Rosemary's Baby '68
Games '67
The President's Analyst '67
The Boogie Man Will Get You '42

Graham Frake
The Truth About Love '04

David Frazee
Everything's Gone Green '06

Benito Frattari
Commandos '73
Taste of Death '68
Mondo Cane '63

Ellsworth Fredericks (1904-93)
Picture Mommy Dead '66
Seven Days in May '64
Tall Story '60
The Light in the Forest '58
Sayonara '57
Friendly Persuasion '56
Invasion of the Body Snatchers '56
Chained Heat 3: Hell Mountain '98

Neal Fredericks
Killer Me '01
The Blair Witch Project '99

Jonathan Freeman
Hollywoodland '06
The Prize Winner of Defiance, Ohio '05
Good Fences '03
At Gunpoint '55
Shotgun '55
Taken '02
Monday Night Mayhem '02
Hitched '01
Ignition '01
Lost Battalion '01
Resurrection '99
Deadly Game '98
Failing Fire '97
Junior's Groove '97
Carver's Gate '96

Lloyd Freidus
Murder in Greenwich Village '37

Henry Freulich (1906-85)
Good Day for a Hanging '58
The 27th Day '57
Bonanza Town '51
Son of Rusty '47
The Courage to Love '00
Resurrection '99
You '42
Blondie in Society '41
Blondie Has Trouble '40
Blondie On a Budget '40
Blondie Plays Cupid '40
Blondie for Victory '42
Blondie Goes Latin '42
Blondie Goes to College '42
Blondie's Blessed Event '42
Blondie Brings Up Baby '39
Blondie Meets the Boss '39
Blondie Takes a Vacation '39
Blondie '38

Silvio Fraschetti
Reactor '85
War in Space '77

Tom Fraser
Enemy at the Gates '00
La Buche '99
Vatel '00
Ronin '98
Seven Years in Tibet '97
Zombietown '07
Frankenstein General Hospital '88
Citizen X '95
The Unnamable '88
Alien from L.A. '67
Hospital '88
The Lover '92
L'Addition '85
Lady Chatterley's Lover '81
Emmanuelle, the Joys of a Woman '76

Karl Freund (1890-1969)
Key Largo '48
South of St. Louis '48
Undercurrent '46
Without Love '45
A Guy Named Joe '44
The Seventh Cross '44
Du Barry Was a Lady '43
Tortilla Flat '42
The Chocolate Soldier '41
Pride and Prejudice '40
Balalaika '39
Rose of Washington Square '39
Letter of Introduction '38
Conquest '37
The Good Earth '37
Murders in the Rue Morgue '32
Dracula '31

Personal Maid '31
All Quiet on the Western Front '30
Metropolis '26
Variety '25
The Last Laugh '24
The Golem '20

Ron Fricke
Baraka '93
Koyaanisqatsi '83

Martin Fuhrer (1956-)
P.D. James: Death in Holy Orders '03
The Gathering '02
Goodbye, Mr. Chips '02
The Sleeping Dictionary '02
Wilde '97

Hideo Fujii
The Adventures of Milo & Otis '89
Milo & Otis '89
Irezumi '83

Tak Fujimoto
The Happening '08
John Adams '08
Breach '07
The Final Cut '04
The Manchurian Candidate '04
Signs '02
The Truth About Charlie '02
The Replacements '00
The Sixth Sense '99
Beloved '98
A Thousand Acres '97
That Thing You Do! '96
Devil in a Blue Dress '95
Grumpier Old Men '95
Philadelphia '93
Gladiator '92
Night and the City '92
Crooked Hearts '91
The Silence of the Lambs '91
Miami Blues '90
Cocoon: The Return '88
Married to the Mob '88
Sweet Hearts Dance '88
Ferris Bueller's Day Off '86
Pretty in Pink '86
Something Wild '86
Swing Shift '84
Melvin and Howard '80
Where the Buffalo Roam '80
Cannonball '76
Death Race 2000 '75
Badlands '74
Caged Heat '74
The Nest '88

Michael Gallagher
Bloodfist 7: Manhunt '95
Bloodfist 6: Ground Zero '94

Tom Galligan
The Dude Bandit '33
The Three Musketeers '33
Boiling Point '32
Local Badman '32

Mark Anthony Galluzzo
R.S.V.P. '02
Magenta '96

Brendan Galvin
Blood & Chocolate '07
Flight of the Phoenix '04
Thunderbirds '04
Bookies '03
Veronica Guerin '03
Behind Enemy Lines '01

Robert Gantz
Assault on Precinct 13 '05
Mindhunters '05

Rodrigo Garcia (1959-)
Body Shots '99
Gia '98
Four Rooms '95

Ron Garcia
The First $20 Million is Always the Hardest '02
Deliberate Intent '01
Baby '00
The Runaway '00
Mutiny '99
Small Vices: A Spenser Mystery '99
The Great White Hype '96
Twin Peaks: Fire Walk with Me '92
El Diablo '90
Disorganized Crime '89

Greg Gardiner
Welcome Home Roscoe Jenkins '08
The Game Plan '07
She's the Man '06
Herbie: Fully Loaded '05
Son of the Mask '05
New York Minute '04
Biker Boyz '03
Elf '03
Big Trouble '02
Men in Black 2 '02
Orange County '02
To End All Wars '01
Dean Koontz's Mr. Murder '98
Where's Marlowe? '98
Homegrown '98
The Apocalypse '96
Somebody's Waiting '96
Boys Life '94
Suture '93

James Gardner
Hustle '04
Naked City: A Killer Christmas '98

Lee Garmes (1898-1978)
A Big Hand for the Little Lady '66
Abdulla the Great '56
D-Day, the Sixth of June '56
Desperate Hours '55
Land of the Pharaohs '55
Actors and Sin '52
The Lusty Men '52
Detective Story '51
Our Very Own '50
Caught '49
My Foolish Heart '49
Nightmare Alley '47
The Paradine Case '47
The Secret Life of Walter Mitty '47
Love Letters '45
Guest in the House '44
Since You Went Away '44
Forever and a Day '43
Footlight Serenade '42
The Jungle Book '42
Lydia '41
Angels Over Broadway '40
Dreaming Lips '37
Smilin' Through '33
Shanghai Express '32
Strange Interlude '32
Dishonored '31
Scarface '31
Disraeli '30
Morocco '30
The Show Off '26

Andres Garreton
Darkdrive '98
Total Reality '95
Intimate Relations '95

Marcello Gatti (1924-)
The Switch '76
The Black Belly of the Tarantula '71
Burn! '70
The Battle of Algiers '66

Gaetano Antonio "Tony" Gaudio (1885-1951)
The Red Pony '49
Love from a Stranger '47
I've Always Loved You '46
A Song to Remember '45
Days of Glory '43
The Great Lie '41
High Sierra '41
The Man Who Came to Dinner '41
Brother Orchid '40
The Fighting 69th '40
The Letter '40
Juarez '39
The Old Maid '39
The Adventures of Robin Hood '38
Amazing Dr. Clitterhouse '38
Dawn Patrol '38
Kid Galahad '37
The Life of Emile Zola '37
Anthony Adverse '36
The Story of Louis Pasteur '36
The Mask of Fu Manchu '32
Hell's Angels '30
Little Caesar '30
The Gaucho '27
The Notorious Lady '27
Kismet '20

Eric Gautier (1961-)
Into the Wild '07
A Guide to Recognizing Your Saints '06
The Motorcycle Diaries '04
The Housekeeper '02
Esther Kahn '00
Intimacy '00
Les Destinees '00
Pola X '99
Those Who Love Me Can Take the Train '98
Irma Vep '96
Love, etc. '96
My Sex Life... Or How I Got into an Argument '96
One Hundred and One Nights '95
The Favorite Son '94
Undercurrent '99

Carlos Gaviria
A Gun, a Car, a Blonde '97

David Geddes
The Messengers '07
Nearing Grace '05
Halloween: Resurrection '02
Fatal Error '99
Don't Look Down '98
My Husband's Secret Life '98
A Call to Remember '97
Killing Mr. Griffin '97
The Colony '95
Incident at Deception Ridge '94
Call of the Wild '93
When a Stranger Calls Back '93

Luke Geissbuhler (1970-)
Borat: Cultural Learnings of America for Make Benefit Glorious Nation of Kazakhstan '06
Alchemy '05
Mail Order Wife '04
Acts of Worship '01

Alessio Gelsini Torresi (1951-)
The Emperor's New Clothes '01

Lu Gengxin
The Blonde '92
The Emperor's Shadow '96
Ermo '94

Dominique Gentil
Moolaade '04
Winged Migration '01

Laszlo George
Tarzan and the Lost City '98
Dangerous Ground '96
Cry, the Beloved Country '95
Model Behavior '00
The Stepsister '97
Last Flight Out: A True Story '90
Swimsuit '89
Vanishing Act '88

Dejan Georgevich
Satan's Little Helper '04
Love Thy Neighbor '06

Henry W. Gerrard (1894-)
Of Human Bondage '34
Little Women '33
The Most Dangerous Game '32
Beggars of Life '28

Merritt B. Gerstad (1900-74)
Watch on the Rhine '43
Bulldog Drummond's Secret Police '39
Strike Me Pink '36
A Night at the Opera '35
Imitation of Life '34
Freaks '32
The Mad Whirl '25

Maury Gertsman (1907-99)
Invisible Invaders '59
The Creature Walks among Us '56
To Hell and Back '55
Red Ball Express '52
Double Crossbones '51
Singapore '47
The Brute Man '46
Dressed to Kill '46
She Wolf of London '46
Terror by Night '46
Jungle Captive '45

Ebraheem Ghafouri
Osama '03
Kandahar '01

Rodney Gibbons
Eye '96
Natural Enemy '96
Screamers '06
My Bloody Valentine '81

Gerald Gibbs (1907-90)
Devil Doll '64
Quatermass 2 '57
X The Unknown '56

Paul Gibson
Paris Is Burning '91
The Refrigerator '91

Sue Gibson (1952-)
Mrs. Dalloway '97
Hear My Song '91

William Gibson (1914-)
Macbeth '05
Wolf Creek '05

Peter Gilbert (1957-)
Prefontaine '96

Alfred Gilks
The Secret of Dr. Kildare '39
Sky Parade '36

Pierre Gill
Beyond the Rocks '22

Dan Gillham
The Thing About My Folks '05

Paul Gilpin
In Desert and Wilderness '01

Xavi Gimenez (1970-)
The Abandoned '06
The Machinist '04
Darkness '02

Aldo Giordani (1914-)
Amuck! '71

Blasco Giurato (1941-)
Terror of the Steppes '64
Atom Age Vampire '61
Too Bad She's Bad '54
The Worker and the Hairdresser '96
A Pure Formality '94
Cinema Paradiso '88

Irving Glassberg (1906-58)
Tarnished Angels '57
The Black Shield of Falworth '54
Ride Clear of Diablo '54
Duel at Silver Creek '52
The Lawless Breed '52
The Strange Door '51
Casbah '48

Ken Glassing
Brigham City '01
Southern Man '99

Hone Glendinning
The Hooded Terror '38
Ticket of Leave Man '37

Pierre William Glenn (1943-)
And Now Ladies and Gentlemen '02
Coup de Torchon '81
Loulou '80
Avalanche '78
Small Change '76
The Judge and the Assassin '75
Day for Night '73

Bert Glennon (1893-1967)
Crime Wave '54
House of Wax '53
Rio Grande '50
Copacabana '47
The Red House '47
Dive Bomber '41
They Died with Their Boots On '41
Our Town '40
Stagecoach '39
Dimples '36
Lloyds of London '36
The Prisoner of Shark Island '36
Scarlet Empress '34
The Half Naked Truth '32
Are Parents People? '25

James Glennon (1942-2006)
Good Boy! '03
United States of Leland '03
About Schmidt '02
Local Boys '02
Blonde '01
Dead Simple '01
Life Without Dick '01
Madison '01
Playing Mona Lisa '00
South of Heaven, West of Hell '00
Election '99
The Runner '99
Best Men '98
Citizen Ruth '96
Lifeform '96
Mojave Moon '96
My Very Best Friend '96
Mrs. Munck '95
High Stakes '93
In the Deep Woods '91
Smooth Talk '85

Paul Glickman
The Stuff '85
God Told Me To '76
Tracks '76
Dracula vs. Frankenstein '71

Richard C. Glouner (1932-98)
Awakening of Candra '81
The Savage Bees '76
Payday '73
Moon of the Wolf '72
The Dunwich Horror '70
The Gay Deceivers '69

Agnes Godard (1950-)
The Intruder '04
Strayed '03
Friday Night '02
Beau Travail '98
The Dreamlife of Angels '98
The New Eve '98
Nenette and Boni '96
I Can't Sleep '93

Michael Goi (1959-)
Witless Protection '08
Red Water '01
Echo of Murder '00
Forbidden Sins '99
The Fixer '97

Stephen Goldblatt (1945-)
Charlie Wilson's War '07
Rent '05
Closer '04
Angels in America '03
Path to War '02
Conspiracy '01
The Deep End of the Ocean '98
Batman and Robin '97
Striptease '96
Batman Forever '95
The Pelican Brief '93
For the Boys '91
The Prince of Tides '91
Joe Versus the Volcano '90
Lethal Weapon 2 '89
Lethal Weapon '87
The Cotton Club '84
The Hunger '83
Outland '81

Eric Goldstein
Dr. Dolittle 3 '06
Dr. Doolittle 3 '06
Break a Leg '03
Mr. Barrington '03
Shelter '98
Naked Souls '95

David Golia
Street Corner Justice '96
The Rosary Murders '87
Horror on Highway 5 '86

Juan Carlos Gomez
Dark Blue Almost Black '06
El Bola '01

Carlos Gonzalez
Arachnid '01
The Breaks '99
The Omega Code '99
Wishmaster 2: Evil Never Dies '98
Original Gangstas '96
Mutant Species '95
Victim of Desire '94

Frank B. Good (1884-1939)
Thunder Mountain '35
Dude Ranger '34
The Wizard of Oz '25
The Van '77

Pliny Goodfriend (1891-1981)
Fast Bullets '36
The Midnight Phantom '35
Skull & Crown '35

Irv Goodnoff
Touched '05
James Dean: Live Fast, Die Young '01

Russ Goozee
Universal Soldier 2: Brothers in Arms '98
Universal Soldier 3: Unfinished Business '98

Gerald R. Goozie
Cybermutt '02
Hostile Intent '97
Specimen '97
Fata Combat '96
Electra '95
Street Law '95
The Escort '97
Invisible Dad '97
James Dean: Live Fast, Die
Young '97
The Corporation '96
Friend of the Family 2 '96
Scorned 2 '96
Sexual Roulette '96
Vice Girls '96
Centerfold '95
Femme Fontaine: Killer
Babe of the C.I.A. '95

Seth Gordon
Hit Me '96
Fall Time '94

Mark J. Gordon
Invisible Mom '96

Vyacheslav Gordanov
Peter the First: Part 2 '38
Peter the First: Part 1 '37

Michael Gornick
New York Doll '05
The King of Kong: A Fistful
of Quarters '07

Michael Grady
Bug '06
The Dead Girl '06
Factory Girl '06
Around the Bend '04
Wonderland '03
The Last Man '00
Day of the Dead '85
Creepshow '82
Knightriders '81
Dawn of the Dead '78
Martin '77

Guillermo Granillo
The Crime of Father Amaro
'02
Deep Crimson '96
In the Middle of Nowhere
'93

Arthur Grant (1915-72)
Satan's Sad sts '69
Demons of the Mind '72
Dynasty of Fear '72
Blood from the Mummy's
Tomb '71
Taste the Blood of Dracula
'70
Frankenstein Must Be
Destroyed '69
The Devil Rides Out '68
Dracula Has Risen from the
Grave '68
The Mummy's Shroud '67
Frankenstein Created
Woman '66
Plague of the Zombies '66
The Reptile '66
The Witches '66
Tomb of Ligeia '64
Paranoiac '62
The Phantom of the Opera
'62
The Curse of the Werewolf
'61
The Abominable Snowman
'57

Gary Graver (1938-2006)
Quigley '03
The Long Ride Home '01
The Capital Conspiracy '99
Death and Desire '97
The Net 95
Invisible Dad '97
A Rookie of the Year '93
Unforgiven '92
Deceived '91
Heartbreak Ridge '86
Bird '88

Mark W. Gray
Firetrap '01
Sand Trap '97
Back to Back '96
Dark Rider '91

Aldo (G.R. Aldo) Graziatti (1902-53)
Twist & Shout '84
Othello '52

Richard Greatrex
Flawless '07
Run, Fat Boy, Run '07
Big Nothing '06
The Detonator '06
The Upside of Anger '05
Connie and Carla '04
I Capture the Castle '02
A Knight's Tale '01
James Dean '01
Save the Last Dance '01
If These Walls Could Talk 2
'00
Shakespeare in Love '98
Mrs. Brown '97
Blue Juice '95

Robbie Greenberg
Wild Hogs '07
Even Money '06
The Santa Clause 3: The
Escape Clause '06
A Guy Thing '03
Marci X '03

Guy Green (1913-2005)
Dirt Boy '01
Relative Strangers '06
Sweet Dreams '85
Swamp Thing '82
The Lathe of Heaven '80
Papa's Delicate Condition
'63
Girls! Girls! Girls! '62
G.I. Elues '60
The Buccaneer '58
When Worlds Collide '50
High Lonesome '50
The Big Cat '49

Jeffrey Greeley
Dandridge '99
Winchell '98
Fools Rush In '97
Sunset Park '96
Under Siege 2: Dark
Territory '95
Free Willy '93

Frank Griebe (1965-)
Perfume: The Story of a
Murderer '06
Heaven '01
The Princess and the
Warrior '01
Run Lola Run '98
Winter Sleepers '97

Garett Griffin
Lover's Knot '96
Space Marines '96
Fists of Iron '94

Loyal Griggs (1906-78)
Camille 2000 '69
The Greatest Story Ever.
Told '65
In Harm's Way '65
The Slender Thread '65

Jaems Grant (1952-)
Strange Fits of Passion '99
Head On '98
Jigsaw '90

Moray Grant (1917-77)
I, Monster '71
Vampire Circus '71
The Horror of Frankenstein
'70
The Vampire Lovers '70

John and Julie '55
Captain Horatio Hornblower
'51
Madeleine '50
Blanche Fury '48
Oliver Twist '48
Great Expectations '46

Jack N. Green (1946-)
Immortal Battalion '44
Man in the Mirror: The
Michael Jackson Story '04
Sidings '04
Creator '85

David (Robert) A. Greene
Are We Done Yet? '07
The 40 Year Old Virgin '05
Serenity '05
A Man Apart '03
Against the Ropes '04
50 First Dates '04
Secondhand Lions '03
Seduced: Pretty When You
Cry '01
Space Cowboys '00
Girl, Interrupted '99
True Crime '99
Absolute Power '97
Midnight in the Garden of
Good and Evil '97

Barry Gravelle
Ice Spicers '07
Requiem for Murder '99
Home Team '98
The Lost World '98
Sir Arthur Conan Doyle's
When Justice Falls '98
Bleeders '97
Face the Evil '97
Sci-Fighters '96
The Witchboard 3: The
Possession '95

Wolfgang Grasshoff
Nuclear Conspiracy '85
No Time to Die '84
Spare Parts '79

Adam Greenberg (1939-)
Snakes on a Plane '06
Collateral Damage '02
The Santa Clause 2 '02
Inspector Gadget '99
Rush Hour '98
La Bamba '87
Near Dark '87
Three Men and a Baby '87
Once Bitten '85
Private Manoeuvres '83
The Big Red One '80
The Uranium Conspiracy
'78

Mutz Greenbaum (1896-1968)
Roaring City '51
The Lost Continent '51
Mask of the Dragon '51
Danger Zone '51
Kentucky Jubilee '51
Leave It to the Marines '51
Nine Lives '57

Jack Greenhalgh (1904-71)
Pier 23 '51
Savage Drums '51
Sky High '51
Fear in the Night '47
Heartaches '47
Money Madness '47
Danny Boy '46
The Mask of Dijon '46
The Lady Confesses '45
Shadows of Death '45
White Pongo '45
Dead Men Walk '43
Law and Order '42
Junior '94
Cave '93
Sister Act '92
Toys '92
Ghost '90
Terminator 2: Judgment
Day '91

David Gribble (1946-)
Jesse Stone: Death in
Paradise '06
Jesse Stone: Night Passage
'05
The World's Fastest Indian
'05
Ike: Countdown to D-Day
'04
Chill Factor '99
The Quest '96
Nowhere to Run '93
Fires Within '91

Peter Greenhalgh
His Fighting Blood 35
The Traitor '36
Rogue of the Range '36

Karen Grossman
The Big Turnaround '88
Microwave Massacre '83

Francis Grumman
The Slayer '82

Ennio Guarnieri (1930-)
Callas Forever '02
Francesco '93
A Family Matter '91
A.D. '85
Silent Rebellion '82
The Cassandra Crossing
'76
The Inheritance '76
The Garden of the Finzi-
Continis '71

Alexander Grusynski (1950-)
Nancy Drew '07
This Christmas '07
Deliver Us from Eva '03
The In-Laws '03
The Brothers '01
Two Can Play that Game
'01
Dick '99
54 '98
Angus '95
I Like It Like That '94
Threesome '94
Stone Cold '91

Shana Hagan
My Sweet Victim '85
Bad Dreams '88

Eric Haase
American Pie Presents: The
Naked Mile '06
The Lather Effect '06

Rob Hahn
The Stepford Wives '04
The Scorpion '01
Loser '00
In and Out '97

Ron Hagen (1947-)
After Innocence '05

Bert Haines
Steamboat Bill, Jr. '28
College '27
Battling Butler '26
The General '26

Burnett Guffey (1905-83)
The Great White Hope '70
The Learning Tree '69
The Silencers '66
The Ambushers '67
Bonnie & Clyde '67
How to Succeed in Business
without Really Trying '67
King Rat '65
Good Neighbor Sam '64
Birdman of Alcatraz '62
Kid Galahad '62
Homicidal '61
Mr. Sardonicus '61
Let No Man Write My
Epitaph '60
Gidget '59
Me and the Colonel '58
The Strange One '57
The Harder They Fall '56
Tight Spot '55
The Violent Men '55
Human Desire '54
Private Hell 36 '54
From Here to Eternity '53
Sirocco '51
In a Lonely Place '50

Manfred Guthe
Twitches Too '07
Twitches '05
Poltergeist: The Legacy '96

Carl Guthrie (1905-67)
The Gunfight at Dodge City
'59
House on Haunted Hill '58
Lady Godiva '55
Long John Silver '54
Francis Covers the Big
Town '53
Francis Goes to West Point
'52
Bedtime for Bonzo '51
Storm Warning '51
Caged '50

Carlos Gusi
Fatwa '06
In the Flesh '97

Brian Gurley
Delta Force '86
Secret of Yolanda '82

Yevgeni Guslinsky
See Eugeny Guslinsky

Eugeny Guslinsky
Termination Man '97
Marquis de Sade '96

Kurt Grigoleit
Naked in the Night '58
The Third Sex '57

Allen Guilford
The Legend of Johnny Lingo
'03
Aberration '97

David Gurfinkel
Under the Domim Tree '95
Blink of an Eye '92
The Crazy Stranger '98
Mondo '96

Eric Guichard
Paris, je t'aime '05
Himalaya '99
The Woodsman '04
Is Paris Burning? '66
Macron '70

Xavier Perez Grobet
Music & Lyrics '07
Monster House '06
Nacho Libre '06
Nacho '05
Chasing Papi '03
A Painted House '03
In the Time of the Butterflies
'01
Tortilla Soup '01
Before Night Falls '00
Santitos '99
Esmeralda Comes by Night
'98

Marcel Grignon (1914-90)
The Beast '75
The Shepherd of the Hills
'41

Jacques Haitkin
All the King's Men '49
Knock on Any Door '49
Reckless Moment '49
The Climb '07
The Stupids '95
Poltergeist: The Legacy '96
Shut Up and Kiss Me '05
Hell's Gate '01
The Ambulance '90
Shocker '89
To Die For '89
Cherry 2000 '88
The Hidden '87
A Nightmare on Elm Street
2: Freddy's Revenge '85
The Kovak Box '06
Take My Eyes '03
Vacas '91

Making the Grade '84
A Nightmare on Elm Street '84
House Where Evil Dwells '82
Galaxy of Terror '81
Long Shot Kids '81
The Private Eyes '80

Conrad L. Hall (1926-2003)
Road to Perdition '02
American Beauty '99
A Civil Action '98
Without Limits '97
Searching for Bobby Fischer '93
Tequila Sunrise '88
Black Widow '87
Incubus '82
Marathon Man '76
The Day of the Locust '75
Smile '75
Electra Glide in Blue '73
Fat City '72
Butch Cassidy and the Sundance Kid '69
The Happy Ending '69
Hell in the Pacific '69
Tell Them Willie Boy Is Here '69
Cool Hand Luke '67
Divorce American Style '67
In Cold Blood '67
Harper '66
The Professionals '66
Incubus '65
Morituri '65

Conrad W. Hall (1958-)
The Longshots '08
Two for the Money '05
The Punisher '04
Panic Room '02
A Gentleman's Game '01

Geoffrey Hall
Shadow Man '06
Kidnapped '05
Dirty Deeds '02
Chopper '00

Jess Hall
Hot Fuzz '07
Stander '03

Harry Hallenberger (1877-1954)
Louisiana Purchase '41

Ernest Haller (1896-1970)
Dead Ringer '64
Lilies of the Field '63
Married Too Young '62
What Ever Happened to Baby Jane? '62
Men in War '57
Plunder Road '57
Rebel without a Cause '55
Humoresque '46
Saratoga Trunk '45
Dark Victory '39
The Roaring Twenties '39
Four Daughters '38
Jezebel '38
King of the Jungle '33

Doug Hallows
Kill Your Darlings '06
Mr. Fix It '06
The Iris Effect '04
The Badge '02
Bark! '02
Outside Ozona '98
Subterfuge '98
Lured Innocence '97
Perfect Crime '97

Fenton Hamilton
It's Alive 2: It Lives Again '78
It's Alive '74
Black Caesar '73
Hell Up in Harlem '73

Victor J. (Jimmy W.) Hammer (1957-)
House of Cards '92
Going Under '91
Lean on Me '89

Peter Hannan (1941-)
The Gathering Storm '02
Longitude '00
Not Without My Daughter '90
How to Get Ahead in Advertising '89
A Handful of Dust '88
The Lonely Passion of Judith Hearne '87
Withnail and I '87
Dance with a Stranger '85
Insignificance '85
Monty Python's The Meaning of Life '83
Dangerous Summer '82

Kazutami Hara
Akira Kurosawa's Dreams '90
Godzilla 1985 '85

Alain Hardy
Sensual Partners '87
Revenge in the House of Usher '82

Russell Harlan (1903-74)
Hatari! '62
To Kill a Mockingbird '62
Pollyanna '60
Sunrise at Campobello '60
The Day of the Outlaw '59
Operation Petticoat '59
Rio Bravo '59
King Creole '58
Run Silent, Run Deep '58
Witness for the Prosecution '57
Blackboard Jungle '55
The Thing '51
Gun Crazy '49
Red River '48
A Walk in the Sun '46
The Kansan '43
Twilight on the Trail '41
Renegade Trail '39

Virgil Harper
Sweet Insanity '06
Miracle at Sage Creek '05
Tremors 3: Back to Perfection '01
The Event '03
No One Sleeps '01
Ripper: Letter from Hell '01
Beefcake '99
Defying Gravity '99

Irek Hartowicz (1951-)
Music Within '07

Harvey Harrison
R.P.M. '97
The Witches '90
American Gothic '88
Salome's Last Dance '88
Castaway '87
Cheech and Chong's The Corsican Brothers '84
Cheech and Chong: Still Smokin' '83
The Burning '82

Thomas M. Harting
Single White Female 2: The Psycho '05

Walter J. (Jimmy W.) Harvey (1903-)
Race for Life '55
Black Glove '54
Blackout '54
Heat Wave '54
Paid to Kill '54
Terror Street '54
Unholy Four '54
Three Stops to Murder '53

The Gambler & the Lady '52
Scotland Yard Inspector '52
A Stolen Face '52
River of Unrest '36

Kiyoshi Hasegawa
Samurai Reincarnation '81
Phoenix '78

Kim Haun
Body Strokes '95
Friend of the Family '95
I Like to Play Games '95

Robert B. Hauser (1919-94)
The Frisco Kid '79
Mean Dog Blues '78
Twilight's Last Gleaming '77
Walking Tall: The Final Chapter '77
Le Mans '71
Willard '71
A Man Called Horse '70
Soldier Blue '70
Hail, Hero! '69
The Odd Couple '68

Yuri Haviv
Double Agent 73 '80
I Spit on Your Grave '77

James Hawkinson (1962-)
The Hitcher '07
Progeny '98

Robert Hayes
The Last Sentinel '07
Welcome to Paradise '07
Pit Fighter '05
Witches of the Caribbean '05
Devil's Knight '03
Body Armor '06
Werewolf '95
Mind, Body & Soul '92
Driven to Kill '90
Hardcase and Fist '89

James Hayman
Buffy the Vampire Slayer '92
Blades '89

George Heath
The Fighting Rats of Tobruk '44

Brian R.R. Hebb
Humongous '82
July Group '81

Antoine Heberle
Paradise Now '05
The Girl from Paris '02
Under the Sand '00

Matthew Heckerling
Left in Darkness '06
Crazylove '05

Dan Heigh
Whacked! '02
The Basket '99
Matter of Trust '98
Laws of Deception '97
Navajo Blues '97
Pie in the Sky '95
It's My Party '95
The Nutt House '92

Bernd Heinl
Milwaukee, Minnesota '03
The Little Vampire '00
The Extreme Adventures of Super Dave '98
Wicked '98
Johnny Skidmarks '97
Julian Po '97
The Last of the High Kings '96

Wolfgang Held
Crazy Love '07
Teeth '07
Disappearances '06
Poster Boy '04
Undermind '03
Fallout '01
Maze '01
The Tic Code '99
Floating '97
Ripe '97

Dogs: The Rise and Fall of an All-Girl Bookie Joint '96
Wigstock: The Movie '95

Otto Heller (1896-1970)
I'll Never Forget What's 'Isname '67
Alfie '66
Funeral in Berlin '66
The Ipcress File '65
Woman of Straw '64
Victim '61
Peeping Tom '60
The Sheriff of Fractured Jaw '59
Who Done It? '56
The Ladykillers '55
They Made Me a Fugitive '47
Mr. Emmanuel '44
De Mayerling a Sarajevo '40

Peter Hendry
1915 '82
Love Under Pressure '78

Peter Hennessy (1916-)
Cat Girl '57
Time Lock '57

David Hennings
Strange Wilderness '08
Ice Princess '05
Underclassman '05
Breakin' All The Rules '04
You Got Served '04
Blue Crush '02
Boycott '02
Cheaters '00
Meet the Deedles '98
Tom Clancy's Netforce '98
Very Bad Things '98
Asteroid '97
D3: The Mighty Ducks '96
Titanic '96

Gilles Henry
Moliere '07
Priceless '06
Apres-Vous '03
Van Gogh '91

David Herrington
Carry Me Home '04
A Killing Spring '02
Verdict in Blood '02
You Stupid Man '02
Blues Brothers 2000 '98

Karl Herrmann
Missing Pieces '00
Kounterfeit '96
America's Dream '95

John Herzog
A Cry in the Wild '90
Heavy Traffic '73

Gregg Heschong
Crackerjack 2 '97
Hello Mary Lou: Prom Night 2 '87

Sid Hickox (1895-1982)
Battle Cry '55
Them! '54
White Heat '49
The Big Sleep '46
God is My Co-Pilot '45
All Through the Night '42
Underground '41
The Wagons Roll at Night '41
A Slight Case of Murder '38
San Quentin '37

Ken Higgins
Hot Millions '68
Cop-Out '67
Georgy Girl '66
Darling '65

Jack Hildyard (1908-90)
Lion of the Desert '81
Emily '77
The Message '77
The Beast Must Die '75
Puppet on a Chain '72
Topaz '69
Villa Rides '68
Casino Royale '67
Modesty Blaise '66
Battle of the Bulge '65
Circus World '64
55 Days at Peking '63
The V.I.P.'s '63
The Road to Hong Kong '62
The Millionairess '60
The Sundowners '60
The Devil's Disciple '59
Suddenly, Last Summer '59
Another Time, Another Place '58
The Bridge on the River Kwai '57
Anastasia '56
Summertime '55
Hobson's Choice '53

Richard Hilliard
Horror of Party Beach '64
The Lonely Sex '59

Erwin Hillier (1911-2005)
The Valley of Gwangi '69
Happy Go Lovely '51
I Know Where I'm Going '45
Butler's Dilemma '43

Sinsaku Himeda (1916-97)
Vengeance Is Mine '79
Proof of the Man '77
Tora! Tora! Tora! '70

Harvey Hines
Kid from Gower Gulch '50
Silver Bandit '50

Milas C. Hinshaw
Mystery Mansion '83
Dream Chasers '82

Paul Hipp (1938-2006)
Psycho from Texas '81
The Incredible Two-Headed Transplant '71
Superchick '71
Corruption '70

Julien Hirsch (1964-)
Lady Chatterley '06
Changing Times '04
Our Music '04
In Praise of Love '01

Gerald Hirschfeld (1921-)
Coma '78
The Car '77
Two Minute Warning '76
Young Frankenstein '74
Cotton Comes to Harlem '70
The Incident '67
Fail-Safe '64

Daf Hobson (1951-)
Othello '01
Sword of Honour '01
Welcome to Sarajevo '97
Go Now '96

Winton C. Hoch (1907-79)
The Witching '72
The Green Berets '68
Robinson Crusoe on Mars '64
Five Weeks in a Balloon '62
Voyage to the Bottom of the Sea '61
The Young Land '59
Missouri Traveler '58
Jet Pilot '57
The Searchers '56
Mister Roberts '55
The Halls of Montezuma '50
She Wore a Yellow Ribbon '49
Tulsa '49
Melody Time '48
Three Godfathers '48
Dive Bomber '41
Dr. Cyclops '40

Zoran Hochstatter (1955-)
Body Chemistry 4: Full Exposure '95
Demolition High '95
Almost Dead '94

Hard Bounty '94
Night Fire '94
Home for Christmas '93
Revenge of the Nerds 3: The Next Generation '92
Not of This Earth '88

Ken Hodges (1922-93)
No Sex Please—We're British '73
The Ruling Class '72

Carl Hoffmann
Faust '26
Dr. Mabuse, The Gambler '22

Florian Hoffmeister
Five Days '07
The Hamburg Cell '04

Henner Hofmann
Warden of Red Rock '01
Immortal Combat '94

Siegfried Hold
M'Lady's Court '73
Apache's Last Battle '64

Adam Holender (1937-)
Carlito's Way: Rise to Power '05
Stateside '04
Road to Riches '01
A Price above Rubies '97
Wide Awake '97
8 Heads in a Duffel Bag '96
I'm Not Rappaport '96
Smoke '95
Fresh '94
To Kill a Priest '89
Street Smart '87
Idolmaker '80
Panic in Needle Park '71
Midnight Cowboy '69

Keith Holland
One of Them '03
Blind Heat '00
Bloody Murder '99
Hindsight '97
Trucks '97
Dark Secrets '95
Carnosaur '93

John Holosko
The Jesse Ventura Story '99
Face Down '97

Bodo Holst
Beyond Fear '93
Pushed to the Limit '92

Ernest Holzman
Cora Unashamed '00
Double Edge '97
Love Jones '96

John Hooper
The Scarlet Pimpernel 3: The Kidnapped King '99
Catherine Cookson's The Dwelling Place '94
Buddy's Song '91

Nathan Hope
Fear '05
Mimic 2 '01
Nice Guys Sleep Alone '99
The Prophecy 3: The Ascent '99

John Hora
God Said "Ha!" '99
Matinee '92
Gremlins 2: The New Batch '90
Gremlins '84
Twilight Zone: The Movie '83
The Howling '81

Louis Horvath
Mesmerized '84
Strange Invaders '83
Strange Behavior '81
Black Samurai '77
Brain of Blood '71

Alan Hostetter
The 24th Day '04
Orwell Rolls in His Grave '03

Byron Houck (1891-1969)
Seven Chances '25
The Navigator '24
Sherlock, Jr. '24

Tom Houghton
State Property 2 '05

The Lookout '04
Fire Down Below '97

James Wong Howe (1899-1976)
The Old Man and the Sea '9C
Hombre '67
Seconds '66
Hud '53
Molly Maguires '70
The Heart is a Lonely Hunter '68
Funny Lady '75
Song Without End '60
Bell, Book and Candle '58
The Last Angry Man '59
The Old Man and the Sea '58
Sweet Smell of Success '57
Picnic '55
The Rose Tattoo '55
Come Back, Little Sheba '52
The Fighter '52
Baron of Arizona '51
Passage to Marseilles '44
Air Force '43
The North Star '43
Hangmen Also Die '43
Yankee Doodle Dandy '42
Kings Row '41
Strawberry Blonde '41
Abe Lincoln in Illinois '40
City for Conquest '40
Torrid Zone '40
Oklahoma Kid '39
They Made Me a Criminal '39
The Adventures of Tom Sawyer '38
Algiers '38
Fire Over England '37
Prisoner of Zenda '37
Under the Red Robe '36
The Guyana Tragedy: The Story of Jim Jones '80
Mark of the Vampire '35
Manhattan Melodrama '34
The Thin Man '34
Chandu the Magician '32
The King on Main Street '25
Peter Pan '24

Matt Howe
Blood Relic '05
Desolation Angels '95
Parallel Sons '95

Gil Hubbs
Flowers in the Attic '87
California Girls '84
This is Elvis '81
Enter the Dragon '73

Roger Hubert (1903-64)
Paris Holiday '57
Portrait of an Assassin '49
Children of Paradise '44
Eternal Return '43
Napoleon '27

Andrew Huebscher
Believers '07
Chasing Ghosts '05
Window_Theory '04

Michael Hugo
The Mountain Men '80
The Bastard '78
The Manitou '78
Bug '75
Head '68

Alan Hume (1924-)
20,000 Leagues Under the Sea '97
Eye of Destruction '90
Shirley Valentine '89
A Fish Called Wanda '88
Lifeforce '85
Just Like a Woman '95
Annie: A Royal Adventure '95
Runaway Train '85
A View to a Kill '85
Supergirl '84
Octopussy '83
Return of the Jedi '83
Caveman '81
For Your Eyes Only '81
The Watcher in the Woods '81
The People That Time Forgot '77
At the Earth's Core '76
The Land That Time Forgot '75
'73

John Huneck
Big Brother Trouble '00
Charlotte Sometimes '02
Walking on Water '02
The Invisibles '99

Robert Humphreys
Nora's Hair Salon '04
Dopamine '03

John Hunek
Diamond Men '01
Kiss of the Vampire '89
Dr. Terror's House of Horrors '65
Carry On Cowboy '66

J. Roy Hunt (1884-1972)
Gunplay '51
Riders of the Range '50
Storm over Wyoming '50
I Walked with a Zombie '43
Call Out the Marines '42
The Flying Irishman '39
Panama Lady '39
Room Service '38
Without Orders '36
She '35
Dancing Mothers '26

W. Mott Hupfel, III
The Savages '07
The Notorious Bettie Page '06
Boys Life '94

Shane Hurlbut
Semi-Pro '08
Swing Vote '08
Something New '06
We Are Marshall '06
Waist Deep '06
The Greatest Game Ever Played '05
Into the Blue '05
Mr. 3000 '04
crazy/beautiful '01
Drumline '02
The Skulls '00
The Rat Pack '98
Played '05

Peter Hyams (1943-)
A Sound of Thunder '05
The Musketeer '01
End of Days '99
The Relic '96
Sudden Death '95
Timecop '92
Stay Tuned '92
Running Scared '86
Contact '84
2010: The Year We Make Contact '84
Capricorn One '80
1:1.14 '03
Drumline '02
The Daytrippers '96

Tom Hurwitz
Our Brand is Crisis '05
Subway Stories '97
Creepshow 2 '87
Wanted: The Perfect Guy '86

Peter Hyams
Howling 3: The Marsupials '87
The Alice '04
The Last Bastion '84
Return of Captain Invincible '83

Louis Irving
Working Girls '87
Eat Your Heart Out '96
The Settlement '99
Eban and Charley '01

Judy Irola (1943-)
Act of Aggression '73

Silvano Ippoliti (1923-)
Caligula '80

David Insley
Cry-Baby '90
Hairspray '88
Polyester '81

John Inwood
The Daytrippers '96
Six Ways to Sunday '99

Arthur Ibbetson (1922-97)
Santa Claus: The Movie '85
The Bounty '84
Sell Out '76
When Eight Bells Toll '71
Willy Wonka & the Chocolate Factory '71
The Railway Children '70
Inspector Clouseau '68
Where Eagles Dare '68
A Countess from Hong Kong '67
Die! Die! My Darling! '65
Murder at the Gallop '63
Murder She Said '61
Whistle down the Wind '61
The Horse's Mouth '58

Slawomir Idziak (1945-)
Harry Potter and the Order of the Phoenix '07
King Arthur '04
Black Hawk Down '01
Proof of Life '00
The Last September '99
Love and Rage '99
Gattaca '97
I Want You '98
The Journey of August King '95
Trois Couleurs: Bleu '93
The Double Life of Veronique '91
The Decalogue '88
From a Far Country: Pope John Paul II '81
Contract '80

Tony Imi (1937-)
Chaos & Cadavers '03
Victoria & Albert '01
Rancid Aluminium '00
The Abduction '96
Dalva '96
Shopping '93
Carolina Skeletons '92
Wired '89
Enemy Mine '85
A Christmas Carol '84
The Slipper and the Rose '76
Edward the King '75
It's Not the Size That Counts '74

Takeo Ito
Drunken Angel '48
The Men Who Tread on the Tiger's Tail '45

Paul Ivano (1900-84)
The Naked Flame '68
Black Angel '46
Slightly Terrific '44
Dangerous Passage '44
Dark Mountain '44
Gambler's Choice '44
Queen Kelly '29

Stefan Ivanov (1954-)
Marion Bridge '02
Genealogies of a Crime '97

Fred H. Jackman, Jr. (1913-82)
Viva Knievel! '77
Harum Scarum '65
Earth vs. the Flying Saucers '56
Coroner Creek '48
The Prince of Thieves '48

Marco Isoli
Desperate Crimes '93
Evil Clutch '89

Levie Isaacks
Bring It On: In It to Win It '07
Dead Men Can't Dance '97
North Shore Fish '97
The Dentist '96
Marshal Law '96
The Dogfighters '95
The Expert '95
The Texas Chainsaw Massacre 4: The Next Generation '95
The Wharf Rat '95
Leprechaun '93
Spontaneous Combustion '89
Saturday the 14th Strikes Back '88

Peter James (1947-)
27 Dresses '08
Cheaper by the Dozen 2 '05
The Pacifier '05
And Starring Pancho Villa as Himself '03
Bride of the Wind '01
Meet the Parents '00
Double Jeopardy '99
Paradise Road '97
Last Dance '96
Silent Fall '94
Alive '93
My Life '93
Black Robe '91
Driving Miss Daisy '89
The Irishman '78

Andrew Janczak
Caddie '76

Maris Jansons
Subway Stories '97
Double Play '96
The Halfback of Notre Dame '96

Anthony C. "Tony" Jannelli
All I Wanna Do '98
Lovelife '97

Julius Jaenzon
The Phantom Chariot '20
Treasure of Arne '19

Igor Jadue-Lillo
The Hitchhiker's Guide to the Galaxy '05
Disco Pigs '01
The Low Down '00
The Newton Boys '97

Daniel Jobin (1949-)
Varian's War '01
It's My Turn, Laura Cadieux '98
The Hanging Garden '97
Lilies '96

Jorgen Johansson
Death Games '80

Ron Johanson (1949-)
Freedom '82

Andrew Jackson
The Strongest Man in the World '75
I Love You, Goodbye '74
Don't Be Afraid of the Dark '73

Jeong-hun Jeong
Three... Extremes '04
Oldboy '03

Peter C. Jensen
Ratas, Ratones, Rateros '99

Harry Jackson (1896-1953)
The Halls of Montezuma '51
Ticket to Tomahawk '50
Mother Wore Tights '47
Greenwich Village '44

Donald G. Jackson (1943-2003)
Roller Blade Warriors: Taken By Force '90
Hell Comes to Frogtown '88

Fred W. Jackman (1881-1959)
Killer Diller '48
Devil's Pond '03
Man of the Century '99

Matthew Jensen
Unknown Island '48
Yankee Doodle in Berlin '19

Robert C. Jessup
Death of a Gunfighter '69

Peter Jessop (1930-)
Lady Vengeance '05

Julius Jaenzon
Charlie Chan on Broadway '37
Think Fast, Mr. Moto '37
Charlie Chan at the Race Track '36
Charlie Chan at the Opera '36

Jon Joffin (1963-)
Gilachi '88

Thomas Jewett
Fast Money '96
Serial Killer '95
Scanner Cop 2: Volkin's Revenge '94

David C(lark) Johnson (1962-)
Alien vs. Predator '04
Resident Evil '02

David Johnson
Public Enemy '31
Steamboat Bill, Jr. '28
Battling Butler '26
The General '26

Johnny E. Jensen
Material Girls '06
The Game of Their Lives '05
Wisegirls '02
The Flamingo Rising '01
The Ladies Man '00
Morgan's Ferry '99
Rosewood '96
Three Wishes '95
Grumpy Old Men '93
An American Story '92
Rambling Rose '91

Manfred O. Jelinski
Nekromantik 2 '91
Der Todesking '89

Devereaux Jennings (1884-1952)
Helltown '38

Bruce Douglas Johnson
Harold and Kumar Go to White Castle '04
Scorched '02
The Contaminated Man '01
Drowning Mona '00
Happy, Texas '99
Perfect Assassins '96
Cadillac Ranch '96
Red Ends '98

David Johnson
The Prophecy '95
Public Access '93

Hugh Johnson
Eragon '06

Frank Johnson
The Mill on the Floss '97
The Very Thought of You '98
Hilary and Jackie '98
An Ideal Husband '99

Matthew Jensen
Parker '84
Schizo '77
House of Whipcord '75
Frightmare '74
Flesh and Blood Show '73
The Harder They Come '72

Robert C. Jessup
Lady Vengeance '05
Oldboy '03

Igor Jadue-Lillo
The Phantom of the Opera '43
The Wolf Man '41
Man Made Monster '41

David Johnson
Resident Evil: Extinction '07
On a Clear Day '05

Jon Joffin (1963-)
Porky's Revenge '85
Silent Rage '82
Deadly Blessing '81
Race with the Devil '75
Creature of Destruction '67
Mars Needs Women '66

Thomas Jewett
Wilbur Wants to Kill Himself '02
Kira's Reason—A Love Story '01

Ron Johanson
Mikey '92
New York '99
Aftershock: Earthquake in New York '99

The Chronicles of Riddick '04
G.I. Jane '97
White Squall '96

Kirsten Johnson
Darfur Now '07
This Film Is Not Yet Rated '06

Shelly Johnson
Sky High '05
Hidalgo*'04
Jurassic Park 3 '01
The Last Castle '01
Durango '99
A Season for Miracles '99
Quicksilver Highway '99
Saint Maybe '98
Alien Nation: Millennium '96
Alien Nation: Body and Soul '95
Hitz '89
Jack's Back '87

Dusan Joksimovic
The Keeper: The Legend of Omar Khayyam '05
The Wounds '98
Pretty Village, Pretty Flame '96

Lawrence Jones
Strange Relations '02
In His Life: The John Lennon Story '00
The 10th Kingdom '00
Reckless: The Sequel '98

Richard A. Jones
Wanted '98
Turn of the Blade '97

Jon Jost (1943-)
The Bed You Sleep In '93
Slow Moves '84

Mario Garcia Joya
Strawberry and Chocolate '94
Alias, La Gringa '91
Letters from the Park '88

Ray June (1895-1958)
Court Jester '56
Above and Beyond '53
The Secret Garden '49
Night Must Fall '37
Wife Versus Secretary '36
China Seas '35
Horse Feathers '32
The Bat Whispers '30
Alibi '29
Through the Breakers '28

Jeffrey Jur
The Eye '08
You Kill Me '07
Last Call: The Final Chapter of F. Scott Fitzgerald '02
My Big Fat Greek Wedding '02
Joy Ride '01
My First Mister '01
Panic '00
How Stella Got Her Groove Back '98
Funny Games '97
Horton Foote's Alone '97
Unforgettable '96
The Last Seduction '94
Dirty Dancing '87
Soul Man '86
Screen Test '85

Hans Jura
Little Mother '71
The Lickerish Quartet '70
Therese & Isabelle '67
Carmen, Baby '66

Jurgen Jurges (1940-)
Time of the Wolf '03
Code Unknown '00
Funny Games '97
Faraway, So Close! '93
Germany, Pale Mother '80
Fear of Fear '75
Ali: Fear Eats the Soul '74
Effi Briest '74
Tenderness of the Wolves '73

Emmanuel (Manu) Kadosh
The Christmas Miracle of Jonathan Toomey '07
The Lost City '05

Modigliani '04

Mahmoud Kalari
Boutique '04
Gabbeh '04

Ernst W. Kalinke (1918-)
Mark of the Devil '69
Strangler of Blackmoor Castle '63

Steven Kaman
Mob War '88
Search and Destroy '88
Firehouse '87
Hangmen '87

Janusz Kaminski (1959-)
Indiana Jones and the Kingdom of the Crystal Skull '08
The Diving Bell and the Butterfly '07
Munich '05
War of the Worlds '05
Catch Me If You Can '02
Minority Report '02
A. I.: Artificial Intelligence '01
Saving Private Ryan '98
Amistad '97
The Lost World: Jurassic Park 2 '97
Jerry Maguire '96
Schindler's List '93
Class of '61 '92
Homicidal Impulse '92
Cool As Ice '91
Wildflower '91
Grim Prairie Tales '89

Adam Kane
Resurrecting the Champ '07
Skinwalkers '07
The Man '05
Redeemer '02
The Last Debate '00
The Life Before This '99
Calendar '93

Stephen M. Katz
A Death in the Family '02
Her Majesty '01
Return to Cabin by the Lake '01
Gepetto '00
I'll Remember April '99
Baby Geniuses '98
Gods and Monsters '98
Mrs. Santa Claus '96
Letter to My Killer '95
My Summer Story '94
18 Again! '88
Last Resort '86
The Blues Brothers '80
Kentucky Fried Movie '77
Las Vegas Lady '76
Pom Pom Girls '76
Switchblade Sisters '75

David Katznelson
Driving Lessons '06
The Queen's Sister '05

Boris Kaufman (1906-80)
The Brotherhood '68
The Group '66
The Pawnbroker '65
The World of Henry Orient '64
Gone Are the Days '63
Purlie Victorious '63
Long Day's Journey into Night '62
The Fugitive Kind '60
Twelve Angry Men '57
Baby Doll '56
Patterns '56
On the Waterfront '54
L'Atalante '34
A Propos de Nice '29
Zero for Conduct '33

Lloyd Kaufman (1945-)
Stuck on You '84
First Turn On '83
Waitress '81
Squeeze Play '79

Judith Kaufmann (1962-)
Unveiled '05
Nico Icon '95

Stephen Kazmierski
Dedication '07
Two Weeks '06
Transamerica '05
A Hole in One '04
Love in the Time of Money '02
Skins '02
Tart '01
You Can Count On Me '99
The Bumblebee Flies Anyway '98
The Myth of Fingerprints '97
Grind '96

Michel Kelber
Phedre '68
It Means That to Me '60
The Hunchback of Notre Dame '57
Beauty and the Devil '50
Devil in the Flesh '46

Alfred S. Keller (1911-89)
Homesteaders of Paradise Valley '47
Under Colorado Skies '47
Wild Frontier '47
G.I. War Brides '46
Rio Grande Raiders '46

Wallace Kelley (1902-82)
Paradise, Hawaiian Style '66
The Nutty Professor '63
Who's Minding the Store? '63

Nina Kellgren
Wondrous Oblivion '06
Solomon and Gaenor '98

Roy Kellino (1912-56)
Johnny Frenchman '46
Nine Men '43
I Met a Murderer '39

Shane Kelly
A Scanner Darkly '06
Urbania '00
Delivered '98

Ken Kelsch
The Black Widow '05
Testosterone '03
'R Xmas '01
It Had to Be You '00
Invisible Child '99
Dying to Get Rich '98
The Imposters '98
New Rose Hotel '98
Rear Window '98
The Blackout '97
A Brooklyn State of Mind '97
Montana '97
Subway Stories '97
The Funeral '96
The Addiction '95
Big Night '95
Condition Red '95
Killer: A Journal of Murder '95
DROP Squad '94
Bad Lieutenant '92
Driller Killer '79

Victor Kemper (1927-)
American Pie Presents Band Camp '05
Eddie '96
Jingle All the Way '96
Tommy Boy '95
Beethoven '92
F/X 2: The Deadly Art of Illusion '91
See No Evil, Hear No Evil '89
Clue '85
Pee-wee's Big Adventure '85
The Lonely Guy '84
Mr. Mom '83
National Lampoon's Vacation '83
Xanadu '80
And Justice for All '79
The Jerk '79
Coma '78
Eyes of Laura Mars '78
Magic '78
Audrey Rose '77
Slap Shot '77
Dog Day Afternoon '75
The Reincarnation of Peter Proud '75
The Gambler '74
The Candidate '72
The Hospital '71
They Might Be Giants '71
Husbands '70

Nils Kenaston
Borough of Kings '98
Day at the Beach '98
Mob Queen '98

Francis Kenny
Cover '08
Edison Force '05
Getting Played '05
From Justin to Kelly '03
Finder's Fee '01
How High '01
Kingdom Come '01
Scary Movie '00
She's All That '99
A Night at the Roxbury '98
Something About Sex '98
Bean '97
Harriet the Spy '96
A Thin Line Between Love and Hate '96
Coneheads '93
Wayne's World 2 '93
New Jack City '91
Heathers '89

John Kenway
My Uncle Silas '01
Dr. Bell and Mr. Doyle: The Dark Beginnings of Sherlock Holmes '00

Glenn Kershaw
At First Sight '95
A Kiss Goodnight '94
Sins of the Night '93
Fatal Skies '90

Rolf Kestermann
Casual Sex? '88
Surf Nazis Must Die '87

Scott Kevan (1972-)
Cleaner '07
Stomp the Yard '07
Deepwater '05
The Hollow '04
Plain Dirty '04
Cabin Fever '03
The Job '03
The Trip '02

Darius Khondji (1955-)
Funny Games '07
My Blueberry Nights '07
The Interpreter '05
Wimbledon '04
Anything Else '03
Panic Room '02
The Beach '00
The Ninth Gate '99
In Dreams '99
Alien: Resurrection '97
Evita '96
Stealing Beauty '96
The City of Lost Children '95
Seven '95
Delicatessen '92

Gary B. Kibbe (1941-)
John Carpenter's Ghosts of Mars '01
John Carpenter's Vampires '97
Escape from L.A. '96
In the Mouth of Madness '95
Village of the Damned '95
Double Dragon '94
RoboCop 3 '91
They Live '88
Prince of Darkness '87

Jan Kiesser
Luna: Spirit of the Whale '07
Beowulf & Grendel '06
Fido '06
Now & Forever '02
Rare Birds '01
Dr. T & the Women '00
Holiday Heart '00
Trixie '00
The Dress Code '99
The Baby Dance '98
Such a Long Journey '98
National Lampoon's Dad's Week '97
Bad Moon '96
Georgia '95
Man with a Gun '95
Mrs. Parker and the Vicious Circle '94
Clean and Sober '88
Fright Night '85
Choose Me '84

Shawn Kim
Smiley Face '07
Ghetto Dawg '02

Jeffrey L. Kimball (1943-)
Bonneville '06
Glory Road '06
Be Cool '05
The Big Bounce '04
Paycheck '03
Star Trek: Nemesis '02
Windtalkers '02
Mission: Impossible 2 '00
Stigmata '99
Wild Things '98
The Specialist '94
True Romance '93
Jacob's Ladder '90
Beverly Hills Cop 2 '87
Top Gun '86

Adam Kimmel
Lars and the Real Girl '07
Capote '05
Beyond Suspicion '00
Jesus' Son '99
Monument Ave. '98
Almost Heroes '97
Subway Stories '97
Beautiful Girls '96
Bed of Roses '95
New Jersey Drive '95

Mike King
Don't Tell '05

Rory King
Dirty Laundry '07

Sven Kirsten (1955-)
School's Out '99
Beyond Desire '94
Play Time '94
Teresa's Tattoo '94
Mistress '91

Alar Kivilo (1953-)
The Lookout '07
The Lake House '06
The Ice Harvest '05
Normal '03
Hart's War '02
The Glass House '01
Frequency '00
A Simple Plan '98
Weapons of Mass Distraction '97
Gotti '96

Eugen Klagemann
The Merry Wives of Windsor '50
The Marriage of Figaro '49
The Murderers Are Among Us '46

Rainer Klausmann (1949-)
The Invasion '07
Downfall '04
Head On '04
The Experiment '01

David Klein (1972-)
Clerks 2 '06
Novel Romance '06
Tattoo, a Love Story '02
Wish You Were Dead '00
Chasing Amy '97
Mallrats '95
Clerks '94

Vladimir Klimov (1949-)
Out of the Cold '99
The Thief '97

Benjamin (Ben H.) Kline (1894-1974)
Bull of the West '71
Munster, Go Home! '66
Holiday Rhythm '50
Operation Haylift '50
Last of the Wild Horses '49
Tough Assignment '49
Rolling Home '48
Shoot to Kill '47
Trail of the Mounties '47
Detour '46
Before I Hang '40
Two-Fisted Law '32

Richard H. Kline (1926-)
Meet Wally Sparks '97
Double Impact '91
My Stepmother Is an Alien '88
Howard the Duck '86
All of Me '84
Death Wish 2 '82
Body Heat '81
Star Trek: The Motion Picture '79
The Fury '78
Who'll Stop the Rain? '78
I Wonder Who's Killing Her Now? '76
King Kong '76
Battle for the Planet of the Apes '73
Harrad Experiment '73
Soylent Green '73
The Mechanic '72
The Andromeda Strain '71
Camelot '67
Hang 'Em High '67

Edward Klosinski (1943-2008)
Gloomy Sunday '02
Trois Couleurs: Blanc '94
Kill Cruise '90
The Decalogue '88
Mother of Kings '82
Man of Iron '81
Illumination '73

Thomas Kloss (1956-)
Showtime '02
Palmetto '98
Fear '96

Douglas Knapp
Assault on Precinct 13 '76
The First Nudie Musical '75
Dark Star '74

David Knaus
Red Shoe Diaries: Swimming Naked '00
Bird of Prey '95

Nicholas D. Knowland
Piano Tuner of Earthquakes '05
Joseph and the Amazing Technicolor Dreamcoat '00
Institue Benjamenta or This Dream People Call Human Life '95
Manigault '96
The Invaders '95
Barbarians at the Gate '93

Wilic West '33

Bernard Knowles (1900-75)
Sec'et Mission '42
Gasiight '40
Young and Innocent '37
Sabotage '36
The Secret Agent '36
The 39 Steps '35

Cyril Knowles (1905-61)
Secret Mission '42
King Solomon's Mines '37
Doe '88

Fred W. Koenekamp (1922-)
Flight of the Intruder '90
Listen to Me '89
Welcome Home '89
Alice in Wonderland '85
Buckaroo Banzai Across the Eighth Dimension '84
Two of a Kind '83
Wron, Is Right '82
First Monday in October '81
The Hunter '80
When Time Ran Cut '80
The Amityville Horror '79
The Champ '79
Love and Bullets '79
The Swarm '78
The Bad News Bears in Breaking Training '77
The Domino Principle '77
Fun with Dick and Jane '77
Islands in the Stream '77
The Other Side of Midnight '77
Embryo '76
Doc Savage '75
The McCullochs '75
White .1ine Fever '75
The Towering Inferno '74
Uptown Saturday Night '74
Papillon '73
Rage '72
Billy Jeck '71
Beyond the Valley of the Dolls '70
Patton '70

Karl Kotler (1940-)
Echo Fark '86
The Children of Theatre Street '77

Hajime Koizumi
War of the Gargantuas '70
Godzilla vs. Monster Zero '68
Dagora, the Space Monster '65
Ghidrah the Three Headed Monster '65
Godzilla vs. Mcthra '64
Attack of the Mushroom People '63
King Kong vs. Godz lla '63
Gorath '62
Mothra '62

Lajos Koltai (1946-)
Being Julia '04
The Emperor's Club '02
Max '02
Taking Sides '01
Sunshine '99
Malena '00
The Legend of 1900 '98
Out to Sea '97
Mother '96
Home for the Holidays '95
Just Cause '94
When a Man Loves a Woman '94
Woman '94
Born Yesterday '93
Wrestling Ernest Hemingway '93
Meeting Venus '91
People '63

Mobsters '91
White Palace '90
Homer and Eddie '89
Hanussen '88
Gaby: A True Story '87
Colonel Red '84
Time Stands Still '82
Mephisto '81
Angi Vera '78
Adoption '75

Setsuo Kobayashi (1920-)
Normagi Pass '71
An Actor's Revenge '63
Fires on the Plain '59

Douglas Koch
The Bronx is Burning '07
Last Night '98

Shigeru Komatsubara
Dr. Akagi '98
The Eel '96

Avi Koren
When Night is Falling '95
Kidnapping of Baby John Doe '88

Fred W. Koenekamp

Gabriel Kosuth (1958-)
Hellraiser: Hellworld '05
Return of the Living Dead: Rave to the Grave '05

Simon Kossoff
Dead Gorgeous '02
The Scarlet Pimpernel '99
The Scarlet Pimpernel 2: Mademoiselle Guillotine '99

Carl F. Koschick (1949-)
Go for Zucker '05
Agnes and His Brothers '04

Laszlo Kovacs (1933-2007)
Two Weeks Notice '02
Miss Congeniality '00
Return to Me '00
Jack Frost '98
My Best Friend's Wedding '97
Multiplicity '96
Copycat '95
Free Willy 2: The Adventure Home '95
The Scout '94
Say Anything '89
The Toy '82
For Pete's Sake '74
Five Easy Pieces '70
Blood of Dracula's Castle '69
Easy Rider '69
Rebel Rousers '69
Mantis in Lace '68
Targets '68
Hell's Angels on Wheels '57
Incredibly Strange Creatures Who Stopped Living and Became Mixed-Up Zombies '63

Pete Kozachik
Tim Burton's Corpse Bride '05
James and the Giant Peach '96
The Nightmare before Christmas '93

Sergei Kozlov (1964-)
Border Blues '03
The Lion in Winter '03
House of Fools '02
The Quickie '01
Jason and the Argonauts '00

Leland Krane
Confess '05
Giving It Up '99
Under Hellgate Bridge '99
The Odyssey '97

Gunther Krampf (1899-1950)
The Ghoul '34
Pandora's Box '28
The Hands of Orlac '25
Nosferatu '22

Milton Krasner (1904-88)
Beneath the Planet of the Apes '70
The Sterile Cuckoo '69
The St. Valentine's Day Massacre '67
The Singing Nun '66
Red Line 7000 '65
The Sandpiper '65
Goodbye Charlie '64
How the West Was Won '63
Love with the Proper Stranger '63
The Courtship of Eddie's Father '62
The Four Horsemen of the Apocalypse '62
Sweet Bird of Youth '62
Two Weeks in Another Town '62
The King of Kings '61
Bells Are Ringing '60
Home from the Hill '60
An Affair to Remember '57
Bus Stop '56
The Girl in the Red Velvet Swing '55
The Seven Year Itch '55
Demetrius and the Gladiators '54
Desiree '54
Garden of Evil '54
Three Coins in the Fountain '54

Robert Krasker (1913-81)
Trap '66
The Collector '65
The Heroes of Telemark '65
The Fall of the Roman Empire '64
Billy Budd '62
Birdman of Alcatraz '62
El Cid '61
The Story of Esther Costello '57
Trapeze '56
Alexander the Great '55
Romeo and Juliet '54
Senso '54
Another Man's Poison '52
Cry, the Beloved Country '51
The Third Man '49
Odd Man Out '47
Brief Encounter '46
Caesar and Cleopatra '46
Henry V '44

Richard Kratina (1928-)
Fourth Wise Man '85
Brainwaves '82
Make a Million '35

Henning Kristiansen (1927-2006)
Royal Deceit '94
Babette's Feast '87
Pelle the Conqueror '87
Parallel Corpse '83

Eric Kress
Flickering Lights '01
Tr'e Kingdom 2 '97
Tr'e Kingdom '95
'96

Les Krizsan
Monkey Business '52
Phone Call from a Stranger '52
People Will Talk '51
All About Eve '50
No Way Out '50
Rawhide '50
Three Came Home '50
House of Strangers '49
The Set-Up '49
The Accused '48
Up in Central Park '48
A Double Life '47
Egg and I '47
The Farmer's Daughter '47
Something in the Wind '47
Dark Mirror '46
Without Reservations '46
Along Came Jones '45
Scarlet Street '45
The Invisible Man's Revenge '44
Woman in the Window '44
Good Bye, Lenin! '03
The Trio '97
El Diablo Rices '39
Carnival Lady '33

Toni Kuhn (1942-)
The Prodigy '98
Like A Bride '94
Homework '90

Willy Kurant (1934-)
Poola Tang '01
The Baby-Sitters' Club '95
White Man's Burden '95
A Business Affair '93
Day of Atonement '93
China Moon '91
Trade Secrets '86
Tuff Turf '85
French Intrigue '70
Mystery Trooper '32

Ellen Kuras (1959-)
Be Kind Rewind '08
The Spoilers '42
Buck Privates '41
The Bank Dick '40
The House of the Seven Gables '40
The Invisible Man Returns '40

Edward Kull (1886-1946)

Howard Krupa
1999 '98
Kicked in the Head '97
Rhythm Thie' '94

J. Henry Kruse
The Duke Is Tops '38
Silent Valley '35

Alvin Kuchler (1965-)
Proof '05
Code '03
The Mother '03
Morvern Callar '02
Lucky Break '01
The Claim '00
Ratcatcher '99
Jimmy & Judy '06
Cock & Bull Story '03
Gang of Roses '03
Players '03

Ben Kutrin

Tom Krueger
Committed '91

Svein Krovel
Elling '01
Self-Defense '83

Jules Kruger (1891-1959)
Sidewalks of London '38
Pepe Le Moko '37
Napoleon '27

Robert B. Kurrie (1890-1932)
Trouble in Mind '86
Powwow Highway '89
Grand Isle '92
Waiting to Exhale '95
Woman Undone '95
Lakota Woman: Siege at Wounded Knee '94
Homecoming '96
Infinity '96
Afterglow '97
Taboo '99
Universe: Super Nova '97
Universe: I Worship His Shadow '97
Universe: Giga Shadow '97
Ta es from a Parallel Universe: Eating Pattern '97
Married? '07

Toyomichi Kurita (1950-)
Tyler Perry's Why Did I Get Married? '07
Madea's Family Reunion '06
First Daughter '04
Cookie's Fortune '99
Afterglow '97
Homecoming '96
Lakota Woman '94

Luigi Kuveiller (1927-)
New York Ripper '82
Deep Red: Hatchet Murders '75
A Lizard in a Woman's Skin '71

Khasan Kydyraliyev
Beshkempir the Adopted Son '98

Christopher La Vasseur
Descent '07
2B Perfectly Honest '04

Jules Labarthe
Descent '07
The Arousers '70
The Velvet Vampire '71
Lady in Red '79
Saturday the 14th '81
Battle Beyond the Stars '80
Humanoids from the Deep '80

Flavio Labiano
See Flavio Martinez Labiano

Daniel Lacambre
'68 '87

Edward Lachman (1948-)
Magical Mystery Tour '67

Serge Ladouceur (1952-)
Mambo Italiano '03
Bonanno: A Godfather's Story '99
Savage Messiah '02
The Rudy Giuliani Story '03

Alex Lamarque
Crimson Rivers 2: Angels of the Apocalypse '05

Kjell Lagerros (1961-)
Ambush '99
Like It Never Was Before '95

Rick Lamb
Mexican Blow '02
Hell's Belles '95
The Love Machine '71

Ken Lamkin
Big Bad John '90
Texas Guns '90

Sabine Lancelin
Belle Toujours '06
I'm Going Home '00

Ardy Lam
Dreaming of Rita '94
Angela '94
Unzipped '94
Swoon '91

Charles B(ryant) Lang, Jr. (1902-98)
The Spectator '04
The Son's Room '00
Elective Affinities '96
Traveling Companion '96
Caro Diario '93
Palcmbe:la Rossa '89
Devil in the Flesh '87

Giuseppe Lanci (1942-)
Eternal Sunshine of the Spotless Mind '04
Coffee and Cigarettes '03
Analyze That '02
Personal Velocity: Three Portraits '02
Blow '01
Bamboozled '00
The Mod Squad '99
Summer of Sam '99
Just the Ticket '98
I Shot Andy Warhol '96
If These Walls Could Talk '96
Postcards from America '95
Crime Story '93
Supercop '92
A Bullet in the Head '90

Edward Lachman
London Kills Me '91
Portfolio '88
Less Than Zero '87
True Stories '86
Desperately Seeking Susan '85

Sabrina '54
The Big Heat '53
Salome '53
Sudden Fear '52
Ace in the Hole '51
Fancy Pants '50
September Affair '50
The Great Lover '49
A Foreign Affair '48
The Ghost and Mrs. Muir '47
Blue Skies '46
The Uninvited '44
So Proudly We Hail '43
The Shepherd of the Hills '41
Sundown '41
The Ghost Breakers '40
Midnight '39
Spawn of the North '38
You and Me '38
Angel '37
Souls at Sea '37
The Lives of a Bengal Lancer '35
Death Takes a Holiday '34
Gambling Ship '33
She Done Him Wrong '33
A Farewell to Arms '32
No One Man '32
Vice Squad '31
Tom Sawyer '30

Martin Langer (1959-)
Sophie Scholl: The Final Days '05
The Tunnel '01

Bryan Langley
Lassie from Lancashire '38
No. 17 '32

Norman G. Langley (1935-)
Jekyll and Hyde '90
House of the Long Shadows '82
Die Screaming, Marianne '73

Reggie Lanning (1893-1965)
Carolina Cannonball '55
Abbott and Costello Meet the Keystone Kops '54
Sands of Iwo Jima '49
Lights of Old Santa Fe '47
Rainbow over Texas '46
Sioux City Sue '46
Silver City Kid '45
King of the Cowboys '43
Bells of Capistrano '42
Man from Cheyenne '42
Frontier Vengeance '40
Gaucho Serenade '40
Days of Jesse James '39
Zorro's Fighting Legion '39
Heroes of the Hills '38

Roger Lanser
As You Like It '06
Strange Bedfellows '04
Till Human Voices Wake Us '02
Maybe Baby '99
Kings in Grass Castles '97
Prince Valiant '97
Billy's Holiday '95
A Midwinter's Tale '95
Much Ado about Nothing '93

Vilis Lapenieks (1931-87)
Rainbow Bridge '71
Planet of Blood '66
Hollywood after Dark '65
Night Tide '63
Eegah! '62
Hideous Sun Demon '59

Jeanne Lapoirie
Time to Leave '05
They Came Back '04
8 Women '02
Confusion of Genders '00
Under the Sand '00
Set Me Free '99
Water Drops on Burning Rocks '99
Full Speed '96
Les Voleurs '94
Wild Reeds '94

Stevan Larner (1930-2005)
Partners in Crime '99
Forbidden Choices '94
Guilty Conscience '85
Fatal Vision '84
Twilight Zone: The Movie '83
Rehearsal for Murder '82
Caddyshack '80
A Rumor of War '80
The Buddy Holly Story '78
Roots '77
Badlands '74
The Student Nurses '70

Federico G. Larraya
A Place Called Glory '66
A Fistful of Dollars '64

Jean-Claude Larrieu
Paris, je t'aime '06
My Life Without Me '03
Oriana '85

Joseph LaShelle (1905-89)
Barefoot in the Park '67
The Fortune Cookie '66
Kiss Me, Stupid! '64
The Honeymoon Machine '61
The Apartment '60
Career '59
The Long, Hot Summer '58
The Naked and the Dead '58
Crime of Passion '57
I Was a Teenage Werewolf '57
The Conqueror '56
Marty '55
River of No Return '54
Dangerous Crossing '53
The Jackpot '50
Come to the Stable '49
Road House '48
Hangover Square '45
Laura '44

Jacek Laskus (1951-)
The Whole Shebang '01
Common Ground '00
The Devil's Arithmetic '99
A Soldier's Sweetheart '98
Elmore Leonard's Gold Coast '97
The Garden of Redemption '97
The Undercover Kid '95
Stepfather 2: Make Room for Daddy '89
Parting Glances '86

Walter Lassally (1926-)
The Ballad of the Sad Cafe '91
The Deceivers '88
The Bostonians '84
Pudd'nhead Wilson '84
Private School '83
Heat and Dust '82
The Private History of a Campaign That Failed '81
Danger in the Skies '79
Great Bank Hoax '78
Hullabaloo over Georgie & Bonnie's Pictures '78
Wild Party '74
Run, Stranger, Run '73
Savages '72
Something for Everyone '70
Zorba the Greek '64
Tom Jones '63
The Loneliness of the Long Distance Runner '62
A Taste of Honey '61
Beat Girl '60
A Matter of Dignity '57
Girl in Black '56

Andrew Laszlo (1926-)
Star Trek 5: The Final Frontier '89
Poltergeist 2: The Other Side '86
Remo Williams: The Adventure Begins '85
Streets of Fire '84
Thief of Hearts '84
First Blood '82
The Funhouse '81
Southern Comfort '81
The Warriors '79
The Man Without a Country '73
The Owl and the Pussycat '70

Ernest Laszlo (1905-84)
Logan's Run '76
Showdown '73
Airport '70
Daddy's Gone A-Hunting '69
Star! '68
Luv '67
Fantastic Voyage '66
Ship of Fools '65
Baby, the Rain Must Fall '64
Four for Texas '63
It's a Mad, Mad, Mad, Mad World '63
Judgment at Nuremberg '61
Inherit the Wind '60
Tormented '60
Attack of the Puppet People '58
While the City Sleeps '56
The Big Knife '55
The Kentuckian '55
Kiss Me Deadly '55
Apache '54
Naked Jungle '54
The Moon Is Blue '53
Stalag 17 '53
Vera Cruz '53
The Star '52
The Well '51
D.O.A. '49
Impact '49
On Our Merry Way '48
The Road to Rio '47
Two Years before the Mast '46
Pace That Kills '28

Philip Lathrop (1912-95)
Deadly Friend '86
National Lampoon's Class Reunion '82
Foolin' Around '80
Swashbuckler '76
Airport 75 '75
Hard Times '75
Earthquake '74
Mame '74
The Gypsy Moths '69
They Shoot Horses, Don't They? '69
I Love You, Alice B. Toklas! '68
The Cincinnati Kid '65
The Pink Panther '64
36 Hours '64
Lonely Are the Brave '62
The Monster of Piedras Blancas '57

Andrew Lau
See Wai Keung (Andrew) Lau

Tom Lau
The Bodyguard from Beijing '94
The Heroic Trio '93
Twin Warriors '93

Wai Keung (Andrew) Lau (1960-)
Once Upon a Time in China III '93
Wicked City '92
City on Fire '87

Paul Laufer
The Cell '00
Frankie Starlight '95

Dan Laustsen (1954-)
Wind Chill '07
Silent Hill '06
Darkness Falls '03
The League of Extraordinary Gentlemen '03
Brotherhood of the Wolf '01
Running Free '00
Heart of Light '97
Mimic '97
Nightwatch '96
Emma's Shadow '88

Charles Lawton, Jr. (1904-65)
A Raisin in the Sun '61
Comanche Station '60
Cowboy '58
Gunman's Walk '58
Last Hurrah '58
3:10 to Yuma '57
The Long Gray Line '55
Kill the Umpire '50
The Nevadan '50
The Lady from Shanghai '48
Getting Gertie's Garter '45
Big Store '41

Vernon Layton
My First Wedding '04
Seed of Chucky '04
I Still Know What You Did Last Summer '98
High School High '96
The Englishman Who Went up a Hill But Came down a Mountain '95
Under Suspicion '92

Jean-Yves Le Mener
The Visitors '95
The Fatal Image '90

Marcel Le Picard (1887-1952)
'Neath Canadian Skies '46
Trouble Chasers '45
Ghost Crazy '44
The Invisible Ghost '41
The Pioneers '41
Zis Boom Bah '41
Roll, Wagons, Roll '39
The Shadow Strikes '37
America '24

Yorick Le Saux (1968-)
5x2 '04
Swimming Pool '03
Sitcom '97

Sam Leavitt (1904-84)
The Man in the Glass Booth '75
Evil Roy Slade '72
Star Spangled Girl '71
The Passing of Evil '70
Desperados '69
The Wrecking Crew '68
Guess Who's Coming to Dinner '67
Murderers' Row '66
Major Dundee '65
Advise and Consent '62
Diamond Head '62
Cape Fear '61
Seven Thieves '60
Anatomy of a Murder '59
Pork Chop Hill '59
The Defiant Ones '58
Hot Rod Girl '56
An Annapolis Story '55
The Court Martial of Billy Mitchell '55
The Man with the Golden Arm '55
Carmen Jones '54
A Star Is Born '54
The Thief '52

Pavel Lebeshev (1941-2003)
Prisoner of the Mountains '96
Anna '93
The Ascent '76

Henry Lebo
We'll Meet Again '02
Ebenezer '97

Claude Lecomte
Le Grand Chemin '87
The Women '68

Philip Lee
Protecting the King '07
Terminal Error '02
Route 666 '01
From Dusk Till Dawn 2: Texas Blood Money '98
Spoiler '98
Galaxies Are Colliding '92

Pin Bing Lee
See Mark Lee Ping-Bin

Robert Lefebvre (1907-89)
I Am Frigid... Why? '72
Her and She and Him '69
Please Not Now! '61
Voulez-Vous Danser avec Moi? '59
Casque d'Or '52
Beethoven '36

Jason Lehel
Bob the Butler '05
Conspiracy of Silence '03

Richard Leiterman (1935-2005)
The Spree '96
Watchers '88
Ticket to Heaven '81
Who Has Seen the Wind? '77

Claude Lelouch (1937-)
Les Miserables '95
A Man and a Woman '66

Jacques Lemare
Dishonorable Discharge '57
There Goes Barder '54

James (Momel) Lemmo (1949-)
Maniac Cop 2 '90
Maniac Cop '88
Fear City '85
Vigilante '83
Madman '82
One Down, Two to Go! '82
Ms. 45 '81

Ryszard Lenczewski (1948-)
My Summer of Love '05
Anna Karenina '00

Denis Lenoir
88 Minutes '08
The Clearing '04
Demonlover '02
Uprising '01
Meat Loaf: To Hell and Back '00
Steal This Movie! '00
Mean Streak '99
La Separation '98
Late August, Early September '98
Thursday '98
The Secret Agent '96
Carrington '95
The Separation '94
Acting on Impulse '93
Daddy Nostalgia '90
Dingo '90

Dean Lent
Phat Girlz '06
Fast Sofa '01
Catfish in Black Bean Sauce '00
Drowning on Dry Land '00
Jack Frost '97
Lover Girl '97
When Time Expires '97

Miklos Lente
Ordeal in the Arctic '93
Happy Birthday to Me '81
Suzanne '80

Don Lenzer
Rush It '77
Road Movie '72

John R. Leonetti
Dead Silence '07
Death Sentence '07
I Know Who Killed Me '07
The Perfect Man '05
Raise Your Voice '04
Honey '03
The Woods '03
The Scorpion King '02
Joe Dirt '01
Detroit Rock City '99
Spy Hard '96
Mortal Kombat 1: The Movie '95
The Mask '94

Matthew F. Leonetti (1941-)
What Happens in Vegas '08
The Heartbreak Kid '07
Pride '07
Accepted '06
Fever Pitch '05
The Butterfly Effect '04
Dawn of the Dead '04
2 Fast 2 Furious '03
Along Came a Spider '01
Rush Hour 2 '01
Species 2 '98
Star Trek: Insurrection '98
Mortal Kombat 2: Annihilation '97
Fled '96
Star Trek: First Contact '96
Strange Days '95
Angels in the Outfield '94
Dead Again '91
Another 48 Hrs. '90
Hard to Kill '89
Action Jackson '88
Red Heat '88
Dragnet '87
Commando '85
The Jagged Edge '85
Weird Science '85
Fast Times at Ridgemont High '82
Poltergeist '82
Breaking Away '79
Prime Time '77
The Bat People '74

Jean Lepine
Coast to Coast '04
A Different Loyalty '04
Charms for the Easy Life '02
Whitewash: The Clarence Brandley Story '02
To Walk with Lions '99
A Cool, Dry Place '98
Habitat '97
Woo '97
Beyond the Call '96
Ready to Wear '94
A Home of Our Own '93
JFK: Reckless Youth '93
Bob Roberts '92
The Player '92
Vincent & Theo '90

Andrew Lesnie (1956-)
I Am Legend '07
King Kong '05
Lord of the Rings: The Return of the King '03
Lord of the Rings: The Two Towers '02
Lord of the Rings: The Fellowship of the Rings '01
Babe: Pig in the City '98
Doing Time for Patsy Cline '97
Babe '95
Two If by Sea '95
Temptation of a Monk '94
Fair Game '85

Elgin Lessley (1881-1944)
Tramp, Tramp, Tramp '26
Seven Chances '25
The Navigator '24
Sherlock, Jr. '24
Our Hospitality '23

Pierre Letarte
The Audrey Hepburn Story '00

John Leuba
Friends and Family '01
Swimming '00

Alain Levent
Daughter of Keltoum '01
Franz '72

Moshe Levin
Axe '06
Motel Blue '98
Hard Justice '95

Peter Levy
The Reaping '07
Lonely Hearts '06
Torque '04
Under Suspicion '00
Mafia! '98
First Do No Harm '97
Dangerous Minds '95
Sugartime '95
The Boys of St. Vincent '93

Lost in Space '98
The War at Home '96
Broken Arrow '95
Cutthroat Island '95
Judgment Night '93
Ricochet '91
Predator 2 '90
A Nightmare on Elm Street 5: Dream Child '89

Shawn Lewallen
The Last Confederate: The Story of Robert Adams '05
Sergio Lapel's Drawing Blood '99

David Lewis
Leprechaun 4: In Space '96
Fatal Pulse '88

David Lewis (1916-2000)
Killer Bud '00
Atomic Dog '98
Children of the Corn 5: Fields of Terror '98
Chairman of the Board '97
The Proposition '96
The Set Up '95
Witchboard 2: The Devil's Doorway '93
UHF '89

Herschell Gordon Lewis (1926-)
The Psychic '68
Something Weird '68
Color Me Blood Red '64
Moonshine Mountain '64
2000 Maniacs '64
Blood Feast '63

Denis Lewiston
The Centerville Ghost '96
Nightmare '91
One Against the Wind '91
The Sign of Four '83
The House on Straw Hill '76

Pierre Lhomme (1930-)
Le Divorce '03
Cotton Mary '99
Mon Homme '96
Cyrano de Bergerac '90
Camille Claudel '89
Maurice '87
This Sweet Sickness '77
Sweet Movie '75
Army of Shadows '69
The King of Hearts '66

Matthew Libatique (1969-)
Iron Man '08
The Number 23 '07
The Fountain '06
Inside Man '06
Everything is Illuminated '05
Never Die Alone '04
She Hate Me '04
Gothika '03
Abandon '02
Phone Booth '02
Josie and the Pussycats '01
Requiem for a Dream '00
Tigerland '00
Speed or Life '99
Fi '98

Stephen Lighthill
The Crying Child '96
Evil Has a Face '96
The Perfect Daughter '96
Open Season '95
Spirit of '76 '91
Break of Dawn '88

Doug Liman (1965-)
Go '99
Swingers '96

Jong Lin
Bend It Like Beckham '02
What's Cooking? '00
Eat Drink Man Woman '94
The Wedding Banquet '93
Pushing Hands '92

Edward Linden (1891-1956)
Yank in Libya '42
Range Busters '40
Trailing Double Trouble '40
West of Pinto Basin '40
Slaves in Bondage '37
Rough Riding Ranger '35
King Kong '33

Karl Walter Lindenlaub (1957-)
The Chronicles of Narnia: Prince Caspian '08
Georgia Rule '07
Because of Winn-Dixie '05
Guess Who '05
The Banger Sisters '02
City by the Sea '02
Maid in Manhattan '92
One Night at McCoo's '01
The Princess Diaries '01
Isn't She Great '00
The Jackal '97
Red Corner '97
Independence Day '96
Up Close and Personal '96
The Last of the Dogmen '95
Rob Roy '95
"Long Island Lolita Story '93
Universal Soldier '92
Ghost Chase '88

John Lindley
Catch and Release '07
Mr. Brooks '07
Reservation Road '07
Bewitched '05
The Core '03
The Last Shot '04
The Good Son '93
Sneakers '92
Father of the Bride '91
Field of Dreams '89
True Believer '89
Shakedown '88
The Serpent and the Rainbow '87
The Stepfather '87
Killer Party '86
Girls of the White Orchid '85
Pleasantville '98
You've Got Mail '98
Michael '96
Money Train '95
I Love Trouble '94

Lionel Lindon (1905-71)
Generation '69
Pendulum '69
The Meanest Men in the West '67
Boy, Did I Get a Wrong Number! '66
Dead Heat on a Merry-Go-Round '66
Grand Prix '66
The Trouble with Angels '66
McHale's Navy Joins the Air Force '65
All Fall Down '62
The Manchurian Candidate '62
The Young Savages '61
Alias Jesse James '59
I Want to Live! '58
Lonely Man '57
Around the World in 80 Days '56
Conquest of Space '55
A Man Alone '55
Casanova's Big Night '54
Destination Moon '50
Variety Girl '47
Welcome Stranger '47
The Blue Dahlia '46
Monsieur Beaucaire '46
O.S.S. '46
The Road to Utopia '46
Going My Way '44

Philip Linzey
Cabin by the Lake '00
Turbulence 3: Heavy Metal '01
Life-Size '00
Evidence of Blood '97
Bloodknot '95

Jerzy Lipman (1922-83)
Dead Pigeon on Beethoven Street '72
Knife in the Water '62
Kanal '56
Lotna '64

Harold Lipstein (1898-1974)
Hell is for Heroes '62
No Name on the Bullet '59
Pal Joey '57
Walk the Proud Land '56
The Private War of Major Benson '55
A Generation '54

Gerry Lively
In Enemy Hands '04
Cutaway '00
DNA '97
The Brylcreem Boys '96
Friday '95
Showdown '94
Return of the Living Dead 3 '93
Warlock: The Armageddon '93
Hellraiser 3: Hell on Earth '92

Greg Littlewood
SLC Punk '99
Sweet Jane '98
The Real Thing '98
Skinner '93

Angelo Lotti
Venus in Furs '70
The Lion of Thebes '64

Art Lloyd (1896-1954)
Project: Eliminator '91
Waxwork 2: Lost in Time '91
Lobster Man from Mars '89
Wexwork '88
The Flying Deuces '39
March of the Wooden Soldiers '34
Laurel & Hardy: Be Big '31

Guy Livneh
Eye of the Dolphin '06
Kids in America '05

Sam Lowry
See Steven Soderbergh

Emmanuel Lubezki (1964-)
Children of Men '06
The Assassination of Richard Nixon '05
The New World '05
Lemony Snicket's A Series of Unfortunate Events '04
Dr. Seuss' The Cat in the Hat '03
Ali '01
Y Tu Mamá También '01
Things You Can Tell Just by Looking at Her '00
Sleepy Hollow '99
Meet Joe Black '98
Great Expectations '97
The Birdcage '95
A Little Princess '95
A Walk in the Clouds '95
Reality Bites '94
Twenty Bucks '93

William Lubtchansky (1937-)
The Duchess of Langeais '07
Va Savoir '01
New World '95
Jeanne la Pucelle '94
Every Other Weekend '91
La Belle Noiseuse '90
The Woman Next Door '81
Comment Ça Va? '76

William Luff (1872-1960)
Juggernaut '37
She Shall Have Music '36
Department Store '35
Scrooge '35

Walt Lloyd
The Air I Breathe '07
Superstar '99
Three to Tango '99
Dark Harbor '98
Feeling Minnesota '96
Private Parts '96
Empire Records '95
Frank and Jesse '94
The Santa Clause '94
Short Cuts '93
Kafka '91
Pump Up the Volume '90
To Sleep with Anger '90
Down Twisted '89
sex, lies and videotape '89
The Wash '88
Dangerously Close '86

Bruce Logan
Botched '07
Jake Speed '86
The Company of Wolves '85
Kiss Tomorrow Goodbye '00
Tron '82

Bryan Loftus
The Company of Wolves '85

Paul Lohmann
Lust in the Dust '85
Mommie Dearest '81
Meteor '79
North Dallas Forty '79
Nashville '75
Trilogy of Terror '75
Scream of the Wolf '74
The Last Temptation of Toxie '89
The Toxic Avenger, Part 3
The Toxic Avenger, Part 2 '89
The Toxic Avenger '86

Jacques Loiseleux
The Stranger: Kablooah '95
A Nos Amours '84
Hell's Angels '69 '69

Ulli Lommel (1944-)
Devonsville Terror '83
Brainwaves '82

James London
The Toxic Avenger, Part 3:
The Toxic Avenger, Part 2
Troma's War '88

Bert Longenecker (1876-1940)
The Red Rope '37
The Jaw Rides '36
Fighting Caballero '35
$50,000 Reward '25

Gordon C. Lonsdale
High School Musical '06
Houdini '99
The Last Don '97

Julio Macat
Because I Said So '07
Blind Dating '06
Wedding Crashers '05
Catch That Kid '04
Bringing Down the House '03
Ballistic: Ecks vs. Sever '02
A Walk to Remember '02
Cats & Dogs '01
The Wedding Planner '01
Crazy in Alabama '99
Home Alone 3 '97
My Fellow Americans '96
The Nutty Professor '96
Moonlight and Valentino '95
Dr. Ace Ventura: Pet Detective '93
Home Alone 2: Lost in New York '92
Home Alone '90
Out of the Dark '88

Syd Macartney
Transmutations '85
Party! Party! '83

Dietrich Lohmann (1943-97)
Deep Impact '98
The Blue Hour '46
The Peacemaker '97
Quiet Days in Hollywood '97
In the Lake of the Woods '96
The Machine '96
A Couch in New York '95
Color of Night '94
Knight Moves '93
The American Soldier '70
Love is Colder Than Death '69

Yang Lun
Red Firecracker, Green Firecracker '93
Ju Dou '90

John MacBurnie (1892-1956)
Missourians '50
Night Riders of Montana '50
Pioneer Marshal '49
The Carpetbaggers '64
The Sand Pebbles '66
Alvarez Kelly '66
MacKenna's Gold '69
Border Saddlemates '52
Silver City Bonanza '51
Thunder in God's Country '51

Joe MacDonald (1906-68)
The Young Lions '58
Will Success Spoil Rock Hunter? '57
House of Bamboo '55
Broken Lance '54
A Woman's World '54
How to Marry a Millionaire '53
Niagara '52
Pickup on South Street '53
Call Northside 777 '48
Dark Corner '46
My Darling Clementine '46

Guy Maddin (1956-)
Careful '92
Archangel '90

Glen MacWilliams (1898-1984)
Lifeboat '44
A Wing and a Prayer '44
Blue, White and Perfect '42
The Gorilla Man '42
King Solomon's Mines '37
First a Girl '35
Evergreen '34
Oliver Twist '22

Jingle Ma (1939-)
Tokyo Raiders '00
Mr. Magoo '97
Jackie Chan's First Strike '96

Russell Lyster
Ringmaster '98
Styx '00

Chester Lyons (1885-1936)
Mad Love '35
Under the Pampas Moon '35

Edgar Lyons (1894-1950)
Dick Tracy: The Spider Strikes '37
The Fighting Trooper '34

Glen MacPherson (1957-)
Rambo '08
16 Blocks '06
Rebound '05
Walking Tall '04
My Baby's Daddy '04
All About the Benjamins '02
Friday After Next '02
Exit Wounds '01
Camouflage '00
Romeo Must Die '00
The Real Howard Spitz '98
Wrongfully Accused '98
Behind the Lines '97

Franz Lustig (1967-)
Don't Come Knocking '05
Land of Plenty '04

Igor Luther (1942-)
The Tin Drum '79
The Handmaid's Tale '90
The Man Who Wouldn't Die '42

Bernard Lutic (1943-2000)
Lumumba '01
I Dreamed of Africa '00
The Luzhin Defence '00
The Quarry '98
My Life So Far '98
Colonel Chabert '94
Boyfriends & Girlfriends '88
Entre Nous '83
Le Beau Mariage '82
The Aviator's Wife '80
Death '96

Laurent Machuel
Merci Docteur Rey '04
Sex is Comedy '02

Thierry Machado
Winged Migration '01
Microcosmos '96

Peter Macdonald
Shag: The Movie '89
Hamburger Hill '87

Jack MacKenzie (1892-1979)
Return of Dracula '58
Isle of the Dead '45
Jungle Woman '44
Three Lives and Only One

Kenneth Macmillan (1939-)
Dancing at Lughnasa '98
Almost Heroes '98
Inventing the Abbotts '97
Mr. & Mrs. Loving '96
Circle of Friends '94
Of Mice and Men '92
King Ralph '91
Henry V '89
A Month in the Country '87
Smiley's People '82
Pack of Lies '87

Lon Magdich
Relax... It's Just Sex! '98
Equal Impact '96

Yonezo Maeda (1935-)
Minbo—Or the Gentle Art of Japanese Extortion '92
A Taxing Woman '87
The Funeral '84
The Family Game '83
Tales from the Gimli Hospital '88

Simon Maggs
Take Me '01
The Wyvern Mystery '00
Barry Mahon (1921-99)
Master's Revenge '71
The Beast That Killed Women '65
Paul Maibaum (1951-)
NightScreams '97
Tornado! '96
Down, Out and Dangerous '95
Stephen King's The Langoliers '95
Shooters '89
Rex Maidment
Cider with Rosie '99
Second Sight '99
Rebecca '97
Gallowglass '95
A Dark Adapted Eye '93
Enchanted April '92
Antonia and Jane '91
David Makin
Jump In! '07
Say Uncle '05
Touch of Pink '04
Held Up '00
Dog Park '98
Kids in the Hall: Brain Candy '96
The Wrong Guy '96
Harry Makin
Dark Side '02
It Seemed Like a Good Idea at the Time '75
Chishi Makiura
Shogun Assassin '80
Zatoichi: The Blind Swordsman and the Chess Expert '65
Michael Maley
No One Sleeps '01
Farmer & Chase '96
Jan Malir (1948-)
Up and Down '04
Divided We Fall '00
Denis Maloney
The Moguls '05
The Zodiac '05
Final Approach '04
Interstate 60 '02
Liberty Stands Still '02
Luckytown '00
No Vacancy '99
One Small Hero '99
Bad Manners '98
Bikini Med School '98
Highway Hitcher '98
Body Count '97
Bikini House Calls '96
Illegal Affairs '96
The Winner '96
Wolverine '96
Baja '95
Desert Winds '95
Witchcraft 7: Judgement Hour '95
Witchcraft 8: Salem's Ghost '95
Floundering '94
Natural Causes '94
Alvaro Mancori (1923-)
Espionage in Tangiers '65
Mole Men Against the Son of Hercules '61
Guglielmo Mancori
Black Cobra 2 '89
Manhattan Baby '82
Thor and the Amazon Women '60
Sandro Mancori
Escape from Galaxy Three '81
Liberators '69
Joseph Mangine
Alligator 2: The Mutation '90
Sword & the Sorcerer '82
Alligator '80
Mother's Day '80
Teodoro Maniaci
The Perfect Holiday '07
.45 '06
Inside Deep Throat '05
Party Monster '03
Searching for Paradise '02
The Business of Strangers '01
Luminous Motion '00
The Tao of Steve '00
Claire Dolan '97
Tarantella '95
Isidore Mankofsky
The Heidi Chronicles '95
Out of Sync '95
Hard Lessons '86
Better Off Dead '85
The Jazz Singer '80
Second Coming of Suzanne '80
The Muppet Movie '79
Chris Manley
Gracie '07
The Big Empty '04
Dahmer '02
Endangered Species '02
The Stickup '01
Robert Louis Stevenson's The Game of Death '99
Running Woman '98
Laurence Manly
Dangerous Curves '99
Spacejacked '98
Anthony Dod Mantle (1955-)
Brothers of the Head '06
The Last King of Scotland '06
Dear Wendy '05
Manderlay '05
Millions '05
Dogville '03
It's All About Love '03
28 Days Later '02
Vacuuming Completely Nude in Paradise '01
Julien Donkey-boy '99
Mifune '99
The Celebration '98
Aiter Mantxola
Lisboa '99
Vincenzo Marano
Butterfly Wings '91
Lucie Aubrac '98
Portraits Chinois '96
Alain Marcoen
The Child '05
Rosetta '99
La Promesse '96
Gunter Marczinkowski (1927-2004)
Barry Markowitz
Sonny '02
All the Pretty Horses '00
Daddy & Them '99
Two Girls and a Guy '98
The Apostle '97
Sling Blade '96
J. Peverell Marley (1901-64)
Life with Father '47
Charley's Aunt '41
Sleepers West '41
The Count of Monte Cristo '34
King of Kings '27
Brick Marquard
Foxy Brown '74
This Is Not a Test '62
Jacques "Jack" Marquette (1915-99)
Scandal Sheet '85
A Home of Our Own '75
More Dead Than Alive '68
Frankie and Johnny '65
Creature from the Haunted Sea '60
Attack of the 50 Foot Woman '58
The Brain from Planet Arous '57
Horacio Marquinez
Anything But Love '02
Dummy '02
G '02
Loving Jezebel '99
Stranger than Fiction '99
Eye of the Storm '98
Ten Benny '98
Oliver Marsh (1892-1941)
Dancing Lady '33
Night Flight '33
Rain '32
Sadie Thompson '28
Charles A. Marshall (1898-1985)
Air Force '43
Night Flight '33
Michael Marshall
Ginger Snaps Back: The Beginning '04
The Twilight of the Ice Nymphs '97
Michael Marszalek
2069: A Sex Odyssey '78
The Invisible Terror '63
Jack Marta (1903-91)
The Trial of Billy Jack '74
Walking Tall '73
You'll Like My Mother '72
Duel '71
Cat Ballou '65
Earth vs. the Spider '58
Beginning of the End '57
Sunset in the West '50
Far Frontier '48
Bordertown Gunfighters '43
Texas Legionnaires '43
Red River Valley '41
Southward Ho! '39
Wall Street Cowboy '39
Larceny On the Air '37
Public Cowboy No. 1 '37
King of the Pecos '36
Otello Martelli (1902-2000)
Boccaccio '70 '62
Where the Hot Wind Blows '59
What a Woman! '56
Il Bidone '55
I Vitelloni '53
Anna '51
Variety Lights '51
The Flowers of St. Francis '50
Bitter Rice '49
Pascal Marti
Paris, je t'aime '06
A Loving Father '02
L'Ennui '98
F. Smith Martin
Hard Vice '94
Zipperface '92
Arthur Martinelli (1881-1967)
In Old New Mexico '45
The Devil Bat '41
Double Trouble '41
Gangs, Inc. '41
Motorcycle Squad '41
Revolt of the Zombies '36
Supernatural '33
The White Zombie '32
Flavio Martinez Labiano (1962-)
800 Bullets '02
Bones '01
Harlan County War '00
Dance with the Devil '97
The Day of the Beast '95
Joseph Mascelli (1917-81)
The Thrill Killers '65
Incredibly Strange Creatures Who Stopped Living and Became Mixed-Up Zombies '63
Wild Guitar '62
Raffaele Masciocchi
The Ghost '63
Magnificent Adventurer '63
The Horrible Dr. Hichcock '62
Mario Masini
Padre Padrone '77
Allegro Non Troppo '76
Private Lessons '75
St. Michael Had a Rooster '72
Steve Mason (1954-)
Harsh Times '05
Venom '05
The Wendell Baker Story '05
Basic '03
Rollerball '02
Bootmen '00
BASEketball '98
Buddy '97
That Old Feeling '96
Strictly Ballroom '92
Stelvio Massi (1929-2004)
The Case of the Bloody Iris '72
Fistful of Lead '70
Gunslinger '70
Sartana's Here... Trade Your Pistol for a Coffin '70
Place in Hell '69
Rudolph Mate (1898-1964)
Gilda '46
Cover Girl '44
Sahara '43
They Got Me Covered '43
The Pride of the Yankees '42
To Be or Not to Be '42
The Flame of New Orleans '41
It Started with Eve '41
My Favorite Wife '40
Seven Sinners '40
Love Affair '39
The Real Glory '39
Stella Dallas '37
Come and Get It '36
Dodsworth '36
Vampyr '31
Passion of Joan of Arc '28
Tibor Mathe (1943-)
Simon the Magician '99
Woyzeck '94
James Mathers
The U.S. Vs. John Lennon '06
St. Patrick: The Irish Legend '00
John Mathieson (1958-)
August Rush '07
Kingdom of Heaven '05
Stoned '05
Matchstick Men '03
Hannibal '01
K-PAX '01
Gladiator '00
Love Is the Devil '98
Plunkett & Macleane '98
Twin Town '97
Bye-Bye '96
Pigalle '95
Clark Mathis
Meet Dave '08
Norbit '07
Rocky Balboa '06
Happy Endings '05
In the Mix '05
The Perfect Score '04
Ready to Rumble '00
Christian Matras (1903-77)
Lola Montes '55
Nana '55
The Earrings of Madame De... '54
Fanfan la Tulipe '51
L'Idiot '46
Grand Illusion '37
Thomas Mauch (1937-)
Fitzcarraldo '82
Stroszek '77
Aguirre, the Wrath of God '72
Signs of Life '68
Shawn Maurer
Epic Movie '07
Date Movie '06
The Honeymooners '05
Johnson Family Vacation '04
Boat Trip '03
Like Mike '02
Bring It On '00
La Cucaracha '99
The Big Empty '98
Bandwagon '95
Tim Maurice-Jones
Envy '04
Human Nature '02
Snatch '00
Lock, Stock and 2 Smoking Barrels '98
Joe C. Maxwell
Zarkorr! The Invader '96
Malevolence '95
Robert Maxwell (1923-78)
Sweet Sweetback's Baadasssss Song '71
Girl in Gold Boots '69
Rebel Vixens '69
The Astro-Zombies '67
Bradford May
Darkman 3: Die Darkman Die '95
Darkman 2: The Return of Durant '94
Target: Favorite Son '87
Harry J. May (1924-85)
J.D.'s Revenge '76
Friday Foster '75
Detroit 9000 '73
Mike Mayers
The Jimmy Show '01
Joe the King '99
Two Family House '99
Broadway Damage '98
Meeting Daddy '98
Whatever '98
Cafe Society '97
Lewis and Clark and George '97
Changing Habits '96
Denise Calls Up '95
Spanking the Monkey '94
Alfredo Mayo (1911-85)
The Method '05
Mondays in the Sun '02
Burnt Money '00
Women '97
Wild Horses '95
Kika '97
High Heels '91
Donald McAlpine (1934-)
The Chronicles of Narnia: The Lion, the Witch and the Wardrobe '05
Anger Management '03
Peter Pan '03
The Time Machine '02
Moulin Rouge '01
Stepmom '98
The Edge '97
William Shakespeare's Romeo and Juliet '96
Nine Months '95
Clear and Present Danger '94
Mrs. Doubtfire '93
Medicine Man '92
Patriot Games '92
Career Opportunities '91
Parenthood '89
Predator '87
Down and Out in Beverly Hills '86
Moscow on the Hudson '84
The Tempest '82
Breaker Morant '80
My Brilliant Career '79
The Odd Angry Shot '79
Don's Party '76
Ted D. McCord (1900-76)
A Fine Madness '66
The Sound of Music '65
Proud Rebel '58
South Sea Woman '53
The Damned Don't Cry '50
Treasure of the Sierra Madre '48
Action in the North Atlantic '43
Trail Drive '33
Dynamite Ranch '32
Tombstone Canyon '32
Fightin' Ranch '30
Malcolm McCulloch
Two Hands '98
Kiss or Kill '97
Sam McCurdy
Doomsday '08
The Hills Have Eyes 2 '07
Outlaw '07
Cold and Dark '05
The Descent '05
Preaching to the Perverted '97
David McDonald
Horror Hospital '73
The Harder They Come '72
Michael McDonough
Diggers '06
Down to the Bone '04
Seamus McGarvey (1967-)
Atonement '07
Charlotte's Web '06
World Trade Center '06
Sahara '05
Along Came Polly '04
The Hours '02
Enigma '01
Wit '01
High Fidelity '00
The Big Tease '99
A Map of the World '99
The War Zone '98
The Winter Guest '97
Butterfly Kiss '94
Barney McGill (1890-1942)
Charlie Chan in Shanghai '35
The Bowery '33
Bureau of Missing Persons '33
Employees' Entrance '33
The Mayor of Hell '33
Svengali '31
Walter McGill
Quicksand '01
Oliver Twist '00
Aldrich Ames: Traitor Within '98
John McGlashan
Captain Jack '98
The Buddha of Suburbia '92
Clarissa '91

Jack McGowan
Deranged '74
Children Shouldn't Play with
Dead Things '72

Patrick Mcgowan
Deathdream '72

Martin McGrath (1956-)
Show Me '04
Fire Serpent '07

Kieran McGuigan
The Other Boleyn Girl '08
Bleak House '05

Austin McKinney
Rockin' Road Trip '85
Axe '74
Free G'ass '69
Bullet Down Under '94
The Sinister Invasion '68
Pit Stop '67

Robert McLachlan
Black Christmas '06
Final Destination 3 '06
King's Ransom '05
Cursed '04
Willard '03
The One '01
Final Destination '00
High Noon '00
Impolite '92

Nick McLean
Short Circuit '86
The Goonies '85
Cannonball Run 2 '84
Stroker Ace '83

Geary McLeod
Who Made the Potato
Salad? '05
Carmen: A Hip Hopera '01
Cement '99
Black Circle Boys '97
Dinner and Driving '97

Stephen McNutt
Back Point '01
Out of Time '00
Inferno '99

Glen McPherson
See Glen MacPherson

John McPherson (1941-2007)
*batteries not included '87
Jaws: The Revenge '87
Hot Pursuit '84

Steve McWilliams (1954-)
Nc Safe Haven '87
Revenge '86

Graeme Mears
Cyberolty '99
Future Fear '97

Suki Medencevic (1963-)
Connor's War '06
The Great Water '04
Hunter's Moon '97
Embrace of the Vampire '95
Poison Ivy 2: Lily '95

Teresa Medina (1965-)
The 24 Hour Woman '99
Female Perversions '96
Things I Never Told You '95
Reflections in the Dark '94

George Meehan, Jr. (1891-1947)
The Desperadoes '43
Inside Information '34

Phil Meheux
Casino Royale '06
The Legend of Zorro '05
Around the World in 80
Days '04
Beyond Borders '03
Bicentennial Man '99
Entrapment '99
The Mask of Zorro '98
Goldeneye '95
No Escape '94
The Trial '93
Ruby '92
Highlander 2: The
Quickening '91
Criminal Law '89
Renegades '89
The Fourth Protocol '87
Morons from Outer Space
'85
Beyond the Limit '83
Experience Preferred... But
Not Essential '83
The Final Option '82
The Final Conflict '81
The Long Good Friday '80

Sharon Meir
Peaceful Warrior '06
Coach Carter '05
Mean Creek '04

William Mellor (1904-63)
The Greatest Story Ever
Told '65
State Fair '62
The Diary of Anne Frank '59
Compulsion '59
Wild in the Country '61
The Best of Everything '59
Love in the Afternoon '57
Peyton Place '57
Giant '56
Back from Eternity '56
Bad Day at Black Rock '54
The Affairs of Dobie Gillis
'53
The Naked Spur '53
Across the Wide Missouri
'51
A Place in the Sun '51
Westward the Women '51
Love Happy '50
Too Late for Tears '49
The Senator Was Indiscreet
'47
Commandos Strike at Dawn
'43
The Great Man's Lady '42
My Favorite Blonde '42
The Road to Morocco '42
Wake Island '42
Birth of the Blues '41
The Road to Singapore '40
Sky Parade '36
Wings in the Dark '35

Mark Melville
Attack of the Sacretooth '05
Asylum of the Damned '03
The Darwin Conspiracy '99
Dilemma '97

Erico Menczer (1926-)
The Innocents Abroad '84
Rulers of the City '76
Dead Are Alive '72
The Cat o' Nine Tails '71
How I Learned to Love
Women '66

Chris Menges (1940-)
Stop-Loss '08
Notes on a Scandal '06
North Country '05
The Three Burials of
Melquiades Estrada '05
Criminal '04
Dirty Pretty Things '03
The Pledge '00
The Boxer '97
Michael Collins '96
High Season '88
Sry People '87
Singing the Blues in Red '87
The Mission '86
Marie '85
Comfort and Joy '84
The Killing Fields '84
Local Hero '83
Danny Boy '82
Warlords of the 21st
Century '82
Gumshoe '72
Black Beauty '71

Peter Menzies, Jr.
The Incredible Hulk '08
Shooter '07
When a Stranger Calls '06
The Great Raid '05
Man of the House '05
Four Brothers '05
The Great Raid '05
Kangaroo Jack '02
Miss Congeniality 2: Armed
and Fabulous '05
Lara Croft Tomb Raider '01
Bless the Child '00
Disney's The Kid '00
The General's Daughter '99
The 13th Warrior '99

Raffaele Mertes
Jesus '00
David '97
Moses '96
Samson and Delilah '96
Fluke '95
Joseph '95
Abraham '94

Jacques Mercanton (1909-)
Mr. Hulot's Holiday '53
Jour de Fete '48

Manuel Merino (1918-2001)
Count Dracula '71
The Castle of Fu Manchu
'68

Russ Meyer (1922-2004)
Beneath the Valley of the
Ultra-Vixens '79
Supervixens '75
Motor Psycho '65

Rexford Metz
The Midnight Hour '86
Every Which Way But Loose
'78

Richard Michalak (1954-)
Children of the Night '92
Body Chemistry 2: Voice of
a Stranger '91

Jan Michalik
Gordy '95

Mark Mervis
Amy's O '02
Standing on Fishes '99
Billy's Hollywood Screen
Kiss '98

John Mescall (1899-1962)
Dark Waters '44
The Black Cat '34
The Leatherneck '28

John Metcalfe
Rawhead Rex '87
Xtro '83
Trespasser '81
Inseminoid '80

Russell Metty (1906-78)
Ben '72
Cancel My Reservation '72
Omega Man '71
Change of Habit '69
Madigan '68
The Pink Jungle '68
The Secret War of Harry
Frigg '68
White Tiger '68
Rough Night in Jericho '67
Thoroughly Modern Millie
'67
The Appaloosa '66
Madame X '66
Texas Across the River '66
The War Lord '65
The Thrill of It All! '63
The Interns '62
That Touch of Mink '62
By Love Possessed '61
Flower Drum Song '61
The Misfits '61
Midnight Lace '60
Portrait in Black '60
Spartacus '60
Imitation of Life '59
A Time to Love & a Time to
Die '58
Touch of Evil '58
Battle Hymn '57
Man of a Thousand Faces
'57
Written on the Wind '56
All That Heaven Allows '55
Crashout '55
Magnificent Obsession '54
Because of You '52
The World in His Arms '52
Yankee Buccaneer '52
Buccaneer's Girl '50
Bagdad '49
Al My Sons '48
Arch of Triumph '48
You Gotta Stay Happy '48
West of the Pecos '45
Master Race '44
Seven Days Ashore '44
Forever and a Day '43
Dance, Girl Dance '40
No, No Nanette '40
Frot es on Ice '39
Bringing Up Baby '38
The Great Man Votes '38
Sylva Scarlett '35

Russ Meyer (1922-
The Jaunter '77

Rexford Metz
Sylva Scarlett '35

David J. Miller
Footsteps '98
Virtual Combat '95

Ernest Miller (1885-1957)
Rocky Jones, Space
Ranger: Renegade
Satellite '54
Square Dance Jubilee '51
The Steel Helmet '51
Thundering Trail '51
Last Bullet '50
Motor Patrol '50
Man of the World '31
Monte Carlo '30
The Love Parade '29
Human Hearts 22

Anastas Michos
Perfect Stranger '07
Freedomland '06
The Forgotten '04
Duplex '03
Mona Lisa Smile '03
Death to Smoochy '02
What's the Worst That
Could Happen? '01
The Big Kahuna '00
Keeping the Faith '00
The Educator of Little Tree

Gregory Middleton
Slither '06
Cake '05
Between Strangers '02
The Snow Queen '02
After the Storm '01
Mr. Rice's Secret '00
Suspicious River '00
Better Than Chocolate '99
The Five Senses '99
Rupert's Land '98
Wounded '97
The Invader '96
Kissed '96

Peter Middleton
The Alchemists '99
Extremely Dangerous '99
The Waiting Time '99
Body & Soul '93

Pierre Mignot (1944-)
The Latte of Heaven '02
Nonega: God's Favorite '00
The 6th Day '00
P.T. Barnum '99
No '98
Sous Sol '96
Hiroshima '95
Vanished '95
Mouvements du Desir '94
Ready to Wear '94
Boy in Blue '86
Secret Honor '85
Erotique '94
Virgin Machine '88

Michael Mileham (1947-)
The Bank '01
The Boys '98

Tristan Milani
Thank you, Mr. Moto '37
The Phantom of the Opera
25
The Road from Coorain '02

Arthur C. Miller (1895-1970)
Prowler '51
The Gunfighter '50
A Letter to Three Wives '49
Gentleman's Agreement '47
Anna and the King of Siam
'46
The Razor's Edge '46
The Keys of the Kingdom
'44
The Purple Heart '44
The Mark of Zorro '40
The Rains Came '39
The Little Princess '39
The Little Colonel '35
The Ox-Bow Incident '43
The Song of Bernadette '43
How Green Was My Valley
'41
The Blue Bird '40
Brigham Young:
Frontiersman '40
Johnny Apollo '40
Little Miss Broadway '38
Rebecca of Sunnybrook
Farm '38
Wee Willie Winkie '37
Heidi '37
Stowaway '36
Pigskin Parade '36
Bright Eyes '34
Panama Flo '32

C. Kim Miles (1973-)
Falling in Love Again '80
Runaways '75
Alien Agent '07
Blonde and Blonder '07
A Dennis the Menace
Christmas '07
Shock to the System '06
Chasing Christmas '05

Alec Mills (1932-)
The Ghastly Ones '68
The Rats Are Coming! The
Werewolves Are Here! '72
Catherine Cookson's The
Rag Nymph '96
Catherine Cookson's The
Moth '96
License to Kill '89
The Living Daylights '87
On the Third Day '83

Andy Milligan (1929-91)
Man with Two Heads '72
The Ghastly Ones '68

William J. Miller
Lost Boundaries '49
Carnegie Hall '47
Blind Fool? '40
The Trap '22

Charles Mills
Karla '06
Baby Boy '01
Jackie's Back '99
Body Count '97
How I Spent My Summer
Vacation '97

Victor Milner (1893-1972)
Jeopardy '53
Carrie '52
Unfaithfully Yours '48
Wonder Man '45
The Story of Dr. Wassell '44
Reap the Wild Wind '42
The Palm Beach Story '42
The Princess and the Pirate
'44
The Lady Eve '41
The Monster and the Girl '41
Union Pacific '39
College Swing '38
Bulldog Drummond
Escapes '37
The Plainsman '37
The General Died at Dawn
'36
The Crusades '35
Cleopatra '34
The Song of Songs '33
One Hour with You '32
Trouble in Paradise '32

Murray Milne
Dead Alive '93
Meet the Feebles '89

Doug Milsome
Dracula 3: Legacy '05
Second in Command '05
Dracula 2: Ascension '03
Return of Wildfire '48
Standing in the Shadows of
Motown '02
Dungeons and Dragons '00
Highlander: Endgame '00
Purple Vigilantes '38
Jeepers Creepers '39
Come on, Cowboys '37
Cowboys from Texas '39
Back in the Saddle '41
Sundown Kid '43
California Joe '43
The Three Musketeers '33
Virtue's Revolt '24
Johnson County War '02

Virgil Miller (1887-1974)
The Woman in Green '45
The Mummy's Curse '44
Charlie Chan at Treasure
Island '39
Charlie Chan in City of
Darkness '39
Mr. Moto Takes a Chance
'38
Mysterious Mr. Moto '38

Pierre Milon
Heading South '05

Dan Mindel
Mission: Impossible 3 '06
Domino '05
The Skeleton Key '05

Stuck On You '03
Spy Game '01
Shanghai Noon '00
Enemy of the State '98

Charles Minsky
That Russell Girl '08
Keeping Up with the Steins '06
You, Me and Dupree '06
The Producers '05
The Princess Diaries 2: Royal Engagement '04
Raising Helen '04
Welcome to Collinwood '02
Tomcats '01
Guinevere '99
Looking for an Echo '99
Dear God '96
Kazaam '96
Pretty Woman '90
April Fool's Day '86

Virgil Marcus Mirano
Coastlines '02
Ulee's Gold '97

George Mitas
Searching for Bobby D '05
Lie Down with Dogs '95

Subrata Mitra (1930-2001)
Shakespeare Wallah '65
Charulata '64
The Big City '63
Devi '60
Aparajito '58
Jalsaghar '58

Kazuo Miyagawa (1908-99)
Kagemusha '80
Tokyo Olympiad '66
Zatoichi: Master Ichi and a Chest of Gold '64
Yojimbo '61
Enjo '61
Ugetsu '53
Rashomon '51

Yoshio Miyajima (1910-)
Kwaidan '64
Harakiri '62
The Human Condition: Road to Eternity '59
The Human Condition: No Greater Love '58

Hal Mohr (1894-1974)
The Last Voyage '60
Underworld, U.S.A. '60
The Wild One '54
The Member of the Wedding '52
Rancho Notorious '52
The Second Woman '51
I'll Be Yours '47
Lost Moment '47
Song of Scheherazade '47
Because of Him '45
The Climax '44
Salome, Where She Danced '45
The Monster '25

Amir M. Mokri (1956-)
Vantage Point '08
National Treasure: Book of Secrets '07
Lord of War '05
Taking Lives '04
Bad Boys 2 '03
The Salton Sea '02
Don't Say a Word '01
Coyote Ugly '00
An Eye for an Eye '95

Freejack '92
Queens Logic '91
Pacific Heights '90
Eat a Bowl of Tea '89

Peter Mokrosinski (1953-)
Evil '03
Speak Up! It's So Dark '93

William H. Molina
The Last Assassins '96
Where Truth Lies '96
Destination Vegas '95

Mike Molloy (1940-)
The Fourth Angel '01
Shiner '00
Noah's Ark '99
All the Little Animals '98
Welcome to Woop Woop '97
Bliss '96
Scandal '89
Link '86
Return of Captain Invincible '83
Shock Treatment '81

Sandro Moncori
Adios, Sabata '71
Return of Sabata '71
Sabata '69

Carlos Montaner
Friends & Lovers '99
Breakaway '95
Lap Dancing '95

Pierre Montazel (1911-75)
Antoine et Antoinette '47
The Fantastic Night '42

Joe Montgomery
Bar Hopping '00
Hugo Pool '97

Felix Monti
Holy Girl '04
Assassination Tango '03
Four Days in September '97
O Quatrilho '95
Of Love and Shadows '94
A Shadow You Soon Will Be '94
I, the Worst of All '90

Vincent Monton (1949-)
Paperback Romance '96
Street Hero '84
Road Games '81
The Night After Halloween '79
Blue Fire Lady '78

Luc Montpellier
Poor Man's Game '06
Confessions of a Sociopathic Social Climber '05
The Saddest Music in the World '03

Mario Montuori (1920-)
The Messiah '75
Goliath and the Dragon '61
The Wide Blue Road '57

George Mooradian
The Hitcher 2: I've Been Waiting '03
Crazy as Hell '02
Winter Break '02
Bats '99
K-911 '99
Made Men '99
Love Kills '98
Postmortem '98
Mean Guns '97
Nemesis 4: Cry of Angels '97
Adrenalin: Fear the Rush '96
Nemesis 3: Time Lapse '96
Omega Doom '96
Ravenhawk '95
Spitfire '94
Brain Smasher... A Love Story '93
Nemesis '93

Richard Moore (1925-)
Annie '82
Myra Breckinridge '70
Winning '69

Wild in the Streets '68
The Wild Angels '66

Ted Moore (1914-87)
Clash of the Titans '81
Priest of Love '81
Orca '77
Sinbad and the Eye of the Tiger '77
The Man with the Golden Gun '74
Golden Voyage of Sinbad '73
Live and Let Die '73
Diamonds Are Forever '71
Psychomania '73
Shalako '68
The Last Safari '67
A Man for All Seasons '66
The Amorous Adventures of Moll Flanders '65
Thunderball '65
Goldfinger '64
Day of the Triffids '63
From Russia with Love '63
Dr. No '62
Let's Get Married '60
The Trials of Oscar Wilde '60
The Gamma People '56

Pierre Morel
War '07
Unleashed '05

Adriano Moreno
Knocks at My Door '93
Shoot to Kill '90

Donald M. Morgan
Back in the Day '05
Bojangles '01
For Love or Country: The Arturo Sandoval Story '00
Sally Hemings: An American Scandal '00
The Thin Blue Lie '00
A Lesson Before Dying '99
The Rage: Carrie 2 '99
The Wall '99
Kiss the Sky '98
Miss Evers' Boys '97
The Rage '96
Born to Be Wild '95
Excessive Force '93
Dillinger '91
Double-Crossed '91
Christine '84
Starman '84
Used Cars '80

Ira Morgan (1889-1959)
Fog Island '45
Mr. Muggs Rides Again '45
Girls in Chains '43
Three Legionnaires '37
Modern Times '36
The Vampire Bat '32
The Great Gabbo '29

Ken Morgan
Catherine Cookson's The Black Candle '92
Catherine Cookson's The Fifteen Streets '90
The Maze '85

Kramer Morgenthau
Feast of Love '07
Fracture '07
Full of It '07
Godsend '04
Cuban Blood '03
Mayor of the Sunset Strip '03
Empire '02
Green Dragon '01
The Man from Elysian Fields '01
Cowboys and Angels '00
The Big Brass Ring '99
Wirey Spindell '99
Dogtown '97

Mark Moriarty
Johnny Was '05
The Fever '04

Prom Night 3: The Last Kiss '89

John Morrill
The Dark '79
Kingdom of the Spiders '77
A Boy and His Dog '75
The Brotherhood of Satan '71
Hideous Sun Demon '59

Mark Morris
Texas Payback '95
Hangfire '91

Nic Morris
The Criminal '00
Firelight '97
Masterminds '96

Oswald Morris (1915-)
The Dark Crystal '82
The Great Muppet Caper '81
Just Tell Me What You Want '80
The Wiz '78
Equus '77
The Seven-Per-Cent Solution '76
The Man Who Would Be King '75
The Odessa File '74
Dracula '73
Lady Caroline Lamb '73
Sleuth '72
Fiddler on the Roof '71
Scrooge '70
Goodbye, Mr. Chips '69
Oliver! '68
Reflections in a Golden Eye '67
The Taming of the Shrew '67
The Hill '65
The Spy Who Came in from the Cold '65
Of Human Bondage '64
The Pumpkin Eater '64
Lolita '62
The Guns of Navarone '61
The Entertainer '60
Our Man in Havana '59
The Key '58
Look Back in Anger '58
Heaven Knows, Mr. Allison '57
Moby Dick '56
Beau Brummel '54
Indiscretion of an American Wife '54
Beat the Devil '53
Moulin Rouge '52
The Golden Salamander '51
Captain Boycott '47

Reginald Morris
A Christmas Story '83
Porky's 2: The Next Day '83
Porky's '82
Empire of the Ants '77
Welcome to Blood City '77
Second Wind '76
Black Christmas '75

Kevin Morrisey
Headless Body in Topless Bar '96
Killer Tomatoes Eat France '91

David Rush Morrison
Stephanie Daley '06
Love for Rent '05
Double Bang '01
Fanci's Persuasion '95

Robert L. Morrison
Backstairs at the White House '79

Paul Morrissey (1939-)
Heat '72
Trash '70
Flesh '68

Andrei Moskvin (1901-61)
Don Quixote '57
Ivan the Terrible, Part 2 '46

Edgar Moura
Tieta of Agreste '96
The Fable of the Beautiful Pigeon Fancier '88

Eric Moynier
The Boynton Beach Club '05
Snakeman '05
Sueno '05

Sead Muhtarevic
Brown's Requiem '98
The Beneficiary '97
American Strays '96
Hard Drive '94

David Muir
And Now for Something Completely Different '72
Lust for a Vampire '71

M. David Mullen (1962-)
The Astronaut Farmer '07
Akeelah and the Bee '06
Shadowboxer '06
The Quiet '05
When Do We Eat? '05
D.E.B.S. '04
Northfork '03
2 Brothers & a Bride '03
Infested: Invasion of the Killer Bugs '02
Jackpot '01
Devil in the Flesh 2 '00
Alone with a Stranger '99
Perfect Tenant '99
Twin Falls Idaho '99
The Night Caller '97
Cupid '96
Dead Cold '96
The Fiance '96
Shadow Warriors '95
Lipstick Camera '93

Robby Muller (1940-)
Coffee and Cigarettes '03
24 Hour Party People '01
Dancer in the Dark '99
Ghost Dog: The Way of the Samurai '99
The Goalie's Anxiety at the Penalty Kick '71
The Tango Lesson '97
Beyond the Clouds '95
Breaking the Waves '95
Dead Man '95
Mad Dog and Glory '93
When Pigs Fly '93
Until the End of the World '91
Mystery Train '89
Barfly '87
The Believers '87
Down by Law '86
Repo Man '83
Saint Jack '79
The American Friend '77
Kings of the Road—In the Course of Time '76

Maximo Munzi
The Christmas Card '06
Bound by Lies '05
Mystery Woman: Mystery Weekend '05
Love's Enduring Promise '04
Momentum '03
Scorcher '02
Backflash '01
Out of the Black '01
They Crawl '01
The Guardian '00
The Stepdaughter '00
Judgment Day '99
Good Luck '96
Blondes Have More Guns '95

J. (James) Michael Muro
The Last Mimzy '07
Rush Hour 3 '07
Flicka '06
Crash '05
Roll Bounce '05
Open Range '03

Fred Murphy (1942-)
Drillbit Taylor '08
RV '06

Dreamer: Inspired by a True Story '05
Secret Window '04
Freddy vs. Jason '03
Auto Focus '02
The Mothman Prophecies '02
Soul Survivors '01
Stir of Echoes '99
Witness Protection '99
Dance with Me '98
A Family Thing '96
Metro '96
Faithful '95
The Fantasticks '95
Murder in the First '95
Jack the Bear '93
Scenes from a Mall '91
Enemies, a Love Story '89
Five Corners '88
Full Moon in Blue Water '88
Best Seller '86
The Dead '87
Hoosiers '86
The Trip to Bountiful '85
Eddie and the Cruisers '83
Q (The Winged Serpent) '82
Heartland '81
Impostors '80
Girlfriends '78

Michael D. Murphy
Beach Girls '82
Silent Scream '80

Paul Murphy (1954-)
October Sky '99
Under the Lighthouse Dancing '97
Mighty Morphin Power Rangers: The Movie '95
Tunnel Vision '95

Nicholas Musuraca (1892-1975)
The Blue Gardenia '53
The Hitch-Hiker '53
Where Danger Lives '50
Mysterious Desperado '49
Out of the Past '47
The Spiral Staircase '46
Bedlam '45
Forever and a Day '43
The Ghost Ship '43
Call Out the Marines '42
Cat People '42
Hurry, Charlie, Hurry '41
Smashing the Rackets '38
Village Tale '35
Cheyenne Kid '33
Smart Woman '31
Inside the Lines '30

Sead Mutarevic
See *Sead Muhtarevic*

Oleg Mutu
4 Months, 3 Weeks, 2 Days '07
The Death of Mr. Lazarescu '05

David Myers (1914-2004)
Hard Traveling '85
La Vie en Rose '07
Paris, je t'aime '06

Mutsuo Naganuma
The Hidden Blade '04
The Twilight Samurai '02

Tetsuo Nagata

Asakazu Nakai
Ran '85
Dersu Uzala '75
High & Low '62
Throne of Blood '57
I Live in Fear '55
Seven Samurai '54
Ikiru '52
One Wonderful Sunday '47
No Regrets for Our Youth '46

Armando Nannuzzi (1925-2001)
Frankenstein Unbound '90
Maximum Overdrive '86
Silver Bullet '85
La Cage aux Folles 2 '81
La Cage aux Folles '78
Chino '75
Ludwig '72

Waterloo '71
Porcile '69
Mafioso '62
Il Bell'Antonio '60

Leon Narbey (1947-)
Whale Rider '02
The Price of Milk '00
Desperate Remedies '93

Hiro Narita (1941-)
The Darwin Awards '06
Dirty Pictures '00
I'll Be Home for Christmas '98
Shadrach '98
Conceiving Ada '97
Sub Down '97
The Arrival '96
James and the Giant Peach '96
The Rocketeer '91
Star Trek 6: The Undiscovered Country '91
Honey, I Shrunk the Kids '89
Never Cry Wolf '83

Toichiro Narushima
Merry Christmas, Mr. Lawrence '83
Double Suicide '69

Mohsen Nasr
An Egyptian Story '82
Alexandria... Why? '78

Guillermo Navarro (1955-)
Hellboy 2: The Golden Army
Pan's Labyrinth '06
Zathura '05
Hellboy '04
Imagining Argentina '04
Broken Silence '01
The Devil's Backbone '01
Spy Kids '01
Stuart Little '99
Jackie Brown '97
Spawn '97
Dream for an Insomniac '96
The Long Kiss Goodnight '96
Desperado '95
Four Rooms '95
From Dusk Till Dawn '95
Cronos '94
Cabeza de Vaca '90

Ronald Neame (1911-)
This Happy Breed '47
Blithe Spirit '45
In Which We Serve '43

Andre Neau
Waiting for the Moon '87
The Return of Martin Guerre '83

Louis Nee
Utopia '51
Vampyr '31

Sol Negrin (1929-)
Happy Hell Night '92
Amazing Grace '74

Peter Nelson (1959-)
A Tale of Two Pizzas '03
Pipe Dream '02
Ed's Next Move '96

Jan Nemecek
Murder Czech Style '66
Who Wants to Kill Jessie? '65

Alex Nepomniaschy (1955-)
Take the Lead '06
10th & Wolf '06
The Prince & Me '04
Narc '02
A Time for Dancing '00
It's the Rage '99
Never Been Kissed '99
The Alarmist '98
The Associate '96
Mrs. Winterbourne '96
Safe '95
Lisa '90
Poltergeist 3 '88
Last Resort '86
Wanted Dead or Alive '86

Harry Neuman
See Harry Neumann

Harry Neumann (1891-1971)
The Wasp Woman '59
Flight to Mars '52
Riding the California Trail '47
Lawmen '44
Marked Trails '44
The Man with Two Lives '42
The Fatal Hour '40
Tomboy '40
Mr. Wong, Detective '38
Prison Break '38
Mysterious Mr. Wong '35
The Dude Bandit '33
Tarzan the Fearless '33
Local Bad Man '32
Boiling Point '32
The Prairie King '27
The Phantom Bullet '26

Mathias Neumann (1965-)
In the Name of the King: A Dungeon Siege Tale '08
BloodRayne '06
Alone in the Dark '05
Heart of America '03
House of the Dead '03
Blackwoods '02
Sanctimony '01

Thomas Neuwirth
The Locket '02
True Women '97

Robert New
Riding the Bullet '04
The Chosen One: Legend of the Raven '98
Lionheart '90
Big Bad Mama 2 '87
Night of the Creeps '86
Prom Night '80

John Newby
Desert Saints '01
Alien Fury: Countdown to Invasion '00
The Defenders: Taking the First '98
The Defenders: Payback '97
The Christmas Box '95
The Disappearance of Kevin Johnson '95
Operation Intercept '95
The Fence '94
Red Sun Rising '94

Harry Newmann
See Harry Neumann

Yuri Neyman
Civil Brand '02
Milo '98
Spirit Lost '96
Roseanne: An Unauthorized Biography '94
Back in the USSR '92
Red Riding Hood '88
Liquid Sky '83

Peter Ngor
Sex and Zen '93
Mr. Vampire '86
Operation Condor 2: The Armour of the Gods '86

Meredith Nicholson (1913-2005)
The Amazing Transparent Man '60
Missile to the Moon '59
Frankenstein's Daughter '58
She Demons '58

Rex Nicholson
Perfume '01
Allie & Me '97
Plump Fiction '97
A Modern Affair '94

Ramsay Nickell (1963-)
Chaos Theory '08
Let's Go to Prison '06
Pretty Persuasion '05
The Medicine Show '01

John M. Nickolaus, Jr. (1913-85)
The Terror '63
Attack of the Giant Leeches '59
Night of the Blood Beast '58
Showdown at Boot Hill '58

Alfonso Nieva (1960-)
Stranger in Paso Bravo '68
Emerald of Artatra '67
Hawk and Castile '67
Dr. Orloff's Monster '64

William Nobles (1892-1968)
Romance on the Range '42
Bad Man of Deadwood '41
In Old Cheyenne '41
Nevada City '41
Sheriff of Tombstone '41
Adventures of Red Ryder '40
Carson City Kid '40
Drums of Fu Manchu '40
Mysterious Doctor Satan '40
Young Bill Hickok '40
In Old Caliente '39
South of the Border '39
Frankie Moon '39
Dangerous Holiday '37
Dick Tracy: The Spider Strikes '37
Roamin' Lead '37
S.O.S. Coast Guard '37
Wild Horse Rodeo '37
Doughnuts & Society '36
Winds of the Wasteland '36
No Man's Range '35
Sucker Money '34
Law and Lawless '33
The Lone Avenger '33
The Drifter '32
Mystery Trooper '32

Eric Van Haren Noman
Montana Sky '07
Brave New Girl '04
Brush with Fate '03
These Old Broads '01
The Truth About Jane '00
The Color of Courage '98
What the Deaf Man Heard '98
Robin Cook's Terminal '96
An Unexpected Family '96
Blue River '95
A Mother's Prayer '95
Too Young to Die '90
Hero and the Terror '88

Christopher Norr
The Hottest State '06
Into the Fire '05
One Last Thing '05
Second Best '05
Guarding Eddy '04
Nick and Jane '96
Nueba Yol '95

Crescenzo G.P. Notarile
Timecop 2: The Berlin Decision '03
Bullet '94

Ben Nott
Tha Company '07
See No Evil '06
Salem's Lot '04
Counterstrike '03
The Outsider '02

Danny Nowak (1959-)
Lemonade Joe '64
Dead in a Heartbeat '02
The Big Hit '98
Bone Daddy '97
Hard Core Logic '96
Probable Cause '95
Abducted 2: The Reunion '94

Vladimir Novotny (1914-97)
The Shop on Main Street '65

Jehane Noujaim (1974-)
Control Room '04
Only the Strong Survive '03

Carl Oakwood
Human Desires '97
Mutual Needs '97
The Big Dis '89

John O'Brien (1962-)
Vermont Is for Lovers '92

L.W. O'Connell
Decoy '46

Flesh Gordon 2: Flesh Gordon Meets the Cosmic Cheerleaders '90
Underground Agent '42
In Old Kentucky '35
Charlie Chan in London '34
Maker of Men '31
A Girl in Every Port '28

Victor Nunez (1945-)
Coastal '05
Without Evidence '96
Gal Young 'Un '79

Sven Nykvist (1922-2006)
Celebrity '98
Private Confessions '98
Curtain Call '97
Kristin Lavransdatter '95
Something to Talk About '95
Only You '94
With Honors '94
Sleepless in Seattle '93
What's Eating Gilbert Grape '93
Chaplin '92
Crimes & Misdemeanors '89
New York Stories '89
Another Woman '88
The Unbearable Lightness of Being '88
The Sacrifice '86
Agnes of God '85
Dream Lover '86
After the Rehearsal '84
Fanny and Alexander '83
Star 80 '83
Cannery Row '82
Twice '81
From the Life of the Marionettes '80
Willie & Phil '80
Hurricane '79
Starting Over '79
Autumn Sonata '78
The Serpent's Egg '78
Pretty Baby '78
Face to Face '76
The Tenant '76
The Dove '74
Scenes from a Marriage '73
Cries and Whispers '72
Siddhartha '72
One Day in the Life of Ivan Denisovich '71
The Touch '71
First Love '70
Hour of the Wolf '68
The Rite '69
The Passion of Anna '70
The Shame '68
Persona '66
The Silence '63
The Winter Light '62
Through a Glass Darkly '61
The Virgin Spring '59
The True and the False '55

Azusa Ohno
Body of Influence 2 '96
Hostile Intentions '94

Daryn Okada (1960-)
Baby Mama '08
Harold & Kumar Escape from Guantanamo Bay '08
Just like Heaven '05
Mean Girls '04
Paparazzi '04
Cradle 2 the Grave '03
Dr. Dolittle 2 '01
Good Advice '01
Joe Somebody '01
Texas Rangers '01
Lake Placid '99
Senseless '98
Black Sheep '96
Big Bully '95
Leo Tolstoy's Anna Karenina '96
Phantasm 2 '88

Julio Ortas
Ratter K'd '68
Hercules vs. the Sons of the Sun '64
One Step to Hell '67

David Odd
My Boy Jack '07
Persuasion '07
The Line of Beauty '06
The Bells '26
Byron '03
The Lost World '02
All the King's Men '99
Our Mutual Friend '98
Retribution '98
Girls' Night '97
Touching Evil '97
A Merry War '97
Fire '96

Bruno Nuytten (1945-)
Jean de Florette '87
Manon of the Spring '87
Detective '85
Possession '81
Barocco '76
The Best Way '76
Going Places '74
Life Is a Bed of Roses '83

Rene Ohashi
Jesse Stone: Sea Change '07
Saint Ralph '04
Jesse Stone: Stone Cold '05
Highwaymen '03
Wes Craven Presents: They '02

Philip Ogaard
Kitchen Stories '03
Aberdeen '00
Zero Degrees Kelvin '95
Cross My Heart and Hope to Die '94

Arthur Ornitz (1916-85)
Wilma '77
Death Wish '74
Law and Disorder '74
Blacksnake! '73
Serpico '73
House of Dark Shadows '70
Minnie and Moskowitz '71
A Thousand Clowns '65
Requiem for a Heavyweight '62

Giles Nuttgens (1960-)
The Good Night '07
Water '05
Bee Season '05
If Only '04
Young Adam '03
Asylum '05
Swimfan '02
The Deep End '01
Battlefield Earth '00
Alice in Wonderland '99
The Turn of the Screw '99
Earth '98

Ronald Orieux
The War Bride '01
The Passion of Ayn Rand '99

Yaron Orbach
The Ten '07
Fabled '02

Jim Orr
A Family Affair '01
Totally Blonde '01

Tim Orr (1968-)
Pineapple Express '08
Snow Angels '07
Year of the Dog '07
Come Early Morning '06
Trust the Man '06
Undertow '04
All the Real Girls '03
Raising Victor Vargas '03
George Washington '00

Michael D. O'Shea
The New Guy '02
Sorority Boys '02
Big Momma's House '00
Here on Earth '00
The '60s '99
Swann '96

Miroslav Ondricek (1934-)
Riding in Cars with Boys '01
The Preacher's Wife '96
A League of Their Own '92
Funny Farm '88
F/X '86
Amadeus '84
Silkwood '83
The World According to Garp '82
Ragtime '81
Hair '79
Slaughterhouse Five '72
If... '69

Woody Omens
Harlem Nights '89
Coming to America '88

Ruben O'Malley
Deceit '05
Love, Ludlow '05

Peter Olsen
Robot Stories '03
Ultrachrist '03
Kaaterskill Falls '01

Harald Gunnar Paalgard
The Inheritance '07
The Last Lieutenant '94

Gerald Packer
Twist '03

Gyula Pados (1969-)
Evening '07
Basic Instinct 2 '06
Fateless '05
Kontroll '03

Luc Pages
A Tale of Springtime '90
I Like Bats '85

Louis Page (1905-90)

Krysztof Pakulski

Riccardo Pallottini
Fearless '77

Paul Onorato
Nowhere to Hide '87

Pallottini
- Emmanuelle on Taboo Island '76
- The Killer Must Kill Again '75
- Black Hand '73
- Lady Frankenstein '72
- 1931: Once Upon a Time in New York '72
- In the Soup '92
- Street Hunter '90
- Fatal Mission '89
- Harlan County, U.S.A. '76
- And God Said to Cain '64
- Castle of Blood '64

Ernest Palmer (1885-1978)
- The Womaneater '59
- Broken Arrow '50
- Uneasy Terms '48
- The Dolly Sisters '46
- Meet the Navy '46
- Murder in the Footlights '46
- Pin-Up Girl '44
- Something for the Boys '44
- Sweet Rosie O'Grady '43
- Springtime in the Rockies '42
- Thunder Birds '42
- Blood and Sand '41
- Four Men and a Prayer '38
- Stand Up and Cheer '34
- Cavalcade '33
- Hoopla '33

Cecilio Paniagua
- Lisa and the Devil '75
- Mission in Morocco '59

Bob Paone
- Judge & Jury '96
- Basket Case 3: The Progeny '92

Phedon Papamichael (1962-)
- 3:10 to Yuma '07
- The Pursuit of Happyness '06
- 10 Items or Less '06
- Walk the Line '05
- The Weather Man '05
- Sideways '04
- Identity '03
- Moonlight Mile '02
- America's Sweethearts '01
- The Million Dollar Hotel '99
- Patch Adams '98
- The Locusts '97
- Mouse Hunt '97
- Love Crimes '92
- Poison Ivy '92
- Prayer of the Rollerboys '91
- Body Chemistry '90
- Dance of the Damned '88
- Phenomenon '96
- Unhook the Stars '96
- Unstrung Heroes '95
- While You Were Sleeping '95
- Dark Side of Genius '94
- Cool Runnings '93
- Wild Palms '93

Andrij Parekh (1971-)
- Half Nelson '06
- The Treatment '06
- Speak '04

Andy Parke
- Grizzly Mountain '97
- Future Force '89
- Operation Warzone '89

David Parker (1947-)
- Child Star: The Shirley Temple Story '01
- Amy '98
- Mr. Reliable: A True Story '95
- Malcolm '86

Phil Parmet (1942-)
- Blue State '07
- Halloween '07
- The Dog Problem '06
- Lonesome Jim '06
- The Devil's Rejects '05
- Dallas 362 '03
- American Gun '02
- 13 Moons '02
- Hard Cash '01
- Animal Factory '00
- Black & White '99
- Love and Action in Chicago '99
- Flipping '96
- The Last Days of Frankie the Fly '96
- Four Rooms '95
- Under the Hula Moon '95
- Nina Takes a Lover '94
- Two Small Bodies '93

Feliks Parnell (1953-)
- Lip Service '00
- The Nurse '97
- Poison Ivy 3: The New Seduction '97
- Smalltime '96
- Serpent's Lair '95

Aiace Parolini (1920-)
- Alfredo, Alfredo '72
- Sicilian Connection '72
- Super Brother '68

Barry Parrell
- A Woman's a Helluva Thing '01
- Zebra Lounge '01
- The Minion '98

Greg Patterson
- TripFall '99
- Paper Bullets '99
- Fatal Passion '94

Peter Pau (1952-)
- The Forbidden Kingdom '08
- Shoot 'Em Up '07
- The Promise '05
- Crouching Tiger, Hidden Dragon '00
- Bride of Chucky '98
- Double Team '97
- Warriors of Virtue '97
- The Phantom Lover '95
- The Bride with White Hair '93
- Naked Killer '92
- The Killer '90

Justo Paulino
- Beyond Atlantis '73
- Mad Doctor of Blood Island '68

Stanley Pavey
- The Runaway Bus '54
- The Belles of St. Trinian's '53
- My Son, the Vampire '52
- Dead of Night '45

Goran Paviceric
- The Second Front '05

Pier Ludovico Pavoni (1927-)
- The Triumph of Hercules '66
- The Hit Man '60
- Mill of the Stone Women '60

Robert Paynter (1928-)
- Strike It Rich '90
- The Secret Garden '87
- Little Shop of Horrors '86
- Spies Like Us '85
- The Muppets Take Manhattan '84
- Superman 3 '83
- An American Werewolf in London '81
- The Final Conflict '81
- Superman 2 '80
- The Nightcomers '72
- Chato's Land '71
- Lawman '71

Homayun Payvar
- Daughters of the Sun '00
- The Taste of Cherry '96
- Life and Nothing More... '92

Kenneth Peach, Sr. (1903-88)
- Puffstuf '70
- Demon with a Glass Hand '64
- It! The Terror from Beyond Space '58
- Sons of the Desert '33

Glen Pearcy
- Outfoxed: Rupert Murdoch's War on Journalism '04
- Uncovered: The War on Iraq '04

Daniel Pearl (1951-)
- Aliens vs. Predator: Requiem '07
- Captivity '07
- Pathfinder '07
- The Texas Chainsaw Massacre '03
- Amazon Women on the Moon '87
- Hiding Out '87
- It's Alive 3: Island of the Alive '87
- Return to Salem's Lot '87
- Invaders from Mars '86
- Getting Wasted '80
- She Came to the Valley '77
- The Texas Chainsaw Massacre '74

Brian Pearson (1967-)
- White Noise 2: The Light '07
- The Butterfly Effect 2 '06
- School of Life '06
- Devour '05
- Karate Dog '04
- Stealing Sinatra '04
- Urban Legends 2: Final Cut '00
- Eye of the Killer '99
- Tall Lights Fade '99
- Bounty Hunters 2: Hardball '97
- Listen '96

Christopher Pearson
- Tideland '05
- The Order '01

Nicola Pecorini (1957-)
- Recipe for Disaster '03
- Harrison's Flowers '02
- Rules of Engagement '00
- Fear and Loathing in Las Vegas '98
- Double Down '01
- Sabretooth '01
- Blood Surf '00

Edward Pei
- Primeval '07
- Helen of Troy '03
- Anne Rice's The Feast of All Saints '01
- Little Richard '00
- Possessed '00

David Pelletier
- The Tooth Fairy '06
- Blood Angels '05
- Before I Say Goodbye '03
- He Sees You When You're Sleeping '02
- Lone Hero '02
- Jill the Ripper '00
- New Blood '99
- Bram Stoker's Shadowbuilder '98
- Mask of Death '97
- Downhill Willie '96
- Moving Target '96
- Live Bait '95
- The Killing Man '94

D.A. Pennebaker (1925-)
- Only the Strong Survive '03
- Moon over Broadway '98
- The War Room '93

C.M. Pennington-Richards (1911-2005)
- A Christmas Carol '51
- The Hidden Room '49

Jean Penzer (1927-)
- Notre Histoire '84
- Buffet Froid '79
- Get Out Your Handkerchiefs '78
- The Two of Us '68
- Love Play '60

Richard Pepin
- Avalanche '99
- Deadly Target '94
- Repo Jake '90
- Emperor of the Bronx '89
- Mayhem '87
- The Newlydeads '87

Richard Perez
- Outfoxed: Rupert Murdoch's War on Journalism '04
- Uncovered: The War on Iraq '04

Georges Perinal (1897-1965)
- Tom Thumb '58
- Bonjour Tristesse '57
- A King in New York '57
- Saint Joan '57
- Three Cases of Murder '55
- The Fallen Idol '49
- Nicholas Nickleby '46
- The Life and Death of Colonel Blimp '43
- Spitfire '42
- Dangerous Moonlight '41
- The Thief of Bagdad '40
- The Four Feathers '39
- The Challenge '38
- Rembrandt '36
- Things to Come '36
- Sanders of the River '35
- Catherine the Great '34
- Private Life of Don Juan '34
- The Private Life of Henry VIII '33
- A Nous la Liberte '31
- The Blood of a Poet '30
- Under the Roofs of Paris '29

David Perrault
- The State Within '06
- They Call Me Sirr '00
- To Catch a Yeti '95

Harry Perry (1888-1985)
- Hell's Angels '30
- Wings '27
- The Vanishing American '25
- Shadows '22

Henri Persin
- Your Turn Darling '63
- The Longest Day '62

Jorgen Persson (1936-)
- A Song for Martin '01
- Faithless '00
- Digging to China '98
- Les Miserables '97
- Jerusalem '96
- Smilla's Sense of Snow '96
- The House of the Spirits '93
- The Best Intentions '92
- The Women on the Roof '89
- My Life As a Dog '85
- Elvira Madigan '67

Reinhart Pesche
- Fascination '04
- Fascination '04
- Woman, Thou Art Loosed '04
- The Apostate '98

Don Peterman
- Dr. Seuss' How the Grinch Stole Christmas '00
- Mighty Joe Young '98
- Get Shorty '95
- Speechless '94
- Mr. Saturday Night '92
- Point Break '91
- She's Out of Control '89
- She's Having a Baby '88
- Planes, Trains & Automobiles '87
- Star Trek 4: The Voyage Home '86
- Splash '84
- Flashdance '83
- When a Stranger Calls '79

Dennis Peters
- Faith '90
- Body Beat '88

John Peters
- Family Tree '00
- Campfire Tales '98
- Double Tap '98
- Sweethearts '97
- Shameless '94

Curtis Petersen
- Safe Harbour '07
- The Wailer '06
- The Confessor '04
- Detention '03
- Gone Dark '03
- Rock My World '02
- Road Rage '01
- Under Heavy Fire '01
- My 5 Wives '00
- The Proposal '00
- The Hunted '98
- My Teacher Ate My Homework '98
- Silver Wolf '98
- The Ticket '97
- Bloodhounds 2 '96
- Dead Ahead '96
- Sabotage '96
- ShadowZone: The Undead Express '96
- Expect No Mercy '95
- Iron Eagle 4 '95
- Death Wish 5: The Face of Death '94
- Tiger Claws '91
- Abraxas: Guardian of the Universe '90
- Dragonflight '90

Barry Peterson
- Jumper '08
- Starsky & Hutch '04
- Dark Blue '03
- Hollywood Homicide '03
- Rider of the Law '35

Gus Peterson (1893-1969)
- Lady in the Death House '44
- Rollin Plains '38
- Sing, Cowboy, Sing '37
- Tex Rides with the Boy Scouts '37
- Charley's Aunt '25

Aleksandar Petkovic (1929-2000)
- Vukovar '94
- Man Is Not a Bird '65

Victor Petrashevich
- Love Thrill Murders '71
- The Projectionist '71

Jacek Petrycki
- The Healer '02
- Shot in the Heart '01
- Europa, Europa '91
- The Interrogation '82
- Fever '81

Wally Pfister
- The Dark Knight '08
- The Prestige '06
- Batman Begins '05
- Slow Burn '05
- The Italian Job '03
- Insomnia '02
- Laurel Canyon '02
- Scotland, PA '02
- Rustin '01
- Memento '00
- Object of Obsession '95
- Secret Games 3 '94
- Stranger by Night '94
- Secret Games '92
- Lower Level '91
- The Unborn '91

Bruno Philip (1956-)
- A Woman Hunted '03
- Nowhere in Sight '01
- Heavy Metal 2000 '00
- Dead Silent '99
- The Arrival 2 '98
- Captive '97
- Snowboard Academy '96
- The Scorpio Factor '90

Alex Phillips, Jr. (1935-2007)
- Luminarias '99
- Dreaming About You '92
- Forbidden Homework '92
- Born in East L.A. '87
- Number One with a Bullet '87
- Murphy's Law '86
- To Kill a Stranger '84
- Cabo Blanco '81
- High Risk '81
- Fade to Black '80
- Devil's Rain '75
- Bring Me the Head of Alfredo Garcia '74
- The Swap '71
- Remolino de Pasiones '68
- Yanco '64

David Phillips
- Beer League '06
- Lift '01
- The Basketball Diaries '95
- The Little Death '95

Frank Phillips (1912-94)
- Midnight Madness '80
- The Black Hole '79
- Pete's Dragon '77
- The Island at the Top of the World '74
- Bedknobs and Broomsticks '71

Garry Phillips
- Candy '06
- Catch a Fire '06
- Better Than Sex '00
- The Monkey's Mask '00

Roberto D'Ettorre Piazzoli
- Curse 2: The Bite '88
- Sonny Boy '87
- Piranha 2: The Spawning '82
- Tentacles '77
- Forever Emmanuelle '75

Joseph Pickering
- The Incredible Journey of Mary Bryant '05
- Idiot Box '97

Andre Pienaar
- How She Move '08
- Restless Spirits '99

Tony Pierce-Roberts
- A Slight Case of Murder '99
- Made of Honor '08
- Home of the Brave '06
- Doom '05
- De-Lovely '04
- Underworld '03
- Dinotopia '02
- The Importance of Being Earnest '02
- The Golden Bowl '00
- The Trench '99
- Paulie '98
- Jungle 2 Jungle '96
- Surviving Picasso '96
- Haunted '95
- The Client '94
- Disclosure '94
- The Remains of the Day '93
- Howard's End '92
- The Dark Half '91
- White Fang '91
- Mr. & Mrs. Bridge '90
- Slaves of New York '89
- A Tiger's Tale '87
- A Room with a View '86
- A Private Function '84
- Moonlighting '82
- Tinker, Tailor, Soldier, Spy '80

Mark Lee Ping-Bin (1954-)
- Flight of the Red Balloon '08
- Three Times '05
- In the Mood for Love '00
- The Vertical Ray of the Sun '00
- Flowers of Shanghai '98
- Goodbye South, Goodbye '96

Guiseppe Pinori (1928-)
- Corrupt '84
- The New Gladiators '83

Tomislav Pinter (1925-)
- Transylvania 6-5000 '85
- Montenegro '81
- Steppenwolf '74

John Pirozzi
- Broken English '07
- The Hillside Strangler '04

Robert Pittack (1899-1976)
- Queen of the Amazons '47
- Strange Impersonation '46
- Goin' to Town '44
- Pennies from Heaven '36

Larry Pizer
- The Proprietor '96
- In Custody '94
- Murder in Coweta County '83
- Timerider '83
- Phantom of the Paradise '74
- Isadora '68
- Morgan: A Suitable Case for Treatment '66

Tomas Pladevall
- Rape '76

Robert Planck (1894-1963)
- Royal Wedding '51
- Above Suspicion '43
- A Woman's Face '41
- Strange Cargo '40
- The Man in the Iron Mask '39
- The Duke o' West Point '38
- Red Salute '35
- Our Daily Bread '34
- Jane Eyre '34
- Be Yourself '30

Franz Planer (1894-1963)
- Breakfast at Tiffany's '61
- The Nun's Story '59
- The Big Country '58
- The Pride and the Passion '57
- The Caine Mutiny '54
- 20,000 Leagues under the Sea '54
- The 5000 Fingers of Dr. T '53
- Death of a Salesman '51
- Cyrano de Bergerac '50
- Champion '49
- Criss Cross '48
- One Touch of Venus '48
- I Love a Bandleader '45
- The Marriage of Figaro '49

Karl Plintzner (1911-)
- Intrigue and Love '59
- The Merry Wives of Windsor '50

Mark Plummer
- Pulse '06
- Head Over Heels '01
- Albino Alligator '96
- The Waterdance '91
- After Dark, My Sweet '90
- Two Moon Junction '88

Rui Poças (1966-)
- Two Drifters '05
- C Fantasma '04

Gabor Pogany (1915-99)
- Night Train Murders '75
- Torture Train '75
- Bluebeard '72
- Double Face '70
- Two Women '61

Clifford Poland
- Hello Down There '69
- Force of Impulse '60

Mathieu Poirot-Delpech (1959-)
- Paris, je t'aime '06
- Cote d'Azur '05
- My Life on Ice '02
- The Adventures of Felix '99
- Jeanne and the Perfect Guy '98

Gideon Porath
- Power Play '02
- Breach of Conduct '94

Gene Polito (1918-)
- Cheech and Chong's Up in Smoke '79
- The Bad News Bears Go to Japan '78
- Westworld '73

Sol Polito (1892-1960)
- Sorry, Wrong Number '48
- Now, Voyager '42
- Sergeant York '41
- Santa Fe Trail '40
- The Adventures of Robin Hood '38
- Angels with Dirty Faces '38
- The Charge of the Light Brigade '36
- Petrified Forest '36
- 'G' Men '35
- 42nd Street '33
- Picture Snatcher '33
- Playing Around '30

Christophe Pollock
- Alias Betty '01
- In Praise of Love '01
- Up/Down/Fragile '96
- For Ever Mozart '96
- Marie Baie des Anges '97

Marco Pontecorvo (1966-)
- The Last Legion '07
- Firewall '06
- Eros '04

Gordon Pollock
- City Lights '31
- Queen Kelly '29

Hang-Seng Poon
- Jet Li's Fearless '06
- Kung Fu Hustle '04
- Formula 51 '01
- Jackie Chan's Who Am I '98

Bill Pope (1952-)
- Spider-Man 3 '07
- Spider-Man 2 '04
- Team America: World Police '04
- The Matrix Reloaded '03
- The Matrix Revolutions '03
- Bedazzled '00
- The Matrix '99
- Zero Effect '97
- Bound '96
- Gridlock'd '96
- Clueless '95
- Army of Darkness '92
- Darkman '90

Dick Pope (1947-)
- Honeydripper '07
- The Illusionist '06
- Man of the Year '06
- Vera Drake '04
- All or Nothing '02
- Nicholas Nickleby '02
- Thirteen Conversations About One Thing '01
- Topsy Turvy '99
- Career Girls '97
- Swept from the Sea '97
- Nothing Personal '95
- Secrets and Lies '95
- An Awfully Big Adventure '94
- Naked '93
- The Blackheath Poisonings '92

Roland Price (1893-1966)
- The Bride & the Beast '58
- Son of Ingagi '40
- Marihuana '36
- Silent Code '35

Robert Presley
- Beowulf '07
- The Polar Express '04

Tom Priestley
- Delta Farce '07
- Barbershop 2: Back in Business '04
- Surviving Christmas '04
- Barbershop '02
- New Best Friend '02
- Undercover Brother '02

Jack Priestley (1926-93)
- Rage of Angels: The Story Continues '86
- The Final Cut '95
- House of Cards '93
- The First Deadly Sin '80
- Across 110th Street '72
- Born to Win '71
- Where's Poppa? '70
- Blood and Steel '35

Anthony Pun
- Robin-B-Hood '06
- A Knight in Camelot '98
- Hot Touch '82

Cynthia Pusheck (1964-)
- Loving Annabelle '06
- Three Days of Rain '03
- Three Days of Rain '02

Ian Punter
- Every Woman Knows a Secret '99
- Tails You Live, Heads You're Dead '95
- A Vow to Kill '95
- Weekend at Bernie's '89
- The Dog Who Stopped the War '84
- Johnny Mnemonic '95
- The Stranger: Kabloonak '95

Mark Putnam
- No Way to Treat a Lady '68
- The Subject Was Roses '68
- A Man Called Adam '66

Allan Pyrah
- Catherine Cookson's The Secret '00
- Catherine Cookson's The Wingless Bird '97

Munn Powell
- The Sasquatch Gang '06
- Napoleon Dynamite '04

Roger Pratt (1947-)
- Harry Potter and the Goblet of Fire '05
- Troy '04
- Harry Potter and the Chamber of Secrets '02
- Iris '01
- Chocolat '00
- The End of the Affair '99
- Grey Owl '99
- The Avengers '98
- Twelve Monkeys '95
- Mary Shelley's Frankenstein '94
- Shadowlands '93
- The Fisher King '91
- Batman '89
- High Hopes '88
- Brazil '85
- Meantime '81

Andreas Poulsson
- The Boy Who Could Fly '86
- Strange Brew '83
- Blood Beach '81
- Dead and Buried '81

Brian Probyn (1920-82)
- Badlands '74
- Frankenstein and the Monster from Hell '74
- The Satanic Rites of Dracula '73
- Witness to Murder '98 — Sex and the Other Man '95
- She's the One '96
- Living in Oblivion '94
- Sleepwalk '88

Frank Prinzi
- Sidewalks of New York '01
- No Looking Back '98
- 200 Cigarettes '98
- The Real Blonde '97
- The Grave '96

Fortunato Procopio
- The Devil and Daniel Johnston '05
- King of the Jungle '01
- A Brother's Kiss '97

Francois Protat
- Seizure '74
- Snowballin' '71

Roger Racine
- Time at the Top '99
- Whiskers '98

Pasquale Rachini
- Incantato '03
- The Best Man '97
- Heaven '99
- The Ugly '96

Stephen Posey
- Pick a Card '97
- Penitentiary '82
- Slumber Party Massacre '82
- Friday the 13th, Part 5: A New Beginning '85
- Hellhole '85

Nils Post (1960-)
- New Beginning '85

Steven Poster (1944-)
- Southland Tales '06
- Mrs. Harris '05
- Daddy Day Care '03
- Stuart Little 2 '02
- Donnie Darko '01
- Color of Justice '97
- RocketMan '97
- Roswell: The U.F.O. Cover-up '94
- The Cemetery Club '93
- Life Stinks '93
- Rocky 5 '90
- Next of Kin '89
- Big Top Pee-wee '88
- Someone to Watch Over Me '87
- Strange Brew '83

Robert Primes (1940-)
- Bachelor Party Vegas '05
- Sleeper Cell '05
- Baadasssss! '03
- The Sandy Bottom Orchestra '00
- Money Talks '97
- My Antonia '94
- The Hard Way '91
- Bird on a Wire '90

Rodrigo Prieto (1965-)
- Lust, Caution '07
- Babel '06
- Brokeback Mountain '05
- Alexander '04
- 21 Grams '03
- 8 Mile '02
- Frida '02
- 25th Hour '02
- Original Sin '01
- Amores Perros '00

Pascal Rabaud
- Idlewild '06
- Paris, je t'aime '06
- Bossa Nova '99

Jean Rabier (1927-)
- The End of Violence '97
- Carried Away '95
- Leaving Las Vegas '95
- Vanya on 42nd Street '94
- The Ballad of Little Jo '93
- Freddy's Dead: The Final Nightmare '91
- Blood & Concrete: A Love Story '90
- The Cry of the Owl '87
- The Story of Women '88
- Violette '78

Simon Raby (1961-)
- Heaven '99
- Le Bonheur '65
- Umbrellas of Cherbourg '64
- Cleo from 5 to 7 '61
- La Femme Infidele '69
- This Man Must Die '70
- Cold Sweat '71

Andreu Rebes
- Beyond Re-Animator '03
- Nico and Dani '00

Don Reddy
- Benji: Off the Leash! '04 ·
- Benji '74

Richard L. Rawlings (1916-92)
- DC 9/11: Time of Crisis '04
- Blackheart '98
- Parting Shots '98
- Charlie Muffin '79

Frank Redman
- Gruesome '47
- Dick Tracy's Dilemma '47
- Dick Tracy Meets Gruesome '47
- Dick Tracy, Detective '45

Ousama Rawi (1939-)
- The Story of the Christa Klages '73

Itzik Portal
- Bonjour Monsieur Shlomi '03

The Thomas Crown Affair '99

David Quaid
- Gold of the Amazon Women '79
- Pretty Poison '68

Dick Quinlan
- Santa Claus Conquers the Martians '64

Declan Quinn (1957-)
- In the Spirit '90
- Moonshine Highway '96
- Curse of the Starving Class '94
- Rising '02 — Get Rich or Die Tryin' '05
- Vanity Fair '04
- Cold Creek Manor '03
- Hysterical Blindness '02
- In America '02
- Monsoon Wedding '01
- 28 Days '00
- Flawless '99
- This Is My Father '98
- One True Thing '98
- 2 by 4 '98
- Kama Sutra: A Tale of Love '96

Claudia Raschke
- Mad Hot Ballroom '05
- Kiss Me, Guido '97
- No Way Home '96
- The Last Good Time '94
- Thank You & Good Night '91

Joel Ransom
- Angels Fall '07
- The Seeker: The Dark Is Rising '07
- Ice '02
- Taken '02
- Freeway 2: Confessions of a Trickbaby '99
- The Second Awakening of Christa Klages '73

Kevin Rafferty
- The War Room '93
- Roger & Me '89

Elemer Ragalyi (1939-)
- An American Rhapsody '01
- Dostoevsky's Crime and Punishment '99
- Jakob the Liar '99
- Mary, Mother of Jesus '99
- A Knight in Camelot '98
- The Hunchback '97
- Ms. Scrooge '97
- Rasputin: Dark Servant of Destiny '96
- Trilogy of Terror 2 '96
- Catherine the Great '95
- A Kid in King Arthur's Court '95

Martina Radwan
- Flannel Pajamas '06
- The Killing Floor '06

Michael Reed (1929-)
- McKenzie Break '70
- Fiction Makers '67
- Prehistoric Women '67
- Dracula, Prince of Darkness '66
- Flowers of Reverie '84
- Daniel Takes a Train '83
- The Phantom of the Opera '89
- Mesmer '94
- The Thomas Crown Affair '99 — Edge '93

David Quaid — This World, Then the Fireworks '97 — Tales from the Crypt Presents Bordello of Blood '96

Dr. Jekyll and Ms. Hyde '95

Clark Ramsey
- The Choppers '61
- The Flaming Urge '53

Franz Rath (1932-)
- The Promise '94
- Marianne and Juliane '82
- Sisters, Or the Balance of Happiness '79
- The Pirates of Silicon Valley '99

Earl Rath
- Raid on Rommel '71
- Shoot Out '71

Tami Reiker
- For One More Day '07
- Mr. Woodcock '07
- Pieces of April '03
- Disappearing Acts '00
- The Love Letter '99
- The Gorgon '64
- Swifty '35
- Valley of Wanted Men '35
- Arizona Terror '31
- Sunset Trail '32
- Range Law '31

Arthur Reed
- Fighting Renegade '39
- Six Gun Rhythm '39

Michael Reed (1929-) — Girl '98 — High Art '98

David Rakoczy
- Asylum '07
- Doomsday '07
- Doomsdayer '01

Jose Ortiz Ramos (1911-)
- The Brainiac '61

Arthur Reinhart (1965-)
- Tristan & Isolde '06 ·
- Crows '94
- Children of Dune '03
- Far Harbor '96

Stephen Reizes
- Marked Man '96

The Curse of the Crying Woman '61
Creature of the Walking Dead '60

Hit Woman: The Double Edge '93

Reizes

Lana in Love '92

Ricardo Remias
Fast Gun '93
Nam Angels '88
Demon of Paradise '87

Peter Reniers
Bloodsucking Pharoahs of Pittsburgh '90
Two Evil Eyes '90

Ray Rennahan (1896-1980)
Terror in a Texas Town '58
Seventh Cavalry '56
A Lawless Street '55
Rage at Dawn '55
Arrowhead '53
Pony Express '53
At Sword's Point '51
Great Missouri Raid '51
A Connecticut Yankee in King Arthur's Court '49
The Paleface '48
The Perils of Pauline '47
Unconquered '47
Duel in the Sun '46
A Thousand and One Nights '45
Up in Arms '44
For Whom the Bell Tolls '43
Blood and Sand '41
Louisiana Purchase '41
That Night in Rio '41
Down Argentine Way '40
Drums Along the Mohawk '39
Gone with the Wind '39
Wings of the Morning '37
Becky Sharp '35
The Cat and the Fiddle '34
Mystery of the Wax Museum '33
Doctor X '32
Toni '34

Claude Renoir (1914-93)
The Spy Who Loved Me '77
French Connection 2 '75
Pearl '78

Marc Reshovsky (1957-)
Most Wanted '97
Set It Off '96
Red Rock West '93
Sorority House Massacre '86

Scott Ressler
Hollywood Chainsaw Hookers '88
Sorority Babes in the Slimeball Bowl-A-Rama '87

William Rexer
The Accidental Husband '08
I Think I Love My Wife '07
The Groomsmen '06
Fierce People '05
Prime '05
Book of Love '04
Looking for Kitty '04
Lisa Picard is Famous '01

Brian Reynolds
Boss of Bosses '99
Murder at Devil's Glen '99
With Friends Like These '98
Gang Related '94
Guarding Tess '94

Buster Reynolds
Hoodlum '03
The Gods Must Be Crazy '84

John Rhode
Devon's Ghost: Legend of the Bloody Boy '05
Born to Lose '99

John Rhodes
The Purifiers '04

Edmond Richard (1927-)
16 Years of Alcohol '03
That Obscure Object of Desire '77
Phantom of Liberty '74
The Discreet Charm of the Bourgeoisie '72
Chimes at Midnight '67
The Trial '63

Zack Richard (1975-)
Bram Stoker's Way of the Vampire '05
Up for Grabs '05

Jack L. Richards
The Beast Within '82
My Brother Has Bad Dreams '72

Robert Richardson (1955-)
The Good Shepherd '06
The Aviator '04
Kill Bill Vol. 2 '04
Kill Bill Vol. 1 '03
The Four Feathers '02
Bringing Out the Dead '99
Snow Falling on Cedars '99
Fast, Cheap & Out of Control '97
The Horse Whisperer '97
U-Turn '97
Wag the Dog '97
Casino '95
Nixon '95
Natural Born Killers '94
Heaven and Earth '93
A Few Good Men '92
City of Hope '91
The Doors '91
JFK '91
Born on the Fourth of July '89
Eight Men Out '88
Talk Radio '88
Wall Street '87
Platoon '86
Salvador '86

Ross Richardson
Unearthed '08
Unearthed '07

Robert Richman
Metallica: Some Kind of Monster '04
My Architect: A Son's Journey '03

Anthony B. Richmond (1942-)
The Comebacks '07
Good Luck Chuck '07
Employee of the Month '06
John Tucker Must Die '06
Just Friends '05
A Cinderella Story '04
Dirty Dancing: Havana Nights '04
Dumb and Dumberer: When Harry Met Lloyd '03
Shade '03
The Sweetest Thing '02
Legally Blonde '01
Someone Like You '01
Cherry Falls '00
Men of Honor '00
Agnes Browne '99
Ravenous '99
A Walk on the Moon '99
Rough Riders '97
Bastard out of Carolina '96
First Kid '96
Playing God '96
Full Body Massage '95
The Immortals '95
Tales from the Hood '95
The Sandlot '93
Candyman '92
Sunset '88
The Kids Are Alright '79
The Eagle Has Landed '77
The Man Who Fell to Earth '76
Don't Look Now '73

Tom Richmond
The Ex '07
Right at Your Door '06
Palindromes '04
Tanner on Tanner '04
House of 1000 Corpses '03
The Singing Detective '03
I'm with Lucy '02
On Guard! '03
The Chateau '01
Chelsea Walls '01
Hardball '01
Knockaround Guys '01
Gun Shy '00
Waking the Dead '00
First Love, Last Rites '98
Slums of Beverly Hills '98
The Twilight of the Golds '97
johns '96
Mother Night '96
Homage '95
Killing Zoe '94
Little Odessa '94
Love and a 45 '94
A Midnight Clear '92
Heaven Is a Playground '91
Pastime '91
I'm Gonna Git You Sucka '88
Stand and Deliver '88
Straight to Hell '87
Chopping Mall '86

Antonio Rinaldi
Five Dolls for an August Moon '70
Danger: Diabolik '68
Kill, Baby, Kill '66
Planet of the Vampires '65

Lisa Rinzler
The Night Listener '06
The War Within '05
Lighting in a Bottle '04
Rick '03
Love Liza '02
Welcome to Collinwood '02
Pollock '00
Three Seasons '98
Tree's Lounge '96
Dead Presidents '95
Menace II Society '93
Guncrazy '92
True Love '89
I Was a Teenage TV Terrorist '87

Leif Rise
To the Shores of Hell '65
The Starfighters '63

Gunther Rittau (1893-1971)
The Blue Angel '30
Metropolis '26

Neil Roach
Category 7 : The End of the World '05
Category 6 : Day of Destruction '04
Gracie's Choice '04
The Whole Ten Yards '04
The '70s '00
Mama Flora's Family '98
Lone Justice 3: Showdown at Plum Creek '96
The Summer of Ben Tyler '96
Harvest of Fire '95
The Substitute Wife '94
Lone Justice 2 '93
To Dance with the White Dog '93
Devlin '92
My Name Is Bill W. '89
Silent Rage '82

James Robb
Ernest Goes to Africa '97
Ernest in the Army '97
Thieves of Fortune '89
The Outcast '84

James Roberson
Tough and Deadly '94
Wyatt Earp: Return to Tombstone '94
Visions of Evil '75

Jim Roberson
The Hunting of the President '04
Shadow of Chikara '77
Town That Dreaded Sundown '76
Winterhawk '76

Jacques Robin
Life Upside Down '64
Double Agents '59

Jean-Francois Robin (1943-)
On Guard! '03
Chaos '01
Nora '00
The Ice Rink '99
Rogue Trader '98
Metroland '97
The Serpent's Kiss '97
The Leading Man '96
Nelly et Monsieur Arnaud '95
A Scandal in Paris '46
Suite 16 '94
Betty Blue '86

George Robinson (1890-1958)
Francis in the Haunted House '56
Abbott and Costello Meet the Mummy '55
Abbott and Costello Meet the Invisible Man '51
Abbott and Costello in the Foreign Legion '50
House of Dracula '45
House of Frankenstein '44
Son of Dracula '43
The Falcon Takes Over '42
Frankenstein Meets the Wolfman '42
The Mummy's Tomb '42
Overland Mail '42
If I Had My Way '40
The Son of Monte Cristo '40
Charlie McCarthy, Detective '39
East Side of Heaven '39
Son of Frankenstein '39
The Tower of London '39
Service De Luxe '38
Dracula's Daughter '36
The Invisible Ray '36
Postal Inspector '36
The Mystery of Edwin Drood '35
Great Expectations '34

Claudio Rocha
Mrs. Palfrey at the Claremont '05
The Maldonado Miracle '03
On the Air '95
Red Shoe Diaries: Strip Poker '96
Talk of Angels '96
Orlando '92

Eliot Rockett
Dirty '05
Frankenfish '04

Alexei Rodionov (1947-)
Yes '04
Passion in the Desert '97
The Velocity of Gary '98
The Whole Wide World '96
In the Shadows '98
Skipped Parts '00
Four Dogs Playing Poker '00
Crocodile '00
The Specials '00
Nightstalker '02
Rampage: The Hillside Strangler Murders '04
Come and See '85

Robert Rodriguez (1968-)
Planet Terror '07
The Adventures of Sharkboy and Lavagirl in 3-D '05
Sin City '05
Once Upon a Time in Mexico '03
Spy Kids 3-D: Game Over '03
Spy Kids 2: The Island of Lost Dreams '02
El Mariachi '93

Bill Roe
The X-Files: I Want to Believe '08
Elektra '05
Where the Truth Lies '99
Hostage High '97

Guy Roe (1903-59)
Godzilla, King of the Monsters '56
Silver Star '55
Armored Car Robbery '50
Try and Get Me '50
Behind Locked Doors '48
Human Gorilla '48
Railroaded '47
A Scandal in Paris '46

Nicolas Roeg (1928-)
Walkabout '71
Performance '70
Petulia '68
Far from the Madding Crowd '67
Fahrenheit 451 '66
A Funny Thing Happened on the Way to the Forum '66
The Girl Getters '66
Masque of the Red Death '65

Derek Rogers
Resident Evil: Apocalypse '04
Crime Spree '03
Cypher '02
New Waterford Girl '99
Cube '98
The Fishing Trip '98

Owen Roizman (1936-)
French Kiss '95
Wyatt Earp '94
Grand Canyon '91
Havana '90
I Love You to Death '90
Vision Quest '85
Tootsie '82
Absence of Malice '81
Taps '81
True Confessions '81
The Electric Horseman '79
Straight Time '78
Network '76
The Return of a Man Called Horse '76
The Stepford Wives '75
Three Days of the Condor '75
The Taking of Pelham One Two Three '74
The Exorcist '73
The Heartbreak Kid '72
Play It Again, Sam '72
The French Connection '71

Glenn Roland
First Strike '85
Ilsa, Harem Keeper of the Oil Sheiks '76

Gernot Roll (1939-)
Nowhere in Africa '02
Beyond Silence '96
Maybe...Maybe Not '94
Kaspar Hauser '93
Terror Stalks the Class Reunion '93
Heimat 1 '92
Heimat 1 '84

Sonja Rom (1969-)
Attack Force '06
Extreme Dating '04
Tiptoes '03

Andy Romanoff
Something Weird '68
A Taste of Blood '67
Jimmy, the Boy Wonder '66

George A. Romero (1940-)
Season of the Witch '73
Night of the Living Dead '68

Ilan Rosenberg
Turbo: A Power Rangers Movie '96
Baby Love '83

Charles Rosher (1885-1974)
Jupiter's Darling '55
Kiss Me Kate '53
Young Bess '53
Scaramouche '52
Show Boat '51
Annie Get Your Gun '50
East Side, West Side '49
Neptune's Daughter '49
Song of the Thin Man '47
The Yearling '46
Ziegfeld Follies '46
Yolanda and the Thief '45
Little Lord Fauntleroy '36
Broadway Melody of 1936 '35
What Price Hollywood? '32
Dance Fools Dance '31
Laughing Sinners '31
The Tempest '28
My Best Girl '27
Sunrise '27
Sparrows '26
Little Annie Rooney '25
Tess of the Storm Country '22
The Love Light '21
Pollyanna '20
Daddy Long Legs '19

Charles Rosher, Jr. (1935-)
Heartbeeps '81
Nightwing '79
The Onion Field '79
3 Women '77

Ann T. Rossetti (1966-)
Voices from a Locked Room '95
Go Fish '94

Fausto Rossi
The Slasher '72
Scarlet Forces '68

Harold Rosson (1895-1988)
No Time for Sergeants '58
The Bad Seed '56
Singin' in the Rain '52
The Red Badge of Courage '51
Command Decision '48
The Hucksters '47
Thirty Seconds Over Tokyo '44
Boom Town '40
The Wizard of Oz '39
As You Like It '36
The Ghost Goes West '36
The Cat and the Fiddle '34
The Scarlet Pimpernel '34
Red Headed Woman '32

Andrea V. Rossotto
The Hunt for Eagle One: Crash Point '06
Sci-Fighter '04
Extreme Limits '01
Poison '01
Venomous '01
Ablaze '00
Against the Law '98
Carnosaur;3: Primal Species '96
Vampirella '96

Giuseppe Rotunno (1923-)
Sabrina '95
The Stendahl Syndrome '95
The Night and the Moment '94
Wolf '94
Regarding Henry '91
The Adventures of Baron Munchausen '89
Rent-A-Cop '88
Casanova '87
Julia and Julia '87
And the Ship Sails On '83
City of Women '81
All That Jazz '79
Orchestra Rehearsal '78
Amarcord '74
Love and Anarchy '73
Fellini's Roma '72
Carnal Knowledge '71
Fellini Satyricon '69
The Secret of Santa Vittoria '69
Anzio '68
Candy '68

Spirits of the Dead '68
The Bible '66
The Organizer '64
The Leopard '63
Bocaccio '70 '62
The Corruptor '99
Maraia '98
Pinocchio '96
The Adventures of

Denis Rouden
Deep n the Woods '00
Don't Let Me Die on a
Sunday '98

Philippe Rousselot (1945-)
The Brave One '07
The Great Debaters '07
Lions for Lambs '07
Charlie and the Chocolate
Factory '05
Constantine '05
Big Fish '03
Antwone Fisher '02
Planet of the Apes '01
Remember the Titans '00
The Tailor of Panama '00
Instinct '99
Random Hearts '99
The People vs. Larry Flynt '96
Mary Reilly '95
Interview with the Vampire '94
Queen Margot '94
Sommersby '93
A River Runs Through It '92
The Miracle '91
Henry & June '90
The Bear '89
We're No Angels '89
Dangerous Liaisons '88
Too Beautiful for You '88
Hope and Glory '87
The Emerald Forest '85
Moon in the Gutter '83
Diva '82
Peppermint Soda '77

Monty Rowan
Chronicle of the Raven '04
The Feminine Touch '95

Ashley Rowe (1959-)
Shattered '07
Starter for Ten '06
Alfie '04
Chasing Liberty '04
Calendar Girls '03
The Governess '98
Still Crazy '98
B. Monkey '97
24-7 '97
Sister My Sister '94
Widow's Peak '94
Unexplained Laughter '89

Danny Ruhlmann
Little Fish '05
The Night We Called It a
Day '03
In a Savage Land '99
The Nugget '02
Spartan '04
Confidence '03

Mauricio Rubinstein
Bernard and Doris '08
Puccini for Beginners '06
Sorry, Haters '05
King of the Corner '04
Casa de los Babys '03

Soumendu Roy
Forgive and Forget '99
Falling for a Dancer '98
'00

Kevin Rowley
Bedrooms and Hallways '98
When Brendan Met Trudy '00
Mad About Mambo '00
The Affair of the Necklace '01

Killby Inches '99

Joseph Ruttenberg (1889-93)
Speedway '68
The Oscar '66
Harlow '65
A Global Affair '63
Butterfield 8 '60
Green Mansions '59
Gigi '58
The Reluctant Debutante '58
Somebody Up There Likes Me '56
The Swan '56
Kismet '55
Brigadoon '54
The Prodigal '55
Julius Caesar '53
Prisoner of Zenda '52
The Great Caruso '51
The Miniver Story '50
Side Street '50
That Forsyte Woman '49
The Valley of Decision '45
Adventure '45
Mrs. Parkington '44
Gaslight '44
Madame Curie '43
Presenting Lily Mars '43
Mrs. Miniver '42
Random Harvest '42
Woman of the Year '42
Dr. Jekyll and Mr. Hyde '41
Two-Faced Woman '41
The Philadelphia Story '40
Waterloo Bridge '40
On Borrowed Time '39
The Great Waltz '38
The Women '39
Three Comrades '38
A Day at the Races '37
Fury '36
Woman in the Shadows '34
Struggle '31

Off the Map '03
No Good Deed '02
Focus '01
The Crew '00

Richard Rutkowski (1966-)
How to Eat Fried Worms '06
Interview with the Assassin '02

Ward Russell
Cruel World '05
The X-Files '98
The Last Boy Scout '91
The Man from Planet X '51
The Green Promise '49
Days of Thunder '90

John L. "Jack" Russell
Psycho '60
Girls' Town '59
The Indestructible Man '56
The Beast from 20,000
Fathoms '53
Invasion U.S.A. '52
Government Agents vs.
Phantom Legion '51

Lawnmower Man 2: Beyond
Cyberspace '96
The Last Time I Saw Paris '54
Reel Life '79
You Light Up My Life '77
Eat My Dust '76
TNT Jackson '75
The Big Bird Cage '72
The Walls of Hell '64
Raiders of Leyte Gulf '63

Stephen St. John
The Guardian '06
Holes '03
Ran '85
Dodes 'ka-den '70
Attack Squadron '63
High & Low '62
Sanjuro '62

Anthony Salinas
Blood Orgy of the She-
Devils '74
The Doll Squad '73
Lulu on the Bridge '98
Love! Valour! Compassion!
'96

Alik Sakharov (1959-)
Lights in the Dusk '06
The Man Without a Past '02
Ariel '89
Leningrad Cowboys Go
America '89

Takao Saito (1920-)
Rhapsody in August '91
Akira Kurosawa's Dreams
'90

Virginie Saint-Martin (1965-)
Thomas in Love '01
An Affair of Love '99

Felipe Sacdalan
Where Is My Friend's
House? '87
Through the Olive Trees '94

Farhad Saba
The Hills Have Eyes '77

Eric Saarinen
Rooster: Spurs of Death! '83

Robert Saad
Anne of Green Gables: The
Continuing Story '99
They Came from Within '75
Hard Part Begins '73
The Rainbow Gang '73

Robbie Ryan
Red Road '06

Ellery Ryan (1949-)
Glengarry Glen Ross '92
Dying Young '91
Liebestraum '91
In Too Deep '99
The Seventh Sign '88
House of Games '87
Surrender '87
At Close Range '86
Where the River Runs Black '86
That Eye, the Sky '94
Running Delilah '93

Paul Ryan
Spin '07
Big Bad Love '02
Thomas and the Magic
Railroad '00
Widowers '99
Box of Moonlight '96
Other Voices, Other Rooms '95
Where the Rivers Flow
North '94
Fraternity Vacation '85
This Is Not a Love Song '02

Giuseppe Ruzzolini (1930-)
Firestarter '84
Life of Verdi '82
Arabian Nights '74
A lionsarian '73
S'nort Night of Glass Dolls '71
Porcile '69

Mikael Salomon (1945-)
Far and Away '92
Backdraft '91
Arachnophobia '90
The Abyss '89
Always '89
Angel Baby '95
Cosi '95
Torch Song Trilogy '88
Zelly & Me '88

Sergio Salvati (1938-)
Red Riding Hood '03
Wax Mask '97
Puppet Master '89
Spin '07

Amnon Salomon
The Milky Way '97
The Adjuster '91
Speaking Parts '89

Geno Salvatori
Dadcy Day Camp '07
Outlaw Trail '06
Terror Beach '75

Francisco Sanchez (1925-)
Klima, Queen of the
Amazons '75
Zombie '80
Gates of Hell '80
The Black Cat '81
The Beyond '82

Bernard Salzmann (1957-)
The Android Affair '95
The Color of Evening '95
Deadly Past '95
Bad Blood '94

Rodolfo Sanchez
Beach Hotel '92
Kiss of the Spicer Woman '85

Gregory Sandor
Pixote '81
Forty Days of Musa Dagh '85
Forbidden Zone '80
Sisters '73
Fury on Wheels '71
The Hooked Generation '69
Born Losers '67

Tino Santoni (1913-)
The Girl with a Suitcase '60
Verdi '53
Young Caruso '51

Sandor Sara
25 Fireman's Street '73
Sinbad '71

Vic Sarin (1945-)
Partition '07
Cold Comfort '90
Bye Bye Blues '89

Paul Sarossy (1963-)
All Hat '97
Charlie Bartlett '07
The River King '05
The Wicker Man '06
Where the Truth Lies '05
Head in the Clouds '04
The Incredible Mrs. Ritchie '03

Aldo Scavarda (1923-)
Before the Revolution '65
L'Avventura '60

Roberto Schaefer
The Kite Runner '07
For Your Consideration '06
Stranger Than Fiction '05
Stay '05
Finding Neverland '04
Monster's Ball '01
Best in Show '00
Everything Put Together '00
Waiting for Guffman '96

Marco Scarpelli (1918-95)
The Mercenaries '62
Uncle Was a Vampire '59

Malik Hassan Sayeed
Belly '98
He Got Game '98
The Players Club '98
Cold Around the Heart '97
Girl 6 '96
Clockers '95

Edward Scaife (1912-94)
The Dirty Dozen '67
Khartoum '66
Trial & Error '62
On the Fiddle '61
Curse of the Demon '57
Sea Wife '57
A Kid for Two Farthings '55
Captain's Paradise '53

Nancy Schreiber (1949-)
Nevada '97
The Nines '07
American Gun '05
Loverboy '05
November '05
Buying the Cow '02
Book of Shadows: Blair
Witch 2 '00
Shadow Magic '00
Never 2 Big '98
Your Friends & Neighbors

Tobias Schliessler
Hancock '08
Dreamgirls '06
Friday Night Lights '04
The Rundown '03
Bait '00
The Guilty '99
Hoods '98
Legalese '98
Outrage '98

Javier Salmones (1953-)
Four Last Songs '06
Rated X '00
My Father, My Mother, My
Brothers and My Sisters '99

Ammon Salomon
Butterfly '98
Twice upon a Yesterday '98
Jerry and Tom '98
Pete's Meteor '98
Mistrial '96
Picture Perfect '96
The Sweet Hereafter '96
Affliction '96
Exotica '94
Blood & Donuts '95

Yasushi Sasakibara
The Mystery of Rampo '94
Violent Cop '89

Masaru Sato (1928-99)
The Wolves '71
The Battle of the Japan Sea '70
Godzilla vs. the Sea
Monster '66

Harris Savides (1957-)
Zodiac '07
Margot at the Wedding '07
American Gangster '07
Last Days '05
Birth '04
Elephant '03
Gerry '02
The Yards '00
The Game '97
Illuminata '98
Heaven's Prisoners '95

Hendrik Sartov (1885-1970)
Orphans of the Storm '21
Way Down East '20

Jens Schlosser
The Intended '02
Time Trackers '88
The Terror Within '88

Ronn Schmidt
The Mist '07
Star Kid '97
Lord of Illusions '95
Men of War '94
Double Cross '94
Sin and Redemption '94

Aaron Schneider
Simon Birch '98
Kiss the Girls '97
Dead Girls '90

George Schneiderman (1894-1964)
Steamboat 'Round the Bend '35
Doctor Bull '33
Pilgrimage '33
Four Sons '28
Hangman's House '28
The Iron Horse '24
A Foo There Was '14
'36

Wolfgang Schmidt
See Ray-Dennis Steckler

Jorge Schmidt-Reitwein (1939-)
Nosferatu the Vampyra '79
Woyzeck '78
Every Man for Himself &
God Against All '75
Heart of Glass '74

Charles E. Schoenbaum (1893-1951)
Good News '47
Junior Army '42
It Happened in New Orleans '36

Howard Schwartz (1919-90)
Just Looking '99
Haunted Honeymoon '86
Fletch '85
Amityville 3: The Demon '83
Arthur '81
The Celluloid Closet '95
Girl in the Cadillac '94
King of Comedy '82
Path to War '02
Visions of Light: The Art of
Cinematography '93

Fred Schuler (1940-)
Gamebox 1.0 '04
A Public Affair '62
The Devil & Max Devlin '81
Batman '66
The Big Bounce '69

Viktor Ruzicka (1943-)
Martha and I '91
Cobra Verde '88

Odd Geir Saether (1941-)
Inland Empire '06
Edvard Munch '74
The Shooting '66
Ride in the Whirlwind '66
The Struggle '58

Timo Salminen (1952-)

Philip D. Schwartz

Nancy Schreiber (cont.)
The Vanishing American '25
Nevada '27

Charles E. ...

Free Willy 3: The Rescue '97
Mandele and de Kerk '97
Volcano: Fire on the
Mountain '97
The Limbic Region '96
The Escape '95
Bulletproof Heart '95
Carryman 2: Farewell to
the Flesh '94

Denis Rouden
The Disappearance of
Garcia Lorca '96
Two Bits '96
A Far Off Place '93
Mr. Jones '93

Ellery Ryan

Duets '00
Lakeboat '00

The Man from Planet X '51
The Roman Spring of Mrs.
Stone '03

Survival Island '02
High Voltage '98
King Cobra '98

John Schwartzman (1960-)
The Bucket List '07
National Treasure: Book of Secrets '07
Meet the Fockers '04
Seabiscuit '03
The Rookie '02
Pearl Harbor '01
EDtv '99
Armageddon '98
Conspiracy Theory '97
The Rock '96
Mr. Wrong '96
A Pyromaniac's Love Story '95
Airheads '94
Red Surf '90

Xaver Schwarzenberger (1946-)
Querelle '83
Veronika Voss '82
Berlin Alexanderplatz '80

Lawrence Schweich
Come as You Are '05
Tequila Body Shots '99
Wind River '98

Eric Scott (1958-)
The Dark Dancer '95
The House on Todville Road '95

Chris Seager
Wild Child '08
Closure '07
The Walker '07
Alex Rider: Operation Stormbreaker '06
Archangel '05
White Noise '05
State of Play '03
Suspicion '03
The Way We Live Now '02
Lorna Doone '01
Frenchman's Creek '98
Ghosts of Mississippi '96
The American President '95
Beyond Rangoon '95
The Paper '94
The Firm '93
Lorenzo's Oil '92
The Doctor '91
Dead Poets Society '89
Gorillas in the Mist '88
Rain Man '88
Children of a Lesser God '86
The Hitcher '86
The Mosquito Coast '86
Witness '85
Careful, He Might Hear You '84

Christian Sebaldt (1958-)
Bratz '07
Crossover '06
Resident Evil: Apocalypse '04
Feardotcom '02
Race to Space '01
Galgameth '94
Illicit Dreams '94
Inevitable Grace '94

Revenge of the Red Baron '93

Edmond Sechan
Blue Country '77
Love on a Pillow '62

Jeffrey Seckendorf
Finding Home '03
Judy Berlin '99

Hiroshi Segawa
Under the Flag of the Rising Sun '72
Face of Another '66
Woman in the Dunes '64

John Seitz (1892-1979)
Invaders from Mars '53
Sunset Boulevard '50
The Great Gatsby '49
The Big Clock '48
On Our Merry Way '48
The Lost Weekend '45
Double Indemnity '44
Five Graves to Cairo '43
This Gun for Hire '42
Sullivan's Travels '41
The Four Horsemen of the Apocalypse '21

Andrzej Sekula (1954-)
Vacancy '07
The Pleasure Drivers '05
American Psycho '99
The Break '97
Cousin Bette '97
Four Rooms '95
Hackers '95
Across the Moon '94
Oleanna '94
Pulp Fiction '94
Reservoir Dogs '92

Jonathan Sela
Dreamland '06
Marilyn Hotchkiss' Ballroom Dancing & Charm School '06
The Omen '06
Soul Plane '04

Dean Semler (1943-)
Get Smart '08
I Now Pronounce You Chuck and Larry '07
Apocalypto '06
Click '06
Just My Luck '06
The Alamo '04
Bruce Almighty '03
Dragonfly '02
We Were Soldiers '02
XXX '02
Eye See You '01
Heartbreakers '01
The Nutty Professor 2: The Klumps '00
The Bone Collector '99
Gone Fishin' '97
Trojan War '97
Waterworld '95
Last Action Hero '93
The Three Musketeers '93
The Power of One '92
City Slickers '91
Dances with Wolves '90
Young Guns 2 '90
Dead Calm '89
Farewell to the King '89
K-9 '89
Cocktail '88
Young Guns '88
The Lighthorsemen '87
Mad Max: Beyond Thunderdome '85
The Coca-Cola Kid '84
Razorback '84
The Road Warrior '82

Lorenzo Senator (1974-)
Lake Placid 2 '07
Return to House on Haunted Hill '07
Alien Siege '05
Manticore '05

Ken Seng
League of Ordinary Gentlemen '04
Zombie Honeymoon '04

Enzo Serafin (1912-)
The Lady Without Camelias '53
Voyage in Italy '53
Story of a Love Affair '50
Musica Proibita '43

Ben Seresin
A Good Woman '04
Circus '00

Michael Seresin (1942-)
Madhouse '04
Straight into Darkness '04
Vlad '03
Dark Asylum '01
Retro Puppet Master '99
Witchouse '99

Eduardo Serra (1943-)
Blood Diamond '06
Comedy of Power '06
Beyond the Sea '04
Intimate Strangers '04
Girl with a Pearl Earring '03
Passion of Mind '00
Unbreakable '00
The Widow of Saint-Pierre '00
What Dreams May Come '98
The Swindle '97
The Wings of the Dove '97
The Jew '96
Jude '96
Grosse Fatigue '94
The Hairdresser's Husband '92

Leon Shamroy (1901-74)
Planet of the Apes '68
Caprice '67
The Glass Bottom Boat '66
The Agony and the Ecstasy '65
Do Not Disturb '65
The Cardinal '63
Cleopatra '63
Snow White and the Three Stooges '61
North to Alaska '60
Beloved Infidel '59
The Bravados '58
The Robe '53
The Snows of Kilimanjaro '52
With a Song in My Heart '52
David and Bathsheba '51
Cheaper by the Dozen '50
Prince of Foxes '49
Twelve o'Clock High '49
Daisy Kenyon '47
Forever Amber '47
Leave Her to Heaven '45
State Fair '45

A Tree Grows in Brooklyn '45
Buffalo Bill '44
Greenwich Village '44
Wilson '44
Crash Dive '43
Stormy Weather '43
The Black Swan '42
Roxie Hart '42
The Great American Broadcast '41
Moon over Miami '41
That Night in Rio '41
Down Argentine Way '40
Lillian Russell '40
Tin Pan Alley '40
The Adventures of Sherlock Holmes '39
Made for Each Other '39
The Story of Alexander Graham Bell '39
You Only Live Once '37
Wedding Present '36
Kiss and Make Up '34
Thirty Day Princess '34
Wayne Murder Case '32

Douglas W. Shannon
The Arrangement '99
Blowin' Smoke '99

Yaron Sharf
The Bubble '06
Yossi & Jagger '02

Henry Sharp (1892-1966)
The Young Land '59
The Woman Who Came Back '45
Ministry of Fear '44
Tomorrow the World '44
Dr. Cyclops '40
Campus Confessions '38
It's a Gift '34
Six of a Kind '34
Duck Soup '33
Strangers in Love '32
The Iron Mask '29
The Black Pirate '26
Don Q., Son of Zorro '25
Soul of the Beast '23

Steve (Steven) Shaw
Children On Their Birthdays '02

Roger Shearman
Lone Wolf McQuade '83
An Eye for an Eye '81

Lawrence Sher (1970-)
Dan in Real Life '07
When a Man Falls in the Forest '07
Grilled '06
The Chumscrubber '05
The Dukes of Hazzard '05
Life of the Party '05
Club Dread '04
Garden State '04
Killing Emmett Young '02
Kissing Jessica Stein '02
Shark Attack '99
On the Border '98

Eugene Shlugleit
3 Ninjas Knuckle Up '95
The Wolves '95
Twogether '94

Eugen Shufftan (1893-1977)
Lilith '64
The Hustler '61
The Horror Chamber of Dr. Faustus '59
Bizarre Bizarre '39
Metropolis '26

Eugene Shufftan
See Eugen Shufftan

Eugene Shugleit
See Eugene Shlugleit

Daniel Shulman
The Son of the Bride '01
Love Walked In '97

William Sickner (1890-1967)
The Undead '57
The Finger Man '55
The Mummy's Ghost '44
Raiders of Ghost City '44
Gang Busters '42
Junior G-Men of the Air '42
Overland Mail '42
Flash Gordon Conquers the Universe '40
Space Soldiers Conquer the Universe '40
The Green Hornet '39
Savage Fury '35

Jerry Sidell
Sleep Easy, Hutch Rimes '00
Acts of Betrayal '98
Trading Favors '97

Allen Siegler (1892-1960)
The Black Room '35
Parisian Love '25
The Plastic Age '25

Newton Thomas (Tom) Sigel (1961-)
Leatherheads '08
Superman Returns '06
The Brothers Grimm '05
X2: X-Men United '03
Confessions of a Dangerous Mind '02
X-Men '00
Brokedown Palace '99
Three Kings '99
Apt Pupil '97
Fallen '97
Blood & Wine '96
Foxfire '96
The Trigger Effect '96
The Usual Suspects '95
Blankman '94
Salmonberries '91

James Signorelli
Black Caesar '73
Superfly '72

Johnny (John W.) Simmons
Collected Stories '02
The Killing Yard '01
Three Strikes '00
Asunder '99
Once Upon a Time . . . When We Were Colored '95

Geoffrey Simpson
Romulus, My Father '07
The Starter Wife '07
Last Holiday '06
Under the Tuscan Sun '03
Glitter '01
Center Stage '00
Life '99
Oscar and Lucinda '97
Some Mother's Son '96
Shine '95
Little Women '94
The War '94
Mr. Wonderful '93
Fried Green Tomatoes '91
Celia: Child of Terror '89

Andreas Sinanos
Weeping Meadow '04
Eternity and a Day '97

Geza Sinkovics
The Last Seduction 2 '98
French Exit '97
Undertow '95
Delusion '91

Sandi Sissel
Tyler Perry's Meet the Browns '08
Going Upriver: The Long War of John Kerry '04
Barney's Great Adventure '98
Soul of the Game '96
Camp Nowhere '94
Dragstrip Girl '94
Full Eclipse '93
The People under the Stairs '91
Drug Wars: The Camarena Story '90
Heavy Petting '89
Salaam Bombay! '88

Santosh Sivan
The Mistress of Spices '05
Bride & Prejudice '04
The Terrorist '98

William V. Skall (1898-1976)
Rope '48
Life with Father '47
Song of Scheherazade '47
Billy the Kid '41

Adam Sliwinski
Meltdown '06
The Deal '05
Possessed '05
Air Bud 5: Buddy Spikes Back '03
Mindstorm '01

Douglas Slocombe (1913-)
Indiana Jones and the Last Crusade '89
Indiana Jones and the Temple of Doom '84
Never Say Never Again '83
Raiders of the Lost Ark '81
Julia '77
Rollerball '75
Jesus Christ, Superstar '73
The Music Lovers '71
Boom! '68
Fathom '67
The Fearless Vampire Killers '67
The Blue Max '66
The Servant '63
The L-Shaped Room '62
Circus of Horrors '60
The Smallest Show on Earth '57
Kind Hearts and Coronets '49
Dead of Night '45

Michael Slovis
Seven Seconds '05
The Foreigner '03
Half Past Dead '02
The 4th Floor '99
Scarred City '98
The White Raven '98
Crash Dive '96
Breach of Trust '95
Malicious '95
Party Girl '94

Arturo Smith
Psycho Beach Party '00
Race '99
Body and Soul '98
Nowhere '96

C. Davis Smith (1930-)
The Amazing Transplant '70
Bad Girls Go to Hell '65
Heroes Die Young '60

Chris Smith (1970-)
The Yes Men '03
American Movie '99

Doyle Smith
Scorpio One '97
Widow's Kiss '94

Gavin Smith
Ginger Snaps: Unleashed '04
Ice Men '04
My Louisiana Sky '02

Glen R. Smith
Rebel Rousers '69

Jeffrey Smith
Are You Scared? '06
Missing Brendan '03

Keith L. Smith
The Wash '01
Luck of the Draw '00
The Sex Monster '99
Diary of a Serial Killer '97
Love to Kill '97

Larry Smith
Elizabeth I '05
Fear X '03
The Target '02
Eyes Wide Shut '99
Go West '40
At the Circus '39

Leonard Smith (1894-1947)
National Velvet '44
Billy the Kid '40

Devil Doll '36
So This is Africa '33
The Wizard of Oz '25

Roland Smith
Savage Land '94
The New Adventures of Pippi Longstocking '88

S. Douglas Smith
The Net 2.0 '06
Black Cadillac '03
Joyride '97
Stormy Nights '97
The Secret Agent Club '96

Vladimir Smutny
Kolya '96
Dark Blue World '01

Edward Snyder
Jaws of Justice '33

William E. Snyder (1901-84)
Smoke '70
The Conqueror '56
Creature from the Black Lagoon '54
Second Chance '53
Flying Leathernecks '51
The Loves of Carmen '48

Piotr Sobocinski (1958-2001)
Trois Couleurs: Rouge '94
The Decalogue '88
Trapped '02
Angel Eyes '01
Hearts in Atlantis '01
Twilight '98
Marvin's Room '96
Ransom '96

Witold Sobocinski (1929-)
Frantic '88
Hands Up '81
Everything for Sale '68

Morten Soborg
Brothers '05
After the Wedding '06

Steven Soderbergh (1963-)
Ocean's Thirteen '07
Bubble '06
The Good German '06
Ocean's Twelve '04
Full Frontal '02
Solaris '02
Ocean's Eleven '01
Traffic '00
Schizopolis '97

Jaromir Sofr (1939-)
My Sweet Little Village '86
Closely Watched Trains '66

Yuri Sokol
Warm Nights on a Slow-Moving Train '87
Cactus '86
Man of Flowers '84
Lonely Hearts '82

Bing Sokolsky (1963-)
Mammoth '06
Black Cat Run '98
Doing Time on Maple Drive '92

Rosalio Solano (1914-)
Vintage Model '92

Leonardo Solis
Jailbird Rock '88

Tamas Somlo
The Girl '68
The Red and the White '68

Barry Sonnenfeld (1953-)
Misery '90
When Harry Met Sally... '89
Raising Arizona '87
Throw Momma from the Train '87
Blood Simple '85

Leonard J. South (1913-2006)
Hang 'Em High '67
The North Avenue Irregulars '79
Family Plot '76

Mike Southon
Beneath '07
Air Bud 6: Air Buddies '06
Sorted '04
MXP: Most Xtreme Primate '03
Replicant '01
The Duke '99
RKO 281 '99
Air Bud 2: Golden Receiver '98
Air Bud '97
Snow White: A Tale of Terror '97
The Final Cut '96
Roommates '95
The Run of the Country '95
Emily Bronte's Wuthering Heights '92
Little Man Tate '91
Goldeneye: The Secret Life of Ian Fleming '89
Gothic '87

Peter Sova
The Proposition '97
Donnie Brasco '96
Feast of July '95
Fatherland '94
Jimmy Hollywood '94
Good Morning, Vietnam '87
Tin Men '87
Diner '82

Theodor Sparkuhl (1891-1946)
Murder, He Says '45
Blood on the Sun '45
The Glass Key '42
Star Spangled Rhythm '42
Wake Island '42
Beau Geste '39
If I Were King '38
Internes Can't Take Money '37

Milan Spasic (1946-)
How Harry Became a Tree '01
Cabaret Balkan '98
Unseen Evil '99
Blood '00

Scott Spears
Witchcraft 11: Sisters in Blood '00
Too Good to Be True '98

Brenton Spencer
Where's the Money, Noreen? '97
Eight Days a Week '97
Hybrid '97
Night Shade '97
Magic Island '95
American Boyfriends '89

James Lawrence Spencer (1958-)
The Killing Club '01
100 Girls '00

Jorge Stahl, Jr. (1921-2003)
A Rumor of War '80
Zachariah '70
Black Knight '01

Alberto Spagnoli
Island of Blood '82
The Blob '58
Ramto 3 '88

Thomas E. Spalding (1926-96)
Lady of the Evening '75
Shock '79
Farny Hill '83
The Man Who Haunted Himself '70

Buddy Squires
After Innocence '05
The Boys of 2nd Street Park '03

Chris Squires
On Edge '03
Lola and Billy the Kid '98
True Crime '95
Nam Angels '88

Decha Srimantra
Bangkok Dangerous '08
The Tesseract '03

Terry Stacey
The Nanny Diaries '07
P.S. I Love You '07
Friends with Money '06
In Her Shoes '05
Winter Passing '05
The Door in the Floor '04
American Splendor '03
Just a Kiss '02

Ray Dennis Steckler (1939-)
Rat Pfink a Boo-Boo '66
Wild Ones on Wheels '62
The Thing with Two Heads '72

Eric Steelberg
Quinceanera '06
Juno '07
Numb '07

Jack Steely
10,000 B.C. '08

Robert M. Stevens
Kickin' It Old Skool '07
Cecil B. Demented '00
The Day After Tomorrow '04
Stealing Harvard '02
Black Knight '01
Just Visiting '01
Rock Star '01
Austin Powers 2: The Spy Who Shagged Me '99
Bowfinger '99
Godzilla '98

Jack Stevens
Laurel & Hardy: Chickens Come Home '31
Laurel & Hardy: Another Fine Mess '30
Beau Hunks '30
Laurel & Hardy: Blotto '30
Laurel & Hardy: Brats '30
Laurel & Hardy: Night Owls '30
Laurel & Hardy: Men O'War '29
Laurel & Hardy: Below Zero '30
Laurel & Hardy: The Hoose-Gow '29

George Stevens (1904-75)

Tony Spratling
Edge of Sanity '89

John Spooner
Merlin's Apprentice '06
White Coats '04

Robert Steadman
The House Next Door '01
Dancing in Twilight '05
Blood Crime '02
At Any Cost '00
A Face to Kill For '99
The Man Who Captured Eichmann '96
Return to the Blue Lagoon '91
Above the Law '88
Acapulco Gold '78
Executive Action '73

Pieter Stathis
Insecticidal '05

Michael Spiller (1961-)
No Such Thing '01
Drop Dead Gorgeous '99
Henry Fool '98
The House of Yes '97
Niagara, Niagara '97
Flirt '95
Walking and Talking '96
Amateur '94
Search and Destroy '94
Hand Gun '93
Simple Men '92
Age Isn't Everything '91
Surviving Desire '91
Trust '91
The Unbelievable Truth '90

Dante Spinotti (1943-)
Deception '06
The Contract '07
Slipstream '07
X-Men: The Last Stand '06
After the Sunset '04
Pinocchio '02
Red Dragon '02
Bandits '01
Family Man '00
Wonder Boys '00
Goodbye, Lover '99
The Insider '99
The Other Sister '98
L.A. Confidential '97
The Mirror Has Two Faces '96
Heat '95
Kansas City '95
The Quick and the Dead '95
The Star Maker '95
Blink '93
The Last of the Mohicans '92
The Comfort of Strangers '91
Frankie and Johnny '91
Hudson Hawk '91
Far Game '89
Beaches '88
Crimes of the Heart '86
Manhunter '86
Basileus Quartet '82

John Spooner
Absolute Beginners '86
My Beautiful Laundrette '85
Everybody's Famous! '00
Balzac: A Life of Passion '99
The Count of Monte Cristo '99
Hombres Complicados '97
Antonia's Line '95
Romance & Cigarettes '05
Bobby Jones: Stroke of Genius '04
The Exorcism of Emily Rose '05
Letters from Iwo Jima '06

Frank Stanley
10 '79
Car Wash '76
The Eiger Sanction '75
Thunderbolt & Lightfoot '74
Magnum Force '73

Ron Stannett
Dr. Dolittle 4: Tail to the Chief '08
Wedding Wars '06
Brother's Keeper '02
In a Class of His Own '99
The Sweetest Gift '98
C.H.U.D. '84

Oliver Stapleton (1948-)
The Water Horse: Legend of the Deep '07
Casanova '05
An Unfinished Life '05
Nic Kelly '03
Buffalo Soldiers '01
Pay It Forward '00
The Shipping News '01
The Cider House Rules '99
William Shakespeare's A Midsummer Night's Dream '99
The Hi-Lo Country '98
The Object of My Affection '98
The Designated Mourner '97
One Fine Day '96

Matt Steinauer
Slayer '06
Voodoo Moon '05

Raymond N. Stella
The Hoax '06
The Thirst '06
House of the Dead 2: Dead Aim '05
Honey, We Shrunk Ourselves '97

Peter Stein
The Con '98
The Hot Spot '90
Necessary Roughness '91
Pet Sematary '89
Graveyard Shift '90

Gerard Stern
Paris, je t'aime '06
Wasabi '01

John Stephens
Sorcerer '77
Boxcar Bertha '72
Billy Jack '71

Mack Stengler (1895-1962)
Hopalong Cassidy: Dangerous Venture '48
The Ape Man '43
Clancy Street Boys '43
Spotlight Scandals '43
Bowery at Midnight '42
King of the Zombies '41
Sky Bandits '40
Yukon Flight '40

Ken Stipe
Motives '03
Epoch '00

Rogier Stoffers (1961-)
Disturbia '07
The Bad News Bears '05
School of Rock '03
Quills '00

Witold Stok (1946-)
Century '04
Close My Eyes '91
Two Deaths '94
The Match '99
Among Giants '98

Dan Stoloff
Wedding Daze '06
Miracle '04
Tumbleweeds '98
Gargantua '98

John Stokes (1961-)
Journey to the Center of the Earth '99
Silent Predators '99

Tom Stern (1946-)
Rails & Ties '07
Flags of Our Fathers '06
The Last Kiss '06
Million Dollar Baby '04
Mystic River '03
Blood Work '02

Alan Stensvold (1908-81)
The Invisible Strangler '76
Cotter '72
Private Navy of Sgt. O'Farrell '68
Eight on the Lam '67
Thunder Road '58
Character '97

Clifford Stine (1906-86)
The 'Burbs '89
That Funny Feeling '65
The Brass Bottle '63
Abbott and Costello Go to Mars '53
It Came from Outer Space '53
The Mighty Quinn '89
Blitz '85

Harold E. Stine (1903-77)
Crazy Horse and Custer... "The Untold Story" '90
The Poseidon Adventure '72
M*A*S*H '70

Rod Stewart
Time Code '00

Patrick Alexander Stewart
Hotel '01

Jacques Steyn (1954-)
Warhead '96
Live Wire: Human Timebomb '95
Terminal Impact '95

Vittorio Storaro (1940-)
Dominion: Prequel to the Exorcist: The Beginning '04
Exorcist '05
Goya in Bordeaux '99
Picking Up the Pieces '99
Bulworth '98
Tango '98
Little Buddha '93
Dick Tracy '90
The Sheltering Sky '90
Ishtar '87
The Last Emperor '87
Peter the Great '86
Ladyhawke '85
Reds '81
1900 '76
Apocalypse Now '79
Last Tango in Paris '73
The Conformist '71

The Bird with the Crystal Plumage '70

Michael Storey
Walter and Henry '01
No Alibi '00
One Kill '00
Locked in Silence '99
Blacklight '98
Elvis Meets Nixon '98
Summer of the Monkeys '98
In His Father's Shoes '97

Archie Stout (1886-1965)
The High and the Mighty '54
Hondo '53
Island in the Sky '53
The Sun Shines Bright '53
Big Jim McLain '52
The Quiet Man '52
Fort Apache '48
Angel and the Badman '47
Abilene Town '46
Captain Kidd '45
Dark Waters '44
It Happened Tomorrow '44
Beau Geste '39
The Hurricane '37
Hopalong Cassidy Returns '36
Three on the Trail '36
Desert Trail '35
Hopalong Cassidy '35
Paradise Canyon '35
Lucky Texan '34
Man from Utah '34
The Star Packer '34
Trail Beyond '34
Badmen of Nevada '33
Riders of Destiny '33
Sagebrush Trail '33
West of the Divide '33
Law of the Sea '32
Police Court '32
Riders of the Desert '32
Two Fisted Justice '31
The Return of Dr. Fu Manchu '30
The Sea God '30
The Ten Commandments '23

Harry Stradling, Sr. (1902-70)
On a Clear Day You Can See Forever '70
Hello, Dolly! '69
Funny Girl '68
Moment to Moment '66
How to Murder Your Wife '64
My Fair Lady '64
Gypsy '62
Parrish '61
A Summer Place '59
The Young Philadelphians '59
Auntie Mame '58
Marjorie Morningstar '58
A Face in the Crowd '57
The Pajama Game '57
The Eddy Duchin Story '56
Helen of Troy '56
Guys and Dolls '55
Johnny Guitar '53
Androcles and the Lion '52
Angel Face '52
Hans Christian Andersen '52
I Want You '51
A Streetcar Named Desire '51
Tension '50
The Barkleys of Broadway '49
In the Good Old Summertime '49
Easter Parade '48
The Pirate '48
Song of Love '47
Holiday in Mexico '46
Till the Clouds Roll By '46
Picture of Dorian Gray '45
Bathing Beauty '44
The Human Comedy '43
The Corsican Brothers '42
The Devil & Miss Jones '41
Suspicion '41
The Lion Has Wings '40
My Son, My Son '40
They Knew What They Wanted '40
Clouds over Europe '39
Jamaica Inn '39
The Citadel '38
The Divorce of Lady X '38
Pygmalion '38
Knight Without Armour '37
South Riding '37
Carnival in Flanders '35

Harry Stradling, Jr. (1925-)
Caddyshack 2 '88
Blind Date '87
A Fine Mess '86
Micki & Maude '84
Buddy Buddy '81
The Pursuit of D.B. Cooper '81
S.O.B. '81
Carny '80
Prophecy '79
Born Again '78
Convoy '78
Go Tell the Spartans '78
Damnation Alley '77
The Greatest '77
The Big Bus '76
Midway '76
Special Delivery '76
Bite the Bullet '75
Mitchell '75
Rooster Cogburn '75
Bank Shot '74
McQ '74
Man Who Loved Cat Dancing '73
The Way We Were '73
1776 '72
Support Your Local Gunfighter '71
Little Big Man '70
There Was a Crooked Man '70
The Good Guys and the Bad Guys '69
Support Your Local Sheriff '69
With Six You Get Eggroll '68

Walter Stradling (1875-1918)
Amarilly of Clothesline Alley '18
Stella Maris '18

Ivan Strasburg
A Raisin in the Sun '08
Fatal Contact: Bird Flu in America '06
The Hades Factor '06
Shooting Dogs '05
Live from Baghdad '03
The Mayor of Casterbridge '03
Bloody Sunday '01
The Corner '00
Britannic '99
The Murder of Stephen Lawrence '99
New World Disorder '99
Deacon Brodie '97
The Theory of Flight '98
Moll Flanders '96
The Affair '95
Sharpe's Eagle '93
Sharpe's Rifles '93
Rita, Sue & Bob Too '87

Christopher W. Strattan
Code of Honor '82
Kill Squad '81

Walter Strenge (1898-1974)
Mr. Walkie Talkie '52
Rodeo King and the Senorita '51
Before Morning '33

Karl Struss (1891-1981)
The Rebel Set '59
The Fly '58
Kronos '57
Mohawk '56
Limelight '52
Mesa of Lost Women '52
Rocketship X-M '50
Mr. Ace '46
Journey into Fear '42
The Great Dictator '40
Rhythm Romance '39
Thanks for the Memory '38
Double or Nothing '37
Waikiki Wedding '37
Go West, Young Man '36
Rhythm on the Range '36
Goin' to Town '35
Belle of the Nineties '34
Dr. Jekyll and Mr. Hyde '32
Island of Lost Souls '32
Abraham Lincoln '30
Be Yourself '30
Coquette '29
The Taming of the Shrew '29
Battle of the Sexes '28
Sunrise '27
Sparrows '26
Affairs of Anatol '21
Dr. Jekyll and Mr. Hyde '20

Charles Stumar (1891-1935)
The Mummy '32
Werewolf of London '35
The Raven '35
Uncle Tom's Cabin '27

John Stumar (1892-1962)
Return of the Vampire '43
The Claw '27
Head Winds '25

David G. Stump
What Love Is '07
Killer Pad '06
Daddy's Boys '87

Jens Sturup
How to Go Out on a Date in Queens '06
Two Days '03
Stuart Bliss '98
Fun '94
Witchcraft 2: The Temptress '90
Witchcraft '88

Ramon Suarez
The Silence of Neto '94
Private Passions '85
Red Kiss '85
L'Amour en Herbe '77
Memories of Underdevelopment '68
Death of a Bureaucrat '66

Kohei Sugiyama (1899-1960)
Gate of Hell '54
47 Ronin, Part 1 '42
47 Ronin, Part 2 '42

Tim Suhrstedt
The Brothers Solomon '07
Idiocracy '06
The Last Time '06
Little Miss Sunshine '06
Relative Strangers '06
Clockstoppers '02
Frank McKlusky, C.I. '02
The Hot Chick '02
Pumpkin '02
Summer Catch '01
Whatever It Takes '00
Major League 3: Back to the Minors '98
Office Space '98
The Wedding Singer '97
To Gillian on Her 37th Birthday '96
Getting Even with Dad '94
The Favor '92
Traces of Red '92
Don't Tell Mom the Babysitter's Dead '91
Men at Work '90
Rainbow Drive '90
Bill & Ted's Excellent Adventure '89
Capone '89
The Chinatown Murders: Man against the Mob '89
Mystic Pizza '88
Mannequin '87
Critters '86
Ratings Game '84
The House on Sorority Row '83
Suburbia '83
Android '82
Forbidden World '82

Bob Sullivan
Outfoxed: Rupert Murdoch's War on Journalism '04
Uncovered: The War on Iraq '04

Brian Sullivan
Little Secrets '02
Route 9 '98
Coyote Summer '96
Just Like Dad '96
Wish upon a Star '96

Igor Sunara (1955-)
Somewhere in the City '97
The Keeper '96
Tales of Erotica '93
For Love or Money '88

Bruce Surtees (1944-)
Joshua '02
American Tragedy '00
Dash and Lilly '99
Just a Little Harmless Sex '99
The Lady in Question '99
Murder in a Small Town '99
That Championship Season '99
The Substitute '96
Corrina, Corrina '94
The Stars Fell on Henrietta '94
The Crush '93
Run '91
The Super '91
Men Don't Leave '89
License to Drive '88
Back to the Beach '87
Out of Bounds '86
Psycho 3 '86
Ratboy '86
Pale Rider '85
Beverly Hills Cop '84
Tightrope '84
Risky Business '83
Sudden Impact '83
Firefox '82
Honkytonk Man '82
Escape from Alcatraz '79
Three Warriors '77
The Outlaw Josey Wales '76
The Shootist '76
Night Moves '75
Lenny '74
Blume in Love '73
High Plains Drifter '73
Conquest of the Planet of the Apes '72
The Great Northfield Minnesota Raid '72
Joe Kidd '72
Dirty Harry '71
Play Misty for Me '71
The Beguiled '70

Robert L. Surtees (1906-85)
Thin Air '00
Bloodbrothers '78
Same Time, Next Year '78
The Turning Point '77
A Star Is Born '76
The Great Waldo Pepper '75
The Hindenburg '75
Oklahoma Crude '73
The Sting '73
The Cowboys '72
The Other '72
The Last Picture Show '71
Summer of 42 '71
The Arrangement '69
Sweet Charity '69
Doctor Dolittle '67
The Graduate '67
The Lost Command '66
The Collector '65
The Hallelujah Trail '65
Mutiny on the Bounty '62
Ben-Hur '59
Les Girls '57
Raintree County '57
The Swan '56
Oklahoma! '55
The Long, Long Trailer '54
Valley of the Kings '54
Escape from Fort Bravo '53
Mogambo '53
The Bad and the Beautiful '52
The Merry Widow '52
Quo Vadis '51
King Solomon's Mines '50
Intruder in the Dust '49
That Midnight Kiss '49
Act of Violence '48
A Date with Judy '48
The Kissing Bandit '48
Our Vines Have Tender Grapes '45
Thirty Seconds Over Tokyo '44
Two Girls and a Sailor '44

Peter Suschitzky (1941-)
Eastern Promises '07
A History of Violence '05
Shopgirl '05
Spider '02
eXistenZ '99
The Man in the Iron Mask '98
Mars Attacks! '96
Crash '95
Immortal Beloved '94
Naked Lunch '91
Where the Heart Is '90
Dead Ringers '88
Falling in Love '84
Krull '83
The Empire Strikes Back '80
Valentino '77
Lisztomania '75
The Rocky Horror Picture Show '75
All Creatures Great and Small '74
That'll Be the Day '73
The Vengeance of She '68

Wolfgang Suschitzky (1912-)
Theatre of Blood '73
Get Carter '71
Entertaining Mr. Sloane '70
Ring of Bright Water '69
Ulysses '67

Misha (Mikhail) Suslov
Suspended Animation '02
Prancer '89
Black Moon Rising '86
Nobody's Fool '86
Smokey & the Judge '80

Maida Sussman
Stricken '98
Ivory Tower '97

Darko Suvak
True Blue '01
The Landlady '98
Stir '98

Rob Sweeney
Canvas '06
Harry and Max '04
Blue Car '03
The Street King '02
The Sleepy Time Gal '01
Big Eden '00
I'm Losing You '98
Color of a Brisk and Leaping Day '95

Adam Swica
Diary of the Dead '07
Weirdsville '07
Bruiser '00

Attila Szalay (1961-)
Dodson's Journey '01
The Void '01

Hubert Taczanowski (1960-)
National Lampoon's Van Wilder 2: The Rise of Taj '06
Deathwatch '02
Tadpole '02
How to Kill Your Neighbor's Dog '01
Turn It Up '00
Buddy Boy '99
Chicago Cab '98
Eden '98
The Maker '98
The Opposite of Sex '98
The Young Poisoner's Handbook '94

Carlo Tafani
Lucky Luke '94
Troublemakers '94

Renato Tafuri
The Church '98
Dial Help '88
Berlinguer I Love You '77

Wong Ngok Tai
Once Upon a Time in China II '92
Operation Condor '91

Ken Talbot (1920-93)
Doomwatch '72
Hands of the Ripper '71
Girl Hunters '63
The Stranger from Venus '54
Old Mother Riley, Headmistress '50

Fred Tammes (1937-)
Face '97
Mad Love '95
Priest '94
Catherine Cookson's The Man Who Cried '93
The Whistle Blower '87

Masaki Tamura (1939-)
Tampopo '86
Himatsuri '85

Ciaran Tanham
Northanger Abbey '07
Bloom '03
Bobbie's Girl '00
Borstal Boy '00

Philip Tannura (1897-1973)
The Flying Saucer '50
Hi-Jacked '50
Strange Illusion '45
Footlight Glamour '43

Jean-Jacques Tarbes
My New Partner '84
Le Gitan '75
Queen of Diamonds '70
Borsalino '70
La Piscine '69
Honor Among Thieves '68

John Tarver
Earthstorm '06
Serial Killing 101 '04
Shallow Ground '04
Seventeen Again '00
The Art of Murder '99
The First 9 1/2 Weeks '98
Stonebrook '98

David Tattersall (1960-)
Speed Racer '08
The Hunting Party '07
Next '07
The Matador '06
Zoom '06
Star Wars: Episode 3—Revenge of the Sith '05
XXX: State of the Union '05
Lara Croft Tomb Raider: The Cradle of Life '03
Die Another Day '02
Star Wars: Episode 2—Attack of the Clones '02
The Majestic '01
Vertical Limit '00
The Green Mile '99
Star Wars: Episode 1—The Phantom Menace '99
Soldier '98
Con Air '97
Mr. Toad's Wild Ride '96
Moll Flanders '96
Theodore Rex '95
Radioland Murders '94

Gale Tattersall (1948-)
Ghost Ship '02
13 Ghosts '01
The Jack Bull '99
Pushing Tin '99
Virtuosity '95
Hideaway '95
Tank Girl '94
The Commitments '91
Wild Orchid '90

Aria '88

Alfred Taylor
Killer Klowns from Outer Space '88
Fatal Games '84
Mutant '83
The Swinging Cheerleaders '74
Spider Baby '64

Christopher Taylor
Nobody's Baby '01
Death Benefit '96
Glory Daze '96
Live Nude Girls '95
Inside Monkey Zetterland '93

Gilbert Taylor (1914-)
The Bedroom Window '87
Losin' t '82
Flash Gordon '80
Dracula '79
Star Wars '77
The Omen '76
Frenzy '72
Macbeth '71
Quackser Fortune Has a Cousin in the Bronx '70
Repulsion '65
Dr. Strangelove, or: How I Learned to Stop Worrying and Love the Bomb '64
A Hard Day's Night '64
Seven Days to Noor '50

J.O. Taylor (1887-1974)
King Kong '33
The See Lion 21

Ronnie Taylor (1924-)
Sleepless '01
The Phantom of the Opera '98
Popcorn '89
Sea of Love '89
Opera '88
Cry Freedom '87
The Hound of the Baskervilles '83
Tommy '75

Manuel Teran
Mercy '00
Petts Freres '00
Red Shoe Diaries: Four on the Floor '96
Before the Rain '94

Ubaldo Terzano
Black Sabbath '64
Blood and Black Lace '64
The Whip and the Body '63
Black Sunday '60

Ted Tetzlaff (1903-95)
Notorious '46
I Married a Witch '42
The Road to Zanzibar '41
Remember the Night '40
Easy Living '37
My Man Godfrey '36
The Princess Comes Across '36
Hands Across the Table '35
His Greatest Gamble '34

Ellis Thackerey
See Bud Thackerey

Bud Thackery (1903-90)
Jaguar '56
Phantom Stallion '54
Trader Tom of the China Seas '54
Iron Mountain Trail '53
Shadows o' Tombstone '53
Outcasts of the Trail 49
Son of Zorro '47
Alias Billy the Kid '46
King of the 'orest Rangers '46
The Phantom Rider '46
Santa Fe Uprising '46
Federal Operator 99 '45
Manhunt of Mystery Island '45
The Purple Monster Strikes '45

Gary Thieltges
Sticky Fingers '88
Eating Raoul '82
Thief '81

Armand Thirard (1899-1973)
Love on a Pillow '62
Sois Belle et Tais-Toi '58
And God Created Woman '57
The Night Heaven Fell '57
Diabolique '55
Wages of Fear '55
Beauties of the Night '52
Utopia '51

John Thomas
Sex and the City: The Movie '08
The Hunley '99
Hi-Life '98
The Last Days of Disco '98
Dead Man on Campus '97
Kicked in the Head '97
Still Breathing '97
Freeway '95
Norma Jean and Marilyn '95
Paookaville 95
Barcelona '94
Metropolitan '90

Jamie Thompson (1962-)
Eternal '04
Tracked '04
Cyborg 2 '93
Freaked '98
Desire and Hell at Sunset Motel '92
Circuitry Man '90

Stuart Thompson
At War with the Army '50
Variety Girl '47

William C. Thompson (1889-1963)
The Sinister Urge '60
Night of the Ghouls '59
The Astounding She-Monster '58
Plan 9 from Outer Space '56
The Violent Years '56
Bride of the Monster '55
Daughter of Horror '55
Jail Bait '54
Glen or Glenda? '53
Project Moon Base '53
Pin Down Girls '51
Demon for Trouble '34
Maniac '34

Alex Thomson (1929-2007)
Love's Labour's Lost '00
A Shot at Glory '00
Executive Decision '96
Hamlet '96
Black Beauty '94
Cliffhanger '93
Demolition Man '93
Alien 3 '92
The Krays '90
Leviathan '89
Date with an Angel '87
The Sicilian '87
Labyrinth '86
Raw Deal '86
The Keep '83
Excalibur '81
The Cat and the Canary '79
Doctor Phibes Rises Again '72

Donald E. Thorin (1934-)
Head of State '03
Dudley Do-Right '99
Mickey Blue Eyes '99
The First Wives Club '96
Nothing to Lose '96
Ace Ventura: When Nature Calls '95
Boys on the Side '94
Scent of a Woman '92
Lock Up '89
Tango and Cash '89
Midnight Run '88
The Golden Child '86
Against All Odds '84
Purple Rain '84
Bed Boys '83
An Officer and a Gentleman '82

Volker Tittel
CryWolf '05
12 and Holding '05
L.I.E. '01

Eduard Tisse (1897-1961)
Ivan the Terrible, Part 2 '46
Ivan the Terrible, Part 1 '44
Alexander Nevsky '38
Que Viva Mexico '32
Ten Days That Shook the World '27
The Battleship Potemkin '25
Strike '24

Romeo Tirone
The Front Line '06
Cowboys & Angels '04
Halfmoon '95

Arthur L. Todd (1895-1942)
Sing Me a Love Song '37
Alibi Ike '35
Monkey Business '31

Gregg Toland (1904-48)
A Song is Born 48
The Bishop's Wife '47
The Best Years of Our Lives '46
Kid from Brooklyn '46
The Outlaw 43
Ball of Fire '41
Citizen Kane '41
The Little Foxes '41
The Grapes of Wrath '40
The Long Voyage Home '40
Intermezzo '39
They Shall Have Music '39
Wuthering Heights '39
The Cowboy and the Lady '38
The Goldwyn Follies '38
Dead End '37
History is Made at Night '37
Beloved Enemy '36
Come and Get It '36
Strike Me Pink '36
These Three '36
The Dark Angel '35
Les Miserables '35
Mad Love '35
Splendor '35
Roman Scandals '33
Kid from Spain '32

Roland H. Totheroh (1890-1967)
Monsieur Verdoux '47
The Great Dictator 40
Modern Times '36
City Lights '31
The Gold Rush '25
The Circus '28
The Kid '21
A Woman of Paris '23

Mario Tosi
Red, White & Busted '75
Frogs '72
Carrie '76
MacArthur '77
The Betsy '78
The Stunt Man '80

Carlos Toriaschi
Brain Drain '98

Bruce Torbet
Brain Damage '88
Basket Case '82

John Toon
The Jane Austen Book Club '07
Glory Road '06
Sylvia '03
Rain '01
Broken English '96

Emil Topuzov
Megasrake '07
Mosquitoman '05

Luciano Tovoli
Murder by Numbers '02
The Closet '01
Titus '99
Desperate Measures '98
The Dinner Game '98
Before and After '95
Single White Female '92
Reversal of Fortune '90
Unsane '82
Suspiria '77
Bread and Chocolate '73
Bandits of Orgosolo '61

Clive Tickner
Appetite '98
The Magical Legend of the Leprechauns '99
Loch Ness '95
Split Second '92
Hidden Agenda '90

Frank Tidy
The Boys Next Door '96
Chain Reaction '96
Getting Away With Murder '96
Peace '94
Under Siege '92
The Butcher's Wife '91
Slipstream '89
Hot Pursuit '87
One Magic Christmas '85
The Grey Fox '83
Spacehunter: Adventures in the Forbidden Zone '83
Bad '94
Black Fox: The Price of Peace '94
Black Fox: Blood Horse '94
Black Fox: Good Men and Bad '94

Gary Tieche
Bad Love '95
Dead Weekend '95
Out There '95

Augusto Tiezzi
Conquest of Mycene '63
Hero of Rome '63
Girl Under the Sheet '61

Jiri (George) Tirl (1947-)
Left 3ehind: The Movie '00
Revelation '00
Tribulation '00
The Heist '89
Stee Dawn '87

Peter Thwaites
Janice Beard '99

Erling Thurmann-Andersen (1945-2002)
Insomnia '01

Sokei Tomioka
War of the Wizards '83
Godzilla's Revenge '69

Shinji Tomita
The Adventures of Milo & Otis '89

Aldo Tonti (1910-88)
Milo & Otis '89
Escape from Death Row '73
The Family '70
Cast a Giant Shadow '66
Barabbas '62
The Unfaithfuls '60
Nights of Cabiria '57
War and Peace '56
The Miracle '48
Ossessione '42

John Toll
Tropic Thunder '08
Gone Baby Gone '07
Rise Blood Hunter '07
Elizabethtown '05
The Last Samurai '03
Captain Corelli's Mandolin '01
Vanilla Sky '01
Almost Famous '00
Simpatico '99
The Thin Red Line '98
John Grisham's The Rainmaker '97
Braveheart '95
Legends of the Fall '94
Wind '92

Leo Tover (1902-64)
Strange Bedfellows '65
Island of the Blue Dolphins '64
Sunday in New York '63
Follow That Dream '61
Misty '61
From the Terrace '60
Journey to the Center of the Earth '59
Between Heaven and Hell '56
The Conqueror '56
Love Me Tender '56
When Willie Comes Marching Home '50
The Heiress '49
My Friend Irma '49
The Snake Pit '48
Dead Reckoning '47
China '43
Bahama Passage '42
The Major and the Minor '42
Star Spangled Rhythm '42
Young and Willing '42
Never Say Die '39
Bluebeard's Eighth Wife '38
Love in Bloom '35
College Humor '33
I'm No Angel '33
No Man of Her Own '32
Lost Squadron '32
Bachelor Apartment '31
The Lady Refuses '31
The Royal Bed '31
State's Attorney '31
The Silver Horde '30
Vagabond Lover '29

Jean Tournier (1926-2004)
The Fiendish Plot of Dr. Fu Manchu '80
The Ultimate Weapon '97
Me '70
Moonraker '79
The Day of the Jackal '73
The Holes '72
Start the Revolution without Me '70
The Train '65

Bert Tougas
Changing Lanes '02
Any Given Sunday '99

Salvatore Totino (1964-)
The Da Vinci Code '06
Cinderella Man '05
The Missing '03

Eric Trageser
Already Dead '07

Luciano Tresatti
Season for Assassins '71
And God Said to Cain '69
Diary of a Rebel '68
The Bloody Pit of Horror '65

Sergei Trofimov (1961-)
Day Watch '06
Night Watch '04

Jan Troell (1931-)
Hamsun '96
The New Land '73
The Emigrants '72

Oberdan Troiani
Tower of Screaming Virgins '68
Hercules against the Moon Men '64
Othello 52

William G. Troiano (1914-83)
She-Freak '67
The Wic World of '66
Batwoman '66
The Slime People '63

Brandon Trost

Alan M. Trow
He Was a Quiet Man '07
The Salon '05
Chaos '05
Grim '95

David Trulli (1951-)
Bloody Murder 2 '03
Face the Music '00
Dementia '98

Shinya Tsukamoto (1960-)
Tetsuo 2: Body Hammer '97
Tetsuo: The Iron Man '92

Brian Tufano (1939-)
I Could Never Be Your Woman '06
Once Upon a Time in the Midlands '02
Last Orders '01
Billy Elliot '00
East is East '99
Virtual Sexuality '99
A Life Less Ordinary '97
Element of Doubt '96
Trainspotting '95
Shallow Grave '94
Middlemarch '93
War Party '89
Dreamscape '84
The Lords of Discipline '83
Quadrophenia '79
Heavy Metal '81

Christopher Tufty
The Theory of the Leisure Class '01

David Tumblety
Brooklyn Lobster '05
Sweet Land '05
Hit and Runway '01

Andre Turpin (1966-)
Maelstrom '00
Because Why? '93

Gerry Turpin (1925-97)
Hoffman '70
Oh! What a Lovely War '69
The Last of Sheila '73

Masaharu Ueda
Ran '85
Kagemusha '80

Matthew Uhry
Mission '00
Trailer, the Movie '99
Murders in the Doll House '79

Frantisek Uldrich
The House of Usher '06
The Perfect Husband '92
Adelheid 69

Alejandro Ulloa (1926-)
El Barbaro '84
Vatican Conspiracy '81
Fury '78
Autopsy '74
Bad Man's River '72
Pancho Villa '72
Horror Express '72
The Diabolical Dr. Z '65
Companeros '70

Derick Underschultz
Carolina Moon '07
Santa Baby '06
Knights of the South Bronx '05
The Twelve Days of Christmas Eve '04
Danger Beneath the Sea '02
Power and Beauty '02
RFK '02
Jason X '01
Sins of the Father '01
Mr. Rock 'n' Roll: The Alan Freed Story '99
Thrill Seekers '99

Geoffrey Unsworth (1914-78)
The Great Train Robbery '79
Tess '79
Superman: The Movie '78
A Bridge Too Far '77
A Matter of Time '76
Royal Flash '75
Murder on the Orient Express '74
Return of the Pink Panther '74
Internecine Project '73
Zardoz '72
Cabaret '72
Cromwell '70
The Assassination Bureau '69
The Magic Christian '69
2001: A Space Odyssey '68
Half a Sixpence '67
Oh Dad, Poor Dad (Momma's Hung You in the Closet & I'm Feeling So Sad) '67
Othello '65
Becket '64
The 300 Spartans '62
Flame Over India '60
The World of Suzie Wong '60
A Night to Remember '58
Simba '55
The Sword & the Rose '53
Made in Heaven '52
The Clouded Yellow '51
Trio '50
Blanche Fury '48
Scott of the Antarctic '48
Meet the Navy '46

Sergei Urusevsky (1908-74)
I Am Cuba '64
The Cranes Are Flying '57

Jost Vacano
Hollow Man '00
Starship Troopers '97
Showgirls '95
Untamed Heart '93
Das Boot '81

Joseph Valentine (1900-49)
Joan of Arc '48
Rope '48
The Possessed '47
Heartbeat '46
Magnificent Doll '46
Tomorrow Is Forever '46
Guest Wife '45
Shadow of a Doubt '43
Saboteur '42
In the Navy '41
Nice Girl? '41
The Wolf Man '41
It's a Date '40
My Little Chickadee '40
First Love '39
Mad About Music '38
The Rage of Paris '38
That Certain Age '38
100 Men and a Girl '37
The Moon's Our Home '36
Next Time We Love '36
Three Smart Girls '36
Night of Terror '33
Myrt and Marge '33

Charlie Van Damme
I Want to Go Home '89
Melo '86

One Sings, the Other Doesn't '77

Theo van de Sande (1947-)
Beauty Shop '05
Yours, Mine & Ours '05
Little Black Book '04
Out of Time '03
High Crimes '02
Double Take '01
Little Nicky '00
Big Daddy '99
Tuesdays with Morrie '99
Blade '98
Cruel Intentions '98
Volcano '97
Wayne's World 2 '92
Body Parts '91
Miracle Mile '89

Paul van den Bos
Diary of a Mad Old Man '88

Jules Van Den Steenhoven
A Flight of Rainbirds '81

Eddy van der Enden
The Gambler '97
Crimetime '96
Lie Down with Lions '94
Daughters of Darkness '71
Traffic '71

Charles Van Enger (1890-1980)
Sitting Bull '54
Bela Lugosi Meets a Brooklyn Gorilla '52
Abbott and Costello Meet the Killer, Boris Karloff '49
Abbott and Costello Meet Frankenstein '48
Buck Privates Come Home '47
It Ain't Hay '43
Night Monster '42
Cracked Nuts '41
Man from Montana '41
Never Give a Sucker an Even Break '41
Half a Soldier '40
The Phantom of the Opera '25
The Marriage Circle '24
Seven Years Bad Luck '21
The Last of the Mohicans '20

Sean Van Hales
Love or Money '01
Different for Girls '96

Kees Van Oostrum (1953-)
A Perfect Day '06
Gods and Generals '03
Cupid & Cate '00
A House Divided '00
Drive Me Crazy '99
You Know My Name '99
William Faulkner's Old Man '97
Stephen King's Thinner '96
Degree of Guilt '95
Journey '95
Down Came a Blackbird '94
The Enemy Within '94
Gettysburg '93
Scott Turow's The Burden of Proof '92
Long Road Home '91

James Van Trees (1890-1973)
Angel on My Shoulder '46
A Night in Casablanca '46
Baby Face '33

Walther Vanden Ende (1947-)
Joyeux Noel '05
No Man's Land '01
A Dog of Flanders '99
Left Luggage '98
The Eighth Day '95
Farinelli '94
Toto le Heros '91

Gerard Vandenburg (1932-99)
Heimat 2 '92
Spring Symphony '86
The Vampire Happening '71

Checco Varese
Prom Night '08
Under the Same Moon '07
The Aura '05
A Separate Peace '04
Fidel '02
Night at the Golden Eagle '02

Henry Vargas
Tollbooth '94
Unlawful Passage '94

Mark Vargo
The Day the World Ended '01
Play It to the Bone '99

Carlo Varini
The Chorus '04
L'Eleve '95
The Big Blue '88
Subway '85
Le Dernier Combat '84

Alex Vendler
These Girls '05
Melvin Goes to Dinner '03
The Bible and Gun Club '96

Gordon Verheul
Impulse '08
Heaven's Fire '99

Rene Verzier
Eddie and the Cruisers 2: Eddie Lives! '89
Of Unknown Origin '83
Death Ship '80
Rabid '77
The Little Girl Who Lives down the Lane '76
By the Blood of Others '73

Jean-Louis Vialard
Inside Paris '06
Tropical Malady '04
The Sea '02

Mark Vicente
Slow Burn '00
Dish Dogs '98
Uncorked '98
Midnight Blue '96

Robin Vidgeon (1939-)
Mr. Corbett's Ghost '90
Nightbreed '90
The Fly 2 '89
Parents '89
Hellbound: Hellraiser 2 '88
Mr. North '88
Hellraiser '87

Ronald Vidor
Crossfire '98

Sacha Vierny (1919-2001)
Catherine Cookson's Tilly Trotter '99
Catherine Cookson's The Round Tower '98
August '95
The NeverEnding Story 3: Escape from Fantasia '94
Lady Chatterley '92
The Belly of an Architect '91
Prospero's Books '91
The Cook, the Thief, His Wife & Her Lover '90
A Zed & Two Noughts '88
Drowning by Numbers '87
Love Unto Death '84
The Draughtsman's Contract '82
Beau Pere '81
Mon Oncle d'Amerique '80
Stavisky '74
Belle de Jour '67
La Guerre Est Finie '66
Muriel '63
Last Year at Marienbad '61
Hiroshima, Mon Amour '59

Franco Villa
Hired to Kill '73
Hit Men '73
Shoot the Living, Pray for the Dead '70

Reynaldo Villalobos (1940-)
Bordertown '06
Juwanna Mann '02
Not Another Teen Movie '01
Love and Basketball '00
Return to Paradise '98
An Alan Smithee Film: Burn, Hollywood, Burn '97
Hollywood Confidential '97
Loved '97
Romy and Michele's High School Reunion '96
Telling Lies in America '96
Roosters '95
A Bronx Tale '93
American Me '92
Sinatra '92
Major League '89
Punchline '88
Desert Bloom '86
Blame It on Rio '84
Ballad of Gregorio Cortez '83
Risky Business '83
Prime Suspect '82
9 to 5 '80
Urban Cowboy '80

Leopoldo Villasenor (1941-)
Hostages '80
The Werewolf vs. the Vampire Woman '70

Joseph Vilsmaier (1939-)
The Harmonists '99
Brother of Sleep '95
Stalingrad '94

Amy Vincent (1959-)
The Mystic Masseur '01
The Camomile Lawn '92
Business as Usual '88

John Visconti
Junction 88 '47
Mistaken Identity '41

Paul Vogel (1899-1975)
Return of the Magnificent Seven '66
The Rounders '65
Village of the Giants '65
The Wonderful World of the Brothers Grimm '62
The Time Machine '60
Wings of Eagles '57
High Society '56
Interrupted Melody '55
The Tender Trap '55
Rose Marie '54
The Student Prince '54
Clown '53
Angels in the Outfield '51
Go for Broke! '51
The Black Hand '50
Battleground '49
Lady in the Lake '46
Wide Open Faces '38
Fit for a King '37

Ted Voightlander (1913-88)
Agatha Christie's A Caribbean Mystery '83
Agatha Christie's Sparkling Cyanide '83
Night of the Lepus '72

Peter von Haller (1961-)
Anatomy '00

Wedigo von Schultzendorff
All the Queen's Men '02
Hollywood Ending '02
Igby Goes Down '02
The Hollywood Sign '01
The Thirteenth Floor '99
No Strings Attached '98

Nicholas Josef von Sternberg (1951-)
Killing Moon '00
Jungle Boy '96
American Cop '94
Body Shot '93
Out of Sight, Out of Her Mind '89
Final Justice '84
Tourist Trap '79
Kill Alex Kill '76
Dolemite '75

Mario Vulpiani
Castle Freak '95
The Bloodstained Shadow '78
Watch Me When I Kill '77
The Grand Duel '73
La Grande Bouffe '73

Steven Wacks
Diplomatic Siege '99
Convict 762 '98

Thaddeus Wadleigh (1964-)
Who Killed the Electric Car? '06
Loco Love '03
Terror at Tenkiller '86

William Wages
Supercross: The Movie '05
Fallen Angel '03
SuperFire '02
Down in the Delta '98
Buffalo Soldiers '97
Riders of the Purple Sage '96
Children of Fury '94
Love Potion #9 '92
A Thousand Heroes '92

Fritz Arno Wagner (1894-1958)
Kameradschaft '31
M '31
The Threepenny Opera '31
Diary of a Lost Girl '29
Warning Shadows '23
Nosferatu '22
Destiny '21

Roy Wagner
Bachelor Party 2: The Last Temptation '08
A Thief of Time '04
Coyote Waits '03
A Rumor of Angels '00
In the Company of Spies '99
The Pest '96
Nick of Time '95
Drop Zone '94
Another Stakeout '93
Mortuary Academy '91
Disaster at Silo 7 '88
A Nightmare on Elm Street 3: Dream Warriors '87
Return to Horror High '87
Witchboard '87

Sidney Wagner (1901-47)
The Postman Always Rings Twice '46
Bataan '43
Whistling in the Dark '41

Keith Wagstaff
The Gold & Glory '88
The Man from Snowy River '82

Ric Waite (1933-)
The Triangle '01
Ratz '00
Truth or Consequences, N.M. '97
Last Stand at Saber River '96
Andersonville '95
On Deadly Ground '94
Out for Justice '91
Marked for Death '90
The Great Outdoors '88
Adventures in Babysitting '87
Red Dawn '84
Class '83
Tex '82
The Long Riders '80

Kent Wakeford
Last Lives '98
Loser '97
Power 98 '96
Wedding Bell Blues '96
Some Folks Call It a Sling Blade '94
The Ghost Brigade '93
Hold Me, Thrill Me, Kiss Me '93
China O'Brien '88
Alice Doesn't Live Here Anymore '74
Mean Streets '73

Ralph Waldo
Cain's Cutthroats '71
Wild Wheels '69

Brad Walker
The Deadbeat Club '04
American Nightmare '00

John Walker
A Winter Tan '88
The Body in the Library '84

Joseph Walker (1892-1985)
The Marrying Kind '52
Born Yesterday '50
Harriet Craig '50
It's a Wonderful Life '46
Mr. Winkle Goes to War '44
Tales of Manhattan '42
They All Kissed the Bride '42
Penny Serenade '41
His Girl Friday '40
Only Angels Have Wings '39
Joy of Living '38
Lost Horizon '37
Mr. Deeds Goes to Town '36
Theodora Goes Wild '36
It Happened One Night '34
Lady for a Day '33
American Madness '32
The Miracle Woman '31
The Fighting Stallion '26

Mandy Walker (1963-)
Shattered Glass '03
Lantana '01
The Well '97
Love Serenade '96

Enrique Wallace
Doctor of Doom '62
The Robot vs. the Aztec Mummy '59

Chris Walling
Sol Goode '01
Blue Ridge Fall '99
Thick as Thieves '99
Wicked Ways '99
Crosswords '96
Solo '96

David M. Walsh
Carpool '96
Taking Care of Business '90
Fatal Beauty '87
Outrageous Fortune '87
Summer School '87
My Science Project '85
Romantic Comedy '83
Private Benjamin '80
Seems Like Old Times '80
California Suite '78
Foul Play '78
Rollercoaster '77
Murder by Death '76
My Father's House '75
Cleopatra Jones '73
Sleeper '73
Evel Knievel '72
Everything You Always Wanted to Know about Sex (But Were Afraid to Ask) '72
I Walk the Line '70

John Ward
Love, Honour & Obey '00
Final Cut '98

Mark Wareham
Introducing the Dwights '07
Murder in Greenwich '02
Dr. Jekyll & Mr. Hyde '99

First Daughter '99

John F. Warren (1905-2001)
Tom Curtain '66
The Cosmic Man '59
The Daughter of Dr. Jekyll '57
Zero Hour! '57

Gilbert Warrenton (1894-1980)
Operation Bikini '63
Panic in the Year Zero! '62
Atomic Submarine '59
Sunset Range '35
Here Comes Cookie '35
Mesa of Lost Women '52
Sins of Jezebel '54
The Love Trap '29
The Plastic Age '25

Norman Warwick (1920-94)
The Creeping Flesh '72
The Final Programme '73
Tre Abominable Dr. Phibes '71
Dr. Jekyll and Sister Hyde '71

John Waters (1946-)
Female Trouble '74
Pink Flamingos '72
Multiple Maniacs '70
Mondo Trasho '69

Bogus '95

Philip Alan Waters
Jane Eyre '96
Urban Menace '99

David Watkin (1925-2008)
Cyborg '99
Night Falls on Manhattan '96
'84
Yentl '83
Chariots of Fire '81
The Object of Beauty '91
Hamlet '90
Memphis Belle '90
The Good Mother '88
Last Rites '88
Masquerade '88
Moonstruck '87
Joseph Andrews '77
Robin and Marian '76
To the Devil, a Daughter '76
The Three Musketeers '75
The Four Musketeers '75
Mahogany '75
The Boy Friend '71
The Devils '71
Catch-22 '70
The Charge of the Light Brigade '68
How I Won the War '67
Mademoiselle '66
Help! '65
The Knack '65
White Nights '85

Michael Watkins
Heart and Souls '93
Point of No Return '93

Harry Waxman (1912-84)
Find the Lady '76
The Pink Panther Strikes Again '76
The Wicker Man '73
Vampires '74
Not Tonight Darling '72
What the Peeper Saw '72
Endless Night '7'
Wonderwall: The Movie '69
The Day the Earth Caught Fire '61

The Swiss Family Robinson '60
The Gift Horse '52

Henry Waxman (1939)
The Anniversary '68

Jesse Weathington
Tracks '05
Interlocked '98
Mom, Can I Keep Her? '98

George Webber
The Muppets' Wizard of Oz '05

Samuel Weil
See Lloyd Kaufman

Yossi Wein
Sepia Cinderella '47
Murder on Lenox Avenue '41

Ben Weinstein
Conspiracy '97
Wet Hot American Summer '01

James Welland (1961-)
The Hound of the Baskervilles '02
The Last Minute '01

Harold E. Wellman (1905-92)
Muscle Beach Party '64
Atlantis, the Lost Continent '61
The Invisible Boy '57

Philippe Welt
...e Bonheur Est Dans le Pre '95

Harold Wenstrom
Madame Butterfly '95
The Lost Patrol '34
The Saphead '21

Egon Werdin (1954-)
An American Werewolf in Paris '97
Mute Witness '95

Byron Werner
Death Valley: The Revenge of Bloody Bill '04
Starkweather '04
Sam & Janet '02

Brian West (1928-)
Ellen Foster '97
Treacherous Crossing '92
84 Charing Cross Road '86
Agatha Christie's Murder with Mirrors '85
B coctbath at the House of Death '85
The Lonely Lady '83
Billy Two Hats '74

Frederick E. West (1903-84)
Terror in the Haunted House '58
Invasion of the Saucer Men '57

Ken Westbury
Jack Higgins' Midnight Man '96
Jack Higgins' On Dangerous Ground '95

Charles S. Welbourne (1907-79)
Tre Three Stooges Meet Hercules '61
Revenge of the Creature '55
Creature from the Black Lagoon '54

Jan Weincke (1945-)
Inside '06
Twist & Shout '84

Howard Wexler
The Last Stop '99
Coffee Date '06
Hope Ranch '02
Newsbreak '00

Studs Lonigan '60

James Whitaker
Crossing Over '08
King of California '07
Running Scared '06
Thank You for Smoking '06
The Cooler '03
The Book of Stars '99
Let the Devil Wear Black '99
The Monster That Challenged the World '57
Guns of Fury '49
Whistling in Brooklyn '43
Sherlock Holmes and the Secret Weapon '42

Lester White (1907-58)
Slaughter's Big Ripoff '73
Silent Running '71
C.C. & Company '70
Toral Toral Toral '70
Yours, Mine & Ours '68
Women in Love '70

Charles F. Wheeler (1915-2004)
Death Valley: The Revenge of Bloody Bill '04
Truck Turner '74
The Best of Times '86
Condorman '81
The Last Flight of Noah's Ark '80
The Cat from Outer Space '78
Centerfold '95
Over the Wire '95
Die Watching '93
Picasso Trigger '89
Hard Ticket to Hawaii '87
Banzai Runner '86
Reform School Girls '86

Frank D. Williams
The Dragon Painter '19
Tillie's Punctured Romance '14

Haskell Wexler (1926-)
Silver City '04
61* '01
Limbo '99
The Rich Man's Wife '96
Mulholland Falls '95
The Secret of Roan Inish '94
Canadian Bacon '94
Sweepers '96
Danger Zone '96
Operation Delta Force '97
The Babe '92
Other People's Money '91
Blaze '89
Three Fugitives '89
Colors '88
Matewan '87
The Man Who Loved Women '83
Coming Home '78
Bound for Glory '76
One Flew Over the Cuckoo's Nest '75
Girma Shelter '70
Medium Cool '69
The Thomas Crown Affair '68
In the Heat of the Night '67
Who's Afraid of Virginia Woolf? '66
The Loved One '65
The Best Man '64
A Face in the Rain '63
Angel Baby '61
The Hoodlum Priest '61
The Modern Adventures of Tom Sawyer '59

Donald Wilder
Spring Fever '81
Meatballs '79

Jo Willems
Rocket Science '07
30 Days of Night '07
Hard Candy '06
London '05

Billy Williams (1929-)
Stella '89
The Rainbow '89
Suspect '87
The Manhattan Project '86
Dreamchild '85
Eleni '85
Ordeal by Innocence '84
Survivors '83
Gandhi '82
Monsignor '82
On Golden Pond '81
Saturn 3 '80
Eagle's Wing '79
The Silent Partner '78
Voyage of the Damned '76
The Wind and the Lion '75
The Exorcist '73
Night Watch '73
X, Y & Zee '72
Sunday, Bloody Sunday '71
Women in Love '70

James Wilson
Old Mother Riley's Jungle Treasure '51
Old Mother Riley's New Venture '49
Echo Murders '45
The Dummy Talks '43
Salute John Citizen '42
The Living Dead? '33

Catherine Cookson's The Black Velvet Gown '92
Magic Moments '89
Ballman and True '88

Tony Westman
Of Season '01
The Last Stop '99
Needful Things '93
The Deserters '83

Harry Wild (1900-61)
Gentlemen Prefer Blondes '53
The Conqueror '56
Son of Paleface '52
His Kind of Woman '51
Big Steal '49
Pitfall '48
Nocturne '46
Murder, My Sweet '44
Tycoon '47
So This Is Washington '43
Stage Door Canteen '43
Legion of the Lawless '40

John Wilcox (1905-79)
The Legend of the 7 Golden Vampires '73
Au Pair Girls '73
The Last Valley '71
The Evil of Frankenstein '64
Nightmare '63
Waltz of the Toreadors '62
Expresso Bongo '59
Carve Her Name with Pride '58

Joseph M. Wilcots (1939)
Hell's Kitchen NYC '97
Roots: The Next Generation '79
Roots '77

Jack Willoughby
Bog '84
The Giant Spider Invasion '75

Derek Wiesehahn
The Reception '05
Video Murders '87
Mountaintop Motel Massacre '86
Loving '70

Lisa Wiegand
Eating Out 2: Sloppy Seconds '06
Little Athens '05
Fish in a Barrel '01
Outta Time '01
Eastside '99

William F. Whitley
Beyond Tomorrow '40
Queen of Outer Space '58
Cat Women of the Moon '52

Gordon Willis (1931-)
The Devil's Own '96
Malice '93
The Godfather, Part 3 '90
Presumed Innocent '90
Bright Lights, Big City '88
The Pick-Up Artist '87
Perfect '85
The Money Pit '86
The Purple Rose of Cairo '85
Broadway Danny Rose '84
Zelig '83
Pennies from Heaven '81
Stardust Memories '80
Windows '80
Manhattan '79
Comes a Horseman '78
Interiors '78
Annie Hall '77
All the President's Men '76
The Drowning Pool '75
The Parallax View '74
The Godfather, Part 2 '74
Bad Company '72
The Godfather '72
Up the Sandbox '72
Klute '71
Little Murders '71
End of the Road '70
Loving '70

Andreas Winding (1928-77)
A Slightly Pregnant Man '79
La Scoumoune '72
Ramparts of Clay '68

Romain Winding (1951-)
Seventh Heaven '98
Sweet Revenge '98

Stephen Windon (1959)
The Fast and the Furious: Tokyo Drift '06
House of Wax '05
Anacondas: The Hunt for the Blood Orchid '04
The Tuxedo '02
The Diamond of Jeru '01
Rodgers & Hammerstein's South Pacific '01
Deep Blue Sea '99
The Patriot '00
Firestorm '97
The Postman '97
Hotel de Love '96
Country Life '95
In Pursuit of Honor '95

A Midsummer Night's Sex Comedy '82
Pennies from Heaven '81

Ian Wilson (1939-)
A Christmas Carol '99
Savior '98
Swing '98
The Island on Bird Street '97
Erik the Viking '89
Wish You Were Here '87
A Midsummer Night's Dream '96
Niagara Motel '06
A Way of Life '04
I'll Be There '03
Below '02
Back to the Secret Garden '01

Willy
Le Schpountz '38
Harvest '37
The Chess Player '27

Nigel Willoughby
The History of Mr. Polly '07
The Magdalene Sisters '02

Bill Wong
Caracara '00
Invasion! '95
Blackjack '97
Once a Thief '96
Dream Lovers '86
Zu: Warriors from the Magic Mountain '83

Wing-Hung Wong
The Accidental Spy '01
Organized Crime & Triad Bureau '93
Twin Dragons '92
A Bullet in the Head '90
The Killer '89
A Better Tomorrow, Part 1 '86

Arthur Wong Ngok Tai

Zack Winestine
Tie Rook '99
Strawberry Fields '97

Glen Winter
The Next Step '95
MVP (Most Valuable Primate) '00
Horsey '99
Premonition '98

Peter Woeste
Stargate: The Ark of Truth '09
Video Voyeur: The Susan Wilson Story '02
Jennifer Stolpa Story '94
Mortal Sins '92
Candyman 3: Day of the Dead '99

Jerzy Wojcik (1930-)
The Deluge '73
Pharaoh '66
Ashes and Diamonds '58

Michael G. Wojciechowski

Ben Wolf
The Young Girl and the Monsoon '06
Bad Company '02
The Mexican '01
A Perfect Murder '98
Hide and Seek '05
Pirates of the Caribbean: Dead Man's Chest '06
The Fan '96

Darius Wolski (1956-)
Pirates of the Caribbean: At World's End '07
Pirates of the Caribbean: Dead Man's Chest '06
Pirates of the Caribbean: The Curse of the Black Pearl '03
Crimson Tide '95
The Crow '93
Dark City '97
Romeo Is Bleeding '93

Oliver Wood
The Bourne Ultimatum '07
The Bourne Supremacy '04
Step Brothers '08
The Dish '01
Subterano '01
Ultraviolet '06
The Medallion '03
Double Vision '02
Gen-X Cops '99
Knock Off '98
Erotique '94
Crime Story '93
The Hunter '93
Iron Monkey '93
Once Upon a Time in China '91
Heart of Dragon '85

Graeme Wood

Freaky Friday '03
National Security '03
The Adventures of Pluto Nash '02
I Spy '02
U-571 '00
Mighty Joe Young '98
Face/Off '97
Switchback '97
Celtic Pride '96
Two Days in the Valley '96
Mr. Holland's Opus '95
Terminal Velocity '94
Rudy '93
Sister Act 2: Back in the Habit '93
Bill & Ted's Bogus Journey '91
Die Hard 2: Die Harder '90
Nasty Hero '89
Joey '85
Don't Go in the House '80
Honeymoon Killers '70

Ralph Woolsey
The Great Santini '80
The Iceman Cometh '73

Bruce Worrall
Innocents '00
Ronnie and Julie '97
The Heist '96
Profile for Murder '96
Tracks of a Killer '95
Hard Evidence '94

David Worth
Shark Attack 3: Megalodon '02
The Prophet's Game '99
True Vengeance '97
Lady Dragon 2 '93
Lady Dragon '92
Any Which Way You Can '80
Bronco Billy '80

Lothrop Worth (1903-2000)
Billy the Kid Versus Dracula '66
Jesse James Meets Frankenstein's Daughter '65

Dewey Wrigley
Wings in the Dark '35
Hell's Angels '30

Peter Wunstorf
Hollow Man 2 '06
Total Recall 2070: Machine Dreams '99
Invasion of Privacy '96
Double Happiness '94
Heartstrings '93
Tomcat: Dangerous Desires '93

Alvin Wyckoff (1877-1957)
Blood and Sand '22
Affairs of Anatol '21
Male and Female '19

Reg Wyer (1901-70)
The Little American '17
Burn Witch, Burn! '62
Masters of Venus '62
Dentist in the Chair '60
Four Sided Triangle '53
Spaceways '53
Trio '50

Manny Wynn (1928-75)
Smashing Time '67
Girl with Green Eyes '64

Steve Yaconelli (1941-2003)
Blue Sky '91
The Temp '93
The Phantom of the Opera '90
The Karate Kid: Part 3 '89

Kazuo Yamada
Samurai Banners '69
Son of Godzilla '66
What's Up, Tiger Lily? '66
I Bombed Pearl Harbor '60
Samurai 3: Duel at Ganryu Island '56

Hideo Yamamoto (1960-)
The Grudge '04
Graveyard of Honor '02
Audition '99
Fireworks '97

Kazuo Yamazaki
The Hidden Fortress '58
The Lower Depths '57

Yutaka Yamazaki
Nobody Knows '04
After Life '98

Katsumi Yanagijima
Shutter '08
The Grudge 2 '06
Zatoichi '03
Dolls '02

Katsumi Yanagishima
Brother '00
Kikujiro '99
Sonatine '96
Boiling Point '90

Jun Yasumoto
Samurai 1: Musashi Miyamoto '55
Samurai 2: Duel at Ichijoji Temple '55

Herman Yau (1961-)
Tsui Hark's Vampire Hunters '02
Time and Tide '00

Steve Yedlin
The Dead One '07
Brick '06
Conversations with Other Women '05
Dead Birds '04
May '02

Robert Yeoman (1951-)
The Darjeeling Limited '07
Martian Child '07
Red Eye '05
The Squid and the Whale '05
The Life Aquatic with Steve Zissou '04
CQ '01
Double Whammy '01
The Royal Tenenbaums '01
Beautiful '00
Down to You '00
Dogma '99
The Pentagon Wars '98
Permanent Midnight '98
Rushmore '98
Dogwatch '97
The Substance of Fire '96
Bottle Rocket '95
Coldblooded '94
The Linguini Incident '92
Drugstore Cowboy '89
Dead Heat '88

Pyotr Yermolov
My Universities '40
My Apprenticeship '39
My Childhood '38

Hou Yong
The Road Home '01
Happy Times '00
Not One Less '99
The Day the Sun Turned Cold '96

Frederick A. (Freddie) Young (1902-98)
Sword of the Valiant '83
Richard's Things '80
Rough Cut '80
Sidney Sheldon's Bloodline '79
Stevie '78
Permission To Kill '75
Luther '74
The Tamarind Seed '74
The Asphyx '72
Nicholas and Alexandra '71
Ryan's Daughter '70
Battle of Britain '69
You Only Live Twice '67
Doctor Zhivago '65
Lord Jim '65
The Seventh Dawn '64
Lawrence of Arabia '62
Gorgo '61
Solomon and Sheba '59
Indiscreet '58
The Inn of the Sixth Happiness '58
Island in the Sun '57
Bhowani Junction '56
Betrayed '54
Knights of the Round Table '53
Ivanhoe '52
Treasure Island '50
Conspirator '49
The Winslow Boy '48
While I Live '47
Bedelia '46
Contraband '40
Goodbye, Mr. Chips '39
When Knights Were Bold '36
The Speckled Band '31

Robert M. Young (1924-)
The Plot Against Harry '69
Nothing but a Man '64

Lu Yue
Xiu Xiu: The Sent Down Girl '97
Shanghai Triad '95
To Live '94

Vadim Yusov (1929-)
Anna '93
Solaris '72
Andrei Rublev '66

Haris Zambarloukos
Mamma Mia! '08
Sleuth '07
Venus '06
Enduring Love '04

Wieslaw Zdort
The Decalogue '88
Without Love '80

Peter Zeitlinger (1960-)
Grizzly Man '05
Invincible '01

Massimo Zeri
Bottoms Up '06
Beretta's Island '92

Fei Zhao (1961-)
Warriors of Heaven and Earth '03
The Curse of the Jade Scorpion '01
Small Time Crooks '00
The Emperor and the Assassin '99
Sweet and Lowdown '99
The Horse Thief '87

Xiaoding Zhao
Curse of the Golden Flower '06
Riding Alone for Thousands of Miles '05
House of Flying Daggers '04

Yuri Zhelyabuzhsky
Aelita: Queen of Mars '24
The Cigarette Girl of Mosselprom '24

Howard Ziehm (1940-)
Cop Killers '73
Flesh Gordon '72

Jerzy Zielinski (1961-)
Fun With Dick and Jane '05
Dodgeball: A True Underdog Story '04
The SpongeBob SquarePants Movie '04
The Lizzie McGuire Movie '03
Who is Cletis Tout? '02
Bubble Boy '01
Galaxy Quest '99
Teaching Mrs. Tingle '99
The Third Miracle '99
Home Fries '98
Washington Square '97
That Darn Cat '96
Powder '95
Houseguest '94
Swing Kids '93
The January Man '89

Bernard Zitzermann
The Blood Oranges '97
Angels and Insects '95
La Ceremonie '95
L'Enfer '93
The Music of Chance '93
The Favor, the Watch, & the Very Big Fish '92
November Moon '85
I Married a Dead Man '82

Vilmos Zsigmond (1930-)
Cassandra's Dream '07
The Black Dahlia '06
Melinda and Melinda '05
Jersey Girl '04
The Body '01
Life as a House '01
Mists of Avalon '01
Playing by Heart '98
The Ghost and the Darkness '96
Assassins '95
The Crossing Guard '94
Maverick '94
Intersection '93
Silver '93
Stalin '92
The Bonfire of the Vanities '90
The Two Jakes '90
The Witches of Eastwick '87
The River '84
Blow Out '81
Heaven's Gate '81
The Rose '79
Winter Kills '79
The Deer Hunter '78
Close Encounters of the Third Kind '77
Obsession '76
The Sugarland Express '74
Cinderella Liberty '73
The Long Goodbye '73
Scarecrow '73
Blood of Ghastly Horror '72
Deliverance '72
Images '72
Hired Hand '71
McCabe & Mrs. Miller '71
Deadwood '65
Incredibly Strange Creatures Who Stopped Living and Became Mixed-Up Zombies '63
The Sadist '63

Marcel Zyskind (1979-)
A Mighty Heart '07
The Road to Guantanamo '06
Tristram Shandy: A Cock and Bull Story '05
Code 46 '03
In This World '03

The **Composer Index** provides a videography for any composer, arranger, lyricist, or band that has provided an original music score for more than one film now on video. The listings for the composer names follow an alphabetical sort by last name (although the names appear in a first name, last name format). The videographies are listed chronologically, from most recent film to the first. If a composer provided music for more than one film in the same year, these movies are listed alphabetically within the year.

Barron Abramovitch
Profile for Murder '96
Tracks of a Killer '95
Hard Evidence '94

Anton Abril (1933-)
Return of the Evil Dead '75
Terror Beach '75
Pancho Villa '72
Tombs of the Blind Dead '72
The Werewolf vs. the Vampire Woman '77

André Abujarrura
Innocent Voices '04

Neal Acree (1974-)
Carandiru '03
They Crawl '01
Venomous '01
Ablaze '00
Critical Mass '00
Militia '99

Bryan Adams (1959-)
Color Me Kubrick '05
Spirit: Stallion of the Cimarron '02

Tree Adams
The Bronx Is Burning '07
Poor White Trash '00
No Money Down '97

Barry Adamson (1958-)
Gas Food Lodging '92
Delusion '91

Richard Addinsell (1904-77)
Waltz of the Toreadors '62
A Christmas Carol '51
The Black Rose '50
Blithe Spirit '45
Dangerous Moonlight '41
Gaslight '40
Fire Over England '37
South Riding '37
Seven Days to Noon '50

John Addison (1920-98)
The Phantom of the Opera '90
Something in Common '86
King and Country '64
Agatha Christie's Thirteen at Dinner '85
A Cry from the Streets '57
Genevieve '53
Grace Quigley '84
Strange Invaders '83
Eleanor: First Lady of the World '82
Love's Savage Fury '79
The Bastard '78
Pearl '78
A Bridge Too Far '77
Joseph Andrews '77
The Seven-Per-Cent Solution '76
Swashbuckler '76
Ride a Wild Pony '75
Luther '74
Sleuth '72
Cry of the Penguins '71
Start the Revolution without Me '70
The Charge of the Light Brigade '68
The Honey Pot '67
Smashing Time '67
A Fine Madness '66
Torn Curtain '66
The Amorous Adventures of Moll Flanders '65
The Loved One '65
Girl with Green Eyes '64
Guns at Batasi '64
Tom Jones '63
The Loneliness of the Long Distance Runner '62
A Taste of Honey '61
The Entertainer '60
Carlton-Browne of the F.O. '59
Look Back in Anger '58
Lucky Jim '58
Reach for the Sky '56
Seven Days to Noon '50

Brian Adler
Ordinary Sinner '02
Hostage High '97

Larry Adler (1914-2001)
Genevieve '53

Jeff Alexander (1910-89)
Clambake '67
Gun Glory '57
Jailhouse Rock '57

Mark Adler
The Far Side of Jericho '06
Fatal Contact: Bird Flu in America '06
Marilyn Hotchkiss' Ballroom Dancing & Charm School '06
The Rat Pack '98
Ernest in the Army '97
Decoy '95
Slam Dunk Ernest '95
Henry & June '90
Eat a Bowl of Tea '89
Break of Dawn '88
The Unbearable Lightness of Being '88
Heat and Sunlight '87

Yashushi Akutagawa (1925-89)
An Actor's Revenge '63
Fires on the Plain '59
Gate of Hell '54

Damon Albarn (1968-)
Ravenous '99
Ordinary Decent Criminal '00

Robert Alcivar
Blind Witness '89
Naked Lie '89
Hysterical '83

Life of the Party '25
When Do We Eat? '05
Leo '02
Focus '01
Cupid & Cate '00
Apartment Complex '98
One Kill '00
Elvira's Haunted Hills '02
One Night '97
True Heart '97
Luminarias '99
Midnight Blue '96
Down Twisted '88
Angel 3: The Final Chapter '88

Cameron Allan
The Nutt House '95
Jericho Fever '93
JFK: Reckless Youth '93
The Good Wife '86
Midnite Spares '65

Billy Allen
See William Allen Castleman

Peter Allen (1944-92)
Kiss Me Goodbye '82
Arthur '81

Peter Allen (1952-)
A Dennis the Menace Christmas '07
Shock to the System '06
Ripper: Letter from Hell '01
Crackerjack 3 '00
Escape from Mars '99
Escape Velocity '99
The Silencer '99
Chained Heat 3: Hell Mountain '98
Dead Fire '98
Crackerjack 2 '97
Act of War '96
Dangerous Prey '95
Crackerjack '94
Cyborg 2 '93

Van Alexander (1915-)
Strait-Jacket '64
Platinum High School '60
Girls' Town '59
Jaguar '56

Hossein Alizadeh (1951-)
Gabbeh '96
Turtles Can Fly '04

Eric Allaman
Witless Protection '08
Letter Days '04
Westward the Women '51

John Altman (1949-)
The Queen's Sister '05
The Reagans '04
Shall We Dance? '04
Amen '02
The Roman Spring of Mrs. Stone '03
The Matchmaker '97
Pronto '97
A Royal Scandal '96
Bhaji on the Beach '94
Funny Bones '94
Bad Behavior '92
Devlin '92
Hear My Song '91

Armand Amar (1953-)
Blame It on Fidel '06
Days of Glory '06

Alejandro Amenabar (1972-)
The Sea Inside '04
The Others '01
Butterfly '98
Open Your Eyes '97
Thesis '96

Daniele Amfitheatrof (1901-83)
Heller in Pink Tights '60
The Last Hunt '56
Storm Warning '51
O.S.S. '46
The Virginian '46
Splendor in the Grass '61
The Young Savages '61
You Gotta Stay Happy '48
Singapore '47

Captain Boycott '47
Odd Man Out '47
Immortal Battalion '44
On Approval '44

Fidel '02
King of Texas '02
Mr. St. Nick '02
The Lost Empire '01
Boss of Bosses '99
RKO 281 '99
Vendetta '99
Legionnaire '98
Little Voice '98
Tracked '98
The Garden of Redemption '97

Joseph (Joey) Altruda
Comic Book Villains '02
Slackers '02
Slaves of Hollywood '99
Shake, Rattle & Rock! '94

Elik Alvarez
The Proud Family Movie '05
Yu-Gi-Oh! The Movie: Pyramid of Light '04

William Alwyn (1905-85)
The Swiss Family Robinson '60
Carve Her Name with Pride '58
Madeleine '50

David Amram (1930-)
The Arrangement '69
The Manchurian Candidate '62

Chris Anderson
The Box '03

Lars Anderson
Treasure Island '99
Hellraiser: Hellworld '05
Deranged '01

Laurie Anderson (1947-)
Monster in a Box '92
Swimming to Cambodia '87
Something Wild '86

Michael Andrews
Walk Hard: The Dewey Cox Story '07
Paris, je t'aime '06
The TV Set '06

Unaccompanied Minors '06
Me and You and Everyone We Know '05
Cypher '02
Orange County '02
Donnie Darko '01
Out Cold '01

Gerard Anfosso
Blue Country '77
Cousin, Cousine '76

George Antheil (1900-59)
The Pride and the Passion '57
Daughter of Horror '55
Actors and Sin '52

Pete Anthony
Love Songs '99
Run for the Dream: The Gail Devers Story '96

Paul Antonelli
China O'Brien '88
Out of the Dark '88
Princess Academy '87
Women's Club '87
Avenging Angel '85

Louis Applebaum (1918-2000)
The Mask '61
Lost Boundaries '49
The Story of G.I. Joe '45

Philip Appleby
The Wyvern Mystery '00
Butterfly Collectors '99
Nothing Personal '95
Maria's Child '93

Tito Arevalo (1911-2000)
Mad Doctor of Blood Island '68
The Ravagers '65
The Walls of Hell '64
Raiders of Leyte Gulf '63

Dario Argento (1940-86)
Dawn of the Dead '78
Suspiria '77

Steven Argila
The Thing About My Folks '05
Memron '04

Eddie Arkin
Pretty Smart '87
Hardbodies 2 '86
Modern Girls '86

Harold Arlen (1905-86)
Gay Purr-ee '62
A Star Is Born '54
The Farmer Takes a Wife '53
Cabin in the Sky '43
At the Circus '39
Strike Me Pink '36

Martin Armiger
Introducing the Dwights '07
The Wedding Party '97
The Crossing '92
Sweetie '89
Young Einstein '89
Two Friends '86

Craig Armstrong (1959-)
The Incredible Hulk '08
Elizabeth: The Golden Age '07
World Trade Center '06
Fever Pitch '05
Must Love Dogs '05
The Clearing '04
Ray '04
Love Actually '03
The Magdalene Sisters '02
Kiss of the Dragon '01
Moulin Rouge '01
Best Laid Plans '99
The Bone Collector '99
Plunkett & Macleane '98
Orphans '97

Stefano Arnaldi
How Harry Became a Tree '01
Tea with Mussolini '99

David Arnold (1962-)
Hot Fuzz '07
Amazing Grace '06
Casino Royale '06
Venus '06
Stoned '05
The Stepford Wives '04
2 Fast 2 Furious '03
Changing Lanes '02
Die Another Day '02
Enough '02
Baby Boy '01
The Musketeer '01
Zoolander '01
Shaft '00
The World Is Not Enough '99
Godzilla '98
A Life Less Ordinary '97
Tomorrow Never Dies '97
Independence Day '96
The Last of the Dogmen '95
Stargate '94

Harry Arnold
Invasion of the Animal People '62

Malcolm Arnold (1921-2006)
David Copperfield '70
Battle of Britain '69
Africa Texas Style '67
The Great St. Trinian's Train Robbery '66
The Heroes of Telemark '65
The Chalk Garden '64
The Thin Red Line '64
On the Fiddle '61
The Pure Hell of St. Trinian's '61
Whistle down the Wind '61
No Love for Johnnie '60
Tunes of Glory '60
Solomon and Sheba '59
Suddenly, Last Summer '59
The Inn of the Sixth Happiness '58
The Key '58
The Bridge on the River Kwai '57
Island in the Sun '57
Blue Murder at St. Trinian's '56
Trapeze '56
I Am a Camera '55
The Sea Shall Not Have Them '55
Devil on Horseback '54
The Sleeping Tiger '54
The Belles of St. Trinian's '53
Captain's Paradise '53
Curtain Up '53
Four Sided Triangle '53
Hobson's Choice '53
A Stolen Face '52
Wings of Danger '52
No Highway in the Sky '51
Eye Witness '49

Norman Arnold
Reel Paradise '05
Shot '01

Bruce Arntson
Ernest Rides Again '93
Ernest Scared Stupid '91
Ernest Goes to Jail '90

Leon Aronson (1945-)
Bounty Hunters 2: Hardball '97
Jack Higgins' Midnight Man '96
Jack Higgins' On Dangerous Ground '95
Eddie and the Cruisers 2: Eddie Lives! '89

Jorge Arriagada (1943-)
Klimt '06
Our Lady of the Assassins '01
Comedy of Innocence '00
Time Regained '99
Shattered Image '98
Genealogies of a Crime '97
Three Lives and Only One Death '96
It's All True '93
The Disenchanted '90
On Top of the Whale '82

Eduard Artemyev (1937-)
House of Fools '02
The Odyssey '97
Burnt by the Sun '94
Anna '93
Double Jeopardy '92
The Inner Circle '91
Close to Eden '90
Homer and Eddie '89
Siberiade '79
Stalker '79
A Slave of Love '78
The Mirror '75
Solaris '72

Bent Aserud (1950-)
Mendel '98
The Other Side of Sunday '96
The Specials '00

Howard Ashman (1950-91)
Aladdin '92
Beauty and the Beast '91
The Little Mermaid '89
Little Shop of Horrors '86

Spring Aspers
Rebound '05

Edwin Astley (1922-98)
Digby, the Biggest Dog in the World '73
Vendetta for the Saint '68
Fiction Makers '67
A Matter of WHO '62
The Phantom of the Opera '62
Let's Get Married '60
The Womaneater '60
To Paris with Love '55
Devil Girl from Mars '54

Michael Atkinson
Heaven's Burning '97
Backlash '86

Georges Auric (1899-1983)
Therese & Isabelle '67
The Innocents '61
The Testament of Orpheus '59
The Crucible '57
Heaven Knows, Mr. Allison '57
The Hunchback of Notre Dame '57
The Night Heaven Fell '57
The Story of Esther Costello '57
Abdulla the Great '56
Gervaise '56
Lola Montes '55
Wages of Fear '55
Rififi '54
Orpheus '49
Beauty and the Beast '46
Dead of Night '45
Eternal Return '43
A Nous la Liberte '31
The Blood of a Poet '30

William Axt (1888-1959)
Libeled Lady '36
Tarzan and His Mate '34
Dinner at Eight '33
Laurel & Hardy: Hog Wild '30
Laurel & Hardy: The Hoose-Gow '29
Don Juan '26
The Big Parade '25

Charles Aznavour (1924-)
Mauvais Sang '86
Sweet Ecstasy '62
Daniella by Night '61
Dishonorable Discharge '57

Chris Babida
Fleeing by Night '00
The Phantom Lover '95

Luis Bacalov (1933-)
Assassination Tango '03
It Had to Be You '00
Woman on Top '00
Children of the Century '99
The Love Letter '99
Polish Wedding '97
The Truce '96
Entre-Nous '83
The Postman '94
City of Women '81
Rulers of the City '76
The Grand Duel '73
A Bullet for the General '68
Catch as Catch Can '68
Django '68
Empty Canvas '64
The Gospel According to St. Matthew '64

Burt Bacharach (1928-)
Isn't She Great '00
Arthur 2: On the Rocks '88
Night Shift '82
Arthur '81
Together? '79
Butch Cassidy and the Sundance Kid '69
Casino Royale '67
After the Fox '66
Alfie '66
What's New Pussycat? '65
The Sad Sack '57
The Blob '58

Pierre Bachelet (1944-2005)
Emmanuelle 5 '87
The Perils of Gwendoline '84
Black and White in Color '76
Emmanuelle, the Joys of a Woman '76
The Story of O '75
Emmanuelle '74

Chris P. Bacon
Angels Fall '07
Blue Smoke '07

Michael Bacon (1949-)
Loverboy '05
Losing Chase '96

Angelo Badalamenti (1937-)
The Wicker Man '06
Dark Water '05
Dominion: Prequel to the Exorcist '05
Before the Fall '04
A Very Long Engagement '04
Dangerous Liaisons '03
Auto Focus '02
The Lathe of Heaven '02
Secretary '02
Suspended Animation '02
Mulholland Drive '01
The Beach '00
Arlington Road '99
Forever Mine '99
Holy Smoke '99
The Straight Story '99
The Blood Oranges '97
The Last Don '97
Invasion of Privacy '96
Lost Highway '96
The City of Lost Children '95
Witch Hunt '94
Hotel Room '93
Naked in New York '93
Twin Peaks: Fire Walk with Me '92
The Comfort of Strangers '91
Wait until Spring, Bandini '90
Wild at Heart '90
Cousins '89
National Lampoon's Christmas Vacation '89
Parents '89
A Nightmare on Elm Street 3: Dream Warriors '87
Tough Guys Don't Dance '87
Weeds '87
Blue Velvet '86
Across the Great Divide '76
Law and Disorder '74
Gordon's War '73

Wally Badarou (1955-)
Boesman & Lena '00
The Lunatic '92
Kiss of the Spider Woman '85

Klaus Badelt (1968-)
Premonition '07
TMNT (Teenage Mutant Ninja Turtles) '07
Poseidon '06
16 Blocks '06
Ultraviolet '06
Constantine '05
The Promise '05
Catwoman '04
Basic '03
Ned Kelly '03
Pirates of the Caribbean: The Curse of the Black Pearl '03
The Recruit '03
Equilibrium '02
K-19: The Widowmaker '02
The Time Machine '02
Invincible '01

David Baerwald (1960-)
Around the Bend '04
Hurlyburly '98
Loved '97

Tom Bahler (1943-)
Gordy '95
The Object of Beauty '91
Cold Feet '89
Fast Forward '84
Mary, Mary, Bloody Mary '76

Tadeusz Baird (1928-81)
Lotna '64
Passenger '61

Mischa Bakaleinikoff (1890-1960)
20 Million Miles to Earth '57
The 27th Day '57
Earth vs. the Flying Saucers '56
Blondie Hits the Jackpot '49
Jane Eyre '34

Buddy (Norman Dale) Baker (1918-2002)
The Puppetoon Movie '87
The Devil & Max Devlin '81
The Fox and the Hound '81
The Apple Dumpling Gang Rides Again '79
Hot Lead & Cold Feet '78
No Deposit, No Return '76
The Shaggy D.A. '76
A Tiger Walks '64
The Apple Dumpling Gang '75
The Bears & I '74
Superdad '73
Napoleon and Samantha '72
Million Dollar Duck '71
The Gnome-Mobile '67
Monkey's Uncle '65
The Misadventures of Merlin Jones '63
Summer Magic '63

Michael Conway Baker (1937-)
Savage Land '94
The Portrait '93
Showdown at Williams Creek '91
Loyalties '86
One Magic Christmas '85
The Grey Fox '83
Silence of the North '81

Richard John Baker (1949-)
The Tooth Fairy '06
The Wailer '06
Beneath Loch Ness '01

Richard Band (1958-)
Curse of the Puppet Master: The Human Experiment '98
In the Doghouse '98
Hideous '97
Head of the Family '96
Robo Warriors '96
Zarkorr! The Invader '96
Castle Freak '95
Magic Island '95
Dragonworld '94
Prehysteria 2 '94
Puppet Master 5: The Final Chapter '94
Shrunken Heads '94
Dollman vs Demonic Toys '93
Puppet Master 4 '93
Remote '93
Trancers 3: Deth Lives '92
The Pit & the Pendulum '91
The Resurrected '91
The Arrival '90
Crash and Burn '90
Doctor Mordrid: Master of the Unknown '90
Puppet Master 2 '90
Puppet Master 3: Toulon's Revenge '90
Arena '89
Bride of Re-Animator '89
Puppet Master '89
Prison '88
The Caller '87
Dolls '87
The Eliminators '86
From Beyond '86
Terrorvision '86
Troll '86
Ghoulies '84
Re-Animator '84
Zone Troopers '84
Dungeonmaster '83
The House on Sorority Row '83
Metalstorm: The Destruction of Jared Syn '83
Mutant '83
Parasite '82
Time Walker '82
The Alchemist '81
Day Time Ended '80
Dr. Heckyl and Mr. Hype '80
Laserblast '78

Brian Banks (1955-)
Graveyard Shift '90
Internal Affairs '90
Young Guns '88
Nice Girls Don't Explode '87

Don Banks (1923-80)
I Killed Rasputin '67
The Mummy's Shroud '67
Torture Garden '67
Rasputin the Mad Monk '66
The Reptile '66
Die, Monster, Die! '65
The Evil of Frankenstein '64
Hysteria '64
Nightmare '63

Tony Banks (1950-)
Quicksilver '86
The Wicked Lady '83
The Shout '78

Roque Banos (1968-)
The Kovak Box '06
El Crimen Perfecto '04
The Machinist '04
The Other Side of the Bed '03
800 Bullets '02
Sexy Beast '00
Goya in Bordeaux '99
Second Skin '99

Claus Bantzer
Drachenfutter '87
Ruby's Dream '82
The Uprising '81

San Bao
Big Shot's Funeral '01
The Road Home '01
Happy Times '00
Not One Less '99

Jonathan Bar-Girora (1962-)
Bonjour Monsieur Shlomi '03
Time of Favor '00

Jack Baran
Great Balls of Fire '89
Barfly '87

Lesley Barber

We Can't Live Here Anymore '04
Hysterical Blindness '02
Marian Bridge '02
Luminous Motion '00
Mansfield Park '99
You Can Count On Me '99
Los Locos Posse '97
A Price above Rubies '97
When Night Is Falling '95

Gato Barbieri (1934-)
Strangers Kiss '83
Firepower '79
Last Tango in Paris '73

Juan Bardem
Swindled '04

John Barnes (1920-2000)
Don't Be a Menace to South Central While Drinking Your Juice in the Hood '95
Better Off Dead '94
CB4: The Movie '93
Babe's Kids '92
Daughters of the Dust '91

Charles P. Barnett
Headless Body in Topless Bar '56

Nathan Barr
Shutter '08
Hostel: Part 2 '07
Rise: Blood Hunter '07
Beerfest '06
Hostel '05
The Dukes of Hazzard '05
Club Dread '04
Plain Dirty '04
Going Greek '01
Red Dirt '99
Too Smooth '98

Jeff Barry
Idolmaker '80
Love Thrill Murders '71
Hello Down There '69

John Barry (1923-2006)
Enigma '01
Mercury Rising '98
Playing by Heart '38
Swept from the Sea '97
Cry: The Beloved Country '95
The Scarlet Letter '95
The Specialist '94
Indecent Proposal '93
My Life '93
Chaplin '92
Deception '92
The Public Eye '92
Dances with Wolves '90
Masquerade '88
Hearts of Fire '87
The Living Daylights '87
Howard the Duck '86
Peggy Sue Got Married '86
The Jagged Edge '85
A Killing Affair '85
A View to a Kill '85
Out of Africa '85
The Cotton Club '84
Mike's Murder '84
Until September '84
The Golden Seal '83
High Road to China '83
Octopussy '83
Svengali '83
Frances '82
Hammett '82
Murder by Phone '82
Body Heat '81
Legend of the Lone Ranger '81
Inside Moves '80
Night Games '80
Raise the Titanic '80
Somewhere in Time '80
Touched by Love '80
The Black Hole '79
The Corn Is Green '79
Game of Death '79
Hanover Street '79
Moonraker '79
Willa '79
The Betsy '78
Star Crash '78
The Deep '77
First Love '77
The Gathering '77
The White Buffalo '77
Eleanor & Franklin '76
King Kong '76
Robin and Marian '76
War Between the Tates '76
The Day of the Locust '75
Love Among the Ruins '75
Shampoo '75
The Man with the Golden Gun '74
The Tamarind Seed '74
A Doll's House '73
Diamonds Are Forever '71
The Last Valley '71
Mary, Queen of Scots '71
Murphy's War '71
They Might Be Giants '71
Walkabout '71
Monte Walsh '70
Midnight Cowboy '69
On Her Majesty's Secret Service '69
Boom! '68
The Lion in Winter '68
King Rat '65
The Knack '65
Thunderball '65
Goldfinger '64
Séance on a Wet Afternoon '64
Zulu '64
From Russia with Love '63
Dr. No '62
The L-Shaped Room '62
Beat Girl '60
Never Let Go '60

Les Baxter (1922-96)
The Beast Within '82
Born Again '78
Switchblade Sisters '75
Devil & Leroy Basset '73
Frogs '72
Torture Chamber of Baron Blood '72
The Big Doll House '71
Cry of the Banshee '70
The Dunwich Horror '70
Hell's Belles '69
Terror in the Jungle '68
Wild in the Streets '68
Dr. Goldfoot and the Bikini Machine '66
Fireball 500 '66
Beach Blanket Bingo '65
How to Stuff a Wild Bikini '65
Bikini Beach '64
Black Sabbath '64
The Comedy of Terrors '64
Muscle Beach Party '64
Pajama Party '64
Beach Party '63
Battle Beyond the Sun '63
The Invaders '63
Operation Bikini '63
The Raven '63
X: The Man with X-Ray Eyes '63
Panic in the Year Zero! '62
Samson and the 7 Miracles of the World '62
Tales of Terror '62
Goliath and the Dragon '61
Master of the World '61
The Pit and the Pendulum '61
Black Sunday '60
Goliath and the Barbarians '60
Usher '60

Lionel Bart (1930-99)
Black Beauty '71
Oliver! '68

Steve Bartek (1952-)
Get Over It! '01
Novocaine '01
T're Crew '00
Srow Day '00
Meet the Deedles '98
Remy and Michele's High School Reunion '97
Cabin Boy '94
Coldblooded '94
Guilty as Charged '92
Past Midnight '92

Dee Barton (1937-2001)
Death Screams '83
House of Death '82
Thunderbolt & Lightfoot '74
High Plains Drifter '73
Play Misty for Me '71

Richard Baskin
Utoria '81
Welcome to L.A. '77
Nashville '76
Buffalo Bill & the Indians '76

Kevin Bassinson (1951-)
Honeysuckle Rose '80
100 Girls '00
Eight Days a Week '97
Beanstalk '94

George Bassman (1914-97)
Wombling Free '77
Ride the High Country '62
The Joe Louis Story '53
The Postman Always Rings Twice '46
Abbott and Costello in Hollywood '45
The Clock '45
The Canterville Ghost '44
Best Foot Forward '43

Cabin in the Sky '43
Whistling in Brooklyn '43
For Me and My Gal '42
Panama Hattie '42
Babes on Broadway '41
Big Store '41
Lady Be Good '41
Go West '40
Too Many Girls '40
Babes in Arms '39
E:erybody Sing '38
A Damsel in Distress '37
A Day at the Races '37

Tyler Bates
Doomsday '08
Halloween '07
300 '07
See No Evil '06
Slither '06
The Devil's Rejects '05
Dawn of the Dead '04
You Got Served '04
Baaadasssss! '03
City of Ghosts '03
Conviction '02
Joe and Max '02
No Good Deed '02
Night at the Golden Eagle '02

Walter Baumgartner
Sensual Partners '87
Ilsa, the Wicked Warden '78
Inn of Temptation '73
Sex Adventures of the Three Musketeers '71
The Beast Within '82

Alexandre Beaupain (1974-)
Love Songs '07
Inside Paris '06

Christophe Beck (1972-)
Drillbit Taylor '08
Charlie Bartlett '07
Fred Claus '07
License to Wed '07
The Seeker: The Dark Is Rising '07
Year of the Dog '07
Garfield: A Tail of Two Kitties '06
The Pink Panther '06
School for Scoundrels '06
The Sentinel '06
We Are Marshall '06
Zoom '06
Elektra '05
Ice Princess '05
The Perfect Man '05
Two for the Money '05
Yours, Mine & Ours '05
A Cinderella Story '04
Garfield: The Movie '04
Little Black Book '04
Saved! '04
Taxi '04
Without a Paddle '04
American Wedding '03
Cheaper by the Dozen '03
Dickie Roberts: Former Child Star '03

The Event '33
Just Married '03
Under the Tuscan Sun '03
Interstate 60 '02
The Skulls 2 '02

The Black Sleep '56
Wetbacks '56
Monika '52

Camille Bazbaz
Priceless '06
Après-Vous '03

Jeff Beal (1963-)
The Russell Girl '08
The Company '07
Hostile Intent '97
Killing Mr. Griffin '97
Crosswords '96

Giuseppe Becce (1877-1973)
The Blue Light 32
The Last Laugh '24

Michael Bearden
The Visit '00
The Arrangement '99
DROP Squad '94

John Beal (1947-)
Alien Fury: Countdown to Invasion '00
Killer Party '86
The Stone Boy '84
Under the Volcano '84
Lookin' to Get Cut '82
The Funhouse '81
The Man with Bogart's Face '80
Defiance '79
Zero to Sixty '78

Andrew Belling
Starchaser: The Legend of Orin '85
The Deerslayer '78
Zoltan... Hound of Dracula '78
Wizards '77
End of the World '76
The Killing Kind '73

Richard Bellis (1946-)
One Special Night '99
How the West Was Fun '95
Where's the Money, Noreen? '95
The Spider and the Fly '94
Blind Man's Bluff '91
Double-Crossed '91
Stephen King's It '90
Fallen Angel '81
Breaking Up Is Hard to Do '79

A Shining Season '79

Roger Bellon (1953-)
The Christmas Card '06
Hidden Places '06
Murder Without Conviction '04
Break a Leg '03
Hitman's Run '99
The Last Don 2 '98
My Husband's Secret Life '98

The Last Don '97
The Unholy '88
Waxwork '88

Marco Beltrami (1966-)
Princess Academy '87
Captivity '07
The Eye '08
3:10 to Yuma '07
Live Free or Die Hard '07
Tr'e Invisible '07
The Omen '06
Red Eye '05
The Three Burials of Melquiades Estrada '05
Underworld: Evolution '05
XXX: State of the Union '05
Cursed '04
Flight of the Phoenix '04
Hellboy '04
I, Robot '04

Stealing Harvard '02
The Tuxedo '02
Bring It On '00
The Broken Hearts Club '00
Guinevere '99
Thick as Thieves '99
Scream 3 '00
Mimic '97
Scream 2 '97
Inhumanoid '96
Scream '96

Bob Belden
Three Days of Rain '03

David Bell (1954-)
Three Days of Rain '02
Scream 3 '00
Scream 2 '00
The Watcher '00
The Minus Man '99
Tuesdays with Morrie '99
The Faculty '98
The Crow: Salvation '00
Dracula 2000 '00

Frank Becker
American Kickboxer 1 '91
Terminal Bliss '91

Herman Beeftink
Forbidden Sins '99
One Small Hero '99
Dish Dogs '98
I Like to Play Games '95

Gilad Benamram
Chaos Theory '08
Pretty Persuasion '05

Vassal Benford
Class Act '91
The Faculty '98
House Party 2: The Pajama Jam '91

Arthur Benjamin (1893-1960)
Fire Down Below '57
Wings of the Morning '37
The Scarlet Pimpernel 34

Wayne Bell
The Texas Chainsaw Massacre 4: The Next Generation '95
The Texas Chainsaw Massacre '74
Eaten Alive '76
Return of the Soldier '82

James Bennett
Poison '91
Swoon '91

Daryl Bennett
Four Weddings and a Funeral '94
Enchanted April '92

Richard Rodney Bennett (1936-)
Swann '96
Equus '77
Permission To Kill '75
Murder on the Orient Express '74
Lady Caroline Lamb '73
Nicholas and Alexandra '71
Far from the Madding Crowd '67
The Witches '66
The Nanny '65
Billy Liar '63
Heavens Above '63
The Wrong Arm of the Law '63
Only Two Can Play '62
The Mark '61
The Devil's Disciple '59
Indiscreet '58

Warren Bennett
Chaos & Cadavers '03
Wuthering Heights '98
Perfect Game '00
The Stars Fell on Henrietta '94
Captive Hearts 87

Jean-Marie Benoit
Seducing Docto- Lewis '03
King of the Airwaves '94
Jesus of Montreal '89

David Bergeaud
Th3e '07
Anonymous Rex '04
The Badge '02
Prince Valiant '97
Donor Unknown '95
Twe ce Dead '88

David Benoît (1953-)
The Eye '08

Cary Berger

Terminator 3: Rise of the Machines '03
Blade 2 '02
The Dangerous Lives of Altar Boys '02
The First $20 Million is Always the Hardest '02
Resident Evil '02
Angel Eyes '01
Joy Ride '01

Eating Out 2: Sloppy Seconds '06
Cleopatra's Second Husband '00
Full Tilt Boogie '97
Suture '93

Tal Bergman
Sasquatch '02
Kill Me Later '01
Dancing at the Blue Iguana '00
Wedding Bell Blues '96

Michael Berkeley (1948-)
Twenty-One '91
Goldeneye: The Secret Life of Ian Fleming '89

Irving Berlin (1888-1989)
Le Bal '82
There's No Business Like Show Business '54
Annie Get Your Gun '50
Easter Parade '48
Second Fiddle '39
Alexander's Ragtime Band '38
Carefree '38
On the Avenue '37
Follow the Fleet '36
Top Hat '35
The Cocoanuts '29
Hallelujah! '29

James Bernard (1925-2001)
Frankenstein and the Monster from Hell '74
The Legend of the 7 Golden Vampires '73
The Scars of Dracula '70
Taste the Blood of Dracula '70
The Horror of Dracula '58
Across the Bridge '57
The Curse of Frankenstein '57
The Devil Rides Out '68
Dracula Has Risen from the Grave '68
The Quatermass 2 '57
Quatermass 2 '57
X The Unknown '56
The Quatermass Experiment '56
Torture Garden '67
Dracula, Prince of Darkness '66
Plague of the Zombies '66
The Gorgon '64
Kiss of the Vampire '62
The Hound of the Baskervilles '59

Jean-Michel Bernard
Be Kind Rewind '08
The Science of Sleep '06

Charles Bernstein (1943-)
After Innocence '05
The Day the World Ended '01
Earth vs. the Spider '01
Miss Evers' Boys '97
The Ticket '97
When Danger Follows You Home '97
Bloodhounds 2 '96
Dead Ahead '96
Rumpelstiltskin '96
Excessive Force '93
Final Appeal '93
The Sea Wolf '93
Payoff '91
Caroline? '90
Drug Wars: The Camarena Story '90
Ivory Hunters '90
Too Young to Die '90
The Allnighter '87
Dudes '87
The Man Who Broke 1,000 Chains '87
April Fool's Day '86
Deadly Friend '86
The Long, Hot Summer '86
The Rumor Mill '86
Chase '85
Secret Weapons '85

Heavy Metal '81
Honky Tonk Freeway '81
Stripes '81
Airplane! '80
The Blues Brothers '80
The Great Santini '80
The Guyana Tragedy: The Story of Jim Jones '80
Saturn 3 '80
The Chisholms '79
Meatballs '79
Zulu Dawn '79
Bloodbrothers '78
Little Women '78
National Lampoon's Animal House '78
Slap Shot '77
From Noon Till Three '76
The Incredible Sarah '76
The Shootist '76
The Old Curiosity Shop '75
McQ '74
Report to the Commissioner '74
The Trial of Billy Jack '74
Cahill: United States Marshal '73
Amazing Mr. Blunden '72
Big Jake '71
See No Evil '71
Doctors' Wives '70
Walk in the Spring Rain '70
The Bridge at Remagen '69
The Gypsy Moths '69
True Grit '69
I Love You, Alice B. Toklas! '68
The Scalphunters '68
Thoroughly Modern Millie '67
Will Penny '67
Cast a Giant Shadow '66
Hawaii '66
Return of the Magnificent Seven '66
The Silencers '66
The Hallelujah Trail '65
Sons of Katie Elder '65
Baby, the Rain Must Fall '64
The Carpetbaggers '64
The World of Henry Orient '64
The Great Escape '63
Hud '63
Kings of the Sun '63
Birdman of Alcatraz '62
To Kill a Mockingbird '62
Walk on the Wild Side '62
By Love Possessed '61
The Comancheros '61
Summer and Smoke '61
From the Terrace '60
The Magnificent Seven '60
The Rat Race '60
The Buccaneer '58
Desire Under the Elms '58
God's Little Acre '58
Kings Go Forth '58
Some Came Running '58
Fear Strikes Out '57
Men in War '57
Sweet Smell of Success '57
The Tin Star '57
The Ten Commandments '56
Never Wave at a WAC '52
Sudden Fear '52

Leonard Bernstein (1918-90)
On the Town '91
West Side Story '61
On the Waterfront '54
On the Town '49

Peter Bernstein (1951-)
Mail to the Chief '00
Atomic Dog '98
Dying to Get Rich '98
Rough Riders '97
Canadian Bacon '94
Nightbreaker '89
Remote Control '88
The Alamo: Thirteen Days to Glory '87
Morgan Stewart's Coming Home '87
Miracles '86
Broken Badge '85
The Ewoks: Battle for Endor '85
Kicks '85
My Science Project '85
Bolero '84
The Ewok Adventure '84
Summer Fantasy '84
Surf 2 '84
Club Med '83
Hot Dog... The Movie! '83
National Lampoon's Class Reunion '82
Silent Rage '82

Reinhard Besser
Heart of America '03
House of the Dead '03
Blackwoods '02

Peter Best (1943-)
Doing Time for Patsy Cline '97
Country Life '95
Muriel's Wedding '94
Crocodile Dundee 2 '88
High Tide '87
Crocodile Dundee '86
Sound of Love '78

Harry Betts
Cheech and Chong's Nice Dreams '81
Big Mouth '67

Ryan Beveridge
Boy Culture '06
Inside Man '06
L.A. Dicks '05
Frankenfish '04
Rampage: The Hillside Strangler Murders '04
Nightstalker '02
Taboo '02

Amin Bhatia
Detention '03
Under Heavy Fire '01
Once a Thief '96
Anything for Love '93
Just One of the Girls '93
Ordeal in the Arctic '93
Black Ice '92
Iron Eagle 2 '88
Storm '87

Nick Bicat (1949-)
Carrie's War '04
Suspicion '03
Stella Does Tricks '96
The Passion of Darkly Noon '95
Framed '93
The Hawk '93
The Reflecting Skin '91
Strapless '90
Stealing Heaven '88
Wetherby '85
A Christmas Carol '84
To Catch a King '84
Oliver Twist '82
The Scarlet Pimpernel '82

Arnold Bieber
Smoke '93
Small Time '91

Keith Bilderbeck
Stir '98
Voodoo '95

Edward Bilous
Just One Time '00
Dead Broke '99
Sleepaway Camp '83

Rene Marc Bini
Grosse Fatigue '94
Weep No More My Lady '93

Ulf Bjorlin (1933-93)
Vibration '68
Elvira Madigan '67

Stanley Black (1913-2002)
Maniac '63
The Day the Earth Caught Fire '61
The Battle of the Sexes '60
The Flesh and the Fiends '60
Jack the Ripper '60
Black Tide '58
The Crawling Eye '58
Time Lock '57

Damon Blackman
Cradle 2 the Grave '03
Exit Wounds '01

Wendy Blackstone
Love Walked In '97
New Jersey Drive '95
Tales of Erotica '93
Only You '92
Eddie Macon's Run '83

Ruben Blades (1948-)
Empire '02
Q & A '90
The Story of Fausta '88

Alan Blaikley
The Body in the Library '84
The Flame Trees of Thika '81

Howard Blake (1938-)
My Life So Far '98
A Midsummer Night's Dream '96
A Month in the Country '87
Amityville 3: The Demon '83
The Lords of Discipline '83
Amityville 2: The Possession '82
Flash Gordon '80
The Riddle of the Sands '79
S.O.S. Titanic '79
The Odd Job '78
The Rainbow Gang '73
An Elephant Called Slowly '69

Terence Blanchard (1962-)
Talk to Me '07
Inside Man '06
Waist Deep '06
She Hate Me '04
Dark Blue '03
Barbershop '02
People I Know '02
25th Hour '02
Bojangles '01
The Caveman's Valentine '01
Glitter '01
Original Sin '01
Bamboozled '00
Love and Basketball '00
Next Friday '00
The Truth About Jane '00
Summer of Sam '99
The Color of Courage '98
Free of Eden '98
Gia '98
Eve's Bayou '97
Get On the Bus '96
Til There Was You '96
Clockers '95
Assault at West Point: The Court-Martial of Johnson Whittaker '94
Crooklyn '94
The Inkwell '94
Sugar Hill '94
Trial by Jury '94
Malcolm X '92
Jungle Fever '91

Ralph Blane (1914-95)
Athena '54
Good News '47

Larry Blank (1952-)
That Championship Season '99

Arthur Bliss (1891-1975)
Abandon Ship '57
Things to Come '36

George Blondheim
Summer of the Monkeys '98
The Halfback of Notre Dame '96
Man with a Gun '95

Red Scorpion 2 '94
Whale Music '94
Heartstrings '93
Gate 2 '92
Bye Bye Blues '89

Michael Bloomfield (1944-81)
Andy Warhol's Bad '77
Medium Cool '69

Frankie Blue
Redeemer '02
Dracula: The Dark Prince
Return to Cabin by the Lake '01
Cabin by the Lake '00
Out There '95

Chris Boardman (1954-)
Blood Crime '02
The Dress Code '99
Payback '98
Tales from the Crypt Presents Bordello of Blood '96
The Color Purple '85
Prime Target '91

Michael Boddicker
Freejack '92
F/X 2: The Deadly Art of Illusion '91
The Adventures of Milo & Otis '89
Milo & Otis '89
White Water Summer '87
The Adventures of Buckaroo Banzai Across the Eighth Dimension '84
Get Crazy '83

Todd Boekelheide
Ballet Russes '05
Spin '04
The Outsider '02
Digger '94
Nina Takes a Lover '94
Exposure '91
Hearts of Darkness: A Filmmaker's Apocalypse '91
The Blood of Heroes '89
Dim Sum: A Little Bit of Heart '85

Ed Bogas
A Christmas Without Snow '80
Race for Your Life, Charlie Brown '77
Heavy Traffic '73
Payday '73
Fritz the Cat '72

Geir Bohren (1951-)
Mendel '98
The Other Side of Sunday '96

William Bolcom (1938-)
Illuminata '98
Hester Street '75

Bill Boll (1965-)
The Low Life '95
Some Folks Call It a Sling Blade '94

Claude Bolling (1930-)
The Bay Boy '85
The Awakening '80
Willie & Phil '80
California Suite '78
Silver Bears '78
Intruder '79
L'Annee Sainte '76
Le Magnifique '76
Le Gitan '75
The Passenger '75
Catch Me a Spy '71
Borsalino '70
The Day and the Hour '63
The Hands of Orlac '60

Jay Bolton
Mom's Outta Sight '01
The Kid with the X-Ray Eyes '99
Stormy Nights '97

Scott Bomar
Black Snake Moan '07
Hustle & Flow '05

Bernardo Bonezzi
(1964-)
Gaudi, Afternoon '01
The Double McGuffin '79
For the Love of Benji '77
Hawmps! '76
Benji '74

Marc Bonilla
Matador '86

Bono (1960-)
The Million Dollar Hotel '99
In the Name of the Father '93

Simon Boswell
(1956-)
Tim Man '07
The River King '05
Close Your Eyes '02
The Sleeping Dictionary '02
Wicows '02
Born Romantic '00
Circus '00
Jason and the Argonauts '00
William Shakespeare's A Midsummer Night's Dream '99
Deacon B'ocie '98
The War Zone '99
Cousin Bette '97
Dad Savage '97
Dance with the Devil '97
Photographing Fairies '97
The Android Affair '95
Hackers '95
Jack and Sarah '95
Lord of Illusions '95
Second Best '94
Shallow Grave '94
Dust Devil '93
Love Matters '93
The Turn of the Screw '92
Hardware '90
Santa Sange '90
Dangerous Obsession '88
Karate Warrior '88
Demons 2 '87
Creepers '86

Perry Botkin (1933-)
Windmills of the Gods '88
Weekend Warriors '86
Silent Night, Deadly Night '84

David Broekman
(1899-1958)
Frankenstein '31
All Quiet on the Western Front '30

Richard Bronskill
National Lampoon's Golf Punks '99

Timothy Brock
Diary of a Lost Girl '29
Faust '26
The Show Off '26

Jon Brion (1963-)
The Break-Up '06
Eternal Sunshine of the Spotless Mind '04
Punch-Drunk Love '02
Magnolia '99
Hard Eight '96

David Bridie
Tempted '01
In a Savage Land '99
River Street '95
That Eye, the Sky '94

Euel Box
Benji the Hunted '87
Eloise at the Plaza '03
Bobbie's Girl '02

Christopher Brady
(1967-)
Pressure '02
House Arrest '96

Goran Bregovic
(1950-)
Carried Away '95
The Shadow Conspiracy '96

Alan Brewer
Come Early Morning '06
Tom betone '33

Peter Brewis
The Tall Guy '89
Micrms from Outer Space '85

Danny Brenner
Rhythm Thief '94

David Bridle
Divided We Fall '00

Ales Brezina (1965-)
Up and Down '04

Leslie Bricusse
(1931-)
Tom and Jerry: The Movie '93
Babes in Toyland '86
Willy Wonka & the Chocolate Factory '71
Scrooge '70
Goodbye, Mr. Chips '69
Doctor Dolittle '67

Mel Brooks (1926-)
The Producers '05
The Twelve Chairs '70

Andre Brummer
(1916-2006)
Pippi Goes on Board '69
Pippi on the Run '70
The Thrill Killers '65

Bruce Broughton
(1945-)
The Show Off '26
Rat Pfink a Boo-Boo '66

Larry Brown
Don't Tell '63

Christian Bruhn
Broadway Melody of 1936
'35

Nacio Herb Brown
(1896-1964)
Singin' in the Rain '52
Broadway Melody of 1938
'37
Broadway Melody of 1936
'35
Broadway Melody '29

Chico Buarque
(1944-)
Possible Loves '00

Alexander Bubenheim
(1962-)
In Hell '03
Night Train to Venice '93

David Buchbinder
Whole New Thing '05

Paul Buckmaster
Mean Streak '99
The Maker '98
Murder in Mind '97
The Last Word '95
12 Monkeys '95

James Brown (1933-2006)
Black Caesar '73
Slaughter's Big Ripoff '73

Leo Brouwer (1930-)
A Walk in the Clouds '95
Like Water for Chocolate '93
Up to a Certain Point '83
Death of a Bureaucrat '66

Jerry Brunskill
Pistol Whipped '08
Sleeping Dogs Lie '06

Joanne Bruzdowicz
(1943-)
Vagabond '85

BT (Brian Transeau)
(1971-)
Catch and Release '07
Stealth '05
Underclassman '05
Monster '03
Driven '01
The Fast and the Furious
'01

George Bruns (1914-83)
Herbie Rides Again '74
Robin _ood '73
The Aristocats '70
The Love Bug '68
The Jungle Book '67
The Absent-Minded Professor '61
101 Dalmatians '61
Babes in Toyland '61
Sleeping Beauty '59
Davy Crockett and the River Pirates '56
Davy Crockett, King of the Wild Frontier '55

Robert F. Brunner
(1938-)
Amy '81
The North Avenue Irregulars
'79
Gus '76
The Strongest Man in the World '75
The Castaway Cowboy '74
Now You See Him, Now You Don't '72
Snowball Express '72
The Barefoot Executive '71
The Boatniks '70
Smoke '70
The Computer Wore Tennis Shoes '69
Never a Dull Moment '68
Blackbeard's Ghost '67
Lt. Robin Crusoe, U.S.N. '66
Monkeys, Go Home! '66
That Darn Cat '65

Kenneth Burgomaster
Hero Wanted '08
End Game '06

Geoffrey Burgon
(1941-)
Longitude '00
Cider with Rosie '99
When Trumpets Fade '98
A Foreign Field '93
Robin Hood '91
Turtle Diary '86
Bleak House '85
Brideshead Revisited '81
The Dogs of War '81
Monty Python's Life of Brian
'79

Chris Burke
Search and Destroy '88

Johnny Burke (1908-64)
Welcome Stranger '47

T-Bone Burnett
(1948-)
Don't Come Knocking '05
Walk the Line '05
Divine Secrets of the Ya-Ya Sisterhood '02
O Brother, Where Art Thou?
'00

Justin Caine Burnett
(1973-)
Dungeons and Dragons '00

Ralph Burns (1922-2001)
The Josephine Baker Story
'90
All Dogs Go to Heaven '89
Bert Rigby, You're a Fool
'89
Sweet Bird of Youth '89
After the Promise '87
In the Mood '87
Penalty Phase '86
A Chorus Line '85
Moving Violations '85
Perfect '85
Ernie Kovacs: Between the Laughter '84
The Muppets Take Manhattan '84
Side Show '84
National Lampoon's Vacation '83
Star 80 '83
Annie '82
Kiss Me Goodbye '82
My Favorite Year '82
Pennies from Heaven '81
First Family '80
Make Me an Offer '80
Urban Cowboy '80
All That Jazz '79
Movie Movie '78
New York, New York '77
Lenny '74
Cabaret '72

George Burt (1929-)
Fool for Love '86
Secret Honor '85

Carter Burwell (1955-)
In Bruges '08
Before the Devil Knows You're Dead '07
No Country for Old Men '07
Fur: An Imaginary Portrait of Diana Arbus '06
The Alamo '04
Kinsey '04

Ben Butler
The Insurgents '06
Heights '04

Artie Butler (1942-)
Grease 2 '82
O'Hara's Wife '82
American Dream '81
She's in the Army Now '81
Sizzle '81
Angel on My Shoulder '80
Sextette '78
The Rescuers '77
Rafferty & the Gold Dust Twins '75
For Pete's Sake '74
Harrad Experiment '73
What's Up, Doc? '72

Edmund Butt
24 Hours in London '00

David Buttolph
(1902-83)
The Horse Soldiers '59
Lone Ranger '56
Crime Wave '54
South Sea Woman '53
House of Wax '53
Fathoms '53
The Beast from 20,000 Fathoms '53
Long John Silver '54
Rope '48
Boomerang '47
My Darling Clementine '46
13 Rue Madeleine '46
House on 92nd Street '45
Crash Dive '43
Guadacanal Diary '43
Immortal Sergeant '43
My Favorite Blonde '42

Roy Budd (1947-93)
Diving In '90
The Spy Who Loved Me '77
Sinbad and the Eye of the Tiger '77
Welcome to Blood City '77
Get Carter '71

Incredibly Strange Creatures Who Stopped Living and Became Mixed-Up Zombies '63
Monster from the Ocean Floor '54

Christopher Brady
(1967-)
The Lost Son '98
Train of Life '98
A Chef in Love '96
The Serpent's Kiss '97

David Brockman
Scrooge '70

Michael Brook (1952-)
Into the Wild '07
An Inconvenient Truth '06
Who Killed the Electric Car?
'06

Welcome to Blood City '77

The Ladykillers '04
Intolerable Cruelty '03
Adaptation '02
The Rookie '02
Searching for Paradise '02
Simone '02
A Knight's Tale '01
The Man Who Wasn't There
'01
Before Night Falls '00
Book of Shadows: Blair Witch 2 '00
O Brother, Where Art Thou?
'00
What Planet Are You From?
'00
Being John Malkovich '99
The Corruptor '99
The General's Daughter '99
Mystery, Alaska '99
Three Kings '99
Gods and Monsters '98
The Hi-Lo Country '98
Velvet Goldmine '98
The Big Lebowski '97
Conspiracy Theory '97
The Jackal '97
The Locusts '97
The Spanish Prisoner '97
The Chamber '96
Fargo '96
Fear '96
Picture Perfect '96
The Celluloid Closet '95
Rob Roy '95
Airheads '94
Bad Company '94
It Could Happen to You '94
And the Band Played On '93
A Dangerous Woman '93
California '93
This Boy's Life '93
Wayne's World 2 '93
Waterland '92
Barton Fink '91
Doc Hollywood '91
Miller's Crossing '90
Checking Out '89
The Beat '88
It Takes Two '88
Pass the Ammo '88
Raising Arizona '87
Psycho 3 '86
Blood Simple '85

Charlotte Sometimes '02
Crime and Punishment in Suburbia '00
Buddy Boy '99
Rio Diablo '93
Gang in Blue '96
Elvis Meets Nixon '98
The Wall '69
Suburbia '83

- Jacquot '91
Killjoy '81
Return of Frank Cannon '80
One Shoe Makes It Murder
'82
Desperate Lives '82
The Blue and the Gray '82
The Prodigal '83
M.A.D.D.: Mothers Against Drunk Driving '83
Ice Pirates '84
The First Olympics: Athens 1896 '84

The Monster Squad '87
Square Dance '87
The Boy Who Could Fly '86
George Washington: The Forging of a Nation '86
Sweet Liberty '86
Silverado '85
Young Sherlock Holmes '85
The Cowboy & the Ballerina
'84

The First Olympics: Athens 1896 '84
Bill '81
Heart Beat '80

The Rescuers Down Under
'90
The Monster Squad '87
Murder '93
So I Married an Axe Murderer '93
Honey, I Blew Up the Kid '92
Stay Tuned '92
All I Want for Christmas '91
Narrow Margin '90
The Old Man and the Sea
'90
Bets's Wedding '90
Big Shots '87
Harry and the Hendersons
'87

Don Juan, My Love '90
Women on the Verge of a Nervous Breakdown '88

David Bowie (1547-)
The Buddha of Suburbia '92
Labyrinth '86

Roger Bourland
(1952-)
New Jack City '91
Night Life '90
The Trouble with Dck '88
The Wolf at the Door '87

Richard Bowers
A Woman Hunted '03
Facing the Enemy '00
The Perfect Nanny '00
The Nurse '97
Dead Cold '96
The Fiance '96
Open Fire '94
The Arrival 2 '98
These Girls '05

Ned Bouhalassa
Adam & Steve '05

Roddy Bottum
I'm Reed Fish '76

Frederic Botton
The Housekeeper '02
Queen of Diamonds '70

Joseph Brooks
(1938-)
If Ever I See You Again '78
You Light Up My Life '77
The Lords of Flatbush '74
Invitation to the Wedding '73

Harvey Brooks (1899-1968)
I'm No Angel '33
The Duke Is Tops '38

Ruel Box
Eambil I '06

Buttolph

This Gun for Hire '42
Thunder Birds '42
Wake Island '42

R. Dale Butts (1910-90)

David Byrne (1952-)
Pittsburgh '06
Young Adam '03
Married to the Mob '88
The Last Emperor '87
Something Wild '86
True Stories '86

John Cacavas (1930-)
Perfect Murder, Perfect Town '00
My Sweet Victim '85
Shooting '82
Silent Rebellion '82
Airport '75 '75
The Satanic Rites of Dracula '73
Heat '72

John Cale (1940-)
American Psycho '99
Somewhere in the City '97
Basquiat '96
I Shot Andy Warhol '96
Primary Motive '92
Something Wild '86
Who Am I This Time? '82
Caged Heat '74

John Califra
My Brother '06

Darrell Calker (1905-64)
The Amazing Transparent Man '60
Terror in the Haunted House '58
Savage Drums '51
The Flying Saucer '50
Big Town '47
Big Town After Dark '47
Shoot to Kill '47
Underworld Scandal '47
Renegade Girl '46

John Cameron (1944-)
To End All Wars '01
Mr. Corbett's Ghost '90
The Secret Garden '87
The Mirror Crack'd '80
A Touch of Class '73
The Ruling Class '72

Bruce Campbell
Plan 9 from Outer Space '56
Mister Drake's Duck '50

James Campbell (1946-)
Elvira, Mistress of the Dark '88

Xavier Capellas (1962-)
Beyond Re-Animator '03
Faust: Love of the Damned '00

John Caper, Jr.
Equinox '71
He Lives: The Search for the Evil One '67

Claudio Capponi
The Fever '04
My House in Umbria '03
Jane Eyre '96

Al Capps
Stroker Ace '83
Cannonball Run '81

David Carbonara
Giuliani Time '05
The Guru '02
The Young Girl and the Monsoon '99

Gerard Carbonara (1886-1959)
Shadows of Tombstone '53
Too Late for Tears '49
Far Frontier '48
Son of God's Country '48
Sioux City Sue '46
The Kansan '43
The Shepherd of the Hills '41
Dr. Cyclops '40

Sam Cardon
Little Secrets '02
Brigham City '01

Jeff Cardoni
American Pie Presents: Beta House '07
Firehouse Dog '07
American Pie Presents: The Naked Mile '06
Bonneville '06
Just Friends '05
Love for Rent '05
April's Shower '03

Philip Carli
Evangeline '29
Peter Pan '24

Robert Carli
A Killing Spring '02
Verdict in Blood '02
Road Rage '01

Hoagy Carmichael (1899-1981)
Hoppity Goes to Town '41
College Swing '38

Ralph Carmichael
The 4D Man '59
The Blob '58

John Carpenter (1948-)
John Carpenter's Ghosts of Mars '01
Halloween: H20 '98
John Carpenter's Vampires '97
Escape from L.A. '96
In the Mouth of Madness '95
Village of the Damned '95
Body Bags '93
Halloween 5: The Revenge of Michael Myers '89
Halloween 4: The Return of Michael Myers '88
They Live '88
Prince of Darkness '87
Big Trouble in Little China '86
Christine '84
Halloween 3: Season of the Witch '82
Escape from New York '81
Halloween 2: The Nightmare Isn't Over! '81
The Fog '78
Halloween '78
Assault on Precinct 13 '76
Dark Star '74

Simon Carpentier
Nightwaves '03
Time at the Top '99

Paul Carr (1934-)
Lady Audley's Secret '00
Janice Beard '99

Nicholas Carras (1922-2006)
10 Violent Women '79
The Doll Squad '73
Girl in Gold Boots '69
High School Caesar '60
Missile to the Moon '59
Frankenstein's Daughter '58
The Female Jungle '56

Gustavo Cesar Carrion
Arizona '86
Remolino de Pasiones '68
Yanco '64
The Brainiac '61

Gaylord Carter (1905-2000)
Docks of New York '28
Last Command '28
The Wedding March '28
Running Wild '27
Old Ironsides '26
The Ten Commandments '23
Shadows '22
Spiders '18

Kristopher Carter
The Modern Adventures of Tom Sawyer '98
Boys Will Be Boys '97

Ron Carter (1937-)
The Guys '02
Blind Faith '98

Tristram Cary (1925-)
Blood from the Mummy's Tomb '71
The Prince and the Pauper '62
Time Without Pity '57
The Ladykillers '55

Carles Cases (1958-)
Darkness '02
Food of Love '02
Beloved/Friend '99
Caresses '97

Patrick Cassidy (1956-)
The Front Line '06
Salem's Lot '04
Broken Harvest '94

Teddy Castellucci
Are We Done Yet? '07
Just My Luck '06
Little Man '06
My Super Ex-Girlfriend '06
The Longest Yard '05
Rebound '05
50 First Dates '04
White Chicks '04
Anger Management '03
My Boss's Daughter '03
Adam Sandler's 8 Crazy Nights '02
Mr. Deeds '02
The Animal '01
Good Advice '01
Repli-Kate '01
Little Nicky '00
Big Daddy '99
Deuce Bigalow: Male Gigolo '99
The Wedding Singer '97

Mario Castelnuovo-Tedesco (1895-1968)
The Loves of Carmen '48
And Then There Were None '45

William Allen Castleman (1922-2006)
The Swinging Cheerleaders '74

Matthieu Chabrol (1956-)
Comedy of Power '06
The Bridesmaid '04
Merci pour le Chocolat '00
The Swindle '97
La Ceremonie '95
L'Enfer '93
Betty '92
Madame Bovary '91
The Story of Women '88
The Cry of the Owl '87

Frankie Chan
Chungking Express '95
Fallen Angels '95

Kwong Wing Chan (1967-)
Three ... Extremes '04
Vampire Effect '03

Gary Chang (1953-)
The Diary of Ellen Rimbauer '03
Path to War '02
Sniper 2 '02
Stephen King's Rose Red '02
Range of Motion '00
Locked in Silence '99
Stephen King's The Storm of the Century '99
A Bright Shining Lie '98
A Soldier's Sweetheart '98
Double Team '97
George Wallace '97
The Island of Dr. Moreau '96
The Substitute '96
Twilight Man '96
Andersonville '95
The Avenging Angel '95
Against the Wall '94
The Burning Season '94
Children of Fury '94
Fatherland '94
The Last Ride '94
The Walking Dead '94
The Last Hit '93
The Nightman '93
Sniper '92
Under Siege '92
Murder in New Hampshire: The Pamela Smart Story '91
The Perfect Weapon '91
Death Warrant '90
Miami Blues '90
A Shock to the System '90
The House of Usher '88
Sticky Fingers '88
Firewalker '86
52 Pick-Up '86
3:15—The Moment of Truth '86

Charlie Chaplin (1889-1977)
A Countess from Hong Kong '67
A King in New York '57
Limelight '52
Monsieur Verdoux '47
Modern Times '36
City Lights '31
The Gold Rush '25
The Circus '19

John Charles (1940-)
The Sound and the Silence '93
A Soldier's Tale '91
Iris '89
The Quiet Earth '85
Utu '83

Peter Chase
Happenstance '00
Portraits Chinois '96
Mina Tannenbaum '93

Tom Chase (1965-)
Little Nemo: Adventures in Slumberland '92
Syngenor '90
And God Created Woman '88
976-EVIL '88
Catch the Heat '87
Creature '85

Jay Chattaway (1946-)
The Ambulance '90
Red Scorpion '89
Maniac Cop '88
Invasion U.S.A. '85
Missing in Action '84
Vigilante '83
Walking the Edge '83
Maniac '80

Steven Chesne (1960-)
The Trip '02
No Turning Back '01

Paul Chihara (1938-)
Romance & Cigarettes '05
Noble House '88
The Bad Seed '85
Impulse '84
Survivors '83
The Children of An Lac '80
The Bad News Bears Go to Japan '78
I Never Promised You a Rose Garden '77
Death Race 2000 '75

Edmund Choi
The Dish '00
Down to You '00
Wide Awake '97

Jason Christopherson
The Crow: Wicked Prayer '05
Epoch: Evolution '03

David Chudnow (1901-2002)
The Jackie Robinson Story '50
Hopalong Cassidy: Dangerous Venture '48
In Old New Mexico '45
The Iron Crown '41

Danny Chung
Happy Together '96
Organized Crime & Triad Bureau '93

Frank Churchill (1901-42)
Bambi '42
Dumbo '41
Snow White and the Seven Dwarfs '37

Alessandro Cicognini (1905-95)
Summertime '55
Umberto D '55
Too Bad She's Bad '54
The Bicycle Thief '48

Stelvio Cipriani (1937-)
Voices from Beyond '90
City of the Walking Dead '80
The Bloodstained Shadow '78
Thundersquad '85
Fearless '77
Tentacles '77
The Boss Is Served '76
Mt'Lady's Court '73
What the Peeper Saw '72
The Frightened Woman '71
Twitch of the Death Nerve '71

Chuck Cirino
Fire Serpent '07
Inner Sanctum 2 '94
Sorceress '94
Body Chemistry 3: Point of Seduction '93
Sorority House Massacre 2: Nighty Nightmare '92
Bad Girls from Mars '90
Beverly Hills Vamp '88
Not of This Earth '88
Big Bad Mama 2 '87
Deathstalker 2: Duel of the Titans '87
Chopping Mall '86

Eric Clapton (1945-)
The Story of Us '99
Lethal Weapon 4 '98
Nil by Mouth '96
The Van '95
Lethal Weapon 3 '92
Rush '91
Communion '89
Lethal Weapon 2 '89
Homeboy '88
Lethal Weapon '87
Edge of Darkness '86
The Hit '85
Wonderwall: The Movie '69

Nigel Clarke
The Thief Lord '06
The Little Vampire '00

Stanley Clarke (1951-)
First Sunday '08
Roll Bounce '05
The Transporter '02
Undercover Brother '02
Undisputed '02
The Red Sneakers '01
The Loretta Claiborne Story '00
Romeo Must Die '00
The Best Man '99
Rocky Marciano '99
Down in the Delta '98
B.A.P.'s '97
The Cherokee Kid '96
Dangerous Ground '96
Eddie '96
The Road to Galveston '96
Sprung '96
Panther '95
Poetic Justice '93
Watch It '93
What's Love Got to Do with It? '93
Final Shot: The Hank Gather's Story '92
Passenger 57 '92
Book of Love '91
Boyz N the Hood '91
Cool As Ice '91
The Five Heartbeats '91

Alf Clausen (1941-)
Half-Baked '97
Number One with a Bullet '87

Siobhan Cleary
Dangerous Curves '99
Spacejacked '98

Nels Cline
Welcome Says the Angel '01
Hard Drive '94

George S. Clinton (1947-)
Harold & Kumar Escape from Guantanamo Bay '08
The Love Guru '08
Bury My Heart at Wounded Knee '07
Code Name: The Cleaner '07
Big Momma's House 2 '06
Deck the Halls '06
The Santa Clause 3: The Escape Clause '06
The Big Bounce '04
Catch That Kid '04
A Dirty Shame '04
New York Minute '04
44 Minutes: The North Hollywood Shootout '03
Austin Powers in Goldmember '02
The Santa Clause 2 '02
Joe Somebody '01
3000 Miles to Graceland '01
Ready to Rumble '00
Red Shoe Diaries: Luscious Lola '00
The Astronaut's Wife '99
Austin Powers 2: The Spy Who Shagged Me '99
Lansky '99
Black Dog '98
Wild Things '98
Austin Powers: International Man of Mystery '97
Mortal Kombat 2: Annihilation '97
Trojan War '97
Beverly Hills Ninja '96
Beyond the Call '96
Business for Pleasure '96
The Last Days of Frankie the Fly '96
Red Shoe Diaries: Four on the Floor '96
Red Shoe Diaries: Strip Poker '95
Delta of Venus '95
Mortal Kombat 1: The Movie '95
The Viking Sagas '95
Amelia Earhart: The Final Flight '94
Brainscan '94
Mother's Boys '94
Hard Promises '92
Lake Consequence '92

Through the Eyes of a Killer '92
American Ninja 3: Blood Hunt '89
Got'am '88
The Jon of Africa '87
Platoon Leader '87
Wild Thing '87
Avenging Force '86
The Boys Next Door '85
Cheech and Chong: Still Smokin' '83

Rene Cloerec
The Red Inn '51
Devil in the Flesh '46

Charlie Clouser (1963-)
Dead Silence '07
Death Sentence '07
Resident Evil: Extinction '07
Saw 4 '07
Saw II '06
Deepwater '05
Saw II '05
Saw '04
Wes Craven Presents: They '02

Elia Cmiral (1957-)
Missionary Man '07
Pulse '06
The Reading Room '05
Wrong Turn '03
Somebody Is Waiting '96
Ronin '98
Stigmata '99
Apartment Zero '88

Robert Cobert (1924-)
Trilogy of Terror 2 '96
Nightmare at 43 Hillcrest '74
Scream of the Wolf '74
3 Ninjas: High Noon at Mega Mountain '97
The Norliss Tapes '73
The Night Strangler '72
The Night Stalker '77
Strange Case of Dr. Jekyll & Johnson '95
Mr. Hyde '68

John Coda
Monster Man '03
Race to Space '01
Love to Kill '97

Barry Coffing
Enemies of Laughter '00
Total Force '98
Love to Kill '97

Leonard Cohen (1934-)
Love, etc. '96

Michael Cohen (1977-)
McCabe & Mrs. Miller '71

Serge Colbert
Derailed '02
The Body '01
Spiders 2: Breeding Ground '01

Graeme Coleman
Father Goose '64
Better Than Chocolate '99
Breach of Trust '95
Bulletproof Heart '95
Malicious '95
Perfect Crime '97
Foolish '99
Soul Food '97

Jim Coleman
Acts of Worship '01

Lisa Coleman (1960-)
The Unbelievable Truth '90
Something New '06
Juwana Mann '02
The Third Wheel '02

Michel Colombier (1939-2004)
Swept Away '02
Werden of Red Rock '01
Innocents '00
Screwed '00
Prcs & Cons '99
The Thomas Crown Affair '99
New Jack City '91
Color of Justice '97
Meet Wally Sparks '97
Woo '97
Barb Wire '96
Foxfire '96
The Program '93
Deep Cover '92
Loverboy '89
Cut Cold '89
Who's Harry Crumb? '89
Fever '91
Diary of a Hitman '91

Phil Collins (1951-)
Tarzan '99
Brother Bear '03

Bill Conti (1942-)
Rocky Balboa '06
Coast to Coast '04
Avenging Angelo '02
Napoleon '95
Spy Hard '96
8 Seconds '94
The Next Karate Kid '94
The Scout '94
The Adventures of Huck Finn '93
Blood In ... Blood Out '93
By the Sword '93
Rookie of the Year '93
A Captive in the Land '91
Necessary Roughness '91
Year of the Gun '91
Backstreet Dreams '90
The Fourth War '90
Rocky V '90
The Bear '89
The Karate Kid: Part 3 '89
Lean on Me '89
Lock Up '89
Murderers Among Us: The Simon Wiesenthal Story '89
The Big Blue '88
Cohen and Tate '88
For Keeps '88
The Gold & Glory '88
A Night in the Life of Jimmy Reardon '88
Baby Boom '87
Broadcast News '87
Happy New Year '87
I Love N.Y. '87
Masters of the Universe '87
Prayer for the Dying '87
Big Trouble '86
The Boss' Wife '86
F/X '86
The Karate Kid: Part 2 '86
Nomads '86
North and South Book 2 '86
Beer '85
Gotcha! '85
North and South Book 1 '85
The Karate Kid '84
Mass Appeal '84
Unfaithfully Yours '84
Bad Boys '83
The Right Stuff '83
The Terry Fox Story '83
I, the Jury '82
Rocky 3 '82
Split Image '82
That Championship Season '82

Rick Conrad
Watchers 2 '90
Amityville 4: The Evil Escapes '89

David Connor
The Dark Dancer '95
The House on Todville Road '95

Michael Convertino (1953-)
Straight into Darkness '04
Liberty Stands Still '02
Dance with Me '98
Guarding Tess '94
Milk Money '94
The Santa Clause '94
Aspen Extreme '93
Bodies, Rest & Motion '93
A Home of Our Own '93
The Hidden '87
Mistress '87

Carmine Coppola (1911-91)
The Godfather, Part 3 '90
The Outsiders '83
Apocalypse Now '79
The Black Stallion '79
The Godfather, Part 2 '74
The People '71
Tonight for Sure '61
Napoleon '27

Normand Corbeil
The Contract '07
White Noise 2: The Light '07
Human Trafficking '05
Before the Fall '04
A Different Loyalty '04
Hitler: The Rise of Evil '03
The Statement '03
Extreme Ops '02
Seduced: Pretty When You Cry '01

Ry Cooder (1947-)
My Blueberry Nights '07
Primary Colors '98
The End of Violence '97
Last Man Standing '96
Geronimo: An American Legend '93
Johnny Handsome '89
Trespass '92
Crossroads '86
Alamo Bay '85
Brewster's Millions '85
Streets o' Fire '84
Paris, Texas '83
The Border '82
Southern Comfort '81
The Long Riders '80

Stewart Copeland (1952-)
I Am David '04
Deuces Wild '02
On the Line '01
Boys and Girls '00
Skipped Parts '00
Made Men '99
She's All That '99
Simpatico '99
Legalese '98
Pecker '98
Very Bad Things '98
West Beirut '98
Four Days in September '97
Good Burger '97
Little Boy Blue '97
Welcome to Woop Woop '97

Aaron Copland (1900-90)
The Heiress '49
The Red Pony '49
The North Star '43
Our Town '40
Of Mice and Men '39

Don Costa (1925-83)
She's Having a Baby '88
Talk Radio '88
Wall Street '87
Out of Bounds '86

Jerome Coullet
He Loves Me ... He Loves Me Not '02
Deep in the Woods '00

Michael Convertino (1953-)
Snow White: The Fairest of Them All '02
Bad Love '95
Corrina, Corrina '94
Pie in the Sky '95
Inside Monkey Zetterland '93

Rick Cox
Bram Stoker's The Mummy '97

Noel Coward (1899-1973)
In Which We Serve '43

Michael Curb (1944-)
The Big Bounce '69
Thunder Alley '67
The Wild Angels '66

Carlo Crivelli (1953-)
The Spectator '04
Marie Baie des Anges '97
Elective Affinities '97
Devil in the Flesh '87

John Corigliano (1938-)
The Red Violin '98
Altered States '80
Revolution #9 '01
Homicide '91
Hand Gun '93

Billy Corgan
When a Man Falls in the Forest '07

Lanny Cordola
Now You Know '02
Fish in a Barrel '01

Frank Cordell (1918-80)
God Told Me To '76
Ring of Bright Water '69
Khartoum '66

Stephen Cullo
Proximity '00
Belly '98

Xavier Cugat (1900-90)
Bathing Beauty '44
The White Zombie '32

Michael Csanyi-Wills
Me Not '02

Douglas J. Cuomo (1958-)
Crazy Love '07

Vladimir Cosma (1940-)
The Closet '00
The Dinner Game '98
The Favor, the Watch, & the Very Big Fish '92
'Very Big Fish '92
My Father's Glory '91

Dale Cornelius
Strange Bedfellows '04
Till Human Voices Wake Us '02

Elvis Costello (1954-)
The Courier '88

Bruno Coulais (1954-)
Himalaya '99
Microcosmos '96
The Crimson Rivers '01
Winged Migration '01
The Count of Monte Cristo '02

Jerome Coullet
Oliver Twist '00

Hoyt Curtin (1922-)
KISS Meets the Phantom of the Park '78
Mesa of Lost Women '52

Michel Cusson (1957-)
The Rocket '05

Michael Covertino (1953-)
Gardens of Stone '97

Rene Cloerec
'79

Charlie Clouser
Bones '01
The Rat's '01

Elia Cmiral
Battlefield Earth '00

Joseph Conlan
Mortuary '05
Moscuitoman '05
Finding Home '03
Miracle Dogs '03

Betty Comden (1915-2005)
On the Town '91
It's Always Fair Weather '55

Alberto Colombo (1889-1954)
Go for Broke! '51
Dangerous Holiday '37

Eric Colvin
Morte Walsh '03
Bar! '02
Crossfire Trail '01
Life-Size '00
Model Behavor '00

Cy Coleman (1929-2004)
Family Business '89
Power '86
Garbo Talks '84

Lionel Cole
Asunder '99
Spirit Lost '96
Devonsville Terror '83

Ray Colcord
Wish upon a Star '96
Operation: Delta Force 3: Clear Target '98
Operation Delta Force: Deadly Reckoning '97

Along for the Ride '00
On the Border '98

Serge Colbert
Colossus: The Forbin Project '70
Les Assassins de L'Ordre '71

John Coda
Gang of Roses '03
Spider's Web '01

Leonard Cohen
The Terror Within '88
The Nest '88
The Drifter '86

Rico Conrad
Napoleon '95
Bushwhacked '95
Dorothy Day Story '96

Composer Index   1879

Cusson

My First Wedding '04
Cruel and Unusual '01

Miriam Cutler
Stolen Childhoods '05
Lost in La Mancha '03
Bikini Med School '98
Bikini House Calls '96
Illegal Affairs '96
Witchcraft 7: Judgement Hour '95
Body Parts '94
Night Fire '94
Beyond Fear '93
Pushed to the Limit '92
Witchcraft 2: The Temptress '90

Richard Cuvillier
Humanity '99
The Life of Jesus '96

Burkhard Dallwitz (1959-)
Paperback Hero '99
The Truman Show '98
Zone 39 '96

Roger Daltrey (1945-)
Buddy's Song '91
The Kids Are Alright '79

Ikuma Dan (1924-2001)
Attack Squadron '63
I Bombed Pearl Harbor '60
Samurai 3: Duel at Ganryu Island '56
Samurai 1: Musashi Miyamoto '55
Samurai 2: Duel at Ichijoji Temple '55

John D'Andrea
Boiling Point '93
Beyond the Law '92
Child's Play 3 '91
Swimsuit '89
Body Slam '87
Savage Streets '83
Grambling's White Tiger '81

Oswald D'Andrea
Capitaine Conan '96
Every Other Weekend '91

John Dankworth (1927-)
Gangster No. 1 '00
10 Rillington Place '71
Accident '67
Fathom '67
Modesty Blaise '66
Morgan: A Suitable Case for Treatment '66
Darling '65
The Servant '63
Saturday Night and Sunday Morning '61

Jeff Danna (1964-)
Chicago 10 '07
Fracture '07
Silent Hill '06
Tideland '05
Resident Evil: Apocalypse '04
The Gospel of John '03
The Kid Stays in the Picture '02
Green Dragon '01
The Grey Zone '01
O '01
Baby '00
Boondock Saints '99
New Blood '99
Uncorked '98
The Big Slice '90

Mychael Danna (1958-)
Breach '07
Fracture '07
Surf's Up '07
Aurora Borealis '06
Little Miss Sunshine '06
Lonely Hearts '06
The Nativity Story '06
Capote '05
Tideland '05
Water '05
Where the Truth Lies '05
Being Julia '04
Vanity Fair '04
Shattered Glass '03
The Snow Walker '03
Antwone Fisher '02
Ararat '02
Green Dragon '01
Hearts in Atlantis '01
Monsoon Wedding '01
Bounce '00
Felicia's Journey '99
Girl, Interrupted '99
Ride with the Devil '99
The Confession '98
8mm '98
Behind the Lines '97
The Ice Storm '97
Kama Sutra: A Tale of Love '96
Lilies '96
The Sweet Hereafter '96
Exotica '94
Still Life '92
The Adjuster '91
The Big Slice '90
Erik '90
Speaking Parts '89
Termini Station '89
Family Viewing '87

Carl Dante (1950-)
Cypress Edge '99
The Creeps '97
Cannibal Women in the Avocado Jungle of Death '89
Slave Girls from Beyond Infinity '87

Mason Daring (1949-)
Honeydripper '07
Silver City '04
Casa de los Babys '03
Sunshine State '02
Say It Isn't So '01
Where the Heart Is '00
Limbo '99
Music of the Heart '99
A Walk on the Moon '99
The Opposite of Sex '98
Cold Around the Heart '97
Evidence of Blood '97
The Ripper '97
Hidden in America '96
Prefontaine '96
Letter to My Killer '95
Lone Star '95
Getting Out '94
The Old Curiosity Shop '94
The Secret of Roan Inish '94
Fathers and Sons '92
Passion Fish '92
City of Hope '91
Wild Hearts Can't Be Broken '91
The Laserman '90
Little Vegas '90
Off and Running '90
Day One '89
Eight Men Out '88
Matewan '87
Osa '85

Mohammad Reza Darvishi (1955-)
Osama '03
Kandahar '01

Peter Dasent
Heavenly Creatures '94
Dead Alive '93
Meet the Feebles '89

Shaun Davey (1948-)
Ella Enchanted '04
The Tailor of Panama '00
Waking Ned Devine '98
Kings in Grass Castles '97
Twelfth Night '96

Martin Davich
Mad Money '08
Jackie, Ethel, Joan: The Kennedy Women '01
La Cucaracha '99

Hal David (1921-)
What's New Pussycat? '65
The Blob '58
The Sad Sack '57

Howard J. Davidson
Romance and Rejection '96
Death Games '80

Iva Davies
The Incredible Journey of Mary Bryant '05
Master and Commander: The Far Side of the World '03

Victor Davies (1939-)
For the Moment '94
The Last Winter '89

Carl Davis (1936-)
The Great Gatsby '01
Topsy Turvy '99
A Dance to the Music of Time '97
Pride and Prejudice '95
The Return of the Native '94
Widow's Peak '94
The Trial '93
Catherine Cookson's The Black Velvet Gown '92
Frankenstein Unbound '90
The Rainbow '89
Scandal '89
Hotel du Lac '86
Murrow '86
Forbidden Passion: The Oscar Wilde Movie '85
King David '85
Silas Marner '85
Champions '84
The Far Pavilions '84
Sakharov '84
Weather in the Streets '84
Praying Mantis '83
The French Lieutenant's Woman '81
Man Friday '75
Catholics '73
Rentadick '72
I, Monster '71
Naughty Knights '71
The Only Way '70
Napoleon '27
The Eagle '25
The Thief of Baghdad '24

Don Davis (1957-)
The Marine '06
The Matrix Reloaded '03
The Matrix Revolutions '03
Ballistic: Ecks vs. Sever '02
Murder in Greenwich '02
Behind Enemy Lines '01
Jurassic Park 3 '01
The Unsaid '01
Valentine '01
Antitrust '00
House on Haunted Hill '99
In the Company of Spies '99
The Matrix '99
Universal Soldier: The Return '99
Route 9 '98
The Lesser Evil '97
Not in This Town '97
Robin Cook's Invasion '97
Warriors of Virtue '97
Weapons of Mass Distraction '97
The Beast '96
Bound '96
In the Lake of the Woods '96
The Perfect Daughter '96

Miles Davis (1926-91)
Dingo '90
Siesta '87
Street Smart '87
Frantic '58
Torso '73
Sicilian Connection '72
Sting of the West '72

Guido de Angelis (1944-)
Faith '90
Body Beat '88
Devilfish '84
A Blade in the Dark '83
Ironmaster '82
Mountain of the Cannibal God '79
Shark Hunter '79
Inhibition '76
Chino '75
The Legend of Sea Wolf '75
Spaghetti Western '74
Street Law '74
Zorro '74
Torso '73
Sicilian Connection '72
Sting of the West '72

Maurizio de Angelis (1947-)
Faith '90
Body Beat '88
Devilfish '84
A Blade in the Dark '83
Ironmaster '82
Mountain of the Cannibal God '79
Shark Hunter '79
Inhibition '76
Chino '75
The Legend of Sea Wolf '75
Spaghetti Western '74
Street Law '74
Zorro '74
Torso '73
Sicilian Connection '72
Sting of the West '72

Lex de Azevedo
The Swan Princess 2: Escape from Castle Mountain '97
The Swan Princess '94
Baker's Hawk '76
Where the Red Fern Grows '74

Marcello De Francisci
The Last Sentinel '07
Pit Fighter '05

Luchi De Jesus (1923-84)
Friday Foster '75
Bad Charleston Charlie '73
Detroit 9000 '73
Slaughter '72

Christopher De Marco
The Toxic Avenger, Part 3: The Last Temptation of Toxie '89
Troma's War '88

Francesco De Masi (1930-2005)
Formula for a Murder '85
Lone Wolf McQuade '83
New York Ripper '82
The Arena '73
Challenge of McKenna '70
Fistful of Lead '70
Sartana's here... Trade Your Pistol for a Coffin '70
Island of Lost Girls '68
Rattler Kid '68
Taste of Death '68
An Angel for Satan '66
The Triumph of Hercules '66
The Lion of Thebes '64
Magnificent Adventurer '63
Sort of Hercules in the Land of Darkness '63
Colossus of the Arena '62

Jessica de Rooij
In the Name of the King: A Dungeon Siege Tale '08
BloodRayne 2: Deliverance '07

Francois de Roubaix (1939-)
La Scoumoune '72
Daughters of Darkness '71
Honor Among Thieves '68
The Last Adventure '67
Le Samourai '67

Aldo De Scalzi (1957-)
Harem '99

Manuel De Sica (1949-)
Cemetery Man '95
Men Men Men '95
The Icicle Thief '89
Bye Bye Baby '88
Hostages '80
The Garden of the Finzi-Continis '71
Twist '57

De Wolfe
Jabberwocky '77
Monty Python and the Holy Grail '75

John Debney (1957-)
Meet Dave '08
Swing Vote '08
Evan Almighty '07
Georgia Rule '07
The Ant Bully '06
Barnyard '06
Everyone's Hero '06
Idlewild '06
Keeping Up with the Steins '06
The Adventures of Sharkboy and Lavagirl in 3-D '05
Cheaper by the Dozen 2 '05
Chicken Little '05
Dreamer: Inspired by a True Story '05
The Pacifier '05
Sin City '05
Zathura '05
Christmas With the Kranks '04
The Passion of the Christ '04
The Princess Diaries 2: Royal Engagement '04
Raising Helen '04
Welcome to Mooseport '04
The Whole Ten Yards '04
Bruce Almighty '03
Elf '03
Dragonfly '02
The Hot Chick '02
The Scorpion King '02
Snow Dogs '02
Spy Kids 2: The Island of Lost Dreams '02
The Tuxedo '02
Cats & Dogs '01
Heartbreakers '01
Jimmy Neutron: Boy Genius '01
The Princess Diaries '01
See Spot Run '01
Spy Kids '01
The Emperor's New Groove '00
Running Mates '00
Dick '99
End of Days '99
Inspector Gadget '99
Komodo '99
Lost and Found '99
Relative Values '99
I'll Be Home for Christmas '98
My Favorite Martian '98
Paulie '98
I Know What You Did Last Summer '97
Liar Liar '97
Carpool '96
Doctor Who '96
Getting Away With Murder '96
The Lazarus Man '96
The Relic '96
Chameleon '95
Cutthroat Island '95
In Pursuit of Honor '95
Sudden Death '95
Houseguest '94
Little Giants '94
White Fang 2: The Myth of the White Wolf '94
Gunmen '93
Hocus Pocus '93
Praying Mantis '93
Jetsons: The Movie '90
The Further Adventures of Tennessee Buck '88
Seven Hours to Judgment '88
The Wild Pair '87

Marc David Decker (1951-)
Bikini Island '91
The Dark Backward '91
The Invisible Maniac '90
Tale of Two Sisters '89

Christopher Dedrick
Waking Up Wally '05
The Saddest Music in the World '03
Torso '01
Walter and Henry '01
The Courage to Love '00
Junior's Groove '97
Race to Freedom: The Story of the Underground Railroad '94

Georges Delerue (1925-92)
Rich in Love '93
Man Trouble '92
American Friends '91
Black Robe '91
Curly Sue '91
Mister Johnson '91
Joe Versus the Volcano '90
A Show of Force '90
Cadence '89
Steel Magnolias '89
To Kill a Priest '89
Beaches '88
Biloxi Blues '88
Heartbreak Hotel '88
Her Alibi '88
The House on Carroll Street '88
Memories of Me '88
A Summer Story '88
Twins '88
Code Name: Dancer '87
Escape from Sobibor '87
The Lonely Passion of Judith Hearne '87
Maid to Order '87
A Man in Love '87
The Pick-Up Artist '87
Queenie '87
Conseil de Famille '86
Crimes of the Heart '86
Platoon '86
Salvador '86
Sword of Gideon '86
Women of Valor '86
Agnes of God '85
Amos '85
Arch of Triumph '85
The Execution '85
Maxie '85
A Time to Live '85
Aurora '84
Mesmerized '84
Silence of the Heart '84
The Black Stallion Returns '83
Confidentially Yours '83
Exposed '83
La Passante '83
Man, Woman & Child '83
One Deadly Summer '83
Silkwood '83
The Escape Artist '82
La Vie Continue '82
A Little Sex '82
Partners '82
Rich and Famous '81
True Confessions '81
The Woman Next Door '81
The Last Metro '80
Richard's Things '80
An Almost Perfect Affair '79
A Little Romance '79
Dear Detective '78
Get Out Your Handkerchiefs '78
Le Cavaleur '78
Love on the Run '78
Dear Detective '77
Julia '77
The Slap '76
Dan Candy's Law '73
Day for Night '73
The Day of the Dolphin '73
The Day of the Jackal '73
Two English Girls '72
The Conformist '71
The Horsemen '70
Women in Love '70
Anne of the Thousand Days '69
The Brain '69
The Two of Us '68
The King of Hearts '66
A Man for All Seasons '66
Viva Maria! '65
Contempt '64
The Pumpkin Eater '64
The Soft Skin '64
That Man from Rio '64
Muriel '63
Cartouche '62
Jules and Jim '62
Shoot the Piano Player '62
Time Out for Love '61
Love and the Frenchwoman '60

Love Play '60
Hiroshima, Mon Amour '59

Joe Delia
Carlito's Way: Rise to Power '05
Bought and Sold '03
The Tao of Steve '00
Fever '99
No Looking Back '98
The Blackout '97
The Substitute 2: School's Out '97
Freeway '88
China Girl '87
Ms. 45 '81
Driller Killer '79

Eric Demarsen (1938-)
Le Cercle Rouge '70
Army of Shadows '69

Gary DeMichele (1942-)
Off the Black '06
The Secret Lives of Dentists '02
'02

Thomas DeRenzo (1956-)
Bossa Nova '99
The Onion Field '79

Eumir Deodato (1942-)
Control Room '04

Claude Desjardins
Full Disclosure '00
Captains Courageous '95

Alexandre Desplat (1961-)
Vera Drake '04
The Golden Compass '07
Lust, Caution '07
Syriana '05
The Upside of Anger '05
Birth '04
Girl with a Pearl Earring '03
Firewall '06
Lies & Alibis '06
The Queen '06
The Valet '06
Casanova '05
Hostage '05
The Painted Veil '06
The Luzhin Defence '00
Love, etc. '96
Innocent Lies '95
A Self-Made Hero '96

Andrew Dickson (1945-)
Vera Drake '04
All or Nothing '02
Someone Else's America '96
Secrets and Lies '95
Naked '93
Meantime '81

Pierre Desrochers
Maelstrom '00
La Deroute '98

Robert Diggs See The RZA

Loek Dikker (1944-)
Rosenstrasse '03
The Babysitter '95
Tre Escape '95
Bocy Parts '91
Slow Burn '86
The 4th Man '79
Pascali's Island '88

Vince DiCola
Rocky 4 '85
Transformers: The Movie '86
Sci-Fighter '04

Antonio Diaz Conde
Night of the Bloody Apes '68
Doctor of Doom '62
The Robot vs. the Aztec Mummy '59
Senora Tentacion '49

Neil Diamond (1941-)
The Jazz Singer '80
Jonathan Livingston Seagull '73

Joel Diamond
Anima '98
The Believer '01

Ron Di Iulio
Mountaintop Motel Massacre '86

Paul Di Franco
Body Chemistry 4: Full Exposure '95
House on Haunted Hill '58
The Tingler '59
13 Ghosts '60
Mr. Sardonicus '61

Von Dexter (1934-)
Exorcist 3: Legion '90
Xanadu '80
Night of the Creeps '86

Barry DeVorzon (1934-)
The Warriors '79
Hard Times '75
Dillinger '73

Frank DeVol (1911-99)
The Longest Yard '74
Emperor of the North Pole '73
Ulzana's Raid '72
Caprice '67
Guess Who's Coming to Dinner '67
The Dirty Dozen '67
Cat Ballou '65
Good Neighbor Sam '64

Pino Donaggio (1941-)
Crazy Little Thing '02
The Doe Boy '01

Francois Dompierre (1943-)
Stardom '00
It's My Turn, Laura Cadieux '98

Thomas Dolby (1958-)
Gothic '87
Feve: Pitch '85

Klaus Doldinger (1936-)
Palmetto '98
Me and Him '89
Fever '88
The NeverEnding Story '84
Das Boot '81

Adolph Deutsch (1897-1980)
Deception '08
Iron Man '08
Mr. Brooks '07
Ask the Dust '06
Open Season '06
Black: Trinity '04

Robert Emmett Dolan (1906-72)
King Kong vs. Godzilla '63
The Three Faces of Eve '57
The Great Gatsby '49
My Favorite Brunette '47
The Bells of St. Mary's '45
Murder, He Says '45
The Major and the Minor '42
Birth of the Blues '41

James Dooley (1976-)
Bachelor Party 2: The Last Temptation '08
Daddy Day Camp '07
When a Stranger Calls '06

Steve Dorff (1949-)
The Junction Boys '02
Dudley Do-Right '99
Blast from the Past '98
Dancer, Texas—Pop. 81 '98
Coyote Summer '96
Breaking Free '95
The Undercover Kid '95
Murder So Sweet '93
Pure Country '92
Kiss Shot '89
Pink Cadillac '89

John Du Prez (1946-)
Tattoo, a Love Story '02
Fascination '04
Mr. Toad's Wild Ride '96
Teenage Mutant Ninja Turtles 3 '93
Mystery Date '91
Bullseye! '90
Teenage Mutant Ninja Turtles II '91
'88

Marc Donahue (1953-2002)
After Midnight '83
Opposing Force '87
Murphy's Law '86
Lies '83

Donovan (1946-)
84 Charlie MoPic '89
Brother Sun, Sister Moon '73

George Dreyfus (1928-)
The Fringe Dwellers '86
Tender Mercies '83

Ludek Drizhal (1966-)
Voodoo Moon '05

Pete Droge
Slayer '06

Robert Jackson Drasnin (1914-84)
Murder Once Removed '71
The Tattered Web '71
They Call it Murder '71
Ride in the Whirlwind '66

Carmen Dragon (1914-84)
Invasion of the Body Snatchers '56
The Strange Woman '46
Mr. Winkle Goes to War '44
Henry V '89

Elizabeth Drake
Japanese Story '03
Road to Nhill '97

Robert Duncan
Fallen '97

Adam Dorn
The Defiant Ones '58

Ivan Dorochuk
Universal Soldier 2: Brothers in Arms '98

Patrick Doyle (1953-)
As You Like It '06
Eragon '06
Nanny McPhee '06
Harry Potter and the Goblet of Fire '05
Secondhand Lions '03
Calendar Girls '03
Quest for Camelot '98
Great Expectations '97
Bridget Jones's Diary '01
Donnie Brasco '96
Hamlet '96
Mrs. Winterbourne '96
A Little Princess '95
Sense and Sensibility '95
Exit to Eden '94
Mary Shelley's Frankenstein '94
Carlito's Way '93
Much Ado about Nothing '93
Needful Things '93
Indochine '92
Into the West '92
Dead Again '91
Shipwrecked '90

Joseph Dubin
Stage Door Canteen '43
42nd Street '33

Al Dubin (1891-1945)
Monty Python's The Meaning of Life '83
The Jolson Story '46
Harriet Craig '50
From Here to Eternity '53
Salome '53
Picnic '55
Pal Joey '57

Jack Curtis Dubowsky
Rock Haven '07

Anne Dudley (1956-)
Under One Roof '02
The Gathering '02
Lucky Break '01
Monkeybone '01
The Miracle Maker: The Story of Jesus '00
The 10th Kingdom '00
Pushing Tin '99
American History X '98
The Full Monty '96
The Crying Game '92
The Miracle '91

Antoine Duhamel (1925-)
The Girl of Your Dreams '99
Ridicule '96
Belle Epoque '92
Daddy Nostalgia '90
Twisted Obsession '90
3ed and Board '70
Weekend '67
Pierrot le Fou '65
Stolen Kisses '68
Mississippi Mermaid '69

George Duke (1946-)
Never Die Alone '04
Good Fences '03

Tan Dun (1957-)
Hero '03
Crouching Tiger, Hidden Dragon '00

George Duning (1908-2000)
Goliath Awaits '81
The Man with Bogart's Face '30
Abduction of St. Anne '75
Arnold '73
Honor Thy Father '73
Pat Garrett & Billy the Kid '73
Terror in the Wax Museum '73
Yuma '70
Any Wednesday '66
Critic's Choice '63
That Touch of Mink '62
The Devil at 4 O'Clock '61
All the Young Men '60
The Last Angry Man '59
1001 Arabian Nights '59

Kyle Eastwood (1968-)
Rails & Ties '07
Letters from Iwo Jima '06
Flags of Our Fathers '06
Million Dollar Baby '04
Mystic River '03

Clint Eastwood (1930-)
Grace is Gone '07

David Dundas (1945-)
Withnail and I '87

George Duning (1908-2000)
Advertising '89

Randy Edelman (1947-)
27 Dresses '08
Balls of Fury '07
Underdog '07
The Last Time '06
Son of the Mask '05
Connie and Carla '04
A Season on the Brink '02
National Security '03
Shanghai Knights '03
Gods and Generals '03
Surviving Christmas '04
Osmosis Jones '01
Head Over Heels '01
Passion of Mind '00
Shanghai Noon '00

Brian Easdale (1909-95)
Peeping Tom '60
The Red Shoes '48
Black Narcissus '47

Bob Dylan (1941-)
Masked and Anonymous '03
High Stakes '48
Hi-Jacked '50

Kiril Dzajkovski
The Great Water '04
Dust '01

Arie Dzierlatka
Mon Oncle d'Amerique '80
Messidor '77
Chloe in the Afternoon '72

Paul Dunlap (1919-)
Naked Kiss '64
Shock Corridor '63
Hercules '61
The Three Stooges Meet Hercules '61
The Angry Red Planet '59
The Rebel Set '59
Blood of Dracula '57
The Steel Helmet '51
The Last Continent '51
I Was a Teenage Werewolf '57
The Finger Man '55
Shack Out on 101 '55
Guns Don't Argue '57
Crime of Passion '57
Down to Earth '47
Man from Colorado '49
Lust for Gold '49
Jolson Sings Again '49
Down to Earth '49
Her Husband's Affairs '47
'49
Three to the Show '55
Tight Spot '55
Queen Bee '55
Picnic '55
The Man from Laramie '55
The Eddy Duchin Story '56
3:10 to Yuma '57

Bell, Book and Candle '58
Cowboy '58
Houseboat '58
Pajamas '84
Monty Python's The Bullshot '83

Manhunt for Claude Dallas '86
A Private Function '84
Oxford Blues '84
She'll Be Wearing Pink Pajamas '84
Ruster's Rhapsody '85
Cannonball Run 2 '84
Stick '85
Swiss Conspiracy '77
Christa Klages '78
The Second Awakening of Night '78
What Ever Happened to Baby Jane? '62
Under the Yum-Yum Tree '63

Black and White As Day and Night '78
The Quick and the Dead '87
Convicted '86
The Never-Ending Story '84
A Father's Revenge '88
Me and Him '89
Gothic '87
Temptation '08

Back to the Beach '87
Personal Services '87
Love with a Perfect Stranger '86
Once Bitten '85
My Best Friend is a Vampire '88
A Fish Called Wanda '88
A Chorus of Disapproval '89
UHF '89
Turtles: The Movie '90

Edelman [Randy Edelman]
Daylight '96
Diabolique '96
Down Periscope '96
Dragonheart '96
The Quest '96
The Big Green '95
Citizen X '95
While You Were Sleeping '95
Angels in the Outfield '94
Billy Madison '94
Greedy '94
The Mask '94
Pontiac Moon '94
Beethoven's 2nd '93
Dragon: The Bruce Lee Story '93
Gettysburg '93
Beethoven '92
The Distinguished Gentleman '92
My Cousin Vinny '92
Drop Dead Fred '91
V.I. Warshawski '91
Shout '91
Come See the Paradise '90
Kindergarten Cop '90
Quick Change '90
Crazy People '90
Strike It Rich '90
Ghostbusters 2 '89
Troop Beverly Hills '89
Animal Behavior '89
Dead Man Out '89
To Die For '89
Triumph of the Spirit '89
Feds '88
Twins '88
Scandal Sheet '85
When Your Lover Leaves '83
Red, White & Busted '75
Executive Action '73
Snatched '72

Roger Edens (1905-70)
Take Me Out to the Ball Game '49
Good News '47
Till the Clouds Roll By '46
Go West '40

Greg Edmonson
Lucktown '00
Blue Ridge Fall '99
Undercover Angel '99
Frog and Wombat '98
Last Lives '98
Turn of the Blade '97

Stephen (Steve) Edwards
Feast '06
Undisputed II: Last Man Standing '06
The Upside of Anger '05
Audrey's Rain '03
Hellraiser: Hellseeker '02
No Sleep 'til Madison '02
Hard Cash '01
U.S. Seals 2 '01
Cowboys and Angels '00
Luck of the Draw '00
75 Degrees '00
The Substitute 4: Failure is Not an Option '00
Bridge of Dragons '99
K-911 '99
The Patriot '99
Cold Harvest '98
High Voltage '98
T.N.T. '98
Bloodsport 3 '97
Diary of a Serial Killer '97
Conspiracy of Fear '96
Illegal in Blue '95
Project Shadowchaser 3000 '95
Night Siege Project: Shadowchaser 2 '94
The Camomile Lawn '92

Robert Een
The Rook '99
Mr. Jealousy '98

Cliff Eidelman (1967-)
He's Just Not That Into You '08
Sisterhood of the Traveling Pants '05
The Lizzie McGuire Movie '03
Harrison's Flowers '02
An American Rhapsody '01
Witness Protection '99
One True Thing '98
The Beautician and the Beast '97
Free Willy 3: The Rescue '97
Montana '97
If These Walls Could Talk '96
Now and Then '95
My Girl 2 '94
Picture Bride '94
A Simple Twist of Fate '94
Untamed Heart '93
Christopher Columbus: The Discovery '92
Leap of Faith '92
Star Trek 6: The Undiscovered Country '91

Ludovico Einaudi (1955-)
This Is England '06
Doctor Zhivago '03
Light of My Eyes '01
Not of This World '99

Richard Einhorn
A House in the Hills '93
Closet Land '90
Blood Rage '87
Dead of Winter '87
Sister, Sister '87
Eyes of a Stranger '81
The Prowler '81
Don't Go in the House '80
Shock Waves '77

Hans Eisler (1898-1962)
A Scandal in Paris '46
Hangmen Also Die '42

Konrad Elfers
Pippi Longstocking '69
Funeral in Berlin '66

Danny Elfman (1953-)
Hellboy 2: The Golden Army '08
Wanted '08
The Kingdom '07
Meet the Robinsons '07
Charlotte's Web '06
Nacho Libre '06
Charlie and the Chocolate Factory '05
Tim Burton's Corpse Bride '05
Spider-Man 2 '04
Big Fish '03
Hulk '03
Chicago '02
Men in Black 2 '02
Red Dragon '02
Spider-Man '02
Planet of the Apes '01
Spy Kids '01
Family Man '00
Proof of Life '00
Anywhere But Here '99
Instinct '99
Sleepy Hollow '99
A Civil Action '98
Modern Vampires '98
A Simple Plan '98
Flubber '97
Good Will Hunting '97
Men in Black '97
The Frighteners '96
Mars Attacks! '96
Mission: Impossible '96
Dead Presidents '95
Freeway '95
To Die For '95
Dolores Claiborne '94
The Nightmare before Christmas '93
Sommersby '93
Army of Darkness '92
Article 99 '92
Batman Returns '92
Darkman '90
Dick Tracy '90
Edward Scissorhands '90
The Flash '90
Nightbreed '90
Batman '89
Beetlejuice '88
Big Top Pee-wee '88
Hot to Trot '88
Midnight Run '88
Scrooged '88
Summer School '87
Wisdom '87
Back to School '86
Pee-wee's Big Adventure '85
Forbidden Zone '80

Jonathan Elias
Pathfinder '07
A Guide to Recognizing Your Saints '06
Leprechaun 2 '94
Morning Glory '93
Far from Home '89
Parents '89
Rude Awakening '89
Shakedown '88
Two Moon Junction '88
Vamp '86
Almost You '85
Key Exchange '85
Tuff Turf '85
Children of the Corn '84

Boris Elkis
The Godson '98
Bugged! '96

Duke Ellington (1899-1974)
Paris Blues '61
Anatomy of a Murder '59
Cabin in the Sky '43

Alan Elliott (1964-)
Let's Go to Prison '06
Seeing Other People '04
Borough of Kings '98

Bill Elliott
Carry Me Home '04
Sticks '98
Stand-Ins '97

Jack Elliott (1927-2001)
The Jerk '79
The Man Without a Country '73
Support Your Local Gunfighter '71
Where's Poppa? '70

Don Ellis (1934-78)
Ruby '77
French Connection 2 '75
The French Connection '71

Marc Ellis
Adam Sandler's 8 Crazy Nights '02
Master of Disguise '02
Assault of the Killer Bimbos '88

Warren Ellis (1944-)
The Assassination of Jesse James by the Coward Robert Ford '07
The Proposition '05

Timo Elliston
Rapturious '07
Blood Relic '05

Keith Emerson
The Church '98
Best Revenge '83
Nighthawks '81
Inferno '80

Stephen Endelman (1953-)
Redbelt '08
Home of the Brave '06
The Net 2.0 '06
Phat Girlz '06
Knights of the South Bronx '05
The Blue Butterfly '04
Evelyn '02
I'm with Lucy '02
Bride of the Wind '01
Blue Moon '00
Earthly Possessions '99
Two Family House '99
Finding Graceland '98
Witness to the Mob '98
Kicked in the Head '97
The Proposition '97
City of Industry '96
Ed '96
Keys to Tulsa '95
Cosi '95
The Englishman Who Went up a Hill But Came down a Mountain '95
Flirting with Disaster '95
Jeffrey '95
The Journey of August King '95
Postcards from America '95
Reckless '95
Tom and Huck '95
The Desperate Trail '94
Imaginary Crimes '94
Household Saints '93
Operation Condor '91

Koji Endo (1964-)
Three ... Extremes '04
Gozu '03
Graveyard of Honor '02
Audition '99

Paul Englishby
Miss Pettigrew Lives for a Day '08
Confetti '06

Charles Engstrom
Coastlines '02
Ulee's Gold '97
Ruby in Paradise '93
A Flash of Green '85

Brian Eno (1948-)
The Jacket '05
Clean '04
Fear X '03
Buddy Boy '99
The Million Dollar Hotel '99
Neil Gaiman's NeverWhere '96
Dune '84
Sebastiane '79
Land of the Minotaur '77

John Entwhistle (1944-2002)
The Kids Are Alright '79
Quadrophenia '79
Tommy '75

Micky Erbe
Blackjack '97

Leo Erdody (1888-1949)
Detour '46
Strange Illusion '45
Dead Men Walk '43
Girls in Chains '43

Sebastien Erms
A Summer's Tale '96
Rendezvous in Paris '95
A Tale of Winter '92

Bengt Ernryd
The New Land '73

Jim Ervin
Uncovered: The War on Iraq '04
The Man on the Train '02
Ripper Man '96

Harry Escott
A Mighty Heart '07
The Road to Guantanamo '06

Ilan Eshkeri
Closure '07
Hannibal Rising '07
Stardust '07
Layer Cake '05

Pascal Esteve (1961-)
Intimate Strangers '04
The Widow of Saint-Pierre '00
The Man in the Iron Mask '97

Asher Ettinger
Brave New Girl '04

Francois Eudes (1974-)
Who Killed Bambi? '03
Joan of Arc '99
High Tension '03

Evan Evans (1975-)
Newsbreak '00
TripFall '00
Wicked Ways '99

Ray Evans (1915-2007)
Red Garters '54
The Lemon Drop Kid '51

Harold Faltermeyer (1952-)
Kuffs '92
Fletch Lives '89
Tango and Cash '89
Beverly Hills Cop 2 '87
Fatal Beauty '87
Fire and Ice '87
The Running Man '87
Top Gun '86
Beverly Hills Cop '84
Fletch '85
Thief of Hearts '84

Sharon Farber
Dark Justice '00
They Call Me Sirr '01
In a Class of His Own '99

Guy Farley (1963-)
The Christmas Miracle of Jonathan Toomey '07
The Flock '07
Cashback '06
Land of the Blind '06
Submerged '05
Modigliani '04
Sorted '04
Darkness Falls '98

Jim Farmer
Double Whammy '01
The Waiting Game '99
The Real Blonde '97
Box of Moonlight '96
Living in Oblivion '94
Johnny Suede '92

Robert Farnon (1917-2005)
Shalako '68

Robert Farrar
Terror at Tenkiller '86
Don't Look in the Basement '73

Chris Farrell
The Hazing '04
Shakedown '02
Hard As Nails '01

Ricky Fataar (1952-)
The Efficiency Expert '92
High Tide '87

Louis Febre
Dead in a Heartbeat '02
Swimfan '02
A Woman's a Helluva Thing '01
First Daughter '99
Dean Koontz's Mr. Murder '98
Little Bigfoot '96
Last Man Standing '95
Rage '95
Serial Killer '95
Two Bits & Pepper '95
Fists of Iron '94
The Force '94
The Secretary '94

Jack Feldman
Thumbelina '94

Tony Fennell
Megalodon '03
Within the Rock '96

George Fenton (1950-)
Fool's Gold '08
Last Holiday '06
The Wind That Shakes the Barley '06
Bewitched '05
Hitch '05
Mrs. Henderson Presents '05
Valiant '05
A Fond Kiss '04
Imagining Argentina '04
Stage Beauty '04
Deep Blue '03
Sweet Home Alabama '02
Sweet Sixteen '02
The Navigators '01
Summer Catch '01
Bread and Roses '00
Center Stage '00
Lucky Numbers '00
Anna and the King '99
Entropy '99
Grey Owl '99
Dangerous Beauty '98
Ever After: A Cinderella Story '98
Living Out Loud '98
My Name Is Joe '98
The Object of My Affection '98
You've Got Mail '98
Carla's Song '97
The Crucible '96
In Love and War '96
Multiplicity '96
Heaven's Prisoners '95
Land and Freedom '95
Mary Reilly '95
George '94
Mixed Nuts '94
Born Yesterday '93
Groundhog Day '93
Ladybird, Ladybird '93
Shadowlands '93
Final Analysis '92
Hero '92
China Moon '91
The Fisher King '91
Memphis Belle '90
White Palace '90
The Dressmaker '89
The Long Walk Home '89
We're No Angels '89
Dangerous Liaisons '88
A Handful of Dust '88
High Spirits '88
White Mischief '88
White of the Eye '88
Cry Freedom '87
Saigon: Year of the Cat '87
Clockwise '86
84 Charing Cross Road '86
The Company of Wolves '85
The Jewel in the Crown '84
An Englishman Abroad '83
Gandhi '82
Hussy '80

Allyn Ferguson
High Noon '00
All Quiet on the Western Front '79
The Man Without a Country '73
Support Your Local Gunfighter '71

David Ferguson
Catherine Cookson's The Gambling Man '98
Hostile Waters '97
The Woman in White '97
A Dark Adapted Eye '93
Dead Ahead: The Exxon Valdez Disaster '92
A Fatal Inversion '92
Tailspin: Behind the Korean Airline Tragedy '89

Jay Ferguson (1943-)
Paradise, Texas '05
Tremors 2: Aftershocks '96
Double Dragon '94
Gleaming the Cube '89
A Nightmare on Elm Street 5: Dream Child '89
Race for Glory '89
Bad Dreams '88
Johnny Be Good '88
License to Drive '88
Pulse '88
Best Seller '87
The Patriot '86
Quiet Cool '86

Ralph Ferraro
Flesh Gordon '72
The She-Beast '65

Gianni Ferrio (1924-)
Blood for a Silver Dollar '66
Flances '63

Paul Ferris (1941-95)
The Conqueror Worm '68
Blood Beast Terror '67

Cy Feuer (1911-2006)
Sundown Fury '42
Bad Man of Deadwood '41

(continued from previous page)
Nevada City '41
Adventures of Red Ryder '40
Carson City Kid '40
Drums of Fu Manchu '40
Come on Rangers '38
Heroes of the Hills '38

Nico Fidenco (1933-)
Doctor Butcher M.D. '80
Trap Them & Kill Them '77
Diary of a Rebel '68

Brad Fiedel (1951-)
Eden '98
Mistria '96
Rasputin: Dark Servant of Destiny '96
Destry '96
Johnny Mnemonic '95
True Lies '94
Blink '93
The Real McCoy '93
Striking Distance '93
Gladiator '92
Straight Talk '92
Terminator 2: Judgment Day '91
Blue Steel '90
Forgotten Prisoners '90
Cold Sassy Tree '89
Immediate Family '89
Perfect Witness '89
True Believer '89
The Accused '88
Fright Night 2 '88
Weekend War '88
The Big Easy '87
Bluffing It '87
Hostage '87
The Last Innocent Man '87
Let's Get Harry '87
Eyes of Fire '84
Children in the Crossfire '84
Calendar Girl Murders '84
Mae West '84
My Mother's Secret Life '84
Right of Way '84
The Terminator '84
The Serpent and the Rainbow '87
Cocaine: One Man's Seduction '83
Brotherhood of Justice '86
Desert Bloom '86
The Midnight Hour '86
Compromising Positions '85
Fraternity Vacation '85
Fright Night '85
Girls of the White Orchid '85
Into Thin Air '85
The Baron and the Kid '84
Murder in Coweta County '83
Nowhere to Hide '83
Born Beautiful '82
Hit & Run '82
Night School '81
The People vs. Jean Harris '81
The Day the Women Got Even '80
Hardhat & Legs '80
Just Before Dawn '80
Playing for Time '80
Deadly Hero '75

Mike Figgis (1948-)
Cold Creek Manor '03
Time Code '00
Hotel '01
Miss Julie '99
The Loss of Sexual Innocence '98
One Night Stand '97
Leaving Las Vegas '95
Liebestraum '91
Internal Affairs '90
Stormy Monday '88

David Findlay
Nowhere in Sight '01
Dead Silent '99
Captive '97
Eye '96
Day '91

Sylvia Fine (1913-91)
Court Jester '56
The Secret Life of Walter Mitty '47

Peter Fish
Intimate Betrayal '96
Wigstock: The Movie '95

Neil Finn (1958-)
Rain '01
Mitty '47

Gunther Fischer (1944-)
Bear Ye One Another's Burden... '88
Solo Sunny '80

Simon Fisher Turner (1954-)
I'll Sleep When I'm Dead '03
The Eternal '99
Claire Dolan '97
Croupier '97
Nadja '95
Loaded '94
Blue '93
Edward II '92
The Garden '90
The Last of England '87
Friday '95
The Pirates of Silicon Valley '99
Love Song '00

Frank Fitzpatrick
Jump In! '07
Paid in Full '02
Love Song '00
The Pirates of Silicon Valley '99

Patrick Flynn
Tennessee's Partner '55
Pitfall '48

Claude Foisy
Sunday Too Far Away '74
Stealing Home '88
The Secret of My Success '87

Pierre Foldes
Cécilie '76

Ruy Folguera
The Broken Chain '93
A Thousand Heroes '92
Repossessed '90
False Witness '89

Robert Folk (1949-)
200: A Space Travesty '00
We'll Meet Again '02
White Noise '05
Friday '95
St. Elmo's Fire '85
The Breakfast Club '85
Collected Stories '02
A Death in the Family '02
The Secret of the Lark '01
The Song of the Lark '01
Above the Law '88
A Prayer in the Dark '97
Hero and the Terror '88
I'm Gonna Git You Sucka '88
Repossessed '90
False Witness '89
The Gods Must Be Crazy 2 '89

Charles Fox (1940-)
Hard to Kill '89
One Man Force '89
Short Circuit 2 '88
Christmas Comes to Willow Creek '87
Love at Stake '87
The Longshot '86
Seventeen Again '00
Lost in the Bermuda Triangle '98
Tarzan and the Lost City '98
Triangle '98
Menno's Mind '96
Public Enemies '96
Solo '96
Wolverine '96
The Surgeon '94
Stephen King's The Stand '94
Love Child '88

Keith Forsey (1948-)
Twin Sisters '91
Crazy Moon '87

Lou Forestieri
Sherlock: Undercover Dog '94

David Foster (1949-)
Tennessee's Partner '55
Pitfall '48
The Little Rascals '94
If Looks Could Kill '91
Listen to Me '89
Fresh Horses '88
Stealing Home '88
The Secret of My Success '87

Louis Forbes (1902-81)
The Bat '59
Slightly Scarlet '56
Pearl of the South Pacific '55

Sherman Foote
It Takes Two '95
Parents '89

Jess (Jesus) Franco (1930-)
Tender Flesh '97
The Diabolical Dr. Z '65

David Michael Frank
The Last Warrior '99
Billboard Dad '98
A Kid in Aladdin's Palace '97
Odd Jobs '85

Carlo Franci (1927-)
Erik, the Viking '65
Hercules against the Son of Medusa '64
Hercules against the Moon Men '64
Medusa Against the Son of Hercules '62
The Wide Blue Road '57

Neal Fox
Killer Tomatoes Strike Back '90
Return of the Killer Tomatoes '88
The Incident '67

Gerald Fried (1928-)
Roots: The Next Generation '79
Roots '77
The Baby '72
The Grissom Gang '71
Too Late the Hero '70
The Killing of Sister George '68
Machine Gun Kelly '58
The Young Lions '58
Barbarian and the Geisha '58
Paths of Glory '57
The Killing '56
Killer's Kiss '55

Gavin Friday (1959-)
Get Rich or Die Tryin' '05
In America '02
Disco Pigs '01
The Boxer '97

Terry Frewer
Head in the Clouds '04
Black Point '01
The Inspectors 2: A Shred of Evidence '00
Out of Time '00
The Last Stop '99
The Inspectors '98
Possessed '00

Ian Fraser
First Monday in October '81
Zorro, the Gay Blade '81

Arthur Freed (1894-1973)
Broadway Melody of 1938 '37
Broadway Melody of 1936 '35

Michael Franks (1944-)
Cockfighter '74
Zandy's Bride '74

Jason Frederick (1970-)
Four and a Half Women '05
2B Perfectly Honest '04

Christopher Franke (1953-)
Green Street Hooligans '05
What the #$*! Do We Know? '04
Seventeen Again '00
Going Under '91
Out for Justice '91
Showdown in Little Tokyo '91

Benjamin Frankel (1906-73)
Battle of the Bulge '65
The Night of the Iguana '64
End of the Affair '55
A Kid for Two Farthings '55
The Importance of Being Earnest '52

Marco Frisina (1954-)
Jacob '94
Abraham '94
Joseph '95
Samson and Delilah '96
Moses '96
Trick '99
Bush's Brain '04

David Friedman (1923-)
A Wing and a Prayer '44

Hugo Friedhofer (1901-81)
Private Parts '72
Homicidal '61
Boy on a Dolphin '57
Soldier of Fortune '55
Above and Beyond '53
Vera Cruz '53
Hondo '53
The Marrying Kind '52
Ace in the Hole '51
Three Came Home '50
Body and Soul '47
The Bishop's Wife '47
The Best Years of Our Lives '46
Lifeboat '44
A Wing and a Prayer '44

Dominic Frontiere (1931-)
Rescue from Gilligan's Island '78
Color of Night '94
Danielle Steel's Palomino '91
Cease Fire '85
The Stunt Man '80
Brannigan '75
Hang 'Em High '67
Incubus '65
Seven Thieves '60

Gary Fry
Trancers 4: Jack of Swords '93
Last Mercenary '82
Scorpion with Two Tails '82
Zombie 4 '80
Trancers 5: Sudden Deth '94

Shiro Fukai
The Reading '07

Parmer Fuller
Get a Clue! '05
Spirit of the Eagle '90
Saturday the 14th Strikes Back '88
Saturday the 14th '81
Time Trackers '88

Lewis Furey (1949-)
Night Magic '85
American Dreamer '84
National Lampoon's Christmas Vacation 2: Cousin Eddie's Big Island Adventure '03
The Peanut Butter Solution '85

Nathan Furst (1978-)
Already Dead '07

Fabio Frizzi (1951-)
Zombie '80

John (Gianni) Frizzell (1966-)
Primeval '07
Black Irish '07
Beneath '07
Alien: Resurrection '97

Giovanni Fusco (1906-68)
The Eclipse '66
La Guerre Est Finie '66
The Red Desert '64
The Trojan Horse '62
L'Avventura '60
Hiroshima, Mon Amour '59
Il Grido '57

Dorothy Fields (1905-74)
Joy of Living '38
Swing Time '36

Jerry Fielding (1922-80)
Escape from Alcatraz '79
The Gauntlet '77
The Bad News Bears '76
The Enforcer '76
The Outlaw Josey Wales '76
The Killer Elite '75
Bring Me the Head of Alfredo Garcia '74
The Gambler '74
Junior Bonner '72
The Mechanic '72
The Nightcomers '72
Straw Dogs '71
Chato's Land '72
Johnny Got His Gun '71
Lawman '71
Hard Frame '69
The Wild Bunch '69

Adam Fields (1965-)
Meeting Daddy '98
Lovelife '97

Magnus Fiennes (1965-)
Theodore Rex '95

The Lady Without Camelias '53

Story of a Love Affair '50

Peter Gabriel (1950-)
Rabbit-Proof Fence '02
The Last Temptation of Christ '88
Birdy '84

Pascal Gaigne
Dark Blue Almost Black '06
Broken Silence '01

Serge Gainsbourg (1928-91)
Menage '86
The French Woman '79
Good-bye, Emmanuelle '77
Le Sex Shop '73
Too Pretty to Be Honest '72
French Intrigue '70

Vincent Gallo (1961-)
Get Well Soon '01
Buffalo 66 '97

Douglas Gamley (1924-98)
The Beast Must Die '75
The Land That Time Forgot '75
And Now the Screaming Starts '73

Craig Stuart Garfinkle
Ghosts Never Sleep '05
Gabriela '01

Robert Garrett
Eye of the Stranger '93
Roller Blade Warriors: Taken By Force '90
Roller Blade '85

Mort Garson
To Kill a Stranger '84
Beware! The Blob '72

Georges Garvarentz (1931-93)
A Wind from Wyoming '94
The Little Girl Who Lives down the Lane '76

Claude Gaudette
Virtual Combat '95
Illicit Dreams '94

Mark Geary
Steel City '06
Loggerheads '05

Lynne Geller
The Adventures of Sebastian Cole '99
1999 '98
Denise Calls Up '95

Lisa Gerrard (1961-)
Layer Cake '05
Salem's Lot '04
Whale Rider '02
Ali '01

Joseph Gershenson (1904-88)
Man in the Shadow '57
The Monolith Monsters '57
The Creature Walks among Us '56
Francis in the Haunted House '56
Abbott and Costello Meet the Mummy '55
All That Heaven Allows '55
Revenge of the Creature '55
Abbott and Costello Meet the Keystone Kops '54
The Black Shield of Falworth '54
Abbott and Costello Go to Mars '53
All I Desire '53
Francis Covers the Big Town '53
Francis Goes to West Point '52
The Lawless Breed '52

George Gershwin (1898-1937)
The Goldwyn Follies '38
A Damsel in Distress '37
Shall We Dance '37

Ira Gershwin (1896-1983)
Funny Face '57
A Star Is Born '54
An American in Paris '51
The Barkleys of Broadway '49
Rhapsody in Blue '45
Cover Girl '44
Girl Crazy '43
Lady Be Good '41
The Goldwyn Follies '38
A Damsel in Distress '37
Shall We Dance '37

Irving Gertz (1915-)
Curse of the Undead '59
Plunder Road '57
I Behold His Glory '53
It Came from Outer Space '53

Michael Giacchino (1967-)
Speed Racer '08
Ratatouille '07
Looking for Comedy in the Muslim World '06
Mission: Impossible 3 '06
The Family Stone '05
Sky High '05
The Incredibles '04
Sin '02

Carlo Giacco
December Boys '07
Murderous Intent '06
15 Amore '98

Michael Gibbs (1937-)
Being Human '94
Century '94
Hard-Boiled '92
Close My Eyes '91
Legal Deceit '95
Iron & Silk '89
Breaking In '89
American Roulette '88
Heat '87
Housekeeping '87
Madame Sin '71
Secrets '71

Richard Gibbs (1955-)
Cleaner '07
John Tucker Must Die '06
The Honeymooners '05
Barbershop 2: Back in Business '04
Fat Albert '04
Johnson Family Vacation '04
My Baby's Daddy '04
Love Don't Cost a Thing '03
Step Into Liquid '03
I Spy '02
Like Mike '02
Big Momma's House '00
28 Days '00
The Book of Stars '99
The Jesse Ventura Story '99
Ten Things I Hate about You '99
Dr. Dolittle '98
Dirty Work '97
Music from Another Room '97
First Kid '96
That Darn Cat '96
At First Sight '95
Blind Justice '94
Dangerous Indiscretion '94
Amos and Andrew '93
Barbarians at the Gate '93
The Chase '93
Fatal Instinct '93
Son-in-Law '93
Three of Hearts '93
Clifford '92
The Gun in Betty Lou's Handbag '92
Ladybugs '92
Once Upon a Crime '92
Passed Away '92
Bingo '91
A Killing in a Small Town '90
Say Anything '89
Sweet Hearts Dance '88

Herschel Burke Gilbert (1918-2003)
I Dismember Mama '74
Sam Whiskey '69
Project Moon Base '53
The Thief '52

Glover Gill
Before Sunset '04
Waking Life '01

Vincent Gillioz
Seance '06
Headhunter '05

Scott Gilman
Extreme Dating '04
Outta Time '01

Marcello Giombini (1928-2003)
Reactor '85
Mandinga '77
War in Space '77
Emmanuelle on Taboo Island '76
Panic '76
Jungle Inferno '72
Sabata '69
Knives of the Avenger '65

Lim Giong (1964-)
The World '04
Goodbye South, Goodbye '96

Ricky Giovinazzo
No Way Home '96
Combat Shock '84

Michael Paul Girard (1954-)
Sweet Evil '98
Witchcraft 9: Bitter Flesh '96
The Perfect Gift '95

Claudio Gizzi
Andy Warhol's Dracula '74
Andy Warhol's Frankenstein '74

Scott Glasgow
Hack! '07
Chasing Ghosts '05

Philip Glass (1937-)
Cassandra's Dream '07
No Reservations '07
The Illusionist '06
Notes on a Scandal '06
Going Upriver: The Long War of John Kerry '04
Secret Window '04
Taking Lives '04
Undertow '04
The Fog of War: Eleven Lessons from the Life of Robert S. McNamara '03
The Hours '02
The Truman Show '98
Bent '97
Kundun '97
The Secret Agent '96
Candyman 2: Farewell to the Flesh '94
A Brief History of Time '92
Candyman '92
Mindwalk: A Film for Passionate Thinkers '91
Powaqqatsi: Life in Transformation '88
The Thin Blue Line '88
Hamburger Hill '87
Mishima: A Life in Four Chapters '85
Koyaanisqatsi '83

Albert Glasser (1916-98)
Tormented '60
Attack of the Puppet People '58
Giant from the Unknown '58
Monster from Green Hell '58
Teenage Caveman '58
The Amazing Colossal Man '57
Beginning of the End '57
The Indestructible Man '56
Invasion U.S.A. '52
Guns of Fury '49
Tough Assignment '49
Law of the Lash '47
The Monster Maker '44

Richard Glasser (1947-)
Kickin' It Old Skool '07
Find Me Guilty '06
Poolhall Junkies '02

Patrick Gleeson
In Self Defense '93
The Bedroom Window '87
Deadly Illusion '87
Stacking '87
The Children of Times Square '86
The Zoo Gang '85
The Plague Dogs '82

Nick Glennie-Smith (1951-)
A Sound of Thunder '05
We Were Soldiers '02
Attila '01
The Man in the Iron Mask '98
Fire Down Below '97
Home Alone 3 '97
The Rock '96

The Goblins
Sleepless '01
Unsane '82
Alien Contamination '81
The Bloodstained Shadow '78
Dawn of the Dead '78
Suspiria '77
Deep Red: Hatchet Murders '75

Erik Godal
What Love Is '07
Axe '06
Subject Two '06

Lucio Godoy (1958-)
The Aura '05
Mondays in the Sun '02
Intacto '01

Ernest Gold (1921-99)
Gore Vidal's Lincoln '88
Safari 3000 '82
Tom Horn '80
Marciano '79
The Runner Stumbles '79
Fun with Dick and Jane '77
Cross of Iron '76
The McCullochs '75
Betrayal '02
The Secret of Santa Vittoria '69
Ship of Fools '65
A Child Is Waiting '63
It's a Mad, Mad, Mad, Mad World '63
Pressure Point '62
Judgment at Nuremberg '61
Exodus '60
Inherit the Wind '60
On the Beach '59
The Young Philadelphians '59
The Screaming Skull '58
Unknown World '51

Murray Gold
Death at a Funeral '07
Casanova '05
Miranda '01
Beautiful Creatures '00

Barry Goldberg
Best of the Best 3: No Turning Back '95
Hometown Boy Makes Good '93
Return of the Living Dead 3 '93
Beverly Hills Brats '89
Flashback '89
Powwow Highway '89
Three for the Road '87
Thrashin' '86
The Trip '67

Stu Goldberg
Impulse '08
Afghan Knights '07

Billy Goldenberg (1936-)
18 Again! '88
Johnnie Gibson F.B.I. '87
Dress Gray '86
Rage of Angels: The Story Continues '86
Guilty Conscience '85
Love on the Run '85
For Love or Money '84
Dempsey '83
Prototype '83
Rage of Angels '83
Reuben, Reuben '83
Rehearsal for Murder '82
Awakening of Candra '81
The Best Little Girl in the World '81
Callie and Son '81
Jacqueline Bouvier Kennedy '81
All God's Children '80
Crisis at Central High '80
Father Figure '80
The Cracker Factory '79
The Family Man '79
The Miracle Worker '79
Scavenger Hunt '79
King '78
A Question of Love '78
The Domino Principle '77
Helter Skelter '76
James Dean '76
The Lindbergh Kidnapping Case '76
Queen of the Stardust Ballroom '75
Busting '74
I Love You, Goodbye '74
Reflections of Murder '74
The Passing of Evil '70
Change of Habit '69
Night Gallery '69
Silent Night, Lonely Night '69

Elliot Goldenthal (1954-)
Across the Universe '07
The Good Thief '03
S.W.A.T. '03
Frida '02
Final Fantasy: The Spirits Within '01
Titus '99
In Dreams '98
Batman and Robin '97
The Butcher Boy '97
Sphere '97
Michael Collins '96
A Time to Kill '96
Batman Forever '95
Heat '95
Voices from a Locked Room '95
Interview with the Vampire '94
Roswell: The U.F.O. Cover-Up '94
Demolition Man '93
Golden Gate '93
Alien 3 '92
Drugstore Cowboy '89
Pet Sematary '89
Cocaine Cowboys '79

Jerry Goldsmith (1929-2004)
Looney Tunes: Back in Action '03
Star Trek: Nemesis '02
The Sum of All Fears '02
Along Came a Spider '01
The Last Castle '01
Disney's The Kid '00
Hollow Man '00
The Haunting '99
The Mummy '99
The 13th Warrior '99
Deep Rising '98
Mulan '98
Small Soldiers '98
Star Trek: Insurrection '98
U.S. Marshals '98
Air Force One '97
The Edge '97
L.A. Confidential '97
Chain Reaction '96
Executive Decision '96
Fierce Creatures '96
The Ghost and the Darkness '96
Star Trek: First Contact '96
City Hall '95
Congo '95
First Knight '95
Powder '95
Bad Girls '94
I.Q. '94
The River Wild '94
The Shadow '94
Dennis the Menace '93
Malice '93
Rudy '93
Six Degrees of Separation '93
The Vanishing '93
Basic Instinct '92
Forever Young '92
Matinee '92
Medicine Man '92
Mr. Baseball '92
Mom and Dad Save the World '92
Blue Desert '91
Love Field '91
Sleeping with the Enemy '91
Warlock '91
Gremlins 2: The New Batch '90
Not Without My Daughter '90
The Russia House '90
Total Recall '90
The Burbs '89
Criminal Law '89
Leviathan '89
Star Trek 5: The Final Frontier '89
Rambo 3 '88
Rent-A-Cop '88
Extreme Prejudice '87
Innerspace '87
Lionheart '87
Hoosiers '86
Legend '86
Link '86
Poltergeist 2: The Other Side '86
Explorers '85
King Solomon's Mines '85
Rambo: First Blood, Part 2 '85
Gremlins '84
The Lonely Guy '84
Runaway '84
Supergirl '84
Psycho 2 '83
Twilight Zone: The Movie '83
Under Fire '83
The Challenge '82
First Blood '82
Poltergeist '82
The Salamander '82
The Secret of NIMH '82
Cabo Blanco '81
The Final Conflict '81
Masada '81
Night Crossing '81
Outland '81
Raggedy Man '81
Alien '79
The Great Train Robbery '79
Players '79
Star Trek: The Motion Picture '79
The Boys from Brazil '78
Capricorn One '78

Coma '78
Damien: Omen 2 '78
Magic '78
The Swarm '78
The Last Hard Men '76
Logan's Run '76
The Omen '76
Babel '75
Breakout '75
MacArthur '77
Twilight's Last Gleaming '77
Breakheart Pass '76
The Cassandra Crossing '76
High Velocity '76
The Terrorists '74
One Little Indian '73
Papillon '73
Shamus '73
Culpepper Cattle Co. '72
The Other '72
Pursuit '72
Rio Lobo '70
Tora! Tora! Tora! '70
Justine '69
100 Rifles '69
Bandolero! '68
The Detective '68
Planet of the Apes '68
Sebastian '68
Film-Flam Man '67
Hour of the Gun '67
In Like Flint '67
The Blue Max '66
Our Man Flint '66
The Sand Pebbles '66
Seconds '66
The Trouble with Angels '66
The Agony and the Ecstasy '65
In Harm's Way '65
Morituri '65
A Patch of Blue '65
Von Ryan's Express '65
Rio Conchos '64
Seven Days in May '64
A Gathering of Eagles '63
Lilies of the Field '63
The List of Adrian Messenger '63
The Prize '63
The Stripper '63
Lonely Are the Brave '62
Stars Lonigan '60
The Detective '54

Joel Goldsmith (1957-)
Helen of Troy '03
Chameleon 3: Dark Angel '00
Diamonds '99
Shiloh 2: Shiloh Season '99
Inferno '98
Double Edge '97
Kull the Conqueror '97
Shiloh '97
Vampirella '96
Blood for Blood '95
One Good Turn '95
Home for Christmas '93
Man's Best Friend '93
A Woman, Her Men and Her Futon '92
Across the Tracks '89
Ricky 1 '88
Watchers '88
Crystal Heart '87
No Safe Haven '87
Banzai Runner '86
The Man with Two Brains '83

Jonathan Goldsmith
Island of Blood '82
Laserblast '78

Joel Goodman
Disorder '06
Undermind '03

John Goldstein
For Better and for Worse '92
Hot Chocolate '92

William Goldstein
The Miracle Worker '00
Just Like Dad '96
The Quarrel '93
Shocker '89
Blood Vows: The Story of a Mafia Wife '87
Hello Again '87
Bad Guys '86
Saving Grace '86
Getting Physical '84
Up the Creek '84
Remembrance of Love... '83

Vinnie Golia (1946-)
Highway Hitcher '98

Peter Golub
The Great Debaters '07
Sublime '07
Wordplay '06
American Gun '05
The Laramie Project '02

Miles Goodman (1949-96)
Larger Than Life '96
Sunset Park '96
Til There Was You '96
Dunston Checks in '95
Lip Service '00
Dangerous Evidence: The Lori Jackson Story '99
Must Be Santa '99
Dead Silence '99
Getting Even with Dad '94
Indian Summer '93
Kissinger and Nixon '96
Heads '93
Stand Off '93
Palais Royale '88
Miracle at Moreaux '86
The Guardian '84
Visiting Hours '82
Blankman '94
He Said, She Said '91
What about Bob? '91
Opportunity Knocks '90
Problem Child '90
Thompson's Last Run '90
Vital Signs '90
K-9 '89
Staying Together '89
Traveling Man '89
Dirty Rotten Scoundrels '88
La Bamba '87
Like Father, Like Son '87
The Squeeze '87
About Last Night... '86
Blind Justice '86
Little Shop of Horrors '86
Passion Flower '86
Poison Ivy '85
Teen Wolf '85
Footloose '84
High School USA '84
The Man Who Wasn't There '83
Tabta for Five '83
Having It All '82
Jinxed '82
Lookin' to Get Out '82
Last Cry for Help '79

Gil Goldstein
Simply Irresistible '99
I Love You, I Love You Not '97

Osvaldo Golijov
Youth Without Youth '07
The Man Who Cried '00

Ronald Goodwin (1925-2003)
Unidentified Flying Oddball '79
Candleshoe '77
Force 10 from Navarone '78
The Littlest Horse Thieves '76
The Little Mermaid '75
Frenzy '72
Battle of Britain '69
Where Eagles Dare '68
Murder at the Gallop '63
The Trials of Oscar Wilde '60

William Goodrum
Spaceman '75
Slumber Party '57, '76
Wham-Bam, Thank You

Jim Goodwin
Darkorive '98
A.P.E.X. '94

Mack Gordon (1904-59)
Mother Wore Tights '47
That Night in Rio '41
Down Argentine Way '40
We're Not Dressing '34

Christopher Gordon
Salem's Lot '04
Master and Commander: The Far Side of the World '03

Alain Goraguer
Village of the Damned '60

Michael Gore (1951-)
Superstar '99
Mr. Wonderful '93
The Butcher's Wife '91
Defending Your Life '91
Don't Tell Her It's Me '90
Broadcast News '87
Pretty in Pink '86

John Gonzalez
The Underground '97
Tiger Heart '96
Hologram Men '95
Street Crimes '92
Bikini Summer '91
Final Impact '91
Sunset Strip '91
Repo Jake '90
Mayhem '87
The Newlydeads '87
'01

Joseph Julian Gonzalez
When Good Ghouls Go Bad '01

Howard Goodall
Bean '97
Mr. Bean's Holiday '07
The Return of the Borrowers '96
The Borrowers '92

John Graham
My Brother's War '97
American Strays '96
Bloodfist 6: Ground Zero '94

Ron Grainer (1922-81)
Omega Man '71
Hoffman '70
To Sir, with Love '67
The Moon-Spinners '64
A Kind of Loving '62
The Mouse on the Moon '62
Nous '92
Smiley's People '82
Comic Act '98
Paperback Romance '96
Lust and Revenge '95
Siam Sunset '99
Noah's Ark '99
Shiner '00
Last Orders '01
Innocence '00
Terms of Endearment '83
Fame '80

Stephane Grappelli (1908-97)
May Fools '90
Going Places '74

Richard Grassby-Lewis
Owning Mahowny '03
Love and Death on Long Island '97

Allan Gray (1902-73)
Stairway to 'Heaven' '46
I Know Where I'm Going '45
The Challenge '38

Stephen Graziano (1954-)
Highlander: Endgame '00
Contagious '96
Ruby Jean and Joe '96

Adam Gorgoni (1963-)
Starting Out in the Evening '07

Gerald Gouriet
Men of War '94

Louis F. Gottschalk (1864-1934)
Hercules vs. the Sons of the Sun '64

Coriolano Gori (1927-82)
The Uranium Conspiracy '78
Fistful of Death '71

Mark Governor
Uncle Sam '96
Notes from Underground '95
Masque of the Red Death '89

Patrick Gowers (1936-)
Specimen '97
Triggermen '03

Terence Gowan
Hollywood North '03
Street Heat '98
Armistead Maupin's More Tales of the City '97
Bonanno: A Godfather's Story '99
Napoleon '03
Nuremberg '00

Paul Grabowsky
Empire Falls '05
It Runs in the Family '03
Last Orders '01

Richard Gregoire (1944-)
The Four Horsemen of the Apocalypse '21
Orphans of the Storm '21
The Three Musketeers 21

Louis F. Gottschalk
The Man with Two Brains '83

Bernard Green (1908-75)
The Brass Bottle '63
Zotz! '62

Johnny Green (1908-89)
They Shoot Horses, Don't They? '69
Alvarez Kelly '66
Bye, Bye, Birdie '63
The Great Caruso '51
Royal Wedding '51
The Inspector General '49
Something in the Wind '47
Easy to Wed '46

Philip Green (1911-82)
Girl Hunters '63
Victim '61
Who Done It? '56

Walter Greene (1910-83)
The Brain from Planet Arous '57

Harry Gregson-Williams (1961-)
The Chronicles of Narnia: Prince Caspian '08
The Number 23 '07
Shrek the Third '07
Deja Vu '06
Flushed Away '06
Seraphim Falls '06
The Chronicles of Narnia: The Lion, the Witch and the Wardrobe '05
Domino '05
Kingdom of Heaven '05
Bridget Jones: The Edge of Reason '04
Man on Fire '04
Shrek 2 '04
Team America: World Police '04
The Rundown '03
Sinbad: Legend of the Seven Seas '03
Veronica Guerin '03
Phone Booth '02
Spy Game '01
Shrek '01
Chicken Run '00
Light It Up '99
The Match '99
Antz '98
Enemy of the State '98
The Replacement Killers '98
Smilla's Sense of Snow '96
Deceiver '97
The Borrowers '97

Lawrence Nash Groupe
Resurrecting the Champ '07
Cleaved: The Legend of Sasquatch '05
The Contender '00
Deterrence '00

Adolph Green (1915-2002)
On the Town '91
It's Always Fair Weather '55

Louis Gruenberg (1883-1964)
Quicksand '50
All the King's Men '49

Jean Jacques Grunenwald (1911-82)
Diary of a Country Priest '50
Antoine et Antoinette '47
Monsieur Vincent '47

Rupert Gregson-Williams (1966-)
Made of Honor '08
You Don't Mess with the Zohan '08
Bee Movie '07
I Now Pronounce You Chuck and Larry '07
Click '06
Over the Hedge '06
Hotel Rwanda '04
Crime Spree '03

Johnny Green (1908-89)
The Brass Bottle '63

D.W. Griffith (1875-1948)
The Struggle '31
The Birth of a Nation '15

Mario Grigorov
What a Girl Wants '03
Strange Relations '02
Extremely Dangerous '99
Virtual Sexuality '99
Urban Ghost Story '98
Shadowboxer '06
The Attic '06
The Insurgents '06

Andrew Gross
Christmas in Boston '05
The Prince & Me 2: Royal Wedding '06
The Prince & Me 3: Royal Honeymoon '08

Anthony Grimaldi
All I Want '02
The Jimmy Show '01
Joe the King '99

Charles Gross (1934-)
Eyes of a Witness '94
Air America '90
Turner and Hooch '89
Sweet Dreams '85
Prime Suspect '82
A Rumor of War '80
Blue Sunshire '78
Valdez Is Coming '71

Guy Gross
The Extreme Adventures of Super Dave '00
Dead Simple '01
Buying the Cow '02
Off the Lip '04
Cut '00

Dean Grinsfelder
8 Heads in a Duffel Bag '96
Overnight Delivery '96

David Grisman (1945-)
Stonebrook '98
P.S. Your Cat is Dead! '02

Ferde Grofe, Jr.
Rocket to X-M '50

Dave Grusin (1934-)
Selena '96
Hope Floats '98
Random Hearts '99
In the Gloaming '97
Mulholland Falls '95
The Cure '95
The Firm '93
For the Boys '91
The Bonfire of the Vanities '90
Havana '90
A Dry White Season '89
The Fabulous Baker Boys '89
Clara's Heart '88
Tequila Sunrise '88
The Milagro Beanfield War '88
Ishtar '87
Lucas '86

Grusin

The Goonies '85
Falling in Love '84
The Little Drummer Girl '84
The Pope of Greenwich Village '84
Racing with the Moon '84
Scandalous '84
Author! Author! '82
Tootsie '82
Absence of Malice '81
On Golden Pond '81
Reds '81
My Bodyguard '80
And Justice for All '79
The Champ '79
The Electric Horseman '79
Heaven Can Wait '78
Bobby Deerfield '77
The Goodbye Girl '77
Mr. Billion '77
The Front '76
Murder by Death '76
Eric '75
Three Days of the Condor '75
The Yakuza '75
Fuzz '72
The Great Northfield Minnesota Raid '72
Shoot Out '71
Generation '69
Tell Them W... Boy Is Here '69
Winning '69
The He... is a Lonely Hu... '68
Div...raduate '67
...hole Number 3 '67

Jay Gruska (1953-)
Outlaw Justice '98
Trapped in Space '94
Mo' Money '92
Wheels of Terror '90
Sing '89
Shadow Dancing '88
The Principal '87
Traxx '87

Barrie Guard
Shameless '97
The Toxic Avenger, Part 2 '89
This Is Spinal Tap '84

Christopher Gunning (1944-)
La Vie en Rose '07
Prince of Poisoners: The Life and Crimes of William Palmer '98
Firelight '97
The Affair '95
Catherine Cookson's The Glass Virgin '95
Under Suspicion '92
When the Whales Came '89
Cold War Killers '86
Charlie Muffin '79
Running Blind '78
Hands of the Ripper '71
Twinsanity '70

Steve Gutheinz
Glass House: The Good Mother '06

Heras
Like A Bride '94
Mary, My Dearest '83

Jim Guttridge
Wishmaster 4: The Prophecy Fulfilled '02
Big and Hairy '98

Omar Guzman
Esmeralda Comes by Night '98
Forbidden Homework '92

Manos Hadjidakis
Sweet Movie '75
The Pedestrian '73
Blue '68
Topkapi '64

Richard Hageman (1882-1966)
...he Wore a Yellow Ribbon '49
Fort Apache '48
Angel and the Badman '47
The Shanghai Gesture '42
If I Were King '38

Francis Haines
Conspiracy of Silence '03
Another 9 1/2 Weeks '96
Split Second '92

Chris Hajian
The Take '07
Running Red '99
Dead Silence '98
Subterfuge '98
Riot '96

Karl Hajos (1889-1950)
It Happened in New Orleans '36

Jim Halfpenny
The Song of Songs '33
Beggars of Life '28

Erwin Halletz (1923-)
Fanny Hill: Memoirs of a Woman of Pleasure '64
The Third Sex '57
Liane, Jungle Goddess '56

Dick Halligan
Fear City '85
Go Tell the Spartans '78

Marvin Hamlisch (1944-)
The Mirror Has Two Faces '96
Open Season '95
Frankie and Johnny '91
When the Time Comes '91
The Experts '89
Little Nikita '88
The January Man '89
Three Men and a Baby '87
A Chorus Line '85
D.A.R.Y.L. '85
A Streetcar Named Desire '84
Romantic Comedy '83
I Ought to Be in Pictures '82
Sophie's Choice '82
The Devil & Max Devlin '81
Pennies from Heaven '81
Ordinary People '80
Seems Like Old Times '80
Ice Castles '79
Starting Over '79
Same Time, Next Year '78
The Spy Who Loved Me '77
Prisoner of Second Avenue '74
Save the Tiger '73
The Sting '73
The Way We Were '73

The World's Greatest Athlete '73
Fat City '72
Bananas '71
Kotch '71
April Fools '69
Take the Money and Run '69
The Swimmer '68

Jan Hammer (1948-)
The Corporate Ladder '97
Beastmaster 3: The Eye of Braxus '95
A Modern Affair '94
I Come in Peace '90
K-9000 '89

Wolfgang Hammerschmid
Mickey Blue Eyes '99
Mandragora '97

Oscar Hammerstein (1895-1960)
South Pacific '58
Carousel '56
The King and I '56
Oklahoma! '55
Carmen Jones '54
Show Boat '51
State Fair '45
Lady Be Good '41
Show Boat '36
Sweet Adeline '35

Herbie Hancock (1940-)
Livin' Large '91
Harlem Nights '89
Action Jackson '88
Colors '88
Hard Lessons '86
Jo Jo Dancer, Your Life Is Calling '86
A Soldier's Story '84
Death Wish '74
The Spook Who Sat by the Door '73
Blow-Up '66

E.Y. Harburg (1896-1981)
Can't Help Singing '45
Cabin in the Sky '43

Hagood Hardy (1937-)
Anne of Avonlea '87
Anne of Green Gables '85
Wild Pony '83
Forbidden Love '82
Mazes and Monsters '82
Dirty Tricks '81
An American Christmas Carol '79
Anatomy of a Seduction '79
Home to Stay '79
Klondike Fever '79
Second Wind '76

John E.R. Hardy
Rancid Aluminium '00
Hedd Wyn '92

John Harle (1956-)
Take Me '01
Butterfly Kiss '94

Leigh Harline (1907-69)
Strange Bedfellows '65
7 Faces of Dr. Lao '63
The Honeymoon Machine '61
The Facts of Life '60
The Girl in the Red Velvet Swing '55
House of Bamboo '55
Savage Wilderness '55
Black Widow '54
Broken Lance '54
Pickup on South Street '53
Monkey Business '52
His Kind of Woman '51
I Want You '51
Big Steal '49
It Happens Every Spring '49
They Live by Night '49
Mr. Blandings Builds His Dream House '48
Tycoon '47
Nocturne '46
The Road to Utopia '46
Having Wonderful Crime '45
Isle of the Dead '45
They Got Me Covered '43

The Pride of the Yankees '42
Blondie Has Trouble '40
Snow White and the Seven Dwarfs '37

W. Franke Harling (1887-1958)
Penny Serenade '41
The Invisible Man '33
No Man of Her Own '32
Trouble in Paradise '32
Monte Carlo '30

Don Harper
The Lion King 1 1/2 '04
Beyond Suspicion '00
Houdini '99

Scott Harper
The Magnificent Seven '98
Roseanne: An Unauthorized Biography '94
Reborn '81

Johnny Harris
Ravenhawk '95
Man in the Wilderness '71

Peter Harris
Happy, Texas '99
Elmore Leonard's Gold Coast '97

George Harrison (1943-2001)
Shanghai Surprise '86
Time Bandits '81
Let It Be '70
Wonderwall: The Movie '69
Yellow Submarine '68
Magical Mystery Tour '67
Help! '65

John Harrison
Day of the Dead '85
Creepshow '82

Deborah Harry (1945-)
Rock & Rule '83
Polyester '81

Jimmy Harry
Party Monster '03
Intern '00

Daniel Hart
Carmen, Baby '66
Nude on the Moon '61

Lorenz Hart (1895-1943)
I Married an Angel '42
Too Many Girls '40
Babes in Arms '39
Evergreen '34
The Merry Widow '34
Hallelujah, I'm a Bum '33

Hal Hartley (1959-)
No Such Thing '01
Henry Fool '98
Flirt '95
Amateur '94
Simple Men '92

Richard Hartley (1944-)
The Lion in Winter '03
Don Quixote '00
Mad About Mambo '00
When Brendan Met Trudy '00
Alice in Wonderland '99
All the Little Animals '98
Rogue Trader '98
Curtain Call '97
The Designated Mourner '97
A Thousand Acres '97
The Brylcreem Boys '96
Playing God '96
Stealing Beauty '96
Rough Magic '95
The Van '95
Victory '95
An Awfully Big Adventure '94
Princess Caraboo '94
The Rector's Wife '94
The Secret Rapture '94
Catherine Cookson's The Man Who Cried '93
The Good Father '87
The Impossible Spy '87
Dance with a Stranger '85
December Flower '84

Parker '84
Shock Treatment '81
The Rocky Horror Picture Show '75

Richard Harvey (1953-)
Luther '03
Two Men Went to War '02
Arabian Nights '00
Animal Farm '99
The Magical Legend of the Leprechauns '99
Captain Jack '98
Jane Eyre '97
Melissa '97
Paper Mask '91
Cause Celebre '87
In the Secret State '85

Bo Harwood
Happy-Birthday to Me '81
Opening Night '77

Jimmie Haskell (1936-)
The Dogfighters '95
L.A. Bad '85
Night of the Lepus '72
Zachariah '70

Paul Haslinger (1962-)
Prom Night '08
Shoot 'Em Up '07
Vacancy '07
Crank '06
Turistas '06
Into the Blue '05
Sleeper Cell '05
The Girl Next Door '04
Bring It On Again '03
Underworld '03
Blue Crush '02
crazy/beautiful '01
Picture Claire '01
Cheaters '00

Harley Hatcher
Cain's Cutthroats '71
Satan's Sadists '69
Wild Wheels '69

Marvin Hatley (1905-86)
Who Killed Doc Robbin? '48
Laurel & Hardy: Night Owls '30

Tadashi Hattori
One Wonderful Sunday '47
No Regrets for Our Youth '46
The Men Who Tread on the Tiger's Tail '45

Roy Hay (1961-)
Styx '00
Pterodactyl Woman from Beverly Hills '97
Precious Find '96

Fumio Hayasaka (1914-55)
I Live in Fear '55
Sansho the Bailiff '54
Seven Samurai '54
Ugetsu '53
Ikiru '52
Rashomon '51
Scandal '50
Drunken Angel '48

Todd Hayen
When Time Expires '97
The Invader '96
Panic in the Skies '96
Shooters '89

Isaac Hayes (1942-)
Shaft '00
Truck Turner '74
Shaft '71

Lennie Hayton (1908-71)
Battle Circus '53
Singlin' in the Rain '52
Side Street '50
Battleground '49
The Hucksters '47
Till the Clouds Roll By '46

Richard Hazard (1921-2000)
Bela Lugosi Meets a Brooklyn Gorilla '52
Radar Secret Service '50

Alex Heffes
Imagine Me & You '06
The Last King of Scotland '06
Dear Frankie '04
Touching the Void '03

Neal Hefti (1922-)
Barefoot in the Park '67
Oh Dad, Poor Dad (Momma's Hung You in the Closet & I'm Feeling So Sad) '67
Lord Love a Duck '66
Sex and the Single Girl '64

Leonardo Heiblum
Trade '07
In the Pit '06
Maria Full of Grace '04
The Maldonado Miracle '03

Reinhold Hell (1954-)
One Missed Call '08
Blood & Chocolate '07
Paris, je t'aime '06
Perfume: The Story of a Murderer '06
The Cave '05
George A. Romero's Land of the Dead '05
Sophie Scholl: The Final Days '05
Swimming Upstream '03
Big Shot: Confessions of a Campus Bookie '02
One Hour Photo '02
Tangled '01
The Princess and the Warrior '00
Winter Sleepers '97

Ray Heindorf (1908-80)
The Music Man '62
No Time for Sergeants '58
Wonder Man '45
The Roaring Twenties '39

Nona Hendryx (1944-)
Preaching to the Choir '05
Gospa '94

Ben Heneghan
Breeders '97
The Proposition '96

Joe Henry
Knocked Up '07
Jesus' Son '99

Christian Henson (1971-)
Severance '06
Chasing Liberty '04
The Great Challenge '04

Paul Hepker
Rendition '07

Matthew Herbert
The Intended '02
Human Traffic '99

Jerry Herman (1931-)
Mrs. Santa Claus '96
Mame '74
Hello, Dolly! '69

Bernard Herrmann (1911-75)
Obsession '76
Taxi Driver '76
It's Alive '74
Sisters '73
Endless Night '71
North by Northwest '59
The Three Worlds of Gulliver '59
The Seventh Voyage of Sinbad '58
Vertigo '58
The Birds '63
Marnie '64
Cape Fear '61
Mysterious Island '61
Psycho '60
Journey to the Center of the Earth '59
The Bride Wore Black '68
Fahrenheit 451 '66
The Man Who Knew Too Much '56
The Trouble with Harry '55
A Christmas Carol '54
Garden of Evil '54

Anthony Guefen
Assassin '86
The Stuff '85

Andrea Guerra (1961-)
The Accidental Husband '08
The Pursuit of Happyness '06
Hotel Rwanda '04
Facing Windows '03
Angel of Death '02
Angela '02
His Secret Life '01

Christopher Guest (1948-)
Waiting for Guffman '96

1886 VideoHound's Golden Movie Retriever

(Bernard Herrmann, cont.)
Beneath the 12-Mile Reef '53
Five Fingers '52
The Snows of Kilimanjaro '52
The Day the Earth Stood Still '51
On Dangerous Ground '51
The Ghost and Mrs. Muir '47
Anna and the King of Siam '46
Hangover Square '45
Jane Eyre '44
The Magnificent Ambersons '42
Citizen Kane '41
The Devil & Daniel Webster '41

Nigel Hess
Ladies in Lavender '04

Boo Hewerdine
Love or Money '01
Every Woman Knows a Secret '99
A Woman of Substance '84

Werner R. Heymann (1886-1961)
They All Kissed the Bride '42
To Be or Not to Be '42
That Uncertain Feeling '41
The Shop Around the Corner '40

Tom Hiel
Fever Pitch '96
24-7 '97

Richard Hieronymous
The Invisible Strangler '76
Angels Hard As They Come '71

John Hill
Tar '97

Hilmar Orn Hilmarsson (1958-)
Beowulf & Grendel '06
Mists of Avalon '01

Peter Himmelman (1960-)
A Face to Kill For '99
Liar's Poker '99
A Slipping Down Life '99
Dinner and Driving '97

Dickon Hinchliffe
In the Cut '03
Devil's Island '96
Cold Fever '95
Children of Nature '91

David Hirschfelder (1960-)
Irresistible '06
Aquamarine '06
Kidnapped '05
Beastmaster '82
American Pop '81
Better Than Sex '00
The Weight of Water '00
Hanging Up '99
Elizabeth '98
The Interview '98
Sliding Doors '97
Dating the Enemy '96
Shine '95

Joe Hisaishi (1950-)
Howl's Moving Castle '04
Dolls '02
Spirited Away '01
Brother '00
Kikujiro '99
Princess Mononoke '98
Fireworks '97

John Hodian
101 Ways (The Things a Girl Will Do to Keep Her Volvo) '00

Michael Hoenig
Girls School Screamers '86
Blades '89
The Contaminated Man '01
Eye of the Killer '99
Terminal Justice: Cybertech P.D. '95
The Amy Fisher Story '93
Shattered Spirits '86
Koyaanisqatsi '83
The Groundstar Conspiracy '72

Paul Hoffert (1947-)
Mr. Nice Guy '86
Fanny Hill '83
Outrageous! '77
Vengeance Is Mine '74

Joachim Holbek (1957-)
'02
Heart of Light '97
Junk Mail '97
Nightwatch '96
Breaking the Waves '95
The Kingdom '95
Medea '88

Mark Holden
Body Armor '96
Ava's Magical Adventure '94
Beyond Desire '94

Lee Holdridge (1944-)
Puerto Vallarta Squeeze '04
The Twilight of the Golds '97
Two for Texas '98
Gunfighter's Moon '96
Holiday Affair '96
Buffalo Girls '95
The Yearling '94
Call of the Wild '93
Heidi '93
Running Delilah '93
The Story Lady '93
One Against the Wind '91
Back to Hannibal: The Return of Tom Sawyer and Huckleberry Finn '90
Old Gringo '89
Born in East L.A. '87
Moonlighting '85
Transylvania 6-5000 '85
Splash '84
Agatha Christie's A Caribbean Mystery '83
Mr. Mom '83
Beastmaster '82
American Pop '81
WinterHawk '75

Deborah Holland
Out There '95
Circuitry Man '90

Andrew Hollander
Waitress '07
Anything But Love '02
I'll Take You There '99
Wrestling with Alligators '98

Frederick "Friedrich" Hollander (1896-1976)
We're No Angels '55
The 5000 Fingers of Dr. T '53
Born Yesterday '50
A Foreign Affair '48
Here Comes Mr. Jordan '41
Remember the Night '40
Bluebeard's Eighth Wife '38
Angel '37
Desire '35

David Holmes (1930-)
The Blue Angel '30
Braveheart '95
Casper '95
Jade '95
Jumanji '95
Mad Money '08
Charlie Wilson's War '07
The Spitfire Grill '96
I Am Legend '07
The Lookout '07
Michael Clayton '07
The Water Horse: Legend of the Deep '07
Halloween 5: The Revenge of Michael Myers '89
Halloween 4: The Return of Michael Myers '88
They Live '88
Michael Myers '95
Big Trouble in Little China '86

Ocean's Thirteen '07
The War Within '05
Ocean's Twelve '04
Code 46 '03
Stander '03
Analyze That '02
Ocean's Eleven '01
Buffalo Soldiers '01
Resurrection Man '97

Rupert Holmes
No Small Affair '84
Jack the Bear '93
A Far-Off Place '93
Bopha! '93
The Pagemaster '94

Nigel Holton (1952-2006)
The Pelican Brief '93
The Man Without a Face '93
Searching for Bobby Fischer '93

Toshiyuki Honda (1957-)
Minbo—Or the Gentle Art of Japanese Extortion '92
A Taxing Woman '87

Arthur Honegger (1892-1955)
Harvest '37
Crime and Punishment '35
Napoleon '27

Nicholas Hooper
Harry Potter and the Order of the Phoenix '07
The Chatterley Affair '06

Tobe Hooper (1946-)
The Way We Live Now '02
The Heart of Me '02
State of Play '03
Bloodlines '05
The Texas Chainsaw Massacre 2 '86
The Texas Chainsaw Massacre '74

Anthony Hopkins (1937-)
Slipstream '07
August '96

Kenyon Hopkins (1912-83)
Lilith '64
The Strange One '57
Twelve Angry Men '57

James Horner (1953-)
The Spiderwick Chronicles '08
All the King's Men '06
Apocalypto '06
The New World '05
The Legend of Zorro '05
Flightplan '05
Troy '04
The Forgotten '04
Beyond Borders '03
House of Sand and Fog '03
The Missing '03
Radio '03
The Four Feathers '02
Windtalkers '02
A Beautiful Mind '01
Iris '01
Dr. Seuss' How the Grinch Stole Christmas '00
Enemy at the Gates '00
Freedom Song '00
Bicentennial Man '99
Deep Impact '98
The Mask of Zorro '98
Mighty Joe Young '98
The Devil's Own '96
Ransom '96
To Gillian on Her 37th Birthday '96
Apollo 13 '95
Balto '95
Braveheart '95
Casper '95
Jade '95
Jumanji '95
Legends of the Fall '94
Clear and Present Danger '94
Jack the Bear '93
A Far-Off Place '93
Bopha! '93
The Pelican Brief '93
Searching for Bobby Fischer '93
Swing Kids '93
Patriot Games '92
Sneakers '92
Thunderheart '92
Unlawful Entry '92
Once Around '91
My Heroes Have Always Been Cowboys '91
An American Tail: Fievel Goes West '91
Class Action '91
Another 48 Hrs. '90
I Love You to Death '90
Dad '89
Field of Dreams '89
Glory '89
Honey, I Shrunk the Kids '89
In Country '89
Cocoon: The Return '88
The Land Before Time '88
Red Heat '88
Vibes '88
Willow '88
*batteries not included '87
Project X '87
An American Tail '86
The Name of the Rose '86
Off Beat '86
Where the River Runs Black '86
Aliens '86
Cocoon '85
Commando '85
Heaven Help Us '85
The Journey of Natty Gann '85
P.K. and the Kid '85
Volunteers '85
Star Trek III: The Search for Spock '84
The Stone Boy '84
Between Friends '83
Brainstorm '83
The Dresser '83
Gorky Park '83
Krull '83
Something Wicked This Way Comes '83
Testament '83
Uncommon Valor '83
48 Hrs. '82
A Piano for Mrs. Cimino '82
Star Trek 2: The Wrath of Khan '82
Deadly Blessing '81
The Hand '81
The Pursuit of D.B. Cooper '81
Wolfen '81
Battle Beyond the Stars '80
Humanoids from the Deep '80
Lady in Red '79
Up from the Depths '79

Richard Horowitz
Drowning on Dry Land '00
Three Seasons '98
Broken Trust '95

Vladimir Horunzhy (1949-)
Original Gangstas '96
Stephen King's The Langoliers '95
Blink of an Eye '92
Point of Impact '93
Three Men and a Little Lady '90
The Sheltering Sky '90
Lakota Woman: Siege at Wounded Knee '94

James Newton Howard (1951-)
The Dark Knight '08
The Happening '08
Michael Clayton '07
I Am Legend '07
The Great Debaters '07
Charlie Wilson's War '07
Blood Diamond '06
Freedomland '06
Lady in the Water '06
RV '06
King Kong '05
Batman Begins '05
The Interpreter '05
Collateral '04
The Village '04
Hidalgo '04
Peter Pan '03
Dreamcatcher '03
Unconditional Love '03
Signs '02
Treasure Planet '02
Big Trouble '02
Unbreakable '00
Dinosaur '00
Vertical Limit '00
The Sixth Sense '99
Runaway Bride '99
Stir of Echoes '99
Snow Falling on Cedars '99
A Perfect Murder '98
The Devil's Advocate '97
My Best Friend's Wedding '97
The Postman '97
Father's Day '96
The Juror '96
One Fine Day '96
Primal Fear '96
The Trigger Effect '96
An Eye for an Eye '95
French Kiss '95
Outbreak '95
Just Cause '95
Restoration '95
Waterworld '95
Wyatt Earp '94
Junior '94
Intersection '93
Falling Down '93
The Fugitive '93
Dave '93
Alive '93
The Saint of Fort Washington '93
Diggstown '92
Glengarry Glen Ross '92
American Heart '92
Grand Canyon '91
Guilty by Suspicion '91
My Girl '91
King Ralph '91
The Prince of Tides '91
Flatliners '90
Pretty Woman '90
Marked for Death '90
Coupe de Ville '90
Somebody Has to Shoot the Picture '90
Three Men and a Little Lady '90
Tap '89
Major League '89
The Package '89
The Image '89
Five Corners '88
Promised Land '88
Some Girls '88
Campus Man '87
Off Limits '87
Russkies '87
Head Office '86
Nobody's Fool '86
Never Too Young to Die '86
Tough Guys '86

Alan Howarth
Bats '95
Braveheart '95
Casper '95
Jade '95
Jumanji '95
Wildcats '86
8 Million Ways to Die '85
Alone with a Stranger '99
Yourself '99
The Dentist 2: Brace Yourself '98
The Dentist '96
Halloween 6: The Curse of Michael Myers '95
Halloween 5: The Revenge of Michael Myers '89
Halloween 4: The Return of Michael Myers '88
They Live '88
Big Trouble in Little China '86
Christine '84
C.H.U.D. '84

David A. Hughes (1960-)
Bob the Butler '05
The Long Weekend '05
New Best Friend '02
One More Kiss '99
Lock, Stock and 2 Smoking Barrels '98
Stiff Upper Lips '96
Solitaire for 2 '94

Gary Hughes (1922-78)
The Dark Knight '08
A Challenge for Robin Hood '67
The Viking Queen '67

Tony Humecke
The Dead One '07
November Conspiracy '06
The Feminine Touch '95

Don Hulette (1937-)
Greedy Terror '78
Breaker! Breaker! '77

Nina Humphreys
Warrior Queen '03
Sword of Honour '01

Steve Hunter
Cyber Bandits '94

Robert Hurst
Brown Sugar '02
The Wood '99

Zakir Hussain
The Mystic Masseur '01
In Custody '94

Terry Huud
Civic Duty '06
Paranoia 1.0 '04

Jeehun Hwang
The Lemon Sisters '90
Leader of the Band '87
Midnight Clear '06

Tor Hyams
100 Mile Rule '02
The Substitute 3: Winner Takes All '99

Dick Hyman (1927-)
Sweet and Lowdown '99
Everyone Says I Love You '96
Mighty Aphrodite '95
Alan & Naomi '92
The Lemon Sisters '90

Abdullah Ibrahim (1934-)
No Fear, No Die '90
Tilaï '90

Akira Ifukube (1914-2006)
Godzilla '54
Godzilla vs. King Ghidorah '91
Terror of Mechagodzilla '75
Yog, Monster from Space '71
War of the Gargantuas '66
Destroy All Monsters '68
Godzilla vs. Monster Zero '65
Ghidrah, the Three Headed Monster '65

Ifukube

Zatoichi: The Blind Swordsman and the Chess Expert '65
Godzilla vs. Mothra '64
King Kong vs. Godzilla '63
The Burmese Harp '56
Godzilla, King of the Monsters '56
A Quiet Duel '49

Alberto Iglesias (1955-)

The Kite Runner '07
Volver '06
The Constant Gardener '05
Bad Education '04
Take My Eyes '03
The Dancer Upstairs '02
Talk to Her '02
Sex and Lucia '01
All About My Mother '99
Lovers of the Arctic Circle '98
The Chambermaid on the Titanic '97
Live Flesh '97
The Flower of My Secret '95
Tierra '95
Outrage '93
The Red Squirrel '93
Vacas '91

Shinichiro Ikebe (1943-)

The Eel '96
Rhapsody in August '91
Akira Kurosawa's Dreams '90
The Ballad of Narayama '83
Kagemusha '80
Vengeance Is Mine '79

Neil Innes (1944-)

Erik the Viking '89
All You Need Is Cash '78
Monty Python and the Holy Grail '75

Akira Inoue

Lensman '84
Young Master '80

Ashley Irwin

Naked City: Justice with a Bullet '98
Entertaining Angels: The Dorothy Day Story '96
The Expert '95
Secret Games 3 '94
Stranger by Night '94
Undercover '94
Secret Games 2: The Escort '93
Sins of the Night '93
Deadly Rivals '92
Fair Game '85

Pat Irwin

Bam Bam & Celeste '05
But I'm a Cheerleader '99
Breathing Room '96
Sudden Manhattan '96
My New Gun '92

Bjorn Isfalt (1942-97)

What's Eating Gilbert Grape '93
My Life As a Dog '85

Mark Isham (1951-)

Freedom Writers '07
Gracie '07
In the Valley of Elah '07
Lions for Lambs '07
The Mist '07
Next '07
Reservation Road '07
The Black Dahlia '06
Bobby '06
Eight Below '06
Invincible '06
Running Scared '06
Crash '05
In Her Shoes '05
Kicking & Screaming '05
Racing Stripes '05
Miracle '04
Twisted '04
The Cooler '03
Highwaymen '04
Impostor '02
Moonlight Mile '02
Don't Say a Word '01
Hardball '01

Life as a House '01
The Majestic '01
Save the Last Dance '01
Men of Honor '00
Rules of Engagement '00
Trixie '00
Where the Money Is '00
Body Shots '99
October Sky '99
At First Sight '98
Blade '98
Breakfast of Champions '98
The Defenders: Taking the First '98
Varsity Blues '98
Afterglow '97
The Defenders: Payback '97
The Education of Little Tree '97
The Gingerbread Man '97
Kiss the Girls '97
Fly Away Home '96
Gotti '96
Last Dance '96
Night Falls on Manhattan '96
Home for the Holidays '95
Miami Rhapsody '95
The Net '95
The Browning Version '94
Losing Isaiah '94
Mrs. Parker and the Vicious Circle '94
Quiz Show '94
Safe Passage '94
Timecop '94
Fire in the Sky '93
The Getaway '93
Made in America '93
Nowhere to Run '93
Romeo Is Bleeding '93
Short Cuts '93
Cool World '92
A Midnight Clear '92
Of Mice and Men '92
A River Runs Through It '92
Billy Bathgate '91
Crooked Hearts '91
Little Man Tate '91
Mortal Thoughts '91
Point Break '91
Reversal of Fortune '90
The Beast '88
The Moderns '88
Made in Heaven '87
The Hitcher '86
Trouble in Mind '86
Mrs. Soffel '84
Never Cry Wolf '83

Peter Ivers (1946-83)

Eraserhead '78
Grand Theft Auto '77

Steve Jablonsky

The Hitcher '07
Transformers '07
The Texas Chainsaw Massacre: The Beginning '06
The Amityville Horror '05
The Island '05
Steamboy '05
The Texas Chainsaw Massacre '03

Corey A. Jackson (1968-)

Left in Darkness '06
It Waits '05

Howard Jackson (1900-66)

Merrill's Marauders '62
Sergeant Rutledge '60
A Slight Case of Murder '38
The Great Gabbo '29

Joe Jackson (1954-)

Queens Logic '91
Tucker: The Man and His Dream '88
Party! Party! '83

Sidney James

Strange Fruit '04
Tube Buster '99

Leos Janacek (1854-1928)

The Unbearable Lightness of Being '88
Don's Party '76

Chaz Jankel (1952-)

The Rachel Papers '89
D.O.A. '88

Alaric Jans

The Winslow Boy '98
Things Change '88
House of Games '87

Pierre Jansen (1930-)

Violette '78
A Piece of Pleasure '74
La Rupture '70
La Femme Infidele '69
The 317th Platoon '65
Les Bonnes Femmes '60

Werner Janssen (1899-1990)

A Night in Casablanca '46
The Southerner '45
Guest in the House '44

Maurice Jarre (1924-)

Uprising '01
I Dreamed of Africa '00
Sunshine '99
Sunchaser '96
Fearless '93
Mr. Jones '93
School Ties '92
Solar Crisis '92
Fires Within '91
Only the Lonely '91
After Dark, My Sweet '90
Ghost '90
Jacob's Ladder '90
Chances Are '89
Dead Poets Society '89
Enemies, a Love Story '89
Prancer '89
Distant Thunder '88
Gorillas in the Mist '88
Moon over Parador '88
Wildfire '88
Fatal Attraction '87
Gaby: A True Story '87
Julia and Julia '87
The Murder of Mary Phagan '87
No Way Out '87
Apology '86
The Mosquito Coast '86
Solarbabies '86
Tai-Pan '86
The Bride '85
Enemy Mine '85
Mad Max: Beyond Thunderdome '85
Witness '85
Dreamscape '84
A Passage to India '84
Samson and Delilah '84
Top Secret! '84
Coming Out of the Ice '82
Don't Cry, It's Only Thunder '82
Firefox '82
The Year of Living Dangerously '82
Young Doctors in Love '82
Lion of the Desert '81
Taps '81
Enola Gay: The Men, the Mission, the Atomic Bomb '80
The Last Flight of Noah's Ark '80
Resurrection '80
Shogun '80
The Black Marble '79
The Magician of Lublin '79
The Tin Drum '79
Winter Kills '79
The Prince and the Pauper '78
Users '78
Jesus of Nazareth '77
March or Die '77
The Message '77
The Last Tycoon '76
Shout at the Devil '76
The Man Who Would Be King '75
Mandingo '75
Posse '75
The Island at the Top of the World '74
Mr. Sycamore '74
Ash Wednesday '73
Mackintosh Man '73
Life & Times of Judge Roy Bean '72

Plaza Suite '71
Red Sun '71
El Condor '70
Ryan's Daughter '70
The Damned '69
Topaz '69
Five Card Stud '68
The Fixer '68
Isadora '68
Villa Rides '68
Night of the Generals '67
Gambit '66
Grand Prix '66
Is Paris Burning? '66
The Professionals '66
The Collector '65
Doctor Zhivago '65
The Train '65
Behold a Pale Horse '64
Judex '64
Lawrence of Arabia '62
The Longest Day '62
Sundays & Cybele '62
The Horror Chamber of Dr. Faustus '59

Maurice Jaubert (1900-40)

The Green Room '78
The Man Who Loved Women '77
Small Change '76
The Story of Adele H. '75
Bizarre Bizarre '39
L'Atalante '34

Gordon Jenkins (1910-)

The First Deadly Sin '80
San Fernando Valley '44

Merrill Jenson

The Red Fury '84
Three Warriors '77

Geir Jenssen (1962-)

Kill by Inches '99
Insomnia '97

Peter Jermyn

The Climb '87
Self-Defense '83

Elton John (1947-)

The Road to El Dorado '00
The Lion King '94
Friends '71

Carl Johnson

Piglet's Big Movie '03
Gargoyles, The Movie: The Heroes Awaken '94

J.J. Johnson (1924-2001)

Cleopatra Jones '73
Shaft '71

Laurie Johnson (1927-)

The Lady and the Highwayman '89
It's Alive 3: Island of the Alive '87
Anatomy of Terror '74
Captain Kronos: Vampire Hunter '74
One Deadly Owner '74
And Soon the Darkness '70
Dr. Strangelove, or: How I Learned to Stop Worrying and Love the Bomb '64
First Men in the Moon '64
Tiger Bay '59

Nathan Johnson

Blue State '07
Brick '06

Adrian Johnston

Becoming Jane '07
My Boy Jack '07
Kinky Boots '06
Friends & Crocodiles '05
Gideon's Daughter '05
Lassie '05
If Only '04
Byron '03
The Mayor of Casterbridge '03
Shackleton '02

This Is Not a Love Song '02
Tipping the Velvet '02
Almost Strangers '01
Lawless Heart '01
Me Without You '01
About Adam '00
All the King's Men '99
Robert Louis Stevenson's The Game of Death '99
The Turn of the Screw '99
I Want You '98
Our Mutual Friend '98
Touching Evil '97
Welcome to Sarajevo '97
Jude '96

Arthur Johnston (1898-1954)

Sidewalks of London '38
Pennies from Heaven '36
Belle of the Nineties '34
Murder at the Vanities '34
College Humor '33

Bobby Johnston

Wristcutters: A Love Story '06
I Walk the Line '70

Alain Jomy (1941-)

The Accompanist '93
The Little Thief '89
The Best Way '76

Dan (Daniel) Jones (1924-)

Four Last Songs '06
Jericho Mansions '03
Max '02
Shadow of the Vampire '00
The Weekend '00

Jeffrey Alan Jones

Serial Killing 101 '04
Crack Up '97

Kenneth V. Jones (1924-)

Tower of Evil '72
Tomb of Ligeia '64
Dentist in the Chair '60
The Horse's Mouth '58
Sea Wife '57

Quincy Jones (1933-)

Get Rich or Die Tryin' '05
The Color Purple '85
The Wiz '78
Roots '77
The Getaway '72
The New Centurions '72
The Anderson Tapes '71
Dollars '71
Honky '71
Man & Boy '71
Brother John '70
The Hot Rock '70
They Call Me Mr. Tibbs! '70
Bob & Carol & Ted & Alice '69
Mirage '66
Walk, Don't Run '66
The Pawnbroker '65
The Slender Thread '65

Ralph Jones

Love Letters '83
Slumber Party Massacre '82

Rickie Lee Jones (1954-)

Subway '85

Terry Jones (1942-)

Mr. Toad's Wild Ride '96
Monty Python's The Meaning of Life '83

Tim Jones

Bobby Z '07
Karla '06

Timothy S. (Tim) Jones (1971-)

Attack of the Sabretooth '05
Sniper 3 '04
Amazons and Gladiators '01
The Forsaken '01
True Blue '01

Killer Instinct '00

Trevor Jones (1949-)

Around the World in 80 Days '04
I'll Be There '03
The League of Extraordinary Gentlemen '03
Crossroads '02
Dinotopia '02
The Gathering Storm '02
From Hell '01
Thirteen Days '00
Cleopatra '99
Molly '99
Notting Hill '99
Desperate Measures '98
Merlin '98
The Mighty '98
Dark City '97
G.I. Jane '97
Brassed Off '96
For Roseanna '96
Lawn Dogs '96
Talk of Angels '96
Gulliver's Travels '95
Loch Ness '95
Richard III '95
Hideaway '94
Kiss of Death '94
Cliffhanger '93
In the Name of the Father '93
Blame It on the Bellboy '92
Chains of Gold '92
Crisscross '92
Freejack '92
The Last of the Mohicans '92
Defenseless '91
Murder by Moonlight '91
Arachnophobia '90
Bad Influence '90
By Dawn's Early Light '89
Diamond's Edge '88
Dominick & Eugene '88
Mississippi Burning '88
Sweet Lies '88
Angel Heart '87
Labyrinth '86
The Last Place on Earth '85
Runaway Train '85
Nate and Hayes '83
Those Glory, Glory Days '83
The Dark Crystal '82
The Sender '82
Excalibur '81

Wilfred Josephs (1927-97)

All Creatures Great and Small '74
Diel Diel My Darling! '65

Phil Judd (1953-)

Amy '98
Mr. Reliable: A True Story '95
Rikky and Pete '88

David Julyan

Outlaw '07
The Prestige '06
The Descent '05
The Last Drop '05
Rory O'Shea Was Here '04
Insomnia '02
Memento '00
Following '99

Bill Justis (1926-82)

The Villain '79
Hooper '78
Smokey and the Bandit '77

Jeppe Kaas (1966-)

Adam's Apples '05
The Green Butchers '03
Flickering Lights '01

Jan A.P. Kaczmarek (1953-)

Evening '07
The Visitor '07
Finding Neverland '04
Soldier's Girl '03
Lost Souls '00
The Third Miracle '99
Aimee & Jaguar '98
Washington Square '97
Bliss '96

Bert Kalmar (1884-1947)
Duck Soup '33
Animal Crackers '30

Peter Kam
Tokyo Raiders '00
The Accidental Spy '01

Camara Kambon
The Cookout '04
Biker Boyz '03

Michael Kamen (1948-2003)
What Dreams May Come '98
Lethal Weapon 4 '98
From the Earth to the Moon '98
Iron Giant '99
X-Men '00
Frequency '00
Band of Brothers '01
Open Range '03
First Daughter '04
Against the Ropes '04
Event Horizon '97
Inventing the Abbotts '97
The Winter Guest '97
Jack '96
101 Dalmatians '96
Die Hard: With a Vengeance '95
Mr. Holland's Opus '95
Stonewall '95
Circle of Friends '94
Don Juan DeMarco '94
The Three Musketeers '93
Last Action Hero '93
Splitting Heirs '93
Wilder Napalm '93
Shining Through '92
Blue Ice '92
Lethal Weapon 3 '92
Hudson Hawk '91
Robin Hood: Prince of Thieves '91
The Raggedy Rawney '90
Die Hard 2: Die Harder '90
The Krays '90
The Adventures of Baron Munchausen '89
License to Kill '89
Road House '89
Renegades '89
Rooftops '89
Action Jackson '88
Die Hard '88
Homeboy '88
Adventures in Babysitting '87
Lethal Weapon '87
Someone to Watch Over Me '87
Suspect '87
Rita, Sue & Bob Too '87
Edge of Darkness '86
Highlander '86
Mona Lisa '86
Shanghai Surprise '86
Brazil '85
Lifeforce '85
Angelo My Love '83
Dead Zone '83
Pink Floyd: The Wall '82
Venom '82
Polyester '81
S*H*E '79
Stunts '77
Between the Lines '77
The Next Man '76

Tuomas Kantelinen (1969-)
Mindhunters '05
Mother of Mine '05

Artie Kane
Devil Dog: The Hound of Hell '78
The Bat People '74

John Kander (1927-)
Chicago '02
The Boys Next Door '96
I Want to Go Home '89

Bronisław Kaper (1902-83)
Lord Jim '65
Somebody Up There Likes Me '56
Them! '54
Lili '53
The Naked Spur '53
The Red Badge of Courage '51
Malaya '49
The Secret Garden '49
Act of Violence '48
Gaslight '44
Above Suspicion '43
Bataan '43
Keeper of the Flame '42
White Cargo '42
A Woman's Face '41
A Day at the Races '37

Elliot Kaplan
Cry Blood, Apache '70
Finnegan's Wake '65

Sol Kaplan (1919-90)
Over the Edge '79
The Spy Who Came in from the Cold '65
The Victors '63
Salt of the Earth '54
Niagara '52
Tales of Manhattan '42

Dana Kaproff
Murder at Devil's Glen '99
Dead Air '94
When a Stranger Calls Back '33

Fred Karger (1916-79)
Fastest Guitar Alive '68
Frankie and Johnny '65

Eleni Karaindrou (1939-)
Weeping Meadow '04
Eternity and a Day '97
Ulysses' Gaze '95
Landscape in the Mist '88

Fred Karlin (1936-2004)
Thank you, Mr. Moto '37
Think Fast, Mr. Moto '37
Charlie Chan at the Circus '36
Charlie Chan at the Race Track '36
Charlie Chan in Egypt '35
Charlie Chan in Shanghai '35
Steamboat Round the Bend '35
Charlie Chan in London '34
365 Nights in Hollywood '34
Doctor Bull '33
The Black Camel '31

Brian Keane
Hometown '96
Stephen King's The Night Flier '96

John Keane
Born Innocent '74
Yours, Mine & Ours '68
Westworld '73
The Autobiography of Miss Jane Pittman '74
Greased Lightning '77
The Beautiful, the Bloody and the Bare '64
Teenage Gang Debs '66
Teenage Mother '67

Steve Karmen
Born Innocent '74

Al Kasha (1937-)
Rescue Me '93
The Closer '91
The Fat Spy '66

Laura Karpman
Carrie '02
Taken '02

John Kastner
Brotherhood of Murder '99
Dash and Lilly '99
Unfinished Business '98
Doing Time on Maple Drive '92
A Very British Coup '88
Cash '93

Fred Katz (1919-)
Sex, Love and Cold Hard Cash '93

Emilio Kauderer
A Place in the World '92
Savage Instinct '89

John Kauderer
Sea '60
Creature from the Haunted Sea '60

Arthur Kempel (1945-2004)
Stray Bullet '96
The Arrival '96
Behind Enemy Lines '96
Riders of the Purple Sage '96

Bernhard Kaun (1899-1980)
The Black Legion '37
Petrified Forest '36
Bureau of Missing Persons '33
Employees' Entrance '33
The Kennel Murder Case '33

Edward Kay (1898-1973)
Decoy '46
Bowery at Midnight '42
King of the Zombies '41
Phantom of Chinatown '40
Tomboy '40
Up in the Air '40

Norman Kaye (1927-2007)
Vincent: The Life and Death of Vincent van Gogh '87
Lonely Hearts '82

Samuel Kaylin
Charlie Chan at Treasure Island '39
Mr. Moto in Danger Island '39
Mr. Moto Takes a Chance '38
Mysterious Mr. Moto '38
Mr. Moto's Gamble '38
Mr. Moto Takes a Vacation '39

Victoria Kelly (1973-)
Black Sheep '06
The Ugly '96

Paul Kelly (1955-)
Full Tilt Boogie '97

Dominic Kelly
The Lather Effect '06

Kevin Kiner
The First Nudie Musical '75

John Kimbrough
Pizza '05
Winter Passing '05

Mark Killian
Lover Girl '97
Trojan Eddie '96
Small Faces '95
A Vow to Kill '94
Hideous Kinky '99
The Break '97
Bombshells '00
Land of Promise '74
Illumination '73
Family Life '71
Dracula '73

Bruce Kimmel (1947-)
Ratings Game '84
The Creature Wasn't Nice '81

Jerome Kern (1885-1945)
Can't Help Singing '45
Cover Girl '44
You Never Were Lovelier '42
Lady Be Good '41
Joy of Living '38
Show Boat '36
Swing Time '36
Sweet Adeline '35
The Cat and the Fiddle '34

Wojciech Kilar (1932-)
We Own the Night '07
The Pianist '02
Zensta '02
The Ninth Gate '99
Portrait of a Lady '96
Death and the Maiden '94
The Silent Touch '94
From a Far Country: Pope John Paul II '81
Contract '80

Larry Klein
Sugar Town '99
Grace of My Heart '96
Mr. Walkie Talkie '52
Silver Star '55
Lonesome Trail '55

Johnny Klimek (1962-)
One Missed Call '08
Dracula 3: Legacy '05
Paris, je t'aime '06
Perfume: The Story of a Murderer '06
The Cave '05

Kevin Kliesch (1970-)
Dracula 2: Ascension '03

Kevin Klinger
Afterschock '88
Necromancer: Satan's Servant '88

Leo Klatzkin (1914-92)
Look Who's Talking Now '93
Look Who's Talking, Too '90
Look Who's Talking '89
Breaking the Rules '92
Trading Mom '94
Surf Ninjas '93
Father and Scout '94

Greg Kendall
Drive Me Crazy '99
BardwAgon '95

Rolfe Kent (1963-)
The Hunting Party '07
Reign Over Me '07
Failure to Launch '06
The Matador '06
Thank You for Smoking '06
You, Me and Dupree '06
Just like Heaven '05
The Last Shot '04
Mean Girls '04
Sideways '04
Freaky Friday '03
Legally Blonde 2: Red White & Blonde '03
About Schmidt '02
40 Days and 40 Nights '02
Happy Campers '01
Kate & Leopold '01
Legally Blonde '01
Someone Like You '01
Nurse Betty '00
Town and Country '01
Gun Shy '00
Election '99
Oxygen '99
Slums of Beverly Hills '98
The Theory of Flight '98
Citizen Ruth '96
Dead Connection '94
Final Combination '93

David Kitay
Over Her Dead Body '08
Because I Said So '07
Shanghai Kiss '07
Smiley Face '07
Art School Confidential '06
The Darwin Awards '06
Date Movie '06
Relative Strangers '06
The Family Plan '05
The Ice Harvest '05
The Family Stone '05
Harold and Kumar Go to White Castle '04
Bad Santa '03
How to Deal '03
I Witness '03
Ghost World '01
The Stickup '01
Tomcats '01
Dude, Where's My Car? '00
Loser '00
Scary Movie '00
Can't Hardly Wait '98
A Night at the Roxbury '98
Clueless '95
Roosters '95

Chuji Kinoshita
The Human Condition: Road to Eternity '59
The Human Condition: No Greater Love '58

Basil Kirchin (1927-2005)
The Freakmaker '73
The Abominable Dr. Phibes '71

Thomas Knak
Reconstruction '03

Jurgen Knieper (1941-)
Allegro '05
The Promise '94
The Bride '85
December Bride '90
River's Edge '87
Wings of Desire '87
Local Hero '83
Comfort and Joy '84

Mark Knopfler (1949-)
A Shot at Glory '00
Metroland '97
Wag the Dog '97
The Princess Bride '87
Cal '84
Comfort and Joy '84
Local Hero '83

Gary Koftinoff
The Confessor '04

Krzysztof Komeda (1931-69)
Rosemary's Baby '68
The Fearless Vampire Killers '67
G2: Mortal Conquest '98
Breakout '98

Robbie Kondor
The Suburbans '99
Happiness '98

Joseph Koo
Fist of Legend '94
A Better Tomorrow, Part 2 '88
Return of the Dragon '73

Zygmunt Konieczny (1937-)
Landscape After Battle '70

Herman Kopp
Nekromantik 2 '91
Der Todesking '89
Nekromantik '87

Rudolph Kopp (1887-1972)
Vengeance Valley '51
Mystery Street '50
The Crusades '35
The Sign of the Cross '33

Brian Koonin
Mr. Nanny '93
When Angels Fly '82

Mark Korven
Shake Hands With the Devil: The Journey of Roméo Dallaire '04
Cube '98
Curtis's Charm '96

Erich Wolfgang Korngold (1897-1957)
Kings Row '41
The Adventures of Robin Hood '38
The Prince and the Pauper '37
Anthony Adverse '36
Captain Blood '35
Man of Iron '81
Man of Marble '85
Possession '81

Andrzej Korzynski (1940-)
Man of Marble '85
Man of Iron '81
Possession '81
Everything for Sale '68

Harald Kloser (1956-)
10,000 B.C. '08
Dresden '06
Alien vs. Predator '04
The Day After Tomorrow '04
Targeted '02
One Hour Photo '02
The Princess and the Warrior '00
Winter Sleepers '97
Singing '87

Richard Kosinski
Bloodstorm: Subspecies 4 '98

Black Scorpion 2: Ground Zero '96
Carnosaur 3: Primal Species '96
Lifeform '96
The Pest '96
Black Scorpion '95
Demolition High '95
Magenta '96
The O.J. Simpson Story '94
Exit '95
Freaked '93

RFK '02
Sins of the Father '01
The Tunnel '01
Kiss Tomorrow Goodbye '00
The Harmonists '97
The Thirteenth Floor '99
Quiet Days in Hollywood '97
The Blonde '92
Excessive Force 2: Force on Force '95
Demolition University '97

Magic in the Mirror: Fowl Play '96
Spellbreaker: Secret of the Leprechauns '96
Vampire Journals '96

Joseph Kosma (1905-69)
The Testament of Dr. Cordelier '59
Children of Paradise '44
Grand Illusion '37
The Crime of Monsieur Lange '36

Irwin Kostal (1911-94)
Pete's Dragon '77
Charlotte's Web '73

Ivan Koutikov
Undead or Alive '07
The Haunting of Hell House '99

Joe Kraemer
Ten 'Til Noon '06
The Thirst '06
An Unreasonable Man '06
House of the Dead 2: Dead Aim '05
Mystery Woman: Mystery Weekend '05
The Hitcher 2: I've Been Waiting '03
A Time to Remember '03
Way of the Gun '00

Robert Kraft
The Mambo Kings '92
Hudson Hawk '91

Raoul Kraushaar (1908-2001)
Billy the Kid Versus Dracula '66
Jesse James Meets Frankenstein's Daughter '65
Sitting Bull '54
The Blue Gardenia '53
Invaders from Mars '53
Sky Liner '49
Blast of Silence '61

Amanda Kravat (1966-)
Never Again '01
Wirey Spindell '99
Fall '97
If Lucy Fell '95

Jan Krenz (1926-)
Ashes and Diamonds '58
Kanal '56

Meyer Kupferman (1926-2003)
Fallen Angel '99
Requiem for Murder '99
Dead End '98
Goldstein '61
Little Men '49

David Kurtz
Alien Nation: Millennium '96
Alien Nation: Body and Soul '95
Alien Nation: Dark Horizon '94

Teddy Robin Kwan
Full Contact '92
City on Fire '87

Milan Kymlicka (1936-)
Sir Arthur Conan Doyle's The Lost World '98
Sci-Fighters '96
Legends of the North '95
Margaret's Museum '95
The Paperboy '94
Psychic '91

Simon Lacey
Me & Mrs. Jones '02
The Railway Children '00

Francis Lai (1932-)
Les Miserables '95
Marie '85
My New Partner '84
Cat and Mouse '78
Emmanuelle, the Joys of a Woman '76
Insanity '76
By the Blood of Others '73
Killing in the Sun '70
Love Story '70

Jim Lang
Hey Arnold! The Movie '02
In the Mouth of Madness '95
Body Bags '93
For Love or Money '88

Arthur Lange (1889-1956)
Pride of St. Louis '52
Along Came Jones '45
Casanova Brown '44
Woman in the Window '44
In Old Kentucky '35

Johnny Lange (1905-2006)
Flying Wild '41
Up in the Air '40
Six Gun Rhythm '39

Clive Langer
Brothers of the Head '06
Still Crazy '98

Bruce Langhorne
Fourth Wise Man '85
Melvin and Howard '80
Hired Hand '71

Brian Langsbard
The Specials '00
Johnny Skidmarks '97

Daniel Lanois (1951-)
The Million Dollar Hotel '99
Sling Blade '96
Camilla '94

Tito Larriva
Just a Little Harmless Sex '99
Dream with the Fishes '97

Nathan Larson (1970-)
Little Fish '05
A Love Song for Bobby Long '04
Palindromes '04
The Woodsman '04
Dirty Pretty Things '03
The Chateau '01
Prozac Nation '01
Storytelling '01
Boys Don't Cry '99

Alexander Lasarenko
Pipe Dream '02
The Business of Strangers '01
Dinner Rush '00

Jeff Lass
Partners '99
Matter of Trust '98
Laws of Deception '97
The Student Affair '97
Hard Vice '94
Vegas Vice '94
DaVinci's War '92

Alexander Laszlo (1895-1970)
Atomic Submarine '59
Attack of the Giant Leeches '59
Night of the Blood Beast '58
Rocky Jones, Space Ranger: Renegade Satellite '54
Dangerous Passage '44
One Body Too Many '44

Jim Latham
Tweek City '05
On Edge '03

William Lava (1911-71)
Dracula vs. Frankenstein '71
Zorro's Fighting Legion '39

Angelo Francesco Lavagnino (1909-87)
Stranger in Paso Bravo '68
Chimes at Midnight '67
Hero of Rome '63
Gorgo '61
Esther and the King '60
Roland the Mighty '56
Othello '52

Raul Lavista
Simon of the Desert '65
The Exterminating Angel '62
Daniel Boone: Trail Blazer '56

David Lawrence
High School Musical 2 '07
High School Musical '06
Getting Played '05
Jiminy Glick in LaLa Wood '05
National Lampoon's Van Wilder '02
American Pie 2 '01
Life Without Dick '01
Company Man '00
American Pie '99
Hi-Life '98
Steel Sharks '97
Moving Target '96
Alone in the Woods '95
Sleep with Me '94
Skeeter '93

Stephen Lawrence
Red Riding Hood '88
Alice Sweet Alice '76

Maury Laws
The Return of the King '80
The Hobbit '78

Alan Ari Lazar (1967-)
Two Days '03
Purpose '02
Billy's Hollywood Screen Kiss '98

Maurice Le Roux
See Maurice Leroux

Adrian Lee
The Medallion '03
The Reckoning '03

Bill Lee (1928-)
Mo' Better Blues '90
Do the Right Thing '89
School Daze '88
She's Gotta Have It '86

Byung-woo Lee
The Host '06
A Tale of Two Sisters '03

Jon Lee
Afghan Knights '07
Who's Your Caddy? '07
The Tooth Fairy '06

Eric Leeds
Giant Steps '92
Giant Steps '92

Michel Legrand (1932-)
And Now Ladies and Gentlemen '02
La Buche '00
Madeline '98
Ready to Wear '94
The Pickle '93
Dingo '90
The Jeweller's Shop '90
Switching Channels '88
Never Say Never Again '83
Yentl '83
Atlantic City '81
Falling in Love Again '80
The Mountain Men '80
A Slightly Pregnant Man '79
Roads to the South '78
It's Good to Be Alive '74
The Three Musketeers '74
Brian's Song '71
The Go-Between '71
Summer of '42 '71
The Young Girls of Rochefort '68
Band of Outsiders '64
Umbrellas of Cherbourg '64
Duke of the Derby '62
Eva '62
My Life to Live '62
Cleo from 5 to 7 '61
Keep Taking Baby '61
It Means That to Me '60
A Woman Is a Woman '60

Franz Lehar (1870-1948)
The Merry Widow '52
The Merry Widow '34

Jed Leiber
Blue Chips '94
Love Potion #9 '92

John Leipold (1888-1970)
The Desperadoes '43
Twilight on the Trail '41
Campus Confessions '38

Bruce Leitl
Man in the Mirror: The Michael Jackson Story '04
Ebenezer '97

Christopher Lennertz (1972-)
Alvin and the Chipmunks '07
The Comebacks '07
The Perfect Holiday '07
Dr. Dolittle 3 '06
Dr. Doolittle 3 '06
The Deal '05
The 4th Tenor '02
Undercurrent '99
Running Woman '98
Baby Face Nelson '97
Humanoids from the Deep '96
Spectre '96
Piranha '95
Suspect Device '95
Unknown Origin '95
Midnight Tease '94

John Lennon (1940-80)
Le Bal '82
Let It Be '70
Yellow Submarine '68
Magical Mystery Tour '67
Help! '65
A Hard Day's Night '64

Patrick Leonard
With Honors '94
Nowhere to Hide '83
On the Run '83

Valentine Leone (1975-)
At Close Range '86
Nothing in Common '86
Asylum of the Damned '03
Backflash '01

Cory Lerios
Boiling Point '93
Beyond the Law '92
Child's Play 3 '91
One Crazy Summer '86

Alan Jay Lerner (1918-86)
The Little Prince '74
Paint Your Wagon '69
Camelot '67
My Fair Lady '64
Brigadoon '54

Cesar Lerner
Lost Embrace '04
Nine Queens '00

Maurice Leroux
Le Petit Soldat '60
Les Mistons '57

Oscar Levant (1906-72)
Nothing Sacred '37
In Person '35
Gambling Ship '33

Sylvester Levay
Flashfire '94
Dead to Rights '93
Hot Shots! '91
Stone Cold '91
Navy SEALS '90
Courage Mountain '89
The Tracker '88
Burglar '87
Mannequin '87
Cobra '86
Howard the Duck '86
Invaders from Mars '86
Creator '85
Where the Boys Are '84 '84

Andres Levin
El Cantante '06
Feel the Noise '07

Geoff Levin
Who Made the Potatoe Salad? '05
Darkwolf '03
One of Them '03
Extreme Honor '01
Jimmy Zip '00
Perfect Assassins '98
Gang Boys '97

James Levine
Delta Farce '07
Running with Scissors '06
A Little Inside '01

Michael A. Levine
Adrift in Manhattan '07
Wonderland '03

Krishna Levy (1964-)
8 Women '02
Dad On the Run '00
Artemisia '97
My Sex Life... Or How I Got into an Argument '96

Louis Levy (1894-1957)
The Lady Vanishes '38
Young and Innocent '37
The Secret Agent '36
The 39 Steps '35

Shuki Levy
Turbo: A Power Rangers Movie '96
Blindfold: Acts of Obsession '94
Trapper County War '89
Fatal Games '84

Herschell Gordon Lewis (1926-)
This Stuff'll Kill Ya! '71
Moonshine Mountain '64
Blood Feast '63

John Lewis
Kemek '70
Odds Against Tomorrow '59

Laurie Lewis

Michael Lewis (1939-)
Deadly Target '94
Theatre of Blood '73
The Man Who Haunted Himself '70

Paul Lewis
The Maze '85
Murders at Lynch Cross '85

W. Michael Lewis
Hot Child in the City '87
Ballad of Gregorio Cortez '83
Revenge of the Ninja '83
Shogun Assassin '80
New Year's Evil '78

Blake Leyh
Outside the Law '95
True Crime '95

Daniel Licht
Frederick Forsyth's Icon '05
Video Voyeur: The Susan Wilson Story '02
Off Season '01
Soul Survivors '01
Cabin by the Lake '00
Cowboy Up '00
Hendrix '00
Splendor '99
Permanent Midnight '98
Bad Moon '96
Stephen King's Thinner '96
The Winner '96
Children of the Corn 3: Urban Harvest '95
Hellraiser 4: Bloodline '95
Woman Undone '95
Acting on Impulse '93
H.P. Lovecraft's Necronomicon: Book of the Dead '93
Final Embrace '92

Max Lichtenstein
Puzzlehead '05
Tarnation '03

Ivri Lider
The Bubble '06
Yossi & Jagger '02

Jacobo Lieberman
Trade '07
Maria Full of Grace '04
The Maldonado Miracle '03

Jimmy Lifton (1955-)
Powder Burn '96
Mirror, Mirror 2: Raven Dance '94
The Takeover '94
Mirror, Mirror '90

Joseph J. Lilley (1913-95)
How to Commit Marriage '69
Paradise, Hawaiian Style '66
Girls! Girls! Girls! '62
Sailor Beware '52

Hal Lindes (1953-)
Quicksand '01
Forgive and Forget '99
Gunshy '98
Reckless: The Sequel '98
Kiss and Tell '96
Band of Gold '95
The Infiltrator '95

Mort Lindsey (1923-)
Real Life '79
40 Pounds of Trouble '62

Michael Linn (1952-95)
Snapdragon '93
American Ninja '85

Michael Lipton
Heroes of the Heart '94
Invasion of the Space Preachers '90

Alan Lisk
R.P.M. '97

Zdenek Liska (1922-83)
Adelheid '69
Murder Czech Style '66
The Shop on Main Street '65
Death Is Called Engelchen '63
Fabulous Adventures of Baron Munchausen '61

Jay Livingston (1915-2001)
Red Garters '54
The Lemon Drop Kid '51

Andrew Lloyd Webber (1948-)

The Phantom of the Opera '04
Jesus Christ Superstar '00
Joseph and the Amazing Technicolor Dreamcoat '00

Lowell Lo
Shaolin Soccer '01
Naked Killer '92
The Killer '90
Prison on Fire 2 '91

Brian Lock
The Land Girls '98
The Gambler '98

Robert Lockhart
Inspector Lynley Mysteries: A Great Deliverance '01
Cold Comfort Farm '94

Andrew Lockington (1974-)
How She Move '08
Journey to the Center of the Earth 3D '08
Skinwalkers '07
Cake '05
Saint Ralph '04
Touch of Pink '04

Joseph LoDuca
Boogeyman '05
Devour '05
Brotherhood of the Wolf '01
Young Hercules '97
Hercules the Legendary Journeys, Vol. 1: And the Amazon Women '94
Hercules the Legendary Journeys, Vol. 2: The Lost Kingdom '94
Hercules the Legendary Journeys, Vol. 3: The Circle of Fire '94
Hercules the Legendary Journeys, Vol. 4: In the Underworld '94
H.P. Lovecraft's Necronomicon: Book of the Dead '93
Army of Darkness '92
Lunatics: A Love Story '92
The Carrier '87
Evil Dead 2: Dead by Dawn '87
Thou Shalt Not Kill...Except '87
Crimewave '85
Evil Dead '83

Frank Loesser (1910-69)
How to Succeed in Business without Really Trying '67
Guys and Dolls '55
Hans Christian Andersen '52
The Perils of Pauline '47
Hoppity Goes to Town '41

Frederick Loewe (1901-88)
The Little Prince '74
Paint Your Wagon '69
Camelot '67
My Fair Lady '64
Gigi '58
Brigadoon '54

Henning Lohner (1961-)
In the Name of the King: A Dungeon Siege Tale '08
BloodRayne '06
Hellraiser: Deader '05
The Ring 2 '05
Incident at Loch Ness '04
Mimic 3: Sentinel '03
A Brother's Kiss '97

Frank London
Everything Relative '96

Steve London
That Beautiful Somewhere '06
Shallow Ground '04

William Loose (1910-91)
Mystery Mansion '83
Dream Chasers '82
Johnny Firecloud '75
Supervixens '75
The Swinging Cheerleaders '74
Blacksnake! '73
The Big Bird Cage '72
Rebel Rousers '69
Mission to Death '66

Peter Lopez
Dirty '05
Dead Birds '04

Robert Lord (1900-76)
Pumpkinhead 4: Blood Feud '07
Pumpkinhead 3: Ashes to Ashes '06

Michael Lorenc
Brute '97

Daktari Lorenz (1962-)
Nekromantik 2 '91
Der Todesking '89

Jacques Loussier
The Five Senses '99

Alexina Louie (1949-)
Last Night '98

Richard Lowry (1964-)
Dark of the Sun '68

Mundell Lowe (1922-92)
Tarantulas: The Deadly Cargo '77
Everything You Always Wanted to Know about Sex (But Were Afraid to Ask) '72
Billy Jack '71
Satan in High Heels '61

Dario Lucantoni
Traveling Companion '96
Acli's Descent into Floristella '87

Eric Lundmark
Quigley '03
The Landlady '98
No Strings Attached '98
Bleak House '05
Like Father Like Son '05
Under the Greenwood Tree '05

John Lunn (1956-)
P.D. James: The Murder Room '04
Cambridge Spies '03
Once Upon a Time in the Midlands '02
Sirens '02
Lorna Doone '01
Get Real '99

Donal Lunny (1947-)
This is My Father '99
Eat the Peach '86

Deborah Lurie
Sydney White '07
Drop Dead Sexy '05
Imaginary Heroes '05
Sleepover '04
Whirlygirl '04

Evan Lurie (1954-)
Interview '07
Lisa Picard Is Famous '01
The Whole Shebang '01
Happy Accidents '00
Joe Gould's Secret '00
Office Killer '97
The Monster '96
Tree's Lounge '96
The Night We Never Met '93
Johnny Stecchino '92
Doomed Love '83

John Lurie (1952-)
Animal Factory '00
Clay Pigeons '98
Excess Baggage '96
Manny & Lo '96
Get Shorty '95
Mystery Train '89
Down by Law '86
Permanent Vacation '84
Stranger than Paradise '84
Variety '83

Lelio Luttazzi (1923-)
The Sisters '76
Joyful Laughter '60

Steven Lutvak
Mad Hot Ballroom '05
Anything But Love '02

Elisabeth Lutyens (1906-83)
Dr. Terror's House of Horrors '65
Paranoiac '62

Danny Lux
Lucky Seven '03
Halloween: Resurrection '02

Bruce Lynch
Hope Ranch '02

Allen Lynch
Stolen Summer '02
Mr. Klein '76

Randall Lynch
Mosquito '95
Rain Without Thunder '93
The Vector File '03

Egisto Macchi (1928-92)
The Rose Garden '89
Diary of a Mad Old Man '88
Padre Padrone '77

Neil MacColl
Fever Pitch '96

Galt MacDermot (1928-)
Mistress '91
Hair '79
Cotton Comes to Harlem '70

Don MacDonald
Dr. Dolittle 4: Tail to the Chief '08
Fido '06
Suspicious River '00
Kissed '96

Mader (1958-)
My Louisiana Sky '02
Steal This Movie! '00
Morgan's Ferry '99
In the Soup '92
Sons '89

Michel Magne (1930-84)
S.A.S. San Salvador '84
Cold Sweat '71
The Monocle '64
Any Number Can Win '63
Love on a Pillow '62

Cliff Magness
Body Shot '93
Beretta's Island '92

Stefano Mainetti (1957-)
Silent Trigger '97
Sub Down '97
Sons of Trinity '95
Hidden Assassin '94
Interzone '88

Hans-Martin Majewski (1911-97)
Brainwashed '60
The Bridge '59

William V. Malpede (1965-)
Dog Gone Love '03
Fast Sofa '01

Nikos Mamangakis (1929-)
Kaspar Hauser '93
Heimat 2 '92
Heimat 1 '84

Bob Manet
Lakeboat '00

Barry Manilow (1943-)
Thumbelina '94

Hummie Mann
Meat Loaf: To Hell and Back '00
Thomas and the Magic Railroad '00
After the Rain '99
Naked City: A Killer Christmas '98
The Pebble and the Penguin '94
Sticks and Stones '96
Dracula: Dead and Loving It '95
Cool and the Crazy '94
Fall Time '94
Girls in Prison '94
Jailbreakers '94
Runaway Daughters '94
Benefit of the Doubt '93
Robin Hood: Men in Tights '93
Year of the Comet '92
In Cold We Trust '91

Mark Mancina (1957-)
August Rush '07
Shooter '07
Asylum '05
Tarzan 2 '05
Brother Bear '03
The Reckoning '03
Training Day '01
Bait '00
Beyond Suspicion '00
From the Earth to the Moon '98
Return to Paradise '98
Speed 2: Cruise Control '97
Moll Flanders '96
Twister '96
Assassins '95
Bad Boys '95
Fair Game '95
Money Train '95
Monkey Trouble '94
Speed '94
True Romance '93

Henry Mancini (1924-94)
Married to It '93
Son of the Pink Panther '93
Tom and Jerry: The Movie '93
Never Forget '91
Switch '91
Fear '90
Ghost Dad '90
Peter Gunn '89
Physical Evidence '89
Skin Deep '89
Welcome Home '89
Sunset '88
Without a Clue '88
Blind Date '87
The Glass Menagerie '87
A Fine Mess '86
The Great Mouse Detective '86
That's Life! '86
Lifeforce '85
Santa Claus: The Movie '85
That's Dancing! '85
Harry & Son '84
Better Late Than Never '83
Curse of the Pink Panther '83
The Man Who Loved Women '83
Second Thoughts '83
Trail of the Pink Panther '82
Victor/Victoria '82
Back Roads '81
Condorman '81
Mommie Dearest '81
S.O.B. '81
A Change of Seasons '80
Little Miss Marker '80
The Shadow Box '80
Nightwing '79
Prisoner of Zenda '79
10 '79
Family Upside Down '78
House Calls '78
Revenge of the Pink Panther '78
Who is Killing the Great Chefs of Europe? '78
Angela '76
The Pink Panther Strikes Again '76
Silver Streak '76
The Great Waldo Pepper '75
Once is Not Enough '75
The White Dawn '75
The Girl from Petrovka '74
99 & 44/100 Dead '74
Return of the Pink Panther '74
That's Entertainment '74
Oklahoma Crude '73
The Thief Who Came to Dinner '73
Sometimes a Great Notion '71
Darling Lili '70
The Molly Maguires '70
The Night Visitor '70
Bachelor in Paradise '69
The Party '68
Two for the Road '67
Wait until Dark '67
Arabesque '66
Moment to Moment '66
What Did You Do in the War, Daddy? '66
The Great Race '65
The Pink Panther '64
A Shot in the Dark '64
Charade '63
King Kong vs. Godzilla '63
Man's Favorite Sport? '63
Soldier in the Rain '63
Days of Wine and Roses '62
Experiment in Terror '62
Hatari! '62
Mr. Hobbs Takes a Vacation '62
Breakfast at Tiffany's '61
The Great Impostor '61
Never Steal Anything Small '59
Touch of Evil '58
The Last Unknown '57
The Creature Walks among Us '56
Rock, Pretty Baby '56
Us '56
The Benny Goodman Story '55
Far Country '55
To Hell and Back '55
Creature from the Black Lagoon '54
The Glenn Miller Story '54
It Came from Outer Space '53
Horizons West '52
Lost in Alaska '52

Johnny Mandel (1925-)
Brenda Starr '86
Deathtrap '82
The Verdict '82
Caddyshack '80
Being There '79
The Last Detail '73
M*A*S*H '70
Pretty Poison '68
Harper '66
I Want to Live! '58

Harry Manfredini (1943-)
Aftershock '88
Necromancer: Satan's Servant '88
Allin '06
Endangered Species '02
Hell's Gate '01
Hidden Agenda '99
The Omega Code '99
Catherine's Grove '98
A Gun, a Car, a Blonde '97
Wishmaster '97
Dead on Sight '94
Final Friday '93
Deepstar Six '89
Friday the 13th, Part 6: Jason Lives '86
House '86
Swamp Thing '82
Friday the 13th, Part 2 '81
Friday the 13th '80

Jim Manzie
The 24th Day '04
Milo '98
Leatherface: The Texas Chainsaw Massacre 3 '89

Kevin Manthei
The Offspring '09
Blood Surf '00
Lurking Fear '94
Night of the Demons 2 '94

Franco Mannino (1924-2005)
Conversation Piece '75
Driver's Seat '73
The Ghost '63
I, Vampiri '56
Beat the Devil '53

Clint Mansell (1963-)
Definitely, Maybe '08
Smokin' Aces '07
Wind Chill '07
Trust the Man '06
Doom '05
Sahara '05
Suspect Zero '04
11:14 '03
Abandon '02
Murder by Numbers '02
Sonny '02
The Hole '01
Knockaround Guys '01
Requiem for a Dream '00
Pi '98

David Mansfield (1956-)
Broken Trail '06
Diggers '06
Stephanie Daley '06
Transamerica '05
Get a Clue '02
A Good Baby '99
Songcatcher '99
Dark Harbor '98
Road Ends '98
The Apostle '97
Floating '97
The Ballad of Little Jo '93
Me & Veronica '93
Desperate Hours '90
Miss Firecracker '89
The Sicilian '87
Heaven's Gate '80

Gianni Marchetti
SS Girls '77

Dario Marianelli
Atonement '07
The Brave One '07
The Color of Freedom '07
The Return '06
V for Vendetta '06
The Brothers Grimm '05
Pride and Prejudice '05
Shooting Dogs '05
In This World '03
I Capture the Castle '03
The Warrior '01
Pandaemonium '00
I Went Down '97

Veigar Margeirsson
How You Look to Me '05
Mind the Gap '04

A.L. Mariaux

See Jess (Jesus) Franco

Mariano Marin (1959-)
Open Your Eyes '97
Thesis '96

Anthony Marinelli (1959-)
Dreamland '06
Memory '06
Mayor of the Sunset Strip '03
American Gun '02
Borderline '02
Lone Hero '02
15 Minutes '01
Hotel '01
The Man from Elysian Fields '01
Quicksand '01
Just One Night '00
Slow Burn '00
Time Code '00
Gideon '99
God Said "Ha!" '99
The Runner '99
Hoods '98
Scarred City '98
Don King: Only in America '97
Sink or Swim '97
Flynn '96
Masterminds '96
Two Days in the Valley '96
Underworld '96
One Man's Justice '95
Young Guns '88

Richard Markowitz (1926-94)
The Shooting '66
A Face in the Rain '63

Rick Marotta
Just the Ticket '98
Painted Hero '95

Branford Marsalis (1960-)
3 A.M. '01
Once in the Life '00
Mr. & Mrs. Loving '96
Sneakers '92

Jeff Marsh (1961-)
Unspeakable '02

Phil Marshall
Hoot '06
Confessions of a Sociopathic Social Climber '05
Kiss Toledo Goodbye '00
Trial by Media '00
Rupert's Land '98
Trial and Error '96
Kicking and Screaming '95
Noises Off '92
Full Moon on Blue Water '88
Inferno '01
No Vacancy '99
Wind River '98

Jack Marshall (1921-73)
Munster, Go Home! '66
The Giant Gila Monster '59
Missouri Traveler '58
Thunder Road '58

George Martin (1926-)
Live and Let Die '73
Yellow Submarine '68
Help! '65
A Hard Day's Night '64

Hugh Martin (1914-)
Athena '54
Good News '47

Peter Martin
Where the Heart Is '90
Piece of Cake '88
Hope and Glory '87

Cliff Martinez (1954-)
First Snow '07
Wicker Park '04
Narc '02
Solaris '02
Traffic '00
The Limey '99
Out of Sight '98
The Underneath '95
King of the Hill '93
Kafka '91
Pump Up the Volume '90
sex, lies and videotape '89

Richard (Rick) Marvin
Eulogy '04
Gracie's Choice '04
The Battle of Shaker Heights '03
Brian's Song '01
Desert Saints '01
Lost Battalion '01
Protection '01
U-571 '00
Dead Men Can't Dance '97
Escape Clause '96
Galgameth '96
3 Ninjas Kick Back '94
Save Me '93
Interceptor '92
3 Ninjas '92

Bill Marx (1937-)
Count Yorga, Vampire '70
Hollywood after Dark '65

Harvey W. Mason (1947-)
Deadly Outbreak '96
Only the Strong '93

Roger Mason
Dead Letter Office '98
Joey '98
Crime Broker '94
Crimebroker '93

John Massari (1957-)
Retro Puppet Master '99
Redemption: Kickboxer 5 '95

Michael Masser
Stir Crazy '80
The Greatest '77

Muir Mathieson (1911-75)
The Big Sweat '90
Killer Klowns from Outer Space '88

Samuel Matlovsky (1921-2004)
July Group '81
Games '67

Sasha Matson
Red Surf '90
Bloodfist '89
Lobster Man from Mars '89
Daddy's Boys '87

Stuart Matthewman (1960-)
The Astronaut Farmer '07
Life Support '07
Northfork '03
Jackpot '01
Twin Falls Idaho '99

Peter Matz (1928-2002)
Stepping Out '91
Torch Song Trilogy '88
Lust in the Dust '85
The Private Eyes '80
In This House of Brede '75

Billy May (1916-2004)
The Front Page '74
The Ballad of Andy Crocker '69

Brian May (1934-97)
Dr. Giggles '92
Bloodmoon '90
Darlings of the Gods '90
Death Before Dishonor '87
Steel Dawn '87
Cloak & Dagger '84
Stage Fright '83
Treasure of the Yankee Zephyr '83
The Road Warrior '82
Escape 2000 '81
Gallipoli '81
Killing of Angel Street '81
Road Games '81
Mad Max '80
Survivor '80
The Night After Halloween '79
Patrick '78

Daniel May
Chopper Chicks in Zombietown '91
Fatal Skies '90
Zombie High '87

Curtis Mayfield (1942-99)
Return of Superfly '90
Piece of the Action '77
Sparkle '76
Superfly '72

Toshiro Mayuzumi (1929-97)
The Bible '66
Good Morning '59

Jon McCallum
Loco Love '03
Grizzly Mountain '97
Little Heroes '91
Project: Eliminator '91
Soultaker '90
Surf Nazis Must Die '87
Terror Eyes '87

Dennis McCarthy (1945-)
The Prince and the Pauper '07
Die Mommie Die! '03
Alien Fury: Countdown to Invasion '00
In His Life: The John Lennon Story '00
Letters from a Killer '98
Breast Men '97
McHale's Navy '97
Star Trek: Generations '94

John McCarthy (1961-)
Turbulence 3: Heavy Metal '01
Careful '92

Paul McCartney (1942-)
Le Bal '82
Let It Be '70
Yellow Submarine '68
Magical Mystery Tour '67
Help! '65
A Hard Day's Night '64

Craig McConnell
Animal 2 '07

John McCulloch
UKM: The Ultimate Killing Machine '06

Garry McDonald (1948-)
Moscow on the Hudson '84

David McHugh (1941-)
Changing Habits '96
The Hidden 2 '94
Tales of Erotica '93
Daddy's Dyin'... Who's Got the Will? '90
The Dream Team '89
Three Fugitives '89
Mr. North '88
Mystic Pizza '88
Go for the Gold '84

Jimmy McHugh
Dancing Lady '33

Rich McHugh
Boa '02
Lost Voyage '01

Tim McIntire (1943-86)
The Killer Inside Me '76
A Boy and His Dog '75

Michael McKean (1947-)
A Mighty Wind '03
Waiting for Guffman '96
This Is Spinal Tap '84

Mark McKenzie
Saving Sarah Cain '07
The Ultimate Gift '07
The Lost Child '00
Durango '99
The Disappearance of Garcia Lorca '96
Dr. Jekyll and Ms. Hyde '95
Frank and Jesse '94
My Family '94
Warlock: The Armageddon '93

Stephen McKeon
Cowboys & Angels '04
Borstal Boy '00
Falling for a Dancer '98
The Nephew '97

Robert F. McNaughton
Ed Gein '01
Henry: Portrait of a Serial Killer 2: Mask of Sanity '96
Henry: Portrait of a Serial Killer '90

Joel McNeely (1959-)
I Know Who Killed Me '07
The Fox and the Hound 2 '06
Pooh's Heffalump Movie '05
America's Heart and Soul '04
Stateside '04
Holes '03
The Jungle Book 2 '03
Uptown Girls '03
Return to Never Land '02
Sally Hemings: An American Scandal '00
Lover's Prayer '99
The Avengers '98
Soldier '98
Virus '98
Zack & Reba '98
Buffalo Soldiers '97
Wild America '97
Flipper '96
Vegas Vacation '96
Gold Diggers: The Secret of Bear Mountain '95
Radioland Murders '94
Squanto: A Warrior's Tale '94
Terminal Velocity '94
Iron Will '93

James McVay
Snap Decision '01

Peter Meisner
Urban Justice '07

Gil Melle (1931-2004)
Fatal Vision '84
Blood Beach '81
The Organization '71

Peter Melnick
Mermaid '00
The Only Thrill '97
Grand Avenue '96
Lily Dale '96
The McMartin Trial '95
Arctic Blue '93
L.A. Story '91

Michael Melvoin (1937-)
Bloodsucking Pharoahs of Pittsburgh '90
Big Town '87

Wendy Melvoin (1964-)
Something New '06
Juwanna Mann '02
The Third Wheel '02
Foolish '99
Hav Plenty '97
Soul Food '97

Jaime Mendoza-Nava (1925-2005)
Forty Days of Musa Dagh '85
Psycho from Texas '81
The Boys in Company C '77
Shadow of Chikara '77
Ballad of a Gunfighter '64

Alan Menken (1949-)
Enchanted '07
The Shaggy Dog '06
Home on the Range '04
Noel '04
Hercules '97
The Hunchback of Notre Dame '96
Pocahontas '95
Life with Mikey '93
Aladdin '92
Newsies '92
Beauty and the Beast '91
The Little Mermaid '89
Little Shop of Horrors '86

Johnny Mercer (1909-76)
Darling Lili '70
Days of Wine and Roses '62
Li'l Abner '59
Dangerous When Wet '53
The Harvey Girls '46
You Were Never Lovelier '42

Stephin Merritt (1966-)
Pieces of April '03
Eban and Charley '01

Wim Mertens
Molokai: The Story of Father Damien '99

Michel Michelet (1894-1995)
The Indian Tomb '59
Impact '49
Outpost in Morocco '49
Lured '47

Franco Micalizzi
Forever Emmanuelle '75
Private Lessons '75
Macabre '69
Fiesta '95

Pat Metheny (1954-)
The Falcon and the Snowman '85

Micki Meuser
Deeply '99
Obsession '97

Marcus Miller (1959-)
I Think I Love My Wife '07
Breakin' All The Rules '04
Deliver Us from Eva '03
Head of State '03
Serving Sara '02
The Trumpet of the Swan '01
Two Can Play That Game '01
The Run of the Country '95
Three Wishes '95

Mario Migliardi
Shoot the Living, Pray for the Dead '70
Tower of Screaming Virgins '68

Cynthia Millar
Brown's Requiem '98
Digging to China '98

Philippe Miller
Cote d'Azur '05
My Life on Ice '02
Jeanne and the Perfect Guy '98

Randy Miller
Hitched '01
Family Tree '00
Living in Peril '97
Without Limits '97
Darkman 3: Die Darkman Die '95
Darkman 2: The Return of Durant '94
And You Thought Your Parents Were Weird! '91
Black Magic Woman '91
Witchcraft '88

Robert Miller
Teeth '07
Red Doors '05

Don Miller-Robinson
Risk '00
Erskinville Kings '99

Mario Millo
Wrangler '88
The Lighthorsemen '87

Sheldon Mirowitz
Johnson County War '02
Outside Providence '99

Paul Misraki (1908-98)
Alphaville '65
Your Turn Darling '63
Les Bonnes Femmes '60
And God Created Woman '57
Death in the Garden '56
Plucking the Daisy '56
Femmes de Paris '53
Crazy for Love '52
Utopia '51

Richard G. Mitchell
A Good Woman '04
Grand Theft Parsons '03
The Tenant of Wildfell Hall '96

Bob Mithoff
Class of Nuke 'Em High 3: The Good, the Bad and the Subhumanoid '94
Sgt. Kabukiman N.Y.P.D. '94
Seedpeople '92
Class of Nuke 'Em High 2: Subhumanoid Meltdown '91
Dragonfight '90

Vic Mizzy (1922-)
The Munsters' Revenge '81
Halloween with the Addams Family '79
How to Frame a Figg '71
The Love God? '70
The Reluctant Astronaut '67
The Ghost and Mr. Chicken '66

Moby (1965-)
Southland Tales '06
Double Tap '98

Cyril Mockridge (1896-1979)
Donovan's Reef '63
The Man Who Shot Liberty Valance '62
Flaming Star '60
Tall Story '60
Rally 'Round the Flag, Boys! '58
Desk Set '57
Will Success Spoil Rock Hunter? '57
Bus Stop '56
I Married a Woman '56
Solid Gold Cadillac '56
River of No Return '54
A Woman's World '54
The Farmer Takes a Wife '53
The Girl Next Door '53
Belles on Their Toes '52
We're Not Married '52
Follow the Sun '51
Let's Make It Legal '51
Love Nest '51
Cheaper by the Dozen '50
Ticket to Tomahawk '50
Come to the Stable '49
Father Was a Fullback '49
I Was a Male War Bride '49
Road House '48

Composer Index

(continued from previous page — Cyril Mockridge)
Miracle on 34th Street '47
Nightmare Alley '47
Dark Corner '46
My Darling Clementine '46
Colonel Effingham's Raid '45
The Ox-Bow Incident '43
The Fighting Sullivans '43
The Undying Monster '42
I Wake Up Screaming '41
Sleepers West '41
Brigham Young: Frontiersman '40
Johnny Apollo '40
Lucky Cisco Kid '40
Michael Shayne: Private Detective '40
Everything Happens at Night '39

Mark Moffatt
Back o' Beyond '95
High Tide '87

Charlie Mole
I Really Hate My Job '07
The Secret Life of Mrs. Beeton '06
The Importance of Being Earnest '02
High Heels and Low Lifes '01
An Ideal Husband '99
Othello '95

Fred Mollin
Inferno '99
Thrill Seekers '99
Spring Fever '81

Paddy Moloney
Agnes Browne '99
Under the Sun '98

Thom Monahan
Hijacking Catastrophe: 9/11, Fear and the Selling of America '04
Peace, Propaganda & the Promised Land '04

Hugo Montenegro (1925-81)
The Ambushers '67
The Wrecking Crew '68
Charro! '69
Too Hot to Handle '76

Michael Montes
Whipped '00

Osvaldo Montes
Firehouse '87
Hangmen '87
A Shadow You Soon Will Be '94
The Dark Side of the Heart '92

Guy Moon
These Old Broads '01

Hal Mooney (1911-95)
Bull of the West '71
Raid on Rommel '71
The Meanest Men in the West '67

Dudley Moore (1935-2002)
Wild Thing '87
Sorority Babes in the Slimeball Bowl-A-Rama '87
Diving In '90
The Brady Bunch Movie '95
A Very Brady Sequel '96

Mike Moran
Cynthia '68
30 Is a Dangerous Age, Cynthia '68
Bedazzled '68
The Hound of the Baskervilles '77
Six Weeks '82

Lucien Moraweck
Bloodbath at the House of Death '85
Sherlock: Case of Evil '02

Patrick Moraz (1948-)
The Man in the Iron Mask '39
International Lady '41
Two Weeks to Live '43

Fernando Garcia Morcillo
Voodoo Black Exorcist '73

Mark Morgan
Hawk and Castle '67
Shark Attack 2 '00
Where the Day Takes You '92

Sophia Morizet
Mosquitoman '05
Possessed '05

Giorgio Moroder (1940-)
Midnight Express '78
American Gigolo '79
Cat People '82
Scarface '83
Flashdance '83
The NeverEnding Story '84
Let It Ride '89
Fair Game '89

Jerome Moross (1913-83)
The Valley of Gwangi '69
The Big Country '58
Proud Rebel '58

Andrea Morricone (1964-)
Capturing the Friedmans '03
Here on Earth '00
Liberty Heights '99

Ennio Morricone (1928-)
Fateless '05
R.ipley's Game '02
Mission to Mars '00
Vatel '00
Bulworth '98
The Legend of 1900 '98
The Phantom of the Opera '98
Lolita '97
U-Turn '97
Nostromo '96
The Star Maker '95
The Stendahl Syndrome '95
Disclosure '94
Wolf '94
In the Line of Fire '93
Beyond Justice '92
City of Joy '92
The Big Man: Crossing the Line '91
Bugsy '91
Husbands and Lovers '91
The Palermo Connection '91
A Time to Die '91
Everybody's Fine '91
State of Grace '90
Tie Me Up! Tie Me Down! '90
Casualties of War '89
The Endless Game '89
Fat Man and Little Boy '89
La Cage aux Folles 3: The Wedding '86
The Mission '86
Cinema Paradiso '88
Frantic '88
Python Wolf '88
A Time of Destiny '88
Rampage '87
The Untouchables '87
The Scarlet and the Black '83
Sahara '83
Butterfly '82
Treasure of the Four Crowns '82
The Thing '82
Nana '82
White Dog '82
La Cage aux Folles 2 '81
Le Professionnel '81
Lovers and Liars '81
So Fine '81
The Tragedy of a Ridiculous Man '81
The Island '80
Windows '80
Almost Human '79
Days of Heaven '78
La Cage aux Folles '78
The Chosen '77
The Exorcist 2: The Heretic '77
Orca '77
The Desert of the Tartars '76
The Inheritance '76
Moses '76
The Human Factor '75
Leonor '75
Night Train Murders '75
Salo, or the 120 Days of Sodom '75
Autopsy '74
Arabian Nights '74
La Grande Bourgeoise '74
Le Secret '74
Master Touch '74
My Name Is Nobody '74
The Tempter '74
Alonsanfan '73
Massacre in Rome '73
Sonny and Jed '73
'Tis a Pity She's a Whore '73
Bluebeard '72
A Fistful of Dynamite '72
Who Saw Her Die? '72
The Black Belly of the Tarantula '71
The Canterbury Tales '71
The Cat o' Nine Tails '71
Dirty Heroes '71
Divine Nymph '71
A Lizard in a Woman's Skin '71
Sacco & Vanzetti '71
Short Night of Glass Dolls '71
The Bird with the Crystal Plumage '70
Burn! '70
Cold Eyes of Fear '70
Companeros '70
The Decameron '70
The Family '70
Two Mules for Sister Sara '70
When Women Had Tails '70
Red Tent '69
Danger: Diabolik '68
Once Upon a Time in the West '68
Partner '68
Teorema '68
The Rover '67
The Good, the Bad and the Ugly '67
The Battle of Algiers '66
Before the Revolution '65
For a Few Dollars More '65
A Fistful of Dollars '64
Gunfight at Red Sands '64

John Morris (1926-)
The Lady in Question '99
Nerds in Paradise '87
Murder in a Small Town '99
Only Love '98
Ellen Foster '97
Scenes from the Class Struggle in Beverly Hills '89
The Adventures of Rocky & Bullwinkle '00
Rugrats in Paris: The Movie '00
The Royal Tenenbaums '01
Sugar & Spice '01
Welcome to Collinwood '02
Sorority Boys '02
Thirteen '03
Rugrats Go Wild! '03
A Guy Thing '03
Good Boy! '03
Zissou '04
The Life Aquatic with Steve Zissou '04
Envy '04
Dead Gorgeous '02
B. Monkey '97
How to Eat Fried Worms '06
Men '97
Dead Man on Campus '97
Breaking Up '97
Faperhouse '89
Christabel '89
The Witches '90
Rushmore '98
The Rugrats Movie '98
Quicksilver Highway '98
Happy Gilmore '96
Castaway '87
Nerds in Paradise '87
Revenge of the Nerds 2: Nerds in Paradise '87
How I Learned to Love Women '66
Best Men '98
It's the Rage '99
Drop Dead Gorgeous '99
200 Cigarettes '98
The Big Squeeze '96
The Last Supper '96
Bottle Rocket '95
The Birdcage '96
Navajo Joe '67
Secret Agent 00 '67
West '68
The Decameron '70
Hellbenders '67
Return of Captain Invincible '83
The Coca-Cola Kid '84
Young Einstein '89

William Motzing (1939-)

Rob Mounsey
Dangerous Passion '95
Working Girl '88

Michael Muhlfriedel

Mark Mothersbaugh (1950-)
The Dog Problem '06
How to Eat Fried Worms '06
The Big White '05
First Descent '05
Herbie: Fully Loaded '05
Lords of Dogtown '05
The Ringer '05
Confessions of a Teenage Drama Queen '04

Bob Mothersbaugh (1952-)
200 Cigarettes '98

Thomas Morse
The Sisters '05
The Big Brass Ring '99
The Apostate '98
If I Die Before I Wake '98
Solitaire for 2 '94

Boris Morros (1891-1963)
The Big Broadcast of 1933 '38

Van Morrison (1945-)
Moondance '95

Trevor Morris (1970-)
The Hills Have Eyes 2 '07
The Last Angel '04
Beyond the Clouds '95

Gerry Mulligan (1927-96)
I'm Not England '96
The Final Programme '73

Dominic Muldowney (1952-)
Bloody Sunday '01
King Lear '98
Sharpe's Eagle '93
Sharpe's Rifles '93
Catherine Cookson's The Black Candle '92

John Murphy (1965-)
Crossing Over '08
Sunshine '07
Basic Instinct 2 '06
Miami Vice '06
Guess Who '05
The Man '05
Millions '05
The Perfect Score '04
All About the Benjamins '02
City by the Sea '02
New Best Friend '02
28 Days Later '02
Vacuuming Completely Nude in Paradise '01
Lock, Stock and 2 Smoking Barrels '98
Snatch '00

Lyn Murray (1909-89)
Snow White and the Three Stooges '61
Prowler '51

Sean Murray
Firetrap '01
The Legend of Cryin' Ryan '98
The Bridges at Toko-Ri '55
The Last of Mrs. Lincoln '76

Romano Musumarra (1955-)
After Sex '97
L'Elee '95
Faceless '88

Michael Musseau
Material Girls '06
The State Within '06
The Prince & Me '04
The Twelve Days of Christmas Eve '04
Dead Gorgeous '02

Stanley Myers (1939-93)
The Summer House '94
Heart of Darkness '93
Serafina! '92
A Murder of Quality '90
Rosencrantz & Guildenstern Are Dead '90
Iron Maze '91
Sammy & Rosie Get Laid '87

Jennie Muskett
The Real Howard Spitz '98
Stiff Upper Lips '96

Michael Nesmith (1942-)
Timerider '83
Northville Cemetery Massacre '76

Fredric Myrow (1940-99)
Plan 10 from Outer Space '95

Mario Nascimbene (1913-2002)
The Messiah '75
Commandos '73
Blaise Pascal '71
The Vengeance of She '68
Barabbas '62
The Girl with a Suitcase '60
Room at the Top '59
The Vikings '58
Love in the City '53

Peter Nashel
No End in Sight '07
The Night Listener '06
Wedding Daze '06
The Deep End '01
Dot the I '03
Pan's Labyrinth '06
The Devil's Backbone '01

Lou Natale (1950-)
Hustle '04
The Man in the Attic '94
Snowbound: The Jim and Jennifer Stolpa Story '94

Miki Navazio
The Sticky Fingers of Time '97

Javier Navarrete (1956-)
Pan's Labyrinth '06
The Devil's Backbone '01
Undefeated '03

Roy Nathanson
Raising Victor Vargas '03

Blake Neely (1969-)
Starter for Ten '06
First Daughter '04
OnLine '01
Title '00

Chris Neal
Around the World in 80 Ways '88
Jack Be Nimble '94

Roger Neill
Chameleon 2: Death Match '99
Acts of Betrayal '98
Bottleneck '98
The Taxman '98
Mercenary '96
Savage '96
An American Summer '90

Willie Nelson (1933-)
Stagecoach '86
1918 '85
Honeysuckle Rose '80
Ruckus '81

John Neschling (1947-)
Kiss of the Spider Woman '85
Pixote '81

Renato Neto
Sitcom '97
Kill Me Later '01
Dancing at the Blue Iguana '00

Eric Neveux (1972-)
Carnage '02
Three Blind Mice '02
Intimacy '00
Of Freaks and Men '98

Ira Newborn (1949-)
Bad Manners '98
BASEketball '98
High School High '96
The Late Shift '96
Mallrats '95
Naked Gun 33 1/3: The Final Insult '94

Eric Neveux
R.S.V.P. '02
St. Patrick's Day '99
Ulysses '67

Fredric Myrow (1940-99)
Frightmare '74

Brain Donors '92
Innocent Blood '92
Naked Gun 2 1/2: The Smell of Fear '91
My Blue Heaven '90
Short Time '90
Cast the First Stone '89
Uncle Buck 89
Caddyshack 2 '88
The Naked Gun: From the Files of Police Squad '88
Amazon Women on the Moon '87
Dragnet '87
Planes, Trains & Automobiles '87
Ferris Bueller's Day Off '86
Wise Guys '86
Into the Night '85
Weird Science '85
Sixteen Candles '84
All Night Long '81
The Blues Brothers '80

Alfred Newman (1901-70)
December 7th: The Movie '91
Airport '70
Nevada Smith '66
The Greatest Story Ever Told '65
The Man Who Shot Liberty Valance '62
The Best of Everything '59
Bus Stop '56
Love Is a Many-Splendored Thing '55
The Seven Year Itch '55
There's No Business Like Show Business '54
How to Marry a Millionaire '53
With a Song in My Heart '52
All About Eve '50
No Way Out '50
When Willie Comes Marching Home '50
A Letter to Three Wives 49
Pinky '49
Prince of Foxes 49
Twelve o'Clock High '49
Call Northside 777 '48
Sitting Pretty 48
The Snake Pit 48
Roxie Hart '42
Son of Fury '42
Ball of Fire '41
Blood and Sand '41
Charley's Aunt '41
How Green Was My Valley '41
Week-End in Havana '41
Brigham Young: Frontiersman '40
Foreign Correspondent '40
Johnny Apollo '40
Lillian Russell '40
The Mark of Zorro '40
Tin Pan Alley '40
Beau Geste '39
Gunga Din '39
The Hunchback of Notre Dame '39
The Rains Came '39
The Real Glory '39
Stanley and Livingstone '39
They Shall Have Music '39
Wuthering Heights '39
Dead End '37
The Hurricane '37
Stella Dallas '37
Come and Get It '36
Dodsworth '36
The Gay Desperado '36
These Three '36
The Dark Angel '35
Les Miserables '35

The Count of Monte Cristo '34
The Bowery '33
Mr. Robinson Crusoe '32
Rain 32
City Lights '31
Street Scene '31
Tonight or Never '31

David Newman (1954-)
Welcome Home Roscoe Jenkins '08
Norbit '07
Are We There Yet? '05
Man of the House '05
Monster-in-Law '05
Serenity '05
Scooby-Doo 2: Monsters Unleashed '04
Daddy Day Care '03
Dr. Seuss' The Cat in the Hat '03
Duplex '03
How to Lose a Guy in 10 Days '03
Death to Smoochy '02
Ice Age '02
Life or Something Like It '02
Scooby-Doo '02
The Affair of the Necklace '01
Dr. Dolittle 2 '01
The Flamingo Rising '01
Duets '00
The Flintstones in Viva Rock Vegas '00
Nutty Professor 2: The Klumps '00
102 Dalmatians '00
Bowfinger '99
Brokedown Palace '99
Galaxy Quest '99
Never Been Kissed '99
Anastasia '97
Out to Sea '97
Jingle All the Way '96
Matilda '96
The Nutty Professor '96
The Phantom '96
Big Bully '95
Operation Dumbo Drop '95
Tommy Boy '95
The Air Up There '94
Boys on the Side '94
The Cowboy Way '94
The Flintstones '94
I Love Trouble '94
Coneheads '93
My Father the Hero '93
The Sandlot '93
Undercover Blues '93
Hoffa '92
Honeymoon in Vegas '92
The Mighty Ducks '92
Bill & Ted's Bogus Journey '91
Don't Tell Mom the Babysitter's Dead '91
The Marrying Man '91
Other People's Money '91
Paradise '91
Rover Dangerfield '91
The Runestone '91
Talent for the Game '91
DuckTales the Movie: Treasure of the Lost Lamp '90
Fire Birds '90
The Freshman '90
Madhouse '90
The Applegates 89
Bill & Ted's Excellent Adventure 89
Disorganized Crime 89
Gross Anatomy 89
Heathers 89
Little Monsters 89
The War of the Roses 89
The Kindred '87
Malone '87
My Demon Lover '87
Throw Momma from the Train 87
Critters 86
Vendetta 85
Frankenweenie 84

Emil Newman (1911-84)

Hondo '53
Island in the Sky '53
If I'm Lucky '46
Greenwich Village '44

Lionel Newman (1916-89)
Myra Breckinridge '70
The St. Valentine's Day Massacre '67
Do Not Disturb '65
Move Over, Darling '63
Let's Make Love '60
The Girl Can't Help It '56
Love Me Tender '56
There's No Business Like Show Business '54
Dangerous Crossing '53
Gentlemen Prefer Blondes '53
Bloodhounds of Broadway '52
Don't Bother to Knock '52

Randy Newman (1943-)
Leatherheads '08
Cars '06
Meet the Fockers '04
Seabiscuit '03
Monsters, Inc. '01
Meet the Parents '00
Toy Story 2 '99
A Bug's Life '98
Pleasantville '98
Cats Don't Dance '97
James and the Giant Peach '96
Michael '96
Toy Story '95
Maverick '94
The Paper '94
Avalon '90
Awakenings '90
Parenthood 89
The Natural '84
Ragtime '81
Cold Turkey 71

Thomas Newman (1955-)
WALL-E '08
The Good German '06
Little Children '06
Cinderella Man '05
Jarhead '05
Lemony Snicket's A Series of Unfortunate Events '04
Angels in America '03
Finding Nemo '03
Road to Perdition '02
The Salton Sea '02
White Oleander '02
In the Bedroom '01
Erin Brockovich '00
Pay It Forward '00
American Beauty '99
The Green Mile '99
Meet Joe Black '98
The Horse Whisperer '97
Mad City '97
Oscar and Lucinda '97
Red Corner '97
The People vs. Larry Flynt '96
Phenomenon '96
Up Close and Personal '96
American Buffalo '95
How to Make an American Quilt '95
Unstrung Heroes '95
Corrina, Corrina '94
Little Women '94
The Shawshank Redemption '94
Threesome '94
The War '94
Flesh and Bone '93
Josh and S.A.M. '93
The Favor '92
The Linguini Incident '92
The Player '92
Scent of a Woman '92
Whispers in the Dark '92
Career Opportunities '91
Deceived '91
Fried Green Tomatoes '91
Naked Tango '91
Heat Wave '90
Cookie 89

Men Don't Leave 89
The Great Outdoors '88
Prince of Pennsylvania '88
Less Than Zero '87
Light of Day '87
The Lost Boys '87
Jumpin' Jack Flash '86
Desperately Seeking Susan '85
Girls Just Want to Have Fun '85
Gung Ho 85
The Man with One Red Shoe '85
Real Genius '85
Grandview U.S.A. '84
Reckless 84
Revenge of the Nerds '84

David Nichtern
Spirit of 76 91
The Big Picture 89

Chris Nickel
Insecticidal '05
Savage Island '03

Bruno Nicolai (1926-)
The Case of the Bloody Iris '72
Your Vice is a Closed Room and Only I Have the Key '72
Adios, Sabata '71
The Case of the Scorpion's Tail '71
The Scorpion's Tail '71
Gunslinger '70
The Gentleman Killer 69

Roberto Nicolosi (1914-89)
The Hit Man '60
Revenge of the Barbarians '60
Thor and the Amazon Women '60

Lennie Niehaus (1929-)
Comanche Moon '08
For One More Day '07
Blood Work '02
Space Cowboys '00
The Jack Bull '99
True Crime '99
Absolute Power '97
Dogwatch '97
The Fixer '97
Midnight in the Garden of Good and Evil '97
Never Too Young to Die '86
Ratboy 85
Pale Rider '85
Sesame Street Presents: Follow That Bird '85
City Heat '84
Tightrope '84

Jose Nieto (1942-)
Mad Love '01
Jealousy '99
Passion in the Desert '97
Guantanamera '95
Of Love and Shadows '94
Running Out of Time '94
The Perfect Husband '92
The Best Intentions '92
The Inside Man '84

Harry Nilsson (1942-94)
Popeye '80
The Point 71

Stefan Nilsson (1955-)
A Song for Martin '01
Jerusalem '96

Jack Nitzsche (1937-2000)
The Crossing Guard '94
Blue Sky '91

The Hot Spot '90
The Last of the Finest '90
Mermaids '90
Revenge '90
Next of Kin 89
The Seventh Sign '88
9 1/2 Weeks '86
Stand by Me '86
Streets of Gold '86
Stripper '86
The Whoopee Boys '86
The Jewel of the Nile '85
The Razor's Edge '84
Starman '84
Windy City '84
Breathless '83
Without a Trace '83
Cannery Row '82
An Officer and a Gentleman '82
Personal Best '82
Cutter's Way '81
Cruising '80
Heart Beat '80
Hardcore '79
Blue Collar '78
Heroes '77
One Flew Over the Cuckoo's Nest '75
The Exorcist '73
Greaser's Palace '72
Performance '70
Village of the Giants 65

Tom Noonan (1951-)
The Wife '95
What Happened Was... '94

Erik Nordgren (1913-92)
The Emigrants '72
The Devil's Eye '60
The Virgin Spring '59
Wild Strawberries '57
The Seventh Seal '56

John E. Nordstrom
Nearing Grace '05

Per Norgard
Royal Deceit '94
Babette's Feast '87

Alex North (1910-91)
The Last Butterfly '92
The Penitent '88
The Dead '87
Good Morning, Vietnam '87
Death of a Salesman '86
Prizzi's Honor '85
Under the Volcano '84
Dragonslayer '81
Carny '80
Wise Blood '79
The Word '78
Rich Man, Poor Man 76
Bite the Bullet '75
The Passover Plot '75
Journey into Fear '74
Once Upon a Scoundrel '73
Pocket Money '72
Willard '71
A Dream of Kings '69
The Devil's Brigade '68
The Shoes of the Fisherman '68
Who's Afraid of Virginia Woolf? '66
The Agony and the Ecstasy '65
Cheyenne Autumn '64
Cleopatra '63
All Fall Down 62
The Children's Hour '61
The Misfits '61
Spartacus '60
Hot Spell '58
The Long, Hot Summer 58
Stage Struck 57
The Bad Seed '56
The King and Four Queens '56
The Rainmaker '56
Daddy Long Legs '55
I'll Cry Tomorrow '55
The Racers '55
The Rose Tattoo '55
Desiree '54
Les Miserables '52
The Member of the Wedding '52

Viva Zapata! '52
Death of a Salesman '51
A Streetcar Named Desire '51

Craig Northey
Dog Park '98
Kids in the Hall: Brain Candy '96

Julian Nott
Wallace & Gromit: The Curse of the Were-Rabbit '05
P.D. James: Death in Holy Orders '03
Gentlemen's Relish '01
My Mother's Courage '95
A Man of No Importance '94

Michael Nyman (1944-)
The Libertine '05
Tristram Shandy: A Cook and Bull Story '05
Nathalie '03
The Claim '00
The End of the Affair '99
Ravenous '99
Wonderland '99
Gattaca '97
The Ogre '96
Carrington '95
Mesmer '94
The Piano '93
The Hairdresser's Husband '92
Prospero's Books '91
The Cook, the Thief, His Wife & Her Lover '90
A Zed & Two Noughts '88
Drowning by Numbers '87
Cold Room '84
The Draughtsman's Contract '82

Molly Nyman
A Mighty Heart '07
Hard Candy '06
The Road to Guantanamo '06

Arion Ober (1943-2004)
Crimewave '85
Eating Raoul '82

John O'Brien (1962-)
Vince Vaughn's Wild West Comedy Show '06
Made '01

Richard O'Brien (1942-)
Return of Captain Invincible '83
Shock Treatment '81
The Rocky Horror Picture Show '75

Oscar Cardozo Ocampo (1942-2001)
Deathstalker 83
Funny, Dirty Little War '83

Erin O'Hara
Day Zero '07
Sicko '07

Patrick O'Hearn (1954-)
Silent Tongue '92
White Sands '92

Phil Ohman (1896-1954)
Dick Tracy vs. Cueball '46
Renegade Trail '39

William Olvis
Steal Big, Steal Little '95
Separate Lives '94
Red Rock West '93
The Comrades of Summer '92
29th Street '91
El Diablo '90

Yuji Ono (1941-)
The Castle of Cagliostro '80
Murders in the Doll House '79
Proof of the Man '77

Steve O'Reilly
Into the Fire '05
Into the Fire '05

Norman Orenstein
Diary of the Dead '07

Stir o' Echoes 2: The
Homecoming '07
Cube: Zero '04
Gone Dark '04
American Psycho 2: All
American Girl '02
Cube 2: Hypercube '02
Danger Beneath the Sea '02
Prisoner of Love '99
The First 9 1/2 Weeks '98
Sanctuary '98
Mask o' Death '97
Bounty Hunters '96
Downhill Willie '96

Robert G. Orpin
Girls Are for Loving '73
Ginger '72

Buxton Orr (1924-97)
First Man into Space '59
Corridor of Blood '58
Fiend without a Face '58
The Haunted Strangler '58

Riz Ortolani (1931-)
Incantato '03
The Best Man '97
The Story of Boys & Girls '91
The New Gladiators '83
Love by Appointment '76
Escape from Death Row '73
Confessions of a Police
Captain '72
Dead Are Alive '72
Don't Torture a Duckling '72
Madron '70
McKenzie Break '70
Liberators '69
Anzio '68
Apache's Last Battle '64
Castle of Blood '64
The Seventh Dawn '64
Mondo Cane '63

Mark Orton
The Real Dirt on Farmer
John '06

Atli Orvarsson
Babylon AD '08
Vantage Poin '08

Jason Osborn
The Triumph of Love '01
High Season '88

Yoshihide Otomo (1959-)
The Day the Sun Turned
Cold '94
Summer Snow '94
The Blue Kite '93

Nicholas O'Toole
Outfoxed: Rupert Murdoch's
War on Journalism '04

John Ottman (1964-)
Fantastic Four: Rise of the
Silver Surfer '07
The Invasion '07
Superman Return '06
Fantastic Four '05
Hide and Seek '05
Imaginary Heroes '05
Kiss Kiss Bang Bang '05
Cellular '04
Gothika '03
X2: X-Men United '03
Brother's Keeper '02
Eight Legged Freaks '02
Point of Origin '02
Pumpkin '02
Trapped '02
Bubble Boy '01
Urban Legends 2: Final Cut
'00
Goodbye, Lover '99
Halloween: H20 '98
Apt Pupil '97
Incognito '97
Snow White: A Tale of
Terror '97
The Cable Guy '96
The Usual Suspects '95
Public Access '93

Marc Ouellette
The Sign of Four '01
The Hound of the
Baskervilles '00

Blair Packham
Hollywood North '03
Triggermen '02

Jose Padilla (1889-1960)
Cuban Blood '03
Ibiza Dream '02
Private Manoeuvres '83

Jimmy Page (1944-)
Death Wish 3 '85
Death Wish 2 '82

Gene Page (1940-98)
Blacula '72
Brewster McCloud '70

Alan Parker
Alex Rider: Operation
Stormbreaker '06
Victoria & Albert '01
Britannic '99
Oktober '98
Rhodes '97
The Phoenix and the Magic
Carpet '95
What's Eating Gilbert Grape
'93
American Gothic '88

Jim Parker (1934-)
Dr. Eell and Mr. Doyle: The
Dark Beginnings of
Sherlock Holmes '00
A Rather English Marriage
'98
Moll Flanders '96
The Final Cut '95
Body & Soul '93
House of Cards '90
Mapp & Lucia '85

Clifton Parker (1905-89)
Damn the Defiant '62
Sink the Bismarck '60
Sea of Sand '58
Curse of the Demon '57
The Gift Horse '52
Blanche Fury '48

Al Pellegrini
Victoria & Albert '01

Heitor Pereira
Illegal Tender '07
Suburban Girl '07
Ask the Dust '06
Blind Dating '06
Curious George '06
Two Weeks '06
Nights '04
Haven '04
Real Women Have Curves
'02

Jorge Perez
The Monster Demolisher '60
The Criminal Life of
Archibaldo de la Cruz '55

Tyler Perry (1969-)
Madea's Family Reunion '06
Diary of a Mad Black
Woman '05

William Perry
The Innocents Abroad '84
The Private History of a
Campaign That Failed '81

Alexander Peskanov
Killing Hour '84

Antonio Pinto
City of Men '07
Love in the Time of Cholera
'07

Coleridge-Taylor Perkinson
A Woman Called Moses '78

Michael Perlstein
Winterbeast '92

Michael Penn (1958-)
The Last Kiss '06
Melvin Goes to Dinner '03
The Anniversary Party '01
Boogie Nights '97

Steve Pecile
Prison Break '39

Jan Pawluskiewicz
The Kidnapped King '99
Possession '81

Don Peake (1940-)
Hard Justice '95
The Hills Have Eyes '77

Art Phillips (1955-)
The Myth of Fingerprints '97

John Phillips (1935-2001)
Brewster McCloud '70

Stu Phillips
Battlestar Galactica '78

Nicola Piovani (1946-)
Avenue Montaigne '06
Pinocchio '02
In Love and War '01
Running Free '00
The Son's Room '00
Life Is Beautiful '99
A Month by the Lake '95
Caro Diario '93
Fiorile '93
Jamon, Jamon '93
Night Sun '90
Palombella Rossa '89
Good Morning, Babylon '87
Intervista '87
Ginger & Fred '86
Kaos '85

Nicholas Pike (1955-)
The Contractor '07
Riding the Bullet '04
Fear.dotcom '02
Return to Me '00
Delivered '98
Star Kid '97
Telling Lies in America '96
Attack of the 50 Ft. Woman
'93
Blank Check '93
Perfect Family '92
Sleepwalkers '92
Mission Manila '87

Franco Piersanti (1950-)
Don't Tell '05
Without Evidence '96
Lamerica '95
Mille Bolle Blu '93
The Stolen Children '92
The Station '90

Piero Piccioni (1921-2004)
Three Brothers '80
Swept Away... '75
Seduction of Mimi '72
Light at the Edge of the
World '71
Camille 2000 '69
Murder to Sale '68
10th Victim '65

Martin Phipps
Persuasion '07
Sense & Sensibility '07
The Gay Deceivers '69
Hell's Angels on Wheels '67
Dead Heat on a Merry-Go-
Round '66

Michael Pavlicek (1956-)
The Scarlet Pimpernel '99
The Scarlet Pimpernel 2:
Mademoiselle Guillotine
'99

Van Dyke Parks
Private Parts '96
The Company '03
Charm's for the Easy Life
'02
Harlan County War '00
Shadrach '98
Oliver Twist '97
Casual Sex? '88
Club Paradise '86
Popeye '80

Stephen Parsons
Conspiracy of Silence '03
Another 9 1/2 Weeks '96

Arvo Part (1935-)
Fast Girl '07
Red Lights '04
Gerry '02

Antony Partos
Garage Days '03
Walking on Water '02
Soft Fruit '99

Johnny Pate (1923-)
Every Girl Should Have One
'78
Bucktown '75
Shaft in Africa '73

Shawn Patterson (1965-)
The Bible and Gun Club '96

Alex Pauk
The Five Senses '99

Arnotz Plessner (1962-)
Road House 2: Last Call '06
Deal of a Lifetime '99

Michael Richard Plowman (1965-)
Alien Agent '07
The Invitation '03
He Sees You When You're
Sleeping '02
Butterfly Collectors '99

Iggy Pop (1947-)
Repo Man '83
Rock & Rule '83

Zoe Poledouris (1973-)
Teenage Caveman '01
Cecil B. Demented '00
The In-Laws '03

Jocelyn Pook (1960-)
The Merchant of Venice '04
How I Killed My Father '03
The In-Laws '03
Time Out '01

Conrad Pope
The Rising Place '02
Pavilion of Women '01
The Set Up '95
Project Metalbeast: DNA
Overload '94

Steve Porcaro (1957-)
Carolina Moon '07
Cougar Club '07
Montana Sky '07
Up in the Air '40

Michel Portal (1935-)
The Machine '95
Dr. Petiot '90
Max, Mon Amour '86
The Return of Martin Guerre
'83

Lew Porter (1892-1956)
Flying Wild '41
Texas Trouble '41
Billy the Kid in Texas '40
Lightning Strikes West '40
Range Busters '40
Rosalie '38
Born to Dance '36

Cole Porter (1891-1964)
Evil under the Sun '82
High Society '56
Panama Hattie '42
Lonesome Dove '89

Giantfranco Plenizio (1931-)
Django Strikes Again '87
And the Ship Sails On '83

Edward Plumb (1907-58)
Peter Pan '53
The Woman Who Came
Back '45
Bambi '42

Terry Plumeri
The Last Letter '04
Lloyd '01
Route 666 '01

Basil Poledouris (1945-2006)
The Legend of Butch &
Sundance '04
Crocodile Dundee in Los
Angeles '01
Cecil B. Demented '00
For Love of the Game '99
Les Miserables '98
Starship Troopers '97
Switchback '97
Breakdown '96
Celtic Pride '96
The War at Home '96
Free Willy 2: The Adventure
Home '95
It's My Party '95
Under Siege 2: Dark
Territory '95
Lassie '94
On Deadly Ground '94
Serial Mom '94
Free Willy '93
Hot Shots! Part Deux '93
Lone Justice '93
Wind '92
Harley Davidson and the
Marlboro Man '91
RoboCop 3 '91
White Fang '91
Flight of the Intruder '90
The Hurt for Red October
'90
Quigley Down Under '90
Farewell to the King '89
Lonesome Dove '89
Wired '89
Cherry 2000 '88
The Spellbinder '88
Split Decisions '88
No Man's Land '87
Iron Eagle '86
RoboCop '87
Flesh and Blood '85
The Amazons '84
Conan the Destroyer '84
Making the Grade '84
Red Dawn '84
Protocol '84
Conan the Barbarian '82
Summer Lovers '82
Single Bars, Single Women
'84
The Blue Lagoon '80
Defiance '79
Big Wednesday '78
Whale for the Killing '81

The Pogues
Straight to Hell '87
Sid & Nancy '86

Rachel Portman (1960-)
Sisterhood of the Traveling
Pants 2 '08
Infamous '06
The Lake House '06
Because of Winn-Dixie '05
Oliver Twist '05
The Manchurian Candidate
'04
The Human Stain '03
Mona Lisa Smile '03
Hart's War '02
Nicholas Nickleby '02
The Truth About Charlie '02
The Emperor's New Clothes
'01
American Women '00
Chocolat '00
The Legend of Bagger
Vance '00
The Cider House Rules '99
Ratcatcher '99
Beloved '98
Home Fries '98
The Other Sister '98
Addicted to Love '96
The Adventures of Pinocchio
'96
Emma '96
Marvin's Room '96
Palookaville '95
A Pyromaniac's Love Story
'95

Portman (cont.)
Smoke '95
To Wong Foo, Thanks for Everything, Julie Newmar '95
War of the Buttons '95
Only You '94
The Road to Wellville '94
Sirens '94
Benny & Joon '93
Used People '92
Antonia and Jane '91
Where Angels Fear to Tread '91
Fruit '89
High Hopes '88
Young Charlie Chaplin '88
Sharma & Beyond '84

Randall Poster
The Pink Panther '06
The Bad News Bears '05
Fun With Dick and Jane '05
The Life Aquatic with Steve Zissou '04
Kiss Me, Guido '97

Sally Potter (1947-)
Yes '04
The Tango Lesson '97

Yuri Potyeyenko
Day Watch '06
Night Watch '04

Andrew Powell (1949-)
Rocket Gibraltar '88
Ladyhawke '85

John Powell (1963-)
Dr. Seuss' Horton Hears a Who! '08
Hancock '08
Jumper '08
Stop-Loss '08
The Bourne Ultimatum '07
P.S. I Love You '07
Happy Feet '06
Ice Age: The Meltdown '06
United 93 '06
X-Men: The Last Stand '06
Be Cool '05
Mr. & Mrs. Smith '05
Robots '05
Alfie '04
Mr. 3000 '04
The Bourne Supremacy '04
Stealing Sinatra '04
Agent Cody Banks '03
Gigli '03
The Italian Job '03
Paycheck '03
The Adventures of Pluto Nash '02
The Bourne Identity '02
Drumline '02
Two Weeks Notice '02
Evolution '01
Eye See You '01
I Am Sam '01
Just Visiting '01
Rat Race '01
Shrek '01
Chicken Run '00
Forces of Nature '99
Antz '98
Face/Off '97

Reg Powell
Poison Ivy 3: The New Seduction '97
Forbidden Zone: Alien Abduction '96
ShadowZone: The Undead Express '96
Baja '95
The Pathfinder '94
Pet Shop '94
Test Tube Teens from the Year 2000 '93
The Banker '89

Pray for Rain
Car 54, Where Are You? '94
Floundering '94
Straight to Hell '87
Sid & Nancy '86

Roberto Pregadio
Invincible Barbarian '83
Place in Hell '69

Zbigniew Preisner (1955-)
The Beautiful Country '04
It's All About Love '03
Between Strangers '02
Aberdeen '00
Dreaming of Joseph Lees '99
The Last September '99
FairyTale: A True Story '97
The Island on Bird Street '97
Feast of July '95
Elisa '94
Mouvements du Desir '94
Trois Couleurs: Blanc '94
Trois Couleurs: Rouge '94
When a Man Loves a Woman '94
The Secret Garden '93
Damage '92
At Play in the Fields of the Lord '91
The Double Life of Veronique '91
Eminent Domain '91
Europa, Europa '91
The Decalogue '88
I Like Bats '85

Tony Prendatt
Loving Jezebel '99
Colorz of Rage '97

Don Preston (1932-)
Blood Diner '87
Eye of the Tiger '86
Android '82

Andre Previn (1929-)
Rollerball '75
Jesus Christ, Superstar '73
The Music Lovers '71
Paint Your Wagon '69
The Fortune Cookie '66
Inside Daisy Clover '65
Dead Ringer '64
Goodbye Charlie '64
Kiss Me, Stupid! '64
One, Two, Three '61
All in a Night's Work '61
Bells Are Ringing '60
Elmer Gantry '60
Designing Woman '57
Silk Stockings '57
The Catered Affair '56
Fastest Gun Alive '56
It's Always Fair Weather '55
Kismet '55
Bad Day at Black Rock '54
The Girl Who Had Everything '53
Give a Girl a Break '53
Kiss Me Kate '53
Small Town Girl '53
Cause for Alarm '51
Kim '50
Tension '50
Three Little Words '50

Charles Previn (1888-1973)
The Ghost of Frankenstein '42
Buck Privates '41
The Wolf Man '41
If I Had My Way '40
Junior G-Men '40
My Man Godfrey '36

Alan Price (1941-)
Britannia Hospital '82
O Lucky Man! '73

Henry Price
See Andre Brummer

Jonathan Price
Rustin '01
Bloodstream '00
Vampire Night '00
Merchants of Death '99
Vampires of Sorority Row: Kickboxers From Hell '99

Michael Price
Wild Child '08

Lethal Dose '03

Prince (1958-)
Girl 6 '96
Batman '89
J.D.'s Revenge '76

Sergei Prokofiev (1891-1953)
Ivan the Terrible, Part 2 '46
Ivan the Terrible, Part 1 '44
Alexander Nevsky '38

Craig Pruess
The Mistress of Spices '05
Bend It Like Beckham '02
What's Cooking? '00

Xiao-Song Qu
Pushing Hands '92
Life on a String '90
The Horse Thief '87

Donald Quan
Cybercity '99
Falling Fire '97
Future Fear '97
Carver's Gate '96

Peer Raben (1940-)
Eros '04
2046 '04
Querelle '83
Veronika Voss '82
Berlin Alexanderplatz '80
The Marriage of Maria Braun '79
Despair '78
In a Year of 13 Moons '78
The Stationmaster's Wife '77
I Only Want You to Love Me '76
Satan's Brew '76
Fear of Fear '75
Tenderness of the Wolves '73
The American Soldier '70
Beware of a Holy Whore '70
Whity '70
Love Is Colder than Death '69

Trevor Rabin (1954-)
Get Smart '08
Hot Rod '07
National Treasure: Book of Secrets '07
Flyboys '06
Glory Road '06
Gridiron Gang '06
The Guardian '06
Snakes on a Plane '06
Coach Carter '05
Dominion: Prequel to the Exorcist '05
The Great Raid '05
Exorcist: The Beginning '04
National Treasure '04
Torque '04
Bad Company '02
The Banger Sisters '02
American Outlaws '01
The One '01
Rock Star '01
Texas Rangers '01
Gone in 60 Seconds '00
Remember the Titans '00
The 6th Day '00
Whispers: An Elephant's Tale '00
Deep Blue Sea '99
Armageddon '98
Enemy of the State '98
Jack Frost '98
Con Air '97
Homegrown '97
The Glimmer Man '96

Paul Rabjohns
Cash Crop '01
The Last Minute '01
Children of the Corn 5: Fields of Terror '98
The Colony '98

Karyn Rachtman (1964-)
Pulp Fiction '94
Reservoir Dogs '92

Stephen Rae
The Road from Coorain '02
The Well '97
Dead Heart '96
Blackwater Trail '95

Robert O. Ragland (1931-)
Top of the World '97
Alien Chaser '96
Plato's Run '96
Warhead '96
The Fear '94
The Raffle '94
Messenger of Death '88
Rooster: Spurs of Death! '83
Brainwaves '82
Q (The Winged Serpent) '82
Only Once in a Lifetime '79
Project: Kill! '77
Grizzly '76
The Thing with Two Heads '72

A.R. Rahman (1966-)
Water '05
Warriors of Heaven and Earth '03
Lagaan: Once upon a Time in India '01
Earth '98
Fire '96

Ralph Rainger (1901-42)
The Big Broadcast of 1938 '38
Waikiki Wedding '37
Ruggles of Red Gap '35
Here Is My Heart '34
Kiss and Make Up '34
Little Miss Marker '34
Six of a Kind '34
She Done Him Wrong '33

David Raksin (1912-)
Night Tide '63
Separate Tables '58
Big Combo '55
Suddenly '54
The Bad and the Beautiful '52
Pat and Mike '52
Forever Amber '47
The Secret Life of Walter Mitty '47
Laura '44
The Undying Monster '42
San Quentin '37

Ron Ramin
Meltdown '06
Fatal Error '99
Rent-A-Kid '95
Christy '94

Kennard Ramsey
Freeway 2: Confessions of a Trickbaby '99
Ringmaster '98

David Raskin (1912-2004)
Daisy Kenyon '47
The Man Who Wouldn't Die '42

Eldon Rathburn (1916-)
Canada's Sweetheart: The Saga of Hal C. Banks '85
Who Has Seen the Wind? '77
Railrodder '65

Roy J. Ravio
Fire on the Amazon '93
Terrorgram '90

Satyajit Ray (1921-92)
Distant Thunder '73
The Adversary '71
Days and Nights in the Forest '70
Shakespeare Wallah '65
Charulata '64
The Big City '63
Two Daughters '61
Jalsaghar '58

Chris Rea (1951-)
Parting Shots '98
Parting Shots '98

J.A.C. Redford (1953-)
Grace & Glorie '98
What the Deaf Man Heard '98
D3: The Mighty Ducks '96
A Kid in King Arthur's Court '95
Bye Bye, Love '94

D2: The Mighty Ducks '94
Heavyweights '94
Extremities '86

Les Reed (1929-)
Parting Shots '98
Creepshow 2 '87
The Girl on a Motorcycle '68

Alan Reeves
To Walk with Lions '99
For Hire '99
Bleeders '97
Jack London's The Call of the Wild '97
Natural Enemy '96
A Young Connecticut Yankee in King Arthur's Court '95
Young Ivanhoe '95
Dr. Bethune '90

Niki Reiser (1958-)
Nowhere in Africa '02
The Trio '97
Beyond Silence '96

Brian Reitzell (1966-)
30 Days of Night '07
Stranger Than Fiction '06
Friday Night Lights '04

Joe Renzetti (1941-)
Blondes Have More Guns '95
Basket Case 3: The Progeny '92
South Beach '92
Basket Case 2 '90
Frankenhooker '90
Child's Play '88
Wanted Dead or Alive '86
Diary of a Teenage Hitchhiker '82
Dead and Buried '81
Tut & Tuttle '81
Exterminator '80
The Buddy Holly Story '78

Graeme Revell (1955-)
Pineapple Express '08
The Ruins '08
Street Kings '08
Awake '07
Darfur Now '07
Planet Terror '07
Bordertown '06
Goal! The Dream Begins '06
Goal! The Dream Begins '06
Man of the Year '06
The Adventures of Sharkboy and Lavagirl in 3-D '05
Aeon Flux '05
Assault on Precinct 13 '05
The Fog '05
Harsh Times '05
Sin City '05
The Chronicles of Riddick '04
Walking Tall '04
Daredevil '03
Freddy vs. Jason '03
Open Water '03
Out of Time '03
Below '02
Collateral Damage '02
High Crimes '02
Human Nature '02
Blow '01
Double Take '01
Lara Croft: Tomb Raider '01
Dune '00
Pitch Black '00
Titan A.E. '00
Bats '99
Buddy Boy '99
Gossip '99
Idle Hands '99
The Insider '99
Three to Tango '99
All I Wanna Do '98
The Big Hit '98
Bride of Chucky '98
Dennis the Menace Strikes Again '98
Lulu on the Bridge '98
The Negotiator '98
Phoenix '98
The Siege '98
Chinese Box '97
The Saint '97
Spawn '97
Suicide Kings '97
The Craft '96
The Crow 2: City of Angels '96
Fled '96
Race the Sun '96
The Basketball Diaries '95
From Dusk Till Dawn '95
Killer: A Journal of Murder '95
Strange Days '95
The Tie That Binds '95
Down Came a Blackbird '94
No Escape '94
Street Fighter '94
Tank Girl '94
Boxing Helena '93
The Crow '93
The Crush '93
Ghost in the Machine '93
Hard Target '93
Hear No Evil '93
Body of Evidence '92
The Hand that Rocks the Cradle '92
Love Crimes '92
Traces of Red '92
Till There Was You '91
Until the End of the World '91
Child's Play 2 '90
Psycho 4: The Beginning '90
Dead Calm '89
Spontaneous Combustion '89

David Reynolds
Heavens Fall '06
Cruel Intentions 3 '04
How to Make a Monster '01
She Creature '01

Tim Rice (1944-)
Jesus Christ Superstar '00
Joseph and the Amazing Technicolor Dreamcoat '00
The Road to El Dorado '00
Evita '96
The Lion King '94
Aladdin '92

Freddie Rich (1898-1956)
A Walk in the Sun '46
Stage Door Canteen '43

Craig Richey
The King of Kong: A Fistful of Quarters '07
Friends with Money '06
The Gymnast '06
Lovely & Amazing '02

William Richter
Net Games '03
Social Misfits '00

Hualampong Riddim
The Judgement '04
Last Life in the Universe '03

Nelson Riddle (1921-85)
America at the Movies '76
That's Entertainment, Part 2 '76
The Great Gatsby '74
Batman '66
Marriage on the Rocks '65
Paris When It Sizzles '64
Robin and the 7 Hoods '64
Four for Texas '63
Lolita '62
Ocean's 11 '60

Stan Ridgway (1954-)
Spent '00
Race '99
Speedway Junky '99
Futurekick '91

Ralph Rieckermann
Loaded '08

Hugo Riesenfeld (1879-1939)
Roarin' Lead '37

J. Peter Robinson
It Happened in New Orleans '36
Hell's Angels '30
Alibi '29
Evangeline '29

Ned Rifle
See Hal Hartley

Tony Riparetti
Postmortem '98
Mean Guns '97
Adrenalin: Fear the Rush '96

Nicholas Rivera
Fast Money '96
Nemesis 3: Time Lapse '96
Omega Doom '96
Spitfire '94
Brain Smasher...A Love Story '93
Bloodmatch '91

David Robbins (1955-)
Guilty by Association '03
Dead Sexy '01
Godmoney '97
Little Witches '96
Saturday Night Special '92
Project A '83

Peter Manning Robinson
The Prime Gig '00
The Cradle Will Rock '99
Everything That Rises '98
Savior '98
Dead Man Walking '95
Fast Getaway 2 '94
Twenty Bucks '93
Bob Roberts '92
Cries '91
The Believers '87

Richard Robbins (1940-)
The White Countess '05
Le Divorce '03
The Mystic Masseur '01
The Golden Bowl '00
Cotton Mary '99
Place Vendome '98
A Soldier's Daughter Never Cries '98
The Proprietor '96
Surviving Picasso '95
Jefferson in Paris '94
Maurice '87
The Remains of the Day '93
Howard's End '92
The Ballad of the Sad Cafe '91
Mr. & Mrs. Bridge '90
Slaves of New York '89
Sweet Lorraine '87
A Room with a View '86
Heat and Dust '82

Milan Roder
The Lives of a Bengal Lancer '35
The Song of Songs '33

Nile Rodgers (1952-)
The '70s '00
Where the Truth Lies '99
The Con '38
Family of Cops 2: Breach of Faith '97
Flypaper '97
The Stepsister '97
Sometimes They Come Back... Again '96
Beverly Hills Cop 3 '94
Blue Chips '94
Earth Girls Are Easy '89
Coming to America '88

Richard Rodgers (1902-79)
Rodgers & Hammerstein's South Pacific '01
The King and I '56
Cinderella '64
Flower Drum Song '61
South Pacific '58
Pal Joey '57
Carousel '56
Oklahoma! '55
Words and Music '48
State Fair '45
I Married an Angel '42
Too Many Girls '40
Babes in Arms '39
Evergreen '34
Dancing Lady '33
Hallelujah, I'm a Bum '33

David Rose (1909-90)
Please Don't Eat the Daisies '60
Operation Petticoat '59
The Princess and the Pirate '44

Ann Ronell (1905-93)
Love Happy '50
The Story of G.I. Joe '45

Andrew Rose
Campfire Tales '98
Carnival of Souls '98
Plan B '97

David Rose
Whisper '07
The Quiet '05
Slow Burn '05
Urban Legends: Bloody Mary '05
Category 6: Day of Destruction '04
Shelter Island '03
Exit Wounds '01
The Crowd '00
Black Cat Run '98
The House of Yes '97
Trading Favors '97
White Squall '96
Lipstick Camera '93

Nino Rota (1911-79)
Hurricane '79
Death on the Nile '78
Orchestra Rehearsal '78
Amarcord '74
The Godfather, Part 2 '74
Love and Anarchy '73
Fellini's Roma '72
The Clowns '71
The Godfather '72
Waterloo '71
Romeo and Juliet '68
Spirits of the Dead '68
Fellini Satyricon '69
The Taming of the Shrew '67
Juliet of the Spirits '65
8 1/2 '63
Boccaccio '70 '62
La Dolce Vita '60
Rocco and His Brothers '60
Purple Noon '60
The Leopard '63
War and Peace '56
Nights of Cabiria '57
White Nights '57
The Great War '59
The Jazz Singer '80
Spy in Black '39
The Four Feathers '39
La Strada '54
Il Bidone '55
Mambo '55
Anna '51
The White Sheik '52
I Vitelloni '53
Submarine Attack '54
The Valley of the Eagles '51
The Hidden Room '49

Renzo Rossellini (1908-82)
Open City '45
Man with a Cross '43
Teresa Venerdi '41
Era Notte a Roma '60
Generale Della Rovere '60
Voyage in Italy '53
The Flowers of St. Francis '50

Robert Rodriguez (1968-)
Sin City '05
Kill Bill Vol. 2 '04
Once Upon a Time in Mexico '03
Spy Kids 3-D: Game Over '03
Spy Kids 2: The Island of Lost Dreams '02
Spy Kids '01

Milton Rosen
King Kong vs. Godzilla '63
Yankee Buccaneer '52

Leonard Rosenman (1924-2008)
Levitation '97
The Color of Evening '95
Mrs. Munck '95
Ambition '91
RoboCop 2 '90
Star Trek 4: The Voyage Home '86
Cross Creek '83
The Car '77
Battle for the Planet of the Apes '73
Beneath the Planet of the Apes '70
Hellfighters '68
Fantastic Voyage '66
Hell is for Heroes '62
Pork Chop Hill '59
Lafayette Escadrille '58
Rebel without a Cause '55
East of Eden '54

Heinz Roemheld (1901-85)
The Monster That Challenged the World '57
Jack & the Beanstalk '52
Loan Shark '52
Kill the Umpire '50
The Lady from Shanghai '48
On Our Merry Way '48
Mr. Ace '46
A Scandal in Paris '46
The Male Animal '42
The Wagon's Roll at Night '41
The Roaring Twenties '39
A Slight Case of Murder '38
San Quentin '37
The Black Cat '34

David Rosenblad
Living & Dying '07

Laurence Rosenthal (1926-)
Master Spy: The Robert Hanssen Story '01
Wild Iris '01
The Man Who Captured Eichmann '96
Meteor '79
Who'll Stop the Rain? '78
A Home of Our Own '75
Rooster Cogburn '75
Death Sentence '74
Satan's School for Girls '73
The Miracle Worker '62
Requiem for a Heavyweight '62

Eric Rogers (1921-81)
Die Watching '93
Ministry of Vengeance '89
No Sex Please—We're British '73
Carry On Cowboy '66

Michael Rohatyn
The Ballad of Jack and Rose '05
Duane Hopwood '05
Forty Shades of Blue '05
Personal Velocity: Three Portraits '02
The Delta '97
Angela '94

Inherit the Wind '99
The Echo of Thunder '98
The Member of the Wedding '97

Alain Romans
Mon Oncle '58
Mr. Hulot's Holiday '53

Jeff Rona (1957-)
Whisper '07

Philippe Rombi
Joyeux Noel '05
5x2 '04
Swimming Pool '03
Under the Sand '00
Criminal Lovers '99

Sigmund Romberg (1887-1951)
Up in Central Park '48
Deep in My Heart '54
The Desert Song '53

William Ross
September Dawn '07
The Game of Their Lives '05
Ladder 49 '04
Tuck Everlasting '02
The Girl from Paris '02
Her Majesty '01
Life with Judy Garland—Me and My Shadows '01
My Dog Skip '99
Black Sheep '99
The Evening Star '96
My Fellow Americans '96
A Smile Like Yours '96
Tin Cup '96
The Amazing Panda Adventure '95
Cops and Robbersons '94
Look Who's Talking Now '93
Thumbelina '94
One Good Cop '91

Elvin D. Ross
Madea's Family Reunion '06
Diary of a Mad Black Woman '05

Robbie Robertson (1943-)
Any Given Sunday '99
Jimmy Hollywood '94
The Color of Money '86
King of Comedy '82
Raging Bull '80

Eric N. Robertson (1948-)
Full Disclosure '00
Captains Courageous '95
Black Fox: Good Men and Bad '94
Black Fox: The Price of Peace '94
Millennium '89

Scott Roewe
The Crazies '73

Bruce Roberts
Flawless '99

Leo Robin (1900-84)
Gentlemen Prefer Blondes '53
Two Tickets to Broadway '51
The Big Broadcast of 1938 '38
Waikiki Wedding '37
Here is My Heart '34

Andy Roberts (1946-)
Face '97
Priest '94

Bruce Rowland
Zeus and Roxanne '96
Andre '94
Lightning Jack '94
Lost in America '85
The Man from Snowy River '82

Peter the Great '86
My Name Is Bill W. '89
Catherine the Great '95

Miklos Rozsa (1917-95)
Eye of the Needle '81
Last Embrace '79
Time After Time '79
Providence '77
Golden Voyage of Sinbad '73
The Private Life of Sherlock Holmes '70
The Green Berets '68
The V.I.P.'s '63
Sodom and Gomorrah '62
El Cid '61
Ben-Hur '59
The King of Kings '61
A Time to Love & a Time to Die '58
Something of Value '57
Bhowani Junction '56
Lust for Life '56
Tribute to a Bad Man '56
Diane '55
Green Fire '55
The King's Thief '55
Moonfleet '55
Men of the Fighting Lady '54
Valley of the Kings '54
All the Brothers Were Valiant '53
Julius Caesar '53
Knights of the Round Table '53
Young Bess '53
Ivanhoe '52
Quo Vadis '51
Adam's Rib '50
The Asphalt Jungle '50
The Miniver Story '50
East Side, West Side '49
Madame Bovary '49
Command Decision '48
Criss Cross '48
The Naked City '48
Secret Beyond the Door '48
Brute Force '47
A Double Life '47
The Red House '47
The Killers '46
The Strange Love of Martha Ivers '46
Because of Him '45
Blood on the Sun '45
Lady on a Train '45
The Lost Weekend '45
A Song to Remember '45
Spellbound '45
Dark Waters '44
Double Indemnity '44
The Woman of the Town '44
Five Graves to Cairo '43
Sahara '43
So Proudly We Hail '43
The Jungle Book '42
To Be or Not to Be '42
Lydia '41
Melody Master '41
Sundown '41
That Hamilton Woman '41
The Four Feathers '39
The Thief of Bagdad '40
Knight Without Armour '37
The Divorce of Lady X '38
Spy in Black '39
The Squeaker '37
Thunder in the City '37

John Rubinstein
The Killer Inside Me '76
The Candidate '72
Jeremiah Johnson '72

Donald Rubinstein
Bruiser '00
Knightriders '81
Martin '77
The Seagull '75

Harry Ruby (1895-1974)
Duck Soup '33
Horse Feathers '32
Animal Crackers '30

Steve Rucker
Little Nemo: Adventures in Slumberland '92
And God Created Woman '88

Arik Rudich
God's Sandbox '02
Shell Shock '63
Syngenor '90

Pete Rugolo (1915-)
This World, Then the Fireworks '97

David E. Russo
Alone With Her '07
Sparkler '99

Gus Russo
Brain Damage '88
Basket Case '82

Willy Russell (1947-)
Shirley Valentine '89
Mr. Love '86

Patrice Rushen (1954-)
The Killing Yard '01
Cora Unashamed '00
America's Dream '95
Hollywood Shuffle '87

Marius Ruhland
The Counterfeiters '07
Anatomy '00

Carlo Rustichelli (1916-2004)
Black Hand '73
Alfredo, Alfredo '72
Angus '95
Shaking the Tree '92
Blood and Black Lace '64
Conquest of the Steppes '64
Conquest of Mycenae '63
Giants of Rome '63
The Whip and the Body '63
Divorce—Italian Style '62
That Long Night in '43 '60

Michel Rubini
Nemesis '93
Manhunter '86
The Hunger '83
Happy Birthday to Me '81
Motel Hell '80

Lance Rubin
The Jungle Book '42
The Thief of Bagdad '40
Spy in Black '39

Joseph Saba
Knots '05
Two Ninas '00

The RZA (1966-)
Blade: Trinity '04
Kill Bill Vol. 2 '04
Kill Bill Vol. 1 '03
Soul Plane '04
Blade 2 '02
Ghost Dog: The Way '99

Arthur B. Rubinstein (1938-)
Nick of Time '95
The Hard Way '91
The Stranger '87
Stakeout '87
Blue Thunder '83
WarGames '83
Best of Times '86

Texas Guns '90
The Heist '89
Catch the Heat '87
Creature '85
976-EVIL '88
A Nightmare on Elm Street 4: Dream Master '88
Remo Williams: The Adventure Begins '85

Danny Saber
Played '06
Blast '04

Craig Safan (1948-)
A Season for Miracles '99
Degree of Guilt '95
Major Payne '95
Mr. Wrong '95
Money for Nothing '93
An Inconvenient Woman '91
Capone '89
Blade 2 '04

Journey to the Center of the Earth '96
North Star '96
The Best of Times '86
Lost in America '85
WarGames '83

Hahn Rowe (1961-)
Spring Forward '99
Clean, Shaven '93
Nick of Time '95
The Hard Way '91

The Last Starfighter '84
Nightmares '83
Fade to Black '80
Acapulco Gold '78
Good Guys Wear Black '78
The Bad News Bears in Breaking Training '77
The Great Texas Dynamite Chase '76

Ichiro Saito
Zatoichi: Master Ichi and a Chest of Gold '64
A Geisha '53 ·

Kojun Saito (1924-)
An Autumn Afternoon '62
Tokyo Story '53

Ryuichi Sakamoto (1952-)
Silk '07
Femme Fatale '02
Taboo '99
Love Is the Devil '98
Snake Eyes '98
Little Buddha '93
Wild Palms '93
Emily Bronte's Wuthering Heights '92
High Heels '91
Tokyo Decadence '91
The Handmaid's Tale '90
The Sheltering Sky '90
The Last Emperor '87

James T. Sale
The Box '07
Music Within '07

Peter Salem
Nancy Drew '07
Grind '03

Hans J. Salter (1896-1994)
Come September '61
Follow That Dream '61
The Gunfight at Dodge City '59
Abbott and Costello Meet the Mummy '55
The Far Horizons '55
Creature from the Black Lagoon '54
Borderline '50
Love from a Stranger '47
The Brute Man '46
Dressed to Kill '46
Magnificent Doll '46
Can't Help Singing '45
His Butler's Sister '44
The Invisible Man's Revenge '44
The Mummy's Ghost '44
The Amazing Mrs. Holiday '43
Hold That Ghost '41
It Started with Eve '41
The Wolf Man '41
The Mummy's Hand '40
The Tower of London '39

Conrad Salinger (1901-61)
The Last Time I Saw Paris '54
Till the Clouds Roll By '46

Ralph Sall

Bennett Salvay
Peaceful Warrior '06
Jeepers Creepers 2 '03
Jeepers Creepers '01
Love Stinks '99
Rites of Passage '99

Leonard Salzedo (1921-2000)
Sea Wife '57
Race for Life '55
Unholy Four '54

Jeremy Sams (1957-)
Enduring Love '04
The Mother '03
Persuasion '95

David Sanborn (1945-)
Lethal Weapon 4 '98
Lethal Weapon 3 '92
Lethal Weapon 2 '89

Bernardo Sandoval
Daughter of Keltoum '01
Western '96

Anton Sanko
One Last Thing '05
Saving Face '04
Scotland, PA '02
Dee Snider's Strangeland '98
Eye of the Storm '98
Ripe '97
An Occasional Hell '96
Live Nude Girls '95
Sex and the Other Man '95
Girl in the Cadillac '94
Party Girl '94

Dana Sano
The Man '05
Monster-in-Law '05
Little Odessa '94

Gustavo Santaolalla
Babel '06
Brokeback Mountain '05
North Country '05
The Motorcycle Diaries '04
21 Grams '03
Amores Perros '00

Frank Sanucci (1901-91)
The Pioneers '41
Stunt Pilot '39
Prison Break '38

Chris Saranec
Hourglass '95

Philippe Sarde (1945-)
On Guard! '03
Strayed '03
Alice et Martin '98
Lucie Aubrac '98
Les Voleurs '96
Nelly et Monsieur Arnaud '95
Ponette '95
The Favorite Son '94
Revenge of the Musketeers '94
Uncovered '94
Ma Saison Preferee '93
L627 '92
The Old Lady Who Walked in the Sea '91
Lord of the Flies '90
Lost Angels '89
Music Box '89
I Married a Dead Man '82
Beau Pere '81
Coup de Torchon '81
Ghost Story '81
Loulou '80
Buffet Froid '79
The Devil, Probably '77
Madame Rosa '77
Spoiled Children '77
Barocco '76
The Tenant '76
The Clockmaker '73
La Grande Bouffe '73
Cesar & Rosalie '72

Kevin Sargent
Fakers '04
Crush '02

Masaru Sato (1928-99)
The Silk Road '92
Forest of Little Bear '87
Irezumi '83
Toward the Terra '80
Nomugi Pass '79
Samurai Banners '69
Son of Godzilla '66
High & Low '62
Sanjuro '62
Yojimbo '61
The Bad Sleep Well '60
The Hidden Fortress '58
The Lower Depths '57
Throne of Blood '57
Godzilla Raids Again '55

Jordi Savall (1941-)
Jeanne la Pucelle '94
Tous les Matins du Monde '92

Carlo Savina (1919-2002)
The Sicilian Connection '85
Perfect Crime '79
Fury '78
Lisa and the Devil '75
And God Said to Cain '69
Samson Against the Sheik '62
Beauty on the Beach '61
Girl Under the Sheet '61

Nitin Sawhney (1964-)
The Namesake '06
Pure '02

Paul Sawtell (1906-71)
Faster, Pussycat! Kill! Kill! '65
Island of the Blue Dolphins '64
The Last Man on Earth '64
Jack the Giant Killer '62
Misty '61
Voyage to the Bottom of the Sea '61
The Cosmic Man '59
The Fly '58
The Hunters '58
It! The Terror from Beyond Space '58
Kronos '57
Stopover Tokyo '57
Rage at Dawn '55
Another Man's Poison '52
Kansas City Confidential '52
Gunplay '51
Armored Car Robbery '50
Riders of the Range '50
Storm over Wyoming '50
The Clay Pigeon '49
Mysterious Desperado '49
Raw Deal '48
Dick Tracy Meets Gruesome '47
Dick Tracy's Dilemma '47
T-Men '47
Mr. Winkle Goes to War '44
Manhunt in the African Jungles '43

Walter Scharf (1910-2003)
Blind Ambition '79
Walking Tall '73
Ben '72
Journey Back to Oz '71
Willy Wonka & the Chocolate Factory '71
The Cheyenne Social Club '70
Funny Girl '69
The Nutty Professor '63
Pocketful of Miracles '61
The Bellboy '60
King Creole '58
Loving You '57
Rock-A-Bye Baby '57
Three Violent People '57
Buccaneer's Girl '50
Casbah '48
Fighting Seabees '44

Johnny Lee Schell
The Forsaken '01
Outside Ozona '98
Black Day Blue Night '95

Vladimir Scherbachov
Peter the First: Part 2 '38
Peter the First: Part 1 '37

Dominik Scherrer
Dracula '06
Scenes of a Sexual Nature '06

Prof. Peter Schickele (1935-)
Oh! Calcutta! '72
Silent Running '71

Lalo Schifrin (1932-)
Rush Hour 3 '07
The Bridge of San Luis Rey '05
After the Sunset '04
Bringing Down the House '03
Rush Hour 2 '01
Rush Hour '98
Tango '98
Money Talks '97
Scorpion Spring '96
Manhattan Merengue! '95
The Beverly Hillbillies '93
F/X 2: The Deadly Art of Illusion '91
The Dead Pool '88
The Fourth Protocol '87
Black Moon Rising '86
A.D. '85
Mean Season '85
Doctor Detroit '83
The Osterman Weekend '83
The Sting 2 '83
Sudden Impact '83
Tank '83
Amityville 2: The Possession '82
Class of 1984 '82
The Seduction '82
Buddy Buddy '81
Caveman '81
The Big Brawl '80
Brubaker '80
The Competition '80
The Nude Bomb '80
When Time Ran Out '80
The Amityville Horror '79
Boulevard Nights '79
The Concorde: Airport '79 '79
Escape to Athena '79
Love and Bullets '79
The Cat from Outer Space '78
The Manitou '78
Day of the Animals '77
The Eagle Has Landed '77
Rollercoaster '77
Telefon '77
St. Ives '76
Sky Riders '76
Special Delivery '76
Voyage of the Damned '76
The Four Musketeers '75
Kelly's Heroes '70
The Beguiled '70
Hell in the Pacific '69
The Brotherhood '68
Bullitt '68
Coogan's Bluff '68
Cool Hand Luke '67
The President's Analyst '67
Murderers' Row '66
Murderers' Row '66
The Cincinnati Kid '65
Joy House '64

Eban Schletter
Coffee Date '06
Dumb and Dumberer: When Harry Met Lloyd '03

Norbert J. Schneider (1950-)
Brother of Sleep '95
Stalingrad '94

Alfred Schnittke (1934-98)
The Ninth Day '04
The Ascent '76
Commissar '68

Galli Schoen
Festival at Cannes '02
Deja Vu '98

Rudolph (Rudy) Schrager (1900-83)
The Last Voyage '60
High Lonesome '50
Great Dan Patch '49
The Green Promise '49
Coroner Creek '48
Fear in the Night '47
Swamp Fire '46

Walter Schumann (1913-58)
The Night of the Hunter '55
Africa Screams '49
Buck Privates Come Home '47

Paul Schutze
The Siege of Firebase Gloria '89

Arthur Schwartz (1900-84)
The Band Wagon '53
Dangerous When Wet '53

David Schwartz
You Stupid Man '02
Two of Us '00
My Little Assassin '99
Magic in the Water '95

Stephen Schwartz (1948-)
Gepetto '00
The Hunchback of Notre Dame '96
Pocahontas '95
Pippin '81
Godspell '73

Garry Schyman
NightScreams '97
Robin Cook's Terminal '96
Tornadol '96
Revenge of the Nerds 3: The Next Generation '92
Hitz '89

Gary Stevan Scott
3 Ninjas Knuckle Up '95
Play Nice '92

John Scott (1930-)
The Mill on the Floss '97
Rudyard Kipling's the Second Jungle Book: Mowgli and Baloo '97
The Scarlet Tunic '97
Deadly Voyage '96
Detonator 2: Night Watch '95
Walking Thunder '94
Becoming Colette '92
Ruby '92
Lionheart '90
Winter People '89
Shoot to Kill '88
The Whistle Blower '87
Mountbatten: The Last Viceroy '86
Inseminoid '80
North Dallas Forty '79
The People That Time Forgot '77
Billy Two Hats '74

Patrick John Scott
Sinful Intrigue '95
Cop-Out '67

Tom Scott (1948-)
An Unexpected Family '96
A Mother's Prayer '95
Deconstructing Sarah '94
Percy & Thunder '93
Final Notice '89
Soul Man '86
The Sure Thing '85
Stir Crazy '80
Conquest of the Planet of the Apes '72
Firehouse '72

Vincent Scotto (1876-1952)
Pepe Le Moko '37
Cesar '36
Fanny '32

Humphrey Searle (1915-82)
The Haunting '63
The Abominable Snowman '57

Eckart Seeber (1963-)
Bram Stoker's Shadowbuilder '98
The Prisoner '90

Maurice Seezer
Get Rich or Die Tryin' '05
In America '02
Disco Pigs '01
The Boxer '97

Brad Segal
Crazylove '05
National Lampoon's Holiday Reunion '03
Isaac Asimov's Nightfall '00

Misha Segal
Santa Baby '06
A Girl of the Limberlost '90
The Phantom of the Opera '89
The New Adventures of Pippi Longstocking '88
The Last Dragon '85

Bernardo Segall (1911-93)
Moon of the Wolf '72
Loving '70
The Great St. Louis Bank Robbery '59

Gregorio Garcia Segura
Icebox Murders '82
The 317th Platoon '65

Ilona Sekacz (1948-)
Wondrous Oblivion '06
Solomon and Gaenor '98
Mrs. Dalloway '97
Under the Skin '97
Antonia's Line '95
Northanger Abbey '87

Gyorgy Selmeczi (1952-)
Flowers of Reverie '84
Daniel Takes a Train '83
Time Stands Still '82
Angi Vera '78

Dov Seltzer (1932-)
The Mummy Lives '93
Hanna's War '88
The Uranium Conspiracy '78

Albert Sendrey (1911-2003)
Bloody Wednesday '87
Father's Little Dividend '51
Royal Wedding '51

Jean-Marie Senia (1947-)
Diary of a Seducer '95
Cross My Heart '91
Red Kiss '85
Man in the Silk Hat '83
Jonah Who Will Be 25 in the Year 2000 '76
Celine and Julie Go Boating '74

John Sereda
When a Man Falls in the Forest '07

Eric Serra (1959-)
Arthur and the Invisibles '06
Bulletproof Monk '03
Chasing Christmas '05
Jet Lag '02
Rollerball '02
Wasabi '01
The House Next Door '01
Mindstorm '01
The War Bride '01
The Messenger: The Story of Joan of Arc '99
The Fifth Element '97
Goldeneye '95
The Professional '94
La Femme Nikita '91
Subway '85
Le Dernier Combat '84

Luis Maria Serra
Brain Drain '98
I, the Worst of All '90
Condemned to Hell '84

Rosino Serrano
The Crime of Father Amaro '02

Santiso '99

Steven Severin (1955-)
London Voodoo '04
The Purifiers '04
Sasquatch '02

Larry Seymour
Stranger than Fiction '06

Patrick Seymour
Anne Rice's The Feast of All Saints '01
The Simian Line '99
Critical Choices '97
End of Summer '97
Tricks '97
Scorned 2 '96
Night Eyes 4: Fatal Passion '95
Parallel Lives '94
Chantilly Lace '93

Paul Shaffer (1949-)
Blues Brothers 2000 '98
Postcards from the Edge '90

Marc Shaiman (1959-)
The Bucket List '07
Hairspray '07
Rumor Has It... '05
Alex & Emma '03
Patch Adams '98
Simon Birch '98
George of the Jungle '97
In and Out '97
One Night at McCool's '01
61* '01
Jackie's Back '99
The Out-of-Towners '99
South Park: Bigger, Longer and Uncut '99
The Story of Us '99
My Giant '98
The American President '95
Forget Paris '95
City Slickers 2: The Legend of Curly's Gold '94
North '94
Speechless '94
Sister Act 2 '93
The Addams Family '91
Misery '90
When Harry Met Sally... '89

Ravi Shankar (1920-)
Wonderwall: The Movie '69
The World of Apu '59
Aparajito '58
Pather Panchali '54

Theodore Shapiro (1971-)
Semi-Pro '08
Tropic Thunder '08
Blades of Glory '07
Mr. Woodcock '07
The Devil Wears Prada '06
Idiocracy '06
The Baxter '05
Fun With Dick and Jane '05
Along Came Polly '04
Dodgeball: A True Underdog Story '04
Starsky & Hutch '04
Old School '03
13 Going on 30 '04
View from the Top '03
Love in the Time of Money '02
Heist '01
Not Another Teen Movie '01
Wet Hot American Summer '01
Prince of Central Park '00
Stare and Main '00
Girlfight '99
Six Ways to Sunday '99
Restaurant '98
Safe Men '98

Jamshied Sharifi
Clockstoppers '02
Down to Earth '01
Harriet the Spy '96

Francis Shaw
Evil '03
The Fourth Protocol '87
Big Red '62

Harry Shearer (1943-)
A Mighty Wind '03
Waiting for Guffman '96
This Is Spinal Tap '84

Ed Shearmur (1966-)
88 Minutes '08
Dedication '07
Epic Movie '07
The Ex '07
The Starter Wife '07
Factory Girl '06
The Bad News Bears '05
Nine Lives '05
The Skeleton Key '05
Laws of Attraction '04
Sky Captain and the World of Tomorrow '04
Charlie's Angels: Full Throttle '03
Johnny English '03
The Count of Monte Cristo '02
Reign of Fire '02
The Sweetest Thing '02
K-PAX '01
Charlie's Angels '00
Miss Congeniality '00
Things You Can Tell Just by Looking at Her '00
Whatever It Takes '00
Cruel Intentions '98
The Governess '98
Shot Through the Heart '98
Species 2 '98
The Very Thought of You '98
Girls' Night '97
The Hunchback '97
The Leading Man '96
Tales from the Crypt Presents Demon Knight '94

Jonathan Sheffer
The Cement Garden '93

Bert Shefter (1902-99)
The Last Man on Earth '64
Jack the Giant Killer '62
Misty '61
Voyage to the Bottom of the Sea '61
The Cosmic Man '59
It! The Terror from Beyond Space '58

David Shire (1937-)
Blood Hounds of Broadway '89
Convicted: A Mother's Story '87
On Valentine's Day '86
Wanted: The Perfect Guy '86
'night, Mother '86
Short Circuit '86
Return to Oz '85
Oh, God! You Devil '84
2010: The Year We Make Contact '84
Max Dugan Returns '83
The Night the Lights Went Out in Georgia '81
Only When I Laugh '81
Paternity '81
Fast Break '79
Norma Rae '79
Old Boyfriends '79
The Promise '78
Straight Time '78
Raid on Entebbe '77
Saturday Night Fever '77
All the President's Men '76
The Big Bus '76
Harry & Walter Go to New York '76
The Hindenburg '75
Farewell, My Lovely '75
The Conversation '74
The Taking of Pelham One Two Three '74
Tell Me Where It Hurts '74
Class of '44 '73
Showdown '73
Steelyard Blues '73
Skin Game '71
Summertree '71
Zodiac '07
The Tollbooth '04
Ash Wednesday '02
Thin Air '00
Mystery '99
Rear Window '98
Horton Foote's Alone '97
Ms. Scrooge '97
Last Stand at Saber River '97
The Heidi Chronicles '95
The Kennedys of Massachusetts '55
Larry McMurtry's Streets of Laredo '95
One Night Stand '95
Tecumseh: The Last Warrior '95
Sarah, Plain and Tall: Winter's End '99
Small Vices: A Spenser Mystery '99
Looking for Richard '96
Sarah, Plain and Tall '91
Sarah, Plain and Tall: Skylark '93
Sidekicks '93
Bed & Breakfast '92
The Habitation of Dragons '91
Backfire '88
God Bless the Child '88
Jesse '88
Monkey Shines '88
Vice Versa '88

Leroy Shield
Laurel & Hardy: Be Big '31
Laurel & Hardy: Another Fine Mess '30
Laurel & Hardy: Blotto '30
Laurel & Hardy: Perfect Day '29

Michael Shields
Ice Men '04
Ginger Snaps '01

Nathaniel Shilkert
Esther and the King '60

Howard Shore (1946-)
The Departed '06
A History of Violence '05
The Aviator '04
The Lord of the Rings: The Return of the King '03
Gangs of New York '02
The Lord of the Rings: The Two Towers '02
Panic Room '02
Spider '02
The Lord of the Rings: The Fellowship of the Ring '01
The Score '01
The Cell '00
High Fidelity '00
The Yards '00
Dogma '99
eXistenZ '99
Analyze This '98
Gloria '98
Cop Land '97
The Game '97
Striptease '96
The Truth about Cats and Dogs '96
Before and After '95
Crash '95
Moonlight and Valentino '95
Seven '95
White Man's Burden '95
The Client '94
Ed Wood '94
Nobody's Fool '94
M. Butterfly '93
Mrs. Doubtfire '93
Philadelphia '93
Sliver '93
Single White Female '92
Prelude to a Kiss '92
Naked Lunch '91
The Silence of the Lambs '91
Quick Change '90
An Innocent Man '89
She-Devil '89
Signs of Life '89
Big '88
Dead Ringers '88
Moving '88
Heaven '87
Nadine '87
Belizaire the Cajun '86
The Fly '86
Fire with Fire '86
After Hours '85
Places in the Heart '84
Videodrome '83
Scanners '81
The Brood '79

Ryan Shore (1974-)
Numb '07
Prime '05
Call Me: The Rise and Fall of Heidi Fleiss '04
Harvard Man '01
Lift '01

Lawrence Shragge
Merlin's Apprentice '06
The Christmas Blessing '05
DC 9/11: Time of Crisis '04
Brush with Fate '03
The Christmas Shoes '02
My Sister's Keeper '02
The Snow Queen '02
The Triangle '01
The Audrey Hepburn Story '00
A House Divided '00
Missing Pieces '00
The Wrong Guy '96
Blue River '95
You Know My Name '99
The Sweetest Gift '98
William Faulkner's Old Man '97

Leo Shuken (1906-76)
Sullivan's Travels '41
The Flying Deuces '39
Miracle of Morgan's Creek '44

Garry Sherman
Alice's Restaurant '69
The Heartbreak Kid '72

Duncan Sheik (1969-)
A Home at the End of the World '04

Richard M. Sherman (1928-)
The Slipper and the Rose '76
Bedknobs and Broomsticks '71
Chitty Chitty Bang Bang '68
The Happiest Millionaire '67
Mary Poppins '64
Big Red '62

Robert B. Sherman (1925-)
The Slipper and the Rose '76
Bedknobs and Broomsticks '71
The Happiest Millionaire '67
Chitty Chitty Bang Bang '68
Mary Poppins '64
Big Red '62

Alan Silvestri (1950-)
Beowulf '07
Night at the Museum '06
The Wild '06
The Polar Express '04
Van Helsing '04
Identity '03
Lara Croft Tomb Raider: The Cradle of Life '03
Lilo & Stitch '02
Maid in Manhattan '02
Showtime '02
Stuart Little 2 '02
The Mexican '01
The Mummy Returns '01
Serendipity '01
Cast Away '00
Reindeer Games '00
The Replacements '00
What Lies Beneath '00
What Women Want '00
Stuart Little '99
Holy Man '98
Practical Magic '98
The Parent Trap '98
Contact '97
Fools Rush In '97
Mouse Hunt '97
Volcano '97
Eraser '96
The Long Kiss Goodnight '96
Father of the Bride Part 2 '95
Grumpier Old Men '95
Judge Dredd '95
The Quick and the Dead '95
Clean Slate '94
Forrest Gump '94
The Perez Family '94
Richie Rich '94
Cop and a Half '93
Grumpy Old Men '93
Judgment Night '93
Sidekicks '93
Super Mario Bros. '93
The Bodyguard '92
Death Becomes Her '92
FernGully: The Last Rain Forest '92
Stop! or My Mom Will Shoot '92
Father of the Bride '91
Ricochet '91
Soapdish '91
Predator 2 '90
Young Guns 2 '90
Back to the Future, Part 3 '90
The Abyss '89
Back to the Future, Part 2 '89
Who Framed Roger Rabbit '88
Outrageous Fortune '87
Overboard '87
American Anthem '87
Predator '87
The Clan of the Cave Bear '86
Critical Condition '86
Delta Force '86
Flight of the Navigator '86
No Mercy '86
Cat's Eye '85
Fandango '85
Summer Rental '85
Romancing the Stone '84
The Amazing Dobermans '76

Carly Simon (1945-)
Piglet's Big Movie '03
Postcards from the Edge '90
Working Girl '88
Heartburn '86

Louis Silvers (1889-1954)
Meet the Navy '46
Jesse James '39
Dimples '36

Sheila Silver (1946-)
Dead Funny '94
Alligator Eyes '90

Shel Silverstein (1932-99)
Payday '73
Ned Kelly '70

Carlo Siliotto (1950-)
Under the Same Moon '07
Have No Fear: The Life of Pope John Paul II '05
The Punisher '04

Lev Shvarts
My Apprenticeship '40
My Universities '39
My Childhood '38

Zoran Simjanovic (1946-)
Cabaret Balkan '98
Tito and Me '92
When Father Was Away on Business '85

Marty Simon
No Alibi '00
Stranger in the House '97
The Ultimate Weapon '97
Marked Man '96
The Wrong Woman '96
George's Island '91
Scanners 2: The New Order '91

Claudio Simonetti (1952-)
Masters of Horror: Jenifer '05
Opera '86
Demons '86

Tim Simonec
A Rumor of Angels '00

Mike Simpson
Stick It '06
Suicide Kings '97

Marlin Skiles (1906-81)
Queen of Outer Space '58
An Annapolis Story '55
Flight to Mars '52

Frank Skinner (1897-1968)
Madame X '66
Shenandoah '65
Portrait in Black '60
Battle Hymn '57
Man of a Thousand Faces '57
Tarnished Angels '57
Away All Boats '56

She's Out of Control '89
Downtown '99

All That Heaven Allows '55
Because of You '52
The World in His Arms '52
Bedtime for Bonzo '51
Double Crossbones '51
Francis Goes to the Races '51
Harvey '50
Francis the Talking Mule '49
Abbott and Costello Meet Frankenstein '48
I'll Be Yours '47
Black Angel '46
Canyon Passage '46
The Flame of New Orleans '41
The Amazing Mrs. Holiday '43
Saboteur '42
Sherlock Holmes and the Secret Weapon '42
Back Street '41
Never Give a Sucker an Even Break '41
The Wolf Man '41
My Little Chickadee '40
Seven Sinners '40
Destry Rides Again '39
First Love '39
The Tower of London '39

Cezary Skubiszewski
After the Deluge '03
Strange Fits of Passion '99
Lilian's Story '95

Rod Slane
Revenge '86
Blood Cult '85

Ivor Slaney (1921-98)
Varian's War '01
The Boys of St. Vincent '93
The Strange Case of the End of Civilization As We Know It '93
Death Ship '80
The Terror '79
Blackout '54
Heat Wave '54
Scarlet Spear '54
Terror Street '54
Unholy Four '54
Three Stops to Murder '53
The Gambler & the Lady '52
Scotland Yard Inspector '52

Christopher Slaski (1974-)
Piano Tuner of Earthquakes '05
Beyond the Sea '04

Michael Small (1939-2003)
The Golden Spiders: A Nero Wolfe Mystery '00
Poodle Springs '98
Mountains of the Moon '90
1969 '89
Black Widow '87
Jaws: The Revenge '87
Orphans '87
Brighton Beach Memoirs '86
The Postman Always Rings Twice '81
Plenty '85
The Naked Country '85
Eleni '85
Iceman '84
The Winds of Jarrah '83
Barbarosa '82
1915 '82
The Chant of Jimmie Blacksmith '78
Circle of Iron '78
The Devil's Playground '76
Picnic at Hanging Rock '75
The Cars That Ate Paris '74

B.C. Smith
Beer League '06
Ellie Parker '05
Kids in America '05
Standing Still '05
A Thief of Time '04
Coyote Waits '03
Skins '02

Joseph Smith
Animal Instincts '92
Secret Games '92

Michael W. Smith (1957-)
The Second Chance '06
Joshua '02

Paul J. Smith (1906-80)
The Parent Trap '61
Pollyanna '60
The Great Locomotive Chase '56
20,000 Leagues under the Sea '54
Fun & Fancy Free '47
Snow White and the Seven Dwarfs '37

Stanley A. Smith
The Gospel '05
Catfish in Black Bean Sauce '00

Neil Smolar
Varian's War '01

David Snell
Billy the Kid '41
The Secret of Dr. Kildare '39

Mark Snow (1946-)
Private Fears in Public Places '06
Another Woman's Husband '00
Dirty Pictures '00
Crazy in Alabama '99
Disturbing Behavior '98
The X-Files '98
Down, Out and Dangerous '95
Frame by Frame '95
A Good Day to Die '95
Treacherous Crossing '92
Alien Nation '88
The Flamingo Kid '84

Johan Soderqvist (1966-)
Things We Lost in the Fire '07
After the Wedding '06
Brothers '05
Like It Never Was Before '95

Stephen Sondheim (1930-)
Sweeney Todd: The Demon Barber of Fleet Street '07
Gypsy '93
Dick Tracy '90
Postcards from the Edge '90
Sunday in the Park with George '86
Sweeney Todd: The Demon Barber of Fleet Street '84

Reds '81
Stavisky '74
Gypsy '62
West Side Story '61

Sonic Youth
The Heart Is Deceitful Above All Things '04
Demonlover '02

Lodovico Sorret
See Tom Noonan

Matt Sorum (1960-)
Now You Know '02
Fish in a Barrel '01

Ondrej Soukup (1951-)
Dark Blue World '01
Kolya '96

Tim Souster (1943-94)
Traffik '90
Slugs '87

David Spear (1953-)
Mortuary Academy '91
Ratings Game '84
The Creature Wasn't Nice '81

Eric Spear (1908-66)
The Stranger from Venus '54
The Shadow Man '53

Mischa Spoliansky (1898-1985)
Happy Go Lovely '51
The Happiest Days of Your Life '50
Mr. Emmanuel '44
Secret Mission '42
King Solomon's Mines '37

John Sponsler (1965-)
The Stray '00
Y2K '99

Robert Sprayberry
Bodily Harm '95
Widow's Kiss '94
Quick '93
Where the Red Fern Grows: Part 2 '92
Video Murders '87

Willy Stahl
Dark Mountain '44
Navy Way '44

Ringo Starr (1940-)
Let It Be '70
Yellow Submarine '68
Magical Mystery Tour '67
Help! '65

Michael Stearns (1940-)
Temptress '95
Baraka '93

Andrew Stein
Death Sport '78
Hollywood Boulevard '76
Premature Burial '62
Atlas '60
Dinosaurus! '60
King Kong vs. Godzilla '63
Shame '61
This Island Earth '55
It Came from Outer Space '53

Ronald Stein (1930-88)
The Rain People '69
Spider Baby '64
Dementia 13 '63
The Haunted Palace '63
The Terror '63
Legend of Tom Dooley '59
Attack of the 50 Foot Woman '58
Invasion of the Saucer Men '57
Reform School Girl '57
Sorority Girl '57
The Gunslinger '56
It Conquered the World '56
The Phantom from 10,000 Leagues '56
Day the World Ended '55

Fred Steiner
Black Brigade '69

Hercules and the Princess of Troy '65

Max Steiner (1888-1971)
Those Calloways '65
Spencer's Mountain '63
Rome Adventure '62
Parrish '61
Cash McCall '60
Ice Palace '60
The FBI Story '59
The Hanging Tree '59
John Paul Jones '59
A Summer Place '59
Darby's Rangers '58
Marjorie Morningstar '58
Band of Angels '57
China Gate '57
Escapade in Japan '57
All Mine to Give '56
Death of a Scoundrel '56
Helen of Troy '56
Run of the Arrow '56
The Searchers '56
Battle Cry '55
Hell on Frisco Bay '55
The McConnell Story '55
The Caine Mutiny '54
King Richard and the Crusaders '54
By the Light of the Silvery Moon '53
The Desert Song '53
Trouble along the Way '53
Miracle of Our Lady of Fatima '52
Springfield Rifle '52
Distant Drums '51
Jim Thorpe: All American '51
On Moonlight Bay '51
Caged '50
The Flame & the Arrow '50
Adventures of Don Juan '49
Beyond the Forest '49
Flamingo Road '49
The Fountainhead '49
White Heat '49
Johnny Belinda '48
Key Largo '48
My Girl Tisa '48
Silver River '48
South of St. Louis '48
Treasure of the Sierra Madre '48
Winter Meeting '48
Life with Father '47
Pursued '47
The Beast with Five Fingers '46
The Big Sleep '46
Cloak and Dagger '46
The Man I Love '46
My Reputation '46
Night and Day '46
A Stolen Life '46
Tomorrow Is Forever '46
The Corn Is Green '45
Mildred Pierce '45
Rhapsody in Blue '45
San Antonio '45
Saratoga Trunk '45
The Adventures of Mark Twain '44
Arsenic and Old Lace '44
Passage to Marseilles '44
Since You Went Away '44
This Is the Army '43
Watch on the Rhine '43
Captains of the Clouds '42
Casablanca '42
Desperate Journey '42
In This Our Life '42
Now, Voyager '42
The Bride Came C.O.D. '41
Dive Bomber '41
The Great Lie '41
Sergeant York '41
They Died with Their Boots On '41
All This and Heaven Too '40
City for Conquest '40
The Letter '40
Santa Fe Trail '40
Virginia City '40
Dark Victory '39
Dodge City '39
Each Dawn I Die '39

Gone with the Wind '39
Intermezzo '39
Oklahoma Kid '39
The Old Maid '39
They Made Me a Criminal '39
The Adventures of Tom Sawyer '38
Amazing Dr. Clitterhouse '38
Angels with Dirty Faces '38
Dawn Patrol '38
Four Daughters '38
Jezebel '38
The Sisters '38
Kid Galahad '37
The Life of Emile Zola '37
A Star Is Born '37
That Certain Woman '37
The Charge of the Light Brigade '36
Follow the Fleet '36
The Garden of Allah '36
Little Lord Fauntleroy '36
Alice Adams '35
Break of Hearts '35
I Dream Too Much '35
The Informer '35
Roberta '35
She '35
The Three Musketeers '35
Top Hat '35
Anne of Green Gables '34
Bachelor Bait '34
The Gay Divorcee '34
Kentucky Kernels '34
Little Minister '34
The Lost Patrol '34
Of Human Bondage '34
Romance in Manhattan '34
Spitfire '34
Ace of Aces '33
Aggie Appleby, Maker of Men '33
Ann Vickers '33
Cheyenne Kid '33
Christopher Strong '33
Diplomaniacs '33
Finishing School '33
Flying Down to Rio '33
King Kong '33
Little Women '33
Morning Glory '33
Son of Kong '33
Topaze '33
A Bill of Divorcement '32
Bird of Paradise '32
The Half Naked Truth '32
Little Orphan Annie '32
Lost Squadron '32
Melody Cruise '32
The Most Dangerous Game '32
Way Back Home '32
What Price Hollywood? '32
Bachelor Apartment '31
Cimarron '31
Kept Husbands '31
State's Attorney '31
Check & Double Check '30
Dixiana '30
Half-Shot at Sunrise '30
Last Command '28

Steven Stern (1967-)
The Assassination of Richard Nixon '05
My Date With Drew '05
Single White Female 2: The Psycho '05
D.E.B.S. '04

Cat Stevens (1948-)
Bloody Murder 2 '03
Big Brother Trouble '00
Hangman '00
Bloody Murder '99
Deep End '70

Leith Stevens (1909-70)
Crazy Horse and Custer: "The Untold Story" '90
The Interns '62
Crashout '55
Private Hell 36 '54
The Wild One '54
The Hitch-Hiker '53
The War of the Worlds '53
When Worlds Collide '51

Destination Moon '50

Morton Stevens (1929-91)
Act of Piracy '89
Alice in Wonderland '85
Backstairs at the White House '79
Banjo Hackett '76

David A. Stewart (1952-)
Space Chimps '08
Alfie '04
Cookie's Fortune '99
Beautiful Girls '96
Showgirls '95
The Ref '93

Gary Stockdale
The Aristocrats '05
Picasso Trigger '89
Dance of the Damned '88
Necromancer: Satan's Servant '88
Hard Ticket to Hawaii '87

Georgie Stoll (1905-85)
Where the Boys Are '60
The Seven Hills of Rome '58
Holiday in Mexico '46

Morris Stoloff (1898-1980)
Song Without End '60
The Jolson Story '46
His Girl Friday '40
Theodora Goes Wild '36

Christopher Stone
Skeletons in the Closet '00
Phantasm 4: Oblivion '98
DNA '97

Richard Stone (1953-2001)
Victim of Love '91
Pumpkinhead '88

Michael Storey
Wavelength '96
Just Like a Woman '95
Coming Up Roses '86
Another Country '84

Herbert Stothart (1885-1949)
Undercurrent '46
They Were Expendable '45
National Velvet '44
Thirty Seconds Over Tokyo '44
The White Cliffs of Dover '44
Cairo '42
Mrs. Miniver '42
Random Harvest '42
Waterloo Bridge '40
The Wizard of Oz '39
Camille '36
A Tale of Two Cities '36
Wife Versus Secretary '36
Anna Karenina '35
China Seas '35
David Copperfield '35
Mutiny on the Bounty '35
A Night at the Opera '35
Night Flight '33

Oscar Straus (1870-1954)
The Earrings of Madame De... '54

Barbra Streisand (1942-)
The Mirror Has Two Faces '96
Nuts '87

Marc Streitenfeld
American Gangster '07
A Good Year '06

Charles Strouse (1928-)
Annie '99
Bonnie & Clyde '67

Joe Strummer (1952-2002)

Grosse Pointe Blank '97
When Pigs Fly '93
Permanent Record '88
Walker '87
Sid & Nancy '86

Marty Stuart (1958-)
Waking Up in Reno '02
All the Pretty Horses '00
Daddy & Them '99
Gypsy '93

Jule Styne (1905-94)
Gypsy '93
Funny Girl '68
My Sister Eileen '55
Gentlemen Prefer Blondes '53
Two Tickets to Broadway '51
The West Point Story '50
Anchors Aweigh '45

L. Subramaniam
Mississippi Masala '92
Salaam Bombay! '88

Michael Suby
The Butterfly Effect 2 '06
The Zodiac '05
The Butterfly Effect '04

Harry Sukman (1912-84)
Salem's Lot '79
Song Without End '60
Forty Guns '57
A Bullet for Joey '55

Mauri Sumen
Condition Red '95
Zombie and the Ghost Train '91

Andy Summers (1942-)
Motorama '91
Weekend at Bernie's '89
End of the Line '88
Down and Out in Beverly Hills '86

Mark Suozzo (1953-)
The Nanny Diaries '07
The Notorious Bettie Page '06
American Splendor '03
The Last Days of Disco '98
Nick and Jane '96
Barcelona '94
Metropolitan '90

Ron Sures
Siblings '04
The Perfect Son '00
The Life Before This '99
Restless Spirits '99
Conquest '98
Body of Influence 2 '96
Long Day's Journey Into Night '96
A Man in Uniform '93

Bruce Sussman
The Pebble and the Penguin '94
Thumbelina '94

Jiri Sust (1919-95)
My Sweet Little Village '86
Closely Watched Trains '66

Elizabeth Swados
Killing Floor '85

John Swihart
The Longshots '08
The Brothers Solomon '07
Full of It '07
Bickford Shmeckler's Cool Ideas '06
Employee of the Month '06
The Great New Wonderful '06
The Sasquatch Gang '06
Think Tank '06
Napoleon Dynamite '04

Kurt Swinghammer
Say Uncle '05
Ginger Snaps: Unleashed '04

Jules Sylvain (1900-68)
The True and the False '55
June Night '40

Stanislas Syrewicz
Extreme Ops '02
Strictly Sinatra '01
Nora '00
Shocking Fish '98
Jack Higgins' The Windsor Protocol '97
Jack Higgins' Thunder Point '98
The Lair of the White Worm '88

Taj Mahal (1942-)
Outside Ozona '98
Zebrahead '92
Sounder '72

Toru Takemitsu (1930-96)
Rising Sun '93
Rikyu '90
Black Rain '88
Himatsuri '85
Ran '85
Dodes 'ka-den '70
Double Suicide '69
Face of Another '66
Kwaidan '64
Woman in the Dunes '64
Harakiri '62

Joby Talbot
Arctic Tale '07
Penelope '06
The Hitchhiker's Guide to the Galaxy '05

Frederic Talgorn (1961-)
Mothers '07
Heavy Metal 2000 '00
The Devil's Arithmetic '99
Delta Force 2: Operation Stranglehold '90
Edge of Sanity '89

Zdenko Tamassy (1921-87)
Colonel Redl '84
Mephisto '81

Tangerine Dream
Rainbow Drive '90
Miracle Mile '89
Near Dark '87
Shy People '87
Three O'Clock High '87
The Park is Mine '85
Vision Quest '85
Firestarter '84
Heartbreakers '84
Kamikaze '89 '83
The Keep '83
Risky Business '83
Wavelength '83
Thief '81
Sorcerer '77

Graham Tardif (1957-)
Dance Me to My Song '98
The Quiet Room '96
Alien Visitor '95
Bad Boy Bubby '93

Michael Tavera
Drowning Mona '00
Silent Predators '99
Girl '98
The Land Before Time 6: The Secret of Saurus Rock '98
The Land Before Time 5: The Mysterious Island '97
The Land Before Time 4: Journey Through the Mists '96
The Land Before Time 3: The Time of the Great Giving '95
The Land Before Time 2: The Great Valley Adventure '94

Barry Taylor
Attack Force '06
The Detonator '06
Seven Seconds '05
Kept '01

Jeff Taylor
Help! '65

Stephen James Taylor
Happy Hour '03
Amateur '94
Disney's Teacher's Pet '04
Boycott '02
Finding Buck McHenry '00
Holiday Heart '00
Passing Glory '99
Why Do Fools Fall in Love? '98
Nightjohn '95
The Glass Shield '95
The Piano Lesson '94

Bob Telson
Life According to Muriel '97
Rosalie Goes Shopping '89
Bagdad Cafe '88

Nicolas Tenbroek
The Moguls '05
Isaac Asimov's Nightfall '00
American Ninja 4: The Annihilation '91

Dennis Michael Tenney
Tick Tock '00
Leprechaun 4: In Space '96
Pinocchio's Revenge '96
Leprechaun 3 '95
Witchboard 2 '93
Doorway '93
Witchboard '87

Richard Termini
States of Control '98
Mac '93

Mikis Theodorakis (1925-)
Iphigenia '77
Serpico '73
Z '69
Phaedra '61

Maurice Thiriet (1906-72)
Fanfan la Tulipe '51
L'idiot '46
Children of Paradise '44
The Fantastic Night '42

Ian Thomas (1950-)
Bloodknot '95
Hostage for a Day '94
Boulevard '94

Mark Thomas (1956-)
Moondance '95
Moondance Alexander '07
Hot Tamale '06
Doogal '05
Agent Cody Banks 2: Destination London '04
Hoodlum & Son '03
Dog Soldiers '01
The Big Tease '99

Stuart M. Thomas
Angels Fall '07
Blue Smoke '07

Eugen Thomass
Spare Parts '79

George Aliceson Tipton
Hit Lady '74
Phantom of the Paradise '74

Marc Anthony Thompson
Brother to Brother '04
Urbania '00
Spark '98

Richard Thompson (1949-)
Grizzly Man '05
Sweet Talker '91

Ken Thorne (1924-)
Love Comes Softly '03
Right at Your Door '06
Love, Ludlow '05
Mean Creek '04
The Mothman Prophecies '02
The Rules of Attraction '02
Waking the Dead '00
Arlington Road '99

Martin Todsharow (1967-)
Agnes and His Brothers '04
Guys and Balls '04

Isao Tomita (1932-)
The Hidden Blade '04
The Twilight Samurai '02

Peter Tomashek
Final Approach '04
Destination Vegas '95

Tomandandy
P2 '07
The Covenant '06
The Hills Have Eyes '06
The Return '06
The Furaway '00
A Lesson Before Dying '99
One Man's Hero '98
Calm at Sunset '96

Yann Tiersen (1970-)
Good Bye, Lenin! '03
Amelie '01

Ton That Tiet
The Dreamlife of Angels '98
Carnosaur 2 '94
Night of the Warrior '91
Buffalo Boy '04
The Vertical Ray of the Sun '00
Cyclo '95
The Scent of Green Papaya '93

Timbaland (1971-)
30 Years to Life '01
Rome Must Die '01

Michael Timmins
Niagara, Niagara '97

Nikolai Timofeyev
The Inspector General '52

Dimitri Tiomkin (1899-1979)
The War Wagon '67
36 Hours '64
The Guns of Navarone '61
Town without Pity '61
The Alamo '60
Rio Bravo '59
The Young Land '59
The Sundowners '60
The Old Man and the Sea '58
Gunfight at the O.K. Corral '57
Night Passage '57
Friendly Persuasion '56
The High and the Mighty '54
Dial 'M' for Murder '54
Angel Face '52
High Noon '52
The Thing '51
Strangers on a Train '51
Cyrano de Bergerac '50
Champion '49
D.O.A. '49
Home of the Brave '49
Portrait of Jennie '48
Red River '48
The Long Night '47
Angel on My Shoulder '46
Duel in the Sun '46
It's a Wonderful Life '46
The Bridge of San Luis Rey '44
Shadow of a Doubt '43
The Corsican Brothers '42
A Gentleman After Dark '42
The Westerner '40
Mr. Smith Goes to Washington '39
Only Angels Have Wings '39
Spawn of the North '38
Lost Horizon '37
Mad Love '35

Stephen Trask
Feast of Love '07
The Savages '07
American Dreamz '06
In the Land of Women '06
A Hole in One '04
How to Lose Your Lover '04
In Good Company '04
Camp '03
MTV's Wuthering Heights '03
The Station Agent '03
Hedwig and the Angry Inch '00

Fiachra Trench (1941-)
The Boys and Girl From County Clare '03
A Love Divided '01
Moondance '95

Ernest Troost
Fallen Angel '03
The Home Front '02
The Seventh Stream '01
Beat '00
Terror Tract '00
The 4th Floor '99
The Settlement '99
The Hunted '03

Ed Tomney
Persons Unknown '96
Safe '95

Colin Towns
The Order '03
Crimson Rivers 2: Angels of the Apocalypse '05
Goodbye, Mr. Chips '02
Catherine Cookson's Secret '00
Catherine Cookson's Tilly Trotter '99
Essex Boys '99
Maybe Baby '00
The Waiting Time '99
Retribution '98
Catherine Cookson's The Wingless Bird '97
Catherine Cookson's The Dwelling Place '94
The Puppet Masters '94
The Blackheath Poisonings '92
Clarissa '91
Catherine Cookson's The Fifteen Streets '90
Fellow Traveler '89
Getting It Right '89
Bellman and True '88
Vampire's Kiss '88
The Buccaneers '95
The Crow Road '96
Tide of Life '96
Born of Fire '87
Knights & Emeralds '87
Rawhead Rex '87
Slayground '84
Full Circle '77

David Torn (1953-)
Lars and the Real Girl '07
Dracula 3: Legacy '05
The Scent of a Woman '75
Hired to Kill '73
Hit Men '73
Friday Night Lights '04
Believe in Me '06
Mikey '92

Cleri Torjussen
Two Women '61
Down & Dirty '76
A Special Day '77

Tim Truman
Angel's Dance '99
Good Luck '96
Marshal Law '96
Retroactive '97

Brian Tyler
Bangkok Dangerous '08
Rambo '08
Aliens vs. Predator: Requiem '07
War '07
Partition '07
Annapolis '06
Bug '06
The Fast and the Furious: Tokyo Drift '06
Constantine '05
The Greatest Game Ever Played '05
The Big Empty '04
The Final Cut '04
Godsend '04
Paparazzi '04
Bubba Ho-Tep '03
Children of Dune '03
Darkness Falls '03
Timeline '03
Frailty '02
John Carpenter Presents Vampires: Los Muertos '02
Last Call: The Final Chapter of F. Scott Fitzgerald '02
Nobody's Baby '01
Four Dogs Playing Poker '00
Panic '00

Tom Tykwer (1965-)
Perfume: The Story of a Murderer '06
The Princess and the Warrior '00
Run Lola Run '98
Winter Sleepers '97

Jonathan Tunick
I Am the Cheese '83
Sketch Artist 2: Hands That See '94

Toshiaki Tsushima (1938-)
The Birdcage '95
The Street Fighter '74
The Slime '68

Marc Tschantz
The West Wittering Affair '05

Armando Trovajoli (1917-)
The Family '87
Down & Dirty '77
Boccaccio '70 '62
Assassination in Rome '65
Mole Men Against the Son of Hercules '61
The Libertine '69
The Reluctant Agent '95

Christopher Tyng
Bookies '03
The Diamond of Jeru '01
Seven Girlfriends '00
Anyway '98
The Associate '96
Cadillac Ranch '96

The Canterville Ghost '96
Tremors '89
Dead Heat '88
South Central '92
Six-String Samurai '98
Final Justice '98
Sirens '99
Simon Sez '99
The Bumblebee Flies Anyway '00
Camp '03
'33

Kazaam '96
Crosscut '95
The Little Death '95
Across the Moon '94
National Lampoon's Attack of the 5 Ft. 2 Women '94
Unveiled '94

Steve Tyrell
These Old Broads '01
20 Dates '99
Once Upon a Time … When We Were Colored '95
Out of Sync '95
T Bone N Weasel '92
Getting It '92

Nerida Tyson-Chew
Anacondas: The Hunt for the Blood Orchid '04
Visitors '03
Mr. Accident '99
Under the Lighthouse Dancing '97
Brilliant Lies '96
Twisted '96
Sorrento Beach '95

Deddy Tzur
Heaven's Fire '99
Termination Man '97
The Final Cut '96
Snowboard Academy '96

Giovanni Ullu
Emmanuelle, the Queen '79
Emmanuelle's Daughter '79

Shingeru Umebayashi (1951-)
Curse of the Golden Flower '06
House of Flying Daggers '04
2046 '04
Zhou Yu's Train '02
In the Mood for Love '00

Pierro Umiliani (1926-2001)
Lady of the Evening '75
Five Dolls for an August Moon '70
Welcome Stranger '47
The Road to Utopia '46
The Bells of St. Mary's '45

Jean-Louis Valero
Big Deal on Madonna Street '58

Teo Usuelli (1930-)
Amuck! '71
Saul and David '64

Steve Vai (1960-)
P.C.U. '94

James Van Heusen (1913-90)
Journey Back to Oz '71
Robin and the 7 Hoods '64
Diabolique '55
Nana '55
Beauties of the Night '52
Casque d'Or '52
Fanfan la Tulipe '51

Melvin Van Peebles (1932-)
Tales of Erotica '93
Sweet Sweetback's Baadasssss Song '71
Watermelon Man '70

David Van Tieghem
Eye of God '97
Working Girls '87

John Van Tongeren
Twitches Too '07
Twitches '05
Malibu's Most Wanted '03

Kenny Vance (1943-)
The Heart of Dixie '89
Hairspray '88

Vangelis (1943-)
Alexander '04
Francesco '93
Bitter Moon '92
1492: Conquest of Paradise '92
Third Solution '89
Antarctica '84
The Bounty '84
Blade Runner '82
Missing '82
Chariots of Fire '81

Ross Vannelli
Children On Their Birthdays '02
The Void '01
Wounded '97

C.J. Vanston
For Your Consideration '06
A Mighty Wind '03
Best in Show '00
Almost Heroes '97

Varouje
Expect No Mercy '95
Fearless Tiger '94

Didier Vasseur
A Business Affair '93
Face the Music '92

Ben Vaughn
The Independent '00
Psycho Beach Party '00
Lewis and Clark and George '97
Black Mask '96

Rene Veldsman
Queen's Messenger II '01
Woman of Desire '93

Caetano Veloso (1942-)
Orfeu '99
O Quatrilho '95

James L. Venable
Superhero Movie '08
Clerks 2 '06
Scary Movie 4 '06
Venom '05
Eurotrip '04
Jersey Girl '04
Scary Movie 3 '03
Jay and Silent Bob Strike Back '01
Iron Monkey '93

Michael Vickers (1941-)
At the Earth's Core '76
Dracula A.D. 1972 '72

Joseph Vitarelli
John Adams '08
And Starring Pancho Villa as Himself '03
My Architect: A Son's Journey '03
Nobody's Baby '01
Excellent Cadavers '99
Kissing a Fool '98
The Pentagon Wars '98
She's So Lovely '97
Commandments '96
Evil Has a Face '96
The Substance of Fire '96
The Invaders '95
Tall, Dark and Deadly '95
The Last Seduction '94
Big Man on Campus '89
How I Got into College '89

Alessio Vlad (1955-)
Callas Forever '02
Tea with Mussolini '99
Besieged '98
Jane Eyre '96

Roman Vlad (1919-)
The Ghost '63
The Horrible Dr. Hichcock '62
Where the Hot Wind Blows '59
I, Vampiri '56
Beauty and the Devil '50
The Walls of Malapaga '49

Henny Vrienten (1948-)
Left Luggage '98
The Vanishing '88

Popul Vuh
Cobra Verde '88
Fitzcarraldo '82
Nosferatu the Vampyre '79
Heart of Glass '74
Aguirre, the Wrath of God '72

Gyorgy Vukan
Hanussen '88
The Fifth Seal '76

Waddy Wachtel
Strange Wilderness '08
The Benchwarmers '06
Grandma's Boy '06
Dickie Roberts: Former Child Star '03
Joe Dirt '01

Tommy Wai
New Police Story '04
Drunken Monkey '03
Time and Tide '00

Tom Waits (1949-)
Big Bad Love '02
Night on Earth '91
Down by Law '86
Streetwise '84
One from the Heart '82
On the Nickel '80

Adolfo Waitzman
Flying from the Hawk '86
Blue Jeans and Dynamite '76

Rick Wakeman (1949-)
Bullet to Beijing '95
Creepshow 2 '87
Crimes of Passion '84
The Burning '82
Lisztomania '75
Kangaroo '86

Nathan Waks
My Brilliant Career '79

Adam Walacinski
Pharaoh '66
Mother Joan of the Angels '60

Dana Walden
Killing Obsession '94
Molly and Gina '94
Wyatt Earp: Return to Tombstone '94
My Mom's a Werewolf '89

W.G. Snuffy Walden (1950-)
Homecoming '96
Homage '95
Stephen King's The Stand '94
The Good Fight '92
The Chase '91

Shirley Walker (1945-2006)
Black Christmas '06
Final Destination 3 '06
Final Destination 2 '03
Willard '03
Disappearance '02
Final Destination '00
Asteroid '97
The Crying Child '96
Escape from L.A. '96
Turbulence '97
It Came from Outer Space 2 '95
Batman: Mask of the Phantasm '93

P.T. Walkley
The Groomsmen '06
Looking for Kitty '04

Oliver Wallace (1887-1963)
Big Red '62
Nikki, the Wild Dog of the North '61
Old Yeller '57
Peter Pan '53
The Adventures of Ichabod and Mr. Toad '49
Fun & Fancy Free '47
Dumbo '41

Rob Walsh
The Darwin Conspiracy '99
Revenge of the Ninja '83

Jeff Walton
Paper Bullets '99
Hybrid '97
Invisible Dad '97
Invisible Mom '96
Prey of the Jaguar '96
Attack of the 60-Foot Centerfold '95
Jack-O '95
Fatal Justice '93

William Walton (1902-83)
Battle of Britain '69
Hamlet '48
Henry V '44
The Foreman Went to France '42
Spitfire '42
As You Like It '36

Gast Waltzing (1956-)
The Enemy '01
New World Disorder '99
Octopus 2: River of Fear '02
Shark Attack 3: Megalodon '02
After the Storm '01
Crocodile 2: Death Swamp '01

Michael Wandmacher (1967-)
Never Back Down '08
The Killing Floor '06
CryWolf '05
From Justin to Kelly '03
On the Borderline '01
Modern Vampires '98
The Legend of Drunken Master '94
Twin Dragons '92
Fists of Fury '73
Chinese Connection '73

Nathan Wang
The Final Season '07
Flight of the Living Dead: Outbreak on a Plane '07
The Game Plan '07
She's the Man '06
Come as You Are '05
Jackie Chan's Who Am I '98
Natural Causes '94

Thomas Wanker (1973-)
Dresden '06
RFK '02
The Tunnel '01

Kenneth Wannberg
Vanishing Act '88
Blame It on Rio '84
The Philadelphia Experiment '84
Losin' It '82

Stephen Warbeck (1953-)
Flawless '07
Alpha Male '06
On a Clear Day '05
Proof '05
Two Brothers '04
The Memory of a Killer '03
Birthday Girl '02
Captain Corelli's Mandolin '01
Charlotte Gray '01
Billy Elliot '00
Quills '00
Very Annie Mary '00
A Christmas Carol '99
Heart '99
Mystery Men '99
Shakespeare in Love '98
Mrs. Brown '97
My Son the Fanatic '97
Different for Girls '96
Element of Doubt '96
Brothers in Trouble '95
Sister My Sister '94

Edward Ward (1900-71)
Cobra Woman '44
The Phantom of the Opera '43
Cheers for Miss Bishop '41
Dance, Girl, Dance '40
The Son of Monte Cristo '40
Night Must Fall '37
Wife Versus Secretary '36
The Mystery of Edwin Drood '35

Harry Warren (1893-1981)
Marty '55
The Barkleys of Broadway '49
The Harvey Girls '46
Yolanda and the Thief '45
That Night in Rio '41
42nd Street '33

Mervyn Warren (1964-)
A Raisin in the Sun '08
Honey '03
Marci X '03
A Walk to Remember '02
The Wedding Planner '01
Steel '97
The Wharf Rat '95

David Waters
Body and Soul '98
Rescue Me '93

Mark Watters
Doug's 1st Movie '99
Aladdin and the King of Thieves '96
All Dogs Go to Heaven 2 '95
The Pebble and the Penguin '94

Franz Waxman (1906-67)
Cimarron '60
Sunrise at Campobello '60
Beloved Infidel '59
The Nun's Story '59
Run Silent, Run Deep '58
Peyton Place '57
Sayonara '57
Spirit of St. Louis '57
Mister Roberts '55
Rear Window '54
The Silver Chalice '54
Stalag 17 '53
A Place in the Sun '51
Night and the City '50
Sunset Boulevard '50
Sorry, Wrong Number '48
The Paradine Case '47
Humoresque '46
God is My Co-Pilot '45
Objective, Burma! '45
Air Force '43
Woman of the Year '42
Dr. Jekyll and Mr. Hyde '41
Suspicion '41
Boom Town '40
The Philadelphia Story '40
Rebecca '40
Strange Cargo '40
Honolulu '39
Three Comrades '38
Next Time We Love '36
The Bride of Frankenstein '35

Roger Webb (1934-)
Riders '88
Boy in Blue '86
Au Pair Girls '72

Roy Webb (1888-1982)
Teacher's Pet '58
Marty '55
Second Chance '53
At Sword's Point '51
Fixed Bayonets! '51
Flying Leathernecks '51
Where Danger Lives '50
My Friend Irma '49
Out of the Past '47
Notorious '46
The Spiral Staircase '46
Bedlam '45
Dick Tracy, Detective '45
Fighting Seabees '44
Murder, My Sweet '44
The Seventh Cross '44
Zombies on Broadway '44
The Ghost Ship '43
I Walked with a Zombie '43
The Leopard Man '43
Cat People '42
I Married a Witch '42
The Magnificent Ambersons '42
Abe Lincoln in Illinois '40
My Favorite Wife '40
Love Affair '39
Room Service '38
Inside the Lines '30

Matthias Weber (1961-)
Crossover '06
Alien Siege '05
D.R.E.A.M. Team '99

Paul Francis Webster (1907-84)
The Alamo '60
Calamity Jane '53

Konstantin Wecker (1947-)
The White Rose '83
Sisters, Or the Balance of Happiness '79

Craig (Shudder to Think) Wedren
First Love, Last Rites '98
High Art '98

Cynthia Weil (1937-)
Syriana '05
All Dogs Go to Heaven 2 '95

Kurt Weill (1900-50)
The Three Penny Opera '62
One Touch of Venus '48
The Threepenny Opera '31

Larry Wellington
The Wizard of Gore '70
Just for the Hell of It '68
She-Devils on Wheels '68
The Girl, the Body and the Pill '67
Gruesome Twosome '67
2000 Maniacs '64

John Welsman
In His Father's Shoes '97
The Baxter '05
P.S. '04
School of Rock '03
Laurel Canyon '02
Roger Dodger '02
Wet Hot American Summer '01

Brahm Wenger
Snow Buddies '08
Air Bud 6: Air Buddies '06
MXP: Most Xtreme Primate '03
MVP (Most Valuable Primate) '00
The Duke '99
Air Bud 2: Golden Receiver '98
Air Bud '97
Hollow Point '95

Guo Wenjing
Riding Alone for Thousands of Miles '05
Blush '95

Rick Wentworth
The Alchemists '99
How to Get Ahead in Advertising '89

Lars Johan Werle (1926-2001)
Cherry Falls '00
Sweet Jane '98
Back to Back '96

Jim West
Hour of the Wolf '68
Persona '66

Walter Werzowa (1960-)
Lady Dragon 2 '93
Lady Dragon '92

Paul Westerberg (1959-)
Open Season '06
Singles '92

Tim Westergren
Defying Gravity '99
The Last Best Sunday '98

Nigel Westlake (1958-)
Miss Potter '06
The Nugget '02
Babe: Pig in the City '98
A Little Bit of Soul '97
Babe '95
Children of the Revolution '95

Robert Whaley
Blood Brothers '97
Joe the King '99
The Jimmy Show '01

Harald Wheeler (1943-)
Lovel Valour! Compassion! '96

Bill Whelan (1950-)
Some Mother's Son '96
Dancing at Lughnasa '98
Straight out of Brooklyn '91
Two by Forsyth '86

David Whitaker (1931-)
Dr. Jekyll and Sister Hyde '71
Sword & the Sorcerer '82
With a Friend Like Harry '00

Daniel White (1912-97)
Revenge in the House of Usher '82
Female Vampire '73
Rites of Frankenstein '72

John Clifford White
Macbeth '06
Romper Stomper '92

Stacy Widelitz
Prayer of the Rollerboys '91
Phantom of the Mall: Eric's Revenge '89
Return to Horror High '87

Jean Wiener (1896-1982)
A Gentle Woman '69
Grisbi '53
Rendez-vous de Juillet '49
The Crime of Monsieur Lange '36
The Lower Depths '36

Frederik Wiedmann
Return to House on Haunted Hill '07
Beneath '07

Scott Wilk
Plain Clothes '88
Valley Girl '83

K. Alexander (Alex) Wilkinson
Avalanche '99
Stealth Fighter '99
Inferno '98
Double Edge '97
Pure Danger '96
Street Corner Justice '96
Forbidden Games '95
The Sweeper '95

Marc Wilkinson (1929-)
The Fiendish Plot of Dr. Fu Manchu '80
If... '69

David Williams (1971-)
Manticore '05
Benedict Arnold: A Question of Honor '03
Asylum '01
Supernova '99
Shelter '98
Wishmaster 2: Evil Never Dies '98
Phantoms '97
The Prophecy 2: Ashtown '97
Children of the Corn 4: The Gathering '96
The Killing Jar '96
No Way Back '96
The Prophecy '95
American Yakuza '94

Alan Williams
Soul Assassin '01

John Williams (1932-)
Indiana Jones and the Kingdom of the Crystal Skull '08
Memoirs of a Geisha '05
Munich '05
Star Wars: Episode 3—Revenge of the Sith '05
War of the Worlds '05
The Terminal '04
Harry Potter and the Prisoner of Azkaban '04
Catch Me if You Can '02
Harry Potter and the Chamber of Secrets '02
Minority Report '02
Star Wars: Episode 2—Attack of the Clones '02
A.I.: Artificial Intelligence '01
Harry Potter and the Sorcerer's Stone '01
The Patriot '00
Angela's Ashes '99
Star Wars: Episode 1—The Phantom Menace '99
Saving Private Ryan '98
Stepmom '98
Amistad '98
The Lost World: Jurassic Park 2 '97
Seven Years in Tibet '97
Rosewood '96
Sleepers '96
Sabrina '95
Nixon '95
Schindler's List '93
Far and Away '92
Home Alone 2: Lost in New York '92
Hook '91
JFK '91
Home Alone '90
Presumed Innocent '90
Stanley and Iris '90
Always '89
Born on the Fourth of July '89
Indiana Jones and the Last Crusade '89
The Accidental Tourist '88
Empire of the Sun '87
Superman 4: The Quest for Peace '87
The Witches of Eastwick '87
SpaceCamp '86
Indiana Jones and the Temple of Doom '84
The River '84
Return of the Jedi '83
Superman 3 '83
E.T.: The Extra-Terrestrial '82
Monsignor '82
Yes, Giorgio '82
Heartbeeps '81
Raiders of the Lost Ark '81
The Empire Strikes Back '80
Superman 2 '80
Dracula '79
1941 '79
The Fury '78
The Deer Hunter '78
Jaws 2 '78
Close Encounters of the Third Kind '77
Black Sunday '77
Star Wars '77
Family Plot '76
Midway '76
Missouri Breaks '76
The Eiger Sanction '75
Jaws '75
Conrack '74
Earthquake '74
The Sugarland Express '74
The Towering Inferno '74
Cinderella Liberty '73
The Long Goodbye '73
The Man Who Loved Cat Dancing '73
The Paper Chase '73
Tom Sawyer '73
The Cowboys '72
Images '72
The Poseidon Adventure '72
Pete 'n' Tillie '72
Fiddler on the Roof '71
Daddy's Gone A-Hunting '69
Goodbye, Mr. Chips '69
The Reivers '69
The Sugarland Express '74 (?)
Sergeant Ryker '68
A Guide for the Married Man '67
Heidi '67
Valley of the Dolls '67
How to Steal a Million '66
The Rare Breed '66
None But the Brave '65
The Killers '64
Gidget Goes to Rome '63
Diamond Head '62

Patrick Williams
Meredith Willson (1902-84)
The Music Man '62
The Unsinkable Molly Brown '64

Hal Willner (1957-)
Theremin: An Electronic Odyssey '95
Kansas City '95
Finding Forrester '00
Normal '03
Criminal '04
Hollywood Homicide '03

Nancy Wilson (1954-)
Elizabethtown '05
Vanilla Sky '01
Almost Famous '00
Jerry Maguire '96
Say Anything '89
Footsteps '98

Joseph Williams (1950-)
Category 6: Day of Destruction '04
Category 7: The End of the World '05

Ken Williams
Mo:entum '03
Judgment Day '99
From Dusk Till Dawn 2: Texas Blood Money '98
Never-2 Big '98
Body Count '97
Embrace of the Vampire '95
Poison Ivy 2: Lily '95
Firelight '03
Crash & Bynes '99
The Crimson Code '99
In the Company of Men '96

Patrick Williams (1939-)
Power and Beauty '22
Blonde '01
Jesus '00
The Thin Blue Lie '00
A Cooler Climate '99
Change of Heart '98
A Knight in Camelot '98
Julian Po '97
My Very Best Friend '96
That Old Feeling '96
A Weekend in the Country '96
The Grass Harp '95
Kingfish: A Story of Huey P. Long '95
Getting Gotti '94
Blind Spot '93
Geronimo '93
The Cutting Edge '92
Jewels '92
Cry-Baby '90
In the Spirit '90
Violets Are Blue '86
All of Me '84
The Toy '82
Used Cars '80
Breaking Away '79
Cuba '79
I Wonder Who's Killing Her '76
Sssssss '73
Evel Knievel '72

Paul Williams (1940-)
The Muppet Christmas Carol '92
The Muppet Movie '79
The End '78
The Boy in the Plastic Bubble '76
Bugsy Malone '76
A Star is Born '76
Phantom of the Paradise '74

Alex Wurman (1966-)
Twin Warriors '93
Once Upon a Time in China III '93
Bernard and Doris '08
The Nines '07
Run, Fat Boy, Run '07
Talladega Nights: The Ballad of Ricky Bobby '06
A Lot Like Love '05
Anchorman: The Legend of Ron Burgundy '04
Criminal '04
Confessions of a Dangerous Mind '02
Thirteen Conversations About One Thing '01
Sleep Easy, Hutch Rimes '00
No Vacancy '99
Play It to the Bone '99
Normal '03

Arthur Wright
Dolemite '75
Dolemite 2: Human Tornado '76

Wai Lap Wu
Angels One Five '54
The Woman in Question '50

Lyle Workman (1957-)
Forgetting Sarah Marshall '08
Superbad '07
The 40 Year Old Virgin '05
Made '01

David Wingo
Great World of Sound '07
All the Real Girls '03

Ari Wise
Schoo of Life '06

Peter Wolf
The NeverEnding Story 3: Escape from Fantasia '94
The Hollywood Sign '01
Weekend at Bernie's 2 '93

Raymond Wong (1948-)
Kung Fu Hustle '04
Shaolin Soccer '01

John Wooldridge (1919-58)
Angels One Five '54

James Wong (1940-2004)
The Tic Code '99
Who's the Man? '93
Bloodfist 5: Human Target '93

Michael Wolff (1954-)
The Code '99

Debbie Wiseman (1963-)
Tokyo Cowboy '94
Freeze Frame '04
The Truth About Love '04
Othello '01
Dead of Night '99
The Guilty '99
Wilde '97
Female Perversions '96
Haunted '95
Tom & Viv '94

Stanley Wilson (1915-70)
The Beatniks '60
Iron Mountain Trail '53
Government Agents vs. Phantom Legion '51
Border Saddlemates '52
Silver City Bonanza '51
Night Riders of Montana '50
Pioneer Marshal '49
Radar Patrol vs. Spy King '49
Missourians '50
Thunder in God's Country '51

Danny Wyman (1945-)
The Lawnmower Man '92
Hell Night '81

Gabriel Yared (1949-)
1408 '07
Breaking and Entering '06
The Lives of Others '06
Shall We Dance? '04
Cold Mountain '03
Bon Voyage '03
Sylvia '03
Possession '02
Autumn in New York '00
The Next Best Thing '00
The Talented Mr. Ripley '99
City of Angels '98
Message in a Bottle '98
The Wings of the Dove '97
The English Patient '96
The Lover '92
Camille Claudel '89
Romero '89
Clean and Sober '88
Betty Blue '86
Trade Secrets '86
Moon in the Gutter '83

Neil Young (1945-)
Neil Young: Heart of Gold '06
Dead Man '95
Where the Buffalo Roam '80

Victor Young (1901-66)
China Gate '57
Around the World in 80 Days '56
The Brave One '56
The Conqueror '56
Run of the Arrow '56
The Tall Men '55
Johnny Guitar '53
Shane '53
The Quiet Man '52
The Star '52
The Lemon Drop Kid '51
Our Very Own '50
Rio Grande '50
Gun Crazy '49
My Foolish Heart '49
Sands of Iwo Jima '49
The Big Clock '48
Emperor Waltz '48
Unconquered '47
The Blue Dahlia '46
To Each His Own '46
Two Years before the Mast '46
Love Letters '45
Frenchman's Creek '44
Ministry of Fear '44
The Uninvited '44
The Story of Dr. Wassell '44
For Whom the Bell Tolls '43
The Outlaw '43
The Glass Key '42
The Great Man's Lady '42
Reap the Wild Wind '42
Young and Willing '42
Arizona '40
Rhythm on the River '40
Breaking the Ice '38

Christopher Young (1954-)
Sleepwalking '08
Untraceable '08
Ghost Rider '07
Spider-Man 3 '07
Lucky You '07
The Grudge 2 '06
Beauty Shop '05
The Exorcism of Emily Rose '05
An Unfinished Life '05
The Core '03
Runaway Jury '03
Shade '03
The Country Bears '02
Bandits '01
The Glass House '01
The Shipping News '01
Sweet November '01
Swordfish '01
The Big Kahuna '00
Bless the Child '00
Wonder Boys '00
The Gift '00
In Too Deep '99
Entrapment '99
The Hurricane '99
Judas Kiss '98
Hush '98
Rounders '98
Urban Legend '98
Hard Rain '97
Bright Angel '91
Rapid Fire '92
Dream Lover '93
Judicial Consent '94
Species '95
Tales from the Hood '95
Virtuosity '95
Norma Jean and Marilyn '95
Murder in the First '95
Copycat '95
Unforgettable '96
Set It Off '96
Head Above Water '96
Murder at 1600 '97
The Crazysitter '94
Barbarian Queen 2: The Empress Strikes Back '89
The Fly 2 '89
Eat 21 '88
Hellbound: Hellraiser 2 '88
Flowers in the Attic '87
Hellraiser '87
Invaders from Mars '86
Barbarian Queen '85
The Power '80
The Dark Half '91
Last Flight Out: A True Story '90
Nautilus '99

Dwight Yoakam (1956-)
South of Heaven, West of Hell '00
Chasers '94

Peyman Yazdanian
Summer Palace '06
Crimson Gold '03

Eric Wurst / David Wurst
Walking Tall: Lone Justice '07
French Exit '97
Eat Your Heart Out '96
The Foreigner '03
Agent Red '00
Mach 2 '00
Rangers '00
Counter Measures '99
Final Voyage '99
Nautilus '99
Restraining Order '99
The White Raven '98
The Haunted Sea '97
Scorpio One '97
Crash Dive '96
The Last Assassins '96
The Death Artist '95
Dillinger and Capone '95
Machine Gun Blues '95
Where Truth Lies '96

Richard Yuen
Bloodmoon '97
The Bride with White Hair '93

Once Upon a Time in China II '92
Wicked City '92
Chuen Yung-Yu
The Mighty Peking Man '77
The Mighty Peking Man '77
Stephan Zacharias (1956-)
Downfall '04
What to Do in Case of Fire '02
Lee Zahler (1883-1947)
The Mask of Diijon '46
I Accuse My Parents '45
The Lady Confesses '45
Boss of Rawhide '44
House of Errors '42
The Great Plane Robbery '40
Flaming Signal '33
Woman Condemned '33
Aleksei Zalivalov
Window to Paris '95
Sideburns '91
Geoff Zanelli (1974-)
Disturbia '07
Hitman '07
House of D '04
Marcelo Zarvos
The Air I Breathe '07
You Kill Me '07
The Architect '06
The Good Shepherd '06
Hollywoodland '06
Ira & Abby '06
The Boynton Beach Club '05
Our Brand Is Crisis '05
The Door in the Floor '04
The Mudge Boy '03
Kissing Jessica Stein '02
Tully '00
Paul Zaza
Superbabies: Baby Geniuses 2 '04
Now & Forever '02
The Fourth Angel '01
The Base '99
Grizzly Falls '99
I'll Remember April '99
Baby Geniuses '98
Hot Blooded '98
A Brooklyn State of Mind '97
Double Take '97
Face the Evil '97
Porky's '82
Prom Night '80
The Ex '96
The Rage '96
Red Blooded 2 '96
Iron Eagle 4 '95
The Club '94
My Summer Story '94
Spenser: Pale Kings & Princes '00
Blown Away '93
To Catch a Killer '92
From the Hip '86
A Christmas Story '83
Stag '97
Eric Zeisl (1905-59)
They Were Expendable '45
Bataan '43
Boris Zelkin (1971-)
Miracle Dogs Too '06
Height of the Sky '99
Lies and Whispers '98
Guy Zerafa
Megasnake '07
Exiled '06
Replicant '01
Redline '97
Sabotage '96
Gladiator Cop: The Swordsman 2 '95
Jiping Zhao
The Emperor and the Assassin '99
The King of Masks '99
The Emperor's Shadow '96
Temptress Moon '96
To Live '94
Farewell My Concubine '93
The Story of Qiu Ju '91
Ju Dou '90

Lin Zhao
Electric Shadows '04
Together '02
Aaron Zigman
Sex and the City: The Movie '08
Tyler Perry's Meet the Browns '08
Bridge to Terabithia '07
Good Luck Chuck '07
The Jane Austen Book Club '07
Martian Child '07
Mr. Magorium's Wonder Emporium '07
Pride '07
Tyler Perry's Why Did I Get Married? '07
Akeelah and the Bee '06
Alpha Dog '06
ATL '06
Flicka '06
Step Up '06
Take the Lead '06
10th & Wolf '06
In the Mix '05
The Wendell Baker Story '05
The Notebook '04
Raise Your Voice '04
Crown Heights '02
John Q '02
Hans Zimmer (1957-)
The Dark Knight '08
Kung Fu Panda '08
August Rush '07
Pirates of the Caribbean: At World's End '07
The Simpsons Movie '07
The Da Vinci Code '06
The Holiday '06
Pirates of the Caribbean: Dead Man's Chest '06
Batman Begins '05
Madagascar '05
Wallace & Gromit: The Curse of the Were-Rabbit '05
The Weather Man '05
King Arthur '04
Shark Tale '04
Spanglish '04
Thunderbirds '04
The Last Samurai '03
Matchstick Men '03
Something's Gotta Give '03
Tears of the Sun '03
The Ring '02
Spirit: Stallion of the Cimarron '02
Black Hawk Down '01
Hannibal '01
Invincible '01
Pearl Harbor '01
Riding in Cars with Boys '01
An Everlasting Piece '00
Gladiator '00
Mission: Impossible 2 '00
The Pledge '00
The Road to El Dorado '00
Chill Factor '99
Prince of Egypt '98
The Thin Red Line '98
As Good As It Gets '97
The Peacemaker '97
The Fan '96
Muppet Treasure Island '96
The Preacher's Wife '96
Smilla's Sense of Snow '96
The Whole Wide World '96
Beyond Rangoon '95
Broken Arrow '95
Crimson Tide '95
Nine Months '95
Something to Talk About '95
Drop Zone '94
The Lion King '94
Renaissance Man '94
Two Deaths '94
Younger & Younger '94
Calendar Girl '93
Cool Runnings '93
The House of the Spirits '93
I'll Do Anything '93
Point of No Return '93
True Romance '93
A League of Their Own '92
The Power of One '92

Backdraft '91
Regarding Henry '91
Thelma & Louise '91
Bird on a Wire '90
Chicago Joe & the Showgirl '90
Dark Obsession '90
Days of Thunder '90
Fools of Fortune '90
Green Card '90
Pacific Heights '90
Black Rain '89
Burning Secret '89
Driving Miss Daisy '89
Paperhouse '89
Prisoner of Rio '89
Twister '89
Rain Man '88
Wonderland '88
A World Apart '88
The Story of O, Part 2 '87
The Wind '87
Zero Boys '86
Insignificance '85
Success Is the Best Revenge '84
Moonlighting '82
David Zippel
Mulan '98
Hercules '97
Carl Zittrer
A Christmas Story '83
Porky's 2: The Next Day '83
Porky's '82
Black Christmas '75
Deranged '74
Children Shouldn't Play with Dead Things '72
Deathdream '72
Enes Zlatar
Grbavica: The Land of My Dreams '06
Go West '05
Rob Zombie (1966-)
The Devil's Rejects '05
House of 1000 Corpses '03
John Zorn
The Treatment '06
Protocols of Zion '05

The Video Sources section provides full contact information, including address, phone, fax and toll-free numbers, as well as web site address and e-mail when available, for mail order and retail resources for videos reviewed in this book. They are listed alphabetically. Some of the videos have no currently known distributor, but copies may still be available. Others are **On Moratorium**, meaning their distributor, or more likely, their producer, has pulled them out of circulation for a certain amount of time. These videos may still be available from local or mail sources because they were distributed at one time. Many video stores still provide an ordering service. If your local video store doesn't have a title you want, you can ask them to order it for you, or you can find someone here who will. To find additional web-based and specialty distributors, please check our **Web Site Guide**.

A-PIX ENTER·AINMENT INC.
200 Madison Ave., 24th Fl.
New York, NY 10016
206-284-4700
Fax: 206-286-4433

ACORN MEDIA PUBLISHING
801 Roeder Rd., Ste 700
Silver Spring, MD 20910
800-999-0212
Fax: 301-608-93·2
Email: info@aco·nmedia.
com HomePage: www.
acornmedia.com

ADM1T ONE VIDEO
PO Box 66, Sta. C
Toronto, ON, Canada M4A 2M3
416-463-5714
Fax: 416-463-5714
Email: admitone@
sympatico.ca
HomePage: www.
adm1tonevideo.ccm

ANCHOR BAY ENTERTAINMENT
1699 Stutz Dr.
Troy, MI 48084
248-816-0909
800-786-8777
Fax: 248-816-3335
HomePage: www.
anchorbayentertainment.
com

ARTISAN ENTERTAINMENT
2700 Colorado Ave., Ste. 200
Santa Monica, CA 90404
310-449-9200
Fax: 310-255-3730
HomePage: www.
artisanent.com

THE ASYLUM
1012 North Sycamore Ave.
Los Angeles, CA 90038

323-850-1214
Fax: 323-850-1218
Email: asylumitr e@aol.com
HomePage: www.
theasylum.cc

BIJOU VIDEO
1349 N. Wells
Chicago, IL 60610
312-943-5397
800-932-7111
Fax: 312-337-1270
HomePage: www.
bijouwo·ld.com

BMG ENTERTAINMENT
1540 Broadway
New York, NY 10036-4039
212-930-4000
HomePage: www.bmg.com

CINEMA CLASSICS
167 7th Ave.
New York, NY 10014
212-243-4905
Email: colassics@
cinemaclassics.com

CINEMA EPOCH
10940 Wilshire Blvd., 16th Fl.
Los Angeles, CA 90024
310-443-4244
Email: info@cinemaepoch.
com HomePage: www.
cinemaepoch.com

THE CINEMA GUILD
130 Madison Ave.
New York, NY 10016-7038
212-685-6242
800-723-5522
Fax: 212-685-4717
Email: info@cinemaguild.
com HomePage: www.
cinemaguild.com

CINEQUEST
United States

408-995-5033
Fax: 408-995-5713
Email: info@cinequest.org
HomePage: www.
cinequestonline.org

COAST TO COAST VIDEO
1938 Nostrand Ave
Brooklyn, NY 10011
718-859-8464
800-221-3420
HomePage: www.

CRITERION COLLECTION
210 E. 52nd St.
New York, NY 10022
HomePage: www.
criterionco.com

CRITICS CHOICE VIDEO & DVD
PO Box 749
Itasca, IL 60143
800-993-6357
HomePage: www.
ccvideo.com

CULT EPICS
PO Box 461556
Los Angeles, CA 90046

CULT FILM STORE
2272 Colorado Blvd. Ste. 1118
Los Angeles, CA 90041
Email: cultfilmstore@
yahoo.com HomePage:

DIGITAL VERSATILE DISC LTD.
15210 Keswick St.
Van Nuys, CA 91405
Email: info@
digitalversatiledisc.com
HomePage:

FACETS MULTIMEDIA, INC.
1517 W. Fullerton Ave.
Chicago, IL 60614
773-281-9075
800-331-6197
Fax: 773-929-5437
Email: sales@facets.org
HomePage: www.
facets.org

FANGORIA
1372 Broadway, 2nd Floor
New York, NY ·0018
HomePage: www.fangoria.
com

FIRST RUN FEATURES
The Film Center Building
630 Ninth Ave., Ste. 1213
New York, NY 10036
212-243-0600
800-229-8575
Fax: 212-989-7649
Email: info@
firstrunfeatures.com
HomePage: www.
firstrunfeatures.com

GOODTIMES ENTERTAINMENT
16 E. 40th St.
New York, NY 10016-0113
212-951-3000
Email: information@
goodtimes.com
HomePage: www.
goodtimes.com

GRAPEVINE VIDEO
PO Box 46161
Phoenix, AZ 85063
602-973-3661
Fax: 602-973-2973
Email: jbhandy@
grapevinevideo.com
HomePage: www.
grapevinevideo.com

HART SHARP VIDEO
380 Lafayette St., Ste. 304
New York, NY 10003

212-475-7555
Fax: 212-475-1717

HBO
1100 Ave. of the Americas
New York, NY 10036
212-512-7400
Fax: 212-512-7498
HomePage: www.hbo.com

HEN'S TOOTH VIDEO
2805 E State Blvd.
Fort Wayne, IN 46805
260-471-4332
Fax: 260-471-4449
HomePage: www.
henstoothvideo.com

HOME VIDEO LIBRARY
Better Homes & Gardens
1716 Locust St.
Des Moines, IA 50309-3023
515-284-3000
Email: support@bhg.com
HomePage: www.bhg.
com

HOUSE OF MONSTERS
1579 N. Milwaukee Ave.,
Gallery 218
Chicago, IL 60622
Email: naschy@
thehouseofmonsters.com
HomePage:

LUMINOUS FILM & VIDEO WURKS
PO Box 289
Hampton Bays, NY 11946
631-728-3111
Fax: 631-728-3311
Email: Frec@lfvw.com
HomePage: www.lfvw.
com

MIKE LEBELL'S VIDEO
75 Freemont Pl.
Los Angeles, CA 90005
HomePage: www.

Thousand Oaks, CA 91360-3901
805-494-7199
805-424-2593
Fax: 305-496-6061
HomePage: www.
montereymedia.com

MOVIES UNLIMITED
3015 Darnell Rd.
Philadelphia, PA 19154
215-637-4444
800-668-4344
Fax: 2·5-637-2350
Email: movies@
moviesunlimited.com
HomePage: www.
moviesunlimited.com

NAVARRE CORP.
7400 49th Ave. N.
New Hope, MN 55428
763-535-8333
800-728-4000
Fax: 763-533-2156
Email: info@navarre.com
HomePage: www.
navarre.com

NOSTALGIA FAMILY VIDEO/HOLLYWOOD'S ATTIC
PO Box 606
Baker City, OR 97814
800-784-3362
Email: info@
nostalgiafamilyvideo.com
HomePage: www.
nostalgiafamilyvideo.com

RHINO ENTERTAINMENT
10635 Santa Monica Blvd., 2nd Fl.
Los Angeles, CA 90025-8300
310-474-4773
Email: drhinc@rhino.com
HomePage: www.rhino.

MONTEREY HOME VIDEO
566 St. Charles Dr.

Screen

SCREEN PIX HOME VIDEO
1219 1/2 W. El Segundo Blvd.
Gardena, CA 90247-1521
Email: catnip@superior.net
HomePage:
213-687-8262
800-422-2241
Fax: 213-687-8425

THE SHOOTING GALLERY
609 Greenwich St., 7th Fl.
New York, NY 10014
HomePage:

SHOUT! FACTORY
2042-A Armacost Ave.
Los Angeles, CA 90025
310-979-5618
Email: info@shoutfactory.com **HomePage:** www.shoutfactory.com

SINISTER CINEMA
PO Box 4369
Medford, OR 97501-0168
541-773-6860
Fax: 541-779-8650
Email: scinema@qwest.net
HomePage: www.sinistercinema.com

SOMETHING WEIRD VIDEO
PO Box 33664
Seattle, WA 98133
HomePage: www.somethingweird.com

SUN VIDEO
15 Donnybrook
Demarest, NJ 07627
201-784-0662
Fax: 201-784-0665
Email: hs@methodsworkshop.com

TAI SENG VIDEO MARKETING
170 S. Spruce Ave., Ste. 200
South San Francisco, CA 94080
415-871-8118
800-888-3836
Fax: 415-871-2392
Email: webstaff@taiseng.com **HomePage:** www.taiseng.com

TAPEWORM VIDEO DISTRIBUTORS
27833 Hopkins Ave., Unit 6
Valencia, CA 91355
661-257-4904
Fax: 661-257-4820
Email: sales@tapeworm.com **HomePage:** www.tapeworm.com

TARTAN VIDEO
8322 Beverly Blvd., Ste. 300
Los Angeles, CA 90048
323-655-9300
Fax: 323-655-9301
Email: info@tartanvideo.com **HomePage:** www.tartanvideousa.com

THOMAS VIDEO
122 S. Main
Clawson, MI 48017
248-280-2833
Fax: 248-280-4463
Email: vgmr@thomasvideo.com **HomePage:** www.thomasvideo.com

TIMELESS VIDEO INC.
10010 Canoga Ave., Ste. C8
Chatsworth, CA 91311-0946

VENTURA DISTRIBUTION
c/o First Look Studios, Inc.
2000 Ave of the Stars, Ste. 410
Century City, CA 90067
805-498-7800
HomePage: www.firstlookstudios.com

VIDEO ACTION
800 W. 1st St., Ste. 1606
Los Angeles, CA 90012

VIDEO COLLECTIBLES
PO Box 385
Lewiston, NY 14092-0385
800-268-3891
Fax: 800-269-8877
Email: info@collectablesdirect.com
HomePage: www.collectablesdirect.com

THE VIDEO COLLECTION
PO Box 2284
South Burlington, VT 05407-2284

VIDEO CONNECTION
3123 W. Sylvania Ave.
Toledo, OH 43613
419-472-7727
800-365-0449
Fax: 419-472-2655

VIDEO OYSTER
81 Ludlow St.
PO Box 1012
New York, NY 10002-1012
212-979-6800
Fax: 212-989-3533
Email: videooyster@rcn.com **HomePage:** www.videooyster.com

VIDEO SEARCH OF MIAMI
PO Box 16-1917
Miami, FL 33116
305-279-9773
888-279-9773
Fax: 305-598-5265
Email: vsom@aol.com
HomePage: www.vsom.com

VIDEO VAULT
113 S. Columbus Street
Old Town
Alexandria, VA 22314
800-VAU-LT66
Fax: 703-836-5720
Email: flix@videovault.com

VIDEO YESTERYEAR
2 Ridgedale Ave.
Cedar Knolls, NJ 07927
203-744-2476

THE VIDEOFINDERS COLLECTION
National Fulfillment Center
PO Box 27054
Glendale, CA 91225-7054

VIDEOPREVIEW COLLECTION
Santa Monica, CA 90405

WELLSPRING MEDIA
A Division of Genius Products, Inc.
2230 Broadway
Santa Monica, CA 90904
310-453-1222
Fax: 310-453-0074
HomePage: www.wellspring.com

The Internet is an important resource for movie information, appreciation, and (especially) obsession. For your web surfing enjoyment, we have compiled a comprehensive list of many of the top entertainment websites that will expand your movie knowledge. If you're looking for information on how to make your own film, there are sites for that, too. The guide is divided into seven categories: cult movie resources; film magazines; film studios; filmmaker resources; film reviews; general entertainment; and video outlets. The sites are listed alphabetically within each category, and each site includes name and URL address information. The general information websites briefly describe what you can expect to find. Just as you can spend hours flipping through *Videohound*, you can spend hours cruising the web with the sites listed below since a majority of these homepages can link you to other sites on the web.

CULT MOVIE RESOURCES

Alamo Drafthouse
www.alamodrafthouse.com/
Web site devoted to a chain of Austin, Texas movie theatres that Entertainment Weekly calls "the best theatre in America." Check out their unbelievably cool theme screenings and Quentin Tarantino-sponsored film festival movies.

Alien Almanac
http://www.alienalmanac.com/
Caters to fans of fantasy, horror, and scifi movies.

Animated News
http://www.animated-news.com/
Animation and CGI news (not Japanese anime).

Animation Insider
http://www.animationinsider.net/
More Animation and anime news.

The Animation Podcast
http://animationpodcast.com/
Weekly interviews and artists in the Animation Industry.

Anime and Manga Resources List
myhome.shinbiro.com/~merope7/anime.htm
Huge list of Anime/Manga general info, series breakdowns, image galleries, and more.

Anime Daze
http://www.animedaze.com/
Animation news, reviews, and FAQ.

Anime Mojo
http://www.animemojo.com/
More Anime news.

Anime News Network
http://www.animenewsnetwork.com/
Yet more Anime news and a handy encyclopedia of anime related terms.

Anime News Service
http://www.animenewsservice.com/
And still more Anime news.

Anime Tourist
http://anime-tourist.com/index.php
Anime news and reviews. Didn't think there were this many Anime sites, did ja?

The Asian DVD Guide
http://asiandvdguide.com/
Rejoice, O ye fans of asian cinema!

Asian Movie Database
http://www.asiandb.com/
A database of all asian film, not just the genre films so many in the states love.

ASIFA Hollywood Animation Archive
http://www.animationarchive.org/
Blog dedicated to archiving animation for the benefit of the public and the industry.

Astounding B Monster Web
www.bmonster.com
Covers all genres of B-movies; includes reviews, top-ten lists, interviews, etc.

B-Movie Central
http://www.bmoviecentral.com/
Reviews and articles on classic B Movies. Also has links to many other genre sites.

Bad Cinema Diary
http://www.cathuria.com/bcd/
Illustrated reviews of bad, low budget, and just plain unexplainable movies.

Bad Movies
www.badmovies.org
Reviews bad movies in a good way (clever, funny, witty). Includes reviews by visitors to the site. Rating system is from five teardrops ("pinnacle of bad movies") to a skull ("this is gonna hurt, lots.")

Badazz Mofo
http://www.badazzmofo.com/
Weblog of pop culture.

Best Horror Movies
http://www.best-horror-movies.com/
Site made for fans of horror films.

Beyond Hollywood
http://www.beyondhollywood.com/
Reviews of asian, horror, foreign, and genre films. Beware popups.

Blaxploitation
http://funkmasterj.tripod.com/blax.html
List of sites and articles written about the genre.

Bloody-Disgusting.com
www.bloody-disgusting.com
Interviews, reviews, features–anything your sick little mind might want to know about the Horror film genre

Bob Burns
http://bobburns.mycottage.com/
Bob's web site has a lot of neat stuff, but none quite as neat as his amazing links section.

Boll Bashers
www.bollbashers.com
With movies like Bloodrayne and Alone in the Dark, German wunderkind Uwe Boll is challenging film director of all time. This web site is devoted to those who gleefully bash Dr. Boll in any way that they can.

Bottom of the Barrel
http://www.bottomofthebarrel.net/
News and reviews of truly the most godawful B movies of all time.

Brian's Drive-In Movie Theater
http://www.briansdriveintheater.com/index.html
Has Photos and information on B movie actors/ actresses from the 30's to the 80's. Also has a very extensive links section.

Brimstone Pit
http://www.living-dead.com/
Science Fiction and Horror film database.

British Horror Films
http://www.britishhorrorfilms.co.uk/
Site dedicated to British horror movies. There really aren't enough of them you know.

Bruce Campbell Online
www.bruce-campbell.com/
Home page of the Tom Cruise of cult movie actors, Bruce Campbell, the star of director Sam Raimi's Evil Dead series. Site features frequently updated Bruce-News, a filmography, and a schedule of public appearances

Buried
http://www.buried.com/
Horror film and fiction news, reviews, and interviews.

Carfax Abbey
http://www.carfax-abbey.com/
The Horror Film Database.

Cartoon Brew
http://www.cartoonbrew.com/
Cartoons and animation resource site.

Cinema Strikes Back
http://www.cinemastrikesback.com/
News, reviews, interviews, and film festival reports. Specializes in genre, cult, and foreign films.

City on Fire
http://www.cityonfire.com/
Reviews of Hong Kong and martial arts cinema.

Classic Horror
http://classic-horror.com/
Reviews of classic and modern horror movies. Also has small profiles of famous actors, directors, and effects artists in the genre.

Classic Horror Film Board
http://monsterkidclassichorrorforum.yuku.com/ bmonsterkidclassichorrorforum
Bela Lugosi demands you visit the forum. You will look into his spoooky hypnotic eyes.....

Classic Scifi
http://www.classicscifi.com/
Contrary to the site's title it also reviews modern scifi movies.

Cold Fusion Reviews
http://www.coldfusionvideo.com/
Reviews of B-movie and genre flicks.

ComicBookMovie.com
http://www.comicbookmovie.com/
Page devoted to comic book films.

Comics2Film
http://www.comics2film.com/
Blog on comics in film and television.

The Cult Movie Den
www.geocities.com/Hollywood/Boulevard/4802/
Provides valuable information on past, present, and future cult movies

Cult Movies Info
www.cultmovies.info/
Offers searchable reviews and summaries of cult movies, categorized into such sub-groups as European Horror Cinema and U.S. Horror Directors

Cult Sirens
http://www.cultsirens.com/
Dedicated to scream queens, and the leading ladies of exploitation films.

Dark Angel's Horror Realm
http://usersites.horrorfind.com/home/horror/realm/
British site for news and reviews of horror films, including a history of the genres battles with censorship.

Dark Hollywood
http://richlabonte.net/darkhollywood/
Classic mysteries, noir, horror, and Hitchcock.

DavidLynch.com
www.davidlynch.com/
Membership site hosted by Emperor Weirdo himself, David Lynch. Contains original films and content as well as a daily weather report from Lynch.

Dreams: The Terry Gilliam Fanzine
www.smart.co.uk/dreams/
Managed by Phil Stubbs, this is the ultimate online resource for anything having to do with ex-Python and notorious film director Terry Gilliam

E. Favata's Comic Book Movies
http://www.efavata.com/CBM/
News and rumors of current and upcoming comic book films.

Eccentric Cinema
http://www.eccentric-cinema.com/
Lists upcoming cult films on DVD, reviews, and even has a store.

European Film Review
http://www.erratica.co.uk/
If you like European exploitation cinema, you'll like this site.

Extraordinary Movie and Video Guide
http://www.emvg.net/
Reviews and interviews focusing on amateur, genre, independent, and underground films and film makers.

Faces of Death
www.facesofdeath.com/
If you're itching for production information on the Faces of Death video series, then look no further.

Fantastic Movie Musings and Ramblings
http://www.scifilm.org/
Sci-fi, fantasy, and horror movies. Has reviews, and upcoming movie and DVD news.

FEARnet
http://www.fearnet.com/
Has a rotating selection of streaming horror films. Also has news, trailers, and behind the scenes stuff.

Flubtitles
http://www.flubtitles.com/
Bizzarely mistranslated dialogue from HK cinema.

Frankenstein
http://www.frankensteinfilms.com/
Dedicated to all things Frankenstein, especially movies.

Giant Monster Movies
http://www.giantmonstermovies.com/
Database of giant monster films from all over the world. Also has the infamous Today in G-History archives.

Girls With Guns
http://www.girlswithguns.org/
For the action heroine fan in everyone.

God Among Directors
http://www.godamongdirectors.com/
Series of web sites devoted to such indie luminaries as Quentin Tarantino, John Woo, Robert Rodriguez, Martin Scorsese, and Kevin Smith

Godzilla Asylum
http://www.freewebs.com/godzillaaslum/
Reviews of giant monster films on DVD with an accent on the Big G...

Godzilla Temple
www.godzillatemple.com/
A home page devoted to the glory of the world's finest man-in-suit, Godzilla. Showcases reviews, audio and video clips, and an exhaustive Godzilla FAQ

Gynoid Gallery
http://gynoid.dreamhost.com/
A list (and image gallery for) films with female androids in them.

Hammer House of Horror
http://www.fortunecity.com/lavendar/judidench/339/
Fan site for the classic Hammer horror films.

Harvey Deneroff
http://deneroff.com/blog/
Blog on animated films from around the world.

Henshin Online
http://www.henshinonline.com/
News and reviews of Japanese fantasy and sci-fi films.

Holywood: Christian Entertainment Reviews
http://www.bettybowers.com/holywood.html
Mock film reviews from Betty Bowers and he Landover Baptist Church, themselves a parody of religion.

Hong Kong Movie Database
http://www.hkmdb.com/
Database of Hong Kong cinema in Chinese and English.

Horror Asylum
http://www.horror-asylum.com/
Reviews of horror films and DVD releases.

Horror DVDs
http://www.horrordvds.com/
Upcoming horror film releases, links, and a neat forum.

Horror Movies.ca
http://www.horror-movies.ca/
Massive Canadian horror film site.

Horror Movies That Suck
http://www.horrormoviesthatsuck.com/
Reviews of bad horror films.

Horror Stew
http://www.horrorstew.com/
Horror clips and articles.

Horror Wood
http://www.horror-wood.com/
Webzine devoted to classic and cult horror movies, and site of the Monster Bash movie festival.

Horrorfind
http://www.horrorfind.com/
A search engine dedicated to all things horror, including films.

Horrorhound
http://www.horrorhound.com/
Horror movie news and reviews.

Horror Movies!
horrormovies.com
Everything you ever wanted to know about horror flicks: films, cast, crew, locations, makeup, etc.

House of Horrors
http://www.houseofhorrors.com/
Horror film news, reviews, and interviews.

Japanese Horror Movie Database
http://www.fjmovie.com/horror/
In English and Japanese.

Joe Bob Report
www.joebobbriggs.com/
Home page of the most prolific bad movie critic of our time, King of the Drive-In, Joe Bob Briggs Site features archives of Briggs' reviews of schlock classics and his hilarious Ultimate B-Movie Guide

Kaiju Direct Website Directory
http://www2.arkansas.net/gsraptor/guide.html
A list of websites devoted to Japanese sci-fi and fantasy film.

Kaiju Fan
http://www.historyvortex.org/KaijuFan.html
A very thorough giant monster history site.

Kaiju Headquarters
http://www.kaijuhq.org/index2.html
Hail Godzilla!

Kaijuphile
http://www.kaijuphile.com/
Portal to 5 other websites on giant monsters.

Keyframe
http://www.keyframeonline.com/
Information resource for animation in all its forms.

Kung-Fu Cult Cinema
http://www.kfccinema.com/
Reviews and news on asian films with an emphasis on martial arts and fighting films.

Ladies of the Evil Dead
www.ladiesoftheevildead.com/
Site run by the three actresses who all died horrible deaths in Sam Raimi's original *Evil Dead*. Granted, they're no Bruce Campbell, but they will sell you suggestive pictures and happily show up to your nerd convention for a price.

Love and Bullets
http://www.loveandbullets.com/
Reviews of Hong Kong films with an emphasis on...

Last Drive-In on the Left
http://www.lastdriveinontheleft.com/
Incredibly fun site if you're a fan of drive-in cult and horror movies. Has upcoming DVD releases and reviews, ads, and trailers.

Love HK Film
www.lovehkfilm.com/
Fans of Jackie Chan and John Woo will love this comprehensive site, which offers copious information on the Hong Kong film industry. Includes an update of new Hong Kong films, filmographies, interviews, reviews, and a searchable database of Hong Kong actors and actresses

Lurker In The Lobby
http://www.thslurker.com/
Reviews of films and television shows inspired by the works of H.P. Lovecraft.

The Midnight Eye
http://www.michighteye.com/
Reviews of Japanese cinema, and interviews with directors.

The Missing Link
http://www.missinglinkhorrorclassics.co.uk/
British site devoted to horror films from the 50's and before.

M.J. Simpson
http://www.mjsimpson.co.uk/
News and reviews of horror and scifi films by former staff writer for SFX magazine.

Mondo Digital
http://www.mondo-digital.com/
DVD, video, and theatrical reviews of horror movies and unusual films (especially foreign ones).

Monster Island News
http://www.monsterislandnews.com/
Film news and forums for the comic book, sci-fi, and Godzilla fan in you.

Monsters A-Go-Go
http://www.monstersagogo.com/
Monster movie blog and reviews.

Mothra's Shrine
http://www.geocities.com/Tokyo/Island/2295/main.html
Site dedicated to everyone's favorite giant Japanese moth.

Muppet Central
www.muppetcentral.com
The coolest and most comprehensive fan-made resource to Jim Henson's ageless creations, *The Muppets*

No Place for a Woman: The Family in Film Noir
www.lib.berkeley.edu/MRC/noir/
Reports on the implications that film noir has had on society. The author, John Blaser, pinpoints the role that women and family have in this genre. Subtopics include "Pro-family Messages in Film Noir" and "Women's Anti-Family Function in Film Noir."

Origins of American Animation
http://memory.loc.gov/ammem/oahtml/oahome.html
Library of Congress site chronicling the history of Animation in the states.

Pit of Horror
http://www.pitofhorror.com/
Covers horror film news, and reviews some films.

Planet of Dinosaurs
http://www.wsu.edu/delahoyd/dinosource.html
Your resource for dinosaurs in movies.

Polish Movie Posters
www.polishposter.com/
Check out this archive of original movie poster artwork from Poland and marvel at how scary Polish advertising can be. Their *Weekend at Bernie's* poster looks like something out of *Eraserhead*.

Prison Flicks
http://www.prisonflicks.com/
Ummm...yeah.

Professor Neon's TV and Movie Mania
www.vortex.com/ProfNeon.html
Covers a gamut of information on film, television, radio, and the cable industry. When it comes to films, the Professor leans more to sci-fi, cult, and weird stuff.

Pulp Movies
http://www.pulpmovies.com/
Inspiring and informational blog on cult cinema.

The Pulsing Cinema
http://www.pulsingcinema.com/
News on foreign horror and crime films.

Science Fiction Cinema
http://www.geocities.com/Hollywood/Lot/2976/SFFilmResources.HTML
A guide to sci-fi films on the web.

Science Fiction Filmsite
http://www.umich.edu/umfandsf/film/
Uses stills and clipz to analyze the realm of science in scifi movies.

Sci-fi Japan
http://www.scifijapan.com/
News and reviews of oriental sci-fi, horror, and fantasy films and dvd releases.

Sci-Fi Movie Page
http://www.scifimoviepage.com/
Sci-fi movie reviews, articles, scripts, and trailers.

Sci-Fi Trivia Real
http://www.realmovietrivia.com/
Insider trivia and neat info on popular science fiction movies.

Scifi-Movies
http://www.scifi-movies.com/
Huge database of science fiction films and television series.

Scifispace
http://www.scifispace.com/
Movie reviews and a directory of stores selling sci-fi stuff in each state!

Sciflicks
http://www.sciflicks.com/
Massive database on sci-fi movies.

Shivers of Horror
http://www.shiversofhorror.com/
Forum for horror movies, and a second site devoted to the Friday the 13th movies.

Shock Cinema
http://www.shockcinemamagazine.com/
Online version of magazine catering to fans of bizarre and unconventional cinema.

Stomp Tokyo
www.stomptokyo.com
Reviews and salutes all manner of schlock and trash cinema on a 5-David Hasselhoff scale.

Superhero Flix
http://www.superheroflix.com/
Covers all superhero and comic related films and television.

Superhero Hype
http://www.superherohype.com/
Comics and some horror movies on the screen and DVD.

Tabula Rasa
http://www.tabula-rasa.info/
A history of horror in Australia, including horror movies.

They're Coming To Get You Barbara
http://www.theyrecoming.com/
Horror film reviews by two sisters who are fans of the genre. They also have some of the most disturbing cakes of all time

The Ultimate Gangster and Crime Film Website
http://www.geocities.com/mikemckiernan/
Title says it all.

Toho Kingdom
http://www.tohokingdom.com/
Oriental film news and reviews.

Underground Film
http://www.undergroundfilm.org/
Underground and independent films.

Upcoming Horror Movies
http://www.upcominghorrormovies.com/
Trailers, image gallery, reviews, etc.

Vampyre's Online
www.vampyres-online.com
Regularly updated database of almost every vampire film ever made, including such obscure treats as *Blacula Lives Again!* and *Wanda Does Transylvania*.

The Video Graveyard
http://www.thevideograveyard.com/
Horror movie reviews and trailers.

FILM FESTIVALS

ACB Sacramento Film and Music Festival
www.sactofilmfest.com/
A centerpiece for the arts community of Sacramento and a celebration of both visual and musical works from around the world

ACE Film Festival
http://www.acefest.com/
Presented by New York Foundation for the Arts.

Adelaide Film Festival
http://www.adelaidefilmfestival.org/index
International film festival held in Australia.

AFI Los Angeles International Film Festival (USA)
www.afi.com/onscreen/AFIFEST
Features attractions from this huge film festival held every October. Also lists synopses of the films appearing each year

African Diaspora Film Festival
nyadff.org/
Highlights the works of African-American filmmakers.

After Dark Horrorfest
http://www.horrorfestonline.com/
Three day festival premiering horror films nationwide.

Angel Film Festival
http://www.angelfilmfestival.org/
Competition for Independent Short Films in Islington, London.

Anima
http://folioscope.awn.com/wordpress/index.php?cat=63&language=en
Annual European cartoon and animation festival.

Animex
http://www.animex.net/
International festival of animation and computer games.

Ann Arbor Film Festival
aafilmfest.org/
Not-for-profit festival showcases independent and experimental films.

Annecy International Animated Film Festival and Market
http://www.annecy.org/home/?PageID=1
Click on the small British flag in the top left corner for the English language site.

Antelope Valley Independent Film Festival
www.aviff.com/

Arab Film Festival
http://www.aff.org/
Californian festival of Arabic film.

Arizona State University Art Museum Short Film and Video Festival
http://asuartmuseum.asu.edu/filmfest/index.html
Short films from directors with varying levels of experience.

Ashland Independent Film Festival
www.ashlandfilm.org/
Supports independent film and film education.

Aspen Filmfest
http://www.aspenfilm.org/index.cfm?flash=true
Indie and short film festivals.

Atlanta Film Festival
http://www.atlantafilmfest.com/
Features animation, shorts, docs, narrative, and full length films.

Atlantic Film Festival
http://www.atlanticfilm.com/
Festival for International and Canadian film.

Austin Film Festival
www.austinfilmfestival.com/

Bangkok International Film Festival
http://www.bangkokfilm.org/
Annual festival held by the government of Thailand.

Beirut Film Foundation Mideast Film Festival
http://www.beirutfilmfoundation.org/
Festival encouraging young filmmakers in the Middle East.

Belize International Film Festival
http://www.belizefilmfestival.com/
Showcases Caribbean and Central American film.

Bergen International Film Festival
http://www.biff.no/2007/index.php3?Eng=Ja
Annual filmfest held in Norway.

Berlin Film Festival
berlinale.de/
Lists production information on all the films featured in this festival.

Bermuda International Film Festival
http://www.bermudafilmfest.com/
Annual film festival and charity event.

Bicknell International Film Festival
http://www.thebiff.org/
Utah's festival o' bad movies.

Bicycle Film Festival
http://www.bicyclefilmfestival.com/
Festival celebrating the bicycle in film, music, and art.

Big Bear Lake International Film Festival
http://www.bigbearlakefilmfestival.com/
California event showing indies, shorts, animation, and documentaries.

The Big Dam Festival
http://www.thebigdamfilmfestival.com/
Independent film festival in Quincy, Illinois.

Big Island Film Festival
http://www.bigislandfilmfestival.com/
Narrative independent filmfest in Hawaii.

Big Muddy Film Festival
http://bigmuddyfilm.com/
Independent film festival held in Illinois.

Blogging Sundance
http://www.bloggingsundance.com/
Blog for the festival.

Boomtown Film and Music Festival
http://www.boomtownfestival.com/index/Home.html
Festival of films and music held in Beaumont, Texas.

Boston Irish Film Festival
www.irishfilmfestival.com/

Boston Motion Picture Awards
http://www.bostonawards.com/
Promotes independent films and filmmakers.

Boston Science Fiction Film Festival
http://www.bostonsci-fi.com/
Annual event playing at various venues in Boston.

Bratislava International Film Festival
http://www.iffbratislava.sk/2007/index.html
Film festival held in the capital of Slovakia

Cajun and Zydeco Film Festival
http://www.bayouprod.com/
Celebration of Southern Louisiana culture held every year in Saulieu, France.

Calgary International Film Festival
www.calgaryfilm.com

Cannes Film Festival
www.festival-cannes.fr/
Searchable site with each year's film schedule, a FAQ, and jury and press information

Cartagena Film & Television Festival
www.festicinecartagena.com/

Chicago Asian American Showcase
http://showcase.faaim.org/FilmFestival/app/user/Home
Promoting Asian American films.

Chicago International Film Festival
www.chicagofilmfestival.org
Answers questions in the area of awards, entries, juries, and transportation.

Chicago International Children's Film Festival
www.cicff.org/

Chicago Lesbian and Gay International Film Festival
www.reelingfilmfestival.org/
Offers a rundown of films featured in this alternative film festival.

Chicago Underground Film Festival
www.cuff.org/

Chris Awards
www.chrisawards.org/
Columbus International Film and Video Festival.

Cine Las Americas
http://www.cinelasamericas.org/
Latino film festival in Texas.

Cine Sin Fin
http://www.alabrava.com/
Chicano film festival in East L.A.

Cine Tropical
http://www.cinematropical.com/
Open air celebration of Latin American films, food, culture, and music.

Cinecon
http://www.cinecon.org/
Hollywood event screening silent and ealy talking films.

Cinefest Sudbury
http://www.cinefest.com/
Annual Canadian film festival.

Cinevent Classic Film Convention
http://www.cinevent.com/
Annual event in Columbus, Ohio.

Cinema St. Louis
http://cinemastlouis.org/
10 day festival showing foreign film, shorts, documentaries, and American Indie movies.

Cinema Rome Filmfest
http://www.romacinemafest.it/romacinemafest/
Annual Roman film festival.

Cleveland International Film Festival
clevelandfilm.org

Danville International Children's Film Festival
http://www.dicff.org/
Films by and for children.

DC Shorts
http://www.dcshorts.com/
Short film festival in Washington, DC.

DC Independent Film Festival
www.dciff.org

Dead By Dawn
http://www.deadbydawn.co.uk/
Annual UK horror festival held in Edinburgh.

Denver International Film Festival
www.denverfilm.org
Besides information on the entries, this site offers insight into the Denver Film Society

DepicT
http://www.depict.org/
Competition for films with a running time of 90 seconds or less.

Digital Gun Awards
http://www.digitalgunawards.com/
Competition for films made within 3 days.

The Directors Cut
http://www.thedirectorscut.org/
International filmfest in New York screening short films, trailers, and documentaries.

Donostia Horror and Fantasy Film Festival
http://www.donostiakultura.com/terror/
Genre festival in San Sebastian, Spain.

Dundee Mountain Film Festival
http://www.dundeemountainfilm.org.uk/
UK's longest running mountain film festival.

East Lansing Film Festival
www.elff.com/

Edinburgh International Film Festival
http://www.edfilmfest.org.uk/
Originally began as a documentary festival after WWII, EIFF is now the worlds longest running film festival.

Edmonton International Film Festival
http://www.edmontonfilmfest.com/
Annual independent film festival in Canada.

Eerie Horrorfest
http://www.eeriehorrorfest.com/
Held in (are you ready for it?) Erie, Pennsylvania.

Emergeandsee
http://www.emergeandsee.org/cms/website.php
London based event showing student films.

Epic Summer Film Festival
http://www.epicsummer.org/
Festival held each summer for short outdoor adventure films.

Everett Womens Film Festival
http://www.everetttheatre.org/filmfestival.html
Washington event featuring films by women directors.

Fairy Tales International Queer Film Festival
http://www.fairytalesfilmfest.com/
Canadian event presenting films by and/or about the gay, lesbian, bi, transgender, and twin spirited community.

Festival Focus
http://www.festivalfocus.org/
Database of film festivals.

Festival of Fantastic Films
http://fantastic-films.com/festival/
Manchester film festival showing scifi, horror, and fantasy films.

FIFA
http://www.artfifa.com/
Festival of films about art.

FIKE
http://www.fikeonline.net/
International short film festival in Evora, Portugal.

Film Festival Deadlines
http://www.coolbae.nl/filmfestivals/filmfestivaldeadlines.html
Calendar of deadlines for major film festival submissions, and a database of festivals.

Film Festival Server
http://www.filmfestivals.com/index.shtml
Searchable database of international film and video festivals.

Film Festival Source
http://www.filmfestivalsource.com/
Directory of film festivals, indexed by category, title, or country.

Film Festival Today
http://www.filmfestivaltoday.com/
Magazine covering the film festival circuit.

Filmfest Zlin
http://www.zlinfest.cz/index.php
International children's film festival.

Filmfest DC
http://www.filmfestdc.org/
Premieres international cinema in Washington DC.

Film Your Issue
http://www.filmyourissue.com/index.shtml
Short film competition wherein the contestants make films about a political or social issue important to them.

Filmfest Munchen
http://www.filmfest-muenchen.de/
Annual summer film festival in Germany.

Flickerfest
http://www.flickerfestival.com.au/
Australian international short film festival.

Flicker Richmond
http://www.rmicweb.org/flicker/
Richmond chapter of the Flicker Festival.

Flicker Los Angeles
http://www.flickerla.com/
LA chapter of the Flicker Festival.

Flicker New York
http://www.flickernyc.com/
New York chapter of the Flicker Festival.

Flying 5 Film Awards
http://www.flyingfives.co.nz/
New Zealand indie film competition for films or videos of 5 minutes or less.

Fort Williams Mountain Film Festival
http://www.mountainfilmfestival.cc.uk/
Festival from the Scottish highlands focusing on mountain based films and photography.

48 Hour Film Project
http://www.48hourfilm.com/
Film competition for films done entirely within 48 hours.

Frameline
http://www.frameline.org/festival/index.aspx
San Francisco based international gay and lesbian film festival.

Fredrikstad Animation Festival
http://www.animationfestival.no/indexeng.shtml
Nordic and Baltic that highlights international and local animated films.

Free Form Film Festival
http://www.freeformfilm.org/
Traveling collection of outsider film and video works.

Freeze Frame
http://www.freezeframeonline.org/
International festival of children's films held in Canada.

French Film Festival UK
http://www.frenchfilmfestival.org.uk/
British festival of French cinema.

Frightfest
http://www.frightfest.co.uk/
Annual fantasy and horror film festival in London.

FW:FWD
http://www.fwfwd.org/
Online exhibit of winning films from a competition for viral short films.

Full Frame Documentary Film Festival
http://www.fullframefest.org/
Large Documentary fest in the states.

Fukuoka International Film Festival
http://focus-on-asia.com/e/index.html
Focuses on Asian films.

Galway Film Fleadh
http://www.galwayfilmfleadh.com/
Along with this film festival, Galway hosts Irelands only film market.

Goteborg International Film Festival
http://www.goteborg.filmfestival.org/filmfestival/
Festival of features, shorts, and documentaries held in Sweden.

Harlan Jacobson's Talk Cinema
http://www.talkcinema.com/
Shows independent and foreign films before their release.

Harmony Film Festival
http://www.harmonyfilmfest.com/2007/
Short film festival dedicated to promoting peace and harmony.

Havana Film Festival in New York
http://www.hffny.com/2008/index.php
New York festival celebrating Latin American film.

Hawaii International Film Festival
www.hiff.org/

Heartland Film Festival
www.heartlandfilmfestival.org/

Holland Animation Film Festival
http://haff.awn.com/
Biennial international animation festival.

Hollywood Black Film Festival
http://www.hbff.org/
Annual festival highlighting the works of black filmmakers.

Hollywood International Student Film Festival
http://www.isfhollywood.org/
Student films from elementary school to college.

Hong Kong International Film Festival
http://www.hkiff.org.hk/
Film Festival in Hong Kong

Hong Kong Jewish Film Festival
http://www.hkjewishfilmfest.org/
Asia's festival of the Jewish culture.

Hope and Dreams Film Festival
http://www.hopeanddreams.com/
New Jersey competition featuring short, documentary, animated, and feature films.

H.P. Lovecraft Film Festival
http://www.hplfilmfestival.com/
Promotes cinematic adaptations of weird tales from professional and amateur filmmakers.

Huesca Film Festival
http://www.huesca-filmfestival.com/
Argentinian short film festival.

Hull Film Festival
http://www.hullfilm.co.uk/
Short film festival in UK

Human Rights Watch International Film Festival
www.hrw.org/iff/
Highlights films dealing with the worldwide struggle for Human Rights

Humboldt International Film Festival
http://www.humboldt.edu/filmfest/
Student run film festival at HSU showing Super 8 and 16mm short films.

IF Istanbul
http://www.ifistanbul.com/en/
Indie film festival held in Istanbul.

Image Out Rochester Lesbian & Gay Film & Video Festival
www.imageout.org
Highlights films dealing with gay and lesbian issues

Imagenation
http://www.imagenationfilmfestival.org/pages/main.htm
Year-round film festival promoting independent art-house films about the African Diaspora.

Image+Nation
http://www.image-nation.org/2007/index-choix.php
LGBT festival held in Montreal.

Images Festival
http://www.imagesfestival.com/
Experimental film festival held every spring in Toronto.

Independent Film Festival of Boston
http://www.iffboston.org/
Indie filmfest held in, of course, Boston.

Independent Lens Online Shorts Festival
http://www.pbs.org/independentlens/insideindies/shortslens/
Annual online festival of short films from the PBS series.

Indianapolis International Film Festival
http://indyfilmfest.org/
Midwest filmfest screening feature and short films.

Indiefest
http://www.indiefestchicago.com/
Combines a film festival, screenwriting contest, film and script markets, and a 10 day party.

The Indie Gathering
http://theindiegathering.com/
Independent film festival in Cleveland, Ohio.

Indian Film Festival of Los Angeles
http://www.indianfilmfestival.org/
LA event showcasing films about India.

Inside Film Online
http://www.insidefilm.com/
Festival news, listings, and articles.

Inside Out
http://www.insideout.on.ca/current2007/index.htm
GLBT festival in Toronto.

International Buddhist Film Festival
http://www.ibff.org/
Films about Buddhist culture, history, etc.

International Experimental Cinema Exposition
http://www.experimentalcinema.com/
Experimental film festival and workshop.

International Festival of Cinema and Technology
http://ifct.org/
Touring film festival that seeks to showcase undiscovered films.

International Film Festival Innsbruck
http://www.iffi.at/
Austrian festival showing contemporary and classic films.

International Film Festival of India
http://iffi.nic.in/
Annual festival and competitions held in Goa, India.

International Film Festival of Kerala
http://www.keralafilm.com/
Annual film festival held in India.

International Hamburg Short Film Festival
http://www.shortfilm.com/index.php?id=shortfilmcom&L=1
Film festival and workshop.

International Short Film Festival Winterthur
http://www.kurzfilmtage.ch/en/index.html
Short film festival held in Winterthur.

International Wildlife Film Festival
http://www.wildlifefilms.org/
Film festival dedicated to wildlife and it's conservation.

International Womens Film Festival Dortmund/Cologne
http://www.femmetotale.de/indexe.html
Films by women, or featuring women.

Internationale Kurzfilmtage Oberhausen
http://www.kurzfilmtage.de/
Short film competition from Oberhausen Germany.

Inverness Film Festival
http://www.invernessfilmfestival.com/
Scottish film festival that shows international films as well as gaelic language films.

ION International Short Film Festival
http://www.ionfilmfest.com/
Promotes digital and short films.

Israel Film Festival
http://www.israelfilmfestival.com/iff07/
Showing subtitled films in LA, New York, and Miami.

Italian Film Festival
http://www.italianfilm.com/
Held every year in Marin County, California.

It's All True
http://www.itsalltrue.com.br/2008/index.asp
Brazilian international documentary film festival.

Ivy Film Festival
http://www.ivyfilmfestival.com/
Film festival for students, run by students.

Jackson Hole Wildlife Film Festival
http://www.jhfestival.org/
Nature festival in Grand Teton National Park.

James River Film Festival
http://www.jrfilmfest.com/
Baltimore festival showing classics, independent films, and new movies.

John Hopkins Film Fest
http://www.hopkinsfilmfest.com/
Indie film and video festival in Virginia.

Juneteenth Film Festival
http://www.juneteenthfilmfestival.com/
Celebrates diversity and promotes the history of Juneteenth.

Kansas City Filmmakers Festival
http://www.kcjubilee.org/
Competitive indie festival.

Kansas International Film Festival
http://www.kansasfilm.com/
Shows independent and classic cinema.

Kansas Silent Film Festival
http://www.kssilentfilmfest.org/
Annual silent film festival in Wichita, Kansas.

Karlovy Vary International Film Festival
http://www.kviff.com/en/news/
Held in the Czech spa town of Karlovy Vary and usually includes a visit by Czech President Vaclav Havel.

Kingston Canadian Film Festival
http://www.kingcanfilmfest.com/
Showcases strictly Canadian films.

LA Femme Film Festival
http://www.lafemme.org/
Focuses on works by female filmmakers.

Lake Arrowhead Film Festival
http://www.lakearrowheadfilmfestival.com/
Screens vintage films.

Last Remaining Seats
http://laconservancy.org/remaining/index.php4
Classic films shown in downtown LA.

Latino Film Festival of the San Francisco Bay Area
www.latinofilmfestival.org/

Leeds International Film Festival
http://www.leedsfilm.com/
Features and shorts from around the world, along with music, comic art, and more.

Lesbian and Gay Film Festival of Toronto
http://www.insideout.on.ca/current2007/index.htm
Promotes and showcases LGBT film and video.

Leuven Kort Film Festival
http://www.kortfilmfestival.be/
Flemish and European shorts, music videos, and animations.

Locarno International Film Festival
http://www.pardo.ch/index.jsp
Annual Italian event.

London Canadian Film Festival
http://www.londoncanfilmfest.com/
Contemporary Canadian cinema.

London Film Festival
www.lff.org.uk/

London Lesbian and Gay Film Festival
http://www.llgff.org.uk/
LGBT festival in London England.

London Lesbian Film Festival
http://www.llff.ca/
Celebrating lesbian film making in Canada.

Lone Pine Film Festival
http://www.lonepinefilmfestival.org/index.asp
Festival featuring movies filmed in or around Lone Pine California.

Long Island Film Festival
http://www.lifilm.com/
Indie film festival at Long Island.

Long Island Gay and Lesbian Film Festival
http://www.ligff.org/
Has a "Make your own gay movie" contest.

Los Angeles Film Festival
www.lafilmfest.com/

Los Angeles International Short Film Festival
http://www.lashortsfest.com/videolist.asp
International short filmfest held in LA.

Los Angeles Italian Film Awards
http://www.itafilmfest.com/
Annual festival promoting Italian films.

Los Angeles Latino International Film Festival
www.latinofilm.org
Co-founded by Edward James Olmos, this festival awards cash prizes to outstanding American, Latin-American, and Spanish filmmakers.

Lost Film Festival
http://www.lostfilmfest.com/
Traveling festival of underground films.

LUCAS
http://www.lucasfilmfestival.de/
Children's film festival held in Frankfurt Germany.

Lund International Fantastic Film Festival
http://www.fff.se/english/index.asp
Scandinavia's largest fantasy filmfest.

Madcat Women's International Film Festival
http://www.madcatfilmfestival.org/
Independent and experimental films by women.

Magnolia Independent Film Festival
http://www.magfilmfest.com/TheMag/The11thAnnualMagFilmFest.html
Held in Mississippi.

Main Line Film Festival
http://www.mainlinefilmfestival.com/
Short film festival held in Wayne, Pennsylvania.

Maine International Film Festival
www.miff.org
Includes 100 screenings of new, old, and student films in a non-competitive, free-spirited atmosphere.

Maine Jewish Film Festival
http://www.mjff.org/
Features and documentaries on Jewish themes.

Majestic Theatre Silent Film Festival
http://www.majestic.spiderweb.com.au/
Silent film festival held in Australia.

Malibu International Film Festival
http://www.malibufilmfestival.org/
Held every year during the American Film Market.

Manhattan Short Film Festival
http://www.msfilmfest.com/
New York based festival.

Mardi Gras Film Festival
http://www.queerscreen.com.au/j/index.php
Gay and Lesbian film festival in Australia.

Margaret Mead Film and Video Festival
http://www.amnh.org/programs/mead/mead2007/index.php
Largest ethnographic/documentary film festival in US.

Maryland Film Festival
http://www.md-filmfest.com/
Features restored classics, indies, docs, shorts, and full length films.

Maui Film Festival
http://www.mauifilmfestival.com/
Annual film festival in Hawaii.

Melbourne Film Festival
http://www.melbournefilmfestival.com.au/
Annual international Australian film festival.

Melbourne International Animation Festival
http://www.miaf.net/
Showcase for animated films in Australia.

Melbourne Queer Film Festival
http://www.melbournequeerfilm.com.au/
Features, shorts, and experimental films.

Meniscus Film Festival
http://www.meniscusfilms.com/
Promotes independent films and filmmaking.

Method Fest
http://www.methodfest.com/
Indie showcase in Burbank California.

Miami Gay and Lesbian Film Festival
http://www.miamigaylesbianfilm.com/
Gay film and video festival in Florida.

Miami Latin Film Festival
www.miamifilmfestival.com/

Milan International Film Festival
http://www.miff.it/
Italian film festival.

Mill Valley Film Festival
http://www.mvff.com/
Sponsored by California Film Institute.

MIX NYC
http://www.mixnyc.org/
Experimental gay and lesbian film festival.

Molodist International Film Festival
http://www.molodist.com/en/
Annual festival held in Kyiv, Ukraine.

Monaco International Film Festival
http://www.monacofilmfestival.net/
Film competition held in Monaco.

Montreal World Film Festival
www.ffm-montreal.org/HHindex.html
Offers a rundown of the festival in both English and French.

Moondance International Film Festival
www.mcondancefilmfestival.com/
Promotes and encourages the best work in screenwriting, filmmaking, stage plays, radio plays, TV scripts, musical scores, lyrics, libretto, musical videos, puppetry theatre, and short stories.

Mountainfilm Festival
http://www.mountainfilm.org/
Celebrates cultures of the mountain communities.

Moves
http://www.movementonscreen.org.uk/
Arts group exploring movement through film, video, and installations.

Museum of Television and Radio TV Documentary Festival
http://www.paleycenter.org/events/ss-07fall/ny-doctest.htm
Showcase for television documentaries.

Muskegon Film Festival
http://www.muskegonfilm-festival.com/
Michigan event showing features and student films.

Nantucket Film Festival
http://www.nantucketfilmfestival.org/
Shows films of various length and genre, studio or indie.

Nashville Independent Film Festival
http://www.nashvillefilmfestival.org/
Tennessee festival showing films of all genres.

New Jersey Film Festival
http://www.njfilmfest.com/
Indie, classic, international, and experimental films.

New Jersey Jewish Film Festival
http://www.njjff.org/
Jewish themed festival in the Garden State.

New Orleans Film Festival
http://www.nuff.no/
Features, shorts, documentaries, and music videos.

Newport Beach Film Festival
http://www.newportbeachfilmfest.com/
Features, shorts, documentaries, and animation from around the world.

Newport Film Festival
http://www.newportfilmfestival.com/
niffmovie2007.htm
International features, shorts, documentaries, and classics.

New York City Independent Horror Film Festival
http://www.nychorrorfest.com/
Indie horror movies.

New York Expo Film and Video
http://www.nyexpo.org/
Nations longest running independent short film festival.

New York Film Festival
http://www.filmlinc.com/nyff/nyff.html
International features and shorts.

New York International Childrens Film Festival
http://www.gkids.com/
Showcase of childrens films.

New York International Independent Film and Video Festival
http://www.nyfilmvideo.com/
For independent, low budget, and non-mainstream artists.

New York International Latino Film Festival
http://www.nylatinofilm.com/
Films made by, featuring, and/or about the Latino community.

New Zealand International Film Festivals
http://www.nzff.co.nz/
Films from around the world.

NextFrame
http://www.temple.edu/nextframe/
University of Film and Video Association's touring festival of international student films.

Niagara Indie Film Fest
http://www.niagaraindiefilmfest.org/
Showcase for Canadian independent film and video.

Noir City
http://www.filmnoirfoundation.org/
Classic film noir movies in San Francisco.

Nordic Youth Film Festival
http://www.nuff.no/
Films by young people for young people.

Northampton Independent Film Festival
http://www.niff.org/2007/
Celebrates independent filmmaking.

Northwest Film and Video Festival
http://www.nwfilm.org/
Foreign, classic, experimental, and independent films.

NSI FilmExchange
http://www.nsi-canada.ca/filmexchange/
Short and feature films from Canada.

NYC Midnight Movie Making Madness
http://www.nycmidnight.com/
Competition for digital films.

Ohio Independent Film Festival
www.ohiofilms.com/

Omaha Film Event
http://www.omahafilmevent.com/
Presents screenings of classic films.

One World International Human Rights Film Festival
http://www.jeoensvet.cz/ow/2007/index.php?leng=en
Features films on the themes of human rights and freedoms.

Orbister Film Project
http://www.filmmm.com/eng/index.asp
Free internet film competition. All films and filmmakers go into their database.

Ottawa International Animation Festival
http://ottawa.awn.com/
Largest animated film festival in North America.

Out in Africa
http://www.oia.co.za/
Gay and Lesbian festival in Johannesburg.

Out On Film
http://www.outonfilm.com/
LGBT film festival in Georgia.

Out On Screen
http://www.outonscreen.com/
Vancouver Queer film and video festival.

Out Takes Dallas
http://www.outtakesdallas.org/index.asp
Gay and Lesbian Film Festival from Texas.

Out Takes-New Zealand
http://www.outtakes.org.nz/
Gay films in New Zealand.

Outdoor Film Festival at NIH
http://www.filmfestnih.org/
Picnic and film festival to benefit charity.

Over The Fence
http://www.overthefence.com.au/
Australian comedy festival.

Ozark Foothills Film Fest
http://www.ozarkfoothillsfilmfest.org/
Festival sponsored by the Foothills Film Society.

Palm Beach International Film Festival
http://www.pbifilmfest.org/
Showcases student and international films.

Palm Springs International Film Festival
http://www.psfilmfest.org/index.aspx
Has both an feature and a short film festival.

Pan African Film Festival
http://www.paff.org/
LA festival showing African American themed films.

Park City Film Music Festival
http://www.parkcityfilmmusicfestival.com/
Dedicated to music in film. Has screenings, and a competition.

Perspektive
http://www.fitame.de/index2.php?lang=en
International human rights oriented film festival held in Nuremberg.

PhillyFests
http://www.phillyfests.com/home.cfm
Annual event put on by Philadephia Film Society.

Phoenix Film Festival
http://www.phoenixfilmfestival.org/pages/
Annual film event in Arizona.

Picture This Film Festival
www.picturethisfestival.org/
Highlights films for, by, and about people with disabilities.

Philadelphia International Gay and Lesbian Film Festival
http://www.phillyfests.com/piglf/home.cfm
Largest Gay and Lesbian film fest on the East Coast.

Philadelphia Weekend Film Festival
http://www.weekendfilmfest.com/
Weekend long film festival highlighting the films of a specific actor or director.

Pioneer Valley Jewish Film Festival
http://www.pvjff.org/
3 week event in Massachusetts.

Pittsburgh Lesbian and Gay Film Festival
http://www.plgft.org/
Annual celebration of LGBT films.

Planet in Focus
http://www.planetinfocus.org/
Environmental film and video festival based in Toronto.

Polish Film Festival in LA
http://www.polishfilmla.org/
Also has info on other Polish events and films.

Portland International Short Short Film Festival
http://www.zonkerfilms.com/
Films of 10 minutes or less.

Portland Underground Film Festival
http://www.clintonsttheater.com/puff/
Shows experimental and underground films.

Portobello Film Festival
http://www.portobellofilmfestival.com/
Primarily British independent films and video.

Port Townsend Film Festival
http://www.ptfilmfest.com/
Independent film festival in Washington.

Projections d'Argile
http://www.fifav.fr/?lg=EN&PHPSESSID=6373d4cad3bac1b6b72308ac8d3c2c4f
French festival of films about ceramics and glass.

Providence Latin American Film Festival
http://www.latin-americanfilmfestival.org/
Competition held in Rhode Island.

Pusan International Film Festival
http://www.piff.org/intro/default.asp?lang=eng
Annual festival held in South Korea.

Q Cinema
http://www.qcinema.org/
Fort Worth's Gay and Lesbian film festival.

RAI Festival of Ethnographic Film
http://www.raifilmfest.org.uk/
Film festival sponsored by the Royal Anthropological Institute.

Raindance Film Festival
http://www.raindance.co.uk/site/
Independent festival by filmmakers for filmmakers.

Real to Reel Film Festival
http://www.ccartscouncil.org/realtoreel/
Independent film festival in North Carolina.

Red Bank International Film Festival
http://www.rbiff.org/
New Jersey film festival showing documentaries, animation, foreign, shorts, and features.

Red Rock Film Festival
http://www.ophilia.com/
Utah film festival showing movies of all genres.

Red Shift Festival
http://www.rsfest.com/
Dedicated to Russian filmmakers and animators living abroad.

Reel Affirmations
http://www.reelaffirmations.org/
International gay and lesbian film festival in Washington DC.

ReelWorld Film Festival
http://www.reelworld.ca/
Toronto festival showcasing diverse types of film and video.

Reggio Film Festival
http://www.reggiofilmfestival.com/
Italian short film festival.

Rehoboth Beach Independent Film Festival
http://www.rehobothfilm.com/Festival.html
Sponsored by the Rehoboth Beach Film Society.

Rencontres Internationales Paris Berlin
http://www.art-action.org/enindex.htm
Film, art, and music festival in France and Germany.

Reno Film Festival
http://www.renofilmfestival.com/
Gambling and movies. MWUHAHA!!! But seriously, avoid the gambling...

Revelation Perth International Film Festival
http://www.revelationfilmfest.org/
Australian festival showing works from the indie, film fest, and underground

Reykjavik International Film Festival
http://www.filmfest.is/?L=1
International film and documentary festival.

Rhode Island International Film Festival
http://www.film-festival.org/
International film festival in Providence. They also hold a horror festival.

RiverRun International Film Festival
http://www.riverrunfilm.com/2007/home.asp
International festival for indie films in North Carolina.

Rochester International Film Festival
http://www.rochesterfilmfest.org/
Independent film festival in New York.

Rocky Mountain Women's Film Festival
http://www.madcatfilmfestival.org/
Annual festival profiling films by and about women.

Roger Ebert's Overlooked Film Festival
http://www.ebertfest.com/
Annual spring festival of movies that Roger Ebert has seen.

Roma Independent Film Festival
http://www.riff.it/
Indie film festival in Italy.

Rosebud Film and Video Festival
http://www.rosebudact.org/
Held in Washington, DC.

Rossland Mountain Film Festival
http://rosslandfilmfest.com/go/
Canadian film festival focusing on local artists.

Rotterdam International Film Festival
http://www.filmfestivalrotterdam.com/default.aspx?Id=10313b28-bba9-41ef-9432-4777e0546dfc
Shows worldwide independent and experimental films.

Roxbury Film Festival
http://www.roxburyfilmfestival.org/
Showcases films written, produced, or directed by persons of color.

Rural Route Film Festival
http://www.ruralroutefilms.com/
Specializes in films dealing with rural locales and people.

Sacramento Film and Music Festival
http://www.sacfilm.com/
Shorts, features, student films, and music videos.

Sacramento Film Festival
http://www.sacramentofilmfestival.com/
Premieres films that haven't been seen in California before.

Sacramento French Film Festival
http://www.sacramentofrenchfilmfestival.org/
Canadian festival celebrating historic and modern French cinema.

Sacramento Horror Film Festival
http://www.sachorrorfilmfest.com/
Californian horror and scifi film festival.

Sacramento International Gay and Lesbian Film Festival
http://sigllf.org/
Canadian film festival for gay and lesbian film.

St. Barth Film Festival
http://www.stbarthff.org/2007/welcome.html
Films covering the Caribbean experience and life.

Salon Des Refuses Atlantique
http://rejectsalon.tripod.com/
Film festival of films rejected by the Atlantic Film Festival

San Antonio Underground Film Festival
http://www.saflim.com/
California film competition.

San Diego Asian Film Festival
www.sdaff.org/

San Diego International Film Festival
http://www.sdff.org/
Competition for documentaries, short films, and music video. Also presents films by Native American and Women filmmakers.

San Diego Latino Film Festival
http://www.sdlatinofilm.com/
Celebration of Latin film, art, and music.

San Diego Women's Film Festival
http://www.sdwff.org/home.html
California's longest running women's film festival.

San Francisco Asian American Film Festival
http://www.asianamericanmedia.org/
Films about the Asian American experience

San Francisco Black Film Festival
http://www.sfbff.org/
Festival celebrating African-American cinema and the African cultural Diaspora.

San Francisco Independent Film Festival
http://www.sfindie.com/
Features American indie films and short animation.

San Francisco International Film Festival
http://www.sffs.org/
Sponsored by the San Francisco Film Society.

San Francisco International Lesbian & Gay Film Festival
http://www.frameline.org/festival/index.aspx
Annual celebration of diversity in SF.

San Francisco Jewish Film Festival
http://sfiff.org/site/pages/index.php
Shows international jewish films and also has a database of films online.

San Francisco Silent Film Festival
http://www.silentfilm.org/
Annual celebration of silent films in California.

San Luis Obispo International Film Festival
http://www.slofilmfest.org/2008/index.shtml
Competitive event in California.

San Sebastian Film Festival
http://www.sansebastianfestival.com/
Annual European festival.

Santa Barbara International Film Festival
http://www.sbfilmfestival.org/
Shows features, shorts, animation, documentaries, and indie films.

Santa Cruz Film Festival
http://www.santacruzfilmfestival.com/
Indie film festival in California.

Santa Fe Film Festival
http://www.santafefilmfestival.com/
Premieres new local and foreign films and has several mini-festivals.

Sao Paulo International Film Festival
http://www2.uol.com.br/mostra/31/
Held yearly in Brazil.

Sapporo Shortfest
http://www.sapporoshortfest.jp/
Annual short film festival held in Sapporo, Japan.

Sarajevo Film Festival
http://www.sff.ba/default.aspx?itemid=&lang=en
International showcase of films.

Sarasota Film Festival
http://www.sarasotafilmfestival.com/
Also shows movies and holds events year round.

Savanna Film and Video Festival
http://www.scad.edu/filmfest/
Independent festival in Georgia.

Sci-Fi-London
http://www.sci-fi-london.com/2004web/about.htm
Science Fiction and fantasy film in Britain.

Scinema
http://www.csiro.au/scinema/
Science films from students and professionals.

Scottsdale International Film Festival
http://www.scottsdalefilmfestival.com/
Arizona festival that premiers newer films.

Screamfest LA
http://www.screamfestla.com/
SciFi/Horror film and screenplay festival/competition in LA.

Scrittura e Immagine
http://www.scritturaeimmagine.it/englishhome.html
Italian festival of films inspired by literary works.

Seattle International Film Festival
www.seattlefilm.com/
Enables you to look at photo stills from the festival, listen to audio speeches, and check out some internet broadcasts

Sedona International Film Festival and Workshop
http://www.sedonafilmfestival.com/
Independent film showcase and workshop

Seoul Net Festival
http://www.senef.net/senef2007/intro.php
Korean showcase for digital film.

SF Shorts
http://www.sfshorts.org/
Short films from around the world.

Shadow Documentary Film Festival
http://www.shadowfestival.nl/
Documentary film festival held in the Netherlands.

Shanghai International Film Festival
http://www.siff.com/Article/index.asp
Annual event held every June in China.

Sheffield International Documentary Festival
https://sheffdocfest.com/
Documentary festival held in the UK.

Short Cuts
http://www.shortcuts.in/
Premiers shorts and documentaries in India.

The Shoot Out
http://www.theshootoutboulder.com/
Competition of short films produced within 24 hours.

Short Shorts Lounge
http://www.shortshorts.org/
Japanese born short film festival

Shorts Film Festival
http://www.shortsfilmfestival.com/
Australian festival of short film.

Shriek Fest
http://www.shriekfest.com/
Scifi/horror film festival in LA.

Sidewalk Moving Picture Festival
http://www.sidewalkfilm.org/
Shows narrative features, documentaries, shorts, and a competition for teens.

Silent Clowns Film Series
http://www.silentclowns.com/
Show of silent comedies presented by the New York Historical Society.

Silver Lake Film Festival
http://silverlakefilmfestival.org/
Independent and alternative films from the world over, plus it highlights local LA filmmakers.

Silverdocs
http://www.silverdocs.com/
Documentary festival sponsored by the American Film Institute and the Discovery Channel.

Singapore International Film Festival
http://www.filmfest.org.sg/index.php
Shows features, shorts, animation, and documentaries.

Six Minute Cinema
http://www.sixmincin.com/
Digital competition for films 6 minutes or less.

Slamdance Film Festival
www.slamdance.com/

Slapstick
http://www.slapstick.org.uk/
Classic silent film comedies.

SNOWYfest International Film Festival
http://www.snowyfest.com/
Competitions for international and local films at Australian ski resort.

Sound Unseen
http://www.soundunseen.com/2007/
Underground films and documentaries about music.

South Asian Film Festival
http://www.thirdi.org/festival/
Indian arthouse classics, documentaries, and independent films from South Asia.

Sport Movies and TV International Film Festival
http://www.sportmoviestv.com/
Italian celebration of sports related film.

Sprout Film Festival
http://www.gosprout.org/FilmFestival.html
Film and video devoted at developmental disabilities.

Stockholm Film Festival
http://www.stockholmfilmfestival.se/
International Swedish film festival.

Straight 8
http://www.straight8.net/
Competition to make a three minute film on one cartridge of Super 8, editing in camera only. The results are shown at Cannes and other film festivals.

Studentfilms
http://www.studentfilms.com/
Online showcase of student short films.

Stuttgart International Festival of Animated Film
http://www.itfs.de/
Competition for animators 30 or younger.

Sundance Film Festival
http://www.sundance.org/festival/
Official site may not be as exciting as actually rubbing elbows among the hot talent, but it does come close. Sections include a daily report, listings of films competing, and a guide for getting around. Also has an archive for past festivals.

Sundance-A Festival Virgin's Guide
http://www.sundanceguide.net/
Online companion to a guide about the festival.

Swindon Film Festival
http://www.swindonfilmfestival.co.uk/
Annual UK film festival.

SXSW
http://www.sxsw.com/
South by Southwest is an annual film, music, and multimedia festival held in Austin, Texas.

Sydney Film Festival
http://www.sydneyfilmfestival.org/indexllash.asp
Showcase for local and international films in Australia.

Syracuse International Film and Video Festival
http://www.syrfilm.com/
Film competition in New York.

Tahoe Reno International Film Festival
http://www.t-riff.org/
Film festival that also holds educational workshops and short film productions.

Taiwan International Ethnographic Film Festival
http://www.tieff.sinica.edu.tw/
Films about the aboriginal peoples of the world.

Tampa International Gay and Lesbian Film Festival
http://pridefilmfest.com/
GLBT film festival from Florida.

Teddy Award
http://www.teddyaward.org/
Gay and Lesbian film awards in Berlin.

Telluride Film Festival
www.telluridefilmfestival.org/
Clint Eastwood calls this film festival the "best", and who are you to argue with the Outlaw Josey Wales?

Terror Film Festival
http://www.terrorfilmfestival.net/
Scifi/fantasy/horror festival held in Philadelphia, PA.

Texas Fear Fest
http://www.txfearfest.com/
Texas based horror festival.

Thessaloniki International Film Festival
http://www.filmfestival.gr/default.aspx?lang=en-US&page=448
Annual fall event in Greece.

Three Rivers Film Festival
http://3rff.com/
Showcases documentaries, films from Pittsburgh, American independents, shorts, classics, and international movies.

Tiburon International Film Festival
http://www.tiburonfilmfestival.com/
California event promoting heightened cultural awareness.

Tirana Film Fest
http://www.tiranafilmfest.com/
Albanian festival with shorts, fiction, documentaries, and animation.

Tokyo International Lesbian and Gay Film Festival
http://www.tokyo-lgff.org/2007/e/index.html
Festival is in Japan, but most films are open to English audiences.

Toofy Film Fest
http://www.toofy.com/
Colorado festival for indie filmmakers only.

Torino Film Festival
http://www.torinofilmfest.org/
Italian shorts, documentaries, and premieres.

Toronto International Film Festival
http://www.torontointernationalfilmfestival.ca/
Take off to the Great White North and enjoy one of the largest film festivals in North America

Toronto Online Film Festival
http://www.torontoonlinefilmfestival.com/
Feature films, shorts, animation, commercials, and music videos.

Toronto Jewish Film Festival
http://www.tjff.com/
Films, documentaries, and shorts about Jewish culture and identity.

Transdimensional Short Film Festival
http://www.tdfilmfest.com/
Specializes in short films that are absurd, odd, or funny.

Tranny Fest
http://www.trannyfest.com/
Transgender film and video festival.

Traverse City Film Festival
http://www.traversecityfilmfest.org/
Founded by Michael Moore.

Trenton Film Festival
http://www.trentonfilmfestival.org/
Narrative films, documentaries, shorts, foreign movies, animation, and experiments.

Tribeca Film Festival
www.tribecafilmfestival.org/
Co-founded by Robert De Niro in 2002, this uber-trendy lower Manhattan film fete has evolved into one of the most respected festivals in the country.

TromaDance Film Festival
www.tromadance.com

Tropfest
http://www.tropfest.com/
Worlds largest short film festival held in Australia.

Tucsonfilm
http://www.tucsonfilm.com/
Annual short film festival in Arizona.

Twin Rivers Multimedia Festival
http://www.twinriversmediafestival.com/
Festival encompassing film, video, and internet media formats.

UK Jewish Film Festival
http://www.ukjewishfilmfestival.org.uk/
Features Jewish short films and features, and holocaust education.

United Nations Association Film Festival
http://www.unaff.org/
Documentaries about human rights, the environment, racism, homelessness, war, and women's issues.

USA Film Festival
http://www.usafilmfestival.com/
Nonprofit dedicated to recognizing excellence in film.

Uppsala International Short Film Festival
http://www.shortfilmfestival.com/
Swedish short film event. Click on flag in top right corner for English version.

Urbanworld Film Festival
http://www.uwff.com/Urbanworld/Home.html
Features the work of high school filmmakers.

US International Film and Video Festival
http://www.filmfestawards.com/
Competition for documentary, educational, corporate, student, and entertainment films.

Vail Film Festival
http://www.vailfilmfestival.org/
Dedicated to American indie films, showing features, shorts, documentaries, tv pilots, commercials, and sports.

Valladolid International Film Festival
http://www.seminci.es/default.asp
Annual Italian event.

Valley Film Festival
http://www.valleyfilmfest.com/2007/main.jsp
Indie filmfest in San Fernando Valley.

Vancouver Asian Film Festival
http://www.vaff.org/
Forum for North American Asian filmmakers.

Vancouver International Film Festival
http://www.viff.org/
Large competition for international and Canadian film.

Vancouver Jewish Film Festival
http://www.vijff.com/
Canada's longest running Jewish film festival.

Vancouver Latin American Film Festival
http://www.vlaff.org/
Canadian festival for Latin American cinema.

VCU French Film Festival
http://www.frenchfilm.vcu.edu/
French films premiered in Virginia.

Venice Film Festival
www.veneziafilmfestival.com/
Includes information on the film festival, as well as news on other cultural activities happening in Venice.

Victoria Independent Film and Video Festival
http://victoriafilmfestival.com/
Competition in British Columbia.

Viennale
http://www.viennale.at/
International film festival held in Austria.

Virginia Film Festival
http://www.vafilm.com/
Weekend long annual event in Charlottesville.

Visions du Reel
http://www.visionsdureel.ch/
International documentary festival in Switzerland.

Vistas Film Festival
http://www.vistasfilmfestival.org/
International event for Hispanic cinema in Texas.

Viva Film Festival
http://www.vivafilmfestival.com/
Spanish and Latin American film festival in Manchester.

Washington DC Independent Film Festival
http://www.dciff.org/
Annual competition for indie films.

Washington Jewish Film Festival
http://www.wjff.org/
Celebration of Jewish culture, films, and filmmakers.

Webcuts
http://www.webcuts.org/2007/indexde.html
Annual internet short film festival from Berlin.

West Virginia International Film Festival
http://www.wvff.org/
West Virginia's Official State Film Festival.

Westchester Film Festival
http://www.westchesterfilmfestival.com/
Annual showcase of films of 60 minutes or less.

Westport Youth Film Festival
http://www.westportyouthfilmfest.org/
Features the work of high school filmmakers.

Where Is The Love
http://www.whereisthelove.ro/index.php?l=ro
Romanian international short film festival.

Wildscreen
http://www.wildscreen.org.uk/
UK event promoting nature films.

Wild and Scenic Environmental Film Festival
http://www.wildandscenicfilmfestival.org/
Nevada celebration of environmental and adventure films.

Wildlife Film Makers
http://www.wildlife-film.com/
Festival and website dedicated to wildlife filmmakers worldwide.

Wildlife Vaasa
http://wildlife.vaasa.fi/
Finnish competition for nature films.

Wild West Film Festival
http://www.wildwestfilmfest.com/
48 hour film competition in Kansas.

Williamsburg Brooklyn Film Festival
http://www.wbff.org/
Festival for new independent filmmakers.

Wine Country Film Festival
http://www.winecountryfilmfest.com/
Open air film screenings in California with food and wine events.

Woods Hole Film Festival
http://www.woodsholefilmfestival.com/
Cape Cod event for New England based independent film makers.

Woodstock Film Festival
http://www.woodstockfilmfestival.com/
Concerts and independent films.

Women Make Waves Film/Video Festival
www.wmw.com.tw/

Women's Film Festival
http://www.womensfilmfestival.org/
Benefit for he Women's Crisis Center in Windham County, Vermont.

WorldFest
http://www.worldfest.org/
International independent and short film festival in Houston, Texas.

Worldwide Short Film Festival
http://www.shortfilmfestival.com/
Annual short film event in Toronto, Canada.

Yamagata International Documentary Film Festival
http://www.yidff.jp/home-e.html
Documentary festival held in Japan.

Yorkton Short Film and Video Festival
http://www.yorktonshortfilm.org/
Canada's oldest short film festival.

Zagreb Film Festival
http://www.zagrebfilmfestival.com/
Croatian festival for shorts, documentaries, and features.

Zanzibar International Film Festival
http://www.ziff.or.tz/
Large cultural event in East Africa.

Zinebi
http://www.zinebi.org/
International festival of documentaries and short films held in Spain.

FILM MAGAZINES

Animation Journal
http://www.animationjournal.com/
A scholarly journal on animation history and theory. Yikes.

Animation Magazine
http://www.animationmagazine.net/
Magazine on animation.

Box Office
http://www.boxoffice.com/
One of the first trade publications to go online, reporting the latest on current films and films in production.

Cinefex
www.cinefex.com/
Online version of the renowned special-effects magazine. Offers synopses of articles, back issues, and a cover archive. Issues are indexed by artist, company, and film name.

CinemaSpace
cinemaspace.berkeley.edu/
Journal dedicated to all aspects of cinema and new media. Covers such areas as film theory, criticism, multimedia lectures, and the film program at UC Berkeley.

Empire Online
www.empireonline.co.uk
The web companion to the U.K.'s coolest film magazine

Entertainment Weekly
http://www.ew.com/ew
Vast amount of content from the best-selling movie, TV, and pop culture weekly

Fangoria
www.fangoria.com
Scream in terror thanks to original content and reviews from the world's leading horror film magazine

Film Threat
www.filmthreat.com
The irreverent film magazine may be out of circulation, but this site is the next best thing.

Frames Per Second
http://www.fpsmagazine.com/
Reviews and articles on animation.

G-Fan
http://www.g-fan.com/
Magazine and site devoted to Japanese giant monster films and their loving fans.

The Hollywood Reporter
www.hollywoodreporter.com/
Provides the latest scoop on all major studio happenings.

iF Magazine
http://www.ifmagazine.com
Online magazine for indie filmmakers. Provides news, movie reviews, and columns.

Millennium Film Journal
mfj-online.org/
Presents articles about independent, experimental, and avant-garde cinema, video, and, more recently, works that use newer technologies. Also has an archive for past issues.

Movieline
www.movieline.com/
Online version of the entertainment and interview magazine.

Premiere
www.premieremag.com/
Online version of the leading entertainment magazine

Rue Morgue
http://www.rue-morgue.com/
Magazine devoted to horror in culture and entertainment.

Screen
http://screenmag.com/
magazine devoted to bizarre cinema, mostly in the horror genre.

Shivers
http://www.visimag.com/shivers/
UK magazine devoted to horror in entertainment.

Time Out
www.timeout.com/
Provides a rundown of many cultural and art events happening around the world.

Variety
www.variety.com
The classic trade magazine brings industry news, reviews, and box office info to the web

FILM STUDIOS

Dreamworks SKG
www.dreamworks.com/
Browse info on upcoming movie, TV, and music projects from one of the best-known studios in Hollywood

Fine Line Features
www.finelinefeatures.com/
One of the leading studios of independent films presents information on upcoming releases and offers enlightenment to budding filmmakers.

Focus Features
www.focusfeatures.com
Check out the home page of one of the major players in modern independent cinema. Includes a link to their more commercial arm, Rogue Pictures

Lionsgate Films
www.lionsgatefilms.com/
Takes you behind the scenes of their latest releases and gives you a glimpse of future films.

MGM Lion's Den
www.mgmua.com/
Home of the re-vamped *ShowGirls* site, also has coverage on the huge distributor's large slate of theatrical releases. Divided into MGM's niches, such as MGM television and home video.

Miramax
www.miramax.com/
Walk into a smorgasbord of Miramax's post-Weinstein delectables. Click on their week's specials and get a glimpse into their upcoming and current releases.

MPI Home Video
www.mpimedia.com/
Answers questions on availability for MPI video releases.

New Line Cinema
www.newline.com/
Displays their current and upcoming releases.

Newmarket Films
www.newmarketfilms.com/
Up-and-coming indie studio responsible for releasing everything from *Passion of the Christ* to *Memento*.

Paramount Pictures
www.paramount.com/
Click on any of the film icons to receive information on production and cast.

Pixar Animation Studios
www.pixar.com/
There's a reason why Disney bought Pixar–they've consistently put out the best animated movies of the past twenty years. Click around their web site and 'earn volumes about how they develop their award-winning CGI animated features.

Sony Classics
www.sonyclassics.com/
Focuses on Sony's independent releases and offers links to other sites.

Sony Pictures Entertainment
www.sonypictures.com/
Sony (which includes Columbia and TriStar) gives you the latest on their crop of films. Along with film and studio information, you can enter their contests to win movie t-shirts or trips to a Hollywood premiere.

Troma
www.troma.com/
With its #1 citizen, Toxie, welcoming you, indulge in the finest in camp cinema. Features information on such classics as *Toxic Avenger, Class of Nuke 'em High* and *Sgt. Kabukiman NYPD.*

Twentieth Century Fox Home Entertainment
http://www.foxhome.com/foxhomemain.html
Promotes the studio's library of films which includes such mega hits as the *Star Wars* and *Die Hard* trilogies on DVD. The site is divided into a time line enabling you to browse through their collection, beginning with the 1920's and continuing right on to the present.

United International Pictures
www.uip.com/
Comes in a variety of languages and has materials on their films which can be downloaded.

Universal Studios
www.universalstudios.com
Learn all about the upcoming films and awesome theme park rides of Universal Studios

Walt Disney Studios
http://home.disney.go.com/index
Divided into nine categories where you can find the latest on Disney books, home video, movies, music, shopping, software, television, theater and more.

Warner Brothers
www.movies.warnerbros.com/
Get the latest on WB's films, TV programs, music, merchandise, DC comics and kid's programming.

Weinstein Company
www.weinsteinco.com/
Powerful producer brothers Harvey and Bob Weinstein left Miramax (the Disney arthouse wing they founded) and formed their own production company. Check out the inside info on their upcoming releases.

FILMMAKER RESOURCES

Adrienne Shelly Foundation
www.adrienneshellyfoundation.org
Founded in memory of actress/director/writer/indie icon Adrienne Shelly by her husband Andy Ostroy. Goal is to fund and mentor female filmmakers.

American Film Institute
www.afi.com/education/
The American Film Institute created this site to further its cause of finding talent that will prolong the life of art and film. The site lists the various courses, study facilities, and grants that this non-profit organization offers.

American Zoetrope
www.zoetrope.com/
A virtual tour of Francis Ford Coppola's Zoetrope Studios, which offers screenwriting contests and seminars as well as post-production information

Assn. of Independent Video and Filmmakers (AIVF)
http://www.aivf.org/
Resource that offers information on festivals and self distribution.

The Clay and Stop Motion Animation How-To Page
http://www.animateclay.com/
Tutorials and community based around stop motion animation.

Cyber Film School
www.cyberfilmschool.com/
Want to become the next Quentin or Spike, but can't afford film school? Try this informative and entertaining venue that teaches the tricks of the trade in areas such as screenwriting, cinematography, and producing.

Daily Script
www.dailyscript.com/
Don't know how to write a blockbuster screenplay? Check out this online archive of hundreds of TV and movie scripts and see how it's done

Film-Makers.com
www.film-makers.com
Offers hundreds of links to film resource sites.

Filmmaking.net
www.filmmaking.net/
Features a comprehensive film schools database and an internet filmmaker's FAQ

Independent Film & Television Alliance (IFTA)
www.ifta-online.org/
Formerly known as the American Film Marketing Association, this group speaks to those who exclusively license, distribute, and produce independent films.

Industry Central
http://www.industrycentral.net/
Links to film industry related sites.

KORDA
http://korda.obs.coe.int/web/searchaide.php
Database for public funding and support schemes for films made in the European Union.

Mandy's Film and Television Production Directory
www.mandy.com/
An international geographical listing of film technicians, facilities, and producers. Helpful site for anyone looking for a film crew.

Screenwriter's Online
www.screenwriter.com/
Invites novice screenwriters to interact with industry veterans.

Screenwriter's Utopia
www.screenwritersutopia.com/
A screenwriter's one-stop resource site. Learn about the format and structure of scripts, how to market your script, network among your peers, receive tips from the pros, and become informed of the latest events and seminars.

Script Zone
www.ScriptZone.com
Offers script consulting and analysis services, providing solutions to creative problems and analyzing strengths and weaknesses in a script

Stop Motion Animation
http://www.stopmotionanimation.com/
Tutorials on stop motion animation and puppet making.

Trigger Street
www.triggerstreet.com
Founded by scary character actor Kevin Spacey, this site allows fledgling screenwriters and directors to solicit feedback on their works

FILM REVIEWS

Attack of the 50 Foot DVD
http://www.50footdvd.com/
Covers and reviews cult, horror, and sci-fi films on DVD.

Back Row Reviews
http://www.geocities.com/stjamespl.geo/backrow.html
James Dawson reviews films that, well, mostly suck.

Chip Remington's World of Movies
http://www.chipremington.com/
Slightly mocking reviews of films by a slightly mocking man.

Choice Review
http://movie-review-sites.choice-review.com/
A review site that reviews movie review sites (say that one fast a few times).

Choking on Popcorn
http://www.chokingonpopcorn.com/
Originally the blog of two friends who decided to review whatever film they watched it has now expanded to include a review team.

CinemaReview
http://www.cinemareview.com/
Includes detailed synopses and content ratings, and sometimes images from the film.

Classic B-Movies on Video
http://www3.sympatico.ca/bmovieguy/
Reviews of classic B films, and where you can find them on tape or DVD.

Cranky Critic
http://www.crankycritic.com/
Rates movies in a way that will speak to people: i.e. was the film worth the price of the ticket it cost to see it.

Crazy for Cinema
www.crazy4cinema.com/
Straightforward, down-to-earth reviews by an ardent movie fan.

Deep Focus
www.deep-focus.com/
Offers up five years worth of reviews by New York cinephile Bryant Frazer, listed alphabetically or by grade.

Digital Monster Island
http://www.digitalmonsterisland.com/
Reviews of giant monster movies on DVD.

DVD Cult
http://www.dvdcult.com/
Cult films on DVD and an awesome links section.

DVD Drive-In
http://www.dvddrive-in.com/
Reviews and announces upcoming sci-fi, horror, and cult films being released on DVD.

DVD Maniacs
http://www.dvdmaniacs.net/
Cult films on DVD.

DVD Movie Guide
http://www.dvdmg.com/index.shtml
Reviews upcoming films on DVD.

DVD Review
http://www.dvdreview.com/
DVD (and high definition DVD) news, reviews, and easter eggs.

The Film Hobbit
http://www.filmhobbit.com/
Not all Hobbits go on adventures about Rings. Some tear Hollywood a new one instead.

Four Word Film Reviews
www.fwfr.com
Movies summed up in four words

Friday and Saturday Night
http://www.geocities.com/fridaysaturdaymovie/
Self described as "potentially intelligent film reviews."

Haiku Movie Reviews
www.wunderland.com/WTS/Ginohn/poetry/HMRlist.html
Movie reviews (really short ones) in Haiku form.

Kids in Mind
www.kidsinmind.com
Reviews movies with an eye toward whether or not they're suitable for the kiddies. Offers a sex, violence, and language rating system for parents.

The Man Who Viewed Too Much
www.panix.com/dangelo/
A New York screenwriting student with a soft touch for the art house fluff and mediocre gems, like Joe Versus the Volcano.

Metacritic
www.metacritic.com
Compiles and provides links to new and recent release movie reviews from various magazines and newspapers, creating an overall rating (on a 1-100 scale) based on the consensus of the reviews. Also reviews DVD/video releases, music, books, and video games in the same way.

Mrs. Giggles
http://www.mrsgiggles.com/movies/index.html
Reviews by what we assume is someone's persnickety grandma...

Movie Deaths Database
http://www.moviedeaths.com/
Film reviews and a database about death in Hollywood films. Two subjects that naturally go together.

The Movie Mom's Guide to Movies and Videos for Families
movies.yahoo.com/mv/moviemom/
Created by movie critic and mother, Nell Minow, who gives critiques and advice on how to get children to watch movies that aren't doused in violence.

Movie Reviews by Joan Ellis
www.joanellis.com/
Film critic Joan Ellis puts her acerbic and astute observations on the Internet as she examines the cultural innuendoes in current film.

Movie Review Query Engine
www.mrqe.com
Allows you to search on any movie and find all available reviews appearing in the Usenet group rec.arts.movies.reviews

Mr. Cranky Rates the Movies
www.mrcranky.com
The joke here is that this guy doesn't like any movie, hence the name Cranky. His rating scale is based on bombs and his followers (scale names Lizard, and Philm Pham, just to name a few) are as nutty as his reviews.

Onion A.V. Club
www.avclub.com/
Spin-off of the popular satirical newspaper that features movie and DVD reviews, filmmaker interviews, and more

The Onliner
http://www.theonliner.com/
Sardonic movie reviews done as only the British can do them.

Out Magazine Movie Reviews
www.out.com/
Online version of the magazine that includes movie reviews and commentary on gay and lesbian cinema.

Roger Ebert
http://rogerebert.suntimes.com/
Newspapers, books, television, now Ebert storms the web. Offers his newspaper film reviews, with a searchable archive that goes back to 1985.

Rotten Tomatoes
www.rottentomatoes.com/
Collects reviews of newly released movies from various newspapers and ranks the overall critical reaction to the film.

Teen Movie Critic
www.dreamagic.com/roger/teencritic.html
Teenaged movie buff from Minnesota offers his thoughts on current theatrical releases. Also has a link to a listing of many video rental stores around America.

VideoHound's Golden Movie Retriever
movieretriever.com
Our very own web site! The Hound's famous reviews, plus community features and blogs from the Editors of VideoHound's Golden Movie Retriever

The Voice of Reason
http://www.thevoiceofreason.com/ComedyMovieWatch/
Most very definitely not entirely serious movie reviews.

The Weekly Blurb
http://weeklyblurb.com/
Sarcastic spin-doctor style reviews of mainstream films.

Women Studies Film Reviews
www.mith2.umd.edu/WomensStudies/FilmReviews/
Movie reviews with a feminist angle written by Florida radio personality Linda Lopez McAlister and film scholar Cynthia Fuchs.

GENERAL ENTERTAINMENT

Academy of Motion Picture Arts and Sciences
www.oscars.org/
Site proves that the AMPAS does more than just hand out gold statuettes every year. This homepage reveals this organization's dedication to spreading the love of film around the world. Includes information on AMPAS's various fellowships, educational, and historical activities.

AGP Film Credits Database
http://www.agpfilms.com/
Database of film credits for the curious who'd like to know who helped make and support films as well as who starred in them.

Ain't It Cool News
www.aintitcool.com
Get the latest on upcoming releases before they even hit theaters with website originator Harry Knowles's inside scoop on their test screenings. He's the geekiest of web master film fanatics, but his information is usually fairly reliable.

American Memory
lcweb2.loc.gov/papr/mpixhome.html
Collection of historical film stock that can be downloaded from the Library of Congress. Time frame is from 1897 to 1916 and includes such archival footage as President William McKinley's funeral and "actuality films" showing panoramic views of old San Francisco policemen and firemen in action.

Angry Alien Productions
http://www.angryalien.com/
Movies re-enacted within 30 seconds....with bunnies. We'd like to say more, but we're speechless.

The Big Cartoon Database
http://www.bcdb.com/
Like IMDB, but for cartoons.

The Black Film Center/Archive
www.indiana.edu/bfca/index.html
An academic reference devoted to sharing resources on black cinema.

Black Films
www.blackfilm.com
Provides a forum for filmmakers, scholars, and organizations to discuss and express their artistic views. Includes info on upcoming releases, films in production, casting calls, jobs, and film festivals. There's also a gallery of film clips.

Black Flix
www.blackflix.com
Highlights the contributors of black movie stars, filmmakers, writers, and directors whom mainstream reviews and web sites often overlook.

Blockbuster Entertainment
www.blockbuster.com
Explores all the goodies the rental chain has to offer as well as their latest contests or sweepstakes.

Bob World Film Database
http://freespace.virgin.net/b..world/
Continuing the tradition of quirky movie databases Bob World is all about films in which the female lead has a "bob" hairstyle.

Box Office Guru
www.boxofficeguru.com
Classic site devoted to box office results. See what came in first this week or check out their database of film grosses for over 2,700 movies

Box Office Mojo
http://www.boxofficemojo.com/
Similar to the above.

Box Office Prophets
http://www.boxofficeprophets.com/
Blogs, reviews, and research tools for movie buffs.

Bright Lights Film Journal
http://www.brightlightsfilm.com/index.html
Film blog and articles.

British Movie Musicals
http://myweb.tiscali.co.uk/britmusical/
Covers musicals made in Britain or with British involvement from 1929 to present.

Britfilms
http://www.britfilms.com/
The official online database of British films.

Bugs Bunny Burrow
http://www.bugsbunnyburrow.com/
Site devoted to classic cartoons.

Celluloid Dreams
http://www.celluloiddreams.net/
web site for the Celluloid Dreams radio show. Features interviews, reviews, and interesting movie topics.

Cine Fantom
framework.xsit.v2.nl/archive/archive/node/text/ default.xsit/nodenr-132348
Examines Russian experimental films and videos.

Cinema Confidential
http://www.cinecon.com/
News, reviews, interviews, and gossip. Also has trailers for upcoming films.

Cinema Sites
http://www.cinema-sites.com/
Directory of film and television related sites.

Cinemaniac
http://frank.mtsu.edu/jpurcell/Cinema/ maincinema2.htm
Collection of links to cinema related sites online.

Cinematic Happenings Under Development (CHUD)
www.chud.com
Offers gossip, news, and previews on upcoming films and projects in development.

CineMedia
http://afi.cinemedia.org/
Archival site directory to films and media

Cinemorgue
http://www.cinemorgue.com/
List of actors/actresses who have died onscreen with descriptions of the events. Kinda creepy.

Clamen's Movie Information Collection
http://www.cs.cmu.edu/Unofficial/Movies/ README.html
One man's personal collection of links to film related sites.

Classic Film and Television
http://members.aol.com/MG4273/film.htm
Fun and educational film site.

Classic Film Guide
http://www.classicfilmguide.com/ classicfilms.html
Reviews of silent and classic films, along with a FAQ.

Classic Films
http://www.geocities.com/classicflicks2000/
Very nice geocities site for classic films. It seems closed to updates for now, one can only hope it will reopen soon. The archives are still worth the look.

Classic Hollywood Biographies
http://www.classichollywoodbios.com/
Also has many magazine covers featuring stars of the times.

Classic Movie Favorites
http://www.classicmoviefavorites.com/
Impressive effort by one tireless fan.

Classic Movies
http://www.classicmovies.org/
Articles, links, and a forum.

Classic Noir Online
http://www.classicnoir.com/
For fans of classic films and film noir.

Cliffhanger Corner
http://members.tripod.com/fedora2/
Fan page devoted to the old cliffhanger serials.

ComingSoon.net
www.comingsoon.net
Presents news, features, interviews, and images of upcoming movies, updated daily

Couch Cowboy
http://www.couchcowboy.com/
Classic cowboy films.

Counting Down
www.countingdown.com
Posts gossip, news, and features on upcoming movies.

Cowboy Pal
http://www.cowboypal.com/
Silver screen cowboy films.

Creepy Classics
http://www.creepyclassics.com/
Lists upcoming classic sci-fi and horror films on DVD. Also sells them.

Dark City
http://www.eskimo.com/noir/
Dedicated to all things noir.

Dark Horizons
www.darkhorizons.com
Movie rumors are aplenty here and it's updated regularly. The site is regulated by Garth (yes, Garth) Franklin, an Australian entertainment journalist.

Dart Movies
http://www.crowsdarts.com/movies/movies.html
A list of films (and the specific scenes in them) that involve throwing darts.

The Darkside of the Web
www.darklinks.com
Specializes in shedding light on the bizarre and creepy in film

The Deadbolt
www.thedeadbolt.com
This ultimate hub site collects daily links related to the coolest in movies, music, entertainment, and more-plus they offer their own original reviews, features, and interviews. One-stop shopping for internet media addicts.

Defamer
www.defamer.com
Frequently updated blog-style gossip rag, airing out all of Hollywood's dirty laundry

Dermatology in the Cinema
www.skinema.com/
Proof that anything can go on the Web. Exposes how skin afflictions are handled in films. Broken down in three categories: "Representation of Evil", "Actors with Skin Findings", and "Realistic and Sympathetic Portrayals." Informative and healthy.

Digitally Obsessed
www.digitallyobsessed.com
Provides information, reviews, contests, and inside information on new DVD releases.

Don Markstein's Toonopedia
http://www.toonopedia.com/
Cartoon Reference site run by the former editor of Comics Revue.

Drive-Ins
http://www.drive-ins.com/
Drive-In movie theater database.

DriveIn Movie
http://www.driveinmovie.com/mainmenu.htm
List of Drive-Ins and some of their history.

Drive-In Theater
http://www.driveintheater.com/index.htm
Lists all remaining drive-in theaters by state and county.

DVD Demystified
http://dvddemystified.com/
Home of the exhaustive DVD FAQ, a guide to everything you wanted to know about DVD's and a lot of things you had no idea about.

DVD Easter Eggs
www.dvdeastereggs.com
Shows how to get to hidden features, or "easter eggs," that are hidden in some DVDs.

DVD File
www.dvdfile.com
Get the 411, in exhaustive detail, on all current and future DVD releases.

E! Online
www.eonline.com
Filled with tons of entertainment news, this is a fun site to visit come Oscar time, thanks to their habit of creating online games at the expense of the stars not nominated

East Meets West Video
http://www.geocities.com/eastmeetswestvideo/
Fan Page dedicated to Chambara (samurai sword) films and Westerns. What more could you need?

Egghaven 2000
http://www.eggheaven.com/
Shows easter eggs (hidden features) in a variety of products, including easter eggs.

The 80's Movies Rewind
http://www.fast-rewind.com/
Reviews, trivia, plot synopses, and more in this homage to eighties cinema.

The Electronic Urban Report
www.EURweb.com/
Supports the positive images of African Americans in film and offers the latest celebrity news on the top black stars.

Fake Film Database
http://www.appallingtrash.com/
Database of movie parodies.

The Felixes
http://www.thefelixes.com/
Devoted to skewering the Oscars.

Fiction Into Film Database
http://www.fifdb.com/
Database of films and television based on fictional works.

Film and Video Resources
www.lib.umich.edu/filmvid/
Created by the folks at the University of Michigan School of Information and Library Studies, this site leads you to many of the textual resources available that deal with film and video. Organized according to reviews, filmographies, discussions and other databases.

Film Crew Online
http://www.filmcrewonline.com/
Remember those guys from Mystery Science Theater 3000? They're baaaaaaack....

Film Forum
www.filmforum.com/
Showcases the latest releases in New York's leading independent movie house. Offers premiere information on independent features and repertory programming.

Film Incoherence
http://members.aol.com/Loig7/ filmincoherence.htm
Study of logical inconsistencies in films, in French and English.

Film Jerk
http://www.filmjerk.com/
Despite the name, they seem like nice people.

Film Monthly
http://www.filmmonthly.com/default.htm
News, reviews, and articles. Has an emphasis on genre films.

Film Noir
http://www.crimeculture.com/Contents/ Film%20Noir.html
The Crime Culture websites historical guide to film noir.

Film Noir, Suspense, and Classic Action Movies
http://www.suspense-movies.com/
Huzzah for Carol Landis!

Film Resources on the Web
http://www.duke.edu/kenneth/filmsite.html
Links to movie resources an sites on the web.

Film Sound Cliches
http://www.filmsound.org/cliche/
Popular movie sound clich's and logic flaws, and some articles on sound in films.

Filmjabber
http://www.filmjabber.com/
A blog with movie and film reviews, trailers from upcoming films, and photos and posters.

FilmScape
http://www.filmscape.co.uk/
Games and quizzes involving movie quotes and taglines.

The Filmmaker's Exam
http://www.rinkworks.com/filmmaker/
Test yourself to see if your movie is a stinker.

Films 101
http://www.films101.com/
Database fo films chosen by critics and filmmakers to be the best in their genre.

FilmSpot
http://www.cinemaspot.com/
Site listing film related resources and sites.

Find Your Video Store
http://www.myvideostore.com/content/store/ search.html
Enter your zip code into their search engine to find movie stores in your area.

A Fistful of Westerns
http://home.earthlink.net/braithwaite/
Website specializing in the old spaghetti westerns.

555 List
http://home.earthlink.net/mthyen/
Mind numbing list of all the fictional 555 numbers used in movies.

FlixFind
http://www.flixfind.com/Weblog/
Directory of links to (mostly) current films.

Flubs of Jurassic Park
http://www.bigwaste.com/library/jurassicflubs/
Several pages of mistakes from the dinosaur movie.

The Flying Inkpot's Incredible Movie Links Page
http://inkpot.com/movielinks/
Gotta love the name.

The Force
www.theforce.net
Articles, gossip, news, fan submissions on all things Star Wars.

Former Child Star Central
members.tripod.com/formerchildstar
Whatever became of those ex-kiddie celebs? Doin' time? Stemmin' for change? Find out here.

ForMovies
http://formovies.com/
Movie news and trivia, and a directory of local video stores allowing users to search them for a specific title.

Gamers Movie Classics
http://www.gamersclassics.com/
Collection of movies sorted by genre. Click on he icons by each one's name to see quotes or hear audio clips. Also has some one word reviews of recent films.

German-Hollywood Connection
http://www.germanhollywood.com/
Site about the impact the Germans, Austrians, and Swiss have had on Hollywood and it's films with essays on everything from Noir to Tarzan.

Glamour Girls of the Silver Screen
http://www.glamourgirlsofthesilverscreen.com/
Images and profiles of famous actresses from the 40's to the 60's.

Gods of Film Making
http://www.ambidextrouspics.com/
Bios of filmmakers.

Golden Age Cartoons
http://www.goldenagecartoons.com/
Central site for 7 dedicated carton historians who have banded together.

Golden Silents
http://www.goldensilents.com/
Bios and film clips from Hollywood's Silent Age.

The Golden Years
http://www.thegoldenyears.org/
Films from 1939 to 1969.

Go2flix
http://www.go2flix.com/
Links to films playing now, upcoming theater and DVD releases, Oscar info, etc.

Hard Boiled Mysteries
http://www.geocities.com/Athens/6384/ filmnoir.html
Film Noir fansite.

The Hollywood Thirties
http://www.geocities.com/Hollywood/Lot/4344/ index.html
Discusses film and hollwood history in the 1930's.

The Hot Button
www.thehotbutton.com
Critic Dave Poland discusses Hollywood gossip, future films, and weekly box office reports.

Hollywood Elsewhere
www.hollywood-elsewhere.com
Movie journalist Jeffrey Wells posts articles on upcoming films, the movie industry, and the vagaries of Hollywood.

Hollywood Online
www.hollywood.com
Feast your eyes at movie trailers, movie trivia, movie chat, vote on the latest contest, or check out some real estate in California.

Hollywood Sign
www.hollywoodsign.org/
Offers snapshots and a historical overview of the world famous Hollywood sign

I Know the Ending
http://www.iknowtheending.com/
Humorous synopses of films consisting of 2 sentences that give away the ending.

IGN
www.ign.com
Testosterone fueled site focuses on sci-fi, wrestling, and video games. Movie fans will find interviews, features, opinions, and trivia in three film areas.

The Incredible World of Bowling Noir
http://members.aol.com/bobbuttman/bowlingnoir/ bowlingnoir.htm
Film Noir and....bowling?

IndieFilms
www.indiefilms.com
An easy, inexpensive way to distribute any feature, short, or documentary film you've made. Allows independent filmmakers to make contact with potential investors and distributors.

IndieWire
www.indiewire.com
Up-to-date info on the latest in independent film festivals and wide releases

The Irish Mafia
http://www.irishmafia.us/
Site devoted to Spencer Tracy, James Cagney, Ralph Bellamy, Lynne Overman, Frank McHugh, Pat O'Brien, and Frank Morgan.

Insultingly Stupid Movie Physics
www.intuitor.com/moviephysics/
Rails on scenes from movies that disregard the laws of physics and explains why they're impossible. Lists generic "bad movie physics," examples of cliches that show up in movie after movie, as well as serious scientific gaffes.

International Film and Video Center
http://www.ifvc.com/home.htm
Film database, links to film festivals, and they produce their own films and documentaries.

The Internet Entertainment Network
www.hollywoodnetwork.com/dealmaking/ index.html
Enables you to become a member of the Screenwriters, Producers, or Writers Network. Divided into various sites like deal-making, box office, in-production, and script sales.

The Internet Movie Database
www.imdb.com
The mother of all entertainment databases. Users can frequently update the information and submit their own film reviews. With thousands of movies stored in its database, you can search by title, actor, director, country, and even by character name.

Jam! Movies
jam.canoe.ca/Movies/
Canadian movie site with daily entertainme ̓t news and information.

James Bond
www.klast.net/bond/
Bond arrives, shaken not stirred, onto the internet. Includes a rundown of every Bond film, villains and their famous lines, Bond trivia and links to other Bond sites

Jerry Beck's Cartoon Research
http://www.cartoonresearch.com/
Comprehensive resource for animation.

Julie's Cinematic Slip-Ups
http://www.geocities.com/Hollywood/2549/s.ips.html
Julie takes on Hollywood.

Kung Fu Cinema
http://www.kungfucinema.com/
Because Kung Fu movies rock!

Latino Review
www.latinoreview.com
Film news, rumors, and interviews directed towards the English-speaking Latin-American audience

Locate TV
http://www.locatetv.com/
Type the name of an actor, film, or TV show into their search engine and it will tell you where you can see it on DVD, television, or online.

Lumiere
http://lumiere.obs.coe.int/web/search/
Record of annual film ticket sales of films released in Europe since 1996. Entries include a breakdown by individual country.

Martin's Film Noir Page
www.martinsfilmnoir.com/
Extensive site on the popular genre of film noir.

Meredy's Place
http://www.meredy.com/
Classic movie trivia site.

Media Resource Center
http://www.lib.berkeley.edu/MRC/level2.html
List of resources for movie fans and makers.

Medium Rare
http://www.mediumrare.org/
Website devoted to quality film and television that is often overlooked.

The Midnight Palace
http://www.micnightpalace.com/
A forum, articles, and reviews on films from before 1956.

Moderntimes
http://www.moderntimes.com/
Has, among other things, a history of how B films began to exist.

Motion Pictures Association of America (MPAA)
www.filmratings.com
Tells what a film is rated and why it received that rating.

Mov.ie
http://mov.ie/
Links to the official sites of movies.

Movie-A-Minute
http://www.rinkworks.com/movieaminute/
Humorous synopses of films.

The Movie Cliches List
www.moviecliches.com/
A vast list of common film stereotypes and instances that stifle logic. Divided into over fifty topics including bodily functions, minorities, teenagers, and wood. A growing site since people can submit their own materials.

Movie Mistakes
www.movie-mistakes.com
Identifies mistakes of continuity, fact, and omission in movies.

Movie Musicals: From Stage to Screen
http://www.geocities.com/TelevisionCity/Studio/8849/moviemusicals.htm
Reference site for those curious about stage musicals later made into films.

Movie Poopshoot
www.moviepoopshoot.com
No, it's honestly a web site. Started by indie marketing genius Kevin Smith, this site offers a menagerie of film, TV, DVD, and general pop culture geek-related information

Movie Poster Web Page
www.musicman.com/mp/mp..html
No, you're not seeing double. This one is a catalog of movie posters available for sale. Includes foreign films.

The Movie Posters Archive
www.filmsondisc.com/movieposterarchives.htm
An online vault of old movie posters, categorized by lead actor

The Movie Show on Radio
www.lifestyletalkradio.com/movieshow/
Site for the syndicated Movie Show on Radio. Includes info on air times and stations that carry the show in various markets, as well as profiles of the hosts.

The Movie Sound Page
www.moviesounds.com/
Download various sound bites from famous flicks and link to other sites.

Movie Theology
http://www.cmu.ca/library/faithfilm.html
Directory of websites offering film information from a Christian perspective.

MovieClicks
http://www.movieclicks.com/index.shtml
Whenever a film is released now odds are it also has a website. This site helps you find those websites.

Movies.com
http://movies.go.com/
Trailers, clips, and reviews of upcoming films. Also reviews films coming out on DVD.

Moviepooper
http://www.moviepooper.com/
Collection of spoilers revealing the ends of movies.

MovieTrailer
http://www.movietrailer.tv/
Online directory of Movie Trailers.

MovieWEB
movieweb.com/
Groups together info from every film studio and offers production data and still photos of their new releases. Also offers the latest box office statistics.

Musicals 101
http://www.musicals101.com/
A history of musical theatre and film.

National Filmographies
http://www.rosland.freeserve.co.uk/filmbooks.htm
Lists sites providing information on world cinema.

Netflix
www.netflix.com/
The coolest mail-order DVD rental service around. Browse through their 75,000 title movie catalog and enjoy DVDs delivered right to your mailbox.

New York Film Annex
http://www.nyfavideo.com/index.htm
Dedicated to genre films of all kinds.

The Ninja Dojo
http://www.ninjadojo.com/
Ninja and samurai films.

Nitpickers
www.nitpickers.com
Points out mistakes, omissions, and equipment sightings in movies.

Not Starring
http://www.notstarring.com/
A database of your favorite stars and the movie roles they didn't get.

NothingButMovies
http://www.nothingbutmovies.com/
Links to film related resources divided by category.

The Old Corral
http://www.b-westerns.com/
B movie westerns. Strange cowboy get-ups included

OpenFlix
http://www.openflix.com/
Listing of films in the public domain and how to get them.

Original Gangsters
http://www.dirtysquatters.com/evocrim/og/
Gangster movies in all their glory.

Pathfinder
www.pathfinder.com
Created by Time Warner, this site links to their variety of magazines that check the pulse of popular culture such as People, Vibe, Groove and Entertainment Weekly.

The Picture Show Man
http://www.pictureshowman.com/
The history of films from 1890 to 1960.

Planet Indie Independent Film Directory
http://www.planetindie.com/
Blog and directory of sites about independent film.

Popcornq
www.planetout.com/popcornq/
Dedicated to showcasing films dealing with gay and lesbian issues.

Prelinger Archives
http://www.archive.org/details/prelinger
Archive dedicated to the collection of historic films that haven't been collected elsewhere.

Projections
http://www.futuristmovies.com/
A site dedicated to films depicting the future.

Pulp Phantom
ulink.net/crossroads/phantom/
What if Quentin Tarantino had written Phantom Menace? Animated series shows you what it might look like.

Ravin' Maven
http://www.themave.com/
Collection of mini-sites devoted to classic actors and actresses.

Razzies
www.razzies.com/
Visitors can vote for the "Golden Raspberry Awards" for the year's worst films and performances.

Real Movie News
http://www.realmovienews.com/
News, reviews, trailers, etc.

Reel Classics
http://www.reelclassics.com/
Classic films, actors, filmmakers, and more.

Reel Faces
http://www.chasingthefrog.com/reelfaces/reelfaces.php
Looks at films based on real life events and people and compares them to actual events.

Running in Films
http://www.runningmovies.com/
A very comprehensive database of films that contain scenes of running. No seriously.

Scary Duck
http://scaryduck.blogspot.com/search/label/Condensed%20films
Clever and funny synopses of films done in L33tspeak

The Serial Squadron
http://www.serialsquadron.com/
The cliffhanger serial appreciation society.

Shobary's Spaghetti Westerns
http://spaghettiwesterns.1g.fl/
Even has a bloopers section!

Silent and Sound Cliffhanger Serials
http://www.themaverick.us/home/serial.html
Lists serials by year, A-Z, and by studio.

Silent Era
http://www.silentera.com/
Scads of info on Silent Films, including what is available on DVD.

Silent Ladies and Gents
http://www.silentladies.com/Ladies.html
Large image galleries of silent film stars, and profiles of the studios of the era.

Silents Are Golden
http://www.silentsaregolden.com/
Devoted to silent movies, and the idea that they are...well, you know

The Silent Western
http://xroads.virginia.edu/hyper/hns/westfilm/west.html
Chronicles the history of the old silent westerns.

Slipups
http://www.slipups.com/
Highlights amusing oopsies in film.

Smoke Free Movies
http://pages.videotron.com/abc/films-movies/
Listing of films where there is no one smoking for those offended by cigarettes. In French and English.

Snopes: Movies
http://www.snopes.com/movies/
Snopes is the ultimate hoax and urban legends reference page, and thankfully for us they have a movie section.

The Sport Psychology Movie Database
http://www.geocities.com/sportsmovies/
Database for movies depicting sport psychology themes.

Sports In Movies
http://www.sportsinmovies.com/
Dedicated to sports films and their fans.

Spout
http://www.spout.com/
Community for discussing movies, and you can buy them as well.

Surf Classics
http://www.surfclassics.com/
Site devoted to lobby cards and posters for surf movies from the 60's.

Teddy Blues Bunkhouse
http://www.wildwestweb.net/
Extensive source on the old west and westerns.

Temporal Anomalies In Time Travel Movies
http://www.mjyoung.net/time/
Now this site is fun.

Theater Hopper
http://theaterhopper.com/
Web comic about movies with some film reviews.

Those Golden Movie Musicals
http://www.classicmoviemusicals.com/
Dedicated to classic musicals.

Todd Gault's Serial Experience
http://www.serialexperience.com/
The old cliffhangers have many fans.

Toons At War
http://www.toonsatwar.blogspot.com/
Blog exploring the history of Walt Disney Studios during WWII

The Top 100
movieweb.com/movie/top25.html
Anxious to see if a certain movie has broken any box office records during its opening week? This site provides the box office ranking of all current releases. Updated every Thursday.

U.C. Berkeley Film Studies Science Fiction Page
cinemaspace.berkeley.edu/Resources/scifi2.html
*For avid sci-fi film buffs, site has separate pages for such classics as **Blade Runner**, **Star Trek**, **Alien**, **Star Wars**, and other genre related sites.*

VaRaces
http://www.varaces.com/
The Movie Car Chase Database.

VideoHelp
http://www.videohelp.com/
Ostensibly a site on how to make your own DVD's, it also has reviews of DVD players, specifically how to access the hidden menu's that will allow you to play DVD's of any region code.

Volkswagens in Film and Video
http://vwfilms.net/
A bug lovers guide to the appearance of VW's in the media.

Wallywood
http://www.wallywood.co.uk/
Movie goofups and some occasional neat trivia submitted by readers.

Welcome to Silent Movies
http://www.welcometosilentmovies.com/
News on silent films available on VFS and DVD, and articles of various sorts.

The Western Posters Page
http://www.westernposterpage.com/
Seller of reproductions of posters from the classic western films.

Westerns
http://www.lewestern.com/
The Western movie internet database.

What a Character!
www.what-a-character.com
Provides bio info, photos, filmographies, obits, and trivia on those character actors who you know you recognize, you just don't know their name (or vice versa).

Where Did They Film That
http://www.wheredidtheyfilmthat.co.uk/
Location listings for films shot in the UK or Ireland.

Whoops! Movie Goofs
http://www.jonhs.com/moviegoofs/
Alphabetical list of films with some tragic errors, and explanations of them.

Women In Animation
http://wia.animationblogspot.com/
Professional non-profit group established to help the advancement of women in the animation industry.

World War 2 On Film
http://www.geocities.com/warmoviedatabase/
For our war film fans!

The Worldwide Guide to Movie Locations
http://www.movie-locations.com/
Photographic history of the locales of movie shoots. Can be searched by place, film, or cast member.

Yahoo Upcoming Movies
movies.yahoo.com/mv/upcoming/
Provides info on upcoming releases (including release dates, cast, and crew), as well as movies in production or scheduled for release in the next 1-2 years.

VIDEO OUTLETS

Action Is My Reward
http://www.actionismyreward.com/
Comics, DVD's, action figures, and more.

ADV Films
http://www.advfilms.com/
Popular anime provider.

Amazon.com
www.amazon.com
The largest online store on the internet, with a huge DVD catalog and options to pre-order releases or buy used copies of out-of-print movies

Anchor Bay Entertainment
www.anchorbayentertainment.com/
One of the leading independent suppliers of movie and TV DVDs, particularly known for their horror catalog

AnimEigo
www.animeigo.com
Japanese animation and classic samurai films, including extensive translation notes on cultural quirks in the film that would otherwise be lost on western viewers.

BBC America Shop
http://www.bbcamericashop.com/
For your British tv and film needs.

Best Video
www.bestvideo.com
With over 24,000 titles, you can search their inventory via various topics and subject categories. Also includes brief monthly reviews of current releases

Big Rock Media
http://www.bigrockmedia.com/
Sells movies on DVD and VHS, and music CD's.

Big Vision Entertainment
http://www.bigvisionentertainment.com/
Specializes in several niches, most notably wrestling and mma.

Bombshells
http://www.bombshells.com/
Profiles and picture galleries of actresses from the 30's to the 50's.

Captain Bijou
http://www.captainbijou.com/
Video and DVD sales, and all sorts of posters and memorabilia.

Carpel Video
www.carpelvideo.com/
If you're only interested in purchasing blank and recycled video tapes, then you've hit the jackpot with this site.

CD Universe
http://www.cduniverse.com/
Primarily a music seller, but it also carries DVD's.

Central Park Media
http://centralparkmedia.com/
Japanese anime and asian pulp cinema.

Christmas Movies
http://www.christmasmovies.us/
Xmas films only, other holidays need not apply.

Cinematrix Releasing/Unknown Productions
www.unknownproductions.com
*Distributes the films of Unknown Productions, including **Vampires of Sorority Row** and **Club Dead***

The Criterion Collection
http://www.criterion.com/asp/
Collection of classic and contemporary films considered to be important.

Critics' Choice Video & DVD
www.ccvideo.com
Online ordering service. Includes new release, upcoming releases, classics, kids video, and bargain sections.

DDD House
http://www.dddhouse.com/v3/index.php
English language version of the Asian site. Carries DVD, VCD, games, and other stuff. Please make sure to pay attention to the Region Code and Format of your order to ensure it plays on your DVD player.

Deep Discount DVD
www.deepdiscountdvd.com
Online ordering service, with a lowest price guarantee, for DVD releases

DVD Asian
http://www.dvdasian.com/
Specializes in asian films (and not just from Japan and China). Please make sure to pay attention to the Region Code and Format of your order to ensure it plays on your DVD player.

DVD Concept
http://www.dvdconcept.com/
Sells Region 1 and 2 DVD's. Please make sure to pay attention to the Region Code and Format of your order to ensure it plays on your DVD player.

DVD Mega Packs
http://store.dvdmegapacks.com/
Packs of films or shows in the public domain, usually about 50 movies for 25 bucks. Quality varies.

DVD Plus
http://www.dvd-plus.com/
Large DVD seller in Canada.

Draculina
http://www.draculina.com/
Magazine publisher that also carries some niche horror and exploitation films.

DVD Empire
http://www.dvdempire.com/

Facets
http://www.facets.org/asticat
Distributor to hard to find art, cult, and foreign videos. Please make sure to pay attention to the Region Code and Format of your order to ensure it plays on your DVD player.

Family Home Video
shop.famvid.com/catalog/
Online ordering service for over 25,000 titles that are also linked to the Internet Movie Database.

HBO Home Video Online
www.hbo.com
Along with information of their productions released on video, this site includes program summaries, sound and video clips, and celebrity photos.

Image Entertainment
http://www.image-entertainment.com/
Films of all kinds, many of which are hard to find.

iNetVideo
http://www.inetvideo.com/store/home.php
Sci-fi movies, music, and games.

J Son
http://jpanimation.com/store/
Anime and Japanese products.

Kino on Video
www.kino.com/
International showcases a breadth of films from world cinema.

Manga Video
www.manga.com/
Spin-off retailer site offering comic books, soundtracks, and fan club information.

Mondo Macabro DVD
http://www.mondomacabrodvd.com/
Foreign horror and exploitation film.

Movie Gold Mine
http://www.moviegoldmine.com/
DVD's and VHS tapes, some hard to find.

Moviesville
http://www.moviesville.com/
English language version of Chinese site. Please make sure to pay attention to the Region Code and Format of your order to ensure it plays on your DVD player.

On Reel.com
www.reel.com
Video distributor based out of Berkeley, California that categorizes films under uncanny subcategories. Hmmm, that sounds familiar. Holds over 85,000 titles.

Out of Print Movies
http://www.outofprintmovies.com
They will search for out of print films for you, but they don't claim to be cheap.

PicPal: Picture Palace
picpal.com/
Enormous online catalog that has a comprehensive and searchable database for its 36,000+ titles. Also has special features including a magazine rack and a place for international cinema.

Rare Hollywood
http://www.rarevideo.com/
Specialists in finding rare and out of print films. They also sell Hollywood memorabilia and posters.

RightStuf
http://www.rightstuf.com/rssite/
Importer of Japanese merchandise, films, and anime.

Robert's Hard to Find Videos
http://robertsvideos.com/
Video catalog searchable by genre as well as format.

Russ Meyer Films International
http://www.rmfilms.com/
The man who gave many large busted women their first acting roles.

Scarecrow Video
http://www.scarecrow.com/
Rare and hard to find films for sale or rent.

Sci-Fi Station
http://www.scifistation.com/
Classic and modern science fiction films and collectibles.

Science Fiction Continuum
www.sfcontinuum.com/
Guide to a diverse collection of sci-fi and horror films as well as animation, television and UFO documentaries on video and DVD. Please make sure to check the Region/Format to make sure it plays on your DVD player.

Silent Film Sources
http://www.cinemaweb.com/silentfilm/
Resources for finding silent films.

Synapse Films
http://synapse-films.com/
Horror, scifi, indie, and cult films.

Tampoo
http://www.tampoo.com/
Videos, DVD's, CD's, and video games.

Tartan Video USA
www.tartanvideousa.com
Surf the web site of the distributor responsible for bringing some of the freakiest films from Japan, Hong Kong, Korea, and the rest of Asia to the good ol' US of A.

Tempe Entertainment
http://www.tempevideo.com/index.html
Direct to video horror and scifi movies.

Thomas Video
www.thomasvideo.com
Having difficult finding that obscure, and admit it, disgusting film you remember seeing when you were younger? Well, take all inquiries to Thomas Video, who specializes in those hard to find videos. Site also includes monthly spotlights on such indie pioneers as Mario Bava, Larry Cohen, and Japanese director Seijun Suzuki.

Turner Classic Movies
http://www.tcm.com/index.jsp
Aside from it's catalog the site also has trailers and clips from classic films.

The Video Collection
http://www.videocollection.com/
Video sales, searchable by genre.

Wolfe Video
www.wolfevideo.com
Online video outlet specializing in gay and lesbian themed films.

Xploited Cinema
http://xploitedcinema.com/catalog/index.php
Imported cult, exploitation, horror, and arthouse dvd's. Please make sure to pay attention to the Region Code and Format of your order to ensure it plays on your DVD player.

Zoom Movie
http://www.zoommovie.com/
Asian films, and Japanese animation. Please make sure to pay attention to the Region Code and Format of your order to ensure it plays on your DVD player.